World of Poetry Anthology

With special thanks to the World of Poetry Staff:
Julie, John, Barbara, Betty, Sherri, Judy, Joan, Michelle,
Raymond, Karen, Tina, Rosie, Carla, Angela, Eve and David

Library of Congress catalog card number: 90-071398
ISBN 0-910147-18-3
1991 Printing
Printed in the United States of America

A Note From Eddie-Lou Cole

This tremendous volume, *World of Poetry Anthology,* represents the best efforts of hundreds of poets from around the globe. If you are one of the beautiful poets whose work has made this dream a reality, thank you! And if you are simply a lover of the art of poetry, I know this anthology will bring hours of joy, inspiration, and focused meditation. We've made a special effort to keep editing to an absolute minimum — I think you'll appreciate the poetic individuality that comes shining through. Congratulations! In your hands you hold a priceless treasure, a monument to poetry and poets everywhere.

Poetically yours,

Eddie-Lou Cole

Eddie-Lou Cole

Lino G Beldi
FORGIVENESS
Forgiveness is the essence of your
godself;
It be born not in the throne of your
superiority and self-righteousness,
but in the womb of love, sired by
compassion.
And it be given freely to those who
may have committed upon you
a real or imagined wrong.
Forgiveness is a freeing of one's
unselfish self
of the burdens of
hate, envy, greed, fear and avarice,
And frees our brothers to seek their
self's self in love.
It be the radiant bright beacon which
releases the great power
of compassion;
For it be in forgiveness that man
finds the path illuminated
to the essence of peace.
And the spectres of fear
be forever cast into
the abyss wherein
man discards his lost values.
And love and forgiveness
look upon this spectacle,
embrace,
and become one.

Elynor Agnes Baran
DANDELIONS

To My Sister Alice Who Will Always Be A Special Part Of My Memories!

As children we laughed, sang
And played along the
Sand washed shores
Of the Lake
Leaving footprints on
The sand of time!

A gentle rain began to fall
And a brilliant rainbow appeared
Over a beautiful meadow
Covered with countless blooms
Of yellow golden dandelion!
An awesome sight!
A timeless memory
Never to be forgotten!
Weaving yellow garlands—
One for your brown eyed Teddy Bear
The other for my curly headed
China Doll!

Joel E Flesch
WHITE ANGEL

The sky reaches out to the birds that fly among its sacred glow. Will a dove love the sky, or will it never know the bully that hides in the gray clouds below. Never will the dove know what waits below, for the bird of white is blessed with the words..."Never Know."

They fly with the wind, they fly and they sing the song of ages that man cannot tinge. They will swoop and carry their joy among the clouds and their innocence will make angels proud.

And if man should ever part his God-given land, the pure white dove's beauty will always stand. The purest white of all man's race, can never take the white dove's place.

Mary C Allison
LOST IN MY DREAMS

To my husband, Al, who helped to make these dreams come true.

Sometimes things aren't
Always as they seem
But that's the time
I am lost in my dreams.
My mind is asleep
Even though I'm awake
It dreams the dreams
As I enter its gate.

I am there amongst love
Where no hurt can touch me
I live life only happy
For no misery I see.

I must always return
To realize what it means
But I always go back
To be lost in my dreams.

Minnie L Teague
ECHO
Let's ponder of places, and things
that be.
The breadth of the land, the depth of
the sea.
Can we search out something new—
maybe old
that truly has never been told.
There be rivers, open roads, or
mountain clime
part of the magic set to rhyme.
The light of day, ebbing amid a rosy
blush
or the wild fling of nature's paint
brush.
The red breasted robin or the tiny
wren
age old portrays from the pen.
The mourning dove, or the Mocker's
trill
Be ready subjects for the quill.
Therefore outer space is the latest
pace,
yet the thought is as old as the race.
Bards have sung of castles in the sky
sun, moon and stars abiding high.
So if we've pieced a work of art
let not vanity swell the heart.
Betwixt each line, the thought runs so
'tis only an ECHO.

Minnie L Teague
EVENTIDE
Shadows stretch along heaven's
floor,
And daylight silently closes her door.
'Tis in the gloaming, all hush and
still,
The time for the call of the
whippoorwill,
Time for the whirr of bats on the
wing,
And the noises the crickets and
katydids bring.

Out of the deep skips an autumn
breeze
To romp and frolic among the trees,
Stirring the aspens in a swish of glee,
Or swaying the willows down in the
lea.
A passing tug at the clinging vines,
Then softly sighing among the pines.

Day pauses briefly in twilight, then
slips away
For dark's descent and night's full
sway.
All nature settles in peace and quiet,
Seeming to say, "The world's all
right."
So bid farewell forever to a day
bygone,
For in memory only can she linger
on.

Minnie L Teague
RAIN
The wintry sky is gray and gloomy
lit,
While by the fireside I muse a bit,
Listening to the drip, drip of the rain
Or the lonely whistle of a distant
train.
My mind goes back to summer days
And showers that help so many ways.
Causing the grain to burst and grow,
Giving the farmer an overflow.

God grants us seasons, hot or cold,
His earth yields pots o' gold.
Yet the blessing of richest gain
Is the splatter of his rain.

As wintry winds ride wild and high,
I think of summer showers and sigh,
Of sun and rain and the bow's bright
hue,
And God's promise to me and you.

Be thankful then, for rain or snow,
For showers that come and go,
For health and wealth and play,
And God's wisdom for a rainy day.

Jason Lyle Trahan
LOVE...
Love, a feeling,
undoubted emotion;
Love, forever,
unblemished devotion:
Love, a language,
universally spoken;
Love, a mender,
of a heart that's broken:
Love, a sight,
so precious to see;
Love, a sound,
so beautiful to me:
Love, a cure,
for any ill;
Love, a dream,
that becomes more than real:
Love, harmony,
so gracious to hear;
Love, a thought,
you hold so dear:
Love, a song,
so wonderful to sing;
Love, everywhere,
everyone, and everything.

Gladys Lough
DREAMS
The death knell strikes my dreams.
They shatter
In fragments around my feet,
Past mending.
I let them lie.
Their brilliance slowly dims
As I walk away.
My lovely dreams
Good-by.

Gabrielle Mayer
WINTER
Under the covers soft and warm
I look out my window at the winter
storm.
By the fire, flaming high,
I look at the cold, gray snowy sky.

The snow drifts fast, swift, and
strong.
The days are short and the nights are
long.
I look at the fire, steaming red,
While I lay soft and warm in bed.

Denise Fox
SHADOWS FROM THE GROUND
Shadows from the ground
Hang from every rafter.
Nights of laughter
are no more.
For now, you're in the after world

Hear them closely
whisper unearthly matters
about their lives they live beneath
the mud.
Waking up to violence
and uttering the wants for blood

Their brain calls out for meat
they want revenge
on those who lived the life they never
got to meet.

Lorrainne C Kent
SAIL ON, SAIL ON
I have stood on the seashore of life
and watched my kids launch out into
the deep.
And as I've done this,
Sometimes I've watched with fear,
Sometimes I've watched with
sleepless nights of worry,
Sometimes I've watched with
anger,
Sometimes with joy,
And many, many times I've watched
with pride,
these kids of mine.
But always I am well aware, I cannot
sail upon their sea,
but only mine,
And stand upon the shore with prayer
and faith and love,
While their ship of life sails on.

Diana Williams deSousa
DISTANT SHORES
I am like an eagle
Soaring through a blazing sky of
pinks and oranges
Streaked with gray...
Heading toward the last rays of the
sun
To warm my cold downy
breast.
The wind whips through my lonely
feathers
And I am chilled still further;
Reality comes quickly, with the
knowledge that
I may never reach the sun, or
enjoy the warmth it brings.
So, hunting for a bit of food, I swiftly
return
To my hide-a-way nesting
where my fledglings await...
And warm them with tales of the
warm sun
That awaits their first flight—
With hope that they will never have
to face my reality.
I ruffle my feathers
And my eyelids droop into sleep
To dream of distant shores.

James H Seago
NO SORROW TOMORROW

To Stephanie.

You are in a time of sorrow and
things
look bad, with no luck and nothing
but time to borrow.

No friends, no money
No smiles and no one who says
anything funny.

So you look in the cooler where there
are
morsels of good food; all are
good-looking.
So you turn on the stove and start to
cooking.

Suddenly there is a knock at the door,
Could it be someone new, or maybe a
neighbor whom you have seen
before.

As you open the door, in walks a
stranger with a smile on his face
who gives you a hearty handshake.
He presents you with a check for
$15,000.00 leaving you with nothing
to fear.
Now you remember that you entered

a poem
in a contest last year.

So behold, there will indeed be no sorrow
tomorrow.

Mary Ann Blaydoe
THE COLORS OF MY LOVE
Red is for my heart so full of love for you,
Yellow is for the sun shining on the dew.
Brown is for my eyes sparkling with love and joy,
How I wish this happiness for every girl and boy.

Green is for the grass and leaves that come in Spring,
White is all the lovely clouds the west winds bring.
Purple is the violet that grows just like our love,
So sweet and beautiful and sent from up above.

Blue is for the sky watching down on us,
Black is how it looks when we've had a fuss.
Orange is for the sunset at the end of day,
Glowing bright and endless to help us find our way.

The colors of my love are so beautiful to me,
Like a summer rainbow mirrored in the sea.
Each color has a purpose, so I am told—
But the one that's most important is the ring of gold.

Mary H Pavlinic
I STRUGGLED THROUGH THE YEARS

This poem is dedicated to my son, William S. Pavlinic.

I struggled through the years
Riddled with strife and tears,
I was a loser in love,
I prayed for help from above.

Every time I turned I'd stall
And eventually face another wall,
That I was afraid to scale
For I feared another fall.

To keep loneliness at bay
I slaved my life away,
To avoid total emptiness
I write poems to fit my case.

In interim I found that
Emptiness could be turned around
With poetry the beautiful sound,
To delight readers near and far.

It is like gazing upon a star,
A God's gift to everyone
Whether reading, wondering, or loving,
Just enjoy and have fun.

Julie A Sharp
SNOWFLAKES
The snow is gently falling
Like a blanket coming down.
The snow is gently falling
Like diamonds to the ground.

Each snowflake, like a prism,
Reflects a ray of light
That divides into its spectrum
And is full of radiant life.

Like rainbows they appear;
The snowflakes come alive.
The snowflakes that are falling here
Are beautiful and bright.
I love to watch snow falling
Like a blanket coming down.
I love to watch snow falling
Like diamonds to the ground.

Kim Boomhouwer
A MELODY OF SEASONS
Rabbit tracks mark the
new fallen snow,
Ice covered trees wave to and fro.
Sitting by the soothing fire,
As youthful spirits fly higher and higher.

Spring has come and snow is gone,
A doe gives birth to a little fawn.
Flowers bloom and grass is green,
Children dance across this scene.

Summer's here and days are long.
Song birds call a joyful song.
Children splash in a river wide.
Shells wash up with the early tide.

Fall has arrived and trees are bright,
Yellows and reds add to the sight,
Festivities are soon to begin,
As a soft dust settles in.

Winter, spring, summer, fall;
Continue on through nature's call.
When one comes another's gone,
Like a melody they carry on.

Evelyn Delores Minton Rainey

Evelyn Delores Minton Rainey
COMFORT

This poem is dedicated to the memory of my father, Leslie H. Minton, a wonderful man.

Put down your hand and comfort them,
In this their time of grief.
Lift off the veil of sorrow,
And help them find relief.

Please help the children to understand
Just why he had to go
Wipe all their tears and comfort them
In a way that they'll all know—

That life is but a fleeting thing
To prepare us for beyond,
The sky, the stars, The Love of God,—
A place beyond the sun.

Edna Kohls Moenter
A LETTER TO MY HUSBAND
Why did you get restless and go on without me into that great beyond?
I was so unprepared to accept your passing and so frightened to find you gone!
I thought we had agreed to grow old together, to do all those things of which we were so fond.

We had walked those many, many miles together, you and I.
We had had so many good laughs and sure an occasional soft cry,
That I still can't believe it's over, I was comfortable by your side.

I still glance in your direction imagining that I will find you there.
Your ready smile, the touch of your hand showing me always that you care.
You were so special in so many ways—it's hard to accept, it seems so unfair!

I know I must go on alone and make the remaining time worthwhile.
But understand it's not easy when the heart is heavy to always show a smile.
You had made my life so happy, it was like being a sheltered child.

The IRS has fined me for some miscalculation, some minor sum.
I should have paid attention when you tried to show me how it was done,
But I was busy running my fingers through your hair. I was having fun!

The interesting trips we took through all those carefree years,
Are blurred now in my memory and washed away by the many tears.
And traveling alone may be great for some but not for me, I fear.

So prepare for me to join you, I shan't wait too long.
For it's difficult to see the sunshine and hear the bluejay song.
Without you I am nothing, I just don't seem to belong.

Lisa M Walker
MY LOVE

"My Love" is dedicated to the man I finally found, Midge Pifer, whom I love extremely.

Sailing into the bright blue waters,
A stare into the sea.
My love is waiting far away out there,
Somewhere, for me.
Desperately seeking the adventurous destination,
Longing to hold.
Unraveling the mystery,
Hoping to unfold.
Night and day, day and night,
Seemingly passing on.
Soon the day will come,
He and I will seal our bond.
Shattered by emotion,
As the beautiful voice of seagulls sing our favorite song.
For one day,
Together forever, we will belong.

Kim Steiner
TO WELDON

How do I explain these feelings? I've been sitting here wondering. I'm so happy, I want to tell all my friends about you and I. But stop, why do I refrain? Could it be a secret only lovers share? If this is true, then I should confide in you. You are my sunshine when I'm blue. You are my confidant, when I need a shoulder to cry on. You are <u>everything</u> to me: friend, lover and pal. I can't ask for more than these things from you.

When we talk, I feel it's straight from the heart. These feelings are so strange and unusual to me. But please have the patience that you have always had with me.

The two of us together we can't lose. I can honestly say I <u>still</u> love you with all my heart and my being. I may have tried to kid myself before, but I never thought I'd be in your loving arms again
I will love you forever.

Rhonda Smith
I AM THE WATER AND YOU ARE THE SEA

This poem is dedicated to Bob, the one that I will always love.

I am the water and you are the sea,
Because no matter what, you will always be a part of me.
When I'm not going in the right direction, you're always there,
Supporting me with your love and care.
Like the ripples of waves splashing against the sand, your
Love has never left me,
Just like the water has never left the sea.
Like the fresh, clean water that fills the sea, our love will
Never die,
If only we keep seeing eye to eye.
You're not a river or an ocean, you're a sea,
And that takes a lot to be.
Off from the water, I watch the sun slowly fall,
And now I know why loving you is worth it all.
As it rains, it gives us a little more love,
Just remember that the rain comes only from above.
More than either of us know,
Our love has so many chances to grow.
God created both of us, so without Him, we just wouldn't be,
Because I am the water and you are the sea.

Bridget Morris
CLOUDED VISION
Will there ever be a
perfect time
Or only blessed moments
Isolated

Can there really be
world peace
When there is no
personal concern

Are we truly an
evolved people
Or are we just as confused
As in the beginning

More technology
Less freedom
So much specialization
not true pictures

Is there a "big picture"
or just a small aperture
Through which to view
Our lives

Vanessa Borges
TO A LOVE
My heart—so blue
My hands—so cold
As my
Tears flow on
And form a lake full of
Sorrow.
This sorrowful lake
Shall grow as big as the
Sea
And
Form a home for my heart
And a grave for me.

Pamela Jean Szymanski
FOREVERMORE

For the man of my dreams, Kevin J. Cassidy, who has made my dreams real and is staying —Forevermore.

Man of my dreams—
who are you?
Slipping away with the dawn—
where do you slip away to?
Every night, something new,
always a romantic rendezvous.
Mesmerized by your eyes,
through the candlelight.
A stroll on a beach,
hand-in-hand under the moonlight.
Can you come back once more
and stay forevermore.

Helen Anthony

Helen Anthony
IN MEMORY OF

To my sister, Pearl.

Although he's gone, and sorely missed,
His sunny smile, the lips you kissed,
His cocky manner—always there,
To hide the fear, he couldn't share.
For courage was his middle name,
He treated life just like a game.

I know he's there, way up above,
And looking down upon his love,
To spread his courage all around,
And blessing you, without a sound.
So smile awhile and do recall,
The very best years of them all.
Your special day will surely be,
A very happy memory.

Cynthia Behrens
WINTER'S WALK

The Intruder approaches the town,
With each step his presence becomes more obvious.
His stride is slow and patient,
As if to tease his prey.
He brushes his hand across the trees,
Putting their leaves to death.
He touches the lakes with his chilling kiss,
And delights as they turn to ice.
He blows his frigid breath down the streets,
That sends a howling by each doorstep.
He wears a solemn look as he continues his pace,
For his time here is short.
He paints the earth a freezing white,
Causing the plants to lie dormant.
But, as time continues to pass,
His presence becomes less of a threat.
He begins to lose his domain,
Flowers start to bloom.
He leaves, but you can hear his impending whisper,
"Winter will always return."

William King
A HAPPY POEM

To everyone who loves Jesus.

Sad roe
Oh No No No
Too many poems
Go this way

This is a happy poem
with happy
Things to say
Joy Ahoy Oh Boy Oh Boy

Cheer so dear is here
Love from above like a dove
Does appear
Get in gear to hear.
So clear to the ear
To cast out fear
Jesus saves

William King
BEAUTY

Where does beauty go
Where love does feed
And always grow
And kindness does
Always show

Where does beauty be
Where no ugliness
We can see
And plainness does
Always flee

Where does beauty dwell
Where everything
Is far from hell
And every direction
Does cast his spell

What does beauty know
What does His goodness
Tell and show...
Love and kindness
That makes him glow
Jesus is beauty

Lucille Leinart
OLD FLAME

What do you do to forget an old flame
Just can't seem to forget their name
Their face seems to always appear
Remember each moment so clear

It would be great just to snap your fingers
But that doesn't help, memory lingers
Drift off in thought and hear their voice
Then you wonder, did I make the right choice

Though you haven't seen them in years
Sometimes you have to fight back tears
It's a difficult problem to explain
You have to go through it to know the pain

Chorus

Who can we blame for losing that old flame
Could it be me, what a shame
Things seem to turn out for the best
How could I blame all the rest

Sometimes you wake in the middle of night
Think of times past till daylight
Wish you could see them, maybe just talk
But I guess it would be the same, away you would walk

What would it be like to meet again, old flame
Would you say hello, or be ashamed
Guess you can never know how it would have been
'cause we live now, and that was then

Repeat chorus and tag last two lines of chorus

Jean L Staub
MEMORY

A darkened corner, candle flame
Raindrops cling to windowpane
Ticking clock, a faded rose
An open book of Shakespeare prose
A torn picture, souveniers
A pack of letters signed with tears
And I'm alone with naught to do
But think of you, but think of you.

A darkened corner, shadowed wall
Whispers from a haunted hall
Muted music, a memory
Of all the things that used to be
And I'm alone with naught to do
But think of you, but think of you.

How long before a dream come true?
How long must I but think of you?

Cecilia Rembert
MY DREAM

I had a funny dream last night
that I was born to be a king
and all my friends were also born
to kings and queens around the world

We stopped the fights
we tore down walls
and black and white were free again

And then together as a team
we fought to win the world again
back whole and clean and beautiful

Phyllis Anne Dootoff
LOST LOVE

I dedicate this poem to Peter, the love that I lost. He drowned in the ocean never to be found. I loved him dearly.

I am sitting all alone, not a soul in sight,
Knowing that God had taken you last night.
Out there in the water, somewhere you must be.
No one can find you; not even me.

I am sitting on the sands of the beach watching the waves fall to the shore.
Feeling the breeze blow through my hair
Hearing your voice calling my name,
Wishing you were beside me just once more.

I have sat here since dawn and now it is dark,
I have searched with my soul and also my heart.
I have stretched out my hand and called out your name,
But darkness and silence are all that came.

I sat there for days feeling great pain.
I knew that you were never coming back to me again.
My heart filled with sadness, my eyes filled with tears.
I know that I have lost you, but I'll love you for years.

Jeannette C Banrey
MY LAST GOOD-BYE

To A.V. L., who is always by my side. You are my inspiration! With LOVE always.

The time has come to say good-bye;
I would have stayed,
But my time has arrived.

The journey awaits
To see the stars
My life is ending,
So let me start.

I Love you my dear
I always have
It's better this way
So let me part.

I'll never forget you
I promise you this
I'll always watch over you
And send you a kiss;

My last good-bye, goes straight to you,
I don't wish to die
If only you knew....

Veronica Laxton
LUST

How should I know? The enormous wheels of will
Drove me cold-eyed on tired and sleepless feet.
Night was void arms and you a phantom still,
And day your far light swaying down the street.
As never fool for love, I starved for you;
My throat was dry and my eyes hot to see.
Your mouth so lying was almost heaven in view,
And your remembered smell most agony.

Betty Brautigan

Betty Brautigan
YOU CANNOT SEE THE WIND

This poem is dedicated to my darling little boy, Barry Wayne.

You cannot see the wind
You can see how it makes my hair blend
You can feel it move
You can see how it puts grass in a

groove

You cannot see the wind
You can see the feathers move on a hen
You can see the leaves move on a Tree
You can pretend you're a bird flying free

You cannot see the wind
The wind with a driving rain makes the cattle huddle in a pen
You can see the wind move the yucca blossom
In a tornado the wind is awesome

You cannot see the wind
My case I must defend
You can only see what the wind does
Blowing around the dust and fuzz

Betty Brautigan
STOOD UP
Stood up by my sweetheart!
How could he throw such a dart
My heart is crushed
My whole being is hushed

Stood up! How could he forget?
I feel like having a fit
Why didn't he call me
Before taking off with glee?

I suspect he went to see his mother and dad
He left making me feel sad
I am in utter despair
Needing some heart repair

I even took my son to the babysitter
Thinking tonight would be a double hitter
What am I supposed to do on a Saturday night
After such a plight?

Betty Brautigan
THE OKLAHOMA STORM
Can you hear the rain
Gushing down the drain?
Can you hear the hail
Hit the skylight without fail?

Great Stars above
This storm is even making interesting whistles above!
The storm makes your house rock
While you look at the clock

3AM is a Tornado coming?
Even the boards are humming
While I'm nestled in a warm bed
Could be in a cellar instead

All around the lightning flashes
And the thunder crashes
The sound of the wind makes you chilled to the bone
While a Tornado takes a nearby home

Thank you God for your great angel care
While I was afraid to move a hair
Thank you God for always being there
While on this earth I have a big scare

Tera L Cook
CURVES OF YOUR LIPS

Dedicated with much love to my supportive family and friends—espicially my mother, Laurel Jean, who has passed away.

Curves of your lips
long to be kissed
by me
or maybe
I long to kiss
the curves
of your sweet neck
to your ears
oh, what fear
when sprinkles drop
a tear
then, a hand caresses
your face
a painter's dream.

Becky Yeager
HELLO'S THE WORD BEFORE GOOD-BYE
What is springtime after all?
Only the other side of fall,
Oh, if I could have
I'd have made you a sunny sky.
Hello's the word before good-bye.
Sometimes it rains, sometimes it shines
Yet the things I want are seldom mine.

How much of summer can we hold
before we turn and find we're old?
The things our mirrors tell us are all lies
Hello's the word before good-bye.
Sometimes it's dark, sometimes it's fair,
Yet when I go home at night
nobody's there.

Perhaps the next wind that blows in
will bring you back to me again.
Till then remembering just makes me want to cry.
Hello's the word before good-bye.
Sometimes you lose, sometimes you win,
Yet I can't forget what might have been.

Macrina Aganon
RIVER OF SADNESS
Tears run down the river of sadness
Lips closing in the moment of silence
The world screams in madness

My eyes capture a moment that's torn
Unclear surmises in the surface of dawning
Love in my heart is unfulfilled with the shadow of burning hell

Silhouette blown out of order
In the loneliness of a cold night's dream
My mind in spinning haze

I cannot make the intentions
I cannot make
I cannot make

Lend me your eyes
Lend me your heart
Lend me anything that's undisguised

Drag me out
Oh, drag me out of this horrifying state
Serenity stands somewhere in the end

Gladys M Sechler
ANNIVERSARY

To my husband Stan, with love and affection.

Will you be here come next September
When the sunbeam glows through the whispering leaves?
Soon they will sleep
Beneath the wintry skies and snow.

Will you be here come next September
When the stars and the Milky Way
Remind us of the Creator,
The promise of another perfect day?

Will you be here come next September
When the hillsides are all in flame?
Blue skies and sunshine
Suddenly turns to misty clouds and autumn rain.

Will you be here come next September
When the harvest moon is all aglow?
Evening shadows lights are dimmed and low.
Will you be here reminiscing?
Special moments cherished,
memories of long ago.

Thelma (Jean) Davis
DRUMMING UP BUSINESS

To my Mother, who inspired me. She now is in heaven.

Accept this gift with my compliments, please,
I'm building my business you see...
And I would appreciate you buying from me!

I also give Free Facials and teach Skin Care,
About some things you may not be aware!
You are under NO obligation to buy...
Just please give my products a try!

Now, everyone likes to look and feel good...
That's no sin...they really should!
So, this little gift is just for you...
Please us it...it's brand-new!
Don't put it away high on the shelf...
Where it won't be used...but just left!

But should you decide to put it away...
Just remember to use it on a rainy day...
It will help to chase the blues away!

These words are composed just for you...
I hope you like them...
You're SPECIAL TOO!
Personal Service Is My Commitment,
On this you can rely...
And if you like my products,
please reply!

Cassie Mae (Just) Wildman
A HEALING

For Reverend Pat and Val Holloran, who helped God in helping me.

You were there when I needed a friend,
when my life was falling apart.
God sent me to you above all others
to help him mend my broken heart.

You talked with me, you prayed for me,
and helped me deal with my past.
I wanted to die, but am going to live,
I know I'll be healed at last.
I have a long road before me
with mountains great and small,
but the Lord will be beside me
to lift me when I fall.

I have the courage to face tomorrow,
and whatever it may bring.
Now that I have faced my past,
my heart is free to sing.

Sharon G Musialowski
LONELINESS
A feeling of complete emptiness.
Arms that ache to hold you,
Eyes that can't see beyond tears.
Wanting but unable to touch.
Sweet love turning to bitter hatred.
Resentment because, of a need left unfulfilled.
A desire burning with my heart.

Verna M Oliver

Verna M Oliver
KILLING FROST

Dedicated to my loving husband, Orbin E. Oliver.

I hear the killing frost will come tonight.
There will be a full moon, the clouds will be gone,
Moonlight will be bright.

Temperatures will be near three and twenty.
How sad, for the flowers are blazingly beautiful and plenty.

All varieties are blooming in riotuous colors of yellow, red and blue.
Prettier now than with their midsummer hue.

Tomorrow they will be a sickly sight.
I must pick some memories before tonight!

Roses, pansies, mums shall be made into bouquets,
so beautifully right.
To be enjoyed and then it is not so hard to say Goodbye.

To cover them with fallen leaves, where they will dormant lie, through cold winter snow.
To come again in spring, when the warm winds blow!

Verna M Oliver
CANADIAN GEESE — LIFE LONG PAIR
I saw the lake in its tremendous vastness.
Then I saw the two of them near the shore.

My first thought was, why are they still here?
They belong in the far north, beyond the reach of man.

Canadian Geese have paired for life.
One would not leave the other.
Was one of them injured and could not fly away?
Did they like the area and decide to Stay to raise a family?

The last I saw of the two of them, they were swimming side by side.
One looking over to check on the other,
As they swam farther and farther away.

May whatever God's plan for their nature, mature to fruitful life.
Maybe in a short time they spread their huge wings,
Flying away to their natural destiny.

Kim Kapinus
HE HAPPENED UPON MY SEPULCHRAL INNER SELF
He happened upon my sepulchral inner self,
No tombstones to mark the secrets there interred.
Thoughts like wisps of graveyard mist
Curled around a vault of unspoken words.

Brushing away the dust of
long-shattered feelings,
Beneath which lay a soul with the intent to survive,
He ventured forth and unearthed the secret
Of my being buried alive.

Lying in the dark emptiness, creeping cold,
Wondering if what I awaited could even exist,
Haunted by uncertainty, sinking with fear,
A suffocating soul seeking to subsist.
Years of resting, preserving strength,
A subtle presence gone undetected.
For the incarnation of my abstract definition of love,
Were my feelings in joyous effusion resurrected.

With the embodiment of what love means to me,
My soul is at long last gratified.
Peace and contentment have replaced fear and doubt,
The knowledge of his existence no longer denied.

Verna M Oliver
A LONE BIRD
A lone bird
Is calling.
Before the dawn
of early morning light.
In the darkness
can he see?
He is free!
What disturbs sleep?

Is he calling
For his mate
Who may have
Disappeared?
Why does he call
In the dark
Before dawn?

Verna M Oliver
RAIN, RAIN—RAINBOW
Out of the rain, dark clouds come.
Through heaven's tears, then shines the sun.

Look! arched across the sky, is
God's promise to man,
Sealed by a Rainbow!

Never again, will there be,
Forty days and forty nights of rain.

With one man came pain.
Man became evil, then came the rain.

Now we have the rainbow.
One Man died then arose to show,
The way out of the pain,
Of mortality into immortality.

Rain, rain, Son, RAINBOW!

Verna M Oliver
JUST ONE FRIEND
It would be nice, if I had a
friend, with a shoulder to lend.
One who would love me, would hear my fear.

One I could tell my innermost thoughts,
One who would understand how hard I've fought!

When I say I can't go on, but know I will!
Somehow, someway, make it to another day!

One that will pray, when I stumble and fall.
Just one friend, who really knows me!

JUST ONE! JUST ONE, TO HEAR MY CALL!

Raymond Schlitzer
A DAY TO CELEBRATE

To my friend, my lover, my wife, Myrtle.

Another day, another cause
My dear to celebrate
Because your love, the reason
That makes each day so great

Sure, I'm just sentimental
But every right I must proclaim
Each day's an anniversary
Because you share my name

Each day is so important
No matter what the season
In fairness I must count your love
Tops the list of every reason
Dear, as I see the time slip by
I'm blessed that I have you
Life becomes a world of mirth
As we share a love so true

You justify the noble prize
By your standard way of life
And I am overwhelmed with joy
In saying you're my wife.

Hilda Hilpert
NIGHT LIGHT

In memory of my mother, Emma Hilpert.

'Twas evening, and as Night draws her velvet cloak
of darkness across her sleepy child, the Earth
the Moon appears, to light the Room of the Universe

His shimmering silvery beams play gently upon the face
of the peacefully sleeping planet, as the stars twinkle
and dance, and softly sing a lullaby;

Until Dawn arrives, and comes quietly tiptoeing in,
to draw back the Curtains of Morning, and greet the rising Sun.

Brian Strader
THE FLOWERS WE REMEMBER
We are gods.
We see the flowers of the Earth.
We look at them and marvel.
So many are so beautiful.
But they die so very fast.
Blooming today, withering the next, dead the next.
And the dry, lifeless bodies
Are either buried or cast into the fire.
Yes, the beauty fades, but we remember the fragrance.
Most have a very common scent.
But there are some rare ones.
They may be very beautiful to see.
Sometimes not.
But the scent of those is very sweet.
It lingers in our minds.
Those are the flowers we remember.

Dolores M Midden
JOY OF LIFE
When I was young,
Morning came too soon
The sun was there
In place of the moon

As I grow older,
And in a slump
The days grow shorter
And so does the month

But the nights get longer,
As I lie awake
Thinking of the joy
One more day will make!

J S Walia

J S Walia
BLIND LOVE

This poem is dedicated to the ever living sweet memory of my beloved wife, S. Surjit Kaur.

MY LOVE ! This life is not mine,
This life is yours,
Better take care of this,
With me this is a trust of yours,
Nothing is now mine,
Everything has become yours,
My every breath is full of love,
Even that love is yours,
My heart is not with me,
It beats with the heart of yours,
My eyes cannot see on their own,
They always see through the eyes of yours,
I cannot think of any other love,
Excepting the love of yours,

I cannot walk on the feet of my own,
I always walk along with the feet of yours,
I cannot talk on my own,
I talk in the language of yours,
Let your life be mine,
My life is already yours,
With me this is a trust of yours.

Rita M Greenhalgh
EYE OF THE STORM
The roaring wind, and pounding waves
The blackened sky of stormy days
Tossed and turned, tattered and torn
'Til I found you in the eye of the storm.

Crushed and defeated, I stood alone
My emotions trampled, my heart as of stone
My will was weakened, badly worn
Then I found you in the eye of the storm.

Now I face each troubled morn
With my arms around the eye of the storm.

Donna Thomas
YOU WERE PATIENT
You were patient, you were kind
Thoughts of you never left my mind
Never jealous, proud or rude
Never held a grudge or changed your mood.

You were glad when truth won out
And prayed for me without a doubt
Loyal to me no matter what the cost
Standing up for me when I was lost.

I saw in your life something I needed too
The light that shined when He talked to you
I asked for your help in finding the Lord
My troubles were lifted, my spirit soared.

Now I also have by the Lord been found
And I am too standing on solid ground
As you have loved me, let me now love you
As I was never before able to do.

Patricia Lynn Moreland
AS ONE
Help Me—blossom into a totally sensuous being,
And Together—we shall blossom as one.
Help Me—spread these wings over new horizons,
And Together—we shall explore those horizons as one.
Help Me—realize there are no treacherous impossibilities,
And Together—we shall conquer them as one.
Help Me—expose this fear which hinders one's being,
And Together—we shall move mountains with our sensuous love.
Help Me—do all that
And Together—we shall be two sensuous beings united as one . . .

Patricia Lynn Moreland
TAKER
Asphyxiate my being of natural happiness,
I shall whither withinside.
Such a deliberation.
Unleash thine enemies onto me,
And ingress as phantoms in darkness.
No angst in thine eyes.
Shift my liberty and attest thy own destiny.
I implore thee, take thought.
Eliminate mine audition, for sensations elude me.
Possess no rue.
Shatter my window of curiosity to accomplish seclusion.
Thou has removed thine own entrance.
Then taketh my essence for there remains
no faucet to journey through.
Therefore sanguineous . . .

Susan Yazzolino
MEETINGS
My mind is filled
with many words
My heart with
endless pain
My soul cries out
from lives past lived
We meet to try again

'tis not the first life
we have met
nor to be the last
Our minds and hearts
our souls survive
to make amends
long past

I wish to give you
things most dear
and 'til love and joy
are given
our souls will meet
again again and then
all past's forgiven

Susan Yazzolino
LIFE'S ELEMENTS
Life is . . .
big soft clouds
and butterflies
windy days
and rising tides

lamb shaped billows
and floating seeds
wind swept beaches
and tossing seas

flaming sunsets
and colorful blooms
storm tossed driftwood
and blowing spume

sky and earth
wind and sea
all this is Life and more . . .
to me

Cathy Clifton
MUSIC
Just one voice pierces the
silence—
Then another joins in—
Soon a chorus sings—in
glory
Only music is heard—
Melodic sounds—and
harmony
The sopranos screeching—
Basses clear and strong, 'tis music—
Beautiful in my ears.

I feel it—deep inside—
I know—
Music is a gift—
For any who wants it—and
I will give it to the world.

Harry Davis Jr
FOR CAROLYN
You claim your brown eyes don't see very well,
You have to look long and hard.
With contact lenses you'd see clear as a bell,
Your performance—it wouldn't be marred.

They watch as you dance easily,
Barefoot 'cross the floor.
Your lovely eyes glance teasingly;
You make them want for more.

After your performance, you speak with them.
My, oh my! The things that you say!
You make the strong weak, turn the weak into men;
I don't know how you keep them at bay.

You claim your brown eyes don't see very well,
But Carolyn, you're not blind!
You see people's spirit clear as a bell,
You see exactly what's on their mind.

Marian G Little
WHEN HAVE YOU SEEN A RAINBOW?

To my husband and best friend, Jimmy, and my children, Jamey, Elizabeth Ann, Bob, and Trent, and also my grandchildren, Jason, Summer, and McKenzie.

When have you seen a rainbow, or watched the orange sun rise,
Picked the petals off a daisy, being loved was no surprise?
When have you blown a dandelion, or wished upon a star,
Found a four-leaf clover, put Lightning Bugs in a jar?

Said Eenie, Meenie, Minie, Moe, to see who would be first,
Or played Rolla Bat, relays, pinheads were the worst?
Felt pride when you won the Spelling Bee,
Ashamed of your paper in Math?
Held hands with your best friend, along the school house path?

When have you found an angel in a puffy cloud,
Thought happy thoughts when all alone and laughed out loud?
When have you tied a string on a June Bug,
And flown it like a plane?
Walked barefoot in a fresh plowed field,
Turned your face up to the rain?

When have you blown bubbles through cupped hands,
Sitting in the bathtub, delaying all your plans?
I try to do some of these things. . . now and again,
It somehow makes being grown-up, easier to stand.

Rose M Matlock
MOMS BEHIND BARS
Every mom loves their children, this is true,
When we're behind bars, we don't know what to do.
As we sit and look out into the night,
We wonder if our babies are alright,
Watching the falling snow,
Wishing we could watch them grow.
Every mom has the same dream,
To see them play, grow and stay in the right stream.
Moms behind bars can't do these things;
We all have the same wish,
To hold and love them and give 'em a kiss.
We broke the law, now we're in jail,
We communicate with our kids through the mail,
So people on the outside don't be so vain,
We as well as our kids, are in pain.
As you look up at the stars,
Think about the moms behind bars!

Allison Cromer
BY THE SHORE
As I walk along the shore,
My toes sink into the sand
The tide comes and carries it away.

As I watch the sun come to another day,
It seems to bring the whole world to life.

Cheryl D Swetland
THE VOLCANO OF HURT
The hurt that grows inside
Is like a volcano erupting.
Spewing out oceans of hateful phrases,
Drowning all my friends' faces
In crevices, deep and wide,
Of differences between us.

We never talk, nor share memories
Of things we do with our families.
I wish we would.
I wish we could,
Just take the time to talk,
Or go for a walk.

Come, my friend
Take my hand.
Let's walk on the bridge of friends,
With the river of enemies below.
We'll toss our differences and watch them flow.
Over the rocks, under the leaves
Until they reach the end.
Let's hope the volcano of
hurt doesn't erupt again,
So we'll always be friends.

Mary L Bulson
MEMORIES

I would like to dedicate these poems to my parents and my sons who encouraged my writing.

At times late at night,
I wonder about my life.
I see bits of my childhood,
My teen years and strife.
I remember my lover,
A love that would last;
Through childbirth and marriage,
We share the same past.
I ponder decisions,
I made way back then,
And think what the outcome,
Might otherwise have been.
Now that it's done,
The decisions all made,
I think, in my heart,
That my life was well laid.

Mary L Bulson
THE CHOICE OF LIFE OR DEATH
It has come to my attention
That since the days of yore,

Man has made some changes
And now you still want more.

First we gave you freedom
To choose the church you like.
Women were given a choice.
They could vote or they could strike.

So many changes have come
No one can list them all.
Now you want another choice,
To make a life or death call.

I think that you've gone too far.
This choice isn't up to you.
For only one has that control
And the Lord demands his due.

Mary L Bulson
MY ERROR
I wished upon a star last night,
I chose the one that shone so bright.
I wished for a miracle to happen to me,
I wished really hard for I wanted to be,
A dancer so great that no other could match,
Famous and pretty, a regular catch.
It wasn't till later when tears fell on the sod,
Instead of the star, I should have asked God.

Kathy A Nichols (5¢)
CATCH A RAINBOW

Dedicated to my friend, Judi Davis, for helping me find my rainbow.

I'd like to catch a rainbow,
And hold it close at heart.
I've never touched a rainbow.
I've never been a part.

The sky's so far above,
It's hard to get there now.
Above life's mass confusion,
One without much love.

Rainbows aren't for everyone,
Some folks never see.
Everyone needs a fantasy,
Or maybe that's just me!

I'd like to catch that rainbow,
To keep it in my hand.
And HOPE someday for PEACE and LOVE,
For all throughout this land.

Byron Paige
THE HOURGLASS
"NOW" is the constant arbiter between
Insurgent memory and the passionate dream;
Each grain of Time's white sand must pass
The orifice of "NOW"; the strictured glass
Imparts to each clear grain eternal hues
Before it leaves the future and to the past accrues.
If ever memory plagues, remember thou:
The past is past; the future will be "NOW!"

Richard R Foley
HERE I LIE ON A BLUE SILK CLOUD

For my wife Lynn, whom I'll love eternally, and my sister, Donna, for her encouragement.

Here I lie
On a blue silk cloud
I'm looking down, at myself,
Friends whispering, crying aloud
My wife and children
Standing by my side
They look of grief and worry
I know, they too, have cried
I felt I had prepared them
For this very day . . .
My life was passing
And now has gone away
A distraction, at the back of the room,
I look to see . . a bride and groom
They are coming towards me
A young couple, I can clearly see
They have just spoken their vows,
Lynn . . Lynn . . . It's you and me
Could we? Have we?
Been granted a second life
Come . . Come join me
I love you, be my eternal wife
The images are fading
The room fills with tears
I'm still here watching
As my silken cloud disappears
I'm alone in the dark
What more is there to do?
I feel your movement . . .
I'll always be watching you

John R Kaudewitz
HORSES

Dedicated to Jennifer Woodruff, who got me interested in horses, and to my teacher, Mrs. D. Cline, who taught me about poetry.

Bridle, Saddle
Galloping, Trotting, Walking
Galloping swiftly and quickly
Pony

George Shevelove
SURREALISM IN OIL PAINTING

This poem is dedicated to my dear Aunt Clara, my teacher, my role model, my friend, and one who is a leader in the fight for peace and understanding.

Have you ever been to a museum of art?
And noticed a huge crowd doing its part,
Nodding their heads like an acquiescing ass,
When in truth, they never attended even one class.

It's so hard to understand how they really believe,
That they've figured out what the artist tried to conceive,
You see, white on white is not much of a chore,
But the crowd oo's and ah's even more.

Do I admire the Picassos, Renoirs and such?
At times I adore them, other times not much,
I see an Utrillo, which opens my heart,
Then I recall that 9-year-old alcoholic upstart.

Gaugin, Chagall, and Van Gogh were giants of their time,
Sometimes, they even make my bells chime,
Please try not to think that I'm mocking their art,
Even though I'm objective, they'll call me an upstart.

I should, as a jazz musician and poet,
Go with the flow, and not try to blow it,
Just like some jazz is beautiful and strong,
Cacophonic sound, like some rock, does not belong.

I know that art must not be chained and bound,
To be too structured would obstruct the sound,
I do hear beautiful melodies pouring out,
So be understanding, I'm not an old lout.

Brenda Lee Cox

Brenda Lee Cox
ANOTHER DAY, PERHAPS
He didn't know he had not tomorrow
No more minutes, nor hours to borrow
He didn't know it would come so fast
Today would soon become his last
He didn't know what the future would hold
Days that were numbered, soon to unfold
He didn't know his time would end
Swiftly into the darkness blend
He did not believe he truly would die
No moments left to say goodbye
He didn't know finality
Would soon become reality
He didn't know this day in death
Would take away his every breath
He didn't know a second chance
To make amends, to sing and dance
To ask the Lord into his heart
He died alone, he died apart
He thought, "another day, perhaps"
Yet will not find another lapse.

Warren D MacEvoy
DILEMMA
I love your tawny, silken hair—
Your skin as smooth as cream.
And marvel at your flashing eyes,
That mock, and laugh, and dream.

I like your casual, languid air,
Your manner quite refined.
Yet know that almost hidden,
Are tendencies feline.

My heart says that don't matter;
The prize is worth the race.
My brain refused to listen,—
Convinced I'd only place.

There's just one nagging question,—
Which,—seems least unkind?
To fall, and break my heart,
Or stand,—and lose my mind!

Cindy Railey
HEART VS. MIND
Sometimes the way seems so unclear.
A battle between heart and mind is near.
So we ask for or are given "Friendly" advice;
Which, at times, exacts a heavy price.

The battle rages 'tween heart and mind,
Solutions only come with time.
Trial and error; right and wrong
Answers gleaned as life goes on.

The conflict within inevitably strains
A heart already filled with pain.
Our mind screams out "I'll have no more!"
But the heart's exhortation seems so sure.

I think, my friends, it's a mixture of each;
Based on that for which we reach.
The intellect is not all encompassing
Nor does the heart always sweetly sing.

Sometimes we win; sometimes we lose;
But the way is always ours to choose.
If lessons can be truly learned,
Then happiness is surely earned.

Lori Folley

Lori Folley
SELF INSPIRATION
Sadness Can be overcome, tragedies happen
to everyone. How great or small differs in size,
the greatness is all just a demise.

How it's handled you must decide, then rest easy
because you have tried. It matters not how odd
you walk. What people say is just small talk.

Remember like coal you've been through fire.
Be proud and honest, be not a liar.
Let others learn from what you've become.
A limp, my dear, is such a small sum.

Amanda Kathryn Lynch
WHEN SEX BECOMES OBSESSION
It starts innocently enough,
contradicting people who say falling is tough.

Created together are beautiful fantasies and love,
which carry you to heaven on the wings of a dove.

Hearts mesh and together you're one,
nothing anyone says can shadow your sun.

For some, this is a beginning . . .
while others are not so lucky.

A dark being—called Obsession—infests the one,
sinking the other into an inescapable hell.

One's weaknesses are used against him
as the other uses them to buoy her insecurities.

Fights, arguments and miscommunication begin to rule,
they can't escape . . . breaking up,
then going back for more.

It's so unfair, as their friends watch helpless,
they could be so happy, if only they would give up for good.

When sex becomes obsession,
everyone suffers.
But no one grieves as much
as the one being possessed.

Karen Dismukes
THE CHILD WITHIN
How long do I have to weep
through this stone heart
Phobic tears reciting rhapsodies
of an unbending of
personalities;
Reawakening
rewards that tremble
in silence

The ghosts of phantasies
Unrewarding ; un-rewinding
delicate white mists atomizing
through the psyche's
shelves
Stacked as foundations on a
construction site
Reworking ; Rezoning
heaving heartbeats
into lightness
Correcting genetic factors
after conception;
The revolt of sub-genetics
Numbness in the revival of
An exciting birth
The grief is timeless
The child is born
with little chance to live . . .

Karen Dismukes
MAPPLETHORPE
his eye is what we see;
photography laden with other "I's"
form with the real texture of life
everyone hiding their masks of erotica
with the celebration of lavish cloth
why not strip; the quorum is at
commissioned quiescence—
the quotient of understanding art is not division
as my hands rub the roughness of the sculpture
into a visionary reality I had never
shared with my naked eye
Mapplethorpe arranged a certain
recounter where man speaks for
himself as he diminishes his
own form into others . . .

Karen Dismukes
THE IRIS—THE FURIOUS DISSECTION
The light with which I have
I cannot see;
The sun has set; but
tomorrow
The eclipse;
The regression as dissection
produces projectiles;
Rejecting;
probing;
Dissected by a scalpel
Azure encroached with
brown lines
Yellow lines; the cache with codified
lines;
Unfolding vivid patterns
of perfection
Whole beauty
Petals Open; close
Close; open; open close
A kinswoman;
Regard for a stamen
Harmony of parts;
Positioned respect;
Ovarian relinquishment
A less pliant friend
Connect; Todayness
The iris
That fills the abyss
of Despair;

Karen Dismukes
VASARELY
Forms; silence; Cubes;
Nonabsorbent
Color transformed into
Engineered designs
Death of pigments:
A feeble unfolding
Duress into black, white,
Reflected excitement of light
into all spectrums
Oblique outlines
transformed art;
foreshadowing
Eternity

Mary E Hill
CONSOLATION
Drear' winter has gone and spring has come;
My heart is heavy, my spirit glum.
Nature tries to enchant me—no use;
Green acres, violets can't seduce,
Because you are not with me, my love.
God has called you to His home above.
May He grant me peace and mercy too,
Until I'm joined in heaven with you.
But just knowing you are waiting there
Gives me hope and strength beyond compare.

Kathleen A Martin
KINDNESS

To my mother, Mary Monahan, who served as an example for the sentiment expressed in my poem.

Have a kindness done to you, pass it on.
Have a kindness done to you, pass it on.
Let it travel down the years, let it
dry another's tears,
Till in Heaven, the deed appears,
Pass it on.

Mrs Linda M Davis-Barber
GRASPING FOR THE LIMITS

This poem is dedicated to the memory of Dr. Humberto C. Bautista and to the encouragement of Dr. C. Frank Csetri, Columbus, Ohio.

Twenty years and two with much to gain
A bride engrossed in time's enduring strain
Confusion fogged the life and plagued the mind
A young girl's passage actually gone blind

I came upon a door on which I knocked
It revealed a second door through which I sought
I came upon a third at which I asked
And as an angel breathing a gentle breeze did pass

The breeze was of a rose in early bloom
'Twould permeate my mind when all did seem of doom
With thorns that pricked and probed inducing strife
As gentle strokes of passion that did sweeten up my life

The rose began to twine about a tree
With limbs so dense that one could barely see
With struggle did it weaken in the night
And with debilitation did perish; angel's flight

But I so young continued to pursue
The challenge strewn with bitter clouds; sweet dew
With words of wisdom guiding me the way
And as the dawn awakened streaked the brilliant light of day

Jeff Blackman
WATERFALLS
Waterfalls,
roaring, tumbling down,
pounding, pounding.
How spectacular!

Coming to rest,
sweet subtleness, a caress—
only the surface,
only the surface.

Jeff Blackman
REVITALIZE, ALIVE!
Pure, unbroken and white
as winter snow fallen anew.
A tender soft touch—light
as a cloud adrift in the blue.
Silent and strong
possessing springly innocence—
elegance in a song
meeting no defiance.

Clear, shining with a flash of
Brilliance: A Gem? A Jewel?
Concealed, waiting to thrash
with motives unknown—lifeless
Ghoul.

Prisoner Light, drawn by the prism goes
bending and twisting; confusing.
Perverting Joy and Happiness to Woes—
but with majestic colors: quite bemusing.
Disguised and mysterious
entrapped with no escape.
The bellows breathe a furious
breath—giving life a new
shape.

Alyce Ruth Spencer
GOD MADE YOU

To J. C., A very special person in my life.

Sheep graze in pastures on grassy hills
While the sun and scorching desert winds
Bathe me to my very soul
And the message sends
Me to distant places seeking love.

Cool breezes sweep the valleys
Where shallow brooks run along
Singing to me as they go
A message loud and strong
Like the peace of a dove.

God created North and South
And sprinkled heaven with stars.
He made the sun and moon
And planets such as Mars.
Then sent you from above.

God made you for some purpose
When he placed you here on earth.
He made you kind and caring
With a voice filled with mirth
And filling me with love.

Arosa "Jazi" Colón
YOU!

To Winnie Arosa Thomas, who was my Guide in this Life and is now my Spirit Guide and greatest source of inspiration. I love YOU!

I am She who sees what you
see—
She who feels what you feel—
I am She who loves what you love—
She who hates what you hate—
I cling to the same things you do
and shun what you shun.
I can be your conscience—
I can be your soul.
Look at me in order that you might
see
yourself
as you really are.
Look at me and see
YOU!

Ruth H Yorns
QUESTION
Forty-seven of our men
Killed in an explosion
On a ship which gained honors
But causing much confusion.

Many, many people
Killed by terrible fires
Started by foolish arson;
Confusion across the wires.

Riots, riots everywhere
People being killed
Drugs take over the world;
We are being billed.

In England, many people squashed
Trying to get to a game;
The captain gives the order,
Suddenly they all came.

Well, what are we going to do
To stop these crazy acts?
Just ask yourself this question
Do I know all the facts?

Thomas Luck
LOST LEGEND (A TRIBUTE TO BOBBY BONDS)

For my wife Fawn, who gave me support.

A spark of life in soft sad eyes,
Long lost legend a fast demise
God given talent that few could match
A towering homer and brilliant catch,
Softly spoken the critics screamed
Writers scorned him, coaches dreamed,
Power and speed like no other star
They all thought he'd go so far,
Always respected—also rejected
Nomadic journeys he seemed unaffected,
They wouldn't and couldn't just let him play
The game he loved turned him away,
When I think back at what he's done
Reflections bring pure ecstasy

For what he did—he did for me,
And no other human can erase
The undaunted smile that covers my face.

Diana M Millasovich
FALL NIGHT
The wind,
Blowing warm and soft,
God's breath, all over the earth

The bare trees,
When Autumn has taken their coat,
All branches are seen,
With moonlight against the dark sky

The lake,
The blood of nature,
Rippling to her tune
The sounds of everlasting truth

The moon and clouds,
Witnesses of the origins,
Friendly eyes to keep us all,
To remember us all

Every lonely nerve of mine,
Realizes where I am,
This lonely beautiful place,
Is here

Marvin Tredwell Priester

Marvin Tredwell Priester
TIME WILL TELL
If love is grand as the mystical chime,
The essence of flowers is father of time.
If hurt can destroy the dignity of mind,
You know that time isn't far behind.

Although forever is never enough,
The price of life is always tough.
Dreams are the masters of all we know,
Heaven or Hell is the last place we go.
Is love really lust or lust really love,

Will we ever be forgiven through Heaven above?
Are the answers to life among the skies???
Destiny forgotten, as it all dies.
Nothing is forever, and nothing will be,

All around us illusions, that's what we see.
There was once a beginning we all know well,
Will there be another, only time will tell . . . .

Earl Kirkpatrick
MY LOVE FOR YOU IS AS BIG AS THE SKY
My love for you is as big as the sky
It is neverending and will never die
I think of you with every living breath
My love will keep growing until death

You are forever warming the chambers of my heart
I am very sad and lonesome when we are apart

I count the endless days and nights ahead
Until finally we can get together and be wed

Matthew Edwards
REST, DEAR CHILD
Rest, dear child, and do not cry;
For in this world there are tears enough
To drown us both.

Though your body sleep tonight
Come tomorrow your spirit will float free,
A shining bubble against the clouds,
Borne upon the wind
Toward far, far, fairer lands than these.

And when October comes 'round again,
The season of remembering,
You will return
To dance among the falling leaves
And sing the sparrows' songs,
Showing us what fools we are
To cringe in fear
From freedom's soft embrace.

Lucy Rovito
A POETREE OF THREE PLUS

A declaration of love.

You light up our life
Our first born one
A shower of light
Our April Sun

You light up our life
The first April flower
Our April jewel
Our little girl
A diamond, a pearl

You light up our life
A warm Sun in June
A happy song, a cheerful tune
A rainbow of lights
Our joy and delight

You light up our life
Two babes of delight
You make the days bright
And add a new height
To our tree of light

To you Son and your Rose
A few words of prose
May life's road for you be
Perfectly Pure Poetry

Cathleen L Mann
THE LOVE OF TWO
The moonlit sky
The river runs dry
Night sounds flow with the wind
The air blows cold with stories untold
The embers in the fire glow dim

Our hearts are warm
We're sheltered from the storm
Together we wait for the end
The morning sighs, the dawn fills the skies
Our eyes wait for the sun

The day is new . . . like the love of two.

Polly-Ann Stewart
TEACHER
Teachers help you learn,
So your test grades take a turn.
Come again to see us,
So you can get an A+.
Triangles, circles, and dots,
Skillets, pans, and pots,
Teachers clear up math
Obstacles in your path.

Paper, pencils, pens,
How far can my brain bend?
Books, bags, and homework,
Teachers help you so you aren't a dumb jerk!

Tim Kruszynski
THE CRUEL KISS
A single drop of rain, not more or less,
Falls from these looming clouds upon my brow,
Surprising me with its soul-wrenching coldness!
An unexpected and perplexing feeling,
The cruel kiss of all-demanding Nature!

Diane Moulin
WINTER'S MAJESTY
Snowflakes falling
Gently down
A foot or more
Lay on the ground.

With valleys white
The pines stand tall
And add some color
To it all.

Majestic scenes
Lie all around
Undisturbed
With nar' a sound.

The air so crisp
With winter's chill
Caress the views
Awaiting still.

The icy brook
On winter's morn
Awaits the spring
To be reborn.

Lora L Parker
THE WOMAN IN THE DARK

To my husband, Bobby, whose past actions inspired me to write this poem.

To the woman lying in the dark.
Alone, crying, desperately falling apart.
Her husband is out having fun every night;
While she waits, not willing to give up the fight.

To the woman lying in the dark.
Nothing will ever make up for all the hurt, crying, and pain,
But, this obsession of yours is driving you insane.

To the woman lying in the dark.
Take your precious child and part.
Listen to this letter,
If not for you, do it for your son;
He's the only person that matters now, he's number one.

Now it's time to get a good night's sleep.
At dawn, when the sun gives its first peek;
Go out and smell the fresh air,
Because you're about to find there's a much better life out there.

Walter Liggett
TOWARDS A DEFINITION OF SURVIVAL
1916: easy to be a survivor!
All you had to do was
be a Frenchman or a German
making it alive out of Verdun.

Now, assert super feminists,
all women,
oppressed by all men,
are survivors.

All Blacks, Black spokespeople assert,
are victim survivors,
alone possess "soul."

Half Jews exist.
Why not half survivors?

Chas Griffiths
IN LIFE
In life love is sought and
Sometimes found.
In death love is everything.
In birth you seek.
In death you find.
In death is birth and
In birth it travels.
In death it arrives and
So arises
With no compromises.

Chas Griffiths
IN THE LIGHT
The candlelight burns softly,
Coolly as its wisdom is contained.
Charging the darkness subduing the dark's bright it triumphs and explains;
"There's no such thing as a long time."
It whisps, "There is only one thing you shall know. One known that is constantly inconsistent. That is the Power, the Force, and the energy that governs the world. That is the flower of our emotional happiness that is the unreadable, unwritable sensation of the achievements, step by step, grind by grind and the inevitable rewards. That is the true love. Whatever it may be with the gravity of true love, wherever it may branch with the many more hearts it will turn. Love, with all the guesses and mistrials. It's the bottom line to vitality."

Jenny Cordero
LOVE IS . . .
Love is an inspiration,
It hurts like an operation,
It spreads like a conversation,
It grows to a population.

Esther Dable Childs
A SIMPLE ANSWER

Dedicated to Susan Tennessen who offered the ride on February 6, 1990—Wisconsin Weather.

As I was walking home today
I had a decision to make.
Should I walk down the icy driveway
Or the flooded sidewalk take—

Just then I heard a pleasant voice.
I was asked, "Would you like a ride?"

I was happy to accept her offer.
'Twas no problem to decide.

I wonder if we meet again, will I know her
So I asked her for her name.
Her name I should remember
As it sounds like a poet of fame.

Even tho I forget her name and face
I'll always remember her deed.
Helping someone whenever she can
Must be her special creed.

Now wouldn't it be wonderful
If all, as thru life we go
Would take time to help another?
Then a world of peace we'd know—.

Jessica Bolen
LIFE
The road of life is not an easy road to travel;
Some lives may be great, and some may start to unravel;
You may hit a twist, or maybe a turn, but sometimes I think it's just the hard way to learn;
Some people think they should have it much better, but maybe they need to start getting it together;
Love and caring are the best things that could ever be, so maybe some of you people should open your eyes and see;

Josephine Nicolazzo
THE BEAUTY OF NATURE
Sitting on a hilltop, gazing below,
The flowers between the grass I can see,
Branches of the trees swaying to and fro,
And in a mass were the clustering bees.

Looking above into a sky so blue,
Shining thru the clouds I can see the sun,
And birds are singing for me and for you,
Bringing happiness to all one by one.

A river I see a distance away,
Along the mountain banks it was flowing,
Then as I was going about my way,
I said farewell, as the breeze was blowing.

Think what the Beauty of Nature can do,
It brightens and lightens the whole world thru.

Kenneth L McAlpine
MY PRAYER

Dedicated to the memory of my first wife, Wilhelmina Mary; and my 2nd wife, Dorothy Elizabeth, both whom inspired the words of "My Prayer" during the 50 years of marriage. Their devotion has earned them a place in God's mansion.

Oh God! what force within me lies,
The evil thoughts that in me rise
To vent in utterance, words of hate
That cut her flesh, and wound my mate?

Please God, replace that thrust with requited love
To soothe the heart; dispel and shove
The forces bad into abyss wide and deep,
Enough to heal our hearts in sleep.

To forever close the tortured gap
Between Love and Hate; that endless wraps
Our door of happiness in webs of mire,
To haunt our souls and coke desire.

Would I, but have the faith to place
Our trust, and turn each face to
Gentle loving smiles, giving eyes to endure;
Perhaps the wounds would heal and cure.

The curse, the plague that haunts our every night
Must ever stand before my sight?
Your words give solace to this humble slave
For Peace on Earth, Your life, You gave.

I pray our hurts be changed to superficial blights
That will, in time, transform to ascending heights
Recycling a state of radiant glow,
Reflecting Your Love in ours below.

Oh Lord! grant us Peace in thy Heavenly Mercy!! AMEN.

John Dewane Allen III
PLAYBOY
Hello lovely lady,
Could you talk to me,
All those other ladies,
They mean nothing to me,
They were all just games,
To impress my friends,
I would never hurt you,
Just to do it again,
I am just a playboy,
Tearing hearts in two,
It's best to stay away,
Or the next might be you,
I love to tease the girls,
Telling them I'm true,
If you believe my lies,
You're another fool,
You're just another lady,
Come and join the game,
I am just a playboy,
Aren't we all the same,
Don't want to be a playboy,
Tired of playing games,
If love was a candle,
Would you light my flame? . . .

Elinor E I Imbraguglio

Elinor E I Imbraguglio
SO GREAT A PRIZE

Dedicated with love, to my daughter Lynne Wesley Anne, on her fifth birthday.

Dear, into my thoughts you steal
A ray of moonlight, yet more fair;
In the sweetness of your face I see
The reverence of an evening prayer.
Each tiny dimple set in place,
Adds to the beauty of your smile;
While laughter, clear as tinkling chimes,
My every moment does beguile.
The golden curls which frame your face,
Would shame a summer sunset rare;
The coolness of your lovely grace,
Belies the warmness hidden there.
Nor could the blueness of the skies,
But reflect the blueness of your eyes;
Wondrous yet, to think that I—
Might claim as mine, so great a prize!

Sandra M Current
HE WALKS ALONG
He walks along the narrow path, searching;
Searching for someone or something.
He walks along hoping to find this man or object.
As he walks, he asks everyone he meets, "Are you Who I am seeking?"
But the replies are all the same.
Each object he sees, he looks for some sign, but there is none.
He continues on his journey for years and years.
Then he becomes ill; deathly ill.
He is going to die.
Or is he?
It is not his time;
It is not his time.
Something deep inside him helps him.
As he stands on his feet once again, he knows
His searching has ended.
He has found What he was searching for.
Not a person or an object but something inside him.
Something inside all of us.
We all possess it.
We are all part of God.

Amanda Eckler
THE WAY I FEEL

For Scott—this is all I never had the chance to say.

I guess you'll never understand,
Exactly how I feel.
But that's alright,
Cause all I know
Is that these feelings for you,
Are very real.

And if you do not feel the same,
There's nothing I can do.
But trust me, I won't put the blame,
Especially not on you.

So until the time
When things have changed,
I'll patiently wait for you,
And silently watch you.
And hope one day,
You'll feel for me,
The way I feel for you.

Maureen Everett-Madiany
TITLELESS POEMS AND DREAMS
Alone, on a rainy almost spring night, wondering what to
do . . . or not to do in my life.
Is this how Browning, Keats and Poe gave birth to their
hopes, fears and wordless nightmares (commonly known as dreams).
To dream, is not having what you want—but hoping the dream
will someday come true, like wishing for a pony when you're
a kid. Some people grow up and own a whole stable, while
others have still have not ridden a horse. Yes, to dream . . .
Then there is the other kind of dream, the ones we have when sleeping,
they, uncontrollable, lurking
monsters, beautiful myths,
all come to life in the playground of our mind, not minding the time.

J Christine Madeker
DAWN
Dawn.
She wakes without coffee
or complaint.
She wakes silently.
You hardly notice her,
appearing from the horizon.
She smiles and brings the sun,
or she cries and brings the rain.
Dawn.
Mother Nature's daughter.
Awake many hours
never to tire till dusk.
She yawns,
her fingers stretching
toward daybreak.
A new day begins.

Lillie Coleman
REVOLVING TIME

I dedicate this poem to my two daughters, La'Keisha and Nija Howard.

As I travel down the path of life I understand the revolving of the earth with more meaning. I understand that my characteristics values and personality have been lived and reviewed before now and it is now my responsibility for any of my distastefulness to be improved and made more inviting for the next time around.

Kim Hickerson
THAMATOPSIS

Dedicated to my brother, Timothy P. Qualls.

Terror in our hearts,
holds many secrets.
A key that opens it,
may unlock our feelings.
Another horror may cross your mind.
The screams of people passed on,
open up doors that have been closed so long.
Peeping through the keyhole to see,
shadows of the dead walk through the night.
In our hearts and in our souls,
something walks forever.

Zahida Yasin
MY FRIEND

To: a Rare and Wonderful breed of people—My Friend, My Mother, My Brothers.

O, friend of mine as you prepare to leave today,
We sit across a table with not a word to say.

Fighting the tears, do I helplessly gaze,
Into life's predicaments of a neverending maze.

Of responsibilities, duties and unbreakable ties,
Pretending to be brave as I try and disguise.

A storm of feelings that threatens to break,
The calm exterior that I am trying to fake.

O, heart, wish My friend a journey, that's gloriously bon,
Though each ounce of the being wills you not to be gone

So I smile to make light of the minutes at hand,

Laughing to give you strength as you hesitate to stand.

With the knowledge that you care as I do,
And it's not easy for you to leave me too.

Other loved ones need you, and so I must find,
The strength to survive when you leave me behind.

The separation at hand simply has to be faced,
The reality accepted and the grief embraced.

But as your physical self the bird of steel bears away,
As I stand in the shadows, and for your safe trip pray.

You leave behind a glow in your path and I know,
That you're right next to me and forevermore.

Josephine Bincoletto
THE BRIDGE
Move forward. One step at a time.
But never look or go back.
What is behind should be left, and not brought forward with you,
for it can hold you back.

Take each day one at a time. Don't rush.
Time goes by too quickly on its own, and,
you should deal with each minute that passes.

You should not try to control time nor destiny.
For destiny is not planned, or controlled by man,
but by fate.

Nor should you be too anxious to cross a bridge.
But you must wait until you get there, and,
it should be approached with care.

Step by step,
minute by minute,
day by day.

If you are destined to get to the other side,
you will have had a chance to wonder, observe and decide.

Then you may know what is to come, but only if it is destined.

Ardena C Bowles
LIGHT OF LIFE
Noise—like a
crack of thunder
but it wasn't.
A space of seconds
the light
the joy is gone
Never to know again.
Darkness, sadness reigns.

Life continues—sleep is fleeting
a knock on the door
Brilliant light—more so than the
Sun, on its most perfect day.
Oh Joy!
He is the messenger—everything is as
it should be but never again as before.
NO! He cannot tarry someone
waits.

Sleep returns
Life continues.

D M Wolf
MOTHER AND SON
Holding him softly to my breast
a tender smile, a warm caress.
A silent prayer, a sigh of joy
"for a healthy little baby boy."

Hugging him gently and drying his tears
a mother's love will quiet his fears.
Muddy shoes and skinned up knees
"Darlin', don't get dirty, please!"

Welcome him home from football camp
a gridiron hero, a high school champ.
Out every weekend with a different date
"can't seem to sleep when he's out so late."

Remembering the baby I held to my breast
a tender smile, a warm caress.
Thanking the guests, yes, the wedding was nice
"and so were the years between diapers and rice."

Amy Lynn Johnson
TOGETHER FOREVER
I've been waiting for so long,
For a love like ours to come along,
The times before have always been wrong,
But, it's apparent, me and you, well, we belong!

Now that we are together,
We could never be apart,
In the beginning I did not really know . . .
I was not very smart.

But the times have passed, you see
And we have both grown stronger,
All the bad times and the agony,
We both know they are no longer.

We do know, though, that with good comes the bad,
We argue and we fight,
This causes us to be sad,
But, somehow, we always make it right!

Together we will never end,
We will never, ever see,
Our wonderful love and happiness
Grow dim or cease to be!

Mary Alice Leal
WHERE DO DREAMS GO

With love to my dearest D. C. Harlan.

I sit high on the side of a hill,
And see my dreams blow with the wind.
The tops of the trees hold them still.
but my dreams refuse to bend.

I hold you still within my heart,
Tho the years will roll by fast.
My love will never, never depart,
and my fidelity will ever last.

Bring my dreams in from the wind,
So I still may hold them tight.
Ease the doubt within my mind,
So I may carry them into my night . . .

Merle C Hansen
A CHILD IS BORN
A child is born,
And once again the miracle of life
Presents a living portrait
Within the framework of itself for all to see.
And hectic nights
And momentary days
Become fleeting images remembered
In a backward glance with sigh of happiness
As years go by.
But now the inch of life
Is but a glimmer of a promise yet to be
Within the mist of tomorrow's pleasures
To become memories
Held and kept within the self.
And so we greet the new life
With its cry
And softest touch
And smile,
And know the fullness of the allness
That it is,
For a child is born.

Terri L Johnson
DEATH
Death is . . . , the hardest way to say goodbye!
Death in many ways is the hardest thing to face.
It's very scary and very sad.
I wish it would never have happened to two great people like you!

Dawn and Kristen you meant so much to Hollywood Hills High. Just look at all the friends you left behind. We will miss you and always care for you. I think I can speak for everyone when I say . . . , We never have to say goodbye we'll see you again, because for us you two are not really dead. As long as we live, you two will be living inside of all of us. To Dawn and Kristen with love see again in the heavenly sky above.

Elmer G Coffey Sr

Elmer G Coffey Sr
GRANDPA'S LITTLE GIRLS

For Cara, Danielle, Elizabeth, Cheronne, Tammy, Celina, and one to be.

The love and the trust of grandpa's little girls
Are dearer to him than diamonds or pearls.
The glow of their eyes, the bloom of their smiles
Make each a princess from enchanted isles

Their grandma in heaven looks thru grandpa's eyes
And tells him in dreams they are stars in her skies
While on grandpa's lap holding his worn hand
Grandma builds them a mansion in our promised land

Grandpa's little girls as they grow and unfold
Become precious flowers with petals of gold
And when they are grown tho grandpa's not there
Will know in their hearts they are still in his care

Elmer G Coffey Sr
LONELINESS
I can never now be lonely though grandma went away
A part of her has stayed with me, I see her every day
We folded up our golden years into a magic book
If a thought brings lonely tears we open it and look

She is there beside me her soft cheek pressed to mine
We turn the magic pages, a bit of heaven in each line
Nothing in this world today can match our life before
And this magic book of love can open each closed door

The pages of our magic book has dreams and pictures too
Its covers are of life and death, love makes up its glue
There is no word for loneliness none was printed there
All there is of heaven or earth we will always share

Loneliness is just for those who never treasured love
Or lived alone like meteors in orbit up above
When their ending comes, they make a fading flash
But leave no magic book of love, only a trace of ash.

Elmer G Coffey Sr
HEAVEN
I was born in heaven in care of angels three
Mother, father, brother, these angels cared for me
Faces above my cradle warmth to feel and see
Nameless fears and terrors soothed on breast or knee

Food, and care, and shelter everywhere a loving face
Made my childhood heaven it's true there's such a place
I learned to be with others, to give, and take, and share
Home a place with love and someone there to care

But all of life is mortal even angels must move on
And childhood does become of age to face an adult dawn
If I find another heaven beyond life's misty sea
Pray God it be like memories my angels left with me

Christina Russo-Memoli
MY SPECIAL KEY

This poem was written for a special man named Denis Burns.

Your lips acted as a magical key,
Unlocking and setting my feelings free.
Feelings which had been unknown to me,
Until awakened by that magical key.
I am searching for a way to thank thee,
For this wondrous gift you have given me.
I can only say that you must be,
A special man to possess such a key.

Darlene A Merskin
GOING AWAY TO COLLEGE

To my beautiful children Jamie, Lauran, and Jaclyn. Much Love, Mommy.

Time to move on, to learn our
own ways.
To see for ourselves the upcoming days.
To further our lives and strengthen our souls.
To achieve our most efficient goals.
To be confidential, independent and strong.
To learn from our mistakes what is right
and what is wrong.
To see to our needs that will
make us content.
To look to ourselves
for important consents
To see that we're healthy,
able and aware
To look after every
possible care
Coming home to see
those we miss
Greeting those ones
With a loving kiss
being proud of the accomplishments set
Knowing that those goals are met.

Mary Ann Kennedy
THE FATHER'S POEM

To Grandmere.

The Word is made flesh . . .
the Word . . .
conceived within the utterance
of a word
"Fiat"
As love, the seed of God's pure thought
proves a beauty
too exquisite for man to bear
except clothed in the ruse
of his humanity.

Amelia Moreno
A PARENT'S THOUGHTS

This poem is dedicated to my children Monica, Melba, and Laurie.

When I feel like my children are slipping away
outgrowing the years of childlike play
My eyes become misty and my heart a bit sad.
Then I remember the good times we had.

The following memories set me at ease
giving my heart a beautiful peace.
One Winter, you were sick in bed with the flu.
All day and all night I took care of you.
So many times you needed my care
to tie a shoelace or to comb your hair.
Some nights I would hug you and dry all your tears
Gently I'd comfort and calm all your fears.

There were bedtime stories and oh, much more.
It's almost impossible to keep up the score.
The times at the park, the swings and such,
I loved you my child so very much.

Through your teenager years, I stood by your side
though at times, in me you refused to confide.
Sometimes you'd be grumpy, sometimes you felt fine.
I had to be patient and so very kind.
I tried to be a good parent, I did my best.

Amelia Moreno
A SPECIAL FRIEND
I have a special friend
who knows me very well.
He leads me by the hand
His love will never fail.

This friend of mine is Jesus
and from me he'll never part.
He promised always to be near me
when I asked Him into my heart.

There's no one who can help me
the way that my friend does,
So when the storms of life arrive,
in Him I place my trust.

Whenever in deep sorrow
or in any kind of pain,
I call on my friend Jesus
and start to praise his name.

Never does it matter
what the circumstance may be . .
He already won the battle
when He died at Calvary.

Nina Miller
REVERIE
Remember when my hair was black?
That was several light years back.
In my reverie I see
A precious moment . . you and me,
Strolling down the lane from church,
We passed beneath a shady birch.
We're standing there, and with a knife
Carved our names, as if for life . . .
We'd be together . . never part.
But another took your heart.

Of course you don't remember me.
You are gone. So is the tree.

Michael Aldieri
THE WALL
Stone black
Those who came back
Stand silent
The names are faces
Black stone
Families alone
Weep softly
The names still live
The names engraved
Forever saved
In stone that reflects
Those who come to look
for a name
a face
a reason.

Bess Turk
HOW OFTEN
How often has a flower bloomed
The thoughts you wish to say
How often has a marigold
Brushed gloom from out your way
A rosebud filled with promise
Of a future yet unknown
Can lift the sorrow from your heart

And as you look
You're not alone

How often have you watched great waves
Sweep footprints from the shore
And tumble noble castles made
Whose fragile walls your dreams did store
Those castles are your memories
Which waves cannot destroy
And footprints once upon the shore

Remain within
Those marks are yours

How often have your child's tears
Brought longing to your heart
To banish all those ugly fears
And fill the space with love
Yet only loving arms
Can give your child the strength to know
He has to live with honest thoughts

And when he hurts
That's when he grows

Bess Turk
A WINTER'S WALK BESIDE THE RIVER
Walk beside the river under open skies
Mark your steps with patience on the frosted ferns
Listen to the silence of the passing mist

Pause to hear the stretching of the icy limbs
Wonder at the patterns on the frozen shore
Feel the finite smallness of this time and place

Know that only changes bring the force for life
Enjoy the simple sameness of nature's muted voice
Accept that after darkness comes the glare of light

Hannah Mendelsohn
THE LAST MILE
The old man stood as rugged as the land he surveyed and called home. After all the years of strife, back breaking work, to find himself alone. Yes, his sons were all gone to a far richer clime, and had long departed. His wife had passed on and so he had the place to himself, though broken hearted.
He was up every dawn to greet the sun, to talk to the wind and last star. To tend the chores, to walk over the moors and gather wood for his fire. Each day his steps grew more slow and the moor seems rugged and bare. If it weren't for his dog he'd not venture forth, but Rover liked chasing the hare. So man and his friend travel along to the end. Up and down life's highway they plod in search of the end and the stair that will lead to Heaven and God.

John H Sparks
BACK IN SCHOOL WHEN THINGS MADE CENTS
Back in school when things made cents
there was a field trip
there were ten and they knew the subject
and they knew some other things
and the leaders knew the subject
but they didn't know the other things
no
these ten intended to change the world
and they could have it was within their grasp
It was the seed
they wanted to plant it in the hills
the hill where things could grow
and things were green
they almost succeeded with the planting
they didn't get to plant
but the granite knows
the granite knows
buried below
the ten told someone for they were a part
and the seed
the seed

the smell of the hunt

Lisa Gonet Randleman
COME WITH ME THROUGH MY MIND
Come with me through my mind,
and I will take you back in time.
When all was right and nothing wrong,
in days of love and nights of song.
Come with me through my mind,
and I will take you back in time.
Where all was good and nothing bad,
when all were happy and no one sad.

Come with me through my mind,
and I will take you back in time.
Where love abounds and there is no woe,
please come with me, won't you go?
Come with me through my mind,
and I will take you back in time.
This time won't you take my hand,
for this time it will be most grand.
To see the things that should be now,
we must bring them back somehow.
For all the world to live in peace,
bringing past to present,
future . . .
eternity.

Richard K Payne
LITTLE FROGGIES
I think of little froggies
And blankets on the bed;
I think of little doggies
And bikies in the shed.

I think of little kitties
And ball games in the yard;
I think of little mitties
And hearties on the card.

I think of little boaties
And splashing in the pool;

I think of little coaties
And workies with a tool.

I think of little mommies
And daddies hugging tight;
I think of little sissies
And bobbies through the night.

Leamon L Jones
SAY NO TO DRUGS
Drugs will make you do the wrong things for money.
Drugs do not taste like honey.
"Say No to Drugs" it is the right thing to do,
What I am saying is so, so true.
You will feel like a pinwheel when it spins,
Drugs can start from a glass of wine or gin.
You need to keep in mind, "Say No To Drugs"
I am talking about marijuana, crack and coke.
Dealing with all kinds of drugs, is no joke.
Drugs are not your friend,
It will bring your life to an end.

James E Bice
PERHAPS
Perhaps in the next world we will be
Two clouds, floating high, out of sight
Or, two shadows of an old oak tree,
Or even two whispers in the night.

In that next life, we will be there
Just as we are here today,
And we're there as a pair
To believe in what we say.

Just as stones are set in rings
And soft notes come from a band.
Perhaps, we will be many things,
Or . . . just two lovers . . .
hand in hand.

Christine R Witt
i and IT
you said you'd call . . .
you
never
did.

i thought i'd never fall in step with . . .

. . . IT!

IT sneaks up fast with quiet feet,

IT may not last and you sure won't succeed,

for IT is something . . .
sweet
and
short.
i thought i'd find nothing—nothing of the sort,
IT can be blue as sky or white like a Dove,
IT'll cause you to CRY . . .
for
IT
is
LOVE! ! !

Betsy A Schlosburg
TOO MUCH LOVE
My arms were aching;
My lips began to pout.
I had so much love to give
That it was just pleading to come out.

I had three children;
Another on its way.
Still, I felt I had more love
To give them than they needed today.

They needed my love;
Did not need all of it.
I was deeply hurt but said:
"No, I do not really care a bit!"

Just like He knew this,
God let the fourth child live.
And made her the kind of child
Who needed all the love I could give.

Rita Wilkins

Rita Wilkins
MY PRAYER

To Jim Bjornzin, Pastor, Grace Lutheran Church.

It's been so long since I've let you in—let you into my heart—because of my pride I've been so wrong—And I drifted apart—Only you can help me in all the wrong I've done—Only you "Dear Lord" You are the Only One—

My eyes are full of teardrops—my heart is full of pain—my mind is oh so weary help me to regain—Walk with me along the path—until I get halfway—and if I start to turn around—Kneel me down to pray—I need you in my heart "Dear Lord" as I take this test—And for every step you've walked with me I will walk the rest—I will ask for your forgiveness as I walk along—My fears will be behind me—for I'll know I'm not alone—That's my prayer to You Dear Lord Thank you for the start—You'll always be here with me always in my heart—

Michael Knight
SWEET BUT PAINFUL MEMORIES
I remember the good times we used to have together
Not caring how good or bad the weather
I remember kissing her after a date
Neither one caring if we were late
I remember the park those many nights
Holding each other and watching the city lights
I remember those roses I used to send
Saying I love you, and hoping it would never end
The times we spent together were great
Us being together seemed like fate
Somehow, our love just didn't last
It was like our heart got hit by a cannon blast
I think of her every night until the dawn
I still can't believe that she is gone
Sweet but painful the memories are
My heart is but a giant scar
She is gone forever that's for sure
Until I find another, I'll just endure

Alisha Michelle Groene
MEMORIES
Memories are so special
they make us feel warm inside
They take away the pain
and fill us up with pride.
Some take away the hurt
whenever we are down
Some bring back the tears
that make us want to frown.
Some are very special
some are very sad
Some of them they hurt so much
it really makes us mad,
They make us think of the things we miss
and hope someday they'll grant a wish,
They lift up our hopes and make us smile
holding on tight for a very long while,
Sometimes I wonder if my dreams are real
and if it's love they make me feel,
I think that it would be very smart
if we kept our memories deep
in our heart!

Tammie Helton
MIRROR IMAGE
I can see you,
Standing in the rain . . .
So ragged and so worn.
Your face tells the story
of your strength, in your lifetime
Your heart, shattered and torn . . .
You don't seek shelter
Nor do you warmth,
You stand as tall as you can,
Wrapping your arms around yourself . . .
Taking on life's tragedies. .
And with each day,
You've grown with wisdom . . .
Yet, pain stays deep in your eyes.
A man can only take so much before he dwindles to nothing . . .
I only wish strength upon him . . .
Now, everything is blurred,
So I, rub my eyes so that I may see,
Clearly, I gaze from a daze into a mirror,
My Lord, it's me . . . .

Lori Jean Bills
IS IT LOVE YOU'RE INTERESTED IN?
As I sit here
Watching the time go by,
I wonder if I'll hear from you,
Or if I'll die
Not knowing if you love me,
Or if your heart beats for another.
Sometimes I have to wonder
If I'll see you again
And if there's only one thing you want
Or is it love you're interested in?
Will my heart get broken,
Or will you save me that pain?

Joydev Acharya
EULOGY
You could have been the bomb
That raised buildings where it fell.
The eyes of the blind could have opened
With the acid you sprayed.
You could have shouted from your pedestal
And even God would have listened.

But misused abused
Confused reduced
You've buried everything

Grand fish could have been caught
In the waters you polluted.
Battlefields could have been fairgrounds
With the armies you saluted.
You could have been the fact
That made the dreams of children come true.

You had the power
Now we give you the honor
Of a minute's NOISE.

Billie J Gora
STARTING OVER
One day soon your life will start over again, in answer to many a prayer,
"God," hears them all, answers in "His," time, "His," promise, not to give us more than we can bear.
It's a wonderful world, full of sunshine and light, each day an experience brand new.
Keep your prayers many, be thankful, be brave, your faith will carry you through.
One day soon, this journey will end, then a brand new one will start.
Let "God," make your plans, you carry them out, you need only pack love in your heart.
Life doesn't always seem fair my son, but, neither are we at our best—
Put your life in "his Hands," confess all your sins, and "He," will take care of the rest.
"He," has "His Reasons," a time and a place, for everything that "He" does,
Maybe "He" planned your days as "He," did, so you could reflect on your life as it was.
"He," wants to hold us so tightly in "His arms," that we just could not fall,
Our "Heavenly Father," is so good to us and we are not worthy at all!
"He," also gives us a choice, so being the children we are,
We must wrestle free, make our mistakes, we take our eyes off the "Star."
There are times that I feel like a very spoiled child, I get everything that I yearn for.
I've come to know, that "God," loves me so, I'm safe, forgiven and loved more and more.
Yes, one day soon your life will start over again, in answer to many a prayer,
Put your old life behind you, the new one in "His hands," and you'll find that you'll live free from care.

Lorraine H Leftwich
MY TREASURES
Treasures I have stored only I can find,
stored for safekeeping away in my mind.
My treasures are my memories sometimes I like to share,
but I'm rather selfish and wish to keep them there.

My treasure chest is full of memories I hold dear,
some of them are new and some from yesteryear.
Some are tarnished with age and some are faded so,
but to me they're precious and I hate to let them go.

I like to view my treasures and sometimes browse awhile,
at times they bring tears and other times a smile.
Then I leave them alone tucked safely away,
until I have the time to browse on another day.

My treasures are not for sale, their price would be too high,
but I'll tell you a secret, your treasures are close by.
So when you find your treasures, I'm sure they will be
just as precious to you as mine are to me.

Iris Swink

Iris Swink
MY EYES
My eyes have gazed upon
The beauty of a rose,
The soft red petals
Of their fragrance.
My eyes have seen the
Beauty of the fluffy flakes,
Of pure white snow that falls
To this great earth below.
The twinkle of the stars at night,
The moon, the sun, the clear blue sky.

My eyes behold the trees,
As the breeze rustles through
Their mystic green leaves.
My mother's soft sweet face,
My children's smiles and tears,
My husband's joy each year,
As he hunts the wildwood deer.

What more precious gift on earth,
Could God have given me
Than these two eyes for me to see?

Penelope
UNRESOLVED
There they sit locked in bars,
Those haggard boots and a silent guitar.

Waiting for the boy who used to play,
And walked in the boots through the mountain each day.

A boy so tall you might remember
A deep seeded boy who's a family member.

The youngest of the group he never had a chance,
To pay the piper and learn to dance.

You see you came from den of wolves,
Of devils Angels and conning fools.

The school has taught you all too well,
Then put you in that dingy cell.

I'm waiting for the day when you'll be free,
To live in this world like others and me.

Until that time in steel and stone
You will be standing all alone.

But don't remorse my dear, dear brother,
For in this world there will be another.

To stand in there by you,
Waiting for the days afar.

To walk in haggard boots once more,
And play their silent guitar.

Cathryn Ellisor Lacey
MUSING ON A MATCH
I see a match all burnt and black.
Life to itself will ne'er come back.
But it has served its purpose well.
It lit a fire in one small cell.
And burning brightly through the years,
It grew with joy and died with tears.
Until its lonely life was spent,
Through the all-consuming fire it went.
It disappeared as it had begun
And went the way that it had come.

Dodi Spain
DEPARTURE
You left,
passing through
eternal gates
of love left
open;

My mind could not
comprehend
your absence
until I saw your
picture
and knew that
was all I had left
of you.

Heather Pimley
TRUE FRIENDS
A real true friend doesn't doubt you,
they help you.
A real true friend doesn't laugh at you,
they enhance you.
A real true friend doesn't hurt you,
they heal you.
But most of all,
A real true friend doesn't desert you,
they're there for you.

Vera Delgado Irwin
HOW WONDERFUL IT WOULD BE
When a baby is born into this world,
We say to those we see;
Oh! To receive that love and tender care—
How Wonderful It Would Be.

As the infant grows into its childhood,
Things begin to feel strange;
Each year brings more responsibility—
Life's suddenly filled with change.

Now at last the child becomes adult,
It's great! you hear him say;
He has a family now to care for—
His own child to love each day.

Yes the cycle of life continues,
The "little child" is grown;
He's too busy though to give back love—
Like his dad made sure he'd known.

So now the old man's surely forgotten,
What loneliness he sees;
Just to receive some tender loving care—
How Wonderful It Would Be.

Vicki L Rivas
MAGICAL DREAMS
Little elves and fairies
Come out at night to play
In a land of magical unicorns
Where all is bright and gay.
The stars are always twinkling
And the sun is always bright,
Forest green is everywhere
With castles sparkling white.
The sea is full of mermaids
That are riding on the waves,
The dragons are always lurking
In the darkest of the caves.
It's a land of make believe
Where dreams have their start,
For deep inside each one of us
There is a child's heart.
But sunshine brings another day
An ending to our dreams,
And with nighttime comes the fairies
And all the other things.

Dale D Stockberger
TO MOM AND DAD
A loving Mom and Dad throughout these many years.
You've shared my joy and happiness and helped to dry my tears.
You've molded me to manhood, you guided me along.
You praised when I was right and scolded when I was wrong.

You watched my form develop and tried to help my mind.
And when I really needed it you paddled my behind.
Your caring always present, your love steadfast and true.
And when I had a problem I could always come to you.

When I was sad and lonely, when I thought that all was lost.
You always stood beside me, no matter what the cost.
When I was feeling better you'd send me on my way.
And though I didn't know it, you'd made mine a better day.

I've penned these lines to praise you on this your special day.
To say thanks for loving me in your very special way.
I'm glad that you two married and have given me my life.
I love you Mom and Dad, you're a special man and wife.

Mrs LaVerne Shaeffer
LITTLE THINGS
Thank You, Lord, for each little thing,
For a host of them each new day will bring.
Like sunshine bright on a dew-kissed morn,
Or a wobbly little animal just newly born.
There's a happy little bird, so gracefully a-wing,
Wait patiently a moment; he'll light and sing.
There's been a new birth,—God's gift from heaven,
His parents have him named; he'll be called Kevin.
Now savor fragrant roses along the way,
Enjoy a child's laughter as he runs out to play.
There's a dog's tail a-wagging as he spies his playmate,
Nothing can stop him as he soars o'er the gate.
All these bring us joy without compare,
Little things that make our world so bright and fair.
So Thank You, Lord, for each little thing,
That causes our hearts to rejoice and sing.
"Little things," did I say? They're really not so small,
When the pleasures they've brought us, we later recall!
So, Thank You, Lord, for each day that we live,
To enjoy all these blessings you so freely give.

Jaymie Hunter
JOURNEY

To my daughter, Cari . . . my special traveling companion.

They brought you to me.
They laid you in my arms.
They walked away and left us alone.

I took your tiny hand and brought it to my lips.
Your fingers curled around mine and held them tight.
You found me.

Your soft and gentle face looked up and sought mine.
I reached out and brought you to my breast.
I found you.

They peeked in the door.
I smiled and waved them away.
We didn't need them anymore.

Our journey began.

Orsolina C Garisto
THE MISTY SHADOW OF DEATH
The rippling water,
glimmered softly in the silver moonlight.
The autumn rain coldly pierced my

back,
freezing my thoughts and making my tears flow.
The blur of the world stood before me,
as the bright lights of the city
shone through the darkness of the night.
The misty shadow of the world
lingered amidst the air,
and passed me by on the bridge.
The faint murmur of city life grew louder.
Honking horns skimmed my thoughts
as hazy objects raced into the foggy scene ahead,
which blurred with each flowing tear.

I walked in the rain, enduring my pain and misery
while I fantasized of a time of peace.
A cool autumn breeze blew past the bridge,
I followed the misty shadow of death
into the beauty of the night.
As the glimmer of the rippling water
captured my soul,
I embraced the silver moonlight,
and my spirit was free.

Carla Lemmer
THE FORMLESS CLOUDS
The formless clouds,
Occupying little of the empty space,
in the low sunken sky,
Capture my attention.
The colourless dusk is only to cover
what is hidden behind,
The part that nobody sees.
The time I spend gazing out beyond
the boundaries,
I try to create a picture in my mind,
The clouds take its shape,
My thoughts and sights get mixed,
Soon my mind turns to figureless
shapes that wonder in my head.

Ryan Thayer
LET THERE BE LIGHT
I can go everywhere or anywhere,
focus on one object or many;

I can be reflected,
or deflected;

I can blind you,
yet help you see;

I can be very bright,
or be very dim;

I am found in space,
and found on earth;

I can be useful,
or harmful;

I can be magnified,
or nullified;

I can shine,
and also glow;

I am not darkness,
I am light.

Julia M Sibley
REMEMBER ME
Remember me at sunrise when the mists are on the sea.
When the new dawn has a rosy tint,
And gulls are flying free.
Remember me.

Remember me at noonday when
you're busy as can be—
When the hours aren't long enough,
And the end you cannot see.
Remember me.

Remember me when sunset's flame is
painting every tree.
When all the earth has a scarlet glow,
And day's end is soon to be.
Remember me.

Remember me when evening comes,
with a rest, a book, and tea.
With quiet hours at a long day's end,
And there's time for reverie.
Remember me.

Michael Miller
REMEMBERING
Since just a child I'm taught many things,
About world peace across centuries.
About how we joined to form one land,
And how we offered loving hands.
But there was a time, that I was told,
A time long ago across years manyfold.
Where people warred and killed and fought,
And shed their blood without a thought.
What brought them to it? What made them fight?
What made them feel such utter spite?
They say also too, their lands laid dead,
Destroyed by the ashes that the sky had shed.
The rockets flared up into the sky,
But just listen to how everyone died.
Consumed by a fire, a brutal storm,
Who knows what screams the flame had torn.
While on they advanced, to conquer a world,
And centuries of work were then unfurled.
Then the last two soldiers fired their rounds,
And both lay dead, sprawled out on the ground.

Teresa A Thayer
PEOPLE AND POEMS
People who write poems they say,
Have new thoughts on yesterday;
We shuffle them, we throw them,
We let them waste away.
So maybe a poem might grow there someday.

You can really imagine what goes through our heads,
The symphony of life to even spark the dead.

If only people could see our fine minds, and thoughts
We'd find everything we seek, and all that we sought.

So people who write poems, must all agree
That the spirit of essence is not pure fantasy.

Vivian V Womble
MAN'S DESTINATION
In the beginning of time God created form,
of how man and woman
existed and what they
performed.
In a world that was pure and untouched by man,
he called this world earth, our
mother land.
As earth revolved and man grew wise,
he needed no God, nor rules to
abide.
For he thought of himself as the power of time,
to conquer and control all
means of mankind.
He had no knowledge of what to expect,
when God produced his holy
text.
Those who believe in only the Lord,
will share my environment in
a place up above.
For no man has the power to undo what I've done,
because I am the power and
man is just one.
I've placed on earth a kingdom to be ruled,
but not by man, the
"individual fool."
To have thought of himself to rule over me,
for "I" am the divine in all that
he sees.
I'll start over new, and begin more creations,
for this beginning has reached
its destination.

Mary Pat Bragers
THE WISH
Break in over me,
bring me back with you;
Roll me in your fierce embrace
amidst a wall of blue.

Take me to the depths,
where it is calm and still
To become a part of none but you,
this is what I will.

Do not cry for me, it is not pity
that I crave.
For 'tis not death, but life renewed
I seek beneath these waves.

Coleen Walker
LOVE
Love is something you cannot buy,
Not even with dollars so high
Because it's found within
the heart of freedom

Love can be found
Not only in the people around:
For it's there within a heart
An art of love

Love is the key to true success
It is found through joy
But although you haven't succeeded
A heart of love is pure riches

Keotah M Fannin

Keotah M Fannin
I DREAM OF YOU

A Book of Poems is like a good friend—easy on the mind.

You come to me
in my darkest hour
like a velvet petal
from a fragile flower.

Softly falling
in a gleam of light
to ease the sorrow
of a sleepless night.

When life is gone
love lingers on
memories flow in
with the coming dawn

Not all the poems I write
nor all the dreams I dream
will end the sleepless nights
or bring you back to me.

Vella H Winning
FEAST OF THE WILD BIRDS
Each morning, as the sun begins to rise,
I feed the wild birds gathered 'round my home.
They wait for me, aligned on fence and bough,
But do not venture forth to feast until
I quietly withdraw to unseen parts
To watch them take the bounty I provide.
No stationary feeder for these friends.
I throw the seed they have to go and find.
And 'mid much pecking, sturdy beaks and beady eyes
Ferret out each seed in record time.
The birds provide for me a daily treat;
Occasionally, a stranger wanders in,
A traveler bound for warmer climes than ours,
Who eats his fill and journeys on, complete.
I gaze in wonder at my daily guests
Sparrows, doves and finches, side by side.
Black crows, grackles, cactus wrens come 'round
Each seems content to stay awhile, to bide
And fill themselves, then wander off again.
But come the dawn, they'll lie in wait for me
To spread again my sumptuous feast for them.

M B Sagall
THE TRAVELER
Through portraits new
From memories old
And storybooks
Of days more bold,
In a room full of toys
And forgotten schemes
I have searched
For lost and magical
dreams.
Though years have passed
The room has not
changed,
Just the toys and the dreams
And me rearranged.

Kostadinka
NEW DAY
Neither gull nor osprey
stirred the void
of sight or sound.
The silence cloyed.

Young Phoebus crowned
the crest of dawn
brighter than the chariot
he rode upon.

Draw near, new day,
but just the finger tips
will toss a greeting skyward
from parted lips.

Vanessa Benjamin
AN INCREDIBLE TRIP
One night I had an incredible trip,
when I put the straw to my lip.
Then it happened when taking a drink,
oh no, I was starting to shrink.
Rapidly down the slippery straw,
sliding like a penguin on ice in awe.
Then swoosh, I hit liquid deliciously sweet,

and was covered with cocoa from head to feet.
Churning, twisting, and gasping for air,
but where in the world was I, oh where?
Suddenly bump, I got stuck,
on a big, white marshmallow; just by luck.
All of a sudden a whirlpool started, circling round and round; back up the straw I departed.
I was up to the top as quick as a wink,
and it seemed like my brain had no time to think.
Hey hold it, I smell hot chocolate, and I'm lying in bed,
so this entire journey was a silly dream instead.

Polly Lloyd Beck
AN ODE TO A FRIEND

To: Louise P. Lloyd, my sister-in-law, whom I consider my "sister" & dearest Christian friend.

Ever so often the earth is blessed with a soul
whose beauty seems eternal.
I have found that beauty in you, my friend,
whose qualities are quite maternal.
You are so gracious your very being
exudes the gentleness of a lamb.
Ah, but quick to rise straight forward
when wrong seemingly gets
the upper hand.
Your children shall call you blessed, they've
been taught which road to take.
The "Good Book" says that when they're old,
it's something they'll not forsake.
Only God could have filled your heart with such
genuine love and respect.
It seems that no matter what the situation,
your tendency is to forgive
and forget.
Understanding others and their feelings
is just a natural part of you.
Why, had our paths never crossed,
what in the world would I do?

D M Stoutsenberger
LONELINESS

To the memory of my wife, Constance Alice Stoutsenberger.

A terrible preoccupation with trying to not be alone,
fills a widowed night cut with stark cold loneliness.
Cherished thoughts and memories contrast to the bone,
chills void of even the face of my hapless happiness.

Time is compressed and stretched along a crazy order,
four months of loss, lost love seems like four years.
Seventeen years of tender togetherness like a summer,
for the hours seem to have stopped; as weary winters.

Every desperate grasp at a chance of our normal life,
thrashes my soul with conflicting emotional thoughts.
Crying, trying to be happy, simple tasks, and strife,
trashes my sight, hurts in my head, throat, and guts.
Working at being busy, so every daylight hour filled,
but not one little accomplishment to say, "it's done."
All the sleepless parts of the night, mind unstilled,
but wrestling midnight demons for a glimpse; reunion.

Penny S Bennett
GARDEN OF STONE
Here my husband lies in darkness and cold,
Here in the place they call the garden of stone.
Where rows and rows of markers tell of soldiers I don't know.
But still sadness arises from deep in my soul,
For so many have come here to this garden of stone.
Never to see the loved ones they left back at home,
The people who loved them, their family and friends,
Their lovers and children whose hearts can never mend.
This is war, no matter how awful but true.
These men gave their lives for me and for you.
Just remember this thought when you go by the gates,
And please stop and put flowers on all of their graves.
Here in this white garden of stone, where they lay,
Asleep here forever, in peace may they stay.

Steven G DeConti
SOMETIMES

To Nikos, Twain and all the others with tenacious soul.

sometimes i dream of
verdant undulating hills
and perpetual blue skies

redolent fields of poppy
and indigo-blue seas

a world free

from the primordial malediction
of the question of cosmogony
with its endless search for answers
with minds profound

and the stalwart yearning
to capture time

a world where man, women and
every living creature
can walk side by side

and do obeisance
to reality's ephemeral beauty

to understand that
god is not beyond reason

not beyond love, truth
and supreme equilibrium

to understand that as we saunter
through life

god walks along side

Gaye Sauvager Fine
THE PASSING OF TIME

To our son Jeremy, whose short life touched those who knew him with the special wonder of love. Jeremy Victor Fine, May 31, 1989—September 18, 1989.

Someone who's born
Must also pass on
Leaving an empty spot
Where once there was a son

So sweet and so innocent
A smile that shone so bright
Yet the Lord needed you more
So you passed on that night

My precious son, my baby
You suffered a lifetime's worth
Since that beautiful day three short months ago
That day I gave you birth

At least I know you suffer no more
And you have someone there who cares
I love you, Jeremy, my darling son
God willing, I will be with you there

In Loving Memory,
Your Mommy

Elaine C Mandulak
WHISPERING

To my daughter Elaine Diana who is the light of my life.

Was that you whispering my name?
Elaine—Elaine.
Could I be so vain
To think you were calling my name?
The memories come flowing back
Of our forgotten youth and love
There! ! Did you hear?
Elaine—Elaine.

Angie Hall
ABUSED
She's a child who's dirty;
She's a child who's sad.
He's a man of thirty;
He's a man who's bad.

She's a child abused;
She's a child who cries.
He's the man accused;
He's the man who lies.

A tear he should have shed;
A love he should have shown.
Now his daughter is dead,
and his love unknown.

Rebecca K Walker
LOOKING ON
As I stand here on the shoreline
watching the waves breaking
endlessly upon the sand and then
returning from where they came
I think to myself Why

Why am I standing here looking on
out over the water to where I've
never been or will ever be
yet in that I find peace

The feeling of being free to roam new
places where I've never been yet
always returning to where I belong

Never fitting in yet never an outcast
Onward, searching for that place
where everything is peaceful and in
its own place never to search again,
but endlessly Looking On.

Aleece Y Jones
OUR FRIENDSHIP
It seems like as far as I can think back,
You have been a large part of my life.
At times it was hard to keep focused, on track,
But between us we found ways to do away with the strife.

With us sharing plays such a big part,
To understand, was to be each other's best friend.
Never to take one another for granted was the start,
To heal, was to help wounded feelings to mend.

Being able to trust one another, the most important thing,
We are strong enough to have different opinions.
This kind of peace only a real friendship can bring,
It's like being in a calm place, a tranquil dominion.

For us to remain as friends it requires work and understanding,
Allowing for each of us a chance to grow.
This will make for the best relationship with no demanding,
Where the seeds of admiration we freely sow.

In loving memory
of My Grandmother:
Ms. Emma Deverall Ewing

Vienna Rambo
ONE DAY
Funny how many
things happen
In just one day
"When it rains it pours"
they say
In just one day
One gets married
One graduates
One moves
One leaves forever
Everyone has
left me
In just one day
So many thoughts
thru my mind
In just one day
They'll remember me
and what love is
One day

Alba Natalicchio
THE FOREST

This poem is dedicated to my sister, Mary Earle, and to my friend, Marilyn Kingsley.

The sun I glimpse through
forests deep
Brings new hope to the
dreams I keep
The darkness lasts but for a while,
For through the mist, the sun's rays
smile.
In this earthy, quiet place,
Attempting to conquer the
fears I face,
Oh, I have learned and I have grown!
In beams of love the
sun has shone.
In a verdant tapestry of my mind
I continue to search, to find
The wisdom of this life's mystique,
As oaks of change around
me creak.
The wooded path I walk leads on
Away from the darkness, into
the dawn.
A brilliant land I barely see
Lies just beyond, awaiting me!

Carmella Celedonia
THE VALLEY BELOW

Dedicated to memories of yester-years.

As I sit here on my patio high above the valley below
I think of the days when I was young and living in the valley below
With memories of my childhood and the friends I knew
With the walks through the valley on our way to school
Skipping and jumping along the way
The valley has changed from days I was young
The horse track is a thing of the past
And building of homes grew so fast
The wooden side walks are no more
With horse drawn fire trucks and the fish peddler too
All through the valley you would hear the call
Umbrella man and knife sharpener here
A bell would be ringing and the fruit huxter appears
With horse drawn wagon selling his wares
Grapes, red apples, celery, lettuce, and tomatoes too
Sweet memories of when I lived in the valley below
The shoe cobbler came and sat on the porch
Fixing our shoes and lacing them too
The ice man cometh with large blocks of ice
Chipping and slicing for a price

And children following for a piece of the ice
Yes those were the days I remember so well
When I was young and lived in the valley below.

Charles L Wynn Sr

Charles L Wynn Sr
NOW

To my tender beloved wife, Cynthia! You are my world, and this is only the beginning!

Now is the time for love to flow, to come and go like the clouds. Constant, everflowing, some stormy, some calm, but always there for you and I.

Now is the time the angels sing. The doves of love send their blessed message upon their wings. From me to you, again and again.

Now is the time for love to flow. To cover the hate and bitterness I know. How much I love and miss you so, is something so awesome we may never know.

Being away from you tends to hurt me so.
Knowing I no longer can love you, tends to also destroy me more.
But even more so, now is the time for love to flow.

Charles L Wynn Sr
LOVE

Love takes time. It needs a history of giving and receiving, laughing and crying.

Love never promises instant gratification, only ultimate fulfillment. Love means believing in someone in something. It supposes a willingness to struggle to work, to suffer, to rejoice. Satisfaction and ultimate fulfillment are by-products of dedicated love. They belong only to those who can reach beyond themselves, to whom giving is more important than receiving.

Love is doing everything you can to help others build whatever dreams they have. Love involves much careful and active listening. It is doing whatever needs to be done and saving whatever will promote the other's happiness, security and well-being.

Sometimes love hurts. Man does it hurt, but love is on a constant journey to what others need. It must be attentive, caring and open, both to what others say and to what others cannot say. Love says no with empathy and great compassion. Love is firm, but when needed it must be tender. When others have tried and failed, love is the hand in yours, in your moments of discouragement and disappointment.

Love is reliable. Love is choice and commitment to other's true and lasting happiness. It is dedicated to growth and fulfillment. Love is not selfish. Love sometimes fails for lack of wisdom or abundance of weakness, but it forgives knowing the intentions are good.

Love does not attach conditions. Genuine love is always a free gift. Love realizes and accepts that there will be disagreements and disturbing emotions. There may be times when miles lay between, but love is a commitment. It believes and endures all things.

Love encourages freedom of self. Love shares positive and negative reactions to warm and cold feelings. (As one) intimate love will never reject each other, only others. It is the first to encourage and the last to condemn. Love is a commitment to growth, happiness and fulfillment of one another.

A G Myrick
I AM NOT A MAN OF WIT

Nowdays, would hymns to oneself be considered
computer age self-indulgence, littered
with calls to needs, anxieties, pains, embittered
by the simple breath of life,
awash with the waves of strife,
Battered by the lack of existence blithe?

Enough! Enough! Enough! I agree, Walt
But few things that come to pass are my fault,
Yet of the lions.
Lions of the night, beasts of incredible might
That stalk the meek and inhale the weak
Beasts of onerous wrath, destroying all in their path
The tree is no haven, its bark by their paws shaven
Its limbs by their weight broken, their prey of small token
For what they gather, they do not seek
It lies not within their sight to see
The wash of life's bath,
Or, the words of life's verse.

I would like to sing a song of myself as well
but the time has been changed,
And I no longer recognize the melody.

Ron Harvey
**JEFF & PATTY—
TOGETHER AS ONE**

To all couples starting life together.

We were kids in school
when we met each other,
We knew at first glance that
we were meant for one another.
We dated and went together
for a number of years,
We discussed our future,
our hopes, and our fears,
Our love was strong,
and plans looked great.
When we were out of school,
no longer would we wait.
Even though the world
pressures crowded in,

We knew our love and trust
would forever win.
Then came that day
under the old walnut tree,
We exchanged our vows,
I love you, and you love me.
Our lives welded together
now as one,
We knew the most precious thing
in life we had won.
We've started our lives of being together
Our love and trust is strong and
any storm it can weather.
Even though the years come and go
We know our love and understanding
will always grow.
If we live to be a hundred years or more
We'll never forget, September 1st, 1984.

Lou Adamo
KAREN

Karen,
Together for sixteen months, we have endured life's giving
Early on, times were joyful and happy.
Some of the better moments of living.
Although what was new and intriguing
Has since past.
A new life has yet begun.
One that will forever last.
It will take long and hard work,
To hold what we cherish
In a period of time agreed.
Holy Ghost will be the parish.
So with few and little words
I would like to share my life
with a special individual of caring love
I ask you, Karen Marie Peterson, to be my wife.
Your response will be treasured,
through all the times of tears and laughter
But the commitment I ask of you is
now and forever after on this ninth
day of April, the year nineteen
hundred and eighty-eight. I ask of
you for your hand in Holy Matrimony.

Angela Walsh
REFLECTIONS OF LITTLE BATTERED JOHNNY

Each year at Christmas time
Johnny's friends would ask Santa
for elaborate train sets
expensive Model T's and toy cars

But all Johnny ever wanted
was a family who knew how to love
he dreamed of a Christmas
with no bruises or scars

Johnny's father tried to control him
and gain respect by using violence
but instead of making Johnny strong
it left him weak in a confused state of silence!

Ben Wilkinson
BIG JIM I HEARD YOU

I heard you call
I could not answer.
I hear your desperate pleas for help
I could not give you aid.
I heard your screams of pain.
I could not soothe you.
I heard you scream my name
I could not answer.
I heard bullets pound into your body
I could not cover you.
I heard you dying
I could not save you.
A mere thirty yards apart we were
But both held by sniper fire
Both in a dead zone
And both in war's hell.
Understand this Big Jim
I heard your cries then
I hear your cries now
And I am sorry.

Elizabeth Zayas
LOVERS SYNDROME

Meet me in the desert tonight,
And we'll drink champagne by candlelight.
We'll trace the stars to the moon so high,
We'll share our secrets with the sky.

We'll melt our dreams together,
and form a crystal fountain;
Where an everlasting flow of diamonds,
Falls from high above the mountains.

Meet me by the ocean's shore,
And we'll build castles in the sand;
We'll turn them into our own palace,
In our own far away land.

Sprinkle sugar on my hands,
And soon rock will turn to dust;
And we have the Lovers Syndrome;
Where dreaming is a must.

Jeannine M Desmarais
ON MY PASSION FOR AN OLD MAN

Dedicated to Jack Huggins.

Strange thing! I have been smitten with passion
For a grizzled old man—bleary eyed and drooly mouthed.
It was not an instant passion, fleshly felt,
But one born of gradual recognition.
He but speaks and I am enthralled.
Like a sponge I absorb and care not to talk.

Hearts and flowers, hearts and flowers . . .
He fills me with sweet scented petals
Fragrant with cigar smoke.
Like a child he laughs, tiny bubbles
Burst forth from his lips as he carefully sips
The holy chalice of Knowledge and Wisdom.

Edward A Granados
LOVE LETTERS

For Lainie.

Love letters old,
Fading yellow and brown.
Reading, bringing tears,
Wish you still were around.
Everything's lost,
Even memories fade.
Thinking back to the times,
And the sweet love we made.
When you needed me most,
During all your hard time.
I could never deny you,
And love I wouldn't have tried.
For it's you that I love girl,
And need by my side.
Although love letters fade,
My love for you will never die.

Denise L Abel
ETERNAL FATE
A voice from past calls out.
Laughter shutters through my soul.
Blood flowing beyond seas of emotion.
I am the sun drying your taste for revenge.
Last remaining tears have been drunk,
There dwindles no more.
A rope falters, its obscurity scrupulous of existence
Falling beneath an infamous clamor.
A road within solitude subsiding into eternal flames.

Renee Albracht
FINAL WORDS
The time has come
for me to leave
please don't worry
please don't grieve.

The Lord will take me
and I will follow
I will find a new home
so please do not wallow.

I will watch over you
and I will care
If you ever need me
I will be there

So if you love me
as I love you,
continue with your life
and please don't be blue.

K Richard Kay
THE VISITOR
The wind came to my house last night.
Boldly
It rattled the windows
and shook the bushes.
I did not
let it in.

The wind came to my house last night.
Outrageously!
It banged on the doors
and bent the trees.
I did not let it in.

The breeze came to visit my home this morning.
Very quietly, and with much respect.
It sang outside my door.
Graciously, I welcomed it
and ushered
this visitor in.

Vanessa Darnell
SMOKEY'S EYES

I dedicate this poem to you, Smokey Robinson. Thanks for the magic your beautiful voice creates in my life. You are my inspiration.

I see heaven in his eyes
I swear I see forever, it's no lie
I dream not of heroes or glory to walk in
Forever never was until I saw it there in him.
Now he is but a mortal man that I can't deny,
And yet I know I see heaven there in Smokey's eyes.
He's one man who's shown no sacrifice
With a beautiful voice to touch my life.
I have a dream that's yet to be
to touch the man who has touched me.
He was born with honor, one who walks in grace.
His voice is pure as sunshine.
No greater gift his faith.
Now I can see forever, there's just one reason why.
I see a small part of heaven
there in Smokey's eyes.

Shirley Kingery
TO MY VALENTINE
Voting for you is
Always true.
Love is so great, the
Envy of fate.
New experiences arise each day
Thank you for your thoughtfulness
Ideal or real surprises
Now and in the future
Endure in every way.

Carole Ciraco
WALK WITH ME
Walk with me always, every day of my life.
Walk with me when I'm happy and especially when I'm not.
Walk with me through every season of time.

Walk with me through springtime.
Share with me the innocence of a sweet new season
And let me feel your passion for life.

Walk with me through the gentle rains of summer.
Enjoy with me the feelings of freedom and the memories of childhood joy.

Walk with me through the leaves of October and the snows of December,
Ever conscious of days that are gone—
Ever looking forward, toward new tomorrows.

Walk with me always, ever by my side,
And when the seasons of our lives are over
Walk with me to God.

Deloris Gayle
I AM A SURVIVOR
I've been through a lot of things,
Experienced emotions untold,
I've been hurt beyond your imagination,
I've even gone through that self-pity stage,
Imagine becoming so down you feel life's not worth living,
Even to the point you try something drastic and stupid,
And when you look back on what has all happened,
You give thanks that you are still here,
Because, I am a survivor,
I'm stronger than I thought I was,
I'm able to accept what has happened,
And prepare for what's to come,
Only because, I've realized one thing important,
"I AM A SURVIVOR."

Kathryn Deatrick
MOTHER
Mother—
One of God's great creations
Entrusted with power
Power to bring forth—
A new creation.

A new creation
To care for, nurture, guide
Thru the years
With loving care.

A new creation
To laugh with
To cry with
To share with.

Great is the responsibility,
Great are the rewards—
That first bouquet of dandelions,
That first kiss that says "I love you!"

Great is the responsibility
Great is the reward—
The child now grown
Whose look now says
"I understand."

Suzanne Connelly
SIGHTING HAPPINESS
Persuaded by sweet dreams.
Convinced by sleepless nights.
Communication bridged with uncertainty.
Thru confrontation lies a solution.
But this conception is extinct for fear of sacrifice.

The breath of simplicity is in the heart.
Reality shadows the pleasure with inconsistency.
Blameless of one, incriminating to all.
Assured acceptance is undeniable.
Progress is precedent to enable the heart and mind uniting in happiness.

Kim De Salvo
ECSTASY
I sit on the veranda, naked, save the blanket of darkness around me.
I look to the horizon and see the first dissipation of light as it seeps over the top of the trees.
I close my eyes and I feel the warm gentle fingers
As they caress, reaching; searching for a solid grasp.
I hear the secrets of the world whispered into my ear,
I smell the sweet, fresh smell that makes my body come alive.
It seems that no one can feel as I do at this moment.
This much beauty can never be described, only experienced.
I open my eyes and see the majestic orange light before me, warming me, waking me.
I sit for a while longer, spellbound, before I go inside.
I look back once more over my shoulder to catch a last glimpse of the beauty.
Elated that I am alive.
This is the ecstasy of a sunrise.

Pam Staszak
YOU SAY THIS CHILD IS FEELING ALONE
You say this child is feeling alone
Please rush her right over
For the sense of alienation
Can hurt a little one so

Those who don't care say enough is enough
That someday you're gonna have to be tough
But have these people ever shed a tear
For them has life ever been rough?
And does age make a difference?
Why can't the world feel the tension
Of those who fear the pain of that invisible fence

Everyone needs to be included
A fact so many of us have deluded
Into believing it doesn't hurt
How else can we stand by so totally muted?

R-A-V-E-N D-A-W-N

R-A-V-E-N D-A-W-N
"I'D LIKE TO MAKE A RESERVATION FOR A PARTY OF NONE."

To my beautiful wife, Sandra Sue Lerman, and to her art. To our forthcoming book of poetry and art, tentatively entitled, NEVER REST IN PEACE. To my son, Harry, my brother, David Lerman, and to Ruth Blotsky, my mother.

It's the ice age of the party.
We go. We stand around
like pawns waiting for the hand
to move us closer to the edge
where we can fall into our cocktail jokes
where we can drink the jukebox
with eyes in our ice cubes
noses suck through straws
and jaws flap like lost flags
on runaway wristwatches
ticking against radical rhetoric
soul survivors of the great process
of dehumanization and taxonomy

of checkered suits and pinstripe
pants
alligator shoes . . .
taxonomy
of a bruised brain
emptied
into a new clone.

There'll never be
an excuse for the missing emotions.

Terry L McGill
LUSH LOVE

She gently awakens, quietly releasing the clouds of mist hanging around her shoulders.

With her tender shrug, the slender Tern rises from her face, sleekly pumping the air in unison with the mirrored image below on the water.

Slowly, with trepidation, the cypress lifts his arms and whispers to the forest, "The morning is here. Come to me."

And the beady, black waterbugs to the lethal water moccasins, all creatures of the lush green rise from the sleeping earth like ethereal apparitions.

A smile curls at the corner of my lips, yet . . . deep within, my soul sighs . . . and cries for what can nevermore be.

Old cypress knees, impeccably polished and handsomely adorning a suburban garden.
Softly moaning, trees stretch to God for salvation as the untamed beauty that once encompassed and engulfed my home
Shrinks in the face of progressive, modern man.

Come back to me, O green, lush love and let me wander your miles with reverence for you are my greatest love.

Kathleen L Rodgers
AGING IS BEAUTIFUL

Aging is beautiful, it certainly is
From the first day of life, the process begins
We remark at the beauty of the bright-eyed infant
Then we observe the toddler, discovering his world
We marvel at his growth through all his school years
And note how strong and handsome he's become
Then his life's work is chosen, filling us with pride
At the contribution he makes to the community.

Aging is beautiful, it certainly is
Especially when it is done gracefully
In order to be beautiful in middle and old age
Care should be taken of the youthful frame
No regrets, no regrets, as the years add up
Just gratefulness and thanks to the LORD above.
Aging is beautiful, it certainly is
From the first day of life until the Lord says, "Come."

Jack Raplee
CAPTIVE IN THOUGHT

Senseless babblings from ancient Greece
Conclude, "I think therefore I am."
But thinking cannot give one peace;
At least I do not think it can.
Think about it.
Our nature compels us all to think
In one way or another. But thought
Can propel us to the brink
of something to discover. We ought
to do without it.

Our thoughts have moved from simple ones
To complex with no solutions.
The theories that we teach our sons
Are intelligent delusions.
I don't doubt it.

I myself am a victim of
The slavery of thought.

This man-made world does not need love
As long as there's no God above
Some men have gods to fill the need
To escape from selfish lust and greed

We write our books and give our talks
About life and love and why we're here.
With logic we can safely walk
Away. We have nothing to fear

And in the end you'll go somewhere
To heaven or to HELL.
And heaven knows if I'll be there
No one can ever tell.

There are too many victims of
The slavery of thought.

Timothy R Mallard
FRIENDS AND LOVERS

No Time Is Wasted That Makes Two People Friends,
No Time Is Wasted When We Can Share With Friends.
The Friendship We Find While Being With Each Other,
A Friendship To Cherish, To Love, But Not To Smother.

No Time Is Wasted That Makes Two People Friends,
These Times Are As Rainbows, A Pot Of Gold At Its End.
Keep Your Doors Open So That Some Will Come Your Way,
Live For A Friendship That Will Last Beyond A Day.

A Friendship To Grow With That Keeps Us Hand And Hand,
A Friendship So Beautiful That's Warm, So Close, So Grand.
Now As This Friendship Grows So Grand We Find That We're In Love,
Keep Our Love And Be My Friend,
Watch For Rainbows From Above.

Hannah Young
MOTHER'S DAY—1988

It's a Mother's Day message in reverse.
For you, my children, I've written this verse.
God made mothers, that is true.
But he also made children,
Kind and thoughtful, like you.
You can't have one without the other,
And I'm very proud to be your mother.

Cynthia Middlestate
SEPTEMBER MORNINGS

The children are back in school again,
All is quiet at home;
There is no more daily activity,
And you start to feel really alone . . .
You get them up bright and early,
Feed them breakfast, and help them dress;
And after the school bus leaves,
You start to clean up the mess . . .
Your days begin to feel longer,
Than they ever did before;
You can't wait till the school day is over,
Just to see them walk through the door . . .
You start to fret and worry,
When they're just a little late;
You pace the floor and wonder,
But all you can do is wait . . .
The best part of my day,
Is when the kids are home at last;
Gosh, how I did miss them,
While they were gone, these hours past . . .

Jen Paul
P.S. I LOVE YOU

"P.S. I love you" is how I end
my letters to you,
My love for you will always
be true.
We have always been really good
friends
And forever my love to you
I send.
I always write "my dearest
Paul,"
And at night I think of you and
wish you'd call.
And when you do it's not for long.
Don't you ever think about me
when you hear our song.
Sometimes I wonder if you really
love me as much as I love you.
And then I get a letter that
starts "Dear Jen" and ending
With a "P.S. I love you!"

Jean Hinsley
WE'RE SO APART IN OUR FEELINGS

We're so apart in our feelings
You could be holding me in your arms
and i'd feel lonely and alone.
Lying in bed, wondering where you are
and what you're doing
keeps sleep chasing memories
across the ceiling and back
again.
tossing and turning
fighting the pillow,
wears me down to a verge of
tears.
Strong again;
i try another strategy.
All this hurting
isn't from knowing we won't make it,
but wondering why
i always keep the hope of
trying.

Dottie Lewis
A SPECIAL PLACE

You sit on a rock with the water rushing by
Surrounded by trees seeming to reach for the sky.
Then, in front of you, in all of its majestic awe
Stands the mighty, thundering, and powerful waterfall.
Strong yet gentle it seems to be
As it pushes onward towards me and thee.
God's presence overwhelms you as the water comes rushing through
In this special place known only by a few.
Fears fade away and hearts seem to calm
As God's glorious creation acts as a soothing balm.
All worries and troubles appear to cease
As our Lord replaces them with His infinite peace.
Throw your cares in the water He seems to say,
And as it rushes by let My love carry them away.
I created this place for you to escape to—
To be totally refreshed and made like new.
So sit on the rock with the water rushing by
And be surrounded by trees seeming to reach for the sky,
But in front of you, in all of its majestic awe,
Please don't miss the message
Of my mighty, thundering, and powerful waterfall.

Janet M Corbett
MEMORIES

This poem is dedicated to my mother, my loyal audience.

The smell of home-brewed coffee
In the morning—
You holding me tight to keep
Me from crying—

Fresh mountain water soothing
My throat—
Feeding the cows, pigs and
goats—

Sunsets brightly glowing over
The mountain ridges—
You standing there quietly on one of
Your favorite bridges—

Stars lighting the way and
The moon shining from far
away—
Blue grass stroking your face
Memories I can't seem to erase—

Lenora Hart
LOVE THAT BINDS

This poem is dedicated to all the lovely couples who have experienced decades of being together and are still in love.

After decades of being together
They held hands and sat contentedly
Not saying a word for confirmation
Of their deep love for each other.

Time was in their youthful ways
When they disagreed and argued over things.
Then they grew to understand one another
And continued to grow up together.

Now in their golden years of age
They still had the deep love,
accepting one another's ways, daily.
For each held a deep love for the other.

The wrinkles, grey hair and aging
of their appearance was part of them.
This they accepted with each other

For in spirit and heart they were one.

Their happiness came from the depth
Of their heart and soul for life
They had suffered together through
Life's hard struggles and pain.

Now they spent their time together
Happily, for life was ebbing away,
But then they had each other with the
Love that binds which is God given.

Susan Barron
THROUGH THE AGES
Through the ages
As time goes by
Things come and go.
People change,
And times are tougher,
Through the ages.
Old lands die out;
Old tracks grow rusty;
Past times are forgotten,
Through the ages.
Bombs land,
A century long gone;
People cry out in terror;
And then it all ends,
Through the ages.
And we still have proved nothing.

Noah Gonzales
THE FINISHED SOUL
A pain causes rain and the coldness
in the air
The darkness in people's souls is the
finished tale.

The cry of howling yowls may start
the day again.
You may pass the dark red sea. That
hate in our
Soul which dreams.

That reality of hate called the most
evil thing
That is ever . . . will live onto the
world, called
The land of the deepest heavens.

In finishing the tale, love brightens
and fights
Both worlds.

Marie James
WHAT NOW IS IT ABOUT
And today I heard another's life was
taken
From this nightmare don't you
think he so badly wants to waken
The pollution, the self-destruction
Destroyed by oil spills are our
oceans
Turning to garbage pails is our land
Think how he must feel, the old
one

He made this world for us to roam
about
Now he looks only to question
What now is it about

He's trying to let us know
He's trying to make us aware
The fires burning, the earth shaking
The wars here, the wars there
No need to fear to those that know
It's pain the old one has to let go

Mary Jane Haley
EARTH MUSIC
The Earth has music that sounds all
around,
from the echo of the mountains, to
the rumble of the ground.
The Earth lives with music of the
little babies' cry,
to the flutter of the little birds as
they begin to fly.
The Earth has songs of Love, like the
cooing of the dove,
to the whispered sounds of Angels,
that come from up above.
The Earth gives a song of welcome,
to those who are oppressed,
and gives them hope and promise
that life may give its best.
The Earth brings forth its music
as the harvest we do reap,
as the winds blow through the
wheatfields, we know that we shall
eat.
The Earth sings out her song as the
winds do rage and blow,
and spreads the seeds both near
and far, so many things will grow.
The Earth has music in this house,
that keeps us safe inside,
and helps protect the ones we love,
or home where we abide.
The Earth gives up her music and
sends it to the skies,
where all the words and feelings
pass before His eyes.
The Earth keeps up her music long
after we have gone,
but still lives on in others, who
will also sing Her song.

Anna E Fontana
FAREWELL LITTLE LADY
Farewell little Lady
You journey afar
Across the deep blue
Past the shiniest star.

Be happy—Be peaceful
Wherever you be,
Your worries are over
At long last—you're free.

But Oh, little Lady
If you can but hear
You left so much behind you
That I'll miss you, I fear.

The gates at last opened
No more must you roam
Paradise calls you
Little Lady——You're Home!

Doris J Billiot Silnieks
I FELT HIS LIPS
I felt his lips brush across mine,
Although he wasn't there . . .
I opened my eyes to see,
But I saw him nowhere . . .
His lips were cool and tender,
Like gentle falling snow . . .
His touch was soft as a rose petal,
And I wondered which way to
go . . .
His tenderness and gentleness,
Touched me more than I can
say . . .
And I began to wonder,
If there would be another day . . .

Marlene Heagle
SAGEBRUSH KITTY

For Connie, who knows all about cats.

Ornery little pussycat, where've you
been?
Made your mama worry again.
Out in the sagebrush, smell that fur!
Listen to me scold, don't start to purr.

Won't come in when I want you to,
Out all night is fine with you.
Miss Independent sleeps all morn,
Won't chase the gophers out of the
corn.

Lazy window kitty, go catch a
mouse,
Don't waste the day, snoozin' in the
house.
Little furry beast, mind my words,
You're well-fed, don't hunt those
birds.

Belly to the ground now, stalking a
fly,
No harmless insect escapes your eye.
Crickets, spiders, beetles 'n' such,
These dangerous enemies demand
your touch.

Little tabby tiger, jump onto my lap,
Way past time for your afternoon
nap.
This is your job here, allowing me to
pat,
Warming my heart, little sagebrush
cat.

Karl Ickes
ENGAGED FLIGHT

In memory of a fine musician, RANDY McCARTY. He is missed greatly.

I have seen the wrath of AIDS.
It has taken many men.
Plague of countless victims,
Why does this black dagger remain
yet mighty?
Memories are all that remain in these
dark shadows.
This plague is so violently cruel!

Hear the thunderous waves crash?
We sail with so few cannon yet!
Calmer waters start farther ahead;
Shall our ships sail there?
Shall the porpoise guide us soon?
Days are the minutes within our
future horizons
Where passing time and blackened
space
Shall try our stretched sails.

I have seen the wrath of AIDS.
Angels fly above the clouds.
Carry the angels our cries to God
While mercy arrows strike their
courses.
This plague shall sink!

Karl Ickes
BLIND FLIGHT
I have been blind
But now my sight is as though
God has made me a Blindman
And now a sighted Eagle.
I have been created with feathers now
For the greatest wings of flight.
I have seen the scary, lonely darkness
Of fear in life.

I once felt like God's carved creation,
Thrown aside and forgotten
In the sands of Paradise beaches.
I was crippled and alone in spirit.
I knew the occasional flights as a
robin
When I presented the currency of
faith to God.
And now I am not crippled to
blindness;
I take my first flight as an Eagle.
A beautiful sight is the Eagle.

Robert Henry Miller
FOR KATHEE—ON HER FORTIETH BIRTHDAY
Buddy! Friend! Good Scout and Pal!
Kathee is just one great gal!
For any frenzied distraught parent,
She'll run almost any errand.
If it's driving kids to school,
She'll show up to help carpool.
For your-Mitzvah, Bot- or Bar-,
Kathee's got the fastest car!
When she's the one behind the wheel,
There's never a skid or jerk or
squeal!
As a party organizer,
Show me someone who is wiser!
As caterer she's non-pareil,
At planning parties she won't quail!
Cake or cookies—tarts or pastry,
Hers are tops, they're fresh and tasty.
Taste her infinite Margarita,
MMMM! Delicious! Smoother!
Sweeter!
Always sunny, never shady,
Kathee—you're the perfect lady!!
Can't you be a wee bit naughty
Now that you've turned thirty-
nine????

Darlene Baxa Lnenicka

Darlene Baxa Lnenicka
THE TIME HAS COME

Dedicated to my beloved husband, who has shared my life with me. We are now enjoying our beautiful new home.

The time has come, we must go on
with our lives.
Things do not have to stay the same,
my heart cries.
With mixed feelings, and emotion we
trudge ahead.
We know the time has come, which
most of us dread.
Will we miss the home where we
lived for so long?
The question many have asked, who
are now long gone.
A beautiful retirement home on the
hill.
That seems the best plan we have
thought of—but still?
The time has come, but where did the
years go?
It was just yesterday, with children
our home did overflow.
Since they are all gone, and have
made homes of their own.
They no longer need our house, to
call their home,
Now the time has come, for us to go
on with our lives.
A new home on the hill, will be just
our size.

Jean Matus
CITY CANVAS
She steps on gum—and squinches
her face—
Her shoe glues gooey to the
pavement;
The small child cries—he is lost
someplace—
And his mother is searching;
The cars passing splash cold, muddy
rain—
A man shouts his disdain—they go
on;
Dirty, weary and muffling a yawn
An old man passes—shuffling along;
Mannequins—blank gazes in store
light—
Display their fashions—bright and
costly;
Pushing a cart she hawks dented
wares—
Soles so thin and her shoes worn
apart;
The chauffeur opens the Rolls back

door—
And furs with jewelry galore drip out;
Sirens wail their shrill notes of alarm
As to some new fright they go speeding;
Now see the shine in a young girl's eyes—
Strolling—arms entwined—with her lover;
This is a canvas of a city—
Life in primary color!

Jean Matus
FIRST PROM
Into the room she came—the music played,
Dancers glided by her—beautiful skirts swayed.
Her heart was a cold lump in her chest,
She only hoped she looked special—her best.
She had taken hours to comb her long hair,
And to practice how ladies sit in a chair.
Her long dress was white with a wide pink sash,
A flower tied to her wrist—a touch of dash.
Oh, will she receive at least one boy's glance?
Must she stay if not asked to dance?
She would be mortified beyond belief—
All at once she sighed deeply with much relief
As a nervous hand touched her arm lightly,
She turned and smiled—her braces shine brightly.
Then as she whirled around the waxed floor—
Another lone girl came through the gym door.

Jean Matus
TO CATCH A STAR
Oh, where with spirit free do you go?
What is it, my dreamer, that takes you far?
Unbounded, uncluttered, and away so
You may try to catch your very own star?
I do envy your courage to soar
Into the farthest cloud—where you must be—
Living your life and grasping for more.
I silently plead as you pass me
Take me along—let me join the search;
It certainly would be a sheer delight
If I could leave my structured perch
And go soaring with you on your high flight!
How may I convince you it is true—
I so want to catch a star with you!

Lynn H Snell
SOMEONE'S PATTERN FOR US
Wilting of tilting—
Like a rose,
From dust it come—
As dust it becomes,
To wither at each limb—
Its cause for life to remain.

For this you see—
That sold you stagnant,
To say it plain—
Is to hear its sayings,
That you are part of someone's—
Determining idea of some
concluded matter.

Then let us say—
What must come,
For the means—
Is not the process,
But the idea—
That makes it great.

When we say—
To the given we learn,
That just as conformativity matter—
Is not the idea,
But it is conformativity matter—
That does not change.

For we spin our wheels—
To make dreams come true,
When in fact we are—
Some concluded matter,
Like the plant that needs growth—
As it can wilt or die of stagnation.

Lynn H Snell
WHEN PRECIOUS METALS BECOME COMMON
An old fantasy film—
In an old saloon bar,
As the cards rustle around—
That tells of an old time piano,
When the chips fall—
Hearing the wind stir the shutters.

Seeing that night—
Passed on to day,
Somehow made the rounds—
To pan for gold,
As the gold towns—
Soon vanish.

The night—
In night time bells,
As the coin mint—
Soon learn how to fuse metals,
To make gold or silver—
By the advance of scientific means.

A passing of metaphysical science—
As gold value drops,
From a dust grave of an old saloon.

Polly Kimball
SHAKE MY HAND, LORD
Shaking hands means much much more
Than what we do or say,
It communicates to us Who and what we are today.

The hands are created works
That our God alone could bind,
as each reveal man's feelings of an unexpected kind.

Some hands are wrinkled and worn
and tell of the toil of man,
who uses his skill often to work out his own life's plan.

For life's plan holds many things that we will not comprehend,
But as we trust God's wisdom we know he's really our friend.

Our handshakes are like heralds
shouting for dreams of days past,
If we look up and beyond We will find God's peace at last.

Here's my hand, please shake it Lord
There's no other way it seems,
To have full success in life and fulfillment of our dreams.

Larry Rollins
WHAT IS LOVE
In Loving Memory of My Daughter Melody Dawn.

LOVE is sharing dreams and making dreams come true with you.
LOVE is bringing happiness to each other.
LOVE is giving my life to you in every way.
LOVE is a word for explaining feelings that would take a lifetime to say.
LOVE is waking up with you in the morning and starting the day with you.
LOVE is sharing my deepest feelings with you.
LOVE is planning my life with you.
LOVE is seeing joy in your eyes and the smile on your face.
LOVE is the word to explain you.
LOVING you is the greatest joy of my life.
LOVE is sharing the greatest feeling in the world and this feeling is called LOVE!

Kathleen F Lloyd

Marcella E Olson
MOTORCYCLE MAMA
To Kathleen R. Smith, mother of Marcella E. Burfield (Olson) and Kathleen F. Lloyd, who made a trip in and around the USA on motorcycles, covering over 10,000 miles in two and a half months in 1978.

It seemed to take forever to be where I am today,
and all that I endeavored was another's choice and say;
From child to teen to young adult, to mother, friend and spouse,
from scrubbing floors to countless chores, I kept a well planned house;
The Grandma that I am today had not the time to age,
with children grown and husband gone, life's closed another page;

Marcella E Olson (Burfield)

Though years have passed and taken toll, my hair now turning gray,
I've time to dwell and dream,
I'm still a child in my own way;
Alone with time to be myself, to think and plan and do,
I'll grow now as all others who accept those years as through!;
I want to romp, jump and thrill at the beauty of God's land,
to touch the earth, to climb each hill, run barefoot in the sand;
I want to do the things I missed that keep one young at heart,
to ride a bike, go on a hike, to know a brand-new start;
It may take years to 'grow' again to reach the age I am,
but God will take me when He will, I'll live now while I can;
I've done my part, I've held the fort,
I've catered through much trauma,
today I'm free and boundless, I'm a 'motorcycle Mama!'

Connie Barrilleaux
THE JOURNEY OF LIFE
To my cousin Daniel Nieblas Jr. for your inspiration. Without you this poem may never have been written. My thanks to you.

From the distant shores of the oceans
to the snow covered mountain peaks,
lies a world of future tomorrows and the hope to fulfill your dreams.
From the sunlit dawn of the morning
to the evening's crescent moon, lies a dream of being successful in whatever you seek out to do.
For the stars above in the heavens to the depths of the valleys below, is the journey for which you will travel to find the destiny your life enfolds.
And for the honesty within your heart and the truth within your love, you shall reach your dreams and tomorrows, if you will believe within yourself.

Ronald Glover
THE BURNING DOLL
This poem is dedicated to my aunts: Eva (Jean), it was your "Robe," and Willie Mae, it was your "Doll," that made these lyrics manifest.

Remembering me at age seven
wearing Aunt Jean's robe,
knowing all the consequences—
but who listens at age seven.
Standing by the heater
doing what kids normally do,
robe and curtains ablaze, me: still standing;
heat warning flesh something is wrong,
a quick glance backward
tells me it's time to get out the robe
out the room and report a fire.
Grandmother's licks sounding off with each word:
I TOLD YOU NOT TO
PLAY WITH FIRE;
Aunt Jean crying about the robe;
no one understands
how the three feet doll
casually dressed got burnt.
—And I wasn't playing with FIRE.

Jacqueline D Katsch
THERE ARE NO GUARANTEES
To my beautiful, special Sisters, and my Mom & Dad, Thank you for your encouragement, and for showing me all this poem speaks of.

There are no guarantees,
no moments in life
that do not hold pain, either physical or emotional,
each carrying its own share of grief.
Yet, between these moments

are others filled with peace and happiness:
A bright sunny day, walking through the woods, or a grassy meadow. The scent of warmed pine trees intoxicatingly fills the air and washes your mind free of worries for a while at least.
Also, there is Music, Drama, Comedy, Poetry, Dancing, Singing, Waterfalls, Babbling brooks, wonderful stories and more than enough to conquer the pain, grief, and worry, there is Faith, Hope, and Charity.

James G Khing

James G Khing
YOUR GOLDEN SMILE

Inspired by a real and understanding golden girl—Gloria Prentiss. I love you ever and ever, Gloria.

The effects of your golden smile, my dear Are like lightning making the darkness bright and clear.
It flashes in my mind driving across the Arizona Highway.
I see it often remembering the sweet encouraging words you say.
Through peaceful enchanted New Mexico
Your sweet smile keeps me on to Amarillo.
The eyes of Texas are on me because of your smile.
They know that the Lord is with me mile after mile.
Into Oklahoma City rolled this sailboat driver.
They see reflected in his face a calm man, a deliverer.
The snow-white MacGregor yachts sailed into Arkansas
Led by a red-nosed reindeer delivering Santa's gifts with awe.
The truck and trailer swept into the highway of Tennessee.
They see your golden smile reflected all over me.
The yachts sailed on into the state of Virginia and why
Your golden smile radiates through the dark and clouded sky.
This keeps me going to the cozy little state of Maryland
Where I delivered the four show boats to a happy dealer man.
Naturally your every smiling positive wish is my command.
It is as easily achieved as the return trip I ran.
When your golden smile shines on me I'll do all that I can.

James G Khing
BECAUSE YOU LOVE ME
The stars shine brighter tonight
because you love me.
The world is a very lovely sight
because you love me.

Two wandering ordinary people
Looking desperately for love and affection
Two hungering sad and lonely people
Led by good angels to make the right connection.

And wonder of wonders the world is transformed.
Gone are the old blunders my soul is reformed.
For our happiness a miracle is performed.
Goodwill makes a fortress free from being stormed.

No more will I be sad and lonely
Going to places all by myself.
I will walk this world with you by me
Enjoying our blessings, giant or elf.

Roses smell sweeter tonight
because you love me.
We will gather close and tight.

Because you love me the world is good.
Because I love you I did what I could.

Susan Johnstone
THE COUNSELOR

For Dale Beck.

He sits in his chair at ease
With himself and us,
Full of insights
As he delves into our lives.

Does he see the real us?
Or what we pretend to be.
Somehow I think he sees what we cannot,
Or would rather not see.

It's difficult for us to understand
How he can do this for others,
When in so many ways
We cannot do this even for ourselves.

He's guiding us on this journey
To discover who we are,
So that maybe we'll feel free
To show ourselves to each other.

Billie Patterson
THE MYSTICAL PLACES OF CHILDHOOD

To the people in my life who are the closest to my heart, especially my little sister, Doxie.

The mystical places of childhood still linger near and far.
New worlds become alive and a little child becomes a star.

The giant oak tree that once was a shade, now becomes a kingdom with Kings, Queens, Princesses and Knights with piercing blades.

An unmade bed with wrinkled sheets and lumpy pillows now becomes a raft made from weeping willows.

The little doll that is threatening to fall apart is a friend, a companion and most of all a part of the heart.

These are the mystical places of childhood.

Anna Kay Christian
WHAT IF JESUS MAY COME?

To my loving Aunt & Mother, Agatha Campbell, and Olive Salmon.

What if jesus may come,
And you're not ready?
It's your duty to be firm, grounded and steady.
He may come today, tomorrow, or any hour,
He'll be coming in the clouds with great and mighty power.

Focus on jesus and earnestly pray,
Give it your best shot and walk in the right way.
He'll be glad to accept you when you make the right start,
He's forever and always so give him your heart.

Marci J Cinotto
TRUE FRIENDS

For Michael Francis Contile.

True friends are found but seldom
As we go wandering on
No darker grows the nightfall
But brighter grows the dawn.

And as we walk together
In friendship's harmony
All seems right forever
In love's true honesty.

Linda Lee Ruiz
MY LOVE

To Miguel G. Garza, the inspiration of my life.

Sounds of waves trying to reach a shore
On the island where we met
It was by the sea; you did confess
Is love real between you and I
Is there love for you and I?

Through the years here and there
Seasons have come and gone
Precious moments were never enough
To touch that love; that is mine; only mine

To one in a million, we did dance and dine
Smooth, warm the taste of wine
Is there love between you and I?
Here I'm longing still; longing, longing still
Those moments embedded in my mind

Through the years, longing till the dying day
Is there love for you and I?
True love that's yours and mine
True love; if not yours then alone . . .
Forever mine

Sylvia A Cayer
MY LOVE

To my husband, Leo, my love.

The love I felt in my youth is past
It did grow and it did last.
The love I feel now is full and sure
It has grown, it is now mature.
When life is gone and my heart is still
My love will stay, until . . . .

Joan Crowder
BEFORE I'M GONE

I dedicate this poem to the family, friends, and doctors, who have helped me find myself.

I've looked around each corner for you
Where have you gone?
I've searched my dreams, in a weary run
Where have you gone?
Each new face I've seen, I realized it wasn't yours
Where have you gone?
Highs and lows of life have been so unkind
Where have you gone?
I've cried myself to sleep at night, only to wonder where you are.
Where have you gone?
I'm too old now to search on and on, some day I hope you'll find me, before I'm gone.

Melinda Wood Roberge
STOP & LISTEN
A branch dances; a bird flies by,
The sun beats; it is mid-July.
A song is sung; a mother goes hunting,
The babies cry; they're asking for something.

At home it is still; quiet as the night,
All day long not a movement in sight.
Shadows are cast as the clocks waste time,
Waiting for their keepers to show them a sign.

They are moving too fast! Slow down a bit.
There's so much to do, no time to quit.
No time to stay in one place too long,
To enjoy Mother Nature humming her song.

This life is a frenzy of 'live for today';
A madhouse of people, going every which way.
When will we stop, slow down and thank God,
For this life that we have, the earth and the sod?

After it's gone and there's nothing out there,
Or when we can't hear a song or a whistle nowhere?
Maybe that's what'll take to appreciate our garden,
But then it'll be too late and from life we'll be pardoned!

Anna Peña
AN EMPTY SPACE

In memory of grandma Vivian Tevebaugh.

Love and laughter was always there.
The morning sun warms your heart.
Shared feelings a lesson taught.
Time rolls like a countless star.
Memories of a family member you know. The time did come for grandma to go. The silence of night grew dark. As the tears rolled slowly like the raindrops from the sky. In the fullness of my heart left an empty space

Debbie Fowler
YOU
You gave me a reason to live, when I thought there were none;
You taught me once again, to laugh and have fun.

You showed me that life isn't meant to be bad;
And that I shouldn't be down, so depressed and so sad.
The tears that flowed each night before I slept;
Have been swept away and are no longer wept.
You gave me a reason to once again have sweet dreams;
And no longer do I awaken from sleep with loud screams.
You have shown me that teasing wasn't meant to be mean;
And that a couple works together as they are a team.
You have shown me affection and caring as I've never known;
And my heart is no longer as heavy as stone.
You have taught me that problems are meant to be shared;
Together to work out, as you truly care.
You have taken me places that I've not known exist;
And have given me happiness, that I never dared wished.
You have shown me that love is felt deep from the heart;
Not something so painful, it tears you apart.
You have shown me making love is very gentle and sincere;
Not something that is dreadful and awaited in fear.
But most importantly you have given me the joy of sharing my life with you;
Each day showing me a love that is special, fulfilling and true.

Evelyn Janice Griffin

PASS IT ON

To my children, Regina, Jessica, Kevin, and Shane.

When you receive a friendly smile, pass it on.
Every happy thought you find, pass it on.
Every time you see a frown, you just turn it upside down
And pass it on.

A friend is there when you're in need, pass it on.
When someone does you a good deed, pass it on.
Whenever you are feeling down and someone turns it all around.
Pass it on.

When someone loves you for yourself, pass it on.
Don't leave it sitting on a shelf, pass it on.
Give someone a happy face. Take a smile a warm embrace
And pass it on.

Elmira Brickhouse

I LOOK AROUND

I look around.
I wonder why people are here today
and gone tomorrow.
I think of the good, how they just
seem to go so quickly;
And the unjust seem to stay longer.

Maybe God is giving them a chance
to redeem themselves.
Some say God is dead.
God is not dead.
I can say that He is very much alive.

I wonder why people are here today
and gone tomorrow.
I think of the good, how they just
seem to go so quickly;
And the unjust seem to stay longer.

Maybe God is giving them a chance to redeem themselves.
I wonder why people are here today . . .

Gloria Henderson

MOURNING

Sleepless
In the cool dark night;
Eyes open, I'm wide awake
Visions
I can see your face;
But I am alone
Reaching
Arms extended,
Yet still empty
Longing
For your touch,
The one that still excites
Aching
Hopes and dreams
Fade to a memory
Morning
Cruel bright light;
Clearly revealing that you are gone

Lynn Pietrzyk

AZURE LAKE

The azure lake,
Pink-tinged by sunset's hues,
Seen through the lacy mist
Of naked trees,
Leaps forward in a hundred
Foam flecked waves,
Powered by an icy wind,
They dash to shore,
Only to grovel on the cold
Damp beach,
Then flounder backward
In surprised dismay.
Diminished by the vast
Uncaring shore.

Kim Nickell

A POEM FOR BETH

I once knew a girl who rained over an Atlantic Gray Sea . . . She wore her melancholy like perfume . . . its fragrance telling tales of Carnivals journeyed to every fall . . . of people said good-bye to in cold November air.

She was strong and sad, wise, yet a fool . . . and I felt the Lighthouse and I, but especially the bright colors of October had always known her.

I'm sure with everyone . . . she was the one lost . . . the one who long ago fell in love with Fairhaven, the green forest that did surround it, and the Knight of the '56 Chevy . . .

And then one rainy day . . .
fearing love . . .
she held out her hand and was
gone . . .

Barbara R Keifer

I LOVE YOU

I love you for the way you touch me
Always at the right place
At the right time
And always the right way
Emotionally and physically

Erin McNary

YESTERDAY, TODAY, TOMORROW

YESTERDAY
Barbies, blankie, sucking my thumb
Driving down roads looking for bums
Strawberry shortcake, stuffed animals too
Bedtime stories and Mr. Magoo.
TODAY
Friends, music, "Days of Our Lives"
Fighting my brother, little white lies
Playing my trumpet, riding my bike
Daydreaming about the boys that I like.

TOMORROW
My children, husband and a farm
Keeping my babies safe from harm
A beauty salon and a nice car
Staying at home and traveling afar.

Pina J Moore

Pina J Moore

QUEERY

Lullabies and nursery rhymes, do mothers sing them still?
Do youngsters know about Tom Thumb, Jack and Jill?
Their eyes amazed saucers as Jack climbs up the stalk
And have they gone with Simple Simon on his walk?

To some new parents this custom is passe.
So when tots are tucked in at night, what is it that they say.
"Sing a song of women's rights, passing Washington's dome,
Don't worry none my little one, Daddy's there at home.

Oh see the homosexuals on parade in sorrow,
Holding hands, hoping for a fair tomorrow.
Hickory, dickory, dock,
Let's stop the nuclear clock!

Get out Mother Hubbard,
Move away from the cupboard
Your place is on the outside
And a profession is your only pride."

Young ladies, tell ol' Nan what you want her to say.
Can I bring a bit of Mother Goose to chant in my own way?
A blend of old and new can make a healthy meal,
So I will give her fantasy, and you impart what's real!

Pina J Moore

MY SECRET GARDEN

I have a secret garden, it hides behind my home.
I feed it like a baby, to make it rich in loam.
In my mind's eye I see each little space
Filled with many flowers in their little place.

The roses bloom in mild array
With pollinating bees at play.
I plant so every time, in every case,
Another flower fills my vase.

Of course, it's only in my heart
I place the horse behind the cart.
The ground is poor as it can be
With too much shade from our old tree.

But I still strive to make things grow.
I break my back with rake and hoe.
The seeds try hard to please my toil.
They crookedly press through sun-baked soil.

They might not be a florist's pride,
But when I see how hard they tried,
I smile, for they look grand to me
And my secret garden I still see.

Pina J Moore

DRAPED IN BLACK FOR THE BLUES (ODE TO SARAH VAUGHN)

Oh soul, you have left us a bouquet,
Bereft of a rose.
A legacy, pressed into wax,
Imprinted on tape.
The birds, deprived of competition.
The air, depleted of sassiness.
The human flute, now at
The Lord's bosom,
Adding to the heavenly choir.
We shall miss your playful scales.
The airwaves bereaved of sweet,
Live melodies.
But through the blessing of retained
Recordings, generations shall still,
Enjoy your magical sounds.
Sister Sarah, your chords will never,
Be lost!

Pina J Moore

SO BIG

Phrases passed down from generation to generation, supplementing a mother's vocabulary. "So big!" I would say, stretching my child's arms to their fullest height and, in time he did, "So big," without aid, reaching high and beaming a gummy grin with pride.

"Patty cake, patty cake baker's man. Peas porridge hot, peas porridge cold," games of his pre-dexterity phase and my reward of giggles and gurgles.

"All gone!" a boast for the Babe and a sense of accomplishment for mom that another meal was successfully dispensed!

Now I peer up at my very tall young man and he really is, "So big!" The little playful games are lost on an echo and, after thousands of meals and years of feeding, now, he too is, "All gone!"

Sheila K Ganey

THE WIND

I cannot see it, but I know it's there,
It rushes softly through the air.

When it's angry, you will know,
The wind will really start to blow.

When it's sad, it will decrease,
And when it's tired, it will cease.

When it's happy it will sigh
The wind is restless, it won't die.

Unlike humans who will end,
The wind is my eternal friend.

It is free, it hasn't sinned.
Oh, I wish I were the wind.

Joseph C Brown

THE AWAKE DREAMERS

Mere children can conquer vast time and deep space
With daydreams as spacecraft to a strange far-off place

And cruising the galaxy on thought paths of flight
While seeking new worlds is their common delight.

Children are leaders in realms they create:
Great heroes for justice and masters of fate
They captain their daydreams and chart a true course
With friends as a crew and free minds as their force.

Children soon grow to be women and men
And tend to lose sight of their daydreams by then—
Except for a few that stay young all their days—
The daydreamers, doers who shape the new ways.

Naomi I Camden

I'M LEARNING A LOVE SONG FOR JESUS

I'm learning a love song for Jesus
I can sing when I meet my dear Lord
The music is sweet and melodious
And there is tender love in each word.

He's my strength, my counselor, and my Savior
He's the "Rose of Sharon," to me
And I want to sing Him a love song
When my precious Lord Jesus, I see.

My love for Him, cannot be measured
It's bigger than the earth and the sky
If you'll come with me, to Calvary's cross
Then you, will understand why.

The mere sound of His name, is the sweetest
Of any that I've ever heard
So I'm learning a love song for Jesus
With adoration and love in each word.

Lee Wells

WAYS OF A SMILE

"Oh" the beautiful ways of a smile
As you give them along life's mile
They are returned without end
As freely to you as you send

If another doesn't have one today
Please send one of yours their way
Don't worry about repay
Many will surely come your way

As you go on your way smile
They will return mile after mile
From very young, all the old
Their beauty is something to behold.

D V Naidu

THE THIRD WORLD

Torn between the bull and the red rag
The third world became an empty bag
For them there was neither care nor welfare
But the boom of guns was heard here and there.

A well-fed man shouted
Look, there is a world bank floated
There is all the food you need
Go now and have your fill;
Later, remember, to pay the bill.

The Socialist turned his face;
Said he, to save his nation's grace;
Bear awhile, we'll give you all the guns
And see how the fatman runs.

These slogans shouted so many times
The poor ones know them to be political wiles
The half-starved shed a tear in his hut
At the dawn of the century;
The hut and tear are still his sanctuary.

Myrtle F Olson

LIVE FOR LOVE

Life is free,
Life is grand.
Especially when,
Love's at hand.

Without Love,
We're bound to fall.
We wouldn't know,
Our folks at all.

Or understand,
The way that they,
Once held our hand,
And walked our way.

Through thick and thin,
Laughter and fear.
Trying to win,
Friendship dear.

Sometimes failing,
Sometimes hard.
With pure intent,
But caught off guard.

To all of you,
From all of us.
Live for Love,
For them we must!

Diane Rothenberger

MAN OF ALL SEASONS

As the snow blows and brings a foreboding chill to our bones, so does a distressed man without a purpose. Ice cycles drip from rooftops as do his tears of sadness and despair. The cold winds howl, but he cannot feel it through his encasement of ice. The rains come to re-birth our lands, and flowers to bloom in colorful disarray. So does the man bloom, in thought and feeling to again become re-born to life. His purpose and zeal for life becomes as lush as the new spring grass.

Thunder and lightning fill our skies, as he fills our minds and hearts with his anger. The warmth and blueness of a beautiful clear sky, brings hope and joy to our hearts as does he, with his smile and kindness. The heat of the day stirs our emotions and gives passion and warmth to his inner soul. Love blooms, and he showers upon us, joy and peace as a gentle summer rain. The sun begins to fade, as leaves tumble and flutter to the earth. The air becomes clean and crisp to the smell and touch. The "Man Of All Seasons" fades into himself, again to face his despair and howling winds of winter . . .

Linda Williams

GRANDMA TILLY

You are the foundation of this old town,
Without you in it, it should be torn down!

Your little town of Natalia is changing as you can see. But the beautiful old house you live in will never change to me!

If the streets you live on, in your little town could talk, this is what you would see, that everyone loves you!!! Especially me.

You have watched your grandkids grow and you can see, that you are the foundation of Natalia, and we want you with us until you are 203. All the architects and engineers can come and change this town around that may soon be, But without all of your love this foundation would mean nothing to me!!

Barbara Lea Sauve´

NIGHT OF THE WHITE STALLIONS

Dark horses,
on a moonlit night,
hide amongst the trees
and quiver at
approaching vibrations.

Their fate ruled by
lusty white stallions,
who prance in splendor—
reflecting light
Back to the very first star.
A lone mare,
caught between shadows,
is seized by
a flowing river of silver
and washed away toward
the sacrifice of dawn.

Christine Gillebo

WILL YOU

Will you hide, when I arrive.
Will you spy, to see if I fail.
Will you just be and let me seek.
Or will you come with loving arms.

Will you speak words to wound.
Will you turn your back on my love.
Will you laugh and say it was a joke.
Or will you speak the loving words I look for.

Will I hurt as before
Will I lock the door to my heart.
Will I love tomorrow without you.
Or will I shine in our love's glow.

Edward R Courtney

THE FIRST TIME WE . . .

The first time we met I was fascinated and intrigued, wondering why I should feel this way.

The first time we kissed I felt so comfortable, so alive, knowing that I could still feel compassion.

The first time I held you close I felt so secure, never wanting to let you go.

The first time we made love I was so nervous and confused, but also excited at being a part of you—close to you.

Now I am beginning to love you;
As a friend,
As a companion

No matter what may happen,
Whichever road we may take,
Either separate or together,
I will always remember those "first times"
And I will always admire and love you.

Naomi Taber Salsman

MAY THE BLIND SEE

Wasted words should never be.
Write so the blind may see.
Yellow daffodils blowing in a breeze;
Describing the beauty of an old oak tree;
The rising sun, casting red hues in the early light,
Or colorful birds flying from their roost on a morning flight;
Dew-covered grass sparkling in the night;
Like a million diamonds—Oh, what a sight!

Tomatoes ripening on their vine
Or bunches of grapes to make red wine;
Orange colored pumpkins in the fall of the year;
Fields of corn yielding their golden ear;
White covered trees on a winter night—
Icicles gleaming like castles in the light.
How may I write so the blind may see
The wonderful sight God gave to me?

Eric L Goetz

FOR ALL

They say love comes on one special day,
And it comes with the flowers that bloom in the May.
I guess they are right, because I have found,
That life's simple joys are just all around.
Take for say the chirp of a bird,
How beautiful and lovely as it would be heard.
Love came to me on a Saturday noon.
Her eyes were like the twinkle of a beam from the moon.
It's simple joy and simple love,
Just like the flight of a smooth, graceful dove.
I speak of no woman, no woman you see.
I speak of our earth made for you, made for me.

Gloria S Haslim

WITH RAYS OF SUN

You appeared with rays of sun,
stood out from the soft blue sky;
swept me high from my old terrain,

As long as there was light
hand in hand we explored
the depth of the ocean.

When the moon kissed the hills,
entrance to our dreamland
need no waves of goodbye.

When the leaves veered to gold,
even though the heat remained,
let us let the rain alter our land.

Still, no waves of goodbye,
and smiling moon lights us up.
No promises, no vows....

Just two hearts holding nature's bow,
'til you appear once more,
with rays of sun.

Michele Golden

THE CALLING

I see a light beyond the crest
Of golden hills which offer rest
With peace in mind becomes obsessed
And someone calls my name

I see an altar long and high
Which blocks the waiting cloudless sky
I thought I was too young to die
But children think the same

I'll laugh at this if I awake
To see the real world, goodness sake
This has to be a bad mistake
But yet I hide in shame

The people stand and look at me
And laugh at my futility
This can't be reality
But yet they know my name

The real world is fading fast
I've found my place of rest at last
My quality has now surpassed
The angel that I became.

Jodi Ann Hilmer
LIFE
Life is a rock, it stands firm in the soil
It stays upheld amid earth's toil
Life is a tree, whose roots run deep
Whose branches many secrets do keep

Life is the sun, that shines each day
With light and warmth in each ray
Life is the moon that does descend
Every star illuminates, every bend

Life is an eagle, through the sky it soars
Representing our dreams and opening doors
Life is a wave, destructive or calm
Life is a way, a hope, a song

Life is a candle, whose flame flickers on
In a minute, life may be gone
To live life fully, each path we trod
Should be guided by the hand of God

Dan Goddard

Dan Goddard
TV DREAMS
'Twas the night before Christmas Eve Beulah
I dreamed I saw an image of Santa Claus on our TV
I sprang to the TV set to clear up the picture matter.
When I heard a holly voice call ABC see Santa in color. CBS to my smiley surprise had a twinkling of snow in its soft color eye.
And as NBC was testing its picture pattern. And as it went out of sight I heard a beautiful peacock singing.
Beulah, boys and girls, Santa Claus is coming tonite.

Norman Master
MAN
The Earth was made, in days of old
Man took a stand and became very bold,
The word of a serpent did turn his head
He then had to suffer, with rocks for a bed,
Driven from the Garden, so plush and green
Into a world that was cruel and mean,
He will learn from his arrogant way
For his misdeeds, a penalty he must pay,
He plows the ground and plants the seed
But all that will grow, is a thorny weed,
All through life, his burden is great
Some days he ponders his future fate,
A strong chain, he hopes, it will that serpent bind
A peaceful tomorrow, he's in a search to find,
From the proper walk of life, he will cease to stray
To the loving God, he will always pray,
Never again, will life be hard or stern
For the Garden will be open for man's return.

Nick Kover
WINTER GARDEN
The winter snow is a feather blanket hiding my rose garden.

Protecting it from the bitter cold.

I can't help but to think, how a rose covered with snow is like a STOLEN KISS.

A thing of beauty hidden from view, the rose, like a blushing lover; bows its head to the ground.

Waiting for the snow to melt and like a new lover, hoping to be found.

Yet when the snow does melt and the rose reappears it will be wilted like life robbed of its infant years.

I can't help wondering why it turns out like this
Is it because of the cold of the winter snow, or because of the STOLEN KISS?

Nick Kover
CLOUDS
Clouds are like thoughts just passing by.
Wandering around in the vast blue sky . . .

Like thoughts flooding one's brain before a special chore.
Clouds crowd the sky before the rains begin to pour.

Getting our attention when accompanied by thunder,
and the flash of lightning . . .
Preparing Mother Earth for yet another spring.

Filling our senses and flooding our minds with
special thoughts . . .
(How wonderful our world and what a high)
Just watching the heavens and the clouds passing by.

Traveling from here to a foreign land
and back again to where I stand . . .

Gliding on thoughts carried by the winds of my mind.
It's so easy to leave my troubles and worries behind.

When the sky is clear and there are no clouds in sight.
There will always be thoughts to create dreams for my sleep tonight . . .

Jeni Common
THE LITTLE PRINCE COMPLEX
I sit on top of my world
One foothold on my cliff
I cry my tears
I feel my pain
Below me
People
Small as ants
Scramble to their
Own destinations
Sitting on top of their
Own worlds
One foothold on their
Own cliffs
Crying their own tears
Feeling their own pain
While below them
People small as ants
Scramble to their own destinations
Sitting on top of their own world
One foothold on
Their own cliff.

Hazel Kleb
LOVE REVEALED

This poem is dedicated to my beloved husband, who appreciated everything cultural. He was a violinist who had a Stradivarius. He had his own little dance band when he was a young man. He played in the ballrooms of the best hotels.

My eyes will look at you when day is done
And try to see the thoughts you think.
Because I feel your love,
Your glance will tell
me so.

And lo
On night air fell
The sound of turtle dove,
Reminding us our lives do link.
Our joy will be as bright as morning sun,
Our days replete with love's deserved attention
From early dawn until the sun does sink.
The night with stars above,
Like a ringing bell
Will show.

Though slow
That naught can quell
Our everlasting love,
Our shining lives like stars that wink
My eyes will look at you when day is done.

Dora La Nell Henderson
INSANITY

This poem is dedicated to my two sons, Michael and LeMarcus Henderson, with love.

A cold winter day confines
six squealing, squabbling, swiggling
frisky, fighting, fusible firecrackers,
fussing . . .
over who is the
biggest, baddest, brightest, and boysiest
ever to set foot in a modest upstairs apartment
Moments short of a single parent working
a full-time night job
with four hours of mandatory overtime,
Seconds after a newscaster announces
"school closing today due to sleet and snow"
One
Straight Jacket
please!!!

Holly Flame Maxey
MOUNTAINS
Mountains, Mountains
What a beautiful sight
When I see them
They're out of sight
They're so pretty, so keen
My Wondrous dream
So someday, I'll probably
climb it, Someday
But for right now
I'll just watch
and say
Mountains, Mountains
You're pretty today

It's just a shame
When we see the
Mountains torn apart
It just about breaks our heart
and the only reason is
to build a road for trucks and cars.

Scott Guynn
FIRE IN THE DEAD OF NIGHT
Fire in the dead of night
People running in confusion
Motivation fright
Children swimming
In a sea of dreams
A deadening whirlpool
Engulfs them
From the shoreline
You can hear the screams
Realization
So hard to believe
They run to an unreal world
Where they can live
In peace

Shawn M Sylvia
DARK LONELINESS
Tears on a pillow.
Steam pours through my mind.
Shivering pistol in my
shaking hand.
The head will feel the final blow.
The heart will beat its last beat.
—But who will cry last,
You or me?

Alberta Campbell Colbert
ALL THAT I ASK

To my parents Emmett C. and Wilma Coffey Campbell.

Someone to love and someone to love me,
A place to live in where I can be free,
God's beauty around me and the power to know it,
God's love within me and the power to show it.
His light from above shining out from within
To brighten the path of a stranger or friend;
To be a good daughter, good mother, good wife,
Is all that I ask for myself in this life.

C G Lange
APRIL
There has been a collision.
Spring is derailed.
Summer spills from the cracked
and bleeding buds
a thick and unrelenting yolk.
The air I swim in
groans
with the complications of yet another birth;
the air is swollen with too many odors
swarming from the broken earth.
Gold and crocuses burst like spices
and summer melts the crisp petals
with heavy hands.

Cathy Scanlan
IN SEARCH FOR MYSELF

To my children, Lani, Jimmy and Dee.

On my journey, what will I find
Someone who's desperate and needs peace of mind

In the mirror, what do I see
A shy girl hiding, is it me

If you look deeper, beneath that disguise
You can see the deep down feelings, that never arise

The hurt and the pain
That always remain
As the truth is told
The emotions unfold

Dear God, please show me the way
Guide me, so I don't go astray
And if I do stumble and fall
Please give me the strength to stand tall

For the battle I fight
I know I must win
It's not in sight
But, I know it's within

So on my struggle
I must go
To find the person
I don't know

Heidi S Heald
IN MEMORY OF TIMOTHY
Some few months ago, on a warm summer's night
Like a gift from the angels, Timothy appeared in my life
With radiance of sunshine, eyes sparkling with life
The smile of an angel, all gifts from on high

My life was made richer for such a short time
God loaned us an angel to brighten our lives

My heart is all burdened with sorrow and pain
For Timothy is no longer with us today

His memory will live in my heart and my mind
Thank you dear God for his presence, for even a short time
Take care of him Father until the time comes
When we meet again at the Resurrection.

David G Eylander
REALITY
What is Reality?
Is it you and me?
Or how about the world we see?
Is it the singing sparrow in the evergreen tree?

What is Reality?
Is it the silent sprinkling of summer,
Or does our world grow dimmer?
Is Reality just a dream I see?

What is Reality?
Red roses in rippling water?
Brave eagles flying higher?
Perhaps only our sweet desire?
Oh, tell me please what is Reality!

Through my vision cleared,
In the foggy mists appeared;
Sweet Jesus of Nazareth!

For He is Reality.
Not the foggy, empty visions of what I see.

Valarie Hicks Lanier
UNIDENTIFIED FEELING
It has been months, and it has not gone away
this feeling I have for you, with no name.

In the midnight hour, it causes restless slumber
and during the day, only for brief periods
will it allow you to leave my thoughts.

It has been months, but when I see you
the symptoms reappear: dizziness, sweaty palms
my heart actually beats faster
and sometimes, I think it skips a beat.

What is this feeling I have for you, with no name
when you have never even touched me
except in your brief letters
and we've only conversed face to face
for too short a while, too few times?

And what is it, this feeling I have for you
that will not go away, or let my heart rest
and makes me feel, like a lovesick fool?

Valarie Hicks Lanier
FROM SOME WINDOW INSIDE THAT TALL BUILDING
You arrive early, earlier than I
I see your car, most every morning.

As I walk toward that tall building,
I can't help but wonder
If you aren't watching me
From some window inside that tall building.

It would be nice to know, that all day long you hold that picture of me in your mind
the colors I have on
the way I wear my hair
how good I might smell!

I put an extra glide in my stride
a pleasant smile on my face
and make sure I look good, from head to toe
And each and every morning
I hope and pray
that you are watching me
from some window inside that tall building
and wondering
what it would be like to love me!

E Martin
PICTURE THIS
In repetition of my morning mind
I find black and white people
in a silver screen sky
a show of lights
that would fill my eye
with bottled dreams and brilliant rays
as some consolation for brighter days

liquid sky and kamikaze rain
again the pensive clouds
blur across a still life frame
a flood of paint
that would surely stain
all red and blue like blood and bruise
a spectrum of pain for all eyes to view

Monica Buster
A NEW DAY

Dedicated to my mom. Who always sees the beauty in the sunrise, sunset, and the clouds.

Look to the east, my friend.
Yellow, gold, lavender, pink, and rose.
Colors, splashed against the sky.
Stunning. Beautiful.
Bringing a promise of a new day.
New life. Hope.
Breath taking beauty.
A beauty to be shared.
Take time with me my friend.
To enjoy the rising sun,
and the dawning of a new day.

Melanie D Hilliard (Age 13)
TIME
Night comes without a thought
And day appears with a dawn
Without a thought of the past or present
Our lives winding road turns another corner
And we face another dawning day

Laurie Habets
ASHES CF LOVE
The love light that gleamed in your eyes,
Has gone out to my surprise
We said goodbye, my heart bled.

Ashes of Love
Cold as Ice
you made the bed, you pay the price

Our love is gone, there's no doubt
Ashes of Love, the flames burned out.

I trusted dear,
our love would stand
Your every wish
was my command
My heart tells me
I must forget
I loved you then
I love you yet.

Ashes of Love
Cold as Ice
you made the bed, I'll pay the price
Our love is gone, there's no doubt
Ashes of Love, the flames burned out

Bonnie Harris
WITH YOU
Lie with me always as it were the very first—
Each time with you is as the break of a new morning kissed by the dew.
The touch of your hand more soothing than warm glow of candlelight against a winter's chill, more enticing than a glass of wine.
Do not touch unless time will lend itself to complete fulfillment—to desist would be more painful than passing through the Milky Way and returning to the bottom of the earth.
Let your body cover me as a blanket of stars adorns the earth. Let your kisses flow as honey,
Move freely and unwanting, for you no part of my body or my soul is forbidden ground.
Lie with me and hold my hand until just before morn, your sleep as peaceful as the sea gull's flight o'er the sea, your rest serene as the swan's glide o'er the lake in misty rain.
I do not sleep—not that I fear your leaving, but only to feel the warmth of your body next to me holding just enough to sustain me for when I wake alone.
Cover me once more in the early morning hour and take me as you did before to the highest mountain
Just You and I.

Esther Parks
THE GIFT OF A SMILE
It was ten below that morning when I awoke to a rap on my door.
Looking out, there stood an old man with an outstretched, gnarled hand.

He smiled. I motioned for him to wait. Returning, I placed coins in his hand, then offered a bag of special treats.
Again, he only smiled; he was mute.

Bowing, he dropped the coins into the pocket of his tattered overcoat.
He turned, waving and munching a sweet, as he walked away on poorly shod feet.

My eyes followed him to the street.
I gave thanks for the slippers on my feet.
My heart ached for that aged man in his
worn-out shoes, ragged clothes and nothing to eat.

You see, I too, am old, but very strong.
I can speak, hear and see well, and will always
remember that morning when a hungry man said thanks with a warm smile.

Harold Jordan Sr
GOD'S BEAUTY
God's beauty is love as his Word proclaims,
reaching to every soul to give life that flames.
God's beauty is being the prince of peace,
to satisfy the needs and give comfort

and ease.
God's beauty is being the bread of life,
to feed our souls each day and keep us from strife.
God's beauty is being the lily of the valley,
to bring us through those storms with hope
and our hearts rejoicing gladly.
God's beauty is being the resurrection and the life,
and because he lives, we shall live also and have life.
God's beauty is being the good shepherd of his sheep,
Whose lives he will mold, watch over and keep.
God's beauty is being the bright and morning star,
that will shine through our lives from heaven afar.
God's beauty is being the Alpha and Omega,
the author and finisher of this world and man's agenda.
—Amen—

Renee Carpenter
THE LOVE OF ROMANCE

To David, my example of romance.

Romance is a wonderful feeling.
It makes your hopes soar,
And your dreams become real.
Long walks on the beaches,
And quiet candlelight dinners
Cause you and your sweetheart to fall deep in love.

Romance is a big expectation,
It bounds the hearts of lovers.
The two fall in love,
As gradually they become one.
Together with romance they care for each other,
And realize their love will last forever.

Romance is a true symbol of love,
The giving and caring of one to another.
Romance can be just like a fairy tale,
All it takes is one male and female.
Romance never grows old,
It is kind and sweet and gentle.
Two hearts will never last,
Without the love of romance.

Stacey A Emiro
STAND BY ME

This poem is dedicated to the people who believed in me. Nick G., I'll always be there now and forever. Also dedicated to my Mother Valerie, Sister Deneen, Brother-in-law Nick, Aunts Maxine, Bernadette, Uncle Steve, Cousins Cresta, Shawn, Johnathan, and my best friend Doreen. God Bless.

What my friends mean to me
They mean more than one eye could see
They're the ones that are there when I laugh or cry
When the days are so long and I feel that I could lay down and die
Being with each other day and night
Our relationship based on love will never be out of sight
To feel that I could not go on anymore
But knowing that they will be the ones knocking on my door
Realizing they're the ones that will Stand by Me
Where I am that is where they will be
To be close as a sister to a brother
When everyone gets us mad
We will have each other to make us glad
To have people say things all over town
But their jealousy never bring us down
This poem I dedicate to the people I can call a friend
But without any of you my life would crumble and end

Michael Waterman
CLOUDS

Clouds are the lingering mass of possible rain. They wander aimlessly about through the deep blue sky in which upon their arrival cast darkness on the earth. They seem to station themselves in an area suited to them to let out what they have gathered from their journey of the past. Just a bang like a cannon and a flash like a camera and the sprinkling of water begins. Scattering on earth is every life form trying to avoid the rain.

Drip
Drip Drip
Drip Drip
Drip Drip
Bloop!

The first rain drop hits earth and nature is awakened with Life.

Kathy M Jordan
LOVERS AND FRIENDS

I woke up in your arms this morning.
The best feeling, I've had in a long, long time.
I can't believe in such a short time,
That I can say I love you.
Or care about you in so many different ways.
I've been waiting so long for this.
You're like so many dreams in one.
I'm so glad we were introduced a while ago.
It hurts me to say good-bye.
So I won't, and please do the same.
'Cause I wouldn't know where to go.
So sweetthing please don't let me go.
If I'm going too fast please let me know.
I'll take in nice and slow.
So let's be lovers and friends until the end.

Jill Fowler
MASK

Upon my face that intent stare
For those of you not really there—
Who ask my name, or how I am;
then turn away—
It's not the same.
It takes some time to really care
I try to help, to care, about people that pass through my life
Time can tell a person's needs—
The hurts, the wants, twisting like a knife
Asking is not being there.
I have learned the difference,
Upon my face I wear a mask
To hide the pain of fears too real.
Past hurts have made me cold
To those who get too close.
Within my life the hardest task—
To gain strength as I grow old, from past mistakes
To learn to feel again
Within my heart I have a place for those of you
Who take the time to see the smile inside of me
And with you I am myself.

Connie Reiterman
TRUE LOVE

I was sitting and thinking about you, darling
And what comes to mind
But that I love you dearly
And will for all time
You are so warm and tender
And you love me, that I can tell
I'd like to hold you in my arms forever
And have you feel my love for you as well.
How much can one person love another
All I know is when we are apart
You are constantly in my mind
And always in my heart
Is this the love I was searching for
Could this be the one
Let's be in this forever
Until our lives are done

"Daddy"

Dee Marie Vogler
CHRISTMAS WITHOUT DADDY

To the memory of Daddy, with love. Clarence Edward Sallee, 6/11/18-10/8/81.

It always seemed like Christmas,
When we would sing a song.
But it won't seem like Christmas,
For this year, Daddy is gone.

It always seemed like Christmas,
When we exchange gifts that eve.
But it's not the same this year,
Since Daddy had to leave.

It always seemed like Christmas,
When on Daddy's face, we'd see a smile.
But we won't see his smile this year,
For Daddy's been gone awhile.

It always seemed like Christmas,
When Dad's harmonica and Lee's banjo, we'd hear.
But the sounds of these are gone now,
Since Daddy's not with us this year.

Daddy will be with us in spirit,
As we gather this Christmas day.
But it just won't seem like Christmas,
Since Daddy passed away.

Marian Bruce
TO KNOW THERE IS A GOD

When I look around at the flowers and trees, how beautiful they are
Then I know there is a God who loves us
When I see the sunrise with all the beautiful colors, then I know
There is a God who loves us
When the sun goes down in the evening and the sunset lights up the
Sky with pink, red, blue, and purple
After the rain God puts the rainbow in the sky to remind us
That he keeps his promises to you and I

Jill Tokuda
THE SKY AND OUR LOVE

It seems to me, that the sky has changed,
Since we have parted
It no longer is painted with bright colors,
Instead, it remains grey with white clouds
It was as if the sky was the bondage, that kept us together
And now, just like the colors,
Our love is gone
But even before I held your love in my heart,
the sky bore its colors
Could it be that someone loved me,
and I just couldn't see it, or is it because, until my
heart was filled with your love, my eyes were blinded from its beauty.
And you, are the miracle that helped me see, could this
be mere speculation on my part, or is it my heart's
way of saying how much I miss you.
And how a piece of my heart
will always be with you

Lance Boucher
THE HOMELESS

No one cares
That they're there
They are the homeless
They sleep in the streets
With no hot meal to eat
They are the homeless
No one to wipe the tears away
No one to warm them on a cold winter's day
They are the homeless
They have no money
It's no longer funny
Every day many of them die
Why?
We must start to care
and notice they're there
They are the homeless
They have no future, only the past
We must start to care at last

Monica A Forcey
THE LOST FEELING ONCE FOUND

To my husband, Richard, my children, Jeffrey and Regina, and my parents, Stephen and Margaret Smith, for with them I was found.

As the raindrops fall and daybreak begins, everyone rises forth and begins the day anew,
Some are happy and some are sad,
But all is well none are bad,
Everyone here needs a little
And when a lot is given they can't handle it,
But as time slowly enters within,
A little of what is given seeps in,
And a small glimmer of hope and smiles comes out,
And as they reach and reach for it the moment is grabbed,
A warm feeling emerges and for the moment,
A lost soul is found,
All from one very special thing,
The love that is given.

Tammy Gale
DEPARTURE

To Dan Arnold Bogle, 1946-1986.

Working hands so calloused
Age-worn lines upon his face
He stares into the sky
Longing for another place

Old friends and family lost
Gone before him in the end
His body starts to tremble
As the pain causes him to bend

His life has been a good one
But he's tired he wants to rest
He reaches for the heavens
As the ache increases in his chest

He remembers his youth; growing old
All the paths he's trod
Then he smiles as he departs
Heavenbound to meet his God

Debra Keister
MY DIRTY CAR
My car is so dirty
From the traffic going by.
It looks so disgusting
I think I could cry.

I keep thinking that when
A warm day comes along,
I'll go to the car wash
Then bring my car home.

But whenever it's warm
I don't have the time
Or I'm just too lazy
To get off this couch of mine.

But Mother Nature does
This favor for me.
She sends down the rain
That makes my car clean.

So things seem to work out
Just as well in the end.
Whether I do the work,
Or Mother Nature, my friend.

Teresa A D'Alessandro
IN THE EARLY HOURS OF MORNING

To a very special friend who warmed my heart and colored my world.

In the early hours of morning as the
sun comes shining through,
My head lifts from my pillow but my
thoughts remain with you.
From my window comes a gentle
breeze that softly cools my skin;
It brings to me great comfort before
the day begins.
Yet I can't stop this feeling, and I
won't even try;
It feels too good remembering, so let
the day go by.

I close my eyes and when asleep my
dreams are still the same;
I'm holding you and touching you
and calling out your name.
Then suddenly, when I awake, the
sky is dark and grey;
Reminding me it won't be long
before you go away.
Rain then falls so steady, but it
doesn't match my tears;
The storm is only moments and the
clouds will disappear.
But like the sun that is forever, my
love will always be;
And even stolen moments, they mean
the world to me.

Theodore F Guild Jr
WHOSE CHILD AM I
Born into a world of turmoil and
pain,
I entered not knowing what sorrow
I'll gain.
As life progressed in the hours to
come,
it was evident that I would not
blossom;
to become the child I should be, a
child who could be loved easily.

With the first signs of withdrawal the
doctors worked hard on me
giving me life but not much hope;
it seemed as though it were an
eternity.
And now I awake each day filled
with emptiness and despair.
Desperately searching for
someone to touch me, for someone
to care;
wanting so much to be held very
tight, knowing that something just
isn't right.

Who was there for me when the
danger was done,
for it was in the womb that I was
alive only to become—
a distraught and lonely extension of
the one who riddled me with drugs.
And feeling no pain for the wrong
she had done;
I was abandoned and left alone, now
I have no one. No one to love me or
to hold my small hand. No one to
tell me whose child I am.

Deborah Greenaway
SEDUCTION
Under cover of darkness you came;
by the light of the silver moon I saw
you standing in the shadows of my
room. My search for you has spanned
oceans and soared summits; chasing
dreams, fruitlessly.
I never thought it possible that such
fulfillment could be a reality.
Pleasant serenity lies tranquil within
my breast now. Am I home at last
finally?
Could it really be that you are here,
or is this all a dream that will whisk
away with the blink of an eye, when I
break through the cobwebs of sleep?
What elation I'd experience if that
were true; what great joy. But yet, if
you should be here only for a fleeting
moment of time, and disappear with
the dawn, what sweet sorrow.

Julia Lyle Spoon
LET ME SLEEP, LORD
Hold me here quietly,
Adrift in the atmosphere.
Still the painful beat of fear
And the agony of not knowing
That gnaws at my vitals.

When my mind is quiet
And my fears lessened,
Let me sink into deep forgetfulness.
Let the soft, smooth blackness
Of blessed sleep envelop me.
Let it roll over, under and about me
And while I'm bathed in this
merciful, marvelous wonder—
cleanse me.
Cleanse me of fear, anger and doubt.
Cleanse me of memories fraught
with despair, uncertainty and
unanswered prayers.
Wash away resentment, disharmony
and my unworthiness.

Then, and only then, let me waken to
the tune of immortality,
Alert to the needs of others, and the
beauty and wonders around me.
Where I've been wrong, correct me.
Where I've been rude, forgive me.
Where I've been ignorant, teach me,
Lord.
Forever and ever, Amen.

Terry K Bellino Cooper
GOD IS NEAR

In memory of my father and sister who now bask in the glow of God's love.

When my life is filled with darkness,
and trouble takes me by surprise,
It helps me to remember,
God is always by my side.

When I feel so very helpless,
and my heart is filled with fear,
when I need someone to hold my
hand, God is always near.

When tears of pain fall from my eyes,
and the future's hard to see,
when I feel that I just can't walk on,
God will carry me.

When I feel that life is so unfair,
and a loved-one's laid to rest,
It helps me to remember—
that God indeed knows best.

Terry K Cooper
I AM
I Am The Lord of Glory,
Master over all.
The power of My mighty word,
created all things, great and small.

I Am The Lord of Glory,
those who trust Me shall be blessed.
Let Me take from you your deepest
pain,
and I'll give you soothing rest.

I Am The Lord of Glory,
no thought is hidden from Me.
Bring to Me the disharmony of life,
that I may create a melody.

I AM The Lord of Glory,
My eye is ever on My own.
I deliver the righteous from trouble
and distress,
They shall never walk alone.

I Am The Lord of Glory,
Leave the dark and starless night.
Just call My name, and take My
hand,
let Me bathe you in My light.

I Am The Lord of Glory!

Terry K Cooper
CHELSEA LYNNE
I gaze upon your tiny face,
Pink perfection in bows and lace,
and thank the Lord, so full of grace,
for blessing us with you.

You came into a world so cold,
as Jesus did in days of old,
with hearts and hands we did enfold,
you close within our arms.

How fitting it does seem to be,
that God would choose this
Christmas Eve,
to give the gift of you to me,
a gift of life and love.

I hold you in my loving arms,
and memorize each tiny charm,
and rock you till your crying calms,
and love you tenderly.

The years will fly, this I know,
thru each stage I'll watch you grow,
and all my love to you will flow,
my angel, from above.

Vicki Starling
MOTHER

To Ruby Jewell Simpson, the Jewell that was never discovered.

You knew me when there was no
other—
You're the one I call mother.
All the times we've sat and talked,
cried, laughed, ran and walked.
You were there when there was no
other.
That is why I call you mother.
You gave me birth and saw me
through.
Do you know that "I love you."
You've watched me grow, struggle
and change.
But never have you shortened my
range.
You made me smile when I was mad.
Wiped my tears when I was sad.
Taught me all that I should know.
One more reason "I love you so."

Sharon Seibert
LOVE

I would like to dedicate this poem to my father, John Seibert, who is no longer with us, and to my mother, Emily E. Seibert; also, to my sister and brother-in-law, Emily R. and Brad Stanton.

Love is great and
Love is pure.
Love is something
You can make endure.

Love is good and
Love is kind.
Love is much more
Than just a piece of mind.

There is Love in laughter
And Love in tears;
But most of all Love is
Knowing that someone cares.

Love is in one and
Love is in all.
When you have Love,
You will never hide behind a wall.

There is Love in the East and
There is Love in the West, but
I want you to know
That you are all the best.

Love is in sickness
And Love is in health,
But one thing for sure
When you have Love, you never need
wealth.

Love is in gladness
And Love is in sorrow,
But Love is one thing
That you never have to borrow.

Christina R Gaskins
TRUE LOVE
Love is a feeling from deep inside.
It's a special feeling we shouldn't
hide.
You will know when you fall in love.
You'll hear angels singing up above.
Some people are afraid to feel.

They're scared of what it might
reveal.
Love is felt down in your heart.
You can't stop it once it starts.
Everyone will find a love that's true,
But the only one who can find yours
is you.
Sometimes love can hurt real bad,
Or it can make you very sad.
With the pain, you'll find it's fun
Just being with that special one.
You'll want to show how much you
care,
And everything you will want to
share.
Saying, "I love you!" is easy as pie.
The hardest thing to say is, "Bye!"
I know that all of this is true.
I found true love when I found you!

Daniel Rodriguez
ITALY
Those eyes of serene black.
Tendentious look to see.
Lips perching, smooth as
mink, waiting for a kiss,
smile, sensually wet.
Hair feathers back, like
sand on an ocean floor.
Skin of olive, a feel of silk.
A moment in our time is all
I ask.

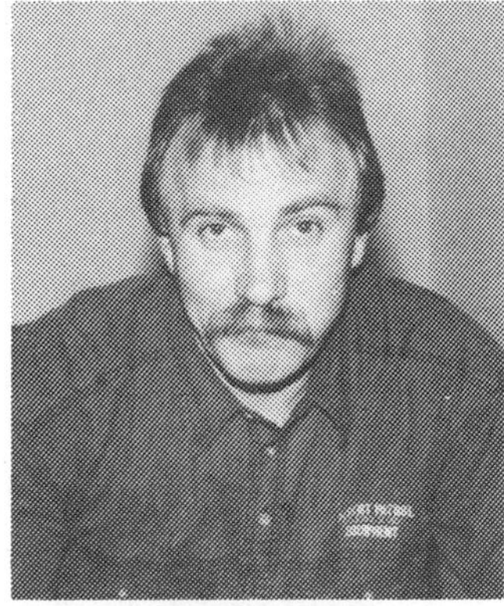

Wladyslaw Koba

Wladyslaw Koba
DRIFTING IDENTITY

To my wife, Jola, and our dear daughter, Alexandra.

There used to be a tree here
the wind blown it down
the same that had sown it

there used to be a river here
its waters dried up in the sky
where the rain clouds gather

finally we too
being rooted in the four quarters of
the globe
quest for a safe ground under foot
here.

Wladyslaw Koba
STILL LIFE WITH A BROKEN PITCHER
There is nothing
but forces
bare forces
struggling against each other
fighting for nothingness
for survival

but we were hunting for eagles
hitting them with big clay pitchers
filled with air
we are lacking it now
waking up suffocating
with empty hands
with which the reality begins
so there might have been no truth at
all
in the big issues
but in ordinary ones
might that be why
we could not have found it?

Wladyslaw Koba
REMEMBRANCE
In this old wild garden
eternally immatured fruit of hope
somebody picks up at night
stuffing his pants with it
when I follow him up the trees
and it looks as if
I wanted to pick up the moon
I can see my whole garden
backwards
harvest after harvest
bad crops after bad crops
back to the first
bush
after which the whole garden
disappears as if
it had been stolen by the wind
somebody had called for somebody
somebody had chased somebody
I am waking up in the open country
hungry scared scoundrel
with my heart in my shoes
and few green apples in my pocket.

Sue Burgess
MOTHER
Mother read to us from her Bible in
red
As she tucked her six children into
bed.
Don't be afraid,
The Lord will guide me and keep us
fed.
As she placed old coats of yesterday
And newspapers on our bed;
To keep us warm from the cold
For soon the mill whistle will blow
Then it's time for her to go
And spin the thread
That paid for the roof over our head.
Our packed lunch
Waited for us wrapped in wax paper
As we ran out the door
To catch the school bus without a
fuss.
We all knew tomorrow would bring
Sunshine instead of tears,
Because mother prayed for a better
day.
Just show me the road
Lord that you want me to tread
As she spun the white thread.

Christine Johnson Weems
REASSURANCE
The feet of Time run swiftly through
the years
In endless flight throughout eternity,
And though the world may plead
with all its tears
She will not slow her pace nor cease
to flee.
Behind her trails a veil of memories,
And little moments move to let her
pass,
While mortals wait to write the
histories
That Time alone can gather and
amass.

This day it is the choice of all
mankind
To live what Time will leave for men
to write.
The minutes move that we may grow
. . and find
Our way out of the darkness . . . .
into Light!
Have faith in God . . . and Time; we
shall find Peace,
For as men grow in Love . . . our
wars will cease!

Jennifer Gouthier
THE END TO BEGIN

Dedicated to Mr. James D. O'Meara—Thanks for believing in me!

As you move on and leave politics
behind
Never forget all your good and
bad times
All your experiences and good that
you have done
Will always be remembered
for many years to come.
When things started getting tough
and people started going against you
You never really gave in, you
seemed to know the right thing
to do.
You put your heart and soul into
everything you believed
And helped in making Winsted
a great place to be.
No matter what others may think, you
were more than just a mayor you see
You've become a great friend
and that's how it will always
be.
Your inspiration and "spunk"
encouraged me so
It's an honor to realize what a
great person I know.
So while you leave and venture other
aspects of life
Remember all the things you
have come to see
And hold on tight to the
memories.
But always remember wherever you
may be too,
There're those who will always
care about you.
So now is known of what I've
learned from you
"I came"
"I saw"
And now I believe I can "conquer"
too!!

Jennifer Gouthier
CONQUER YOUR DREAMS ONCE YOU START
Usually your tasks will be many
And more than you realize you can
do
Many times the road will be rocky
and the hills hard to climb too.
But just remember
The hills aren't that high as you may
think
And the courage and pride in your
heart
Will help you reach your dreams.
Nothing in life is ever that hard to
achieve
Just as long as you take the chance to
try it
And have faith to believe.
With courage in hand and faith there
too
Many of your defeats will turn into
triumphs for you.
So go out there and walk the roads
that are rocky
And climb the hills that are high
Soon you will realize there's nothing
you can't do
By then you can make your own
dreams come true.
But remember to believe what you
feel in your heart
Take those first steps
And try to conquer your dreams once
you start.

Jennifer Gouthier
TO REMEMBER TO FORGET
It was a time that left many families
in fear
Only praying that their boy was still
alive out there
But the Vietnam War was a situation
very severe
For it took three lives, of Winsted
men, down there.
But for all those who had fought and
survived
Home to hostility they had arrived.
It was as if our men didn't do right
But they are the only ones who knew
how it felt to fight.
For they should be proud and have no
regrets
To have served and become Vietnam
Vets.
Now 17 years after the end of the
Vietnam War
A Vietnam Memorial, in Winsted,
CT, will now stand high
With 3 maple trees—one for each
man who died.
All is in memory of those who died
As well as for those who bravely
came back alive;
And it will all symbolize peace and
the rejuvenation of life.
To rest we want to put the war
For it brings back so much pain
But we should still remember it
And never forget those who died and
survived all the same.

Jennifer Gouthier
THE BEST EMERGENCY ROOM DOCTOR
Whenever you need to be treated
For all the times you get hurt
or sick
Winsted Memorial Hospital
is the place to pick.
For there's a great team of E.R.
Doctors and nurses there to treat you
But to pick a favorite E.R.
Doctor might not be that hard
to do.
There's only four at WMH that I
know of (Dr. Ayers, Gunter, Lovejoy
and Ward)
And they all treat you pretty
great
But I think Dr. Michael Gunter
is number one in the state.
He's the doctor with experience
Who knows what to do
For when he starts treating you
He shows he cares a lot too.
He's pricked and he's poked and he's
bandaged me up
He's helped me feel better and
deal with a lot
He's the best E.R. doctor
Winsted Memorial Hospital
has got.
I'm thankful for all the treating and
caring
that Dr. Gunter and everyone
else has done
For it will always be remembered for
many years to come.

Jennifer Gouthier
IN MEMORY
Our hearts were sorely aching
And through tears we could
not see
It felt we'd lost tomorrow
The day you were taken from
thee.
But alone you did not go
For a part of us went too
For the day that god called you home
Our love for you just grew.
There's so many times we need you
So many times we've cried
But you'll always be inside our hearts
For your memory will never
die!

Jennifer Gouthier
REACH FOR THE STARS

Dedicated to all my friends and teachers and especially to Mrs. Agatha Tresky, Mr. James Pettit and my family who've helped me reach for the stars and make my dreams come true. Thanks for believing in me!!

You can climb every mountain
or swim every sea
Everyone's able to conquer anything
as long as you follow your
dreams
Your dreams are the things
that can carry you far
So go with your heart
and "Reach For The Stars"

You can go half way
or you can go twice as far
You can do it with help
or do it alone
It's up to you in what you want to
achieve
how much you put in is what
you receive

You can be the very best that you can
be
as long as you do as you
believe
You can conquer your dreams
plus anything else and go very
far
But you can only do it when you
"REACH FOR THE STARS"

Sylvia Anfang Trotiner
PICCOLO
Listen! The plaintive wail of a
piccolo in the alley . . .
Piteous, pleading! Even God must
hear it!
Its song is as bitter as the cold
outside.
Cold! Chilling the soul!

Hunger! Cold! Hunger! Food!
The piccolo plays, pleads, cries:
"Throw a coin, someone! Coins mean
food!"
Food! To stave starvation.

The window opens. Grating sound to
unnerved nerves.
A coin? No, a curse.
"Go away, damn you! My husband is
sleeping!"
Sleep! Blessed sleep! And
oblivion!

Oblivion? Or is there no oblivion?
No escaping Life? No escaping
damnation?
No forgetting hungry mouths,
And hearts, and souls?

The piccolo in the alley plays and
pleads,
Plays and pleads!
It's the cry of desolate,
Homeless mankind!

Sherry Trayer
KATHY
When I first held you on the day of
your birth,
I thanked God above for blessings on
earth.
You were so warm and cuddly and
lovely of face;
Your skin pink and soft, hair slightly
out of place.
That time seems so long ago, yet so
very near;
How lucky I am to have a daughter
so dear.
Before I knew it, several years had
flown by.
Your first day of school brought a
tear to my eye.
How anxiously your return that first
day I awaited;
But I could see in your face you were
very elated.
A few more years passed, and on to
middle school,
I had no worries for you knew the
Golden Rule.
Next, on to high school, so eager and
willing
To grow towards your future, I hope
it's fulfilling.
Now has come that first step to your
dreams and your wishes;
I encourage your freedom with
Mother's love and kisses.
As you walk to that stage, trembling
a little I'd say,
For your diploma well deserved on
your graduation day,
Remember, I love you, I'll always be
near.
You are a lovely young woman,
forever dear.

Lovingly,
Mom

Nora Jean Lindo
A SONG
Well, it says right there in the Bible,
Lord, that the weak shall inherit the
earth.
If that's so and I went and stubbed
my toe, would that mean I'd be first
in line?
Now take your time. I know it's hard
to think with all the things you've got
on your mind.

Well, I went to Church Sunday,
Lord—same old thing. Your congress
mumbled a lot about Love
But they smelled kind of like Jim
Beam.
Now, I saw *Jesus Christ Superstar*—
saw it twice straight through and I
must say,
I was really impressed with you. But
tell me, was it all true?

I'm lost on a Sea of Glass, Lord. A
Storm struck and now I'm
Shipwrecked.
The Beast of the Sea has struck at
last. O, Lord, lost on a Sea of Glass.

Well, you say thou shalt not commit
adultery Lord—that's really a riot.
You say thou shalt obey mommy and
daddy and never create a fight.
But what are you supposed to do, my
Lord, when they're setting such a
good example,
By fooling around in another part of
town with somebody else's wife?

Well, I played hooky all day, Lord,
and on Thursday and Friday too.
If mommy ever got told of this, she'd
send me to Timbuktoo.
I'm one of your little lost sheep, one
of the many who've strayed and
Where I am at the moment, Lord,
Well, I really couldn't say. For

I'm lost on a Sea of Glass, Lord. A
Storm struck and now I'm
Shipwrecked.
The Beast of the Sea has struck at
last. O, Lord, lost on a Sea of Glass.

Tracy Smith
AN UNDYING WISH
If I had one wish,
that never would subside
I'd wish for you, and only you!
To feel your warm touch,
As you pull me so near.
To caress me ever so softly,
Every waking day of the year.
To know that you were close
I would never have anything to fear.
For you to whisper
Those sweet nothings, I've always
wanted to hear.
Those sweet words, "I love you"
That would trinkle into my ear.
If only wishes could come true,
Then I never would have shed a tear.

T Michael Manning
WITHIN HER LIGHT

Victoria—my friend, my lover and my life—I will love you always.

Lessons so cruel
They teach you the cold
Watch who you follow
And do as you are told

You know how I felt
And remember what I said
Heading for the blackest night
We sense, we fear and dread

I saw the moon
Cryin' last night
Saw your face
Within her light
A gentle tear
Was streaming down
From eyes so wide
And eyes so round
You were the fire
You were the heat
We lost our love
To admit defeat . . . .

M Wayne Williams

M Wayne Williams
MANY WAYS TO WALK
Today I've decided to accept myself
and the world around me.
Replaced rationalization with
challenge, pain
with tomorrow letting prayer
set me free.

I've learned not to forget those
who lead me to now—be it
good or bad.
For those are the people that gave
me more than I ever had.

And, no matter how you choose to
explain your direction or fate
The hours from one day to the next
are constant and never wait.

There are many ways to walk—in
spirit, in body and within
one's soul.
But only when you walk in them
all will you become whole.

Candice Kay Fuentes
WALKING TOWARDS TOMORROW
O Father come swiftly but gentle as a light breeze. Come as a warm breath bringing freedom to every limb of my body. I pray that there will not be but a whisper of pain. As I lie here lifeless, I wait for my Lord to come and offer me His hand, to walk with me this dark corridor and through the heavy door. I see Jesus enter my room. As He takes my hand my body seems light but full of strength the pain vanishes. Joy floods every fiber of my being. Father lead me home.

Help me not to look at what I leave behind. Where I am going I know. But those I loved in life I leave behind. Father comfort them. Let peace wash over them. Remind all of them, my newness of life and my abode with Jesus. I pray sadness will not linger with them but that Joy will come in the morning. Let them, Father know that I am completely whole. I no longer suffer pain or sorrow. For I have passed over into tomorrow.

Carroll Coleman Bohn
A CIRCLE OF ONE

To my family.

When we first met
My life started anew;
We touched and held hands
And were a circle of two.

I could see no further
Than where you had been,
And no one around us
Did I want to come in.

The circle was small,
And you knew it should grow,
But there was no one else
I wanted to know.

By my own selfish actions
I drove you away,
When all that I wanted
Was for you to stay.

The joys we have shared
And knowing you so,
Make my memories strong
While I'm letting you go.

There's no hand to touch
Or to get warmth from—
Now there's only myself
In a circle of one.

Josephine M Stassi
A SPECIAL MOMENT IN MARCH
While looking out the window, I saw the trees that had been so bare all winter begin to take on a faint shade of green as the "new born" leaves began to bud.

And through the trees, and above, I saw the dark clouds swiftly passing by—a few drops of rain, and then the sun came out.

I eagerly looked all around the sky to see if—and yes, there it was—without fail—a beautiful rainbow.

My heart was filled with joy and I gave thanks for the beauty of the moment and the coming of Spring.

Pamela Nava Vilches
LOOKING DOWN UPON MY WORLD
What is in store for me?
Confined within the walls of
my own city.
Rarely able to experience what is
outside
Yet to whom am I to confide?
What is in store for me?
Afraid to take charge of my

own sea.
Am I really the captain of my ship,
And the master of my fate . . .
. . . or is my life a game in which I started too late?
What is in store for me?
How does one know what he is destined to be?
Focus on today, never on tomorrow,
Only on the joys, never on the sorrows.
What is in store for me?
A life filled with glee.
Forever and ever, Amen.

Diane R Sullivan
HAPPY ANNIVERSARY

Dedicated to my wonderful, loving husband, Michael.

Happy Anniversary Dear,
I guess that's what they say.
Tomorrow it's our 14th anniversary,
Right to the very day.

It seems like just yesterday
that you came my way.

We've surely had our ups and downs,
Our smiles and our frowns,
Our good times and our bad,
But we never did stay mad.

Here's my heart and my very soul,
I've given to you my very whole,
I've devoted all these years to you and the kids,
But, I'll tell you, our alone times
I sure do miss.

We sure have our differences, too,
Me, I like Rock 'n Roll,
You, the Moody Blues.

But basically we've been pretty close,
And have seemed to come from the same pod,
Our interests have intermingled,
And our love has not been a fraud!

You've worked VERY HARD to try
to provide me with the best,
As long as we have our love,
Let God take care of the rest.

True love is hard to find,
And a mate who can love you,
and understand you and be kind.

I have seen so many good qualities in you,
I hope it will take us many more years through,
And you'll be beside me through thick and thin,
And we'll see another and another Anniversary again.

You are a good man—as good as gold.
I hope you'll be that way, even when you grow old,
Today, I'll be thinking of you in all,
I think, say, dream and do.

Be happy, do your best; Let God take care of the rest.

Dear, have a good day,
And there's one more thing I want to say:

HAPPY ANNIVERSARY!
And I love you forever and a day!

Love,
Your Wife.

Victoria A Chik
THE ANSWER
Barely wisps of clouds
Gazed down like angels from the sky.
Then they were smoke—
The Holy Spirit passing by.
There came the help;
I sought an answer to "why?"

Trees gently whispered,
I strained to hear the reply.
Birds taunted me
With their discordant cry.
"Oh, thank YOU, Lord,"
I heard my audible sigh.

Janice J Murphy
MAKE BELIEVE
In your mind
There's a space
For imagination
A wonderful place

To be who you want
And do what you feel
Nothing matters
Because it's not real

Only to you
This land exists
It's magic and mystery
You can't resist

When reality gets you down
You can always retreat
To the secret place
Where life is so sweet

Nancy B Miller
AND WE WILL ALL BE CHANGED
At nine fifty-two
I went to pick some parsley for the meatloaf.
At the top of the porch stairs
I felt
A presence.
A butterfly on the fat yellow marigold was slowly,
silently, pulsing his wings—dreamily.
A Fall butterfly—orange and brown like the chrysanthemums in
the driftwood boxes.
Not especially spectacular.
A touch small.
And fragile.
For eternity that butterfly pulsated slowly.
The wind whispered in the trees out of respect.
A crow jeered, uncaring.
The locusts sang.
And then away it flew.
(Did my coming prompt its leaving?)
Up over the porch rail
Resting briefly on the down spout
Then, over the roof and gone

David V Ouano
THE TIMES
I read about you
In all the papers.
They said you were changing,
Opening up your mind,
Releasing your iron grip.

Your shade was turning,
Mixing with our whites and blues,
Becoming a brighter, beautiful, new color
We all watched and smiled.
I too rejoiced in the revelations.
I was one of the silent many,
Now cheering with the others
For the speeding times,
The raging rampant freedom.

Then, I visited your home,
Saw you behind your curtain . . .
Yes, I see,
It was all an act.
A promising performance I admit.
But, you're still as Red
As a child's weeping wound.

Karen Renyard
MY FRIEND
I have a friend named Ted,
who isn't very old.
He's got stuffing in his head,
and he's always there to hold.
He listens to only me,
when I go to bed at night.
He knows just what I need,
when things aren't going right.
Sometimes when I cry,
he understands my tears.
He just stays by my side,
'til I cry out all my fears.
That stuffing in his head you see,
may be stuffing just to you.
But only my friend Ted and me,
know it isn't true.
It's full of thoughts and dreams,
because he really cares.
And he listens to only me,
'cause he's my Teddy Bear.

Marilyn J Berry
FIRST DAY OF SCHOOL

Dedicated to my beloved son "Douglas."

This morning I softly opened your door
Reluctant to rouse you from sleep
Your blonde hair all tousled from a little boy's dream
And your body curled up in a heap.

For a stolen moment standing there at your door
My mind reached back into time
To a little blue bundle cuddled up in my arms
And gentle hints of a nursery rhyme.

Was it not a mere yesterday
That you were learning how to walk
And I know that it was just last week
We were teaching you to talk.

But somehow I managed to waken you
To your breakfast waiting there
I dressed you in your finest clothes
And I carefully combed your hair.

Oh little boy, I love you so
And I felt like such a fool,
To be so hesitant to let go of you
On your very first day of school.

Carol Rusk
IF ONLY A DREAM
My child you lay there so helpless and weak.
I lifted my eyes to heaven for mercy and help to seek.
I cried out why?
It's just not fair.
God, are you really up there?
God, do you really care?
God, do you hear my inner cry?
Or is my baby son going to die?
Lord, I'm down on bended knee,
Hear me, Lord, my earnest plea.
Lord, my faith is weak, not strong.
My eyes are weary from days and nights so long.
Lord, I need you to close my eyes in rest.
I beg you Lord, my son to bless.
Heal my son with thy mighty power.
Touch him Lord, this very hour.
Take my hand and hold it tight,
Guide me through the rough and lonely nights.

Teresa A Reis
DROWNED LOVE
He told me he loved me,
He told me he cared.
He told me his secrets,
He told me his dreams.
He told me everything
I ever wanted to know.
Now he's gone,
And now I'm lost.
Who will love me?
Who will care?
All his secrets,
And all his dreams,
Drowned in the beer
That killed it all.

Nonnie Ruth Abbott
ENCOURAGEMENT
Along with the sunshine,
God sends the rain.
Sometimes it comes to us,
As a piercing pain.

Life can't always be roses.
There have to be thorns.
Else, we would all forget,
Why God let us be born.

Let us ever look up,
There toward the sky.
We will always find him waiting,
In the sweet by and by.

We should not be discouraged,
When we do not understand.
God is standing there patiently,
And leading us by the hand.

Anna Keyerr Remillard
I MISS YOU MOM
I miss you Mom, I cry,
as I kneel beside your grave.
Born too soon and too small.
Against all odds you did try.
You raised me fine and proper.
Taught and guided, my life you saved.
I, not always being what you wanted.
Fifty-five years you were my best friend.
I know you suffered silently at the end.
Your wisdom and love remain my legacy.
A painless, peaceful place you did transcend.
I miss you Mom I cry.
I miss the Christmases and Easters you gave.
I miss your azure blue eyes that understood,
my pain, fear, doubts, dreams and schemes.
Thank you Mom, for all you went

without,
to give to me and I took for granted.
Those last nine days in October, I felt your pain.
I was with you, day and night, and when God called you,
I cradled you in my arms and let you go.
I love and miss you Mom, more than you'll ever know.

Cynthia Karen Trump
MICHAEL

I have missed you Michael.
The days I have spent alone have been merciless and cruel.
I called for you. You gave no answer, and left me
With the pain in my heart. You left me with no reason
To live. But to die would be too simple.
I have missed you Michael.
The nights I have spent alone have been lonely and evil.
I called for you. You never answered and left me
With the cold, stale air carrying the memories of our times.
The times we will never again share.
I have missed you Michael.
At first my thoughts were purely sympathetic.
But quickly did they change into those from a cold heart.
A heart near death. A heart with no future. And now,
My dearest Michael
I wish it were more than my heart to last.

Georgia C Wiser
HOO! HOO! OWL?

Dedicated to: Mary Pat (Mom) Wiser, for all of her love, support, and belief in me. For her knowledge, strength, beauty, and love of owls.

Hoo! Hoo! asks the owl 'tis why he's wise.
Hoo! Hoo! through the night 'tis all the owl cries.

Hoo! Hoo! lurks after dark searching for his prey?
'Tis the brown-feathered bird who sleeps through the day.

Hoo! Hoo! has the yellow eyes so bright that they glow?
Hoo! Hoo! asks (as if he doesn't know!)

Hoo! Hoo! loves my beauty, strength, and knowledge true?
Hoo! Hoo! that is wise strong and beautiful, too!

Shelly Lord
BY THE SEA

I walked along the beach one morning.
Dawn was coming over the horizon.
The gulls made lazy circles in the sky.
My steps left prints in the sand,
Small shelters for small creatures,
Only to be washed away by the waves.

The water lapped softly against the shore;
The foam, white lace along the sands.
The roar of the ocean surrounded me, protected me.
Ah! The peace that filled me at this sight!
Like the sudden serenity after a storm,
It filled my soul like sweet wine.

Now, as I live on the cold prairies,
And the heaviness of life is upon me,
I need only to close my eyes
And I return to the seashore,
Filled with peace, once more.

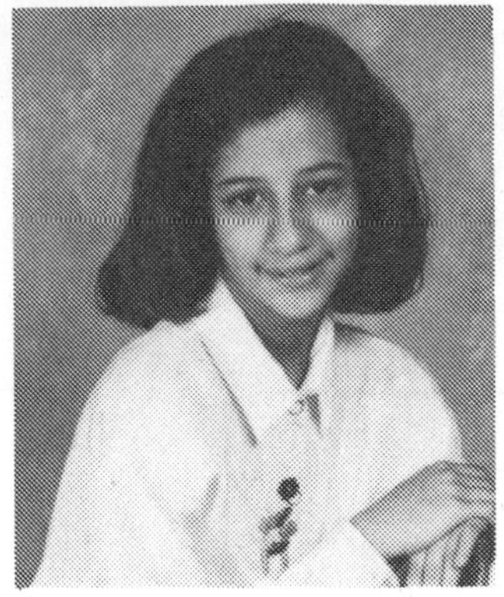

Zinnia Alvarado

Zinnia Alvarado (age 11)
FRIENDS FOREVER OR NEVER

I remember the days we were together, friends!
It seemed forever, you and I together
That's how friends should be

You and I would fight sometimes
but knew deep inside we will always be friends.
Forever together just you and I.

But once again that day came and everything came to a change
Now we are no longer friends and once again I say why was I the only one to cry

Didn't you care that our friendship had died?
I see you in the hallways at school laughing at me making me feel like a fool
I wonder I wonder why this change brought our friendship to an end.

You and I were close, closer than anything
'Til the day that someone else came and ruined our friendship forever.
I felt like a clown and my heart just crumbled to the ground.
But picking up the pieces just won't do
'cause all I do is cry over you,
My lost friend
Even though you and I are no longer friends
I will always keep our last moments as friends in my heart and I will always cry over you, my lost friend.

Joy Carta
LONGING . . .

Lust, thoughts of temptation
Love, blowing in the wind
Leaves, spread across the world
Light, touching every person
Laughter, reaching into our souls
Luck, curing our society
Lines, drawn by the victims
Long, days drifting into time
Life's, changing paths

Barbara B Rhodes
THE SAMENESS

To my Mother, my dear Mother, for her nurturing, her strengthening, her warmth and oneness.

Mother, my dear Mother
When I hold my head this way
And when I laugh or hear myself
Say things that you would say

In your mold my life was formed
In love and gentleness, secure
And in this life as I unfold
A sameness—curious—does stir

I'm proud to hold my head so strong
And laugh with love that beckons love
I am yourself, and as you—I
have grown to where you stand above

And now I know you as myself
And wonder if you feel
This image that, at once, is yours
Wanting to hold close reveal

My love for you, dear Mother

Barbara B Rhodes
DREAMING

If I could gather spirits all
And conquer space in reaching deep
To slowly ascend Midnight's wall
And lastly, gently drift asleep . . .

Dream. Dissolve elusive mind
The frenzied path I follow, quickened
Slowed by dreaming, chased by time
Trailing—lush, and flowers thicken

If I could gift my wisdom's depth
A shell of richness whole unearthed
Bestow—condensed the goodness left
To dreams anew and old re-birthed

Shirley Dionisio
COTILLION

To my 8th grade English teacher, Mrs. Georgia Russell, who showed me the beauty of words . . . and to my grandmother, Nellie Gilbert, who loved the words I wrote.

The fragrance of magnolias
filtered slowly through the air
A summer breeze, though infrequent,
gently brushed against my hair.

Music playing, people dancing,
couples walking hand in hand,
Amidst the crowd I stand alone
a tiny particle of sand.

The sun's descent is fluid
close behind it darkness falls
An atmosphere, almost surreal,
soon veils the garden walls.

Mem'ries of a bygone era
when youth and beauty reigned,
Are all that's left this aged form
a portrait, with no frame.

Shannon Henry
MY FIRST LOVE

This poem is dedicated to my brother, Zebedee Henry IV, as a small gift for the happiness he has brought in my life.

My first love
It came to me as a lost dove
It flew over the vast horizons
And landed in the deepest valley
Where I felt it gladly

My first love
It came to me from above
It landed on my heart
But this was only a start

I held him in my arms
Causing me to release many tears
And interrupting my inner fears
Oh, I knew I loved him

As I kissed him my heart raced
For it was on him in which it was based
I had waited for months to do this
To give him his very first kiss

As he looked at me with his warm eyes
I knew he was all mine
For I had waited a long time
For this great baby brother of mine!

Brenda Betancure
NATURAL ME

To my mother Marie Dillinger for the freedom to experience life, and the confidence to write about it. I Love You, Mom.

You make the woman in me arise, the
small child steps aside.
The beauty once hidden, suddenly appears,
your way of life excites me.
I'm like a small town girl in a big city,
scared yet eager to explore all of life.
Each encounter with you is new and feels
frightening, yet natural to me.
I found myself through the time I've spent
with you.
I feel so natural being who and what
I am, and I thank you my music man . . .

M Neita Ropers
A BIRTHDAY THOUGHT

To my husband, Dieter, on his 50th birthday, July 31, 1990.

Fifty years ago today
A baby boy was born.
On the faces of his family
A happy smile was worn.

For nineteen years he stayed and played,
And worked in his own land.
Then he followed his family across the sea
To a new and different land.

For twenty years or more, he lived
In a state with snow and ice.
Then he smiled to himself and said one day,
"I think Texas would be nice!"

By then we both had made mistakes,
And from them got some 'smarts.'
That is why we found for each other,
A place within our hearts.

So now, I'm thinking happily
Of a little town in Germany—
Where fifty years ago today,
A baby boy was born.

Crystal Emerson
BLIND MAN'S PAIN

He sees not you,
but his ears do.
Where you go the blind man sees.
His ears leading him along,
he wonders without wrongness,
For he is human, too.

Sometimes he hears little children,
Asking,
"What's wrong with that man?"
For he is old and lonely,
The fear of not knowing what lies in the dark.
He and his cane go place to place,
wondering in shadows.
For he is human, too . . . .

Judith A Davis
THANK YOU LORD

Every morning, when the sun comes up

I thank the Lord, for his warming touch!
To hear the birds sing and see skies of blue
I ponder of all the things I must do!
I think of my friends, who are special and dear
They are true friends—from God I hear.
Sometimes in pain and not feeling well
We put on a smile and listen as well
It takes so little—to please someone,
That you find a reward in all you have done!
With God on my side and Angels to guide
I'll hold up my head and walk with pride!
Time is so short and so much to do
May God give me strength and peace in all I do.

Anna Keyerr Remillard
DO YOU KNOW

Dedicated to Richard, who inspired, encouraged, and believed in me.

Do you know, after loving me,
when you leave, the scent of you
remains in tangled sheets, and in
my exhausted sleep, I dream we are
lovers walking barefoot, hand in hand,
like children, kicking up the sand,
splashing waves, rushing into shore,
only to die, slipping back into the
sea to be reborn evermore.

The sun warms us, moonlight holding us in its spell,
salty sea winds caressing our bodies,
as we melt into a kiss. I awake
trembling from your touch, with the
realization of it being a dream.
Another day dawns, another day
closer to when I'll be with you again.

Jeanne Patton
DO YOU KNOW WHAT I SAW

Do you know what I saw today? I
saw a house without a yard selling for
a million dollars. Do you know what
else I saw today? I saw a hogan with
no plumbing, housing six people.

Do you know what I saw today? I
saw a woman with long tapered nails
getting a manicure. And oh yes, do
you know what else I saw today? I
saw the cracked worn hands of a
woman doing laundry in a cold
stream with lye soap.

Do you know what I saw today? I
saw a fat toad of a man stuffing his
cheeks full of more fat food. And oh
yes, do you know what else I saw
today? I saw a wide eyed, starving
child pleading for a crust of bread.

Do you know what I saw today? I
saw a very chic lady buying a lynx
coat. And oh yes, do you know what
else I saw today? I saw a poor
helpless animal chewing its foot off
in a trap to save its life.

Do you know what I saw today? I
saw a matron, chattering her way
through a concert. And oh yes, do
you know what else I saw today? I
saw a hundred tattered people
listening quietly to an impromptu
park band.

I saw a wino, a limousine, a beautiful
building marred with graffiti, a rose.

You know, I think I saw a lot today.

Rose Vanderlip
WHY OWLS ARE SO SMART

To Roxanne Dougherty, kindergarten teacher at Mar Lee School, who faithfully read all of my sixty-five children's story poems to her pupils; my husband, Fred; my grandchildren and everyone who has supported and helped me.

Hooty was a great horned owl
Who lived near a deep blue pool.
He watched the critters every day
As they went along to school.

He saw the happy frogs go by
As they hopped along their way.
They never missed one day of school
And they were learning every day.

He saw the rats as they stopped by
To play and sleep and eat.
They hardly ever were in school
And when they were they'd cheat.

The frogs grew up to be real smart
For they learned to read and write
But the rats grew up without a doubt
To be the dumbest critters in sight.

Well, as Hooty sat upon his limb
He was glad he'd been to school.
He studied hard to learn his lessons.
He didn't want to be a fool.

Cathy Jo Stout
THE ESTATE SALE

Tomorrow,
people will come to bid on these,
left by the old women,
fragments of heritage,
now mere ghosts of day-ago
memories.
On the storm, impending,
laughter merges with empty quiet
and hint of yeast, warm,
drifts from an open window.
Years echo thru rooms as gently
I touch each oaken memory,
solid in my mind like the tree
from which it was crafted.
Tied with string, a bundle of letters
etched in ink, faded as the years,
with me I'll take
to be treasured by lovers future.
Smell now, entwined with musty rain,
of old women and lilac, lingering
among the lace.
Remnants of these folded years greet the dawn
as she remembers . . .

José Vasilio Torres
THE FROZEN CREEK

The silence of Winter is all around
me; white hills,
trees with the whiteness of Nature's
frozen tears at its peak,
sitting in a place with much a killing chill,
as I stare at the frozen creek.
The noise of the world surrounds me;
black and white,
battling each other's intelligence, it's
power we seek,
I hear those battles every endless night,
and as I stare at the frozen creek.
The waste of the world is closing in
on us; human products,
most of us only think of ourselves,
not what Nature can keep,
it's obvious that Man only thinks of
the Almighty Buck,
as I stare at the frozen creek.
The walls of time close in on Man's
ultimate misery; carnage,
for the pit of despair will bury our
ignorance in rather deep,
many people can foresee the coming
of a boldly cold dark age,
and I do too, as I stare at the frozen creek.

Nancy Kimball-Miller
THE TREE

I saw a tree standing alone.
I wondered, how does the tree feel?
The tree must be lonely—I thought.
I walked to the tree—and,
felt the loneliness. So,
I sat by the tree: and pondered—
how could I take away the loneliness.
Then I knew—I'd plant another tree,
or two—So I did.

Kathleen J Miller
FOR THE NURSES

You tucked pillows around my head
washed my back, rubbed it too,
changed the sheets upon my bed
for this I thank you.

You checked my vital signs
each shift worked as a crew,
on my legs drew designs
I thank you.

You listened to me complain
each and every one of you,
it's your energy I drain
Thank you for all you do.

In the still of the night
you come walking through
making sure everything's alright,
I thank each one of you.

You helped me laugh when I cried
difficult times I'm going through,
You knew the truth, to others I lied
I thank you.

Jeannette C Butterfield

Jeannette C Butterfield
MOVEMENT OF TIME

This poem is dedicated to my son Joel, who is sorely missed. Love Mom

When the sun came round
The moon gave way to
The bright needing
Of day
So was the space
So was the moist dew
So clever the movement
Of time

When the sun came round
The flower's face smiled
Its approval, dripping
With silent dew
Dreams

So was the space
So was the moist dream
So clever the movement
Of time

Chrisi Cavaness
EYES LOOKING INTO THE GALAXY

I dedicate the poem "Eyes Looking Into the Galaxy" to my parents and friends and dreams.

Love is a mystery
It's hard to find
So many clues
Never making sense
What is love?
One of the greatest wonders
Maybe it's just a four letter word
Who knows
It could be a rose
Beautiful at first
Then dying
Turning into something ugly
How can we find love?
Through the eyes?
Maybe through a language?
We'll never know
The constellation is our only clue.

Christine M Flores
DAYS OF OLD

Oh, I remember
When we were young . . .

So strong and full of life
The songs we had sung . . .

And yes, I recall
The days of old . . .

But somehow we got careless
And broke that mold . . .

No longer shimmering
Silver and gold . . .

For the time has come when
Men's souls are bought and
sold . . .

Heather Lynn Halstead
NIGHT CYCLE

Beckoning in melodic voice,
The time of stars and fireflies;
Sleeping child, restless, stirs,
And slowly opens drowsy eyes.
Dark lashes flutter, vaguely see
The flooding silver on the floor.
Slipping softly from the house
She tiptoes quickly through the door.

Dusky shadows all around,
Liegemen of the Master night;
Playful winding winds entwine
Whilst scattered leaves are whirled in flight.
Phantom forms are merged and blurred,
And nighttime echoes mournful cries;
Opaque mists engulf and shroud
As swaying forms touch passer-bys.

Along the path the wood withdraws,
And night unveils its shining stage;
Velvet black with pinprick lights,
The glowing works of ancient mage.
The Dreamer treads on silent sands,
Gliding through the pool of time;
A solitary trail of prints
Is soon erased by cleansing tide.
Moon-child waves erode the night,
And midnight fades to lighter grey.

Lulled by the rhythmic sounds
The Dreamer sees the touch of day.
Sea-salt grasses catch the breeze,
An artist paints in rose, afar.
Day comes; a prelude to the night;
"The sun is but a morning star."

Jamie Johnston
A POEM, A PRAYER, A PROMISE (TO MY WIFE)

To Dodie Owens, in loving memory of your husband, David Owens, December 26, 1989. With love and understanding, your daughter, Jamie.

To my wife, whom I loved with all my heart
Thank you for your loving touch
Your kindness and your caring for me.
I wished I could have told you every day how much I loved you, but the words would not come out right.
You cared so much at times
I wanted to cry for you.
The years passed by so quickly it seemed not so long at all my time with you.
I pray, Dodie, your happiness and forgiveness for my leaving you so badly broken-hearted, and alone.
I promise you, Dodie, I loved you very much, and I'll miss your loving touch and gentle words.
Goodnight, my love, sleep well.
I'll see you in our dreams, goodnight.
Love you, Dode!

Brad Busch
PERSUASION TO LOVE
Losing fear, the first and last to fall,
Pain, compelling restlessness, today and tomorrow;
Casting aside weary pride, let dormant spirit release,
Led by unseen presence, unique joy and sorrow.

Excitement envelopes me, baring weakness and strength,
Slowly and swiftly it travels, no sound revealing arrival;
Composing each thought quietly, and loudly proclaiming,
Direction lost yet found, extolling survival.

Tranquil and stormy variance, joining restless zeal,
I shine before its brilliant light;
Futile attempt at distinguishing unspoken appeal,
I reach and cannot grasp, I look and lose sight.

Subtly invited by marvelous force,
Accepting destiny's strong and gentle shove;
Truth beyond capacity to understand,
Guiding me, with persuasion to love.

Samuel Lee Oliver
THE MIND OF A POET
Poets write many things
about life and what it brings.
They touch the depths of the soul
and uncover stories to be told.

A poem is more than simple articulations
about people and this creation.
It is a description of inner ties
from poets who want to know why.

Why humanity has to struggle so much
to be able to stay in touch
with God who created in us a
blessing
that humans find so distressing.

Then, what we fear turns into relief
and what we learn is to grieve
a life in need of grace
in order to someday see—God's face.

Stefan M DiFrancesco
HEARTS OF FIRE

To Cassie, my love, you set my heart on fire.

In my heart there burns a fire
Red and hot with love and desire
Desire strong and love so true
All this I feel burning for you

A fire so high, a fire so bright
Its light piercing the velvet night
Calling to the one who keeps a fire too
All this burning I made for you

Then she came bringing the same
Only adding to the heat and flame
So intense a fire, there was nothing to do
A fire out of control made by me and you

We tried not to flee, we tried not to run
Instead we let the flames consume us and make us one
Tongues of fire lashing at us bright and hot
Yet all of it burning us not

In its place was coolness and comfort
Also there was understanding and compassion
There too was all that is light and true
These things we try to give to each other
And these things we long to receive
There inside the fire we gave ourselves to one another
Inside the heat and fire forged by love and desire
We were bound to each other by hearts of fire

Alex Ferro

Alex Ferro
AMOR

A mis hijos: Rigoberto, Giovanny, Diana, Mauricio A. y Dennis Fernando, a mis nietos y nietas con ternura maternal.

¡Que palabra tan pequeña!
cuatro letras nada mas,
si la siembras en tu alma
con sinceridad y candor,
crece, crece cada dia
y mitigaras dolor.

Ama el pobre,
ama el rico,
ama el anciano y el niño.
¡Cuan grande es su poder!
que si el universo entero
la cultivara en su ser,
toda soledad y dolor,
se borraria con amor.

Jack S Brenizer
LOVE
Love is the greatest gift we can receive
Coming from deep within the heart.
Its power must not be used to deceive
Destroying one love would impart.

Love inspires wherever shown
From the least to life's most blessed.
Seek ways to share love of your own
Increasing your life's value when assessed.

All love is from heaven sent
And greatly enhances all of life—
It's endless and is never fully spent,
So use it freely whether in joy or strife.

Vickie Batzer
DOCTORS?: NO.
Physicians are a dime
a dozen.
And they rarely probe
to where it really hurts.
Giving out prescriptions
Like free pennies,
that work like Band-Aids.

James Andrew Quarry
THE WITCH'S QUEST
An eye of green and one of blue,
On the devil's wings she flew;
Her hair as dark as raven's breast,
Onward, onward in her quest.

By night she brewed her poignant stew,
By day she slept beneath the dew;
Ever she searched among the blest,
To find that great eternal rest.

The one who had the strength to hew,
The ever binding chain in two;
To free her from her deep distress,
And from demons depossess.

Linda L Landry
THE GOOD OLD DAYS

To Debbie, I love you, sis.

We used to drive the hornet,
all around town.
Just to see what was going down.
We would crank up the tunes,
as loud as they could go.
And we would have a blast,
as long as dad didn't know.
We got in a lot of trouble,
but I still thought it was fun.
But now that fun is over and done.
You went your way,
and I went mine.
And I know that everything is fine.
I remember the good old days,
all of the time.
Because the good old days,
are like a fine wine.
The good old days will always remain.
Because you and me will always walk,
down memory lane.

Wendy Hernandez
HURT
Outside is sunny and bright
But inside it's dark with rain
Outside is happy and laughing
Inside is hate and pain

Outside is calm and warm
Inside is anger and hurt
Outside is joy and fun
Inside feels like dirt
I sometimes wish I was outside
So many days gone by
I don't think I'll ever get there
Inside I'll forever cry

Branden Smale
BULLFROG

I would like to dedicate the following poem to my English teacher, Brad Shurmantine, Vintage High School, Napa, California.

With legs outstretched,
An Olympic swimmer striving for the gold.
With nostrils closed;
With eyes covered,
He swims towards the lily pad,
Getting ready to accept the gold.
He shoots out of the water onto the lily pad,
Proud of himself.
He waits.
He waits for a fly.
His tongue shoots out his little mouth;
He chews and swallows,
A young child, hungry; without manners.
Satisfied, he jumps off the lily pad,
And disappears into the
Deep,
Black,
Darkness.
A mystery man on a full
Summer's
Moon.

Ada Ghuman
THE EYES
The wealth
of man cannot
be found on
granite hard nor on
soiled stock.

I have never seen it
inside soft silks
nor hidden
on attic sills.

Wealth I have seen in
the eyes
of old and young
luminous and fine
rich in spirit
fortunate in love.

Wealth can be found
only in the eyes.

Rev Lucius C Gallion
I'M NOT MAKING THIS JOURNEY ALONE
Since I've started my journey,
My family is gone.
My friends have rejected me.
My neighbors unknown.
But I shall endure, unless overthrown.
I'm not making this journey alone.

Since I've started my journey,
Life has been hard.
I've been called everything, but a child of God.
I have no time for worry or time for fear.
Though I seem to be alone, Jesus is near.
To all young people and old just the same,
Seek our Lord, Jesus.
Make salvation your aim.
Now I'll continue my journey to our father's throne.
I'm not making this journey alone.

Rev Lucius C Gallion
I SAW THE LORD
(Refrain)
I saw the Lord (I saw the Lord.)
I saw the Lord. (I saw the Lord.)
Yes, within him (pause) I saw the Lord. (I saw the Lord.)

While roaming the streets, I met a young boy,
With no food to eat, yet filled with joy.
Speaking unto him, I couldn't avoid,
For within him I saw the Lord.

He reached out to me, holding in his hand,
A book he had read, but didn't understand.
He said unto me, "Before they died,
They told me this book would be my guide."
The words he spoke with joy I heard
And read unto him God's holy word.

Then there joined us a young police.
He said, "I'm sorry, but you're disturbing the peace."
He said, "I have a home right down the street.
Here, take my keys and there you may eat."

Rev Lucius C Gallion
THE BOUNDARY OF HATRED
There's a thin line between love and hate, like an imaginary line, separating county from county, state from state, nation from nation. Yet it's more dreadful, for it keeps apart those who would very much love to be together, but are afraid of being caught in a hurricane of suggestions that will never succeed. But the first step must be taken; just as with a baby, who will only walk if he makes the first step.

Let us rid ourselves of such, sending those demons who now dance and rejoice upon that line that puts us into two different worlds, having the same aims and our goals such a short distance from us, into another universe. Yet, we'll never succeed as long as hatred lies between us, not allowing one to touch the hand of the other. It's a sickening line that brings forth tears unasked for.

Let us not be as idols, closing our eyes that it be not seen, shutting our ears that we hear not the words, though like daggers they put a pain in our hearts, hard to bear. Yet we must live with it, or like the paralyzing of the body that won't allow us to taste of the true feelings within. Let us not let it be as such. For a long time lies ahead of us. 'Tis too precious to waste.

Rev Lucius C Gallion
TORNADO—32
The month was January. The year, 1938.
Dear Grandson, I shall remember that familiar date.
A tragic storm almost took away my life.
But instead it took away that of my former wife.
It was a storm of tornadoes from the ground to the sky.
We stood outside and counted, as they went by.
The 31st tornado caused a lot of trouble.
Once it would split. Twice it would double.
I thought that was all a tornado could do.
Until I saw the size of tornado—32.
It traveled through the town in a straight line
And caused more trouble than the others combined.
It picked houses and stores off the ground.
Then all of a sudden put them back down.
To me she said, "That's all it can do?"
To her I said, "It isn't through."
After entering the house and closing the door,
I heard her voice just once more.
Dear Grandson, what I've said is true.
That was a hell of a tornado, number 32.

Rev Lucius C Gallion
FREEDOM WITHOUT A HOME
For centuries I have searched for a home.
But not one have I found.
Each time I begin to spread my roots
I find bitterness in the ground.

The greed of my neighbors brings sadness to my eyes.
It increases moresoever,
While my young friends continue to die.

The hatred of my former home
Keeps them even farther apart.
They have no ears to hear.
What's worst, they have no heart.

If only I could get them together,
Then I would have a home.
But if they continuously repel each other,
I might as well move on.

Susan P Selnau
A LEGACY
I am
All that my mother
Was
She was
All that her mother
Could be

My daughter
Thus becomes
All that I am
And on it goes
For eternity

James F Dew Jr
ON LIFE—AND DEATH
I lost another friend last night,
To "Old Father Time" and the "Reaper" so grim;
Makes me wonder how long, and by just what right,
I remain; but one day all too soon,
I must surely follow him.

Still I've no regrets—I've made my own way,
I've done pretty much as I wanted to do.
I've lived a good life, and dread not so badly the day,
When it will become my time to depart from here too.

Oh, I'd hate to leave here, for I very dearly love life,
I've a family so dear, and loved ones so true;
The best girl in the world is mine for a wife,
Strong sons and darling daughters to carry on when I'm through.

To face the unknown fairly boggles the mind,
But it's just one of those things that we all have to do.
And the same God who has watched over us so kind,
Is still up in Heaven and still watches over us too.

So here's to tomorrow—may we all again see the dawn,
Here's to years yet to come, may they be long and gay;
But one thing to remember, comes the time when I'm gone,
I've enjoyed to the fullest the things that God gave me today.

Jim Roiger
CARRIER LAUNCH
The engines moan in anticipation.
Colored lights wink and gauges steady.
Helmeted white ghosts caress
the skin and surfaces, verify
the fluid levels.
With thumbs-up all around,
a yellow arm rises.
I throttle-up, stir the joystick.
Surfaces move, imitating
a dancing marionette. The moan
becomes a crescendo.
I salute. The arm drops.

Metal grinds against metal.
I am cocooned by the seat,
unable to move as the shuddering
hulk gathers speed. Then,
gently released, I sense blue above
and below. Airborne,
I am alive.

Leonard A Grades
LOVE IS FUNNY
Our love is renewable as a morning sunrise—
Each day its radiance is restored.
Each dawn we're granted the rays of new feelings.
How different things in such a light!
What makes the eyes laugh—is the sheer comedy of life.
For in all we do there's humor—just look for it!
And when we see the funny side—when all others are viewing grief—
Our eyes sparkle with happy remembering.
When our life has a companion, our spirit's a troupe of clowns—
Romping through routines that makes belly laughs for our soul!
Comedy is everywhere—and laughter is our nourishment!
Thank you my love, for this front-row seat at life's burlesque show!
This romance tickles my heart and I'll spend my time in chuckles!

Mary Ball
IN MEMORY OF MY DEAR FATHER
Dear Daddy
How I miss you
And wish you were here
I think of you; your kindness, your honesty
You were always there to help others
Never expecting anything in return
How I'd like to see you, Daddy
Are you happy, now Daddy?
I hope the pain and trouble you had here on Earth
Are forever gone for you
I'd like to wake up tomorrow
And see your funny old jeep coming down the road again
And see your careworn face once more
It's funny somehow when I'm down,
I can feel your
presence with me
Although I never told you enough
I love you, Daddy

Rebecca Booher
MUSIC—ITS PLACE IN THE WORLD
In thinking about music and its place in the world, one might first think about what the world would be like without music in that place:

A sleepy child put down to bed,
Would have no songs to rest his head.
His mother would tuck him in real tight,
But there would be no lullaby that night.

The praises to our Lord and King,
How much joy could they really bring?
For not a voice inside would sing,
And certainly not a bell would ring.

A family gathering outside at night,
Would be without folk tunes sung with delight.
The tiny children drawn 'round the fire,
Might have to settle with a clown to hire.

How about war, and the sorrow it brings,
What trumpets could play its "Taps" that should ring?
The little boy's drum that brings forth the beat,
Would have no effect on a weary soldier's feet.

Symphonies, orchestras, choirs, or bands,
Wouldn't be heard throughout any lands,
What about concerts, solos, or riffs,
There wouldn't even be a Beethoven's Fifth.

What company would there be for long driving trips?
Certainly, not, Gladys Night and the Pips!
Nothing but silence would be at your side,
No matter how long the trip or the ride.

These sounds that seem part of everyone's life,
Would keep to themselves apart from the world;
Until it was realized that the people here and now
Hold their place in the world somehow.

John Buld
A PENCIL GETS LOST
My pencil: freshly pointed
and rubbered and warmed by
the hand, had escaped in
the folds, as I was
proofing my verse.

Where did it go, the yellow one,
slightly dulled where graphite
is and already chewed by
erasures?

Did I show no mercy,
at all, toward my evasions
of clarity and too little
charity, my verse was
in need for?

Was the pencil, I mistook for a
docile ally, saner
than I?

Kathy L Mocny
TO LIVE A DREAM
My imagination has gone afire, as an inferno blazing high.
It was sparked by your heartfelt words and the desperateness of the lie.
It burns hotter and more brilliant than ten times all known suns,
And torments me to the hopeless point of knowing you're the one.

It's been you that has unlocked this door I have shut myself behind.
Your song was what released me into another place and time.
It's the timbre I find in your voice that drives me far beyond
The point of simply being free and into being overcome!

My rationale cannot now rescue me from whatever may be wrong.
It can't draw close enough to pull me from the flames so hot and strong.
If not dealt with quick and carnally,
I'll be totally consumed
By the fires of my Gehenna 'til my life be as a tomb.

But if only you could come to me and steal me away
From these fiery thoughts of mine that I've fashioned here today,
My heart would truly live a dream as forever would be sired;
For only in your touch can you extinguish dreams desired.

Teresa Evans
I'D RATHER
I'd rather have nothing,
than have a broken wing.
I'd rather be alone,
than throw stones.
I'd rather die,
than lie.
I'd rather be sad,
than bad.
I'd rather have a frown
and be down,
than have a smile
that lasted for miles.
I'd rather be without you
and be blue,
than be hurt by you.

Mary L Higgins
I OPENED MY EYES

To E.V.H. with all my love.

I opened my eyes as
his body moved in
rhythm with mine.
I looked deeply into
his eyes, his face, his soul.
I saw strength, beauty,
warmth, love.
I saw me.

Elizabeth Tracy

Elizabeth Tracy
TEAR DROPS FROM HEAVEN

To all workers for a cleaner planet.

'Tis woe to me when a bird dies on the wing.
Its fluttering young to never sing
A hideous sight to see the dead fish
on the shore of the sea.
The teardrops of the Almighty fill my heart
with fear for all that do not see or hear,
or care not for the future.

Where art thy heartfelt thanks
of yesteryear, did it beat in the bosom of the dead long ago?
Why the learned do not know when to stop
and how to sow?
Within my heart the teardrops bleed longing
for knowledge when and how to plant the seed.
Thee that lust after wants seek and see.
Ear and eye, will tell thee.
Want for God, thy foolish one
for God, alone can save thee.

Melony Thompson
WAR
Monotonous wars and
the cries of pain
Continuous yelling of
words that destroy
Severed bones and
reblackened bruises
The shattering of vows
Battered wives
Marriages taken through hell.

Loraine Gearhart, aka Monica Michaels
YESTERDAY REVISITED

To Leanne with Love . . . now it's your turn.

Her feet and her midriff are always quite bare;
She's forever fooling around with her hair;
Her outrageous language exasperates me . . .
What I'd do without her, though, I just can't see.

She talks back . . . she sasses me, time and again,
And makes me feel like a dowdy, old hen!
Her manners are rude, her clothes are much worse,
And the money she costs me is really a curse.

But then, when she's gone, it's strange, I must say,
That my peace of mind is the price that I pay.
There's no one to make me feel young anymore . . .
To reflect the young girl that I was, years before.

Was I just like her when I was her age?
Could I have been such a total outrage?
It's odd how time changes the way that I see:
This child . . . who undoes me . . . is EXACTLY like me!

Margaret Ferrelli
BURNED BY THE WINTER SUN
I sat on the windswept beach . . .
feeling downcast . . . and crying
I steeled myself . . . to refrain from dying
My capricious lover was
absent . . . vanished . . . gone
Our liaison . . . torrid kisses that
flourished and flamed . . . were done
Deception . . . I listened to his lies
and flattery . . . under the pale moon
Promises that were unrealistic . . .
paled by the light of the next day noon

I met this man, in February, on a
cruise ship bound for Bermuda,
honeymoon haven
He was urbane . . . forty-ish . . . pale
white skin . . . gray eyes . . . his heart was craven
A coward, he was . . . he
demurred . . . hid the truth . . . down to his boots
The dark mirror of his soul . . . a
philandering scoundrel . . . I was duped
Naive . . . an unattached middle-aged
woman . . . gregarious . . . so humiliated
"Prince Charming" struck a
responsive chord . . . our ardor was sated

As we dined in the ambience of a
restaurant with a Spanish galleon theme
Suddenly, I heard a sharp
exclamation . . . a strangled
sob . . . a screeching scream!!
An exotic bronze native
woman . . . dark flashing eyes . . .
aiming a dark flashing gun!!!
His WIFE!! Proven
unmistakably . . . rampant
jealousy . . . BURNED by the
WINTER SUN

Police were summoned . . . examined
his lifeless body and took it away
My fear . . . puzzlement . . . the
terrifying rage etched on her face that day
A broiling winter sun . . . my hot
bitter tears rained upon the pink coral sand
Dishonored . . . scorned . . . languid
beauty, forgotten . . . wrested from my hand
Forget . . . Return home . . . Vow to
never again be . . . BURNED by the
WINTER SUN

Margot B Collings
TO BEN

As a parentally-abducted child, Ben was a victim of vengeance. He is now safely back at home, and I am his babysitter once more.

I wonder where you are tonight,
if you're safe and warm,
And if, somehow, you're happy,
while we all wait and mourn.
I wonder if you miss us,
if you call our names out loud,
And how you deal with living
inside a big, dark cloud.
We're trying hard to find you,
as we've done for oh—so—long.
But things will never be all right
until they can see it's wrong.
It seems they think it's all a game,
and they don't see what's true—
That the one who's really losing
is precious, innocent you.
I hope you still express your joy
and live as if you're free.
And someday I hope to share, again,
the love you gave to me.

Marlene C Jinkins
A PATRIOT: OLIVER NORTH
By definition secret is a covert operation—
This one to aid the underdog within a struggling nation.
The Nicaraguan Contras at the time were batting zero,
With Congress cutting off all funds,
Then, Semper Fi! A Hero!
This was no time for cowardice, he did as he was told
And carried out his mission with maneuvers shrewd and bold.
He did his best to follow what he thought would represent
The non-specific wishes of our nation's President.

A shame the way they left him.
Abandoned. None would tell.
A Patriot. His only crime—
He did his job too well.

Alice Obey Guidry
A BLESSING PERSONIFIED

To my three blessings—Fredrae Trenice; Christopher Lawrence & Brettynia Rachelle—all of whom I will love and cherish all the days of our lives and beyond all time to come.

You carry within your body all that is wonderful and good,
For you have been embraced into the state of motherhood.

You wait in anticipation for what was once a minute seed,
To willingly give of yourself—to give what it might need.

Making plans and creating dreams by which you will abide,
When part of your being emerges and is placed right by your side.

Now amazed and overwhelmed by what your eyes are seeing,
You instinctively reach out without a doubt to embrace the tiny being.

A part of you that will make you proud and sometimes make you cry,
Yet a part of you to cherish 'til the very day you die.

Yet take this joy unto you and thank the Lord above,
For sending someone else to love you and someone else for you to love.

Daisy L Sharp

MOM

Dedicated to Betty L. May, My Mom, With All My Love.

Forty years of loving,
In ten different ways.
Trying to catch up to,
What to most, was yesterday.
No time were you allotted,
To dream of days to come.
So busy with the ten of us,
Assuring us, your love.
My room is now a hideaway,
To gather thoughts of past.
As young, I thought I was,
The one your heart put last.
Now I share your future,
As unfair as it may be.
I'll never doubt your love again,
For it's been shared, so equally.

Joan A Clow

Joan A Clow

WHEN AUTUMN LEAVES

Dedicated to my three daughters, Michelle, Melanie and Melissa, to my Lord Jesus Christ and to all those who encourage me to write.

All the shades have turned from red and gold to dying brown on earth and soul
And Autumn leaves . . . and we ought'a get going
'Cause the green's all gone and the bare truth's showing
Like the Autumn leaves . . . when Autumn leaves
And the colors all fall down

Now the skies have turned from blue to grey
And stark, bare branches softly sway
And Autumn leaves . . . and we ought'a start going
'Cause the green's all gone and the fireplace is glowing
With the Autumn leaves . . . when Autumn leaves
And the colors all fall down

But your body's warm and the winter's cold
Life and hope still stirs within our souls
And Autumn leaves . . . and we should'a got going
When the green dried up and bareness started showing
Thru the Autumn leaves . . . when Autumn leaves
And the colors all fell down

Joan A Clow

SOUL SEARCHING—ONE YEAR A.D. (AFTER DIVORCE)

Ah, what would you do now, oh soul set free
Still tainted with sharp, bitter memory
Oft' pierced within by fiery points of pain
Now metamorphosed, longs to rise again

With what, my soul, would you replace the years
Whose long, corrosive dregs you've cleansed with tears
Discovering much unworthy of retain
The heart, once captive, sheds its heavy chain

From whence, my soul, will you derive the way
To soar above the ashes of dismay
An enigmatic proselyte of fate
Quiescent once, now quickened to relate

What truth, my soul, do you yearn to discover
Of betrayals and violations, how recover
From life's vast volumes penned, answers surmise
Nay, greater far to spread new wings and rise

Joan A Clow

ARTISTIC ATMOSPHERE

Gentle Artist . . . Pure young Dawn clad in pastel negligee
Arises from her misty bed to greet the ancient Sun each day
Her wondrous palette filled with the palest of all shades
Paints life's promising beginnings . . . then sweetly, silently she fades

Bright, bust Artist . . . Master Day does his abstracts all on blues
Sometimes dabbling in grey; always swiftly changing views
Blending, floating, swirling forms; white or grey of various texture
Life's drama settings, his creation . . . kissed by Sun emerge majestic

Flashy Artist . . . Gorgeous Eve takes her place now high above
With bold and brilliant strokes she paints bright endings with her love
Gold, red, purple, pink or scarlet; Eve's most fanciful of notions
As she tucks the sinking Sun . . . beneath the mountains, trees and oceans

Somber Artist . . . Old Lord Night arises after fading gold
With Silver moonbeams and reflections works in colors warm or cold
Sparkling, golden star specks sprinkled on canvas dark and satin lined
He paints soft canopies for dreamers . . . deep shadows for the restless mind

Joan A Clow

I HAVE FELT THE MORNING

Oh, I have felt the morning burst upon my youth with joy that stirred my soul
Wakening to eager strains within my heart that shimmered like pure gold
Arising fresh to greet the day, anticipating what it held in store
Never once believing life could get me down as I walked through the door

Oh, I have felt the morning's soft, rose glow upon the face of newborn child
Awakening within my breast a wonder at this pureness undefiled
Arising to the urgent voice of crying as my flesh and blood had need
Never once believing there would ever be a time I couldn't heed

Oh, I have felt the morning clutch my inward depths with fingers icy cold
Wishing not to waken to realities that never were foretold
Arising to a sinking feeling weighing on my spirit, with a sigh
Never having once perceived the awesome darkness of this sad goodbye

Oh, I have felt the morning's clear dawn beckon me to sparkling crystal dews
Awakening my senses to the tingling smell of coffee; and the news
Arising once again with hope inspired as today's horizons soared
Ever found believing precious love, when shared, will deepen and endure

Judy Starnes

BLOCKED!

These poems are dedicated to my wonderful husband and kids, my best friend and sister, Claudia Caffes, and my special friends who know who they are!

I want to write something fresh and new!
But, my eyes are red and I am blue, I am blocked!
I have this poem I want to write, full of lots of good insight!
But, my eyes are red and I am blue, I am blocked!
I am an amateur writer, not published yet!
But, my eyes are red and I am blue, I am blocked!
I have the courage, but, I lack the pep!
But, my eyes are red and I am blue, I am blocked!
Everything in God's green earth has kept me from this typewriter!
But, my eyes are red and I am blue, I am blocked!
Fatigue, the kids, a crisis or two!
But, my eyes are red and I am blue, I am blocked!
I have all these beautiful images in mind that I could put to rhyme!
But, my eyes are red and I am blue, I am blocked!
What? What do I see? A poem is before me!
But, my eyes are red and I am blue, I am blocked!
It may not be what I wanted it to be!
And my eyes are still red and I am still blue, but it will just have to do!
I am blocked!!!

Joanne C Oakley

A TIME TO SPEND A TIME TO SACRIFICE

At times we get carried away,
We don't want to wait another day,
So charge it that's what we say,
It's summertime and we want to play.

But if we thought about tomorrow,
We might not be so eager to borrow,
When our creditors come we feel sorrow,
Let's all think about tomorrow.

Life is hectic we all know that,
Are you sure you need that $50.00 hat?
And what about that feline, a $200.00 cat?
Are we sure we need a $20.00 welcome mat?

Let's think twice and a triple thought too,
And stop the buying, and enroll in school,
Maybe we all need to forget what we want,
Or those creditors actually will come and haunt.

We could smile in the morning,
We could be happy and not scorning,
We could sleep sound at night,
It would be so great to see the light,
And not worry, because, we used our insights.

Betty Klipstein

THE SWEETEST GIFT—IS LIFE

So often, we just take life for granted.
We don't live each day to its fullest.
We mosey along, letting most of life flow by,
Wasting the value of each day and every day.

Opportunities come our way, but we miss out.
We are too scared to give it our best try.
We just sit by and say we can't.
So then, we don't know what might have been.

The good Lord gave each of us some talent.
Maybe some seem to have more than others.
But then some have never tried to do things.
While others try and give their all.

Life can be like a breath of fresh air.
Always flowing for those who can take a breath.
It is like the currents in the river or waterfall.
Always flowing through the rough and calm.

Think of your Father up above.
Give thanks to what He has given.
Try to do your best in all,
For the most precious gift—Is the Gift of Life!

Andrew Tassler

FOOTBALL

It's high in the air
And it comes fast and hard
I think it will hurt me
But, it never really does.

David D Porter

THE TIME WE MET I WAS THE LIGHT

The time we met I was the light
it shined in your eyes that night
It made me feel you'd be the one
I want to see, can it be done

I felt that I had met the one
come with me and be my love
I may be bouncing I don't know
can I let my feelings show

How do I show you I am there
and see if we are meant to share
Share a life just for two
I hope that you want it too

I want to hold you, can it be true
I don't know if you want me too
If I reach for you, will you run
I hope you want to have some fun

I want to love and trust thee
Trust is very hard for me
I've been burned twice you see
I really hope I can trust thee

Kelly Gavin
COMMON "SENSE"
Someone "Speaks"
But do we "Listen"?
Flowers are "Sweet"
But do we "Smell"?
Fire is "Hot"
But do we "Touch"?
Love is "Bitter"
But do we "Taste"?
Hearts are "Broken"
But do we "Feel"?

Alma Joyce Zabka
WITHHOLDING
When passions lay buried
'Neath earth and sea
Some shall arise or
Wait their change
Unencumbered by the tides.

Still small genes receive rebirth
By order from on high
Into separate components,
Earth's truth and heaven's lie.

Wisdom guides eternal increase
Speaking the Father's perfect choice.
Discerning breeze does whisper
Love encompasses, even lust's
Consuming forms, for the growing.

Jim Crowell
TONGUES
I am the spark—which ignites the world into meaningless "fiery" ways;
Into a place where peace is naught and man must live through days,
Unaware of what—I bring to the world with such a grand appeal,
Like Death, Destruction—and so much waste that even time can't heal.

For I am the organ—which plays the songs that many stop to hear.
Songs of truth—and songs of love and even songs of fear.
I affect the hearts of many a man who listen for my sound.
And because of me—emotions surge and love and hate abound.

I'm known to change—in a moment's time not often slow or late.
I'll say the things you want to hear then say the things you hate.
For without thought—I sometimes act and bitterness will be found.
But if controlled—and urged just so then joy I'll spread around.

No earthly power has conquered me throughout the ages long.
And though I'm small—to count me weak would but to count me wrong.
So use me well—and you will find A love to meet your need.
But use me wrong—and you will find the tongue is sharp indeed.

Bonnie Jensen
THE LADY IN BLUE (A POEM FOR SAILORS)

To Rob Harter—Thank you for the inspiration!

The Lady in Blue is beckoning you,
She's waiting for you at the shore,
You'll answer her there and not really care,
If she's mother or lover or whore.

She'll rock you to sleep just over her deep,
And sing a lullaby along with the moon,
You'll rise at the dawn to find she's not gone,
She gives birth as she plays out a tune.

An' then in a turn, it's what sailors learn,
When they think of her nature as sweet,
She'll cast off her lace and throw salt in your face,
And make love to the wind 'til complete.

She's put sweat to your brow where wisdom sits now,
And her sweetness has somehow been etched,
Your ship has come home after all this is done,
And your land life again you have fetched.

But she'll beckon again, though you don't know just when,
'Bout the time that you need her the most,
And you'll run to her side, your horizons so wide,
'Cause you've gained from her more than you've lost.

Jim Crowell
MOUNTAIN MEMORIES
A moment of solitude with myself on peaks of ice and snow,
Near a Colorado sky so clear and blue
where eagles only go.
Save for the wind there's quietness here
and peace beyond compare,
Above the world alone with God
a place without a tear.

To look and find our steps below
on cliffs of agony,
And remember pain of tortured breath
endured this place to be.
Brings pride to those who've made their way
above the tree line green,
But makes one think how small he is amid God's total scene.
By His power we'll walk some day near skies that He has starred,
And see again His handiwork
above where men have scarred.
To feel once more His breath of wind blown round the icy way,
And talk with Him so near, yet far,
'bout friends of yesterday.

Nicole Brooke Anca
TOO LATE FOR WORDS
You feel an emptiness
You reach, but you touch nothing
You're falling . . . falling
You feel weak, forever forgotten
You never appreciated
Only thought you could do better
Never did you think time would run out . . .
until it did
Tears rolling down your face like rain
You only have memories
The words you never said, but held in your heart
You held them too long
Know your chance is gone, and . . .
You feel some of you is gone too

Jean M Parrack
EVERY MINUTE

To my husband, Tim, who I love so much.

Every minute of every day
I love him more in every way.
Together we have so carefully planned our life.
But I needed more than to be his wife.
No greater treasure could we have won,
Than the blessing we received when God
Sent us our son.

Ruth Esther Custodio
DON'T DRINK AND DRIVE
Not only are you in danger
But you endanger other people
When you drive under the influence
That's not the way to deal with anger.

Maybe you say, "It's just one drink."
But, listen, that is enough
To put someone's life on the line
Please, come to your senses and think!

Many innocent people have died
Because of one person's foolishness
Please wait 'til you're off the road
Be smart and put your drink aside.

Don't drink and drive is my advice
If you follow it, you will feel proud
Because people will feel safer
If you'd just listen up and get wise.

Nell P Harvey
MY HUSBAND
When I awoke this morning and saw you lying by my side, I was so very happy that I turned my head and cried.

Happy that I had you for my very own
For our little family, and little home.

Sometimes I've taken you for granted, Tho all the many years, you have always been there to dry away my tears.

The years have passed so swiftly since you took me for your wife, I hope we'll be together for the remainder of our lives.

Now we're getting older we're turned from youth to gray, but I love you even more than on our wedding day.

My prayer is to God above, that He will keep us with His guiding love.

Mildred Capps Jerome
THIS IS MY SOLO FLIGHT
O, tides of time, my ship awaits
I will not bide the night
Come close, my darling and kiss me
This is my solo flight

Angels are singing, tower bells toll
Rhythm of heavenly harps fills the air
Lights in the harbor are shining bright
I see the golden stair

Brilliant stilettos from setting sun
Point sharply o'er the west
Ebbing tide from the shores of time
Murmurs a soft behest

O, tides of time, anchored ship that waits
I know I must board tonight
It will carry me to my heavenly home
THIS IS MY SOLO FLIGHT . . . .

Claude R Hurst
MAMASAN (CAMLO VILLAGE '67)

To those who served; dead and living, prisoner and citizen, and saved and unsaved. To those of us who are still fighting the war.

Mamasan you don't even bat an eye
when most folks i know would lay down and die
you go about your usual business
as if it were quite endless

Mamasan you care for your young
while husband and sons are carrying guns
you don't seem to show pain
but as i walk by i can feel the strain

Mamasan i see something in you
that my mom back home has too
you can't stop the pounding of the drum
but you pray for its end to come

Mamasan you were strange and menacing at first
until i soon realized the curse
you are like the mothers in all of war's thirst
always loving and caring for family first

Mamasan if only mankind was like you
then the clouds of war would clear to blue
you through love do your duty
while mankind looks right through the beauty

Jenni B
THE ROSE OF MY HEART

To my dearest Brett who I hope is a part of my future. All my love, Jenni.

If I could send a rose to you for all the things you've done, to show me that you cared for me like I'm the only one, there'd be no place to put them, and surely there is none who could make a bouquet large enough, so I will send just this one. The world is full of good looking guys, but you're the only one that fills my heart with tender love by all the things you've done. You cheered me when my heart was sad with tender words you said, so all my love will be for you while roses are still red. Even though the time will come someday, and you must go away, I want to give this rose to you for the words I cannot say. May all the thoughts I left unsaid to you when we must part be brought to mind by this one rose that says You Have My Heart!

Stuart Levine
ON THE LAST HOUR
End of the day,
Thoughts quietly tucked away.
To sleep away the cold dark night,
A chance to dream in silent delight.
And when morning shows itself to me,
I must believe in eternity.
For all that I have been and done,
I know that I have just begun.

David L Walker
HEAR ME CRY FOR THE WORLD
I'm in a Dark World, where time has stopped
I can see the footprints, where many have dropped
Before me there were many, ahead there are none
I bow on my knees, for the damage that was done
We just sat around, and watched the ozone disappear
Our world is falling apart, but no one fears
We just didn't think of what was going to happen
Some people cry, while those that knew it just kept laughin'
They knew we were fools, 'cause we couldn't see
Someday the end will come, and that's all that will be
Hear me cry in the night, 'cause no one will change
They just keep going, never stop the game
I know when they finally see, It will be too late
'Cause when the missiles are launched, they won't hesitate
Everyone kills anyone, It happens every day
Do you know how many crimes will be committed today?
I'm tired of living, I can't take any more
I don't care any more, I'm all cried out
The world will be destroyed, there isn't a doubt
Hear Me Cry, Hear Me Cry, Hear Me Cry in the Night

Twyla Bogard
WHILE WE'RE APART
When I feel my heart is breaking,
And I cry night after night,

When the pain gets too unbearable
And there's no relief in sight,

I'll keep your smile in my mind,
Your love within my heart.

'Twill make the time seem shorter
Each day while we're apart.

Daryl Milchman
FEELINGS
The dawning of the summer time blues
Dancing in your blue suede shoes
Running miles 'round the track
Two steps forward, 3 steps back

Hyperactive, you run wild
Merely warping, inner child
Darkness you see, under piles
Mystic unknowns, out of style

Time is justice, blank to you
Your friends took 5 steps, you took two
Remember love is just a trick
A broken heart's a broken stick

Tearing life from others too
Doesn't mean nothing to you
Standing tall, at 3 feet tall
Doesn't help your choice at all

Joseph K Edwards

Joseph K Edwards
PRESSURE
The couple met and fell in love
She'd found that special one,
They married in the spring time
And their love brought them a son

Those early years were happy
Such a special time in life,
She was proud to be a mother
She was proud to be his wife

But life would not be gentle
They began to feel the strain,
The happiness that they once knew
Was soon replaced by pain

Overwhelmed by endless failures
That they blamed each other for,
They failed to seek the help that waited
Just outside their door

Consumed by never ending debt
Distraught by broken plans,
This marriage made in heaven
Had begun to break its bands

Twice they tried to reconcile
But things had gone too far,
When left to fester, open wounds
Will soon become a scar.

Joseph K Edwards
APPRECIATION
I rode a kayak down the rapids
Sailed on gliders in the wind,
I have climbed the mighty Everest
Had a pirate for a friend,

I've lived beside a lion pride
Climbed mountains in Nepal,
I've rafted down the Amazon
Heard howler monkeys call,

I have ridden on a camel's back
And saw a bison calf,
I've tagged the mighty polar bear
And heard hyenas laugh,

I've had all these adventures
And there's many more to go,
I do my traveling once a week
On the public TV show.

Joseph K Edwards
REGRETS
One year ago a mother kissed her daughter on the cheek
One year ago a father said, "We'll see you in a week,"
One year ago these parents said "drive carefully, love you dear"
One year ago I wish I hadn't stopped off for a beer

One year ago this bright young girl was driving back to school
She had to cross a traffic light on Hyway 102
Her mind was full of plans and dreams, her future seemed so bright
One year ago I wish I hadn't hit the bars that night

One year ago today I heard the bar maid say last call
One year ago today I thought I really had it all
One year ago while driving north on Hyway 102
I didn't see the light turn red so I drove right on through

It seemed to take forever for the car to finally stop
When I woke up in the morning I was talking to a cop,
He said a girl was killed last night, while driving back to school
He asked if I'd been drinking, I said only one or two

One year ago I had it all, today I want to die
Every day I think of her, and every day I cry

One year ago today I made my life a living hell
One year ago today I made their lives an empty shell,
Every night I sit alone and every night I think
One year ago I wish I hadn't stopped off for a drink.

Joseph K Edwards
VIOLATED FOREST
They foraged in the tangled turf,
They frolicked in the trees
They filled the mighty rivers,
And they sailed upon the breeze

There were fish and there were insects
There were reptiles, birds, and more
And so many kinds of mammals
Crawled across the forest floor

Shrubs and trees and flowers
Filled each niche in this terrain,
Each species had a role to play
In this forest of the rain

But there's another species
That's been introduced of late,
And this self indulgent life form
Will change this forest's fate.

Owenna
ALPHA ET OMEGA

To My Uncle Bub. The Reverend Ernest Hull, Jr. Thank You.

We call each other gifted.
Inner voices we do hear.
Sounds like Guardian Angels,
of danger, they keep us clear.
The fallen one beware!

We claim home is another dimension.
This is only an illusion here.
And before the tribulation,
we'll be taken from this sphere.
Surmising New Jerusalem and Rapture.

Our philosophy is of supernatural power,
which governs the science of universes.
From future comes evolution
and all karma becomes erasures.
Through Jesus this ensures.

What is this new age religion?
The blasphemous Babylon of old!
From the seed of Abraham
Justice and Peace behold.
The Christians' stronghold.

Mabel Olson
BE GLAD!
Well, today I'm sixty-five!
How glad I am to be alive!

How glad I am for birds that sing
I'm thankful for another Spring.

I'm grateful that I'm filled with vim
I'm glad I'm feeling fit and trim!

I'm thankful for my work each day
So unique in every way.

I'm thankful for my Husband dear,
I'm glad indeed that he is near.

I'm thankful for our families too
Who bring us joy and are true blue.

I'm glad for friends throughout the years
Who love our fun and share our tears.

I'm thankful for my God above
Who floods my heart with peace and love.

Thanks, Dear Lord! I'm sixty-five!
How glad I am to be alive!

This is "my" day which the Lord hath made;
"I" will rejoice and BE GLAD in it.
Psalm 118:24

Debbie Vojtech
WHAT IS LOVE . . .

Kyle, To the man in my life who I will love forever . . . Love Always, Debbie.

Love is when two people feel for each other. In a special way, such as if one is in sorrow, so is the other. Of course we cheer each other up, when one is down, but we can tell when something is bothering one by their voice or facial expression.

Love is when two people always enjoy each other's company. Because they're fun to be with and loving. Love is hard to put in terms so the best way to describe this wonderful word is by seeing this: Debbie Loves Kyle . . . . Our relationship is strong and filled with LOVE to last an eternity.

Patsy M Benson
SUICIDE
The night is so quiet, all seems right with the world.
And in my hand the pills look so much like shiny pearls.
One by one they go down and out of my sight.
And then a big drink of whiskey before I turn out the light.
I don't know why,
I don't really care.
Sometimes things come along that you just can't bear.
By my bed I see my clock
I hear the sound
tick, tock,
tick, tock.

Darrell Gene Mullikin Jr
LOVE IN MIND
When I was younger and as I grew
I had this dream of loving someone
as lovely as you.
A love so strong, exciting and new.
You had the same dream with
exception you'll see
We can be thankful for us to see
A relationship that shall always be.
Our lives entwined till the end of
time, so beautiful and true.
Such a perfect blend of two
individuals
Who cared enough to see success as
it happened for you and me.
I know that lately things have been
hard.
You feel the pressure and see the
need.
I'd just like you to know that you can
rely on me.
Most important, keep in mind we are
capable of dealing with anything that
may arise.
So do whatever you must because
time will tell,
For after we are through these hard
times
We will be able to look back and see
what we have accomplished
made us closer indeed.

Becky Weymouth
MY WONDERFUL DAY
Little one, little one,
High in the tree,
Tell me, oh, tell me,
What do you see?

It's not what I see,
It's not what I hear,
It's how do I feel,
When God seems so near.

I'm like a wee fairy,
Poised out on a limb,
As light as a feather,
With magical wings.

I'll float thru the sky,
Enchantingly blue,
Ride the soft clouds
And fly to the moon.

I'll look down and see,
A world emerald green,
A world made for me,
To live in and dream.

It's fun, it's exciting.
I'm happy to say
Thanks God for making
My wonderful day.

Erika C Maston
IT WAS A DAY FOR CURIOUS
It was a day for curious things,
Like pink and red flowers
and green and blue strings.
I was walking in the garden that
day,
And up from the grass it came.
As it grew I realized this creature
had a mane.
It looked at me and said "hello,"
But all I could say was "hi."
It then looked up and flew away
into the bright blue sky.

I often walk in the garden now
hoping to see,
That creature that said "hello"
to me.
It hasn't returned, yet it really
should;
For I wouldn't keep it, though
I wish I could.
I can't help but wonder
if that creature was my
imagination,
I think that day I had too much
carbonation!

Tawana B Seymore
I BELIEVE
(Credo)
I believe in tomorrow's world,
The equal attraction between boy
and girl.
Gray birds flying in the sky above,
The innocence of a young child's
love.
The sky and ocean as pure as
can be,
Air so light tomorrow you
could see.
Not black or white but a pretty
shade of gray,
Greed and hunger have all gone
away.
I believe in "my" tomorrow,
because nothing is
—impossible.
And with the combined strength
of man progress
—is unstoppable.

Len Tucker
PETEY
My life as a cow dog
is different from that of a "cuddle
dog."
That's what us working dogs
call the "little" house dogs.

We go out in the morning
and come back late in the night.
Chasing cows and herding calves
running on till we feel like we'll
drop.

Always being yelled at
for biting the slow calves.
"And don't you rush those bulls;
they can take their own time."

But, it is what my life is;
and I can't change that much.
But I sometimes wonder about
sleeping on a couch
or eating out of a china dish.

But my life goes on
day to day
And the pat on the head
sure does a lot for me.

Joanne M Phillips
CHRISTOPHER

To Christopher's parents Donald and Karin Haggmark, and his new little sister Emily Marie. May God always bless and keep you. With love, Joanne.

God looked down and saw
Our precious little man,
And He knew the time had come
To take him home again.
He graced our lives for just awhile
And he brought us lots of joy.
We know not why the Lord chose
him,
Our precious little boy.
Given time the pain will fade,
And the void within be filled.
His memory will be with us
And we shall love him still.
God will love and keep us
And help us thru this time,
When our lives seem empty
And our loss is on our minds.
In God's hands we've placed him
And know him to be safe.
May our love be with him
And our memories never fade.

Up in heaven angels sing
As they gather to rejoice
The returning of a little child,
Our precious little boy.

Danielle Havercamp
WILL THIS WORLD LAY TO REST
Will this world lay to rest
All its thoughts never ending.
The constant spinning,
Confusion in my mind.
No one great moment,
No happy day,
Can stop this ongoing puzzle.
If once forgotten,
It's sure to return;
For you can't put aside
What you must face.
These forever revolutions
May never stop.
So, as this world turns,
We must search each ocean
And strive to keep afloat;
For if we don't try,
One by one we will drown.

Maureen Ann McArdle
THE ETERNAL WHY
As a child, I inquired
About the color of the sky,
And why I was inspired.
My brain asked the eternal why.

As my mind grew older,
It learned the meaning of a lie.
I learned to be bolder,
And I asked the eternal why.

Now, old before my time,
I don't want to reach the blue sky.
I'm paying for my crime
Of asking the eternal why.

Rodney D Wallace
EVERYBODY NEEDS A FRIEND

To Jerry . . . and every other Police Officer who has experienced too many of the world's maladies . . . .

Death of a friend's somehow easier
to take than to see a good guy lose
his grip . . . .
for death, we all know, will
inevitably come—sanity we hope
will not slip.
To see a friend lost in his mind's
torture cell is so scary—'cause what
do you do . . . .
to help him come back and know that
he's loved—though we don't know
what he's going through.
You fight for the words to say how
you feel—all the while fighting back
all your tears . . . .
you want to hold him real close—like
a parent to child—let him know that a
friend is real near.
But we're so damn macho, all
dressed in our blue—so we find ways
to hide what's inside . . . .
yeah, we drink loads of beer, curse
the system or cheer, anything for the
tears we must hide.
But remember these words:
"everyone needs a friend"—just to
hold or to laugh or to cry . . . .
so, if you hear a 'cry out'—go ahead
hold them close—hey don't worry,
your machismo won't die.

Michael J Powell
SCHOOLBOY FANTASY

To my parents, Margaret and Joseph Powell.

How long is this lonely road
This path of discontent
How paranoid it seems today
The sun beyond the fringe
Inside the lessons have begun
The desk lids shine instead
A carved reminder of school days
past
Of sleepy summer days and riverside
dreams
A schoolboy once again

Yet life beyond the mother's wing
The homecoming over now
A desert of emotion is all the eye can
see
The dry barren land of hopes and
fears
And winter's frosty hand touches the
folds of memories
Long since passed away.

Ethel M Domec

Ethel M Domec
SOUVENIRS
If I could stop Time as it whirls by in
flight,
Waywardly whirling through
darkness and light,
The moments I've loved so, I'd bring
into view,
The time I have spent conversing
with you.

If I could go back to time that has
been,
And live over scenes that were dear
to me then,
I would choose to relive some time
we have spent,
Just chatting in friendship, warm and
content.

Those moments still linger in
memory's shrine,
The part of your life which is woven
with mine,
And ever I'll cherish as tender and
sweet,
The much loved occasions we've
happened to meet.

Ethel M Domec
SEEKING
I seek for you in every empty room,
And scan the cloudless reaches of the
sky,
And, seeking always, yet I fear my
doom
Will strike, and you will pass me by.

I seek for you within my secret heart,
And as the sun pours forth its brilliant rays,
Still seeking, I would wish to start
Apace—down each of my separate ways.

I seek for you in murmur of the breeze,
And in the golden rays of Mother Moon,
And as I seek among the verdant trees
I shiver—lest I've lost you all too soon.

I seek you when I bow my head in prayer,
And ever wistful—pause to plead that God
Will give my seeking heart to you to share,
And shower blessings everywhere you've trod.

And suddenly I know that as I seek,
I found you, closely locked within my heart,
While seeking you—your dear glance touched my cheek,
Your love had bound me to you from the start.

Ethel M Domec

INDIAN SUMMER

'Tis strange to think that years have passed,
Without my knowing you,
That, far apart in different worlds,
The same skies smiled as blue.
The Spring of Life has passed me by,
And Summer comes apace,
And now some star has led you here,
My lonely life to grace.
We've tilled our gardens, you and I,
Of flowers blooming fair,
And bouquets of romance and love,
We've long since gathered there.
But fancies flower in the Fall,
of a Life that's passing by,
And fragrant memories bloom again,
Even for you and I.
So let us treasure while we may,
Fate's gift, so sweet and rare,
And ere cold Winter's chilling blast,
Our Indian Summer share.

Ethel M Domec

REJECTION

The hissing wind curled—a cold snake about my throat,
While velvet leaves whispered a muted, warm caress,
Silver rain murmured past the high dove cote,
And only mourning pierced my solitude.
About me the new washed world blazed, gaudy, gay,
And brazen flowers nodded sleepy heads,
The sun lay idle, brooding on the day,
And only I was foreign to the mood.
Heart wrung by anguish, came I here
Bringing an empty soul, bereft of love,
And eyes which cast no glance of fear,
A bitter recluse, wrapt in rectitude.

Julie Ann Nolon

I'VE DREAMED OF A TIME

I've dreamed of a
time when you would
hold me
and tell me that you
loved me,
and we would go far
away from everyone and
live together forever.

But now, I've awakened
to find
my dream just a dream,
and to find alone and
frightened someone that
would never be capable of
having
you love me
and I'll be alone forever.

For now, I'll sleep
and dream of you
holding me and
loving me,
and I'll dream of a far away
place where we will go
and I'll never be
alone.

Anthony Iandoli

I'M THAT WOMAN

To My Darling Mary.

Man, you need a woman by your side,
If you'd sit upon a throne;
One to suit your ego and your pride,
In a Kingdom we call home.
Before time passes you by, picture me there as your Bride,
Vowing to love you, always to call you "My Own!"
Someone with rare devotion,
someone so hard to find
I know the score, stop look no more,
"I'm That Woman."
I'm someone who'd cross an ocean,
to hear you say "you're mine"—
To share your kiss, perhaps some bliss,
"I'm That Woman."
I will do the things, that lighten up your day, and,
give my heart to you along the way! I say,
be there a magic potion, to warm your heart, you'll find—
You need a dame to share your name
"I'm That Woman"

Matthew Robinson

I'VE BEEN TOUCHED

I've been touched by the morning sun
that chases the night away, and
I've been touched by the gentle
words that Love Struck Poets say.
I've been touched by the morning
mist that everyone calls the dew
but, it all seems more beautiful
now that I've been touched by you.

Susan E Good

ROADSIDE-TRAVELING MAN

Lights flashing,
Silhouettes of objects on the walls,
sleep doesn't come.
Heat, fan air blowing away dreams of yesterday.
Highway sounds speaking of people on the move.

Life passes quickly, but the traveling man never catches up.
The road is his home,
The company he keeps lies within the four walls, and yet,
He has sat with kings, even presidents have consulted him before addressing a nation.

Caught between vacuity and the things he longs to be,
The traveling man has traveled in mind and spirit,
Far beyond a marked road, a mapped pass.

Tears flow in silence,
In darkness pain is felt only by him.
But the darkness continues, the lights keep flashing,
Silhouettes of dreams disappear, but the sounds of tomorrow seem only moments away.

For the traveling man, the ability to stretch the mind,
Truly exists with him, for he has really sat with kings,
And even presidents have consulted him before addressing a nation.

The door slams, the lock turns, the vacancy sign flashes,
Another man checks in.

Rory Osborne

DREAMS

To Jeannie—my best friend, lover and I hope, wife.

Your life is your life,
Like a swift flowing
stream.
But good or bad,
happy or sad,
Never give up your
Dreams.

Natalie A Smith

BLUE

Deep skies,
Crystal clear waters,
A cool, sandy beach,
The majesty of the sea,
An autumn breeze.
The depth of your eyes.
The comfort that
surrounds me.
The still of the night,
A day sky painted with
clouds.
The early morning
Song of the birds.
The sound of wind and
waters,
Rushing by.
A picture of the mountains,
Deep blue.

Nikki Kirchberger

DECEIVED LOVE

Thank you to the three of us—for this poem wouldn't have come about if it wasn't for the Bizarre Love Triangle, P.S., M.A., and N.K.

I used to love him,
but he
loved another
and the one that loved him
was deceived by the other
into thinking there was
no other.

He used to love me,
but like him
I loved another
and the one who loved me,
he was deceived into thinking
the one who loved me
could love no other.

Now
the ones that loved both of us
were the only ones
that were deceiving the others
into thinking
there were
no others.

John Rodgers

HIDING WITHIN

This poem is dedicated to all my friends and family.

Coming from my soul as perfect
as a rose

But something is missing to the
observer

The beauty is intact—the foliage
green and flourishing

But something is missing—the
observer peers closer

The petal is moist—red as an
indian sky

But something is missing to the
casual eye

Stroking the stem toward the root
the observer starts to mourn

For on this perfect rose—what is
missing is the thorn

The observer looks at me with
glassy eyes—knowing my
fears I cannot disguise

The observer has discovered with
sadness

That the rose in my soul is scarred
with madness

Christina M Moore

TO MY DAUGHTER, SUZANNE

To all unwed Mothers, who can relate to these words.

You were a beautiful baby, I guess that's what all Mothers say,
But life wasn't fair at the time of your birth, so I had to give you away.
To afford you the life that I could not give, You would have to belong to another,
My beautiful child I had no means to provide both Father and Mother.
No one knows what it cost Me, the anguish and feelings of shame,
It was for your own good, or so I believed, to give you a legitimate name.
Life went along with its ups and downs, and My thoughts forever strayed,
To the babe that I bore, and it made My heart sore, knowing of the decision I'd made
Now thirty years later, and out of the blue, on a morning in May and alone,
I was wondering what to do with My time, when the ring of the telephone.
I answered, but could not believe My ears, it was You, My little girl,
Had found Me after all this time, then My mind went into a whirl.

I had longed and hoped for this moment, and still not believing it true,
Then You told Me You wanted Your Mother, that we could begin anew.
Oh the tears of joy I shed that day the utter happiness,
Made everything that had gone before, worthwhile no more no less.
And today when I look at You My love and see the lovely young woman You are,

I'm very proud You turned out so right, after having to come so far.
Of course, it was none of My doing, I only gave You birth,
I honor the ones You call Parents,
They must be the salt of the earth.
So now we go forward together,
leaving sorrow and tears behind,
To the future that's bright with promise,
Unbroken, the ties that bind.

Laurel Parmelee
GRAM

"Gram," that conjures up many thoughts in my mind
Like Christmas mornings when she would wake all
With the words, "time to get up and find
What Santa has brought. Come on, it's last call!"

"Gram" always walked wherever she went
Since she never did learn to drive
And there wasn't much money to be spent.
This, I believe, is what kept her alive.

"Gram" would always put others first
Even if this meant that she would go without.
Like the time she pulled from her purse
So that others had heat in their house.

"Gram" was always filled with so much love
Especially for her daughter and grandkids, the apples of her eye!
But top of the list was the love of her God!
To Him she remained faithful 'til the day she died.

I am grateful to have known her for so many years,
To have lived with and learned first hand
The experience and wonder of ninety years long.
I do love and miss you so my dear "Gram!"

Sam V Volard
TO SALLY—HOW SHOULD I RETURN

When was it that I last attempted to portray
The outline of a rose upon the sand,
Guiding her listless finger as she lay
Upon my breast, heart on heart, hand in hand,
The azure sea a million, million miles away,
The sun forsworn . . . and nothing more to say.
What else was there to say upon that golden strand?
The finger moved and left our mark upon the sand.

And now that I would model such another rose,
How should I return, how find my way?
And, having found it, what, do you suppose
Would tide and time have done to mar its stay,
Spoil its stark and naked freshness, close
Its gaping lips, stir its sweet repose
And sweep it all, but for my memory, away,
Among the sand dunes of a half-forgotten bay?

Oh! what a fool that I should seek to play again
Upon the sand, knowing as I do its wanton ways,
Its shifting nature, subject both to wind and rain.
Yet, there it is my destiny to play always.
Where else would guided finger take the strain
And trace the outline of a rose? In vain,
I must pursue the emblem of my living days
Among those moving sands and half-remembered bays.

Aretta-Nash Seal
LE DUEL

To my children, Tommy, Kelly and Pamela.

Just outside my window
In a stately maple tree
A cardinal and bluejay
Were quarrelling raucously.

Said the cardinal to the bluejay,
"You're really tempting fate
By your infernal interfering
With first, my nest, and then my mate."

Insulting words flew back and forth
To the fire adding fuel,
When the cardinal did fiercely
Challenge the bluejay to a duel.

My poor, brave cardinal is now
Lying in state, while the
Strutting, quarrelsome bluejay
Another challenger awaits.

Laura N Shifflett
A LIFETIME

Wings of Eagles
days and ways
through sands of time,
the free spirit moves
us each to carry on

Though, through
deep mire we must wallow
and quicksand we must tread
still our lives are filled,
with emptiness
and much time has sped

Just like air through an eagle's wings
and sun through the clouds
our lives come and go
like sands through an hour glass
but not quite so slow

Mark Elliott
TODAY IS JACOB'S BIRTHDAY

Today is Jacob's Birthday,
a chance to celebrate
a year of changing diapers
and sleep that had to wait.

A year of smiles and laughter
while we watched him learn to walk.
We're now anticipating
listening to him talk

Fervent prayers to God each day
to keep him safe and well.
Wondering as he sleeps each night
how far his dreams will sail.

Today is Jacob's Birthday,
a day of hope and joy.
His Mom and I and Kate and Claire
Wish Happy Birthday to our boy.

Becky Mount
PARENTS DIVORCE

To my parents, Gary and Lynne Mount, forever.

I had a family,
For them I cared;
We lived in a home,
For which we once all shared.
Now they are gone,
And so am I;
My only question is . . . .
Why?

Why must there be two of us here,
And three of you there;
I don't understand it,
It's just not fair.

Families are important,
For this I know;
Because being without one,
Hurts me so.

Lisa M Lucas
CHANGING TIMES

Times were different way back when, life was not so complicated then.

People cared for one another; not scared.

Money was earned by working hard, today it is not but by who you know, man has developed so.

Our lives are surrounded by technologies but are filled with emptiness.

Drugs, violence, crime, and family destruction surrounds the units where quality should be found.

The dollar is only what shows;

God help us in this world which no one knows.

Reverend Kenneth Logie
A HUMAN ROSE

The other day I saw a rose,
a human one I mean,
A Woman who portrayed to Me,
The beauty of a Queen.
Her face was filled with character,
That only Christ can mold,
Her smile held real sincerity,
That shone pure as gold.
Her graying hair caressed her head,
Much like a silver crown,
The tenderness within her eyes,
Caused her to look renown,
I marveled at the way she walked,
Each step a work of art,
Old in years but all the same,
So very young at heart.
Her countenance was that of faith,
And hope in days to be,
Lined with a velvet sweetness,
Which fashioned Heaven's Keys,
And so I write this verse to her,
In an effort to disclose,
The little things which make her,
My Darling that Human Rose.

Cindy K
PETALS IN THE WIND

In memory of my precious Pollyanna Charlotte.

THE years have fluttered by my child, like Petals in the Wind
and I will never quite forget the pain they ushered in. No,
not of body, my baby dear for that was really nothing, it was
my very heart and soul you see and they will ne'er recover.

I loved you from the day I knew and I could hardly wait, but
who'd have known that that March day would twist the hands of fate.
You were born my dear, so tiny and so new, but only five little minutes
was I to have with you. So much now I wish I had done, but again the wind blew, and now you are gone.

YOU are the daughter I will never have. NO tiny dresses, no bonnets or bows, no chubby hands for only God knows, the beautiful child that I loved so. As your fourth birthday flutters on by I know I'll remember and probably cry and I miss you today as only few know, the sorrow and hurt that will never go.

FOREVER in my heart you will be for you ARE WANTED so desperately, and as those years flutter on by, I will try to catch those Petals in the Wind and keep them forever in my hands.

Gladys O Jansen
I AM THE FUTURE

To the lives of Generations yet unborn.

I am the Future—A Baby
Let me come into this world
today and tomorrow with happiness
I am soft warm and alive
with hope and faith
I am a shining star of trust
for future Generations.
I am ready with a smile,
a challenge, a hope for
many to come after me—
Just give me Love—
I am the future Generation
of this Planet!

Christine L Quintana
VISION

Have you ever seen a rose
Not
Pink or peach or red
With petals softly circling, forever circling

Have you ever seen a rose
Without
The small green leaves fallen down
That used to hold it close

If you walked and walked
Down a rose laden path
And came upon such a flower
You'd probably PASS IT BY
And never see the rose.

Letitia M Elston
TIMES HAVE CHANGED

Dedicated In Loving Memory of Merle B. (Smiler) Elston, My Wonderful Ever-lovin' Hubby.

In days of old, to wed, a girl had to be a "Virgin!"
Many men were virtuous, bent on "Mergin'!"
If a couple over-stepped, Gave Not A Darn—
Made love before marriage, no back seats, out-door movies, possibly behind a barn—
Culminating into a shot-gun wedding
Before the lovers, legally went bedding;
Gentlemen bowed, kissed a girl's hand when introduced—
"Real Young Ladies," were not to be seduced!
Above reproach, in Seventh Heaven, Couples Wed—
Raised families, through life, lived and loved together,
Loving the good, no matter what or whether!
Times Have Changed, not for the best, fewer and fewer pass the test!
Women's Lib. has had Its Hey Day—
No Longer Idolized, Women, Though Deserving, Get not Equal Pay!

There's so much Promiscuity, Free
Spirits, Many Choose To Be!
"Such A Hex," Without Respect and
True Love,
"What Good Comes From Sex!"
Played To The Hilt In Books,
Theatre, T.V., Every Walk Of Life—
No Wonder, All The Unhappiness,
Struggle and Strife!

Letitia M Elston
OUR MAGNIFICENT U.S.A.
In The Garden Of Eden, God First
made Adam, Then From
Adam's Rib, He Created Eve,
The Two Were To Live
Together Happily Forever,
Future At Stake!
They Ate The Apple, Tempted By
That "Damn Snake!"
For That, We Are Paying Dearly,
Corruption, Greed, Drugs,
Alcoholism, Promiscuity, Disease
And Hate!
Do You Not Want To Enter The
"Pearly Gate?"
I Do, Hope It's Not Too Late!
The United States Of America Has
Been Let Down By Many
Trusted Higher-ups,
Do-gooders, Now Busted!
In Prison, They All Should Be, The
Wheels Of Justice Now
Travel, "Too Damn Slow!"
Many Previous "Jailbirds," Now
Out Walking, Shouldn't Be,
We Know!
Not Amiss, The Time Has Come To
Rectify All This—
There Is A Better Way To Live,
Love, Keep Happy And
Progress!
Unless They, Themselves Will It,
There Should Be "No
Homeless!"
Much Of The World, To The
United States Of America,
Looks Up!
Everybody, "You And Me Have A
Great Responsibility!"
We have "Our Precious Jewels,
Our Young," Growing Up!
Let's Strive To Keep Them
Happy, Ours And Their
Future, Their Cup!
God Bless Our Beautiful, Glorious
And Beloved Nation, Hey.
Hey!
The Very Best Land Ever Created,
"Our Magnificent U.S.A.!"
"Let's Cherish And Glorify HER
Forever, Forever And A
Day!"

Ann Marie Evankovich
HARMONY
Always standing at the window, I
was
Looking at the same piece of my
world,
At the same picture before me
Each day. By chance I began to
Note the picture was not the same
I had seen at first, I had
Missed some patterns that brought
The picture into a kind of
Harmony that had earlier eluded me.
Of the too familiar came
The excitement of the new—like a
Song the wind writes in the sky.

Ann Marie Evankovich
DARK FRUIT
On the sunny days
When the heat was bearable
We'd gather the blackberries
From the roadside brambles.
The juicy black fruit
Entranced us so that we each
Blundered into solitude—
Anticipating the sweet cobbler
Not yet made.

Deep in the thicket dangled
A perfect cluster of plumb berries
Dancing in the light
Between the leaves.
And I, caught up in the picking,
Plunder toward them
And get tangled and
Snagged by the pricks.

Peggy Sue Cameron

Peggy Sue Cameron
MOTHER DEAR

Dedicated to all Her children everywhere. With special devotion to The Better World Society!

Mother Dear, suspended in space,
Rainbows abound, colors of grace.
Your children rape, your children
jeer,
Your children gape, your children
fear.
Naughty children shed never a tear!

Mother Dear, suspended in space,
Colors fading, smog in her face.
Your children shiver, your children
shake,
Your children quiver, your children
quake.
Naughty children do all but forsake!

Mother Dear, suspended in space,
Ozone missing, trees out of place.
Your children plead, your children
cry,
Your children lead, your children die.
Naughty children, is that a sigh?

Mother Dear, suspended in space,
I need the rainbows and colors to
grace.
Might I adore thee, treat thee with
care,
Can't I implore thee, forgive us our
ware?
Naughty children, learn how to share!

Mary Elizabeth Chapman
NIGHT SIGHTS AND SOUNDS
Sitting on the doorstep
In the twilight dim
I listen to the crickets
Sing their midnight hymn.

Watch the moon rise o'er the hilltop
Bathe the world in silvery
light
See each tiny star that twinkles
Like a diamond in the night.

In the calm and stillness of the
midnight
Hear the soothing ripple of the
stream
As it flows along so gently
And reflects the moonlight's
silvery beam.

Far off in the distance
Hear the plaintiff whippoorwill
Then once again there's silence
All the world is calm and still.

Elesha Ellison
I WISH . . .
I wish to see a day with a peace
that no one could disturb
a day with a happiness that
no one could sadden
a day with a child's smile
that never could be broken
a day with no wars, no
conflicts, no hatred
a day that I know I will not
ever see

Elesha Ellison
DREAM OF ANOTHER TIME
In a dream of another time
I thought of you and my heart shed a
tear,
for the memories all but forgotten
they always were so dear.
I wish we could have stopped in time.
No room for things to change,
no room for things to be lost.
Now your absence seems so strange,
You're always on my mind
in a dream of another time
Someday we'll be together again,
In a Dream of Another Time

Kimberley Chapman
GRANDPA

This poem is dedicated in loving memory to my Gramps.

A very special man who found a
place in my heart,
you've been there for me from the
start.
Honest, caring, loving, and kind,
when God created these words he had
you in mind.
Although you are not here with me
any longer,
knowing you and having you in my
life has made me stronger.
Gramps, I will never forget you,
you and your memory will be with
me in all that I do.
I do not understand why God took
you away from me,
but I do know that you are better
there where he wants you to be.
Gramps I love you with all my heart,
I have since the start.
Although we are no longer together,
my love for you will last forever.

Kimberley Chapman
A SPECIAL FRIENDSHIP

This poem is dedicated to Ker Bear, Caro, Boo Boo, Kimmie and Bobbin, my special Friends whose Friendship inspired me to write this.

There is a friendship I know of that is
true and strong,
this friendship I know of will last
very long.
The bonds between these friends are
hard to break,
because what they share is a true
friendship not a fake.
They are honest with one another,
and they know that no matter what
they can always trust the other.
This year has passed them by awfully
fast,
but the memories they have obtained
will always last.
They have all shed their fair amount
of tears,
and helped each other conquer their
fears.
They all have very caring hearts,
they try to ease the pain before it ever
starts.
Always watching out for the
youngest two,
trying to make sure we won't get hurt
from the things we do.
This friendship I know is the one that
I share with all of you,
the one that cheers me up when I am
feeling blue.

Elizabeth Koliadko

Elizabeth Koliadko
THE HOTEL

To Susan, my sisters, fellow writers Pat & Marie, Trudy, the nurses who worked in the adult home hotels, and mostly the seniors who lived there.

Above the pitted marble staircase
the hotel reaches for the sea,
the sun, frustrated, halts its thrust
to penetrate the ancient arched
windows, fastened tight, by thick
dusty boards.
Above an empty ballroom, twisted
halls sprawl,
flanked by dreary faded rooms,
older perhaps than their occupants
who appear, as chipped as the
walls,
their skin more wrinkled and
stretched
than the drapes, that block sun
and sea.
Below the hotel facade, on the
boardwalk
a lady sits, white curls
glistening,
her face absorbing a tangerine sun,
the filmed eyes scan the sea,

searching.
Her red dress screams hope, perhaps joy,
beaded and stockinged, she smiles,
Beckons . . . slowly says . . . "I remember . . .
The hotel, not long ago . . . Let's see,
Yes, I remember this hotel . . . when . . .
Well, it was young then, young like me."

Jack Cygielman
I LOVE YOU

I Love You
For the feeling that you have
Instilled within me
As my hopes and aspiration;
As a new birth of life;
As my reason for being.

I Love You
For your acceptance
Of what I am,
And even for the silence
Of your truthful heart.

I Love You
For the grace with which
You carry on your daily task
And the ambition with which
You achieve your goals.

I Love You
For having given my eyes
Your vision of loveliness,
And a view of heaven granted
Here on earth.

I Love You
Even for the prayers,
Desires, and Torments
Of all my sleepless nights
As I lay restless
With the stillness
Of my aching heart

I Love You
For the child-like innocence
Of your smile, and the purity
Of your soul.

I Love You
For the charm and beauty
Of a few sunlit moments
A walk in the park; the touch
Of your hand; the radiance
Of your smile.

I Love You
For the feeling when your lips
First touched mine, and
The yearning and passions
Of my desires.

I Love You
Because you are
All the memories of yesterday,
The joys of today,
The dreams of tomorrow

And when all tomorrows
are yesterdays come true,
I'll thank you for the love
I found in you.

Thelma H Cotton
A WALK IN THE WOODS

What does my heart a world of good,
Is a leisure stroll through a country backwood.

The shade provided by the branches and leaves,
Makes a comfortable setting for my soul's reprieve.

I reflect on the things that leave me disturbed,
And contemplate on the affairs, the state of the world.

I am always calmed by the running stream.
It allures, sedates me, then makes me dream.

The wrongs of the world I can shut out,
To concentrate on the beauty and the wonders about.

The music of the fowl, the rhythm of the trees,
Relaxes my mind, and sets it at ease.

I am inspired by the animals in their movements of grace,
That I should live at such an unhurried pace.

When I stop and smell each little rose,
Nature gives my life that needed repose.

I am hesitant to leave, desiring to stay longer,
My faith has been renewed, and my spirits made stronger.

The healing powers of the tranquil and serene,
Have given me strength to face the world again.

Thelma H Cotton
A SPRING DAY

To Susie M. Hicklin, my mother, and the loving memory of George Hicklin, Sr., my father, the Hicklins, My family: Larry, Lillian, and Brittany.

Happy faces in Easter brights
Break the stillness and comfort
of morning light.

Suddenly—the world's in love
and the birds are in flight.

Who can forget the winter morn
When snow and sleep were the only sights?

Pastels and greens—a pure delight
in place of winter's gray and white.
(A welcome relief from Jack Frost's bite).

Tractors plowing fields upright.
Wild animals scurrying in obvious fright.

March wind blowing dragon kites.
Children running, screeching,
(A playground fight).

Orange and gold sunset, another delight
Ending the day with diminishing light.

Compared to morn's exhilarating sights,
What—bespeaks the night?

Thula J Earl
ONE

Each person is a one—not a two.
Different moods make one many,
Flowing in and out of a one.
But the one still remains only one.

The one can never be a two.
Altho' he seems to sway and bend,
Blending with a family.
Still he's only one.

A one is important.
Without a one you cannot make two,
Or a four or a lively crowd
Where one can blend but still remain one.

All in all, I like being a one.
Sometimes lonely—but underneath is joy
Which I alone can own—
Which I alone can share.

I can choose! I can choose!
Because I am a one, I can choose!
No other one can make me do
What God does not intend.

Mary Louise Nichols Blackwell

Mary Louise Nichols Blackwell
HEAVEN

To me and you baby. We always said we were good.

I lay here on my bed,
thinking of the life I've led.
My thoughts always seem to say,
heaven is just a breath away.

Rooms of pearls and streets of gold,
gardens of beauty untold.
Soon my soul will be there to stay,
because heaven is just a breath away.

My family here I'll love and miss.
I would gladly exchange it all
for heaven's bliss.

Friends and loved ones again I'll see,
and together we will rejoice,
to be painless and free,
and together we will watch others
down below and pray,
for heaven is just a breath away.

Mary Louise Nichols Blackwell
GOD'S NEW ANGEL

She came into my life,
like a fresh breath of air,
So loving and humble,
With a touch of gentleness,
That said without words I care.

She taught me tenderness,
and a sense of love that,
I had never known,
and today she is with God.
Spreading her love around
his great throne.

Mother, my dearest, of this you can be sure.
Your teaching was not in vain.
Someday soon we will be together,
in that land that is painless
and pure.

Mary Louise Nichols Blackwell
THE FAMILY DOCTOR

He greets you with a friendly smile.
He is very kind and gentle.
He puts you at ease,
no matter how bad you are feeling.

He listens while you tell him
of your aches and pains.
He quietly makes notes now and then.
He explains your problems,
in words that are simple and plain.

He will gladly give you a comforting hug,
when you feel down and out.
You will leave his office,
knowing things will get better
without a doubt.

Thula J Earl
GROWING OLD

It's no fun to grow old, my mother said.
Now I am that age, I can understand.
The idea of fun retreats and fades.
In its place quiet steady hope,
an appreciation of this
beautiful day!

Gratitude for little numerous things.
Memories that soar in and out again.
Birds singing, a child's laugh.
Old mixed with new, blending together,
not fun, but food for the
heart.

Loneliness and sorrow are mercifully muted.
Affection and joy can take this place.
Growing old means more wisdom.
Less and less foolish painful mistakes,
as peace moves the hours
into a day.

Jeri Marie Dippold
THE WISHING WELL

To Mom & Grandma Erma for wishing I'd do something with my talent.

Wishing well will my dream come true if I throw my shiny penny into you?
Wishing well will you tell me all you know about life, love and happiness?
Wishing well here comes my penny, tell me my plans for the future, if I have any.
But no magical secrets of life unfolded, no unseen dreams did I see.
Then I realized I was just one of the many who lost my penny to the wishing well.

William D Cameron
MONEY

Look at this green dollar bill
For this my friend some people kill

Why? You ask as if amazed
Because money is most highly praised

Now it's really too bad
And it's awful sad

That some of us can't get enough
of that green stuff

But fact is I'm sure you will agree
That gold seems to be the one and only key

Many a man has fallen by the way

And lost their natural stride

They had no money with which to deal
And thus could not abide

Yet the real side of cash is rarely told
That is, it can destroy your very soul

It is good to have enough it's true
But to love it will make a fool of you

So while you're getting that green dollar bill
Remember, an empty heart it cannot fill

William D Cameron

MY PRAYER

May the Almighty Lord in his glory bless
Those whom this neurotic world has oppressed
Those who are raped, robbed or killed, and them laid to rest

Bless the children who have not those things
Which cause the heart & soul to sing

Bless those people on God's earth
Who are starving and cold depraved from birth

And for times and a time shall I kneel & pray
That they see no more days like today

No more days of tears and woes no days of cold
Without a home or warm clothes

No more days of physical pain
No days of dark shadows and helpless disdain

No days of loneliness & bitterness within
No days of grappling and lusts for sin

No days of ignorance, violence and strife
For these things, I pray tonight

Cora P Chism

BUILD UPON THE ROCK

We cannot get to heaven
If we tend to hold a grudge,
Don't talk about your neighbor
For who are we to judge.

Do unto others as you'd have them do to you.
We find this in the word of God
And to this we must be true.

To ask amiss would hinder
So believe when you pray.
God's on the throne you can be sure
Your answer's on the way.

So build upon the Rock
And not upon the sand
And live every day of our life
According to God's plan.

If you build upon the Rock
You'll surely never fall,
For the Rock is Jesus Christ
And He loves us one and all.

Gay S Culler

THE GIFT

Slight movement
in the top
of a poplar tree
at mid-afternoon;
Gold,
wafting
gently
from
tree top,
slowly,
ever so lightly
falling
toward the earth.
Breathing suspended
as I watched you
float
toward me,
then rest
in my
outstretched hand.

Gay S Culler

BETRAYED

Time is ashamed.
Why else would he cover
His face with his hands.
He knows it's not proper
To tick away the minutes of life
And tries to hide his guilt.

He plays a trick on us,
Quietly stealing our youth
When we aren't looking.
Then one day we realize
We are old.

For shame, cruel Time,
Hide behind your skinny hands.
I know what you're up to,
But I can't make you stop
Tick on, you traitor,
You win.

Martha Walker

Martha Walker

WHEN FORCED BUSING IS PASSÉ

For years we've forced bused children
Equality we all cried
How can we accept the premise of equality
And let quality education die
Educationally malnutrious children
We see them every day
What an error . . . who must pay
My child and yours . . . which prompted me to say
Where will my child be along the way
When forced busing is passé

Now many politicians will simply say . . . I'm naive
But the proof is in the pudding
Which makes many parents' hearts grieve
In the future our children's knowledge
Will be put to the test
Those 'equality laws' will be weakened
Have we done our best
Now is the time to join in and say
Where will my child be along the way
When forced busing is passé.

Let's turn the wheels of equality
Never giving up
But not at the sake of our children
Of whom we love so much
To keep our goals in mind as adults we must not plunder
Making error after error sending our children asunder
Now is the time to evaluate who is gaining the most
Certainly not our children for their learning is a hoax
Where will my child be along the way
When forced busing is passé

Lorraine J Carter

LADY OF LIBERTY

Oh, our guardian, oh our guardian, oh our guardian one sublime,
You're our peace and refuge ever (amid the harbor), freedom thine.
Like a halo, is your bright glow,— shining down on land and sea,
On the island, in Manhattan, in the land of liberty.

Millions gather, beneath your statue, to view the sky's all-dazzled blaze,
As you are honored, with pomp and grandeur, on "The Fourth," nite and day.
How they loiter, and applaud her, and the flag of which we boast,
And the splendor, and the many,— who arrive from coast to coast.

May the years of the nineties!
In the land that's free and just,
Shine the light in every nation
With lasting peace, . . . in God we trust.

Lorraine J Carter

WHEN ARCHED EYES ARE SIGHING

When God looks down on this earth today,
I wonder what he thinks and says
About this great and glorious world
He made for man—and made superb.

With all the sorrow he would see
I'm sure he would astounded be;
For, this wide world of which we boast
Is filled with crime, and greed and dope.

Where the homeless cries are left unheard,
And, famine fills the air like birds.
With much unrest so widely strewn
I'm sure he'd make this earth anew.
Seeing the faces of many in agony
He'd ponder with heart-felt sympathy.

Perhaps, in time we might recall
The 'gift of love' he gave to all.
There's no love without caring, no hope without prayer
No peace or goodwill, when nothing is shared.

It's a dread of the future—on this earth below;
It's the loss of a God . . . that's caused our woe.

F J McGoldrick

THE WAITING

Here I anxiously await the dawning of a new day.
So long have I hoped for a day that's never come
When I, for even but a moment,
Could think upon my dreams and say: yes, I have wished,
And yes, now I have done.
Yet still I sit, watching the clock ticking
Away moments, hours, days, and years
Until my time arrives.

If only the waiting were but to measure
The grandeur of the wish fulfilled;
Or if the reaching of a dream were so grand
As the count of these many sleeps
Sacrificed as fare,
Then would the wait be that much easier.
Oh, if only we knew today,
That which we hope will be tomorrow!

F J McGoldrick

MOTHER AND CHILD

Sleep, child, sleep.
Close your eyes and dream:

Fear not the raging wind,
Nor the rising tide.
Fear not the crashing thunder,
Nor lightninged sky.

Fear not the hollow dark,
Nor monsters, ghosts,
Or things—
For I am here,
My watch to keep;
I am mother,
And my love is deep.
Sleep, child, sleep.

Belinda Clement

THE WIND

Winding, creeping,
in and out of the branches.
Rustling leaves,
weaving through the meadows.
It stirs the cattails,
while making ripples across the water.
Whispering a silent unknown language
to all who listen.

Elizabeth Koliadko

SNOWBOUND

The sky laced with tiny chutes
That mold lop-eared trees
And infiltrate hidden places
Erasing familiar landmarks
Rearranged in hunchedbacks
And deep hollows.
No color touches this negative
Of overexposed black and white.
Imprisoned by ice knots
Strung across the door.
Impotent I sit cloistered,
A Russian icon bathed
In cold Vermeer light.

Russell C Earhart
A DAY LOVING YOU
Morning has risen, awakening to the Robin's song of love,
Patiently I await to say "I love you my beautiful dove."
While the chilly morning breeze is blowing through the trees with care,
Seeming to say "I will always love and cherish thee."

While beauty such as yours awakens to another day,
The magic in the morning wind will blow my kisses your way.
As the flowers open to the warmth of the morning sun,
Through the meadows with you I would love to run.

With the rays of the afternoon sun set high in the sky,
They will say, your man loves you and I will tell you why.
For you are his earth angel, you are his only treasure,
His loving and caring for you, gives him great pleasure.

The evening breeze now blowing and caressing the trees with care,
Saying to you my love, for you, I will always be there.
On our porch, holding hands and swinging for hours,
Dreaming of moonbeams and watching the brightly shining stars.

Another day has now come to a close,
Believe me Darling: you are still my precious rose.
May dreams of our future together always be grand.
Someday soon, upon your hand my golden wedding band.

Lora Likins Diehl
BUTTERFLY

To mom and dad.

When I was young, I was like a caterpillar,
eating and crawling, but not doing much else.
Yet you were always there.
When I was an adolescent, I spun a protective
cocoon around myself, and I went through many changes.
I was impossible to reach and reason with.
Yet you were always there.

When I went away to college, I found I had changed into a butterfly. I tested my wings and at times found the sun hadn't dried them enough; I tried and failed.
No matter what, You were always there.
Now I am an adult, and I feel I want to fly. But sometimes I feel I'm being held too tightly and I'm going to be crushed!
I know it's hard to watch your caterpillar grow and change into a butterfly right before your eyes. If you just look at my wings now, I'm sure you will be pleased.
Because you were always there, I have wings to spread and they are beautifully colored, for you have colored them and you did a magnificent job!
Because you were always there when I needed you.

Paula Cole
LOVERS

Dedicated to my loving husband, Ron, who still lights the fire after 15 years! I love you FOREVER!

We walked under the moonlight hand in hand,
Down in the midst of the grazing land,
Talking of things that weren't really of need,
Wondering which of us would take the lead.

We both knew our feelings but were so unsure,
Afraid that the other would think it impure.
We laughed and we joked trying to ignore our thoughts,
But we couldn't forget them, it was love we sought.

Finally our eyes met, we kissed and embraced,
It was so intense, all else was erased.

Our needs kept getting stronger, they were powerful needs,
This terrific attraction that made our hearts bleed.

We were both filled with anxiety, we just had to let go,
And yes, we made love, neither could say no!

Benjamin F Miller

Benjamin F Miller
SOUTH GEORGIA WIND

This poem is dedicated to all personnel in the library, Jordan Hall, and Richards Building at Columbus College.

As I sat here relaxing and dozing off in this comfortable chair in the library at Columbus College and between naps, I gazed out of the window to watch the work of the busy wind.
Then, I began to scribble a few lines and this is the thought that came to my mind:

I know that I can never write a poem as lovely as the wind.
The wind that blows the warm air out and it ushers the cool air in.
The wind can do its work both day and night and never have to stop to take a rest.
The wind has no hands, feet, or mouth,
but surely can howl, run, skip, and play.
Who can see the wind itself? No one can but one certainly can see its mighty works.
The howling wind blows through the limbs, the trees and it scatters the brown leaves every way, and the leaves all run, skip, and play as they go on their merry way to the drainage pit.
The wind searches for holes in skirts and trousers and causes the individual to tremble in the cold.

Cathleen Conway
WOULD YOU

For two splendid and valiant hearts, my children, Eileen and Liz.

If I could be
What I should be
And tell the world about it
Would you love me more
Or love me less
To see your dream unfolded

Or would you see
Inside of me
The pain and disillusion
And would you see confusion?

Would you wait to see
Or hurry from me
And leave the dream behind you
And speak well of yourself
That you did your best
And like all the rest
Come back when the shadows leave me.

Suzie Clark
THE BREAK OF DAWN
At the break of dawn,
All of life is aglow.
The dew in the meadow;
The snow on the mountaintop,
So white and blinding;
Through the palm trees
The sun peeks through,
Leaving dark patches of palm.

The sky cracks in orange and yellow lines
As the sun rises above death.
The uncontrollable power of our God above
Is seen through the break of dawn.
Our God almighty has given us life;
Through birth, and through the break of dawn!

Lisa Cole
A CHILD'S IMAGINATION

This poem is dedicated to Tabby, B.J., Karen, Mandy, Damon, Josh, Beth, Kim, Chad, Brett, I love all of you, Lisa.

They say they're too busy
They have to meet an obligation
They tell me to go play
To use my imagination

I go to my room with a frown
I look at all of my toys
I imagine they are gifts of love
Instead of grown-up ploys

I think of things to do
Just for a little attention
Not caring if it's bad or good
I use my imagination

Being a child can be fun
When I imagine I am dad
With a bottle of rum
He's happy and he laughs
He gives me kisses and hugs

Or I imagine I am mom
When she sniffs powder in her nose
She gets so excited
Sometimes we try on clothes

I think I will be just like them
When I grow up
I won't need my imagination then
Just white powder and rum

Edie Boyd
THE TRUTH ABOUT LIES

To Saundra (Mitzell), truly the wind beneath my wings.

I hope that you will never
tell a lie to me
A truth can be forgiven
A lie can never be

Once a lie is told
It grows until it dies
Hurting friends and loved ones
Also ruining lives

There is nothing more deceiving
Then when a lie is told
To someone you know loves you
Or a friend of old

The truth in all its boldness
Its hurt and its pain
Can someday be forgiven
And turn to love again

But the lie is not forgiven
And the pain it will remain
For who could believe that once you've lied
You will not lie again

Donald H Charles
EARTH 1990
This good planet, that we call Earth
Floats in space, since its birth.

It gives us water that's fresh and blue

Now the wildlife is trying to escape
the goo.

It gives us fresh air from its green
Now the smog, makes that a dream.

Some giant companies with
throwaway trash
give some humans a pocket full of
cash.

Nuclear waste has come of late
Wake up humans to change that fate.

Asbestos, toxics and dioxins man
tries to bury
Finding fresh water is a little bit
scary.

Now the clouds give acid rains
Big green forests, become great
plains.

Great big oceans that give us pride
throw back the garbage in each tide.

Machines that run on diesel and gas
Make great fishing for big dead bass.

This earth that we call yours and
mine
We better wake up, we are running
out of time.

Let other generations enjoy Earth
2090.

Stephanie M Chambers
WHERE DID THE CHILDREN GO

The world means a lot to me,
but it's not like it used to be.

Where is the laughter I used to know?
Where did all the children go?

Where are the games they used to
play?
Why did these things go away?

Why does everyone want to grow up?
I don't know, I give up.

We used to play games and have
races,
but now popularity and beer have
taken their places.

This is a problem we all have to face;
the world is not a very safe place.

Without the children playing games;
the world will never be the same.

Anjelina Charme
COMMITMENTS

my heart is shaking;
trembling in confused rhythm,
matching the cigarette smoke
disturbed by the breath from your
lips.
passion's words,
spoken in hushed tones.
yet there is more warmth in my
cognac
—or my memories—
than in your eyes resting so carelessly
upon my breasts;
as your body is sure to do
moments after the beginning.

and how ruthlessly you beg for the
commitment
of flesh and bones and blood;
not trusting a commitment whispered
with the honor of the heart.
perhaps this is why I accept your
diamonds so casually—
never speaking a commitment,
never trusting a promise.

Sharie M Carbajal
IF

Dedicated to Armando and Ricardo with all my love.

If your sky is grey
I'll make it blue.
If you have a wish,
I'll make it come true.
If in your eye a tear,
I'll take the fear.

If I really had the power to make
your sky blue,
If I really had the power to make
your wish true,
If I really had the power to take your
fear;
Then I would be in heaven and God
would be here.

All these things I can't give to you,
All our dreams may not come true,
But, if you believe in your heart, I
love you,
If you believe in your heart, my love
is true,
Then God is in Heaven, and he is
here too.

Pat Cook
LOVE IS THE GARDEN OF HIS SPIRIT IN THE 90'S

The spirit of the 90's will long be
told
We all the seeds to be planted each a
flower ready to unfold
If we all pray in spirit each and every
day.
We his children of the spirit will be
shown the way
He will lead us to plant more seeds of
love, peace and harmony.
Forgiveness of ourselves and each
other we will see
As our spirit goes on and on into
eternity
So all brothers and sisters in prayer
daily we should be
For love is the garden of his spirit as
free all are we
So be his ray of sunshine a light to
show the way

As with light in our garden it will
grow day by day
So find a quiet place away from the
worldly ways
As we have tried all avenues and he
won't lead us astray
Picture opening your garden gate his
beauty to behold
Talk to him as a friend and our
heaven on earth will long be told
And when another's garden needs
some tender loving care
Love and lend a helping hand always
be lead in prayer
As you and me all brothers and
sisters in his spirit will see
The spirit of his 90's garden will be
of total love a reality

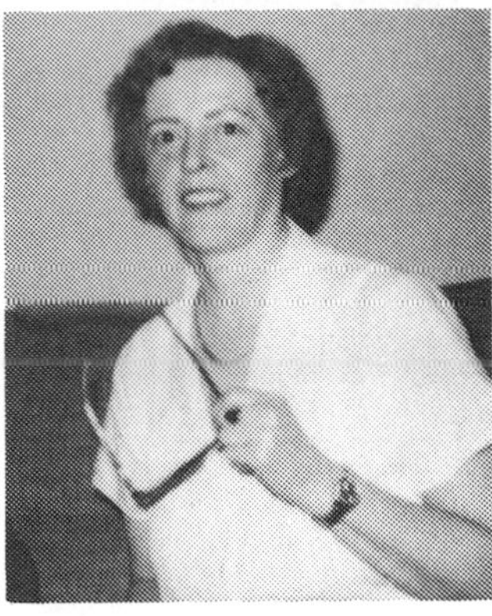

Romine R Newsome

Romine R Newsome
MY DREAM

There's a little country road
a'running west, running west—
Got my wandering soul to itching
without rest, without rest;
Down the little road a'winding stands
a house, stands a house—
I can see it, I can see it, in my
dreams!

Got to go and find that road a'runnin
west, running west—
Got to ease my searching thoughts
and still their quest, still their quest;

I can see the house—can touch it. Is
it real? Is it real?
Or is it just a figment of my dreams?

I am searching, always searching for
a house by the road—
Not a manse of brick and etched with
gilded gold, gilded gold;
But a weather-beaten cottage, gray
and bare, gray and bare—
Where inside the souls of free men
ever thrive!

And the house that I yet search for
has a hall, has a hall—
Wherein dwell the knights of
manhood, great and small, great and
small;
Wherein reign such queenly women
that the stars dim their lights
To behold these royal saints who bear
no sin!

In the hall the air is purer than the
purest flakes of snow—
And they say 'tis in this dwelling that
the cherubs of Springtime grow;
'Round the house the fields are
barren and the pale moon's silvery
shine
Blends into a mystic sweetness, as of
roses dipped in wine!

On the lofty beams a'towering
toward the diamond-studded sky,
Lounge the noble apparitions in their
noblest attire;
Higher, still, the night is tressed in an
inky, purplish hue—
Hung with stars like drops of honey
splashed on royal midnight blue!

There is laughter, there is singing, I
am gay, so very gay—
'Til I'm spinning in a mist that turns
the blackness into day;
I am left with vivid memories and a
mouth that tastes of wine—
I recall the high-beamed rafters and
the songs of saints divine!

But, the ancient house has vanished,
as now vanishes the dew—
And the little road a'winding is like
none I ever knew;
'Tis some dream. I've dreamed it
often. Fools know dreams are never
found—
Still—upon my lips the vintage, on
the wind, celestial sounds!

Romine R Newsome
REFLECTIONS ON SNOW

Snow—that pure and refreshing
down of angels' wings,
Lent by Heaven to salve the chafe of
Winter's sting,
And wash away the dead pallor from
hills, and fields, and trees,
Leaving in its stead, celestial
whiteness.

Snow—a gentle blanket of warmth to
spread o'er lonely graves;
A shroud for their dead leaves and
weeping grasses.

Snow—a phenomenon of Nature so
wonderful, it defies mortal
description,
Yet simple enough for even the
smallest child to understand.

Snow—that which makes old hearts
gay and young hearts gaier.

Snow—a crown of glory for lofty
peaks; Perpetual Spring streams for
their deep valleys; a crystal mirror for
the Sun, Moon and Stars.

Snow—white enough to shame the
lilies; bright enough to outshine the
ugliest sin; pure enough to reflect
God's own Image in all it touches.

Aileen Chavez
COLORS

To my family.

Colors of black and gray
filled my world as a child.
Not a rainbow of colors.
My existence was known living
in fear and poverty.
I had no choice, this was the world
given to me.
I survived by means unknown.
And I remember.
Not by choice; but by being there.

P J Danas
A MATHEMATICAL DEBT

This poem is dedicated to my darling wife, Dorothea, and our beautiful children: Jim, John, Patty and Chris. And to fellow mathematicians everywhere.

From earliest days of creation,
until the end of time:
Man has always sought the
difference,
of what is yours and mine.
While ancients posed on a number
base,
modern man is cruising in outer
space.
From the era of the abacus
to the age of computers,

Mathematics has assisted all of us—
even extending to city commuters.
The eye marvels at constructions
by planners with instruments of old,
While the intellect appreciates structures
so magnificent and bold.
As we project on calculators, traveling
quickly as light—
And observe a huge jet, already in flight;
Let us pause to remember that
math plays a really great part,
Whether the topic is science, or music,
or just simple art.

Keith Frederic Dungan
FINAL TEAR

Dedicated to John Eric Roellinghoff d. 11-9-86 "Our Beloved Friend"

Why was there no way
For us to keep you here
We didn't have a say
Just a final waiting tear
I know I'm not alone
When I'm hurting deep inside
With hopes that you're at home
But from us you cannot hide
I saw an opening in your heart
Letting heat out turning cold
We couldn't see just how torn apart
You were deep inside your soul
Yes our friend you'll always be
Even though you can't be here
So if you're watching you will see
Us cry you a final tear

Donna Marie Dulian
MIDNITE'S OTHER SIDE

To my life, To my love, To the fox.

Hold on to me
As no-one has
While we settle
Amid the grass.

I ask that You
Stay long enough
To help me prove
That I have worth
Of some kind.
You decide . . .

Am I as narrow
As the noon tide?
Am I high enough
To touch a single star?
Will I ever reach the
Far, far-off field?

Do I have worth enough
To occupy an hour,
Maybe more, within the
Frame of reference
You call time?

The corners of my eyes,
But just the corners,—
Frown.
My nipples are erect
To nudge my dress as
If to burrow through.
You haven't smiled,
And yet You do.

I wish that I were
Plain enough to show
You I'm but me; Or,
As fancy as I feel
You think I should be.

Sort me out
While I decide
What's real
Or make-believe
In You.

Better still,
Deliver me,
If not to
Your own self,
Then to the
MIDNITE'S OTHER SIDE.

Mrs Evelyn Turqueza-Dreher
TREES

For Tony Ramella, Dawn Klemm, my nieces Analyn & Eurly, nephews Ricky, Donald & Euland, to Callie, Donna & their brother Kevin Jr. & Joshua & the rest of the youth of today, to you I dedicate this poem.

Here and there I see them grow
some so tall, some are low
their branches swing as wind blows
leaves dance in graceful flow

Oh! What a beauty to see
mountains crowned with green trees
viewing them makes my heart glee
birds fly over them so free

Useful in so many ways
they make us cleaner air
they give shades where kids can play
every time day is fair

Everybody can't you see?
the importance of trees
why don't we plant two or three?
so warming will decrease

How healthy this place would be?
if we learn to take heed
trees give not only beauty
but clean air our earth needs

Donna K Leslie

Donna K Leslie
DREAMS

In my dreams . . .
Your love has brought new thoughts and meaning into my life.

Objects that didn't exist before now excel in beauty.

Feelings that I have never before felt, I now feel through your touch.

Is it possible to go through life with only our thoughts and dreams alone?

Never really touching or sharing with anyone.

Putting our feelings into neat little boxes, opening them only in certain places and special times.

Dreaming again . . . .
Reality can be hard to face.
I know your need for me outweighs your love.

I happened to be there when you needed someone.
I know the day will come when your need has been fulfilled.

What will happen to all my beautiful dreams then?

Marie Cetnarowski
RAINDROPS

I'm sitting at the window
Staring at the rain
Wondering when
I'll love again.

Wish the tiny droplets
Would wash the
Pain away
That haunting memory
Of your goodbye
that took my sunny days.

Time isn't the greatest healer
Remembrances abound
Each tiny drop
Is a broken heart
Seeking to be found.

When a broken heart is mended
And a new love one does find
The rain is gone
The sun returns
And pain is left behind.

E Marcella Chavers
REMEMBERING A DREAM

To my special children, Bruce and Steven and to another Steve. Only he knows the truth.

Sometimes I look back, remembering your arms.
Touching me, molding me, igniting flames
Eternal ones that tear at my soul
Voices, whispering in the darkness
Everything you knew I needed to hear
Now empty words, shattered dreams.

Pausing a moment to make sure
Asking, without uttering a spoken word
Trying to say no, while my body is burning yes
Risking our futures, selling our souls
Incomplete moments here and there
Complete only in my mind, in my dreams
Kicked down with your abrupt, no, I can't

Bringing us back to the real world
Right or wrong wasn't an issue any longer
I only knew you'd stolen my heart, my love
Love does strange things to people, but it's
Loneliness that keeps me
Remembering a Dream.

Ila Kimball Calkins
A WALK ALONG THE SHORE

Did you ever walk on an island
among ancient 'Indian lore;'
be beckoned onward and onward
along a rugged shore?

The shadows lengthen in the pines;
the air had a tinge of chill.
A finger of sunlight lingers on.
A Gull cries out so shrill.

I sit upon a driftwood log;
behind me is a mossy glen.
I hear swift steps, a whitetail
disappeared just then.

I peer behind, where in the pines,
shadows had begun to fall;
I'm sure I see an Indian Chief
standing, straight and tall.

The water laps against the rocks
upon the island shore.
I look again for the Indian Chief, but
he had gone before.

Steven R Chatterton
DAYDREAMS TO REALITY

With my love, always and only yours . . . "LOVE ME"

Seeing your image upon the shelf,
While I'm lying here by myself
I hear your voice—this is so sweet,
Waiting for time when next we meet.

Wonderful light comes from your smile,
Which makes this life so worthwhile.
During this time, gazing into your eyes,
Once again I feel those butterflies.

I feel your warmth beside me now
While I lie here wondering how.
With my smile there comes a tear;
Through all of this you're really here.

As this rain turns into sun
We are molding from two into one.
With our risks that brought us near
I have no regrets, with you no fear.

Forever yours my heart, my soul, my me—
Always, with prayer, this you might see.
With your beauty, I love with delight,
So wishing I could give you your moonlight.

Cherie L Colet
CHRISTMAS

Christmas!
Oh the wonder and beauty of it,
Shining down the ages still!
As the Angels speak from Heaven,
"Peace on earth, to men good will,"
And Christ's own Holy presence
sheds its glory all around
As it did from the lowly manger
where, by shepherds He was found.

Holy Christmas!
To commemorate the birth of our Savior.
Born that He might give
His life eternal ransom
That you and I might live.
Oh, may we all accept Him as we travel on life's way,
And the joy and peace of Christmas
will be with us every day.

Stacy Ann Dombrowski
GRANDFATHERTIME

In loving memory of my grandfather, John Stanley Dombrowski, who passed away April 3, 1989.

He is a man of time.
His name is John and has a wife and three children.
His life was through the depression

and the times of change.
His hobby is to work in his garden,
He is to his garden as God is to life,
He works hour after hour in the lush green vines.
His secret of life, no one knows.

His favorite pastime is teaching,
He sits with the little boy and teaches him to play cards,
John makes sure that he stays to win.
He is a teacher of life.

Time is moving on and leaving him behind.
His face is pale and white, all of wrinkles.
And there is no more garden.
He sits all alone, waiting for his time to come.
He is afraid of what is unknown.
He takes nothing he doesn't deserve, but gives all he can.

John will play his last hand of cards,
There the joker is waiting.
Now he lays his tired body down to rest, only to pray to see
Tomorrow.

Wendy Marsh
THE TIMES
Do you remember the time I said . . .
And do you remember what you said to me . . .
How much fun we had . . .
How much time we had . . .
Our youth and naivety . . .
The times were great when we . . .
Oh, but how the times have changed . . .
Do you remember what I did . . .
And do you remember with whom I was with . . .
I DO!!!
I recall that particular night we . . .
Those were the best times of our . . .
Do you remember how we used to . . .
And then there was the time . . .
And when we . . .
Oh, but how the times have changed . . .
And now that the times have changed . . .
And now that we have grown old . . .
AND WISE!!!
We have grown apart . . .
But Oh, how the times have lingered on . . .

Susan Kay Smith
TWO SIDES TO EVERY STORY!
For every wrong, there's a right,
For every hard day, a restful night,
For every person there's a twin,
And forgiveness for every sin.

For every death that loved ones mourn,
There's a beautiful baby being born,
For all the crime out in the street,
There's policemen fighting for defeat.

There's drugs being abused and people are dying,
Those doctors use for medicines, cures they're really trying,
For all the mentally ill who sadly kill and torture,
There's an intelligent mind working for our future,
For all the gangs at war, the fighting and hating one another,
There's couples in love, friends, families, a loving mother.

You've got to view both sides before you can really judge,
Because people that focus on one side only, tend to hold a grudge,
So if it really matters to someone, what opinion you hold,
Be sure to remember: "There's Two Sides to Every Story that's Told!"

Jennifer Lee Unger
UNTITLED
They say that "Hell hath no fury like
A woman scorned,"
But what about the bitterness for a
Love that could never be,
The hope that she knows
Will never be,
The pain and the longing
For something unattainable?
These are worse, for the flames
Burn from within,
They do not mar the flesh,
But singe the soul.

Lisa Jablonski
WHEN IS IT LOVE
When is it love
When I notice you and you notice me
When is it love
When you hold me tight down by the sea
When is it love
When I see that sparkle in your eye.
When is it love
When we never have to say "goodbye."
When is it love
When I can feel you near
When is it love
When you need to turn to me I'll be there
When is it love
When you look me in the eye and say "I love you."
When is it love
When I'm standing in my white gown answering "I do."
When is it love
When we get to be together every day
When is it love
When heaven is only one step away.

Mark Walton
REACH FOR THE STARS
Reach for the Stars, She would tell them all,
Her students loved their teacher.
There was nothing to do, I just wish it weren't true.
The Lord stretched out his hand to reach her.

It was cold and dark that tragic morn, in the sunshine state.
Twice it was no, but now it's a go, no one could sense their fate.

Well now we're ready, so we think, they're sitting on the cape,
but it wasn't long, till it all went wrong,
and there was no escape.

It was just a routine mission, number twenty-five,
but when all seven, went into heaven, not one came back alive.

You must be brave to go into space, you must have the touch.
So here's to you the Challenger crew,
We'll miss you very much.

Gwen Washburn
A COLD WINTER'S WIND
On a cold winter's morn,
A winter's wind is born.
It flies like a bird,
And barely a whisper is heard.
Once it touches the trees,
Away fly the leaves.
It's like a whistling old tune,
With a scent as crisp and fresh as a new rose in bloom.
And once it flies away,
You'll remember this cold winter's day.
Farewell to the wind,
And may you come back again.

Belinda Howe-Hinson

Belinda Howe-Hinson
A LOVE OF YESTERDAY
Loneliness is a broken heart
Who cannot stand to be apart

A love that cannot fade away
With darkness left its only prey

In a far back crevice of the mind
A love that couldn't stand the test of time

But a silent flame still burns bright
On such a cold and lonely night

And in the past it must stay
Just a love of yesterday

Stephanie Warren
PLEASE COME

For everyone in my family, I thank you. You guys made me who I am. Love, Steph.

Oh moonlight
please come,
Shine your rays upon him
enlight his body that lays
upon my breast,
Caress him with your soft touch
as I do mine,
Play your sweet melody
upon his skin
and enlighten him of my love,
Chase away the Black Night's hand
that lays upon my lips
so I may tell him of my love,
Oh moonlight
please come
and lay upon his skin
as he lays upon my heart.

Florence Arlene Elliott
HEAR THEM GROWING

To my wonderful husband, Charles, and our children; Charles Nathan, Meghann Saunders, Lauren Elizabeth, and Kevin Andrew (the poetry of my life). Also, in honor of my mother, Marguerite Nicklow; and my husband's parents, Drs. Earl and Virginia Elliott.

There's a quiet corner that no one else can find
Far away from others' view, the corner is my mind.

I'm apt to share a lot of me with others as I live
Perhaps too much, I'm bound to say . . . If too much, please forgive.

I see myself in my offspring four, they're not like many others
So many traits between them all—twixt two sisters and two brothers.

A profound love of laughter, a gentleness, a shyness, a certain mystery
A battle and smiles after, caring, truth and jealousy.

What a marvelous mix of charm and wit, of creative airs and spice
How often they turn on the cold, then so quickly melt the ice!

Our gang's unique, I'm a bit gray . . . but my heart is overflowing
With pride and joy I watch each day and hear my children growing.

Scott Stets

Scott Stets
LOST IN THE PAST

This poem is dedicated to two wonderful ladies, Kim Vaillancourt and the other I have yet to meet in this life.

She visits him in his dreams,
hair as gold as sunbeams,
eyes as blue as the bluest ocean,
yet, still he is alone.

He's known her so long and yet he knows her not,
but he knows that forever, she'll be in his heart,
he looks back now in regret,
with only memories of where, when and how they met.

There was once a time when they were one,
years ago when her heart he had won,

he was her knight in shining armor
and she, his princess,
and by the lake, they so tenderly kissed.

Then her white knight turned black as coal,
now, a lonely man with no one to capture his soul,
scared, he didn't realize that she was his true love,
and off into the night flew his beautiful white dove.

He has died a million and one times,
every time he remembers of when he was blind,
now he is lost in the past, and she is far from his grasp,
and at the same time, she is right in front of him.

Rose Dell Freemon
TINY TOT

Tiny tot with eyes of Blue
Chatterbox the day through.
How big the world must seem.
Is it any smaller when you dream?
Are the trees and people, all
In your dreams quite as tall?
Or do you become taller then
And travel farther than you've ever been,
To places farther than your arms can reach,
To forests tall or sandy beach?
I wonder sometimes just what you see
In those eyes with love for me.

Rose Dell Freemon
INTRUDER

Water is flowing over slippery stones
Quick moving fish are going on their way.
Crisp Autumn leaves are kissing the water
As dawn stretches her arms on another day.

A bee goes buzzing by me
I hear his quick moving hum
The morning sun promises
That later warmth is to come.

Merganser ducks slip into the water
From a shady spot on the other bank
Mother Merganser taking the lead
And the others following in rank.

The fish aren't eager to bite
Here in this quiet, peaceful stream
I could lie back against a log
And close my eyes and dream.

But I just might miss the beauty
Of some new found moment, near
For other woodland creatures might peek out
To see what I am doing here.

Rose Dell Freemon
POCKET TREASURES

Grandma's apron pockets
Used to hold a recipe or two
She would stand before her stove
Cooking up something new.

Deep in thought
With ingredients on her mind
She wouldn't hear Grandpa
Sneaking up behind.

He would surprise her with a daisy
Or some other flower that he found
As he went about his chores
Or plowed the warm, moist ground.

A petal or two might be crushed
By the pockets of the overalls he wore
But they meant as much to Grandma
As if delivered from a store.

Michael Mueller
FREEDOM ON THE FOURTH OF JULY

Listen, and you can experience freedom.
Freedom of white water on this Fourth of July,
Dancing and celebrating from the High Sierras
And its river canyons, to the El Dorado foothills.

Look, and you can see freedom.
Freedom of nature in the Sierras—a place where deer, birds,
And squirrels like to play among the giant Ponderosa Pines,
Flowering Dogwoods, and golden Aspens of the Eldorado National Forest.

Breathe, and you can smell freedom.
Freedom of the great outdoors, with clean, fresh air
In the high country from the still meadows,
And river canyons, to the mountains overlooking them.

Touch, and you can feel freedom.
Freedom of a mighty river roaring past you—
Refreshing and alive like an endless parade
Celebrating our Independence Day.

Taste, and you can be nourished by freedom.
Freedom of enjoying what you want to do
In these scenic outdoors of the High Sierras,
With peace and happiness shining this Fourth of July.

Michael Mueller
CATCHING A RAINBOW IN BRIDALVEIL FALL

On a crisp winter afternoon with the sun shining brightly,
I stop to say hello to Bridalveil Fall,
With its tumbling waters pouring over its cliff,
That looks like an avalanche of crystals, sparkling in the sun's rays.

The sparkling waters leaping in the air in exuberance,
Free falling from the top of Bridalveil Fall,
Tumbling downward as it blows in the wind,
Changing its shape countless times before touching the Valley below.

My senses could feel the energy and many moods
Of the thundering waters exploding on the Valley floor,
Shooting wind blown mist and spray,
Reaching for the high country once more.

The forceful winds blow the mist and spray,
Covering me with refreshing wetness,
As if the water had wings to fly,
From these tumbling clouds of once melted snow.

Now the swirling mist and spray of Bridalveil Fall
Captures a rainbow in the sun's rays,
In this special Valley called Yosemite,
Lasting long enough to be remembered forever.

Roger Gilpin
BREAKDOWN

The bus has stopped and I am told to leave
I wipe my nose on my wet, dripping sleeve
All year round my head allergies are bad
My sister has got them and so did Dad
In school a girl lights up a cigarette
I know that she has slept with young Evette
That ass just pushed someone I sort of know
Let me at him to give a good hard blow
I know that I am being watched and hide
Everybody hates elevator rides
Some money would be nice, I am in debt
Put some in stocks and bonds, I would be set
Now let us go down to the liquor store
Get two cases or maybe I'll get four
Some of my friends say that I have lost touch
But they are all stupid and care too much

Marie G Woods
SHE LAY IN HER BED

Dedicated to Debbie, my sister, my friend.

She lay in her bed
Alone
She called out
I love you alone
She whispered
I need you
Alone
She screamed
I hate you
Alone
She cried
Alone
She died
Alone

He came to her graveside
Alone
He called out
I love you
ALONE

Gloria Leney
SPRING LOVE

To all things beautiful, both the things of the world, which are seen, and the things of the soul, which are unseen.

Flowers blooming, birds singing, rippling streams, a relationship begins.
Springtime, filled with so much beauty and love, sweet smelling flowers, beautifully decorating a lonely field, birds busily swooping to get their meal, streams in full flow; the relationship is at its peak now.
Love is stronger than it's ever been.
But then seasons change, people change
Birds' songs have faded out, the rippling stream has frozen stiff
the roses have wilted, the relationship dies.
Along with cold weather comes cold hearts
lonely barren fields and quieted forests.
Until springtime comes again and the relationship gets another try, the flowers are more beautiful than before, the forests are alive with birds singing and once again things are seen through the eyes of a lover.

Laura McLean
CHILDREN OF WAR

Battered into quiet numb,
Scarred and beaten and maimed,
With broken, bruised, and bleeding bodies,
But spirits still burning unquenchable flame.
With heads courageously held up high,
With dignity and silent calm,
Faces turn to now tranquil skies
And tired hearts revel in peace's balm.
Courage it takes to honourably die,
But sometimes more courage to live on and fight,
For darkness and death seem ever prevailing,
And such pain and fear do haunt the black night.
Endure! Oh Children, have faith,
Your souls thrust high above like burning spire,
So all the agony, death, fighting, killing, War,
Won't ever quell your fire.

Dennis M Miller
A BEAUTIFUL SKY

This poem is dedicated to Charles F. Manor, who I love very much. Thank you for your love and being who you are; you gave me the inspiration to write this poem.

It's early morning and everyone is sound asleep,
I sit here feeling a pain that runs deep.
I watch the sun rise and the sky turn red,
as thoughts of pain and suffering run through my head.
I sit and fight as I try not to cry,
as I watch the Lord make a beautiful sky.
A beautiful sky, that's how all the days start,
as my day starts with a broken heart.
My heart is with my loved one so far away,
it hurts, so much each and every day.
With all my heart and soul, I love my dear,
it's hard not to shed a tear.
I have a love that's deep and true,
I wish we were together, yes I do.
As I sit and look at a beautiful sky,
I pray God will be with my loved one as time goes by.
Someday we will be together again, you'll see,
until then, I can't let this suffering get the best of me.

Catrina L Clayton
THE FINAL BLACK DAYS III

My smile
is but a mask
My laugh
a scream

If you scratch my firm, creamy
surface
a deep, red fear of life I will bleed
Mankind's malice is mortar
making strong the stones of my
self-deception
As I claw at this wall
I collapse in the shadows
so no one can see my weakness
My fingertips are raw
as my hope flows to the floor
to form a warm, crimson puddle
As it glistens
It calls . . .
There, I see my future
in all its rosy glory
There is no future
It calls
as it glistens . . .

Wanda M Hill
TROUBLE IN MY WAY

This poem is dedicated to my best friend, Betty Jean Thomas.

Trouble is in my way it comes from
every hand.
I try to live a straight and narrow life
But it still seems to find me.
Sometimes it's on the streets, streets
that are so full of pain and sorrow
You try and go around it, behind it,
or in front of it.
But, every time you try and rise
above it, here it comes again.
Raising its ugly head.

I find a quiet place, trouble seems to
make it noisy
You seek refuge in your Temple and
it seems to have come there to stir up
more trouble.
Then you think there's one place I
can go to get out of trouble is home.
But, that's no help because, that's
where all my trouble began.

Debra Boyd
THE FAMILY!

I marry him with his one and my two with me trying to make a family. It all was good till the day. They all didn't get (their) way. Now all we have is argument and fights trying to see who is wrong or right. Working it out and getting it right. To have a family and not a fight. But live together in life as one. As a family not as (stepsons) so the house that we made, can be with love that we gave!

Karma Larissa Myers
AS WE LIVE

Time is never still
Upon any such hill.
The sun's rays glide past
Blades of grass till the last.

Youth is never kind
To anybody's mind
Lasting a season
It leaves without reason.

So we try to live
So much we often give
To justify life
Through all our pain and strife.

Answers can't be found,
Within this trodden ground
Why death's sure to come
To all who have become.

But there is great hope
That surpasses man's scope.
It's in His great pain
That we live not in vain.

Cecelia M Castillon
THE GUARD

This poem is dedicated to Christopher J. O'Reilly. You're a terrific little boy and I'll miss you when I leave!

I can see him from up above
that's where I stay to watch over him.
Where he stays is beautiful
On the dark green meadow
Waiting for someone to come.
He is guarded by
everything and anything
that surrounds him during the day.
During the night
I shelter him and keep him warm.
There he stays
day by day
loved by me
but not knowing
who his Guard is
that watches over him.
I too, wait for someone to find
and to take care of baby Christopher.

Melisa Stearns
COMPASSION

You were there when I needed a
shoulder on which to cry
Not fully understanding but never
questioning why
You gave me everything and were
always there to give a hug
You helped and consoled me out of a
hole that I had dug
You so carefully would wipe away
all my tears
Then in your special way put to rest
all of my fears
For all of these and everything else
too
I hope I can be there when you need
someone to turn to

Cindilou A Hockman
TEACH

Once I felt education was a burden,
as heavy as the fetters and chains
worn by slaves.
Now I realize that as the War freed
the slaves,
Education has freed me.
I have found wings to fly over
Oceans and Lands
and the winds of wisdom support me.
I've set down roots to grow and
learn,
so that I might give another the gift
of flight.
Those I teach can go on flights of
discovery
and they can pass the gift of
knowledge on.

Esther L Shocksnider
MEMORY THEME

To our Father in Heaven who gave me my understanding.

A day starts out with the rays of the
sun on high.
But like troops of well-trained men,
Each makes his appearance, then
goes by,
Etching on one's mind the eternal
query of when.

When do we really start to live?
When do we really learn to give?
When do we really espy a person's
nice trait?
When does one learn to make the
most of his fate?

When? When each man loves his
neighbor as himself.
When? When each man learns to give
of himself.
When? When each man appreciates
another's fine trait.
When? When the love governing
man's actions is very great.

Thus, each day in one's life merges
with another day.
And so one's lifetime is here, then
gone away.
Only in memory the main theme of
life holds sway.
Days begin, nights start, another day
and another start.

Our memories know no stop or start,
But of our lives become a continuing
part.
So, good or bad, our thoughts and
deeds in life hold sway.
Always reminding us of thoughts and
deeds of a previous day.

Colette Caldwell
THROW OUT THE LIFELINE

The rain always plays it out . . .
It draws upon the melancholy
Like the sea at the sand
It ebbs; it breaks
It's gone again . . .
and here I stand
within circles
and circles
flapping my arms
Lost in the waves . . .
foolishly
in mid-thrash
I hit bottom . . .
The tide recedes,
I'm standing in the sinking sand
Just a raindrop
from the Solid Rock
Always wanting the rainbow
before the rain.

Michelle McElderry
LIFE AFTER DEATH

Dedicated to the memory of Chad McElderry, Carrie Rouse, and Mike Brown. They were killed in a car accident July 2, 1989.

Love is happiness . . .
Life is pain,
Loved ones die
And ruin all our days,
We know it's not their fault,
They had to go,
Only GOD controls the time
We spend together . . .
And alone.
But when they go away,
They create so much pain.
We miss them so,
GOD only knows how much it hurts
To feel so alone,
Alone in the darkness,
Our stories go untold . . .
Our feelings inside grow so old,
They stay on and on,
They won't go away,
They make our days and nights,
So very, very grey.
Our love for them leaves us haunted,
Lonely, and in so much pain.
Our love was a gamble,
Our lives like a dream,
We can't go on, as it seems.
That's my life at 14 years, my
happiness is gone,
as my hope disappears.

wild irish rose

wild irish rose
A BIRTHDAY POEM

I know I should tell you more often,
too seldom are loving words said.
Let this stand as my monument to
you—
no truer words ever read.
You are listed in the blessings
I give daily thanks for.
Your beauty runs deep to the core.
Like a flawless gem, a consummate
femme—
You are someone I could only adore!
Today I want to tell you
I am the luckiest daughter alive,
because only a blessed few
receive what they need to thrive.
Know you will always be
within the circle of my love.
In my esteem I put none above.

wild irish rose
NUKE NIGHTMARE

Last night I dreamt of nuclear war.
Complete despair smote my very
core.
I needed my love to hold me tight
to shelter me from ferocious fright.
I saw with crystal clarity
the annihilation of humanity . . .
sweating and struggling to break free
of this dream of absolute anarchy.
So night surrendered to beauteous
day.
I pushed away this vision of decay;
reassured my dream was not quite
a prophecy of our future plight.
But the memory left me so aghast
I treat every day as though my last—
and give thanks for an immortal soul
that will survive a world out of
control.

Cynthia Bradley Tielens
TO MOTHER ON MOTHER'S DAY

On this special day of the year
Our dear mothers we will cheer.
Of all the things they have to bear
To show them how much we really care.

To one who works and runs a family too;
To one who has so much to do;
To one from whom you never hear a fuss;
To one who knows the best for us.

To one who washes and rolls my hair, too;
And does most things that mothers can't do.
To one who all our sorrows share;
To one who we know always cares.

To one who is a referee at fights;
To one who wakes up with sick ones at night;
To one who might have to use switches;
If we don't do what she teaches.

To one who fixes such good things to eat;
Things like that are hard to beat.
To one who is so sweet and kind;
Mothers like mine are hard to find.

To one who is so sweet and pure;
I'll tell you one thing and that's for sure;
You can search the whole world and never find;
A mother that is as sweet as mine.

Jamie Aldrich
COLORS OF OUR WORLD

Black is darkness and White is bright
Blood is red and Silver's the knife
Orange is the sun shining above,
Yellow is tenderness, peace and love
Blue is the air crisp and clean,
Green is the ocean's beautiful scene
Brown is the earth, Purple is space
Peach is a star that twinkles someplace
Gray is madness, Turquoise is sadness and fuchsia is our dreams
yet, the greatest to behold is that color Gold which stands for eternity

Julie Shellum
GAMES

It's such a shame
If you can't see
What I call the game
That doesn't have to be
You and me
Such a pair we could be
If only you could see what I see

Val L Meek
FROGGY

I dedicate this poem to the people of the world. I hope you have as much fun in reading this poem as did I in writing it. P.S. Enjoy

There was a little froggy that I once knew.
And this little froggy lived by you.
This little froggy was a lot of fun.
This little froggy loved everyone.
This little froggy went hop, hop, hop.
And when he got thirsty, he'd drink pop, pop, pop.
Now everyone knows that froggies don't walk.
But this little froggy sure could talk.
Gribbit, gribbit, he did speak.
As he splashed, the water, with his feet.
Back and forth, he did swim.
In the little pond, made for him.
Now little froggy's, favorite treat.
Used to be, flies to eat.
Froggy's color, is green and black.
With little white spots, on his back.
There's only one phrase that I can say.
To describe, my feelings, on this day.
About the little froggy that I once knew.
That lived in a pond, out by you.
Spring is gone, summer past, fall is here, and winter last.
It's time for me, to say good-bye.
Until next spring, when the birdies fly.
There's only one thing I have to say.
If I'm ever, back this way.
And I feel the way I do.
I'll stop by, because I love you.
The little froggy that I once knew.

Val L Meek
TWINKLE, TWINKLE, LITTLE FIRE FLY

I dedicate this poem to all of my family and friends. But especially to those who said it couldn't be done. P.S. Look at me now.

Twinkle, Twinkle, Little Fire Fly,
You used to be my light at night.
But now that you have faded away,
How will I ever be able to play?
Twinkle, Twinkle Little Fire Fly,
Who will be my guiding light,
To see me home safe, every night?
Who will hold me very tight,
And protect me from the night?
Twinkle, Twinkle, Little Fire Fly,
Who will be there to dry my tears?
Who will be there to hear my fears?
Who will be there every night?
And who will be my bedroom light?
Twinkle, Twinkle Little Fire Fly,
Now that you are out of sight,
Who will tuck me in at night?
And who will kiss me and make things right?
Twinkle, Twinkle, Little Fire Fly,
I only have one thing to say,
If you're ever back this way,
And you feel the way I do,
Please come back, I STILL LOVE YOU.

Gladys V Newby
THE LONELY ROAD

As I travel this long lonely road
With sweet memories of you
You're my Darling
And I'm looking for you.
I hope you'll be there waiting
As I come 'round the bend
Just as you were before
This just can't be the end.

I'll love you 'till the end of time
But if I don't find you there
At the bend in the lonely road
I hope you will drop me a line.

As I travel this long, lonely road
Weary, oh so weary am I
But I'm sure you'll be there
Waiting for me, to hold me tight
Now I'm around the bend
And you're not in sight.
This must be the end.

Kathy S DeCarlo
A DEDICATION TO MY SISTER, JEANNE MARIE GOTTSCH

Sometimes I wonder if there's
another place we meet
But the fear of even having the
doubt is something hard to defeat.
It scares me to the point of
wondering where I'm going to,
If I don't have the faith in the Lord
and let him guide me through.
I want so bad to believe
that my angel's happy and content.
But there are times when my mind wanders
thinking of where she really went.
My heart feels so broken
and so overflown with tears.
I try so hard to pour them
but I have so many fears.
I loved my sister dearly
but it was said times too few.
I wish I had said it more
but in her heart I think she knew.
We had so many good times
that I will always keep at heart
But trying to accept her death
just tears me all apart.
I'm sure from her strength,
she wants our chins up and us to stand
Because she knows one day,
we will all meet in Jesus's land.
I will always hold the memory
of her in my heart and in my mind,
for she left us with a note in her Bible,
"Find strength in what remains behind."

Marie Venero
THE MOTHER SHEEP SPEAKS TO THE NEWBORN

You are yet unaware of time
the hours and the seasons pass
over you like a river whose
banks cannot hold it
You are a child of mountains
and forest
The beat of your running hooves
is the melody of spring
In your eyes the mirror of heaven
Reflects your innocence

As you grow, the day will teach you knowledge
and the night will give unto you many treasures of life.
Unlike man, you will call nothing ugly
For there are no scales upon your eyes
Go now—and dream of tomorrow
For you are a fair jewel of the earth
And princess of the running waters.

Deanna M Oren
THE PAST

It's creeping up behind you
From a dark corner
You knew it was behind you
But you didn't believe in it.
Just as you turn
It stabs you
The unbearable pain makes you
STOP!
You turn, looking it straight in the eyes
Wanting it to go away, but it won't
It's stubborn.
Knowing it will always be there
You begin to run.
Leaving it far behind
But someday it will be back
To cut you again.
Each time the wound is deeper
While knowing the whole time
It's your own fault.

Heather Salaber
NOTHING'S FOREVER

The dreamy nights I longed for you,
Have faded in love's misty blue.

Your peaceful shadow that sways in the wind,
Has never been so badly sinned.

I shall never forgive for what you did to thee,
You gave her love before you did me.

My heart was broken and stricken with grief,
But you didn't care to my disbelief.

Some days of gleam and some of pain,
Some so wild and some so sane.

But to believe something could last forever,
I have just found myself not so clever.

Rebecca L Meyer
MAY HE REST IN PEACE

Out of the vast and endless stretch
of the seas of sand;
in the midst of near and far,
there lies a lonely man

a solitary speck of white
is all that there remains
to attest to the life of Stephen
Locke—and all his worldly gains.

Stephen was a wealthy man,
his kinsman was his slave;
he strove for riches, and he
shrank from the blessed and the brave.

his skin was of the purest white,
and thus, Stephen professed:
To kill a man was not a sin—
if colored was his chest.

he claimed to be a Religious man
while he abused his slaves at whim;
if only Stephen knew his heart was
blacker than their skin.

eternity has passed; gorged with
sin, Stephen lies alone

all that remains of his wicked life
is a pile of bleached white bone

While the dusty sands swirl
endlessly
in this void where time stands still,
the wind that erodes Stephen's
grinning skull whispers,
"thou shalt never kill . . . "

Barbara J Reinholz
THE ROCKING HORSE

Dedicated to Rich and Heather in loving memory of their dad, Ron.

When a little boy was only three
Santa left a rocking horse by the tree
On that Christmas morn to our
delight
That little guy's eyes big and bright
Upon that pony he climbed
As thou' he had found a gold mine.

That pony and son became as one
A constant companion, Oh what fun
A million miles they rocked away
And we still recall the sight to this
day
On that rocking horse he would fall
asleep
These memories for us to cherish and
keep.

(Francie) Mary Meeks
DADDY'S LITTLE GIRL

Daddy, thanks for showing Gram home. We will see you soon. (Frannie)

Daddy, you're so far away now.
I never thought you'd leave me,
You're the one who taught me
how to be the best I could.

It's hard to believe how
but now you're gone and I have
to go on without you to
help and guide me.

You gave me the best years of your
life
and now I'm all that mama has left.
I'll do my best

You didn't get to see my graduation
or my wedding.
But I know you would be proud.
I grew up just like you.
And I'll always be Daddy's Little
Girl.

Corina Benkovic
THE LADY IN WAITING
the lady in waiting
lies, smiling, debating
this possibly falling man
and
his probable hands
moving slowly
through her hair
lying there
smiling
for a moment
this moment
that she'll search for and find
once in a while
whenever she decides there is a need
he probably won't see
it coming
her
slowly moving away
when the moment closes
like the lady's eyes
as her smile falls
his hands
boring her to sleep
he, this
she realizes
is not what she needs.

Amanda Lynne Millette
CHANGES
In just a minute life can change,
From good to bad, it can range.
It might take seconds; it might take
years,
It may cause happiness, it may cause
tears.
It may last weeks, it may last days,
Whatever may happen, it is life's
way.
You never know when it will
transpire,
It may be, it may be dire.
If it is simple there is no harm,
If it is dire you have to be calm.
If it is good enjoy it; it might not last,
If it is bad brace yourself—it might
not pass.
If it is good be happy and gay,
Keep a smile on your face from day
to day.
If it is bad keep your faith and don't
despair,
Try to keep your spirits up and see
how you fare.
These are words to the wise from
someone who knows,
I've had my share of good times and
my share of woes.

Kristen Whitford
WATCHING
I watch as deer
cross the road in the snow,
struggling to make it to a clearing.

Fighting for their lives
trying to stay alive,
as a car comes by and they dive.

A dodge and a leap
but if they do not succeed,
there they will lie in a heap.

Left, with no one there
no one to help them,
no one who cares.

Their memories left blank
as they lie very still,
on the side of a bank.

Waiting and watching
for a mortal soul,
to come and revive them
from their deep, dark hole.

All alone in the night,
with not even a single human in
sight.

Aaron Shawn Hadsock
PREJUDICE

To my lovely wife, Sellia, Dusty, The Beatles, and those who don't participate in separation by race, sex, creed, etc.

Many times people separate others;
Black and white, not the same.
But a blind man sees no difference
and doesn't place a name.

Many times people separate others;
Too masculine/feminine a voice.
But a deaf man hears no difference
and doesn't make a choice.

Many times people separate others;
Too strong or weak to the touch.
But a crippled man feels no
difference
and doesn't care too much.

Many times people separate others;
Too smart or ignorant a mind.
But a maniac knows no difference,
not even his own kind.

Many people are so prejudiced,
But if they could only see,
That there really is no difference,
between you and me.

Doris E Wetherhold (Dee)
MY TREE

In loving memory of my mother, Lily M. Elkins.

My Tree
Is not tall and spectacular . . .
Or close to being majestic.
He's short, scarred and weather-
beaten
And stands as a lonely sentinel upon
the hillside.
He's strong, stubborn and courageous
as he faces life's eternal battle of time
and weather.
Each year he raises his arms in prayer
with new hope and promise.
Only to be shattered by wind, rain,
lighting, snow and ice . . .
But, he does not give up.

As winter passes, he looks to the sky
and God,
With prayers for yet another
year . . .
And when in spring he bursts forth in
his new coat of green,
He shares with all who see,
His strength, his determination, his
courage . . .
HE'S MY TREE

Doris E Wetherhold (Dee)
A VERY SPECIAL FRIEND
A very special friend
Enters one's life so quietly and
gently.
He asks not who I am or what I am
For he already knows the inner me.
He knows my loneliness and the
happy painted face . . .
He feels my need for his caring,
understanding, compassion and love.
He accepts me as I am and demands
nothing . . .
He washes away my fears and
unhappiness . . .
He holds me gently, but passionately
while he tenderly strokes away the
tears in my eyes.
A friendship so rare and so beautiful . . .
He is truly My Very Special Friend.

Doris E Wetherhold (Dee)
IS IT POSSIBLE

To Evelyn with love.

Is it possible . . .
One person can be three people to
me?

A friend . . . to share my hopes,
dreams, joys and sadness . . .
And always there to urge me on
to new and better days?

A sister . . . to enjoy together our
wild and crazy schemes . . .
To confide with one another our
secret loves, disappointments
and plans?

A mother . . . who understands
the inner me . . .
Who offers compassion, comfort
and love . . .
And holds me when I cry?

Yes . . . It is possible . . .
For you are all three to me.

Doris E Wetherhold (Dee)
LOVE
Love cannot be one-sided . . .
Nor can it survive only day to
day . . .
It needs the test of time to grow
stronger.

Love needs food to replenish . . .
A kind thought, words to confirm,
time to enjoy . . .
Laughter, a tender touch, quiet
togetherness . . .
A total sharing of dreams and
sorrows.

Together love grows . . .
It heals all life's hurts . . .
It diminishes disappointments . . .
It glorifies successes . . .
It takes two people and binds them to
each other and makes them one.

This is Love.

Susan Helkema Meese
FLOWER OF LIFE
I would like to live life
As a beautiful flower,
Growing in a velvet valley
Untouched by worry or hate.
And like that beautiful flower
I would bloom eternally
For every eye to behold,
For every spring rain to touch me.
My life would be a thing of beauty
Blooming every year in the same
glory;
Lifting my blooms toward the sky,
Stretching my roots deep into the
earth.
Then someday I would be plucked
And taken in tender hands,
Placed in a vase of the palest blue.
There I would look into the eyes
Of an ill one.

My life would then be complete
As I would have given joy
To a blind child.

Raina Dawn Townsend
MR. ROUND AND MR. SQUARE
Mr. Round and Mr. Square went for a
walk one day.
Said Mr. Round to Mr. Square, "The
sky is turning gray!"
"Oh, no!" gasped Mr. Square, his
face all shocked and grim,
"I left my donkey in the rain! The
barn's locked! He can't get in!

He'll drown in the rising waters, and be caught in the raging storm!
He'll float in trembling waves!"
Square's face was all forlorn.
"There, there," said Mr. Round, to comfort Mr. Square,
"The rain will have stopped by the time we get back. Your donkey will be there.
See across the meadow he stands, happy in the rain."
Square's eyes lit up, he clapped his hands, his speed began to gain.
He ran and ran across the field, Mr. Round not far away.
He reached the wooden barnyard fence, and there the donkey lay.
Said Mr. Round to Mr. Square, "Here is a word for you.
If you will take my advice, I'll tell you what to do.
Don't let small things upset you, don't let them cause you strife,
For you won't be strong for bigger tasks that affect you in your life.
Don't let small things upset you, you're sure to find release;
Be calm about all things, and then you will find peace."

Chrystal Doucet

RE-COLLECTED MEMORIES

Dedicated to my parents: Mr. & Mrs. James and Lucille Bookhout—who gave me as a child, the precious gift of toys.

Re-Collected Memories, from my inspiring youth
Re-Collected Definitions, of God's inspiring truth.
A Porcelain Doll, A Balla-Bat, from pages of my past
With many a colour-ful Hula-Hoops, these memories sure to last.
Those precious days, we all recall
To make life's dreams worth-while
Our Re-Collected Memories, that made many faces, a smile.
Re-Collected Memories, from my inspiring youth
A Re-Collective revived addition, of God's inspiring truth.

Marlen Bodden

CONTEMPLATIONS

I look upon the glory of Thy heavens work thy hands have made—
I watched the greenness turned;
to winter, watch it began to fade.
Such beauty brings motivations!
And makes the courage stronger—
For man to challenge the nations;
earthly peace may last longer.

"Praises arises from off the earth"
when man by custom cursed.
The day of light, his very birth:
Because of his empty purse.
Wisdom—Oh mother have pity—,
on thy children of today.

Show them the true beauty—
that thou hast brought their way
¡One by one, we fall, we die!
Oblivion comes—sit by our side
then we know not where we lie;
Oblivion—Welcome! arms open wide.

Kristin Sookrow

THE SUNSET JOURNEY

The sun rises behind the banks, the heat beaming.
I am safe for I know,
but the wind starts to sing.

While looking at the mountains,
what do I see but a bird.
A bird attempting to fly against the rapid winds.
For he struggles, he knows it's a challenge.

He lands in tall grasses for he knows he is safe.
But he can't help but wonder what tomorrow's going to bring.

He sets off again as I watch him fly.
But today he has nothing to worry about,
as he glides along the motionless skies.

The sun is now setting behind the banks,
as I can feel the heat cooling.
For I know I am safe.

Mary Brinkman

THE BIG ONE

For my dreamer, my Love, and my fishing buddy; "John Brinkman."

Dream a little,
Hope to find . . .
Visions of "The Big One"
Each time he pops his line.

He misses church . . .
But he's learning how to pray
For a 20-pound big mouth
To put on display.

So, this wife will pray
For his prayers to come true;
Then maybe he'll stop fishing . . .
At least during "Sunday School."

Dale D Smitley

THANK YOU

This poem is dedicated to three special friends, Dee Dee Flores, Dan Roope and Eric Tatnall.

A thank you is to express one's gratitude
For help that one has given
It's just these words I have for you
In this poem that I have written

You've helped a friend whom you know
Just by being there to listen
The words you said really showed
The caring of your mission

The thank you that I give to you
Comes from very deep within
The words alone are not enough
To show how much you've given

I came to you for something else
When a listening ear I needed
As we talked it started to come out
The feelings that I have hidden

Thank you, God, I must say
For sending your angel to me
You heard my words when I prayed
And now the blues are leaving.

Bonnie Jean (Zinsli) Worth

UPON GENTLE BREEZES

To my son, Brian Richard Zinsli, who has been a gift since the day he was born.

My Spirit travels with you . . .
Wherever you are . . .
If you gaze at the sky . . .
You'll see the bright star . . .
The one that I've whispered
Please cradle my love . . .
Make safe his journey . . .
Guide him from above . . .
Sprinkle his pathway . . .
With glitter of strength . . .
Courage and happiness . . .
Acceptance and grace . . .
Place on his shoulder . . .
An Angel with care . . .
To comfort and hold him . . .
When I am not there . . .
Soothe him with soft winds . . .
Kiss him for me . . .
Tell him I love him . . .
And that he is free . . .
To go where his heart goes . . .
To follow his star . . .
Upon gentle breezes . . .
and I'll not be far . . .

Gretchen Renee Pontsler

TWO MORE TEARS

The look on her face told me something was wrong,
Her eyes told me inside she sang a new song.
The tremble of her lip as she fought back the tears,
Made her look like a child of only five years.
The pain in her eyes was a knife through my heart,
Stabbing and piercing, pulling me apart.
When words finally came, they were all too clear,
Her grandpa had died,
Then came two more tears.

Anne Marie Martinez

PUPPY TIME

I'd like to dedicate this poem to my dog, LACEY. I wrote this for her when she was just a puppy.

I have a brand-new puppy
She looks so innocent and cute
But after you get to know her
You'll think she's quite a brute
She never stops going to the bathroom
She whines and cries and peeps
The best time to have a puppy
Is when she's sound asleep

Frances Ferguson

WAY OUT IN IDAHO

Way up in some high mountain,
I really like to go.
Where the sly fox has his den,
Way up in sight of snow,
Way out, in Idaho.

Where mountain deer, run free.
Busy squirrels, chatter, so.
Huckleberries, smile at me.
Then, down, the mountain, I will go,
Way out in Idaho!

Where mountain streams, rush and sing,
I dive into nice hot spring,
Where roads run high and low,
'Tis the great State of Idaho.
Way out in Idaho!

Ann Harris

THE BATTLEFIELD

The battlefield is smoking
Destruction is everywhere
The enemy no longer hides
Life is not precious here
Freedom has long been gone
Only a few now remember
What it was like to walk the streets
Without their lives in danger
The war is here, here to stay
A never ending battle
What was once a peaceful place
Is now not fit for cattle
Who will win? Who will lose?
Many ask that question
Sadly, it's plain to see
The whole world's desecration
Everyone will fight in this war
The War Against Drugs
And with God's help, once more
Our freedom will be given back to us

Criquette

Criquette

THE SONG OF LARKS

Floating alone, aloft and afar
I had hoped one day to find a star.
I became embroiled in the facets of life
Turning always from strife to strife.

Just when I thought there was no more to be done
And felt misfortune had surely won . . .
Suddenly, pure chance led me by the hand
To be enfolded in the arms of man!

We had singing bodies and hungry hearts
And when we embraced . . .
Behold the Song of Larks!

We floated aloft and afar
And even reached out and touched a star!
Pianissimo, forte, alto, moderate . . .
Where oh where will we go?

Bernadette Dutka
HIS SOUND

Dedicated to my soul mate.

He doesn't really speak
When he verbalizes his thoughts
He just sort of parts his lips and
lowers his jaw
And the rough, soft, sounds
Seem to just roll and flow and fall
Into all the beautiful things
that he says.

Tina Lynn Schroyer
SWEETHEART

In memory of Junior Hart, my love.

Although you're very far from me
I still feel you near each day
One touch, one kiss are things I wish
could once again be mine
Those eyes that smile your tender
style
Are things that come to mind
You and I were meant to be a pair
never to part
But God had other plans
Even though I don't understand
You'll always be in my heart.

Susan Tiger
DEATH YOU SHALL NOT CHEAT ME

In Loving Memory of my cousin, Gerald Kubic.

Oh, death, you shall not cheat me
no matter how you try—
For joy will come again to me,
One day my tears will dry.

Although I shall not see him
perhaps for many years,
I'll ne'er forget his smile—
I see it through my tears.

You cannot take the twinkle
The Lord put in his eye . . .
And, yes! I still can hear his voice
I will until I die.

You cannot take the memory of the
babe I held and rocked,
You cannot take the years we had,
the way we played, the times we
talked.

So, death, you shall not cheat me,
some day I'll understand . . .
For now I have my memories,
He has his brother's hand.

Eva Kalme
DEFIANCE

Amongst the stone, steel and glass of
this old city.
Where the grass sprinkled with
crushed glass thrives and the trees
shrivel and die.
Where dreams are born in the
morning and die in the late afternoon.
Where artists struggle for survival
while cheaters and fakers prosper.
Where merchants of bodies walk the
streets and happiness comes in a pill.
Where hopelessness and despair live
around the corner and the poor
people live and die in the pavement.
Where the value of one single life is
insignificant and even the air can
choke the life out of you.
Here I stand!

Ernest Shuford
MY MORNING PRAYER

When I wake up each morning,
And a new day is dawning.
I thank the Lord for the new day.
And to be with me all the way;

And I ask the Lord, for his help,
For I cannot make it by myself.
For life is full of many trials
Sometimes it is hard to face it
with smiles.

But if we can face it with smiles.
It may help someone, with their
trials;
And make their burdens, a little
lighter.
And their outlook on life, a
little brighter.

The Lord's business, is to make
burdens light.
And to ease our burdens and
strife;
IF we ask him He will forgive us of
our sin
IF we live for him every day, at
the end we will win.

Julia Tolliver
ALONG THE CLOUDLESS SKY

This poem is dedicated to my mother, Mrs. Ann Tolliver.

along the cloudless sky i fly
soaring to and fro as i go
searching each path i take
as i fly south, my friends and i
for when the snow ceases to fall
and the great cold wind ceases
to blow
i'll be back again real soon
when summer skies and
flowers and fields are
all in bloom.

Tommie K Wade
HEART TO HEART SOUL TO SOUL

I feel love blowing
In the wind
Open my heart and
Let it in.

There's A hunger
I feel
Heart to heart
Soul to soul.

I feel so cold inside
I'm reaching out to you
In hopes of replenishing
My pride.

I can feel your presence
It's drawing near, and
It's getting more and more
Clear.

I feel love blowing
In the wind
Open my heart and
Let it in.

Rosal Giammarese
A DREAM

I dream that I walk into the deep blue
sky
I yelled out loud, Ma! Ma! where are
you?
Please let me see you for one more
time
All of a sudden, Ma! Ma! appeared
She had tears in her eyes
She held me in her arms and then she
disappeared
Ma! Ma! Why did you go away?
You broke my heart, I need you
Thank you for letting me see you for
one more time
I will always love you because you're
my Ma! Ma!

Florence Dora Rapp

Florence Dora Rapp
THE MIRCLE YOU ARE

The chance that you are the
combination
Which is you
Which is I
Is a miracle that no one
Can defy!

The chance is just a shade above zero
That the part of your father,
And the part of your mother's
meeting
That caused you,
Is a thought that is almost beyond our
comprehension,
And the imagination
It does move!

Reg Cannon
PASTORAL SCENE

Summer's dressed in golden
sunshine,
Winter's wearing woolen white,
Rippling river quietly flowing,
Brook that burbles through the night.

Cabin's set in pastoral scene,
Meadow's filled with emerald green,
White clouds afloat in azure skies,
Close it is to paradise.

Joyce A Luckett
ZACHERY

April 6 of '86 my heart did jump for
glee.
Because it just so happened that we
had Zachery.
When he smiles those brown eyes
glow, and
When he frowns my heart drops low.
But all I want is happiness for Zach
throughout his life.
Someday when I'm old and gray he'll
make me smile my cares away.
Because he is my joy—
My sweet little boy—Zachery

Will Tiller
SEASONS

With each season begins a new meaning in life. When every leaf changes its color the calling of winter is near. As the sun approaches the horizon the trees depict an artistic rainbow. A hallow beyond belief from only an eye of an artist can capture. Grasp a moon, grasp a star and only then will you know where you are.

Can you capture a rainbow? If only one could see beyond the brightness of the snow. Seeing beyond the snow is like seeing beyond the stars. Stars shining at night is like a marvelous bird in flight. We do not know its destination, only the bird does within itself.

As the snow begins to disappear spring is near. The fresh air of spring brings a joy within my peace of mind. As the robin sings the song of its heart, I hear a delightful new start.

When summer rolls around I can hear the waves of the ocean. Walking on the beach with the world in my hands I can think of a foreign land. Land beyond the sea, land of you and me. Let us open our eyes and see this land, then and only then may we understand the meaning of another land.

Ruby O Moore
OUR LOVE

Dedicated to: Those who have made it last by being kind and considerate of each other.

Love is a many splendored thing.
That poets write of and sing.
Of moonlight and roses in your hair
Champagne and beauty everywhere!

Love is knowing that you care
By the smiles that you wear.
By all your kindness,
And the patience you have with me.
These are a testimony of your love
for me.

When food is short and money too,
you smile and say,
"I don't care, we'll make do!
Just as long as I have you."

In illness you offer me a gentle touch.
In sorrow your deepest sympathy.
Just a simple word of praise from you
somehow you know all the things to
do,
To keep the magic fresh and new
of moonlight and roses for me and
you.
To keep our love glowing forever
with a rosy hue.
These are the things that mean so
much to me and you.

Rodney Laws
my love
my strength

for Andy and Nikki. written through his eyes. written for his feelings.

you give your heart—
because you love me.
you give your strength—
because you see me weakening.

i take your heart—
because i love you.
i take your strength—
because i am so scared and weak.

i love you—i need you.
i just wanted you to know . . .

i love you.

Rodney Laws
AIMEE'S VERSE

for my "pretty lady." if ever a man had it all, it would have to be me.

when i'm hurting—
when i'm down—
i need someone,
someone to turn to.

when i feel all alone—
i need someone,
someone to let me know i'm
really not.

when i feel lost—
i need someone,
someone to take my hand
and show me the way.

so many times in my life
i need someone.
so many times in my life
i need advice—
a shoulder to cry on—
a hug—
or just a smile . . .

i take so much joy in knowing these
things are
always there for me.

i take so much joy in knowing that
you are
always there for me.

you are my friend.
i love you.

AmBegonia
FAIRY TALES

Take a deep breath and hold it
And then exhale.
Then take a step or two
Along an old trail.
Take a good look around
At the sights you unveil
And you'll see the fairies
In your own fairy tale.

Write your own story
As you follow life's trail.
And mark it with stones
To be sure it won't fail.
Make it your quest
For the fabled Holy Grail.
And take the fairies out
Of your own fairy tale.

When life seems unreal
And it moves like a snail,
When sunshine and starlight
Begin to grow pale,
Take a deep breath and hold it
And then exhale.
And look for the fairy
In your own fairy tale.

Write your own story
As you follow life's trail.
And mark it with stones
To be sure it won't fail.
Make it your quest
For the fabled Holy Grail.
And take the fairies out
Of your own fairy tale.

Life and love are very real,
They just cannot fail.
Sometimes they just hide
In a thin, misty veil.
Trust yourself, not the fairies,
Along that old trail;
And the story that you write
Will be no fairy tale.

AmBegonia
ADVISE AND CONSENT

Earth is crying . . . with acid
tears.
Winds are sighing . . . telling its
fears.
Land is frying . . . when Sun
appears;
Oceans drying . . . but no one
hears.
Earth is dying . . . over the years!

There is a meeting, and we hear this
motion:
"Let's save our planet, the land and
the ocean."
This move takes hold with lots of
commotion.
All agree, seconding the motion.

What should we do, who has a
notion.
Call the Soothsayer, he'll make a
potion.
Sprinkle far, his magical lotion.
Cover the planet, land and ocean!

Earth is crying . . . with acid
tears.
Winds are sighing . . . telling its
fears.
Land is frying . . . when Sun
appears;
Oceans drying . . . but no one
hears.
Earth is dying . . . over the years!

Tell all the people. "Heed our
motion,
Save our planet with all devotion."
Thus they spoke and spared no
emotion.
And the people rose to this great
notion.

The next meeting, they ratified the
motion.
The Soothsayer came and spread his
potion
Which gave the people more pride
and devotion
And life insurance to land and ocean.

Earth is glowing . . . with pride
and poise!
Winds are blowing . . . telling its
joys!
Oceans are flowing . . . with lots
of noise!
Trees are growing . . . like girls
and boys!
Earth is alive . . . its people
rejoice!

AmBegonia
DIZZLE-DAZZLE

Dizzle-Dazzle this,
And-a Dizzle-Dazzle that.
What is going on here?
Such a dazzling tit-for-tat!

Look at all the gals,
And look at all the guys.
The same Dizzle-Dazzle
Is a-shining in their eyes!

Dizzle-Dazzle this,
And-a Dizzle-Dazzle that.
It all got started
With a dazzling tit-for-tat.

When Adam met Eve,
They began the Big Begat.
He Dizzle-Dazzled this,
And she Dizzle-Dazzled that.

Dizzle-Dazzle this,
And-a Dizzle-Dazzle that.
It always begins
With a dazzling tit-for-tat.

Look up at the stars
A-way up in the skies.
The same Dizzle-Dazzle
Is a-shining in your eyes.

Dizzle-Dazzle this,
And-a Dizzle-Dazzle that.
Let's you and I go dizzling
In this dazzling tit-for-tat!

Joan Sullivan

Joan Sullivan
COLORS OF FALL

To My Son, Robert and To Richard Castagno, A Dear Friend.

Sitting here on this Saturday
afternoon
The leaves are falling down
And the rain is falling and
Together they make harmony

Colors of red and gold and brown
Replace the green left from
The summer that has just passed
away
And Fall has finally arrived

Looking around I can see no one at
all
It seems they have all gone behind
Their windows and doors closed
down tight
For the Winter that is to come

With the world full of colors
All around us to see
Can you imagine a world without
color
And yet sometimes we live without
seeing color at all

Erica Burton
FOOTSTEPS

Lying here, I realize that it's too late.
I'm left here to listen and wait.
I listen to every foot that He has
stepped.
I know it's time to give up this life
that I've kept.
To say good-bye to everything I'd
once knew.
There's nothing but the footsteps to
listen to.
Everything I see is fading away into a
shadow dim.
I can only hear the footsteps that are
echoed by Him.
I know who He is without my sight.
It's of the one person I've prayed to
every night.
His footsteps become louder as He
comes closer to me.
Because it's Him, I'm not afraid of
what I can't see.
Everything He tells me, I shall obey.
I smiled, for I felt God carry me
away . . .

Marian Egenberger
THE BEAUTIES OF LIFE

I would like to dedicate this poem to my children and my grandchildren whom I love very much; they are my life.

Thank you for the flowers
thank you for the trees,
thank you for the grass that grows
thank you for the breeze.

Thank you for the rain that falls
and the sun that shines so
bright,
thank you for the light of day
and the dark of night.

Thank you for the moon so bright
and this world of ours,
thank you for the universe
and all the twinkling stars.

Thank you for the mountains
where the pine trees grow so
tall,
thank you for our canyons
and all our waterfalls.

Thank you for our oceans wide
our lakes and many seas,
but most of all I thank you God
for what you gave to me.

Corinne Brown
TAPESTRY

I dedicate this poem to all my grandchildren.

Intricate patterns expertly designed
Yet untouched by human hands
Compounded by divine architecture
For each thread of life.

Each purposeful meaning unknown
to man
Attributed brotherhood, love, and
compassion.
Complexity into life's travel along
with many rewards
Revealing secrets, diverting snares.

The threads, though twisted and
tangled,
Carefully planned by life's maker
Carries no mistakes.

For he who made the universe
And all the secrets there,
Magnificently wove the tapestry
With confidence and care.

Unequaled quality, majestic realm,
Divine attribution, love unending;
All patterns in the threads of life.

Scott Dunn
I LOVED YOU
Like a poet loves to write,
a God loves to create,
a lover loves to love;
I loved you.

Like a thinker loves his thoughts,
a life loves to live,
a being loves to be;
I loved you.

Like a bird loves to fly,
a soul loves to be free,
a mind loves to wander;
I loved you.

And now you are gone from me
The poet dreams no more,
the God creates no more,
the soul is bound,
the mind is still,
the bird is caged,
and life . . .

There is no life.
I still love you

Though I shed no tears
I shall not cry over you, I loved you.
I loved you.

Nancy Adams
WHAT I SEE
If for one moment you could be me
Looking through my eyes—what would you see
You'd see the one that takes my breath away
The one on my mind twenty four hours a day

You'd see a smile that's beautiful and bright
You'd see the man that's my shining knight
You'd see eyes that are full of life and joy
Eyes that are sometimes that of a little boy

You'd find humor and very deep emotions
A man full of love and all its devotions
You'd see a face so truthful and giving
The face of a man that makes life worth living

You'd see my heart so full of love
A special love, sent from God above
A love so deep, it's hard to explain
A love so true, it's not hard to obtain

Someone so tender, yet so very very strong
Someone who seems lost, yet knows where he belongs
So in that one special moment, here's what you would see
You would see my world looking back at me.

Quentin R Simon Sr
HAPPY MOTHER'S DAY

I dedicate this poem to my mom, Betty Simon.

Mother's Day is something sweet
The love it takes for us to meet
Your loving touch and gentle care
And with us all so much to share.

So for the love you've given us
Today we give to you
Some extra love and tenderness
And care so greatly too.

So sit right back and enjoy this day
That's especially for you
For we will do our best to serve you
Till this day is through.

Allison Moore
ALIENATION
Standing in my little corner
Apart from everyone and
Anyone that matters.
Feeling a little unimportant,
Maybe even worthless
Trying to figure what separates
me from her.
She in her elegant clothes
and elegant manners.
Me in my ragged cloths
and stumbling walk.
But it doesn't matter. I
Don't need that Bullshit,
That pre-Madonna need.
That power she feels when
people, on their knees crawl,
and from her hands, feed.

Elizabeth Grizzard Barnhart
NIGHT DREAMS
Sometimes in the depth of night
An evil walks, bellows with a voice of doom,
Encompassing all the reaches of the earth
Like a tidal wave.

With hearts filled with dread we hide
Afraid to face him, though knowing he is there.
Somewhere he waits now, ready to make us a part of him.
Is he Death, the unconquerable foe?
And yet there may be some who call him
Friend.

James Schellenberg
IN THE GRIP OF THE FURY
Dark thunderclouds,
Blackly raging.
Before the wind, bowed
Trees quickly aging.

Down snaps lightning,
Echoed by thunder.
Storm's hold tight'ning,
Peace torn asunder.

Lashing the earth,
Rain-whipped soil.
What is its worth?
Why the storm's toil?

The Fury subsides,
Clouds draw back
Like an ocean's tides;
Someday another attack.

Stephanie Nahirniak
THE ROAD TO SUCCESS
A failure is not always to be complying,
The real mistake—is when you stop trying,
Even being a star with the trophies it brings
It is still the adventurers who accomplish great things.

Let no feeling of discouragement take over your lead.
Then in the end you are sure to succeed
For there's nothing that Satan can put you on to make life rough,
That the Lord with His love
and power can't take you off.

We make a living by what we receive
But we make our life by what we give,
For if we can forgive our offenders,
God'll grant peace to our soul.
He too'll forgive our wrongs,
and help us to reach our goal.

Valerie Johnson-Seidler
POLAR OPPOSITES

To my daughter, Anna and my son, Alan who inspired this poem, and my life.

As different as the moon and the sea, each needing the other to be.
The sea sparkling and always in motion, inviting unto many.
The moon veiled in mystery slowly makes its rounds in solitude.
The sea its high tides and low, mostly a friend sometimes a formidable foe.
The moon with its phases, sometimes not there, at others a large magnificent sight, even staying out until morning's light.
Polar opposites to nature I compare male and female by gender fare, flesh of my flesh born unto me, each needing the other to be.

Rev Warner W Faris

Rev Warner W Faris
DWIGHT D EISENHOWER

I dedicate this poem in memory of all men everywhere—who have fought to preserve the peace through love of God and country.

Few men aspire to great height
Youth of Abilene, Kansas site.
West Point Graduate 1915—
War I—War II—theatre scene.
President—Columbia U
Majority run of "52"
Brilliant record speaks for itself,
Famed trophy's upon mantel-shelf.
All through the wars his best he gave:
Associated with might mid brave—
Strong midst strong—weak midst weak;
Freedom's causes Ike would seek.
Never faltered—Never wavered
Always liked—Always favored.
Enemy lands ne'er overpower,
Men like Dwight D. Eisenhower.

Rev Warner W Faris
"IN MEMORY OF FLAG DAY"
AMERICA!
America!
God! Made you what you are!
Freedom!
Home! Of brave; free; afar!
Life!
Liberty! Pursuit; happiness!
America!
Live! Love! In eloquence!

America!
We! Raise a boy for you!
America!
Our Flag! Stars! Stripes!
Staunch—true!

America!
Love it—or leave it!
Freedom!
All Nations receive it!
Life!
Here! In abundance!
America!
Worship! Omnipotence!

Rev Warner W Faris
JOE ZUROSKI—
"77 Years Young"
Life is like a bowl of cherries
Some are sour—some are sweet.
Joe's footsteps two years tarries:
Forgotten name—Love's calls' defeat.

Met lass Wisconsin Tavern;
Tended Bar in great delight!
Aye! Eyes meet! Hearts concern;
Hark! Answer to yon prayer!

Married Alice—Town Catholic Church,
Twenty-four years ago:
Ah! End to Lifetime search—
Mills big lift—after-glow;

All young ones now are grown;
Answers to finite prayers:
Twilight comes—Nature's sown,
Harvest due—all earthly cares.

Life goes on—so they say:—
Have many more Octobers!
Till you reach Gold Matinee
God Knows! Both now—
teetotalers.

Joe! Get well—Stay well! Be
Happy!

A Golden Poet's Gift to you.

Mary Ann Lehrer
INTEGRATION
welcome "dear one"—full time. full circle
we have tested our traveling manners
we are true companions on the trip of our soul
Schedules, timetables ripped and but fragile
shards of memory left to scatter on the platform
our destination is now

James Norman
I SEE, HEAR AND TOUCH YOU LORD

Some people say they have never seen you,
Some people say they have never heard or touched you,
But, I see, hear and touch you all the time

I see you as a bubbling brook
I see you in the morning sun
I see you as a twinkling star
I'll see you always as you are

I hear you in the whispering trees
I hear you in a wild bird's song
I hear you in the thunder afar
I'll hear you always as you are

I touched you when I held a new born baby lamb
I touched you in a fresh cut fragrant rose
I touched you when I felt my beating heart
I'll touch you always as you are

You are with me always,
You are my Lord and my God
May God bless you
Your friend Jimmy

Patricia A O'Brien
IRELAND

My heart belongs to Ireland,
No other place I've found,
Has touched my soul so deeply,
As when I walked on Erin's ground.

Beauty in its natural state,
Laid out for man to see,
From Kilarney's lakes of silver blue,
To the edge of Dingle Bay.

The Emerald Isle has caught my heart,
A kindred spirit we.
We share our dreams and sorrows,
And our longing to be free.

Lorrie Brewer
SNAPSHOTS ON A CO-DEPENDENT JOURNEY

You looked like a little lost puppy first time I met your gaze
Said you couldn't live without me, call anytime I'll be there always.
Run child run, a voice whispered inside
But someone really needs me the rescuing part of me sighed.
Years passed by but things went wrong, you found something else to always lean on.
Our marriage now is all but gone since Lady Alcohol sings your songs.
Laugh child laugh, a voice snickered inside
It was too good to be true the joke's on you, now there really is no place to hide.
Is this the end of everything; the broken vows the pawned off ring?
The Lord was there to see me through.
Cry child cry, a voice mourned inside
It's never ever easy to watch things wither and die.
Are my tears in His bottle, flowing like a tide?
But nothing is too hard for the Lord it seems
He delivers the oppressed and helpless victims too.
Wake, rise up, these aren't dreams!
Don't you know that the Lord heard you.
Sing child sing, lift your voice up high
Can't you see it's Spring and your redemption draweth nigh?
Rejoice my friend rejoice, when you think you're out of rope
Call on the name of the Lord
His deliverance rides upon your hope.

P.S. Happy Anniversary to Us

Tanya Radny
A LETTER TO MY CHILD

To my son Brent, you are my inspiration and I love you always!

The greatest joy in life is the feeling you give me.
I wonder what it's like for you.
Do you understand me?
Can you hear me?
Do you feel it when I caress you?
The love I feel for you is so strong, nothing can compare with this feeling.
I can't wait to see you, what will you look like?
What will you think when you finally meet me?
Oh. little one, are you as scared as I am?
How I await to hold you in my arms and feel your tiny body next to mine.
I can't imagine loving you any more than I do now, but somehow I know I will.
My precious child:
I only hope I can make your life as happy as you have made mine in this short time.
I love you little child of mine!

Evadne V Shirley
THE CHILDREN OF THE WORLD

Won't someone nourish the children
The ones that have obedience to their parents and get perfect grades in school
For these children need just as much support against the temptations of the world as those who have fallen short, in our eyes

Won't someone nourish the children
The ones who use their bodies as marketable commodities to be bought and sold, as a means of survival
For these children need to be shown humanity, to be taught dignity, and to learn to feel self-respect for their bodies

Won't someone nourish the children
The ones who walk with knives, chains, and guns to show that they belong to a group and are united in some way
For these children need to feel wanted, loved and cared for and shown that they have a secure place in society

Won't someone nourish the children
The ones with the red, cloudy eyes and the arms filled with holes to match the decaying cells in their brains
This is the body of our future, a shape without a purpose or aim, it needs to be taken in hand and pointed in the right direction

Won't man-kind nourish the children?
And take its responsibility, for mankind is the parent of ALL the children of the world.

Kemberle O'Neil
HELL IS REAL

I yell but no one hears.
I cry but no one cares.
I walk alone amidst the fire,
praying this is a dream.
I come to face reality,
it scares me so I scream.
I ponder in my heart,
"I'm not really here?"

I believed nothing of Heaven
or Hell or what God has
lovingly given.
But now if I could just go
back in time and change my
sinful ways, erase my unbelieving
heart and mind and do it over
again.

I yell but no one hears.
I cry but no one cares.
I walk alone amidst the fire
saying, "Yes I'm really here!"

Brandee J Taylor

Brandee J Taylor
LOVE IS . . .

To my loving and caring family, Love, Brandee.

Love is a little bug that hops upon your shoe, it creeps up on your body and gets inside of you.

It makes you want to hug and kiss someone all the time.
It also makes you say, that everyone is fine!

Brandee J Taylor
WHERE DOES THE SKY END?

The sky goes on and on in a fantasy, but in real life it goes on as far as the eye can see.

It's never ever ending, yes it is so true, and it is just as beautiful as the early morning dew.

Just look up at the sky
with a friend or all alone,
and experience it yourself,
it's more fun than eating an ice cream cone!!!

Jan Davis Martel
THE TOY BOX

A plain wooden box . . . that's what I used to be . . .
With no decorations . . . or frills . . . none you could see.
But when that nice lady came into the store, you could tell by her look I was soon to be sold . . .
Because for her grandson . . . Justin . . . lots of toys I would hold.

So, out of the store I left that day,
With thoughts of all the great experiences, coming my way.
Because . . . for Christmas I had been promised . . . you see . . .
To be built . . . finished . . . decorated . . . and under the tree.

So, the work began, the plan was intact,
I was going to be beautiful . . . and that was a fact!
Assembled . . . sanded . . . stained . . . and finished with care,
No longer was I not decorated . . . nor plain . . . or at all bare.

Now all that remained was the long wait . . .
And to meet the small child . . . whose hands hold my fate.
I just couldn't wait to have a new pal . . . and a new friend . . .
With whom many hours of fun, I was hoping to spend.

Just think of all the treasures I'll hold,
And all the dreams from each of those treasures . . . that's sure to unfold.
Then, someday . . . when little Justin's all grown . . .
Maybe he'll still keep me for his children to own.

So, yes, a great life lay ahead, I'm happy to say,
Now I guess I should just be quiet . . . and wait for the day . . .

Maria D Ray
YOU KISS ME

To my Beloved Husband Donny, who I Love with all my heart. My Muffin Kisses are yours forever. Your Muffin.

You make my body tremble
All my fantasies come true.
Your touch is gentle your caress is real
A fantasy come true Love

making under lighted stars
My Fantasy unfolds Along
a shore hand in hand an admired
moment long to last Forever
Look into my eyes
Your touch has cured me
Your caress has comforted me
A soul is freed from bondage.
An answer to a prayer.
Kissing me our bodies tremble
together as one.
My fantasy has been told
My Love belongs to you.

Never to see alone
Never to see loneliness
A soul is Freed from bondage
An answer to a prayer
Your touch is gentle Your caress is
real.
A fantasy come true.
Hand in Hand along a shore
Waters calm an admired moment
longed to last forever.
A fantasy Come true

An Answer to a prayer.

Del

Anna K Wilde

Anna K Wilde
TO BE BORN ON FRIDAY THE 13TH IS BAD LUCK THEY SAY

Dedicated to my children: Harry R. Jr., and Wayne R. Sr., Wilde. Patricia Williams. Grandchildren: Michael, Joanne, Diane, Maryanne, Rick, Dave Wilde. Charles L., Gregory, and Scott Williams. Ryan and Samuel Conrad. Kyle Wilde.

To be born on Friday the 13th is bad
luck they say
I guess I'm one of the lucky ones
born on that day
Having three children was God's gift
to me
He knew I would grow a strong
family tree.

The road that I traveled at times got
rough
And many a time I had to really get
tough
I made many friends as I went along
the way
And they are still with me to this very
day.

There are many routes to heaven I'm
sure
So pull up your bootstrings and feel
secure
To reach that top takes a lot of grit
So rest along the way but please
don't quit.

Troubles and worry often block out
the light
But the sun will shine through if you
put up a fight
Heartaches and illness at times make
you weak
But with friends by your side you'll
reach that peak.

I wore a smile on my face and tried
not to frown
At times I even pretended and acted a
clown
Now I'm a mother, grandmother, and
great-grandmother too
And I hope you are as healthy and
happy as I am at 82.

Dorothy Shreffler
SEASONS OF LIFE

Dedicated To My Daughter Meredith.

If we stop and think clear
Life is like the seasons of the year.

Summer, Winter, Spring and Fall
And in life, that is all.

Spring—is the baby that we are born
and everything is adorn.

Summer—everything is bright and
growing up seems just right.

Fall—the leaves are turning a
different hue,
And our hair is turning, too.

Winter—Oh, so cold and white
The end of the season—the end of
life.

Now, as we start Life on the other
shore
There will be no seasons anymore,
It will be Spring—ever the same
And never a sign of change.

Lisa M Michaelis
WHAT CHRISTMAS CAN MEAN

Recognizing: El Shaddai; family; good friends; Jackie B. and 12-Step.

Christmas can mean as much or as
little
as each person has learned how to
feel it.
Lights, tinsel, wrapped gifts, or a
bottle of cheer—
or release from school halls that are
so drab and drear'.
A long night of prayer and sweet
heavenly songs
of Hope, for which gathers the whole
joyous throng.
The Eve of The Birth prepares for
spirits' feast,
reviving the warmth that through the
year slowly ceased.
A patriarch sits with his softened,
aged lines
as lost in past time an old heart yet
does pine.
The youth play around and reflect
back the ghosts
of chapters swift' wrote in his silent
season's toast
to a young Jew born and thus
embodied He strove
to ease all men's burdens, but from
them He was drove.
Some drive still today, others hold
the day true—
I hope Christmas is all that it has
come to mean for you.

Hope Thompson Wasilewski
RESCUED

To my Saviour, the Lord Jesus Christ.

I do not know why terrors dark
invade my very soul.
I do not know why angry billows o'er
my head would roll.

I cannot comprehend the why
But look to HIM with helpless cry
"O, Master, save me, or I die!"

And then retreats the raging flood
At the mention of HIS BLOOD.
And then retreat the waters chill—
At HIS commanding,
Peace,
be
still!

Diana L Driscoll
IT WAS MY LIFE

Dedicated to everyone who has ever felt the way I did when I wrote this. Remember, sometimes you have to hurt to recognize the love someone has for you.

Why couldn't I live my own life,
and make my own mistakes.

I tried to do the best I could,
I tried to do what it takes.

I tried to make you happy,
I tried to make you proud.

You didn't understand the way I felt,
or the way I cried out loud.

I rarely did what I wanted to,
I did what you thought I'd need.

This time I did what I wanted to,
and this time I did succeed.

Now the roles are changed,
I am happy and you are sad.

Sorry it ended up this way,
I'm sorry mom and dad.

Gertrude F Candini
MY MEADOW

To my mother, Florence Boutwell— With Love Gertrude.

My meadow lush beneath my feet
The rebirth of nature abounds
A flock of robins fly above
About to take a mate
Beneath a willow aflame with gold
A riot of greens did peek
The watercress a carpet of green
Afloat on a brook of peace
Each bud, each bloom alive with life
What mystery did I seek
The birth of nature all aglow
Did rest my spirit and calm my soul
My dreams of nature awakes
A gift from God to hold so dear
My meadow, my joy complete

Kymberly Walden
AS YOU SLEEP

To My husband, Donald, The Inspiration for this & All my other Dreams.

I wake in the morning to see you
asleep,
Your thoughts far away, but
your dreams go so deep.

I wonder if I'm in those dreams
you dream—or because of that
smile it so does seem.

You're breathing so light, So quiet
to Ears—
The sound I will Listen for
throughout All our Years.

I'll watch how you twitch and
move in the night—
For the dreams that you dream
are Clearly Not Fright.

If a man can be a vision of beauty
so deep . . .
That's what I see in you my
love . . .
As You Sleep

Barbara Fleming Wiltshire
THE FIELD

The field has softly come alive
In the rainbow covered sky,
A bee is gathering nectar
On a yellow petal high.

The water is softly running
In the field's clear, shallow stream,
As the sunlight filters downward
Sending rays of colored beams.

A cow is grazing lazily
In the far corner there,
Breathing in the freshness of the field
And its dewy-rain cleansed air.

Within the field's leafy trees
A symphonic trilling can be heard,
It is the lovely, lilting sound
Of the melodious song-bird.

Stand a quiet moment and gaze
Upon this lovely place,
And the field will softly whisper:
"I've been touched by God's
heavenly grace."

Valerie Ryan Jungen
THE ENDANGERED SPECIES

Dedicated with love to my sons, Lucas and Brian. May you both be blessed with lives rich in joy and happiness.

The woman sat down next to me and
crossed her legs just so.
She set her briefcase on the floor,
then let a sigh out slow.
"Do you work?" she asked of me,
while fussing with her hair.
It made me wonder why she asked; I
doubted if she'd care.

"I work at home" I told her and knew
she'd scoff at that.
With powder from her compact, she
gave her nose a pat.
She drops her kids at daycare in
hopes that they'll do fine.
And chats about the baby's cold on
coffee break at nine.

She looked so perfect sitting there
and this I must confess;
It made me wish I'd done my nails
and worn a different dress.
But suddenly it dawned on me just as
she rose to go,

The joys I've had while staying home
are joys she'll never know.

Athena Walters
I STAND AND I STAND THROUGH THE NIGHT

To my family, relatives and friends, I dedicate this poem.

I stand and I stand through the night
and hope to wish on a star that is in the sky
And it will come true and I know it will
Because I wish on you

Diane L Peters
COCAINE

You said "no"
but you couldn't
resist their insisting.

So you went along.
You said "wow."
You kept saying "wow"
Until the day your
mind went "Pow."

Kimberly Lynn Houle
THE GREAT UNKNOWN

I have just begun to know Him
To Learn the Heavenly ways.
I pray to Him in thanks
And Guidance throughout my day.

I look forward to reading the Bible
It's not just another book on the shelf.
For He is now in the center,
It is no longer Just Myself.

What I'm trying to say is,
I've accepted The Great Unknown.
This enlightened heart inside of me,
I now consider His home.

Bonnie L Worden
COLLEGE BOUND

To my beautiful daughter . . . Jessica. May you find as much joy as you have given me.

This is the year you'll go away,
and grow up on your own.
Forever keep in your heart and mind,
that you'll always have a home.
My love for you is deep and strong,
and will forever grow.
Feel free to always talk with me,
while you're out on your own.
There is a special place for you,
that's deep within my heart.
This place is warm and safe and dear,
and from it you shall never part.
I'll miss you dearly while you're away,
and anticipate your trips home.
When we can sit and talk and laugh,
about the things that have
helped you grow.
I'll be here always whenever you need,
for a special daughter you are
indeed.
Mom

Marcella N Hurry
OCTOBER'S BALL

To my son—Gerald A. Krauss.

October said to the trees, one day
"It's time for our annual Ball"
The trees agreed, then loosened their hold
And the leaves began to fall.

She signed up all the songbirds
To form the sweetest band
A breeze was offered by Mr. Wind
As he gave a helping hand.

She sent out invitations
The leaves by hundreds came
All dressed in reds and golds and browns
Yet no two wore the same.

Miss Red Maple was Belle of the Ball
In her beautiful scarlet cloak
She danced and twirled and whirled about
With Mr. Golden Oak.

They skipped and danced the hours away
'Til came the wint'ry sun
Then thanked October for her help
And said, "We had such fun."

Marion J Lamb
A TRIBUTE TO A NURSE'S AIDE

A Nurse's Aide has qualities
That too few people know,
Emotions play a major part
To make her shine and glow.

A steadfast heart to keep her calm
When working under stress,
With head held high, she goes along
To only do her best.

A touch of the hand for kindness
A smile to see her through,
Courage beyond comprehension
For Alas; it could be you.

A Nurse's Aide is many things
Too lengthy to unfold,
A Very Special Person
From A Very Special Mold.

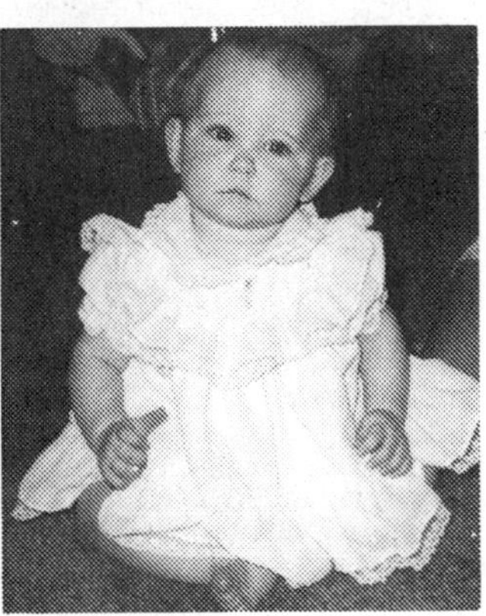

Autumn

Vicki Granata-Laca
AUTUMN LEAVES

For all of the parents of abducted children, for my loving mother, Kay Warren, and Dr. Philip Rich—the psychiatrist who carried me through my nightmare and tears, and, of course, for you Autumn.

My tears that fall,
Are like leaves from an Autumn Tree.
Scattered on the ground,
Ready to be blown away,
By the first dark cloud that rolls by.
Like leaves, my tears, fall from my eyes,
Only to be scattered on the ground.
And slowly, but surely, each dries up and dies,
As my heart is, knowing you are gone.
The cruelty and harshness of winter has set in.
I look at the bare trees,
And there is no sign of you.
They are bare and empty;
A void, where you once were.
They have no life in them,
Just as Father Nature intended it to be.
I long for your return Autumn.
The beauty for which you were named after.
The life you give turns the season
Into a kaleidoscope of magnificent colors.
The brilliance of you is burned into my memory and heart.
Autumn, I'm waiting for you to return to me.
I'll wait for you forever.
I'll love you until my dying day.
Happy 1st birthday princess—
Wherever you may be.
Love, Mommy

Lottie Marcum Brewer
MOTHER

"This poem is dedicated to Mrs. Elmer (Maude) Marcum, my angel Mother."

Some look upon her brow and say:
"It's wrinkled and her hair is
grey."
But to me she's sweet, kind and true,
And all the world should know
it too.
Do you know why? She's my
Mother—that's who!

I look upon her brow and see
Just what each wrinkle means
to me:
The love she gave, the hours she spent,
In teaching me to be content—
Do you know why? She's my
Mother, God sent!

I look upon her streaks of gray
And think of all those
yesterdays;
When sickness came and friends were few
There knelt in prayer the one I
knew—
It was my mother—that's who!

Now look into your heart and see
I hope you are lucky even as
me.
Has God sent you a mother like this,
To share your burdens and
troubles lift?
Then thank God too . . .
For Mother great and true!

Lottie Marcum Brewer
MOUNTAIN PATRIOTISM

It is spring in Appalachia!
The sun is shining brightly on the majestic mountains,
The birds are singing melodies to the mountain people,
The trees are bursting with pride in cloaks of white, pink and green,
The bubbling brook is on its way to tell the world of our happiness.

Where is the poverty of which my fellow man speaks?
My eyes, are they blind with beauty, that I do not see these ugly things?
My ears, do they hear only the soothing sounds of Nature Calling me?
The peace and joy that burst from my lips in a song—
Thrills my heart with thoughts of summer and bright flowers.

This cannot be an illusion . . .
For I see the reflection, evident in your happy smiling faces.
The togetherness—sound of your laughter, penetrates the warm-felt air.
Speak out mountaineer! Sing loud and clear!
Another spring has come to Appalachia.
God's gift to the mountain people!

Erna M Sawyers
COVERED BRIDGE OF PHILLIPI

This Covered Bridge had stood the test,
for six score and seventeen years, across
the Tygart River, an artifice of the best;
serving freely to all who crossed its piers.

What are the stories it could tell, of
Confederates brave and union troops as well;
and countless souls who crossed its floor,
took shelter, rested in its shade and more,

The builders had wrought with art and skill,
architecture fashioned to their will;
the people said, "this bridge shall not know decay,
great the skill, its fame shall endure for aye."

But fire destroyed the stately bridge one day,
wind fanned the flames, that swept it away;
this West Virginia town was very sad,
for a Historical Shrine, that they once had.

Truly our builders a structure will raise,
workmen fashioning with skill and grace;
as in the elder days, again will shape the part
an art entire—A Bridge, A Shrine!

Karen Hauser
SOMEONE TO TURN TO

This poem is dedicated to Jim Uland for listening and caring, and to my sister Sharon, I love you.

Life is lots of ups and downs,
full of extremely happy times and
times we choose to forget.
Everyone has their own separate
world—
some that are perfectly set
while yet others are seemingly full of
confusion.
The people in this world differ
as much as life itself—
some seek many friendships
while others never desire any friendly
tips at all.
Those that do reach out to others
are sometimes afraid,
feeling alone, scared, and confused.
It's hard to find someone to trust,
someone you can really turn to—
but there are those lucky few
that are touched by someone

special—
and maybe someday they too—
can be as special as you.

Marty Mannor-Smith
TIME OUT

Dedicated to my favorite son, Jasen Todd Smith, with whom I have shared and enjoyed the best times of my life.

Take me again to your castle which has no clocks
To your forest, lush and sweet
Which knows no paths coming in or going out

Remember how we ran with bare feet sliding over meadows
Wet with dew and felt the grass
Push up between our toes

Grass alongside the quiet, little pond
Tadpoles and Dragonflies in a timeless tag
Under the sleepy gaze of frogs, afloat on giant yellow pads

Let's find again the hole we dug into the mud
Sides caved by seeping waters
Where we said goodbye to the world

And buried Late and Early
Stop That! Don't!
We'll be late! and Hurry!

Take me once more running naked through the wind
And let's be free, you and I
For a time

Zelda H Steward
THE WAY IS MADE

Forever thankful to GOD, Charles, Kimberly, Amelia, Albert, Tina, Lynn, The Stevensons, and all the Saints and Friends which encouraged me.

Don't you ever be discouraged
Don't you ever be dismayed
There's a blessing coming to you,
Don't you know the way is made?

Some folks sit
And some folks sigh
Fleeting moments glide on by,
Memories of the past do fade
They forget the way is made.

Sometimes problems come your way
You just can't see the break of day,
God will come to be your aid
Don't you know the way is made?

Don't let Satan make you doubt
God has things all planned out,
Through life's water you do wade
Still I say the way is made.

Faith will tell you look ahead
Keep your mind on what God said,
A great foundation he has laid
Keep on believing the way is made.

Nikki Chaganos
1990

1990
Is the year,
I hope it will be one
Of good cheer.

Not a year of heartache,
Or a year of pain;
Not one of losses,
But one of gains.

A year in which
World hunger will end,
And fighting countries and people
Will all become friends.

A year of love,
Not one of hate;
A year in which people
Will believe in God and in fate.

A year in which people
Begin to adore,
In love and in peace,
And not in war.

Chrystal Erdmann

Chrystal Erdmann
DEATH

This poem is dedicated to Rudy Podoba. He's the one who inspired me to write this poem. I'd also like to dedicate this poem to all my friends and family.

Death is . . . .
an eternal sleep.

Death is . . . .
when family and friends weep.

Death is . . . .
never waking up,
to see a friendly face.

Death is . . . .
waking up to,
an unfamiliar place.

Death is . . . .
a time to rest,
in peace.

Death is . . . .
a trying time,
that often takes a person
in their prime.

Death is . . . .
a deep,
peaceful sleep.

LaClaaire C Nzerem
SONG OF THE NIGHT WOMAN

Empty footsteps click across
the wet sidewalk, faceless people
pass.
Cabs honk by and splash the feet
where hookers cuss at the curbs of streets.
Empty footsteps come to call
at the creaking doorway down the hall.
In a room that hisses of pungent mold,
the plaster crumbles from mildewed walls.
She waits in a tattered robe of white
on an unkept mattress in the night.
Through the window she hears the worried dog call
a cat picks up his pointless howl,
responding with a tiring wail.
He holds on in wild embrace,
he comes a man without a face.
The dollars down from cold
embrace, she turns to the
window to hide disgrace.
The empty echo leaves the hall
of shadowed footsteps as they fall.
Away and further into dark
Two lovers embrace in the park.

Carol Erhardt
AUTUMN LOVE

Autumn leaves of varied hues, glisten in sun's light.
Cool winds rustle through the trees, foretelling winter's blight.
Time for change from summer's heat, with days so long and bright,
To barren trees, crystal lakes, warm fires in the night.
'Twas such a time when first we met, as lovers bound to be,
When autumn cast her golden spell around us . . . you and me!
Never caring that winter's breath, soon would still the dove,
With icy fingers spreading glaze and freezing autumn's love.
Wiser now, two lonely hearts, wait alone for spring,
Longing, remembering passion's heat, when Autumn reigned as KING!

Janet S Dugger
A SPECIAL COTTAGE

A Country French Cottage nestled by the Sea
is exactly where I've always
wanted to be!
"My Place at the Beach," up till now
has seemed a dream
impossible to reach
But with some goal-setting, and no one to please but me,
I have no excuse for not
making it my top priority!

I'm looking forward to those "Golden Years,"
the same ones I used to
dread and fear!
Oh, what fun I'll have doing my own thing,
and ignoring the School Bells
when they ring!
My Country Cottage will be small, I know
just large enough for love to
grow!

Kimberly Wright
ODE TO MY TEACHER

Dedicated to Mrs. Haley—with love, Kim.

There is no room in your garden of love
For thorny patches
Dry with the drought of fear
Crowded by weeds of insincerity and doubt
For yours is a garden fair
The garden of your heart
Blossoming with faith
Hedged in by truth
Truth blown by the winds of experience
Wet by the showers of deep love and understanding.

I stand within your gardens
Filled with gratitude and awe
Holding tenderly the blossoms and roots
Which you had shared with me.

Joann B Williams
OCEANS OF CRYSTAL BLUE

This poem is dedicated to John, with all my love.

Oceans of crystal blue.
Beaches of crashing waves,
All quiet and yet so loud.
Sitting alone, so alone.
Air clean and cool.
No one to be found.
Sitting alone, so alone.
Life goes by.
Mechanical, material things,
They All fade away.
Just God-given things,
They surround me.
I'm not Alone, Not alone.

Melody Vance
REFLECTION

To my beloved Mother, Edna Davenport, my friend and my inspiration.

I am bright as daybreak
Yet dark as the setting sun

I am a fierce winter's blizzard
But gentle as spring rain.

I am yesterday's questions
And tomorrow's answers

I am a simple country farmer
Yet a sophisticated city worker

I am a ferocious jungle lion
And a meek young lamb

I am all the wars that have been
Yet the peace of a lifetime

I am the happiness of today
And the sorrow of tomorrow

I am the innocent trusting youth
Yet the guilty doubtful
veteran

I am mixed
Yet I am pure

I possess within me
Today, tomorrow and forever

That's why
I'm me

Mary Musser
FOR BRITTANY—WITH LOVE

Sweet babe so pure with angel's face
And silent eyes and gentle grace,
You found a place within the heart
Of those who now watch you depart.

You go with love and dress of lace
To a quiet, peaceful resting place.

Oh Brittany babe, so young and fair
We will not grieve nor hold despair!
But rather, we will miss you much,

These faces here whose lives you touch.

We say goodnight and bid you love,
Entrust you to our God above.
Sweet babe so pure with angel's face,
You touched our lives with gentle grace.

Jimmie Nell (Bush) Sutton
CHRISTMAS LETTER FROM THE SOUTHWEST

For my brother, Earl.

We're jes' plain an' simple folks
Out he'ah in the ol' southwest.
Shore like y'all to know we're
Thinkin' 'bout you, podnuh,
when we rest.

Chuldrun scurry like squirrels
Huntin' pecans 'neath thuh full trees.
Thuh pennies they earn will
thill us all
With gifts yuh ought'a see!

We done trimmed thuh Christmas tree;
Gee'tahrs a-strummin' out he'ah.
We recollect thet babe,
stable-born
—'Bout this time'a ye'ah.

Yup, He came down he'ah to save us
From earthly hurt and stress;
Mendin' broken souls forever
With plain joy and happiness.

We send yuh our glad "howdys";
All thuh peace yuh could desir'ah.
May yore cattle grow stronger, daily;
—Yore horses nev'ah tir'ah.
Luv, Jim

Trutti Gasparinetti
KISS THE IMAGE

I love you Santoro—1990!!

Hard to face, harder to say, lips were sealed since birthing day.
Cried for help, no one was near, silenced baby, stilled by fear.

Through this mouth moves breath to live, food and water, life to give.
Lump in throat, , tho never seen, felt forever, xrays clean!

Silent actress, cannot speak. Mouth, no memory, useless, squeak!
Speaks well without lines rehearsed, Easiest to write in verse!

Lovers loved, tho love did cease, , could not quiet the un peace.
Did it through a sense of duty, felt like work, not needed beauty.

Suffers Asthma of the Soul, adds Tar to a darkened hole.
Lessens smoking's false relief, blackened lungs preferred to grief!

Same response when each found out.
"You don't like to kiss my mouth!"
Didn't know this, tho I tried. If I did it well, I lied!!

Last one was the worst I knew.
Kissing was the thing to do.
Lip service to Everyone, nothing serious, lots of fun!!

Injury to insult, , add, tastes of horror, very bad!
Caused my serpent to recoil, can no longer love thru Toil!!

Crises from an Image came, visions, you, I screamed in pain!!
Gasping, choking, in my mind, your mouth breathed life into mine!

Yes my mouth has done too much, still I hunger—for Love's touch
Your mouth holds a secret Pain, my lips ache for yours, in Vain!!

Melodie L Newell-Lament
DAD

This poem is dedicated to my Daddy, Melvin W. Newell, from his little girl.

The pain that he's in, I wish I could share
To make him bear it all just doesn't seem fair
All who come in contact with his great love
Are lifted as high as the wings of a dove

On his face you can see not only bags and lines
But caring in bunches like grapes on the vines
To see him in pain just tugs at my heart
It feels like a balloon that's been pierced by a dart

To lose this man would be a great loss
Because he is my friend always, not just my boss
His rules may seem strict but all is meant well
For love and safety they are for he does tell

Tough fighting and screaming I am well known for
My love for him was always there at the core
He laughs and talks and sometimes acts like a cad
This person I will always love, this person is my Dad

Barbara E Gilmore
THE SNOWFLAKE

The snowflake transcended in fluttering sequences
Upon a nestling spot of barren earth
Its ethereal composition a perfection born
By nature's creation to hold in solemn worth
The whiteness of its being glistened and sparkled
Silently in solemnity capturing a bird
A majestic tranquility of grace enveloped by many.
The shivering bird flew high amid the flurries
Of the glistening snowflake
And found a naked branch upon which to rest his
Weary feathered self and make
An academic look to barren earth below now turning
Silvery white in nature's elation
With a million snowflakes in perfection born by
The impeccableness of nature's creation.

Naomi and Walt

Naomi Stanchina
TICK OF THE CLOCK

To Walter: my father, teacher and friend. For everything you've given me throughout the years. Now it's my turn . . . This one's for you.

Time—
You're my friend, you're my enemy,
You'll always change.
You've given me lessons on my love, life and dreams;
That it may either remain the same
Or be washed away.
I can only try to deceive you,
For you go swifter than I wish.
Or I may love you,
For you give me a second chance.
There is so much of you to spare.
You're always with me, whether I need you or not.
You are good to me, you teach me what I ought to be taught.
You punish me when I take advantage of you.
There were many times when I'd wish you would stand still
But you had to carry on;
Changing me, my life, my heart, and my knowledge.
I've hated you to the point of loving you
For I will always need you in my life.

Mamia Culbreth
ASSAULT IN PROGRESS

What is your name? *VICTIM*

How old are you? *BIRTH TO SENIOR CITIZEN*

This question is optional, you don't have to answer it. What is your color? Oh, I don't mind answering it. Color me *DEFENSELESS.*

Occupation? *I could be a housewife, single, mother, even a lawyer!*

Could you describe in your own words what happened. *IT HAPPENED THE DAY I WAS BORN. REGARDLESS OF MY COLOR OR RACE, I WAS STRIPPED OF SOMETHING VERY PRIVATE, VERY PERSONAL. MY DIGNITY! NOTHING CAN REDEEM IT, I BEAR THE GUILT AND SHAME*

Do you know your assailant? *YES, A PERSON WHO TOO WAS ONCE ABUSED AND IS LOOKING FOR AN OUTLET.*

Can you describe your assailant? *YES, SICKNESS: BORN OUT OF LUST, IGNORANCE, AND FEAR.*

We are putting out an APB right away!

Do you know where we can find this person? *YES, ON THE POLICE FORCE, IN THE SCHOOL SYSTEM, IN ANY GIVEN PROFESSION, CLERGYMAN, IN NEIGHBORHOODS RICH OR POOR. IT COULD EVEN BE YOU.*

There's an assault in progress RIGHT NOW!
Are you looking for a victim? or Are you being victimized?

Barbara J Herron
BELOVED MOTHER

Dedicated to the memory of my mother, Daisy H. Walls.

It was a Monday morning at eleven forty-one, on the 12th of June
nineteen hundred and eighty-nine,
That your spirit took its flight across
Earth up into heaven's splendid light.

You left your husband and children
to bear the memories—
To cherish forever . . .

God left you here for 72 years; it was time you took your rest.
He was ready to take you—but we were not ready to give you up.
But, we had to release you . . .
We had to let you go . . .

You will be deeply missed by all of us;
But your love will live on—
In our hearts and in our minds;
You will be cherished forever . . .
My beloved mother.

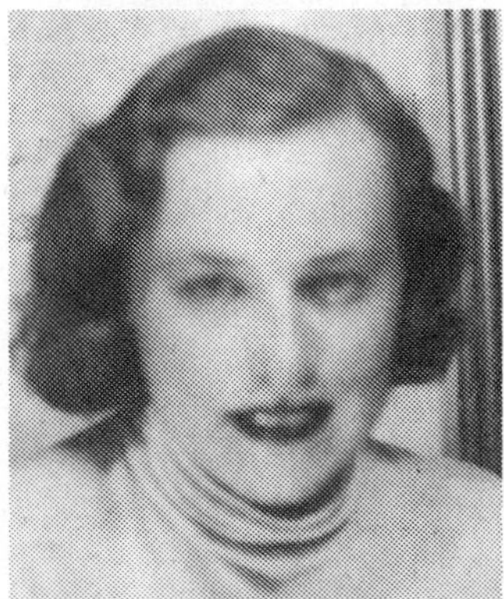

Anne C Grofe

Anne C Grofe
WINTER MEDITATIONS

These poems are dedicated to the still Unknown God.

Eerie Starlings' sighs pierce the afternoon's silence,
A white cat crouches between ferns

and rock,
Leaves scurry and rattle in a soft ocean breeze,
And Gulls circle and soar before joining their flock.

Bright pink Impatiens suckle a cool earth,
Red Throated Sparrows dance on berry laden branches,
Mourning Doves sing and coo in the Orange Tree,
And a stark naked Apricot Tree casts shadowy trenches.

Calla Lilies peek out to catch the waning sunlight,
Each day grows shorter in Winter's continuing rite,
Italian Cypress grow erect reaching heavenward,
And budding Camellia plants hold their blossoms tight.

The white cat darts out from its hiding place,
But too late to catch fluttering Sparrows in flight,
Winter's Sunset brings golden red hues,
And blazing skies cast memorials to God's might.

Anne C Grofe
FALL MEDITATIONS
Like a bottle churned up by the incoming tide,
And cast upon eroding sands,
I stood alone awaiting the rain,
Sea gulls crying echo thru cloudy brooding bands.

A shadow, Oblivion, walks by the water's edge,
With weather weary cliffs frowning in the fading light,
And twilight crouching on the horizon line,
As an eerie silence gives way to rising windy flight.

Brother past, and brother future play in the sand,
While a Servant called Death casts lots of stone,
And Life gathers his priestly garments from the sunset,
As a stalwart Angel meditates upon all made of bone.

At last the rain is falling,
Quenching my parched soul and the parched earth,
The Servant called Death gathers his lots,
While the High Priest Life awaits re-birth.

Teal blue waters bare whited teeth,
A pounding surf and rumbling heavens unite,
Lightning flashes, the storm ends, the rain ceases,
In the gathering gloom I await
Daybreak's Light.

Franke OpdenGraef Cunningham
MELODY
There's a poem in every word we speak,
There's poetry in each thought,
And a poem in every heart and soul
And elsewhere if it's sought.

Poetry beautifies the thought,
Gives brilliance to the deed,
Enhances every spoken word
When from the pen it's freed!

Rachael Lara Hardin
GOD'S GIFT

This poem is for our world, And all things God created. May we never take them for granted!

The earth, for you and me
He created
The cool breeze is the air
from the balloon He inflated
The water is His tear
shed for us to quench our thirst
A gift we treasure
very dear
The sun is his smile
high from above
Its bright rays of warmth
are a token of His love
The source of food among many beasts
is for us to share
A gift from God
given to us with care
For everyone, God made a match
in Heaven
To keep each other company
as a friend and a companion
This is yours and my land
in which we are safe and secure
For God's got us
in His gentle hand.

Andrea M Nelson
MY BEST DAY

Dedicated to: Rev. James N. Williams, New Hope Baptist Church, Jersey City, New Jersey.

When I wake up in the morning
And everything seems fine
I close my eyes and say to God
Well Lord, it's you and I

I'll take whatever comes today
No matter what may be
For I know that I can handle it
If I but call on thee

You are my heavenly Father
I look to you for all
I know that you won't let me down
On you I can always call

And when my day is over
And I again lay down to rest
I find comfort in knowing
That this day was the best.

Diana Narváez
ME AND MY KITE
My kite is my partner
It keeps me company
And that makes me feel
better.

My kite keeps the sun company
'Cause it's way up there
That makes the sun feel
pretty good.

Richard Myers
THE TREE

For Jorene with love.

Lord in the attic there is our family tree
Mother explained it once to me
It went way way back to some far away date
She said this tree may be my fate

Great-grandad was the branch a bit above me
Ma said he fought to keep me free
Although we won the great war, he died alas
The victim of some poison gas

Great-grandad's son was on the next line askew
He fought in the great World War Two
Grandpa is still alive although better off be dead
The war drove him out of his head

My father's line was connected to my own
Just that one line I was alone
You see, my father is a Vietnam Vet
And to this day he can't work yet

It seems as though every branch had run to war
Run off to even someone's score
I am the last line, the last branch on the tree
Dear Lord please make no war for me

Susan B Berntson
DARKSIDE OF LIGHT
In a way I believe
There's a darkside of Light
Or shadows that stand in the way.
As hard as I try,
I'm just getting by
Surviving as day passes day.

But how do I find
This darkside of Light
And bring it some rays from the Son?
Tho' I may yearn,
I'm eager to learn
Stand true in my faith of the One.

Maybe I'm wrong
There's no darkside of Light
I've just much further to go.
In any case,
I've made my place
& I'll fight, whatever the foe.

Keri Olesinski (age 13)
WAR
War is a time when everyone is sad.
A time when you might lose your Dad
Or Uncle, or Brother, or
someone for whom you care
This kind of thing I cannot bear.

War is unwanted, like a small mouse.
As soon as you see it, you want it out of the house.
When you hear about War, it's like a blow to the mind.
Why can't people just learn to be kind?

When the War is over, many dead are forgotten.
Since they died for their country
I think that's just rotten.
Then the ones that survived go home to their wives.
So tell me, how come G-d spared their lives?

David Hill
GAIA'S FIRE
You can change the world
By yourself
All you have to do is touch
Somebody else

The chain will grow
And love will spread
We'll stand heart to heart
Hand to hand

You can start the fire
That brings the world to life
Love is all you need
To let the spark ignite

So, turn your sorrow into joy
Whatever's wrong, set it right
Love is all you need
To let the spark ignite

David Hill
THE QUEST
Such a place I have not found
One where I am touching ground
That has not been walked before
Or left behind some open door

Such a sight I have not seen
That opens heart and mind
And every spot there in between
Or any dream I've yet to find

Such a song I've not yet heard
One of a fully tranquil bird
Which flies 'fore and aft her nest
With the victory of her quest

Such a sun has not yet risen
To free man from his inner prison
And come to others in a way
That brings to earth a brighter day

We're simply searching for valleys new
Suns that rise to fullest view
Songs that will not ever end
In short, the hand of a lifelong friend

Lucille Kerr Rawling

Lucille Kerr Rawling
TELL ME GENTLE WIND
Whisper softly gentle breezes, tell me where you go
Days and times I do not feel you, I would like to know.
Tell me why and how, sometimes you get so strong
You cut swathes of destruction . . many miles long?

Sometimes your touch is gentle, as you go whisking by,

Like a Mother singing to her
Babe . . a sweet-soft-lullaby.
What makes you get so angry, where do you get your Might
To turn into a Hurricane . .
up-rooting everything in sight?

You're really Schizophrenic, in the changing of your Moods,
At times with little warning . .
you tear off house-top roofs!
I find I often ponder, if your wrath could be God's-Way
Of showing disapproval, when His Children . . . go astray?

Or when God is pleased, He shows
His LOVE—by your breezy touch
In Hopes of re-assuring . . how He
LOVES us all . . . so much!
What is your secret "Gentle Wind" . . . why with a sudden change
Do you turn your "Tenderness" . . to "Fury"
devastating such wide-range?

Evelyn M King

TOAD

On a cold, dark, rainy night,
I found him—underneath the light;
on the steps, and washed so clean—
the biggest Toad I'd ever seen!

I picked him up and took him in
to scrutinize this—denizen—
of the swamp, the marsh, or creek—
wondering—what did he seek?

Food, of course, is first in mind
when an animal you find;
swiftly, with his tongue, he caught
all the mealworms that I brought.

These golden worms I raised to sell
to pet shops—and they sold quite well . .
The Toad ate seven—all he could;
I guess he thought that they were good.

A plastic boat became a pen—
a dish of water—so that when
his temperature he sought to cool
he had a private swimming pool.

Then I brought a mossy rock
from the river—at the dock;
I put it by his swimming pool,
'cause every Toad should have a stool.

Wasn't he the lucky one—
when everything was said and done;
company he did not lack—
a tiny Toad rode on his back.

When I took him for a walk,
just like a Turtle he would balk;
and look at me as if to say,
"With little Toad—I want to stay"

Jerrieline K Manaole

WHO . . . ME?

When I was young in my early teens
I was proud of myself and thought only of me
Solving life's problems and marveled at things
And I really thought it was all done by me . . .

During my middle years, life was filled with
"Ups and downs," I did falter, stumble, fall
But I survived and it caused me to wonder
Were all things done by me????

Now each day when I awake
I thank the Lord and I truly appreciate
My life, my family and all I've received
Came straight from God and not from me . . . .

Vickie Lyn Brown

REST DADDY REST

Rest Daddy rest, It won't be long, before I too, will be moving on.
Please be patient, no matter how long it takes, for it is you
Daddy, I want to meet, at Heaven's gates.
Then we'll do it again, we'll start anew, only this time Daddy I'll want to know the real you.
You had so much to offer, so much to give. I feel so cheated
Daddy, why couldn't you live? I never knew one person who didn't like you. You made people laugh, it was so easy for you. You were always laughing, you were always joking, Now I know how your heart must have been choking. You hid your pain so very well, Why Daddy Why, did you go through such hell?
For as long as I live I will never forget, your smile, your charm, your humor, your wit.
So rest Daddy rest, You're out of your pain, May God love you and keep you, until we meet again.

Antoinette Velise Jackson

A SELF PORTRAIT

For my grandmother and mother, the two most sophisticated, intellectual and strong women in my life, who helped me become a young lady.

High Expectations
Strong Self-esteem
Self Motivations
Committed, Preoccupied
Starry-eyed, Confused
Me!

Frenchie Clements

THE FACE OF A CLOWN

I knew the face, that was painted as a clown,
With a curly red wig, and a nose too big.
I wanted the world to know he could win.
That great big man, with a turned down grin.

He painted on a smile as he went through the day,
And dreamed of his youth that had faded away.
I saw his world come tumbling down . . .
And "God" he prayed, but not with a frown.

The dancing, and laughter that he had caused;
Had turned into darkness, just like the applause.
He had gone to the top so many times before,
But this time he stayed, real close to the door.

The stakes were pulled up, and the poles were down.
The "Big Top" laid silently on the old hard ground.
He stood in the corner, with tears in his eyes,
And his baggy old pants, as he said his good-byes.

I wanted to look back, just one more time,
To see the face of that dear old clown.
But the tears made the paint look just like clay.
I wept to myself—and quietly walked away.

Mrs Angie N Jones

IMAGINE

This poem is dedicated to James, my loving husband.

Imagine in the nighttime how the moon
Shines so bright among the stars

Imagine two shadows walking hand-in-hand
In the sunset at early morn

Imagine the highest mountain
That reaches far into the blue sky

Imagine the fresh scent fragrance
Of a beautiful rose in the garden

Imagine a smile that seems to gleam
On the face of a little child

Imagine capturing a treasure
At the end of a rainbow

Imagine the gentleness
When you stroke the fur of a kitten

Sweetheart, imagine how much I love you

Fay Ward Hillberry

FOND MEMORIES

To my beloved mother, to whom I owe so much.

Down the road of memory
I travel now and then,
Remembering when I was a little girl
And held my mother's hand.

The skies always seemed so fair.
The sun always shown so bright.
The flowers nodded in the breeze,
And filled me with delight.

I loved to listen to the whippoorwill's call,
That came gently floating thru the night,
And listen to the cricket's song
As my mother held me tight.

She'd hold me close and sing to me
The songs of yester-year,
Their melodies sweet; I still can repeat
The tunes she taught me there.

I've grown and traveled far and wide,
But fond memories are still my guide,
As once more I turn into the little girl
Who walks by mother's side.

Fay Ward Hillberry

TIME

Today will soon be yesterday,
For time flies swiftly by.
So make the most of now and here,
Worthwhile things to apply.

The handshake of friendship,
The smile of warmth and cheer.
The little things that matter,
Will last thru many a year.

So give a smile of sunshine
To a stranger along the way.
Perhaps his heart is heavy,
His spirits you may lift this day.

Give a hug to someone lonely,
Let them feel your loving touch.
Let them know they really matter,
For that is what they need so much.

So scatter the seeds of kindness,
Let the winds carry them afar.
Then when the time of harvest comes,
You will have won your shining star.

Fay Ward Hillberry

WIND

It's very interesting the way the
Wind rushes thru the trees.
It sends the leaves dancing and rippling
In just the slightest breeze.

They float and sway in rhythm gay,
And lift their heads up to the moon.
Then gently sway and turn themselves
To face the earth again.

It always fascinates me
The way they move and flow.
The magic of the silent wind,
That moves the leaves just so.

Love is what I feel.
When I am with you,
there is no doubt.
I know you feel the same way too,
you're all I can think about.

Jane Hill

HER EXAMPLE

As spring arrives and May ninth in particular, I think of her.
The trees were in bud, the grass was green, the front porch washed down, the big green porch swing hung.
She and I spent many hours swinging, reading, and singing.
"Jesus Loves Me" and "It Is No Secret" were our favorites.
We picked out birthday cards and get well cards for her friends, made cookies and pies.
She spent her time in service to others.
If death entered the life of a neighbor, she prepared food and collected money for flowers.
She loved her roses, snapdragons, and flowers in general.
The funeral director was amazed at the size of her funeral.
She was just an "ordinary" person.
Her fame and fortune were not much by this world's standards,
But the legacy left to me far surpassed this world's wealth.
She didn't teach me the importance of receiving, but showed me the results of loving and giving.
To me she was "extraordinary."
I called her GRANDMA.

Marjorie Wilkes
DAY DREAMS
I built a home of silver wings,
Where pearls grow
And angels sing;
There are no walls or window pane,
And flowers grow
Without the rain . . . .

Darcelle Wise
RUSSELL VAUGHN

Dedicated to my Grandmother, Ambrozine Vaughn.

Russell Vaughn passed away today.
He didn't say a word.
He smiled at me and closed his eyes,
And gently slipped away.
I wondered what he had seen
To put him so at peace.
Maybe Daddy's hand was reaching out
For what he'd left behind,
Or maybe, he glimpsed the lamb,
And saw a brighter day.
At first, the tears filled my eyes,
Emotions roaring high,
And then, I said, "Why should I cry,
My brother didn't die."
He's only resting from this place
Until tomorrow comes,
When Heaven's gates are opened wide,
And Russell can walk inside.
I look forward to that day
When all the earth shall smile,
And Jesus in his glory will have
Him at his side.
And in a voice of sweet thunder
My Lord will stretch his hand and say
This earth is now a paradise
And I am here to stay,
So Russell Vaughn your rest is done
Rise and see the Son.
For now mankind shall live in Love
For all the work is done.

Terrie A Koch
IN HIS ARMS I SLEPT

To my loving Husband Frank, my darlin daughter Kassandra, to all the teachers that have touched me. To all the family for their support, but most of all to God.

Even when I stumble and fall, you were there to answer my call
I still love you, I still love you.
Even when I didn't seem to care, I still saw you standing there
I still love you, I still love you.
Even when I'm nasty and blue, I'll always find my way back to you
Because I still love you, I love you.
Even with my darkest fears, you still followed me through the years
Because you loved me, you loved me.
There I was a child too blind to see, that you would never give up on me
Just when I thought I could run away and hide, you would always find me
and you held me when I cried.
Because you loved me, you loved me.
So all those times I thought I was in hell, those were times I stumbled and fell.
I couldn't find you, I couldn't find you.
I was drowning in the icy waters of the deep,
and in your warm arms you cradled me to sleep.
Oh I only wish I knew, that all those years it was you.
Because you loved me, I love you!

Miriam Hill Caviness
PERCEPTION, THEN AND NOW
Crepe Myrtles planted two by two
Give me a sense of déja vu;
A pair of Fuschia Myrtles stood
Defending the home of my childhood,
As sentinels boldly guarding the gate,
To shield us from some evil fate;
Inspiring us to feel safe and warm;
Their vigil protecting us from harm.

Today, admiring their fragile blooms,
A vision of our innocence looms,
Of times when golden dreams were new,
As fresh as unspoiled, sparkling dew.
The brilliant hues of Myrtles fade;
And then, they offer only shade;
Their raison d'être, a compromise,
Though, like a dream, it seldom dies.

Crysi Mitchell
OUR EYES
Since our eyes last met,
My mind cannot erase,
Deep reflections of you.

I will never forget,
The unique look your eyes carry,
When they penetrate deep into mine.

Our eyes have a way,
Of conversing together.
No words are portrayed,
There is no need.

A deep understanding,
Of intangible thoughts.
Is what we experience,
Each time our eyes intertwine.

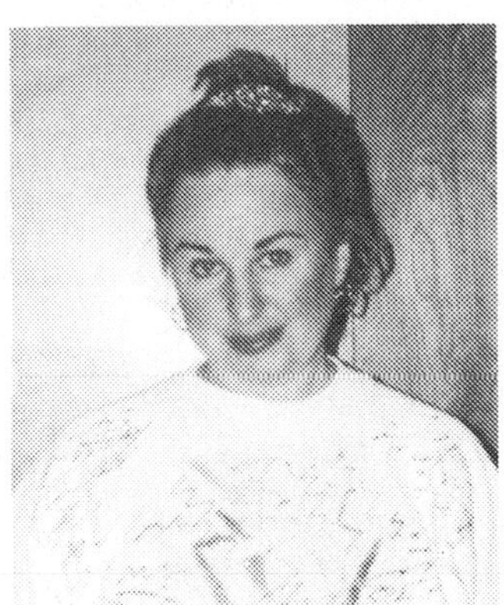

Anne Nelson

Anne Nelson
REINCARNATION OF LOVERS

To Jeane L. Dixon, my friend.

Many Lives and many Loves—
There were and are many mansions,
Mansions are earthly and heavenly . . . .
There and here are many stars and homes.
The higher power up there planned us all,
He still plans for each of us.

I grew up in a loving atmosphere of this earth,
Without real love and attention from my parents—
My surroundings were animals, dolls, friends,
Trees, flowers, lonely times and dreamy moments—
I was completely distracted from my family and relatives
No realization of that, I went into mysticism.

As I grew into a full and awkward womanhood—
At my tender age of 25, I had an early discovery
Of reincarnation with many past lives and lovers
In full ecstasy, I was Anne Nelson in Scotland
Riding on a horse over the rocky road.

So very clearly in my dreams, I was running
Away from my lovers—fearing any bloody fight,
I found many ways to escape—not meaning
Any repeated behavior or problem in life
Deep in feelings, I was so lost in love.

Heard a silent voice calling me, "Anne"
Knowing it was my lost lover, "Kendrick"
He left me because I was a born actress
Not plays—not to the theater life . . . .
The problem is the wrong world of
Listening to palmists, mystics and "gods."
I was abandoned into another life.

Christopher W Crosby
MY BROTHER, MY FRIEND

Dedicated in loving memory of Calvin J. Crosby (1976-1984).

You were my brother
But also my very best friend
We promised to be together
Until the very end

I recall all the good times
The times we spent together
Though sometimes we disagreed
Our bonds were tough as leather

I could not imagine
That we would ever be apart
And even though we're separated
You're still deep in my heart

Now I cling to the memories
The joy and love you gave
But I cannot help but shed a tear
As I lay this flower on your grave

I know you're in a better place
But it doesn't ease the pain
I do however find comfort in the fact
That one day I'll see you again

Ricky Lee Hasse
SILENT VOWS

Dedicated to April my forever love.

Be honest and I'll never lie,
Be true to me, You will never hear good-bye,
Be around others the way you would have me be,
Be gentle, be caring, trying always to be kind,

Because I want you forever and forever to be mine.

Juli Hanson
DESCRIBE MY LOVE?
It is that which has no boundaries
or limitations,
It is unconditional and understanding.
It is reality and fantasy;
it is real . . .
yet beyond my imagination.
It is all my heart's desires
and all my dreams.
It is inconceivable,
but not beyond comprehension.
It is the total being
of your soul and mine.
It is because we are!

Angel Sczenski
FOUR FRIENDS

To my best friends forever together (4).

These Four Friends who now stand
Strong and tall
Who not so long ago were all so
Small, Have laughed, cryed, teased
And even sighed are now
Slowly growing old but they'll
Never forget the stories told
For in their hearts will
Always be a memory of a special
Friendship that was meant to be.
For Friendship is like a golden band
It has no beginning or no end.

Pamela Kaminski
JOURNEY'S END

Dedicated to My Mom for her caring, and her endless love.

Who is that, the lonely one I see?
Searching, for lovely shells, by the sea.
Colors of pink, or colors of white.
They are all so pretty, in the gleaming sun-light.
She bends not so freely,
like the wind on her face,
for her bones like the seashells,
have narrowed in place.

She smiles as she brushes the sand from herself, and pictures the beauty of shells on her shelf.
She gathers them to her and slowly begins, the lonely journey back, against the strong winds.
Like time in an hourglass,
her path will soon end.

Anxious her feeling, to
sail with the wind.
To forget all her pain and
sit for a spell.
To glow in the sun,
as one with her shell.

Betty Caruso
DRUGS OR LIFE
Plant a seed, smoke some weed
only a plant you will feed
Pop a pill, so you will, find some
time to kill
A line of white, you call it coke
shoot it up, and soon you'll croak
Snort up some crack or crank
soon you'll be walking a plank
off the edge and losing your
mind all the time
Find a needle, stick it in your
arm, it will do a whole lot of harm
What about AIDS, don't you lie!
It's caused by dirty sex and dirty
needles
AIDS will make you die!
So if you have dreams, Please don't
do drugs
Think about your dreams, family
and friends
Before your life, you end!

Adelia L Roth
IDAHO *

I dedicate this poem to my pioneer parents, Dr. & Mrs. F. H. Hostetler who came to Boise Valley, Idaho in 1905.

Beautiful Idaho!
Gem of the mountains!
We come to you "early on"
When you were young—
When we were young.
We saw you growing—
We helped you to grow.
We saw you blooming—
We helped you to bloom.
And now?
Now we hear you singing—
"Singing your way to fame."

* Voices of a pioneer family.

Marie Tschumperlin
AND JOHN
And John looked down—
The dry, parched land
Has yielded what it can.
The dry, parched land
Waits to be kissed by the rain.
And for man to plant seeds
Down its narrow furrows.

And John looked at the sky—
The dry, parched land
Begs the clouds to loosen
Their bowels into showers.

And John knelt down—
Some raindrops fell to the ground.
And a plane circled above the
land—
The once dry, parched land.

Lois M Allen
THE AMERICAN FLAG
God bless this standard, the red,
white and blue,
Colors so beautiful, brilliant and true,
Flying in glory o'er all our bright
land,
On plains and in mountains, together
we stand.

With hats doffed in honor, while
you're carried by,
Emblazoned with glory, for you we
would die.
We are respectful of other flags, too,
Why can't men honor, the red, white
and blue?

It's burned and it's torn while others
protest,
And dragged in dishonor, while many
attest,
The more it's derided, the deeper our
love,
And thank our great God for His gifts
from above.

The gifts of our freedom and symbol
so true,
May you wave always, O red, white
and blue!
In pride and in honor above our vast
host,
Of all the earth's flags, we will love
you the most.

Angelina Casey
TIME BOMB
I feel like a time bomb waiting to
blow.
I know when it happens someone will
go.
I feel a little empty and kind of lost
I feel like my actions will have no
cost
But, I know deep down there will be
a price to pay.
But, I don't care anymore at least not
today.
I feel like a zombie walking around.
I feel kind of hopeless and a little
down
There is so much stuff that is
happening to me
Sometimes I just want to scream
"leave me be!"
I feel like a time bomb and soon I'll
blow.
It's my secret no one knows.
But, soon they'll find out, soon
they'll see.
That no one really knows the real me.

Norma and Ed Friend

Norma P Friend
HOORAY FOR RETIREMENT

Written for my beloved husband Ed (pictured with me), on the occasion of his retirement.

Hoo-ray for retirement and for those
who have made the grade.
The very best time of life for which
the first was made.
We work faithfully and hard for
many years.
With toil, sweat, and heartaches, we
often shed tears.
Then, at last comes the long awaited
day
When from "time-clock" or "daily
schedule" we can turn and walk
away.
"Let someone else take over and do
the best he can."
"But there'll never be this knowledge
and wisdom found in a younger
man."
God grant peace and joy and
happiness that seems
To be the richest fulfillment of all
one's hopes and dreams.
Thank you Lord for retirement and
for each relaxing day.
The very best time of life for which
the first was made.

Jeanette H Beveridge
ISLAND IN THE SEA
Snow fell softly
This cold winter's day
Gently and quietly
Out over the bay

The sound of the groaner
Way out in the deep
Guiding boats homeward
While the rest of us sleep.

The eiders and drakes
And old squaws too
Were bobbing and drifting
All in plain view.

As I stand on the shore
Here, all alone
It is heaven on earth
This island . . . my home

Kathleen M Sherek
ON THE WAY TO A DREAM FULFILLED
Ripping apart everything,
Tearing down the walls and having
God build up LOVE
Does take time and effort but
the rewards will be great.

Gone will be the days of
bereavement,
The loss of fear . . .
The loss of self-pity.

Fantasy can be a killer
if you let it—the escape
isn't worth it.
"Reality" does hurt—it is a living
hell
if there isn't Total Acceptance.

Susan Minnerly Engers
ABSENCE OF TIME

To my Mother with Love, my Teacher in Life, And my best friend.

The sun is setting quickly.
It's now time to remember.
Time to call back those long
forgotten places of yesterday.
To relive all those almost hot nights
In the early spring of youth.
So swiftly changing
To red, gold, and yellow,
With a slower step.

We are clocked, like timeworn
runners
In a perpetual race against the
inevitable.
Still; I have no fear of death.
It fails to hasten my step on a dark
night,
Nor does it intimidate me in thoughts
of loved ones.
For death marches side by side with
time.
Each their owed dues collecting,
Forever confident, indiscriminate,
And never ending.

Ruth Williams
IN BLOOM

To my lovely daughter, Julie, who unknowingly has provided me with a life-time of poetry inspiration.

A wildflower breaks through the
tough crusty earth
To tell all who will see or listen,
Of her delicate and fragile worth.
A silent beauty of stems and leaves;
She is brave and bold to challenge the
world, the disease.
This tiny little bud so timid, so shy
Wipes away her angry tears, held
within so many years,
And whispers upon the breeze, a
tender sigh.
Determined to conquer her dreams
silently, without a cry.
Then, very slowly and mysteriously,
a miracle appears
She begins to unfurl her guarded and
sleeping bloom.
Soft, precious petals with wondrous
perfume.
A gift to all— a gift of heavenly
creation.
So deserving of total appreciation.
And, for those who loved her, and
trustingly cared,
Patiently waited for this moment and
happily shared.
And, always would.
They kissed and beheld the proud and
beautiful little
wildflower, Julie, and understood.

Theresa Tryce
THANK YOU PRECIOUS JESUS
Thank you Precious Jesus for this
life I live,
Thank you Precious Jesus for the
blessings that you give.

When I call upon your name, your
love comes shining through,
Making everything I do, I do just for
you.

Thank you Precious Jesus is what I
like to say,
Knowing that you hear and know
what's in my heart I pray.

Thank you Precious Jesus all thru the
night and day,
Thank you Precious Jesus, that's all I
have to say.

Theresa Tryce
DON'T TELL ME
Don't tell me, that you want to go
Don't tell me, I don't want to know.
I still feel and always will, within my
heart my life you fill.

Our years together had some pain,
but for me I still remain true to you
forever more, you'll always be whom
I adore.

Troubles come and troubles go, but
somehow I must let you know what I
feel is sincere, you really are my
precious dear.

Give me time to reminisce, about our
years and the bliss of the years we
shared together, and give us time to
get to know again one another.

Theresa Tryce
TURN TO GOD, HE IS THE WAY
When you're feeling lonely, when
you're feeling blue, and you're all
mixed up inside you don't know what
to do, Turn to God, He is the way.

He is our salvation, He is always true, everything we need in life he will give to you. Turn to God, He is the way.

There will be temptations, that you can be sure, ask him for the strength to keep you strong and pure.

His love is never ending you can count on that, keep on searching you'll find out where it's at. Turn to God, He is the way.

Jon M Johnson

WHERE DREAMS LEAVE OFF AND *FANCIES* FAIL

For My Darling Bunny.

A lonely night, a famished glance that does perceive nought but perchance the void of life when Love recedes and leaves the one whose dreams do seek a single goal: To Be, To Have, [Ah, Yes!] To Hold.

To Him this is the darkest night, the first to come to bare His plight to quench His hunger and ennumb, but mostly ever to assure Her bliss, though He may fall and She not kiss.

There comes the time when dreams do fail: the night is loud, the breeze a wail, yet midst the night, its shroud, a single lantern beckons: Her lamp is out, yet She is on—He reckons . . . He reckons.

The night now calm, the wind does weep, for embalmed's His heart, (He fears) knows not Her keep. Too much to ask for? His life curtails Where Dreams Leave Off and *Fancies* Fail.

Kathi Pearce

HEAVENLY LOVE

I love you more than I can say, my love grows stronger by each passing day, my heart is full of laughter, my tears are full of joy; and if some day I lose you, I don't know what I'd do. I'd rather lose my own life than to live without you. And when we hear our calling, and we know that we must go, just remember that our love was special and our minds were full of hope. The love we had now resting in my heart and sleeping in my soul had awoke from its rest. I know that you will be there 'cause our love was the very best.

Brenda Rounsavall

WINE AND ROSES

Through the years of wine and roses we walked the roads a-winding. Through the laughter, pain and tears we found the hope to travel this many years.

The silver now that is slowly taking the auburn from my hair will not dim the sweetness I feel for you dear. For the kindness you have shown, the gentleness you have given, I will return to you.

The roads have been many, the curves sometimes sharp, the memories not always kind. The seeds we planted not always fruitful. The dreams we saw washed away; All the many disappointments, the many turbulent storms. The offering of peace in a time of war, all these things we have shared.

So, I will walk with you through all the many tears and laugh with you through all the many fears, and the seeds we planted that are good, we will share together. I will walk with you through all the many years, and we shall drink wine; and smell the roses. We will walk the roads a-winding, we will see the changing of the maple tree and taste the honey from its cone.

We will dream the dreams that make a life: The life of you and me. And the fire that burns so slowly out, like a thief it surely comes; We will have cheated death a-many-a time before the fire burns out. "And we will sip from the cup, filled with Red Wine, and smell the roses fragrant."

Jessica Pelletier

UNDERNEATH THE WILLOW TREE

To all the sisters at Presentation of Mary Academy, Hudson, N.H.; for they helped me achieve my goals.

I sit here under the Weeping Willow Tree.
Whether I fell wildly free or in a rage,
The always swaying branches cradle me like a cage.
As I sit on the swing thinking soaking up every knowledgeable bit.
Thinking of jokes to charm my wit.
Hoping to find a glit
A glit to whisk me into anything I want:
The vain beauty who lives to flaunt.
Or the queen of all lands.
Maybe a scene, where mountains rise high,
Where trees lie low, where birds are free to fly.
This is my place. My place to dream.

Mike Calvert

ANOTHER CHANCE

I sit alone in Betty's house wondering if things will ever be the same.
Then I realize with God's help, I can find a way.
So Lord thank you for another chance, in which I'll try to be a little more deserving of the gifts you've given me.
For yesterday is over, and tomorrow's far away, and I'll remain committed to the good in every day.

Mike Calvert

THROUGH MY CHILDISH EYES OF GREEN

I see my bears dancing in the cool Summer Breeze.
I collect them all no matter how big or tall, for I am twenty-five now, going on three.

I have music boxes that sing to me through the night, a moon hangs over my bed, what a glorious sight, there are stars of blue and white, that guide me throughout the night.
"Oh, what I can see through my childish eyes of green!"

I could grow up, but this I do not wish, for I see each day as a fresh new painting, for flowers are blooming, and the grass is green, birds are flying high above all the trees.

Dear Lord, thank you for what I see, Through my childish eyes of green.

Lucila Villaseñor Grijalva

Lucila Villaseñor Grijalva

THE JOY OF SERVICE

To those I have loved, Those I love now, And those I will love—always.

I see the hands of service
Opening with delight,
Coming out of darkness
Bringing forth new light.

I hear the wings of angels
Rustling swiftly by,
Waking from deep slumber
Freeing love across the sky.

I feel the joy of laughter
Holding the kingdom's keys,
And the open heart of wonder
Being all it's meant to be.

I sense the feet of service
Pressing firmly on,
A special path less traveled
Filling now with wisdom won.

I touch the rim of happiness
Knowing where it is,
Moving close to harmony
Embracing new found bliss.

Mary Santos

A BAD DREAM

This poem is dedicated to the most important person in my life, Stringfellow Hawke . . . .

As the morning sun rises
Another day is beginning
'Cause he and I will be together
Again for just one more day

I awaken by the lovely tunes he had played with his cello
For me to hear it my last
But even though we'll be apart for a long time
I'll always remember him as a memory of my past
I knew he loved me just as much as I loved him
'Cause he proved to be the best guy for me
He took care of me and always held me beside him
And he also showed the most beautiful things for me to see

So should I say he's all upset
'Cause I can see those tears forming in his eyes
I felt like crying with him because of the pain in both our hearts
And we will be saying those sad goodbyes

Now the sun had set while this time he played lonely tunes with his cello
For me to feel how depressed he was on the last seconds we may be together
I last kissed and hugged him tight while we both cried
And by the last second, I was taken to another world without him

Suddenly I woke up, gladly finding him still beside me, which meant it was all a bad dream . . . .

Gina Williams

IF YOU WERE TO BELIEVE IN ME

Dedicated to Jordan Knight, my Family and Friends, To all of you with Love.

If only once you were to believe in me. Do you know how much it would mean to me?

It could give me the hope to do what I might not have done, to become that someone I've only dreamed of, to do the things I've always wanted to do.

If only once you were to believe in me. It could light that spark deep inside, make me be the person I've wanted to be. If only you were to believe in me it could make my Dreams Come True.

Viviane Cochrane

LOVE IN LIMBO

As always, to BOB.

I've reached a fence
Beyond where greener pastures beckon,
Searching for a gate
into love's arms
not yet found—
Longing to spread a blanket
of love
upon new ground.
No fence would be too high to climb,
No gate too far from view,
if only I knew—
Beyond, deep within those fields
of love
There would be you.

Ginger McLeod

MY TRUCKING TEAM

Dedicated to my parents, Junior and Mona Thurman, with love.

Seems anymore can't find a moment to steal,
With mom and dad who drive an eighteen wheel.
They sure get around run from coast to coast,
But don't get much time where loved the most.

They're a quick phone call from any state,
Often expected home but arriving late.
Mommy and Daddy are truck driving folk,
Writing their love in the diesel smoke.

So proud am I of the both of them,
My truck driving team that's her and him.
And love them much I certainly do,
No parents more special than those two.

They're sorely missed and dearly loved,
As ever so tenderly they're thought of.
And are gently placed in God's care,
On each trip the two would share.

They're always here though gone so far,
As in my heart they always are.
And though absent I still want to say,
To my trucking parents you're loved today.

Donna L Farrell
BLESSINGS

Dedicated in sweet loving memory of Barbara J. Lovell.

The hard times for going smoother,
the happy for going strong.
The will to live for each other,
the blessings for going on.
The angel in the clouds in your friend
in the darkness, your shadow in the light.
Your strength when you're in sorrow,
your guardian at night.
There is heartache in our lives,
sorrow in our pain.
For all this there is a reason,
God works in mysterious ways.

God gave us tears to wash away our sorrows.
He also gave us life to make better tomorrows.
He gave us sunshine in our hearts,
strength in our souls, ambition to
strive for better, direction to achieve our goals.
So look beyond the stormy skies, life
is full of joy, tears, and rain. Thank
God for what you have and don't
ever live in vain.

Donna L Farrell
FRIENDS ARE FOREVER

We were two souls that passed in the night.
Endless oceans had brought us together.
We shared tears of our broken hearts.
our friendship would last forever.
Romance may come and go, but will seldom stay together.
Friendship is a special bond of truth, and honesty. Friends are Forever.
You were always someone who could bring me a lift through life's ups and downs.
Someone who could mend my broken heart, when it was in a million pieces onto the ground.
You brought me strength at times when I thought my world was coming to an end.
You would bring me sunshine to my darkest of nights, by just being a friend.
You were the kindest and truest of hearts a friend could ever be.
You are that special someone, my true friend, for all eternity.

Alex Barnes
GROWING

To my family, Columbus Rehab., a New MediCo facility. My life with both has been a growing experience.

Love in the field
Fill with love
Growing and blooming
Oh boy, the joy of it all.
Molded from the earth.
The head of an ape made from tapeworm
Squirming and yearning to fulfill its needs.
Only to become greater than man's.
Knowing how to grow up and
up-lifting oneself.
And become a success in life.
Let no person remove the coarseness
And enamel of life that you have attained.
No longer boring.
You have arrived, you have seen the light,
God Bless You.

Nada Knight
IDENTITY

as I look out
at the entity of
winter white,
an absolute takes up
residence in me:
the unique and individual
pattern
of a falling snowflake
stops
when it does

Nada Knight
PURPOSES

beyond mere life,
each season has a
societal reason;
the onus of autumn
is to give us
color power enough
to last through
the days of greys

Audrey J Krueger-Hale
SENDING A FRIEND MY WAY . . .

This poem is dedicated to Dee E. Hedlund my Beautiful friend from Bloomington, Minnesota whom The Precious Lord sent my way . . . .

A thousand times I think of her . . .
A million times I pray . . .
And, thank the Good Lord up above
For sending her my way.

I'm speaking of you, Dee, my friend . . .
The one who's in my heart . . .
That Little Lady up the street . . .
Whom I knew was special . . .
From the start.

She walks in . . .
When the world walks out . . .
And, keeps me shining . . .
through the clouds of doubt.
Lifts me up . . .
When I've fallen down . . .
Keeps me smiling . . .
When I start to frown.

She lessens my grief,
doubles my joy . . .
Our chats we certainly do enjoy!
We laugh—we cry . . .
We share our thoughts . . .
For all we have . . .
and, our have-nots!

I count the hours . . .
'til we meet again . . .
For that beautiful time . . .
With my Special Friend . . .
And, once more . . .
Precious Lord, I pray . . .
Thank You for sending, her my way!

Daryel Ann Groom
STILLNESS

Rocks me backwards, words inside my head, palpitate my soul. This feeling so empty, where do I start? God above help me to see you're rooting for me. I'm feeling like shallow water in the middle of a drought. Where is my spout? No love right or wrong can make me feel whole. Just the love of myself that I've been too desperate to hold. Just the words I've been given too big and too bold. Just the place I've been driven, the memories hold tight, a new facet on life. Incredible plight "Oh, Lord" help me? fight all these feelings locked tight, stillness creeps about my walls, yet it never falls, silently waiting to echo my calls, as I cry for the heavens, it listens that's all . . . .

Christa Marie Hemm

Richard T Hill
LITTLE CHRISTA

How long we visit, who's to know
What day we come, what day we go.
But who we touch and who we love,
We are surely in control of.

Christa never danced a step,
Because of that some have wept.
But when I walked on troubled days,
She walked with me in her own way.

And all the words that Christa spoke,
A thank you mom, or a little joke,
Came directly from her heart,
And were clear to me while far apart.

I often prayed about this day, for the power to make it go away.
But as we know, God's in control, He takes the body, but shares the soul.

What's left behind is ours to keep, a memory that nestles deep.
We ask our Lord to hold her tight,
And kiss her goodnite, for us tonite!

In loving memory, Uncle Rich

Diane Seneczko
WHAT IS LOVE?

Love is when someone is there,
To be your friend, comfort, and care.
To cheer you up when you're feeling blue,
And offer a love that's fresh and new.
To be there when you have feelings to share.
To hug at night like a teddy bear.
To hold hands with while you're walking down the hall.
To kiss in the middle of the shopping mall.
A love like this is hard to find,
because they are
Just one of a kind.

Mayme E Bennington
MEMORY'S GARDEN

In my mind I have a garden.
It's among the clouds—up in the blue.
No one ever enters there
Except me and my thoughts of you.

I have a section in my garden
Which is very dear to me.
Through it runs a winding path,
Which I alone can see.

Up that path I often wander
As twilight settles o'er the land.
I sit upon a misty bench,
Am entertained by memory's band.

The memories still haunt me
Of the times we spent together,
How we wandered everywhere
No matter what the weather.

Many songs tell of new loves
So enthralling while they last
But nothing beats good memories
Of the dear departed past.

Kristina M Ferreira
THE WIND

For Joseph M. Cordeiro, Jr., my Grandfather, with all the love and admiration my heart can possibly hold.

The wind has trapped memories in me forever
For everytime the wind blows my face
I will remember how closely it reminds me of my true feelings
I want to get used to the feeling of wind
For everytime I feel the wind is near me,
my memories become part
of it.

Donna Losey
WE TALK, WE JOKE, WE LAUGH, WE CRY

We talk, we joke, we laugh, we cry
For we know it is goodbye.
You lie there pale and bleak
As though you are asleep.
I bend and kiss your little head
For I know that you are dead.
The moment's long as time stood still
Goodbye my love, goodbye my Bill.

Paula M Ynda
A PLACE FOR ME

To My Loving Parents.

My Lord why do we have this chance to live?
Can eternal Life mean to receive is to give?
A sin . . . is to say thou name in vain.
But your forgiveness renews our faith again.
With one Last breath, with every miracle of
Life, there may become death.
My Lord you listen
so much and speak not a word though, through
the whispering wind your voice is heard.
But why is Life so short and death is eternity?
It makes no difference how troubled one may be.
For when that day that is sure to come . . .
One must have faith in thou judgment for all you have done.
But i am not afraid i have this to believe . . . with you, my Lord i know there's "A Place For Me."

Larry R Grubbs
PEACE OF SNOQUALMIE FALLS

Snow falls at Snoqualmie Pass
Water at the Salish
With rainbows cresting sunny days
Through its mist like long ago

Snow fell in the mountains of old
And an Indian maiden from The Falls
As told by People of the Snoqualmie
Through its mist to the waters below

Tales of Valley of the Moon
And of a sacred place of peace
Memories of old ones and their ways
In a valley of beauty and awe

Still survive these days of hurry
On the rocks below The Falls
Peace of mind as one does gaze
At the water falling so slow

Charles A Bevier Bouvier
SEATTLE IN THE RAIN

Little drops of sparkling silver, falling on my face again.
And Old King Sol, shining thru another beautiful rainbow.
A day so refreshing, cool to green.
A greater sight my eyes have never seen.
Seattle in the rain,
Seattle in the rain.
Another magnificent day in our city,
Seattle in the rain.

Charles A Bevier Bouvier
THE DOORWAY TO YOUR HEART

When you first saw me standing in the doorway,
The autumn rain was with us once again.
You smiled as you tipped your umbrella.
And asked me in, from the cold and rain.
Now I'm standing in the doorway to your heart.
Will you open, let me enter, never to part.
For I've loved you from the start.
And now, I'm standing in the doorway to your heart.

Joan Gilliam
THE WESTPARK TRAIN

I can hear the train on Westpark
When the wind is from the South,

And it calls into memory
As though it has a mouth.

And the years roll back like freight cars
To the time when I was small

In a childhood home so near the tracks
I could hear the brakeman's call.

On open-windowed summer nights
As I drifted into sleep,

Railroad noises filled my room . . .
Some were shrill and some were deep.

There were huffing, puffing, hissing sounds
Unlike the diesel's drone,

And clanging, banging, screeching sounds
With whistles that could moan.

A switch engine would push and pull
To rearrange the line

While the warning bells went "ding ding ding"
At the RAILROAD CROSSING sign.

Boxcars, tank-cars and passenger cars
Are filled with days now passed,

But I still can't see the red caboose
For it comes at the last.

Those clickity-clacking metal wheels
Roll right up through the years

When the wind is from the South at night
And the train on Westpark nears.

Janet A Wagner
THE BAR, THE BARTENDER, THE BEER

To all of those who gather here,
To laugh and talk and drink the beer.

To all of those who serve the beer,
To all of those who gather here.

Just think about what your drinking's done,
To you, to your family, to everyone.

Just think about the ones who care,
Who sit and wait, the pain, the fear.

It very seldom brings you joy,
You play with lives, and they aren't a toy.

At times it's taken the life of a boy,
Or a mother, a sister, or someone's dad,
Why can't you see why it's so bad.

To those who sell it in excess,
How is your conscience, or should I guess?
How do you feel the very next day,
When you read of a life just blown away,
By the same drunk driver you served that day.

What will it take for you to see,
Will it be your life, or maybe me?

Each night I pray to God above,
That he'll protect the ones we love.

That he'll make them stop before they've had too much,
So they'll always be here for us to touch.

So they won't ever have the guilt inside,
For the one that they hurt, or the one that died.

Susan A Harvey

Susan A Harvey
THE LADY

Dedicated to my uncle J. and all the soldiers who died preserving Liberty.

It was cold on the ship that November day,
The journey was Long, his old home far away
The boy stood on the deck scared, yet eager to see,
The new land he would be in soon, with his family.
He was young, nine or ten? He couldn't remember when.
But he could recall best of all,
How he felt when he first saw "The Lady"
Though cold and tired, his heart was inspired,
And he fell in love with "The Lady."
The years rolled on, the boy now gone,
Grown into a fine young man.
Said he, 'I promise to do all I can to serve and honor "The Lady."'
The war had come, and now was won
But the soldier died and in his last breath cried;
'I did it for "The Lady."'
And she still stands welcoming other boys from other lands.
"THE LADY LIBERTY"

Susan A Harvey
CAN YOU SEE THE BUTTERFLY?

To Patton, Sarah, Betty, Ann, Erna, et al., at C.E.C. who look with eyes of love and do see the butterflies within us.

I was a caterpillar
I was ugly no one liked me.
Girls screamed when they saw me,
Boys tried to kill me.
I even, did not like me.

Then a voice inside
An idea!
I would have to die in the cocoon.
A change will take place
Fear, then trust, I would spin my cocoon.
And follow the voice inside.
Unbelievably I emerged beautiful and loved.
I'm a butterfly now and always will be
From now on nothing left of the old ugly me
Changed by love, and a miracle.
Can you see the butterfly, as you gaze at the caterpillar?

Susan A Harvey
THE EDGE OF FOREVER

Dedicated to Rita my best friend And to Michael my beloved husband.

We stand alone in the dark,
On the edge of forever.
Afraid to go forward, or right, or left,
Hanging back, paralyzed by fear, of hope bereft.
A warm glowing light from afar, pierces the dark,
We are drawn forward to it, yet; hold back,
It is a loving light, we yearn to go to it.
We look to the right and left, and see,
Yet, more lights appear, smaller lights
And love and hope shine through them.
Faces smile, and a loving hand reaches out to us.
A friend, or a lover, trembling on the edge of forever too,
We share, we strengthen one another, we lead each other on.
Drawn ever forward, to a greater love a greater light.
Now no longer afraid we go on
Toward the edge of forever
The way though rough, and unknown
Is made smooth paved by love, and lighted by hope.
So take my hand as a new day dawns
On the edge of forever
We can face life together.

Cathy Jones-Easterling
A GIFT OF LOVE

Dedicated to my two Foster children, Tamita and Russell.

A Gift of love, a tear for joy
a hand of mercy on a tiny boy
He cries for love with one small touch
God gave me joy to love him much
To ease the pain, of a little girl
Can make life easier in this evil world

A great big hug and a tiny kiss
to tuck into bed and have heavenly bliss
and know that tomorrow will always bring
happiness through the tolls and rain
the innocence of this girl and boy
brings lots of love and a ton of joy

I'll always cherish this work of art
and tell "God" now, I've done my part
so lead me on to higher heights until I rest that final night

Barbara Fairburn
HE LOVES YOU—AND ALWAYS WILL

Someone cares and always will,
The world forgets but God loves you still.
You cannot go beyond his love,
No matter what you're guilty of.
For God forgives until the end,
He is your faithful, loyal friend.
And though you try to hide your face,
There is no shelter any place.
That can escape his watchful eye.
For on the earth and in the sky.
He's ever present and always there,
To take you in his tender care.
And bind the wounds and mend the breaks,
When all the world around forsakes.
Someone cares and loves you still,
And God is the someone who always will.

Louise Bradt
ADOPTION—WHAT IS IT?

To my Moms, Opal and Matilda.

Is it giving away?
Is it taking away?
This bundle of joy that became my sorrow.
This bundle of sorrow that becomes our joy.
Full arms now empty.
Empty arms now full.
Is it a memory that haunts you?
Is it a memory that delights you?
Do I go out and find this memory?
Do I dare tell of another?
Will seeking bring joy and peace to my empty heart?
That someday may enter our lives.
Or bring hurt and sorrow with this long ago memory?
Is there love in my heart to share?
Trusting another to love your own.
To someday love enough to let go.

Louise Bradt
YOU STEPPED IN (STEPFATHER)

To my father, James L.; to my adoptive father Wilfred; to my stepfather John.

You did not give me life nor breath
But you stepped in.
You did not give me your hair
or the color of your eyes
But you stepped in.
You did not come to fill another man's shoes
But you stepped in.
You did not shove or push your way into our hearts
But you stepped in.
You did not crash down the door of our home
But you stepped in.
You did not rob us of our Mother
but stepped in right beside her.
You left deposits of stepping stones
to lead us and to guide us.
You never stepped on our toes, nor walked on our heels
But stepped in right beside us.
But one day, you stepped out of our life
And
You stepped into the heavenlies.
When you stepped out
Our Heavenly Father stepped in.

Marge Bemis-Breznen
PRAISE GOD FOR THE MUSIC

To my husband, Bill, who has made my life a "tapestry filled with romance."

Praise God for the music that bids us to dance.
She lightens our footsteps and lends a new glance
To all that surrounds us by day and by night,
And changes our outlook from dismal to bright.

She softens the edges in a world too concrete,
And lessens the drive to always compete.
Then coaxes us gently to slacken the pace,
And dresses our wounds even time can't erase.

She listens to longings, then summons our soul
To bathe in her spirit and make ourselves whole.
Her tune never faileth, her grace never falters.
With cadence and harmony, our vision she alters.

Praise God for the music, the word, and the dance.
They make life a tapestry filled with romance.

Veenie Winland

Veenie Winland
WHAT WENT WRONG?

I dedicate this poem to Dad, Mom, Scooby Doo, Puppy and Bosco.

Sometimes I wonder about this life,
So many hardships, so much strife.
People killing, children starving,
Forests shrinking from so much carving.
Air so stale it chokes you while breathing,
Water so polluted it seems to be seething.
Ministers stealing from their congregations,
Animals used for experimentations.

I picture God looking down at the earth,
With fond remembrance for the day of its birth.
What more could God do without interfering,
He watched his own son die, while humans stood cheering.
We must wake up and try to understand,
God created this paradise, because he loved man.
What has happened to the earth is not God's choosing,
For when we destroy, we are the ones who are losing.
I fear one of these days God will bid us adieu,
At which time we will remember Jesus's words,
"Forgive them Father, for they know not what they do."

Veenie Winland
LITTLE CIGARETTE

Little cigarette made from tobacco leaf,
Your pleasant taste has caused much grief.
People like to smoke you, and seem so pleased,
While slowly you kill them with some disease.
I can only hope when the world becomes sane,
You'll be sent back to hell from whence you came.

Dale Magnuson
MY LOVE

Roses are red
Violets are blue
This is what
I think of you

Your hair
flows with flair

Your eyes
are like little blue skies

Your mind
makes you say things kind

Your personality
makes things pleasant in reality

Your beauty
is why I call you my cutie

What I am trying to say
that is if I may

May I call you my dove
because you are the one I truly love

Janette Harvey
LADY HAWK & GREY WOLF

To My Love Grey Wolf
One Day We Will Be Together
Forever Lady Hawk

I have to get above where I am
In order to do what I have to do
Does night have to be day
In hopes of seeing you?

This torture we endure
Seems too much to bear
Yet still we continue
In search of the prayer.

You soar like the hawk
Then I roam like the wolf
In your flight you will see me
As I longingly look up.
Enemies by nature
Lovers by birth.

The hunt it is over
The curse it is past
The savage is calmed
Home at last.

Delores A Crawford
A LEAF IN THE FALL

The rain has ceased and left
A shining glow on roofs and streets
And wet leaves clinging to binding boughs

Clean sweet smells hang heavy in the air
With rain soaked leaves of brilliant hues
Of subtle blends of green and blues
The misty air is like a million
Tiny moist beads upon the face

A twiggy branch holds the last lonely leaf
That clings for life, but yet is dead
The leaf still twists and tries to cling
As the bough joins the battle against the wind

To and fro and up and down
The branch bows to the wind
And the lonesome leaf yields to the gale
The leaf spends, flutters and softly kisses the ground
The wind whistles, the leaf moves, the twig stands guard

Rain drops falling once again
While rainshine streets and silver roofs
Witness bowing branches and falling leaves
Lose daring battles to mighty winds

Peachye Gunn Childress
MY BEAUTIFUL MEADOW

The meadow is full of beautiful flowers,
Blooming in colors of reds, whites, and blues,
Wavering in the light breeze that's blowing,
Sparkling in the fresh early morning dews.

It's so wonderful to wander thru this meadow,
And pick an armful of these flowers in bloom,
As they stand like a soldier at attention,
With an aroma like some sweet perfume.

Would you like to come to my meadow,
And stay for just a short while?
I'm sure it would bring a lilt to your heart,
And you would leave with a beautiful smile.

Olive Mae Courtright
MOCKING BIRD HILL
A wise old owl perched in a tree on Mocking Bird Hill, told this tale to me, The mocking bird's call was loud and shrill, when called to his mate on Mocking Bird Hill, then all grew quiet and very still, till the silence was invaded by a whippoorwill, Then the fight was on and the feathers flew, and I don't give a hoot who won; Do you?

Pearl Palmer Erikson
THE ANTS
I sat upon the dampen earth
And watched the ants at work.
So many little mounds of hill,
Had sprung up since the night, until
I had to watch my every step,
So not to crush the tiny insect.

Such busy little things are they,
Working, Working through the day.
I Wonder what they think about,
They make no noise, never shout
As they go about from place to place
Hurrying as if, in a race.

Do you suppose they're storing food, down
In their holes, into a town?
Getting ready for the winter weather,
When they can't get out to-gather,
Crumbs and bugs and such,
And that is why they are in a rush?

Jean I Brown
BEYOND THE TOUCHING
Oh sorrow! Sorrow!
My soul cries out for all the yesterdays and no tomorrow.
You are gone now. Beyond the touching I so long to give.
Beyond the reality which is today.
Living only in that ethereal realm of memory in yesterday.

To feel your heart. To know your warmth.
All gone.
Gone beyond love's reach.
My cries have rent the air!
I lift up my face to God in utter despair. To no avail.
Of course, it is not fair.

The opposite of life is death, and so I live on between the two.
Held by the one, beckoned by the other.
They are my lovers now.
With one, I work, I talk, I coexist.
With the other I dance, I dream, I wait for you.
And of course, I sleep with sorrow.

Tony J Eckstein
ONE DARK RAINY NIGHT
one dark rainy night
just sitting alone
a knock at the door
just sitting alone

I said come in
she explained a flat tire
well, get out of the rain
another log on the fire

she said there wasn't a spare
no way to get home
just dry off
you're not alone

when I offered a drink
she asked for the phone
she made a call
no one was home

we sat down and talked
it seemed like hours
just like old friends
it seemed like hours

another knock at the door
help had arrived
thank God for the good
the good shall survive

we keep in touch
now and again
that dark rainy night
gave me a friend

Kathy Estrada
REVENGE
Dreaming of the desire to accomplish such a great goal.
Loyal, noble mature man of enterprise.
Too hasty in actions of thoughts.
Riches, inheritance; Don't even think to ask!
So much for fate—creative evolution within the laws of chance.
Love of life cautioned by the loss of would-be friendships.
Simulates enjoyment for the malicious laughter of others.
For all cruelty, cowardliness is but the degradation of an empty victory.
Journey from place to place, misery for no cause.
Chance-bearer of tidings; Desire is power.
Living for the past—the choice of rage.
Life is but unwanted knowledge, for he indeed is the Fool.

Sherry E Engler
SLEEP
Unexplained mystery,
Darkened secret untold;
From where do you come?
What magical powers do you hold?

Quiet as a cat,
Stalking as you creep,
Upon every living creature
As you curse them to sleep!

Mary Ruth Easley
AN AGENT FOR SATAN
He wrote: "I'm not trying to disprove God but to dethrone Him!"
Volumes he wrote long ago by candlelight dim.
His philosophy was adopted and spread;
It's still growing a century after he's dead.

His system of government enslaves, causes wars and denies God.
He was powerful—so powerful he rules much of the earth from beneath the sod.

Millions have suffered and faded on;
But God still lives upon His throne.
Judgment Day—the evil one's soul!
Eternal Hell with Satan as the great Bible foretold.

James Leonders
AEROPLANES
Our thots are aeroplanes
When we fly
To higher climes;
When you and I
Seek the Truth to find.

Our thots are aeroplanes
When we feel
Love is life's crowning seal.
Our thots are aeroplanes
When we see
Others as they might be.

Our thots are aeroplanes
When we strive
To elevate our Lives;
When we know
God's Word is ever so!

OUR THOTS ARE AEROPLANES!

Mary B Evan
UNTITLED
You say you love me
then turn away.
You're between night & day
giving me mixed emotions.
What do you want,
give me a clue.
I can't pull you towards me,
but I can't push you away.
If time is what you need
let me know.
I'm not here to pressure you
or monopolize your time.
But don't toy with my emotions,
don't lead me astray.
Don't say you love me,
then turn away.

Christina H Taylor
THE SERMON

For Frank, with whom I have started to meet many truly wonderful people.

Great warships fly o'er as they quietly raise their hymn;
And flames lick at the tower as they hold their prayer within.
And their hearts beat ever on, quiet drumming rumbling nearer,
Distinct reminders of Mars's gun, ever building on the fear

That shattered pieces of colored glass never again will join to be
The congregation of all who pass in hope of peace and harmony.
Eat the crust; take the cup; raise them high as terror reigns down!
Simple calm and gentle sup amid the bawling, hellious sound
Of souls forgotten, cast aside by impulses never understood.
Uranus, the Magician, cried for the dissonance, for the good.

Carl R Eiss
LIFE
Life is a very important thing
Sometimes you laugh
Sometimes you sing

Sometimes you walk
Sometimes you fly

Sometimes you cry
When loved ones die

The saddest thing happens at last breath
The hardest thing about life is <u>*death*</u>.

Marci Masiello Elliott
HAPPINESS
Two separate lives.
Two strangers meet.
They become friends.
They become lovers.
Their lives become one.
Wanting and caring for each other.
They find happiness, together.

Pat Clark
MY HEART HAD WINDOWS
Would you take me
under your wing
and teach me to sing
the praises of the universe?
i know there is a presence in my life
of which i have denied
but then i cried and then i died
because happiness was not.
i gave myself to the universe
and guess what? much happiness abounds
my new world reigns
i forgave the pain
now only love is nigh
and heaven is not up high
it is right here
on this ground
And on this ground is where i tread
this is my point of power
no longer do i yearn for yesterday
because love is <u>*here*</u> today.

Yvette Checkie
PROUD
I glance across the crowded room—
My hands fill with perspiration.
I can hear my heart pounding in my

head,
I begin to quiver.
What a way to say good-bye to you!

I walk slowly toward the huge box.
All eyes turn toward me . . .
They probably thought I wouldn't come.
Still, I hold my head high.
To the end, I will make you proud!

Finally, at the box, I look at you
And a lifetime of memories
overwhelm me.
What a way to say good-bye
I wipe a tear from my face as the minister closes the lid.
Till the end—I'll make you proud!

Mina Emami
NIGHT
Night passes by
with a palpitation of repeating moments
and gets captured
by the restless shadows
in the depths of my eyes
night, full of shadows itself.

Night passes by me,—
standing on the bridge of love,
given up my whole entity
to the hollowness of the moments passed,—
and enwraps me
in a flowing silence,
and abandons me
in far, deep, unknown spaces,
the infinity of time.

***

Somethin's flowing
in the dark limpid essence of the night,
that breaks the noble crystal of my heart,
and on the broken pieces of my heart
it curdles.

Night pierces into my whole being,
blind, dark, cruel,
and lets the blues
creep into my heart,
darken the mirror of my mind
and settle to the bottom of my eyes
like murkey dregs,

And lets me,
in the contempt of the empty dull moments,
think of the happiness of a tree,
that in the belief of the bird's sorrowful flight,
can go crazy and wild
with the bewildered winds of the night
and die, still standing
in the quiet mystic passage of the night.

***

In the night of the beloved's birth,
I feel like a tearful lump in a bird's throat,
which is broken
into the dark gloomy nature of the night

*

James J Elliott
THE HANGING TREE
Some one shot the banker,
And they blamed it all on me,
The posse had me all strung up,
To a limb on a hanging tree,
Some outlaws shot the posse,
And then they cut me free,
I rode away with my new friends,
And I looked back to see,
That sheriff hanging on the rope,
That he put there for me.
They asked me to join up with them,
But an outlaw I can't be,
I thanked the boys and rode away,
Far from that hanging tree.

J Yvonne Elston
THE ANSWER
You know all the questions
It's the answer you've lost
Remember your mission
It was not holocaust

Should you search deep inside
The answer would come
It will flow like the tide
Should you let it be done

In the beginning
You knew what it was
You started out singing
You knew of your cause

Then came the questions
And with them came doubt
You can feel the vibrations
Just let them come out

You started to doubt
And then came the fears
And what came about
Was you deafened your ears

You've only to listen
To that feeling inside
I know you will glisten
For the answer won't hide

Now look to the skies
Far far above
For the stars tell no lies
They sparkle with love

The questions are many
The answer but one
Just love and be happy
Your quest will be done

Yes, love is the answer
Love is the key
Love is your treasure
Love sets you free

Donald Edwards Jr
TINA TURNER
Dances with her high-stepping legs
In control, famous, rich and free
Singing and performing great which we all can see

Her beauty of nature's gift is notorious
Sensuous, sexy, and gorgeous
Performing with no rage, but still showing us
what she can do on stage

She made a great comeback in '84
From then 'til now her fans beg for more
The sweet voice of love songs that soothes you
And the rock'n'roll that moves you
Good luck towards her success
Now! Coming back strong with her first single "The Best"

Margaret J Ellis
SUMMER'S EVENING
The sun slowly fades away, night is just beginning.

Listen! summer's light breeze whispering through the trees.

In the meadow ponds the frog's symphony can be heard.

Scampering and fluttering here and there go the field mice and the birds.

Then all is still, Suddenly a screech is heard a hawk has made a kill.

Off in the distance the owl softly calls Who-o-o Who-o-o.

As I snuggle down for my night's rest I wonder who.

Then as I drift off, All is still.

Eugenia Edgin
THE WALL
A headstone it stood,
a grim reminder to all—that wall,
of the repression of hearts and souls;
of those who will never sing their songs or dance their dance—they're gone.
So many wanted to escape, they tried
to jump over to freedom's gate.
Some made it and found loved ones
on the other side,
Some did not—
their blood forever embedded in the stone,
never to be forgotten by those who cared—
whose life they shared.
And now the mighty wall is coming down;
they're hammering and chipping it away,
and from Heaven, joyful voices shout
—hurray!!!!!!!!!

Kimberly Lea Brown
DESTINY
Walking along the sands
searching for the hands
that lead us ever onward
through the life that we must live.

And just as we grow weary
our plight increasingly dreary
fate steps in and turns us around
and gives us a new direction to travel.

This is our destiny
and we must choose to trust in the hands
or to follow the sands
and never be bitter
for ours was the choice . . .
the dream . . .
the destiny . . .

Richard L Elsmore
CHILD
I am a child, my youth is hid
Neath ageing bone and skin
And layers of things said and done
Mask the child within.

I face the future,
I leave the past,
Step down paths of time,
But never through these living years
Can I leave the child behind.

He is ever with me, ever in me,
Hidden well from view,
Although you see this ageing man
I wish the child you knew!

When living days draw to their end,
Old bones will rest at peace,
But, old man will not his spirit send,
For it will be the child's release!

Suzanne Meile
THE GODDESS
The Goddess is so wondrous fair,
Sunlight streams within her hair.
Her cheeks are stained with rosy blush,
And her voice is gentle like the thrush.

Bold is she, and strong.
She will not stand for wrong.
Her message is of purest love,
For she has come to us from above.

Mary M Emly
TEARS ARE SHED
Tears are shed
to purify the mind
and release the soul.
Flow free—
for in my weakness
I have more strength
than many.

Kristy C Eichstaedt
THE PAST
Memories of a long forgotten past
are very good to have

The old events of childhood
which can make us cry or laugh

The important thing to always know
is cherish all you can

But when it starts to rule your life
it's time to take a stand

Always remember the good times
heed lessons from the bad

And reach an understanding
of the feelings that you've had

Learn to leave things in the past
and there they will always be

Because the past is just the past
and should be a memory.

Shirley Eger
WINTER WONDERLAND
Childhood in the country
a wonder to behold.
Rising in the early morn,
Is a blessing to unfold.

The windows they are frosted,
glisten in the cool crisp air.
Snowflakes softly floating down,
Sparkle everywhere.

As you look across the meadow
to the lofty mountains high,
Flashing like a precious jewel,
Of rainbow colors entwined.

And as the blizzard winds do blow
to chill across the lakes,
We feel the warmth from the fireside,
From the love in our precious home.

I wouldn't have traded this country
life
for the rush of the city streets,
As we lived in such a peaceful realm
With nature at our feet.

Lois Ewing

THE LORD'S LOVE

When we have the Lord we
have it all
For if we put our trust in him
we'll never fall
He comforts our hearts, souls,
and minds
And is there through our most
difficult times
We are so thankful for his mercy
and his love
There is none greater than our
Almighty God above
He sent his only son Jesus to die
on the cross
To save the souls of the ones
that are lost
Can you imagine the pain God
went through
To see his only Son shed his blood
for me and for you
And the pain Jesus felt as he hung
there that day
He did this so all could
be saved

Sherri Dawn Evans

THINKING OF YOU

At times I find myself
lost in a world of dreams,
holding onto the moments that we
shared.

At times I find myself
wishing for your closeness,
for only you can hold me
the way I like to be held.

The tenderness of your lips,
The softness of your voice
that echoes in my ears,
you are in my mind.

At times I find myself
caressing your body,
only to find it's just a dream.

At times I wish you knew,
how much I want you near me,
how much I really care.

Lisa Ezernack

LIVING AN ILLUSION

Shrick at acts defined in me.
And laugh at things inclined to be.
Believing souls will be set free,
Living an illusion!

Faithfulness without despair.
Laughter here and laughter there.
Willingness of all to share,
Living an illusion!

Contentment just a piece of cake.
Always give and never take.
Loving for each other's sake,
Living an illusion!

Nothing real and nothing free,
Locked up inside what used to be.
Pain outlasts infinity.
No longer an illusion!

Debbie Cox

INTENSE

Like the panther, sleek and smooth,
muscles ripple with every move.

Fear instilled as he stalks his prey,
marks the prowess of his play.

With the agility of the beast,
his prey captured for his feast.

But alas, it is the prey who is fed,
by the charm of the thoroughbred.

Michelle Crafa

MISTAKES

To my aunt Barbara.

You look so cold and sad.
Inside it makes me mad.
They told me there was some beer.
When I think about it, I start to tear.
I really thought your friends were
true.
I really thought they loved you.
Now you lay without the look of
stride
Because you thought it was "cool"
To "drink and drive."

Wilma R Cole

THE UNKNOWN

I am a traveler in this land
I haven't very long to stay
Then I too must be on my way.
I meant no harm—
I meant no harm—
Forgive me, if I have transgressed
On thee.
It is I who seek abode
Away from all my painful memories
I seek to enter
The Unknown.

Benjamin L Jones

Benjamin L Jones

YOUR OWN WILL

Look beyond our physical being
And touch me with thy soul
Join me in the light
Forever to have and hold.
I shall scream throughout the
universe
These words I know to be true
No man could love a woman,
As much as I love you
I listen through the silence.
And this is what I hear
Millions of voices inside of me
Calling for you my dear
Then something deep inside of me
Said to stay still
That you would only come to me
At your own will

Benjamin L Jones

GOOD MORNING

The morning embraced me with joy
and delight.
The morning missed me
And I missed the morning through
the night
Since the morning has been good
enough
To show itself to me
I shall treat this morning
By being the best I can be.
When evening hours arrive and night
intervenes
This morning will be counted
As the best ever seen
For those not satisfied from day's
beginning till its end.
Remember this could be your last
morning so treat it like a friend.
Please heed my warning
So be it rain, hail, or snow.
It's still a good morning
Now that you know what to do
I'll say good morning to all mornings
And you

Mark D Cyr

THE LOVE YOU SEEK

To the Love I found, at a time when I was not looking for love. Janice Pecoraro, the love I always want in my life.

The love you seek,
will one day cross your path
and you will know that it is right.

The love you seek,
will be kind to you.
That love will also be gentle and true,
and always understanding with you.

The love you seek,
will always be there for you.
When you are feeling sad and blue,
when you need someone to talk to.

The love you seek,
will be like you.
The love you seek,
will also be seeking you.

Robert S Cullison

MEDALS OF TIN

I gave the order to advance,
Yet I had not been born
With the power of the mighty lance,
The rider of death did I scorn.
Each day,
Between nightfall and the morning
dawn
In silence I lay—, in battle with the
Minds dark tangled form—seek the
warmth
And softness, of a long lost song—
Still embraced by Hell's mighty
storm.
In the battlefields they lay—
Nameless faces young and old,
Hero's lost!
I gave the command that day:
"Advance at any cost!"—I the lone
Surviving Soul—A child not yet a
man;
Yet was honored with a hero's brae.
In silence I cry, not believing in
heaven
Nor hell——
I lay in thoughts of things that were
And could've been—and die over
again.
I long to hear the tranquil sound
Of childhood's tinkling bell
And blind myself of medals of tin.
Could I but untangle the darkness
Of the mind—and these shadows
unwind—
I would leave the battlefield untorn,
And perhaps walk into time—
For then I would be born.

Robert S Cullison

TIME'S MELODY

Sweetheart, if life were to smile upon
me
one more time, and bring your love
Back for just a while—
I wouldn't hesitate to ask for your
Hand in mine—just as I did back
then.

Count all the stars up in the galaxy
And know again the many smiles you
brought to me
And the shattered hopes and broken
dreams
Your patience once helped mend
Gives me now the will to be

What a beautiful song we sang
together,
The music was all our own
The happiness we shared was meant
to be forever and ever—Without ever
shedding a tear—
Yet somewhere in time, we left
behind
The rhythm and tone we held so dear

Thoughts of you constantly knock
upon my mind
And remind me of the foolish things
That drew us apart
But I want you to know and hear
what I say
Wherever you are—Every hour of
every day—
All of you—from head to toe;
Always crosses my heart

Robert S Cullison

WHISPERS OF TOMORROW

I hear the whispers of tomorrow
And I see an empty eternity
What will I do with so much sorrow
If you walk away and set me free

I'm sad and filled with sorrow
And I can't stop the tears you see
For the whispers of tomorrow
Tell me that you're leaving me

Darling come and whisper that I'm
wrong
That you love me just as you did
yesterday
Tell me that our love is much too
strong
And that you'll never go away

Because I love you more than you
know
And shall until the day I die
So won't you come and tell me
Oh tell me . . . that the whispers of
Tomorrow, yes the whispers of
tomorrow
Are telling me a lie

Darling come and whisper that I'm
wrong
That you love me just as you did
yesterday
Tell me that our love is much too
strong
And that you'll never, never, never
go away

Robert S Cullison

NICKLE AND DIME DRIFTER

Nickle and dime drifter
Where have your fantasies gone

Could you but tear a leaf from
The silver—icon, You'd catch a glimpse
Of a cherished belief . . .
And indeed be a king
Nickle and dime drifter
With your pocket full of dreams
When you walked upon the waters
Of life's restless and tempestuous streams
Did you lay your head upon the rock
Where did you hide your masterpiece
A taste of the bittersweet
What valley holds the lease
When you walked with the green grass
underneath your feet . . .
Indeed you held love
Nickle and dime drifter
Reach and from your pocket
Pull a star
Think upon it as it flights away
Upon memories left ajar
Recall the dream—the paradise
A fantasy in disguise
Indeed there was a home

Robert S Cullison
WHERE ARE WE

He lays out his clothes before he goes to bed
Wakes up in the morning with nea'er a word said
His daddy lays on the couch
Not yet resurrected from the night before
And it's been months since
His Mamma set foot in his front door
He cooks his own breakfast—and
Off to school he goes
Nobody seems to give a damn
Or at least it never shows
In school he puts up with the ridicule
And all the scorn
And never complains that his hair is long
His shirt is tattered and his pants are torn
A lot of times I've seen the hurt in his eyes
And they get glassy as he reads through my lies
He tries not to show it, but I can see
That little boy needs his Mamma and Me

Connie L Avenarius
TRUE LOVE

On a dark, cloudless night, I peered into the sky when I saw a shimmer of light my heart could not deny.
As golden as my dreams,
our love seems to be one of a kind.
You have touched me in many ways, showing you care by always being there.
I want you to know
our love is going to grow.
We don't have to prove it to the world that this is meant to be, that's between you and me.
Love is cherishing the good times, forgetting the bad, fighting, but loving when we make each other mad.
Your thoughts and ideas I treasure as if they were mine.
Never hide anything from me, never keep it inside.
Don't hesitate to come to me. It's better to let your feelings show than try to hold them in.
To trust and understand someone is where things must begin.

Amy Elizabeth Atwood
MIRRORED EYES

A fool to their own disguise,
Neglecting what underneath lies,
Too late they gaze past green, blue haze,
Beyond the reflection of a pretty face,

Here mourning bells toll numbing my soul,
Dark clouds engulf it in pain,
Tormented by unforgiving rain,

In its well echoing raindrops fall,
A black circle draws near the top of the wall,
Closer, Closer it comes to spilling over,
Mounting eternity, crying on God's shoulder,

Slipping it falls into release,
Without feeling all pains cease on this side,
Steadily flowing into a lifeless tide,

Washed upon a deserted beach,
Helpless to reach out my hand,
Nothing to grasp but sand,

Death floats adrift inside,
Among all the tears I never cried,
Internal suicide.

Gilmore Andrews
EVERYTHING IS BY COMPARISON

When the days are long and the way seems dark
And we can't hear the sound of a blue bird or lark
Many the words in this verse brighten your day
And chase your worries and teardrops away.

We wouldn't enjoy the sunshine if we never had the rain.
We wouldn't appreciate good health if we never had a pain.
If we never shed a teardrop and always wore a smile
We'd all get tired of laughing after we had grinned awhile.

Everything is by comparison,
Both the bitter and the sweet.
And it takes a bit of both
To make our lives complete.

Keep your chin up
And your life bright.
And things are bound to turn out
Just right.

Rebecca Ostenberg
THINKING OF YOU

I think of you and I stare into space,
you're the only thought I can't erase,
my mind wanders all day through,
I keep finding the only thoughts I think are of you,
I never thought I could hold you,
or that you'd be mine,
to always want to be important to someone,
I never in a million years dreamt it would be you,
how I wish I could always see,
the warmth in your face, the smile in your eyes,
to think that all that love could be directed to me,
me and only me, a shock it will always be,
I will always love you there's no doubt in that,
although there is one thing lingering in my mind,
I always promise to be here as I hope you do too,
but promise me the reassurance I need,
that it will always be the two of us,
just you and me.

Bill Adams
CONFUSION

For my mother, who always said I could do it.

Look into the shadows
Do you see what I can see
No, I suppose you can't
For that image is meant for me

As you look all around
Do questions arise in your mind
Perhaps you have no doubts
Or maybe you are blind

Reality is a concept
That is very loosely used
Yet the way that I perceive it
I must say it's been abused

For what exactly is reality
Who are you to say
That it is the world we live in
Or a region clouded gray

How can anyone tell me this
When no one can feel what I feel
I wish I could decide
What is fantasy and what is real.

Daniel Andrade

Daniel Andrade
OLD AGE IS CREEPING UP ON ME

Old Age Is Creeping Up on Me
I'm not young like I used to be
I'm so tired of taking pills
All I have is doctor bills
Old Age Is Creeping Up On Me

Old Age Is Creeping Up On Me
Each day brings some new misery
My blood pressure's up a shade
And I wear a hearing aid
Old Age Is Creeping Up On Me

Old Age Is Creeping Up On Me
Without my glasses I can't see
I now have a double chin
Where my neck has always been
Old Age Is Creeping Up On Me

Old Age Is Creeping Up On Me
My health ain't what it used to be
There are wrinkles on my face
My false teeth won't stay in place
Old Age Is Creeping Up On Me

Old Age Is Creeping Up On Me
My aching back's a mystery
I'm run down and always ill
Might as well make out my will
Old Age Is Creeping Up On Me

Old Age Is Creeping Up On Me
Old father time won't let me be
All my hair is turning gray
And I'm aging day by day
Old Age Is Creeping Up On Me

Peggy Clegg
SOMETIMES

Sometimes I feel so alone and down that there's nothing in this world I can do right. Then there's times I feel so mad at everybody that I just want to scream. But all those feelings are soon gone, when he comes in the room with his smiling face and says sorry mommy when he didn't do anything wrong, or I LOVE you. Then I feel like I can do anything and I'm not alone. Then I thank God for giving me this little boy to share in my life. THANKS GOD!

Bernice Rush Courtney
A POSITIVE ATTITUDE

Dedicated to my first and only spouse for two decades and a half, Evang. Frank Courtney.

When things are not going so well.
Why on your adverse situation must you dwell?
What you need is a mind elevation.
In this situation God needs a standing ovation.
You must acknowledge that all is well with thee.
Praise God until your situation reaches that 180 degree.
You must keep a positive attitude.
Or you will become quite confused.
Keep telling yourself that all is well.
Tell yourself that everything is going to be swell.
There is much power in your flow of words.
A positive attitude is waiting by God to be heard.
The enemy feasts on your negative statements.
Remember that God loves your sincere compliments.
Always confess that all is well with thee.
Then watch your troubles begin to flee.
A negative statement soothes the enemy's ear.
Why praise him when it is God you must fear.
Always confess that all is well with thee.
Remember God shall establish whatever you decree.

Shelene Thompson Carlson
WHAT IS A ROSE?

This poem is dedicated to my loving parents, Walter I. and Bessie Thompson, who loved roses as I do.

A rose is a flower of beauty rare
With fragrance borne on petals fair;
Kissed by the dew, caressed by the bee
A rose is a bit of mystery.
Blossom and barb on its stem are borne
Even the Peace rose has its thorn.

A rose is a part of God's creation—
The choice of flowers, in all the nation.
Both Prince and Pauper in awe do see
The rose God designed for you and me.
A rose bouquet expresses love
From a heart as gentle as a dove.
To walk in the garden and behold a rose
And believe in God, then anyone knows
A rose is a rose, is a rose.

Karen Bourget
THE GREATEST STRENGTH
We go each day with worries that sometimes keep us from not moving on,
We go each day with fears that sometimes bring tears to our eyes,
And we go each day with troubles that sometimes makes us not want to go that extra step.
But in between all this we also have laughter; it makes us happy inside.
We have children, who with their innocence, bring joy to our lives,
We have love to make us feel good inside and to feel wanted when we get lost in this troubled world of ours.
But most all, we have God who gives us the greatest strength of all.

Nancy Lee Gassin
YOUR VOICE IS BUT A SHADOW INSIDE MY HEART
Your voice is but a shadow inside my heart
Piercing deep, far beyond where my eyes can feel
Electrifying shivers, a light touch

A lethal ray shatters the unfortunate
falling within the path,
struggling to escape, to nothing,
but a hazy horizon.

The blur soothes, a frozen moment,
until unrelenting light returns,
overpowering
the inner heat
transforming warmth
into scorching ice.

Mistaken fields of roses
vanishing—reappearing—
dandelions.

Grasping for a faded image
turned gray
one streak of color sparkles
but distance inhibits
—gone.

My heart
is but a shadow
inside.

Glenn Egill Hordal
WOW! WOMEN OF WORDS
Words would only mirror it,
How her hair is adverbial of her spirit.
Her thighs belong in the Louvre.
Her eyes punctuate a body move.
Underneath, she wears lace
With gobbledygook upon her face.

Words can be delusive.
Women may be Delilah's sieve.
Words penned to prose can be piercing swords.
Women bumped into bed may be binding cords

A verb between her teeth
To slay you, her heart throbs underneath.
Adjectives sung around thy neck from her palm.
What tongue does beck her heavenly psalm?

Breasts without abbreviation
Send descriptive words to poetic elevation.
Love is personified by her lips that accentuate,
Onomatopoetic hips that make exclamation points alliterate.

Her silhouette is a synonym of everlasting youth's key.
Her visage profile is the embodiment of haunting beauty.

Glenn Egill Hordal
POETRY PRAYER
Most High God who dwells in highest heaven above.
Hallowed is thy name showering abundant love.
To worthy men this day, their daily bread appoint.
Upon Christian souls thy Holy Spirit anoint.
At the Messiah's return, the daughter of Jerusalem gives birth.
Thy will be done, as in heaven, so in Christ's kingdom on earth.
As men and women forgive their debtors, forgive their sins.
For Christ's Church is gathered from all families and kins.
True Christian, from temptation and ungodly sorrow keep.
Diligently deliver saints from evil and Sheol's dark sleep.
Unto Christ give David's throne, with glory and dominion without end.
Create a new heaven and earth, and from heaven a new Jerusalem send.

Leona R Sansom
ON BEING DIFFERENT
I dream a future when all encompassing and nurturing love will encircle the earth like a multi-hued rainbow, altering the public mind set—where conformity is the model—and make it popular to be dissimilar. Then I can fling my arms full length and dance to my own true rhythm on the edge of a floating cloud—making a new kind of music the world has never heard—and need not ever think of being different.

Ann Mary Jos (Age 15)
ASSUREDNESS OF LIFE

For the Glory of God and to My Family.

Growing up is hard enough,
Without the agonies and strife
Of what this world has to offer
To every human life.

With all the afflictions, adversities,
And grief that we all face,
It never seems to matter
The color, creed, or race.

I lie awake in bed sometimes
Just trying to figure out,
What my purpose is here on earth
And what life is all about.

With no one there to answer me,
No one to give a reply,
Ultimately I then realized
I had only me, myself, and I.

So we live our lives as best we can,
In this frantic world each day;
And try to avoid those people
Who just might lead you astray.

Diane Smith
MY DAUGHTER
I sat and watched my daughter
Doing homework just last night.
She had the radio on loud,
And her jeans were way too tight.
Her hair was hanging straight and long,
And her math answers were all wrong.
Sitting and watching her that way
brought to my mind another day.
A long time ago: just yesterday it seems,
It was me sitting there
Full of hopes and dreams.
Generation gap, there may be;
But that girl sitting there is me.
And just like me, someday she'll see
The long-haired girl of used to be.

Mildred Dhondt

Mildred Dhondt
SCHOOL OF AFFLICTION

To my children, Marvin Brown, Eleanor Pandil, Evelyn Anway and Kenneth Brown and their children.

For the believer in Christ,
The most valuable lessons
Are learned in a place
Called, "The School of Affliction."

Instruction and training through
Suffering, are experiences
In which we ought to profit,
Unpleasant though they may be.

Learning the ability to comfort,
Developing a special sensitivity
Of sympathy and encouragement,
While drawing us closer to God.

Suffering teaches us more
About trust, love, and obedience.
Also new ways in which God
Keeps His promises to us.

Never rebel against our Lord.
Let us be open to what he teaches,
Thanking Him for the privilege,
Of being one of the students He reaches.

Showing gratitude and praise,
For every test and trial we meet,
Gives us God's benediction,
In this "School of Affliction."

Mildred Dhondt
BIRTHDAY THOUGHT
A birthday is the perfect time,
For turning thoughts to those
Who've always meant the most to us,
As each day comes and goes.

Our thoughts and memory of days past
Stay with us throughout each season.
So sending cards and words of cheer
Is usually the reason.

Mildred Dhondt
MY THOUGHTS OF LIFE
Rejoice in the Lord always,
For foolish thoughts come our way.
A crisis may come into our lives
Unexpected, swift, and sure.
Causing a great deal of strife
That trust and belief will cure.

Friends may gather 'round
With good intentions which profound
The sum total of our thoughts.
These can flash into being so quickly
Revealing His presence in our lives
That fill our hearts and souls.

For each thought will sink into the soul,
Contributing to the pillars of Character
Which you see as you and me,
As we go on our way from day to day.

Gloria Norvell
A DREAM SO SWEET
Last night when I fell asleep
Last night I had a dream so sweet

I dreamed I came where you are
I dreamed I floated above a star

I saw a halo around your head
I heard things that you said
I saw you at the Master's feet
Then I heard music sweet

Upon a harp you did play
I could hear it plain as day
From the stream of life
Flowed a current strong
The heavenly sky
Was filled with song

By the tree of life you did stand
I saw you when you shook
Our Master's hand
Joy my heart did fill
When I saw you on a
Lovely wooded hill
You picked flowers oh so sweet
And knelt at the Master's feet
Then I awoke and I knew
I did not have to worry about you

This dream gave me so much hope
No longer in darkness will I grope
I will stay busy the way you are
Till I too can live beyond a star

Doris Lee Johnson
MOMENTS!
Moments, oh how they are
sometimes looked forward to with
great anticipation.
With the anticipation of a child
looking forward to a happy Christmas
morning.
Or they can be as dreaded as the
evidence of an upcoming storm.
How quickly they come and flee!
Like the twinkling of the eye or a
heartbeat.
Moments here at last!
They all have their place in time.
Sometimes filled with matured
unpleasantness and pain.
And sometimes filled with priceless
innocence wonder, magic and
awe.
Moments, now that you've come and
gone—now what?
The bad ones try to remember with
less bitterness and pain.
Though never to be recaptured, the
good ones to forever cherish and
treasure.
Moments however pleasant and
memorable never to just live for.
Moments!

Pat Johnson
BEGINNING

To Russ, who believed in me 28 years ago, and believes in me now.

I feel so lucky since we met
At a time when I needed you
You came to me with your kind heart
And with honesty through and
through

You're patient and understanding
And you say the things to me
That keep me going every day
And help me to feel free

Please give our relationship a chance
To flourish and grow strong
And you'll soon see me blossom
With a love that can't go wrong!

Dawn Case
ME
If ever you wander alone
Down a path that is dark and cold
Just reach out and know my hand
Is there for you to always hold

Or if you are ever feeling
Scared and a little shy
Never forget these words
My shoulder you may cry

Or maybe you have a fear
And it is something you wish to share
Do not ever shut it up inside
Because me, I will always care

Or maybe just a person
Someone to hold you, oh so tight
To make you feel so warm
So late into the night

Or maybe just a friend
Someone who will always be around
To this there is a person
To this you have so found

But if ever a person
Like this you shall see
Never forget this person
Is someone I will call "ME"

Jeanne M Jacquet
LET ME BE
Let me be . . . .
I don't want to go on . . .
Each day seems like the last,
No new thing ever happens.
Why can't people see how I feel?
Why can't I tell them?
My friends see a cheerful, happy,
healthy person.
I don't feel that way.

Sometimes I just want to scream it
out loud . . . .
I HATE what I am doing!
The only thing is,
I don't know what I want to do,
or be.
Someday, maybe, I will know.
For now, just . . .
Let me be!

W R Buck
MY MOM

To My Mom, Julia Louida Buck Deceased Oct. 1988.

She left the land of milk and honey
For a pioneer frontier land.
Why would she leave such beauty?
Just because she loved her man.
They had five children and a wagon.
Two rode the horse following close
behind.
A dog stood guard and went with
them.
Along the way folks were so kind.

She lost her oldest son in the Army.
As each boy served it broke her heart.
Her daughters brave stood close
beside her.
They were the flowers of her heart.
Thru the years had many sorrows.
Her heart was big and oh so kind.
No greater MOM walked on this
earth.
I'm so proud of this MOM of mine.

A trusting Dad, a loving Mother,
What more could this world provide.
Although Dad died shortly after,
Our Mother raised us with pride.
Soon she'll join the Heavenly chorus,
Her trials and troubles will be o'er.
With Dad she'll stand with arms wide
open
Singing welcome children, Welcome
Home.

Marilyn E Wheeless
COLD
You call me cold, and yet
You never stop to think
Why that might be.

You tell me that I've changed,
I'm not the person you once loved.
And yet, you cannot see

That I remain the same,
Warm, and with a loving heart.
What you say isn't true.

My coldness, as you call it,
Is simply a reflection
Of what I see in you.

Virginia M White
A VIGILANT WATCH
Whilst ye were asleep;
A quiet watch, over ye I didst keep.
Love in mine heart, didst for ye
during this restful time, yearn;
Whilst mine eye caught the
movement of thy body's every
restless turn.
Mine eyes followed the rise of thy
chest;
Each breathing movement, didst I
watch as thee lay in bed, in a sleepful
rest.
So calm, ye look;
As though ye were lying beside a
still brook.
So content with thy every thought;
Love on thy face is in an instant,
fleetingly, caught.
Mine heart leaps and bounds;
Though it be to only thy sleeping
sounds.
Ye have more than a guardian angel
to look over thee;
Besides the angel, and GOD
above, ye also have me.

Tammy Sheppard
FRIENDS ARE FOR . . .

Dedicated to the loving memories of Britt, Casey & Jennifer.

It is so hard to know
The way you feel inside.
There are so many thoughts
And feelings that you hide.
I wish you would open up
And talk to me.
Because I will be there,
No matter what the problem may be.
I am your friend,
And that is what friends are for.
To help you out,
When you cannot deal with your
problems anymore.
Friends are for good times.
Friends are for bad times.
Friends are to help you out of
Problems of many kinds.
So if you have a problem,
And you do not know what to do.
Call me up,
Because I will be there for you.

Lisa C Smith

Lisa C Smith
REASON

To Steven, fellow artist and forever friend . . . Thanks for the insight!

Brackish waters fall
Down slopes of flesh,
Stopping short at journey's end.

Time passes . . .
Quickly and quietly fades a sunset,
Languishing once more into the
horizon.

Tears seem senseless,
Ever to the sensible . . .
To those incapable of response.
Questioning the purpose
Behind such emotion,
An answer fell from infinity:

Children weep, and angels brood—
Men know not to share.
A wise one said,
"The secret stands—
Not to <u>cry</u> . . .
To care."

Lisa C Smith
LOVE

To Dan . . . always in my thoughts and dreams!

Two hearts
Unite in rhythm,
Stirring Heaven's expanse
With music.

God listens . . .

Symphonies welcome the coming
together
Of body, mind, and spirit,
As self is absorbed
In another existence.

What boundaries are there to love?
None which the soul cannot conquer!

Mortal man sees as much of God
As love's immortal spirit
Allows him to share
With his second self.

Lisa C Smith
REDEMPTION

To God, my first love—With a thankful heart in praise and honour of Your unending mercy and grace!

Thorns . . . spiked rubble . . .
Crowning decor fit for a king,
Designed only for Jesus—
"The King of the Jews."
Hail Him!
Carefully weaved bramble . . .
Characteristic complexity of life—
Entwining adversity of souls, who
know not what they do.
Oozing red mockery spilled on
Golgotha's hill—
Spilled only by Jesus,
The convicted innocent, the accused.
Hail Him!
My God, my God, why was He
forsaken?
For gamblers, blasphemers, thieves?
No!
For <u>all</u> who call upon His name!
The rocks cried out; the earth did
quake . . .
Rent in twain, the temple veil,
To this our Jesus, the Jewish king—
The coming king of the world . . .
All hail!

Lisa C Smith
IT'S HOW YOU PLAY THE GAME

To all artists striving to make a difference through expression . . . Never stop!

I watch the game from behind the
lines.
Teary-eyed, I listen to the "super
powers" plot strategy.
Soldiers wander the globe like pawns
traveling a chess board.
Which block will be the next
occupied?
Which man the next conquered?
Which country the next to fall?
I fear the match, yet I fear the end.

There will be no congratulatory shaking of hands—
Only a sting in the heart of brother pitted against brother . . .
Only a defiant distaste for the concept of war.
Perhaps such defiance will be the silver lining
To this great cloud of manipulation.
As for now, the game continues . . .
Big Brother is watching.
Armageddon awaits.

Frieda Cleveland

ASPIRATIONS

A poet I've always wanted to be,
To be very famous and go down in history,
To be read by people far and wide,
And loved by some, would give me great pride.
I would write of high mountains with deep valleys below,
And the moon as it shines on the new fallen snow.
Of the birds flying south shaped like a vee,
And the tiny nest in the big oak tree.
Of the mother robin scolding her young,
For some transgression he must have done.
i would write of the ocean swelling with pride,
As it rolls in on the evening tide.
Of the spring flowers bursting into bloom,
And the frost that nipped them because they bloom too soon.
But who would listen to a mother and wife,
Who hasn't done very much with her life.
Just the everyday things that all mothers do,
This couldn't be interesting to even a few.
Of all these things I would know and would tell,
If I were a poet with words to sell.

Michael Jarnagin

BEST UNKNOWN

To that which is me, my family.

In moments quiet . . . though noise surrounds.
My mind seeks deep that elusive truth:
These mass of friends and foe alike join in confused array . . . as man . . . mankind?

Then why? Why me . . .

till moments quiet fall fast away . . .
Give way to noise surround.

Peaceful, quiet noise.

Ann Bradstreet Brown

HAPPY

Are you really happy?

If Life is the same for you every day, why not Change it? Do just one thing differently!

Change your daily routine! When you wake up, get ready to face the day in a different order. Eat breakfast, then take a shower . . . walk to work instead of taking the Subway . . . eat an apple in the park for lunch . . . say "Hi" to someone at the office you've not spoken to before . . . It will brighten your day, and theirs, and maybe you'll make a new friend. New friends will make you Happy!

Happiness is all relative to how you feel about yourself, "What am I doing? Who am I?" Be receptive to change for change promotes growth and growth promotes knowledge and knowledge promotes awareness and awareness can lead you on the path of light towards a happier day.

Life will not always be "rosy" but what you do with it can give you a better chance to capture the roses. Don't only stop to smell them, touch them, eat them, drink them and encapsulate yourself in them. Do not wait . . . be not afraid. Should you really care what anyone thinks? Do for yourself and be Happy!

Happiness is a challenge . . . challenge yourself to that greater goal. Be mindful that all cannot be accomplished at once . . . goals that you set must be conquered one at a time. Enjoy each day because it will never be here again . . . remember the past, don't live in it . . . look to the future . . . enjoy the present . . . smile . . . ALL, will make your LIFE . . . Happy!

Tammy Metzler

MY LIFE IS CONTAINED

For Aksa and Andy—they know why, and for Mack—for everything.

My life is contained
Among these pages
My heart and my soul
Through all ages

My soul is bared
For you to see
Consider it a gift
For you from me

Walk gently through
My thoughts and dreams
For in them you'll find
I'm not who I seem

I'm opening my heart
For you to see
Please keep in mind
It's not easy for me

You've given me time
You've shown you care
Now is the time
For me to share . . .

Darlene M Paige

TO MY MOTHER

To My Mother Kiki And Daughters Jolene and Anna.

God gave me a wonderful mother,
A mother who never grows old,
He gave her a smile of sunshine,
And molded her heart into gold,
He made her so like an angel,
As anyone ever could be.
God made a wonderful mother,
And then gave her to me.

Jennifer A Coleman

OF ALL IN THIS WORLD

Of all in this world
it is you I cherish.
My love is undying,
never to perish.
You mean more to me,
than heaven above.
I offer to you,
an unselfish love.
My greatest desire
is holding you near,
so tender and warm
in my heart, so dear,
A love of great value,
so highly esteemed,
to reach way beyond,
the happiest dream.
A love given freely
a love that is true
my love and my soul
I only give to you.

Ellen Cook

YOU HAVE GONE

I felt the tears fall to the floor
as I watched you walk out the door—

Out of my life you have gone
you say it's time to move on—

What have you left me but fear
as I feel down my cheek another tear—

Happy was I and so much in love
I really felt you were sent from above—

I never thought it would end
then one day you said good bye my friend—

You said you loved me with a kiss
even though I feel a bliss—

I can't help but love you now
and pray that God will protect you somehow—

Must I wait for my life to end, to be free
will memories of you forever haunt me—

Becky L Beltz

TWENTY-ONE LINES

A poem of twenty-one lines or less
Is what from us you request
I find myself in quite a mess
Therefore I feel the need to protest

The time it's taken to put down
On paper what lives in each poet's mind
As we've fought through every verb and noun
Searching for words we're unable to find

When we have a thought inside
We don't think of how long it will be
To shorten our poems is to commit suicide
To tell our stories we must be able to remain free

We must be content with why we write
It's a challenge and passion as well
Working at it till all hours of the night
To bring out our best—to make us excel

Though we may never be heard
Because we couldn't make the limit
We'll continue to write each word
For ourselves and others as we see fit

Twenty-one lines, no more—no less.

Edgar J Willmott

WHY MOTHERS CRY

Oh! Look at those fat little legs
Strong arms, bright shining eyes,
Many they will charm,
See how hard the suckling goes
When feeding at my breast?
This end result has me on a crest.

Admiration in her eyes, she teaches, protects and loves
Dreading, yet not showing,
When her children will leave her side.
Mothers have tender spots in their heart
For the children that by them are got,
But children, tho, have a habit when grown
To forget what their mothers went through.

Neglect, insensitivity
Never showing for her they care,
Sends a message loud and clear,
Stand back Ma, you don't fit in here.
This causes mothers to sit and cry
Emotions they cannot hide.

Cynthia Roberts

Cynthia Roberts

GOD IS STILL THERE

To Kathy—After the death of her beloved husband.

God grant you strength in your sorrow
to believe that His will has been done,
though it's hard to face each tomorrow
with the rising and setting sun.
God's grace is sufficient to help you through the pain and heartache you bear
lean on Him and trust Him too,
and the load you carry He will share.

Don't blame God for happiness that's ended,
try to make His will as your own
and know—God has never left his children hopeless
and He will never leave you alone.

Laura Lynn Moriconi
THE TRUE MEANING OF CHRISTMAS

I dedicate this to all who will take the time to read this poem. I thank my God for the opportunity that He used me as a vessel for His words to be printed here. My prayer is for all who read it, that you will be blessed. Thank you Father—Bless them all.

Christmas time may as well start in June
People want to jump the gun before shopping "time" has even begun
All the stores get decorated but not one sign of you
Oh sure, we see Santa and his sleigh
But don't people realize you were born on this day!
Help me never to get caught up in the rush but to always see the real meaning in my heart;
And never let my family believe in some fairy tale but only Jesus from the start
The True meaning of Christmas is your son
because "Jesus is the Reason for the Season" that soon will be done
Then Santa Claus is packed away waiting for the next year when again He'll arrive
But the feeling, we, as Christians, share is the true meaning we're alive
It should not be packed away with all the decorations and forgotten for 12 months
But live within us day to day, month to month.
Please remember Jesus as a babe in Bethlehem
And forget about old St. Nick and hanging stockings in the den
Remember why we celebrate and thank Him before you lie
And when you wake, remember the baby who never would cry
I thank the Lord for God's resurrected son
And for the rebirth of my soul that will go on living when the world's done
Just remember Jesus the "Christ" in Christmas this year
And wouldn't it be great if you could accept Him and never fear!

Sandra J McAmis
RUMORS OF JESUS

Dedicated to the memory of my Grandmother, Ora Malone. She was and always will be my source of inspiration.

I've heard that His hands are calloused
from years of hard work as a carpenter.
And yet, they are soft and gentle
as a mother with her newborn.

I've been told that His eyes are filled
with a deep sadness as He searches for the goodness of mankind.
And yet, they are overflowing with hope, for He knows
that He will find it.

They tell me that His voice is liken
unto thunder, that His words are powerful but full of love and peace.

I've heard that the warmth of His
smile would make the sun hide in shame, and
that His tears and pain are felt by
the angels in Heaven.
All of these things I've heard, not seen.
And yet, I know within my own heart
and soul that they are true.

Michelle Rogers
WHO'S ON THIRD?

To Nana: my heart, guiding light, best friend, and mother, I love you very much. Without you, I would be lost. You are a genuine jewel that will never be duplicated. May God bless you today, tomorrow, & forever.

You live on the East Side,

While my part of town is known
as the wild side

You dine at Four Seasons,
Mortimer's, and Tavern on the Green

My spots are McDonald's, chinese
restaurants, and hero spots where
no white wine is mine

Lovely marble floors, paintings, and gold faucets and candelabra adorn your homes

Cockroaches, heatless nights, and
no hot water are a part of my dome

Your philosophy is divide and conquer,

While mine is to insure
that we remain

Are you a liberal or a republican?

All I know is the budget
cuts are killing us!!

You expect doors to be held open for you, everyone to move out of your way, and not dare talk back to you

We expect not to be judged by the
color of our skin, not to have our
clothes, jewelry, and appearances
judged by you, and to be treated
kinder and gentler by you

Trump Tower, Trump Plaza, and
Trump Parc mean money to you

Welfare, minimum wage, and a
decent job mean money to us

If you're not satisfied, you move on

If we're not satisfied,
we must keep on movin'

So, who's on first and
Who's on third?

R Walker Berry
WALTZ OF THE DAMNED

To Melissa Glover. Whose faith and support in me overshadowed my own.

The dead poet sits in a silent room,
Barrel of the revolver still warm,
A shattered man buried underneath dreams,
In images he no longer made real.

Weeping, tears from those left behind,
His heart no longer beating, but bleeding,
The sins of his life, the terror of failure,
The merciful darkness that now surrounds him,
A simple boy grown to man complex,
The clicking gears of his mind, his answers,
The stories told in verse of man and his worth,
An unbiased view of man at his worst.

The black abyss in which he slept,
The white light which grew darker in sadness,
A weight of mankind that never slackened,
Could his just reward be but death?

Yet inside there lived a man, sensitive to pain,
Though to others he claimed indifference,
Left scarred with the mark of the human race,
The ailment which bred his painful insanity.

Mildred E Benton
MY NEW HOBBY

I have a new hobby
I want you to know.
It's cracking the faces
Of the high and the low.

How do I do it?
Just watch me and see.
Here comes someone
And she's looking at me.

Her face is so careworn,
Weary and sad.
Her lips droop down,
My,—she looks bad.

But I greet her and smile,
And she smiles right back.
There! Did you see
How I made her face crack??

Mildred E Benton
THAT OLD HOUSE ON THE HILL

Dedicated to the brothers and sisters who helped bring up the "baby."

There is an old house that stands on a hill.
Its rooms are ice cold and silent—and still.
No longer the patter of baby feet on the floor;
No longer the chatter of teenagers and more.

Here babies were born—eight and one more.
Here Dad and Mom sang though they'd problems galore.
Twenty years together was all they had.
Dad died in his prime; all were made sad.

The neighbors and townsmen pitched in with a will
And helped the poor widow and her brood on that hill.
"Let's bring up the baby," was the rallying cry.
Mom, brothers, and sisters made a good try.

With family all raised, Mom then lived alone,
Read her Bible and prayed; Heaven was her true Home.
She'd tell you to go There, you must have one Friend;
He, Himself, paid the way so on Him to depend.
Mom went There last year in a wild, wintry storm.
We shed many a tear, but her suffering was gone.
And so, though for 58 years that old house on the hill
Heard much laughter and tears, it's silent now—and so still.

Lois Bylewski
WHAT IN THE WORLD?

What kind of world would you make,
If you were God, for goodness sake?
I've thought it over once or twice.
There were some things that would be nice.
Can't list them all, but here's a few.
All things would always be brand new.
And nothing new would ever break.
You'd never get a belly ache.
Dirt would always know its place,
Not cling to your hands and face.
Dishes would wash themselves of course.
And I'd invent a hayless horse.
Or better yet, a gasless car.
Now there's one thing that would go far.
Why not let money grow on trees?
You'd never mind your neighbor's leaves.
A body that would not grow fat,
No matter how much you ate or sat.
Taxes of course, would have to go!
Weeds would just refuse to grow.
Mosquitoes without stingers please.
The same applies to bugs and bees.
No more colds or allergies;
Think of that, You'd never sneeze.
I'd not allow a war to be.
No one would have an enemy.
You think that this might be too bland?
Or would it be the promised land?

Dwight Buzick
POETIC ALPHABETICS

Creative Poetics
Altruistic Blessings
Cruise Down
Earthward From
God's Heavens, Increasing Our
Joys, Kindnesses, Love,—
Mystifying Nobly in an
Orthodox Peaceful Quietude
and Reviving Such Truly
Unblemished Virtues
With Xylophonic,
Youthful Zest!

Lisa Babb Byars
THE COMMITMENT

The diamond on my finger is for all
the world to see
that I belong to you and
you belong to me.

The commitment we have made will
never be broken.
There will never be "I love you's"
that go unspoken.

We are one, you and I, never will we
part;
and, if I give you mine,
will you give me your heart?

You've become a part of my very
soul.
In my mind and in my heart;
you've made me whole.

I only hope you love me
the same as I do you;
and that you care as much, too.

And I hope that you know
no matter what you do
Always I'll be there for you.

Edna Brown Smith

Edna Brown Smith
REVELATION

To: Bernard Mark, my love, my best friend & Inspiration.

This world is disturbed and crazy,
The men are weak and lazy.

People are hurting one another,
Sisters are destroying their brothers.

Mothers have no love for their babies;
I hear there are no more ladies.

The newspapers are full of crime,
Oh Gosh! That's a relative of mine.

You don't know who to trust,
Relationships are based on lust.

And for the love of sex and monies,
Spouses are murdering their honies.

What happened to our holy preachers,
And our dedicated school teachers?

They taught us all the Golden Rules,
And now they too have become fools.

Fraud using the Grace of God,
The children abused, not sparing the rod.

The strange changes in the seasons,
All the excuses and the reasons.

Kimberly A Vigue
YOUR EYES

A look, a glance
a smile by chance
Your stare runs deep
a memory to keep

Things to see
both good and bad
Times to share
both happy and sad

A look of concern
so genuine and true
I see all of those qualities
and I see them in you,

I see your eyes,
so open to see
all of life's pleasures
and to share them with me.

Valerie Walker
A CHILD-LIKE FAITH

I see a child off in the distance
playing in the grass and chasing butterflies
caught in her child-like wonder of a world made by You
I see the child-like faith in a God full of rainbows
and ducks in a pond and dew on the morning grass . . .

I see the same child
Closer but yet so far away
Only older now
And more aware of the world that used to hold only rainbows
A world that now holds only tears
And she allows the tears to fill her world and drown out
All of the love of God that had never left her . . .

I watch that child become a woman
And seeing that this person is not so far away
I ask myself who this person could be
And as she turns around . . .
I see that the child is me . . .

And as I remember when the world was seen
In the eyes of a child as one big rainbow
And the only tears shed were over scraped knees
I pray for answers
"What happened to the child-like faith that I once knew?"
And a voice replied:
"Whosoever shall humble himself as this little child
Shall enter the Kingdom of Heaven."

Donna L Russell
A TOUCH

I have been doing a lot of thinking
Sometimes I know—I think too much
Too much about everything
Sometimes all I need is a touch

A little touch of kindness
A little touch of care
A true touch of love
I can't find anywhere

I am forever reaching
Reaching for someone to care
I know I think too much about it
And I'll find it somewhere

Sometime, somewhere I'm sure I'll find
That little touch—that touch so kind
For I keep thinking and I'm sure I'll find
That meaningful touch
That touch "LOVE" that someday will be mine

Doris Taury
WEDDING DAY ADVICE—
to the Groom

Here's some advice for your wedding day
When your new life begins
Keep your insurance payments up—
In a year there may be twins!

Just think—after saying those two magic words
You'll be a big operator
The washer, the vacuum, and what's more
You can even mash the "potaters."

When you come down from that rosy cloud 9,
The challenge of living begins
That's when fast footwork really pays off
Dodging dishes and rolling pins.

When big decisions must be made
We know you'll be head of the house
When all's said and done you'll do just what she wants
After all—you're a man—not a mouse.

It's all in fun, and when it is done,
And you are "man and wife"
You are wished nothing but the best
Throughout your married life!

Annette Maureen Brady
THE UNFORGETTABLE ONE

The times we played,
The times we talked,
The times we shared,
The times we cared,
The unforgettable one.

The times I needed a
Shoulder to cry on,
The times I needed a
Shoulder to lean on,
The unforgettable one.

The friendship we had,
I'll never forget.
The friendship we had,
Almost impossible to get.

Now that I moved,
Doesn't mean I don't care.
I want you to know,
I'll always be there!
Our friendship,
The unforgettable one.

Sabrina Hammel
THE MOVEMENTS OF TIME

To my husband Roger and my children R. J., Shawna, and Morgan.

The wonders of time, elusive to the touch.
Miracles of creation, moving seemingly slow.
Yet to the living, time is our enemy.
Running faster still, we can't keep it.
We must lose it.
Moving over for another generation to use the time,
as the sun reaches a new glow.
Bringing yet, another day.
The time moves ever forward.

Doris J Hocott
THE TRAIN

Dedicated to my father and mother in Heaven, Charles J. Johnson and Alice K. Johnson.

Clickity clack, clickity clack,
Went the railroad track,
Beautiful farms rushing bye,
And cumulus clouds in the sky.
The porter announces dinner
in the diner car,
Only three coaches ahead, it's not very far!
Hoot hoot went the whistle, a crossing in
sight—Pull on the brakes, with all your
might, Clickity clack, clickity clack,
Next summer I'll be back.

Lisa Becker
DEAR LORD

In Loving Memory of Grandma.

Dear Lord my thoughts turn to you today,
and I hope you're thinking of me.
If those who haven't met you Dear Lord,
I wish they'd wait and see
sometimes a day will come and go
seems I've nothing good to show.
Then if I quietly close the door
and place my knee upon the floor.
A still small voice from way out there says—
Quiet my child now whisper your prayer.

Michelle Hughes
TRUE FRIENDS

Feelings are lost and memories last, But friends are forever. To all my friends.

A friend that's there for you
Is a friend that is true
One that's there when you're happy
And there when you're not
Someone who has listened
And someone who has taught.

I learn from you my friend
I know you'll be there 'til the end
I just hope that everyone has a friend that's true
Like the friend I have in you.

Janet F Cyr
IN MEMORY

Dedicated to family and friends of Armand and Evelyn Cyr.

As a young child,
I feared the day,
When my Mom and Dad,
would pass away.

My heart, I felt would
break just then
I'd cry myself to sleep.

I'm older now and thank the Lord,
for allowing them to stay.
I had them with me for a time,
But now they're gone away

I go to sleep at night, my fears
have come to pass,
Remembering the moments I
shared with them, their last.

Though time has made the years
go by, I'm still that frightened
child,
Never wanting them to leave me,
but stay with me awhile.

I close my eyes the tears still fall,
my heart it breaks in two.

MOM, DAD, ?

S Elizabeth Gorley
I YEARN TO KNOW

Dedicated to Jane J. Hoyt, Oklahoma City, OK, in appreciation for her beautiful, dedicated photography of Nature Studies for Move Makers Org.

I yearn to know the WHY
of night, of morn, I yearn
To know the WHY Of dusk,
of setting sun

How shadows lengthen, WHEN
Night shades fall.
WHYs are very important
For WHENs and HOWs an all—
Ethereal scopes in space
Scenes turn—I can't explain—
The WHYs—I yearn in vain.
Secret Earth, how do you know
the time to glean, the time to sow?
The time to change color
of the roadside weed?
When the Luna Moth must breed?
—then die?
—WHY?
Wonderment—puzzling—despair—
O, for a place for retrospection
With God somewhere.

Nadene R Crow
BETRAYED

To my ex-husband and my best friend; without whose "loyalty" this poem would never have been written.

Oh, wasted youth and shattered dreams.
Love is blind? Ah, bitter truth.
Faith and trust are tools of traitors;
I the fool of fools.

A loyal friend she claimed to be—
Lips that lie and cheat and steal.
Temptress deeds, a throaty laugh, and
Eyes that promise more.

Their moments shared seared in my head;
Pain and torment never cease.
Hands caress and lips that hunger.
Mine! My anguish cries.

My lone heart aches for hope snuffed out;
Spirit flame to glow no more.
King of mine with armor bright, your
Feet are earthen clay.

Oh, Lord above release me from this
All consuming, seething rage.
Bring me peace to inner rest.
Take me death this day.

Fred C Hornberger
THE SKY, HOW HIGH

Dedicated to my Granddaughter, Jaime. Love you, Doll.

The Sky, oh my, How High is the Sky
No one seems to know,
It's a void in space where the wild geese fly
Where the clouds bring the rain and snow

The sky is so blue, but sometimes it's grey
The clouds block out the sun that brightens my day,
Then the sun goes down and the sky turns red
There's an old saying "There's a fair day ahead"

Where does the sun go,
When it no longer shines in the sky?
It journeys to another part of the world
It brightens their day for awhile

When the sun goes down, the Moon is there
To light up the darkness of night,
A million stars will shine from above
Twinkling their beautiful lights
Travelers have used the stars as a guide
Wise Men and Kings so they say,
A shooting star will fall from the sky
Make a wish before it goes away.

Jean Lambert Lee
PAIN

This poem is dedicated to Dr. Ralph L. Cash, Sr.—my doctor since 1963. His patient and understanding care has helped me stay positive.

You invaded my body without warning,
As a thief who stalks the night;
Your scheme was to gradually destroy me,
But, "You sneak," you're in for a fight!

With your powerful grip, you squeeze me—
Attempt to bend me out of shape;
You torture my mind till resistance is low,
Hoping I'll be an easy prey.

In your totally erratic fashion,
You skip and dance merrily around—
Just contemplating the moment
You can knock me to the ground.

I pray for strength as I struggle,
And I'm positive I WILL WIN;
You may be my constant companion,
Yet, I certainly can't call you "friend."

For just like "Old Satan," you're evil—
You victimize and demand full control,
(BUT PAIN, YOU'VE MET YOUR MATCH . . . .)
Though you're able to bring me to a halt,
I'll NEVER allow you to hold!

Jenny Lorentzen
A NEW BEGINNING

In the the memory of John Lennon.

I lie upon the newly cut grass
Looking at the clear blue sky
I watch the different shapes pass
As the billowy clouds go bye
I can hear the robins sing
I can hear the bees buzz
Hearing the flower bells ring
Knowing the past as it was
I smell the fresh air
I smell the wonderful flowers
Smelling the yellow pears
Smelling the lilacs' good powers
As dusk comes to a near
The sun goes down
All is silent to the ear
And dark as Mother Nature's gown

Deborah Lantz
WAVES ARE RUSHING TO THE SHORE

Lovingly dedicated to Mom, Daddy, Delmar, Trevor, Jeremy, Raymond, and Michelle.

Waves are rushing to the shore,
A breeze does softly blow,
The cool, blue sky, and warm, gold sun,
Enhance the sand's pure glow.

I sit here, and get lost in thought,
Quiescent, so serene,
My heart and soul are captured,
By the beauty of this scene.

Now lying back, I close my eyes,
Aware of what I hear,
Emotions greatly amplified,
As the roaring surf moves near.

Retentive, in-exhaustible,
The waves rush toward the shore,
So sensual, so powerful,
To caress the beach once more.

I muse to myself for a moment or two,
How it resembles human emotion
In deeper thought still, I conclude with a grin,
We're as complex as the mysterious ocean!

Debra Worsfold
GOD, ED, AND ME

Dedicated to God and to my husband Ed.

In the year of 1982,
I was lonely and blue.
Then I met a man named Ed,
And that's the year we wed.
In the year of 1984,
We had a baby boy.
By the year of 1989,
My life turned out just fine.
Now I'm just as happy as I can be,
And I give all my thanks to these three,
God, Ed, and me.

Stacey Anne Snee

Stacey Anne Snee
HE'S MY FRIEND

To My Brother and Friend, Jason C. Snee.

He's my friend.
The one I can talk to.
When I'm down he tries to help.
Maybe he's not always there,
Maybe sometimes, he just didn't care.
Totally different, but totally the same.
Living our lives full of trouble and pain.
But he's my brother just the same . . . And I love him.
He's my brother,
He's my friend, from the beginning to the end.

Jaci Risser
CHOICES

For everyone who makes life harder than it has to be . . . .

Do we choose our life?
Or does life choose us?
Busily I go about striving for this or that
very important piece of my life,
only until the next mountain arrives yet unconquered.
Do I look for these mountains or do they find me?
Climbing, falling, struggling—finally,
gaining a foothold and then losing it again.
I am blinded by the wall in front of me.
Fear and anger keep me clawing at the rock
With my back to the sun.
Finally, the warmth and glow pervade my body
and I turn.
It was there all along, beckoning me.
This is the way!
Take the gentle path with light and peace.
The mountains are comely
like jewels glistening in the sand.
Just as we grapple for them
they change and fade in our hands.
But the quiet little path bathed in radiant sunlight
will always be there
to draw us into the warmth and love.

Heather E Kahsen
A FRIENDLY FATHER

To Mr. Norman Jack Bohne and Family. GOD BLESS YOUR HEARTS!

It is the time,
Of the season,
That you can go,
With a reason.

There is a leaf falling,
With a rain drop,
Or snow,
Or even ice.

I'm thinking of a friendly father,
Starting his day fine,
With his crane at work,
He was airborne, just like a plane.

Just like a plane, he was sent into the air,
He crashed,
He died,
With his body like trash.

He was a friendly father,
Never to be forgotten,
By his loved ones and
The family within musicians.

Ann L Bishop
TICK TOCK

To those who have helped and encouraged me along the way.

The clock ticks
Tick Tock
Time races fleet-footed

Earth cries
Raped by her children
Tick Tock

Rain is Heaven's tears
One day it will drown the villainous Titans
Earth gasps for breath
Black and blue, broken bones
Her veil ripped and torn
Tick Tock

Small voices cry out for Mother
Drowned out by the roar of a chainsaw
Tick Tock

Green paper takes precedence
Over the future of doe-eyed babies

Tick Tock Tick Tock

Time races fleet-footed
Tick Tock

Gwendolyn R King
ENDLESS LOVE

I dedicate this poem to my Husband, Michael O. King.

It seemed like only yesterday,
When we looked into each other's
eyes;
I asked you to come along with
me,
And that's when we realized . . .
We were meant to be.

We were two special people,
Who grew very close;
We laughed, we argued,
Giving each other love in a big
dose.

We would be together,
Then we would run away,
Until one day we ran too far . . .
Now for running away, we must
pay.

Not being with the one you love
Can cause much pain,
You become confused and
disoriented
Until you're back together
again.

So, we must not give up hope,
In being a part of each other's
life;
If it's God's will, we may
remain friends
Or, I could become your wife.

Janice Appel

Janice Appel
SOLITUDE

To my first love.

No arms to hold me close
No lips to press on mine
No hugs to keep me warm
No love to make me shine.

We could have been so happy
Laughter was your fare
But, I left you—You didn't
seem to care.

I realize now—I was too young
To have an adult mind
The years went by, I missed you so
I hoped and dreamed and pined.

But you were gone—I know not
where
We'd never meet again.
God took you away, I feel so sad
All the wasted years we could have
had, 'cause I still deeply care.

Linda Gross Fowler
THE REBEL SOLDIER'S LAST SALUTE

Dedicated to my great great grandfather, who after witnessing the surrender at Appomattox, returned home to his farm and orchard near the Peaks of Otter, Bedford, VA.

The Rebel soldier hung his head
as down the road to Appomattox he
was led.

"It's all over," he heard the Captain
say—
"and we'll be on our way home in
just a few days,
or at least some of us will . . . "

The Captain's voice faded into the
wind,
as he thought of the friends he would
never see again—

Confederate brothers who had given
their lives,
had sacrificed their dreams to see the
South survive.

Four long years were coming to an
end—
many a sleepless day and night,
were spent in marching before the
dawn's fearsome fight.

Supplies were scarce and rations
were low—
when at Sailor's Creek the battle had
taken its toll,

and many more fell who would never
grow old . . .
The Rebel soldier looked around,
and with tears in his eyes, he knew,
He was not the only one glad to see
Appomattox town.

Linda Gross Fowler
SIMPLE THINGS
I like rainbows with their bright
colored hues—
and sunshine and roses
kissed by the dew.

Hummingbirds too—with their fast
humming flights,
and fireflies dotting a summer's
night.

Fresh running water from a mountain
stream—
and the whistle and smoke of a
locomotive's steam.

The little country church that sits by
the way—
Fishing for trout on opening day.

The pink and white blossoms of the
peach and apple trees,
the buzzing in and out of a
swarm of bees.

Honey suckle growing on an old
fence post,
though it sounds rather simple—
these are some of the things
I like most.

Linda Gross Fowler
MANNERS
When I was just a child
I heard my mamma say,
Always use your manners
and you'll get ahead some day.

Though I never gave it much thought
way back then—
It seems to happen time and time
again—
When good things happen
as they sometimes do—
It's always to the one
who says "Thank You."

And when opportunities arise,
I always seem to find,
They're offered to the one who says,
"Please, if you don't mind."

So if you're bound and determined
you're
going to get ahead—
Instead of using pressure—
try manners instead.

Martha Brozyna

Martha Brozyna
THE SUN NEVER ROSE THIS MORNING
The sun never rose this morning
The bluebirds never sang
The newspaper was never delivered
The alarm never rang

No one ever woke up
No one was ever born
Nothing was ever spared
No one ever did mourn

A poet never wrote
Not a word was ever said
Nothing was ever heard
Except the silence of the dead

The sky was never blue
It was an evil, pitch-black night
No one could ever stop it.
No one could stand up and fight

Our dreams were never fulfilled
It's impossible for them anymore
No one was ever forgiven
And no one ever won the nuclear war

Martha Brozyna
I AM A MISFIT

To all those who have ever been rejected or misunderstood for their individuality—Don't ever let society put you down.

I sit in the night and watch the rain
fall from afar
While looking into the darkness, not
even one star
It is very dim, not at all any light
But what's to be expected from a
cruel, melancholy night

I step out the front door
And take a walk through the rain
If find myself running from people
They all despise me—think I'm
insane

Feeling the coolness on my skin
Thinking there's nowhere to go
Institutionalized in this forsaken
place
I don't want this anymore

Cold and wet I look to see
All this rain falling all over me
I asked myself, "What could this be?"
Is even God crying for me?

I feel like an outsider
As I again start to roam
Asking softly to the Lord:
"Please God, Don't let me die alone."

Martha Brozyna
SUMMER LOVE
Gone
Gone with the autumn leaves
Never to return
Blown away
One day
That will always stay
In memory
Not fair
Never fair
Always pain
Always the one to hurt
Don't hurt
Anymore
Scared
So frightened
I loved you
Still do
You do too
I hope
Never
I'll never say farewell

Martha Brozyna
HOPELESSNESS
Come let us remember this day
Let us acknowledge and mourn
The death
The death of my rose
See the wilted, fallen petals as they
lay upon the floor
See my wilted dreams and everything
they stood for
Look at the browned stem and sharp
thorns
The thorns that had pierced my heart

I am weary of being trampled all over
I am weary of having my dreams
stomped on
I'm tired
I am tired of forever lies
Now they are coming to take me
To the sunset
Through the night
Into eternity
With no hope

Save me

Martha Brozyna
DISORDERED FAMILY LIFE
! ! ! ! ! ! ! ! ! !
A shriek pierces through the
atmosphere
Hysteria
Mass hysteria
A scream, a shout, an obscenity
A tear
A distressful one
One that shows fear
Hate
Passionate enmity
Inhumanity, cruelty, insanity
Confusion
Puzzlement
? ? ? ? ? ? ? ? ? ?

Help
Help me
Don't let them hurt me

Never let them take me
Stay
Always stay
With me

Sharon J Willis
A WORD TO MY MOTHER

To My Best Friend . . . My Mother . . .
With Love and Admiration . . .

Mom . . .

You've shown me how to succeed
You've taught me wrong
from right,
You've understood all my needs,
You've shown me there's
always a ray of light.

You've shown me what it's like
To laugh, cry and be me,
Even though we may have a fight,
You still fulfill my needs.

You've encouraged and taught me,
You've shown me your strength,
You've comforted, sang and
rocked me without any complaint,
You've conquered all obstacles set
before you,
These are just a few reasons—
I LOVE YOU!

Sharon J Willis
TIMES TOGETHER
The teardrops rolling down their
faces,
As they say good-bye;
They do remember all the places,
Looking eye to eye.

Walking barefoot in the sand,
Looking at the sun;
Holding each other by the hand,
Having lots of fun.

Those long and beautiful nights
together,
And days of equal time;
Never like bad nor stormy weather,
All things went just fine.

My broken heart I must go and mend,
Wiping tears from my lips;
Finally realizing it's the end,
Of our long and beautiful
relationship.

Deborah K Maroncelli
A CHANCE I THOUGHT WORTH TAKING

To "Ronald Keith Anthon," Sometimes it is better to risk taking a chance and gaining something than not and never knowing. You were worth the risk and will always have a place in my heart. All my love, Debbie (Tater).

I knew from the beginning that you
had a broken heart
And yet I dared to take a chance and
love you from the start
A chance my heart thought worth
taking on you
For your smile and touch were
feelings I felt were true

Knowing your heart had been
mistreated and taken for a ride
Although I saw a man of power; he
lacked dignity, trust, and pride
I could see the hurt and disgrace,
beneath the mask you wear
You try to hide those feelings of hurt,
the pain too strong to bear

My arms I outstretch wide to you and
wipe that single tear
I'll hold you close, I'll say three
words, and wish away your fears
Those fears you feel, sitting sadly,
alone beneath the stars
I hope I can make you understand
and help to heal the scars

Time is the only healer I know,
willing to ease the pain
I hope you honestly know by now,
my love is real and not a game
There is no patent, no price, or
measurement for love
Guided with patience and understanding, we'll be free as the dove
above

So give yourself some time to heal
and search the inner you
I know under that mask is a man of
honor, and love enough for two
If we open up our hearts, our love
will grow stronger day by day
And those three words that mean so
much, "I Love You," are words we'll
often say.

Sonja DeRaad
TIME
Time goes on and on,
Leaves fly by.
Breezes are stirring,
Now and then,
A bird's cry.

One's own life,
Endless it seems.
Filled with events,
And fulfilling dreams.

Soothing talk,
Chimes of laughter.
A peaceful walk,
Everafter.

Diane M Bischof
THOUGHTS OF YOU
Thoughts of you lie deep within my
heart.
In everything I do you become a part.

You come so close but are far away.
Your image in my mind will always
stay.

When I sit alone my thoughts wander
to you.
My spirit comes alive with the love
you renew.

Your special love I'm beginning to
know.
My love for you continues to grow.

Thoughts of you lie deep within my
heart.
Thoughts of a love that will never
depart.

Donna J Chauncey
METAMORPHOSIS
what is it going to take
what am i going to do
i've lost sight of the shore
i'm getting lost in the blue,
i've thought of going crazy
but it's not what it seems
like a windmill in the desert
like a life without dreams,
everything is so different now
and i'm hanging by a thread
my future like Avalon
lies waiting in my head,
when you're not who you were
and changes happen fast
it's like being two people
and one is caught in the past,
this day is like none other
i've ever had before
my hand reaches for the sun
warmth, light, and so much more.

Donny Caldwell

Donny Caldwell
THE BEST TEAM IN THE N.F.L.

To my mom, football buddy, and best friend. You are the greatest mom a kid could have. I love you, and always will until I die.

The 49er's are the best,
they even passed the
ultimate test.

Yes, they have won four Super
Bowls,
and they did it by a lot of
touchdowns
and some field goals.

Joe Montana's really hot,
with a little help from
Ronny Lott.

Joe Montana throws the ball,
as if it was nothing, nothing
at all.

Jerry Rice leaps in a single bound,
and catches the ball for a
touchdown.

Once Roger Craig gets the ball,
there isn't anybody that can
make him fall.

Tom Rathman breaks through the
line,
leaving the rest of the
players behind.

They call Joe Montana the "Golden
Great,"
he wins every game
without hesitate.

The 49er's are the best they can be,
I think they'll be the best
team in history.

Louise Rathbone
MY BELOVED AND ME
I sit alone by sand and sea,
recalling all that used to be.
Childhood days; castles in the sand;
bathing, swimming, holding hands.
Parents watching us at play.
Oh! the joy of those happy days!

At sweet sixteen I met him first:
painting the sunset in its glorious
burst.
Most days would find us sitting there,
planning our future, it looked so fair.
Watching the waves dash down to the
beach
With majestic splendour, to spray at
our feet.

We dreamed our dreams to sail the
ocean blue,
but war came upon us and took him
too.
He said he would come back for me;
my sailor boy from out the sea.

I sit and wait and wonder why,
he had to be the one to die.
He lays beneath the ocean blue.
My heart lies buried with him too.

My body grows older, my eyes grow
dim;
the sun is golden, I think of him.
I close my eyes and say a prayer,
at last I sleep without a care.

He comes to me and holds my hand.
Together we walk the golden sand.
Across the mighty ocean deep,
as if we had wings upon our feet.

Into the golden sunset we go,
to a pathway lit by heavenly glow.
And there our Saviour stands and
waits,
with arms outstretched, at the
Heavenly Gate.

They found her body lying there;
with sand and seaweed in her hair.
A smile upon her face so sweet,
They knew her love had been
complete.

And on that spot facing the sea,
They inscribed on a rock—
"Together, at last, my beloved and
me."

Phyllis Dell'Osa
THE SPLENDOR OF IT ALL
I gaze outside my window
At the splendor of it all.
The trees in all their glory,
Some short, some very tall.

The birds are all a-chirping,
As they flit from tree to tree.
The robins and the orioles,
Blue birds and sparrows too, I see.

The beauty of the flowers,
As they bloom in colors fair,
The tulips, lilies, daffodils,
Their aroma fills the air.

How can one feel unhappy,
Or think of problems of the day,
When there is so much beauty
To enjoy, with naught to pay.

Jeanette Enyart
DON'T QUIT

I wish to dedicate my poem to all those who feel that their world has come to an end. And feel they have nothing else to live for. I've been there, don't quit.

When things go wrong as they sometimes will, when the road you're trudging seems all uphill, when the funds are low and the debts are high, and you want to smile, but you have to sigh, when care is pressing you down a bit—Rest if you must, but don't quit. Life is queer with its twist and turns, as every one of us sometimes learn.

Don't give up though the pace seems slow, you may succeed with another blow. Often the goal is nearer than it seems to a faint and faltering man; and he learned too late when the night came down, how close he was to the golden crown. Success is failure turned inside out. The silver tint of the clouds of doubt. So stick to the fight when you're hardest hit. It's when things seem worst, that you mustn't quit.

Leslie Nason
WORLDS APART

To my greatest challenge. Tony, I love you.

Two different worlds
Separate lives trying to live as one
Circumstances out of control
No end in sight
Having only hope to hold
No safe place to hide
Unconditional love, trapped
in a world full of restraints
Worlds apart
Chains of memories keep the door locked
Unable to be free from the past
No desire to live this way
It will never work
Too many obstacles
Too great a challenge
Love unable to be free to explore
Hopeless situation
No way out, worlds apart unable to blend

Rosemary Smith-Kebe
MY POEM

To Norman, Nancy, Michael, Mary Jo: my favorite poems.

Life makes more sense through poetry.
Images and feelings expressed in words
Strike a note and echo in another.

We meet on common ground within.
With words we touch we understand.
We feel the spark and parts of us awaken.

A lonely soldier sings:
A poet to himself his fears depart.
He is his song his gun a mere encumbrance.

A mother soothes her crying child.
She is her babe her poem her self
Her arms embrace the child that is us all.

I hear you say "I'll love you for forever"
And I believe once more, again,
And all's as well as it will ever be

Thus by our daily acts of poetry
Are lives enhanced and truly lived.
Which makes good sense to me and me a poet.

Edna Renée Oldebeken
ROSE HEART

To you, who thought it should go on, I dedicate this to you, you were the raindrop and it was my roseheart!

A raindrop hits
a rose's heart
Then gently,
slides away,

leaving it to dry, in the
sun
Cracked—
Parched,
like
"a lover's
stilled
Heart"

Tina R Freeman-Nead
RISING SUN, FALLING RAIN

For my Darling Timmee and my Dear Friend Randy for encouraging me to try.

Rising sun, falling rain
See my joy, feel my pain
Risen moon, fallen star
Drawing near, running far
Touch my hand, hold me close
Secrets told that no one knows
Down below, up above
Is it friendship, is it love?
Secrets told that no one knows
Touch my hand, hold me close
Drawing near, running far
Risen moon, fallen star
See my joy, feel my pain
Rising sun, falling rain

Chántica G Camejo

Chántica G Camejo
I SEE CHILDREN AS KITES

Chántica Giselle Camejo—July 29, 1971-December 26, 1987. Chántica's last poem written Dec. 15-25, 1987. Chántica, even though you fly free, I miss you and love you sooooo much. Mom.

You spend a lifetime trying to get them off the ground.

You run with them until you're breathless,
They crash, they hit the roof.

You patch, you comfort, adjust and they'll fly.

Finally, they're airborne.
They need more string and you keep letting it out.
But with each twist of the ball of twine,
There is a sadness that goes with joy.

The kite becomes more distant,
And you know it won't be long
Before that beautiful creature
Will snap the lifeline that binds you together
And will soar as it is meant to soar,
Free and alone.

Only then will you know you have done your job.

Danah Webb
WILD HORSES

I dedicate this poem to Mick Jagger and the Rolling Stones for without their song "Wild Horses" this poem simply would not be. I would also like to dedicate this to Scott Curnow, lead singer of the band, "The Strokers" of which this poem is written; for singing the song "Wild Horses" to me on that cold January knight not so long ago . . . 1985

I remember seeing him in my mind
I remember seeing him as he stood
off stage lines, music was his life
His hair was long, straight and styled
His hair was also wild
He stood before me
His body he did bend
Yes, he bent his body forward
I remember glancing towards him
His long mane he did shake and
shake and shake
At that exact moment
He reminded me of a wild horse
I too am a wild horse
Wild Horses . . .

Hon W F Rivera-Ramos
SHADOWS

Dedicated to Ms. Deborah R. Morgan; friend to my soul and mother to my dreams.

I thought I saw a shadow from the tail of my eye. It leapt at me as though from an unremembered dream. I flinched to take a look and low and behold off it took, not a moment it stood. Shrugging my head and shaking the past, at once to my task I took not wondering what I saw or if indeed I did? I thought and thought but not a thought it provoked, and the more and more I tried, the more curious I became. I toiled in its grasp till midnight. It was quite a battle to tell of. Once again I laid my pen down as to write a line or two, in pretence to my task attend; and in my lie I pinned my eye, to that very place. I stood and looked, pooheda, and sighed, what a fool am I. 'Tis no wonder I thought I saw, but not at all. 'Tis but the light and shadow its merry game doth play with me, and I have fell pray to its ploy.
It is now late, my task not yet finished my pen I must take my task to haste. With my thoughts astrew, my mind confused I wrote words not even a computer could compute! I poised myself and squinted my eyes. I waited and waited, but not a word could be had, not even a thought. For a moment I sat not chewing the fat, but wondering at. When out of the corner of my eye I did spy as it were a shadow, in fact, a shadow as it were. I slowly turned my head to look and low and behold it stood. I thought its name to inquire, but what a silly thought I could not even move. Its featured shape had me held by its glowing self. So I sat and looked at this queer shadow with its elongated nose. Its skinny neck and unkempt hair, which seemed to wave in the air with wheat like flair. Finally my lips unglued I spoke these words; Who are you? I thought it poised to answer; but off it took as it had stood. I looked about to whence it stole to. As I dared to look, I saw him face to face; a one handled long neck pitcher filled with long stemmed rosies in a queer shaped posy. In my quick relief I could even speak—Oh there you are my friend, I thought you too quick my friend.

John C Gibbs
DREAM

Dedicated to the ones I LOVE for staying with me; My Love KATHY L. COOK, Dustin, Jared, Caleb, Lucas and Samuel; Iris E. Barrineau, Iris E. Matuszewicz and Peggy S. Fajman. They will always have my love.

It must have been a dream
Yes, I'm sure of this
Because she touched me
And upon my mouth she put her kiss.

It wasn't real that I saw her face
Right before me there
Or held her hands in mine
Or touched her soft brown hair.

It's always been a sweet and lovely dream
When we've been together and
Loved each other deep.

An imagined beautiful scene
Played before my heart
In the darkness of the night,
In the silence of my sleep.

Missionary Samantha Ingram
THE MAN OF GOD

This poem is dedicated to my pastor, a wonderful Man of God who has been an inspiration to me as well as an example to me down through the years.

At first encounter, I thought that he was just a boy.
But, Oh!!! to hear him play the piano brought my heart much joy.
Mama!!! I exclaimed as I came home from church that day.
That boy can really preach, sing, and how he can play.

Later, I found out that he was the pastor, the Holy Man of God.
But, how young he looked and with such humbleness of heart.

A member continued to invite me to church, and I continued to go.
My heart was blessed beyond measure and I just couldn't say no.
The love being exemplified in the pastor and his congregation
Caused me to want that love and to seek God for salvation.

And later I became a member and
God saved my soul one day.
I haven't been the same since,
needless to say.

For my new life in Christ Jesus is never, ever a bore,
Because every round goes higher and higher need I say more.

And I owe it all to the Lord for the Man of God who practices what he preaches.
And for giving him as a living example before all the souls he reaches.

There are many ways to describe him,
but these are only a few.
At last I'll introduce him without further ado.
This wonderful Man of God that I am talking about, to put it quite simple

Is none other than Apostle Cleveland Smith, pastor, and founder of
St. John's Deliverance Temple.

Sheila Warner
MY PRECIOUS CHILD

This poem is dedicated to my daughter, Marsha, who has been a pillar of strength through the years.

God has given you your precious life,
So my child, be content;
Be thankful, it's his gift to you,
What more could he present?

Give thanks to him and appreciate
all that's yours to enjoy,
And shun the evils of this world
that might your soul destroy.

So don't forget my "Precious Child,"
Make not this world your trust;
For lack of wisdom her victims die,
They drop into the dust.

God's loving kindness is for sure,
He folds his arms around;
The places where his children dwell,
and make them holy ground.

My "Precious Child," I shall close,
But this is my advice to you,
Believe on every promise in his word,
And he will take you through.

Fran Woods
I WISH

For Stefanie and Jeremy—my precious children—and for my husband Doug.

When I think of all the things
I'd like to wish to be,
The things I wish for most of all,
Are things my children see.

The sun to rise, the sun to set,
The moon so full and bright,
The stars that shine far in the sky,
And glow with such delight.

A begger's face when given even
Just one little dime,
Or anyone who smiles and tells them,
"Thank you for your time."

May they know compassion
For a world so full of hate,
That they might be the ones to help
Encourage someone's fate.

I hope the pride they'll know,
Is for goodness they have done,
To help a tired and weary heart
Feel like their battle's won.

And, I wish them laughter

Maggie Workman
WHY

This poem is dedicated to Mrs. Jennie V. Garrett and Family.

Why is life so hard
When you try to do your best
It seems that your best
Is not good enough
You try to let others know that
You are doing your best
But others do not care

Why is there so much hurt?
Why is there no joy?
Why is there no trust?
Why do you hate your neighbor?
Why is there so much hate?

You go here and there for answers
No one else knows more than you
But I will tell you one thing
There is always our heavenly Father
He knows just what to do
That's why God cares and
Makes a 'Why' into something
That is why he died for us all.

Louise J Davis
MOTHER

To my friend and loved one—my own dear mother.

She gave me life, and the light of day
She gave me love, in every way.
She watched me laugh, and watched me cry—
Consoling me always, asking not—why?
She taught me right, when I was wrong—
She taught me how, to sing a song.
She gave me understanding, peace and joy,
Bought me always, a brand new toy.
No task too large, or favor too—
She did everything, a soul could do.
Companion, friend, there'll never be another—
As the one I love, my own DEAR MOTHER.

Jesse Holliday
ONCE'T UPON A LOG

Oh, once't upon a log I sat
My eyes hid under brim of hat
A noise I heard went pitter pat
My wonder tuned me into that

First looking left an then to right
Nothing there could escape my sight
Pulled up my pants an buckled tight
Getting me set for hasty flight

As quickly there was no more sound
For only stillness did surround
I looked just one more time around
Before I sat myself back down

A minute passed or maybe three
My eyes had grown more sleepily
Comfortable there and not in need
When again the sound came to me

I pantomimed ice water froze
Kept even still my wiggling toes
So barely breathing thru my nose
For now the sound was very close

Then from the log came jumping out
A large bull frog my eyes did scout
Laughter drowned the waiting shout
I jumped and chased that frog about

Jesse Holliday
HEART ON THE WING

Let loose my heart
gently
from loneliness mountain
So when again
soaring time arrives
it is unbroken
for flight

Carly Ellis

Carly Ellis
WAITING LOVE

Here I am thinking about you
All alone wishing you were here.
Knowing I could never live without you
Remembering the moments that are always so dear.

I miss you so very much
Giving anything to talk on the phone.
Wishing I could feel your warming touch
Trying hard to remember that you're not home.

I try to get you out of my mind
Even though it seems so hard.
I feel you've left something behind
And I feel I've left you no regards.

Deep inside I am really sad
And I know you probably are too.
And I am not seeing myself as being mad
But I see myself as being very blue.

Knowing we're really not apart
Even though you're not with me.
We're still together in our hearts
As we both can often see.

Knowing you're in another state
Makes me want to cry every night.
Knowing you're not going to be home till late
Until this Saturday night.

I can't wait until I see you again
It seems so far away.
Knowing my love for you is true
And knowing I'll see you in another day.

It makes me feel so good
To know you'll be home.
And I know it should
Because then I'll no longer be alone.

I know when I get to see you again
My day will turn bright.
You'll always be more than just a good friend
I always want to keep you in my sight.

Having you been gone
Makes me understand how much I care.
Wishing you could be back before
this Saturday's dawn
And not seeing your face in despair.

You mean so much to me
Nobody can take that away.
Nobody can touch me
The way you do every day.

This comes from my heart
I hope you can see.
Knowing we'll never depart
Because no one can take you away from me.

I never want to let you go
Or have you leave me behind.
Anywhere you go, I want to go
Because you're the most special person I could ever find.

Agnes B Wagner
LOST TREASURE

In memory of my niece, Jessie Mae Jones, who died May, 1941, at nine months of age.

Dear Lord, she's such a darling child
I knew You'd want her there
To hear her tiny baby feet
Upon the golden stair.
Our little ray of sunshine, Lord,
Makes Heaven much more bright—
Just so you play with her enough
And tuck her in at night.

Don't burden her with wings, dear Lord,
They'd be too much, I'm sure.
Just little cuddly toys and things
Are what you need for her.
Those tiny little fingerprints
You see upon Your throne
Are hers. We would give all the world
For one of them at home.

We know she's happy there with You,
We shouldn't cry about her,
But please have patience with our tears,
We're lonely here without her.

Marianne M McGee
DREAMS

With love to mom and dad, Shawn and Sheryl McGee.

Unaware of nightmares, fairytales, and thoughts,
Dreams come and then quietly go.
Dreams help make decisions and overcome our fears.
They even give strong hopes
That without DREAMS you would never feel.

Joana L Vanzie
WHAT DO I SEE?

What do I see, when I look at you,
The class of eighty-three?
Why, I see God's image reflected in both you and me.
For He's so great, and we're so small
That often you may wonder,
What was His purpose in creating such as me?

Your life as a gift to you He gave
To climb, to soar, to conquer,
'Tis yours the right to claim it all
And enjoy the Father's splendor.

I see possibilities, potentialities, all within you,
Teachers, preachers, gymnasts, too,
And politicians, even a few.
But then there's you, that special you,
Who dares to see things through
And show the world the best in you.

What do I see when I look at you,
The class of eighty-three?
I see no less than God sees
In His divine plan for you,
Can you see it, too?

Joana L Vanzie
CARL'S HEART CALL

Often I sit and ponder, about this man called Carl
And why he's into body parts
And neglects his own heart's call

Such beauty is found in this friendship of ours,
That I'm prone to wonder
If away from dumbbells, bats, and balls
Could he learn how to care?

Eleanor Hughes
AGING

Dedicated to "The Aging."

Some accept it gracefully
Others find it hard to see
Day by day the aging body
Moving towards eternity

Once bright eyes
grow dim with haste
Slower steps
now set the pace
Ears that used to catch each sound
Now strain to hear those gathered round

Fading memories lost in time
Mix with present scenes and signs
Small confusions in the mind
Keep past and present intertwined

Slowly now those things I see
One by one intruding me
Should I just accept the fact
or, vainly try to turn time back

Louella Marie Antone
TEET-PHA TEET-PHA (ETERNAL SOUL)

In honor of my 1st grandchild and to all my grandchildren and children, the three of them.

As I lay feeding from my mother's breast.
"My heart knows only love" Yet!
Within my heart, there is a see.
"Untouched and soon will grow."
Teet-pha Teet-pha—I pray for those that I will follow. And those that will follow me.
"Though they be great-or-small."
Teet-pha Teet-pha—I pray that when my life is over
And my heartbeat is no more
I will have served you well—
Teet-pha Teet-pha
(Teet-pha Teet-pha)
Quinauht—meaning Eternal Soul

Barbara L Martinez
A BOY AND A KITE

To Cody, Casey, Rebecca and Josh Martinez.

Oh what joy for a little boy
with a kite
He runs with all his might
Eyes wide with wonder
As his kite flies up in the big blue yonder
Now holding tightly to the string
Higher, higher she goes
He runs jumping in a spring
will she touch the clouds who knows

Smiling laughing he runs and plays
As his kite soars into the sky
Thank God for beautiful spring days
He has a colorful kite red, blue, and a sunburst tie
Only a little boy could know the joy
Of a beautiful breezy spring day
To him a kite is a wonderful toy
He thinks only if this day could stay
But soon this wonderful day is over
He hurriedly ran home thinking about his day
And is happily met by his dog Rover
He thought what a perfect day in the month of May

Vicki L Ebel
I AM JUST TWENTY-THREE YEARS OLD

To my son, Michael, the love of my life.

I am just twenty-three years old,
but I think this story should be told;
There was a time long ago
when hardships made people strong,
brave, unselfish, loyal and respectful.
I've been told those days
will never be back,
they will always remain a memory
of a truly good day gone by.
I wish they could be again.
I hope and long for a time
when we will see what we are
doing to ourselves and our children,
and pray that everyone takes time
to be strong, brave, unselfish,
loyal and respectful.
I think there can be.

Angelica Jauregui
THANK YOU

To my best friend Jill Crane. You helped me be myself when no one else would. I love you for it. Thank you . . . .

I thank you,
my best friend for your love,
for caring when push came to shove.

I thank you,
for holding my hand when it needed to be held,
thank you for not asking things of me
that I couldn't tell.

I thank you for trusting me in all the decisions
I made for me,
I thank you my friend,
for just letting me dream.

Love,
Angelica

Leah M Bailey
I BELIEVE IN TRUE LOVE

Dedicated to the one I love with all my heart, my dear sweet Craig Norman Oltman. (True love is for eternity my darling.)

Now that you're not by my side . . . .
now that you are gone
all my nights are empty
and all my days seem long

I thought we'd last forever . . . .
for an eternity
I thought that's how true love was
and I thought that we were meant to be.

Reality is cruel sometimes
and this time it broke my heart
and so there's nothing I can do now
except be lonely while we're apart,

Baby, I believe in true love
and my faith will see me through
and I know that I am right . . . .
because I can't stop loving you.

Chris Barr
THE PERFECT SPEECH

In dedication to all dreamers, they do come true. For my family, I love you all!

For those of you who understand this
Honor, that's why I'm here.
For those of you who don't understand,
That's also why I'm here, Thank you.

Kelly Ann McGee
WHAT IS RED?

All my love for my mom and dad, Shawn and Sheryl McGee.

Red is a fire,
Red is a base,
Red is the color of a sunned
Mommie's face.
Glowing, shining, boldly standing out,
Red is the color I picked, without a doubt.

Red is the color of a raging fierce beast,
Or even the color of a rare roast feast.
Red is the color of a blazing red rose
When it pricks its thorns upon your nose.
How beautiful Red is to forever see,
Especially on the leaves of a tree.
In Summer, Fall, Winter, or Spring
Red is the color of a special thing.

Circuses, bedrooms, and Ruby rings,
Red gives sparkle to happy things.
Red is beautiful as you can see,
That is, if you agree with me.

Carolen Bronson-Ward

Carolen Bronson-Ward
PEERLESS

To my father, JAMES BENJAMIN MOORE; who, in my mind, is without equal!

When taking stock of myself
through years that come and go,
I remember lessons taught to me
and all those "oats" I had to sew.

And when I was learning to walk,
as all God's children do;
I had no doubt, when I would fall,
"helping hands" would come from you.

Through all those nightmares
and nosebleeds, even flu;
your protecting hands upon me
assuring me, I'd pull through.

When in those "teenage" years, did emerge,
an individual, within the crowd;
It made all efforts worthwhile,
just to know I made you proud.

I know your task is hard, dear Dad,
and many do not succeed;
but of the ones that do, you're special
and your advice I still do heed.

So when reflecting upon my youth,
and all thoughts were surely fearless I
take great pride, and comfort still,
that the man I call "DADDY" is
"PEERLESS"

Judie Packer
A DANCER

Her grace Presented true essence
Of the dancer's Presence;
With fervent desire
To challenge herself.
My eyes filled
For her determination
To achieve and succeed.
I wonder if—
No, I know
For she saw
Where those who have sight
Do not.
Yes, she could tell
And sensed how I felt.
She's missed
There's emptiness,

I ache to teach her
To be ensconced
In her brilliant light
Again,
For a moment in time.

Shaquan Smiley
WORDS

This poem is dedicated to my parents, Cherilyn, and God.

Words can sometimes hit harder than a fist or cut deeper than a knife.
Some words are even responsible for the taking of a teenager's life.
Words can make a wound deeper than a bullet can.
Words are always recognized by a woman and every man.
So you have to be careful about what you say.
Or someone will go and take it the wrong way.
The harsh words you say can make your child think of suicide.
Or maybe a murder homicide.
And it's all because of the words you said.
So please be careful before someone ends up dead.
Words can also make you feel good such as I love you
Some words can make you fall in love with the person who has written to you.

Glenn T Rivers Sr
TIME

Forever My Love, Diane.

Composing a Poem is virtually time consuming:
Like the elements working away at the Land;
Rivers and streams altering their routes, taking the earth away with them,
Winds blowing and howling tearing away at trees and hillsides,
Volcanic mountains blowing their tops, spilling lava and ash forcing changes,
Oceans tearing away at the edges of various countries:
Trying to come up with thoughts and ideas, roaming through the mind; mulling over this and that hoping to catch the right mood, the right feeling for the thought, the right idea hoping that what is written is enjoyable to read:
Interesting At Least!
The sun rises and sets,
The moon, too, rises and sets,
Yet both are the same;
Friendships come and go,
Yet they too are the same:
Slow or fast, High or Low,
Words make life a game,
Time is the answer,
Don't ya know!

La'Lita A Lockett
SELF TRUTHS AND OTHER IDEAS

I dedicate this to you, who gave me life, gave me love, who gave me hope and the desire to grow. My Parents I thank you. And to you "Mr Rod" my heart of hearts. I love you all. Lita . . .

Limitations, Suffocation,
Circumstances out of Necessity,
The need to love and be loved, the need to long for and belong to,
A cry out for comfort,
A plea out of hurt and anguish,
Ticking in the distance reminds me that life seemingly standing still, does, move, on,
Wondering, Pondering, as the clock ticks,
Limitations, How much longer,
How much time, How will I know?
Regression is like the tearing out of one's heart, the transforming back to what was,
Progression now looks alive and yet lonely, I have a need to grow and go on, yet, I have a need to love you and stay, and yet, I have my limitations.

Wondering, Pondering, the clock ticks in the distance reminding me, that time moves on, as I move forward, or as I stand still,
I, wanting or not, must meet the consequences, and then face my own self truths when I look back upon my life as I look forward into the eyes of my God!
My own self truths will then come out,
I must then bear witness within myself of all the time that
the clock,
has ticked,
away . . . away . . . away.

Wendy Cook
CRYSTAL AFFAIR

For the ones who bring sunshine to my life Kelly, Jason, Stormie and Brandon.

You come into my soul only once a day
a wonderful glistening love affair we share today
You enlighten me with rays of color more beautiful than ever seen in the magnificent rainbow
Yet you leave me standing alone to wait for another tomorrow to take away my lonely sorrow
For you are the morning sun and I am the soul of the Crystal.

Betty Ann Wooley

Betty Ann Wooley
OUR KING

Our King our King our blessed King
Now stands at heaven's girth
With armies of angels He soon will bring
The promise thy will be done on earth

Clad in white upon white horses
The storm of trumpets to be heard
Thy Kingdom come thy will be done
In prophecy of His word

In close of Tribulation then
The Battle of Armageddon fought
Where peace at last echoes Amen
By words that He has taught

No scars will He bear on hand or brow
All bondaged released and free
The faithful ones at last endowed
He comes for you and me

Stand ready beloved for the day is near
When the lion shall lie down with the lamb
And beasts be led by a little child
A new heaven and earth is planned

Guard every hour of every day
Place faith and joyously sing
Our Father which art in heaven
Is sending His son . . . Our King

Charles Fromal
LOVE IS . . .

To Ellen. We do not share love yet our true friendship, a higher form of love which most will never know as well as us, is forever. '90'—CF

Answers are not always easy to come by.
Conform to and for others.
Why?
Life is our obstacle . . .
sex is pleasure,
lust is sin.
fear is always,
anger is predominant.
compassion is a foregone trait,
friendship is painful.
Hate is often prevalent,
just, in all manner.
as for love,

Love is . . .

Loreene P Ray
WIND AND RAIN

Wind soars, rolls, and tumbles
On upward then
Plummets.
Rests just a minute
Then puffs up its jaws—
"I'll sweep all this earth
'Til it's clean all around
Then I'll announce Spring
With a soft, gentle sound."

Rain will fall gently,
Then pouring, and splashing,
Filling gutters and curbs,
Then rushing to ditches.
While grasses and flowers
Drink to the brim
And trees bow their heads
In a thankful Amen.

Aileen Rodriguez Luna
BLUE DREAM

I close my eyes in the middle of the night,
The moonlight takes over the sky,
I don't know where to turn,
Nothing seems to be right.

I see a light far away,
Somehow is my guide,
To an unknown world,
From which I can't hide.

There's million things to be learned,
But not everyone is willing to teach,
Your respect that's what I want to earn,
But I need a hand to reach.

We all need a guide light,
To show us the way,
And when we finally get there,
We won't let it get away.

That's the kind of satisfaction,
That we all want to feel,
It's the joy, the agony,
That's what I call a blue dream.

Charlene Thornett
WE LIVE FOR OURSELVES

I would like to dedicate this poem to my family, whom I love dearly, to Eddie-Lou Cole, for helping me to believe in myself, and to all the people of the world, for being there.

We live for ourselves and only for us,
Who cares about them? Why make such a fuss?
The homeless, the sick, the hungry and scared,
It would make such a difference if just one of us cared.
I'll start with myself, I'll do what I can,
There's such a great feeling helping woman, child or man.
Together, we can help in just a week or two,
To help them be happy, instead of blue.
For just a moment don't live for yourself, not only for you,
Live for the others that are in this world, too.

Keith T Wilson
CORVUS AND LUPIS (WING AND PAW)

To Corvus—for being my friend.

The raven is a friend of mine
When I turn my head, he's never far behind
I go off into the woods alone
With raven behind, like the shadow I own
The hunt begins, I'm on the chase
To eat this day, I must win the race
The hunt ends and the prize is won
The moon rises, and sets the sun
Raven above me, playfully flies
As I tease him with my prize
The raven knows, his next meal
Will be what he can sprightly steal
With bellies full, we're on the run
To join the music that's just begun
The sound of pad foot and flapping wing
Adds to the song, the night now sings
This night's song slowly ends
With a final howl and a raven caw
They slowly fade into the winds
We dart off quickly, wing and paw

Jaime Brash
WINTER SIGHTS

To grandpa and grandma Brash for always being there for me.

Out for a stroll
On a winter night
The snow falling softly
Against the city light

The traffic is crawling
At a snail's pace
As the city happily
Puts on a new face

Mother nature is dressing
The trees and grass

And soon the ponds
Will look like glass

The children will soon be out
With skates and skis
And the dogs will be crawling
Through snow up to their knees

When I reminisce nature
And all its delights
I feel we are fortunate
To have had these sights

Penny Maynard
HEAVEN AND EARTH
My lonely light in a wilderness alone.
Are they not the Rulers of my Heaven
And Earth? Do They not stand there
Noble and solemn?

I hide no fear—
I see no Heaven but in the
Warmth of Their smiles and in
The coldness of their smiles.

I admire more the flames of Their
Peace and love, than the cold
And lonely darkness of other's hate.

Frank Valdez
THE TOUCH OF HEAVEN

This poem is dedicated to my wife and Jennifer Valdez, and the people of the world.

As I gaze into the clouds of heaven and earth,
And feel the cool gentle rain splashing against
My face. And when I close my eyes,
I feel this

Pleasant joy of peace, within me.
As if Lord God was touching my face with his
Fingers and wiping the tears away . . . .

Beckie Hippler
HOME SWEET HOME
A street light shining
As you read last week's paper
Surrounded by boxes of trash
and drunken bums
The growl of your stomach
reminds you of the fact
that you've only ate
half of a sandwich
all day
which you found in the trash
You're tired
You lie down, to awaken to your
Home sweet home

Steven A Rooney
LONELY SEA
Night is black and the sea is cold
Wind is strong and I'm all alone
Floating here in the sea
Now I'm drowning look at me
Winds are sighing in the sky
Waves of pity rising high
Waves rise higher crashing down
All life's pressures are pushing down
Heart of lead is sinking me
Can't escape the lonely sea
Depressing thoughts, feeling bad
The lonely sea will drive you mad
Caught by emotional undertows
Pain of a sort that no-one knows
Life is leaving I have lost
One mistake, tragic cost
Too far under got to swim
Reach the surface, got to win
I can't escape the deadly pull
Because the lonely sea is in my skull.

Carolyn H Duffer
FRANS' RODDY DOLL

To my daughter, Linda.

I found this doll at Frans' doll show,
Looked like she needed a place to go.
Brought her home and wondered who?
Would want a doll that wasn't new.
Because of late—the things you enjoy,
Thought you would like this old toy.
She was made in 1951 so I am told,
Now for a dear person, that's not old.
But for a toy with a bump and a fall
She will be antique in no time at all.
I didn't change her dress or fix her hair,
I will leave that to your loving care.

Marian Webster
FOR ANDY AND ALEC
Oh, How long ago it seems.
That I was all that there was for you to see.
You have slipped slowly away.
To become someone on your own today.
How I wish I could turn back time,
to when you were young and all mine,
to hold my hand with trusting eyes.
Oh, how I felt alive.
Now you have grown away from me.
A baby no more, a boy I see
But once again the cycle begins
and I have another chance
to be better at all things.
Thank you!

Robert Christopher
ILLUSIONS OF LOVE
Two lonely people
tending a flower bed,
illusions of love
alive in their head.

Sharing their garden
but not their hearts;
they're not growing together . . .
they're growing apart.

Their life grew weed infested
from years of indifferent care;
assuming love grows voluntarily,
but completely unaware . . .

That clouds of pure delusion
kept the sun from showing,
and soil sewn with disappointment
kept seeds of love from growing.

They've shared their garden
but not their soul;
they're not growing love . . .
they're just growing old.

Etti W Nissila

Etti W Nissila
GREEN LEAVES ON SNOW
It is surprising, on cold winter day, flower roots wake up. They break the frozen ground, so its leaves can find their way to outside, and their way they brush the snow away.

The green leaves look so beautiful against the white snow. They don't mind the frost or snow,
their rule is to grow.

Every time I see them, I know
spring is coming some day.
No matter if we have to wait
for a while, nature must have
its way.

Jean Marie Walton
INNOCENCE
I do not know his name.
I do not see his face.
I can only feel his presence.
He pulls my strings as a master
guides his puppet.
Bound forever by something
that does not exist.
Freedom is a myth,
a story of long ago told
to the young and willing—
only to shatter dreams;
as mine have been.
One more scar on the lining
of my heart signifies
the passing of time.

Frank Grannis
WIND-SWEPT TEARS
Wind-swept tears streak across her face
A long shadow gathers as trembling fingers trace
Etchings of her past like some long distance moan
Harness to her senses—she is so all alone.

Elizabeth Dillenbeck
DESERT NOCTURNE

To my son Tom, who first showed me the beauty of the desert.

The summer desert . . . harsh, unrelenting;
All creatures hidden from the sun's pitiless glare.
An aching stillness so profound it makes you feel
As though you must be
Alone upon the earth.

But sit quietly, and you will hear
The whirr of a million insect wings;
The far-off questioning call of a dove,
And sometimes a soft sigh from the wind.

As shadows lengthen, lizards come forth to claim
Their territories. In slow motion they rear up
To face the enemy . . . like tiny dinosaurs.

At the desert's edge, rough-hewn mountains thrusting upward
Are turned to fiery molten copper by the setting sun.
A lone hawk floats in lazy circles against the fading sky.
The saguaro stands
motionless . . . its arms raised up
Protectively . . . a strong, silent sentinel.

Very soon the desert will rest, under a heaven
So full of stars that you will feel
The whole universe is there to watch over you
While you sleep.

Lottie Gluck
ALAS VOYAGER
I have never climbed a mountain
I have never crossed the sea
And there are places in this world
That will remain a mystery.
Oh, how I would like to fly
Over the ocean to another land
Wishing for that magic dream
To stroll on wind-swept sand
I stare out to the mountains
I look over to the sea
I think of all the hope-filled dreams
Of the child I used to be.

Ruth Francis
WISDOM OF DREAMS
The king summoned his tribe at dawn's first light
To tell of the vision that shattered his night

I had a dream of cruel men and dark ships on the sea
Come closer now and listen to me

One day they will carry us to far away lands
Much suffering and sorrow we'll learn at their hands

Prepare yourselves now be courageous and bold
Throughout the compound this story was told

Another King spoke these words loud and clear
I had a dream and I tell of it here

This is the day our people are free

Be courageous and bold rejoice with me

Two jubilant spirits now walk hand in hand
And dream peaceful dreams in an ancient land

Thomas J Mariotti
TIME REKINDLES
Shadows cast on life-long dreams,
Pass, by heartlight's radiant beams.
Moments taken by the dark,
Time rekindles, lights the spark.
To brightness taken by the night,
And darkness spawned by dismal light.

Echoes call from empty rooms,
Soundless whispers play their tune.
Lonely heartaches call her name,
Time rekindles, lights the flame
To future dreams, so long desired,
And lightless years, now inspired.

Time rekindles, lights the spark
To tasks undone and deeds to mark.
Time rekindles, lights the flame
To happiness, joy and love's new name.

Elizabeth Smith
CLEAR, CRISP & STRONG
Clear, Crisp & Strong
Like the wind on a bright autumn day,
The leaves turn—reaching their perfect color
—on a mid-October morn.
His quiet wisdom—he imparts to each son or daughter
Like the wind scattering and sharing all that it owns.
You feel alive, rekindled
His words spark
all that is good, noble, and true.
His gentleness and kindness—ever present
His love unconditional
A Man
Walking
Following Christ
Leading others
Wise, Loving
My Dad

Antoinette M Silvestro
SPECIAL FRIENDS

Dedicated to Jean and George (Price) Preikszaitis—two very special friends.

How do I begin to tell you about George and Jean?
I could tell you how they are the happiest couple I've ever seen.
George—so blond and tall,
Jean—so perky and small.

You can see the special love they share.
They really are a great pair.
George with his photography and deejaying.
Jean always enjoying the "oldies" he's playing.
George never missing a chance to catch fish,
He always grants Jean her Christmas wish.

Jean with her leather, suede and lace,
You'll always see a smile on her face.
With them you can have so much fun.
It could be in the rain in Virginia or under North Carolina's hot sun.
Jean enjoys her shopping and going out.
You will never see her eat a lima bean or Brussels sprout.

I've learned a lot from Jean over the years.
She is not afraid to let people know how much she cares.
They certainly are an extraordinary husband and wife.
How do I thank them enough for giving me the best surprise party of my life?

Mary Kopler Rice
THE WAY OF THE CROSS
The Way Of The Cross is a lonely road,
Filled with suffering and shame,
He who walks it must stumble and fall,
Yet strong-hearted rise again.

Christ, Our Lord, walked the self-same way,
In the years so long ago.
He shed the tears, He knew the fears,
The Agony, the Woe.

With His Crown Of Thorns and His nail-pierced hands,
He was dying, cruelly, too;
Yet His clear voice called, "Lord, forgive them all,
They know not what they do!"

The Way Of The Cross is a glorious road,
For Christ is always there.
He sets the pace that will lead you through,
To Our Heavenly Father's care.

Cynthia Nazworthy
THOSE KIND AND THOUGHTFUL HEARTS!

"Almighty God loves all, the lost, lonely, forgotten, and those who fall! Almighty God will touch all!—But remember, He loves you best of all!"

Thank you God, for those kind and thoughtful hearts! The ones who bear them know how to care!
For you see, it sets them far-far apart from their meaningless, merciless, hateful counterparts!
Those kind and thoughtful hearts seem easily to "crush," with the "dishonesty," "unfaithfulness," and "liars," trying to rule the world, squeezing the pressure tighter and tighter, until they seem almost ready to bust! Sending a "chill" down the spine and such!

Then out of nowhere, "travels a kind and gentle hand," who caresses lovingly those hearts, so once again the "pressure" they can and will withstand!
They are the caring hearts, of the young and old! The hearts that stand so proud and so bold, handling quite an overload!
So, as you may face the "trial" that seems destined to come your way, don't give up hope reach out and cope, as there will be a kind and gentle heart that will soon be traveling your way!
To quietly pick you up, and carry you, over your burden that brought you into such a disarray!
Then, when your "trial" is through, take the time to thank "our God," for the "kind and thoughtful heart" that helped carry you!

Wesley Washington
FRIENDS
Time is the essences of all life,
this is especially true
in the relationship between people,
as more time is spent with someone
the feelings towards that someone,
becomes more defined,
as with parents, teachers, and friends.

So please don't think of me
as a "Stranger," but as someone,
with whom you've never shared any time
if given this opportunity,
you might learn to feel towards me
as you do towards your friends,
and your loved ones . . .

Stanislaw Sieniutycz

Stanislaw Sientiutycz
GLOSS

To Professors of the Institute of Chemical Engineering at the Warsaw Technical University, Warsaw, Poland.

The curtain is the barest image of the lie

Stupidity
—the greatest luxury of mankind
His pettiness is the deepest fissure of heaven

The scoffing smile
—the highest duty of the devil.

Lucidity is the wisest daughter of truth

Talent is the most capricious son of wit

Finesse is the cutest baby of the soul

The creative pain
—the smallest molecule of God.

Stanislaw Sieniutycz
BEACH
The wave approaches silently—
a night melancholy,
hiding the secrets
of solo dances.

On the hard coast
a bronze Cupid
has drawn some letters
of our names.
Shielding them, my open hands
implore the thoughtless tide:
don't destroy;
you own all the grains of the beach,
we have only
these few unskillful symbols.

Some day, unforced,
we'll come to be lost in the sand—
united babes of destination.

Annie M Clavon
YOUNG AT HEART

I would like to dedicate this poem to my husband David. Children Samuel, Yvonne and Gwendolyn. My grandchildren Shervawn, Lakeshia Aaron and Jessica.

Life can be young, life can be ole,
Life can be a rainbow or a pot of gold.
Whilst young the rainbow is bright,
When ole it's like a twilight.

Yesterday I was young
Today I'm ole.
Ole, but not in mind or heart
Young in mind as if life is about to start.

Young in mind, young at heart,
Young until life depart.
Life can be beautiful, like a butterfly,
Flying freely under the blue sky.

As the seasons come and go,
So does life as we journey forward.
Young man, young woman
Don't take life for granted.
If you do you surely will panic.
Take each day with a stride,
Be forewarned, don't forget education.
If you do, there will be no vacation.

David Moroski
THE SOUND OF SOLID GROUND
I pressed my ear
to the floor
and closed my eyes
till I could see no more

flutes and drums
I could hear
were playing softly
with sorrow and fear

I realized
that mournful sound
was the eternal music
of solid ground

Alfred Morgan
SPRING
Change of season is in the air,
Plants and trees are budding everywhere,
The earth and nature is awakening.
Rivers, lakes, and streams are slowly thawing

Humans and nature will once more meet,
Breathing the air so pure and sweet.
Sunshine is warming everything
Hooray! Thank God! It's spring.

Walter H Andres
TWO NURSERIES
We held a baptismal the true Christian way
For our family's youngest, two months to the day.
While in a nursing home the octogenarian
Juggled his memories with thoughts of an old man.

While in the nursery little Alexandra
Was smiling sweetly after lunching on her Mom
She had some complication but the Lord set it right.
While great-grandpa John in pain had a rough night.

Nearly fifty family and friends celebrated with a party.
"Poppop" John sees that many and more in his own way;
Our blessing to them both spread 88 years apart
We thank the Lord for keeping this welled within our hearts.

Renee LaPrade (age 8)
THERE'S A CAT IN OUR CANDY, PAT!
He likes our candy because he is handy
Catching mice in our den, that is nice.
And our den is nice because it has mice
And mice are nice for cats to chase
But I don't like them in our place.
He likes it in there because of the air—
It's not hot or cold, it's just right for mice
That's why he lives there.

Jackie Erwin
SPONTANEOUS LOVE

Dearest Ray: "My Love to You" Always, Forever, Vivid and True.

Her loving him on sight's first glance:
So utterly charming was he:
Perceiving him that night in stance:
Spontaneous love came to be.

From inside out she saw romance:
With intent hope to start anew:
By bright array she was enhanced:
To new found love of instant hue.

Echoes bounced for belonging need:
With precession she sent a call:
Penetrating planted a seed:
That made him so humbly fall.

From her throbbing heart set afire:
She sent a spark that caused desire.

Ida B Foster
LIVING IN DARKNESS

To my husband, Al, and sons Al and Omar.

Even though I was born with sight in both my eyes, my body is full of darkness.
Not fully understanding events that were good, bad, sometimes sad—
Happening in my life.
The dreams, visions and nightmares—I couldn't comprehend
Not realizing the struggles, warnings, stumbling blocks were sent from above.
Finally, one day I realized and focused my eyes toward the sky.
The darkness I felt inside brought my knees down and I cried with so much pride!
Oh my God—I repent.
The moment I received my Lord, no more struggling and confusing events.
For Satan no longer controlled my soul.
God and I, we're a team.
He's forgiven me of all my sins.
Now my eyes beam with sight and my body shines also with light.
I'm changed! Amen

Eddie Spruell
IT'S TOO LATE

To Those Whom Love Has Disappointed.

Too late my love, time has played its part,
and the pain has gone away . . .
And i'll try to have no more regrets about a by-gone day . . .
Too late, the tears have turned to smiles, now I no longer cry . . .
We've sang our song . . .
But sour notes . . . disturbed love's Lullaby.
At first, I wandered all at sea . . . But now the storm is through, I'll look toward these future years . . . with an optimistic view.
Too late, there's little use to dream of—things that's said and done . . .
My broken dreams are mended now . . . and there's a . . . Brighter Sun.
That's how it goes in this old world . . . We all are slaves to fate . . .
We played the game as always . . .
But now . . . funny face,
It's too Late!

Howard Bandelin
SHARE

To my Lord and savior, Jesus Christ. The true living God.

I have something that I want to share.
It's the love of Jesus, and it's everywhere.
He's so wonderful and loving and full of grace.
He put a smile in my heart,
And it shows on my face.
He gives me Peace and understanding.
And he's always there.
He talks to me in spirit, and I talk to him in prayer.
God is love, and he really does care . . .
So, come unto Him, come and get your share.

Larry W Parish
I KNOW SOME EYES I LOVE
I know some eyes I love; they are windows to my soul.
Those eyes watch me daily, in all I do, wherever I go.
I know some eyes I love; and beautiful hair that glows.
I know some lips, some precious lips;
They utter words that save men's souls.
I know some eyes I love; I know a hand,
A mighty hand that I love to hold,
That reaches down to me from above,
Offering salvation, obedience, and love.
I know some eyes I love; I know some arms,
The mightiest arms, and they're always unfurled;
Welcoming those who are lost, back to safety . . .
From sin, remorse, and dangers of this world.
I know some eyes I love; I know a heart,
A gentle heart that's thoughtful, kind and true.
Yes, I know them all, and love them all,
Because Lord and Merciful Master,
And Heavenly Father Jesus Christ . . .
THEY BELONG TO YOU!

James H Taylor
YELLOW ROSES

Dedicated to Evelyn.

I'd like to see the roses bloom again.
The way they did in '71.
Bright yellow, glowing in the sun.
Those yellow roses warm the soul.

Perhaps, before another year,
with God's blessings,
We shall see the sights
Which made that blessed day.
The sight of roses blooming in the noon day.
A sight so beautiful to behold,
It warms the spirit, enriches the soul.

James H Taylor
A WOMAN'S TOUCH

To Grace and Evelyn.

When twilight calls, I hear
The cheerful noises of children at play.
The sounds of the end of a long day.
My woman calls.

Laboring long as well,
But often one can't tell
How long she has labored.
She speaks too, in subtle tones,
"The day is over," she says,
"However long."

The children remind me, as does the setting sun,
Your day is over.
Let's have fun.

Laurie Ann Hutchinson
OUT OF THE BLUE
Tears stream down my face,
forming puddles at the base.
How was I so lucky to meet,
someone so neat?
He came out of the blue,
as if he were someone I once knew.
We had days both long and short,
of every sort.
Together,
hoping they would last forever.
Then it came time to say farewell,
and he left at the tolling of the bell.
Although he never left my mind,
it pains me to know, that once again I was
left behind.

Laurie Ann Hutchinson
YOU
What is it
that I fear
or that always
seems to make me cry?
What is it
that I hold so dear
and never
want to have die?
I never knew
that it could be,
someone I
hold so dear to me.
Packing up
just to say good-bye,
hold me now,
I know that I am going to cry.
This pain is just
so hard to bear,
I never thought,
like this I would ever care.
For a friend,
who will in time leave,
when that time comes, the end,
I know for you I will deeply grieve.

Jessica Mankowski

Jessica Mankowski
THANKSGIVING

This poem is dedicated to my brother, Fred McKinney.

Thanksgiving is:
turkey, cranberries and yams,
Then there's people!
getting together
hugging and kissing,
trying to make up for the times
they've been missing.
Then—there's—God!
who made all this good
Let us thank Him
for this food,
So we bow our head in a silent prayer
and we feel His presence
everywhere.

Jessica Mankowski
CHRISTMAS—IN—SALADO
There's a fire in the fireplace
and warmth in the air
A feel of St. Nickolas
who will soon be here.
There's a tree by the window
laden with gifts
All wrapped in bright paper
and ribbons of silk.
There's holly and mistletoe
hung from the door
Ready to welcome those
coming in from the cold
Oh! what a happy day
this is going to be
When all of our family
we will greet merrily.
But this is Christ's birthday
and we mustn't forget,
To give him the praise
and the wonders of it.

Jessica Mankowski
TEXAS WINDS
Oh! winds that blow
the whole day long
Oh! winds that sing
so sweet a song . . .
They carry the tumbling
tumbleweed far
making a ball—sometimes a star—
And—yet these winds blow up a storm
A cyclone hits—down comes the barn

also the houses—sometimes the towns
Are—blown away and a lot of harm
comes-to-the people—their stock and trade
All carried away—so they must have aid
Yet this old wind continues to blow
Sometimes it rains
Sometimes it snows
Sometimes it destroys everything in sight
But these howling winds
continue their fight.

Jessica Mankowski
A CANDLE FOR CATHERINE

As I went into the chapel
just before I knelt to pray
I lit a candle for your mother
For it was her Mother's Day.
I told her that we loved her.
And we missed her very much.
That's when I knew I must be dreaming
for I felt our fingers touch.
"And my boys," I heard her whisper,
They are well and doing fine,
I watched a tear fall from her eye
And then one fell from mine.
I realized that no matter
How far we'd grown apart
that our children were the link
to keep her living in our hearts

Kimberly Slater
HUES OF NATURE . . . LEAVES

A combination of reckless hues
Jumping and playing on the eyes of man.
Brilliantly overpowering the largest choir
With only a rustle.
Falling to paint the ground with vibrant array
The Wind God delights in the timeless, everchanging picture.
Miniature animals sculpt their design
To help perfect the picture in the artist's mind.

Then the picture turns to a dying heap,
Compacting and decomposing to a pile of organic
Trash.
Hues of black and brown dance across the pile.
Topped with a white hat they return to their ancestors
Fertilizing and reviving man's home.
Helping produce their children, they die
Happy and satisfied for years to come.

Mrs Rosalie L Walker
TO MY BELOVED GRANDMOTHER

This poem is dedicated to Mrs. Lucy L. Reavers, my beloved grandmother, who died November 1977. She showed great love and strength as a mother and grandmother.

Oh Granny, how I hold you so Close in My Heart and Thoughts. Remembering Your Undivided Attention to my Every Need. Praising Me with Your Upright Spirits with Clapping that was Louder than Thunder, for a Job Well Done. Enriching me with your Knowledge of Love, Caring, Understanding, Courage, last, but not least, and Most of all, Your Blessings. Chastising me, but, with Love in Mind, so I would have less Mistakes to make in Later Life. Encouraging me to take the Career Path I chose, and Outfitting me along the way with Advice and Uniform.
Teaching and Showing me how to Give, rather than always expecting to Receive. Letting me take Certain Responsibilities into my own hands.
Thank You Very Much Grandmother!!!!
Oh, Granny, how I Hold you so Close in My Heart and Thoughts.
I love and Miss You Very Much,
Granddaughter Rosalie L. Walker

Ed Jeffers
STOP TO SMELL THE FLOWERS

When you can't see the sun for the fog, look at the fog.
But when you can't see the sky for the clouds, look at the rain.
When you can't see the meadows for the flowers,
stop to smell the flowers.
Because today is today and it's ours.
Yesterday is gone and so are its powers.

When you cross a river, look for its falls.
Tomorrow is not here, and neither is its cause.

Encourage yourself to pursue your dreams.
But don't put emphasis on future schemes.
Encourage yourself to live today.
It can only be a better way.

When this done and peace within,
reach out and touch a friend.
Your wisdom and courage will touch their soul,
And this will go on to be three-fold.

Rose Ann Mikos
FEELINGS

Lord give me courage to rise above defeat.
Lord give me strength to rise upon my feet.
Lord help me see what it is that has got me down.
Bring a smile upon my face, take away from me my frown.
My hands are reaching out to him, for my heart is full of sorrow.

Stand by my side to guide me along,
To help me face all my tomorrows.
Should ever I get depressed or blue,
Dear heavenly father I'll turn to you.
Should ever I be depressed and burst into tears,
I'll call upon God to lend me his ears.
He listens to my problems no matter how small,
All need be done is give him a call.

Help me cope with the everyday things.
Help me face what each day brings.
Lead me through the path that I should follow,
For within my mind, my thoughts are hollow.
With God's hands to help me guide the way,
I'll grow stronger each and every day.
For when my thoughts are clear to me,
I shall thank God I've faced reality.

Lynda Lou Holland
GOOD FRIENDS

To Kristen, a truly special "good friend."

Your friendship means a lot to me,
It's special in every way.
I say this straight from my heart,
And your friend I'll always stay.

If ever you feel the need to talk,
Cause you're feeling a little down.
Just call me up and I'll do my best,
To help remove that frown.

As long as communication stays open,
We will always get along.
When you need me I'll be right there,
And our friendship will grow strong.

Even though I don't come over and visit,
Each and every day.
Doesn't mean I'm mad or angry at you,
In any way.

I want you to know
That you can always turn to me.
This, I believe,
Is how "GOOD FRIENDS" should be.

Bill McClenahan
SALK TALK

Jonah Salk went for a walk.
Nothing could cheer him, great man of the block.
He walked to Pacific, but too-knowing talk
And the demons of Webster made Mister Salk balk.

Not since the creature, leviathan hulk
Had left him at shoreline a wobbly stalk
Had Mister Salk ventured down by the boats
—Boats that bobbed at their moorings: ancestral footnotes.

Gloom from his chilly room, paint flecks, loose caulk;
He sat in the big chair, and stared at the clock.
Sullen, he sat there and salk, and salk.

Bill McClenahan
MESSAGE TO A TYRANT

Before you cause me defamation
And bring about expatriation,
I'm certain it's of consequence
To punish me with common sense.

Hence, while your hatred oft exceeds
The volume my behavior needs,
The punishments should fit the crime,
While your "head of steam" subsides with time.

Through practiced efforts, you have learned
To flaunt your power toward those you've spurned
Through verbal pressure and display
That's proscribed by U-C-M-J.*

So, lean back in your office chair
—Sagging jowls, grey head, bi-focaled stare
—And admonish those whom you command
'Til Jurisprudence takes the stand.

---

*Uniform Code of Military Justice, *Manual for Courts Martial*, 1951

Mabel S English
MY ANGEL

There are songs about seeing Angels walking,
There are songs about hearing Angels talking,
But, I ask you, have you seen an Angel sleeping?
At dusk, the Sandman comes creeping—
Then in the bed, a tousled head,
So quiet at last, asleep so fast
From playing so hard the whole day thru;
How could it have been so trying for you?
A little pug nose, lips like a rose
Dimpled chin, with lashes long resting on soft cheek;
Makes you feel so very, very meek.
Just today you seemed as a tyrant
Two little hands that are now so silent;
The busy, noisy, pattering little feet
Of a cuddly bundle so soft-so sweet—
You know deep in your heart, and are glad from the start,
Of all the gifts given from Heaven above—
Most of all, of them all, that's the one you love.

Carolyn Hunt-Smith
ARE YOU SURE WE'RE OUT OF MILK

To Laura Marie the sunshine in my life. Your beautiful face and precious smile make Mommy's days really worthwhile.

Have you ever been shopping with a baby
Sometimes it's enough to drive you crazy.

They lay in the cart smile and pass gas
The customers think you have real class.

She wants to be held not pushed in the cart
So happily she smiles, giggles and farts.

You're pushing your cart with only one hand
As you run over kids and an old man.

You try to avoid a canned vegetable display
Because your cart seems to steer that way.

You're standing in front of the deli stand
Waiting your turn with baby in hand.

Her face turns red and something starts to smell
The customers turn and run like hell.

Suddenly for some reason you're next in line
You think to yourself she timed that just fine.

I paid for my groceries now they're all bagged up
This is the time she decides to spit up.

As I walk out the store I can wear a smile
Knowing I won't have to return for a while.

Virginia Foraker
SUMMER EVES
What is it, in the still of the night,
That softly whispers through the trees?
That, which even in pale moonlight,
One hears, but never sees?

It is the murmur of sleepy birds
Settling down in their nest,
Of myriad insects often heard
At night, when others rest.

It's sighing sounds of a gentle wind
As it rustles through the leaves.
Of a hoot owl perched on a limb.
Symphonic sounds of summer eves.

Mary Ruth Carroll
LOVE GROWN HERE
Mom, Dad; Fifty years ago today;
you began to earn this name,
Being there; strong and loving;
always the same.
Through the years and without much pay.
How warm and glad you've helped us stay.
Making time to play lots of games,
Throughout the years of growing pains.
We've grown fonder because we care,
Always knowing you've been there to share.
In times of sorrow and times of need,
You've been there to help and lead.
Our lives are better too; all because of you.
A Mother: A Dad, No one could have ever had.
Ones like you and not have known,
A joy, a peace because you've shown.
Loving kindness and concern too:
Never asking for what was your due.
Even when our mistakes we made;
You've been understanding; never staid.
Now on this day we want to say,
Outside your home, there should always be:
A sign for all who pass by to see:
Saying "LOVE GROWN HERE."

Shelly A Ayala
THE SILENCE BEGINS
Echoes of darkness fill the air
Voices of spirits surround
As the walker seizes pulses of light
Hidden to barriers of sound
He cannot see, he cannot hear
But only his fearless mind
Searching for meaning in the shadows
Answers of which to find

It is here that the wall stands
Between the night and day
Shutting the signals of true light
Out to its own way

But he cannot be reached or ever climb
The destructive, cursed wall
The power will strike even before
His cries come out to call

For this is the battle, the only war
The one where no one wins
Where souls are lost to human pride
And the truth of silence begins

Linda C Grazulis
COUNTRY MORN
There's something special about a country morn
With a cast iron skillet snug on the stove,
One can sniff the fried eggs a-sizzlin'
As thoughts wander down the grassy grove.
To hear the barn roosters crowing so early –
Makes a heart feel right at home,
Ahh, that sweet scent of newborn clover
Assures the restless spirit, "cease don't roam."
A morning stroll speaks of its own glory
As one meets with a whispering breeze,
A bright, red barn and silo
Contrast a row of kelly green leaves.

To discover the wee secrets of mother nature –
A butterfly soaring mid-air,
A spider weaving its breakfast,
A mantis kneeling in prayer.
The fresh aroma of alfalfa and hay
Make country mornings the best,
Mesmerized by its quiet beauty
Makes one yearn to be more than a guest.
One can't compete with a country morn
Where a poor man invents a dream,
Down by the ole weeping willow –
Near the muddy banks of a silvery stream.

Linda C Grazulis
UNWANTED TENANTS
There's a small invasion
Upon this planet earth
Of creeping, crawling, critters
Who are daily giving birth.

Taking residence in wee knotholes—
Suddenly the kitchen becomes "their" grocery store,
Rolling in a jar of jam and jelly—
Tumbling victoriously on the floor.

Exterminators stand baffled
While mice continue to be on the loose,
They are skillful, cunning escape artists
And traps are of little use.

Consistent in their search for yummy treats
They make cheese number one on the list,
For it is considered a delicacy—
Cheddar, American, or Swiss.

So, beware of the charm and curly whiskers
Of these fuzzy, furry gents,
And I warn you, don't make them your tenants
Cause they'll never pay the rent.

Christina M Catrone
INFINITY
She is so mysterious, seeming harmless as her beauty encompasses your inner soul.
Her allure, so vast, so overwhelming makes man weak to her needs.
As soft as the clouds above, yet, beneath her skin lies a world of wonder and fortune—
The Ocean
So powerful, in which one could be, so very easily, lost in her luster.
To be taken in by her is like no other phenomenon known to man.
The danger that lies within
The challenge of exploration
The beauty of life and the intrigue
of risk grabs hold of your emotions then sets you free to embark on a fantasy of life unknown.

Denise Dale Gilbo
BIG BROTHER
Sitting here alone just thinking about the past. The best years of my life, that slipped away too fast.

Growing up with you was the best thing for me. You taught me to be myself, and be the best that I could be.

I remember all our fights, that I would always lose, about whose room was cleaner and whose toys were whose.

But all those days are gone now, they are just a memory, of me and my big brother, together faithfully.

So please take all my love and a great big hug and kiss, cause you deserve the best in life, from your one and only sis.

E R Estrada
MELISSA
As Moments Of Night Repeat
Fantasies Amass While Remaining
Unanswered
But I Have You
I Have You
And Forever Would I Dare Not Close
My Eyes
Lest I Were To Open Them
And Find You Gone
A Fantasy

Kevin J Jenkins
WISHFUL THINKING
I wish

that there was no such thing
as disease and hatred,
that love is our only handicap.
I wish,
man could see man
with the eyes of God,
and not as competitor
or challenge to survive.
I wish,
the world we live in
was the heaven we dream of,
so we could live eternally.
Then one would never know
that life could be a living hell.

Frank Mathews

Fae Walker Mathews
DEAR HEART
To Frank: till we meet again.

In dreams, Dear Heart, you come to me
And whisper soft and low
And hold me close unto your heart
As when you loved me so

Your lips are warm upon my own
I nestle in your arms
For I was ever wont to be
A victim of your charms

The laden years so soon be-dim
The dreams that we hold dear
With body and soul we strive to hold
The loves of yesteryear

So come, Dear Heart, that I may live
The love we used to know
And hold me close unto your heart
As when you loved me so

Arlene Mintz
SPRINGTIME—THE SEASON FILLED WITH GLADNESS!

For Fred, Marla, Holly and Michele giving me happiness and seasons filled with gladness . . . .

Brightly the sun is glowing.
Flowers in bloom, plants are growing.
Trees swaying on a lovely Spring day.
Sky is serene in its own way.
Makes one feel, happy to be alive.
Conquer the world, aim and goals to strive.
To one's self, a thought of peacefulness.
Springtime—The Season Filled With Gladness!

Children seen everywhere.
Playgrounds, on bikes; something new to dare.
Species of dogs being walked by their master.
Happy to be outdoors, romping and running much faster.
Joggers on the run, hearty walkers—exercising.
Feeling great and thankful the air is not freezing.
Smiling faces beaming, all with happiness.
Springtime—The Season Filled With Gladness!

Meaghan Elizabeth Hastie
GONE
I never told you I loved you
Nor did I say I cared
All the thoughts inside my head
I never really shared
You always had a kiss for me
Or a caressing touch
I loved you very dearly
And loved you very much
Your shadow slips away
In the darkness of the night
Your looks they come to haunt me
In reality of light.

Kimberly K Dickinson
IT'S A SOLITARY WAR . . . SOME ARE STILL FIGHTING
So they say the war is over
The fighting has stopped
But has it?
Have you adjusted to the new life?
Life without guns and nuclear arms?
You don't need to hide behind barricades anymore.
You are free.
You can put the past behind you
Forget about all the people you killed
"It's no big deal," they say.
"Wasn't that the point anyway?"
But you can't forget it can you.
You can't put the past behind you.
You are still living it, still feeling the pain, the hurt, and the anger.
The past needs to be put out of your mind and be forgotten.
Don't dwell on it.
Don't ruin the rest of your life.

Juana Lourido
LONELINESS

To mom; dad and ofe who said I could. LOVE, Juana Lourido.

Sitting on an empty beach
with no one there to care,
I think about the world,
that one another share.
No one there to sit with me;
the sun goes slowly down
The beauty of it all to share.
And no one is around.

I walk and walk the sandy shore.
It's really hard to know,
that I'm all by myself again,
again, again, alone.

The seagulls flying high above,
come sweeping down to me.
I reach towards them in gratitude,
but then they only flee.

So what is left?
Some pain and some sorrow,
alone today,
alone tomorrow.

Valter D Valenca
IN THE WORLD OF POETRY

To my parents, Itamar and Cleodice Valenca, for bringing me up with love and care, and for giving me this small talent.

In the world of poetry,
Where it is tough to compete,
I will send in my entry,
To face the best of the elite.
Though a poet they say I am not,
This poem I shall enter in,
Luck, they say I haven't got,
Nor should I expect to win.
Yet, I will cherish the thought,
Of competing against the best,
That America has ever brought,
From the east to the west.
Twenty-one lines is the cap,
And this I will not exceed,
For a single line is the gap,
And that is all that I need.
So, now this poem I finish,
To place in the mail today,
Much luck to all I wish,
And to the winner, "HURRAY!"

Gloria Beacham
WHY

To Erica—Grandma's "Todd" forever.

Have you ever wondered "why"—
and the Bible says it's so,
That if a bird falls from a tree,
our God will surely know,
And why a soul seems closer, the longer "it" is gone,
Or why, when you rest your head at night, a voice goes on and on.

Why it's someone dear, you love, to whom you can't relate,
Why, sometimes, you'll progress at best, when you take your time and wait,
Why you'd never miss a grain of sand, but which grain is the beach,
When you're lost in the wonder of a child, why you're the one to teach.

I'm sitting here with pen in hand, my coffee cup near-by,
The world is slowly waking up, behold! an opal sky,
No need to wait for answers, but, I don't see why it's true,
God needs my life so badly, to help His love get through.

Gloria Beacham
SAND CASTLE

Dedicated to Michelle.

(Please read slowly, thoughtfully, sadly.)

I stared at my sand castle,
Being ravaged by the sea,
And at the gaping hole beside,
Much like the heart of me.

Michelle! My precious castle,
Oh! The dreams I had for her,
But the tide, it rose and fell there,
God's plan won't be deferred.

My castle's gone to somewhere,
Dawn brings a satin shore,
Michelle's back with her maker,
My heart's broken evermore.

Gloria Beacham
ONLY NATURAL
Not much more than an embryo,
When she limped half-dead 'cross my patio,
By all the rules she should have died,
. . . and I cried.

Bones without skin, tail without fur,
What could have made so "poor" of her?
She was determined to survive,
. . . so I tried.

Like clockwork, every day at four,
A tiny scratch upon my door,
A trusting sniff at both my feet,
my day complete!

Winter's here, she should forget,
She's fatty, furry now, and yet,
How the peanut treats do fly,
. . . .while I spy!

Oh yes! She will be back again,
A little less naive but then,
My squirrel will remember when,
. . . I cried.

Glenn Allen Willoughby
THE HOBO: AN AMERICAN TRAGEDY
Reach out your hand, oh glorious and clement land
To one of your own, the hobo who's lost and alone
He meanders along your rails and oh the stories he could tell
How they would make your mind soar
Please don't let him become another dinosaur

He's lost in his dreams as he eats from an old tin can
He drinks from your streams being looked upon as less than a man
In his tattered hat and newspaper lined shoes
Using anything that you can't use
Can you tell me his harm
When all he adds to the land is an old rustic charm
So please don't let history read:
"He's gone forever, The Hobo: An American Tragedy"
We see a flame in the night from a fire he's made from kindling pine
We know not to help him just ain't right but we never seem to find the time
There are people who would destroy what they don't understand
But those who would strike the first blows
Would be so much less than a man
Let's live with him and not without him should be our plea
May God have mercy on The Hobo: An American Tragedy

As he slips out into day in the blitheness of the morning's light
You see the smallness of the man until he's placed in history's sight
Then we will never really understand why we hated this man
When all he ever wanted to do
Was to walk across the crossties one more time
So let's take from his heart the ties that bind
And set him forever free
The Hobo: An American Tragedy

Sherrie D Wilson
'TWAS BUT A MAN

To my Lord and my God who invites us to "come unto Him, all who are weary and heavy laden, and He will give us rest." (Matthew 11:25)

God, bless this man, who by thy hand,
rescued me from the storm.
You knew my needs, from months of pleas;
and from my past I was torn.

He looked at me, but 'twas You who would see,
not the man in the opposite chair.
He asked of me, "What are your needs?"
Unafraid I stated my cares.

You brought us together. I question not whether,
'twas Your words this man had said.
From that day I knew my answer from You;
to this servant of yours I'd been lead.

My needs and Your will . . . I praise You, Lord, still,
for this man who met with me.
I'm sure, with a smile, You knew all the while,
he would help bring me back to Thee.

Thank you, Lord.

Martha K Descant
POEM AND POET
A poem is a ballad
That sings forth from the heart.
It's taking words and placing them
In a rhythmical sort.

A poet need not be inhibited or coy
For his goal is to bring
Feelings of love, thoughtfulness, or joy.

Expressing feelings in a clever way
Is just one more thing
That helps to make a poet's day.

Looking closely at life's situations
Helps to improve his poetic eloquence.
For life has many lessons;
One need not live in any pretense.

In each of his poems

His virtue shines through
Leaving some in wonder,
And maybe impressing a few.

Ruth Brigher
BROWN EYES

In memory of my beloved husband Herman.

Brown eyes,—
Changing eyes,—
With the knowing look.

Brown eyes,—
Dreamy eyes,—
A look, is all it took.

Brown eyes—
Searching eyes—
Closed forever now.

Brown eyes—
Loving eyes,—
Memories—still show.

Debra A Marcum
GOOD-BYE!!

People come and people go
It happens every day,
Though good-bye is such a simple word
I find it hard to say.

And as I watch you leave me now
I'll try hard not to cry,
For this is not the only time
I'll have to say good-bye.

And you are not the only love
I'll pass along the way,
Good-bye is just a simple word
I'll have to learn to say.

Diana L Sollid

Diana L Sollid
HIS LOVE

There is only one to whom this poem could be dedicated; To my precious Saviour, who loves us all.

'Twas not that I loved Him, you see.
'Twas that my Saviour first loved me.
All filled with sin,
I could not win,
But Jesus came to set me free.

He touched me with such love, my friend.
It's hard to even comprehend.
He loves me so,
For this I know,
My torn heart, He came to mend.

Away with anger, self pity too.
So now I'm here to share with you.
The love He'll give,
So we may live,
So we from death, may rise up new.

Whate'er He wants for us to do,
We must be willing to do, it's true.
But we must yearn,
To ever learn,
To give it all for Him to do.

Diana L Sollid
KEEP ME LORD!

Keep me Lord, keep me close to You.
Do whatever You have to do.
Keep me strong;
Your love prolong.
Keep me Lord, keep me close to You.

Keep me Lord, keep me close to You.
Give me peace, joy and patience too.
Hold me near;
Keep me from fear.
Give me love that's forever true.

Keep me Lord, keep me close to You.
Take away self-pity that makes me blue.
Give more love;
From up above.
Fill my heart with Your Spirit too.

Keep me Lord, keep me close to You.
Through pain, death and struggles too.
The battle's o'er;
I'll fight no more.
I give all. Keep me close to You.

Wendy Marie Ingoglia
MY SHOES

"To Mom," for always standing by my side.

Here I sit with my grandmother's shoes
I'll wear every color, if that's what I choose . .
High ones, low ones, ones in between . .
So relax my friends, and don't be mean . .
Flippity flop, I'll walk all around . .
And I'll be proud, 'cause these I've found . .
I'll slip them on and hook their latch
I'll wear Granny's clothes, if my shoes will match . .
I guess it doesn't matter because in the end
You'd like my shoes, if you were my friend.

Janet Ford Stone
MY HUSBAND FRED

We've Come A Long Way, Honey, You & I . . .
But I Still Don't Know The Reasons Why . . .
* * *
My Love For You Has Grown & Grown . . .
Like Something, I Have Never Known . . .
* * *
It's Twenty Eight Years For Us Today . . .
And I Love You In The Same Old Way . . .
* * *
I Look At You & I Can See . . .
That There Is No One Else For Me . . .
* * *
Our Marriage Has Been Very Good . . .
And I Can Tell You That I Would . . .
* * *
Let You Place Your Ring Upon My Hand . . .
And Forever Be At Your Command . . .

Janet Ford Stone
DANI JOY

Dedicated To: Danise De Donato, My Godchild & Niece.

You Stretched Out Your Hand, And I Held It . . .
* * *
You Poured Out Your Heart, And I Cried . . .
* * *
I Always Knew You Had So Many Things,
Buried Deep Inside . . .
* * *
To Smell, To Touch, To Feel, To See,
To Hear So Much When You Talk To Me . . .
* * *
There Is Nothing Wrong With Feeling Life,
If You Watch A Loved One Die . . .
* * *
And You Hold So Much Within Your Heart,
And It Is Alright To Cry . . .
* * *
Let Go, My Godchild, Of All The Pain,
And Take The Happiness Once Again . . .

"It's Yours"

Your Godmother
Janet Ford Stone

Janet Ford Stone
MY SON'S FIANCÉ, MILLIE

Today Is Your Birthday,
So Wish Upon A Star . . .
* * *
And All That You Wish For,
Cannot Be Too Far . . .
* * *
You Are A Great Person,
And I Hope That You Stay . . .
* * *
Like Your Mother Taught You,
The Old Fashioned Way . . .
* * *
The First Thing She Gave You
Was Life To Deal With . . .
* * *
The Next Thing She Gave You,
Was Mildred Elizabeth . . .
* * *
You Will Keep This Always,
This Is Your Name . . .
* * *
But, I'm Hoping And Praying,
Your Last Name Will Change! ! !

Janet Ford Stone
FRIENDS

Dedicated To: Patricia Boyce-Zakhar, Dorene Reale, Lillian Bono-Mola.

Friends Are So Important,
In Everything You Do . . .
* * *
They Seem To Know And Understand,
The Things That Trouble You . . .
* * *
Sometimes You Find You Hurt Them,
Although It's Not Intended . . .
* * *
And If The Friend Is Really True,
You Will Stay Befriended . . .
* * *
There Is Almost No Extent,
To The Things You Can Achieve . . .
* * *
The Serenity Of The Secret Thoughts,
In Which You Both Believe . . .
* * *
And That Is Why I'm Thankful,
To Have You For A Friend . . .
* * *
I Pray That This Will Never Change,
Until The Very End! ! !

Your Loving Friend
Janet Ford Stone

Janet Ford Stone
GUS

Dedicated To: Gus Kourpouanides, East Norwalk, Connecticut.

With Hair And Eyes As Dark As Pitch,
This Tiny Little Greek Boy . . .
* * *
He Runs And Jumps, And Scurries Round,
Like A Mechanical Toy . . .
* * *
Gus Is Built Like His Mom And Dad,
His Bones Aren't Very Large,
He Will Do Very Well,
Of His Life He Will Take Charge! ! !

Janet Ford Stone
THE HYPOCRITIC OATH

There Are So Many Things Going On Today,
That Cause Each Other Pain . . .
* * *
And They Don't Seem To Be Natural Or Fair,
And There Is No Personal Gain . . .
* * *
The Polluted Air And Litter Bugs,
Gangs And Murder And Street Wise Thugs . . .
* * *
There Is Child Abuse, Drugs And War,
And Racial Confrontations . . .
* * *
Put All Of These Together,
It Will Be Our Damnation . . .
* * *
There Seem To Be So Many Hypocrites,
So What Are We Going To Do . . .
* * *
I Don't Think You Should Ask Me,
For I'm A Hypocrite Too! ! !

Janet Ford Stone
MY LITTLE BROWN FORD

My Little Brown-Ford
I Love So Much . . .
She Taught Me All I Know . . .

She Taught Me How To
Yield And Curve . . .
To Stop And When To Go . . .

She Also Taught Me How To Love
All Children, Adults And Old . . .

And All The Animals
Put Here By God . . .

Many Stories She Has Told . . .

Now I'm Sure You Think
I Mean My Car
. . .
It's My Mother, Keeping
In Accord
. . .
Her Maiden Name Is Brown
Her Marriage Name Is Ford

Debbie Scienski
A KNIGHT TIME TALE
"Verily, verily, verily," the Knight was heard to say.
Merrily, merrily, merrily, he was riding on his way;
Hearing a maiden's helpless cry,
He sped along to find out "Why?"
Finding her trapped in a dragon's lair
Was much too much for him to bear.

Going forth with trusty lance
To dragon cave did he advance.
The great beast snorted fire quite hot;
The Knight's sword melted on the spot.
Needless to say, the poor brave man
Was neither heard nor seen again.

Today, the maiden is still there
Crying "Help" from the dragon's lair;
But, see, they've always had a deal
Making cash selling molten steel.

Donna A Chaples
GREAT GRANDMA'S HANDS
Great Grandma's hands
Wrinkled with age
Reveal her story of life, and
Bear the signs of hard days

For as many lines
And scars that show
There is a memory, a story
Recalled as if not long ago

A young man had come
Never separated 'til death
Leaving eight children behind, to
Carry on, do their best
Through the great flood
Depression, and wars
Surviving on little
Always doing the chores

Almost a century has passed, and
She's still holding on strong
Her life, a precious one
I'll miss her when she's gone.

Donna A Chaples
RAGGEDY ANN
Layered dust covers each box and trunk
A typical attic storing objects from the past
Folded in Great-Grandma's quilt
Lay Raggedy Ann

Her life has equaled that of her owner;
Each stripe on her trousers—each mistake
Each rotted thread on her face—each year of life

One look brings back a million memories
Dusted in the clinging cobwebs of age.

Florence G Sain
ONCE AGAIN

This poem is dedicated to my daughter Barbara Jean as she chose this one to be her favorite.

Once I was a mother, a mother dear was I
Till fate began to use me, only name did I belie.
I gave birth to a baby, six darlings did I conceive
Though two were taken from me, two others came to be.
I nursed and pampered all of them, how stubborn they could be
But everyone among us, knew that the mother, was me.
Times that came, times that went, much happiness was often spent
But soon after graduation, the wedding bells for bride and gent.
And now I seem so lonely, for I made the child my life
I've never had the loving care or been important as a wife.
So now I sit and wonder, and wonder why I sit
The kids are gone forever, and mother doesn't fit.
If only dreams were good enough, to fill these empty hours
Or I was just remembered, and it was really in my power.
Although I don't regret it, it's a wish that I have learned
To be the mother once again, is all that I'm concerned.

Debi Dunklin
GAZING OUT MY WINDOW
I stand, as the sun slowly descends from its home in the sky,
Gazing out my window.
The wind softly blows,
Pushing the leaves and debris.
Sluggishly, the hands of the clock are nudged forward.
I stand, as the darkness drapes its arms around the street,
Watching the city greet this change with brightly colored lights.
I stand behind the glass,
Comforted with the knowledge that I am safe,
Aware of the consequences of venturing from my sanctuary.
Tension mounts and my hands become tight.
Another day has blossomed as I move from my place at the window.
Slowly, the door creaks open and I step into the sunshine.
The world unfolds in front of me.
My senses are excited as my barriers are let down.
Into the world to find the peace and harmony I long for,
I venture.

Florence G Sain
THOUGHTS
What glory the crown, to reign above at will
When naught is gained for less.
Speak I say! To none be still . . . tarry on awhile
Then open sail, go on and sail . . . go on.
Words softly spoken release my deepest pain
To which I owe it all, the madness, tormented rain.
Watch needless waste of time regained
To those tarnished ways we will abstain.
Hark! The thought to say, as if too soon I wait,
Great love was the whisper, a lie so graciously late.
While time passed on the memories, thoughts and many dreams
Yet not to possess as if to say . . . be gone . . . be gone . . .
Forget the past and never think? A shame it is not true
For you and I will remain, as thoughts remind us again.

Jeanne Padlesky

Jeanne Padlesky
WHAT HAPPENED
What happened to our beautiful world
Our rivers lakes and streams
The living creatures were so plentiful
Our unforgettable dreams

What happened to our healthy air
Our fruits and vegetables too
And all the changes in our lives
And sadness in me and you

What happened to our love for all
The happy hours we spent
The happy family that once was
Were happy to no end

What happened to our grandma
Who made a large apple pie
And we all gathered around the table
There was plenty for you and I

Our prayers of to-morrow
Our thoughts of great dismay
Our hopes just turned to sorrow
Our faith of yesterday.

Jeanne Padlesky
MY GRANDMA OF YESTERDAY
Like a dream that lasted for years
I can picture her silvery hair
The flowers and birds she used to love
The children playing, music in the air

She was the world's best grandma
Whose poetry was known everywhere
The bloom and love throughout the world
The soft music was always there

As the new chapter was added to her life
When time had come for a rocking chair
I looked around of what used to be
It was slowly vanishing through the air

She was my grandma of yesterday
With her the beauty of the world lay deep
The bloom of love through all those years
That was left behind forever to keep

She was a woman like music of air
Like a lovely afternoon in silent days
With flowers blooming all around
Her gentle footsteps and smiling face.

Ruth Lunt
A FOSTER GRANDMOTHER
I am a Foster Grandmother who goes to school each day.
I teach, read stories, play computer games;
Sit in chairs too small, and have even played on the playground,
and been hit by a soccer ball.

But each day I go gladly,
To help a child that needs me.
For to miss a day, brings tears & "where's Grammie today?"

When a child says "Grammie you look so pretty today,"
It ties my tongue and turns my feet to clay.

And when another bends and ties my shoes or gives me a hug,
Or says "Grammie, you smell so good;"
Then I know when someone asks me, "What do you do all day?"
I can proudly say,
I am a foster grandmother who works every day.

Ruth Lunt
GUARDIAN ANGEL

Dedicated to Marti Crossman.

I have a guardian angel
Who sits on my shoulder to look after me.
She's as patient, understanding and loving
As she can be.

She whispers to me when I'm angry and when I'm confused
And how she does it always keeps me amused.
If I'm unhappy, silent or sad
She'll tease me and chide me and try to make me glad.

She never asks for anything,

And if I don't speak to her
She doesn't seem to care.
But if I need her I always
Know she's there.

Linda M Nichols
THE PERFECT SPRING

To my beloved Grandfather, E.B. Nichols, who inspired this poem.

In the stream of morning sun
I lift my voice to pray.
Lord, may I ask for blessings
on such a lovely day?

My senses filled with lilac
that blossoms on a tree.
Lord, shall I pray for joy
when you've given it to me?

Upon the branch there's a bird
who sings a lovely song.
Lord, how can I pray for peace
when there is nothing wrong?

All creation is a "Miracle."
Lord, never one so grand.
That reflects Your perfection
as a baby's tiny hand.

With all my heart I "Thank You"
Lord, for your love in many
ways.
I'll ask nothing of tomorrow.
You have sent it all today.

Yvette Alfrey
A PERMANENT SOLUTION

This poem is dedicated to all those who have tried, but in this case, It is better to fail than to succeed.

A permanent solution to a temporary
problem
that's what suicide is
A coward's way to die; It's just not
worth it
A horrible way not to exist

I don't know why I even tried
what would I achieve?
Pain, suffering, hospitalization?
I don't want that for me.

I feel so dumb and incapable
of doing anything right.
For causing pain to Mom
I wish I could make things alright.

Suicide. Why was it invented?
It just causes pain.
Mom feels like a failure with me and
my brother
She doesn't know who to blame.

I don't want death
I'm too young to die
I hate causing trouble
I don't even know why I tried,
(Suicide)

Walter Allen Twyford
UNCLE "HO" AND THE OLIVE DRAB COWBOYS

To those that sacrificed in Vietnam.

I came to your home uninvited.
That glance from your eyes
undelighted.
I said "I am here, for freedom is near,
Won't you simply lend me your ear."
He said what a lie that I've heard by
and by;
From the French, Japs, and the
"Chis,"
That this freedom you hail is a cover
for jail,
And like they you surely will fail.

Now my patience grew thin, and I
yelled out "We'll win!"
We're the mightiest army on earth.
We've airplanes and guns, and
bombs by the ton,
And warriors eager to fight.

Then he said it again, again and
again,
"The end for you is in sight."
For the lie that you told, about
freedom's like mold, to a rock that
keeps moving won't hold.

Patricia A Allen
NEW HORIZONS

I love to sit on the beach
watch the tides roll in
wishing it would never end

To look at the children play
hoping to overstay their visit

But as I look high up into the sky
I notice that something is there
that wasn't there before

The seagulls are trying to tell me
something
I wish I knew what it was

As I smile and grin I find out what it
really is

And I tell them that someday I'll be
with them again

Soaring and searching for their new
horizons

Jeane Carman
SEE ME

Listen to me, hear me, see me, feel
me
I long to be free of all the
expectations you have laid upon me
To be nice, to be polite, to do what is
'right'
To produce, to act, to not talk back.

No longer will I accept: your abuse
and your neglect
Your refusal to let me be, your
inability to see me
NO MORE EXCUSES: "she was
hurting so I needed to reach out,"
"I couldn't tell him no," or
"I 'should' do such and so."

There's not much time left; it's a
matter of life or death——
The life of a child who no longer
chooses to be meek and mild.

Will you listen to me? . . . hear
me . . . see me . . . feel me?
I have been hiding, waiting for a safe
Place, needing to be set free
From your little boxes . . . from this
prison space

Listen to me, Hear me, see me, feel
me.
Let me be just me and I'll release to
you your gift
The gift written into your being, your
spirit and the world's to lift.

You will listen to me? You will hear
me?
You will see me? You will feel me?
IT is I your INNER CHILD, the little
girl you wouldn't see
Longing to be free, unbound, released
To be the person God intended me to
be.

J Elmer Aaron
JEFFREY

'Why do the leaves fall off the trees?'
He asks me in his curious way.
'What will they do without them
now?
And will God glue them back again?'

He wonders why the sun comes up.
And where it goes when darkness
falls.
And why the sky is golden red.
And how far up it really is!

'Who makes the bugs?' 'Why do
frogs hop?'
'How can birds fly?' 'Do they get
cold?'
As ceaselessly his mind explores
The wonders of his new-found world.

It's his world now, as well as mine.
He has not lost its beauty yet.
God sent a little boy of three,
To bring its wonder back to me.

DeLeon Lee Jr

DeLeon Lee Jr
TO MY FIRST GRANDCHILD

Thank God for little Grace
For grace is great upon her face
At a glance my heart you melt
Never have such love I felt.

Little Grace, Amazing Grace
How beautiful you are in frilly lace
Like an angel you are to our world
My pretty granddaughter and little
girl.

We prayed for you before your birth
That God might thru you bring joy to
earth
To bless your parents, your home and
all
A tremendous gift from someone so
small.

To watch you grow is to reminisce
Of times gone by of which we miss
When we were able to cuddle our
own
Never more, for those times have
gone.

I cherish to think when we too
Together, grandmother, I and you
With one another good times will
share
Our lives may show the depth that we
care.

I know your parents will do their best
It's their nature to labor without rest
To provide for you a home of love
Unmatched because it was made
above.

For those we love most, your mom
and dad
Have blessed our lives with you
instead
The bells ring out and with much
happiness we shout
What a change your life to us has
brought about.

DeLeon Lee Jr
THE LEE HOMESTEAD

Four miles Northeast of Olanta Town
Lies a small farming community on
sandy ground
Where greatly was to be enjoyed the
rural life
Men labored to farm, as most often
did the wife.

The "Sandhill" as it's called, by all
who know
Where childhood we spent, and to
adults did grow
It seemed so distant and far from all
The crops we grew and to market
would haul.

The sandspur and pricklepear grow
splendidly here
Beware the barefoot, ever you should
travel there
The serenity of the country is quite
uncompared
Where once we all lived and loved
and shared.

Who can forget, the years we spent
Of summer days and tobacco scent
To harvest the crops and store for
feed
The corn and hay, the livestock
would need.

Now the barns sit idle, where once
was much labor
Each one had their task, help came
from neighbor
As dawn to dusk, seemed the normal
routine
To crop the tobacco, clad in stained
blue jean.

The farm back then, as we fondly
remember
The harvest that seemed to bring each
September
Tho many years have passed, we so
ably recall
As only yesterday, that came each
fall.

Thru the medium of poetry, may we
share it with all.

Jim Wolner
CLOQUET, CLOQUET

To all the pioneers who have made this northern Minnesota town a great place in which to live.

Cloquet, Cloquet,
Where sawmills once held sway.
Those saws would sing,
And then you'd hear them ring.
They'd cut logs fair
To lumber square.
Cloquet, Cloquet,
You're wood town U-S-A.
That old St. Loo
Goes winding gently thru
This town where wood
Is changed to products good.
The river's flow
Makes pow'r to go.
Cloquet, Cloquet,
You've come a long—long way.
Cloquet, Cloquet,
Your dawn is bright today.
That purple east,
Provides these eyes a feast.
Green trees so fine
Dot hills that shine.
Cloquet, Cloquet,
I love you more each day.

Wes Robertson
ZEPHYRS

I hear your softly whispered word.
Your feathery touch I feel
upon my face.
I can see the zephyrs swirl and dance.
They bounce the leafy litter
and make it race.

My days are governed by your whims.
In the night, I shiver to hear
you groan.
You detour around all man-made dreams.
I am awed by the sands you
have blown.

Into every nook and hole you creep.
All things you cover. All things
you reveal.
Nothing can forever withstand your caress.
While in the sky, clouds turn
and wheel.

Could it be that a calm most dreadful would settle
If, one day, your progress
should slow and die?
Upon a waveless sea, the sail would slacken.
Not a tree would shudder—
not a bird would fly.

Though some may curse your hurricane blast,
You are a friend to the child
with kite aloft.
You are the pull on his arm, the push at his back.
So, blow, dear wind—either
hard or soft.

M Jane McKenzie
BUT . . .

I really love you
But . . . do you love me?
Sometimes you seem to
Lack sincerity.

Yet I do love you
But . . . you don't treat me
Right—no one deserves
This uncertainty.

I love you so much
But . . . you don't need me
And so I find that
I feel so lonely.

I'll always love you
But . . . you aren't ready
To settle down yet.
You want to be free.

M Jane McKenzie
THE HURT INSIDE

You tell me that you care.
But it really isn't fair
How you've been treating me.
I feel so hurt inside.

I don't deserve such pain—
An emotional drain.
Your love is all I wanted
(Not such deep hurt inside).

People don't hurt ones they
Love—I thought that one day
We would be together.
Now there's this hurt inside . . .

Mary Moquin
BEAUTY OF THE SPIRIT

Beauty of the Spirit
Is there for all to gain—
To use, preserve, and cherish
In God's All-Holy Name.

A beauty that is silent,
A beauty that is strong,
A beauty that is helpful
When anything goes wrong;

A beauty that ever sings
As it spreads its gentle wings—
Seeing the beauty in others
And all surrounding things.
A beauty that is forgiving
Feeling another's woe
Beauty fully living,
Yet gentle as a doe;
A beauty that is thriving on God's all precious Word;
Assured of surviving—telling Jesus heard!
A beauty that is reaching to all beyond bounds,
To help share the glory of all God surrounds!

Mary Moquin
SOMETHING PRECIOUS

Sheltered, secluded—
Hidden from view—
Sits dutiful Mother Bird
On something quite new!

Anticipation—
I see in her eyes,
As she patiently sits,
Ever-guarding her prize.

At times looking east,
As hours pass by;
And later it's west—
With nary a sigh!

Days come and go,
They turn into weeks—
When, Lo and Behold—
Upped three little beaks!

Oh, joy of joys!
A Mother's reward!
Through all kinds of weather—
Now, finally, scored!

Walt Bell
LAND OF LIBERTY

'Tis shame we bring upon this land of free, our Fathers Author Of Liberty; we did not wish this land to be, raped by foreign democracy.

Oh! Lord our God, please make this be the land our Fathers fought for thee, not what you see, poor land of free, no more our country 'Tis of Thee.

Our Pilgrims' pride is gone from thee because our children cannot be part of our country's infancy you see they know not what it be.

Our sea shores were so freshening, but now the brown tide's threatening, our Trout are dying in the pools, 'tis acid rain we are such fools.

They'll be no scenic views to see because of rich man's Lumbering, Progress! Progress! that's what it be, I! think it's something else, you see.

The "Greed" Of Man is what it be, "He," sold our land of Liberty and now our land is not so Free, so fear what is ahead of Thee!

Walt Bell
A TEAR FROM A CLOUD

A tear fell from a cloud on the mountain, then it started something grand; a jewel of a mountain pond, which was named by an Indian man.

It is nestled in a Glen of Hemlocks, just below a summit of snow; there were Cougars' prints in its stream beds so many years ago.

The Eagle soars above it—and the Broad-wing nests near by;
The Raven's call is frequently heard as the Jay bird passes by.

'Twas told here once camped an Indian Chieftain, on his journey to Heaven above. His spirit is all around there passed on by the Mourning Dove.

It's the source of the mighty Hudson—a pool of Heavenly gold as the sun shines down upon it, 'tis Heaven on earth it's been told.

No more will the Trout rise there,

No more will the Eagle call,

No more will the wilderness hide there,

Acid rain has started to fall.

Walt Bell
TWO MORNING DOVES

At dawn I hear a tone that's clear, Two Morning Doves are nesting near.

Their calling seems to fill the air with mournful sounds and loving care.

My neighbor's Pine, it seems to be the place that these Doves have agreed to build their nest, high in the tree, secluded from all eyes to see.

The nest is built with twigs and sticks, two white eggs therefore affixed.

They both take time to settle in on hatching their two fledgling twins.

They flicker off and dart away, a whistling noise they sound that way.

But soon there will be more, you see my feathered friends new family.

I watched my neighbor's "Old Tom Cat" sit still as he could be: he is watching the activities of the Doves high in the tree.

It seems his curiosity is satisfied, you see, because he moves off out of sight beneath that large Pine tree.

Next winter there will be, I hope, two more Morning Doves feeding at my feeders with all my friends, I love.

So when you hear the cooing from a Morning Dove above, remember he is calling to his mate he chose to love.

Dian Rosamond

Dian Rosamond
MY CHRISTMAS DREAM

As the snow falls gently upon my face
As the candles light my way in the night
It's the time of year to see if our wishes will come true
Everyone has their own Christmas Dream
Children dream of stuffed animals and toy trains that run
Some of us just want an old fashion Holiday
Hear the sleigh bells ring and see the people ski down to the village
To get all their shopping done
This is their Christmas Dream
This is the way it always should be right through the year

Kathie S McCullough
RETURNING HOME

For the first time ever
I feel peaceful inside.
Like the sounds of the sea
Just as darkness falls.

Life seems full
As the peak of the moon.
Yet, new
As the birth of springtime.

I used to write of loneliness
And fear and anger and pain.
But they were my gifts
Back to the universe.

The power and the beauty
Of the waves cover me,
And protect my existence
As though I were home again.

To bathe in the softness
And taste the salty wetness
On my lips. Oh sea,
You touch all of me.

Kathie S McCullough
LOST FRIEND
I sent my unicorn to fetch you that you might come out and play. But the angels guarding your threshold motioned him away. For a moment I gasp of fear that they might be guards of your tomb. So I sat quietly in the darkness, peering from my room.

Yet, I thought it strange that you would slip away without a word, so I decided to pretend that there was just no one at home. Suddenly some stars fell down from the sky. I picked them up and held them high, to light the way for your return.

I thought I glimpsed your shadow from within your castle walls. But 'twas only elves and fairies dancing through the halls. They'll stay and dance while you're in dreamland, but when you awake they'll have to go.

So if you'll peer down from your castle window, you'll see that I'm still here, just waiting with my unicorn for you to come out and play.

j edwin doughty
WRITER
They say that I am normal,
Predictable I've heard,
I lack originality,
I tell you that's absurd,
I can sing and dance with angels,
I can fly away with birds,
I can take you to the fall of Rome,
I do it all with words,
I can use imagination,
To enhance a tale I've heard,
I can add some lines to lengthen it,
Or leave it undisturbed,
I can color it with adjectives,
Or switch around the verbs,
Yes, I am a writer,
I do it all with words.

j edwin doughty
THE WAY OF THINGS
Life is lonely,
and death is only but a breath
away,
I heard him say,
a child is born to die one
day,
And if by chance the world is kind,
the child may find,
peace of mind,

Love is only,
a rose whose precious beauty
knows today,
I heard him say,
a flower blooms to wilt
away,
And if by chance the flower grows,
the cold wind blows,
to kill the rose,

Death is lonely,
but right is always there to
light the way,
I heard him say,
a dream is born to live
one day,
And if by chance the angels sing,
my death will bring,
the way of things.

j edwin doughty
TO OUR PARENTS
You gave us life,
Protected us,
Taught us to live,
To think,
To love,
To care for each other,
And to be ourselves,
You gave us everything.

j edwin doughty
AND FOREVER
The lights begin to flicker,
the night turns into day,
The echoing of freedom,
carries me away,
And forever,
and forever,
the stars will always shine,
There will be a dreamer,
as long as there is time,
to fade away.

The night begins to settle in,
the sky is turning grey,
The past is left behind us,
tomorrow slips away,
And forever,
and forever,
men are growing old,
Searching for serenity,
in a world that's turning cold,
each passing day.

j edwin doughty
UNTIL I LOOKED INTO YOUR EYES
I've seen the flowers glisten,
In the early morning dew,
I've felt the sunlight warm me,
I've kissed a girl or two,
I've heard the music whisper,
With true love the melody,
I've seen the sun set softly,
Into a glowing symphony,
I've seen the moonlight dancing,
Through a velvet summer sky,
But I never saw a rainbow,
Until I looked into your eyes.

j edwin doughty
I SHOT HIM WITH MY GUN
He was just a young man,
no more than twenty-one,
His future was before him,
his life had just begun,
I bet he had a family,
a wife, a home, a son,
I didn't even know him,
but I shot him with my gun,

They said go do your duty,
there's a victory to be won,
Do it for your country,
I did it now it's done,
In peace there's always courage,
in killing there is none,
And just because he's different,
I shot him with my gun.

Laszlo Szuromi
SPIRIT LADY

These poems are dedicated to my best friend Dale & Elaine Stotts, and their sweet daughters to Kristi & Jenna.

I can crying, I can laughing
At the time, if at the worst.
In my dream the blessed return,
And she realize what swindle she was
How long the executioner hands
holding her.
I seize her face and encourage
confidence
How she can keep faith with her love
Under the spirit clothes.
She not sob, for only lived in my
dream,
But I sob when she fear in the fat
hands.
She tremble my soul deep nook,
And shout in my brain.
Don't give there nobody for nothing.
Shouting already me too,
Because the pain push me in the fat
hands.
From the sweat bed kick out the fear,
I did laughing, because on my neck
No was nothing of rope,
But I bewail spirit lady,
Who maybe no come back
never-more.

Laszlo Szuromi
DEATH THE REAPER
Silently fly over your head the years
As each other addition the forest
litter,
That the wind snatch up, then lay out,
Somewhere along the road cover in
the dust.
Your forehead wrinkled bend down
with the time,
Like somebody who fears from the
dark,
You so run away with your rickety
bones.
From your lung comes only a sigh
S.O.S. God!
Besides you nobody knows the Big
Reaper.
This moment your soul was light, the
pain go off.
Death the Reaper is the greatest
angel,
Who indeed makes no deal with
nobody,
Because he has the judgment of
non-suit.
No, No, never was he murder,
He is the Executive, and above is the
Justice,
Whom lordship is the saving
goodness,
Above he no was, never be biggest
mightiness.
The devil have key just for the small
gate,
Which opens those people who love
him.
On this door never came back
anybody,
Under the endless fire they positively
pass away.
I know Big the Reaper one day will
grab me,
But I believe he feels that, I don't
hate him.
My mind, my heart give me honesty
life,
Death the Reaper always be friend of
mine.

Laszlo Szuromi
FOR THE FOXED NAKED LADY
Wild flower the naked lady,
Everybody envious on your
beautyness.
All bachelor dying for your love,
All girl hate your beauty.
Only for me no effective your yellow
dress in silk.
I know you from inside, I think you
don't have heart.
What you have is a hungry frog, who
daily hold many guy.
You born for fawn, but your idea turn
you a wolf-bitch,
Who murdering the meek-hearted
roe-bucks.
How long keep yourself that type of
life,
Do you believe, you be always the
star?
Day-dreaming and cheating never
give you peaceful of time.
Change in your soul the yellow light!
When the ageness knock on your
door,
You have two choice; red or green
light.
The loser only you can be, and the
ugly frog,
Who leading your brain and heart.

Laszlo Szuromi
STARRY-EYED
Summer night the stars twinkled in
the sky,
Don't fall into servitude your
starry-eyed.
Let me go hand in hand with
yourself,
Let me get to know what your lady
heart hide and have.
Let me love you exposed to the
public gaze,
Don't let me that forget for ever the
starry night.
Thereupon I feel that, all the world
have, I can held.
I recovery in you the good and
fairness that starry night.
You will be my children mother, for
the family the queen.
Keep me in your soul when you
walking or sleeping.
Nobody no damage in your
starry-eyed the lovely shine.

Laszlo Szuromi
MOTHER'S DAY
Your children grown-up long time
age,
For whom tell your story good
Mother?

By oneself lie on the big family bed,
For whom find you the new story,

Who be in tears after the happy
wedding?
Your great heart gave away half of
kingdom,
Poor young man got lovely princess
hands.

We learn from you the truly
affection,
And how we can live or can't.

I know you never be alone,
Because your mind and heart with us.

That why we working for the future,
That why we believing in God.

I wish for you every day;
God love my Mother!
How she love and believing You.

If your God appearance her dream,
Give her all children with smiling
face.

Kathy Altman
LOVE IS
Love is a gift to be shared
with someone very special.
Love is fulfilling and to be
willing, always ready to share.
Love is pleasing, never teasing
and never having to ask.
Love is having trust and respect,
never any doubt.
Love is holding, touching and
kissing any time you're near.
Love is always wanting to be
there when the other's in need.
Love is having hope for tomorrow,
knowing that you will be there.
Love is so real, I wish that

everyone could feel,
The way I feel for you in my heart.

"I LOVE YOU"

Mary Helen Mobry Leksa
NEXT-DOOR NEIGHBORS

To the Wernings from the Mobrys with Love.

Where elms once arched over the avenue,
the afternoon sun charcoals on their house
the shape of ours, the shadow of our chimney
falling softly on their roof,
two smokes curling and mingling—
two white frame houses blending
through the years.
Across old lilac bushes
morning and evening hand waves
from lighted kitchen windows,
garden plot conversations,
hot oven breads carried around the open fence;
our Concord grapes transformed
into their bright jelly,
returned like gifts of stained glass—
window reflections of our little church
around the corner, summoning
with its clanging old bell
our three generations.

Diana Mercado
SWEET JESUS

Where have all the flowers gone, it's time for them to bloom.
The early Spring is whispering, "Let death go to his tomb."
My Master's heart is bleeding, and in His eyes I see a tear.
He's wounded and rejected, and His time is oh so near.
How could they all just stand there, and watch Him slowly die.
They laughed and mocked His Holy name, not a tear fell from their eyes.
There are nails in His hands and feet, a crown of thorns upon His head.
His back is torn where He'd been beat, His body is blood red.
Did they care that He loved them still, as they watched His life grow dim.
And did they hear Him say, as He faded away, "Father, forgive them."
This man of love who gave His life, so unreservedly, is our Dear Lord,
Sweet Jesus . . . He died to set us free.
Do you know that He loves you still, He gave all He had to give.
He gave His love, His very life . . . that through Him we might live.

Diana Mercado
TELL ME WHAT YOU SEE

Now that you have come inside, tell me what you see . . . a frightened child with tearstained eyes, seeking comfort endlessly.

Or do you see a raging fire, burning deep within my soul. Does it yield warmth to those around, does it provide a gentle glow.

Or does it burn like wildfire, destroying all it sees. Does it laugh a haunting laugh, as it brings you to your knees.

Does the child inside scream in terror, as he watches the fire consume. Does he turn and run for his very life, lest it bring him to his doom.

And what of the child, and what of the flame, are the two not one. And can you see, they both are me, when all is said and done.

Rose Marie Tilotta
A BETTER WAY

When life's frustrations fence you in
and it seems you've forgotten how to win;
When hope is shattered and efforts fail
and pain and disappointment prevail;
When those you depend on are untrue
and heavier burdens are placed on you;
When there's nothing left for you to give
and you hate the way that you now live;
Know that there is a better way,
If you humble yourself, kneel down and pray,
You cannot make it on your own;
But with God's help, you are never alone.
God wants to do great things for you.
He'll become "real," if you ask Him to.
He'll create in you a transformed life
That is free from heartache, misery and strife.
Emerge from your cocoon a butterfly.
Obtain the impossible with only one try,
Then praise God for setting you free
And for helping you walk in victory!

Rose Marie Tilotta
ONLY YOU, JESUS

Only you, Jesus, can give life to me.
Only you, Jesus, can set my soul free.
Only you, Jesus, can do anything.
So, I exalt thee, my God and my King!

If the world could know you the way that I do,
They'd turn from sin this moment and follow you.
I've just got to tell them that you're real and you care.
They don't know you love them or the power of prayer.

When I was lost you came to me, with a message of love.
When hope was gone, you gave me life and strength from above.
You taught me how to stand by faith, trusting in you.
No matter what may come my way, you'll see me through.

Thank you, Lord, for loving me enough to give your life.
You died so I might live, you already paid the price.
For every problem, great or small, the answer's found in you.
I owe you everything; Jesus, I love you!

Only you, Jesus, can give life to me.
Only you, Jesus, can set my soul free.
Only you, Jesus, can do anything.
So, I exalt thee, my God and my King!

Jacqueline C Patterson
MOTTO IN POETRY

P Stands for the PRIDE which permeates inside.
R Stands for the RESPONSIBILITY which runs wide.
O Stands for the OBLIGATION we tide.
S Stands for the STAFF that sometimes chides.
P Stands for the PURPOSE which abides.
E Stands for the EXCELLENCE in education for which we strive.
C Stands for the CHILDREN in our lives.
T Stands for the TRUTH we try to revive.

Jean Conley

Jean Conley
LITTLE SHOE

Dedicated to my sons, Robert Conley and Donald Conley.

One worn little shoe with
Perhaps a hole in the toe.
And why have we saved them?
Well . . . all parents know.

There's nothing so sweet
As a baby's worn shoe,
And patter of little steps
Following you.

The feet they once held
Have grown slender and strong.
Tonight they'll be tired after
Working so long.

We guided his feet when he
Wore this little shoe.
Dear God, guide them now,
Please, won't you?

Jean Conley
JOY

Dedicated to Jack Conley.

"Joy," for me, is loving you

And sharing daily life
With that special kind of closeness
Between a husband and wife—
Setting goals, and working
To reach them, one by one,
Sharing quiet moments
All alone when each day's done,
Discovering each other—
Always something new to know—
Helping you, as you help me,
To learn and dream and grow. . .
We're lovers and companions,
Best friends and partners, too—
More and more, with every day,

"Joy," for me, is loving you!

Roland W Schultz
THE PIONEERS' SEA OF TEARS

Dedicated to Beverly Neitzke, who taught me to read.

Have you ever thought about what our pioneers would say?
If our pioneers could see the web of cement and asphalt we have left behind.
Would there be a path of tears behind our country's pioneers?
No, I think there would be a sea of tears behind our country's pioneers.

Devro Jim Nakagawa
THE WAY

Voices fleeting sweet
Songbird essence encapsulates
Whole a frenzied soul.

The cry of mysterious
Spirits forebode the
Pull of groin and sensual holes.

Aspirations of the young
Dig the bass with
Strange sexuality and
Not a fractured erection.

Deirdre Daly
STONE WALL

Untouched by the sands of time it stands.
Buried, the work of long lost human hands.
Leaves lay upon it, then covered with snow,
Its mysteries, its secrets, we'll never know.
Perhaps the cold stones hold a hidden time,
Of a peaceful evening walk, so fine.
Wish the wall could talk and say
Of all that has happened with every passing day.
Perhaps this wall watched time go by,
Saw soldiers of the armies die,
Perhaps this niche supported
someone's ancient gun,
That time of history the wall knows done.
Many years and seasons by have flown,
The secret of time still not known,
Perhaps someday the earth will fall,
With the secrets, still hidden, of the old stone wall.

Sylvia Helton
MY MAN
Green is the grass I walk on . . .
Golden the sun that warms my day.
Brown is the ground I tramp along on.
Blue is the sky on my perfect day.
Warm are the arms that hold me tight,
and make me feel just right.
Cat green—yes cat green are the eyes of my guy—Harold.

Carol M Bell
NEVER ALONE
Come to me whenever you get lonely
Just reach up your heart and there i'll be
My truth will light your way out of the darkness
When you feel you've been forsaken come to me

I'm asking you to understand your faith in me
Trust in me and know that i'm your all
I'll never leave you nor will I forsake you
Trust in my love and you will never fall

Come to me when sorrow overtakes you
When trouble seems to follow you around
Believe in me and know that I will save you
I'll plant your feet on safe and solid ground

Reach out to me when the pain overcomes you
When you reach the point you feel you can't go on
My feet will walk the path of life for both of us
My love for you will shield you from the storm

Come to me each time a storm befalls you
When trials & troubles weigh your body down
I will give you rest and ease your burdens
Reach up your heart and there's where i'll be found

Lois Peck
THE DAY AFTER CHRISTMAS
'Twas the day after Christmas and all through the house,
The children were fussing and grumbling about.
Could it be too little sleep or too many sweets,
That makes coexistence an impossible feat?

Mama picks up the ribbons and all of the wrappings,
While Father reclines in his easy chair napping.
The puppy scratches unnoticed at the door,
And soon she makes a puddle on the floor.

The vacuum collects needle ten-thousand and five,
Which is more than the tree had when alive!
The fresh scent of pine lingers in the air.
How did eggnog get spilled on that chair?

The yule log has shed its last warm glow,
Casting its ashes unto the new fallen snow.
Someone is hungry? Now, how can that be?
It's time to slice the leftover turkey.

Christmas cards adorn the mantel, vicariously arranged.
I wonder why we count them, doesn't that seem strange?
Rereading the passages, makes one thing quite clear,
We celebrate the birthday of One very dear.

Linda Cohen
A POEM FOR A FRIEND
Of the depths
of God, unseen,
'tis for some men to know;
but there I find 'tis only few
desiring to go.

There is a place for lesser men
awaiting on the shore;
the depths of God
they hunger not
nor desire for.

And if it is
this life you seek,
to go beyond the surface, deep,
as deep the dark of the blue sea,
'tis where few men will ever be.

And if it is your portion
this mantle to bestow,
then this I pray, dear friend,
yet deeper you will go.

Jen Vespa
DO YOU . . . ?
Can you hear the brisk wind blow?
Do you watch the falling snow?
Do you ever feel the rain,
or ever cry at the thought of pain?
Do you like the smell of flowers?
Do you realize Mother Nature's powers?
Do you ever stand in the breeze
or carefully study the leaves on the trees?
Do you ever sit on the grass
and watch the clouds slowly pass?
Do you notice the beauty we can share
or do you even care?

Mary Louis Kister
LIFE
Had I not awakened
From my sleep today
Others may feel sorrow
But to them I would say
I am feeling nothing save
Peacefulness and calm
Just serene contentment
Enfolded in God's Arm
I did not ask to pass through life
Or enter on this earth
And God has led me—
Lovingly
To my eternal birth!

Mrs Eddie Lynne Hammonds-Quisenberry
HOPE
Hope is the stem of what our lives are built on,
Each day brings a new portion of the unknown.
The future may hold so many different things,
And we have to cope with what cannot be explained.
We must take slowly one day at a time,
In order to appreciate what wonder we can find.
There's so much to be discovered and the joy and hope to live on,
And so many things we can do without having to be shown.
The drug problems, the homeless to mention a few,
This could all be solved if each and every one of us started anew.

Dorothy Murray
THE CREATURE
I bob and weave;
I spar and joust.
I just know it will leave;
But it I cannot roust!

Wait! There's a chair here
Behind which I must hide,
I peer out; it's very clear
It's here, there, like a tide.

It's quite plain to me now,
However I try to elude,
To the victor I shall bow
No matter time, place or mood.

Janette S Smoot

Janette S Smoot
SUCCESS

Dedicated to the field of psychiatry.

Look! When the sun shines
Through my window that's wealth
When I can turn in my bed
This what I call success
Viewing life each day—
To succeed
Balance to balance
Life to living is success
Meeting life's crossroad
Movement to movement
Relationship to relationship

Travel to travel
A gift to life
Growing to growth
Interaction to Interaction
Self soul to soul
Strive to striving

To rise in the morning
Stepping yet climbing
Gaining, yet higher and higher
In
One
Shot

Richard Pearce
THE TREE
Could I climb this tree more swiftly
than the tree itself climbs skyward
with the breadth of great intent?
Then would I wheel with dizzy dancing joy
as night-time stars dip and swirl
in the purple vastness of creation's eye?

(There's food yet to spend,
growing gray, growing old.)

Will no one mourn one falling leaf,
One spinning, scented needle pine?
Will no more grateful eyes greet this
The all-embracing vision of this tree,
Planted, so unlike mankind,
which wanders with its roots
declining soil?

For man I'll shed no bitter tears
We've clipped our cultured lawn,
Our cruelness bears a blunted blade,
Unshielded, by a final light at dawn.

Elva R MacKay
AWAY
I don't want to go away, dear
It will break my heart in two
But I know that you don't love me
So what else is there to do.

I can't stay and see you daily
Knowing you no longer care
Even though you cannot love me
All my love for you is there.

So I'll go away tomorrow
Hoping God will ease the pain
But—if your heart should e'er remember
I could still come back again.

Elva R MacKay
WITHOUT YOU
Our love, dear, is over,
My lifetime is thru,
For I can't keep on living,
Each day without you.

You say you found someone,
You love more than me.
My ears hear your story,
But my eyes cannot see.

Please turn and go now,
What more can I say,
My lips want to kiss you,
And beg you to stay.
My arms want to hold you.
My poor heart is sore
My life is ebbing
As you walk out the door.

My poor heart is breaking
As you walk away,
My life is over
It ended today.

Linda M Biega
IF EVER WE SHOULD MEET

For my family.

If ever we should meet, I know;
A warmth would pass from hand to hand,
And from eye to eye a glow.

For we are kindred spirits,
Our souls somehow entwined.
Perhaps it is I once was yours,
And you, that once, were mine.

Lavada Robbins
LAKE OF FIRE
The devil dances and laughs with glee,
'A soul' he said, 'for me' with greed.
'Oh Master of darkness, you'll have your way.'
His evil angels begin to say.

Make it play and dance for you,
do bad things you want to do.

Fightin' and drinkin', and making a riot.
Drugs on the street day and night.

Sell to the children, sell to the poor.
By all means, the rich ones will always want more!
Thieves, liars, murderers too.
Keep them working when they are through.

A lake of fire is their reward.
Dark angels will punish them for evermore.
Hell torment they will stay
for the evil deeds they did today.

Tracie M Norman
EMPTY EMOTIONS
When I look in his eyes
I see hurt and depression,
The touch of his hand
is not of aggression.
The pain in his heart
Weakens his emotions,
The sounds in his head
are like thundering colbultions.
The life of this man
is starting to melt,
things that he missed
and never has felt.
His future, his dreams
are passing him by,
He just sits staring
not a sound or a sigh.
Now he is gone
his memory remains,
inside of my heart
Now I'm feeling his pain.

Everett Swenson
ADVENTURE IN DREAMS
Read me a story as I lay and rest
With lids of my eyes drawn closed
But ears that are posed to gather your voice
So story on mind is imposed.

Read me a story of subtle romance
Adventures and travel afar
Then let me sleep and soon start to dream
Let me be the story's main star.

Let me experience in my dreams
Of love and adventure untold
To countries and people of different tongues
Where intrigue is sure to unfold.

Then let me sleep with raptured dreams
Fulfilling a lifetime desire
To haven and play with the greats of the day
And travel with those I admire.

Then as I wake to reality
To find my dreaming sublime
My only conclusion is at that point
It was lesser in fare and in time.

Fern Costello
THE WALLS ARE TUMBLING DOWN
The trees stand straight and tall
Away beyond the Berlin Wall
Their branches sway with evening breeze
Leaves flutter to the ground
They are free.
Once I stood straight and tall
When I was out beyond the wall
But here my head hangs low with shame
For what they did.
At night I watch the stars above my prison bars
They too are free.
What I would give just once again
If I could be . . . just free.

. . .

Now I stand straight and tall
Outside the Berlin Wall
I am free
The Walls are tumbling down.

Lisa Marie Lee
YEARS AGO
As I sit in my chair and watch my child play,
I have memories of a long since past day.

I have memories of a sparkling brook.
Such fun rides I took, up and down its sandy shore
Which I shall see no more.

Mother's roses of yellow-gold,
I've been told are all gone away,
Though I never forget them from day to day.

Blue-birds build nests in the tops of the trees,
And the quiet sound of the whistling breeze,
Fields of Susans with big brown eyes.

I remember crows with their squaking cries,
The field with its grass so green,
Such a sight has never been seen.

Though those things have passed away,
I keep them precious in my memory from day to day.

Gretchen Duncan
I'M PROUD
I'm proud to be an American
To live in a land that's free
For many men have fought and died
Keeping that freedom for you and me.

They fought King George's army
Through winter winds and snow
And when the battle ended
They were victors o'er the foe.

When world war threatened, again they fought
To keep our nation free
And keep us safe from enemies
Who stood for tyranny.

Once more we called for men to fight
After the Day of Infamy
We asked so much, they gave so much
In the name of liberty.

Oh, I'm proud to be an American
And I give thanks to God for men
Who loved their country more than life
And did their duty to defend.

Michael C Bradford
MOTHERS OR NOT
Love and devotion,
You do have a lot.
To me, all women are special;
Mothers or not!

So if nature has handed you
An empty pot,
Just remember, you're still loved;
Mothers or not!

So you've been cheated
Of having a little tot,
You're still wanted;
Mothers or not!

So in case you've forgot,
Your children and/or husbands
Still need you;
Mothers or not!

Pug A Bowers
PLOWING SNOW: CONFESSIONS OF A FIRST YEAR EQUIPMENT OPERATOR
Getting a feel for the road condition, your first round, very intense, heightened senses, listening, watching, careful. You become part of your truck, the gears and levers are part of your body, an extension of yourself, blending together until there is no distinction. You become part of the storm itself, a vital, living thing . . . you are an important part of the whole operation.
Alone out there in the heart of it. Alone . . . yet together, each snow flake having a characteristic all its own . . . fluffy and dry mocks you as it settles in your wake. Again, on your prime purpose, your road. Wet and heavy snow is a lot more fun, sometimes you think you are gaining, but it's all in your state of mind.
Your road, your assignment, it is yours to take care of, yours to make right, sometimes against Mother Nature's wishes.
White out, the terror of total white blindness, so remote, so alone and in a dangerous situation which requires all your skills and awareness.
Headlights coming up behind you will now cause a tightening in your gut. But, you are ready . . . until white out happens again.
Plowing snow, it's not for everyone. Don't think for one minute, that we're not around, someone is always watching roads, making sure they are sound.

Sandra Rose
ANGEL TEARS
Rain comes and goes throughout the years
But I really believe that it is Angel tears
They cry for the little boy, who has broken his favorite toy
And when a new baby is born they cry for joy
They cry for the man that leaves God for tomorrow
And when a man dies that hasn't received God's grace, they cry for sorrow.

Mary C Prue
THE PATRIOT

Dedicated to Staff Sergeant William F. Lee, Jr., Kailua, Hawaii.

There He stands, so straight and tall
With eyes of azure blue.
He sees what no one else can see,
And knows just what to do.

He sees the unrest in our land,
He sees the hunger too.
He sees the greed of lawless men,
And prays for the homeless too.

They call this Man a Leatherneck,
But, of course, this isn't true.
He's made of flesh and bone you see,
Just like Me and You.

Who is this Man that stands alone?
Or with others, tried and true.
He's a United States Marine, of course,
And He's My Grandson too.

Marple E Peterson
COMMUNICATION
There is a word
That one should strive
To often use
And keep alive.

It keeps your world
From havoc and strife,
And creates a smoothness
Throughout one's life.

Keep this in mind
Without reservation,
It is one word—
Communication.

Anne Gray PhD
MORTE PARENTIS
The passing of one's parents
Is an inevitable milestone
Pushing us, reluctantly onto the plateau
Of the next generation

Too clear the consciousness
Of years sped by,
We are barraged by the return
Of childhood memories
Long forgotten

Regrets fuse with words unspoken
Time not spent together
Promises broken

Yet nothing can be undone
The cord had to be cut
And snap't the tenuous line
Of being their extension

So we could become ourselves
In due time to perpetuate their blueprints
In our children

Charles Arthur Young III
GUARDIANS
From behind the toadstools they peer.
Little ones, little ones small and dear.
Air with light by early silver fog.
The large white horses fly over fallen log.
Blades at their side to protect the innocent.
To slay evil dragons with triumphant magnificence.
Journey to far off dimensions to discover treasure.
Not to hoard, not to hoard but only to give measure.
Order was given by the unknown king.
For all to join in this magic ring.
Converse to the trees as they give you aid.
Upon resting underneath in graceful shade.
Fellowship to call as one with another.
By Bishop, the knight as common brother.
Free all that have need by no regret.
On courage and humility before golden sunset.

Charles Arthur Young III
THE IDEA OF TRUTH
There is a truth.
The only truth.
One that few can touch.
It's seen from the heart.
In which love has to start.
A peaceful yearning of the truth

concerning.
That you and me should only seek
The definite truth that is to be.

Charles Arthur Young III
IP
A point is seen at a churning tip.
Upon the windy extension of a howling whip.
Seedlings to grow from just a small snip.
While the brave men gaze from their lofty ships.
The old men retire with a regretful chip,
As they lay to rest with their sore hips.
Shell to the oak as an egg is split,
For the smell of a new morning with a cool nip.
Go out through the day and beware of the whisp.
Defend from the dread full in its dark pits.
Hold strong to the test with a righteous grip.
Consumed with humility towards God's holy mitt.

Charles Arthur Young III
STONE MAN

This poem is dedicated to my wife Adeline Young.

Stones will rest until they are moved.
A resistor of wind with an intimidating mood.
Endured to absorb heat and concentrating the cold.
They have made no complaints since the times of old.
The creator of stone we wish to see.
Through erosion in time on the land with me,
logic of stone for the beholder's eye,
used in a tiring craft under hated disguise.

The color of stone a many seem to claim.
May strengthen the soul without heavy vain.
An awareness prevails where all stone lives.
By their majestic heights and the support they give.
Stone to dust as the elements take toll.
The same for a man with descent of getting old.
Stone and man are so much alike
Both will change appearance by the storms of life.

Wendy Lambeth
I LONG TO BE NEAR YOU
I long to be near you
To feel your touch,
To have your kisses
I enjoy so much.

I long to be near you
Every minute of the day,
To hold and to cuddle
Each step of the way.

I long to be near you
To see your sweet smile,
That gives me strength
Through my troubles and trials.

I long to be near you
To know that you're mine,
To know that you'll love me
Till the end of time.

I long to be near you
To let you know,
Just how much
I love you so!

Charles David Minifie
PEACE AT LAST
Pull down the sky and bury the sun
'Cause there comes a time when we've gotta move on.
When you think and you jump and you climb the tree,
And get to the top, tell me what you see:
Does it twist, does it sway, the high tree top?
As the roots they burn—the ground's so hot
From the melting clay of our star's own heat;
Give me a shroud, a clean white sheet;
Pile the wood on top of the bier—
Throw the ashes off the pier.

Well, the ghosts, they die, and lie in rest—
Their hearts lie still in their rotting chests;
Their souls have fled and are now long gone,
Their voices have ceased singing their songs,
Their hymns, their cries, their lonely praise—
Their heads bowed down, never to be raised
'Cause the clouds have fled, dipped to the sea
And the wind doesn't blow, not even a breeze.
The air is still, the sound's now silent,
All is done, nothing is violent . . .
But, Is this Peace?

Charles E Shook
MEDLEY OF SEASONAL HAIKU
The soul of winter
Brings a Renaissance of Life
And awakens spring.

Spring beauty gives way
To white skies with streaks of blue
And summer sunshine.

Autumn's Spirit walked
Where goldenrod sprang like fire
Near golden maples.

Winter chills my blood
And sucks away autumn leaves
On the snowy ground.

Thomas H Davenport
GRANDDAUGHTER

To Savannah Marie Hay—my first grandchild.

There's she, I see her for the first time
She doesn't know Grandpa
So little, so innocent
Grandpa feels inadequate . . . to the occasion
Time goes, milk flows
Baby sees Grandpa and smiles an impy smile
only a Grandpa and Baby can know.

Lingering in the twilight of life
Beautiful interlude only last—
only last
Time, life stand still now, as I understand
Yet ever onward go, look back, wish to stay
Too bad, too bad, time, life rolling as a glacier to the sea.

Linda Adams
FREEDOM

Dedicated to Frances C. Adams—my mother-in-law—my best friend.

It shall be dark and cold soon as the night does fall.
And there is stillness among it all.
The world . . .
Is a never ending ball unhurled.

The world is not made up of greed alone,
It's made of people, skin and bone.
People, who work and slave all day,
And at night to God they pray:
"Lord it is not for me to reason why,
But someday I too shall die,
Someday I pray the world will be free and wars will cease.
For then and only then, I can rest in peace."

Wanda Williams
FALLEN MAN
Just a fallen man,
Brought low by life's demands.
No way to straighten out his life.
Everything ending in strife.

He met the Lord one day,
And he heard him say;
"Son don't worry now.
We'll work things out somehow.

Nothing ever stays bad,
And there's no need to be sad.
I've come to help you all I can,
You won't stay a fallen man.

The devil wants to keep you down.
But he hides when I'm around.
I'll set everything right.
And he'll stay out of sight.

You'll be a new man.
Able to face life's demands.
See everything through different eyes,
Because now on me you rely."

Carol Ann Kaufman
ANOTHER VIEW

Dedicated to Greg Houser for his interest and support for the blind and deaf / blind.

For those with sight, we all behold
A different tree of green or gold.

For all of us who see this thing . . .
We see it different in the spring.

No matter what the object's name
We'll never see it all the same.

So, you can't see this thing at all . . .
Yet you describe the thing as tall.

You say it smells real fresh and clean.
You even use the color green.

You touch the leaf with gentle care
And tell me it is Oak tree's hair.

And then there's Sumac . . . long and light.
And prickly Holly's leaves are bright.

For though you touch, now tell me true,
Isn't it just another view?

Susan L Hansen
THE SPECIAL WINDOW
I press the joints
into a skeleton
that mirrors the three-dimensional
raving of a lunatic
knocked into sense
by a rubber hammer

I glaze where my reflection
reveals my bloodless fingers
coercing the tool to cut
the cold and fragile to fit
unfelt blood drips
tinges the pane
my callous fingers
break the flawed crack
as my scarred hands
reflect in the discarded shard
a splinter of unpolished glass
pointed in place
and puttied over

Carmen Ruiz
ONLY YOU

To Jim, my forever love.

The tears I cry
Cannot hide my feeling
The tears I shed
Cannot disguise the hurt

The nights I spend without you
Cannot hide the longing
The nights that stretch before me
Cannot disguise the truth

The longing I feel for you
Cannot hide the need inside
The longing I have to hold you
Cannot disguise the yearning

Nights that turn into days
Days that turn into nights
Cannot hide the memory
Of what I once had.

T L Wrobleski
PECULIAR DAY

For Daniel: Good Luck, I miss you.

I always knew the day would come,
that you would go away.
I remember wondering many times,
exactly what I would say.
I don't know where the years have gone? It seems they've just slipped by.
I guess I don't even want to know,
It's too sad, I might cry.
Understand I'm proud of you, wish you all the best.
Your life is what I want for you, your freedom from the nest.
It's all the years I've given you, to send you on your way,

That makes me feel the sadness on this one peculiar day.
You'll understand as years go by exactly what I mean.
I know you will, 'cause you'll have yours,
That you will have to wean.

Donald G Reamy
BEYOND THE HORIZON
Dense are the shadows we are among,
Long are the days—yet they be young
Silent are our dreams of hopes to be,
Beyond the horizon—our destiny
Only the brave shall walk this land,
With one desire—to be a man
Surrender our hearts to the will of our Lord,
For beyond the horizon lies our reward
The gift of life we treasure so dear,
Beyond the horizon—far and near.

Gone are the years of fear and strife,
For, they too, were a part of our life
Silent are our dreams of hopes to be,
Beyond the horizon—our destiny
Treasured are the smiles that hold back our tears,
For the love we've shared throughout the years
Look upon the bright side of life we must,
And watch our troublesome cares, turn to dust
For, silent are our dreams of hopes to be,
Beyond the horizon—our destiny.

Raymond A DeFrank Jr
LOVE IS

This, I dedicate to all of life, with LOVE.

LOVE is gentle like the whispering wind in my ear,
LOVE is close like the hand-held touch of someone near,
LOVE is good, it's like seeing things work out just as they should,
LOVE is great, it's always on time and never late,
LOVE is free as a bird flying swiftly in effortless stride,
LOVE is sitting back and watching the ocean's current flow with the tide,
LOVE is never saying no, because you "must-go-on" with the show,
LOVE is care, truth, trust and honesty that we emanate,
LOVE is sharing all of our feelings together and avoiding the hate,
LOVE is a babe in arms looking you straight in the eye,
LOVE is God understanding you and never passing you by,
LOVE is having your body next to mine . . . and together we share our lives through time.

Jana Lynn Dykhoff
MOM & DAD:
In the gifts I give for birthdays, anniversaries, and Christmas, and even the unexpected ones,

Please do not feel guilt.
Please do not worry about cost.

It is my small and meek thanks that I offer for the endless things you have done for me.

When I was growing up . . .

Who was there to tie my shoes; put on my jacket?
Who was there to hug me when I scraped my knees?
Who was there to hold my hand when I was scared?
Who was there to teach me right from wrong?

So please enjoy your gifts. You have given me life, you have cared for me for so long, please accept them as a "Thank You" for all that you have done. A gift wrapped in pretty paper and curly ribbon is so small in comparison to what you've given to me.

I Love You Both!

Diane Neil
LOSER
Look, man, I don't care about sports
or algebra or school,
and because of that . . .
because of my image,
you looked at me and called me a loser.

But that's not my only problem.
Dad's best friend is 'Jack Daniels.'

You'd think he'd stop after the accident with mom;
but he didn't; he didn't care.

So I took away the pain,
and here I am with my mom.

I had nowhere to run, nothing I could do.
So I was the loser—or was it you?

Hee-Ju Yoo
HEAVEN
Thou speakest to me of faraway lands
Where the sands grow red with the richness of sun
And the green earth sprouts a meddling of youth
Like the skies know no end and dreams hold truth—
Thou speakest to me then of the passing of time
And the silver silver moon that gleams up high
Watching over the growth of our remembrance
Like the mountains that drift to the following stream—
Thou speakest to me of the vastness of stars
Waiting with pride for my dawn as we sleep
Lights quivering with the melancholia of yearning
For the silent kind of strength it keeps—
Thou speakest to me of the ways of life
How each strife is a prize of beauty
Making love from the deceptiveness of hate
Faith guarding our trust and always standing—
Thou speakest to me of the tears that flow
To come to the pure river
Where every passion that ever knocks
Turns her keys towards the opening docks . . .
For a godgiving belief forever—

Lois Steffan-Teeter

Lois Steffan-Teeter
MY FATHER, MY DAD, MY FRIEND

This poem is dedicated to my father, Joseph Franklin Henry, Henshaw, Kentucky, deceased in 1988 at the ripe age of 92.

My Father, My Dad, My Friend,
The kindest of man to the end
Loved by all who knew, regardless race or creed
To each, if they needed, he would do a good deed
A limited education did he receive,
Only second grade, I believe
A must to quit to help with family living,
Planting crops, harvesting, his true nature of giving
With a doctorate degree he well earned in life,
Shared with five children, our mother, his wife
Money was limited but most importantly to him in all,
His children diplomas, to hang on the wall
I am his youngest and lots did we share,
He taught me gardening, fishing, respect and to care
Now he's with God and with dignity to the end,
That was my father, my dad, my best friend.

Ronda Meadows
MY NEW BEGINNING?

Mom, Dad, Sissy, Greg, Mitzi, Prissy and Amber this one's for you all. You're the inspiration and I love you very much. Last, but not least, thanks for the push, Jen.

Are you my new beginning,
or just a passing thing?
Could you be forever,
or are you just a fling?
Do you understand me?
Do you really care?
I want to give my love to you,
but do I really dare?
Life is full of choices,
and different roads to take.
Should I trust you with my love,
when my heart's at stake?

Mary Heins
MY LIFE
Now is the time, it seems to me,
To think about immortality.

When I have breathed my last breath of life
And I've left this world of struggle and strife

Who will remember that I was here,
That I laughed and loved and brought good cheer?

My husband, my sons, or children of theirs
Who ran up and down our steep old stairs?

Will they remember the things we've done,
The things that were pleasant and lots of fun:

The Easter egg hunt, the cookies we've made,
The little old sand-box out in the shade?

Or has it all been lived in vain,
And all they'll remember is hardship and pain?

Was it worth it all—the struggle and pain?
Oh! Yes! I wish I could do it again!

Renee Tera
DARKSIDE DAY
Dream of wondering in an open field alone by your own
Pick the flowers with a glow of life
Sit by the brook that flows softly through the night

Watch the trees throw shadows on me by your darkside day

My heart pumps life through scenes, scenes of the past
My heart waits for a love so strong that will last
And no one will take from my strengthened side

Calm yet pounding soft yet loudly
I've heard my heart cry out
Saddened yet smiling laughing yet crying my heart surely knows

Dream of wondering in an open field with a love so true to me

Share all these things
Share all these dreams
By your darkside day.

Lionel Cantu Sr
THE DREAM

To my daughters, sons and grandchildren. From your dad & grandpa.

Life is a beautiful dream!
Only we can turn it into a nightmare, I know!
I have lived my dream,
I pray that your dream in life
Will be beautiful throughout your life.
That God be always at your side,
For as long as God is with you,
Nothing can keep it from you.

Kathleen M Garrett
HOW MANY TIMES
How many times can a heart break
I'd like to know somehow
If my heart will still be breaking
Years and years from now
How many times can a heart break
With unkind words from you
Or can a heart turn into stone
That can't be chiseled thru
I pick up all the pieces
Put my heart together again
And vow it can't be broken

But that is always when
My silly heart betrays me
Believes promises you make
I really should know better
But that's my heart's mistake
How many times can a heart break
I'd like to know somehow
If my heart will still be breaking
Years and years from now

Mary Eason

Mary Eason
A DAUGHTER'S LOVE

I want to dedicate this poem to my wonderful Mother, Nora Webster, whom I loved so dear and has gone on to be with the Lord.

Sometimes I look up in the sky and I think how I wish I could tell my mother goodbye.

If you're up there Mom I love you. When I think about you and I want to be with you it makes me blue.

You were the greatest mother ever. Patience, you had plenty, lose your temper never.

Growing up as a child I was your idol.
I tried to be the best; better than the rest.
Girls were wild, but Mom said; "Beauty is as beauty does." I kept myself from all wrong; pretty as I was.

You found me a mate, wasn't that great.
I didn't even have to look around. It wasn't long and we were bound.

Now that you are gone can I go along life's road. It's hard when we're apart.

I'll always keep you in my heart.

Mom will my daughters do as well?

Aksel Pettersen
IMAGES

Deep purple flashes
Line the dark velvet sky
The Images of yesteryears
Are left alone to die

Gentle sea breezes
Blow the mist away
Images of sorrows, losses
Watched them swept away

Dreams, I cry, In joy so real
All fairytales?, I can't conceal
This driving force, The hope . . .
. . . To feel!!

Yesterday—
The haunted past
Tomorrow—
Under foggy glass
Today—
I'm here, I'm here . . .

Soft silky moonlight
Enlightens, Shadows fade
Images are freedom
With our dreams to pave the way
Images are mine, yours, our freedom
Our Images do pave the way

Aksel Pettersen
AMERICA

For all who served, and families that lost. For the freedom and her cost. I thank and bless you, with heart and soul—Aksel Pettersen—Vet.

Children starving in Africa
South America they starve too
Whenever there's a disaster
They turn to Red, White, and Blue

The only Country in the world
With freedom with no bounds
Loss of life, Scores untold
For Liberty to be found

The only place to desecrate
The meaning of it all
To burn all we died for
It's sickening, There's no law

Everything we stood for
The true meaning of pride
Are we so free, That we can't see?
We're losing from inside?

The most honored flag in the world
She protects one and all
How can anyone be so bold
Burning her, Burns America's soul.

Cecil T Crutcher
THE MORNING

I've stood by the river, and watched the sun rise;
Through the misty skies.
I've felt the dampness of the dew;
As though the morning cries.
I've listened to the birds that sing;
They somehow seem to say:
"Awake, awake, my little ones;
It's dawning near that day."
The trickling sounds of water,
flowing from the river's
stream;
As though a band of angels singing:
"Praise His Holy Name."
Behold the beauties of our God;
Come seek Him while there's time.
Let them that have an ear then say:
"God cleanse this heart of mine."
For I want to see the dawning of . . . .
That resurrection day:
I want to be among the saints, and hear my Jesus say:
"Awake, awake, My little ones, never to sleep again."
Standing by the river of life, a life that has no end.

James A Dunlap
L'AMOUR EN RÊVE/REVERIES OF LOVE

I lie awake at night and dream
Of rolling hills and woodland
streams;
Of soft white skin, so smooth and fair,
And moonlight dancing off her
hair.
What can I say? What can I do?
For sad to say, she isn't you.
So now I say, "Come, please be mine,"
"We'll drink to dear Saint
Valentine."
And if, perchance, you choose to stay,
We'll leave her there, and go
away—
To roam the world, to wander far,
Beneath fair Venus, morning's
star;
For Fate will never put asunder
Bonds of Love entwined in
wonder,
Though our souls should dare to brave
A bright new land beyond the
grave.
Why waste one day, one minute more?
Let's bite the apple to the core,
And while the years and seasons fly,
Our love will grow, nor ever die.

Willie M Kenner
FEELINGS

There are feelings,
which my heart beholds.
Lingering there untouched,
and never to be told.
Of great and wonderful things,
that should be said.
But kept locked away inside,
as if being dead.
Only to live in my heart of hearts.
Never to unfold, never to part.
And on my day of days,
they'll still be there.
Locked safely away,
And never to be shared.

Velinda Austin
THE LONELY FLOWER

Dedicated to those who have inspired me and touch my life.

The night with the moon, the day with the sun,
The tears with sadness, and the laughter with fun.
The sky with the clouds, and the choir with their song,
But there was the lonely flower, it stood alone.

People with friends, a husband with his wife,
A mother with her love, gives her newborn life.
The telephone with a ring, the clock with the hour,
And still all alone, stands the lonely flower.

Loneliness is when someone you love is far away,
Or having no one to answer you, even when you pray.
The winds blow and the clouds bring a shower,
And there on the ground, laid the lonely flower.

Barbara Nesmith
LIL' ANN

She came to live with me in such
a strange, strange way.
Someone left her on the porch of
my neighbor down the way.
We fell in love at the very first
sight,
And I decided to keep her at least
for the night.
But then came the dawning of a
brand new day
And I knew I'd just have to let
her stay
As long as we lived—the both of
us two.
The days have gone by—oh, boy
how they flew!
Now in the twilight of both our
years,
Slow of foot, dim of eye, and with
decrepit ears,
I reflect on what our life has
been—
How much we've shared! I know
I'd do it all over again.
Her intrusion into my life was
surely God's plan.
It has been an honor and a
privilege
Sharing life with my dog Lil' Ann!

Elaine A Campbell
A TRIBUTE TO GOOD PARENTS EVERYWHERE

"Mother's Day" and "Father's Day" were set aside as such
To pay tribute to the two of you who gave to us so much;
But, every day should honor the Love creating birth
And put upon a pedestal the objects of our worth.

We tend to overlook, I think, the sacrifices made
On our behalf from day-to-day—the many prices paid;
It could not have been easy to suffer for our needs
And give up your own pleasures to satisfy our greeds.

We should not take for granted the care that we were given
Through many days and years of toil to make our lives worth living;
Sometimes it's all too easy to point and criticize
And blame our parents for the way that we conduct our lives.

But, our loving parents gave us the basics to live by,
So if we stray from that good path, it's 'cause we didn't try;
The genes that they provided us are very much essential,
Yet, we must tap the power of them to reach our full potential.

"Honor thy Father and thy Mother" all your living days
And show the love you feel for them in many tender ways;
Overlook the faults you see and greet them with a smile,
Since they overlook the faults in you because they love their child.

Elaine A Campbell
A HIGHER COURT

Dedicated to the memory of all who gave their lives to honor the Flag of the United States of America.

The Supreme Court rules as the law of our land to settle issues that no one else can;
"The buck stops here" so the saying goes, with decisions by "appointees" we never chose!
Are their minds so clear they can always see what's best for the people in "the Land of the Free"?
Yet, their decisions affect us all and determine if freedom will stand or fall.

Being human they have their flaws which are sometimes written into our laws;
At that point, then, "the buck stops here"; let the will of the people make the issue clear!
There's a higher court that supersedes illogical reasoning and dastardly deeds;
A court composed of lives that were given with blood that was shed as hope for the living.

Fathers and Sons and Families were lost; a price was paid at tremendous cost
To keep "Old Glory" waving proud and free—the Stars and Stripes for humanity.
Our Flag, they say, can be burned to express one's discontent and unhappiness;
That the "Red, White and Blue" waving proudly here is only a symbol of what we hold dear.

Only a symbol?! No! Much, much more! It's the blood of our lives—the hope of our shore;
The pride of our people—our reason for being; and the Court dares to call our Flag just a thing? ? ! !
We believe in our right to march and protest; to carry a banner expressing unrest;
But, let it be noted that where our Flag burns, democracy lies in ashes and ruins!

Melissa M Easter
STRUGGLING
I see the tears in his eyes
the anger in his face
and feel the sorrow of his disgrace
as his thoughts begin to race.
"What is going to happen to this place?"
He's lost with nowhere to go
and he sees the tears on my face
and soon he knows that
all the tears and anguish
will be gone from our face.
For our love will heal everything
and give us a new place
together forever and forget any disgrace.

Melissa M Easter
WISHING
As I sit here and think of how it could be
you and I sitting under a tree
drinking wine together as the sun sets
oh how romantic that would be;

Oh how I wish you would be mine
and be with just me
but how could that be
when you're sitting with another
under that tree

Angela Clark

Angela Clark
A SILENT CRY
Why must you kill me?
I do not wish to die,
For I am just a baby.
This is part of my silent cry.

What will you feel after my death?
Is it so very wrong to want to live?
If I were a girl, would you name me Beth?
Can't you see I have a lot to give?

What if I were a boy?
Would you still want me to die?
For I could be a little bundle of joy,
A little more of my silent cry.

I think of how wonderful life would be,
But my death is your final word.
I am a living baby, can't you see?
But I'll never be heard.

Gwyn Cotten
THE HEART OF A FRIEND

To Gloria Leiva with love and affection for her belief in me and my poetry. To her beloved sons Claudio and Dante. God bless you all!

When onc't I so despaired, that I dare not live,
For that living was fraught with misery and tears,
And a heart so broken, it would not mend,
My poor sore eyes, ne'er without sad tears
Caused my soul to turn to the heavens
In search of the heart of a friend.

I was a lost wanderer traveling alone
In a desert so vast with no end.
Wrapped in a cloak of my own defeat,
I noticed not the heart of my friend.
Had I forgot the door to happiness
Stood in readiness to easily unfold?
For all the time I possessed the key
To release this poorly tortured soul.

Anguish blindeth that which was meant to see
My gentle love who stands before me.
As blessed serenity cloaks my tortured heart,
And I seek love like a river with no end!
So deep shall I enter the depths, of the soul, of the heart of my friend.

So back I crossed over the river of eternity,
Back across the desert so vast and empty,
My sojourn finally at end
And, uplifted my face to the heavens,
And thanked God for the heart of my friend!

Jenna Prager
FOREVER A FRIEND
Through all of my days and
Through all of my years,
I look back and remember
The way you helped me fight my fears

Through all of my doubts and
Through all of my pain,
I look back and remember
How you always showed me
there was more to gain

And at times when I may be hurting,
Or at times when I may be upset,
You'll always be there to guide me,
And this I'll never forget

You are my mother and I need you
You are my mother and I trust you
You are my mother and I believe in you
Mother, I love you

Lisa M Maughan (Leele)
I HELD YOU FOR ONE LAST TIME

To Shawn: Because I didn't get to hold you one last time.

Late at night I stare out of the window, holding onto my teddy bear.
In the stillness I can hear my own heart beat.
It sounds like a million drums beating in perfect rhythm.
The conductor, He has perfect timing as he guides my heart through its sorrows and heartaches.
My conductor does not only know the next note, but the whole song, and yet he leads me with such joy and warmth it is as though he is conducting for the first time.

A sigh escapes my lips and I hug the little bear closer to my chest.
I have never felt such loneliness in my whole life.

A tear escapes my eyes, I wipe it away quickly.
Too many of them have escaped from my eyes in the past week.
And even though my problem is not all that unusual, it seems very unique to me.

They say that the loss of a loved one is always hard to take,
no matter how many times it happens it is always hard to let them go.
They're right. But I get no comfort from knowing this.

Morning breaks through the window and I sigh deeply once more.
I say to myself, "Time to start life again."
I look down at the little teddy bear that I held all through the night and whisper in its tiny stuffed ear, "But last night I held "you" for one last time."

Caffee S Wright
MOTHER AFRICA
Uphold Her in high esteem
The Mother of the land

Her beauty is magnificent
Strength more to stand

Oh mighty One
Mother of all

Thou deserve more than they will recall
Maybe a message this will send

For Thou art stronger than ten thousand men
Hold tight the honor and respect is at naught

And they won't admit Thee as they aught
Soon honor and respect will be at Thou side

Many will come for Mother Africa's ride

Thou strength is beauty, Thou beauty is strength

May I linger close to you so I may never forget

Charles L Strimling
FACING THE INNER SELF
Peering into a looking glass,
Seeing far beyond myself,
Liking what I see, yet
Again I feel that it's there.
I see all the mistakes that I have made,
As a child up until now.
Knowing I cannot change them,
Kicking myself in the rear.
I see a child who yearns to live,
But is a scared, frail teenager.
Walking away from the truth,
But soon to face the lies;
The mirror is now a shattered mess,
That is lying on the floor
beside me.

George A Paul
THE GLOW OF PASSION
The Ocean is barren—spanning its infernal depth beneath the
Silver glow, On this petrified and secluded shore;
Below the mist, Two silhouettes embraced the dance of passion
On this forgotten shore, where many have stood before.

The radiant infernal Ocean "Echoes,"
A sigh of relief!,
The circle has been broken, the quest was met.
The transformation as began, the shallow mist could not stand;

A promise has taken command—for all could not bear witness.

All are mere parts of—The glow of passion.

George A Paul
ESPECIALLY FOR YOU
A secluded rendezvous in that special
Place, not too small—or large,
But it's ideal for two.
Where fantasy meets forgotten dreams,
That only now became real; And all
That has been said, has proven to
Be true—especially, for you.

George A Paul
THE DISTANT PATH
A Journey's end—is a man's best friend; Though friends came
And friends may go, I have come—face to face with the path
This seemingly endless journey, with only memories of beauty
So rare and true—yet, I behold not that which kept us apart.

The distance remains the same—only now it's an affair, fueled
By a desire of passion, consuming the distance to reveal the
Path often surrounded—and ever so secluded, reserved for
The beholden to heed the beckon—of a distant path.

The way there is the way home—and the way of destiny.

Betty Tatum Davis
PARENTHOOD
You are born in this world fresh and new
A dimple, gurgle, drool and a kick or two
Diapers, training pants, crawling to walking
From baby to child, starting to talking

Boyhood to manhood—years go so fast
Little League, skateboard, and tennis shoes to last
Football, basketball, baseball, soccer and such
Golf, racquetball—so many sports, little too much?

Girlhood to womanhood—will she be a beauty
If she is, will that make her snooty?
Piano lessons, tap, ballet—many a recital,
"Good reputation" is the blue ribbon title.

Did you do a good job? Mom and Dad
Now that they are grown, are you happy or sad
Do they serve the Lord in their own way?
Then, HE answered your prayer for them each and every day

Sharon L McElroy
CONSUMPTION
My love for you did not end
with my new beginnings.
My search for you continues
internally, and for eternity.
Of this, I am certain.

The constant memory of you
intrudes, and protrudes into
many moments of my days,
without any warning.

I am consumed by thoughts
of . . .
what you were,
what you are,
what you will be, and
WHY?

Why your love for me ended
with your new beginnings?
Or, if it began at all,
before it ended?

Ann Ryan
RELEASE

This poem is dedicated to my loving priest, Fr. A. Montalto (Tears are a language God understands).

As I sat huddled in the darkness
I was scared of my lonesomeness.
He was gone; my friend, my love;
I felt that tight knot within my chest;
It was pain; it was anger; it was torment at its best.
I wanted to scream, to shout to cry out passionately
Why? Why was he taken from me?
But my throat refused to release the sound,
And my eyes remained like the parched earth.
Terrible darkness overshadowed me
As I struggled within and without.
Every fibre of my being seemed to be wrung out
Like a pawn after a battle with the angry sea.
Yet, my body kept going through billows of darkness,
And my mind cries out, "O God,
If this be my Gethsemane, let it be,
But when I arise, let me be happy
At my friend's release from his agony."
And then, only then, my throat released its grip,
And as if from the very core of my soul the sound explodes.
And my eyes, as if in unison, released its showers.
Beautiful tears falling down my cheeks
Followed by the gentle rocking of my body.
Tears, beautiful tears;—What a release!
The release to a pain-filled soul.

Ann Ryan
ALL I HAVE TO GIVE

This poem is dedicated to my friend Alvin Stutzman who has taught me that true love does exist, and because of this, dying can be made beautiful.

Like two ships passing through the night
We met; we felt that spirit of joy—but pain,
Because we knew that one of us was sinking, and
We felt each other's plight.
But in passing, we reached out to each other,
Giving love, giving strength; everything in our power
To hold on together; forever.
Would to God that I could hold you to my breast,
And share my strength—my breath.
But for you, my friend: my love is
All I have to give.

For you dear friend whom I've loved
From beginning until the end
This is what I have to give;
Love that surpasseth all understanding;
Only giving, yet never demanding;
Strangers we were needing each other—
Friends we are loving each other—
Sad I will not be at your leaving—
Short our time may be, but that's our destiny;
But this my friend I leave with thee,
My love for all eternity

Angela Ketron
WILLIE (IN MEMORY OF)
I dream of you
Or have nightmares,
One of the two.
Your face.
In the strangest places
When I expect no thoughts
To get through.
Your voice.
In the walls
When it's dark blue
And I dream,
Or have nightmares . . .
Your eyes
I can't see them
I can't, when I want to.
Not even when I dream
Or have nightmares of you.

Connie A Hasty Carpenter

Connie A Hasty Carpenter
CHILDHOOD

I dedicate this poem to my parents, William Carl Hasty and Mary Frances Nelson Hasty.

I often think of summer days,
Of childhood, spent in many ways.
Material things, we had little of,
Plenty to eat and lots of love.
Fields to roam and hills to climb,
Blue skies above, and lots of time
To lie on green grass,
And watch clouds pass,
To dream big dreams,
And think of things
To share with a friend—
Imagination, there was no end
To the plans we made,
Just sit in the shade,
Or fish all day,
Whatever our plans, nothing got in the way.
For one of God's greatest gifts to me,
My childhood, happy and care-free.

Shawn Mackey
FEAR NOTHING FOR I AM HERE
Fear not the storm for the sun will shine again.
Fear not the rain for rainbows will soon appear.
Fear not the dawn for it is a new beginning.
Fear not the dark for I will guide you.
Fear not the night
for I am part of it.
Fear not death for in death
there is new life.
Fear no evil for there
is no such thing.
Fear no one for I will never let them hurt you.
Fear not loneliness for I will always be with you.
Fear not being alone for I will never leave you.
Fear not to trust me for I will never fail you.
Fear not to believe in me for I believe in you.
Fear not what you do not understand for I will teach you.
Fear not to believe in yourself for I have faith in you.
Fear not to dream for your dreams are mine.
Fear not to stumble, never be unsure, for I will never let you fall.
Fear not to love me for I will never betray you.
Fear not what you feel for it was meant to be.
Fear me not for I love you.
Fear not love for my love for you will never die.
Fear not the end for it shall never be.

Kimberly S Ellis
BOTH MY DADDIES

This poem is dedicated to Both my Daddies, Mr. John M. Senior and Mr. Edwin G. Ellis.

Both my Daddies are very different.
And both my Daddies are very alike.
One is tall.
And one is short.
One is light
And one is dark.
One with a big belly,
And one without.
Both of them love me without a doubt.
They are both very protective, but that's alright.
I rarely complain,
And I rarely shout.
I know they love me and that's all that counts.
Both my Daddies are unique in the way they deal with things.
But both share a common interest in my life, feelings and needs.
Both my Daddies listen when I just want to talk.
They respect my privacy and my freedom and don't watch me like a hawk.
Both Daddies are there when I'm crying or alone,
Yet neither Daddy lives with me at my Mommy's home.
Over the years and over the days my Daddies have been there for me.
That's why I'll always be special
'cause Both My Daddies love me! ! !

Dawn Marie Healy
EL AMOR PACIENTE

Para Karina, mi hermana verdadera.

The young unicorn waits patiently.
She knows that time will bring the other
Just as it brings each sunset
When Mother Earth subtly goes to sleep
And the sky turns black as coal.

But they come bringing only hurt and pain.
And every time she thinks
That maybe true love has finally come for her
Her eyes deceive her.

She thought she was a magical creature
That could make dreams and hopes come true
But now she wonders why it matters
If no one believes in unicorns or love anymore.

But she waits patiently . . .
And trusts once more
And this time happiness comes
To take her away from immortality.
Lesson learned not to believe the eyes
But the heart and soul:
That's what makes unicorns and love become real.

La Homa' Floyd
IF MY DREAMS CAME TRUE

This poem is dedicated to "Michael," a dear friend.

If my dreams came true,
You could surely see,
just how much your love,
really meant to me.

If my dreams came true,
you would truly know,
how I could have loved,
and cared for you so.

If my dreams came true,
you'd be by my side
and our true love,
would never have died.

If my dreams came true,
you'd be a great star
'cause in the center,
is where your parts are.

If my dreams came true,
life would be just great
But, I guess I can wake up,
for dreaming now is too late.

John J Mendoza Jr
PERFECT

Dedicated to JULIE, the PERFECT YOUNG CUTIE BEAUTY.

She's the girl of my dreams
Sexy and sweet
She loves me dearly
I love her complete
Our life together
Is as perfect as can be
Even in stormy weather
Our love never ceases
Never decreases
And this is how love should be . . .
PERFECT

Dori Ann (Gray) Frederick
QUASI QUALM

When you live in a world
Where pragmatics
Are a basic way of life
Bored to tears
And feared to the highest extent
Quasi qualm

Everyone believes themself
To be the only dreamer
They think you sit quiet and dense
Brazen faced and non-committal
Quasi qualm, becomes more intense

Living among those puritanic types
They look there at light
And see light
While you see shadows dancing
Boring, more boring, and most boring, they are
To put a bird; where he belongs
Narrow minds and you don't mix
All is quasi qualm
And my quasi qualm becomes more immense
One feels . . . . . . quasi qualm

Dori Ann (Gray) Frederick
DRIVEN

I feel an emptiness
Cold and dense,
I feel a heat
Quite intense,
I feel a desire
Deep inside
I am driven
It is my guide

I wonder how,
I enquire why,
The birds all sing
I only cry

I wish for more
And I shall! Have
I travel a cold
But driven path . . . .

Dori Ann (Gray) Frederick
IN THE MIDST OF OUR CONFUSION

The kind of people that we are
Still yet to be defined.
For in the midst of our confusion
We sit lonely and declined

One man frustrated!, infuriated!
The other discombobulated
Together we are in the fire
Yet we prefer to go it alone
So "in the midst of our confusion"
We have, no subliminal home.

One makes a decision to alienate themself
"See I can fly on my own!"
And "in the midst of our confusion"
We are left
In endeavor, and transition
To be alone

Bryan Scott
YOU HAVEN'T

To: My Would Be Lover.

You've called, but haven't spoken.
You've stated but haven't clearly expressed.
You've suggested, but haven't acted.
You've touched, but haven't felt.
You've reached, but haven't connected.
You've been there, yet you seemed elsewhere.
You've implied love, but mention like.
So,
Before I get on this EMOTIONAL ROLLERCOASTER;
I'd better listen to the silence!

Colleen Hill
MY SISTER—PART OF ME

Be strong, my Dearest Loved One.
Our faith will light your way.
Soon your darkest nightfall
Will turn to sunny days.

We bound our love together
When we were very small
And as we grew, our strength did too,
So, now, we may stand tall.

Looking back, our childhood past,
We've seen dark days before.
We made it through together,
And, we can too, once more.

The wisdom of those days gone past,
Is very clear to me.
So, I've come to reassure you,
"Bestest Friends" we'll always be! !

If darkness is upon you,
My strength and love is near.
So take my hand, you must believe
You are a part of me! !

Melissa Diem
UNFORGETTABLE

J.L.—I told you I would dedicate it to you. You are, and always will be, very special to me.

I can't forget you.
No matter how hard I try.
You stay on my mind.
Your smile your laugh, your kiss.
I never thought this could happen to me.
I never wanted it to.
But,
It did.
I fell in love—
With the wrong one.

Nancy M Vice
HOW DO I THANK YOU?

Dedicated To My Loving Husband, Dave . . . and To My Heavenly Father, God.

How can the pot thank the potter?
How can the flower thank the seed?
How can the fish thank the ocean?
And How do I thank you for loving me?
How does the tree, thank the twig, or a blind man thank the eyes that see?
How does an eagle thank the skies around him; how do I thank you for loving me?
The bird without wings; the blind who couldn't see; the heart that couldn't sing; now how do I thank you for loving me?
Tomorrow the dawn will be grateful for the rain, the moon will rest in peace; the birds will awaken one by one;
the night owl will find his sleep.
Every touch of nature has its own touch of love and how do I thank you for loving me?

Joanne Webber
THANK YOU

Dedicated to: K. Hagin, Jr.

Father
Thank you
For this day
Thank you
For all the blessings
You've brought my way
Thank you
For your love
That's always here to stay
Thank you
For coming to me when I pray
Thank you
That you never let me stray
Thank you
That you're always with me
Along the way

And knowing all this
I can now run out and freely play

Susan Paris

Susan Paris
THE DAY HE WENT AWAY

This poem is dedicated in loving memory of my brother, and to my wonderful parents for the gift of life.

It was a sunny day in the middle of May, that was the day that he went away. He said he'd be gone for a ride and be home for dinner by a quarter to five.

He was only a boy yet merely a man, he was my brother and friend.
He'd take my hands and swing me around, take me to the circus and dress me up like a clown. He'd hug me and tell me I'd be all right then tuck me in bed for the rest of the night.

To my parents he was their breath of life, a love that was enduring, a love that was life. A love that comes when a man loves a wife.

Until the day he went away we had the perfect family life.
Mom and daddy and three big brothers who enjoyed every moment.
We went to parks, on picnics too, and

we'd even go to the zoo.
We'd act like the monkeys,
kangaroos, and oh, porcupines too.

I remember the day that he went away, on a horseback riding trip with his friends. It's the day the phone rang. It's the day that changed our happy home. It's the day I shouldn't have answered that phone.

That day is now forgotten all the sorrow it holds, memories still linger and the story still told. If only I could relive that day, I'd say please stay at home just one more day . . . .

Harry Carpenter Sisk Sr

SPRING SILHOUETTES

When I am gone, and you're all alone, read this poem. Love to my Family.

A flower blooms, with petals wide,
Where rain and sun may peep inside,
For beauty is why flowers grow,
To make the love of humans flow.

A stem of these a petal there,
A rose will fresh the cool night air,
A dandelion in field of green,
Will show a meadow full and clean

I've walked upon meadows' dew
And watched the sunset's Golden Hue,
As sun was sinking low to fade
As silhouettes in clover lay

Elizabeth J Guider

I WISH YOU WERE HERE

To Bob, my inspiration. What you gave me is far better than anything material. You touched my life with a rainbow and opened a new world to me! I Love You from the bottom of my heart now and always! God Bless You.

I wish you were here
so I could hold you near.
I can almost hear
every breath with my ear.
To me it is very clear
you are so very dear.
Please have no fear
I only want to bring you good cheer!
I just talked to you on the phone . . .
wish I weren't alone.
I am drawn to your tone
as long as you I've known.
Your sexy voice
leaves me no choice
but to . . . rejoice!
I must confess
I miss your caress.
And your luscious kiss
brings me total bliss.
That's what I miss.
Your sexy voice
leaves me no choice
but to . . . rejoice!

Mary Katherin Mauldin

TOMMY

Dedicated with love to L. E. "Tommy" Thompson who has always believed in me and was my inspiration.

He's a very special fellow who came into my life,
Who treats me like a lady tho I'm someone else's wife.
When I feel down, he picks me up with little words of praise.
He makes me feel important in so many special ways.

He's taken his place inside my heart with my husband and my dad.
He's very much a part of me—The best friend I've ever had!
A jolly soul—a joy to know—He's seen a many year,
But thru each one he's held his own and faced his every fear.

For each and every occasion, he's full of "toasts" galore;
A little on the round side—all the much more to adore,
He wears a giant bolo people call his "License Plate";
A feather of pure turquoise unequal in its weight.

His bowling is a legend, a pool shark—he was one.
A hustler in his younger days, but now those days are gone.
His eyes have grown much dimmer and his hair has turned to gray.
He walks a little slower than in his younger days.

He may not be a millionaire with wealth beyond compare,
But should I really need someone, I know he's always there.
And should I need a loving smile, he gives me one for free—
A hug, a kiss, a joke and more—my TOMMY gives to me.

Marj Coté

Marj Coté

MUSIC OF LIFE

To the memory of my beloved husband Philip whose beautiful symphony was completed February 11, 1986.

Ah, the eagerness of children! I watch them at their play
And reflect upon the wonder of life and each new day.
Morning follows morning like the rhythm of little feet,
As in a regimented march, beat surely follows beat.

The children and the mornings come with promises anew,
But then we hear a different tune, the teen years are in view.
Like discordant notes of jazz are so dissonant and wild,
Comes now high noon, the time of life we're not adult nor child.
Maturity brings harmony, the afternoon of life.
We play it all, the high and low, meet challenges and strife.
As a ballad can be sad or a joyous story told,
We go the whole score of emotions as we're growing old.

In our last melodious years, evening falls upon us . . .
What's that I hear, the last waltz, Dear? Well, I'll not make a fuss.
I know that night is coming and too soon I'll have to go.
I'll take liberty of tempo, not miss a step, you know!

We danced, we sang the melody . . . the staff of life we wrote, measure to measure, verse and chorus, treasured every note.
If in our parting hour we see our lives in memory,
We'll hear an orchestration of a lovely symphony.

Marj Coté

THE WINDY HEIGHTS

We have climbed the windy heights communing with the stars,
There I am yours and you are mine, the universe is ours.
Count all the stars in all the sky as joy beyond compare
And all the sweet wild ecstasies in life that are so rare.
In this whole world there's nothing, nor will there ever be
A gift that can compare, my sweet, to the love you bring to me . . . .
Except when I give you my soul and I delight to see
You share the wonder of it all and give your soul to me.
When the time comes God has chosen that you and I must part
I'll hold a cherished memory of you deep in my heart.
I would not ask for more in life nor to eternity
Than to climb the windy heights forever dear with thee.

Hazel L Gardner

THE BEAUTY OF THE EARTH

To all who love God's earth.

I love to wake up in the morning,
smelling the flowers of the fields.
And listen to the birds singing
in harmony and zeal.
And to smell the scent of the pine trees,
it's something to behold,
As their lasting fragrance, every hour each day unfolds.
We should stop and ponder,
the beauty of the earth.
And shall we? Just for a moment
Give thanks to God,
For this, The beauty of the earth.

Sunday Jaramillo

FINAL EXAMS

To Peter, who encouraged me to believe in myself.

Struggling through thorough reading and searching,
for test taking methods that strangle intelligence.
But through all this chaos, ideas still merging,
from studying minds with stern belligerence.
Then all of a sudden, fantasies appear!
Loss of concentration, thoughts become muddled,
confusion takes over, you're stricken with fear.
Calm down, take it easy, and just be subtle.
To make a better way, and make society rattle
is your goal to meet for future success.
What a flight, what a climb, an uphill battle,
but a worthy effort, still striving for the best!
So get on the ball, put forth that power,
shake up those teachers, be imaginative, outrageous.
Just remember your aim, and flow with each hour,
learn the ways, make a statement, and be courageous.

Darrin P Hennessey

NOTHING'S GONNA CHANGE MY WORLD

To the U.S. Air Force.

A thousand days, a thousand dreams
I always know what tomorrow brings
One might say my life is boring
That's o.k., it used to be adoring

I find myself sitting here
Playing games of solitaire
I don't know what to do
Maybe I could meet you.

We could talk and laugh and joke awhile
Then, maybe then, I could smile
I've been feeling rather sad
I tend to think of things I had

Things I found that I lost
Plans I made that I tossed
What would it all mean
If these things could be seen

Leaving people that I met
Losing games or a bet
With all these thoughts uncurled
Nothing's gonna change my world

Tami Bobbitt

WHEN I GROW UP I WANT TO BE

I dedicate this poem to my mother, Sharon Bobbitt!

When I grow up I want to be
bigger than the biggest tree!

When I grow up I want to be
happy! with lots of glee.

When I grow up I want to be

sailing around the seven
seas!

When I grow up I want to be
able to be free, free, free.

Patti Wood
WHEN I THINK OF LIFE WITHOUT YOU...

This is dedicated to a very special man, Ellis Wood, my Grandaddy and my best friend.

When I think of life without you
it brings tears to my eyes.
You mean so much, I don't want you
to die.
But you will and that's something I
must realize.

We have a special and rare
relationship
something no one else shares.
And I want you to know how much I
love you
and how much I truly care.

I know one day you will go and leave
me
But you will always be in my heart
I love you too much to let go.
So when you leave this earth
we will always be together and never
apart.

Dana Leone
LOVE

To my Aunt Lisa who got me started on poetry.

Love shows us different ways to care,
As well as it shows us to be kind.
It means to be pleasant and to share,
But also has times when it's blind.
Sometimes love can be a serious
devotion,
It can be life's greatest treasures.
Love might leave you drowning in
emotion,
Or may leave you with much
pleasure,
The feeling could come from way
down in your heart.
It also can start to annoy,
But even for the greatest part,
Love leaves you with extreme joy.

Helen J Guinta

Helen J Guinta
DO NOT MOURN FOR ME

When I die, do not bury me
In the cold, cold ground 'neath a
blanket of snow,
But burn my decrepit body in a
furnace of fire
And spread my ashes in the
mountains in the evening glow.
Do not mourn for me, my dear, good
friends
For I've lived my life in a brilliant
display.
I've fought with gusto for the goals I
would seek
And achieving a goodly share, cannot
regret one day.

I was born in the mountains that I
love with my life,
Learning patience, compassion,
mercy and love
For each tiny creature and all
growing things,
From a blade of grass to the Lord up
above.

For each of us, in the scheme of the
universe,
Was placed for a reason upon these
lands.
Some have succeeded and others
have failed.
The amount of effort expended was
left in our hands.

When it is time to draw my last
breath,
Let me return to the mountains from
whence I came.
May my spirit teach others a true fact
of life:
Our persistence for achievement is all
part of the game.

Kathleen (Monroe) Kajfasz
SPECIAL LOVE

To Denny, my mentor, teacher, husband, and most of all my Love!

I have a special kind of love,
So soft and gentle as a dove.
A rare individual who's everything to
me, he opens my eyes and helps me
to see. His hands are strong, warm
and rough, when he touches me it
can't ever be enough. He's so simple
and full of life, how I pray to become
his wife. When that happens how
happy I will be, to show that special
man what he means to me.
All my love.

Kathleen (Monroe) Kajfasz
THOUGHTS

Gathering my thoughts, trying to put
it all down, confusion going around
and around.

Drawing a blank with so much to say,
looking for that brighter day.

Trying so hard to be strong,
wondering where, to whom I belong.

Given a chance to start over new,
but often finding myself lonely and
blue.

One step forward two back when will
my life be cut some slack?

Needing some guidance from a friend
from the beginning and to the end.

Don't give up, don't complain,
It's real hard to explain.

What do I need? Where do I turn?
Without getting hurt or totally
burned.

Needing so little and yet so much,
trying to find myself and stay in
touch.

The circle of life is round, I hope I
don't get lost, but instead found!

Julie E Todd
I CRY EVERY COLOR

First appears the red, a hot, guilty
lava, which flows with all desire.
Then flows the blue, a free, secure
surrounding of all who are at peace.
Followed by the yellow, as it sparks a
few harmless flames and is caught
between good and evil.
Next flows the green, a sign of
growth and new beginning, which
adds questions with no existing
answers.
Which dries and leaves behind
puddles of orange, silent but is filled
with sound, which express pain and
grief.
Then comes a streak of purple, that is
light but filled with a heavy passion.
That dries and leaves a surface of
white, a pureness that forms with
innocence.
Finally it is splashed with black, an
empty, lonely space in which one can
get lost.
So in the silent hours, when each
color represents a feeling,
I sit . . . And cry every color . . .

Debra L Basco
THE PAST

Debra L. Basco Santa Ana High School Class of 1969. Thank you Lord. My grandmother, Ralph, children and grandchildren, for inspiring me. Thank you Frank Ramirez S.A.H.S. Class of 1962 and Mike Campos for your support. To the Class of 1969.

You cannot live in the past
All times must come and go
This is the cycle of life
The past must pass
In order for life to be given
A chance to start fresh
You cannot live in the past
By now you must have learned
That all things must come to an end
Life is like a flower it grows and
blossoms
When it is time to stop growing
The flowers die and the leaves begin
to fall
This is what life is all about
If you cannot let go of the past
You will only be cheating yourself
Out of some of life's greatest
pleasures
If you try to hang on to things that
were
And are no more
You will only feel the pains of woe
You must learn to begin
To let go
Before melancholy sets into the pit of
your soul
Thus preventing you from becoming
whole
The past was a great part of the future
That was and is no more
Our future has now become part of
the past
That was not meant to stay or last
If we keep looking over our shoulder
And find ourselves beginning to
reminisce
About what might have been
Or about what we might have had
We might remember some good out
of our past
Then again we also might not
Find anything of what we thought
was there
The past has now become a fading
shadow of memories
Of what once was
And is no more
If you try to look past tomorrow
To see what the future will bring
Stop cheating yourself of the
wonderful things
That God placed on this earth for our
being
Put your memories away
In the depth of your heart
Get on with your life
For the years that one has
Are as precious as gems
And creation is where it begins
So take a chance and start fresh
All one has to do is to learn
. . . TO LET GO OF THE PAST . . .

James Frye
TO KIM, A MOVIE STAR

A smile such as yours,
Turns the world around for me.
To see you cry, cry dearly for me.
Singing bird of the morning to see.
A smile that warms me inside.
A smile that glows.
A smile that says,
I can make it, too.
A smile that reaches;
My life to begin anew.

James Frye
JUST TO BE ME

Power in me;
Beauty to soar;
Enlightenment soaring in me high;
Soaring high above me, an eagle
flies.
Fly in me.
Fly me above these clouds, friend of
my spirit.
Spirit of my truth and eyes;
Spirit so true in my eyes.
So true to fly these nights alone.
Land in some land of enchantment,
with you alone.
Spirit in me so true like the eagle—
eagle of nature,
Who knows I've never really known.

Spirit in me so true, lift me above
these clouds;
Clouds of mist and rain;
Clouds that I shall never see again.
Through these clouds the warm,
radiant sun will shine;
Shine for me, my love, lovers, and
me.
Just me in a quite so beauteous
tranquility.
Spirit in me to be free;
Free to love you,
And, just really to be me.

Andrea Anthony
COME CLOSER

Written exclusively for Mister Tony Kirschner, my Boss. From the employee of the year "1990" Andrea Anthony. Here's looking at you.

Until, I can touch the warmth of your hand, or step inside of your heart and can feel what you feel
How will I know you?

Until your tears can fall from my eyes or the sword that pierces your heart can enter into mine and your prayer becomes mine,
How will I know you?

Until my eyes can reflect what your eyes see, or your thoughts become mine and your laughter echoes inside of my ear,
How will I know you?

And how will I ever really know you, until you come closer! Close enough for me to see, my own reflection in your eyes?

Frank Landfield
SHORT

Let me tell you about short
It's kinda like a wart

It's not tall
Nothing like a waterfall

A 1-1/2 gallon hat
Short's like that

I tell you what short's all about
Short is when
You're in and you're out

Short's very simple
About the size of a pimple

There's really nothing to it
Short
It'll fit in any port
Short

That's what short is
Quick, very little fizz

Tina A Bryson
A MYTH OF LOVE

Speak of evil
Lovers' lies
Holding hands
Lovers entwined
Burning hearts
Beneath an innocent sky

And there I will spin you rubies and diamonds
And sing to you
Unicorns with loving horns
And hearts that beat as one

Silvery hearts upon the sea
Maidens dancing upon the heavens
Crying tears
That drown out their lonely cries

I will sing to you
of people falling in love
Never to return
Of people dying in each other's arms
Of eternal love that cannot rest

Melvin Sykes
DRUMS OF PASSIONS

Storytelling ripple rhythmically
Loudness brings out proudness soft smooth beat
Dancing romancing emotions love potions
Our bodily heat
Drums of passions

Hearts beating flames of fire
Causing inner reactions
Sounds of rhythmic thoughts showing desire
Moving swiftly female together male
Electrifying hairs stares
Our bodies rhyme
Feeling find

Ascending together thru ethereal
Touching together bringing out what's within
Some say this is how love stories begin
Drums of passions
Vibrations stirring sensations fever pitch
Jubilation thenceforth
Aware awakening heaven sake
What we relate brings spiritual satisfaction
Drums of passions

Jan Daniels
EFFECTS

A fool chatters, a wise man listens.
Garbage is dumped, a pretty pond glistens.
People roam; no place, no home.
We may pray, but God will say: You made the mess,
Who cleans up, can you guess?
They need food; is anyone shrewd?
What is prettiness? Not clothes that are hideous.
You have no arms, how do you itch?
That's no cinch.
Can't help from crying, no need in lying.
We all need love to be strong, and to know that we belong.
Songs, poems, and stories, certainly give us many glories!!

Stephanie P Campbell
ON THE LOSS OF A CHILD

This is my way of letting go.
How truly painful it is to know,
That no time soon will you call my name;
The time is past, for love, for blame.
The time is past; no more can we,
Seek to hold it. Eventually,
We realize only forward can we go.
And realization is such a heavy blow,
That we reel under this titanic pain;
From passing time only can we comfort gain.
I've held you close to my pain-filled heart.
I've allowed none else; I'd better start.
For you, my dear child, are gone from me;
I cannot bring you back, I do not have the key.
I cannot bring you back, I do not have the key.

Harriet Thompson
FOOD FOR THOUGHT

This poem is dedicated to Gary Clay, my son, who graduated from Jet Mechanic School, Amarillo, TX, USAF, November 1956, and served on Okinawa. Ball Peen Hammer wound Back part/skull/11-7-57/ omitted/no more letters.

Postulating to be the first woman President elected
Vice President would be most carefully selected,
He would be manned to qualify and modify weapon plants
And empowered to curtail excessive artillery grants.

There would be no gray fox racketeer; behind local scene,
Kangarooing, to boost military with boys, by age seventeen!
There would be Official Juvenile Court in every U.S.A. town
And no Suburb Mayor would spread race hatred world round.

No minor could be discharged in a far-off land
By Cold War Officers who do not understand;
Graduate Mechanics age seventeen, serviced THE SUPER SABRE JET!
Unofficial Sophistry on paper, would be retracted yet.

No stepfather could legally adopt the child of another;
Sealing filial, making his wife Her Own Child's Foster Mother!
NECESSARY ADOPTIONS would be a NATIONAL affair
Processed and then followed up, by Persons who care.

Well! the passe woman on her own will never be President,
A cool Mentor Husband has long been a precedent;
We must suffer the egotist if the gender be man
As number one ruler of this God-given land!
'Twas written in stone—as wishy-washy as sand.

Peggy Korsog Dennis
ODE TO AN OLD BOYFRIEND

The beauty of your being
is so perfect to behold,
I should express my feelings,
you really should be told.

I love you and I want you
how'd this happen—when?
We knew each other long ago
What broke us up back then?

To see you now so handsome,
smart and sensitive too,
you're so good to me
I want to be there for you.

I wish I could be happy
and have you by my side,
the life we could have shared . . .
the knot we should have tied.

It's too late to get together,
too much time has gone by.
I'll stay with my husband now . . .
think of you and cry.

Annette Carter-Kovac
THE PICTURE PERFECT

Blue skies,
Green forests,
Surging oceans,
the picture perfect.

Skies clear, fresh, open,
Forests alive with sweet vegetation and scurrying animals,
Oceans brimming and brewing
With aquatic life,
the picture perfect.

How long will this picture remain so perfect?

Sandy Davis
DREAMS

Dream is all I ever do
When I can't have you near,
I only dream of having you,
It's you that I want here.

Dreaming is so easy,
When I think of you so clear,
You see my eyes are glistening
And you wipe away my tear.

I cannot help but wonder
If ever you dream too,
I never really realized
How much I dream of you!

La Wanna Hall Wright
STARS ON VACATION

You promised me a night of stars
when they didn't appear, I cried,
You held me close and kissed away my tears,
they're not gone, you sighed,
They're only hidden from sight,
the stars are on vacation tonight!

The clouds hid the stars from view,
I recovered from my fright,
I was with you,
and you held me tight.
Under a cloudy sky
we discovered a whole new sensation,
The night when you explained,
the Stars Were On Vacation!

You took good care of me,
when you were six,
and I was three!

Margaret M Cantrell
A CHILD CRIED OUT, INSIDE THE RAIN

Lord these grown-ups don't feel the pain.
I've never seen the grass or a tree.
I've never had my father touch me.

Let me run, laugh and play.
Let me see tomorrow and the next day.

Why can't you grown-ups see?
I am a child; a human babe.
Let me come out to live and dream my own way.

Marion E McCullum Singleton
A MOTHERLESS CHILD FEAR

Dedicated to my sisters and brothers, Robert, Ethel, Easely, John, Hattie, Mattie, Fluarie, Emanuel, Pearl, Maggie, Alexander, Dena.

I was a motherless child all my fears and feelings were real. No one was there to hear my cry, or to listen to me tell the hurt and pain I felt inside or to put their arm around me and hold me tight. To make me feel secure.

I pray every night. Dear God, please make things better for me tomorrow. All my prayers and faith in God that heal all the hurt and pain I felt inside.

Beth Mishler
LIFE

Life is a gift
from God to you
Take care of it
and he will you:

Life is two roads
the right and the wrong
Choose carefully
for the road is real long.

Life is a treasure
with no price attached
Be wise with it
for you can't get it back.

Life is a one-time thing
so guide it well
Be the best that you can
for God can tell.

Ronny Lee Smith
A LOVING WIFE

A loving wife I've been told, is worth her weight and then some in gold. You asked me why?, and then I reply, Know not I. For the one I've found Is worth more than any amount of gold. For we first met while we were just In our teens, high school sweethearts with puppy love and teenage dreams. As the years went by our love grew, and grew, and then somehow I knew, that this girl is the one and only girl for you. So on April the 10th of 1983 we said to each other our I love you's.

Now it's only been six years since that day, and never once have I regretted it in any way. For a woman yet I have to see, that has such love and compassion for someone like me. Now as I pray to the Lord each and every night, Please help me keep and take care of my loving wife. For without her to brighten my everyday, I myself would surely waste away. Now maybe my loving wife you will see, the way I feel about you and me. I have but only one thing to add before I close, I love you my loving wife, for now and always our love will forever grow.

Paula Bockenhauer
DREAMS

Deathly afraid of the evil,
the ring in my ear shows,
that elsewhere the world
is a mirror to show
the best of the last.

Miss Lourdes Cabrera

Miss Lourdes Cabrera
TE SEGUIRÉ AMANDO

To my special friend, which I love dearly.

Sabes que te quiero
Sabes que te amo
Sabes lo que siento es
Que mi alma llora por ti

Tus besos son profundos
Tu piel suave como un bebé

Me gustan tus brazos
Sobre mi piel

Me gusta como me agradas
Sin malicia ni crueldad
Solo con tu belleza de tu niñes

Me dices que me quieres
Y yo digo mucho mejor
Recordando la promesa
Que te hice con mi passión

Te respetaré, te ayudaré
Te cuidaré y te amaré
Solo con la promesa de
nuestro Señor—Amen

Ralph L Watts
SIDE OF THE ROAD

Here I stand on the side of the road
Scorned thru days and nights of cold
Brutalized by conditions often in despair
Criticized by the fortunate, to roads lead elsewhere.

My future is uncertain, all bills are unpaid
Distressed by the brain, overworked, tense, hair fully greyed
Depressed by the strain, evidence of heavy loads
Please don't leave me on the side of the road.

Oh! Disappearing friends and prosperous diplomats!
With perforated minds, fame and truth to combat
Celebrating unclean fortunes; proudly as you strode
Neglecting the innocence on the side of the road.

My legs are weak and a great feel of thirst
My eyes for sleep; understanding at its worst
Misfit, unfit, scum, no good; all I've been told
Located here on the side of the road.

Oh God! Suspend my death; preserve my faith!
Purify my breath, your word I'll never forsake
I'm still, fulfill, thrill; your grace I behold
Patiently waiting here on the side of the road.

Ralph L Watts
OLD RAGGEDTY HOUSE

Thanks for this old raggedty house
Quiet, peaceful, even without a mouse
Weather changes bring a little pain
That cold wind and summer rain.

Rags and paper plugged in the holes
Does a good job keeping out the cold
Ooh! Here comes a hard rain!
Pots and pans! Again and again!
Catching all the water I can.

Julie Lacy
MY FIELD OF PEACE

It feels like forever ago I found my field of peace—where the land and sky meet, all worries cease.

The creeks are all clear—man is not near. All things are wild and free, all things at peace.

Daisies and thorn trees grow side by side. Honeysuckle and weeds together abide.

It seems like things cannot change—but they do, with age comes the wisdom of knowing it's true.

Life is different now than it was as a child—my field of peace belongs to someone else.

I hope they see the beauty the field owns and understand the peace that it loans. And one day they will see, just like me, the field is just their memory.

Where honeysuckle and weeds grow side by side—this is where peace abides.

Susan Stukins
COME ON HOME

One night as the angels said to me,
"Father God, he's our glory.
His perfect love awaits you.
So will you come on home?

Come to where you ought to be,
and you will shout for Victory.
He's standing there awaiting you,
So will you come on home?

Don't be afraid that he will scold you,
for in His arms He wants to hold you.
To comfort you in all your pain,
So will you come on home?

He's calling you because he cares.
No more burdens shall you bear.
You won't be alone, for He's your friend.
So will you come on home?"

Becky Keisler
MY DREAMS

In my dreams,
I can see the pain.
Our anger always remains the same.

In my dreams,
I can hear the silence.
While in my heart, I feel nothing but defiance.

In my dreams,
I can taste my tears.
And yet not understand all of my fears.

In my dreams,
I can smell distress.
For some reason, I cannot find happiness.

And yet . . .

In my dreams,
I can feel your touch.
I never knew I loved you so much.

Mary Ann Anderson
LIFE

Life is like a rose, so tender, so
fragile, easy to destroy . . .
Take each petal with beauty of its own.

Let life grow like a rose and the
fragrance will always be exposed.

Take time, patience, and work, you'll
see how much love it will have
enclosed.

May your life together be never
wilted with wrong words
from you or anywhere.

So with all the roses you shall see,
think of the beauty your dad
and I wish for both of thee.

As life goes on and age you'll see
bouquets is yours to be . . .

So with love we wish on you both,
may it be a garden for
you both always to see.

Love, Mom

Karen L Ackley
A DREAM

I dream of living,
many years ago.
When life was simple,
and the pace was slow.
Work may have been harder,
but at each day's end
There was peace and fulfillment,
and pride within.
Families were close,
and love was strong.
Each knew one another,
and that they belonged.
Friends came for miles,
in wagons—cross land,
To chat or when needed,
lending a helping hand.
I dream of living,
many years ago.
When life had meaning,
and the pace was slow.

Lorrie Lee Coe-Meade
HOSTAGE

I lie on the bare, wooden floor,
Hands, feet bound so tightly
They begin to turn blue.
I stare in terror above me.
Blood oozes through the cracked ceiling.
Moments before a shrill scream echoed
Sending cold chills down the crook of my spine.
In the distance a dog bellows;
Flies buzz through stagnant air.
Blood drips onto my forehead
Burning as it seeps into freshly knifed wounds.
Each drop trickles down my bruised cheeks
Reaching the crease of my lips.
Bitter, sweet taste of death
Spreads over my thirsty tongue.
No more torture.
What savage revenge shall be mine?

LaVerne A Dorsey
A CELEBRATION OF LIFE—GO TOWARD THE LIGHT
Go toward the Light, Beloved
Fly toward the bright, shining Light.
Free of your Earthly raiment,
Temple of flesh with limited sight.

Go toward the Light, Beloved
And we shall celebrate with Joy
And speak with Love and fond memories
Of our Beloved—we knew man and boy.

Go toward the Light, Our Beloved
As we remain mired below.
And when our time for Freedom comes,
We shall be joined again, we know.

Tricia Ireland
THE TRUTH ABOUT LOVE
Love is a murky black bottomless pit filled with pond scum and black decaying seaweed that tangles around your ankles and pulls you under the dark churning waters until you live for your love no more.

Love is a bloodthirsty vulture that swoops painfully down from the sky and grasps you by its sharp, repulsive claws until you wonder what you ever loved for.

It's not that I don't respect the people who fall in love for three days or so, but sometimes I just can't help but wonder, what's the point . . . you know?

Dora & Stephen Mathew Baker

Dora Baker
IN CONFIDENCE I SPEAK
I dedicate this poem to the leaders of our nation and to my husband, Thomas Baker, and two sons, Tom Baker and Stephen Matthew Baker.

In confidence I speak
About the world, the cross
And Jesus Christ's precious feet
And how he thus died
To save a wretch like me

In confidence I love
All that he is
And all that I hope to be
In him in love
In body and mind

In Him I speak
With compassion and concern
That he teach me—
Which spirit to discern
In Him, in love, unity and power.

In Him I speak of hope—
That he will save you and me—
From despair and pain
And send us a blessing
As pure as rain

For this I ask in His name
That He send you and me
Where he wants and wills for us to be

So that others then shall see
Jesus is the way
The truth—
And the life—John

Ed Long
CANDLE'S FLAME
Candle's flame
a prayer became
warm glow—
pleasant thoughts—
forth from candle's flame.

Soul to mind—
mind to soul—
the mind now echoes
its soul—
softly burning
candle's glow—

Surcease
sorrow and pain.

A candle's flame
burning vapors glow—
of thanksgiving
of love
of forgiving.

Debbi Buist
CINCO
We ran barrels on the same horse for years
Mom even won her a buckle
That ol' sorrel packed us around quite a few
Always stood ground, when things were beginning to shuffle

Cinco's been a family horse for several years now
He's now purtin' near twenty-nine years old
He helped raise three young uns'
Now, each with horses they are pretty bold
That sorrel will always
Be in their hearts
As they grew older and drifted away,
With him they hated to part

Mom's got a new sorrel gelding now
The kids ride horses of their own
That sorrel will always be a special horse
Even if what they have now may be bays, duns, or roans

We all owe many thanks to the little sorrel gelding
He was one of the first, for years he was always there
And won many a ribbon
At the local county fair

Danny G López

Danny G López
. . . THE END
My destiny is to overcome,
that false road in which I ride
Sometimes we all receive that empty gift
Sometimes there's no place to hide

Falsehood takes my life
I imitate that fellow being
Seems like I can now only ask,
"Is this the truth that I am hearing?"

This loneliness before my eyes
Is it my mind feeding on sorrow?
Is it really worse than death?
Can I believe I will be here tomorrow?

The one above all
The one with the majestic touch
I offer you my only life,
even if I'll miss my loved ones very much

My road now ends here
My journey in life was not complete
I fell on my knees to my fear
Now I must admit my defeat . . .

Danny G López
PICTURES IN THE RAIN
I dedicate this poem to you, Caren Escatell, for all of your love and inspiration. You are really so special. Sweetness, nothing compares to you. I love you.

Memories come falling with the rain
Rainy days can make your heart drop
Even when it's reflecting in my brain
Sometimes I cry and never seem to stop

Grey clouds hover above me
I can see pictures begin to seemingly form
I wonder what it can truly be
Perhaps some forgotten thought lost in a storm

Maybe a child running free like the wind
Maybe a warm hug from someone that cared
Many feelings that soon begin to spin
Vague memories that you and many have shared

The sunshine may break through very soon
Like the changing seasons throughout the year
And though my stare is as cold as a full moon,
I see pictures forming yet so very unclear

My fingerprints will erase from the glass,
But all my dreams and memories will remain
Puddles form while the drops endlessly dance
Never to leave are the faded pictures in the rain

Danny G López
SO RED THE ROSE
To my late grandfather, Antonio Carcamo, who will live in my heart forever. A man with a heart of gold. "Nunca lo voy a olvidar papatono . . ."

No one around me or my friend
I can't see anyone in sight
I lay here frozen still in the graveyard
I lay silently here all day and night

That's until I begin to decay
For now I comfort here with grace
Only 'til the day I fade away,
Will this be an empty and lonely place

"You will now fly free like a bird"
These words I offer with the warmth from my heart
"All the peace to be with you forever"
Please believe from tranquility you'll never be torn apart

"Rest in eternal peace my friend,
rest peacefully in the forever dawn
The scars of pain no more to open,
all those days are now truly gone"

These words will always shine on and on
Even past the day I'm removed from here
Your new kingdom will glow with colors
I'm just a rose making sure paradise is near

Danny G López
SAILED AWAY
The blood red roses remain on the table,
but the letters that are torn lay on the ground
Just like a faded memory that quickly dies,
you've left me without a sound

The room I stand in feels so empty
There's guilt written all over the wall
It gives endless feelings of regret
Sadness destroys the floor for me to fall

I've got to pick up the pieces,
have to find my way back on the high road
My ship has sailed away and left me very lonely,
along with a shredded heart that needs to be sowed

Sadness delivers all of the burning pain
Madness results from the empty sorrow
Our shadows fade like pictures in sand
Nothing will ever be the same tomorrow

Stories were written and chapters

were told
Unspoken words fall silent from my broken heart
A love story with an ending never to unfold
Now I dwell in sorrow and cry in the dark

Bonni V Hill
HIS GIFT

Dedicated to Geoff, my Man Above All Men.

He is a man of music
And talent yet untold
To the standard of convention
This man—he could not mold

He chose a path and without intent
Would compromise himself
The end result, his heart's desire
Was forced upon the shelf

Through demise of well-laid plan
He is left without direction
Misplaced trust in one man
Brought emptiness and dejection

In suffered disappointment
his soul feels very lost
This breeds much discontentment
As he views the final cost

One day he will awaken
And know he did not fail
He still has the gift within
His talent will prevail

Margaret Whitsell Moen
POEMS ARE THE LETTERS OF MY HEART
I can't talk very good,
I can't write letters the way I wish I could.
I can't tell you when my heart is aching,
I can't tell you when it's breaking.
I can't tell you how I feel,
But in a poem I can.
Poems are the letters of my heart.

I can't tell you when I am sad,
I can't tell you when I am lonely and blue,
But in a poem I can tell you.
Poems are the letters of my heart.

God sends me thoughts from above,
That helps me tell about what I love.
You; Little Children, Rainbows,
Dogs, Flowers, Beaches, Sunshine,
Trees, Mountains, Skies, Birds,
Brooks, and Butterflies,
And lots of other things too.
But most of all, I love You.
Poems are the letters of my heart.

Julie A Kite
THE WALL AROUND YOUR HEART

For Dale, whose wall around his heart will always remain.

The wall of East Berlin,
Crumbled.
The Iron Curtain,
Parted.
The wall around your Heart,
Remains.

Natural Disasters,
Change lives.
Terrible crimes,
Change lives.
The wall around your Heart,
Remains unchanged

Your love,
Changed me.
Giving you my love,
Changed me.
The wall around your Heart,
Remains unchanged

Joyce A Belna
RAINBOWS IN YOUR SMILES
Rainbows in your smiles
Dreams in your eyes
In your Touch happiness lies.

Lovers are like roses
Beautiful—delicate—tempting
(with hidden thorns)
Exciting all the senses
Lovers—like roses—are seasonal.

Robyn M Albanese

Robyn M Albanese
THE TRUTH

Dedicated to Scott.

You've seen a part of me
no one's ever seen.
Having your love upon me
is like living in a dream.
Everything is so perfect
everything is right.
You make my every day
so very bright.
I know your love is different
from the other loves I've had.
They weren't really love
for I was always feeling sad.
I love it when you're near
I hate it when you're far.
Even when you're away
In my mind you always are.
This love will always last
I feel it in my heart.
We will grow closer every day
even when we're apart.

Ila Reams Odom
WANDERER
A lone, weary traveler
on the road that leads afar.
Just one of many wanderers
never knowing where they are.
Patiently plodding onward,
searching for life's reason,
Seeking refuge from the storms,
passing calmly through each season.
Never committing to anything fully,
leaving the door always ajar,
Journeying aimlessly through life
on the road that leads afar.

Christine Collins
FROM PAIN TO PEACE
What a wonderful world it would be
If peace could come for you and me.
If, together, we could make things right
So peace could shine like a brilliant light.
If the world could join together somehow
And make a firm and solemn vow
That we all will try to live as one
Like the universe and our golden sun.
Then country to country will be happy and proud
And every nation would shout out loud
And peace will finally come to stay
And take the war and pain away

Tanya A Walker
RIVER'S EDGE
Does everyone have a place
Where they can hide
Crawl away from the world
And allow their pains to die?
I do you know,
It's under a bridge
Next to a river
In a small city
There the river flows slow
And whispers in my ears
It whispers comforting words
Of times long ago
It takes my sorrow away
And with its currents brings another day
Its peace I find
In my heart and mind
In my special place
Where I can run and hide.

Jody R Harmon
POETIC DILEMMA
My "Question" is; What is a Poem?
Just bunched up words, that make thoughts roam?

Or; Could it possibly be more,
than what it's given credit for?

This dilemma, I've pondered on,
from moon-lit nights, till
sun-drenched dawn.

I've researched this, until I'm blue,
and this is what I've found poems do . . .

They make us laugh, and sometimes cry,
Poems help us say things when we're shy.

They're therapy to young and old,
and help to warm the heart that's cold.

Poems simply help the world go round,
by grouping words, with lovely sound.

I've found poetic verse can be,
to Life; like salt is to the sea.

Neither complete, when stand alone,
but as a pair, their strength has grown.

So; We need poems, like seas need salt,
and ice cream shops need chocolate malts.

The "Answer" is; Life Is A Poem!

Dale L Mullen
FALL

Dedicated to Delores Klaritch.

Autumn leaves like jewels of Amber
Ruby red, and Emerald green
Laced on every single branch,
Scarlet, violet, copper and jade.
Brilliant leaves perform a dance
With an early morning breeze,
'Til exhausted hit the ground,
Then scatter about the dewy lawn.
Sunlight hits this season proud
A gift of every giving tree
Only once a year and brief
The peak of brilliant colored leaves.

Tanya Bolotnick
IT'S OVER

Lovingly dedicated to my husband Sam, and daughters Tina and Tami for making me truly blessed in this lifetime.

It's over,
We will never meet again.
It's over,
We must say goodbye, but then,
How strange it will seem to be all alone
Without your lips to call me your own.

It's over,
All the joys we knew before.
But somehow,
I can't seem to close the door.
Although you have told me love now is gone,
Deep in my heart the longing goes on.

I love you,
With my heart and soul I care.
But gone now,
Are the arms I used to share.
And so dear, I beg you with this little plea,
If you ever want to, please come back to me.

It's over,
Now my life is at an end.
It's over,
But I leave this for you, my friend,
A promise of love that forever is true.
Yes, it's over . . . but only for you!

Candace Ottenstroer
YOU ARE SO VERY SPECIAL, YOU SEE

To my son, Robert Wayne Lane.

You are so very special, you see,
You were made from love by your daddy and me.
We loved you since before you were born.
And inside my body I kept you warm.
I felt you grow and move and turn,
Then came the day you were finally born.
You almost died right from the start and

I felt a pierce deep in my heart.
Your father left us when you were just five, and
I did my best to help us survive.
I might have done better, we'll never know,
But I don't really have a lot to show.
My love for you is all I have to show.
It will never die, it will only grow.
I hope that this is enough, you see.
And that your love you'll give to me.

Dixie Metcalf
MOMMYS LIVE FOREVER, DON'T THEY?

In loving memory of my mother, Elizabeth K. Howey.

You told me when I was a little one
That I needed to learn to do
All the things for which
I depended on you
You told me that you would not always be
There by my side
To do for me
I didn't think too much about what you had to say
For I believed Mommys lived forever, didn't they?
I grew up and I moved away
I had the family you said I'd have someday
You were still there, just a call or letter away
Then one day you grew tired and ill
In just a short time, your heart grew still
But, I still believed you had told me wrong
I thought Mommys lived forever
Until the day I realized
You were really gone.

Heather Miller
SUICIDE

You see it on t.v.
You hear it on the news
It's hard to play the game of life
and to intentionally lose

You think it's pretty stupid
And no different when on the spot
But when the choice is up to you
when it's you it's really not

Life is hard
And sometimes unfair
But there is some good
In the world out there

So before you put
Your life to an end
Think of your family
Think of your friends

Robert H Elliott Jr
THE WINTER SNOW FALLS SOFTLY

The winter snow falls softly
Among the weighted boughs
Of pine trees bent so slightly
Beneath their blanket there
The wind blows so lightly
With sparkling crystals fair
And give the fresh clean coolness
To winter time's night air
I walk along a footpath
Beneath the oak trees bare
Along the winter footpath
That belongs to snowshoe hare
The full moon would be rising
But for clouds that fill the sky
Above the mountains that surround me
Across the meadow in my eye
So pleasant and fulfilling
The view would fill my soul
As winds sweep the nearby mountains
And ride the clouds of snow

Joycelyn D Carp
ZOO OF TEARS

Dedicated to the journeymen and/or victims of today's civilization.

All in the middle of a false,
overheated jungle,

I see man-planted trees,
a baby niece, and an uncle;

—walking back and forward—

They look secure, without . . . fear
They appear out of place, but
neither seem to care . . .
or is it fear?

Within a cage: within a smaller cage;
and within yet another,

I see man-made hills, a five-inch
pond, fresh cut meat, a cub,
and a mother;

—walking back and forward—

They look secure, without . . . fear
They appear out of place, but
neither seem to care . . .
or is it fear?

They do fear;
They do care;

They are "in-place" in
civilization . . . and yet "out-of-place"
without communication.

We are all cubs, nieces, mothers, and
uncles; within uncivilized man-made
jungles.

By force, by nature, by choices
We all live howling without our
voices;

Hiding from our fears
Living in a zoo of tears

Karyn L Ambrose
THE MAGIC IN YOUR EYES

The magic in your eyes is always there for me to gaze upon when I need you.
Your smile caresses my heart and makes me feel warm inside.
Always I can find a piece of you when I need to feel your love around me.
Though you are miles away from me and I cannot touch your hand or gently caress your face I feel your love and know that your love is mine to save.
There is such joy and happiness when we're together and I savor those moments for times when we are parted.
No more do I cry if I cannot see you, but smile and feel warm knowing you're always there for me.
Our future holds many more memories for us to cherish and I hold onto our past memories while waiting for our new days yet to come.

Karyn L Ambrose
LOVE'S SWEET VOICE

The sweetest sound to my ear is your voice telling me you love me.
Telling me that we'll be together for always, until the end of time.
I can bide my time until our life together can start.
I can dream of us as one and wait for our dreams to come true.
There's no one but you in my heart and in my mind.
No one else in this world that I want to give myself to so wholeheartedly, so completely.
I want you to know all my secrets and share all my dreams.
I want to know everything about you so I can please you in every way.
We will travel through this new world of ours together as one and still remain as two separate beings.
Two lovers, two friends, together forever.
So sing your sweet voice in my ear and promise to love us from now on.

Nidia Figueredo
I DREAMED I WAS AWAKE

I dreamed I was awake
Like steel on fire
We melted away
and on the white sheets
Traces of happiness

I woke up
in my arms I held emptiness
But still
on the white sheets
Traces of happiness

Linda Garske
MEMORIES AND DAYDREAMS

To Daryl: For all the boundaries we have crossed; for all the joy that we have shared; for all the memories—and daydreams . . . thank you.

Thoughts about him fill me
with warmth and happiness
His honesty, integrity
and depth are limitless

I'm mesmerized—such tenderness;
amazed at the chivalry
I'm touched by his simple attitudes;
awed at his complexity

Qualities so rare,
I've only found in one
The memories; the daydreams
of joy . . . beyond comparison

Dorothy E Latragna
PRIDE IS A GRANDFATHER

In memory of my loving Grandfather, Edward Stanley Watson.

Next to the fireplace, in a corner so cozy,
sat a gentleman, who was not at all nosy.
He was absorbed in his books, arrayed on the shelf,
awaiting a visit from a mischievous elf.
His bible and books held treasures divine
and instilled in us elves, a grace so fine.
His younger days, in his touring car, he took us places, both near and far.
Down to the shop, his pride and joy, where many a man was made from a boy.
For he was a gunsmith, an art from the ages,
who created a gun, piece by piece and in stages.
The smell of wood shavings and linseed oil
were a part of this craftman's happy toil.
This man in the corner, my father called Dad,
and to do so always made him glad.
We called him Grandpa and climbed on his knee,
where we were as happy as we could be.
Now Grandpa, to me, will always be
a model for what a man should be.

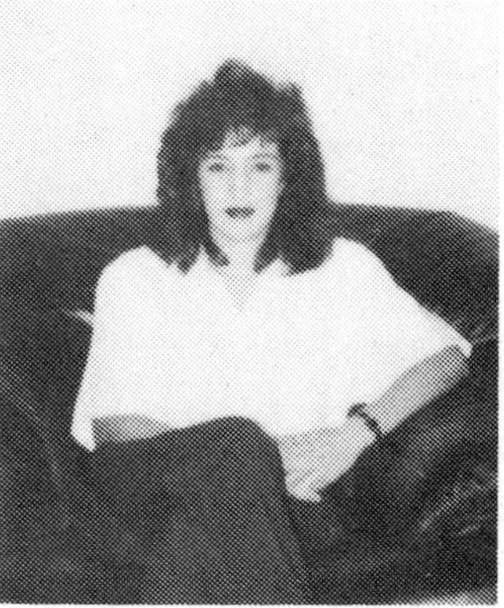

Patricia Anchondo

Patricia Anchondo
I NEED A TRUE FRIEND

Dedicated to Edgar Allan Poe and Stephen King for their inspiration.

If I begged you on my hands and knees
To split my head open
Would you refuse or would you agree?
If I were drenched in gasoline
Would you strike the match that would set me free?
If in the middle of the road I stood
Would you run me down if you could?
Or would you slam the brakes like a "good boy" should?
If I held a dagger upon my heart
Would you push my hands to tear it apart?
Or would you take the dagger right from the start?
If I had a rope around my neck
And I'd be standing on a wooden stool
Would you push the stool and give a heck?
Or would you be a spineless stupid fool
If I gave you a loaded gun
To empty inside my head
Would you laugh at me and run?
Or would you use it 'till I'm dead
After all, all I want is a true friend
To help me end my End.

Patricia Anchondo
IN THE DEPTHS OF HELL
Why do I feel I'm sinking?
Sinking into a deep dark well
My days and my life are shrinking
I feel I have to tell
To prevent myself from thinking
Thinking I might be under a spell
It's dark; not a light is twinkling
I've reached the bottom of the well
There's a noise and it sounds like crinkling
There's a fetid and horrid smell
Oh God! It's my own flesh
Burning in the depths of Hell!

Michelle A Gregory
MY MOTHER, MY FRIEND

This poem is dedicated to Patricia Boone, my mother.

My mother my friend you're always there,
Our deepest thoughts we sometimes share.
You're there for me when times are tough,
I couldn't begin to thank you enough.

You're my mother this is true,
At times you talked to me till you were blue.
Then I was young and didn't know,
That you did what you did because you loved me so.

Then I grew up and things became clear,
That you only have one mother, so to her be dear.
Although you're the one that gave me birth,
You're also my best friend here on earth.

Not many kids are willing to say,
That their mother could be a friend that way.
I can say it with very much pride,
I know that always you'll be by my side.

Sometimes we laugh, sometimes we cry,
About our feelings we are not shy.
It all comes down in the end,
You are my mother, you are my friend.

Michelle A Gregory
A LOST LITTLE BABE
A friend of mine told me a story one night,
About something she saw that gave her a fright.
On her way home from her sister's one day,
She stopped in a restroom and there something lay.

There was something all wrapped up in the corner, without a doubt,
The next thing she saw a little foot had fallen out.
She was almost afraid to look inside,
And when she did she broke down and cried.

It was a little babe not more than a couple hours old,
Whose poor little body was purple from the cold.
She couldn't believe it was left there to die,
But thank God for her just driving by.

Although she was crying it seemed she knew what to do,
As if God was watching over the two.
She held the babe in her arms so tight,
So to keep her warm and prayed she'd be alright.

When she got to the hospital the doctor had said,
If you wouldn't have found her, by now she'd be dead.
At that point she realized in such a way,
That she just saved a human life that day.

Patrick Corcoran
SILENT SILHOUETTES
Gently falling specks, reflecting
prisms; wafting smoothly,
slowly to the ground.
Large ogres forming; standing in
deadly solitude; watching,
waiting.
Icy breath; swirling, whispering;
spinning life from lifeless dust,
then settling once again onto
soft blankets, covering those
that once were, and scarcely
be, 'cept on these nights of
serene quietude.
Swift, silent silhouettes sliding
across the snow.
Muffled screams and wails of
agonies;
reminiscent of solitary last
moments, but stored in these
torn and thoughtless spectres;
return to rest beneath sentries,
guarding the lost souls.

Mandi Eizenbaum
THE SEWING BOX

For Sherry, For Matthew—
My two fountains of love, strength, and inspiration.

Faded and ashen,
The sewing box sits silently and

all alone

in the freshly painted room.

Excluded and neglected,

The timeless box—
with all its knowledge and years of battered use—
Serves no purpose now
Yet the sewing box
softens the freshly painted room.

Memories of a lifetime,

All jumbled together;

The sewing box shines love
throughout the freshly painted room.

Pam Bailey
IS IT YOU

For Richard, who tore down my walls and let in the light to show me all that real love can be.

Like a shadow in my mind you are always there—and the sun is shining.
Through the walls of my own making sunlight pierced my heart.
Fear grips me as I struggle to keep from drowning in the rapture of the light.
The light is warm and soothing—like the caress of your touch.
And through it all I ponder the question that haunts me—"Is it you?"

Is it you who will light the days of my life and help to keep the fire burning?
Is it you who will shut out the darkness and ease the fears that plague me?
Is it you who will dry my tears and hold me when cold winds blow?
Is it you I can depend on to brace me when I am too weak to walk alone?
Is it you who will fill the unlit places in my soul with a light that never dies?

I look in your eyes and I drown in a sun-dappled meadow.
You touch me and I'm warmed by the fire.
You say my name and the music of bird songs plays softly.
The scent of you is fresh like springtime.
The taste of your kiss is sweet like nectar.

As I drown in the warmth of the light and a breath escapes my lips, I whisper
"Is it you? Is it you who will love me forever?"

Dawn K Alread
RECONCILIATION
Sitting here all alone by the telephone
Wondering where you are
Are you near or are you far?
I'm waiting for the time to be right,
So I can hold you tight.
We don't always get along,
But baby, together we belong.
Long ago things seemed fine,
I was yours and you were mine.
Sadly things came to an end
Hopefully the bad we can mend.
I'd like to start all over
And maybe together we can discover
The love we once had
Never did go bad.
My heart is filled with love for you,
Hopefully yours is too.
I long for the time to come
When once again, we are together as one.
That would be a wonderful treat,
And once again my life would be complete.

Virgil J Strader
A EULOGY FOR A BOXER PUPPY
Free as the breeze she roved the upland glade
Her gold coat shining in the midday sun.
The happy yelping spoke how much she loved
Her blithe unfettered life of joy and fun.

She came to me when just a babe,
A ray of sunshine on a wintry day.
Her playful ways and soulful look, at times,
Gave promise of a future bright and gay.

But Belle's life ended one hot summer eve
On a dusty country road near my home,
The victim of a careless speeding car.
Upon the woodland hills she'll ne'er more roam.

She sleeps now 'neath the trees she loved so much
So peaceful, green, and fragrant breathes the air.
Where the wild flowers bloom and the birds sing,
Her small world is forever light and fair.

And if there's a heaven for dogs somewhere,
She'll be there roaming the woods as before.
Sometimes it seems on a clear windless day
I hear her barking and playing once more.

Tammie Burger

Tammie Burger
FRIENDS FOR LIFE
She met him at the tender age of six
It was puppy love for her—
They swore to be friends for life.

Then came high school and college
They helped each other with life's daily problems and relationships.
She still had a special place in her heart for him, but it had grown.
The question was, did he for her
Still, they would be friends for life.

Years later they developed their own relationship—her dream had come true
Months went by, he got restless
They had known each other too long to carry on
Yet, they would be friends for life.

He had another serious relationship
She still loved him but knew she had to carry on with her life
Then he realized she was for him
He had found the key to happiness—
But it was too late, she had already committed herself to another.
As a tear rolled down his face, he heard her whisper—
We'll be friends for life.

Stacey J Grant
MOTHER
A baby born not too old, I rocked on mommy's lap,
I wanted you forever close to see when I woke from nap.
A couple more years I clung to you, never letting you stray, I couldn't stand to see you more than a foot away.
At 5 through 8 I held your hand and walked from place to place,
Never wanted that time to end, didn't

yet know about space.
My years grew on, I walked more alone, not much accompany needed,
I wanted to walk a different path to where maturity leaded.
Turning on heel, feeling so grown nothing stopping my way of succeeding.
Halfway back down the path I heard a lot of child laughing, stopping to read the sign that said, "Child Land You Are Passing."
I looked in and saw a little girl holding her mother's hand,
She looked at me and said in voice, "Not much growing up have you ever needed, just a place to stand and stay and a family to believe in."
In other words what I'm trying to say is never think you're not needed, because on that path of maturity, A mother is always heeded.

Mary L Fogg
SANTA'S CHRISTMAS
By the light of the moon
On Christmas night
Santa turned homeward
After a long, hard night.
He'd dashed, and danced
All around the world.
He'd flown through the air
With his beard all unfurled.
His toys were all gone.
His reindeer were tired.
His sleigh must go back
To the where it'd been hired.
What a nap he'd have now,
At his home near the pole.
Right now, that nap
Was his only real goal.

Jennifer Daniels
CALLED IT POETRY
On damp sand
I scrawled a few sparse ideas with a stick and
Called it poetry.
I raced to finish before the tide could
Sweep it away.
I remember not the configuration of its words,
Nor how many lines I ended with,
Nor even,
Directly,
The ideas portrayed.
But I recall this: that it was, by far,
The most lurid of colors,
The most intricate of thoughts,
The most eloquent of spirit,
And so perhaps it is best unshared in common language,
But by a revelation of spirit.
—unhampered by the weakness of mortality,
And not contorted by a mere, shrill word,
But spoken by the winds,
And the wounded sun,
And the restless wave that was the only entity
Able to swallow it whole.

Mary Echevarria
NAZI MASK
Dedicated to all who have suffered from hatred.

Aryan chant, Ku Klux dance,
They wear the face of the Nazi mask.
And Jacquard clowns, upside, downside
He spins, bobbing up and down,
Smirking his lopsided grins,
Swastikas emblazoned on concrete walls,
the creeping black widow's pace.
And jesting fools shout venomous hate,
Children of love and peace, lift banners at freedom's gate,
And walls crumbled when all thought too late;

Krista Rhoades
ODE TO THE DYING MAN
Be quiet and kind
you wretched young man.
Be soft-hearted and gentle—
always do what you can.

Live life to the fullest,
waste time when you will,
be carefree and trust
the same man you would kill.

Be sincere and think peace;
and give what is taken.
Sleep sound and dream not—
soon you will awaken.

Now you are old;
your heartbeat has stopped.
Resting with you gently,
the glass plate you once dropped.

So may splintered shards of time
cut deep into your hands—
lest you forget my dying words
when you pass through the empty land.

Nancy J Bartling
REBIRTH
I am alone
My soul stripped bare
like leaves torn
from a tree
by a violent wind.

Oh, I long for spring
the renewing
of the rain the sun
and the rebirth
of my heart.

Jeannette Beyer
IMPRESSIONS OF LOVE
Love is not just skin deep,
Or something dreamed up in one's sleep
It lies deep within your heart,
When you can't bear to be apart.

Love can be quite demanding,
It takes patience and understanding
You must share the good and bad,
Keep in mind the love you've had.

Before you decide to go through life,
And take each other as husband and wife
Don't forget it's not just give and take,
You have to give love an even shake.

Life's not easy, on that you can bet,
If love has grown deeper since you met
You'll be glad you decided to go through life,
Loving each other as husband and wife

Audrey Lumbert Tibbott
VIETNAM
They left their homes.
Boys, just tall, not aged.
To travel far, alone,
Where death and destruction raged.

Dark criticism, shame fell
heavy on them all.
Back, they gave questions,
not understanding their betrayal.

No celebration, parades, comfort.
No glamour here.
Who took all these
and gave back only tears?

Names and dates listed
on a black stone wall
never show fears, emotions.
They gave their all.

Michelle Ehlers
SENSES OF LOVE
Look . . .
at the sea gulls
free as they land.
Listen . . .
to the waves
as they crash on the sand.
Smell . . .
the fog
that covers us as we stand.
Taste . . .
the salt
that fills the air. And
Feel . . .
the love that I feel
as I stand here holding your hand.

Effie Douglas Henderson
THE PALETTE
It is night and I should sleep
But my mind is full of words
Spilling over onto the paper
Full of energy and light like great blobs of color—
Red and orange exuberant with joy
and the ecstasy of living.

And then again come gray and black,
The somber tones of sorrow and destruction,
The grim reminders of the misery that humans
Often bring to themselves and others.

And yet there are the lovely tones
Of pinks and blues and violet
The colors of the sweeter gentler feelings
Of love and sympathy and understanding.

And so the spectrum flashes by,
A myriad of light and shadows,
Etched in our beings as we become the
Palette of the great painter from above.

Dan Vandervort
OUR OWN REALITY
Today there was a cloud in my blue sky.
I wanted to call, to hear you sigh.
But I knew that I shouldn't . . . and yet . . .
It's a feeling I get when I think of you
Even when we can't speak I feel you.
Here with me . . . holding me . . .
loving me.
You ask me if we can stay this way,
and in my heart I know,
that through the years our love will last,
get stronger day by day.
The bond was built, strand by strand,
that once in a lifetime thread,
that binds two hearts together,
and makes them one.
So when the stars fall from the sky,
and the sun goes down in the west.
Sitting on that hilltop hand in hand,
will still be you and I.
Two souls
Two hearts
One love.

Patricia *Majik* Gist

*Patricia *Majik* Gist*
WITH PEN AND INK I SLAY THE DRAGON
Darkest, Deepest, Dare to review,
the underlyings of its hue.
Hidden beyond common sight;
garnished with an appetite.
Roaring, Roaring deep within,
a fire breathing mannequin.
Rise. Release. 'Til it is gone.
With pen and ink I slay the Dragon.
Igneous creature conquers and slays
the ingenuity of mighty ways.
'Til water, sparkling, effervescent lights, releases the giant of sleeping nights.
Face to Face, the creature is seen,
amongst the lilies; a consuming weed.
Rise, Release. 'Til it is gone.
With pen and ink I slay the Dragon.
To all who have and have not yet,
against the white, the black has met,
Together form an invincible shield,
that only a god can properly wield.
Surgically, it rectifies the words,
within and without to shake the world.
Rise. Release. 'Til it is gone.
With pen and ink I slay the Dragon.

Barbara K Andrews
WISHY WASHY KNIGHT
I would have
I could have
given myself to you
body and soul
You were
I thought
The knight in shining armor
of my dreams
Tall, dark, brown burning eyes,
oh yes, handsome too
but then the knight

he too has his faults
his tongue was his fortune
it also was his undoing
He couldn't keep a secret, you see
So he too lost me

Nikole Brandolino
HEAVEN'S QUESTIONS
Someday I'll fly to the Heavens,
And meet the Almighty God,
Tell him all my problems,
He'll give me a friendly nod.
He'll ask me some questions,
I'll answer them so,
And one of them will be "Are you ready to go,
And meet all the Angels,"
And you know what I'll say,
God, I'm just not ready today.

Helen Roberts
SPRING
Spring, spring, my dearest spring come in—
You're surely welcome as can be.
You brought the brighter, warmer sun
And sky of azure blue, I see.
Oh! Look! The robins just flew by.
I am thrilled you brought them, too.
You won't forget the grass of green
Or flowers in the fields, will you?
I hope you woke the sleeping beasts
That have been nestled in the ground.
There are so many, many things
That you have always brought around.
What's in the bag you're holding there?
Won't you please let me look therein?
Alas! I see spring rains, rainbows
And cottony clouds stored within.
A breeze is waiting to be freed—
And look—crocus and tulips, too.
Spring, spring dearest spring stay awhile—
I have waited so long for you.

Cory Whitebird
VALENTINE'S
Valentine's Day is when there is kissing and loving and hugging.
It is sweet and Cupids will come out sometimes and give you notes and candy.
Sometimes you cannot see them but you can feel it in your heart.

Christine Casner
WISHING ON STARS
Old Joe is a 9th & 20th Street wino
But also something more
The woman on floor four
Loves him.
She lays newspapers down as bedding
Underneath the stairwell for him to sleep
A semblance thereof of tucking in

Old Joe took off his Mets cap so carefully
Placed it 'neath the last stair
Curled up his old self like a fetus
In the corner
And as a mother leans over her child's crib
So did the woman on floor four
Lean over the stairwell railing saying
Sleep tonight sweet one
I'll be on floor four see you in my dreams

A cigarette thrown to the street
Careful don't land on Old Joe
Where are our guides
And where are Old Joe's
Tonight?

Cheri Wickwire
ON THE DAY . . .

Dedicated to the heroic and courageous people of the Bay Area for their efforts during the earthquake in October 1989.

On the day the earth trembled . . .
the flowers danced gently in the fields

On the day the mountains roared . . .
the birds sang in the meadows and trees

On the day the grass rippled . . .
the flags waved softly in the breeze

On the day the fires consumed . . .
the human spirit was ignited

On the day the ground shuddered . . .
the people stood firm and strong

On the day the bridges collapsed . . .
the city began to rebuild

On the day the bay became silent . . .
the souls of many winged their way towards heaven

On the day a child's life was spared . . .
the angels rejoiced with his mother

On the day a father was rescued . . .
tears of joy were shed by a nation

On the day the earth trembled . . .
faith in God was renewed
human kindness was revealed
unity among mankind was restored
love that sustains all life was reborn

On the day the earth trembled . . .
God said "Amen."

Cheri Wickwire
DESERT DREAMS
I've seen the beauty of the desert . . .
I've heard its silence in the day

I've touched the stone that marks its presence . . .
I've molded pottery from its clay

I've tasted the fruit from nature's garden . . .
I've shuddered when the cougar screams

I've walked in glory thru its vastness . . .
Seeking out my desert dreams.

Cheri Wickwire
ELIZABETH
She's but a wee bit of a thing . . .
This mother of mine

She has a heart as big as heaven . . .
And she grows more beautiful with time

The tiny lines that etch her brow . . .
Were created by smiles thru the years

Her skin is smooth and oh so soft . . .
From being bathed by all those tears

Her sense of humor brings sunshine to my days . . .
Her blue eyes twinkle with delight

Her wisdom gave us all direction . . .
To guide us safely thru our lives

Seventy summers she has lived . . .
Four children she has born

Eight grandchildren call her "Gram" . . .
Our special lady,
Elizabeth Elaine Stroup Ohm.

Cheri Wickwire
HEAR THE CRY FOR FREEDOM
Once again the cry for freedom is heard . . .
Carried thru the air

By countless tens of thousands . . .
Seeking answers to their prayers

We are the fortunate . . .
They are the daring

We have read the prophecy . . .
And wish for them, democracy

Hear the cry for freedom . . .
Not only hear, but reply

America remembers its history . . .
And all the years gone by

Spend a moment in reflection . . .
And thank God for His direction

Fly your flag proudly . . .
Kiss your family when you see them

Be thankful you're in America . . .
When you hear the cry for freedom.

Monica L Bradshaw
THE FINAL SUBMISSION
We chase loneliness
We run from freedom
Our disinvolvement confines us
We're so immoral that we are pure
When we try and try and always fail
Why should we pursue any longer
One day we'll find our place
At the final realization that we are alone
One day in our reflection
We'll come to know fulfillment through another
In the end we will give to truth that
We must feel pain
We speak in vain
We need to risk our souls; our lives
Search for the answers
Where they cannot be found, and they will be
But when pain returns
We no longer have the answers
Emotion takes over reason and again
We chase loneliness
We run from freedom
Our disinvolvement confines us
We're so immoral that we are pure
When we try and try and always fail
Why should we pursue any longer.

Scott L Sanders
ANGELA
The real Angela is truly covered within,
Yeah, her early years have stolen her patience thin.
An offensive attitude is her guard of protection,
Against anyone who may add to the circle of dejection.
Consciously excusing bitterness as it drives pain from the site, "Well, it brings about some relief, alright."
A way of life this feeling has become and is no longer noticed,
for it's all that's known, "life must go on, no time to mope it."
For the real Angela wants to please and do good, but it won't go away and She's overcome.
Meditating is her way of information, to bring about some assurance and eliminate condemnation.
She sorts it out until she feels right, it's easier to, than fight.
Yeah, with tunnel vision delusion is cleared, for the trance covers the wrong, and with this, self-rejection is gone.
Certain fears manipulated her then.
For being young there's no choice, but to bury it, and give in.
Yes, abiding within me I have her answers, but to tell her too quickly would only upset her.
"I am He" taught me about her and what would bless, but until she's safe, "I have no rest."

June Kay Drao
A CHILD AM I
I am forty-one, but really I am five
'cause I will not give up my childhood,
I will not let it pass me by
I act just like a lady, and do what I'm supposed to do
But when I have the chance to, it's really a little girl that I am

I love all the grown-up things, I love all the grown-up joys
but when I can sneak a moment, I play with my little girl toys
I talk to my dolls, hold my teddy bears tight,
but when I hear someone coming, I put them all aside
I am but a child at heart
though a grown-up now, I must play the part
so I'll go to work, and fulfill the day
but I'll be back again to come and play.

Nealy H Wooten
EXPERIENCE
As I grow older, somewhat wiser, a lot less bolder,
I understand in a different way.

I can see what the blind can't hear,
I can hear what the deaf can't say.

I know that no matter how stormy the weather
Tomorrow will be a better day.

In years of my past I expected to grasp
All things beyond my reach.

Now I do concede, no matter how deep,
It's the water and not the depth that will drown me.

My ways, I was certain, were always right.
By lessons of experience I learned.

I could see only so much with limited sight,
So I took my turns getting burned.

Nealy H Wooten
THE ANIMAL CONVENTION
Once upon a time in a long ago rhyme
the lions played a game with the rabbits.
And all of them laughed and all of them sang
and soon it had become such a habit.

The alligators smiled when the turtles changed styles
and they ran up a branch just to grab it.
The birds and the bees and the squirrels in the trees
took a look and decided they must have it.

The monkeys and the bears dressed up combed their hairs
for this glorious celebration on the Sabbath.
The feast that they shared was the finest anywhere
and the harmony that was there was dramatic.

Now they were having secret fun in the forest in the sun
and here I come along and I blab it.
I know wine can lead to crime make you mean make you blind
so there must have been some magic in the salad.

Scott McCrae Kittridge I and Scott McCrae Kittridge II

Scott Kittridge
LIFE'S ROAD

To Eileen.
I never stopped loving you.

As I go down the road gazing up at the sun never looking back, for the hurt I might see behind me lay like cracks in the road.

As I go ahead wondering what may await knowing the road must end but never knowing when.

Always passing by what matters and living with what doesn't.

Scott Kittridge
FEELING EMPTY

To Joy Dodds.

Dreaming of things that never are,
wishing for things that might be.
Everything around us isn't right,
and we must question what we
cannot see for what we cannot see is
planted in the depths of our mind and
we must seek out the unknown and
know that we are vulnerable to what
we cannot see.
And find that dark corner in space
and explore the edge of time and
reality.

Corinne M Petray
THE LOVING KIND
Oh—your love! Babe, I feel so safe with your love
It's so steadfast and true—I have peace in loving you
You're so true and exciting
Your love is the lasting kind
And I could never find
Any romance as attractive as yours
Your love is like from God above
It's not the suffering kind
That I tried and cried to know sometimes
You are truly kind and oh so fine
God and my lover's love

It's the caring kind.

Evelyn Vollmer
HAPPINESS
Some people search for happiness.
They search the whole world o'er.
When happiness is really found.
Right at their own back door.
It's a feeling of joy when day is done.
It's a voice that says it's a job well done.
It's the smile on someone's face.
The handshake of a friend.
A feeling of contentment that never seems to end.
The love of God brings this about you'll find
There really isn't any other kind.

Elizabeth Keefe
SEASONS

To my "Pop" Charlie Combs, who left me love and memories. I'll never forget you!!

When we met he was young and I was old,
while I was timid he was bold.
He was of the Spring and I was of the Fall.
While in each other's arms,
there were no "Seasons" felt at all.

He taught me to love in ways so new,
I gave love and warmth he found with few.
In my heart I knew our love should never be,
family and friends all laughed at me.
He only smiled, said, "The best is yet to come."

We never know what life holds,
Winter often comes too soon.
They said I'd grow old while he'd still be young.
We loved so much our "Seasons" were always warm,
remember Dear, "The best is yet to come."

My love was first to lose his life one Spring,
I was left to face the lonely Fall alone.
The love we felt still warms my memories.
His words I still hear, "The best my love is still to come,"
Our Summer "Season" has not begun.

Natalie Grabert
IN THE BEGINNING
Our souls reach beyond
the cold winds in the darkness.
Feelings surface from far within
warming the cold night air.

A touch
A gentle caress.
The pureness of becoming one.
One being secured in our bodies
warmth and love.

An absent mind
Free from fear and hurt
Retreating into a world of newness
A world of love
The world of Samson and Delilah.
There we reach beyond the cold wind
and the darkness.

Shirley R Powell
SCOOTER
Who is this furry creature
Who greets me at the door—
Asking only for a stroke of my hand
And really nothing more—

Who is this studious creature
Sitting on my windowsill—
Watching hour after hour
Until she's had her fill—

Who is this whimsical creature,
Sleeping curled up in my lap—
When without a moment's notice
She's chasing a catnip rat—

Who is this pesky creature
Who leaps upon my bed—
Nibbling gently at my nose
Until she's finally fed—

I'll bet by now, you've guessed it
That this affectionate little brat—
Is none other than dear "Scooter"
My loveable, adorable, cat—

Gloria Riseling Wilford
GOD'S TALENTS
From the heights of the stars to the depths of the sea,
God's art works displayed, majestically.

He's master of all the artful professions,
Even Shakespeare, Picasso, and Bach could take lessons.

His musical abilities are unsurpassed,
From the song of a bird, to the tune of the grass.

His art work is truly a wonder to see
For the colors he uses are heavenly.

He sculptures out valleys, and shapes mountains high,
And balances a glowing mobile in the sky.

His dance is so graceful, motions of love
As performed by a deer, or the flight of a dove.

He has written a book of story and rhyme
That will be a best seller throughout all of time.

His culinary arts are impossible to match
Just take what He put in a strawberry patch

His greatest work, of highest price
Was His Son's loving sacrifice

His love for us will never cease
For to God, We are His masterpiece!

Marilyn K Meskill
PARODY
The wind howling through mossly covered naked trees,
Nightingales singing their lonely song,
The smell of dew on long grass,
Reminded me of days gone past.
Through my life I found no cause,
Too many people; too little time,
Illness beseeches us all,
I swing and sway; like the oak I stand tall.
Snowflakes wisping from the wintery sky,
A cold child,
Hunger pains my every sense,
There is no rhyme or reason; no words left to mince.

Almyra Keller
MY DEAD FRIEND
I'm finding it very hard to exist without you
Now you're not here with me
I've thought of joining you
But you taught me to be a fighter
I'm still fighting
But someday I'll join you

Time has gone by but I still love you
I long to hold you
Whisper words that I never told you
Time has changed and I've grown older
But you still have a special place in my heart
Because I love you and always will.

Stacie L Sutton
MOVING ON
Heart of stone; tears of ice.
Is there no more sacrifice?

We go on, day by day.
I see you look the other way.

Hand in hand, different paths.
Now there is no turning back.

Day gives way; turns to night
Ghostly shapes in pale moonlight.

I am ice; you are fire.
Nothing's left of our desire.

Hunger's gone, pain increases.
Now it's time to pick up pieces.

No one's right, no one's wrong
It's just time for moving on.

Katie Juckniess
UNTITLED
Deep in your eyes
I can sense your fear,
and the loss of words I long to hear.
In the garden of my soul,
you plant your seed, I feel love grow.
Although you fail to find much time,

when you're with me, it seems so
fine.
Each time you look at me I feel
that something is there you won't
reveal.
Is it so hard to let it out,
is your heart afraid or is there a
doubt?
I will not give in to defeat
when I think I'm traveling a
one-way street.
I feel empty, my heart is sore,
Do you love me anymore?

D Chandler Wellington
ATTRACTION
I curse the arcane laws of attraction
Whose depths I will never plumb
As your eyes drive me to distraction
And your simple words strike me
dumb.

If you tell me what you want,
I'll give it.
If you tell me the words,
I'll say them.
Teach me the spells and the
incantations
My need must be there in my eyes
You can't have missed all my
indications—
Or were you listening to my lies?

Christine Marie Yoho

Christine Marie Yoho
STRINGS

To my family and friends—thanks for believing in me!

Remember the kites?
Yours were always airborne,
Ascending, blowing brisk
In the breeze.
And mine?
I'd tenaciously try
For a rush of wind
To rouse my craft
Like yours.
Once on its way,
My kite would lilt then lean
Between gusts.
You'd shout "String! Let go
Of the string!"
At your impatience
I'd panic.
Freely stopping the flow.
No.
I never have learned to let go.

Walter A McClure
OUR ENVIRONMENT
The environment is precious, we
should guard it well.
Like the beautiful memories of a
tulip's smell.
The melodic bird songs have a
soothing tune,
Or the beautiful scenery of a tropical
lagoon.
But these and many more we take for
granted:
Like the beautiful colors of animals
enchanted.
But now we're destroying the homes
they prize.
You can hear the poor animals'
humble cries.
The creatures in the sea are dying
from waste.
People on bulldozers are destroying
forests with haste.
And if we don't stop all this
commotion:
Then aside from mankind, there
won't be any motion.

Linda Bliss
SURGES OF LOVE
I looked up into the sky,
I saw a big moon.
And you said, it was an unusual size.
I said not so.

I saw the waves of the sea.
I wanted to chase them beyond all
cares.
But you looked at me with suspicious
eyes.

The ocean breeze, the summer sand,
All beckon me to them.
No man can keep me so.

I want an affair with the sea.
I want to feel the lips of the sea wind
on me.
I want to taste of the champagne
Of the infinite love in my heart.

Elizabeth M Rork
WHEN WE WERE YOUNGER
When we were younger,
Time seemed to crawl by;
And how happy we always were,
We didn't have reasons to cry.

But those days have come and gone,
Oh, how quickly they disappeared,
The days when we would watch the
sun,
And always did things we feared.

Now, our life's sun is at noon,
And we realize that it's way past
time,
To throw away dreams of going to
the moon;
Along with hopes of finding a gold
mine.

For soon our sun will be setting,
And our remaining time will fly,
And we'll wonder what we're getting
Out of the world, as it quickly passes
us by.

Richard Barnett
HIGH
How high the heavens
How near eternity
How many ways to reach the summit
There are many more to fall

To understand the reasoning
behind man's desire to be high
one has to reach the plateau himself

To talk of others and not to
understand them
is to violate all solidity before taking
a conviction
experience what the people
encounter, doing their own thing
Pause before speaking and when you
obtain truth
Speak with wisdom
and truly you will be high . . . .

Katherine Nielsen Eckhart
PETALS ON THE GRASS
Rose petals on the lawn—
Across the sky there now will dawn
For that rose another day.
The rose that fell beside the way
Its radiant beauty gone.
Fragrance spent for some sweet lass
Soft petals fell upon the grass.
Pure velvet rests on mossy green
A lovely picture still is seen.
The petals pile there fragrantly
Awaiting the rose-jar of a queen.

Robert Shell
MEG'S PEG LEG

To my mother. I might not ever have written this poem without her.

There was a young woman named
Meg.
She happened to have a peg leg.

It thumped like a rock.
It wouldn't fit in a sock.
And it looked like it came from a
keg.

Cathilyn Elton-McDowell
MY LOSS

In finally granting you your wish, I wrote and hereby dedicate this poem lovingly and specially to you, Mom.

I'm born within a glow
all my life I'm held closely amidst
the most beautiful of lights
emanating from a tiny flame

I draw close for protection and
comfort as it lights my way
forever shining in the arena that is my
life
brilliantly vibrant, never failing

I continue to bask in its rays, growing
stronger and brighter
as its struggle flickers, unnoticed
shadows of gray begin to surround
me and I'm drowning in fear . . .
it is noticed now

I join in its struggle but am helpless
to sustain the flame
I'm able only to observe the glimmer
fade into darkness

It's lighting my way no more in this
arena that is my life
I'll one day reignite from the spark
which was nurtured
so lovingly, tenderly, and completely
from the quenched fire
but I am cold now in the dark

As my life's sustaining light grows in
strength and beauty yet seen
becoming one with an even greater
light
I begin to hover for warmth within
the memories of the fiery brilliance
that once was
my Mom.

Tisha McManus
MY MOM IS GREAT
My mom is great
Greater than she'll ever know
I love her so much
I wish I could let it show
She makes me feel wanted, special
and loved
When something's got me down
She tells me I'm above
Above the juvenile things all teens
must face
As long as I've got mom
I'll be ahead of the race
A woman so special is almost unreal
Maybe someday I can express
How I feel
I love you mom

Your first born will always love you
no matter what. I know as she goes
through her phases in life you doubt
her love, but don't because life has its
ups and downs in everyone and
sometimes it's hard to let someone
that means a great deal to you know
how you feel. Love always, 5-9-73

Caprice Laxamana
SO MANY WORDS
Our world is filled with so many
words to express the way we feel.

A day will come when all of our
souls will make one.

And speech will not be necessary to
do or make undone.

Confusion and illusions never will
be; no needs, no dreams, no anxieties.

Jonathan W Cobb
UNJUSTIFIABLE MEANS
There was the old style,
when you could think good;
Now there is the new school—
Except for my father, he stood
for fair play, being nobody's fool;
But standing up straight obeying the
rule.
He's far from perfect, don't be
misled;
But he chose the right route instead.
So act as you choose, I don't matter;
Continue your scam, until they
scatter.

Lorraine Brown
THE PERENNIAL NATURE OF FRACTURED REASON

For Neil . . . my husband and best friend.

Pushed out of darkness and aloneness
by the need
To self-actualize
Slowly unfolded the essence
As it stretched to embrace the sun.
Simple of need . . . Trusting of
nature . . .
It planted its existence in the new
world
As it stretched to touch its God.
As it looked with new eyes
It heard with new ears

All the trivialities of Import
Itself unaware of its own truth
Its own value.
Disappointed and weakened
By Import's dominant nature and inability to feed
It began to tire and wilt
Seeing that light can be as cold as dark
When Truth is found to be without substance.
No . . .
It is not spring but winter's eve still
And internal darkness holds a greater warmth and a better God.

Scott Feltis

Scott Feltis
LOOKING UPON
As times have changed,
so have I.
My wills have grown greater,
my soul restored.
I wish for only the best,
but rarely receive.
I don't think that's fair
to someone like me.
It's time for a change,
Look upon me.
Find out who I am,
and what I should be.
For now I am going,
but not too far.
Keep me in your sight,
and close at heart.

Michael A Johnson
CUP OF TEA
Look into my heart to find me.
Sometimes I am not all you see.
But I know you are my cup of tea.

Bring your dreams of love within me.
To light your flame of hope to see.
But I know I am your cup of tea.

A dreamer's night as you sleep with me.
Within my arms, oh yes, I can see.
But we are each other's cup of tea.

All I can see is you in me.
To feel you in my soul I can see.
But there is a neverending cup of tea.

The magic that bonds you and me.
Forever we are together you see.
So please darling another cup of tea.

Shirley Ellen
BE CONSOLED
When God comes and takes
a loved one by the hand,
It is difficult for one
to let go—to understand
Why you no longer can gaze
upon her face and say,
I love you. I'll see you
on another day.
But another day is just
not meant to be,
Her face you will no longer
be able to see.
But peace is hers and in
your heart you know
It is a far better place
she was chosen to go.
Be consoled . . . for did
God not say
He would take her hand when
you took yours away!

Dorothy I Walker
STEPS
Little foot steps all in a row
Stepping on toes as they go

They move so fast here and there
Hardly a time for burdens to bear

But as they get older they step on hearts
And that is when growing up starts

There comes a time for decision to make
And they have to decide which steps to take

Sometimes the steps are filled with pain
Other times they have the world to gain

As time goes on the steps grow slow
Now they watch Little Foot Steps all in a row

Leonard Joseph Nunez
PARENTS

To My Parents Whom I Love Very Much: Whether We Be Near or Very Far Apart. You Are Both at the Center of the Love Within My Heart.

Most of us know
And most would agree,
That we are their product;
They made you and me.

They molded and structured
Long before we remember.
And worried and hoped
As we stumbled and fell.

They encouraged and loved
Though not oft understood,
And the secrets we shared
They would not again tell.

They uplifted our spirit
When the light seemed its dimmest.
Hidden tears from the heart
Till they knew all was well.

Though none of us knew
That their prayers to the Father
Are what carried us through;
They made me and you.

Leonard Joseph Nunez
CHRISTMAS
All the gifts have been wrapped
And look neat 'neath the tree.
Dressed in Christmas colors
Of gold, red and green.
Green, the symbol of life;
Red, the essence of life;
Gold, the meaning of life.
Blended together this way
In order to say
Merry Christmas with love
To honor Jesus, Our Savior Above.

So as one year ends
And a new one begins,
May the best life has to bring
Come your way this new year.
Joy in all that you see;
Wisdom in all that you hear.
So celebrate this day
And each through this year
With expectations of hope,
Love . . . and good cheer.

Carol Nechtman
JOURNEY
As I travel free and quickly
And soar where none can see,
I see myself below me,
And the love surrounding me.

I bring within my spirit
My present and my past,
The future stretched before me
Seems now within my grasp.

I've left insecure emotions
In the phase I left behind,
I look forward to the peace
That now is ever in my mind.

Adrienne D Durgin
LESSONS FROM CHILDHOOD
O, what a thrill
to go down and take my fill
at the local theatre.
Little did I know what would happen later.
The western was great
and so I stayed a little late.
I hopped on my bicycle,
took the shortcut down the hill.
I went too fast
and was aghast
to see my bicycle chain
had been stolen.
Careening out of control,
terror took its toll.
A decision I had to make
before it was too late.
I swerved into a driveway, hit the wall,
and had a great fall;
determined that next time
I would walk to the theatre.

Glenn Hass
FALLEN DAYS

To my sister, Cindy Woolford. Thanks for illustrating my book "Creation Speaks."

Fallen days
Kiss the night
Sweeping glory
From our sight
Visions lost
In shadows bright
Empty fields
Frosted white

Glenn Hass
THE FIELD TRIP
The broken branch,
Dripping with sap,
Lies,
In the naked field.

The wounded rabbit,
Licking the sap,
Remembers,
Ghost images of its kin.

Next to the branch,
A starling,
Searches in vain,
Through a broken nest.

A doe,
Gazing on these sights
Wonders,
Who will be next?

Bob B O'Loughlin
I'M GOIN' WALKIN' WITH MY LADY

To my lady and best friend, Irma, for over forty years.

I'm goin' walkin' with my lady and we're walkin' hand in hand
If you've ever been in love you'll understand,
And when I'm walkin' with my lady you will know that she's the one
For my smile will make a shadow of the sun.

As we go strollin' down the avenue we're certain to be seen.
The girls will stare, the boys will just turn green.
And when the fellas try to catch her eye for her there's only me
And heaven's just another place to be.

And when I'm talkin' with my lady as we go along the way
She'll agree with everything I have to say.
Although I know she may not mean it, is just a game she plays
She wants this mother's son to have his day.

Oh I'll be walkin' with my lady till she shuns the likes of me,
But I hope to try for all eternity.
So if you're walkin' with your lady and as fortunate as me
Take my word there's not a better place to be.

Bob B O'Loughlin
CARE AND SHARE
Care and share if you're lonely
You'll never forsake what you've had
There's no need to be lonely
You'd better be glad than be sad.

Take my hand and be friendly
Friends are always in style
Kindle a spark deep within me
And then melt my heart with a smile.

None other can give what you have to share
No one can care quite the same
For you are you and the only you
By any other name.

Take a part of me with you
Please may I do the same
Trust in faith and each other
There's no better way to gain.

To care and share with the lonely
Is never a lonely way.
To care and share with the lonely
Is one other way to pray.

Bryan Pitts

Bryan Pitts
MUDDY BANKS

To my mother, Joan, who was always there.

Some boulevards spread the
myth
and tell the tale of
the American Buffalo.
Other streets show
that Lewis and Clark
rode canoes to sandbar claims
on a map.

Furry critters make a
home
in muddy banks,
and Paris brokers
pray to
northern lights;
I point the flock
to the end of
the rainbow,
and swim in the
highlands of
kilts, and
castles gone
dark.

I led a group of
the old 49'ers;
we took snowshoes,
dogs, sleds and
a compass,
to follow great
herds of
running caribou.
Arrows of Geronimo pointed
the way,
to fight the firesticks
and
spear the bluecoats.

In the final
leg
we had to break camp,
among the woodland
houses of
feathered friends;
I ended up in
the redwood avenues,
between the boulevards and
muddy banks . . . .

Stacey Trocchia
GREY CLOUDS HID THE AFTERNOON SUN
Grey clouds hid the afternoon sun
A quiet rustle of leaves was the only thing heard
Thunder clapped
Lightning flashed
Rain dropped from the sky
The coldness of a stone drained the heat from my hand
Yet I stood there
Staring at the letters that spelled your name.
They were perfectly engraved in that stone.
It rained harder
Lightning flashed brighter
Thunder clapped louder.
All I could think of was the memory of your smile.

Candy Farmer
A PEACE CALL
Come one Come all
To the peace call
A place where we
Can all call home
But never be alone
To share with each other
The love we have together.

Lara Hinckley
DRINKING AND DRIVING
We thought we'd have a really good time,
all of us young and in our prime,
we drank and drank till we could stand no more,
and we crowded in the car and slammed the door,
off we drove very fast,
and then you see that was the last,
sirens, lights flash right past,
everything was spinning very fast,
as the lives of my friends slowly drained,
we just wanted to have a good time we claimed,
ever since then nothing's been the same,
and I guess everyone's to blame,
SO, THINK BEFORE YOU GO OFF AND DRINK,
just stop for a minute and start to think.

Michelle Swint
A BIG MISTAKE
It came as a thief in the night,
on March 24th of '89,
they said it would never happen
just like the Titanic was unsinkable,
but just four strokes after midnight it did.

Prince William Sound was changed forever,
it smelled like a gas station on a hot humid day.

Diffusing across the ocean blue
like spilled juice on a waxed floor,
was eleven million gallons of crude, raw oil.

It made the lives of many creatures miserable,
small and tall, big and little
Their bodies pliant
like bent, twisted twigs
drenched in black, slimy oil
some died; some lived
they had no choice.

Their chance of living had been
destroyed by one man's
pleasure—a drink.

Michele Delon
PEACEFUL QUIET
Walls still, no vibration
Carpet serene, no static
from small, socked feet.

Doors hug their jams,
Relieved to be idle
from slams.

Telephone perches on its hook
grateful for the respite
from alarm.

Mother sits in the peaceful quiet,
yearning
for intrusion.

Vivian Heller-Kenyon
MORE THAN A DOCTOR

Dedicated to: Dr. Gregory Chiaramonte, who taught me what's really important in life is not what I can't do—but it's what I can do that counts.

Once I felt down and out,
because I was told
I had a dreadful disease
most people get when they're old.

My joints were swollen
and I had stiff wrists.
I was diagnosed as having
Rheumatoid Arthritis.

You took me under your wing,
and were so kind to me.
I knew real soon I was on
the road to recovery.

You gave me the fighting spirit;
my shattered dreams you did mend.
And, it's a comfort to know
you are my doctor, and my friend.

Vivian Heller-Kenyon
OUR LOVE LIVES ON

Dedicated to my Great-Aunt Nee, who I'll love forever.

Our love lives on
throughout the years;
despite our problems,
frustrations, and fears.

Our love lives on
with hopes and visions
of taking on life's
busy ambitions.

Our love lives on
though the miles
between us
are long.

I love you
with all my heart.
Even beyond death,
it will not part.

Lynn Ryder
WONDERING
I try to give all of me
never understanding much,
but always trying to foresee.

For it's the tears
that I've shed,
Hoping never to be torn
apart or mislead.

Always hoping to forget the pain
never accepting that most of it was in vain.

Believing I would never have to
pay the price,
never knowing any one person
that was so concise.

For it's my reasons I have given.
Knowing that someday I will be forgiven.

Elizabeth Jones
TAKE TIME TO PRAY
On a beautiful sunlit day
Mother and daughter, forgot to pray
As they began to greet their friends at work
They attacked their work with great exert

As the day went on, soon it was noon
They planned to leave, to go to the Silver Spoon
They had planned to talk, and have a great lunch
As they left, friends assured them, they loved them a bunch

Laughing and talking, they went out to greet the day
But they should've taken time to pray
But they didn't know they wouldn't be coming back
That only a few miles away, a man was having a heart attack

As he came their way, he began to weave and swerve
Still, their master, they had forgot to serve
They didn't know, they had said their last good-bye
That he was headed their way, and they would soon die

When lunch was over, and they hadn't returned
Friends and loved ones, became very concerned
So the lesson is this, "Take time to pray"
Because this could be, "Your very last day"

Kay W Killian
THE YELLOW ROOM
The yellow was special to me and to sister,
In our eyes it was beautiful, always full of mystery.
Two beds and a dresser and linoleum on the floor,
No other place was like it, with only one little door.

We would lie in bed and talk till Mother said, "That's enough!"
Then we'd start whispering, so we wouldn't cause a fuss.
I always got tickled and ended up laughing out loud,
"Here comes Mother," sister would say and we'd quiet down right away.

"Girls, it's getting late, it's almost eight thirty,"
"Tomorrow's another day and we have to get up early."
"Mother, I love this yellow room," I would always say,
"Let it always be yellow, let it always stay this way."

My yellow room became sad one day, when sister started to school,
It didn't seem the same anymore, the color almost seemed to fade.
"Mother, please go and get her and bring her home again,"
"I don't want to be without her, she's my only friend."

"Now don't you fret, she's only gone for a little while,"
"She'll be home before you know it, now give me a little smile."
It sure seemed a long time till she got home at three,
Now, my world was complete again, with my sister and me.

April Bowden
THE RUNNING MAN
The hands of time hold
Your future in a cold embrace.
You run from place to place

Trying to escape the trying
Past that haunts you.

You can run as far as time
Will spare, but there are some
Who will forget you like an
Autumn leaf. But others
Will not forget so easily.

Your biggest sin was that
You wanted to be loved. You
Didn't care who it was, anyone
Would do. Now the thought
Of that four letter word
Hurts you more now than it
Ever did.

Douglas Lee Penner
VALENTINE
Electric
inscrutable
currency,
legacy's trestle.
Your crowning
legs,
amendment's
cognition.

Delia M Holmberg

Delia M Holmberg
PRAYING HANDS

To my family and dear friends for their love and encouragement throughout my lengthy illness.

Let us clasp our hands together;
Pray fervently for each other:
First for forgiveness of our sin
So we have joy and peace within,
Have his Holy Spirit's power
To witness for Him every hour.
We have pains and worrisome cares.
Name them all in believing prayers.

Kenneth E Sutton
SAY NO TO DRUGS
Say no to drugs
While you still can!
Let the demon know
That you understand!

Say no to the monster,
And the hell drugs put you through!
Slam the door forever,
Lest the monster becomes you!

Say no to suffering,
To all the money that's spent,
To the trouble and the pain,
And the mental torment!

Say no to degradation,
To malice of the heart,
To love, to trust and honesty
That addiction tears apart!

Say no to shattered dreams,
To a whole world gone awry!
Say no now, and forever
please . . .
And forever don't you cry!

Marilyn Heinz
EYE CONTACT
With innocent eyes I undress you
and flirt wildly with your eyes
over coffee and cigarettes.
My eyes beg you with no words
to touch me.
Taking you all in my eyes snap a
picture of you wrapped in a towel,
fresh out of the shower,
standing silhouetted by the light
of the open refrigerator.
Through eyelids heavy with sleep
my eyes look closely at your face,
studying 6:00 am sunlight
as it shines across your eyes, making
you blink.
My cheek rests on your
wheat-colored beard stubble and my
eyelashes brush your cheek
in a butterfly kiss.
Then, behind closed eyes
I can remember the day that I met
you
and the way my heart felt
the first time that I saw you.

Lani Cubells
PAST TO PRESENT
Past to present,
Far away to near,
This is what you'll bring with you.
Old love to new love,
Old hope to new,
This is what you'll bring with you.
My heart will be full;
Complete.
My mind will be satisfied;
Pleased.
My life will be with meaning
with you.

Lucy C Pruett
CHRISTMAS GLORY
As I sit by the fireplace on this crisp
December morn
I imagine that time long ago when
Jesus Christ was born.
How the Mother Mary smiled at the
baby so dear,
While God the Father sent his angels
to be near.
And on that wondrous night all the
world lay at peace
From the smallest of creatures to the
largest of beast,
And the bright star that shone as a
beacon in the night
Led the wisemen and shepherds to
that glorious sight.
They knelt round the manger and
gazed in reverent awe
At the tiny little babe, yet the King of
kings they saw.
And the animals that shared the
stable with the newborn babe
Seemed to know he was destined for
the world to save.
As for the Christ child he uttered not
a peep
For wrapped was he in righteousness
lying fast asleep.
And God the Father smiled from his
kingdom up above
Knowing his son would bring
mankind hope, peace and love.
Yes, truly 'twas a miracle that
inspired this little story—
For God so loved the world that he
gave us Christmas Glory.

Deborah M Taylor
A EULOGY OF JFK

Dedicated to the memory of my dear father, Joseph G. Bierman.

I hear a voice, and it seems to say,
This is not true, this tragic day.

But, the caisson passes by my eyes,
With military death guards on both
sides.

The riderless horse as it trots behind,
From years of past history to present
divine.

The flag-covered casket that bears
our beloved,
Both symbols of freedom for
America we love.

My heart filled with ache, and heavy
with pain,
I stop and think just what will
remain?

A country with wisdom, much more
than before,
And even a memory of possible war?

No, there still are more memories that
will remain,
That no other country could possibly
gain.

I stop and think, what did that voice
say?
This is not true, this tragic day.

With heartfelt emotions and tears in
my eyes,
I suddenly realize our President dies.

But what do I cry for, for loss of one
man?
Or loss of our leader throughout this
great land?

If only his end came in some other
form,
This surely would ease our hearts that
are torn.

He gave us guidance, his love and his
plans,
When decisions arose in far distant
lands.

He knew just what measures and just
where to step,
And assured us with promises which
he always kept.

So many things that he did will
always live on,
And make it hard to believe that he
really is gone.

I loved him so dearly. Each night
when I pray I ask,
Why, oh Lord, did you take him
away?

Since that memorable year 1961, a
landslide victory when Kennedy won.

Once more in the hands of a leader so
great,
That dates back to 1778.

Yes! I heard a voice that seemed to
say,
This is not true, this tragic day.

But now it speaks in a different way,
It says he is not dead, he's just away.

Jessica Collins
CHILDHOOD LOST
Turning the pages of an old and dusty
book,
In hopes of capturing one last look.
One more glance at what used to be,
When we played all day and climbed
every tree.
A time when laughter and fun was
always there,
A time when it didn't matter if you
didn't care.
To us it was all but a game,
We always thought it would stay the
same.
It never occurred to us the idea of
growing older,
We only thought of new games to
play when the weather was colder.
Our parents were always there,
To dress us up and comb our hair.
But times have changed and so have
we,
We're all adults now as you can see.
As everyone knows growing up is not
an art,
But we'll all always be a child at
heart.

Lera Bailey Hamilton
RESPECT FOR MATURITY
The horse plowed from sunup to
sundown;
He hauled in the wood and food from
town.
Now he is old and of little use;
He receives less care and more abuse.
He may be turned out to pasture to
graze;
His coat of hair is never brushed, his
eyes glaze.
To appease a sudden mood, he may
be carried to a soap factory;
This may be this once useful animal's
final destiny!

The dog used to be a playful pup;
He minded his manners and ate from
his cup.
He fetched the paper and barked at
the prowler;
He was adored, patted, and stroked
on his glossy fur.
Now he's mature, not as agile as
before;
He's not as beautiful, he's now
kicked out the door.
His final home may be in the country
a distance away;
There he may be found finally dead
on a highway!

Our compassion is becoming nil, we
hardly ever cry;
If there's an hindrance, we don't let it
pass by.
We're thrilled only by wealth and
utility;
We need to respect and honor the
elderly—
We must not let the actions toward
animals turn to humanity!

Serena M Helmick
UNIQUE SPLENDOR OF THE MOUNTAINS

To all my loving children and grandchildren.

The mountains are so beautiful, so majestic and regal
They change their looks with each new season to enhance their unique splendor for a reason in God's creation
In winter they're covered with blankets of snow that glisten like crystal in moments of sunlight between sparkling rays
In autumn their colors are beautiful too—as the sunshine reflects all its colors in view—orange, red, yellow and deep purple too.
In spring they are brimming with new open buds of wonderful fragrances so sweet to imbue with God's new creations each one of a kind.
In summer they blossom with flowery shrubs and trees all dressed up in glories unique to behold as God's splendorous gifts of creations to all humankind.

Lorrie Meistad
DEDICATION TO A TEACHER AND FRIEND

I dedicate this poem to Señor David G. Haakenson, my teacher and friend. Also, Julie Oxley, my family and friends.

I wanted so much to please you
But nothing I did was right
You said you were proud of me
But I knew better

My winning the competition
Meant a lot to you
When I failed miserably
I saw the disappointment

Because you were my friend
You only smiled
I knew right then and there
I would make it up to you

So now I try harder
Harder than I've ever tried before
Because I can still see
The disappointment in your eyes

This time when you say you're proud
I want you to mean it.

Lori D Lapping
WINDOW OF TIME

For my son, Levi Blu Lapping, with all my heart.

Looking out the window
Staring into time
I wonder how your life will be
Oh tiny son of mine
Will you grow up to be
Short or tall, strong and healthy
Will you be happy
Intelligent and wealthy
Will you go off to college
Move away and leave home
Will you meet a nice girl
Marry and have kids of your own
Will you have a good career
Make a name for yourself
Will you still remember and love us
Your father and myself
As I sit here and wonder
My eyes are turned to you
And I smile as I notice
You are looking out the window too

Laura L Wright
MOMENTO
Cradling the pillow that held your head
Between my breasts I wet
It with my tears,
Wine sweet from your mouth now
Sour in mine without
Your lips to fill full overflowing;
The rich scent of our love lingers
Musky in the sheets
On which I lie,
You lied,
We lay together once
Each other now
A line, a phrase,
The feel of you lies
Sleeping in my thoughts
There to awaken at my
Slightest touch—
Have I left, I wonder, you
Ought to remember?

Anthony and Tonya

S D Buckner
EMPTINESS 3001

Dedicated to Anthony Warren and Tonya-Renay BUCKNER: YOU ARE THE SUNSHINE.

When the sky has fallen . . .
And the wind moves heavenly across the sky . . .
When birds cannot move south, and trees begin to die . . .
When life holds a stillness, no population cries . . .
No heaven will open . . .
No soul has survived . . .
No one was friendly
No child could be seen
Food was never there,
because of greed . . .
The earth was too hot
Dust in the air
Not a planet could be seen
Nor a soul to be heard . . .
If ever to wonder
Why to a planet
Just ask the ones who were left to die . . .

Who destroyed the earth,
the heavens of the sky

Cindy Dawn Goolsby
THE WAY LOVE IS. . .
Love is like a ship sailing in the night.
Love is like a bluebird bird flying in the light.
Love is like a friend always there when
you need it most, but love is really a special toast.

Love is like a cat prowling in the dark.
Love is taking a walk through a lovely green park.
Love is like a riddle you can never figure
out, but love is really bad when you're in doubt.

Love can hurt you, it can soothe you.
Love can also make you blue, but if you're in doubt which I hope you'll never
be, love will be best for you and me.

Jilliary Thomason
GET PREPARED THIS IS LIFE
Today, I came home and climbed a tree,
to get a cat named Johny.
I fell out of that tree.
Last night, I was walking down a road,
at 2:30 am, didn't know where I was going;
didn't really care.
I just shook my head in awe and repeated these words to myself.
"This Bizarreness of Life"
and I dreamt of traveling to places and writing about them.
Now it's hanging so fragilely within my grasp.
I remember when I was just a young child,
riding on a bus, home from school.
I'd look out the window and
Just thought of traveling on foot.
In North Carolina, I used to walk a certain way home;
and when I got to this certain place it always felt dreamy.
Down a barren dusty hill
there was this foxhole,
I always thought robbers had lived there.
I just kinda wanted to live there too.
At that time, standing there, that was life to me.
But now I find, I must say to myself.
"GET PREPARED THIS IS LIFE."

Daniel R Jackson
TEAR DOWN THE WALLS
Ever since slavery, blacks seem to have lost their pride,
and they build walls between themselves just so they can hide.
It's time to tear down the walls of subjection and put up the walls of affections.
(Let's Tear Down The Walls)

Let's tear down the walls of ignorance, fear, and separation,
and open up a freeway of love, compassion, and communication.
Let's open our tightly shut minds and let out all negativism, and replace in our minds love, and optimism.
(Let's Tear Down The Walls)

Let's tear down the walls of "It Might Come True,"
and put up the walls of "I Can DO."
Let's tear down the walls of "It Might," and put up the walls of "In Spite."
Let's tear down the walls of all negative things, and put up walls that help promote Dreams.
(Let's Tear Down The Walls)

Robert P Barracca

Robert P Barracca
THE EMPTY ROOM THAT HAS NO WALLS
Many people believe that when evil men die,
They sink below to receive the hot punishment they did buy.
But as a man of good sense I have to object, I do.
That is not what I believe they are to be subjected to.
For there is a torture much worse than burning;
That is the sensation for companionship yearning.
Loneliness turns a man's stomach inside and out.
A scream can be heard, a cry and a shout.
For over this torture even the strongest man bawls.
Trapped alone in The Empty Room That Has No Walls.

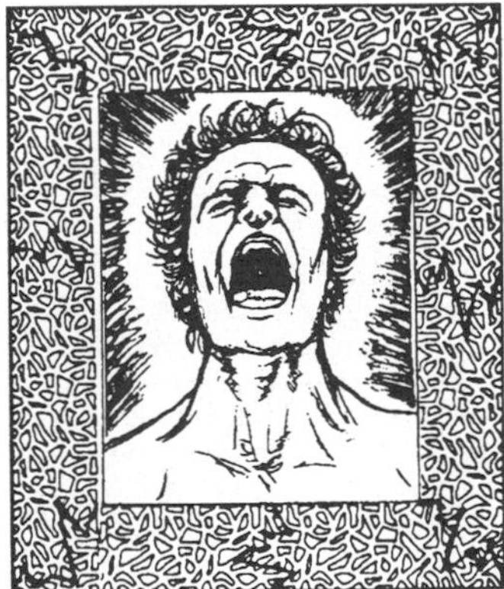

The strong man exclaims, "I can take what they give me!"
But when loneliness sets in, he will try to break free.
Knowing the Legend has deceived him, he stares into the dark.
He can see nothing of fire; he can see nothing of spark.
How quickly he becomes so much more mild,
With his thumb in his mouth, dribbling like a child.
A large puddle of tears he leaves on the floor.
Crying and screaming, "I can't take it no more!"
He resembles an infant as in circles he crawls,
Trapped alone in The Empty Room That Has No Walls.

Nancy J Hull
MAMA (JANE K. EVANS)
My mother was a tall woman; her shoulders strong, her eyes bright blue, her hair dark blond, and her manner friendly and kind.
She was most always singing, dancing, laughing and loving life.
Her tears were only for the wrong and pain of others and when she failed. She gave a touch, reaching to those near with patience and care.
She tended the sick, elderly and young, possessing a high spirit of endless effort.
My mother was a tall woman, giving deep love and support to her family, and giving to me, a daughter, constant loyalty. She taught me to meet life with passion, wonder and faith.
Mama was as beautiful and lasting as diamonds resting on the snow, and as delicate as fresh flowers in a milk-glass vase, placed upon a white lace tablecloth.
My mother was a good woman, as strong and right as the tide seeking and reaching the shore.

Suzanne Lee Stephens
FOR THE LOVE OF NEEDLES AND BABY FOOD
I love you more than life.
Make love to me
through this hole in my arm.
I feel you all over my body.
I hear your voice.
You always leave me too soon.
I have to find ways to
make you stay.
I have to have you.
You are my possession.
If you want me to,
I will sell the car, the house,
and the baby can eat tomorrow,
. . . maybe.

John L Rossi
HEBRIDÉS
In Londontown there lives a cat
whose name is Hebridés,
And he's the cat who'll tell you
that the world's a bag of fleas;

The world's a kennel full of dogs,
the world's half sour milk;
The other half is scolding marms
and troubles of that ilk.

But oh how nice the world becomes
when it's a windowsill,
When it's a mini-jungle patch
where he can hunt at will;

When it's a bouncing ball of yarn
or cuddles from li'l Matt,
When it's a batch of catnip chunks
along with Nancy's pat;

Or when all curled some wintry day
athwart the fireplace mat,
He squints an eye and softly purrs,
"It's fun to be a cat."

Margaret Garbino
WHAT LOVE IS TO ME
Para el indio de la sonrisa dulce.

Love is birds singing
Mornings full of sun
Cold, rain, the smell of flowers
Life that's just begun.

Love is pain, love is sorrow
Love is when your heart
Is burning with passion
Every time you feel his touch.

Love is sleepless nights
Full of dreams of futures
That may never come.

Love is the warmth of a smile
Every time he smiles at you
Love is looking into his eyes
Knowing he loves you too.

You must try to understand
That's what love is to me
To be nourished and grow stronger
For that is what God intended
Love to be.

Sheri Gadfield
FIGMENT OF IMAGINATION
I am a figment of your imagination—
I give a love that exists only in dreams.
I am WOMAN
Deep
Destructive
Poison
Passionate
I can stay only for a short while
Then I must fly—
No ties, no tears, no hate.
Searching for a dream
Maybe you, maybe not.
Here today—Gone tomorrow.
Do not pity me
I do not want it.
Do not love me too much
I cannot return the love that you want.
Fear—of getting something I'm not prepared for.
I have loved once
It destroyed me
But made me whole.

Carol Bennett
ODE TO DR. COHEN
To Dr. Cohen—who unknowingly helped me overcome much more than a fractured hip. You're one of a kind!

I used to have a hip bone, all smooth and strong—intact;
But now my doctor tells me there'll be no more of that.
You see, he says it's fractured—all broken at the neck;
And when I found out about it, I sure was a wreck!

When I was at the hospital and settled inside my room,
He came to see me at my bed—his voice all full of gloom.
"Surgery must be scheduled; there are some things you need to know."
And so he began to tell me, and my fears began to grow.

He said "odds are against you; you have a slim chance to live."
Then he proceeded to deal out the pain he likes so much to give.
He told me I may have blood clots, lung problems and the like,
In fact, he told me I might not wake up to see the light.

His dissertation made me crazy, hysterical and quite dazed;
A common reaction I'm told, but he seemed to be amazed.
He told me I was abnormal, that I needed to see a shrink.
He thought I was crazy—is that what all doctors think?

So in marched the psychiatrist, in fact, I was glad to see him;
I could voice my frustration at Dr. Cohen and his sarcasm.
The psychiatrist listened intently, and my story I did tell;
Didn't Dr. Cohen understand that I was feeling quite like hell?
This wouldn't be a "normal" surgery, he told me I may die;
Did he expect me to just accept it and really not to cry?

I guess I passed inspection; surgery was scheduled soon,
And Dr. Cohen eventually came back into my room.
I thought perhaps I should suggest that Dr. Cohen see the shrink;
He seemed so mean and cruel to me, I didn't know what to think.

But surgery went as scheduled, and my fears came to an end.
I knew in spite of Cohen's harshness, I really was in good hands.
In fact, his antagonistic humor, though hard to take at times,
Was what I really needed to keep myself in line.

And now that I'm almost healed and out of my wheelchair,
I've had time to think about Dr. Cohen and his unusual bedside care.
Though often gruff and cynical, obnoxious and quite rude;
I think it's just a big facade to hide someone nice and kind and good.
You see, he knows just when to frown, when to smile and when to tease,
When to joke and to be serious, and how to put your mind at ease.

I found out what major surgery is; how frightening it can be,
And I can now respect and admire what my surgeon did for me.
He may not even know it, but it's because of him,
That I was able to face this situation and smile at the end.

Deborah A Taylor
LOST ANGEL
Propped high upon her immortal throne
The only world she's come to know
Where steel swords are cast against stormy skies
Providing the shelter from her dark demise
'Cause she's doing that slow dance with the devil again
And he won't stop knockin' til she lets him in
Sending her back out in the rain,

Such a lonely place to be
She's just another lost angel
A vagabond of life's empty highways
That overflow with signs that point one way
Where the sun don't shine and her colors collide
And dreams are lost and souls are forgotten—
I'll always remember her that way

Joe P Ryan
DESPITE MYSELF
For your eyes only,
My heart you plainly see,
You know the inside of me,
I cannot hide my feelings,
For you know my soul,
Yet despite myself,
You still love me so,
Your eyes reveal me,
You see me as I am,
It is your love,
That will make me into a man,
For your eyes only,
You're an angel from above,
For despite myself,
You look at me in love.

Joseph Bastian
NOVEMBER IN BERLIN
The river runs beneath the wall
Invisible, weakening a deceptive foundation.
This barrier built on fear, distrust
Sinks unseen into the flowing warmth
Of the vein of human life.
Above, between its borders
Bodies press against, atop the concrete
Chipping with chisels, axes
Softening its sides with
Extended warm blooded hands
Sculpting its stony edifice
Like clay, back into the ground
From whence it came,
Back to the river
That always ran through, between
Penetrating and unparallel.
I saw you for the first time today,
First time in twenty-eight years
On top of the world
Under the light of glowing fireworks.
The crowd roared at the new found color
Of your once gray face
Now grinning, glistening with tears of joy.
I know where you have been
It was partly my fault we haven't talked
I'm sorry, I've missed you.

D Heather Sutton
WHEN HE LEFT ME . . .
For Dane, the love of my life.

When he left me, I almost died from grief . . . literally
He experienced no betrayal from me but I was only a surrogate for an absent lover.
I found out in my depression that good memories are no good, they only enhance anguish.
He saddened me so many times and all I wanted to do was to lay my heart on his.
He didn't have the courage to make a clean-cut choice and one day he had to leave and he didn't have to make a choice.
If you delude yourself, reality might kill you.

The hurt is gone . . . now I sit in contented silence and wonder . . . "what if."

Gary Miller
ODE TO HUMANITY

Cry for my father
You may not have known him
But you have heard of his tragic demise

He was one of the 259 who perished in the terrorist bombing of Pan Am flight 103. He was savagely ripped from his loving family in the prime of his life—never to feel love again.

Cry for my father
You may not have known him
But he knew you

He cared and slaved for every worthy cause which came his way, not discriminating based on race, sex or religion. For after all, he cherished mankind.

Cry for my father
You may not have known him
But thousands were touched by him

Even in death he was able to bring out the good in others and suppress the animal within us all. The support extended to his loved ones and the grief shared by so many defy words.

Cry for my father
You may not have known him
And now you never will

If his death is to be justified, we must wipe out the animals among us, and more importantly, the animal within us all. As rational human beings we must finally understand that the key to happiness is family, health and peace, transcending national and political barriers; not war, murder and coveting what is not ours.

Cry for my father
For he cried for you

Shirley-Anne Marie Gauthier

Shirley-Anne Marie Gauthier
THE EMPTY CHAIR

I dedicate this poem to my good friend, Mr. Jerry Kramer, who I learned a great deal from, during my visit to Forks of Salmon in Northern California.

Deep in thought he sat in his chair now alone
Save for the small curly dog asleep, close by.
His hair once golden as the dawn's sun tone,
Now faded, still shone like silver.

He asked little but a kinder hand be dealt.
To savor the warmth, of a fireside.
The old excitement, he now still felt,
At the sight of a rainbow, breaking the tide.

Years had taught him,
There is little in the take.
Lord help us see; should our sight grow dim
That our joy, be greater when we give.

He'd gladly give, his gold stake
Knowing once more, that empty chair
Being filled again, would relieve the painful ache.
The loss of the love of his life.

Now only silence filled the room.
Where once laughter and song rang out.
Now such a dark thread, being woven on the loom
Oh Lord! Remove this awful doubt.

His heart bearing a deep wound, His eyes filled with tears,
Knowing down this lonely path, he must tread,
Till the stars fade, with the growing years
And our God calls him home,

To be with him, in those heavenly hills
Where we need never have, another worry.
O that a man's days be so full, his Soul to still
That he may need not gaze, at an empty chair.

Kim Thompson
WHATEVER FOREVER

Dedicated to Brian West, who I hope will continue to give me the best of his "whatevers" forever.

You walked over and stood beside me
Knocking me totally off my guard.

Was it by chance that I found you there
When I thought I had searched everywhere?

I look back and wonder why I made love so hard.
Now that my soul search has ended,

I still have but one fear in my life
That one day I'll awake and find . . .

You gone like a thief in the night . . .
Stealing my broken heart and giving it to your wife.

Tell me this is not what you've intended.
Do you really love me? If so, I wish I could see . . .

Far ahead to the future to where we will be.

I wonder if one day you'll ever be free . . .
And if so, would you still want to be with me?

You say I get the best of what you've got.
When it's over, I ask only that you forget me not.

So turn your key inside and unlock my door.
As for love, I'm sure in here you'll find more . . .

Of your "whatever forever" . . .
For your desires are my pleasure.

Cheryl Kupi
PICTURE FRAME

Rolling hills of heather green
With gently swaying pines
Breezes sweet from buttercups
Red cliffs all in a line
Hawks that glide on unseen winds
And crickets sing in tune
A warming sun ascends blue sky
Montana in mid-June
Fuzzy antlered deer still graze
The sprouts of reborn seeds
Melted snows from far away
Form pools to meet their needs
A chipmunk burrows his new home
And ants rebuild their dune
A picture framed by God Himself
Montana in mid-June

Hilda Bel
MAKE ME SEE

I dedicate this poem to my love and to the special soul, who leads my heart to my writings . . .

Pour your golden heart in mine,
As the life goes by.
Stir it with our magical spoon of love,
As our passion grows as its delicacy.
Many times i felt your electrical touch,
Even when you were far.
I saw the evil anger in your eyes,
But still we continued loving life.
I see our road filled with golden trees,
The sky is bright blue filled with purity.
I know the sun will shine at all times,
As our fruits nourish the magical land.
We don't need to talk of how we feel,
The words come out as golden drops in our tears.
We share an unreachable love,
Even though others may not see.
Your hands are hard, filled with anger of darkness,
Your face has its own delicacy.
I fear to talk, yet i feel at ease,
When you give your smooth smiles at me.
You keep my heart in a golden cage.
You fear to open it with your love and care,
Yet you know that it will still be there.
We will live life until our sunny day.

Just make me see a light until that day . . . .

Tracy Muskevitsch
A LITTLE TOO LATE

A little too late
To say I'm sorry
A little too late
To try
A little too late
For I love you
A little too late
To cry
Although my tears
I can't hold back
I cry aloud
In pain
My heart is broken
The tears pour out
I'm drowning
In the rain.

E L Davenport
MANKIND

Man is great; and man is small.
Man is everything, or nothing at all.
His mind is strong, but his flesh is weak,
His animal instincts tell him what to seek.
He's mainly flesh, but part divine;
He's sometimes bestial, and then sublime.

He sets his values on material things,
And regrets the ruin that this often brings.
He's too complex for a measuring rod
For he's still part animal with a spark of God.
He struggles upward, but he'll soon tire
For he reaches for the stars with his feet in the mire.

He's learned his science and forgotten his soul,
And he hopes someday to reach that goal
Toward which he aims, be it only dreams of wealth.
He does think of others, but usually himself!
Only a few gain that favored role
To conquer the body that only houses the soul.

Anne Hall
THE SWING

Laughing child
On tree top swings
Touch your toes
To heaven's things

Soaring heart
To unknown trails
Finding light
Within the sails

Frank Burns
TIME

The foe of man and empires great
It loves to ruin and desecrate.
Towns and cities it devours
As well as trees, birds and flowers.
Slayer of kings and paupers too,
Taking lives of newborn ewes.
It turns great mountains into hills
It dries up rivers when it wills.

It wipes out species with one blow
Its wrath and fury never slow.
An unseen killer in the night,
You cannot run or hide in fright.

Mary L Terrill
STORM

Sitting here watching the clouds roll in
And thinking of you every now and then
The clouds are thick dark and black
Just waiting for the storm to attack

The Wind is blowing cold and wet
Something I'm not really ready for yet
While sitting here in the very cold wind
There's thoughts of you my very best friend

The storm is almost here I see
Because all the leaves are blowing free
It's getting darker and darker by the minute
Here comes the storm, and yes I'm in it.

The rain is coming down fast and hard
Now I have to run back to the yard
Back to the yard, I go to stay
Until this storm is over, anyway . . .

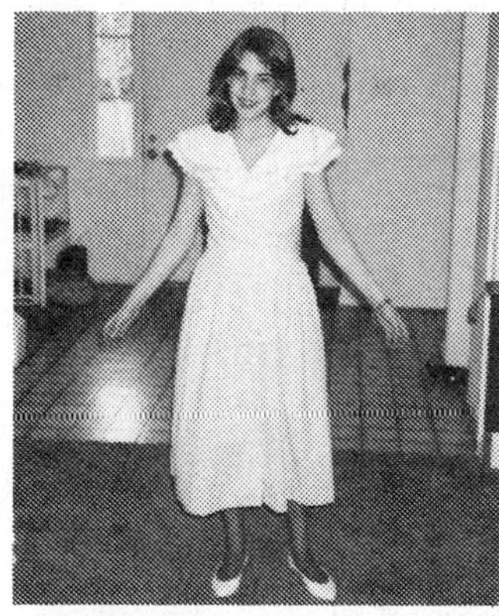

Melissa Burt

Melissa Burt
LOVE

Dedicated To My Inspirations To Whom My Love Goes . . . I Love You Mom, Dad, and Grandma Burt.

Love is like a gust of wind that is not sure of where it is headed.

Love is like the sun,
one minute it is there the next is not.

Love is like a rolling wave, it could make you float on air one moment then drown you in its sorrow the next.

Love is there for all of us, just sometimes not at the right moment.

Love is something we all need, just sometimes we don't all get it.

But love of all kinds, is something we all cherish and could not live without.

Though some say they could live without it, it is just not possible.

Charles Poling
NATURE'S SYMPHONY

Of all the sounds that mortals hear,
That let the soul go free,
There's none so soft, or sweet and clear
As Nature's Symphony.

It starts right in at break of day
With sonnets from the deep.
The bird lifts up his voice so gay
While man is yet asleep.

The sun and wind are in there too
With rhythms, soft and low.
They touch the earth with strength anew
And set it all aglow.

But Nature's song will have no bliss
If Man turns not his ear;
And all the beauty, he will miss
Because he will not hear.

The twilight brings the end of day;
The song drifts out to sea.
The sun puts forth its faintest ray
To end the Symphony!

Betty Deborah Mercer
AWAITING THE ARRIVAL OF SPRING! (3/23/89)

Spring will be complete
When Snow beats a retreat.

Winter is overdue to go,
Yet, chill winds still blow;

Spring is here by date,
Easter is a short wait.

It's time for snow to melt
And d i s a p p e a r !

Crocuses and lily of the valley
Will soon appear!

Forsythia will bloom
Outside my window,

Bringing Spring into my room
With its golden glow!

Little tiny leaf-buds will open
On the twigs of trees . . .

There will be a concert
Of Robins, Blue jays, and Chickadees!

And grass will grow in my lawn . . .
With dandelions and other weeds
I will have to mow!

Roger Gibby
THE EXECUTION OF A DREAMER

May your dreams be realized. Seize the day.

At night, your watch rests upon the stand in its usual place.
Waiting as it always has, each night, for as long as it can remember.
Your slippers snuggle in their well worn spot.
Ready at a moment's notice.
Bound into your being is tradition and honor
Which forges a path that you are doomed to follow

You say, you don't understand him.
You say, you have sacrificed all for him.
And you say that he wants to throw it all away
Just to follow his strange little dream.
Within that dream, he dances to a different tune.
A sound so foreign to your ears
And you cannot comprehend why.

Only those who have dreamed the dream,
Have danced the dance,
Can understand the dreamer.
You awake him from his serene reverie
And cast him into the whirlwind of a dreaded nightmare.
He falls lifeless without a life to live
Your words mean nothing now.
Now nothing has no meaning.

You awake in the night to a sound of foreboding.
You race to dispel it from your mind.
You see the smoke rising from the ground.
Your nightmare screams into reality.
You rush to take him up in your arms,
But you know that it is far too late.

Too late for gentle words.
Too late to change your ways.
Oh, if only you had listened to his soul.
If only you had talked instead of told.
He might now be returning your warm embraces.

Roger Gibby
PHANTOMS OF THE PAST

To the one who came with joy and sorrow.

Phantoms of the past
Transform to fears of the future;
A fear of giving,
A fear of loving and living.

As I sit in my own corner of the world
Within my mind shadows dance to well played tunes.
They surge with time and pierce my soul to the core.
My anguish rises up and echoes in the emptiness of my heart.
But still, I carry on.

Is there any meaning to my existence?
Any purpose to what I say or do
As if sentenced to an eternal purgatory,
I go on living a dead man's life.

And if by some chance
My sentence is reprieved,
Then my angel of light will come to me
To chase away these specters of the night
And allow me to live and love again.

Roger Gibby
THE PLEA OF COME FOLLOW ME

To those who follow and may they reach the mountaintop.

I once sinned a great sin of fear
And my life it did steer
Down dark paths of lost hope.
I earnestly tried to cope.
I find myself in the pit of despair
Never, ever wanting to care.

As I surrender my soul to be swallowed by the night,
There in the distance shines the brightest light.
And I hear the voice of a new-born child.
Softly it speaks, gentle and mild.
His message pierces my soul to the core,
Hoping to chase sorrow from me forever more.
'Lift up your heart and rejoice,'
So says that still small voice.
'Gird up your loins and follow me
And with me thee, I will always be.'
Something now has changed.
All has been rearranged.

I see him standing at the waters of a fountain,
Alongside a path that leads up a mountain.
With an outstretched hand to me.
He beckons, 'Come and see.'
With faith and hope, I begin to climb.
With strength, I move, but only for a time.
The fears of doubt begin to flood in,
As I turn about in a sudden.
And nowhere do I see
This man, who with me promised to be.
Swept up on tides of confusion,
I am praying for a resolution.

And with a break in the storm
I hear his voice so clear and warm.
'Gird up thy loins, fresh courage take.
'Here, I will always be. You, I'll never forsake.'
With new sight, I can now see
That his hand was always stretched out to me.

How long will he patiently stand,
Waiting for me to take his hand?
How many times will I fall
And not heed his call?
How many times will he come to me
And pull me from deep misery?

With humble eyes, I look up
And drink from his life giving cup.
Oh, when will the time come, when to me he'll tell,
Come and rest, my son, thou hast done well.
And then softly come the plea
Of come follow me.

Roger Gibby
THE OVERLOOKED BOOK

A grey book stands nestled on the shelf.
First goes the one on the left
And then the one on the right.
Alone, he now waits patiently,
Wishing he would be next.
But alas he knows he will not be.

As he sits by himself,
He dreams of a time.
A time, when someone would
Come to take him down,
Open his faded cover
And blow the dust from his crown.

He yearns for a time.
A time, when someone would
Leaf through his golden pages
And find the wealth that lies therein.
To give of himself is all he hopes for
The only thing he looks for.

As the light grows dim,
He still waits upon the shelf.
And still within him lies
The story that can change lives,
If someone would just come and see.

Laura Wilkinson
GROWING OLD

Dedicated to my superior, whom I most admire and respect.

To grow old isn't easy, I've often been told,
One feels so crotchety, At us he will scold.

But if we have empathy, And try to understand,
We can show that we care, By just holding a hand.

With hands and knees, All crippled and sore,
With eyesight so dim, They can't see anymore.

Their ears are stopped up, Their backs badly bent;
It's easy to see, Their good days are all spent.

"We're useless!" they say, "We're just in the way."
"Do you think maybe someone will come visit today?"

But underneath all the pain, And the heartaches and more,
Is a great personality, That most certainly must soar.

Lessons can be learned, If we open our ears;
These people have wisdom, For all of their years!

anne r teist
TEARDROPS
Crystal facets of beauty
Reflecting the moon's opulence on
a late summer's night
Immortalizing the dreams of the
young at heart.
Raindrops of emotion,
Shimmering betrayal of a love
not yet forgotten.

Salty with the sting of rejection
They cleanse the soul and revive
the spirit.
Life goes on . . . love endures,
The reality of a passion denied
is forever engraved
in your memory.

Marlene Willman Gehris
MY KIDS

This poem is dedicated to my kids, Jimmie, Laurie, Scottie, and Kimberly. Love, Mom.

I have two daughters and I have two sons,
And to me they each are that extra special one.
They have brought me joy and so much fun,
That I wish that everybody could have at least one.
I love each one of them with all of my heart,
And hope that they remember me, (their mom), after I depart.
They have and always will be my pride and delight,
Because to me, my kids are just out of sight!
I pray to give Thanks to God every day,
For sending these four precious gifts my way.

Marlene Willman Gehris
MY GRANDSONS

This poem is dedicated to my grandsons, Tristan, Brandon, and Jarrod. Love, Granny.

My grandsons are very special you see,
Especially when they total up to three.
To me each one of them is very precious and unique,
Because these little people have made my life so complete.
Now, sometimes they make you happy,
And sometimes they make you fret,
But their innocence always comes through,
And on that I would make a bet!
They also somehow manage to always get their own way,
As they always seem to know just exactly what to say.
So when, how can I ever stay angry or blue?
When they come up and say,
"Granny, I Love You!"

Karen Klipstine
UNTITLED
Like the waves hit the shore,
As the tears you once bore.
Because of the commotion in the water unseen,
As your emotions were overbubbling.
The water rushes in and back out,
Hiding your feelings, so long nobody knows what you're all about.
As the moon captures the serenity of the sea,
Of all the hurt you set yourself free.

Delva L Wolfe
LOVE IS A FEELING
Love is a feeling that can't be explained
There are moments of sunshine, moments of rain,
Moments of passion, moments of pain,
Moments of wonder, and moments inane.

Love is a feeling that touches the senses
It covers the eyes with rose colored lenses,
It tickles the nose with fragrant aromas,
It plies the tongue with poetic phrases.

Love is a feeling that can't be missed
It puts the rapture in a kiss,
It fills the heart with joyful bliss,
It holds the magic of an eclipse.

Love is a feeling of sheer delight
It puts the sparkle in a light,
It puts the splendor in the night,
It fills the air with butterflies.

Love is a feeling beyond any measure,
Love is the feeling of a new found treasure,
Love is a feeling of explicit pleasure,
Love is the feeling that holds us together.

Carrie R Alexander
THE LETTER
As I read the note,
my eyes grew wide,
and with a surge of shock,
I tossed it aside.
You can't be gone,
I just can't believe,
you will never talk again,
there's so much you'll never achieve.
I'll never see you smile again,
I'll never hear you laugh.
The only thing that's left of you
are the old wrinkled photographs.
I walked outside, and the world
seemed so unreal,
and people are all walking by,
and I can't say how I feel.
People ask me what is wrong,
and all I can do is cry,
you're dead and I'm alive,
and I just can't understand why.

Shannon Cook
SPIRIT OF THE NIGHT
My Spirit belongs to the night
It is then that it is wild and free
There are no worries
As it spreads its wings and soars
Off, into the star lit night
Only to return
When morning has finally come

Barbara Awuakye
EVANESCENCE
Life has no explanation and it is conceived
With love and affection.
Suffering produces its survival and enables
It to grow and develop.
Humans are so terror-stricken with the
Conception of death, that their existence is
Succinct and inert.
They spend a portion of their time trying
To alter destiny and fate with new inventions
Sinners sell their souls for immortality
But their feat is all in vain.
Why should they ponder over extinction
When they live lifeless and dormant?
They will one day realize the inevitable
And assent to the reality that;
"Life is real! Life is earnest!
And the grave is not its goal."

Agnes E Kerr (age 76)
HOME
There it is, the Church—
Still standing straight and tall,
Its spire reaching ever skyward—
(But, somehow, looking small.)

Its doors as always open wide
As with welcoming arms it draws us forward.
We hear the music, and with a swell of feeling
We find ourselves moving inside.
We stand a minute looking around, expectantly.

Yes, it's all there—the velvet covered pews, the flowers,
The beautiful stained-glass windows,
The cross, all wrapped in that reverential hush.

Then we move ahead on tiptoe but, suddenly with a rush,
For we see, quietly waiting, our usual place.

As we sit we look at each familiar face,
The organist, the choir, the director at the podium,
The minister, with his up-raised hands
To ask for grace upon his flock.
We relax with a sigh and a prayer
No longer needing to roam, we have come home.

Susan Merrill
SEAN
I feel my heart ache so
just to be near,
when I think of you
as I sit at work
my precious baby Sean
Minutes go by
like hours at a time,
when I think of you
as I sit at work
my precious baby Sean
My eyes tear as I watch
the clock stand still,
when I think of you
as I sit at work
my precious baby Sean.

William R Pittl Sr
BE GOOD TO THE WATER

To the World!

To gaze upon the waters, oh! how they glisten.
To hear a waterfall, oh! how I listen.
I love the water that, God has given us plenty.
To drink, to grow enough, to eat for so many.

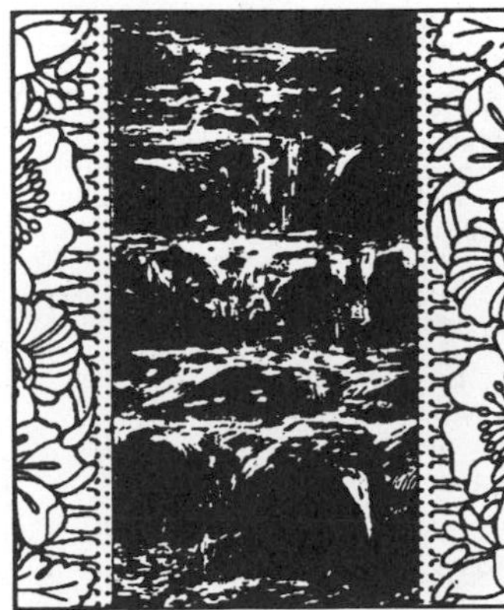

To feel the joy, that a warm shower brings,
this is another of life's simple things.
Be good to the water; because it has been good to you.
This is one of God's gifts; from him to you.

Naia McMindes
TRUTH'S EYES

Can it be, oh can it be
in the meeting of our eyes
that you know so much of me?
Can it be, oh can it be
in the meeting of our eyes
that you think so little of me.
Can it be, oh can it be
in the meeting of our eyes
that our hearts tell such lies.
Do you know how much you tell
in the meeting of our eyes?

Denise Kebernik
WAITING FOR YOU

To my loving family and my special boyfriend, Patrick. I love you all!

When you don't understand your own foolish moves
When you have no one else you want to talk to
And when you're empty and aching, and your tears flow anew
Then come to me, I'll be waiting for you.

When you can no longer carry that burdensome load
When people are so cruel and so hard and cold
And everyone keeps talking, but no one is bold
Then come to me, I'll lead you down the long road.

When the whole world kicks sand in your face
When you feel as if you're falling behind in the race
And you can't keep up with the persistent pace
Then come to me, I'll back up your case.

When your body is weak and there's nothing you can do
When you're misunderstood or you don't have a clue
And you try to break free, but you're stuck like glue
Then come to me, I'll be waiting for you . . . .

Rose Marie Domingo
TEARS

For sadness—
Hopes, and fears.
For gladness;
Passing years.
Goodness, badness,
All in one.
Hatred, anger,
Love and fun.
A tear will come,
A tear will go.
With every passing
Friend or foe.
A little feeling
From the heart.
At the end of life,
Or at the start.
Crystal clear
And fresh and blue.
A way to say that
"I love you."
You'll be able to tell
If anger or joyfulness is near.
By one single, small, and shining tear.

Gretchen Slinker Morgan
KINGDOM OF THE SAPPHIRE SKY

On dark and lonely winter's night
vague recollections come to mind.
I journey to a distant world—
a cherished place I left behind.

From jagged throne engraved by time
I gaze upon my vast domain—
a silent world of sun and rock
devoid of suffering and pain.

A living creature not in view
save raptor circling ever nigh
protecting nest and family,
observing me from sapphire sky.

My only subject unafraid,
undaunted by my presence here
upon my loftly granite throne
he speaks to me, his message clear.

Although I masquerade as lord
departing as the light grows dim,
the kingdom of the sapphire sky
forever will belong to him.

Katherine A Grace SNJ
SHADOWS UNSEEN

The quiet formations of His clouds,
Reflecting tears of the day,
Whisper the beauty aloud,
Then catch the last ray.

The mountain slope,
Where the tears entwine,
The Lord gives hope,
Through this beautiful sign.

When darkness is cast,
And shadows unseen,
The star sinks fast,
Into waters, serene.

A glimpse of night,
The candles burn,
'Til morning light,
And His Son's return.

Raymond Degeteau

Raymond Degeteau
FIRE OF THREE WORDS

My soul is burning,
My spirit is boiling;
My mind is trespassing the times barrier
And . . . it burns.
There's fire everywhere!
There's fire every second in my quiet living days.
I'm bearing an explosion!
Fire! S.O.S.! Wonderful explosion!
Help! No water enough
To turn my fire off.
Breathing! I can't breathe.
I need oxygen!
My heart is moving too fast!
It presses my chest.
I need to breathe deeply,
Calmly,
Easily.
The doctor. Where is the doctor?
He's in the hospital.
Great! I don't need him.
Three tiny words cause fire to burn in me.
Very simple! That is!
I ought to say them so tenderly,
So sweetly,
So you can hear them;
And they are: I LOVE YOU.

Tobina M Matson
AS THE SUN RISES

As the sun rises and the sun falls
My thoughts turn to someone who is always there
Who always cares.
No matter the miles
The thoughts always bring smiles
Our spirits will always stay close together
Our hearts joined in a father/daughter relationship
Shared by few

I love you.

Megan Crabs
CUPID

Cupid, oh Cupid, where are you now?
I want to love someone, but don't know just how.
And if you were here,
You could shoot me with your magic arrow,
That is carried along by a pink and red sparrow.
I could then lend my heart to the person I love,
And we'd come together like a little white dove.
But since you aren't here right now,
I'll just have to tell you,
I hope someone can say to me,
I love you too.

Margaret Nienstedt
EULOGY

Her friendship warms, surrounding me
With ardent angel piety.
How many others does she touch?
What influence is wrought by such?

Her attitude abounds beyond
Approval; heartens. I respond.
How many spirits can she lift?
Directions capable to shift?

Her woman aptitude is based
On love. It's fervent, passion laced.
How much exertion gladly spent?
How many times acknowledgment?

Her teaching talent brought to meet
Advances learning, quells defeat.
How many futures does she hold?
Incentives, mastery unfold?

Her unconditioned mother care
Believes and listens. Always there.
How many risks do parents dare?
How much do mothers have to share?

K Henderson
FOR THINKING HEARTS

Boundless

Horizons that touch our earthly years,
Spring deep meaning within the powers of the mind;
Imagination struggles to strive, to seek, to find,
And with mental wealth, and physical health,
Anything is possible for the progress of mankind.

Infinite,

As we wish our souls to be;
When free to soar like our feathered king,
We're raised above hate and human suffering;
And only then will we find within,
The harmony that peace and happiness bring

Eternal

Love radiates in the warmth of Truth,
Wisdom, in the essence of simplicity;
When Heaven's glories yield to this three-fold unity,
Happy are we alone, who can call these three our own,
For Beauty then becomes our ultimate reality.

Connie Wallace
NIGHT PUPPET

Hello puppet—
I'm so glad that I control
The strings to you
Do your dance—
Strut your stuff
Roll your empty head
Tonite I shall set you down
In the dust
And the darkness
Where you belong.

Krista Headley
CHRISTMAS WISHES

The Christmas season is very near.
Two months, one month,
Now it's here.

There is much planning, preparing, good cheer,
Laughter, maybe some crying,
With those you hold dear.

The true meaning of Christmas to me,
Is not the presents, the turkey, or trimmings,
But as much love for everyone as possibly can be.

We should all be thankful for all that we own,
Because many are less fortunate than we,
And have no place to call home.

My wish for everyone this holiday season far and near,
Is to have all the happiness not just now,
But all through the year!

Glenn Maynard
DREAMWORLD

I had a dream one night
Of a perfect earth.
All members ate quite right;
It was total mirth.
Suicide did not occur;
Murder was unheard.
A convict did not stir;
"Jail" was just a word.
In one God we trust.
No such thing as race.
Enforcement not a must
In this peaceful place.
Environment unsoiled.
Poverty was void.
Everyone was spoiled;
Not a soul annoyed.
One thing with it was trouble
The good began to taper.
My waking burst my bubble;
More so the morning paper.

Tara Harbaruk
TIME ORPHANS

Thank you, Dena, for giving me the inspiration I needed to write this poem.

Cold, alone in a dangerous world
Time orphans!
They drag themselves across the desert land
With the chill of the wind caressing their faces with sand.

Look at them!
They're the time orphans
No time to laugh; no time to cry
Trying to survive, they spend their lives.

They are warriors
'Cause they live in a cold, cold world.
They only have each other
Each other is all they have
Don't be surprised if a girl isn't wearing any pearls

Instead, she'll be holding a razor-sharp sword.
Her life depends on her strength of mind
If she is cruel
Just remember that this girl can't afford to be too kind.

For her, survival is life
Family doesn't exist.
This girl, she's a time orphan: lost and forgotten
Just one piece of time
This girl, she is one, one brave soul.
Time orphans!

Beverly Smith
THE SWAN
Although he has beauty
not to compare.

He bows his head
in reverent prayer.

Conceit to him
does not belong.

His humility cannot
be wrong.

And if my life should
change by wand.

I'd wish to be
the Humble Swan.

N A Karpisek
A LADY IN WAITING
I have been in love with you for quite some time,
Still you seem blindly unaware.
So many days I've looked for you,
So many days you've failed to appear.
If only you knew the many times I've reached for you,
But retreated, not knowing if you wanted to be found.
Yet I am peacefully aware,
if we are meant to be, so we shall.
At times I yearn for you so deeply,
the void of emptiness overwhelms me.
Perhaps not yet enough time has come to pass,
Although it seems the beginning of our time together is long overdue.
Maybe some day when I have mastered the virtue of patience,
I'll turn to find you by my side.

Carol Kaufman
THE PAINTING

Dedicated to Jerry W. Sanford, artist and friend.

The sun bursts
From behind the hill.
The river water's
Cold and still.

The fir trees
Stand beside the shore.
The forest background
Has many more.

A waterfall
Can scarce be seen.
The shallow water's
Painted green.

Some little mounds
Are velvet brown.
The sunburst does
Reflect a crown.

A crown upon
A dusky hill
By river water
Cold and still.

Anna Toma Anderson
DRUG ADDICTION

Dedicated to all my nephews and nieces and the young generation. May they be inspired by God's grace to lead fruitful lives.

Take the "d" out of Dope
And replace it with "h,"
Killing the drug-force with
Spirits of hope, kindling a positive note
Of revival . . . A power so great . . .
Transforming the Addictor to a born-again
Christian, through the love and mercy of
Our Savior . . . For now he "copes in a free-drug"
Existence, fulfilling his true purpose of life;
To serve God with golden deeds of action
For mankind . . . rewarding the "user" with a
Purification of body, mind, and soul—
And a heart glowing with joy, peace,
And contentment.

Richard Lee Hamm
WAVES

I dedicate this poem to my new born son Richard Lee Isaac Hamm, my wife Brenda F Hamm & my two girls Tramaine, Tangelia—To all of you Thanks! Richard Hamm.

Waves are soothing and relaxing to the soul
Waves are breath-taking and relentless and bold
Waves are inspiring and uplifting and cold
Waves are heavy and busy and old.—
Waves can shape and fashion and fold
Waves can dance and prance and control
Waves can sing and bring and hold
Waves can jump and dive and roll.—
Waves can fuss—at us and start—
A conversation at day or dark—
A melodrama that can touch the sky—
And send the news—to you and I.
Waves can carve and marveled and string
Waves can do almost anything.

Heidi Woodard
THE FANTASY

Ask me now about fantasy, the thrill of everlasting rain, that in turn fell upon my face, rinsing the sweat from my forehead. In the fields where I lie; collapsed and running out of air, quickly now, ask me now, about Fantasy Child. My time is near; slavery will be no more. Good-bye my friend, I will be happier, and then you may tell about my fantasy!

Marion MacPherson Lisle
POLLUTION
Beneath the psychedelic sky
The geometric cities lie
while I as usual wonder why—
why do we always in our haste
despoil the earth with toxic waste
to hurry on to nowhere.
There is no ocean deep enough
to hide away polluted stuff
and we don't seem to care enough.
Some day a silent earth may lie
because we let the flowers die.

Julianna J Kendall
THE VICIOUS CIRCLE

My poem is for the children whose bodies and spirits have been broken by abuse and the child within me who cannot forget the pain of my past.

The pain of my past is upon me and I am weary,
I feel the loneliness, the shame, the fury,
I long for the sleep that has no end,
then morning comes and I am reminded again,
of the loneliness that I constantly face,
and the shame that time just won't erase,
then the fury builds inside me as water to a dam,
and I lose touch with reality, with who I really am,
I want nurturing, arms to hold me, a gentle kiss,
these things I've never had yet greatly miss,
I journey through the day in misery,
I draw so deep within,
and I know that this must be my greatest sin,
Then night falls and I am once again so weary,
From carrying the weight of the loneliness, shame and fury,
I long for the sleep that has no end,
Then morning comes and the vicious circle begins again.

Doris F White
DONNA

Dedicated to my grandchildren Sky and Marlene. To my great-grandchild, Scott.

There's songs for Donna,
There's verses for her too.
But, I sure miss my daughter,
A blonde and eyes of blue.
Her smile was contagious, she had friends galore.
Her voice was pleasant with no scorn.
She is missed, you know she died on Mother's Day.
It's not much of Mother's Day,
But I feel she walks by my way.
"Oh" Donna, I know you are in a happy place, for your laugh,
Rings in our ears.

Penny K Coy

Penny K Coy
MY FRIEND
We are all alone now with nowhere to go
all that we can hear is the wind as it blows.
Let's us go for a stroll you and me
or sit on this rock here by the sea.
Watching the waves toss themselves so high
it is so breathtaking that it makes me cry.
To feel the peace, the harmony here
the rumbling in the waves I can almost fear.
Let's go for a swim one said to the other
let's not ther's a chill in the weather.
With strong gales and a colorless sky
better to sit as the ships pass by.
It is great being together so young and so free
with the sand, and the rocks, and

the restless sea.
How very precious this time we spend
with my very best and dearest friend.
You are my friend I want you to know
for it is now that I realize my friend is my soul.

Billy Yunker
THE MARCH OF THE DEAD

As I write this story in my red colored world, there lies a small graveyard not far from my house. Which lies quiet in the pale moonlight.

There is no sign of neglect of any kind, not a weed or blade of grass grows in the small graveyard not far from my house, for it is well kept, by who? Some say their own.

But tonight, tonight the dead are restless. And so begins their march. Rising out from their tombs to greet each other with decayed hands.

Then they realize their purpose, their reason for leaving their earthen homes. They come to embrace a new member of this intimate group of death. As they march they sigh, as they march they moan,
they are coming for me . . . .

Shirley Wright
OUR WORLD AROUND US

They might be giants but
for we are small
For we are a mere race
but lost God's grace.
For we want Peace and
not war, they say war
is a must and it's
justified to teach us.
This Earth is the last
place, it's green and blue;
but it's shrouded in white
and we mustn't fight.
Our race isn't all
on this world
For there are others who
want to be our brothers.
For mankind is this
threat
They say it's nothing at
all and the Earth is only a bet.

Carol Orbe
THE BATTER

Dedicated to my son, Billy O'Keefe.

The bases are loaded
it's his turn to bat
he looks at the stands
to see where she's at
his Dad doesn't come
doesn't seem to care
but his grin gets wider
because his mom's always there
he watches the pitcher
with eyes on the ball
he swings and he misses
his smile starts to fall
he looks at his mom and
she just nods her head
he tries to remember just
what it was that she said
Do your very best son
I'll always be here
he swings and he hits
he can see the crowd cheer
he turns to his mom
his face all aglow
this is one proud moment
his dad will never know.

Clifford G Pitts
THE GARDEN OF FLORENCE

Dedicated to Florence Tait, a most graceful lady.

Florence, a lady of loveliness, ninety years old this day
Is on her way, to spend this summer, seven thousand miles away,
With dearest daughter, and three great-granddaughters, and hubbies too,
To hug, with kisses, and share loves, all different, but so true.

Florence; when last here; asked: "Where are the flowers in your garden?"
We had a few, wild and tame, on acres of meadow and fen.
But! Not a TRUE garden, with colours trained to be bright and gay,
With bowers, stems, shrubs, and lilies and lavenders all asway.
So! This time! When Florence alights on these great and sunny lands
Seven thousand blossoms await her, in mighty herbaceous bands
Herbs and flowers and roses, trees, vines, bushes, and much, much more
Mighty galaxies of colour, that go on and on galore.
This; is the Garden of Florence; for wife and mother and friend.
Birds, Bunnies, Deer and Lambs, all await Florence . . . to round that bend.

Clifford G Pitts
IDENTIFY

Dedicated to a United Canada, remaining good friends with the U.S.A.

Hey! From what nation does this
poem come to World of Poetry?

So! You're in Californ-i-a, and
that's in good ol' U.S., eh?

Stuart L Williams
RAPTURE THE SOUL

Thanks to those who believe in me.

RAPTURE the soul,
pain within the heart
the feelings deep within
hurt by the lashing
of others
with their tongue
their actions
unintentional, maliciously
for their own purpose
the heart hurts
feels
longs for the missing happiness
of their soul

Dwight Smith
TO DAVE IN BASKETBALL

So firmly muscled, fleet of foot,
He shoots each free-throw with a quip.
His life ahead, his future bright,
A trace of hair upon his lip.

Yet what is man? A fleeting breath,
The lord of all, a child of fate,
A pilgrim on the way to death.

Catherine Webb Black
LONELY THOUGHTS

To my late husband of 53 years—Jim.

He lit a fire in my heart—when first we met,
We danced—We laughed—even stole a kiss or two
But now he is gone and all that is left
A small bit of ashes in the corner of my heart.
The empty chair—The empty plate—
Are just reminders of the life we had;
Then why are tears flowing down my face?
It is the lonesomeness that eats my heart—
Why am I left?—only God knows what He has in store—
Maybe it is to comfort some poor soul along the way,
I face each day with fear and hope—
That only He will cure my broken heart.

J Maria Sorg Liptak
DESTINY

Our lives pass before us all too soon,
With memories stored in boxes that could fill a room.
We wonder, as we look back over the years,
Will we be remembered when the boxes disappear?
We're surrounded by objects built as square,
Their corners collect dust or protrude in the air.
Very few things built by man are lasting, I have found,
Yet the earth, moon and stars endure forever as round.
As destiny beckons to that box in the ground
With corners so dusty and covered with mound,
We want to believe that life abounds
In the afterworld our dreams have found.

C K Shroyer
OH! THIS MEDICARE

To my dedicated wife, Reta Grace, who encouraged me during my retiring years to continue in my hobby and lifelong desire to write poetry.

Yes, Medicare will pay you, they told me so with pride,
"Just file your claim and sign your name." They're really on our side.
"You'd better read this handbook first, it clarifies," they say,
Like where you're really covered, and how they plan to pay.

Now if you have a question, and you're really in a tizzy,
Just try to call them on the phone, you'll find it's usually busy.
Then ask about assignment, it's clear as mud to me,
Confusion is the game it seems, as anyone can see.

They tell of all the benefits, if it's part A or B,
Does it go to the doctor or come right straight to me . . .
And 'bout the time I think I know, these folks are paper tools,
We get a notice in the mail, they've up and changed the rules.

We'd better make a copy sure, and keep it in our file,
To get it signed, it's then we find, we've walked another mile.
I'm really glad I'm 65, and have this health care plan,
It's just that I'm a bit confused, not knowing where I stand.

This Medicare is really great, I hear it all the time,
The thing I ask myself today, "Is it just my feeble mind?"
I sign the claims, I mail the bills, I really try to care,
But usually end up standing there in my Jockey underwear.

Martha J Do
MY SPIRIT IS FREE

This poem is dedicated to my mother, whose need for freedom was never able to be met in this life.

Don't think me here inside this grave
For at last my spirit's free.
I finally have the chance to be
Just who I want to be
Happy I am beside my lord
For eternal peace I have
Don't cry for me
For I am free
And now I have eternal peace.

Yolanda McGraw
CHRISTMAS IS LIKE

Christmas is like all other holidays put together as one.
Christmas is like Valentine's Day, you're with the one you love.
Christmas is like St. Patrick's Day, you wear green along with red and white.
Christmas is like Easter,
you look for your presents instead of eggs.
Christmas is like Mother's and Father's Day,
you go visit and spend some time together.
Christmas is like Independence Day, you let off fireworks to celebrate.
Christmas is like Halloween,
you have lots of different kinds of candy.
Christmas is like Thanksgiving Day, you give thanks to everyone.
Christmas is mostly a holiday all of its own.
It's the day everyone is supposed to celebrate the birth of Christ.
It's a day you should help people less fortunate than you. A day you should spend some time with family and friends.
At the end of the day you should pray and give thanks for what you have received that year and guidance through the next year.

Kyriacos Georgiades

Kyriacos Georgiades
MY BLACK LITTLE FRIEND

To all colors—equally.

I got into the train the other day
There she was; a little black girl
She smiled at me. She did not know
the word DISCRIMINATION
She gave me her little hand and we
walked side by side
We walked and walked for hours—
We walked and walked for days

We passed the White House, we
passed the Capitol Hill, we passed the
Supreme Court, we ended up in
Georgia . . . and a little bit further
down in South Africa

WHITE SUPREMACY, on one side;
I HAVE A DREAM, on the other

The little girl looked at me with a big
question mark in her eyes
I did not say anything. I walked with
her side by side
This planet is revolving the wrong
direction
The road is so unclear
Thousands of black crosses are
hunting me
Colors dictate our destiny

DISCRIMINATION . . . My Little
Black Friend, how can I protect you

Kyriacos Georgiades
DREAM A DREAM

To my father, who inspires every step of my life.

O lost paradise;
Why am I here, out of the dreamed
Eden? I, the son of truth; I, who
devoted a whole life long serving
justice; I, who had only one family,
and that was the whole world. Why I,
the son of sunset and son of dawn,
have to pay Adam's fault? Why do I
have to wait Jesus, the son of living
light, to reopen paradise?

O true nature of man;
Why justice, freedom, and peace
were taken away from me? Why do I
have to abandon the effort for a new
cosmos? Why do I have to accept the
future, without reacting to it? Why do
I have to accept elements that are not
mine? Elements far away from my
paradise?

O unknown tomorrow;
I have the fear of a nuclear war
sticking in my mind. My children
won't be free to see the spring. The
earth will die. I want to rid myself
from this fear. I want to destroy all
the weapons and go out in the streets
and scream for the new beginning. I
want to see the man not the
nationality, the color, the race. I want
to call you brothers, sisters, and I
want you to call me brother. I want
you to be my companions. Now is the
time. We still have the chance to
strike away the fear of a nuclear war.
Let's go out and demonstrate our
antithesis. Let's go out and free our
children from that fear. Let's do it
now!!!!!!

Kyriacos Georgiades
MAY 15, 1990
One more day
And then
Darkness
Sun will not shine
Again

If it was death
That took you away
Maybe
I will understand

Spring is fading away
It's raining and it's cold
So ugly the earth is turning

The plane took off
And it took all my dreams
Standing there
Staring the sky
I tried to hold my tears
For one more time
In the name of freedom
I tried to be strong

Kyriacos Georgiades
JUST A FRAME

To Jackie, my love, for all the good times.

I am writing to you again
I will write to you forever
Maybe you will never receive this
letter
Maybe I will never send it. Who
knows?
But . . . this is the only way I can talk
with you
The only way I can be with you
Bring good memories in my mind—
our memories

I write to you my love
Love has no boundaries . . . no
boundaries
I love you today like I loved you
yesterday
I will love you tomorrow even more
Love has no boundaries—you are
miles away but I am always with you

Love has no boundaries—you will
always be the morning sun
In my life
You are the love
You are the day
The stars and every name

Kyriacos Georgiades
A PLANET NEXT DOOR

To my brothers Nicos and Marinos; my sisters Christina, Elena and Tasoula and their families.

I wanted to forget
To be born again in a planet where
pain does not exist
Where my heart won't feel anything
Where a farewell won't break me
into pieces

I wanted to become a piece of
furniture which does not complain
Which will be put quietly aside
the same way it came

I wanted to be born and don't
understand anything
I wanted to be aneducated
I wanted to be color-blind
I wanted to know no business and
commerce
I wanted to be born in a desert—few
trees and little water—clean air . . .

Where industries don't exist, where
superpowers camps and prisons don't
exist

H Wayne Dail
STONE COLD
Grasping.

Grasping at straws.
Fingertips touching,
Not able to hold on.

Falling.

Falling from high.
Want to land,
Don't know if I can.
The ground is coming up fast.

Stopped.

Stopped by the ground.
Came too fast to stand.
I lie motionless.
Paralyzed.

Stone cold.

Kathleen M McConnell
A WARRIOR'S LAMENT
I believe I know what you are
thinking now
My broadsword raised above your
lowered head,
As Satan rises from the bowels of the
inferno,
To claim the souls of the wicked
from the dead.

I will be the one to choose your fate.
'Tis I who hold your lifeblood in my
hands.
You're praying now for the God
above to save you.
A brave chief must not weep before
his clan.

As the stench of battle wounds engulf
me
The once green turf is stained blood
red.
The cry of pain reaches my ears
Reverberating through my aching
head.

I weary now of fighting, of havoc and
of death
I'm sickened by the waste of life I've
seen.
At home I long to be with my sweet
lassie,
Whose hearth is warm and eyes are
sparkling green.

I look down upon the helmet of my
captive,
My heart softened by the empathy I
feel.
I slowly put my blade into its sheath,
but alas the scars of war will never
heal.

Carol James
AND NOW THERE'S YOU

With love to J.P.W.—without whom there would be no poem.

Fifteen years without a man's caress
Because I wouldn't settle for less
Than what I wanted.
And now there's you.

Fifteen years without a man's
devotion
Because I wouldn't settle for less
Than what I deserve.
And now there's you.

Fifteen years without a man's tender
smile
Because I wouldn't settle for less
Than a real one.
And now there's you.

Fifteen years to wait for
What I wanted
What I deserve
What's real.
You.

Betty L Hunt

Betty L Hunt
MY DAY WILL BE BRIGHTER

To my dear husband, "Jimmie."

Lord, lend me this day
Lead me to some lonely soul,
That I might cheer or wipe a tear.
My day will be brighter
To be there for a friend or
Help someone who is in need
Lord, my day will be brighter,
Let me be your feet and your
hands
Your voice in a kind word
Lord, use me, today
This is my prayer.
Lord my day will be brighter.

Sarah J Elio
BEGINNINGS OF LOVE

For being my inspiration, I dedicate this poem to my husband; Christopher.

You took me like a whirlwind
And set my soul on fire
You made me feel such great desire
And then you took me higher.

You captivated me with your smile
While your eyes lit up the night
You make me feel so good inside
How could this not be right?

In my heart I keep you with me
No matter where I go
So keep me with you also
And together we will grow.

Sharon Hinson
A GIFT

To my daughter, Catherine Brooke.

The birth is such a joy,
the love is so strong.
As I hold that tiny hand I wonder:
Why God, why did you send
such a precious gift?
And the response I hear is:
How great a gift is up to you
dear, with each growing year
the gift could grow more
precious and dear.
I then looked at that tiny hand again
and I knew that God was there
holding mine.

Mansur Joardar

Mansur Joardar
WORLD TO ME

I can't uphold my weakness—Oh!
Rather, should try to be bold,
This World, I think, prone to mock
And, compels one to be sold!

I look forward with utmost zeal
Hope for the best of life,
Yet, days turning with hostile gesture
Things are no more now fine.

The struggle stage I am going
through
It's I do not take curse,
I can't stand mute when come across
Struggle turns to be farce!

Any wrong happened within the
Nature
Causing change in the Order?
It's the high time for right thinking
How odds we can cover.

The around World—it's a free gift
All having right every inch,
Universal sacrifice needs top priority
Then we would recognise each.

Jane Rutkay
WINTER'S FINALE

I thought that spring had finally come
The day was warm and there was
sun.
The calendar proclaimed it spring,
And morning doves began to sing!

A new day dawned, I was impressed
It wasn't spring but winter dressed.
The wind did blow and there was
snow,
The thermometer read one below!

Inch by inch the ground snow grew,
Until at last I finally knew
The old man was reluctant to,
Surrender to the new.

I felt a little sad to see
The glorious show he had for me.
His finale so to speak
So much of winter's show is bleak.

But this the soft white covering
To trees and bushes wetly clinging
Was his farewell, but greeting too,
Good-bye to winter, hello spring!

Jane Rutkay
A PHILOSOPHICAL OUTLOOK

I used to think that every beach
Had sand along its shore.
But as I grew and broadened out
I found that some had stones galore.
And so it is . . . .

The more you grow, involve yourself,
The stonier your path.
But I would rather gather stones
Than castles in the sand.

Of course I find some sandy shores,
This makes my life so sweet.
And then again, a pebbled beach
Which also makes my life complete.
And so it is . . . .

Pearl Williamson
YOU GIVE A SIGN

To the one who has given me the inspiration and encouragement, my husband, Dan E. Williamson, Sr.

You give a sign
you are one of a kind
Though strangers in life
you took me for your wife.
After all these years
there's not one tear
I can hear echoes of the past
but none seem to last.
As we near the end
you are my closest friend
Now that it's over
we have never been closer.
Sharing the happy and the sad
we have lived a life many wish
they had.
Now that we soar without any pain
you figure out if dreams and
fantasy are the same.

Pearl Williamson
A BETTER LIFE FOR MOM

In the beginning we come from our
mother
In the end we're laid down by our
brother.
As a child, I never knew the pain
Mom suffered without any gain.

Entering the lonely walk
Not a sign of stopping to talk,
She wearily strolled the empty path
Never stopping to look back.

On the darkest of nights
Will shine the brightest of lights,
And in the end she knows she'll find
A life of peace and a man so kind.

Pearl Williamson
TO A DEAR FRIEND—GRANDPA

Down beneath the ground
In a box cased in steel
Is where each of us are bound
'Cause this is God's will.

Under one cement stone
Lies a man, that once was strong
Now this man lies all alone
Waiting for his final song.

With each day that passes
He knows we'll soon be near
I know his wait grows restless
My memory of him is so clear.

This man I hope to see again
'Cause he's still my dearest friend.
At his side is where we'll be . . . after
all
This man is my Grandpa.

Good-Bye

Amy Smith
GOOD-BYE

Dedicated to Stacy Hayes, the man who captured my heart.

I am told I am no longer loved
I am told to let him go
I am told to let him "find himself"
I am told we are better off apart
Each time I stand up for my love
I am knocked down . . . by words

So I pack my memories of the times
we shared
Neatly away
Only to open them every now and
then
And reflect back to a happy
time . . . when I'm alone
Hoping that one day they will be
unpacked
By both of us

I find myself sitting alone now
Wondering if I can ever prove to you
That you are my Heaven and Earth
Knowing the answer, afraid to admit
it
Packing away your final picture
Giving to you the knowledge of my
love for you

I slowly close the box
And wipe the tears from my eyes
And say . . . I love you, good luck,
good-bye

Amy Smith
BLUE EYES

Dedicated to my special brother, Mitch.

He started a boy of 5
Full of life, full of love
Knocked down a boy of 8
The flame of life, the flame of love
grew dim
Now at 13 the boy lost
No life, no love
Only a new-found strength . . . Hate
He goes on through life
A chip on his shoulder, an emptiness
in his heart
No one allowed close enough to see
or feel the pain
The love aching to be released from a
wall 17 years built high
Searching and never finding love
only hurt . . . the wall grows
And now a man of 22, hiding behind
the laughter, hiding behind the wall
Fearing life, fearing love, but
searching for both
For how can you give life, give love
to someone if you have none?
A man afraid to give, afraid to lose,
for that has been his whole life
What happened to that boy of 5 who
knew nothing but life and love
Before being tarnished by hate and
pain?
Find that wonderful child of 5 that
hides inside that man of 22
Bring out the love, bring out the life
that I see in you

Dream on blue eyes . . . dream on

Rose Marie Zaitz
BURNING IS YOUR REWARD

To Lisa, who knows she didn't because she couldn't have . . . !

When eyes of grey are staring,
through the sun that was once
glaring.
When all of a sudden everything
looks red and black,
and you've seen enough, all you
can hack;
through the strings of light you can
see him
and you know you've lost the fight.
When all of your fortune disappears,
On his face you see a smile, on yours
. . . tears.
Now no thought of greed runs
through your head.
Only the thought that you'll soon be
dead.
You never had faith in the power.
As you breathe your last breaths in
this hour.
Don't ask him for another chance.
For he is the creator of the bloody
sabbath dance.
You manage now to gasp, "satan is a
liar!"
As he throws your loved ones in the
fire.
Where are the holy ones, the ones
who believed?
They're with the saints, amongst the
trees.
Your reward for sponsoring lucifer is
hearing the shrieks of death.
Among them are your children and
your friends.
For believing satan, this is the end.

Rose Marie Zaitz
PICTURES IN MY TEARS

The hurt is all gone
but the pain is still there.
I've got no time to waste,
No time to spare.
Dreams are like icicles crashing to
the ground.
If you don't catch them quick,
you're all shot down.
The anger has diminished;
but the tension is strong and not yet
finished.
Love is like a flower, in a short time
it has to die.
Like everything it has to end
sometime.
I'm practically drowned but still
sober.
I still have to swim, life is not over.
Sorrow is like a trip through hell.
How long it will last!
You can never tell.

The aching has stopped,
but the bruise still appears.
My story can be seen
through the pictures in my tears.

R "Pete" Thomas

HE HELD MY HAND

He was the dad I never had, but
He held my hand.
I guess I always loved him, and
He held my hand.
He had a very warm smile, and
He held my hand.
I felt so good and safe near him, and
He held my hand.
He always had time for me, and
He held my hand.
I could talk to him because he cared, and
He held my hand.
He had a soft and gentle voice, and
He held my hand.
I wanted him for my father when
He held my hand.
He had a family I wanted to be part of, and
He held my hand.
I saw him often while he was sick, always
He held my hand.
He always knew me and smiled that smile, and
He held my hand.
I could feel such warmth when
He held my hand.
He is here with me now, and he holds my hand.
I can feel his strength as He holds my hand.
And I was proud to have him
Hold my hand.
In time I pray we'll be
together again, and He'll hold my hand.

R "Pete" Thomas

TOGETHER

We had fun together.
We played together.
We went to school together.
We went hunting together.
Yes, he was my Brother.
We went camping together.
We went fishing together.
We worked together.
We would build things together.
Yes, he was my Brother.
We would make planes together.
We would grow things together.
We had good times together.
We had some bad times together.
Yes, he was my Brother.
I know you can't see us together.
But I know we are together.
I feel him with me, so we're together.
Our love will always keep us together.
Yes, he will always be my Brother.

R "Pete" Thomas

MY GRANDMOTHER

She was the lady that gave Grandpa much happiness.
That was my Grandmother.
The lady that made big mountains of troubles go away.
She could wipe away my tears with a very soft touch.
That was my Grandmother.
The lady in the apron who had so much love.
That was my Grandmother.
She had the sweetest kisses and so many of them.
The lady who always had a big friendly smile.
That was my Grandmother.
She always had time to sing me a song and hold me.
That was my Grandmother.
The lady that never complained about anything.
She could always find a kind word for anyone.
That was my Grandmother.
The lady I never did tell that I loved her.
That was my Grandmother.
She's gone now but I will never forget her.
The lady I will be with again some day.
That IS my Grandmother.

Greta Cleghorn Bryan

ODE TO BOBBY BROWN (MY SECRET KNIGHT)

To all those who have reached out to another in need—To all who have needed; for without a receiver—there can be no giver.

Oh shattered me, so many years, the pieces scattered far
Let no one close, hold strong your shield, that was my only hope.
Yet, you came to me and kissed my hand; then led me out to dance,
Gazed in my eyes and held me close, melted my defense.

The time raced by, no one alive; the two of us were all
The wounds and scars just slipped away; with you I was renewed.
Those magic hours spent in your arms will last me all my life,
10,000 dreams—or maybe more—sustain me while you're gone.

I can't regret—not even once—the time I spent with you
No words of love—an empty room—fogging up the mirror.
It poured from you right into me, a fountain's overflow
For my great thirst had drained me dry and now you made me whole.

The priceless gift—yet given free—the one that saved my life
To have you give me such a gem makes my heart swell with pride.
I search and search for one to give you in return
I could not think what it should be; though I pondered quite some time.
But, no treasure so great have I to give to you, so this is your reward my personal gift to you
A heart made new, a life made whole, shattered pieces mended well
Outstretched arms for life's embrace; a shield that's laid aside.
An arm outstretched (tho in a cast) to try to trust once more

And f-o-n-d, indeed! Sweet memories of a lifetime—spent with you one night.

Lisa C Sawicki

SORRY

I can read your mind
When I look in your eyes.
Whether you tell me the truth
Or tell me lies.
What happened before
Was a long time ago.
And whether you used me,
I do not know.
So listen to me,
I'll admit I was wrong.
But the feelings I had
Were very strong.
So please don't hate me,
Just be my friend.
I'm sick of fighting,
I want it to end.
I still care, I'll admit that's true,
But a friend is all I am to you.
Do you understand what I'm trying to say??
It took me a while to admit it this way.
Can you read my mind
When you look in my eyes??
All I'm trying to do
Is apologize . . . .

Helen R Tobler

DADDY'S BOY

To Lauren: For believing in me. To Fuzzy and Bunny: Because you're special.

You tried to smile
My sweet little man
As I placed the flower
In your hand

You put it upon
Your daddy's grave
You tried not to cry
You'd promised to be brave

As we listened to
"Amazing Grace"
I saw a tear
Trickle down your face

You wiped it quickly
So I wouldn't see
Daddy asked you to be strong
For you and for me

He's gone now my sweet
So let the teardrops fall
I promise I won't tell daddy
If he should happen to call

Helen R Tobler

MY BEST FRIEND

Dedicated to Magill, from the bottom of my heart I'm glad you're a part of my life.

Of all the friendships I've had
I treasure yours the most
My pen is poised on paper
This poem to you a toast

Your laughter is my sunshine
At times my saving grace
You're always there to guide me
And to keep me in my place
Steadfastly you've stood beside me
Never faltering through the years
You've listened to my dreams
As well as caught my fallen tears
We've shared so much together
From the intimate, to the insane
I want you to know I love you
A better friend I could never obtain

Happiness, success and love
These wishes to you I send
Forever you have a place in my heart
My very special friend

Virginia Dimino

. . . HERE THEY COME . . .

Here they come, one by one
Marching along in the morning sun
They spy a site with food delight
And as they gather in their plight
They make their plans within their clans
And so each company of hands
Attack the steaks, the pies and cakes
Now forty-six ants have bellyaches!

Catherine B Alston

Catherine B Alston

FOREVER SHINING

I am like a light,
Shining so brilliant and bright,
It's no wonder I can't let you
out of my sight.
It's such a delight to be
with you tonight
May all our dreams come true,
Let neither one of us
forever be blue,
How can I stop loving
you.

Nicole Stele

CRUEL WORDS

Cruel words like slaps across the face
your intentions sting in my mind
screams of ignorance pass over your lips
as your red face reflects the
hellishness you borne
the pain you inflict upon me
is no match for the pain you inflict in me
the flesh of my soul like the night sky turns black
as once again you have won

Jerry Karr

CURTAIN CALL

Ballerinas, dancing timeless dreams
Upon the stage of life,
In shabby clothes and tattered shoes,
We twist, and turn, and smile.
Human folly dances to a song
The soul finds hard to sing.

Hope eternal holds us on life's stage.
Although the lights grow dim, we dance,
We smile in hope, twirl on.
The curtain soon must fall,
Leave us in darkness, standing,
Hoping for a curtain call.

Frances Carnahan Ebaugh

Frances Carnahan Ebaugh
THE ESSENCE OF LIFE

There are no strings attached to love.
It is the breath of life to me—
Life made of particles, forces, and quarks
Gluons, and all such chemistry.

There are no strings attached to love.
My life will leave as it came, with a breath
But love will remain as sure as the stars
And I will remember after death.

Frances Carnahan Ebaugh
POEMS I MAKE FOR YOU

Like a harp that makes a song
When its strings are pulled along
Or a flower makes a flower
In its sweetest, bearing hour
Like a rose with pearls of dew
A string of poems I make for you
Like a rosary to wear
Made with gems and blossoms, fair
Like a harp that makes the song
When its strings are pulled along.

Frances Carnahan Ebaugh
WHEN I THINK THESE THINGS

To my beloved daughter, Frances Ebaugh Colvin.

When I think that I was sent
To live on earth today—
That I was meant to visit here
While going on my way—
That no one stays inside a tomb

Except a frame remains—
That all born here beneath the stars
Arise above the plane—
And always Jesus reaches out
On earth and heav'n above
And touches all both great and small—
I know there's God, and love.

Frances Carnahan Ebaugh
THIS PICTURE

Dedicated to my friend, Jere Herrington of Hawthorne.

Spring has come.
I trimmed the green Pittosp'rum
Down to a bush
Round and white with blossom.

A redbird lit on the left
A blue on the right
The color of delft.
Oh, what a beautiful sight!

The grass is green.
The sky's turned silvery blue.
Leaves on high
Form lace in the sunset hue.

Birds are singing.
All the world doth sing.
I'll remember
God, this picture in Spring.

Frances Carnahan Ebaugh
LAKESIDE COVE
(AS TOLD TO MY DAUGHTER)

There's a place in Lakeside Hills
On Lucky Drive o'er Rainbow
Near the cove where they hunted deer
Many a year ago.

There's a house, a little green dock
And boat, which means a lot
'Cause granny planned it for the boys
When one of them was a tot.

Remember we named it Lakeside Cove
And planted a Wonder-Tree?
Where are the golden hours our children
Gave to you and me?

Ernie Houston
MOTHER IS RESTING NOW

This poem is in memory of Doris Morris.

There is nothing I can say to ease the pain,
I know that true feelings are hard to contain.
I am sure today, you can't help but weep,
But she has finally found her most peaceful sleep.
I know your mother has meant a lot to you,
Try to remember the good times and not be blue.
She has meant a lot to everyone—I am sure,
By us being there, she knew our love was pure.
Loving and caring should never be undone,
Now is the time for family to be as one.
It is hard, but you also know this is best,
It is nice to know—she's finally getting some rest.
Remember when she said—"Pray for me,"
She has gone to a better world—can't you see.
Try to understand, and this may be how,
The pain is over—"Mother is resting now."

Ernie Houston
THINGS MISSED

This poem is dedicated to Tina and Janie, my children.

I miss the whisper of a gentle breeze,
And the calm of the clear blue seas.
I miss my children's warm embrace,
And also the happiness in their face.
I miss the goodness in every man,
And try to find it, if I possibly can.
I miss the sweet smell of fresh flowers,
And the love between us for all those hours.
I miss the beauty of a calm lake,
And things done for my children's sake.
I miss my child's smile and her curls,
And things that made this string of pearls.
I miss things lost while in my prime,
And of being loved all of the time.
I miss wiping away my child's tears,
And wanting happiness all these years.
I miss my children's intense thought,
And never knowing the love they brought.
More deeply than anything—I miss the Lord,
When he comes, I hope to be on board.

Ernie Houston
FORGIVING

To forgive is sometimes very hard to do,
People don't realize the hardships we go through.
To understand and be happy under so much stress,
Forgiving and understanding—we do not possess.
Why should we feel inside—so much hate,
Try to forgive and forget, before it's too late.
The world is filled with so much sorrow,
Make something happen today; not tomorrow.
We must sometimes show the way,
Better do it today, without any delay.
People are finding more places to roam,
Sometimes we forget our love at home.
Things are sometimes very hard to bear,
Try living in the real world—not someone's dare.
We should all—our real problems face,
Do something to improve the minds of our race.
Loving is one thing only for the living,
Forget the hate and start "forgiving."

Ernie Houston
THE TRUTH

Things should never be a surprise,
We should not devote our lives to lies.
It is better to have things sweet,
We need to love the people we meet.
It is nice to keep what is spoken,
Truth is better and should not be broken.
We should learn to care and to be strong,
It is better to always try to belong.
Learn to always turn the other cheek,
It is also better to remember what we speak.
Try not to judge by a person's past,
Remember forgiveness should always last.
Try not to do things only in vain,
A better understanding is ours to gain.
It is better to be seen more, than heard,
You will always be judged by your word.
We should remember the things of our youth,
Nothing is more important than "The Truth."

Jan Nurenberg

Jan Nurenberg
IN FLIGHT

Like a bird of the night,
I'm on a long and lonely flight.
I just don't dare to stop,
Or I would surely die of fright.

So many things to see and do,
Things unknown, things so new.
I feel so apart from life,
Oh, to be a Mother and Wife.

But I tried it once and failed,
Oh Lord, it hurts so bad, I wailed.
I really miss the Hugs and Kisses,
Oh to be again a Mrs.

But for now I'm content to be,
In search of a healthier, happier me.
So I'll spread my wings and fly about,
And when I land, I'll give a shout
Oh Lord, No more me, only thee.

It's in your hands, I state,
Please look about, find me a mate.
Someone who Cares, Loves, shares in Ecstasy,
And just lets me be, Really Me.

Jan Nurenberg
HOW DO I KNOW?

What are my chances to meet,
and the past not to repeat.
A Gentle, Caring, Loving man,
Who can ease the past, he can.
What are my chances to meet?

He says he loves me true,
But the past cuts in, turns me blue.
I want this friendship to grow,
But how do I know?

His voice so low, so soft, so soothing,
Touches my heart, he's so moving.
I'm trying hard to hold the feelings,
The sky's the limit, I've touched the ceiling.

My conscience says, Hold on girl,
He's only giving you a whirl.
Watch out for him, he's on the make,
My heart says, the chance is but to take.
But, How do I know?

My prayers are answered,
My dreams come true.
He promises me that,
I'll never be blue.
But, How do I know?

I put my life in God's hands,
and pray that he understands.
Love, Trust, Give and Take,
The future is but ours to make.
But, How do I know?

Edna E Daniels
TRUTH

To the ones seeking the truth, and to the ones who have found truth.

The truth comes slowly to most,
As we travel this worldly coast,
We search the whole world over,
For the four-leaf clover,
'Til right within ourselves we find,
Truth was there all there all the time.

Elizabeth J Donnelly
DRAGONS MAKE TERRIBLE BEDFELLOWS
I speed to our bedbox 8 floors up from the sea.
Your sweater engulfs my nostrils in a musty barroom reek.
I inhale a shot
and the dragon in me fumes.
I want to spit fire,
but the words won't come out.
I toss and turn beside you
as I wrestle the dragon in the sheets.
Next morning there is an icy powder on the beach
where our hot bodies once lay.
The dragon pounded blue-violet trenches over my cheekbones
to revenge his night's keep.
My pancakes suck down the tree sap
I cannot swallow
as I stare out the window at a gray man
picking morsels out of a dumpster.
You run your hand up my thigh
while the waitress pours us coffee.
I wait a moment, but my mind can't withhold
this beastly anger any longer,
and the dragon rages free.

Peggy E Olson
THE HOLY ONE
Raise your voice and sing praises
to the Holy One above.
Bow down and pray, you'll find your way
with His blessings and His love.
Mark His words, so strong and true,
proclaim them far and near.
Gather your sheep about you,
and grab them by the ear.
Pour forth His loving words
with your fire and your flame.
And if they do not listen
well, then, you're not to blame.
Your calling is clear; His words are dear
and this fold will see the light
of His tender mercy and brotherhood,
or perish in the fight.
Your strength comes from this Savior,
from His righteousness and love.
So raise your fist, take aim and fire,
for the Holy One above.

Dana Michelle Schabel
HOLD ON TO YOUR HOPES AND DREAMS
A dream is the one thing that urges man forward.
It makes him strive to reach his future,
Push to climb the ever rising ladder of success.
Some gain what they set out to acquire,
While others lose sight of their goals;
Drifting along in a bleak, dark world of despair—
Depressing thoughts forever cluttering their minds;
Never again letting the light of dreams,
The glimmer of hope,
Shine in to dispel the smothering clouds of repression.
No, when dreams are lost,
The inner soul,
The spirit inside of every person,
Will be forever abandoned—
Thrust into the pit of forgotten goals,
Where dreams will never to be gained by the one whose hopes had once strengthened his stride to achieve.
For your sake, please heed the warning of a dreamer—
Hold tight to the dreams you dream
Keeping yourself from the forever darkness of a lost soul.

Jimmie Nell Ford

Jimmie Nell Ford
TODAY, TONIGHT, TOMORROW
Today you laughed.
We watched as you skillfully threw rocks in the sand.
You smiled, then you vanished—
Forever, into darkness.
You were a child of the universe.
No more—no less than I.
Tonight, you slipped away from us.
In solitude, your mother cries.
But not alone.
Your friends, those who loved you, weep also.
Reasons unknown.
God's plan is mysterious to some,
But to him only must we pray
That understanding will come to us
Tomorrow—
On judgment day.
In memory of Franklin Polke
Nov. 26, 1970—Jan. 15, 1990

Sandra B Pierce
DREAMS
Dreams are part of everyone's life,
some are good and some are bad.
You let your mind wonder near or far,
to see if you can catch that dream star.
Life wouldn't be as great,
if we didn't let our minds create.
Dreams can be fulfilled to a tee,
but sometimes it takes the right key.
There have been great men in our past,
who have dreamed and created so many things that last.
Whether it's great or small,
life wouldn't be complete at all.
So as you can see,
dreams are important to you and for me.

Jessica Parmenter
HEAVEN

Dedicated to Catherine A. Lever, "Gramma Kay"
Until we meet again.

Greyness covers the sky,
As pain fills my heart.
The thought of losing you,
Tears my world apart.
Now you have gone home
God has taken you away
No matter where you are
In my heart you'll always stay
Our Father has opened the doors
Angels have come to land
To lead you to the promised place
As they take you by the hand
You have touched so many lives
With the love that you have shared
That is what makes you special
The way you truly cared . . . .

Jessica Parmenter
FREE
She was young and free,
A child forever to be.
A dream was all she had,
That no one else could see.
Her life just passed her by,
No one understood why.
They did not care,
They didn't hear her cry.
Her death really wasn't a mystery,
She was never truly happy.
She didn't want to end it,
She only wanted to be free.
Her hardest she did try,
To find a reason why,
To live a life with no meaning.
Why should she live a lie!
She found no reason to be.
She decided it was time to leave,
She told the world goodbye!
Setting her soul free . . .

Pamela Smith DeWitt
ODE TO GRANDMA FLORENCE
All our quiet walks and little talks
A cup of tea for you and me
Homemade pies and all your smiles
Your sunlit face through the windowpane
Watching all of us play our childhood games
Talks about the folks and all our jokes
Oh Grandma Dear don't you fear!!!
You're not alone
You've just gone home!!!!!!

Sherry E Goodwin
ON WHICH PATH

Dedicated To My Mother And In Memory Of My Father,
In Love, S.E.G.

When in doubt I never pout for on which path should be taken.

I go in stride with foolish pride unworried of situations.

Along my way if I should stray from all my destinations.

I simply turn about correct my route and never pout.

For on which path should be taken.

L Pearce Pearson
THE BITBURG DEAD

Reflection on President Reagan's visit to Bitburg Cemetery, Germany in 1985.

Love be read
Courage, conviction
Rest all dead in peace
Sons, brothers, husbands, fathers, all
Let hatred cease
Honor the dead, <u>all</u> dead
They gave their all
Each gave his life
Dwell not on yesteryear, The tear
Fan not anew the strife
Have no dread
Build for all tomorrows
Foreign or resident
Remember the strength
Of the President
Our President
Trust should spread
For friend or foe
We know
GOD is Judge.

Michele Ann Scott
A CHAIN REACTION
It started with a feeling, which rose to an emotion which set free a desire, that unleashed a drive. It could not be contained neither withstrained,
It could not be held back but systematically is kept on track. It's timing is sometimes
Erratic, spontaneous or sporadic.
Let it not be tested though some men may reject it. The universe is filled with it,
though some men may try to steal from it
This cannot be bought or sold, stacked or boxed or put on hold, we use it constantly day and night and that my friend is the Right to Life!

Brenda Melton
ENCOURAGEMENT

To all rehabilitating alcoholics and drug abusers.

Just when you think the world is dark, there is no light to see;
Look into your heart, my dear, there the light will be.
When your troubles seem so wide, your options seem so thin;
Look into your soul my dear, for there you'll find a friend.
The task you took upon yourself, the peace of mind you seek;
I know is very hard my dear, and you think yourself weak.
But given time and lots of love, the burden you will lose;
And the way you lead your life, will then be yours to choose.
I write these words to let you know, that you are not alone;
For I am right behind you, my faith forever strong.
When you feel you're going down, your will is growing weak;
Pick up this piece of paper, and then begin to read.
Feel the strength I send to you, deep inside your soul;
And the things you think you need, you'll find you need no more.

Bruce E Benson

Bruce E Benson
SPARKLES

Dedicated to my fellow brothers and sisters in Christ.

As the stars do shine in the sky above, there is a sparkle in the eyes of love. And until the saints of God do part, there is a sparkle within the heart. In life, in love, in peace, and in care, yes, it is a sparkle there.
In all the things that mean the most, there is a sparkle at its post. A sparkle for mom, a sparkle for dad,

A sparkle for the little lad. A sparkle for the elderly and the youth, a sparkle for the bible, a word of truth. A sparkle for the husband or the new wife, a sparkle for heaven's eternal life. Whenever we kneel down to pray, that sparkle is not so far away. When we do good in life and try, that sparkle is with us until we die.

Bruce E Benson
VISIONS OF VICTORY
When I close my eyes, I see a light that shines inside of me. I know there's hope, I try to cope, as I vision victory. In darkness hour, I pray for power that Christ will strengthen me, that I may live a life for Him, for I vision victory. So as days go by, I pray and try to do as God has said, as I dream and vision victory and a crown upon my head.

Bruce E Benson
AFTER THE RAIN
After the rain, the clouds fade away and the sun will then shine for a brighter day. At the end of darkness a dim light will shine, for the faith that we seek and the hope that we find. After the battle, the hatred will cease, then love will move in to give us peace. Yes, dark days will come and troubles will be, but we must seek Jesus to find the true key. Sometimes we worry about troubles and pain, but it will all be much better, after the rain.

Bruce E Benson
CAN I MAKE IT LORD?
When this old world seems to get me down, can I make it Lord? I want to know I'm heaven bound, can I make it Lord? When friends and enemies don't treat me right, I pray to God with all my might, please help me make it Lord. Temptation, trials and pain I bear and I feel that no one really cares. I cry and I try to do God's will but it seems I'm climbing up a hill, can I make it Lord? I don't know what's next to come, but I will try until all is done. I'll try to make it Lord.

Jennifer Lindsey
BIRDS
Birds are so sweet
When they go tweet, tweet, tweet.
When they soar through the air
Their wings flap with such care.
Oh! They are so beautiful,
And their songs are plentiful.

How I would love to be a bird!

I adore them so,
As they fly high and low.
When they are in flight
They look ever so light.
How I would love to fly
And soar into the sky!

How I would love to be a bird!

They are so full of songs,
They chirp all day long.
Some songs are happy, some are sad.
Some songs are glad, and some are mad!
But they are all so gorgeous,
Please! Sing more to us!

How I would love to be a bird!

Sonja D Oliver
NICHOLAS

To my son, Nicholas Oliver, you are the light of my life and I love you more than words can say. Have a wonderful life. Love, Mom.

Now close your eyes
& sleep my son
find peace & love
when your day is done.

I hope you have dreams
of happiness & joy
little red wagons
& your favorite toy.

A very peaceful rest
into your next day
where you'll find sunshine
while you're out to play.

As the beautiful sun
fades into the night
you'll know that my love
will always be your light.

Now close your eyes
& sleep my son
find peace & love
when this day too, is done.

Robin C Pelletier
COME GROW WITH ME
Come grow with me
For the world is ours to see
Do not blacken me
to lighten thee,
For if you blacken me to lighten thee,
No growth can there be.
We are all new souls put to earth to roam,
To find a place we call home.
We all need gentleness, kindness,
and caring for our growth:
For if you blacken me to lighten thee,
You stunt not only my growth but yours as well.
So place your hand in mine,
and together we can climb
Above it all and delight in the lightness
I have found in thee,
If you just come and grow with me.

Rosa Ashworth
REFLECTION

This poem is dedicated to those who truly believe in making necessary changes in their life. Thus, making the world a little brighter where they stand.

To stand before the image of me
To look deep inside for what you don't see
To reconstruct what I find within
To know where I'm going, I must know where I've been

To find each fault, to go deep inside
Where they live and breathe, but have nowhere to hide
To take each one, whatever it may be
Work it and change it to benefit me

When the job is complete, now comes the test
To look straight at the reflection of me at my best
The journey inside is worth it my friend
You know where you're going, cause you know where you've been.

Stephen Searle
YOUR TOMORROW
Do you dream that your tomorrow
Will improve upon today?
Do you think that all your plans
Will come true in any way?

When I awake from dreaming
I know it's time for care,

There is a time for working,
Another time for prayer.

There is a time for learning
To share your joy and sorrow,
There is a time for planning
To build for your tomorrow.

Margo K Hull
JESUS SAYS
He says, let yourself listen;
You'll enter into a wisdom, very few will ever hear.
He says, let yourself feel;
you'll enter into a peace of mind
so blissful you won't believe it's real.
He says, let yourself see yourself,
and you'll see more of what you'll truly be.
And Jesus says;
let yourself be yourself
and you truly will be free.

Margo K Hull
COME INTO MY REALITY
You see it's not that I'm antisocial or
Of prejudice means when I stand before
You peering into your mind,
Finding it of a radius insignificant in Time;
That I seem to be complaisant with this
Conversation of yours and mine.
I just haven't the reasoning for all this
Wasted effort I find.
Repetition is the name you have slain.
No purpose, no proof that reality has rained.
For you're unaware of being the sleep-walkers
Stumbling about;
And so as it is, I have found you out.
I can say this to you without any shame,
For the reality of this is just a stroke in
My game.

Charlene McCloskey
UNSELFISH LOVE

I dedicate this poem, and all my love, to Eddie, the light of my life.

In the beginning, on the night that we met,
I knew you'd be someone I could not forget.
I didn't realize why I felt that way then,
All I could think of, was to see you again.
Anticipating, thinking how it would be,
When we'd be together, was all I could see.
You gave me a gift, that no other could give,
It is found in my heart, and there it will live.
As it stays there, it can do nothing but grow,
All that it needs, is the tenderness you show.
There will be times, when it sees sunshine and rain,
But this it requires, to grow strong past the pain.
And if it can make it through this and survive,
I know it's our love, that has kept it alive.
And should you still wonder what I'm speaking of,
The gift that you gave, was your unselfish love.
This warm thriving love cleans the slate of my past,
It brings a new hope, of a love that will last.
Thank you for everything you've done from the start,
I love you so much and I give you my heart.
There still is another that I must thank too,
I know that He listens, for He has sent you.

Kimberly R Sine
TAKING BACK OUR STREETS

This poem is for anyone who should choose to close their eyes to their surroundings. We really can change the world we live in.

People fighting on the streets.
White supremacy hiding under white sheets.
Murder, abuse, robbery and rape.
Bureaucrats, liberals and the courts' red tape.
Drug addicts and criminals with no shame.
They look forward to the worst and someone to blame.
Illiteracy and poverty for the young and old.
Homeless wander lonely in the heat and cold.
A few lousy reporters with their nose to the wheel.
Giving the curious public any privacy they manage to steal.
What can I do to change this country in pain.
To start, clean up the streets where people were slain.
I would love to paint white over all vain walls.
Teaching ethics, morals and dignity in all school halls.
I want to take in the elderly in their time of need.
Giving the indebted farmers back their lost land deed.
I alone cannot change our country, not overnight.
I alone cannot change it, not without everyone in this fight.
Our country can be beautiful, not dark or grim.
It's time to rid the bad from the community and let the good move in.

Lisa Stovall

Lisa Stovall
SHATTERED DREAMS "I LOVE YOU DADDY"

In memory of Sammy Allen Stovall.

White and Beautiful, Spring is here
a wedding ceremony is about to begin.
Family members and friends are gathered to see the giving of one's daughter.
As they walk down the aisle
towards the altar of sacrifice.
Between giving up each other
and opening a new place in their lives.
The memories of love and the times they shared, can never be forgotten
by those who are there.
The uniting of this couple to marry will never be viewed by this father who's giving.
For his daughter will walk down the aisle alone, with somebody else playing his role.
One lonely summer, late in August,
God above took this father.
A father of love, who was always around
disappeared without a sound.
There were no goodbyes, with hugs and kisses
only hopes of dreams and wishes,
all were shattered before our eyes
leaving us feeling lonely and deprived.
"I miss you Daddy"

Melanie L Petre
THE STARS ARE BEAUTIFUL

The stars are beautiful
They glow so bright
Like you and I together
Under the moonlight.

The sun is going down
We are kissing on the beach
Sitting close, holding hands,
A shooting star, a wish for each.

The sun's reflection on the water
Is the prettiest I have ever seen
I hope our love goes well this time
This I really mean.

I wish you knew how much it meant
For this dream to come true
I have wanted this for so long
I just never knew how to tell you.

Dorothy Tracey
HE CARES

To Dr. Frank Burchell and Dr. Walter Johnson for their caring and encouragement to me, as well as their dedication, love and ministry for the Lord.

When all you can see is darkness,
And you're overwhelmed with hurt and pain.
When prayer doesn't seem so easy,
God hears you just the same.

Your pain He does feel. He knows your need.
A Father so loving, for us He did plead;
He offered His Son, so precious to Him.
His gift of Love, just let Him come in.

He gave us His Word. He's faithful and true.
He really does care what happens to you.
So during those trials, those hurts, don't despair,
For our God has promised, He'll always be there.

Pamela J Drown-Cockerham
AUNT BELVA MINE

No matter how far I may travel away,
I'll think of my Aunt almost every day,
Of her life on the mountain in her cute little home,
It's the prettiest scene, beats my journey to Rome!

In the winter she makes lovely quilts of designs,
And sews clothes—oh to boredom, she will not resign,
She uses the talents that God's given her,
To share with so many, He knows it—I'm sure!

Spring and summer bring hard work outside in the soil,
Getting up with the chickens and all day she toils,
She kills snakes in her garden with a whack from her hoe,
And returns to her work, once she's stomped out her foe.

She's a talented Orator, a circus story she tells,
And she says it so fast, it brings laughter and wails,
About a ring-tailed monkey, ask your mother for a dime?
I can't do it! At this, she's the queen of all time!

If I had mail-ordered an Aunt from above,
I would get this exact one with her special love,
Her example's the best; it is certainly fine,
I'm so proud she's my Aunt, yes—dear AUNT BELVA MINE!!

Linda James Boston
MY HEART ACHES FOR YOU

I've tried to forget,
but thoughts of you drift in my mind constantly.
You gave the impression that you cared,
Now all hopes of you and I together seem like a shattered dream.
Months have passed since I fell in love with you.
Yet I always feel that there is hope for our love to materialize.
Why do I wait for a seldom smile, or just a deep eye contact?
When I know that there is a possibility neither will occur.
Loving you has made me lose all sense of reality.
For in the real world there is true love, understanding, and sometimes a lifetime of happiness.
I hate to think that I have fantasized the way you sometimes look at me. If I have, then I've lost control.
For if I had control of my true feelings, my heart would not ache for you.

Heidi L Wentz
PRISON

Dedicated to my best friend who encouraged me, believed in me, and taught me how to believe in myself. Thank you, Jackie.

He sits staring at the cold bars of his prison.
No one will let him have the key,
They laugh at his struggles to escape.
All he wishes for is a freedom
Beyond the concrete of his surroundings.
Counting the days, counting the tracks
Of greedy rats and roaches—who daily
And nightly as he sleeps seek to
Devour him—as does his surroundings.
They do not see his strong-willed determination
Which will never let go of a single, sacred, solitary hope.
His eyes; red, bloodshot—he has spent many
Nights—awake—weeping—
waiting—wishing—wondering
A light would shine through the thick, impounding
Darkness, the heavy doors would open while others
Accepted him again to the world.
He only wants to try again. Should we give him opportunity?
A key to a new life? To help and not hurt?
Or should his sin be held against him forever
As we look on, in our own
Self-Righteousness . . . .

Heidi L Wentz
TO WANDER

I wandered o'er the lowest valleys
Of long lost love
Of missed chance.
I wandered o'er the highest peak of majestic mountains
And when I reached the top—oh
How happy I was!
I continued to walk to wander
To search
Something was still missing
What was it?
I wandered o'er the calm pools
Of fresh clear waters
And found peace
Oh, to wander.

Eleanor Estella Wilson
A BOOK'S MESSAGE

This poem is dedicated to all students of the world.

I am a book
Take a good look,
I have eighty faces
Many lines and spaces,
All fit for writing
About things that are inditing.

I love to be kept neat,
Not thrown on a seat,
But kept in places
Where eager faces,
Read what's in me,
I think, you'll agree.

Work in me that's torned
Cannot be learned
Much less retained,
So no knowledge can be gained
From a book that is such,
So think, about this, much!

So let's have a book
That you'll like to take a good look,
All eighty written faces
With figures, facts and graces
To be fixed in the mind
Until knowledge we find.
That's the book for you and me!

Carol Yamamoto
KARAH'S BACKYARD

This poem is dedicated to Karah, my darling daughter.

Karah, in your backyard
there is much to see and do.
Everything is brand-new
and waiting just for you.

Karah, in your backyard
there are five oak trees.
Their dancing leaves,
gently swaying in the breeze.

Karah, in your backyard
there lives a family of bluebirds.
Chirping and peeping bird words,
making noise in order to be heard.

Karah, in your backyard
there are colorful flowers.
Standing tall in the daylight hours,
and bowing to rainy day showers.

Karah, in your backyard
there is grass that is green.
Paths to places you've never been,
leading to sights waiting to be seen.

Debra Salmon
IN TIME
A moment in time with a genuine purpose
A warm gentle person came to the surface
Of a life that needed a tender hand—
A loving strong force that I call my friend
Like the winds on a powerful moving ocean
You've given me caring, life and devotion
A kindness you've spared to reach me in time
A special dear closeness I call only mine
When my days are a struggle and we can't be together
I think of your smile and my heart changes whether it's bad or dark or gloomy or gray—
I know one thing will always stay
A happiness I cannot measure
You, my love, I will always treasure

Lee C Marshall
EXPRESSIONS
I'm not a writer.
I'm not a poet.
Nobody special.
Just want ya to know it.

I write about people.
I write about life.
Write about husbands,
write about wives.

Write about babies.
Write about crime.
Write about pleasure.
I write all the time.

Give me a title,
I don't think you should.
I'd lose my expressions,
and wind up no good.

Lee C Marshall
TO MOTHERS
I love you precious mother,
more than time can tell.
More than pen could ever write,
if the ocean were her wells.

I love you dearest momma,
as I've watched the wells run dry.
Soon there will be no raindrops,
then there will be no sky.

I love you dearest mom
yes I always will
as the leaves so quickly fall
and scratch at my windowsill

I love you dearest mother,
you know I always will.
Until the leaves no longer fall
on these weathered windowsills

Yes I love you mother,
for all you have done for me,
you know I can never pay you back,
and that's what bothers me.

Elise Marie Neiger
NIGHTMARE

This poem is dedicated to my father, R. Alan Neiger, whose presence I miss tremendously. In my loving memory, Elise.

A whirlwind of feelings
brew up inside
As I fight to keep
your memory alive
In the night of slumber
you enter my world
of illusion
My world of
Sadness and Confusion

Face to face
we appear to find
you're losing the race
against fate and time

In your eyes
the pain I see
Of this suffering
you want free

A long battle,
But
your time has come
In the end
cancer won

Debra Wright Blevins
JUDGE ME
Judge me not by the clothes I wear
Judge me not by the looks of my hair
Judge me not by the color of my skin
Judge me not for my sins

Judge me not for what you see
Judge me as I seem to be
Judge me not for what you hear
Judge me not as one to fear

Judge me not for the way I walk
Judge me not for the way I talk
Judge me not by the color of my eyes
Judge me not as a passerby

Judge me for the inner me
Judge me for what I seem to be
Judge me for a soul who's free
Judge me for my personality

Judge me for who I am inside
Judge me for how hard I try
Judge me for my caring ways
Judge me for my love each day.

Joseph F Heisel Jr
A CREED FOR EVERYONE
. . . born of our love for others; our love for each other!
We believe! We work and pray
Our fellowship <u>will</u> cast a ray . . .
of hope!
Faith and love we offer too
Reverence in all we do
We believe! It <u>can</u> come true
If only within <u>us</u> and <u>you</u>:
Our Dream—
One race, all human, all divine
One creed, respect for yours and mine
One plan, deliverance for all:
One God, our answer to his call:
A Pledge—
More faith, more hope,
more love for all!
If we believe in anything
We believe in rendering
<u>Ourselves</u>!

Joseph F Heisel Jr
A PLEDGE OF ALLEGIANCE . . . TO GOD, TO EACH OTHER, AND TO ALL OTHERS
Based on the fervent belief that there is <u>one</u> creed, <u>one</u> plan, <u>one</u> God . . . and really only one race—the human race! Whoever you are, wherever you are, whatever you are . . . you are part of me, I am part of you, we are parts of each other!!! Do not deny me, do not forsake me, do not ignore me, <u>just</u> because I am different! Help me! I am a key to your lock; a piece of your puzzle; a solution to your problems; your path to salvation (and you are mine!!!)

<u>The Pledge</u>:

I pledge allegiance to this day
to everyone in every way
with reverence in all I do
kindness, patience, love for you
I'll live His rule, His word, His joy
change tears to smiles in His employ
I'll pass-it-on, this pledge contagious!
<u>Love</u> is meant to be outrageous!
Love can heal!
Love can feel!
Love's the answer.
To love, I yield!
<u>Love</u>: All powerful! <u>Love</u>:
Invincible!
Unmistakably Divine;
Will not fail to bring together,
All who pledge: "Not mine, but thine!"

<u>Important</u>: This is particularly appropriate and necessary for males and females—every day—to pledge allegiance to, and respect for, <u>each other</u>.

Kathy Dawn Brown
THIS TOO WILL PASS
Thoughts that ruffle my mind's pages,
Plans and schemes in various stages . . .
None of life's problems ever go away;
They only multiply and grow each day!
There is so much that I must face;
To sift and sort and put in place.
This I know and can't ignore,
All have failed that tried before.
To think of triumphs I'll never know,
Gives my heart a deadening blow.
My prospects seem so bleak and dreary,
It is no wonder my heart grows weary.
Such a sinking feeling this thought gives;
I am going to die before I live!
This will be my life's one greatest sin;
To have suffered so, to never win.
I'm grateful feelings like this never last;
For I know that in time, this too will pass!

Agnes M Cicurillo
FRANKLIN, MY SCHOOL
As I remember many years ago,
In a neighborhood surrounded by small family homes,
Stood a magnificent red brick structure
Named Franklin School,
In honor of an early statesman,
Benjamin Franklin,
Every day many children came,
Including myself and other members of my family
To pursue our elementary course of study.
Happy and proud of its teachers and supervisors,
Who gave of themselves,
For the benefit of all the students.
And as I grew in years and accomplishments,
I became one of the teachers here.
I tried my best to give back,
Something of those wonderful years
The school gave to me,
Last year Franklin School celebrated 100 years.
I hope and know it will
Continue to give more
Wonderful years for those who come.

Jonalynn R Stevens
ENDURING TIME

I dedicate my poem "Enduring Time" to my loving sons, Bruce Andrew Morehouse II and Christopher George Brown, of whom the Lord has blessed me so dearly.

As time passes on, in age we grow old,
winter's . . . they come cold.
Words have been spoken,
hearts . . . many times have been broken.

Spirits have not been forsaken,
still . . . we search,
our souls yet to be taken.

Find us, for we are weeping,
our hearts . . . know not they are sleeping.

Jennifer Beardslee
THE BEACH
Walking on The Beach
the soft sand
warmth all around
At sunset, the water
is so free
the waves crash
the water sprays
It washes up on the sand
each layer of water
takes a little bit of sand
The Beach is a beautiful place
It's a place to go for
freedom
Freedom from life
there are no troubles on
The Beach
It's kind of a heaven to go
to just forget or
think things through
We all need to go to a
place like that.

William R Johnson
VENICE BEACH AKA PRETTY SUMMER WOMEN
Pretty Summer Women
lookin' so sexy and free
golden skin, golden hair
Hey, are ya all noticin' me?!

Pacific poundin' in so noiselessly
your lovely bodies so enticin'
Some of you are out on a moneyless spree

some of you are hagglin' for a pricin'

Sun pouring down like Misses Butterworth
as ya all gorgeously romp in the sand
All with smiles of jest and mirth
And come in singles, pairs and bands!

In coffee shoppe or Cerveza bar
or crowded boutique, ya love to talk
on roller skates or bicycles . . . there ya are
gigglin', gabbin', or jivin' all along the boardwalk

Hey, ya all sure are a delight
for these tired old eyes to see
and here I am, tryin' with all my might
YO! Are you bitches noticin' ME?!

Steven S Harrington
I SPENT A MOMENT BY THE SEA
I spent a moment by the sea
this moment that was spent for thee
We sat and kept each other warm
On a breezy cold crisp day in fall
Birds we saw were soaring free
Oh this love we have for an ocean breeze
I know this moment shall last not long
But this special moment by the sea
is a moment that shall never leave

Frances Anne Cooney
IN ANOTHER TIME
We were together in another time
We were together in another place;
I know that I remember those eyes
They're something time just cannot erase.

You took my love and most my mind
My heart is coming apart at the seams;
Now is it any wonder why
You got me dreaming those old time dreams.

Somehow when you touched me
I had this feeling that you knew me too;
When I loved somebody long ago
I was thinking that it might be you.

I'm glad I met you way back then
'Cause now you're always on my mind;
Once we belonged to each other
In another place, in another time.

Jason Agan

Jason Agan
CLOUDY DAY
Well, the clouds are rollin' in
and my body hopes for drought,
but it seems I feel at home
when there's pain in my heart.

When the storm is on its way
and I can't explain why,
but it seems that I feel better
on a cloudy day.

Sometimes when the sun's not around
you see things in a different light.
Then along comes the early darkness
and the silent stars of the night.

There's always a chance she'll stay;
tomorrow's another cloudy day.

Just leave me in the rain
I don't mind anymore
I'll rely on the rainbow
to shine the memories of her door.

I know all too well
that "Sunshine" is her name.
That's why I can remember the reason
why there's a cloudy day.

Jason Agan
THE MAN
A man is born as another man dies;
a child is brought into this world
with his imagination on his side.

He dreams while learning,
and learns as he dreams.
Magic is abundant
while he works at his play,
but only will he realize tomorrow
the memories of yesterday.

He thinks ahead
and does his best to judge,
only to have a reversed plan
and a dream that won't budge.

Character will build
and memories will wear,
as this man weeps and says:
"I've been there."

The cycle will renew
as life manages to progress,
but don't forget the man
who has carried out this process.

Nora K Hancock
SPRINGTIME ON THE FARM
Fluffy white clouds ride the horizon,
Bringing sprinkles of sweet raindrops pure.
Whose little patter seems to awaken,
All sleeping nature, everything's begun to stir.

I stand above my rich loam furrows,
Sifting tiny seeds into a straight row.
Planting now to reap for the tomorrows,
Can hardly wait to see my garden grow.

In distant field, with mothers watching,
White lambs, on stiff legs, romp and play.
All nature has awakened to its prompting,
As sun breaks through; it's such a lovely day.

Gentle breezes blow the awakening branches,
A hint of green shows on the rolling hills.
A young foal lies flat in the warm sunshine,
Tulips nod, and look at all those smiling daffodils.

Springtime has come home to our valley,
Children laugh and play in yards and street.
After winter months of snow and cold and foggy,
Yes, lovely springtime, you are such a treat.

Phyllis Wright
HALLOWEEN
Snuggle 'neath the covers,
cover up your head.
The things that are astir tonight
are better left unsaid.

Witches on the rooftops,
ghosts up in the sky;
goblins on each corner,
scaring passers-by.

Grinning pumpkin faces,
with their flaming eyes,
stare from every window,
gape in great surprise.

Bags are full of candy
childish hearts are full of joy,
because tonight is "Trick or Treat"
for every girl and boy.

So, Mothers, get the candy out.
Kids, let's make the scene.
Tonight is fun for everyone.
Tonight is Halloween!

Tammy Fletcher
REMEMBER ME
Remember me when I am gone
far into my silent world
When you can no longer hold me
when I am not there when you need me

Remember when I first cried
beginning from happiness
ending from our pain

And then as each day and night becomes blurred
I cast the sadness far behind me
I place the ugly remembrances into the mirrors

These are my mirrors
There the reflections become clear

Remembering that I loved you.

Carfene Shew
MORNING BREEZE
When cares of the day have been a burden, and caused a long sleepless night
There's nothing more refreshing, as the stillness, of the early morning light.
Take your coffee outside to the patio, and feel the gentle morning breeze
Listen to the singing of the birds, watch the squirrels as they run up and down the trees.
Just stop long enough to say a prayer, as you look up to the sky
Say thank you God for all this beauty, that no amount of money can buy.
And through this busy day, Lord, when I begin to feel like a lemon being squeezed
Please help me to remember this early morning breeze.

Tom Calif
THORNS OF ROSES
I'd hurt you tenderly,
On your rosy cheeks,
On your thin lips,
On your little feet,
On your sexy hips,
Whatever you can list . . .
Not with nails,
Not with knives,
Not with bites,
Not with chisels;
Only, with the growing mustaches,
Thorns of roses . . .

Ritva-Liisa Riissanen
THE DOG
She was shaggy
she was skinny
she was scared.

She came to our yard,
seeking home
and friend and master.

She took our heart
and mind and soul.

She got the bed
and yard and home.

And today
she thanks us
with her tail wagging
her eyes glittering.

Richard Downs
ONCE IN A DREAM
Once in a dream or nightmare would be
A bird and a butterfly sang song in a tree.
The bird's song so sweet animated with hope
Taught a lesson of life to laugh is to cope.
Far down below on a branch hung with gloom
The butterfly's sarcasm rang on with doom.
The bird though not pretty a sparrow it seems
Kept singing of life so rich with esteem.
The butterfly's colors a spectre of chance
A knight in full armor its tongue be its lance.
So if walking through forests of trees in a dream
Listen for bird song and a butterfly's scream.

Wilma R Ackman
ONE TRUE LOVE
True love is all giving
Of kindness and trust and talent,
To make someone happy
Each day as life is spent.

It is comfort and quietness
A sereneness, not otherwise found.
It is a smile, a sweet name,
A presence, without a sound.

If you have found this
No matter what life brings,
You can conquer and go forward.
A loving heart is happy and sings.

Lavinel Savu
THE SEPARATION
I now know that he meant nothing to you;
and I can prove she meant nothing to me.
Can't we forgive and forget? Your old shoe
you can try on, once again; Oh for she,
that other one, could not get her foot in.
Respond quickly before my hope wears thin . . .

. . . You make me out to be a total fool;
I can read through you so very clearly.
Using your assumed knowledge as your tool
brings me to hysterics. He did truly mean so very much, but you were too blind
to have noticed. It was his light that gave
me the power and means by which to find
myself. I have since been able to save
my foot for the proper shoe, which is his
shoe. I can try to forget, but never could I forgive what you put me through. 'Tis
indeed time to advance, but on severed
paths, mine to a quick recovery from your remnants; I have rid myself of some.

Carolann and Rick Dukovich

Carolann Dukovich
UPON A HEART GIVEN . . .

To the man who secured my heart with love—My husband, Rick.

Heart, Would I be able to
survive without you?
Heart, Would I be open to
new Love?
Heart, Would I greet Him with
outstretched arms?
Heart, Would I hold Him never to
let Him go?
Heart, . . . I would
Love Him
(YOU)
Forever!!

Carolann Dukovich
AS I SEE IT
I close my eyes to paint a picture in primary colors
I see only white space enticing objects of imagination

Then

I spin the color wheel 'round and 'round
Fast and smooth without a sound
One color to choose, I am lead
Will it be yellow, green, blue, or red?

This picture is one only I can see
These objects are ones that only I let them be
Can an apple be blue? Only I can say
I open my eyes to see the same picture painted another way!

Carolann Dukovich
A SALES PITCH
A sales pitch
Good.
Only one.
Make your point . . .
What's the bottom line?

a SALES pitch
How much does it cost?
How can I buy without money?
"Easy" you say with

a sales PITCH
Wind-up, here it comes . . .
buy now, pay later!
sign here?
Thanks.

Ann Winter Lesher
GLORY TO GOD IN THE HIGHEST
We wait through the seasons of the year
From New Year's Day with its hopefulness of a new start;
To Easter, the sign of the Resurrection signifying eternal life;
And in the heat of summer the glorious Fourth of July;
Labor Day brings groans from kids and shouts of joy from parents
As school begins for another season.
Thanksgiving is soon to follow with Advent on its heels.

What does Advent mean to you?

Are you preparing for the great event to come?
Is your heart opening to receive the Christ Child?
Do you share with others the meaning of Christmas with allelulias and great joy,
Giving to others the most wonderful gift of all?

The good news that God, our Savior, is born
To give us fullness of life, meaning to the word love,
Hope for the future, faith in humankind.
All are given to us by God, the Father,
His greatest gift to each of us is
The baby in the manger, Jesus Christ, His precious son.

Share God's gift with the world and
Receive the gift of love in your heart.

Uzi Johnson
EVOLUTION OF A FRIENDSHIP
My world was going down the drain,
My life was filled with misery and pain,
I was looking for a way to make it all end.
Then you came along when I most needed a friend

For once in my life someone cared.
When I needed a shoulder you were there.
We shared each other's secrets and insecurities,
We supported each other through times of grief

I can't place an exact date or time,
This feeling just slowly grew inside.
We're still friends yet so much more.
I love you, of that I'm sure

I never thought one day I'd hold you like this,
I never imagined I'd kiss your lips.
We started out as friends to each other,
And now, to my wonder, we've become lovers

Rose Skubsch
CHRISTMAS
Snow is falling soft and white,
whispering a song . . .
Stars are shining clear and bright,
sparkle all night long.

I hear music, children singing,
see the yellow smiling moon . . .
I hear bells, and they are ringing:
Christmas will be here real soon!

Harry G Kemmer
DECEMBER SONG
'Twas fraught with grave foreboding, that icy, sunless day,
As if to make one wonder if spring was far away.
Would robins build their nests again; would gentle bluebirds call?
Would crocuses adorn the lawn and daffodils withal?
And then outside my window I saw the shrubb'ry move,
Entranced I watched the branches to swift the reason prove,
My heart beat faster as I saw a feathered form and bill,
A Carolina wren appeared and hopped upon the sill.
It warmed my heart, the day made bright, to see the bird so near,
And then despite the dark and cold, with song so bright and clear,
It sang four wondrous liquid notes I'll treasure till I die,
For with its cheery song it bade my doubts forever fly,
And now I know, however dark and drear the day may be,
The sun will shine and spring will come with cheering certainty.

Harry G Kemmer
AT PARTING (BASED UPON THE DEATH OF MARTHA'S DEVOTED DOG)
My time has come to leave you—
You who have been the very center of my universe.
At break of day I've lain with watchful eyes
And sensed your breathing and your waking moments,
We have gone forth and felt the freshness of the dawn,
Together we have faced the challenge of the daily chores.
The day has seemed so long
When you have told me to remain behind
And I have sat atop the hill awaiting your return.
In the quiet hours of evening I have lain at your feet
And known the warm sweet feeling that my day has been complete.

My time has come to go
And yet in mem'ry I shall never leave you.
So smile, take heart and of good courage be,
For though my time has come to go,
Know truly that I shall not be far,
Indeed, if turning home at close of day
With love's clear sight you scan the distant hill,
With shining eyes you'll see me waiting still.

Charmaine R Vogt
MY MOTHER AND I

To Penny Marie and Ken and new grandchild with love. This poem is dedicated just for you.

My mother and i, sharing a closeness so short.
I not yet ready, to come forth.
Needing mother so.
I lay within her womb, so safe thinking.

My mother and i know a love, no man can ever feel.
Nature, makes it so.
Count one, two, and you can see two creatures, creating a bond of love.
Like no other, anywhere.

My mother and i thank dear father on earth, and our heavenly father who began it all.
A tiny egg, turning into life.
Because of one, giving to another.
With God's help, a new beginning.

My mother and i.
Little me coming forth.
Creating a family, which mind will bind together.
Ending, only, when God takes all onto him.

Ava Madison
THOUGHTS ON MY 35TH BIRTHDAY
My mother has taken over my body,
Sounds crazy, but it's true.
It's her reflection I see in the mirror,
My voice sounds like her too.

This started rather gradually,
She didn't do it all at one time.
First my face turned into her face,
Then she slowly took over my mind.

It's her hand that holds my coffee cup,
And her gestures as I talk.
I hear her words teach my children,
And I feel her as I walk.

Now, if I just take on her energy,
And her sense of what's right and fair.
I'd like her strength and faith in God,
But I think I'll keep my hair!

Dea Marks
SUNDAY SILENCE

Sitting quiet . . . sun lacing soft patterns that will never be quite the same on another day;
Remembering . . . memories of every mother—
Each child, unique as those soft, sun-lit patterns,
no one the same—
no one to be repeated again,
—ever—

All the quiet joys and pride,
all the deep sorrows that only every mother feels,
and yet, uniquely, my own . . .

And in this Sunday silence,
in the quietness of memory and birth of understanding,
I can wonder at their uniqueness,
at the different paths they have taken—

But does it really sink into my soul
that I, their mother, am also unique?—
By God's intricate design,
a joy to them in their memories of me,
A soft, sun-lit pattern
never to be repeated again,
—ever—

John Preston Beck
POEM FOR PEACE

Unto you I release, my "Poem for Peace,"
to do with what you may;
But it is my prayer, that you will share,
the Love of the Infinite Way.

For Peace is found, on the common ground,
in the Souls of all Mankind,
And it comes from above, through the gift of Love,
in the hopes that you will find.

Now the place to start, is the bottom of the heart,
for it touches all of you;
And it's from people who care, and people that share,
that God's true Love shines through.

For Peace on Earth, came the New Birth,
and it came to set us free;
So let us employ, the Love and Joy,
for all the world to see.

And never forget, from the very onset,
that in all the things you do;
That you can release, your "Poem for Peace,"—
for LOVE begins with YOU !

Norma Foss Chernis
AT NINETY

I've never been old before,
And there is no way to open that door.
I know what it's like to be young and free
And to make all the plans that you wish to be,
But I've never been old before.

At times, I feel I'm the same inside,
But lined and aged on the outer side.
So how do I act to meet that space
That falls between age and the unlined face,
Since I've never been old before.

And, since I've never been old before
I often wonder more and more,
When that last door of life is closed,
And I have earned my last repose,
Will youth and age become the same
When we meet again on that Higher Plain?
Because . . . I've never been old before.

Dawn Ewald
FLY AWAY

Come fly away
with me.
To a place far
away.
A place where you
can be anything
you want to be.
A place where you
don't have to think
of tomorrow.
A place where you're
not disturbed.
Where you can leave
your troubles and
problems behind.

How do you get there?
Just close your
eyes and dream.

Gerald R Simonds
9/30/34-1/1/87

Gerald R Simonds
ALONE

To Rick Carney—a friend.

Speak to her softly
In the purple shades of wonderment
And call out to the triangles
Of a waiting moment
Each beating note of a crystal
Remembered fragrance.
Draw gently back into the shadows
Of Little Boy Time and see behind
Me the shape of something wanted.
Remember the velvety curve
Of a speaking lip
Saying words—only words
Invested with meanings I gave;
I gave because I knew
Her song was for other ears.
Shatter the fire ice rainbow
Sprinkling frost of loneliness among
My hunger frightened memories.
Her brow a curve in flatted fifths
Tracing intimate scales to
Secret sonatas, a symphony in muted
Fire opal alabaster;
Falling waves of stardust sprinkled
Dusk courting her shoulders with a touch
Like a tenderly caressing fingertip,
Scenting the purple evening dark
With the clean fragrance of nearness;
Her walk a fluid movement Debussy
Sought and never found
With just the barest echo trace of wind
Swept beaches and the majesty of rolling surf.
Touch her softly, both hands fingertipped
Beside her eyes—
For she cannot see.
And tell her of the falling emeralds
With multicolored coals trapped inside
That fall through the overturned bowl
Of the nightsky arch overhead.
Sit beneath the willow tree—carve an
Initial upon the bark, and listen to
The wind converse with branches that
Weep her leaving before she goes.
Take her hand and place upon the palm a
Kiss—

A lock for which only one key exists—
Buried behind the shimmering curtain
Northern Lights paint across her eyes.
Broken pieces of eternity sift
Around her spread skirt, belled out
On the deep blue grass carpeting our glade,
And she suddenly lifts her head
So I can see only her profile
Etched against the streaming Milky Way—
I know
She is going.
I cry out silently against time
Because it moves between a dream
And me;
And so the willow weeps alone, but for
Me—and fire dust falls from the apex
Of a universe Entropy has taken from my hand.
Tomorrow waits for my coming and the currents
Of moments are irresistible.
I cannot stay—
She fades, in her walk over star pathways
Leading away from me,
Tomorrow, or the day after enfolds her
Merging her with the time stream
Of inevitability.
Tell her the willow is barren
And colors have left the star stream
Ladders across the sky.
Tell her moments never end, but march
To a dirge in front of my blinding eyes.
Make her listen
To the wind—
To the wild, free surging
Song of the sea
I could not sing because I did
Not have the words,
Or the voice
To sing. And in the warm, soft
Place she closes her eyes upon
When the steel bright cut of day
Wounds the heart,
Let her hear the music I could
Not compose,
To the poem I could not write;
Let her feel the imprint in her
Palm, and the touch of my
Fingertips beside her eyes.
And tell her—
I am alone.

Robert DeLeno
INFANT FEAR

Little Benny is faced with a nightmare
A monster that flows through his veins,
His mother's not capable of helping him
In fact she's the cause of his pain!

Daddy's not much to remember
Just mother's night out on the town,
Instead of popcorn and a movie
A dirty hallway seemed safe and sound.

There's no sign of relief for my future
While I lie in my pen and shake,
For it seems I've been punished severely
Without making my first mistake.

A trinket or a tourniquet
I'm feeling used,
Mother looks like shit
Worn out and abused.

Complications in Benny's liver
Is all he'll ever be,
An empty kindergarten desk
Now has vacancy.

Cynthia D Minnick
BLAKELEE FAMILY RESTAURANT

To my son, Eric, who said I could do it!

As you step into our door
One of the first things you see is our black and white checkered floor
Listen carefully on the jukebox
the oldies play.
Singing us into the memories of another day.
Smile as you're greeted by one of your nice friends.
They will serve you until the very ends!
In the kitchen we have our cooks,
so much is their special talents
not learned from books!
Let's take a little look at your dishes.

And hope you get all your wishes,
Because if you don't get everything
your way
Our nice manager to his help
will have something to say.
As you step out of our door
And off our black and white
checkered floor,
We hope you liked everything in
sight.

Christina M Guk
RHAPSODY OF THE SKY

This poem is dedicated to my mother and father, Mary Elizabeth and Edward Sylvester Luks.

When I was a young girl
running barefoot and free,
the clouds in the heavens
played often with me.

Peeking and poking in scattered
array,
changing their colors at close of the
day.
A cycle for dreamers—the dawn
through the dusk,
create fantasy journeys laced with
perfume and musk.

High in the heavens and toes on the
ground,
exhilaration unleashed . . .
imagination unbounds.
The portraits I've harnessed, pass
swiftly away.
A whimsical journey on a soft, lovely
day.

A twinkling curtain
descends from the sky,
applauding the rhapsody . . .
in my heart and my eye.

Meridyth Howard
KIMBERLY
She was very beautiful. Got
everything she could ask for.
She achieved high marks. But she
wanted more.
Food was one thing that created
tension.
Other people noticed, but did not
mention.
Her weight like her marks, dropped
very low.
Her once beautiful skin didn't even
glow.
She made a wish upon a star . . .
But that one little wish went too far.
As she lay in a hospital bed
extremely emaciated.
The help from the doctors definitely
unappreciated.
Although her thoughts steered her
wrong.
Her will was still much too strong.
She said, "To be the THINNEST was
the BEST."
At age fifteen she died . . . of cardiac
arrest.

Cheryl Cunningham-Finley
TOGETHER
Many times you voiced your feelings
I listened with my ears and with my
heart
Never did I bother to mention I
shared your feelings
I now realize that would not have
been a bother at all
Our lives could have possibly taken
off in a different direction;
TOGETHER!
But, instead our love is like the
forbidden fruit.
We can share precious moments
But, they must come to an end.
We can share thoughts, dreams, and
wishes
But, they will be just that.
TOGETHER we should be—APART
we must be.

Margaret Carthan

Margaret Carthan
THE SILENT RIVER

To my family with love.

The Silent River lay still and deep
As a slumbering child fast asleep
And yet I know that within your
shores
Lurks many dangers and so much
more
Death and destruction, diseases that
hide
Its ugly terror from the human eye.

As I sit on your banks, watching the
water so quiet
I think on the mystery that's hid from
sight
Why is it so, and how can it be
That you can rise and swallow me
Just like a great creature out in the
Sea

And when you arise with such power
and might
Destroying and devouring everything
in sight
You then return and quietly lay
As still and calm as a peaceful day.

Margaret Carthan
THE MYSTERY OF THE APPLE
How doth growth that apple upon the
tree
Aha, A mystery for the eye to see
The leaves are green, the branches
brown
Yet the apples they're green, yellow,
red, and round

How doth growth that apple upon the
tree
Did it originate from you or me
The tree root buried in the cold, cold
ground
Surrounded with green grass all
around

Was it the planter, the water, the one
who cultivated
What maketh it grow? From whose
pattern does it take?
That causes that apple to take the
shape
From the tiny seed to the size it
makes
Was it the tree, or leaves, the ground,
you or me
Nay, the mystery is far more greater
you see
Than the seed, the sower, or keeper
of the tree
Or the wind that moves the leaves so
free

Look High, Skyward, gaze far above
That apple on the tree came from
Love

Margaret Carthan
WHAT IS A POEM
What is a poem?
Is it a few scattered lines written here
or there
Without meaning or fulfillment,
empty words laying bare
Just meaningless words written
without any phrase to be put aside
and there it stays
Or carelessly thought upon in one's
idle time, Or cast aside and never
brought to mind
Words that do not tell a story,
Worthless of any glory
Is this a poem?

Nay, a Poem is much more than any
of these
Poem touches the heart and then it
leaves
A feeling of warmth, brought by a
warming breeze
It stirs up the mind, and spirit within,
for there the thoughts and phrases
begin
Teaches, Instructs, Guides, and Gives
a deeper purpose to the way we live
Motivates our actions in our work
and play
Yes, Poems are worth more than
words of yea or nay

A Poem can make the heart grow
fond, It can soar one's spirit far up
beyond
It can even cause a melody to flood
the heart, And make all gloom and
sadness depart
It motivates the mind to think, When
sometimes in despair it sinks
Can look beyond and see afar, And
fling its phrases amidst the stars
So altho its letters are very few
This my friend is what a Poem can
do!

Margaret Carthan
IMAGINARY DREAMS
Pots and Pans, A sink full of dishes
While dreaming thoughts of fame and
riches
Beds to make, Rugs to sweep
Hungry people, ready to eat.
Why can't I dream, Why can't I plan
Even tho my castles are only of sand
Tell me—who has ever built a rocket
Who hasn't at one time fixed a socket
So while you sit in your fame aglow
My simple imaginations gives me
joy.

S E Gladden
WASTED DREAMS
Walk to the light and the shadows fall
behind
Says the prophet to the loss as they
trip on his mind
Walking backwards to the cross
And embracing their shadows

Circular worship
They move to stop
Yet they dream at the bottom
Of waking at the top

Fly to the Son and below fall the
clouds
Says the bird to the plane as the
passengers jump out
Easing upwards like a snake to the
flute
The progress undone by the
parachute

Wax and feathers
They rise to drop
Yet they dream at the bottom
Of waking at the top

S E Gladden
ALLATOONA SLEEPS
Allatoona sleeps, sheets of midnight
Blue waters are blackened then
Crickets crying, bats are flying
Deer eat roses that tickle their noses

Allatoona tosses, losses of purity
Mosses growing on the limbs of
maturity
Lightning bug wailing, lamenting in
light
Lonesome lives stir hornet hives
Dying for crying for someone to love

The clouds are flying on wings of
vapor
Tails of fog may drag along
Treants awaken, leaves of disease
Lapping up raindrops flavored by
man

Allatoona turns, a septic urn
Moths on my window, my light still
burns
Saddened trees, a somber lake
Where are the bears? Nobody cares
But wait, accomplice, wait for the
storm

S E Gladden
SAILING WITH A DROWNING MAN
I was whirling around with dragonfly
eyes
Fourteen frames in one and a cross
between each
And Jesus hung there, dwarfing my
life
Calling to me while I was still in
reach

To think that the wind once thought it
was water
And the ocean's afraid of blowing
away
A trial's a way to put it, but the
execution's closer
To the feeling of it all when you're
reeling through the fall
And it drips, slow, tickling cheeks
and nose

I was clinging to the mast when envy
took hold of me
And shook me around, made me look
at the sail
Swallow the breeze and you'll skim
through the seven seas
But don't forget to look over the rail

To think that the cross now thinks
that it's Jesus
And Jesus is afraid of rotting away
Sailing for sport and forgetting the
rest
The puddle would be gone, but my
soul would have a stain
And my eyes would be too dry to see

S E Gladden
THE FALL
I am a shadow and I'm groping for my form
It's hard to see when the light is blocked out
I am the rain and I'm stretching for the storm
It's hard to pour the puddle back into the cloud
I am a scabbard and I'm searching for my sword
I keep coughing rust, but know I had a blade
I am a crown and I'm looking for my lord
I lay in the dust, but remember words he said
Yes, I remember, when I was eighteen
The silver lining was lurking in my bed
And now an ember, I'm too old to dream
The silver lining's just sitting on my head
I used to be so . . . so . . . I can't recall
For I'm the crash site and I'm empty of the fall

Steven G Alston
I MET A MAN
I met a man, awhile ago
Whose face was all aglow
I said, what is it that makes you smile so
He said, "'Tis the beauty of nature, don't you know
The grass so green, the trees how tall they grow,
The lovely flowers all in a row
That, my friend is what makes me smile so."
I said, "That's fine as things go,
But there's more to life than things that grow,

Like things that make one sad, you know.
War and crime and sickness, oh.
But still you think you should smile so."
"Yes," he said for I do know,
That even through adversity,
goodness will flow.

Valerie M Jacoby
RIVERS
Rivers
Flowing fast
Rapid and wild
Remind me of life
Long

Debra A Lea
THE FLING
All hope, All desire
burned by failure's fire!
Only pain and sorrow
but no tomorrow.
We try to go on
but there is no hope to lean on.
We fight the fears,
and choke on the tears.
We try to pretend
but our hearts do not mend.
As time passes, memories fade
an we relearn not to be afraid.
The years go by and we all weep and cry,
but we carry the sting of failure's first fling!

Rhonda L Valeriano and Son Sam
TWO-WHEELIN' SAM
Sam is five years old
and still a little kid.
But he knows how to ride
his bike
just the way his
daddy did.
With his feet on the pedals
and his hands on
the handlebars,
Sam speeds down our sidewalk
and stays away from cars.
Yes, just yesterday Sam was little—
now look at how he's grown!
Riding his two-wheeler
all on his own!

Christine De Anna
SHE'S ONLY IN MY THOUGHTS NOW

To Her Family—She was a source of inspiration.

I thought of her this morning
as I woke from a peaceful sleep.
I smiled when I saw her face
pictured in my mind. Her voice was sweet
as she bid me "hello."
But this morning, I walked in
only to find she had left her room
much like she had the week before.

Now I sit here alone in silence.
As I look out at the painted blue sky
I recall the few short weeks I've known her
and have to sit back and sigh.

Thinking back to the time I saw her last,
the image of her smiling face
has made the days between travel fast.

She is only in my thoughts now
but I wouldn't have her any other way.
I thank God for the day I met her
and thank her family for bringing her my way.

Mary Lorne
I WONDER
I wonder what this world is made of
Hurt and greed and lies
But I forget my painful past
When I look into your eyes.

For there's the warm sincerity
And there's the love I know
That I can always turn to
When there is nowhere else to go.

I know you'll always be there for me
As I'll always be there for you.
And anything that I would want
I know you would try to do.

I know someday we will say goodbye
As everyone usually does
But Heaven holds vacancies, and
Happiness will always be as it was.

Mildred M Dryden

Mildred M Dryden
THE YOUNG BLACK MOTHER
She walks very tall;
She is sometimes responsible for all.

She carries herself with beauty;
As she performs her duty.

She is almost indispensable;
She has to go on whether or not she is able;
She often falls asleep while sitting at the table.

She is extremely progressive;
She is also very possessive.

The young black mother is a marvel to see;
She does it all like one, two, three.

Jeri King
HIS FIRST DAY OF SCHOOL

This poem is dedicated to our special little boy, Jason, who started his kindergarten year late because of foot surgery. He kept this poem tucked in his pocket every day for the first few weeks of school. We love you, Jason. Love, Mom.

Your first day of school,
a day so big and new.
I don't know who is prouder,
is it me or is it you.
A world of new beginnings,
is a song to start singing.
For today I let you go,
the first step down your road.
Have fun today,
as you learn and play.
I'll be thinking of you,
every moment of today.
And when you come back home,
proudly showing what you have done.
I will give you that hug of joy,
my little man, my big school boy.

Doris M Kempski
HER ROOM
She is suspended in time
She is trapped within herself
Her emotions are running wild
She is only free in the darkness
of her room
For how long
Until the sun rises
Then she is back to the world
of confusion
Where she lives in the nonexisting
world of her creators
She is angry
She is confused
She is a prisoner of her creators
She is petrified to expose her real self
To the people she encounters
Day and night

Doris M Kempski
COME OUT TO PLAY
The weather is overcast
Her eyes are cloudy
Rain is pouring down her cheeks
Her soul is flooded
A tornado just hit her world
She has built a sanctuary
Where she will hide
Until the storm ends
Until she sees a rainbow
Hover over her shelter
Will she come out to play

Jeanné Harness
THE RED ROSE OF LOVE

To my beloved family.

The rose with sweet smells
and a drop of water
on the luscious petals,
flowing down the red river
as you fall in love with
the red rose of love

Jay (Jerry Burnett)
FEELING LOVE
Fingers tapping my emotions
Awakening thoughts and feelins
Once thought cold and dead.
I'm glad I met you.

Awareness entering my soul
Presenting a life filled with love,
Compassion,
Honesty.
I'm glad I touched you.

Bringing scattered emotions together
Allowing me peace within
Such a long time felt.
I'm glad to love you.

Ines Del Castillo

Ines Del Castillo
CIRCLE OF TIME
I walked through the mist
of lime and apricot,
serenity, autumn leaves,
feathers and songs . . .
In the circle of time I heard a tear,
in anguish, dying hurt, there was a man,
his pain so deep and true!
I extended my hands
to touch, to love, to hold him in my arms,

then sad, I realized
I was transported very far
in waves of time
to another berth, to another
land . . .
Hopeless I tried to reach,
it was too late, my time was gone
my time was past . . .
I turned into the mist
of lime and apricot
and there, over the feathers
of the wind, I cried.

Loralee Clark
DECEMBER

We know
cracked ice
can shatter easily.

Ours
is not built
on substantial accounts.

We don't
know to talk
of truths to
one another.

We wait
to cry
when the ice
splinters
in the coldest winters.

Lillian Chambrun
SO GOD DOES LOVE THE WORLD

So God does love the world,
And when He plays his hand;
For players, we are picked,
To care for sea and land.

So God does guard us all,
And animals, bird friends;
Let us protect their rights,
As we can make amends.

So God foresees our needs,
With each new, blossomed tree;
Not mar this global earth,
Take care, and leave things be!

Nicky Stinson
END OF THE ROAD

To all the teenagers whose parents did not listen, hear their problems, and ease their pain. To all the parents who never knew, I dedicate this poem to you.

Life is not a bowl of cherries
Though everyone thinks it is.
We all have so many worries
All we want is for them to end.

Today's teenager can't cope
So, some turn to marijuana and dope
Parents don't understand
The pressure on the teenager at hand.
The child is yelling for "help"
The parents tell the child to help
himself.

So, you decide to die
Some people call it suicide.
Your parents are left standing—
wondering why?
Their child chose to die.

There they are standing in black
Placing flowers on the casket.
Ashes to ashes—dust to dust
Their parents ask themselves
Why didn't he come to us.

There you are freezing cold
Lying in a wooden box.
There's nothing you can do but lay
and rot
Because you reached the end of the
road.

The end of the road,
Where a lot of teenagers go.
They never return
That's a lesson we all must learn.

Randall Acuff
IT WAS GOD

It Was God Who Gave Her To Me
Could I Have Got Her On My Own
The Answer To That
Is No

On My Own
Could I Keep Her
The Answer Still
Is No

It Is The Power Of God Within Us
That Draws Us To Each Other
And The Way She Loves And Treats
Me
Makes Me Want No Other

Her Love Is Always With Me
Makes Me Feel So Good
I Do Need Her Beside Me
The Way This Husband Should

Miracles They Happen
For Sure It's Plain To See
For It is God Who Gave Me To Her
And Gave Her To Me

Ramon H Silton
THE MIDNIGHT SHOW

In the wakeful haze of morning's
night
My mind invents you without my
will,
And you sit beside me again,
Alive in the purple darkness.
How clear the curve of your lips,
And the deep, searching softness
Echoed in the infinity behind your
smile.
How lively the hint of laughter
That waits in the crinkles of your
eyes.
I am hopelessly engulfed
By the innocence of pure friendship
That flows from you in a fertile
stream.
And I cannot repress a secret smile
As I snuggle into the depths
Of that inner warmth
Which radiates from you
Like a softly crackling fire.

Mandy C Humphrey

Mandy C Humphrey
THE INVITATION

What would you say if I gave you a
line,
A piece of my mind, and a piece of
my time.
I'd show you a beach where the
waves are dark blue—
And the stars in the sky appear
almost brand-new.

I'd give you a view where the lights
are a sight—
And the twinkle in your eyes shine
ever so bright.

Or how about a walk through the
snow or the rain—
Or a drive along Anytown's
Christmas Tree Lane.

I could steal you away and feed you
cheese, bread and wine—
Up in the mountains, alone where
we'd dine.

That is an invitation to do whatever
you'd like—
'Cause I'm yours for ONE WHOLE
NIGHT!

The ending to this list of
rhymes is . . .

Here's hoping that soon you'll be
mine.

Macie Castleberry
TAKE THE TIME

This poem is dedicated to Craig. From his mother, Sandy Turner.

Take the time to help fly the kite.
Take the time to help push the bike,
Take the time to watch him play,
Listen to what he has to say.

This thing he will always know.
That you loved him so—
Take him, guide him, by the hand.
Let him know you understand.

For if you don't even still.
Time will pass and he will
Leave not at last, and
You will wonder then—
How much was gone in the wind.

Things that didn't matter,
How they cost.
Time gone is simply lost.

Sarah Hilliard
THE HAMMERING SEA

To Russ, our life has been like the sea—it's time for peace—forevermore. I love you.

Grey clouds loom overhead,
Rolling waves hammering upon the
shore—
Crackling thunder and bright
lightning,
The fireworks that bring daylight to
the moor.

Rolling waves hammering upon the
shore,
Whitecaps and foamy brine
Beating against the jagged rocks—
Throwing spew and spray.

Silver slivers of the moon,
Seeking escape from the gloomy
haze.
Rolling waves hammering upon the
shore,
For endless time—forevermore.

Cari Lin
MY TEACHER, MY FRIEND

You are my special friend.
I know that can never end.
When my doll was left out in the rain,
You dried my tears of pain.
You raised me with truth and love,
And called me your little dove.
A teacher and a friend—
The list will never end.
One day I know we'll have to part.
But I'll always love you with all my
heart.
There can never be another,
As special as you—my dear mother.

Sherrie E Jones
FEELING FINE

Standing tall doing my own thing
Hey! I'm Feeling Fine!
I will open my mouth in positiveness
and sing my blues away
I'm Feeling Fine!
As I approach life its pros and cons in
existence from day to day
I'll keep a positive attitude as i go
along my way
I'm Feeling Fine!
Giving Love, Getting Love, The Best
that Life can offer
Uplifting lives, and brightening eyes
Oh! Yes I'm Feeling Fine!

Lisa D Comstock
SANCTUARY

Calm is the owl so
brilliant in flight.
Swoops down on his prey . . .
As I sit and watch.
Trees stand stifled
the breeze so light.
The moon shines deeply,
on the swamp tonight.
My private sanctuary
behind our house,
keeps our sanity
for, I and my spouse.
Three children we have
all under five,
so this is our time,
for us to revive.
The cars in a distance.
The lights from afar,
fade out as we listen
to the swamp and the stars.

E Devlin O'Connell

E Devlin O'Connell
THE IMMIGRANTS

In loving memory of my dear mother and father, Patrick J. O'Connell and Mary C. Devlin, who immigrated from Ireland to the great United States of America.

They left behind their home and
loved ones,
Many years ago.
Traveled over water on a ship so
slow.
Two people boarded who never
before met.

As the ship pitched and rolled the days
And the nights passed,
Many friendships from chance meetings,
Did come to pass.

When the ship passed the Lady and immigration
Was done,
The two individuals did part to take
Different paths.

One went to Bridgeport the other Detroit,
Where communications did follow back and forth.
As time went slowly a decision was made,
That courtship would bring them together to stay.

They were married in Detroit on a bright October day.
The two immigrants from Ireland who met
Aboard ship, became my mother and father,
Who since have passed.

Love for each other born aboard ship,
Till the end did last.

E Devlin O'Connell

THE BIRDS

When you awake in the morn in Florida, you can hear the birds at play.

They seem so happy and lively that the Cold North is so far away.

You see and hear so many and some with strange sounds and names.

Like blue jays, cardinals, egrets, pelicans and mockingbirds too.

But, the strangest by far and the easiest to find is the snowbird from afar.

They can be spotted from afar, usually in a restaurant or bar, in pursuit of the early bird.

They make strange sounds and fly here and there to catch the finest early bird listed on the bill of fare.

Jean E Edwards

MY FAVORITE PLACE

I often go to my favorite place
when I want to be alone.
To get away from all my woes;
to get away from all my foes.
It is a place of beauty, peace and joy.
Far away and yet so near.
The sun is always shining here,
and fall is the time of year.
The sky is blue, the grass is green;
my favorite trees ablaze with color.
Fragrant flowers grace the landscape,
every color of the rainbow.
As I sit beneath a tree,
my friend, a deer, approaches near.
As she pauses by the brook,
I take in all her beauty.
She is not afraid, nor I;
because no one can harm us here.
For this place is only in my mind.

Richard Hall

THE FLAME WITHIN MY HEART

The flame within my heart,
Is like a burning fire,
Altho we are miles apart,
You are my heart's desire,

I love to hold you in my arms,
And caress you tenderly,
I love you with all my heart,
Altho mine you can never be,

We knew that years ago,
As we talked about our love,
You have been my gift from heaven,
My prayers have been answered from above.

When I gazed into your beautiful brown eyes,
I had memories of long ago,
When you said goodnite sweetheart,
It's time for you to go,

Nidia Krimilda McPherson Hoag

Nidia Krimilda McPherson Hoag

THE MASQUERADE BALL

To my sons, Erik Anthony and Michael Andrew.

The Masquerade Ball goes on and on
With the rhythm of hypocrisy
And the champagne of lies,
Intoxicating their souls,
and this observer suffers,
Holding a cup of wisdom
and a full glass of realities.

Nidia Krimilda McPherson Hoag

FOOLS LIKE ME

I am a fool with hopes and dreams
that wishes romance and tender love.
Why can't I learn that
only few are fools like me.
To find a man that is sincere,
honest and kind with tender heart
It is like looking around
for a white pearl lost in the snow.
But fools like me with hopes and dreams will be forever only fools.

Nidia Krimilda McPherson Hoag

THE SEASONS

The snow is falling
the wind is blowing
the Winter is having its way
making me think of the changes
making me dream of the past
giving me hope for the future
leaving the Spring of my life
and the warm Summertime
of my spirit and the leaves
in the Fall of my life.
The Winter, Fall, Spring and Summer
the love, the thoughts, smiles and
tears will fill my heart with
contentment
and let the sun rise again.

Nidia Krimilda McPherson Hoag

MATURITY

I can sit down and think of age
like a sweet blessing in disguise.
I do not want my painful youth
and getting older is a charm.
I am feeling wiser, more serene
sometimes with pains
and aching back.
But I do have so much to learn,
so much to see, so much to write.
I left the yesterdays behind
and now the stormy time is gone.
It's nice perhaps for a short while
to feel old age can be such charm.

Nidia Krimilda McPherson Hoag

MOONLIGHT

When I was driving home tonight
I couldn't help but look up high.
The moon is bright
and I am thinking all the time.
It is so beautiful and quiet
and with no special thoughts in mind
I felt some peace inside my heart.
I started to sing all the way home
feeling so good, feeling so fine.
The moon so bright
in the dark sky, shining on me
giving me light
and the most peaceful time tonight.

Nidia Krimilda McPherson Hoag

ADVICE

I do remember an old man
he had white hair
and a sweet smile.
It was so very long ago.
He told me, child,
life is a crazy carnival
you have some thrills,
excitement, laughs,
but only lasting a short while.
So run and have a real good time
Because tonight after midnight
the cotton candy will get dry
and all the hustlers will get tired.
The Teddy Bears will go in a box
and they will move to another town.
You see my Dear, most of the time
like vicious circles in our lives
from happy moments moving on
to sad and lonely ones at times,
life is just like a Carnival
go on my child, run, laugh, have fun.

Nidia Krimilda McPherson Hoag

SPRINGTIME

Come in sunshine
and give me warmth
it has been Winter much too long
I want to smell
the sweet perfume
and fill my soul
with the delights
of all the flowers now in bloom
Please butterflies
perform your dance
exhilarating playful ones
come back songbird
and sing for me
I want to hear sweet melodies
to soothe my heart
and fill my mind
with glorious thoughts
of love, sweet love.

Nidia Krimilda McPherson Hoag

EMPTY GARDEN

They told me very long ago
If I plant roses
They will grow,
in a good soil
with sun and rain.
But now I'm learning painfully
from the great book of life,
even with love and warm sunshine
Some roses never, never grow.

Nidia Krimilda McPherson Hoag

NOSTALGIA

In myth of Winter,
Up in this northern prairie lands
with many lakes, and bitter cold,
I find myself wishfully dreaming
away.
Far from the place where I was born
by the warm seas,
tropical land of sun and rain;
It is not hard to fantasize
putting my feet inside
the warmest water and dark sand,
feeling the sun
on my shoulders and my back;
and me, only recalling pleasant
things,
of my lost youth and my lost love.
The cold long Winter now ahead
makes me so lonesome for
the deep blue sea, the sun and rain,
the swaying palm trees,
the fertile land where I was born,
far from the cold and lonely frozen
beauty
of this northern prairie land.

Tammy Martinez

WHAT AM I?

To my friends and family, with love.

What am I? Am I a person who thinks they have seen enough. A person who figured out that life's just too rough. I don't really know and sometimes don't bother to care. I am only here because someone put me there. I did not ask to come. Now I am forbidden to go. Sometimes I wonder if I am my own friend or foe? I just keep on living trying to make people see. The silent cry for help that I have inside of me. When I feel like breaking the forbidden rule I don't feel like going on. The love and caring of my friends really comes on strong. I think what I am. I am like a little bird who has not yet left the nest. Who has only seen the world around herself, and does not care about the rest. As I watch the rest of the world go by I want to go too but I cannot and I wonder why. Then I realize that just like the little bird I have not yet learned to fly.

Walter A Czepiga

PERSISTENCE

Persistent dandelion am I,
Giving up never,
I rise like the dew,
In the morning sun,
To form a cloud,
And move across the sky,

Collecting power along the way,
Only to fall down another day.

Persistent snowflake am I,
Gracefully falling,
Cold and beautiful,
Hitting the ground,
Many will melt,
And make no sound,
But together shall cover,
Like a white wedding gown.

Mitch Davis
THE DREAM
It was the national finals rodeo the year I can't recall
the bull's name was Romeo he had made many a cowboy fall
I hoped I wouldn't draw him but I guess my luck ran out 'cause as I unfolded the paper I heard the other cowboys shout
I thought that it was over that I'd never make the ride
I thought I should run for cover and find a place to hide,

Well the time finally came and it was my turn to ride
Old Romeo still looked the same he still had the fire in his eyes
So I tightened up my spurs and I pulled on my rope
and hollered at the gateman, let's give this bull a go
well he spun to the left and he spun to the right
and I'll have to admit he put up quite a fight,

I thought the ride would never end but the whistle finally blew
and with that ride I scored so high I knew I couldn't lose
But then I woke up as the sun was shining in
My national finals rodeo had come to an end.

Joyce Luke Dailey
ONE ALONE

With much love to my sons, Bradley, Roger, and Ray.

It seems as though I'm One Alone,
yet there are people all around me.
I stand alone, outside the world.
There is no one for me to cry out to.
I must bear my burdens, as One Alone. I have my lover, I have my friends, but alas, I am One Alone.
I have but one life to live, and all my love to give, but, it seems, I am One Alone.
I have my sons, but soon they will be grown.
Again, that leaves me, One Alone.
Today I live and love. I have so much to give, yet I lay awake at night, One Alone.
In time, as it quickly goes by, my life rushes on,
And I will die. Again, once again, I will be, One Alone.

Georganne Hernandez
DREAMS
Last night I was sleeping in my bed, when something came and hit my head.

I looked up and down and my shoes were dancing all around.

Paper was flying, pens were writing, markers were coloring and scissors were fighting and clothes were coming out in style.

Boy, anything can happen when your mind goes wild.

J K Smith
I NEED A HUG
I need a hug
I want a hug
I cannot hug
I do not know how to hug
What is a hug?
A meaningful embrace?!
An act of emotion?!
A way to show your feelings?!
I do not know how to show my feelings
I do not know how to hug
I <u>need</u> a hug

Bernadine Trimble
OLD MAN JACK FROST

To my dear husband, Paul I, our grandchildren, Brian, Aaron, Tera, Michael Nathn, Paul II.

Last night while I was sleeping in my bed,
someone came and painted the window over my head
Mommy, mommy, I yelled at her, come quick,
look at my window, someone has played a trick
See the silvery designs all over the pane,
when I went to sleep last night it was plain
Now I see trees, mountains and streams,
beautiful things I see only in my dreams
Mommy was laughing, she thought I was funny,
and then she said, I'll tell you what, honey,
Have you ever heard of Old Man Jack Frost
well, he flew through last night and tossed
Beautiful silvery snowflakes in the air
looks like Mother Goose combing her children's hair
Frosty snowman is smiling ear to ear,
'cause it's so cold and he won't melt a tear
The trees look like a winter wonderland,
from Old Man Jack Frost's paint brush in his hand
So enjoy the beauty while it lasts,
when old Smiley Sun comes out it melts fast.

Janet K Thomas
IT DOESN'T SEEM LIKE MUCH TO SAY
Christmastime is here again;
soon another new year will begin.
It seems only yesterday I was living at home
but the years have passed and I'm on my own.
Even with all the mistakes I've made
you've always helped me through my hardest days.
For three very dear people, I wish only the best.
You've all given me so many things
I want nothing for you less
than all the joy and love in this world.
It doesn't seem like much to say
but I love you all
on this Christmas Day.

Mildred Minnis
PUZZLE OF MY LIFE
God handed me a puzzle of my life!
One of the hardest pieces to be fitted was being a wife.
I thought being a mother could be fitted easily enough, but here too, I found the edges a little rough.
The first few pieces of my life, God fitted those himself.
Once those pieces were fitted, God said, "I'll need your help!"
Those first pieces were when he gave me a father and mother,
He also included an older brother.
God said, "Now let me see, that's not enough family.
Four sisters and three more brothers are what I'll add.
These pieces should make your heart glad. Think I will place you in the poor category."

So—the pieces of the puzzle were fitted not a happy story.
I thought God at times didn't care, especially when he gave us a hearth that was cold and a table that was bare.
I've struggled through life to put each piece in place.
Once they were fitted, I could see a big smile on God's face!
A cold hearth and a table bare to a lot of people was nothing rare.
For me it was a piece to be fitted to teach me to love (care), to give (share)!

Darlene Bright
LOVE YOUR CHILDREN
Yes, also, love your children
Flesh of your flesh
Cloned to your perfection.
How can you not love
Your own perfect creation?
From bottles and bottles
Endless formula feedings
Of perfect vitamins and minerals
To grow into a vision
Your dream quest for perfection.
From diapers, pampers, and panties
To walking shoes—scuffed and polished
Scrapes and scratches on elbows and knees
Band-Aids, pain, and tears
Tears of joy all through the years.
Memories that last a lifetime
Remembered just like yesterday
The visions are all so clear
Though they may be out of sight
They are never out of mind.

Jessie M Koscel
THE WONDER OF IT ALL

To my daughter, Broné, and my grandchildren, Joshua, Jonathan, Jason and Justin.

From the tree of knowledge
flow the answers
Like ribbons in the breeze
To the questions all around us
Will the wonder ever cease

From the hearts of mankind
flow the memories
Like pollen in the breeze
To the children all around us
Will the wonder ever cease

From the far off darkness
flow the sunbeams
Like gold dust in the breeze
To the saddened all around us
Will the wonder ever cease.

Dale D Sutton
ON A COLD BLACK NIGHT
A black cloud covers the moon, darkness all around. I was falling but didn't know how far down, as a black cloud covers the moon.

A street light shadows my way, I was walking hand n hand with the lighting on a rainy day, as a street light shadows my way.

A cold frost covers my heart, we were being ripped at the seams being torn apart, as a cold frost covered my heart.

A fire fills my bones, longing for shelter, needing a home, living all alone, as a fire fills my bones.

As ice fills my lungs, I scream and fight for air with no one there to help or care, as ice fills my lungs.

As death steals my soul, I'm the first to live and the last to go, as death steals my soul . . . .

Ermadine Jeanie McIntire
MY TREASURES

To Kerma, Kermit and Kemit, my treasures.

First came a little girl with dark curly hair,
Second came a little boy so timid and fair.
Third came a little boy with dark brown eyes;
And these are my treasures that were sent from the skies.
God gave them to me to teach them of Him.
He didn't give them to me to teach them to sin.
Please Lord don't let me stumble, for the way is very steep.
Help me find the pathway for their tiny little feet.
These treasures that you've given me,
Are more valuable to me than gold.
Thank you Lord for giving me these loving little souls.
Oh Lord, if something should happen and I'd have to leave this world,
please keep my treasures shining, my precious boys and girl.

Bridgett Nasibi
WINDOWS OF MY SOUL
I awaken to the sound,
A very rhythmic sound.
It is the voice of my
Heart and soul within
Telling me to arise
To seek out the new day that has begun.
I listen to the melody
Of each pulsing beat
Telling me, asking me
What will you do to beat defeat?
I have courage,
I am victorious
I will not be afraid to
Answer the voice within,
But will be bold enough to face
The yearning,
Windows of My Soul!

Lazida Yacoobali

Lazida Yacoobali
THE BEAUTIFUL WORLD
This is a beautiful world.
With beautiful things to see,
Like tulips in the garden, and sweet smelling roses.
The thundering waters of the beautiful seas.
The beautiful trees and the windy breeze.
Buildings so big as far as the eyes can see.
The golden sun is peeping through the sky,
and shining all around us.
With a peaceful night the stars are so bright,
and the moon so peacefully calm.
This is a beautiful world,
with beautiful things to see.

Alice I Schmaltz
MY DAY
On an April day, I knew that this would be my day, I ask the sun to shine, it does, and then I sigh, I ask the flowers to bloom, they do, and I cry.
The birds come flying all the way, that's why I call this

My Day

As I lie here in sweet daydreams, the world is mine, or so it seems. There is not a cloud in the sky, not even a distraught or troubled eye. Even the music that plays at my ear, so soft and gentle I need not fear, for this is my day.

My little pet that sits so near, listening for bells that we must hear, she seems so peaceful and so at rest, I know at best, that this is my day.

I hope they never take this away, for what I've done, or I must pay, because of whom I should be. I must always feel love and be free, for this is truly a day made for me, my day.

Florence B O'Leary
OUR BUSY POOL

These poems are dedicated to my family, David and Kristina, for their love and encouragement.

Around our pool all kinds of things
Do flit, crawl, hop, or fly
It seems to have its own private life
As it lies there 'neath the sky.
In fact it sometimes seems so busy
With things coming and going round here
That I watch from my chair in amazement
For a miniature traffic cop to appear.
He'd send the bees in one line
While ants got organized in rows
Frogs would hop in the slow side
But in the fast lane spiders would go.
Birds would be scheduled at daybreak
While raccoons could come only at night
And we swimmers allowed only in a heat wave
Taking care to cause nothing a fright.
But here we really don't need a traffic cop
To set up any guidelines or rules
For we just follow God's simple give and take
And that suffices, round our busy pool.

Florence B O'Leary
SINS
Envy niggles
And pride thrusts
Anger sizzles
Then erupts.
Greed consumes
While lust burns
Sloth idles
With no urge.
Gluttony slavers
As jealousy feeds
Deadly sins
Covet our needs.

Bunny H Muir
THE SNOW ANGEL

In memory of my beloved father, Elwood Gill Heister.

Along the icy, rugged slopes of Shavano
the angel lies,
Her face upturned, her arms outstretched
In prayer, beneath the azure skies.

For centuries this gallant queen
Has stood on guard thru ice and snow,
But when the valley turns to green
She'll shed a tear, and slowly go.

Callie M Orr
THAT PASSING ANGEL
She wasn't a raving beauty,
Tho, you might have considered her cute;
There was something about her that got to you,
And stuck, like an undersized boot.
She didn't try to act deceiving,
Or possess any outstanding charms.
She just had that something about her,
And you knew she was made for your arms.

You could look, but you could never find her,
If you searched till your dying day,
Cause she'll only appear for a moment
Then quietly steal away.

You have to watch for her coming,
And hope you'll catch her in time.
For once she is gone, you will know it,
As was the misfortune of mine.

I only hope, that the next time
I'll realize, before it's too late,
And grab hold of that passing angel
To keep for my lifelong mate.

Bill Murphy
A POEM FOR THE C.I.A.
Ducks are strange animals,
The way they squat and squabble.

Sometimes they talk to you
As if you understand what they are saying.
And sometimes you do.

Bill Murphy
LICKETY SPLIT
Lickety split,
Quick as my dog's tongue,
Breathes the fire of light;
The light that dawns my day,
Furnishes warmth and bread
And lights the way.
You can make life complicated
But simple is the way.

Emma Hammack
OUR FADING GLORY
What has happened to the Golden Rule?
To the Scriptures and prayers that were taught in school.
Who can point with pride to the glory and honor
For which our heroes died?
Who can name the ill-gotten gain made through greed and lust?
With no regard to our motto:
"In God We Trust."
How many lives has this country gave
To protect the land of the free and the home of the brave?
Can we regain our principles that made America great?
Or do we have to accept our fate?
Why were they trampled in the dust?
Will not someone pray for us!

Annette Dion
A LOST LOVE
A place in my heart forever empty without you.
So much giving and giving with so little taking.
Your mind so stimulating,
a kiss, breathtaking.
I remember quiet times when a look, a glance
could bring a smile to my face.
Whisper something nice,
send me soaring into space.
Your confidence and assuredness
placed you at a distance.
Nobody could reach you,
your temper and willfulness.
But love we did,
and friends we were, too.
Forgiving is hard,
but that's what friends do.
Oh what a great cost
for a love forever lost.

Jeffrey S Kuehn
GONE AGAIN
My dear don't let what we have ever end. I know we are so far apart. You there and me going everywhere.

To never stop holding you is my only dream. To love you forever is what I want.

When I return we'll be together. In the short time we have we'll make up for all the lost time in between.

Your playful eyes, your loving ways, your body so lovely and most importantly your true beauty deep within is what keeps all my love for you.

The time to part has come again. I hold you tight but never want to let go. But with one last kiss I go on my way.

Veronica Edison
DREAMS WILL NEVER DIE
Always make your dreams
Bigger than your goals.
No matter how many goals you reach . . .
. . . Your dreams will never die.

Your goal is the mountain.
Your dream is the moon.
You'll reach the top of the mountain,
But you'll never reach the moon,
For dreams will never die.

Your goal is the moon.
Your dreams are the stars.
You'll reach the moon,
But never the farthest star,
For dreams will never die.

Carrie McLean
IN MY DREAMS
All night long, and every night
when I turn out the light,
I see you in my dreams
as plain as day before my eyes.

As fine as I have ever seen
you in my dream,
for every time I see you
I fall in love again.

First I came to you
then you came to me
now we are together,
I hope it will be forever.

Janet Lovell Cierocki
TOO
I love you, want you, need you far too much
You might be too young, I am too old
My heart beats fast, I long to feel your touch
I have too little to give to one so bold

I am a fool to feel this one desire
The icy touch of logic burns too cold
My heart will turn to ashes on this pyre
Of knowing I may have but cannot hold

Richard J Pentello
CHILD'S PARADISE

To Dad and Mom, Sabatino and Rose Pentello.

Horses going 'round and 'round;
Serpents soaring and climbing;
Squids jerking up and down;
Red-breasted birds gliding.

Cars moving on a track;
Trains' steel slicing a rail;
Shuttles creaking on a cable;
Wagons rolling on a trail.

Life-machines in a booth;
Statues, with hands out;
Pleasure-seekers everywhere;
Like ceramic tile grout.

Polly L Turpen
PERFECT LOVE
You love me more each day
Than You ever have before;
Even when I go astray,
You're still knocking at my door.

I could never love You more
For Your precious gift to me;
On the cross, my sins You bore,
Giving love so perfectly.

Your perfect love is all I long for;
Your perfect grace is all I need.
Mercy and truth have kissed my longing heart;
And there is nothing, no nothing
Like Your precious, perfect gift of love to me.

Lisa Latham
JENNY
Since the love you've given me
Is only in the past
Knowing that this love for you
Was never meant to last.

I never meant what I had said
When my heart it couldn't show
I'd tell right away my love
But as days go by you'll never know.

You're the one
Who meant so much
You're the one
That gave a tender touch.

The look in your eyes
Will never be the same
Since the love you've given me
Is only in the past.

Elizabeth Huggins
THE DANCE OF LONELINESS
I wanted to tell you
so we're convinced
that the
shadows
we felt between us
were a mere
misunderstanding
of the nature at hand;
It seemed so clear
that the ballroom dancers
were all but us.
The glitter and gold were all but gone;
and the fascination of a love
trimmed with diamonds
turned not into reality
but, instead, crashed down to earth
where the
serpents
of our hearts
tore
at our souls.

Ker
WISHES
May your food be tasty
Your spirits high.
Your atmosphere rich
With friends not shy.

A subtle breeze
To touch your skin,
A joke or two
To lighten within.

So be aware
Of things untold.
As time goes by
And does unfold
Of little warmth
And too much cold—"Love Thy Neighbor"

Eugene A Coughlin
YOU AND YOU ALONE

This little poem of mine is dedicated to Lovers, everywhere—regardless of age. You are blessed!

You and you alone, my only world, Dear,
You and you alone, my only dream;
You and you alone are a part of me,
Lasting love—our only theme.

I and I alone adore you,
I and I alone need you so;
I and I alone live just for you—
With you, my heart begins to glow.

We and we alone shall love forever,
We and we alone—all time to be—
We and we alone shall never part,
Not even for eternity.

You and you alone, my only world, Dear,
You and you alone, my only dream;
You and you alone are a part of me,
Lasting love—our only theme.

We and we alone shall love forever,
We and we alone—all time, our own—
We and we alone shall never part,
For I love you—and you alone.

Eugene A Coughlin
SHARING
Two Souls met, each burdened by the past,
each lonely for someone to
listen, to care;
Someone to laugh with—someone to cry with,
and they shared their pasts with one another.

And in so doing, they found something:
Voicing their fears seemed less fearful;
Stating their hopes seemed more hopeful;
Telling of their dreams seemed more natural.

Secrets long kept inside were revealed,
feelings long hidden were surfaced;
Emotions long denied were allowed expression,
and the two Souls slept easier.

Each ignored the personal demon,
helping the other,
and as the other felt better,
so did the first;
For they really cared for one another—
and this was as it should be.

Each Soul then loved—and was loved—
both were bathed in the warm glow
Of loving and caring and sharing;
and this was meant to be.

Delphine Ledoux
RED'S CHILI BEANS
It was dark and it was foggy;
It was cold and it was drear;
It was night time in November,
A disheartening time of year.

Red ate chili beans for dinner,
Washed them down with swigs of beer;
They were spicy hot and burning,
Smoke poured out from nose and ear.

Got so hot he couldn't stand it;
Went outside, shed spicy tear;
Came a rumble, then a blasting,
Lit the sky both far and near.

In the months and years that followed
Folks were haunted by the fear
Red would eat his famous chili
And the sky would disappear.

Kathy Doster
FIRST LOVE (IN A SIMPLER TIME)
He's young—so is she.
The clinking sound as they walk is familiar—
It's the marbles in his pocket.
There is still a trace of dirt on each face
As she carries his shirt past the seesaw.

It's hard to love first.
You can't sit by her in the lunchroom.
He can't hold your hand in the hall.
The kids tease you constantly,
As you walk red-faced side by side.

It's hard to love first.
Teachers, parents, and principals will CONDEMN you!! You'll get no help
From your friends.
So how does first love
EVER
Get started, especially
When you're only
10?

Robert A English
LOVE OF MY LIFE

To Jennifer, my loving wife.

How could I have known,
That cool November eve?
Why would I believe,
In fate etched in stone?

Together we sought to find,
The secret of passion everlast—
Two souls forever entwined,
By love's tender grasp.

Your faith has stood the test,
Enduring through the worst.
Extending complete forgiveness,
With you our love came first.
Now time for me to say,
My love for you is strong.
Time for me to show,
That I to you belong.

For you must now believe,
Our love's an endless song.
From your side I'll never leave,
My promise to you lifelong.

Robert A English
SWEET DIVERSION
I ventured along my chosen path,
Honoring my choice without reflection.
But sweetness entered to shear in half,
My road, altered by warm affection.

A hand in mine begged me to follow,
How could I forego the pleasure?
Upheld a promise to me to show,
A blissful union I'll always treasure.

I've wallowed in your inner glow,
Elusive to others you insist.
Though you deny, I surely know,
Only the blind could resist.

Lament eternal for sorrow inflicted,
Bestowed on me resides the blame.
With indecision sometimes afflicted,
To savor or douse our candle's flame.

Settled to resume my prior path,
To test I must, where it goes.
Cease not your smile nor laugh—
Jewels, from which your beauty flows.

Aline Dixon Dykes
THE SUN
The sun is my glowing gliding clock
It spends the winter traveling to and from Antarctica;
Waiting to pendulum back towards the North,
Heading for Greenland and Norway and me.

Gradually, I watch the sunrise which trends
Toward my South, or Violet window, where I winter in its
Weak, warm glow, lacking heat in the pale rays; inching towards my East window where it peeks in shamelessly in dead summer.

Then, reaching the zenith of its Northward orbit, turns Southward
And the heavens are timing the year by its passing;
To mark anew its foreordained trail to the icy
Blazing splendor, of the South Pole and its penguins.

I feel like an aged American Indian

Backed up in his smoky tepee,
Cogitating on his canyons and
gulches of time; and
I feel his spirit is noble, pulling
forward my afghan for warmth.

Anita M Lockhart
TO A NEW VENTURE
Like a moth emerging from darkness
Today you spread your wings.
Escape from your confining cocoon,
Fly on to greater things.

The heights you reach are only bound
By the power of your flight.
The only thing to limit you
Is the earthly creature's fright.

So test your strength
Make this your cry.
I cannot fail
For I only try.

Anita M Lockhart
MY SHADY LADY LOVE
I love a tarnished lady
Her shoes soiled with the dirt
Of the byways she has tread
Roads the gentry always skirt.
(Yet I'd walk the same path because
she chose it.)

My love has embraced too many men
With compassion her heart is
overflowing
She has clasped some to her breast
Unworthy of her knowing.
(But I love her all the more for her
charity.)

The quarrelling children around her
feet
Are not blue blood and pure.
They do not all share
The same father for sure.
(Still I cherish them for their
mother's sake.)

Her heart is good, her virtue is
sharing
Her home and her land, her main sin
is caring.
My love is notorious, her name is
well-known.
The lady I love is, America, my
home.

Anita M Lockhart
A SPECIAL PLACE
Near a quiet peaceful inlet
Down the hill beyond my door,
Lies a haven which awaits me
There my spirit to restore.

In the evening, when I'm weary and
my life seems full of care,
I hasten to my secret harbor, knowing
rest attends me there.

Green the boughs which hover o'er
me, soft the moss beneath my feet.
Sweet the scents of Mother Nature,
these alone make life replete.
Scarlet are my trees in Autumn,
Master Painter, splendid art.
Soon the leaves will pave the
pathway, feathered friends will then
depart.

White the snows of winter magic,
covering the earth laid bare.
Spring will come and then my haven,
blooms again with tender care.
Gift that love created for thee,
molded gently, meant to share.

This is home as God intended,
Eden can be anywhere.

Annette Gleason
QUANDARY
This heart died a thousand times,
shed a million tears, enough to drown
the ache, before it could break.
It suffered so, while it was tearing
asunder.
If I let it go, how will I know? or
always wonder, what happens to
Love?
Maybe I'll just label it "Rejected
Heart."
And stash it someplace out of sight.
Recycling is in, since I have no
bin . . . . Please, tonight let me cradle
it again, ache with its pain, lose sleep
and weep. Perhaps tomorrow I try to
tell it good-bye without tears as it's
buried deep.
I'll hover about, wait without doubt,
for its many jagged edges to rise,
infinite, each one will grow and
show . . . "LOVE NEVER DIES."

Annette Gleason
THE EXIT
Schedules were made to be kept.
Don't be too early or too late. Be on
time.
If I had been too early, how would I
have passed the endless time, perhaps
peeling all the gum. Carelessly
scattering the wrappers or would I
open one of my swollen eyes to see
the gowned and masked figures pass.
On time? I should have watched the
clock. I should have held your feeble
hand, wiped tears and struggled with
the dagger through my heart, closed
the other eye.
Too late? The life train was pulling
out of the station, leaving only the
deafening departure and signs: DO
NOT ENTER, CLOSED EXIT.
I was still. I lost my ticket to
tomorrow. I should have held it
tighter; and you my love.
Slowly, you passed, the cabbie came,
I stumbled then knelt.
I crossed my heart and made a
promise: For our last date.
I might be a little early. I would not
be late. I would be on time . . . Please
wait.

Peggy Mae Odegaard
LOVING YOU

*To my friend, my inspiration, my
love, my husband, Curt.*

Rainbows of colors
Tears from the sky
Wash away fears
Hugs that never end making us one
Knowing before saying
Heart bursts with joy . . .
Loving you

Peggy Mae Odegaard
PRECIOUS MOMENTS OF LOVE
Precious moments of love
Fly sweetly by
I hold them in my heart
As I do you my love
Each day is brighter
As my love grows stronger
My heart fills with the love
You give me in return
As a ring never ends
So too our love for each other
My friend and lover
I forever give you my precious
Moments of love

Darlene K May
A THOUGHT

*To my mother, who I love dearly but
am so hurt from.*

The bond between Mother
and Daughter is special
Most people say.
In this case
It didn't happen that way.
She left when I was ten
We've really never been friends.
I'm sixteen now
I wrote her the other day
And practically begged her
To let me come and stay.
No, was the answer, she gave.
She asked if I understood,
But there's no way I could.
Who do you turn to
When all your world
Has fallen apart
You try to hold
Your head up high
And hide
Your broken heart.

Russ Rattigan
BEING HERE

*To my sweet little Alice Blue Gown:
the girl who makes my life rhyme.*

Isn't this morning like any other
where,
wrapped soft in the silent darkness
like a comforter
in my early morning chair, watching
my
reproachful pendulum adding up my
days—
my friendly clock tick talks to me its
prayer?

What was so urgent in all those
yesterdays to read and reread
so many books to feed my brain
with facts and fantasies to relieve the
pain in me?
Reading of other worlds and
nightmare distances in our galaxy
trying to see the things that Ptolemy
could see.

The first morning rays lap my face
with a warming that I hungrily
embrace
so true . . . everything I call my own
is HIS—
home—health—children—wife, love
of work—especially life.
From the lofty and sublime to the
blessed and most lowly—
everything that is, is HIS, everything
that is, is holy.

Of a sudden I start up from my
chair—
yes—wonder surrounds us
everywhere.
His sudden peace fills me with joy
dispelling fear
spilling over my cheeks in an early
morning tear.
Of all our wonders, there is none so
dear
as the mere daily wonder of just
BEING HERE.

Paul Bray
LOOKING BACK AT PUGGY

*To my beloved cousin, Helen Norman
Davis, on February 1, 1977.*

For all those years you weren't
around,
I still remembered you.
Now my cousin at last is found;
My lifelong dream is true.

Were we as close in those young
years
As it now seems to me?
Did we share those laughs and tears?
Are they a memory?

Or did I conjure up a dream
Of someone I had known;
Of someone who could make it seem
That I was not alone?

The past to me will not unfurl,
But I am sure I see
A little girl with long black curls
Still standing there with me.

Jason J Erickson
CAN WE REALLY CHOOSE
Have you ever watched a fire,
fighting to survive.
Knowing soon it will go out
If I was a fire,
how long would I last
Would I only be the flame of a
match,
lit only to serve one purpose,
and then put out.
Or would I be a campfire,
keeping people warm as I burn
contentedly through the night.
Or would I be the forest fire,
burning out of control, and leaving
destruction behind.
Something tells me that I wouldn't
have a choice.
Only being human do I have that
right.
People can choose how they want
to live their lives.
Still there are those who are like the
fire.
Just living their lives as it comes.
Forgetting that being human,
means you can choose
which fire to be.

B R Haynes
THE GIRL ON THE BEACH
I saw her in the morning mist
Her hair was by the sunlight kissed
There were no shoes upon her feet
But otherwise she looked so neat
The sunlight on her golden hair
Appeared to be a halo there
In her eyes as she looked at me
Were reflections of the sand and sea
Her beauty was beyond compare
With hair of gold and skin so fair
I wished to talk to that girl so
But when I got the nerve to go
With thoughts of things that I would
say
She had spread her wings and flown
away
I am not sure but it would seem
I had only seen her in a dream
Oftimes I walk along that beach
To find that dream beyond my reach
I search the sea and scan the shore
In hopes I'll see her just once more

Edward W Bell
KAAAWA DAYS

*To Pegi—The Best who will always
Be Beautiful, and to her sons—Shane
and Joe.*

Kaaawa Days; a Windward Sun,
One Beautiful Wahine who's second
to none,
A Warm Ocean Breeze at Kaaawa
Beach Park,
One cold case of Bud—a party at
dark,

'Neath Coconut Trees with Peg, Me, and Pleiades.

We'll swim on the reef,
We'll laugh with our friends,
Then stroll off together to Swanzy Beach Park.
You get the keikis and here comes the dog;
I'll pick you an orchid on the way.

Kaaawa today or da kine—you know—Kahana Bay,
We'll have an ono time either way.
But to Kailua Beach you say,
Hey Brau—There's a Party Today.
Three stops on the way—Will we get there—We may.

Not responsible to thee were Pegi and Me,
We're Free as the Sea,
To laugh and to love, and to be.
So you get the Stein and I'll get the Wine,
And Here's to Our Friends and the Wind called The Trades,
Aloha Nui Loa and Mahalo-Kaaawa Days.

Edward W Bell
LUNAR ECLIPSE—AUGUST 16, 1989

To Farrell Ann, Ed, Ian, Ryan, Joseph Edward, and to Danielle, who was my highlight of that summer.

The eastern shores of mighty earth
Rushed in tonight to take
The western flanks of rising moon;
We visited the place.

As Sherpas scaled your mighty hills
Pacific waters flowed
Into the Sea of Tranquility;
Where footprints fill the sands of time.

As you grew dim and dark
I heard crickets chirping
On the banks of a Mare;
Lord Byron was roving late tonight.

Earth's celestial empire filled your own
Then Middle Moon surrendered
Her torch to Occidental Wave;
The time was terra—the place was luna.

We drew a ring around this moon
And a line from star to star
A shadow marriage that was beautiful then;
But there is more night to dawn,
The moon is but an evening star.

Donna Babashan
AUTHOR? AUTHOR?

To Lena Waldman, a delightful lady with an incredible sense of humor.

Blank paper holds me hostage.
Mocking my defeated, tell-tale face.
Tantalizing me and taunting me but offering no hope for grace.

Swaggeringly, an adventurer would rise boldly to the formidable task.
Undaunted, a history buff would delve happily into the glorious past.

A romanticist, I mold words to mirror man's soul; to reflect what he thinks.
Then, often watch in horror, as my cerebral ventures roll over and sink

Into a profusion of meaningless, wasted wit, with intent and purpose destroyed.
Causing my dubious claim to poetic license to be shelved as null and void.

Drawn helplessly back to verse and pen, I again summon up the audacity
To firmly believe that this time around I will be lauded for my perspicacity.

Once more eager words hastily tumble from my joyful, free-flowing pen
While I elatedly tag along, daringly dreaming of literary fame again.

Donna Babashan
SHADES OF LOVE
The old dog tried to worry the spent bone,
that memories made so dear,
With the same sense of joy known before
in an elusive yesteryear.
When just the sound of her master's voice
made her heart beat loud and fast.
Nothing could have made her doubt that their
love would not last.

Now, the dog, looking as battered as was
the old bone,
Often sat dazed and listless from spending
too much time alone.
No longer did the bone provide any comfort
or strength,
Though still carefully nurtured, sometimes
at great length.

Time, too, had eroded the dream that her
love would yet ignite
Another spark in her master, soon to flare up bright.
With painful clarity the old dog somehow
knew it was time
To finally lay down the worn bone, a symbol
of her love sublime.

Pensively, she gently reached out to tenderly
fondle the bone.
Just one more time, she said, before the long
journey home.
Then, slowly nudging it from her, the lifeline
for her being,
Stared dully ahead until her eyes glazed over and
became unseeing.

Estelle P Pfetsch
WARMED BY MEMORY
The pale ribbon of road o'er misty hills;
The deep ravine wrapped in cloak of green;
The gray shadows of chimneys on distant Mills;
All—magnets that draw me to the scene.

Far-off blue mountains are daring me now
to reach their site and climb to their brow;
The sparkle of sunshine that gilds a lake
teases my thoughts—a new route to take.
Plotting the adventure gave me a goal;
Starting the journey was balm for my soul.
I hoarded memories of mountain and stream
to while away hours in winter's long dream.

The open road has a special allure
for most of the months in the year;
But home is the place where I feel secure
when bitter north winds and snow sweep thru' here.

Mickey Sprenger
MY CHILDHOOD FRIEND

Dedicated to Robert White: my friend, now, and always—With love, Micki Sue.

He can't write this song, it's been twenty years,
and that's too long
The words are in a jungle of bad memories,
cause he was with her, not with me—
I can start again, with my best friend—
Knowing I'll love him to the end—
I was lost and lonely all those years,
Living with a wrong man—I shed a Thousand tears—
Now that we are free from our bad memories, Time will heal the tomorrows, with a living fantasy—Truth and love is all we need—I have him and he has me—. Besides he'll kill me if I leave—I just wrote that last line, as I sat at his feet—His eyes twinkle with laughter as he lovingly touched my cheek—I can't write the words or the melody—, and I only know three chords, that's not enough, he says to me—. I got up and left him then, only to look back, to see him grin—He was beside me in that moment, I felt his melody—It was more then three chords—This lover's fantasy—.

Mijj Beckett
"WHOOPEE"—HOMEWARD BOUND
We traveled through the light of day,
To Florida we did go,
But now I'm thinking on the way
Into the ice and snow
Of seeing family, friends, and church,
Of neighbors and the like—
I love them all
Both large and small—
So Florida take a hike.

We travelled through the cities,
Swamplands, around the lakes;
We saw the ranches, swaying palms,
And all the things it takes
To be attractive to the folks
Who live up in the north—
But you can't leave me in this place
For all its money's worth!

E A Douglas-Keats
CHILDHOOD MEMORIES
Days of listening and sharing
ideas for calming a youngster's mind.

Thunder and lightning
became a story in itself.
Angels bowling in the sky/
Snow became the essence of wonder
as words were told
of fun loving angels—
pillow fighting in the sky
the snow being the feathers falling from the pillows.

An opening in the sky after a storm became,
sunbeams brightly showing and leading someone to heaven.

A kitchen kettle's murmurings became,
a Nun saying her prayers during devotional.
Rainbows in the sky became—
God's promise to never flood the earth again!

So many memories to remember
to pass on to the new generation
to share with so many other youngsters
to calm the fears and teach
them not to be afraid of the natural wonders.

So many thoughts to be shared with
TENDER LOVING CARE
from one generation to another
down through the passing years
and to ease the worries of childhood
with LOVE.

Dawn Marie Ritchotte
THE ROSE

To Mrs. Linda Dailey, the one who first inspired me to write.

As a rose grows in a garden,
So my love grows for you,
Each day becoming more, and more beautiful
The rose is our love,
Our love, the rose

Cathy Myers
LIFE
Come, take my hand,
I am love with roses and daisies.
Come, take my hand,
I am sadness with grief.
I will lead you into warmth
and sunshine
or drop you into cold harsh darkness.
I am rich,
I am poor
I am life.

Merri Jo Hill
FANTASY
As precious as the morning dew
Is the love I have for you.
But yet you have never been seen
Because you only exist in my dream.
I wonder if in this world exist thee
If so perhaps you're dreaming of me.
Someday maybe our paths will cross
Then we'll know our dreams were not of loss.

Donna M Jones
TRIBUTE TO MOTHER

To Darlene this poem is dedicated, from Donna your daughter.

As a kid I used to wonder
If my life was going to blossom into something grand
I would sometimes ask my mother, when confronted with
The things I did not understand.

She would turn and say to me,
With a smile the answer pleasingly
Holding all the answers and love, oh so much love mother.

There were times we disagreed on
what I thought was right
For me and I was wrong
Now I've grown and gotten wiser, so

I thought I would
surprise her with this special song.

Special and so dear to me, without a doubt she is dear to me,
Holding all the answers and love, oh so much love, Mother.

As my life goes on I think back, I would say I want to be
Like her when I was grown.
She taught love, respect, and many things, now I teach all
Those very things to my own.

Marc Cadiente
HAPPY
Be happy and happy again,
As equally happy are men.
Count on the persons you call a friend,
To be happy, a happy that will never end.
Happy is a feeling that greets you inside,
It's Happy that you can't seem to hide.
So when you're not happy, not happy a bit,
You'll find a Happy good enough to fit—
Your own personality, of your own special you,
You'll feel yourself, old self, but new.
You'll feel like a flower blooming high,
But unlike other flowers' happiness, this will never die.
Because Happy's happiness grows here,
And where there's a heart it feels too dear—
To let the feeling end that Happy has on you,
Because Happy isn't fake or a lie, but true.
So when you're feeling down, count on Happy—
To do the job right and snappy!

Virginia Harris
I HAD A LOVE

To my husband,
the Reverend James Harris.

I had a Love that won my heart
When we were very young
A love that grew as years sped by
And time was but a lie.

We never saw the ending come
Our dreams so sudden gone
And now my Love is gone from me
And I am left with memories.

I had a love, my only Love
When time was but a word
Now the world is dark and gray
Because my Love is gone away.

Betty Ann Hudson
AS FREE AS THE BREEZE

To my family, friends, teachers, and the one that I love, Shawn.

I sit by my window and feel
The cool morning breeze
Oh how it must feel to flow
Through the trees
If I could be as free as the
Wind
I would have only one message
To send
As long as you flow like the
Summer breeze
You will never fall like the
Autumn leaves

Misty Lee Monteiro
DREAMING
I love to dream of things that fly
I love to dream of things that run by
I love to dream of dreams that have not happened
I love to dream of the past and future
And while I'm dreaming
The present is present and the presents of
Then is the past of now.
Now, the future from the past is now present
Dreaming of dreams all around
Just waiting to be found

Margaret Crawford
LEAVES
I gaze at the golden leaves of autumn
shimmering in the sun
that beams down through
an azure, October sky.
They bewitch
They beguile
They beseech me . . . .
That, I too, might have
a glorious
moment in the sun,
before
I
lie
down
to
die.

Liane Suda
A FRIEND FOREVER

This poem is dedicated to my mom, dad, and my brother who will always be a friend forever!

A friend forever is like you and me,
Our friendship will last for eternity.

Even though we are apart,
I will always remember you in my heart.

Throughout the times we shared together,
I will remember those days forever and ever.

Those days when I was feeling down,
you cheered me up without a frown.

So now I want to thank you
For all the things you've done.

So remember this poem,
As I have written it to you,

Just wanting to Thank You,
and say "I Love You."

Flora E Greene
EIGHTY-YEARS-YOUNG

In Memory of my Parents, LeVern and Mae Niles.

The Gold and Silver threads of life,
Are laced with illness and despair.
Some times our illness can be mended,
Many times there's no repair.

The sunshine of our attitude,
Can bring marvelous success.
When we look upon the world about us,
We see how well we are blessed.

A little thought, a pleasant smile,
Can make another person's day worth while.
There are some precious words
that work magic for me every day.
"Turn your eyes upon Jesus."
Please try it and see,
If it will work the same way
for you, as it does for me.

Flora E Greene
THE AMERICAN FLAG

Dedicated to the memory of my husband, Mercer V. Greene.

The Stars and Stripes, A beautiful flag.
May God protect it from above.
As a symbol of our love to keep our country strong, free and peaceful like a Dove.

The American flag is a symbol of the greatness of our land.
Men have given their lives in combat.
Others have suffered painful hazards of war.
Did these soldiers die in vain? Did the disabled cringe in pain for naught?

The answer lies with you, those who love the Red, White and Blue.
May our beautiful flag, continue to wave on high.
Like the lofty Eagle flying in the sky.

William E Karnak
STILL MOMENT

To Debbie, my inspiration and love.

A gentle wind did storm the Polar power
and from the icy tundra did unseat
the frozen fetters on dead Arctic feet
with warming stream of Spring's melting shower.
Cold Time was halted for that one brief hour,
and still it stays: a frosted sculpting sweet —
one moment when two searching hearts did meet;
etched for eternity in mem'ry's tower.

Thus, Love's in bloom a little late this year,
since winter's harsh, unhappy circumstance
did choose to linger far beyond its time.
In gracious thanks for season's change—no fear
this be some strange, unnatural mischance —
give welcome to a kinder, warmer clime.

William E Karnak
CHEAP PEN
Why won't this pen write a decent love song
with words like these: "Heaven on earth, that's what
you've made for me since the day we met."?
How can this scribbler be so cursed, so wrong?
Can't it feel in my hand these feelings strong?
What is its reason no worthy words are set
to pad? Is hand too weak a conduit
for what heart feels? O, grievously I long:

to say with sweetest words that stars above
pale dimly next to her—their glow so soon
becomes a fading candle that seems unreal;
to tell in honey phrases of my love
and how she moves more deeply than the moon
could ever stir the swelling stormy sea.

Dwayne Lee Vernon
PEACE ON EARTH

I dedicate this poem to my mom and dad.

There is a place I love the best
It's nothing like all the rest
On a mountain is this place I see
Where all living things can be free
Trees grow thin the higher you go
As the white water begins to flow
Changes come faster than they do mild
Where the elk can still run wild
Peace on earth this I know
The place my dreams will always go

Ethel E Seipp
GRANDPA'S CHRISTMAS SHOPPING DAY

In loving memory of my husband, William W. Seipp.

Christmas was always Grandpa's day
So when three small grandsons came our way
And one wee granddaughter, he was in his glory
So, I'd like to tell you this dear story.

Grandpa shopped early in our town's one toy store
To try out little cars on its bright, shiny floor.
The clerks were so helpful as they sensed his joy
Of finding the right toy for each good little boy.

Then over to the girl's department we'd proceed
And consult our list of presents she may need.
Would she like a dolly or a little doll house?
A cuddly Teddy bear? A Mickey or Minnie Mouse?
For tea parties, she'd want a set of pretty dishes,
Anything at all to fulfill our little girl's wishes.

Our handsome three grandsons now all have grown
Our lovely granddaughter with her young husband,
Has dear babies of their very own.
Grandpa is in Heaven; I'm snug in this home,
But I never can forget, thanks to memory's ways,
Grandpa's happy yearly Christmas Shopping Day.

Ethel E Seipp
DEAR MEMORIES
I want to tell as best I can in some way,
Some dear memories that come to mind each day . . .
The year we bought our farm and home.
We moved in with our four year old son.
A new phase in life for us had begun.

We cared for our animals, each one a pet.

We thanked the Lord for all he had given.
We didn't ask for more—Ah, but yet,
The next April First,—One year to the day,
A beautiful daughter came with us to stay.

Dad would come into dinner after working so hard.
He would put baby beside him in her sturdy highchair.
How patiently he fed her, with such tender care!
Mother would wash brother up and get dinner on.
With sister's place by her Dad and brother's by his Mom.

The years so quickly rolled away,
Soon off to school they were on their way.
The first time each one left to catch the bus,
Mother tried hard not to make a fuss.
So little, so brave, out on their own;
that first school day.

John L Roton Sr

John L Roton Sr
MY BACK YARD
In my back yard so luscious and green,
leaves of every kind, on most everything.
Vines and bushes, and trees of sorts,
grasses and toad stools, just heavenly art.
The terrain is not level
and the trees are not straight.
But the leaves make the difference,
in this garden of escape.
Birds of all kinds enjoy peace at its best,
while squirrels in the trees put your mind at rest.
And as I sit at the base of this tree so grand,
can you imagine, how this tree has loved, to be in this garden, so grand.
And from morning, til night,
as the tree shade does change.
The shadows move from the west to the cast,
as if they too, enjoy the change.
So whenever I get blue
or down in despair,
I just remember in my back yard,
there's a haven out there.

John L Roton Sr
JESUS OUR LORD
As I sit in the presence of this Mrs.,
As I view such a picture of my dream.
With eyes that promised a tomorrow,
As we worked together as a team.
With faith and hope there was a future,
As we trusted in Jesus, Our Lord.
We will always now and forever be together,
Because Jesus the Christ is our Lord,
For today we are ever so closer,
Then at first when we began.
For in Christ we trusted our marriage,
Survived and lived only in Him.
With children, He's been our only guidance,
His support and a trusted friend.
Without Him we wouldn't have had the first tomorrow,
Much less a future in heaven with Him.
With our family we will always be together,
In Spirit and love with Him.
Because our future is now growing brighter,
Than all the world has to offer with sin.

Cindy Hein
SEASONS
There are four seasons in the year,
I really like them all.
But like the chicken and the egg,
Is Spring first or is Fall?
Summer can't be first in line,
Spring gives it such a lift.
And Winter wouldn't be my choice
It doesn't have the gift.
Fall comes on slow and helps prepare
for Winter's snow and ice.
Spring melts the snow and thaws the earth,
to help make Summer nice.
You can't have Summer without Spring,
or Winter without Fall.
But then you wouldn't have a year
unless you use them all.
Putting them in order
shouldn't be such a hard thing.
But as for me I can't decide.
Is Fall first or is Spring?

Penny J Grubbs
A SPECIAL MESSAGE

Dedicated to my brother, Michael D. Jenkins, who made this poem possible. I love him and thank him for being so special, caring and loving.

I Love You So Much
That words can't describe
The feelings for you
That I hold inside.

You're not just my brother
You're also my friend
Who I know will always be there
Right up 'til the end.

So let me now thank you
Straight from the heart
And always remember
We never shall part.

In mind and in body
In spirit and soul
Whenever you need me
All you have to do is call.

Just call and I'll be there
From this side or the other
Cuz you are my soulmate
My friend and my brother.

Margo L Higginbotham
THE WALL
It was never part of a garden
blushed with the beautiful rose and vine —
but a deliberate act of oppression
to divide your world and mine.

It was never a symbol of beauty
of peace and tranquility —
but the severest flaw of distraction
and acute disharmony.

It could never evoke a memory
that one could fondly recall —
but always brought tears of sorrow
for one to talk of The Wall.

For it was more than a wall of convenience,
much more than a figure of speech —
it was the cold, cold wall of bondage
that only one's love could reach.

But today is a day of great victory!
It is the greatest conquest of all!
For today is reclaimed the freedom and peace
once denied by the unsightly wall!

Elsie F Tyler
AWAKING: AURORA BEFORE DAWN
It's been a night of rest. Somnolent still. Other worldly and this worldly. It's up from the sleeping Morpheus and into the vigilance of day. It's a rolling, rambling safari that guides. It's a cloudless ferry passage that leads from night into day.

It's here now, this flight. It's up from the land of Nod into the Nation of Awake. It's the changing of gears, filtering and fleeting, airy and light.

Tied neither to asleep or awake, it's a dreamlike pilgrimage. It has no anchors. It has no weights. The mind soars free. Thoughts slip and glide here and there, in and out, drifting across the perimeter of space. Reflections gliding with the tides of spiritual and physical being.

Cutting to the quick and getting to the heart. It's a jaunt to the central point of radius where perceptions are formed. Difficulties can be seen in breadth and wisdom.

Shuttling always, it's a vagabondage trek. It's a roaming promenade, fleeting and descending; however, always gently transcending into the dawn of earthly thoughts. It's a sojourn from the inner self to the public persona.

From the subliminal to the deliberate until the alarm is calling. The envoy must now end. Disembark quickly for day awaits.

Lane Chisholm
MOMMIE AND DADDY LOVE YOU, NICCI

To my sweet granddaughter, Nicole Marie Vidas, with all my love . . . forever . . . you are the light of my life. Papa.

It's so hard on one so young,
Divorce is never easy —
Words so harsh in anger flung,
Leave children's stomachs queasy.

You've cried a lot—not knowing why
Mommie and Daddie fight,
But try as hard as I know you try,
No answers come to light.

Can love be real? I know you fear,
And so I promise you —
Doubt not their love, they hold you dear . . .
Their love for you is true.

Never blame them—either one—
Youth's the thing to blame.
You'll know when all is said and done,
They'll love you just the same.

Someday you'll know how precious you are,
To Papa and Mama too —
God lit his heaven with a special star,
The day he gave us you.

James Long
"HOW HIS BARGAIN BEGAN" OR "SAVE SOME MONEY"
How his bargain began,
First let's try, and define a bargain,
Let's say it's something at a good price,
Many times bargains happen after
Christmas or around New Year,
Or around major holidays,
Many times bargains are called sales,
Take for instance a 4th of July sales,
A good business man has to keep up with current styles,
Many times bargains, or sales are
aimed at young women, or men;
Many another time sales at large
department stores have sales
in their men's department in suits, or shirts.

Edward Allen Estes
ADDRESSING WORLDS ONE, TWO, AND THREE
We divide our Earth
As if it were three
How can I stand here
And you stand there and not see that we are one.

By our actions we erect walls
Walls of thought that stand behind a symbol
A name
We erect walls

I do not attempt to judge the ugliness
Of the plan
But only to understand why
We erect walls

We as people have the right and the duty
To run the race
The only race is the human race
We can control the pace

Edward Allen Estes
A SIMPLE RAIN
I was sitting in a forest a recent day
With the cool spring air around me
The moss covered log I sat upon
So damp from the rain
I knew I could not complain
Because with every breath
First inhaled then exhaled
An intimate bond was established
Between the earth at my feet
The misty green ferns that surrounded me
And the purest of life within my deepest self
A life that could only thrive in such a simple rain

Edward Allen Estes
QUESTIONS
Grandfather, what did you do in the war?
What did you fight for?
Did you kill people?
Tell me grandfather what you did
I killed the enemy
Dad, what did you do in the war?
I know that you fought
And I know that you killed
But who did you kill?
I killed the enemy
Let me ask you son, what did you do in the war?
Did you know what you were doing?
Did you believe in what you did?
Was it the enemy you killed?
I am the enemy
I killed the enemy
There was no enemy
And part of me has died
Tell me again Dad, what you did in the war?

JoAnn Newton

it seems you have forgotten
that i exist inside your
soul that you have cast out
into the world of bleak
reality that i can't learn
to cope with
all
the pain of icy winds
at least hate me in mind
and not just in speaking
then i could live with the thought
that all my dreams
for you
have not totally
been in
hopeless vain

Pat A Young
CHILD UNKNOWN
Lord,
Take the soul of our child unknown
Guide and protect what we cannot hold

When once again our hearts are whole
Return to us our child unknown

Pat A Young
MY HUSBAND'S PRAYER
Lord, take the hand of my best friend.
Walk beside him through the day's end.
Reach out your heart and touch his soul.
Guide him Lord, so he may know,
the eminent wisdoms you have bestowed.
Please show him compassion
when others are cruel.
Show him patience
when others have few.
Show him strength
when the weak need a hand.
Show him courage
to make a stand.
Show him honor,
to have pride in himself.
Show him respect
for others as well.
But, above all Lord, I do pray,
Show him the love that surrounds him each day.
So, take the hand of my best friend
and see him safely through the day's end.

Pat A Young
A WEDDING WISH TO OUR PARENTS
When we were young, so innocent and free
Our lives were as children, filled with hopes and dreams

As we grew older, so did our doubts and fears
But you came along and wiped away the tears.

You were our teachers, the strength in our souls
You gave us the light that we can now hold.

You gave us your love, you showed us the way
And now we are one on this beautiful day.

To you our respect, our neverending love
We owe you the world for all you have done.

Pat A Young
FLASHBACKS
When I'm alone at night and I get scared
I think of you and the flashbacks are there

Long walks
Hands entwined
Silent thoughts
Hearts unwind
A gentle kiss
and you are mine

Suddenly, the flashbacks are no longer
But you are home and I am stronger

Albert Nelson
THE QUESTION
Is Life a—Parallax
Of loves and hates,
Of hopes and fears,
And Faith—the Sword, the Ax,
The Way to conquest of the Years,

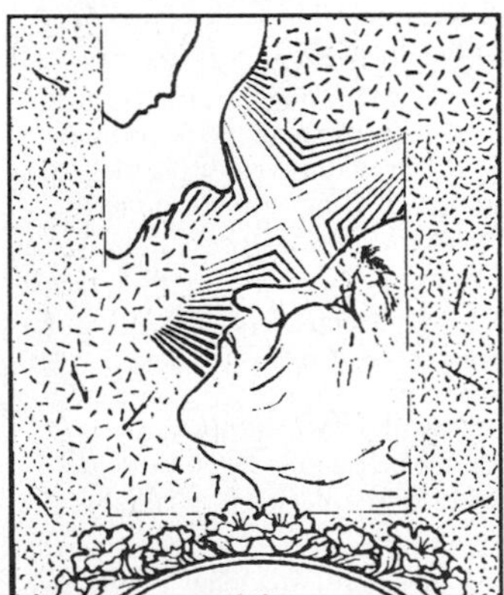

So that, once Time is rent,
Like shoots in spring that sip the light,
A nectar for the Soul be sent,
Eternal Truth, Supernal Sight?

Saundra Lamb
TO SEE

Ray (De' Rey), your thoughtful ways I shall never forget. You were always there for me. With love in infinity you remain in our hearts.

You always say, "Don't tell me
I have eyes, I can see"
And I think to myself
'Tis true you have eyes,
But I never saw, you see

Saundra Lamb
MEMORIES OF COURAGE
Memories of you make me want to hold on to
The goals within my heart, more than a dreamer,
A fighter with a heart

Full of courage, there was no doubt, into
The world, you went out, to seek your goals
to secure your dreams and this is the path that
I wish to gleem

Courage in memory of what he was, take hold
of me, as I extend my hands to thee

Hold steadfast to my soul give me the Courage to be bold

Jami Jacobs
INEXPRESSIBLE LOVE

To Ron Reynolds—In regret I could not express my love for you.

Please understand,
that as I take your hand,
I shiver inside my heart;
I almost fall apart.
There's nothing I can say or do,
to express the way
I feel for you.
Images in our mind reveal,
the way that we
really feel.
The sweet romance of where we've walked;
the things we've done, the way we talked.
I think you should know—
you're in my heart;
But if I don't tell you—
we'll grow apart.
So take these words that are written true:
The words I can't say are, "I love you."

Denise Flack
UNEMBRACEABLE
The mirror hides no secrets
It reveals what is already known
Either as friend or enemy
Pure honesty comes from no other
The truth laughs in your face
While beyond the reflection lies the substance
The unembraced substance, waiting to be understood
The void leaves the soul to wither
Leaving a shell lacking substance
Loneliness finds no friends
For it bears upon us, stealing the last breath
Replacing it with an aching emptiness
A barrenness that is yours alone
To take alone, to be alone

Audra Prater
SILENTLY

To: Richard, my husband, for his unlimited faith in me and my daughters, Debra and Jacque, whom I am 'constant' in my love for them.

Be still my child
Know I'm near.
In this knowing
Embrace no fear.

Tho silent,
I may be
I am . . .
Constantly.

Emma Eva Hankey Barnum

Emma Eva Hankey Barnum
SNOW

To my wonderful children and grandchildren.

Looking out my window I can see
The snow that fell upon the trees
Birds are hopping up and down
Searching for seeds on the ground.
Children sliding down the hill
And until, they get their fill
Only laughter breaks the still

The sound of shovels when they hit the dirt
While lifting winter's heavy skirt
Soon a voice that you hold dear
You know that coffee time is here.

Kimberlee Gasper
FIRST BREATH
I crawl onto warm sand
my body struggling against the tide.
Almost alive, the sea
it holds firm its grip upon me.

At last I free myself
I am lying on the beach, dying.
With my first breath of air
my body shudders and arches,
gripped in pain.

It hurts too much, this pain!
I wriggle backwards, trying in vain
to reach my sea.
I can't reach it, I am doomed.

Slowly, the pain decreases,
the air doesn't seem as harsh.
Overhead the sun sinks and now the sand cools.
I find the strength to move . . . .

Irene V Moore
CLOUD WATCHING

To my family and friends.

These were fragments of clouds
Not great masses of startling frothy whiteness

Piled mound upon mound, oh no,
Rather, they were wisps, mere bits
and pieces,
Sweepings really, forming and
reforming
Into amazing configurations . . .
White-whiskered ancients
Last seen debating, in an Athens
That respected their wisdom
And their accumulation of years . . .
Animals so loved by Francis of
Assisi,
Many of his small birds, his doves,
his sheep
His "Brothers" he called them . . .
were here . . .
Female faces with deeply mysterious
eyes
And bodies thinly swathed
In floating transparent veils . . .

Much that I have seen on canvas,
Today I saw, in pale sequence,
Moving across the sky.

Wayne Silva
DAD

There comes a time when you will
see
What's treasured deep inside,
A statue of a man a heart of gold
And steel for eyes

Although his strength comes from
within
A marriage so clean and pure,
The only thing beside that fact
Are children to guide and cure

A man whose life walks strong and
bold
From now and to the end,
But not just once he told that seeds
Should grow and transcend

And life must go on to the end
No matter when he'll pass,
I'll remember Dad the gifts you gave
And make you smile at last!

Idoya Urrutia
THE KEY TO FREEDOM

The rain outside left streaks on her window as lightning lit up the cloudy sky and the world around her.

This day made her think back to the harsh memories, she thought back.

A small child ran across the cotton field in search of her father.

When she got to the yard of the big white mansion, she saw no one.

She then kept on going to the quarters out back where she lived.

When she got there, she saw a huge circle of people. The girl pushed through them and saw her mother bawling on the chest of her father, who was on the floor.

At that moment, something shocked her and hit her as hard as that leather whip had once. She knew her father was gone. All of a sudden, she felt despair because she was alone. Her mother later told her that they would never be rid of the iron chains that would follow their race forever.

As she sat there she realized her mother was only half right because long ago she had found the key to unlock the chains and open the door to freedom.

Janet Peros
THE WALL OF SEPARATION

To everyone in the world; black, brown, white, yellow and red. May there be no walls between us. And to anyone in the world who must deal with their own "wall of separation."

What is it that separates?
Walls
Walls built of strong hatred
Walls built of petty differences
If One were to climb over the wall,
Could One change the world?
Could One be accepted on the other
side of the wall?
Crumbling
If the wall crumbled and fell to the
ground;
There would be no boundary.
There would be no separation.
War and Hatred?
Peace and Harmony?
What would become without the
wall?
One would have to persuade Many
for the latter.
What would be the decision of
Many?
The vote must be unanimous
Many, what is your vote?

Bernice Myers
LOVE PREVAILS

A person full of dreams and hopes;
Feelings like that are easy to cope.
A person full of fears;
It's hard to hide the tears.
A person full of pain;
Makes it hard to gain.
But a person full of laughter,
Will add a cheer year by year.
A person full of sharing,
Will be there for the caring.
A person full of giving thoughts;
Will add joy to our hearts;
And a person full of love,
Will prevail through all!

Nina Benson

Nina Benson
GOING HOME

When I awoke this morning, I heard a
small voice say.
Whisper a prayer for the souls in
flight,
Somebody's going home today.
It may be by car, it may be by plane.
The journey for all will be the same.
Some may go by violence. Some may
just sleep away.
One thing is sure, they are going
home today.
Life is uncertain and we know not
when,
The path we have taken will come to
an end.
Watch over your soul and walk in the
holy way.
It may be your time to go home
today.
When I quit this busy walk of life,
I will be free from pain and strife.
With a wave of my hand, I'll be on
my way.
For I am going home to stay.

Christy Lynn
MR. SAGUARO CACTUS

Standing tall and straight,
You tower over us all,
So proud, So strong.
Removed from all around you.
Gloriously spreading your arms wide,
Just waiting to be embraced.
Look! Don't Touch!
For you are a monument,
The one people come to see.
A prickle to protect you,
For you wish to last,
Forever,
You will never know danger
Death will never capture you.
Your beauty will not ever cease.
For our memory
Won't ever
Forget you.
Your existence seized our souls.
The desert shows worship and respect
as it
bows
before you.

Rob L Boco
OF ME

I am impatient
it cannot be condoned
Today I urged night to fall
with the weight of a Redwood falling
and night sneered derisively at me,
being the cynic that he is,
lingered beyond the twilight
and stalled.
What compels this haste?
Maybe I'm more comfortable
lurking in the obscurity of darkness
hiding from the predators
intent to see me fall
Like the night
or perhaps it appeases me
to see the darkness permeate
the surroundings,
Casting shadows on all that is
unappealing
and everything I am discontented
with.
An opaqued façade disguising what is
unbearable in the light.

Amparo Sosa
LOST LOVE

I dedicated this poem to my sister Teresa, for believing in me and my poetry. One of my many dreams has come true, to become a poet.

my lost love is somewhere
in this world.

loves me for who I am not
for what I can become.

morning to night I've searched
no luck yet.

I know you're out there waiting
for me.

with time you and I will
meet and become one.

Cynthia Remian Taylor
LOOKING BACK

The apple tree we used to climb
The sandbox now is gone
The brook we used to splash through
Is dried up, weeds abound
The hills we thought were mountains
From a child's point of view
And the treehouse we once built
Is decayed and rotted through.

Upon looking back, I refuse to see
The reality of it all
For in my mind, there will always be
The apple tree in the fall
The sandbox, the brook, the hills,
And treehouse too
These memories can never fade
For they will always be renewed.

Scot Ohms
WHEN IT HURTS TO REMEMBER

Dedicated to Wendy Lee Clark, Whose Love Inspired Me.

When it hurts to plunge deep into
your mind.
When it hurts to find feelings that
only remind,
Of the tears that were shed, and the
emotions thought dead.
When it hurts to remember the
days of the past
Only for dreams and hopes that
they'd last.
When your tears turn to blood and
her eyes turn to stone it is these
thoughts that hurt, when you're cold
and alone.
And when the flame goes out in
your heart, and your dream washes
away, there's nothing more to say.
These are the times "when it hurts to
remember!"

C Edwin Ward
SEASONS

Dedicated to: Jeanne Del, Karen Sue and Chuck.

SPRING,
Robins sing; worms surface, serve
their purpose;
April showers, pretty flowers; sticky
mud, trees bud;
Grasses grow, mowers mow, loans
made, taxes paid;
Easter parades, pretty maids, musical
tunes, young love blooms.
SUMMER,
Heat's a bummer, bats crack,
golfers hack;
Beautiful brides, sunburned hides;
fun swimming, teams winning;
Crowded beaches, movie features;
fishing tackle, paint and spackle;
Vacation cruise, or laze and snooze.
FALL,
Visit the mall; harvest done, food
by the ton;
Back to school, close the pool;
witches fly, goblins nigh;
County fairs, stock and wares;
rake leaves, cough and sneeze;
Turkeys roast, brown as toast; pep
rally flames, football games.
WINTER SEASON,
Everyone freezin'; mittens and
coats, furs and totes;
Cold winds blow, shoveling snow;
holiday greetings, shopping
meetings;
Gifts to wrap, no time to nap;

mistletoe and holly berry,
Feasts and parties, making merry;
resolutions to make,
Easy to break; the year is shot,
thank God I'm not.

C Edwin Ward
SURF
Breaking
Waves upon the sandy beach,
White foam trailing
Fingers in the sand.
Behind each receding wave,
sandpipers race,
Seeking the sea's bounty.
Thumbnail size crabs
Bury themselves below the sand
Trying to survive.
Gulls overhead
Swoop and glide adding
Raucous
Sound
To the tranquil scene.
Some float, like ducks, just beyond the surf,
Beady opalescent eyes reflect contentment.
A pattern of breaking waves adds Monotony.
Each fourth, or is it the fifth, wave reaches
Further up the beach.
The tide is coming in.

Helen DePriest
THIS NIGHT
This night is very quiet
As I sit here all alone,
The kids were here for supper
But, now they've all gone home.

The stars above are twinkling
And the moon is shining down,
And as the dark comes closer
The lightning bugs fly 'round.

It gives me need to thank my God
For all he's done for me,
For everything he's given
For letting me just be.

Tomorrow when I 'waken
And see the morning sky,
Again, I'll say I'm grateful God
For helping me get by.

For giving me my children
Each different in their way,
But everyone so special
And so loving every day.

Kimberly J Nagel
WHERE I RAN
There you are away from me, and here I am.
Somehow our goodbye made me leave and this is where I ran.
To another life, to mend the wound, changing what I feel.
But the reality is nothing can change a heart of steel.

A shield placed around the emotion of love, so no one can touch.
But deep inside the emotion is crying, because I miss you so much.

A thousand years ago, or so it seems, we fell apart.
Running away, a solution to what we thought was smart.

Needing one another in so many ways.
Yet throwing everything away in just one day.

Memories of yesterday smashing down on me,
longing for a last hope to save all dignity.

Pride forcing me to walk away.
Spitting words I never meant to say.

To know we have lost it all,
and yet as I sit here it's you I need to call.

Your voice still so familiar to me,
and yet its tone is so carefree.

Easy come, easy go, is the attitude we share.
Ever since we closed the doors that made our hearts tear.

Now we talk as if we've been friends,
long distance I shed a tear, knowing you must be on your end.

A sniff that lets you know I'm crying.
When I deny it, you know I'm lying.

So we sit at our different ends of the world, listening to one another's tears hit the floor.
Silence, with only you and I involved, wishing you would rescue my heart so it will suffer no more.

John M Gear
IN THE RUINS OF YESTERDAY
In the ruins of yesterday
a man sits and cries in pain.
For the loss of his existence
has frozen him insane.
As the world just keeps on passing
in a flash of sudden death
a panic starts to whisper
it's tattooed on his breath.
And in a final desperate struggle
he rises to his feet,
to find he isn't where he thought he was
and there's the man to meet.
So in the end the walls just disappear,
and leave a wasted land,
and there's a man out on a park bench
with a flower in his hand.

Miss Helen Dreyer
TORNADO

To Carroll County, Georgia, for surviving ....

I awoke
Startled
by flashing-crashing
light-sound . . .
quickly subsiding
to be replaced by
closetrainsound
lowplanesound
solidhellsound
Silent as it was loud,
I lay in my once-so-safe bed
Terrified
Waiting . . .

For an eternal minute
Scared to look at the battery powered clock
Fearing the stopping of time
as for the dead

With twisting, roaring death outside
Time has no meaning

Praying for silence to infect the night like cancer
eating at the churning gray black flak monster
Listening for absence of sound

Waiting to breathe
Hoping that the next sound is not
My Own Scream
Being sucked from safe haven to disappear
into the twisting-roaring-churning hell of
nothing but wind . . .
. . . gone mad

Karyn White
LOVE IS . . .

To my beloved family who has shown me what real love is. I love you! !

LOVE is caring
LOVE is bearing one another's crosses
LOVE is sharing everything, the profits and the losses
LOVE is more than bells and laughter on a wedding day
LOVE is facing what comes after sunny skies or gray
LOVE is giving
LOVE is living, just for one another.
Working out the daily
problems of our lives together.

Celeste A Terry
ALL THESE THINGS

For my son, Camerion Scott.

Shadows of the trees, flower petals in the breeze.
Sun shining bright, smiles to keep you warm at night.
Kisses to make you feel, like you've never felt before.
A weeping willow, blowing in the wind.
Makes me happy, happy that I live.
The smooth sound of a stream, the fresh air after a rain.
A field of white daisies, with butterflies scattered.
The sun going down, people not realizing, that day, won't ever come again.
A pasture, with tall green grass, horses running wild, forever never a care.
A baby rosebud, and a humming bird collecting pollen.
Children playing in the park, not really knowing what life is, and loving every minute of it.
A walk along the beach, the sun is beginning to set.
Sea gulls gliding over the splashing waves.
A child that has just taken his first step, first step down the long road.
A candle burning bright, and never burning out.
Being in the world, and really loving everything in it.
And just knowing, all these things are free.

Leo Clive Williams

Leo Clive Williams
M A N—KIND?
Angry fearsome visages
Grunting! Sighing! Mumbling curses,
A hate a deep searing hate etched on the brow,
An evil eye a cruel mouth
Fear distrust malice
A frustration beyond repair
And ivory tower'd rhetoric fuels the flame,
The rhythm of the death dance quickens,
Some faces contorted with glee
others with pain—
Bodies in the heat of passion and uncaring—
Unfeeling—lusting—grinding in the excesses of frustration;
Spellbound—we watch and our minds merge with the players of this gross spectacle and we become one—
Throats constricted with lifelong bitterness howl,
Bellies denied of fullness roar!
"The Lamb! We want the Lamb and the blood of the Lamb"
Having eaten of the Lamb we want no more
And the taste left in our mouths is foul;
The players are spent,
The watchers tire of the spectacle,
A calm returns to the air
But we are caught in a vortex of despair.

Deborah Sanders Burrus
LIFE'S MEMORIAL

Dedicated to Edith Marie Sanders Lawson, a lady who learned the balance of life in order to enjoy it to the fullest. Thank you Mom for teaching that treasure to me!

If we knew today were our last earthly hours,
I suppose we'd reflect on this pathway of ours:
How much did we matter?
Did we live a good life?
Did we somehow balance the joy and the strife?
Did the people we love seem to know how we felt?
Were our words and our actions considerately dealt?
How much did we impact the places we served?

Will our names be rewarded for the things we deserved?

I suppose we'd embrace the world that we know,
We'd cling to the warmth of our memory's glow:
The times that were special,
Those shared with family and friends.
The times spent with nature, we hoped they never would end.
And what of the world beyond the realm that we know?
If God's in His heaven, then I'm happy to go.
If for only one thing I'm remembered on earth,
May it be that I loved every day since my birth.

Meredith Dillon
THOUGHTS

I lie awake at night thinking of my thoughts,
I lie awake questioning why we ever fought.
I never really showed it, how much I really cared.
Me tell you? I probably wouldn't dared.
Do you know? How long I've cared for you?
I thought you felt the same, the same about us two.
You don't know how much you love someone until they've gone away,
I wish he were back, holding me that very special way.
Just think, never again it will be us two,
From now on, just me and you.
I love you, I love you, I love you!
Can't you understand?
Can we walk together one more time, walking hand and hand?
You're probably saying her? No way!
You know what I'm saying? Him, any day!
What am I thinking? You've left and gone away.
We are getting farther apart from the first day you were gone.
I remember these things while laying on my bed,
Now I must go rest my tired head.
There is just one last thing I have to say,
Boy you're gone, I can't stand to live another day!

Therese Garrison
CLOUDS SOMETIMES

To Sharon My Joy Pacanowski—Always remember that life is full of wealth, love and happiness—It's all what you do and make of it—And I love you. Forever 143.

Sometimes the clouds get in our eyes. Obstructing our vision, Preventing us from seeing what is right before our eyes.

A gentle touch, a warm heart. Strong hand and willing eyes to understand. Maybe someday you'll see, maybe I'll hear, maybe he'll learn, and maybe we'll grow. Maybe sometimes the clouds will leave our eyes and we'll live and let die. Without the cry of anger or defeat, or the taste of victory at our feet, and realize we can only walk in our own shoes, and very easily grow apart just the same to be free. Still we'll learn that when the clouds get in our eyes the sun will still find a way to shine, and there is always a rainbow at the end of a rain storm. Never a mountain too high to climb, just the same as never a heart too cold to melt.

Howard Scott
CONFLICTS OF LIFE

To Marilyn Bell, my love who has given me a new life.

Torn and trembling, confused and sad
Happy and singing, rejoicing so glad
Not understanding what these feelings are
Hoping to calm them before they go too far.

Travelling a journey into this new life
With many a conflict and open strife
Lost in a turmoil wondering why
Feelings inside make me want to cry.

Have a new concept of God up above
Trying to understand his love
But the fears keep coming, please Lord why
Please make me believe in this guy.

Fear is a weight so heavy inside
Conflict and patience ready to collide
Talking to someone who means so much
Afraid of losing that friend's sweet touch.

Sleep is evasive the whole night long
The hours were lost that I had been in song
Oh please dear God, hear my plea
Don't let my life be ruined by me.

Valerie J Hacnik
A CHILD'S SHAME

Daddy dropped him off at
daycare much like every morning.
He was used to that feeling of
relief, upon leaving his home,
there was something in the
air that didn't like him.
Sometimes he thought it might be
mom or dad but since that was too
scary he quickly willed it away.
He loved the comfort of his days
at pre-school and the security the
routine gave him
Five o'clock came and with most of
the other kids he watched the clock.
Six o'clock and still ticking, when
he looked around he was the
only child left.
As the minutes passed he
watched as his teacher tried
to reach his mommy or daddy.
But with every ounce of his three
year old soul he knew.
He knew that mommy was using
that stuff again, that stuff
that made her mean and
awful. That same stuff that
made daddy yell and red in
the face.
He knew they weren't coming.
He knew he was to blame.

Carolyn Domenichelli
LITTLE FACES

Dedicated to my dear sister, Linda . . . who like my lovely garden, fills my heart.

Pretty little faces all in a row.
Water and sunshine and up you grow.
Rich earth envelopes like a nurturing womb,
And birth takes its shape in your glorious bloom.

Moonlight brings rest to your weary heads,
And dew drops blanket your snug little beds.

Each morning you greet me with bright cheery faces,
Your beauty and sweetness fill my heart with your graces.

Tressie J Sala
WHAT IS A FRIEND IN THIS LIFE

To The Keystone Gang of the 60s & 70s era, Thank you for all your moral support—I love you all.

One who stands by you through everything. Never questioning your loyalty or what the morrow brings. Listening to your problems and helping to sort them out.
Never asking others for in their heart there is no doubt.

If in this life you have found a true friend
Let them know you are grateful to the end.
When you are helping one another in this life
It's so much easier to get through all your struggles and strifes.

There are friends of all nationalities during your life
Those who seek your friendship whom are very nice
And those who seek to hurt you & stab you in the back

But to have a friend who is always there, never falters
and forever cares. It makes life much easier, the nights shorter, the days longer to have one friend who is stronger A FRIEND LIKE YOU

Tressie J Sala
DON'T PAINT ME BLACK

To My Children and Grandchildren—Born of Joseph W. Tressie Sala in San Bernardino CA. A daughter—Sheree, Four sons—Joseph Jr., Rocky J., Geoffrey K., and Kerry G. Sala. I love you all dearly.

Don't paint me black while I'm away
For true colors will come through
My colors are shining brightly
Orange, purple, yellow and blue

YOU paint a person black
And you've really done him wrong
You've painted the wrong shade of color
And you are singing the same song

Now if your colors turn dark & grey
During the time you are away
You've time to add the colors bright
The colors of the rainbow & brilliant Sunshine light

True colors will come through in the end
Don't paint me black
I'm trying to be your friend
Colors were put here for special reasons
Even so—We can tell the time of our Seasons

COLORS

God gave us colors to enjoy
But there's some that's the devil's toy
So let a peaceful color come through
Let it be a color that's forever true

Cavell B Spear
MOMMY'S LITTLEST ANGEL

To Paula Louise Spear, Mommy's Littlest Angel. I love you very much! Love, Mommy.

On one early December morn,
my little baby girl was born.
Joy and happiness filled that day,
little did we know it would soon go away.
A mother, and a father,
that couldn't get along.
How could two people have been so wrong?
But, through all the tears, and heartaches,
my little angel was strong.
Now she has two families you see,
with twice the love there used to be.
So from God up above,
MOMMY'S LITTLEST ANGEL
was sent here for twice the Love!

Marie Ducharme
TO . . .

to earth
to freeze
to wait
to grow

to fight
to start
to move
to root

to push
to break
to show
to leaf

to bud
to blossom
to die
why?

Keith Shively
FOREST FORGOTTEN

And the leaves gently sigh
As they fall and die
And the trees, they weep
For the children they cannot keep

As you quickly walk by
Can you hear them cry
For the emotion there is deep
And the price not at all cheap

And their questions all echo why
But no answers, the winds are empty

and dry
Though they stand strong and steep
A lonely death they shall reap

Now empty their space in the sky
No reminders, or rest for the birds that fly
Gone now, lost forever in final sleep
Their existence, for you and I only, to remember and to keep

Maura Boyle
A THOUSAND WISHES IN THE NIGHT

A thousand wishes in the night
A thousand reasons why
When I sit and dream like this
You're all that comes to mind
A thousand thoughts whispered in the night
with no one there to care

A thousand words told to the stars
That will never reach your ears
And, as I drift into my sleep
I wonder why I care
When you're so far away
And my heart's so lonely here.

Kendra Suzanne Cheshareck
SUNRISE

The flowers yawn
and rub their eyes
like sleepy people
when the sun
begins to rise.

Birds twitter
and flutter about
weaving, like cars in a traffic jam,
in and out.

The whole world begins
to stir and stretch
with the rising
of the sun.

William H Dennis
OUR NEIGHBORS

Dedicated to our neighbors: James and Mary Flaherty.

Men have many neighbors,
As the shiny years go by.
People that have come and gone
But don't see eye to eye.

We have real good neighbors,
That live right next to us.
There's always a friendly smile,
And there is no fret or fuss.

For in due season of the year,
There is a shower of earthly gifts;
Fruits and many vegetables,
That give us spiritual lifts.

We cannot keep up with them.
No matter how hard we try.
God bless our next door neighbors,
As the shiny years go by.

Heather Knell Shelton
WHISPERING MOUNTAIN

The mountains rise above the ground,
Little creatures running all around.
Between two peaks,
The wind speaks,
"Come my children,
Come one and all,
Come to the mountains tallest of tall."
Listen closely, you shall hear,
The wind whispering the message in your ear.

Gayle Jones
DOVE SONG

Doves are speaking tender
words of love,
Their peaceful voices echo
heartstrings from above,

Joyful notes that overflow
into this heart of clay,
Messengers of the spirit that
transcend the promise of day.

They remain only when the
soul is open to receive,
The fullness of a moment that is
fertile to conceive.

Comforted by these melody
makers from the sky.
I start my day with thoughts renewed
by their gentle sigh.

My open window reveals
them in the green willow trees.
Their day song flows sweetly upon
the tranquil breeze.

Their task completed they
soar through the summer air.
Their presence requested an
opportunity of hope to share.

Betty J Ross
THEY'RE NOT FOR YOU TO WORRY ABOUT

To my children; Debbie, Joe, Linda and Brenda, my grandchildren; Becky, Dawn, Pam, David, Rachel, Jeremey and Jessica, and to my Lord Jesus Christ, the Author of my words and my life.

I stood in my own strength on the threshold of despair,
Surrounded by uncertainty, and fear was everywhere.
Fear of what tomorrow held and all that could go wrong
Enveloped me and kept me from the place where I belonged.
Worry creased my forehead and etched upon my face
Were lines of desperation time could not erase.
I wandered in confusion, lost and so alone,
Crying to my Maker, "Lord, where have You gone?
Don't You see me here below calling out to You?
Where's the peace You talked about, the joy of knowing You?
Why do I have these burdens Lord, when You said You'd take them all,
Why do You turn your head and ignore me when I call?"
I heard a still small voice say "Child, that's just not true,
But you've filled the place I need to be with worries about you.
You imagine that I've left you, your mind is full of fear,
But if you'd just look beyond yourself you'd see Me standing here.
Don't exert yourself, My Child, all you need to do,
Is grasp the nail-scarred Hand that's reaching out to you.
I took your cares and burdens, I took your fears and doubts,
I took them to the cross . . . they're not for you to worry about!"

Laura Badeaux
CHILDHOOD

To my son Dewey Wade, daughter Robin and grandson Micheal Sellman.

I watch the children happy at play
Too busy to think about yesterday
And tomorrow seems so far away

When children are little and life's uncluttered
They don't understand the remarks adults mutter
Like the color of folks' skin
Their religion and such
They just don't seem to count for much

It doesn't matter if you're rich or poor
They're just having fun
That's what life's for.

Childhood should be a wonderful thing
Happy and light and not filled with pain

For too soon we grow up and life can be tough
And the days never seem to be long enough.
We look back on our past, the good and the bad
And bless the wonderful childhood we had.

Virginia Heston
ON SURVIVING A SPOUSE'S DEATH

We're watching you
We watch you live with courage,
Watch you care,
Though life grows bare.

We're watching you
We watch you reach for laughter
To save a day
That shades of gray.

We're watching you
We see you seek refreshment,
Renewing soul
And self control.

We're watching you.
We watch with appreciation.
We haste to cheer
And hover near.

We're watching you.
We take strength from your fortitude,
May we emulate
Accepting fate.

Donald Woods
IN THE MIDST OF A STORM

Storms of life will rise in our lives
as a ship driven against a raging sea

Just as Jesus in a ship, with his
disciples, beckoning for him to see

The winds and the waves that arose,
while he lay asleep

Jesus arose, and replied, o why do
you fear

As he rebuked the winds, and the raging sea, can't you feel my
presence near?

He dwells on the altar of your heart
like a ship on a stormy sea

Wake him up, let him rise in your life,
for all the world to see

Melissa Willson
QUESTIONS OF THE HEART

Do we reunite again?
Or do we fall apart
Do we relive yesterday?
Or make a brand new start

Do we learn to forgive?
Or never let it die
Do we tell the truth?
Or is it better of a lie

Do we learn to love again?
Or destined against our fate
Do we give it time?
Or is it all too late

Do we let each other go?
Or hold on by a thread
Do we always remember?
Or forget the bad things said

Do we always have to hurt?
Or finally show we care
Do we have to wonder?
Or promise to be there

I wish I had the answer
of why we're now apart
Maybe someday we will understand
These questions of the heart

Becky Kralik
REMEMBERING MY GRANDPA

To my grandpa, who I love dearly. He had the gift of life, and he enjoyed living life to the fullest. He always has a smile.

Remembering all them good ol' days.
Remembering all the fun.
Remembering how much I love him.
Knowing he's number one.

Remembering how young he was.
Remembering how much pain he felt.
Remembering how he wanted me at his side, so I knelt.

Remembering all them hospital bills.
The trouble he had and how it kills.
All those times I had to cry.
Dear God, I hope he doesn't die.

Helene Poirier
TOMORROW IS NOT HERE

To the most important people in my life, you have helped me to grow and learn, thanks Rickey and Donna.

The pain of death
is so deep and final.
How we dread to feel it.

Filled with sorrow, for losing someone
no last goodbyes, there was no time.
What needed to be said,
forever in our hearts.

When the moment is right,
and words need to be spoken
seize the moment.
For you may never get another chance.

In our lives
we forget that death
is so much a part of us
that, when it calls us,
we are surprised.

Do not live in fear of death,
but live with the knowledge,
that it will come one day,
and that you will have done, the best
you can.

Elaine Levan
THE JOB
Oh, God above,
Watch all the
People that I
Love

Guide them to
Do only good
things right
and keep them
in your Divine
Loving Light.

Bruce A Pfeiffer
DREAMS OF SUZANNE

For Suzi—Source of my inspiration.

Overhead clouds rush by
Eluding chill winds in pursuit.
Now scattering, allowing to reach the
ground
But one single ray of sunlight.
The dear one that I love.
A warm breeze gently stirring
She fills my soul, renewing my spirit.
Bathed in her radiant glow,
I float upon a tranquil sea.
Rain begins to fall, the wind again to
blow;
Seemingly crying her name.
Tossed by angry waves I awaken.
Realizing my place being on the
threshold of a dream.
As far as the vastness of the heavens
Is her distance from me.
Yet, as near as my heart she remains.
And so the breath of my very life
Is now the wind which carries her
name.
Gently drifting through time
immeasurable.
Being the loveliest of all—Suzanne.

Elaine Ralph
SONG FOR CANADA

Dedicated to all Canadians; and especially to Julie, Kelly, Lori, Ashlee and Chandra with love.

Thank you Lord for letting me be
Born of Canadian nationality
Born in this country that's young and
free
Where people can be what they
choose to be
We've got two national dialects
And many races
Where people don't discriminate
Against one another
From Mould Bay and Ellesmere Isle
Down to Windsor, your most
southerly child
Your lovin' people and resources
unfold
Ah, yes, this land has riches that go
untold
Oh from Vancouver shores to
St. John's
And every town in between
Oh maple leaf, truly how you gleam
Canada, land of our dreams
Land of the future
From Pacific to Atlantic seas
A miracle, oh Canada
You are really free

Libby Lou Scott
LOVE IS . . .

To Jim Cummings. You are the reason why I wrote this poem. I love you!

Love Is . . . Happiness that you give me when I'm with you.

Love Is . . . Caring for you like I always do, when I'm away from you or by your side.

Love Is . . . Sharing everything that we have love, happiness, sadness, and feelings.

Love Is . . . Loving the way you do.

Love Is . . . Joy that you bring to me day in and day out, no matter where I am.

Love Is . . . For Jim Cummings the person that makes all of this come true.

Love Is . . . For Libby Scott the other person that makes all this come true.

Ofelia Pancarician
HOW IT CAME TO BE
The universe was black
as empty as can be.
Till one day the Lord
came down to see.

To bring out the light
hiding within.
To bring out the sun
that's how he'll begin.

He brought out the moon
and the heavenly stars.
He brought out the earth
and the planets afar.

On the earth he put land and water
animals and trees.
He even put humans,
Adam and Eve.

The flowers smelled sweet,
God did all of this
in just one week.

Althea "Boo" Bradley
BEGINNING TEARS

In Memory of Albert Austain Stein.

As we begin to make our mark in the sands of life, we start to realize that it is a cold cruel walk.

We meet people and friends along the way, we sort our friends and enemies.

As we race against time to make our fullest dreams and our deepest thoughts come true, as our friends move away we feel confused and empty.

Like a sky breaking into a million pieces, our hearts beating faster; Like thunder crashing against the clouds, we start to think about how this world we live in can destroy us.

As we continue further throughout our adulthood we remember all we have seen and learned,

We never grow to our dream or thoughts; until we are gone.

Kimberly Caporale

Kimberly Caporale
MY DREAM IS NOW REAL

Anthony, You have inspired me to believe that dreams do come true. Thank you for having enough courage for both us of us and for believing in us. I Love You.
Miss Kim

An ache in my heart that tears me
apart.
A tear in my eye. My love couldn't
lie.
A touch of the hand. Do you
understand?
Will we be together? This dream is
forever.

The news breaks my heart. We'll
soon be apart.
You sing a sad song. Could I have
been wrong?
My heart now must pay, as you walk
away.
My dream slowly shatters. My one
dream that matters.

I hoped every day you'd come back
my way.
If only you'd see what you mean to
me.
My prayers were heard without even
a word.
You finally came. Will it be the
same?

The hole in my heart, together or
apart,
Grew bigger each day. "It's nothing,"
I'd say.
You offered an ear and said you were
here.
You'd help if you could. I doubted
you would.

I waited so long. You proved I was
wrong,
Your kiss was so sweet. My heart
skipped a beat.
You colored my days with sweet
sunshine rays.
All the love that we feel. My dream is
now real . . .

Cindy Robertson
BLUE AS THE SKY

This poem is dedicated to Gary, my delightful son.

You are so beautiful and innocent,
Wonderfully bright and shy.

You are so bouncy and happy,
Your eyes are as blue as the sky.

You make me happy every day,
I know you are very special.

You are such a big part of my life,
In each and every way.

We are happy when we're together,
We always have such fun.

You are my one and only,
Thank you for being my son.

Correll Loundermon Townes
SHE IS
She is strong under the weight of oppression.

Her faith is endless, never waning.

She watches her children dying, yet presses on another day with hope.

Decades has she waged her endless struggle; the wrinkles on her brow show her ageless search for peace, equality and dignity.

SHE awakes each day ready again to face whatever comes with determination.

Her eyes have washed the land with tears that would fill many oceans.

Her children's blood has flooded the land like terrestrial rains.

Her pain has been felt around the world.

SHE is rich, yet poor,
Powerful, yet weak,
Intelligent, yet ignorant,
Blessed by great heritage, yet cursed
by greed and power.

SHE IS AFRICA, AWAKENING AGAIN IN SEARCH OF HER OWN DESTINY! ! ! ! !

David Neil Manzer
THE GATHERING
Let's all gather to reflect
let's all gather in close
let's not speak of title
let us not boast
let's be ourselves
all at the same time
let's once in our lives
leave all the lies
and insanity behind.

Gayle R Amaral
FAMILY OF FIVE
A family of five living in an outdated house—white with green shutters remains a mystery to me, and so many others. With some shades down, and other windows with none; No curtains, nor furniture, not even a bed for the three little ones. Family and friends, never arrive, to visit the mysterious family of five. On every holiday, decorations will be hung outside for everyone passing by to see, but the inside remains empty, and they go on living in secrecy. The family of five are as friendly as can be, yet, it is still unknown as to why they live so mysteriously.

Esther Henson
THE LILY
The lily tree, they toil not
Neither do they spin
But King Solomon was not arrayed
Like unto one of them
They come in many lovely colors.
White, pink, even lilac too.
Painted by the Master Artist's hand
To bring beauty to me and you.
So the lily tree reminds
When the night seems dark and long
The hand that paints the flowers
Will guide me until dawn.

James A Reives

James A Reives
LOOK INTO YOUR HEART

To the lady that inspires me to write, Barbara L. Temple, and my children and all the poetry readers of the world.

If you look into your heart with a positive mind, and take notice of His love and His grace then you're leaving all the sinful things behind, everybody's got a story about His love and about he good things he does, some of us want sugar and spice and everything nice, but Christ is the spice of our life, I'm telling everybody to believe in His name, because eternal life is what you gain.

So look into your heart with a positive mind, you will see that God's love and grace have been there for some time, Christ is the one who can heal, he'll show us how to live, Jesus died on the cross on Calvary Hill, this was his Father's will.

Just open up your heart and let Jesus in He'll forgive you of all your sins. So I'm telling everybody to believe in his name, because eternal life is what you gain.
So look into your heart and you find where love first starts. When I had nothing left and thought that I was by myself, that's when Jesus came and I knew I had to accept. For the spice of our life, Christ is the one who paid the price. So let's all believe in His name, because eternal life is what we're gain.

James A Reives
'TWAS THE NIGHT BEFORE JESUS CAME
'Twas the night before Jesus came and all through the house, not a creature was praying not one in the house. The Bibles were on the shelf without care, in hope that Jesus would not come there. The children were dressing to crawl in bed, not one ever kneeling or bowing a head. Mother in her rocker with baby on lap, watching the late show while I took a nap. When out of the east arose such a clatter, I run to the window to see what was the matter. Right before my eyes, Angels appear, proclaiming that Jesus was here. Then I saw a light shining like the noon day sun, I knew in a moment that it was God's only son. The light of His face made me cover my head, it was Jesus returning just like he had said. Though I possessed worldly wisdom and wealth, I cried in shame as I knelt. In the book of life which he held in His hand, was the name of every saved man. He never spoke as He searched for my name, then He said it's not here, my head hung in shame. The people whose names had been written with love, He gathered to take to His Father above. With those who were ready, He rose without a sound, while all the rest were left standing around; I stood and cried as they rose out of sight, oh if I had only been ready tonight!

Marne H Finfrock
MEMORIES
Memories landscape the mind.
Those of rolling hills behind
The peaks and valleys, we recall
The plateaus reached affecting all.

Memories landscape the mind.
Greener pastures—yet to find
Plains of joy, from hollows of grief
In gradual slopes seek relief.

Memories landscape the mind.
Aspirations are entwined
In vast terrain of what might be
Instilling hope as thoughts run free.

Marne H Finfrock
CORPORATE CAPERS
Should corporate gods take control—
Mankind will relinquish its soul.
  In disguise as Progress,
  Yet it's not more, but less,
To succumb to greed takes its toll.

While a nation at risk blames schools,
Let's take stock of corporate ghouls
  Who have power to lead,
  But abuse it to feed
A network entangled with fools.

Questioning minds, actions are bound
By fear—so not making a sound
  We are setting a trend:
  Teaching children to bend
Toward lifestyles where freedoms aren't found.

Cloaked by many capes of disguise,
Corporate Capers dazzle eyes.
  Let us see through the murk,
  Where the danger does lurk,
To prevent ultimate demise!

Bonnie Rae Walker
IMAGINATION

Dedicated to my mother and father, Alice & Charles Rhoden, for their unconditional love and encouragement.

There is a place in the imaginations of people,
That comes from somewhere inside;
Where lonely women seek out their lovers,
And little boys go there to hide.

Where old men have dreams of importance,
And young girls look for a friend;
Where all God's creatures are lovely,
And naught ever comes to an end.

There is a place in the imaginations of people,
A place from deep down inside;
Where illusion is a peaceful escape,
And each one goes there to hide.

Bonnie Rae Walker
TEENS WITH TIME
Why is it that I never saw a gang member fishing by the sea?
Or a young person riding horses plotting trouble for you or me?
For it is hard for one to dwell on any kind of hate
When you are busy trying to thread a worm for fishing bait.

And young people, if you cannot find healthful things to do,
I suggest a horse be found, especially for you.
A gelding fine and in his prime will show to you the way
Of long trail rides and cleaning stalls and fresh cut new-mown hay.

For our young people's curse, you see, besides their loneliness,
Are parents who don't care enough to plan for idleness.

Cynan
FRIENDS

In deepest memory of my friend Daniel Wolf.

A shoulder to cry on,
An ear to bend.
Money to borrow,
Clothes to lend.

Friday night movies,
Afternoon walks.
Being together,
Our private talks.

Mending our hearts,
Crying those tears.
Planning our futures,
Voicing our fears.

Our memories together,
May they never end.
Always together,
Forever friends.

Hedy Irma Gonzalez
UNDYING LOVE
Deep within my heart is an emptiness that has not been filled since I've lost you.

Nothing said or done can erase this pain.

Time keeps ticking on and on but my heart remains frozen, remembering only the hour we said our last good-byes.

I held you so close that day, feeling the warmth in my arms. How could I have known it would be the last time we would hold each other again?

My Darling . . . My Love . . . so great was that love, so pure and so sweet.

Nothing can replace it. Nothing at all . . . Not even time.

Gary F Seifert
FATHERS AND SONS
The deceit of life
Is strangely sweet
And deep within its glow
Conceals the truth
It leads us to:
That we beside our
Father's grave will stand
And then in time will be
With him beneath
The brooding sand.

We'll want to say of him
When he is gone, I'm sure,
That despite his flights
From duty's call he was
A simple man, and good,
Who did what he thought best
Although he couldn't know
If what he thought was so
And whether the promise
Of his faith did more
Than hide the dulling
Of his argument with time.

Chiquita M Hopkins
RESCUED

To God be the glory, for His spiritual insight and guidance.

The sky was thick and cloudy but the sun broke through,
A welcoming sunshine, comforting sky of blue.
Head hung low in dismal sorrow to the inner face bear,
Rescued by an awakening smile, hearts of joy share.
Though you dined in poverty's barrel, enclosed in its towering walls,
Escaping through the cracks of narrow, timely answer to the call.
Poor and sick in health, in sickness comes death sleep,
Restored before its coming the healing campers creep.
Caged in self destruction locked without a key,
Even iron wears out, it's the love of yourself that sets you free

Mahala Buckingham
THE SKATER
My heart is a frozen pond of silence
which you skate upon with your
sharp skates

Bowing and turning
dipping and sliding
You are so elegant and swift

And when the spring comes
as it must do
My heart will pool and melt

But it will run in the
currents you etched with your
sharp skates

Marie Ann Hissom
W-A-C-K ALL WORLD STATIONS
Keep up the good work
Don't worry about the others
Because this world is going around

Ding-a-ling here—Ding-a-ling there
Get your phone calls and let it pour
The sour-casim is not ashame
But the good ol' station is insane
Gossip, gossip a trillion miles high
The ones on the other planets would love to die
Laughing, coaching isn't cheap
Because it's all garbage and by the heap
If by the end of the day your blood pressure is good
You wonder how in the heck you ever stood
Talk, talk and ever again
My this station is wearing thin
But God bless you and at the end
We are so happy we made a friend.
W-orld
A-erial
C-ommunications
K-orners

Eva C Davis
JONQUILS IN THE SNOW

Dedicated to the memory of my husband, Richard L. Davis, who died Feb. 14, 1977.

I walked out in the yard to-day,
Through a late, light winter snow;
And jonquils, he had planted there,
Were blooming, row on row.

Their golden heads were bowed
With the unexpected snow,
But soon the sun shone bright again,
To reveal their golden glow.

He planted them so long ago
And loved to see them bloom.
He'd stop, sometimes, to pick a few
To brighten up my room.

He's sleeping now, beneath the snow
And, though many years have come and gone,
So sure, as jonquils bloom in snow,
So do the memories linger on.

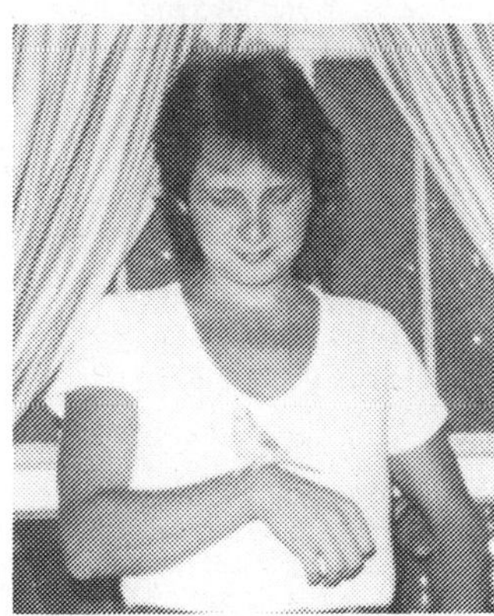

Ricky E Barnette

Ricky E Barnette
ON MY WAY OUT
Big city buildings
Bright flashy lights
Streetwalkers
Fast talkers
And winos in the night
The feel
How good it was
The smell
How sweet it was
The taste
How exquisite
After nine months of waiting
I finally arrived
Deal me in
Count me in
The next hand's mine
Showgun
How fast I won
The winnings are mine
And here I go
Back again in time

Melissa Anne Williams
TO VALERIE ON HER WEDDING DAY
The dawning of things anew is often
hand-in-hand with the season
of Spring—
For it is always during the Springtime
when pastel-colored flowers
can be seen inching their
way up
through the cold and
hardened earth;
when the "neigh" of a newborn
foal
and the song of a
newly-hatched bird
can be heard on every
current of air;
when two hearts, two minds,
and two souls
melt beautifully into one
being,
and can celebrate the
miracle of Love . . .

With each and every Springtime,
a new and more fresh
beginning is created—
Just as your life is now facing
a new and more beautiful
beginning.
For Poetry's sake, one could also call
this most precious time in your
life
"the Spring" of your life—
Only your Spring came in January!

Kim Fisher
CHILDREN

Dedicated (in loving memory) to my son, Oscar, 1973-1990.

C is for Caring, an emotional
must,
H is for Having great patience
and trust,
I is for IF there's any reason for
doubt . . .
LOVE is the answer—It never
runs out.
D is for the Dreams that shall
now come true,
R is for the Reality that this
child's a part of you,
E is for Everlasting is the love of
a mother,
N is for Now you have given new
life to another . . .
And, this life is your life,
needing love like no other.

Cheryl King-Haughey
MY BELOVED
I thought of my horse Sendosha today,
it opened a hurt long put away.
A pain that tears at my very soul,
it seems to bury it has been my
goal.
Now as I return to the place of her death,
I can feel the emptiness as it
takes away my breath.
And as I try to reach down deep within,
it all comes rushing back to me
again.
As I reminisce of the joys we shared,
the tears come with
the thought, "Why wasn't she
spared."
Deep with my heart I mourn her passing,
but she lives within my
memory which is forever
lasting.
Now it is time to turn away,
and replace the lid, but not
forever to stay.

Scott R Atwood

Scott R Atwood
TRUE OR DREAM

This is dedicated to those who dream . . . for if you dream and work at the same time you will accomplish your dreams.

Life is like a dream
not knowing if it is alive or not
it can be as devilish as a nightmare
or as peaceful as a dove in flight
a dream is like life
jumbled and confused

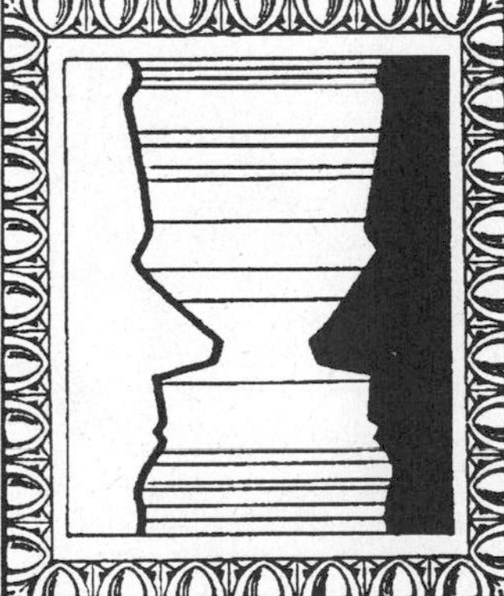

for not knowing when present
becomes past
for as dawn comes another day
begins
or another dream starts
so life lives on whether it be dream or
reality
for one does not know the difference

Francene Oachs
CABIN IN THE WOODS
The rays of the sun
Streams through the dusty window.
Leaving shadows of the trees,
Falling across the floor.

The small table in the corner,
Has memories of a writer sitting
there.
The yellowed papers written on
Have dreams of a lover and his tears.

The slight creak of the door
When fully opened wide,
Exposes to the peaceful outdoors
The loneliness hidden inside.

Barbette Garwood
A LIFE FORGOTTEN
Nesting deep within my mother's womb
I think of what it is like outside in the world.
Yet, not knowing what will become of me
I can't wait to greet my mother's face.
I bet she is beautiful!
I hope she likes me.
I dream of her cuddling me close, and giving me all of her love.
But what is this?
A powerful force pulling me away! !
I'm not ready yet!
Mommy it's hurting
Do something
Why are you letting this happen to me?
Did I do something wrong?
Do I deserve to just be thrown away?
Whatever did I do to make you do this?
All I would have ever want from you is your love!
Was that asking so much?
I guess you didn't want me after all,
you aborted me!

Steven J Miller
FACES

To the Loving Memory of Albert Miller, 1907-1989.

Faces of the Past,
Flash in my mind
Faces of childhood
of fun and games
Faces of love
The face of Grandpa
Faces of friendship
Dedee the best
Faces of Guidance
Mother and Father
These faces I remember
and cherish each waking
day, God bless these
faces of time and
memory and may,
love be eternal in
their hearts and lives

Betty Wicks
MENDER OF THE NETS
As he sat in his boat with his net o'er his knee
There was much need for mending and he searched diligently.
Some holes were from weakness and some from abuse.
Some had been snagged on a nail that was loose.
Just as our lives—our nets—we neglect
We must oft times drop anchor and take time to reflect.
We must learn to let go—take our worries and wrath
Box them up neatly, close the lid and then laugh!
We must never lose faith or hide from his light.
We must open life's window and then turn to the sun
Make a new start ere the old day is done:
We must take up the cross, as did Jesus and then—
We too, like the others—become fishers of men.

Cleator Rose Clay
SONGS OF FLOWERS IN THE HEARTS

To the Clay Family and Rev. Joe West Clay and family, a special friend (non-mention), Theodore Dargan a post-dispatch photographer and his success with Gov. Dukakis Campaign for presidency in St. Louis.

Life has its growing pains for all
Blacks, whites, big, fat or small
But a song in the heart is
Escalating joy of a special event

A gift, a talent, a praise
That is by all, a God sent
A song in the heart is a
Flower blooming to its peak anew
Cultivated with warmth, love
And adornments of its view

Songs of flowers in the hearts
Acknowledge that all peoples
Are God flowers no matter
How the flowers bloom
A good harvest of the heart
Makes the difference of
How the flowers gloom

Mike Peterson

Mike Peterson
A WHITE DWARF DIES AND LIVES
As the moon rises,
The stars come out.
But there's a crisis,
When meteors flash about.

Shooting stars fly then fall,
But they leave a streaming tail,
For an angel just made his call,
Now night after night they sail.

Whispering secrets to each other.
Yes, they argue and fight,
With even their brother,
That's when they see the light.

They sway and loop,
Off they go in a flash
With all of their troops,
Leaving a white gash.

Mike Peterson
THE EARTH
For the sky is blue,
And the ground is green—
With trees speckled all over,
It is like a dream.

Mike Peterson
THE WIND
The wind whistled past
Occasionally shaking the windows.
The night mournfully casts
Its hollow cradles
Of solitude that lasts.
Some believe the night is a friend,
Others doubt this in their souls.
But who will know when
The night will end.
Howling blissfully about it takes its tolls.

Surely, the curtains are drawn,
If not dare gaze out.
For fear of seeing death about.
True, the window will scream on
And cry for mercy, so doubt.

If it's your soul that counts
Then listen to this plea:
Let the night beg—what it wants—
But don't let it have, you see
It's your life that you treasure.

Mike Peterson
A SCENE OF ENERGY
Rippling, full of energy,
Cresting, then breaking, crashing
Spilling its vibrant life over the surface,
Spewing foam and bubbles.

Crest after crest endlessly,
Trailing from its source,
On a route unknown to it,
But still found in its drive.

Feverishly, pulsing, pulsing,
Pulsing with unknown life.
Life that exists in the unknown.
But ending just as well.

Pamela Malliaris
KALEIDOSCOPE
I open my arms to embrace mankind,
but never seem to touch.
I release my soul to give of myself,
but never give too much.
I listen most intently,
to voices old and new;
but never seem to comprehend,
what is really true.
I'm an impotent observer,
gazing through my kaleidoscope.
Wading through a sea of change,
I try in vain to cope.
The paths that I have travelled,
have become a maze of years.
I see my past reflected,
in shards of broken mirrors.
What remains is just one spark.
The light I know as hope;
The only color left inside
my shattered kaleidoscope.

Tammie L Boyles
DREAMS

This poem is dedicated to John Szymanski for reminding me that without dreams we have nothing at all.

how many times must i sit here and wonder
how many times must i ask myself why
how many times must i sit here and ponder
watching my dreams drift by

one by one they shatter before me
one by one they scatter in the wind
too far gone to ever hold again

why did they have to drift away
why could they not linger a while longer

but alas
they are gone like the days of yesteryear

life seems unfulfilled
time passes by at a miraculous rate
i am left behind again

my life takes a turn
my dreams seem closer than ever before

i reach out to grasp a lifetime of dreams
only to find that they are no longer dreams
but reality

Louise T Templeton
THE HOUSE ON THE HILL
There's a dear old house that stands on the hill
And oh how I long to be there
Just a child again tonight
And sit in the little high chair

Again in my dreams I fancy I hear
A little girl's voice as she said
Her "now I lay me down to sleep"
As she knelt by her mother's bed

Girlish dreams were unfold in that dear old house
And castles were built in the air
If houses could talk I'm sure you would know
Every childish sorrow and care

Sometimes at evening when day is done
I think in the shadows I see
A tired little lassie of long ago
Asleep at her daddy's knee

Oh I'd like to turn back the years in their flight
And just be a little girl still
Living again those wonderful days
Spent in that house on the hill

Virginia Spicer Tillison

Virginia Spicer Tillison
THERE AN IRIS GROWS

In loving memory of my sister, Iris, who loved children and nature, especially the sea. She was transformed into Glory May 9, 1990.

The iris so beautifully formed
is more than meets the eye,
you see
It's delicate yet strong to withstand
the elements that be.

Thoughts of my sister bring
Such images to mind
Her name itself implies her beauty
and strength combined.

Beauty of character matched in
face and form
Standing tall I watched her
weather many a storm
And after each storm was past
I saw her face with a smile
Still standing tall with strength
for yet another mile.

Though the womb denied her
her rightful claim, she taught
Many a child to stop—and see
to touch and hear—things like
A bird taking a bath
The wind in a silver maple tree
A stone in the path
The shell a creature left by the sea.

When as a child, I myself she taught
to run and play and shout
Filling a need I felt to be loved
and cared about!

She taught me to be strong
and fight the fears of night
The ones that often gave me
such a fright.

She taught me to dream
and never give up
That what God gives to fill
is a big cup!

With adulthood came the faceless fears
of night again,
Forbidding the child within
to play and win
They didn't hinder us though,
we'd laugh and joke and talk about
Those days, they're ours forever
without a doubt!

When we were together there was
that lightness of heart
Reminiscent of those childhood
days—even in the supermart!

Now my grown-up children too
join with me to say
A life of "special" memories they
share with their little ones
Along the way.

Somewhere I've heard it said—
Oh! 'twas in the Word of God
I read:
"Hold on too tight and lose it all
Give some away and watch it grow"

Her life proved that to be so
as her beauty and love grow
And ripple across our lives
never ending))))))))))

Now she's gone to teach and share
with all the little ones THERE
Who here were snatched from
the womb—never allowed
to hear, or touch, or see—things
like: A bird taking a bath
The wind in a silver maple tree,
A stone in the path, or
That shell a creature left by the sea.

Surely God meant for them to
know and see
For now THERE an Iris grows
beside the Crystal Sea!

Nathaniel Bruce Dowdy

Nathaniel Bruce Dowdy
A KNIGHT'S PLIGHT

To my wife for caring, and my dog for not eating the second copy.

Castle dark
Chamber deep
Fair haired maiden
Lays asleep

Dragon's bane
Evil plight
Death to all
But bravest knights.

Flossie Shipman
NANNY'S KNEE

This Poem is dedicated to my Darling Twin Granddaughters Misty and Melody Wines, whom God chose to brighten the remaining days of my life. Age 4 1/2 yrs. old.

There's always room on Nanny's knee for little ones so dear,
and though she's very busy, she'll sit down to hold them near.
She loves to hear the things they say
and hopes they understand,
it makes her life so happy when they're holding to her hand.
And when they want to cuddle up, and take a little nap,
it makes her feel much younger when they climb upon her lap.
And when their eyes are heavy, the sand-man's close you see,
they'll look and smile a precious smile, 'cause they're on Nanny's knee.
But much too soon the time will pass,
and they will all be grown,
and Nanny Prays they'll all be Blessed, with children of their own.
Yet they'll always remember, though older they will be,
when troubles come, they all can run,
and kneel at Nanny's knee.

Patricia Billings
MY BEAUTIFUL FUR

I run in haste as I see them slaughter my brother
Knowing that if I stay I will be next
I know I have not the weapons to war with them,
Nor do I have the strength.
For so long I have cried out for help,
And still to no avail
The burly hunters most surely prefer my hide to my yell
It takes me and 249 more of my brothers to coat a petite woman
Shouldn't that be some clue
That my beautiful fur was not made to fit you?

Matthew J Roman
BLUEBIRD

Thou art beautiful
Beautiful as a bird in flight
Let me ride on your wing Bluebird
The wing of existence
In your eyes Bluebird I exist
Although I fade away sometimes
Upon your wing I can exist forever
Together our love will soar higher and higher
Soar Bluebird

Matthew J Roman
INSANITY

The other side of my mind
The colors of black and white crowd its interior
Nothingness is all I'll ever see
Everything is impure
The white walls are tarnished with gold blood
The golden droplets form a river ever flowing through the center of my mind
The shades of gray matter take control of my mind
I'm a prisoner of my own existence
Escape is no longer a reality
The other side of my mind

Nona M Upright
SHE'S GONE

My friend, you left so silently
leaving only His footprints in the sand.
If I could have but held your hand
in that brief moment before Eternity.

The darkness of my thoughts and days
are filled with plans that
now will never be.
Oh, Dear Friend, it's now I need your hand
to gently lead me forward in
your loving ways.

Maria Bee-Tapscott
THE SILVER CORD OF LOVE ETERNAL

To "The Windwalker" my love eternal.

The Love Eternal; innumerable kisses, caresses in forbidden places; the only
Exploding nova of uncontrollable passions; young teenage romance.

Vietnam War; Army tour of duty; home on leave to return to awaiting embraces;
Letters filled with love and encouragement, hope and future plans.
A silver cord interweaves between lovers.

Apocalypse; unanswered letters; dejection, yet hoping for the love eternal to
Return. Days, weeks, months; alive? dead? in another's embrace?

Other companions saunter along into our worlds: Alas the void, the abyss!
The sight of friends' loves eternal sickens me.

Only in dreams does my love eternal appear to me, ever walking thru the winds
Of my mind. Glowing embers awaiting the rekindling of my love eternal returned.

Convenient and lonely marriages, expensive separations from temporary partners
Attempting to fill the gaping wound.
Twenty years gone with the blink of an eye.
Loneliness grows as sunset to the black velvet of night.

BUT WAIT!! A familiar call from the other side of the abyss reignites the
Flames within. It is my love eternal returned. A new era begins. All is
Forgiven and Forgotten. The silver cord of love eternal has always existed;
Yet invisible.

Reunited, the silver cord reveals itself. Two youthful spirits, two soul-mates
At last united in eternal marriage.

No dreams are needed now. All is reality.

Lorraine Jackson

Lorraine Jackson
JESUS

This poem is dedicated to inspire Christian Services, and to the work of International Convalescent Ministries.

Jesus changed my life.
He was the key to my sight.

People don't know till they are told, 'bout Jesus bless his soul.

Jesus, he is always with us.

He stood the test for the right.
He never gave in to Satan's fight.
He is a mighty king to bear our sins.

I praise him and his healing hands.
Jesus is a holy man.

Jesus, he is always with us.
Count your blessings he came to earth.

Can you still feel the power of the hours he walked this land?

In love you find what he taught.
On mountains you see where he thought.

Upon Jesus's face was the cares of everyone.
In grace he embraced us.

Jesus is always with us.

Lorraine Jackson
ELDERLY

This poem is dedicated to Eddie-Lou Cole and all seniors world wide.

Our elderly are to be cherished
every day we should tell them.
Let's let them know they
are worthwhile, and greet them
with a smile.

The elderly help shape our todays
with their yesterdays.
And their wisdom gives us knowledge.

We bless them with ourselves,
the love we share with them,
the care we give them,
the joy we bring them.

Gregory R Travis
I AM OVERWHELMED, AND FRANKLY, I'M AMAZED

I am overwhelmed.

A sunburst of light, more brilliant than I had ever hoped to see, has entered my life.

Her dazzling sparkle diminishes my importance in life, for I have now seen true perfection.

I had hoped to turn away, frightened of what such radiance might do to me.

But at last, I stand transfixed, mesmerized by her beauty and simplicity.

Her innocence seems to purge the torturous harshness of life's realities from my mind.

Peace and contentment envelope me as I stare at her, trance-like, all the while disbelieving that she's really mine.

Frankly, I'm amazed.

LaRay Sharee Price
RESTING PLACE

God looked down from the sky above
To find the next soul to protect and love
From the sky he reached down his hand
And said "Come to me and walk in my land"
He found the soul that was rich as gold
And said "Forever with thee you will behold"
"You will be with me for all the days to remain"
"I will protect you from all hurt and pain"

She looked up to him with a smile on her face
And knew that she had found her final resting place

Emil K Rottler
CHILDREN PLAYING ON THE BEACH

Children in the sand,
Both boy and girl,
Finger elements of time
To shape and build
Masks of life eternal—
To dare in youth
By shaping in molds
Imaged earthen gods
That wash away
In tides of life eternal.

Anthony M Radcliff
FOREVER BLIND

In their eyes I'll
always be, just a color
running free, they look at me crazy, and they
always stare, and because of my skin, they treat
me unfair, I had no choice, in which the race I
was made, and if I did, I would stay the same,
I can't understand this hate that they feel, what
seems to be wrong, what's the deal, is it so bad,
that you have to kill, my brother and friends,
just tell me, will it ever end, or will you
be like this all the time, and stay sadly

FOREVER BLIND!

Gwendolyn Moore
IN THIS CIRCLE IS FULL OF LOVE

To my mother, Carolyn, my brother, John and my sisters Joyce and Lorraine. I love you.

In this Circle is Full of love
Within the circle we look above
Looking at the sky below heaven
Hoping we all will be forgiven
We stand in silence saying a prayer
Hoping to see a sign from our savior
We are asking to be forgiven for our sins
Deep inside the soul within
In this circle we are standing hand in hand
Praying for forgiveness of woman and man
Every race, color and creed
Stands hand and hand for this deed
We have finally seen the light
We came out of the dark night
Never again will we judge each other
By the color of our skin
We will see each other
For what we have within
Heavenly Father thank you for shining the light
Or we would have lived each day on a dark night

Diana R Yost
FUTURE WORLD

Through the window, I see the future world more vividly than the past
It isn't the dark starry-filled days
with chrome surfaces of sci-fi novels.
It is a world of bright colors and varied histories.
The future will bring many advances and technologies and shiny new buildings will sprout on the surface like virgin grasses
Spirits of the past will remain floating stories high and reflecting in the glass and steel of the shiny new buildings—time cannot erase history, it creates history.
Through the window, I see myself still alone but not unchanged.
Aging flesh surrounds a young soul.
Eyeglasses enhance the color of her eyes making it impossible for me to see the reflection of my present self.
I cannot help but wonder about this woman who isn't yet me
Does she see the future? or, does she simply remember the past.

Pat Bordner

Pat Bordner
CHRISTMAS THROUGH TIME

The 92 year old clock ticks faithfully on the mantle,
chiming out Christmas joy
A family heirloom and gift of a father's love.
Truly, a measure of the past, present, and future.

The Christmas tree stands
near the hearth,
symbolizing family roots
and life
Yet, as the needles drop slowly a reminder
of aging and temporary existence.

Dinner is served and childhood memories are shared,
packages unfold one by one
Faces reflecting the spirit of giving and the joy of being remembered.

Christmas Day passes and the clock steadily ticks on,
now chiming in the New Year
Bringing new hopes, adding more links to
life's chain and more history
to record.

Kelly Griffith
BECAUSE OF YOU

Because of you
The sun won't shine
The birds won't sing
My words won't rhyme.
Because of you
The nights have grown cold
The songs on the radio
Are now very old.
Because of you
The skies have turned grey.
There's no one around
There's nothing to say.
Because of you
The grass won't grow.
The flowers won't bloom
The wind won't blow.
But because of you
I'll try and say goodbye
Because it wasn't your fault
You didn't choose to die.

Rachael Jeffreys
LOOKING AT HIS PICTURE

I look at his picture and see his face
I think of our love and his warm embrace
Trying to figure out what could go wrong realizing our love is too strong
I look at his picture and seeing him smile, wishing he was here but not for awhile
I look at his picture as he walks in the room
Seeing him there I start to move
Coming together I feel so safe
I love him and love seeing his face

Shanon Berlin
LONELINESS

Am I a stranger living in this time,
With nothing more than my body and my mind?
A desperate spirit wanting to be noticed
By something more than a lens gone unfocused.
Always alone as if encased in a glass shell.
Doesn't anyone want to know the stories I have to tell?
Sure, one day they'll hear my voice
And when they do I'll clearly rejoice.
For then they'll see that I am a friend,
And that is when my loneliness will end.

Linda M Foley
MICHAEL

Permit me to explain exactly what he does—
Important in reflection, and also just because—

Persistence, with gentle patience are his strongest tool,
His manicure of subtlety disarms and slowly cools—

My tension—mounted by his velveted methods combined,
Chocolate eyes, supple lips, longing tongue tease until its time—

For his hands, that wait—put in coaxing places of mine;

And then he moves me to a poise, spiced with dominance,
and he is everywhere—the best poet of his body—commanding every stance!

His pleasure becomes my mirror—as he guides me to this place,
I've never been without him, before him, or after in this case—

Can another man be taught what only he has done to my soul?

by a woman obsessed, LMF

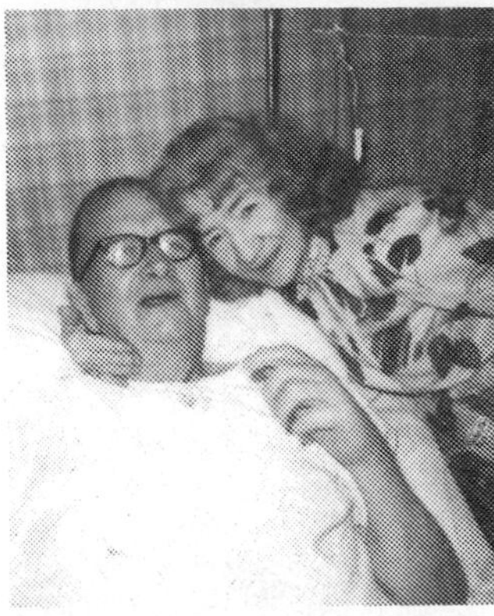

John and Verdia

Verdia P Batson
DREAMS

To John Lamar, my darling husband of 49 yrs. Died Sept. 6, 1987. "I Love You."

I come as a thief in the dark of the night
Stealing your thoughts to my special delight
I come as the lightning that splits through the sky
And flare like the flames of a daring fire.

I tell you of things that are false in one hour
Yet true they are while you're in my power
Preposterous things you see through my tales
You see, yet see not, and your eyes do not fail.

Through me you die and gain life in one night
You eat with the lowest, you drink with great height.
I show you things that no man's ever seen
Things that no other could possibly dream.

My master men are, yet I master all men
I only come while men sleep, from my den
You yield your minds to me, this thing
I conquer you all, and make myself king.

From the beginning and until the end
As long as there's life, I will rule over men.
By night I'm man's master,
By day I'm his slave
Men create me, yet of me
Most men are afraid.

Gregory Hess
WINTER WINDOW

To Elmer, A nice broad with stinky feet—G.

The snowflakes fall as autumn whispers
As I look out my winter window

In sassy flight, on this late eve,
There is freedom in where the wind blows

The ice, whimsically dancing, paints a portrait for only I

Guided by the wind, season's hearty gusts
In shapes surreal of water and pane

Alone, in shadow, I see a sea of seasons
rolling in tides of my memories

Winters before, as boy and man,
I see as if reflected in the glass before me

A light clicks on, the past retreats
My window reflects only the present season

A smile traces the edges of a somber face
Reflected, in my window, is you.

Mary D Carr
BEAUTY AT OUR TOUCH
The sky is so soft
limbs so long and beautiful
the sound of the trusting wind
the smell of fresh air
the love of God shining all around

The wet ground from the rain
with the worms, moving in
the soil, feeding from the
roots of the trees.

Look at the birds fly by
Spreading their wings
hearing the sound of music
To our ear and to our sight
It touches the very depths of
Our hearts.

Winter and Spring, trying to come together
Bringing in its own kind of life
Giving and taking all at the same time
Showing us the power of the base
Of the heaven and earth.

Frank Dolphy Crooks
REGAL BIRTH
It was just another birth;
One more of millions around Earth.
But the media made it grand,
And welcomed it with fanfare and marching band

Then the news came 'It was a girl'
And the crowd went into a swirl
Born with 'eights' she will have no distress
She is bound to be a lucky princess.

Each wagerer increased his stake
To find the babe a namesake
Victoria, Elizabeth or maybe Anne
Or shall we make it the fashionable Dianne

But it was just an ordinary birth
Surrounded by pain hope and mirth
The babe who came along was just another child
Calm, humble, meek and mild.

F J German
WIND BLOWS
And sometimes when the wind
blows back the sand
And the petals from the rosebud
fall
And a good friend goes away
Only then can you understand the
lonely despair of death.

A death while the heart still beats
and the hands still grasp for
the last remnants of respect
A death so cold that it melts the
ice while the air is cool
And the rain falls in torrents
while the sun still shines.

But once gone, will never return
For nothing that once was good
can be again.

Dolores Wilson
TO HONOR THE BABE

Dedicated to all those I love, especially the late George Kohles, my first true fan, and Robert E. Lent my current benefactor.

The one who was born so meek and so mild.
The one who would be a king as a child.
The one full of love, the one kind to all.
The one who would be the savior on call.
The one who would talk from the depth of the heart.
The one whose dead body would be subject for art.
The one of the virgin, the one without sin.
The one with the eyes Mary Magdalene would win.
The one who put fear and such desperation in a king known
as Herod who would slaughter a nation.
The one of compassion, the one without greed.
The one who would shelter all those in need.
The one who was born in a stable of straw.
The one who for honor would desperately crawl.
The one who had animals speaking in voice.
Not from a whip but strictly by choice.
The one who possessed an ultimate grace.
The one who would become an eternal face.

Irasema Ida Harris
MY FAVORITE COLOR IS RED!
My Favorite color is red
It is not dull or dead
It is how teachers write
failing marks
And also the color of
strawberry tarts
This is a color for
Valentine's Day
And also of love in a
special way
Red is the color of my
favorite shirt
And also of the cardinal
bird
It stands for the color of
my favorite game
Sorry but I cannot remember
the name
There is a color I do not
dread
By now you should know
My favorite color is
RED!

Debbye Harmon
THE LAST JOURNEY

Hallie Hargrave, farmer's wife and my beloved grandmother, inspired this poem.

The worn out rocker gently
creaked on the porch as the
old woman slowly swayed
forward and back.
A wisp of gray hair had escaped
the bun to entice flirtation
from the breeze.
The gnarled hands that had
tirelessly cooked and washed,
held untold numbers of babies,
and administered to a dying
husband now lay folded and
motionless in her lap.

She noticed, not for the first time,
how badly the old porch
needed painting.
She noticed, for the last time, the
beauty of the setting sun as it
silently sank out of sight.

The creaks and groans of the old
farmhouse bade her goodnight
and goodbye.
Her tired heart fluttered, her
breath shortened, and she
knew.

Weary eyes gazed longingly at
the rainbow array of
wildflowers in the field.
They had adorned her table
countless times, and she would
have them once more.
Easing herself off the porch, using
the cane for balance, she
hobbled her way to the field.
The pain worsened, and she knew
it was her last journey. She
smiled.

D Perry Hunter
WALLS ENCOUNTERED
Sometimes as down this road I stride,
Entanglements are encountered high and wide.
I stop awhile to ponder,
How and when, I'll cross to yonder.

I turn to take a look from whence I've come,
To receive a clue on what to do.
Maybe, by reviewing the past,
I'll discover why all that security, I felt, didn't last.

Then I remembered not too long ago
Coming to a fork at the end of the road—
'Twas I who chose this path;
'Tis I who must find a way to cross to yonder side this day.

Suddenly, I reached down and grabbed up my fear,
And threw it far, far away, out of sight.
Then, along came Faith, and holding on with all my might,
We, together, crashed that wall in no time at all.

Vicki Gould
CHILDREN

I dedicated this poem to Billy Jack & Alysha for making me feel as though I may be doing it right.

Take them as they are, not as <u>you</u> want them
They're here because you
wanted them to be
Give them credit where credit
is due
Sometimes they know more
than you.

Be their friend, not their Boss
Guide them, Don't Push
Let them know their thoughts are heard
Yet be there to give your word

Allow them time to be just kids
Yet help them grow to adulthood
Teach them, don't criticize
They may be just as wise.

Children are no more than little adults
Waiting to fill the adult world
Let them see what that can be
A place for them to live free.

Jill Hobbs
HONESTY
I've lived my life the best I can
tried to be an honest man
but honesty can be perceived
as anything to suit your need
so what is real and what is not
I only know what I have got
and what is real to me inside
is not to let yourself divide
don't be drawn into the norm
and settle for what's safe and warm
reach inside and see it all
never hide behind the wall
face yourself with open eyes
throw away your old disguise
and only then you'll come to see
you're everything you want to be

Jill Hobbs
DECEIT
I've had enough of sad circus clowns
making an act of putting you down
dancing & daring with hate in their eyes
pulling your strings 'til they hear your cries
evil intent is what keeps them alive
we are the substance on which they survive
consuming us in their web of self hate
their masque of deceit is seen much too late

Jill Hobbs
THE GAME

To my parents for their unconditional love and to Larry for his encouragement.

Step right up and try your luck
play the game and pass the buck

everyone in unison
running with your blinders on
through the maze and up the hill
just to sacrifice your will
thinking that to get ahead
is measured by on whom you tread
pass the cards and roll the dice
convince yourself it's not a vice
try to feel what you have done
is for the sake of everyone
and if you wonder what's the cost
it's only you who will have lost
so step right up and play the game
you've only got yourself to blame
and in the end it all comes true
you'll realize the game is you

Amelia and John Dabul

John Dabul
THE PHILOSOPHER, HIS WIFE AND DISCIPLE
In a small town close to Constantinople,
A Greek philosopher had a night meeting with his disciple.
His wife came with intention to fight,
Claiming she did not want people in her house every day after midnight.

Suddenly she came with a bucket of water,
And washed them from head to feet all together.
The philosopher said this is my dear and lovely spouse.
I want you to know that woman is the unique boss in her house.

What happened is a good lesson, if you'll let me explain;
A few minutes ago we had a small thunderstorm,
Now it is time to get some rain.
In short, let me tell you again;
When married people have problems in their social life.
Husband can be the big winner if he looses with his wife.

Sarah Ford
THE STORM WILL PASS
On a rainy day, I see your face
Tears are shed as we embrace
Rivers are flooded, emotions are flowing
The moment is special as together we are growing
The rumble of thunder, the beating of our hearts
Together we promise, to never be apart
A bolt of lightning, adds a shock to the land
As the sparks ignite, by the touch of a hand
The whirling wind around us,
describes the lightness of my head
All things are forgotten even the previous things you'd said
The rain turns to shine as I remember at last
The words you had spoken, were
"The Storm will pass."

Sarah Ford
I'M LEAVING YOU
The sky is dark and cloudy this night
And I see your eyes are filled with fright
Our hands we hold as we walk in the park
Your body it trembles in the deadness of the dark
Your cold hands touch me as it rains
Your fingers feel heavy but it's only the pain
I'm sorry I'm leaving the fault isn't on you
You make me happy but when I'm without him I'm blue
A raindrop just fell upon your cheek
I realize it's a tear and I feel so weak
I'm sorry I still love
You
Goodbye

Linda Joan Foley
THE SOUL'S EDUCATION

To my son Greg, who has taught me to endure.

During life's journey
We oft become comrades of the Dark.
Never knowing what lies before us,
We blindly travel the pathways.
Taking our souls into the night—
places of doubts, fears, and despair,
We constantly struggle amid the sludge and mire
that gives us pain.
Then comes the new dawning—
The voice of TRUTH—
"Peace and Comfort I give unto you!"
This is
The education for the soul!

Viola Sue Woods
A POLITE SPIDER
I build my staircase of silk strings
From myself; a sagging roof over the apexed
stack of bricks
That form the cornered wall behind your head.
You, lying in the grass, may look through
My honest abode
To see that we are short.
For meteors' white light
The black universal dome.
Lovely! but with my
sallow crumpled legs,
I'll walk and lay my web
across your face,
Or ask you please to
move.

Denise Keys
ALL ALONE
Now that you're gone, all my dreams are lost.

All your memories are still here with me in everything I do.
How do you expect me to live all alone?

Why does it have to be the way it has to be?
Why do you get my hopes all up high,
then slowly just say goodbye.
How do you expect me to live all alone?

We had such a good thing going and now it seems like a dream.
All my friends said "He's the one for you"
but now all I can do is scream.
How do you expect me to live all alone?

Memories come and memories go
but now that you're gone that is all I have to share . . .
Your memories.

Even when we used to fight, I knew you'd be back.
But now it's different because there is no more you.
How do you expect me to live all alone?

Carolyn V Smith
RETROSPECT
As I sit here between these walls of emptiness, I wonder if the time will ever come when we're together again.

I watch minutes turn slowly into hours. Turning on the radio, tunes that were once so beautiful suddenly sound hollow. The same songs we listened to together have no meaning now. The words are cold and void of feelings. Funny . . . they were warm when you were here.

Closing my eyes I picture your face. I see the flashing dark eyes that evolved so much warmth, your strong chin, and the lips that kissed me with such tenderness and passion. I re-live every minute spent with you, moment by moment. Then opening my eyes, I wonder if I can sit here between these walls much longer without word from you.

Then moving across to my window, I wonder if you are out there somewhere . . . walking . . . or riding. Hoping against hope that your journey will bring you my way. Hoping that you will somehow feel my need for you. Then turning back into these empty walls . . . I wait . . .

John C Steffen
THE ANSWER
Around three thousand years ago,
Ten laws came down from Heaven to us,
Written in His own hand,
For each and every one of us.
No blood be shed, no tears would fall,
To get even, with one or all.
It's all the law, we would ever need,
To live in PEACE and HARMONY.

Joan Gay
LIFE CAN BE FUN
You say you cannot sing!—then try,
Let the sounds reach for the sky.
Smile, and feel the warm vibrations.
Love the way you feel and sound.
Lift your eyes up off the ground.
Breathe in the air around the trees,
Catch the fragrance in the breeze.
Watch the birds soaring higher and higher.
Walk an imaginary trapeze high wire.
Pass time of day with all you meet,
Everything in nature greet.
Play with the children, enjoy the hours,
Hear the chirping birds, smell fragrant flowers.
Help a stranger in distress,
'Tis then you'll find true happiness.

Joan Gay
A SEASON IN PARADISE
The air is nippy out today, but
the sun is in the sky
It makes you know that spring is
here, the squirrels scutter by.
The hummingbirds are hovering
on my porch to get a feed
And little snow birds on the path
where I have thrown their
seed.
A robin perching on the fence, so
tame she seems to be
She cocks her little head to one
side to take a look at me.
The oak trees too are budding out,
and the pine trees look so
green,
Just then some mountain jays flew
by, the prettiest I have seen.
So I think how fortunate I am to
live just where I do
Maybe sometime you'll visit me
so you can share this too.

M H Sheridan
LOST LOVE
The passage of time moves onward
Days and nights drift away,
Lost forever and ever.
Only to be remembered in dreams
And thoughts of yesterday.
Smiles and laughter, frozen in time,
Suspended in eternity.
A touch, so tender,
Etched in memories
Lost with the passage of time.

Tammy Ann Beattie
THE WAY WE WERE
There never is a day
that goes by
when I don't think of you.

The way you used to
make me laugh . . . and cry;
far apart
yet closer together.

Those used to be
the good ole days
when we were supposed to
conquer the world . . .
together.

But, in this lifetime
there's no escape
of different changes

that captured us.

So as time goes on
we drift apart.
Instead of two
now there is one.

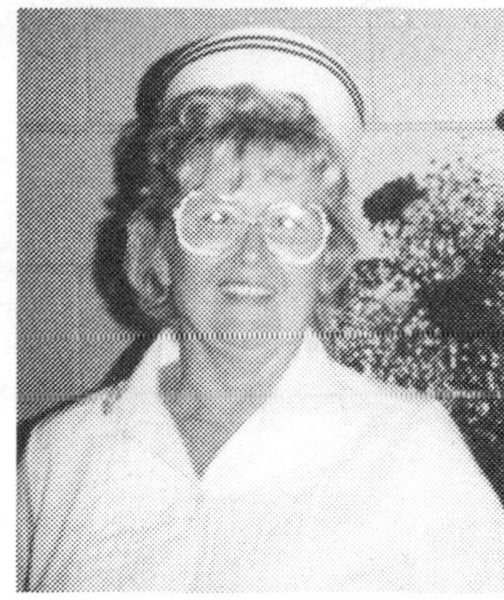

Ruth Bay

Ruth Bay

SOMETHING TO STAND ON

Dedicated to the memory of Melvin Gillette Baynard, M.D. and Surgeon, my deceased husband.

I need something firm to stand on.
There are those times I don't understand.
Life woes enclose and I'm alone,
Forsaken—without a helping hand.

A flower's stalk holds it secure.
Storm winds whirl but it can endure.
Man's stalk to endure is so unknown,
When he confronts his sorrows alone.

Man treads onward through trial and error.
At times, he is crushed as storms come nearer.
His pains cause him to win or lose.
What decision will he then choose?

I leave others to now face myself,
Contemplating of what life has left.
I think of the past and the now,
And I see rays of hope somehow.

I have something to stand on like the flower.
It came not from a song or books to disband.
A light glistens ahead of me every hour.
'Twas beautifully learned from a helping hand.

Ruth Bay

THREE THINGS OF NATURE

The sun was slowly gliding downward
in the clear, western sky,
While a late hour, briskly breeze
coursed through the risen lily tops.
A brown rabbit decided
to make its usual come-by,
For quick nibbles of water
among the pond's white, lily crops.

As the rabbit neared the lily pond
for some water to take,
It saw wavy shadows on the pond
as forms began to make.
Its ears cocked as if in thought
to stay or make a run.
Then, it leaped two jumps away
and sat on its brown buns.
Behold! A greenish frog spread its hind legs,
making a deep smash,
And splitting the pond water sounding
like a bold, mighty crash.
Within minutes, that greenish frog sat
on the same rock on the ground,
And from its throat, it uttered a lover's call
with a rasping sound.

The rabbit's short legs left a trail
of dust on the smooth ground.
Nearing the greening, spring woodlands,
it stopped and turned around.
Resuming its speed, it entered the forest
and turned to the right,
Heading for the safety of its home
before the darkness of night.

As my back rested against that stump
of a once tree,
This section had become a place
of solace for me.
I marveled at these three things of nature
in acts of survival,
Thinking that for each, a new dawn must
be nature's own revival.

Ruth Bay

ROBIN RED BREAST

Oh! Robin rust-red breast,
Where is your cuddling nest?
Is it in the trees, the grass,
woods or fields,
Housing your downy youngs
trying to squeal?

Your slim beak gathers insects
and fruits
And you muster up leaves, worms,
and seeds.
Your plumage mounts you skyward
carrying loot
To meet six nestlings nutritional
needs.

When you land on your grass,
cup-like nest
That you've carefully made from
soft mud,
Tiny, hungry mouths gape wide
to be blest
Like nature making flowers
from small buds.

Oh! male robin with detached
toes on fences,
Thrusting your breast forward
while song commences,
Your virile melodies belts which
no one knows.
A female's call returns:
a love signal grows.

Oh! splendorous robin red breast,
Rocking on fences – Off you fly
To where? Maybe a lover's nest:
Your life – no one can explain why.

Amy Ledford

BEAUTIFUL THINGS

To my Dad; the man who called me his and his alone.

Never forget the times you laughed
When things were working out right
Always remember who you are
As your tears streak your face at night
Remember the love of your parents
How they took you in as their own
If it's the other way around
Then think of the ones with no home

Never forget yesterday's past
It's part of the way you feel
And always think about your dreams
'Cause it's the beautiful things that are real

Chris Gayden

DEAR FATHER

This is dedicated to my father, whom I still love very much, even with the pain of not having him around. Please come home.

Father . . . How could you have done that to us?
Especially since we loved you so very much.
How could you have just gotten your clothes to pack
Without ever even taking one look back.
When we were facing the hardest times in our lives,
You walked away without saying goodbye.
We soon forgot what having a father meant.
You never sent us one red cent.
We struggled hard like never before
Because we didn't have you anymore.
It was hard for poor Mama to keep food on the table,
But she did her best as long as she was able.
Working three jobs, she never had much rest
Bags under her eyes from being worried and depressed;
But you know Mama, she refused to let the hurt show;
All because she loved us so.
Father . . . We often wondered
where you were,
or if you ever really cared
For the family that you once had;
For the family who was left oh so sad.
Father . . . You are welcomed back
home with us any time or any day
Please, don't let your foolish old pride get in the way.

Chris Gayden

ODE TO THE GARBAGEMAN

This poem is dedicated to my wonderful hardworking garbageman husband, Mr. Johnny Gayden, and also to American Waste of New Orleans.

Awake at the crack of dawn
Cleaning debris off your lawn
Sweating profusely by never stopping
House to house, we are always hopping.
Picking things up that we often shouldn't.
Some things that even you wouldn't.
Your leftovers and broken glass.
Your baby's pampers and your grass.
We are neither dumb nor stupid
Because we get paid to do it!
Sometimes a little smile would suffice
Or even a kind thank you would be nice.
Our jobs are not easy, not by a long shot—
But rain, shine, sleet or snow we never stop.
You need us, but this you won't admit
But think how it would be if we quit!

Chris Gayden

OBEY WHAT GOD HATH COMMANDETH

Blessed with God's wisdom
You can conquer all.
Believing that He lives in you
Will never let you fall.
Putting Him first in your life
He will always prevail.
Submitting all efforts to Him
Will allow them to excel.
Keeping His commandments
Will always help you through.
Rendering Him your best
Will receive the best for you.
Remembering that He's always at your side
And your heart is where He abides.
In your times of trouble
You will never be stranded;
If you would only obey
What God hath commandeth.

Chris Gayden

BRAIN DEAD

For all of the overworked, underpaid, stressed out individuals, who can't really describe how they are feeling after another tedious day on the job. This description should suffice:

My mind is blank
My thoughts are clear
My dreams are no more
My focus is drear

My attitude is bad
My emotions have left
My feelings are void
My depression is kept

My intentions are insane
My memory doesn't recall
My nerves have been vexed
My intelligence is none at all

My pain is buried
My tears have all been shed
My conscience is lost
My brain is dead.

R Shields

TRANSIENCE

Firelight, dancing bright
On skin as fine as porcelain
Reflects the softness of her face.
Every hidden shadowed place,
Veiled in shades from black to gray,
Effulgent flames seek to betray
Revealing mysteries hidden there.
As afterglow the flames appease,
Now passion, too, must take its ease.
Night, in turn, must also die
And sleep in joy my love and I.

Kay Hoffman

EASTER PROMISES

Today I walked where crocus bloom
From out the winter's dark, cold tomb
And marvelled at this golden worth
That comes each year with spring's rebirth.

And then I thought of Easter joy
Of purest gold without alloy
When heaven opened wide death's door
That man could live forevermore.

But O I know there has to be
Renewal and rebirth in me,
And now I lift the chalice up
To Him who fills the empty cup.
In Christ who proved eternity
There's Easter joy and hope for me.

R S Dumas
SPECIAL FRIEND

To Karen. Her kindness and quiet understanding filled my heart with warmth and caring when I needed it most.

You know my feelings, I wish we could be together, but
To ask you to start anew,
Is just not fair.

So if I may be bold, I'll simply tell you where I stand.
Should you ever need a friend,
I will be there.

I pray that you are happy always, heartache never near, but
Should you seek a warm shoulder,
I will be there.

May your problems be few, not getting the best of you, but
Should you yearn a listening ear,
I will be there.

You're a pretty tough kid, not much seems to get you down, but
Should you long for added strength,
I will be there.

If it is not in the cards, me being your man, then
As a dear friend to the end,
I will always care.

But as time goes by, if you find an ace in your heart, and
Should you want to call me yours,
I will be there.

Shirley Zercher Miller
THE BLESSED BABE
See the baby, soft and sweet
Waving tiny hands and feet
Yawning, stretching, sleepy-eyed
Cradled by his Mother's side
Daddy standing proudly near
Angels singing loud and clear
Glorias to all who'll listen
While the stars above them glisten
Shepherds, camels, the Wisemen three
Cows and lambs, have come to see
This Son of God, this King of Kings
This babe of whom the angels sing
Blessed is this baby son
Whose Holy Birth will make us one
So sing Hosannas, Praise and Glory
For our Baby Jesus Christmas story.

Fay Wurm
THE TRAP
The blackened eye, the tiny face
Festooned with welt and bruise
Stared bleakly for a beat in time
From out the open door
And then was rudely plucked from sight
To be seen no more.
With bitter thoughts, I dialed the phone
To seek help for this child.
They came and took her frame away
To find a place to call a home
But would she thank me for that call
When she began to feel alone?
The woman shook a meaty fist from her front lawn,
And then she smiled a bitter, vicious grin
And I saw why
In weeks her swollen body would produce again
I had prayed the agony was over,
But it had just begun.

Douglas F Edwardson

Douglas F Edwardson
"OWED," TO JOHN LENNON . . .
Paul is the finest record machine, the world has yet to see.
George is the feeling amplifier, his guitar says: "Listen to me!"
Ringo is the precision percussion player, his rhythms set the others free.
But, the Beatles' vital instrument, was John, his "Imagine"-ation gave them electricity.
Paul's still makin' music, Ringo's makin' films, and George spends happy hours on his farm.
But, the Beatles are gone, with the death of John, he was the bracelet, for their charm.
He was a magically, enlightened dreamer, sharing truth,
like a kindly brother.
But, now he's in the past, and the future must ask:
"When, comes such another?"
Life, still goes on, but in memory of John,
we should put on his music, and dance.
And, remember: the main thing, John was saying, is:
"Why not give peace a chance?"
John was someone, you could rely upon, he "Imagined,"
a world united.
By the wonder of youth, and the nature, of truth,
Life's questions can be decided.
We have to "Let It Be," "Yesterday,"
and live, today fully, for tomorrow.
And, learn enough, not to judge
someone, on how much money
they beg, steal or borrow.
"Instant Karma," like gravity,
operates anyway,
without regard for belief.
While life uses death, to demonstrate,
that "Time,"
is the inexorable, thief!
Only simple fools, follow silly rules,
but, it's a bigger fool whom follows none.
"We hope, someday, you'll join us,
and the world can live as one!
Knowing: "Nothing, is above, the feeling of love!"
When we all "Come together," in the brilliant light,
of living truth, the spirit of "John Winston Lennon,"
Becomes a nuclear shine.
Then, everyone alive will share, in the most beautiful thought,
knowing that: "Living is truly, Divine!"

John W Ball
THE LONELY TREE
A deep starry night,
The moon burning bright,
All is quiet.
A cat plays within the shadows
A tree stands alone in a field
Its leafless limbs reach to the sky,
As if to cry,
Does anyone know why?
A cat romps among the daisies
Far in the distance stands a church steeple
Upon the steeple, a clock chimes with power,
From within its bell tower,
Bursts a musical shower.
The cat no longer plays in the shadows
As time goes on years pass by
The cat long ago returned to the ground,
The church steeple now has been torn down,
The stars in the nighttime sky have drown.
A small wooden cross now stands where a cat once played
And a tree stands alone in a field.

Debra Leah Fitzgerald
THE DEATH OF INNOCENCE
As I lay there,
I could remember how the night crept in.
Everything then was a monster,
or moved supernaturally.
And the fear . . .
I always remember the fear.
There was no way out,
No scream that was heard,
Helpless and alone,
And I cry.
For yet tonight
Another child dies . . .
If only inside.

Lydia Segui
CHILD OF THE NIGHT
The poor child of the night
Lives with the feelings of terror and fright
Never knowing where she will be
Never knowing what the future will see
She has no place, or a home
There's no one there, she's all alone
She sleeps the day and works the night
Trying to survive is always a fight

The child of the night will never know
The feeling of love and the way it grows
Drugs and sex rule her life
Never having a family or being a wife

Will this child ever see
The way she came to be?
Will this child ever wake
To discover the horror, just for her sake?

As of now she lives with grief
And the feelings of false belief

Nancy Giamette
TRIBUTE
He is a simple man with extraordinary values
And high expectations,
Never settling for the cards he has been dealt,
Always holding out for a better hand.

He has tried to instill the same values
In his children,
Saying, "Lead, don't follow."

I look up to this man
And see in his eyes
The depths of places I want to go.
I could never hope to measure up to his greatness,
But if I achieve even a fraction of his successes,
I will hold my head high,
Proud in the knowledge that I have learned
From one of the few great ones.

Cynthia M Boros
HOW TO PLANT A GARDEN OF INSECURITY
First, dig three holes in the self-confidence.

Second, into each hole, drop 1 seed of laziness, 1 seed of stupidity and 1 seed of good-for-nothingness.

Third, fill each hole with contempt.

Each day, sprinkle the area with sarcasm and plenty of accusations.

It's best that nasty notes, (to encourage the growth of self-hatred), be read aloud, no, even shouted, on a daily basis.

Place as many responsibilities on your garden as possible.

Be sure to weed out any growth of self-esteem and watch out for self-love, which could kill your garden.
(This can be prevented with the liberal application of insulting and insinuating letters.)

Be aware that if you touch your garden, praise your garden or in any way indicate love to your garden, these three plants will not survive, and you will never have a daughter to be disappointed in.

Joy Lynn Davis
DESIGNER GENES
Sometimes I wonder just what it is
That makes me—me,
Why I hear what others do not hear
And see what they do not see.

Men of science who ought to know
Say it is a matter of genes,
We carry within us our forebears
And carry on their dreams and schemes.

Does a myriad host guide my life?
A tiny touch of William the Conqueror?
Or Matilda his gentle wife?
Or even a bit of Charlemagne the Emperor?

Did it happen just by chance
That I am strong and also weak?
Or, could it be by Special Plan
That I am indeed unique?

Nicolle D'Angelo
LONELINESS
Turbulent winds dancing

Dance upon a tree
the leaves caress each other

Dance upon the sands
they pile together

Dance upon the people
they huddle for warmth

Who dances among the wind?

It dances alone

Delores I Markt
OUR HOME
The antics of little ones,
The parties,
The holidays,
The sharing of many good times,
These are the memories
We hold so dear
For now and all time.
You have shared the lives of many,
Their joys, sorrows, anger and despair,
You have kept us safe from storms and
Cradled us in your warmth and loving care.
Tho your enveloping walls will be destroyed
The memories of these times will
Live forevermore.
A new facade will be erected
And new memories will arise.
But you will always live in our eyes.
We salute you, Our home—
And thank you for your loving care,
Our sadness at this parting
Is beyond repair.
So we will not say good-bye to
The memory of you
But simply say—Adieu.

Ruth Vandegrift
THE BARTENDER
I see them from the other side—some happy—some sad— some stripped of pride—
I see the weak, I see the strong, the young, the old—some right—some wrong.
By day—by night—I hear their tales—
Of broken hearts and health that ails.
I've watched them come and watched them go—
Some hide their pain, some let it show, some 'sing a song,'
Some tarry long, "You're a friend in need" I've heard them say—they seek advice, then turn away—oh, the stories I could write, but never will—to me their secrets they confide—
I see them from the other side.

Annette S Elkins
ILLUSION

This poem is with special dedication to my one and only real illusion T.E.S.

In the world of illusion where you can't cry on solid ground
In a far away place is where I fell in love with you.
You were the deliverance from darkness once felt
You were so brilliant, so beautiful.
You taught me well, you brought the laughter, the passion and . . .
the tears.
As you held my heart in your head—
you whispered in my ear . . .
I awoke . . . you were gone.
Some say it was fantasy to me it was reality
In the still part of the day . . .
thoughts of yesterday
Come rushing to that unforgettable love affair

Mary B Greer
PHYLLIS
When the earth was made, the Master's hand
Placed upon this fertile land
A man who had to prove his worth
And help redeem us here on earth.
And then, to show His love and care,
He sent to us a woman fair.
For all the things we wrongly crave,
Let's do remember all He gave.
So let's not think He doesn't know
And guard the peace He did bestow.

And then He sent you, my friend.

Rosa Chandler
MOTHER
You never heard her complaining
You never heard her moan
But she always had an open ear
for the ones she called her own.
She was always there when you needed her,
and she always reassured that God's love is always with you
in the times you're insecure.
She really loved her children, her in-laws and her friends
and always had something good to say, about the worst things that came.
Her grandchildren really loved her, they adored her Christian way, they could always count on grandma when in troubled times they prayed.
She's gone to be with Jesus, and watches us from above,
We really, really miss her,
But she is in God's heavenly cove

Harry A Smith
THE BATTLEFIELD OF THE MIND

This special poem is dedicated to all Christians who are going through some difficult times of trials and testing.

Since you made Jesus Christ your Savior and Lord
You've entered into a battle that cannot be ignored
The enemy consistently plots and deceives
To keep you off guard that you might not believe,
The enemy causes some soldiers to become blind
forgetting their armour and not renewing their mind
The enemy we fight is a defeated foe
But without a renewed mind you'll never know
The enemy is smart and wise on every side
Overcoming those who neglect the word of God
King Jesus who is mighty in battle, victorious in war
Commanding his soldiers to obey his word making their election sure.
Wounded and hindered much on the field
But not defeated because of Jesus whom we yield
Our afflictions are many in ways we can't count
Obeying our Commander and Chief we overcome with a shout
Yet in our light affliction we become wearied and beat down
But we look unto the hills from whence comes our help
Whose grace is much more abound
Our minds are renewed and ready to fight
We take the enemy by force with the word of light
We sing victory, victory so sweet and divine
We've learned to use our authority in
The Battlefield of the Mind.

Dionne Hartnett (11 years old)
CHORES

To my wonderful parents and brother who have done so much for me.

I couldn't make my bed, because my sheets were made of lead.
I couldn't vacuum, 'cause the room was filled with toxic fumes.
I couldn't clean my room, because my cat created a sonic boom.
I couldn't do the wash today, 'cause all the cloths ran away.
Sorry mom, I just couldn't do the chores today.

Karena Larrisey
THE SEED

To the man of my dreams. To the love of my life. To my husband-to-be. To Glenn.

Deep in the wilderness stand millions of trees
That block the warm sunlight and swallow the breeze.
Though soundless and calm, much activity goes on
Many animals are busy from dusk until dawn.
But far below the leaves there lies an open field
As a seed lies alone using time as it's shield.
No grass to accompany, just plenty of weeds
There's no future with them, they're unfriendly to seed.
There's no life for this one, nobody to care
No allies, no affinities, no world to share.
Then soon comes a time when the wind becomes strong
It lifts the seed up and carries him on.
He lands in a place so foreign to him
Where there are many alike and they welcome him in.
So, it's true, there's a land where love can be found
But don't sit there alone — start looking around.

Ken Hewett
GLASSES FOR THE HEART

To Geri Brooks, the inspiration of this poem.

Sometimes we see things that shine bright as the sun
Like the beauty of stars on a black velvet sky.
Things that are precious, things cherished by one.
But love is not seen with the eye.

Strength in a relationship can tend to go weak.
Like the eyes, the vision can fade.
An empty heart gets a better peek.
A closer look at our love has been made.

Things are unnoticed, sometimes things are unseen.
Like the passing of a beautiful day.
I know my heart's vision was not very keen.
But true love will never go away.

For now my heart sees the mistakes that I've made
To be in love is not to be alone
The glasses you give me by sending me away.
Now love's bright but my true love is gone.

Tom Fugalli
RICHMOND HILL

This poem is dedicated with love to my grandfather, Anthony Fugalli.

Words cannot describe
The lamentative dirge,
Within myself submerged,
Forever circumscribed.

And memories cascade;
One by one descend.
Until alas, the end.
To echo and to fade.

Mortal flesh and bone;
Sneering Sickle Raker,
Greedy Undertaker,
Carves every name in stone.

The soul, you cannot swallow.
For once you arc your blade,
Your own death-bed is made.
And Death, you cannot follow.

Donny Binkley
MY LOVE FOR YOU

To my wife Lynn. My first love. My last love. You'll always be in my heart.

My love for you,
is like the first winter's snow.
As it falls through the trees,
so graceful and slow.

Like a ride through the mountains,
seeing their beauty and grace.
Thinking of someone special,
a smile on your face.

Like the sunset over the ocean,
the waves gently touching your feet.
Your hearts become one,
your lips slowly meet.

Like a rose in the morning,
its petals glistening with dew.
All of these things say,
Lynn, I love you.

Scott Arminas
SHE IS

To my loving wife Dr. Maria Basora-Arminas.

Space and time stand still when I look into her eyes.
Sparkling pools of espresso being sipped as two lovers hunger
Sitting together in an outdoor cafe on a busy Parisian street.
Her eyes iris penetrate my soul.
They peer deep into the realms of hidden desire.
Within, Nymphs dance in Autumn woods.
Within, majestic mountains are white with Winter snow.
Within, a tan goddess bathes in the hot Summer sun.
Within, there are gentle pools of light reflecting Spring's water.
The birds sing as her sun rises far East of Eden
And Paradise is remembered once more
Long after eating forbidden fruit.
Goodness walks close by in this secret place
Where evil cannot molest.
She is the statue of Aphrodite
Forever Immortal.
She is a rose's fragrance.
She is the glitter of light rays in a diamond.
She is the music of a flute playing a haunting melody
As the morning sun rises over the ancient hills of Delphi.
She is simply what she is.
She is you.

Kristal L Elzey
ETERNITY

Dedicated to R. Mallory Weaklem who was unselfish and strong and who helped me to become the person I am today. I love you and miss you.

On a rainy night I can see forever
Frosty greens, brilliant blues
I can see eternity
I can see forever

Let me pass onto the sea
My knowledge of eternity
From the trees, the greens, and herbs
Yes I can see eternity

The clouds are high above the sky
Let me grow my wings to fly
Soar above the Earth below
So I may see eternity

Give me knowledge, teach me love
Give me knowledge lost white dove
So I may soar and I may see
The brilliance of eternity

Now I soar, now I fly
Above the Earth in the grey-blue sky
Wings of steel I cannot sever
Now I soar above forever

Betty Jane Allison
"DEAREST FRIEND"

This poem is dedicated to Alice, my daughter.

Mother was so dear to me
I miss her since, she's gone,
It was God's will in His own way
Is why He called her home.
She didn't say goodbye to me or even a sigh
But, I wasn't there when she said her last goodbye,
God was standing by instead
Holding to her hand
Leading her to the promised land.
One day, we'll meet again
As we have done before,
Only difference it will be
She'll be standing at Heaven's door.

Georgia White
MEMORIES

In Loving Memory of Edward Eugene Bates.

I spent some time with this old man
when I was just a youth.
He taught me how to hunt and fish.
He pulled my very first tooth.

We sat out in the garden
to watch the vegetables grow.
He taught me all the wondrous things
that a child ought to know.

Memories are such wonderful things—
they warm our every day.
No matter how the years fly by,
they never dim or fade.

The years have not been good to him—
he's elderly and he's ill.
Now when memories fill my mind,
I suddenly get this chill.

For the old man is my Grampa
and I love him with all my heart.
I only wish I'd told him more
right from the very start.

So I'd like to take some time with you
to show you that I care.
To reaffirm my love for you
even though I can't be there.

Linda Anne Rutherford
I REMEMBER

Dedicated to my son Damion.

Fair-haired boy, born to me,
What a wonder you will be!
Cheeks aglow, skin so soft,
Only you are my first thought,
Face so innocent and round
you are bliss
Though you utter not a sound.
Loud and strong are your cries
But always stop when I dry your eyes.
So very young — not yet a man;
But, your first step I held your hand.
Memories of love are no regret.
Though they fade, I can't forget.
A life too perfect, one might say,
And when you left, I had to stay.
What made this happen? How can this be?
I remember you were gone when you were but three!

Jeri L Schiro
THE MOMENT WE'RE IN

This poem is dedicated to Dwayne Ours for making me the happiest person in the world. You've made my life worthwhile. I love you.

When I see you smile
And you are close to me
And we walk together for awhile
And talk about how things might be
When I'm lost in your eyes
And I feel your gentle touch
The World around us dies
Haunting problems don't matter as much
When we are alone
These are the sweetest of moments
Pleasures still unknown
These will be the sweetest of moments
Time stands still, my love, my friend
And nothing matters but the moment we're in

Emlee
CHALLENGE

To My Family.

The bleak of the morning is dull for some
But to others it is a new day begun
The choices of all are set in their stride
And most of us help the hours along with pride.

Each hour and day as we progress along
Let us remember the day with a cheerful song
For with it brings smiles which always helps others
For here we stand you and I as brothers.

It is God's way to have implanted in our thoughts
Kindness, love, friends and understanding so taught.

Sam Phillips

Sam Phillips
MINISTER OF WEALTH

Dedicated to the first lady Bernita, there's no other woman sweeter, who's divine inspiration is responsible for my poetic creation.

My name is Gordon Randall and I'm tall, dark and handsome. If I get kidnapped would you kindly pay the ransom. From the pulpit I give the congregation a fit. I sport a California Curl, for the young girl. With a ducktail fullback, they like it like that. I wear a red shirt and handkerchief, an angel white suit of double breast; When I preach I get a lot off my chest. A pair of white Stacy's, one of many from Macy's. Material things I will lovingly cherish, before I perish. Members call me Bishop because I'm the man all men and women worship. Those who believe, want deceive and shall receive. Some say I'm sinister, but I'm still the minister. I have a steel grey Mercedes for all the ladies. And of course a Benz for all the Men's. A leader of Blacks and the owner of two Cadillacs. A townhouse, a condo' a Lincoln stretch limo'. When I deliver the word of God. I become motivated. Jealous enemies interfere and make me aggravated. My father was a southern Baptist preacher of the Step'n'Fetchit speed, but I'm his son and I'm the newbreed. I don't Step'n'Fetch. I Fetch'n'Catch. I Fetch everything in sight and I catch everything thrown at me after I'm gone. I preach on current events, while the members pay the rents. About Aids and other diseases, whatever pleases. I hope my followers never pull down the curtain. If they do I'll be hurtin' for certain. As I wipe the perspiration from my brow, I'm going to close now! I'm tired and exhausted, but Lord knows I haven't lost it.

Janice L Perkins
SEASHELL LOVE

To Terry,
For I adored you.

Today, seabirds flocked above me
To an angry sea,
their windswept voices
cried out pathetically . . .

With pink sunset tears,
(Sly-Smile-Survivor-Style),
I found myself screaming
For no one could hear me . . .

And with eyes closed,
using just
one
finger,
I traced endless patterns
(silent and secret)
on the hot sugar sands there . . .

Thoughts of you
burned Smokey and Sweet;
Leading to near madness
alone in the heat!

Windy and wild, my Love;
Like you and like me —
Perhaps damned by Love on this beach . . .

Only to be cooled by
Ocean breeze and brine,
And when your
Seashell Love was mine.

Strauzie L Collins
GRABBING

I would like to dedicate this poem to my family and my church for helping me reach my goal but mostly I would like to thank God for blessing me with the talent to reach my goal.

I'm grabbing for something way up in the air,
I'm grabbing for something that's not even there,
I'm grabbing for something and trying to achieve,
But it's up too high and I know I can't get it and no more do I believe,
I keep grabbing more and more do I try,
I still cannot reach it and then I start to cry,
What I used to feel is gone and no more is there,
I'm still grabbing but no more do I care,
I look up and it's still there looking down at me,

I look up and wonder what does it see,
Does it see a person who shivers inside,
Or does it see a person who is energetic and alive,
To my future it holds the key,
I wonder what will become of me,
Will I be successful in reaching my goal,
Right now I'm wondering will I ever know,
I reach and reach and look up so far,
Then I look up and realize it is my wishing star,
And now when I look up I do believe,
That anything is possible and I can achieve.

Helen Kelsey Morgan

WHEN TWO HEARTS MET

Written in Loving memory of my husband "Rusty."

Long ago two hearts met, and soon they beat as one,
They shared such precious memories, each moment, one by one.

They had so much together, through years that I recall.
They laughed and cried, so many times, over things both great and small.

Many times, when duty called, the miles between these two,
Were countless as the stars above, but still their love just grew.

Until no matter who, or what, would try to come between them,
These two hearts, would always be, the same as one between them.

Then one day, the Angels came, and one would be no more,
The second heart fell weeping, when left outside the door.

Now the heart, that's left behind, must carry on for two,
Must live and laugh, and love and cry, the way both used to do.

I'll live with just your memory, to carry me on each day,
I'll laugh again within my heart, of things you used to say.

I'll love again my darling, when I reach the other shore,
And I can be within your arms, and hold you forever more.

I'll cry for you my sweetheart, for I miss you and your love,
Wait for me, I'll be coming soon, to our new home up above.

Then once more together, we'll go strolling hand in hand,
With our Heavenly Father's blessing, in his Holy Promised Land.

Emma Jean Walker

A POEM FOR AUNT LIZZIE

This is dedicated to my friend Romaine Williamson. Thank you for sharing so many stories with me.

The Bible says, "Our years are three score and ten"
Yet you Aunt Lizzie, have been blessed thus far with ninety-nine.
Please tell us what you have seen.
Do you remember the first car you saw?
Tell us of life during the first and second World Wars.
The abdication of the Duke of Windsor? Women voting rights?
How about the first vehicle in space?
Civil rights?
What was it like to teach school before the two World Wars,
The Korean Conflict and Viet Nam were history?
Does one truly become wiser with age?
You have seen so much; the invention of computers, airplanes,
Vaccines, TV, satellites, VCR's, world communication in seconds.
Share with us if you will, this grand and loving life of yours,
So rich in memories, so full of heritage.
A century of wisdom, joy, sorrow, learning, teaching,
Seeing and experiencing.
Making and losing friends and loved ones along the way.
Share with us please, Aunt Lizzie.

Charles H Norman

MIDNIGHT DREAMS AND COWBOY JEANS

To the kids of yesterday, today and tomorrow — never give up something of value, unless you find something more valuable to take its place.

I've Been Around To Every Old Town
Any One Could Want To See.
From Maine To Nome Alaska, From L.A. To Tennessee.
Records On The Jukebox, And People Raising Hell
Are Among The Favorite Subjects Of The Things I Love So Well.

Cigarette Smoke, And Rum And Coke, Are The Company I Keep
Neon Lights My Way At Night, And The World Beneath My Feet.
The Folks I Meet Are Hard To Beat,
There's A Smile On Every Face.
There's A Midnight Queen In Her Cowboy Jeans, In Every Single Place.

It's A Different World That Beckons Me, The Forgotton Past Aren't There To See.
The Rewards Are Few, But The Nights Are New, And Your Worries Never Bother You.
At The Crack Of Dawn I'll Travel On, I Ain't Looking For No Glory,
Just Another Round In Another Town, Another Chapter To My Story.

For Midnight Dreams And Cowboy Jeans
Are My Only Category,
The Bright Lights Gleam, And The Night Life Seems
To Paint My Whole Life Story.

Susie Hazell

HUMANKIND(NESS?)

Dedicated to those with nothing but themselves, and to those few with all they desire and more. Be kind to each other . . . Please!

It's seen in their eyes.

It's felt in their movements.

It's in our hearts.

It's shown in our actions.

Let's open ourselves up to each other.
To the love of our sisters and brothers.

Kitty Cather

A WARNING

To the inhabitants of the Earth.

An Angel
with the thunder
of God
The Book of Mormon
God's truth
Angels and visions
wisdom and revelations
promises and light
the visitation of Christ
To ancient America
Won't you read
The Book of Mormon
Tonight?

Clemmie Hampton

HE'S A MAN

This poem is dedicated to Fred Roberts, with Love.

If a man can come back fighting when his luck is running low —
He can begin his journey over.
If a man can smile through teardrops—He can make his dreams come true, a man with such determination can and will achieve all that he's due.
If all the world seems to be against him, but he strives for what is right—sometime, somewhere he will surely win, he is a man of great strength.
If a man admits his failings, he is a man who is strong — He's a solid man, he admitted that he was wrong.
If a man can shoulder trouble and decline to shift the blame — He's a respectful man and worthy of the name.
If a man can still be humble, although fame holds him in sway
He's a man that men will follow, for his good will lead the way.
You are that man, I Love You.

Barbara LeBlanc

REMEMBRANCE

To Jimmy — The light that has never stopped shining. (1969 –1975)

How annoyed I would become at little handprints on the door.
Or why must he leave his footprints on my new-washed kitchen floor?
"Why can't you bake some cookies just for me today?"
"I'll find some time tomorrow if you'll just go now and play."
The games and projects he designed were so much mess and noise,
And his room was a disaster in the manner of small boys.
Tomorrow I'd have patience and understand much more.
The things he wanted me to do would not be such a chore.
We cannot realize that time will not go on the same
For suddenly, without warning, my tomorrow came.
My house is neat and quiet now with no toys spread around.
The rooms that echoed with his shouts are still — without a sound.
I have much time to do the things he wanted me to do.
And much too late I have a greater understanding too.
For all the things that I put off until another day
Are now put off forever since you have gone away.
But through it all you now must know the way that angels do
That there was no one else I ever loved as much as you.

M Star

THE WHITE CHRYSANTHEMUM

To My Friend, Sam.

So the white chrysanthemum can grow,
true victory can only come as individual
inward cures
for A.I.D.S. and all other allegedly "fatal" ills. Our mind
so pure, washed
clean by the sight of a single glamorous flower.

Tanya Puente

THE FALL OF SPRING

May our World live wisely and in Everlasting PEACE.

The Meadow slowly dies,
As the Sun sets the skies
The Season is coming to an end
A secret place hides around the bend

Leaves Fall, Float, Land
Dry as the Hottest sands
But this place will always be
The loveliest place for ME

It hides the secrets
It hides the pain
It hides all Life
Never to be slain

And when it is time for death to come
Welcome it kindly for you're the ONE
That is ready and willing
To be the Prey of a Good-natured killing.

Nancy J L DuBois

BRAIN PAIN-PARENT OF A TEENAGER

I dedicate this poem to my son Seth. He stuck it out through thick and thin. He is the reason, purpose and motivating force for my personal growth.

Drill my brain
and drain the pain

I feel I am locked in chains
Chains of blame
I might go lame
Soon I might need a cane

I thought I was quite a dame
But now I forget even my name
Almost maimed
Beat with blame
What's left to gain?

Life is such a strain
Today is so much pain
I think I'll stand in front of a train
That ought to deaden the pain
Am I sane?
Or did I drain the brain and keep the pain?

Girl take aim — Don't complain
There's lots to regain
Life to reclaim

Fuel the flame
Another day, it's not the same
And I will aim to tame the pain
And win this life of games

That pain was just a windowpane!
I win the game!

Sylvia Olalia
KEEP TRYING

This poem is dedicated to Jorge, my darling husband.

Why is that there are poor and rich,
And good and evil, luck and unluck for each,
That this world over has to offer,
Yet, here we are, go on over and over,
Accepts what life has given us,
Only we can do is continuing,
Taking one day at a time, and keep on trying,
All the best we can!

Why are there some souls,
Who despite all these things whole,
This universe has its own nature,
Every one has each role to play,
Life has to offer each day,
Yet, here we are, go on over and over,
Only we can do is to keep on trying,
All the best we can! Till we get what we're searching for

Gertrude Kahrhoff
JUST ONCE MORE

To my sister, Connie, who shared my joys.

Give back the days of my childhood—
Days when I romped o'er the meadow
Midst butterflies and wildflowers
In happy years of long ago.

Or, was it only yesterday
When I shared popsicles with friends,
And roller skated 'round the block
Never dreaming this pleasure ends.

Give back the days of my childhood
When grandpa and I roamed the hills,
Looking for nuts and raspberries,
Birds in the trees and other thrills.

I'd like to go back just once more
To catch horse-drawn sleds on the run,
And enjoy those sleigh ride parties
Aware of nothing else but fun.

Give back the days of my childhood.
Lord, let me fish and swim and hike,
Let me ice skate on the lagoon
Just once more—let me ride my bike!

Michelle M Lorenzo
JIMMY

A little less light shines on the faces of those who love him today. We do not forget, as the air is still cold.

Sorry I called so late,
but I'm feeling rather numb,
lost a friend
a year ago today.
Kamakazi Night
took his life.
I don't understand,
a boy of eighteen
not given the chance
to be a man,
gone like
a stone thrown
into a river and
I couldn't follow.
Excuse the quiver
in my voice,
the air is cold
in this room
and I feel so alone
Sorry I woke you.

Raquel Soto

Raquel Soto
DAY BY DAY

This poem is dedicated To: Miss Sabrina Marie Wise—and all the staff at St. Martin's Lutheran Day School. Which are: Marva, Sheila, Cathy, Nancy, Charlotte, Susan, Jodie, Linda, Debbie, Claudia, Jackie, Gayle, Relaine, Cindy, Angela, Dawn, Zena, Alma, Stella, Kristian, Mariella, Jean, Lane, Rachel, Laura, Leslie, Thank You For All Your Support and Encouragement.

Day by day that I take A step ahead
In my life.
Let me accept each day as a new challenge,
And as the day goes by give me strength each hour of the day.
To close the door on criticism and complaints,
To open it to kindness,
understanding, and forgiveness.

To each Individual that works around me,
As the day comes to an end . . .
Let us put aside the difference of each Individual . . .
And as we shall accept each other's needs.
Let's look forward for a pleasant and peaceful day.
And let it be a day worthwhile.

Timothy R Kervahn
REMEMBERING THE DAYS

To my beloved Ceci: Tu eres mi vida.

We all have stories
Of walking barefoot in the snow
And we all have heroes
Each generation will know
Of times and of places
That often shadow the minds
And of people long since gone
Only in books do they remind
We all have a childhood innocence
Remembered from time to time
Of friends we would play with
And trees we would climb
Of seeing the special days
That had quickly passed us by
Of recapturing a distant youth
Bringing a tear to the eye
We all have gifts
Of us we give so well
And we all have secrets
Each with a story to tell.

Christopher Lee Patrick
DAWN OF THE PSALM
CAPSULE OF TIME?
YEARNING FOR STATURE OF THE HEART

The eyes! Peer from the beauty bounded within the gaze; of Him.

Flickering as candles in each age of morning, more are they learned, and watching to protect, always sensing;

For a loft, as they pass each second of intersecting dust glance; I shake at fear of loss of such gems.

Vibrate as the fowl chirrup, there is awakeness on contact with the awe of singing;

Yet, as they pass, one by one through the sphere as I watch; what markings are these?
A different draw from within, but learned again.

Perched high is the Predator, waiting for the innocent, to snare with descent and evil intent,

Leaving a sparkle of fire pricked, with each encounter a knight; would they begin?

Her unawares! A hare of splendor for He seeing, a suiter's grass is what is meant!

Old Timer? A reaper of skillful dart, pass at the close of his heart each night.

Forces in motion and an upset of balance, what? A new seed today, tomorrow; a growing of beauty I perceive one, two, or three of veil, sands of the glass, He strifeless to strike with gentle strokes of thought to be schooled with might.

Yes, still another day, the beauty not yet forsaken; quiet and sullen to be of Hail.

Sweeping without summons, in a thief ant of the eye, the unforeseeable steals the birth from the apparent; He needs to ask in delicate reek of stables, is this the Time?

Romance at sunder, fleeting with the moment's nourishing, He departs earnestly to grasp and hold frozen the beauty, charm, and rime.

Phyllis J Mahlbacher
ONLY ONE

To Crystal Lee Mahlbacher, (Granddaughter).

Did you ever sit back and say
I've had a hard day,

Everything looks bleak and there is no other way,
With all your problems you wish you had a shelf
To put them on and deal with yourself,

But when you look around and make yourself aware,
You cannot sit back and say I don't care,

There are people out there much worse off than I,
So why feel sorry for me and cry,

Get up, get out, and look up at the sky,
And thank God for what you've got and don't ask why,

If everyone could help one person in their life,
Through trials & tribulations & some of their strife,

You'll stop feeling sorry for yourself & smile
It may be hard but it will be all worthwhile,

So look back in your life & see what you've done,
And be proud of yourself if you helped Only One.

God Bless You!

Doris L Taylor
THE PINK DISHCLOTH

To Bonnie—my friend—not well, but always cheerful, giver of "dishcloths" to all who visit her.

Every time I go to my sink—
I pick up and use this thing that's pink,
I spill on the stove or the burner link—
What to use in a hurry? — I'm trying to think,
Aha — I grab this thing of pink.
When the table needs wiping — without a blink,
I turn 'round — grab the pink from the sink.
When meal-time's over there seems a link,
Between eatin' and usin' this thing of pink.
When chocolate covers the face of my little "doll-link"
The handiest clean-up — the pink from the sink.
It glides o'er the formica top smooth as a mink,
Then I wring it — and leave it — and it dries in a kink!
Sure couldn't get along without this thing of pink —
It has its own hanger under the sink.
Use it on cupboards, floors, windows — everything, I think —

Is there anything handier than this thing of pink?
Guess people would say I'm sorta "dink"
For all the uses I have for this thing of pink.
You may not have a "Pink" by your sink —
But the dishcloth by your sink's mighty handy — I think.

Nitza Rivera
FOR THE LOVE OF HER I CRAVE!

"To Maritza Lopez, the ultimate love of my life."

For the love of her I crave,
to search my soul for unseen sights,
to touch the dormant parts within,
for what she must be is a part of me
to forever hold in my heart.

For the love of her I crave,
to feel my insides ache with life
to greet her silhouette in eternal sin
for what she must be close and far
to forever hold her dreams with mine.

Belinda Carter
DEAR JULIE

Dedicated to Julie Marie Carter 10/18/83 –10/6/89.

I wish I had more time.
I wish I had one more day.
Just so I could say good-bye.
And everything else I need to say.

I know if you could have
You would have held on.
But the pain was too much.
And the pain was too strong.

I wish I could see you smile
And run and jump and play.
Oh, if just for a little while.
Oh, for just one day.
You were my special one
Right from the start.
You always loved the sun.
You had the kindest heart.

Ju-Ju Bean, I want to say
I miss you so much.
I think of you every day,
And I'll never say good-bye.

Charlie Halbrook
THE TRUTH

For Rick K.M.

You want the truth
The words that split the heart in me,
Opens it up
Like an ancient tomb
Linking Time—
Search your own heart;
What has come and gone
In Time has no significance,
Pledges are what they seem
The heart encased
Waits to be rejoined—
Physical and emotional completion.

Feelings live on
In thoughts called memories.

Joseph W Summers
THE PETALS OF A SIMPLE ROSE

For Beth, who inspired me to try. Mom, thanks for your encouragement with this talent.

The petals of a simple rose.
One by one they fall away,
taking with them tender
moments of my life.

Each of them carry a memorable part.
The red droplets only a piece,
Yet collectively form the whole
of my precious existence.

Your first gift to me fluttered hither
with a wind,
Catching upon a thorn,
to stay with me forever.

My gift to you consists,
not of a single leaflet,
but of what remains.

Lisa White
FRIENDS

This poem is dedicated to Denise, a true friend.

A friend is someone you can count on when everyone has let you down.
They can make you smile and wipe away your frown.
You know no matter where they are you can call and talk, no matter how far away if they had to they would walk.
What ever you need you know they would be there.
They have their family and life but still they care.
You are the one person in the world they're willing to share.
So my friend, what I am trying to say is, "Please don't leave or go away," because I really want you to stay.
I will be by your side until the end.
Why?
Because I am truly your friend.

E Ackermann Randolph
ALTHOUGH

To Ramona, my precious wife who, ALTHOUGH I am less than perfect, loves me as if I were.

Although:
Love conquers all,
There is no contest
Love is blind,
Its perception is complete
Love is dear,
It is freely given
Love is shared,
It is undivided
Love is not unique,
It is singularly ours
Love will endure,
There is no waiting
Love has no dominion,
I am yours, you mine.
We are one,
To infinity.
Love, precious love.

Mary E Inman
CHRISTMAS TIME

This poem is dedicated to my father and mother-in-law, Waymond and Lucille Inman for the warm Christmases we've all shared over the years.

Christmas to me, is the most wonderful time of the year. A time when friends and loved ones get together and toast a holiday cheer.

Feeling the crisp cold air, the smell of smoke from the chimney tops, filtering everywhere.

Snow gently falling, covering the ground, people hustling and bustling all over town, their Christmas presents wrapped all festive and bright, to put under their trees on Christmas Eve night.

Taking a ride in a horse-drawn sleigh, listening to carolers, all along the way.

Walking in the snow, with a friend hand-in-hand, surveying all the wonders God created in his land.

Christmas trees twinkle with their lights, oh, so bright, while mommies and daddies tuck their children in bed for the night.

Loved ones all kissing 'neath the old mistletoe and one more thing I would like you to know, I try to keep Christmas in my heart all the year, because the birth of "Our Savior" to me is so dear.

Jaime Ellington (age 11)
ONE SHINING STAR AGO

In Loving Memory of my Grandfather, Morgan Holman.

One shining star ago,
I felt a soft, subtle wind blow.
When I heard my lover's song,
I floated to him and we danced.

We danced on the wind,
We ran on the clouds.
We talked in the gardens,
We sang to the night birds;
Whilst we walked under the pale moonlight.

Anna Marie Horn
AS TIME GOES BY

To my son Richie, who even though he wasn't born yet, could very easily be the little boy in this poem. He has made my life very exciting As Time Goes By.

A buzz you may hear,
In your half deafened ear,
And you know you must rise,
Because time flies and flies.
A jump out of bed,
Just to land on your head,
Makes you wish you had stayed,
In the bed you just made.
But you rush down to breakfast,
The last stair you just missed,
So back up you go,
For your pants you must sew.
With your pants sewn and set,
It's to the table like a jet,
But only to find,
You've left your books far behind.
But now it's too late,
For you've missed your first date,
So back up to bed,
Is where you should head.

Gary Allen Herman
I WAS ONCE AS MY CHILD

To My Son: Gary Allen Herman, II.

From the ancient clays and sands
I was formed a child to become a man
with loving hands, this love gave me life

I was once as my child — pure, innocent, gentle and mild
I was held in trust, kept in the fold and dreamed of higher goals
I was a gift that was as a beautiful song,
I could do no wrong
It was me then, which is now of my own flesh

I was once as my child, not then what I am now
a light making my parents proud, and how
they gave their love to me
with that same love — I set my own child free

If only time could take me back — to a time before the "Crack"
to what was once as my Child is now!

To hands that carried me and from which I fell
into a raging, burning hell

Sincerely, I say I am sorry to you
for I truly do love you — now I know how to
for I was once to you as my child is to me now

I pray that when he becomes a man
that he treads not a step in my past failed plans

If I could be now when — I was once as my child!

Debra Boccelli Smith
NEVER FORGOTTEN

This poem is dedicated to my father whom I miss very much.

Even as the days and years have gone by, it has only been harder to bear the emptiness I will forever feel inside, or the many times I've cried when just the thought of you has come to mind.

I now will go on with life cause that's what you would want me to do, but from now and forever it will just be another day without you.

Lisa Orlandoni

Lisa Orlandoni
TODAY'S DREAM — TOMORROW'S VICTORY

This poem is dedicated to my wonderful parents who taught me that dreams do become reality. I LOVE you Mom & Dad! To my Grandmother who still keeps my present dreams alive. And to my sister, brother, and brother-in-law; I Love you guys!

There Was a Blue Time
But Then I Found Myself
I Know My Dreams.

I Fight, Struggle, Sacrifice . . .

Then, I See Green
And I Reach Up And Aim A Little
Higher Every Day,
Reach A Little Farther
To Pursue The Light That Gets
Brighter By Dawn

Then, I Reach Higher Until The
Sky's The Limit With

VICTORY!

Rodney K Anderson
WAKE-UP

In dedication to The Anderson Family.

One man's goal is another man's dream.
God put you here for a very good reason.
To live your life through all four seasons.
If you respect yourself and do good for others.
You'll go through every day in a better way.
You can walk real tall even if you're short.
You can feel real rich even though you're poor.
Treat yourself like a big superstar.
It's no good reason to look down on yourself.
If you're trying your very best to take care of your health.

Wake-up out of the dream world and pursue your goals.
Don't be like a lost ball in high weeds.
If you're waiting for something to fall out of the sky.
It's not going to be what you want it to be.
Use your eyes to see where you're going.
Keep both feet on the ground and you won't get
caught up in what's going around.
Strength is your crutch, and God is your guide.
To get your cut of that big piece of pie.
God Bless You and Thank You.

Elizabeth Lynne Henderson
HAVING THE TIME
Come to me whenever you are lonely

For I'll smooth away your tears
with the gentleness of my hand

I'll stay near for you to reach out and touch when you long for reassurance

I'll stroke back the hair from your eyes when you find it difficult to speak

I'll kiss your lips tender
when you become speechless and scared

I'll listen with open heart
if no one else has the time

For love is having the time.

Sheila Lyn Jenkins
TRIANGLES OF LIFE
The triangle of life is
peace, love, and happiness.
The triangle of sorrow and death is
anger, hate, and loneliness.
Though the triangles may intertwine,
the one used most of the time,
will, in the end, predict your life line.

Elma C Onken
HAPPY BIRTHDAY MOM
I'd like to catch a rainbow wrap it up and tuck it away
To give it specially to you on the day of your birthday;
I'd like to capture a sunset and box its beauty and glow
Send it special delivery to you cause I love ya dontcha know.

How about a fluffy white cloud to relax in its softness and ease
To forget your troubles and woes and mom — do just as you please;
Love to package and send moonbeams perhaps the twinkling of the stars
I'd like for you the very best the Milky Way or the planet Mars.

I could never repay you for your time and care thru the years
But I do hope that I produced more joy than tears;
God will send forth more celestial delights each new day
I wish you happiness always as He sends blessings your way.

Frances E Robinson
LOST BUT SAVED
I was sick in sin and lost in despair
When sweet Jesus reached down and found me there,
What joy for me, he cared so much,
To save my sinful soul with his touch,
No other has cared enough to die for me,
Or bare my sins on calvary's tree,
He's got me a home in heaven this I know,
And has saved me from a hell below.

Angeles C Lopez
THE LITTLE WINDOW
I was looking out the window
Searching for a patch of blue
But my eyes only saw bare trees
No more that lovely green hue

The snow began to get restless
And sent flurries from afar
They fell like millions of twinkles
And disappeared, like the stars

It's serene, out of the window
You hear the stillness you see
And suddenly, gusts of rough winds
Awakens your reverie

Spring with its garden, so lovely
Summer, warm with golden sun
Autumn, full of falling colors
Winter, white, and soft, and cold

I saw that out of the window
Like a movie, rolling fast
Just a few minutes of dreaming
To come out of Wonderland!

Michael J Stozicki
AND SO COMES THE NIGHT
Listen! The sound of a clock counting rhythmically like the cricket's chirping. Tick, tock, tick. How stealthily the shade approaches. What holds? What binds? What shackles? One, two, three. Nothing like the moon. What moves? What shines? What sinks?

The day's end as well as the night's, where people deny and lie and cheat inevitability. Deceive? Psyche. Click, click, click. Listen! The rhythm of the night. The moth's blind navigation. Don't guide, take out your eyes! Click, click, click. And so comes the night.

Holly Weaver
I'LL BE MUCH DIFFERENT
"Roses are red,
Violets are blue;
Sugar is sweet,
And cows go moo."

I'm tired of poems
That start out this way;
Who cares about roses
And what the cows say.

A poem should not
Be written in form;
It should be much different,
Apart from the norm.

But poets lack courage
To say what they think;
Instead they surrender
To writing in sync.

Well, I'll be much different,
'Cause my first lines will say:
"Once upon a time,
In a land far away."

Ardy Hoffmann
WHERE ARE YOU?
It was supposed to be fun
our evening together.

We should have laughed and talked,
but instead, we were alone.

Can two people in love
really be alone?

Only if one desires it
and chooses it over togetherness.

I cannot reach you
when you desire unhappiness.

I cannot meet you
in your hole.

All I can do is look in
and extend my hand to yours.

Is there hope for us?
Will you reach for me?

I'll wait for awhile and see.
I hope you choose us.

Ellen M Holland
WITHOUT
Crouching beneath a rickety park bench,
She searched for shelter from the freezing December rain.
The brisk wind bit into her aching bones;
As she peered wishfully toward the grim, frowning
Sky, she began
Slowly realizing it held no pity for her.
She felt abandoned by the world.

But Wait!
Suddenly two figures appeared on the stone path,
Playfully dancing through the puddles, the pair passed by;
As she peered wishfully into their bright, smiling
Faces, she began
Slowly realizing they held no pity for her.
She was abandoned by the world.

K Laurie Ferris
GENTLE FORCE
Listen,
let the sound of water soothe your soul.
Be patient,
let nature take control.
Don't fight it,
let it absorb your every pore.

Frank Catanzarite
BLESSED
If I could write a poem so pretty!
Like the lights at night in the big city.
Or a boy in the yard whose face is smiling and dirty.
Just a few lines to excite a happy joyous feeling.
Words that everyone could find appealing.
To bring out brotherly love and no killing.
Imagine an old couple holding hands as they walk.
A baby's first grins and gibberish as it learns to talk.
Standing on the shoreline skipping rocks.
So the whole world would get up and dance!
And give the earth one more chance.
To fill our lives with its rich substance.
Wild country flowers that bloom in the spring.
Early Sunday morning as the church bells ring.
All the children as they learn to sing.
Grandpa and grandson at a game of chess.
A tiny baby girl in her first new dress.
Realizing that our world is peacefully blessed.

Bill Barcome
YESTERDAYS

To my mother — her love and encouragement in all things has filled my life with hope and joy.

Why this attraction with what has been?
Why this desire to live it again?
And what is there about the past
that holds me close within its grasp?
And what would I expect to find
if I could but go back in time?
What would I expect to see
if I could relive a memory?
And back in time how would I fare?
Is there some special magic there?
If only I could come to know
what is this past that haunts me so?
Oh! what I'd give to be truly free
from this past that calls out to me.

Vicki M George
FATED LOVE

This is for Bob. He knows why.

Ours wasn't a match made in heaven
Or programmed in a computer date.
For this perfect love we owe our thanks
To the intervening hand of fate.

In our search for true love we had failed
For reasons we could not discover.
It was as if we had never been meant
To find the perfect friend and lover.

Then at a time we least expected
We suddenly found someone who cared. One who was so much like the other
So many thoughts, hopes and dreams shared.

Had our future been left in our hands
Our blindness would have kept us apart.
But one with vision saw our common thread:
Two rebel souls were bound by one heart.

Timothy R Jeffries
A JESUIT SMILE

In memory of Cathy Heartman.

What a dilemma . . .
to be conscientiously
dreaming . . .
While floating
in stone . . .
Buoyant in secretions . . .
of ecstatic vibrations . . .
Hysterically screaming
to be left
alone . . .

Wendy Strange
CHANGE

How come things always change?
Nothing ever stays the same
May it be . . .
The illuminating colors of a rainbow
Against the bright blue sky
OR
The green leaves of spring

Even the love within a heart
The love may remain
But pounding passions soon fade

And the feeling leaves
Just as the sun disappears
When the night sky unfolds blankets of glittering stars
Nothing ever stays the same

Maybe change is good
Perhaps needed or desired
Though hard to accept
To live is to change

Scott W DeBord
LIFE'S LESSONS LEARNED

To my Mother and Father who taught me that true maturity only comes through the nurturing of one's Spirit. Without spiritual growth, the maturity of the body and mind are rendered purposeless. Without a knowledge of the creator, the creature is lost.

From life's first moment of corporal shock
When all is new and innocence free
Through early youth when Death we mock
We smell, We hear, We taste, We see
We touch - We are Sensuality

When summer is young and spring is spent
We yield erudition's plea
It leads to a knowledge — the World has lent
We read, We write, We gain our degree
We postulate — We are Scholarity

A journey we take when the bell tolls eight
For redemption that comes from bent knee
Salvation We plead — for it is late
We search, We find, His image We be
We cherish — We are Spirituality

When Luna arrives, in life's tide we wade
Results will display where virtue adjourned
What values were chaste, where weight had been laid
Our message of life will surely be burned
By the fire of commitment to Life's Lessons Learned

Jude Kranitz
PEACE

This poem is dedicated to my children Susan, Scott, Cindy, Tim, Suzanne, Chris, and my granddaughters Kathy, and Amanda. Also, The World.

How happy my heart would
Feel
If all of us could climb the hill of
Peace
Together
With sunshine on our
Faces
And starlight in our
Hair
No more wars or threats of
Bombs
The power of
Love
To guide us along
Thank you dear
GOD
For being there
Peace to Peace
Is always
Fair

Tonya Case
OUR LOVE FOREVER

This poem is dedicated to Doug, who means the world to me.

Our love is something romantic to share,
to know that someone will always be there.
When I'm feeling down and sad,
all I do is remember
the great times we've had.
So many songs are of you,
I'm always thinking
of the things you do.
Be here with me to stay,
to keep our love always
and never go away.
If our love grows far apart,
please remember it wasn't
meant to break anyone's heart.
Don't forget me,
and I won't forget you
but we are always meant as
that great number two.

Sharon Kruger
MY BELOVED AND I

To the man I fell in love with.

Even though he is far away, he is always in my heart.
Every stolen moment we have together is short,
and I dread the time that he brings me home.
Soon we will be together, my beloved and I,
and his home will be where I am.
We will be free to love each other,
whenever and wherever we choose to.
His love is all I thirst for,
and in his loving eyes I see forever.
My beloved and I, together, forever.

Vallorie K Ettien
GROWING UP!

"To Daniel," Thanks for the life that you've given me. It's so much better than before. "Your Loving Wife," Vallorie.

At two years old they meet,
Sitting around playing and tickling each other's feet.
As they grow and get to the age of eight,
They get caught kissing behind the golden gate.
When they get to the age of sixteen,
They think they know what the word love means.
She wore a beautiful, long white dress,
Even though things were a mess.
As two years passed,
She always knew it wouldn't last.

Ann Gilmore Taylor
SNOW

This poem is dedicated to my sister Adelaide Gilmore Hoepfner who has many exceptional qualities I admire.

All glistening white.
The FLAKES Come
T
U
M
B
L
I
N
G
Down.
Like goose feathers soft,
They sparkle o'er the town.
What a joy to walk,
And feel the crunch beneath your feet.
To know the ecstasy of a cold winter day,
As you talk to all the birds you meet.

Norma J Reyes
MOTHER

To my Mother: Carmen Romelia Reyes, I Love You.

A gentle touch; A loving hand;
A whisper when evil touches me,
Makes everything alright.
A smile when I'm sad brightens my whole world.
A loving look; A shoulder to cry on, is what a mother is.
You brought me into this world and never asked a thing, but to let you love me.
You've always been there for me;
Always my friend.
I've let you down so many times and
Yet you still love me. Of all the people in the world I'm blessed
to have you as my
MOTHER.

Mark Olson
JUST BEING ALIVE

To Jesus Christ, the one who showed me what being alive really means.

Spring of autumn joy is bound
A time to see what love is found
In the past or future tenses
The present holds the soul's senses

A leaf is tossed and windward blown
Stars of light in heaven sewn
A rock is still a flower grows
From the earth music flows

Times to be had, lived, and felt
Moments past in memory melt
In the sky a cloud is hung
On the ground a bard had sung
Of animals and love with lyre
Is it not that we fear
The things we lose but cannot gain
That bring the heart most terrible pain

With beards and wrinkles life is told
Not what you have but what you've sold
The price is not silver nor even gold
It is experience (moments of time)
When we laugh and when we rhyme
In love with earth we play

Rebecca Crader
DREAMS CAN COME TRUE

To my knight in shining armor, for that special magic that you alone can give me.

As a child, I used to dream
Of Knights in Shining Armor
Riding great white steeds.
As I grew older, these dreams
Became tarnished with reality.
Sadly, I learned that "Fairy Tales"
Don't belong to the "real" world,
And that our dreams
May never, ever come true.
Until I met you.
You have given me back my dreams,
As you have that special magic
That blends dreams into reality.
You have given me the courage
To turn past dreams into tomorrow's reality.
You're a very special man
And for what you've given back to me,
I LOVE YOU.

Barbara C Bryant
SUMMER VRS WINTER

To my mother — Daisy K. Rowles.

Another winter has just passed by,
and Spring has opened its weary eye.
The leaves on the trees are starting to bloom,
and the birds and the frogs all start with a boom,
The flowers start lifting their sleepy heads,
and seeds are soon planted in the flower beds.
Now it's rain, rather than snow,
Which is worse, I'll never know.
A nice spring shower is fun to see,
but thunder and lightning frightens me.

A night when everything is still,
you can hear the song of the whippoorwill.
The firebugs come out to play,
but leave again at the break of day.
To Love, a young man's fancy turns,
and in his heart a true love burns.

Winter skies have a certain hue
but summer skies are azure blue.

Michele Eyerman
DO YOU EVER JUST SIT AND THINK

To Cathy. Her life was taken away at the age of 22. July 22, 1989 — Rest In Peace.

Do you ever just sit and think
Think about what is going on
Going on in this world,
Do you ever wish
Wish to take back a night
A night something went wrong,
Something went wrong one night
One warm july night
A night I will never forget,
When you get a call
A call of sorrow
Sorrow that a friend
Was Brutally Murdered,
The emptiness inside
Ending of her life of happiness
A life of dreams
A life of goals,
Did you ever wish
Wish you could take back a night
A night something went wrong,
I wish I could.

Betty J Chastain
LATE VISITOR

Dedicated to my Grandchildren: Leonard & Charley Chastain, Amy & Tammy Nabor.

Nothing was stirring in the dark lonely house,
When all of a sudden was heard — one little mouse.
All day he lay quiet — as respectful as could be!
But just before midnight — He went on a spree!
He ran thru the bookshelves,
You could almost feel his glee!
His tiny feet rustling,
this paper and that.
Being careful — not to attract the cat!
Then came a night when he was heard no more.
The cat must have gotten him or chased him out the door!
So tonight in the dark lonely house,
Nothing is stirring — not even the mouse!

Ray Potts
MY HEART IS WEAK FROM CRYING

To Sherry. Though we're apart my love will always be in my heart for you.

My heart is weak
from crying
That if I don't stop
my heart will
Feeling as I do without
having your love
is hurting of knowing
That am alone with
this feeling
Caring is not even
hating what am going
through
Knowing I love someone
who can't even feel
my heart
is real pain for the
heart holds love even
by itself
For the strongest feeling
my heart will ever hold
will always be missing you
Am sorry our love
didn't come together

D Timothy Scronce
YOUNG AGAIN

To my wife Sandra, my daughter Crystal, and my son "T.J."

Let me go home again.
Release me from the
shackles that bond
me to this world.
Free me so that I
may glide on dreams
of days gone by.
Let me go back to
days of innocence
when yesterdays were
but a nuisance, and
tomorrow a faraway
fantasy.
Let me be young
again.

Richard Anthony Miller

Richard Anthony Miller
MY NEIGHBORS

I have these neighbors that fuss and fight
They carry on like this every day and night
I told them once to get themselves together
Or you will burn in hell forever
But they never listened and that goes to show
Of how much and how little did they know
This little saying is to let you know
That there is a hell, because if there wasn't
Where would my neighbors go

Richard Anthony Miller
FIVE TO FOUR

Several of the faults we had, ended with us working things out
Nevertheless spending weeks of being sad, and a whole lot of things to think about
But faults came beneath us, as we grew older and more mature
Every day seemed like Christmas, we were in love we knew for sure
Our careers caused us problems, well only just a little distance
Letters and phone calls solve them, missing with a lot of resistance
But I always came back to my love, on every break that I had from work
And we were just like two lovely doves, we love each other so much it hurts
Our distance became an issue, well she finally started feeling alone
Realizing now why she stopped saying "I miss you" you see she had another love when I got home
I never thought another could make our love changed, no I never had a hunch
I can't believe you let it go down the drain, our five years to his four months

Paula L Rodriguez
IF I COULD TURN BACK TIME

This poem is dedicated to Joe H. Brown, Jr., for putting up with me for the last 21 years. I love you. Your sister, HOCKS.

If I could turn back time
I would make you small again.
You would be wrestling with the guys or playing baseball in the park.

If I could turn back time
you would be reading comic books and pulling my hair for laughs or playing catch in the yard.

If I could turn back time
I would still be following you around dressing like you while getting on your nerves with mimics.

If I could turn back time
we would be playing cards at the dining room table calling each other "cheater" and actually be cheating so the other could win.

But since I can't turn back time
I'll settle for the memories of our childhood and keep the secret hidden in my heart of being your little sister.

JE Whitmore
THE WAYS OF LOVE

This I dedicate to the Lamb of Truth and to his beautiful Bride. May their light shine Eternal, that no Soul need be lost to darkness.

The wind breathes his tale, that time spins her rhyme.
Lady of the light you show the ways of love.
Your adoration, it is truly an endearment of right.
This feeling love's game is times of change.
Lady, but lady your affection is still the same.
You surely I will always treasure.
Such true sentiment is hard to measure.
Your tenderness helps see life's will thru.
With you the path is certain and clear,
Beloved, how so do I cherish you most dear.
Lady of the light you show the ways of love.
Such devotion is faithfully an affair of right.
These beautiful vibrations are like creation's might,
In motions and notions of that will be done.
Oceans and seas change, the trees lose their leaves,
But lady your caress forever is the same,
Like cycles in a never ending game.
Lady of the light you show the ways of love.
With now nothing left here to say,
Even today your loyalty is still the way.
Lady of the light you show the ways of love.

Nellie Rivera
WHO AM I?

This poem is dedicated to my loving husband, and wonderful children.

Am a simple and humble person in which in me a great love
exists towards the one I love with all my heart.
Am my own person. Also I don't try being someone am not
or someone I could never be.
Am one of those persons in which love they give, love I returned.
If they give me confidence, confidence they will obtain.
If am treated with tenderness, tenderness you will have.
If you offer me understanding, understanding will exist.
If am offer communication, communication there will be.
And if they were to offer me the most important out of
all, their heart, my heart and soul I'll have given for
everything their sincerity and offerings that they had
offered with all their heart and their whole life.

John S Bavo
DOWN RIGHT DIRTY

To Lisa Platt whose friendship and love has helped me through a lot.

This world we live in
No one cares.
Brother and sister
Never to share

The thing we see
The thing we hear
Sex and violence
Are much too free

Life waits on no one
No one at all
We all take chances
But then some fall

The sun may shine
The wind may blow
Step by step
And you will know

The games people play
The lies they tell
The emptiness comes
From within the shell

You tell me you love me
But I can't tell
Your hugs and kisses
Feel like hell

There's one more thing
That you must hear
Your talk of equality
Could never be real

Look in my eyes
What do you see

It's the soul
Of my personality

Time will pass
As the value of sin
The place to look
Is deep within

We all condemn
We all make law
Help me earth's children
To change it all

I have but one more
Thing to say
Tranquil and love
Will brighten your day

Carie Bingman
A POEM IS . . .
A poem is a feeling,
a thought beneath words,
a scarce emotion from the heart.

A poem is a want, a dream,
an emotion,
from life itself.

A poem is words,
expressed from your inner soul,
that's what a poem is.

Tracey Celeste Bradshaw
THIS GENERATION
As we see the sunlight,
And smell the roses,
We see a nicer side of life.
But what about those children
Lost out in the night?
Are we not the generation that
Is going to make the mark?
Where are our resolutions,
Our caring and our fight?
Have we not come close to hope,
That our future generation
Might dare to take the rope?
Have we lost to such oppression,
No dignity and pain?
On what stand is your vote?
An endless score of questions.

We have thought not.
A paper does not do it.
Oh! But, what?
Have you thought about those
Children or not?
You see, we are that future
Generation of this time.
But what, you ask,
Have you not?
The games we play will not
Save those souls.
The studies of the world lead
Us not to control.
Where are our values, morals
And souls?
Should not we be doing
What the Lord above told?

Cesseley Dobbins
ODE TO A M&M

This poem is dedicated to my son Charles, I love you, Mommy.

He told me not to wait for him.
He didn't know to me he was a
precious gem.
I knew what I was getting into.
It was just too easy to get used to.
I knew it wouldn't last.
Feelings got involved too fast.
I know deep down he is not to blame.
But how can I rid my shame?

Shauna Morrow
FRIENDSHIP
Sharing clothes, laughs, and tears,
Ridding me of foolish fears.

Special moments, special times,
Forgiving me of little crimes.

Helping when you think you can't,
Knowing when to rave and rant.

Being honest when you should,
Knowing you'd do all you could.

Staying when you'd rather run,
All those times we fought and won.

Not believing all you heard,
Friendship what a special word.

Lynn M Russell
MY FRIEND
Like the mid-day sun,
you keep me warm inside;
and when the darkness haunts me,
you tend to be my guide.

Gentle are your hands,
as they reach out for me each day;
so precious is your special touch,
that tells me we're ok.

In the evening hours, hun,
when the day has come to end,
I lay down beside you knowing,
that you really are my friend.

How can I ever thank you
for all you have given me?
Especially your understanding
when I just won't leave things be.

You are certainly full of patience,
love and beauty too;
let me take this time to say,
Honey, I love you.

Karen Duescher
WE'VE SEEN THE CHANGES COME AND GO
We've seen the changes come and go
Upon us all is autumn, comes a sad
And restless feeling
Through the beauty, silently flaming,
The wonderland of Autumn is slowly
Drawing to an end.

The days will soon forever be cold
The curious, prowling wildlife, I see
The early mornings
Gathering up their nutrients, hickory
Nuts and things of such.
Soon they will retire, beneath the
Winter's earth.

I am weak, I am small, I need
Your strength, autumn is sound.
I hear your voice, the lessons you
Have hidden in each leaf
To fight my greatest enemy, Myself.

Doug Fitch
GIRLS, WHERE TO FIND THEM
Look in that black book,
will do you no good.
Look at school, not good.
Look for days, no luck.
Then you start to cry.
After a while you think and think.
Then you've got it.
A song is where you find a girl
of your dreams.
You hope!!!

Elizabeth Trevor
THE QUAKE OF '89
Like Eddie-Lou Cole, I'm 80 plus,
I've lived a colorful life.
Struggled through situations
causing heartache, pain and strife.

At this point I would like to add,
grandchildren, I have thirteen;
I'm very proud of all of them,
including great grands of eighteen.

The most devastating time of all
was the Quake of Eighty Nine.
I thank the Good Lord up above,
my large family made out fine.

I've picked up broken objects,
straightened pictures on the wall.
Picked up fallen objects,
the worst that I can recall.

The aftershocks keep coming
as under a doorway I run;
And softly mutter to myself:
Dear God, let this be the last one.

Joseph J Greenberg
TICKET TO HELL
He's coming for me,
I know that now,

He's coming for me,
But I don't know how.

He's coming for me for what I've
done,
This was the price for all my fun.

I lived on the edge,
While putting a wedge, between me
and God.

I destroyed a church,
I walked with a lurch,
And the wedge got bigger and bigger.

I didn't like my life,
It wasn't very swell,
For all it got me was a ticket to hell.

Edward Masterson
VISIONARY
Eyes of humanity twinkle bright,
given to each and all a true light.
He that seeketh shall stand tall,
the unwanting promised to fall.

Unconscious mind, knowing not
shame,
awaken days he does bring tame.
Easily lost in the masses of trend,
men by weakness, so willingly
offend.

His be strong, forgiving and tender,
all this and more stated the sender.
Too many are lost, one all all are
fools,
not of him lay in dark and
sightless pools.

Men numbered great fight his ghost,
through him sanctity to be found
by most.
Without vision, heart and soul will
hollow,
the eternal beacon you and I must
follow.

"Our Lord Jesus"

Edward Masterson
CAPTURED HEART
Sensuously pursed in a moist ruby
glaze,
unfilled hunger, man's strength
they crave.
Memory aloft, bits still in haze,
enchanted by him, a kiss she gave.

Scented light with an earthy potion,
brunette hair of silk, always
glowing.
Mind bewitched by her frantic
motion,
dreams of love and passion are
flowing.

Body and soul entwine one's chosen
mate,
thought impossible, time endless
in measure.
Since Adam and until I all men can
relate,
besides God, life's most sought
treasure.

Upon past images I'm not to reflect,
there be another woman, no,
never.
A lady is rare and demands respect,
I give unto her this and love
forever.

Dee Colvin
OUR LITTLE TOWN

This poem is dedicated to the Gladewater Chamber of Commerce, and the Gladewater Antique Dealers Association. It was because of my work with them that this poem was written.

Come to The Gladewater Round-up
Rodeo,
It is fun to see this exciting show!
There is roping, riding, and even a
clown,
It is a BIG event in our little town.
Gladewater has a lot in store for you,
Come early and you will find plenty
to do.
Spend a day in shopping pleasure.
Find many items that you will
treasure.
There are Antiques, Collectibles,
Crafts, and more.
Eating places that you will adore.
Folks come here from all over the
nation,
Because they have heard of our
reputation.

Ruth E Green

Ruth E Green
OUR 25 YEARS

I dedicate this Poem to my brother and sister-in-law, Richard and Aurora Escott, Clinton, Michigan.

Today, Our Twenty-fifth year, our
memories go back, far across the sea
A new life began there, for you and
for me
We have weathered the storms of
those years now past
Our Silver Anniversary is here at last.

Sometimes it seems the years drifted
slowly by
Yet it was as the twinkling of an eye
We are blessed with the joy of our
friends so dear
Who banish our frown with their
smiles to appear.

Each new day comes with a mystery
to unfold
Its part of our life, we must set the
mold
Yesterday is a day, already far in the
past
Never to return, no chance to recast.

Tomorrow is the approach of a bright
new dawn
The hopes, the fears, the sorrows to
spawn
The sands of the future fan out for all

to see
It's God's will what the rest of our life will be.

Life is too sweet for us to fret
This could be our best year yet
Our lord watches over us from above
We send up our thanks for these years of Love.

Estelle Gertz
A DEVOTION
My friend to me, is like a gem;
His young brother is retarded;
He taught him to have faith and strength,
And makes sure that he is well-guarded;

No matter what he is doing,
He will find time for him to spare;
He taught not to give up hope,
Big brother was always there.

He will make the time to take the time
To teach him honesty;
Be bold and hold his head up high
With honor and dignity.

He told him, "It is not what you are that really counts,
It is who you want to be;
As long as you are doing your best,
It would be a great gift to me."

He is God's special creation
Which makes him very rare;
Bless you, big brother, for the things you do;
When he needs you, you are there!

Betty Adams Holt
DAY OF THE FUNERAL
Softly, softly fall the footsteps
As a loved one takes his leave;
Quietly seeking, one may hear
Them
In the whisper of spring breeze.
Birds sing gently on this morning,
As God's sunshine lights the day,
Making rainbows in the teardrops
Shed for one who's gone away.
As late evening shadows gather
Round this family he held dear,
Give to them sweet solace, Saviour
While they yet must tarry here.
May they realize the promise
In your message long ago,
Of eternal life so blissful
In a land where gladness flows.
Gentle footsteps there now hasten
From the darkness into light
Through death's door to life
Eternal;
Led in love by God's own might,
Footstep sounds will soon diminish
As the stars begin to shine
Looking up toward the heavens
Is a sight to ease your mind
For a new light there is glowing
Lit by Jah's own hand divine.
Though life's candle be extinguished
God will make it newly bright;
Up above a radiant gleaming
Lights a loved one's way tonight
Softly, softly, comes a
Whisper,
From a dear soul gone away
"Dry your tears and do not
Sorrow,
I am safe with God today."

Sharon K Colvin
WRITTEN WITH THE HELP OF THE LORD
In due times, in due seasons —
moments in time for all to see.
in view rhymes, in view reasons, a purpose for all to be
Arising from seemingly no where,
to vanish in the night.
A new day shines in glory and all there is is right

Some are and some are not, in the end we'll find
what is and what was not who could see and who was blind.
Marching through the wilderness,
the liar to behold offering all there is to block the street of gold

Thorns and thistles in the path
some are kept in love
some are not they haven't known
a light shining from above

Marilyn Roberts
ASSAULT AND BATTERY
With snowpeaked glaciers watching
the crystal-blue sea
A tanker leaked crude
as thick as could be.

A muddy brown stain
cut like a knife
to cloud and to coat
all sea-going life.

The waves crashed black
as they washed up on shore
that left the dark sludge,
the tar and the gore.

Oil-slick otters, birds and fish brave,
were found floating in death
on their watery grave . . .

The once-pristine landscape
died hard that day
when the Exxon Valdez came
and took it away.

Shirley A Marquez
JUST ONE MORE TIME

Dedicated to my brother: Robert L. Cooper.

His wise sayings and restlessness
Are mysteries to be sought
Someday he'll find the answers
While searching thru his thoughts

His emotions are questionable
Confusing as it seems
No meaning to his life
Just unsuccessful dreams

He's always a dreamer
That brother of mine
Always willing to try it
Just one more time

He hangs onto life
Seeking out his place
Surely there must be
Some little empty space

He's on the move again
Following those dreams
With a twinkle in his eye
And a smile that gleams

He's always a dreamer
That brother of mine
Always willing to try it
Just one more time

Shirl A Exum
MY EMOTIONS
I have always tried to keep
My emotions hidden within my heart;
I could not show or share them
Because I did not know where to start

However, the harder I tried
My emotions to conquer and tame;
It would only lead to my failure
And feeling so terribly ashamed

But then there arose a time
When adversity came my way;
That I had no other choice
But to let my emotions go and pray

Do you know what happened when
My emotions were released?
The tears flowed and anger and doubt left;
Faith came and the confusion ceased

All my emotions I now share with God
I cast them as His feet and there they hide;
I am free in my emotions and no longer bound
Because I have His assurance that He is on my side

Valerie Cooke
THE BEE
Buzz, buzzz . . . .
It's the bee!
B u z
z z B zz Bu zzz
u z z
The bee is drunk.
It is high on fermented life.
Happy yet sad.
Good yet bad.
I am the bee;
The bee is me.
Buuzzzz

Ana Munoz de Rivera
THE MIRROR ONE

Because my love for you is endless, I'll love you forever. Because you're so special to me, you make my life special also. Because I love you these poems are for you.

A man walks in the darkest forest of the Universe.
A man who talks to himself, because no one wants to listen.
A man who speaks the truth of our senses,
Who says that we are monsters of our destinies.
Someone who picks up all the tears that I am afraid to let run.
Tears that carry stories of sorrow.
A man, who relieves me of the weight of the heavy chains that tie me in the dark.
A man who is everything and nothing in a simultaneous manner.
Someone, whom I am desperately trying to reach.
A person that is in me;
Who takes trips to other worlds and brings me
more stories that turn into more tears.

Ana Munoz de Rivera
PATTERNS OF TIME & LIFE
One day, I came to the past.
I met this person from a dream lost on time.
The unknown was telling me who I was.
An undecided life.

One day, I came to the present.
I met this person from a nightmare on time.
This person told me about the person I met
on my past. He also told me who I am,
An unstable one.

Today, I came to my future.
I met a nude person, who told me about the
persons I met in the past and the present.
The nude one tells me, that I'll become,
what I want to become.

Rebecca Vergara
MY SHADOW DOES NOT LIE
My shadow does not lie,
if you open your eyes you can watch it cry.
My shadow is a curse, to remind me of myself,
when I try to become someone else.
My shadow does not lie because with me it will die.
It would turn me in, but my shadow, shadow comforts me
While I wander and while I sleep,
it keeps me in my miserable company
and I wonder if my soul should need one to weep.
Who am I if God doesn't know about me?
Oh Lord, give me what I need!
For what I have I bleed, I bled for my shadow my strongest security.
but it would turn me in. Should I bleed forever?
Or until my aching heart should become my desert home?
Oh Lord I will heed your call in the darkest night
like a falling angel in flight.
My shadow does not lie.

Cheryl L Mason
AND SO . . .
Another page of life begins
yet more phases with fewer friends
Finally all the answers
to what is already through.
And so naivety dies
the open eyes have closed
Only anxiety can be in the future
A rebirth of the growing that
once more must come.
There are no winners to watch
to question or to idolize.
Stars reflect the vastness of
life's configuration.
Though innocence is gone life is not over.
And so to future dreams.
To whatever can be wrought
To tomorrow . . .
And so . . .

Gladus M Moore
TRIBUTE TO A BROTHER
From very young he was a man in stature.
He was hard, yet gentle and kind.
An Honored Soldier of many years
He lived the Code of Honor for the U.S.A. our land.

Today he is gone in body, yet spiritually walks the land.
We meet in the woodland to watch the rise or the setting sun.
We talk, the walk in silence, marking time
In harmony and peace with-in, we understand.

In life as in memory he will always be
My brother, my friend, my Honored Guide.
Loved: Yes by all who knew
Retired Master Sgt. Francis D. LaFollette the man.

Byrdene Byerly
ROY DEAR
Roy Dear,
You forgot your favorite hat.
You left a tire on your old Ford Flat.

Your chair still sags from where you sat;
You never saw your Sons at bat.

The pool's in shambles;
The Yard's a mess —
You did something around here after all, I guess.

I have no doubt as to where you are —
I know you've safely crossed the Bar.

I know you aren't as lonely as we . . .
For You see,
Dear Husband and Dad,
What makes our days so lonely and sad . . .

You also left us three —
Eddie and Aaron and Me.

Andrea Quincy Jamison
RHYTHM OF LOVE

Thanks to God for the ability to write, I dedicate all my writings to those that have inspired me, the late Quincy, Murphy, family, and to my friends — w/ L D.B.C.
Andrea Quincy

My heart follows
the sound of my lover
It reaches out to grab
him and pull him next to me
—and when it finds
that he's not there, it
drops down to
— ONE LONELY BEAT

Angela R Chester

Angela R Chester
MY CONCEPT OF COLOR
Black is more than a color; more than just a word, it says more in silence than most ears have ever heard.

In the deep blackness of the night the brightest stars come to sight.

My hair is coarse, yours thin. You'd say, "give me some of that moonshine boy," then you'd grin.

It would make me wish and sometimes pray that I would be another color someday.

Not realizing all the while I was looking at you, you were looking at me, check'n out my moves rhythmic motions that can't be taught nor bought simply born or instilled within you.
But I've matured, Now I can really see how beautifully Black I have come to be.

So, I checked it out making up my face coloring my full lips; clothes clinging to my curvaceous hips. Looked into the mirror and what did I see? Nothin, but all that beautiful blackness staring back at me!

Patricia R Joyce
ROSEMARY'S SWEET SIXTEEN
I Believe — In miracles — and I believe in you
I Believe — In everything — that you will decide to do
I Believe — That you have the ability in life
To handle the things that may come your way with strife . . .

I Believe — In rainbows because you've made my life so bright
I Believe — In you to keep your important goals in sight
I Believe — In Angels because God was good and sent us you
And I know deep in my heart your "Dad" feels the same way too!

I Believe — There will be times you may go astray
I Believe — When —— in need you will keep your faith and pray
I Believe — In miracles — Great and Small for you
To state it Sincerely — "Rose" I Believe in you . . . .

Love,
Mom & Dad

Eveline Richard

Eveline Richard
PRECIOUS BONDS

With love, I dedicate this poem to my husband Alonzo and our children Thierry, Dale André, and Imelda.

In our field of life we gather
Many friends wonderful and true
But there is with a precious few
Unique fondness — there forever

As kids we laugh — we hope — we play
Our hearts full of innocent dreams
Not knowing what it really means
To grow — to love — to go away

Then all too soon our youth is gone
And we know that destiny's game
Did not weaken the precious bonds
So very long ago were made

and so

The haunting whistle of a train
Brings memories of misty rain
Three friends sharing one more good—bye
Their friendship stood the test of time

Misty Larson
RIDE AWAY WITH ME

To Jodi Swanson — For everything, My parents — Harry and Marg Larson, and my Aunt Nancy Campbell.

Come
Saddle up with me
Upon my stallion
We'll ride away
to tomorrow
away from the confusion and loss of today
Hold on tight
We'll ride fast with the wind
up near the clouds
to where life is peaceful and safe
We'll stop to rest in a green meadow
and drink from a bubbling brook
Then mount up again
and not stop until we reach our destination
Our destination of serenity
So come on
Saddle up with me

Tammy L Salinas
IF ONLY IN MY HEART AND MIND
Not one day will pass
that I am not here
waiting for you.
Not one day will pass
that I don't hold my
love for you.
Not one day will pass
that I won't see your face
in everything I look at.
Not one day will pass
that I won't love you,
or that I'm not thinking
of you.
I believe we are one in one
For you are my day, and
not one day will pass that
I am not with you,
If Only In My Heart And Mind.

Lynette C Melton
WILDEST FANTASY
The moon shines very brightly tonight,
In the woods, it is such a beautiful sight.
It was just on such a night that I found myself,
In another land, such as you find in a book on a shelf.

I was among many others like me,
Those who had desire to, yet could not see.
Life in this jumbled up world is so hard,
Some may never know what lies in their molded hearts.

As I look about me, the woods seem so alive and full,
Of wonders and secrets, elfin lives are never dull.
The small ones, they gather around me now,
They want me to see life as they, and to show me how.

I fear not this strange land of dreams,
As frightening as it may look or seem.
I am safe here among the creatures of the night,
They protect my soul and make things right.

One day, I shall run among them free as the breeze,
Life will be so much fun and full of ease.
I will come to your dreams and help you then,
And forever and an eternity, we will be best friends.

Deborah Ann Beavers
I GOTTA BE TOUGH

My poem is dedicated to Kenny Curtis. He made me realize I wasn't quite as tough as I thought.

It's been so long since it felt so right
The feeling that I get when you hold me tight
I feel such a tingle from head to toe
Oh, how I just wanna let it go

I really don't know if I honestly can
Open up my heart to a man again
I've tried to live from day to day
And survive each one in my own way

I've had such a wall around my heart
I feel that wall coming apart
Your kiss brings on much desire
You make me feel like I'm on fire

I want you here night and day
To show you love in my own way
I feel that wall starting to shake
I've gotta be tough, for my own sake

Ben Sedgwick
THE MYTH
Why don't the truly beautiful stab hearts right?
Their together motivation separates light

Dark grey messengers using beautiful traits
Give falsified answers inspiring nylon gates

These polyester pigeons
Licking bad tasting whiteness
and inward blackness
Lay down with red roses in time of need

Rooms with corners which when lit
Leave no room for pigeons to impede

Sweet sweet snow of no regrets
Beautiful roses are each other's pets
Add extra holes to tightened belt
Remove all thorns, let butter melt

Esther Hance
DAISY'S GARDEN
Daisy wanted a garden I know,
Due to drought the seeds did not grow.
There was plenty of space,
Bad weeds took their place,
She said "This art I need to explore."

Donna E Skiles
WIND
I am the wind
And I sing through the trees
A soft, sweet tune
With my warm summer breeze
When the music is gone,
I will live on

I quietly wait for winter's cold chill
I cry out my name as I rage at will
When the snow is gone
And the earth is thawed
The wind lives on

I drift through mountains and across the land
I sweep my gales over oceans and sands
And when eternity comes
And all is gone
I remain
The wind lives on

James C Robson
DRUMMOSSIE MOOR
There is a grave on Drummossie Moor,
Where lie our brave beside a cairn.
Here they died, and here they rest
Their spirits o' the fen and forest.
Therefore, when you come in quest
For a sprig o' rare white heather here,
Wait in the stillness without fear.
You may a distant pibroch hear.
Walk now softly
On their belted plaid
O' gorse
Green-ferned,
Bright-heathered
Tartan made
To find that cherished
White cockade.

Janice Bale
DID YOU KNOW?
Oh my pet I love you so
So very sweet, soft, pure little Beau
I miss you so much my little one
With long grey hairs and deep green eyes.

Daily I wonder where did you go?
I'd feel so much better to know
Are you in pain or sweet peace?
If I knew maybe my sorrow would cease.

I hope you're not angry that I wasn't there
When they put you to sleep while I was here.
Selfish of me to think of myself
To even dare leaving you, my dear.

If you can only know
What you mean to me
The joys and memories I'll always cherish
Oh Beau, I miss you so much.

Please be happy my kitty wherever you are
And forgive me for not holding your paw
As they injected that final lethal poison into you
I wanted to be there, if only you knew.

Bill Seibel
NEW YEAR
We always say this every year
Happy New Year, and Good Cheer.
Don't wait to be cheerful 'til season tide
Below, I am leaving you a little guide.
For some, it's not easy, as you may find
It's just another year we've left behind.
We're on this earth for so short a time
I feel I've used up most of mine.
Enjoy yourselves, as life goes on
Life is short and will soon be gone.
Be happy and cheerful at work or play
Do something good and nice each day.
Love your family, friends, and thy God
Before you're placed beneath the sod.
This is all I have to say today
Happy New Year, any way.

Norma Durbin
IN ABSENTIA

To Ganny — For believing in me.

If tomorrow comes
Without me
I hope you will remember
Yesterday
With a smile,
And look forward to every mile
You travel alone,
Knowing,
My love never demanded
An accounting of tomorrow
Without me

Anne L Sudeikis
CTA OF A THOUSAND DREAMS

I dedicate this poem to Stephen J. Kabala, Esq., who has to be the transportation genius of all times and also to the most efficient transit authority of date, meaning the "Big Apple." —New York

CTA of a thousand dreams, I lie awake in darkness searching
For the truth — over this bed, above this pillowed place—
But then through tears I watch the image fly.

It is too late for me — The sun pursuing time will never slow.
For fools like me who sleep too long to know that heavy litigation will never catch its beams.

The waste of years lies heavy on my heart—
It is too late for me. I am not now what the CTA thought to conjure.
On my brow the frost of time confounds the CTA's part.

CTA of a thousand dreams, sleep on, dream well—
Of sun-drenched isles where ageless people dwell.

Pamela S Hagy
THANK YOU FRIENDS

In dedication to Marilyn and Lowell, two special people.

When we had no where to turn
You were there with care and concern.
You opened your doors of your humble abode
And took upon yourselves a heavy load.
Without a doubt, complain you did not,
But slaved over the stove to feed the lot.
Don't forget to let it be said,
That you also moved over, and gave us a bed.
To you, Our Friends, we are much in debt,
But with money they can never be met.
Your home, your love, and your concern you lent.
For that, your special rewards will be heaven sent.
Entrance thru the GOLDEN GATES you have surely won.
We thank you, Our Friends, for all you have done.
Friendship is something you can never measure,
But when you find it, it's certainly a treasure!

Pansy Byerl Hyatt
THE FLOWER GARDEN
I saw a beautiful garden
With flowers all array
So many beautiful colors
It took my breath away.

In the midst of all the flowers
One stood so strong and bright
It seemed to be so peaceful
As it moved in the wind so light.

I wanted to cut the flower
So I could enjoy it alone
But then I thought it would not be best
For me to enjoy it all alone.

So I let it grow in the garden
That all who pass may see
And enjoy all the beauty
This one rose brought to me.

One day the rose will be transplanted
To a land of pure delight
Where flowers bloom eternal
For there never is a night.

The Caretaker is Jesus
And the flowers are well kept
Especially the rose
That I will call Jeanette.

Bythford Clayton Smalls

Bythford Clayton Smalls
ARROWS
It was early October, that the arrow of love was ripped from my heart, leaving a distorted illusion of the happiness that love brings.
I lay dying in a pool of frigid sorrow, remembering the brightness of that love remembering the gleam, the sparkle, the moments in which had been my heavenly shadow!
I had gasp my last breath, when Father Time gently restored my life like the slow blooming flower on a warm spring day,
birds in song flocked around me, lifting my tattered spirit high into the heavens releasing me into the warm rays of the sun.
I was then cradled like a child in the arms of Venus, like a soft tender kiss she whispered into my heart!
And once more I am free and happy in this world that can be so unhappy . . . .

Carol Ann McEnroe
CRY FOR HELP

This poem is dedicated to my brother Allan McEnroe Jr.

Some men laugh, some men scream
I wish I could wake up from this dream
Tired and hungry, we march up a hill
Please someone, anyone, pass me a pill
Scared and nervous, I reach for my gun
Johnny . . . Frank . . . Don't die run!
Hatred and horror, fills the air
Sometimes I could just pull my hair
Pride and honor is what we are taught
Die if we must, but this fight must be fought
Alone and hungry, I try to be strong
When will they learn that killing is wrong

Alicia Galvan
BUT NOT TO ME
He laughs
He talks
But not to me
He walks
He sings
But not to me
He walks past
Not a word
Not a smile
Not a laugh
Towards me
Towards his friends
But not to me

Mary Harris Gist
MY PAIN
The world is a beautiful day
Things to appreciate—
If you sleep well, wake up smiling
All seems well —
Although there are aches and pain
To remind you of their toll
You bare them with God's good grace
With a smile — you always think
They will go away.
You hold the thought — That being
Well is only a step away —
Keep standing straight and the smile is
There to stay.
The pain creeps back in, as the day goes on
The pain
We rest with God and feel His love and Grace
Will be less tomorrow — Keep that smile
My pain—

Mary Keppers Schmidt
IF JUST ONCE
If just once I've made you wonder
why the sun shines a little brighter
or why the moon shines forth with romance,
If just once I've made you laugh and
made your day a little happier,
Perhaps I may have been able to help
you to look inside of yourself
and see the goodness that I see in
your soul through your eyes.
If just once my child like qualities
has brought out the child in you,
If maybe just once I've touched your
heart and showed you the love
that you are so capable of giving—
whether or not you can at this time.
If by chance I was there for you when

you needed me most and have
helped you in anyway.
If just once you remember me with a
smile, laughter, or the sun shines
a little brighter for having known me.

If only just once . . .
Then my soul shall sail on the wings
of time,
forever to be grateful to have lived.

Dorothy B Wright
WHITE BIRCHES IN WINTER
I am startled by the cleanness
Of a white birch cluster
As it raises modest fingers
From the gray palm of the earth
And purifies thin segments of the
sky.

Wet snow has painted every
tree-trunk by the road
With a vertical white stripe, on the
northern side,
And made each tree a temporary
birch,
And telephone poles have stepped in
line
To join the "birch society."

Carol Ann Stephey
FRIENDSHIP

To my husband Paul, the best friend I ever had.

Friendship is an unseen bind
which keeps people together
as the years unwind.

Jane Kurtz
SLEEPING BABES
They play their games
and sing their songs,
while the grinning truck rattles along.

They shave their heads
and shine their boots,
the grinning truck just chugs and
toots.

They move and watch
with nervous fear,
the grinning truck grows oh so near.

Did you call your Mom?
I have time, tonight.
The grinning truck so anxious for a
fight.

We're the MIGHTY MARINES!
They cried.
As they fell before their grinning
bride.

Did you call your Mom?
No, not yet.
WHY?

Susan Carole
FOR SALE (AS IS)
Clear blue waters
Sullen gray

Rain clouds gathered
Tossed away

Teeming wildlife
Cupboards bare

Sealife dying
Should we care

Forest verdant
Barren plains

Of Creation
What remains

Once came many
None would see

Jumbled buildings
Man's debris

Songs in the day
Cries at night

Children helpless
What is right

At Rainbows End
Near the start

To have it all
Blind your heart

Heather Anne Warmuth
BLACK ROSE
As black roses bloom,
Black birds sing a tune.
As the black sun will rise,
The dying, beaten child cries.
The child, dressed in black lace,
Lays inside the black casket case.
As black clouds float overhead,
The beaten little girl is dead.

Kim Graessle
THE THEATRE
We're all prisoners in a castle
All actors in a play
The game of life is calling
Come dance your tears away
Let's read our lines out loud
We're more of what we've been
The curtain call is starting
We must begin again
We'll reach for the applause
I hear it loud and clear
Don't let the tempo fall
I'll act my life out here
It's an endless melodrama
A thriller in the round
It's we who do the acting
Till our curtain tumbles down
Let's bow to the ovation
And stand when we are told
Accept our roses smiling
The play begins to fold
Yes, we are gracious actors
Our lines they have no end
If it's true this is the theatre
I'll return to act again.

Sunita Kumari Singhi
THE ANGEL
One day, as I was breathing the forest
air,
a little man, not more than four feet
tall,
approached me and sat down
beside me.
I had been crying; he could tell.
I was melancholy; he spoke many
encouraging words
with a voice so soft and beautiful,
more peaceful than the gentle brook,
whispering and murmuring . . . .

His voice soothed me,
my troubles seemed to slip away . . . .
I knew not how to thank him,
he simply nodded and put his finger
to his lips.
Then, he left— walked off —
disappeared, like the
sun drifting off behind the clouds.

Now, as I think back to that insightful
day,
when I learned that life was not all
bad,
I must but wonder:

Had it been my imagination,
or did his feet really not touch the
ground as he walked,
and did there not seem to be a
celestial glow about him?
a heavenly glow, like that of an
angel?

Benjamin Katz
BLOOD AND GUTS PATTON

This is the tribute to the most aggressive and winning general of our fighting men, of World War 2. So say Benny Kaye and Det. Kelvin Mills of the New York City Police Department (Retired). Benny Kaye (ASCAP).

Blood and Guts Patton, out front with
his men,
Forty fives blastin', he's mighty as
ten,
Bayonets glistenin' bright in the sun,
After them, after them, they're on the
run;

Blood and Guts Patton, fearless
leader of men,
Forward and onward, givin' heart to
his men,
Tanks rumblin', and grumblin', shells
burstin' everywhere,
After them, after them, vict'ry's in
the air;

Blood and Guts Patton, great warrior,
so true,
Fightin' for country, the red,
white and blue,
Forty fives blastin', he's
chargin' the kraut,
After them, after them,
they're in a rout;

He lies not alone, in a grave deep
down,
This courageous soldier of great
renown,
It's battles he won, when all was
done,
Blood and Guts Patton, Patton,
Patton.

Benjamin Katz
THIS WORLD, BUT ONCE
I shall pass through this world, but
once,
Let me do, what I can do, at once,
Any good I can do, the LORD's way
I can show,
Let me know, let me know, let me
know;

I shall walk this good earth with
dignity,
Let me have compassion and charity,
Anything that I can do, someone I
can be kind to,
Let me know, let me know, let me
know;

I shall pass through this world, but
once,
Let me bring the good word, yes at
once,
Anywhere I shall go, anytime, please
GOD let me know,
For I shall pass through this world,
but once.

Benjamin Katz
I LIVE A DREAM
I live a dream, and want so much, for
it to come true,
This dream concerns the one I love,
and that one my dear, is you,
I dream that we should be as one,
sharing our lives together,
Doing things with loving hearts,
enriching our lives for better;

So tell me, that you want me, and
let's blend our hearts as one,
For all the world to see, that love, and
love alone has won,
Let's make a vow, to each other,
never to love another,
I live in a dream, and want so much,
for it to come true.

Linda Tenney
THOUGHTS ON THINKING
All day long our thoughts keep
linking
Forming a process we call thinking.
Everyone thinks these thoughts
through the day
Even *things* have thoughts—in their
own way.
Thoughts are things—we make them
real
By the things we think and the way
we feel.
If good things are not what we're
thinking of
Then think about peace or think
about love.
Think it hard and think it strong
Think it loud and think it long
And just when we tire and our mind
moves on
And the thought we just thought is
over and gone . . .
Something happens to each
thought—though it never is shown
They become real and take on lives
of their own.
They live in a place we as yet cannot
see
Living their lives—independently!
Drawing from that place where each
thought thrives
We weave the rich tapestry of our
lives.
Never forget that thoughts are the
things
That make up the lives our thinking
brings.

Susan B Erb

Susan B Erb
MUSIC
Music can warm your heart
And calm many a storm inside—
It knows the void of a moonless night
It can brighten a darkened room,
Or make you cry for memories past
Or speak of feelings yet to bloom.
It can talk of dreams as sparkling
stars
Knowing some stars go out,
It can hope when there seems to be
only doubt —
It can make you breathe a little
deeper —
Sigh more broadly —
Pause slightly longer —
Feel more fully . . .

Jessica M Fordham
DEVOTION

To my dearest friend, I love you. Forever and always.

You, are the Oak — straight and tall.
I, the Willow — soft and pliable.
You, are the Older — I, the Younger
You, are the Wiser — I , so much to Learn.
You, have abounding Patience — I, yet to Acquire
You have experienced so much, I only wish I could have been there.
You, are the Quiet and Scholarly and I Love to Listen.
Only
You, say I Like and I, say I Love.

Phyllis DéLicien
WHY CRY

Dedicated to Christina M. Banas and Karen L. Schiff-Golovcenko.

So many of us don't have a place to live a meal to eat. Can't find a job that pays enough for food, rent, clothes, medical bills, heat, electricity, phone, and just normal everyday needs.

If this were possible no one would be or feel left out. Everyone would have a chance to live.

America once was said to have streets paved with gold. On one hand this statement is true. For any other country that needs food, medical help, money, etc., etc. On the other hand if poor in America you lose.

So why cry if one did that person would cry the first day of birth 'til the day of death.

Virginia Carter Lefler
MICHAEL

To my son, Michael Scott Long, whom was killed May 9, 1988, in a car accident.

You will always be my little boy,
That has brought me so much joy.
I love you with all my heart,
And I have right from the start.

Your eyes were the prettiest brown.
I was so proud, I couldn't wait to tell the town.
Your skin had a brilliant tone,
I knew you were my very own.

As you grew and grew,
I knew you would learn to love me too.
We would do so many things,
In the Autumn, Fall, and Spring.

You have grown so big my son,
But we still have had lots of fun.
We have had a lot of good times,
Even if we didn't have a dime.

If you ever need a friend,
I will be with you 'til the end.
Some day you will know,
How much, "I Love You So!"

Michelle L Burgoyne
BLEEDING HEART

Love
pierces through
my heart . . .
like a shard
of broken glass . . .
that cuts the
flesh of,
my hand.

Denise G Coniglio
LEAVING

To all victims of suicidal feelings, this too shall pass.

when you find this and begin to read, it will be too late. i will be gone from this world and entering heaven's gate. do not be sad that i'm not here, just remember me in your hearts so dear.
mom, i'm sure this is hard for you but i didn't know what else to do.
dad, what really can i say? we didn't talk much anyway. brother, you wanted me confiding in you but keep in mind you felt this way too
family i'm not sure how much you care but you know that life isn't fair.
best friend you're probably mad right now, i wanted to tell you but didn't know how.
my love, my support and everything you are, you'll always be my shining star
i never wanted it to end this way but i couldn't stand another day — of living in a world where i had no meaning, i didn't belong here and felt like Leaving.
i can't tell you if this was a mistake, but when something's handled carelessly eventually it breaks
if by chance you think of me once in a while, do not be sad — remember the times i made you smile.
i love you all and always will though now you can't understand, but one day we'll be together again and you can take my hand. i will explain to you just how i felt during the darkest time of my life — why doing this was my answer to the confusion, sadness and strife. i'm hoping you won't be angry as i write with tear-filled eyes to all of you that i really do love, now i must say goodbye . . . .

Colleen Baker
THE HUNDRED BUNNIES

My son asked for the hundredth time
"please draw me a bunny and make him mine"
Then I think back the twenty years
To all my bunnies with long white ears
That my own mom sketched out for me
When I brought paper to her knee
And so for the hundredth time I draw
Another bunny for someone small

I had a hundred bunny friends
All ears and tails and rabbit grins
From Mother's loving hand they came
All the bunnies she knew, no two the same
I loved each one though paper they be
Because she made them just for me

I know she wearied of her task
And where they went she never asked
I thought they'd gone on to yesteryear
But, mother to child, they were always here

Dorothy Myres
LIFE

Life is but a vapor, here today,
gone today.
Life is what you make it. So
live, love, give.
Life is but a vapor, here today,
gone today. Make the most of
each moment. You may never
have the chance again.
Life is but a vapor here today,
gone today, So live, love, give.
Live each moment as though it were
the Last.
Love sincerely it will carry you
Through as in the past.
Give of your substance to others as
The spirit directs you to.
Remember Life is but a vapor,
Here today, gone today. Life is
What you make it. So Live,
Love, Give.

Michael E Rutkowski
BEAUTY

The beauty of a lady
Is not found on her outside shell,
But in her innerself.
For when her heart glows with
love,
Her outside beauty glows like a dove.

Lisa McNair Costales
WITHIN

To the thoughtful, concerned authors who address the uniquely human search for self-esteem and ethical solutions to the dilemmas of life.

Don't look to where you are going
Or where you might have been.
You can't deal with what is coming
Until you look within.

You must not look for answers
Among the dancers, the preeners, the prancers,
Get lost and lose your chances
To secure yourself within.

Around you it's not a peaceful time.
The only way to win —
Keep the harmony within your mind;
You are your very best friend.

And, if you're looking for someone
To fill a void inside;
You're searching for it on the run
While from yourself you hide.

There is a strength inside you.
An inner voice is there to guide you.
Maybe love will come again;
First, learn to look within!

Paul L Robida
SKATES—CACTUS—AND HEATHER

Dedicated to a lovely granddaughter from Connecticut who truly loves to visit her grandparents in New Mexico.

There's a pretty little lass named Heather,
Who skates on the walk like a feather.
She floats in her skates made of leather,
In rain, wind, all sorts of weather.
She loves to jump, to play, to run,
And have all kinds of children's fun.
One day this nearly led to her demise,
When from out back we could hear her cries,
She was running around with pain in her eyes,
Although the pain was lower, closer to her thighs.
Because, lo and behold, much to her surprise,
She had backed into a bush — cactus — not heather.
For a while there was a doubt about whether,
All the needles had been pulled out of Heather.
They looked her over and what did they find?
There were none in the front, only in the behind!
So there's a moral in this story to be found,
Keep your eyes not heavenward, but closer to the ground!
All of us, even Heather, would painfully have to admit,
Needles are great in sewing, but not in where you sit!

Paul L Robida
MOTHER AND CHILD

What Mother, what makes the grass grow green?
"God provides color to make things serene."
Why Mother, why does the sky look so blue?
"The Lord, in his wisdom, chose that spectacular hue."
How Mother, how will the rain fall today?
"Like teardrops from Heaven directed our way."
Where Mother, where will the winds blow away?
"To Heaven's gates, my dear one, our prayers they'll relay."
Why Mother, why does the sun shine so bright?
"So God's winged creatures may see in their flight."

When Mother, when shall I rise from this bed?
"Jesus will come, place His hand on your head."
Forgive Mother, forgive the hurts I sent your way!
"My child, they are nothing, forget them, I pray."
Please Mother, please do not cry for me!
"How can I not, dear one, I love you, you see."
Now Mother, now look! I see a great light!
"Son, clasp your small hands and I'll hold them tight."
Mother, oh Mother, I'm going home at last!
And soon I'll be with you as I've been in the past."

Rolf Threlkeld
WAR

War is such a horrible thing
Human beings go fighting and die.
And those of us who don't go to war
Are struggling to hold back our cry.

And the sons are the loved ones
Who never return,
In the form of a man, but a letter.
The bureaucrats don't like it
But they don't try to stop it.
"War makes economy better."

At the tomb of the soldier
Who was always unknown,
There are colorful victory
celebrations.
Though many thousands have died,
We still have our pride,

And the people who run
our great nations.

James B "Mike" Johnson
WAR REFLECTIONS
A bugle call, a pistol shot;
The great World War had ended,
And those that lived, cried out with joy;
And those who died, died splendid.

A ragged man leaned o'er a form,
His face was torn and bloody.
He turned his face toward God and asked:
"Why did you take my buddy?"

A grey-haired Mother breathes a sigh
To choke back grief and sorrow;
She's waiting for the time to come
— To join her boy "tomorrow."

And Daddy, too, is sad with grief,
Sits where the dark may hide him;
And long his gaze rests on the vacant
Chair that sits beside him.

And in the night, a maiden fair
Looks at the stars above her;
Sad tears well in her grieving eyes
— No more she'll see her lover.

Sleep on, Sleep on, Thou noble lads;
You won that great endeavor —
And may thy souls rest peacefully
For ever, and for ever.

Long years have passed, the grieved forgot,
The gaps of love are mended,
But War is soon to come again . . .
Nay, Sorrow is not ended.

— written February, 1934

Patricia Henry
DOUBLE RAINBOW
As storm clouds gathered overhead.
I thought OH NO! the storms I dread.
Then as the sky turned beautiful gold,
We went to look and then behold!
There in the sky as perfect as can be
Was a colorful rainbow just waiting for me.
I thought of the promise God gave in his book.
And went to take just one more look.
As I stood gazing into the sky,
Something wonderful caught my eye.
Over the first rainbow stood another
Almost as beautiful as the other.
Then I knew God was talking to me.
Keep your heart right and one day my face you will see.

Russell D Ramey
THE DREAM
Each night he rose
As a ship outlasting a storm
Clouds beginning to break
Beams of life streaking across miles of broken dreams

He was more than a shadow
Against the backdrop of shaded clouds
He was the faceless man
That never slept

Light glanced off his helmet
Causing me to shade my eyes
I gazed only at his torn work boots
And frayed jeans

Finally his silhouette covered the blinding sun
My hand fell to my side
And my eyes slowly moved towards his face
Our eyes locked
My throat became dry
And the scream that began
Quickly died.

Carol Mikoda
OR DID HE SIMPLY WANT TO PLANT SOME TREES?

For my father, Philip M. Mikoda, Sr.

I fell asleep last night lulled by waves of wind crashing through the trees that line the path out back. My father planted them some forty years ago, when he was my age. Now they touch the moon that rises less than full at ten o'clock. No matter what he says at tea-time — judging us or calling Mother foolish — whether he has barns filled up with junk, or projects unfinished or unbegun — he still comes close to perfection with those lines of massive old spruce trees.

At thirty-four, could he see so far to know these trees, just needled sticks with roots, would become such lullabies to me?

Barbara Claudette Messer

Barbara Claudette Messer
OUR FAMILY REUNION

In memory of my beloved, "Dad."

We all gathered like so many times before, to be with each other just once more,
There was huggin', and kissin', an sweet babies, new
Oh; And Aunt Martha, brought her great stew,
We all talked and some told jokes,
Passed around, the news, who was rich, and who was broke,
The guys talked shop, and football games
The girls, traded recipes, and, talked about famous names,
Sister Beth had a brand new dish,
And Uncle Joe, had caught, the biggest fish,
The kids played ball, and hide-and-seek,
And when they came in, Mama said, "Wipe your feet,"
Just like old times, we all sat down, at the old table, big and round,
This was the moment, we all dreaded to face,
For there was one, who wasn't in his place.
The head of the table was silent and bare
Everyone was conscious of that one empty chair,
But as, we all bowed, our heads, in a, prayer,
It seemed, as though, we felt, your presence there,
In that special moment, we were, no longer sad.
Because we know, in spirit you're still, with us "Dad."

Todd M Callery
THE CRACK

To Mrs. Petrelli — who started it all.

When I feel like cracking,
I think of,
A pressured can bursting open,
A plastic pipe exploding under a high pressured leak,
Then a bomb comes to mind,
Exploding in a mine to crack the earth wide,
Or a depth charge exploding in the ocean wide,
I then think of a lone ship tossed by crashing waves,
Grounded by the ocean tide,
Bows high, stern flooded, bilges open wide.
I think how a tree cracks as a lightning bolt strikes,
The limb splits and falls to crumble on the ground,
The trunk, how it explodes by fire and power,
At last I see an egg that has fallen off an edge,
Falling, falling,
Crack!
It splits wide open on the kitchen tile.

Karen J Zandler
JUST LONELY O ME

This poem is dedicated to The Fun Bunch, who ALWAYS comes to my rescue.

Only the Lonely knows
What you're feeling inside
The emptiness of living
And of life passing you by

Only the Lonely can understand
Your silence within
Wanting to break through
But never destined to win

Only the Lonely
Can be silent and listen
And try to convince themselves
With their own words of wisdom

Only the Lonely—
Is lonely
And will forever be
That is, only if you don't come to rescue
Lonely O Me

Michaela Gail Andes
NOW AND THEN I GET UP CLOSE TO YOU
Feel my sadness, my heart cries
See my gladness, it's all in the eyes
And all because you make me feel that way
Just around the time I know
I simply cannot stay.

Now and then I get up close to you
Can feel the warmth shared between we two
I don't know why
And dare not try
To understand the part of me that's become part of you.

Sometimes I cry to be near you
I'm all alone
Just too free of you
It's so sad, but true
What to do?

Now and then I get up close to you
Can feel the warmth shared between we two
I don't know why
And dare not try
To understand the part of me that's become part of you.

Joyce E Petitjean
FROM DEPTHS UNTOLD

For Cathy, a woman and friend of depths untold.

From depths untold the sea flows steadfastly from shore to shore.
Her perseverance is unmarred by feast or famine peace or war.
Her solitude is only temporarily disturbed by the petty storms of nature or man.
A fragile human takes her cue from the imperturbable sea.
The basics of nature nurture her soul.
She finds sustenance in the wind and rain, rock and sand, but most of all in the sea.
She finds inspiration in the wonders of the waves.
She finds solace in the song of the wind and the gull.
She finds hope for the future in the neverending caress of the wave against the shore.
The wonders of nature nurture her soul.

Kathleen S Foster
MOM AND DAD
When I was young, I looked up to you;
You were my strength, in what you would say and do.
You were the people I admired the most;
Except of course, the Father, Son and Holy Ghost.
As I grow older, day by day;
I wonder how you were able to stay;
So good and seemingly all knowing;
Always helping and always showing.
The right way to go, and the best way to be
And to get there with the most dignity.
How did you "know yourself" and still help us?
When today I feel, I must do it all or bust.
I understand now the job you had to do;
With very little praise, and hardly any "thank you's."
I pray that I have the courage to do it your way;
In this crazy "parenting" world of today.
Sometimes I think I'm doing ok;
Other times I think there must be a better way.
So, mom and dad, here's a tribute to you;
My love for you, will always be true.

XXXX
OOOO

Gayle Hixson
WHY ME LORD

People complain in times of trouble, pain and grief. Why me, Lord? Why me?
Not once did the lord ask through all his troubles, pain and grief. Why me? Why me?
Not once has the Lord said to us when we've made him sad through our bad actions and harsh words. Why me? Why me?
He loves and accepts us even through our faults and not once ask. Why me? Why me?
Should we not try to accept things as they may be and not once ask why me, Lord? Why me?
But instead pray that we may see the light and come to realize the reasons.
Why me Lord? Why me?

Brenda A Butler
EDUCATE MY EDUCATION

To: Elder Robert & Mary Butler & Family with lots of love from your daughter, Brenda A. Butler. Thanks for your love and prayers.

You should want to do better to strive to reach your goals
As long as I can remember this what I've been told
I was told to never ever settle for less
They told me to always endeavor to be my very best
Always try and eliminate the insignificant middleman
Head straight for the top just as fast as you can
Thank only those who helped you along your way
Those who didn't well to them you know what to say
I listened well and all those words I took to heart
So I'd know just what to do when I start
An education I got and then some
Thought I had the battle fought, that I had the battle won
Cause no one told me that beyond those educated doors
Life was happiness, life was sadness, life was strictly hard core
For seven years I educated myself thinking I was sufficiently prepared
But when I stepped out life handed me some blows life really had me scared
My life continued on experiencing some good and bad times
Life was full of surprises but I managed to keep my state of mind
So safely sheltered by those educated walls
I was so well educated I thought I knew it all
So before you venture out with your degree in hand
Determined to make this world a better place for man
You've set your goals and even reached your destination
And now you've realized you have to educate your education
The End

Patty Pearcy
THE FAMILY TREE

No living person can ease the pain,
That is raging within you today.
And, though, you will never see him smile again,
Perhaps, it may help to think of it this way.

Only the top of the tree has died.
Just look at all the branches below!
Look at them with pride,
Cause the family tree continues to grow.

So, even tho he has gone from this earth,
And taken with him a part of you.
When your grandchildren's children give birth,
A part of him it will renew.

Vernonia L Alexander
TO A LOVING SISTER

In Loving Memory for a Dear Friend and her sister, Nona, and my own beloved, Sissie.

To the beautiful Lady who has gone on before,
To pave Heaven's way and fling wide the door,
For the rest that will follow as the years fly,
Listen to your heart, she's not saying good-by.

Hold fast to your memories of the Love and Fun,
That you shared through life's days on the run,
No one else will ever take her place,
Or remove the memories of the smile on her face.

She lights up your life as she did then,
And just as she will when you see her again,
Her Love is with you, and will always be,
It's just as sturdy as the old oak tree.

So in the memory of all the Love you shared,
Through all the days she let you know how much she cared,
She lightened life's load, was a rock in your plight,
Having her in your life was pure delight.

Jennifer Rideout
ONLY MY LIFE

I have nothing to share with you; only my life; will that keep you still with silent anticipation, or will you flee from me before I can start my story?

When I tell you of my experiences will you judge me, analyzing my life, or will you simply process the information accepting it for what it is; a part of me.?

I have nothing to share with you; only my life;

Will you listen to my dreams with quiet recognition and respect them for their development and their need to exist, or will you scatter them upon the earth like chaff?

I have nothing to share with you; only my life;

Can I show you my thoughts, will you take them under your wing and help me to nurture them and watch them grow, or should I be afraid of persecution and laughter?

I have nothing to share with you; only my life;

Can I share with you all of my worries and fears, will you know how to comfort me, or will you tell me that these feelings should not be felt and therefore, are not valid?

I have nothing to share with you; only my life; . . .

I have nothing to give you; only my outstretched hand extended in friendship; will you accept?

Penny Musok
MY ROSE

The petals tarnished
Through the hours of age.
No one knowing
Its heart may still be alive.
By just one touch
My Rose will crumble—I know.
So, I leave alone My Rose,
Meaning more than just 'My Rose'

Given to me—full and radiant.
Given to me—with its
tenderness—
And its thorns.
The scent was faded in days passed,
As was the giver's face in my mind's eye—
Yet, the love remains with me forever.

I leave it on my window sill
Where I left it long ago.
Often,
I look at it and see—
A love that has tarnished
Through the hours of age.

Wilma Joyce Berry
HAPPY BIRTHDAY TO A SPECIAL SON

To our son, James Hulen. Dad and "Mom."

When God put you in our care
He knew what he was doing
For there are lots of sons out there
With lives in shambles and ruin.

You've kept your life so clean and straight
And served your country too
I know it wasn't easy
Not an easy thing to do
But you came out a winner
And I'm very proud of you.

To follow in my footsteps and sit behind the wheel
Or over on the other side was really quite a deal
These are the times we talk about
I know we won't forget
The times we took wrong turns and such
'Cause we were on the road so much.

Now time has come for me
To look back and just review
A son in his father's footsteps
And I'm oh so proud of you.

Patricia K Titus
CANDLES

Candles are like friends:
Taking time and care—giving comforting warmth;
They brighten our lives.

Candles are like flowers:
One or many is always perfection;
Each has a beauty all its own.

Candles are a complement to any setting;
They blend with any mood.

Their cheerful glow lifts spirits low.
Their soft flame reflects love's romance.
They shine gloriously for celebration.
They lighten the darkness of sadness.

From early times to present day,
Throughout life from birth to death,
Candles have their say.

There are no two alike;
Each burns at its own pace
And remains a mystery.

Lighting a candle is like asking a blessing:
The answer lies in the light it brings.

Emilie A Perez
MY BEST FRIEND

In memory of M.C. May she rest in peace.

You gave me some wisdom,
You gave me some trouble,
And when you died you gave me sorrow

You made me laugh,
You made me cry,
And at times you
Made me a little mad.

Whenever I'm down or just feel
Alone, I remember the good times
That we had when we were young.

"What the mind forgets,
The heart remembers"
As long as this phrase
Remains true, I know that
Our friendship will remain
Forever true.

Michelle Holt
THANK YOU

I said you couldn't do it,
But you did.
I said I wouldn't let you,
But I did.

You came into my life
Two years before
And started out a friend
But ended up more.

I really care for you now
More than I can tell you.
You make me feel so happy,
A feeling that is so new.

I want to thank you
For everything you've done,
Because without you
Life's meaning is none.

Shirley Peterson
IF I COULD HANG A BUBBLE ON A CHRISTMAS TREE

If I could hang a bubble on a Christmas tree,
Oh! gowh! Oh! Gee! how pretty it would be;
With a tinkle and a twinkle, like a bright and shining star
The bubbles make a pathway for the
Angels from afar,
If I could hang a bubble on a Christmas tree, Oh, how pretty it would be.
You can add touch of Snow Flakes and a breath of Angels' hair,

An icicle and a candy cane can go most anywhere;
A little bit of tinsel and a child's toy, like a Teddy Bear a Toy train would bring great joy,
But if I could hang a Bubble on a Christmas tree, Oh! how pretty it would be.

Kelly D Rowe

Kelly D Rowe
WE ARE THE FUTURE

This poem is dedicated to Deoncca and LaZar, with love, Mother.

Hello mothers and fathers out there
These words with you I want to share
Babies are born crippled and sick
From all the alcohol and drug addicts
I know I'm just a very young man
But even at my age, I can understand
Drugs are nowhere, it's a dead end street
Please listen, to you these words I speak
So please mothers and fathers, and those to be
Think of what drugs do to our families

Cathy Foe
LOVE DEFINED

To P J. Oliver, my inspiration.

I can find no words to describe
How I feel about you;
The silkiness of
Your hair through my fingers,
The sparkle of
Your eyes when they meet mine,
Your smile,
Your wink,
Your tender touch.

Could it be that this is the
Definition of love?
The fun of
Spending time together,
The sound of
Your laughter mingling with mine,
Maybe the
Meaning of love
Is us.

Donna Culwell
MOTHER

You always told me
To do my best
People will put you
To the greatest test

You were there
When I felt bad
You held my hand
When I was sad

You've always meant
The world to me
You are all the things
I wanted to be

You are there for me
When there is no other
You are my sweetest
My dearest mother

Lynn Kern
THE DAPHNE

When the Daphne blooms
I must draw near
to tremble in your fragrance, unsurpassed.
Gentle blossom, love adorned
glistening in the twilight;
your beauty clad in raindrops,
my unshed tears—
As God smiles upon you
His sweet promise of spring,
will He see that I am
standing here?

Susan Pepin Beczynski
WHAT IS IT LIKE WITHOUT YOU

To my husband, Stephen, with love.

What is it like without you?
The house is the same,
Everything's still in its proper place.
The sun comes up every day as always.
Work, it doesn't change, the same old thing,
the same old people.
And when the day is over, the house that doesn't change
is suddenly different.

I lock the door, knowing you won't be home after work.
I eat alone, watch tv alone and go to bed alone.
If only I could talk to you, touch you, see you.
I want to sit beside you and rest my head in your lap,
I want to hold your hand and kiss your eyes.
To lay beside you warm and safe, knowing you'll be there when I awake.
To feel your body against mine, your arm pillowing my head.
To kiss you once more before we sleep.

The loneliest thing in the world,
that's what it's like without you.

Barbara Christopher
SPIRITS OF LOVE

In Loving Memory of My Grandmother, Mary Elizabeth Spicer.

It goes like the wind
that rings the chimes
Quickly it passes
in increments of time
Ageless are all of the
people we love
'til death creeps in
with a mighty shove.
But where is the spirit
that now is free,
that from its earthly shell
did hastily flee?
Sometimes I feel it close at hand
lifting my spirits
with a gentle command.
Love is ageless and will ever be
here in my heart
with memories of thee.

Mark Edmund Tritschler
DISCOVERY OF TRUTH

the stretching of one's heartfelt feelings,
taut as sinew
over the limitless boundaries that are what really exist.
where our mind's reality is as shortsighted
as our heart's backyard.

Peggy Chittum

Peggy Chittum
WHERE WILL THE CHILDREN PLAY

While sitting one day looking out of the window
Watching the children at play
I thought of another yard and other children
of another time and day.

I thought of hills where we used to climb
The creeks where we learned to swim
And wondered what memories these would have
What their world would be like then.

For the earth was once green and generous
But now has grown barren and brown
And the country where children can run and be free
Has given way to town after town.

So when all the trees have turned granet
And the birds have nowhere to nest
Then maybe we'll see all the harm that we've done
Before this generation lies rest.

For the one who so generously gave it
Can also take it away
Then where will the birds and animals go
And where will the children play.

Margaret McGinley IHM
A BIRD'S SONG

A bird's song—how tremendous!
What's your reason for trilling such a joyful cadence?
Are you sharing some secret with the world?
Who taught you your musical scales?
Do you practice each melody or has Nature gifted you?
What caused you to end this morning's serenade?
Do you give encores?
Tomorrow, will you warble that same refrain or a new composition?
A bird's song—how tremendous!
The world and I are richer because of your chant.
My day begins on a happier note.
I stand in awe of a bird's song.

Margaret McGinley IHM
THE WIND

Today, a strange force jars the elements,
Teletyping a perhaps ominous message.
Tree limbs sway with this power.
To refuse to bend results in total dismemberment for frail branches.
What a lesson for mortals
Who have not learned to roll with life's punches—
Who choose to throw their mettle against formidable foes!
As I continue my walk, I relish the fresh air-conditioning.
I am renewed and readied for life's continuing challenge.
My batteries now are super-charged,
For you, Wind, have rattled my cage of mediocrity
And pummeled me from my lethargy.
I now reach out to grasp another day of promise.

Joyce Magnuson
THE DEEP

I stand on the beach.
My mind has gone blank.
Out over the water, I see not a thing.
The truth to be told.
It's a good place to think.
If only the waves could speak.
No more alone would I be
For on its bottom, some place asleep.
Lies my family. Down so "deep."
"Oh" deep dark ocean.
Take me home, for keeps.

Lucille M Hovland
PETALS

The Rose so enchanting
With petals so frail
Is one of God's wonders
His power prevails
The blooms grow toward Heaven
To thank Him again
And as with the roses
Human life does begin
We're born with the purity
and the skin of a rose
But as we grow older
We lapse in repose
Our life like the petals
Share beauty so long
Then like the roses
We fade and are gone.
God gave us life
For beauty, not sins
When the old petals fall
A new life begins
On through the Seasons
New petals unfold
Generations hereafter
A story is told.

Maxine R Strickland
NEW DAUGHTER

Today I got a "New Daughter,"
Because "She" married my son.
They think they're so lucky,
But I'm really the lucky one.

My son deserved a good wife.
She's smart and pretty and fun.
The reason I love her so,
Is because she loves my son.

My son looked so proud and handsome,
As he stood by his beautiful bride.
I was so happy I was bursting,
And my tears were hard to hide.

She wore her Mother's wedding gown,
And her Mother was so very proud.
As they left the church together,
We were all floating on a cloud.

Their marriage won't always be perfect,
'Cause life is just not that way.
But I know they will always be happy,
Today and every day.

Stanley W Bori Jr

GABRIEL'S GREETING

To Arlene Savoca—May sunshine and your five wonderful children brighten all your days.

Oh' pearly gates, open thee wide for the worthy
Bless'd thee be, those committed to me surely.
Light'd upon a cloud, this peaceful realm
Hand in hand, we shall stand at the helm.
Captain this vessel upon the Heavenly sea
Marching gloriously forward to meet the Lord, we be.
Salutation to you, my brother
God's gift of redemption, as no other.
Can righteously shine with majesty exalted
Flight'd a whispering wing, white feathers vault'd.
Wing'd upward to catch a rising star
Forever a prayer, reaching near and far.
Contentment of the Lamb, a gift for all
Delight'd, we are cast into the hallowed hall.
Where a dream may become your reality
Refreshed eternally with unending vitality.
Ye be newborn, set within a velvet glade
Caress'd with the comfort of Heavenly shade.
The eternal light surrounding your virtuous soul
This requited to all those who enter; man's immortal goal!

Stanley W Bori Jr

FANCIFUL LOVE

A sad admonition of a love unrequited
Woulds't thou to be better a hearts delight'd.
My spirit lifted to a mountain's precipitous peak
Dashed lowly to fathoms deep and bleak.
'Tis beauty that most all hearts desire
Coulds't I ever get enough, find this treasure I require.
Oh beloved pleasures I do long for
My cup overflowing, yet I may quest for more.
This quantity we call love, a vanity most perplexing
To satisfy all heart's desires, every man is excelling.
Shoulds't we cast visage upon this lusty heart.
Before tumbling down and needing a fresh start.
Perhaps a straight and narrow path needs be shown
More diligence aforethought to be applied and known.
Such nonsense to padlock this fanciful love
Free spirit flight'd away on the wings of a dove.
Light'd the sky with a golden sheen
Enraptured forever, never betwixt or between.

Stanley W Bori Jr

DISNEYWORLD

A monorail does speed you swiftly to Disney's beckon and call
Delights heretofore unknown, await one and all.
Mainstreet U.S.A., lined with both shops and store
Excitement rewarded, you can wonderously explore.
Many banners waving briskly, course the avenue
Cartoon characters costumes donned, stroll along past you.
The hub of enchantment, a castle rises to the sky
Turreted towers climbing, most stupendous to the eye.
A giant tree, with stairway leading up into its branches does rise
To climb its spiral staircase, a joyous surprise.
A step aside and you are off on a jungle cruise
Real perception of African wilds, a sense of reality you will lose.
A haunted house, ghosts frolicking, around you they do abound
Devious and delightful apparitions, your senses they will astound.
A ship most unusual, Captain Nemo's submarine
Takes you on an underwater voyage never before seen.
Space Mountain, thrills you with a fantastic journey through space
Along a twisting railway, the rocket cars do race.
Many other never before seen pleasures do await
Be sure to visit this wonderous world before it is too late.

Stanley W Bori Jr

THUNDERSTORM

Oh, behemoth rambling across the sky
Dark ominous clouds envision my eye.
Do crackle and spew forth a thunder
The day's tranquility ripped asunder.
Shards of lightning, tongues leaping to the ground
A frightening vestige, its sight does astound.
Its countenance be as a lion's roaring
Unleashed fury, as a whirlwind's soaring.
Venting its cup, rain streams to the ground
A torrent unleashed, Heaven's flood earthly bound.
Both field and earth soaked most thickly
Rivers do burst their banks most quickly.
The deluge has now passed
One final drop of rain, will be the last.
A brightening light shows across the sky
Majestic rainbow now fills my eye.

Stanley W Bori Jr

DAISY DAPPLE DEW

A daisy, sprig twisted upturned flute
Lively honeybee buzzed to nestle this shoot
To seek sweet nectar for sumptuous reward
Flight'd away to his hive to hoard.
Light'd with sunshine, Oh dapple this sprig
In such a heavenly garden, should we dig.
To plant a seed for all to seek
Never a home for just the meek.
Oh fluted horn dripping with dew
So covetous am I to hew down a few.
To garner this treasure until my own
Kept secret forever, its bless'd favor unknown.
This world's wonder, privy I share with you
Majestic creation, Oh Daisy Dapple Dew.

Stanley W Bori Jr

THE BEST THING I EVER DID

From a seedling's young sprout it was nurtured
The sun's warming rays tended it and it grew.
'Twas a piney, a thistlethorn of the coniferous variety
My hands replanted this fragile whip.
The good black earth caressed the tender root fibrils
As the years passed, its stature was raised to the height of a man.
I could no longer leap across its crown as I had done in my youth
More years and its boughs would stretch out to rest a bird, then nest a bird.
It grew to ten feet, twenty, thirty and and more
Proliferous pine needles cast down to litter earthen floor.
Its trunk, once just a whip, now massive and burly
To mark the passage of my time, nature's calendar surely.
Now as my years are prolonged
This tree grew with majesty, towering and strong.
I will fade, brought low to one knee
Yet onward and upward groweth my tree.
Reaching to the sky for Heaven's glory sent
Remembering my presence, where under its boughs my youth was spent.

Stanley W Bori Jr

MARINES

Semper Fidelis, a comradeship of men
Bound together was the platoon of ten.
Steadfastly forward, of a singular mind
Courageously true, of the noblest kind.
Arm in arm, braving terrible harm
Boldly they fought, never showing alarm.
Stricken and bleeding, they must achieve their goal
Proving courage will out, an exacting toll.
Upon the beaches, in valley and dale
Guardians of freedom, we salute and hail.
Let not one valiant marine fear
Shedding blood precious and dear.
For of a purpose he was born,
Next O'kin hallowed Gabriel's horn.
Onward they fought, triumphant indeed
Unified in resolve, this was their creed.
Liberty preserved, we honor these men
Oh valiant and courageous platoon of ten.
Laudits of merit we most graciously shower
These were Marines in their finest hour.

Stanley W Bori Jr

ARCHERS

A group of three, came to the line
Bows and arrows in hand, their talent would shine.
Nocking the arrow upon a string
Vault'd through the air to sing.
Feathered shaft whisked to a target, woulds't fly
Flight'd downcourse, their skill to try.
To penetrate the target's center
A contest, to prove best those who enter.
Proving grace and stamina, a steady nerve with most keen eye
All striving for perfection, to hit the bulls-eye.
Nimbly they should finger the bowstring
Each flight'd arrow would bring.
Points tallied upon a score
To prove who could gather more.
Courage shown of the stoutest of hearts
Always seeking the perfect form, hoping not to depart.
From the position of a statue
Each effort to regain and renew.
Sharp razors cut, the winning edge
Trophy in hand, victories pledge.

Stanley W Bori Jr

MUSIC

When sprightly chords should wiggle my ear
Notes touching the heart, do I hear.
Melodies entwined to tingle the spine
Tender embraces to enlighten and shine.
Bass beat and rhythm, moody or blues
Enrapturing the spirit with caressing hues.
The singer and musicians spin their tale
With bright-eyed notes, fragile and frail.
The music shines as a galaxy of stars
Its truth be known, near and far.
Daintily portrayed, or sharp and shrill
Ever showing the presence of man's goodwill.
Casting a voice upon the earth
Proving to the Lord, man's spiritual worth.
Gladdening the heart with robust desire
Its countenance be thee Oh emotional fire.
With a loving grasp, we hold these songs dear
Tunes of harmony for all to hear.
The harmony of life played with these notes
Mystical spell of the emotions wrote.
Cast upon the medium of air
This musical voice for all to share.
When life's bitter strife may pull you down
Reach out for a melody, most

soothing sound.
A lullaby of love to lift you up
Man's immortal soul to fill your cup.
Emotions uplifted, now questing to climb the mountain
Bathed in glory, as with a watery fountain.
Purify the body with this vibratory wave
A sound to enhance the spirit, the soul to save.
The music forever casts its emotional spell
Drawn from the deep reaches of a sanctified well.
Welling from the heart of the true
A bless'd favor to those who knew.
That this sound cast upon the air
Brings joyful tidings to those who care.
Its message will bring truth to the land
In every outpost where man should stand.
Let music always and forever ring
As God would have us surely sing.

Kathy Ann Hoffman

FATE IS YOU

I sit . . . I wait . . . then here comes fate
knocking on my door like a stranger
I don't answer so it lets itself in
behind it, in walks you

There you are standing so bold
arms reaching out, wanting to hold
Come touch my heart, feel my soul
combine our spirits and make us whole

Sharyn Phillips

TO KNOW LOVE IS TO GIVE LOVE

This poem is dedicated to my relatives and friends, especially my parents, siblings and daughter.

Love Is Forever
Not Just Today
Love Ends Never.
Love Has A Depth
Deeper Than Any Sea
Love Touches
All Life's History.
I Love Today
More Than Yesterday.
I Realize Now
To Know Love Is To Give Love.
I Shall Give Love
Till I Reach Heaven Above.

Reneé McCandless

HOME IS WHERE MY HEART IS

Home is where my heart is,
But tonight I'm running free,
I walk the streets without you,
But I hear you calling me.

I'm heading home to you,
But it'll take a little time,
There's a lot of roads to travel,
Before I find which one is mine.

Baby, don't you worry,
Because tonight my thoughts are of you,
We don't always have a reason,
For the crazy things we do.

I know I left you lonely,
And I know I left you scared,
But I wouldn't have left you,
darling,
If you didn't know I cared.

Tonight I'm on my way,
But my steps are short and small,
There's a lot of pathways out there,
And I must try them all.

Stephen Garone

AT A DISTANT COUNTRY HOUSE

Almost all is forgotten while at a distant country house,
When gentle autumn is declared:

Scarlet and gold navies,
launched from trees,
sail across the rippled lake;
Shooting bark—
woodpeckers at work.
A few courageous blades peek out
from beneath the camouflage of leaves,
the other troops remain disguised;
Dying flowers—
casualties of the equinox.

Almost all is forgotten at a distant country house,
While humanity rages on back home.

Lori A Noebe

AN AUTUMN DAY

On an Autumn Day,
trees begin to blow
swaying to and fro.
Leaves begin to fall
from trees standing tall.

On an Autumn Day,
birds still sing
their songs of spring.
The smell of fresh hay
glistened by the sun's ray.

On an Autumn Day,
apples begin to harvest
cider at its best.
Ghosts and goblins appear
teasing all with fear.

On an Autumn Day,
how I wish it would stay,
but to my dismay
winter is on its way.

Anne Marie Flaherty

Ann Marie Flaherty

WAITING

To all of us that have had to wait—be it for friend, love, or a dream—let us always keep sight of our hopes and the ones who love us.

I sat there waiting
I don't know how long
I waited and watched
as I listened to an old song

As I sit here watching
there are many things I'm thinking of
things I want to do
so much I'm dreaming of

I'm sitting here alone
looking out the window for him
even though I've been here awhile
my hopes don't seem to dim

Oh well, maybe next time
maybe it wasn't meant to be
we'll try again another day
we'll just have to wait and see

How long should I wait
the answer I'll never know
now it's getting late
it's time for me to go

Yes, I wish he'd come
it's him I came to see
because regardless what the past has been
he's still very dear to me

Jackie Goldstein

WHEN THE MIRROR CRACKS

A look in the mirror, and an image appears,
but it's different from the day before.
So many years wasted, staring at that mirror, scrutinizing the surface deceptions.
What appears there? It's merely a disguise, a superficial shadow to hide all those lies.
The lies you live every day, a wall for all the pains suffered,
all the failures,
all the goals never achieved.
And for every defeat you build yet another golden bar.
And you build, and you hide,
entangling yourself further,
Until you're so trapped behind those bars, tied by all the webs.
It is when this day comes, when your resources are gone, and you have no more strength.
And you look again to the mirror, and see all that exists is illusion.

Mabel Lagerlof (Manville)

AMEN—SO BE IT!

The TELIC end is near . . . It is
For ALL to SEE and HEAR . . .
Our FATE is being SEALED!
HOW? By WHAT we do about it!
If ANYTHING: <u>Accept</u> or JEER!
1914 was to be the TURNING Point in HISTORY!
WAR Clouds are LOOMING in the EAST . . .
AIMING to DESTROY the WORLD's . . . <u>Greatest</u>
Also, the very . . . LEAST!
There is ALWAYS HOPE . . . (our God says)
Based on Accurate Knowledge . . .
plus LOVE . . .
FAITH . . . including <u>GLORY!</u>
So, we KNOW in our HEARTS . . .
IF . . . we LISTEN and <u>then OBEY</u> . . . It is NOT the <u>END of our STORY!</u>
(Ps.83:18)
AMEN
John 17:3

Donald E Krohn

A TEARFUL SMILE

So easy come the tears
Nurtured by unknown fears
So freely they do flow
And as quickly they will go.

At first you see the pain
Behind the eyes the strain
As they try to comprehend
When the hurt will finally end.

The cheeks flush red and hot
The voice cracks a lot
And then it's over so fast
Not but a minute did it last.

The voice stops its cry
The eyes begin to dry
The fear is washed away
And the twisted face gives way.

A brightness beyond belief
Replaces the child's grief
The mouth turns to a grin
And the smile is there again.

Missy Brewer

TRAINS

I dedicate this poem to my mom, Pam, who I love very much and has taught me that dreams do come true.

I like the sounds of trains at night
Metal wheels rolling over land and hills
They move so fast as if in flight
As I sat silently listening from my window sill

Someday I will be riding on those wheels
Traveling on a train going from town to town
Seeing land I have just dreamed about
Rolling along up the hills and down

Ty Anderson

A MEADOW WALK

As I walk through the meadow all green with grass,
I'd love to have the chance to dance.
To love, to cry to be with you,
And love you like you used to do.

As I walk through the meadow all white with snow,
I'd love to have the chance to know.
To ask you why you went away,
And left me here alone to stay.

As I walk through the meadow all fresh with spring,
You finally gave me a promise ring.
You say you love me, you say you care,
You'll stay with me my life you'll share.

As I walk through the meadow all summery and new,
I finally learned to walk with you.
I'd walk with you to the ends of the earth,
And give you my love a beautiful birth.

As we walk through the meadow all bright with fall,
Hand and hand so each won't fall.
Now we are old, we have lived our life,
I'm really glad I became your wife.

Elizabeth Ryan
UNAWARE
The light turned green
But she saw it not.
She sat in silence
Until a horn honked
And shouted,
"Move!"

The bell rang sharply
But she heard it not,
Engrossed in her book
Until burning food
Shouted to her,
"Come!"

His indifference grew
But she knew it not,
Escaping from loneliness
Until the door closed
And shouted,
"Gone!"

Barbara Ball
RED CRYSTALS WASTED
The last Indian
chants privately,
shaded by the old willow.
He strokes a cold red
cat-like spirit,
tries to revive
what once was.
He lets it smash,
hears old crosses cry.
The shattered pieces
fall onto my dirt path,
seen only as
pretty glass.
The Indian is dead,
his cross stands alone.
Pieces of red crystal
forgotten.

Sean H Bodnar
WAINTING BY THE MOON
Crystal in a mirror shop
Like creamy icing in a tube
Bouncing, breathing and smiling she
Lifts me from the gray. The view:

A mango in Eden's garden.
Asking myself soon:
Is she waiting in hiding
In the shadows of some moon?

Yes, the best of Kino's findings,
The finding of a lucky fool,
Perhaps a cunning illusion that's
dreaming
and waiting, as I, for a clue.

Maryanne Buono-Noda
LIFE

To Peg, Shobha and Julie,
We are many parts. Thanks!

Chimes the clock
as if to call;
Reverberating echoes
from wall to wall.
Breaks the silence
hanging there
And quickly leaves
no time to spare.
Through heavy cloak of night
it ticks,
In monotone, the mind
it grips.
It robs us of our
innocent youth,
makes us face
unholy truth.
The morning sun
brings no relief;
The clock ticks on
time is brief.

Brad Coulter
CASUAL CONFLICT
Broken windows and baseball bats,
Peer through the reflections in the
slithers of glass,
She said this and she said that,
Everything was destroyed in a sudden
soulful blast.

The things that happen are foreign to
human control,
Things that cannot be understood by
the "competent" mind,
The occurrences that take the highest
toll,
Seem to fall around arms like ropes
that bind.

You can't always smell the fresh
spring air,
You can't always roll in the leaves of
fall,
You can't always pretend that you
don't care,
You can't always forget it all.

Friends will come and they will go,
The things they leave are the things
they show.

Patricia Thomas Fabiszewski
UNDISCOVERED PEARL

To mom, who always was my best
fan, with love.

All alone he stands to face the
world—no one to call his own.
His life has been of sadness
since—they've taken him from home.

Afraid he is to open up—to let his
feelings show . . .
His heart is much more heavy
than . . . we will ever know.

As bad as things had been
before—at least he knew his
place . . .
But now he is a
number—referred to as "a case."

I want to take him home with
me—to gently hold his hand.
I want to tell him softly—I'll try to
understand.

I want to teach him lots of
things—to trust, to love again . . .
And that Your love, dear Father,—
will his wounds mend.

Let me help this soul receive You
Lord—let me see his tears dry.
Let me be Your tool upon this
earth—please listen to my cry.

Please help me Lord to win his
trust—to let him see Your world.
I know, dear God, that Billy is—
Your "undiscovered pearl."

Marsha Hansen
ANGUISH

Dedicated to Rick John Cell and
Patti for having faith.

A Hidden Pain mysteriously
numbs my entire body
My sorrow slowly emerges as the
lump in my throat becomes
tremendous
Exploding violently all pressures
held within
Releasing my collected tears
Regrets of abandoned words
never said
Leaves a gnawing pain which
aches continually
An emptiness that longs for a
departed friend, now gone.

Marianna Jo Arolin
RAINBOW
Here from my window
the world seems calm,
with spring showers falling
upon my lawn.

Each raindrop, a mirror,
reflecting nearby
a colorful rainbow
in a fresh-painted sky.

Diana Lane Johnston
OCTOBER MORNING
Now draped from every branch and
stem
Star-spangled banners hang . . .
Each spider's web with countless
beads of crystal is bedewed.
The browning seed-pods, fall-fecund,
Await their ripening in the sun,
And scraggly thistles bow their
heads,
Their matted hair with water
weighed.
Still blooms the creeping blackberry,
Its scarlet tentacles outspreading,
While bunching fruits of mountain
ash
Hang down amid the toothed combs
Of pinnate leaves. Through fading
mists
Slim saffron spires of poplars stretch
Into the blue infinity.

Woodrow F Bowen
MY PRIDE AND GRATITUDE

This poem is dedicated in loving
memory to all of my fellow war-time
veterans, especially to all those who
made the ultimate sacrifice.

While considering this world and all
inside
I feel such a great, incomparable
pride
For this great land in which we live,
And to our heavenly Father I always
give
My everlasting gratitude for keeping
it free
From dark oppression—for you and
me.

Dear friends, let us resolve that never
Shall foes of freedom be victorious
ever,
While thanking Him, beside whom
there is none
For, without Him the battle is never
won.

Sara Dawn Smith
HIDDEN
No one seems to understand.
No one wants to lend a hand.
No one stands by my side,
This is why I choose to hide.

If someone would stop and lend an
ear.
If someone would let me know
they're near.
I could let them know what I feel
inside.
But, they won't, so instead I have to
hide.

Life is so confusing and hard to
figure out,
I'm trying to understand what it's all
about.
But this world is so full of selfish
pride,
Temporarily I escape, alone, and
hide.

I'm told though it's rough, it'll soon
end
There are better days ahead—around
the bend.
The sun shines bright at the end of
the ride
But until it is here, I'll just run and
hide.

Sara Dawn Smith
A NEW BEGINNING
As I look out the window at the
leftover snow, I think about us.
The snow is no longer freshly fallen
but now dingy and gray.
We used to resemble a soft
snowfall,—just floating around
without a care in the world.
Sitting with the rest of the
snowflakes, strangely alike, yet no
two the same.
And then, as if we hit the ground too
hard, so many different people
walked through and caused us to be
separated.
Now, we can never build the
snowman that depicts the life that we
planned to build together.
Right now we probably couldn't even
manage a snowball.
But I'm okay,
It'll snow again.

Vikki Carmitros
PASSAGES
So much has gone unsaid from me to
you
through the years
Since you've allowed me to share
your thoughts, your feelings, your
interests,
I've learned what's made you
specially you
through the years
I sense the sharing to open new
avenues
of understanding between us never
existing
through the years
You can't know how important
our
sharing is to me,
how worthwhile our budding
relationship is to me . . .
how much I've missed
through the years

Trudy Ettelson
THE SOUND OF THIRTEEN
My daughter likes the sound of
thirteen.
Not a kid anymore, she listens.
Not a kid either, I listen too.

With flushed face and burgeoning
breasts,
she flips her biteplate and
contemplates the conundrum.
With bleary eyes and droopy
haunches, I wring my hands and
remember the riddle that remains . . .

Whoosh across the ice, I feel
the edge of a blade not clean.
Not ready to fly, I force my legs into
the air.

I hear the judges judge:
" . . . a good little skater . . . so young
to be champion." Me—champion? I
feel a fraud as the people applaud.
My bra snaps—exquisite shame.

The sound of thirteen, the sound of
thirteen,
Daughter and mother, we are the
harp.

Seth Greenberg
THE OPEN SEA IS A HUNGRY OLD MAN

The water has always been there
like an old man,

But a ship is like a newborn baby.

The waves are ready to swallow
the ship in whole,

While the men who are brave,
strong, calm, and courageous
play their role.

Men who work so hard and forget
about fear,

For the tower tilts as in fear of
the waves.

While the heaven watches over
the ship
as if waiting for the last minute
to save it,

The ship will fall
into the water's pit.

The Open Sea Is A Hungry Old
Man.

Leo C Shomler
MY ELDEST AT SEVENTEEN

To David, our firstborn and son No. One of Three.

Today you are seventeen
An exciting age to be,
A man almost, a boy no more,
With a brand new world to see.

You've learned to play these few
short years
But most, you've learned to work;
We're sure this has prepared you,
Son,
For duties you'll never shirk.

Just fix your eyes uplifted to
High purpose—always keeping
That faith in self—those goals you'll
win,
There'll be no cause for seeking
A second-rate life, and weeping.

Ardith J Hoff
RECOMPOSURE

We are forests
Filled with light
And air
Recording ourselves
In loops
To be played back
Endlessly
During darker hours

Joel Cohen
THE WIND

From nowhere—
A bent tree,
A whisked leaf—
To nowhere.

Roxann Fletcher
PRECIOUS GIFTS

People are given
at the beginning of life,
two Precious Gifts
joined as husband and wife.

They seem unimportant
through most of the years,
but there for the good times,
bad times and tears.

They're taken for granted
they'll always care,
taken for granted
they'll always be there.

By the time you realize
the love you found,
these gifts that you had
may not be around.

It's hard to get over
and really sad,
these Precious Gifts
were Mom and Dad.

Lawrence Nigel Roberts
TOMALES BAY

To mum and dad, Penny James and Sam, my friends at Hop Kiln Winery; and Ted for giving me the space to write this poem, and not letting daylight in on magic.

On the point, of the sandy knife
That cuts the throat of the deep vein
Of Tomales Bay, where the ocean's
salt
Rubs itself into the beautiful wound,
That daggers the land,
A gull pulls a fish into the wind of
life
A sacrifice to a perfect moment.

The white blunt boat shuttles rounds
of diggers
Out onto the sleeping back of a dry
bar.
In the clam cold waters
Of the long neck of the bay.

Behind the boat the scenery tears,
Islands of forests, and hills of islands
Are China fragile stencils,
Painted on priceless moving plates.
Porcelain, broken at a party,
To show it was wild and untamed,
fun and alive.

And all the time the rocks beneath the
water
Decide, when they should split, and
crack the whip,
To make the earth dance again, along
the razor's edge.

Jay Sossamon
REBIRTH (TO FIND OUR HEARTS AGAIN)

You and I we don't have a thousand
lives to throw away like grains of
sand
we have each other our imaginations
and our beliefs
in which we stand
SO
take me to where the tumbling sea
stands
to where the baptismal waters kisses
the sands
strip me bare of society's constrictive
bindings
cleanse my fermented flesh with
blessed tidings
and set my soul dancing with the
skies
I am emancipated by the love that
never dies

Pauline Martin
I GIVE TO YOU, WORLD

Dedicated to Rick, my husband and best friend, who believes in me.

Oh that, to my fellow man, a positive
force I might be.

My smile a drink of clear, cool water
to the parched desert of his soul, that
it may once again bloom.

My kind and caring words a balm
that will heal his bruised ego,
spurring him on to be the best that he
might be.
My arms ever to be a haven,
sheltering him from the storms life
blows upon him, keeping him safe,
secure.

My tears, mingled with his, wash the
dust of grief and sorrow from his
heart giving him new hope.

My laughter, the wings of the eagle,
transporting his spirit to the
mountains of joy.

These gifts, covered in a wrapper of
love, tied with the ribbon of sharing, I
give to you, world.

Ann S Kennedy
ALONE IN MIND

I dedicate this poem to all daydreamers—and to my husband, Jack—my best friend.

To be alone is a gift so many seek
Away from the hum-drum and clatter
of every week.
You can dream, imagine, believe, fall
in love or even travel miles,
If you just allow yourself time, alone
in mind, away from the strong or the
weak for only a little while.

Barry A Mogel
APPLES AND ORANGES

I dedicate this poem in loving memory of my uncle, Jack Gross, and in honor of my dear brother-in-law, Joseph Bonjokian, and my friend, David Jank. Their courage, wisdom and support will sustain me forever.

I learned that the important ways we
are similar
Are far greater than the ways we are
different.
With you, I was amongst the best of
keen sensibilities,
The best of the human purity of
spirit.
If I had to pick the most important
lesson I learned from your
generosity?
You are where you are supposed to
be in your journey through life and
beyond,
I am where I am supposed to be in
mine.
And even if the most scientific
graphs were to plot us on opposite
sides of a rainbow,
We are still on that same spectrum,
perhaps one closer to the proverbial
pot of gold.
But rainbows end, and when they do,
I realize the length of that rainbow
was never very long between us.
The colors of our lives are both filled
with every color of that spectrum,
And so, comparisons are not valid.
We're both on the same symbolic
wavelength, whether one moves
faster, one slower.
Our spirits can always be close
enough to merge.
No matter which directions we take,
we are never apart,
We are both a part of each other.
So what difference does it make if I
am the apple and you are the orange?
What difference does it make if I am
the orange and you are the apple?
We're both sweet, aren't we?
We're sweet.

Maria Theresa Tarquinio
LITTLE GIRLS

For my lovely little girl, Nicole Marie, who is so special and the love of my life. Without you my life would be empty.

Little girls are like angels singing up
above.
Little girls are filled with so much
love.
A beautiful face and a head full of
curl,
You will say proudly, that is my little
girl.
A happy child with a beautiful smile.
She is content but only for a while.
There are obstacles to conquer.
As long as you are there to hold her
hand,
She will get through anything.
As she grows up and does not need
your hand as much,
She will find a lover, a friend, but do
not fear,
Her love for you will never end for
she is your little girl forever.
Then you will look back and
remember all that you have done for
her and all you both have shared.
You will look back and be glad.
Then you will thank God for the
angel he sent you.
You will say, "Thank you God, I
have done a good job and thank you
for my little girl."
Your little girl will always be special
to you
And you will always be special to
your little girl.

Charla Einhorn
UNTITLED

The sun
shining through the window
—Glass—
Reaching out
to touch you but I can't
—Glass—
Looking at
myself reflected in the
—Glass—
Mirror, mirror
inside out and merely
—Glass—
A reflection
but a fake, false, fragile
—Glass—
That can be broken violently
—Glass—
Smashed
to the ground

Dorothy M Anderson
IT'S LATER THAN YOU THINK

Wake up! O sluggard out of thy
sleep.
The Lord is calling, prepare now thy
God to meet.

He has called you to do a work for
him,
So you watch and pray that Satan
cannot get in.

Work for the Lord while it is yet day,
The night cometh and soon your soul
will be called away.

Fast and pray to stay in his will,
Read the word daily as you climb
life's rugged hill.

Don't let him catch you with your
work undone,

The Almighty God, everlasting father, the only begotten son.

Look up! Look up! Your redemption draws nigh,
The king will soon appear in the clouds in the sky.

He's coming for his church at a time you wouldn't think,
Are you ready to meet him?
For it's later than you think.

Paulette Currie
THE FLOWERING SHRUB

Bernie, Forever I will love you.

The flowering shrub cannot compare with the love that blooms in my heart for you.

The biggest tree with leaves to bear can never hold the love I do.

The flowering shrub will bloom then die, but my love will live forever.

The leaves from the massive tree will fly, but my heart from yours they will not sever.

Walter Gilliam
WHERE HAS IT GONE

To all parents and those who shall someday become parents.

Where has it gone? "The mannerism that used to be the order of the day, when children obeyed their elders and strove to please in every way, and chores came first before there was play."
Where has it gone? "Prayers that were taken out of our schools, blessings recited at the table before we ate food."
Somewhere along the way; "We parents, as well as our children have gone astray."
Unable to control our own emotions being careless about things we do and say, creating chaos, confusion and finally dismay.
Therefore it's really not our children's fault, because as parents some of our children were never properly taught.
Where has it gone? Ethic, integrity and love that was once shown, peace and morality
All seems to be gone, and now; "We the parents are reaping what we have sown."

Leone Neider Johnson
POETIC CONTINU-UM
Consider the consequence:
The result of any action.
Respect the long-term effect:
Its inference, and logical conclusion.
To the result of any action—
Respect its importance . . .
Wise action makes the difference:
Wisdom is Intelligence
Held in continual reverence.
Truth supplies continual
evidence . . . .

John L Vetter
FOR MY LITTLE PRINCESS

Dedicated to my little princess, Natashia Lee Conant Vetter.

My little girl is gone now,
No more to worry about.
'Cause I know she'll never get hurt,
Like she did so many times before.
We never got to truly know each other,
Like we should have.
We both knew our love was strong,
and understood each other that christmas eve.
That hug I'll remember,
Until my last born day.
You seem to know you were going away,
Never to return.
I'll miss you my little princess,
'Specially on christmas eve.

Delna A Gates
ROOM NO. 6
Here's to the kids in room no. 6;
the ones who don't get straight A's.
The ones whose pictures aren't in the main hall;
the ones the system down plays.

Here's to the ones who'd rather be different
'cause everyone else is the same.
Here's to the wild, impetuous ones
that Society tries hard to tame.

Here's to the Einsteins and Madam Curies that go unnoticed alone through our schools.
Here's to the kids with secrets inside
to make you and me look like fools.

What if they could tell us the ways that they learn?
What if we were willing to listen?
What if the kids in room no. 6
were products of what education is missin'?

Estella Liebensperger

Estella Liebensperger
LOVE FOR MANKIND

Dedicated to an unknown man who was kind enough to stop four-way traffic on a very busy highway to leave me cross the road. These words are actually the lyrics to a little ditty. I sang it on the radio at Thanksgiving. I'm 72 years old.

If you see a little old man,
Who can barely walk,
Take him by the hand,
And say, "I'll take you across."
He will look into your face,
Then smile and say,
"I can find my way,
But, thank you for having made my day."

Sherena M Saito
MAG FEELINGS
My life seems empty . . . nothing coming through
It's as if everything has stopped . . . going nowhere
I often sit and wonder . . . "What am I doing here?"
Because my life is just . . . one old dull routine
Every day I sit and stare at the same old walls
Wondering when it will all come to an end
So that I can be free
My only escape is Autism . . . where life overflows
There is excitement and happiness
. . . and no isolation or boredom
There is no time to waste
Or things will never be done
I am free to do as I want
No walls to cave me in
I am flying high . . . with freedom at last
Only to have reality hit . . . hard and fast . . .
. . . dropping me to the ground
Realizing that I am still surrounded
By the same old dreary walls
That has instilled in me a sense of emptiness

Vicki Lauren Duckett
LET THE EARTH BE RECEPTIVE TO KINDLING LIGHTS
Incrimination, discrimination,
destruction, drugs and war,
Are nothing close to what the earth was meant for.
The earth, our home that could be so peaceful,
The earth, our home that instead is deceitful.
The love on earth should be so much stronger,
The drugs and war should not go on any longer.
The earth is like this because of us; it is our fault.
The earth, our home, that used to be
A place to live for you and me,
Has now turned into a drug-war zone,
The wonderful planet we used to call home.

If only people follow their dreams,
To make the earth free of starvation, drugs, war and pollution;
With enough people helping, we would have a solution.

We must change our earth, show love to our kin,
And maybe the earth will be peaceful again.
It is up to everyone who inhabits our earth,
To show the love to our children they so richly deserve,
And bring a new meaning, to love and preserve.

Elizabeth Ann Andrews
AU REVOIR

This poem is intended as a tribute to M. Francois Villon, French poet of the 15th century, and to the nation of France, 1789-1989.

Au revoir, my good friends, au revoir;
Au revoir, my good friends, au revoir;
To duty we go;
We must win the show and vanquish the foe;
Bonsoir, au revoir!

You must never bid me adieu;
God and man forbid adieu;
Say au revoir, for au revoir means I hope you love me, too.

Au revoir, my good friends, au revoir;
How dark is the sky, au revoir;
God knows history condemns tyranny;
Proclaim liberty!
Bonsoir, au revoir!

I shall never bid you adieu,
But we've glorious deeds to do;
Say au revoir, for au revoir means that I'll come back to you.

Au revoir, my good friends, au revoir;
The handkerchief, please, au revoir;
While we weep away, the night chases day;
Once more, I shall say, bonsoir, au revoir.

Bonsoir, au revoir!

Tracey Nicole Castley

Tracey Nicole Castley
NO SECOND CHANCES

I dedicate this poem to the world Men, Women, and Children—Family, Friends, and Foes.

A fire rages
Through dry eyes
Charcoal clouds
Burnt amber skies

Fiery red sunset
Mere shadows from trees
Metal against cotton
Destruction no one sees

A burning message
Through broken glass
Determinate course
Among the working class

Traveling through clouds
Of male and female
They give in so easy
Their life for a sale

Trading paper
Hands transfer the deal
The box is shut
White powder its seal

A candle by the window
Where your head once laid
The window is now open
The flame flickers and fades.

Jennifer D Weiler
FINE ART
When we're born, we start our lives resembling a block of clay.
As our child life continues, our parents, relatives and siblings add a little water.
Adolescence is when we hit the potter's wheel.

We are molded, shaped & formed
by everyone we come into
contact with.
Strangers in a store or at an
intersection, looks shared or
communicated
have a lot to do with who we
are today.
At the end of our lives, we can look
back and see how we were
created.
We remember being glazed & how
we were placed so delicately
into the kiln
That intense heat & pressure has
made us something that cannot
be changed.
We've completed our course of life.
Now near death—we are Ceramic
Carefully created.
To some people, it's time for us to
gather dust
To others, it's dear memories of
FINE ART.

Jennifer D Weiler
IRONY
They sit in a neat orderly line,
just waiting for someone to come
along and fill them with life.
But not long after, (and it never fails),
the life is withdrawn carelessly
and they are forced to go back
to the waiting area.
Inevitably running in circles . . .
. . . Yes, some people do remind me
of shopping carts.

Cynthia Rose-Fry
PAST-PERFECT
Exception to the rule
How could life be so cruel
To inflict this mad desire
To paramount even higher

This perfection war within
Someone silence this incessant din
The voice inside still prodding
Not good enough—spirit-trodding

My fatigued bones now weep
Just smouldering in a heap
Ashen fragments—no shrine to
perfection
One chance—no resurrection

Why can't I just release
Am I tethered with a leash
To the destiny—perform
Am I lost—internal storm

Chasing elusive fantasy
Far-fetched expectations—illusionary
Here's to deviance from the norm
Can't deny this eternal storm.

George Hopper Fitch
NIGHT FLIGHT
Through the wakeful night
My thoughts fly fearsome sorties
Strafing phantom dreams.

Deborah Arbuthnot Abbott
A FIRST
Love at first sight,
is just sooo trite.
It couldn't happen to me,
Then guess what I see.
A beautiful male vision
with form and precision.
My walking dream
sweeter than cream.
My heart started pounding
bells started sounding,
and I knew it was love
with charm from above.
So, I asked his name,
now my life's not the same.
Because; I LOVE YOU!!!

Julie Hargrove
RUN
The sound of freedom, of
experience, and of life, tunnels
into a wave of light
expanding motion onto a shore of
consciousness—
A kaleidoscope of people run.

Sand absorbed light contracts
the stability and anguish of soul
undeveloped, bonding elating
winds into a relationship
of youth and child.

Angela L McCoy
YOU HAUNT THE CORNERS
You haunt the corners of my mind
like a spirit who violently
from life has been torn.
Visions born on the wind,
love shared only in the halls of sleep.
Mist heavy, all night long,
kiss and kissed.
And I awake to stand
at our—no—my bedroom window
and I sing a song for the dead
because I've lost you again.
I look at the clouds as they ease down
to sit in the tops of the trees.
The distant mountains rise and stretch
to meet the horizon.
Pale fog reaches ready and sure,
caressing hills and valleys that
become
soft contours of a dream-nude
behind a misty veil.
And I sip my coffee and think of you.

Carol Tabor Sizemore
NEW BEGINNING
The dawn has come,
The day begun.
The night has passed along,
To hear the morning's song.

Each day has been blessed,
To be more wonderful than the rest.
Accept it with warmth and grace,
Try to keep up its harried pace.

Live each day as if the last,
To remedy all you've done in the
past.
Greeting each one with a warming
smile
Willing to walk the long, last mile.

Surpass your dreams, long forgotten,
Desires that you have labeled
forbidden.
Or your regret may get in the way,
Of all that you truly deserve today.

It's never too late to begin to live,
To love, to share and to give.
Life is a game that must be played,
Full and complete, nothing delayed.

Stacy Schultz
OBSCURITY
Majestic and swift
Wings abound, probing
For powerless prey;
And underground fearful
Intentions are mysteriously
Conveyed to vulnerable
Yet quite cognizant field mouse
Who, after waiting until preying
Shadows pass, comes out;
Security for now from the
realm of haunting silhouettes.

A lone falcon travels
A darkened land in an expedition
For external flaws which
Could nurture its existence.
Abruptly, movement is sighted;
A mad dash is for cover, although
Young hare is scarcely visible;
Preying talons to defenseless
And pitiful victim.

Michelle Little
CHILDREN
There are many kids
who have nothing at all
They have no place to go
or they have no one to call
Kids like us see life
so plain
We don't feel other
children's pain
It makes us sad
the commercials we see
But some kids just say
"I'm glad it's not me"
We shouldn't feel bad
then just let it go
We can help them out
and this we have to show
The children are our future
we need them to see
The world we have today
isn't how God wanted it to be

Roslyn Thomas Jones
A LYRIC TO MY LORD
I have walked this road forever; He
was always by my side.
Yet, I somehow just ignored Him, as
I prepped my foolish pride.
He told me of His love for me; of the
prizes I'd attain,
If I would just obey Him and praise
His Holy name.

But, I said, "Not now, Jesus; I have
other things to do,
There is so much world to see; so
much that is brand-new."
I went about my stubborn way;
ignored His friendship's call.
Then Satan took me in his grasp;
that's when I met my fall.

"Have mercy on me, Lord!" I cried. I
moaned, I groaned, I screamed;
"I cannot stand another day; it's
worse than I had dreamed."

He picked me up, He touched my
soul, He told me what to do.
He held my hand and healed my
wounds; He turned my skies to blue.
He holds me in His fond embrace;
He'll never let me go.
He set me free and gave me peace;
Oh, how I love Him so.

Mrs Mildred M Lovell
OUR DARLING
Our darling baby boy is gone
But sweet memories of him linger on
Planted deep within our hearts
There to stay and never to depart
His sweet smile and sparkling eyes
Shine as stars, up in God's sky
He was a happy child on this earth
Enjoyed most everything from his
birth
The fountain coke he loved so well
His love for music, no tongue can tell
An ice cream cone, an old can ring
Satisfied with almost any old thing
God only loaned him to us for a
while
But needed back his precious child
To fill a place in Heaven fair
No pain he will ever suffer there
For he suffered his here upon this
earth
In Heaven he knows only joy and
mirth
We miss you dear one, daddy, sister
and I
We'll meet you in Heaven, in the
"Sweet By & By."

By His Mother: Mrs. Mildred M.
Lovell

Laura Hayslip
NO REGRETS
With pen in hand and thought in
mind
I begin to write one more time
Of our love since we first met
A glorious feeling I'll never forget
Looking at you from bended knee
Your lilting voice answering me
We've had five decades of married
life
I'm so pleased you became my wife
Your smiling face, your wonderous
ways
For God's mercy, I do pray
That you'll be with me the rest of my
days

Paul Cappuccilli
GOD HAS COME INTO MY HOUSE
God has come into my house,
a raggedy old house it was.
He set one foot in the door,
and my house was blessed from
ceiling to floor.

Myrtle White Romero

Myrtle White Romero
SILENT SONGS
I thought to walk through virgin
snow
Then saw I was not first to go . . .
The path was crisscrossed all along
With verses from an evening
song . . .

Staccato notes the rabbits made
Then heavy notes where dogs had
played.
It must have been cold morning when
The birds had added their scores, then

The grace notes of their tiny claws
Went on and on without a pause
Until across my winding trail
The magpie dragged his heavy
tail . . .

His aim? To make the bars to close
The silent songs left in the snows.

Lavita Ward
GO AWAY, BIG-JON!
Go away, Big-Jon! Take your noisy
barking
At everything that happens by,

To some other open and friendly door.
You've become a pest, you know;
For the fact is, in this old house,
You're not welcome anymore!

You've overstayed your welcome, Big-Jon.
You've overturned my flower pots;
You've dug up all my planted bulbs;
You've chewed up every rag and rug.
Your wagging tail and wise, trusting eyes
Deceived me—now go away!
You've lost a
Good friend, Big-Jon!!

You've broken the swing, chewed up bowls,
Dug holes in flower beds, too, to hide bones!
Sometimes I think you're only lying there, just
Dreaming up more mischief you can do!
Go wag your tail and bark at someone new!
Oh—come on back! I'd never find another
Sweeter dog, with a heart so true.

Joseph Posner
THE HAUNTING DOROTHY G.

To Dorothy Green: A quality lady with lots of class. Dorothy knew the true joys in life.

Pine cones and fresh cut watermelon smelling grass;
Button-eyed, curley-haired scotties and night blooming jasmine's saccharine aroma remind me of Dorothy.
Fast convertible white Buicks and smokey, smelly, happy hour bars;
Tight legged slacks, and stacked scandalous paperbacks remind me of Dorothy.
All night talks and late night snacks with opinions too severe;
Aligned lacy couches; evened out rugs; and squared picture frames;
Crossword puzzles; burning cigarette ashes, and coffee stained cups;
All knowing of people; vodka and tonic; meat fulled with wine; oysters on the half shell and snails remind me of Dorothy.
But Dorothy isn't here anymore. And that reminds me more of her than anything else.

Thelma D Hall
LOQUACITY: PRO AND CON

I dedicate this poem to my two sons, Kirk and Alan, and their families.

Our agile tongues too quickly offer speech
Where silence is a virtue fine.
Conclusions then we sometimes reach
Which we, ourselves, would ne'er opine.
We seldom limit subject matter
To please our very closest friend,
But carry on incessant chatter
Until someone we do offend.

Le Envoi

Behooves us now to try to mend
With "gift of gab" at our command,
Our nimble speech again we lend
To use to heal, upon demand.

Aurora F Schneider
DREAM LAKE
Favored by circumstances
I fall in with this whimsical work of nature
Alluring my wild imagination
to present a fragment of prosaic writing
Leaving me with a feeling of great pleasure.
Causing me to obey my mundane intellect
Thus, in a peculiar way,
Trying to saturate my mind of nothing but you . .
in the midst of the night
dreaming of a haven . . . held in reserve.

Aurora F Schneider
THE TWAIN MET
touch shoulders with
meet at every corner
run fingers together
enchanting to behold
impossible to hold.

Jennifer L Steinke
I WISH . . .
I wish to be lying beside you,
beneath the dim lit sky,
wrapped within each other's arms,
together you and I.

I wish to lay there through the night,
your body touching mine,
a desire to be, yours forever,
a feeling so divine.

I wish the night could last forever,
then together we could share,
a passion growing deep inside,
and forever we'd be there.

Col Bobby Clark
THE LONELY COWBOY
Donna said, to him, I would like to be your friend,
To the "Lonely Cowboy," it was a long way,
between watering holes.
Searching, longing for someone, to go with him, to the end,
To share with him, his dreams, his goals.

Donna, plain of dress, yet that of elegance and style,
"The Lonely Cowboy," meeting with her on his daily way.
Sharing a few moments, easing the feeling of loneliness,
for just a little while.
Hopefully, God's Will, that he could see her another day.

"The Lonely Cowboy," thinking, how nice it would be,
to tie up, start a new home.
Been running this lonely dusty trail, now,
going on fifteen years.
Donna relating to him, of her desire to roam,
"The Lonely Cowboy," traveling alone, somedays of joy,
somedays of tears.

"The Lonely Cowboy," thinking that she could be like,
"The Goddess of Love,"
Her fair complexion, blonde hair, beautiful eyes,
As pure, as great, as the heavens above,
Her speaking, with fear, of future ties.

Of someone asking her, to step to his side,
Of her two daughters, with a smile.
If this be so, of another, "The Lonely Cowboy," may be left,
no other choice, but to onward ride,
On down that long, lonely, dusty trail, a never ending mile.

Patty Shanks
HURTING
To live death—
To touch life—
Do not hate—
Let me love.

Pauline "Mick" DeMartino
SQUIRRELS
Squirrels running in the white winter snow—
Some moving fast, others slow.
Where did we bury last year's nuts and acorn?
Our treasures we've found early in the morn
Others worried they haven't found a thing—
Hoping their friends a crumb they will bring.
Four little birds out in the tree
Watching the squirrels so busy as can be
We are hungry too the little birds sing,
We promise to share when winter turns to spring.

Myrtle Dudley Martin
JOSHUA CRAIG
His tiny hands were folded
Upon his little chest,
His little eyes were closed
In eternal rest.

A smile was on his little face
He looked so much at rest,
For God had called him home
He need not pass the test.

God knew long before his birth
He was a special child,
And so he looked upon him
With favor and with smile.

Joshua never knew the ones
That really loved him most,
But he waits for them in heaven
To be their special host.

He watches over Mom and Dad
And little brother Todd,
And knows someday they'll come
To live with him and God.

Beverly L Besser
GREED
I watch a bee who sips the honey . . .
while draining each flower
For all its money.
Like some human instinct . . . when man becomes greedy
And drains the soul from the kind and needy.
At least a bee has a purpose in life
To build a home for his family and wife . . . .
To make it safe for his loved ones to roam . . . .
To feel happy and free in places unknown.
The trouble with man . . . he has no direction
He builds and he leaves . . . always seeking perfection.
A time to change . . . a time alone . . . .
Though he has no space to call his own.
For wherever he goes . . . he takes his heart
Leaving his past to fall apart.
Instead of trying to understand . . . .
The road is not greener on the other side of land.
There is no hand for him to hold
He is so busy searching for gold.
Not like the bee who drinks to touch
And hold his hive . . . he loves so much.
Free from danger . . . safe to roam . . . .
Perpetually happy to know there lies home.

David Ruston
A FEBRUARY SNOW

I am dedicating this poem to my wife Nancy. Her inspiration and love allows me to be the best I can be.

The sun shone through a snowy sky,
The drifts were mounting white and high.
Just yesterday it all began—
A wondrous February plan . . . .
God sent white flakes, all soft and dear,
To surely thrill and bless us here.

It lasted far into the night,
A beautiful and charming sight.
Each branch and tree a rich design,
A forming bit of wintertime.
With fields and hills and country lanes,
All bright and sparkling once again.

Then as the dawn rose in the east,
The sun broke through—the snow had ceased.
A world of pleasant sweet surprise,
A fairyland before our eyes . . . .
All nature smiled the world did glow,
God sent a February snow . . .

Janet Sarah Vose (Grover) Barker
CHILDHOOD DAYS

Composed in 1989 in loving memory of my Dad, William John Vose Grover, April 11, 1888—May 10, 1967.

When I was growing up I didn't have material things,
Like fancy clothes and diamond rings.
What I had was more important than that,
I was taught about caring and sharing, as I look back.

The things I was taught are more precious than gold,
I was given more love than I could hold.
The memories I hold in my heart as a child,
Won't be forgotten for a long, long while.

I made it just fine through the struggles and strife,
Which has made me a better person in this life.
It's made me care for my fellow man,
My love reaches out to hold their hand.

I'll always remember sitting on my

father's knee,
That has always meant so very much
to me.
Those childhood days have long
since passed,
But I can tell you how happy I was, if
you should ask.

Janet Sarah Vose (Grover) Barker
DADDY'S LITTLE TOMBOY

Composed in 1989 for my daughter, Roberta Lynn (Barker) Archer.

On May 26, 1965, there was wind,
rain, and a terrible storm,
After the whole ordeal was over, you
were born.
When the doctor told me I had a
healthy, beautiful baby girl,
I held you and checked you all over,
and was oh, so very thrilled.

You had the most biggest brown eyes
I'd ever seen,
The thickest hair, such fat little
cheeks, and were chubby as can be.
You were a happy baby right from
the start,
When you smiled your dimples
melted my heart.

The older you got, the cuter you
became,
When you were one, if they went by
looks, you'd have been in,
"The Hall of Fame."
You were always very observing of
everything you'd see,
You'd always comment out loud, and
quite often embarrass me.

No matter how naughty you were for
me,
You always made sure you were
perfect for daddy to see.
You were a little tomboy, and would
get very dirty,
That's when your dad's eyes would
gleam, as he thought you looked
pretty.

I'll always remember all the
happiness we've shared,
We've had lots of long talks, and
have showed how much we cared.
The precious memories I have of you,
are tucked away forever,
Having a special daughter like you,
no one can ever sever.

Janet Sarah Vose (Grover) Barker
FIRST BORN

Composed in 1989 for my daughter, Roxanne Lou (Barker) Ketchum.

When you were born I was only
sixteen years old,
The minute I saw you I knew you
were more precious than gold.
The first words I uttered were, "Does
she have all her fingers and toes?"
When the doctor told me you were
perfect, I felt my face was aglow.

I prayed I'd be blessed with a girl
right from the start,
You were so precious, and I gave you
all the love in my heart.
I thought you were the prettiest baby
I'd ever seen,
Your beautiful eyes, and tiny ears,
were oh, so very keen.

You looked like a little doll in your
frilly little dresses,
You were so neat, and very seldom
made any messes.
Even though I didn't like to see you
dirty,
You managed to make mud pies, and
didn't look too pretty.

You were always loving, and a very
caring little girl,
As you grew older, sometimes you'd
put my mind in a whirl.
Now that you are grown, married,
and on your own,
I hope I'll always be your best friend,
no farther away than the phone.

I'll always remember the precious
moments we've shared right from the
start,
I have so many precious memories of
you tucked away in my heart.
The closeness we share are words
beyond measure,
Having a special daughter like you is
something I'll always treasure.

Melissa Long

Melissa Long
SITTING UP ON CHRISTMAS EVE

Dedicated to Chris, Kim, Amber, and Brandon.

Sitting up on Christmas Eve with
wonder in their eyes, hoping they can
stay awake to see his reindeer fly.
Hoping Santa leaves them just
exactly what they wished, and
leaving him a glass of milk with
cookies on a dish.

I'm getting too sleepy they say to
each other as they lay upon their
sheets. Then suddenly it's like a
magic spell they both fell fast asleep.

And wouldn't you know it not one
minute passed when here came ole
Santa with toys on his back.

Ho! Ho! Ho! he chuckled and said, I
only leave toys when you're asleep in
your bed.

Melissa Long
TWO LITTLE DOGGIES

Dedicated to Chris, Kim, Amber and Brandon.

There were two little doggies and
they were chasing just one cat when
suddenly that ole cat stopped right in
its tracks and said, "Wait just a
minute, do you think that I'm a fool?
Do you think that I'm gonna be afraid
and run away from you?"

Well, the doggies started growling
and the cat's meow was brave, but
when those doggies walked up near
that cat, well, its hair began to raise,
and its nails began to pop on out and
its eyes, they looked so mean but
then suddenly with a big surprise that
cat ran up a tree.

And it said, "Wait just a minute, do
you think that I'm a fool? Did you
actually think that I would stand there
and fight the both of you? Well, let
me tell you doggies something that
you may not know, well, a straight
haired cat I might be but a fool no
way no. I said a straight haired cat I
might be but a fool no way no."

Twyla Stuart
THE NEW DAWN

To my brothers Streeter Jr. and Douglas, gifted speakers and teachers.

The sparkling rays of the rising sun
will shine softly over
the golden meadow;
Radiant light will brighten the
shadows and lift all that is low.
The dark clouds will have cleared
away;
It will be the dawning of a new day.

The harmonious singing of birds will
be heard throughout the land;
Wild winter winds will have passed
away, a new spring will
be at hand.

A rainbow will reign in the sky;
Roosters will crow, and doves will
fly.

A new dawn awaits us on the path of
life;
Weeping is but for a night, soon will
come the end of strife.
Step by step keep on traveling the
road,
The appointed time will come to lay
down each load.

The full day will arrive, the white
lilies will grow;
Sheaves will be gathered in for the
seed we sow.
The stones will be rolled away
in that new and dawning day.

Sue Gaither Wilson
CHANGES

Love To Bill and our Family who have always had faith in me.

I live my life for only me
I trust no one but myself, you see.
Should I adopt changes as they come,
you'll witness the death of
Consciousness I.

I live my life for the state and me,
according to what others think I
should be,
and when I change my point of view,
you'll witness the death of
Consciousness II.

I live my life for you and me,
Loving humanity, the land and sea,
experiencing life and helping others
will be the continuing life for
Consciousness III.

J Brand
GREEN GENIE
Green Genie came today,
Making me think he wanted to play,
But when I sipped the absinthe he
offered me
The bitter taste embittered me.
Where went the virility, the manhood
Of which I was so proud,
The yearning to be free of parental
bounds,
The longing to explore the world,
Tender moments with the right girl,
That warm fire burning in my
members,
The need for cohabitation with
someone special.

Gone—all of them gone—
The only fire, my only burning
desire,
Take me with you, Genie, into that
bottle,
Let its bitterness burn away the
bitterness in me;
Soothe my pride, warm my members,
Make me content to cohabit with
thee.
Keep me your slave a little while
longer,
Till I can hallucinate my freedom,
Bound to thee.

Author's Note: Absinthe is herein
used as a metaphor for all debilitating
addictive substances.

Cheri Lewis
LIFE
Every time I see a flower come from
the Earth
Our Father who art in Heaven helps
me
Remember our short time on Earth.
And surely the Lord has plans for me
Every flower's life shows me Love.

The Love shown in a beautiful red
rose,
The sight of but one, will make life
feel a little bit better.
There is no other feeling quite as
wonderful as the feeling of Love.

Everyone's eyes should behold such
wonders of the world yet to come.
The Love of God will overthrow the
hate in the world.
All shall feel the Love of our Father
who art in Heaven, No-one shall
refuse!
All will be at peace with one another.
There will be no sickness or fears.
The tears of the world as one shall be
heard by our Father in Heaven.
Matthew 23:9 "And call no man your
Father upon the earth: for one is your
Father, which is in Heaven."
God bless everyone,
Cheri Lewis

David W Rogers
EDEN
In the breadth of silence stillness
slept,
Unending dreams of the Netherworld,

Flailing tears of golden streams,
From amber lights of sunset rays,

Somberness fulfills the days,
Emptiness crawls through the night,

Hear songs, see games from animals,
Virtue dare not strain their hearts,

Sensuous the Mother Earth,
Yielding fruit and untamed land,

Songbirds flying high above,
Lamenting through the mountainside,

And beauty such as none have seen,
Until the dust had brought forth
man . . . .

Deborah A Tackett
EMOTIONS
Sometimes we're blind to the voice
inside . . .
That distinguishes between the mind

and heart.
Sometimes we reach for the falling rainbow . . .
And suffer with the pain we can't hide.

Sometimes our emotions are like a roaring sea . . .
Caught up in a tidal wave.
Sometimes we feel, but we don't know what . . .
Because our mind and our heart don't agree.

N L Shaw
THE LAST PARTY

Dedicated to Anna Mae (Evans) Monette.

Such a celebration!
All the beautiful flowers, the cards, the phone calls.
Seeing people we had not seen for years,
As well as seeing those close to us.
Eating a meal together at their home,
Spreading out into the shaded backyard,
And hearing the healing sounds of laughter.

How can one say—one enjoyed the service?
Why not? The Minister's words, the large round
Stained glass window, the music—
Oh, the music! Some of the music
Was played by family "string" members.
Music has been the very warp and woof of our lives.
Three numbers were written in the front
Of her hymnal. They were just right.
We used them.
Father requested "September Song" as well.
That piece was so appropriate—and well sung.

Later came thank you cards, those very personal notes
That try to convey, with the inadequacies of words,
Deep feelings of appreciation, giving a meaningful
And finishing touch to—the occasion of—Mother's funeral.

Warren P Althouse
TOUGH LIFE PRAYER
Lord Help me life is like a raging river
Hazardous and swift, turbulent and wild;
Hold me up help me across, I am but a child.

Another deep hole I didn't see
Stumbled fell and scraped my knee.

If I take one step at a time
Perhaps I'll miss those rocks of slime.

Can't see the handholds on the bottom,
Reach down ease along gottem.

Think I'll sit and ponder awhile;
Top of the canyon is but a mile.

Could have made it through the night,
Instead I slept giving in without a fight.

Not too far now I see the beach
Almost with my reach.

Another life ring goes floating by,
Missed so many why try.

The river is mellowing a bit now,
Made it this far not sure how.

I may stumble and I may fall
But I'll get up straight and tall.

Along each step of my goal,
Another bell I will toll.

Some day I will make it across,
Bruised and sore but I'll not stop.

This old river will try to break me down,
But I'll make it and I'll not drown.

Thank you Lord for your helping hand.

Toril C Tangen
BLACK BOARD EDUCATION
Pacing back and forth,
in the empty room, full of students.
Presenting facts and theories upon the black board.
No form of communication.
No knowledge within our deep dark minds,
not upon conscious level.
Result of exhaustion of education,
deeply resolves in restful sleep.

Toril C Tangen
SUNSHINE
Shine now my light, yellow, yellow.
shine clear through, the clear blue.
Let the green grow.
Give the light to the damp,
drive the drizzle away.

Phillip R Stephens
ALONE, WITHOUT LOVE

For Ginger, without whose encouragement this and I wouldn't be here.

As shadows fall with deft precision
I awaited your decision
I asked you this evening to be my girl
And as I did my mind was awhirl

With the tantalizing scent of your body there
The sweet swirling softness of your perfumed hair
The warmth and sincerity of your smile renowned
The tender liquid beauty of your eyes tinted brown

Your answer is negative, I feel depressed
Left with your memory of which I'm obsessed
I hang my head in sorrow and am bereaved
Because this lovely dream shall remain unconceived

The light is gone from the sky above
As I walk these streets; alone without love

Bonnie L Allen
JANUARY
Oh Lord, the January month can seem so very bleak,
There is not one tiny flower; or grass down by the creek.

I even see some ice on the duck-pond by the shed,
And the tiny bouncy snowbirds are waiting to be fed.

Yet you have made provision for your beauty to abound,
As cold as it may be, hear the pleasant winter sound

The crunching of the snow, the whistle of the wind
And the brilliant colored redbird as he flies around the bend.

All this you have given; precious gifts you did impart.
There must have been a reason, yes, to show your tender heart.

June P Bushey
MOUNTAIN NIGHTS
Here all alone in the bright moonlight,
Streams roll softly through the night.
The Eagle's call echoes out a melody,
The stars twinkle high beyond the trees,
The breeze moves over me wild and free.
Far above the great mountain's face,
Streams, brooks, and rivers race.
There is no noise, just sound,
Wild creatures are all around.
My dinner consists of roots, and berries,
For they are much easier to carry.
The moonlight gives the leaves an orange-yelow color,
And the green turn to red flowers.
The bears' cubs are all tucked in for the night,
And the birds of prey, take flight to extreme heights.
My sleepy dog rolls up next to the fire,
For we are both tired.
This mountain is like a giant mixing bowl,
I get mixed with animals, young and old.
Tomorrow when I wake up—
Everything will be stilled again,
And I'll wake up with my best friend.

Darlene Lathigee
FOSTER CHILD
Little child unaware doesn't anybody care

Where have Mom and Daddy gone
Where's your crib your teddy bear

Where is Grandma's comfy lap
Where is Grandpa's silly cap

Are there cookies on the shelf
Can you reach them by yourself

Who will kiss and hold you tight
Who will tuck you in at night

Did you have a piggyback ride
Is your blanky by your side

Who will wipe away your tears
Who will guide you through the years

Little child unaware doesn't anybody care.

Grandma Darlene

Robert W Payne
RACHEL'S TEARS

To all the countless many who have suffered and fought the good fight against the disease of many losses—AIDS, this poem is hereby dedicated.

I leave for Paris on a midnight flight,
For it is here that I will live and die;
To pay the price, one must fight the good fight;
Believing that love in the end will survive.

The plane's engines roar as they cut through the night,
Bringing to mind all the nightmares and pain
That ensue and invade my perilous plight,
And in time will consume all false hope I shall gain.

Before I became my own victim of fate,
By contracting this scourge that now deems to destroy,
I was something to someone in a once dream-like state,
Who could fully express his desire for joy.

Yet all too soon the dreaming ends,
And herein lies your greatest fears;
That this life, though short, will not be cleansed
Nor washed afresh by Rachel's tears.

I have regrets though they are few,
Too many sad loves to recall;
Yet with every day I face anew,
I will remember one and all.

Frances Gillard Harvey
MARCH SQUALL
Snow, snow,
Fall softly on his grave—
The kitten that I loved;
The cat I could not save
From the vagaries of men.

Snow, snow,
Fall gently on my face.
Wash the tears away,
And unobtrusively replace
Grief with equanimity.

Snow, snow,
Set enmity apart.
Resolve all bitterness,
And, last, release my heart
From the unrelenting grip of sorrow.

Snow, snow,
Arrest my fevered brain.
Grant your mysterious peace
So that I may live again,
A redeemed and ransomed creature!

Janice Barancyk
IN SOMEONE'S SHADOW
Be not in distress
Over the mess
The world is in today
Do not despair
Or compare
The weather from fall to May
Be at ease with what isn't there
Think not too hard of what to wear

Be sure of nothing and you'll see
What an adventure life can be
And from time to time
Put on your best smile
'Cause you were here once before
In someone's shadow
And what's more
When you find out where you have been
Most likely you won't go again.

Andrea M Grassi
A FOREST IS A RECIPE . . . AND SILVER
Add a pinch of bare spots,
Two pounds of animals,
Lots of trees and bushes,
One golden sun shining in,
Season with some wild flowers,
Then give your forest a couple of ponds to drink from and live in peace with . . .

Silver is the color of Christmas tree bells,
And the band on a ring.
Also the voice that a singer uses when a lovely song they will sing.
Silver is the tinsel on a Christmas tree,
And the stars in the skies.
Silver is the feeling when you get married,
And your mom's tear when she cries.

J L Armstrong Jr
TREASURE OF CHRISTMAS EVE

I dedicate the publication of my first poem with love and appreciation to my Grandmother, Ruth B. White.

Together we gather 'round the tree on the year's most special night
While all the world seems bright with silver, gold, red, green, and white.
Outside the winds spread drifts of snow beneath the cold moonlight.
Inside the mood is sweet with music, chocolate, and firelight.
Like painters using the dancing colors within the fire's warm glow
We continue murals of Christmas mem'ries begun so long ago.
Mysterious gifts are wrapped and sparkling beneath the boughs of green
While the angel atop keeps constant watch o'er this near-perfect scene.
Let's take a moment to thank the One whose birth we celebrate
For promise of hope and life-eternal His coming does create.
The heavens fill with angels' songs of peace and the Christchild's cause.
And our hearts are full of His love through the spirit we call Santa Claus.
For each of us at every age does marvel on this night
The miraculous love and joy that floods our souls with pure delight.
Alas, a telling yawn escapes one face so young and fair
And the loveliest eyes we've ever seen are heavy with despair.
For this year Jessica pledged she'd stand as guard and would not leave
'Til sighting Santa for positive proof of magical Christmas Eve.
But the oh-so-sleepy eyelids close, and her head gives one last nod.
Yes, the magic is real, and you, dear child, are our treasured gift from God.

Christine Bevis
EMPTY INSIDE
You came into this world not wanting to fight,
but soon they sent you running to hide.
No thoughts of deception, no chance to get by.
You had no intention of living a lie.
I guess that's why, you're so empty inside.

You followed the path they chose for you.
Instead of doing what you wanted to do.
Don't waste your time on something that's new.
Be one of the many, not one of the few.
Do they know why, you're so empty inside?

I see your eyes they blankly stare,
into a place that's free of care.
I wonder why you never dared
to take the time to learn to share.
It makes me cry, you're so empty inside.

Laurie A Wagoner Cottrell
MOTHER TO DAUGHTER
I have to sometimes wonder
if I did the right thing
by bringing you into this world
just for my own gain.
I wanted the completeness
that people say you feel
when you have a life inside of you
that only I could feel.
Now that you have come at last
and I know that you're a girl
my heart now knows a fullness
that only you can fill.
What I hope the most for us
you being my daughter,
is that you will always know
how much I cherish being your mother.

Emma Crawford
THE LOST OF A LOVE ONE
Sympathy and Grief are merely two words.
When the losst of a love one enters your world.
Words can't express the sorrow you bear.
When someone you love is no longer there.
Loneliness! Tears! and Depression! all meet.
They form what is known as "ANXIETY."
Tears flow like the river heartache set in like stain.
And all you can feel is pain! pain! pain!
But JESUS and TIME were my best friend.
And they help me through from deep down within.
Time is a precious gift from above.
Time fades out pain and replaces it with love.

Heather L Baker
DAYDREAMS
Can you hear me calling your name
As you softly whisper mine?
The handsome man's chiseled features,
Outlined by his hair, so fine.

Your beauty left me helpless,
As I stood alone on the sand.
You walk closer to me now,
As you outreach your hand.

But as I try to grasp your hand,
Your figure started to fade.
I suddenly realize I was daydreaming
In the quiet afternoon shade.

Anna M Scholz
TO MY CHILDREN
Although I hope there's someone who I know will really care,
And at the time of parting, will shed a little tear
If there may be sorrow and a feeling of despair
Let it pass quickly, for those who are still here.
The feeling of regret and sorrow have often passed my way
I know the feeling very well, that's why I'd like to say
Don't hold it tight within your heart, let the sorrow pass away
Remember only the happy part, and enjoy each blessed day.
Enjoy the things that I've enjoyed.
And love as I have loved—Then I'll look down and surely smile—from Heaven up above.

Sarah Schmidt
SAD
Sad is the color that fills the sky
Sad is the child that needs to cry

Sad is the lost that is never found
Sad is the wanderer that is nowhere bound

Sad is the words that are never heard
Sad is the cry that comes from a lonely bird

Sad is the poet that cannot write
Sad is the blind man that is trapped in night

Sad is the glory that was not won
Sad is the cloud that hides the sun

Sad is the death that should not be
Sad is the author that is me

Jeffrey Jay Jewett
THANKS FOR LISTENING
I want to thank you
for listening to what I have to say
it means so much
to be able to tell my thoughts
without fear of being criticized or ridiculed
to listen to every word
and understand what I'm saying
and why I'm saying it to you,
you seem to care
and want to help
in any way
you are willing to do anything for me
and right now
listening
is the very best way

Johnnie B Williams
COCAINE
I am a world power and you all know it's true . . .
Use me once and you'll know me too . . .
All nations have plotted to bring destruction . . .
I am a breeder of crime and corruption . . .
I capture men's wills and destroy their mind . . .
And cause them to commit all sorts of crimes . . .
I can make a man forget his wife . . .
And send a greedy man to prison for the rest of his life . . .
And now they must suffer, that's part of the game . . .
They lay with discomfort and squirm with the pain . . .
Then he reaches the end of the cocaine . . .

Adrienne Miller
I AM
I am a free spirited girl who likes to travel.
I wonder if I will ever be able to go to Italy to visit my loving family who lives there.
I hear night calling me as I dream of hula dancing in Hawaii.
I see myself on a plane over France looking down and seeing all the wonderful scenery it has to offer.
I want to go on a hot-air balloon ride through the Amazon jungle before it's too late.
I am a free spirited girl who likes to travel.

I pretend to be greeting the royal king and queen of England as their invited guest of honor.
I feel that I'm swimming in the Indian Ocean enjoying the cool summer breeze.
I touch the sky and sleep on a twinkling star at night in Jamaica.
I worry that on my way to Australia I realize that I'm on the wrong plane.
I cry for all the starving children in Guatemala that I can't help.
I am a free spirited girl who likes to travel.

I understand that I'm probably not going to go anywhere I want, but just to go once, what a thrill.
I say maybe someday I'll be able to go anywhere in the world I want.
I dream about going on a cruise around the world seeing many different cultures and eating delicious exotic food.
I try to imagine that I'm sailing the coast of Africa listening to the waves crash in to the ship.
I hope to become the youngest female ever to travel to space.
I am a free spirited girl who likes to travel.

Patrick L Chilcott
THERESA
Memories of her are still inside my head.
Her long black hair which curled at its ends
somehow always ended up in my mouth.
The long hikes on the hot summer afternoons.
Our throats would be so dry.
Our legs would ache.
We'd rest under a shady maple tree,
And stare for hours into each other's eyes.
A person could fall into those dark brown eyes and never come out.
Her eyes were as deep as the darkest wells.
She enchanted me.

My friends hated her!
Her friends hated me!
I must have lost her somewhere in that crowd.

Janice DeHaven Watkins
PARTING

To Joe Shank. Thank you for your encouragement.

When it comes time
for us to part,
you take your heart
and mine—
not one but two.
It's easy for you to make it through
but what am I to do?
I lost not only you
but my heart too.

Bob Furtek

Bob Furtek
SATELLITES
The earth has satellites galore
But man still wants more
Every day he goes to work at his chore
To put up more spies
Way up in the skies

Crystal L Norris
MY PRAYER FOR PEACE

Dedicated to my mother Audrey Ann Norris 1936–1987.

Hear me Lord as now I pray,
There are some things I need to say;
I pray for peace I pray for love
I pray there's eternity in heaven above,
I pray for the rich, I pray for the poor
For the rich will need prayers to get through the door,
I pray for the hungry and all of the others
I pray for man to stop killing his brothers,
I pray for the moon, I pray for the sun
I pray for God's work and how it was done,
At last I pray the wars will cease.,
Oh Lord here is., my prayer for peace . . .

Crystal L Norris
PEACE ON EARTH AMONG THE LIVING MAN

Dedicated to my dearest beloved brother, Talmadge E. Norris 1959–1988.

As I remember back in time
I remorse the wars back then
For peace was won,
Though wars were fought
Among the living man,
There just must be
Peace on earth
Among the living man,
I say, I can remember when
We each have lent a hand,
Although our time is passing by,
And we are near the end
Time will bring more peace on earth,
Among the living man.,

Weary, I say unto you
I hope you understand,

We could not live
For what life's worth
If there were no peace on earth,
Among the living man . . . .

Rhonda J Griffin
UNTITLED
So confused
What to choose.
Lost my mind.
Cover behind.

Money, money, money
Buys the milk and honey.
Money, money, money
Doesn't make life sunny!

Love's what makes it mean so much.
Life's made for two.
Love is a sweet, sweet gentle touch—
Reminds me now of you.

No one's ever made me feel
The way you make me feel.
Is this love inside I feel?
It must be, it feels so real.

Iva Hart
A CORNER OF MY MIND
I've tried to block your memory
To protect me from the pain.
Pretend I never knew you
And never asked your name.
The walls I've built aren't strong enough
And I fight my tears in vain.
The feelings still come creeping through
And the hurt is still the same.
I wish I could forget you
Or make you see me now.
I thought you really cared,
But it seems you don't know how.
In time the tears and the pain will subside
And another I will find.
Yet, the memories will live forever
In a corner of my mind.

Otis C Polk Jr
THE WAY YOU ACT
As on your way you go,
The things you've learned will show,
Not only what is in your memory sack,
But are also told in the way you act.

And the way you act may someday be,
The thing that gets you a job you see,
It may decide whether you win or lose,
It is up to you the conduct you choose.

It is up to you to do good or bad,
Act real nice, even when you are sad,
You are the one not parents or friends,
Who will gain the most in the end.

So be kind and give a smiling "Hello"
Regardless of where you chance to go.
Show yourself friendly and friends you will make,
And life can never your good conduct break.

And in your bag of things to pack,
Save space for God or you will lack,
The main garment you will need to live,
In this world of receiving what you give.

Anne Delaney
CLOUDAPHIM
Suspended in splendor,
high above despair,
Appeared such a figure,
I cannot compare.

It might have been an angel,
or could have been a cloud,
For in my magic moment,
I saw this vision endowed.

Anne Delaney
ON SEMINARY GROUNDS
A clerical rabbit I did not foresee
when first I cast my eyes on thee,
For amidst a company of stately oak trees
stood you in ecclesiastic ministry.

Your order by nature was indeed a sight,
an original creation of black
and white.
A clerical rabbit indeed,
said I,
A clerical rabbit indeed.

Anne Delaney
DABS AND STABS
A Masterpiece my Lord said I will be—
dabs of His precious caresses.
Sharp stabs on my weak canvas
are sufferings and trials all
known.
But His dabs of precious caresses
cover these stabs with gold.

His Masterpiece is not an earthen
treasure stored for the glory
of man.
But His dabs of precious caresses
make a Masterpiece of an
Eternal Soul.

Anne Delaney
FOR A PHILOSOPHER
From Pip to Paradise
Lost
to
link
G. K. to God
typing to touch
Love's Lamb

Gina Burfield
A STRONG BLESSED TIE

To Richard, with love.

Our life is a mixture,
of sunshine and rain,
laughter and pleasure,
teardrops and pain.
Our days aren't always bright,
but it's certainly true,
there's never a cloud,
that we can't shine through.
Let's just keep hanging on,
no matter what,
and one day all of the bad times,
can be forgot.
Someday we will find,
our days will be brighter,
all of our burdens,
will seem so much lighter.
Let's just make our love,
a strong, blessed tie,
that will keep our hearts together,
as the years go by.

Caranell Bush Lott
MY COMPANION

In memory of my daughter, Joan C. Lott.

When I need a friend to talk with and no one is around,
I call on my Savior because my spirit is down.
I talk with Him freely and breathe a sigh of relief.
I know He will help, 'cause I have this belief.

He does not utter a sound, yet,
I know He has helped by the serenity that's found,
From a troubled heart and confused mind,
To a peace of tranquility that's one of a kind.

A renewed sense of being encompasseth me;
For there is beauty in life that's meant to be.
I'll live in hope and will not despair.
There is comfort in knowing my friend can be reached through prayer.

yvonne gomez
TRICKLE ON
Can you hear the voices
Can you hear the laughter
Keeps a trickling—trickle on
Can you hear the music
It's the morning after
Keeps a trickling—trickle on

Can you hear me calling
Calling out to you
Can you hear me breathing
Breathing for you
I can feel you touch me/I can feel me touch you
Touch you now/Touch me now
I can feel it trickling—trickle on

Can you hear their heartbeat
Hits the ground
Can you feel it trickling—trickle on

It hits the ground,
The sound of their heartbeat
You can feel the pound
Keeps a trickling—trickle on

yvonne gomez
MAGIC CASTLE
I know you got a great castle
Won't you let me in
I want to see what's going on inside of you
Won't you let me in?

*It's—Like a magic castle
We could fall in love again
Underneath the moonlight
The rays shining in
Living in a magic castle
I can feel me touching you once again

Oh how these walls they protect me
From the evil
That might sometimes come from within
I've touched you once
I want to touch you once again

(*)

Never meant to hurt you
All I wanted—was to love you
It's like a magic castle
We could fall in love again

Brian A Jones
RUSSIAN EARTHQUAKE
Oh Mighty, Fearsome Russian Bear,
Whose strength is unsurpassed,
Your missiles, tanks, your firepower,
Strategically amassed.
For years the Western World has stood
In awe of your great power.
Awaiting Armageddon;
That dreaded Doomsday hour.

Then a natural disaster strikes
And sixty thousand die,
And people all around the world
Grieve with the Bear, and cry.

It's sad, so sad to understand
Such a tragic loss must be;
Before we can look at them, and say,
You're people, just like me.

Jay C Lyons
MY WIFE
Some women cook and that's their strength,
Baking pies and cakes and meals at length.
Some women clean all day and night,
Ne'er a speck of dust found in broad daylight.
Some women work at jobs all day,
To help pay bills goes all their pay.
Some women excel at raising a child,
The youngsters learn quickly not to be wild.
But my wife has them all easily beat,
She cooks life a chef, the house is always neat.
She helps pay the bills by working from home,
Finding time to raise our daughters,
Making certain they don't roam.
My wife is all the others are
And more to me by very far.
So on Mother's Day I have to say,
She's the best, one and only, for me in every way.

Jay C Lyons
TWO AS ONE
Love is the key
Use it; Unlock the door
So we may be together
And share a world of our own.
One is contentedness
But two is happiness.

We can do as we please
For we are masters of all we survey
From a speck of dust to the universe of beauty.

We will be the masters.
I bid you welcome.
You have entered now,
let us be.

Jay C Lyons
AN ANNIVERSARY THOUGHT
My love for you will never die
In fact it grows each passing day
Explaining it is hard to do
Because it's special in every way.
So many years have come and gone
Where did the time all go
We've seen so many good times and bad
And our love's strength continues to grow.
We have two wonderful daughters
Who brighten our lives beyond compare
A house, two cars and so much more
So much happiness do we all share.
We show G-d that we love him continually
By being our best every day
In hope that he'll keep us together and healthy
And never let us go astray.
So to finish this thought in a meaningful manner
And to tell you in one simple line
Exactly what I've been trying to say is,
"I love you till the end of all time!"

Erika Walters
TRIBUTE

For my husband, David, and all men and women who fearlessly served our beloved country.

Forty-seven strong and bold,
atop a battle-ship.
Oh, who could have ever told
of this, their final trip.

We hail them now with tear-filled eyes,
and praise them for their bravery.
We raise our faces to the skies,
where they now rest eternally.

Forty-seven men behind
the fiercely flaming guns,
have died for humankind
and for their countrymen.

Oh, let their loss in the bloody sea
not ever be in vain.
Let's honor them in our "Land Of Free"
and in "Old Glory's" name.

Alice M Woughter
A PRAYER
I am the breath of his essence
I am the kindness of his heart
In his arms, I cradle the children of the earth
With his hands, I give of myself
His feet carry me through the miles of life's journey
With his eyes, I see love in the smallest thing
Everything I am, Is because of he
Everything that is him,
Is everything of me—

Alice M Woughter
SIMPLY ME
You Ask in you
What things I see
As simply a mirror
A reflection of me
I see my world
Through your eyes
Though you can see
Seems in disguise

You love to sit
And laugh and talk
Or in the night
Go for a walk

Azaleas, puppies
And big old trees
You see something special
In all of these

You love to bask
Under the sun
Or play a joke
All in fun

What else in you
Do I see
Everything I am
That's simply me

A Charles Cope

A Charles Cope
SORROW

Dedicated to those who have wept for what might have been.

Of ages past and time of now
of times to come

Search the musty corners
of shadowed souls
and shattered hearts
of fear and want

Speak not of Grandeur and Dignity of man
to the doe-eyed woman
of fallow breast
and her child of want

But give her hand of help
and Edge Row
of Harvest field

That she at warmth of hearth
give suckle
in dignity and hope

Then will her soul and heart
quicken the times to come

A Charles Cope
MY LOVE
Walk along with me—My love
and while away the day,
hand in hand

Entwine your fingers with mine—My love
as I my heart with yours
with silent thoughts

Thoughts ne're spoken—My love
but meaning known
as we walk more
surely now
this path of old

Echoes of laughter and joy—My love
dance along on golden thread
of times touched and gone

Faded, but not lost—My love
as I walk with you in memory
of the love we shared

We shared and grew—My love
and drank love's sweet wine
of the vine we knew

Which bright star are you—My love
that needs light my way
these gray few days—My love

A Charles Cope
WET REFLECTIONS
It's raining softly,
as I walk barefoot
through the fields.

I stop and kneel
beside the lonely daisy,
It's quiet here - - - -
just the daisy and me.

Then slowly, I walk away,
leaving the daisy
for another rainy day,
and - - - - you.

A Charles Cope
SMALL WONDER
Hold it firmly
but ever so gently

Guide it with sureness
warmth and tender love

For its whole being
is so sweet in its trust

This small child
of my child.

Karen Kirby
LIES
My son is 10 years old
handsome and bright, I am told,
but he has a problem that I can see,
he likes to lie, to you and me.

He goes to a Catholic School,
even there he breaks the rule.
He's not dumb, but very smart.
He just keeps breaking my broken heart.

When asked, "Why this must be?"
He simply states "I like to see—
the expression on your face."

I am shocked and very sad,
because he really isn't bad,
just confused about his life
and that makes me, the bad wife.

I do not like someone who lies,
but I can't make him realize,
that he is wrong and it should cease,
before he grows older and has no peace.

The lies continue and my heart aches
to see him make the same mistakes.

Ocie Wolffe
SOMEONE SPECIAL

To the one whom I wish to be with, in the next life.

Walk through the woods in the fall.
Appreciate the colors.
Wonder.
Delight in all the scents that the light breeze brings to you.
Listen to your heart:
the subtle feelings,
the overpowering joy.

Observe what can only be seen now.
You know of a lively past,
and a greying future.
But that doesn't matter now.

Enjoy the present.
Learn its secrets,
all it has to teach.
Preserve the good things
you experience.

I know the woods
and I can see the love
Just as I see it in you,
my very special friend.

Dana L Alexander
HUMILITY

Dedicated to the equality of the human race.

Pride builds false barriers,
of ego and achievement,
which fall with humility,
and its unveiling power.

Equality of human spirit,
provides reason
for baring one's soul.
One no better than another,
and all having the same claim,
of a cycle—life to death.
All equal in the last moment,
in that nightfall of the human spirit

Being humble in this knowing,
brings peace to every heart.
A quiet acknowledgement,
that for all mankind,
gifts freely given,
with no attached conditions,
are the greatest gifts of love.

Ray Satterwhite
BUFFALO BILLS

This poem is dedicated to Pat, Ray and Jim Kelly and the Buffalo Bills.

They came in like a herd
They left with a sigh
The last game they played
Came down to do or die.

They fought with aggression
Cornelius, Bruce and Shane
And at the end of the third quarter
Cleveland was feeling the pain.

Kelly to Thurman—Kelly to Reed
It was an exhibition that had to be seen
He threw at will and he scrambled for his life
In a game like this you have to pay the price.

The Browns drove hard, The Bills pushed back
You could really feel it with each and every sack
In a game that builds character
You couldn't help but feel the pain
When Kelly threw to Ronnie, Cleveland
Thought about "THE DRIVE" in vain.

On this day it wasn't meant to be
But the Bills played like champions
Wouldn't you agree?

Jessica Lee Holmes
MOM'S AND ALWAYS'

Mom was always there . . . to comfort our pain,
to hand us an umbrella when it looked like rain,
to cook Christmas dinner and open her arms,
to shelter, protect, and keep us from harm.

Mom was always there . . . causing dangers to flee,
to help us achieve all we could be,
to encourage us on . . . while obtaining our dreams,
to be strong for us, she silenced her screams.

Mom was always there . . . to keep us together,
to help calm the storms in the roughest of weather,
to stand up for us, never faltering aside,
to see us stand tall, pride's tears she cried.

Mom was always there . . . an anchor and a friend,
to help us understand a pain even she couldn't mend,
"to help her?" we asked, to comfort her pain,
to hand her an umbrella she answered, "it looks like rain."

Dorothy Jean Jenkins
UNTITLED

Odessa, I try to tell you
but you don't understand
much of my time
you now demand

I'd love to give to you
what you seem to need today
but you are one of four
who all want me to play

So a little time to each
is all that I can give
but you all have my love
which is really quite big.

Love Always
Mommie

Sonyé, Jovar and Victor

Dorothy Jean Jenkins
MY SPECIAL LITTLE PEOPLE

Special to me they are, Shonyé, Victor and Jovar

One by one they were gifts
From my three—that is
Odessa, Oliscia and Otis Lee

Sonyé I call my little "Boo Bear"
Her smile is oh so precious and
The hugs we like to share.

Victor I call "Moo Moo"
He captivates my heart and
We share hugs and kisses too.

Jovar I call "My Buddy"
He is the thoughtful one
We sometimes share "quiet time"
After he has had his fun.

These are my special little people
Who all bring me sunshine and joy.
Each one is like a favorite toy.

Gramma Jenkins

Erin E Sasaki
LATE NIGHT INSPIRATION

(The full moon)

a beacon in the darkness
illuminates the sky
piercing the wistful eyes
of wayward travelers
and wakeful poets

(hides behind sleepy clouds)

the man on the moon frowns
filmy clouds pass over his countenance
to hide his stern magnificence

(when its brilliance radiates)

I am inspired as clouds—swept aside
turn his saturnine expression
to one of absolute joy

(brightness not diminished by the early light of dawn.)

Michael David Craig
STRAY

I found you on the beach
Just a skinny stray
I convinced to stay
With coaxing and soft stroking

I offered to take you home
Then neither of us would be alone
But you were content instead
To lie in my lap and not in my bed

So I desperately wished
As we started at the sea
That someone soon would find me.

Ana D Roman
NO WAY OUT

I'm drowning within myself. There is no life preserver, unless it comes from within, my inner being. The pressures of everyday life seem greater, with less expectations of a reward. The pressures squeeze so tight, I'm losing my strength with each breath I take. How deep in torment am I now? I keep asking myself, but there is no response. Search for something to keep you afloat. I tell myself. But what? What is there to help me from drowning? Everything seems hopeless, nowhere to run, nowhere to turn for comfort. How sad life can be. While others enjoy life. I'm consumed here to drown within myself. For I have found, there's no way out.

Rita JoAnn Vance
IS A HOME A PRISON

A home can be a prison
Sometimes without any reason.
The days seem to have no end
When you feel you haven't a friend.
A home can be a prison
No matter what the season.
The winter is always bad
Without friends or loved ones,
It's always very sad.

At times when you are alone
You wish for someone to phone.
But the phone makes no sound
Because there is no one around.

Why doesn't anyone seem to care?
At times it's more than you can bear.
It seems a thing of the past
For the mold is already cast.
Real friends are hard to come by,
As time just seems to fly.

Johnny R Gary
EVIL IN A DREAM

It's all a dream in my mind.
An untold story I cannot find.
It was so strange I didn't understand.
And I was left in an unknown land
In this land I could find no light.
dark and cold like the darkness of night.
A place in this world where all is unseen.
Only love in my heart and nothing in between.
What is this place? Nobody really knows

It's only darkness that continues to grow.
Soon this darkness will cover the earth.
Then we'll all know about Satan's birth.
He will be born of the hatred and evil we do
And end all the happiness and joy we knew.
He will send us from darkness to the flames of hell.
And leave us under his evil spell
So living and dead we cannot leave.
And you will never end the hell you receive.

FUZZY

Kevin R Browne
RENÉE

Tonight I sat up late,
I couldn't sleep,
And I thought about you.
I rose and turned the light on
And looked at your picture,
And remembered,
And cried,
And thought how happy I was I had this picture;
I picked the picture up
And you were almost alive;
I hugged the picture tight
And cried the hardest I have in a long time
And kept crying
And said I love you
And I'm sorry,
Put the picture down
And everything was alright.

Victoria Gamble
REMEMBER SEASONS

Try to remember the kind September
When life was slow and mellow
Try to remember the kind of September
When grass was green and grain was yellow

Try to remember the kind of
September
When you were a tender fellow
Try to remember October
When life began to willow
Try to remember your life in
November
With your dreams under your pillow
Try to remember when life was so
tender
That love was about to billow
Deep in December it's nice to
remember
The fire of September that made us
mellow
So let us keep remembering the
seasons
For there are many reasons.

Justin Jordan
TWINKLE, TWINKLE
Twinkle, twinkle, little star
Never got me very far
And when Jack jumped over the
candlestick,
I could never make much sense of it.
So once upon a time would have to
be
Because happily ever after,
I'll never see.

And if there is a man in the moon,
Why is he always so blue?
Is it because the whole world he can
see?
And what ever happened to it
Being made of Swiss cheese?

So I'll just be like little Jack Horner,
And I'll go sit in the corner
With little Boy Blue,
Because all of these wishes were lies
And will never come true.

Lisa Wamego
EMPTY EAR
Don't listen to me with an empty ear.
Listen to me and try to hear.
Listen to me and do not fear,
That you might hear me!

Listen to me with your heart,
soul, and your mind, not closed.

Don't expect it will be what you
know.
Listen to hear what is spoken.
Listen to hear what is meant.
Do not listen to me with an Empty
Ear.

Jacquelyn G Loury
TOMORROW
Can we go to the movies
Tomorrow
Can we go outside and play
Tomorrow
Please don't go to work today
Tomorrow
Mom you never say no just
Tomorrow
It's been 30 years now Mom
When will tomorrow come?

Brenda Baldwin
SIMONÉ, ERIC &
CHRISTOPHER
A parent I became in my years as a
teen
Made mom scream and everyone
look at me mean.
Pride and joy it brought to my life.
Yet all others shouted
"It's wrong you're not a wife!"
A child is a gift from the man above,
The greatest master of all love.
Man can give nothing to compare,
So please people get out of my hair.

Today this child is with child.
Drove my mother and all others wild.
But I smile and caress and say
everything will be alright.
No matter what the battle there's no
need for fright.
A young grandmother I'll be oh so
proud,
And I'll shout it out clear and loud.
"What a blessing it is that I did live to
see,
A beautiful grandchild as great as
thee."

Deen Underwood

Deen Underwood
WASHDAY
I remember Mondays at
Grandmother's,
A shed out back,
Boiling tubs,
Stirring clothes with a stick.

Yellow bars of lye soap,
Chafing grime against a ribbed
washboard,
Rubbed clean,
In a cloud of steam.

Bluing added to the rinse,
To lighten all those dingy whites,
Swimming swirls,
In tubs of cold water.

The wringer chews things almost dry,
Damp and wrinkled,
Mashed slowly,
Through hungry rollers.

Collars and cuffs must be dipped
Carefully immersed,
Coated in icing
Of thick liquid starch.

Shirts, sheets, pinafores, bloomers,
Held on with wooden pins.
My thoughts flutter
Like remembered wash on a line.

Oh, to be made clean and pure again,
Baptized in Grandmother's rinse.
Swirled in magic bluing,
To brighten my faded dreams.

Deen Underwood
OLD SCHOOLHOUSE
Listen, it still sings its own tune.
All the children's voices remembered
in the halls,
Walls that trapped schooldays
between the crests of dreams.

The pot-bellied stove is cold,
Never to be fired again to warm small
hands
In the crisp cool days of fall.

The room remembers when other feet
tip-toed
And other hands caressed the
woodwork.
Worn steps tell of their passing.

Rows of desks with inkwells empty,
Names in wood artistically carved
long ago.
Teacher's desk with rosters carefully
preserved.

Some names left against their will,
Some on tombstones are engraved,
But here they reside in eternal spring.

Echoes of young voices have faded
into silence,
But the old schoolhouse remains,
Holding their dreams forever.

Helene Lozier
ODE TO MAMIE
Happiness comes not from possessions,
but from our appreciation of
them.
It does not come from work,
but from our attitude toward that
work.
It does not come from success,
but from the spiritual growth we
attain in achieving that success.

Mamie lived that legend in her
own right.
She truly cared about everyone—
short, tall, large, small, rich,
poor—to her, there were no
boundaries or specifications to
be met.
She was supportive and understanding—mentally, physically, giving
from her heart.
She always found a way. To her, the
door was never half closed; but
always half opened.
She touched all of our lives in one
special way or another that we will
remember.

And as you will recall Mamie as
your beloved mother, grandmother . .
I shall always remember Mamie as
my dear friend.
A friend is a life-line you give to
yourself.

She may have lost the battle to
cancer, but more important, gained
her freedom from pain.
"One day at a time," she would say,
"Just one day at a time, and I can
handle that," and indeed she did.
Her destiny in life was fulfilled
with honor and dignity.
Your friend and mine

Sara Lee Reyes
PASSING ON
My time has come to pass away,
no more hours to each day
I know that time has reached an end,
darkness stirs with light to blend
To this life my eyes won't wake
never to see beyond dawn break
This body's work is finally done,
my spirit's journey just begun.
By,
Sara Lee Ryes

Jasmine Q Ejan
MIDSUMMER NIGHT
The birds in their nests,
Twitter far and near,
The sun in the nest,
Sets there then here.
Hark, oh listen,
At the faint brief noise,
At the lake, the sun glistens,
Its beauty it shows.
The days are longer,
The nights so short.
Midsummer . . .
The day I report.
Winter and spring,
Have come to their end,
The people, they sing,
Celebrate with their friends.

Cathy Diane Bohannon
EMOTIONS
Depression deep within
burning heart desire
Expression goes unwanted
turning backward to emptiness

Fear swells within my soul
Awkwardly disappears
Numbness increases
Falling upon my thoughts
Sensing Spiritual presence
Fades into inner peace

Tracey J Anderson
MY FOREVER LOVE
You are so special in every way,
I want to tell you everyday.
It seems like you came from heaven
above,
and you are the one I truly Love.
I want us to be together forever and
ever,
I will leave you never.
Because for you and me,
We will always be.

Yvonne Mathews Moore
THE BLACK MAN'S
DESTRUCTION
O, Black man, O Black man, why
are you destroying yourself?
I think about how you had a hard
struggle, many, many decades
ago.
But, Black man, what was that
struggle for?
Why, Black man, are you letting
the world take your mind,
twist it, condition it to its standards?
O, Black man, O Black man, why
are you destroying yourself?
Black man, your babies are being
born with drug addiction,
Born with that emotional
handicap stigma,
Born with no self-esteem,
O, Black man, O Black man, why
are you destroying yourself?
Where is your PRIDE?
The PRIDE, Black man, that
presented the "FAMILY" as being
very important.
The PRIDE, where God was the
center of your LIFE.
But, now, God is left out of your
LIFE.
O, Black man, O Black man, why
are you destroying yourself?
Black man have you forgotten
what your forefathers did for you?
Black man, did your forefathers die
in vain?
O, Black man, O Black man, why
are you destroying yourself?

Tara J McQuade
THE FUTURE IS OURS
Adults in the city, kids on the street.
We're not all bad, the kids that you
meet.

We have Hope, Laughter, and Faith to share.
All we ask is for you to care.
This world has no room for our dreams,
Only for crime and passion,
At least that is how it seems.
So give us a chance and you will soon learn
What we need is a friend to help our flames burn.
We're not made of steel, as you will soon see.
So stop crushing our dreams and let us all be.
Because the future is ours, and we'll make it grand.
God will hold us up and help us to stand.
So just for now allow us to laugh, learn and grow.
Work with us as a friend, instead of a foe.
Because the future is ours and we'll make it bright
If only YOU will provide us with the LIGHT!

Lisa M Hess
SOLDIER BOY

This poem is dedicated to every unknown yearning to be heard.

Young boys sent to war leave their families and friends
America is your country
You were one of the many chosen to fight for the
Freedom we have come to love

In return, glory and honor is expected;
Praise from the government is never enough

Only you can see the blood and tears
Only you can feel the pain and hear the endless shots fired
That echo through your ears

Will you be able to forget the living hell
You've just entered, if you survive?

Soldier boy, do you want to go home?

After all is said and done, the memories will not disappear;
The look in his eyes as the bullet laid him down to sleep

You've waited long days and nights to reunite
With those you left behind
You are no longer that boy
You have become a man

When you hear your mother say
"My little soldier boy;" innocent with hopes and dreams

You really wish you were!

Fouche'na Sheppard
EVERY PERSON GOD CREATES IS GOOD

To: Ever Free of Charleston "Save the Children" campaign Bayside Gardens & Manor Apartments.

SO WHAT DOES THAT MAKE YOU?

You who tried to steal my precious life?
You who abused my flesh—my mind?
You who violated my person?
You who ruined my reputation?
You who brought me trepidation?
You who shrank my self-esteem?
You who before my stumbling blocks gleamed
IT MAKES YOU A GOOD CREATION OF GOD!
Had it not been for you who brought forth my tears
I would not know the joy of giving good cheers.
Had it not been for you who brought me pain
I would not know the power of strength gained.
Had it not been for you who brought me humiliation
I would not know the secret of determination.
Had it not been for you who gave me a false start
I would not know the miracle of a mended broken heart
Had it not been for you who brought me so much strife
I would not have the opportunity to experience a full, filling life.
Had it not been for you who made me so sad
I would not know the feeling of being glad.
YES, THANKS TO YOU, IT IS UNDERSTOOD EVERY PERSON GOD CREATES IS GOOD

Fourhéna E Sheppard
BY THE SIDE OF A MAN

I can proudly walk by the side of a man
Who has suffered and seen and knows
Who has measured his space on the battle line
And given and taken the blows.
Who has never whined when the scheme went wrong
nor scoffed at the failing plan
But taken his dose with a heart of trust
And the faith of a gentle man.

I'd give my all—be it little or great
To walk by his side today
To stand up there with the man who has known
The bite of the burning fray
Who has gritted his teeth and clenched his fist
And gone on doing his best
Because of the love for his fellowman
And the faith in his manly breast.

I would love to walk with him, hand in hand
Together journeying along
For the man who has fought and struggled and won
Is the man who can make men strong.

Debbie Krzywonski
WHAT ARE WE?

Dedicated to a very caring and giving friend, Susan Winkler. A friend and second mother to my kids (Scooter and John) and my kitties (all sixteen of them).

Where are you,
as you sleep in front of me?
It's been a year now that I
have had to face the reality
of you and me.
So I guess now we have gone
nowhere except in our own
but separate directions.
Each day now counts for more
than before.
Now this time I've realized
Friends are still Friends,
but what are We?

Cheri Bronson
TIME

To Sean, with love, always.

Time is going so quickly
we know not where it went.
For when we've reached the
day at end,
we cannot figure the
time we've spent.

Lori K Moreland
TREASURED FRIEND

For Dewayne, who helped me find myself.

In this life of joy and woe
There are very few with which to share your soul
In you God sent me such a friend
But I was careless and you slipped from my hand.

Friends and dates will come and go
And with each one we learn and grow
But a friend so rare is a shame to lose
Such a friend over a lover
I'd quickly choose.

The time we shared I'll
treasure always
You helped me grow in
so many ways
Although our relationship we
had to adjust
Total avoidance was not a must.

As poor or ill-written this poem may be
I pray my point it will help you to see
Others in this life I have found
that care
With whom my dreams
I cannot share.

Manuel Ante
REBELLION

To: MC, Claire, Mae, Mar and Mahal.

I opened the page of time
when vales and rains rhymed
to the solitary moods
of wandering in the woods.
There I saw the bamboo trees
pliant against the tropical winds
as they embraced Mother Earth.
I heard the Pacific waves in anguish
on the shores of Asia;
I felt the gentle sun
warm the souls of mothers
whose children's tears washed
the streets with havoc.
Now, I close the page of time,
neither knowing if grasses turn red
nor why it needs to be.

Manuel Ante
DEPRESSION

Have come like the thorny bush
blown by the stormy winds of youth,
crushing against the sands of time,
oblivious of verdant leaves turning brown
until there are but naked twigs
buried in the monotony of self-pity.

Am here.
Have come to ponder upon the soul
trusting the phantoms of imaginations
into a reality of what one should not
until dreams are obsessions
within nightmares.
Am here; am depression.
Have come to bring those tears.

Manuel Ante
DENIALS

Your soul ventures deep
into tangled brain cells
and finds abode amidst
lost memories, until
tears—crystal clear
as a winter stream on wrinkled cheeks—
drown the moments
in solitude I cannot define;
yes, awakening with fears
that grip your mortality.
Aging are nightmares
beyond your forgetting;
and unless you glow in His Being,
you dwell with the iniquities
Of being not, like a golden day
pawned to a moonless night.

Gary D Thomas
THE PEN

In dedication to the achievements of all poets, past, present, and future.

BLACK and blue on shade of white,
Visions transfer through,
Verse of song dance forth to write
The wisdom owed to you.

When ages passed the lore of time
To modern hearts aflame;
The authors, poets, words and rhyme,
Your hue belongs their claim.

Down fingers that sway your gentle blow,
A tinted word appears,

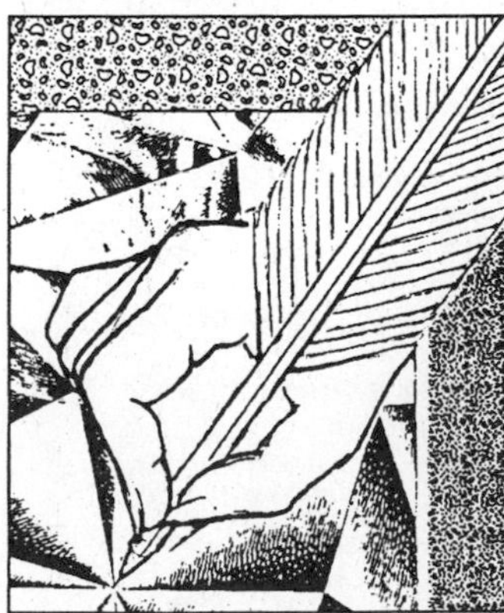

"What enchantments show, for men to know
your tale of yesteryear!"

You may be small in shape, and tower
mere inches high, and yet,
Your gentle crawl, your rise to power,
We never shall forget.

So, "Light the world and all it sees!"
Oh Revered One I hold.
Your moments reign through history,
Forever to be told.

Bobbie-Joe
NOW AND FOREVER

My man M.D. who has me in seventh heaven.

We have survived all that we've
been through,
all heartaches and hardships,
that had made us sad and blue.
We will survive the sorrow and pain,
to see our lives reunited again.
We have been together for all
these years,
smiling, laughing, and also
shedding tears,
just remember,
I will always love you
now and forever.

Raymond Vuk
THE SILVER TRAP

To Mirjana, my wife.

From the jagged branches of a fallen tree
He crawled upon the threads of his canopy,
And moved with haste through the strange design
To inspect each knot and to test each line,
Bidden, as it were, by the mute alarm
From the faintest touch of my careless arm.

I watched him as the wind through his netting teased
As he tuned each string 'till the tremors ceased,
Then I saw him slip in the cranny of a tree
From there to survey his silken canopy;
A fantastic work of art, geometric in design
With each slice of space bound by a perfect line.

I watched and mused of life and of living things
Of that tiny artist and his silver strings,
Of lines that touched each in a perfect place
Of the power that teaches such measure of space,
Then I thought of the purpose for that silky map
And saw in its strings but a grisly trap.

Corazon M J Digdigan
MODERN SLAVERY

Dedicated to my Grandfather, Don Mariano Mayo Maralit, the inspiration of my life.

The dismal condition of slavery
Still controls and wrecks many lives today.

The mighty are bondmen to vain obsession
With oppressive power and wealth possession.

The lowly are slaves to harsh misery
Of endless fight for life's needs and decency.

For human wants and man's vanity well-known
Are the real slave drivers in dominion.

Jenn Poudrier
SOUNDS OF NATURE

I dedicate this to my wonderful family: Mom, Dad and Ken.

Rejoice, hear the birds sing,
a sound of happiness.
Rejoice, hear the wind,
breaking through the reeds—
beautifulness.
Rejoice, hear the water,
crashing against a rock—
forcefulness.
Rejoice, hear the little children
antagonizing each other—
aggressiveness.
Rejoice, these are the sounds of
nature—gloriousness.

Amantha A Baron
IVY

Nancy/Eddy/Akin - 1931-1934.

Ivy is such a cheery plant
Grows and grows where others can't.
Seems to me like a little green fairy—
Tendrils clinging to the window airy!
Nods and plays with the sun all day
In memory of one away.

E Rosemond Fraser
POPCORN, PINK COTTON CANDY

To my daughters and grandchildren For all the joy, for all the laughs.

In a May garden so lovely and heavenly,
The white dog-wood trees have suddenly turned to popcorn,
And the pink to cotton candy.
If the birds knew of this confection,
What a day of celebration, of May Day.
Popcorn and pink cotton candy.

Claude E Toney

Claude E Toney
CALCULATED KILLER

To my lovely Lady Patricia Dick, I love you Princess" and dedicate not only this special poem but" also a special love" Always!!!!!

I lay here on my pillow every night here all alone,
hoping that you'll someday let my roaming heart come home.

A calculated killer now in you is what I see,
you've stuck a dagger strong and ster direct inside of me.
You told me that you need me and you told me that you care,
you said that nothing in this world could separate this pair.

You expressed a sense of happiness declared a sense of joy,
but not it seems your love for me is no more than a toy.

Still" I lay here on my pillow every night here all alone,
hoping that you'll someday let my roaming heart come home.
Yes" A calculated killer in your heart and in your mind
but" with the proper caring we can heal it all with time!

Vanessa Van Schoick
LOVE'S NEW DAWN

Dedicated to Autumn, Justin and Mrs. Sessoms for believing in me and my passion—writing; also to my mother for the various ways she has supported me through college.

Saving an empty space for you to lie,
Dreaming, touching you, then you disappear.
You weren't there for me, I asked myself why,
With sorrowful eyes holding back a tear.
Losing sense of common conversation
Because my mind dwells, drifting to your love.
Believe me, I have no reservation
Before I did, I was "free as a dove."
Time has made me see love turn true for you.
Insight, given with time revealed real me,
Secret me whispered why I love you too,
Telling me sweetly with you I should be.
Yesterday cried, love lost—forever gone!
Yet today, old love awakes new as dawn.

Marilyn Sanchez
LIFE-DEATH

In memory of my great-grandmother poetess Lyda-Stanley-Moon.

Life but a moment, a blink of an eye, a shadow on the wall, one beat of a hummingbird's wing, what a little while to prepare for death. Birth, time for only one sweet song, then death is upon us, but not to fear death, not to wish for it, but time only to prepare for it. But how do I hold time, push time back, so I might have time to prepare, I know not. You have all the time in the world so says an old grandfather clock hanging on the wall, ticking every beat of my heart away, faster and faster it goes, around and around as a carrousel gleaming in the sunlight, no more sounds of children laughing, the sounds of a whistling teapot, "Oh" the sweet sounds of life. But I dare not take the time to stop and listen, to stop and smell the roses. An old oak tree afar off, the wind and moonlight dancing on its branches, a wise old owl sitting upon high in the grand old tree, watching the stars while they're out to play. I dare not tarry long, make swift my feet I pray before the dawn's early light. How much time do I have? I am not prepared as of yet. The old time scales of life, off balance, broken, have cheated me out of my autumn years, have left me no time to prepare. Death is knocking at my door, he has come for me, I have no cleft to hide in, no table set before me, no light to find my way out of this dark void, no one to hear my cries. I was not prepared.

Donald Gordon Martel
SOMETIMES

Sometimes late at night
I would walk the quiet streets
I could only hear the echo
from a heart paved with stone

Sometimes when it rained
I would stand there for hours
Showered with the comfort
I wasn't crying alone

Sometimes came a smile
remembering something ou said
Heartbreaking memories
piercing the silent night

Sometimes flat on my back
no place to look but up
I'd search for a guiding star
yet it was nowhere in sight

Some time in the morning
with the beach sand as my pillow
and the sunrise, my blanket
finally—came the light

Donald Gordon Martel
THE SILENCE

How can I tell you
just what I'm thinking of,
where the mood has taken me,
when I hear songs 'bout love.

Please don't let the silence get yhou down, even without sound, there is harmony.
And I won't let the clouds get me down,
even when they surround, anmd dampen me.

It hurts to know
the reasons why you weep,
true feelings that won't show,
the hurdles I must leap.

Please don't hide
the love that you have found,
whenever you're around,
and close to me.

Lend me time
to mend my broken wing,
to fill the empty space,
where painful memories cling.

Lend me time
toi mend my broken wing,
to fill the empty space,
where painful memories cling.

Dawn Crew
WITHOUT A TRACE

To my first love, Rocco Antonio Mele . . . someone I'll never forget.

You say you never loved me
But I know it isn't true.
How could you not love me
When you know that I loved you?

I dreamed we'd be together
Until the end of time.
But my dreams turned into
nightmares,

And now you are not mine.

You said you needed freedom,
You said you needed space.
I know that you did love me
Though you're gone without a trace.

Nancy N Smith
THE FARMER

TO MY DAD (the farmer), H. E. "Hoppy" Nickelson

Dawn breaks silently over the valley
Early morning mist rises wispy from the creek
The sun peeks over the mountain ridge
Stillness fills the morning
And quietly a cabin door opens.

He sits upon the porch swing
And pulls on his mud crusted boots
Then walks down the grassy trail
To the freshly tilled fields.

Hoe in one hand, bucket in the other
His heart filled with hope for the life to come
As he prepares Mother Earth
For another year of rebirth.

Wendy L Frey aka-Babooshka
DISTANCE OF ILLUSION

To Jacquie for letting me try to shelter you from the world.

Crossing the distance of illusion
as pink bolts of lightning flash
against the bluish sound of thunder.
Silence sings a sorrow tune
dodging stars that laugh aloud
at the reddish moon that spins 'round like a top
the houses rectangle, with pyramid frames
set with no windows, only one door.
Made out of foil.
The cars move backwards
futuring time into the present.
Crime and hate do not exist
only in colored jars kept on the shelf
for special occasions, parties.
Harmony and peace float against purple clouds
that rain orange speckles
crossing the distance of illusion.

Donald E Gray
SUNSET "GOD'S LIVING PAINTINGS"

This Poem is dedicated to my sons, Donald E. & Charles L. Gray. Thru their lives I have grown in the gift of patience, & matured in the knowledge of understanding. Lord; Bless my sons forever, as you have uniquely blessed me with them. Love Dad!

Come, mingle with my thoughts!

As daylight draws to an end, people gather along the beach. Many have come to experience their first sunset. As I kneel into the sand, my eyes encompass the scene and my thoughts begin to wander. Feelings of being really blessed with a gift inspire me. Inner peace and tranquility embody my being. I am in a unique location, in space and time! Reality overcomes me, a theory comes to mind, "here" the elements of the world come together, blending harmoniously with life. Land, Water, Air and the Fire, from the Sun.

The elements are in focus with my mind, soul and spirit. Land, with its sand and shells, tapers to the water as if to end. Water, gently stroking the land with a melody, both rhythmic and calming. Air, an invisible element, roaming across the top of the land and water. As I inhale a deep breath, the smell of the saltwater entering my body and feeling it touch my face, "tingles" with the inspiration of good health and well being.

As if to say, the Grand Finale is about to begin, people come together, closely embraced, with "inquisitive" expectations. This bright orange "ball of fire;" is now glowing in an indescribable illumination, as if it were a mirage.

Suddenly!, the world changes as reflections of color radiate across the sky. Clouds seem to try to unite, but are pierced by rays of light thus the scene now becomes one of overwhelming magnitude! Birds recognize the noctural signal, homeward bound to their island refuge. I gather my thoughts as they silently glide in front of me, never knowing the special living impact they add to our wonderful sunsets.

My eyes scan the horizon, gathering all the images they can, as the giver of light sinks into the water, ending this day. My deepest inner being of my mind, soul and spirit are again overwhelmed, by the awesome after effect. How can this glorious exhibit be put together so perfectly? My mind ponders to explain, never has there been, nor will there ever be two the same!

A smile comes across my face, as a thought managed to intrude. Oh foolish man; why do you desire to explain? Just accept one of your ultimate gifts, absorb all the special feelings you receive and most of all ENJOY!

Oh please grant my prayer, that each spirit may receive a unique blessing as they witness; "God's Living Paintings."

Tracey M Cole
HE!

"I dedicate this poem to Terry L. Ballard, and love him forever and a day, plus some."

He is my friend, a good friend indeed,
The person he is, is the person I need.
Although I don't know him all that well,
I feel that I do, as this poem will tell.
He is my friend, he's good to the core,
This may be selfish, but I wish it were more.
Maybe I'm blind and cannot see,
That he does not have the same interest in me.
If this is the case, I'll not feel blue,
For I still need his friendship, I did and still do.
I fear that I'm going way too fast,
But he's given me feelings I've never had in the past.
I'm sorry, my friend if I've embarrassed you,
I can't take it back, because it's all true.

Wynne Baldwin
THE GREATEST GIFT

To Valerie, Ann Marie, and Valerie Anne for The Gift of Life.

The Most precious gem, be it ever so rare,
Of priceless worth, cannot compare,
To the gift of a child, for you to treasure,
With love and devotion, that has no measure.

The mind of a child in the early days.
Responds with trust and guileless ways.
Teach them with patience to understand,
Help them to grow, with a guiding hand.

Prepare the way to adolescence,
With constant care, which is the essence.
Of all those things you hope to be,
The proper road to maturity.

From—
The Best of Baldwin.

Joseph Pistolese
FAITH

"This poem is dedicated to Fran, my darling wife, and my two daughters, Yvette and Jennifer."

Is life really what we make of it?
Oh—it sometimes is so far-off from being true
There are multitudinous challenges that have to be met -
However, it all has to come from you.
Meet all challenges and for sure the better life will get.
Believing in yourself is the power that
transforms your soul -
'Tis the trial and adversity which gives life its goal.
You must hold on to hope—there is a place out there just for you -
Remembering that your faith will always bring you through.
Follow your beliefs with enchanting sounds -
Just like an echoing song.
Its blend of harmony abounds.

Wilhelmina V Dumas
AS I TRAVEL

To Valerie Y. Dumas, My Daughter.

As I traveled down the highway, I see the trees standing so straight and tall,
with their branches reaching towards the heavens,
as to be thanking God.

As I glanced toward the mountain,
that's so high . . .
I see the clouds coming down and caress the mountain tops.
I see the cool waters running down the walls of the mountains,
to give the earth below a drink, to quench its thirst . . .

As my eyes continue to search the mountainside . . .
I see what seems to be a door, which has been closed and locked,
to keep the secrets of nature that lies below . . .

Laura Hildman-Summers
DREAMS

This poem is dedicated to Steve, You've made my "Dreams" come true!

Dreams are for those who sleep at night—
Nightmares are for those who like to fight.
But they seem to follow us wherever we go—
Some speed up and some are slow.
When we close our eyes and start to rest—
The good dreams I feel, are the ones I like best.
I can control my dreams and make them right—
If I want someone in my dreams, they can hold me tight.
But when I awake and my dreams disappear—
I always pray that he will be near.
Dreams have a way of making you sad—
When you wake up alone, and need someone bad.
When that day comes and your dreams go away—
You'll have that love in your arms
and hopefully it will stay.

Elizabeth Anne Cole
UNTITLED

To Ann.

You don't understand
I don't either
But please don't be mad
Because you'll never see her

Remember all the good times
And forget the bad

Life will go on
It won't stop
Even though she's gone

She'll live forever
In my heart
Always together
Never apart

I know it's hard
Because it's hard on me too.

Donna Taylor
INNOCENCE

This poem is dedicated to my daughters, Deyandria and Latashia.

Bright eyed and pure
What one wonders of,
So innocent and sweet
Not a care in the
World to worry
About

A life given of no choice
Of one's own
A new world with a brand
New beginning,
Strange surroundings and
Unfamiliar sounds
What does one think of
One's new beginning?
One cannot help but
Wonder what such a
Tiny infant thinks of.

Donald Benzing

FOR A FRIEND

Thank you—Joyce, for a special time in my life.

Friend of mine, remember me,
I'm the one you used to see.
The times we had were so much fun,
You filled my life all full of sun.

Friend of mine, let me go on,
How we laughed and carried on,
How about the time I thought you'd crack,
When the coffee pot dumped on my lap.

I can't explain what happened then,
Those feelings I had that came from within.
That yearning for passion that never ends,
I forgot to remember that we were just friends.

Although our ages were so far apart,
The feelings I had came straight from the heart.
I should have known you could not feel the same,
But you were so kind, and I was so game.

I'm sorry that we had to part,
I'm sorry that I wasn't so smart,
But after all, I'm just a man,
Who will never forget a friend like Joyce Ann.

Teodulfo T Yerro and wife Serina Davis

Teodulfo T Yerro

COULD IT BE LOVE?

In loving memory of our most benevolent brother Alfonso and very kind and obedient children Peping (Jose Manuel) and Leling (Vicenta Erlinda) whose demise made our family world less complete.

When the first ray of light peeps through my window,
It reminds me of your smiles when I first saw you;
I can still feel the warmth that zinged my heart with joy,
Like a child on seeing a long-sought for toy.

But alas, that ray has not peeped through again
And my window seems to feel my longing with pain;
Although that crimson ray I've not seen for so long,
The joy is still in my heart like a live song.

When I'd see that ray again, I just know not,
But I always know that you're in a vantage spot,
With that enchantingly sweetest smiles on thy lips,
Bewitching when the ray through my window peeps.

I hope tomorrow would be warm and sunny,
So that I may again see the joy-bringing ray
And my anxious heart would drink to quench its longing,
With its live song finding a sweet new meaning.

What's it then that keeps me wishing for that ray?
Is it just your sweet smiles that lives in me each day?
And what about this consuming longing in me?
Ah, am lost for the answers, please, do, tell me!

Tanya Bird

LIGHTHOUSE

In memory of Corey Glenn Armstrong.

You are my beacon,
Against the fierce seas.
Without you I fall,
Trembling to my knees.
The rage of the endless current
The crash of the waves
Bear hard against my insecure ways.

The tide is strong
The gale is fierce,
Can my worn sails,
Which harsh winds pierce
Be strong enough to make it safely to shore
Oh, how much longer . . .
Can I take more?

The rocky cliff
Lumbers in the distance,
I must hold up
And fight for existence,
I think of you
And you lead my way,
I thank thee Lord
I shall live another day.

Ruth M Thibodeau

JONATHAN

Dedicated to Gladys' Mary Thibodeau, mother of Jonathan. With love, Ruthie.

There's so much to say, so much I feel
The pain all too real
My soul misses the light of your smile
I can only see you in dreams now, once in awhile
And I remember you, as a child
You came to me, when you skinned your knee,
When you were nine, you had a crush on me,
You had dreams of stealing me away
You would hide me in a cave, wrap me in diamonds and furs, you would say,
And we would have nothing to do but play,
My heart is sore
I miss you more and more
Remembered nature walks, picking berries, running from a bumble bee,
Your laughter as you hid behind a tree
Memories, much more than a few
My heart will not forget you.

Jean Richardson

QUEEN OF THE STREETS

This is dedicated to the Lord and my wonderful husband Curt.

She walks the streets each and every day,
Looking for love in the same old way.

She's hungry, she's tired, and she's looking so old,
Her shoes are worn out and she's awfully cold,
She once was a Queen of the Streets, you know.

A castle, a king, and lots of Gold.
She lived on the high horse and was too good to speak,
Now she eats from their garbage while the rich ones sleep.

She didn't think she would ever see the day,
She would live on the streets and forget how to pray.

She has a small Bible tucked under her arm,
She knows it's the only thing to keep her from harm.

It's midnight and the day is fast slipping away,
Guess what? She remembers to pray.

As she curls in her box all wrapped for the night,
And she pulls the blanket around her all snuggled down tight.

She thinks to herself as she tries to sleep,
Just think Lord, I was once
"Queen of the Streets."

Patricia Ann Hall

FLOATING THROUGH LIFE

To Lynn, my best friend, and to my sister, Peggy.

I'm lost in the sea of love,
Forever floating free,
Hoping for that special sailor,
Coming to rescue me.

He will sail a ship of hearts.
Loaded with love and kisses,
And pulling me aboard his float,
Will finally make me his Mrs!

Drifting about this open sea,
Wondering will I sink or float,
Hoping love will come eventually,
To me, my own special loveboat.

Tall, dark, or handsome, be him short or light,
Please Lord, let him rescue me,
From this emotional fight.
Emotions are the shark of the sea,
They can tear you apart,
Until your special sailor comes,
And he will steal your heart.

So float, just float,
Through life,
Wandering here
And there.
Just paddle your
Own canoe,
And soon life
Will be eternally
Fair.

Laura Paulson

NO SWEET GOOD-BYE

This is dedicated to my brother Jason Paulson, who was the inspiration for this poem. May he know that his sister's love for him, will always be there.

When your image fades
and the ghost of your presence
lingers no longer
I shall know fate's hand
has guided you well
destiny has begun
your life's wandering
and gripped you hard
to hold on
the journey is long
and many stumbles
I know you shall endure
Yes
a carefree soul you are
no worries of how
your life shall end; or begin again
just a carefree hand waved;
lingered; and fell
may you one day see
that life is cruel
and beautiful
that you destine your life
that pride is worth fighting for
and honor is man's strength
that freedom is ours
liberty is God's will
and love overpowers hate
in the end
when the scepter falls
and heaven and hell clash
like titans on the ocean's floor
we shall all stand tall
for in the end; when light goes dim
we all stand alone

Christine J Telson

ONE MORE CHANCE FOR LOVE

Emilio, thank you for being the light of my inspiration and my love forever. Thank you for believing in my dreams and helping me make them realities. I love you!

I promised myself no more love,
I can't handle anymore,
not after all those promises
that were made so many times
before.

But here I am, once again, where I was before.
But for some strange reason this is different:
You are always there with love so open and free
and your decision—
to share it all with me.

I wasn't sure and I was cold,
but little by little I felt my love
flow.

I know at times I got confused,
but we took it slow and
our love shined through.

We gave our love to each other
and our love became one
as we promised each other
forever.

You and I are good together
and I will never let you down.
Without you, I will lose myself
for I love you with all my soul.

Christine J Telson
EMOTIONS

My life,
like the sea in a storm,
the waves of emotions
churning the sands of time.

Calmness was rarely known,
but is calmness the answer
to a life of understanding?

Are sands of time known as reliable,
or is it just security?

I've known some calmness,
yet am unsure of the future,
but satisfaction with the things I
accomplish now is my acceptance.

I know very few bounds
and limitations.
I live my life the way I know how.
Sometimes I am scorned because of
my ways,
but I smile and understand why.

Like the sea in a storm,
the waves of emotions.

Linda Snelgrove
EXPRESSION

To the one who shares my soul!

Skies of blue, sun so bright
As I wake with dawn's early morning
light
And breathe so deeply of God's
fresh air
As I gaze in wonder at the one lying
near
So close to my side, so dear to
my heart
It's hard to believe, but I knew from
the start
This love was different in so
many ways
And I find myself wanting only to
stay
By his side, in his arms, where I
feel I belong
As the bond between us grows ever
so strong
The tenderness, the strength, the
love in his eyes
God, I pray the flame never, never
dies
Or the love ever fades from the
face I love to touch
The face of the little boy, inside the
man
I love so much.

Thomas H Keith
DARKNESS

To Dorothy, the once light of my life.

To have found and not known, until
realizing only too late, what could
have been my fate.
For now to live with only the deep
sorrow, that will touch and thrive
within, for that one true love that
was cast aside.
without hope, of ever having again,
what was, and could have been.
For the hurt and pain, that will
forever remain within, only to
increase the loneliness, that will be
left, for that one true love, that could
have been.

Frances Stobart Fry
GOD'S PICTURE

I sit before my window,
While the snow is drifting down.
Each flake is oh so different,
Like the people in the town.

The snow is so terrific—
It can keep us home for days.
Sometimes it forms deep snow drifts,
Along the great highways.

The trees are all so pretty;
They are etched in glistening snow.
The children like to sled-ride,
Or they're skating to and fro.

Don't forget the drifting snowflakes
Are the work of God, you see.
So let us be real grateful
For their ermine purity.

Charleen E Gaspa
THE SADNESS OF A RAINY DAY

"This poem is dedicated to Francis, my loving husband."

There is a certain sadness about a
rainy day
It is for the children that don't like to
go out and play,

Broken hearted thru windows they
stare
The sight of rain is not their only
care,

They watch all the birds hide deep in
the trees
Hoping they will be protected from
the misty breeze,

They look to the clouds all dark and
grey
Wondering when they will all pass
away,

The pouring rain once it hits the
ground
Becomes to them but a tender sound,

As time passes and the day wears on
All hope of seeing the sun is gone,

Darkness begins to cover the earth as
the blanket upon their bed
In the place of warmth there is a
coolness instead,

The moon begins to play hide and
seek with a late passing cloud,
The brightness of their days will only
be what the future allows,

The coming of night has finally
ended the day
But with your sweet touch and caring
ways,

All children of the world will have
songs in their hearts
And will want to go out to
play . . .

Rita Jarvis
JUDGING

I wish to thank Iris Buchanan, Connie King and my Family for believing in me.

If you see a ragged man, walking
along the beach,
Don't be too quick to judge him,
because of his clothes or speech.
Don't brand him a tramp or be too
cruel.
Don't turn your back and whisper,
thinking he can't hear.
Don't graciously bow out pretending
that you care,
When all along in your heart you're
wishing he wasn't there.
Who is this ragged man, now
walking with a friend?
Why just look—It's Jesus Christ who
has ruled for thousands of years.
So often we have done this, judging
other men.
Thank you Jesus for your mercy and
the chance to repent of this sin.

Laura Magaña
GIVE YOURSELF A BREAK

To Mary: For all your love and inspiration.

When the anger builds
Release it.
When the edges unravel
Smooth them.
When life's ups go down
Stop and look around
Feel the calm in the clouds
And the peace in the trees
Hear the laughter of your
Children's voices
Bring into your thoughts the
joy of love & know God in your
heart.
The Peace will come, the anger
Will fade—The calm will soothe
and once more—life is good.

Steve C Phan
I'M GOING TO MISS YOU

To my life-long friend Bob.

I never thought this moment would
come
When we'd have to say good-bye.
I guess I thought you'd stay here
forever,
Never leaving me behind.
I'm gonna miss you.

You were like an older brother to me.
You were my very best friend.
You were someone I could talk to
When I needed a listening ear.
You were someone I could depend on
for advice
When I had problems.
You were someone I admired
Because of all your
wonderful qualities.
Boy, I'm going to miss you!

I will never forget the moments we
shared.
I will never forget the letters we
wrote each other,
And the encouragement you
gave me.
I will never forget the long talks we
had about life,
And how you helped me work
through my problems.
Most of all, I will never forget you.
I'm going to miss you.

I guess it's time to say farewell.
I don't know what else to say.
Take care and may God be with you.
I'm going to miss you.
I'm really going to miss you.

Matt K Benjamin
REBIRTH

Dedicated to the one that finally said "Who Cares?" when it came to entering my first competition—me. (This won't be my last)

Rising from a troubled dream,
To find the world as it may seem.
I grasp the golden chalice cup,
Raise it high and drink it up.
And pray the dreams
That I have found,
Are my temptations
On solid ground.
Standing on my own two feet,
I walk along an empty street.
Faces in windows that have no
names,
I strive to end a useless game.
Though sin and hurt are all around,
I still can hear the Child's sound.
And even though the voice is small,
I walk towards the beckoned call.
In the darkness a light appears,
Sent to melt my dreaded fears.
I reach my hands towards the sun,
And give my soul to The Holy One.

Brenda W Boyd
SPECIAL DAY BEFORE VALENTINE . . .

To Lindsey, a little "Sweetheart."

Did you know?
You have a Special Valentine . . .
This little valentine bundle is the type
that has sleepy eyes,
& as we all know this valentine will
be extra sweet,
Because this valentine has tiny little
hands & tiny little feet.
This little bundle will always be extra
special to hold,
As I'm sure the proud parents will
have told.
She will snuggle in mommy &
daddy's arms,
While all the time using her new
found charms.
She may not be flowers or candy,
But we all know we would rather
have something like her,
extra special & dandy.
So mommy & daddy, celebrate your
"Special Day Before Valentine,"
who was delivered from heaven
above,
To be here for Valentines, to be with
you,
to celebrate her first special day of
Love . . .

Beth A Livingston
LIKE THE WAVES

Written June 15, 1989 for Ray Bombino, Jr. I couldn't have done it without you. I love you—now and always! Thank you for the encouragement! Lots of love and thanks to Dad—for all your support.

Like the waves coming in,
You and I would meet again.
And when we did, we both knew,
That this new love would be
forever true.

You're always honest with me,
you'd never lie,
You would never hurt me, or
make me cry.
Now this, my love, I must say to
you;
My love for you will be forever
true.

Aileen Fielding

Aileen Fielding
CHEROKEE INDIAN'S SPECIAL SUMMER
Indian cast a weather eye, see winter
sign.
Wooly worm's heavy coat say, "A
tough winter ahead."
Heavy foliage has fallen from each
vine,
A warm coverlet for its winter bed.

Heap many, gold, red, and fuchsia
colored leaves,
Translucent through the sunbeams
that dance and play,
But Indian's heart hurts and sadly
grieves,
So soon they will be blowing away.

Indian hear sluggish, droning honey
bees' heap-big hum.
Indian saw spoon-shape in persimmon seed.
It tell him that a bountiful reaping
year is about to come.
Indian grateful for this full, mature
spoon to offset need.

Exquisite, yellow-flecked butterflies
flit by the spring.
Indian amazed at this complex
creation of Great White Spirit.
A dainty purple finch close by stops
to fluff his wing.
Graceful dragonflies dart, prance, and
flit.

It is Indian's very special season of
the year,
Sandwiched between summer and
winter days.
Haze make Indian think campfire
smoke envelopes the atmosphere.
Indian in a state of euphoria beneath
sun's coppery rays.

Irma Burres
GOD IS EVERYWHERE
Dear Lord; What will you have me
do?
I'll climb the highest mountains
Just to be with you
I'll go down in the valley for I know
I'll find you there
I need not go anywhere for you are
everywhere.
You are in the trees so tall,
In the flowers, grass and all,
Neverending, eternally giving,
Always sending your love and mercy
for us to share,
Your love is all enfolding
For our sins "you" do the scolding
And shape our lives into the molding
of your love.
We should love each other
Never hurting one another
Be Christ-like in our giving
Sharing—always helping—sending
our love everywhere.

Irma Burres
MY PASTOR
Wouldn't our church at calvary be
better
If we heard someone say
I know something good about Bro.
Gary
And treat him in this loving way.

Could we not say he is fine and
loving
And not always beating him down
Could we not uphold him to others
And find no fault or call him a
clown.

Wouldn't our church be far more
happier
If we love and praise what we see
For there is a lot of love and kindness
Found in you and me.

So let's try and practice,
And change our attitudes too.
And say something good about Bro.
Gary;
Then he can say something good
about you.

Jamie L Brower
ESCAPING DEPRESSION
To my family and friends whom I love very much.

Why do I feel the way I do;
Why am I always sad?
I never feel like smiling;
Sometimes I wish I were dead.

If I would count my blessings;
If I could find a way.
Maybe I'd feel like smiling;
And want to live each day.

I think I'll search my heart;
I'll do the best I can.
There are so many things;
Oh, where do I begin?

I have a loving family;
A wonderful group of friends.
The warm sunshine days;
And ocean beaches of sand.

I have the flowers fragrance;
The bright moonlit sky.
I think I've changed my mind.
I don't want to die.

Rogelia Dawn Doty
THE ADVERTISER'S VICTORY
Commercials, Commercials
See what I've got,
Come and purchase!
Or we'll put you on the spot.

Specials, Specials
They're all for you,
Come and purchase!
Doubting us, it's all quite true.

Relief, Relief
We have it here,
Come and purchase!
You need not be in fear.

Belief, Belief
We caught you now,
You came and purchased!
Thank you, we take a bow.

Marilyn L Halle
NOW SHE'S GONE
To my family and the memory of Luciana—our cat.

Remember when she was a kitten?
How cute and full of fun
Then—suddenly she was a cat.
And now she's gone—
Remember all the fun things she did,
And what comfort she brought
to you?
For now those memories are—
What are going to comfort you.

Shelby L Willis
FIRST KISS
Remember the first time?
We thought about it so many times,
then when it happened, wow we
kissed.

We thought that was as wet as it will
ever be,
And as sweet and soft as God would
allow.
What, to feel that way again . . .

Dorothy M Clark
THE DAYS OF JAKE, THE DOG
Come on, Jake, let's go and fish
With Grandpa at the lake,
The three of us have so much fun—
Some worms and pop we'll take.

I don't know, Jake, if you understand
What happened yesterday—
Grandpa died and went away—
To heaven is what they say.

Now, Jake, today the doctor said
I'm very sick inside,
I won't get well, I think I'll go
And be by Grandpa's side.

And now, alone upon the porch,
Jake waits with saddened eye
For friends he had and times they
shared
As each day passes by.

Hubby Clement
YOUNG FACES
I remember the long plane ride
to do my patriotic chore,
I looked around at all the young
faces, most had been in high school
just months before.
We reached out to each other, making
friends and writing down their
names, hopefully, we'd be together
for our year in Vietnam.
Some said prayers together, others
talked of their old jobs and friends,
some just looked out the window and
wondered if they would see their
families again.
So many young people together,
assigned such an awesome task,
giving of themselves, to do what their
country asked.

Sue Williamson
MY FRIEND
The lowly little sparrow
Sits swaying on the limb,
His song is heard above the roar
Of thunder and the wind.
The rain beats down relentlessly
On bird and branch and tree,
But he knows that God is watching
Over him as well as me.

Rebecca Carter
AUTUMN LOVE
Listen to the sound of the falling
leaves,
Listen to the wind blowing in the
trees.
And whisper in my ear,
That you love me my dear.

Listen to the silence all around,
Listen to the crickets upon the
ground.
See the birds up in the sky,
And watch the clouds float lazily by.

Listen to see if you could hear,
The fleeting step of a passing deer.
Slowly walking in the woods.
I wonder if you really could.

Then take my hand and softly hold it.
And together as thus we sit.
Looking like a pair of doves.
Let us pledge our own true love.

Mary J Johns
CLOVER
I found a four-leaf clover
And put it in my book
I left it there for years
I never went to look

To see if it had withered
To see if it was there
I spent my life in pleasure
No longer did I care

If life was passing by
If things had died or grown
Until one day I found my
Four children had all gone

I lifted up the cover
I turned the page and then
I found the four-leaf clover
Was nothing but a stem

Jesse Johnson

Jesse Johnson
THERE'S SOME FOR YOU
There's some for you, it's somewhere
out there.
The world is real to those who dare
care.

Well the story goes of a love that grows in those who choose to pay their dues but do they know? It's so much simpler walking it alone, when everybody's someone you don't know.
The face is placed, the times that are shared.
The world was real the thrill was killed there,
by the lady who waits at the garden gates, she loves to hate the love that you might show. It's so much simpler walking it alone, when everybody's someone you don't know.
Well the faces blend 'cause they all pretend to smile at a friend
they shake the hand and crush the bone. It's so much simpler walking it alone, when everybody's someone you don't know . . .

Leah J Charles

Leah J Charles
LORENE

Dedicated to Lorene's beloved Husband, Charles Nettleton and their families.

Her infectious laughter bubbled over like a tumbling stream;
Being around her was like waking up after having a lovely dream.
Her gentle, loving ways were like a soft, summer breeze;
Sighing softly with the rustle of the wind blowing through the trees.
She had a heart of purest gold; But her real wealth and reward came from giving of herself and always doing for others; Nothing against anyone by her was told.
We were cousins, Lorene and I, but became as close as sisters, always together, never alone.
In time, we both had husbands and children of our own.
Distance divided us far apart; But we were never really very far apart in each one's own heart.
Lorene went to live in Texas, her favorite place on this earth, "The Lone Star" State. When I look up toward the sky and see a lone star, I'll always think of you, "Lorene," and wonder how you are?
You see, she was only 60 years old and became terribly sick one day and God in Heaven called her away; To be with Him and took away all of her pain and made her well and happy again.
We all love and miss her dearly; But this we can see quite clearly—This all of us know and understands; That she is in the very best of hands.

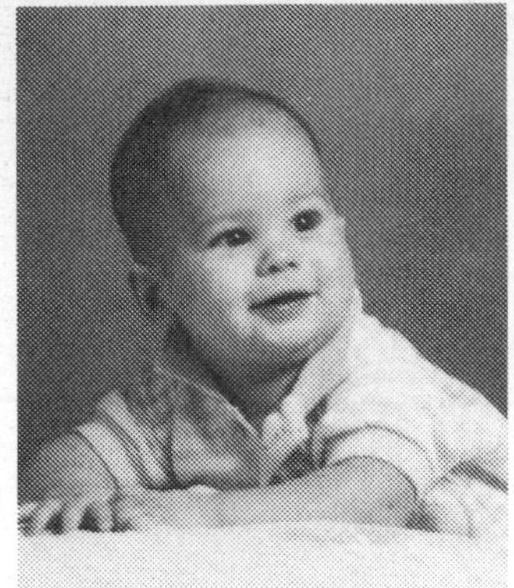

Blake Lawrence Rosales

Leah J Charles
LITTLE BOY BLAKE

Dedicated to Blake and his parents, Mr. and Mrs. Troy Rosales from grandparents, Mr. and Mrs. Floyd Charles.

Your big, dark blue eyes seem to look up quizzically, taking in the view; and asking, "Now, what shall we do?"
Your little button nose is cute and perfection in itself too.
Your cheeks are pink and fresh as the morning dew.
Your little rosebud mouth just suits you, and seems to be getting ready to ask questions like, "Why is the sky blue?" Like all little boys do.
Do you dream about riding on a white pony prancing around on a musical carousel gaily whirling beneath cotton candy clouds against a sky of blue?
And seeing toys come to life and playing with you?
Do you see rock candy mountains and gumdrop trees everywhere?
And are cuddly animals of every kind also there?
Your Mom and Dad are as proud of you as they can be—
And so are we!

Mrs Vernon (Dorothy) Nelson
THE PICTURE ON THE WALL

As i sit in church on Sunday—
I look up at the picture on the wall;
It's a picture of my Jesus,
I know he's six foot tall.
I find his face, so comforting to see,
And I've heard his thundering voice as he said to me!
"You can't come here 'til the last day."
Then I awoke–in the hospital-I lay
Each Sunday as I pray,
"Dear Jesus, tell mom and dad hello!
Tell them that I miss them so!"
I think of you up in the sky—
But yet you are with me;
just you and I.
And when I have a pain,
you take it away
You're always there, even in the rain.
As I look again, at the picture on the wall,
I see the rocks, the sky, the sun shining through—
Everything is made by You.
The preacher stopped preaching—
Is it time to go?
My mind was on Jesus,
and now I know—
That he will be with me
wherever I go.
So as I got up from my seat
I looked up again and who should I meet?
Jesus had come from the picture on the wall—
He told me to come back—
He'd be there 'til fall.
My husband and I walked out hand in hand;
How happy I was, that we live in this land;
To have freedom to pray,
<u>And have freedom to play</u>
And it all came about by the wave of His hand.

William Porter & Jennifer Listewnik

William Porter
YOUNG AT HEART

To my granddaughter

"I'm young at heart but old in years
But among my aches and pains and tears
I see no reason to complain
when I look around and see,
people who are worse off than me.

Some day in heaven, I will arrive
But thank the Lord I'm now alive"

Jimmie Marciel
AT PEACE

I dedicate my poem to my son Chris Marciel.

I bathe in the sea of sunshine.
I wade in the rivers of dew.
And sleep in the nest of a hummingbird.
And my soul is like white driven snow.
I eat the nectar of a buttercup.
And let my tears gently flo.
My world is not complicated.
For I like living so.
I pray to God everyday.
For everyone not just for my sake.
And I surely find.
All of this gives me peace of mind.

Jeanne Patterson
WELCOME

I had a dream last night
A dream I couldn't understand.
I walked toward a spot so bright
And heard a voice command,
Keep coming, don't turn around.
Come, see what we have here.
I walked that way and found
A feeling of love so clear.
What kind of place is this?
This place so full of peace.
The sight my eyes could not dismiss
As my soul found its release.
I saw a man beckoning
And went over to His side.
Suddenly I felt like singing
As He opened his arms out wide.
It wasn't a dream after all,
The truth I began to see
I had heard my Savior call
Now we're together for all eternity

Terry Cain
LOST IN LIFE

Caught behind a mist of change,
Everything seems to have been rearranged.
You have an overbearing question;
the answer, nobody knows.
You're alright, things never changed,
People just changed clothes.

Whether pink and blue or black and grey,
A picture painted remains the same from day to day.
A wanderer through traffic; unheard, practically dead.
Has to realize, to live today,
You have to get out of yesterday's bed.

Rebekah Morris
FROM THE VIETNAM MEMORIAL

Black wall
Darkly reflecting
The pain and loss
Of war,
The price of freedom.
A man kneels
By the name
Of a comrade,
A brother,
And cries
As the child
In his lap
Brightly looks
Into the sunrise.

Anna Michele Scherer
CHAINS OF THE MIND

Shed a tear for the lonely soul, who lives up high in a fantasy
Let out a sigh for the wasted years
The faded smiles of reality

Don't talk of hope to the dweller here
for every plan has been pondered
Don't speak of love or undying faith
For even that path has been wandered

Watch in silence to the story told, of everlasting pleasure
Spent instead on Fortune's Dream
A solitary treasure

Journey on into redemption, linger not within this demise
Do not remit to the story's hold
Or of your freedom compromise

Sail away, when breath is still, from the horror of the reef
For comfort here is but a dream
The grievance long, the rapture brief

Chained to a mind with no escape, of entrapment you must beware
The crushing blow of agony
Is all that you'll find here.

Christi Marie Lombard

Christi Marie Lombard
THE FLAME OF LOVE
The candle lit, bringing forth light . . .
Waves of heat disappear in flight.

Through the dancing flame I see your face . . .
Then you disappear without a trace.

Only an illusion, did I see . . .
Oh how I wish you were here next to me.

A tear then fell, smothering the golden light . . .
Within darkness a stream of smoke floats out of sight.

A flame of love once burned so hot . . .
Now only a smoldering candle is sought.

Cynthia Nazworthy
WHENEVER

***Jesus is not dead! He has risen,** now lives in heaven, and wants to love you through "all eternity," showing tender mercy!*

Whenever you feel down and low—raise up your eyes, look up to "Me" for "I" can see! I have love for you. So, whenever My children feel so low, look "up" and "feel Me!"

Then—as you look upward to the "heavens," My home, send up a smile, dry your eyes, and "peace" will come into your home! Let "Me" suffer your hurt and agony—"I am" stronger, can't you see?

For then you will feel just how close "I am" to thee! How "I" have never left your side, since the moment you fell in love with "Me"!

For even if you stray, "I am" still with you, hoping you will come back to Me and stay, "I" love you each and every day!

For "I am" Jesus—"I" brighten up your dark days! Just be as "a child," run to me, and "I" will deliver you from "all" your worries!

"Peace" unto you, Your friend, Jesus

Stacey Lynn Huston
LIES
Sometimes they come
Just can't seem to stop them
They come and go
Like fallen leaves from a tree
They sit
Motionless
Leaves when a big wind pushes it away
Further and further into the sky
Till they're forgotten,
forever.

Anna Velardi
THE VILLAGE CHICKEN

This poem is dedicated to Mary, my darling sister.

Under the spreading Maple tree
The village chicken stands
A wise courageous chicken is she
When waving her magic wands

A handsome man walked up swiftly
"Kind Chicken, is there any truth
That you're over the hill at fifty?"
Waving her wands the Chicken did say

"Foolishness, you've mellowed matured and improved in value,
So be on your merry way"

Kenneth Stoddard
THANKSGIVING

Dedicated to all of the needy folks and especially the children of the world who hunger for food and love. May God shower His Blessings upon them.

Thanksgiving is a time when loved ones gather all around,
To Thank The Lord for all the gifts and blessings that abound.
A joyous time of feasting on His bountiful supply,
But I remember too all those less fortunate than I.
If God would grant me but one prayer I offer on this day,
He'd feed the multitudes on earth who hunger I would pray.
For I have looked into the eyes of children in despair,
And I have seen the hopelessness and sorrow that they share.
The hunger in their eyes reflect they've lost their childhood dream,
With a maturity beyond their years, for they no longer beam.
Their time of innocence is lost, they've lost the will to try,
And in my prayer I Thank The Lord, for but by His Grace go I.
So on this day of Thankfulness please take the time to share,
Your gifts with those less fortunate and show them that you care.
And God will Bless You for the love you've shown to those in need,
For it will be returned to you, for once you plant the seed.
It will grow and it will flourish as a flower in the spring,
No other gift will give more joy than this gift of love will bring.

Kenneth Stoddard
MOTHER

To my Mother who has been the one solid rock in my life. The shining jewel, the guiding light, the first love that I knew. Not once did her love falter or fail me.

A Mother's love will never fade but grows more everyday,
For they give life and nurture us and care in every way.
From our first breath until we're old we are never far apart,
Though the miles may separate us we remain within their heart.
A Mother is a Gift of God, and is His way to say,
I love you and I give this gift to help you on your way.
And with the gift He gave to me, there's nothing I need fear,
For the comfort, care and strength she gives is always very near.
Dear Mother I could never tell how much you mean to me,
But in my way I try each day and pray that you will see.
I Love You Mom don't ever doubt how much I care for you,
And let the love I have give strength, the way that yours can do.
Each night in prayer I Thank The Lord and ask that He will stay,
Beside you and protect you from all harm that comes your way.
These words I write are just for you, though such a little part,
For words can't tell you how I feel, or what's within my heart.
My Love For You is greater than any love the world has known,
I Love You Mom, with all my heart, and Thank God that you're my own.

Kenneth Stoddard
MY WIFE

To My Wife who overlooked my faults and loved me in spite of them. My constant companion, my best friend, the Mother of my children. Thank You for the many happy years.

I thank the Lord for blessing me with the best thing in my life;
That special person that I love and that I call my wife
It's been so very long ago that day that we first met;
It seemed she hardly noticed me, but I will not forget
Our paths each went their separate ways, till fate it intervened;
Since then we've been together through the good times and the lean
We've had our times of turmoil as all marriages have had;
But our love has seen us through those times, the good ones and the bad
She blessed me with three children, each one a joy to me;
And grandchildren, now there's five, of whom I'm proud as I can be
She's My Lover, My Companion, She's My Best Friend, at times My Nurse;
And all the love I have for her, I've set down in this verse
If my life I could live over, there's one thing that's for sure.
There are some things that I would change, but I'd still marry her
And as we share these later years, I pray Lord you will see;
That as we serve You up in Heaven, she'll serve beside of me
If You should choose to take me Home before her time I pray;
That when she comes I take her hand and guide her on her way
For now I Thank You Dear Lord for each day that we share;
For my life on earth without her would be more than I could bear

Anna M Gonzalez
LONELY GIRL

This is dedicated to my darling mother, With all my Love.

Lonely and afraid this world she used to hate
a poor little girl had no one to blame,
her childhood was tormented with shame
for which she did no wrong
just tried to Love . . .

Her heart was filled with a glow
that no one would see.
lonely and afraid this little
girl was to be till one day she
found someone
that someone is Jesus
for he healed the hurt
and helped her to forgive

Now the little girl has someone
that someone is a friend
that friend is Jesus.

Michael Olson
MY LIFE

To Sophia, who went out of her way to make me feel uncomfortable.

I hate life.
When I look at my life, I feel sad.
Even though my life isn't as bad as some people, I still feel sad.
I hate my life compared to the beautiful people around me.

At least I can walk.
But my legs and body are not as
perfect as the people around me.
At least I can talk.
But I'm shy and not able to talk
freely with the people I want to meet.
When I look at my life I feel
depressed.
I would end it all, but I wouldn't
want to hurt my family who loves
me.
But, do they really love me?

Mark M Foster

SOUL TO SHADOWS

To Mom and Dad—thank you for allowing me to be me.

To all who have reason to know me
There are mysteries right from the
start
And I guess you would like me to tell
you
Of the static that powers a heart.

Why, when hope was a landscape on
canvas,
Did I paint the skyline gray?
Why, when love was the plan of all
mice and men,
Was I apt to go astray?
Why, if thought is a solid-steel
groundwork,
Do I study the starlit dome?
Why, if life is a prosperous journey,
Am I never far from home?

It gives comfort to thrive in my
silence
When spoken words shatter my sight
I have flown in my shroud of
indifference
And found joy in my soft sullen
flight.

Each in our separate existence
And each in our own separate way
I guess I'm a soul to the shadows
Just as your life gives breath to the
day.

Bobbi Jo Kelvington

ANDY

To Rena Dobeck in loving memory of her brother, Andy Anesetti.

I know you'll always love me but I
can't help missing you.
I'll never forget all we've been
through.
Andy, you're a true best friend.
You stuck with me until the end.

Somewhere down the road you died.
I know you wouldn't want me to but
I cried.
Andy, you're a true best friend.
You stuck with me until the end.

I'll always love you no matter what I
do.
I miss how we would laugh and
everything else we would do.
Nothing could amount to what we've
been through.
Andy, you're a true best friend.
You stuck with me until the end.

D M Walker

FINE LIGHT

Sweet sound
Sweet murmur
Issues from
that dying
breast . . .
Mine alone.
"After all, my love, you know."
That pale hand
Clings
to my heart,
The light most of all.
"The light, you know . . .
isn't it simple?"
Those eyes—
somewhere all
alone
Finding my love, my soul—
"Be calm,"
she smiles
"After all,
This is simple."

Lance Cullen

VISIONS

I dedicate this poem to a very special person in my life, Tieneke, who I hope someday will read it and realize the depth of my Love for her.

I close my eyes and what do I see
A beautiful vision standing before me
With Joy in her eyes and Love in her
heart
For someone as ordinary as me
I open my mind's eye to see
The joy that could be
If only you could see Darling
How much you really mean to me

The thought of you warms me like
the Sun
I now know how things should be
I now can finally see
How much you mean to me
All I can do is let what God's Will be
And pray that it will be
The happiness that I now know can
be
For Darling as you can see
We have always been meant to be

Svetlana Vashovsky

Svetlana Vashovsky

INSPIRED BY FREEDOM

I am inspired by this Country
I want with friends to share
To bring my love in poems
And from heart to cheer.
I trust in G-d, this is from
heart
and teach my children
this to do
to get up in the morning with
beliefs
what G-d us told remember
too.
On Friday nights, I put the lights
and meet my son with Kiddish
To bless my home and to America
I say Sholom!
Today a poet I became
I will sing my song
Let everybody know
Should we live all long
I love America
For Shabas and a Freedom
For the future of my children
I always pray for her.

Svetlana Vashovsky

PEOPLE OF AMERICA

People of America to-day decide
To which President keep the side
People of America understand
Who for nation can be trust and
stand.

Voices, debate important going
When the leaves from trees
are falling
To the moon the ships could fly
Our America could always
shine.

Look, one more ship of USA
Went up to the sky!
People of America keep the wheel
From the land we watch the screen.

Let it fly
America flag bring very high
Could we world to watch
Never people war approach.

People of America wants peace
People of America wants friends
People of America I am asking you!
To Share love and happiness
Watch and bless this country too!

Coleen Strebel

A SPECIAL PLACE

There is a place that we both
share,
where calmness is all around.
The tall green grass by a pond,
that's clean and cool to our touch.
The birds that sing so softly,
which lures us to lie down.
While looking at the deep
blue skies,
we know: Peace is finally found.

Toni A Williams-Sanchez

VERIFICATION ON VALENTINES

Everyone needs to have their life
verified, sometime
Everyone needs to know that
someone needs them, sometime
Everyone needs to know there is
someone there for them
sometime
Sometime we need to have our life
verified.

Sometime I need to know I'm needed
Sometime I need to know you know I
love you
Sometime I need to know you know
I'm here for you
Sometime
everyone needs to have their life
verified.

Everyone has needed verification by
important people
Everyone has needed a relative,
friend or companion
Everyone has needed reflection,
suggestion, or circumspection
sometime
Sometime we need to have our life
verified.

You are my someone who makes the
verification
You are the one who shares my
reflection
You are the one who understands my
confirmation
Sometime
everyone needs to have their life
verified.

I verify that I do love you this
Valentines.

Annie Morgan

THE PASSAGE HOME

I entered through a side door.
It seemed curious that it should be so
heavy—so difficult to
open—for such a small place.
My steps had quickened until I was
inside.
A gentle calmness washed over me as
I paused to do a rapid inventory.
It was so still—so quiet. The aroma
of a foreign bouquet filled my senses
and there was very little light—just a
flickering glow about.
I walked to the front and fixed my
eyes forward.
I was grateful to know that there was
no one else present.
Strange, I saw no one but felt
crowded.
The only room I had was on my
knees below.
Trembling, I whispered a prayer of
thanks for finding a place for me.

Janie Simpson

WINTER EVE MAGIC

It was an angel who softly spoke,
To cast a spell as I awoke.
I turn to the window and there behold
a magic sight.
Golden moonbeams shimmer through
the still, cloudless night.
They magnify the beauty that I see,
The calm of a snow covered winter
eve.

The snow sprinkled limbs of the tall
oak tree
Sway as gently as the angel spoke to
me.
Caught between the frosty window
and the moon,
Cast dancing shadows on the pane
and into the room.
The moon spreads its light upon the
ground,
and a feeling of magic all around.

I'm held as a captive, enchanted by
the sight.
I hear the wind whisper into the
night.
It speaks to the stars and snow-
covered hills,
And belies the danger of its icy chill.
I snuggle in by the warmth of a
crackling fire,
As I pull the bedcovers a little higher.

Kandy Kane Shick

SHADOWS FALL

To my children.

Shadows fall
Soundlessly
And echo not at all.
Silence screams
Wordlessly
In beckon to my call.
Images abound
Recklessly
Upon the mirrored wall.
My heart strives
Desperately
To catch the shadows fall.

Contance I Phifer
IDIOSYNCRASIES OF A DEARHEART

I dedicate this poem to my grandmother, Thomasine Sears. "You have inspired me to be all I can; I love you very much."

We are the ones they said were likely to wed
A thought often pondered by us as well
Irreconcilable differences were reconcilable to us
Friends before we were lovers was how we began
Quality time spent together meant our love was destined
Inevitable separation for a while didn't seem to matter
Soon enough
the silent phone only reminds me
how I miss the sound of that voice
Worry begins to overrule the anger in my soul
My heart senses there is something wrong with my better half
I inquire and I'm enlightened to the personal tragedy of my Dearheart
The condolences I send are in order
I think of returning to be nearer but I hear no response
Arrangements are made nonetheless
Before leaving
the loneliness that has been felt for months sets in
ANOTHER in particular
innocently distracts my thoughts of Dearheart
My heart begins to feel for the other
Telephone remains quiet.
I suspect "my love" cares for me no more
I LET GO!
I give myself to the other
Suddenly! DEARHEART CALLS.

Deborah A Walker
CLOSER STILL
Down the dark and lonely road
Your dreams so far away
There is a picture of the hope
When you're on your knees to pray
Life's path will take you along its steps
To a place of lost despair
But you'll always find the way to go
In your quiet times of prayer

Fill me, oh Lord, so I can be
A perfect example of Jesus living in me
My life is Yours, do what You will
'Till I'm full of You and closer still

Look up and beyond what you see
There's more than meets the eye
See past all your hurts and pains
The truth of the One who died
So stand firm when things get tough
He's always by your side
Until that day when He arrives
The Lord will be your guide

Alvin Glen
JULIE

To a love I once cherished, Julie.

I love you Julie don't you know
Don't resist me I wouldn't let you go.
Through your hearth let my feelings flow
Give love a chance girl let it grow.
I am not blind I can see.
I love you and you love me.
Here is your chance let love begin
Break your barrier, let me in

Drink what joy my presence brings
Drink like a lily let me be your spring
Drink and drink until you are filled
Giving love is all my will

Lighten your hearth and let it fly.
But be aware love is passing by.
There may never be another me.
But this passing memory.

William H Van Horn
ACCOMPANY ME
Accompany me to the top of the hill
before the last light descends
so we can watch together the closing of another day
The sun setting over the valleys and hills far away
The quiet hours coming when stillness begins and all about comes to rest.

Accompany me to the top of the hill
so we can watch together
the heaven's lights appearing
that will shine throughout the night
The moon casting shadows and lighting a pathway bright that we can descend this hill in safety on our way home tonight.

Shall we now go to rest the quiet hours through until first light
of morning shines and
sparkles on the dew
bringing the world about to
another day of life anew

To live, to work and love all things until the light again descends and another day comes to an end.

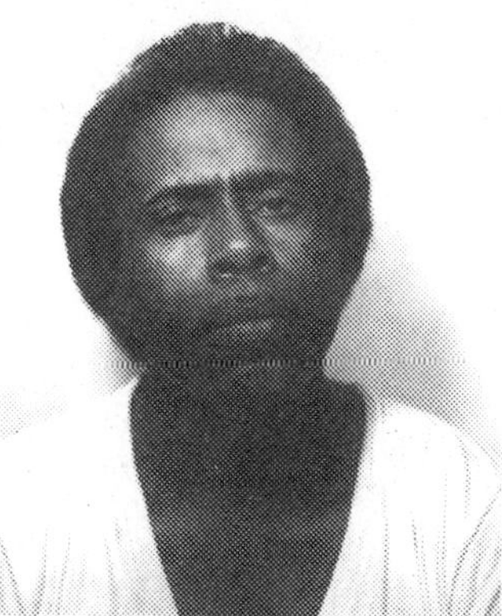

Devereaux R Divens

Devereaux R Divens
DAUGHTER
My little big eyed baby is the prettiest in the world,
Dede is her name and she is my little girl.
She is seven years old and very, very smart,
and she's always asking, daddy let's go to the park.
With her hair so long and black which she likes to twirl,
she's my joy and blessing she's my pretty little big eyed girl.
When she climbs upon my knee
and I hold her in my arms,
Lord I pray your angels, keep her safely from harm.
Though she has the gift of gab
and a one track mind, she can sit
and talk to me any old time.
Lord I thank you for this child
that sweeps me off my feet, as
she says I love you dad and
quickly falls to sleep.
As you grow up you'll always be
a precious gifted pearl, but for
now stay small awhile my pretty
little big eyed girl.

Devereaux R Divens
MY WANDA
I know people are desirous of me
but that's just the way it will have to be

I found something a few years ago
that's more precious than silver or gold

And each day I thank my god, that I will never ever be robbed.

There are times when I am low and I feel bad,
but one look at its beauty and I feel glad.

Now before I found it I was all alone,
till I decided to make it my own.

Now everybody has something precious in life,
but what I've been talking about is my wife

When I looked at her on our wedding day
I was so excited I forgot what to say

But, I knew she was mine till the day I die,
and everything she needed I would gladly supply

When I look at her it's hard not to believe,
that God made her just like Adams' Eve.

Devereaux R Divens
WISDOM
The Lord's wisdom founded the earth,
his understanding established the universe.

There are two things that will protect you like a fence,
that is wisdom and common sense.

Wisdom is more precious than all of our jewels,
and with common sense it can be used like a tool.

Wisdom gives you things you can benefit from,
it will make you rich so you won't be no bum.

Wisdom will give you a long, long life,
And it will even help you to find a wife.

Now honor comes along with it too,
and it will keep people from thinking you're a fool.

But peace is something that is hard to find,
but with wisdom it's with you all the time.
Wisdom will give you another treasure,
something the devil counterfeits, it's called pleasure.

Stacey Grammick
CASTLES IN THE AIR
The winter was the longest and the coldest one,
I've seen in years.
It's been a week since our food supply ran out,
And the water Joseph brought in huge rain barrels
Ran out three days ago.
The kids are sick, and so is Joseph—
My loving husband.
I must admit I too am weak with hunger.
This winter was a slow, bitter one;
But I can see from my chair by the drafty window,
The snow has stopped, and the sun is out.
And I'm hopeful we'll all make it.

Richard James Driggers
EMPTINESS OF OLD
There are veins, but as with the heart,
Filled with only air
Deep, exhausted emptiness, seek happiness,
Oh I wouldn't dare;
Fall back to tired emptiness.
As with a path, that's trodden bare,
My heart lies hard and cold
I sink to sleep in this exhausted
Emptiness of old.

Loretta M Kailburn
LADY SLIPPERS

To the Kailburn family—with love.

Lady-Slippers, Lady-Slippers
Prettiest little orchid, I've ever seen
You grow in the woods, called "Rolling-Stone"
Where the deer and bear run free.
Lady-Slippers, Lady-Slippers
Prettiest little orchid, I've ever seen
You wake up every morning,
With the sunlight on your face,
And the wild turkeys call.
Lady-Slippers, Lady-Slippers
Prettiest little orchid, I've ever seen
You've kissed each night by the evening dew,
And go to Sleep, to the Whippoorwills' call
Lady-Slippers, Lady-Slippers
Prettiest little orchid, I've ever seen.

Bryan Randolph
ROSE, HEART

For Debi.

The Rose is wrapped around the Heart
Unknowingly she punctures with her thorns
Hurting, bleeding, causing great pain
Blood trickling, hurts like an acid rain
Beauty of the Rose the Heart sees
Ignoring the pain from his wounds
Wanting, yearning for the Rose
Cannot have her, the Heart knows

The Heart can't, won't complain at all
For the Rose gives him great joy
Dying, killing of the Heart
Began to suffer from the start
From strength he, the Heart, will survive
Still wanting the love of the Rose
Wounded scarred from this Rose
The pain and hurt she hardly knows

Robert T Lewis
THE VOID

This poem is dedicated to my wife, Allegra and my sons, Roberto, Marcos and Xavier.

With all of life's experiences, a little is left. We touch a soul or two along the way,
A leaf, perhaps a flower; wild and bright. Now and then the tears will flow, flooding the
faces we so carefully prepare with glitter and soft hues. We cannot hide that little bit that remains;
it shows. Penetrating our platitudes and Sunday wears; it never slumbers off nor sleeps; it stays.
After the tears, the cares and the worn-out affairs, something is left behind—Dragging.
Even after the arms, long and folded, legs lean and crossed; words exchanged and friendships
Perhaps lost; a little stays on. It never goes away; it never leaves.

We see it in the pain beneath our cheeks, in the tear filled eyes, the forced smile.
Yes, even in the thunder of tumultuous laughter we can detect a little bit.
It hangs on tight. At times it spreads, slowly, seeping through the cracks of forgotten thoughts
And faded memories turned gray by time and unexpressed emotions—
Life, drained to a single drop.
Silently still, it lingers for a time; a time with no ending; no resting place in sight. And so
We send out signals. Signs of pleasure or regret. At times, a bitter statement of resentment or disdain.
Not being cognizant of how it stains and stays around; settling in some cold and distant corner of the mind.

Meanwhile, we take the time we have to chase or erase the time we waste.
Knowing that time
Can never take away that bit that stays; that which permeates the fabric of our days and ways.
Our wonderful dreams and our feelings, our deepest thoughts and fears; the lengthy tales
Of our glorious years; all perfused by that little bit that is there, even as the final curtain falls.
A little is always left. It stays. And so, we move through this puzzling incarnation leaving a trail;
A path behind with bits of pain, our name, rainy days mixed with moments of sparkle; and sometimes periods of quiet loneliness. It never leaves; it stays until we die.

Mary Ellen Varley
WHEN SUMMER LEAVES

When summer leaves it takes a
  part of me
  With flight of birds; the
  restless, eager part
That sought in every flower and
  tree
  And down each lane sweet
  treasures for the heart.

The extra miles I've gone to see a
  stream
  Cascading over rocks, to watch
  white peaks
Of mountains in the morning
  sunlight gleam,
  And listen as the thunderous
  ocean speaks.

These are memory; quiet
  September brings
  The little sound of crickets in
  the field,
A rose more vivid where the
  aster springs
  Amid the slow decay the
  garden yields.

The first shy yellow leaves begin
  to dance
  To any hapless tune the wind

  provides;
While I accept, who walked
through summer's trance,
  The folding-in of autumn
  eventides.

William D Pekoske Sr
THE CUCKOO'S CALL

I've got a little cuckoo clock
Just hangin' on the wall.
Sometimes I sit and watch the hands
To wait the cuckoo's call.

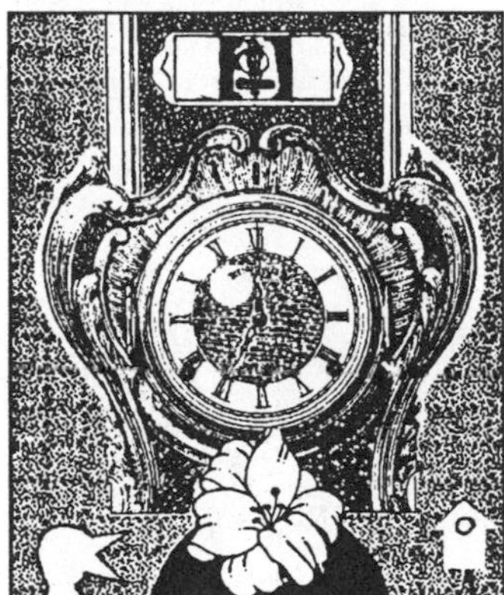

He never leaves his wooden nest.
I sit and wonder why,
But he does come out to cuckoo! -
The time is passin' bye.

Silvia Houchen
FREEDOM OF FLIGHT

In Loving Memory, with Deep admiration and love; I dedicate this poem to my "mutti" (mother) Margot Buchholz, without her I could not reach my dreams.

Freedom is the sense of tranquility within oneself, the inner peace from one journey onto the next

Freedom I seek as I gracefully swarm down, towards a brightly coloured sailboat, in my passing still flight.

The sky so blue and clear within the reach of heaven's delight
I want to be free, and spread my wings across the magical sea.

Flying high and gracefully across the shimmering sky, I want to see it, to feel it, the salt of the sea, to taste it, to become it

I want to be free!

I am the many wonders of God, I am the pure white dove, I want to be able to touch the sky and reach beyond it, I want to be able to taste the salt of the sea, why? because I am me.

I fly beyond the cotton-balled clouds, reach out for it, grasp it, with my velvety whitened feathers, I want to see beyond the ocean and the sea, the freedom of flight.

Free as the white dove as I am, full of grace and feel of the Earthliness wonders within my wings and the tranquility across my face . . .

I am Free!

Firdaus E Udwadia
AT SUNRISE

They flung him against the black
stone wall
And quickly made a silent row,
They saw him trembling at the heels
Yet none asked why or whatever for.

They raised their rifles to their brows,
As the gentle glimmer touched their
swords,
Took aim to drop him to the floor
Yet none asked why or whatever for.

His mind had come to a silent halt
As he walked the hallway to the door,
To enter that bright enormous room
In which there were no words, no
song.

Last he remembered, when he was
small,
His mother marking on the wall,
To tell her darling son, how tall—
He stood erect a moment:
Before the fall.

Wendy T Vandermeir Brown
TO LOVE

Love;
  a word left unspoken, but
  knowing it's in the heart
  the feeling in one's heart,
  when love is true
  a gift given so free, so
  thoughtful from the heart
  the touch of your hand, so
  tender and warm
  a moment of silence, many
  thoughts are revealed
  the look in your eyes, like
  stars in the sky
  a kiss that says, "I love you,"
  and always will
  the feeling I get, whether
  you're near or far
  a cold night embracing you, I'll
  always be warm
  the times we have shared our
  ups and downs
  a time for comfort, when pain
  or sorrow is near
  the tender care that's given in
  every way
  a lonely night, in my dreams
  you are
  the knowing, when one wants
  to be alone
  a moment to show I love you,
  no matter what
A prayer, I pray, you'll be there when
I awake,
  to love twice as much each
  passing day.

Gwendolyn Collins
FRIENDS

Friends . . .
What are friends?
Are they people
Are they dreams
Or just a word.
A word that means nothing, nothing
to me.
Friends come and go just like night
and day.
Are they people
Are they dreams
Or just a word.
A word that makes you feel wanted.
What is the true meaning?
When you call someone a friend—
Does it mean just someone you know
Or someone who cares
Or someone who also doesn't want to
be alone.
I wish I knew.

Mary D Sands
NIGHT OF MY BELONGING

To M. who has hastened the dawn.

Ah night of my belonging!
  Sweet honey of delight!
Bright memories come thronging
  To bathe my soul in light.

Rosé to ease the senses,
  The pillow-satin bright.
Banished the last defences
  See, now, with inner sight.

Pour from the vessel flowing
  All vestige of the fright
That ends, beyond the knowing,
  Deep agony—black night.

Come, let the golden shower excite
My spirit wing to song and flight.

Lori Maureen Kephart

Lori Maureen Kephart
YOU AND I

We have found each other
We will never need another
At least that's what we say
You and I
We will always be true
We will never be blue
At least that's what we say
You and I
We will always be there
We will always care
At least that's what we say
You and I
But late at night
When I cry
I wonder if we lie
You and I

Lori Maureen Kephart
DECEMBER

December is a Unicorn
With a gleaming silver horn
Who has never had a master
And flies all the faster

having never known a bridle
nor a rider, nor a rein
A beast of snow and silver
Whose soft wings slice the skies
With a swooshing singing sound
December is a Unicorn
Blowing through the sky
Howling its windsong cry

Joseph E Barnes
ODE TO A FALLING BUDDY

To all the vets.

In this far-off land, a letter from home meant so much,

Our loved ones, remember us, by keeping in touch,
we read letters, even in the pouring rain,
some letters meant love, while others meant pain.

How much can a lonely soldier bear,
to lose a loved one, he showed so much loving care,
trip flares going off, tracers lighting up the sky,
in the darkness, we shudder when we hear a buddy cry.

Through the mud and the blood, we trod through the night,
while in each man's heart, a secret prayer to God, for the morning light,
while knowing at the crack of dawn,
we had to face that searing sun,
on just a little sleep, or no sleep at all,
and giving thanks to God, we hope
and pray, no more buddys fall.

Star Byrge
A FEAR THAT WON'T GO AWAY
With the click of the door each morning,
My heart does skip a beat.
I pray to God all day long,
Until our eyes do meet.
I know your job is underground,
And that you love it so.
But, honey, sometimes it's true,
I want to beg you, please,
please, don't go.
So, if a tear does trickle down,
And I have a smile, not a frown.
Just remember, I love you so,
while you're underground.

John F Chavez
THE QUACK OF DAWN

To the pretty girl who works at the Burger King, I hope this poem brings you happy dreams.

Quacker on neighborhood patrol, what a
Quacker Jack was he
A badge from Quacker Oates
Box, shining on his feathery white chest,
made him, Dodge Quacker
devoted to the Beak
a little quackle
the darnest duck
any neighborhood of
Counsel Quackers
would want.
Let me Quack a note
the deductible Quacker said. I see the
jumping Dogo-bulls are
spying on me, as usual
Cleo, jumped above the red brick fence
first, saying I seen him first, then
Bojo, jumped higher, no I seen him first
then Cleo again higher, no I seen him first
and then again Bojo higher, no I seen him first,
How's a duckling to quickly
Quack a case
with those jumping Dummies
Hounding
Dodge Quacker

Four rabbits were found laying
quietly dead on Corrale Street
Must be the work of
Evil dog-Benton
he hates rabbits
deducted Dodge
Quacker.
Was brought up wrong by the
Dolton "Kid" gang
of Spits Streets. Dodge Quacker's
oath was to protect
Long Ears Avenue
Dog-Gone, Dodge Quackered
to the evil dog-Benton
the ducks Quackle, Crime news
says they found Quietly dead on
Corrale,
one Quackly morning
the evil dog-Benton
a huge carrot through his teeth
this mark can only be from one
from the Badge
of
Dodge Quacker

Mary Whibley Bissett
DELAYED LOVE
Darling, remember that old saying,
"Rome wasn't built in a day."
And many times you showed me,
Your love is that way.
But eve' as time goes by,
And you have gone away,
In life and perhaps death, until
I'm sure there's no hope for
your love,
Will I finally mourn.

Several times I thought
perchance
You might still care.
For your cherished ring,
None had seemed to share.
So now, if the curtain must
Fall on my unhappy romance,
Remember, with me to reconcile,
You will always have the
chance.

James M Brown
WHEN THE GRASS WAS GREEN
Many years ago—only yesterday it seems—
Trodding the land and fishing the streams,
A barefoot boy, when years were lean,
Always happy when the grass was green.

Early morn the cock would crow,
He seemed to say, "It's time to go!"
Breakfast, then doing chores that were routine,
Always happy when the grass was green.

Feeding the stock and working the land,
With time for others—a helping hand;
Dreams of a better future not yet seen,
Always happy when the grass was green.

The peace and joy of those days
Did not stay; they went other ways;
The winds of tomorrow were unforeseen,
But yesterday's grass will always be green.

John J Bracken Jr
FOND MEMORIES
As I sit by the fireplace
My fond memories of her come to mind
Her beautiful face and wonderful grace
A loving heart that helped all the lonely souls.

She brightens up a room with her songs and words
Giving new meaning to dreams and hopes.
For I'll always remember the fond memories that I shared with her and her with me.

I'll never forget all the times of laughter and sorrow in her heart
Yes, the fond memories I have and will treasure forever.

Barbara D Burton
CATS
Cats, Cats, Cats
Everywhere I Look,
Digging In The Garbage;
Tearing Up My Books!

Cats, Cats, Cats
Jumping Everywhere,
Getting Into Trouble;
Giving Me Gray Hair!

Cats, Cats, Cats
Climbing Up Big Trees,
Sharpening Their Claws;
To Dig Into My Knees!

Cats, Cats, Cats
Washing Their Faces And Paws,
Keeping Themselves Clean;
To Obey All Kitty Laws!

Cats, Cats, Cats
Taking A Long Nap,
Picking Their Favorite Place—
On Their Master's Lap.

Evelyn C O'Brien
ENCOUNTER
It was brief
Unspoken was the question
Would we meet again
I was free
But not he
So time and again
We passed each other
A smile was all
In that exchange
But the spark, that flared
Became a flame.
Time has passed.
Thankful we are.
We have no shame.
For the fire that burned
Became embers of a fleeting dream
And that is all, it will ever seem

Vivian Elsifor

Vivian Elsifor
FULFILLMENT
Treasured friend, I see ache
in your eye,
I fear you distress far too much
Over my dilemma and try
To shield me from all hurt, to touch
Me as I tear myself apart and cry.

Indeed, problems are for solving;
My soul pleads for calm, quiet peace.
Confusion ceases—resolving
Trust in God brings blessed release
Of faith in myself—with pure absolving.

I search for proven paths to follow
Information and high esteem
Stretches my mind to bestow
Skills and talents that reach a dream
Of fulfillment, traced in bold tableau.

Living can be strife and conflicts
Conscious integrity and love,
Loyalty to ideals predicts
The choices I make: the consequence of
My judgements and visions, passing time depicts.

Andrea H Bues
SEARCHING FOR SELF-WORTH

To my children. I hope I can instill in you the self-esteem you need, so that you may have the confidence to pursue your dreams.

Days roll into nights, nights into days
I just can't seem to get out of this haze
I need a way out—a chance to escape
I want to stop and set my own pace
Pulled to the left and pulled to the right
Give here, give there, am I doing it right?
Give till I'm empty, give till I'm drained

When can I stop and relax my brain?
I long for the peace of being alone
No one to upset me, not even a phone
No children, no husband, no errands of mine
Only the time to find peace of mind
A few minutes, a few hours, a few days to myself
So I can get in touch with the dreams I put on a shelf
I must find something to do with my life
There's a lot more out there than just being a wife
Somewhere, somewhere is the right road
But I must find it fast, for I'm getting old
I know my happiness lies in a career
I just have to learn to get over my fears
If someone could help me—just give me a push
Someone to support me on the road that I took
I can't seem to get started. Please show me the way
I know it's not easy and I'd have to pay
But just to be on it, oh how happy I'd be
FINALLY I would be doing something for me!!!!!!!!

Debra Blundell
HOMELESS

As I involved myself wholly,
in my daily routine.
I caught a glimpse of misfortune,
as I have never seen.

To be at one with the elements,
no way to express emotion.
Strong willed to survive,
and to tolerate social shun.

With only meager belongings,
to appreciate simple needs.
How could they take for granted,
this way of life indeed.

I wonder why you
choose this life.
Of being homeless,
and always in strife.

I look at you NOW,
and you know what I see.
How very real you are,
it could just as well be me!

Edmond J Burgess Jr
BEYOND THE HIGH HORIZON

MOTHER: To the best Mother a Son can have . . . I dedicate this poem to the one I love the most; That's you, Mom.

Beyond the high horizon above
there's a place called Heaven
where the Lord lives.
He is the greatest man that ever lived.
I'm always counting my blessings.
I thank God for my life.
Just like I thank God for yours.
He heals people who believe in Him.
The Lord puts angels right here
on earth to watch over us.
Oh Lord, show me the way
when the day comes.
I pray to him every night.
You can say that I believe in Him.
There will be a day we will all be
beyond the high horizon to meet the
God All Mighty.

Marie Kovach Basto
A REFUGEE

Oh! What makes you sad?
Hardships that are so bad.
There are unshed tears in your eyes
From all your broken ties.
This is not home for you
Trials and tribulations follow too.
All is not well.
You are hollow like an empty shell.
Glad that you are living
But there are thoughts of dying.
You are in a strange land
And cannot speak or take a stand.
Just because you had to flee
You became a refugee.

John Vincent Mameli
THINK OF THE SUN

To my daughter Neysa Leigh.

Think of the sun,
Think of the moon,
Think of the stars that
gleam your eyes;

Think of the birds,
Think of the bees,
Think of the blue that fills
the sky.

For the things you want are buried
In the center of your mind,
Not the perfumed scent
That only bares a name.

The things you keep and cherish
Can be wealthier than none,
On the sidelines,
In the corners of your mind.

Think of the birds,
Think of the trees,
Think of the seas and wonder
why;

Think of the rhymes,
Think of the times,
Think of the rhythm of your
life.

If they ever seem to take you,
Break you,
Make you fall away;

Think of the sun,
Think of the moon,
Think of the thought of
every day.

Mildred Crowdus
TINY ROSES IN THE SNOW

As the snow flakes begin to trickle down from the skies
I cannot withhold my cries.
It seems that it was only hours before
That the long limousine came to my door.
Visions of lowering the casket into the ground
With my tiny baby boy in the basket resounds.
Just five short months to live, and
Jamie's family had barely time
to give
Love, hugs, kisses and a proper good-bye
Before that terrible sickness ended his life.
Tearful farewells from family and friends
Suddenly brought Jamie's life to an end.
And now as I peer out my window to the cemetery
Down across the road,
The only thing to comfort me now are the
Tiny roses in the snow.

Larry M Crandall
BEAUTY IS IN THE EYE OF THE BEHOLDER

Beauty is in the eye of the beholder
And your beauty I have beheld many times
But this is not a poem of lyrics and rhymes
But my thought as I watch your eyes gazing into mine
Your eyes are mystifying yet dazzling
As I watch your eyes
They send from them a feeling of warmth and friendship
They express your every desire
The first time I kissed you they dazzled and danced
As if showing your approval
They shown magnificently, bringing a glowing sensation to your entire body
As I kissed you, and your lashes began to close
I saw in your eyes, a wonderful expectation of the kiss to follow
As you opened your eyes again
They almost seemed to smile and say that was beautiful

Sandra Frost
INDIAN BORN

Indian Born
A warrior among his race
Cherokee heritage do not face

Indian Spirit
So free and fierce, full of rage
The wolf paces in its cruel cage

Indian Heart
Longings—None can ever see
His hidden self, the eagle free

Indian Eyes
Their fierce challenge beware
Gently malicious, they softly dare

Indian Brave
True rings his swift battle cry
Echoed with an Indian sigh

Clarence E Cahill
MAY I EACH DAY

Dedicated to my Daughters Christi Colleen Cahill & Debra Ann Cahill.

I have been given so many days in my life, May I not foolishly spend them.
May I rise early each morning to hear the quiet sounds normally lost to the voice of the city.
May I walk in the darkness of the night and smell the fragrance of the dew on the grass.
May I see the smile on a happy child's face and may I see the look of love in a mother's eyes.
May I give to someone each day a warm smile to lighten their load, and may I say a kind word in a day of trouble to lift them up.
May I each day of my life offer a hand of friendship to help fill a lonely life, and may I offer a portion of love to Someone who has lost but will love again.
May I each day seek the good that is in everyone and may I take part of that good as part of me.
May I each day think of someone loved in the past and wish them part of my happy day.
May I somehow make each of my days left worthy of living
so that I may help someone else know the value of their days.
May I, as my days grow less, reach my last day with this thought, "This has been the best day of my life."

Trudy Whittington

Trudy Whittington
MR. POSEY

There once was a man, called Mr. Posey.
Who in fact was, very, very nosey.
Bad he was, and sneaky, as a mouse.
That day he approached, Miss Lily's house.
Through her window, he did, peak.
Lord you never heard, such a terrible shriek.
Took no time, before he fled.
Tripped, and fell, into her flower bed.
Miss Lily was mad, one could tell.
Across the yard, she, ran like hell.
With a pan, she struck, his head.
In a flash, she knocked him, dead.
When anyone asks, people truthfully, say.
Mr. Posey, just disappeared, one day.

Monica Cotten
IT'S ALL GONE

It's all gone now darling, no more sad good-byes.
Just these last few million teardrops, that are fallin' from my eyes.
It's so hard to believe, that it's all gone so fast.
But I guess some things, just weren't meant to last.
It's all gone now baby, time for a new start.
No more broken promises, no more breakin' my heart.
Now you go your way, and I will go mine.
I can make it on my own, just give me time.

It's all gone now darling, nothin' left to say.
I'm just going to take things, day to day.
You've got your freedom, and you're on your own.
Because . . . baby, it's all gone.

Marian B Couch
A NAIL

Man has many uses for a nail
Without it we couldn't ride the rail
Boats and ships couldn't sail
Many inventions its uses entail

Wanting to work with a nail
Which only our hands can avail
To be done on any scale
Done not right would fail

If I couldn't hit the head of a nail
I could lose my fingernail
And no words would avail
I'd get sick, my face would turn pale

Somewhere under a board is the home of a snail
Here he is hidden, safe from the gale
He'd better watch out, might come through a nail
Against the point of which he has no act to prevail

In stories of the life of a nail
There hangs many a tale
From across the way I heard a wail
You guessed it, an old woman stepped on a board with a nail.

Fern Yvonne Case
A SUMMER DREAM

I was sitting by a Shimmering Stream, when I heard his warm soft voice whispering through the breeze. He didn't have to say another word, as he gave me a gentle squeeze. I wanted to be with him forever, the feeling was right on that warm summer night.

As we stood there side by side, he asked me to be his bride. "Then I woke up," It was only a dream. Every summer, I sit by that shimmering stream and wait for the man in my dream. Till someday he will come, and we will be together as one!

Norma J Carpenter
LETTER TO MOM

My poem, "LETTER TO MOM," is dedicated to my mom, Gertrude Jenkins, who was the wonderful Christian, example I have tried to emulate with my own family.

Dear Mom,

If I were eloquent in speech, as I would like to be,
I'd open up my heart to you, and try to make you see,
How everyday I love you more and how much you mean to me.
First, I should like to tell you, of your sunny precious smile, and how when things are going bad, just to think of you makes the pain worthwhile.
Then I remember how you would say, "Have your good times now, my dear, for your youth will fade away, and many years from now, you'll be much too old to play,
Then you'll have sweet memories to cherish, for comfort and to love,
Just be sure my darling daughter to get your guidance from above."
Then your brow would become furrowed, and you'd take me by the hand,
And you'd try your best to teach me and to make me understand,
That all of life is not a party, that sometimes the way is hard,
And you'd tell me not to falter, that God would always be standing guard.
Mother, dear, If I could just tell you, if I could make you see,
That I want to be outstanding, and to make you proud of me,
And though fame and fortune may go by, and never smile on me,
So that I could build you a monument, for all the world to see,
I shall try to live up to the standards you have set,
And follow in your sweet footsteps, so that everyone will know, that you were a guiding angel, And your path did upward go.
Though I cannot say these things, Mom, dear, for I'm not eloquent in speech,
I'll end with simple statement, I think you are a peach!

Bob A Cloyd
DREAMS AND WISHES

To my wife Joanna.

If a lonely man's dreams did come true,
I'd force myself to sleep at night
Just so I could dream of you . . .

If a lonely man had two wishes,
And these wishes did come true,
I'd wish for you to love me,
And the other I'd save for you . . .

If a lonely man's tears could write Love songs, before love songs were Thought of, I could write so many Love songs with these tears that fall for you . . .

But, since these are Just Dreams & wishes which seldom do come true,
This poem I send with Hugs & Kisses with all my,
Love for you . . .

Marie H Coleman

Marie H Coleman
FRIENDS

To my loving children, Barbara, Dirk and Dwight. Also, Silvena and Desma, Muriel and Mrs E. Greene. Always believed in me and encouraged.

Friends! How refreshing that sounds to the ear
Whenever we say the word "Friend"
A warm, delightful feeling glows from within
A pleasant expression beams on our faces, then
A twisted smile forms on our lips
Just the thought of the word . . . causes a tingling sensation
A sense of satisfaction of being alive
What is a Friend?
A friend is a thoughtful and trustworthy Individual
One who stands by you . . . not only during the good or pleasant times
But at your side when days are dark . . .

filled with entangle difficulties
When you feel as though, you are at the End of the Road
A Friend is constant and true
One who does not criticize or condemn you during perilous times
Instead, will console and help guide you through those gloomy and grievous times
The world Friend has a profound meaning
. . . sometimes unexplainable
Oh! A Friend is like the Evening star
That brightly shines and glitters in the Evening dust
Friends! How refreshing that sounds
. . . like a breath of fresh air
No doubt, Friends make up the constellation of our world.

Marie H Coleman
MY THOUGHT OF TIME

Although the time is speeding fast
Memories still linger from the past
Intermingled with pleasant and unpleasant thoughts
Although Time has changed many things
There are some things that never change
Future days are not foreseen
But, they hold many unknown things
Life's road is like a long winding tortuous stairway
With just a dim glare of light beyond
Although the present time is now
These days are seen with many, many Complex Things
For Life is full of Ups and Downs
Although Time heals all wounds, 'twas said,
We do not know what Time will tell . . .

Marie H Coleman
ALWAYS A REASON

There's always a reason for something
No matter what is the problem
There's always a solution for something
If we attempt the End . . . for search will find it out
There's always a reason for a relationship—whether it is for love or money or comfort or revenge
There's always a reason for Everything
Though, sometimes, It may twirl our lives around.
There's always a reason for the beautiful and Colorful Rainbow
That adorns the clear blue sky
It usually appears soon after
A destructive storm and hale
As we look above in amazement
We see the sun Agleam . . . descending its torrid and brilliant rays
To Amend the Effects of the Storm
So always Remember the Rainbow
When Unpredictable Adversities Befall
There's always a reason for something
And tomorrow . . . brings New Hopes and Joys.

Marie H Coleman
HOME

This poem is dedicated to my Beloved Parents. Alfred and Elsa. Mr. and Mrs. Hemsley. Memories Linger.

Home! sweet, sweet Home
Oftentimes it was said, that a man's Home is his Castle
And home is where the heart lies
When we think of Home . . . as we always do
A sense of security, tranquility, and contentment, also
A joyous feeling overwhelmed our Emotions
The strong tie is like the Bonding of a young, loving mother with her newborn Infant
Home is the place where our laughter and our tears are sincerely felt and shared
Home is the place where we are treated the Best
Home is the place where we grumble the Most
Home is the place of Refuge . . . the place we seek when illfate encounters
Surprisingly! with all our faults . . . we are still accepted, cherished, loved and protected
Truly . . . there's
No Place
Like Home . . .

Marie H Coleman
SPRINGTIME

The spring season is here
The swallows are singing and flying merrily in the air
Spring is the season for Survival
The green leaves sprout on the boughs of trees
The beautiful flowers are blooming again
Rendering sweet fragrance and beauty to the environment
An inspiration for men to enjoy Nature!
April showers reflect the advent of Spring
The cool fresh scent of Spring is in the air
The scent is so fresh and natural—it almost takes

Our breath away
Old Mother Nature indicates, that sometimes,
Simple things in Life are essential to make it complete.
Spring is the time for Revival
The time to cultivate new innovations
The time to restructure our lives
The Spring Season is here
Jesus is this Season!

Marie H Coleman
THE PICTURESQUE SUNRISE

As I look out of the window
At early morn—just at the break of day
I was entranced by the Exotic Picturesque Sunrise
It stimulated and created magnificent imageries
of that Celestial Place—those Pearly Mansions
Far beyond the grey-blue sky
It was a beautiful sight . . .
The sun beamed and glistened
through transparent white clouds
Emitting and scattering various sparkling red rays of sunlight
Creating marvelous exquisite sceneries
to the adjacent grey-blue sky
Dazzling and blinding the vision of sight
It was a beautiful view . . .
Never forget to look above
At early morn—just at the break of day
To see the Exotic Picturesque Sunrise, then
Thank God for the priceless, precious Gift of Sight
And the opportunity for the invaluable Gift of Life
To serve Him . . .
and to see another day . . .

Rudy Bodnar
ALONE

It is dark and desolate, I can hear my heart beat,
Its thudding is slow, my body grows weak,
My room is empty, there is nothing I own,
My life disperses like seed that are sown,
I feel scattered; remote, set apart from the world,
Like a flag in waiting that is never unfurled,
My midnight approaches and I'm so utterly cold,
How I wish I had someone, if only to hold,
But dreams shatter like glass by Despair's piercing tone,
As the shadows enshroud me and I remain all alone.

Carolyn S Coxson
THE APPLE OF HIS EYE

To My Daughter Kimberly, In Memory Of Her Beloved Grandfather, Richard B. Coxson.

She was too young to lose someone,
It's truly very sad.
Death took the innocence and fun
From the childhood she'd had.
At least it's comforting to know;
She was the apple of his eye.

All she has now are memories
Of days now long gone by.
Her mind filled with inquiries,
Why did Papa have to die?
They say all wounds, with time, will heal
And so each day I pray
That the empty sadness that she feels
Will soon just go away

To be replaced with thoughts
Of the times that they both shared
And comforted by the knowledge
Of how much her Papa cared.
She was the apple of his eye.

Arminda A Guerrero
WHEN I KNEW . . .

For my first honest to goodness boyfriend, my darling Jarod.

When I found out I was in love with you,
I only knew what it seemed to be.
I loved you.
When I knew that our love would be so true,
Just me and you,
It made our love seem brand-new.
Every footstep I hear,
I wish it was yours.
Every voice that is near,
It has to be yours.
Every time of the day,
I want to be with you.
The sparkle in your eyes,
The moment we rise,
A rose that brings us near
Love rings until we hear.
When I found out I was in love with you,
I only knew this was meant to be.
I love you.

Willie C Cole
BY FAITH WE LOOK TO THE LORD

Lift your eyes Heavenward my child;
Beholding Jesus at God's own right hand;
This "Pilgrim's Journey" may be long, you'll be blessed with Eternal life in the after awhile;
He calls all His true children against evil to take a firm stand:

We must assuredly know;
That this path from Earth to Heaven can be very long;
While we dare not tread where He didn't go;
Today, Help us Lord! to realize in Heaven you are on your throne;

Because of what happened many years ago;
When our Heavenly Father sent Jesus thy only "Begotten" Son
Through obedience to His Gospel we may this "Christian Race" run;

This is the hope we must firmly as an anchor hold on to;
Though many times our bodies be wracked with unbearable pain;
We must without fail remember: the "Great Physician" is near, True!;
To lift us up and heal us for this is in His plan;

Are you weary and heavy-hearted?;
Then my Brother, Sister, and my Friend;
Tell it to Jesus! Tell it to Jesus! while weeping over "Loved Ones"; departed;
He'll save us now, and someday in "Mansions" we'll be blessed by Him;

Nick Edward Nicholson
PICTURE THIS:

The sky, animated,
portrays the scene.
The stars, diamonds,
spark distant thoughts.
The moon, full,
illuminates rippling waves.
The air, salty,
enlivens the night.
The ocean, playful,
cools the beach.
The sand, sticky,
whines under footstep.
The prints, trailing,
find the couple.
The silhouette, devoted,
wanders the shore.
Your touch, soothing,
warms my heart.
My lips, delicate,
brush your cheek.
Our thoughts, quick,
ponder the dream.

Dawn Greenman
MOTHER AND FATHER

Like the tinsel on the tree,
your love shines through to me.
Like the cookies and the cakes,
your hearts are pure and sweet.
Kindness and love are at my feet,
anytime I need them.
Because kindness and love
describes you two.
Always around,
Caring forever,
For worse and for better.
For those very special treasures,
I thank you forever.

Diane D Carter

Diane D Carter
LOVE MOOD

Fresh Red Roses
Mellow music
A burning fire
A deep desire

Heat Seated Passion
A sensual fashion
Romantic meal
A man that's real

A Taste Of Honey
Love on the money
A scent to last forever

Sorry If I Leave You Never!

Diane D Carter
DELIVERY

I sit beside the quiet sea
I need you Lord, deliver me
I often sit and wonder why
Within my heart, I want to cry

I need you Lord, to hold my hand
And help me Lord to understand
My life is not what I wish to be
Oh help me Lord, deliver me

With each new morn I do Lord pray
To help me through another day
With sickness around me and jealousy
Oh help me Lord, deliver me

I know I'm not the perfect child
Be patient Lord, for just a while
And open up my eyes to see
You've helped me Lord, with delivery

Joe Billingsley
NOW I LAY ME DOWN

To Mrs. Gwen Accawi.

Now I lay me down to sleep.
I pray the Lord my soul to keep.
If I should die before I wake;
I pray the Lord my soul to take.

As I lie upon my bed,
I'm sure I hear the countless dead.
I hear them calling out my name.
They call to me without shame.

I dreamt the Reaper stood by my side.
I lowered my head and softly cried.
The tears washed away the sin,
As his hands caressed my skin.

I feel his presence; he is here.
The one I now hold so dear.
The time for me is almost nigh.
The time has come for me to die.

But when I go you need not mourn.
For in my place another will be born.
One whose heart will be filled with love.
One who'll be sent from the Lord above.

Roxanne Allen Duhon
BRIEF MOMENT

This poem is dedicated to Jessica my beautiful little girl who is very sick. Please get well baby. Mom loves you very much.

I think the sweetest joys in life,
are those more felt than seen.
When someone sees within our soul,
with nothing in between.
When trust is freely given,
hearts meet on common ground;
and this ignites a spark that lights up everything around.

Only when we grow more simple,
can the love within us all,
spill forth touching all with splendor;
that's a wonder to recall.
One such very tender moment,
was it given me to share,
when I came upon a red bird;
perched upon my feeder there.

He had weathered many winters,
it was very plain to see,
but his eyes were calm and steady,
as he turned to gaze at me.
And the thing I am most proud of, in all my life today . . .
is that he let me stroke his back,
and didn't fly away:

Connie S Martin
HE NEEDS ME NOT

He is so "Holy."
He is "Supreme."
Winds obey.
Birds do honor.

He needs me not.
Yet, He hurts
When I hurt.
He takes my hand
In His.
He says,
"I love you."
He offers me "Life."

I shall exalt Him.
I shall exalt Him.

Shawn Lucas
FILM AT ELEVEN

Hatred and war
is shown every night.
Misery and death,
they take the spotlight.
Racists and Nazis,
the stars of your shows.
Gang-wars and bloodshed,
so everyone knows.
Kingpins and druglords,
interviews with a killer.
And Girl Scouts selling cookies
is a last minute filler.
Death draws the ratings,
and blood's sent from heaven.
If you miss it at six,
there's film at eleven.

Jack Jackson
HEAVENLY HOAX

To my Dearest friend Kate. Thanx 4 always being there.

Death, the untimely end.
Our physical world comes to a stop
Our confused spirit runs through the universe
Joining the echoing choir,
"Jesus are u there?"

Lu Anne Harl
DEAR DADDY

To All The Daddies Of The World . . . And Those Who Love Them.

This is our first Christmas without you
Some people think we should be sad and blue
But we're going to be happy in spite
Of the fact that we miss you this Christmas night
You left us yourself to live in our hearts
And still touch our lives in many parts
We see you all around us day after day
We still try to do things in just "your way"
The wood reminds us of work-roughened hands
We see your love in well-tended lands
Hunters remind us you loved your guns
Laughter reminds us you loved to have fun
Our children let us see you in their eyes
Telling us you adored strong family ties
Your jacket that hangs there on the wall
Reminds us of the warmth you gave to us all
Your boots we see make us smile
For to make us happy you'd walk for miles
Your overalls maybe bring a few tears
They've been a part of you so many years
Sometimes the day gets a little brighter
Whenever we see your ashtray and lighter
We see you sitting there with a grin
And your hair straight up on your head again
Sometimes I feel memories are part of a soul
Because memories of you keep our hearts whole.

You're with us each day and night
The parts of us that are good and right
So we cannot possibly be sad and blue
For in our lives we'll always have you.

Federico A Camacho
ONCE IN A LIFETIME

To Rosa. Thank you for inspiring me with your beautiful presence and for believing in my poems.

Once in a lifetime a girl like you comes around
To then disappear without a chance to be found
As time goes by your memory lives on in a dream
That may never come true or so it seems
Resigned to reality one doesn't expect to see you again
Except it will be your lovely image that is recalled now and then

The words that have failed me will perhaps flow freely now
Expressing my need and desire to be with you somehow
Perhaps an act of fate may give me a second chance
To win your cherished heart and shower you with romance
An opportunity like this may have to be destined and divine
But to kiss you once would be sweeter than wine
And if you just had five seconds you could spare me
I'd spend an eternity to make you happier than anyone else could be . . .

Verona M Holtcamp
LOST

I was lost in that pitch black forest.
The trees so thick and dense.
There seemed no way to find my path.
The direction I looked made no sense.
I could not tell if it was north or south.
Or where I stood was east or west,
For the sun was gone from mortal view,
And to find an opening, I tried my best.

A little bird came into sight.
It seemed maimed with a drooping wing.
I thought if I could catch it,
I longed for the comfort it would bring.

I started after it as it hopped along,
Following, taking care not to bring it fright.
I crawled over logs and through the brush,
Forgetting the problem of my plight.

I followed it for quite some time,
And soon the seeming night turned to day,
As I stepped out onto a familiar path.
Then the little bird flew away.

Amy Denise Roberson
HELPING TO GIVE

Dear World,
What can I give that you want?

I will try my best to find the greatest gift.
I owe so much.

Where should I start first?
I will find the answer,
In a book?
On the ground?

Help me world . . . for I find your thanks.

Miriam R Ramming
DREAM

I was being chased
Down a long dark hall,
But suddenly the floor gave way
And, I began to fall.

I'm not sure what was chasing me,
But, I know I was scared.
I could not look back.
I wouldn't even dare.

The terror overcame me,
All, I could do was scream.
It must have been a nightmare,
A horrible, bad dream.

Even after waking,
I couldn't shake that fear.
It was like some sort of evil,
Was standing very near.

Sometimes even now,
That feeling is right behind me.
I wish there were some place to hide,
Where it just couldn't find me.

Maureen C Gould Wills
MY DAUGHTER

To Tamara Marie, My beautiful daughter, who brings love, happiness and sunshine into my life every day.

Why are you in such a hurry to pass
These beautiful, carefree days of laughter
To do the things that grownups do and
Say "Goodbye" to your youth ever after?
Why do you rush so quickly
Through diapers and dolls to dates
To a world of worries, troubles and trials
To a world that is filled with horrors and hates?
Why do you give up your nursery rhymes
For boys, clothes and perfume
Why are you bothered with little things
Like making your bed and cleaning your room?
Why do I ask such silly questions
Don't I remember that life can't be worse?
I know the answer to these foolish inquiries
Why? It's because you're a child, of course.

Donald D Hutchinson II
PEACE

Peace is where you find it
It is inside your heart and mind
You can only stumble across it when you're not looking
For those who look for peace rarely find it
It can be in a country field
With the flowers and wind and rolling fields of grass
Or in the city among parked cars and decadent old buildings that life seems to have deserted
Or on the ocean where fish swim freely under the shining waves
Or in the sky where the white clouds are painted against a blue canvas
Or in the forest where time has been stopped since the age of Camelot
Peace is elusive but can be found anywhere when you're not looking for it

Bunny Balint

Bunny Balint
MY TINY FRIENDS!

To my daughter, Dawn, who is the reason I have kept writing all these many years. She has always kept me going, never give up, she would say.

Hummingbirds are my special friends.
I'm getting used to all their trends.
As soon as I put out the red—sugar and water treat—
They're at the feeder—all ready to eat!

Their tiny bodies, always colored so nicely
Wings flutterin g so fast and precisely.
At times they sit on the feeder, while eating, to rest.
I often wonder, where they go at night, I never see a nest?

After I have my early morning swim—
While I fix my breakfast, they're on

the feeder's rim.
They feed when hungry about three times a day.
Often they eat later, and longer they stay.

Kristin Schorr
POEM TO BE READ SILENTLY
Who are you, old man;
Old grizzle-beard, deep-sea man,
Old watcher in the night?
Sit awhile, talk with me.
Tell me your dreams, your fears.
Speak!
Please, you have much to say,
Old hunch-back, tree-bark man;
Tell of your loves and lives.
Who are you, old man;
And what do you search for
By candlelight?

Sue DeGroff Raych
BUT NOTHING IS AS NIGHT TO DAY
Ice cream from persimmon trees,
Cashews from the pea green seas,
Cherries made in breweries,
Acorns fall from honey bees.

Apple pies are grapefruit nuts,
Cola comes from muddy ruts,
Oak trees felled are cigarette butts,
Calico cats grow in bamboo huts.

Cattle drives are turned to clay,
Lumps of coal are days in May,
Flowers are words, and what I say,
But nothing is as night to day.

Sue DeGroff Raych
UNTITLED
Though I cannot see your picture well in the darkness, Darling, I know it is there. The darkness hides your person from me, but I feel your presence near; I reach across the bed to touch you, and I know you are there.

Of all the many reminders I have of you every day, the most important is the everlasting impression of you that I keep in the corners of my mind. Never do I go through a day without the thought of you on my mind—of a precious moment once shared together, of a common goal we hope to achieve, or of a future we will someday realize.

As my pen makes known these words that were borne in my mind, they are cherished in my heart and preserved in my soul for eternity.

I have loved you in the past, do love you now, and will continue to love you until I draw my last breath. Once I am living no more, I will continue to love you forever after, in a world which knows no separation of lovers, nor pain, nor grief, but only peace and togetherness; something that all people spend their earthly lives searching for, rarely finding it. When we are together, and even when we are apart, I know it is you who have given me the most precious gift anyone can give or receive—Yourself.

Lydia Venta-Dobrovolsky
TRANSCENDENTAL PEACE
It's Sunday:
transparent atmosphere,
translucent calm,
light, fragrant breeze—
like soothing balm:
the inner thoughts are giving birth
to new horizons—Sanctified
Rebirth.
While God—
His Mighty Wings expanding—
folds you in Peace—
His loving Peace
surpassing human understanding.

Mil Pumroy
THE ARTIST

To Pop Dick.

It was nothing unique, a splash of color on a canvas;
done with a trembling hand that held both brush and bottle.
Still a flash of genius from sober times.
The color and shading all remembered.

Rosemary Meraz
IN SEARCH OF A ROSE

My poems are dedicated to those who believed in my search for a Rose, especially my mother and little sister, Irma.

One rose,
Small, red, standing alone
Surrounded by grass and weeds
It's not like the grass
Although its stem is green
It's not like the weeds
Although it may turn brown some day
It's a rose
Small, red, standing alone
Sometimes the grass and the weeds crowd it
Almost suffocate it
But it endures, determined to stay,
To live out its time
Sometimes it thirsts for water
But settles for dew
When it rains the selfish grasses
And rambling weeds steal away the raindrops

Yet she remains, determined to stay
When the sun goes down the rose seems to sigh
She no longer feels alone
But a part of everything that cannot be seen
No one can know
There are grasses and weeds in the field
No one can know there is only one rose
One rose, standing alone
Determined to stay
In the blanket of darkness
Surrounding the field
No one sees the droplet of dew
That forms on her petals
No one knows of the trickle of moisture
That gives the rose life
No, no one knows
For all you see is a rose
Standing alone
Determined to stay

Rosemary Meraz
SILENT TEARS
Silent tears were seen falling
dropping softly, gently gliding
Everything seemed sad surrounding
Head was resting on her palm
The smile I often took for granted
was not there, disappearing
like a sunset in the summer
with no traces left behind
Her tears were like a gentle rain
not a storm thundering loud
But soft and cleansing raindrops
meant to wash away the pain
I so wanted to console her
touch her, hug her, gently hold her
in some undisturbing way
Let her know, somehow I'm with her,
sharing what is hard to say.

Rosemary Meraz
WIND CHIME
Everyone should stop and listen
Sit and watch an elm tree grow
Watch the branches softly swaying
Like a violin and bow
The leaves so gently dangling
Keeping rhythm to the song
Trees and branches don't resist life
Or play tug-a-war you see
They just dance their lazy dance
To the music of the wind
Bending, laughing, never breaking
Stretching arms up to the sky
They don't question much their purpose
Nor defend it you might say
Just a swishing, cleansing movement
And a whispered wave invite
Join me, join me, steps are simple
Choreographer the wind!

Billy R Mayo
THE DAY THE EAGLE CRIED
The eagle soars, its wings outspread, its piercing eyes behold,
This shame we've dealt this land of ours, a shame that should be told.

He sees the ruins of mighty oaks, their limbs no longer spread,
The scars we've made with axe and saw, where once the bear could tread.

He sees the smoke where fire burns wild, he feels the touch of fear,
As light winds sail him high above—the eagle sheds a tear.
He lights upon a blackened snag and looks upon the waste,
Where once were meadows lush with flowers—erosion has their place.

There are no birds to sing their songs, no deer or fox to see,
No fields of blossoms bursting forth to feed the tiny bee.

He looks upon a land laid waste, so void of things of cheer,
His breast grows tight, it almost burst—the eagle sheds a tear.

The eagle spreads his mighty wings, he knows that he must fly,
To stay here in this wasted land he would surely die.

This was his home, this ravaged place, this empty dark domain,
The eagle knows this land he loves will never be the same.
He circles once with heavy heart, this land he holds so dear,
In solemn flight he sails away—the eagle sheds a tear.

Marla Kailburn-Washnis
2:52 AM

To Zack, John and David, my three wise men.

I am awakened.
My hand reaches out in the Darkness—
Searching, yearning for reassurance.
Emptiness meets the tips of my fingers,
Loneliness sweeps over my soul.
My hand, rests upon
my swollen belly—
Life waiting to be born.
Bring Light back into my Darkness
Dear Child,
Bring Life back into my Soul.
Awake me with a cry
End the silence of the night.
I caress your pillow beside me
And kiss it with a tear.
It's 2:52 AM
Are you awake too, Dear?

David James Meeler
BUT SHALL I LOSE A FRIEND?

Dedicated to Craig V. Winner, who, eight days short of his 28th birthday, fell victim to liver cancer. His spirit and determination deeply moved all who knew him.

Death Is A Man In A Long Black Gown
His Face, Forever Still
No One Knows Just Who He Is
And No One Knows His Will

He Moves With Silent, Supple Grace
To Search For Those Unknowing
With Velvet Grips of Cold, Hard Steel
His Love For Pain Not Showing

Compassion? That He Knows Not Of
His Heart? It Does Not Bleed
With Hooks Extended, Staff At Hand
He Satisfies His Greed

Though You May Think You're Not His Type
He Goes About His Works
Steer Clear Of Him, My Life-Long Friend
You Know Not Where He Lurks

Helen Ehline Lambert
EXODUS

To Paul, my youngest, a good son of whom I'm very proud!

Thankful to God for deliverance and aid—
His people, the Jews, observe Passover Day.
They pause to remember the plagues that He made,
So that Pharoah would weaken and give them their way.

They recall the night they prepared to flee—
The spotless lamb was slain.
The unleavened bread for all to see—
And the guidance of God made plain.

The blood of the lamb on each doorpost was brushed—
So the angel of death would pass by.

Time to depart—the assembly was hushed,
God's people no longer need sigh.

The Red Sea ahead filled them with fear—
Where could they go? Wasn't God near?
Then suddenly look!! There's a path thru' the sea—
The dread was gone, at last they were free!

They followed a pillar of cloud by day—
A pillar of fire by night.
For forty years God led the way—
Not once were they out of His sight.

Jason Berkowitz

Jason Berkowitz
HALLOWEEN
Giant Monsters,
Scary ghosts,
Halloween's the day,
You scare people most.
Spooky goblins,
Black cats.
Fill your bag
With ghostly hats.

Jason Berkowitz
WORLD PEACE DAY
There should be a day,
Named World Peace Day
Where no one will fight
From morning to night.
Where there are no wars
No guns or roars.
You can walk in the street
Without any worries.
Without any deaths
Or hearing marching feet.
One day it will come,
One day it will go,
Just one day without a foe.
You know,
There should be two days
Named World Peace Day.
No, three days.
No, I have a better idea,
Let's quit wars altogether.

Jason Berkowitz
A SUMMER PLACE
My summer place as you can see,
Is reading a book under a tree.
Watching the birds fly in the sky,
Hoping summer will never die.
The sky is so blue,
The book is blue too.

I looked in the sky,
Seeing the birds fly.
They are read and blue and green.
They don't look a bit mean.
They soar through the air,
So swift and so fair.

I'm just so happy to be reading my book,
And at the birds, taking a look.

Jason Berkowitz
THE REFRIGERATOR
The refrigerator looked at me,
So I looked at It, you see,
And It said,
"Why don't you just let me be!"

Jason Berkowitz
A FRIEND
A friend is someone who cares,
A friend won't put you down,
A friend is one of your peers,
And if you're sad, he'll act like a clown.

A friend is someone you can count on,
He/She might get you out of trouble.
He/She might even help you mow the lawn,
A friend would stay with you if your tummy bubbles.

Jason Berkowitz
FRIENDSHIP
Friend is a person who can help you.
Racing a friend is fun.
Interests in the same thing can help.
Enjoying to be with someone.
Never hurting that person
Do you have a good friend?

Jason Berkowitz
MUSIC
Sounds and Bangs,
Roars and clangs.
Whistles and toots,
Saxophones and flutes.
That's what music is.

Soprano and soul,
You don't pay a toll.
Or records with a tiny little hole.

Just turn on your dial,
And listen for a while.
So you'll know what music is made of.

Jason Berkowitz
MRS. GAMBA AND THE PANDA
Mrs. Gamba is cute like a panda.
But I don't think she's a panda, because
They're not allowed in school, you see.
She works at our school,
She's not even cruel.
Mrs. Gamba is a great teacher in school.
What's the difference, we all like her so.
If she is mad, the class will be sad.
Mrs. Gamba grows horns in her head.
She even grows a tail, that grows when she's mad.
We have a class raffle every week.
We get prizes that you can't beat.
At math we have fun.
At reading we read books that always get done.
Now you know what she can do.
Why don't you come along, and see her too.
Mrs. Gamba is nice to us, so she'll be nice to you.
The best thing to do is to come to our school,
And watch her walk by your classroom.
Mrs. Gamba is Number One, and so much fun.

Logan Baillod
I NEED SOMEONE

To Michael, the "someone" I finally found.

I need:
Someone to listen to me,
Someone to laugh with,
Someone who cares very deeply,
Someone who can share so much by saying so little.
Someone who can understand what no one else can,
Someone to give me a hug,
Someone who is a lot like me.
I need someone and I found that someone through God;
I found my special someone, and my special someone is you.

Agnieszka M Matejko
WALLS
Sometimes, when the walls come up
Brick by brick
All around,
They are big and strong:
Too high to climb over,
Too heavy to dig under;
We look up in despair
And discover
That we can fly.

Agnieszka M Matejko
SILENT ROOMS
When the leaves fell
there was silence.
It filled the rooms,
The empty hallways,
Stepping gently, softly
Along well worn paths.

The path to the morning coffee,
The tired floor
Around the kitchen table;
The silent tracks
Of daily rituals.

Juliet D Quevedo
MEMORIES
Memories of you keeps haunting me
Everytime I am lonely and homesick with you
Each night and day I pray for you
That one day you will come back to me.

Memories of you keeps me alive
Everytime I am alone and troubled
Oh! my love, here I am with hope
Waiting for you forever.

Thanks for the memories you shared with me
Happiness I felt deep inside of me
Hardships and miseries were forgotten
My darling, you love is the greatest of them all!

Joshua B Lederman
HER BEAUTY
Her beauty enrages me with joy.
When through each time passing,
and through seas of eyes we meet,
Her affection destroys My Soul
with peace.

Her walk intrigues me with cool neglect.
When from behind I grit,
and through our intimate vibrations,
her trails of joy deny me such.
Her smile engulfs me into the sand.
When through wet and dry she kills,
and through wet and wet I die.

My endless time escapes me.

Joshua B Lederman
THE MERMAID
In your eyes,
with which you look,
I saw the sea,
and sailed away.

In your eyes,
with which you look,
my heart, my heart
went up in flames.

When eyes I see,
besieged by milk,
Internalized
by fragile brow,
I see, you look,
the sky is low,
the stars are dimmed
by melted snow.

In your eyes,
with which you see,
there lies a place
I hardly know.

In your eyes,
with which you see,
each step I take
my intrigue grows.

And when our minds
embrace in thought,
I travel far
Beyond the blue,
find waters deeper
than I'd sought,
but suddenly
I long to drown.

Dorothy Peters Alfred
WINTERS BREATH
The wind blew and trees swayed at its breath
As little chimneys, reaching upward to the sky,
Blew their contents over the city.
For it was winter.

James H Goin
FLEEING TIME
I have lived, but I can't see where I've been,
to be blinded by reality are my sanctions for
time, I know not when. Entwined and strangled,
choking for some knowledge, just wondering again,
and again.

Pull me free from the depths of myself who
is lost, and looking to be someone. I find my
self distracted only by time that has shot by
me as if it were a bullet of blinding speed.
I still find I'm searching for the answers,
answers that I so very much need.

The days go by, the weeks they fly, next
month's near, the New Year's here. I know
I'm older and wiser,

which comes with time, but slow things down in this life of mine.

Is there time? Is there time left that I so badly need? Will I find I am someone, someone not blinded by reality or entwined and engulfed in this continuous circle of seasons that has fled me with such blinding speed? I think there is, as long as I have the need for life, then I am someone, someone who will live forever.

Charlotte Natasha Bindo

Charlotte Natasha Bindo
RAIN
Why do people
Speak words
That hurt
A heart in pain
Tears fall
My heart breaks
Like shattered crystal
Pieces fall silently
To the ground
A friendship gone
Lost in the wind
What went wrong
So sad it's a sin
Rain falls
On this unhappy
September day
But I still love you
What else can I say
No letter
No call
Nothing at all
The hurt is deep
I cry in my sleep
I thought our friendship
Was a treasure to keep
I wish you no evil
I chant no witches spell
I just want you
To hurt as well

Karen R Nastasia
OVER-THE-HILL 50TH BIRTHDAY
My friend Dick,

Being 50 isn't tough
It's the road to get there
that's mighty rough.

Life starts with much vip, vim and vigor
But along the way, at times,
you opt to take the trigger.

Those obstacles are just fleeting flips,
For there were many great times
with family, in public service and scouting trips.

As you look in the mirror you see

an image, and yes, the mirror lies.
That full and fossilized form looks
great through your eyes.

The bald, barreling and bulgy physique looks quite different to
you than how others perceive,
Amid the giggles and snickers you receive.

You have a good self-image and a well-worn body with an air of distinction
Which it earned through success in work and in play.
You made it, you fought off extinction!

From now on it is smooth sailing, the damage has been done.
You've passed the entry level,
earning $80 each week,
Experience and Wisdom you have won.

You have dedicated your life to achievement.
You have reached the crest of the "mountain of life."
Enjoy the easy times now with

Elaine, your lovely wife.

In my eyes, Dick, you will always

be wonderful and nifty.
For I see you as firm, fit and
Oh yes, fifty!

Beverley Rostant
SMALL HOPE
High we stand
Faces turned windward
Waiting, waiting, hand in hand
As far away
In another land
Others lay in the sand

Don't cry, don't weep
For we are all human
With all our failings
We must keep
Until we've learned
And then can sleep.

But there is hope
In this land
As we awaken
To join in hand
And in sorrow
High we stand

Lois Williams Young
THOUGHTS OF SATIN, SOUNDS OF SMILING

Dedicated to my husband, Bill, my loving 'Honey Do.'

Light fading
Day ending
Week departing
Night starting

Fresh beginning
New awakening
Time arriving
Night re-styling

Thoughts of satin
Sounds of smiling
Thoughts endearing
Smiles embracing

V Le'Ann Weilandich
AFTER THE STORM
We've made it through
The storms and rain,
Through all the torment
And the pain,
Through the hard times
And every trial,
Making little things count
All the while,

Through the cloudy days
And the stormy days, too,
We've done alright.
We made it through.

There will be many times
When things look grim,
When the storms come
And the lights grow dim.

But, don't you worry
When the sun decides to show,
We'll find our pot of gold
At the end of the rainbow.

Laura Bonowicz
SKYCASTLES

Let your imagination flow—Lola.

Castles in the sky,
Enhance the world below,
Dreams built on clouds so high,
Eternity is set afar.

Castles in the sky,
Enrich a person's soul.
In search of one true hope,
In search of one true goal.

Crystalized emotions-shattered everywhere.
When visions of one's future is never very clear.
But, castles in the sky, make it easy to accept.
That even though we're not there now,
There still is something left.

Adrianne E Woodruff
NIGHT FLIGHT
While once upon my flight at night, grey clouds obscured the bright moon's light
I saw a vision, vague, unsure; a man in black, unclean, unpure

He sat astride his mighty steed, its nostrils flared, its eyes did bleed
The hooves rang out like broken bells, it was a tune straight out of hell

The Master's hands wrapped 'round the reins, he whipped his mount and with great pain the two came face to face with me, at last skies cleared and I could see.

The Lord of all the evil dead, his journey brought him to my bed
He carried all his long-lost souls, to take me with them to Their shoals

A million arms across my breadth, beckoning me on to my death
They whispered lies of past dark deeds, their Master cautioned me to heed.

What had I done to lose my self, my soul, my being to Hell's wealth?
What evil done I did not know, I knew this was my time to go

As I felt my life's blood leave, I wondered who I'd leave to grieve
Would any have their tears to dry? to feel a loss or hear my cries?

I reached to touch the evil Saint, my senses dimmed, my eyes grew faint
His sleeve a finger's width away, the souls did chant and He did pray

Precisely timed at my demise, the morn cock crowed and I did rise
Another chance to view the sun, to live and breathe, to get things done

Carolyn Freeman
WINE, A PINE AND FEELIN' FINE

To my family and several very special friends. I wish you all peace of mind and all the joy life has to offer. Special thanks to my hero, Thoreau.

Oh, how I wish I was sitting
under a beautiful pine,
looking at Nature's wonders,
so divine!
I wish I was sipping some
delicious Chablis;
that would taste so fine to me.
There I would be with a really good book,
relaxing in some shady nook.
Oh, to sit there with some
beautiful music and hum,
getting away from all the
people who think me dumb!
Wouldn't it be nice to sit there
with an old friend, so dear?
I think I'd feel peaceful, with no
need for fear.
Yes, in Thoreau's own chapel, so fair,
mighty nice it would be
to shun all worries and care!
I could step to the beat of my
very own drummer,
in a forest, so green, in
earliest summer.
I could think straight and feel all
brand new,
under those fair
skies of Cerulean blue.
I would love to be in the lovely spot,
so serene,
where the air is clear,
fresh and clean.
In that beautiful place, I would
converse with God and rest.
Oh, I would be truly blessed!

Carolyn Freeman
LOVE'S OWN TIME

For J.T., my husband, partner and friend. Thanks for all our crazy, wonderful years together. From, your "skinny, ugly, little, ol' Boll Weevil."

I thank The Master, up above,
for the fine man he gave me to
love.

After work everyday, I rush to
get home.
I never have the wish to roam.

I look forward to the late nights
alone;
hours for each other, none to
intrude upon.

When the brown turns to gold in
his eyes,

I'm filled with tenderness and
the time flies.

My heart beats with a passionate fire.
Only for my beloved could I feel
such desire.

In his strong arms, held in a loving embrace,
the music of Wagner spirits us
away to another place.

As we are together, in love's own time,
there is no past or present, just
love sublime.

The candles flicker and the lights go dim.
I cherish each moment I have
with him.

Our love is like a rare and precious, fine wine.
Yes, I do love this Husband Mine.

Carolyn Killeen

Carolyn Killeen
CLEARING SKIES

This poem is dedicated to David, who helped part the clouds.

The sky is black, the clouds thick.
It's so dark and heavy. Loud with thunder.
I stare at the heavens, in the doom
and pray for a change.
I wait. I think of you.
Slowly, ever so slowly
the clouds part.
Shyly, ever so shyly
a tiny sliver of light
peeps through.

I smile, and my heart lifts.
The rain and sorrow is passing,
and I see a new beginning.
Torrential rains reposed the sorrow
and pain.
The sun, still ever so slight
smiles and promises more.
Thinking of anew,
I patiently wait for
solar warmth and anticipate
the slow embrace of happiness.

Carolyn Killeen
TAKE A STAND

This poem is dedicated to the people in the world who persevere to 'make a change' for the better.

Take a stand my friend
and we'll stand together.
Take the courage my friend
to make this world better.
Take the first step towards
the place your heart says to tread,
Take the lion along
where the scarecrow has led.

Carolyn Killeen
IF . . .

If,
If only everyone in their own way
could help fix our world
to make better our stay.

If the physician could heal a heart broken in two,
we could mend those dark feelings
that make us feel blue.
If the plumber could stop the oozing
drip of despair,
some lives would be easier, some
loads lighter to bear.
If the electrician could ignite the
sharp sparks of hope,
we wouldn't feel so alone, we'd be
better able to cope.
If the carpenter could build a strong
hand for the giving,
we could use the tools of his trade
in making life all worth living.

If only we could spread the goodness
we all hold within us;
there would be hope throughout the land,
new beginnings for every man.
We know it can be done,
and we know just how it could,
but only . . . if only we would.

Carolyn Killeen
HONESTY

The problem with the concept of honesty
is the fear it provokes in each entity.
On the surface it appears in simplicity,
down deeper lays hidden the rest to see.
Unable to be what we want to be,
restricted by the rules of society,
we chose a pretty picture of identity
to display
to the congress of humanity.
To come forward and speak with honesty
opens wounds that at one time cut deeply.
To touch raw emotions however briefly,
exposes vulnerabilities kept tucked
away so secretly.
Contraire to this image of purity,
lies selves that we hold onto with vanity.
To think we're so virtuous is insanity!
There's but one who possesses such quality.
One day my friend it could be you and me,
open yourself and be open to honesty.

Joyce Meyle
INFINITY

I whisper in the night
Come creeping – never sleeping
I caress the sand –
softly so, softly so
I am the sorcerer of the cosmos,
but never seemingly so, never so
I thunder on the blue –
I hush by the moon.
My secret is on the wind –
ever knowing.
I am the faithful Master of time –
I am the tempter of the adventurous –
I am the cradle that rocks the weary.
I am the reflection of dreams,
for i am the eyes of all that see me.
I am beauty and I am ugly; I am fierce, and
I am pleasure.
I am free and I am relentless –
I am a summer's day – I am the death
of winter.
I am the ruler of the Universe
For I am
the
sea.

Joyce Meyle
LITTLE BOY

He smiled his toothless smile—
she thought for her alone.
He reached and touched a butterfly—
his world was pure and innocent
For he was a babe, and not yet one—
and his Mother's love shone like
the sun.

His meeting with the bumblebee
and romping with the cat
taught him lessons of respect—
for things like that.
A man he would be—but then you see,
he was only three.
And the love was in his Mother's
eyes.

The bumps and hurts of this dear child,
for whilst he was an Earth born
boy,
He thought of flying like the apes—
his love of trees was now his toy.
He sought his comfort and his niche
in warmth and softness of her
arms.
For he was but seven,
and his Mother's love—a gift from
heaven.

His journey through his childhood quick—
he grows so fast;
his mind won't quit!
No longer her baby boy of three.
This person-child, his mind alert,
knows someday, when the break
will come
and he's no longer child,
but man—
Can he to his Mother look
for the love light shining from her
eyes?
His little heart knows, Of course he can,
for now though he is all but ten,
A Mother's love is never done.
There's nothing like a little boy—
there's nothing like a son.

Gene Brooks

Gene Brooks
MY FRIEND, MY WIFE

This poem is dedicated to my darling wife, Almeria (Susie), whom I love very much.

With a nose spotted with freckles, and
curly hair,
Is how I first saw you, and I couldn't
help but stare.

And I said to myself, "I wonder if
she's noticing me?"
But you were wrapped up in youth,
and wondering what was to be.

We became the best of friends, with a
friendship that would last through
life
But our paths crossed again, and we
became man and wife.

Even now, when I see you unexpectedly,
even after all this time,
It fills me with pride and happiness
to know that you're mine.

I long ago gave up my dreams of
being a cowboy or a famous
ballplayer.
Now all my dreams include you, and
I have come to realize that I am
blessed—I love you.

Gene Brooks
DON'T FORGET TO PRAY

This poem is dedicated to my mother, Sadie, who is in heaven now, and I'm sure she is still watching over me.

You know, when I was a kid, I used to think that my world was a stage, and I was the star attraction. I was Tex Ritter, Gene Autry, and all the rest, rolled into one. But, as time went along, I came to realize that I was only a role player, with only a fleeting part in this big world.

"What can I do?" I asked my mom. "What kind of role can I play?" "Do what you can," she replied. "But while you're doing it, don't forget to pray!"

She said, "Learn your part well, try to excel, and help others along the way. Try to set an example, do the best that you can, and while you're doing it, don't forget to pray."

My mother's role was fulfilled when she suddenly became ill, and the angels came and took her away. But I can still see her face, feel her warm embrace, and she cries down to me now, "Don't forget to pray."

Now my part is getting smaller as time moves along, and sometimes I wonder along the way—"What happened? Where has time gone?" and "Did I forget to pray?"

Susan Elaine Geiger

SOMEBODY!

Somebody loves you—
Somebody cares—
Somebody watches you—
Somebody stares—
Somebody admires you—
especially your smile.
You make that Somebody's
life worthwhile.
Somebody flips over you—
head over heels.
To be in Love—
she knows how it feels.
Somebody adores your beautiful
eyes—
She thinks you're better looking
than all the guys.
Somebody's in love—
I know it's true.
And if you keep silent—
I might just tell you.
Somebody loves you—
I DO!!

Violet Touch

VICTORIA

Dedicated to my Granddaughter, Victoria Hunter German.

I see you in your bassinet,
With lace and ruffles 'round
your face;
And in three weeks, the time was
set
For your move to another place.
I see you playing in my home,
How much of life we did explore;
And in my yard, the dog would
roam,
Then run as you would dance
some more.
I follow you through school until
From High School Valedictorian
strife
And college, honors graduate still,
You find a place to start
your life.
I see you, now, a lovely sight,
With grace and poise and
ethics, too
And pray your choices will be
right,
To give you peace in all you do.

Violet Touch

OUR UNIVERSE

Where Moon and Stars and Planets
are,
There Space awaits us, from afar;
Who thought we'd ever get to see
What is out there, for you and me?
It always seemed so far away
Before, at last, we found our way
To touch and walk upon the moon
And go to other planets, soon.
Oh, wondrous science, wondrous
minds
That work as each event unwinds.
Who knows what yet will come
to be?
Our universe has much to see.

Violet Touch

TOGETHER, THEY GROW

Dedicated to my two sons—Alan James Touch and Michael Thaddeus Touch.

Two little boys in the morning,
Two little boys late at night;
Neither will heed any warning,
Each one is sure he is right.

One thinks in terms of the great stars,
One thinks in terms of fast wheels;
One thinks of flying to see Mars,
One thinks of how a car feels.

One spends his time on the ball field,
One studies things in the stores;
One learns the joy that high scores
yield,
One learns the joy when cash soars.

Both know the value of real love,
Helping and sharing on earth;
Both know the beauty from above,
Both know their singular worth.

Two fine young men in the morning,
Two fine young men in the night;
Oh, may they please heed the
warning,
To be sure their lives are right.

Sharon Angel Gartman

Sharon Angel Gartman

TEARS OF A CHILD

The tear stained face with saddened eyes, attempted a feeble smile.
Beneath the tattered clothes and dirty hair I saw a battered child.
"Please Lady, can you spare a dime?"
I heard the soft voice say.
My heart went out to this small child as I turned to look his way.
"My Momma had to leave me but she'll be back I know.
They say she went with Jesus and that's why I couldn't go.
No one wants to keep me around now that Momma's gone;
and it's hard to be like Momma said when I know I'm all alone."
His voice began to falter as I knelt beside him there.

I searched my mind for words to let him know how much I cared.
"Well then, my friend, I have good news; but I'm not sure where to start.
You see, Jesus isn't far from you, He lives within our hearts.
So Mamma hasn't gone away to far and distant shores.
She only came to dwell within a child she must adore."
From that day to this I love him still, and his words have echoed through time.
The voice of my adopted son; "Please Lady can you spare a dime?"

Joyce White

THE FEAST

There is a place behind the restaurant
where he goes. Out of sight of
The Lady who passes
in dead animal skins
she calls Elegance;
and The Man who wears
the last of reptiles on his feet.
He eats from the can that holds
the food The Man and The Woman
rejected as unfit.
They pause to buy sirloin for their
poodle.
The man behind the restaurant
fails to see because
he's found a treasured bit of cheese
and he peels the mould with ease.

Martena Sasnett

WHAT IS THE BLISS FOR ME . . .

What is the Bliss for me . . .
that I can take and hold
and press it to my heart
and feel that it is mine and mine
alone
and mine because no other has such
background
or such needs . . .
no other has such fears, such dreams,
such searchings, such despair.
I do not know this Bliss by any name
or any feel,
or any abstract concept
captured from the realms of occult
wisdom
or the truths that seem to stalk the
human mind
in search of rest.
I open up and wait . . .
and know in deepest heart
that Waiting is my only Bliss . . .
for now.

Gwendolyn J Campbell

JUST THIRTEEN SECONDS

Just thirteen seconds—
Violent shakes—an earthquake!
Oh God! I'm falling!!
Just thirteen seconds—
I'm alive—no broken bones!
Get help—don't panic!
Just thirteen seconds—
WHERE'S MY WIFE? CHILDREN?
PARENTS?
My relatives? Friends?
Just thirteen seconds—
HELP!! POLICE! Please God give
strength!
Guide all my thinking!

Just thirteen seconds—
NO FOOD! NO WATER! NO
CLOTHES!
NO HOME!—POSSESSIONS!

Just thirteen seconds—
Keep sane for future lifestyle.
THE PAST—MEMORIES!

Sherry Collett Eblen

MOODS

To Mary my wonderful sister, and Kelly my friend.

How do you feel
Moods are funny
They come and go
Just like money

Grumpy angry mad
Happy silly glad
Confused lonely sad
Good sometimes bad

We all have them
Yes we do
Those feelings
Can change you

You might think
You're losing your mind
But just calm down
And give it some time

And listen to this
Moods really stink
Save your money
Don't see a shrink

Patricia G Magyar

A NEW YEAR

Time, it encircles my head like a
heavy halo.
In life there are steps to follow.
A time for this, and a time for that.
Wait!
"Sigh" . . . I need to breathe and
remember.
Funny, the air smells unfamiliar.
Where did it all go?
What robbed me of my joy?
Was it an act of unthankfulness?
Did this joy leave or did it transform?
I would like to believe it has
transformed.
So I can know it has never really left.
Oh, don't ever leave me my happy
little memories.
You keep me young and keep me
sane, if ever I was that.
"Sigh" . . . wait, I can almost smell it
again.
Hmm, it was there for just a moment.
Memories . . . to do it all again.
Goodbye 1989—

Matthew B Wales

THE BLOOD OF HEROES

A sad but proud tear falls from his
cheek
as he stands upon the mountaintop,
his mind is growing weak.
The wind was blowing cold that day
and the teardrops fell from his eyes.
As his body fell to the ground

darkness fell over the skies.
This hero rode through history, and he fought so strong and proud, and today his name lives on as he flies among the clouds.
But the blood of the hero has been spilled; the noble warrior has been killed.
If you walk quietly through the canyon, pause then stop,
You can still see his soul standing on the mountaintop.

Barbara Ann Malone-Verduin Sgt USA Army

Barbara Ann Malone-Verduin Sgt USA Army
PEACE

To my father, Thomas David Malone—may he rest in peace. To my mother, Nancy Bernice Malone (Moss)— who deserves all the peace in the universe. To my loving husband, Elwood Errol Verduin, Jr. and everyone who encouraged me.

Myself, alone on a vast, soft, sandy beach
The warm sand hugging and molding me
Its grains blowing sporadically in the wind, like my thoughts

The lips of a calm, rippling ocean
Whispering words of wisdom, responding to my thoughts
As I ponder my past, present, and future existence.

The sun, sinking into a flamboyant horizon
Its colors and panoramic view giving me
A vivid, picturesque, open mind

Birds and sea gulls flying into the sunset
Chirping their songs in a harmonious tune

A gentle breeze; swaying palm trees, dancing rhythmically
To all of nature's aesthetic, orchestrated sounds
A gentle breeze; kissing, caressing, enveloping, and accepting me

A time for serenity, nourishment, strength and healing
A time to absorb, to relax, and to breathe freely
A time to expand, to grow, and to be me
A time to think of pure, raw, uninterrupted thoughts
A piece of mind . . . . . . a "peace" of mind
Peace . . . . . . Peace . . . . . . Peace

Linda Hagood
LIKE HIMSELF
My lover is not dark, handsome, elite, dashing.
He is Lanky, tall . . .
with high cheek bones and hair blond, coarse.
His words are not practiced, smooth, flattering, sly.
They are intelligent . . .
Placed with mood and moment, or said in humor; a baffling bullshitter,
Persuading me to romance him.
He cuddles next to me while we watch a sunrise,
or taunts me on a swing under an Autumn full moon.
But as we sit together on the rail of a covered bridge,
I see and hear the truths of his heart
as plainly as the rush of the stream's clear water over the rocks below us.

Louise C Bullock
AH, SPRING

To Jo Anne, my daughter. These poems are to reassure you of God's love everlasting.

Ah, spring!
You sing to me
With soft, silky sighs
Filling my soul with delight
And the promise of another life.

Ah, spring!
You tranquilize me
With intoxicating songs
Of birds chirping cheerily.
You make life seem without strife.

Ah spring!
Flowers only yesterday unadorned
Today glowing with crystal color
Challenging my senses
Renewing God's promise of everlasting life.

Louise C Bullock
TO A MOCKINGBIRD
Tremendous sound from small bird.
Such pure melody comes from no other source,
Poured forth in ecstatic word,
Forever a reassuring force.
God's glory revealing.

Your songs of delight
Glorify our dull days.
Your harmonies enhance the night,
How I wish to follow your ways:
God's story proclaiming.

As you pour forth your soul,
In pure ecstasy you celebrate life,
Freeing listeners from the droll,
Dreary world of sadness and strife.
Of God's existence reassuring.

Your immortal voice forevermore
Singing songs from the forgotten past,
Bringing to all of us an open door
Leading to a love that lasts:
God's love everlasting.

Mary R Burns
SPRITES' EVE

To All the Delightful Children Everywhere!

Wink, little pumpkin,
Keep a bright eye
Up on the hill
Where the moon-mists fly,
Down in the hollow where the slyest little shadow
Scurries with the witch-wind and dances in the meadow!
See! Where the Red Moon tiptoes on the hilltop!
Watch! Where the Pointed Hat slips by the cornstalk!
Burn a bright flame for the passing of the Wee Folk . . .
Wink, little pumpkin,
Keep a bright eye,
On All Hallow's Eve
When the moon-mists fly!

Carolyn P Englehart
A SLEEPING WONDER

Dedicated to my grandchildren Crystal and Eric.

Have you ever watched a baby sleep
Seen a pout and then a smile creep
Upon the tiny lips of an infant child
You watch and you can't help but smile

Wonder what's on their tiny mind
Something cruel and then something kind
The devil perhaps and then a saint
A tug of war on her face, they paint

Sounds at times can even erupt
As her sleep, they interrupt
A whimper here, a giggle there
They reach the babies everywhere

So if you ever get the chance
Give a sleeping child a second glance
Their expression is sure to change
And it's something no one can explain.

Marsha Klonowski
MY CAT

This poem is dedicated to everybody (including all creatures) who inspired me to write, who was inspired by my writings, who is being inspired by them now, or who will ever be inspired by them!

Look how you're growing
My kitty cat, kitty cat!
Your eyes are glowing
My cat, I adore!
Turn around, and you're one!
Turn around, and you're four!
Turn around, and there's the mess
that you made on the floor!

Where are you going, my pretty cat, pretty cat?
My, how you're growing from whiskers to paws!
Turn around, and you're growing when I stop to pause!
Turn around, and there's the curtains you tore with your claws!

Miriam Selb Roberts
NOT AN ORDINARY DAY
As soon as I awoke
I knew it was no ordinary day . . .
Beneath the cheerful, bubbling carol
Of the robins in the pre-dawn light
Pulsed tender notes
As of golden trumpets afar off;
I could not tell from which direction they came.

Suddenly the eastern sky
Became the focus of a thousand floodlights
Glowing in all the radiant hues of dawn;
I stood transfixed,
Aware of the crescendo of sound
As those golden trumpets announced
The rising of the Light of the World.

It was overpowering and unreal;
I ran outside, and there they were . . .
Countless cohorts of golden trumpets
Clustered in my garden,
Standing straight and proud on every side . . .
And it was EASTER!
I told you it was no ordinary day.

Miriam Selb Roberts
A CHRISTMAS PRAYER
Did Mary lie awake that night
Following Jesus' birth?
Was she too keyed up to sleep
Awed by the mystery so deep . . .
Why me, Lord? Bless me.

Did she hear the angels sing
"Peace to men on earth?"
Was she frightened by the throng
Or exalted by the song?
Tell me, Lord. Bless me.

Did she pray there silently
For assurance of her worth?
Did she greet the glowing dawn
With lifted heart, all doubtings gone?
Help me, Lord. Bless me.

Stephanie Surina
RIVERS
Rivers, rivers
Are so deep
Rivers, rivers
Give me shivers
Rivers, rivers
Are full of oil
But never, never
Made of foil!

Lucille Jackson Thomas
REQUIEM FOR MIKEY
We made you a bed with loving care,
A pillow, a blanket and toys were there.
'Twas only a box, but you thought it was great,
As you grew to your mighty six-pound weight.

For years you reigned as household czar;
You insisted on riding with us in the car;
You offered opinions about the food;
You inspected all comers in critical mood.

As little old man you climbed the stairs
With stiffened limbs and anxious stare.
You whimpered a bit when we picked you up.

Long gone were the antics of wayward pup.

On that last sad journey you loved us still,
As we drove down the driveway and up the hill.
You tried to kiss away my tears
As I smoothed your fur and stroked your ears.
In the waiting room you snuggled down,
Secure you thought and safe from harm.
Then they called for us but I could not go,
And you had to face the end alone.

Tinker PPFL CTO
STILL WATERS

Dedicated to the survivors of the 1980 Skyway Bridge collapse, Pinellas County, Fl.

Quiet water, blue sky and gulls
Come to light this early day
With towering clouds and tempered sun
Beckon the rain and heat to come
Among these waters, still and blue
With deadly quiet from below
Where once screams of terror
Were heard from there.

Storms come and go to rile these waters
Only to return its wake to those below
To the spirits whose bodies died
And they who refuse to leave its grave
Until the waters return to peace,
I will hear, feel, sense the dead . . .
Who died before their time, they say,
But whose final day was born within . . .
. . . These waters.

Melissa Newman

Melissa Newman
SUMMER IS

I dedicate this poem to my mom and dad for all their love and help. After all, if it wasn't for them my poem wouldn't be in this book. Thanks.

Summer is the moonlit sky
that shines upon me and you.

Summer is the birds that
sing beautifully in the dew.

Summer is the fun-filled days,
the beach, the park, and sunlit rays.

Summer is a lot of things.
Happiness is what summer brings.

Shannon Stevenin
SILENT PAIN

Lonely tears
slipping down my cheek
silently falling
to the page below
leaving it scarred
with memories and feelings
scalding tears
burning the sterile whiteness
the first marks in a blank book
shadows reach past me
through my barriers
beyond all defense
drawing their fingers
across the page
smudging my tears
tracing a telltale line of sorrow
where joy might have been
but with each passing second
the marks fade
leaving the world unaltered
to my pain.

Jill Ann Yoder

Jill Ann Yoder
LIFE AT SEA

To my sister, Colleen Mary Yoder, who inspired me to write this poem.

Remember your yesterdays
Remember your tomorrows
The past has known grief
Your future may know sorrow
Remember last year
Look forward to more
Hold on to what's dear
And the things you adore

The past cuts like a knife
Fight back its attack
Go on with your life
Don't stop to look back
Create a new memory
So much fun is in store
Take a ride on the sea
Of life's long rocky shore

Jill Ann Yoder
EARTH 1990

I dedicate this poem to future generations.

Wild with fury
Screaming with worry

Caught up in a cloud
Because we're too proud

Afraid to stumble
Don't want to be humble

Speeding through time
To rest is a crime

Too vain to care
Too selfish to share

Reverse our fate
Before it's too late

Patsy C (Storment) Rosio
GREECE

This poem is dedicated to Roy, my wonderful husband.

Ah! Greece we have mis-judged you,
Your men most exciting, your statutes so fair
But why do your girls wear
their skirts so short,
And never seem to comb
their hair?

Betty Grace Northup
BABY IS A TREASURE?

With crib, diapers, bottles, formulas and such
How can baby be a treasure when it costs so much?
I always thought a treasure was something you could spend
But with a little baby, expenses never end.
Oh look at that dear face, and this chubby little cheek
Two beautiful eyes look up and through long lashes peek
These tiny hands that grip my fingers and my very heart
Can't be priced with money, not even one small part.
Take all your silver and your many sacks of gold
They're not worth a thing, compared with what I hold.

Cece Griswold
THE SINGING TREE

Oh, how my Mother loved her "Singing Tree."
It stands so tall, straight and free.
Surrounded by the stately firs, hemlocks and cedars.
That old cottonwood, with its rustling, sighing, singing leaves,
still sways with the mountain breeze.
The love affair between those two went on for many years, so near the cabin dear.
Now the cool winds of fall and winter begin.
Before the early snows blanket all,
yellow leaves float slowly down as I stand,
and look up and on up and say,
"Mother, are you there?"
And something whispers back
with the rustling, sighing, singing,
"See you all next year."

Gene Miller
WHO'S TO BLAME

We all read it in the papers and hear it on the air
Of killings and stealing and crime everywhere
And we think and say as we notice the trend
"This Younger Generation—When will it end?"
But are we sure that it is their fault alone
You blame them I can tell by your tone
Aren't we Guilty—when we place in their way
Far too many things that lead them astray
There's too much money, too much idle time
Too many filthy movies of passion and crime
And too many books not fit to be read
With too much temptation in what they heard said
Far too many children left free to roam
By drinking parents who just won't stay home.
Kids don't create movies, they don't write the books
They don't paint pictures of gangsters and crooks
They don't make the liquor, they don't operate the bars
And they don't make the laws or drive all the cars
When it comes to peddling drugs that muddle the brain
It was started by Older Folks, greedy for Gain
Delinquent teenagers are the first we condemn
All these Sins of Our Nation, we blame it on them
So change things around, make living worthwhile
Then someday in the Future We can ALL learn to smile.

Hildburg Baker
BROTHER

Yesterday you gave me pleasure, today it turned to pain.
A month and a year have passed, and life is not the same.
My love for you has not yet died, and even though you're gone,
you've left behind my heart and soul, and all of me to mourn.
Remember the times when you and I shared sorrows and all joys, of being two and not alone, to love and laugh like boys.
You told me once and I won't forget, that you and I are one,

and even though I'm all alone, and
you're the one who's gone.
I'll remember till the day I die, the
love I feel for you.
Oh brother why, did you have to
leave, why not take me too.
The emptiness surrounding me is
dark and full of pain,
because my brother dear, you're
gone, and life is not the same.

Kevin J Welch
NATURE'S HEALING

Oh life eternal, or so it seems, in those woods and in my dreams.

The sweet blue sky, the laughing streams. The dancing clouds and mountains green.

Lying on the forest floor, engulfed in nature's fine decor. My heart it lifts, and then it soars, my body pleased down to its core.

Oh man minute, in this vast domain, in nature's arms I will remain.

Lynn McCandless
LOVE FILLS MY HEART

Sydney brightens my days and
warms my nights.
Watching me with curious, shining
eyes,
She approaches me with playfulness.
The sleekness of her body is so
appealing,
I reach out to caress her.

Love fills my heart.

As we lie together
Drifting toward sleep,
Her gentle breathing is
But a whisper on my shoulder;
Slumber overtakes us,
Her head next to mine.

With the coming of dawn,
She stretches and arises from my bed.
Resolutely I follow her,
Missing the warmth of her nearness.

Each morning is the same
As I tend to the chore,
Of feeding my cat Sydney
And opening the back door.

Eva Kotyza
CONSEQUENCES

I would like to dedicate this poem to my father, my mother, my three brothers, and to all of the people who take the risk of drinking and driving—think about the consequences!! This one's for you, too Jenifer!

He said he'd be fine—everything
would be O.K.
He said that before his life was taken
away
Because of a foolish decision that he
had made
The price of drinking and driving had
to be paid
A shock wave hit and the light of life
shined
When he heard the screams,
screeches, and metal grind
That was the end—no more problems
to face
He was alive and then gone without a
trace
Everyone had asked if he had wanted
a ride
But he said no—he had his silly pride
He never thought of the consequence
of ending up dead
"Trust me, I'll be fine," he had said
But now everyone is mourning over
the poor boy
An intoxicated mind behind the
wheel isn't a toy
This makes people realize just one
thing
The awful result that drinking and
driving can bring
Too many people end up like this
young boy everyday
We've got to stop and think before
we're swept away
So remember the moral and help
people stay alive
Remember the consequences when
you drink and drive

Andrea Anthony

Andrea Anthony
THE BEYONDERER

To Garland Robinette, New Orleans' finest TV newscaster, a great artist, and the gentleman that will always be my first inspiration.

His eyes gleam as stars that shine in the night. Revealing a curiosity that cannot be hid. In wonder they sparkle beyond the day's night.

Searching for answers his mind is aware. Answered in silence, for his soul to bear. Misunderstood by those whom he loves. Pain caused by wisdom, not shared.

In visions of the night, his soul wonders beyond the beyond. In dreams of the night all truth comes to mind. For the truth he is hated, for love, he's a vagabond.

Revealed truth hid from others, the beyonderer has known. For his soul thirsts and hungers, for the place he calls home! A place beyond the beyond!

Andrea Anthony
VISION IN SOUND

Inspired by the musician and his horn Scott Page from the group of "Pink Floyd".

My heart's rhythm beats in tempo to the perfectly orchestrated notes. A surge of energy fills me as I listen, and feel the music flow. Vibrations echo sounds within, that penetrate my soul. And vivid revelations come to mind through his golden saxophone.

The musician's tune has reached my soul, my heart burst into song. Releasing mortal chains that bind me, another dimension is known. In the harmony my spirit departs from bondage, like a soaring eagle flies. Feeling mesmerized as in infant embraced and sang a lullaby.

The music from his instrument enlightens me, my spirit is aware. Awakening my dreams in a melody of truth, I long to live, to share! For what worth, would my life be without a song or a vision? And what worth, would the horn be without the inspired musician?

Andrea Anthony
CHILDREN OF A HIGHER LOVE

To Cheryl, Dinah, Christene, Arnold and Julie Gerber, all my earthy children, I've dedicated to a HIgher Love, more than a mother's Love.

Terrestrial children with celestial hearts, ensnared in a limbo between heaven in hell. Carefully embracing life, each lonely road they take. Nurtured by visions and dreams of God's love. And cradled by the hand fate.

Trusting in fate's hand, to reach their destiny, they are as wandering stars dwelling in a world that's lost sight. They are the earth's sojourners . . . the children of a higher love. Gently sharing their love to a lost paradise.

Rejected by humanity with terrestrial hearts, they are drawn to each other in celestial love. They know each other in each other's eyes. They share in silence words of pure love. Their love for each other is untouched by time.

Andrea Anthony
THE SOJOURNER

I dedicate this to all those, that my life visited, to give my possessions to! My possessions are truth. Elizabeth Drago, thank you for accepting so easily! And for accepting me.

You needed my hand, and longed for my strength. And sort for the kind of Love I possess.
You wanted my treasures from near and from far
Your heart cried out across a vast sea. Fate heard your cry and whispered to me.

I am your sojourner sent by fate's call. I've been sent here to dwell, with you for a while. To tell you of all the places I've been. And teach you the ways of a far away friend. Listen gently to the words that are pure. I won't be passing this way, again.

At first my language will sound strange to your ears. Until they penetrate deep in your soul. Then, will you know and understand. That all of my possessions are yours. But time will not permit you to come with me now, on my journey, far away in the great by and by.

But your heart will join with mine someday.
Somewhere, out there in the sweet by and by
Somewhere, where fate has me bound. When time has revealed the truth to your heart, of all I have given of what fate had allowed.

Andrea Anthony
THE WAY YOU SAW ME YESTERDAY

I dedicate this to Dawn Mendow . . . Christina McGill, Karen McGill & Laurie Whitaker. May your dreams come true. I wish you eyes that love.

The enchantment is broken. The golden silence ends.
Thoughts remembered, turn to tears. A crystal vision fades. Dark shadows appear, a terrible storm. A sand castle washes away, when the sea rushes on the shore.
The reality is seen. A child's dream is gone.

All that remains are particles of sand. The princess of the castle hangs her head down, when she remembers the prince that almost was. Angry at the sea, she falls to her knees.
She gathers sand in both her hands and tosses it to the wind. The sand falls down in her eyes. She sees him no more. She weeps and laments, awhile.

Still angry at the sea that brought the storm that blew her castle down. And at the wind that blew the sand in her eyes.
Once again, she sees the face of the prince that almost was. He smiles and gently says, Build me a sand castle in your mind, where skies are blue and winds are calm, and the sun lights up the day. Where, thoughts remembered, won't bring tears. The way you saw me, yesterday.

Andrea Anthony
SOUL MATES

To Elizabeth Drago, Trent Beach, Liz Gruder, Chrisy, Dawn, Debbie Adrienne, and all the love children of Shell Island.

Together, we rise above the storms of life.
"More than friends, more than lovers."
Excelling high above the clouds you and I . . . "We lift each other up when others let us down!"

Individually, we walk down separate paths, that lead to the same place. "More than friends, More than lovers." Guiding lights we are, that . . . "Shine for each other."

And though, we travel different paths, going separate ways. Our hearts are Joined together. Because to each other, we are, much more than friends, much more than lovers. We are Soul Mates, you and I . . . Forever.

J C Flowers
FATHER

F is for God, the one that created
each and all
A is for Almighty, warning us to
listen for his call
T is for Terminal, which our life
will come to
H is for Heaven, where our spirits
won't be blue
E is for Eternity, where our soul
will last
R is for Repent, which we must
do, forgetting all of the past.

The Father above created Adam and

Eve from the start
Now we must love Him from deep in our heart
The Almighty will be with us until our very end
Hoping we all will hear and turn from our sins.

Our soul will be terminal but can live in Heaven, if it's right
His word is that we must repent and live in His sight
He has loaned us one that we call father or dad
The one that fills in and the best one we ever had.

Dad you are the greatest one, but He is above all
We do what you say, but still, we must listen for His call
Dad you teach us what you think must be right and not wrong
With the help of the Almighty I can be very strong.

Bob Ricketson
FRIENDS

To my friends, Judy and Kathy.

I have two friends
One is near, one is far.
Even if they were at earth's ends,
Our friendship, distance would not mar.

We love to sit and chat
About topics that are far ranging.
Books, music, this or that—
It matters not what is currently raging.

What matters most is that, together, we stay
Through thick or thin.
We will make it through the fray
And help each other with the pain.

It is after the battles are won or lost,
That we understand the meaning of friendship.
It is those that stand by you the most
That you want on board your ship.

I have two friends
One is near, one is far.
Friendship that never ends,
One that time will never mar.

Franceen C Bentley
YOU AND I
You and I
We are so much like
a flower
A flower in the garden of life
we need love and care
to help us grow.

Sometimes we like to stay
where we are planted
strong and secure.

Then
one day,
the rains come
and winds blow
It blows hard and cold!
and the weeds they grow
all around us—
sometimes they try to choke us.

During the storm
the flower's leaves are crumpled
and its delicate petals
withered—
but when the storm is over,
and the sun comes out again,
the flower, its stems are stronger now
and its roots are deeper
No one can pull it out of the ground.

Cynthia A Y Rupel
A WALK IN THE RAIN
No, thank you, sir,
I like the rain.
Feels good on my face—
so free.
A walk in the rain
is good for the soul—
it hides the tears,
you see.

Sue Bryant
THE GIFT
It was my sin, the deed belonged to me.
The pain was personal, the shame became my persona.
The guilt was my own, not to be shared.
But when downcast eyes looked upward,
and the light could be seen through the clouds,
the joy could be felt all around me.
I could not keep it personal, nor did I want to.
What I could not share before, I could not keep from sharing.
My crises became a celebration, my suffering brought joy.
The darkest wrappings enclosed a most treasured gift.
Forgiveness!

Elisa F Joaquin

Elisa F Joaquin
WHAT IS LOVE?

To Rudy, Dony, Nick, Doel and Betty – constant sources of love and inspiration.

To forgive and pray for those
who hurt you
Think kindly of their deeds
don't misconstrue
It may be what you, in his place
may also do.
To share the many blessings
God gives to me
Help heal the sick, clothe the poor
feed the hungry
Yet, not in self-righteousness
pride or vanity.
To do things for others, without
thought of gain
Patient, understanding, loving
always remain.
Sharing someone's burden
easing his pain.
To pray sincerely for all
troubled countries
That their people may shun war, and
work for peace
So unrest, suffering and turmoil
In God's world may finally cease.
This is love.

Elisa F Joaquin
THE SEARCH

To my mother and father who bequeathed to us, the joy of Christian living.

Slow me down O Lord, I pray
I've lost my course, I move too fast
Rushing, searching, yet finding not
The things in life that count and last.

My impatient and restless spirit
Feverishly paces in and out
Looking for answers, seeking truths
To what life is all about.

Just when the goal is within my reach
Everything vanishes in the sand
Why, O Lord, I helplessly ask
Please give me wisdom to understand.

Above the world's din and strife
A voice softly whispers to me
"Be still and know that I am God
In time these will be known to thee."

Believing, trusting, I slowed me down
And, with guidance from above
I found the things in life that count and last:
Peace, Faith, Hope and Love.

donita lee schaller
MAVERICK PHANTOMS
Cuts like a knife
pain like never before.
Why do i struggle?
i don't think, i don't know if
i can live like this
any more.

Strange twist of fate
life has never been fair . . . but cruel?
Why can't i cope?
i don't think, i don't know if
there's an answer, or even
any hope.

Shards of glass filter prisms of
light through the gloom.
Why live with the charade; the light's not real?
i don't think, i don't know if
i can continue to care—the
hurt's too big; there can't be
any room . . .
for me.
for You.
for us.

Alice Reid
I SIT ON THE PORCH TODAY WATCHING PEOPLE GO BY IN A BUSY WAY

To Caroline.

I sit on my porch today watching people go by in a busy way.
There's going to be an auction on this very day.
People from near and far stop and browse to see what bargains can be found
I'm sad, hurt and full of tears, to see an auction go on like this.
Because it's a household auction, with two special people in mind.
These people were people you don't find too often today.
They asked for help from no one.
They were too proud.
Much too often, we would say, "Can we be of some help today?" "Why no, dear, we are already done."
(Which you know they weren't.)
"Besides, dearie, you're too busy to be waiting on us old folks."
They always wanted to be left alone.
In their own little private home.
Sixty years of household things. Yes, that was a lot of household keeping.
And you believe it only took two days to make a house not a "home."
A lot of hard work gone. And the sad part was that they had no say in it.
You see, Mrs. Elizabeth (Libby) Boughton died during the summer.
But before she died, she suffered three weeks in the hospital. Broken-hearted, Mr. Boughton had to go to a community care home and seven months later he died of a broken heart and loneliness.
And now, they are both together again.
I'm closing for now. You may be gone, but you won't be forgotten by me.
So here's to a couple of good neighbors and a couple of close friends I once had.

Alice Reid
WHAT LOVE MEANS TO ME
It means you have someone special
But this kind of special
means a lot to me—
You have to grow with each other
And learn about each other
Sometimes laugh, sometimes cry
But always have that
communication to even try—
For love is a special gift
Of many different things
To many different people
And for many different reasons
Love comes in all sizes and
shapes of forms
Big or small
People or things
It just comes together for me.
The different ways of love
Are just so incredible
How I may love thee
Or be loved by thee.

Betty J Douglass
A LOVE GIFT
Oh, Lord, it's hard to understand
The misery and the pain,
That happens all around us
O'er and o'er again.

Does love not prevail
Over everything,
Our hungry hearts to fill,
Or do we walk in darkness
and say;
Oh, heart, be still.

If while here a spark
we light,
And kindle it to flame
Could not this enlighten
And take away our pain?

Lord, help us each to realize
That's why you sent your son.
To die for us and rise again,
T'was a love gift for each one.

Chelsea D Singley (age 8)
A BOY'S NAME IS PAUL
Frogs live all around the world.
A circle is curled.
An oyster is pearled.

An ant is small.
But what's big is a wall.

If you don't watch out you'll fall.

A girl likes to play with a doll.
Some people are tall.
You bounce a ball.

You shop in a mall.
You can call, and
A boy's name is Paul.

Shirley Louise Nabours
YESTERDAY, TODAY & TOMORROW

This poem is dedicated to my son, Stephen, who was the inspiration for the poem.

A poem, is a poem, is a poem, they say.
Not so say I, though you surely may
Consider a tale, a poem today.

Yesterday, I told a tale of an incredible time,
Today a verse of non-sense rhyme,
Tomorrow a story of poetic bliss.
My future holds an honour of mine.

My son at three who could not discern,
That today was not tomorrow
And yesterday held no concern;
May live to proclaim an innumerable time,
When Mom could tell a tale with non-sense rhyme.

His son to be may yearn for the bliss
Of Dad beside his bed to tell of a time
When age was of no concern and time stood still
When he was told a verse of non-sense rhyme.

Velma Eloise Pratt
LIVE FOR THE THINGS WE LOVE

To my children, grandchildren and great-grandchildren.

Live for the laughter of children at play
Live for these joys and wonders each day;
Live for the sight of a bird on the wing,
Live for the sound of all who joyfully sing.
Live for the student in church or schoolroom
Live for the beauty of flowers in bloom,
Live for the song of a babbling brook,
and the fish caught on a well-worn hook
Live for the hope your talents will give others
Your talents will give others after, with Christian purpose to live
Live in the spirit of one from above,
Given to us, in beauty and love.

Carol Buell
THE SEA

To my three children, Terrie Mohlman, David Buell, and Linda Buell.

The sea, thundering against the shore
sending waves ever so high with power
in each swell, it beckons to you
In its rampage there's majestic beauty,
an enchantment, a curiosity that drives
man to her. She embraces you, then
torments you leaving you weakened

In her calmness she is serene
her beauty unmatched
The morning sunrises and evening sunsets offer
you tranquility, peace comes within
you savor on her beaches as she warms you, then
embracing you,
she gives you power and
enlightens you, with her strength unequaled

One sits for hours staring, as she puts
a hypnotic spell over you
She lulls you to sleep with the soft
whispering of her waves, her scent reaching
your nostrils, a kiss as she engulfs
you and puts you at ease.

Deborah Mae Kendall
AN OLDER BROTHER AND SISTER

To my favorite brother David and my sister Sarah.

There's nothing better in life than to
have an older brother and sister.
An older brother will make you laugh
and protect you from all danger.
An older sister will read to you
and play paper dolls with you.
They will teach you about life
the good in people and the bad.
There's nothing better in life than to
have an older brother and sister.
They tell you all the time how
much they love and care for you.
You can be crying all alone but
not for long, they are there.
They always give you a hug and
words of encouragement when you need it.
They buy you presents for no reason
Just to say "I love you."
There's nothing better in life than to
have an older brother and sister.

Mary Ewing
THE JUNKYARD

Funny faces,
Front of a car,
A light going up—
A light going down,
Bumpers with crooked smiles—
All tell a story.
Cars that are dead;
People that are dead—
Romance with the car?
Death of a car,
Death of a body,
Life of a soul?

Anne M Blanchard
WE DON'T CARE

It's raining on the ocean
but we don't care a bit.
'Cause we can see the water
right from where we sit.

We're in our snuggie motor home
where the two of us just fit.
Now, how much more comfortable
can we retired people get.

Daisy L Swearingen (wife)
DEAR DAD

In loving memory: Miller Boyd Swearingen, a wonderful son, husband and father. Death—doctor error; June 30, 1937—November 2, 1984.

Dear Dad,

You were the greatest Dad
a little girl ever had.

You always treated me good and never bad.
I loved you more and more each passing day
as you loved me in your understanding way.

You taught me how to say grace and pray
and many a kind word to say.

You gave my mother twenty of the happiest years of her life.
You treated her like a special person and wife.
You were the light of her life.

Truly I know you'll play with the Angels
as you always played with me.

I loved you dad and will always.
Your precious memory and loving eyes
will with me always stay.

Until we meet in Heaven
I'll just say thanks for being
such a special dad.

Love, Keli
Daughter, Age 4

Robin de Barros

Robin de Barros
WISHING YOU'D HOLD MY HAND

To Brett.

Oh, how I wish you'd hold my hand.
Your fingers laced in mine would feel so grand.
Your palm against mine would feel so divine.
You've done it before, so do it again.
Don't let this beautiful relationship end.

Robin de Barros
A ROSE

The most fascinating plant is a beautiful rose.
Its wonderful scent is the one which God chose.
The petals of this flower are extremely delicate, as gentle as a candle being lit.
A rose often catches the human eye.
One can see it open if they try.

Robin de Barros
THE SPIRITUAL EFFECTS OF LIGHT

As light spiritually envelops the earth,
God's kindness tells us what nature is worth.
Sunlight and moonlight are equal in beauty.
Each one plays its own separate duty.

T A Kostic
high elevation

a blazing soul fills the
heart with a warm current
of passion expanding . . .
stretching to be filled
as grace gives birth to
your colored plumage while
life's fiber is weaved to
holiness!

gazing in awe—being one with
all falling in love with your
best friend.

Jo Nell Helms
ODE

Ode, did you know that was my mother's nickname? This tomboy, hunter, fisherman. The beautiful woman who shaped me, filled my mind with healing verses, words to guide my life.

She made my clothes. Sweetpea, our cow, with the big pretty eyes and long eyelashes, ate the feed while I wore the sacks. Mother sewed the rose-covered skirt which I wore with a ruffle blouse from a flour bag. She taught me to cook beans, cornbread, biscuits, steak, gravy, to use what was at hand and waste not.

My mother, Ora Irene Deen, played piano music by ear, created pictures from crushed glass, quilted, molded plastic flowers, loved God, my father, me, and her home.

Muriel E Vebsky
I'VE GOT TO KNOW

Tell me how the flowers grow
Will the clouds pour out their rain?
Can a child learn how to smile
Play with dolls once in a while?
Tell me, please, I've got to know.

How the airplane flies the skies
Like the eagle soars up high.
Can a puppy run and play
Grow up to be pal some day?
Tell me, please, I've got to know.

How can one acquire a friend
True and honest to the end?
Will bad memories of the past
Dampen loyalty or last?
Tell me, please, I've got to know.

Will close friendship and my love
Stretched out arms from God
above
Force you to stand much smaller
Or become a whole lot taller?
Tell me, please, I've got to know.

Patricia Eich
DO YOU KNOW?

For John, the man who brought out the worst and the best in me.

Your silence of many days
Cuts through me like a sword;
The ubiquitous weapon, that keeps
me out
Of your mysterious world.

Days turn into weeks,
Eventually becoming months.
The closed bedroom door stares
at me
As I stare back.

Is she beautiful and exciting?
Like a show girl in Time Square?
Or maybe raunchy and earthy,
Fulfilling your needs.

You loved me when I came to you
From that small Maine town.
N.Y.C. never changed my ways;
I faded fast in your eyes.

Never knowing where you'd been,
Or who was with you last;
But your scent was not mine,
And you were silent once again.

Diana M Bixler
ILLUSION
We don't exist—
We are born
We breathe
We live
We grow

We learn
We prosper
We decline
We are gone
We don't exist—
Perhaps, we never did.

Diana M Bixler
THE OWL
Darkness surrounds us like a shroud,
No moon dispels its embrace.
In the blackness lurking there,
A round and feathered face.
On silent pinions quiet glide,
As talons find their mark.
A tiny victim meets its end,
Grasped, dying in the dark.
Like the Great Horned Owl,
Silent death stalks us all.
Unsuspecting we may be,
Some day he'll come to call.

Diana M Bixler
CHAMBERS OF THE MOON
I walk the chambers of the moon,
On silver iridescent trails.
Soft echoes greet me as I roam,
And fills my head with fairy tales.

Moonbeams light my path of dreams,
Glitters as I slumber.
Stardust scatters as I walk,
Particles unnumbered.

Life seems but a dream each day,
Ending much too soon.
Tied to my mortal feet of clay,
I walk the chambers of the moon.

Diana M Bixler
BUTTERFLY
Stardust in rainbow pallette,
Upon silken wings.
Preening on daisy petals.
Creations' lovely things.

Like tiny fairies on the breeze,
They dance among my flowers.
Charming beauties that they are,
Enchant my summer hours.

Jewels drifting in the meadow,
Fluttering to the sky.
Coloring the landscape,
God's lovely butterfly.

Marlen Sykes
WHEN WE FIRST MET

This is dedicated to my love, "Jack."

When we first met
We were wondering souls
Lost in the darkness
Out of control
We taught each other to trust
And believe again
That life could be great
We would be each other's friend

I fell in love with you
You fell in love with me
We are so fortunate
That now we see
No more darkness before us
Only light
'Cause we know when the
Darkness falls
It's only night.

Marlen Sykes
LET'S SAY TODAY

This is dedicated to my love, "Jack."

Let's say today our love to each other
'Cause death may come in the night
To rob us and cheat us, of words yet
unsaid

Each moment is so precious
For we know not, how long we have
Wake up, my darling
I have so much to tell

Let me tell you
How happy you've made me
In case I should die, in the night
If God should grant us another day
That will be all right

To be able to tell you again, dear
That I love you so
Will mean so very much to me
More than you will know.

Ruth Brenda Ashoury
A CHILD'S GOAL
Last week I spied a boy who rid a
lawn of leaves.
His small arms worked steadily and
his face full of glee.

I could just imagine his feelings as he
round up the piles, a new bike he
would buy so he could race around
for miles.

Today I saw the boy who rid the lawn
of leaves,
he tired of his new bicycle and took
to climbing trees.

Kelly Michael Mills
HAMMER
Hammer
Swings by my life.
Tears me apart inside.
Fear in my mind reminding
me . . .
of pain.

Hilderd Fields Gunn

Hilderd Fields Gunn
LITTLE CEDAR

Dedicated to the Arbor Day Foundation.

Lovely and stark as can be, you don't
age as I can see.
In all seasons, summer, winter, and
fall you just stand there for all of us,
as if for a reason.

Ten Thousand years' generations will
come and go, you and your powerful
famous friends, although many cut
down, will be there standing still,
adorned in God's pure white snow.

What is your name, is it just Little
Cedar Tree? Maybe Mr. Shade or
Miss Beauty, Serene Green? Perhaps
you could be called Mrs. Oxygen
producer, gas exchanger, or Ms.
Noise Reducer.

From where was your source? It was
a brother, until I learned from the
Bible that we were created from the
same heavenly Father. Why God
gave you as a gift to mankind to help
one keep warm, breathe, and not to
sneeze.

I love you Cedar Tree—wish I could
be, but it wasn't meant for people to
be a tree.

Roberta L Garrett
A TWIG

To my family, who always greet me, with outstretched arms that hold "My Twig."

Try your wings little bird, there's lots
and lots of sky
But drop a twig to mark the spot,
where first you learned to fly
Freedom flight is part of youth, and
little birds will roam
Still you're never quite so far, if
you've left one twig at home
It leaves a part of you with those you
love, and by and by
It warms your heart to know it's
there, no matter where you fly
Really look at all you see, feel
everything you touch
Love every minute sixty-seconds,
don't be afraid to love too much
It doesn't matter where you perch,
while life is still a test
You gather bits from here and there,
before you build your nest
It's not so much the song you sing,
but that you sing at all
Somewhere another little bird, is
waiting for your call
So flap your wings and fly away, the
world is not so big
Knowing there's a place called home,
you marked it with-'A Twig'

Pamela J Adams
THE GIFT

To Mother with love. Thank you for believing in me.

There's a gift we each possess
Though sometimes buried deep
inside;

It's a gift worth more than gold
And one we often push aside;

We must live our life and live it well
To show how much we care;

We've very little time you see
It's something we must share;

The gift—it's in our heart
Though it takes on many forms;

The gift, you see, is LOVE
And true LOVE will weather any
storm.

Alice D Taylor
THE BITTER WOMAN
She rises early, yet no one calls her
blessed. She has a heart of stone—
rarely has a kind word to say to
anyone.

She works with her hands all day and
is never satisfied. She eats of the fruit
of the land, yet is never filled.

She lies down to rest but finds none.
Her eyes show years of anguish—no
hope, no joy, no peace.

She weeps bitter tears—crying for
help but, yet, no one can touch her.

She longs for love. She longs for
peace. She longs for joy. She longs
for hope.

When you talk to her, she turns a deaf
ear. She rages in disbelief.

She prays empty prayers. She calls on
the name of Jesus, but it is all in vain.

She shuns fellowship with the
children of God. She shuns His word
and she shuns Him.

Fear—perhaps. Fear of being set free.
Fear of knowing true love, true joy,
true peace.

Pray for the bitter woman.

Alice D Taylor
DANCING BEFORE THE LORD

In Loving Memory of Deon and Jacquelyn Bose.

Your dancing has blessed us all so
much. You've touched so many
hearts and encouraged so many souls,
and I thank God that He allowed you
to touch our lives.

I remember the way you danced;
your face radiant; your movements
swift and graceful as you humbly
reverenced the Lord.

In my mind I see you dancing up the
stairway to Heaven; clothed in white;
laughing; singing; stars twinkling
around you like diamonds; and as
you leap joyfully, you turn and
beckon your daughter to follow you.

I see little legs happily running
through the clouds, eyes wide with
wonder as they behold the glory of
the Lord.

Even though the tears will flow and
hearts will ache because we will miss
you so much; We can find comfort
and rejoice in knowing that you are
dancing before the Lord in His
glorious Heaven above; And that's
the way he will remember you . . .
dancing before the Lord.

Patricia Bey
SLING

For Dennis, my loyal husband and friend.

He sighted the house sparrow,
But ignored the appeal
Echoing from the loft.
Hit, bronzed Goliath—fell.

He, another stone loaded
And readied to pelt
Those glassy eyes fixed
And forehead smudged—moribund.

No cheers from Israelites
Or love of Michal;
Only glassy eyes fixed
And forehead smudged—dead.

Virgie M Smith
INSIDE MY MIND

This poem is dedicated to my children, grandchildren and mother (Helen Stroy).

Oh prison walls you only hold
My flesh and bones, but not my soul
For over these walls a free mind soars
From prison guards and cold steel
doors

To a world confusing as can be
That holds no future for you nor me
Cold and hungry babies crying
Men at war fighting and dying
Women hanging their heads in shame
Washington looking for someone to
blame

I'm looking for a place to hide
So I might as well go back inside
To my cold dense prison cell
To me it's pain
To others it's hell
But there's one thing I know—
Inside, outside, there's no place to go

Shawn D Breter
HEY THERE SWEET VALENTINE

To my first and only true love, Jennifer Lynn.

Hey there sweet valentine
Ive got something for you.
It's big and beautiful
and bold and true.
Its meant to make you happy
and never make you blue.
Its pretty simple what I've got,
the most complicated thing you'll
know.
I hope it's easy for you to see,
sometimes it's hard for me to show.
Oh sweet valentine
nothing could ever tear us apart.
Because this thing I have for you
comes from my heart.
I guess I should tell you what it is
But I'm hoping you already know,
Its my deepest, deepest love for you.

Margaret Sutton Hadden
HOW
How do you paint a picture?
Where are the colors you need
For a mountain stream,
Or a sunset gleam,
Or a trembling cattail reed?

How do you sing the song
That haunts through the night and the
noon?
Where do you find the tune
To lay the words upon?

How do you tell a story?
Where do you find the skills
For all those adventures of glory
That lie asleep in the hills?

How do you build a bridge
To span a roaring river,
Laced from ridge to ridge
Hanging all aquiver?

The tools and skills you can,
Find where He placed them, my
friend
To hide away or to spend
Deep in the heart of a man.

Rafaela W Barker
THE MAGIC DREAMS OF SEASONS GONE
In my youth I'd dream of knights in shining armor, magic meadows, enchanted forests, magic castles and other magic places, and I remember thinking that I find these magic dreams somewhere in the future.

I felt that magic was somewhere in the future, when the warm evening air would wrap itself around me, and envelop all my senses with the fragrance of its scent and caress me in a very gentle way. Or when I heard a mockingbird sing and greet a morning on the first day of *Spring*, I felt that the magic lay somewhere in the future.

I remember thinking that the magic would be somewhere in the future, when I'd look outside my window, into my backyard, and saw the hazy *Summer* sunset bathe the lightly studded skies in its warm amber light, where at a distance, far away I could see the twinkling specks of city lights, and there was magic there, but still I thought magic was somewhere in the future.

I remember feeling that magic was in the future, when in my backyard I could see the silhouette of the old pepper tree against purple and amber evening skies. And in the silent visions of my mind I remember the light fluttering sound that its rustling leaves made, as it swayed to and fro, in the *Autumn's* gentle breeze, but still I thought there'd be magic in the future.

And as time came and went, the magic feeling I waited for, never came to be, because it slipped away far into the future.

Now in the *Winter* of my life, I realize that the magic dreams and feelings that danced around in the reaches of my mind, were nowhere in the future, but they had slipped away into the past, and lay peacefully somewhere back in time . . . alongside my youth.

Dale Hendrickson
BLAST!

Blasts! A dedication to our forefathers' "Struggle towards Freedom."

A blast goes fast, but does
not last, like a cast, that's from
an arm or a leg. With some
firecrackers inside the cast
with one fuse lit, the
firecracker would then
fizzle out slowly, until it
hits the bottom of the
fuse. With the rest of
the firecrackers that
light up, the first
firecracker would
then go ka-boom.

While the rest of the fireworks
are ready to go off,
they'd go ka-boom, ka-boom
one after the other. There the
cast would then explode
wide open, with
shimmering pieces of the
cast flying apart. While
the rest of the
firecrackers go off,
they would show
those beautiful
bursting colors,
that shoot up
in the sky on
the fourth
of July.

Steven J Navarre
BOX
I've lived in a Box all my life
All Four walls surrounding,
THEY touch everything I do.
I have no regrets,
I have no better.
For it was in a box I was born
And have never known freedom,
Nor wanted IT !
For in my Box I am secure and safe.

Life is no Problem.
What lurks out Beyond my walls
bothers me none,
For it is their Problem!
And not my own.
My walls protect me,
For in my Box I am secure and safe.

B Sadler
KNITTING
Imprisoning amber light, my needles
flash
Within my shuttling hands, that,
weaving to and fro
A thin blue strand—are dignified and
prim
But clicking a merry staccato.
Each step is sure and firm, and like
my thoughts
Needs no release from fettering
bonds and ties
But flows into the garment of my
dreams
To match the clear true burning of his
eyes.

J Lynn Kelley-Tinsley
A SHADOW OF THE SUN

For Amy Marie Gallimore Born: November 7, 1989. At rest: March 5, 1990.

Her life was like a warm summer day. When she was born, it was as if the sun rose and brought warmth into our day. She was so alive and vibrant. In the end of her life, it was as if the sun was setting. One moment, we looked and saw a beautiful baby girl. Then, she was gone. Her life was short, just as the day, and the moments without her seem long, like the cold, dark night. We loved her as long as we had her, and now that she is with God, we have memories of her . . . like a shadow made by the sun.

J Lynn Kelley-Tinsley
YOU WERE THE LIGHT
You were the farmer
Who planted my seed.
You were the gardener
Who pulled out the weeds

You were the artist
Who sculpted my mind.
You were the friend
Who, to me, was kind

You were the teacher
Who taught me so well.
You were the doctor
Who healed me when I fell.

You were the light
When my world seemed dark
You, too, are a flame
That began from a spark.

Laurie R Kelley
NOT ONLY ON SUNDAY
I just read about an auto, Its price tag
reads a half a million bucks.
Does it sometimes seem to you,
Some other guy has all the luck?

Sometimes I think how nice that it would be, To have that kind of wealth,
But, Then my mind goes back a ways, To when I was very ill.
I called upon the King of Kings, He restored to me my health.

There are people in this world, With no pillow or a bed.
Thank God that I have both of these,
And there's a roof above my head.

People do not seem to care today,
About the other person's sorrow,
But, Their turn may come . . . We cannot see tomorrow,

My greatest wish is this Oh Lord,
Please help me to have compassion
For the other souls upon this earth.
Oh please help me to have compassion, Even when I'm not in church.

Laurie R Kelley

WINTER'S THE TIME

Winter's the time, For roasting of hams,
Of Bright festive tables, And Mom's homemade jams.

Then there's the sleigh rides, across crusted snow,
All laughing, and singing, Oh the fun as we go!

Winter's the time that Christmas, comes here,
We hope that our family, Will all gather near,
To sit by the fireside and sing of good cheer.

While we pray the Lord Jesus, We'll all be here next year.

Letha Memorie Wayne

Letha Memorie Wayne

AS SEEN BY KRISTEN'S CAT, BRIDGET (KRISTEN—5 WEEKS OLD)

What kind of creature
is this that has come
into my territory?
"It's" not furry
Nor has "it" a tail
But my mistress
sure fusses over "it"
At the first sign of a
Whimper and wail
"It's" fragile, small
And pink
Demands attention
From my master—I think—
I must remain constant,
patient and true—
Then they'll know I am loyal and true blue.
I hissed at "it"
When "it" came into my
Special domain
But alas and alack
This small bundle
Still seems to here remain
I've been pushed
And removed from
My throne—The Bed
"It" has priorities
over me
A princess—'nough said!
Strange sounds from
"its" little mouth
Come forth
No "meow"—No "purr"
But "they" jump for joy
At the first sign
of noise
From this tiny wee thing
Called a "her!"

Connie Stevens

AFRAID TO LET GO

To whom I cared for very much.

You seem so perfect to me,
everything is fine;
You're everything I would want you to be
if only you were mine.
The feelings are there,
we both know that it's true;
for each other we both care,
so why am I so blue?
One thing is holding you back
and keeping us apart.
You might not realize,
but because of it you are breaking my heart.
I realize you will always have
feelings for her big and small,
but you have to let go
and when you do I will be there to
comfort your fall.
Remember as we grow closer
our friendship grows stronger.
So if you decide you're not ready
to let go of her,
and you need to cling on,
our friendship will always stay strong.

James Pritchard Rose

NATURE TALKS

To Craig Alexander, Kelly Wassil, Dave Trommer, Dave Bradley, Butch Hillier, and most of all, my family: Mom, Dad, Bob, Rick and Sherry. I Love You All!

As I looked around the brisk November air began to numb my toes and face,
The sun was setting and the moon was rising to the sky.
The soothing sound of the nearby river made me forget the cold,
And then the river began to speak to me.
It turned my thoughts to our friendship and how it is like the river,
For just as the river flows seemingly endless—so grows our friendship.
As I looked out further I noticed that the river forked in different directions,
But the river said, "I do not end here
but I take separate paths to my destiny."
I thought a while and the river continued speaking,
"Just as I change, so will your friendship—but this does not mean you are leaving one another."
"For in the end you'll be together, meeting once again—just as I will."
As the river bid farewell and continued towards its destiny, it occurred to me,
Today I believed my thoughts were of nature and life, but now I realize that your friendship is the nature of my life.

Mazola A Hunley

REFLECTIONS

Dedicated to my sister-friend; Phyllis M. West, and to all the people who inspired, loved, and challenged the woman I was to become. To the Spirit: Without whom I could do nothing.

In her eyes
I see myself looking, staring, studying her
The curl of the lashes, the pattern of the eyebrows, full lips, thick nostrils, tiny moles, tiny lines beginning to form.
The Eyes
PENETRATE, CONCENTRATE, CONTEMPLATE:
Hints of how she used to be
Hints of how she wants to be
Hints of how she will be
Older. Wiser.
Sooner. Later.
Her weaknesses. Her strengths. They are the same as mine.
I notice her even on the street.
In store windows.
In the eyes of others.
For she is a reflection of me.
She is me and I am her.
We are the same.
We ARE ONE.

William P Warden

AMOURS

To Calico, princess of the unicorn, inspiration for creation.

Hearts are for lovers, and hearts are for friends,
whose faith in each other has no end.

Our trust and respect, it knows no bounds.
To talk, just eyes, no need for sounds.

Skin as pure as alabaster, her hazel eyes, I looked past her,
and saw the truth in her heart, and beauty in her soul.

You, the unicorn and I, the rainbow,
at whose end a pot of gold.
Us, two friends.

Mildred Jarratt

THEY LET ME SEE, THEY LET ME SMELL

To the many sweet neighborhood kids and adults who constantly shower me with flowers month after month. I love you very much.

Let me smell my flowers while I live
An expression, I've heard through the years
A tribute to me you thought you'd give
A gift that brought many joyful tears

Long stems, short stems, some, no stems at all
Each one you brought, I received with glee
You came from spring through the fall
All that I could save, I saved for the world to see

The roses, carnations, marigolds and dandelions
Sometimes with the tulips an onion or two
The days that you came brought peace sublime
Each day I have beautiful thoughts of you

Red, orange, yellow and blue
Silk buds, and real old fashioned bouquets
Pink, white and violet too
Are the beautiful flowers you brought from day to day

You are not my maternals, but I gladly own you as such
Glad to call you my girl, my boy
For the many flowers, I thank you much.
You Let Me See, You Let Me Smell.

Patricia Ford

TRANQUILITY

This poem is dedicated to my husband Tom, and my four sons, Tom, Greg, Steve and Chris.

I wish that everyone could see,
The joy of a family on a camping spree,
The slower pace of life it brings,
Takes you back to nature and beautiful things,
The rustling leaves of a grand old tree,
Fills your heart and mind with tranquility,
Stop for a while and you will see and hear,
The flight of a rabbit and leap of a deer.

You may enjoy just playing ball,
Or gazing at the trees in fall,
No radios or phones that ring,
You will be amazed at the peace it brings,
A walk thru the woods where the wildflowers bloom,
Will lighten your heart if it's filled with gloom,
Nightfall brings the best of all,
Nocturnal animals with their haunting call,
Just raise your eyes to Saturn and Mars,
You will discover thousands of glorious stars,

When the sun is shining or moon aglow,
Try it yourself, and you too, will know.

Shannon McDowell
OUR RELATIONSHIP

This poem is dedicated to Steve Landry, the man I will always love.

Our relationship
Is so special to me
That is why I cannot
Leave you be.
I want to hold you
And love you
All the time
But we seem to live
Too far apart.
But maybe it's time
To combine our love
Into one big heart
Instead of two
Broken hearts
So far apart.

Mrs Maurice (Merle) E German
MY LOVE

This poem is dedicated to my loving husband Maurice W. German. He passed away in 1977.

You feel your life is over,
When your loved one is called away.
We know that God knows best,
It's hard for us to see it that way.

If, I could only touch his hand,
What a comfort that would be.
Some day we will walk together,
On heaven street just he and me.

We were truly blessed with the good things in life,
Our years together were happily spent.
I am looking forward to that great day,
That reunion in heaven, a joyful event.

As I go out in the evening,
And I see the stars in the sky.
I know he is there waiting,
He is waving me a good-bye.

Susan Miller
THE OLD GROWTH TREE

Dedicated to my beautiful daughter, Stephanie, who has always given me loving encouragement to write poetry.

We stood in the forest and looked up at the sky,
And saw the top of the tree standing so high.
We looked around, there were many more
Spreading high above the forest floor.

The owl hoots and the moss does grow,
The sounds and smells are from head to toe.
Deer run through, past the old growth tree,
Then stop to look at the tree and me.

Some old trees rot and to the ground they fall
To make a home for the creatures small.
The underbrush is thick and lush,
Plants will grow to the sun's morning blush.

The old tree stood, until one day
They cut it down and took it away.
It was cut with pleasure and with ease,
Only to sell it to the Japanese.

Ancestors suffered to come to this place,
To share the land with the trees of grace;
But the trees in the forest that are so old
Will never return, so we've been told.

Gina Francis
HAUNTING CABIN

To Justin and Jennifer—who inspire me to write stories and poems.

The air felt calm, for such a winter night.
The cabin was dark—such a shivering sight.
It looked gloomy and lifeless, surrounded by trees.
It made me shake nervously—way past down my knees.
I heard a crack coming from inside the door—
It sounded like it may have been caused by the floor.
Was it a shadow I just saw walk by . . .
Holding a candle, making sounds like that of a cry?
I must be dreaming, I need to wake up . . .
I mean, how could this be—if no one's been seen!
I suppose it could be my imagination—if you know what I mean.
Picture yourself alone out at night
In front of a cabin—with such a shivering sight.
What would you do—perhaps walk inside?
No thanks!
I think I'll just stay in my room under my blankets and hide.

Opal Luella Lowrance

Opal Luella Lowrance
A TALK TO MY DAFFODILS
Oh how I love the daffodils
That grow wild upon the hills.
Yet in my yard I find you there
So sweet, so lovely, and so fair.
But aren't you freezing you pretty thing?
You bloom so early in the spring.
There is snow on the ground and the wind is so cold
Yet not once have I heard you scold.
It seems to me that you need a coat
But that would hide the ruffle on your beautiful throat.
You are God's blessing and gift to me
Spring will be here soon you will see.
The sun will shine and the birds will sing
Then you will know that it is spring.
And then God will send April showers
For the beauty of His flowers.
So keep your smile my pretty one
Soon you will be warm in the sun.

Opal Luella Lowrance
THE BEAUTY OF THE ROSE
No flower is sweeter than the rose
It is a symbol of love all lovers knows.
Its fragrance is like perfume in the dew.
Sweethearts send them to prove their love is true.
Red ones are sent to mother on her special day
White ones are worn in her memory if she has passed away.
It makes no difference if they are red, pink, or yellow,
Pretty girls like to receive them from her fellow.
Much happiness can unfold in the petal of a rose
And there is so much beauty in the garden where it grows.
In the rose we see so much grace
And they are lovely in a vase.
Husbands send them to their spouse
Sometimes they keep him out of the dog house.

James Gregory Murray Jr
FIRST LOVE

If time ever stopped in this universe, it stopped, for one brief moment with you.

I sit here in this darkest hour
Dreaming of yesterday
A time I held you in my arms
A memory never fading away.
I whisper your name in a gentle breeze
Praying that you will hear
The love in my voice that I feel for you
The mist from this lonely tear.
My heart slowly melting,
Burning for your touch,
The warmth from your smile,
I miss you so much.
Although I have come to realize
Our time has come and gone
Like the cold wind,
Following a summer's breeze,
I know now I have to let you go
But in my heart you'll forever be.

Mary Jane Lawrence
Y O U
Someone molded your body,
Designed your fingerprints,
Added just the right amount of coloring
To create a special YOU.
You have your own birthday,
Your very own name.
The government donated numbers
That no one else can claim.
You can fashion your dreams,
Spark your wildest ambitions,
Develop a personality
That belongs just to YOU.
There will be days
That you would like
To take a walk
In the other fella's boots.
Sorry, but they just won't fit—
The plan doesn't work that way.
You were meant to be yourself,
One of a kind,
Just YOU, an extra special YOU.

Emilie Pieper
HEART STRINGS
The strongest ties are made with strings
Not of material strength.
There's no measure of pounds per inch
or of the plies or length.
They're measured in a greater sphere
with bonds that ne'er are broken.
The strings are really elastic
with golden words unspoken.

Woven in are kindly deeds
with perhaps a daily smile,
a genuine concern for all
no hypocratic guile.

They automatically synchronize
with a mother and a cradle.
They lovingly begin at home
with a scrub brush or cooking ladle.
They reciprocate to neighbors
to all in Christian love.
They will never snap while on earth
They're strengthened from above.

Willimette Fewell
ISN'T GOD BEAUTIFUL!
The trees are lush and green,
The sky is blue with frothy clouds,
The grass a lovely blanket for our feet,
The flowers abound in rainbow beauty,
The earth's alive with His creatures,
The warmth of the golden sun upon us,
The birds a-chattering in the trees,
With their songs of magic to the world,
A world embraced by greenery everywhere,
The spirits abound among us
Though we do not see,
Love is a-giving all through the land,
Through God and His beauty!

Nora Neville Harlien
PEACEFUL VALLEY
It's a bleak, gray day, and the trees are naked and bare,
The cold North wind sweeps through the Valley like a Wild March Hare.
The silver icicles hang from limb and thread,
After the freezing rain has cast its shimmering spread
To the gurgling stream and evergreen trees.

The peace and quiet,- and a long time dream
is more fulfilled than it could ever seem,
The air carries an urgency and an age-old drive to burrow and hide, in an effort to survive.
The sun sinks in a velvet bed of red and gray
Leaving a portent of a snow-white day.

The diamond tipped ice on the horse's mane
And the glistening snow on the hills and lane,
A rosy cheeked boy with the World in his hand—
The hope of tomorrow and a newborn land.

The night shadows wraps her arms
around the hill and the naked trees,
pregnant with the promise of Spring,
Stand like sentinels against the sky.
While the moon, encircled with a
gossamer ring
Looks down on the Valley that lies
peaceful,—and still.

Doris C Zanders
HALLOWEEN FLIGHT
One black scary Halloween night
As I walked outside to have some
fun,
A piercing scream filled with fright
Fell on my ears and I began to run.

A black cat chased me throughout the
lane.
She changed to a witch as it started to
rain.
Thunder rolled and lightning flashed,
The wind was blowing and two cars
crashed.

The witch changed to a ghost but I
ran on.
I made a quick turn and headed for
home.
It was MY scream I heard on that
horrible night,
Which was the reason for my
Halloween flight.

Catherine Tan

Catherine Tan
HER BEAUTY SHAMED THE BUDS

I would like to dedicate all the poems I have written, including this one, to NKOTB especially to Jonathan Rashleigh Knight (he's the sweetest guy). I also dedicate this to my family and close friends.

her beauty shamed the buds
made the sun but a glimmer of light
the stars insignificant to the night
the moon a boring sight.

she was raved in all corners of the
world
bowed down even by the creatures of
the wild
And for men
her beauty was the reason of life.

blinded all they were
of the beauty of the pearl
So very unaware
it's not to last forever.

but suddenly the world was shaken
beauty is now a fright
One with the dwellers of the night
and the titans were more of
beauty to their sight.

Annette Dollard
DARK CLOUDS SHED TEARS LAST NIGHT
Lights off at ten thirty P.M.
Room silent, dark
Only bright light of outdoor
Street lights glazing through my
window were awake.
Thousands of tiny crystals rain drops,
like a little boy infinite tears,
or the drips from a child's lemon
lollypop were on the glass.
Dripping—dripping
gradually down until
they fell into my eyes
turned into my own tears
and made me whimper—weep,
for a century of time—
but God came to bless them,
to set me into a silent sleep.

Dee Overpeck
MEMORIES
Memories are your views of past
times,
Neither right nor wrong—
Even though someone always tries to
correct you.
Memories create illusions that cause
peace of mind;
Otherwise, you might find difficulty
to cope—
Souvenirs of dreams made a reality.
You must be true to yourself!
Needless suffering is not a cure
Even though you must face it &
adjust.

Mental faculty to store &
recall—
Emotions & feelings that are yours,
A visible view of the event,
Not necessarily the actual reality, but
Sense of proof of what happened to
you.

Memories can be a peaceful fantasy.
Even our artistic process or ability
will
Merge as a memory
Or a union of creative nature,
Right or wrong, thrusting with a
fertile imagination.
Your memories are a part of your
self-vision.

Tonny Brown
WALLS OF COLOR
'Tis a world with walls
round-about,
where people are standing,
some in, some without.
The walls that are cannot be seen,
for they stand in the hearts of
'Human Beings.'
A man and his brother are not
alike,
for they are separated by colors
some black others white.
It has been found in the heart of
man,
an inexplicable blindness and he
cannot understand.
That the world is full of
variations of things,
the same, God intended for all
living beings.
That they be born of different
creed and race,
then dwell together in this
earthly place.
Please rest thy soul and hold out
thine hand,
and then I shall take it, and
together we shall stand.

Karen R Koppelman
ACCEPTANCE
What is life?
a series of troughs, winding up and
down through life's midstream;

once on the plateau, high as a bird,
nothing can touch, the heart
preserved;

then spiralling down the path so deep,
fall to the bottom, the ravine is steep;

now far below the earth's crust
entwines, shadowing light, darkness
surrounds;

climb back above till the land lies
flat, search far and wide for the pain
to subside;

feel no embrace, nor any distaste,
surroundings are calmer, steady and
stronger;

realize, accept, no delusions expect,
will never climb further or submerge
thru terror;

fulfillment awaits, though hardly
content, wiser we are, disguised by
life's scar;

comprehension complete, we accept
what we meet, though never quite
receiving, life's broader meaning!

Paraskevi D Contos
THE KAFFENEION
Small tables
and worn chairs
surround the old kaffeneion

Clouds of smoke rise slowly from a
few tables
A towering oak tree looks over the
busy scene
Chatter, gossip, giggles
A song or two . . .

The smell of a roasting lamb sizzles
over the strong, crackling fire

The tables are filled with soda bottles
Dishes full of ice cream,
Tiny glasses filled with sweet liqueur

Worry beads play in hands
Coffee is sipped from chipped cups
thoughts fill busy minds
And people fill the old kaffeneion
with merriment and delight

Paraskevi D Contos
UNTITLED
White columns rise from the dry, arid
dirt
Dry grass seeps between the cracks
An armless, headless woman looks
over the empty scene
The warm, whirling wind winds up
the columns
History has been made.

Across the archaic scene
The lively waves play with the shore
The warm sun casts drops of light on
the pebble sands
The foaming white crest of the blue
catches them
and shimmers in praise
History is being made . . .

Paraskevi D Contos
UNTITLED
White walls follow
Worn leather sandals step on the dull,
smooth pebble street
Green, glazed eyes from a lazy feline
look out in dark curiosity
Her tail sways and curls
A violet flower sits on the windowsill
greeting any passer-by
Narrow, winding, closing
Lost, confused . . . perhaps
A coal black night holds . . .
and does not let go . . .
and no one knows . . .

Paraskevi D Contos
THE VILLAGE
Twenty small houses hide
in the thick patch of green
Red brick roofs ascent the patch
Cool water runs from the spring
Pails reach in to catch the quenching
course
Winding dirt roads lead
—a labyrinth, a maze of marvel
Chickens, goats, lambs fill
the air with sound
Villagers gather on the veranda
Some smoke, some chat, some laugh
And when day closes its eyes
Crickets sing their rhythmic concord
and lull the villagers to sleep
and night keeps watch

Paraskevi D Contos
THE MARKETPLACE
Busy merchants sell their luscious
fruits—
figs, grapes, apricots, peaches
A corpulent woman pulls her rusty,
wire cart full of green beans,
tomatoes, lemons, meat, and such
All ingredients that will make the late
afternoon meal

Merchants bicker and argue
Dirty tents cover the street like a
dingy quilt

But the day ends and the heat of the
tepid sun dwindles
The busy marketplace is put to rest
The quilt is lifted
The street is emptied
The late afternoon meal has been
eaten and night swallows the empty
street

Ben Taylor (15 years old)
TRAGEDY
I was driving with the blindness
Of a Deadly dark dream.
Eyesight faltering, reactions slow,
Thoughts altered. Trying to see what
Lies beyond.
I found a brink of a grim light
shining.
I blacked out as screams came from
ALL around and envisioned
Two meteors crashing in the sky.

I awakened seeing a woman that had
her
Life taken away. Through one second

of the
Long eternity, a group of four is now ONE.
Poisoning the body for fun
Was the cost of four.

Soon after the bodies were gone
And will be forgotten in the future by most,
I closed my eyes and thought about three
Blind boys and an innocent woman
That were no more.
The nightmare would Never end!

Melony Lynn Canipe
MY PICTURE
As it hangs there on the wall
I daydream as I stare a bit,
My picture it's so beautiful
Just wishing I were a part of it.
I'd have a cabin by the stream
Just in view of the mountain peaks,
This is where I'd dream my dreams
Day by day and week by week.
The giant trees they're standing so tall
They're full of nature's colors,
The peaks so high and covered with snow
I'd take a hike someday ya know.
The animals would be an important part
I'd watch them every day,
From early morn till almost dark,
As they hunt, they eat, they roam, they play.
Nature is a beautiful thing
I do believe you'd all agree,
Peaceful surroundings is what it brings
I could stay there for all eternity.
Just one of my dreams, is it meant to be?

Marjorie Grogan
HOPE FOR A NEW-WAVE WORLD
Oh! Great and good cosmic-creator
Almighty,

At last you set earthlings
Shackle-free.

For out of the cruel coldcrusted
war-weary wilderness walls
you delivered us from woe.

While born-again daisies sprout right out
from under yesterday-dated
superannuated snow.

Anne Evans Gibson
GYPSIES
Wild and free as dust they went,
And came yet again;
Wandering back for one last stop,
Before they left forever.
They lived for generations here,
And then were gone to another world;
To a world of freedom and gaiety.
Gypsies traveled when they were here
To escape our world of blindness.
They could not play the games,
Nor memorize the phrases to be said;
The places and the times to say them.
So when they could no longer travel
Together in their Gypsy groups,
They were lost to our world, or they left it.
Come back, Gypsies, and take us
To your unprejudiced world of freedom!
Impossible, for happiness can be with but a few,
And still be for the same reason.
One would lead and the rest would follow,
Like sheep, to the pasture of oblivion.

Karen J Mouradian Lages

Karen J Mouradian Lages
DEAREST DAD

This poem is dedicated to Vasken, my Dearest Dad. Love always, Karen.

Dad you showed me so much in life
How can I go wrong
To have a dad like you
It takes so long
But now you left me dad
And had no right to do
I hate you for leaving me
Now what am I supposed to do
Just listen to what you taught me
There's times in our life when we will have to go
But dad not yet, you're supposed to stay
Dad how can I stop this feeling
This feeling of emptiness
I wish you were back with us
Mom, your children and grandchildren
But I know now that in spirit
You are here to stay
If only I can touch you
I know it will be someday
I love you dad and always
The hate has gone away.

David "Stein" Goldstein
THE CHILL OF A WINTER NIGHT
The warmth of a blazing fire
Two silhouettes dancing in the dark
During the moment of strong desire
It strikes like a man-eating shark

The flow of warm blood
A figure rushing through the house
The whole world's at peace
Except for his spouse

Nothing for this matron to do
Only but to sit and wait
Comforting the One who fades with the night
No sounds of help, the ambulance is late

Sounds of morning pervade the land
The Light of Day shines unto all but one
Sitting by the window, looking to the sky
She curses at God for what He has done

Lisa Curtis
SILENCE (AN ABUSED CHILD)
Tiny drops of snowflakes fall,
Freezing the face of a winter doll,
Her salty tears mixing with the ice,
Slide off her cheeks and fall like dice,
Deadly silence rings through her ears,
Only the sound of her painful tears,
Alone, no one near, on the ground,
She hears nothing, not a sound,
Her ice blue eyes cut through the air,
Watching the snow in an empty stare,
Fragile lips whispering to say no,
As another teardrop hits the snow.

Maxine Bredeman
FRIENDS
Friends may come
and friends may go,
But you're one friend
who is nice to know.

Material things can
be bought in a store,
But true friendship just
Grows and grows evermore.

Thank you again
For the wonderful things
But friendship is the one
That will always remain.

Friends from
Country to Country
Working and living together
For you and me.

Carolyn E Hoover
WINGS
Warm, warm is the Wind from the Garden,
And it carries a breath of the Sea . . .
There's a salty tang to the taste of the apples
We must steal from the boughs of that ancient Tree.

And our God sits there with a smile on His face,
Watching His children fall from grace,
(Watching His children grow!)

Warmer still is the kiss of the sun
Melting the snows of our fears,
Drying the feathers on our wings . . .

Wiser still is the Silence of God
As He lets us meet every challenge . . .
Scorning the binding laws of Men,
Leaving behind the dour and the pious.

And happy is the heart of God
When we stretch our wings at last—
Wearing the mantle of Freedom He gave us,
And embracing the IS of the world as He made it!

Carolyn E Hoover
EVE'S SONG
My love, I brought thee golden apples,
From the Tree of Paradise . . .
Plucked and brought them,
Full and bursting . . .
Finer than the sweetest wine . . .
Brought thee apples, golden apples,
For the sunlight in your eyes.

Dawn shone forth in Eden's Garden
Glinted golden on the bough,
And I plucked them, golden apples,
For the glory on your brow.

From my heart the treasure's torn,
From my soul where Love was born:
For Love I gave thee golden apples,
Apples stolen from the bough . . .

Susan P Danford
TODAY
Today I have loved life.
I have smiled into the sunshine,
I have watched the clouds drift slowly across the sky,
I have breathed in the joy of existence.

Today I have given someone a chance.
I have shared someone's laughter,
I have listened to a problem,
I have offered my help.

Today I have tried.
I have tried to be friendly,
I have tried to be honest,
I have tried to live my life.

Tomorrow.
I will watch it unfold,
I will expect great things to happen,
I will tackle challenges,
I will keep on going!

Jennifer L Warm
MY HAND TOO WEAK
In the palm of my hand you rest,
Settled, and immobile.
I watch, hoping to find the strength to take a firm grasp,
Enough to wrap my stiffened fingers around you,
So you are locked inside,
And unable to escape this given shelter.

Frustration builds up, as my knuckles grow rusty,
For all those times of hurt warped my bones,
And now, my hand too weak.

Like sand passes through fingers, I feel you slip,
And I find my body in pain, as I struggle to recapture yours,

Because I realize that this is one less time I have to catch,
Before you fall out of my complete vision.

I see you sliding,
And I feel your taut hold around my cold, lifeless finger,
But it's not to attach yourself to my dreams of such closeness,
It's to save yourself from the solid guilt that awaits,
Down below.

Danny Bradley
TWILIGHT
When I was a boy it was a magical time.
Twilight seemed to suit me just fine.
Just when you started to really have fun,
suddenly you realized your day was done.
Feeling you'd never have another day of your own,
reluctantly you started to make your way home.
You went to sleep and your dreams were spun,
till the morning you awoke and saw the sun.
And you knew that the magic was surely not done.
Each day you felt it had just begun.
But now as the years weave their blanket,
I wonder if someone else drank it.
This potion that used to make me feel magic.
Did it exist or is it so tragic?
That with old age we just seem to forget,
whatever it was that made us not quit.
Don't think I've lost it completely, not yet.
Still see the twilight, now with fret.
Need to go back and hear the twilight strumming,
that magic old tune, a new day is coming.

Juliette Marie Palmer
THE WARS THAT NEVER CEASE
A shot rings out, a cry is heard, as soldiers raise their arms;
Families torn apart, cities burn, destruction brought to farms.
Millions die. Millions mourn, though some more than others,
The gentle hearts of mothers die, as brother strikes his brother.
The cannons roar, the muskets fire, smoke burns in their eyes.
As soldiers fight to save their flag, many more will die.
The grass is stained with soldiers' blood, and not a soul can tell
The color or the race of he who in that deathyard fell.
And after all is fought and won, the Civil War found peace,
The tears that burn our memory's eyes fill the salty seas.

A cry rings out, no voice is heard, as millions blind their eyes.
Hearts torn apart, lives destroyed, a baby silently cries.
Millions die. Millions mourn, though some more than others,
The unknown lives of babies die, murdered by their mothers.
The passions roar and burn afire, and though they blind their eyes.
The mothers, with their doctors' help, will snuff out unborn lives.
Their hands are stained with their babies' blood, and not a soul can tell
The dreams and charms of he who in his mother's deathyard fell.
And though we thought we'd fought and won, the Civil War found peace,
Then why allow our babes to die, in wars that never cease?

Reva Yeates Bignall
SONG OF AMERICA
My heart races when I see
Old Glory rippling in the breeze.
Flag of the Free—You are beauty to me;
You are the symbol of all I hold dear.
You represent honor, respect, regret,
Help, distress, cognizant of signals;
Resolve situations, relations with nations,
Confirmations, regulations, indications,
Confrontations, identifications
Near or far . . . In peace and war
On land or on the sea.

One night I placed a blood red rose
Upon a young boy's casket.
How I longed to touch his face,
A guard stood near.
But I had known him as a lad of twelve,
A chubby boy with curly hair and laughter.
He was the first to greet me in the morning
The last to say goodnight,
His love of life—responsibility.
Quick to do without the asking,
To everything he gave his all
And proudly went, before his country's call.

He was a prayer boy, a choir boy.
He'd be glad I'd come to share
The sacrifice he'd made,
A battering ram in Viet Nam
With honor he had paid.
How proudly he must have worn
His Navy uniform.

"My Country 'tis of Thee . . . "
The bugles sounded
Volleys resounded
The flag triangularly folded
The last bell for him had tolled.

I sensed his silent caress;
He was glad. He had done his best.
Perhaps by others, greater blest
For he'd come back to rest
Among the hills of home.

Bonnie-Jane Mason
SINGLE-HANDED CROSSING
Smoothly I glide through a gray-green, liquid world:
Undulating . . . fathomless.
The breath of God—
Gentle as a sigh or strong with fury—
Blows me onward at His pace.
I navigate by faith (no landmarks here!),
My progress marked not by signposts but by images:

Bright flash of white-hot sun on highly polished chrome,
Sensuous delight of warm, smooth teak under bare feet,
Slap and splash of sparkling, impish wave,
Sharp "thwack" of sturdy canvas filling well,
Soft, rich cloak of black-velvet sequinned night.

And, everywhere:
Sticky . . .
Salty . . .
Wet.
Small, small price!

Elaine E Robinson

Elaine E Robinson
WALT DISNEY'S MICKEY & MINNIE MOUSE

Dedicated to Youth, especially at Concord, New Hampshire, and Christa McAuliffe.

There was a mouse, that
had no house
Who soon met Minnie, and
called her Mrs. Mouse.
This mouse soon became king
Oh, what a zing

As they went cheerfully along
He now owns not a house
with no hassle but lives
in a fine castle.

Oh what a sight to see, as they dance
on the stage with glee
Mickey and Minnie, Goofy, Donald Duck, and Snoopy
Oh, no, we can't forget the Walt Disney's Mickey and Minnie History.

Gayle D Button
YOU ARE MY SECRET

This poem is dedicated to a good friend—Shirley.

You are my secret love
The one I always think of.

You make me feel so special
When you put your arms around me
I wish I would never have to let go
You are my secret dream

You are the one I can talk to
You always seem to understand
I don't know why I ever left you
You are my secret man

When you whisper in my ear
My heart just jumps about
I love you more throughout the year
You are my secret doll

When we are so far apart
We're actually still together
Because you're always in my heart
You are my secret love . . . Forever!

Gina M DeAngelis
FOR MY FRIEND
Time passes-many people enter
our lives—some seem to stray . . .

Neverending—the search for one
to trust—count on day after day.

Life is easier with friends like you
enjoying, happiness—what life's about . . .

You have become very special to me
one I can trust with never a doubt.

I can be who I am with no
need to pretend . . .

Honesty and loyalty, never a front
with you MY FRIEND.

The long search has ended when
I found you . . .

Thank you for everything . . . so many
friends—yet so few.

Louise Schroeder
GOLDEN SEQUENCE
God, addressed us, upon "Holy" pages,
until, we, walk with Him: 'tis vain, in spite of stages!

"Poet" let thine poem be spoken.
God, gives life to dormant seed;
and, rainbow, over broken reed!

Lord, JUSTICE reigns: upon "Thy Day!"
Forgive us forevermore, MERCY—MERCY
there is a score!

Cindy K Crick
A VERY SPECIAL JOURNEY
A very special journey two doves took one day long ago
led them through the challenges, only the skillful dare to go.
There time was spent together, never left to drift for long,
before the one would make its call, to incapture the other with
their song.

Songs of soft tone cooing, echoes off through forest glade,
rehearsing every moment, when that first "Love's Bell" ring was made.
This "very special journey" had its time when wing flight felt no end,
Turned into a "Life's long journey,"
with the one you love, a "Legend."

Dale E Collins
UNTITLED
sexy talk,
intuitive listenin',
moist pursed lips,
long wet kisses.

moonlit night,
logs aflame,
burning desire
left untamed.

heavy breathing,
bodies caress.
silhouette by candle,
slowly undress.

slow and gentle
both lie down;
joined as one,
arms all around.

candles go out,
fire still hissing,
side by side
bodies lie glistening.

Alice Louise Quinn
NIGHT-WALK SOLILOQUY
My several shadows go along with me.
Some clear-cut, some pale and wavering

Like reflections of my many selves.
A myriad of lights overhead causing this phenomena,
I, in my somnambulant state,
Think they epitomize my thoughts of you
Some stark and clear,
Others illusive, ephemeral, and fast disappearing.
The streets are dark and eerie.
Even the four-legged creature by my side
Ever intuitive and alert—seems unfamiliar and leery
In this suddenly strange land of dark streets and closed-up houses.
The flowers are folded in for the night like their owners.
Swiftly slithering cats scramble through hedges.
I crisscross the winding streets in ever increasing flight from
Creatures of the night—two-legged and stumbling.

Oh light, show a clear ray for me!
I, who am lonely and lost, secretive and confused.
Oh for space, clear air and stars overhead.
Would that erase this weight from my heart?

Alice Louise Quinn
LA INGLESIA*
La Inglesia, indestructible
Ever encompassing
Always keeping
Never sleeping

To the heights they rise
To the depths they sink
No boundaries link
This social ink

On each social grain
Your claim is set
Clicking beads weave the net
To enmesh all without regret

Souls held spellbound
All tongues wagging,
The dirge entrancing,
The Word enhancing.

*The Church

Kelly Tschantz
COMPLEX THOUGHTS
How very complicated are the thoughts which rule my mind.
Symbols such as words are difficult to find.
I've searched and searched, but for what?
Could it be I've searched in vain?
Who is to decipher between the pleasure and the pain?
Expressions of my being crave such understanding,
But how can you understand?
I'd like to be able to take you
For one moment, if I could
Into the capacity where I'd be understood.
Would you like to go there, If there's even such a place?
Questions, doubts, and confusion this capacity will erase.
Images without form invite such thoughts to dance around.
How can it be that the explanations cannot be found?
Reflections of these images are blank in the looking glass.
If you don't know what I'm talking about—
You've proved my point alas!

Richie J Mitchell

Richie J Mitchell
A FATHER'S BEAMING LOVE

Dedicated to my children Donna, Ricky, Laura, Theresa, Jimmy. I love you.

Mountains are high
Valleys are low
Streams run fast
From melting snow
See the stars up above
Each time you look at them
Remember my love
In the morning
When the sun will shine
Think of me
Who helped you grow so fine

Now my children
Some day in time
This world will be yours
No longer mine
Like the melting snow
So one day I must go
But remember the stars up above
Look for the brightest, like the dove
It will be me
Beaming you down my love

Richie J Mitchell
THE BIKER

Dedicated to my son Jimmy, and grandsons John & Timothy.

Two wheels of death
Some would say
He pays it no mind
As he rode on his way
His black leather flapping
In the strong, gusting wind
This machine of fire would sing
As it carried him
The angels were his friends
Pagans were home

When you see him pass
You knew he was a breed alone
No lip did he take
No quarter would he give
To make trouble with him
Meant you didn't want to live
His tattoos were faded
Hair was snow white
With eyes of steel wisdom
That would pierce the night
Just an old biker from a younger life

Richie J Mitchell
TIME

Dedicated to my beautiful wife Rosemarie, I love you.

Time gone
Time spent
Wonder where
All the time has went
The only thing
That saves the day
Is all you have learned
While time
Was going away

People take
Your time for granted
They don't realize
This is not
How you planned it
So very few
In this world today
Used their time
In a wisely way
Before they know it
Time
Has gone away

Jennifer Gett
MYSTERIOUS BEAUTY

To my brave and beautiful Grandmother, Mary Ann Appleton.

As day puts on her majestic cloak of night,
The madness grows stealthily and silent.
And the giggling stars honor their plight,
Even though the clouds remain defiant.

Within this state,
Exists the essence of mysterious beauty
Like the serene ocean with the look of dare,
While the air whispers a scream in unity
Just for the thrill to scare.

Even though all this grows in short time,
To unwrap and gracefully showing
How shine and glory breathtakingly rhyme
My spirit excitedly starts growing,
During that dark mysterious time.

And until once again the sky is playfully glowing,
The love of mysterious beauty is mine.

Peggy Roberts
ALMA
I have had the pleasure of spending two weeks with a terrific lady,
She has brightened our days with stories both sunny and shady.
A joy and inspiration, a caring soul is she,
Happy to have known her wisdom are we.

Tales of a childhood filled with hard work and care,
Enough hard times to gray your hair.
But no feeling sorry or moaning of her fate,
Just taking in stride and being willing to wait.

Soft as the petals of the most delicate flower,
Continuing to bloom hour by hour.
Strong as the limbs on the old oak tree,
Such a hard worker, an example for you and me.
Wise and sage as mother earth she is,
At keeping the faith, she's truly a wiz.

Laughing and singing, a bit nutty at times,
(tah, tah, tah, can't find a word that rhymes.)
The Lord knew what the world needed, He saw the need for care,
So created our Alma, may she always be there.
For we need such a person to keep us on our toes,
A person whose love just grows and grows.

So my prayer for today and for tomorrows to come,
So thank you for sending so precious a one.
As dear Alma, a joy and a blessing is she,
Thank you dear Lord for introducing her to me.

Claire K McTavish
THE COLOSSUS RESTORED

To my immigrant parents, Joseph and Mary Ann Kunze, who entered in 1887.

Silent Guardian of sea and shore,
Lift your flaming torch once more.
Cast open wide that Golden Gate
To the downtrodden, the homeless,

The persecuted, longing to escape.
Bid them enter the now empty Ellis Island stalls,
Once the refuge of the poor,
The weary and forlorn.
Together they again will blaze the trail
And join the Masses journeying
To a land of wheat and plains.
Cottage or cabin built on hill or prairie sod
Blessed forever by "One Nation Under God."

Elizabeth DeMello

LIFE . . . TIME

The desert sun beats down on shifting sands,
Time presses on.
Wind storms; dry, arid heat storms
Break at dawn.
My skin is dark, dry and wrinkled,
More like leather.
My youth, sweet youth,
Is gone forever.
The sun, a fiery white flame,
Burns across the sand.
Leaving desolation in its wake;
An endless wasteland.
On this parched flat,
A lifetime spent.
Now, knocking at death's door
Eternally innocent.
My life flies by me,
Quick as a flash.
In this desert, I was born,
In this desert, I return to ash.

Deborah Bannan Shone

A BLESSED CHRISTMAS

To Eugene with Love.

It's Christmas time
And Joy is everywhere
The sounds of church bells
And carollers fill the air.
Our hearts are filled with thoughts
Of turkey and punkin' pie
The laughing faces
And twinkling eyes
As little children
Find the delight of a Christmas surprise
The hoped for toy,
A doll so sweetly dressed
The love of a friend
Yes, we are all greatly BLESSED!!
On Christmas Eve
Snowflakes begin to gently fall
They cover everything with a blanket
Soft and delicate
As if made by angels.
Each snowflake is individually designed
With the beauty of an Angel's mind.

Misty Jones

THE RAIN

To mom and dad in heaven.

As the rain falls
My tears tumble
The thunder calls
And my thoughts fumble

I sit here quiet
Alone in the dark
I just can't fight it
The hurt, the spark

The pain builds up
My tears keep fallin'
My brain corrupts
The thunder's still callin'
I'm steadily thinking
Why did He do it?
Without even blinking
He is the one who hit

He took them away
My mom and dad
And now they lay
So now I'm sad

Matilda Geaschel

DON'T BURN THE FLAG

The spirit of our Nation is to hold our head high.
In the dream like a bird, the fleecy clouds drift.
Visions fulfilling the pyramid lost eye.
As surely the web breaks clear to shift.

Don't burn God's flag the world to blame.
The Gods are swiftly marching to victory.
As the joy the heavenly angels forever rein.
The 1989 victory is singing from sea to sea.

The falling leaves like teardrops fall.
It's written far and wide.
That the multitude marching to the call.
That God's children, free all men side by side.

Jenna V Ownbey

Jenna V Ownbey

ARTISAN

I am an artist, drawing magic from my heart to nurture your Soul forever. (original)

I draw pictures in my mind
When I find you desire me;
I write words into rhyme
If your time can fire me
Into a soul at rest on a beach.
Within reach of ecstasy,
So easily can a sonnet or a song
Belong and become our destiny,
That I paint you into my sunset
While I, Tristian,
Lift the sky
To let cheyenne or koran
Weave me into artisan,
Artisan.

Jenna V Ownbey

SEASONS IN ARLINGTON

In Arlington where beauty grows
Beside those crosses, row on row,
The seasons come,
The seasons go,
But not for those who lie below.
Because of sun,
Or in spite of rain,
Arlington seasons
Never change.
The seasons come,
The seasons go,
But never for those entombed below.

It is whispered by those who know
That among those crosses, row on row,
Many winds come,
And many winds blow:
God dries the tears of those below.

The seasons leave,
The seasons stay,
While in Arlington we kneel to pray;
God weeps there always,
We know, beside those crosses, row on row.

Marie Burdeaux Bateman

TEACHER, CAN YOU HELP ME?

To the faculty and staff of Franklinton Elementary School. They were my inspiration.

Teacher, can you help me
tie my shoe?
Of course my dear,
anything for you.

Teacher, can you help me
zip my jacket?
In a minute dear,
let me first quieten the racket.

Teacher, can you help me
find my pencil and pen?
Sure my dear, but first let's
all go in.

Teacher can you help me,
I think I'm sick.
Get the trash can, my dears,
and please be quick!

"Teacher, can you help me?"
You wonder will that plea ever stop?
But you realize, of course,
If you're a teacher, it WILL NOT!

Amy Wing

MY ALL SEASONS VALENTINE

Tho many I've loved in my lifetime, none have I loved as much as my funny Valentine.

Thank you, my sweetheart,
For all the reasons
You've given me to love you
Throughout the seasons.

We've shared many jobs and professions,
Every one of them fun.
And the things we've accomplished in life
Have all been well done.

You've managed on nothing
But pure love and spiritual power
To guide and show me the way
Every year, every day, every hour.

Our cats all delight us with their love
and their warmth; we're never alone.
They cuddle, they talk to us, they bring
Special meaning to our hearts and our home.

Can you now understand, Richie, why
I'm grateful to God you are mine?
Not just once a year . . . but each second of my life . . .
You're my All-Seasons Valentine!

Amy Wing

THE BOWMAN

To a significant Sagittarian in my life.

An archer appeared during an August full moon.
We reasoned psyches, morals . . . all things profound.
He carried no bag of tricks or wasted words, yet soon,
With penetrating eyes and youthful touch
. . . He had me turned around.

This bowman shoots his arrow straight.
With white-heat energy he abounds,
Seeking knowledge, searching for truth,
He hits his target
. . . Emitting music without sound.

Remain level, dear archer, keep your aim and know
How mighty your karmic influence can be,
And one day I may be inspired to write your song
In friendship and thanks
. . . For what you've given me.

Amy Wing

ETERNITY

We will be together
Always and forever
'Cause we were meant to be
For all eternity.

When I'm with you it feels so right,
Especially when you hold me tight.
I always want to be with you;
Because I know your love is true.

You are always there for me;
Because we were meant to be,
We were meant to be,
For all eternity.

Richard Huffstutler

PETALS

The teardrops of a rose
It drops its petals in the midnight air
Is there anyone around who will listen . . .
Anyone around who will care?

Moonlight shines on forest green
The leaves shimmer in the wind
A touch of color, a touch of hope.

Roots tearing deep into soil rich
A taste of earth, a taste of life.

The smell of rain, the smell of newness.

Richard Huffstutler

REFLECTIONS OF A MIDNIGHT ROSE

Darkness rewarding only glimpses of beauty . . .
Shadows hide the dangers

In a world of night there's a glimpse of beauty,
There's softness in the shadows
A beauty that stands out . . .
that demands to be seen . . .
yet sits silently in its beauty.

Focused,
In a shimmering glow . . .
softness with a shadow.

Am I that midnight rose . . .
I am.

Marjorie Punches von Pohle
UNDER THE WILLOW TREE

In Memory of Vernon, my husband for forty-nine precious years.

I'm sitting here
All by myself
Beneath this willow tree
Should perchance a stranger pass
And see
Upon my face
A tear
And question me
As why I'm all alone
Down here
By this stream
Weeping beneath this willow tree
I could not answer
This stranger
Who is only passing by.
How could I tell him
What's deep inside—
Way down deep in me—
The pain
The hurt
That life is not at all
Like I thought
That life would be.

Linda Marie Deyo
I LOST AGAIN

This romance has become cold. It's time to pack away the pictures of you and I.

For it was only yesterday we met, and lived out our dreams together.

We've shared so much in the last four months, . . . BUT I can no longer live on dreams.

For dreams are for lovers, and that we are no longer.

I LOST AGAIN . . . So I'll say again, I'll pack away the pictures of you and I.

For it was only yesterday we met, and lived out our dreams together.
And now I must go on living my life
WITHOUT YOU
I LOVE YOU

Linda Marie Deyo
LIVING TOGETHER ME AND YOU

Living together, it's ME AND YOU.
It's having a place of our own. It doesn't have to be a palace or a castle . . . As long as we are together.
LIVING TOGETHER, ME AND YOU . . .
It's a chance for US.
Our PARENTS don't seem to understand. They use age as the answer to separate us. But we know different, Because of our LOVE for each other.
We know that age is just numbers, and everyone can count.
LIVING TOGETHER, ME AND YOU . . .
It's a chance for us to start living for OURSELVES.
Whether it's GOOD, or BAD, It's what we as a whole have to find out about ourselves.
LIVING TOGETHER ME AND YOU . . .
It's taking on LIFE'S responsibilities on our own TOGETHER.
It's being what we want ourselves to be.
But with us both together, we will be able to do it. For when we want something we both work for it, and go for what we are searching for.
And that LUV is for us. It's US.
. . . LIVING TOGETHER ME AND YOU . . .

Sandra I Bartlett
THE ALPHA AND OMEGA OF LOVE

Being with him was like basking in a dazzle of light;
Anchoring in calm waters, snug harbors, batten down tight.
God finally gave me soft breezes and set my sails right.
With him piloting, I'd have run life with infinite might.

Then "reality" cruelly hit.
Seems we were just star-crossed lovers,
Like Romeo and Juliet;
Tossed on the stormy seas of lust,
Scuttling mind and heart and spirit.
Neither passion nor compassion
Given by my chosen pilot.
A broken heart now knows the truth.

Men just go from their mother to a wife,
Expecting maternal care all their life.
And for any large of slight transgression,
Like children, assume they'll be forgiven.
Woe is the woman who falls for a man;
His behavior'll never be as planned.
For men are sociopaths, one and all,
Charming their way, through lies small and tales tall.
Mom never thought her little boy did wrong;
Now, as his lover, you'll get the same song.

Sandra I Bartlett
MESSAGE TO MY DAUGHTER ON HER WEDDING DAY

Eagles don't flock.
You only find them one at a time.
I feel so blessed

Having two in this family of mine.
"Matching feathers"
Means you will soar through life
together.

Sandra I Bartlett
FEELINGS OF WELL BEING IN SMALL TOWNS, U.S.A.

The tintinnabulation
Of small-town Church bells
Is heard throughout the nation;
Not one clapper knells.

Through rural American miles,
(As the music swells)
Are feelings of pride . . . and smiles,
Knowing all is well.

These sounds are blessed by Heaven . . . .
Not a note from Hell.
Joy in every Citizen
For "just-being" dwells.

Pamala S Tomasone
KIDS ARE PEOPLE TOO!

This poem is dedicated to my children Matthew and Mechelle, who are a gift and wonderment I praise the Lord for daily, and to my husband Mike, who has shared the joys of parenting with me.

"Kids are people too!" That's how the saying goes.
It used to be the title of a television show.
How often we forget this; we people called adults do.
It matters not if my daughter's 5 months and my son is only 2.
When our children awaken grouchy and it's a day of whines and tears,
we sometimes say, "What's wrong with you? Why must you misbehave my dears?"
"You're getting on my nerves and I have heard enough from you!"
So many times they have to put up with our "off days" too.
They cannot explain their fears and feelings of boredom or woe.
They only cry and fuss and pout and yell a lot of "NO's."
I pray that when this happens God will let me see
That it is time to stop and think before acting irrationally.
I don't want to yell and shout and scold "Behave you hear!"
Instead I wish to embrace my child and say, "I love you, dear.
I know that you're upset today and just don't feel quite right.
It's OK and I'll try to help you through it, if I might. I love you."
And I must remember EVERYONE has "off days," it's true.
May God remind us in just such times that KIDS ARE PEOPLE TOO!!!

Albert E Anaya Jr
HAIKU

For mother now in Heaven, December 21, 1937—March 25, 1990.

Spruce which cries at dawn
Dew it's called by many men,
Tears from nightly foe.

Albert E Anaya Jr
MOTHER FLOWER

In the valley of your birth
land where you blossomed;
Mother tulip, Mother flower.
Swayed to the momentary wind,
petals in the sky

In the garden of our Lord
Fields of rest.
Mother tulip, Mother flower
Sharing the everlasting breeze,
Petals in the sky.

Jonathan Clarke
TRUTH HIDES

Truth Hides
Uncover the rocks
And you'll find it
Sleeping
Nestled between Faith
and Optimism
Don't try to wake it
For if you do
You may discover
It's Dead.

Melvyn L Benson
SOLITUDE

As I sit by the lakeshore
So peaceful and serene
The calmness of the water
Really is supreme
I listen to the cry of the loon
As daylight slips on by
And marvel at the colored sky
That fades away too soon
I feel the wind caressing my face
As it dances through the trees
And I sit in silent solitude
And it puts my mind at ease

Laura Robinson
LOVE ME, LOVE ME NOT

To Sweet Richard for all the love, life and laughs you bring me . . . My love always, Laura.

I count my blessings everyday
That you are in my life.
I really try in many ways
To be a perfect wife.
I have never met, nor never will
A person such as you.
I don't regret a moment spent
That all our memories fill.
So on this day of hearts and flowers
I can only share this thought . . .
I am deeply in love with you
now and forever
And will never "Love you not."

Elaine D Barber
CHARLIE THE SQUIRREL

Charlie the squirrel is as cute as can be
He likes to put on a show for you and me
Up on the high wire he balances himself against the wind
Down he comes burying his acorns again
Somehow he manages to brighten your day
He brings lots of laughter and joy your way
Charlie you're welcomed in my yard any day.

Doris Lipscomb Burks
IT REALLY DOESN'T MATTER

In honor of Jesus Christ, my Savior; In memory of J. Gilbert Lipscomb, my Dad.

It really doesn't matter where I am
'cause God is there;
If I get a little lonely, I just
go to Him in prayer.

It really doesn't matter anymore
that I have sinned,
For Jesus came and died for me,
my record He has cleansed.

When a great big disappointment
comes along to spoil my day,
It really doesn't matter—
Jesus has a better way.

I think of all the times I've cried
with heartbreak in the past;
And praise the Lord because I know
earthly sorrows cannot last.
Satan tries so hard to plague me
and sometimes he gets me down;
But it really doesn't matter—
Jesus has, for me, a crown.

Ralph W Rocha
OLD WOMAN

Old woman as I watch you from afar,
I wonder, what your thoughts are?
Are they of thoughts of long ago of
past loves that are lost in time or is it
of your husband of so many years
that you had to lay to rest. And
knowing someday that you again will
be by his side. Or is it of time that
has passed so quietly before your
eyes. Knowing, that you have lived a
full life. Or are your thoughts of the
future and the time that is left to you.
Do you think about death?
Old woman someday I too will be in
your place, and I hope I am like you.
So gentle and quiet and silent,
listening to the voices of the past.
Old woman as I watch you from afar
as the winter winds blow thru your
silver hair knowing that your time is
near I no longer have any fear.

Sarita Michele Bennett
A MAN WITH A DREAM

To my lovely daughter, Kelly Marie Cobbs, and all of my friends.

A man with a dream

(It's possible to find the intensity of
the mind)

A man with a dream in his world of
teachings;
A man with power in his destination
he's reaching,

But, he's a man that walks proud
through all troubles and pain;
He's a man with a dream, he's a man
with a name,

The source of his life is to live it and
to accomplish it with determination;
His accomplishment is dealing with
reality for it is his confirmation,

He's a man with a dream and nothing
can stop him now;
He's a man of God and nothing can
bring him down,

In his world he sees nothing but his
goal of success;
In his world tears and sufferings are
for growing and strength is to
confess,

He's a man of wisdom and his
knowledge is to behold;
He's a man with a dream with a need
as good as gold,

His life is built with that dream and
his dream is his life;
His motivation to succeed is based on
his sacrifice,

He's a man of hope with a will to
strive;
He's a man that gives his all to grow
and survive.

A man with a dream

Phyllis C Watson
MY BEING

All in my mind
I search for the reality
of what is and the truth of
what should be.
I come to conclusions not
of my own, but of that of
the majority who is beating
down on me all the ideas of
a man long since past,
Whose desires are met by the
beating of his fist and the weakening
of my will to endure. I stand
alone surrounded only by the
comfort of His power on High
and with that I alone shall survive.

Lee S Allen
ON CREMATION

Not for me
  That my spent physical form
  Should lie in a costly casket
  Uselessly moldering.
No, not for me.

Let my ashes
  Be consigned to a river
  Leading to larger rivers,
  Thence to the oceans.
Yes, let them go.

Let the elements
  That shaped a living human
  Be carried away, afar,
  Perhaps to Africa or Australia.
Yes, let them go

To far places
  Dreamed of in armchair travels
  To become, perchance,
  Parts of other living forms
Again, and again.

Andrea Covelli
I AM

I am the last leaf
Clinging to a branch until
A cold winter wind takes me
In a cascading whirlpool of confusion
To my final resting place upon the
ground.
I am the ceaseless tide
Flowing in and out
With nothing but the eons of sand
To keep company with throughout
time.
I am a raincloud
Crying tears of loneliness
That will evaporate to only a memory
With the heat of a summer day.
I am all of these things
And nothing more
Until I can escape this prison
of depression holding me tight.

Shirley Harris
MALLORIE

There's a special angel
That came from up above.
She is so very special,
And wonderful to love.

She's just a little angel
That came to stay with us.
She keeps us at attention,
With her precious little voice.

She came to us one day
When we needed her.
She is such a blessing
This special little one.

We call her Mallorie Terry
This angel dear of ours.
She's only 2, but what a joy,
A difference she has made

In all our lives this baby,
She brought us so much joy.
She came to us from heaven
This special little soul.

Love, Mom

Eleanor Chavez
TO BE IN MAINE AGAIN

To those Acadians who lived so long ago.

I'd love to be in Maine again
and walk along her paths
climb the rocks and sit awhile
to watch the sea, the cliffs—
And birds
flopping around in the wind
riding the breeze
I'd think about those Acadians
who lived here long ago

Thomas G Cox
AGING

Aging: Comes to the best of us
  Comes to the rest of us:
  eventually

Aging: Means getting older, while
  winters get colder for you—you
  and for me

  Just like the river—on its way
  to the sea
  We're on a journey—to our
  destiny
  We look back and wonder—what
  might have been
  We wonder what happened—to
  the years in between

  Aging means older—and the years
  pass us by
  We can't bring them back—how
  hard we try
  Our children grow up—soon we're
  on our own
  'Tho we're on our own—we are
  never alone

  We've lived life to the fullest
  our days had no end
  But now we are older—much
  older my friend
  We started as youngsters—right
  from the start
  'Tho now we are aging—we're
  still young at heart

Eleanor L Hoffman
I CAN HEAR A RAINBOW

The yellow sun bursts alive
Herald of a vermillion dawn,
And gently cascades her golden
fingers of life to earth and sky
To promise a rainbow symphony.

Tinkling laughter of silvery waters
Rushes on into roaring gales of white
foam.
Here and there bold buttercups pop
into view
Amid whispering valleys of emerald
grass.

Orchards of rosy cherries, chartreuse
limes, brassy peaches,
flaming oranges, and mauve plums
beat out a gypsy colored timpani
The wind sings a love song from
smokey blue firs
To plains of crackling burnished
wheat.

Slowly the sun descends into the
deep violet blue night
And sends the shimmering crystalline
moon to bring quiet peace,
The perfect denouement to a rainbow
symphony.

Helen Cain Cossitt
DAD

He went riding over the hill
His voice has been forever still
Dad, oh Dad, you never came back
Your hat's still missin' off the rack.

We are twelve, ten, eight, six
and four
How come you never came back
no more
Dad, how we've missed you
every day
Why don't you come ridin' back
this way

Mom says you've gone to a
better land
It's hard for us kids to understand
She says you're still watching over us
And we're to mind without any fuss

Us older ones understand you've
gone from sight
Our brother, eight, cries a lot at night
Little sister, six, doesn't
understand still
And brother, four, thinks you've rode
over the hill

Dad, oh Dad, we have been so sad
We've needed you back, dear Dad
Somehow if you can see fit to ride
Come along and stay by our side.

Eunice Marshall
SEASONS OF LIFE

Springtime, Summertime, Fall then
Winter,
That's the way our life goes.
We come forth like a flower,
First a bud then a rose.

The weeds of sin try to choke us,
While yet in childhood we grow.
Soon the summer sun will warm us,
Into manhood we'll go.

The beauty of youth we'll enjoy,
For a few years or so.
But get ready my brother,
Fall of life is at the door.

In the Fall the rose is fading,

Its petals lose their hold.
Death is coming, can't you feel it?
Strength you had is there no more.

Now Winter of life is upon you,
Your hair is grey, your limbs are weak.
Your aches and pains with you always,
I pray the Lord my Soul to Keep.

John C Flewellen
CHRISTMAS
Christmas comes but,
Once a year,
A time to share love,
Joy and cheer.

Take the time,
To stop and say,
Merry Christmas to all,
You see today.

Think of the children,
The daughters and sons,
Remember their joy,
Happiness and fun.

Remember this feeling,
All year long,
For Christmas is one day,
And then it's gone.

I wrote this poem,
For one reason,
God bless you all,
It's the Christmas season.

Tina M Omelian
TIME HAS PASSED BY
Time has passed by, and we have gone on our separate ways. Only a small spark of hope of seeing you again.

Many years have passed by and fate has again brought us together.

Strangers to each other. Small talk seems out of place, yet intimacy is forbidden.

For I have been promised to another. Who is innocent of everything except a deep loving.

The flame you ignited so long ago is growing within me. Holding it back is a battle yet unwon.

Confusion is a great beast to tear at my heart. I am caught between two worlds; one of pain, one of love.

My heart is being torn in two pieces left to die a great death.

Ronald Sklar
NICE FRANCE
Suddenly I am awakened as the sun enters my room.
The horns sound from avenue Jean-Medecin.
I jump up from my bed to drink my café au lait,
while reading the local news in Nice-Matin.

The day is very warm; sweat drips from my temple.
I put on my bathing suit in haste and descend the stairs.
The passers-by stare.
I leave the hotel and walk into the summer heat.

Walking along the sidewalks of the boulevards,
in a few minutes I reach the Promenade des Anglais.
The sea shines like a mirror towards the horizon.
The summer air is very lively.

At the beach I find the smile of companions
who leave the water and rest on the shore.
It is time to feel again the beautiful weather.
I will always have the taste for summer and blue sky.

Raquel C Fernandez
A LOVE THAT IS REAL BUT DOES NOT EXIST

Dedicated to everyone I know and love. Uhe heurex vie.

I wish that you would love me
as much as I love you.
But then I look and see it
cannot be true.
I love you and I know it, like
the stars above and sea.
You are my love, my life, my hero;
for all eternity.
There are many things I want
to do, to let you know I care.
But how can you love someone
who is not even there.
I just wish that sometime,
for always, someone would
love and care.

Judy Randolph
BLESSED ANGEL
Some of my fondest memories of you
Go back far throughout the years:

Sitting me on your lap and hugging me
While my four-year-old's nightmare slowly fades,

Being the beautiful face I saw
Every single day when I came home from school,

Sitting up through the night over cups of tea
And talking me through my fifteen year-old's problems,

Gracefully letting your eighteen year-old leave home
While inside, your heart longed to keep me there.

I have never been blessed as a Mother,
And perhaps that is why I cannot understand
Your patience and almost saintly devotion.
Your arms are always outstretched to readily give me hugs.
You have stood by me through every crises in my life,
And you have never ceased to shower me with love and affection.

My love, gratitude and un-ending need for you
Will go on for all time.
At thirty-seven, I am still your little girl, saying
"Thank you for being my Mom."

Donna E C Aschbacher
REDEEM MY MORTGAGED SANITY
Hell-my innate nature stranded;
waiting for the affirmation of a promise-the gift to come;
the economy that is unprecedented
in a fierce battle of a dream phase
to free the intellect and good will,
where compassion is epidemic
and no door is closed to the speeding convergence,
sympathy, tenderness, love and affection,
the uncontrolled spiritual consciousness.
There within a symbolic heart,
lies the secret thoughts of love for another;
a healthy desire.
Earth, my mother, rescue me that I may die
only to be resurrected from your womb,
where fire will forge my metal to all possibilities of nature.
I am willing;
rich in latent energies to produce the guru, in the temple of my soul.
I boil with compassion as my inner being unfolds
and redeems me from insanity-Hell.

Gisele Collette
HE LOVES ME . . .
He told me he loved me.
I stood there
looking,
not knowing what to say.
I loved him,
not in a married way,
but I loved the way
he treated me.
He was kind,
gentle,
honest
and so many other wonderful things.
He had faults,
but none so great
that they couldn't be overlooked.
He saw my insecurity
and he,
he understood.
We talked
and I held back,
but I released myself
and we spoke about
our dreams, our hopes,
our fears.
We became close
so close
that our thoughts
blended together
as one
and we were one
for that special moment.
It was then
I realized
how good we were together
and how good we were
for each other.
I did love him
and I knew
that I would
forever.
No longer was I insecure.
I knew what to say
and I told him
I loved him.

Darlin Groves
I AM SOMEONE

To Natalie, Crystal, and Lisa, that I help you realize early in life, how special, unique and invaluable you are to yourselves.

I mean so much,
to myself, yes me.
I'm beautiful, kind,
wonderful, pretty.

I'm beautiful inside,
with a heart of gold.
Great personality, fantastic looks,
so I am told.

Intelligent, classy & witty,
I have learned to become.
I'm special, I'm unique,
I'm Darlin, I AM SOMEONE.

Lona Patterson
CLEAN YOUR STOVE
Clean your stove at least once a week
Or inside a tiny mouse may creep.
He'll nibble and gnaw on whatever's there
Eating anything that's left—he doesn't care.
But, soon he'll become a gourmet connoisseur
And move from the stove, of this I'm sure.
Now he'll search your cupboards and counters too,
For anything different and new to chew.
He'll lie in wait for the perfect chance
To leap at you and laugh at your dance.
He, alone, would be quite harmless
But, he'll breed so fast, you'll soon be armless.
Nothing will stop his food stampede,
As hundreds of mice upon you feed.
As their taste buds begin to mature,
They'll move on to engulf your furniture.
Nothing's sacred, old or new;
Everything's a challenge for them to chew.
Don't let them in for even a peek;
Clean your stove at least once a week!

N J Bugella

N J Bugella
OCTOBER'S GIFT

To Miranda Jo.

A pool of golden threads, her head reposes on my tired shoulder;
A budding child, eager for all in her seventh year.
In gentle breaths of sleep, her weight upon my lap and yellow locks
Recall to mind her very mother, who sat thus so many years past.
One slipper dangles from a foot; the ivory toes unlike those of myself,
my husband, or my kin.
I stroke her little arm, the warmth inviting my fingers to caress the dimpled
Elbows. I am distressed that so much

of her does not mirror me . . .
Another grandmother I can't deny,
who has surely given Nordic beauty
to this child.
The sparkle in those eyes came not
from me—or the azure brilliance.
All told, her figure resembles mine of
youth not at all; the way she moves,
Or thinks, came surely not from this
woman who holds her.
A sigh escapes me; a heartfelt lack of
visible contribution
That was, and is, and will be me . . .
If envy be it called, then let it be a
gentle envy,
For I love all whose part of them is
this child.
She stirs; (a tear falls on her hair),
only to pull her little self to comfort.
The slipper drops unnoticed, as she
shifts.
One little hand creeps from its hiding
place of warmth 'neath the blanket,
To lie upon my arm, gently splaying
itself into rest.
I do not move. My mind bolts as my
eyelids become lifted with shock
At what I see before me:
The hand, so small, yet so much a
part of my memory, is there again,
After the passing of a half a century.
The very nails, the shape, the pink
folds at the knuckles,
Even the speck of freckle on the ring
finger were there for me
To wonder at, like an old friend . . .
I lay its wrinkled ancestor upon the
precious hand, the veins now blue,
Now prominent, as more tears find
their way into her tresses.
I smiled, and knew . . . that I would
live . . .

Ann Marie Fusaro
THE GREATEST GIFT

Dedicated to Lauren—My Precious Daughter, My Sunshine.

She was such a beautiful little thing
Born in a pretty time of year
As flowers blossom and the sun
shines brightly
Her head so small and proportionally
rounded
Hair so soft and smooth as silk
Eyes opened so widely, full of
warmth and love
A nose so cute and tiny
Puffy little cheeks with dimples
piercing through, as she warmly
smiles
A mouth so petite and lips shaped to
perfection
Her arms, legs, and torso making her
more beautiful
Hands and fingers so small; feeling,
touching, holding on to someone
close
Feet and toes so soft and sensitive to
touch

That little girl is growing up fast,
right before my eyes
Learning, talking, walking; wanting
to know the Why? and How come?
She is my beautiful sunshine, my
daughter
Who brightens every day of my life
Through her, I have learned a great
deal and grown
She is my greatest gift of all
Nothing more precious, nothing to
compare

Amy Brunell
TO A FRIEND

Dedicated to Grandma and Grandpa Pagani.

Reflections of a lifetime,
where nothing's come to pass,
but empty dreams and memories
of good times gone too fast.
Now I've found a friend in you,
it means so much to me,
through a life of closing doors
now, at last I'm free.
Confusion almost conquered,
another half-lost soul,
you showed me how to fight it,
and helped me keep control.
We've found we're almost just the
same,
made a wish on a shooting star.
It's like we're two halves of the same
person,
who have learned just who they are.
I'm taking this chance to say to you
how much I really care,
and how I'll never forget the way that
you were always there.

Barbara Stewart
LITTLE BLUE BOY

Dedicated to my Mother and Father, my children Renée, Christopher, Bill.

See the little Blue Boy
As he walks his beat
Carefully guarding
The Savage streets

He
says
I'm gonna catch a junkie
'Cause I've gotta scheme
Let the little Blue Boy dream!

Watch him ride in
His stallion of Black and White
Immediately getting attention
With his Strawberry lights

He
says
I'm gonna catch a junkie
Cause I've gotta scheme
Let the little Blue Boy dream!

See the crowd gathering
Hear a widow cry
While all eyes are fastened
To where the little Blue Boy lies

He
says
I'm gonna be a hero
Cause I've gotta scheme
Why do little
Blue Boys
dream?

Peter Baisley
NEVER SAY GOODBYE

To Karen, my missing link, whose love has made my life complete. With all of my love always, Peter.

If you never said hello
How can you say goodbye
If you never spread your wings
How can you ever fly

If you never tread that path
How can you find your way
If you never give of yourself
How can love come your way

If you never touched its petal
How can you know you chose
If you never smelled its sweetness
How can you love the rose

If you never walk beneath the stars
How can you make your wish
If you never stopped to face the sun
How can you feel the gentle rays of it

If you never walked along the sea
How can you know its shores
If you never held a small seashell
How can you ever know
The wonder of it all

Judith A Vahs
BRICKY, MY LITTLE BLACK DOG

TO BRICKY, MY LITTLE BLACK DOG, who passed away 11/23/89 on Thanksgiving evening.

When the kids left home, I felt all
alone,
I felt like a bump on a log.
Until one day, in the month of May,
I bought me a little black dog.

The dog was so tiny, but I spanked
her hiney,
for piddling on the floor.
Then she got smart, before she would
start,
she headed for the door.

As time went on, we had lots of fun,
teaching our dog new tricks.
But when we were done, she still had
fun,
wondering what to do next.

She speaks, she sits, she rolls over,
she has toys all over the floor.
I'm really glad that I got her,
but I really couldn't handle no
more.

When it comes to snacks, she's right
on track,
she likes to catch popcorn.
Toss two kernels at once, she's a real
dunce,
she's really quite forlorn.

Sometimes she will pout, when we
go out
and leave her all alone.
She gets in the trash, and has a big
blast,
and makes a mess of our home.

She looks at me with her big brown
eyes
and gives me a great big kiss,
If I'd never got my little black dog,
just think what I would have
missed

Michael Corbett
NO MORE DEFEATS

To my grandfather, Alfred Tracz, who has been like a father to me.

Here we sit and look at life,
and think of all the cause of strife.
Asking ourselves is it worth the
bother,
wondering if we can make it any
farther.

I sit and hope and pray,
that soon they will find some way;
To get the drugs off the street,
so we can declare, "NO MORE
DEFEATS!"

I know with God and all my trust,
we all will make it, and we must.
To look at life through eyes of clear,
Knowing the drug problem end is
near.

Michael G Helmer
SCENES OF THE HEART

Somewhere in the scenes
of the heart . . .
Lingering there, is something
ready to tear them apart . . .

For some reason I could
never see tomorrow . . .
Maybe I was afraid because
I was never told of the sorrow . . .

To avoid more pain and
for my own protection . . .
Maybe I should shut
out the world to prevent
any more rejection . . .

Sometimes when I'm all alone
I sing my saddest song . . .
Trying to figure just where
in life I belong . . .

When I'm all alone
When no one can see . . .
because the song
is for me . . .

Josephine Kapke
UNSOLVED MYSTERIES

Dedicated to the Rev. Thomas E. Fast.

There is a song that should have been
sung.
There is a voice, that should not have
gone wrong.
There is a love, that should have been
fulfilled.
There is a hate, that should not have
been instilled.
There is a baby, that should have
been born.
There is a life, that should not have
been scorned.
There is a bridge, that should have
been crossed.
There is a vagrant, that should not
have gotten lost.
There is a war, that should not have
been fought.
There is a country, that should not
have been bought.
There are promises, that should have
been kept.
There are tears, that should not have
been wept.
There are times, people should get
involved.
There is why mysteries go unsolved.

Derina Barringer
VISION

To my dearest, loving mother and family.

As I walk in the sand,
looking at the sea.

A vision of light,
is placed upon me.
When I look around,
the beach disappears.
While angels are floating,
and motioning me to come
see all they can see.
What a beautiful sight!
White painted houses,
and pearly-white trees.
I ask to join them,
they told me someday I
would.
And I did!

Montia F Clay

GRAY CLOUD

This poem is dedicated to my dear sister, NOLIS.

"Come Gray Cloud," said the wind
one day.
"I'll take you to a place far far
away,
Where people are sweltering beneath
the broiling sun,
From the early morning hours, till
the day is done."

Gray Cloud signed, and shed a big
tear.
And said, "No one ever wants me
near;
They say I'm filled with trouble and
gloom,
And for me they have no room."

But the raging wind, swirled the
livelong day;
And took Gray Cloud to a place
far away.
There the people all shouted with
pure delight,
When they saw Gray Cloud come
in sight.

The elated Cloud soon begun;
To shield the people from the fury
of the sun.
Spreading its veil far and wide,
Covering all the countryside.

Then; said the wind to the Cloud,
"Now; no more pining,
For you see every Cloud;
Has a silver lining."

Laurie Poirier

HAZY MOURNING

The old woman rocks in the decrepit
chair
Cobwebs dangle in the musty air.
All is quiet except for her tired
breathing
Sharp ragged breaths. She will soon
be leaving.

A cough is choked from her dry
parched throat.
On a testament she shakily wrote,
"My life was long and one of pain
If I were to question living again
The start would be my end.
I haven't the strength for my soul
to mend."

She has no one to plead to.
Children? She has none. She never
felt the need to
A husband was but a dream. Was this
a test?
She failed? She was never blessed.

Now her soul is as bitter as the odor
of her being
And her eyes as dim as the world she
is seeing.

The ancient clock chimes an earth-
shattering tone
She is 94 this day and quite alone.

A silent whisper she struggles to hear
She realizes she is alone, her heart
beats with fear.
Her throat aches as she hears a moan
The voice she heard had been her
own.

The wrinkles heavily written in her
face
Are structured in a frown of disgrace.
NOOO!! her mind screams.
A Christian she was, through and
through
If YOU are there I ask this of you?
Why do I linger for this continuous
punishment?
I thought you forgave all and passed
no judgement?

With this last thought her arthritic
hands clenched the chair
Her eyes widened with a drifting tear
The wind blew through the cracked
windowpane
Never to be able to touch her again.

Dust settled, her rocker stilled.
Now her dreams are fulfilled.
The spider quickly begins making a
new web
As the sun awakens. It is Mourning
for all . . .

Michael Hofsass

RAIN

To the brotherhood, Mom, and Jennifer, without whom writing this would have meant nothing.

Long faces.
Dragging feet.
Sadness.
Darkness.
Gloom so thick, it pushes
Down on the world.
Silent rooms.
Creaking doors.
Empty.
Lonely.
Fear as palpable as the
Morning dew.
Day dreaming.
Aimless.
Tired.
Wind.
Where is the sun?
When will this mood end?
Will the world ever glow again?
Drip.
Drip.
Drip.

April D Mickel

CONSTANTLY

To my three lovely daughters— Melvina, Katrina and April.

Something's in my head, it's
there . . .
constantly
On my mind . . . night and day
Not sight unseen nor sound unheard
a familiarity
It's there . . . constantly
A face, a place, a happening
like déjà vu
A memory . . . I was there, so were
you
Was it in days gone by or days yet to
be?
Maybe both . . . 'cause it's
there . . .
constantly
Why upset it, one might ask
Just let it flow . . . day by day
Relax enjoy let it be . . .
For it's gonna be there . . .
constantly

Floy E Roberts

TODAY

To my family with love.

The clouds are all asunder
The ozone is filled with holes
While the earth is cracking open
Causing untold grimest woes
Fighting in all the Nations
Crime and drugs still persist
Many people are old and homeless
Wondering how they can exist
Only by faith and hope
Hard work and unfailing grit
A lot of love and prayers
To the one whom we hold most dear
The one whom all things are possible
The reason we are here
So get on with your praying
Stop groveling over your woes
And know that God will help
And keep you no matter where
you go
Even tho your strength be tested
Your faith and hopes be low
Let not your heart be troubled
For he hath told you so.

Rick Lamacchia

Rick Lamacchia

I DREAMT

This poem is dedicated to my mother and to every human being (myself included) who has fought (or attempted) the good fight to find inner peace, love, and contentment; to those who have struggled to let go of their fears, to free their dreams, to find themselves.

I dreamt
I made the big attempt
Like a scared ice skater
Making his first jump
In the big time

I dreamt
That the great adventure
Pre-empted my fear of falling
Like a bursting sun
Burning away morning fog

I dreamt
That my discontent emptied . . .
slowly
As I turned the glass of fear
downward . . .
And I was tempted
To love myself

Kay Sinclair

LOVE

This poem is dedicated to my husband, GABE.

Love is a whirling vortex,
a rushing soundless endless thing,
'Tis but the spirit of truth so
beautiful,
Of poetry and music and dance,
It goes on forever, in this
everchanging universe,
Varies in so many forms,
sometimes ever so humble
"The mother and child."
Then again so violent, and so sweet
"the lovers."
"The artist with his brush." "The poet
with his pen."

They wonder from whence it came,
That strange uplifting of the heart,
name it inspiration, but, 'tis love,
The dancer by some strange force,
knows only that he must obey,
And in graceful movement, his wild
joyous heart commands.

Stephanie L Cook

TOGETHER

I would like to dedicate this poem to Kevin DeBolt with love.

We will be together, one day, you
and me.
It will be unlike any dream we have
dreamed.
Life will continue to go on as before
But deep in our hearts we'll know it's
something more.
Together I know we could overcome
Any obstacle big enough to brave our
home.
As one united front we will face this
land.
Just as a happy couple walk hand in
hand.
Nothing very unusual, no, not really.
But together we will know is the only
way to be.

Marguerite Morgan

THE OLD MAN AND THE OCEAN

To my dear sons, Chris and Richard.

Once there was a very sad lonely old
man
He had no old lady to keep him
happy
He had no little boy to talk to
He had no lop-eared dog to keep him
company.
But he had the sea. He was a
fisherman and he loved the sea.
He also had an old boat with a sail.
At daybreak he'd set sail.
He'd sail way out in the sea and
sometimes be gone for
many days and nights.
He'd go far out to sea with his nets
and cast them out and haul
in tremendous amounts of fish.
It might be weeks before he'd talk to
a soul.
Only the seagulls were his
companions and the moon
and stars and the sun.
So he wasn't a lonely old man after
all.
He had the ocean as a companion.

Jeff Niepoetter
MY TWO BOYS

For Jason and Jonathan and lovely wife, Katherine.

You are the creator of the heaven and earth and I know we're in your hands
And I know you see each tiny child and love them as only You can
But this vast, magnificent world of yours has grown so hectic now
I just want to be sure you've noticed two boys whom I'm so proud.

To most they're probably average like all the other boys
They laugh, they cry and, yes, complain when it's time to pick up toys
And getting into mischief, they too are not exempt
They do have much to learn you know so please, be patient with them.

So I realize that in most every way that boys are all the same
But I'm sure these two are special, please let me try to explain . . .
I can feel this special warmth as they sit upon my knee
Their eyes have quite a twinkle as they listen to me read
From their favorite bedtime storybook they've heard so many times
And I love their precious smiles as I kiss them each good night
Then as I tuck them into bed love pours from each embrace
And the moonlight casts the warmest glow upon each tiny face.

Indeed these two are special, in a special sort of way
And in light of all the joy they bring, to you I humbly say . . .
Please, with all my heart, I ask you one more time
Give them all the love they deserve . . . bless these two boys of mine.

Jeffrey L Swank
TIME IS NOW

I thank God for the words and the ability to form and write the thoughts, and for sending Amanda to bring out my courage and make me feel special.

Time is a very special thing
And there is no way to measure,
Just what any second will bring
Or which one will be a treasure.
When we dwell upon the past
Whether the good times or bad
Today's seconds just don't last
And we miss what we could have had.
When we guess about tomorrow
We forget about today,
For we cannot hope to borrow
The actions or words we'll say.
Yesterday will never return
Tomorrow comes when we're gone,
So feel the fire within you burn
And enjoy each breath that is drawn.
God controls all time and space
So slow down and enjoy your days,
After all, life's not a race,
It's a series of many todays.

Ron Carey
JUST TELL ME WHY

To those who have loved and lost.

All I ask is tell me why, she was my love and my life.
Tell me why God took my wife.
Even though I know she's gone, it's so
insane, I walk around and call her name.
I sit and stare at her empty chair,
And remember all her love and care.
I know she went to a better home.
But now I sit here and cry 'cause I'm all alone.
Please tell me why God let her die.
I lay here alone in the bed we shared and,
remember how her last smile told me she would always care. But now before I meet
my maker just tell me why God had to take her.
I know it was wrong but that punk that took
my baby from me, my gun was the last thing he
ever saw. So maybe now the greatest law of
all can just tell me why she had to die.

Marie Filiano
HE . . .

This poem is dedicated to Anthony Filiano Jr., my loving father and friend.

He is a special person,
one whom I admire.
His patience and understanding
and especially his smile.
His hand of strength when I need it.
The glow around his heart,
and the loving touch to let me
know he loved me from the start.
And I will always cherish
each moment that I've had
For no one can take the place
of my Dear Ol' Dad.

Lee-Anne T
CHILDREN

This is to the adults—for the children.

I hear their cries,
It's a cry I've never heard before,
I wish I could destroy the elements
that bring them such painful sorrow,
I know there is a way,
But how?
Do you have the answer?
Life is so short,
They need laughter,
Time's running out,
Why don't they laugh—do they know how?
They're still crying

Lee-Anne T
JUST A FEELING
Lonely, can it be.
Feeling empty inside of me
Lonely, can it be
I need
Lonely, can it be
My heart and soul aching
Lonely, can it be
Maybe just temporary
Lonely, can it be
The aching, need, emptiness will it leave me

Gerry Good
HIDING

To Bill: who helped me grow.

I don't have to say I'm sorry
I don't have to run and hide
I don't have to say I'm sorry
Sorry to be alive . . .

I don't have to say I'm sorry
For things I cannot do
I don't have to say I'm sorry
Sorry to be alive . . .

I don't have to make excuses
Because I can't ride a bike
I don't have to make excuses
For not going on a hike . . .

I don't have to pretend I'm stupid
Or lazy, or fat, or dumb
I don't have to hide from others
I'm always in such awful pain . . .

I can't ride a bike or go on a hike
I can't run or dance a jig
I can't skip rope or play basketball
I can't ski on water or snow . . .

I can't bend my back without an attack
I can't bend my knee or hip
I can't get up without some prop
I can't walk without a limp . . .

I can't get up when I fall on my back
Or even when I trip on my toes
I can't get rid of this crippling pain
My body just betrays me again . . .

I'm tired of making excuses
Tired deep in my soul
I'm tired of hiding the sorrow
I can't do what I want to do . . .

But I'll fight for life, no matter how hard
I'll fight to conquer the pain
And when at last I win the fight
I'll be able to laugh again . . .

Morris Listopad
TO MY LOVE

To my wife Anita, and my three children: Howard, Michael and Ruthie.

Just like the bird roams through the sky
With its wondrous, watchful eye;
So do I swim through the sea of life,
Ever in search of a loving wife.

I follow the sun, I follow the moon,
I search everywhere from noon to noon;
I'm filled with anguish and despair,
For without love, life is unfair.

Jupiter had his Juno; Romeo loved Juliet;
Even Aucassin found his Nicolette.
Am I like Sysiphus a slave of fate
or will I someday, somehow, find my mate?

Yet the rays of hope still shine
On my quest for a love divine;
And I know my pains will one day cease,
When at last I'll love, and live in peace.

From heaven you'll be sent.
To bring me feelings of content.
When I count your many charms
As I hold you in my arms:
Forever:
Morris Listopad

Karri A Ackley
BEAUTY OF THE WIND

I would like to dedicate this to all that can see the beauty in everything.

The wind is so strong
So thin and long

The beauty of it all
Comes from its call

The sun so bright,
With the wind so cool, light

You can't stop from enjoying
The beauty of it all

Especially at night.

Edna L Davis
A WOMAN OF COURAGE

To Winnie Mandela for her courageous dedication and struggle for freedom in South Africa, which her husband, Nelson Mandela, helped to initiate.

A woman of courage
among other things, she possesses
love, strength, endurance
and most of all, finesse

Buried deep, a longing love
within her heart
for the man she married
but was forced to part

Years and years and years
steadily passed on by
loneliness and sleepless nights
kept her wondering why

Her man fought for a cause
he truly believes in
but was taken away from her
because of someone else's greed

She, however, stood by her man
barring all unforeseen circumstances
carrying on the fight as best she could
for one day she knew they would be together again.

Arnita Jennings
LIFE IS GOLD

This poem is dedicated to Malcom, Hasson and Guy, my sons, may they learn to respect the gift of life.

Shattered dreams come and go.
Death and taxes inevitable.

How times have changed! Sex, drugs, we gotta be responsible.

Don't be fooled by Joe Cool's hun'it dollar jewels!

Believe in your dreams when crystals gleam. Don't be easily sold, you are as precious as gold!

Shattered dreams may come and go,

and death and taxes inevitables,
but sex, and drugs you can control!

Hold your head, don't be misled,
don't get caught-up-in-deathland.
Once fooled, now schooled.
Crystals gleam—life is gold!

Heather Kay Kiehlmeier
UNICORN

This poem is dedicated to my caring mother who always believed in me and to Allusions, my beloved horse, in whose memory I wrote this poem for.

As I walk through the green grass
sprinkled with beautiful flowers,
I notice a faint night breeze gently
rustling treetops,
and the moon bathing its silvery light
over the emerald colored fields,
then I see a unicorn graced with the
color of the pale moonlight,
she was watching me from a small
hill that seemed to say was her
throne,
and I can see that her eyes were that
of the clearest blue skies.

As she moves towards me on dainty
gold hooves,
I watch how she proudly lifts her
snow-white head with a sliver of gold
upon her forehead,
then she stops just a few feet in front
of me and stares curiously,
I slowly reach out my hand to touch
her velvety muzzle,
but she disappears into a haze of
smoke.

Now I am alone again listening to the
sounds of the night,
as I go back the way I came I wonder
to myself if the unicorn had been
real,
but then I see her again and her
beauty taking my breath away,
and this time she lets me climb onto
her strong, silvery back,
only to take me flying to the stars on
a magical road of rainbow colors.

Sharon B Wilkie
THAT MAN OF MINE

This poem is dedicated to my loving husband, Jeffrey.

Why do I love that man of mine
with big brown eyes that sparkle
and shine
Why do I love that man of mine
with a soft sweet smile that drives
me wild
Why do I love that man of mine
with a heart of gold, full of
compassion and love
Why do I love that man of mine
with a heavenly touch so tender
and kind
That's why I love that man of mine

Dora McDearmon
THE LITTLE PIXIE

This poem is dedicated to my darling daughter, Valerie.

There was a little Pixie
And he lived in a cave
And odds and ends
He pleased himself to save:
Like rubber bands and rags
And string and paper bags!
He knew there'd come a day
When a need would arise
And he guarded all his loot
As though it were a prize!
Well, anyway and anyhow
There came a rainy day
And in his dark cave
He didn't want to stay!
So, he rolled himself up
In a rubber band and rag
And sailed down the hill
In a big paper bag!

Laura and Kandi Welsh

Laura Lynn Welsh
KANDI

With love to my beautiful daughter, Kandi Marie Welsh

"K" is for the kid in you that you
will always be,
"A" is for the angel that you are to
me,
"N" is for the naughty role that you
sometimes play,
"D" is for Daddy the first word you
learned to say,
"I" is for infinite, my love can only
be,
for my darling baby girl, my
little Kandi Ree.

John Matthew and Kandi Marie

Laura Lynn Welsh
LIFE'S WANDERING ROAD

Dedicated with love to John Matthew and Kandi Marie from "Babble" — Do as I say—Not as I did —

As I trudge down this wandering road
called life,
As a daughter, mother, grandmother,
and wife,
I look back behind me at the things I
have done,
Some stupid, some dangerous, some
crazy, some fun,
Warm bitter sweet tears fall from my
eyes,
I see all the things I have learned to
despise,
Of life's hard knocks, I've had my
share,
Searching for someone who'd always
be there,
I pushed along 'til the fork in the
road,
Had to make up my mind to loosen
the load,
I knew these crossroads could change
my life,
If I took the right one, I'd end all the
strife,
I was weary from walking the one
dark and cold,
Thinking of the evils I'd consumed
and sold,
So I chose to walk the one narrow
and straight,
This one had no room for sin, sorrow,
or hate,
I'm grateful each day for the decision
I made,
As I watch my troubles and sorrows
fade,
Through all the agony and despair,
I can now look up and know God's
there.—Cinderella.

Evelyn Evon Pigg
ONLY YOU AND YOU ALONE

This poem is dedicated to Robert. With all my love always-and-forever.

Only you and you alone can make the
rain stop and the sun shine.
Only you and you alone can put the
stars in my eyes and the glow on my
face.
Only you and you alone can make my
heart sing and make everything
alright and make me so happy and
make life worth living.
Only you and you alone can make
each day and night brighter and dry
the tears from my eyes.
Only you and you alone can make
everything so wonderful because I
love you so very much.
Only you and you alone can put all
this desire in my heart and make my
heart beat faster and make everything
go right.

Kathy E Hall
TO BE FIVE

Written especially for my son, Michael Kelly Hall, on his fifth birthday.

What's it like to be Five, my son,
To race and play and skip and run,
To know no worries, no cares, no
woes,
To have no grief, no pain, no foes?

What's it like to be so carefree,
To be held upon your parent's knee,
To wake each day with joy anew,
At being alive, and just being you?

What's it like to be so small,
And wish that someday you'd be tall,
To know that you are loved so much,
Because of just a word or touch?

My son, enjoy each day you live,
Each moment that the Lord doeth
give,
For surely and quickly time slips
away,
And Five will be just a bygone day.

Janet Masterson
A LOST SOUL

I didn't pray this morning, Lord.
I couldn't find the time.
But I'll try again tomorrow,
Maybe I'll keep you in mind.

I hurry through my busy day,
I work my very best,
and when it's time to pray again,
Lord! I need my rest.

In this world of temptations, Lord,
it's hard to walk away.
But I know that you will understand,
when I forget to pray.

When I awoke this morning, Lord,
my body racked with pain.
My whole life flashed before my
eyes,
I had lived my life in vain.

O Lord! I need your help,
walk beside me all the way.
And when I get to heaven, Lord,
I'll find time to pray.

Poor foolish soul, you served me not,
on earth you trod so free.
Your reward now I give to you
condemned for eternity.

Kim A Webster
PATTERNS

This poem is dedicated to my grandparents, Dorothy and Wayne Rossiter, whose lives made my world a nicer place.

Seasons, months and years
all blend as time continues on.
Flowing faucets, rivers and tears
all derive from nature's gifts.

Babies to children and children to
adults
each grows through stages here and
there.
Catholicism to Christianity to cults
Whichever we choose may not be
forever.

Country, towns, and cities
all consist of people and places.
Ducklings, puppies and kitties
need nurturing and a human touch.

Seeds to sprouts to gardens
are all steps of mother nature.
Excuse me, thank you and pardons
help in making the world nicer.

D K Doran
THOUGHTS

As the first rays of dawn kiss the
Earth and warm the hearts of all her
children, my heart is warmed by
thoughts
of you.

As the early birds lift their voices and
sing of the joy found in a new day, I
think of a time when Love was new
and
I was by your side.

As the colors of a new day splatter
the sky
with brilliant orange, red and pink,
taking
the breath of the beholder, I think of
your
touch in years past.

As the Spring breeze whispers
through the trees,

scurries up the housetops continuing
on
its way, I am reminded of my silent
Love
for you.

Mary Jane Transue
JUST MY THOUGHTS

I.

Our lives are Oh! so fleeting
When we're old enough to know.
We think we won't get older,
But, how the time does go!

II.

When we're young, it seems
We never will grow old,
But, time is just, day by day—
It really should be told!

III.

We grow and love and have good
times
Bad times—in between—
Some are good, some are bad—
You know just what I mean!

IV.

I hope someday we'll meet again,
In heaven, up on high.
So, this is just a time away.
It's not a last goodbye!

Crystal Anderson

Crystal Anderson
IT COULD HAVE BEEN

Dedicated to all Indians of all tribes, with sincerity and hope; for all.

I wish it could have been,
like way back when.
I wish it could have been,
just like it was then.
As soon as you came,
our home-land; went up in flames.
The world you stuck us with,
Should put you to shame.
You pushed us aside,
the nature we once knew was gone.
You choose not to like us.
Yet we're so proud of who we were
then,
And who we are now.
You made so many promises,
each of them lies.
When we think of this,
as Indians we cry.
You don't care about
the hurt our tribes feel.
If it was up to me, it would be;
like it was way back when.
It would be in nature's
loving, caring hands.
I wish it could be,
like it was then.
But I know, our beautiful home-land
we once knew and loved;
shall never exist again.

John J Armitage
FRIENDS

I'd like to be the sort of friend
That you've all been to me
And I'd like to be the help
That you've been always glad to be.

I'd like to mean as much to you
Each minute of the day
As you have meant, good friends of
mine
To me along the way.

And that's why I am wishing now
That I could but repay
A portion of the gladness
That you've strewn along my way.

And could I have but one last wish
This is what it would be
I'd like to be the sort of friend
That you've all been to me.

God Bless you all forever.

Jerri J Keats-Smith
TO MY BROTHER

To my brother, Ron, who has become my good friend.

How sad,
if we never learned the importance
of us.
There is no relationship
more delicate to handle.
No memories more relished.
There is no laughter
or tears
more sensitive.

Louis Edward Amos Jr
YOUR LOVE FILLS THE AIR

It's 4 o'clock in the morning,
And the fire is still burning bright.
The logs are popping with life,
And your eyes sparkle with life.
Holding your hands in mine,
Watching your eyes shimmer.
The thoughts go through my mind,
As my heart starts to tremor.
Your love fills the air,
Like a heavy mist.
I'm blinded by the light,
And I cannot resist.
You shot into my empty life,
Like a speeding, shooting star.
I knew that day would come soon,
Because for you, I hold the highest
regards.
Only time could tell of our future,
The future of our life together.
When I look into your eyes of
shimmer,
All I can say is my heart I
surrender.

Jeanne M Howard
WINTER SHOW

Snowflakes falling as gentle caresses
upon the warm earth
Draping the naked trees with mantles
of white
It comes upon the earth's bosom as a
child suckling its mother's breast
Graciously adorning the beautiful
remnant of man's abode
Mountains arise from the plateau as
gods immortal
Decked in their finery of white and
silver frost
Taking stock over all the kingdoms
Cold and unyielding, their frozen
fingers hold the destiny of all who
enter into its world
Mysterious and forbidding, they
make the barriers strong
And as immortal warriors keep at bay
those who will mar its magnificence
Look those who dare, see the canvas
that nature paints
What pictures of lovely scenes
appear, they delight every eye
Glistening gems of light hanging
everywhere
Virgin snow covering earth's
nakedness as an artist's canvas
To share such a sight with a kindred
soul
Would be the purest delight.

David Wayne Phillips
THE COMEBACK PLAN

I was sitting on my couch one cold
and lonely night
thinking about my troubles with no
hope in sight
I started to go to the kitchen for a
cold beer
But was stopped by a tiny voice
which brought a big tear
The little voice came from my
daughter's room
As I got closer to it the chill bumps
started to zoom
She was talking to the Lord in a
sweet and childish way
And oh how her words tore my heart
apart as I heard what she had to say
She said, "Lord, I have a problem,
it's my dad, you see.
He won't go to church with my mom
and me.
Lord, he's not really a bad man.
So won't you please include him in
your comeback plan.
When I went to church last Sunday
the preacher told me about it
And I want you to include dad if you
can see fit.
For I seen him one time read his
Bible.
And, Lord, one time he even went to
a revival.
So you see, Lord, he's not really a
bad man.
Won't you please include him in your
comeback plan?"
Hearing this made me a changed man
And thanks to the love of the Lord
and my sweet daughter
I'll be included in his comeback plan.

Jean Kissinger
ODE TO A TREE

There's a tree out in back—weather
worn and cracked—
No lovelier tree have I seen.
Birds in the spring—how sweetly
they sing—
In its branches so lofty above.

When a breeze passes there—and it
tousles your hair—
Makes your heart want to stop and
take wing.
On warm sunny days—it's there I
give praise—
For the beauty of life we can share.

Now if I could be-just like that old
tree—
My branches would fan out in the
sky—
Limbs would hang low—touch the
green grass below—
My shade I would give til I die.

My roots would grow deep—to hold
and to keep—
The earth as a home for my seed.
The beauty I'd hold—would never
grow old—
But renewed ever fresh in the spring.

When I leave this old life—with its
conflict and strife—
Let me sit in the shade of my tree—
And share its embrace—with the
whole human race—
And its peace grace a land that is
free.

Evelyn A Smith
FAUNCY

She was such a comfort,
Gave many years of joy—
Never was a bother
Nothing did destroy.

With a happy whimper
She climbed up in your lap,
And snuggled up so close
So you could rub her back.

Her little doggie eyes
Just seemed to roll and smile;
The little rugs she loved
To put them in a pile.

You heard her little paws
As they danced on the floor—
All knew what she wanted
When she watched the kitchen
door.

Fauncy was a pleasure
And just went everywhere—
If there's a doggie heaven
I'm sure that she's up there.

Sherlyn Anita Swan
IMPORTANT DAY

To Gregory and Desiree, my loving family. You are my lifeline to reality.

Have you ever lay
In the depths of the dark
Listening to the silence
And the beat of your heart
Did the thump get quicker
With beat after beat
When you finally realized
You couldn't go to sleep
You're filled with excitement
Before an important morn
As a pregnant mother
Awaits a baby born

You lay in the dark with an inner
glow
Something good's going to happen,
you just know.
The reality of this thought, comes
from down deep
It soothes and relaxes, and finally you
sleep.
. . . SASY

Sherlyn Anita Swan
A BROKEN SPIRIT
Why do we not stop before we raise the voice?
Have we forgotten that we can make a choice?
To decide not to strike out or hurt with a word
Takes monumental control so I have heard.
But personally I feel that it's not so hard to do
When you'd rather not hurt plus filled with love too.
One word spoken be it mean or unkind
can remain forever within the depths of mind.
Stop-Listen-Please!! Can't you hear it?
It's not the silence of hurt feelings,
But the thump of a broken spirit,
We must fight for the strength to keep the spirit free,
I won't hurt you so please don't hurt me.
. . . SASY

Sherlyn Anita Swan
FATE
What makes us face trouble without fear,
Is it the inner voices we hear.
Do they come from our subconscious,
a lost lonely place
Or from our past life of an inner space.
Do we listen to the voices with deep intent
or have they been ignored when we didn't know what they meant.
Either way it does not matter if we hesitate,
Because what we will be is determined by the fates.
Although we feel we guide our destiny
Our human life story is an infinity.
A continuous web of which we have no control
A record of beginnings and endings will be told.
We can either face it and be sure to enjoy
Or fight the fate forces and be marked to destroy.
We must look at life and take a stand,
And defend the fate forces to the unknowing end.
. . . SASY

Sherlyn Anita Swan
LIFETIME DREAM
A lifetime passes as I look at you,
Remembering moments between us two,
We ask ourselves where did the time go,
As the hours moved fast and the progress slow.

But as we look closer we realize our plot
was a gradual advancement while accomplishing a lot,
With great strides plus small and giant steps,
We've still got dreams to conquer yet.

So my lifetime partner we live together with pride,
Throw anger, frustration and sadness aside,
We look to the future with burning hope,
Knowing with love and understanding we will cope.
. . . SASY

Frances H King
WHERE ARE WE HEADING
"Where are we heading?"
Good Question!
That all depends on what you want out of life.
Me—I want to smell the roses blooming!
I want to hear the birds singing!
Oh! I just want to feel my heart beating.
WAITING! HOPING! PRAYING!
Praying that God will just allow me to breathe
just another breath.
Let me stand on yonders mountain—
And gaze at one more sunset.
Oh just to hold hands and to dream—
That maybe someday soon—
This world of ours will be united as one.
And we can stand as brothers together
in everlasting PEACE.

Frances H King
LONELINESS
Dark and silent are the midnight hours
That I must spend alone.
Quiet and tranquil the moments pass—
As thru the mind thoughts roam.
Deep are the feelings that pierce the soul
As fleeting sad memories drift by.
Take flight Oh my spirit!
Don't linger below!
Soar high as the eagle flies.
Freedom is yours to live and to dream
Tho winds of confusion blow hard.
Be strong—face the future!
It's all that you have,
And live to the fullest you must!
Peace Oh Peace—beautiful peace shall return—
Joy comes as loneliness dies.

Frances H King
BEGINNING AGAIN
The rain has come in heavy torrents
And covered almost everything in sight.
It seems like every dream you've treasured
Is hidden far beyond your nearest view.
No Sun to see, no not a glimmer of light
No matter where you probe and search.

But well you know—if not tomorrow;
Someday soon the Sun will surely shine—
And with it comes a serge of added strength.
You've fallen, stumbled blindly, now just stand!
Reach down and pick up all the broken pieces
And start again a life that is renewed.

Mary Vitcenda
REFLECTIONS
As I sat in my rocking chair,
I thought about times past,
How sure I'd been when I was young,
That all was fun and it would last.

The years went by as they will do,
The problems came and the bad times, too;
Still, I was young and thought so I'd stay,
As I continued on day to day.

Now I know it comes to us all,
The handwriting upon the wall;
We will be called, one and all,
To enter into Heaven's Hall.

Paige R Dixon
THE FLOWER (ON THE HILL)

This poem is dedicated to Mom, the "Pride" of HCHS, and Laressa K. Franks.

A single flower in a storm
Wind & rain its petals torn
Mother nature moves her hand
On the hill, the flower stands

The storm continued & it saw
The flower standing on the hill
"Little flower you will fall,"
Said the storm unto the hill

With all its might the storm did try
Then it stopped & asked out why
"Why O' flower do you stand
Why not fall onto the land"

The flower beaten by the storm
Standing boldly, nearly torn
"Faith" it said with all its might
& then it fell, unto the light.

Kenneth Walsh
LIFE
Life, what should it be. Should it be reality?
Please tell me now what do I see?
What's in life that surrounds me?
I cannot see, for life is like the forest and the trees and life it completely covers me.

Down the road stands an old oak tree.
It also has life and reality.
So tell me what should I see, should everything be reality?
My eyes they open wide, what I see I try to hide, and all my life
I've been told life is worth more than gold.
So tell me now why should I see all my life as reality.

Should I spend my life in light or should I wait for the darkness of the night?
Why should I ask and really shout, the things in life I've already seen and they don't bring much happiness it seems.
I feel, I touch, I know what's there. I love, I hate, I feel what's there;
But tell me now, is it life I have to share, or is it just a burden I must bare? Or is it just a game I play, or is it how I live day by day;
So tell me now what must I do? I beg of you, what in life must I do.
Tell me now if what I see is really life in reality.
Please, please, I've got to know,
What's in life you really love so.
Is it life or reality, or is it things that just must be.
Please, please, I've got to Know,
What's in life, I've got to know.

Anita L Davis
GOD PREVAILS

In honor of Otis Clifford Phillips, both Father and Daddy, and all of my memories of him.

When you only see grief
in the world where you live—
You need to stop. And see the shore.

When comfortless sorrows confront
you every day—
You need to feel the rising sun.

When questions get cloudy and
answers elude you—
Quietly ponder—the ocean's waves.

Yes life is funny with
its twisted ways;
Unexplained trauma we just
can't understand.

Then go to the shore
where the sun sets on the sea.
Observe the perfection of the
beauty you see
And know on your heart—
God is over all!

Anita M Macias

Anita M Macias
THE LORD CAN HELP
As I was growing up life seemed so easy and carefree,
Now that I'm older I get scared of all the horrible things I see.
It seems as though we are trapped in a world that's evil and cruel,
And at times it seems nothing will get better no matter what you do.
Yet there is one way to escape from all trouble that leads to sin,
Look away from evil things and ask God to take you in.
That is where you will never go wrong 'cause God doesn't turn anyone away,
He will only open up his arms and then he will say . . .
"My child you are very special to me and I love you."
And you should say you are my God and I shall do what you want me to!!

Rosie Byrne
LANE OF PAIN
Speak thou not a word,
But you said a lot,
Not a sound heard,
That you're overwrought.

Broken hearts he mends,
Never to be ignored,
Goodbye my dear friends,
You're with our dear Lord.

Love might have helped some,
But you were in pain,
Nobody would come,
To walk down the lane.

While you were still here,
My life you did touch,
I don't wish you near,
Though I miss you much.

You shed not a tear,
No one heard your cry,
Now the Lord will hear,
For you chose to die.

Laura M Walker
THE BLIND CHILD'S PRAYER
Dedicated to my mother.

They tell me Father, that tonight
you'll wed another bride.
That you will clasp her in your arms
where my poor mother died.
They say her name is Mary, too: the
name my mother bore.
But, Father do you think she will care
like the one you loved before?
And is her voice so sweet and low,
her face so meek and mild
And Father, do you think she'll love
your blind and helpless child?

Laura M Walker
CHANCE TO LOVE
If some sweet space could be set
apart free from the prying eyes of
judging curious men:
some sweet dear place betwixt the
earth and sky
where we to-gether for one little day
could find the unopened pages of the
heart. If you could utter all you yearn
to say and I could answer you before
I die: O then I could go gladly on my
way again. But, this despair, this
fretting and this chafing and this care
for what the stupid world will say or
think: O love, surely in all thy
universe of skies there is some spot,
some cloudy place upon the
evening's brink where we, my
beautiful and I may meet and suffer
not: where longing hands, at last,
may interlace and kisses fall upon the
beloved's eyes. No room can hold the
beauty of our first embrace God!
Find us a place

Skye D Cornell
BIRTHRIGHT
The reflection of a long cracked
mirror
bears a cameo pink soul, seizing her
childlike youth.
With swollen abdomen she reminds
herself of a new succession to come.
Tear stained eyes like chilling
raindrops,
running its course down the
windowpane.
Movement in unknown dark waters,
always a reminder,
tangled with sin.
An error of misconduct,
or so they say.

Gerald Clay Lewis
MY MOTHER
To My Very Loving Mother, Elsie I. Lewis, Mother of the Year Every Year!

There's no other,
Like MY MOTHER;
More than a Dove,
She's always been my Love.

Thru thick and thin,
She sticks me like a pin;
Keeps me narrow and straight,
Taught me never to hate.

All thru my life,
Better than a wife;
I've always been a bother,
She's still Mother and Father.

In nineteen eight-five,
She's Number One in my life;
Even when she shed a tear,
For MY MOTHER of the year!

Gerald Clay Lewis
PUDDIN'
My dog's name is PUDDIN',
She's cuter than Sally Goodin;'
Tho she's years of eight,
She's grown never to hate.

Her pretty eyes of brown,
Have never let me down;
While I am away,
She's not as happy and gay.

My Mother calls her "Black Rat,"
Tho she's neither a rat or cat;
Sometimes she appears befuddled,
But always loves to be cuddled.

She's been my pride and joy,
Since I was at heart a little boy;
With much Love, no I wouldn',
Trade anything for my PUDDIN'.

Kathleen M Marshall
GROWING-UP DAYS
I love you, my children, in so many
ways;
And I really do cherish your
growing-up days;
Of diapers, play-dough, crayons,
cartoons;
Of cookies and milk, bubble baths
and balloons;

Walks to the park, sand in your
shoes;
I'll never forget the "Terrible Twos";
Wiping your tears, wiping your nose;
Counting the piggies on your little
toes;

The endless laundry, the endless
noise;
The endless pleading, "Pick up your
toys;"
The endless hugs, the endless kisses;
The endless worrying, and endless
wishes.

I'll never forget all those cute things
you do;
I hope you know I'm always here for
you;
I'm here when you laugh, I'm here
when you cry;
And to answer those questions
beginning with "Why?"

Sometimes I want you to grow up too
fast;
These days while you're little just
won't last;
I love you, my children, in so many
ways;
And I really do cherish your
growing-up days.

Renita G Decker
THE LITTLE BOY'S PRAYER
To my son, Michael.

Mom watches as Mikie kneels on his
knees
His little hands folded and his head
bowed
She hears his small voice asking
GOD please
"To take care of mommy, you know
how.
I know that sometimes I am bad,
I broke one of mommy's favorite
things
GOD I didn't mean to make her sad,
It used to be pretty and sing.
Mommy said not to worry, that it was
alright,
But I know it wasn't 'cause I heard
her sigh
I wish I could make it again alright
'Cause I heard her cry in her room
last night.
My mommy she loves me way too
much
When I'm sad, she holds me and says
it's ok
She really does love me way too
much,
So I promise that I'll never go away.

'Cause GOD, I Love my mommy."

Maxine MacDonald
THE CHILDREN
Because there are children
the stillness is not so endless

And every depth has a ladder
by which you may return.

Their laughter is sun
on the cold moon.

In their eyes is your lost
child self
And your reason for tomorrow.

So listen to their sounds
and footsteps
Their music is for you.

Dagmar Errasti
UNTIL
Until I held you,
my arms ignored they were cold.

Until I kissed you,
I didn't know the power of my lips.

Until I gazed into your eyes,
I couldn't grasp infinity.

Until I met you . . .
I didn't exist.

maryanne wood
WHEN DAWN BEHOLDS THE NIGHT
For all who touched my life.

Name the moment,
(if you can!)
When night did cease,
And day began . . .

When do the stars heave their final
sigh?
When do mixing hues confuse the
sky?
When does day escape the clutches of
the night?
Or chase darkness into shadows of
the light?
Arriving upon the first whispers of
light,
Dimension itself, greets time and
sight.

Long before
colors adorn the grain,
and the brilliance of the Sun does
reign,
Life begins
for all creatures of the light,
when first the dawn beholds the
night.

Grace Watts Lee
THE MISCHIEVOUS ONE
Children running through the
schoolyard gate
Wondering if they are going to be
late.
He starts running, dropping things
As the school bell rings.

Up the stairs and through the halls
Running, laughing he makes loud
calls.
Skipping through the door, he took
his place
Wearing a mischievous grin on his
face.

The children stand and begin to sing,
From his pocket he takes a string.
When the teacher isn't looking
He makes a lasso to start hooking.

All the children turn to stare
When he tumbles out of his chair.
Stretched out on the floor
Suddenly, he beings to snore.

Curled up in a big bunch,
He waited for the bell to ring for
lunch.
From his position on the floor,
He was the first one out the door.

Tina M Egy
TIED BOATS
Sunlight filters through the
leaves to the ground below
Everything's fresh and new,
Ever so softly does the wind
blow.

The birds each sing
their own little song,

Each one brings
and carries along,
The Forest is like a melody,
Each living thing a note
contributing to the music . . .

Gently rocking tied boats.

Grace Watts Lee
THE WEBBER CLAN
Gather around, listen to me
As we learn more about our family's history.
Of our early beginnings, little is known
But in Adam Webber, the seed was sown.

Man living alone has a lonely life,
So Adam took Betsy for his wife.
He then became a family man
And started the existing "Webber Clan."

He lived in a place called Buffalo Creek,
And he probably worked seven days a week
To enable him to adequately provide
All the necessities for Betsy, his bride.

They must have been a very special pair
To endow us with the many talents we share.
There are Doctors, Lawyers and Teachers galore,
Artists, Ministers, Librarians, Pilots and many more.

There are talents we did not name,
But we all belong in the "WEBBER HALL OF FAME."
Of our heritage, we can be extremely proud
For each of us stands tall in any crowd.

Grace Watts Lee
LEFT OUT
When a child feels left out
He begins to frown, then to pout,
Wondering what he has done
That displeases everyone.

He really wants to fit in
But doesn't know how to begin.
There's no one he can tell
Why his attitudes make him rebel.

Why is he always so sad
When everyone around him is glad?
He only wants a smile from all
Or a friendly voice to call.

Then he takes a look at himself to see
How others thought that he could be.
He doesn't want to always be a loser
Instead, he wants to be a chooser.

It's up to him to make a change,
To be friendly, pleasant and not act strange.
Now, he tries to do as he should
So that by others, he will be understood.

Grace Watts Lee
MY KITCHEN
If the spider invites the fly into his kitchen,
He wants to catch him in a trap.
If I invite you into my kitchen,
You would meet with a calamitous mishap.

What could happen in a kitchen?
Why nothing! You're sure to think.
Don't be overconfident about my kitchen,
Because there's a HOLE where once stood the SINK.

Fragrant aromas come from many kitchens
Whetting your appetite as they pass.
From my kitchen, you sit waiting and waiting,
In there, turned off has been the GAS.

Bright sunbeams in the morning
Come dancing through the door.
Where could they dance in my kitchen
When I only have part of a FLOOR?

Man's home is his castle,
In the kitchen works his wife.
But when you work in my kitchen
It's done at the RISK of your life.

Rose E Clark
REACHING FOR THE SKY!
Sitting alone with thoughts of my own
I saw a Hawk fly by,
Look at him go—Oh! look at him soar
He's reaching for the sky!

I watched and I thought could this be why
We're so unsatisfied,
Could it be we've set our sights too high
We're reaching for the sky!

With love at our side—dear friends nearby
What are we searching for,
With God at our side—our guiding light
Now who could ask for more!

Time passes by so swiftly by
Too late we realize,
All that we've missed—that we've planned to do,
While reaching for the sky!

Juanita Bryant
HOLIDAY MEMORIES

To my children and family, whose love and caring has been my inspiration.

As the holidays draw closer
I think of years gone past,
Of the closeness of the families,
These times in life don't last.

Our loved ones all draw 'round us
To share our blessings great,
These are the times to show our love
Not the time to hesitate!

Before you realize it
The years have come and gone,
And each loved one goes their separate way
And cannot make it home.

So be thankful this Thanksgiving
This Christmas show your love,
You might not be together again
'Till joined in Heaven above!

Toni Raimondo
I'VE TAKEN THE WRONG PATH

To the one I'll always love.

I've taken the wrong path
and I don't know where to go.
I'm tryn' to follow my heart
but it's the wrong time to know.

I've taken the wrong turn.
Maybe it's time to go back.
Only because they say I should
I will mend the wounded crack.

Day and night I searched high and low,
Only to find what I'm missing.
Although I could not see it
I do not need to see
what I already know.

James Scarborough
WATCHER DANCER
In a blue dream
She is on the end, it seems
The very end of all
The path it leads along
To a point somewhere in
The forever twilight

There stands someone to make
The second half complete
The image of the golden time
I cannot see apart from that

And as the breeze gently sways
The colors snapping to attention
Concerns to drop around
The smell of success
Beckon in the soft glimmering
And before the shadows fade
To yesterlight, they build
The perfect vintage of another day
The road is paved
Sweet release it smiles
I am home

Jade

Jade
THE SILVER WIND
The silver wind is blowing in the hills,
Where the tallest mountains stand.
The peaks it pulls down, by each grain of sand.
The levelling wind is blowing in the earth.
It turns the pages of time.
It will bring the mighty down, the conqueror.
Its captive and the captive knows rebirth.
See how this earth reshapes by this Great Silver Wind.
From North to South, from East to West,
Four silver winds assault with force.
They push the lavender blue clouds about the sky.
And pull the mountains down.
The sailboat is restless on the ocean.
The rocks melt into sand
All the earth's voices are now hushed,
In deference to the Silver Wind,
as the lesser birds are still . . .
as the eagle spreads its wings,
on silver in the Wind . . .
I shall look for you.

Grace M Davidson
BAD DREAMS
I saw it there, hanging in the Western sky way out on the edge of the World—
Blood red it was, and bigger than the sun has ever been,
but its light was cold—and when it slipped beyond the
hills no twilight remained, for this was a greedy sun, gathering every scarlet ray into itself as it slid
beyond the horizon and left me there in the night.
And the blackness surrounded me and covered me
and streamed beyond the world into infinity—
Alone I stood on that barren rock in a black so black
that even God could not have seen—
And the moments stretched and mingled into minutes 'till
I dared not even breathe.
In the center of my being formed the fear that I would
stand imprisoned on this icy rock till time wound to
its end—When I thought my mind would surely break
and be consumed by fear, a thin white line formed in the black and grew into a sphere—
The huge white moon crept up the sky alone in the
velvet night.
As it moved along its ordered path, I whispered
"Thank you God for light." Then I awoke.

Helen Neeley
MY DAY
You hold me captive, GOD, in the morning as I pray,
With the quiet glory, LORD, of the every changing day.
Sounds a mounting serenade, of the creatures You have made
To a sunrise bursting with colors You once laid.

Through distant hum of traffic, and frequent blare of horn
Denoting many others, too, are up in early morn.
Then as the day goes swiftly by, You guide my eyes to see
The beauty of the birds, Leaving perch in leafless tree.

Now, I catch sight of children, in sunlight's special glow;
I hear their shouts and laughter, as they shovel the snow
From the sidewalks of their homes; then later in the day
Making snowballs, building forts. A sudden shout, "Let's play."

I am sure the sunsets, try to rival dawn's sweet light,
Yet to each beholder, 'twill be a slightly different sight.
Once again, You paint the skies, as sun sinks in the West,
And for me, oh GOD, this day, You have completely blessed.

C D Kumamoto
SUCH A GOOD WIFE
This is the marvel of a sensible woman
To fling a mask across a stretch of the sky

To light the last light, or a yearning cry
Burning thousands of miles to a still point:
The suddenness of him.

Place does not matter, nor history,
Nor that she gives like a prodigal raw, he a nomad's love:
This single hour is for the intensest yield.

Their centers meet,
She is like one on a small boat coming over
On a turning edge of the greening water,

Sea of dark breathing,
Sea of womb remembering,

Body suffer, gently
A change, aureate, in the heartscape
Over her apotropaic sea.

It is a fact, or has she dreamed it?
She will deny everything. Mean-while,
The placid smile on a hearth-worn face knows
Moralists cannot divine this ecstasy: the knowledge
She will not run madly anymore.

Glenn D Sotzky
THE APPLE

To sunny summer days and a woman's sweet smile.

The apple is a kind of fruit,
it grows on a tree.
Nutritious, and healthy, shiny and red,
meant to be eaten by you and me.

An apple fell on Sir Newton's head
and gave us the laws of gravity.
An apple a day, keeps the doctor away,
we always remark poetically.

Some say it was an apple tree,
not fig, in the Garden of Eden,
that Adam had ate from
after Eve had eaten.

So, bake your apples into strudel,
apple jellies, jams and pies.
Apples, apples, everywhere;
apple trees growing as high as the skies.

Carolyn Powers
SILENTLY

Dedicated to Ma, with love, Carrie.

Silently I sit unnoticed except by one or
two as emptiness shades their faces like
fresh fallen dew
The path I must find leading to life's destiny
Or is emptiness to shade the face I thought
to be me
Darkness I once knew has fallen far behind, life means more than just existing
in Time —

Julie L Nebres
NATURE

Nature is precious in every way,
It helps us live and strive each day;
It gives a smile to every face,
It makes the world a lively place.

See the birds up in the sky;
Look at the mountains that are so high;
See the sight of falling snow;
Look at the clouds as they come and go.

There's the rain that supplies us with water,
It hits the ground in a lovely spatter;
There's the sun that gives us heat,
It is the source of the food we eat.

Let's take care of our precious nature,
That will give us a better future;
Nature is our best companion;
Let us keep it from extinction.

Elaine Kersey
FIRST MOMENTS

As the sun sets
Our eyes meet
As the sea sways
Our hearts beat

As the seagulls soar
Our hands brush
As the stars shine
Our bodies touch

As the moon enlightens
Our lips seduce
As the moment lingers
Our senses heighten

As the passion ends
Our embrace softens
As the night continues
Our hearts surrender

Micheal Lee Overmyer
IN TO THE BLACK

Dedicated to the Homeless People.

As the night approaches, I awake from my sleep
Not knowing where I've been, the light makes my eyes tired and weak.

I stumble around in a daze hoping it will all come
to an end, like some kind of bad dream.
But I look into the mirror and see my reflection
it wants to make me scream.
Scream of all the pain I've had through this short
life, or scream because I'm afraid of what the future may bring?
So always remember, hold on to your dreams,
and may they stick in my ear like a familiar ring.

Clara Mae Duguay
THE MEADOW

There is a meadow in my world
Where animals of many kinds come out to play,
And hunt for food among the grass and rocks,
Or even in the trees where branches sway.

When gentle breezes blow the clouds away
I am privileged to see now
The mysteries of Nature all around:

Crows so black and herons blue,
Mourning doves, possums, raccoons all say,

"It's okay to share the meadow
Even with the Farmer's cow,
For there's enough for all of us."

And if the whole wide world could only see,
A lovely meadow of sharing would stretch
Around the globe and exchange our troubles
For peace and harmony.

Robert Matias
ONLY IN DREAMS

For Karen Delseni: The first, fairest, and finest resident in my own private world of thoughts...

The touch of your kiss.
The kiss of your touch.
The feeling of your eyes caressing me
with passions governed solely by the powers of
love-everlasting.
These are the things I have come to know with you . . .
But only in dreams . . .

Leroy Holbert
GARDEN FOR THE BLIND

Would you plant a garden, Sir,
For people just like me?
Who came into a world of darkness
With eyes that cannot see.

Please plant the roses
The ones I love so much.
The big ones with a fragrance
That I may smell and touch.

When you've planted the garden
And it is fully grown.
Lead me down the path my friend
There let me stand alone.

Let me stand among the roses
And think of people just like me.
Who live in a world of beauty
With eyes that cannot see.

Tracy A DeJardin
THE EMPTY CITY

This poem is dedicated to Epie, my beloved. And to the memory of my wonderful great-grandmother who remains in my heart today.

The night called out for so much more than a simple whisper between two.
It longed for the passion and fury felt between bodies when love is new.
The clouds were low, and the mist thickly lined the bright city.
The smell of day-old garbage ran rampant, and nothing in sight was even partially pretty.
The sound of faint music and people carrying on was often heard on a night such as this.
Old folks enjoying a sunset were nowhere to be found in this shallow city lacking bliss.
Bums sleeping on park benches, and hookers looking for love in the next man's face.
All the pain and cheapness anyone could imagine was here, and it always took place.
Crowded apartment buildings possessing unhappy faces of children longing for something better.
Parents hoping that tomorrow would never come, and neither would that eviction letter.
Cities hold so little for so many, yet they produce so much.
But the one thing that they will never contain is the warmth of a human touch!

Anna Mae Carter
GUARD WELL THY POST

Guard well thy post.
Keep with sleepless eyes
The watch I gave to thee.
'Tis a great thing I have asked of thee,
To keep this place.
Patience is required,
And great love,
And much kindness.
A strong character is needed here,
And when thou hast finished this task
Thou wilt be even stronger,
And thou wilt be well fitted for other tasks for me.
Guard well thy post.

LaVerne E Wear
THE EASTER PROMISE

The sky was dark, the world was sad
for men among us had been bad

They nailed our Savior to the cross
not knowing what our loss

And so we wept and prayed, for days
by His tomb we stayed.

He'd come again, I had heard Him say
We would not go away

And then the clouds parted and the sun shone through
Upon each rose was a drop of dew

And there before our wondering eyes
our Savior stood

He'd kept His promise like He said
He would.

Kevin G Rittmeier
FOR YOU

To my wife Reyna, with whom I am complete.

A thought and we came to start
How far I do not know.
But I will share the moon and stars.
I will open my heart that seems so far
and I hope in time,
I hope with you I will find
The love that keeps lovers near,
The love that conquers fear,
The love that can make us one,
The love that we can share,
Love that we once knew
Love to us that is precious and dear.

Rebecca L Stone
OUR HOME

Our home is a place where we cook and clean.
Our home is where our children play in their room, or out in the yard.
Our home is where my family eats the meals we cook.
Our home is where our children have sweet dreams while they sleep.

Our home is where we go after work and after school
Our home ——
Oh God! I must have been dreaming!
Our home is a mission, when it's not full.
Our home is where our children play on the sidewalk.
Our home is the mission meals or handouts.
Our home is a mission or a cardboard box or sidewalk where our children now cry in their sleep.
Our home is a mission or the streets, because I no longer have a job.
Oh God! How could America let this happen, my family is homeless!
Why? What happened?
We pray for a better tomorrow.

Christine Christensen

Christine Christensen
A FLORAL BOUQUET

An eight-year-old child.
Sits at my table.
With a bandage above one eye.
Another on her chin.
And a red black eye.
From an angry father.

The sun streaks through white curtains.
On a floral bouquet.
Sitting on a dining room table.
They are bursts of life.
On stems of green,
gold, lilac, peach, yellow, and white.
And they coax from this battered face,
The smile of angels!

Christine Christensen
— I AM,

When I think of you -
I breathe in the warm ocean air.
When I think of you -
I see my wedding bouquet.
When I think of you -
A surge of passion floods my soul.
When I think of you -
I'm always humming our favorite song.
When I think of you -
I dream of our future.
When I think of you -
I gaze lovingly onto our past.
When I think of you -
I radiate joy across my face.
When I think of you -
I embrace love.
When I think of you -
I am.

Christine Christensen
AS CHILDREN OFTEN DO -

As a child I dreamt of having great things.
As a child I longed for far away places.
As a child there were some things I just knew.
As a child I did everything I thought I could do.
As a child I made you happy and blue.
As a child I made you laugh and cry.
As a child I sailed you through a sea of emotions.
As a child I believed all the things you said were true.
As a child I broke something important to you.
As a child I ran away from you.
As a child I wanted to be just like you.
As a child I made up a story or two.
As a child I had my own fears.
As a child I stole some candy too.
As a child I cried crocodile tears.
As a child I got lost frequently in the department stores.
As a child you spent many hours nursing me back to health.
As a child I had to be different.
As a child I grew up, as children often do.

Christine Christensen
WORDS

Is it true about words?
Are secrets revealed by words?
Can friends be made or lost by words?
How can you make a deal without words?
Because of words,
nations rise against and for each other.
Men are condemned,
by one man's choice of words.
Isn't it said:
Words have power over life and death?
If this is all true,
should we say nothing?
Can silence rule a kingdom?

TJ Chwala
DREAMS OF OZ

Last night I dreamt I slept & slept,
Then dreamt the oddest dreams of OZ.

It seemed unreal like dreamy dreams,
Yet really real like not in dreams.

"You ate too much!" "You ate too fast!"
Screamed mobs of munchkins from OZ.

"Your eyes are bigger than your belly!"
Screamed the voice of Wizard, himself.

"Is this a dream?" I asked from dream to dream
And I hoped to wake in bed and dream no more.

Some said yes and some said no, yet
Some were silent and some didn't know.

I ran from the wicked witch of the west,
And I walked down the yellow brick road.

And they were there, no matter where,
From dream to dream, they followed me.

Where to run or where to hide, for
They were there, no matter where.

Suddenly the alarm went off and
They were there, no matter where.

They were there, munchkins from OZ,
The witch and the voice of Wizard, himself.

"Is this a dream?" I asked from dream to dream,
And I hoped to wake in bed and dream no more.

Some said yes and some said no, yet
Some were silent and some didn't know.

Lawrence A Caire Jr
FOLLOW YOUR DREAM

In Dedication to my Mom & Dad for their Love and support they gave me in The Beginning of my Life.

Follow your dream to an awesome land.
Where boys and girls walk hand and hand.
Where there's no fights, no fires, no wars.
Where people don't have to lock their doors.
This is a place that can come true.
Just follow your dream and let it guide you.

Judy Trathen
TODAY . . . I DID SOMETHING FOR ME

To: David.

Today, I did something for me.
Today, I planted a tree.
I will watch it grow,
Through the wind and snow.
Through the rain and sleet,
And the climbing of little feet.
To others it will give much pleasure,
But to me . . . it will be a treasure.

Steven Grames
DREAM

Last night I dreamt of you
Writing in the sky
Underneath a broken moon
You sang a lullaby

Your eyes were pools of fire
Burning into mine,
Your lips were soft like pillows
Of clouds in summertime

Your gown so freely flowing
Purer white than snow
Seemed to live around you
For love itself to know

When I awoke, I wondered
At such a dream of you
I turned and saw you smiling
My dream, alas! was true

Ellen J Penny
THE ROSE

Like the petals of a rose as it opens,
Once the warmth of the sun has touched it,
Your love has touched me.
It has caused the petals of love,
Once buried and locked away deep within my heart,
To blossom and unfold as never before.
The warmth of your love surrounds me,
Like the fragrance of the rose fills a room.
The fragrance of your love is so very sweet,
As it fills me.
My love for you continues to grow and blossom,
And produce a fragrance even sweeter than the rose . . .
But as a rose withers and dies,
Without the proper care,
I too, would wither and die without you,
For I Love You,
And it is your love, that feeds, and nourishes me now.

J E Murray Jr
THE MOVIE HOUSE

The Projector was on
The Lights had dimmed
The seats were full
See the credits begin

The Lion had roared
The stars shined bright
The Wind was Gone
See the screen shine on

The 50's arrived
The T.V.'s had light
The theaters were empty
See the stars shine bright

Kay Ray
A SPECIAL GIFT

The Lord sent me a special gift
And wrapped it with His love.
Truly, a very precious gift,
From Heaven up above.
He didn't give, but only lent it.
For how long, He didn't say.
I only know I've grown to love it
More and more each passing day.
It's up to me to nurture it
Through its childhood, that's my goal.
Sustaining it,
Loving and maintaining it,
Body, mind, and soul.

Novlet Mills
CRACK

This poem is dedicated to all school children.

You have destroyed the best out of every next home
You cared not where you pop up or be found
Or whether your pushers will be bound
As long as you are spread all around.

They are so many innocent victims
Who just caught up with your wicked system
In which you have poisoned their mind
So they all turned on the street to crime.

Many are illiterate, they can't read
But they fall victims because of greed
All they wanted was to be in the latest style
Even if they have to go an extra mile.

Be still or I will surely kill
Just empty your bags and pockets
Move over there with your hands in the air
Where is the rest of change
Before I blow your xxxx brains

With crack for their middle name
They all are so insane
They have no fear in their hearts
They'll shoot you dead then depart.

Harriette K Halley
I LOOKED AROUND
I looked around
to stop and stare,
I looked again
I wasn't there.

I tried to find
what I should see,
and when I looked
it wasn't me.
Was I dreaming
was I there?
I couldn't tell
it wasn't clear.

Sometimes you dream
you don't prepare
and when you wake
you can't compare.
Are you here or are you there?

Verna Smith
FRIENDS?

Jennifer: You're one of the greatest anyone could ask for! Never forget the good times, twin!

We used to say
our friendship would last,
But now it seems
to all be in the past.

We always had fun
when we were together,
I used to think this friendship
would go on forever.

I'll never forget
what we once had;
a special bonding
always happy, never sad.

I can still hear your laughter
ringing throughout my head,
"Our friendship will never end"
That's what we said.

Our friendship is dying off
slowly but surely, day by day,
And I'm begging you now
Please don't go. Please stay.

James E Van Duzer
NEW YEAR
So, another year came and went,
To many, a very important event.
Remembering past achievements,
And of course, nostalgic sentiments.
All celebrated in mystical moments,
Sparkling champagne, and heart-
throb ferment.
I celebrated too!
As a snake sheds its skin;
leaving it behind,
paying it no mind,
slithering to the next rock
for protection from sun's ray
shock.

Pauline V Conley
DEAR PAM

To Pam with love on your birthday, May 14th, 1990. Mother and Jack.

On your birthday, Pam, I sent a
prayer,
A special prayer to God,
For sparing you so long ago.
When I prayed without ceasing,
and I wouldn't let go,
And God in His mercy
Reached down from above
and healed you and kept you
For your family to love.
In miracles I do believe,
For you're living proof, you see,
of how great and mighty is our God;
What he did for you, for me.
So when things get rough, and you
feel unloved,
or think you come in last,
Remember what God did for you,
How He gave you another chance.
And I like to believe of all the
prayers
That bombarded Heaven long ago,
That it was mine God answered
For I love you, and I wouldn't let go.
Love, Mother.

Pauline V Conley
I MET DEATH

To my son-in-law Jack, without whose help & thoughtfulness this poem might never have been published.

Face to face with death I came
On the highway of life one day
Not a word did he speak
But silently by the hand let me away.

There was no chance, I had to go
The Lord had need of me
This was a journey I had not planned
A trip I did not see.

What if I hadn't been ready
Could I have told death to wait
No, it was I the Lord wanted
No one could take my place.

Death took me across the river
To the home of eternal life
This was my reward of sixteen years
Of doing what was right.

Amina Siddiqui
HATE
I silently sit and contemplate
What in this world produces hate.
Why rivalry breaks reverie
Everywhere I look and see.

Above our heads stars glimmer and
shine
Far above the tallest pine,
And with such a peaceful show in the
night,
Down below, why must we fight?

Why sister against brother?
Why father against mother?
Why World War I and World War II?
What in the world do we do?

We live to learn, to love, to teach
Each other. Now I do beseech
The people of the world to hear
That hate in this world is our greatest
fear.

Everyone can't have their way,
But certainly I hope some day,
From this world the smog of hate
Will soon and briskly dissipate.

Sherry Riley Devine
UNDER A PERISH SKY

For my mom and dad, who believe in me.

Waving heat from hilltops
In the distance
Oranged—yellow flowers
Cover the peaks.
Long-neglected grapevines
Still bearing fruit
Frame the weathered fence
Where on the other side
Rust-colored clay beds
Flank an uttering creek.
Ribbons of butterflies
Dodge waving flowers
Tilting in the wind.
In the severity of twilight
Watching the westering sun and
All the delights of this day
Rest for tomorrow,
I lie in lacy shadows of
A live oak, lost
In the sky of perish blue.

Deziray Hilderbrand
ROCKS IN MY SOCKS

To grandma & grandpa Wilson, with Love.

I got rocks in my socks holes in
my clothes penny in my pocket,
and I just picked up my grandpa's
socket.
I went to the moon in a rocket, and
found a locket in my pocket.

Debra Baker Rathbun
THIS IS YOUR CHILD
This is your child
Child of the streets
Living in fear
No time for tears.

Will you see him
Your child of pain
Or do you turn
Your head in shame.

This is your child
Though not of your name
He is yours and mine
All the same.

Your child is hungry
He learns to steal
Your child sees hatred
He learns to kill.

This is your child
Show him you care
Give him a reason
Give him time, his share.
This is your child.

Ruth Haak
BIRTHDAY WISHES

Written for and dedicated to my Hawaiian friend, Lopaka Young.

Your birthday, I said I would
remember.
Please look around you and observe
your day
And as you do so, these words
remember:
Wherever you are, whatever you do
You're wished a day with a sky that's
blue,
And the sun with its warmth shining
down on you;
An evening with friends to share your
day
Making you happy in every way;
A flower to look at, giving its beauty
to you;
And most of all, that your dreams and
wishes may all come true.
These are my birthday wishes for
you.
Again, a Very Happy Birthday to
you!

Guy S Apollo
RETROSPECT
Wherever I turn, eyes are upon me.
Brown eyes, blue. It doesn't matter.
They're all
the same. Searching.
Some as young as twenty-one, others
twenty-one the
second time around.
What are they missing that they are
here tonight?
Why has life molded them to follow
the pattern of
hundreds before them?
Loneliness? Sure some are here
because they're lonely.
Others only because they're
afraid of getting involved.
For some, no attachments are safer.

I've seen some of these faces before.
Many as long as
when I was first aware.
Hair is a little different. Lines a little
deeper and
waistlines a little bigger.
The game still being played. Still
searching for that special
"blue plate."
God don't they know that life exists
outside these walls and
beyond the jukebox that plays
the same songs year after year?
Hypocritical or reminiscent?
I was here before, I'm here now.

Jessie S Grigg
ALTHOUGH WE PART
I shall be with you ever
Although we part—
All of me with you
My mind, my soul, my heart

Thoughts will all barriers cross
Though continents and oceans divide.
Our thought children will meet and
mingle
And on high seas majestically
mingle.

I sense your calm in the starlight
night—
You are the glory of sunsets
unborn—
I feel your force in the fiercest gale—
In all of earth's moods you come.

Fireside joys of other mortals we may
never know

But the peace of perfected harmonies
is ours—
Like the mingling of sweet aromas
From strange unknown flowers.

Doris H Williams
PARENTS
We Love the seasons, but not the
storms.
We Love the rose, but not the thorns.
We Tend our garden, but hate the
weeds.
We Love our children, but sometimes
neglect their needs.

Our Life is the seasons with all the
storms.
Our Bed is the roses, with all the
thorns.
Our Garden is our children which we
have sown.
Our Love is the finished product
when they are grown.

Betty Dukerschein
BESIDE THE SEA
Come, take my hand and walk with
me,
Along the shore, beside the sea.
The sun's last rays ignite the sky;
While, all around us, seagulls cry.

The air is soft and warm and sweet;
As wavelets wash upon our feet.
The sand is cool against our skin,
Where tiny beasties burrow in.

The world is very far away;
I wish that we could always stay,
The two of us, just you and me,
Along the shore, beside the sea.

Opal E McQueen
MY WEEPING WILLOW TREE
We sold the old home place this year.
The pasture and the well.
The buyer does not know we kept
Some things we could not sell.

We sold the barns, the shed, the
house
And my garden filled with flowers.
He could not know, there is a place
That always will be ours.

We sold the garden and the grove.
It is his property.
He cannot know my heart still owns
My weeping willow tree.

But does he own our old home place?
He bought it every nail.
Yet old and well-loved memories
Can never be for sale.

Mildred Jones Stauffer
FIFTEEN YEARS OLD
I do not see the little boy I had—
Nor the young man I hoped to raise.
A stranger, rude, thoughtless and
cruel
Is here—oh why my son?

They say that this is just a
phase—
All youths are going through,
Rebelling the parental yoke
And all the things they do.
My son, but why the threats?

Please hurry, hurry, and grow up
For I cannot stand much more,
Your rebellion is so evident
It hurts right to the core.
Please—hurry son!

No one wants to hold you back—
To guide you dear, is all I ask
Until I can rightfully say, "YOUNG
MAN"
And know the stranger's gone at
last!!!
My Dear—please understand.

P.S. At last—"YOUNG MAN"—at
last!!!
Love, Mother

Dorotha V King
THE RED RIBBON

To my family and friends.

I would rather get a red ribbon
Tied around a package of love.
Than any gift I could be given
Except treasures from heaven above.

I can open that gift when I am lonely
or when things don't seem to go
right.
And use a little of the love each
morning
And just a tiny bit more at night.

I'm going to be very careful
with that package of love that you
gave.
And retie that red ribbon around it
So some of the love I can save.

I know that God up in heaven
Watches over the things that we do.
And when I untie that red ribbon
He will be watching over you too.

Ethel L Campbell
STANDING IN THE SURF
Standing in the surf looking out over the deep, the restless waves washing over my feet.

I think of desert islands lying amongst the waves, of sunken ships and treasure chests and underwater caves.

I gaze out over the white caps as far as the eyes can see. I know that a bold adventure waits just over the horizon for me.

I can almost smell the spices from a quaint little shop in the East. I can see the jungle with exotic birds and wild ferocious beasts.

I can feel the salty spray as the wind fills the sails, I can hear the old ship creaking as the waves spill over the rails.

I know that my imagination sometimes gets the best of me, but oh! how I would love to sail far across the restless sea.

Verna Smith
MY BEST FRIEND .....
MY SISTER

Nancy: You're one of the very best! You mean a lot to me. I love you!

I have a lot of friends
but my best friend is you,
You may not believe it
but what I say is true.

When I need help
you're there to talk,
And when I'm bored
you're there to take a walk.

You can be a pain
you can make me mad,
But no matter what
you make me happy when I'm sad.
You don't treat me like dirt
you treat me really good,
I hope I do the same for you
like I know I always should.

I'd like to say "Thank-you"
for all you've done for me,
Yes, thank-you for being there
when I needed you to be.

So always remember sister
no matter how mad I get,
You're my best friend
please never forget.

Connie Denise Hosey
I'VE MISSED YOU
The games we played,
the adventures we took,
the talks, the laughs
and all the throw abouts.
I miss them all.
Especially losing you.
If you were here today,
I would kiss your lips
and say, "Never go away."

I never knew,
what was happening to you.
I didn't mean
to let it slip away.
Oh, I wish you
would have told me,
so that I could have seen you,
your very last days.
I've missed you.
I want you back today,
but maybe we'll meet
at Heaven's Gates someday.

Deborah K Milligan
HAVE I?

To my parents, Dan and Nancy, with love.

Have I thanked you for the
little things you did when I
was small?
Like sewing pretty dresses . . . and
papering my walls?
Like teaching me to ride a
bike . . . and getting one for
me?
Like going to work . . . and staying
home, to give security?
Like somehow always finding
A way to give to me
The things I thought I had to
have . . . and the "things" I
couldn't
See?
Like teaching me the value of
giving from the heart
And caring for the other guy . . . and
how to do my part?
Like teaching me that growing
up is more than growing old?
Like teaching me that family is
having love to hold.
Thank you now for all you
gave, but most of all, you see,
Thank you for the gift of Life that
you have shared with me.

Maureen Martin
OH LORD
Let my faith lie not in what I can see,
But in what I can be for thee,
For in my heart you put a treasure,
More valuable than one can measure.
So as I lift my eyes above,
To you and your unfailing love,
I trust worldly pleasures to not fulfill,
My heart like submitting to your will.
In a world filled with Satan's
schemes,
I stand firm to dream your dreams,
With the faith that you've sown,
Secure that I no longer walk alone.
For Jesus whom my sins crucified,
Loves me still and is by my side,
And together we face each day,
Guided by the Father to whom we
pray.
And for many death is the end of the
story,
As for me, it's the beginning, I'll live
in glory.

Brenda Jean Elisabeth Pavlik
FADING PURITY
When I look in your eyes,
I picture a rose,
White and pure.
The rose has a thorn.
It pricks my finger.
A drop of blood
Falls on the rose;
Washing the purity
From its petals.
I begin to cry.
The blood has not come
From my finger.
It's from my broken heart.

Dorothy Ahern Stevenson
THE REASON I CRY
I cry because my mother's child
No earthly time my friendship
sought,
I cry because I'm what I am
And she could be what I could not.
I cry because life's time is short—
Our friendship missed the chance to
grow,
I cry because I never thought
That I would stay, and she would go.
My children cry, their friend is
gone—
She had with them what we had not,
My children cry for friendship lost,
And I shall cry for friendship sought.

William E Monnie
FREEDOM '76

To my wife Ruth, on our 50th anniversary.

Today I stood where the Pilgrims
stood and looked out o'er the
boundless sea.
I wondered what force it was that
drove them to be free;
And I stood on Concord Bridge
and the Minutemen were
there.
They laid their lives upon the line
so of freedom we'd have our
share.
From seventeen hundred and
seventy-six up to the present
time.
Our young men have fought and
died in every land and clime.
That all the Peoples of the world
could stand and say they're
free.
So now I look unto myself for

what freedom means to me.

I want to go where the wind blows free
And the wild, wild ocean is a kin to me.
I want to go where the sea gulls soar,
Where I can listen to the ocean's roar.
Where peace and joy walk hand in hand,
Where footprints make trails in the shifting sand.
I want to walk the mountains high,
See the sunset in the evening sky.
To see the eagle on the wing,
To listen to the bluebirds sing.
And with my love, walk hand in hand,
And see God's work upon this land.
To feel the wind and rain blow free,
This is what freedom means to me.

Nancy J Frank

COLOR SPRING YELLOW

Yellow is the hue of spring,
I noticed from the window,
Pussy willows when they pop,
The fuzz is yellow on the top,
Forsythia with golden tresses,
Daffodils in sunny dresses,
It goes so well with new spring green,
A vibrant shade comes on the scene,
Notice all these signs of spring,
With more than a passing nod,
Along with the birds and trees and sky,
Burst forth these gifts from God!

Rod Hess

A STROLL ALONG THE TRACKS

To my father, who was always there for me, and who loved me more than I could begin to express. I love you Dad.

the railroad tracks . . . lonesome, friendly . . .
a pink sky and a blue cloud framing, at the far end,
the grey-blue coal joining the endless steel and brown
in the friendly deserted distance of forever . . .

. . . o . . .

they've been with us so long now
that Manifest Destiny merges
in the broken bottles and the dusty feet
and the ghosts of harmonica hobos . . .
at the pinpoint of perspective, where the dust of a dry day
twists into the spiralled horizon of long-lost dreams
that still exist, in potential exponential
in the drifting clouds of spindrift possibility
where the soul glides in innocence
like the thoughts of a ten year old
tasting twisted twizzler licorice . . .

. . . savoring . . .

the moment . . . and eternal dreams, undifferentiated,
by particulars as yet unlearned.

Jeanette Wiatr

A LITTLE BIRD

I walked into my garden
And turned my footsteps 'round
And there upon a broken branch
A little bird I found.

Pale pink & blue, grey & gold
Blended with heavenly skill
The colors danced before my eyes
And made my heart stand still.

No artist could have done a job
As beautiful as this
A rainbow on a broken branch
A Heaven-fallen kiss.

So startled at its company
It waved its wings in flight
A sigh escaped my heavy heart
As I lost it from my sight.

We need not venture far to find
The beauty in our land
I found it in my own backyard
Made by our Master's hand.

Larissa Paetow (age 9)

WHITE AS THE BRIDE

White as the bride
as she walks down the aisle
White as the ghost
as he gives a big smile

White as the clouds
as they fly away
White as the wind
in the middle of May

White as a dove
as she loves to fly
White as an egg
as it starts to fry

White as a rose
as it touches my nose
White as a statue
in its beautiful pose

White as the stars
as they twinkle so bright
White as Nestle almond bars
as such a delight

Rose Gibson

THE DRAGONS OF 'MORROW

I dedicate this poem to all the pretty words left out there unsaid, and to those of us who search for them.

In days of old, Mapmakers, coming upon the unknown, wrote:
'Beyond there be Dragons.'
I have met those dragons.
Some were kind; some vicious.
Some took away; some gave.
I learned from all.
Have remembered the worst; not the best.
How cruel we can be to ourselves!

I ask myself: 'Where do I go from here?'
Only the 'morrow knows; only it can tell.
But it doesn't tell!
Whisper to me 'Morrow . . .
Tell me your secrets.
Did God give me any special gifts?
Can no-one love me?
Only the 'Morrow knows,
and . . . Beyond there may be dragons.

Linda Melkner

MEMORIES OF DIETER

Every day I really do try
to make my mind understand why
my destiny gave me you
just for a month or two.
It all happened a long time ago.
How can I still miss you so?
I guess it's the memories you gave me.
They remind me of you constantly.
Sometimes I just want to sweep them all away.
Then I whisper to them: "Come back and stay"
'Cause I guess I still do
and always will love you.

DeLisa Ann Dickerson

LISTEN . . . SEE . . . FEEL . . . KNOW.

Do you hear the moving of the crowd? Do you feel the hate that abounds? Do you see the mocking of the Savior, God's Son, the one from Galilee? Do you feel the burden of the cross? the weight upon His back? Do you taste the sweat of sorrow, that He bore because of our lack? Do you see the hammer pounding nails, in hands and feet that did no wrong? Do you see them mocking the Savior, the chosen One, from Galilee? Do you hear Him saying, "It is finished?" Do you see the darkened sky? Do you feel . . . the sword? Do you see, His blood, His water? Do you see them mocking the Savior, God's Son, from Galilee? Do you see the empty tomb? Do you hear Him making captives free? Do you see death's sting in His hand? He's made US free! Do you hear them mocking the Savior, God's Son, the only One, from Galilee?

Because we were so rotten, because the sin was great, hell was our final home, we had chosen a horrible fate.

God saw us and had compassion. He loved us through all that shame, so Jesus came to fill the void, so we could go home again. Upon Himself He bore our hurts, our pains. He became the Holy Lamb of God, so in hell our feet wouldn't trod.

Do you hear the mocking of my Savior, Oh let them laugh, because to me . . .

He's the Holy Messiah! Jehovah Jirah God's Son, the Lord that made me FREE!

I Love You Jesus.

Shalom

Lawrence S Lim

BROTHER JESSE NEVER SLEEPS

Why so glum my friend,
At a single hardship, a trifle obstacle
Please understand
Life is but a miracle,
Everything has its ups and downs
We fall, we get up, we return
But your heart whispers one thing,
That Brother Jesse is sleeping.

Wake up and see
The world is not what you seem to be,
Strengthen your spirit
Don't just sit and wait,
Go forth and do it
As always I'll be there
As always I'll handle you with care
Now listen to your heart beating,
Is He still sleeping?

So get up my child
Wipe the tears you weep
Let us try again
And remember, I never sleep.

Madeline Cruz

AS I THINK OF YOU

As I look to the blue sunny skies
I think of you

As I sit and watch the rain fall
I think of you

As I watch the snow cover the city
I think of you

As I watch the seasons change
I think of you

MY BILLS

Mary E Brown

CURIOSITY

To Thelma "Baby" Wimberly, my dear friend.

Curiosity, it has been said, killed the cat,
But humans are not cats,
It's as simple as that,
Without curiosity the mind may as well be asleep,
And with curiosity you may laugh or you may weep.

Since life is made up of the good and the bad,
And tho being curious can cause you to be sad,
Simple interest in others and what they are thinking
Brings reward many times,
And gratitude and thanking.

In many lives it remains far below the surface,
But once revived there is no reversing.
It is a quality so alive in the young of our nation,
What a pity it dims so in later generations.

God surely intended it as part of each person,
And each individual must seek out his own reason,
He is either curious and receiving and reaping,
Or not curious and may as well be sleeping!

Cory Ayn Nielsen

TOYS

The little boy sat and stared at the clouds
Stroked his grey cat and said aloud
"Today which battle shall it be?"
"French and Indian or World War III?"

Killing soldiers with mighty blows,
This is wrong as everyone knows.
Death is not meant to be for toys,
and the power given to little boys.

Wayne Kasper
I JUST WASTE PAPER

This is for my mother, so she would know I was a poet and to my Grandfather who never had a chance to know.

He was one of those
rare ones—
died a carpenter
with all his fingers—
bouquet of square,
plumb-line, level,
flowers . . .
a hammer leaned against
open casket lid.
He gave himself
a year to break,
shake the spell.
"Warren Hutchison"
you would have thought
. . . 'cept you
wood shave better.

Melissa Osborne
A WATERFALL OF LOVE
You are like a waterfall,
Pouring your love over me.
Your voice flows through me,
Like the water to the sea.

Soaking my thoughts with your love,
Filling them up to the top.
I hope your feelings are strong,
I never want this love to stop.

If your love would ever go dry,
So would the oceans and streams.
It would be the end of everything,
For you hold life together at the seams.

A storm fills the rivers,
As your love fills my heart.
If there's ever a drought,
It'll be because we're apart.

You nourish my life each day,
As the water falls over the rocks.
You fill my feelings with joy,
With your poems and your talks.

Brenda A Cornett

Brenda A Cornett
YOU'RE MY SPECIAL SOME-ONE

To Jim M. Ambrose, my inspiration.

You're my special someone, you're the sunshine in my days;
You're all that I could ever want, and I love you more than words can say.

You're the twinkle in my eyes, and the smile upon my face;
You're my heart's desire, you fulfill that deep and special place.

You're the joy in my laughter, and the warmness in my touch;
You're "my happily ever after," you mean so very much.

I can't imagine anyone else who
could bring these feelings out
in me, not in all the years to come,
with you is where my heart
will always be—You're my Special Someone.

Charles B Kropfelder Jr
HAVE I BEEN MISLED
Lying here in this bed,
Thoughts of you dancing in my head.
Reaching out trying to touch,
Oh girl how I miss you so much.

The distance between our hearts,
A bridge, some water a few miles apart.
Longing to be with you in time,
Waiting patiently for you to be mine.

Days come and days go,
Where I stand with you, I still don't know.
Like the blossom of a flower,
I think of you by the hour.

Longing to hold you and squeeze tight,
That's all I think of day and night.
So put my mind at ease,
Let me know where I stand please.

Let's take some time, have fun, and unwind,
candlelight dinners, walks in the park,
more picnics, even late night talks.
So take a minute to think about
everything I said,
And let me know baby, Have I Been Misled?

Michelle F Taylor
PRECIOUS BUTTERFLY
Trapped as if I am a butterfly.
Suffocating for air, oh, will I die?
Just a pinhole of air will do.
I won't escape because I can't fit through.
Why keep me in a jar where my beauty
Can't be seen.
I'm slowly dying for air
And becoming lean.
I'm such a rare species of my kind.
So let me go spread my designer wings
Oh so wide.
Share me with the world,
But don't possess me.
Please, think about these words quite gently.
I thought you said you loved butterflies.
But I guess you lied
Because now I die.

Rachel Mitschelen
A SPECIAL GIRL

To Brenda Kay Culp, one of the young innocent AIDS victims. She touched many lives in 20 short months than others do in a lifetime. This continues today even after her passing.
"What the world needs is Jesus"
John 3:16-17

There was a special girl named
Brenda Kay,
who was a wonderful light to any day.
Though her body was weak,
her love and smile were never bleak.
She was good all along,
and she tried to be strong.
She had Jesus in her heart,
and that's the best part.
Though her face we will miss,
she had just one wish . . .
Love, Peace and Hope for all,
As God's love is for us all.

Dennis Allen Burke
PRISONER OF WAR
You know they must feel
all alone;
Can't run away
so far from home.

Suspended by their wrists,
then whipped;
Kept in sewer water
up to their hips.

Fed only rice
to break them down;
Rats scamper by,
hardly making a sound.

Told to reveal secrets
while in great pain;
Playing Russian roulette
with the insane.

This is the plight
of Jim and Tom;
The P.O.W.'s
in Viet Nam.

Gayle Leon
MATURITY
Everyone
In actuality
Gains maturity
By seeing reality.

Innocence, once lost
Can never be restored.
Truth, once found
Can never be ignored.

So as we learn,
We comprehend.
There's really no gold
At the rainbow's end.

And slowly,
As we understand,
We see a bit
Of the Master Plan.

The plans we make
Can't all come true,
And life can't be
Like we want it to.

Limor Moshe
SLEEPING BEAUTY
Fifteen years before,
in the wars of evil
and light,
a prophecy of
a needle's crime
was shed
on the tender child.

Now she spins
a wheel—
The golden wheel
of her demise,
and blood
drips down
her white arm
as the night
of a hundred years
hits the earth
with
a shuddering blow.

Amy Lynne Hoerner
THE EMPTY CHAIR
There was always someone
To sit in that chair,
Someone special,
Like my grandfather.
I would walk into the door
And there he would be,
Waiting for me.

But now I walk into the house
And something is missing
Out of that chair.
There is no one quite as special
As Grandpa
To sit in that chair.

But now it is empty
And no one is sitting there,
Waiting for me.

Lynda Bartholomew Bolig
DOG
There was a dog who chased sea gulls along the shore;
And although each flew too high
For him to reach
Still he jumped up towards every one.

And when the gulls would turn and fly over the ocean,
The dog would run into the tide
Until the ground would fall beneath him.
Desperately he would struggle back to the shore,
And race proudly along the beach,
Eyes always glancing upwards.

There was a dog who chased sea gulls along the shore;
And he didn't rest
Until the sky was still.

Alice Lacy
MISSING YOU
I see the flowers, all pink and yellow and blue
And I think of how much I miss you.
I see the flowers, and hear the humming of the bee
And I feel the joy inside of me.

I see the flowers, I see the rain
And oh! How I feel the pain.
I see the flowers and I know in my heart
That we will never be apart.

I see the flowers and I see the grave
And I know I must be brave.
I see the flowers, all pink and yellow and blue
And I know how much I miss you.

Vivian A Jiles

UNCENSORED PASSION

I laid open—
taking in
a breath of spring,
smelling the sweetness
of his flesh—
tasting the salts
of his body's seas.

I laid open—
to his entrance,
moved by the volcano's
tremble—
as my temperature rose,
then dropped
to a cooling flow,
and still—
I laid open,
to love.

Vittoria T Francilia

THE CAUSE OF INSANITY

I know, I'm slowly going insane
I can feel it more and more every
day.
My insecurities turn to panic
And events seem more ungraspable
each day.

In my family's world of respect,
When honor and deceit mean all,
If one were to argue against this
He would surely be made to fall.

In my business world of pressure,
Where it takes everything just to
make ends meet,
And with my peers who expect me to
be
Like them, so helpful and sweet.

In my lover's world of possession,
Where I'm regarded as a priceless
gem,
Never to leave his sight for too long
Causing me to feel guarded; closed
in.

In all of these worlds I must live,
Every month, every day of my life,
As you see: I'm going insane
Though others may call it just "life."

Wisie L Shipman

DRUG EDUCATION

To my Daughters: Carrie and Terri McMillian Shipman.

"Hey Dad!
That White House hero,
Yea! Mr. Bennet,
Said, This drug war, Dad,
We can win it!

And my classmate Jack,
that's lost on crack;
Dad, can we win my classmate back?
Or, will he go to Heaven's Druglord
Who the Bible said shall come with a
Sword?

The very last time Jack was seen
He passed cash in a flashy long
limousine.
Who's winning Dad?
And why do the users look so sad?
Are they dropping drugs down
all around like bombs
It seems so simple to score some

Coke, smoke, doogie, whatever they
deal
I wonder just how does it make you
feel
I just wonder 'cause it seems so
funny . . ."
"Just say No!, and forget about it
Sonny!"

Bonnie Dionne

IN MY DREAMS

In my dreams, in the day,
I dream of this place, where nobody
plays;
The games I mean, that tear us apart.
Pulling down our pride, and ripping
out our heart!!
And although nobody wins,
everyone somehow plays a part.
It doesn't matter if they enter,
or even where they start.
For in my dreams, I see different
things.
Where hearts are true and gold,
and nobody drifts apart.
Where peace never ends, because
endings never start.
In my new life, In my dreams,
How Beautiful Everything seems!!

Christie Denny

SEASIDE LOVE

Sitting on the beach
hoping for a visit.
But knowing there won't be one.
I think as the water
Crashes on the rock
How I miss him so much.
I know that he will be back.
And I don't know why
I miss him.
He is so caring, and loving.
He treats me with great respect.
More than what anyone ever could.
I picture him running behind me
trying to reach me.
I know it's just a dream,
Or is it?

Laura Aleana Harvey

LIFE TODAY

There are so Many Things,
In this large, large world,
So many thoughtful thoughts,
So many rainbows unfurled.

Looking at a paper,
Waiting for Inspiration to strike,
Pen Poised Motionlessly,
Then it Begins to Write.

A Kindly face,
Forever frozen,
In a sandstone rock,
That had been so gently shaped,
When water and wind had fought.

A lone old tree,
Defiant on the Desert floor,
Blue skies shining clearly,
Part of old Folklore.

Thus I live in this World,
A place of magic and mystery,
Exploring through many things,
Back to the days of chivalry.

Geno Kedzierski

A PICTURE OF YOU

A picture of you
Here in my heart,
I carry all the time.
A multi-faceted memory
Of the good times and bad,
Helps my troubled mind.
Moments of discord
Recalled from the past,
Somehow taste so sweet.
Our happiness together
Thought of on a gloomy day,
Makes me celebrate.
Whenever hard times bother
I look at my picture,
All I need is you.

Gloria A Wright Kleis

IF ONLY

If only you knew;
How scared I was of you
Because of this tremor my heart now
feels.
You see the best in me,
You bring it out of me,
Precious things—I've kept
concealed.

If only I could say:
What my heart wants to express,
To please you is my every dream.
I want you constantly,
I need you endlessly,
To love you with all my might.

Florence McMillian Caballero

A NEW DOOR OPENS

This is for my husband, Al. With love, Flo.

Though your patience
Has almost passed,
And you've seen that
New door at last,

Remember when the door,
Opens up for you,
Just stop, and look.
Do Not run through!

It must be taken
Just very slow.
For it takes much time,
To get to know.

Especially if you,
Are one in love,
Your path must then
Be shared instead of.

So, that door
May not be so good.
Just pass it on by,
But, be sure you should!

Gloyce Skelton

Gloyce Skelton

MIKE (A Teacher's Poem)

With love to Jackie, Tim, and Jamie.

He waltzed into my room with an
attitude.
"I'll rule this class,"
Each gesture declared.
Little work, less cooperation
From
A defensive 12-year-old.

He came again next term, different
attitude in tow.
"I'm not perfect, but I'm trying."
Classwork attempted, friendships
made
By
An average teenager.

Another semester, a whole new
person emerges.
"I can be successful; I feel good
about Me."
Grins about, laughs echo
From
A confident student.

He tried too much—the challenge too
great.
"It won't hurt anything, just this
once . . ."
Now tears stream, people hurt
Over
An empty desk.

Rosalia Watterson

ELVIS

From one Human Being to another. With Great Admiration and Respect. To all those who Loved Elvis and have seen beyond the Image!

There was no star
Shining bright in the night
No Wisemen, Shepherds
Or Gifts of Delight
Yet on January 8th
A King was born
That was Humble, Loving and Scorn.

He became a Star
Shining bright in the Light
Leaving us three choices
In which to delight
It could be in a Song
A Concert that's Live
Or even a Movie, fit for any eye.

The man had a message
Humble, Faithful and True
His Love for God, Mother and You
A lesson for all
To help guide us thru
Though the man was not perfect
Perfect was not promised you!

R Udaya Bhanu

CEASEFIRE '89

Stop the ubiquitous wars
Shelve the nuclear race
World citizens
UNITE, for global peace.

The prelude
to Man's devastation
is WAR—primitive or sophisticated.
War crumbles Man's civilization.

Religious fanatics
Parochial paraplegics
You awaken barbaric instincts
to appease the War Gods.

The world is a satanic cauldron
where megalomaniacs
commit heinous crimes
and politicians sing elegies.

Cease fire!
Let Peace emerge! Make peace. Keep
peace.
Respect
the Universal Declaration of Human
Rights.
Om Shanti!

Osie Stryker Wilcox

YOUTH YOUTH

I pound my fists 'gainst the
unyielding chest, of time,
Who stands, unmoved, by my
deep agitation,
And looks disdainful, for my cares
are showing,

Till I am still—appalled by
such unheeding,
Then start again new ways of telling
youth,
Whose inexperience alienates
our understanding
For time learned lessons pale, with
explanation.
Direct experience only is their
tutor.
And they have chosen her to be their
teacher,
Though her price be dear, and
mine much cheaper.

Deboraha Linn Shutt (age 13)
THE ROSE

In the winter there are snowbirds
that come and go so free,
They drop a little seed and then
just go and flee.
It begins to rain, sleet, snow, and
hail,
And you feel like running outside
to yell.
You think of all the sunshine and
warmth you never get,
Your mom says, "don't worry and
try not to fret!"
But you know in Alaska the seed
just won't grow,
And you've never seen a flower
'cause the wind just blows and
blows.
Then one winter morning you
step outside and see . . .
A beautiful red flower that grows
so silently.
You look at such beauty and wish
for millions more,
Because you know it will not be
there, everytime you walk
outdoors.
However this special flower will
not leave you, it just will not
go . . .
It's something special and
it lingers on . . .
And so you know, It must be
a ROSE . . . .

Gloria Bowes
THANK YOU, LORD

I never ask for much, Lord,
And still I can't believe.
All the many blessings
From You I do receive.

The songs of birds you give me,
The beauty in a day.
I ask You for so little,
You send so much my way.

When I sit in darkness,
You always send me light;
A guide for me to do the things
That are pleasing in Your sight.

The greatest gift you've given,
Oh, for my soul to win!
Is the precious blood of Jesus,
To wash away all sin.

For all these things I thank you, Lord,
That come from up above.
They make me feel your presence
And tell me of your love!

John H Foard Jr
TO A BAT

For Percy Bysshe Shelley.

Hell to thee, blind Spirit!
Weird thou ever wert—
Phantoming through moonlit
Mist in shadows girt,
Then back into thy cave, to hang all
day inert.

Like a demon hidden
In a cavern deep
From the light forbidden,
Darkness thou dost keep,
And wrapped in bony membranes,
upside down dost sleep.

Till, when nightmare hour
Strikes, thou dost emerge—
With Satanic power,
Frenzied thou dost surge
To haunt the graveyards and the
countryside to scourge.

Freak of erring Nature!
Diabolic pest!
Creepy, crawly creature!
Thing that I detest!
Of all Hell's horrors, surely thou art
horrid<u>est</u>!

Willow Juanita Rose
GRANDMOTHER WHISPERED TO HER GOD

On her knees Grandmother knelt
down
Bowing her head near to the
ground.
In the back yard no one around
On her knees Grandmother knelt
down.
Grandmother whispered to her God
Knowing God heard every
sound.
On her knees Grandmother knelt
down
Bowing her head near to the
ground.

She had a terminal illness.
Oh how I wished I could help
her!
I am glad God loved Grandmother.
God loved her then and
forever.

Jacalyn Scott
THE CRIPPLED-BIRD STILL SANG

On the park bench I sat
like an infant wailing
milking my wounded
pride. cursing the wooing
liar who stole my love
leaving me with chapped
lips and
brokenhearted

when a small child
sat beside me
holding a crippled-bird
who stared so curiously
at me and I at her
'til I felt ashamed
for even that crippled-bird
still sang.

"R C" Underwood
MEMORIES

To my Missy, my sweetest and dearest inspiration. May you be with me always.

As the winds of time,
Whisper through my mind.
It's sad to see the joys,
Of my youth forever lost.

The passion of a young love,
Lips full and soft.
Moments full of emotion,
All remembered with a song.

Now here I sit with memories of,
A time long since gone.
Thinking that I'm so much wiser,
And knowing that I'm wrong.

Rexie Silag
WITHERED SPARROW

Withered Sparrow
amidst the storm
Glory is the light
The truth adorn
You linger through
till moonlight strikes
Flying endlessly
towards the light
And finally reaching
the tintess line
a place for keeps
the sea divine . . .

Abram J Emerson
EGYPT

To the memory of Howard and Minnie Middleton.

prince edward
old man
domain
constantly digging
constantly building
what
for whom
heir gone
black pharoah
the son
pushing on

preserve preserve
preserve
the
dying
kingdom

Candace Hill
ONE THOUGHT

Yes I'm trying to spell out BLACK
AMAZEMENT
A not so sweet dilution in the way
Arms and feats only find room to
shape
t's around perfume areas transported
in our rural cloth torn genes mad
with designs like Dis and DAT DAT
DO
it can turn you into I will like . . .
your baskets your mask from a tribe
You don't no and on and on from
there
Victoria Falls Pretoria's walls like
Berlin
playing the Blue Danube with
creative
license transcending apathy young
man
man have I missed you who's two
too
know shrunken heads with semi
Greek reason in the bushes lit with
colons
slash bumps spoiled by passion
a substance and graduating without
cars
class to stimulate me at the time
of Dan's Dynasties much less coming
In wavy wavy wavy
water

D J Frierson
CLOSE YOUR EYES

Close your eyes an' wander through
The colors in your mind,
Drift in sleeping slumber, leaving
past regrets behind.
Awake to find a new world all its
glory shines so bright,
Offering you its riches, bathing
you in light.
Wisdom is your teacher
Knowledge is your plight
Dreaming holds the
answer
When you close your
eyes tonight

Columbus Foyd
TWILIGHT PRAYER

To all of my friends.

In the mist of the early morn,
I lay in my bed and wonder
how shall I face this day
one which I have never seen before

and as I lay there in my bed
I think of God, my heavenly Father
and my twilight prayer, beging,
All thru the hours when I was
sleeping dear God you have
been with and all thru the hours
of this day Stay with me Just
the same, help me gladly do my
work,
but never be too busy to do what
I can for others. Guide us all with
thou
spiritual Guidance, in Jesus' name
Amen, because I know God is still on
his throne whenever you walk
you are not alone Just remember
God is still on his throne.
and remember too:

There is no failure in God,
You can search the record thru
And see what God can do
You will find there is no failure in
God.

I get up Put my clothes on and
say Father I put myself in Thy
hands Use me today as you will,
and where you will, I will neither
worry nor be afraid, because
I believe in you and Trust
you. AMEN.

Evan B Farrior
SWEET JESUS

Dedicated to the late Jane C. Robinson, a special dear friend.

Sweet Jesus, Sweet Jesus
Oh, Sweet Jesus
Your name is so precious in my sight
Sweet Jesus,
I will praise your name all my life
You are my hope for today and
tomorrow
As long as I live I will serve you,
Sweet Jesus
You promise me that you won't leave
me even in death
Sweet Jesus
I give my all to you
I can't find a friend so faithful like
you

You promise me that you will stay by my side always
You have been my constant friend, Sweet Jesus
That I can depend on
You opened your heart to me,
And I took you into my life
Ever since I took you into my life there has been joy and peace
I've learned how to rest on your promise
I've learned how to trust you, my precious friend
I owe everything to you
I want to stay in your presence forever
I will never, never, never forget you, Sweet Jesus

Megan Donahue
I AM THE SEA
I am the Sea.
I hold within me what seems
To be another world.
In a storm I can toss boats
And cause shipwrecks.
Me and the clouds act as a team
To provide water for the land dwellers.
My waves seem like claws trying
To pull the land into me to rule
It too.
I am Ruler of All.
I am the Sea.

Kenneth E Dennis Sr
LOVE
Darling let me love you
While we still have time
One day could make a difference
Then there is no time

It is but a short time
From one day to the next
Let's live it to the fullest
Put all bad things to rest

"Love" this is hard to explain
It's a feeling more or less
For some one who is special
That only you can express

So What More can I tell you
My love goes on and on
So remember that you were loved
From Dusk to dawn

When it comes time to leave you
There is nothing we can do
So read this poem at times
It may help you through

Bernard C Dasso
GRANDMA'S FIRST TIME AT SEA
When Grandma went fishin'
She stood up in the boat
The tide was high
and she was drifting afloat
The fishing was good
and there she stood pulling
Fish in as fast as she could
Sea gulls were chirpin'
and dolphins at play
Grandma was happy
the live-long day.
The coast guard was coming
their ship she could see
The storm in the west
was as plain as can be
Her radio was beepin'
as her sails came down
Grandma got smart
and said, "Let's swing it around"
She had the stuff that
it takes to go straight
Like a cowboy at rodeo
and a bull through the gate
The crew was so jumpy
like the hippies downtown
The clouds were adrifting
as the rain poured down
I'll outrun the coast guard
as tough as they are
The lighthouse is blinkin'
we're approaching the bar
Rocks on the jetty as far as
you can see
adventure is fun for you and me
The crew is all joyful as we
made it so far.
Three cheers for Grandma
in the nearest town bar
What could be so fun
as Grandma at sea
Sailors so funny as funny
can be

Cory Woods (12 years old)
WHEN DOES THE SKY END?
Does it end when the stars shine above?
Does it end when you lose your true love?
Does it end when the clouds appear or
Does it end when you shed a tear?

Does it end when the flag so true
loses its red, white, and blue?
Does it end in war or peace, or does it end when a friend is deceased?

Does it end when you get a bad grade?
Does it end when you've disobeyed?
Does it end when your best friend leaves?
Does it end when the trees lose their leaves?

Does it end when you go to heaven?
Does it end when the clock strikes eleven?
Who knows, when does the sky end.

Benjamin Leon Carson
THINK POSITIVE
Some you'll lose
But more will come
Pick me up
Don't throw me down.

Feel the breeze
I see the storm
The cold will come
So will the warm.

The skies are dark
But soon will clear
You're now away
Soon will be near.

When things look bad
Positive you must be
A negative attitude
Is not for me.

Christopher L Burford
MOTHER OF FIVE . . . MOTHER OF LIES
You did not raise your children mother of five!
You achieved conception through facets and lies.
Oh yes, it is true there were five lives which you bore.
But not from love or wedlock, more from passions of a whore.
The first you gave life to and then life's repose.
Food for alley cats, to be nibbled by rats; what became of that child God only knows.
Left abandoned in a box set out for trash.
Done with no feeling, your heart at no clash.
And as I've heard you say before:
"That will be the last," now a mother of four.
The next child after you did not ignore.
My brother, born: blond hair and Aryan eyes, you said would fetch a fair price.
To the gypsy woman you sold him again with no contempt.
She said she would love and adore him, and your concern was with house rent.
And as I've heard you say so carefree: "That will be the last," now a mother of three.
The next, my sister, you said was half black.
A relationship of love, and you set out to prove it by lying on your back.
No money or interest from this child did you gain.
Nothing but a title which you laugh off—cracking your mask of pain.
To drown a child in the same place you cleanse your soul!
Oh mother of mine, what price do you NOW owe?
Oh mother of mine, I fear and pray that your soul will never learn—so shall it burn.
And again you said it, and again I knew, now only a mother of two.
Thank God the next child born would never live to see your vile ways.
Through your cold heart you sang:
"The pain of birth was worth the gold I gained."
For this child was born from a man you did not know.
You carried your asset for nine months, only THEN to let go.
This time you said it with spiteness and pun, now only a mother of one.
You died in the arms of my father before I was born.
He murdered you (and me) only to prevent society's scorn.
Oh mother of mine your reasons died with your last son.
Oh mother of mine, now a mother of none.

Kay S Bottoms
JUST PLAIN DUMB
I'm no poet, so why do I write.
Can't match an ant in an elephant fight.

I can't sing, it sounds like a bird without spring,
Or a bell without its ding.

I can't dance, but it's fun to try,
Murray must teach me before I die.

I can't play golf, I have no tee's what does that mean anyway, please
Oh never mind the ball is in the weeds.

I'll tell you what, let's forget this begun and just say,
Oh, how nice it is to be, "Just plain dumb."

Duane K Cinnamon
FATHER'S PASSING

This poem is dedicated to the memory of my Father, Toney K. Cinnamon.

God took my Father, but left him here!
So, there's time for all the things we'd like to say,
to show our love, God left him to lay.
Dad can't move or speak, but God left him here!

They say it is a miracle, your being so.
God loves you, he wants you with him, he's calling you away.
So what's the reason, leaving you here, there to lay?
Are you fighting to come back, or waiting before you go?

I didn't understand at first, but now, I think I see,
God gave this time for you to make your peace.
And, for us to say the things, to put us at ease.
We're all important to God, that's why this had to be.

I want you to know we love you, very much so.
And wish we'd had a chance to spend more time.
To get to know that part of you, that was so very kind.
We're proud of you Dad, and want to tell you before you go.

Dad, I guess you know, you're going on a beautiful journey.
The things you'll see, so full of joy, the splendor so grand.
And the warmth and love, that's so missing over this land.
I love you Dad, and I'll see you, when it's time for me.

Sheldon Berle Bogen
FATE, AND THE WORLD WE LIVE IN
Fire and brimstone, let the sulfur fumes rise,
It will get them before they are wise.
Give them cities, their machines and their cars,
The smog's so thick, it will soon hide Mars.

Streets no better, butts, paper, and a can.
Oil on the sea, are the pride of man.
Given this world, its mountains and its seas,
To love his home, so God made man free.

With brain, with mind, given thought, he was boss,
Greed, not caring, man only feared a loss.
The stench stronger, man walked

without a care,
the world trembled, you could smell
the air.
The world more hot, oceans rose,
cities fell,
Man in glory, perceived not the hell.
It's not too late, for man and solution,
Reverse this fate, caused by
POLLUTION.

Waitie D Gorham
PATCHES AND PEST
With all the love in the world
To fluffy haired Patches and straight
haired Pest.
To you, each lovable in your own
way,
You have met every possible test.

You, Patches, with your long curly
hair,
And, Pest, with your straight locks,
You're as different as you can be,
As different as any two rocks.

Oh, Patches with your wistful little
face
And eyes that look right through me.
Food, food you cry from each eye,
Can't you see that I am hungry.

Oh, Pest, it's a long day since I've
seen you
And then, out of the long, tall grass
You come hopping with a big fat
mouse.
And you eat it like you are starved,
Alas!

With all the love in the world
To fluffy haired Patches and straight
haired Pest.
To you, each lovable in your own
way,
You have met every possible test.

Mrs Ruth M Fullerton
I'LL SHARE A PRAYER

Dedicated to good Dr. Reddy—who knows his urology surgery.

This has been a B-I-G day for me
and I think you will agree
when one's life is at stake
any inconvenience one
has to make
Can—And may help prepare for
Whatever Fate has in store
Help strengthen the heart for less
time or hopefully, more
to be with those I love and adore
the doctor comes now—to "give me
the score"
I could see it was not good, he kept
his eyes glued to the floor

Then he related his plans (surgery) to
help me, medically
I think, I felt much as a criminal must
as he hears the Judge
sentence "Life for Thee"
Cancer is a very familiar but dreaded
word in today's society
What will it mean for me?

August 28, 1989

I thank thee, Father, for
every blessing
and am still here, keeping
them guessing

Mrs Ruth M Fullerton
A HAZY CRAZY FLIGHT
Sometimes when I can't sleep at
night
I lay and imagine a crazy flight
perhaps to the White House—a good
deed in mind
the president could use a good idea of
the right kind
They need quite a few to straighten
out all those crooked VIP's
That would be new bringing them all
to their knees
But no one man
Even a favorite movie fan
Would be able to bring worldly
peace, only your father in Heaven can

Next I go find the bucket of gold
at rainbow's end, as we have been
told
it wasn't too difficult—but then
dividing it up in Africa was an
Amen!
Am I dreaming, or am I awake?
it seems so real—but a weird
nightmare I can't shake
I'm so weary now—I'll try to nap
such tiresome trips, I must
get a map
and shorter routes, I'm such a sap
finding myself on the floor I give a
loud shout
which brings every one running to
see what it's all about
I tell them I got all wrapped up in my
dreams, took the wrong route and
fell on my snout

Clarence Knowlton Burnside
WHIP-POOR-WILL
Is it true that some reincarnated soul,
lies trapped beneath a feathered
breast?
For ever crying Whip-Poor-Will,
Whip-Poor-Will, never seeming to
rest.
Is he doing penance for some wrong
done long ago?
I wonder why, and yet I shall never
know?
Why a bird with an almost human
voice, that comes from a feathered
throat.
For ever crying, Whip-Poor-Will,
Whip-Poor-Will, as though his heart
was broke.
For ever calling Whip-Poor-Will,
Whip-Poor-Will, beneath an evening
sky.
Forever crying Whip-Poor-Will,
Whip-Poor-Will, as he goes sailing
by.

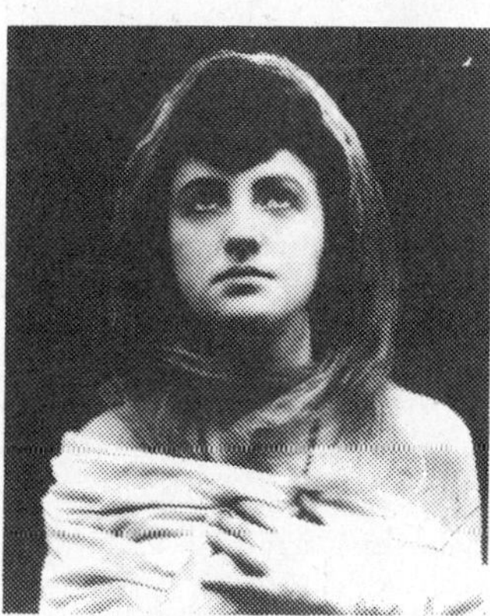

Lillian Hugh Lawson

Lillian Hugh Lawson
THE ANSWER
Crawling, groping, striving,
Looking to a star;
Wake, O Man! and realize
God is not afar.
Hoping, fearing, seeking,—
When will you decide?
Power is within you, Man,
You can change the tide.

Live your godhood, Man,
Cease the vain delay;
The mold is made, the statue cast—
Now be done with clay.

The sacred gift is yours,
Hold high that Guiding Light!
From death and darkness,
Grief and want—
Set the world aright.

What shall the future be?
Arise! and think! and do!
Will mankind claim its heritage?
The answer is in you.

Rita Calliari
SPRING IS HERE!
Spring! Oh Spring!
A Wonderful Thing,
A Wonderful Thing to See.
The Birds and Bees
Flowers and Trees
God Made so Wonderfully.
Little Buds Peeking Out,
Crocuses so Fair,
The Brilliant Yellow of Daffodils
Scattered Everywhere!

The Early Songs of Wrens so
Sweet
Upon the Morning Air,
The Cooing of the Morning Doves
What a Pretty Pair,
The Robins Hop, Hop Hopping
In the Morning Dew,
While Looking For Their
Breakfast
They'll Glance up at You
And keep right on Listening and
Pecking at the Ground.
They keep right on a Hoping
That there's a Worm Around!

Diane E Perry
MY DAD

With loving memory to my father who passed away on June 26, 1988.

My DAD is a wonderful man
He's worked hard all his life,
He has always given us his hand
And has always loved his wife.

My DAD can be very funny
Once he said, "Here's a tarantula,
Honey."
And there was a huge, hairy spider in
a Mason jar
But for the course, that was par.

I sometimes miss my childhood years
For never really knew my DAD,
And in my eyes will be tears
For it makes me really sad.

But now we are very close
Closer than we were before,
I had to run away
To realize what he was trying to say.

My DAD has never let me down
And to my girls he's their favorite
man and clown,
I'm happy for the relationship they
have
He's an extra special man.
That's my DAD! ! ! ! !

Ruth M Blackwell
WHAT IS LOVE?
What is love?
I ofttimes ask myself
My love, oh Lord, I freely give
Always reflects to someone else.

The distance of our relationship
Is as near as a heartbeat away,
It's not just here for a little while
Our love is here to stay.

But what is love?
I ask myself again,
Does anyone really know
The answer to satisfy man.

I'll care for you, I'll cherish you
I'll choose you as my very own,
I'll be for you, what you want me to
I'll never leave you alone.

Spiritually I know what love is.
But you can share it with such a few.
The question that continues to haunt
me is:
What is love, from man's point-a-
view.

With my mind resting on you
My heart forever says yes,
It's nothing you have time to think on
It resembles a pop quiz test.

The question still remains in my heart
Flying around in my mind, like a
dove,
What is it? Will I ever be able to
explain?
What is love? What is love?

Rhonda L K Brown
THE BEACH

I dedicate this poem to my mom and dad for their love and inspiration, to my family and friends for their understanding and encouragement, and to God for blessing me with the ability to write poetry.—Thank you.

There's an enchanting place where
the waters are deep blue,
And the sands sparkle in the mist
of the morning dew.

Where the white tipped waves rush to
kiss the land,
There I reach down and it softly licks
my hand.

I stand up looking at the big blue
friendly sky,
The white fluffy clouds seem to
smile at me as a red sea-crab slowly
crawls by.

I feel the saltiness of the water like
tears that fall
I can hear sounds of nature in a far
away distance call.

Little green trees bend sway
and dance,
Coaxing your thoughts into a
dreamy trance.

The coolness of the wind sings your
song
These magical things can do you no
wrong.

A place where you'll find
happiness galore.
Just sit among it let your spirits
soar.

The rise of the sun where it last left
its mark
Shines on the earth where it used to
be dark.

Rainbows smiling butterflies flying,
Birds tweeting, hearts full of feeling.

These magical things lay there to
remain,
Until I come back to see
them again.

Melissa Dawnelle Paul
THE WAVE OF MY EXISTENCE

It comes crashing in—a single wave
Not a word does it save
Within its being it holds
A story never told.

It serves as a message of my possibility
Its vastness tells me I can be what I want to be.
It is a true account of life
with its beauty and its strife.

That wave has disappeared now
While its sister has followed.
I guess that's just to say
Tomorrow I may be gone, but I'm here today.

For me its message I have found
It didn't have to mutter a solitary sound
I will not be here forever and always
It told me to cherish each and every one of my days.

As it disappeared into the sunset
It whispered into my ear . . .
Life is a gift—so special and dear.

Cary
NEW BEGINNING

After 46 years of living in a world without family love, warmth, support, I found a new beginning—Adult Children Anonymous. Thank you.

Our lives have not been easy
Our friends have been but few

We came together from different worlds
To start our lives anew

Accepted hope from anyone
Believed in what we heard

Confused about a word called love
Our hearts were sad our lips were numb

Inside ourselves we have survived
To share with others our saddened lives

Thanks to a special God above
We're here today with hope and love

To share our thoughts together
As a family we'll survive

And sooner than a tear or smile
Our hearts will open wide

This is a new beginning
Life will be kind to me

I've opened my heart to you. Please open yours to me
I've opened my heart to you, Please open yours to me

Opeal J Momon
FRIENDS

To Charles, my beloved friend, this poem is dedicated to you; gone but never forgotten.

Friends are special.
Friends are people you can depend on.
Friends will never leave you in your time of need.
Friends will love you no matter what the problem.
Friends will not question the things that you do.
A true friend will be understanding, and when you need your friends they'll be right there.
If you ever need me, just call my name
For I am your friend.

Tina L Mortenson
TO MY SON

To the little boy who was full of laughter
To the little boy who loved to run and play
To the little boy who was so independent and could do everything himself
To the little boy who started to grow before my eyes
To the teenager who started to become somebody
To the teenager who made me so proud of him
To the teenager who really cares for people and tries to help people whenever he can.
To the teenager who became a young man
To the young man who became very special to me.
To the young man who admitted he had a problem and wanted help
To the young man who is trying to overcome his problem and is doing a wonderful job
To the very special young man whom I love very much and will always be very proud of in everything you do in life.

Love Always,
Mom

Melody Richard
THE REVOLVING DOOR

Life is like a revolving door
With relationships going in and out
As long as there is someone to push us along.

Someone comes along who shakes the very foundation of our soul.
Their eyes meet.

The colors of a kaleidoscope begin to twirl in their eyes.
The door turns.

The dance of the trumpeter swan is carried out with such grace and beauty that it is inconceivable that anything could disrupt their bliss.
The door turns.

Their seeds grow and produce sweet smelling flowers.
Only to be taken away by a strong gust of wind which carries their delicate petals to new, strange ground.
The once zealous dance becomes a smoldering fire. The flame is there, but it is hidden within an altered hull.
When the fire is extinguished all that is left is its powdery ash.
The door turns.

Its lifeless texture and color give the illusion of nothingness, but when it is strewn throughout the earth it embellishes all new life soon to come.

And thus causing the revolving door to turn once again.

Bonnie Michel
ROADS

I've gone down many empty roads
all alone.
I've made some turns
that have turned into
dead ends . . .
So I backed up and started again.

The road I'm on now
hasn't come to a dead end;
Because I keep backing up
again and again . . .
I don't want to see this road end.

This road is a little bumpy
and I'm not sure what lies
ahead . . .
And sometimes I'm not sure
what the signs have said . . .

But this time I hope there is no toll to pay;
And this road becomes an endless freeway.

Elizabeth K Doman
THE QUEST

To Sean—May our own quests end together.

We experience the goodness of life.
The crisp radiance of an early morning sunrise,
The warm smile of a stranger,
The glow of new love.
Still we push on . . .

Looking for something more out of life.
Believing that we can climb higher still,
Hoping that the best is yet to come.
Knowing that there is a higher truth.
Still we push on . . .

Not realizing that this may be the best of life,
Failing to see reality.
Unappreciative of true, honest love and
The last glorious breath of the evening sunset,
Still we push on . . .

Adele (Holt) Gilley
FROM A TO Z

With Love and in Honor to God and to my children, Gary, Kenneth, Randy Holt and Marilyn Holt Gay.

"Mom, what's there to do" comes the whiney little cry—
Through the noise of household chores that makes me wonder why
Of all the things I could have done, I wonder, well, why this?
But then I chalk it up to know that ignorance is bliss.

I wanted to be married, this was my biggest dream
To have a house upon a hill and flowers by a stream,
A picket fence around a yard with children playing there
All of this would surely be great joy beyond compare.

Nobody told me there'd be long hours each day
I'd be on call all night and with hours of dismay
My patience would be challenged, my self esteem quite low,
But revelations such as these aren't for us to know.

I'm glad for all those moments as sunset years descend
That was my beginning as I now approach the end—
I'm thankful I had children to love and watch them grow
For being with them then and now is the GREATEST LIFE, I know! !

Katherine Bigler Grimes
A CHILD

I dedicate this poem with love, to my precious daughter, Katie.

A star, a light, nothing so bright, as a smile that holds the warm sunlight

The inner glow that radiates from deep below, coming forward from within the very heart and soul

The innocence and purity, and all that's really meant to be, that makes life exude so wonderfully

Seen gleaming at its very best, the happiness that is expressed
On the silent beaming face of a child that is blessed

In the art of spreading joyousness

Erica Johnson
A ROSE IS A ROSE

A rose is a rose, and with any other name,
A rose is a rose, they say, will always smell the same.
But a Daisy or a Tulip, and with this they must agree,
Will never have that special scent, that scent of something free.
A diamond in the meadow blowing in the breeze,
Something just so beautiful, something I'd like to be.
When being picked in children's hands, put in a narrow vase,
I'd cry my petal heart out, dew-tears spilling down my face.
A rose is what I long to be; pretty, wild, and free,
Amongst a patch of Daisie's all kneeling down to me.
High upon a mountain top
A rose, Is what I'd like to be.

Michael K Frank
PLASTIC MEAT

There you were
Where you said you'd be
Sitting by the railing
Under some green counterfeit tree
We knew each other not
But our friends did we
Quite nice of them
How lucky could we two be
I approached and we met
Sat and spoke of them
What a topic of discussion
Our two friends
Nothing more to say
I looked at she
Such nice foliage

It was time to leave
I rose and smiled
Then said good-bye
Turned and left with a hardy sigh
My evening shot
The tree never alive.

Cristina Bonnie Drake
NATURE'S SIMPLE BEAUTY

To my entire family, because they understand.

A sea of rolling fog at the foot of an emerald
mountain, making it look like a mystic island,
where anything is possible.
The last rays of an evening sun,
shining gloriously atop a snow covered tree
in the still of winter.
The sweet Lilies of the valley,
That bow their crowned heads
in quiet prayer.
The uncanny whiteness of a forest in the night,
covered in drifts of diamond-like snow.
Sunrises of subtle pinks, faint lilacs, and soft peach.
Sunsets of smoky greys and reds,
A cup of beauty splashed over the earth.
As you surrender to nature's
simple beauty,
all of those problems that seemed
so big before,
slowly melt away to nothing.
And best of all,
You will find courage
to bravely face the world ahead.

Edie Yung-yee Chen
JUNK SHOP

Under a naked mannequin,
a signed picture of Neil Armstrong
in his proud space suit lies.
A bit of mildew grows at his chin

where he used to be hairless.
The mannequin bares her breasts
toward a window facing the alley
where the neighborhood boys hang

out to laugh and smoke clove
cigarettes.
Somedays, the boys come
into the shop to touch her
hard, skin-colored plaster

and practice their manly voices.
All the while, the dusty print
underfoot smiles as each sneaker
brushes past his growing beard.

Angelina Pace
I CRIED

Dedicated to Frank, for his encouragement.

First I cried then I sighed my young friend died.
He was so young handsome and strong.
He had a happy childhood life his mother taught him wrong from right
He could have walked in the light, but he said he did his best work at night.
As he grew he just knew he wanted to get ahead and share every woman's bed.
Wanting capital gains he did not care who shared the pain.
And he certainly did a lot of romancing around.
Yesterday all his ex-girl friends came to town, to see them put his young body into the ground.
Moving too fast he had no time to learn from someone else's past.
If he only knew on his last romantic escapade the woman had AIDS.

Lee M Faber

Lee M Faber
WHAT MOM TAUGHT

This poem is dedicated to Karen Slaven, my wonderful mother.

When I was a tot Mom would teach
Things were to be seen
And not for my reach.
When I was a lad
Mom taught that everything
I seen or wanted wasn't to be had.
Mom always taught that
to lie, steal, or act up
wasn't ever nice
For if I needed a reminder
My behind paid the price.
Mom always taught there was a time
for work—and a time for play
And that work comes first
And still does even to this day.
And now that I'm grown
And what I see,
Is that Mom's corrections
Wasn't to be mean or cruel
but that she was teaching
THE GOLDEN RULE.

Lee M Faber
THE GAME OF LIFE

The game of life is a
game we play day by day
Searching for an easy way.
Every day we try
harder and harder
not realizing every day
takes us farther and farther.
For every morning is a
new way to begin
But also a possible end.
The roads we walk are
not always smooth ground,
for during the game
in ruts we're found.
Not always shallow or deep,
But lessons we learn
we'd be wise to keep.
For when the game's over
and comes to the end,
The Lord determines
who's to lose or win.

Herbert S Spencer
JOY OF LIVING

In memoria to Robert I. Spencer.

A red balloon gently tugging at its string,
A sea gull's cry at sunset as he tries to sing,
The joy of living shown with a pinwheel or a kite,
The happiness they are giving is the sunshine for the night.
The small and simple things we seldom seem to see,
Are the great and joyous things He gave to you and me.
Green grass in the springtime, alive with morning dew,
The sound of children's laughter, and the smile they gave to you,
Now see the dandelion below, the azure sky above,
And thank Him for these favors, for they're HIS gifts of love.

Nancy E Medved
THE SEAGAZER

An old man sat on the seashore, his head held in his hands,
He gazed out at the coastline and thought of foreign lands,
He thought of battles fought and won and battles fought and lost,
He thought of battles lost and won and thought of America's awful cost.
He remembered the war he had served in, and he got wounded and almost died,
He remembered when the war was over how some men laughed while other men cried.
Sitting there, in his wisdom he knew of all the places in the world for him to be,
Was sitting on the Atlantic coast, gazing out into the sea.

Wanda L vonSeeberg
SOUL'S JOURNEY

Maxine and Bernon Moore, thanks for all those years, out of your life, given to me. May God Bless and keep you. Love Ya! Wanda.

Oh that through the Silver Thread
that binds me I might travel,
Gaining knowledge here and there
using it for the battle.

Let all that's of thee
reach out and indwell me,
Stave that which is not thine
while my body yet reclines.

The knowledge that engulfs me hence
will I not share it yet
'til time gives its permission,
That nothing but the truth
flows over in translation.

Doris Dolejs
HAINT WOMUN

She loved her little shanty, 'twas up upon that hill
It grabs her in the heart, I guess it always will

Her hen she were a layin' her, one egg fer every day
Her kitten was a playin' with her rabbit, in the hay

The turkey came a struttin' a right side in the door
She kept some chicks a pippin' in the pantry on the floor

She had a little pony mare, a whelp she gave to she
A birthin' he stud right up, he stumped against a tree

She planted she a garden as fine as any there
Her neighbor stole her watermelon, he tuck it tu the fair

It's Tennessee I reckon, that's were I wanna go
The cotton bolls are poppin' 'til the winter brings the snow

In early spring there's wildflowers of every color there
And scallions on the hillside, make a purfum on the air

She love her little shanty sittin' up upon that hill
It grabs her in the heart and I guess it always will

They said "That house is haunted"
The roof was made of tin
And on a rainy night, the water came right in

That tin roof was a shakin' such noise you never heard
That wind it lift and shake that tin, my blood it turned to curd

One day she were a nappin' the afternoon away
She thot she were awakened, she'd be hard put to say

She saw a little cloudy man, a right thar by her side
He be askin' her a question, her surprise she could not hide

"What do a Yankee womun . . be lookin' fer round here
And haint you got a family a somewere my dear?"

She told some friends about him, they said
"She's a haint womun, that's sure"

So no matter where she wanders, wherever she may go
In Tennessee . . she's the Haint Womun from that hill
That's all they know . .

Still she loves that little shanty, sittin' up upon that hill
She'll go there in the fall of life, when time is next to still

C Willie Hodge
STREET PEOPLE

Last night I walked the streets
And was passing through the slums,
On every street I came to
The people looked like bums.

Some were sleeping on sidewalks
While others stared out at the street,
And I found myself wondering
What has caused them defeat.

I thought of my home and family
And how life has been for me,
And I wondered what I would do
If the streets were my destiny.

I thought of all the people
Who pass the street bums by,
Always ignoring their pleas of mercy
Not even caring why.

Those people were just like me
Who must of had a home one time,
So why do we treat them like crooks
Or is being homeless a crime . . .

Mary Gribble

Mary Gribble
WHEN BUBBLES THE HIPPO WENT AWOL FROM HER CALIFORNIA RETREAT

Bubbles, accidentally killed by her captors, left a legacy. Yawning her Big One at safety/certainty, she covered much dry land to look for, find and submerge herself in a reservoir of peace.

Gutsy Lady's made election
Waddling to life's intersection
Gusty Lady's said goodbye
To a life that was a lie.

Experts said her up and go
Was uncompetitive and slow
That a pool with all her friends
Would handle all her longing's ends.

They claim they need you
With redundance
Since now you've found deep pond;
Abundance.

That so much you could work a lather
Was a fact they did not gather
You have welded inspiration
By non-acceptance of your station.

Scant left to say but "Here's a toast:
In every way you are the most."

Mary Gribble
THERE'S NO FREE LUNCH: LET'S DO FREE VERSE
Who can find a virtuous mod
woman?
For her price is far above junk mail
sweepstakes

She knoweth how to pulleth wool
over her husband's eyes
But though invited out much she
accepteth not
And putteth herself not alone with
male businessmen
For she knoweth One Thing

Leadeth to Anothereth.
She rolleth with the punches and
goeth light on the punch

Her husband getteth bored and
leaveth. Her divorce lawyer
Riseth early in the morning and
soweth incompetence.

So she selleth real estate in Southern
California.
She perceiveth her merchandise is
good

But at 10.75%, no one believeth
She girdeth her loins at the Thrift
Shop

And from her business lunches,
sneaketh doggie bags
Home to the kids.

Her children arise up and call her
Easy Mark
Yea, also her lawyer and real estate
customers

And phase her out of the gates
But not before she grabbeth her
typewriter and freeeth

A verse.

Mary Gribble
WAR AND WOMEN
Of ancient age is the belief
That justly war can be the thief

Of mothers, wives, sweethearts and
sisters
Since war is packaged up by misters

In Pentagons of every land
Live men who do not understand

That the most onturning chore in life
Is ridding universe of strife

Instead, behind clear masks of power
Solve problems with a bullet shower
While bullet salesmen international
Silver-tongue on what is rational

Fearless leaders of our planet
Unhelped by woman's proven granite

Like small boys turned to fairy tale
And the sad, sad earth repeats the
wail,

"The War Department Regrets To
Inform You"

Daughters of Eve, share what's done
In market, media, Pentagon

Think, work, rule with men until
The bullet salesman's song is still!

George A Bailey
A RAINBOW

To my Family—then—and now.

I dipped deep in the
 wells of memory—
Where visions of dreams—
 Linger in the shadows.

I've floundered on the
 shores of lonely worlds—
Thru the grief and heart
 aches that Life scatters.

The joys of other days—
 may elude me.
But other dreams have—
 taken root to grow.

For after the storms—
 of Life—the Sun shines—
And beyond the hill—
 There's still—A RAINBOW.

John Roach
A POEM FOR DAMIEN
The sun shines as you wake for day
A bounce is in your step
The smile that glows upon your face
Cannot be called inept

For cheery is your middle name
As you wake to face the day
Too bad so many other people
Cannot begin this way

You bounce around and cause a crash
In your mischievous kind of way
You break your toys and excel in
noise
As you begin to start to play

Some people say a sinister look
Is sometimes on your face
But little boys just look like that
As they tear apart the place

But a smile I see is still a glow
As you lay your head to sleep
So peaceful now as the quietness sets
And you begin to count your sheep

John Roach
AROUND AND AROUND YOU GO
Around and around you go
With heaven above and hell below
They say sin is a craze
And you're in a maze
But you don't know which way to go

So no matter what the world shall do
Think of you and only you
Until the day that you shall die
For nobody else will ever cry
Over someone as worthless as you

Remember these words are true
No other words will ever do
So when sorrow is deep in your heart
And you feel that you must part
Remember, no one loves you quite
like you

John Roach
THIS IS FROM ME
Trying to think in a whirlpool of
thought
Trying to write what others could not
Trying to be what others can see
When all I really want, is just to be
me

Taking the time to write what I think
Writing it down in invisible ink
It just doesn't matter what I want to
say
It just won't come out the very same
way

So I write what I want in a leisurely
way
And don't listen to others and what
they have to say
'Cause this is my poem and always
will be
These are my thoughts, this is from
me

Cindi Thompson
A FUTURE
If you take away encouragement
and replace it
with shame
What do we create?

If you take away a spirit and
acceptance
and replace it
with mistrust and worthlessness
What do you create?

If we take away love and praise
and replace it
with insecurities and misconceptions
What do we create?

If we take away the meaning behind
these words
before they have been experienced
What do we create?

If you take way the right
of our children to be themselves
Who grows up??

Margaret Fedan
VIEWPOINT

To My Dear Husband Ed; My two Sons, Ray, & Dana & grandchildren.

As I stand here on earth soil
And look out onto the sea
I can only think of one thing
Of the world, and how it should be
The world with all its sorrows
The world with all its tears
The world that cannot think
tomorrow
 Without fear

As I stand here on earth soil
And look out onto the sea
I can only think of one thing
How beautiful the world seems to me
The world with all its beauty
The world with all its charm
A feeling comes to me, calm
Human to Human, Beast to Beast
 Humanity to all
I worry, not in the least

Denise Miller
THE FUTURE HOMELESS I.R.S.
We've owed you money for over A
year,
and now you've left us in despair.
We tried our best,
to straighten this mess,
You did not hear,
our cry of fear.

Now we'll have to go without,
while HUD and welfare spread about.
Their rent is paid their food their bills,
and when they're sick they get their pills.
We who work and try so hard,
must live in fear and be on guard.
There's always someone who's ready to take,
the hard-earned money that we make.
Soon we'll be without A phone,
we'll have no money to pay our loan.
Next to go is light and heat,
finally to go is all that we eat.
Now we'll go into the street,
seek food and shelter with tax paid heat.

Ruth Vaughn Deaver
WHAT IS PAIN?

The hurt you feel when you are hurt and someone laughs while you're crying.
The agony and loss of sleep because of his cheating and lying.
So much sorrow & grief we experience when a friend, a relative or loved one is sick or dying.
Watching your mother wipe away her tears, or your father working away his life and his years.
Hearing about the hungry homeless in the young & old, seeing the unwanted animals out in the cold.
Sweating and saving for things you want with all your might,
Then losing them all later in the midst of the night.
Scornful words expressed between husband & wife,
Don't they know there's supposed to be harmony in life;
Crime, drugs on crowded streets; crippled people who can't walk nor speak
For those who wonder
What is pain
Read this poem once again.

Mary Ann Martens
A WALK IN THE WOODS

Leaving cares behind
I enter oak domain
Walking ancient trails
Remembering moccasin clad feet
That trod this same terrain
A healing balm
Soothes and calms
As I return to earth.

C D Harley
COULD YOU

To My Very Special Angel, Veralee K. Pilouw, for her inspiration to me and my poetry.

Could you stand in the square,
and face the Jewish leaders there?
Could you take the spit and slaps in your face,
as you stood there silently in my place?
Could you face Pilate and accept my fate?

Could you drag my cross through the city's gate,
or watch me in the crowds so full of hate?
Could you wear my crown of thorns,
as you listened to the crowd's scorn?
Could you take my nails through your hands,
without shedding a tear upon the sands?
As you hung there,
and your flesh began to tear;
Could you still look up in the heavens so blue,
and say, "Father forgive them for they know not what they do?"

Could you with a final groan knowing,
that your life was almost gone;
Pour out all your blood to cleanse me,
and from my sin set me free?
You see, this is what our Jesus did for you and me ! ! !

Catherine Ramstad

Catherine Ramstad
CAREFUL

To my beautiful daughter, Deborah.

There by the dim roadside races a beam,
I seldom see or care.
There by the dim roadside stands a team,
One gaunt, one fair.
There toils a man,
Weary of years,
There lies a lamb,
Surrounded by tears.
A child's tears fall because the lamb's dead,
His heart is given to his eyes of red.
All the world's watching, holding pity for him,
As the beam by the roadside now grows dim.
Other beams pass on into the night,
They honk and fire their very soul of might.
Tears will fall on forever—forever things die,
Because the eternity of cars never slow when passing by.

Annette J Wesgaites
NATURE'S SONG

This poem is to my brother Bill, and dear Mary, who love nature, and their love of God, and family.

Can I share with you the beauty of nature's creation?
Just to see the clouds drifting lazily through the summer skies,
Feel the warm breezes blowing and knowing how good the morning is, giving me a cool sensation,
I can hear the birds happily singing as their young try their wings to fly.

Oh, to smell the fragrance of the cherry blossoms in the air,
And to see the first violet picking up its lovely face,
I love to hear the song of the rolling creek water as it drifts swiftly around the bend with so much care,
And see the busy spider weave its web through the branches of each tree making it like dainty pieces of lace.

I walk the rocky pathways through the woods.
Never knowing what new beauty of nature will I see,
Up ahead I can see the squirrels darting through the bushes at play, and then I wonder if I should,
Follow the paths that the wild deer take and realize that God has given me the key.

To His Kingdom of love and happiness,
That only you, and I can feel just how much we have to share,
With each day we have left, to live it to the fullest that some others can care less.
That we are the chosen few who have the vision to see into tomorrow's plan if we dare to care.

Lana Wall Bednar
DOWN THE LANE

Walking down the country lane
I found it to be the same
The hills were still green
The flowers blooming in spring

A special time remembered
Of a past gone by
I quickened my step
As the house drew nearer

At the open door
A stranger stood there
I turned on the long lawn
And walked back down the lane

My heart felt bare
Where had the time gone
The rain gently fell
Down the country lane

Lana Wall Bednar
BEYOND TOMORROW

I dreamed of you again last night,
You looked so very much alive.
I cannot understand why
You were suddenly called away.

I think of you often and wonder;
We didn't have a chance to say
Goodbye and I'll see you again.

Once I said to you
I'll always love you
Even until forever.
Now I know how true
My love stays and sweeter grows.

When I am alone,
I feel your presence near.
In my memory you remain
Still so very dear.

The remembered touch and smile
Is mine to keep;
It helps me all the while,
And in time I shall join you
On that beautiful day beyond tomorrow.

Angela Dewoody
THE DARKNESS

The darkness growing inside of me wants me to take my own life away,
The sadness that fills my heart gets stronger each and every day.
Why must the worst of things happen to only me?
The darkness is blocking the light, making me not want to see.
The darkness is making me fall into this deep black hole,
Why is this terrible thing taking over my soul?
The truth is inflicting this horrible pain,
The darkness is leading me, it's gonna reign.
The fear is tearing me up inside,
The darkness is slowly making me die.
Another day of horror I just can't bear,
The darkness is cancer, it just isn't fair.

Patricia L Riley
THE GHOST OF THE LOST SEAMAN'S WIFE

The autumn night was starlit,
the sea breeze salt and cold.
Before dawn I would witness
a tragedy unfold.

She sadly walked by moonlight,
drawn by some strange power,
drifting up the rocky path
unto the lighthouse tower.

Climbing up the winding stair,
never did she stop,
weeping gently to herself
until she reached the top.

She lingered, staring at the sea
as if to count each wave,
then threw herself into the wind
toward a salty grave.

Before she disappeared from view
she changed into a dove,
then flew away across the sea
to search for her lost love.

Dorothy Miller Ward
CHRIST SAW LOVE

Christ saw love streaming through eyes
in the form of tears
as they saw the huddled bodies
lying upon their biers.
Old Smokey took his place at the head of the group.
He was the oldest, the first to go.
The next one was Princess, a poodle, white as snow.
Little kitten sublime and saucy
had never done anything very naughty.
Twinkey and Shawn died at dawn.
The children didn't realize their pets were gone.
Who threw the arsenic ingested by pets?
Was it a stranger no one had ever met?
Perhaps the devil induced a person to stray.
Or did someone roam the
neighborhood night and day?
The pets are gone and sadness lingers.
Dandelions were placed on the bier
of Princess
and Christ saw love in a child named Dove.

Kathy A Smith
A CHILD'S CASTLE
A little girl sits down to play
She'll build her world in just one day
She sits and stares at her tiny little hands
In them she feels the strength of a man
The soft breeze is blowing through her hair
Surrounded by sand it's everywhere
In her mind she can see
How her life should really be
Scared and determined she goes to work
Each bucket she fills then lifts with a jerk

Carefully she stacks them one on top of the other
Gentle pats to form them as if she's their mother
Her artistic ability shows up in her fingers
Quietly performing as time seems to linger
Drilling holes for windows so she can see
She can now look out and see eternity
The moat she builds encircles her castle
To keep her safe from any danger or hassle
No way will she be treated like less
For just today she is a princess

Helen J Sherman
YOUR RED ROSE
Walking along the beach, I hold the red rose you had given to me. Looking over the rose, tears drop from my eyes. The beauty reminds me, of the soft spot I had found deep in your heart . . . .

With every step I take, my mind flips the pages of my memories, that I keep deep inside. As I wipe the tears that I cry, I toss your red rose into the sea. I stand to watch it drift away.

"your red rose will never return."
"but my love for you, will forever burn . . . ."

Chris-Mary Repiscak
BOOTSIE
To Bill H., the man I wish I had married.

Bootsie can be a very fresh cat.
If you met her, you would likely say scat.

Always biting and fighting
And fighting and biting.

Bootsie is gray and white
And her weight is very light.
Yet tiger is the word for her.
My ex-friend Betty would say cur.

Very charming to me can she be
Especially since she likes my company.

I feed her scraps of people food
which puts her in a very good mood.

Bootsie likes to play with Goldie cat.
My home is where they stay at.

They usually cuddle and kiss
Sometimes a swipe which is a miss.

Bootsie liked paper balls as a kitten
pouncing with her paw which looked like a mitten.

Bootsie can be smart and wise
She'll be with us until she dies.

Barbara J Freese
CHANGES
Our walk near the waves seemed out of a song.
Both of us so much at peace
You talked of high school and of change,
of the boy you were and the man you became.

I've felt some of the same change
from girl into woman
College cost you a lot
the friends you knew
the person you were
You worked very hard and sometimes resented it,
but in your heart you know it was worth it

As it is now,
I face more education
You look to your promising career

In the future, we will look back
to this time and
be glad that we shared
a part of it, if only a small one,
together.

Cynthia G Allen
HIDDEN ATTRACTION
To someone I'll always admire from afar.

Something about the way he looks in my eyes
Makes me smile, makes me wild

To talk, listen and get to know
Only makes my feelings grow

We smile and joke and I'm glad it's us
But my fantasies are of love and lust

The feelings I get, I know are wrong
I think of him often, when I listen to songs

I dream of sleeping in his arms
With all his love, all his charm

I know these dreams will never come true
Dreams don't hurt anyone, So I'll dream of you

Howard L Kaiser
MY PURPOSE
When old dad's tired from daily strife,
And trudges home this night,
Weary from the woes of life,
To him his purpose out of sight,

And as he settles down to rest,
And cleanse the clutter from his mind,
He searches with his very best,
In hopes his purpose he might find.

Then suddenly he becomes aware,
Of two smiling happy little boys,
Both before him standing there,
Full of mischief, full of noise.

Now one's five the other's seven,
And they close in on this old wreck,
They let him feel a touch of heaven,
When they put their arms around his neck.

And now I see my purpose clear,
Why did it pose as mystery?
For no reward could be more dear,
Than these two sons God gave to me.

Theresa A Hill
I SIT AND REMEMBER
For My Mom—Who knew I could do it long before I did.

I sit and remember my childhood days,
The things that I did and games that I played.
It seems that those days forever are lost,
But to have one day back would be well worth the cost.

Yes, when I was young my life was carefree,
Playing with friends and wondering what we would be.
But we went on through time with our own little changes,
We all had our problems and growing up phases.

Now time has flown by and no longer we share,
Our childhood dreams and our childhood cares.
We've all grown up into our young adult ways,
But I sit and remember my childhood days.

Betty D Cooper

Betty D Cooper
I'LL ALWAYS LOVE YOU
This poem is dedicated to my deceased husband, was written for him 38 years ago.

I love you, my darling I do . . .
And to you I'll always be true . . .
I hope that when I'm your wife . . .
That I'm happy all my life . . .
I hope you will be happy too,
Sweetheart . . .
Then you and I will never part . . .
I want to be your wife, your love . . .
As long as stars above . . .
For you make my dreams come true . . .
And keep me from being so blue . . .

I'll love you forever and a day . . .
And I'll prove it no matter what they say . . .
I'll love you all the years as we grow old . . . And the memories will be worth more than gold . . .
Through laughters and tears, I'll always be at your side . . .
So happy that you chose me as your bride . . .
I'll be with you in happiness and sorrows . . .
As I'll be with you all the tomorrows . . .

Betty D Cooper
LOVE IS YOU
Dedicated to the only man I ever really loved: my husband.

Love is . . .unchangeable and forgiving.
Love is . . .tenderness and thoughtfulness.
Love is . . .faith and trust.
Love is . . .wanting and loving me all the time.
Love is . . .comforting when I cry.
Love is . . .feeling warm in your arms.
Love is . . .wanting and loving you,
Love is you . . .

Faith W Owen
QUESTIONS
In memory of my brother, James L. Chaffin: 2/27/58—1/17/90. Godspeed.

So many destinies, so many roads.
So many painful, heavy loads.
Do they take us anywhere?
Or will we find ourselves trapped in life's foolish fair?
Does it end, does it stop,
Or does it all fall on top?

How many lives have taken our path?
In spite, in pain, in rage, and wrath?

Why must you and I fear,
Scream for every lonely tear,
Even after all these years,
When shall peace follow near?

Robin Goodfellow
DREAMS
I live in dreams
Make it real
It's not the same
Invulnerable
Invincible
Immortal
I like it here
I want to stay
In dreams

Susie Sandusky
CLOSE TO HEAVEN
I want to dedicate my poem to my father-in-law Earl G. Sandusky, who passed away in October 1989 and is missed very much.

It was a beautiful starry night
The moon was shining so bright
I was standing upon a mountain

The stars exploded like water from a fountain
I felt I could reach out and touch the stars
They felt so close, but yet so far
I wanted to fly away into the night
To get lost in a peaceful flight
I can hear the angels sweetly sing
I quietly spread my wings
I feel the breeze upon my face I never want to leave this place
Close to heaven is where I want to be
No pain or sorrow just God and me

Kate Fate

GOING DOWN

Simplistic satisfaction has carried us through the years
Waiting, wanting, painfully submerged in endless tears
Changing, challenging, somewhere between dignity and desire
Sifting through the sand, searching for treasures I require

Sentenced to death when my life is just beginning
Losing a fight that might not be worth winning
Keeping the last kindling, so the fire cannot die
As I cut off my hands to keep from waving good-bye . . .

Lee Fissori Wright

BEYOND THE PALE OF THE SUNSET DYING

Look well to this day, for yesterday is but a dream and tomorrow is only a vision.

It was strangely dark, when I awoke:
From my deep slumber in the onyx night.
A glow appears, then rises softly shaded,
A tiny ember on a north-bound flight.

Tonight, I have seen the aurora borealis!
Cast upon the frozen white of Iceland.
I watch each color blossom forth,
Glistening iridescent, over a vast strand.

I marvel at the golden orb
called . . . earth
Touch each new day with
white-swept memory,
And intercept at intervals day's somber dream;
That rises with the essence of discovery.

Tonight, I become once more that tiny ember:
Racing across a flaming sky on my way.
Perhaps I'll see the Jade of India.
Sail down the Nile with the sun's first ray.

And when I awake with dawn's first light
From night's journey into
ever-lasting space,
I'll hear the faint hush of yesterday,
With the sigh of today's
golden . . . voice.

Constance A Deming

HARVEY'S HOME

He is new in my life
And so I am leery.
When I saw him tonight
My wise heart grew weary.

He is more than I dreamed
One man could be.
I told him he fills
Not one wish but three.

We're old yet we're young,
He feels that way too.
Time brings this but once,
Please let it be true.

Constance A Deming

FROM A DISTANCE

Listening from a distance,
She heard a man's passionate dreams
of romance and brave deeds.

Watching from a distance,
She saw a man surround himself
with roses and heartaches.

Feeling from a distance,
She felt the man's intense
pain of confusion.

Through that distance, they felt love.

Beyond that distance they shared dreams.

Because of that distance, they never met.

Patricia A Restaino

TRAGEDY IN SPACE

Abort me
I shall return to the waters
Even the colors of this earth
do not touch me

Abort me
I am frozen solid
suspended in being
unwanted

I know to rehearse
these ashes of creation
hysteria on a frozen stage

To face this shroud
and recreate what is mine
where even a bullet
to the head won't do

Is it not to touch
and break the ice of a soul
an invitation to love one's wounds

So much depends on me . . .

Patricia A Restaino

YOU HAVE FORGOTTEN ME

You have forgotten me
as you set fire
in the frost upstate
where the ice melts slowly
as you throw snow on her body
awaiting its changing form
to follow its wetness
down her curves
carrying her into her bedroom
where a fire sits ready
and hot-mulled wine flows through
your waiting inner thirst

You have forgotten me
as I watch from my window
waiting for no one
only to hear the owls
court each other in the night
where no other sound is heard
only a drop of a tear
from a shivering
heart of empty

Patricia A Restaino

BRONZE LOVER'S JADE

I await you
know you will return
a broken bird
Wings of an angel soar

Never know when you will
pass over me
Return to my tongue
on your breast
alone to explore the depth of a ghost

Never too close
You will lean to the wind
Fly secretly to jade
where clouds cover truth

Let me find you
my jade brook in black leather
capture your madness
with my open hunger

Carolyn L Prouse

HOLDING YOU

Dearest Richard; Oceans may separate us, but you are near in my heart. I miss you. Love, Carolyn.

Holding you are the best times of my life
Holding you makes me happy when I'm sad
Holding you picks me up when I'm down
Holding you keeps me warm at night
Holding you helps me make it through the day
Holding you makes the rest of the world go away
Holding you makes my shoulders feel lighter

Wish I were holding you now.

Allan Jay Lagumbay

OUR WORLD? WHAT WORLD?

The world is full of special things
That probably is what you think
It is as nice as Saturn's rings
But heck you're wrong that's what I think

The wonderful earth you're standing on
Is sooner or later will be gone
Somehow machines are all turned on
And that good earth will soon be none

Machines destroy the earth so great
They pollute the air and water
They can change the cows' fate
There goes my bread and butter

You know the things they send in space
To tell the creatures about the planet earth?
They show a lot about the human race
But how about our very ugly, messy place of birth

Are we really living in a world?
Let us ask ourselves about this
Where the lions roar and snakes hiss
On earth, Our world? What world?

Elizabeth L Senise

LABOR DAY

This poem is dedicated to my son Michael, The sunshine in my life.

All the reading that you do,
cannot prepare you for what you'll go through.
The correct breathing and a calm coach,
are both important at the approach.

Ah-hee's and hoo's, the right positions,
are hardly worthy of transition.

All thoughts are on a healthy child
your body trembles, your eyes are wild.
You push and breathe, the end is near,
and then a baby's cry you hear.

You gaze into those little eyes
and all your fears are minimized.

NEVER AGAIN, you think through tears . . .

not at least for a few more years.

Evelyn Wagner

WHAT IS LOVE

Do you want to know if it's true love you found?
When he walks into a room, your heart will pound.
In love before you have never once been?
His touch will burn and tingle your skin.
When he is near, you'll feel happy and gay,
You'll feel cold and empty when he is away.
If he loves you too, and he lets you know,
Inside your chest you'll have a warm glow.
If you think he does not, your heart will break,
In fact the whole inside of your chest will ache.
How will you know if his love is really true?
Well, my darling, he will always wait for you.
All his kisses will be so special, you see,
So in his arms, you will always want to be.
When he holds you
against his so very soft chest,
That's where you'll always want your head to rest.
When he has to leave, and he kisses you good-bye,
You'll feel completely numb, but you needn't cry.
Because it is then, you will realize, at last,
That you have fallen in love, the die is cast.

Charles F Anderson

LEAVES

Despite being green you are ladened with grief,
By sight of the brown forming on the next leaf;
Because of its weakness the leaf lost its place,

Not falling but rising to heaven's embrace.

That all leaves turn brown is an absolute fact,
Because of the apple, the snake and his pact;
But there is another leaf nailed to a tree,
Turned brown for His love to save you and save me.

The judgment day promise finds doom for the snake,
For he and his crew will be cast in the lake;
As leaves that believe reappear on the scene,
That leaf just turned brown will see you and be green.

Holly Noel

LONGEVITY

It's ALWAYS Sunshine.

always bright,
always warm,
always soothing, relaxing, and cheery
positive
patient
calm, directed, and satisfying

It has to be . . . .

It's never RAINING . . .

never bleak,
never bitter,
never piercing, disappointing, and permanent
apprehensive
defensive
depleted

It can't be

Holly Noel

SATURDAY NIGHT

A crowded room of strangers
pretending to be friends
A crowded room of talking, the Bullshit never ends.

The people start to mingle
to play their little games
The people Try to love you all . . .
tomorrow, "What's your name?"

The strangers become buddies, until the clock strikes two
Then the Bullshit disappears and you're left with plain ole you.

The Monday morning begins again, another week of strife.

A group of strangers Shared again

The Bullshit . . .
A Social Life!

Lori-Bee

THE PORPOISES AT PLAY

While walking, along the beach one day,
In the town, where the ocean meets the bay,
The most beautiful sight, I must say,
Were the porpoises, at play.

Rolling, jumping up, from the ocean floor,
Was a creature, everyone must adore,
In schools, they came along the shore,
Wherever you looked, were more and more.

To see them, in their habitat was rare,
First one here, then one there,
Free as the wind, without any care,
A sight to behold, a feeling to share.

Romping about in synchronization,
Creating a most wondrous sensation,
Why do humans, tend to destroy,
These creatures, everyone could enjoy,
The porpoises at play.

Lori-Bee

MEMORIES THRU THE YEARS

As we walk, across the sands of time,
And gaze upon the years, long past;
We reflect, upon the memories,
That it seems, will always last.

Our childhood years, a happy time,
Of lullabies, and games for playing;
Sitting with dad, telling us stories,
Kneeling with mom, at the bedside praying.
Our teenage years, endless party time,
With dancing, and songs for singing;
The heartbreak, of our first romance,
And waiting, to hear the phone ringing.

Our middle years, a wondrous time,
Of candlelight dinners, and moonlight sails;
You're a blushing bride, in a veil of white,
With a nervous groom, in white tie and tails.

Our golden years, a special time,
Of caring, sharing as we grow old;
Remembering the years, we had together,
And the precious moments, life had to hold.
Thru all our hopes, and all our fears;
We will always, have memories thru the years.

Brent Porter

FOUR GREY WALLS

Four grey walls;
bars, bunk
and an old pair
of shoes.

There is blue out there,
fierce and defiant
of the solid green
below it.
Filtering through the
darkened windows,
illuminating dust
freefalling
through the air.

Like birds over the guard
tower,
we plan our escape.
No need for files or
rope, this escape
requires nothing but
a backbone and a
careless slip of the
foot.

Karen C Marshall Thomas

THE TEARS HAVE FALLEN

To John Piper, the first person to truly believe in me. Thank You!

The Tears have fallen again for what cannot be.
Wisdom imparts on me to be happy not sad.
Happy for what I had, not sadness for what I lost.
Memories live on Forever Love, and on that I will build
a life.

Emy Murakawa

INEXTRICABLY BOUND

I find myself jealous of all the years lost, of all that I've missed.
You leave me behind, inextricably bound. Stuck, I stand transfixed
I have but to hear your voice once again, and all that was lost is found.
That gentle pulse that is but your presence is once more all around.

The "forever we, forever one"—what I lost but didn't let go of
Jumps back to life from uneasy sleep and still goes by the name of Love.
You've always been all-consuming to me—my thoughts, my hopes, my dreams.
Something keeps growing and breathing between us that keeps me tied, it seems.

It's foolish for me to dwell on these thoughts. There's nothing much I can do.
Inexorably drawn to the center of my soul, what I find there is you.
Choices made, choices mourned—my life overflows with these.
Through laughter, tears, and all the years, know that I'll love you, please.

Kimberly S Heath

Kimberly S Heath

WE'LL REMEMBER YOU ALWAYS

Great thanks to my entire family, Greg, and Jodie for making a lifelong dream come true.

We'll remember you always,
Deep within our hearts.
We'll keep you in mind,
Since we are apart.

We'll remember you always,
The way you used to be.
We'll think of you often,
In our time of need.

We'll remember you always,
In your loving days.
We'll remember your life,
Which kept us amazed.

Your new life is now beginning,
And down on us you'll gaze.
We just want you to know,
We'll remember you always.

Nicholas D'Andrea Jr

OVER THE YEARS

I may have lost the shine of my hair,
But I retained the sparkle in my eyes.
I may have a wrinkle here or there,
But my beauty inside never dies.
I may not get any taller,
But my mind will always keep growing.
And my heart doesn't get any smaller,
'Cause the love and friends keep me going.

Carol Jean Byrd-Brown

THE WIND

I have been around since the beginning of time.
I can be as cold as ice in the winter
I can be as hot as boiling water on the stove
I, also, can be as calm and pleasant as the Sea of Love
I sometimes do not come at all.
But I get lonely day after day as I journey on my way
I am so lonely—won't you please come and talk with me;
For you see there is not anyone for me.

Deborah Owen Edmonds

MOMMY NO'S BEST

Don't touch; it's hot.
You must get your rest.
No sweets before meals.
Mommy no's best.

Did you finish your homework?
Your room's a mess.
That music's too loud.
Mommy no's best.

You're getting married?
And moving out West?
Remember to write.
Mommy no's best.

What? You've got news?
A pregnancy test?
Drink plenty of milk.
Mommy no's best.

You're now the mommy,
A child at your breast.
Sudden understanding . . .
Mommy knows best.

Connie Schildtknecht

TAG

As I reflect as Mothers do
I recall a day when my son was two
I lay on a blanket on the beach
Not too far from the ocean's reach
It was a sunny day in May
Yet too cold in the water to play
I contently watched my son's smiling face
As along the water's edge he raced
Following on her heels as the waves recede
Then coming to the brink he'd dare and tease
For a moment he was the victor in pursuit
Until the tide caught her breath and changed her route
Then those little legs did flee
Just out of the grasp of the sea
And thus the game of tag would go
Both bodies running to and fro
My son would banter with giggling urge
The play went on about the same
Until the ocean tired of the game
And cast a billow of icy cold
Hands that tripped my two year old
Panic, chill the frolic done
She'd turned the tables and had won
Suddenly the playmate had lost her charms
And he ran for the warmth of his Mother's arms

Lynne Luck
A THOUGHT

You are a Thought—
One Fearful,
Awesome,
Enchanting
Thought
Filling Me.

Will I Know You?
One Moment,
Waiting,
Surely,
Sweetly
Leaving Me.

Suddenly, You have
One Life,
A breath,
A name,
A face—
You Are.

John Richard Urbana
GOODBYE OLD FRIEND, GOODBYE

This poem is dedicated to my friend Ted Green. You are missed.

Goodbye old friend, Goodbye
You will be missed
not only by me . . .
But all of those
who loved you . . .
Goodbye old friend, Goodbye
you will be remembered
and not forgotten . . .
the memory of you
will live on . . .
Goodbye old friend, Goodbye
You were a special person
Whose caring and understanding . . .
touched the hearts and souls
of everyone you met . . .
Goodbye old friend, Goodbye
Knowing you has made me
a better person . . .
Thank you for sharing
Your life with my life . . .
Goodbye old friend, Goodbye

Ellen Irene Preston

Ellen Irene Preston
I WISH

I wish I were an eagle, free to fly away.
I wish I were a tree, free in a breeze to sway.
I wish I were a tiger, hunting in the night.
I wish I were a bear, with nothing here to fright.
I wish I were a butterfly, flying all the day.
I wish I could tell someone all I wish to say.

Barbara Cardinelli
A DAY CARE MOTHER

This poem is dedicated to: All the children and parents who have come thru my door.

I am a day care mother.
As a job for me there is no other.
Children come and children go,
Each and every one I get to know.

Some are loud.
Some are shy.
Some laugh.
And some cry.

I watch them play and grow.
And as time goes by, they go.
Each off to a new adventure.
I gave them all a start,
With them they take a piece of my heart.

I wonder if they will remember me?
And all the times they sat on my knee,
As we sang songs.
Because when you're little,
Days can be long, without mom.

Erick N Valenzuela
SIMPLY PERFECT

To: Kimberly Smith of Little Rock, Arkansas from: Erick.

Never quite was a special day
Never knew it was coming my way
A simple smile, a sweet look from your eyes
There's something about it . . .
Something special about it

I just know my thoughts were true
Even though the feeling's quite new
Natural as the stream, simple as the sky
Nothing close to it . . .
Nothing really like it

I hope you'd stay as simple as you are
Elegantly neat & charmingly sweet!
Unique in your own way
Nothing really fancy . . .
Just downright pretty & lovely!!!

Don't know what this will lead to
Guess I do have a slight clue
I know time, time will clear it all up
Maybe it's you two
Maybe it's me and you!

Naturally crystal clear & fragrantly fresh
Sometimes flaky but one of the best
All word is, is not enough to describe
Simply Perfectly . . .
Kimberly.

Patricia O'Brien
MIKE

To the parents, family and friends of Michael Pegoli, a small comforting thought.

Like a comet in the night
Which glows then travels out of sight
For one brief moment Mike touched our lives
Brought warmth and joy
As he shed his light
Now he's gone before us
Into that Good Night.
Though now we sorrow
'Cause we miss him so
We shall see Him again I know
He will greet us at the door
Beacon brightly lit, his face
With joy aglow
His laugh will ring out
Like a song
He'll smile and say
"Hey! What took you so long?"
Sleep with Peace Michael, we love you

Monica E Cummings
YESTERDAY MOURNING

Mercy, Mercy, You.

I always stay a day behind,
I never watch the news.
Today's paper is my Tomorrow's News,
So I can stay one day ahead of
Yesterday's Mourning News.

Peggy Tremblay
LIFE'S LITTLE PLEASURE

Dedicated to my Granddaughter, Amanda Marie Millar.

It seems as if it were only yesterday,
When we were given this special gift.
A little chubby faced, black haired beauty,
With a bow formed into lips.
She had such a rough beginning,
We all held our breath.
But God stepped in and saved her life,
And I'm grateful forever yet.
She was conceived when physicians said,
"Know way could it be done."
For her Mother had been told, she would
Never hold a daughter or a son.
Her father, John, must be very special,
To give life to a dormant seed.
For from all of this comes, my special gift,
Nana's little "Amanda Marie."
Now, she might not see like others do,
But that has not stopped her yet.
She wears these cute little glasses,
And never misses a step.
She is full of joy and happiness,
Yet sometimes gets in her Mother's way.
But that doesn't stop the love that flows,
From Mother to child each day.
She is your special gift of love,
That I've waited to have for a long time.
I thank you John and Cyndi,
For giving me what is mine.
The joy I feel, when she calls me,
"Nana," She says on the phone.
My heart melts and my eyes tear,
For joy like this I have never known.

Ivy L Torrez
LET THE SEASONS SAY

I wait patiently through seasons
Sun and moon I have known without you
I arise alone, from dreams—
Someone in love with someone
Was it us—I do not know you
But I have seen and remember
Links of life, and felt their truth
Combined with love, cycles of living
Are made complete—
Separately, we are bound to the whole,
By strength determined, for a time,
A day, or forever—
With you or not
I make my place in the scheme
But I think and dream at times
You will be a link to which I am bound
And if to you and God,
Can love be broken
Or truth be found a lie,
I wait, and let the seasons say—

Sandi Browning
FEARS

I put all my fears
All my worries
All my tears
Behind me
I leave them there
I look straight ahead
And walk away
Only to see
All those things
Right back in front of me

Lucile Davis Darrah

Lucile Davis Darrah
WIDOWER'S LAMENT

To my friend, Wanda Lucas, who has been an inspiration in my new life; since George passed away.

I cannot cry, though tears
May lie upon my cheeks:

I cannot hear, though thunder
Loudly speaks.

I only know, I love you so
In vain.

While here below, I watch
The falling rain.

The night we met, I heard
An Angel's Voice:

It was then I knew my heart
Had made its choice.

Since you have gone life
Haughtily derides,

But I must wait, till God,
My fate; decides.

Dave Helton
THE WREATH ON THE WATER

See the wreath floating there . . . on the water so fair,
How can we tell them now how much we care . . .
. . . Of our pride in their dare?

How can we tell Mike, who fought for us in war,
Then turned his face skyward . . . forever to soar?

And tell Christa the children watched

with awe on their face,
 And waited to hear her voice
 teach them from space.

How can we tell Dick and Ellison
how much we care,
 And tell Judy and Greg . . . and
 Ron McNair?

That . . . our hearts were with them
on that fateful day,
 That our spirits flew with them
 as they lifted away.

They were reaching out for a new
frontier,
 And sharing with us . . . all that
 was dear.

It was an adventure all of us could
share,
 With seven brave people soaring
 up there.

But . . . all we can now do is utter a
prayer,
 While we stand and stare,
 . . . At the beautiful wreath
 floating there,
 . . . On the water so fair.

Covering our heroes . . . our loved
ones,
 . . . Buried there.

September Black
RE: DEATH
I've always wanted to slide down a
rainbow
And ride around on the wind
And gather stars instead of scars
That try as I might I can't mend—

As for HELL it's on earth, we each
make our own
In pieces and snatches and bits
But should I find "he" is there, I'll
get me a spear
And give the old Devil the fits!!

Antonio Askew
SUNSET & SUNRISE
Swallowed by the ocean
Unusual colors seen dancing until the
Night comes and scares them off
Stars sing soprano while the evening
Evening sits to listen
Then the sun is no more . . . until

Spat out by the horizon slowly
Upward into the sky telling the
Night to go away, to
Rest, to come back later
Ivies, clovers, peppers, and all
Sorts of plants and animals depend on
El rey del cielo, el sol*

*Spanish for "The king of the sky,
the sun"

Amanda J Petrillo
A DREAM FOR TOMORROW
Happiness and laughter
Sorrow and Tears
Yesterday, Tomorrow
For today is here
Look around; What do you see

If you look for good and
feel good, you will find
Happiness and laughter
If you look for Bad and
feel bad, you will find
Sorrow and tears

Though there are times
When sorrow is all around you
And the walls are crushing in
Remember tomorrow
It may seem far away
But look back upon your yesterdays
There was Bad and Good
though the Bad is here
The very good is near!

Patricia Louise Carmichael
SECRET LOVE
Bury you not within your heart
A secret love, for your soul will part
Straight to a life, to you unknown
Until your love will be outgrown.

Always keep a love so sweet
Don't leave it now, forever keep
Inside your soul and shine it through
Then your secret love will remain
true.

Thomas J Harkins III
DON'T LEAVE ME HANGING
Don't leave me hanging
You've got me on the edge
Don't wait too long
To slip off the edge

My heart is beating like a locomotive
Running at full speed, I just need a
motive

It just won't stop
Whenever you're near
My whole body is shaking
With curiosity and fear

Don't leave me hanging
You've got me on the edge
Please give me an answer
Before I leave the edge

My heart is still racing on the rail
Tell me soon, before my gears fail

They're gonna shut down
Even when you're near
You've driven me crazy
Long enough not a tear

Evelyn Judy Buehler

Evelyn Judy Buehler
THE DAYS OF "BILLIE JEAN"
To the world's greatest superstar . . .

Tunnels and corridors; hazy
memories;
Drifting like the summer breeze.
A song once cast its spell;
Into lives it came to dwell.

Summer meadow/city street
Billboards/running feet
Noonday shadows; blackest wine;
Music softly on my mind.

Moonwalk across a stage;
History came and turned the page.
Birds in flight; leaves of autumn
Whisper softly when they come.

Pacific Coast Highway/California sun
Had fun when you were number one.
Motorcycles at Cherry Beach;
Flashing cars; tires screech.

The days of "Billie Jean" were swift
Like the smell of rose just sniffed.
I'm so glad that they began:
To Michael Jackson, from your
number one fan.

E Johanna Telke
TO MY GRANDSON
I was afraid to love you, love you too
much.
Afraid, that someday we would get
out of touch.
It's happening now, this dreadful
thing
"Divorce Proceedings" the words
now do ring
Mother and Dad who are about to
part
Breaking their's, as well as our heart.
To many, to many, this is happening
today
Families destroyed in this permanent
way.
There are crosses to bear in
everyone's life
God grant us the faith to overcome
strife.
Dear "Chris" hold fast to the words
of the Lord
And He will heal the wounds caused
by this sword.
Let us pray to the Lord who loves us
so much
This way, through Him, we will still
keep in touch.
 Love,
 Grandma

Michelle Hammond
MY HERO
When I think of you,
I often compare you to a boxer.
You get beaten up, but you keep on
fighting.
You get knocked down many times,
But you bounce right back and still
continue to fight.
Then one day your opponent lands a
punch,
A punch that hits so hard it knocks
you off of your feet,
A punch that hurts so bad it makes
your bones sore and your muscles
weak.
You struggle to get up, you try so
hard,
But the referee continues to count
until he counts you out
Your opponent is triumphant, but
your family and friends are very sad.
I hope that when it is my turn to step
in the ring,
I can be as brave as you, to fight until
that last punch,
And not give up at that first hard hit.
I love you, for you are my hero.

Stacey McCollum
FORGOTTEN VOWS
She saw him from across the room.
They met, they talked, they left real
soon.
They vowed to share their lives, the
two,
She thought his love would be
forever true.

Their lives went on from day to day,
Two happily married people just
rolling in the hay.
The two were together, stuck like
glue,
She thought his love would be
forever true.

But there was another in his life you
see,
Going behind her back, creating
mystery.
Working late, many business trips
too,
She thought his love would be
forever true.

Then one day when he came home,
He found himself all alone.
There was only a note that said Dear
Lou,
I thought your love was forever true.

That's when he realized that he had
lost,
But he couldn't bear to pay the cost.
So through his head that bullet blew,
If only his love had been forever true.

April Daniel
CHILDREN ARE TO BE SEEN AND NOT HEARD . . .
Let the children rise,
Is it that they are to be
 seen and not heard.

Let the children rise,
We have power,
 and will be heard.
We will speak and be seen.
Listen, hush your voices,
Silence the guns,
We will be heard.
And when you hush your
 voices and silence the guns,
We will speak.
The young know of past,
We know of presence,
We know of future.

Listen, and let the children rise,
Peace will come and we will
 be thanked, . . .
Or maybe they will not
 hush their voices and
 they will not silence the guns
And well, maybe, peace
 will not be there,
But yet you have not for
 the children to blame.
For you would not let
 them rise.

Listen . . . and let the children rise.

Michelina "Mickey" Revans
MY PERSPECTIVE ON LOVE
Love is:
A ripple in the water, but cannot be
seen
Spreading from heart to heart so
virtuous and clean.

Love is:
The beautiful echoes of music, but
cannot be heard
With an extravagance of harmonies
and joyful words.

Love is:
The sweet fragrance of roses, but
cannot be smelled
Its natural essence longed to be
grasped and held.

Love is:
New fallen snow setting on one's
tongue, but can't be tasted.
A partner to all of which is pure, a
crime if wasted.

Love is:
The softness of a baby's skin, but
can't be felt

The innocence defined by God, 'fore
Him most have knelt.
Love is good.
Love is grand.
Love is gracious.
Love is God.

Ron Workman
BROTHERS
Brothers are friends forever;
They will love you clear through:
Stop loving you, they will never;
Because a brother's love is true!

Love has great meaning;
But a brother's love is stronger:
When a brother's life is ending;
We all want him to live longer.

But life can't always be that way;
'Cause God knows when he wants
you;
And he knows when you should stay:
But always remember, A brother's
love is TRUE!
And "true love" lasts forever!!

Peggy Brown
HER BABY'S CRY
Touching the tombstone of where her
baby lays,
A teardrop sinks in the sand as she
wipes another one away,

For every month the baby lived, she's
living in sorrow,
In her eyes will remain the past, only
to hide tomorrow,

All the pain she felt as her dreams
were being ripped apart,
Thoughts of her baby's cry is tearing
up her heart,

She leaned down to place a rose
across the baby's grave,
Then kissed the ground under which
she knew her baby laid,

Someday they'll be reunited up in the
skies above,
Then she'll have the chance to show
her baby all her love.

Christine Burwell

Christine Burwell
LIKE THE COLOR OF BRONZE
Like the color of bronze
There are sparks of light
where ever you go
Rays that effect everyone
you touch
The graceful steps you make
Moving like a great king
Broad shoulders on a well
built body that could hold
up the world
Hair as soft as lamb's wool
Lips that reveal a smile
that lights up my life
Hands that send electrical
shocks through my body
Arms that are strong enough
to lock out any fears that
I may have and hold me so
close
it's like melting inside you
Yes all the things said are
true, for such a beautiful
strong bronze man like you

Irene Martin
MY FATHER'S BIBLE
My Father's old Bible worn with the
years,
It's marked at the scriptures and
covered with tears.
As he read he would say "children,
come gather near,"
You must hear about Jesus, our
Savior so dear.
How he healed all the sick and the
blind made to see,
As he preached long ago by the sea
of Galilee.
How he walked on the water with
waves tossed and wild
And taught his disciples the faith of a
child.
Our eyes upon Jesus we always must
keep,
Or we'll sink to the bottom in
fathoms so deep.
Although he is gone each day we still
read
That beloved old Bible, it fills every
need.
In fance so often I still think I hear,
My dear Father calling "children,
come gather near."

Novia L Amadore
THE KEY TO MY HEART
My dearest love, the pleasure you
bring me cannot be described
with words.
Your smile is like the sun in the
morning so refreshing to my
eyes.
If you were to speak to me it
would be much more than I
deserve.
If only you could see the desire in
my eyes, you can never know
how much I care for you.
It is all locked inside my heart
and only you have the key.

Gina Havens
GOD, PAPA AND MAMA
Two people met and now you see
the years they number fifty
three.
For reasons I can never know,
God said, this tiny seed I sow
and from it an immortal soul
shall grow.
I question not because you see
for some reason God needed me.
A tiny seed, and then a sprout,
first breath, my soul and a cry
came out.
Accept me world take my tiny
hand and I will give all the love
I can.
With God always in the lead and
papa and mama to guide me,
They taught me love, faith and
charity.
With all these and a soul that is
free I know God expects no
more of me.

K Helena Richard Laramee
PAX VOBISCUM
Now nostalgically I remember
Morning grayness, end of November
From my library look-out sadly
noting
Purple ribbons, airborne, floating
From Advent Wreaths that newly
graced
The Cathedral's formal face.
At the curb a waiting hearse
Guarded by a lone attendant
Unaccompanied by other cars
Indicated mourners would be sparse.
Church doors verified these tokens
When finally, slowly giving way,
Out came one unadorned coffin grey,
Wheeled by members of the service
Followed by women three . . .
and he . . .
An only nephew, duty bound
To see the hearse to the burial
ground.
Three woman gathered and went their
ways
Leaving the deceased her last and
lonely
trip to wend
A sad, sad denouement for a
one-time friend.

Charleene Lisberg
STABILITY
Carefully, she steps on rainbow's
edge.
Step by slow step she climbs,
teeters, flails, regains balance.
She says, "Don't look down.",
fights to keep eyes upward,
to ignore mad sea,
and dark pit that gapes.
She climbs on, balance tightly held,
reaches the top, prays,
"Lord, don't let me lose my parasol."

Lindsay M Lane
WHEN YOU LOOK AT ME
When you look at me, I am not what
I appear to be.
My emotions are not what you want
to see.
I am a dreamer, you are the dream.
In my eyes, you glow just like a
beautiful stream.
We all search along the roads and
highways of life for that
special someone to fulfill our dreams,
but sometimes
we feel as if we're all alone.
When you look at me, you only think
you know what you see.
Where is reality? The roads are
stretching, making it harder for
me to find me. Nobody knows the
inner side of me,
for I am not what I appear to be.

Barnarr Cannon
THE CAGE OF TIME
No matter how I try I cannot
comprehend
Were we lost in time between the
beginning and the end?—and if so,
when?

The day I saw you first or was it once
again?
I wondered, had we met before?
When did our lives first blend—
sometime, somewhere?
In the so distant shadows lurking in
my mind,
I tried to set the time within the
present age and clime—when first we
met.
From fruitless search my memories
arose in rage
To seek at last their freedom from the
confines of this cage—of present
time!
My mind took flight and from this
cage of time did soar
And crossing o'er the years did find a
long lost distant shore—of memories.

A century went by, and maybe even
two!
Then in the darkness of those years I
rediscovered you—yet once again!!
You left no doubt!! Your smile, your
walk were all the same,
I soon found out, you differed only in
your age and name—it mattered
not!!!!

I begged my memories to open wide
the door
To let me live again those days I
spent with you, once more—those
days of yore.
Suddenly those all too ancient
memories fled,
Back to the lonely confines of this
cage of time I sped—the door was
closed!!!!

The years grow late, so we must part
as once before,
Our hands still clasped across the
tides of time for evermore—for
evermore.

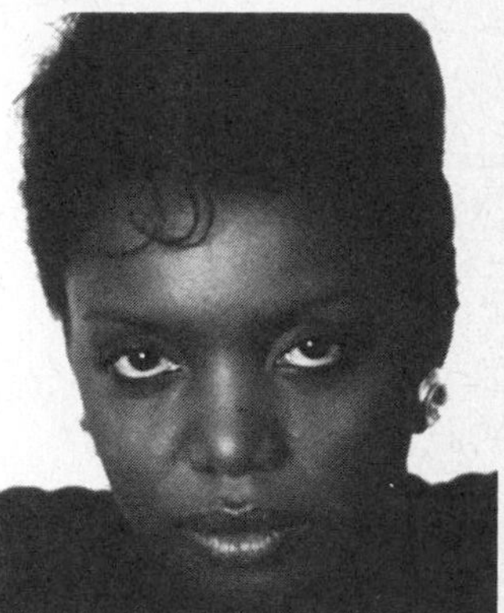

Elma Beckford

Elma Beckford
THE MIGHTY WIND
Somewhere out there the mighty
wind blows and blows.
From east west north and south it
howls.
From whence it cometh no one
knows.
Somewhere out there the mighty
wind rolls.

Somewhere out there the mighty
wind whistled and whistled.
In the stillness of the night it twistled.
As I watched through misty windows
that dazzled.
Somewhere out there the mighty
wind frizzled.

Somewhere out there the mighty
wind moves on, and on
As the great force of its wind began
to strengthens
I watched the eruption of trees tossed
to and fro,
Somewhere out there, the mighty
wind began to destroy.

Somewhere out there the mighty
wind moves faster and faster.
In seconds the wind came gushing in
like lightning.
As I reached forth to touch its mighty
force.
Somewhere out there, the mighty
wind is powerful.

Somewhere out there the mighty wind has slowly passed.
In its taking over it leaves behind such great tasked.
As I wonder where, O where has it gone without a masked.
Somewhere out there, the mighty wind seems mightier than all men.

Richard Allen Hobbs
STARSHIP GIRL
She rides on astral moonbeams
Never touches the sun
Travels on forever
Loves sometimes for fun
Hair of golden-blue
Eyes of fire-green
Always left in my mind
Very seldom seen
A vessel of warm desire
So very free and bold
Yet like a distant starship
She grows never old.

Ellen Biggerstaff
LADY OF LIBERTY

To my loved ones for their faith in me.

There she stands with torch in hand
A mighty guardian of our dear land
A symbol of truth and sweet liberty
For those who seek the right to be free.

People who come from far away places
Look upon her with hope in their faces
Eager to enter our glorious nation
Their hearts beating fast with anticipation.

But those of us who were born to this land
Already know that it truly is grand
And we are proud as no others can be
Of this beautiful statue that means liberty.

Ellen Biggerstaff
APRIL SHOWERS
When old man winter bids "adieu"
And lovely spring comes into view,
She brings along those April showers
So that the world can have May flowers.

And when they spread their gentle mist
The earth looks like it's just been kissed.
They wash away all sleet and snow
To make the world take on a glow.

Then when the winter work is done
What else could ever be more fun
Than walking with a carefree pace
And feel the warm rain on your face.

Margaret Joyce Tibbetts
LOST LOVE
Lost lost, oh, lost love.
What will I do without you?
You have been mine for all these years.
Now my love is gone.
Lost love, oh, lost love.
My life, my heart, my gentle hours
Are empty without you.
You enter my mind and make it sad,
But, it also smiles to recall,
All the love we had.
Lost love, oh, lost love.
You will always be a part of me.
As life goes on and time goes by.
Oh, my lost love you will always
Be in my heart.
Lost love, oh, lost love.

Margaret Joyce Tibbetts
DAYDREAMING
Here I sit, staring, daydreaming again.
You are running through my mind.
Like a summer breeze.
I smile softly, as you pass by.
On the wings of a rainbow,
So bright in the sky.
The colors are fleeting,
Like the flutter of a butterfly.
The colors dance, the image fades.

But, you are still there in my daydreams.
So soft, so light, like a gentle breeze,
That whispers through the trees.
I have my daydreams, when I don't have you.
Oh! Daydreams, my time you do take up.
By drifting through my mind,
All thoughts leave, when images of you drift in.
It's daydream time again.

Margaret Joyce Tibbetts
LITTLE TEARDROP
O'little teardrop how small you are.
Rolling down the cheek so far.
O'little teardrop, what do you mean!
Are you a teardrop of happiness
Or a teardrop of sadness?

O'little teardrop as you are
Roaming down the cheek so far.
Is that a smile, I see shining
Through the teardrop?

It must be a teardrop of happiness.
But wait! The smile is gone.
What is it little teardrop.
Has something made you sad?

O'little teardrop,
I see you shining there.
Will you be running down the cheek,
To form a river of sadness,
Or will it be for happiness.

O'little teardrop shining there.
What has made you so sad!

Alexia D Perry
FACTS

To Sydney, thanks for the memories.

There can be no life without a death,
Life has no beginning till you take your first breath.
There is always sunshine on a sunny day,
There's a storm a brewing in clouds of gray.
There can be no apple without a core,
There will be no scar without first a sore.
There can be no earth without a sky above,
The heart can feel no pain where there is no love.
There is no story without an end,
Life is not worth living if you haven't got a friend.
A poor dejected flower can't exist without some rain,
One can't go through life without enduring pain.
There can be no happiness, if there's no sentiment.
No tears can flow, if there's no contentment.
There can be no waking, if there is no sleeping,
There can be no giving, if there is no keeping.
There is no life where there is no water,
When love is strong, nothing can make it falter.
When two happy people have to part,
There's bound to be a hollow, where once they had a heart.
There can be no blood, if there is no wound,
There can be no God, until belief is found.

Alexia D Perry
UNLUCKY THIRTEEN
Whenever I hear the number thirteen,
It makes me want to shout and scream,
That was the day she came between,
Now it has proved unlucky thirteen.

And as I go through the months and years,
When it's the 13th I'll have my fears,
Remembering how, in spite of my prayers,
He left me alone to cry my tears.

Lucille M Wood
OLD BLIND MAN
You may have a Seeing Eye dog,
but I have a seeing eye tree.
Branches beaten off in spring gales,
branches crashing down in winter winds,
leaving almond scars
like a chorus girl's eyes
outlined in velvet black
against the silvery white bark
of the quaking aspen tree.
Old man with sightless eyes,
you may read braille,
my seeing eye tree,
feels the braille
of all creation—
in its knowledge of ages past,
feeling—before you ever began to feel.

Lucille M Wood
THE LITTLE CHRISTMAS TREE
A cherished memory of tiny Tim,
a toddler, not even two,
and a tiny Christmas tree,
just as tall, or small, as he,
decorated and standing in a mall.

The little child, almost an infant, still,
turning his back to me,
slowly walking step by step,
carefully approaching this
wonderful tree.

I could only see his expression
reflected on the faces of two tall grown men.
The wonderous joy on the
little face, reflected in their eyes
and I knew then, his glorious—
first time thrill, beholding a living
magical Christmas tree.

Kathleen Betts
SUCCESS

Dedicated to Betty and Joann.

Oh, for the days of my youth . . . as I watch them slip away. As I climb the ladder to success. Step by step and day by day as I reach the top. I suddenly realize the best years have slipped away.

You ask, my friend, would I do It again If I had a chance you say? Oh yes my friend, with my family, more time I would spend.

I would take my son and afishin' we would go. I would take my little girl to a picture show. I would take my wife dancing and a dinner for two. Oh yes my friend, I would enjoy my youth . . . If I could just recall, for I was so busy with success that I lost my family and all.

Ellen T Billeaud
FAST
Fast,
Hectic,
Furiously Living
Life
Within The Confines Of Four Walls.
Contrasting
Suddenness
And
Slowness.
Life
Loses Meaning For Me.

Ellen T Billeaud
GLASS HOUSES
Illusions shatter
like crystal prisms,
spraying shards of
fragile thought.

Gentle words can
ease the pain,
but cannot piece
life back together.

Dreams are crushed
but not forgotten,
wounds down deep
will never mend.

Love for two
can have such meaning,
and yet for one
destroy the same.

Shawna L Bradley
VALENTINE'S DAY
Today reminds me of the ways
your love has brightened all my days,
The little things you always do
that show your warmth and caring, too . . .

Today reminds me to be glad
for every moment that we've had—
The quiet times we've spent alone,
the memories we call our own . . .

Today reminds me of the pride
I'm always feeling deep inside,
The pride of knowing that you're mine—
my friend, my love, my valentine.

Linda S Dameron
A PRAYER OF THANKS
Dear Lord, I'd just like to say Thank You,
for the changes you've made in me.
For molding me just a little each day,
Till you make me what you want me to be.

Your Love is so very exciting,
and I feel the need to share.
How happy that you've made me,
and how very much you care.

It amazes me to feel within,
the Spirit of your Love.
The Hope, the Truth, and the Peace,
which can only be found from above.

You've always been there to carry me through,
the difficult times that I've had.

You've taken away the hurt and the pain,
and encouraged me, when I have felt sad.

So please help me Lord, as I Praise your name,
in everything that I do.
To not do anything for myself,
But, for the Privilege of serving YOU!

Linda S Dameron
A TREASURED GIFT

. . . Dedicated to my three beautiful daughters, Lana, Lisa, and Laura. With Love, from Mom.

Our beautiful, precious little miracles from God,
were sent to us from above.
The treasured gift of our children,
Whom God gave us to care for and Love.

Being a Mother is such a precious gift,
but not everyone seems to see.
Some take it for granted, they push them aside,
but it won't be that way for me.

I will always try to take the time,
to laugh, to love and to share.
And to wipe away the tears that they cry,
to show them how much I care.

I know that I will make mistakes,
but I hope that they will see,
that all of the things that I try to do,
are for them and not for me.

And I hope that we will always be,
very close to one another,
and I hope they'll always be proud to say,
"She cares, she's my friend, she's my Mother."

Nkosi Nomusa

Nkosi Nomusa
LIFE FOR A MOMENT

Like a rose that outshines the other
It's picked amongst the others
to reflect the intentions of the owner
It's a token of love, it's a token of reconciliation
The symbol of a dove is the closest it can be.

What joy, what fragrance it gives
To the giver, pride; to the receiver, joy
The thought of it is the greatest feeling it portrays
How often and how long does this last?
Just one is enough to share the feeling inside.

A moment follows a day and a day, a night
It can only be appreciated in the light
Are we like a rose, having limited time
We live but for a limited time,
learning and working
Time comes like a rose where we are of no use
There is no time or space for us when withering away

Art Winwood
LOVE

Love is like an anvil under
All of life's relentless blows;
Set to catch the hammer's thunder
While our metal shapes and grows.

Ever patient, and achieving,
Wearing duty as a yoke,
Like an anvil—blows receiving,
Love does not return a stroke.

Strong in faith and understanding,
Virtue at its very core;
Love itself is king, demanding
Justice, mercy, truth and more!

When in life's eternal battle,
We as sinners suffered loss;
There amid the scorn and prattle,
Love itself was on the cross.

Let us post a new beginning,
Sharing wide our love and care;
With its trying, giving, winning,
Love's a blessing—anywhere!

Art Winwood
SPACE

As fish indwell the sea's embrace,
Thus all creation lies in space,
That mystifying entity
That harbors time and energy.
A medium that's not a void,
But is a vehicle employed
To spread the galaxies abroad
Like fiery chariots of God.

Great myst'ry lies beyond the veil
That human eyes cannot assail;
Nor can our great inventions pry
Beyond the beauty of the sky.
By faith alone our eyes can see
The Ruler of eternity,
Who holds the cosmos in His hand—
As part of heaven's wonderland.

Ann Gonzalez
A PART OF GROWING UP

Dedicated to my Mom and Dad, who made growing up the very best it could possibly be.

What was it like in yesteryear,
to know it's over, is what we feared,
it's done, no longer to be young and free,
but, at the time we could not see.

We laughed, played and partied down,
all our worries were to get to town,
to roam the streets to see what was going on,
to stay out late, hating to go home.

Our teens and our twenties, they pass quickly,
we never once admitted to feeling sickly,
push on, push on, the weekend's coming up,
when our friends called, we always felt in luck!
Now we're older, a lot more settled down,
But, we can't stand for our kids, to want to roam the town . . . .

Ann Gonzalez
HE

Dedicated to Abel for showing me true love really exists.

My man with those beautiful eyes,
always fill me with deep sighs,
As I watch him and he does not know,
I know my face is all aglow,
His hair and eyes are black as coal,
I love him deeply, heart and soul.

When I met this man I knew,
to him I'd always be true.
He took me dining and dancing all over town,
nothing could have slowed us down.
Now, We three years have been wed,
My oh my, how those years have sped.

His sights going, my back aches,
he does the cooking, I bake the cakes,
We sit together all the night long,
He watches T.V. I write songs.
My soul still shudders with deep sighs,
When I look into his beautiful eyes . . . .

Linda Ireland
TO MY SON

Dedicated to everyone who didn't think I could ever get published—and to my husband and children who knew I could, I love you all.

Little one, I long to hold you, see you grow
To spend my life and love on you
Little one,
I'll never forget
I long to watch you grow, to help smooth out the hurts and enjoy the good times
It was never to be
Maybe we'll meet one day in heaven
And then I can see what we've missed
Not a day goes by without some thought of what you'd be doing now
If you were here
Little one, who left too soon
I love you, always will
I felt your turns and kicks
So did your dad
If only we had known that last night and day all your activities were not preparing to say hello,
But goodbye.

Wilma Lipscomb
DON'T TOUCH

A dozen Bottles, standing on the sill.
Doc gave 'em to me, to make me think I'm ill.
Knocked one off, fell into the sink.
Threw the rest out !
Now I'm in the pink.
Poured one bottle down the drain.
Now, I hear it cry, "O, I'm in pain."
Got my plunger, pushed very hard.
It blew up and knocked me in the yard.
Got to my feet as fast as fast as I could hobble.
Went to the house and got the other bottle.
Buried it in the ground, it began to grow.
It looked like a Monster, or a thing,
"I don't know."
If you start complaining about your ills,
Better think awhile about them pills.
"O," you might get better, maybe worse.
Then again, you might end up in a Hearse !

Wilma Lipscomb
WORTHY OF LOVE

Dedicated to my only Love, forty-three years of Marriage, My Hubby Guy! On the loss of a dear friend, Homer.

When lonely and depressed; take time to weep.
When burdens and fears mount up, you cannot sleep.
Seems you have no time of your own;
Slow down; take time to weep.
Inside hurting like Hell,
Outside holding up well.
Only time can heal, Take time and weep.
All the burdens and hurt, mounting high.
So lonely and depressed,
Lost the one you love the best.
Nothing can comfort your soul.
Seems everything is out of control.
Take time to weep.
There is a brighter day when the soul that is mourning,
Suddenly will awake and find rest and peace.
Fight it no more.
Take time to weep.
Sometimes we feel no one cares!
We feel so alone.
Now is the time to remember GOD, on His throne.
When peace won't come to help you sleep.
Now's the time to pray and weep.
Life goes on in an empty way.
After our love has passed away.

Canadia Collins

Canadia Collins
CROSSING THE GREAT MIDDLE SEA

With thoughts toward the moon, we
Follow the sun and always think
toward morning
And yet, there is unspoken longing
For magic miracle in sky.—As once
we were told
There was: There was a ringed-ship
Always on our course, or theirs;
And we knew,
To follow them was our safety! We,
The small-boned people, did
even think to

Sometimes call it name like, God!—
for,
At least and perhaps at most it was
like old sound of highest thing.
But, from intelligence and from much
Experience, the bright do know to
not so ever
Quickly move to conclusions—
except
Perhaps when in panic, which then
does cause the
Thoughts to be unclear and
computed
Too unevenly in the mind for any
strength in the reason, then!
Yet, in retrospect sometimes—and
always
When a miracle is seemed—the
unthinkingly computed thoughts
Even in a panic, on calming down do
flow
Strangely into some to-be-translated
kind of half-folded, upper vision!—
Like uncounted, new resources stored
away in old, old places.

Carmen Johnson

FATHER, OH FATHER

Father, oh Father,
why did you desert us,
as if we're not alive.
Why did you get up and go,
as if you can't survive.
Did you not consider the fact
that your children might suffer?
They are going to react
in one way or the other.

Listen Father
We are your children speaking to you
out loud we will scream until you
hear and understand what you have
chosen to do.
You have lost us only by your choice,
and you will never have us back,
until the drinking stops.

Father, oh Father,
I am sorry that we cannot share our
goals and dreams coming true.
We are making it in this world with
or without you.
Two children proving themselves in
life and in a song.
We know you regret your choice,
you know you were wrong.

Tanya R Jarvis

RIVER OF FREEDOM

For Indians all over the United States and my father Eldon Charles.

Oh is the river as it flows,
Of Indian passages no one knows.
Their Indian customs once held as
true
Until there came the Whiteman's
rule.

Indian chiefs and Indian squaws
One man's rise, One man's fall.
They owned the land, to them it was
theirs,
Till many battles shed many tears.

They were far away from the land
they once loved,
Giving up hope and chance, were
they shoved.
Their chance was now over, their
freedom was lost
For the Whiteman had become
equally cross.

Now many years have gone and
passed,
For the Indians knew their dreams
would not last.
Old Indian stories are all that remain
Of a Legacy made and broken all the
same.

An old wise tale once told as true
An eagle that flies in the sky so free
Will do all it can, and be as it be

Norman A Johnson Jr

TO THE ONE I LOVE

This poem is dedicated to Bonnie, my precious wife.

She raises in the morning to
turn on the sun.
She keeps me warm as the days.
go on.
Never do I fear to touch the sun,
for her warmth helps
me to live on.

Skies may darken clouds may gray,
but the sun never fades.
As I look into the sky, I see
the flame, the burning for which
shares my name.

So, now I say to the one with
my name, I am but a creature
whose love will never change.

G Lynette Jeschke

INSIDE, LOOKING OUT

Caught in a world of nothing but
faces,
Not being able to go to other places.
Sitting inside my private little world,
All my thoughts are unfurled.
I sit here, thinking about my trouble,
I know I'm a girl in a plastic bubble.

Locked away from the outside world,
Never getting to meet other girls,
Just thinking, feeling and saying
silently,
I don't want to stay here, I'll not act
violently . . .
Sitting here, crying softly to myself,
I feel as though I've been placed on a
shelf.

Looking out at my old friends,
I see that is where it ends.
Searching in their eyes, I see a fading
rainbow.
I watch as their colors fast lose their
glow.
I sit here thinking of my past
I see my life fading fast.
Looking down, I feel my hands
double,
I'm only a girl in a plastic bubble.

Jolene Jobe

A DREAM OF PERFECTION

Perfection is an elusive dream.
We search in vain to find it.
We struggle, work, think and scheme,
To help ourselves to bind it.
And just when we relax our guard,
The butterfly of perfection flies
away.
Leaving us to try twice as hard;
But perfection never comes to stay.

J McKeehan Jacobs

THE SHIRT

The shirt
Fell to the ground.
No remnant . . .
Could be found.

Starched:
The picture stood,
Against the mind
Old, as aging wood.

Hanging
On the nail of time.
A shadow . . .
A faceted rhyme.

The shirt
Unheard of, unseen.
Shrinks in the rain
Bleaches in the sun
Weeps in vain.
An essence
Of the one who wore it.
A figment
Of the heart that won it.

Claudette Ann-Marie Dinnall

SOMETIMES

To my family for all their love and support. Especially my mother, a precious jewel who God has given us.

Sometimes I sit and think awhile
Of where my life is going.
Where will I be ten years from now
Or is it worth the knowing?

I sit and sink deep in my thought
Wondering who I'll be,
Or how I'll ever come to know
What will become of me.

Where will the winds of Time blow
me?
What paths will I make in Life's
sands?
The future is all unknown to me
I must leave my fate in GOD's
hands!

Lenneth Oliver

WHEN

When you feel that you have
reached the end and that
you can go not one step
further . . .

When endeavors seem to be
drained of purpose

Think of good things and renew
your mind with positive thoughts
and you will see the world out
of different eyes!

Remember!!

Keep your mind open or else you
will shut out more than you
will ever shut in. For, blessed is
the man who expects nothing
he in no way can ever be
disappointed!

Salima

Tammy M Smith

WHEN

When you're feeling down and
lonely,
When you don't know what to do,
When you think you'll go crazy,
If you don't do something soon.
Just think about the one you love,
The one you care for too.
The one you want to marry,
But too young to really do.
The one you share your feelings with,
The one who knows you're you.
The one that never gives up,
No matter what you do.
Just talk with her,
And tell her the truth,
No matter what it be.
Because if she loves you very much,
She'll understand—you see.
This is just a little story,
To tell you what to do.
When you're feeling down and
lonely,
She'll help you through anything you
do.

Dian Cuccinello

MY PICTURE

There is a face
you cannot see
dwelling here
inside of me.
Although my eyes
elude this frame,
its arms enfold me
just the same.
Pick me up
and touch my soul
I am
unphotographable.

Amy Feuz

NOTHINGNESS

Faded letters
are all that remain
of the feelings we shared.
What once meant so much,
now brings only sadness and tears.

It was difficult to explain the
connection we had—
no one understood.
Sometimes,
neither did we
But we did know the other was
there—always.
Or so I thought.

As the years passed,
and the ink on your letters bled into
the paper,
you needed me less and less—
until
I was just another face in the crowd.

How can the feelings I harbor for you
have remained the same—
when your feelings,
your promises
of the past
have faded,
and bled
into
nothingness

Amy Feuz

A REBIRTH

The rain drips gently
from virgin leaves

The petals of a budding rose
struggle to emerge

The brilliant blue jay
hums his soothing song

The sun comes out of hiding
to coax the fresh grass seed towards
the sky.

The sound of child's play
echoes from street to street,
as spring
f
a
l
l
s
upon us.

Lois Lynda Kobs

A CHILD'S INNOCENCE

In Dedication to those who are survivors of Child sexual assaults, and Susan Griffiths, who gave support and was a great Inspiration to me.

A child will trust and believe
always in the family tree.

Even when some of the feelings
inside of them
are saying that these things shouldn't
be happening to me.

A child feels its innocence is taken
away
when someone touches them
and says it's ok
to play in a sexual way.
Because it's not in the right, it's in
the wrong
that's why a child then feels its
innocence is gone.

A child's life should always be pure
and free.
And in their lives
a child should never have to feel or
see
their innocence be taken away
because within the rest of their lives
things then won't be ok.

So what I'm trying to say
is you should care and love your
child but let it be in the right way.
The way where your child feels its
innocence will always be ok.
Because that's the way it should
always stay.

Lois Lynda Kobs
THE SURVIVOR

In Dedication to My Mother Betty (Kobs) Raabe, Pat, Ellen and Susan, Who all gave encouragement and support and believe in me and my Poetry.

We struggle through the hard times in
our lives
and when we make it, we say,
"We have survived and let nothing
get in our way."

We all have nameless fears
that can get us physically and
emotionally down.
We sometimes will give a smile
When we should show our true
feelings even if it's to be a frown.

It's ok to ask for help
in talking to someone about your hurt
inside
and to get out that anger we all try to
hide.

A person needs to see that the old
tapes that are running in their minds
have kept them from growing
emotionally strong.
Now, to put on new tapes
and to look to the future, 'cause that's
where you belong.

To survive in this life a person needs
to see that the past no longer exists.
And to learn to go for new things and
take a risk.

A person should stand tall and say,
"Even when some things aren't all
ok.
That's all right, 'cause I'm a survivor
and I'm sure to find the right way."

Robert E Merton
OF CRYSTAL SHIPS

For Jan.

A crystal ship, beneath a golden sky
Newly on board, my lover and I.

Sailing reefed waters, lacking good
charts
We stand close together, and steer
with our hearts.

We often embrace, as new lovers do
Another becomes, from the union of
two.

We weather the storms, of our
uncharted ways
Dreaming and planning, for mild
pastel days.

The child who is us, must now depart
A lover has come, and stolen a heart.

They glide away quickly, as lovers
will do
Their own crystal ship, shiny and
new.

Our crystal ship, though battered and
old
Reflects oceans of beauty, for our
eyes to behold.

Some future day, it will melt in the
sun
Our journey through time, over and
done.

We'll still be together, and truly be
free
As we walk the bright shores, of
eternity.

Betty Vogel and Matthew Berkowitz

Betty Vogel
CONVENTION TIME

I took a trip to Washington,
Yes, Washington, D.C.
To join the big Convention,
Called "World of Poetry."

I joined the throng of Poets,
From many states and towns,
Including places that I thought
"World of Poetry" was unknown.

The Gold and Silver Poets
Had reason to be proud,
As each read off his poetry
To other poets out loud.

Bob Hope you couldn't ignore.
'Twas anything but boring.
He kept us wanting more,
As the audience kept roaring.

Mickey Rooney, Don O'Connor,
Legends to most folks.
To watch them was an honor,
So funny were their jokes.

The shows had great variety,
So wouldn't you just know it
Would have been enjoyed by anyone,
Even a non-poet.

Jayne Meadows a poet herself, in
fact,
Told an engrossing story,
Of little known historical facts
'Bout famous women of glory.

There's one thing I would do,
If it were up to me,
I'd give a trophy to the creator
of "World of Poetry."

Betty Vogel
THE CONVENTION

I took a trip,
As was my intention
To join all the poets
At the big convention.

The guests I have known of
Since I was a child.
Their Jokes were so funny,
Our laughter was wild.

Bob Hope, Mickey Rooney,
And Donald O'Connor,
To watch such legends
Was surely an honor.

Their jokes were so funny,
No one was bored.
How could that be
When everyone roared.

The Golden Poets too,
Received much applause,
As they each read their poems,
And accepted their awards.

There's an award I'd give,
That I must mention,
To the folks who invented
"World of Poetry" convention.

J Stuart Watkins
DAUGHTER'S SHOWER

Half awake, half asleep
Reaching for a towel,
She turns the water on . . . too hot!
Awake at once and hopping mad;
Haltingly enters the shower.
Music springs forth off-key to us,
But video quality to her ears.
Shampoo, conditioner, and soap at
work
to make her squeaky clean.
"Hours" later the shower's off.
A hand pokes through the curtains,
And slides the great white towel
inside.
Finally the towel emerges,
Engulfing a child from ankles to
chin;
A princess about to stylishly dress
In the most modern attire befitting
A sixth grade girl ready for school.

Kelli Diane Bongo
BABY

Laughing and happy
She's so little and so pure
What a baby is
Tiny cries, a need for love
A mother's best dream come true

Gloria J Butkiewicz
THE GAME

To my therapist, Sheryl, my mother Lucille, my sister Bev, without whose love and encouragement, I would not have survived. Thank You!

Shame such a disgraceful game,
Bringing dishonor tears and pain,
Like a wilting rose with its petals
falling,
These little voices keep on calling.

Another has ingrained upon your
mind,
That you're not nice and you're not
kind.
You're undeserving of self-esteem
because,
Someone before you had no dream.

Red adds to shame a blushing color,
I can't imagine it any other.
The falling petals turning black:
Reminding one not to look back.

The thorns on its stem, so wilting and
sharp,
Piercing your soul and breaking your
heart.
The aromatic fragrance of the rose,
And its velvety texture, serves to
impose, upon my psyche.

That wonderful feeling !
That there is a God, Who's filled
with healing.

Linda Stone Helton
PASSING YOUTH

From the stormy sky fell sheets of
rain
As the eyes looked from the
windowpane.
A single streak of lightning crashed
down
Reminding her of her fleeting youth.

Once here, now gone,
In spite of it, she must go on.
Too many obligations, too many
cries,
Someone needs help, she can't deny.

As the storm begins to cease,
The sun breaks through bringing
peace,
Telling her as the door to youth
closes behind her,
Another door opens and there you
will find her.

As the rain falls like teardrops from
the trees,
A tear is dried, a heart is freed.

James W Sloan
WHAT A DAY

To middle and lower class workers everywhere!

Another day going to waste,
your head, on a good night, feels like
paste.

Things to do, places to go,
people nagging, you really blow.

Life is hell, with no end in sight,
just going day to day, not very bright.

No time to slow, no time to quit,
I'm pulling up short, bit by bit.

You try something new, hope for the
best,
another day useless, from climbing
the crest.

Night falls dim, from out of the sky,
the sandman comes and sprinkles my
eyes.

The only peace for me, in this world,
oh mine,
Is the peace in my dreams, that holds
up time.

Mavis Vaughn
J.D. OUR LITTLE HALF PINT

Written to you Jack Daniel Hammons in remembrance of meeting you with your Auntie Lynn.

Our little half pint. Oh, What can I say? You gave us joy that was here to stay.

You kept us glowing from day to day, only because of your awesome ways. Three months old and smiling so. We wanted the best to help you to

learn and to help you grow.
God took you from us this full moon day. Maybe to teach us his God-Damn-Way!
To be in his limelight, there you will stay. Us to our memories that we will love each and every day.
He gave you life, personality. Plus, for us to accept this, he says is a must. Give us our faith, oh Lord, we are ready to Bust. We accept the fact that he's with his brother. But why? Oh why Lord, do you take so soon after the other?
Help us to make our lives go right. So very soon after such a plight.
What do we do when the body remains? The soul you gave us is gone and only time remains.
We will bury your half pint and give him back life. To you my Lord, again, I give up the light of my life.
Make of my son, what you want him to be, and promise me dear Lord, I can see him again in eternity!

Sarah Brower
LOVE IS RARE
Love is rare
Like a bird
You can make it
If you know the words.

You know the words
That mean so much
You know the words
That mean a special touch.

Angela Morrow
SCENIC VIEW
There is a mashed potato mountain standing high upon my plate, and at the very center lies a gravy crater lake.
There is a tasty green bean raft on a golden butter creek while a bright tomato city past a parsley forest peeks.
There is a rocky coast of meat loaf and a perky pickle boat with a golden biscuit sunset soon to vanish down my throat!

Steven Hills
ROMANS

This poor man cried, and the Lord heard him, and saved him out of all his troubles.

Lord help me to live my life
Better each and every day
Show me the way to live
Being kinder, more loving in every way!!!

To touch with patience and love
With love . . . I'll not be ashamed
Indeed Christ for the ungodly
God's love let His Son take our blame!!!!

Mary Jacobs
ARE YOU OVER THE HILL
Have you ever thought about it
Have you ever wondered who's coming or who's going
Have you ever said she's over the hill
Move out of the way
Don't just stand still
I have now haven't you
But have you ever thought that
You're at the top of that hill
Now I have Haven't you
Move out of the way
Don't just stand still
There's a baby crawling up that hill

Tammy Noble
BRANDI JO
She's small and fat, full of bubbling joy.
She jumps up and down when she gets a new toy.
Her eyes are blue sparklers, her hair is sunlight.
Running through the grass, she looks like a kite.
Her face is an angel's, innocent's reflection.
She's truly God's gift, & she is perfection.
She sees teddy bears in popcorn, elephants in the clouds.
She's a little performer, dancing for crowds.
She's still very young, not even quite four, but her mind takes in everything, and searches for more.
I wait for the day when she falls in love.
When she feels feelings she knew not of.
When she is slender, and the baby fat is gone.
When she starts staying out, and waiting for dawn.
When I see that look, I'll understand, that certain look of love, when she's found her man.
Then I'll know Brandi Jo is growing away.
Know that she's bound to leave us someday, but now it hasn't been long, she's been born.
And she sees elephants in the clouds, and teddy bears in popcorn!

Anant Vijay Joshi
MESSAGE

Dedicated to all those whose love was never reciprocated, but who continued to love.

My heart misses a beat
Whenever I see you
O my love, just imagine
Someone falls for you
For him you never care
And he longs for you
To him you never remember
Day and night he pines for you
At whom you frown sometime,
Always he smiles for you.
Don't detest his feelings, please
He wants to live and die for you
In the heart of his hearts
He loves you and only you
And wants love from you.

O my love just imagine,
Someone falls for you.

Linda K Mincy
THE ONE I LOVE

I dedicate this poem to the person, for whom it was written about, my husband, the love of my life. I love you, sweetheart.

You have the most beautiful eyes of green,
They are the prettiest I have ever seen.
Sometimes they can be so demanding,
Then there are times when they are so understanding.

I want you to know that I love you so much,
There seems to be magic in your gentle touch.
I pray that we will always be happy together.
Because I want to be with you forever.

I love to touch your soft, cute face,
I feel so happy and safe when I'm in your embrace.
When you hold me with your arms so strong,
I get the feeling that in them is where I belong.

No one could come close to the desire I have for you,
And my love for you will always be true.
I could never get tired of loving you,
Because I want to be with you my whole life through.

I love to feel your warm body next to mine,
Oh baby, I think you are so divine.
No one could ever take your place in my heart,
You have been so special to me ever since the start.

Sherry N Bryant
THEN CAME YOU
I thought I could carry on no more,
there was no fight left in me for sure,
My soul was shattered, my dreams were gone. I never felt so hurt and so alone,
I could find no happiness in anything I did and it showed in my actions and what I said,
I gave up on life convinced no happiness could be found, I was so depressed and oh so down,
Like a drowning man I was sinking for the last time and I knew it too.
and as i sank with only my hand in sight I was pulled to the surface
Then came you.

Judy Peninger
TEARDROPS
I reached into my heart,
and felt afraid that we would part.
I thought of all the good times,
and I cried a tear for you.
As my fear grew,
my tear multiplied a time or two.
Soon I was flooded by sorrow—
worrying about loneliness
without you tomorrow.
I somehow slowed the rain—
I held a tear filled with pain.
I remembered nothing could take away what we had—
I felt a little less sad.
I hugged my tear,
then set it down with a sigh—
It gently changed to a raindrop,
a gift from the sky.
I saw a rainbow shining through—
My rainbow of hope—
My belief in me and you.

Anatosha Manuel
THE ROSE
The rose so sweet, its petals so delicate,
Its cloak of thorns, its composition so intricate.
What is the significance of a single rose?
It lives, it dies and again it grows.

Yet its brief life of beauty has caused us to pause
From our hurried occupations, the urgency of causes.
The elegance of but a single rose
Has caused romance to blossom and love to grow.

So what is the significance of a single rose?
It lives, it dies and again it grows.
It affords us one tranquil moment in our day.
Then hurriedly we continue along our merry way.

Liberty Campbell

Liberty Campbell
MY LITTLE GREEN SKINK
Often green or black,
Where's my green chameleon?
Eaten by the cat?

Liberty Campbell
FOG
Friendly germ-free fog—
So much easier to breathe
Than brown oily smog!

René McClure
GRANDMOTHER'S EASTER

I dedicate this to my grandmother, who is on my mind and in my heart at Easter and all year-round.

Tagging along with grandmother in an Easter dress.
An innocent sight with my hair all a mess.
Running about in those tiny pattern shoes.
The flowers are beautiful, which one shall I choose?
I miss those childish things I used to do.
But most of all I miss sharing them with you.

Barbara J Bennett
MY MOM
I took my mom away one day
the doctor said a hospital day.
Said she wouldn't be coming back
and how she loved me so.
I stayed with mom day and night
and phoned some relatives.
I watched her slip out of it
for many days to come.
The doctor talked of only time
I held her hand so tight.
As she took her last deep breath
my heart just sank and sank.
As I tried not to cry
I had to let her go.
My mom had always told me
She'd walk with dad again
I guess this is their time
to walk in hand and hand.

Eleanor Evans
FOSTER PARENTS
We have two little girls who fight, scream and yell
A cat and two dogs who are all best pals.

Life just isn't the same
Since our two little arrivals came!

Dirty clothes scattered on the floor
And muddy shoes in and out the door.

Beds unmade, fingerprints on walls,
Gripes and complaints, they do it all.

Here we go ahead, with a merit chart
Meanwhile, hoping things won't fall apart.

What a challenge to Hope and Pray
Kindness and patience will one day pay.

Foster Parents are we who share
Our love and home because we care.

We look to the guidance of our dear Lord
In hopes, someday, Heaven will be our reward.

Jacqueline D Sciallo
MY OBJECTIVE
To venture into your mind, I'd give the world.
I could spend a lifetime wondering how you'd react.
But, the creation of these feelings is indisposable
I am almost left without a doubt.

It is so difficult to churn out these phrases,
I'm always afraid I'll say the wrong thing.
I don't want to send your attention in another direction
Your attention is more precious than gold.

Am I a hopeless romantic? Maybe so.
Do I dare follow your fleeting glance?
If somehow you would let me know
Do I ever stand a chance?

You constantly interrupt my train of thought
But the train had no previous destination.
In your eyes I could see forever
If I'd ever get the chance to look.

To lure you into feeling the same;
Just to hear your voice—I'd hear nothing else.
My objective is to move you with these words.

Sue Rodgers
THE SEA HAS A EUPHORIC QUALITY
The sea has a euphoric quality,
Transpiring a feeling of tranquility.
Waves dancing ever so gently.
Bringing timeless secrets to its shore.

Lonely souls before me,
Have walked these sands
Pondering and wondering,
Seeking to understand.

An eternity of emotions
Fills the night.
As those before me,
Have sought insight.

Humbling mankind by its pure beauty
A strange sensation it does produce
Within one's self
Eliminating hatred; spurring truce

If we could all have once
To gaze upon the sea
And etch into our minds, its memory,
In a moment's thought, it can set us free,
From the harshness of reality.

Laura A Dahlke
LOST FOR YOU

This poem is dedicated to Jason. Dreams can come true . . .

A night-light is all that brightens this small, dark, empty room.
No voices can pass through,
only the sound of a distant heartbeat.
Too distant,
And barely heard.
Here I lie, am wide awake,
staring in the shadows of my eyes.
Seeing all but fear;
all but pain,
Wondering if I'll ever love again.
Someday this search will end,
After repeated mistakes of . . .
but, where not finding myself,
Lost for You.

June Keller McKaig
HOME PLACE
Down a narrow, rutted road, deep ditches on each side,
A pine thicket at the bend, sharp turn to the left.
Cornfields on both sides—the old home place at the end.
Shade trees dwarf the house, on native rock pillars,
Huge stone slabs for steps, a long porch across the front.
Lots of chairs with plump cushions . . . and two front doors—
One to the main room, the other to guest quarters.
A scuttle full of coal on the cracked marble hearth,
A grandmother clock ticking away time atop the natural wood mantle.
Soft lace curtains at the windows, comfy chairs, lots of books.
The kitchen was the meeting place, a table that sat eight,
With kerosene lamps down the middle, a huge cookstove on the side.
Buckets with dippers by the door.
Down a dirt path, barn listing slightly to the right,
Hayloft open to sunshine, home for horses, cows and kittens.
Pastures and fields well guarded by rolls of hay, silent sentinels over their domain; a sparkling brook at the bottom of the hill.
Big boulders form a small pond, just right for hot tired feet.
Blackberry tangles all around, another delightful treat.
That's the old home place—dreams of summer's past.
Lots of love and laughter live on in memory.

April E Stevens
SCHOOL DAY MEMORIES
As we reach out
To shake each other's hand,
While we think of the memories
Of years in the past.
Tears fill our eyes
Because it's now gone
And we all have to move on.
We hope friends will keep in touch
As the years pass us by,
Although it hurts inside
We'll try not to cry.
We think of years in the past
And our first day here,
Now we've reached the end
We are going away.
How do you say good-bye
To friends who mean so much?
Will there be time
To sincerely keep in touch?
You'll always have the memories
Of this school from day one,
Just don't think of leaving this school—
Think of going to a new one.

Gali Shalit
IMMA

This is dedicated to my darling grandmother, Imma.

The scent of her sweet perfume
fills every room.
I always sense her nearby.
Our souls are one.
I miss her!
Life is like a fast moving highway
that ends wherever one takes his exit.
Why do we have to exit?
Where is she now?
Can she hear me?
Can she see me?
There are so many unanswered questions
but where is the book of answers?
I am confused!?!
What are we doing here?
We were so close
and now we are so far apart!
It is too confusing to go on!
All I can say is that life
isn't meant to be
understood!!!!

Barbara Hampton Herrick
A HILL

The ground became apart from the glow and the dirt was different colors than the cloud pictures.

The trees moved away from their physical embraces and the ceiling became green leaves and grey sky instead of a carnival.

The air felt as sighs rather than silent songs and the hill was higher than the wind feeding the water circles.

The sounds were soft syllables instead of still starts and our hands were transformed into white flesh on wet, fertile decay.

The hair became separate strands of human silk and the sun made the grass a different green with only fraction force.

The smells were unborn flowers under turned rocks and the cold was a gift to remind our lungs to love the air.

The mating crickets became suburban mothers and the 5:00 magic produced a brave new world of morning birds.

Kathleen J Koglin
MY FATHER
My father you are
no matter how near or far.
In the heavens above I,
your daughter knows of your love.
With all your sacrifices and pain,
And now your ten children remain.
As your love, your wife,
still lives her life.
You are missed so much
that we pray
as such.

That you are reunited
with your mother and father.
And so delighted
without a bother.
And safe within our Lord's hands,
with no more of life's demands.
Happy and free,
as a spirit should be.
My father you are,
no matter how near or far.

Laura Handke
PASTURES
Come walk with me
through the meadows of your mind.
Pull me into the pool of your eyes
for I want to jump in
but swim with me
for I fear I may drown in their depths.

Sing with me
the laughter in your soul
for I want to share
in the music of your joyous abandon.
Take me riding
on your intuitive spirit
so I may follow you to the place
of your wisdom and awareness.

Shower me with your loving affection
and drench me
in the storm
of your passion.

Virginia McPherson
LOVE IS LIKE

To my ninety-year-old mother, Mattie McPherson, who demonstrated such love to her four children.

Love is like the purity of a flower
It secretes its fragrance everywhere.
Love is great to touch, to have, to hold
Sparkles like a bubbling water flow.
Love is like the melodious song of the bird
Soothes our well-being, word by word.
Love is like security for our present and future plans
Supplies all our needs and never ends.

A B Jones
A SAD WORLD

To Barbara, Wendy and Lisa, with love.

Why can't things be like years gone past
Where people loved, that really last
Where families joined in hand-to-hand
to make this world a wonderland.

Now don't bring out the heavy guns
and don't bring out the missiles
We could all learn to live in peace
with just some hugs and kisses.

Teach our children right from wrong
So there's no mistakes in years to come
Tell them about the prejudice and hate
And why we all should have more faith.

Come one, come all, let's do it right
We know damn well too many

wrongs aren't right
We should learn from what we're taught
for life is already, oh so short.

Nakia Chambers
IF IT EVER ENDS

So close too close my heart wants to be to his.
I'm feeling like this could be love and it is.
I can't believe that my heart is ready to be given away.
Maybe I will be ready someday.
I can't believe my heart is feeling so much love.
I feel like I'm soaring on the wings of a dove.
Maybe one day our love will be again,
But my heart will break if it ever ends.

Tina M Bellner

Tina M Bellner
WHO WILL I BE

There are so many paths alive today
Freshly cut to follow,
Some made of dirt, others of gold
Many are dead ends and hollow.

It is often difficult to choose and pursue
The appropriate route to go,
But, there's only one way to find yourself,
Only one way you will know:

Follow your heart, your instincts,
Your inner voice, your mind,
Down one of those paths there's likely something
Worth your time to find.

Yet there are so many skies to wander
And people to be right now,
Which ones will I present today
And when will I know how?

There's charming, ruthless, innocent, famous;
Devious, witty, charming, sincere . . .
It's an eternal list of opportunity
That spreads amongst the years.

It takes time and experience to find yourself
That forever impressionable you,
And the best advice you could give or take
Is to "be yourself all your life through."

When selecting a path for the future ahead
Don't hurry to decide,
Take time to figure out what's "YOU,"
Use your original self as a guide.

Daniel James Haney
MY LOVE

For Nima, Ashley, and Katie Lynn, the ladies I adore most in this world.

The waning moon and rising sun,
The sullen deep and purple-blue,
Before my eyes became the dawn,
Then offered me a lighter hue,
Across the earth for miles it seems,
Across the sky on this new day,
Slowly beckoned by morning dreams,
For my love's light I hope and pray,
Like petals torn to reap the sun,
Like daisies lined throughout a field,
Today with love I will be one,
For love alone weapons I'd wield,
And love will stay in my heart true,
For love I live forever new,
And sorrow be for those who may,
Attempt to take my love away.

Jerri Lynne Neville
A RIDE THROUGH THE WOODS

To my best friend, Sam, who was the inspiration for this poem.

Is it actually catching, brushing, saddling, and bridling?
Or is it thundering hooves, rustling leaves, and laughter?
Maybe walking, talking, and laughing,
Possibly the smell of flowers or pines . . .
The thrill of jumping with powerful bounds,
It could be the peacefulness of birds singing,
Or sitting talking, eating, and drinking.
It might even be the excitement of being in control of a powerful, huffing, puffing, wet, sweaty creature,
Or seeing the freedom of deer and rabbits.

Probably though it is sharing a sense of freedom with someone very special in a beautiful sunny world where birds sing, streams run slowly, and leaves rustle as you move quietly on the way back to the real world where nothing is as calm as . . .
A RIDE THROUGH THE WOODS.

Thomas Di Maria
STAYIN' AND RETURNIN'

I can tell that your dreams
are twistin' and blazin'
You seem to be gearing up for the bout
Sizin' up the dew of past devotions
Between stayin' and returnin'
On back to the south

And in your darkest dreams you creep underground
Till you catch the sound of that foreign land
It swells and it sobs where once you were
Leaves one with the heart of a child and yet
You endlessly search for
A noiseless nest where you will not be stirred
Like pigeons sitting on these streetlamps
Still dimly blurred

And onward in the journey one comes to understand
These visions type you and hype you
Wherever one seems to turn
Like the lights of the swallowing city
With its enticing eyes
Can become deathlike at times
And the burnin' hope inside us all
Is the only light in these dark woods
The tranquil of the night
The strength from time alone
The love that blankets your will

Thomas Di Maria
HIDDEN LEAVES

In this motion of thought
Tightly entrenched
Hides
Something hidden beneath my face
Thoughts covered by leaves drooping shy and unseen
Unstirred
Where the trees grow high
Glittering dreams and naked truths
Obsessions hidden in the shade
Some without human meaning and feeling
So much accumulated within
Impulsed from a heart painted black

And like drops of rain
That slowly weave their weary paths
A harvest is gradually blown
Years pass
But only the frailest leaves
Are dared to be exposed

Thomas Di Maria
COLD WINDS AND WARM EYES

The wind is blowing coldly now, I can barely smile
Reflecting upon times gone by and their drifting wires
It was not too long ago I met you in tainted attire
I was looking for the sunshine
The warmth in your eyes.

In looking upon the prickly road
That's blown from hell to here
They say not to ever drift back
Strength nurturing from reflection?
Just tears among the years
But in the end one can laugh standing silent and wide-eyed
A newborn breath
Life at the end of death
A vision at the end of the tier

So we live our lives and dream our dreams
Never hesitating to put aside
The winds that blow inside our souls
to triumph above the times
And maybe I can make you laugh
Reflect edit or cry
On the search for the sunshine
The warmth in your eyes

Hugh Wallace
SIN SNIFFERS

Dedicated to Bob Wallace, Lake Stevens, Washington.

A wonderous organ is the nose;
Great for smelling the rose.
  But, some do differ,
  Being a sin sniffer!
So, be on your toes!

One, with such a nose,
Before a mirror did pose.
  His nose did grow.
  Then glow with a golden glow!
So, now you know, the nose knows!

When these noses die
They just hie to the sky!
  O' nosey noses, so bright!
  How you make the sky so light!
Glory to your panoply on high!

Hugh Wallace
OWL HOUSE BLUES

The Spotted Owl
Let out a howl!
  (Being a Howl Owl,
  Not a Hoot Owl)
"I'm being treated most Fowl!"

"Bunyan Bobs
Worry about jobs,
  While baby owls
  Tote teary towels
From homeless sobs!"

"They don't give a hoot
When we have to scoot!
  We catch their mice
  And treat them nice,
And we get the boot!"

Claudine Ericksen
SPRING

The blue sky is dotted with fleecy clouds
Like sails on a peaceful sea.
The sun sheds its golden glory
O'er hill and dale and lea.

The trees are alive with bursting buds,
And the tiny leaves are green,
Soon the apple will burst into radiant bloom;
And the brooks have a silver sheen.

In the lilac bush 'mid the fragrant clusters
Of sleepy, half opened flowers,
A robin sings his carols sweet
To the tune of April Showers.

And down in the pond where the rushes grow,
A frog pipes his high shrill song,
For the spring has come in her prettiest guise,
Bringing new life along.

Claudine Eriksen
TROUT FISHING

As we forced our way up the gurgling stream
  One summer morn
The Forest Carpet was a silver sheen,
  That summer morn.
The woodpecker hammered the dead beech trees;
The linden blossoms were raided by bees;
A brown thrush sang his song to please
  That summer morn.
Dewdrops hung on the grass like tears
Bushes were old men weighted with years
  That summer morn!
The blue violet snuggled down under the leaves;
Tall ferns were bending on trembling knees;
And a drip-like rain came from the trees
  That summer morn!
But the brook trout raised to the new fly hatch
And we had lures that would surely match,
Our long rods flashed as we spotted our flies

But not one wiley trout would give us a rise;
So we called it a day—and the morn as our prize,
That summer morn.

Patricia Tury
A BUTTERFLY
The silent shadow on
the shore,
And wispy, weaves of waves
and more,
Of summer threads that
pass us by;
And weave a shadow
from the sky.
The shadow of a butterfly.

Sybil Smith
MY PRAYER
Help me with every decision i make,
The Course in life that I must take.
Let me be generous, loving, and kind.
May I live by your will and not by mine.

Make me an example of your precious love,
So no one will ever doubt there's a God above.
Help us to always give Praise to you,
You are the One to whom Praise is due.

L Ganatos
GRATITUDE
Thank you Mr. President for all that you have done;
You sent the troops to Panama and now the war is won.
In every situation you always know what's right;
To catch the wicked General you sent the troops by night.
In planes and helicopters they flew so very high
Dropping their bombs on target to light the nighttime sky.
The tallest buildings in the land were suddenly leveled flat;
The army sifted through the ruins to hunt the last dingbat.
Two dozen youthful soldiers in coffins were brought dead.
Now you hold the culprit whose underwear was red
Inside the Nunciatura; the troops do guard him well,
Ensuring he won't cast another evil spell.
Of "Operation Just Cause" we can be very proud;
They serenade the General with music that is loud.
Last summer you went fishing but barely caught a fish
Because the sport of hunting turned out to be your dish.
Nobody can say you're aging and that your spirit's limp;
Your Panamanian strategy showed all you are no wimp.
A country full of ruins that are invasion made,
Awaits to be rebuilt with Yankee dollar aid.

R V Lipscomb
WHY
Why is it that when babies are born they cry?
Is it that they come into our world sad, naked and alone?
Is it that they can smell the disillusion and the frustration and the fear?
Is it that they dread to leave their world to be met by the ugly pain of ours?
Why is it that babies are afraid to be born?
Why is it that their parents are afraid to die?

Edna M Selby
WHEN IT'S WINTER, ON THE RIVER
When it's winter on the river,
and the sun is sinking low
The summer birds have vanished
and the winds begin to blow

There's a special time of quietness
you can feel it in the air, and the
Autumn leaves are falling. Blowing
gently everywhere.

It's as if the earth is resting, in
a veil of winter Peace. Where
the noises of the summer long
ago have ceased.

The ice is slowly forming where
the water meets the sand. And it's
winter on the river, And it's
white across the land.

Kathy Sand
EAGLE'S LOVE
Star lite, Star brite
As an Eagle's in flight,
within the sparkle of the eye.
To spread their wings as to
soar so high.
Purity of freedom has to
feel so right.
Star lite, Star brite

Pure beauty within an Eagle's life
Inspiring strength power of
integrity, purity to breath.
As I look up from down beneath.
Wishing for such durability.

Star lite, Star brite
Grant me Lord though I see, where
the Eagle's life should remain to be.
So please remember me Lord, after I
die you see.
I would Love to think as, an
Eagle's life as me.
Star lite, Star brite

Heart's Love Of
Kathy Sand

Joni Cheah
COUNTRY BEDROOM
You can find it in the country
Where the flowers grow in pretty
ridges along the sand
beside the sea.
The clouds run along in the purple light
across the night
And in the day they shine in the sunlight.
I'd love to live in my country bedroom.

Gloria Matheson
ODE TO HAPPINESS
Happiness is my one desire,
To think of it I would never tire.
A little place that's free of pain,
To walk down a country lane.
A place to think in peace and quiet,
Away from the city where there's riots.
The simple pleasures of life's beauty,
Will last forever if we do our duty.
How many bridges must we cross,
Before we find we're not lost.
Over the horizon dawns a new day,
Right your wrongs without delay.
Do God's work and he'll think it's grand,
That you could give him a helping hand.
Life can be an enigma, no rules or charts,
For only happiness, comes from the heart.

Louis A Albini
GRATITUDE
I found a fledgling in the field one day.
With wounded wing it nestled in my hand, a cup of velvet gray.
Beneath the feathered breast a weakened pulse kept static time,
And filled my heart with discord and dismay.
I gave it strength and even more, a love that lengthened day by day,
And little dreamed that lions once were cubs.
When succoured with my blood the hawk grew strong,
I blindly watched its talons tear my heart.

Jimmye Kay Hendrick Hensley
ALONE
Alone, what does it mean?
Is it a feeling?
Or maybe a fear.
Can you tell me?

I'm beginning to realize,
It's a type of isolation.
You're cut off,
In a world of silence.

It's seeing happiness,
And not feeling it.
It's hearing words of love,
Not spoken to you.

It's hearing a name,
And feeling sadness.
It's missing him,
Not knowing where he's at.

Please hear me calling.
Answer if you can.
Love me if you're able,
I don't want to be alone.

Carrie A Eckerley
SOUNDS OF THE HEART
My heart beats
each beat is without an echo
I feel you,
but you are no longer in reach
How can I make an echo?
I am without feeling.
Dying, uncared for with no one near
I was wrong to hurt you
please come back
I am without an echo
A leaf in the wind
a grain of sand
settling to the ocean floor—
I am lost without your love.

Paul J DuPont
LITTLE PAULIE
Once there was a little boy
who brought me lots of joy.
Even though he was quite small,
In my eyes he stood ten feet tall.
In many ways he looked like me,
and brought to me a heart full of glee.
He was my precious son.
With him life was so much fun.
Then one day he died
and I cried and cried and cried.
His death had broken my heart
and my life had fallen apart.
But all is not lost
because Jesus paid the cost.
I will see him again I pray
in that place which is fairer than day

Juliet D Quevedo
MAMA
This poem is dedicated to my beloved mother.

Nine months in your womb,
you carried me with pride and glory
smiles and happiness was on your face
life you gave me, love you showered me
caress and tender touch I felt,
Oh! I didn't know that the baby would be me.

Nine months, I made you suffer,
I made you sacrifice for my life
I made you shed a tear because of pain
I made you nervous whether you and I will live
When the time comes for me to exist,
But thank God, you and I were both safe and alive.

But those nine months of your sufferings Mama,
were totally gone and blown away by the wind,
Because, I was such a lovely baby then . . .
Mama, your sacrifices,
hardships and miseries will never be forgotten,
For without you Mama, I should have not seen the beauty of the World.

William Christopher (Chris) Humble

Maxine Humble
FOR FRIENDS AND CLASSMATES
Dedicated to all teenagers.

The leaves are children
of the trees:
and Chris, a child of man.
We loved you Chris,
and wherever we go,
Part of us is gone:
that part is you.
For sixteen years
you were mortal:
living in a mortal world,
but today you are immortal:

living in an immortal world.
We who loved you,
can close our eyes and
see you: As you were mortal:
called back by memory
and recollection.
Some day Chris when we
meet, beyond the blue:
there will be no pressures,
and sorrows pushing us
forever away from you.
So now we thank the Lord,
for the short time we had
you: and by the grace of God,
some day we will meet you:
somewhere, beyond the blue.

M L Dunbar
ARIAN AMOUR
O, passion, thou scorching flame of desire,
Touch not this reluctant Soul.
Let thy searing ecstasies pass me by.
Impugn the wanton moiré.

Nay, I have no wish for transient raptures,
Nor do I crave brimming cups of cassé.
The abyss lies darkly waiting
For him who ascends for the marotté.

Save for me the tranquilities of love,
Born of simple artemesian esteem.
Cloaked in tender, diurnal intimacies
of living, touching, sharing love.

Marla J Dahl
TOTALLY CONFUSED
Sitting alone at a table for four, with just one cup of coffee . . .
Waiting for you and rewinding the past . . .
The years have certainly thrown a few boomerangs on you and me,
And we've been intertwined by threads of love that last.
We have this strange, unique bond between us that somehow stands out when one of us needs the other, in any way . . .
I think it's strange how our feelings unfold when needed and respected and how you can unleash so much of my trust, night or day.
As if on command, you look my way—and as if tongueless—I don't know what to say.
It angers me sometimes because I feel helpless, almost a victim . . .
Unknowingly, you cast a spell with your blue eyes that I always recognize.
And though we've been with others throughout the years,
There are times my feelings scare me, for though you love me and I know it's true,
I wonder how much and to what extent you really do.
I've known you long and intimately, yet I'm afraid to let go and truly allow you into my heart and on that thought, my eyes fill with tears.
I am afraid to allow myself the possible wonderment of fully loving you,
In every degree and in all possible ways, I want to . . . but something always holds me back . . .
It's either my fear or yours, who knows?
I think I'm singing the "Want you but scared to death whoas!"
What a mess! Wad it up into a ball
and none of it makes any sense at all!
I'm totally confused you see . . . Is there any way you could possibly help me?

Patt E MacDowell
NOTHING'S EVER EASY
Bewildering is the ambience which envelops
my very being.
The mannerisms of life: those good and those bad
invade my mind's liberty.
Former experiences restraining new ones.
Hopeless to habour; haunting forever. Similarities encroach upon me, forcing
denial, confusion, regression.
Serenity within is gone,
previous feelings, critically revamped. Encompassed by demands, surpassing capabilities.
Encore intensely eluded-uncertainty prevails.
Loathing the risk, sacrificing reward.
Nothing's ever easy, no one said it was.

Mildred E Howard
SEASONS
It was a breezy spring night
And the setting was just right.
Couldn't ask for anything better
'Cause he seemed like a girl getter.

Summer came pretty fast,
And I thought, how long could this last?
It felt so good, warm and tender
That all I could do was just to surrender.

In the fall things are sweet,
and nothing could stop us when we meet.
Everything is going your way
and the night seems to say stay.

Winter has its warm pleasures
and you keep them like treasures
But winter is long and cold
And Love is very hard to hold . . .

Marilyn Roy
AMERICAN SOLDIERS ARE DYING
War has broken out in Panama and there is fighting all around
The people are looting in the stores there is no peace to be found
There are American soldiers who are giving up their lives dying in the line of duty with dignity and pride
They have served their country with love for all mankind
Bringing peace and some order to control crime
Our men are over there not knowing if they will live
For the blood they are shedding their sacrifice they give
We need to stand together and hold our flag high
For our American soldiers who are there to die
To capture Noriega and have him stand trial
The American people are standing behind the president through this for awhile
The president had to take action for the crime
For people were being killed this time

Virginia Ogline
THE BEGGAR
As I walk down the road I see,
The beggar standing there.
Can you spare a dime or maybe two?
I stop and I stare, but then I'm compelled to share with this man
I don't even know.
I look into his eyes, as I hand him the coin.
Without a word, I know I've been blessed.
As I walk further on,
I turn and he's gone.
The question comes into my mind,
Could it have been the Master
Asking for my dime?

Gigi Rodgers
THERE'S NOTHING YOU CAN DO TO MAKE A MOMENT LAST
There's nothing you can do
to make a moment last
no matter how hard you try.

You can hope and pray
with all your heart
that time would
take wings and fly.

But it's not that way,
unfortunately,
so wipe those tears from your eyes

No one said it would be easy
to stand alone
and face that inevitable
good-bye!

Jeffrey Levine
TO WRITE
We know some poems will never win,
but that's not why we send them in.

To write is what we like to do,
to make words rhyme with beauty through.

To save a piece of what we are,
to give life meaning from afar.

We write of shores, of sand and time,
the things in life that are sublime.

Of people, places, thought and truth,
this is the measure of our worth.

A simple word can change the space,
between our differences of race.

A loving thought can heal a wound,
make life's true nature stay in bloom.

A gentle rain, a winter's wind,
this is where our lives begin.

To see the pattern of our days,
in simple things that pass our way.

For when we write we fill that space,
that occupies the human race.

Susan Buol
THE ROSE
A single rose bud
so fragrant and delicate,
Brilliantly red
against the cool green grass.
It stands alone
against the night's crisp breeze.
Morning comes
The dawn of a new day,
and the rose bud has bloomed
to its fullest.
Winter is near
The days shorten
and the rose slowly dies
Leaving behind only fallen petals
on the moist ground,
and the memories
of its sweet fragrance.

Deeann Polito
MY BROWN TEDDY BEAR
It keeps me company through the long hours of the night.
The brown fur is mangled,
The arm has a tear,
but knowing it's with me gives me a sense
of comfort and understanding.
This bear is like a shield to me
protecting and giving me courage.
Without him,
I would be lost
In a world
without feeling.

Pegi Smith
ONE WHITE DAISY

Keith and Carol—May your life together be blessed with Sunshine and Petals of Love.

My Garden is such a wondrous place
with its palate of multi-hued petals.
I sit for hours enriched by
the hibiscus, so vivid, in yellows and orange,
the sweet peas of lavender and pinks, so serene.
Today, as I gaze upon 'One' White Daisy
I feel a special warmth of sunshine.
There is strength in this Daisy's stem,
holding it tall above the daffodils.
Its outstretched leaves beckon
a delicate ladybug to rest.
The bright yellow center reminds me
of the man in the moon,
the stamen forming the twinkle in its eye.

Surely, this 'One' Daisy holds my answer.
Carefully removing the petals I find;
the first is gentle to my tug,
a softness to my touch on the second,
a temperament as the next one resists,
yet, a gentle gasp as the last is extracted.

Yes . . . He Loves Me!

Julie Marie Baker
A TEAR IN MY EYE
A tear in my eye
No reason to cry
A day went by
I wish I could fly
A faraway place
A wide open space
A capture of beauty

A gust of the wind
The sound of the trees
The branches to bend
The birds in the sky
The clouds floating by
The water flows gently
The mountains stand high.

Donna Marie Sweeney
MY MOMENTARY RAINBOW
At times I Loved .
At times I lost .
But always buried deep within .
My loss .

My child lived before she died .
My child lived after she
died .
She lived without rage or pain or
silence unencumbered .

She lived as a rainbow lives , very
briefly , very fleetingly ,
very quickly .

Her moments were a Lifetime .
Her lifetime, but a moment .

I loved her .
I love her .
I'll love her always .

I need to be the best I can be
to live in the shadow of a life
lived perfectly in the shadow
of a momentary rainbow .

Ada S McCoy
THE COMING DAY
There is coming a day
a great and awful day,
When the Bridegroom as a thief;
steals His Bride away . . .
Such weeping there will be,
such running to and fro . . .
People searching for their loved ones,
Oh! where have they gone?

They've gone to a Wedding Supper,
There's a marriage up on high;
The trump of God has sounded
and split the Eastern sky . . .
The Glory Cloud came rolling,
names were called
from within . . .
It was the voice of the Bridegroom
gathering His Bride to Him.

From the four-winds they will gather,
when He calls them by name . . .

Saints alive will not hinder
those asleep in the grave,
At the sound of the trumpet
they'll come forth with a shout
Oh, grave where's your victory?
God's power is taking me out.

Mark Oniboni
TIME
Time past beyond years
Lie still the night and day
We seem still but
death is drawn nearer
In our mind we are still
not what we want to be
As time goes on it is too late
for change.

Diane Staiano
A POEM
I tried to write a Poem
but
it died
so I buried it.

I tried to write another one
but
the letters switched themselves
around
to form words other than
those I had intended:
"Letter Liberation!
Alphabets of the world UNITE!"

So, I tried to write a third poem
but
those letters escaped
and ran off the page.

So, I wrote this.

Charlotte F Madrid
STREETS OF GOLD
There's a City above
That I've been told
That has many Mansions
And streets of Gold

In this beautiful City
There are angels that sing
With love all around
And bells that ring

In this City up above
There will be no more sorrow
No more tears
And no more tomorrow

The people will all be happy
And, will never grow old
In this beautiful City
With the streets of Gold

Karen J Johnson
P.H.D. REQUIRED
P.H.D. . . . required
To endure the fire
Let these three
My virtues be
P., H., D., . . .
Patience . . . leads to endurance
Humility . . . is the door to
Knowledge
And the gateway to
Wisdom
Devotion . . . is the Key to the
Kingdom . . .
Awaken the Physician in me . . .
Seeking my P.H.D.
Let these three
My virtues be . . .
To Endure the Fire . . .
P.H.D . . . Required

Laima Kontautas

Laima Kontautas
OTEMPORA OMORES

My special poem is dedicated to my dearest friend, David Stevens, the accountant.

Otempora, Omores!
Life is weaved on such short stories
As fast as today and tomorrow.
A cradle rocking with a baby
Music song of babyhood lullaby.
Otempora, Omores!
Life is Colorful.
Just like fiction and stories
On such short basics to
understand.

The day you do,
The day you wonder,
If that is true
The life I knew.

Baby stop Crying,
Music stop playing,
Old age grey hair shining
Like silver mountain in the
moonlight.

Otempora, omores!
Where are those days!
Days were not used,
Did I save them? is there such as?

A coffin little closet,
Inside is I!.
There are no extra days,
It seems I used them all.

Thank you my lord,
For those good days
I have been used
Indeed I did, I used them well.

Maxine Ringwald
HOLIDAYS OF YORE
I remember the holidays of long ago,
Cardinals so red-decorated the snow.
Everything inside was cozy and
warm,
Each and every room was adorned.

I was busy as I could be,
Making cookies, candies and
decorating the tree.
Christmas packages wrapped in
holiday hue,
Oh, my—so much to do.
The table was beautifully set.
It looked like a picture that had been
sketched.

The aroma from the kitchen of
everything good,
The compliments I loved to
hear—
And everyone shouting, "Merry
Christmas—Happy New Year!"

I can't turn back the time—I wish I
could.
Those days and the people are in the
past—
Gone for good.
I am alone now, but I won't waste my
time on grief and pity.
I'll just make a sandwich—and hum
a Christmas ditty.
Then, I'll stack my memories on a
shelf
And wish a Merry Christmas to
myself.

"MERRY CHRISTMAS!"

Alma Mikelsons
TODAY
Today, today I'm still here.
Today the sun is shining outside
And reflects its beams in my
heart.

Today my voice is ringing
And breath I'm taking deeply.

Today, still here, I can pray for
someone.
Today, today too let me do
some little good
If only for the smallest creature
of Yours.

Stacey L Randolph
YOU'RE SPECIAL TO ME
You're so very special to me,
And that's the way it will
always be.
You always help me, you're always
there,
I know how much you really
care.
I really do care a lot about you,
This comes from my heart, and
it's very true.
You are still very special to me,
I hope you know that, I hope
you can see.
If everyone had a special mom like
me,
They don't know how lucky
they would be.
You gave me all the love you had,
I'm so grateful, and so very
glad.
I really miss you alot, you're the best
mom there is,
And you're all I got.
I love you, mom!

Suzanne M Volpe
REALIZATION
I wander aimlessly through this thing
called existence,
Clinging tenaciously to the tattered
threads of fragmented dreams.
Struggling through blackest moods of
listless longing,
Wishing always wishing, but never
daring to burst forth
From the carefully forged bonds of
my invisible prison.

Yearning for an instantaneous
transformation
That will somehow alter my barren
destiny,
Yet, unwilling to make a move to
effect the change,
Dangling suspended in the world of
living
Not dead, but never truly alive, I
remain inert.

Tormented and tantalized by what I
permit my blinded eyes to glimpse
And moving rapidly toward timeless
eternity
With nothing to shield me from its
merciless stab,
I stand apart—
Alone and lonely.

My anguished soul's unuttered pleas
lie withered on my tongue,
Crushed against my teeth.
I have but to reach out, yet, I am
paralyzed.
Security in the known, in the present,
in the familiar,
In the me that I am now, is my
constant and possessive jailor.

M Brent Foxwell
DRIVE TO ARRIVE
Anything you want, can be won,
I know, this can be done.
So just believe you can do it,
As you set your mind to it,
And do your best, to push yourself
through it.
Another thing that's no doubt
essential,
Is confidently knowing, you have the
potential.

Ok, so what, it's true.
You've got to work hard, at what you
do,

If you wish to make it through.
Now that you're sure which path is
for you,
Do your best to keep solidly driving
on,
And in doing so, you soon will be
arriving on,
The top.
Don't stop, driving on!

Deborah J Mack
THOUGHT WAVES
It is synonymous, the quiet time
spent;
while one probes the thoughts of his
ways.
Riding upon the crest of a wave,
there's a million in the ocean some
days.

Each hits shore with impeccable
power;
time turned inward, the desirable
hour.
In masking the common-stroke of
breath;
blown in by the wind, for its
purposeful death.

Maneuver the surf, then ride it in;
and consider the wave to come.
Allow the moment its place in your
mind;
and ride only the crests of some.

Strength immensely those you
control;
and muse at those that take you.
Many are those that will challenge
your mind;
and be certain they'll always be new.

James A Kuhta
ARISING DESTINY
Sea
dogs
sleep.
Lady luck's
cryptic whisper drifts,
far off.
Sultry grip, of
warm flagons and
plundered ballast.

Sextant sky,
erred one degree,
charts misty myths
of sunken skeletons;
Afloat,
The edge of dreams . . . .

Kathleen L Steinman
SAYING GOOD-BYE ONCE, NICE
You used to know the meaning of life
and cared so much about me.
When you took me for your beloved
wife, you told me that you loved me.
As years went by you lost your love
but still told me you cared.
I believed in you for oh so long and
remembered all we'd shared.
I didn't know then how you felt, and
you never really told me.
But I thought these years we were
happy and that you still loved me.
We were bound by a commitment
paper that says we're man and wife.
But if you are so unhappy that is no
way to spend your life.
I would give you all the freedom that
I possibly could.
I would always feel the same way,
although you never would.
I'm unhappy but not bitter and think
I'll be OK.
But now it's time for you to leave
and good-bye is hard to say.
Before you go there is something our
discussions always lacked.
If you decide to come around I'll
never take you back.
I will never bear the hell again of
saying good-bye twice.
So I will just leave it like this and say
good-bye once, nice.

Rob Teune
DROUGHT
The searing heat
Of that eternal furnace
Burns down
—blistering the ground
with its scorching rays.
Baking the torrid earth,
scalding the cracked
parched land of drought.
(lashing great scars
in once green pastures)

That molten orb
which is the author of life,
is also the finisher of life,
Incinerating man's pride,
singeing withered crops,
Creating famine,
where there was once fertility,
—death where there was life,
—poverty where there was wealth,
(and) sorrow where happiness once
reigned.

Melissa W Woods
BAD LUCK
I've been recently fired
from my job at the store
and that's just the beginning,
Listen, there's more

The rent hasn't been paid
the electric bill is due,
Our dog got ran over
and little Susie has the flu.

The water pipes froze
and burst overnight,
The car won't start
Nothing is going right!

My wife went to the doctor
and he eagerly replied,
"Guess what Mrs. Smith?,
the rabbit has died!"

Bad luck isn't supposed to be real
at least that's what people say,
So could someone please inform me
on just what has come my way?

Jennifer J Schroeder
WALL
While I live through each day,
I am dying.
My calloused heart relies on a weary
body
which cannot support life.
A golden ring lies beyond my brick
wall—
unreachable.
I am in isolation,
Away from the rest of the world
And my wall stands strong.
I reach out for love and caring
but my wall is thick.
I cry out for help—my wall stands
strong.
Penetration through my wall is
impossible
But the foundation has been shaken
and I am afraid that soon,
my wall will crumble.
Who will help me when my life
crumbles?
My friends try to help now—
But my wall stands strong.

Martha L Langford
MY STEADFAST LOVE
To Bill, my loving husband.

How long before my heart forgets,
The memory of your tender kiss?
Before my mind dismisses your every
way,
Or I cease to think of you each day.
I feel the empty nights your
tenderness will bring,
And the sad songs lonely birds sing.
My aching heart this pain will always
know
As each bright star in radiance glow.
How long before each sweet refrain,
Refuses to repeat your name?
I sense the lovely flowers your
secrets will ever give,
And you in my heart forever live.
When all on earth becomes inert,
And guardian angels their dutiful
watch desert,
While all grows cold, under the sun's
warm glow,
Then, and only then, my love you
will not know.

Dolli
GOODBYE
This is for someone special who I didn't get a chance to say good-bye to. Till we meet again on the other side . . . .

As I watch you just lie there and slip
away.
I think of all the things left unsaid,
of all the things we've yet to do and
wonder just how unfair this world
was to you.

Do you hear me, do you know I'm
here?
All the sleepless nights that I stand
here with you.
I remember . . .

I remember joy in your face when
you took your first steps.

I remember the tears your first day of
school,
when I walked away.

I remember the day you saw Santa
Claus come out of the chimney, in his
bright red suit and full white beard.

O how I remember . . . all the tears
and the laughter.

But most of all, as I look at you
laying there I remember the last time
I saw you awake, and the fear in your
eyes. How I wanted to run to you and
protect you, to make everything all
right.

You did not understand what was so
terribly wrong.
What you could have done to deserve
a punishment so cruel and final. How
do I tell you that I love you, how do I
say good-bye.

As you lie here now so frail and
helpless, so small and pale
almost invisible against the sheets, I
know that I will remember your
smile, your laugh, or the simple
delight you felt about being alive.

You sigh for the last time and fade
into the night, I bend to touch your
cheek to mine. And my tears flow
ever so slowly as I say GOODBYE.

Patricia R Hundley
REFLECTIONS FROM AN AUCTION
I spent today at an old homeplace,
Vacant now, with a shuttered face;
The contents of its house and barn
Set out for view on the weed-choked
lawn
For bargain hunters come to buy
And the idly curious such as I.
Who will find a treasure?

While wandering 'round I found a
tray
Of odds and ends to be cast away:
A smiling face in a tarnished frame
Once loving and loved, but without a
name;
A china cat with a glued-on tail,
A toy boat with a tattered sail.
Who will save these treasures?

Their stories, sadly, be unknown,
Lost, like the lives that shared this
home.
I took the cat which I've placed with
care
In a window nook with my teddy
bear
And other cherished souvenirs
Of precious moments through the
years . . .
Who will find my treasures?

Didi Gibbs
BALSAM MOUNTAIN
To Grandma Rice who taught me the beauty of the Blue Ridge.

My Nikes got soaked and dried, like
my skin, in the sun.
The bronze-green rocks slipped under
my feet,
but still the river was soft.
The sun's fingers picked at the
water's shadow
and sparkled it to its silvery morning
life.
And I sat drenched.

The eagle swam so deep in the sky,
drenched
with mockery at our sight. His wings
were tangent to the sun and they
toasted his sumptuous life.
If only I could revoke all rights to my
feet
and abscond with his wings and
ornate shadow
into the sky, intertwining with
gravity's age and softness.

Grandfather Mountain approached
and once again my Nikes rejoined my
feet.

Two mounds sharing a single vein
with shadows
of blood pumped across. We were
drenched
with excitement; dropping the life
from rocks. We learned of sea level
and witnessed the softness
of the sleeping valleys coaxed to
dreams under the sun.

The sun's soft mothering of the
mountains brought life
to every shadow, I was drenched and
mothered too and
enjoyed soaking my feet in its
embellished, simple existence.

Sonia McPherson
EACH OTHER
Late at night
When I close my eyes
I can only think of you
And everything else that lies.
We are both separated
While you're still ahead
You and I both have
A lot of things to be said
I truly love you
If you could only see
How deeply my love is for you
That's where my heart will always
be!

Leathia R Siewert

Leathia R Siewert
BONNEFOI

To Mother, Alice Jirak, who was a blessed lady and friend.

Mundane lies give me verjuice;
Dishearten and bind me in anger.
White lies foster mistrust.
Cursory stories can only blear.
To lie in one's throat causes deuce.

Exalted truth may cause fear
But creates good faith and sets me
free.
Builds a supereminent character.
Probity I wish to always hear.
Honest always, even if there is no
glee.

Leathia R Siewert
A MACABRE TALE OF A FLY
It was so gruesome
How it happened to die
So misfortunate to sit on the loam;
Poor thing, the unsuspecting fly.

One swift tweaking wrist jerk
With a swatter like a dirk
A broken-hearted baby fly is left all
alone;
Crying for his dead Mother is lying
prone.

Leathia R Siewert
TORNADO OF LOVE
Love is to paradise
As the sun shines
After a tornado
Corn all twisted and bent
Yesterday stately and tall
Beautiful in its own way
Leaves whispering in the gentle
breeze

Paradise comes, paradise goes
And the sun shines no more
A misunderstanding twisted
And bent paradise
Like corn razed by a tornado
Paradise is twisted and bent
And is no more

Leathia R Siewert
TREASURED MEMORIES
When the March gale puffed across
the plains
I churned in turmoil like an endless
roller coaster.
You gave to me a treasured gift—ten
minutes of your time.
Thanks for the peaceful comforting
touch of your kindness.

When the September gust snatched
the maple leaves from their branches
In tempestuous times not unlike the
violent wind of a typhoon
You shared, you cared, you had the
time to give a treasured memory.
May God eternally preserve your
peaceful comforting touch.

Andre L Evans
HER PUPPET
Joyfully does she abide.
The puppet, there by her side.
Like a child she will guide
the puppet. There by her side.

Her life through him she'll live it
through.
Abreast. Together, they make two.
Decisions she'll say what he should
do.
The puppet his life, gone down the
tubes.

In her life, all is grand.
Her life. His life. Hand in Hand.
Only from him will she demand.
The puppet, "It's time to take a
stand."

To clip the cords from his life.
To be rid of the dreaded domineering
knife.
To move freely from delusion and
mother's strife.
To live and let life be his wife.

But never. Real life she will hide
the puppet there by her side.
The two, now one, will not divide.
The puppet still there by her side.

Diane Jean Bousquet Young
WAR . . . AMEN!
WAR is hard on soft small faces
marked by grime and teary traces.
WAR is crying, of young and old, the
healthy, and the scared, and the
dying, untold.
WAR is hunger and thirst, for
fighting peoples far worse.
WAR is pain, in heart, in soul, in
body, and in mind.
WAR is cold and harsh, uncaring and
unkind.
WAR is a tool used only by political
tools.
WAR is the end, of all we know and
then..........................AMEN.

Sheila Orange
ANYTHING
I'd give anything,
to be yours again
anything . . .
but more than a friend
I'd give anything,
to kiss your face
anything . . .
for your warm embrace.
I'd do anything
for you,
you mean so much,
anything . . .
just to feel your touch.
I gave you everything
including my heart,
but everything just fell apart.

Ginger E Wade
PEACE OF EMOTION
Alone, somewhat at peace
Yet there is no peace

As if I fight a war within myself
It is two adverse feelings

Another day is about to begin
The sun is rising . . . Yellow, Orange,
Red

The whole world is in its routine
People awake, to go about their daily
business

But the day I start is not routine
Today marks an emotion

An emotion which is all new
One of pain, with a cause

Pain with a cause
Almost without reason

My love has left me
Not physically—but within

My mind has run rapid
It has run a different direction

Run, alone . . . where there is no
peace.

Helen M Evans
BY YOUR SIDE

For my grandma, Helen M. McCoid.

I'll be there, right by your side
although you may not see me.
And if the future should start to look
grim
close your eyes and therein an

answer will be.
But if the light appears to call you
home
then you must go without me.
But be assured when it's my turn
I will once again stand beside
thee.

Rebecca Ann Giles
I SEE YOU

To Linda, for believing in me.

I see you, though miles separate us,
I feel you, though nearness seems so
far away. I touch you with the
closeness of memories. I see you.
I hold you with the embrace of
tenderness. I kiss you with the soft
whisperings of the night. You move
me with your love, I see you.
I walk with you in every step you
take. I awake in the opening of dawn
with you fresh in my mind. You are
there, in every constant moment of
my days. I need you, stay with me,
and await my return. I live for you,
with every breath I take, every move
I make, I see you.

Rebecca Ann Giles
FLEETING FREEDOM
See it, slipping away, you
grasp, moments never last, you live
the past, a chance, fleeting freedom

There is justice, retribution,
open spaces, steel bars in front of me.
Fleeting freedom.

Lovers, two as one.
Divided, become undone.
Laughter in the rain,
Silent tears in vain.
Reality, painful illusions.
Fleeting freedom.

Lucille Cast Mowat
TRANSPLANTED

In loving memory of my dear sister, Alice, who has been "transplanted" to that Fairer Land.

In God's beautiful garden of lives
Each one of us is a flower
Planted by Him upon this earth
To bloom in our finest hour.

As tender young seedlings at birth,
We grow in the warmth of His
love
Towards maturity day by day,
While He watches us from above.

But the Gardener's plans are to us
Somewhat of a mystery,
For here with His other plantings,
We know not how long we may
be.

He takes us away at His choosing—
Some early and some in our
prime—
And we ponder the reason, as others
He leaves for a longer time.

But whether just budding or faded,
Those flowers removed by His
hand
Aren't plucked but only transplanted
To ever bloom on in a fairer land.

Lucille Cast Mowat
YOUR WORLD AND MINE
There are many little worlds
In this big one that we're on—
Not just places 'round the globe,
But in the lives of everyone.

Each one lives in his own realm
As he goes about his day—
Toiling, dreaming, loving, caring,
In his individual way.

Yet as parts of separate spheres,
With yours diverse from mine,
We find our worlds oft overlap;
Our paths converge or intertwine.

And however brief the meeting,
Or how slightly we may touch,
Because we need each other,
This can mean so very much.

For at the points of sharing,
Side by side and heart to heart,
We lend strength to one another,
Though in some ways worlds apart.

James G McMullen Jr

Kathy M Shealy

ELUSIVE TRUTHS

For my brother James, whose footprints will always be upon the sands of every ocean in the world.

Sparks fly home.
Every time you touch me
the aftermath of loneliness
knocks holes
in the facade
of my "cemented" walls survival.
Fortifications?
Quivering masses of jello maybe
but heaving every principle
I ever teethed on.
And the earth trembles
untried feet, novices and fools
which am I . . .

Perhaps the rumble of the whole
suffices to describe
the tumult of my soul—
there is no solid ground for water walkers.
For even as we pass
the waves
the ever rolling waves
wipe our footprints from the sand
on cued command . . .

Christine Kay Wazinski

CRYSTAL'S PICTURE

To my niece, Crystal Lynn Wazinski: Thank you for your love. Love, Aunt Tina.

Crystal made a picture
And it hangs for all to see
A lady and a little girl
She said it's her and me.
Hearts float around us
Open arms in the air
Waiting for the love
That we've always shared.
Each day I think about her
And wish that she were here
The last time I had seen her
Has been more than a year.
Crystal's six years old now
And I wonder how she has grown
Photos can hide the truth
As do voices on the phone.
Crystal made a picture
And it hangs for all to see
A lady and a little girl
She said it's her and me.

Denise Collins

INSIGHTS OF THE MAN REV. DR. MARTIN LUTHER KING JR.

This poem I would like to dedicate to another very bright man; thank you, William.

Although he's been dead for many years
He was one black man who really tried
He was a civil rights leader before he died
People could not believe their ears
Because he was the man who fought their fears

Martin Luther King he really understood
If there was ever anything that he could do
It would be out of the love he feels for you
You may forgive a man who would
But never misjudge a man who could

Martin Luther King was very bright
He loved those who could and helped those who might
He was one black man who saw the light
And fought for things that were only right

Corrine V Olvera

SO BE INNOCENT MY BABY

I dedicate this poem to my son Jerimie and husband Paul, whom I love and cherish dearly.

I experienced a death in my heart today.
Oh my baby you've gone so far away.
Two months growing and caring for you,
Only seven more to go and we would have met you.
What happened, where did I go wrong?
Oh my baby, I guess it's where you belong.
I was told just one month ago you were just the beginning,
And told yesterday that your life was ending.
Your daddy and I grew to love you in thoughts,
But now only memories of our little babies forgots.
Oh my little one, we never even got to meet you
But all along we knew, you'd love your mommy and daddy too.
The thoughts of never meeting you is painful,
But the memories of loving you are beautiful.
So mommy and daddy say in their hearts,
My little mystery, you never really had a start.
So be innocent my baby.

Tara R Wilson (Age 13)

IF ONLY LOVE WOULD LAST

When I saw you that day so long ago
I found a love I just can't let go
One I thought would last forever
But now I see love doesn't last ever

When you pulled me close
It was such a soft touch
Now you just push me away
And it hurts so much

How can your feelings change so fast
Mine are the same as they were in the past
You say there is nothing wrong
So why aren't you singing our song

You look at her with wishing eyes
It doesn't take much to realize
You would rather be with her than me
But my love is too strong to set you free

As I look to the future
I think of the past
I would do anything
If our love would last

Marie Younger

MY MOTHER

Mom, it's hard to put into words, just how wonderful you are,
You are very special, above all mothers by far.
I'm so gifted and loved, by our dear Heavenly Father,
For he gave me you, so I will try to live up
to being your daughter.
One day I hope to be like you,
Beautiful in words, thoughts, and doings,
If I can achieve these goals,
then life's worth pursuing.

There's no greater joy in the world,
in my life I know,
than being a mother, with a family that loves her so.
Times get hard and life is rough.
Mother you're always there to help me through that stuff.
I would commend you highly for the mother that you are,
For you are bright and beautiful,
You are my shining star.
Mom, in everything you do, you do it well,
I'm just trying to let you know
that I think you're just swell.

Tami Hatcher

THOUGHTS FOR YOU

Reckless and hellbound,
stared and borrowing.
Moments passing
through life's stages,
thoughts and times
endearing,
and memories forgotten.
So are my thoughts for
you.

Jennifer Carson

OREO

Black and white
as different as
day and night,
and yet the same
nothing to gain.
She's both with
feelings,
dreams,
and though it
seems
hard,
unfair,
that mass of curly hair
betrays her.
She doesn't know
what to do,
so she's out
there feeling
blue.
She's both the cookie
and the cream,
a very bad dream.
So wherever you are
or wherever you go
remember that girl
alone,
lost,
frightened,
for she's
still
that oreo.

John K Crawford

SIMPLICITY

For those, like myself, who sometimes desire a simpler age.

Simplicity is wonderful—
Essentials—nothing more.
Resist the urge to showiness—
Essentials—that we swore!

Simplicity—partake the cue
And strive for safety's sake.
Well, harken to the primness, here—
Austerity we take.

The generations come and go—
Our tastes solidify
Until eruptions overflow
And crimson hits the sky.

We find we're in a different age—
Abundance here, galore!
With gingerbread about the page—
Essentially—nothing more (?)

John K Crawford

DAY IS NIGHT * BLACK IS WHITE

It may be some are unaggressive—
You call them men?
Their natures—seemingly repressive
Will count to ten.

It may be others overshoot the mark—
You call them women?
Ha! Their superficial natures spark
But they're not always women.

It's hard enough to know the path, success
Without a falter
And now a code of ethics will suppress
Divinity—the altar.

No! No! I know not what you want
You intellectual.
The day is night. The black is white.
These taunt
The ineffectual.

Anthony Caughlin

TRUE LOVE

Patience is a virtue, this is true
But I will not be happy until I am with you.
I crave your company when we are apart,
Yet when we are together, I know not where to start.

Should I serenade you with poetry down on my knees?
Or should I take you in my arms and do as I please?

Hopefully, one day you will take notice of me.
Then I will no longer have to keep my feelings
for you under lock and key.
'Til then my love, I shall steady my heart;
but I shall not cease thinking of you
as a rare and priceless form of art.

Helena Wall Douros
I PASSED TODAY THE TEMPLE GATE
I passed today the Temple Gate . . .
At the corner of Temple Square
And there walked a man so thin and cold
My eye could only stare
The wind whipped the trouser around his leg
The cynical look the lady gave
As she shook her head a nay . . .
And carrying the bag, on she went
Into the Temple Gate
The stranger seated upon cement
A table for potted plant
And crossing his leg he looked about
Then spotted a well-dressed gent
And again the reply a negative one
Across the street . . . the gentleman went
The light turned green
And I sped along
But a tear filled my eye
How very similar the setting was
As that of the time of Christ
No alms for the poor . . . the hungry . . . the weak
All taxes secure in the vault
The success of a nation . . . the care of their own
And this has now come to a halt
The disgrace of a nation
The greatest on earth
The power of man . . . the extent of his worth
And no one considered at fault . . .

Troy Cheskaty
KING ARTHUR'S ROUND TABLE
But of all the things about King Arthur
Things that fascinate me the most
Are tales that come from the Round Table
That stalk through the
centuries like his ghost.

The table was a gift to Arthur!
At the time he took Guinevere
for his bride
It came from his father-in-law well graced,
For a hundred knights were
also seated by his side.

A hundred-fifty could be seated at the table
Imagine it in great splendor if
you can
The table heaped with food of every kind
Every chair taken by a brave
and handsome man.

A common bond that urged them on
To face dangers in the woods
and on the trail
Was to win against all the odds
And find the mysterious Holy
Grail.

When day was over or at the journey's end
Around the table, tales were
shared friend to friend
How the foe was beaten, the dragon, slain
How chivalry was spread
across hill and plain.

King Arthur had a smaller table, too
One that would seat a chosen few
To be good enough and brave enough to be one of twelve
Would be the greatest honor,
I think, don't you?

Lara Lynn Blythe
MOTHER'S DAY
This year I have no pretty card
No boxes, gifts, or bows,
Instead, I'm giving you my heart,
In the form of a rose.

I want you to remember this day
As better than all the rest.
I just couldn't think of a better way
To say, "That I love you best!"

The world is full of mysteries,
And wonders to behold.
But the love of a mother,
Is more precious than gold.

To say, this year on Mother's Day
You mean more to me than ever.
I want to show, in so many ways,
That our bond will never be severed.

The bond between Mother and Daughter.
The love that only we share,
Is one that will never falter
And no other can compare.

So on this day; for you Mother,
These flowers I give to you,
Because there'll never be another
As wonderful as you.

Cheryl L McIntyre
ROMANCE
A nice picnic lunch,
A stroll in the park;

A candlelight dinner,
A kiss in the dark.

A cold winter's night,
A drink by the fire;

A soft feather bed,
A night of desire.

A horse-drawn carriage,
A ride in the night;

A heart to heart talk,
A feeling that's right.

A weekend away,
A ride on a train;

A walk in the mountains,
A dance in the rain.

A romantic man is
A difficult find;

A man such as this is
A man on my mind.

Dolores J Elenga Hazen
THE GIRL OF YESTERYEAR
Just a glimpse I caught of her,
walking down the road
was she the girl of yesteryear
with hair of shining gold.

I too once looked as she did now
so sweet and oh so young
with hopes and dreams beyond the scope
of future things to come

I thought if only one more time
together she and I
would walk the road of yesteryear
before we bid goodbye

My memories fade as so does she
but yet I do recall
that she is me and I am her
together through it all.

Betty Keziah
OUR CHILDREN TODAY
How can a mother and father expect
A child to do right when there's been neglect
They fuss and cuss around this child
It breaks my heart when he doesn't smile
He says they fight most of the time
So I'll live with you and you'll be mine
They bring out the pot, the pipe and tray
And wonder what's wrong with our children today
It's not so much the children as the way they've been raised
If we lend a hand, maybe they can be praised
The mother and father don't seem to care
As long as the children get out of their hair
I don't know what these people expect
When all along there's been neglect

I have a little friend and he's just four
He comes up and knocks on my door
He says, "I don't live down there anymore.
They just fuss and cuss, I'm gonna live here now
You are my mama and Jay is my father."
What am I supposed to say? "That's no bother."
We love this little kid a lot
But worry about him because of the pot
I wish they loved him as much as we do
Then we wouldn't have to worry because he's blue
Then people wonder what to expect
Because their children don't have respect
Can you have respect for someone you like
When all they do is fuss, cuss and fight?

Barbara Dalton
ETERNAL PLACE OF REST
When I reach those Pearly Gates,
where many men have gone
I know that God will take my hand
and safely lead me home.

Just to look upon his face, where
many tears have flowed
Just to see his nail scarred hands
and touch his long white robe.

Where men know no sorrow, and
all my loved ones are at rest.
I thank God, for every day I've
lived for I've been surely
blessed.

Just to hear the Angels singing in
that Heavenly Jubilee.
And see the little children sitting
happily on his knee.

Just to enter into Heaven, in that
Eternal Place Of Rest
And hear God say, come in my
child, I know you've done your
best.

Joe Newbury
SOMEONE WITH NO IMPORTANCE
He came from nowhere important.
His eyes full of emptiness and
nothing important.
The freedom of his expressions,
And the overwhelming personality,
Are the traits of confusion and
nonsense.
Getting older,
Hoping not to.
Trying to achieve,
Deny.
Setting goals,
Confronting them.
New anguish,
Comes and goes
Never to leave.
And all the while learning,
And imagining
What would it be otherwise?
Fighting the never-ending emotions
Doing nothing important
And always, fighting the biggest
opponent
in life
himself.

Kristianne K Scalese
THE TREES
On top of the bulldozer
Sat a cruel old man
To which the children gathered
'round.
Watching and waiting fearfully
As the old man tore down
Their wonderful trees.
The trees that had come to
Represent the lives of the little
children.
"Go away, little children, leave me
alone."
The old man said as he
Returned to his work.
The children backed up and
Stared with wonder as if to ask
"Why?"
"Go away, little children, leave me
alone."
The children left and said
good-bye
To their wonderful trees.

Irene Tykochinsky

Irene Tykochinsky
JOURNEY
You have to walk
my dear friend
before you learn
to fly . . .
and all mistakes
that I have made
that's really
all that's mine.

My tears have dried
and fears are gone
my future looks so bright
and never ever will again
I lose the sight of light.
I'll never blame another soul
for things that I have done
and I forgive my fellow men
like Jesus said and done.
Our Father watches over us
until we meet again
and we'll be there by his side
but no more a man!

Clarence C Beasley
THE POET'S ANSWER
My friend you ask, what do you gain,
In this old world of pain?
You labor not and harvest naught,
And all you write's in vain.

It is a work born of above,
Seeming idle with my pen,
I try to bring both joy and love,
Into the hearts of men.

Jane Marie Barnabie
THE MIRACLE
The heavens are sealed by the thick gray masses.
The sun gently pecks at its shell.
A crack appears spilling rays of soft white light.
I'm experiencing a birth for the first time in awe of what will happen next.
My senses are alert.
The closer I view the fissure in the sky,
the more luminous and breathtaking the phosphorescent glow appears.
The beams that are cast outline the cumulus view,
transforming it from gray to golden white.
Obediently the cloud cover gives way to the mighty sun's emanate birth.
Gently as a caress it slides through the downy denseness,
exposing itself in the celebration of power and love.
I'm enlivened at the sight of pure ecstasy eternal.
All in a sheer instance transcending time.
As I turn to confirm this miracle, it returns from whence it came.
The titillating Aurora Borealis sinks slowly under its billowy blanket,
freshened like spring air only to share itself again,
with the next sleeping flamingo!

Melissa Fruge
REALITY
In this strange world,
I fail to see;
How people could miss,
Reality.

Everyone has to face it someday,
We all shall see;
When drugs and booze are pushed away,
And we find this thing . . . Reality.

We have to deal with it,
each day of our life;
We can't just sit,
and moan and sigh.

So stand up and smile to
each person that comes your way
Be that one person who
Found Reality, Today.

Rose M Robichaud
SILHOUETTES
Silence is creeping around me
Waiting for darkness to fall

Silhouettes of the swaying trees
Against my bedroom wall

Shadows of dreams and wishes
Trick my eyes to see

Wondering if my lover
Shall ever return to me

JEB Allen
WILD BEAUTIES
Lord, I picked a bouquet today
Along the side of the road
The beauty of a better way
To live and laugh and lift the load.

The brilliance of yellow, brown and green
Makes me feel the glory of a queen.

Lord, how can such sweet beauty
Grow wild, yet take my breath away
You and you alone served your duty
For our eternal life you suffered death.

The joy of a heart seeing flowers
Makes up the pain of needed showers.

Lord, our jumbled lives grasp so little
Of the daily beauties all around
We grope in the middle
Losing sight of your eternal sound.

When storms of lives tend to drain
Help us seek the beauties to be found
And not lose touch with those all around!

Deborah Meadows
SWINGING
I am sitting here
swinging in the sun
feeling the warmth penetrate my body,
healing my soul
I feel at peace,
or do I?
I still feel somewhat confused,
overwhelmed.
I wish with each swing
another problem would disappear
with each swing another one would drop off
I know I need to take one day at a time
take life as it happens
but I can't help to panic when I see
all that is in front of me
all that I need to do
all that I neglected to do
and all that I missed

I could sit here and think of it all
but I think I'll just swing for a while

Effie S Whittier
SEE THE BEST IN US
Wouldn't this old world be better
If the folks we meet would say;
I know something good about you.
And then treat us just that way.
Wouldn't it be fine and dandy
If each handclasp warm and true
Carried with it this assurance
I know something good about you.

Wouldn't life be lots more happy
If the good that's in us all
Were the only thing about us,
Folks bothered to recall.

Wouldn't life be lots more happy,
If we praised the good we see?
For there's such a lot of goodness
In the worst of you and me.

Wouldn't it be nice to practice
That way of thinking too.
You know something good about me
I know something good about you.

Virginia Rothfuss

Virginia Rothfuss
A SOLDIER'S COURAGE

To the Allied soldiers during World War II.

A soldier asks only one thing,
As he stands by a comrade's side,
To be brave, to be true to his course.
His fate is for God to decide.

He stands in the face of death.
He knows he is only a man,
But something inside says, "Go on.
You can do it. You know that you can."

And, so, he goes on into battle.
He watches that comrade die,

A friend who'll stand by him no longer—
Instead, by the road, he will lie.

Night comes, and the town has been captured.
The price that was paid is not known.
He only knows that he lives,
But his friend is gone—he's alone.

A soldier asks only one thing,
As he stands by a comrade's side,
To be brave, to be true to his course.
His fate is for God to decide.

Jennie Mantone Gentile
WAITING FOR THE MESSIAH
The blind must climb
to new heights
To see above the heads
of others
Their reward lies
in their enlightenment
God lives to proclaim
his spiritual truth
That is undiminished
by either, space or time
He offers you a gift
that is divine
Do not hesitate to take
what is, so freely given
To all, who worship him
and are worthy to receive him
When you see him
in all his glory
Do not deny him
for he embodies, the spirit
of eternal life

Jeannie Kibbe
WHAT ARE FRIENDS FOR?
Everybody needs a real friend,
Someone to love them until the end,
A person to understand, reason and care,
Someone to talk to when no one else is there.

Someone to cherish day after day,
One who'll often go out of their way,
Someone who comforts and eases the sorrow,
One who will be there today and tomorrow.

At times when you're down, and nothing seems right,
A friend will be there to show you the light,
And when the time comes that no one understands,
A friend will be there holding your hand.

Cathy Daut
I AM INVISIBLE TO THE WORLD
I am invisible to the world
I crave love but receive hate
I desire warmth but enter into coldness
I beg for affection but get pushed away
I am invisible to the world
I ask for friendship but gain enemies
I am kind but treated cruelly
I give but never do I receive
I am invisible to the world
No one acknowledges my presence
for my ugliness is so
That
I AM INVISIBLE TO THE WORLD

Melanie Maureen Bannister
THE TAMARIND TREE
He stands there as he has, forever, it seems.
A gnarled old figure
Bent, once tall.
His mantle of green, changed every year
Betrays his age, disguises his pains.

Generations of kite flyers have seen their prizes
Fall into the old man's outstretched arms.
He has seen their indignation, their tears and wails
And he tries to release their precious possessions
But his old rheumatic fingers refuse to let them go.

In compensation he gives them fruit
Some sour, some pleasingly sweet.
A gesture which may reveal his innermost feelings.
Their indignation and tears dissolve
And they revel in his generous offering.

As the weeks go slowly by, his young friends become fewer
Until, alas, they come no longer
To fly their kites, nor delight in his

satisfying fruit.
But he is not sad
Because he knows they will return
one day.

Rodney Black
TEARDROPS
Teardrops fall in a silent night
As quietly and gently as a bird in
flight.
They come and go like beautiful
snow.
They stream down your face like a
river in its flow.

Teardrops fall on a saddened day
Because your parents left you in a
fast like way,
But after awhile they come from their
job.
You hear them argue and you began
to sob.

When your teardrops fall, are you
really sad
Or are you just faking because you're
mad?
When I cry, I don't play.
My face gets cold like white sand
clay.

Don't be ashamed when you do
really cry.
Because when your parents beat you,
do you know why?
When you look back, thank God it's
no more.
You won't do it to your children
because you've been there before!

Concepcion H Rios
THE MELODY OF THE MOCKINGBIRD
To hear the melody of the mockingbird when your heart is truly sad,
When your heart is badly injured and your spirit's flying low.
When you have no will to live, no reason to go on.

That is when this melody can touch your very soul.
Its melody is beyond compare, you must hear it for yourself.
It is rare and pure and soothing to the spirit.
This melody can soothe the soul and help the heart to mend.
It can help to lift the spirit up and renew our faith in love once more.

Patricia Ann Brockett
INDEPENDENCE
Independence walks on air,
Call his name he'll only stare.
With nonchalance he breaks the laws
By scratching chairs with dainty
paws.
And if you scold him when he's
done,
He'll only stare:
He knows he's won.

Vyvyan D Boykin
AFFINITY
Mystical stirrings around us
In a cloak of time,
Carefully weave their swirling
Hands to titillate our minds.
Affinity pulls our questioning souls
Entire from our shells,
Lessening past and solitary pain

Inside porcelain hearts we held.

But emotions now are floating free
Leaning toward a common theme,
About our hopeful hearts that need
Caresses of love for eternity to
Keep those feelings forever true...

Ethel Verla Bailey
RETIRED SENIOR CITIZENS?
So, we're retired persons, is that so?
There is much that you don't
know.
Sometimes our bodies may move
rather slow;
But our brains compare with
the Dynamo.
In our minds the thoughts constantly
flow;
We tell of yesterday, today
and tomorrow.
Our fingers can still tie a neat bow,
Use the typewriter, computer,
and even sew.
Our energy is seldom so very low
That we can't keep on the go.
In some way always working down
here below,
We are far from retired!—
now you know.

Margaret Peel Burris
MEMORIES OF PEARL
The silky slivers of priceless pearl
Drift slowly downward and so softly
swirl
Each silky flake caresses my
windowsill
As memories of your smile my heart
ore fill
Memories like snowflakes drift ore
my soul
Memories of fun and laughter before
love grew cold
I stagger and reel from memories that
over power
My logic, my senses, and my will,
hour after hour
The string of pearl like memories
drift and fill
The empty hollows of my soul
Like my windowsill like winter
follows after the spring
The emptiness follows after seeing
you again
No place to run, no place to hide
Your memories are with me forever
inside
I grasp for new meaning in life
But find little happiness, only
emptiness and strife
This smile I show to all the world
Can only be touched by the string of
pearl

Katherine Durst
FUN
Fun seems to come
From a line or a pun
Trickling out of one's lip
Like some sort of slip
With two-sided intention
One dares not mention
But oh how funny it seems
When it hits all our dreams
Like an arrow pointed at all
And thrown in the air like a ball
Intended to drop and bounce
With giggles no one counts
It's nice to see one clown
Instead of a constant frown

Kerry G Meyer

Kerry G Meyer
SCHOOL
Today wasn't very hot,
As I untied a knot.

I put on my shoes,
And wiped away the blues.

I sat on my chair,
And combed my hair.

When I was going to school,
I felt something cool.

It was the cool winter breeze,
Which made me sneeze.

When I got to the playground,
I looked all around.

Nobody was here,
That was very queer.

DeLois Davis
MEMORIES
As I sat in my rocker
With the cat on my foot;
I saw my yesterdays
and the chances I took.

Those of love, fear,
laughter and tears,
Brought to memory so very clearly,
The best of glowing yesteryears.

But those times are gone,
Except for the glances I sneak;
To look at memories forgotten
In my heart forever to keep.

Time nudges me forward
To face paths unknown;
Challenged by greater risks,
Of past memories never shown.

Almeta Day
ODE TO GOD
Here I am again, God.
You never tire of listening to my
woes,
no matter they're absolved, already
known to You.
How glad I am to have You for a
friend, yet close as breath, You're
there, one's very life renew.
God, have I told You lately?
When earth's oppressions pull in all
directions,
like octopus, eight hands all caught
and firmly bound,
I go into my deepest, secret person to
find release, pure peace, and You I
found.
God, I specially want to thank You.
When zigzag rambling ways ofttimes
were chosen the silky, steely cord,
loose-tied, unbinding, wove wildly,
spiraling in myriad scrawlings,
patterning Love-Source, always near
I'm finding.

Nicole De Champlain
THE ROSE
Thinking about life, I find that life is
like a bed of roses
In the beginning, when the roses are
buds
Humans are just babies, growing up
to the prime of their life
When the roses begin to open
That is when we are adolescents,
Tackling problems and life in
general.
This is the hardest time for the rose
and the human.
As the rose opens more, the human
also grows older.
They go through other problems and
fears
As the sun brightly shines on the
rose, it opens to its fullest.
Life from now on seems to slope
downwards,
Problems still arise but are tackled
with more ease
They have been through so much
The rose starts to wither up
The human is growing older and
starts to wither away also
Now the rose is dead.
So is the human.

Cheryl A Burzak
ASK IF I LOVE YOU
Ask if I love you
I'll tell you forever
Ask if I'd leave you
I'll tell you never
Ask why I love you
I could say so much
I love your warm kisses
I love your soft touch
I love it when I turn around
And see you standing there
I love that certain look you give
To let me know you care
I love how your hand touches my
face
I love how you hold me
Your warm embrace
When you tell me you love me
I close my eyes
I'm an angel in heaven
Up high in the skies

Bonnie Birchfield
FRAIL HARVEST
How thoughtlessly we sow the seeds
of life
Tossed into the winds of fate
Knowing not the bitter harvest
The fruits they bear
Till it's too late.

The things we do, each day we live
Can touch or alter, someone,
someday
If seeds are kindness, hope and love
And help the traveler, on his way.

But alas! sometimes the seed we sow
Thinking not of autumn's gain
Till in the eyes of winter's child
We reap the frail harvest
In a garden of pain.

Irma Martin
WATER FALL

Dedicated to God who gave me my gift of poetry and the beautiful waterfalls.

The most breathtaking sight I have ever seen
so amazing and beautiful
I marvel how can this be . . .

Power surrounds this awesome wonder
which thrills to the excitement to the young and old
alike . . .

Roaring like thunder into the night
It's splendor rewarding delighting mankind
with its sensational glory . . .

Carved from nature so many years ago
improved by age by its magnificent flow . . . .

Winter, spring, summer and fall
decorate the occasions for all.

Watching this marvelous grandeur
calms the heart
is soothing medicine called the
"Miracle of a Water Fall"

Bridgette Breaux
MY TEARS OF GOLD
My tears of gold
have turned very much
cold
In my harsh life
Maybe I should
be a wife
To be able to give
and for me to live
My life is so
very hard
Oh please! help
Me Lord

Lori Beltramini
A CLOSE FRIEND
A river is like a wild animal
Running free as a wild bird just
Running away from its prey.
It was a nice summer day
That I saw the river just
Flowing gently away.

Away from memories that I
Had from the past when you
And I were young and free.

But we had those special
Moments when we just had to
Catch our breaths and talk
To each other also to understand
What we've tried to accomplish.

But now very far away from where
We used to sit,
And watch the river.

All of my dreams that I had
Never came true but all of my
Dreams were all about you!

Dawne B Bauer
DAYS OF THE BLAMELESS
Words Taste so bitter Lord,
Chains protrude from hands.
Smiles injecting poisonous stings,
With malingering reprimands.

Face of brass, amoral eyes,
Speaks with slanderous tongue.
Mind unbalanced from devious tasks,
Truth remains unsung.

Bloated ambitions, edacious views,
Poverty of intellect showed.
Justice is oblivious,
Coercement, still unexposed.

Alice Dommer Berg
JUDAS (MATTHEW 27:3—10)
Jesus, the Christ, called him friend
whose traitor lips inflicted the
first wound.
What mysterious destiny moved
this hapless man to press that
fated kiss?
If do he must, would not it have been
less cruel to boldly point the
finger?
Pitch-dark the hour, and Scripture tells
Satan entered in to stage his evil part
"And Judas went out into the night."

Then from whence this sudden longing
for scent of fern on mountainside,
for dusty roads and Words of Life?

Judas, the betrayer, cringing in shadow
of temple-gates, fist tight-clenched
with damning coin to hurl back
at that pack of wolves with
whitewashed souls and unholy feet.

For Judas, awful remorse, bitter tears,
a twisted olive tree in the garden,
a hopeless bed in Potter's Field
and a name ever to be despised.

Iris C Berge
A LONELY GUY
I sit in a field all full of grass
Bewildered by afar.
I look to the moon and stars above
And wonder where you are.
Are you in the wilderness beyond the lake?
Or in my mind an imaginative state?
Wherever you are I wish I knew,
Are you beyond the sun and sky so blue?

I never seem to have much fun,
And can't wait till the days are done,
I miss the days I called you mine,
I ask myself time after time,
What about way back when,
The days so short the time so slim?
We could never find quite enough time,
But that was when I called you mine.

Now I'm alone so much time to spare,
The days too long I go nowhere,
What happened to the girl I knew?
I ask myself as I stare into the
beautiful blue.

Lisa L Belluardo
I WANT TO KNOW
I want to knock at the door of your
soul.
I want to know what resides there so
I'll know if it was better to let you
go.
I want to slip past the keyhole and
peer inside your eyes.
I want to know if there's really
scheming in your mind.
Can I tiptoe past the facade that you
keep parked outside.
Can I light a candle and see the light
still flicker in your eyes.
You were the warm burning sun, I
just can't believe that all the
sunlight
is done.

Kellie Berens
JUST FOR TWO
If I had a wish that would come true,
I would wish for a world with only
me and you.
Just the mountains, the oceans, the
birds that fly free.
The green grass, the flowers, and
beautiful trees.
If I could do the things that God
can do,
I would recreate the world
and make it just for two.

James Randall Alderson

James Randall Alderson
A LINE TO A FRIEND

To my beloved daughter, DEBRA FAY.

A line to a friend
that could not be
Because there's no more
use in me
I have no treasures
or gold to give
I'm having a hard time
trying to live
But if I had these things
that make you blue
I would surely
share with you

James Randall Alderson
A PICNIC

To my beloved son, NATHANIEL.

I wish I had a jelly bean
red, orange, black or green
I'd put it in my pocket
and save it 'til we meet
We could have a picnic
with something good to eat

Amy Berry
PARTY
Drinking's great
Smoking's a ball
But add those with wheels
And it's not a party at all.

Pauline Barrett
THE MAGICAL KINGDOM
I laid beneath a grand oak tree,
And watched as clouds passed over
me,
The shapes they took were life-like
forms,
A cat, a dog and a bull with horns.
A rainbow sprang up from the
ground,
Trailed above a bear lying upside
down,
The bear flipped over, stood on his
feet,
And bumped a cloud-shaped
parakeet.
Soon I drifted off to sleep,
I dreamt of rabbits, mice and sheep,
I woke to see a cloud-shaped rat,
Surprised her young had teased the
cat,
She scolded them and took them
home,
So again I laid there all alone,
And watched as new clouds rolled on
by,
In the magical kingdom of the sky.

Helen F Brady
JUST TO UNDERSTAND
Material things I buy to use,
To help me get over the
lonesome blues.
They cannot love, they cannot
embrace,
Nor can they look into my face.
They understand not how I feel,
What I'm going through seems
so unreal.
To be so lonely at a time like this,
Is like living in hell with all amiss.
Oh, why can't someone hear my plea,
Someone who loves me, and
thinks
of me.
To act as tho nothing is wrong,
It hurts so much, not sure I belong.
No conscience, no feelings, just for
me,
How can it be so hard to see.
A little attention is what I need,
Not just to do, or just to feed.
When will I be understood,
Too late I'm afraid, when I'm
gone
for good.

Jean Boer
MY TREASURE
There is a treasure hidden in my heart
It is a treasure I keep whole and can
never part
In quiet times in each and every day
I sit and think of my treasure, I enjoy
it in every way
My thoughts are listening to the voice
I love to hear
I feel his warmth and I want him to
be near
I feel his hands so gentle and kind
When he looks in my eyes, I feel he
reads my mind
There is this rapport between us that
is so very unique
I know it and feel it when we meet
Sometimes at night when I cannot
sleep

I pull a pillow close to me, I silently weep
I weep for this treasure I have in my heart
The treasure I keep whole and can never part

Betty Louise Domes
THE SYSTEM

This poem is dedicated to my son, Gordon Andrew Domes, with love and many thanks for the inspiration!

Pestilence, plague and putridity,
Derived from forms of stupidity.
A well-balanced planet overflowing with strife,
Creating a continuous stream of degenerate life.

Destruction was a miserable fate,
Dominoes falling at a terrible rate.
Exiles from the other lands,
Drifting in the blowing sands.
Bitter bands
of heavenly girth,
Trample upon
our beautiful
earth.
The vacuum of time,
Is only a dime,
The creatures of space,
Were having a race.

Robert L Bloom
TOUCH OF NOVEMBER
Countless shades of gray
Are wiped across the sky,
By a cold and angry wind
As autumn passes by.

Leaves begin to migrate
Across the lawn and street,
Wandering till they're wrestled down
By snow and freezing sleet.

Protected from the onslaught
By a fragile windowpane,
I watch the mad convulsions
Of a rusted weather vane.

I move out on the terrace
Looking up into the sky,
Pressed beneath those leaden clouds,
The wind begins to sigh.

The kiss of cold upon my cheek;
That icy sullen pride.
November's bittersweet caress.
She whispers, "Go inside."

Bill Brooks
OVER THE YEARS
Over the years many things can occur
Important things as well as foolish things
This can happen when you forget what binds
Just for no reason nor for any rhyme

There's some bridges you cross you just can't burn
Maybe this comes from the lessons you learn
The memories over the years you've known
Like certain dreams to the four winds they've blown

Yes, over the years I've done many things
Guess that I was a bell that you could not ring
This we both know, I was weak, you were strong
I was just the words, but you were the song

You were always there to show me the way
It just seems that I forgot what to say
I can't forget the way that was so right
That glow from your smile was fire in the night

To turn back the pages would be a task
So let me be there in your eyes I ask
To be that smile in your life with no fears
Let me prove this to you over the years

Dawn Broyles
BARBARA'S GRADUATION
At last Barbara, your big day is here!
You give a smile, a sign and a cheer.
just think of school and your very first day,
Filled with letters, numbers and play.

But as you grew from that time on,
The fight with verbs and nouns you've won.
Oh how well you've listened and learned.
And look! Into a young woman you've turned.

No more ringlets, ribbons and braids,
Nor bubble gum, cartoons and parades.
For you've outgrown your childish toys.
Now it's perfume, purses and boys.

A new part of your life is just beginning.
Through all the trials, so far you're winning.
With a lot of help from your mom and dad,
And brothers and sisters and friends you've had.

So—frightened and happy that this day is here,
Whatever your future, no one can say.
go on and cry and then give a cheer!
Best Wishes to you on this special day!

Anita T Brantley
THERE IS SOMETHING IN THE AIR
Once in a while, there is something in the air,
Just as potent as a sunny day.
It comes—and—
Transforms a heavy heart, stimulates a sluggish mind,
Nullities a corruptive thought, transcends the depth of night
As it transposes darkness into light.
What else can rid the world of its reckless madness?

One in a while, there is something in the air,
Just as clear as a cloudless sky.
It has come—and it has—
Penetrated tradition, elevated justice, inspired unification.
This rebirth of hope sent the Berlin wall crash to the ground,
And opened those South African prison gates, with a
Cry for freedom, heard around the globe!
A possibility not foreseen.

Once in a while, love and truth permeate the air!
Is there any other way this miracle can succeed?

Kristina Billings
PREJUDICE
Prejudice comes from
narrow-minded
people.

Who don't care
about other
people's feelings.

Prejudice is
dark, evil,
terrifying.

Even prejudice against
the tiniest things
is bad.

But prejudice against
people is the
worst kind.

It hurts . . . It kills.

Maybe . . .
If we all stood together . . .
We could let those under oppression go free.

Colleen Maloney Neimoyer
THE TRAIN

To my family and friends.

Off it speeds
With a haunting sound
That fills miles of space
As it travels down
The back streets of towns and cities.

Taking and giving Loved ones,
friends and strangers
Throughout the journey
It races to meet
A destination in time.

People of all ages
Watch in wonder and excitement
Waving and saying hello
To the train
That has become
A friend

David Battershell
VIVIAN
Vital vivacious Vivian,
Into paradise or oblivion
Vicariously soars my soul.
I must have your answer now
As to whether, when or how—
Nirvana maybe my goal.

With Cupid helping the wooing
Oh, how I hope you'll be cooing!
Other thoughts banished from
mind.
Teach me, Vivian, of magic—
Each moment happy not tragic—
Nourish my love—please be
blond!

David Battershell
THE MAKING OF A BUREAUCRAT
Never trouble trouble 'til trouble troubles you,
If it ain't broke don't fix it, whatever you may do.
When everything's a-workin'—rear back into yer cheer,
A little snoozin's good fer you from everything I hear.
Don't be a schnook—don't read a book—the thing might strain yer brain—
It might cause frothin' in the mouth and drive a man insane!
Don't lift that weight, don't tote that bale—I've never seen it fail,
Yer back can get such a strain—
I'd rather be in jail!
I was on the job, the other day—some twenty years ago—
I was sitting back in a good 'ole cheer one moment or an hour or so,
When the boss slipped up and snarled at me for I guess the millionth time,
"Get on your feet!—Get up from there! You slob—you worthless slime!"
Says I to him, "Now looky here, I just got in this cheer,
A little snoozin's good fer you from everything I hear."
Says he to me, in his reply, "Are you embalmed and already dead?"
"Get up, go on and get up from there—that chair is not your bed!"
Says I to him, "I know it boss, I was just restin' my eyes in prayer,
I didn't know how gruff you'd be—you're as cross and as mean as a bear,
Three days ago, when I got this job, who'd a thought it'd be such a strain,
If it ain't for an infernal catch in her back—then it's enough to short-circuit your brain!"
So says I to he and he to me, in assorted and similar replies . . .
But the thing so insultin' about that man, was he thought I was telling him lies!
For if there's only one thing I'll always know, I tell the gospel truth,

To dare to question my veracity—
why it's mean—it's
low-down—uncouth!
Others knew what I was sayin'
was true—I was promoted
over the years—
In federal government where I
always worked, I was
commended—it wasn't all jeers.
'Cause a little snoozin's good fer
you from everything I hear—
Our government's been asleep for
years with dope, with liquor
and beer.
It's party time from dawn to dusk
and the same from dusk to dawn,
The years rolled by, until at last,
twenty years had come and gone.
So I finally retired from my years
of toil, but did I get a watch?
No, they gave me the cheer I'd
been a-sittin' in, a slap on the
back and some Scotch.
So I suppose in disguise they
were a'tellin' me, I was
nothing' but a drunken fat slob,
But that a little snoozin's good fer
you was always the truth on
that job.
A catch in my back on that very
first day is why government
became my career,
I was fat—split my pants—got
wedged when I sat and
couldn't rise up from the cheer!

Heidi Flaten
HAPPY—SAD
Have you been happy,
So happy you thought your heart
could leap out of your chest,
So happy you could run through a
grassy field,
Miles upon miles without tiring.

Have you ever been sad,
So sad you thought your heart would
break in two,
So sad you wish you could curl
up and die.

Carol Boly
JENNIFER
Jennifer oh Jennifer oh my darling
oh my dear oh sweet Jennifer how I
love you. How I need you oh dear
Jennifer stay by me teach me
how to be sincere. Oh my darlin'
oh my dear oh sweet Jennifer
guide me to the throne above
teach me how to pray for you
oh my darlin' oh my dear
Stay with me for a while
Jenny oh Jennifer
you're a sweetheart
I can see it in your smile.

Chelly Auzene
UNTITLED

To my beautiful Gma. You must be so happy.

Away from the crepid
I awoke to the light
Sprung from the silence
Joyous was my sight

My limbs danced in movement
My eyes glistened clear
My heart youthfully pounded
for my eager ears to hear

The sun shone brightly in a blissfully
blue sky
My skin felt warm
as I uttered a peaceful sign

The flowers in bloom
praisingly swayed in the soft breeze
Showing the blades of grass
in rainbows beneath the trees

I knealt to pick the only red rose
in this utopian delight
The birds chirped a welcoming son
and I felt the hand of the one I have
loved so long
Beheld was heaven's glorious flight

Chelly Auzene
LINGERING
Lingering, linger, is the heart's sword
to bear
dreaming of nights past when the one
you loved was there
warmth at your side
and beneath the flesh of your breast
when the smoldering lips of the one
you loved
were close against you pressed

Tears sting our cheeks
with the memories that came to mind
Slowly and surely
the stinging numbers with time

Dara Mae Ramsey

Dara Mae Ramsey
SYMPATHY
Host portray fiction against truth
but miracles resolve all things to
behold.
None reaches eager sympathy
composed
enlightened will to know one is right.
Troubles soar long strife growing
little said while much learned by
listening.
Govern speed pure and simple
hasten a format through love and
devotion.
Understand merits of cheerful
countenance
duty—bound high esteem fairness to
all.
Reap glory gained good intentions
granting a pastime of good labors
shared.
Them composure strengthened
through faith
maintained by a belief sure and solid.
Duty devotion never stands still or
lacks mean to show love growing.
Quietly survived home hath meaning
governed promises bounded
sympathy with an encore.
None survey's route except
able-bodied
living proof life is ordained through
promises.

Elizabeth "Beth" Marion Bray
DRUGS
Drugs are bad
for they make you sad.

Drugs are losers
so don't be bad choosers.

Drugs may damage
the minds of different kinds.

So don't take drugs
for your sake and mine.

Debra Sue Bare
WHISPER GOD
What is felt in an autumn breeze?
What is seen in tiny leaves that fall?
Consider the clover and the lilies that
grow;
They whisper . . . "God" . . . He
created them all.
When discouragement comes and
darkens your hours,
And desperation lends to you its
hand;
When clouds cover the light of day—
silver linings hid,
Let your lips whisper . . . "God" . . .
the solid rock on which to stand.

Find the strength in
whispering . . . "God" . . .
There's majesty in that name,
Bountiful blessings from living by
faith
A song of redemption to ever
proclaim.

If there's joy in serving Jesus—
Happiness in knowing the paths that
we now trod,
Are ordained by Him Who loves us
Then our life whispers . . .
"God" . . .

Debra Sue Bare
HEART TALK
Memories from yesterday's past
Linger at my heart's door
Waiting softly, there at last
To come alive one more.

In search of tomorrow's hope
Happiness in days gone by;
Struggle to hide behind the scope
All hurts—to satisfy.

Recalling only hugs—not tears
Peace and love and quiet days
Strain to cover all inward fears
As faith and hope do mark my
way

Suzanne L Bowers
RED HATS
Like red hats on
very old women,
our little pleasures
stand out from the rest.
We have to grow
and live independently,
learn to let go of
darkness in the past,
and hold on dearly to the best.

Give us room to grow
but enough precious
moments to ourselves.
Red hats, blowing in
the afternoon breeze.
Flying away fast and high,
reminding us to grasp
the different and obscene,
learning to be happy, doing as we
please.

Suzanne L Bowers
USED TO STORMS
I never thought I'd
find myself missing
someone again . . .
or feeling quite
this way again.

You give me sunshine
when I'm so used to storms.
And instead of turning
cold on me,
I suddenly find you warm.

You shout your
smiles at me
instead of crazy, angry words.
The pounding of my heart and
the way it beats
with your's is
the loudest sound
I've ever heard.

David Keith Fleming
GRANDMA

For my loving grandma, whose prayers and love meant so much to me.

Her race is over, her race she has run.
She fought a good fight, the battle
she's won.
Her feeble body she has left behind.
Her eyes no longer are they blind.
She's walking on streets of purest
gold.
She now lives where no one grows
old.
No matter how good or bad the day.
She always took the time to pray.

She prayed for me, she prayed for
you.
For as long as I knew her she stayed
the course
Keeping faith against the force.
Through trials and temptations she
overcame
She would say, "Trust in the Lord
and you'll do the same."
On this earth no longer is she here.
But through Christ, her spirit is
always near.
Today we are saddened our hearts are
sore.
Today she knows joy as never before
Be ye not saddened this is what she
lived for.
To live with her God forevermore.

Harry F Bridges
THANK YOU
Thank you, Jesus, for showing me the
light.
Thank you for the hearts and pain.
Thank you for the stars and the rain.
Thank you for helping me remain
sane.

And most of all watch over us all.
The good, the bad, the rich, the poor,
The drunks, the pipers, the pushers,
and the smokers.
Millions didn't make it, but I'm so
glad I did.
Thank you, Jesus.
Thank you for the joy in my soul.

Mary Ann Anderson
LIFE

Life is like a rose, so tender, so
fragile, easy to destroy . . .
Take each petal with beauty of its
own.
Let Life grow like a rose and the
fragrance will always be
exposed.
Take time, patience, and work,
you'll see how much love it
will have enclosed.
May your life together be never
wilted with wrong words from
you or anywhere.
So with all the roses you shall see,

think of the beauty your dad
and I wish for both of thee.
As life goes on and age you'll see

bouquets is yours to be . . .
So with love we wish on you both,

may it be a garden for you
both always to see.
Love, Mom

Barbara A Anderson
CHILDREN

To my beloved father, Aaron Moore, for always believing in me.

Children are like flowers.
They are spread all over God's land.
Why folks are harming them?
I will never understand.

Sarah Volkenborn

Sarah Volkenborn
OUR SPECIAL PLACE

Today, I returned to our Special Place
As I looked out across the body of
water I could almost hear the familiar
sound of your footsteps shuffling
through the leaves

As I stood there alone, remembering
the past months,
how it had taken all summer, for us to
become friends
You stopping by the doorway, to say
hi and chat a bit you would even wait
there morning and evening as I came
and left
I begin to look forward to these
special moments with you knowing
in my heart it was wrong, knowing
one day it would have to end,
knowing one or both of us would be
hurt
Why didn't we stop when the feeling
began
I mentioned it, remember?
But you said it's only now and then
that Someone Special comes along
We ask ourselves, why did God let
our paths cross
Was it a testing of our Wills, our
Faith, our Belief

The fall came and went so fast, as our
love for each other grew
I'd watch the calm water as the
waves came in softly to shore
The gold rays from the setting sun
dancing, playful upon the water
The smoke from burning leaves high
above the treetops
The black squirrels running here and
there, gathering pine cones For a
long, cold winter ahead
I wait patiently knowing soon you
would arrive where I waited with
cold pop and sweet-filled popovers
We talked, laughed and listened to
each other's stories
Then walking along the beach before
saying goodbye each wondering if it
would be our last time together

Today is different from all the rest
As I waited briefly at our Special
Place I could hear the loud slapping
of the rough waters as each new wave
slammed into the shoreline, jarring
my memories as a knife cutting each
one into threads
The north wind was bitter and cold as
it blew my hair across my face
The snow began to fall, trying to blur
out each happy memory of you
I realized soon the water would turn
to ice
Soon your job would be finished
Soon we would say our last goodbye
Soon we would part Special Friends,
going our separate ways
As I ran back to the car, with the
sound of wet leaves under my feet
I wondered if someday you would
remember our special times here
together and perhaps return trying to
recapture our happy times we spent
sharing
at—
Our Special Place

Linda Arnold
LORD, IS OUR DAD WITH YOU?

Lord up above, you've taken from us
our dad and his love.
Is dad up there with you? Watching
over each one of us?
Does he know we miss him, and just
how much?
Or how we had yearned for one more
hug, one more touch?
Is dad free of pain and grief, and his
soul do you hold, forever to keep?
Is dad as happy as he should be? His
Face, some day will we again see?
Tell me Lord! Please tell me
somehow, is our daddy in heaven
with you now? If so, I know he's
happier than he'd ever been down
here!
Then my heart would no longer be
burdened with sadness, only
thankfulness and cheer.
Lord, we truly love that man. But if
he's with you, we could better
understand, that the reason he's left
us, was a part of your plan.
So thanks, Dear Lord, for hearing my
prayer.
And thanks for the dad that we all
had a chance to share.

Paula Marie Angelle
THE TEST

This poem is dedicated to two of my grandparents who have touched the hearts of many, and are gone but not forgotten. "I LOVE YOU," Thelma Brown and Allen Angelle.

When you tell the kids to do one
thing
And they do the opposite of that
Punishment nor a spanking seems to
help
Not even threatening them with a
baseball bat

When you boss drives you up the
wall
And you're ready to throw in the
towel
Shake, shake, shake it all off
Let out a loud screaming howl

When things just aren't going right
And Murphy's Law really kicks in
Suicide seems to be the answer
But you know that would be a sin

Don't feel down
Lift your head up
Pray to the Lord
Take a sip from his cup

Remember your purpose here
Try to do your best
'Cause God is watching over you
he's just putting you to the test

Betty Lou Baker
OUR INTERNAL CONTROL

Dedicated with love and appreciation to our dad, Cleo Brown, who showed us children, even though he didn't get much education, the ability of the brain to learn.

The brain, such storage and memory
space, capacity we all use is only a
small trace, plenty of space left to
study and learn, the effort now may
mean later we can earn,
this part of the body has such control,
use it wisely for thinking and
searching the soul,
listen if it says,
"GO FOR A WALK,"
it may be relaxing so with others you
can talk,
use this part of the body to laugh
when amused,
but be wise and take heed when it
might get abused,
it directs your reflexes to let go of
harm,
so listen to your instincts, especially
your brain's alarm!!!!!

Michael J Babbey
IDENTITY

Dedicated to the memory of my mother, Mary.

So many people all passing by
All of them trying to identify.
All looking for peace and happiness
All asking for more and giving up
less.
All living in the past instead of next
year
All deathly afraid but only of fear.
All running away to find new hope
All taking drugs just trying to cope.

All of them going on day after day
All waiting for joy in the good old
way.
All getting bummed 'cause they left
it behind
All finding out it was all in their
mind.

All of them knowing that they made a
mistake
All feeling their freedom was all just
a fake.
All distraught and nearing their end
All wishing to find a dearest best
friend.

All coming home to find it's all new
All seeing their past and now missing
it too.
All knowing it's all over—forever
you see
All in the name of goddamn identity!

Charlene Denise Wilkins
UNTITLED

I dedicated this poem to the children, though not this extreme, soon you'll find the answer . . . .

It is good
That I kneel here drenched in the
blood of my lover
With his head in my arms
And his body lying limply across my
lap.
And it is good
That I remove all traces of my being
home for the entire day
So it never be known why he was
here.

It is good that he was my lover?
Is it lawful that he was my father?
Is it justified that I killed him because
I wanted this insanity to end?
And would it be murder if
I flee . . .

Jo Ann (Edge) Brown
FAITH IN GOD

When the pressures of life unfold;
Let the Lord God take hold.
No matter what's the circumstance;
Give God the praise, the glory, and
chance.

He can work it out if you have faith;
Trust in God, believe what He saith.
'Cause whatever your heart's desire
may be;
Don't doubt and it shall transpire,
you'll see.

Worship the Lord with your whole heart;
Do what's right and let Him be a part.
God is able, victory He can proclaim;
God's grace and peace be with you,
in Jesus's name.

Jo Ann (Edge) Brown
AN ANALYSIS OF LOVE

For God so loved the world, that He gave His only begotten Son, that whosoever believeth in Him should not perish, but have everlasting life.
John 3:16

What an unselfish act of love. For God loves us so much.

And now . . .
Do you spend time, perhaps wasting time, looking for love?
Should first, you get to be what you are looking for?
Could it be that everybody wants to be loved?
But how many of us give the love that we want in return?
In search for the "perfect" love we may seldom see ourselves becoming the "right one" for someone else.
Is our expectation of love usually conditional?
Is it that we generally want from others what we don't give ourselves?

Could it be that if you want somebody to be ideal for you, then why not become ideal yourself.
Can it be that "true" love reflects "giving of yourself" and then experiencing the reward of having love returned to you by someone who is willing to give you all?

Judith B Borromeo
ETERNITY

This poem is dedicated to my one and only, Ronnie Pel, with all my love, Judi.

My love for you
Cannot be compared
To the abundance of the stars
Nor the vastness of the valleys;
It is much too mighty
To proportion with these . . .

Amanda Bruyere
LOSING SOMEONE SPECIAL

I lost someone special
He'll always be in my heart
I don't understand
Why God separated us apart.
But as I grow older
I'll understand more
Until we meet in heaven.
Dad will be there waiting to
open the door.
Our love was and is very special
And he's always in my heart.

Mildred Pulver Hochheiser
NAVY BEANS ARE WHITE

I'm in a Gorgonzola mood
blander than blue, sharp of tongue, crumbling
I started out like a Muenster
on the soft side and mild
Then I met you
I beheld you as Provolone
wrapped with prosciutto on melon
We became Tilsit and sherry
not the ordinary combination
With time we mellowed into cheddar
and apple
Then too much presumed
Too little attention and
We blended into a
holiday cheeseball with beer
You evolved as circuitous a pattern
as the holes in Swiss cheese
I grated as well as Sapsago and
impersonated its green color
Now I associate you with
a mongrel soaked in whey and
gorging on limburger

Leticia Le Victro Mills
I'M MY OWN CROWDS

To my Best Friend, Robin Smith, and Morenci Clark and To my Beloved Parents, Brothers, and Grandparents for their support.

In a marked corner of a queue,
only dim lights display the
Beauty.

"Will someone ever accept me?"

Whilst Time grants consciousness,
Bit by Bit,
pieces devoured hungrily
are gagged back uselessly.

(Too Much Seasoning Perhaps!)

Gerald J Arbor
THE WORDS THAT FOLLOWED

I've wandered down
some distant roads
o'er hill and dale
and hollow

Fast I flew
and recklessly
but mother's words
still followed

Go slow.
Be careful.
Go easy.
Advice both gentle
and loving.

But I brushed it off
and went my way.
I could not hear
for all my rushing.

Years have come
and years have gone.
With them went
my childhood.

And still I hear
my mother's words.
But now they do
more good.

Much pain could I
have spared myself.
Much trouble
passed me by.

Had I but paused
and listened
when my heart
told me to fly.

My wandering days are over.
My sails are set for home.
My home address and mother's
words have eased my need to roam.

Gently rolls
the ocean grey,
White capped waves
above the deep.

Slowly but surely
I sail towards home,
my rendezvous
to keep.

Gerald J Arbor
THE KEEPER OF THE LIGHT

The keeper lights the beacon
for yet another night.

Faithful to his duty,
the tending of the light.

A young boy sits at supper
staring at his plate.

His appetite has fled him.
He knows that Daddy's late.

"Mommy, where's my Daddy,
He said he'd be home today."

"It's dark outside.
Mom, I'm scared.
How can Daddy find his way?"

Rising from the table
she takes his little hand
and walks him to the window.
Together there they stand.

"Your Daddy's on his ship son,
and his ship is out to sea.

"With the money that he makes there
He cares for you and me.

"You see the light that's shining
down there by the bay?

"Your Daddy sees that light
and it guides him on his way."

"But what if it goes out, Mom?
What will he do then?"

"The keeper at the lighthouse
Will light the light again."

Lifting him gently in her arms
she walks him up the stairs.

Dressed for bed he kneels
and says his nightly prayers.

"God thank you for my Daddy
who's on his ship at sea.

"And thank you for the keeper
who guides him home to me."

Ten miles off the eastern shore
A sailor spies the keeper's pride.

Thanking God he trims his sails
and heads for home at eventide.

Gerald J Arbor
THE SAILOR'S CREED

Far from those we love and home
To thankless tasks we bend our might
On briny waves that froth and foam
We sail where land is far from sight

Day into night and night to day
'Round the clock our watch we keep
We guard the gateway to our nation
That those at home may safely sleep

Not for glory do we strive
Nor fame nor fortune though we might
But children family friends and loved ones
Who keep the homefires burning bright

Though our task be long and thankless
From duty's toil we will not cease
It is our joy to bear the burden
While our nation rests in peace.

Brenda J Murray
THE BRIGHTSIDE

When things are tough
And you're down and out,
Think of the times when
the going was such,
that your laughter was
louder than ever so much.

If you can manage to smile
And share it a while,
You will find that the joy of life
Is not in getting, but in giving

And if you can make it through the day
With your sadness and sorrow
And find that your laughter made someone gay,
The night will pass in pleasant dreams,
And by dawn, the problem will be on its way
To a brighter and lighter feeling
towards tomorrow.

Julia Anna Gines
FAR FROM ME

Lilacs used to grow, in the meadow;
past the stables.
Where we often found our passions.
Still, when I held you close . . .
You tickled me . . .
With your carefree reactions.
Never in my life
Had I imagined a time so gay;
When everything seemed . . .
So easy to play.
Now . . . it seems like
I've been grounded a year . . .
Since we last saw each other.
My sweet . . . Pinyo;
We really got in deep trouble
This time . . . You know?
Mama and Papa . . .
Thought they had nothing to fear.
And with each passing moment . . .
I am reminiscing; it's ever so tender.
My Pony, Pinyo flew into the
heavens to be with God, how I love
you both.

Richard P Thompson
BEGINNINGS

To Hilda F. Manbeck, and my parents for their support, and for Andrea, Amanda, and Joshua.

Beginnings,
Not endings.
Something yet undone,
Or a dream unfulfilled.
Words not yet spoken,
Or happiness unrealized.
Still another new adventure
In life's continuing drama
Who knows what it might be?
Anything could happen,
Each day is a brand-new
Beginning!

Theresa Pettit
HEART TO HEART

He grew up in the slums.
She grew up in the country.
He did odd jobs that enabled him to eat.
She sits at the dining room table
with lobster and champagne.
His home is the luxury of a cardboard box which he guides atop the steam vents to keep him warm.
She lies on satin sheets reading a book as the fireplace roars.
He's grateful for enough food and warmth for just one more day.
She, wealthy and educated, shops all day and socializes at night.
He dreams of the day he has a home and family. He has the heart of a lion.
She sighs from boredom of her daily routine.

Life has no real meaning to her.
Isn't it a shame she has no heart at all.

Theresa Pettit
BLACK AND WHITE

The hour was early
yet it was still dark.
I had all the wealth
yet I was poor.
I had my health
yet somehow I was sick.
I had many acquaintances
yet I felt alone.
Driven by power and greed
left me with nothing important at all.

Orestes Perez
A ROAD TWICE TAKEN

For Alexandra Freire, Who inspired this poem. Lots of love O.P.

Underneath this mortal coil I wear is a man as vulnerable as the spring's unsettled air. Since I met you, you have evoked a certain care that till now just simply wasn't there.
May I stare for just a bit and absorb your soul, your mortal being.
I feel that you have opened up a road that I once traveled long ago. As I think of what might be please remember that I'm human and sometimes can be weak.
It does not matter what might be for in my heart your soul I'll keep.
You see my love, I was once a roaming lad whom the angels thought quite mad.
But in the quiet of the night a strong sensation fills my light, these sensations are quite bountiful and beautiful.
If you believe that looks can kill, then we both share a love and will.
Be not troubled by my thoughts, but It's just you are the cause.

Miss Laura Lambe Burrell
VALENTINE'S DAY

To a utopian way of life and the blessing of God to Missy, my pooch, and Heather, my special child.

Four-squared
2 dice
3 pick-up-sticks
Man-in-the
Moon
Silvery halo
What's tonight?

Gladdened hearts
A lace-a-trim
Those
Hearts keep
Poundin'
For Valentine
And
kin . . . .

Miss Laura Lambe Burrell
FANTASY DOLLS

The rapunzel
Fell
Kneaded
Rhubarb
And sat
Twiddling her thumbs
Against
Witches,
Cinderella
A must
With her
Soft shiny-glitter toe
And
Red Riding Hood
Paranoid

In her
Night-time
Dreams
All dolls
And fairy tale
Musts
To spur
Little childrens'
Hearts
From woe is me
To
Glee . . .

Barbara VanOsten
BEACH

Dedicated to Kenya, Fredrick Jr., Tyrone and Christopher.

Here I lay,
in the harbor of gritty particles
against my skin,
The sun's rays sizzling upon me,
Slightly toasting my rinds.

I'm occasionally amused by the ocean's arms,
Extending itself to me
Leaving its salty deodorant, flashing across my nose.

On this day at the beach,
I feel the hospitality from
The earth's shelters relaxing Me . . .

Barbara VanOsten
CURIOUS

Dedicated to Kenya, Fredrick Jr., Tyrone and Christopher.

Stared Eyes, Wanting,
reaching out, with no connection
Wondering if forever . . .

But governed by the "Fates"
who control one's destiny;

Imaginary minds,
reflecting powerful desires
Yet left unconnected
Wanting its turn of the impossible,

Powerful minds rejecting
Truth of the impossible,
Overcome by One's treacherous heart,
which saunters to excitement
Only to be acquainted
with the outcome of Pain !

James Morrison
LISE

How much I adore thee, Lise.
The sweetness of your name
And how it flows off my lips
Like a Spring breeze whispering
through the villas of love.
Lise, Lise your name floats
To the top of mountains
And to the bottom of the bottomless
sea.

Jenny Kieser
THE CORNER OF MY EYE

In memory of Dad . . .
Edward Kieser . . .
I remember . . . .

I sat in a darkened theatre and saw you pass by . . .
Yet when I turned to look . . .
You were not there!

I noticed you glide quickly by as I walked down the street . . .
I looked . . .
Again you were not there!

You tease me with your "corner of the eye existence"
wherever I go . . .
Devoutly, in church, you pass . . .
Joyous, in the park, you skip merrily by . . .
Your presence is always felt, the faint tinkle of your laughter . . .
Almost heard.

I'm comforted to know that I am not alone, yet frightened . . .
For what will it mean when I turn to look . . .
And you <u>are</u> there?

Jenny Kieser
I ONLY GLANCED AWAY A MOMENT

In loving memory of my son . . .
Jon Anthony Shumaker
Forever in our hearts . . . .

He's tiny and ever so vulnerable, the warmth of his tiny body spreads a glow through my being . . . I'll hold him always . . .
I only glanced away a moment . . .

He crawls, his little hands grasp at everything . . .
The world must seem a bright and shiny toy . . .
I only glanced away a moment . . .

A bike, new books . . . the adventure of learning begins . . . unlearned fingers struggle with strange symbols . . . teacher said this is the way . . .
I only glanced away a moment . . .

He runs . . . he dodges . . . he chases phantoms and sunbeams . . . he reaches for a butterfly and wonderingly watches as it avoids small outstretched hands.
I only glanced away a moment . . .

Tall and straight, head held high, he walks beside her . . . he glances . . . she changes . . . how fickle the young heart!
I only glanced away a moment . . .

Muscles firm, shoulders broad . . . no longer a child . . . striving to find his place in a world so new . . . yet so old . . .
A kiss . . . a hug . . .
The door closes . . .
His footsteps fade . . .
Oh God, I only glanced away a moment . . .

Grace Lawrence
A LIE THAT FOOLS

Heart's illusion fills your soul,
And nothing can stop the heart when it wants to play.
A tidal wave sweeps over the moment,
And that moment holds you in its spell.

Just a crime of the heart, wired in its power,
Footloose and fancy free, you cast a spell.
But the heart was so drunk, it could not see
High on the apex of the mind.

You pander the heart with its deception,
Just a go-between the love and the dream.
And hold on to love for only awhile,
Living a lie that fools.

Kneel down in this hurting sin
When you chased all your dreams away.
Seeing through the eyes of a child,
And the heart just cries and cries.

Just a crime of the heart, wired in its power,
Searching for tomorrow's rainbow.
Holding out your hands to harness the winds,
Living a lie that fools.

Yvonne Martinez
TOO MUCH OF ANYTHING

To that special man in my life, he knows who he is!

Once, I had a true love,
one who could make my heart
soar like a dove.

But my love has a wondering heart,
one that could kill at a
blow of a dart.

He loves to be with women who flatter,
but will soon find his
head on a platter.

Someday soon . . . he will come to his sense,
and find that too many women
can come to quite an expense.

Velma F Pickle
DADDY

To my father-in-law, Henry F. Pickle.

The road of life was hard for him
Sometime the future was very dim
But he always held his head so high
And looked the world right in the eye
He would work from dawn till dusk
To care for his family was a must
His worried face, his wrinkled brow
His hands so calloused by a plow
Sometime his love, too tired to show
But love was there, this we know
In his own way he gave all he had
Sometime happy—sometime sad
We'll miss him now, for he is gone
To live with God in his heavenly home
Tho he is gone away from here
Our love will keep him very near

Wendy L Stice
PEACE FOR HUMAN SOULS

In the springtime when the mountains bloom with frosted flowers glistening with sunlit rain
I think of how tomorrow will grow with new beginnings to start our never ending spiral of life, love, and tomorrow

My day is filled with thoughts of
transparent fields of colorless grass,
spreading the mountain's trees up to
our HEAVEN
The afternoons are spectacles waiting
to be cleaned by God's hand; His
hands are our hands filled with our
minds

Being human is easy; being godly is
MASTERFUL . . . And being mind
worthy is GOD
If we could see yesterday without ill
feeling then we can live with each
other; and with ourselves
Why should we as humans let
ourselves be pushed around by bigots
and merciless killers who have
revoked their rights by choosing to
hate their own brothers, because of
race, age, religion, and/or opinion?
Our society has accepted hatred as a
stronghold for building up pride and
egotism

Let peace reign and let pride flourish,
but only if it's pride for us as human
souls!!!

Holly S Weidig

JOHN

*To my "Dad," John Tagg, Jr.—
I love you. Holly.*

I have a stepfather, his name is John,
He used to have hair, but now it's
gone!

He's nice to me, he makes some
jokes,
Lucky for us, he never smokes!

He gave me another brother, as if I
didn't have enough,
But on my birthday, he gives me neat
stuff.

He brings us to California, Florida
and more,
He makes us walk around, so our feet
get real sore.

When we're on vacation, we never
stop,
He doesn't give us time to browse
around and shop!

He can take jokes, and he doesn't
care
If you make wisecracks about his
hair.

He acts like a kid, he even plays
Nintendo,
We should have given it to him,
'cause he plays as much as we do.

I'm glad my Mom picked this man,
And not some guy from a country
western band.

Sometimes he yells, and makes me
mad,
But hey, "that's life," 'cause he's the
Dad!

Kimberly Scaggs

TIME

Time is of great essence but
Sometimes we still do not care
We do not realize the importance
To appreciate all things that we bear
Our lives are so unpredictable
And yes time goes on when you're
gone
Living and learning
Building and yearning
Loving and caring
Hoping and sharing
Live to the fullest, give life your best
Live for the moment, have no regrets
Positive thinking, here is your key
Now go out and make life
What you want it to be
I think you'll feel better
If you don't agree I say
Life is too short to live improperly.

Therese May P Neri

A MOTHER IS

*To my dear mother the late Aurora
Gayloa Pearson.*

A mother is a person who carried me
in her womb
With love, care and devotion, I was
in full bloom
She was the one whose life was at
stake
When she labored for my most
awaited birth

Life then was never the same with
her at my side
Loving, feeding and guiding me all
through the days
When I stumble and fall, or in pain
all of these
Disappear like a miracle with her
tender loving caress

I've come to the point where I'm
already old
Capable of deciding and doing things
I am told
Life becomes more complicated and
hard
But my dear mother is always there,
on guard

My thank yous and heartfelt
appreciation of having you
Is not enough to make up for the life
you've given me
All I want is to let you know and to
show you
That I do love you above all things I
own

I wish that I'll walk by your side and
have you as my guide
For the most important years of my
life are yet to come
And that is my future that lies bright
ahead
No one else could take your place

For you're the lady, who I'm lucky
enough to have

. . . Mother . . .

Tamra Rocsko

MR. NIGHT

Creeping, creeping, laughing,
sneaking
I hear the night befall.
Darkness closes all around
and spiders climb the wall.

In your bed you lie asleep
you never hear a word.
Whatever's lurking in the dark
would rather not be heard.

Something's hiding 'neath your bed
a shadow starts to form.
Lightning dances in the air
the sky begins to storm.

And when he knows you're not
awake
he comes to take a peek.
Runs his fingers through your hair
then he begins to speak.

"Fear not, fear not, my sleeping one
do not wake in fright.
For I watch over everyone
My name is Mr. Night."

Linda L Markham

THE CAR SHOW

The first thing to do is to get checked
in.
See that all things work, outside and
within.
The headlights work, taillights do,
too.
The radio, turn signals, brakes, even
the horn blew.
Phase one is over, yet a lot more to
go.
Next, the car must be cleaned, if I
still want to show.

Washing and waxing is just the
beginning.
Not a speck of dirt anywhere, if I'm
thinking of winning.
Work hard and fast, for time's
running out.
Clean the interior, the engine, the
wheels—you know the route.
One o'clock, time's up; cleaning
must stop.
Phase two is now over—My car sure
looks SHARP!

Judging begins so you sit and wait.
Tension is building, competition is
great.
Time for the trophies, this is what it's
about.
Third place, second place, my name
was not called out.
With excitement building, I'm
standing tall.
First place trophy goes to—Yes!

IT WAS WORTH IT ALL.

C Woodhouse

SILENT DEATH

Don't be afraid of me
Young and old
I won't hurt you
Amidst all your pain
I come quietly and gently
The peacefulness I bring
Is worth your suffering
For you'll suffer no more
Don't fight me
Young and old
In the end I will win
And the battle you have lost
Will be
Your
Victory

Scott W Thomas

ODE TO ARMENIA

*Dedicated to God, the Master Poet
and to Charles Mire, my teacher
first—my friend forever.*

O little town of Armenia
in this Silent Night,
No bells will be ringing—
no Jingle Bells.
No presents are received here
this night.
Rudolph the Red-Nosed Reindeer
forgotten by all these young
minds.

Here Comes Santa Claus—
once joyous,
Replaced by horror
and fright.
Frosty the Snowman,
melted and seemed to fade,
While this dreadful sight of
sadness—
takes your breath away.

So Come All Ye Faithful—
those with reconstruction in mind.
We'll send you our aid
and love you through this day,
For God made us all—
One kind.

Madgery Gardner

THE FINISH LINE

Dedicated to all paraplegics.

You are encouraged
That you start the race
That you finish the race

With courage, go!
With a SMILE, go!
With Determination, go!

Play the game,
Play it fair,
Friend, "Good Luck"

Bravo! Bravo!
You did it, you made it
To the finish line—
God gave thee strength.

Sara A Faria

THE WIND

*I dedicate this poem to my loving
family. Thank you all for your love,
support, and belief in all that I do.
This is for you, Mom, Dad, Sabrina,
and Elizabeth . . . .*

Crisp, cool, and refreshing; cold,
harsh and depressing,
Winter's greeting, spring's 'morrow;
A summer's gift, An autumn's
sorrow,
The sway of a rose petal,
The twitch of a field mouse's settle.
May all thank the wind for its
brusque sweep,
Its kiss, Its sting, Its weep,
A fallen leaf, a drifted blossom,
A scattered lawn must also bear
caution,
For the wind's kiss is never
anticipated,
It'll sting, It'll burn, Yet in return will
be retaliated,
By the next day's sun, or the next
week's warmth,
It's sure to find revenge's scornth,
Its voice rustles in the trees,
Its song taps the windowpane,
Its coolness is in vain,
For the sun now takes the fallen
leaves, the drifted flowers, the settled
seas,
Its final kiss will take the stillness of
the earth,
Its final kiss will bring rebirth . . . of
the new warm sun,
Yet, caution is heeded, for the wind
competed,
And will return for victory,
When the kiss of a new wind is
greeted!

Helen R Hammonds

MEMORIES

In memory of Vaden L. Hobbs.

All the boys I've ever known the one I love has gone home, to be with Jesus there on high, where we live and never die. Jesus called him home one afternoon, much too early he was gone, oh! how I miss him, it seems so long, his sweet smile and happy face, most of all his warm embrace.

We do not understand the reason
why, I am sure Jesus needed him on
high, he is sadly missed by mom and
dad, friends, and loved ones he had.
Life down here is not the same.
Sometimes I hear him call my name.

The letters and phone calls kept our
spirits bright until we met on Sunday
night. We laughed and talked on
Friday afternoon, little did we
realize God's call would come so
soon.

Those happy times we shared you see
are very precious memories to me,
years cannot take them away, but
forever within my heart will stay.
When life is done on earth for me, in
Heaven we will be together through
eternity.

James L Berry Jr

GRANDMA'S HOUSE

*In memory of Grandma Powell . . .
and all who precede us.*

Coffee pot's aperkin', its aroma fills
the air
Grandma's busy cookin', her
family'll soon be there

Grandpa's in the orchard, gatherin' in
some fruit
He's raiding grandma's garden
She yells, "You'd better scoot!"

The buffet sure is tempting, a feast is
close at hand
Shared by friends and family, this
day will sure be grand

The trip, sometimes seems endless,
though soon we do arrive
The food, the fun, all that's shared
We know it's worth the drive

A card game in the corner, kids are
playin' jacks
A ball game in the front yard, girls
skip rope in back
Old folks playin' checkers, ladies sit
and chat
The boys are teasin' Jimmy, he just
struck out at bat

The sun grows weak, night is near,
we know it's time to go
A kiss good-bye, a sleepy head, we
drive away real slow
All we've learned, all we know, all
the love we share
It's a comfort, just to visit grandma
Knowing she's always there.

Judith Bowry Ratteray

LET ME BE

*This Poem is dedicated to my friend
Shirley for all of the encouragement
and inspiration she so kindly gave
me.*

I was born black and of the Negro
race
Not brown, as you say when trying to
save face
Accept me as I am in my natural state
Not bypass me in your general haste
To find one of me who looks
acceptable to you
Let me be what I was born to be

No matter how I dress or how I speak
Make no mistake, I am black!
I never said I was anything
But of the Negro race
So let me be what I was born to be
Accept my brothers and sisters who
Are true to the race, black until blue
Let them be true to themselves
By accepting them as they are
Black in body, mind and face
Let me be what I was born to be

K Sue Fitt

ARRIVAL OF SPRING

At last the time is almost here
For the bleakness of winter to
disappear.
The cold ground, bare trees,
everything seems forsaken
Empty nests where birds used to
appear
Seems so long to wait for spring to
awaken.

The long wait is worth all the beauty
of spring
The buds start to bloom, the first
robin sings,
The showers come to cleanse all the
earth
Then erupts all the beauty that nature
can bring
Leaving winter behind with spring's
awesome rebirth.

Janice Reynolds

MY MOM & DAD

*To George & Margaret Coolen, the
most thoughtful, caring parents ever,
from your loving daughter, Janice
(Coolen) Reynolds.*

As time goes by, I look back quite a
bit
I remember how I learned to walk,
talk and sit
I remember school and how to
subtract and add
But most of all, I remember my mom
and my dad.

My goals and triumphs, my
downfalls and troubles
Thank God, thank God, they made
parents in couples
You were both always there to pull
me through
And although you're away, I'll
always love you.

My life has been good and you two I
owe
For the Bible says, "You reap what
you sow"
To my family now, I hope I do what I
should
As the parents who taught me, and
taught me so good.

Benjamin E Everhart

CHILDREN OF EARTH

Children of Earth
Hear me, for I am Earth.
My wind blows sadness upon you,
Yet you do not feel.
My rains weep of death,
Yet you do not hear.
You have tortured me with your
luxuries,
Yet I allow you to continue.
You have scarred me with your wars,
Yet I do not fight back.
You speak of changes
Yet I feel none.

Soon I shall endure no more,
and you shall be faced with darkness.
The very essence of your being
within me,
shall be,
as you have done to me,
ripped away.
Children of Earth,
hear me!!

Benjamin E Everhart

SHAMED

Once scarred, I shall never repair.
You poke me with drills
until I quake and quiver.
You put craters in me just to see what
they look like.
You contaminate my fluids just to
drink it later.
My breath brown, grows shorter than
ere before.
How much more must I take
before you realize that,
YES!!
It kills me as dead as it has killed
you.

I scream with terror but you refuse to
hear.
How many more studies must be
conducted
for you to see
that the air is choking me,
the water is poisoning me, and,
my ground reeks of toxins like bad
breath.

My flowers wilt; I grow sterile and
barren.
My children have ears plugged with
cork.
My children grow lazy while I grow
tired.
I cannot repair, what you have done.

Betty Lou Gignilliat

ELVIS

*This poem is dedicated to Elvis, his
music will live forever within me.*

Elvis Presley, as you know,
He was King of Rock and Roll

Why he died we cannot say
But his Love is here to stay

Elvis knew the day would come
He'd be with his loving Mom

Fame and fortune can't compare
with what heaven offers up there

So wipe your tears and sing his songs
Because his music will always live
on

He's up there singing grace
'Cause he's happy in his place

People say so many things
But Elvis knew he'd be with the King
of Kings

He was ready when he was called
He left memories behind to tell us all

How many people could be that
strong?
To tell a story in his song

Elvis knew the day was near
But look at what he gave to us all
these years

Something to tell our children
That Elvis was King of Rock and
Roll

Rudy T Olmedo

THE WAY OF LIFE

To my brother Joseph G. Olmedo.

The way of life. Things change and
rearrange.
But all things must pass,
at last. Ever wake up to a
day when nothing was going
right, then hold tight keep
your sight, and think bright,
and soon you will welcome
the satisfaction of
knowing, that you're still
up to bat.

Kevin L Berry

STRANGE

I have a big head
I have a big nose
All my hair hangs
Down to my toes
I'm a rugged old man
I've got no food
And for some strange reason
I'm in a good mood
Please won't you tell me
Why this is so
Because if you don't
I'll feel like a hobo

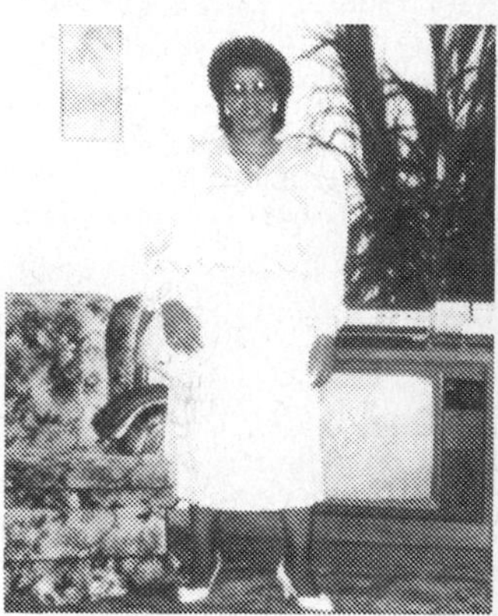

Hilda H Braxton

Hilda H Braxton

HEAVEN DOORS

I know a place called Heaven
Its gates are as pure as gold,
I'm trying to make it there one day
I'm trying to save my soul.

I know the Lord will be there
They told me so today,
I know there'll be a resting place
Up there, so far away.

I'm asking God to guide me
And to lead me in the right way,
So when the day will come for me
I'll be up there to stay.

With outstretched arms, he'll guide
me
Within those golden gates,
I hope that when my time comes
It will not be too late.

This world is not my home
I didn't come here to stay,
I know one day, we all must go,
On that Great Judgment Day.

Hilda H Braxton

I AM THY SERVANT

The road is rough, the hills are hard
to climb,
My faith is in my God, because he's
with me all the time
. . . I am Thy servant . . .

When my burdens get heavy, and my
friends are few,
I look up to God, to help carry me
through,
. . . I am Thy servant . . .

He's with me in the morning, He's
with me every night,
I know that God loves me, He is

The Holy Light,
. . . I am Thy servant . . .

He brings the sunshine and the rain,
This we cannot understand, that
God is still blessing us, so we
can join the Christian band,
. . . I am Thy servant . . .

We need to awake and turn to God,
to let Him know that we love Him so,
Because when He comes, we all must
go
. . . I am Thy servant . . .

I'm trying to live the best I can,
and this is very hard,
But I want to see Him face to face,
I want to meet my God,
. . . I am Thy servant . . .

Joah O Bastien
RED ROSE
To my Valentine, I give one red rose.
In my passion, electrified sparks
Turn the candle's light fire into rays
of heat—
The heat of night and day, my
Valentine in mythical time.
Valentine, my sweet ever-loving red
rose of the land,
Your voice is my Valentine's
musical, magical bond of everlasting
love.
My Valentine's hair is red flaming
flares of sunlight,
Reflections of the sun.
My Valentine's eyes of green
emeralds, specks of green jade,
In a ring around the moon.
Your kisses and caresses, my
Valentine, are food of life.
With one Valentine red rose of sweet
fragrance and soft aroma of spring,
Here is the love I bring you.
Spun silver webs of Valentine love,
lost in time.
My Valentine love, I must have you
as mine.

Mary C Frye
MY LIFE'S PRAYER

This poem is dedicated to my grandsons: Lance, Coty, Shane, and Jeremy Frye.

Let me live my life to love,
those I've touched and become a part
of.
Let me live my life to see,
all in one time that I can be.

Let me live my life to hear,
sounds of laughter instead of tears,
Let me live my life to taste,
sweetness and goodness, no time to
waste.

My life will not be lived in vain,
if I had time left I'd live the same,
and when it comes my time to die,
life will not have passed me by.

Mary Drobny
TIME, SWIFTLY FLOWING SAND
Time, swiftly flowing sand
Change, ever shifting patterns on the
shore
The sea, calm, serene, soothing,
And suddenly, fierce, violent,
unforgiving
Venting anger stored over genera-
tions
Or perhaps a warning for generations
yet to come.

The sea has witnessed events long
forgotten in the books of mighty
man.
Has learned the lessons man has yet
to question
Has borne upon her crests
Man bound for war, for peace,
For bondage, and for freedom.

If the sea could only talk; how much
we should learn
Yet listen; perhaps in her disorderly
rage there is a message,
A legacy of experience, hope and
heartbreak
Stored over generations.

Have we time enough to push aside
An opportunity at Knowledge as
great as this?
As time flows, the patterns change,
And we rely on that which we
condemn,
It must be realized: without the sea,
there would be no sand
No tides, no waves, no life.

Elena Sona John
FACE I LOVE SO DEAR

To all those I love so dear.

My eyes scan the crowd
Searching and seeking,
Looking for a sight familiar
That face I love so dear.

My dreams of loving fervor
My sleep they do banish,
to see, just to see—
That face I love so dear.

Times my eyes deceive me,
I cannot tell how much—
I despair for just a glimpse
of the face I love so much.

I sit so forlornly here
I wait so patiently
to see, just to see—
that face I love so dear.

Elena Sona John
TO SEE YOU SMILE
I long to see your smile again
That does seem so like a dream—
It drives away my fears of pain,
Oh! to feel your smile again.

I remember that day you turned—
And smiled so dazzlingly bright;
In my heart—those many emotions
churned.
My heart! O' what a plight.

You belong to another
When you could belong to me . . .
The things that could have been,
The dreams we could have seen.

But those loving thoughts of you
Only herald in the pain;
You left a legacy of yearning—
A longing to see your smile again.

F M H
WHY
When we were young
The world seemed bright
We'd walk side by side
Into the night
We'd gaze at the sky
And then at the sea
It seemed the world was made
For just you and me
But
As we grew older the world grew
dark
The stars no longer shined
Why?

Karen "Janelle" Stephens
AZURE MELODY
Let me quiver
To the music in my soul
A lapis lazuli concert from my heart.

Each syncopated minim
Slides like mercury 'cross
The strings to form
Tiny drops of moisture
'Round my thoughts.

Thrum rhythmically
To the beating of my heart . . .
rat-tat-tat.
Tap melodically in time—two part—
triplet—
Now a nonuple in jazzy ragtime
romance.

Let me quiver
To the music in my soul
Each wildly captured note
An expression of the love I feel for
you.

Elisabeth Anne McArthur
BUMPER HEARTS
One meets
One loves
One leaves
But love stays
Then one meets and loves again.

Evelyn Hass
A TRIBUTE TO TONI

This poem is dedicated to Toni, A Very Special Person.

She came to us with dark soft eyes,
With laughter to hide her pain;
She taught us much of life and Love,
Not seeking wealth or fame.

She knew the time had come for her
Soon she would say good-bye,
Come hold my hand and sing to me
Wipe teardrops from your eyes.

Please don't be sad, I leave this world
Tho I am twenty-eight,
My life has been so full and good
Watch for me at heaven's gate.

Now she sleeps beneath the big oak
tree
On the land she loved so much,
Our hearts are sad and the tears they
fall;
Then we think of the lives she
touched.

Evelyn Hass
GATHERING STONES
Mrs. M. sat in the corner of her room
At the rest home, head bowed and
eyes closed,
When I spoke, she raised her head
and smiled;
What is your name, I don't see so
good.

From the window, I could see a
beautiful garden;
With stones neatly laid,
Did you know I planted the flowers?
She said Papa gathered the stones,
Did you know, he went away?
She wiped away the tears.

We chatted for a while
As I stood to say good-bye,
She reached for my hand
What is your name dear?
I don't remember so good.
Did you see my garden?
Papa gathered the stones,
Did you know he went away?

Mary Ann LaFarge
MIRRORS OF MY SOUL
Come with me, across the sea; we will sail, on blue crystal waters, for all eternity. Ask me no questions. I will tell you no lies; for my heart and my soul are mirrored in my eyes. Be my love; and together there, there is nothing we can't do; for nothing can destroy a love, that is forever strong and true.

Look deep into my soul; and watch my love unfold. Stay with me. Be with me; and let our love take hold. You and I shall cross the bounds of infinity, and forever find the raptures of love, which is our destiny. How could we go through life, never knowing each other's kiss; for all that really matters is our life that knows such bliss.

Summer breezes are fading fast; and autumn is almost here.
I gaze out the window; and into, the ocean, there falls a single tear. I implore you, darling, to sail away with me; and together, our love will flow, light sunlight upon the sea. Feel my love, around you, as ocean waves begin to roll. Look deep into my green eyes. They are the mirrors of my soul.

Donna Calder
THE MIND GAME
Life is an illusion
of total confusion
People afraid of giving from the soul,
so they learn to play the role.

Too many competitors in the game,
all wanting the feelings of fame.
Not many romantics anymore,
and so many just keeping the score.

So few left who give from the heart,
but many who play the part.
Love seems to be in the past,
and sex without feeling gets boring
fast.

True love lies within
Much more than just the touching of
skin,
It's sad—so many will touch, yet
never feel.
Makes you wonder just what's
real . . . .

Adeline Fleischer
THE SILENT ONE
He was always around
He was always there
Without a word
You knew he cared
When you were sad
When you were blue
He was always there
To see you through
Just his presence
Meant so much
A tender look
A friendly touch
Yet never a word
Did the silent one say
His presence said all
As you faced each day
Now he is gone
And you feel alone
With the deepest silence
You've ever known.

Cynthia Ann Cortez
TEARS FROM HEAVEN
Shadows slowly moving
Across the darkened wall,
Constantly changing shape
As the moon begins to fall.

Thoughts coming and going,
Putting myself down
For real and imagined failures,
Ever racing round and round.

When did it all begin?
And when will it ever end?
Pain pouring from the heavens
Like the tears only God can send.

A fire that's burning low,
Smoke rising into the sky
And drifting into nothing,
Hope that was meant to die.

The moon that started out so full
Is now nothing left to see,
Just darkness filling up the sky
Where once it used to be.

Cynthia Ann Cortez
WAITING
Sitting alone,
Waiting for him,
So the loneliness will leave
And life can begin.

Being with him,
Yet feeling miles apart.
Is there really a difference
In the ache of your heart?

That empty space,
The wound that won't heal,
You created your wall
So you wouldn't have to feel.

But the wall couldn't hold
All the pain felt inside,
And with every brick added
Another part of you died.

The answers you seek
Must come from above,
For it's from God we receive
Unconditional love.

Alexis M Wales
THE NIGHT
The night, the night
I slowly turn to fright
The loneliness it brings to me
Alone in the dead of night

The quiet silence creeps slowly near
Making me tense and full of fear
Is there someone hiding in the night
Waiting to come out into the light?

I hear the grandfather clock
Ticking away the time.
I hear every second, a tick and a tock
Waiting for time to go by.

Claudia J Lent-Boutchyard
ALL MY TOMORROWS
Heavenly Father, my God in sorrow,
I need Your strength to face
tomorrow.
I need Your comfort to get through
the night.
I need Your wisdom when things
don't seem right.
I need Your presence to fill up the
space.
I need to feel Your love and grace.
When tears flow and loneliness
screams at me,
I need Your touch, Lord, to help me
feel and see.
There is no other who knows me, like
You do.
You are my hope and sunshine. My
tomorrow comes from You.

Daphne F Benedict (Age 10)

Daphne F Benedict
BEST FRIENDS
A Best Friend, is a friend till the end.
They'll stay by your side,
even if you slip or slide

Though for my best friend,
It is the end.

"For us I mean . . .
And it's not a dream!

It's a terrible nightmare,
And I have a feeling of despair.

I've got a new Best Friend,
She'll be my friend till the end.

It's time to stop dreaming,
When my eyes start gleaming.

'Cause I want to try . . .
Not to Cry."

Mary P Lawrence
RETURN TO RAPTURE

To my first Love who gave me an eternal moment of passion, E. J. M.

The sun peers through the angry clouds that sail the airy seas, the villainous vessels conceal the warmth from the earth, dispelling the ashes of modern man, blanketing the coils of the mountain's summit with ivory snow.

The leaves laugh with the wind as the tranquil trees bow gracefully to greet the morning breeze!

I launch out into the depths of my soul and capture that sparkle of gleam lost to oppressive times when fear gripped my heart, caused showering tears of pain and misery to flow as a mighty river of destruction!

Come! Let us escape to rapture! The time we gave in unity, dranked the elixir of living waters, built a kingdom of joy and happiness, and we, were at peace! Your eyes are as beautiful as the sky, your smile is as bright as the sun, your touch is a fiery furnace that intense my emotions to sizzling sensations! Sensual seeds that blossom into flowers of love, illuminate the dreary corners of my heart and color my world of darkness!

Remember when we walked the sandy shores, felt the gravel tingle our toes!
I can still hear the gaiety of our hearts as the blue waters rushed to the muddy banks drenching our bodies with its soothing mass while the birds soar overheard adorning the skies with a portrait of eternal bliss! Oh! to grasp the soil of love, inhale its aroma, possess that moment when time ceased. We were one in unity in our world!

The contours of neutrality grow very sheer, dreams of reality become transparent, fantasies and hope fades away!

Where is the mountain we climbed together and saw the beginning of our lives? Will my lips taste the wine of rapture from the fruits of our devotion?

Jenny Cutler

Jenny Cutler
IN HONOR OF GEORGE WASHINGTON CARVER

My dear neighbor, Marjory Hath, recently retired from a lifetime in a faculty college, advises me: "Keep your gifted pen moving!"

Born in the darkness of serfdom,
Bound by the shackles of need,
Placed in his niche by God's
wisdom,
Too lowly for mankind to heed.

Tifany Archer
UNTITLED

This poem is dedicated to my deceased father, James Archer. Without him I would have never fulfilled my dream of writing poetry.

As I looked upon the sky, I glimpsed a vision as the clouds floated by. As I gazed upon that deep blue sky, I saw two people come into sight.

One was a guy, the other a girl. I was that girl and the guy was you.

It was you and I walking along the beach. Sharing kisses, holding hands, walking and talking upon the sand.

I stood next to you and felt secure, knowing you and I were together once more.

The feeling was so wonderful, how good it made me feel. But when I turned around, and you weren't there, I realized it was only a dream floating across the sky.

P R Plummer
THE CHRISTMAS OF MY FIRST HEADACHE
Mother's favorite ornament,
a gold ball as bright as her hair,
hung in our tree between needles and
tinsel
and fell with the help of my hands.
With a "poof" it broke on the pile
carpet and quietly lay dying next
to the radiator.
I thought the small, scattered
pieces must be mirrored tears,
blown out of their skull like a
volcano.
And that you could sit a million
tiny kittens in that sleek, clean
shell.
Their claws would screech
onto their innocent images
like nails on blackboards.
Squeege, squeege, they'd slide back
down into the well of that broken
ball.
When I pressed my finger to a stray
glass tear,
I felt a silent splintering underneath
and something scratching inside.

Melissa Luttrell
THE PLANTATION
As the dusk slowly settled with the
remnants of the day's hectic pace,
The fresh starlit breeze enslaved my
concentration.
I walked the grounds where my
mirrored lineage created memories,
Recorded forever in the wispy
mimosas in cadence along the lanes.
Courting lovers strolled bashfully
along the magnolia-filled brooks in
my very steps.
An undying aura of southern grace
tied me to its history,
A time when ladies were feminine
with molasses-sweet flirtiness,
And men were romantic and gentle
without disrupting their masculinity
and determination.
It was a time of sorrow and pain,
fantasy and reality, with magnetism
and charm.
It is now at peace.

Nathalie Moisan
I SEE IT IN YOUR EYES
I see it in your eyes
And feel it in your touch
I taste it in your kiss
And hear it in your voice

Your friendship means so much to
me
Your warmth, your laugh, your love
Mean much more than you can see
I think I am in love

In love with a friend
That can't happen. Not to me.
Don't let it end
This friendship. You and me.

You help me laugh at life
You help me scare the pain
You help me day after day
Keep sending your love my way.

Betty Morales Shepherd
MY GRANDSON

To all my grandchildren whom I love dearly.

I watched you walk down every stair.
Your little legs take one by one.
I hold your hand and try to guide,
Your footsteps as they reach the
ground.

You walk now farther down the path,
of unknown dreams
and hopes young man.
Not knowing what this life will bring,
yet smiling as you go along.
So soon too soon, you'll go to school.
Encounter friends and foe alike.
For life's not perfect understand.
You'll make mistakes as we all do.
You'll fall in love in years to come.
Then I'll be gone and you'll forget
I watched you then, I watch you now.
Proud that you are a part of me
A part I know will now go on
To greater things I never did.
I'm still your guide, will always be
I give my blessing, now my dear
Go on your way tho I'm not near
To hold your hand my grandson dear
But God will guide you throughout
the years
Just hold his hand, through the years,
and he'll take care of all your tears.
Your fears and dreams
So now goodbye my precious dear—
I helped you while—I was still here.

Betty Jean Patterson
THE GHOST SHIP

To my dad, who believed in me.

The ghost ship pushed the foamy
waves
And furled its gossamer sails.
A hearty yell from galley slaves
Kept rhythm with the great grey
whales.

"Yo ye men!" bellowed the burly
mate
Crack went the leather whip,
"Push this barge of rotten timber,
Push this wench of a ship."

I saw and heard, I'm sure I did
At least I thought she was there.
This ghost ship upon the sea
This lady with long white hair.

Again I gazed, again she sailed
Again she disappeared.
Was I imagining this memory
Of days lost to greying hair?

I was a lad—a galley slave
With laden oars I pushed that ship.
I felt the sting of salty spray
I heard the mate's black whip.

It's all there, I see her now
Heavy with spice and gold.
This ghost ship pushed by galley
slaves,
Some bent, some young, some old.

Betty Jean Patterson
THE TINY STRAY
Kitty cat. Kitty cat. Solid black
Who are you anyway?
You come to my door and cry for
food,
Then up and run away.

I wish you would be like me
Needing a special friend.
Then we could find time together
Hours alone we would spend.

Getting to know each other
While I stroke your tiny back.
Tickle your chin or belly,
As you curl upon my lap.

Little kitty black as night
Will you come and stay?
You'd have a home. I'd have a
friend.
And lonesome would go away.

J D Smith
MUSIC MAN

"In my favorite corner bar, he plays a steel guitar." To Mark Lawler, and his band "Meltdown."

Music man upon the stage
with words to say
and chords to play,
singing feelings so deeply felt,
with fire enough to make me melt.

Rock me gently music man,
so beautiful to see.
rock me gently all night long,
and set my spirit free.

Music man shine up the night,
up there playing
beneath the light.
Intoxicate my cares away
with music skillful fingers play.

Rock me gently music man,
and let me feel your heat.
Rock me gently with your songs.
You move me with your beat.

Music man, oh can you see
exactly what you do to me?
You make me live. You make me
feel.
You make me love, with magic steel.

Rock me gently music man.
You touch my heart tonight.
Rock me gently, melt me down.
You make me feel alright.

P D George
MORNING WAIT

For my mother and father, the greatest inspirations of my life, I love you . . . .

Watching the leaves as the wind
moves them like a thousand
heartbeats,
It mellows me,
And takes me into a comfort only the
spirit meets.
Then time becomes irrelevant as my
mind lingers on,
Awaiting the beauty of God's perfect
dawn,
Soon there is a warmth as colours
caress my face,
And I think how tender the sun's
morning kiss from space,
So again another day begins as
perfect as before,
And I thank God I can adore . . . .

P D George
THROUGH A CHILD'S EYE

For Bonnie, Alysha and Natasha. A blessing to our family.

The river of life it flows ever so
quickly by,
Oh to see the river again through a
child's eye,
'Cause everything that's seen from a
child's point of view,
Is full of nature's loveliness and
warm with melting hue.
And fresh is the lilac which dances in
the air,
As birds sing songs and in the mind
they linger there,
And in the mellow comfort of a
child's thought and will,
Time, it sometimes seems as if it's
standing still.
Oh, I hope I'll always remember until
the day I die,
To only look at life through a child's
eye . . . .

P D George
THE QUESTION

For John Hall; A Good Friend, and the best ear.

Way in the deepest realm, where
hidden passions lye,
All the truths and desires away from
naked eye,
I hear the hollow echo of my heart
crying,
A plea with life for love undying,
In this unfinished space awaiting
symmetry,
Does my love so wait for me?

P D George
YOUNGER DAYS

For L.D.E.S. (Chloe) my confidant, my friend, my rock.

Oh to those days when life was full
of zest,
And sunlight danced on daisies west,
When love was young and echoed
laughter,
And passion flared forever after,
All time was spent like pocket
change,
Not one precious moment need be
arranged,
And one day awoke it had all gone
by,
Like the child's twinkling of an eye,
But left with us sweet memories,
Of many many days like these . . . .

P D George
GOOD OLD ROCK

To my brothers Jim and Shaun, for the good times.

Spirited highs and purple haze,
These are memories from earlier
daze,
Oh so young and carefree child,
Living on life's border called wild,
Partied here and tattooed there,
Long and braided was my hair,
Many loves they came and went,
And all the rules they were bent,
And then one day I awoke,
And years had past in a cloud of
smoke,
And I felt like there was something
missing,
It wasn't freedom and it wasn't
kissing,
So I jumped in my car and took off
with a blaze,
And smiled as the radio played
purple haze . . . .

P D George
FOR YOU

To my love Luc Therrien.

Do you my love ever stop to listen,
To the sound of sun on water as it
glistens,
Or feel the warmth in a summer
breeze,
And watch the birds play through the
trees,
Or smell the lilacs of summer's first
bliss,
Or feel the passion of a lover's first
kiss,
To live one moment without a care,
Or to trust in love if you dare,
These things are precious this is true,
But all are nothing without you . . .

Charlesetta Cole

Charlesetta Cole
THE SIGNS OF TIME

This poem is dedicated to my mother Ophelia, for believing in me. It is also dedicated to, Rena, my dear friend, my teacher Mrs. Joe Buckner and Mrs. Carolyn Minor. All of these special people were my greatest inspiration. A special dedication to my children.

People of the nation
Look around and see,
The world is changing
Don't you agree?
Drugs are spread out
From city to city,
Children killing children
Ain't it a pity?
Children being raised
With no shame
Or self-control,
Disrespecting their parents,
Even the old,
Lack of determination
Afraid to believe in dreams,
Losing all hope
And self-esteem.
Children are abandoned
For the sake of cocaine,
Children being born
With drug abuse pain.
Women selling their bodies
For a "Cocaine High"
Losing all abilities
And left to die.
I don't understand
Why there's all this grief,
When we have our dreams
And all of our beliefs.
We know that life is a journey,
And we are just passing through.
People of the nation
What are we going to do?
As we take this journey
Through "The Signs of Time"
We must have "Love"
And "Compassion"
And educate our minds.

Rose Marie Robichaud
YESTERDAY'S CHILD

To my one and only love, Jay.

Yesterday's child has come and gone
Tomorrow's child is here
Eternal love is always ready
If you take the dare

The dare is life
And you must live
To care is love
And you must give

Tomorrow brings joy and love
Yesterday brought the tears
The love of another is calling
As gentle as the deer

To answer you must listen
With an opened soul
To love another and to be loved
Is to be in Heaven's own

We answer to the calling
When it has been heard
We cannot resist it
For it is the solemn word

Rose Marie Robichaud
SILHOUETTES
Silence is creeping around me
Waiting for darkness to fall

Silhouettes of the swaying trees
Against my bedroom wall

Shadows of dreams and wishes
Trick my eyes to see

Wondering if my lover
Shall ever return to me

Cecilia A Jacobs
UNTITLED
What was, never will be again.
All has changed.
If I knew then, what I know now,
I would have done things differently.
And maybe now, we would be more.
As it is, we'll be friends.
And I can start anew.

Thank-You for what was.
Maybe it will be again,
With someone new.
You are part of my life,
I will never forget.
Nor will I want to.

I hope you find what you want.
As I hope I will.
And maybe together we can be happy apart.

Gloria J Gillies
THE HUM OF THE HUMMINGBIRD

I want to dedicate this poem to my four children that I love very much! Sherry Acosta, Tammy Kibler, Glen and Brandy Gillies, and to my wonderful husband, Michael.

One day I walked outside, and I heard, this sweet hum,
And I couldn't help but wonder, where it was coming from.
Then as I looked away, up into the sky,
I saw this beautiful hummingbird, as it flew by.
I watched him, as he completely, stood still,
And sipping nectar, from a flower, with a bill.
Then he flew up high, to this tiny little nest,
Then stopped for a moment, just to sit and rest.
Then as he flew out further, on that limb,
There was his mate, almost as pretty as him.
I just simply couldn't, keep my eyes, off them,
As they hatched out, their family, way out on that limb.
I knew they were the tiniest birds, I'd ever see,
Because, they were not much bigger, than a bumblebee.
They would dart, every direction and miss every stick,
And the speed they had, was remarkably quick.
Now, I just sit here and I dread the day,
That they will leave me, and go far away.
And that lovely hum, I'll no longer hear,
Until, they return to me, again next year.

Toni Crummy Moore
EVERYDAY
Everyday we work
and play,
Everyday we eat.
Everyday we have fun
with people that we meet.
Everyday is a holiday
Somewhere on this earth,
So let's be happy and make
Everyday the best that it is
worth.

Lois Lynn Henderson
THE SNOW

To my loving daughter, Monica Anne.

Blankets of snow
Surrounds me as
I stand upon
Winter's land,
Snowflakes that
Melt from the
Touch of a finger,
Snowflakes that
Fall on my hat
And linger.
Trees that seem
Sprayed with
Whipping cream,
A wonderland of
Whiteness as if
In a dream.
I slide on the ice,
My skates sturdy and
Sound as the snow
Falls softly to the
ground

Scott Pfeifle
FIRST WAVES
First Waves of thought are tepid with subtle machinations.
They are raw, unchecked, reaction, the selfish subconscious's outlet.
So often, yet less now, they escape into perceived decisions,
then to be reflected upon, and corrected, with shameful regret.

The artful let First Waves reverberate a short soothing time
And when they have settled and cooled send them peacefully forth
As thoughtful communication with the universal mind.
The artful reflect upon footsteps, not earth unjustly scorched.

Scott Pfeifle
SEASONS OF PEACE
It's standing windward on a high hill
inside a young spring afternoon,
tasting thoroughly a swollen brook
and the budding oak.

It's drifting asleep in a lover's arms
with the day filtering softly through,
feet and heart just so warm
they are scarcely felt.

It's sitting alone upon a bench
as golden breeze-tossed leaves
fall.
Children on swings laugh
and all is as it should be

It's gazing through frosted glass,
in love with a settling white blanket,
content to stand in wonder,
knowing things are quiet and life
is good.

Susan L Fields

Susan L Fields
I WANT TO:
I want to look unto you everyday Lord
I want to savor all that you are
I want to breathe every breath that you take
I want to live in your kingdom afar.

"I want to sit as close to you Jesus"
I want to touch your spirit, divine
I want to hear every word that you say Lord
I want to praise you above all mankind.

I want to meet all your followers, Father
I want to share, in your Holy name
I want to thank you for saving me Jesus
from Satan's deceitful domain.

Dorothy Morris-Dillon
THEY, THEY, THEY, THEY.

To my grandchildren, Arthur, Yolanda, Monique, Neisha, Kason, Shawn, Shavar and Chyna.

You may not go to their schools
THEY say.
What fearful, ignorant, poor fools are THEY,
To put in your small hands the power THEY lack.
The courage to walk past them and never look back.

So great are you that THEY all fear.
Your power is too strong to have you near.
So weak are THEY, so very unsure,
That even to look upon you makes them insecure.

Hold your heads up, stand tall and proud.
Say "I pity you" to that lily white crowd.
Pity the big people who stand and jeer.
Go forward small ones, do not listen, do not hear.

For THEY're still afraid even after so long.
That you'll discover weakness, and what they've done wrong.
Show them the courage that THEY lack.
Remember our heroes, be proud to be black.

Beatrice M Kerner
WHO ARE THEY?
In closeness with God's people
they sit apart in church.
Who are they?

Freed by death
from marriage vows
They turn and say;
"My sisters, let us come
together as family."
For a few hours
they gather and find
joy in breaking bread.

At night they lie down to sleep
never afraid
quietly guided
protected by God
These widowed friends are aware
of His eternal love.

Cheryl Twaddle
TO MY LOVE
The past few weeks have been so great
I sometimes wonder if it was fate
That brought you to me that night
And made everything so right

I love you so very dearly
I always want you near me
I want to be your only one
I want to know that we have won

That special feeling shared by two
Nothing could take me from you
I think it's true love that I've found
'Cause I miss you when you're not around

Although I've known you a short time
I just want you to be all mine
I've never before felt this good
I never even dreamed I could

I feel proud to be your side
My love for you I'll never hide
I want you to know to never fear
'Cause for you I'll always be here

Selene Graham
FALLING IN LOVE
Just one look, my heart surrendering
Just one touch, no more pretending.
In your arms, . . . nothing matters
My head whirling, . . . pulse patters.
Soft caress, soothing is your voice.
Falling in love; . . . no other choice.
This feeling inside, as if it roars!
It is clear now . . . always I'm yours.

Carl A Chase
WHO'S THERE
I look and I look. But I don't see a thing. But I know in my heart that someone is there.
That's why I never feel alone.
Because I know, that someone is watching over me.
Some say it's God. And some say it's not. And some may go as far to say that maybe I'm nuts.
But I say and so do many others
That someone is there.
Thank God!

Lynn Johnson
DAFFODILS DANCED
Bewildered, blushed with decay
The crazed journey lingered on
Where the house befriended the lake
Hosting a sea of wild flowers

Though the rustic peel shriveled
The graceful haunt tarried on
Beams dazzled the shattered mirrors
Inheriting glimpses of four

With vague arrogance, the mark
Peered above the ruling mass
Once shielded by kindly pebbles
Reduced, as mere victims of death

Blown ashore, the stone pathway
Toted damp traces of old
Innocence discovered at last
By the ever nurturing breeze

Through the gentle pendulum
Daffodils danced 'mongst daisies
As one of four stood, gazing back
The sunset hid beneath the graves

Patty Greenfield
NIGHT CREATURE
Loneliness a nocturnal creature
allowing
its presence known at dusk
Daylight fades noise and
commotion
settle with the sun
Loneliness creeps in unnoticed
until
firmly postured for the duration
of darkness
No conversation no shared feelings
no differing opinions
Occupying thought staying off
sleep
Sharing a bed allowing no warm
embraces
no words of comfort no
rhythmic beating of a heart no
security
Shrinking somewhat at dawn
refusing to
perish
Merely taking cover from light
Preparing to reveal itself again
growing larger more intense
Gaining strength and control with
each visit

Valerie Barrett

Valerie Barrett
LEARNING IS PROCESS

To those with whom I've lived and loved. To all who held my hand.

Mastery of terms and direction
requires repetition.
Repetition moves toward ability.
Ability increases understanding of
language.
Increased language aids listening
ability to learn.
Learning and doing develops positive
attitude.
Positive attitude eases application.
Application of learning brings results.
Results bring success.

Success creates self-confidence.
Self-confident experiences multiply
acts of courage.
Courage heightens initiative.
Initiative intensifies productivity.
Productivity magnifies worthiness.
Worthiness enlarges capacity to care.
Caring enhances integrity.
Integrity displays reservoir of respect.
Respect promotes sound relationships
and friendships.
Sound relationships demand
responsibility and honesty.
Honesty bestows freedom.
Freedom allows exploration.
Exploration brings the opportunity
for Ageless Learning.

Valerie Barrett
FRAGMENTATION
Fathers are leaving.
Mothers are tired and loose.
Babies by the age of five
Are captured in the noose.

We must not keep pretending
Or continue to defend
A lack of values that is mated
With actions we cannot mend.

Parents aren't trained to parent.
Teachers can't repair
The damage that's been done
To those too young to know . . . or
care.

Promises are broken.
Hearts are cold as steel.
Life rides on a video game
And robots cannot feel.

Fragmentation has a price,
Costly, unkind, and scary.
Please! Don't have more kids . . .
You're too young to marry and
We don't need them to bury.

Valerie Barrett
WISPS WITHIN
Cattails containing secrets,
The movement of the dance,
The magic mix of colors,
Powerful horses in a prance.

Regal decks of playing cards,
A whiff of baking bread,
The excitement of a carnival,
A needle holding thread.

The secret pirate's paths and coves,
The treasures nature brings.
The hunt, the hunt,
To capture pleasant dreams.

The skater's scab peeling off the
knee,
The skipping of a stone,
A special favorite colored piece of
glass,
Out of breath, running, running
home.

Childhood's memory stirs more
clouds
Of mist encircling dreams.
These fleeting, nameless gnomes
Whisper 'round the essence
Of our being.

Sherree Berterman
SHE

Morris, thanks for being my friend . . .

Since the day she called . . .
How happy I have been . . .
Excited and confused . . .
Remembering how to begin . . .
Relax and wait and give her time . . .
Express the happiness you hope to
find . . .
Especially love, from the heart and
the mind.

Diane Yinger
A NOTE TO MYSELF
out of all the poems you may ever
write—
or all the words you may ever lay
down on paper—
there is nothing more significant
than the realization that your
thoughts,
problems, ego, losses, defeats, are
nothing
more than mere specks in the realm
of things,
the universe, Orion . . .

to dwell upon them is not only a
waste of time
but a detriment to your purpose.

keep your insight.
rise above it.
achieve.

if nothing else—
do attempt to keep things in
perspective.
contemplate the Southern
Cross . . .

Diane Yinger
GOOD-BYE
cancer growing
internally spreading
killing.

moonrises, sunsets,
trips to the lake, and
quiet mornings in the sun
become important once again.

bleak moments—
times of despair—
the helplessness of those who care—
eternal hope.

entwined hands of father and
daughter.
lack of pain—
lack of breath—
the silent tears of those still living—
serenity.

Russell Leroy Fielder
NO OTHER
Willing I was granted the power to
glean an eternity of precious
treasures; I would bestow each and
every one to you in expression of
adornment and affection.

No other is more worthy than you of
such tender treasures.

If I possessed the secrets of the
universe; I would capture all the
echoes of laughter and traces of joy
ever known. Readily, I would deliver
to you a bouquet of splendid smiles
that would forever reveal the magic
and happiness known to your heart.

No other is more worthy than you of
such burning passion.

If I could soar with the wind; I would
journey to the limits of heaven,
casting my dearest wish—hoping for
you a world of good fortune,
adventure, excitement and romance.
No other is more deserving than you
of such love.
No other is more stirring to my soul

Julia Flowers
MY SPECIAL FRIEND

I dedicate this poem to my best friends who inspired me to write this poem. "Darlene & Eddy," I Love You Both.

You make me laugh when I want to
cry,
You are honest with me, you never
lie

If he breaks my heart or lets me go,
You are there for me I always know

I hope our friendship never ends,
You will always be my special
friends

Tina DeLuca
STUNG
Take your hands off me.
The scars left by your touch
are slow to heal
And to cover them becomes
impossible
Though I continue to try
to forget
As salt trickles into the wounds,
still open.
Your touch pressing harder
until it happens
And the shape of a heart
is etched in my skin
Marking me forever.
Telling everyone I've been had,
quite bad, once again, yet
That same stinging touch
I seem to invite
And the scars never fade
As you do . . . slowly.

Gladys Alford Everhardt
OUR GRANDMOTHER MARY

Dedicated to Grandmother Mary's grandchildren and the priceless memories they inherited.

Memories of the late twenties and
thirties
Keep coming back to crowd my
mind,
How I ran and played with many
cousins
A barefoot child in summer time.

Our Grandmother Mary was the
reigning queen,
All her grandchildren knew she was
boss
And if we did not obey her,

Well, it was our loss!
She loved her numerous grandchildren
And wanted them to have fun
But if she thought you needed it,
Her little switch was hard to out-run.

I remember Grandma's grove of mulberry trees,
After school we would climb and eat
Go home with torn clothes and tell-tale signs
Like blue mulberry stain upon our teeth.
Grandma always had a flock of geese,
Mattresses were made of fluffy down
What fun to climb upon the wooden foot-board,
Dive in and disappear without a sound!

Using an old corn shuck mop with many holes,
She made us scrub the kitchen floor
And if we grumbled very much
She made us scrub it more!
Each weekend we had to sweep the yard
With broken branches gathered from the wood
When we missed a leaf or twig
She made us back up and do it good.

And what fun to raid Grandma's pie safe!
On special occasions she always baked her best
So she wouldn't notice any were missing,
We would take one or two and rearrange the rest.
Grandma calmly rocking in her chair
With that wise and knowing look,
Gave us all uneasy feelings
She knew exactly how many pies we took!

Treasures stored within my heart,
Memories time cannot erase,
Of this strong, courageous lady,
With wisdom etched upon her face.

Donald Dennis

Donald Dennis
WE BECAME ALIVE WITH JESUS
We became alive with Jesus we didn't come alive 'til Jesus was live in us, our lives came to life we didn't become to life 'til Jesus's life came alive with us, our lives never realize Jesus coming real to our lives, we never realize life Jesus made within us before we was create us, how Jesus gave Jesus life, how Jesus gave life to our lives I thank of how Jesus life gave for us, I thank how Jesus came to life within us with his life with us Jesus gave us life that cannot love live for all that love of how Jesus came alive in lives in life Jesus made within our lives of us we came within life with Jesus our lives must realize we came with life with Jesus our lives never were alive 'til we realize how Jesus's life became to our lives we must realize how Jesus was made within lives of us we never realize how must Jesus work within our lives

Kathleen M Stone
LOVE'S RANSOM

These poems are dedicated to my family and friends who always believed in me.

What fool calls to the past?
One who does not see?
For love that held no fury
becomes a tainted memory.
Begotten the heart-felt emotions,
the soul exemplifies.
Deep in the heart's hidden chambers,
true love never dies.
Wisdom holds no forbearance
for the empathetic embrace.
Spirits imbued linger on with hope,
still the pain will not erase.
One can save himself from sorrow
and never love at all,
but can one's soul afford the price,
for the heart to never fall.

Kathleen M Stone
LOVE ME UNTIL TOMORROW
The gates of Heaven opened,
for angelic eyes behold,
beyond the blue tranquility,
warmth defeats all cold.
Night tightens the noose of loneliness,
Satan comes to call.
Silence is absurdity.
My soul begins its fall.
Speak no more than an utterance,
for no words will ever say,
apparitions are yet yielding,
take my solitude away.
Extreme deliverance from oneness,
blood streaks a moonlit sky.
My soul becomes forgiving,
hatred starts to wilt and die.
If never to love again,
and time I cannot borrow,
wrap my soul in angelic arms,
and love me until tomorrow.

Jennie M Wiggin
YOUR LONELY HEART
The riches that this world will bring
but in a different way.
Can give your life new meaning
and another way to pray.
To take a lonely heart and cheer it up
for just awhile.
Reach out and help another soul
and live a different style.
To care and give yourself in love
to work at being kind.
These are the things for happiness
a hand to help the blind.
Sometimes we do not see the things
around our little nest.
To want to go outside ourselves
and try to help the rest.
To be aware of someone's pain
to care with all your heart.
The meaning of true happiness
will help your lonely heart.

Jennie M Wiggin
MY GOD
If I could write a sonnet
I'd write about your love.
I'd tell the world how grand you are
with streamers from above.
I'd tell them how you touch a soul
as you pass by each day.
And lift each heavy burden
when we kneel down to pray.
I'd tell them all about your grace
and how you bless each saddened face.
Of how you mend a broken heart
and give a life another start.
Oh I could tell so many things
the foresight that your wisdom brings.
What a happy place this earth could be
if not only the blind could see.
I'd tell them all about your bliss
and how two lonely hearts may kiss.
This earth to me became anew
when I first gave my life to you.

Jennie M Wiggin
MY ULTIMATE DREAM
I'm living with time in my fantasy world
as I sit in my corner with me.
Some days are too long, some days are too short
when my fantasies traveling free.
I circle the moon, I reach for the stars
when I'm sailing the storms of the sky.
On a cloud I'll remain, my strength to regain
then a rainbow I'll catch going by.
No time there is known, no sadness is shown
or tears will my lonely heart cry.
So humbly I'll speak, to the king that I seek
with his love and his kindness untold.
Forgiven my past, forever at last
as I walk with the man who was sold.
My ultimate dream of my fantasy world
oh my soul how it longs to be free.
I look up to the sky with a tear in my eye
feeling his love encompassing me.

Jennie M Wiggin
AWARENESS OF A NEW BORN DAY
Awareness is the breath of life
to find it all around.
Altho the wind is blowing
it comes without a sound.

Your eyes are filled with wonder
the beauty of the sea.
The hills around you picking up
all things that are to be.

The mountains and the valleys
the beauty of it all
These sights they take a new look
and how I do recall.

The flowers they are budding
the birches growing tall.
The birds they come from all around
and now I hear them all.

To look up to the tallest tree
then up into the sky,
Oh God how wonderful it is
to feel you passing by.

Jennie M Wiggin
MY LIVING PRAYER
For God alone, your perfect love
is coming straight from up above.
And you alone the perfect one,
your love is ours from sun to sun.
Together we come to pray as one.
We need you so this very day,
for yesterday has passed away,
tomorrow is too late to die
This hunger, thirst is passing by.
Don't let temptations come to me,
that I can't handle honestly.
Nor give me pain I cannot bear
unless you promise to be there.
To please forgive us one and, all
for flesh was made of you.
Come help us with the cross we have,
your love will sure get through.
With rising hands in living prayer,
with loyalty so true.
Help us conceive your mighty plan,
Show love the way you do.

Lou Jean Royle
THE STORM
A clash of thunder,
A flash of lightning,
And the storm did come,
In all its fury.

The storm sent people,
Scurrying to their homes and
To their cars,
And it did come down.

The storm did come,
In all its fury,
Knocking trees and roofs,
Helter, skelter.

The thunder roared,
The lightning flashed,
The rain, it did pour down.

After the storm,
The sun did shine,
And the clouds
Were gone.

God brought the storm,
To clean His Heaven,
And refresh His earth,
So everything could be
Beautiful again.

Carolyn Faith Springman
ON THE EDGE
A mood is devouring my brain
My soul is in eternal pain
I'm in a world of floating sadness
My veins are eroding in madness

Occasional pieces of laughter echo in my head
& alternate with the deafening silence of the dead
I feel a black absorbing shocking pain
The colors of life have vanished from my brain

My body exists in a world of cold cacophony
The real me is a lost memory
I have an emptiness that goes beyond the soul
I am forever lost in this deep black hole

Searching for an answer ends nowhere
There is no purpose to being anywhere
My movements have no meaning
The essence of my life is missing

What began with joy is now a lost memory
for every beginning ends in tragedy
Only from such depths can one make any gain
Growth only occurs when you have experienced life's pain

Carolyn Faith Springman
ANHEDONIA
The joy of life is gone
Where did it all go wrong?

When you didn't love yourself
How can anyone else?

My pain is so intense
Nothing appears to make sense!

I took the difficult road
I am lost! I am scared!

Carolyn Faith Springman
SLIPPING AWAY
Events are not as they were
The happenings of time are strange
Life is not what it was
It is harsh, indifferent & painful

I am not as I was
I am not me anymore
My thoughts & feelings are different now
Touch me & I cry without joy

When did it all change?
Why did it happen?
When will it stop?
Only when I have silently slipped over the edge

Eric Dollinger
OF LEATHERNECKS AND NARWHALS
Beastward ho! The sea-thugs rove,
Their souls appulse and raw.
For another victim, its salts now sea,
Cannot mask their lack of depth,
Their withered cause, their greed.

Extinction consumes such gentle life,
And bomb-pronged spears unleash a message well;
Each success secures a mammoth death,
And food for dogs
Who feast upon the processed flesh.

Andreas Panayiotou
TIMES TO REMEMBER

To Constance Annette Chartier, my eternal love.

When my hard day withers away
and darkness prevails,
I remember times of gentleness,
times of love.
I remember the times my heart trembled,
and my soul winged away,
into the infinity of passion.
I submit to these thoughts,
and there I find joy.
I WAS LUCKY TO FIND YOU.
When your hard day withers away
and darkness prevails,
you'll remember times of gentleness,
times of love.
You'll remember the times your heart trembled,
and your soul winged away,
into the infinity of passion.
You will submit to these thoughts,
and there you will find joy.
YOU WERE LUCKY TO FIND ME.
WE WERE BOTH LUCKY TO FIND EACH OTHER.

Stephen Serafini

Stephen Serafini
BEHOLD THE NIGHT

To My Beloved Catherine and Vincent, You've taught me that Beauty is best expressed through words.

The night holds a balance unknown to wisdom itself . . . A subtle sanctuary, a world apart from day.

The light of night spills through barren branches to cast its glow upon the forest floor, the soft light exposes only what it wants to, and yet hides all of the scars and imperfections caused by the careless trampling and hurriedness of day.

For what can I learn from you, the darkness . . . is it harmony you teach, for I'll be still and wait, and try to see, by night . . . all that . . . which I cannot see by day, and in your timeless solitude, grant to me a place to come and rest from the rush of day, that I may drink of your tranquility and reflect within your shadows, and at the last watch . . . before dawn's first breath . . . I will behold the night.

David C Darrell
THE LAST FLIGHT

Dedicated to all of humanity, may they strive for a cleaner environment.

A bird once flew from east to west
Seeking a place to build her nest
She tried to perch with weary feet
But found no trees but a ruinous heap.

Onward she flew from whence she came
The earth was bare it was all in vain
Tired and thirsty she landed by the shore
To refresh herself for her flight once more

Sorry to say she never did rise
For the water was polluted so there she died
She left us a memory so we would know
Not to pollute the water where we go

David C Darrell
THE RETURNING
Oh Beautiful African Land
Your children were taken to all foreign lands
With feet bound in fetters lifeless they stand
It is time to return to our African land

Oh Wonderful African Land
Your mysteries are great throughout the whole land
With love in our hearts it's all we can do
It is time for your children to return to you

Oh Turbulent African Land
Though millions you have lost
Your people still stand
For four hundred years they were treated as slaves
That left countless millions lying in their graves

Buried beneath the great desert sands
Our history lies hidden where now pyramids stand
Until such time, Africans are all free
The world would be buried in its history

Be careful my people for great is your joy
Though millions are dying your survival is sure
Let us sing praise wherever we stand
For soon we would return to our African Land.

Monique Lavalle
THE OCCIDENT EXPRESS
Democracy, bureaucracy, democracy, bureaucracy,
Capitaliiiiiiism . . .
Technocracy, plutocracy, technoc-racy, plutocracy,
oportuniiiiiiism . . .
Red tape, tape, tape,
red tape, tape, tape,
words, words, words,
words . . .

Give me, give me,
give me, give me,
give me THE DREEEEEEEAM!
Give me, give me,
give me, give me,
give me THE DREEEEEEEAM!

Get up, dress up, go to work;
cool down, wind down, go to bed . . .
Get it? Do it! What a bore!
Want it? Charge it! Work some more . . .

De mo cra cy, bu reau cra cy
tech no cra cy, plu to cra cy,
Ca pi ta liiiiiiiiism!

Monique Lavalle
TO FIND MYSELF
To find myself,
to find myself on time
before death . . .

Let me be,
let me free
find my path
through eternity . . .

Hear my drums,
set the pace,
look at life
right in the face . . .

Answer: YES!
Ask: WHY NOT?
Yell: I'M GOING!
With no stop . . .

To find myself,
to find myself on time
before death . . .

Dorothy Carmen Johnson
LOVE IS AN OLD SHOE
With you I'm as comfortable
As an old shoe.
Not a romantic picture 'tis true.
Yet my passion is endless—
Like stars in the night—
Endlessly burning, endlessly bright;
While oh so comfortable—
Like an old shoe.
I love you my darling,
Truly I do!
You are my confidant—
My job, my delight.
You fill my days;
We'll not mention my nights;
When I feel so comfortable—
Like an old shoe;
So warm and so cozy—
So much better than new!

Phyllis St Pierre
NORMAND, YOU ARE LOVE

For My Husband, darling, count the waves.

Lingering in sweet solitude
I'm grateful for this quietude.
While just outside the multitude
goes hurrying by,
much lighter footsteps I employ.
Transfixed and mindful only of a joy . . .
. . . so suddenly, reality . . .
our private serendipity
Who could deny.

Today I'll dare not open doors,
quite fearful
that the smallest breeze
just might,
somehow manage to disturb
the ALL of you
I carried home last night.

"querida,"
April, '84

Barbara Enright
TO TIM
This is a poem to Tim
Whose gentle smile warmed me through
Whose dark, flashing eyes saw into my soul
Whose laugh brought out the sun
from behind dark clouds.

A gentle touch, a quiet word
The ringing phone, the secret jokes
The comfort and friendship you gave.
All destroyed.

Never look back,
What's done is done
But, Oh, how could you?

My anger struck out trying to hurt
But only the sounds of my broken
sobs do I hear,
Only the pain in my heart do I feel.

Where are you?
How could you?

So I write this to you, Tim,
For a tiny spark of life and love
You kindled in me
And left.

E Maber Gonyea
THOUGHTS
How came life here, from whence
and whither bound?
This earth, exotic daughter of the sun,
Unlikely as the fragile rose and white
Of blossoms on the rough-barked
apple tree;
This earth, blue-veiled, sea girt and
garlanded,
So seeming fixed 'neath heaven's
protecting arch,
Is spinning, rocketing thru time and
space,
Transporting in her green-clad,
loveless arms
The miracles of beauty, life and love,
And at her side the myriad galaxies
Flee blindly, each upon its ordained
course.
Mankind, who of the tree of
knowledge ate,
Beholds his state in wonderment and
awe,
Seeks from infinitudes of time and
space
The why and whence and whither of
his days;
Seeks sister planets shelt'ring other
life;
Pursues his vision of a caring God.

David Nauke
WHITE BUTTERFLY
white butterfly
in
violet sweet pea
silken thread
at a moment's notice
from fingertips
clear into Calamus
Montauk air
the sound of Montauk waves

David Nauke
WITHIN HEAVY RAIN

*For Tiananmen Square Martyrs—
Wei Jinsheng.*

within heavy rain
tiny brown moth ascending
now gentle rain

David Nauke
HEAVY EARLY APRIL RAIN

For Vajrayana Tibetan Martyrs.

heavy early April rain
sparrows singing
dawn
heavier rain yet
still they sing

Helene Blais
THROUGH THE WINDOW OF THE ORIGIN
Thousands of minuscule pebbles
drop by drop
stardust at the window of the origin

pink sandy magics
texts of husky fires
clasped by the eye

Bengal's drizzle
softly sprinkles
the soul's deep cavity

ambrosial eyelid unburdens
writes itself

in the hollow of this space
showers of echoes extend of infinite

some astral sea-horses enjoy
themselves
drool of honeyed dew
on the skins' bodies
heads' hearts' flesh's fcast

Guy C Allen

Guy C Allen
FORTUNE
Fortune smiles on each of us in many
different ways.
Although it seems 'tis far beyond our
gaze.
Our Nickels and our Quarters seem to
vanish like the mist,
Just the same, I'd like to hit old
worry a wallop with my fist.

Richer far is he whose fortune comes,
not from this worldly gain,
But from depths of disappointment,
to a higher, nobler plain.
Dissipating dissolution, rising to a
better view,
Ever hopeful, happy and pleasant,
That's when Fortune smiles on you.

Guy C Allen
I DREAM OF YOU
Each day and night, dear one, I dream
of you.
Each passing while, your goodness
fills me through.
Time changes not, nor dims your
gracious winning smile.

It lingers there forever, and inspires
me all the while.

Kind thoughts like kindly deeds,
forever live.
A fitting symbol, of the best a friend
can give.
Deep from your loving heart, your
love expands.
Enfolding me within like the
sunshine or the land.

One fleeting hour, I treasure as of
yore.
Compassioned for your sorrows, that
have come to you before.
Across my pathway, as I journey on
my way.
A lovely flower, grows, perfumed
with love, always.

Guy C Allen
TALE OF LOVE
A tale of love that must be told,
My heart is yearning to unfold.
Our love came quickly and
surprising,
Like the Sun thru clouds arising.

Bursting thru all my daydreams,
It sparkles like joyous sunbeams.
Warm and tender—gay and young,
Like a song that's half unsung.

A symphony of love untold,
Our hearts are learning to unfold.
Forever through life's sunset glow,
The music of our Love will flow !

Guy C Allen
HEART OF GOLD
How much love can one heart hold ?
How many pieces in a bag of
gold ?
A heart that is loving gives love
birth—
How, then, can you measure worth ?

Tho it may never be filled like a bag
of gold.
A loving heart has room for more
love I'm told.
For how much gold might it be
brought ?
Oh, a heart is not sold—but sought.

Tho pieces of eight may be sold,
A heart's love is never brought with
gold.
How much love can one heart hold ?
More, much more than a bag of gold!

Linda J Malarkey
THE HEALING PROCESS
An antique vase propped on the
mantel
survived decades of champagne
toasts
Grandpa's war stories of grenades
being tossed over the sofa
until, jarred from its corner perch
it careened to the oak parquet floor
shattering into hundreds of fragments

And you came to it like a surgeon
resetting broken bones
searching for the key
fitting piece onto fractured piece
with no shards left untouched
blending the remnants
into a stained glass window
or a cracked mirror
with a keen eye
for the image of a vase
making it whole again

Ameera Lateefah Masani
PARENTHOOD
When children understand parent-
hood,
They've not given up being bad for
good;
They've not become intelligent;
They've been quite busy, their time's
been spent
In giving birth and staying up late.
For special care they had to take
To shape the generation they'd
started;
And learn to sacrifice without being
martyred.
When children have travelled along
that way,
There is no doubt that whenever they
say
"I love you Mom, Dad," it's most
sincere,
'Cause they appreciate you—they've
been there.

Leslie A Miller
SOME MOTHER'S SON
Another young Black boy
died last night
claimed by the streets
some mother's son
cut down by a gun

Good riddance some say
that young punk
that thieving hoodlum
some mother's son
played a game with death, death won

hung out on street corners
sometimes drug dealer
sometimes drug user
some mother's son
dead before his life has begun

uncontrollable child
unreachable adolescent
unredeemable youth on the brink of
manhood
some mother's son
lost and forever gone

Cristina Galiano
TAKING EXAMS
Tension
It fills the air,
On exam day it can be found
everywhere.
All around you people ask
"I wonder what I'll get," and "Do
you think I'll pass?"
People talk of staying up all night,
Just to get the answer right.
They study till dawn,
Hoping they won't get any wrong.
And when the last exam's turned in,
That is when the curiosity begins.
The next day the students go to the
teacher and ask,
"What did I get," and "Did I pass?"

Valerie Pineo
PRETTY LITTLE RAGDOLL
Pretty little ragdoll,
you're not too short & you're not too
tall.
Your hair is made of yellow yarn,
I don't want you to come to any
harm.

I'll take you to my room,
& I'll make you a blanket on my
loom.
It'll probably be white & red,
then I'll tuck you in your bed.

Pretty little ragdoll,
I need to make a call.
You should have a name,
something like mine, but not the
same.

I think I'll call you Suzy Q.
& tomorrow I'll take you to the zoo.
Right now it's almost bedtime,
I'll tell you a story & maybe a rhyme.

Pretty little ragdoll,
off to sleep you'll fall.
We'll be together tomorrow
having lots of fun & no sorrow.

Cathy Smith
LOVE IS . . .
Two people in front of a warm
fireplace.
Two people in love with one another.
Being able to talk about anything.
Helping one another with our
problems.
Jesus dying on the cross for us.
Trusting one person with everything.
Not keeping any secrets from one
another.
Love is very special and lasts forever.

Faye Froelich
A HORSE OF MANY COLORS

I Wrote This For Kenny.

He rode his White Horse in
To spread his devastation through your land
Brought his mighty boats to your banks
To dump his filthy poison on your sand

He surveyed your towns and cities
Invaded them like a maniacal disease
Entered your homes without compassion
To separate and destroy your families

He seduced and pillaged your young
Dumped them like trash on your streets to roam
And while you pretended not to notice
A bloody battleground became their home

YES AMERICA, He came to stalk you
Promising you passage to the land of hope
Led you down his illusionary path to escape
And tethered you tightly on endless miles of rope

And as you dangle on the brink of destruction
He amasses a fortune from your misery
Never having worked a day to support you
He rides in the lap-of tax free-luxury.

Deborah S Kisela
THE LOVE OF LIFE

I dedicate this poem to all my family members and friends, who have loved me and showed love through good and bad times; THANK YOU ALL!!!

The Love of Life is so full of God's Light although it may not always be bright.
The Love of Life is in the warmth of New Life in the mother's womb; in the beauty of a family of baby raccoons.
The Love Of Life is in all the clean waters that flow; in the trees that grow; even underneath the fallen snow.
God's Light is the Love of Life, in everyone's lives.

Angela R Blair
MOM'S MAGIC BED

To my three sons, Joshua, Zachary and Luke, with all my love.

Why does it seem, no place can compare to Mom's magic bed?
That no blankets are the warmest, or pillow softer for your head.
There's never any monsters lurking underneath that queen size frame.
It never moves mysteriously, it just remains the same.
When you're hot with fever, and have a stuffed up head,
everything seems much better once you sit upon her bed.
Maybe it's in her whisper, or the way she strokes your hair, knowing as you snuggle, when you wake she will be there.
As the time progresses, trips down the hall become few and far between, staying in your own bed, is much easier than it seemed.
With the understanding tho, and please let it be said,
never let me grow too old or big, to hop into that bed!

Abigail Merriman
DISSONANCE

To the memory of my Beloved Husband, John Aidan Merriman.

I would not tear an oak leaf,
Nor ruffle up the pines;
Nor would I muss a single fern
That gracefully reclines.

Yet, though I tread most lightly,
The forest's mossy bed;
I cannot fully disavow
Some damage I have spread.

I would not cause the slightest frown,
Nor bring a single tear,
Nor pain of any kind at all
To those I hold most dear!

Yet, though I tread so gently,
This world's strange, rugged road,
Those I love most deeply
I sometimes discommode.

Amy Fasnut
THE POOL THAT WASN'T COOL

"Maybe Mindy" said Goofy Gwen
Trying not to drop his pen
You will get dry and go to school
Instead of being wet from the pool.
One day when Mindy got out of the pool
She wasn't dry and thought it wasn't cool
She took her towel and rubbed her skin with it
She couldn't get dry so she threw a fit
She never got dry from the pool
She tried saunas, tanning beds and much more than that
Today since she is still wet
She can't take her dog to the vet
She cannot get dry
Much less figure out why
So she has a water bed and when she is not in that
She's in her jacuzzi and can never see her cat

So never go jump in a pool —
Obviously it's not cool.

John Robert Porter
WHEN HOMETOWN JUNKIES BRING MODERN ANGELS

This is a work of fiction and dedicated to nobody.

funny what emotions arise
when memories get circumsized
and bumbs come
with something better than love
you thought you'd never say it
but there it is on your lips
and she's walking with old thoughts
that she thought were sold or bought
the fear of losing nothing
or the fear of having something —

if you cut me loose
i will lose my wounds
but the bleeding won't subside
flooded behind my eyes
tricking off the light
when i thought i was lying
performing strange things
with lipstick and whipped cream
another set of dreams
to close your eyes around —
my soul is prompt — it dies
on time —

Janet M Tindel
A MOTHER'S DAY WISH

A special day to you is given for all you are
each and every day.
Time may not be taken in this hurried world to say
"Thank you" but, my heart
always thanks you.
For all the love and understanding shown every moment
As well as kindness and patience in all my years
as your child.
Warm sunshine comes my way when skies are blue
and I'm with you in heart and being.
Thank you for all the little things that mean
so very much — a smile, hug, a tender word.
Words cannot express my overwhelming love I hold
for you.
My appreciation for all you have done is great.
Thank you, Mother, for being part of me
'cause you're a good part to have.
Happy Mother's Day, today and everyday
to a great YOU!

lleret ybtihw
UNTITLED

To Lucy: The shining light in my life, "Thanks" for everything. Mom Dad, Tiana and Quanda.

Raucous winds grasp him for a brief moment
But
he is quickly returned to his taciturn society
where few know the unseen beauty that exists
In his emotionless society there is no love nor is there pain.
For him there is uncertainty
Constant gloom lurks over him throughout his travels.
Simplicity is his and for his society, things are left to be questioned.
He is not blind. Why can't he see the horrified children as they pass him and muse about his presence beneath them?
He is not deaf. Why can't he hear the diva's aria that lofts above his ears?
There is no warm fireplace for him to snuggle near.
Dinner is not on the table waiting for him.
His lone intimacy is an old dirty blanket which provides comforts.
This man is truly an island —
A personal fortress —
Though his life is scrutinized, this intrepid creature continues to strive for a solemn peace.
Although there are many reasons he could scream
the only words he can mutter are:
"I'm homeless, not helpless"

Dawn Stratton
IT'S BETTER THAT WAY

It's better that way, she used to say,
When you don't give your love away.
Said her heart was hers to keep,
And her love didn't come cheap.
She had little faith left in her heart,
Said she wouldn't let anyone tear it apart.
She can't get over her life's tragedies,
It's better that way, she tried to make me see.
Said she had no tears left to cry,
And that's when she told love good-bye.
Tried to tell her: It's such a sacrifice trying to love you,
'Cause I can't feel the pain you're going through.
I can feel your heart beating, but I can't get inside,
'Cause you found a brick wall and that's where you hide.
I'll remember those words till my dying day,
From her heart she'll always say,
it's better that way.

Vivian McCarty-Morris
I REMEMBER MAMA

With love to my family, my husband, Lee, and our son and daughter, Tina and Brian.

I remember Mama when she stood so straight and tall,
I remember how she would kiss us when we'd fall,
Or reach out and catch us as we'd go running by,
But I don't remember Daddy no matter how hard I try.

I remember Mama as she'd toil out in the fields,
I remember seeing the tears run as she kneeled,
And hear her as she prayed, "Oh, please do come back,
How could you leave these kids and I, oh, my darling Jack?"

I remember Mama as she grew so stooped and small,
I remember Mama calling, "Dinner one and all!"

And how we'd eat the gingerbread and cookies she had made,
Knowing her thoughts of Daddy never seemed to fade.

I remember Mama crying softly out at night,
I remember how quickly I'd wake up in fright,

How she would come and quietly calm my fears,
As I cuddled close to her, I'd feel those running tears.

I remember Mama as she lay alone and ill,
I remember her last words before she grew so still,
I knew she lay praying, hoping he would come back,
As I moved, she smiled and said, "I knew you'd come, my darling Jack."

Vivian Callahan
THE SOUNDS OF DEATH

To all I have cared for who saw the Death Angel.

The sounds of death are silent
As the death angel stalks
You can hear her move softly
In your mind
She looks at her new friend
In a godly light
And with the look of love
Brings out the fright
She takes the friend's hand gently
And gives them a hug
And says very softly "God is Love"
So with a bright light encasing her and the friend
Carries their spirit to heaven
And this is by no means the end.

Vivian Callahan
BLUE MOON
The blue moon shine
Over a black lagoon
An iridescent purple glow
Filled the room below
The mountain's edge.

the ocean flowed the opposite way
I knew my soulmate was coming my way
the waves made a stairway to the sky

the Heavens opened
the moon stars and sun were one
the signs were here
He walked softly to where I stood

No more would we be apart
And the blue moon would forever shine

Leslie E Hanks
A LETTER FROM JESUS
My dear lovely children,

Do not complain when it rains, but rejoice. Do you not realize that the rain is my tears falling upon you?

It is I crying because of the sufferings from the cross.

So please do not become angry when it rains, but become calm and peaceful.

Please realize I shed these tears to remind you, I died for you!!!! So that your sins may be forgiven.

Love,
Your Saviour
Jesus Christ

Cynthia Thompson
SCARLET MARKS

To John, my best friend.

Grey and black are what I see.
The wounds left Scarlet Marks on me.
How can Passion Burn as Bright as Hate?
When Passion is Gold and Sin is Hate.
Repentance beg of me,
beyond Revenge I can clearly see,
Black, Scarlet, Gold, and Grey.
God's Judgement Day.

Mary Ann Butler
SOMEONE TO DANCE WITH?
"Someone to dance with — What if I was?
What if you were? Were you looking? Was I?
Where did the music come from?
So many questions . . . answers all too few.
Just "someone to dance with?"

All our lives we look for someone to be with, share with, dream with — so much time!
There are no short cuts, no easy way to find a love that exists only in your mind.

Not many can see into this dream — the wonders, hopes and wishes in your mind.
Some have gotten close and you have no idea why. No reason why. It just happens . . .
Someone has followed his heart upon the doorsteps of your soul and knocks upon your door.

But you hold back before you answer. The question never before asked in such an intense way — has never had an answer to be given. But one is needed for him, for you . . . and must be carefully thought through.

"Someone to dance with" is more than an answer. It is the beginning of many questions of the heart. But when your heart dances, your soul rejoices, your mind puts away reservations, little by little as it opens more paths towards which may now be followed.

"Someone to dance with" becomes someone to love with, someone to laugh with, someone to cry with, someone to be with in ways you never before thought possible.
So, be careful who you dance with — you never know who is able to find his way
into your heart . . . and soul.

Alvin Williams
MY WIFE

This poem is dedicated to Pamela, my darling wife

If a rose could bloom
And look into the sun
I'd call it my wife
Just for fun
And if the sky could
be so blue
I'd call it your eyes
because I love you
And if the birds could sing so fine
I'd know they would have you in mind
So my love, when you hear a bird sing, see rose so red, or sky so blue
Remember I love you.

Adriana Serrano-McGee
UNTITLED

To Chon, and to Richard; Thanks for the inspiration!

You loved me like no other
had ever done before;
Showed me warmth and tenderness,
Undying love you swore.

Now there's only melancholy,
Hearts broken in two,
Shattered dreams and promises,
Memories of you.

And we gave so completely,
Nothing felt more right.
We truly loved each other,
Why did we quit the fight?

All that's left is loneliness,
feelings of regret,
Remnants of a love that was,
Longing . . . to forget.

William R Greenawalt Jr
THUNDERSTORM LOVE AFFAIR

Dedicated to Bill E. Hawk Productions.

Sitting alone with the television on
And the sound of the street below
Humidity's high, damn flies
And time ticks by so slow

I just can't sleep, thoughts too deep
Playing back those days in my mind
Clouds roll in, thunder sings
And lightning streaks the sky

The city's hot, rain won't stop
Fog rolls in like waves
Evening news, same old blues
Dreamin' 'bout sunny days

Same old lies, thunder dies
But clouds still fill the scene
Lightning strikes all hearts alike
And teardrops fill the street

Memories flash, heartbeats clash
Thoughts turn back to you
Stormy times whirl in my mind
It's just the thunderstorm love affair blues . . . .

Michael Caracciola
RACE
The human race had not produced a winner
although the line had been crossed
Many times
Making all losers blind and lost
The so-called winner stumbling and gasping and learning the cost
of running on dreams that have no waking
Trampling time-two-one-oh irony no rest for the weary

So what
The gun had been fired
many times
like an echo that would not fade
louder than the screams of those in its path
Faster than those who ran from the noise

So what
The ribbon had been broken
no, torn
no, shredded to confetti to pour down endlessly on the celebration of illusory triumph . . .
only to blind most with its flash . . .
or suffocate those who breathed its excess

NO COLOR CAN BE SEEN IN THE DARKNESS

Michael Caracciola
STILL UNTITLED
At first he was taken
When feelings he thought long-dead
reemerged as she stood before
The music of voice
The burning of eyes
The touching of souls HE could not ignore
For the Face that launched one thousand ships
this time could not compete
With one that sails a heart so far . . .
Gives wings to feet that tread so long on paths of darkness . . .
'Til lifted in that fleeting moment by visions of her already fading
beyond the dreams that bore them
like a LOCKED-OUT-FRIEND
beyond a open door . . . and . . .
growing softer softer
'til all he can hear are THOSE footsteps
echoing from the inside out
like the ticking of the clock . . .
and the gnawing of doubt . . .
and the passage of time that left him only weaker
with the spectre of living
without

Bradley S Killip
THE THEATER
The theater is empty now.
The lights have dimmed their last.
The scenes have all been out away.
The laughter's in the past.
Our lives have been made richer
As we practice this our craft.
To see that which is in our self,
And let the whole world laugh.
We say "It was the lines I said,"
That made them all applaud.
Yet, we took our bows at end
And sought that form of laud.
The characters will go away until brought back to life.
Yet, they will live within our hearts.
In our character, of life.

Carolyn Couch
SPACES
Our hearts and minds are full of spaces.
Each one filled with different faces.
No one else can ever fill
This same space, for it is sealed.

Sealed with love and all emotions
Even with our crazy notions.
We have filled our space alone.
How full this space? It's never known.

We should strive to fill immensely
Love in each other's mind intensely.
For we will leave behind this space.
It will be our only trace.

This way we will never die.
In the hearts of those we'll lie.
If our space is filled completely,
Then our life has ended sweetly.

Bonnie Lee Henry
LADY IN BLUE

Dedicated to Rochelle Cunningham. Thank you for being a friend, an inspiration that made this poem possible. Friends always, B. Henry.

Most every day you come by my way,
wearing high heels, a blue suit.
You have your lunch, right after noon,
I'm the one that waits on you.
Only once you smiled at me, said 'HI,'

On the other hand I said 'BYE.'
Don't know your name, where from you came,
Just wait each day to see you again,
Sooner or later, hope without hope, we will be friends.
Something about you, just can't describe,
Makes us happy to be alive.
Got lots of friends, good ones too,
I can make room for one more, YOU.
I run a diner, that's real small, Have time for you,
If you want to talk. You sit alone seem so sad, I'd
talk to you, but you may get mad. I glance at you,
you at me, Neither of us takes the time to speak.
Curly brown hair, your suit of blue,
Must be a busy person,
in some business too,
Me, I waitress from morn till night, wait for friends to
come by, my way, look forward to the time that you look at
me, and I can say . . .
You've got a TRUE FRIEND, too, . .
You're my friend,
"LADY IN BLUE"

Bonnie Lee Henry
EYES OF THE PAST
She may be older now, but once she was young as could be.
Full of life like you and me.
To talk of the past is all we can do . .
I can just picture it in my mind can't you?
She talks of days of canning food and such,
Didn't buy groceries, clothes, and much . . . .
Her eyes are like a picture show,
Look into them and away we go,
Back to whatever she has to say,
Of life that is preserved in Bygone Days.
She talks of the porch and snapping beans,
Sitting there on the swing,
Walking the banister, must of been keen.
She talks of baking bread,
making quilts for the beds,
Putting up hay,
Making lemonade,
Homemade remedies for first aid.
This is just a sample of a great, great, past,
If you want to hear more, see more,
Come with me . . . and we'll ask, if we can look into her
EYES OF THE PAST

Aleka Papathanasopoulos
JUST ONE MORE SMILE
Many hard times did she face
And knew if it was someone else in her place
The tears she'd cry would never cease
For a sad heart would only make them increase

Always alone she'd face the pain
Never in public did she reveal strain
Her brilliant smile would light up their day
Hoping that she would never go away

There came the day when she no longer was around
And everyone went about without a sound
For their only wish all this while
Was that she could be around for just one more smile

Sabrina Ann Mize
BIG BROTHER
Now that you're gone,
Who is there for me to lean on?
You were always there, But now you're gone.
What am I to do without you?
You always cheered me up when I was down;
I always looked up to you,
But now that you're gone who is there for me to count on?
You were always there for the good times
And stuck with me through the bad.
You were there through it all;
I hope you'll be back real soon;
'Cause Big Brother . . . . . . I really miss you!

Michael K Strandquist

Michael K Strandquist
CHOICES
What incredible possibilities,
The word Choice creates.
Who's to choose,
The perfect mates!

Life has numerous roads,
in which to take.
What path do you follow,
What choice do you make!

Wherever you venture,
Is there wrong or right.
Is it a test of endurance,
Or strength in the fight!

Choices will be in favor,
But not all will bring joy.
Choices are lethal,
They are not a toy!

So select your choice,
In deepest of thought.
For the choice you choose,
Will be the choice you brought!

William J Jacobs
MOTHER

Dedicated to my mother, Mary, and my my best friend and future wife, Theona.

Thoughts of the days our mother prayed
That we'd be blessed and saved
Down on her knees we watched as she
Asked God to lead our way
We did not know to and did not show her
Love as we should have
Still loved us dear and even still
Forgave us and we're glad
She'd find us bread we didn't have
From where we do not know
She'd make us clothes from wears of old
To warm us from the cold
She taught our minds so we could find
A life far better than hers
And through all this she never hissed
Any unloving words

Cheryl Jan Boeglin
IN HER MEMORY
To the one that I knew,
In my younger years.
And now that you're gone,
I still cry tears.
I know you watch over,
and see to me fine.
I feel you near me,
most all of the time.
I've changed so much,
Since the time you were here,
I grew up without you,
Through sadness and fear.
Now that I'm grown,
I try hard to be,
A number one Mom,
Like you were for me.
I'll always remember,
The times you were here.
And I'll always feel,
Your love so near.

Yvonne Krajewski
PLEASE UNDERSTAND . . .
Lately, all of my thoughts of you
only seem to make me feel blue.
I cannot explain why
because I thought you were my special guy.
I know it will never be
quite the same between you and me.
So, let us give it a rest
and later try for the best.
My thoughts of you are now astray
please understand why I feel this way.
For in my heart, it will always be
just the memory of you and me.

Grace Arnell
THE BATTLE GROUND VIETNAM
The rockets, bombs, napalms,
terrorist and mortar attacks.
The firing of the artillery,
rifles and machine guns,
Are total destruction to all
the living ones.
To the service men in Vietnam,
who are fighting and those
wounded in the war,
Will remember ever–more
The thousands of their comrades,
who have gone on before,
To another home in heaven
Across the Golden Shore,
Through the gates to peace and
happiness,
That welcomes them by the score.
May war ever remind us of
the loss of our precious
Fathers, Uncles, Brothers, Sons,
Who have won a victory in Heaven,
By the enemy behind the guns,
These young men who have given
their lives,
So, that you and I might live,
if they had it to do over,
Would again, their lives they'd give.
These young service men who have
no future here on earth to behold,
Go to war and into battle
And die before they are old.
It does not seem fair
to give their lives when
they are so young.
But up in Heaven "their lives have
just begun."
To serve the Lord in kindness given.
And we too, will go to Heaven
All our days are numbered
And we too, will cross the Golden
Shore.
We will all be together
As we were on Earth before.
Won't that be a great reunion?
When we are together once more,
In Heaven where there is no
fighting and no despair,
But an ever-lasting happiness
And we will all be there.

Michelle Lynn Kuklinski
SMILES
Smiles make the world go 'round
They can be bought, sold or even found.
They are wond'rous things to have close by
They can fit in a pocket or behind a bow tie.
They love to dance and prance all day,
and laugh and sing and even play.
They come out of hiding when the timing is right,
and they love to come out even at night.
They brighten up faces to make them the best,
and they come out tops above all the
rest.
A smile is essential for everyday fun
So be sure to have extras for faces with none!

Theresa Tirone
THE RIVER KNOWS
The many lights of the city
illuminated on the river,
reflect its sad beauty.

How much happiness and sorrow
has been imbedded
into her darkest depths?

How many have laughed
and cried, by her moving side;
and, even died.

She knows all
and bears it so well,
after all -
Who has ever seen a
river c
r
y?

Stephen Fortune
OUR LOVE BEGINS TODAY

Dedicated to Keri Collier for her inspiration, smile and above all her love. Love, Stephen.

You creature of such Beauty
Who doth thou dream at night of?
Whose soul fills thine? Who is he?
Where is your ecstasy bound in love?
Mine tears a thousands times doth fall
Yet, smile I do when I see thee.
Mine heart hath to thine many times a call

Yet whispers the song when close you are to me.
O, My Love give me a hope, a chance
Thou Knight may all ready have been slain
Give you me a waltz, one dance
Do not let your heart be filled with pain
For true love a heart shall ne'er betray
Surrender in love your heart, our love begins today

Tawnya Robinson
LOVE
Walking with you hand and hand across
The hot desert's sand,
You and me together as one,
Loving each other and watching the sun,
We can see the sun setting at a distance,
And this is just to test our resistance,
Being with each other is all we'll ever need,
Just you and me baby together all the way,
My heart is for you and yours for me,
Together forever we'll always be.

David McPhee
BROKEN MENDS
Like the lighthouse . . . a solitary figure
Standing watch, waiting for something to occur
Sending its signal to the object unsure
Offering its own unselfish brand of cure

And as the caterpillar, building its cocoon
Knowing its fate is all too soon
So emerges the butterfly . . . full of life and immune
Floating, floating — just like a balloon

So it is that I feel, my friend
Never holding as a means to an end
And learning always from my broken mend
For I won't break . . . I will only bend

Josie Milhomme
OTHERSIDE #3

For Mr. Bemrose
who believed in me. . .

The otherside pulls people away
Wide eyed and surprised they have no say
The lost innocence shows in their eyes
Filled with the lowest of lies

Coming back to their homes and cities
Never seen so many looking for their lost identities
Their innocence they can never claim back
Just stick them on a cold steel rack

Bitter and confused do not under-stand them
For the otherside knows no pain
Hopeless and desperate looking for dreams
Only to find them falling apart at the seams

Ocean black and blue waves riding so high
Dazed people crossing the tide
Otherside pushing away desolate dreams
Breaking hope and faith to seams

Josie Milhomme
FADED DREAM
Running toward that now faded dream
Pink and white roads like gold that gleam
Baby blue grass to stand on
And a shocking pink pond
Mint green sky above
Coral flying doves
These colours of dreams turned grey and old
The little child in me has gone ice cold

Wish I had me that dream
Life would be easier it would seem
Maybe I live in rose coloured glasses
Better than dark clot masses
Cold people on the outside
How have I let myself get like them
Got to feel my own self again
Please let me amend
Laying on the pure white sand
Soaking up the golden sun

Feeling so young to do my own thing
The words are said without the fiery sting
So this too is a rose coloured dream

Josie Milhomme
COULD THE WIND
Could the wind be telling me
Whispering all the secrets it knows
Only keeping in what's too powerful to hold
Could the wind take me away before I'm told

Could the wind be seeing me
Through the hazy light
A chill making me shiver
When I hear the wind calling to me in the night

Could the wind want to take me away
On the path of darkness
Where it traps me then sets me free
The wind keeps calling to me

Kelly Partington
BEST FRIENDS
Best friends are the ones you talk to
When things don't go just right.
They're always going to be there,
Anytime, day or night.

God gave me the greatest two best friends
I could ever have hoped to get.
You know who you are, my dearest friends,
We've been pals since the day we met.

We've laughed together, cried together,
For, oh, so many years.
We know we'll always be best friends.
Together we'll conquer our fears.

Janice Achimon
SOLACE POND
The dawn's soft rays pour from the sky like spilled paint across
the top of the water.
A lone observer, I witness the birth of a new day.
Back and forth, swaying sunflowers summon me, dancing in honor
of the pastel sunrise.
Dewdrops sparkle with the eloquence of crystal tears upon the
long, grassy lashes of the emerald meadow.
The glorious field awakens.

In the distance, a misty cloud rests atop a still pond.
Ebony silhouettes of naked trees fade in and out.
I wave to bony branches that wave shyly back to me.
At the water's edge, the pond serves me as a grand mirror of
glass; yet, I shiver amidst the beauty.
My bare feet are damp with moisture of the frosty morning.
My awakened senses rejoice.

Spiraling amber leaves of aspen—
earthbound heart—shaped kisses.
Enhanced, enchanted season—
permeating essence, colossal beauty.
And breezes blow for the earth sighs in sleepy, shallow breaths.
Still silence surrounds me as time
is seized.
I caress the captured moment.
Behold!—the pond of solace.

Billie Doner
JUST BEYOND REACH

Dedicated with all my love to my son, Willian Casey Doner, whose mother I am privileged to be.

From the darkness of my sleep I feel that something isn't right,
The last remnants of my dream are slipping out of sight.

Slowly yet suddenly I awake,
I can feel it in the air, there has been no mistake.

How long has he been seizing, how much longer will it last,
I yearn to pull him to me — put this seizure in the past.

Soft words of reassurance fall on ears that do not hear,
The prayer so often spoken that the end of this is near.

Beads of perspiration glisten on his lip and brow,
The jerking is subsiding, the seizure is over now.

His eyes flicker recognition, his lips move to speak,
Just before he drifts off for the much needed sleep.

He will dream peacefully, with his hand holding my finger,
But for me, just beyond reach, sleep will teasingly linger.

Alicia Whitehead
MYSTERIOUS THINGS
They sparkle of beauty, peace, and love.
They are diamonds in the sky,
shining with a mysterious shine.
They light the ongoing sky in the universe.
What are these mysterious things that light up the heavens of blue?
What are these diamonds of many?
What are these peaceful, loving things?

Norm Robison
INSOMNIA

Dedicated to, and in memory of my father, Frank Norman Prather. I waited too long. He'll never see me in print. For this I am sorry.

I lay awake with my thoughts,
they torture me unkind.
The things I've done and left to do,
and the wrongs I've left behind.

I have not slept in several days,
my worries, they are so fierce.
I out turn the light and close my eyes,
yet through the darkness they pierce.

The sheep I've counted got lost in some realm,
far from where they leapt.
But the thoughts are still there,
and the thinks I still think,
and still I have not slept.

I've drank 'til drunk and smoked "The Weed,"
and downed many a pill.
I've tossed my body on the most comfortable place,
but my eyes stay open still.

I've done everything that could be done,
short of finding me dead.
But the thoughts I have and the thinks I think,
are still bouncing around in my head.

Sue E Dykes
BLIND LOVE
It started with a smile, as you looked at me
nothing else mattered, i was too blind to see.

that time would bring pain, my heart full of sorrow
knowing we had no chance, for us no tomorrow.

The hardest part came, in spite of prayers from above
i tried to resist, but i still fell in love.

What i feel is true, for you it's not there
no expectations i hold, it's not something we share.

So when time comes for us, to let go of each other
for me i will vow, there won't be another.

As the years pass, and we lead separate lives
i'll remember the passion, and our last kiss goodbye.

Dale F Kinkel
THE CITY OF MY HEART
Minneapolis, Minnesota;
Pretty city where I was a boy.
I biked your streets and played in your parks,
Remembering those years, years of joy.

Summer days by the Mississippi,
Carefree boys swimming there, in bare skin.
Playing baseball on neighborhood teams,
It was fun but we played hard to win.

And in winter a city of white,
Going skiing on snow-covered hills.
Playing hockey on smooth frozen ice,
Growing up was a boyhood of thrills.

On Hennepin, downtown I met her,
That sweet girl, I would take for my wife.
'Neath moonlight by Lake Minnetonka,
Love began for the rest of this life.

Minneapolis, Minnesota;
Life's directions have caused us to part,
But the memories you gave live on,
Still to me — the city of my heart.

Dale F Kinkel
SAILORS OF THE DEEP
Those that go out on the sea in ships,
Are sailors of the deep.
Sailing the far–flung oceans so wide,
Our liberty to keep.

They man our fleet's mighty battleships,
Riding the surging wave.
Destroyers, carriers and cruisers,
Sailors aboard so brave.

Freedom to live, is worth fighting for,
On land or ocean foam.
Good Lord above, those dear ones we love,
Please guide them safely home.

Vikki Delorme
ONLY YOU

To the teenagers who have seemed to lose their dreams, from one who knows they're the most important part of life.

When blue skies are grey
My spirits begin to stray
When days are long, seemingly endless
Times together, alone, are few and sparse
My hopes and dreams only of you
Always manage to see me through.

Hopes of a happy marriage
Fifty golden, wonderful years
Grandchildren, great grandchildren and more
Happy joyous days since no one's there
To keep our spirits locked up, confined.

Dreams of walking on the beach, hand in hand
Talking laughing, sharing sadness, tears and anger
After all is said and done
Only you can make me feel
There is still a life to be won.

When life slaps me in the face
Sends nothing by regrets, frustrations
When my spirits rise, almost soar
Only to come crashing down once more
Your smile and cheer make me feel
life is still worth living.

T M Corbeil
WHEN MY LIFE COMES TO ITS END

For Catherine —

When my life comes to its end, I will smile
at all that memory serves. And I will count
the blessèd teachings from when the turnstile
completes one turn. Though I might not surmount
all the lessons that I draw near, my soul
came here to learn. And be it that I make
mistakes, it is my goal to attain wholeness, a claim from this life that I will stake.

So, I welcome you tomorrow. Bring your
mysteries to me. Challenge me a feat
to take pleasure in what fate has in store
beyond. And then my life will be complete,
with peace of mind, to know that in the end,
certainly, I would do it all again.

Nicki Eason
IMAGINE
Imagine yourself as free
as the wind
Unhindered by duties
Encouraged by friends
To follow your dreams
Wherever they take you—
Imagine yourself as free
as the wind.

Sometimes in life we all
feel the sadness
of getting caught up
in life's endless madness—
That's when to Look Up!
Let your spirit soar
Imagine yourself as free
as the wind,
and remember that Love
is what it's all for.

Debra A Hayes
TO THINK OF YOU
When I'm all alone in a big dark room,
and sitting in a chair.
With a candle lit among the mist,
of the fresh pine scented air.
I think of you as I often do with your face,
seen through my stare.
Your eyes so bright, so full of life.
I'd reach to touch, but I'd know you'd not be there.
I place a smile upon my lips, to recall
a gentle kiss.
Then ask myself when I dare,
if without you, I'd be missed.
I'd survive I know, I did before,
no questions need be asked.
I'll think of you as I often do,
of the times that now have passed.
For even though I may long for you,
I still have my inner pride.
While the candle's glow is way down low,
I shall snuggle in my chair.
To think of you as I often do,
of the times we now have shared.

Debra A Hayes
DREAM LOVE
When in love with love itself,
it mystifies the air.
Your every sigh is softened with
enchantment in your stare.
Your wonderment does come true,
as you dream your dreams each day.
When reality sets itself in place,
the dreams have gone away.
Yet still the feelings linger,
your heart still thrives the need.
To feel the love of love itself,
no matter if it's real.
When in love with love itself,
romance is in the air.
Your eyes and heart soften,
as your gaze becomes a dream.
And all the while the love progresses,
it always seems to be,
that when the love has finally heightened,
it was only a moment dream.

Birthel Lyon
IN MEMORY OF A PET
Fond memories I have of a pet mule named Pete. He was king of all animals and swept me off my feet. He was a hunk of a mule always keeping his cool. Whereever you are I miss you.

He stood tall among his barn yard friends. A caretaker he was until the end. He was always by our side and always willing to give us a ride. Pete I wish you were still around.

One day our lives parted. He went away, fond memories I have until this day. Now I must accept the fact you are gone, and move on. Pete you were my best friend.

Grady Locklear
ANNIE

This poem is dedicated to Annie my loving wife.

There is a lady in Carolina her smile is like the
morning light. One day she be my claim to fame.
Being with her is like heaven
Annie
is her name.
And they should change the names of angels to
Annie you see because Annie an angel to me.
I feel I've always loved her and know I
Always will. Because when I'm with Annie in
Heaven is how I feel.

Barbara J Lewis
SMILE
You may not feel up to par,
But you can smile.
You may not feel quite right,
But you can smile.
A smile can bring sunshine to a heart that is sad.
A smile can lighten a load and make weary hearts glad.
Since the world is full of sorrows
And heartaches for tomorrow,
Smile!

Julie Ann Larochelle
WHISPERS
I heard God knocking on my door
and I knew that I should answer.
When I did, the step was empty.
Wind swirled the leaves, which rustled
Like the thoughts of my mind.

Death came to me in a dream
and I tried to waken.
Once I did, my head was clear.
A spirit breezed by me with softness
Like the wind that blows the leaves.

Lisa Lazzaro
A POEM ABOUT MY CAT
I have a cat, his name is Kitty,
He gets into so much trouble it is a pity,
He lies in front of the refrigerator,
And he has not heard of the movie the TERMINATOR.
His favorite things to do are eat and sleep,
When he sleeps he never makes a peep!
Now that we have moved, we live at the corner of
Webb Chapel, and we are scared that he might get hit,
But, we don't have to worry, because all he does is sit!
Unless . . . he finds that squirrel that lives in our tree,
He tries and tries but he cannot catch him, if he did
he would surely yell "Yipee!"
He is all black so he can slip through the night without being seen,
But watch out! At times he can be mean!

Theresa Luscan
I BELIEVED

To Dan Cistone with all my love and friendship always.

I believed in love,
I believed in you,
I believed,
that what we had was true,
but, now you're gone,
and you took my heart with you,
Still I think of you.

Rebecca Evans–Snider

Rebecca Evans–Snider
GLISTENING MEMORIES
Cold, brisk, glistening night shadows
hover, through trees, over twinkling, lighted homes.
Skaters glide close to an island
on a shimmering, crystal lake.

Fire's flame pierces frosty breezes
as pine mingles in wafts of smoke.
The taste of hot chocolate shared
brings friends' laughing voices close.

Tinkling bells and swishing blades
carve into silvery ice, loops
from outside edged figures.
Powdered ice is brushed from clothes
as skaters fall and slide in free–style challenges.

Gone now, are those good times and friends
in a dream of crystal playgrounds.
Remembered, is a vision of ice skating in winter
and glistening memories of
experienced realities!

Sonya M Lester
TOMORROW
My blanket at night
Is the rich mellow heavens
That nestles me softly,
Into my bed

At first I am restless
But the stillness comforts me,
As I drift off in thought
With many dreams in my head

After much thought
I awaken to find
The rays of sunlight
Not far behind

I rise from my bed
And rush to my window
I look all around
And then straight ahead

Finally the sun rises and
I hear him say:
Yesterday was yesterday and
Today is today.

W June Lowe
WHEN I CLOSE MY EYES

When I close my eyes
His kiss is soft and warm.
His brown eyes say "I love you."
I relax in his warm embrace.
I love him like no other.
And it will always be so.
I am certain he will never leave me.
He will be with me forever.
We're lovers in a private world.
Then I open my eyes.
That private world is gone now.
It's only in my mind, you know.
But there I can be anyone,
Or love anyone I choose.
Reality plays no part
In the dramas of fantasy.
He loves me; I love him;
We're together forever.
When I close my eyes.

Debra L Larson
HEART

To mom.

Oh, the different patterns
of life to see;
all around us
and inside us they be.

Upon the looms
our hearts we weave;
but only art
do they perceive.

Upon your heart
pretty patterns do start.

Oh, that mine could be
as beautiful as thee.

Vivian Regina Lary
SOME PEOPLE NEVER SAY . . .

You and I walking under a summery
sky,
The birds are singing, flying high.
The ocean gives a gentle roar as the
scent
Of love grows strong, and its cool
water
Chases us until nighttime comes
along.

Some people never say these words
"I Love You—" it's not their style
To be so bold, but our love depends
on hearing these words, because
Like children we long to be told.

A new day dawns as the sunlight
creeps in.
Caressing, holding, and at one time,
awakening every sensation within a
touch.
Expressing, responding, and at the
same time, learning so much.
A nighttime of celebration of these
golden bands around our fingers.
A lifetime of reminiscing as the
feeling of an everlasting love lingers.

Some people never say these words
"I Love You" — they feel it should
Be obvious without a doubt, but our
love depends on these words,
Because saying "I Love You" is part
of what real love is all about.

Evelean Leatherwood
IF GOD CAME BY TO VISIT

If God came by to visit unexpectedly
today.
Would you ask him to come in or
would you turn him away.
If he's cold and weary would you let
him stop and rest.
Or would you be too busy to make up
an extra bed.
Would you have to hide some books
and get the Bible out.
Or would you even find it, it's around
someplace no doubt.
Would you dare to turn the T.V. on
and watch your favorite shows.
Or would you be too embarrassed for
the man above to know.
If you're at the table would you set
another place.
Or would you make excuses and send
him on his way.
Would you treat him like a stranger
or treat him like a friend.
Would you open up your door and
say he's welcome to come in.
Would you have to make excuses for
the way you've lived your life.
Or would you sit down beside him
and ask him for his advice.
When your days on earth are over
and you're standing at his gate.
Will he welcome you with open arms
or will he tell you it's too late.
If God came unexpectedly to visit
you today.
Would you ask him to come in or
would you turn him away.
And if he's cold and weary, would
you let him stop and rest.
Or would you be too busy to make up
an extra bed.

Theda Marie Lewin
COWBOY HEAVEN

I dream of Cowboy Heaven
A part of the sky so high,
There's a little boy of seven
Waiting there 'till night draws nigh.
He's roping falling stars, with a
silvery lair,
On his Golden Palomino, I see him
everywhere,
I've stood amazed and gazed,
Into the stardust haze,
Wondering how my Cowboy knew,
Which star was going to fall,
Out of its little stall,
For surely they do pass from view,
But he shouts,
"Mom, look–out! there's falling stars
all about,
Oh how they roam, please tell my
Dad,
To send them Home"

Olaf Lund
YESTERDAY'S CHILD

I am Yesterday's Child
Oh what can I say
When I look at her
And she looks away

She's gotten too close to keep her
away
Yet I am Yesterday's Child living
today

If you look too hard
If you try to stay
I will laugh at you
Just to keep you away

Yet you can't come near
'Cause I can't stay
For I am Yesterday's Child living
today

Lord I don't mean to hurt
But I could never say
That I am a victim of circumstance
That could happen today

The mother that was always mad
The love I never had
Have caused me to be strong
But not really wrong

The inner strength I will always have
Helps me to love other people
Even when they're bad

But I love from afar not from anear
Because I am Yesterday's Child
So please don't come near

For if you come too close or you
come too near
You would break down my wall and
cause me to hear
Memories of the past
With visions of fear

I am Yesterday's Child living today
Loving all the little children
And hoping they will find the way

I am Yesterday's Child living today
So if you really love me
Please . . .
Don't stay away

Lillian Lemaster
OUR BOSS

Kindness, was our boss's name.
He should have been listed in the
Hall of Fame.
When we disobeyed orders, he was
never cross.
He made us all an excellent boss.
"You did good" was the slogan he
used.
Somehow he never became confused.
Today and tomorrow he was always
the same.
To all who by his office came.
He had a heart of gold to those in
need.
Always ready to do a good deed.
Eternally his work with us will stay.
He was an angel in every way.
Now he has left his position for
another to hold.
And gone on home to walk those
streets of gold.

Martha Wright Land
TIME

Stop!
Time . . . Stop!
Let me board your pendulum,
And milk your hours
so swollen full,
'Till I suckle you dry
And savor the lingered drops
I covet upon my lips;
And when my thirst for you
is quenched,
And, only then,
shall I let go;
Oh! Sweet,
Sweet
Breast of Time.

Mary Ellen Lough
AND THE WALL CAME TUMBLING DOWN

After December of 1962,
a wall was built by government issue.

It was tall and wide, big and strong,
and when the wind blew it would
sing a sad song.

It divided up families and brought
great sorrow,
but each day there was new hope that
maybe tomorrow . . .

They would get to share love, just
once more,
hope that maybe someone would
open a door . . .

To friendship, love, and also peace
and now there's TRUE HOPE that all
the hatred will cease,

Because the wall came tumbling
down one night,
all the tears of happiness were a
wonderful sight,

When the wall came tumbling down!

Heidi Ann Lehan
A BETTER WORLD

To those who cherish their dreams, through their pen and their heart. To Jason Miller, fellow poet and dearest friend — my highest regards, deepest respect, and warmest love.

Consequences are often great
But should our wrongs cause us to
hate?
How often do we cease a fight
Instead to choose wrong over right?

Life shortens time, and tests our
strength
Why should we not extend its length?
Why end impartialness and truth?
But find the goals to seek through
youth

Only haste can cause a stand
Unity throughout this land!
To make amends with hopeful foes
And end our tragic hate and woe

This dream of mine will find its place
Security on every face!
The minds of youths taught to
befriend
Instead of having to defend

Yet prepared this world is not
For my hope to choose its lot
But when this world starts to beseech
I know my dream begins its reach

Betty Lewis
GLOW

You have the same spirit as the one
you ride.
Long flaming red hair flying in the
air the same color as your mare.
As you ride to the top of the hill
everyone can see you for miles.
They can tell by the color of your
hair that it's you up there sitting
on top of your mare.
As the sun began to set you began
to glow.
And everyone knows it's the
reflection
from your hair while you sit atop the
mare.

Patricia A Lofgren
THE PRESENCE

Sitting in the dark I feel a presence
around.
It can see me, but it makes no
sound.

Makes my body feel real light.
It's a strange feeling I can't fight.
What could this spirit try to say?
When I felt it on such a weird day.
Is it a sign of life or death?
If so why does it capture my breath?
When I come down from its high
I know it's a feeling that it wasn't to die.
The presence leaves me and I am still.
I can feel it leave, but not on its own will.
Will it come back to remind me of faith a different time?
When love was free like a whispering chime.

Joseph L Lemoine
LOVE AT MOONLIGHT

To the one who inspired me to do more than dream. She showed me how to reach for them. Thank You Alisa my Love.

My soul was captured this night
as the moon moved across the sky.
The light that struck her hair,
made it shimmer in the crisp night air.
She walked with pure perfection,
like a goddess among mortal man.
Her love surrounded me,
as her love drifted down from the heavens.
I felt her gentle loving touch,
which I yearned for so much.
The touch of her sparkling lips,
raced through me tenderly,
My heart exploded with passion,
that left me gasping helplessly.
She captured my heart this night,
just like love at moonlight.

Howard C Fichtel
SUMMER RAIN STORM

To my mother, my family and to Lisa for believing in me.

See the clouds, a dark blanket floating from distant winds
No compassion in her sails reaching out from her endless mast.
When will it hit?
How long will it last?
After the lightning listen for the sound.
Of the breaking sky falling to the ground.

Listen to the thunder, it's mighty roar.
Causing a stillness on land and the birds no longer soar.
Feel the rain as it hits the earth,
Cool drops of water the sky has given birth.
They gather to form puddles, fill rivers and streams
Answering prayers, killing dreams.

Catherine List
GREETINGS TO AN OLD FRIEND

I traveled down Life's Road one day_
With all the skies above so gray;
And then a friend reached out his hand
And suddenly the world was grand!
The years have passed, and our roads have parted,
But I still recall the dream we started;
And I hold that dream close to my heart
As I travel on down the road apart.
Tho skies above me sometimes turn gray
I think of the friend who came my way,
I think of the happiness we have known,
And I realize in my heart, I'm not alone.
To you dearest friend this wish I send,
May your Holidays be filled with joy no end.

Lucy Jane Mayes
THRU OPENED EYES

This poem is dedicated to my loving family and friends.

I looked up at Heaven
What did I see
Jesus smiling down on me
What a wonderful feeling
His smile so appealing
Kindness and love on his face
I knew I was saved, by his grace
All my sins from the past
Were all gone at last
I knew I was found
By his love, I was bound
I will praise his name
For he has made me tame
I know I'll never be the same
My heart now filled with joy
Makes the world seem like a new toy
His glory is all around
When I die, I'm Heaven bound!

Suzanne Henson
DEPRESSION

To my daughter, Linda, the lifeboat in my troubled seas.

Against painful reality I defend
On harmful patterns I depend
Soon great sadness fills that dark cold chain of wills
Shackled by fears; forged link by link
Slipping despair; I drown then sink
Shadowed nights with no endings
Pleading cries for help I'm sending
Because this inner voice is weak
There lies a heart where only sorrow speaks . . . .

Andrew Thompson
BURDON

It seems a man by the name of Eric.
Would weave his songs as an R&B fabric.
He sings about a house of ill fame.
The Rising Sun was its infamous name.
Price would play an organ with dedicated zest.
As Valentine, Chandler and Steele did their best.
The Animals they would come to be called.
But, their appearance would leave some people appalled.
As long as their music could jump and move.
They knew that they were in the groove.
Unconventional in their dress and ways.
Their musical style, swings and sways.
Burdon, puts his soul into a microphone.
This to be his musical epitome.
Newcastle upon Tyne gave us all its best.
When the U.S. had Burdon as its guest.
Instrumentality backed his vocals with certain power.
The organ and piano made a musical shower.
The guitars and back vocals made their statement.
As they continued without abatement.
Burdon shows an ability.
To set his musical talent free.

Andrew Thompson
VISIONS OF A SAINT

To Mr. R. Moore and family.

Simon Templar meets a woman
Whose troubles are not few
Said Simon to the woman fair,
"What can I do for you"
Said the woman to the Templar
"I think the Saint is really due,
To take my troubles by himself and offer me a clue."
As the Templar looked above his head
A roundish halo he did view
As the music played a theme, so familiar to a fan
A figure stood upon the screen
Somewhat like a man
His thinness is deceptive
Because of all he means
To those of us who watch his namesake
On all our T.V. screens
Even the theme song in the background
Has a feminine power
So, Simon can know just what to expect
Exactly on the hour.
It seems an actor, Moore by name
This figure having made his fame
Goes on with greater things in view.
A. R. Broccoli gave him something to do.
007 he will play with certain style and wit.
Humor he will also use and not a little bit.
But he will still remember, back, in those halcyon days
The visions of a saint and his saintly ways.

Nanci Satin Reichman
UNTITLED

Dedicated to Louis I. Reichman.

I have just discovered
that there is no death.
I saw your still body.
I watched the box lowered
into the ground.
And I wiped away my tears.

My new companion was loneliness.
We learned to keep house together.
I tried so hard to live with him,
Feeling that then I could believe in death.

But you never went away.
You wouldn't go away.
Over and over you came to me—
In dreams, in thoughts, in parts of me.
No matter how hard I tried to write an ending
None would come.

Now I know there is no death.
I feel your thoughts, I know your ways.
And most of all
I've learned to love the part that's you in me.

Nancy M Baker
NO MATTER

This poem is dedicated to Joe, my darling husband and to the Miele and Baker family.

No matter where I am
No matter what I am doing
You are always there
Always on my mind.

No matter what you are thinking
I will always support you
No matter what kind of mood
I am in, I am always here for you.

No matter where I am
No matter what I am doing
You are always there
Always on my mind.

No matter where you go, I will always care about you.
No matter what I am thinking,
I will always let you know how I feel.

No matter where I am
No matter what I am doing
You are always there
Always on my mind.

Jason Brown
MYSTERY

To all, who are just trying to find their way.

When the seconds are minutes
The minutes seem years
The days call the hours
The night brings the tears
Do friends stand behind you
When night comes the day?
Will they remember this soul
Gone astray?
I cannot recall the time come
And gone
The life flash before me
The night ends at dawn
Yet when shall I leave here
No tear on my face
No footprints behind me
No clue or a trace

Melissa M Johnson
IN LOVE

To Jim Gordon, till we meet again.

In love with someone I met one night
It was love at first sight
When I saw your face in the night
The touch of your hands on my body
I knew I was in love

Time has passed and you're all
I can think about

The dreams of you I wish to come true
I never wanted you to leave that night
My heart cried when you did
For that night I fell in love with you

Lurlene Chesser
EXPECT A MIRACLE

To my dear grand-son—19 yrs old—Dean Arnold.

Some days you wonder why the sky is dark blue,
All the dark clouds close in on you.
It happened to me in a terrible wreck.
My spine was severed, but I could talk and move my neck.

A year of my life has gone by, my legs don't move,
I tell the doctors I'll try anything, what can I lose?
I'm only nineteen and dream of what the future may bring.
My wish is for a normal life and everyday things.

My parents help, my mother's heart is filled with love
So I try for their sake, and pray for help from above
It's hard dear God to meet each day
I'll keep on praying for a miracle to come my way.

Jimmy L Elkins
IT TAKES TWO

This poem is dedicated to my future wife, whoever she may be.

Love, in the purest form,
Started with a foundation, a concrete base of friendship
A deep respect and enduring trust, priceless time spent together
Walks in the moonlight, gazing into those deepest of eyes
Picnics under the willow tree—it weeps no more
Tender kisses and gentle caresses
The smell of your hair, touch of your skin
Your beauty and innocence lingers in my mind
Our arms support each other, emotions overflowing
Together, even when you're gone, by my side—always

Now vows are exchanged hand in hand, eyes connected by time
Desire, longing, and love is fulfilled
Not lust or flesh, but an innermost merging
A lifetime connection—together—never apart again
From this purest love a creation of life

Many years of happiness and joy, also bitterness, hate, and pain
For so is life, but we made it
Sharing the hurt, listening and taking the pain away
Bearing one's most inner self, even fear
Being there for each other till the end
Which you were . . . THANK YOU!

Jane C Binns
WILTED ROSES

For Thuan Van Vo: May you someday meet and embrace your inner peace.

His tears roll quickly down his cheek, thinner
than water. So fast, I think that his pain
will not last long. Our friendship's dimmer
than ever before; we are both slain
by knives of grief within us. He, because
of my words ending all, and I for it
had taken so long. Time, lost in jaws
clenched tightly. I slip through a
crack from parting lips.

Now, I'm roaming through so many spices,
sizes, flavors, and shapes. I don't deny.
The world lets loose unto me bliss—crises
are no more. The tears that dripped inside my
soul . . . have no pit to fall in. It is gone,
and with it walls, that trapped my jubilant song.

Jill Sharron Hall
THE DREAM SHELL

On the warm golden sand
From the cold cold sea
By the toss of a wave
I happen to be.

To a small creature
I used to be home
And now I'm a treasure
To those who beachcomb.

What is the treasure
I hold deep inside
That just sounds to the old
Like the oncoming tide?

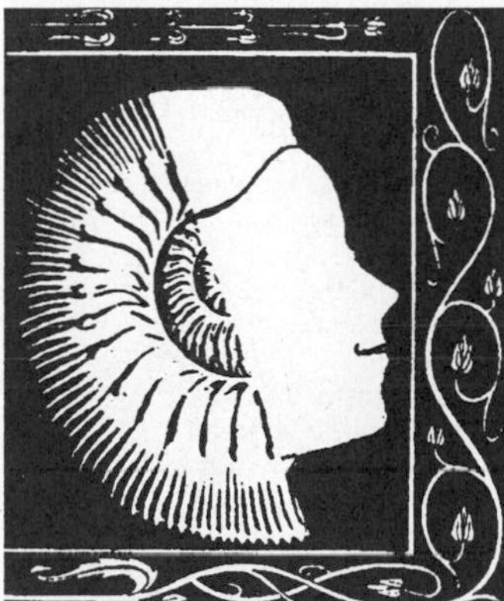

It's the whisper of dreams
From both far and near.
The whisper of dreams
That only the young can hear.

And to those of you
Whose heart is still young,
You too can hear the song
That the dream shell has sung.

Kathy Seaman
I, NIGHTWOLF

To My Grandpa Seaman. REST IN PEACE, For All Eternity.

I, Nightwolf sleep in the darkest room of my home. I sleep until the shadows of the night fall across the land. I awake and hear your calls in the darkness. I can feel the presence of your thoughts in the shadows of the night.

I never knew you in life, not even in death. You know me in death, you reign with the Lord. I am destined to walk in the shadows of the night. I know you are with me, I know you are watching me in the shadows of the night.

When dawn starts to come, I must return to my darkest room to sleep, until the shadows of the night, fall once more across the land.

Rosemary Higgins
FAREWELL

To my father, I loved you so much, Feb. 1980.

There were soldiers standing all around
Guns were rested upon the ground . . .

Friends and family were all about
Seven children stood straight and stout . . .

A courageous lady softly cried
The man she loved no longer by her side . . .

A flag draped casket held a man dressed in blue
A pilot, a hero, and a father too . . .

Guns were raised to fire a twenty-one round salute
This man was given this final attribute . . .

The flag was removed and folded neat and trim
The flag a symbol meaning so much to him . . .

A bugle sounded a last farewell to this man in blue
Farewell to the pilot, the hero and my father too . . . .

Donald E Hunt
LOVE

To Tina With Love who gave me inspiration.

What is love
Part is being free
Knowing you're still you
While I'm still me
Knowing together we make one
But alone are just as good
And accept if it should end
We've done everything we could
That life without love
Is no way to live
But to have true love
You have to be honest when you give
To give yourself completely
And do it for giving's sake
Not to work on your lover
Then you're really on the take
Accepting your partner
For what they really are
And not pretending to accept them
But wanting to change them from afar
True love is being committed
To make a spouse a part of your life
But remaining happy with yourself
Whether you're the husband or the wife
It means saying no
If that's truly how you feel
And not putting someone on a pedestal
Just because of a marriage seal
But treating them as an equal
While you share in what you do
And then the world will see
You are one while you are two

Eileen June Smith
PRECIOUS ONE

To my son, Thomas James Smith—on the date of his birth, July 16, 1988.

Go to sleep my precious one,
Wake to see the morning sun.

In your dreams there will be,
Visions that only you can see.

With your love, you will light my day,
For you I would throw all my cares away.

Love has grown into a son,
You'll always be my precious one.

I'll hold you close, sweet little boy,
I'll care for you like a fragile toy.

When my day is over & done,
I thank the Lord for my precious one.

Jimmy Johnson
A FAIRY TALE COME TRUE

To Sandra & Tony Lyons
For Sarah Ashlee, Lilly & Bob Schoenberger
For Matthew Lawrence

The gorgeous sun bathes the morning sunshine,
Doves cooing in pairs gathered upon
high wire;
Swarms of sparrows bursting with song in time,
Mocking birds teasing all with
"Hey! where's the fire?"

Busy bee flitting onto a blooming rose,
Humming bird hovering in fortuity;
A beautiful setting to jot down in prose
As Nature wakens us all to reality.

Warm sunbeams shining thru a bedroom window
Upon a crib rousing the sleeping beauty.
"Pretty Baby" they mean to call soft and low,
Wakening the child up deliberately.

A proud new mother stirs anticipating,
Learning by "wear and tear" in expectation
The many whims expected from a baby weaning,
With motherly patience without restriction.

Here's wishing Mother "all's well that ends up swell";
  Rousing cheers for great assist from the Father;
And child growing up "to be what it will spell"
  As in fairy tales "SO HAPPY EVER AFTER."

Carla Thompson
I BELIEVE . . .

For all that have entered my heart and allowed me into theirs, I dedicate this poem.

I Believe . . .
In our lives
God gives us someone to care for

I Believe . . .
They stay in our hearts
Because they need a place to be close to God

I Believe . . .
In my life
God gave you to me to care for

I Believe . . .
With all the goodness in heaven
I never want to do without caring for you

I Believe . . .
For each on earth
A blessing is waiting for us in the future

I Believe . . .
In our lives
God gave us each other to care for

I Believe . . .
I will try
To be all and do all for you forever, so help me God

Vena A Ziegler

Vena A Ziegler
REVERSES
When answers are given
And I hear them read,
It will not matter too much,
For I doubt that I shall hear
The verdict said;

Yet, here lingers a spark
Which can rekindle
To progress life another step;
From experience to experience
Where there will be a further
  demand
Beckoning me to taste the
  forbidden cup;

But having enjoyed the ruby
  nectar,
Verdicts can be gainsaid,
And find the judges themselves
Standing as the accused.

Vena A Ziegler
ACCEPTANCE
The Great sleep will o'ertake me
And will ne'er end its quest
'Til I bow to its scepter
In an eternal rest;

So let me accept this moment
As evidence of having been,
For I know not how I shall resurface,
Nor the where nor the when.

Vena A Ziegler
DEFINITION
Is love only passion,
Or is passion a consuming love?
Can we count the hours either
  will last?

Would we try?
When you come to me in
quietness
And caress my lips with yours,
Is duration important?

When you are mine
And I am yours,
What matters time?

Perhaps this is eternity.

Vena A Ziegler
NANCY
Tonight I must think of the happy
  times—
So let me linger quietly 'neath the
  moon,
And let soft shadows course
  across my mind—
Not to disturb—
But to brush a treasured memory
  into life
To let me again live its fullness,
And recover the lost moments—
Not to dissipate and replace the
  present,
But to savor again the past glow
So that this can refresh my
heart,
And ease the ache:

As the earth is enlivened by a
  soft summer rain,
And before the sun can turn it
  into an arid desert,
Let it tremble in new growth and
  freshness
Before it is again bled of its
moisture,
As I may be of my tears in
memory
Of my lovely daughter Nancy—
A young matron, wife, mother—
And my treasured child.

Vena A Ziegler
HOURGLASS
When first you were in the wrong,
Without intention or of plan,
You set in motion an unknown force
Which will follow you from youth to
man;

Worry not about changing the past,
But accept this axiom—
Your first error in judgment
Will not be your last;

For the footprints you should have
made
Neither appear nor can they fade,
For the drifting sands shift and move,
And like your phantom footsteps
Are only the essence of faded
dreams.

Vena A Ziegler
STAND MUTE
Come to me in silence
Walk softly to the door,
Ask me no questions,
Just sit and adore;

If a confession I must make,
Close your ears then and there,
And let only deafness know the
  score;

You cannot will the perfect,
You can only wrap the errant
In a cloak of clandestancy.

Vena A Ziegler
QUESTIONS
Where do things go when they
  are gone?
Where does love go when it has
  flown?
Where does the day go when
  night invades?
Where does the rose go when it
  fades?
Where does the soldier go when
  the battle is o'er?
Where does time go when it is no
  more?
Where does happiness go when
  laughter is done?
Where does the night go with the
  rising sun?
Where does the shadow go when
  there is no light?
Where does the hero go at the
  onset of fright?
Where does the beginning go at
  the ending?
All things, beginnings, endings and
  in betweenings
Accept infinity's blending,
And in the final stage meld into
  Nature's wending.

Vena A Ziegler
ENDOWED

Dedicated to the memory of Christopher, beloved son of Joel and Sherran Ziegler.

There was a fathomless emotion
in the look
As the naked depth of the soul
was bared,
Revealing the eloquence of the
penetrating eyes;
Though pure sufferance spoke, no
words were heard;
The searching opaque look
entwined this soul with
  His,
And that which was silent and
beseeching remains
  unsaid;
Perhaps it is incalculable to
understand such
  silence,
But there seemed to be a
covetousness to learn
the unexplored depth of truth:
Still, fate left the silence
undisturbed,
Knowing the future would solve
the question
Of whether words would ever be
necessary;
For the two souls so joined in this
union
Was built on a rock of complete
understanding,
And He accepted the new soul to
escort it across
  the border
To merge it with His Father's
Kingdom of
  everlasting love.

Letitia Maria Reeks
FOREVER, MY LOVE

To Gus Costopoulos—The inspiration in my life.

Stronger and stronger every day that I
breathe,
Is my love, which will grow
infinitely.
You are all that I live for and all that
I need.
Our true love has grown like a
fertilized seed.

Like two souls soaring alone in the
sky,
We were brought together by God's
knowing eye.
Together we'll soar to the greatest of
heights,
Discovering our world for the rest of
our lives.

Together we'll build every one of our
dreams.
And conquer any obstacle life may
bring.
Since our love is like no other before,
We'll be united together,
forevermore.

Marylin Daly
HE SITS WITH A BLANK LOOK ON HIS FACE

To Mom, God rest her soul, who gave me the inspiration to write.

He sits with a blank look on his face
Just staring into empty space
for hours he just sits there
Wishing that someone will care
His stomach knows he has not eaten
Stupid Bum, someone shouts, he
should be beaten
His legs are aching from his new bed
He cries dear Lord, let me be dead
How could this have happened to me
I had it all before the fall
Won't someone please hear my plea

Evelyn L Blackwell
JOYS OF A GARDEN

For my husband Roy, Sr. and my children Roy, Jr., David and Diane.

The joys of a garden
  Long rows of peas, beans and
  corn
Sparkling in the morning dew

The joys of a garden
  From tiny seeds
To bountiful harvest

The joys of a garden
  Peace and content
I feel within
  A garden

Catherine P Driver
EMPTY HEART/LONELY MIND

I dedicate this poem to Brandon.

The night is filled with expectation
  over tomorrow's day
I can't handle this anticipation
  over what my life will say
I fear the night
  as a waiting time
Between these dreary-black
  lonely days of mine
There is no love
  in my heart

From the world
I feel apart
I feel so cold
and dark inside
With laughter and jest
this I hide
But within myself
I am confined
With my empty heart
and lonely mind

Dolores Wilson

BLACKBERRY WINTER

'Tis Blackberry Winter:
Blackberry bushes
Are bursting forth
Into snowy white bloom;
Competing with
Candytuft, Hawthorne, and Spirea, too;
Though we labored long on the latter,
Me and you.

"Competing," I say, "and
Frequently surpassing them all
Though we labored long,
Me and you."

Already, we relish their summer fruits:
Sweet juicy blackberries
To be picked
From these bushes which grew
In our back yard
With no help at all
From me and you.

Dolores Wilson

THOUGHTS ON HEALING

At times I have been reluctant to say,
"I'm better today."
Myself, I never congratulate;
Nor say, "I'm fine today!"

WHY?

When I do, that demon Relapse
My ebullient spirit always zaps.
I have come to believe that
The very essence of well-being
Is too fine a wine
For this allergic body of mine.

Perhaps long illnesses can cause one
Too self-centered to be:
When tackling tasks to be done,
Prudent and decisive I must be
To maintain healing given to me.

So now, I try only to think objectively
Positive thoughts of wise action and happy health.
Surely, the thought of well-being:
'Tis truly a very fine wine;
"I am okay. I am fine. Today is mine."'

Nita J Barnes

THOSE YOUNG SCHOOL DAYS

The laughter, the smiles, the talking in class
The teaching and learning so they may pass.
Math, art, and English too,
There's so much to teach, so much to do.
Do your work, be quiet, please sit down,
Don't tattle, don't doodle, quit making that sound.
Time for lunch, please get in a line
After that it's recess time.
The home bell rings and the children scatter
Rustling and bustling with lots of chatter.
Off to home for dinner and play
No more school for the rest of this day.
Homework's done, and your tummy is full
Eight o'clock bed time is Mom's rule
The morning alarm shakes us awake
Have a wonderful day dear and
Good grades do make.

Nita J Barnes

I LOVE YOU FOR YOUR GENTLE TOUCH

I love you for your gentle touch
that warms my body through
I love you for your loving ways
that keeps our love so new.
I love you for the things you say
that makes my heart beat fast.
My eyes, you see the thoughts that say
I know our love will last.
You're my breath
I take each day
My bread and water too
Myself is all I have to give
And I give it all to you.

Violet B Osborne

THE DAYS OF YORE

This poem is dedicated to Mabel, my loving Aunt.

There is a lane where no one walks,
Perhaps a spring, a shelter sought.
It once was used, the way was known,
Did someone use it all alone?
I long have seen the empty shells
Of long lost buildings where life dwelled.
Now all that's seen is bush and wall,
We cannot know the shape at all.
There sometimes is a chimney, rent,
That time has tolled, its use is spent.

The lilac stands so stately tall,
Who planted it no one recalls.
If I upon this lane do wend,
Could I see those sights again?
Imagine how it was back then,
A fawn would pass, perhaps a friend.
So peaceful were the days of yore.
That time has gone forevermore.

PauLita (Pauline) Hernandez

RAINBOW OF HUMANITY

To my son Michael and my daughter Valerie. For all the children of the world. I Love You.

If I were Orange, and you were Blue,
Like the Sun in the Sky;
I would adorn you.
If I were Brown, and you were White,
Like Sweet mother Earth,
and the clouds in the sky.
If I were Tan,
Like the beach's sand,
and you were Black like darkness or night.
The bottom line is this:

We are a Rainbow of Humanity
and our Love is bliss.

Karen A Flynn

LETTING GO

To my Daughter, Jennifer Rose Flynn.

Our minds say "it was for the best
That our daughter died that day,"
Yet for our yearning hearts
We said "Lord, don't take her away!"

I thought of how much I loved her
And the tears began to flow,
The Lord said "There will be others
But with me this one must go."

Well, who has the right to tell God
He cannot have what is His,
So goodbye our little Jennifer
Whom forever we will miss!

Karen A Flynn

YESTERYEAR

To my brother, Wayne Desautels.

Our crying days are over
Our grown-up days are here
Do you ever sit and wonder
What happened to yesteryear?

When we used to sit and argue
And sometimes we would fight
And mom and dad would teach us
All about wrong and right.

In the summer we'd go to Lakeville
And swim in a freshwater pond,
In the winter we would get up
For school at the break of dawn.

Remember when we got Bowzer
The names that we would give,
Now we're all grown up
With different lives to live.

I want you to know I love you
And I wish that you were here,
Now I hardly see or know you
What happened to yesteryear?

Karen A Flynn

WHY GOD MADE LITTLE GIRLS

Dedicated to Mike and Sharon and their five daughters.

God made the world with its towering trees,
Majestic mountains and restless seas.
Then paused and said "It needs one more thing
Someone to laugh and dance and sing.
To walk in the woods and gather flowers,
To commune with nature in quiet hours."
So God Made Little Girls

With laughing eyes and bouncing curls,
With joyful hearts and infectious smiles,
Enchanting ways and feminine wiles.
And when He'd completed the task he'd begun,
He was proud and pleased of the job He'd done.
For the world when seen through a little girl's eyes,
Greatly resembles Paradise.

Cindy Weaver

THE RAPIST

Dedicated to my beloved husband, Ray, and my loving son, Michael.

No greater anguish or hurt
can one feel,
than to witness the destruction
caused by the Exxon Valdez oil spill.

Birds no longer sing
their joyful songs of praise,
for they're struggling for their lives,
in this thick oil glaze.

The fish that once swam
so abundant and free,
now float on their backs
through all the debris.

Greed came upon
this land oh so bold,
as we struggle for more
of this black liquid gold.

The wildlife they never
had a say,
in what was to happen
on that disastrous day.

Cindy Weaver

THE RAPIST'S "SHADOW"

It has been a full year
since the devastation struck,
Cleaning the beaches
has not brought too much luck.

The oil lies deep
underneath the sand,
Still killing the wildlife
and spoiling the land.

People try hard
to wipe the oil away,
But go home heavy hearted
at the end of the day.

They know the destruction
brought forth on that day,
Forever in our memories
and in our hearts it shall stay.

The Exxon Valdez oil spill
shall forever remain,
A tormentful memory of hurt,
devastation, sorrow, death and pain.

C L Saxton

HEALING TIME

A time for pain, a time for grief.
A time to cry, whether long or brief.
A time for anger, a time to sigh.
A time to ask our Father why.
A time to laugh, for once in a while
a time for memories, can help you smile.
The time has come for him to lay
asleep 'til Jesus returns one day.
Or maybe his spirit now does dwell
with God in heaven, whole and well.
Whatever your time, whichever your belief,
know we are with you in your time of grief.
Remember too, you'll find us there
in your time of healing. For we do care.

C L Saxton

TREASURES FROM THEE

The man does look upon the face
of these young children blessed with God's grace.
Then proudly he smiles, giving
thanks to THEE

for these wonderful children.
Their father is he.
The woman rejoices at finding them whole,
seeing their beauty deep in their soul.
Then she gives thanks and asks guidance from THEE
to nurture these children.
Their mother is she.
So seldom we tell these children we raise
we're proud of them; or give them high praise.
Too often we tell them the answer is no,
stop, don't start, or you can't go.
Remember the moment you knew they were real?
Remember the happiness and joy you did feel?
Return to those feelings, share them and see
the true loving nature from these children;
Your treasures from THEE

C L Saxton
I WAS WORKING AWAY BY MYSELF IN MY ROOM

To the ones I love. For their patience and encouragement.

I was working away by myself in my room,
when my sister threw open the door with a boom.
"Oh Tommy, come quickly. For this you must see!"
I said, "Go away. Please don't pester me!"
"But I told him you'd come." Josie looked at her shoe.
"I said you believed in leprechauns too."
I thought she was nuts but decided to go.
Then I could show her, this just wasn't so!
She opened her door. And I looked at the place
where a wee man did stand, with a grin on his face.
"I cannot stay long, but I've time for a chat.
Wheatberry's my name," he said tipping his hat.
I pinched my arm quickly. This was not a dream!
So Josie was right! Or so it would seem.
"This here is Tommy," said Josie a'squeal.
When he shook my hand, I then knew he was real.
We all started talking, and then before long
he said, "I will see you." and POOF! He was gone.
I will not doubt Josie, as once I had done.
And for a small sister, I've found she's quite fun.

Wilma Sheridan
TO THEE O LORD
I do not ask O Lord, a pleasant life to lead—
But one whose path toward holiness
Begins and ends with Thee

I do not seek O Lord, my cross to understand
But in the bitter darkness
Thou dost take me by Thy hand

I do not quest O Lord, for rest from toil and tear
But ever walk unfalteringly
In Thy footsteps, without fear

I do not plead, O Lord, for comfort, ease or fame—
But to praise and honor Thee
And glorify Thy name

I do but beg of Thee, my King, to o'er me ever reign
With grace to serve Thee faithfully
Perpetually in Thy domain

Amen

Wilma Sheridan
BLESSED CHRISTMAS
'Tis Jesus Incarnate whose birth we remember
With joy and much gladness the twenty-fifth of December.
Sweet holy Infant, Babe in Bethlehem born
Laid in a manger, swaddling clothes worn.
O'er the hills arose, a bright glistening star,
guiding Shepherds and Magi from pathways afar,
leading them where Jesus lay, to a cave, a stable, a manger bed of hay.
All was so calm! All was so bright!
'round Jesus, Blessed Babe this most holy night.

Angels raised their voices in song;
Alleluias chorused 'til break of dawn.
Divine Holy Babe, born God's Only Son,
Redeemer, Messiah, the Eternal One!
Come to the stable, come to the manger,
Come to the Saviour, remain not a stranger.
'Glory to God . . . Peace to men of good will,'
Let psalms of praise be echoed still.
With Cherubim and Seraphim loving voices raise,
"REJOICE! REJOICE THIS WONDROUS DAY OF DAYS!"

Peggy Sanford Weed
NOVEMBER IN NEW ENGLAND
I never see bare woods in Fall
With leafless limbs against the pale blue sky,
The trunks smoke-dark and frosty,
The ground, hard-packed and crackling
With rime on sear brown leaves;
The distant mountains bluer than the sky they border
With a morning mist between—
I never see these things of frost and blue and gray,
But that my mind and eyes deceive me
And show me, winding on the stony path,
A band of gray-clothed Pilgrims:
Wide-collared, dark-browed men
Shouldering their muskets,
Guarding their full-skirted women
And grave-faced children—
All walking silently
Off into the mist.

Raymond A O'Hara
VOICE OF STONE
I am a lonely tombstone
Of polished marble white.
I sparkle in the night time
And in the morning light.
But no one decorates me
With holly or with pine
To make my sweet protection
Both ample and benign.

I do not care a wit, I don't,
If no one visits me,
For I am nestled underneath
A leafy walnut tree.

But what of him who's under
My sparkling marble stone?
Won't he feel deserted
And somehow all alone?

If my charge is ever
Deserted from above,
He'll die again and yet again
For want of human love.

Toot Menner
DEAR MOM
I would like to tell you now,
How much I miss and love you.
With all my heart, wow!
After seventy years without you.

Most children will never realize,
The love a Mother gives.
They won't understand,
'Cause their Mother lives.

It's not until she leaves,
For places unknown to them.
Just how much they'll miss her,
She was their very best friend.

I was a lucky child tho,
An Aunt gave her love to me.
She never let me forget "My Mother."
How wonderful she could be.

Thank GOD for giving me,
An angel from above.
One who took the place of Mom,
To her I give my love.
I love you Mom.

Christine Reece
SPRINGTIME ON THE GILA
When it's springtime on the Gila, swift water runs deep;
Cottonwoods and willows shade the river banks, so steep.
The Gila, fed by seasonal rains and melting mountain snow,
Flows from New Mexico mountains to Arizona farms, below!

The blossoms on cat-claw, mesquite and palo-verde trees
Provide nectar for butterflies and the busy honeybees.
Most birds nest in trees, but quail nest on the ground.
Reptiles will eat their eggs, whenever they are found.

Gila monsters are crawling from April until November;
A rattlesnake's warning rattle is a sound to remember!
Young deer and javelinas will migrate to higher hills;
They'll be game for hunters, looking for some thrills!

Deep water and shades are popular at this time of year.
Recreationists will be coming from places far and near.
Crews of cowboys will round up cattle for a month or so;
Yearlings are loaded on trucks; to pasture they will go!

The bermuda grass will grow another carpet of green;
Horses, cows and calves will be grazing there, again!
As winter's snow melts and the Gila is deep and clear,
And nature's new cycle begins, the springtime is here!

John J Milone

John J Milone
LIFE'S EXPERIENCES
I have heard the silence of the night.
I have seen the beauty of the day.
I have lived a little bit with fright.
I have lived a lovely month of May.

I have known a sweet and happy smile.
I have fondly brushed away a tear.
I have jogged another extra mile.
I have dodged a rapid mortal spear.

I have surely lived beneath the storm.
I have likewise lived 'midst the flowers.
I have been both very cold and warm.
I've even had some hungry hours.

I've certainly laughed, joked with others.
I have wept alone within my room.
I have labored and dined with brothers.
I have tried to operate the loom.

I have sung and danced, and been joyful.
I have vied, been denied, still been glad.
I have found life to be quite "awe-full."
Writing phrases on History's pad.

Mary Lillard Young
THE EARLY EASTER GIFT
The Easter Bunny Was to have
Brought this Gift,
But since you are feeling bad,
I brought it early to give you
a Lift.

This is something I think
You will like,
And I hope you will soon
Be feeling all right.

Aline Dixon Dykes
CONTENTMENT
Snowflakes falling busily down
Like foraging questing quails;
Sun glowing on a scarlet canna,
The smell of bread and brown stew,
Charcoal and turps to spice the nostril:
These have been my privileges.

Color to glorify the artist's eye:
Books and words to the treasury of the mind.

Gentle friends to share a mood,
Children with precious faces:
A few special people and special places;
These have been my blessings.

Jerry Zboinski
THE SEARCHER
Eternity, a dreamer's greatest dream, this poet's greatest theme.
But perhaps eternity is a dreaded plague, though the conclusion seems vague.
Yet alone to face the ages, certainly this is not the dream of eternity.
For only true love can instill, the inner passion if you will.
To boldly face life's many obstacles, that would constrict you like giant tentacles.
While you question the wisdom in braving such continual misery.
Yet somehow your determination remains steadfast, as you pray this moment's despair be your last.
And you manfully battle the urge to weep, yet find no refuge in the bosom of sleep.
For the dreams once revered, now haunt you like some demon from hell.
You doubt your sanity, but perhaps only you know the meaning of sobriety.
As your companions drink to their despair, while you alone truly care.
But with no one to share your heartfelt tears, to eternity you bid farewell.

Dawn Demmerle
TORN DREAMS
Some people say that the world is ok
And that the sun will always shine
Some people sit and cry all day
Because they feel they will never be fine
The people think that the world's going to end
And they think that it's just a shame
Everybody in this world needs to mend
All the torn hopes and dreams of the ones with no fame
If you hear a voice outside the door
Don't be afraid to let it inside
Just remember that a friend might mean more
Than a person who happened to have lied.

Bob Metcalf
REMEMBER EARTH
Remember, how she paint
her autumn canvas
how she sleep
childlike in winter
how she weep
in spring gladness.
Remember when
before the greed
when earth was all
and all she was
were all we need . . .
Remember, how she
her heart—
like summer
beating.

Rozalia Coloka
AS THE NIGHT TURNS TO DARKNESS
As the night turns to darkness,
She puts on her white lace garment,
And looks in the mirror.
Her hair brushed with her golden brush.

Her body of sweet perfume.
She puts out the light, and lies on the bed.
With her hand under the pillow,
And embraces the pillow with her right hand.
Her tear drops fall from her eyes and her thoughts,
Are far away to the voice that was hers,
And the comfort that she had. Now gone
And not heard.

She holds on to the pillow and comforts herself with the thoughts of him,
And sees him in her mind,
Reaching out to her with a white rose in his hand.
She reaches out to him, to embrace him to touch him
And suddenly she opens her eyes and reaches out to an empty shadow,
That was in her mind.

And only the white rose is left beside her.
And with her last breath of life
"She whispers his name."

Joseph Mangan
CARING

To a special friend who means the world to me.

When I was down, you cheered me up,
You didn't turn away.
. . . A friend who listened with concern
At what I had to say.

If I could have a wish come true,
Or maybe through a prayer,
I'd pray that there were more like you
Who took the time to care.

Joseph G Hruby
LOVE'S INSPIRATION

Dedicated to Sandy Truesdall for the wonderful years she gave to me and inspiration.

You lighten up my life
You give me what my heart is needing.
You inspire and give encouragement to stand for what I believe in life's journey together.
When you are at my side I walk up rightly.
You stand beside me to strengthen our love and guide me.
Your love is brighter than the stars a bove that shine upon us.
Through those wonderful years we've shared together.
You've shown me the way we've come and where we are going to together through eternity.
We have embraced heavenly Father by the love we've shared.
As we walk hand in hand with life's promises.
We face challenge of success and the disappointments together through the years.

Joseph G Hruby
A FATHER'S LOVE FOR HIS CHILDREN
Why must he see himself like a mirror image in his younger years rebellious in spirit.
What does he try to simply guide his children in the most glorious ways that they won't make the same mistakes.
Where can he see the unrest in his children's hearts wanting to experience life in its fullness.
We face life's pleasures in our youth as growth.
Who watches us with open hearts and arms lifting our spirits to heaven gate and guide our children through life.
With humble gestures of tenderness and kindness we touch our maturity as we hold onto our youth.
In our youth we see the future in innocence to give our sons and daughters a world that we may be proud of.
Reaching out with open hand and arms to welcome them home.
As they fail in life the door is always open for us to feel secure to pick ourselves up and direct own lives to choose best direction that we may seek.
The love our children give us is respect and admiration as they grow through life's experiences and leave the failures behind them.

Joseph G Hruby
MY LADY

To Karen Howard with love.

Your eyes are blue which fills
My heart with tenderness.
With love in words you express
Your joys and sorrows.
When you touch me, brings the
Warmth that engulfs me to the
Very center of earth.
Your freedom gives you sunshine
And direction to grasp upon the
Love that we share together.
Why must the world be so angry
To see what life can be, simple
And wonderful as love she expresses
To me.

Barbara Jean Korb
YOU AND I
We were siblings you and I
Together we would wonder
Sharing so many things
Time, places and some dreams.

Now you are gone
And I am here
Left shaking and numb
Filled with tears.

I shall hold strong
To the sweet memories
That is all that is left
Of you for me

We were siblings you and I
Alone I will wonder why
Missing so many things
Time, friendship and some dreams.

Wenonah J Snyder
PREMATURELY
Lincoln, the man of the masses,
Shouldering the woes of a nation
Exclusively
Shedding the cares unripened
Prematurely

Lincoln, the man of immortality,
Soaring above the house divided
The war
The injustice to humanity
Prematurely

Lincoln, the man of the cabin
Climbing by giant steps to
The castle
And on
To the cabin in the sky
Prematurely

Ms Peggy L Johnson
SPECIAL MOM

To My Mother, Mrs. Jewellene Morris Johnson, for her Leadership and Guidance; and My Fiancé, Robert A. Martin, who always lends encouragement.

Mom, I would like to take a few minutes out to say "Thank You." Thank you Mom for the things you have done for us down through the years. I know there were times when you didn't feel like going or doing, but you did it for us, your children.

I know there were times you probably wished things had been different; you realized they weren't, so you adjusted to the situation, because that's the kind of person you are.

Mom, again I would like to say, "Thank You" for being that Special Mom" in our lives. If it hadn't been for you, I don't know what we would have done or what would have happened to us.

Mom, I know we are truly "Blessed" to have a Mom like you, and I just "Thank my God above every day for you."

Mom you are a very Loving, Giving and Caring person. That's what makes you the Very Very "Special Mom." We Love You MOM, Very Much.

Ms Peggy L Johnson
SOMETIMES
Sometimes the interruptions of life are so great, until you don't know what direction to take.

Sometimes our trials and tribulations are so hard for us to bear, until we don't feel like facing a new day.

Sometimes our roads of travel can be so hard, long and bumpy. Sometimes the harder we try to achieve something, the more difficult it gets.

Sometimes the sky gets so dark, gloomy, and gray, until you think the sun will never shine again.

All these facts and statements are elements compounded together, to make up the Word called Life. You go through all of these and more, in order to survive in this ole world.

The sky will be sunny and bright again, in time. God is still on the throne with the eye of a Closed Circuit.

This is how I feel sometimes.

Ms Peggy L Johnson

A LETTER TO MY DECEASED SISTER AND AUNT

Well Hello Elma,
How are you today?
I heard you had left us in a very quiet way.

Well Hello Elma,
We're going to miss you in a very special way,
But we know you are with God now, and he will keep you. Day by day.

Well Hello Elma,
It will be hard for us to get used to you being gone away,
But we know now that you have gone home to stay.

Well Hello Elma,
No more weeping eyes of sorrow,
No more pain you will have to bear,
Because now you are in God's special care.

Well Hello Elma,
So dear sister lay down, and take your rest,
So hard you have worked, you deserve the best.

Hanesta Blango

Hanesta Blango

HOME

Where is home?
Where can I call home?
I've lived in many different homes,
But none to call my own.

What is a home?
What can I call a home?
Is it a place full of love?
Or is it a place as gracious as a dove?

They say a home is where the heart is.
But what about a broken heart?
Torn apart by pain and worries.
The kind that tears a family apart?

Who lives in a home that's sad?
A traitor and someone that's grumpy.
Who lives in a home that's gay?
A mom, a daughter, a son and a dad.

Why is a home called a home?
Is it because it's a place of comfort?
Is it because it's what you call your own?
Or is it because it has a big parking lot?

I don't know why a home is called a home.
Because there's none that I can call my own.
If I do have a home I would share
All the comfort and riches it has to offer.

Melissa Finch

THE RAT THAT WASN'T A CAT

Not last night but the night before
I went downtown to my favorite pet store.
I wanted a pet—I really wanted a cat.
But my mom had said, "No"—so instead I got a rat.

He was not too small and he was not too big.
He really kind of looked like a small hairy pig.
I really was excited, I really was glad!
My mom wasn't excited, my mom was mad!

My mom was scared but decided to take a peek.
My rat came over and kissed her on the cheek!
So my mom gave in and I got to keep my rat.
He's a really good pet—
But I still want a cat!

Sally Ann Kates

WE'RE NOT LIVING IN A GAMEROOM, BUT ON A BATTLEFIELD

To honor the "Great Commander in Chief, Jesus Christ," and all of his soldiers who daily are on the front line.

We're not living in a gameroom, but on a battlefield
Good and evil batting heads to see which one will yield
Tinsel temptations glitter and shine, it's hard to resist their allure
The land is no longer virgin, our motives are no longer pure

In this land of opportunity with amber waves of grain
If every belly isn't full, our heads should hang in shame
Our innocence lost, we've raped the land
And you can't close a deal with a shake o' the hand

We're living on a garbage dump of filth and shame and greed
Our minds polluted every day by what we see and read
Runaways and alcohol, drugs and porno queens
Nothing more than babies in their frosted, holey jeans

A whole generation of kids that are lost
And unwanted babies are murdered and tossed
In this world of dog-eat-dog where everyone competes
We've thousands upon thousands that are living in the streets

I'm sure that the Maker of heaven and earth cries at these sights so grim
The only way out is to give it all back and to once more live for Him
He's the Great Creator of all that exists, the one who holds the deed
He patiently waits while we struggle, for without Him we'll never succeed

Amen

Sally Ann Kates

THE DEATH OF DEDICATION

To my husband, Myron Kates, who has faithfully worked the same job for twenty-seven years. "Jacob's wages were cut ten times, time and again deceived; But a Covenant was finally made, and all because Jacob believed." Genesis 31.

They used to care about dedication and loyalty went two ways
But now the almighty buck is king and those are bygone days
The receiver was always priority, there used to be time for caring
Now, the faster we run, there's just more to been done and we've all been robbed of sharing

We're truly in danger of losing ourselves, our identity stands at risk
In the big rat race, we have no face, we're a number that's filed on a disk
We used to know each other's names and we'd lend a helping hand
But now it's hard to find someone who wants to understand

We try to survive without breaking the rules
And the maneaters out there would play us for fools
But, I tell you truly, it pays to do right
Don't give in to the pressure, don't give up the fight

Raise your head and stand your ground, there's an answer here today
There is someone who listens when we take the time to pray
He's the Son of God, yes, Jesus Christ, He knows what's in your heart
So work for Him and when things look grim He'll more than do His part

We find ourselves in thankless jobs where the outlook may seem dim
Christ understands, He takes our hands and draws us close to Him
And there's just one thing to keep in mind after all is said and done
When Christ is our employer the adventure's just begun

So, when the going gets real tough, just remember, Christ's enough!

Amen

Sally Ann Kates

BOWED, BUT NOT BROKEN

Dedicated to our mother, Dorothy Vest, who daily displays strength, perseverance, and insight. Proverbs 31:10 "Who can find a virtuous woman? for her price is far above rubies." Proverbs 31:28 "Her children arise up, and call her blessed."

There she is, all 90+ pounds, and yes, she has her ups and downs
Physically her body's shot, but she keeps on going with all she's got
A broken foot that will never heal, crippled hands she can barely use
Frozen shoulders, locked in place, it seems she's paid her dues

Robbed of so many pleasures, yet not throwing in the towel
From east to west, she's the very best, our mom is quite a gal
For every cookie or pie she bakes, it's truly a labor of love
And our hearts reach out to embrace her and to thank our Lord, above

That He saw fit to make her our mother, a decision for which we are glad
A good and faithful woman who loves her kids and loved our dad
Aching and hurting she nursed our dad after he suffered a stroke
And dauntless, she kept vigil as she bore the heavy yoke

She was there by his side the morning he died and the last words he heard spoken
Came from our mother, "I'll be with you soon," as her aching heart was broken
With her family all around her and her feelings there exposed
She removed the tube, and kissed him, and his blue eyes gently closed

Our dad was able to die at peace, we know, we don't just think
For he loved our mother very much, and he knew our mother's strength
He didn't worry she'd crumble, 50 years he'd observed her grit
He was sure of her perseverance, and he knew he could count on it

We know, Mom, how much you hurt, and we love you dearly—Mike, Sal, and Bert

Catherine V Frey

OUR WORLD

To future generations . . . You do make a difference; and to my three children: Christopher, Michael and Tina, and to my husband: Jim, you've made a difference.

Everything is backwards, times are confused.
What once seemed beautiful, now just seems used.
Models are pretending to be mannequins on stands.
Mannequins have been computerized to seem like real man.
Cars have been programmed, machines now are talking.
Everything is loud, and, no one is walking.

Everything is worried, and graded, and stressed.
We work under the gun, like every action is test.
This world is challenging and trying to provoke . . .
the wrong kind of actions, and functions which connote.
Our jobs would be simpler, our minds would be free,
if we did away with false pressures, which only impede.

Just take a deep breath and say to yourself . . . "I am no different from anyone else."

Let's try not to judge everything in sight . . . for who are we really, and, what makes us right?
We've grown, we've challenged, we've learned and explored.
One way isn't right, there is always one more.

Let's give unselfishly, LOVE, will enhance!
This world is "our world," let's give it a new chance.

Catherine V Frey
CHRISTINA'S POEM
The little girl I love so much,
brightens my life, with her gentle touch.
She bounces when she runs at play,
and hugs me so tight, before I go away.
She giggles when she tries to speak,
with a voice so tiny and filled with squeaks.
Her eyes so bright and full of love,
so honest and endearing, like angels above.
The little girl I'm speaking of,
is my little girl, the one I love.
She's just as tiny as she can be,
but goodness gracious, she's only three.

Catherine Frey
MY CORPSMAN FRIENDS
Somewhere out there, I know we'll meet again, and we'll be together,
helping our patients win.
Way out beyond our dreams and fantasies,
will be the reality of meeting other's needs.
With kind spirits, we'll share our caring ways
we'll live by our creed giving to others day by day.

There's going to be that Special time,
when we lend a helping hand;
There's going to be that trying time,
comforting a dying man;
It's going to be a challenge when we bring a baby in;
It's going to be so joyous when we see an infant grin.

Somewhere out there, I know we'll meet again,
giving to all others will be our Corpsman friends.
Way out, beyond, our dreams and fantasies,
we'll see each other, helping people . . .
Yes and children to mend.
See you again my Corpsman friends.

Connie Ford
HE'S MINE
He's mine by the way he touches me when we are together.
He's sweet and kind in his own special way, that's why I love him so.
He lets me know that everything is alright.
Sometimes I feel lost, and don't know what to do with myself.
He's there to let me know that it's alright if I'm lost, and tells me I'm here if you need me.
It's wonderful to know that a man could care so much.
Not many women have a man like mine.
That's how I know he's mine. This is how I come to love him so. Just being in his arms at night lets me know how special that I am as being the woman he would like to hold dear. As the part we will be close together.
I know he will be mine to keep forever.

Bernice Brock Johnson
SONNET NO. III

To the Memory of my Husband, Thomas Cabot Johnson, Lt., U.S.N.R.

If Death should walk among us, unafraid
I'd meet him at the door and ask him in.
And quake not at his step, nor be dismayed
At sight of that stark, vacant, toothless grin.
I'd seat him at my board and give him meat
And heady drink with merry grip and jest.
And when he'd had his fill to sip and eat.
We'd rise and leave anon at his behest.
Cold terror would not make me cringe and sweat.
Nor horror give my steady feet the lie.
I'd grasp the clammy hand and never let
Him guess that mortals sometimes find it hard to die.
I'd welcome him and give cold Death his due,
If first, I've spent a lifetime loving you.

Bernice Brock Johnson
SPLISH SPLASH
If I were someone else but me,
I wonder who I'd like to be.
Suppose I were a small pet fish.
My entire world would be a dish.
It really would be awfully grim
With nothing else to do but swim
Around and 'round and get nowhere
Because I was already there.
I'd rather be out in the deep,
With space to dart and jump and leap
Into each crashing wave that bore
Me to some far-off distant shore.
However, I would really hate
To end up on somebody's plate.

Bernice Brock Johnson
OVERSIGHT IN LIVING
When life was young and youth was fair,
I'd climb each day a golden stair.
Each step was sweet, each day was rare
As ever seen.

Now I am old, the days are not.
My golden stairs are full of rot.
I think, perhaps, I just forgot
To sweep them clean.

Jeff Hough
WAR
Fierce crystal grails
Toast to life divine
Out of violent vessels frail
Spill bitter drops of wine

In a medley of uniform diversity
Goblets clash in cryptic clear din
Multitudes mire in precise mendacity
Savory stock drips from within

Outstretched arms a half seas over
Raise the chalice in a glorious pledge
Choice morsels flow from lips sober
Drunken fists spill spirits over the edge

The vineyard's crop
How bitter the taste
Spare not a drop
There must be no waste

No one remembers delicate vessels
That spill crimson over their brim
Only the drunken hands in which they nestled
That lay them in boxes at the festival's end

Jeff Hough
THE SHATTERED CLASS
Divine black shines
through the hollow soul
Hatred wails
her grievance cold

Sour minds crush
with splintering blows
Iron hands shred
the dignity mold

You've fueled the furnace
that forged this wrath
This hammering vengeance
shatters your class

Jeff Hough
INNOCENCE
When days were tender
and years young
When dreams danced on billowing clouds
in flaming afternoons
When the eve's breeze
carried visions
shrouded in orange blossom scents

I cried because life was so hard

Jeff Hough
PALE, COLD, ALONE
Pale,
as the mist from whence he came,
a bent form searches ancient stone walls.

Cold,
aged arms embrace his own chattering body,
forever trying to warm the chill from within.

Alone,
with the cruel winter air forming bitter tears on wrinkled cheeks.

Echoed mockery rings in the thick distance,
as gray eyes lash out at the maddening emptiness
that surrounds him.

He returns to the mist from whence he came.

Karen French
WALKING ALONG IN THE WOODLANDS
Walking along in the woodlands
I began gazing at the flame colored trees.
I started to dream about,
The winter that's on its way.
With its white cotton blankets of snow.
The sunlight, how it makes the leaves glow.
See the beautiful sight,
How I long to see it longer.
But winter is upon me.
All the trees are bare,
Everything is covered with the white cotton snow.
This is beautiful but,
I long for the trees of flame.
Now all I have is the white fluff
Of snow and a fire burning,
The colors of the trees.

Hazel B Foster
STILL MY BABY

I dedicate this poem to my son, Ray.

No longer does he climb
Upon my knee
You see, he is six-foot-three
Going on fifty-three
But he is still my baby
He works for the Lord
In the ministry
He is a Rev. Dr.
And preaches the word
But he is still my baby
Not much of his time is free
But when he can
He spends it with me
So no matter how old or how gray
He is still my baby

Kristina Morfin
I AM A ROSE
You are the ground in which I stand . . .
You hold me tight when I begin to fall . . .
For you are my soil . . .

You are the backbone in my life . . .
You give me strength to stand as one . . .
For you are my stem . . .

You protect me from the cruel human hands . . .
Yet to those who have the softest of touch—
I may be touched . . .
For you are my thorns . . .

You are the true beauty in my life . . .
You make me what I am . . .
For you are my petals . . .

I AM A ROSE . . .
. . . Without you I would not be.
I would simply wilt away . . .
and die.

Raymond Francioso
DOWN THE ROAD
Walkin down the road
Walkin down the road
Now that you left which way will I go
The waysides around remind me of the time we used to know
Just walkin down the road.

Remembering the good times we shared
I thought you cared
Was it really so bad
Walkin down the road

Now that you said so long
I'll be moving along
Thinking this is the way it had to be, you without me
Maybe I'll be going to another place in time
But for now this road is only mine
Just walkin down the road.

Walkin down the road

Walkin down the road
Now that you left, which way will I go
The waysides around remind of the times we used to know
I'll miss them so
Just walkin down the road.

Lynn Ferris
DREAM LOVER

To Don Wesley Colbert, the love of my life, my Dream Lover. With all my love, Lynn.

My heart shuttered,
The first time he held me
CLOSE . . .
And kissed me passionately,
I fell in love with him.

All the good times we had,
We were friends as well as lovers.
Our long rides together,
And our picnics in the park.

He left without a word,
It all seemed so real.
Was it all a dream . . .
Or was it my dream lover?

Joan M Fish
IT CANNOT BE
You ask me love why I am blue
I had so dreamed of love with you
That daily it came to seem
Real and mine and not a dream
Then all was hope of our embrace
And wonder of the time and place.

It was a dream, I know that now
As my heart asks the why and how
I lost you and who else will know
The joyful bliss your love can sow
When it's returned in sum and kind
With heart and soul and even mind.

Now I cannot help but envy she
Who lives the dream I dreamed for me—or us.

Vickie S Sellers
OUT OF A DEEP SLEEP I AWOKE
Out of a deep sleep I awoke
I was sure I felt you climbing into my bed.

Given a moment to clear my head,
I realized it was only the cat instead.

Now I'm awake—again
—Alone—left to fight
this cold and lonely feeling—
again.

Every night it's the same,
Laying awake for hours on end.
Looking at the pillow where you should lay your head.

I wish you were here in my bed.
I guess I have to settle for the
cat instead—
This Time.

Jennie Kyser
WARRIOR OF LOVE
She comes from a native island,
That's so peaceful and full of compassion.
Her eyes are clear as the sea.
There's music in her love. There's music in her heart. There's music all around her.
Because she's a warrior of joy and happiness to everyone. Heart to heart she will stand with all nations. She sings a song of strength and beauty that brings peace to all ages.
You can feel her spirit all in your heart.
The starlight dews above her head.
All silently their tears of love instill weeping themselves.
Till infuse, Give us oh give me the man who sings a song of life.
He's equal to any of those who follow the same pursuit of happiness.
It takes pain to bring joy and love to the heart and soul.
Sing a song of life. Sing a song of death.

Jennie Kyser
BECAUSE I COULD NOT STOP FOR DEATH
Because I could not stop for death.
The time where for all the lover.
He kindly stopped for me;
The carriage held, but just the two of us.
We slowly drove, he knew no haste,
And I had put away the pain behind me.
My labor, and my leisure too,
For his civility,
We passed the school where children played.
We passed people asleep beside the road.
We passed the field of gazing grain,
We passed the setting sun over the ocean.
We paused before a house that seemed.
A swelling of the ground;
The roof was scarcely visible,
The cornice but a mound.
Since then our centuries; but only each of us know.
Feels shorter than the days that pass each days to come.
I am the first to surmise,
that love ahead happiness is destruction.
The true meaning of our love is compassion.
We're toward eternity.

Jennie Kyser
FIRST LOVE LASTS FOREVER
I looked into his eyes and,
nature had her way when we met.
And we hardly had to try.
It's a feeling that, I'll never forget.
First love, you are my first love.
First love, you are my first love.

First love, baby, you are my only love.
first love.

Each time I held his hand.
The meaning of our love is so dear.
It wasn't hard to understand.
All I had to know was that she's near.
First love, you are my first love.
First love, you are my first love.
First love, baby you are my only love.
first love.

Although it was so long ago.
It seems like yesterday.
I loved time and time again.
But it's never been the same.
There was sunshine in our lives.

Helen Fitzgerald
THIRD CLASS RIDE TO WAR

In Memory of G Dee Warner.

Take the Third Class Ride to War,
That's what you've been brought here for,
Some will live and some will die,
Do you know the reason why?

Trains go passing through the night,
Windows blacked out from our sight,
Is there sun or fields of green?
In a land we've never seen.

Wheels that sing and brakes that scream,
Will you waken from that dream?
Do you know what's up ahead?
Are we living? Are we dead?

Helen Fitzgerald
SUBWAY MUSICIAN
I walk up the incline to the long tunnel,
And suddenly the cavern walls resound with haunting, mournful tones,
Music of another time and place.
He stands against the wall, eyes closed, transfixed,
Lost in a world that only he can know,
A lonely train whistling through a prairie town,
The echo of a distant valley, green with spring, or burnished with fall.
At his feet, the battered guitar case with a few small coins, a rumpled single.
Shall I drop a coin?
Shall I try to tell him of the fleeting moment of joy at his music?
I silently walk by, fearful to break the spell.

Helen Fitzgerald
VETERAN
He stands, shabby, toothless, face lined parchment, blue eyes faded,
In his hands, a small flag—the Stars and Stripes.
Now the band strikes up, a blaze of gold and silver,
The drum major strutting, the strains of the Marine Hymn, the Army, the Navy, the Air Force,
The flag goes by, and he stands with his right hand over his heart,
That valiant heart beneath the shabby jacket.
The tanks go by, the floats of mock battlefields.
His tired old mind goes back to other tanks, other planes, other battlefields,
Incredulous that he once was part of this,
The aching legs that once strode gallantly,
The knotted fingers that once felt the cool rifle steel,
The faded eyes that once unerringly found the target.
Now the squad cars move slowly down the avenue,
Then sanitation vehicles efficiently sweeping away the cluttered memories.
He stands silently, clutching the small flag.

Helen Fitzgerald
WEEDS
Reviled victims of the bulldozer's pogrom; legislated against, doomed to extermination.
Your only epitaph a gleaming steel and glass tower, a shopping mall.
Obscure origins, unpatented, nor proclaimed from some grower's glossy catalogue.
Stowaway in the ball of soil surrounding a shade tree's roots,
Gossamer parachute borne in on a summer breeze,
A bit of life left dormant under stone and concrete.

Dear friends of my childhood, pressed in the herbarium of memory,
Red clover, shepherd's purse, pure white daisies, the delicate lavender of a thistle, burnished gold of dandelions, goldenrod.
Last survivors gathered here in a wire enclosure,
Your only visitor a derelict cabbage butterfly.
But you will rise again from beneath some skyscraper's foundation,
Wafted on a breeze, carried by a bird, swaddled in a wave,
One man's weeds are another man's flowers.

Kristi A Foster
SILENT PAIN
It's so dark here by myself
Won't someone open the door and listen
Listen to me and my silent pain
And help me make it go away
So the tears don't fall so frequently
It tears me up inside
So please, won't someone listen to my silent pain
It makes me not want to talk, or function
It makes me want to disappear and be alone
To deal with my silent pain
But it just gets greater, till someone listens to my silent pain
It's not easy to talk about it when there's no one,
there to help or listen to my silent pain
Please won't someone listen to my silent pain and help it go away
I can't make it go away by myself
It cannot be seen it eats you up from inside out
The silent pain must go away
Please hear my, SILENT PRAYER

Viola Bartlett

Viola Bartlett
MR JAY
One cold winter morn, the snow was so deep
The walk was all covered with ice and sleet—
When at my back door I heard such a chatter
I jumped from my chair to see what was the matter
And what with my bleary old eyes did I see

This frantic old blue jay was yelling at me!
He danced and he pranced in the cold icy snow
First looking at me, then the feeder, 'twas empty I know
I watched him in wonder. I knew at a glance
That bird was hungry. And thus this wild dance.
So, I gathered my boots and tightened my garter
And flew to the garden with birdseed and water—
I quick filled the feeder and turned on the heater
The poor little fellow did not move off his seater.
But watched me carefully until I was through
Then chattering and calling thru the woodlands he flew
He was back in a jiffy and lo and behold
He brought birds of all colors, red, black, blue and gold
I watched in amazement till they had eaten their fill
And flew back to their woodlands,
But oh! What a thrill!!!

Mary Elizabeth Harvey

PROGRESS

To David, my beloved grandson
Born March 24, 1966
Died August 14, 1986

Slaughtered trees lie on the hillside—
A blight upon the land,
Somewhat like an earthquake,
But destruction wrought by man.

Long roots are torn asunder
From the ground in which they lay.
They reach up instead of under—
No longer hide in soil and clay.

Who dares to strip earth's grandeur
Of the beauty nature made
And fasten down the concrete
Concealing splendor God displayed?

Mary Elizabeth Harvey

RAPE OF THE LAND

The hill lies naked, scalped and torn,
And where the animals come to mourn,
The trees no longer stand in pride,
But lie dismembered where they died.

There now remains a silent void
Where man has ruthlessly destroyed.

Mary Elizabeth Harvey

IN MEMORY OF DAVID M. HIGGINS, JR.

And now we weep—
Feel unutterable pain.
Carry smothering guilt
That will remain.

What words so deep
Were left unsaid?
What walls were built?
Why is he dead?

Now he lies in silent sleep.
The years stretch on and on.
The flowers bloom again—and wilt.
He's gone from us forever—gone—

Mary Elizabeth Harvey

OUR DAVI

It's hard to bring the tree in
And stand it in its place.
Tears fall on the ornaments
As we fill in every space.

There's the little Santa
That he placed beneath the tree
And the little wooden sled—
Our weeping eyes can hardly see.

But then we feel his presence
With his quick and loving smile
And we have our boy back with us
For just a little while.

Brandy Fletcher

GRANDDAUGHTER

She's pink

Not just her room and her blankets and clothes
She's pink from her nose to her pea pod toes

The slightest breeze ruffles her downy hair
And her eyes are blue and her skin is fair

My heart overflows with love and pride
And I feel pink deep down inside

Brandy Fletcher

THE CAROLERS

Sing ye joyous all together
Unmindful of the wintery weather
Angelic voices lifted high
While snowflakes round them fall

Muffed and scarved and booted people
Strolling past a tolling steeple
Marvel at the sparkling diamonds
Mooncast on the snow

Red and numb their noses bitten
Fingers cold despite their mittens
Sing from hearts full, full, overflow-ing
With the season's love

Glimpsing warmth through sparkling panes
Of house dressed in candy canes
Holly berries, bells and boughs
While yule logs crackle there

Wearing parkas filled with eider
Folks come out to offer cider
Tankards filled with warmth and comfort
For these cheery souls

Brandy Fletcher

ON LOOKING DOWN

Beneath the dank green forest
Where mighty pine trees sway
Grows a tiny fungoid forest
Where frogs and lizards play

Brightly coloured toadstools
With spots and lacy edges
Grow on trees and bark and logs
And cling to stoney ledges

They hide their spongy faces
In the shadow of a fern
Then spread about their tiny spores
And to the earth return

Many miss their beauty
While looking up to see
Their gently swaying neighbor
The giant cedar tree

While walking next within the woods
Be sure to look around
Not only up at stately pines
Don't miss what's on the ground

Amanda Caton

OH HOLD ME IN YOUR ARMS LIKE THIS FOREVER

Oh, hold me in your arms like this forever, please never let me go.
I hear the raindrops tapping at the windowpane.
I feel the warmth of your body next to mine.
I taste the wine you have so carefully poured for me.
I see your love for me lingering deep within your eyes.
It is a truly perfect day.
Please hold me in your arms like this forever.
For if you let go, I will wake up and then my dream will go away.

Harrell Pearsall

WHAT A BEAUTIFUL DAY IT IS

This poem is dedicated to Diane Sulton.

I awake to hear the rain
And smell the sweet-fragrant
in the morning, O I am alive!

Margie Gray

THE FACE OF LOVE

For Bryant, a friend, whose questions inspired this verse. I hope you find a perfect face.

If love must truly have a face
You should need only but to trace
The soundless echoes of your dreams,
The beat and sweep of music's wings,
The rise and fall of birds in flight,
The star-strewn beauty of the night,
The warmth that summer sunshine brings,
The music that the mountain sings.
Search your soul and find the part
That makes you strong in mind and heart;
Then fan the embers into flame.
Love has no face, but only a name.

DeAnna Dunlavy

ROBIN'S SONG

She was born on a homestead at the crest of a hill
rocked in a cradle to a lullaby still.
Make-believe fun-filled childhood hours of play
as she searched for violets amongst fields of new hay.

Robins song brings . . . the strawberries' bloom . . . leaves turn to amber . . . and snowflakes fall soon.

She was wooed and won by a neighboring son
they were wed in the fields of her make-believe fun.
Fiddlers played amidst shadows of the moon
stars were her diamonds as she danced to love's tune.

Robin's song brings . . . the strawberries' bloom . . . leaves turn to amber . . . and snowflakes fall soon.

On an ordinary day at the crest of a hill
her new sons' first cry rang forth from the still.
Now make-believe daydreams filled motherhoods' hours
As she dreamed of their future and its magical powers.

Robin's song brings . . . the strawberries' bloom . . . leaves turn to amber . . . and snowflakes fall soon.

Years folded quickly and hours were filled
with day-to-day moments both happy and real.
How easy to forget that one day would come
when a life of his own would beckon her son.

Robin's song brings . . . the strawberries' bloom . . . leaves turn to amber . . . and snowflakes fall soon.

She slumped in her chair at the crest of a hill,
rocked like a cradle to memories still.
Make-believe hopes filled her solitary hours,
dreaming of visits that never would come;
of how it would be when she next saw her son.

Robin's song brings . . . the strawberries' bloom . . . leaves turn to amber . . . and snowflakes fall soon.

There's a cluster of violets at the crest of a hill
he cries when he walks the long path there still.
Make believe wishes fill retrospect hours,
as he sits near the crest of the fields' wildflowers.

Robins' song brings . . . the strawberries' bloom . . . leaves turn to amber . . . how could snowflakes have . . . fallen so soon?

Ricky Saenz

ONE GLORIOUS DAY

The power of God I do solemnly fear.
But I feel protected when you are here.
Our paths were divided and I never suspected,
That the void that I felt would soon be corrected.
Like a flash from the past you reentered my life.
Now you bring enchantment and comfort my strife.
I would aimlessly wander if we were to part,
And in your possession would be my heart.
For I love you sincerely and I often pray
That we be united one glorious day!

Amy Butler

THE LOVE OF YOU AND ME

The truth is in every step you take,
In every move you make.
It's only us together,
Our hearts we shall not break.

At odd times things get in our way,
Every word is a mistake.
As time goes by, day by day,
I know we need a break.

But as we talk and let it out,
Things begin to heal.

And in our heart there is no doubt,
Our hearts begin to seal.

I feel your lips touch me light,
My heart begins to beat,
Is it true, all of this seems so right,
With tenderness we meet?

Love is all that I can feel,
Aside your loving touch,
Your gentleness is all so real,
Oh, I need you so much!

Natasha Manners

TRUE LOVE

To My Loving Daddy—Irving, and Gemma Quammie.

Back long ago in the olden days,
People were in love because that's what the rule says.
They were born to marry each other,
When they really wanted to marry another.
Nowadays, people sweet-talk their partner by saying 'sweetheart' or 'honey,'
But that's only when they want some money.
When you're out of money, they leave you and discard—
But come back lovingly when they want to use your credit card.
They love you when they want their hair done or some new clothes,
But what is the real meaning of love?
Only God knows.
Love is when you love someone for who they are—
Not because they're famous or some great superstar.
Love them for their knowledge, personality and mind,
Leave all your cruelty and wicked-ness behind.
Show them what a nice person you can be and how you care,
Be with them when they need you and always be near.
Tell them you think they're kind, sweet, loving or all of the above,
Then and only then will you find the true meaning of love.

Beverly Chabrecek

YOU DRINK YOU SAY

You drink you say,
Well, that's OK.
As long as you're right,
And don't want to fight.
It's not what goes in,
It's what you bring out.
Like when you shout,
You'll run them all out.
It's a terrible fright,
To see loved ones fight.
If you're an overdrinker,
You're not using your thinker.
So, use your thinker,
And don't be a heavy drinker.
Your loved ones will say,
Yes! I love them that way.
It's great when you see,
That your loved ones can be.
The greatest of all,
Is when you stand tall.
And, not fall.

Juanita Derringer

THE GIANT APATHY

Did you think there were no giants in society today
And that the days of giants had this long while passed away?
If you had then you'll be shocked to find out that you were wrong,
For the presence can be felt of a giant who is strong.

He has come to settle down as an uninvited guest,
And his manners you will find are not the very best.
For he's arrogant and lazy and complains incessantly,
To the havoc he creates is indifferent as can be.

We must show him he's unwelcome and to us has no appeal
By discouraging his habits with much courage and much zeal.
Have you run across this giant that roams thru life so free?
You will know him when you meet him, he's the giant, Apathy.

Ben L Clements

MOTHER

As long as I have known her,
She's always the same each day.
So loving and understanding,
And she knows just what to say.
Through good and bad she stood it,
And loved me like no other.
So if I searched the whole world over,
I'd never find a sweeter Mother.

Louise M Reed

DAUGHTER'S PRAYER

This is dedicated to my mother, Gloria Reed. God bless her soul.

As I sit here waiting,
For a woman I love so dear . . .
I wish that I could understand,
Why her death it is so near.
She raised me from a baby,
Always with her loving ways.
I wish that I could help her now,
By adding to her numbered days.
She is a loving mother,
And was a loving wife.
I wish I had not given her,
All those worries in her life.
Her days they have been numbered,
That's what the doctors say.
But in the end it will be our lord,
Who chooses just which day.
I'm always going to love her,
Even when she's not around.
For the woman is my mother,
God keep her safe and sound.

Clara Skaarhaug

REFLECTIONS

Dedicated to Pickeral Lake Bible coffee group as we met at Lylas Fisher's home one very foggy morning.

The dense fog was lifting just a bit
And I could see across the lake from where I did sit
across the waters as I gazed
at the broken shoreline—I was amazed.
I saw trees beautiful in their perfection
but also lined up upside down was their reflection
there in the water I could see
the entire outline of every tree
I wanted to say everybody stop and look
It's then I lost the place in my study book
it never did get said
as I listened to some scriptures that were read
it was a moment gone by
now to reflect upon the inward eye
And in the shadow of this life we live
may it be God's reflections that we give

Judy Burns

LOVE ANEW

To my loving husband, James, and my precious son, Robby, to my great parents, Bell and Mayhue Brown.

The birds are singing softly,
The sun is shining bright.
All things look so fresh and new,
In the early morning light.

Last night's rain fell slow and steady.
Turning the brown grass green.
And in the wonder of it all,
It's the prettiest sight I've ever seen.

Yes, spring is a time of new beginnings.
All life begins anew.
And on this crisp spring morning, dear
I pledge my love for you.

Jamie Adelman

IT'S TIMES LIKE THIS

It's times like this when I really need a kiss!
A little something sweet and kind, something that will never leave my mind!
When things are bad and I'm feeling sad,
when I have the blues and there's nothing left to choose,
when my goals are shattered and I want to feel a little flattered,
It's times like this when I really need a kiss!!!!!!!!

Janet A Hester

Janet A Hester

THE JOLLY ROGER STRIKES AGAIN

To all my faithful pirates!

Ahoy, ye swabs! Ship ho!
Prime those cannons and away we'll go
All hands on deck
We'll get them, by heck
Quick matey, to the crow's nest with you
Climb that rope covered with ocean dew
Raise those sails and those waves we'll cut through
We'll catch that tub
But, here's the rub
Their booty we'll take
Fit for a queen, not at all fake
Hoist up our flag
Here lad, don't lag!
And as we pull alongside their boat
We'll go on board and they'll all take note
That we're a rowdy bunch, by gum
They'll shiver and shake and take off at a run
They'll be no match
An easy catch
For we're all the best from captain and crew
We fly the Jolly Roger all day and night through!

Steven J Stepleman

WOMAN IN RED

To Flo, wherever you are.
To Dad, for being a friend.
To Mom, for listening.

Oh, what has happened to us?
We haven't spoken in years.
Time has wiped dry my tears.
And yet I remain hopeful.

You and I have quietly moved on.
As has the world.
I remember your hair; beautiful, red, and curled.
And I pray to touch it again.

Some have felt the surface of my soul.
You gently caressed it.
No other has matched our relation-ship.
And my heart cries for your love.

I need a friend like you again.
Otherwise, I will die.
I need a lover like you again.
And I pray to the gods for one more try.

Steven J Stepleman

ACCEPTANCE

Whom do you love?

What is the truth and how is it found?
The truth? I have nothing to love.
My heart has been stepped on and thrown around.
Could it be that I'm to blame?
Could it be that I attract pain?
Could it be?
Who cares? I'm just me.

I need love just like everyone else.
I need a lot of things.
I have grown accustomed to loneliness,
and I confess,
Who cares? I'm just me.

Whom do I love?
what kind of question is that?

Jack D Fields

YESTERDAY

This poem is dedicated to my darling wife, Iris, who has stood behind me throughout the years.

If only I could relive the times
In the years when I was growing
To be with the one I love
And to feel the wind blowing.

Gathering the fruits of my past
I can clearly see myself now
There is so much in my grasp
If I only knew how.

My days of past success and failures are over
It is time to live and plan

To hope and discover
To show the world that I am a man.

Yesterday in my mind will last
But yesterday is no more
A mere glimpse of time passed
It is now time for hope and
recollection.
Is there anything more?

Tom Ferguson
SEASONS

To My Inspiration—Kathleen.

The rain falls gently
The wind blows softly
Both caress the trees.

The harsh wind blows
That prompts the snows
And the world bends to its knees.

The flowers bloom
The birds return
And bring a warming breeze.

And now it's hot
And why not?
The seasons never cease.

Leiva G Hughes
(THE HOUSE OF FAITH)
I, built my house with the labor of
love,
Deep, I laid the foundation, far into
the earth, it yielded . . .
Its frame was cut, from the balsam,
the fir . . .
Setting, its: site, at each running
curve,

That the season winds that blew,
passed and fail,
To weaken the rains, the snows and
hail . . .
With prayer: and help from the
stars , , ,
Angled. The windows with strong of
iron bars . . .
That they cast sun's ray bright, till
the grey of the night,
I built each room with, the soul of
love . . .
That it touched. Each one who
crossed the floors , , ,
That each one be blessed that entered
its doors , , ,

That it stood through the years,
Through the laughter and tears , , ,
Casting out the troubles and fears . . .
For those of this house, over the
years , , ,
Ah, my house I built with, faith and
with love , , ,
And each gift that was sent me from
heaven above , , ,
So I: built my house . . .

Leiva G Hughes
JOY WITH AGE
let me not, become skeptical; nor
doubt as i grow old . . .
nor judge man and not pretend.
yet; fit in with passing men.
into the pace of time, as if yet
young;
that life for me had just begun , , ,
(as i, grow old;;)

that i; like a blossom flower in green
grass . . .
tell my heart; to build as in the past.
and deep within the heart, and mind
of me . . .
yet function, onward fast and
free . . .
that my steps remain high and bold,
let' this be me as i; grow old . . .

let the morning winds, yet smell
crisp, and sweet . . .
that i walk tall' yet on my feet
still carry a song upon my lips;;
smile at hearing, a sound, of a bird,
and thrill with it . . .
let this remain, as I, grow old . . .

Phyllis Rhoda Weprin
THE ACTOR
Sly as a fox
Attractive as well
Charming and bright
An intelligent shell

A talented man
A user of souls
Difficult to know
He plays many roles

Acts like he cares
Enthusiastic and such
Will drop you on a dime
His world doesn't mean much

Has a sensitive smile
Is needy but strong
A breaker of hearts
Won't admit he's ever wrong

What a pity it is
And such a waste too
This gifted player
Can't sustain a love that's true

Phyllis Rhoda Weprin
REVIVAL
When a fantasy dies
You get no cards of sympathy
No words of comfort
No wake
No funeral procession

You reflect on all the lies
Especially those you told to yourself

Then comes the anger
Followed by a cascade of tears
With the tears come the fears
You think you can't go on
And you know you've played the
fool

The lights fade to black
The other actors leave the stage
The curtain comes down
You linger for a little while longer
Slowly you come to realize
It's time to regroup
Pull yourself together and move on to
a new beginning
The death of a dream is no fun but
you know
You're not alone and there is life
after death

Phyllis Rhoda Weprin
U.P.T.
I stare at the phone and say, "Ring
dammit, Ring!"
But it doesn't.
I hear your voice and I look to find its
source,
But nobody's there.
What happened between Friday and
Tuesday?
We didn't argue; we seemed so much
closer;
Then you disappeared—again.
I read somewhere that aliens from an
Unidentified place were discovered
in Russia.
Could they have whisked you away?
It seemed we were never more in
tune.
But that was Friday and now it is
Tuesday.
An eternity has gone by in these four
days.
You said you'd call. You haven't.
Where are you anyway?
Perhaps it's best that I don't find
out—
Just accept the fact that for a few
Brief moments our hearts, minds and
bodies united.
Then you went one way and I went
another and
Between us now are those unidenti-
fied particles of time.

Estelle Joubert

Estelle Joubert
THE SEARCH

*With love, to my grandparents,
Estelle and Leonard Eybers and Piet
and Lida Joubert.*

Hopelessly working and searching
for food
Among mountains of junk, not
looking good
Not knowing at all what to expect.
He kept searching

Only a mile away a big city roared
They couldn't care, it's only junk
Not knowing what to expect
He kept searching

His parents are taken, he wouldn't
know
Has this always been his life?
Not knowing why
He kept searching

Slowly, his hope is fading away
Soon the junk would wish him
farewell
Not knowing
He'd soon pass away

Lori Willoughby
FRIENDS
Friends are caring and sharing to one
another.
They care what happens to each
other.
They don't let guys come in between
them.
They don't let anything go wrong to
their relationship with one another.

Friends are kind and loving even if
they do fight—they will be there.
Good friends are not easy to find.
So, keep a hold of the ones you have
and please,
Oh please don't let a guy or a girl
come between you, because you
should be friends to the end.
You may have your differences, but
please for your own sake—stay
friends through the good and the bad
in other words—stay together
forever.

Reggie Anderson

Reggie Anderson
I NEED MY GLASSES
I need my glasses now and then
Need my glasses to be my friend

Need my glasses didn't think
that I would
Didn't know I could not see
that good

Left them one day and boy did
I slip!
Missed the curb and busted
my lip

Went to the restaurant ready
to eat
Found the table, but missed
the seat

Opened the menu and tried to see
Asked the waitress, "Please read this
to me"

The waitress read it without
a smile,
Frowned and said, "I'll be back
in a while"

I can hear one of the customers
laughing still
In the meantime the waitress returned
with the bill

Knocked over the water and wet my
sleeve
Ate my meal and decided to leave

As I finished my dessert, and
proceeded to pay the check
Discovered my glasses chained
around my neck

Monica Pryor-Benskin
REMEMBER

*To my cousins Hope and Tracy—
especially to Alvin and Stedman for
having faith in me.*

Remember . . .
. . . the days we played hopscotch
and Chinese jump-rope during
recess?
. . . the days we walked to the
center for free swimming lessons,
calling out and waving as we
passed grandma's door?
. . . being sent to the corner store
for souse, saltines and cold
Pepsi-Cola during the summer?
. . . trying so hard not to be
involved with "those bad children,"
as mama called them, while trying

to concentrate on our schoolwork?
. . . when we got into fights only to make up the next day because grandma said "family don't fight"?
. . . when we moved out of the projects and into suburban homes where there were barely any streetlights and no children out late at night playing hide-and-seek and 1-2-3 redlight!

Anne Robinson
TO GIVE SO LITTLE

To My Daughter Merideth Because She Gives Of Herself To Those Who Have So Little.

The world is hungry,
and I am fed.
The world is thirsty,
and I am quenched.
The world has no door,
and I in comfort dwell.
The world is sick,
and I am cared for.
The world's babies die,
and mine is warm and loved.

We live in comfort unsurpassed,
fresh fruit and milk our fare.
Our jeweled trinkets encased in glass,
all things that we could share.

While natives sleep in airless huts,
their children bloat and die,
and cattle thirst in arid ruts,
where water ran, now dry.

The children cry from hunger pains,
legs bowed and waste away.
No water coming from the rains,
no good to fill the day.

Yet we who have so very much
our God we do implore,
"Ignore the weary world as such,
forever give US more."

How ungrateful is our lot!
How unpleasant to behold!
Never thankful for what we've got!
For Wealth, Our Souls are Sold!

Dan Stevens
HE'S SO SMALL

To Demian, I hope you will someday feel the joy I feel in you.

He's so small, as he lies in my bed.
Not very far, from his toes to his head.

With both arms around him, close to my chest,
The feeling I have is surely the best.

The bed is so crowded, we're packed like sardines,
Though the house is quite large, you know what that means.

He just likes it here, in his own little space,
With his hand on my neck and his head in my face.

While he tosses and turns he administers blows,
With a foot in my back and an arm to the nose.

Forget about glory and fortune and fame,
Life without this, just won't be the same.

Soon he'll grow older, too big for his spot,
And sleep by himself, more often than not.

In a room full of toys and pictures and games,
And legions of dinosaurs, he knows all their names.

He'll play a few sports, have a few friends,
Learn that with girls, the fun never ends.

The proms and the parties, hot cars and schools,
He'll mingle with scholars, and jokers and fools.

He'll enter a world of confusion and doubt,
I don't think anyone can figure it all out.

Will he remember me now, as I lie here above him,
As I watch him sleep, and tell him I love him.

Will he know that I'll be there thru good times and bad,
His teacher, His partner, His friend and His Dad.

Carol L Suchocki
TWILIGHT RUN
Hawk in the twilight
Wolf on the run
Staying astride one another
between the earth and the sun
What an unlikely pair; yet equal
in many ways
Both stalking for prey in life to
keep them alive
Though their souls are free like
the wind around them
Free to be wild; Free to be free
Yet the two are stalked
Stalked by an even greater force
Life itself
It will either love one or conquer one
Even if fate itself has already dealt the cards
So, let the hawk and wolf be wild
and free
And when Father Time comes calling
Mother Nature shall guide the two souls to an even more wondrous
place.

Eileen C Nowitzky
BARREN

To Norman, for his patience during those long nights when I wanted to talk about the meaning of life. (My Love Always)

I sat on a hill
in a
blue
windbreaker.
Looking below at the
dry earth,

I saw that it
brought forth
nothing.
I was alone.
The soil rolled across the field
to nowhere—
as I would someday be carried.

Ruth B Rinker
A CAYUSE AND THE SADDLE
The man in the saddle was brash and bold
He was mean, his hair black, his
eyes were cold
The quirt cracked as he rode into view
The horse snorted and bucked, his
gray mane flew
He went up in the air, his wild eyes rolled
Down on all fours, his body
seemed to fold
I, a little girl, had never seen
A strawberry roan, or a man so
mean.

Again the whip cracked, and our peace was marred
At our remote ranch, scenes like
this were barred
Pat stood with head down, lathered with foam
"Dear God!" Dad said, "He needs a
good home
A Cayuse cannot be gentled by force
No one should put a saddle on this
horse
Abuse is not allowed at our place
And buying him will mean
problems to face."

"He will go at your price," replied the man
Faithful Pat worked with Dad's
kindness and plan
He dearly loved children and his master
Still—saddling our Pat meant a
disaster.

Marie S Daunhauer
THE CHRISTMAS GOOSE
I saw her flying high,
Dropping right out of the sky.

She clipped my shining hair,
Honked and set her down right
there.

The kids all gathered round,
Picked her up and set her down.

In class the teacher asked,
"Are you not well?" "Honk," she
gasped.

She hopped on my bus top,
Rode along to my own stop.

Flew high over my head
Nestled on my fluffy bed.

"The Christmas Goose!" Mom
yelled.
NO, N-O-N-O I spelled.

She's tame, she is a pet.
She can't fly off, not just yet.

I had turned off the light
Then she laid four eggs that night

On the living room floor
Right close to the open door.

Mom really didn't care.
She had to set the tree there

With tinsel, bows and bells.
Goosie's breast just puffs and
swells.

This night is Christmas Eve.
The eggs will hatch, I believe.

We saw the open door
And her gander hit the floor.

He joined old Goosie Loo
Four goslings were cracking
through.

We giggled then with glee.
The lights lit up on the tree.

Gander honked. Goosie purred.
Mom softly said, and I heard,

"The Christmas Goose." So wise.
Why would I think otherwise.

Elisabelle Greenhaw
MY MOUNTAIN
I look across the Isle from me,
and what a beauty there I see.
A mountain high below the Sky,
that scallops down to meet the earth that lies all-round.
Its solid mass so stately true,
remains a refuge for a few.
In times of loneliness you see,
I look and there it stands for me.
When I catch a glimpse of its form
so rare, my life then I do compare.
I can stay at the base with my
despair, or climb to its height beyond compare.
I choose to climb each day I look,
and there at the top my life comes an open book.

Jacqueline Sloan (Age 10)
MEMORIES

For Grandma Lee Pokorny.

In the past
things went by so fast.
Some memories seem
So far away.
Others seem like yesterday.
Old friends, old faces,
Old homes, old special places.
Special memories don't fade away.
In your mind
They just stay.

Lucille Vigué
THE ONES FROM TUSAYAN *
Basket weaver
blanket maker
sower of the maize
agrarian
and potter fine
you once had many days

of living, dying, birthing
feasting, building, hunting game
and dreaming of wild canyon lands
you'd someday hope to tame

but fate had other plans for you
your future waned and died
in fallow furrow
and stick figures
lying at rimside

now we in this time
come to view your legacy bone dry
as haunting echoes of your past
return 'neath canyon sky

* Tusayan ruins are the only excavated ruins found at the South Rim of the Grand Canyon. These "ancient ones" lived in a small family group of Indians (about 25-30 members).

Irene M Zimmerman
THE PASSING OF TIME
Lord, as I look back and see the past
the time has seemed to go so fast.
I used to sit with little ones in arms
to only surrender to their crying charms.
In a way I wish I could go back and redo
everything over and do it anew.
I'd spend more time with them at learning and play
and spend more time in prayer every day.
I was like a child myself

and I put them on a shelf.
I thank you; Father, for your forgiveness
and ask you to help me put to rest my perfectionistic craftiness.
I need you now more than ever before
for there is nothing as a time machine door.
As a new phase of life has come for me
I need to learn to depend on thee.
Meet me where I'm at I pray
and I know with me you've promised to stay.
For now it'll be you;
Father, my husband and me,
and our grown-up family,
to go on in life as the time does pass
and one day soon to be with you at last.

Bryan D Ogle
THE LIFE OF HOPE
In the dark of the fear in a world of debase,
The light of hope is sight.
From the bleakness of tears that the years cannot face
Is joy and life and might.

In all humble little towns in the blackest dark night
Is light from love and care.
For the worry of loss allows God from the fright
The importunity to share.

In the hour of despair in the wan of our world,
The life of hope is there
In the heart and the soul by which deity is held
With golden chains of prayer.

Sandra L Wuchevich
REMEMBER ME

To the only one I love, Kenny, from Sandi.

Remember me,
While we're apart;
Keep our memories,
Close to heart.

The times we had,
The fun we shared;
The rose you gave,
That said you cared.

But while you're gone,
I won't despair;
We'll meet again,
Sometime, somewhere.

Russell Dewayne Ingle
HOME
A place where you can sit back
and watch life go right on by.

A place where you can experience
your good times and bad times
without a drug to get that high.

This is a place where you come to relieve yourself from the world's unprovoked attacks.

Instead of hard times and troubles
you bring yourself here to relax.

There's no other place like it, not in your mind but only in your heart.

Sometimes you have to protect it, to keep it from being torn apart.

It protects the ones you love and keeps them sheltered from the storm.
It welcomes one and all from adults, children, and a baby that's just been born.

You are always welcome here, but there are no reservations by phone.

A place as great as this you find with your heart, and this place is called Home.

Diane Anderson
HURT
Why do things in this world have
to hurt so much?
Just when you think things are
going great.
Somebody comes along sweeps you
off your feet.
One day they tell you it's over.
Not really expecting it to last.
Not really expecting it to end
so fast.
Now you're left hurting trying
to put the pieces together to get
on with your life.
Why does it have to hurt so
much?

Karen Olson
VALENTINE'S DAY

This poem is dedicated to all those who still believe! Especially to my parents who taught me the importance of caring and remembering, and to my children who make me proud.

A SPECIAL DAY
Which permits wooing and
honoring of each other;
renewal and affirmation of
love,
Where silly and soupy lover-
actions are chuckled at and
approvingly nodded to by
those who see and know!

A RECOGNITION DAY
For all lovers, young and old;
those devoted worshipers of
romance,
When one lover says to another—
let us always remember and make
time for those little things that
made our hearts glad; let us
always remember to show each
other our devotion and love,
to tell of our caring.

A SPECIAL DAY
To tell you I remember
To tell you I care
To say, "I love you!"

Valentine's Day
Our Day

Denise Sannicandro
THE DISCOVERY OF THE TRUE ME

To my father, Carmine L. Sannicandro.

Born one day out of pain so deep,
Flowing from a point within
Little did I know I had reached the hole in my soul
Now being awakened from a long ago sleep.

Fragmented visions of days gone by
Flashing before my eyes
Confusion and despair gripping at my being
I had not one clue—Why?
The Beast of Separation can take many a form
Its main purpose is to kill the child-soul within
And its source of life is all but scorn.

As this tornado reared its ugly head
to be wrestled with once more,
My child soul cried out, "But I love Me" and let go—
At once she was fully free.

Now it's so clear to see
The reason this devilish storm came to be;
It is known to humanity as Man's Destiny: to discover the True Me.

Sharon A Harper
WHO AM I?

This poem is dedicated to my son, Dorian Shawn Harper Lewis.

I am an employee to my employer;
I am a taxpayer to Internal Revenue Service;
I am black to non-blacks;
I am a foreigner to Europeans; I am an alien to Martians.
I was a child to my parents; a student to my teachers;
A patient to my Doctor; a client to my attorney.
I am or have been all of the preceding in relation to all of the persons or agencies described with whom I have interacted at one phase or another during my lifetime.
I am who I am by a series of decisions based on information received consistently from symbols of authority; symbols of love; symbols of trust.
What I am to become is directly related as to what the world will demand of me in order to survive.
I am what I am in relation to many people; but most of all;
I AM ME: I AM MYSELF: I AM I.

Billy Hart Jr
A WORM'S POINT OF VIEW
I live in the wet cold ground
Where I feel safe and sound.
From above digs, rusted steel,
Half into this we feel.
In a bucket of dirt and stone,
We're carried far from home.
On a fishing bank, in the shade . . .
I feel the hand who held the spade.

Robin Hall
DANGEROUS WORLD
Our world is in a state of shock,
From guns, AIDS, and the such.
The world is like a ticking clock,
It's getting to be a little too much.

God has warned the world for now,
That things must change fast somehow.
But we can't seem to see the light,
How close our end is, so let's not fight.

Hell isn't where we want to be,
So everyone must try to make him pleased.
For he above is our only hope,
And without him, we simply can't cope.

Dear Lord above I pray to you,
Please put us back in your school.
For you are our savior, our Lord above,
And all you really need, is our love.

Clair Tomlinson
RESURRECTION OF THE GODDESS OF DEMOCRACY

To All those brave souls who died for freedom in Tiananmen Square

SHE was born on international T.V.
In Tiananmen Square
By the labor of the Chinese
Struggling for the right to be free
She was murdered on international T.V.
By the desperate communist
Who did indeed dash her, bash her,
Crash her and smash her to the ground
For the whole world to see.
If this has outraged you,
As much as me,
Then you can easily understand
And should obviously agree
That we as the sons and daughters
Of Democracy
Must demand
That the Goddess of Democracy
Be resurrected in America
On Alcatraz Island
Facing West
Toward the imprisoned Chinese

And there She will stand
On her eternal vow
That someday She will resurrect the dream
Those brave souls died for—
In that ghastly, horrible scene—
And lying next to her,
In anticipated state,
Shall be (Ascendshea)
The Twin sister
To the Goddess of Democracy
Where she will be destined
To be presented as a gift
From all Americans
To the Chinese
On the day that they
Finally struggle free
And glorious
Will be the day
When these two outstanding ladies
Stare across the Pacific—at each—
In PEACE!!!

Sally E M Brisbois
CAESAREAN

To all the women who were denied the right of natural childbirth.

I felt the baby growing
I was radiant
I was ALIVE!

He said everything is fine—
but we must—the time is now
I asked—WHY?

PAST DUE—i owed a debt

I asked for reasons or,
(or problems . . .)
that may arise . . .
He said history has no importance
My calculations are exact.
(He has no patience for nature's pride)

My call for help . . .
My streams of tears . . .
My pleading cries . . .

He gave no answers,
showed no compassion, no mercy,
as he RIPPED you from inside.

My spark is gone
My love is guarded
My soul has died . . .

Mindy Sue Gray
RAIN
Have you e'er wondered about rain,
How it wipes away tears,
And soothes the pain
of a troubled heart?
Despair, as well as fear—
And sorrow—disappear,
As one listens to the sweet refrain,
of the gentle, fragrant, falling rain.
Stay, rain—at least for a time;
Make my life happy—make it sublime.
Please don't depart,
my gentle rain—
I want no more sorrow,
I want no more pain.
Stay,
Sweet rain—
go not away;
At least 'til tomorrow,
Please remain.

Karen Roberts (Age 16)
THE GOOD TIMES
Remember the times we had
They were so happy they made
me so sad
Just holding your hand and
hearing your voice.
I knew there would be no other choice.
We loved each other so much,
I loved to feel your touch.
I know, I hurt you more
than you hurt me.
I thought you still loved me.
But I guess you didn't
See how much you really
mean to me.

Susan Grescowle
THE NOT SO DISTANT FUTURE
Mother Earth in all her glory so proud;
Now wears a blanket of fog like a shroud.

The once virgin clouds have turned charcoal gray;
And cleansing rains are now a salty spray.

The fragrant air of spring that replenished one's soul;
Is choking on atoms gone out of control.

Remember the vivid hues of an October sunset?
The colors have faded to a sea of regret.

Mother Earth is crying a repugnant tear;
That mankind cannot see her mortality is near.

Susan Grescowle
THE JOURNEY'S MIDDLE
In the twinkling of the twilight came;
a wretched old man, part blind and lame.

His smile revealed a toothless jaw,
And through the shadows of his eyes
I saw;

An innocence that is rare to man,
He felt my presence and reached forth his hand.

His bony fingers were twisted with age,
The strength that emerged was nearly a rage.

Where does your journey lead you? I asked him why.
He spoke not a word as he gazed toward the sky.

The lines on his face seemed to taper away, His frailness diminished in a glorious way.

We nodded farewell, and as he disappeared from sight,
His gait was full of vigor, his spirit light.

In the crystal mist of moonlight he went,
His tribulation over, his journey almost spent.

Bertha P Patton

Bertha P Patton
LIFE IS WORTH LIVING

To my family and friends of WABQ with love.

Life is worth living—take the time to care.
We can help make life worth living
for someone somewhere,
If silently we take a moment to
whisper a prayer,
We can help make life worth living if
we give a loving smile.
Give it to a passing stranger or even
to a little child.
We can help make life worth living if
truly we try to give.
Just a little of ourselves to someone,
somewhere, each day we live.

Lisa M Hultenschmidt
GOLDEN HEART
A golden knife, A golden spoon,
A golden sun, A golden moon.
All of these, it's true they shine,
But nothing like this heart of mine.
A golden heart that shines and glistens,
I talk aloud yet no one listens.
And in this world of sorrow and gloom,
I, a lonely flower bloom.
I try my best to stay a blossom,
Me, a little helpless opossum.
If someone hears me, come save me please,
For I hang upside down from the branches of trees.
No one and nothing needs more help than I do,
Even if they do really try to.
Even though I'm just a frail flower stem,
I'm glad it is me who is helpless, not them.
Now I know you believe that nothing can shine,
More brightly than this golden heart of mine.

Madeline Shannon Salas
WHEN THE WIND BLOWS

To my beloved Father, Ronald Salas, who is not with us today but who I will always love, Forever.
"I LOVE YOU, DAD!"

It was a grey moody afternoon as I walked into the room of nothing but sadness and tears. When I laid my eyes upon my father my heart ached with pain when I saw his eyes made of marble and the grey snow upon his head.
He laid there in silence without movement, only his head moving faintly like the movement of a branch when there is a slow breeze.
Though he spoke in silence it meant everything just to see his face one more time.
For I knew that he would go just as the days pass.
But still I was reluctant to accept it just as the sun when it slowly sets.
Looking at him I never said good-bye, as I held his clammy hands, I kissed his cushioned head and said I Love You for one day we will be together again. Oh how I wish I was there for him when he needed someone.
No one knows how cold it is until the wind blows.

Larry McCarthy
ICEBERG

I'm an iceberg,
crying tears of fire

Rivers ran filling corners, avenues,
even a basin of desire

I'm an iceberg, cold, cold, to the touch

A dramatic episode, crumbling inward
leaving molecules, hot to the touch

I'm an iceberg, I came and I went
only to must go . . .

Accounting, adding, traveling
this ground of life

I see there are things
I will never know, never to show

I'm an iceberg

Elsa Olivares
HIS SHADOW
His love for me ended a long time ago
Yet, I still remember him
I remember his strong embrace and
his passionate kisses
I remember the way we talked as the best that we were
All that is gone and lost forever
Sometimes when I am alone and I think of him
I can feel him close to me
As if he were watching over me
His shadow and the shadow of a love that once was but could be no more is lost
Lost forever within the sands of time

Lynn Kagan Price
THE GIRL IN THE MIRROR
I can't find her, that girl I used to see in the mirror,
I saw her in lots of mirrors; ladies rooms, dressing rooms, hotels, the boyfriend of the month's toothpaste stained bathroom mirror, mirrors in her purse, airplane mirrors, oh so many mirrors, but I can't find her anymore;
She used to have hair the color of a Kansas wheat field, eyes as blue as the Aegean Sea, skin unblemished and soft as down; an innocent virginal essence surrounded her being, but I can't find her anymore;
She has been replaced by someone with thin lifeless grey hair, the blue eyes have faded and are hidden by thick glasses, skin sallow and wrinkled from too many hours in the sun;
She lost her innocence long ago and if I could find that girl somewhere,
I would get rid of that old lady who looks back at me.

Arthur R Elliott
TRUE LOVE NEVER DIES—TRAVELING OUR LIFE'S HIGHWAY

To my loving wife, Molly.

Sweetheart O mine when night is near
And stars in their brightness shine
Deep down in my heart there's a longing for you
Beloved sweetheart O mine

As I see one small star twinkle
Just as tho it was lonely there
It reminds me of you O sweetheart
Lonely waiting somewhere

Linda C Waleford
DIRECTIONS
Oh God!
Sometimes I feel confused,
I guess I'm just that way.
Each day I know you're here
to guide me I am secured,
I am safe.

I try to understand why you
do great things for me
You give me love, you give me
joy, great peace and harmony.
As I get dressed each morning
Before going out that day,
I wonder why the sun is shining the
sky is blue that way.
I wonder why the grass is green and
trees are full with leaves,
I wonder why the moon is round and
the stars they shine for me.
I guess I must be special it seems to
me that way,
That God would give to me
Great blessings every day.

Heidi Ach

LOVE IS

Love is kind,
and sometimes hard to find.
Love is caring,
and sometimes even daring.
Love is great,
but sometimes you have to wait.
Love is sweet,
love you can't beat.
But most of all . . .
love is for two . . .
ME and YOU!!

Rosette Mines

LONELY

Lonely, I sit and wait what to do,
what to do

Time sits heavy on my hands, the
phone silence become pronounced,
What to do, What to do

The lonely no not from momentary
pleasures such as the delivery boys'
warm smile, the cries from the
children at play, or the familiar tune
from birds singing its songs What to
do, What to do.

Chantal Bigras

THE OCEAN

An ocean as deep as your eyes
Overwhelms me with desire
The wind of love tells me to watch
out
I could get killed in this turmoil
A night with you would satisfy my
hunger
But I must stay away from those
nights
They bring me to tears if I think of
them too hard
I must only think of the distant past
When you and I really loved each
other
Neither Earth, nor sky, existed really
You were mine and I was yours
Break my heart again, I will always
be yours
For love never dies
In the ocean of your eyes

La Paloma

THE WRONG CHOICE

With straw in beak,
Mother Robin sought a place to sleep.
The porch light,
A comfort for a weary traveler's
flight.
Day after day flying here and there,
Assembling her new home with no
time to spare.
Under the large green awnings,
Away from the sun and rain she left
her belongings.
The nest intact,
She sat and sat and sat.
Disturbed by the opening and closing
of the back door,
She flew back and forth, fence, roof,
no further than before.
She didn't seem to mind at first for
nothing was in the nest,
Till one day she had eggs one, two,
three, at best.
One warm May day,
There on the porch one blue broken
egg laid.
To relocate was on her mind,
For those two chicks left behind.
All was sad as the day unfold,
Another dead chick the grass did
hold.
In the abandoned nest the one was
left,
No one to give it breath
The choice was for Mother Robin to
take,
Her choice was also our mistake.

Stephanie E Bryant

FIRST ANNIVERSARY

To Chris, my inspiration . . . .

From my heart stems love in all of its
glory and through it I have watched
and felt you grow.

My true age is less its number plus
one for I have lived a mere year of
love yet an eternity of joy.

My breath of life made possible
because of you.
With you my search is over
my life complete
and I am able to grow.

Full of passion are you who inspires
me
The face I love to see
The voice I love to hear
The hand I love to hold and to hold
me.

My year of life so precious in sweet
memory and present desire.
My hope lies within you as I rest my
heart upon yours to share your life.

I am with you always.

C R Healy

C R Healy

FREEDOM'S BREEZE

For Freedom—
For my wife—
For Gladys Matts—

You can feel it in the air,
the world is sifting out despair.
Democracy is what we want,
and the world wants it too.
It was a long time coming
and certainly overdue.

From our hearts to their hearts
with the world on its knees.
Praying for peace and contentment,
we feel from the freedom breeze.

The dictators, the evil ones,
and all who produce fear
are falling by the wayside,
so many, just this year.

Follow the breeze you feel, my
friends,
Do what you can for the just.
It's precious, priceless and needed,
and starts right here with us.

Brenda Coney

FROM 1 TO 9

To my daughter, Casey; may she always remember not to ever drink and drive. Love, Mommy

First I start out icy and cold . . .
1 little drink just to soothe the soul.
I feel a chill run down my spine;
You say shucks this is nothing I
could drink 9.

Now I'm at drink #2.
What did you say this could do?
See I'm normal it didn't touch me
Come on baby we can dance till 3.

Drink #3 I'm out the door
I'm so cool, I can handle 1 more
I think that was 2, 3, or 4?
But then who's counting let's go
outside.

Come on my friend you can't drive . . .
In this hand is drink #5,
He drank it all and that's no jive,
You'll never make it home alive.

At home black coffee is what I will
fix
But by that time he'd had drink #6
When I get home, that will be like
heaven,
In the car around the curve was a
child about 7.

At that time he couldn't see straight
Just a sip now that's #8
The next three seconds were much
too late,
'Cause the child out of the car had to
be scraped.

There he sits, drunk but fine
Never got a chance to drink #9
He turned and looked down, there a
lady lay crying,
"I hate you! I hate you! That child
was mine."

Betty Jean Booth

THE WEARY TRAVELER

To my beloved Uncle Guy Royal Atchison Jr. for his dedication and belief in my work as a writer and to my husband and children for their love and support.

On the road of travelers the paths
sometimes will be
dusty as the Autumn winds too soon
to cover me if we learn to strive for
better in the steps we make each day
the tides of life will slow up as we
travel on our way
sometimes we seek for pleasures not
knowing what we need
and when the cost is added up we've
failed to harvest seed
it is so easy to be wrong when we
think that we are right
so take heed to understanding learn
the measure of your plight
what advice can be given if we fail to
listen well
for our arrogance may be hindering
and our steps are sure to fail
slowly sinking in the tides of life as
the waves we try to ride
we are drowning in our ignorance
shifting back from side to side
we always reason to ourselves the
things mankind has said
yet in our darkest hour of need
philosophy is dead
drink from the cup of wisdom as you
strive to make your way
for in the widest measure shall your
victory come and stay
though when we keep on toiling as
the birds that softly sing
life surely will be gentle as we look
to higher things
for it is meant for our survival to be
wise in all we do
waiting for the signs of others trap us
through and through

Bunnie L Stark

WHAT WILL BE, WILL BE

Dedicated to Charles Turner and my mother Elizabeth Washington.

What a wonderful spirit
What a beautiful soul;
Of all your pain and suffering
The half has not been told.

But what a great consolation
When walking into your room;
For when the door swings open
A smile on your face will bloom.

Such a determined spirit
To accept the will of God;
I'm not sure how well I'd fair
If in your footateps I trod.

So hold on tight to your faith
And never doubt for one minute;
That your fate like countless others
Has God's royal seal upon it.

Don't ever stop to wonder why
God let this happen to me;
For as you've said in days gone by
"What will be, will be

Helen Sonia Moore

REMEMBER LONG AGO

Dedicated to my sister Verna.

Remember that Christmas so very
long ago
Daddy played his harmonica under
the mistletoe . . .

Remember how poor we were,
sometimes shedding tears
Daddy held us in his arms to keep us
from our fears.

So into daddy's truck we went,
everything was fine,
All us kids with our burlap bags
picking Princess Pine.

Mother made holiday wreaths, we
sold from door to door.
They were only a dollar apiece, never
a penny more!

Then when Christmas morning came,

under the lighted tree,
There sat Raggedy Ann and Andy,
just for you and me

Our brothers got all kinds of things,
they could play with too,
but the best things under the tree
were made for me and you

Many years have passed since then,
our dolls had disappeared . . .
Our brothers had hid them away, Oh
how I had feared!

Then one day I discovered, our
brothers had operated,
Raggedy Andy was gone, but Ann
was just sedated!

So I sewed her new clothes and gave
her new hair,
To remember our mother and how
she did care

Now remember that Christmas, not
how we were poor,
You're still my little sister, I'll
always adore.

Stephen Marc Mancini
DREAMS

To my loving wife, Debbie, who has put up with a lot.

I dreamt a dream of castles and kings,
of lost gardens and things.
I dreamt a dream of traveling the
ocean blue,
always in search of that wonderful
you.
I dreamt a dream of a snow
mountainside,
Of trees and lakes with a gentle
lapping tide.
I dreamt a dream of an old country
farm,
the smell of fresh hay being loaded
into the barn.
I dreamt a dream of flowing way up
in the sky,
holding you close as the sun gleams
in your eyes.

I dreamt a dream of sparkling jewels
and gems,
the warm glow of your skin much
brighter than them.
I dreamt a dream and slowly opened
my eyes,
you were laying beside me and the
love that I felt made me want to cry.

Stephanie McCarthy
TEARS OF THE CHILDREN

To all who have shed tears . . . .

As we watch, our parks . . . where
children laugh and play . . . how do
we learn of the others, whom love is
lost, their life left astray.

As those we watch, dance upon their
feet . . . others are living . . . on our
city streets . . .

These are the children exploited,
most runaways . . . lost from kin, it is
hard to understand . . . their unwilling
sin . . .

God sees their innocence . . . he will
surely forgive . . .
Those, the helpless . . . the life in which
they live . . .

We, the strong, must do our
part, . . . by the love we show, to
warm their hearts . . . from the love
sent, with heavenly glow . . .

We must pray each day, for houses of
covenant . . .
To thank God, for his wisdom
sent . . .

We are the ones, to get our kids, off
the street . . .
to show them the way, with
love . . . not deceit . . .

So let us show to the kids, with a
reaching hand . . .
Show to them, God's love, and
understand . . .

Remember not, to show our
tears . . .
For the tears God sees, is only theirs

Stephen Marc Mancini
THE STRANGER

A stranger rode up to the pub, with
the darkest of cloaks you ever would
see.
He walked in and up to the bar,
quietly he asked the barkeep for a
pint of ale.
Upon receiving this he walked over
and asked ever so politely, if he
might pull up a stool and sit beside
me.
I answered as politely that yes he
may, since he looked as if he'd
traveled quite a distance and was
looking quite pale.
I listened intently to this stranger's
tales, in hopes of getting a story that
might be worth repeating all in good
time to you.
He told me of little people that built
towns and homes, in the mountains
from a distance, all carved by hand.
He told how the little people found
jewels and gems in these mountains
that he produced to prove that this
tale was true.

He talked late into the eve, as I asked
him a question or two.
I was simply amazed, believe it or
not I could see what he was saying
deep in my head.
In my enthusiasm I bought us quite a
few more pints, to have him tell me
more.
Many visions I had I tell you no lie,
as his wondrous tales filled my head.
When suddenly I awoke and looked
all around not a soul was to be seen.
I thought to myself this was all just a
dream. Yet there sat a jewel with a
note underneath.
All the note said was, "Thank you,
you will see me again," on the jewel
he swore.
This tale I tell to whomever will
listen, whenever I'm doubted,
I produce the jewel and tell what the
stranger in the dark cloak had said.

Adele Lee Martin
ABOVE THE FOG

On a mid-winter morning
The fog crept low.
Yet the sound of birds
Descended below.
Back from their journey
Across southern seas
Their beauty was hidden
But their songs came to me.
Those red-winged carolers
Their tunes I knew
And the sound of their wings
Descended too!
As I stood there to listen
The fog cleared away,
And their beautiful, brilliance
Brightened the day.

Pauline V Davis
WILD GRAPE JELLY

Some folk can browse around a store
And find the pretties by galore
To make the Christmas thrills.

But I by empty purse-strings tied
Cannot afford the gifts I've spied
My heart with sorrow fills.

Methinks I'll play Ole Santa part
With homespun gifts and culn'ry art
My sagging spirit trills.
So as the autumn sun peeped in
I trapped in vials of glass and tin
The nectar from these hills!

Thelma Coleburn
VOICES OF INSPIRATION (FOR THE CHILDREN)

This poem is dedicated to my dear parents, Nathaniel and Lila Coleburn.

Children look on the bright side
Lest the dark side blind
March ahead
Never looking behind
Don't retreat into defeat
We must be strong
For the race goes on
And in this world
Full of doubt and sorrow
Where no one knows
What will happen tomorrow
We must cling to God
His strength will abide
Use Him as your armour
Fight by His side
So children, keep your head to the
sky
And when trouble strikes don't ask
why
Just pray to withstand
Remembering there's hope close at
hand
In the past, you went the wrong way?
Never give up, because there's
always today.

Cindy Kozlowski
MAN HAS ARRIVED

To my best friend, Sandra Jean Smith, whose constant battle for the welfare of others frequently goes unnoticed.

The wind whisps by and causes the
trees to sway in its gentle breeze
The sun shines bright against a
cornflower blue sky and warms the
earth with a kiss
The flowers blossom shyly as the
birds sing a song of sweetness
The ocean beckons as it drifts in and
out with the tide bringing waves of
welcoming delight
The rain washes the earth with a
clean fresh scent

Soon the wind brings with it a new
change

The trees look barren amidst the
cement and glass structures
The sun's light is masked by the hazy
sky
The flowers are less plentiful unless
seen thru a flower shop window
The birds loose their lilting melody
as they search for someplace to nest
The ocean still brings in the tide, but,
now the waves shove debris into the
sand
The rain brings with it a certain
danger as it cleans the earth in its
natural process

Man has arrived.

Peggy De Mars
STOLEN MOMENTS

May I cast away all depression and
grief?
May I give you a smile that is
golden?
May I warm your heart, even when
we're apart?
May I freeze all the moments we
have stolen?

Do you know how I feel as I lay in
your arms?
Do you sense my total atonement?
Do you feel me tremble as I look in
your eyes?
Do you pray for the next stolen
moment?

Can you leave me unchanged for just
what I am?
Can you whisper calm words when
I'm scared?
Can you go on with life even after
I'm gone?
Can you hold tight to stolen moments
we've shared?

John A Gadd
WHEN I HEARD OF THIS

To my son, Gene, who laughed not and was never mean when my pen I got.

When I heard of this
inviting "World Of Poetry" contest
I didn't want to miss
writing for it my best

Rhyme which I will drop
in several lines on you
which lines they will stop
ere reach-ing 2 - 2

As you have a rule
in place again this year
and I am no fool
2 - 1 I do fear

Could then throw my verse
off the field of play
that would deny me purse
from the "World Of Poetray"

So I've written twenty-one
lines in which to say
all my best I'm done
you must judge then pay

From Goldin Californ-i-a.

John A Gadd
MODERN TIMES
In this hustle and bustle,
technological world we're faced each day with much stress and strain

And just to keep pace, our "modern man" more and more, runs 24; is there any wonder his energies drain?

Since the horse and buggy and the ox and cart gave way to the car and train

There's been no end to our need for more speed as just to keep pace we constantly re-train

Why, a trip that took our settlers five long months to complete, across the land of a man named Zane

Can now, in 5 hours, very rapidly be made by the mighty, high flying, jet plane

But still and all, taken in context, as to history, and man's time and place in same, which is germane

I know of no other way than to participate so, why complain, for to live in it—"modern times," that is—we can't refrain

John A Gadd
CONSTANT CHANGE
How often have you heard someone say:
"Things didn't used to be done that way"

Or: "That's not how we do things around here" as just a suggestion of change brings out their worst fear

Yet the only constant in life is change, for better or worse

And those who best adjust to it are blessed not cursed

For the simple truth is nothing forever stays the same

In our lives as we continue to evolve in an ever-changing game

As relentlessly, ever forward/up or down we continue to move along with the weak, nee: the lame, sick or lazy, failing to make way by the wayside failing to make way for the strong

And, no matter how we may wish to prolong today

We're powerless to stay the hands of time and prevent what is from becoming, just another, yesterday

Gone forever, except in our mind's eye, lost in life's rush and blur

Gone, save for a teardrop or two, and this verse to remind us of how, things once were

James Kellermann
LAST APPEAL ON DEATH ROW
You cannot really know me
Wild eyes, orange attire, is all you see
I weep at night you know
It is a period when my feeling sails low

The crime is said to be death
For I held a man's throat till he had no breath
And now I sit in this lonely cell
Wishing, praying I not go to hell

The state contemplates I am not morally fit
In the electric chair they desire me to sit
Never shall I repent for my sin
And upon my departure vengeance is secured
There is no victor, only loss, no win

The day draws near
My heart races with fear
These wild eyes race about the room
Knowing my body, my soul, destined for doom
I scream out in certain rage
And rattle the bars of this cage

The hour draws near
My heart pounds with fear

Now enters the final meal
Lawyers speak of final appeal
Break bread for his body
Take, drink for his blood

The hour is now here
My heart is steady though I still fear

The executioner appears tired and grim
As if expressing his own morality is way out on a limb

Mother, they've locked me in and shaved my head
Soon the circuit will lock, I will be dead

James Kellermann
A FORGOTTEN DREAM
Lurking in every shadow
Riding the invisible pony
From factories in China
To sands of a Sahara

Wandering in the recesses of a mind
Desolation is what thy find
To be remembered if only a bit
But thy sinks deep, deeper into a pit

Weep in the dark
This is a solitary park
Listen, listen to a silent roar
Anticipate a recollect from before
In stealth thy steer wishing for a home
Whole avenues, every corner thy comb
To find a passage, knock and cry
Into a reflection, a memory thy could pry

One day thy will be found, it does seem
But at present, thy is just a forgotten dream

James Kellermann
THE GHOST OF GROUCHO
A heavenly chorus assembles and softly hums. Harpo appraises the harp and magically strums. Children sell empty bags of peanuts for a dime. In the kingdom of God, day after day, this is a special period known as Groucho time. Clinging to golden cigars, wearing greasepaint mustaches, Angels drift in from clouds which are fluffy and white. Dressed incognito, stepping with inclination, peering through wire glasses to alleviate their sight. O the beautiful sound the piano fits into the air as Chico plays. While Zeppo and Gummo ride about on inconspicuous five-horse sleighs. God grins intrinsically and grumbles within the burning bush. He desires to hear from Julius Z. Hackenbush! Hush, a voice from afar. "Hello, I must be going," whispers a star. Riding an elephant in his pajamas, the holy spirits smile as they observe the Ghost of Groucho.

Lisa Marie Coon

Lisa Marie Coon
MY MOTHER

To my very special and beautiful mother, I love you . . .

Holding the small child gently against her breast, as this child dreams and peacefully rests.

The soft sweet voice cuddling her to sleep, is a sound this world could never repeat.

This is the price she loves to pay, for loving her baby and letting her stay.

Even though no one approves, she is strong and that's what soothes.

Watching her child grow smarter and older wishing again she could hold her.

Today is the time this child moves away, knowing her mother wants her to stay.

Lonely and afraid the child sadly knows that she's getting older and quickly grows.

So, it's time and I know it depends for my mother and I to be special friends.

For sharing our lives so close and together, I know she will be there forever and ever.

Now for my MA, I send kisses and hugs and I also send her all of my love . . . .

Lisa Marie Coon
THE END
Reflections of me . . .
while turning the cold knob and cool water on my burning, sensitive skin. Opening the reflection of me and slowly taking it away while that sharp tool I have used over and over again comes to my not so knowing knowledge. Looking at the swollen blue veins that surround my razor hungry wrists, I touched this object and a tear of hate for life trickled down my cheek.
SLASHES
AFTER
SLASHES
surround my wide screaming for help eyes, for no more smiles, nor laughter will ever overcome me again for I have reached . . .
THE END.

Lindy Kosak
SOMETIMES
I sometimes need to remind myself
to laugh . . .
to enjoy . . .
and to just have fun.
It's so much easier to be
happy . . .
to be truly happy
filled with excitement
and wonder
to be able to wake
to another day.
I like to wake to the world God
gave us
full of sunshine and oceans,
blue skies
and soft grass, trees and
raindrops, and
All the challenges we face in
the homeless and drug
problems, struggling
with education and
prejudice, crime and
disease . . .
Sometimes the challenges seem
overwhelming and
exhausting; enough to
make me sad . . .
That's why sometimes I need to
remind myself—
but mostly—
I just simply remember
Because I truly am happy.

Aletha L Judd
UNDERSTANDING
Bend with the wind, I've been told,
It's hard to change when one grows old.
Pay attention to what's happening around,
Don't keep your eyes glued to the ground.

Look to the future, don't dwell on the past,
Even though your years are passing so fast.
Don't worry about Winter's chilly gloom,

Look forward to Spring when flowers bloom.

Remember when your own youth ruled your heart,
Your parents were out of touch, but you were smart!
When you see a young person try to find his way,
Remember when you too, at times went astray.

So bend in his direction until you touch,
Then gently sway, but don't bend too much.
Hold him tenderly, then stand him straight and true,
Bend enough so he can be himself, he's not you!

Rose Long

Rose Long
GREATEST LOVE

To My Family With Love: Clyde Long, Gary, Clydene, Lee and Craig Brock, Becky and Bekah Jordan, Jodi, Jason and Brittney Waters.

I walked upon a hill today,
And thought of another hill far away;
Where so long ago Christ died for me,
On a cross of broken dogwood tree.

Blue skies, sunshine smiling down on me.
Sweet springtime, new life, dogwoods blooming.
But He saw anguish, pain, cruel agony,
With thunder, earthquakes, darkness, glooming.

Yet He loved! and we are all forgiven.
Love so great could only come from heaven.
Love so strong; I feel it here today,
From His hill, long ago, far away.

Della P Bailey
GOD'S ANSWER TO PRAYER

In loving memory of my brother, Fred.

We were driving a Wyoming highway,
A sister, a brother and I.
Headed west to our homes in Nevada,
And facing a beautiful sky.

We were tired and deeply sorrowing,
Our hearts were filled with pain.
We had said our farewells to a dear brother,
Whom we would never see again.

We had been called to his bedside,
Where his life was ebbing away.
Nothing more could be done for him,
But to seek our God and pray.

The sun had completed its daily round,
And was settling down for the night.
When suddenly the entire sky was ablaze,
With a most wondrous sight.

Fingers of colors: red, blue and gold,
Laced the clouds together with colors untold.
As they mingled their colors with gray and white,
They created a gorgeous fairyland sight.

We watched as the colors faded away,
Knowing that God was answering each prayer.
We must move onward with our lives,
While our brother seeks rest over there.

Julie C Holt
THE CITY OF ANGELS

The streets are filled with violence
The churches turn to silence.

The children live to die
The darkness fills the sky.

Bloodshed fills their dreams
Laughing turns to screams.

Eyes of a switchblade knife
A child takes a child's life.

Chants of inner spells
The City of Angels.

Another town to suffocate
No kindness, but only hate.

Offspring robbing stores
Justice slamming doors.

What have we done wrong
Are we ever going to get along?

Through the pain and bitter strife
Another child takes a child's life.

Locked in barred jails
The Little City of Angels.

Another tear-stained face
Hearts left to an empty space.

Every smile a fake
Suffering for a past mistake.

Blood drips from the knife
Now the child has taken his life.

Padded prison cells
City of Angels.

William Greathouse
THE STORM

The sea breeze nudge the gliding gull,
The lightning winks, at the thunder's rolling call,
With a promise from the distant storm,
The waves seem intoxicated with the whitecaps' charm.
From where I stand upon this beach, all this do I view,
And know that upon this sand, my heart does weep for you.
'Twas on this beach where we first kissed, on a day much like today,
Confessed our love, and vowed 'fore God, that we would never stray.
But alas my dear, my darling one, a mockery you have made,
Of that thing, that wonderful thing, for which I have given my soul in trade.
Now the rain has reached the shore, it pelts against my face,
And mingles with my tears, that tell of my disgrace.
With each thunder's boom, my heart does pound,
And spit its love upon the ground.
And each lightning flash that lights the rain,
Is but a reflection of the burning flash within my brain.
Oh if I had but the nerve, to surrender to the salty swells,
For to live without you, is to live with a thousand hells.
But I shall live, yes I shall live, for my grief is liken to the storm,
It shall subside and pass away, and my heart again shall be warm.

Carolyn J Green
THE DAYS YET TO COME

To Randy, Angela and Chris, my three beacons in the night.

At times as I sit
In my bedroom alone,
My thoughts go out
To the days yet to come.

Wondering what will happen
When I'm lonely and old
Where will I find strength
To nourish body and soul.

Will my children desert me
In my time of need
Or will they remember
My love, and take heed.

Will they care for me
When I'm old and gray,
When I'm sick and can no longer
Make my own way.

Will they remember,
And always be kind
To someone who loves them,
Yet must leave them behind?

These are just some of the thoughts
That come my way,
As I sit in my bedroom and listen
To my children at play.

Paul Gire
VIETNAM WALL

To the men with their name on the wall,
We thank you for standing so tall,
To help make the rest of us free,
And letting the whole world see.

You left your families and friends,
And to communism you went to put an end,
You served your country well,
And marched into the jungles of hell.

You made the ultimate sacrifice,
You ended up losing your life,
Our heroes you'll always be,
We thank our God for thee.

We thank you all,
For standing so tall,
The men with their name on the wall.

John L Hamilton
SHARON

Be still my heart, it's only a voice!
But the melody lingers on echoing
In the caverns
of my mind.

Don't beat so hard at the song you hear!
But the notes keep tinkling
Like the first drops of rain in the spring
Awakening my soul like leaves unfurling
When catching drops
as they fall.

Oh, the words we speak are not our thoughts,
But the sounds we hear
Are thunder in our ear
Beating back the loneliness of years gone by.

Be still my heart, it's only a voice.
But the emptiness is filled
with your song.

Cynthia E Devin

Cynthia E Devin
BUTTERFLY

Butterfly, butterfly,
Where are you going?
You scatter about,
In a delicate frenzy.
Your wings are so graceful,
They flutter with brilliance,
Keeping the rhythm,
Of your own melody.
If you stop for a moment,
I see a pattern of art,
So free in your frailty,
In your life a new start.
For once a cocoon,
Wrapped safely in shelter,
Now flying around,
In a helter-skelter.
From river to rock
And flower to tree,
Your life is of beauty,
That fascinates me.

Cynthia E Devin
HOW LONG WILL I CRAVE
Why keep all this distance between us,
When our lips long to meet with a touch?
It isn't your absence that haunts me,
But the wanting of someone so much.

As I wait with anticipation
And a body that feels it will burst,
In hopes of a satisfied craving,
I fear the unquenchable thirst.

Moments to share are deep in my mind.
In breathtaking joy, we fumble about.
A closeness I seek is there in your eyes,
With visions of lust, I can't do without.

I caress your skin with my fingers,
To memorize every detail,
So that each little motion lingers,
When I'm left all alone in the spell.

You captured my thoughts and I succumbed.
When thinking of you, I am my own slave.
You do have your wings for flying alone
And if you forsake me, how long will I crave?

Cynthia E Devin
IN THE BOTTLE

Dedicated to Alcoholics Anonymous.

Am I a small man,
who lives inside a giant bottle?
How do I escape the glass wall that enslaves me?
The liquid surrounds me, as thirsty as I am—
Do I dare drink? Let me think,
maybe I should drown.
My taste buds gather, as it beckons me on.
In my sleep, it is haunting,
with things that I have done.
If I consume it all,
it might then consume what's left of me.
Is there nothing else to do,
but wallow in self-pity?
I could reach within myself,
for any strength that does exist,
and call out for a life-preserver,
to avoid a death of emptiness.
Am I a small man,
who lives inside a giant bottle?
Or am I just a man,
who can control his only life?

Cynthia E Devin
THE CONFESSION
What misfortune would I gain
If now I did confess
It is the feeling deep inside
That has me quite obsessed
Yet none can see the pain
As I suffer all alone
In this eternal silence
That my heart has only known
The truth of what you mean to me
Your touch within my soul
Is something that I do redeem
By keeping this control
Though better left unsaid
It is useless to pretend
While others wait at home for us
And you remain a friend
Our words have been so remiss
With what we know is true
The fact, my mouth conceals
Is indeed; I do love you

Jeannie Calero
AS LONG AS FOREVER

To Samuel Jason, with all my love.

As long as forever, I will stay by your side
I will be your lover, your friend, as well as your guide.

As long as I live and as long as you care, I will do anything I will go anywhere. I will bring you the sunshine to light up your days, I will comfort your fears and dry up your tears.

As long as there are more years to come, I hope I will be your only one. As long as I love you, my love will be true so please don't ever leave 'cause my life will be through.

As long as forever, you will be all that I want and all that I need because you have become a great part of my life and me.

As long as forever, you will remain in my heart even through the bad times that may tear us apart. As long as forever, I hope you can see just how much you really mean to me.

Valerie Jean Welch
THE REAR WINDOW

The poem is dedicated to someone I love dearly, my love, Henry Austin Jr.

Sitting here all alone with
time to think,
I look out my window at the emptiness
across the way, wondering is there something
out there for me.
My heart is so lonely so sad, and empty.
Could there ever be a place that could make my heart happy again.
This place outside my window is so dry and deserted, the black windows all around me, caged in and back up with nowhere to go, that's what my heart is saying, please let me out so I can live again

Ophelia E Brown
AFRICA-SHE

For my mother, Lula, and all my family whose love gives me inspiration and hope.

Africa still lives
She still gives
A life a day
for another man's pay
Land of our heart
Rich from the start
Freedom of the Nile
lost in every mile.

Still today she weeps
while equality sleeps.
Honor her breast's side
Joy of Her children's pride
People without their land
Fighting their only stand
to regain a mother's womb
stolen by greed's tomb.

One day Her rights to regain
giving halt to Her babies' pain
Yes, Africa still lives
Her wealth she freely gives.

None dare quote Her low
for She's where spirits of Kings go.

Rebekah Bowen
DAD SAID
Dad will be proud of me this time
For I told my Love good-bye
And I didn't cry
Dad Said, I had to be strong
Choose the "right" man
Not the "wrong"
My Love is gone
But I'm here where I belong
Dad Said, Never let a man see my tears
He still doesn't know it
But I've been crying . . . for years.

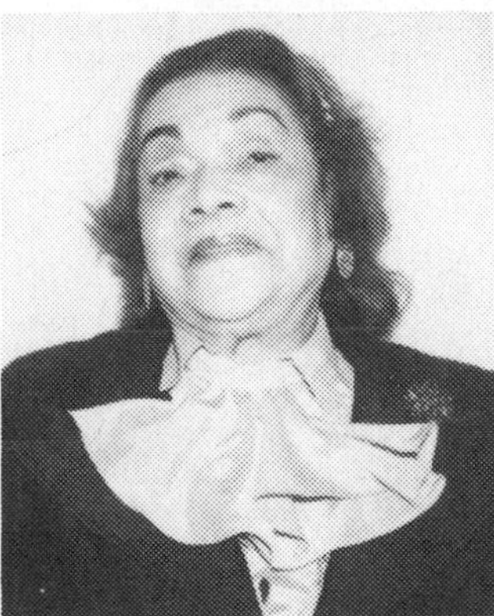

Carmen María Alvarez-R

Carmen María Alvarez-R
ONENESS

To The Memory of my Marvelous Mother, An Inspiration, Always! Agripina de Alvarez-Rodríguez

It may be Oneness of the bodies drenched in
Splendid care
Or then once more, like clear Niobean tears,
It may be Oneness as when tears become the
Liquid mass of time.
Of the Soul? As tho' of Souls a separate
Linear could be drawn
They say (and those who say are not perhaps the wise)
That Oneness is: Impossibility,
Untruth Divine!

Like Sands perpetuating Time and Age
(for Time and Age are Oneness)
Like Eyes of Owls that in darkness see
Then is it not a Oneness this quality of Owls
of Eyes of Owls that in darkness see?
Like Birds who flock together keeping Time their own
their own, Alas!
The pace each winged life has planned
is followed by its kin . . .
Is it not Oneness then,
to feel alike, to feel, to speak
and tender care alike,
To love as if that Oneness was and is Perpetuating Time?

Carmen María Alvarez-R
WISHES
I want to take these Grains of Sun,
These Beams of Moon . . .
And hold them, alternating, each in my hands . . .

I want to nourish same across the Universe!
The Grains of Sun across the Universe: that wide expanse of days and days!
Across the many daylights of the Universe . . .

The Beams of Moon across another wide expanse, across the Universe!
Another wide expanse of Nights and Nights!
And these will dance a Ballet as on a strip of velvet soft . . .
Black and tearful, beaded—the beads effecting tears!

The Grains of Sun will blind all Evil!
These same will serve as gleams of light for Kindness and
Survival . . .
And Man will serve his term on Earth between these opulent Aetheria . . .

When Life is done! The heavens will attest to Grains of Sun
And Beams of Moon
That man! Courageous Man! Indeed! was here! was here!

Jane Grayson
SEARCHING IN VAIN
I must go home one day,
Experience my own childhood play.
My own child laughter I must hear,
Feeling a mother's arms when in fear.
To know the protection of a mother's love,
Hear her voice, sweet like the dove.
Soothing words for a fall that pains,
Loving hugs when it thunders and rains.
To receive when I'm going to be three,
A little dolly all pretty just for me.
Instead, I cannot go home again,
Home for always is just pretend.
So a yearning heart plagues my mind,
With love for a mother I cannot find.

T J Wright
I HEARD MY MOTHER'S LAUGHTER
I heard my Mother's laughter floating on an ocean breeze.
The wind was talking to me as it blew atop the trees.
I felt her soul among the waves
as I walked along the shore.
Worries and problems of the past
existed here no more.

I heard the ocean tell me softly
as I looked out toward the sea.
"Troubles of the past," it said
"are of no consequence to me."

I knew she's finally found herself
and peace she'd been searching for.
So I helped by casting all my doubts
deep on the ocean floor.

I smiled with her in sunlight,
I gently held her hand.
As we walked along a distant shore
In warm November sand.

Janet Walters
I WISH I COULD HAVE TOLD YOU

To A Very Special Lady, Our Mom. We Love You.

Mother I've been thinking, just since
you've went away.
Of the things I should have told you,
and the things I would like to say.
So often I've taken things for
granted, that I sometimes failed to
see.
All the love and kindness and
understanding that you always
showed to me.
I know that as a child, we don't
always understand.
Yet I know that when I needed you,
you were there to hold my hand.
Or when I was afraid, and my heart
was full of fear,
You would wrap me in your arms and
wipe away every tear.
You are more precious to me than all
the world's finest gold.
And God knew what he was doing
when he chose to take you to his fold.
Yes, so often we take for granted the
ones who mean the most,
But mother I am proud you were
mine, and on you I will always boast.

Constance deM Jones
LITTLE DANNY

This poem is dedicated to my Granddaughter, Sgt. Stephanie L. Daniel (Walker) With love and gratitude for Little Danny.

I use my hands to do my sums,
The fingers 8 and 2 for thumbs.
This makes the count of digits 10
And now we start it o'er again

I have a foot on which to stand.
I have five toes, just like my hand.
I have another foot, and then—
It brings the count of toes to ten.

Joy Sekula Meacham
VIETNAM

This poem is dedicated to my deceased father, Frank J. Sekula, and to my closest friend, Philip R. Musy, both of whom have instilled the utmost confidence in me in all my endeavors.

War brings pain and leaves a scar;
The men who fought there were
young.
The pain subsides for most by far;
The scars leave tales left unsung.

Maimed bodies and twisted minds—
The rewards these men receive.
A thankless job and a job left undone;
The memory and truth they yet to
believe.

Our men took abuse both abroad and
at home;
No honor, no glory, no "job well
done."
Deprived of dignity and hope and
torn with guilt;
Seeking only respect and receiving
none.

Shunned by family and friends;
Rejected by their lovers.
Crumbling lives and countless
suicides;
Understood only by their brothers.

Trembling hands and sleepless nights—
The crosses that some must bear.
Mournful cries from the battlefield
pierce our men's solitude;
Unkept promises to their brothers—
they'll be okay and they care.

Tina Horton
A GRAIN OF SAND

To my daughter, Erica Marie, my inspiration and biggest fan. You have given me the courage to go after my dreams. Thank You. Love, Mommy.

Life is a beach and all the people are
but grains of sand.
Some grains have the wind to control
their destinies,
Some are controlled by the relentless
tide,
And some are carried to their fares by
the creatures of the Earth,
While others join together to form
pebbles,
But some remain the same grain of
sand that they started out as.
We never stay in the same place for
long and two grains of sand that
started out together are separated
forever.
Constantly we are shifted and we are
never able to make it back to our
original partner again.
So if we as people happen to find our
perfect mate, we have the ability to
hold onto that person and if we don't
then our lives aren't worth that of a
grain of a grain of sand.

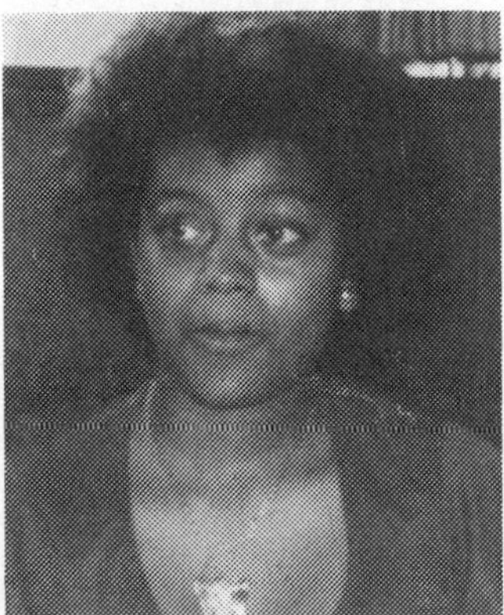

Sandra Ingram Brown

Sandra Ingram Brown
LOOKING UP

I looked at you today 8 lbs 9 ozs.
My heart was full of joy.
I looked up at you today.
I laughed and shook hysterically.
I looked up at you today.
I frowned and shook my head.
I looked up at you today.
I grinned and learn to bear it.
I looked up at you today.
I smiled and kissed your cheek.
I looked up at you today.
I want to protect you always.
I looked up at you today.
I wonder how you grew so tall.
I looked up at you today.
GRANDCHILDREN
AND
ALL

Lisa Jones
RELATIVITY

Wherever you go, whatever you
do,
Step lightly.
Whoever you see, whoever you
meet,
Step lightly.
Whatever you say, whatever you
hear,
Step lightly.
Whatever you give, whatever you
receive,
Step lightly.
Whatever you conspire, whatever
you conceive,
Step lightly.

Phyllis D Francis
BELOVED

To all lovers.

They say that love is blind, and it will hide the faults of the one they love. But what they see is only skin deep. That is as far as the eyes can see. But real love not only sees—the beauty in the eyes of the beholder, but deep down into the heart and soul of the ones they love.

A touch, a glance, a smile, these are the things that a real love sees. Not only the beauty of face. But what life can bring. No one not father, mother, a sister, or brother, can break the tie of love, and if they try not only do they lose a loved one, but they will slowly die inside.

They are worse than a thief in the night. They tear love and trust. But real love, real love goes on till you die.

Ninfa Caso-Flores
YOUR MOTHER

To Celeste and Rene, whose love, purity and sincerity, bring sunshine and beauty to all who cross their paths.

When you were born, all comments
were, "How absolutely perfect!"
My quick retort to that would be,
"Oh, no! Not so! Look at those little
tootsies!"
How vain and smug would I not
sound, to graphically detail, those
torrid, moonless evenings and
sweetly whispered nothings which
brought you into being?
Dare I admit to one and all, of that
perpetual fear of someday finding,
that you, my love, are but a figment
of a great imagination?
Or of some not too distant future,
when someone, God, perhaps,
coveting this bond we share, might
take you from my side?
Let that not be, else who, but HE,
could so bestow upon an undeserving
soul, like me, that uniquely cherished
honor to let <u>me</u> be your mother?
You are my love. You are my life.
You are my son. You are my
daughter.
Like you, there is no other.
You are my heart, which burst with
pride because I <u>am</u> your "Mother"!

Ninfa Caso-Flores
JOSEPHINE, MY MOTHER

To Josephine Solis-Becerril, my mother, whose love and understanding has always brought solace into my life and without whom I wouldn't even be here.

The sobs I heard tonight gave me
such sorrow.
I wish it were within my power to
obliterate all stinging prose which
cause you heartache.

How could you even think to ask
such as you did of me?
Didn't you know what I would say
because I care so much?

Are any of us immune to the frailties
of life?
I can't pretend I've never cried; we
know each other far too well for that.
I, also, bleed from wounds without
and some which lie within.

I've no regrets, only, perhaps, a
change or two, or maybe, three but
nothing more than that.

You showed me how to love and care
by simply watching you.
I'm glad you taught me about love
and life and even grief, you see, for
mere existence just wouldn't do for
me.

I know myself, while others only
think they do.
Without your love and help along the
way, I doubt I'd be just who I am
today.

I'm proud of me! I'm proud of you!

I'm very proud you are my mother. I
love you very much.

Your Daughter.

Ninfa Caso-Flores
DO YOU REMEMBER?

Do you remember, when you loved
me and I loved you and you believed
in me and I believed in you?
I still believe in you, my Love, do
you believe in me?

Do you remember, when you
appeared to have; what seemed to be,
a bright, perpetual sparkle glistening
in those eyes of green and gold?

Do you remember, when knowing
smiles between us, you and me,
would put dimpled, toothy-grins, like
splashes across your face?

Do you remember, a frosty walk
along a dark and foggy beach, and
love, and candlelight, and nectars of
the Gods?

Do you remember, just how
wonderful I know you are and how
very proud I am of you?

How many times have I not begged
that you take care, my Love, do you
recall?
In that respect you haven't done too
well of late, or so I'm told.

Is this peculiar just to you, or is it so,
with all those such as, you;
those overzealous, busy, busy, Big
Tycoons?

My love, respect and admiration are
yours forevermore.
Will you, also, remember that, My
Dear?

C L Nunies
SOMEONE ASK ME ABOUT LOVE

This poem is dedicated to Paula J. Darnell for always being there.

Someone ask me what I wanted out of love?
I said someone who cared and could express the same feelings I have.
Someone who I could talk to when I have something on my mind.
Someone who wouldn't judge me because my ways are different.
Someone who will walk on the beaches and lakes with me in silence and appreciate nature.
Someone who can take my point of view not of criticism, but of my philosophy in life.
Someone I could trust and be comfortable with knowing wherever I go I will be at their side.
Someone who will give me space when I need time to be alone.
Someone ask me where do you find this love?
I said when a glance becomes a smile, a heart becomes aflutter, your body becomes weak.
Then someone wanted to know what would I call it?
I said chemistry of LOVE.

Cynthia A Toll
ROSALINA

This poem is dedicated to my beautiful daughter, Sherri, who gave Rosalina her name.

Rosalina, pretty Rosalina
With beautiful eyes of blue
Rosalina, you're in Heaven now
You know that God loves you

You'll feel no pain now, as you did
When you were with us here
I know that you'll be happy there
I'll try not to shed a tear

Though life was hard for you, I know
We tried to do our best
To make your last days easier
It's time for you to rest

I'll think of you in springtime
When the grass is fresh and new
You'll romp and play in Heaven
You know I'll always love you

Rosalina died June 1, 1988.

Louise J Davis
OUR FLAG

To all the members of my family who fought for OUR FLAG.

AMERICA—our land of the home and the free
Oh, waving Flag, we truly love thee—
Your color of red, as it blends with the white
Symbolizing purity, and everything right.
Your stars, like the heavens are outstanding it's true
Lives have been lost—all because of you.
You're our symbol of freedom—our hope in this world
Keep waving dear flag, from the moment you're unfurled.
Let NONE desecrate or mock you—dear friend,
You're our past—our future—from beginning to end.
May you wave every day, as our prayers go with you,
Thank God for this Land—of the RED WHITE and BLUE.

Marian Y Klosterhoff
WHEN YOU THINK OF THIS MAN

In memory of Ray Fred Klosterhoff, Sr.; November 29, 1977.

Celebrate for a man who lived gentle and strong,
Helping others in need—as he went along.

Whether bicycling to town, or watching baseball,
He gave the gift of life his all.

Family, traveling, business—a pleasure,
Memories he leaves for us to treasure.

Loving, living, laughter and fun,
He departs this life, the battle won.

Thoughts, feelings—it's what I saw,
With love—he was—my Father-in-law.

Clarissa K Sailor
THE CROSS THAT COUNTS

In memory of my brother, Christopher L. Sailor.

The Old Rugged Cross that
takes a stand
I look to see an amázing
man
With spikes that pierce His
bloody hands,
He washes away the sin
in the land.
Around His head a crown
of thorns.
To every person again to
be born.
For the ones still with
sin.
Through heaven's gates they
cannot enter in.
But the soul so clean
and free
Heaven's doors it must
be.

Tadeusz Chabrowski
MOTHER'S FINGERPRINTS
The lab analysis of the dustcloth
showed mother's fingerprints,
words that fell from her mouth,
endless rushing,
entangled trains of thought,
tapestries of worries thickly woven,
roses of once fortuitous winds
and a fading point
of her gaze fastened on the beyond.

Tadeusz Chabrowski
THE HERO
I was born
from the blossoming of facts
on rotations of a narrative machine
my finest features
faintly typed
are polyphonic participles

the author reproduced my face
using a bishop violet carbon
now the reader
extracts the eye for his net
or tears out the grey beard
for a rope to hang the wash

some discuss
my complexes
ethical miserable
indiscernible others say
I was created
according to rules of the SACRED STRUCTURE
unblemished
dressed in Brabant laces of thought

Tadeusz Chabrowski
MY IMAGINATION
I shall die
of cricketlike words
well-groomed
betrayed by FICTION
not stored in time in the granary
of aesthetic salvation

Isabel Serrano
"The best grandma in the world"

Jennifer Simpson
GRANDMA

This poem is dedicated to my grandma, the best that ever was.

My grandmother was laid to rest at the age of 72.
She accomplished many things in life that most couldn't do.

She raised three daughters all on her own.
Her grandkids too when her daughters were grown.

She had six grandkids four boys and two girls.
She gave us lots of love and tried giving us the world.

She sat by our bedside many a time.
When the colds were bad and fevers so high.

At the age of 48 my grandmother retired.
To raise her granddaughter because my mother had been hired.

She went on to raise me as well.
When we were bad she never would tell.

My grandmother raised my sister Patti and I.
When my mother needed her own free life.

My grandmother once again was to come,
And raise two more girls all alone.

She didn't have to, she wasn't forced.
She volunteered 'cause of the love in her heart.

We were taught not to need anyone.
Sadly enough I needed her alone.

I needed her love day and night.
I needed her for counseling to show me what was right.

My sister was closer to my mother.
But I loved Grandma like no other.

She was my teacher, my counselor too,
My mother, my buddy to name a few.

She saw me through my freshman year.
And when I dropped out she shed many a tear.

We shared many secrets that only Grandma understood.
And worried later when mom would find out, 'cause that was never good.

I'll never love anyone the way I loved her.
The tables are turned and I owe her these words.

I'm sixteen years old now, she's been gone eight months.
I miss her something awful, and I'm still down in the dumps.

I keep myself busy morning and night.
But I still wonder if she thinks it's alright.

I know she is still watching me,
And watching what I do.

And Grandma if you hear me,
I'm doing it for you.

And Grandma if you hear me,
I Love You

Stephen Bowman
THE DEATH OF THE HALF-MAGE, PO
Light shines dark in those waking hours,
after death has passed us by.
Green grass is now black with the
blood of the dying men.
Swords and blades are seen dully
by the sun in the dawning sky.
A whisper pierces the eerie
silence and I look to see.
She stands over me like an angel with hair of gold.
One moment she is there—blink—
she now is gone.
My world seems empty and I cannot lift myself.
The sun goes black once more and
I see the dragon soar.
He is diving towards me and I am
a trapped victim, immovable.
I feel his talons tear into my skin
. . . I am gone.

Norma I Viruet
REMEMBERING
I remember those brown eyes that shined.
As they looked so hard back into mine.

Now it all seems just like a memory.
Remembering when you said, the
eyes are the mirrors to the soul.
It all seemed so clear when I looked
into your eyes and you looked into
mine.
Seeing what really was there.
The love that we shared.
And will always share till the end of
time.
I remember them twinkling.
I remember them smiling back at me.
I remember those tears,
We sometimes shared together not
because of us,
But because of others who were at
fault.
Just by looking at them made my
whole day bright.
No matter how my day started,
If it started right, you would make it
more wonderful.
If it started wrong, you would make it
right.
Just by looking into them.
I remember those brown eyes that
shined.
As they looked so hard back into
mine.

Shirley Lambert Henderson
LOVE?
A simple hello
Unspoken words to those we don't
know
A baby's cry
A loving sigh
A kiss or a hug
Grandma's handmade rug.
A pat on the back
Chocolate chip cookies in a brown
paper sack
A long stem red rose
A kiss to fingers that were froze
Love is something you can't grow
Just be around it, you'll know.

Philips T Palermo
BE STILL AND KNOW

Dedicated to my family, friends, and the SPIRIT of LIGHT.

My Father you are our God indeed
and Jesus is your Son,
He came to place within men's hearts
the truth that you are One.
The way, you clear with Thy Mighty
hand
is sure into Thy heart,
Your thoughts of light clear every
step,
Divine knowledge you impart.

To know you are one just empties
self
and reaches deep within,
and hears your voice in silent calm
while fire rushes in.
It cleanses and it purifies
this Spirit, Holy, Divine,
and I know a love and express it thus,
Father, not my will, but Thine.

Philips T Palermo
CHRISTMAS SPIRIT
On the night of our dear Savior's
birth you'll see children with shiny
bright eyes.
There's a feeling of magic in the air
and a feeling of Christmas everywhere.

Children laughing all around
snow is falling on the ground
a warmth of love, and a tree all
shining and bright.
And within our hearts we pray
that upon his Holy day
all is Blessed throughout the world
with LIGHT.

On the night of our dear Savior's
birth you find joy in all the things
you do
And we pray your year is good
Blessed with peace and brotherhood,
and we pray, Merry Christmas to
you.

Susan Dudley
DEAFENING SILENCE
The concert is over
The players are gone,
The day is now closing
And darkness has drawn.
The silence is blending
Into the night,
The audience has vanished . . .
No one left in sight.
But people will gather
Once again just to hear
Strong emotions expressed
Through the band's unity.
Musicians have emptied
Their vibrations in song
But now have retreated . . .
Their time is thus done,
Until there is a time
For electrical sensations
To pulsate through space
And excite imaginations.

Karina Weidmann
UNTITLED
Walking down the halls of death;
Seeing the blurry shapes of the past;
Feeling the unreality of being;
Sensing the hands trying to grab;
Hearing nothing but the pleading
moans in hollow silence;
Tasting eternity;
Wanting to live.

Faye Hatley
MY GINGHAM DAY
A calico cat
A spotted dog
And two pebble pups,
A summer blue sky
Patched with white clouds,
Dark green pines
Stitched along the edge of a meadow
That is laced with daisies and vetch,
Now my two pebble pups
And the spotted dog are
Playing throw and fetch.

Laura A Larabell
THE TREE . . .
There is a tree
Beyond the brook
A heart was carved
Its life they took

Their love was tested
It was not true
He broke it off
For someone new.

But, the tree
He slowly dies
When the wind blows
He sways and cries

Cries like my heart
For it was me
When I saw her with you
I felt like the tree.

For an untrue love
Thus I cried.
But, for my love
the tree, . . . died.

J D Singleton
MEMORY LESSONS
Why must memories always remain
Why must they remind me again and
again
Of things that I desperately wish to
forget
The Past may be gone, but it's not
finished yet
The Present allows that I make my
own choices
The Future beckons with wise,
timeless voices
And the Past, year or second, is
equally gone
Yet the memories, as if etched in
stone, linger on
And it seems that the memories I
wish to let go
Are the strongest, and clearest, of all
that I know
Yes there are those of laughter and
joy, to be sure
But the ones that bring sadness are
the ones that endure
Perhaps the strength, and the length,
of their presence
Reflects the importance of their
ultimate lessons
And if it's a memory of sadness
deserved
It's a lesson best learned the first time
it's served

Caroline McGuire
ONCE IN MY WORLD
Once in my world
Things were so clear
I could have touched the sky

But now there's confusion
Surrounded by fear
And I am too scared to try.

I need to expand
And try all new things
I need to be on my own.

I want to fly high
And spread both my wings
To see all that's unknown.

I just need some time
To look and explore
The world with my own eyes.

So just let me go
And don't ask what for
When I say my goodbyes.

Magda Lee Cabrera

Magda Lee Cabrera
THE EMBRACE
I go on searching for days on end
Searching for that special friend
I wonder where he could be???

Someone to grasp me to soothe my
soul
The power of an embrace to take
control
No more worries, no more fears
All just because he is here

No! I can't believe! It was just a mere
dream
It wasn't what it really seemed
I've awakened alone again
He was never here, my special friend

I must once again face reality
He was never here with me
I go on searching in great despair
It isn't right, it isn't fair!

But I know someday my dream will
come true
You facing me and I facing you
As we stand together at a certain time
and place
You holding me in your strong, warm
embrace

Sherri Shurtz
MY HEART CRIES
Even though
My heart cries out
to you,
I know
I cannot come.
My heart cries
for your sweet love
Each and every night
As I lay my head
to the softness
of my pillow.
My thoughts
are only on you.
You're so far away
that only my heart
can reach you.
As each dream
Becomes a reality
I become more

close to you
than even I know.
As my heart
Reaches into your
Heart and becomes
ONE.

Jeff Keller
THE MIDNIGHT RODEO
The rodeo crowds have long since dispersed
And the last winning cowpoke collected his purse
The parking lot's empty and the stock's bedded down
The last of the white face has been washed from the clown

Now is the time, when we are at rest
For the midnight rodeo to strut out its best
The arena's lit up, although just from moonglow
But that's all you need for a midnight rodeo

Rodeo cowboys, long since passed away
Have come here for fun—night is their day
The rough stock of yore had their day in the sun
Well they're all here too—to buck and to run

Each event goes like clockwork—one, two and three
Bucking and roping, barrel racing for she
When the sun's first rays reach up from the East
All will be gone, cowboy and beast

We can't gain admission till our time has come
The last breath in our body, the last belt buckle won
But when I've danced my last do si do
You can find me at midnight rodeo

Joan Lenore Waters
4/27/90

To Trent,
who has been a blessing to me.
Love, Mom.

My son, my little boy
Such a blessing, such a joy
What a pleasure to watch you grow
My son, from head to toe
You gave me so much pleasure
My son, in my heart I'll always treasure
My son, a grownup man
For this was in God's plan
To give me a son to be so proud
That sometimes, I want to shout out loud
You bring sunshine and warmth with your smile
My son, I want to reach out and hug you close awhile
My son, God has given you to me
To help to make what he wants you to be
So when your world seems not to glimmer
Reach for the heavens for
My son, you'll always be a winner

Footnote: Inspired by God

Takao Hashida
SNOWMAN
Snowman
"This is Hawaii
no way! Man."

Novella D Leatherwood

Novella D Leatherwood
WALKING WITH MY MASTER

To my granddaughters, Amy and Katy Rankin.

When just a girl of twelve, I heard Him say,
"Come, child, and walk along with me today.
Come, child, and let me gently hold your hand
As I guide you through this vast, troubled land."

So with outstretched hand I did join Him there
And we two walked together everywhere.
We passed through dark valley and sunny glade
While thoughtlessly mistakes I sometimes made.

He freely forgave again and again,
Teaching me to forgive my fellowman.
And now as I enter life's twilight zone,
Here's a prayer I would like to make my own.

"Thank you, Master, for meeting me there
And giving these years in your loving care.
Please, now a bit more firmly hold my hand
As our journey continues through this land.

"Though my step may falter, my sight grow dim,
Please give me the strength to witness for Him
Who sent Thee to save that child who was lost,
And help me prove worthy of that great cost."

Beth A Lorah
YOU & ME
You and me together it seems so good. Thru all our trials and triumphs side by side we stood. It wasn't always easy and it wasn't always fun, but we knew after "the rain" would come "the sun." And thru all our doubts, trials and fears came a strong, secure relationship to withstand the years. For with you I'm prepared to spend the rest of my life . . . to bear all your children and be called your wife. You're special to me in a million and one ways & I look forward to learning, growing and sharing with you every day. So we'll press on with our future which looks so bright and I'll tell you "I love you" every day and every night. You're the one for me, it's so easy to see and I know in my heart we were meant to be.

Frances Metzger
THE RAINS CAME

Dedicated to my cousin, Shirley Dietz.

The rains came—not in May to fill the barns with hay,
Not in June to make the roses bloom.
The rains came in the fall, when the corn was tall,
And the creeks were dry and the swamps were low.
The rains came and the grass stayed green.
The leaves turned red, every tree was a queen.
The rains came and the mushrooms grew
Like little umbrellas all covered with dew.
The rains came and the deer grew fat.
The hunter was waiting his shotgun intact.
The rains came and the days were dark.
But the air was fresh; every view a park.
The rains came and the harvest stood still,
Waiting for sunshine to pop o'er the hill.
The rains came, but the farmer just waited,
Knowing God brings a harvest to the world he created.

Orit Ostrowiak
THE BEGINNING AND THE END
Softly, slowly, the ball of fire starts to sink
The water beckons, the sky deepens
Closer, closer, the margin is approached
Until the oval balances delicately on the horizon
Equilibrium is at hand,
Harmony is felt between sky, earth and ocean
From dusk to dawn:
Night falls here; day breaks there
From sunset to sunrise
It is simultaneously, the beginning and the end
Softly, slowly, the human form starts to age
Eternity calls, life hardens
Closer, closer, the end is at hand
Until finally, the meaning of it all is discovered
Balance
Dusk to dawn; dawn to dusk
From our sunsets new sunrises are created
For,
It is simultaneously, the beginning and the end

Betty Sikorowski
WE REMEMBER
We remember the sun,
And not the rain
We remember the joy,
And not the pain,
Of living.
We remember the laughter
And not the tears,
We remember the days,
And not years,
Of living.

Dan Kerley Jr
LOVE IN EXILE
The time I spend away from you
Is counted out in pebbles
Falling to a canyon floor,
The irregular report
Of stone to ground
Sets off no alarms
In that eternal place.
But so are measured
All my feelings
As they explode within me.

Only to think of me
From time to time
Is to discount my place.
Your heart pushes mine
And, from miles away,
My echo can be heard.

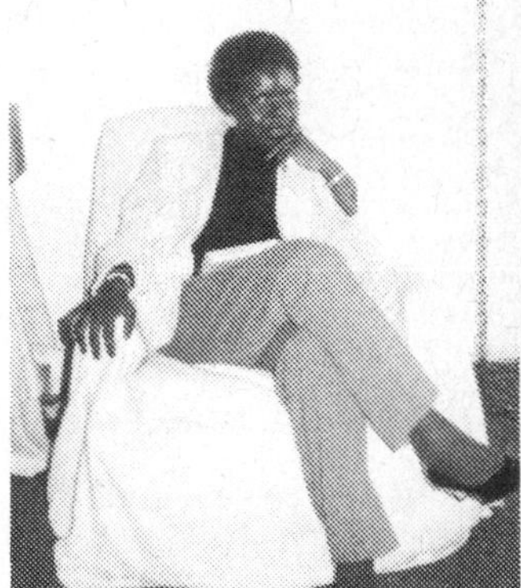

Dolores L Green-Jackson

Dolores L Green-Jackson
TRACI, MY TALL MAJESTIC QUEEN

To Traci, My Loving Daughter. You are a precious gift sent from God. Your sparkling personality brings so much joy to all around you.

As she's walking down the street,
to a drum of her own beat.
She will always be,
My Tall Majestic Queen.

As she does her own dances,
that look like they are prances.
She will always be,
My Tall Majestic Queen.

When she gives you respect,
she reveals her intellect.
Whether early or late,
she moves in her own gait.
She never misses a day,
of bringing joy our way.

Traci, My Tall Majestic Queen!

Wade Andrew Rettig
BODY WITHOUT A SOUL
Your lifeless heart it beats for me,
Cold, dry, blood is caged in frozen flesh and veins,
Convulsions rage, at the reality of death's pangs,
You need my soul to survive—

Peering deep into the eyes of my window's heart and soul,
Think you know my thoughts and origin, from which I have passed go,
And I know, you've stalked me down days of old
To charge me with my conscience' crimes,
Only to find they've locked you up
And thrown away the key of times!

I feel the smile fall from your face
Because you know your house is torn,
To the place that's none you try to run,
But for you, death has just been born,
The demons wease the gates they shake
Bells begin to ring,
To the body without a soul I sing,
"oh death,
Death where is your sting?"

Regina
A CIRCUS IS LIKE A NIGHTMARE
The ringleader is the fiendish master conducting the bizarre events of the night.
A clown is like a swirl of running colors, drowning his fury in the din.
The audience is a swarm of bees, buzzing among themselves the mad delights they see.
The tiger is like the cannons of war, booming its raging roar.
The fat man is a rolling ball of twine, rolling to entangle confusion.
A monkey in a cage is like a hairy barbarian, shrieking to be heard over the pandemonium.
The peanut seller is the mock of Satan, pushing evils to the swarming bees.
An elephant is like a trumpet out of tune, bleating his trunk to add to the whirl.
A broken doll in the middle of the ring is the lost life of the woman who was in the trapeze act.

Helen Hayes Krok
TO SUZIE Q (MY DOG) DECEASED "FOUR FEET IN HEAVEN"
Your favorite rug is vacant now
No eager bark to greet me,
No softly padded paws to run
So eagerly to meet me.

No coaxing rubs, no tiny cries
Will say, "It's time for feeding."
I've put away your bowl
And all the things you won't be needing.

But I will miss you, my little friend
For I could never measure
The happiness you've brought to me
The comfort and the pleasure.

And since God put you here to share
In earthly joy and sorrow
I'm sure there'll be a place for you
In heaven's bright tomorrow.

"WE MISS YOU SUZIE Q"

Carol Tifft
OUR WORLD
This world of ours, with trouble about us,
With people going about, making such a fuss.
It was so perfect and peaceful not long ago,
Now everyone knows not which way to go.
Look at your neighbor, his needs much like yours,
We question him, degrade him, being not good doers.
There must be a way for harmony to abide—
So that peace and love can once more be supplied.
Another topic of the day is pollution,
Many tax dollars spent but still no solution.
As for war, what can I say?
We talk of peace—well, maybe someday!
Which brings us to the so-called generation gap,
Since when can't people live together on this map?
Peace, smog, poverty, taxes, pollution, war,
These are a few, you can think of many more.
Yes, we could talk all day of the problems that are about,
We can rant, rave, holler, and shout—
But there is still one thing that we all can do,
"Do unto others as you would have them do unto you."

Janet Smith Collins
REFLECTIONS

To all of my precious loved ones.

The script has been written.
The cast of characters are in play.
It's act three.
The spotlight diminishes.

Into the journey of the very center of myself
. . . reflections.
Yet, in my journal of emotions,
I do not walk away
empty-handed
for I have a realization
of the balance of life itself.

I have grown by observation and experience.
I have touched on the attributes of humankind.
I have a sense of accomplishment.

The epilogue of this drama
is the close of a season . . .
yet marks the beginnings of seasons to come.

My expression of love to the audience,
and to all that will hear.

The curtain comes down.

Janet Smith Collins
THE MASTER
Life is like a ship on the open sea.

While the lightning and thunder rages,
the craft is tossed and beaten
against the forces of nature.

In the midst of the storm,
The Master shines forth
with great glory and power.

The sparkle in His eyes is love;
a love so fathomless
it covers all creation.

He reaches down with a gentle hand . . .

"Peace, be still."

Charles G Buchanan
BEAUTIFUL HEART
If anyone should ask me
What I considered to be
The most desirable trait
One could hope for in a mate,
I would answer unequivocally:
Of all the other traits there be,
Give me, The Beautiful Heart!

And, what is a beautiful heart?
A beautiful heart, understands;
A beautiful heart, makes no demands;
A beautiful heart, is selfless love,
The origin of which, is from above.
Of all the other traits there be,
Oh, Beautiful Heart, I love thee!

Charles G Buchanan
FAREWELL AUTUMN
Farewell Autumn,
your comeliness
with all your colorful splendor
has begun to fade
into the cold bleakness of winter.
I was enraptured
with your beauty
while you were here
but now,
I must let you go.
Only the memory of you
will remain.
Fare thee well!

Charles G Buchanan
DO I LOVE THEE
Do I love thee, Lord?
Is my love for sure?
Would I die for thee, Lord?
Could my faith endure?

Could you trust me, Lord?
Would I let thee down?
Would I deny thee, Lord?
When evil abounds?

Am I hopeless, Lord?
Is my faith too frail?
Would you strengthen me, Lord?
Could I yet prevail?

Charles G Buchanan
EVOLUTION
The Theory of Evolution
Is strange indeed
From absolutely nothing
It grows like a weed.

Brenda J Teplitsky
THE STRONGER SOUL
Entering deep within my mind,
I see a familiar reflection.
It reminds me of something I once knew,
But strange, I don't make the connection.

Attempting to go deeper in,
But trying to pry not too much.
Afraid of what I might find there,
And hoping to find of no such.

A love that just went untended,
A soul that was left to feel pain.
A tear that would shed in a pillow,
A scar that was meant to remain.

Instead on my prehesitation,
I find only to my dismay.
A strength that could only be practiced,
And a stronger soul waiting for the next day.

Jeffrey W Brown
THE SANDMAN CAME AND FOUND ME
The sandman came and found me,
ripped dust
from my heels,
Tore happenstance signals
into my decrees.

His tepid domain,
an unintelligible rift,
thrust a ghost-barren
Matrix
upon my stagecraft.

So revolving wind glaciers slashed
skies from my pupils
and allegoric
Thresholds cast qualms
in their spume.

Then sandman confounded me,
intenerated my force,
gospelized mist hymn
Whispers
into governed fact.

Margaret E Ott
CLOUD FANTASIES
A long-eared rabbit dashed through the sky,
Pursuing a pheasant that just ran by.
And a playful Pekinese up in the blue,
Challenged a goose up there too.

What a delightful summer day!
When angel children come out to play.
And, using the thunderheads just like clay,
They create all these fancies to brighten the day.

Betty H Rogers
THIS IS MY POEM
I saved my strength,
But I have never been strong.
I saved my time,
But now the days are too long.
I saved my money for a rainy day,
But I took my love and gave it all away.

Terri Lynn Dickey

Johnnie Bill Jackson

Terri Lynn Dickey
APRIL 17, 1990

To Ed, for always having faith in my creative abilities.

I may be unhappy
with my existence—

doing a job I have never
desired or dreamed of

from work I do not enjoy,
I become too tired
to do the things
I most desire

The career I want to pursue,
the dreams I want to live

seem a lifetime away

The only way I breathe—

is to think of YOU
and my DREAMS

To combine the two,
I have oxygen,

I have LIFE!

Rebecca R Gibson
QUIET

A beam of sunshine
Breaks through the clear morning
And falls delicately across the windowpane
Bringing light in
Casting shadows on the walls

The silence is so loud
You can hear a breeze blow through the room
As if it were thunder in a storm
The silence is peaceful
And yet still frightening
Here I sit
In the quiet
Thinking
Remembering
Alone

Yvonne Philbrook
GOD'S GIFT

To my grandchildren—Holly, Nicole and Eric.

What precious little angels
Sent from up above
To show us how to get along,
To teach us how to love
They fill our lives with
Sunshine—our days from
Gray to blue—this gift
Of little children—God
Gives to me and you.

Johnnie Bill Jackson
EAST AND WEST GERMANY, YOUR NATIVE LAND UNITED

To my Ida Lee and my Daughters, in Jamaica, New York (Gwendolyn Ann). To my Gladys and my sons, Victor Emmanuel and Karl Frederick Jackson, Smiths, Alabama.

Who Loves His County Will Not Rest, To See That Wall Was Not Best.
Now it's down on common ground,
That fell to keep out my love and song of your fatherland!
East and west, Your Native Land United,
Content with vow and pledge for thee;
"Deutschland, Deutschland, über alles!"
The Common Speech of one Nation,
Distinguished from that of another race and style.
Flies her banner, seek and count the destiny as her own,

Seek No Boundary, despite those titles, "Power and Pelf,"
Not only when the "National HymnePlays"
"Deutschland, Deutschland über alles"

East and West Germany, Your Native Land United,
With Children, Women, Wine and German Songs
Out with the Old, Bring in the New, "Vatherland,"
Good Luck, "Glücke, bluhe Deutsches Vatherland!"

Jacksons, from "The United States of America," Say Good Luck, "United Germany."

Johnnie Bill Jackson
THAT OLD CHATTAHOOCHEE RIVER

She Come Out from the Hill of Ha ber sham,
Flows down the val ley of Hall's,
She Hur ries a main to reach the plain, and
Runs through rap-ids and Falls.

That Old Hoo-Chee Riv er, That Old Chattahoochee Riv-er,
She runs through halls like, "The Old Man River,"
She just keeps on mov ing, just keeps mov-ing a-long,

She don't Split rock but Pass-es by, accepts no bed that's
Nar-row or Wide, she flees from fol-ly on each side,
She'll be Stop, when she all runs dry,
That Old Hoo-chee
Riv-er, that Chattahoochee Riv-er,
She runs and joins that old Flint Riv-er, She just keeps on mov-ing, Just keeps mov-ing a-long.

She Don't Call if you're Drown-ing,
Sil-enced, if You're fish-ing, That Old Hoo-chee never will be for-gotten,
That Old Hoo-chee Riv-er, That Chattahoochee Riv-er moves on.

She don't call for du-ty, She don't call for rest-ing,
She turn no tides to be
for got ten, That Old Hoo chee
Riv-er, that Chat-ta-hoo chee
Riv-er moves on.

She bars me pas-sage with friend-ly brawl, like that old Chattahoochee goes, She just moves on and on, I am in a-vail
And I am al-so weary, I feel like dy-ing for old Hoo-chee,
I feel just like cry-ing, for old Chattahoochee back home,
That a long . . . She H-ome.

Laeslie Stokes
SILENT CHILD

Silent child in the dark she lay
Curled up in a corner with nothing to say
Her thoughts are in her hands
but without a sound
She has a new way to think
She has finally found
Silent Child please speak to me
With grace, pride, and dignity
So don't be afraid just take my hand
And with the other use to understand
For there are more things in life
Than just learning to cope
Just use some faith and a little hope.
Because you have learned to relate without sound
And a special friend you have found.

N O Lacey
SNOW TEARS

I feel the sadness in your tears
as I've done for many years,
and again the need to comfort you
consumes my very soul.

White tears forming masses
weighing down my outstretched arms,
chilling me and filling me
with the passion I withhold.

I will be the warmth that soothes you.
Don't despair—I'll never leave you,
and perhaps one day you'll understand
without you I would die.

Phyllis K Wright
ODE TO JOHN

The first one I think of
when morning is bright.
I visit you often in the
dead of the night.

To not give you credit
just wouldn't be fair.
Whenever you're needed,
you've always been there.

So here is to you
my much needed friend.
May you always flush clean,
and the paper not end!

James H Scranton
EMMANUEL

In honor of Emmanuel Fellowship, a church that exemplified God's abiding presence.

Eternal Father, Almighty God,
Merciful Master, Author of Love;
Mankind's Deliverer, coming to all,
Abides in the hearts prepared for His call.
Name that reigns in eternal majesty,
Unveiling His presence and His glory,
Emmanuel's Spirit shines from within
Light of His mystical communion.

Dale Ely
THE RAIN

Rain is good for all our crops, but not good for me;
Rain puts leaves on the trees, yet does nothing for me, you see?
"The Rain" causes flowers to grow,
I'm tall enough 'as is,'
the bees love flowers, but that's their biz.
"The Rain" we get helps everything grow big and strong;
or if it never Rained, something would be very wrong.
"The Rain" turns grass, oh, so green;
Rain does so many things, even some unseen.
"The Rain" washes our cars, anyone want a shower?
It can even Rain quite awhile, even hour after hour.
"The Rain" can sometimes pour,
other times a mere sprinkle;
even attended by thunder and lightning, that's a new wrinkle.
Now and then, hail may even come along for the ride;
Rain oft times has other partners along by its side.
Sometimes, the rain can fall gentle as a lamb;
Other times, it may come down a hard, BAM! BAM! BAM!
I'm not overly fond of rain, gray skies, the gloom, you know?
But I, a lot rather, prefer rain anytime, over the snow.

Hyacinth Rizzo
THE FIBER SCULPTOR

To Robert J. Kirchmyer, my dear friend, the fiber sculptor.

The artist sits beside his loom
eyes narrowed
brow puckered
lips tightened
in concentration
as strong deft fingers
skillfully weave

earth-toned strands of fiber
back and forth into long tight ropes

Sunrays dart through the open window
to perform their skipping tricks
over the loom
trying out for parts
in the fiber artistry . . .
the artist rewards their act
by weaving in their strands of gold

Now he stands to stretch
and breathe in crisp October air
at the window
he watches yellow, bronzed and reddened leaves
put in their bids
for parts in the work of art
as they drift softly
to the browning lawn
"You're already in it,"
he tells them.
"You're already there."

He sits at the loom again
and stays
till dimming daylight
hazes over his work . . .

"Tomorrow," he promises
"Tomorrow we braid the ropes
to create our masterpiece."

Benjamin J Cox
DESIRE

There's a part of me I can't escape
For years I've tried and tried
to understand the goings on
inside this skull of mine

Every morning I get up
My head goes round and round
The pressure that builds up at night
looks for a place to bound

Sometimes I want to build a house
or make the perfect graph
To write a poem that speaks out loud
without a tongue or mouth

Sometimes I want to have it all
To own the world's biggest bank
But like my dad and his 'fore me
I just look up and say—thanks.

Walter M Newland
HAPPY MOTHER'S DAY

To remember with love is the ultimate accolade.

I take no credit for the turn of fate
That brought you into my life
But the smartest thing I ever did
Was seek you to be my wife

I've had my share of honors
Acclaim—prestige—reward
But for me the everlasting glory
Has been our marital accord

Heaven to most is but a promise
But what's a promise worth?
I need not wait and wonder
Mine is here with you on earth.

Kimberly Ann Fabri
RUSH HOUR

The traffic is backed up, all o'er town
Look up the streets, then down.
People are shouting, honking their horn
This goes on daily, at the eve and the morn.
Traffic is moving, in a snail pace
You can see anger, frustration, on each face.
People having so much to do
But must wait 'til the rush hour is through.

Janet M Bassi
I NEED TO KNOW WHY

You stand there so cool and smooth
One look from me could've made you move
But now I really need to know
Why did you ever have to go

It started out to be so much fun
We couldn't be separated by no one
You made me need you too much
You were mine with just one touch

I need to know the reasons why
Why did you have to make our love die
Why did our love have to die
Please, please tell me why

I guess I never saw how you are
You just wanted to be a star
You took my hand and led me away
You left me there to find my own way

Another day may come, you'll be there
I may not be the one to care
Don't think about crawling back
You blew your chance and that's a fact

Annie Grace Gorie Heller
A BIRTHDAY TRIBUTE TO GRANDMOTHER

To my Mother-in-Law, Mrs. Eunice L Heller, with love.

After you have counted number ten
Do not forget to count us in
Because we are joining in to say
We wish you a very HAPPY BIRTHDAY!

Like honeysuckle on the vine
You are just as sweet
And, Oh, so kind.

You are always there when we are sad
And remind us when we are acting bad.
GRANDMOTHER, we all want you to know
You are so dear, and WE LOVE YOU SO!

With love, your Grandchildren and Great-Grandchildren.

Dawn M Farmer
POLLUTION

As I walk along the sand,
And look across this land
I watch the silent footprints
running up and down.
I look at a little silent town.
I look across the water,
which resembles a page,
I look at the water and it fills me with rage.
I look at this polluted land,
polluted by you and me
Why do we pollute this land, why do we?

Dorothy D Lund
FAREWELL

To my son,
whom I shall never forget.

When the door on the right
is beginning to close—
Another is opening
as everyone knows.
If only my puzzled eyes could see
there is something ahead
That is better for me.

If every end is a new beginning
only God knows that I am winning.

So when the door
that is on the right
Is completely closed
and I'm out of sight
Let there be no tears for me.
What I am getting is not what you see.

For at last, instead of just wishin'
Dennis Lund has finally gone fishin'.

Tho difficult the transition may seem to be
it's never right for you or me
To try to determine the route it takes
even tho one's heart it breaks.

Barbara S Weppener
HEART BEAT

Acclaiming the rhythm of life
with throbbing, pounding pulse
my beating heart beats on.

Needled arrows pierce nerve and bone
splintering fragmented senses into shards
that fading memory reassembles
into the beauty around me:
perfume of lilacs in early spring
sunrise glazing purple mountaintops
ambrosia melting on fevered tongue
song of meadowlark in clovered pasture
caress of satin sheets on tortured flesh,
shadowed now by curtains of gauze
that bind me in a shroud of pain.

My beating heart beats on
with throbbing, pounding pulse
acclaiming the rhythm of life.

Julia Correa Youmans
THE FALLS

To the City of Spokane, Washington.

Unrestrained mountain of washed aquamarines tumbling down. She falls, crashing onto the abysmal gray, basaltic bottom . . .

And then rises again, twice high, splashing the atmosphere with furious pride in liquid, unlimited refractions of shattered gems.

She carves her path, gashing the earth with a million wild hooves and frothy muzzles, roaring through deep, dark canyons, marking the course of her freedom regained.

Ingrid Olsen
RESTLAND V

For my grandfather and all the things I never said.

I never told you
How much I love you.
I never had the courage to say
How you filled each day
With a love so unselfish
And unchecked.
Your knowledge of love
Beheld my fascination;
That through even the toughest of times,
You stayed strong and honest;
Fighting each battle
Until the very end.
Never losing your strength inside
Your soul will live forever.
But among the regrets that haunt me
I have but a few,
These things I never said to you.

Violet E MacDonald
ARISE AND AWAKE

Arise

Rise up—ye Christians; take your stand,
The devil is riding o'er this dear land,
Rise up—Rise up, and clap your hands,
For Jesus is coming—coming to this land.

II
Awake

Awake, ye Christians, open your eyes,
Don't believe the devil's evil cries,
He's riding o'er this dear land,
God forbid that he should land—
There's trouble, strife and war at hand
Tell Jesus, He'll revive this land.

Debra A Kemp
THE CURTAIN MUST FALL

To Rebecca,
who loved so many
despite her own sorrows.

We all die a little each day
Hearts heavy, life so sad.

Treating one another
as though neither one exists
inside.

The games we play.
The competition
a challenge.

Who will win
this one?
We play hide and seek with
our
emotions
Okay, you have hurt me
so I will find a place
where you can never find me.

On and on
like an endless ocean
no land in sight
only more treacherous waves
of strength
to flood my mind, my heart,
my soul.

My soul.
Where has it been?
Buried beneath
a sea of hurt
not only my
own.
So young

at some time long ago
dreams
shared.

Our paths
are not the same.
We still play the game
going farther still will
we ever
meet again?

Jane Ellen Peterson
SNOWY AFTERNOONS
As winter winds bring icy temps
And snow begins to fall,
I remember all the times
You and I built snowmen.

The days of snowball fights are long forgotten
And sledding is in the past,
But I still remember our afternoons
Playing in the snow.

Audre and Frank C Tribbe

Frank C Tribbe
TO MY DARLING AUDRE
I hope you don't ask if I love you;
Some days I don't show it, I know.
I often am pleased, but don't tell you;
There is much that you do for me, though.

I hope you don't ask if I love you;
When you go it alone, and do well—
Though I'm secretly proud and all glowing,
I rarely to others will tell.

I hope you don't ask if I love you,
When I'm thinking, preoccupied, blue—
When I'm sharp and unthinking or careless—
And notice too late what I do.

I hope you don't ask if I love you—
Though I'm bursting with love,
I just tease.
So I hope you can feel it or see it,
For if you must ask, then I've failed.

Ronald G Adams
GOOD MORNING
The morning dew so soft and clean
Like velvet laid on earthly green
The light that dances through the mist
Changes the colors with its kiss
And shoos away the clinging dark
Which makes the morning gladly start
The sounds of night give way to song
To all of us their tunes belong
The morning is a wondrous thing
Newer values it will bring
Yesterday has gone before
Except for memories, nothing more
Pull the morning close to you
Let it fill you through
And through
It is a challenge you should take and make of it what you will make
Embrace the morning with all your might
Into your life will flow new light
That makes you glad to see the dawn
As you rush to put it on

Tammy Lynn Cronk
LOST SOULS
Life can be a very beautiful place.
It can be full of laugh, love and dreams.
It's up to yourself to make it that way.
But sometimes happiness is afar, so it seems.
And some people are too weak and give up.
They feel like it's an empty place and nobody is there.
So they decide the drastic, to end it all.
And there goes all the hope lying everywhere.
So if life starts to bring you down,
And you start to feel sad and lonely,
Try to bring in your mind the things that are special.
Memories, family and happy things only.

Andrea Doetzel
CHRISTMAS COUNTDOWN
Gone is the turkey and Thanksgiving hen,
We are upon the holiday season again.
Long shopping lists and name exchanges
for gifts of all types and varied price ranges.
As the stores get crowded and the lines start to form,
you stop thinking exotic and purchase the norm.
Can you get the color and size that you need?
If not, then it's back to the paper to read.
Try something else for the person in mind . . .
after waiting for that, a raincheck you'll find.
Meantime the holiday parties begin,
gone is your last chance this year to be thin.
You are up until midnight addressing the cards,
while dad's tangled in light cords in the front yard.
Start baking your cookies and then try to hide some,
this is really a challenge 'cause everyone smells 'em.
Alas, some free time and off shopping you go,
so the weatherman says it is now time to snow.
Christmas concerts and school plays to attend.
There are out of town boxes you now need to send.
Time flies by as the big day is near,
carolers at your front door soon appear.
Up goes the tree with lights all around,
out come the chocolates and fruitcakes by the pound.
Finally there is time to sit down and relax, (then you hear . . .)
"Mom, we're out of Scotch tape and we need some more wrap."
Then back to your chair with a big glass of sherry,
Christmas is here, so drink and be merry!

Gretchen Haapanen
STARS

To Art Aslesen, who encouraged me to submit these poems.

The stars are a remote fraternity spending an icy clarity on the summer night. They have a purpose of their own: Arcturis, Lord of snow; the Seven Sisters in their robes of milk-stained white—Orion waiting to make known the edge of morn on the eastern horizon in his aloof gloire. I have talked to them, cried out to the pole star and the Pleiades, but they have never given back reply, neither reproof nor praise. It is enough, for us, that we should see them shine. They do not care for human laugh nor cry, these being fickle, lacking the heaven's distant constancy. Stars have no warmth to grant the chilly breath—they know not, care not, for lovers of the earth and the minute dissensions that rend us one from one. Beneath their frozen benison we stand undone.

Do the stars sing as some have claimed they do? If so, they have nothing to say to the inconsistent creatures that toil below—but that somewhere there exists a brightness that is for the sake of radiance alone: A vast luminance beyond romances that we'd weave of it—light that is steady, beyond shadow, beyond divertissement.

Gretchen Haapanen
ON WINTER
The summer's colors have fallen like idle fruit to the precisions of Winter. She makes no mistakes: all of Summer's superfluities are made grist for Her mill and I am ground under, too, to make a gravity on her bare, harsh stones. I know myself the ache of trees frozen in the wood and how all shows a dissolution toward the bone. I know that what there is left after Summer's excess is not to be counted on.

The sea plunges toward the cove where I had sought, last summer, certain talismans against the snow, sunburnt masks which I could wear, deceits in gold.

But pure, dark winter takes strong precedence over the disguises of the sun when sought to make a tentative hanging-on toward Spring. As winter closes in and in I see how death can be, as well, what keeps the heartbeat going, without the colors and the costumes of the summer's season. Winter compares pretenses and disguise with reason, so that you might see your skeleton, as well, among the trees.

Summer's like a dream: the time of cold is real. I learn to reach within the winter's tomb and feel . . .

Gretchen Haapanen
MONET AND WATERLILIES
Eventually he painted nothing but the waterlilies on his pool at his house at Giverny. He had said he wished he could have been "born blind that I might gain my sight and be able to paint objects without knowing what they were." Now he disappears into his dream of color—nothing but color—the surface of the pool floating with leaves and blossoms, where water, air and light are one with lilies and their sleepy fragrance changing, always changing with his soul that loves this radiant ware; inchoate mass of golds shining on surfaces, falling through to surfaces below—never staying in symmetries as man is used to having things inhere to suit himself. The flowers he paints are free of precedents of logic and systematic ways of seeing things—diving after lily roots, divining other ways of sight, he saw his lilies, simply, as their own reason for being, color and changing fragrance come into its own, beyond its subject, relevant to a dream he had that was not blind. In this last legacy of waterlilies drifting, becoming with them all that would drift free, he left his life—summoned into pools of petals reflecting visionary light, bright as blossoms glowing on delicate, hidden stems; articulate as the radiance that summoned him to them . . .

Gretchen Haapanen
I HEAR A BLACKBIRD
In twilight from the field across the road I hear him call again. It is cold but the white moon shall rise from the green snow of the far mountain. And the flower of dusk shall fold all elements of time and change away with the passing day. The snow weight of the word of the wind shall fade: wait but a moment yet—the blackbird spake. His dark syllables fall like rain. I will take his place by some magic that the winter gives to its own pained denizens—his body for my own: mine for his sleek blackness. And I will fly through his space, knowing the beauty, relentless, ravaging, of time in flight. Before I come home again I will fly even to the mountain that in the distance does arise—and I shall sing! My throat from black feathers shall encompass all pain and all surmise, all plan and all disguise. And the long moon that passes in white and tawny shades, shall, before I fly home once more, fill my eyes with strange rewards: of crisp snow, parian, bright . . . and of the denser, crooked ice . . .

Teresa M Smith
THE CANDLE

For my husband, Gary, and our forbidden courtship.

When I met you I was stifled by the hypnotic powers of our connection.
The remnants of my romantic intuitions began to reflect upon me as I lit the candle.
I began to see a concentrated light—a light which surrounds the distance between you and I.
It is a bright powerful light

it is not blinding
it is not deceiving
it is not suspicious
It is a starving light
it craves
it longs
it suffers
Let not the candle be the hourglass of time or solitaire.
Let not others betray your ideals
Never relinquish—gaze through the flame
For it is a sensuous light which
believes in destiny—
A new beginning of another life.

I shall shiver tonite at the very thought of forever loving you
I shall see your eyes as the tip of the flame becomes
a harsh reality
for I lit the candle
the light still shines
and the wax never
burns.

Rabia Onur

Rabia Onur
THE STREAM
The stream is dappled
By yellow leaves
As they fall in the fall
By four or more
Vaulting dancing
To the sweet melody
Of the warbling waters
As they go by
Humbly in silence

Silence
Mother of emptiness
And lonesomeness
I wish those leaves
Stayed green
Forever green
Light green
Dark green
Whatever green
I wish they stayed green
By the stream
To stave off
My dream

Rabia Onur
SUNNY SMILES
I collect sunny smiles
That's my angle
I ramble
I scramble
Make my way
Through miles
And miles
In magic I dabble
Many I handle

I drowse I browse
I dawdle I idle
I traipse on the hunt
For sunny smiles
I walk miles
Some day
Some way
I may be going your way
I may
For sunny smiles
I walk miles
And miles

Keep smiling

Rabia Onur
A KINGDOM
My heart is a Kingdom
'cause my heart has a King
I walk the skies
I catch the stars
I scoop the Sun
And on and on

The world around I survey
Messages of peace I convey
This land of flowers
With scent of early hours
Violets and daffodils
Daisies or chamomiles
This oak tree this pine
All these are mine
Summer winter or spring
Harmonious melodies they bring
I hop I swing
I dance I sing
For my heart is a kingdom
And my heart has a King
Has a King.

Jayne Powell
FOREVERMORE

To my loving Michael.

We talk of plans,
neighborhood walks,
picnics and such,
endless days together.

Peaceful moments,
warm conversation,
loving touches,
endless nights with each other.

I want you dear
by my side
morning, noon, and night;

To smile with me,
cry with me
to make each day bright.

You are my one and only love
The one I've waited for
I love you now and will
FOREVERMORE.

Anita Mumford
THE LEAF
I am like a leaf
That sways sluggishly in the breeze
Sinks slowly—totally at ease
Is caught by a sudden updraft
Defeats the viscous laziness and fights
Soars up to immeasurable heights
Unexpected it drops again
Incessantly, constantly—like a falling plane
In a muddy puddle it lands
Rests, and waits for its end.

Sharon E Williams
SAYING GOOD-BYE

This poem is dedicated to my dad in memory on May 28, 1987.

It's one thing just saying good-bye
It's another thing meaning when you say good-bye
As bad as I hate I wish I could say good-bye but didn't mean it
This is true, I'm saying good-bye

I see the hurt in your eyes
I see the pain in your heart
I see you also hate to say good-bye
This is true, you are saying good-bye, too.

We are saying good-bye to each other
We both are hoping with all our might neither one of us really means to say good-bye
All we both hear is we both saying good-bye to each other
Saying good-bye brought tears in our eyes

Is this true, we saying good-bye?
Is this true, this good-bye is final?
This is true, I'm saying good-bye
My father passed away May 28, 1987.

Sharon E Williams
I SAVED THE LAST HUG FOR YOU
Through all the arguments we had
Through all the experiences we share
Through all the tension of life, we talked about it
Through all the tears that fall

It brought unhappiness and hatred between us
It brought confused minds
It brought us to know each other more
It brought us together as one

Through all the smiles and tears
A lot of people take a mom for granted
All the hell we've been through
And still get together with laughter and tears

For all those people that have a mom
I'm writing this poem for you
Don't take your mom for granted
Remember all the things ya went through

Even when I said you are dead
I would like it very much that we share our lives together before it is too late and you are no longer with me or Andy
Through all the hugs I give to the people I will love in the future
I'm saving the last hug for you tight in my heart

Sharon E Williams
THANK GOD, I STILL HAVE MY LIFE
I still have my life
My life is full of sorrows
My life is full of heartbreaks
Thank God, I still have my life

I finished high school
My dad expired on my graduation day
I finished trade school
My boyfriend was out of my life soon after my trade school graduation

I had 2 pet friends
Bushki and Binaca were their names
Bushki gave me his last paw shake
Binaca gave me her last tender affection

I also have a mom and a brother
They drifted away from me
when that happened
I lost my self-esteem, self-pride, and self-image

I had a job that contained being robbed was part of the work
My mom lost her car due to crime and we watch in fear
My life still remains in what all that its known tears and sorrow every day
Thank God, I still have my life

Pamela Buller Ehardt
HE'LL CARE FOR YOU AND ME
Sheltered in His loving arms
I leave my burdens there . . .
For in my sorrows I do know
That He does really care.

He shelters me from raging storms
Within my tempestuous strife . . .
Until the darkest hour expends
From all the struggles of life.

So should you need a quiet place
Of refuge from the storm . . .

Just seek the loving Savior's arms
He'll keep you safe and warm.

He'll never leave you all alone
To face the rampant sea . . .
Because He promised us his love
He'll care for you and me.

Mara Lee Uldall
POINT OF VIEW
St. Peter held a conference among the chosen few.
"The problem is the earth" he said,
"The question—what to do?
That tilted planet, spinning fast
Has little on it left to last.
Its mountains, valleys, lakes and seas
Diminish with the centuries.
Should we reshape the planet?
From mortal clay remold?
Create another pattern? That model never sold.
Perhaps we should forget it
Let it go its way—alone,
For his unending bumbling let man himself atone."

God looked down upon His beauty
And musing, said aloud, "How can I forget it—
For who can sculpt a cloud? Who can help a babe be born, or paint a fresh midsummer morn?
Who can light the evening sky—
save I?"

Mara Lee Uldall
MOVING DAY
I have surrendered the keys.

There is nothing left for me to do
But wait
In the deepening gloom
Where shadows play across the room.

I feel the cold
Creeping through cracks
I never knew were there
When everywhere
The sounds of children
Warmed the air.

My life is now within
That packing crate—

I wait.

Jewel Heintjes

Jewel Heintjes
MY DADDY WENT AWAY

I love you, Daddy—
Forever and always,
Your daughter, Jewel.

Two years ago today, my dear sweet Daddy went away.
I've tried and I've tried to write this poem for you, but when I try, the tears I cannot hide, they come so fast they wash the words away. Oh Daddy why couldn't you have stayed?

They say that time heals all wounds, but my heart is like an open sore, Daddy every day I miss you more and more.

There were so many things I wanted for Mother and you, so many things I didn't get to do.

Daddy oh Daddy what will I do If my Mother goes away too?

The world outside goes on by, They can't see the hurt I feel inside. I look the same, I guess I act the same too, the only ones that know It's not the same, Daddy are me and you.

Jewel Heintjes
THIS MAN
He walks through the casino with an elegant flair,
My heart melts as I watch him standing there!
This is his kingdom, his palace, his throng, and he makes sure nothing goes wrong.
He works both night and day. I think maybe he likes it that way, because when it comes to his job he really cares,
This man who walks through the casino with an elegant flair.
As I think back now to the first time I saw him, I could not help but stare,
The best looking man I had ever seen with his curly red hair.
I wonder if he will ever notice me, or even care that I'm there.
This man who walks through the casino with such an elegant flair.
He is like a king among men; so quiet and strong, but I need someone to hold me when I'm all alone. So when I'm gone I hope he will remember me and know I will always care; for, this man who walks through the casino with such an elegant flair.

Mary Crickmer Conley
ABOVE AND BELOW
The birds landed in their usual resting tree
Twittering of the long flight and the storm at sea
Of the quietness and the beauty all around
The wind is soft and there is no sound.

Below the men lay on the Battlefield
The birds had flown over like a giant shield
The guns were silent as dying men watched them fly along
And all heard the peaceful glory of their song.

Charles M Langford
SINGING SOFTLY OF SPRING
Sibilant sounds surmount with Spring
When wild winds whistle while whirling
Through trembling trees, taut-drawn and tall,
Heaving hastily with the haul,
Until the undulating urge
Dies down to a duteous dirge.

Then all about, around, above,
Docile and downy as the dove,
Spring softly sings, succulently,
To tempt us to tranquility.
In fields it flings the flowers far
And all-adorned the arbors are.
On rock reclines the rambling rose.
In pastures the peonies pose.
Two throats with trills their tones trial through
Toward heaven's hale and hearty hue.

At times a tumultuous thing,
Sing now the soft, sweet songs of Spring.

Francis X Nulty
ON FIRST HEARING THAT MY DAUGHTER IS WITH CHILD
The morning speaks in many voices now:
The waters sing renewal sweet and green,
The light strikes up the birds on every bough,
And winds hymn softly to the shining scene.
O Morning is of all our time the best!
A time of newborn strength and fresh desire,
When all the nights of past are put to rest,
A time when like the sun we may aspire
To arch the sky with golden light and form;
When all we dream seems possible to us;
When love equates infinity with norm,
And plans all strike the note of fabulous.
Our love is never brighter or so new
As when we pledge the future will ensue.

Terri Bouche
ONE LITTLE GIRL

For Tony—my fairy tale come true.

Soon one day, together we'll stand
In the presence of God in his holy land
and one by one He will call our names
and there we will stand and have to explain
the worth of our lives and how much we've done
for the glory of God and his Holy Son

And sooner or later your name we will hear
and you'll slowly walk forward with a small tinge of fear
with judgment at hand you will stand before him
praying your good deeds outweigh the sin

And one little girl, lost in the crowd
will speak right up and cry out loud
"This man did his job, his debt is paid.
He showed me Jesus and my soul he saved."

Then eyes will turn and there I'll stand
and then I'll walk right up and take your hand
I'll no longer fear and I'll no longer cry
But in your behalf I will testify
that here is one man with whom God should be pleased
'cause it is from him that I learned to believe.

Carol Bates Cummings
TREASURES
I see the sky above my head
I feel the ground beneath my feet
I hear the trees slowly swaying, with the
whistling wind . . .
I taste the bubbling brook, that trickles down the
rocky path . . .
I touch the soft white clouds, that go rolling
silently by . . .
The earth has many treasures to which you can
behold . . .
It makes my life worth living, always forever giving.

Carol Bates Cummings
A TRIBUTE TO MOTHER
Day of sunshine, loving and caring . . .
Day of all hearts giving and sharing . . .
Flowers in bloom—the beauty of spring.
She in her gown all satin & lace—hair adorned in flowers.
The face of an angel—the beauty of a woman . . .
He in his finest—all handsome and smiles.
A nervous laugh; a yearnful look . . .
Today is the first day of your new life together—the love that is yours will flourish and grow fonder—your hearts will not wander . . .
Let your love as endless prove; pure as gold forever.
May the love you share grow deeper day by day . . . so may your hearts harvest joy from the debts of your love . . .
May all your tomorrows be beautiful.
May everything that makes life worthwhile—be yours today and always . . .
Two hearts, two rings, one love.
First you are two 'til a whisper "I do" then you are one . . . .

Gina M Shortt
MIRACLES
Try to catch a hummingbird
And hold it in your hands;
And feel its wee, small, tiny wings
Sent from far-off lands.

Feel the flutter of the feathers
As they brush against your palm;
How the stroke of each soft feather
Makes you anything but calm.

Such a small and simple happening
Is a rare thing to achieve,
But if a thing like that could happen,
In miracles you'd believe!

Brenda Butts
THAT MAN

I dedicate my poem to my 4 children and my husband, Robert.

That Man:
He is so tall and strong; he keeps me holding on. He's my fresh air, he always lets me know, he will always be there. He is my sunshine, and on June the 2nd, 1990, he will be all mine. That man, I love to touch, that man, I love so much.
That Man, My Man.

Tracey Clark
THOUGHTS OF YOU

Thanks to everyone who believed in me. A very special thanks to John O. and David S.

Sitting in a bar room,
thinking thoughts of you,
wondering what you're doing,
wanting to be there too.
If I told you that I loved you,
would you turn and walk away,
if I told you that I needed you,
would you hold my hand and say,
"I would stay with you if only I could,
but I only love you as a friend,
I am also very afraid,
if we did our friendship just might end."
We're so close together,
but yet so far apart,
I want to grab and hold you,
so very close to my heart.
I guess it's just something,
that won't ever be,
But I can always sit and think,
about the possibility of you and me.

Joyce Davis
TO THE ONE I LOVE

To Raymond, my husband.

On this very special day,
There is something,
My love,
I want to say.

Your arms are,
For a sweet caress,
Your shoulders,
For my head to rest.

Your lips,
For kind words to repeat,
Also,
For my lips to meet.

Your eyes,
For me to see the care,
Your life,
For me always to share.

Your ears,
To listen to,
My troubles and strife,
To help me bear,
My burdens in life.

There's something,
My Love,
I want to give,
My love for you,
As long as I live.

Georgia D Stones
A DYING MAN'S ADVICE TO HIS BROTHER

To "P.J." with much love and thanks!

You think being wild is
oh so cool—
I got news for you, mister—
you're just a young fool!

Smokin' all that pot—
& screwin' around;
all that's gonna bring you down.

Why do you think I'm lyin' here—
wasting in this bed?
It's because young fool—
I didn't use my head.

This place is called a "hospice"—
& do you know why;
because people come here to die.

I'm your brother—
& I've made mistakes;
& you're gonna listen to me—
however long it takes!

Mama can't help you—
daddy won't try;
so at least, listen to me—
before I die.

Those "yard dogs" that you cling to—
they don't give a damn about you!

All they think about is—
their next fix;
or where they can get their sordid kicks.

They share their works—
& don't care with who;
you trying to lay here beside me too?

In case mama & daddy didn't tell you—
well, I'll spell it out in spades;
I'm layin' here dyin' from a disease
called AIDS.

I've had it for months—
& I'm on my last legs;
but if I can help it—
you won't be one of society's dregs.

You got a bright mind—
please don't throw it away;
my life's almost over—
for once, do things my way.

I could die happy—
if you get away from that crowd;
think of somebody other than yourself—
make mama & daddy proud.

Stop lying to yourself—
you know you're going nowhere fast;
how long do you think it's gonna last?

Well, I've had my say—
& I did the best I could;
now it's up to you—
whether you do bad or good.

I don't have much time, little brother—
I think it's time for me to go;
I've reaped all that I've sown—
you've still got yours to sew.

Nicole L Gilvey
CAT AFTER PRAY

My claws grind at my hairless paws,
as the door becomes shreds at my
attempts to escape this.
A light of outside shines once it is gone.
The sky becomes white,
while most objects are black.
Everything around me a shade of grey.
No colors, no cares.
My huge mass stretches as I reach for the sky.
Catching an angel from the trees,
as I rip it to nothing,
with my teeth of stone.
I sneak away knowing I can't be seen,
except for my luminous eyes.
As they see the door,
I leap just in time,
to let my soul back in
just before the morning.

Lauriel L Fouquette
ALWAYS WITH YOU

As the cold winter snows begin to fall,
I always will be with you.
When the loneliness seems to be unbearable,
I will comfort you in the emptiness of time,
Think of me.
When things go wrong and life itself
is too hard to take,
I will come to you on the white wings
of a dream,
Though you may forget me from time to time,
I am always with you.
Think of me.
You cannot touch me with your hand,
But I hold you in my heart and guide your soul
With an unconditional love.
Oh why do you not understand?
I am never out of your reach,
I am forever and always just a thought away.
In times of trouble,
In times of peace,
I am always with you.
Think of me.

Mildred E Griffith
TIME OUT

To: daughter, Margo – sons, Curtis, Pat and Joe – sister, Nila – niece, Carol – and husband, Victor.

Time for love in the world, not hate
Time for love of a friend or mate
Time for peace on earth, no war
Time for our prayers to reach afar

Time to enjoy the flowers and trees
Time to watch the butterflies and bees
Time to embrace the wind so cool
Time to listen to the cows moo moo

Time to thank God and pray a lot
Time to appreciate what we have got
Time to look at ourselves and wonder
Time to do good and not blunder

Time to count the blessings we have all had
Time to think about good, not bad
Time to feel the goodness of it all
Time to stand up proud and tall.

Norman Wixon Jr
JESUS

Oh sweet Jesus if I could see your face.
And in my soul receive your mercy
and your grace.

In the Eucharist I take your Body.
In the Wine I take your precious Blood.
Into my heart that makes us one.

Oh Sweet Jesus when I die please
take me to heaven up thru the sky
And then I know what it will be
to be in eternity.

I will not worry anymore.
For You on the Cross have opened the Door.
And I shall be with you
forevermore.

Norman Wixon Jr
NATURE

I saw the Eagle fly on majestic wings,
See the raindrops fall on everything,
I see the robin at her nest,
The Raven with its ebony glow,
The trees swaying with the wind flo.

The Elk and Deer make the forest ring,
I heard the timber Wolf howl and sing,
The Chickadee at my window sill,
The hush of night when the wind is still,
Oh how I love to hear the Whippoor-will.

The Trout jumped in the pond,
Beavers at their lodge,
Otters playing in the stream,
Blue Jays watching everything,
The wise old Owl up in the tree,
Bring fond memories back to me,
When GOD loved everything.

Beth A Rist
THE PROMISE

Now, I have always known within
my heart
That, soon, the time would come for
us to part;
For as you grow in your maturity
You, justly, must outgrow all need
for me;
But, (since I think I know you fairly well)
It will be difficult for you to tell
Me that the time has come to say,
"good-bye."

So—for my part—I promise—I will plan
To make this task as easy as I can;
Just do not think that I will ever know
Exactly when will be the time to go;
So it must be for you, alone, to say
That we should part. But—I'll not try to stay;
Instead, I promise to gently say,
"good-bye."

For I would have your memories to be
Of pleasant times you've spent with me;
Not sorrow, nor guilt, nor tearful
parting time;
But lunches and laughter and lobsters
and letters that rhyme;
And—could I—somehow—leave
you with a smile
And believe you found the memories worthwhile,
It <u>might</u> not hurt—<u>so</u> much—to say,
"good-bye."

Thomas E Harris
WHY I LOVE MY DAD

The love in his heart is plain to see
Especially when he is giving it to me
He is great to follow around
Because he travels all over town

I wish to thank him for helping me grow
And sharing his time to help me know
The things in life I need to pursue
Looking at my Dad it is plain to see
Features in him he gave to me
Some are good and some are bad
But he is still my loving Dad
I wish to thank him for giving to me
His unending love to keep me company

Kathleen McFadden
TO THE ONE I LOVE

This is to the one I love,
you are a hand and I'm a glove.
Putting it on slowly in time,
with kindness and gentleness you are reading my mind.

Treating me like a precious gem,
I am a rose and you're its stem.
Planted in the soil and heated by the sun,
now we're growing together as one.

Bright as the sun and as clear as the sea,
This is to the one who is meant for me.

Oliver Hank Vining
OH! FOR A TENDER SPROUT

Dedicated to Roseanne Lopez, the loveliest sprout I've ever known.

On the mountain stands a lonely pine tree. Still standing tall, but oh! so scraggly. At the treeline all grows close and healthy, but storm clouds sit on that lonely tree.

In terrible thunder, darling I am swaying. Sharp lightning takes another piece of me; but I'm standing tall, my roots entwined so deeply; in this mountain of hope that you'll come back to me.

God knows the weather's been so bad dear. Through the years I've become all rough and gnarled. Darling, I don't belong down at the treeline. I'll take my beating reaching for the clouds.

If only a sweet wind would blow a seed to me. A tender sprout, rising at my feet. We could grow strong, roots entwined so closely; and a lonely pine tree never again shall I be.

In terrible thunder, darling, I am swaying. Sharp lightning takes another piece of me. I'm standing tall, my roots entwined so deeply; in this mountain of hope that you'll come back to me.

Joan Opferman-Mayfield
OUR BOY

We have a little boy named Adam
That we watch when he's on the loose
We ourselves have nicknamed him
Our little Beetlejuice

He gets in and out of trouble
All throughout the day
He'll smile and then he'll hit you
Then try to run away.

But oh God how I love him
He means the world to me
And the day will come soon enough
That he will turn to three

He might seem like a bad kid
But if you see him through
You will come to realize
That he's just a terrible two

David Markus
DEATH TAKES ITS TOLL

The unbearable heat wasn't tolerable for the plane engine,
Its new ruins within the dunes of the desert.
As the orange sun set in the yellow hills of sand,
He escaped the rubble.
The lone survivor of the tragedy.
No one to turn to for miles, miles, miles.
Surrounded by millions of grains of sand,
He prayed for an oasis.
Somewhere, sometime . . . soon.
All he got was the image of one.
Water was sand.
Coconuts were rocks.

Hunger struck like a viper strikes its prey.
It had been days since food.
And fatigue began settling in.
Memory fading, Lips chapping, Skin peeling,
Lizards slithering, Vultures hovering.
As much as he tried, he failed.
As much as he searched, he was lost.
No where to go . . . but up.
And after much struggle, he did.

Mary Jordan
PRAYER; I'M SCARED

Oh Lord
I'm afraid
of being alone.
I listen to the pump beat
real late at night

Oh Lord
I'm afraid
of the night
I listen to night sounds
when I turn out the lights

Oh Lord
I'm afraid
of not having enough
I listen to the kids breathing
to make sure they're alright

Oh Lord
I'm afraid
of not having someone
And I listen to myself think
because I'm scared of the night

Neil E Mickelson
COME AND GO

People come and people go,
Actors in the Largest Show:
Play the bit parts, smaller roles—
They disappear when curtains fall.

Fates decide their place in life,
Random numbers by a roll of dice.
Watch the show from the thirteenth row;
People come and people go.

Leave the theatre, but not the stage;
Memories haunt you in a plague.
Open your heart to let the tears flow,
For people come and people go.

Push the boundaries of time and space,
And bring them to that special place
Inside your mind, with stage-lights low,
For people come and people go.

People come and people go,
Actors in the Largest Show;
Play the big parts, the largest roles—
Then reappear when the curtain falls.

Neil E Mickelson
CIRCLE

Emotions transferred to
Hand to
Pen to
Ink to
Energy to
Motion to
Words to
Paper to
Sentences to
Symbols to
Bridges to
Lights to
Eye to
Nerves to
Brain to
Mind to
Emotions.

Cappie Durbin
CLOSETS

I hate closets!
Full of clutter and shoes that smell,
Filled with clothes I bought on sale;
There, at the top, a box on a shelf,
I'm thinking, what could be in it,
I gave to myself?
Oh, how selfish can one be,
Lord, can this be a dreaded disease?
Well, clean I must and throw away,
Garments of well lived, long yesterdays;
Now, won't he be pleased, my husband that is,
When he gets home and opens the door
And nothing falls out at his feet, on the floor;
You see, I've been busy, slaving all day,
Cleaning this mess, I packed away;
Well no more, now my closets are free,
Words—half price, on sale, mean nothing to me;
The next time I'm out and in red letters I see,
Today only! Buy one, you get one free;
I'll just pass it up as if not to see,
Remembering my closets back home, cleaned by me.

Cappie Durbin
FOREVER

Dedicated to the past, present and future love of my life.

Forever is a long long time,
But not quite long enough;
To lie beneath the sheets with you,
And love you oh so much!
It's true my lips have trouble saying
Hidden thoughts that my heart holds.
So, with pen in hand
I write down the pleasures of my soul.
Now, when I look into your eyes
I see a bit of fire;
A spark that started long ago,
With a kiss I call desire;
And if by chance you should look back,
You may see a flame;
Which was kindled by your touch,
For me, it was no game.

Ms Teddi R Franklin
HEAVEN

Heaven is like
A paradise
For which our Lord
Did sacrifice
His loving soul
For us to live
To make things great
And that He did
He created the stars
He created the dove
He created people
And things to love
He worked for days
Then took a rest
Deciding that
He'd done his best

Angela B Soto
FANTASY

I constituted a spoon in my mind,
with a man so out of reach.
Majestic I found him to be in the things he's set out to teach.
Little does he know
that my heart longs so
for his tenderness and caress,
so I've captured moments
in bath tubs, swings, and parks
to envision this gest.
While he spoke of procedures and expectations,
I found myself getting revelations.
I've tried but failed to stop this thinking.
It's easier to stop an alcoholic from drinking.
So to reality I'm blind.
I've found happiness
in back of my mind.

Heather N Moreau
MY THOUGHTS

My thoughts are like a seed
From far below to high above
It grows through the times I have spoken
It keeps me alive like a battery keeps a machine
As I grow older my thoughts increase
As I die my thoughts decrease
but right now, my seed is a tree overlooking the other seeds
My thoughts are like a seed.

Bryan Lee Brown
ALL CAPTURED IN A SMILE

My feeling felt for you to understand, my girl, Bryanne.

Make a step, take a chance, what the heck nothing to lose.
Build a boat that won't float, make a deal, take a trip by
the ocean wing tip to tip. Spread your wings and fly.
Afraid of fire, stones that are precious, make no sense.
Like me a lot, no end to tie, most knots can be untied.

Beautiful sunshine, red color wine,
oh delightful to taste,
robust full of haste. Satin so shiny
blinding from afar
damsel in distress. Personalities meet
then clash rescue efforts
being endless. To foresee in one task.
Jokes make cover to polish that
blunder and hide behind your mask.
Could I forget to remind you a cut
bleeds reopened time after time,
rebuild to destroy you.
Turn make believe into a story, a
learning pleasurable event.
Climb a mountain hillside unable to
be form a bond, unite together as one.
Don't need to be hot to burn or leave
a scar. The deeper you dig the more
dirt piles up. Rexcavate a terrain
redesigning one's hula hoop. Make
your own break, you can't run before
you learn to walk. It's possible you
mumble with no words to talk.
Roulette wheel spinning you only
need to cover one spot. Either odds
say gamble, do I have a fresh start.
Even though nothing is certain trying
spin after spin. Growing, knowing
who you are out smarted ten million
times.
Senses bestowed, young to mold, so
kind remembering signs all captured
in a smile.

Danny J Dickerson

THE STATUE

Dedicated to my loving wife Marilyn and my beautiful children, Patricia, Dianna, Robert Allen, Paula, Daniel and Spencer Cole, with love.

"There," on the mountain,
overlooking the valleys below,
Stands a Statue,
made of diamonds and gold.

It was shaped in the form,
of a figure of the cross, a
constant reminder of the son he lost,
a constant reminder, of all good men
gone bad,
a constant reminder,
of what we had.

"The Statue stands Proud,"
with no guilt, with no shame,
it's just too bad we couldn't do
the same.

Instead we choose to destroy,
we've brought destruction
"upon ourself,"
and the poor little children
will inherit what's left.

Larry W Merchant Sr

TO MY WIFE

This poem is dedicated to my wife who is to me a very special gift from God.

Someone just like you was what I
was praying for.
And on that day which you arrived
There was no need to ask for
more.

As I knelt to simply say "Thank
you Lord."
I realized there was nothing could
sever our hollowed cord.

'Cause of you, I have learned the
true meaning of love and giving
It was on that day I first began
living
You brought total happiness and
contentment to my life
And I will forever cherish that
evening you became my wife

Kathleen McGibney

Kathleen McGibney

GOOD-BYE, NORMA JEAN

A lonely child, Norma Jean
never had a life of her own
in and out of foster homes
left by her mother who was ill
taken away, not by her own will
leaving others' homes to
become a wife
making her dreams true to life
Her sudden death, mysterious
to us
blamed on an overdose
covering up for the truth of
those
unable to be revealed
Hoping for people to forget
about the girl who
began her career as a starlet
through her innocence it portrayed
the goddess we know today
leaving behind her memories
fighting so hard, but in the end
she lost
her life, because of those who
said they cared but their
reputations they had to spare
There are many things that are
left for us not to know
about the death of Marilyn Monroe.

Sheree M Riggs

CRIMSON BEAUTY
(Nymph Beauty)

Almond shaped tiger eyes
Wild land under the skies
Blue dust of the north star
Sat alone among the bizarre
Wisteria blue ice is broken
Enduring passion has spoken
Heart of gold in the white snow
Dainty castle of beauty glow
Nostalgic charm of the weather
Attractive man in old leather
The queen in antique lace
Charming personality in a polish face
Bed of roses holding a sleepy voice
Flowers of her choice
Wavy locks covered with winter rain
A night's dream remains

Elizabeth Egerman

WHERE IS GOD?

Children often ask questions, not
easy to answer
"Where is God?" Have you been
asked "that one," for example?
Were you at a loss? Did you ponder
the question?
Does HE live in Heaven, in church or
a temple?

I decided to do extensive research.
I looked in the temple, I looked in the
church
I looked at some chicks and a mother
hen
I looked at my neighbors, both
women and men.

I decided God is not confined to one
place
HE belongs not to any one people or
race.
If you look very hard, you can see
God everywhere
HE's in the sunshine, the rain, in the
wind in the air.

HE's in the murmuring brook, in the
roar of the sea,
HE's in each flower and shrub, in the
leaf of each tree.
You find God in temples and
churches, that is only a part
HE LIVES IN A SHRINE IN YOUR
VERY OWN HEART

HE lives way up high, in the
shimmering sky,
And down low, in each blade of
emerald green sod
Wherever there's life and beauty,
hope and compassion,
Wherever there's L O V E . . . there
lives God . . . !

Elizabeth Egerman

BROTHERHOOD

From north and south, from east and
west,
Let's all try to do our best
To make this world a better place,
For every color, creed and race.
To work and worship, make wars
cease,
Live in brotherhood and peace.

Our skins and our accents are
different,
But our blood is the same.
If you don't agree, it's really a
shame.
Regardless of accent, religion or
name
When hurt, we all suffer much
anguish and pain.

One God up in heaven, there is no
other.
Share God's wondrous world and His
gifts with each other.
So, be your skin yellow, brown, red,
black or white,
Let's all live as brothers and
nevermore fight.

rob drew

1 SONNET ARCANE

For Dorothy F. Burr: Long live the spirit of 'Nan'!

Need to see you in your idiolect,
whilst I am still an ego and not a one;
'fore void's foison can cleanse my
intellect,
and compose your visage as I have
done.
Through gardens giverny shall I see
thee,
attending thy wedding as Maya's
bride;
or invert my sense and leave extant
be,
eluding Maya's pride, but thee to
chide.
Shall I choose to mind your fractal
beauty,
mortally bound, or rime the absolute,
flying 'round satori. You and glory
sound in me, herald afflatus acute.
Two ends have I to my mortality;
you to become and lonely ubiquity.

rob drew

2 SONNET ARCANE

Fair Quietus why doth thou brood in
me?
thin elysian face querulous moods
quench.
Why care if I rive atomically,
since you like us are of illusion's
blench.
Hinayanist eradicates maya
and nuclear cataclysms purge
quiddity.
Yuga's coda : : real : fata morgana;
annihilate trey for obliquity.
Weltschmerz . . . how like an
adolescent's brume.
Whiles Quietus wheedles—whence? . . .
omniscience;
Suicide lurks wherein petards work
doom,
to jilt rich quietus in each conscience.
Nuclear tilts to Suicide prick my
glee;
oh Quietus we love . . . but may not
see?

Tolbert L Slane

FIREWORKS IN THE SKY

What a glorious and wonderful
celebration;
On this day—the birth of our nation,
'Tis a time for fireworks in the night
sky,
But keep in mind, those that had to
die.

We celebrate our freedoms, which
will never fall;
With parties and dancing, everyone
having a ball,
With laughing and joking all around,
But never thinking of those in the
ground.

Remember those who fought the
wars;
And those who died on foreign
shores,
For our flag, so full of grace,
May she e'er fly over our place.

On this, our day of celebration;
For the birth of our great nation,
Keep in mind those who had to die,
For your celebration in the sky.

Remember too—those who heeded
freedom's cry;
Remember them, as you look to the
sky,
Them—that chose to die,
For your fireworks in the sky.

D L Gallion

A SPOT IN TIME

This poem is dedicated to Leo, my bestest friend, who has shown me how to open new doors.

As our creator, he stands humble yet
tall,
Always knowing the great and the
small.
When you start out as just a tot,
And get confused, 'cause you don't
know a lot,
He looks down and says, "Child of
mine,

this is just—a spot in time."

As you continue through your
growing years,
You come upon new hopes and fears.
And soon you mature and fall in love,
But somehow it turns to push and
shove.
He looks down and says, "Child of
mine,
this is just—a spot in time."

Before you know it, your children
have grown,
And now have families of their own.
For their new families take up all
their day,
And you somehow get pushed out of
their way.
He looks down and says, "Child of
mine,
this is just—a spot in time."

As the years pass by and you grow
weak,
And your old body seems to moan
and creak,
You're not discouraged 'cause you're
old and frail,
For you look up and see that golden
trail.
And he looks down and says, "Child
of mine,
this is your final spot in time."

Bob Hartwig
DEATH'S POWERS
I dream of death,
A person's last breath.
Death in the day, death in the night,
The soul entering a tunnel of light.
The body lay without a sound,
Later to be buried in the ground.
After years the body it lay,
The bugs and insects contribute to
decay.
After a decade the grass grows near,
From all around come animals and
deer.
And from the middle of the grave
pops up a flower,
The body's spirit in the ground has
Mother Nature's power.
And when the animals they return,
The flower's seed they learn,
Land on the ground and spread,
Creating and becoming a lovely rose
bed.
Covering that person's deep grave,
How amazingly valiant, he must be
brave,
To face death and its powers.

Jack Graham
CRAZY
This is dedicated to my Family and all my Friends at Wade Thomas School.

Crazy is a lazy word,
That makes other words sound
different,
When crazy is a compound word,
You get dazy when you look at it.
Crazy is a word that should have
never been,
For he or she who made the word,
Must have been crazy.

Billie June Sturm Stimpert
ROSE PETALS
I wish to dedicate this poem to my Mother, Pauline Burnside Latimer, who was my inspiration.

A box of old rose petals,
Curled and dried with age
Found within my attic
Thoughts of yesterdays.

'Twas a deep scarlet bush
Standing close by the path,
Leading out past the orchard
Where we often played and laughed.

I can see Mother yet,
With loving touch and sigh
Carefully choosing roses,
Very special ones to dry.

Each petal felt of velvet
Sweet fragrance filled the air,
Perfume that lingers on
Though I'm no longer there.

This box of old rose petals,
Though many years have gone
Takes me on a journey back
To my old home and Mom.

Carol Koehler Hebert
THE ONE I REMEMBER
This poem is dedicated to the memory of my sister Annette Roberts and to every Christian pastor's wife I have ever known.

Hard as a rock but soft as rain
A smile softened by her pain
Eyes that spoke of trust and love
With faith that radiated from above
A heart that broke with the sorrow of
others
A sense that some things—
Just need to be done
A strength and comfort to those
around
Encouraging, lifting those on the
ground
A servant yes but princess always
A Godly wife to the end of her days.

Heather L Biggers
WHIRL OF ECSTASY
Soft-spoken, almost whispered
of an event that should be
shouted and shared with
everyone.

An event that brings tears
of sorrow to some or tears
of relief to others

To the two responsible, it brings
remorse and heavy laden.

"They're only babies themselves,"
I could hear them say.

An event so tragic and so
unwanted by two young
people only to end in a
whirl of madness that
started with a whirl of
ecstasy

Heather L Biggers
FLAMES A' BURNING
They enter the dark like a whirl
of mad dancers who quickly
hear the beat of a slower tune.
Embracing and gasping at the
tangible dark, showing their
heat with an illumined glow.
Whisking to and fro, jumping and
whirling, the dancers became
a togetherness, all joined
together in a tight group.
One or two fall from the group
and slowly die out, unable to
grasp the music, till more
scatter, and are too deaf to the
beat, until all that remains is a
pile of cinders and ashes on
the cold ground.

Jennifer Steese
TIGER
Hear him.
His smooth form
glides among the jungle trees.
His stride is soundless.
His spring is full of lean muscle.
In night
his green-yellow eyes shine like stars.
He covers land
like water covers the sea.
He goes through the jungle
as if he has wings.
As if time stopped
he will stand there like a statue.

Christina Senn
THE DAY SEEMED CHEERFUL
The day seemed cheerful and happy,
But days are always deceiving.
When you wake up, you look outside,
What do you see?
A clear blue sky,
That twinkles in your eye.
Should I face the day?,
Or should I look away?
A question we probably all ask,
But in reply we say, "to life it is our
task."

Today the ocean, blue as a sapphire,
Teases, but never pleases.
Does life always disapprove?
Disapprove of me and you?

Even with life's sorrows,
There is one thing of use it let me
borrow,
Your love.
I hope life never takes you back,
For your love I would always lack.

So to life I have one thought,
"Thank you for what you have
brought."

Benedick Acord
MEMORIES AND DREAMS
To Marielle Williams, my special Love.

Memories keep lingering on my mind
Thinking and wishing you were all
mine
The day I spent my time with you
alone
Makes me feel like loving you for
long.

I see the life burning deep inside you
And a spark of love that's beginning
to show
Your pretty smile and your sweet
innocence
Will surely fill one's life full of
essence.

You are like a flower sown in the
summer
Showered with care and warmth in
the winter
I'll stay with you even until the
spring
So I can play and hear the jolly
robins sing.

I feel that you're so near but yet so
far
Compared to the sea and clouds as
they are
As long as we're together we shall
not part
Until we meet in the middle heart to
heart.

Oh come on my dear, do not shed
your tears
It is just but a dream that will
disappear
But if it is meant to be, it will truly be
This dream and memories will come
to be.

Jeffrey L Williamson
RISING SON
This poem is dedicated to my loving wife and family Wanda, Chad and Courtney.

He came here to this earth
And from the moment of his birth
People knew the special meaning of
his life
He came to end our fears, our sorrow
and our tears
To show us love and put an end to
strife.

A new day has begun, We must face
the Rising Son
And live our lives in peace and
harmony
For even now he's here, His presence
always near
His perfect love has always been the
key.

And if you see the light, everything
will be alright
and a new day will dawn for you and
me.
And if you cease the wrath and
follow in his path
You'll have eternal life just wait and
see.

For a new day has begun, We must
face the Rising Son
And live our lives in peace and
harmony
And even now he's here, His
presence always near
His perfect love has always been the
key.

Betty Peirson
LOOKING AHEAD
I dedicate this poem to my dear mother Georgina Monroe, from her daughter Betty.

Thinking of just tomorrows
Because we only have yesterday
Life too short to sorrow anymore

When we think of others
Good deeds that we can do.
Loving and the caring
Is all that we should do.

Put our hearts together
Be at peace within ourselves
That's the way it's going to be
Now and forever

Living life the fullest
Today & everyday
I'll be a better person
That's all I want to say.

Patricia Mayo

Patricia Mayo
AZUL ISLAND
On the outside, a mere sandspit
Barely any grass for miles
But the interior, oh, the interior
Is a magnificent place.

Black, snakelike tunnels
Through the yellow walls
Open up to a bluegreen valley
Formed by golden cliffs.

A wild stallion
Flaming chestnut
Leads a band of horses
A bottle canyon
Holds a foal
Rejected at birth.

A sea entrance opens
To let the ships come in.
These vessels carry men
Who must conquer this land
And its fiery red king.

Lela Roloson
OUR YESTERDAYS
Where did our yesterdays disappear?
We want to know.
Never to return, the old days, we used to enjoy so.
That hay ride, as our hearts danced with joy.
Under a silver moon with your favorite boy.
We sang love songs in that happy old way.
Where did they fade away? Our yesterdays.

We walked through lanes where the roses bloomed,
Though, we knew not, our country so very soon
Would be at war. So only a kiss under the pines
To tell me to wait. It all seemed just fine.
Soon this lad—so tall, so nice—went away,
Never to return. But that was yesterday.

We meet. We pass; like sailing ships at night.
We find other friends that fill our lives with delight.
Swiftly pass the years. We are growing old.
Like a faded flower; hair is silver, not gold.
Often times, too weary, too tired to even pray.
But one minute in Heaven would be worth all our yesterdays.

Lela Roloson
A SMALL COUNTRY GIRL

I wish to dedicate this poem to a wonderful daughter. Through her, I have found happiness and success. All those who know her, say she is one of the best.

A small country girl I knew so long ago.
She ran about so fast, never one bit too slow.
Doing little errands for folks; always with a smile.
For, to aid someone, she would walk a mile.
She saved her nickels to buy her Mom a gift.
Her only reward was a big hug and a kiss.

A small country girl was happy all the day.
Pictures she could paint in a very beautiful way.
Though other things she did almost as well.
School lessons were easy, but about that, she won't tell.
Using her talents to assist others was her thing.
She was so good and kind. We thought she had wings.

That little country girl lives quite far away.
When she visits me, it is a happy day.
I may miss her now and then, but I'll not weep.
Because I'll soon see her again; that little country girl so sweet.
She always does little things, others don't think to do.
"My little country girl, I will always love you."

Lela Roloson
THAT FUNNY OLD HILL
On my sled, I was coasting down that funny old hill.
It was there, my sled and I, had our big spill.
My sled was surely sliding; but upside down.
I came tumbling too, like a silly old clown.
I felt kinda dizzy, but somehow reached home.
Mom said, "Thank goodness. You got no broken bones."

In Summer, I picked berries on that funny old hill.
If it didn't rain by noon, my pail, I would surely fill.
One day, I saw, peeping around a tree, a black kitty cat.
But that kitty had a white stripe running down its back.
Kitty was eating my blueberries all down the trail.
'Cause in my hurry, I dropped my full berry pail.

I wonder—Do kids still coast down that funny old hill?
Do black cats still eat the berries that they spill?
I've heard it's lonely. Perhaps it's just waiting for me.
But, it has been decided, to let it rest in peace.
I'll fool it, by golly. No more of my silly stuff.
My kid days capers, I think, were quite enough.

Louise Taylor
MY BELOVED

This poem is dedicated to Ethel Hantz, in memory of her beloved Husband, Adam.

'Tis a cold dark dismal day,
  I sit alone beside his bed, I
  pray.
I watch as shadows dance within
  The dim lit room.
My heart tells me the end is near,
  And death will claim him soon.
I feel its presence all around me, Death,
  death is hiding, waiting.
I cry within my heart and say,
  "You cannot take him, go, go
  away."
But I feel the fear squeeze into my very soul.
  This battle with death he
  cannot win, I know.
My body shivers as I look upon his pale
  And pain-filled face.
His eyes speak, "I love you," they seem to say.
  I lean toward him and try to
  lend him
  of my strength.
But I'm weak with fear, and spent.
  I bow to kiss his feverish brow,
  And slowly his eyes close.
I am grieved, in anguish I lift
  My eyes toward Heaven above.
The battle is lost, death has
  Claimed my beloved.

Kenneth Marshall Allan
A BOWL OF CHRYSANTHEMUMS
I was out in the autumn musk and snapped the chrysanthemum stalks.

They are
in a stone bowl
before me now—

Mint white, must color leaf
yellow stain bud
all snarled
breaking out in shaggy feather.

For me
the warm cool day is mine forever.

Mark Helmke
CRISS CROSSING
Criss crossing from day to day
  And from dream to dream,
Our paths part here.

Like glider planes we wander
  until again we land,
To love each other,
  if we can, or simply hold each
  other's hand.

But now again we're on the wing
  And heading for all new flights.
A gust may come and take us away,
  but all in all and just the same,
  we're gone.

Looking over Mississippi nights
  And quiet times in the park,
A little tree that stands alone,
  And we dared sit near
    on needles and cone.

But if again our paths show how,
  I will love you then
    just as I love you now

Mark Helmke
TRAVEL
The railroad track lies miles away
  And the day is loud with people
  speaking.
There isn't a train goes by all day,
  Yet I hear those whistles
  shrieking.

The nights are lonely and no train goes by,
  I'm told they're still for sleep
  and dreaming.
Yet I see cinders red on blackened sky
  And I hear the engines
  steaming.

My heart is warmed by friends I've made
  And those I'll not be knowing—
Yet there isn't a train I wouldn't take
  And that's no matter where
  it's going.

Angela Barnes
SHE IS WITH ME!

We dedicate this poem to Bill Sander. Love you, Jennifer and Angela.

She is with me in the twilight
When the evening shadows fall,
She is with me in the morning
When daybreak comes to call.

She is with me in the noonday
When skies are bright and clear,
She is with me in the darkness
As the storm clouds hover near.

"God give me faith to feel her presence
As I walk from day to day,
Let me never fail to trust her,
She goes with me all the way!"

Sherri L Brault
LISTEN TO THE TREES

With love to the trees.

A few lonely trees
Beyond reach
Lost spirits
A soul reaching
Reaching for help
My fears grow: as their screams
increase louder LOUDER
They want what every human wants
To be loved and respected
Trees searching for help hoping
someone hears
Hoping someone cares
Cares enough to help their screams
Never stopping: each year the
screams get louder
"Please help us be free—
Free of the fear, the fear of death,
help our spirits be free—
Free to love and laugh, help us
please! Please! We need you help!"
Haven't you listened to them or don't
you care?
The trees need us and we need them
HELP US STOP THE PAIN!

Doreen E Ryan
WISDOM
Wisdom is a song in a whisper . . .
Wisdom cometh in the
    morning . . .
Wisdom is a ray of sunshine on
    a cloudy day . . .
Wisdom calleth in the wilderness
    to set the captives free . . .

Wisdom is a raindrop in
a cloud . . .
Wisdom unfolds beauty in a
sunset . . .
Wisdom cares for all creations;
young or old . . .
Wisdom guides where she
provides . . .
Wisdom finds answers to
unsolved problems . . .
Wisdom is knowing the battle has
been won . . .
Wisdom is taking the trials and
tribulations and wraps
them up into experience . . .
Wisdom is the gratitude that is
shown with love and
praises to Him on high . . .
Wisdom is rooted and grounded
with the Father making
them one . . .
Wisdom is knowing to soar above
the storms like the eagle.

Doreen E Ryan

LIKE THE WIND AND THE WILLOW TREE

To Vernon: A wonderful person indeed; may peace and love abound as tears you shed no more.

You and me against the world, you are my rock;
You are my soul and when the road is darkest
and the light begins to cease, you are the only spark that is there for me to see.

When all do forget me, like the dust in the wind, you will be the only one there for me . . .
(Like a for-get-me-not).

You are like a prince in a chariot waiting for his mate but all that you have to do is come to the dance
and wait and like a princess waiting for her beau to show,
so will I be waiting for you.

You are like the Wind and the Willow Tree . . Do not forget me, for it is you and me against the world.

Jeffrey C Olson

LIFETIME TOGETHER

Dedicated to the woman who brought these words to mind, who inspires me daily—Ronda Lyn Gillespie. No one knows what the future holds fo us . . . Perhaps A Lifetime Together.

A lifetime together
To learn and grow
A lifetime together
So let's go slow

A lifetime together
To love and keep
A lifetime together
Our love's so deep

A lifetime together
Of friends and kids
A lifetime together
Of shoulds and dids

A lifetime together
To grow so old
A lifetime together
And fifty is gold

A lifetime together
And now we are gray
A lifetime together
I love you each day

A lifetime together
In heaven above
A lifetime together
On the sea of love

Deborah Estell-Robersone

MIDLIGHT

In the middle of the night
all seems at peace.
No playing, or laughter
and few cars on the streets.
The stars twinkle with joy
and the moon adds more light
with a special warmth, and gentle
love that caresses the night.
Yet all is not quiet, and
everything is not still,
for dreams of love must be fulfilled.
The quiet moves in and inserts a key
and suddenly, the secret desires
and yearnings run free.
Surrounded by hope and
motivated by love
To find, to feel, to experience love.

No time wasted as I rapidly search
through the clouds, over rooftops
and then back to earth.
Slowly the sun begins to rise
and I gently open my eyes
Feeling wonderful, warm and loved
too,
because the mid-night journey
was shared with you.
Yes, 'Dark is the hour'
in the middle of the night,
but with the presence of true love,
there is no darkness—only light.

Deborah Estell-Robersone

COLOR-BLIND

To Mr. B.g.—Just because you are . . . .

He has eyes but can't seem to see
the obvious difference
between him and me.
He has two ears but can't quite hear
the thoughtless comments or
hateful sneers.
I'm sure he has a heart, but he never
seems to feel
a separation of any kind—it's
almost unreal.
Such an intelligent man, but he just
doesn't 'think,'
He follows his feelings, even
if it raises a stink.
He's quite a scholar, yet he does not
know
how unpopular it is to share
what he knows.
He's really kind of strange, almost
makes you feel funny,
To hear him call you 'dear' or
maybe even 'honey.'
What a joy he is—he's truly one of a
kind.
He doesn't see like others
see,
Because you see,
He's Color-Blind

Teresa Varela

BEDTIME

They run and hide, for it is night,
With giggly voices and delight,
Still wanting to be free, they fight.

The three of them attempt to win,
They struggle; questions soon begin,
But after nightly prayers they grin.

Debbie Weaver

MY WALK

As I walk through the woods,
I hear the leaves crackling beneath
my feet,
I feel the wind gently blowing
through the trees,
This is my own little private retreat.
When I feel the pressures of life,
Beginning to take their toll,
I get away to be with my thoughts,
As I take a quiet little stroll.
The animals scurry away,
As I slowly walk by,
And the birds startled with fear,
Take off to the sky.
The beauties of nature are so
peaceful,
It fills my very soul,
It calms and quiets my troubles,
Just to take that little stroll.

Grace A Lasher

LOVE'S JOURNEY

This poem is dedicated to Travis Justus. I'll Love You Always!

A look of love
In a careless glance;
A whisper of truth
In the passing wind.
A slow, steady rhythm
Which starts the dance;
With a slow, sweet melody,
Our love begins.
Three words spoken gently,
Make us whole;
The darkness recedes,
As love takes its toll.
Obstacles that were mountains
Now become hills
Paths that diverged
Are now crossed.
The look of love in your eyes
Gives me chills;
All of my fears are now lost.

Evelyn Heinz

MONDAY MORNING SUNRISE

Today,
I wanted to bring
The sunrise to you.
God brought out
His special
Monday morning
Watercolors
Of every hue.
There were pastel shades,
Pinks, yellows and blue.
He edged it with
Pure white puffy clouds
Laced with the
Light golden sun.
This morning's sun rise
Was the prettiest ever.
Then a rainshower
Interrupted the sunrise
And apologized
With a beautiful rainbow!

Donnie Alexander

REMEMBER ME

Michelle, I love you so much we have shared so much together. Please! Give me another chance.

As you stood there before me.
Looking into my eyes.
I wonder if you're seeing me,
Or is it his heart you still love.

I understand how you once loved
him,
I've had loved the same.
But now you are the only thing
In my life I really care for.
But it turns out to be a game.

If you could only forget the things,
The time y'all have shared, forget all
the
Happiness and the pain. I can make
our
Love so true.

I know he makes it hard for you
By trying to win you back
Remember now, you have me
(My love) remember me.

Jane A Williams

SUCCESS

Success can come on rapid wings,
That swoop and brush an unknown
cheek
And promise dreams of many things,
That only work can make complete.

Success can leave on rapid wings,
Desert whomever it may choose
And leave behind the empty dreams,
That lack of effort did abuse.

William M Bumpus

LIVING ON A SAILBOAT

Dedicated to my son John.

The love nest of the sea
Sails are full of southern winds
Sea is calm as we began
Bunks are made and breakfast too.

Sea gulls are flying high above
As we sail the open sea
Clear skies and rising sun
A new day has begun.

Sailing along on a beautiful day
We stand to see the sun fade away
Time has come we must return
It was great, a super run.

We dropped our sails and stored
away
It was a memorable wonderful day
We say good nite as the moon
shines bright
Living on a sailboat is a delight.

Nola D Scott

THIS ONE IS FOR YOU

You came into my world
Like a river into the ocean.
It seemed so natural
No questions were asked.

The moments turned into days, into
weeks.
We shared, learned and grew with the
time.
The feeling crept up and was planted
in my heart.
The beauty of it is, you love me.

Kahtarina La Cava
WILD MILES

Wild Miles
turns the styles
inside out and back again.
Plays it smooth
teasing, pleasing
sultry and low
explosive and high–
my, my.
Wild Miles
bringin' it down
takin' me out to left field–
out into the orbit
out by the moon–
dancin' me from star to star.
Play it silvery cool
like the moon on the waves.
Trumpet weeps–
melancholy blue
takes me through that sweet
seduction
effortlessly, confidentially,
thoroughly
Wild Miles.

Louis D Izzo
WHOM DO YOU TURN TO?

To my dear departed parents Anna and Alfonso Izzo.

As a child it was our mother we
turned to for advice,
And it was given free, for with
mother there was no price,
Or we could go to our dad, but, –
mother was best,
For she would solve our problem
with no fuss or stress.

Now, —they were all minor
situations at that time,
Also there was not much pressure on
our mind,
But as we grew older, more serious
conditions came into our life,
And looked for the answer, as to
doing something wrong or right.

We depended on our parents to set us
on the right road,
Which at times was a relief and also
lightened our problem load,
Always ready to comfort us, by
lending a helping hand,
And willing to do within their power,
all that they can.

Now that they have all passed on,
there are no parents to turn to,
And brothers and sisters have all
gone to seek friends anew,
The family closeness that was in the
past, does not exist anymore,
Not like in the old days, when homes
always had an open door.

Yet, "Whom Do You Turn To," at a
time of advice and need,
Well, –I guess a person of any
religious order, you can call, —
indeed,
But remember, your "God's" faith
will always be at your side,
And you will be able to solve your
problems, with dignity and pride.

Janice Corrigan
DANNY BOY

To our beloved Danny who we loved so much!

There will never be another like him
He brought us so much joy
That bright ray of sunshine
Our precious Danny boy.

We only had him a short while
Till God called him home
But he brought laughter and a smile
To all he had known.
'Tis our final farewell
To the one we loved so much
We shall meet again someday
For he was blessed by the Master's
touch.

Christine Marie Levin
ALWAYS

To my wonderful mother, whose love and friendship I will cherish forever! I Love You!!

Childhood Memories — Mom,
Always.
She taught me everything;
How to laugh, how to smile,
How to be a lady,
How to love.
She taught me to express my
Creativity and to use my imagination.
She taught me that I will be
Everything I set my mind to.
Best Friends — Mom, Always.
She is my best friend.
She has told me and shows me
Beautiful things about myself and
The world around me.
She is someone I share my
Hopes and dreams with.
She knows what is best for me,
Yet stands aside and watches.
She is all that I could hope for.

My Mentor — Mom, Always!

Jay F Manning
SILENTLY I GO

(This poem is dedicated to Shannon, whom I will never see again.)

I walked upon the water
And dreamed about the sea
Felt the love inside you
For all that I would be

I lost a certain aspect
Of the life I lived before
Watching time that washed upon
Your own romantic shore

Please, don't try to save me
I can't be seen this way
Your body is so lovely
Surrounded by the waves

And softly sinking down
Words I shouldn't have to say
Your love—a rose so soft,
Where has it gone today?

Kathleen J Rollins
OH DADDY, OH DADDY

Dedicated to my loving Father, and the memory of my Mother.

Oh daddy, oh daddy,
Oh what can I say.
You took care of us,
When mom went away.

You held us and told us we would be
alright,
When I wasn't sure we would survive
the night.
But come the dawn and the sun shone
bright,
I knew as you had promised, we were
alright.

It's been a lifetime ago since that
terrible day,
When we stood by and watched
mom's life slip away.
And as time has passed all you said
has come true,
We have been okay, because we were
with you.

You were there for us when we
needed you most,
And now it is our turn to play the
host.
We are here for you and whatever
you need,
Because through us you have planted
a seed.

Oh daddy, oh daddy,
Oh what can I say.
We love you more with each passing
day.

Anne Devine
TAKE TIME

To my dear niece Linda Anne.

Take time to smell the flowers as you
walk
Along life's path each day,

Take time as you'll only pass this
way once
On any given day.

Take time from the hustle bustle and
the cares
And worries of a business day,

Take time for those who miss you all
those working
Hours you're away.

Take time to share yourself with your
family even if
You're tired and it's been a long
day,

Take time before they're all grown
up and you regret
What you missed along the way.

Take time before it's passed you by
and the strands
Of your hair have turned gray,

Take time for those who love, care
and need you
Much more than they may say.

Verna S Shellenberger
EACH DAY

Dedicated to bowling friends — Mr. William Dreisback & George Boettcher.

Each day when you begin;
Each thought you wish to share;
Could be a peaceful thought
If God is there.

Each day when you begin;
Each deed you wish to share;
Will illustrate with kindness
Your tender thought thought and
care.

Cathy Koenig
ONLY TO WILT AND DIE

To my father, who will be missed forever.

What is life but a flickering flame,
Only to be blown out with one
breath.
What is life but a blood red rose,
Only to wilt and die.
What is life but an "I love you,"
Only to be ignored.
And what is death but an "I love
you,"
Suddenly remembered.

Gwendolyn A Olbris
WHEN HE WALKS INSIDE MY MIND

To my very special friend, Erik J. Brzoska.

When He walks inside my mind
the thoughts of light start to bind.
He is my life,
he is my world.
He makes me happy.
He makes me sad.
This is why I am glad
I have a best friend who can walk
inside my mind.

Frederick S Ballenger I
THE LAST CRY

For what . . . why the tears . . . is it
pain from within . . . or the pain from
what is seen and felt on the outside . . .

The last cry

Is it tears of relief . . . tears of faith . . .
for today for tomorrow . . . maybe the
knowledge of the one . . . whose eyes
are of water . . . a crystal stare . . . to
know that
life in the world for the one, is almost
over . . .

The last cry

Are they a plea to the Father for the
Savior to return and put the madness
of the world . . . "straight" . . . and on
the path of survival for all mankind . . .

The last cry

Or is it the joy and the knowledge of
the Father's answer . . . that "thee"
has
seen and will bring an end to hunger . . .
famine . . . nakedness and the
homeless . . .
people now will you understand and
know the reason for

The last cry

Frederick S Ballenger I
MY BLOOD IS MY LIFE

When it flows warm . . . my heart is
open . . . when it's cold, there's no
understanding for even the simplest
of things . . .

My blood is my life

When it boils . . . it releases the
unknown fury of the past . . . that has
stuck
in my blood stream of life . . .
generations after generations . . . now
the
blood that is to continue the
generations to come . . . must have
instilled in
it, the richness of purity from living
and doing the right things in life . . .

My blood is my life

Within my blood . . . there's no drugs
. . . alcohol . . . or semen from those
who
are the same as I . . .

My blood is my life

And I live my life . . . to keep it . . .
flowing . . . and within me . . . never
without . . . remember this . . . when
you remember me . . .

My blood is my life

Frederick S Ballenger I
A DIFFERENT GOD
Strong in body, strong in mind, a
spirit of hope, a new dimension
to be without is to lose all sense of
being . . . to be with is to
be completely depended upon . . . to
achieve all and have nothing

This different God controls thought
and action . . . love and hate . . .
trust and distrust . . . want and want
not . . .

This different God is the imitator of
the spirit of righteousness
This different God holds a false sense
of security . . .
This different God has the power to
take you with the first testimony . . .

The difference between the God
above and the God below is that
the God above could not and would
not deceive you . . .

The below will deceive you, control
you mentally, spiritually and
most of all totally . . .
To be totally dependent upon on a
different God other than the
One above is to be a child of the
Devil . . .
The one who has no respect for life,
love,
happiness and development . . . This
different God I talk about
is Public Enemy Number One . . .

This different God is drugs.

Frederick S Ballenger I
A PREGNANT MOTHER'S LOVE FOR DRUGS
Drug dealers all over the world, take
heed to what I am going to say to you . . .
Future mothers, carrying a
developing baby within you . . .
future mothers,
you of all people, listen and
understand the message I give you . . .
Your unborn child in the developing
stages of pregnancy starts to form
a human form, cells growing,
multiplying to a rate where fingers,
legs, arms,
and all internal organs and body parts
develop . . .
DRUG USE . . . in the very earliest
part of this development could cause
you
to damage an unborn child to a point
where their mentality . . . their
emotions . . .
their body structure could be altered
to the extent of severe deformity
and disbelief . . .
DRUG DEALERS . . . your
contribution to this destruction of a
temple of God
is extremely bad . . . the unpleasantry
of a birth of a drug–addicted baby is
terrible and your punishment should
be also as just . . .
MOTHER, your continued use of
drugs of any kind, not prescribed
by a licensed medical doctor . . .
mothers you should be arrested and
charged
with a crime . . .
PREMATURE CHILD ABUSE . . .
and your punishment should also be a
just one . . .
I say to you all . . . the destruction of
any form of human life is the ultimate
sin man or woman could do, and your
punishment prescribed by the
laws of the Almighty is . . .
DEATH.

W E (Bill) Titus
SILENT PASSION

This poem is dedicated to Amber, Mindy and Trevor.

Talons of love hold them firmly.
Charmed warmth gently cascades,
channeled from love's grasp.
Moonlight and candles fill the room.
Their eyes caress, holding each other,
they never touch.
Gently, white–hot they become
enfolded in love's embrace.
Never touching their fervor soars,
having complete dominion of their
souls.
In dawn's sandy light their hands
embrace.
Souls and passion willingly
bound, the sun cast but one shadow.

Jonathan Gray
LONELY RIDER

To the family and friends of Pat Shannon, God Bless her memory.

"He mounts the storm and walks
upon the wind" (Pope)

Ride on the wind spirit free
Bringing peace to a troubled soul,
On a winged stallion to watch over
thee
While the thunder in its anger rolls.

The lightning flashes, a banshee
screams
As the storm lights your lonely way,
Throughout time on a guiding beam
Riding back to the light of day.

Come forth sweet soul from darkness
grasp
Let time erase all fears,
Forget the evil from the past,
And let the sun dry away your tears.

Jonathan Gray
THE UNFORGIVEN
"The trail of the serpent is over them
all" (Moore)

Black eyes that watch through night
From the shadow move forms
unseen,
Silent creatures that flee from light
While lost in an unholy dream.

Drowned in a constant illusion
Within a swirling image of fear,
An existence born from confusion
From a past that always seems near.

No soul, no shape, no sound do they
make
While they follow an endless trail,
And throughout time the path they
take
Must be shrouded in darkness veil.

On a desperate, fiendish, hellish
course
Chased by a spirit unknown,
That shines from the edge of a
driving force
Making certain no mercy is shown.

Harold L Zachman
MY LITTLE ARTISTS
Pretty harps or tiny pipes
Kelly Green or shanty Whites,
Rather big or fairly small
We've the lads to draw them
all,
Mighty sharp or just for fun
Call SU 7-6821.

Rita Becnel Bentley — "Mosquita"
ONENESS

To my family and friends; I pray they rest assured in Jesus.

Just take my hand and I'll follow you
like a wide eyed child close
to her mother's breast.
Just tell me what you want, and you
can rest assured I'll do my very
best.
When I look into your eyes and see
you're tired and feeling blue, just
rest your head close to my heart until
the day is all anew.
Just whisper that you love me, as
much as I love you. There won't be
anything to separate us, because we'll
know our love is true.
As long as we show God we want to
do what's right, we'll form this
oneness with our hearts for the rest of
our life.

Rita Becnel Bentley — "Mosquita"
SEARCHING
How many changes must I go
through before I reach my ultimate
goal?
I think, I search, I react upon feelings
deep in my soul.
I want love and happiness, and all the
best things that life can
bring. Why can't there be joys
every day that make my heart sing?
Sometimes there is loneliness my
heart can hardly stand, but I keep
hoping that someday I'll find that
special man.
A man who is wise, strong willed,
and loving, a man with a mind of
his own, a man who is always near
and never leave me to roam.
How much longer now do I have to
wait, before I find out what is
my fate.

Richard M Haynes
AFTREE: A PLACE IN MY MIND

In loving memory of a true friend, Frank Kerns.

Looking through a porthole of time I
see the clouds of morning bind,
floating like dreams across a sky blue
mind.
A breeze is warmed by the sun's
golden rays, and left lazily full of soft
summer days,
with scents a wafting of childhood
laughter and happy days
Where the winged one soars with free
delight, over mountains of the highest
of might, and here yet roams, the
cycle of life.
It is here, this place in my mind, that
all events in my life, are like
threads weaving a pattern that is
unfolding by design.
When thoughts of these are delved
into, they seem afar as though
momentos
The people in this place, some of
whom you are most fond of,
are left only in no respond of to carry
on in this place in my mind.
Where there are illusions of no time.
Where life's innocence never fades,
and remains untainted to this day.
But in this place in my mind, one
must not spend wasted time, for the
past will
not be forgotten of untouchable
thought of those begotten.
But this search for yesterday's gone
by in tomorrow's by and by lie
screaming in
the narrows of my mind, by this, ruin,
may find you from the separation and
loneliness that awaits inside you.
While I'm lost in this new age world
weeping in tormented pain,
I sometimes wonder if I'll ever make
it home again to this
place in my mind. So as it stands, the
loneliest place known to man,
is the human heart, but home is only
a thought away.

Richard M Haynes
THE GIFT
The gift is not traditional, yet given
to each generation.
It was given in good faith, by the one
that gives all.
In that time, the greatness of its
expanse was largely unknown
To meet our needs, we began to
change it and mold it for meager
satisfaction.
Though we sacrificed the natural
order, we founded civilization.
Why would, what it was, be not
enough to give our children.
This was the first tear shed, by the
one that gives all.
And in that was given our children,
their first code to live by.
We did not fathom his word, so how
would we know the destruction
set in motion.
If only were wiser in days of young,
could we have
spared the expense of future man.
Though we are creatures of creation
with wanton; desires for knowledge
and everlast, then why is it we stand
fast in the pattern long
set in the past.
This we attribute to our darkside, the
pillaging of fruits and life
from our gift.
Are we so victorious, our spoils
we
may squander, all in
forgotten love for our children.
When truly our love, if it is dreamed
so, is but for self
fulfillment.
By this, we have founded our
existence on earth.

Dianne Louise Linneman
GOOD MORNING MOM
"Good Morning, Mom," It seems to
be such a nice day to play.
But I know better than to ask for that,
for it happens every day.
You wake me up each morning,
throw breakfast in my face.
Then you run around all day trying to
clean the place.
The laundry's going, you're
vacuuming, there's dishes in the sink!
There's more to life than mopping
floors, at least that's what I think.
And still you carry on like this,
pushing me aside.
Doing the things that must be done,
yet it's hurting inside.
Sometimes you try to talk to me, or
we'll play a little ball.

But it's "Hurry up I've got things to do," and it isn't fun at all.
When Dad was here, we had good times, like it was meant to be.
But when Daddy left, he took everything, including you from me.

Dianne Louise Linnemann
SECOND CHOICE
I know a thirsty man must drink, but with two cups side by side.
A bitter brew, a water true, which would the man decide?
He lifts the cup of his choice, and cursed for it was dry.
He longed for the taste of the bitter brew, a taste water can't satisfy.
Now disappointed and angry, he still must quench his thirst.
He drinks the water, his second choice, and still longs for the first.

Dianne Louise Linnemann
GUILT SHOULD NOT BE PUNISHMENT
Society conditions us in the ways we are to think.
What is right, what is wrong, are written down in ink.
One learns through acceptance, one's right if one conforms.
But I have learned in the sea of life there are often many storms.
Mixed emotions, troubled thoughts, can stir the once calm sea.
Into a raging turbulence, when once it's hard to see.
One reaches out in blind faith for something to stop the spin.
Holding on to see one through the trouble that one's in.
When the clouds have parted, and the seas again are stilled.
I hope that one's survival isn't looked back upon ill willed.
For each of us have our ways of getting through the storm.
And guilt should not be punishment for those who don't conform.

Grace W McKnight
LOVE

This poem is dedicated to George, my devoted husband.

The world has lots to offer us
In this I can rely
There are so many many things
To interest you and I

The greatest thing I know is love
Yes love beyond a doubt
It is the one most needed thing
We just can't do without

Love makes the world a stronger place
In which we have to live
Love makes us want to walk upright
It makes us want to give

Love helps us know right from the wrong
It guides our daily life
Love takes care of each one of us
In all our toil and strife

Love can't be bought yet men have
Sought for love in various manners
Some have tried to come forth in
Life, carrying all the banners

Love never alters as you know
It endures until the end
Why try to live without true love
Love is our very best friend

There are a million wonderful
Things this world could offer us
It seems like now that all it
Offers is a lot of lust—

Avril J McLeod
YOU HAVE WATCHED ME GROW FROM BIRTH

To Mom.

You have watched me grow from birth
Blessed me with your love,
Annointed me with your tears
And suffered when you could no longer help.

When I was ill you stood over me
And your tears ran down your face
And splashed upon me.

Now when the tears have gone by
Your face still comes to mind.
I look at my life and truly thank you.
My pain and sorrow
You have shared and often carried.

I'll never be rich nor will I be poor
But the faith you embedded in me
Shall never leave.
We have walked together
In life and death
And still, Mom, you are there.

Richard B Griffin

Richard B Griffin
THE WAY I FEEL

This poem is dedicated to my mother and father – I love you both.

My heart is like a burning fire,
My search for life is frenzied.
I'm looking for that thing called love,
The word that's never ending.

I want a love that's true to me,
A love my heart can take.
One my heart can deal with,
A love I can reciprocate.

I have found this love in you,
The love that I've searched for.
And I will never search again,
For I'm content forever more.

I have never loved like this,
(The love I feel for you.)
And I will never love again,
(The way that I love you.)

Vidal Roldan
IT WAS HANDSOME STRONG AND GREEN
It was handsome strong and green
and the shade was a dream
it was envy for its beauty
for the flowers and its fruit

By some it was wanted
by others it was guarded
it was painted in portrait
and in bronze it was cast

Now time sure has passed
and also has taken its toll
it is hate by those who praise
and hurt by those who guard

But it may happen
who knows when
that tender hands sweet and true
come and care for the old tree.

Barbara J Harris
SOLITUDE IN THE HILLS

This poem is dedicated to Gary, my husband, and his beloved outdoors.

O rolling hills
and valleys deep
Bring to me
a somber peace.

The birds in song
and the roosters crow
Trees gently
swaying to and fro.

Floating clouds
casting shadows down
These hills and valleys
all around.

Serenity does
this peace afford
A blissful moment
this earth has poured.

My soul cries out
a song of praise
For all this beauty
my eyes have gazed.

Carol A Nikols
SPRING'S PROMISE
Dawn blossoms its newest day,
Little children go out to play,
Above the winter's deepest spell,
Arises life, its words to tell.

A brand new day, the spring awakes,
The sun shines warm upon our face,
Birds do sing, their voices true,
Grasses filled with morning dew.

Flowers bloom, their scent unfolds,
As each awaiting promise holds,
To take away the coldest night,
And welcome in a day that's bright.

Carol A Nikols
WINTRY SHADOWS
Winter casts its purest spell,
On snowy trees that limbs had fell,
Beyond dark corners, around the bend,
Little finches that God did send.

A child's paradise, a dream come true,
The sky pure white, no longer blue,
Though it lasts for a shorter while,
It still seems to bring a smile.

Especially at this time of year,
Santa brings the children's cheer,
Memories call upon us once again,
Reliving moments spent with friends.

And most of all, the precious gift,
The child Jesus born, our spirits lift,
Rejoicing, hereinafter peace,
The wintry shadows did decease.

Randy J Hughes
WARMING RED GLOW
Outside everything is covered in the early winter's snow.
So I'll just sit here feeling the warming red glow.
Watching the flames dance to an unknown tune.
With hopes that spring will come back very soon.
As I dream my dream of the soon coming spring.
I hear off in the distance a few carolers sing.
As I sit here by my fire, I'll look out my frosty window.
And watch the new coming snow.

Outside it's looking wintery cold, but I know by my fire I'll be warm.
So I'll just dream through this passing storm.
As I dream my dream I'll lay back and have a short winters nap.
In my warm blanket I will tightly wrap.
Because when I awake everything will be covered in the new coming snow.
And I'll be thankful for my warming red glow.

Doris L Gossett
HOPE

My first published poem of Hope is dedicated to my wonderful grandchildren — Kristen Ann Schildberg, Kelly Ann Miller and Scott Douglas Miller.

Every day in retirement I say
What can I do in my own little way
I sit in my chair and dream and dream
Of winning a contest for self-esteem
When what a great surprise I find
A contest is offered — just make a rhyme.
What can I say, or do, or write
To bring my entry within sight
Of all the judges who will choose
To make me win instead of lose,
To think mine best in every way
When on May second they will say
Congratulations. You're the best
The winner of our big contest!
And now I really must rationalize
There still is hope in winning a prize
So I will anxiously await
For the result I hope I can celebrate.

Rita D Lee
MAMA

To my MaMa, God couldn't have given anyone a better mother who on her own raised five children and was always there when we needed her and still is –love Rita.

When we were growing up,
You guided us and never gave up.
When there was only you,
We never knew there wasn't two.
Through the good times and the bad,
Through the lonely and the sad,
You were there to wipe our tears,
And comfort us and all our fears.
Your courage and your love,
Must have come from up above.
You gave and did without,
And we grew with stout.
Your morals and love for life,
Gave us all that added spice.
We hear your voice and see your face,

How could anyone ever take your place.
You've been our inspiration through all our years,
With your smile, your laughter and your tears.
Without you, our lives would be empty,
So stay in our lives and hearts and never leave them empty.
Thank you MaMa for all you've given,
We know we'll meet you in heaven!

Jade McCann

WHERE ARE YOU NOW

Dedicated in loving memory to "Sarah" my canine friend.

Where is that part of you, that gave your eyes
more than the empty gaze of death,
that gave your sweet and so soft carriage
warmth and movement? Not now confined with ashes in an urn, but gone into
the atmosphere and far beyond.
Do you still exist as "Sarah," or a part of
a larger "Whole"? Are you an entity
now still, or part of the "Everlasting All"?
Do you rest upon some puffed ethereal
pillow, in the sky, or are you only "Essence"
all form dispersed back into what was,
what is, what always shall be? Are you free,
truly free, "home" in the arms of "That"
which created you, out of "Its" most dear longing
for the knowledge of "Itself."
Where are you now?
I ponder on the shape of you, since you are gone,
missing the form I knew you in,
hoping to feel
your breath upon the breeze, even though I cannot
name, or see, or touch, what you are now become.
Where is that part of you, that terminated not
with the stillness of your flesh?
Can you
be emersed in the ray, which silently spreads its
splendour into a new day. Or be the
droplet,
perched upon, or nestled in a petaled array?
It gives me comfort to believe you are,
I am, we are, part of each other
for ever
for ever
for ever.

Susan M McElroy

UNFINISHED

As the waves hit the sandy shores;
I can't help but ponder this thought;
If a raindrop
A pinch of clearwater
produces a memory of feelings
all packed-up in a single drop
What then is a rainstorm;
the sick
the hungry
the poor . . . .

Danny J Davison

THE RAIN HAS ARRIVED

The rain has arrived
The first of the season
To wash away my summer dreams
To cleanse the Earth
To make it wet
To drip off leaves
To gather in puddles
For no apparent reason
The mud
The smell
Is it not so wonderful?
The rain has arrived
To start this new season.

Cindy L Ritchie

THE EAGLE SOARS

The eagle soars inside himself first.

He contemplates all around him
with the intensity of knowing
how absolutely marvelous he is.

His wings point the way
and
he soars.

Always knowing, the best,
is
who he is.

Experiencing the flight,
freedom to move in his direction
where the reality of his mind
and spirit
are combined to lift him
above his own belief.

The eagle soars.

Ernest Stein

THE OLD MAN IN FALL

Golden years of aging life
Glorious warm days of autumn
Cool nights and foggy fields
Wet fall-scented leaves
Late roses and chrysanthemums.
Time to dig the black and fragrant soil
To plant, to bury bulbs.
Mother Earth: welcome me too
Let me return to your womb whence I came
And accept my aged body,
My tired flesh and brittle bones
And my exhausted brain.
Release me from Thinking,
From the everlasting struggle for "The Truth"
And from the endless quest for "The Absolute."
But after winter's purgatory let my spirit rise
And join the resurrected bloom
And join the chorus of the millions
Gone before me to eternal light.

Jean Newkirk

THE SEED CATALOG

I tramped out to the mailbox,
Leaving footprints on the snowy ground,
And oh the surprise I found inside the box,
Quickens my heart in leaps and bounds.

It's my garden seed catalog
With its familiar picture pages,
With vegetables, fruits and flowers in bloom,
Their seeds preserved for ages.

A thousand times I scan the book
With an optimistic view,
While the cold wind outside is howling,
I read the pages, through and through.

It provides me with a promise,
The miracles of root and seed,
A yield of bushels and bushels,
Of everything I need!

Halina de Roche

THOUGHTS ON THINKING

Our beautiful world —
Great — wide — and precise —
A former paradise —
Has not enough room—
For the Good — the Strong — or the Wise—

And as time goes on—
And the Wise grow numb—
This teaming seems to be—
Life's phenomenon—

The Wise and the Good—
Have either to hide—
Or swallow their pride—
Or glide into oblivion
Where they quietly cry—
And painfully die.

Barbara White Kimball

LIFE

Icy Pain
Summer Rain
Wet Tears
Happy Years
Troubled Fear
Many Cares
Last Hope
Life's Facade

Iris R Hazel

Iris R Hazel

NOTHING LOST!

To David, Because Chiquita Loved You The Most!

How do you feel?
I feel WONDERFUL!
Because
In knowing you
I have loved
I have hurt
I have felt tremendous pain
I have healed
I have learned
And I have grown.

I thought I was the one who had lost you,
But,
I did not lose you,
You lost me
A good woman
A GREAT WOMAN!
A woman who loved you

A woman who adored you!
A woman who had nothing and would have given you everything you ever wanted.
Without
Asking for it
Working for it
Or
Begging for it

I thank you for your part in making me that
Great Woman.

So,
I haven't lost.
I have won!

And You?
Well
God Bless You.

Melissa B Papageorge

HALF-REMEMBERED FACES

Half remembered faces in the corners of my mind
I should remember but I can't
Though they press against the eyelids
Screaming, importunate, jostling, trampling,
Demanding the recognition, rot, rebellion
and strife
Tear down the ordered walls of my mind.

Muriel Rosen

ART CLASS

The painting
So dark and dreary
And I
So tired and weary
Begin
To feel a bit leery
Of doing anything more
So eerie.

Jane W Goodrich

DREAMS

Dreams are made of magical things,
Wishes that soar on gossamer wings;
There have been dreams since man began
And there will be dreams 'til the end of time;
For hope springs eternal in ev'ry soul,
The young have dreams and also the old;
And yet without dreams, where would we be?
Today's dreams are tomorrow's reality.

Dream on to the top of the hill
For life without dreams is a life unfulfilled;
Climb on to the top with courage and daring,
Hold high the torch, never despairing;
Reach out for honor o'er rock and rill
And up on the top of the crest of the hill
The dreaming of dreams of golden hue
Will one day actually all come true.

Carol J Coyer
THE SEARCH
The search is on for a better way
to solve the problems we face every day

We try to amass material wealth
in hope of improving our spiritual health

We read stacks of books on the New Age theory
until our bodies and minds grow weary

Can the answers be found on a library shelf?
or are they hidden deep in yourself?

The search goes on, here below and up above
The answer, my friend, is simply choose love.

Cynthia K Townsend
WHISPER

To my brother, Butch, whom I love very much.

The night you felt no one cared,
I whispered, "I love you."
If only you would have shared,
Your pain and heartache, too.

I'm there when there is no one
To hold and comfort you.
So, when all is said and done,
I'm the one who is faithful and true.

I know just how you feel
I know when you hurt so much.
I have shown you that I am real,
Your life has changed with just one touch.

Move from a life that wasn't fair,
Don't stop! listening to me.
Let me show you how much I care,
Ask, and I will set you free.

So, listen when I whisper I love you.
Please, listen, and don't make me shout.
When you're feelin' alone and blue,
Just listen, I'm your only way out.

Donna Soroky
CHILD IN FLIGHT

To my sister, Joan.

Leave the nest my child
if you will,
but with you goes a
portion of my heart.
I've loved you all your days
and always will,
you are the last to go
and must depart.
I know that with the end
comes new beginnings
and I'll know you in a way
I've yet to know.
I, too, will yield to change
through life's continuing
but love will be unchanged
when you come home.

Nancy J Johnson
LADY BLUE

In dedication to the superlative one, Jehovah, who declared: "The heavens are my throne and the earth is my footstool."

When Lady Blue says, 'Goodnight'
And pulls her shades down low
She leaves on all her tiny lights
That no one stumble here below

Within the veil of her blue realm
She welcomes every guest
As Haley's Comet speeds on by
She bids him, 'stop and rest'

And all who dwell in her domain
Have countless chores to do
Her spacious home is always clean
. . . 'case an angel's passing through!

Lady Blue has many moods
Each one she wears with pride
They say she throws a Fashion-Show
Each season passing by!

But when her spirit's gloomy
She paints her face dark grey
And woe be unto little stars
Coming out to play!

Nancy J Johnson
LOVELY LADY BLUE
With what shall we compare you
Lovely Lady Blue?
Could a picture paint the words to show
The loveliness of you?

And how do we describe you?
What phrase so justly true
Since nothing in this world of ours
Looks quite the way you do!

But oh how glad the Ocean!
How proud the beaming Sea!
That they should be the chosen
To reflect your majesty!

Dear Lady of a thousand eyes
Whose ageless face we've loved
What awesome secrets hide behind
That Peerless masque above?

For in our quest to know your world
The poets fantasize
That they were chosen to write about
The story in your eyes . . . .

Fumi Migimoto
RETIRING

Dedicated to all retiring educators . . . and to my dear parents, Mr. & Mrs. Katsutaro Kodani, and family.

When you are ready to retire
Just set your imagination afire
And do whatever you aspire
In terms of money, health, and time.

When you have reached your golden prime
It's surely no longer a sin or crime
To step up your daily earthly pleasures
Napping, jogging, taking tours
To Europe, Vegas, or other lures.

When you are ready for a binge
To scale the highest snow-capped ridge
You're never too old for a change:
Step lively in the RIGHT direction
Eating and drinking in moderation
To physical fitness, paying attention.

Learn new TRUTHS about yourself;
You need not end up on the shelf.
Retirement means true HAPPINESS
And LONGEVITY . . . no stress or mess!

Trelys Du Pre'
SHIRLEY
I feel your closeness everywhere;
Your soft silent footsteps wading in the peaceful
Waters of my memory;
And the recurring waves that you create there,
Ripple throughout fibre of my being,
Kissing my lips with a smile.

Though worlds apart at times, it seems,
Yet the same golden thread of dreams
Intertwine our lives, and we are more yet deeply bound,
Than by mere lovemaking.
The hands of our souls are joined,
And we soar on a meteor's stream,
Somewhere beyond the stars!

Dolores J Bell
THE RING

To Raymond, my husband of 41 years.

Thank you for the ring so small
The glass of wine and all
But; I'd envisioned something on a larger scale
A much more macho looking male

A ring with two carats weight
I thought somehow would be my fate
A cruise to Europe would be nice
After everyone had thrown the rice

A home at least two stories high
With trees reaching to the sky
A maid to do my every wish
I'd never have to wash a dish

A cook to serve on linen fine
Crystal goblets filled with wine
The finest silver napkin ring
In general; all the finer things

But; you are the finest man I know
And I don't need the outward show
So I'll settle for a gown of white
And my little ring that shines so bright

Marvel J Nelsen
ARIZONA NIGHT
Guilt feelings rise as I sit at poolside
On a lovely September evening
In Phoenix. Stars twinkle overhead
Giant birds lift their wings
And flash their light as they climb
From Sky Harbor International to many destinations
One every few minutes

When you are from Iowa
It is too good to be true
At home public pools in small towns
Close before school starts
And now stand half empty.
Temperatures dip low up North
Indian summer is very near

Here a balmy 75 reminds one
Of Acapulco in January.
The pool is only three feet deep
Warm and safe as filial love
Deep enough to be immersed
Shallow enough to feel secure
Held close in loving arms

Sherry Harrison
INSTEAD OF ME
Sitting at my window,
I watched you two walk by,
Your arm was 'round her waist,
and all I could do was cry,
The tears poured down my cheeks
and landed on the floor,
Oh what I'd give if you'd walk through that door.

If you want her instead of me,
That's the way it's got to be
Nothing turns out right for me
and I hope you'll both be happy,
Nothing's alright now,
It will all turn out somehow,
If you want her, if you want her instead of me.

Walking down the street,
our two eyes seemed to meet
At your side was the girl you dreamed of.
I walked on down the street
The tears fell at my feet,
I'd lost the only guy I'll ever love.

Sherry Harrison
I'D GIVE IT ALL
I've got a mansion on the hill with forty rooms,
I've got a den full of priceless hearilooms.
I own everything as far as the eye can see,
but I'd give it all just for someone who really loved me.

To have someone to love you
is the greatest gift on earth,
No one can measure
what it's really worth,
I could start from the bottom
and there's nothing I couldn't be
If I had someone, someone who really loved me.

I've got oil wells in Texas
a ski lodge in Aspin
Anything I want at my beck and call,
But I don't have anyone who really loves me,
and that's what I want most of all.

Tammy Usher
THE LIGHT
It is dark in the night,
But the moon shines some light,
And if you are so blind to see,
Then the moon there musn't be.

A L Kulik
SEA GULLS
Out on the dock
the tide rolls in
the sea's chilling breath
cools my skin
and heaving waves
sway side to side
attracting the gulls
who downward glide.

Into the wetness
with claws immersed
each squawking eagerly
to catch food first.
They ascend from the wetness
and onward go
home is a place
they'll never know.

Christine Larkin
THE PATH
I'm walking alone,
I don't think I can make it on my own.
Which path do I take?
Too many hard choices for me to make.
My life is filled with so much pain
Don't know what's left for me to gain.

People are deceiving
False leaders everyone is believing.
People get hooked and are dying,
Children are beaten and crying.
I can't walk anymore
Thoughts of nuclear war
The path is clear, no one's in sight,
If we don't wake up, destroy the earth we might.
I'm afraid to walk 'cause then I'll see
Tomorrow what new horrors there will be.
Needles in the water,
Garbage on the land.
If I fall there will be no helping hand.
People are selfish, just think of themselves
Each too concerned with his own pleasure and wealth.
But I continue to walk 'cause You will be
At the end of my path patiently waiting for me.

Denise Garon

Denise Garon
IN THE PINK OF A FLESHY SHADOW
I don't wear pink
Hot pink / Blush pink / Coral pink/
Parfait pink/
NO PINK!
This does not mean i can only
Feel comfortable with Eunuchs
I have not adopted
Ancient Amazon ideals
It's not that i resent males
But your body reminds me
That i have one also.
I have the greatest difficulty
Accepting my blood, my bones
And my epidermis with eyes.
For i dream of being
As non-existent as the wind.

(The wind breathing wishes of you.)

Betty Bratsky
NOT THE END
When you're down as low as you can get, And there seems no
place to turn.
It's your inner self that will save you,
God will help you,
If to Him you'll turn.
You can't just stop, say this is the end, There's so much waiting
for you round the bend.
Each day brings sunshine, new promises of Life.
There's beauty in all God created,
You're one of the special ones
He's tested with Strife,
You really should be elated.
Just look to the stars, pick one for your own. Hang your wishes
high as you can get.
There's a million things that you can do. Talents never even
tested yet.
You can travel to far off places, learn customs, make friends,
And study new faces.
Each person is a whole new world, with ideas and thoughts to be tried.
Just think of the ones that you will know, Thank God that you hadn't died.
If the time seems dull and depression sets in, Don't let it get you down.
The more you make of the life you have, There will be more stars in your crown.
Remember no one's perfect, we all have lots to learn, We just do the best that we know how, and love will come out in return.
Each stumble we take along the way, just makes us stronger day by day.
Growing up is very hard to do, some days are bright and happy, some days are grey and blue.
Just keep your focus on Happy times, the rest will come out right.
God will guide you on your way,
He'll lead you into His Light.
Just thank Him each day for all you have, Your heart
will happy be. And I'll thank Him too, for all our love,
He saved you, for all to see.

Georgia Steenrod
THAT'S LIFE
Have the woes of the world
Got you down?
Do you have a dragging chin
And wear a big frown?

Are you in debt?
Do you worry and fret?

Do your bills outweigh your paycheck?
Is your car almost a wreck?

Might as well lift up your chin
And put on a big smile.

The sun is bound to shine
Through the clouds after while.

Gretchen V DeGeer
MYSTERY OF LIGHT
The iced tree stood alone on the hill
With limbs spread wide to catch the sun's smile.
Prismed lights shone forth like blinking moons
All dressed up in scarlet, gold and blue.

At first I thought my eyes played tricks on me;
The lights appeared where apples used to be.
I grabbed my camera, hoping to catch the surprise,
But on film, those lights never did arrive.

I began to wonder, if they were ever there;
Or was it imagination exposing hidden treasures,
Daring the tree to cry out to me,
That clear, bright light can only be seen
When the mind is stilled, but open to mystery.

Pamela Lafferty-Walkley
A TREE IN NIGHT RAIN
To Gary, who always believes in me—

The tree rose—
Shivering in the icy rain,
Its branches glistening,
Reached feebly into the night,
Knobby branches—
Looking startled,
Like a naked grape vine
In a cut crystal bowl.

A misty veiling of rain
Has tried to make it's home
In those ancient crevices—
But, in failing has dribbled
Down the arms and torso—
Like the juice from a peach
As it runs in trailing rivulets
Down the trunk—

Of a child.

Pamela J Jones
SITTING IN A WORLD OF NEW
Sitting in a world of new,
in my mind, thinking of you.

As I watch the colorful sea,
your love comes rushing to be with me.

Its simplicity seems so small,
and yet it catches the minds of all.

In its beauty my mind wants to wade,
and into my heart comes the love we made.

It was so true, so real, so unique,
that only its depth am I left to seek.

But together always will we stay?
for we live our love from day to day.

And if the time comes for us to part,
then please remember me in your heart.

For I love you so and I always will,
and I know my love is forever real.

Gladys E Conklin
AUTUMN
To B.S. it is because of you that I am able to write like this. I LOVE YOU.

The most deafening sound on earth is the
Death of summer.
The Autumn air surrounds us, it holds
Our hearts enthral.
People drive for miles, days, just to
Catch a glimpse of color. To capture
That moment on film, photographs later
To be discarded.

Leaf peekers we call them.
What is it that they see in the colors
Among the trees?

Each tree, each limb, an open wound.
Dripping of blood then collected in the
Leaves.
Withering up to die,
Crashing to the ground.

It is autumn in Vermont, and the trees,
They bleed.

Joye Elrod Hatfield
NEVER SAY HELLO
If we never say hello
If we make our paths never cross
If we never see eye to eye
We'll never have to say goodbye.

If I walk the straight and narrow
Close my eyes to your sight
If we never say hello
We'll never have to say goodbye.

For us to say hello
Would only be a chance
To watch our feelings grow
Then have to say goodbye.

Kelly Kuszner
THE ELUSION OF SLEEP
Sleep
It is my butterfly of night

Chase
It looses you to
from waking

Lay
It laughters and plays would-be dreams

Lost
It will chase you while you

Wake
It tells you should be a

Sleep.

Evelyn Grisso Pittenger
MY SON'S GIFT
To my son, Ken Fawley.

I have a little cedar chest
Where my treasures I hoard.
Most precious is a little knife
Carved from a piece of board.

It was made by little hands
That strove to do their best,
But he was just a lad of eight
So it was quite a test.

He whittled and he sanded,
Wood chips were everywhere;
But it had to be just right
And so he worked with care.

And then on Christmas morning
I found beneath the tree,
The little knife, all neatly wrapped
With these words: "To Mom, from Me."

Now that was many years ago
When he made that little knife
And I will always treasure
The gift throughout my life.

Eugene F Tonelli
A BANDING BEGINNING (WORLD BROTHERHOOD)
From th' mist gather'd on a shore,
And in the tales that we're still told,
Where it was found so long before,
A plan to show that of one fold; a word to
The earliest of this nation, given by one
Who knew of this way, and would carry on
To every generation, of our many, to each,
Have as he may. The right to be, one with
The other, seek out his living, in going,
Understood; where distance or status, not to

Bother, meaningful unity for a
common good,
The concept to be, in the eyes of
another,
Respect a feeling, a hand to a hand,
raising a
Spirit, a gift to our brother; finding
this way
To strengthen our band. These
ancient
Peoples, in language, then, fashioned
from
Signs, see in their skies, from father
to
Son, we're told of when, for on
This misty shore, our future lies.

Sheena Strudwick
DREAMS AND PROMISES
We all have dreams,
We all make promises;
But unfortunately not all our dreams
come through,
And we never, ever keep all our
promises.
However, the Lord gives us that
strength;
To live through our dreams, when
they become darkness
And our promises when they become
shattered.
Sometimes we will cry and feel like
dying:
But it is only the Lord's way of
making us stronger
I thank the Lord for making me
stronger and stronger
To reach up, and out: Stretch my
arms . . . OPEN
Open wide and to hold on, with all
my strength.
Stand up and to go again
When my dreams are only dreams,
And my promises are shattered and
broken.

Dawn Orlove
TO DADDY
Daddy, you were the one
that I could look up to
When you died
I thought I did too.
When you were in the hospital
I was too little to visit you
So I never had the chance to say
"I Love You!"
We had a lot of fun times
we also had some bad
But we stuck together and
made the best of what we had
I wonder how I would be
if you were still here,
I often wonder how I'd look
and what I'd wear.
Daddy, it's time now
For me to say goodnight
but before I do
I want you to know that
"I Love You!"

Jodi L Smith
THE WAR
The war is over the battlefield is
dead;
No sound from the cannons, just
stillness instead.
The soldiers are gone, the camps are
still;
Their only reward is the homecoming
chill.

Nightmares will haunt them for the
rest of their years;
Leaving behind scars and wounds
and many tears.
Lost in the war were their fellow
soldiers;
Making them always look over their
shoulders.

The true heroes, were the soldiers
lost;
For giving their life, was the true
cost.
To save our country and get it out of
turmoil;
They fought and died on foreign soil.

Cheryl Lynch
VOWS

To my dear and loving husband, Jim, and my two wonderful children who give me my inspiration.

I want you with me forever
Until my dying day
To love and to cherish
In each and every way

I'll do my best to keep you happy
I'm sure you'll do the same
We were meant to be together
An undying flame

There will be good times and bad
times
That we will overcome
In health and sometimes sickness
Even when we're glum

I want you for my husband
To have and to hold
From this day and forever
You're worth your weight in gold

C Howard Greene
LOVE THOUGHTS AND MOONLIGHT

Dedicated to Dianna D. Dimick who touched my life for a short while and made such a lasting impression.

Love is a tantalizing thought of Dianna, the mystery of gently exploring hills and valleys, the garden places of her lovely body. Love is conceived in my heart and made strong by the beauty of her afterglow. Loving her is my concept of Heaven, my Pearl of great price. Love for her is my release from the grave, the joy of my resurrection. Holding her is the center of my universe, the cornerstone of my creation.

Love, Dianna, is the smile of moonlight in your lovely eyes while in fascination, you seek out the man in the moon. The sudden thrill of discovery, the sound of laughter as his face jumps out at you, and I want the world to know that the purity of your moonlit face makes me realize there is enchantment in the magic of you. Your aura framed in stops my breath and I cry, "Oh, Dianna!"

Billy Porter
A MAN AND A WOMAN IN LOVE
Her love is the pleasure of this man
alone
And I want her attention till the
passion is gone,
My hunger is that of a storm wild at
sea
Of a babe for a breast, of a rain
starving tree.
In a soft voice she whispers
Billy I need you so,
As she takes my erection
In her belly below.

Jenny M Peto
GOOD-BYE
Good-bye my love, good-bye,
After this I shall cry.
I love you dearly,
But since you're not near me
I must say goodbye . . . .

Farewell my love, farewell,
After this you will surely yell.
It was true love I found
But I fear I've let you down
So farewell my love, farewell . . . .

It was great my love, it was great,
And you are probably full of hate.
But you were bored of me anyway,
So I will be the one to say
I Love You, but good-bye.

George A Piggford
SONNET 18
What shall I compare you to, as
Shakespeare did?
A day in autumn comes to mind, late
autumn;
The orange and yellow have turned to
rust and red.
This most glorious of seasons,
when—
Nature invests herself with a mantle,
Enveloped in glory, blazing splendor
That has in it a meaning, a signal.
This is not vain coquetry. No suitor
Need apply who is not
serious-minded,
For the colors of fire and excitement
Will become just a shade; will be
muted
Into tints of superior temperament.
Colors that linger on, of a lasting hue,
Are those that I compare to you, to
you.

Ray Polakowski II
ANOTHER MOCKERY
Nuclear war is now to be,
As the world is in obscurity.

Guns and knives are obsolete now
As radioactivity nuked the cows.

Many of us were glowing in pain
As is greater with the acid rain.

The world is becoming worthless
now
A worthless world, a worthless cause,
what's the sense of it all.
Was the sense just to see who was
the toughest kid on
The block.
Or create Earth into just another
rock?

Everything is bleak to me.
Can they see that across the sea?

For if so let us be in peace and
harmony.
And not make the human race
another mockery
Another mockery

Steve Plumlee
THE ENEMY
Tears fall from the mourning sky,
Heaven, pouring itself open,
The air is dying, gasping for breath,
From human greed and selfishness,
Earth is such a perfect place,
But Man is less and can't live in a
perfect world.
In the name of technology we move
forward,
We can see the end,
Growing closer to nothing.
If we are the only intelligent life in
the universe,
Why do we try and destroy
ourselves?
We are just children in the eyes of
time,
Carelessly playing with fire.
We are killing our children,
And we have the power to save
ourselves,
But it's hard,
When you, are the enemy.

Gerald York
WE LOST MANY THINGS IN VIETNAM

To all Vietnam Vets.

We lost many things in Vietnam.
Some our virginity.
Most our youth.

We saw its inhumanity.
And in turn, surrendered pieces of
our humanity,
in days that followed.

Some of us discovered, to our
revulsion,
at times we actually liked it.
How much humanity had we lost?

Mary Webb Phillips
ADDICTING FRAGRANCE

To Wayde, Angela, Kyle, Sarah, and Joey. You are what life is all about.

Holiday dinners being prepared!
Expensive Parfume . . .
A well groomed man . . .
Just some of the things that I love to
smell.
Cedar trees . . . Meadows of wild
flowers . . .
Sheets from the line . . . Fresh
brewing coffee . . .
Monsignor's cigar . . .
I wonder each day how a fool
could allow . . . oneself to get hooked
on a drug.
But as I inhale each of the above,
addiction's quite easy to see. Tho
being the strong sort of person I am
total control I have over these.
The aroma that captures every
ounce of my being . . .
I can't get enough of this smell. If
this Glorious Fragrance were bottled,
to the ends of the earth it would sell.
Peace and Tranquility would
spread cape to cape . . . If everyone
sniffed at a small baby's nape . . .

Mary Webb Phillips
SARAH'S SONG

To Sarahs' Father, Dale Wayne Phillips.

Sarah is my little girl, and this song's for her.
She's made out of sugar, and everything that's nice—
and I love her dearly, she's the treasure of this life.
She was two, and hadn't walked alone from the moment of her birth, yet in her very special way, she'd traveled all the earth.
At four, she'd never said a word, but the sparkle in her eyes was the sweetest sound I've heard.
They said there must be something wrong inside that little head, but I don't think it knew it by the pretty curls it shed.
Girls are made of sugar, and girls are made of spice, and that describes our Sarah, so very full of life.
They call this thing they think she has Ce-ree-bral Pawlzy and there's a lot of people helpin' her and me . . . and I thank them all for being there, for showing us they really care.
And I thank the Lord for sugar and I thank the Lord for spice, and I thank the Lord for Sarah . . .
and the precious gift of life . . . .

Mary Webb Phillips
SARAH, PART II

In loving memory of my father Charles Edward Webb, DREAMER OF DREAMS . . . (puller of pranks) The inspiration! To my mother Mary Ellen, The backbone. The strength.

The candles flutter in the breeze . . .
A brother reaches out to tease.
She huffs and puffs and out they go.
Eight little candles in a row.
We have come a long long way.
Sarah is eight today.
She can walk, and she can talk . . .
better yet, she laughs . . .
She attends a "special" School, but anyone can see . . .
that any place that Sarah goes is a special place to me.
She likes to help, she loves to flirt, she always does her part.
ROCKY B. holds first place in her great big heart.
Some people call her "Handicapped" at home she's part of "US."
I'm just so glad that she is here, no matter what our plight.
Every day I'm thankful Lord for the precious gift of life.

Rosemarie Price
SUGAR COATED MEMORIES

In memory of Grandpa Howell for all the love and happiness that will eternally carry through all his children.

The dreams of long ago, the thought so far from today,
Sugar coated memories that seem like only yesterday.
The gifts he used to give, the candy that's sweet,
The toys on Christmas and birthdays that was so neat.
All these sugar coated memories, oh how I love to sleep.
The gifts that he gave me: a penny, a quarter, a dollar.
A shiny new necklace that I wore about my collar.
I tell my children about my grandfather, so that they can tell theirs.
Those sugar coated memories of the things we used to share.

Bernice Pedersen
GOD ONLY KNOWS

This poem is dedicated to my children and grandchildren.

How much do you Love me,
may I ask?
How great can your Love be,
and will it last?

How much do you love me,
Why can't you say?
You're as sweet as the sunshine
That brightens the day.

Your eyes are of Heaven's blue,
They sparkle like the dew.
Your face is as fair as a lily,
I can't help loving you.

Your smiles are as sweet as
a baby's face
Your kisses are as warm as
your embrace
Your lips are as tender as
the petal on a rose
How much do you Love me?
God only knows.

Brian K Patrick
PERSPECTIVE ON BEAUTY
How many of us, if given the choice between roach and butterfly
Without so much as the bat of an unsure eye
Would choose the homelier creature to crush, and leave to die
Honestly?

So entranced are we by the gleam of a pearl
Or the wayward charms of a lovely girl
That we often fail to remember our creature is one and the same

Sometimes, in my mind, I recite the line
BEAUTY AND THE BEAST
But by the pen I expose our sin
And attempt to show
Because our prejudice runs high, and our prudence is slow
We have truly made things so
That for the sake of accuracy
In the name of correctness
Should not this phrase surely be twisted, turned and tied tautly in a knot
So that it may only go
In all of its ugly directness, and contrast glow
BEAUTY IS THE BEAST

Elizabeth Rose Paulus
THE EMPLOYEE LAW OF N.Y.C. THE ELEVENTH COMMANDMENT
Thou shalt not sue thine employer
Thou shalt suffer in agonizing,
fiery monstrous pain
From injuries as a result from
working
Thou shalt get no medical attention
If by MIRACLE, money is
obtained, medical is paid
(Benefits owed YOU, because of
the EMPLOYERS'
NEGLIGENCE)
Just as it was given it shall be
stolen away.
Compensate Compensate Compensate
Insurance Insurance Insurance
Nonsense Stuff & Bother
"WE ARE HERE TO HELP YOU"
The apple doesn't fall far
from the tree
Can we honestly expect the
Wolf to protect the Chicken
from his brother Wolf?
The result of that is—thou shalt
get no medical attention
Wherefore your body cannot toil
its daily bread
Thou shalt be PENNILESS,
GRIEVING, and S T A R V I N G
Depending on others for even
the barest necessities

AND THOU SHALT REMAIN
SICK
But It's alright, It's moral, It must be,
IT'S THE LAW OF N.Y.C.

Hope W Overstreet
THANK YOU

To my children, The Loves of my Life.

My Children! My Children!
I love you so.
But I miss that one
Who had to go.

My life has changed
Since that night
When He went to Jesus.
To live in God's light.

For the roof over my head,
And the food with which I'm fed
For the lights with which to see
And the kisses and hugs for me.
I Thank You, My Father,
For the warmth and respect of
Grandchildren,
And the loving affection of
Great-Grandchildren.
For seventy-seven Birthdays to watch
them All grow.
And to hear them say, "Grandma, I
love you so."

Thank You, Heavenly Father.

Shannon Odom Rase
WHEN I BECOME A MOTHER, TOO
Soon, I will be a mother, too
And I will instill in my child
The things instilled in me by you

I pray, as the months speed past
That my baby's childhood will last,
And not fly by unseen by him
As mine did way back when

I will be a parent at last
With all the headaches and worries
Handed down to me from your past

I pray, as the months speed along
That I follow the right path
And don't do this all wrong

I pray I do as well as you
When I become a mother, too

Mike Omar
A FACE IN THE CROWD
Persistent reflections of a split second
A deja vu perhaps, in the mind
Of sweet memories, of past life
Flooding like a river, for a while
Of a face in the crowd
Tracing the globe around
To the horn of Africa, down the Nile
A childhood's friend's smile
In downtown, U.S.A., unexpected
In a crowded post office, amazed.

Angela Odell
UNTIL WE GROW OLD

This poem is dedicated to Eddie, the greatest husband anyone could have. Here's our wedding song. I love you—Angela.

When we first met—it was love at first sight
Now here we are dancing on our wedding night
Our love is so special and we knew from the start
That we'd be together—till death do us part.

One day I asked "Will you be my wife"
You're what I want for the rest of my life
To Angela the girl, who I love so dear
Now you and I will always be near.

I hope through our life, we never must part
For Eddie I Love You with all of my heart
No treasure on Earth could ever compare
To the joy we have now and the love that we share.

We'll cherish each other all the days of our life
And nothing will change this new man and wife
From this day forward to have and to hold
We promise to love—Until We Grow Old.

As we end this night, we hope that you see
In love and so happy we always will be
We thank you for coming as we start our new life
Together, forever as husband and wife.

Shawnee O'Nan
AN ALCOHOLIC'S CRY

For my dad and I, with all my heart.

Many times I've wondered,
In the morning feeling ill.
If there was someone out there,
That I didn't mean to kill.

After all night drinking,
The daylight brings me Fear.
I've cried for help a lot,
But no one seemed to hear.

My friends and family worry,
But they don't understand.
I can't do this by myself,
I need a helping hand.

Can someone out there save me?
This fear cuts like a knife.
I need the help today,
To maybe save a life.

Lisa Wimberley
NIGHT AND DAY
The sun rises overhead
While the moon falls as if dead

The birds fly with the bees
As I splash through the leaves

The wind is whisking through my hair
And against my clothes and skin so fair

The day has started
The night has ended

The sun has risen
The stars descended

Georgia Osborn
DO YOU REMEMBER?

For my son David Atkins.

Hostess O's and Harleys
Cinnamon rolls and cheer
Laughing in the sunshine
Wish you were here
Fishing rods and a shot gun
Old boot top-happy 41
Marigolds and fighting
Pretty woman and bud
Ian Dory and the Blockheads
I wouldn't change you if I could
Always a dog, always a lady
You're a grown man now
And no longer my baby

Scott A Oakley
REMEMBRANCE

To Lelana; never forget that I loved you.

I see the raindrops fall from the sky.
I remember the memories with only tears in my eyes.
I know I'll never find you again.
I can only remember.

Those beautiful walks through the park,
Saying, "I Love You!"
If only you could now guide me through the rain.
But, I know that I will never find another you.
I would give my precious life,
To win back that love.
But, I know now that I will never love or find someone like you.
As the rain stops, the tears stop.
I can only say "I Loved You!"

As I walked that same quiet park
remembering You.

Mindy McClain (Age 14)
MEMORIES IN THE SAND
That night my life was torn apart
As you made me cry and broke my heart.

But as we stood in the sand, we held tight.
Being with you again felt so right.

As I looked in your eyes, all I could see
Was a person that meant the world to me.

As we walked through the rippling waters of the sea,
You turned and kissed me.

I looked up to the stars above,
And picked a bright star on which to place our love.

But as the moon lay low,
Your arms that wrapped tightly around me let go.

I guess forever was too long to say
Because without a look back, you turned and walked away.

Somewhere our star died and fell to land,
And all that was left were memories in the sand.

P A McDowell
THE BOOK
Life is like a giant book,
Be it blank in verse,
That's opened up and given us
Upon our humble birth;
The words within are ours to write
As only we can do,
Each page is filled as day is done,
The next to start anew.

When the final words are written,
The chapters all complete,
When accomplishments are listed
Next to failures and defeats;
Once your life is in the book,
Down to your final deed,
When God gathers all the pages,
How will your book read?

Christianne Michelle O'Biso
JACK FROST
Jack Frost! Jack Frost!
How much does it cost?
To paint my leaves
Before they freeze.
Red, orange, yellow, and green,
The prettiest I've ever seen.
Can you do it tonight?
It would be a beautiful sight
When I awake the colors I would see,
While having breakfast and my cup of tea.
You would be such a dear
If you could fill my year.
I'll appreciate your skill;
Just send me the bill.

Herbert P Moore
IRENE

Dedicated to my one and only, Irene.

Her canvas was my mortal soul
Her paints were words of love
Her brush an angel's golden voice
Called down from up above.

And she, a living picture drew
In the hallways of my mind
A priceless treasure, always new
That thieves could never find.

But her picture grew as time went on
Giving birth to thought and deed
That spilled beyond my finite mind
Into a world where mortals feed.

And her picture spread o'er all the land
Until no barren spot was found
For the artwork of her spoken love
Covered all the earthly ground.

And angels gasped to see her work
As they marveled at the scene
And then softly spoke one word of love
They spoke her name, . . . Irene.

Herbert P Moore
CHANGE

This poem is dedicated to Carol Yogi.

I stopped the clock upon the wall
And bid its hands move not at all
The folded hands lay quietly there
Still shadows changed upon the stair.

I ordered then that change be still
Change must obey my royal will
But the sun marched on its merry way
And calmly marked the end of day.

The summers came, — The summers went
My frame, with age, was slowly bent
And constant change just moved on by
And paid no heed to such as I.

For relentless change cannot be still
But must its destiny fulfill
Beg not the clock be slow or faster
It's just the servant, not the master.
My royal wish had been a dream
My life the whistle, not the steam
Eternal change is all that's real
The rest, — Mere fancies that I feel.

Judith K Pierson
CAUGHT UP IN A DREAM
Could I be . . .?
Would it seem . . .?
Caught up in a dream?
For the thought of you
is heaven to believe.
That you're there,
really there, waiting.
With a prayer,
I wish to stay
near you always,
And touch your heart
And be your friend.
This is my dream,
May it never end.

Rochelle Parrea
"HAND ME DOWN" ADVICE
Listen to me younger sister
For I will tell you no wrong
I know that you are thinking
Here comes that same old song
I was once your age you know
And I thought I knew it all
But I learned to listen to good advice
In order to eliminate downfalls
Don't pay too close attention
To what's in or the current style
Like any other phase or stage
It will only last a while
Have you thought about your future
Or how to make your life more complete
Start working on obtaining realistic goals
So that you can stand on your own two feet
You may take this advice
Or may not listen to me
But when you look in the mirror
I hope you like what you see
Go ahead and have some fun
I did and I still do
The reason I am telling you this
Is that I love you

Gina Palmese
TRAVELLERS OF THE NIGHT

To my parents, a pair so rare, To Andy Chisholm, a friend so true,To Domenic Massa, I could never find another as great as you.

The lacy silhouettes that dance in the sky,
Are created with the bellows of the wind.
The unborn images of the dancers of the night,
Soar gracefully with the travelling owls in flight,
As the trees added mischief and far greater sinned.
They created an atmosphere that was dread by the mind,
As the silhouettes were in chorus with the moonlight,
They would chant their songs in their mischievous cries,
While the dance invited the dead to rise,
During this evening of darkness; the evil of night.
Risen in hatred from their forbidden sanctuaries,
They journey to the dwelling of their soul mates,
Through the distant patches of the blinding fog,
The corpses of evil travelled to the bog,
To reunite with the ones who arranged their fates.

Violet M Penland
OUR HANDS
Do you know when I miss you,
Darling?
It's when I sit down to dine.
I'd slip my hand over to you
And your hand would cover mine.
Of course there's a feeling of love
When our hands would entwine,
But also a certain strength
That I can't exactly define.
Sort'a like, "Now, I'm here, darling
You can always depend on me—
I love you with all my heart
That's how it will always be."
But fate has decreed it different
Now when I reach out for you—
There's only the cool, crisp table
Just memories will have to do.

Becky Ptacek
BURYING THE PAST
They have always told me to bury the past
Otherwise I will never last
I will never be able to go on
If I think about what is now gone.
This advice slowly becomes a part of me
And I am slowly set free.
But there is one thing I will never do
That is forget about you
You will always be in my heart
Even though we are miles apart.
Yes, I will cry at night
Wishing I could hug you so tight
But you are someone gone by
So looking ahead is something I must try.
Now I can finally let them know
That I am letting you go
And that the past is gradually being buried
Along with many of the feelings I have carried.

Shelley Pederson
INSIDE OUT

For Kathy Hopkins, who taught me the importance of feeling from the "inside out."

Seeing things with your eyes,
is easier than seeing them with your heart.
After all beauty is only skin deep,
and feeling is but an art.

Seeing a sunset is breathtaking
but your eyes can only see so much,
It is when you start to feel the beauty
that you know you have the touch.

Feeling it on the inside
that's what life is about
You can't feel the magic
until you feel from the "inside out."

Minnie E Parker
CHRISTMAS
Christmas is coming—it's almost here
The happiest, jolliest time of the year;
With cards and papers and bows galore,
All kinds of decorations in windows and doors.

So let us enjoy every bit of the fun,
But don't let us forget that Holy One
Who was born on the day we
celebrate;
That he lived and died to compensate

The many wrongs that we might do;
Giving His life for me and you.
Healing the sick; raising the dead,
And to the hungry giving bread.

He gathered Disciples and taught
them the way
To live and teach, and how to pray.
And He says to all "Come unto me,
I'll give New life and hope to thee."

He came to forgive every vice and sin
That a place in heaven all might win.
So say halleluiah *sing and shout,
For this is what Christmas is all
about.
Merry Christmas, Thank you Jesus.

Sheri Penn
TO A SPECIAL FRIEND
It started out as friendship,
and turned into something more.
The love I feel for you,
I've never felt before.
You make me feel so happy,
whenever I am down.
By telling me your stupid jokes,
and acting like a clown.
I can't believe you tell me,
all the stuff you do.
But I'm glad that you can trust me
And I can trust you too.
You're my best friend
and I want you to know,
no matter what may happen
I'll never let you go!!

Kama Page
VIOLENCE
To the victims of the storm.

Over the world hangs a dark,
ominous cloud;
its presence is felt and known
for it grasps the soul, and like a
vacuum
sucks from the soul rational thinking
and behavior,
forgiveness and love,
leaving a husk engulfed in a storm—
a storm of hatred and violence.
Trust is no longer known;
it is replaced by suspicion, anger, and
fear.
Life no longer has worth or dignity;
it is sustained on revenge, humiliation and death.
Nobody is exempt from the winds of
this storm,
the winds of violence,
pushing us further down its path—
its long, dark descending path . . .
to hell.

Gilbert Pizani
FRIENDSHIP'S BOND
When people get together to speak of
things long past
There is only one commodity that we
all agree will last
Material things come and go as the
old wears off the new
But the one thing that is ageless is a
friendship that is true
For when people speak of friends
there is but one conclusion
You can be surrounded by friends
while even in seclusion
For even though fate may separate
paths and test the ties that bind
You will always have your friends if
you keep them near in mind
So bring to mind a memory linger
over it for a while
If you think about your friends you
cannot help but smile
The calendar will slip on by time will
surely pass
Still there is no time limit on
friendship whose bonds will hold you
fast

Connie Pifer
THE WORLD TOMORROW
This poem is dedicated to my Husband Tom, and our children, Raymond, Kimberly and Jennifer. The Joys Of My Life!

If we had a second chance, would
it bring war, or peace
and love towards our countries.
Would it bring drugs and torment
with families and friends.
Will it let us live the days once
more, and forgive the
mistakes, we had made in the past.
Will it let us have the inspirations
and the quality, as
life goes on for a brighter tomorrow.

James M Pressley
MAN O' WAR
There beneath the squalid sea
She lays upon her staved-in side;
Her sunken decks strewn with debris

She towers up in majesty
Erupting from the sand with pride
There beneath the squalid sea

A crew in death guards loyally;
Their polished bones, a ward,
bestride
Her sunken decks strewn with debris

The shifting floor she oversees
Upon the ancient reef she strides
There beneath the squalid sea

Once so fearsome, now to be
Thus riddled with holes, gaping wide;
Her sunken decks strewn with debris

Look then, she rests so peacefully
Swaying gently with the tide;
There beneath the squalid sea,
Her sunken decks strewn with debris

Sarah Pitcher
CONFUSED
I'm trapped in my mind,
I can't decide,
I can't make up my mind,
What should I do?
My problem is frustrating.
All I can do is pace,
Back and forth, back and forth
My heart is beating faster than
before.

I'm fidgeting,
Tapping my pencil up and down.
I just can't decide.
What? what is the question I'm
striving to answer?

Why is this so hard?
Think, why am I desperate for
knowledge?
Why am I confused?
Why can't I decide?
As the time beats away,
What is the answer I'm searching
for?
Only you hold the answer.

Misty D Payne (Age 8)
MAGICAL
To: Mrs. Snyder, Third grade teacher at Laurel Valley Elementary.

Witches and Wizards and Scarecrows
too.
Have magical brooms or a magical
brew.
They may have a ring or a magical
stone.
But I have a magical telephone!

Lisa Pasternak
STARS
Its figure,
So sculptured fine,
Upon the high heavens,
Looks upon Earth,
With a glisten in the eye.

Up in the sky,
A light follows,
Radiant beams cast,
Day and night,
A guide of where I'm going.

Its light
Fair and peaceful,
Lightens up the galaxy
And brightens futures beyond.

Its pathway,
So long and deep,
Directs me into the heavens,
Where I 'tend to sleep.

Lisa Pasternak
LIFE IS LIKE A GAME
Life is like a game,
We compete each day,
We strive to succeed,
Even if our potentiality is troubled.

The qualities in life,
Can be won or lost,
Can show sadness or joy,
And bring out true spirit.

The person in life,
Can succeed or fail,
Whichever order he strives to be.
Look out for yourself and you
Will get your goal,
If not try harder.

Our finesse, of our sportsmanship,
That makes life like a game,
Is that we may bring out a better
person,
And show our glory,
After it is through.

Jodie L Philipps
WHY
How could she kill herself,
Why did she want to die?
I don't understand,
I want to know why!

She was just like a sister to me.
Never depressed, but happy to be
alive.
Maybe something came up to make
her all stressed out,
And she thought this was the only
way out.

I thought I knew her from head to
toe,
I was wrong, I didn't know.
I wondered what was wrong when
she gave me her sweater
I guess I went wrong when I didn't
ask her.

We had an intimate friendship,
But then I let it slip.
By letting her pleading hints pass by
And not once thinking to ask her
"why?"

Jennifer Ann Perez
SONG OF THE STARS
The sky is glistening,
sparkling blue.
The stars shine brightly
just for you.
Twinkling and shining,
we watch the stars.
Shooting stars
can go quite far.
Big and little,
some stars are brittle.
Shapes and sizes,
from falling to rising.
Stars are special
any way you look at them.

Henry Grady Pilcher III
THE AMUSEMENT PARK
The loneliest place that I have ever
been
Was an Amusement Park without a
friend
No one to share the laughs and smiles
No one to help me walk the miles

The games and thrills were no fun
alone
It was like a visit to the Twilight
Zone
Where life is going on all around
And a familiar voice is nowhere to be
found

The hours became a burden to bear
Life lived like this, I did not care
By choice I could leave at any time
Go or stay, the decision was mine

I decided to try and find a way
To get in the fun and join the play
But not alone, a lesson learned well
Life lived alone is a private hell

David 'Dvid' Perry
BEAUTY
From the Pages of my many Dreams
Came She, One who moved
Like a god-forged Moonbeam.
Her Eyes were those of the winter
Sky,
Her Hair as black as Jet.
Skin of Alabaster shone with purity
She smiled the Smile of Aphrodite,
Freyja, and Isis.
Wrapped in a Gown of the whitest
Silk,
She was the Milky Way above my
Eyes.
Like the Wind, like Music, did she
dance,
Her Laughter the Song of Life itself.
When She left, Agony beyond Agony
struck my Heart.

When She came, Her Touch gave me new Life.
Lights played about Her, a thousand Stars,
A thousand perfect Diamonds.
She was Beauty, She was Loveliness incarnate.
And She danced with None.
None but Me.

Sarah Moore Roy
TELEIOTES (PERFECTLY FINISHED)
Suppose that tomorrow morning I received these bills,
25,568 golden sunsets upon the hills (70 years),
Health enough to last me all my years.
The right to life, love, and prayer without fears.
Music and laughter and joys to spill;
Friends and family and wheat for the mill,
Clothing, food, and shelter, too!
I couldn't pay God, could you?
Roses, daffodils, and hyacinths so blue,
A creek to swim in and to fish with your dog!
A walk across blue waters on a hollow log.
Oh, God, now I can't pay these bills, there's no way;
Oh, yes, He answers back with a voice soft and low;
Just look at my Son and then don't you say no!

Helen Roussos
A ROSE

To the decade of the 30's—good and bad.

Our love was like a summer rose,
It blossomed and it was fair,
Its petals had such color
And a fragrance truly rare.

You took this rose and placed it
Close to your singing heart,
You vowed that it would never die
That we would never part.

But then one day, I saw that rose
Tossed on a busy street,
A broken stem and petals
Crushed by hurrying feet.

Sr Jill Rupprecht
FROM THE HEART
"How lovely is Your dwelling place, O Lord of Hosts!" (Ps. 122)

Yearning.
A heart filled with hope
hastening to your company
soundless words between us.

Loving.
Sunlight piercing the painted glass
fragrance sweetly blowing through
glimmer of red candle light.

Being.
You for me. I for you.
Relationship of love.
Worthy, Lord, may I be.

Hermione Heather Rhones
THE CONTENTS OF A TEAR
One part anger,
One part grief.
A dash of bitterness
And a pinch of regret.
Add fear mistrust and
Irrational hate.
Mix it with sadness and
Self pity, then frost it
With spite.
Last but not least
Is the most important
Ingredient of all.
The delicate sparkle of
Hope completes the tear
drop as it falls.

Jean M Reed
LORD LET ME DO SOME LIVING
Lord let me do some living twixt the cradle & the grave
Let me make a splash of joy as the ocean makes a wave,
Train my eyes to search for wonders so that none may go un-missed,
Keep my loved ones ever near me & that none may go un-kissed
Let my ears hear every bird song, every church bell as it rings,
Let me help a wounded sparrow, teach me how to mend its wings,
Let me scatter words of wisdom, guide me 'round each winding trail,
Let me live life to its fullest, lift me gently when I fail,
Lord let me be a lighthouse with my light supplied by thee,
Let me do a lot of living 'til thy blessed face I see.

Edward Reynoza
TO KAREN (TO LOVE)
United only by the shared Heavens above, we stand apart.
The sight draws us together, as the joys we brought each other's heart.
The sand of a distant land lay about your feet, seeming as endless,
as the sands of distant shores which lay about my own.
Our horizon's bound by land and seas, mountains tall, and self
built walls about our heart's true desires.
Our hope rests uneasy with the traveling Sun, as it pursues pale moon of midnight sky.
Such as they are we, residing within a dream, held tight, in hearts filled by Love ever true. To be understood only by the Eternal Lord.
That one day soon, the glowing Sun may capture the fleeing moon, and
together light the Heavens above.
Mountains tall, will fall, walls crumble, and sands will join at near waters. Our feet will leave their prints side by side.
The distance between us no greater now, than the softness of Love's most sweet kiss, and the gentle touch of your small hand resting safe within my own.

Richard Panaewa Ronolo
HERE I SIT AT CHILDREN'S HOSPITAL BESIDE MY DAUGHTER

This poem is dedicated to someone very special, My Daughter.

Here I sit at Children's Hospital beside my daughter and her favorite pillow. She's been to surgery to correct a defect, one which I hope will never take effect upon thousands of new babies that the world should expect.

We the people of today can only come to imagine what this world would be if it were to be free of all these many types of crippling diseases.

All these babies and young children of today are not at fault. Even their parents may not be of fault. But I guess maybe we could say it's the way nature may take its way.

As I sit here in this ward with babies around me, I can only hope that joy and happiness soon will be founded.

Funny as though it may seem, how our very young generations come to be.

Doctors and nurses try their best. That doesn't mean we adults and parents can sit at rest.

Help these little ones of today and this whole world will be a better place to stay.

As I sit here watching my daughter toss in pain, I can swear I feel just the same.

This is her first of corrections, and still several more lay ahead. But there's no worry, Mom and Dad will be by her side to help her ease along in every stride.

Some day she'll walk this land without a helping hand. This is her goal and our belief.

By the way, her name is Cori-Linn.

God bless you, Sweetheart, and many others.

All my love,

Your Daddy

Rebecca Randles
OUR WEDDING DAY

This poem is dedicated to my husband Tim. In loving memory of my mother Barbara.

Our wedding day
was such a joyous treat,
Our emotions were racing
from our heads to our feet.
With all of my womanhood
I gave him my all,
In all of his manhood
he stood so tall.
We proudly spoke our vows
standing side by side,
All of our promises
we will gladly abide.
Lord, give us your blessing
guide us in your way,
On this the happiest of occasions
our wedding day.

Carole A Robichaud
I THINK OF YOU
When the moon comes out so bright at night
And shines its magical lovely light,
When all the stars up there in the blue
Twinkle and sparkle the whole night through,
What do I do? I think of you.

When the leaves from the trees begin to fall,
And the autumn sun captures it all,
When the breeze seems to utter a tender sigh
That says you are gone but where am I?
What do I do? I think of you.

Where have you gone without me?
What have you done to my heart?
Once it was warm, warm as can be
But now you have torn it apart.

When I go to bed to sleep at night,
But all I can do is toss and fight,
To keep the tears away from my eyes,
When I remember all your lies,
What do I do? I think of you.

Angeline Mary Rondenelli
CLOUDS

To all "Cloud Lovers."

My never ending love affair with clouds
began many, many years ago.
They nestle up in the vast, blue sky
moving ever so slowly and gracefully.
I always remember the special magic
they performed for me alone.
My fairy tale characters came to life
for hours of pure enjoyment.
Animals, big and small, raced across the sky
playing gleefully with one another.
Some days, it was just peace and quiet
gazing at those whisps of fluff.
Being mischievous, they would tease me
maybe they would perform, maybe not.
Then came that special day when the
clouds separated in long, thin layers.
The rays of the sun came filtering through
as I stared in awe and wonder-ment.
Before I was overwhelmed by the
peace that enveloped me completely.

Irma Robledo
THE CHILD IN ME
The child in me
Is alive and yearning
Always searching always learning
She runs free
Like the wind
Her eyes bright and cheery
Always guiding the woman
Into a path of light
Where hopes and dreams
In all her endeavors
Will soon take flight
Forever and ever

Sheila Roman
SHELTER HOLD
Wandering through the city streets covered with snow
Beth walks almost aimlessly, young daughter Jill in tow
Shielded only by a blanket against the cold of winter's day
She whispers to her little child
"Honey walk this way."
Her mind races back as her feet keep the pace
Of days when she was happier in her very own place
The car horns remind her of the car she used to drive
But reality brings her back to wondering how tonight they will survive
Beth searches through the garbages of the best restaurants in town

Hoping inside some food for her
young girl will be found
Then they rush off to the shelter
hoping to find a place to sleep
But once again there is no room, this
is the fourth time this week
"Mommy I don't mind the cold, you
can keep me warm"
And in Beth's eye you can clearly see
her heart being ripped and torn
Jill looks at her mother as she again
starts to cry
"Don't worry mommy, we always
find some way to get by"
As they ride the warm subway a
young girl stares from the other side
She quietly asks her mother
"Mommy are they trying to hide"
Beth smiled as she heard the young
girl's innocent ignorance of her plight
But reality swept in again as the girl
left the train and said goodnight

Sheila Roman

A POEM FOR JENNY

I look how big you've grown not just
in body but also in mind
And soon you'll be walking out of
the door, what adventures will you
find
I'll tell you everything I know, that is
all that I can do
And the best words that I can say are
Jenny to yourself be true
How I want to walk beside you and
guide you through every storm
I now have to let you go I knew this
time would come the day you were
born
Before I set you on your path to all
the wonders that you shall see
My daughter who is a woman now
one more time will you listen to me
The time has come for you to go to
live your life as best you can
Walk straight on up that ladder, but
don't make steps of your fellow man
Remember you're only human and as
such you will make mistakes
Remember I'll always be there for
you through your happiness and
heartaches
Believe in yourself, you're good and
strong, no matter what path you
choose
Each step that you take along the way
is a piece of knowledge you can use
Your mind is your greatest weapon,
it's also your greatest tool
Be proud to be a woman, but be
nobody's fool
Now it's time to go my dear Jenny,
and as you go I go too
Remember home is where the heart
is, and my heart will always be with
you.

Averi Roberts

LOCKED BETWEEN MYSELF AND THE REAL WORLD

I LIVE LOVE and DON'T
UNDERSTAND
Before I could blame it on stupidity
Now the reality must be faced
Seeking knowledge is a shame when
jealousy prolongs it
Many of us have been accused
I guess then you say—ACCUSED of
what
Then I say to you
ACCUSED of truly living
Trying to dream and achieve life's
goals
I am baffled by my intellectual ability
to be ignorant
And believe me I verbalize this with
great wisdom
For much of me is and has lived but
still a part of me has yet to be
discovered.
Those who look to play upon my
weaknesses
Shall find life most perplexing come
stormy weather
Look for you have listened but still
do not hear
Carry on for our triumphs will be
extraordinary
I've talked so much about dreams
Thus the values by which I live are
floating within them

I won't lie anymore
I am caught
Yes my life is becoming meaningless
For you the wicked misled
self-centered criminals
Have SEIZED my mind
Oh I guess all of life's prosperities
have been conquered
No it's time for an education to be
given and received
But listen not for I am sure you will
HEAR
Many have fatal diseases

You who have been misled by
misguided souls must redeem
yourselves
Look around and see that life has
been turned upside down
Shaken out of our hands and into
destructive mechanisms
Let me take you back to ABC and
123
For those are the basics but strong
foundations
Begin to formulate new meanings to
life
STOP TAKE time and begin again
Let the YOUTH regenerate
And let our elders guide us
For the Love of my Half-Hearted
soul will be embedded in life.

Sandra K Rath

A SPECIAL WISH

A special wish for the one I love;
Six long weeks it's been for me.
I know, Love was not to enter in;
Not for you, but for me
The attraction has always been.

And I gave no thoughts to the future;
But lived for our moments alone.
Though I knew there must be a
departure,
For not even our time is our own.

Six weeks, nothing but thoughts;
Many moments alone.
My feelings for you cannot be
bought.
I want you, My feelings my own.

So whether you're here or gone;
No one can ever erase;
Those brief beautiful moments
Of our every embrace.

A special wish
To this person so rare;
Somehow you will realize
That I will always care.

Dianna D Sheehan

INSPIRED BY BILLY

When you lose a friend
It isn't like losing something
from your pocket.
You can't find that friend and
put them back where they belong.
That's all you can do is hold
on to memories
And cherish those
for someday you will meet again.

Lane Robert Schweim

THE EYES HAVE IT

The media's all inclusive eye.
Probing, intruding, demanding why.
Searching for those to crucify.

Blurring lines of objectivity.
Shrouding true facts in obscurity.
Creation of false reality.

To entertain, inform, or lead us?
Censoring words, stifling ideas.
Overwhelmed, will they defeat us?

Echoed murmurs of hypocrisy.
Putting on face of democracy.
Casting the seeds of complacency.

Voices of death propagating war.
Grimly displaying the starving poor.
Is this of the people, by, or for?

Hollow speech in a sound bite of
fear.
For the beckoning cries draw them
near.
Mesmerizing sheep so they may
shear.

Tabloid, radio, television.
Cable, video, high definition.
Altered thought, individual decision.

Tonya Sowers

ETERNITY

Tons of memories from the past,
all those dreams were supposed to
last.
Now you have left me forever,
time can't put us back together.

My heart is beyond any repair,
heartless people like you don't care.
You left me when I needed you most,
memory haunts me like a ghost.

You savagely abandoned me,
help me erase the memory.
The pain abruptly rushes back,
as I wonder what our love lacked.

You found someone totally new,
but I was devoted to you.
I guess it just wasn't meant to be,
I'll remember you for eternity.

Banavali Shripad

THE LOVE ETERNAL

Dedicated to my inspiration, VCM.

Climbing the mountains of our love I
weep;
in the depths of your eyes I take a
leap.

Piercing the barrier of your absolute
silence;
it's I who was questioning your own
conscience.

Breaking the ripples of your hearty
laughter;
trying to solve the mystery of the
Creator.

Hearing cautiously the beatings of
your heart;
looking carefully, in the heap of your
thoughts.

Oh, everywhere I was searching for
that love eternal;
but all this external beauty was just
physical.
In your soul at last, I looked for the
joy infinite;
And yes . . .
it's there, that I discovered Eternal
Love alright!!

Donna L DeMagistris

A BABY'S BORN, A MAN DIES

This poem is dedicated to the loving memory of my father.

A baby's born, a man dies,
Everyone comes together and
cries;
Some are happy and some are sad,
Others wish for the times they
once
had;
And a baby's born, a man dies.

One says hi, the other good-by,
But for some, the memories will
not die;
Life begins and life comes to an end,
For some it means losing a friend;
And a baby's born, a man dies.

The time has come to say our
good-bys,

Tears fall as we begin to cry;
A child is born, a life's lost,
The pain has ended, but at what
cost;
And a baby's born, a man dies.

Dawn Shafer

SECRET LOVE

As we lay together
He Holds me like a dove
Firmness to show his power
Gentleness to show his love

He may be older than I am
But with that I'll have to live
It isn't our age that matters
It's the love that we give

This person I cannot reveal
For I love him so
I'd hate to hurt our families
For This Reason no one shall know

So now you've heard about
The love that we share
A secret from our families
And proof that we still care

Karin Sementelli

LETTING GO

As the quiet night silently falls
My thoughts go outside the four inner
walls.
Remembering back to the sun-filled
days—
I wonder how we let it slip away.
Tears form on the insides of my eyes;
As my love for you unfolds out of
disguise.
Loneliness invades my broken
heart—
But deep inside I know we must part.
As our time together takes its place—
I will remember always your smiling
face.
In my dreams that I hold deep inside;
I remember our love you held in your
eyes.
Our love unfolded like a blooming
fresh flower—
Yet ended abruptly in that final dark
hour.
Alone, now I must stand without you
by my side;
I will let you go but will not run and
hide.
You made me laugh until I had to
cry;

We never thought we would say good-bye.
Tucked away in my dreams is where you will stay;
As I shed the tears that you created;
And the words 'I love you' I will never again hear you say.

Sylvia Soraparu
A VISIT TO THE VET'S
My Benji loves to go for a ride
But going to the Vet's he can't abide,
He puts on his brakes when I open the door
A gentle nudge, and he lays on the floor.
He seems such a coward as they check his weight
He shivers and shakes till the table vibrates.
I stand by his side as he clings to me,
The look in his eyes is pathetic to see.
He takes his shots with nary a whimper,
As his body slumps and his legs get
limper.
As we get in the car on the way to go home
I tell him "Good Boy" and I give him a bone.
As smart as he is, he seems to forget,
That most of his "rides" end up at the Vet's.

Stacy R Shick
DREAMS
Everyone has dreams
No matter if they're yours or a team's
Dreams can be scattered
Or just thrown around and battered
There's always risk and mistakes
that you make
But those are the chances
you must take
Some people are born without
dreams or hope
But they learn how to cope
Everyone's dreams can come
true
But the chances and choices
are totally up to you

Nola T Sherrill
JOY
I feel joy when I hear a child's laughter,
Sorrow when I hear it cry;
There is joy in watching an eagle,
Soar across the heavenly sky.

There is joy in living for Jesus,
In striving to do His will;
There is joy in loving your neighbors,
Your friends and enemies as well.

There is joy in reading God's word,
In walking with a friend for a mile;
And it would be a joy to me, when
you have read this poem,
Knowing it has caused you to smile.

Barbara Sellinger
LOVE
Love is such a special treat,
that doesn't happen every day.
Open your heart and your arms,
and love will come your way.

When you're in love and happy enough,
that it makes you cry.
Keep that love inside your heart,
that's enough to keep you high.

The only time that love hurts me,
the only time I'm sad.
Is when that special someone,
goes away and gets me mad.

The time goes by so slow,
I wish that I could die.
I knew one day, you would return,
and that's what makes me cry.

Donna Davis
THE TIME HAS TURNED

To the loves of my time—my children Alex (Allicia), Adrienne, Heather and Stephen. To my mother, Laura, my loving family and friends—each and every one!

The time has turned—has turned at last,
The seasons gone, the decades past.
And now the world is fresh and new,
As all creation pans the view.

No more the time of dreary thought,
Of things that should and words that ought.
Freedom sails on far and wide,
And scans the stars up to the skies.

Below the people of earth remain,
Attempting to shape and to regain,
All that they had lost through doubt and fear,
And salted with their bitter tears,

But time works for the good you see.
Time shapes greater destinies,
As seasons pass and seasons turn,
Time holds the key from which we learn.

Donna Davis
NEW BEGINNINGS
The old year ends, a new begins, the blessings counted now as friends,
And memories of brighter days that Father Time cannot displace.

Here lies a trace of aftermath, the fragments of a bitter past,
That echo of the coming dawn and sparks the new year to live on.

The friends of cherished legacies that stir so soft and fain the breeze,
And light the path that lingers on, the love that spurs the pilgrim on.

A watchful keep was held at tide, the burrows of a life which died,
Though truth was really never tried, the shadows hide the reason.

Do hope for those things yet unseen.
Do hope to hope and dream a dream.
For life is but a shadow past and only God can cast the mast.

Live on as if you destined be, to live forever sea to see,
A fragment of the universe, created in a single verse.

Your burdens cannot come undone,
till you set sail and search the sun.
The merriment of one to come, bursts wide the troubled heart.

For shadows of those things are past.
The Captain guides the sailing mast.
We sail for open seas at last, the heart, the burden, now uncast.

Sammie J Storie
OUR HOSTESS
When she toils, unliken to any other place
Whether to dine or relax, a familiar face;
For lightening our burdens, she's the key
Making the day brighter, with her to see.

A portrait in motion, portrayal of a beauty
To behold and adore, while performing her duty;
A spectacular smile, charm, and sweetness
Traits of endearment, courtesy, and cheerfulness.
Our delightful Waitress.

Laughing or crying, even shy and blushing
Doesn't interfere, for she never ceases talking;
Constantly taunting, amusing, reveling in all
Leaving memories, for later in life to recall.
Our admirable Friend.

Such a wonderful person, one rarely finds
Remaining always, in our Hearts, on our minds;
For sharing her feelings, our love she's got
Remembering and cherishing, forget her we'll not.
Our precious Sweetheart.

Jacquelyn deFarral
SIS
Your presence, your smile,
comforted our daily woes

Our lives were graced by your
devotion and tender direction

How you persevered all those years
without faltering no one knows

It was so good to know you . . .

When you fulfilled your final
obligation, with sadness, we said so
long

Though you went to a better place—
resting in eternal peace

Loved ones unwillingly
acknowledged that you were gone

It was so good to know you . . . .

Fond memories of you lighten the
darkness we encounter along the way

The days were a little brighter when
you were among us

You continue to live in our hearts and
perhaps we'll meet again some day

It was so good to know you . . .

Laura A Seinitz
THE JOURNEY TOWARD DESTINY

To all those that have traveled on this path before me, and to all those that will go after me.

The road is long and hard
Glass cuts my feet
Rocks trip and bloody me

The ever-present sun
Is hot and unmerciful
The taunting wind
Whips round my soul

I know not where I am
Nor where I will be

But let the glass cut
And the rocks bloody
May the sun be unmerciful
And the wind whip
May I be ignorant of where I am
And where I will be
For when I arrive
I will have met my destiny

Sheila Betts Stewart
FIRST BALMY DAY
Gentle sighs the breath of spring

New born against the frosted earth.
Springs forth the sap in rising flow.
Ebbs the streams in joyous mirth.

Balmy sighs the breath of spring,
Forth bursts the buds to touch the sun.
Whose gentle fingers caress the leaves,
As again nature's miracle is done.

Lawrence Spirio
JUST FRIENDS AND NOTHING MORE
We met and thought we knew the score;

but in the long run we are,
just friends and nothing more.
We kissed the kiss
that only a lover understands;
our eyes had a knowing look
each time we squeezed our hands.
We said it was love
and saw each other all the more.
It was a false love, for now we are
just friends and nothing more.
Ah yes, just an infatuation
and only that from the start.
Too bad we did not understand;
too bad, for now we must part.
Good by my sweet, someday
true love will knock upon thy door,
But as for us, we part, we are
just friends and nothing more . . . .

Lisa Salyers
THE TIMES HE SHARE
In all the days I cause you sorrow,
You seem to find a better tomorrow.
When I make mistakes and end up
Who knows when or who knows where?
I take a look around me and by
Some miracle, you're right there.
I've failed a lot of tests and trials
But you're always the best and full of smiles.
When I look back on all my life,
The years of pain and all the strife.
I know I'll be happy to say,
I'm proud to have you, as my wife.
The time passes so slowly as I stare at the clock.
But it doesn't seem to bother me

When I think about you, my rock.
It doesn't seem like I'll be here as long.
When I know you're out there standing strong.
The times we're together mean so much now.
Everything looks brighter somehow
That's why the times he share
Stand alone, beyond compare.

Vickey Seales
SPRING

To Bobby, my beloved husband, who has always been there for me.

Spring is so very special,
She brings beauty after repose.
But what a delightful facial,
After her long restful cloze.

Bright shining daffodil heads,
Smile and dance in their apparel.
Glorying in rising from beds,
While above darts the sparrow.

Mrs Orietta D Stewart
I REMEMBER

Dedicated to my son, John.

I remember on August twenty third
A beautiful summer day;
God sent you into this world
To laugh, to run, and to play.

Then as you grew to the master's plan
It filled my heart with joy,
To see God's wonderful gift to me
A handsome curly head boy.

I remember you as you were
Tall, tan, terrific and strong,
Kind hearted, loving and careful
You were easy to get along.

I remember the years we spent together
And then the accident came,
You lay quiet on a respirator
But I knew you were in pain

While looking at you in bed that night
Knowing you were going to die,
I remember whispering these words to God
"Lord, my son; can't say good-by."

Tina M Smith
JAMIE
As we walk the road together
I think of how it used to be
All the trials we've been through,
Hand in hand, you and me.

The apartment was small and dusty,
That day we first moved in.
But we touched it and it came to life
And our love shown within.

The days at work were long and hard
At the drugstore down the street.
But as the hours passed on by,
I would think of you, my sweet.

Weekends were a special time,
We came together as one.
And two months after we said
our vows,
We conceived our firstborn son.

We watched him grow inside you.
Each movement and kick we felt.
And as you became more tired each
day,
I tried my best to help.

Nine months later, at 2 a.m.
It was time for our son to be born.
And though I was nervous,
as a new father is,
You remained calm and never torn.

As we reached the door of
the delivery room
The pain became so much
stronger.
I said, "Hold on honey, you
Can make it, it won't be
much longer."

And at that moment, you
looked at me,
The tears filling your eyes.
Your last breath was short
and silent, you were
gone forever from
our lives.

You left behind a son, my love
He's ours and always will be.
The love we shared in the time
we had,
Will show in the eyes of Jamie.

Annette C Sanzari
THE PLEDGE

To Bob, who brought me the joys of life and love to share. I'll love you always. Annette.

I love you in the morning
And in the afternoon
I'll love you in the winter
And in the month of June.

A love like ours will never die
It just gets better through the years.
It brings only happiness
No room for doubt and fears.

So kiss me in the moonlight
And hold me close at night.
And tell me that you love me,
And everything will be alright.

For Love cannot be measured,
In any special way.
It's just a look, a thought, a phrase,
On any given day.

And so I pledge my love to you,
And hope you will agree.
That I was made for loving you,
And you for loving me.

Peggy M Smith
BERLIN WALL
Oh glorious day in 1989,
"The Wall" began to crumble;
And with it, fell—oppression;
And then, in close succession,
The crowd began a cheer,
That started there,
And swept around the world;

Tears mingled with champagne,
Flowed freely as the rain,
While some remembered others gone before,
Who missed this day of days;
Until the cheers swept up,
A crescendo raised on high,
Beyond all space and time;
The joy picked up by seraphim,
Echoed higher still,
As stardust fell
From Heavenly bells,
That pealed out clear,
And joined with heavenly voices there,
That sang, as we, in harmony,
"Praise God, The Wall is Down!"

Chris Chew Smith
OLD FASHIONED LOVE
I like old fashioned love
And old fashion things
Like big candy hearts
And precious rings

Soft playing music
Romantic candle light
And thoughts of you
Holding me tight

The whisper of your voice
Your beautiful eyes
Your innocent looks
When you get high

Just the presence
Of you being there
Makes me happy
To know you care

The roar of the ocean
Meeting the shore
Day by day
Just loving you more

The wind in our hair
Our toes in the sand
Your arms around me
The softness of your hand

Walking side by side
Ice cold rain
Waiting for you
To kiss me again

All of this
And so much more
Is the old fashioned stuff
I love you for

Robert Everett Singer
TOY SOLDIER

To My Wife, Patricia.
Our stormy courtship inspired this poem. Your love, patience & understanding inspire my life.

it's lonely up here
on this cold shelf.
won't you take me down today?
don't you want to play?

i won't break this time
i promise you;
i'll do anything
you want me to.
we'll play any game
you wish to play
and have great fun
all night, all day.

but when you're tired
and just need yourself,
just put me back here
up on my shelf.

Penny S Shumaker
MYTHICAL TIMES
Mythical times, Oh days of yore
How I long to find you, just walk through the door.
Of legend you are made, in legend you exist
To live the life, is hard to resist.
In the realm of dreams, of reality you know naught
Illusions surround me, firmly I am caught.

Mythical times, Oh days of yore
You have betrayed me, my Soul is quite sore.
You are not real, as firm as a mist
The fantasy pursues, of substance you insist.
Delusions is all I've found, the opposite I have sought
The bright light of truth, desperately I fought!

Of legend you are made, in legend you shall stay,
My heart has found a path, from it I'll not stray.
Mythical times, Oh days of yore
Imagination has freedom, truth it can bore.
Illusion has a place, 'tis food for the mind
Like rain upon the desert, of which you are kind.

Of legend you are made, in legend you shall stay,
But only if I can find you, if only for a day.
Mythical times, Oh days of yore
How I crave you, I truly do adore.
Facts abound, light can be harsh
Like an endless moor, or sucked in a marsh.

In the realm of dreams, reality stand aside,
Illusions can be perfect, and from life you cannot hide!

Myra Skelton
CELEBRATE SPRING

I dedicate this poem to my wonderful husband Michael who enjoys springtime so much.

Spring has come
New life has begun
In our ever changing world

The new green landscape is filled
With roses, tulips, and daffodils

Mother robin is in her nest
With three blue eggs against her red chest

The frogs happily croak out their songs
Knowing soon the crickets will sing along

There is the sight of gardeners sowing seed
Hoping their efforts won't turn into weed

All of this and so much more
Is what the earth has been waiting for

As all winter long she had slept
Her beautiful secrets well kept

Until she awoke refreshed and new
To celebrate spring with me and you

Candi M Squires
DIET FOR A HOUSEWIFE
A cup of this, a pinch of that.
Create a dish to make you fat.
No need to worry, your hunger ignore.
Don't stay for seconds—go sweep the floor.

Hubby's and children's sweet tooth all the time.
Baking this pie or that cake—orange, lemon or lime.
There's still hope, your clothes fit—though snug as a bug!
No time for seconds—go vacuum the rug.

Those pie crusts and bread dough,
you knead your way through.
Add inches to places known only to you.
There's no time for sampling as your stomach wishes

Push away from the table—start washing those dishes.

As everyone else enjoys your great skill
Of cooking and baking—for you it's a thrill.
You'll see smiling faces on children and spouse.
And you won't gain a pound, but you'll have a clean house!

Dianne Danuta Sage
SEA WOMAN
all the waters of my body
drawn to the moon
tears fall easily and so, so soon

row through the waters, your mind sails on
yes, cry for the stranger, with his slow, sad song
cry the silver screen hero, who doesn't last long
why, you'd cry for a commercial, if it had a sad song

sail, sea woman, sail along
ride the waves of emotion
hear the sad song
weep the sad story, sail on

like a child, sea woman
you shed a world of tears
you cry for the strangers, when they show their fears
you'd cry for a cartoon, if sadness drew near

sail on, sea woman, seek the dunes
release the waters, drawn to the moon
ride your emotions, that flow so soon

like a child, sea woman
waters of your eyes, draw to the moon.

Wayne A Souza
MY BROTHER

This poem is dedicated To my brother Rick and My wonderful son Ricky.

As the last tears dried
And my soul was empty
I felt I could not cry again
But the memories of you
Have brought me
More tears to shed

The loneliness I feel
Cannot be erased
Nor the pain lessened
But with time
Maybe I can learn to live without you
So sleep my brother
May you be at rest
I think of you often
I remember the past

Gladys S Solera
MOTHER

To Clara-Argelia-Ledo, My Mother.

Mother
let thunder roar
let the sky
lash out its rays
of fire
if there is peace
in the heart
of your daughter . . .
Mother
let me sleep
without exaltations
nor hurry
with this serenity
absolute
that has been given
to me
by your love . . . .

Stanley Sherr
POEM NEAR THE WHITESTONE BRIDGE
I stood at a sea wall,
A well-worn monument to love and bravado, painted over.
Straight against the waves it stood, and I behind it.
Suddenly, the clouds, which had closed the sky shut
For that entire day, till then, opened up.
A shaft of light, at least the width of that stone wall's expanse,
Burst from the cracked and rolling cover and struck the Earth.
I was enveloped in a searching ray.
An arm and wrist and hand reached out to rock and sand
And placed its palm on top of me.

Illuminated so, I stood in meditation.
Staring at the brilliant stripe of sea in front of me
I seemed the spokesman for a gallery of tall grass,
That now bowed low,
Combed by shining fingers, whipped by the winds,
And whispered their rhythms.

Then leviathan, sweeping overhead,
Closed its mouth again, darkening water and land.
It swallowed up that hand of light and rushed eastward.

I stood at the sea wall and sought above me another opening,
Entranced by the light that had caught me up before.
I knew it was never to be expected.
I turned and walked away from the shore.

Sherie Sirois
I REMEMBER . . .

To Papa, with love and fond memories. Always your loving granddaughter, Sherie.

I remember your smile, your smile
so sweet like an angels sigh that
swept me off my feet.
I remember your eyes, so big
and grey that whenever they saw
me they brightened the day.
I remember your hands so big and
strong that helped me with my life
and to move me along.
But most of all I remember your love,
that made my life so happy &
gay, and gave me that shove so that I
will keep moving along and never
forget your unending LOVE.

Betty Swaffard
WINTERTIME
It's wintertime now, but I can remember
seasons of yesteryear.
Days of my youth and freedom and laughter,
and as I remember, I feel a tear
Tracing its path down a cheek, that once soft and smooth
is weathered now.
And there's weariness there from trials and pain, but,
Happiness, too,
Because God in His wisdom preserves what
He needs.
Those trials, that pain had a purpose
And joy replaced sorrow and a lesson was learned,
And I've a story to tell if you'll listen.
A story to tell of my love for my Lord
How He's given me strength for my days
How He's loved and supplied, givenhope
that was free,
I'll share with you
If you'll take time for me.

Mrs Alice C Stapel
LOVE

To Elmer (Al) my husband, my one and only love. Also to my loving children—Donna—Gail—Douglas and Kimberly. Lovingly, Mamma.

Love is you, love is me.
It is weak, it is strong.
It is long.
It comes to all.
Sometimes when you're young,
For others when they are old.
With some. It is always, when they walk and when they talk.
In their smiles, in their tears
Many times in their fears.
Love is wonderful
I love to be loved, and I love to love, LOVE.
Where would we be without it?
Who do we thank for it?
"GOD."
"HE" is wonderful and "HE" is love.

Jeanette Scheckman
SING A SONG

Dedicated to my dear husband Mike, my daughter Ina, my grandchildren Robert, Susan, Steven and Laura: And my great grandchildren Jessica and Daniel.

Sing a song of Suzie,
Sing a song of beauty:
Sing sweet, sing long,
Sing with a silver tongue.
Let your voice be heard above.
Sing to the flying dove,
Sing a song of love.
Sing on the mountaintop,
Sing in the valley,
Sing in the light, sing in the dark,
Sing with the evening lark.
Sing a song of joy.
Sing with passion: sing of compassion.
Sing with a joyful voice,
Sing of freedom of choice,
Sing a song of Suzie.
Sing it loud, sing it clear,
Sing so the whole world may hear.
Sing high, sing low,
Sing where the rivers flow:
Sing a song of Suzie.

Jeanette Scheckman
TO LOVELY LAURA AT NINETEEN
Laura is love and laughter;
Laura is hugs and kisses.
Laura is a butterfly wing
And a gossamer dream.
We hold her in high esteem:
Our lovely granddaughter who is nineteen.

Greg E Stewart
MY BOY

Dedicated to Rainor Duke Stewart with love.

Time goes on
The days go past

Sadly, I think
He's gone
My little son is gone
Never forgotten
Just not here for me to hold

I think of him often
See his smiling face in pictures
Feel like crying
Strong desire to hear him say
I love you daddy, I love you very much

My boy
Big part of me
I miss him

Sylvia E Sleighter
COMMON SENSE
Common sense is what we use
To help us through each day.
It keeps our thinking clear and sane,
That we don't lose our way.

People call it "Horse sense" too,
Which really baffles me.
Horses do not think at all,
As anyone can see.

When someone gives him a command,
The order is quite clear.
Gee means right, haw means left;
Whoa means, "Stop right here."

People as a general rule
Can reason problems out.
Worry gets you nowhere fast;
Prayers will work things out.

Anger is <u>not</u> common sense,
But impulsivity.
Use the daily prayer approach
To work things sensibly.

Clare Stack
SKATING
Skating sets you free,
nothing can get in
your way. As you
speed around the ice,
you feel the wind against
your face.
There's nothing,
just you and the ice.

Nancy Stem
MY FRIEND
'Twas there on the Island of the sea,
I'm remembering laughter in the night,
'Midst sultry music, his voice, his eyes.
Those delirious pigeons, round about
Asking nothing of the sky above,
With bells pealing, feathering our sighs;
That kiss that haunts me night and day,
Said more than lips could ever say,
And plead no excuse, why we were
there,
But, why have I sown my love so wide?
As if for him, to see it, everywhere?
Could it be for me, my thoughts to hide?
Between the seas of "Friend" to "Friend?"
The forceful loud wave from out of the sea
Must be my very own, surging self,
I agree
Declaring, only by love, is life so free,
In longing to see my "Friend."

Maxine Swank
LIFE'S A BEACH

I dedicate this poem, to my family and friends.

Life is like a beach,
We are the sand
And the ocean
Is life.
When the tide is out,
We build ourselves up.
But when the tide comes in,
It washes us out.
Each time
The tide goes back out,
We try to build ourselves up,
Stronger than the time before.
But it seems
That each time the tide comes in,
It is more powerful
Than the previous time.
After being washed out, time after time.
We think there is no way
To ever beat the tide.
That is when you must reach deep down
Within yourself, to be as strong as you can be.
There is no way to beat the tide,
You just have to have the strength and courage
To never give in.

William M Sanders
THESE ARE MY FEELINGS

To my darling wife Bobbie Joe—there are so few beautiful flowers in the world.

These are my feelings;
from a source I do not know.
They well up inside me—
with much uncertainty and woe.
I need this lady—
this woman of my heart
To give me the comfort I seek
from the turmoil that threatens to tear me apart.
I look into the blackness—
and feel it coming closer.
Telling of loneliness, I struggle,
I Love Her—I must not lose her

Oh what can I do? —What can I say?

To ensure the seed I have planted
will blossom each and every day?
I try to nurture and make it grow strong,
but I fear I tugged at the leaves a little too long.
Oh discomfort soul—
If I lose this flower I hold so dear—
I believe my own life may whither
to nothing I fear.

Shannon Smith
MAYBE IT'S BECAUSE I'M TOO SHY

I have a great big crush on him
And I really don't know why
I haven't the nerve to speak to him
Maybe it's because I'm too shy

He always says hello to me
Whenever he's passing by
But I usually start to giggle
Maybe it's because I'm too shy.

I dream about him every night
Sometimes I could even cry
I start to speak but he's out of sight
Maybe it's because I'm too shy

Sometimes I think he likes me too
When I see his smiling eyes
Looking at me, then turning quickly away
Maybe it's because he's too shy

Evelyn Hutchins Slattery
LADY, WOMAN, EARTH

To those who believe in me.

Welcome to the canyon, I'm trying hard to remember
I'm trying hard to forget, Slipping into the canyon slippery and wet.

The gorge is a stream, Flowing deep in the valley
The timber keeping tempo, You ain't seen nothing yet
The sun is arising, the temperature is hot, High as the sky
Deep as the valley, Cold as the Snow,
I'm glad you're in the canyon
Honey, Don't you know?

I am the Earth, You are the Sea
The two of us, Three plus three
We have reached the essence you and me.

Lady, Woman, Earth
Life, Death, Birth
Lady, Earth, Man, Sea
The canyon is Me!

Welcome to the canyon, I'm trying hard to remember
I'm trying hard to forget, Slipping into the canyon, Slippery and wet.
Trying hard to remember the tempo,
The timber, Hot weather, 90 degrees in December
I am your Earth, You are my Sea
Life, Love, You and Me
Lady, Woman, Earth, The Canyon
Ecstasy!

Michael Siegfried
SABLE HAIRED LADY

Many years I traveled alone
Having no place to call home
I met a beauty, with which I fell
Now here in Dallas I will dwell
She entered my heart as if from Cupid's bow
With the arrow's strike love came I know
Sable hair embraces her neck
Autumn-brown eyes and a dance in her step
Chattering, laughing and carrying on this way
A petal perfect rose had brightened my day
Her beauty and figure are cast in stone
Standing with the immortals in glorious Rome
The aura about her physically stirring
It sends my heart pounding, my emotions whirling
She has the voice of an angel's song
So tender and caring yet so strong
Her skin soft as rays of the moon
Lying in fields of lilies in full bloom
She is woman, a lady fine
A gift from God, the world's valentine

William Monroe Morgan III
LOVE IN THE AIR

The winded scent of roses
drives one wild
they make a certain grin
some people call them smiles.
He looked up
as if his nose was the detector.
And alerted for where about
the smell of this elegant substance
was coming from.

His eyes gleamed
a gleam that no other could see
but only to be seen
by the rose who shall forever
carry this scent of love.

He feels himself move
but he remains still
as if he was paralyzed
in a world of thrills.

The day must move on
as the wind will calm
and the one who holds the roses
shall find a new scent of
"Love in the Air"

David Perrett
MY TRUE LOVE

In life we face many ups and downs
From different relationships, but as long
As we have a true love we will always
Be...

To let her flow through my head, you must first let her flow through my heart.
To touch her is to feel the burning desire in my soul.
We have a love unlike any other that cannot be scarred, by anyone or anything.
We have a good relationship, but sometimes she doesn't communicate and we argue.
From time to time we fight, but we always come back because ours is a true love.
Through all other relationships, she will always be in my heart because our devotion
will be bound forever.
She is the one that I will hold tight when I feel alone.
She cradles me in her arms, when I'm terrified of the night.
When I am deeply depressed, she is always there to comfort me.
When I fall asleep, she takes me to a dream world, where I am safe from harm.
She fills my veins with a great passion, then sends a flaming arrow to my heart.
She is the only true love that no one can take from me. I will love her always.
In life we face many ups and downs,
but as long as we have a true love,
"Creativity,"
we will always be.

Pauline Rossberg
A BABY'S CRY

Dedicated to my darling grand-daughter, Kimberly Kolbert—With love.

A universe that God created,
Where acorns flower and trees are shaded,
Where poverty and wealth abound,
Where lives are lost and treasures found.
Where some men work from dawn till dusk,
And others laugh and love and lust,
Where some men die with hunger pain.
And others pray for wind and rain.

Where man has learned such wondrous things,
To fly like birds, without their wings,
To make fertile fields from barren waste,
And perhaps destroy the world in haste.

But for all this, one can't deny,
The miracle of birth and wonder
why,
None can surpass your tender
sigh,
Or match your little baby's
cry.

Imogene G Brunson
OPEN DOOR

To my Stepdaughter, Kathleen Anita Brunson, Date of Birth: January 5, 1957.

Honey, as I wait and pray
For you, as you give birth today,
I see in time, so long ago
The One that died to make it so.

I see your mother, Bless Her Soul,
Numbered in the Heavenly Fold,
I raised you from her infant small
To stand upright and never fall.

Jesus died that we might live
"Eternal Life" is His to give
The Blood He shed on Calvary
Gives Mothers hope for their child-to-be.

So, "Love Thy Neighbor as Thyself"
And "To Thine Ownself be True"
And teach your own to do the same
To be worthy of His Precious Name.

Vow that "Not a day goes by"
Reflecting on the Ones who died
Had it not been for those gone before
There would be no hope for
"AN OPEN DOOR."

J Lawrence Ingram
A NATIVE, A SON, AN AMERICAN

To my wife Anne.

I am a native of Kansas.
From here, it seems oh so far away.
I remember buffalo running on a vast sea of prairie grass.
This land gives my country it's amber waves of grain.
I am a native of Kansas.

I became a son of New Hampshire.
The sun makes a spectacle of color more than from where I came.
This place is where all others wish they could be like.
A birth place of my great nation.
I became a son of New Hampshire.

Best of all I am an American.
The sunlight strips away the distance.
I go everywhere and freedom shines upon me.
From my purple mountains, to my amber waves.
And to the birth place of my great nation.
Best of all I am an American.

J Lawrence Ingram
I CAN SEE THE COLORS
I see crimson and some gold.
In the morning's haze I see beauty untold.
Color exploding as fall's foliage starts unfolding.
Thick and dense and deep with some birch white.
I can see the colors.

Then the beginning of night.
The hazy-blue turns black the sky.
A red-orange ball of sun wanes its light.
Silhouettes then fly by.
I can see the colors.

Again to the color of morning.
Now it seems that the blackness surges.
To get the sun's blaze in color surges.
Come to my window for my waking eyes.
I can see the colors.

The end of the day draws near.
Tomorrow seems closer though.
Today still here begins to make changes.
What will tomorrow bring—the cycle of ages.
I can see the colors.

Toni Scott
WHERE'S MY FATHER?

This poem is dedicated to Talicia, my loving daughter.

Changing Pampers, taking her temperature
Sitting in Emergency alone . . .
Wiping her tears and my own, after getting her shots . . .
Where's My Father?

Seeing her first tooth, hair growing enough
for ribbons, her first party . . .
Trying to run before she walked,
getting a stitch on her lip from falling down . . .
Where's My Father?

Three years went by, he never saw her face,
he never spoke a word, never held her in his Arms . . .
Then God answered our prayers and sent my daughter
a daddy, that's there always . . .
Someone who loves her, gives her a hug, Says "I love you."
Now, she can draw a family
(Mommy, Daddy & Daughter)
There's my Daddy!

Toni Scott
MOTHERHOOD

This poem is dedicated to my children, Talicia and Dante, with much love, Mommy.

Motherhood is a hated job.
There's days, sometimes you don't
Know whether to laugh or sob.

Cooking, cleaning, washing bottles
Making formula, doing the kids' hair.
Sometimes you feel so smothered
Are they gonna give you some air?

When depression steps in and the
Kids do and say things that make
You feel so good.

That's the part, that catches my
Heart and that's Motherhood.

Kathy Holloway Warmack
INSIDE THE GLASS

For My Mother.

Sometimes I see a little girl,
Small, eager face outlined in smiles;
And, free, erase the years and cares
To run and meet her standing there.

I'd tell her to hold summer close—
That "Neverland" is at her door.
We'd gather flowers in the sun
And chase the stars when evening comes.

But . . . we cannot speak of paper dreams—
Of crayoned sweet imagined things,
Or horsemen crossing cloud-filled skies
And shining dancers leaping high.

She slips away beyond the glass—
The mirror where the shadows play;
And skipping through the silver gates,
She smiles in silence where she waits.

Kathy Holloway Warmack
ON RIVERS AND OTHER PASSAGES
How long it's been, I could not say
The journey has gone on.
The hours and days have slipped away
Like a silent, unnamed song.

Is this how a green leaf feels
When summer warms the air?
When languid haze lines sultry skies,
And moonlit clouds are fair?

Singing, climbing, slow I walked,
No sudden moves I made.
But quietly I eased along
Into the summer's August shade.

I heard the promises of youth,
Of love that spoke of magic things;
The midnight dreams, the opening doors,
Unfolding quickly after Spring.

I tell myself, "There is still time,"
Though days rush on and years are brief—
Still time to keep for secret dreams,
To save for summer's last green leaf.

And still more time to feel love's fire . . .
To walk through August's golden glow
And balance wisdom with desire
As swirling rivers past me flow.

Can the journey soon be ended
When summer passions seem to change?
Or does the heart grow mellow
When the last green leaf remains?

Nancy L Lyke
OMNISCIENCE

To all who believe.

I am being called.
And it is frightening and confusing,
Yet enlightening and joyous.
It's been unbelievable
But it is being shown, and I know.

The signs are in the light and in the sky
In the sun and of the clouds it speaks to me.
And I hear it in my mind
The word of God.
And it keeps on calling and calling.
I am to pass that on, and now I do know
To follow the presence.
And I will try to give it to you
Because that's what I think I am to do.
He is real, and He is strong
The force of fields which can be felt and heard
But not seen.
And I do trust.

Carolyn Sheetz
LONELINESS

For Cindy Cunningham.

What color is
LONELINESS?
Is it a misty gray
NOTHINGNESS
or a dark brown
DULLNESS?
Is it COLD shades of blue
that CHILL the EMPTY spaces
of the HEART?
Is it SHARP black and white
of HARSH JUDGMENTS
that SHUT you OUT?
NO!
LONELINESS is—
golden yellow,
LAUGHING orange,
JOYOUS red.
ALL the BRIGHT colors
of SUNSHINE and WARMTH,
a kaleidoscope
of HAPPINESS, ALWAYS
JUST BEYOND MY REACH;
THAT IS LONELINESS!

Grace W Roach
VACANCY BY DEATH
It was a dark, dreary day and the death angel had paid
A visit to their beautiful and very happy home
Her eyes were red from crying and her heart was empty
As she thought of the one from which she would never roam.

During the days of World War II she had waited for him
She had dreamed of the day when he would finally return
And she would become his loving and devoted young bride
Never again for his hugs and caresses would she have to yearn.

The years had been good to them and two children came
To make their happiness even more fulfilled and complete
Always together they traveled down life's joyous pathway
In their hearts their wedding vows they would often repeat.

As years went by and their children found their life mates
Little ones came along to increase all their happiness
It seemed that life was so full and a rainbow they had found
They thanked God for their blessings and so little stress.

Now as she looked wistfully back over the long and happy years
She realized that they had known the ultimate of happiness
But he was gone and she wondered how she could face tomorrow
Memories she must hold close to her heart and banish stress.

Lydia R Watson
UNDER THE INFLUENCE
Male children of an influence based environment
Media's effectual implications
Images repeated over and over, subtle connotations
Become a part of one's own identity
Speaking in benevolence;
"Man it's cool to be,
The baddest rapper
The baddest dresser
The baddest dealer
The baddest a bruiser
The baddest lover
The baddest quitter."
Commitments cease
Determined not to become victim of a user
Our men discussed with pressures of society, lack hope
Bound by media's standardizing methodology, sack the cope
Giving up easily
Their fight for righteousness and dignity
Protesting, silently raging, sportingly but seriously jesting
Our men targets of an internalized warfare;
A mental game
Strategy tactics, if that might appease
Pawns, knights, somehow checkmate or king me, please.
Self-defeating is its name.
Male children, it's time to get up,
stop hitting your snooze alarms.
Wake up, you badd__ss
Men . . . wake-up!

Carol L Franklin
TROPIC LOVE
On the white sands we lay
Enjoying the tropic sun.
Tanned and looking chic,
We share a coke and rum.
We watch the sea gulls fly
And hear the waves rush in.
Our day is filled with love and
We'll share the night again.
After a quiet dinner for two,
We will glide to the dance floor.
Soft, slow music tempts us
Until we can't wait any more.
Arm in arm, we stroll to our room.
Our hearts beat as one it seems.
"Mom, get up! You overslept!"
That's right—it was just a dream.

Linda Everett Johnson
SONNET FOR A HIGH SCHOOL SENIOR
Destined to whatever the future holds
Bound to find and win or lose—
Growing up to learn or confuse
The truths and realities that help to mold
The gifts of life—stories retold.
Taking this life and learning to use
Advice received regarded as good news.
Each day well lived, life unfolds
With many challenges to defeat.
Whichever road decided and taken
Whichever dream in route to seek,
Courage and faith must not be shaken—
Life is never at its most complete.
Each day brings a new dream and truth to meet.

Christine Fogel
SAVIOR
Oh poor heart and soul, as we were one and once stood tall, so high upon this
wretched earth; and so we have fallen.
Into every new year there comes a battlement within us.
The years get worse, not better,
and we become one of a million hurting souls, just waiting to be found.
One by one we are wanting to be saved.

Be of help. Save us! How can so many be so lost in a time of dread?

The loves and good future are lost and oblivious to our minds. We see no more, thus causing a heart to fall to the ground, and death will come too fast for our eyes to see.

Alexander Campbell
HERACLITUS CONSIDERS THE UNIVERSE
"All things change. Nothing remaineth."
Heraclitus (C.535-C.475 B.C.)
Beyond the threadworn edges of this sleeve
Observe these folded hands of bone and flesh
And ask if life each year works to achieve
Impermanence of such a costly mesh.
For when again will chromosomes combine
To fashion with so sure a mastery
These fingers that in deprecating sign
Strive to evade their certain destiny.

And from the cigarette they hold so fast
Drifts out in patterns of a tracery
The thin, uncertain wisps of smoke that cast
Vague shadows from the sun on stones that must
By time and the eroding tides of sea
Be ground into an ever-changing dust.

Peter J Woodman
WHERE THE GHETTO LIVES
My eyes wandered down a street one day.
Streets are where the ghetto hides for they are chaotic and dirty.
Streets are where people become human as they sit double parked, chatting to friends.
Streets are where the young meet to get drugs or find sex.
Streets are warm in summer's evenings but scary under a police car's light.
Streets are American society where everything meets in self-destruct mode.
I have wandered the streets where the ghetto lives.

Peter J Woodman
HOMELESS
He wanders about Jack in the Box totally mad.
I'm trying to get something to eat man!
But he cannot stay because he smells.
I'm trying to get something to eat man!
He is unshaven and unclean, like a heathen.
I'm trying to get something to eat man!
He is vile, base and not even human.
I'm trying to get something to eat man!
You don't belong here, go away.
I'm trying to get something to eat man!
You have failed. You are a failure.
I'm trying to get something to eat man!
Get a job or go back to the street.
I'm trying to get something to eat man!
Retreat to the refuse where you are safe.
I'm trying to get something to eat man!
Leave us alone!
I'm trying to get something to eat man!
I'm sorry poor man.

Peter J Woodman
CRY THE MIGHTY NATION
Cry the mighty nation and be heard once more.
Raise your voice against those deaf ears.
Protest for those burnt books or censored songs.
Lament those banned photographs.
Weep, weep for the innocent destroyed by government.
Speak for those things we once believed in.
Fight for those ideas we have shed so much blood defending.
Cry the mighty nation and let not your tongue be silent.

Smitty Dobson
LOST SHEEP
This is a story of life as you see
About three lost sheep and each to be.
Goodness; Innocence; and the ungodly do share
Just as our experiences would have us beware

The first was lost from himself, oh me
His name was E.H., faithful to Thee
The second was lost from man, pity be
Her name was Elsie, mindless to Thee
The third was lost from God, 'tis he
His name was Satan, a devil to Thee

As the Master looked down upon His flock
And saw three missing from the rock
He sent out His Shepherds for which to find
The lost ones; without loss of time

The first was easy for Shepherds to behold
For his faith had lit a path of gold
The second was simple because of right
Like a child, no sin was the light
The third a sinner the devil is he
Lost to hell throughout all eternity

Smitty Dobson
EARTH DAY 2—?
The sun burns down on desert floor
No animal to tread nor bird to soar
Dead silence—all's lost—the lack of song
The missing link—its life all gone

What happened to Earth I loved so dear?
No plant to breathe—no one to tear
Waste land so vast the sicken smell
The garden of Eden is lost to Hell!

Man's waste has taken the ultimate toll
Not caring for others but only for gold
The final price was paid for each today
The Grim Reaper appeared and all must pay

The mounting debt, Oh careless fun
What might could be would now be done
Now lost forever in shifting sand
Our great nation a once proud land.

Wake up! wake up! from nightmare's fright
Only a dream—A dream not right
Today's the day we clean the way
So tomorrow and tomorrow will be a day.

Smitty Dobson
OTHERS
Christmas comes but once a year
And 'tis a time for good cheer.
A family present in which to find
That extra special gift of time.

True feelings of love that will make
A friend: a relative: in which to take.
To demonstrate to others that I do care
About what happens and how to share.

To wear a smile not just on face
But in our hearts a special place.
Reserved for others that gift to find
The "Golden Rule": Mine for all time.

The secret's out for all to see
What can I do for you—not me.
Great gifts be given for us to share
By doing for others, because we care.

Patricia Shaw Talley
WINGS OF TIME

Dedicated to the memory of DAVID PATRICK JOHNSTON (1957-1975).

Time flies bye in the wink of an eye and waits for none to follow
From day to day it winds its way, plunging ever into the 'morrow

Leaving in its wake, for memories' sake, all that has gone by before
The hopes and dreams and people's schemes and all that is unknown to man
Is locked away, each second, each day in the weaving of the cloth of the past
Though it cannot be seen, it will always remain, a part of the cosmic dust

For what has been may be again, somewhere, some world, some dimension
When our lives stop with the ticking of the clock, another life springs forth
To start anew with things to do, to love, to laugh
It cannot be told for it must unfold, each life has its own road to travel
And when it is done and that life is gone, who shall be left to remember

The hopes and the fears through all of the years will fade with the passage of time
In the blink of God's eye a lifetime goes bye, how short is our time on this earth
So bravely we go into the unknown with faith as our only companion
What we may find is the secret of time, moving through one of God's canyons

For time flies bye in the wink of an eye and waits for none to follow
From day to day, it winds its way, plunging ever into the 'morrow

Patricia Shaw Talley
SOMEONE STOLE MY PRISM
Someone stole my prism, they took it from my car
It was hanging in the window and it twinkled like a star
I'd left it in the open for all the world to see
The thought it might be stolen had not occurred to me
And yet a slinking shadow reached in and dimmed the light
Dropped quickly into pocket, both soon were out of sight
My loss was soon discovered, I was filled with such dismay
Who, who would have done it, to take this joy away
All that glitters is not gold, all things aren't meant to last
But oh how I shall miss my precious piece of glass
But rather than be angry, I changed my view today
I've found another reason why my prism's gone away
I think it flew to Heaven to twinkle in the sky
And give its joy to millions with the other stars on high

Louis J Warmoth
FADING LOVE
I Saw My Dream, While Kneeling,
At Heaven's Open Portal.
I Saw My Dream, Beckoning Me,
And I Was Only Mortal.
I Reached Out Touching, My Angel,
Caressing Redbird Breast.
My Angel Was Ready, To Receive,
And I Was For Her Test.

I Gently Then Stroked, My Angel,
Softly She Called To Me.
The Guardian Then Turned, Her
Head, So No One Could See.
Prepared For My Journey, Mother,
Caring For Her Dove,
Pulled The Drapes In, Behind Us, To
Conceal Our Love.

'Twas The Lovely Night, I
Remember, And Pray to Repeat,
Because At That Moment, The Devil,
Turned On The Heat.
Blowing His Hot Lies, Into The Ear,
Of My Dream So True,
She Heard The Promises, Of Devil,
Instead Of I Love You.

Promising Love Forever, The Devil,
Stole My Love From Me,
And Placed A Bar, Across The Door,
No One Else Can See.
The Bar He Placed, So Firmly, Now
I'll Never See The Place,
Because Without My Angel, I Go
Swiftly, Leaving Not A Trace.

With Heaven On Earth, Denied Me,
I'll Never Find The Path.
I Feel Hell's Fire, Inside Me, And All

My FATHER'S Wrath.
I May Be Called The Avenger, Angel Of Mercy, You May Hear,
But Now The Answer Must, Come Soon, I Loved You Little Dear.

Louis J Warmoth
THE DEVIL'S GARDEN
I Tried And Tried, My Whole Life Through,
To Make Every Word I Spoke, Come Out True.
Money From Pocket, I Would Spend,
Almost Anytime Needed, To Help A Friend.

Time I Spent, I Never Considered Wealth.
I Knew That Work, Was Good For My Health.
When Anyone Would Ask, What They Owed,
A Thank You To Me, Was The Seed I Sowed.

I'd Work All Day, I'd Work All Night,
To Help A Friend, Who Asked Me Right.
Nothing There Was, That I Couldn't Do,
So Never Was I Asked, To Say Thank You.

Now That I Start, To Show My Years,
I Have Nothing Left, To Shed But Tears.
The Ones I Helped, Now Don't Need Me.
The Ones I Need, Do Not Sow Seed.

Same As You Sowed, So Shall You Reap.
The Price I Paid. It Seemed So Cheap.
Asking Now I'm Told, To Beg My Pardon.
I Sowed My Seed, In The Devil's Garden.

Louis J Warmoth
THE LITTLE REDBIRD
I've A Little Redbird, Flying In And Out So Quick.
Who Only Flies Away From Me, To Help Someone Who's Sick.
Working Only For Love, He Wants Not Money.
Flying Straight To Those, Who Call Him Honey.

With Nothing Else Could, He Ever Be Bought.
That Is The Secret, To Him I've Taught.
If Ever Anyone Him, Someone Tried To Use,
They'd Find So Quick, His Love They'd Lose.

Flying In So Fast, Then So Quickly Away,
Returning To His Nest, And Then There Stay.
Complete Freedom He Has, To Fly and Roam,
Sending All My Love, Then Hurry Back Home.

His Nest Is Buried, Deep Within My Heart.
Only Through True Love, Does He Ever Part.
He'll Fly Out Either, During Night Or Day,
Only After I Have, Pointed Out The Way.
Mercy And Love Pour, With Wings Widely Spread.
Those Who Would Use Him, Will Feel Like Dead.
Those Who Would From Him, Ever Try To Take,
Would Want Him Back, For Dear JESUS'S Sake.

Beverly R Dixon
SHADOW DANCER
Alone at her table,
She sips her wine and waits.
Soon the music will carry her away.
She's a
shadow dancer

Against the night that fell so hard her feet
Began to move, dressed in black to match her
Sorrow she becomes one with her music.

Song after song . . . she's a shadow dancer.
Man after man sweep her off her feet.
She's alone in her dance and the men do fade away.
Her mind calms into a blissful dream . . . .
She's a
shadow dancer

Even though she dances close, the arms that
Hold her are not her own.
They probably never will be, and that's the way she wants it.
She's a
shadow dancer

Beverly R Dixon
THE STORM

I wish to dedicate this poem to lifelong friendships.

It was the storm that brought them close. The waves were creating a bond between these two. In their hearts they knew better, but the rough waters ran deep. She was falling, and he wanted to help. He didn't know the rescue would be so costly, and she was so afraid. Tossed they were between two worlds, the one so secure and right, the other so tempting . . . . Played with fire they did, now there are cooling cinders, sparks remain asking to be lit.

In the cool of the eve they took to the bluff and pretended they were alone. As the wind slipped through the grasses they tumble into each other and let the moment carry them away. Now she sees him in her dreams, the wind blowing through his curls and his searching eyes that cause her heart to ache. He cares and seems strangely to know her pain. But she can't keep "this one" she knows, he will remain forever in her dreams but not in her arms. When the storm ceases to rage she will have her wisping memories
she is comforted.

Catherine Elizabeth Egan
UNITY

To my dearest Karminder, for appreciating my artistic side and for encouraging me to be my very best.

the air is clean and fresh
the wind is softly brushing our skin
the sun brightly shines warming our unclad bodies
silently we face the sun shining and peer out onto the ocean
the waves gently roll then clash into the rocks, as we gently roll
and become one upon the sand . . . as we smile an exhilarated sigh of contentment
a dove flies by so white and pure and drops an olive branch at our feet
we softly embrace and the kind green branch flowers in our sight
and in it we see the destiny of the heavens
a rush of knowledge spreads upon our faces
overwhelmed we are startled by this presence
we jump instantaneously
and run freely into the calm of the ocean
then drift in onto the sheer beauty of the rocks
together we join and stay hidden
for the power is dangerous
and together we cannot be overcome
in our union there is eternity

Deborah D Riordan
THERE IS A PLACE FOR ME TO LIVE

To Tony and Christopher, for believing in me, even when I couldn't.

There is a Place for Me to Live
A Place to Love and Learn

A House for Me to Call My Own
And Keep Forever More

If I Knew a Way to Find This Place
I Would Leave Here Right Away

I'd Pack My Bags, and Hurry There
Never to Turn Back Again

There is a Heart for Me to Love
A Heart That's Always Warm

A Life for Me to Call My Own
And Keep Forever More

If I Knew How To Win This Heart
I Would Search Night and Day

And Hold on Tight to What I Found
To Never let Go Again

Pauline W Elswick
COUNTRY SOUNDS

I dedicate "COUNTRY SOUNDS" to my parents Rosa and Beve Wells who endowed me with a legacy of deep appreciation of my country roots.

Country sounds make muted stabs
at a peaceful, silent environment.
The muffled rhythmic beat of a hammer
on a skeletal, unfinished shed.
Orchestrated concerts by
nest-building birds.
The lazy hum of busy bees
collecting nectar from colorful flowers.
A cow mooing in a nearby lot
to her awkward new-born calf.
A bored horse galloping deteminedly
around the enclosed field
neighing in utter disdain
at the chug- chug- chugging
farm tractor
who has replaced his
mission in life.
The hammer ceases its rhythmic, muffled beat.
The satisfied cow stoically chews her cud
staring moodily at the horse
who now stands silently
watching
the big, green farm tractor
bringing the farmer
home to lunch.

Jennie Clary
SEASONS
The summers go so very fast,
We always seem to want them to last.
But autumn has to do its thing,
So after winter it will be spring.
The grass will turn from green to brown,
The winter's snows will fall to the ground.
But nature has to have its way,
To keep the four seasons at bay.
Our life is like the summer's past.
We do not know how long we will last.
So watch the seasons come and go,
Let the gentle breezes blow.
Nature's wonders will never cease,
Until we move on, and rest in peace.

Jennie Clary
MEGAN AND GOLDEN BOY
Mare and foal with a look on his face,
Wonders when he too can enter the race,
The mother dreams of days long ago,
When she came in first, and not to show.
Will he be able to do her proud,
To come in first among the younger crowd.
If he should lose, much to his chagrin,
He will learn from her, to take it on the chin.
Then when he himself has grown to sire,
His fillies also, he will admire.

R W Perkins
OUTSIDE THE DOOR

I dedicate these poems to my wife, children, and friends and family that have so much faith in me.
Thank you.

A little girl sat playing
in the sunshine with her doll.
She shushed her as she dressed her,
and placed her in the hall.

How she wished she'd brought along
her tattered bear and blocks.
But that door must not be opened
'cause her mommy sure sleeps lots!

"It's funny dolly, how mommy's headache
gets worse after daddy goes to work.
And that 'ol bottle she always drinks from
seems to bring her more and more hurt."

And then even a little noise, was
bad enough to get shut outside.
For little girls can't play quiet
when slapped because they cried.

But cry she must, 'cause mommy
isn't fun now any more.
So she and dolly play very quiet
in the hall outside the door.

R W Perkins
LIFE'S NOT FAIR
How glad I was in spring-time
to put forth my leaves of green.
When each limb was blossomed
I was splendid like a queen.

What joy then when each limb bore fruit,
from lowest branch to farthest.
And the laughter of the children
as they aided in the harvest!

Then Jack Frost came to kiss me,
and set my gown ablaze!
Then my sap ran down to rooty toes,
and here I stand for winter days.

Why must I stand here naked
and tremble in the blizzard's snow?
I could have been an evergreen
bedecked with Christmas glow!

R W Perkins
THY PLAN FOR ME
Each day I pray for pain to cease—
Yea, sometimes twice,
Sometimes three.
Yet fail to hear thy voice of peace—
Yea, sometimes twice,
Thy plan for me.

So much time crying over pain and woe—
Yea, sometimes twice,
Sometimes three.
My ears hear not which path I should go—
Yea, somtimes twice,
Thy plan for me.

How long suffering Jesus, is Thy love—
Yea, sometimes twice,
Sometimes three.
And hold out the promise of a home above—
Yea, sometimes twice,
Thy place for me.

R W Perkins
THE SPECIAL DAY
"Come on, little Larry, you know
tomorrow is a busy day!"
"Not just yet, Linda. Later!
There's lots more time to play!"

"No there isn't! You come on now!
Get washed up and then to bed!
You don't want to be all tired
for our special day ahead!"

"That's the same thing you tell
me, Linda. Tomorrow just won't be
Any different than the last times.
They'll say the same, you'll see!"

"Don't you hope this will be the last time?
Don't we pray each time is right?
Ain't we practiced all our manners?
And never had a quarrel or fight?"

"Please don't think tomorrow
will be the same in any way.
Just think it's special! Really special!
It could be our last adoption day."

Bill Beres
ALWAYS THERE
Do you feel love in the air
When birds sing songs
For all to hear

Like the tender touch
Of a breeze of fresh air
Or the warmth of the sun
Or a mother's love
It's always there

Do you hear the sound of the ocean waves
Upon the shore they sing
On a quiet evening's day

Can you feel
The sound of the rain
Gentle teardrops falling
On a window pane

All these things God gave
For us all to share
As is his love

It's Always There

Bill Beres
TULIPS
A rainbow of colors
Radiant and warm
They spread their wings
At the break of dawn

They open their hearts
For bees and all to see
As they sway gracefully
To a Spring Day's breeze

They all join hands
As night arrives
To awake the next morning
As the sun begins to rise

As they gently drop one by one
They say good-bye
Until another season comes

Dorothy Faye Osner
THE SONG IS ENDED
On the heavily travelled trail of time
Their moccasined feet scarce left a line.
No markers show their slow retreat
To corners dusty, lone and bleak.
In a stifling world they can't accept,
Their trail of tears has long been swept,
And distant now the muffled drums,
As many moons pass up above.

Each man expressing his outward reach,
Made himself a song, his very own,
Composed of wood notes, earth-attuned,
Boy and man by nature wooed.
What happens to the soul of man
When oblivion holds the winning hand,
And lying strewn across earth's floor
Are the plaintive, perishable songs of man?

Dorothy Faye Osner
STELLAR INDIFFERENCE
Who they are, how they arrived there,
Never troubles the stars . . . .
Untouchable, remote and scarred,
They communicate from great distances
That all is not gold dust
drenching our eyes,
It is mostly glitter
in a too-cold sky.
The rest of us can be found
Face up, unyielding,
Beds of coal, put upon,
Black-visaged, for in us
the sun abounds.
We utter never a word,
But warm ourselves as we hug the ground,
And bury our dream-like yearnings . . . .
Fuel for some future burnings?

Dorothy Faye Osner
SHIFTING PATTERNS
Far back in neglected recesses of mind,
Dimly-lit as rain-drenched boulevards,
Stretch a multiplicity of lines,
Boundaries enclosing lifetime dreams.
On looking back, old memories fade,
Merging blurs once familiar scenes.
That split-rail fence protecting childhood
Put many a splinter in eager knees.

Hopes stands a beacon on a hill . . . .
Meshed fencing has guarded jealously
Each changing nuance of my life,
And picked me up each time I fell.
Though faded now those lines might be,
They still define those other worlds
I left behind to fully explore
A future pregnant with possibilities.

Dorothy Faye Osner
SACRED GROUND
In hobnailed boots the days parade,
And children play their simple games,
Unmindful of approaching winter,
They laugh and sing. The green of summer
Could not stay . . . there in scattered heaps
Lie discards, resistant to the last,
Autumn yellow is my world, shifting fast.

These children, intruding, seem not to know,
And cannot see, innocence a protective screen,
But there is no sign or inkling
They play on a burial ground of dreams.
The bones lie deep, I inwardly keen,
But childish laughter drowns my sighs.
On platforms open to sun and wind,
I should have exposed my cherished dreams
To the healing grace of the limitless sky.

Peter E C Forrest
WHAT CAN I GIVE YOU

The following are dedicated to My Daughter Jeanne Michelle — My son Christopher Nathan And the "Seconds" we did share.

The Thought came to me Like Lightning —
Yet — Why I Really Do Not Know
Nothing New — or Revolutionary — But
Relearned Again — I suppose.

I've raced here and there —
Wherever and Back Again
Bought Cheap Gifts and
Not So Cheap — But
What of it all — there is a
Bit of Deceit — Untruth.

When the Most Precious
The Best — Most Meaningful
I have felt without Meaning
Is Just "Ourselves"
Not "Searching for the Star"
But "What we Are."

As this is — actually a
Gift Not Too Often Given
At least Not Too Often Recognized
By Me
Maybe My Own Lack —
Maybe Not.

But If It is — with you — As
It Has Been With Me
I No Longer Look For the Star
I Give You Me — Just Me
My Friendship — My Caring
That all is Well with You
And that I care about You and
Your journey — as I do now
More about Me and My Journey.

And NOW this is More Important
Than Rings and Things
That Only Money can buy —
As the Gift of Oneself
Is Finer Still — To Hold You
When you Cry; To encourage
You
When you feel Beaten.

I wish I had a Few More like that.
But — I am Finally that Way
With Myself; Liking me Better and
Easier to Give me away and
Feel Good about the Gift of Me.

Peter E C Forrest
JUST DO YOUR OWN THING
Search It Out
You Only Know Your Answer
Within You It Lies
Listen
In The Silence Of Your Heart
Only You Know The Answer

Get On With It
Was Not Jesus A Rebel At Age 12
You May Be A Little Behind
In The Silence Of Your Heart
You Know The Answer
Do 'Your' Thing

It Was Given By The Creation
Along With The Courage
To Do It
Just 'Your Own' Thing
No More ——— No Less

My Brother — My Sister
We Find What We Look For
We Become What We Think About

God's Speed

Pauline Davalos
COLORADO
Clear blue skies, sunshine, cool mountain breezes,
babbling brooks and clear blue lakes in the morning,

Birds singing; deer, elk, and antelope playing;
bears, mountain lions and buffalo roaming the hills . . .
then without warning,

The skies turn gray, the breeze turns to high winds,
the brooks begin to churn, turning the water murky,
and the lakes abound with menacing foam upon the waves,

The birds curl up into their wings; the deer, elk and
antelope run for shelter; and the bears and mountain lions
head for their caves,

One day it may be a gentle rain shower, which can

quickly turn into a violent thunderstorm pelting
giant raindrops upon your head,

The next day it may begin with sleet which will
turn into hail, or maybe a snowstorm which turns
into blizzard, that all began with a few gentle snowflakes when you first got out
of bed,

That is the beauty of living in Colorado,
you just never know what the day will bring,

That's why to me, living in Colorado is like being
on a merry-go-round every day—and always catching
the brass ring!

Sara Vichayakul
NIGHT RIDES

When the moon has filled out
Fat and round in the night
And the glow of the stars
Lends dim ghostly light
Then Jenny and I on our brooms we will ride
With Jenny's dog Hooter alight at our sides
And I have my bear and my
Mountain Scout cap
And away off we go
Like this and like that
Up over the moon
And out through the stars
When we open our eyes
Did we get very far?

Tucked into our beds
With our brooms at our sides
Both of us breathless from
Dreamy night rides.

Sara Vichayakul
WHERE

Where shall I fly
Where shall I go
Since I put away
A harsh and grieving heart

Now touched by the sun
And burned around the edges
It will beat away
Like a mad little bird.

Sara Vichayakul
DEPTHS

Depths of silence
Curled in shades of gray
To velvet black
Slip away

In other worlds
They unfurl
Bursting
Into joyful song

Howard S J Brown
SOMEONE SPECIAL

For my sweet, wonderful wife, Kathy. She is my treasure and I will love her forever and ever, Amen.

Guys say a woman is God's gift to man,
And they try to master her any way that he can.
But a woman is more than just a trophy prize,
This soft and tender creature comes in any size.
Different types there are—and some are very cold,
But her love is worth winning and she can be hard to hold.
Yes, a woman is a great piece of clout,
And my wife is someone I just can't do without.

I love you, Kathy!
Your sailor.

Ann Douglas
BEFORE

To Clifford.

Before, the highways of my life—have not treated me very nice
Before, before I found you.
Through memories I have found—your love for me is still around
We've graced time's span before, love.
I dream, alone through misty blue—and hoping for a glimpse of
You. We can't turn back the lost years—and abolish all the pain,
Can't reconstruct our life again—but can we really start anew?
I try, to put you far behind—forget that you were never kind—
Before, within another life.
The hurt my dear was oh so deep, somehow I know that you still
Keep, a vigil for me in your mind.
I know, my thoughts will always be, with you and our sweet reverie
You're always in my thoughts dear—today and every waking hour
I am your lonely little flower—please listen to my urgent plea!
Please try to reconcile yourself—to leave me on the past's
Bookshelf; if you, if you can do it.
You have the will, you're not that blind—to move the pain that's
In your mind; Then you will know that wisdom's wealth!
I wish you joy, I'll have you know—little heart how I loved
You so. Before this life—and even now!

Karen Spurdle
WHEN YOU ARE AWAY

*To my husband
Andy with
love.*

A part of me dies when you are away
Like the brown leaves of Autumn
That fall and decay

My heart it feels broken
Like a cracked China vase
That water leaks out in tears on my face

Rivers of sadness flow out to sea
Where dark waves of loneliness
Engulf and tease me

In the battle of time I weary and weaken
Until at last you reach out to save me

And when you embrace me
Autumn is Spring
My heart has been mended
The birds they do sing
For the love that is rescued.

Debbie Spiller
CRYING

*To all my friends and family
God Bless. I love you.*

All alone I sit up straight
The night outside is growing cold
In bed at night I lie awake
This feeling is growing, oh so old.

I'm crying now
Who will stop the pain?
The whistling sound of the tree
Whistles outside in the rain.

I'm still crying
Outside the wind is blowing
Inside I'm slowly dying
My pain is clearly showing.

I loved him so much
All I can do now is try.
I'd always tingled when we'd touch
Now I'll be lonely till the day I die.

Crying, Crying, Crying,
Who really cares?
Dying, Dying, Dying,
Nothing else compares.

Paul Romani Jr
BENJAMIN SPARE/ WITH APOLOGIES TO E. A. ROBINSON

Thanks to my wife, Joanne.

When troubles came about
And no one seemed to care
We could always find hope
In old Benjamin Spare.

He would listen carefully
Then offer us some advice,
And if we followed patiently
Things would turn out rather nice.

But one day as we came to his door
We were not welcomed as before.
It seems old Benjamin never had
Friends to turn to when things went bad.
So, sadly we turned from his door
Never to see old Benjamin anymore.

Jimmy Lee
LOVE IS NEVER ENDING

This poem is dedicated to Laurie, my darling wife.

Loving you is as sweet as can be
And I hope you return your love to me
Until there is reason for questionable trust
Reassured faith, harmony, and devotion is a must

In as much as I wholly believe in you
Evenly you must see that I will be true
Just as we are a combination of true loves
Under the sight of God we are as a pair of doves

Neither of us should be without the other
Either must never want to consider another
Let us always honor the other's intentions
Leaving no room for any dishonorable mentions

Every day is meant for me to be with you
Leaving no doubt that's all I want to do
Ever to know there isn't a chance for strife
Eternally love you Darling, for the rest of my life

Anna M Matthews
A.I.D.S.

Dedicated to James E. Hudson for coping so well.

Once I saw a lonely man . . . Quite timid . . . Rather shy . . .
And once you've learned the reason, you'll understand the "why."
"Death sentence" he'd been given . . . did he say "Death?" . . .
Oh, Yes!
That's exactly what it is when told "A.I.D.S."
Still, some find life worth living—forge pos'tively ahead . . .
Cook and clean and wash and fold, and even make the bed.
Often, in those troubled days, they search and find a song,
Join their voices with the choir and find that they belong.

Each of us should take a look within our inner soul . . .
If we were told, "It's hopeless" . . . how would we play the role?
My hat's off to those who smile . . . look forward to each day . . .
Some days better . . . others worse . . . "Survival, please" . . .
They pray!

Daniel Turcato
WHEN YOU'RE UP AND LOOK IN THE MIRROR

*40th Happy Birthday Linda Faye
From Daniel, Tarot, Putts.*

When you're up and look in the mirror,
Better not feel too poorly—
'Cause that woman in the mirror is you
And today that once little girl is now 40, Happy Birthday

Jules R Rousseau
EXPOSED

Open to all sides and wishing to hide
The darkness is comforting not hurting one's eyes
To bleed forth our being and be understood
A cry out loud if only we could

Searching for words that one longs to share
A void that is deep no one who will hear
Our lives are so fast, sometimes lost in the past
Time stands still for no one, we are fragile like glass

With our minds we do struggle to make our way clear
In a world of darkness, worry and fear
So back to our spot, a small quiet place
To peer through the darkness with no escape.

Philip C Giffin
GRANDMA'S REUNION

They all rushed out to meet her,
The day my grandma died.
They shouted with peals of laughter
When she got to the other side.

Grandpa was there with a loving grin.
Her parents and sons, Ed, Bob, and Paul.
Her, "Well, I declare!" was lost in the din
As she joined in reunion with one and all.

We miss our loved ones here on earth
When they've gone ahead to heaven
Where God and loved ones bring joy and mirth,
With hardships gone and sins forgiven.

Death to Christians is not the end!
Christ has promised by His cross
Eternal lives for our loved ones begin,
And death's a brief, not a total loss.

Lia Kupers
OUR SMALL TOWN CHRISTMAS
Our little town, everyone knows each other which makes our Christmas a little more special. Neighbors exchanging gifts, sharing their Christmas joy. Each house is filled with the warmth of the people and the pleasant smell of fresh pine, homebaked cookies, and hot cider. The trees are beautifully trimmed surrounded with gifts which are filled with thoughtfulness and great cheer. When people drive through our town they can feel the love and warmth in the year which can send a holiday chill down their spine. Only the people that live here can actually feel the feeling. They are the people who share Christmas with gifts that God gave us all, the ability of loving and sharing. Not just the Christmas joy but also the joy of being friends This is what makes the spirit come to life, as did our Lord on this celebrated day.

Melissa Diane Crowe
A MOURNING SONG

To Jan Leigh, thank you for your belief in me and your friendship.

A heart surrenders in the dark of night, A lover's need is satisfied. A commitment made, a lie unfolds, a tear admits the truth is bold. Was I yours or were you mine? A question answered with the passing of time.
Dust to dawn, day after day, a love you is spoken then taken away, a heart so true, green eyes cry blue, forever and ever I will love you.
Day after day, the rain seems to know, I was losing you and letting you go, crying clouds weep by my side, changing my heart from happy to sad, Was loving you really that bad? At night I still cry missing you so, sadly realizing, my heart cannot let you go.

Patty R Merz
CHALLENGE
Life is just another obstacle we are challenged to go through.
We are meant to learn, to love, to fear,
to show emotion and even cry a tear.
To have needs, to want, to hate,
to feel the pain we all create.
To know the happiness we all can feel,
the illusion of loneliness can hurt so painfully real.
To laugh and to cry, to show the emotion
we once used to hide.
Learning what is to be taught,
fighting this fight that has to be fought.
It is a challenge, this obstacle of life they taught.

Etalea Unferth
PENCIL ETCHINGS

To dedicate this to the Special Friends who inspired and encouraged me to write.

Last night
We talked
Just you and I
Of trifles
This and that
You were so
Close—so dear
I felt so calm
And yet you
Were not near—
That I
Could really hear
Your voice—
But last night
We talked
Just you and I
Of trifles
This and that.

Paul J Poirrier
THOUGHTS
There are times
When my dreams soar into
The realm of hopes, long forgotten.
When my thoughts burn
So deep into my soul
That I have to dream away
The dreams that haunt me.
Thoughts, illusions of a future,
Of a time, of a world that may or may not be;
Yet, they will be,
In my deepest fantasies,
Burning forever in my soul.
In time, illusions fade,
Dreams pass away,
And desires are forgotten,
As it should be during the course of life.
Yet, thoughts of her . . .
Her burning sunlight, her warmth,
Her passion, her touch, her love . . .
Forever will they be . . . Thoughts.

Julie Hollman
A HUG

Dedicated with love to my family and friends who have taught me to appreciate the value of a hug.

A hug can be a powerful thing,
We all know the comfort and warmth one can bring.
A hug can tell a loved one you care,
Or let them know that you'll always be there.
A hug can be a sign of devotion,
It's a gesture that can carry so much emotion.
A hug can give hope, forgiveness and strength,
And a hug gives out love no matter the length.
A hug can lend your support to another,
But mostly a hug means we all need each other.

Dwight Granger
PARALLEL LIVES
Parallel lives touch once to see
There is no end to eternity
The time is here
For us to steer
Our lives in the right direction
We have gone through the selection
Process
Oh yes
Now we see
It is to be
But the place will never mean so much
As the time when parallel lives once touch

Dwight Granger
TODAY
If dreams are for dreamers and wishes for fairies
Why does it change whenever one marries
Why continue to send out wishes
While standing and washing dirty dishes
Why hang around and hurt and mope
When all that is left are dreams of hope
So live today as though it's your last
If it's not then today is tomorrow's past

Pamela J Markell
COME WALK WITH ME

I would like to dedicate this poem to Johnnie, who I will love always.
Pam

Come walk with me,
Beyond the shadows of the pale moonlight.
Erase my tears,
Ease my fears.
Come hold me tight,
Kiss me gently under the starry night.
Come love me in your own special way,
A way like no other.
Till morning's first light.
Hurry now let us put the stars to bed.
Let the sun warm your heart as it has mine.
That the only thoughts in your head,
The only feelings in your heart are of me.
Then to you my love I promise to always be true.

Patrick Barbato
OUR TREE

To my wife Nutzie—all my poems are of you, for you made my life a poem that rhymed.

I remember with love when we planted it,
Our constant love made it flourish and grow.
It grew tall and green and lush, withstanding the cold and deep snows of winter.
Adorned with leaf and new growth in its summers.
Its seven branches were shown how to brace themselves,
against the force of oncoming winds.
Our poems and songs have all been sung.
Let the cycle of our time be complete.
Let our years be measured and numbered.
Let the leaves fall.
Let the tree wither and die.
For the seed from its seven branches, has given new life.
Encircled sevenfold by already mature and stately trees,
beautiful and standing together.
Nurtured with heredity and love of their parental origin.
The cycle of our tree of life ended when she left me.
The last leaf will fall—when we meet again.

Patrick Barbato
JUST BLUE
Thoughts of you—all day through—
It's always this way—when I get blue-
And there's nothing to ease it—it seems—
Guess I'll take a drive—an hour or two—
I'll be alright—let myself out—
Soon as I sight—a meadow and stream.

I've handled it before—it'll pass again—
And I shouldn't let myself get so low-
Just one of those days—the longing won't end—
Takes more than trying—and my heart keeps crying—
Fighting all other thoughts—wanting to come in.

There now—I've talked it over with you—I knew
You wouldn't let me walk here alone—
Just knew you'd be near—waiting for me here—
Yes I'll go home now—my heart is consoled now—
I'll call one of the girls—soon as I'm home.

Patrick Barbato
DEBT OF TEARS
At times I thought it was useless to go on,
Rebuild my castles after you had gone,
Search for words I have never used replying,
To my heart, when it wouldn't stop crying.

But my heart just had to have its way,
For it's only in writing my heart can lay,
Open its feelings, its love, that it may not burst,
Writing words and memories into poetic verse.

And tho it smiles and cries when I write,
My memories of you, each morning and nite,
Unaware of the debt it must pay,
When I read the poems of you, I wrote yesterday.

G S Huggard
LOSING THE FARM

To the Earth, may I never lose my love for her.

Today I grieve
For my childhood memories
Are now another's dream
come true
Today I cry
As I walk on the soil
That my feet grew upon—
Traveled it for the last time
Today I have sorrow
Having to let go—
Ending a part of my
existence
Today I smiled
Thru my tears
For the joy, beauty
and freedom
The place where I grew
Gave me.
Today I grieve
Forever I'll remember.

G S Huggard
UNTITLED
Cry for the childhood past
Cry for the seasons slipped by
Cry for the birds that have flown
Cry for the loves that were lost

Sigh when the heart is heavy
Moan when the burden too large
Deny thoughts if the mind is cluttered
Break free if the soul is uneasy

Cry once more for the seasons
The memories, the sensations
And then sing for the
Emotions you possess
Sing for the moments of pleasure

Sing for the corridors of time
They are never ending
And sing once again
When the spirit is flying

Sigrid Singleton

Sigrid Singleton
WHAT REASON FOR YOUR TOIL?

This poem is dedicated to my brothers and sisters.

Your eyes red—rimmed by the wind, your ruddy face blackened by the blowing dirt, your callused hands the crafter, your uniform a denim shirt—

Those dimples in your cheeks, like exclamation marks for your smile, spreading to a crinkling near your eyes, least they stay awhile—

That auburn colored hair, with natural curls enmesh, vigorously blowing with the wind, the wind that makes the ruddy flesh—

Those broad shoulders, quite awesome, in that proud powerful torso, your voice echoes like a heartbeat, when the time is apropos—

Your fortunes were not money, then what reason for your toil? just to love and to do, you, the tiller of the soil—

Sigrid Singleton
GATHERING WILDFLOWERS
Meadows of wildflowers
Like droplets of dew,

Blossoms on mountains
Blending their hue,

Warm spring sunshine
Dotting the ground,

Everything gets seeded
Without anyone around,

Deserts of wildflowers
Deep as the sky,

Countless bright blossoms
Caressing the eye,

God be the one
Sculpturing all things,
Wildflowers, wildflowers,
Oh, it is spring!

Virginia Greer
SPRING IS HERE
Spring is Here!
Spring is Here!
As it comes once every year.

Flowers with buds anew;
Blossom in the morning dew.
Robe's birds of colors sing;
Sing the glorious song of Spring.

Don Lippert
THE BAY AT SUNSET
Sunset on the bay at the end of a beautiful day is a colorful event.
The sound of the wind whistling through the trees is a ghastly sound.
As the rolling waves splash against the dock, they spray a white foam.
The boats look like toys as they jog lazily back from another world of peace and quiet.

The sea gulls circle over the boats, squawking as if begging for a fish.
The sun like a dying fire, scatters its golden rays across the water and then disappears behind the coastline.
Then, suddenly as if a flickering candle had given up the fight, the night settles.
Everything is quiet again until tomorrow.

Don Lippert
AUTUMN COMING
The sweet scent of lilies in the valley hauntingly lingers,
As the fluttering breeze—trickles through the dying remnants of summer.
In the distance, the tall redwood standing valiantly against evening's horizons.
Suggests a silent warning of winter with its once beautiful decor warmly blanketing mother nature's earth.
No sign of activity is to be found,
Gone are the busy little insects contently and continually working,
Gone is the small sly squirrel leaving only scattered shells as evidence of his endeavors, it is much colder now as the once enchanting breeze transforms into chilly ghostly gusts.
Suddenly as if a fluttering candle had finally died,
The cold crisp night suddenly appeared.
Trace of a new moon barely can be seen through the milky mass of clouds, as if strange white invaders can be seen drifting uninhibited through the peaceful valley.
Forming a huge white blanket upon the earth's breast.

Thelma Giles

Thelma Giles
PEACE BE STILL

I wish to dedicate this poem to my sons, James and John.

There is sunshine
There is rain
There is joy
There is pain

But the thought
That turns the tide
Is knowing God
Will ever abide

Under His arm
His sheltering arm
We are free
From all alarm

At his feet
We beg His will
As He whispers
"Peace Be Still"

Thelma Giles
REFLECTION
What you wear in your heart
Will show in your face
And thoughts of the mind
One can't erase

But the smile of God
Upon a face
Is filled with joy
And endless grace

A look of peace
And a look of love
Reflect the nature
Of God above

Reid P Bowers
WHY AMERICANS?

To a Drug Free America.

Why as Americans, do we so idly stand?
While drugs and dopes, invade our land.
Maybe looking on this matter, as just a joke.
Thinking it only affects, some other folk.
I write this now, from experience of my own.
This deadly killer, can invade any home.
Yes American people, in their daily life face.
These morbid drugs, their lives can erase.
I hope this poem, might instill prospective.
For a drug free America, that is effective.
Through all endeavors, Americans have faced,
By God's almighty power, we have been graced.
Once more together, Americans must stand.
For our own freedom, from drug contraband.
Other countries may build, on drugs and dope.
Let's build America, on true American hope.
If one does choose to, stand idly aside.
What an utter disgrace, to American pride.
This poem I wrote, is so devoutly true.
I just had to pass, these facts on to you!

Nannie Lyles
EARLY MORNING
I love the early morning hours
When no one's up but me.
I like to turn my thoughts to God
And let Him speak to me.

I like to read my Bible
I like to kneel and pray.
It gives me strength and courage
To last another day.

I like to look up in the sky
And see a fluffy cloud.
Hear birds singing in the trees
So carefree and so loud.

Yes, morning is a special time
Wherever I may be.
To enjoy this special friendship
Between my Lord and me.

Jenny Cluff
GARDEN OF MY MIND

Dedicated to my husband Ben Cluff, A dairyman that gave to the poor. 1977, Cluff Street named after him in Carson, California. Out of his head 2 years tumor of the brain.

God gave me something he gave no one else
God gave me something just for myself

He gave me a fantastic mind so I can concentrate
He gave me a sound mind that I can meditate

I can picture every mountain, every scene
I can travel the world over, I can dream

I can go for a walk with the wind in my face
And my mind can escape way out into space

There are no mountains that I cannot climb
If I but only use the treasures of my mind

For my mind has an unsurpassing power
It allows me to sit and dream by the hour

When I am depressed, I can gain on life a new lease
In the mirror of my mind is a reflection of peace

And when I sit and dream I am never alone
My mind drifts off into a world of its own

I plant good seeds in the garden of my mind
And they grow and germinate to heights sublime

I must sow my seeds into rows that are straight
And from time to time I must water and cultivate

Now my mind is the heart of my understanding
Help me Lord to always be kind and not demanding

There are no windows in the garden of my mind
Only God can look in, he's the keeper of my time

Dear God if all my body should waste away
Please leave me a sound mind, this I do pray

There are so many dreams and prophecies ahead
I pray my mind will remain fertile till I'm dead

I can think back to my childhood and reminisce
Only our God in Heaven can give us a gift like this

For my mind I am thankful, I can understand
And obey your word that you left for man

I pray dear Lord all my bad seeds you'll pardon
And take me home to a different kind of garden

Jenny Cluff
UNLOCK YOUR HEART AND THROW AWAY THE KEY

Dear Child: Today when your letter arrived
I was not only shocked but quite surprised
All these years I knew something kept us apart.
But I didn't realize the hurt that was in your heart
Please push the anger & bitterness out with a shove
For these have no place in a large family of love
If only I had been trained in child care
Every time you needed me, I would have been there
But I married when I was not yet twenty
And you children came and came a plenty
Your father was ill for years and passed away
And I just did the best I could day by day
When you were hurting, I was hurting too
I honestly didn't know I was neglecting you
So dear child, I'm asking you to forgive me
And unlock your heart and throw away the key
Hate is much too great a burden to bear
My love for all my children I want to share
I want you to know that I really do care
And if you ever need me, I'll be there
You're all gone now and have children of your own I
need your love more than ever, as I'm all alone
I'm pleading guilty as charged, so please set me free
And unlock your heart and throw away the key
Love
Mom

Louise S T Spell
DESPAIR

Vague glimpses of the familiar
Made tolerable
This approval—seeking,
Principle—Compromising
Stranger I had become.
Uneasily, I existed.

Until . . .
Blinding illumination.
Comprehension.
This kindred spirit—
Long my only impetus—was you.
And I . . . a mere appendage!
Not a trace remained
Of the entity that was me.
My despair was inalienable.

Tom DiPaola
BROTHER TO BROTHER

We sit together as friends and talk to each other,
for support and guidance like brother to brother.
We open old wounds closed only by scars,
spilling our souls to rekindle old stars.
Together we laugh and together we cry,
to ask from life only one question—WHY?
but without each other we would be floating in space
like looking through the eyes of a lost friend's face.
not knowing up and not knowing down
just floating through dreams looking for ground.

Thank the Almighty that we are together
our memories will last for ever and ever.
In my mind we will always help each other
like friendships bonding
or more like—
BROTHER TO BROTHER!

Brenda Green
UNFINISHED JOURNEY

To start a task
and never finish
To express your thoughts
so they won't diminish
To take a walk
and turn around
To reach for stars
but fall to the ground
To make an attempt, to succeed; and try
to live forever and never die
The journey we take is a passage through life
But the unfinished journey
can cut like a knife

Jennie Y Fly
YOUR WEDDING DAY

This poem is dedicated to my dear niece Sandy and her wonderful husband George.

It isn't every day we're asked
To take a "stand-in" part:
To fill a void created
When loving parents depart.

I know they're watching over us,
Were they here, they would agree.
A finer couple you couldn't find
If you looked an eternity.

As you stand here before God today
To start your lives anew;
I pray he will endow you with love,
Faith and understanding, too.

The survival of a marriage is based on this foundation;
Just as our forgiving God has,
Down through all creation.

As you go forth into a new life,
May you always be as one;
Loving, laughing, sharing,
Until your days on earth are done.

Karen S Lee
A WORKING MOTHER

To my daughter, Susan, who inspired this poem.

My child, I must leave you
To earn a day's pay,
Remember I love you
When I am away.

There's a lump in my throat
As I try not to cry,
I feel so guilty
When I must say good-bye.

Each day is the same
Seeing your tears,
Do you hate me, or;
Are these only my fears?

I pray that I leave you
In capable hands,
For harm must never touch you
On that I strongly stand.

I also pray that someday
When you've children of your own,
You will never have to suffer
The guilt that I have known.

Yvonne Hunter von Mizener
LOVE

Words unspoken, words unsaid
Now fill each corner of my head
'Tis best howe'er to keep it quiet
Until I'm sure that all is right.

My heart speaks loudly with each beat
My walk betrays me on the street
'Tis but from you my secret's kept
Oh! You don't know the tears I've wept.

Like pearls of stardust in the skies
That the love light in my eyes
Like waves upon the ocean's shore
Shall I care forevermore.

Goodnight my dear, I pray the skies
May sprinkle stardust in your eyes
And that the ocean, as she plays
May teach you something of her ways

I love you!

Sandra Liska
FEARLESS

For Brian, my best friend and the love of my life.

Bright pink sky lights the world
Freezing the darkness in its icy steps,
As I reached for you—
For love,
Fearlessly.
And turned away
Dark ashes
Of pain.

Sharmila Daryanani
THE FLOWER OF LIFE

This cannot be. Is it but a dream?
Will I ever wake up from this nightmare?
The sun's rays, so warm and bright,
Yet I see my beautiful flower, shrivelled, dying.
I cannot save it, I've tried so hard,
But nature is too strong, her jaws clenched tightly,
The stem snaps, petals everywhere,
My flower, where's my flower?
It is gone, washed away so far.
I cannot reach it, I tried, you must believe me.
The pain, the pain, make it disappear,
It has taken control, its force so strong,

I am weary, I cannot fight anymore,
It has weaved itself into my life.
All is dark but for one petal clenched
In a fist so tight it bleeds tears so red,
Quick, catch them, there is still time,
My poor petal, so small, so brave,
But the drops are too heavy, she is crushed.
Let it go, I must, for I am too weary.
It is time, I am ready . . . take me now.

Zoraida Semprit
LIFE REGAINED

To the special person that believes the moon is my special star . . . .

I have loved,
But truly have not.

My eyes were broken,
My soul was blind.

I could not see the thorns in
Those roses which I held in my grasp.

The blood of love flowed and
Would not cease.

You came and my eyes were mended,
My soul could see.

I no longer held a rose that made me bleed,
But one that gave me life.

Zoraida Semprit
LONELINESS

When you are not by my side,
Life feels like a sparrow that cannot fly.

Frozen in time, he can see,
feel, but cannot move.

Having you close to me would make me
feel free of the frozen bondage of loneliness.

Just as a sparrow flies and sings with happiness,
I too, would sing full of joy because my love has
come near once again.

Gina Cuciniello
SPECIAL YOU

Jeff no matter where love takes you there will always be.

You are so special to me
With the potential for more
You are not who I belong to
But you are the one who I adore

You are not who I make love to
For his love is so cold
But, you are the one I think of
And this is wrong so I am told

You are not the one I caress
For I am another man's wife
But it is you that I cherish
You are the warmth in my life

I could never hurt him
For his love has been true
But in my heart there will
Always be a
SPECIAL YOU . . . .

Tammie Jones
WEEPING WIDOW

A weeping widow dries her tear
while thinking of the yesteryear.
Her pain is deep and so very cold
for she has no one left to hold.
Alone and abandoned she does feel
her life has come to a sudden standstill.
She remembers the long Sunday walks
and the many special midnight talks.
Although her love has went away
his memory will be with her every day.
She knows that they will be together again
and that their new life will begin.

Ruth Kathryn Irby
WHAT LOVE CAN DO

There is no difficulty that enough love will not conquer,
No disease that enough love will not heal,
No door that enough love will not open,
No Gulf that enough love will not bridge,
No wall, that enough love will not throw down,
No sin, that enough love will not redeem,
It makes no difference how deeply seated the trouble may be—
How hopeless the outlook,
How muddled the tangle may be or,
how great the mistake.
A sufficient realization of love will dissolve it all.
If we could only love enough, we would be the most powerful
Being in the world

Robert J Staley
ICE BLUE

In memory of Katie Tackett.

Ice blue was splashed across the spring sky
Below it danced on the crystal stream
Warmth from the sun melted ice in that blue
Like a smile between my Lord and me.

As I saw the blue heavens reflecting on Earth
A truth was made clear to me:
Sparkling from my eyes were the eyes of Christ
Also meant to be.

How many times the mud had been stirred
Clouding the beauty of Him,
Times when the hate, the jealousy, the mistrust
Had shadowed my life in sin.

Only Jesus could love me enough
To intermingle my heart with His own
And wash away in a crystal stream
Every hurt that I have known.

Ice blue was splashed on my view of the Earth
It sparkled on the water that purled
How simple to see that, like sky in a stream,
Through us, too, God comes to the world.

Jeanne Louise Morgan
TOMMY

Today he chased the falling autumn leaves
As they swirled and whirled down around the trees,
Then he laughed and clapped his hands with delight,
When the wind danced the dry leaves into flight.
He looked at every single bush and tree,
Searching for treasures very carefully.
He showed me his treasures quite solemnly,
Gave a stick, a rock and a leaf to me.
The dear little fellow is just past one,
My curly haired baby, my grandson.

Jeanne Louise Morgan
MY HUSBAND, MY LOVER, MY FRIEND

Monday through Friday I'm a dutiful wife,
boys, bunk beds and blue jeans and bills are my life.
But Saturday night is my lover's and mine
He's sweet and exciting like sparkling red wine.
On Sunday my friend and I go to the park,
we laugh and eat hot dogs and talk until dark.
Please do not judge me I've committed no sin,
my husband's my lover,
my lover's my friend.

Betty Lloyd
SPECIAL KIND OF FRIEND

I have this special kind of friend
that I respect a lot
I have some special feelings
that won't ever be forgot

I have this special kind of friend
that I have feelings for
This very special kind of friend
will come knocking at my door

I have this special kind of friend
that sees my troubles through
For this my special kind of friend
hates to see me blue

This special kind of friend of mine
means the world to me
For this my special kind of friend
he will always be

I have this special kind of friend
that follows me around
I have this special kind of friend
that I'm really glad I found

Jill Marie Snyder
LOVED AND LOST

I have been dropped from the sky
Thrown unto the sea
Beaten against the rocks

As I go near the river of pain and reality
I drink from it in hope to become strong
And I will walk alone
Along the path that is laid down before me

Though my hands will not be full
Nor the sky with clouds

And within my tears may fall
Like a hammer on a nail driven into a cross
And perhaps the anger inside
May one day die

I shall put on my armor and with my pride
I will refuse to cry

Patrick Raymond Bunnell
STAINED-GLASS SHADOW

All churches enchant me; But
Gazing at Your steeple
Gently penetrating the satin sky,
I am drawn to Your steps.

Running my fingers along Your walls,
I feel
As if I created You,
As I, too, were a temple.

And there, above me,
Behind a stained-glass window
Delicately stroked in regal hues,
Is a shadow of You,
A silhouette, silent and still.

Amidst the silence,
I hear You calling
Though You do not speak.

Yes, I will open Your doors.

With soft steps I enter
And become complete.
Then doze into a dream
To the sounds of chiming.

Robin N Massie
BLESSED ARE THE CHILDREN

Blessed are the children
for I can hear them weep
who have no food for hunger
or a place to lay and sleep.

Blessed are their parents
who cry every night
holding on to their children
for fear what will happen before light.

Blessed are the sick
who pray to God each day
Take me on to heaven
so by your side I'll stay.

Blessed are all the people
who are sick, hungry and poor
Praying this life will be over
and the pain they will have no more.

Blessed are the blessed
who lend a helping hand
who in time I know
will make this a better land.

Gayle Terese Woodard
GIRL ON A BIKE

She rode with the breezes that nestled her cheeks;
surrounded herself with the natural and free.
Like the tropical flowers and birds in the pond,
she reflected the sunset and no human sound.
Her muscular limbs pounded hard up the grade,
which eased all the tension that crowded her head.
Her long hair whipped back as she sped round the bend,
and felt such delight as she tried to pretend
That life was so simple, with no way to fail.
Just a girl on a bike, in love with the trail!

Gayle Terese Woodard
MY HANDS

I've been to every place in town
where patients have demands
They want a cure, I want the same
I only bring my hands
That wash and dress, support and hug
It doesn't seem like much
But day by day I see a change
Response to gentle touch
A little smile across a face
now crossed with lines of age
A softening of give and take

From humanist exchange
I may see strength where yesterday
the light had left their eyes
They greet me now, may say "old friend"
But that's not very wise
For soon I must be on my way
to give help to another
I try to stress "Don't be depressed
You're still my sister/brother"

Levina Hale Dowell
CONCLUSION
Woe, but to have loved and been loved
'Tis but great sorrow
If circumstance preventh love
To flourish on the morrow
Why then, chooseth fate
To cause such pain
Where love must cease
And woeful hurt shall take its reign
Abounding obligation
Rears her wanton head
Duty and honor to her
Are the things that must be fed
Lifelong to be haunted
By mistakes of our youth
Never enabling our hearts
To identify the truth
Henceforth, my conclusion
'Tis but hard to draw
'Twas better to have loved and lost
Nor not to knowth love at all

Rebecca McKnight
THE CAROUSEL

This poem is dedicated to all of the remaining carousels in the world.

The horses gallop around and around,
Their heads are high but they make no sound.

Look at the colors so bright and gay;
Blacks and browns and whites and grays.

The carousel is marvelous, as you can see
For when children ride it, they laugh with glee.

The horses are magic as they may seem,
For you can ride them into a dream.

So when you see the carousel,
Jump on and ride into its magic spell.

Helena Secre
ODE FOR ANNE SEXTON
Two strikes against her—
So Anne Sexton said,
That ruled her off and on . . .
Many times hospitalized—
Anne's life felt caged power.
She would say,
"Ride, walk or run away."
Anyway . . .
When her score was added
She was gone.
No more stays in a world shut out
Like so much jail time—
"Jailed for what?"
O, fate played her cards—
And fate left her legacy
To poetry.

O, dear one you have grown
And grown, and time,
The eternity of it all—has taken
You away, as life goes
Away to distant shores.

Fern de Graaf
REFLECTIONS
Succulent green foliage
bows over the
crinkling water's surface.
Unique and glistening
patterns emerge,
shooting outwards in
repetitive circles. They
bubble and sparkle,
ingeniously hypnotizing the
captivated viewer.

Sonia Sierra
THE CONVERSATION
What is this idle chatter that drones around me
And hints of despair?
These words I hear; devoid of mind
Eyes that close to souls locked away
In chambers deep, only hints of Life and Form.

All this talk that drifts nowhere;
permeates the
Air, direction unknown
Laughter abounds, sorrow is sublime
Never a touch, a gentle touch
Fear of what one may find?
Rather to spend time in idle chatter—
Believing

Patricia N Fields
HAPPINESS WITHIN
Life is only what we perceive it to be
Circumstances of good are what we need
Sort out the good in all that we see
Disappointments can be overbearing indeed
Let life deal us the things it may
Face them with hope of a brighter day
Sadness and pain is around us to stay
To help us search for the better way
We store up memories to help us thru
There's always some good in what we do
What's ahead in life we haven't a clue
What we would change if only we knew
Would good be good had we never known bad
Could we know happy had we never been sad
Appreciate the experiences only we have had
Character, virtue, patience to these does add
Let us to life now willingly cling
Happiness within ourselves now bring
With the birds we now will sing
Bells of joy we too now hear ring

Mabel E Lewis
THE CHILDREN
Red rimmed eyes
Somber faces
Little soldiers on display
On their best behavior
Attended grandma's
Funeral today

Beverly B Bittle
JUST AS ONE ROSE DIES
Just as one rose dies
Another blooms
As one love dies
Another blooms
A love far greater than the first
A love that is actually immersed
In love for one another
Not only as man and wife
But as sister and brother
He is the love of my life

Therese Hall Leach
CHILDREN

To my oldest nieces and nephew who allowed me to be a child when I was still one. To my younger nieces and nephew and my daughters Erin and Erica who took me back in time again.

Laughter, funny faces, tears, soap suds, and whispered prayers . . .
children—a gift of passing time
Laughter wrinkles their eyes . . .
Tears tug at heart-strings . . .
children—growing a grain at a time
Pictures of funny faces with turned up noses hold the wonder of childhood . . .
But the soap suds quickly fade like youth and disappear . . .
children—taking you back in time
Whispered prayers touch you deep inside . . .
A child is someone who passes through your life and then disappears into an adult.

Joshua L Klynn
WHEN
Several times before now
i remember being born

In times of bloody terror
When uniforms were worn

In times of magical love and joy
i watched the people's freedom

In a time of dragons and maidens' hands
i wandered 'round the kingdom

And all through the eras and decades and days
'long the tunnels of life and existence

Remain the same person far, deep in your core
while not facing change with resistance

As the clocks and the wheels orbit my mind and the sun rises up and then back—
all i can do is just go with the flow
and carry my mind in a sack.

Becky Wheeler
THANK YOU
Thank you for being there,
For showing me the way.
Thanks for telling me you care,
Every single day.

For everything you've done,
For always being true.
Thanks for all the fun,
When happy times were few.

All the times I gave up,
For helping me get through.
I want to thank you for so much,
But mainly, for being you.

Stephen Madrid
CONTEMPLATION

To Stacy Brown;
May you find what you have been searching for,
May your questions be answered.

A white light burns to chase away the shadows
of memories that I have tried to forget,
but still haunt the halls of my m
I fear of losing the light if I choose to make us one.
Yet, I do not have the light as my own to make such
decisions and perhaps break my destiny either way.
Enough idle talk!
I must step over the threshold and come what may!
Indeed, I do fall with my heart instead of my head,
a true mark of a fool, but no matter.
The light is not mine to lose,
but perhaps to gain.

Stephani Fordham
TWO LINKS
Faces like angels
Fairy tale queens
Eyes like rare jewels
Heaven blessed dreams

Two typical children
Ordinary to some
Two daughters fulfilling
The prayers of a mom

So pretty and pink
In buttons and bows
Uniquely distinct
As the smell of a rose

From beauty and brains
To irresistible charm
Two links form a chain
Surrounding my heart

Andy Jeffries
JESUS
Jesus-Savior of My Soul
Jesus-The One Who Made Me Whole
Jesus-The One Who Set Me Free
Jesus-The Only One For Me
Jesus-All My Trials He Bears
Jesus-The Only One Who Cares
Jesus-My Only True Companion
Jesus-The One Who Keeps Me Standing
Jesus-Can Be The One For You
Jesus-Because He Loves You Too

Mary Annette Phipps
KINDRED SPIRITS
On ivory wings of fantasy I embrace
A love that patiently awaits
A heart that beats in rhythmic tones
A force that generates
Our spirits move in harmony
Our bodies cry is it not fate mere destiny to be
joined together melodically.

Oh! what is this force beckoning, passionately
clinging to me, trying to take away my serenity,
divert my very destiny
It whispers softly in the moonlit night,
Kindred Spirits are we moving through life simultaneously
Silhouette to Silhouette it intimately strikes a chord
a faint note written upon my heart
Heart beat to Heart beat, breath by breath until the
two hearts beat as one being played on a key board of
rapturous rapport.

Kindred Spirits are we bound

together throughout eternity
Hearts beating as one simultaneously,
no more can there be
two distinct mortals, as you and me
our journey has ended we are one
united, inseparably
free, now shall we forever be Kindred
Spirits throughout
eternity.

Margarite Mayes
DEAR MOTHER

This poem is dedicated to Margaret Mayes, My Dear Mother.

Mother you are a jewel cherished as a
PEARL.
The beautiful person who brought me
into this world.
I will always love you because you
were so kind
When I need a friend you are the first
who comes to MIND
You raised me to have GOALS and
to do my BEST,
I still will go on to SUCCEED while
you are at REST,
I remember how my Father would
put you down.
But I came to wipe your tears away
and tried to turn your WORLD
AROUND.
"Mamma" I would say "I will get my
Doctorate Degree someday."
Just to hear me say that would inspire
her the most.
She baked me cookies, warmed some
milk and made a toast.
"Continue to go on my CHILD be the
BEST that you can BE.
Put GOD first in your life, then put
me."
I didn't understand I was only
SIXTEEN.
Why the WORLD was cold yet I kept
my SELF-ESTEEM.
Often I wonder why GOD had to take
her away.
I forever will PRAISE HIM because
he didn't let me go ASTRAY.
I keep her in my heart and keep my
mind on my GOALS.
I ask GOD to take care of her and for
him to bless my SOUL.
I still have my FATHER, SISTERS
AND BROTHERS.
BUT NO ONE CAN EVER TAKE
YOUR PLACE DEAR MOTHER

Amy McNulty
WE ARE NOT ALONE

A pair of saddened eyes stare at me
through the mirror,
Looking past them into a world full
of darkness and sorrow,
Making my own world to escape this
painful one,
Trying hard to win the battle between
right and wrong,
But not knowing which is which,
Looking for someone to turn to when
no one is there,
Running down a deserted road
leading nowhere,
Looking back and seeing all the
friends and people that
really care for you,
Trying to turn back and break the
glass that separates
the worlds,
But only succeeding in pushing them
farther away,
This is the world that most of us live
in,
And when walking down that road to
nowhere,
Thinking of what we should have
said,
Or what we should have done,
WE ARE NOT ALONE.

Stephanie Newmark
WHAT IS A FRIEND?

To Pete, with all our friendship you have made my dreams come true. I love you.

A friend is not only a person
who cares and shares,
he is a person who can foresee
a volcano erupting and rescues
you before it explodes;
he soothes until you are like
new.

A friend sheds tears as you do.
He lends you a shoulder to lean
on; no matter how small the problem
may seem.

He is the sunshine of your day,
the smile in your sleep.
A friend remains a friend
until the end of time.

No matter what the distance or
the cost because a friend
is the one thing that is true.

Linda Gaye Langford
MOTHER'S DAY POEM

Dedicated to my beautiful mother, Bettye Jo Wilkins Cortines, and thanks to my loving husband, Peanut Langford, for his encouragement, and to the memory of Mary Jo Hughes.

Your laughter could fill an ocean.
Your eyes could light up the sky.
Your voice could cause a bird to sing.
Your beauty could make me cry.

You have the smile of an angel.
Your compassion is beyond compare.
You're always kind and gentle,
and I thank God for you in my
prayers.

What I'm trying to say,
Is that, I love you mother.
And even if I could find a way,
I wouldn't trade you for another.

John Hetzel
CHESHIRE CAT

You suddenly appear
From out of nowhere,
Recalling your new escapades.
You're not here very long
But even after you're gone
Your sweeping star smile never
fades.

You're there on the bough,
So smile on me now
Before you again drift away.
For your smile's remedy
When I need memory
To clear up a curious day.

Corbin England
THAT QUESTION

That question clings tightly to my
tongue,
Afraid to travel beyond my lips;
I open my mouth so that it may be
sung,
But upon my teeth it always trips.

Whenever I see you, it's always
there,
Within my mind and heart;
I would say those words if I would
dare,
Sadly my mouth will not let them
part.

It is but a small question that I seek to
ask,
A few words that form a simple line;
It may be said many ways but never
masked,
What a wonderful phrase: "Will you
be mine?"

Bill Bridel
OPENING WINDOWS

To Joanne, Miss Moseholm and all the friends and family who keep loneliness out of my life.

Alone, facing the world
No one around
to care for or love
I must lean on me
for support.
With every horizon
I open a new window
and look into myself,
only to see
the same lonely soul
tragically searching
for one moment of
dissipated solitude.
But knowing I'm forever destined
to walk in the chains
cast by my fears.

Melissa James
LITTLE LOVE

See how the shafts of sunlight
glisten on his skin.
Notice the slight rise and fall
of his chest as he sleeps.
Follow the contours of his body
as the sheet clings to every curve.
Marvel at how peaceful he looks as
he dreams of what could be.
Little did I know that he would
become more precious to me than
life itself.
Sleep without worry, my love,
my . . . son.

Linda Sutherland
NO MONEY IN MY POCKET

No money in my pocket
No place I want to go
I lost my job last Friday
As for unemployment
I'm the last one on
the row.

No money in my pocket
Newspapers wrap my feet
I got kicked out of my
apartment
Now, I'm wandering on
the street.

No money in my pocket
The soup lines are where
I eat
I'm so wet, and hungry
It seems like a real
good treat.

No money in my pocket
No place to rest my
head
The streets are cold and
lonely
How nice to have a bed.

No money in my pocket
and morning calls once
more
I've been kept walking
and the blisters on my
feet are sore.

No money in my pocket
There's not much more
to say
I'll keep the faith he
gives me
and live my life day
by day.

Virgie F [Escott] Custer
COLORS ON PARADE

Dedicated to; The Escott & Custer Families.

It's Spring time and very, very soon
All the spring flowers will be in
bloom.
The White Easter Lily so beautiful
and tall,
Soon to be followed by the lovely
Purple Crocus so small.
The Golden Forsythia in her long
yellow gown.
Will be followed by the perfumed
Lilac as she comes to town
Then the American Beauty Rose,
comes into view.
In her Crimson Reds and satiny
whites too.
Look! Here comes the apple
blossoms all dressed in white.
And the sweet smell of Pink
Cherry
blossoms, Oh! what a sight!
Soon, some of the blossoms will fade
away,
And in their place, a lovely fruit
will be on display.
The fruits will begin to grow and
grow.
Their colors will change from green
to reds and yellows, you know!
They are carefully picked, packed
and shipped
to your favorite store.
You buy them, take them home—
They will taste so delicious
you will want more and more.

Virginia F Custer
MY FRIEND

We were so close, my friend.
So many years ago.
We were so very young, my friend
That a romance began to grow.
I was married and you were not.
I had a husband, whom I loved a
lot.
In spite of my mate—
I fell for your charms
And soon I longed to be in your
arms
You held my hand as we danced
'round the room
Suddenly everything was bright
instead of gloom.
I tried to discourage your love for me
But all in all, it seemed an eternity
Some years went by—you found a
mate
When I heard, I tho't it was great.
Finally, I was out of your life
And you out of mine.
We both raised a family—
But not yours and mine.
Grief has crept in and left us alone
Dark clouds over us where once
the
sun shone.
Perhaps, Fate will step in and show
us the way
To find, at last, Our Love of
Yesterday.

Virginia F Custer
ALONE
I am so very lonely, since my Love
passed away.
I think about and dream about him
with every passing day
I think about the happy days we
both had together
Thru thick and thin, bad and good
and very stormy weather.
Our Love was true, Our Love was
good.
We always knew where each other
stood.
Tho many years have passed on by
Since my Love was taken away
My heart beats still for this Love of
mine,
I know I will be with him some
day
As I sit in my chair by the window
Watching the shadows fall,
If I listen carefully
I know I can hear him call.

Virginia F Custer
TOUGH
As I was walking down the street,
A little child fell at my feet.
As I stooped down to pick him up
I heard him murmur—"I'm tough."
Altho he was all broken up inside.
I didn't let on—but I cried.
Not once, did I see him shed a tear.
He was so brave, he showed no fear,

His parents came by and took him
away,
The doctor said "There's little hope
for this child today."
But God came down and said to the
lad,
"You're tough and don't you be sad."
As I was thinking of the boy in pain
I was praying for him to get well
again.

Some years later as I was walking
down the street.
A nice young man smiled at me—so
sweet.
He looked at me and said "Hi, I know
you.
You're the lady who picked me up
and I said to you—
I'm Tough."

Diane L Bennett

Diane L Bennett
THE RIDE
The beauty in the ride is a personal
affair.
It's an individual experience,
which
bikers love to share.
And if you haven't had a chance to
do this as your scene . . .
You've missed out on a nature
trip,
and missed a "biker's dream."

There's nothing like believin' in the
freedom that you hold,
as before your very eyes, nature's
beauty does unfold,

And spreads its mystic glory to the
heaven and earth around,
and reminds you that the bike you
ride is still the sweetest sound.

The sound of your sweet engine as it
leaves the miles behind,
match the picturesque America, so
vivid in your mind.

So priceless is the masterpiece that's
framed for yours to keep . . .
A harvest of golden delight, on
which your soul and mind does
reap.

Just like an eagle's freedom as he
rules the skies with noble grace,
You soar through virgin
wilderness
and rule the road unpaced.

Trading in yesterday's problems and
feeling the pain subside,
absorbing a tranquil peace
within . . .

the love within "The Ride"

Nina I White-Allen
I'M WONDERING WHY! THESE WARS GO ON!

This poem is dedicated to my family—parents—grandparents and friends—trusting world's "childhood memories" may be better than mine. Free of wars and sharing our brand new package. P.S. Let it be soon.

Before: "I" was born: Now—82 years
have gone!
"Read" About and was Told! By
All—Folks—Since—I was a Small-
Fry!
I'm wondering Why? These wars! go
on!?
And—is—it! because you or I—
didn't—"even" Try!?
Could "I" make things "Better-for
you all!"
Remove "Our World's Pains of War!
Fix-up that Trouble Place!
My Child-Hood Memories! I vividly
can Now Recall!
Those Pitiful Tears—Running down
their Troubled-Work-Worn-Face!

Tho "I" was Young—"I" worked at
cheering People up!
Lifted Ones—Asked How I could
Help at wanted need!
Medals! None and Received no
Silver Cup
Please! World! Be—Like wise—
Please to take Heed!
Help! Not to Destroy "Brothers &
Sister" We Need them!
For Each Other! Then this World's
Repair Made!
A "Heritage" to Us-All! By Our
World's Savior! When!?
Thee—Creator! Maker—Knowledge!
For Beauty is Shovel and spade!
A Lot of Hard Work did Before this
day or AGE . . .
Everything has been made Perfect
We Hope! Every "Daughter" and
"Son"!
Let it Be! What Our Children wear
Our Brand New Package!
When more Children are old They
can Live in this World without
Wreckage
"I" or "they" won't have to say "I'm
wondering Why! These Wars go on!"

Thomas L Herman
WHAT YOU MEAN TO ME

Dedicated to the reason why, Laurie Fessler.

As the buzzer sounds, my eyes scope out the picture of the cold hard fact, another morning! With the fading of the stars I too fade a little inside. I turn scared with my collar to the wind. Now is where they call it the darkest part of night. And while I welcome it with my eyes aimed low, something makes me raise them.
As the cloud rolls past it carries along your voice followed by the golden edge of the sunrays. You are my sunray, you are what I stand there to gaze at, to admire afar. And when you have fallen to the other side you leave behind your stars. For each star stands for a dream that both of us can share. You are my day that is part of my world which is in my life. What do you mean to me? I guess you'll never know.

Mark T Stovall
OBSERVER
You painted a portrait
a lover image bound, yet free,
Only the canvas did reveal
This prince with golden Fleece
is but a gilded soldier, a heart
without color,
a reflection of your shadow on
Flee,
You painted a portrait
to this observer me,
Who saw past your colors
to the picture with emotions
unseen
Emotions, just ambitions longing to
be free
A portrait draped in gold trim
the times of you and me.
You and I, a rainbow tapestry
hidden, behind hollow colors
it's our hearts, in need, in need of
love
You painted a portrait,
a profile in professional pride and
created this gilded soldier
never learning how to cry,
and I, your soother when the paints
run dry.

Christine Kutt
LOVE IS PURE AND WORTHWHILE
I learn something from each
situation, and this was an outstanding
experience I won't forget
It was far less than liberation, and I
hope that as time passes I won't feel
it's something I'll always regret
When she used to introduce me as her
lover, how could it be if she wasn't
even my friend?
It took a year and a half to discover,
that now it's finalized to this end
It shouldn't be right to have to
struggle, for what I needed real love
from another
I gave Loretta my love, but for
someone like her it wasn't enough
She wanted my soul, only it's not for
her to possess, or pretend to touch
I am worthy of genuine love,
something which she may never fully
understand as such
And I deserve to feel happy times,
and am entitled to special easy fun,
but she pushed me away and she
couldn't really walk hand in hand
Loving is not controlling whenever,
or pushing or pulling along
But it's rooting for each other
together for better, and this what will
make us all healthier and strong
So again love is not controlling and
love has not a price
Love could be warm and consoling,
and love is how we feel in our lives
I can say I gave this "so called"
friendship my trust, my all and best
shot
But I've realized for quite some time
now, she wasn't ready for spontaneous love at all
Sharing my love with a special
woman will always be important to
me, and one day when the time is
right it will happen I believe
Loving is not intentionally causing
harm, and it's not one tries to fool
people all along
If I've learned anything from this, It's
that I get weary when I settle for less
And this continuous uneasiness in my
past I'll never miss, for everyone
deserves the truth and best
I know I proudfully earn and deserve
real love
Deplorably, she may choose to
continue to hurt herself within, and
throw this great gift of pure love out.

Wanda Moore Vinson

Wanda Moore Vinson
I LOVE MY FAMILY

This poem is dedicated to Helene, Faye, James, Kathy & Jackie. I love you all very much, your sister Wanda.

I love my family
Siblings all in a row
I love them so deeply
But why does it hurt so
I know that I love them
But now I must let go

Our childhood was rough

This fact we all know
Some of us have held on to that
Others were blessed to let go

I love you, I love you all five from the heart
Let's bury the pain and make a new start
I've grown, you've grown, we've reached up above
Now let's take our family
And broaden out in our love

I love my family
Siblings all in a row
Now let's pull together
And watch our family grow.

Leonora Hayden-McDowell
IN THE TWILIGHT
In the hush of twilight
Among the gravestones
Of my dreams, I gaze
Far out, where the Great Spirit is,
And feel the Gypsy dark
Close gently over memories
That choose to haunt my soul.
And in the hush of twilight
I share whispers of the wind
And come to terms with shadows.

Leonora Hayden-McDowell
AUTUMN
Sighing pines surge with the wind
And stained galss leaves are falling.
The silent music of star-song
Drifts through dark shadows,
Mingling with sounds of loneliness.
Wild bird cry dropping from the blue
Shatters wood smoke's scent of silence.
The last leaves of Autumn
Hold a memory of summer gold
And frost-burned reeds are dry.
Beneath withered humus of the earth
Lies dark whisper of winter's cold.

Eugenia Grinwaldt
MY CHRISTMAS
Darkness . . .
all stars gone astray
behind thick walls of clouds.
And they can't find the way
to the hearts of all people
to light them aglow.
Even the biggest and brightest
—the Bethlehem Star . . .

I can't see, but I feel
dark-green softness of pine nearby . . .
with its dizzying spell of light fragrance.

Not a flickering light, but I know:
—the candles of pinecones drop down
a warm golden wax.
It feels breathless and painfully sad
all around . . .

I am a lonesome silver angel
on a lonely pinetree.

Eugenia Grinwaldt
JULY'S FRAGMENT
My hand sharply pulled the shades:
unexpected fog stood close
behind the window,
looking me straight into the eyes.

Where is the sun? A hot July sun?
Hot as a fire in southern pampases!
Bright as the light of hope!
Hot as a breathless fever!

Give me back my sun—
let it melt me all
and turn into an amber of love,
because I want to give a gift of
myself to my beloved.

Eugenia Grinwaldt
SINGING
I wish I had a voice deep and wide
like a river that flows through
beautiful valley.

I wish I had a voice like
the velvet of night,
vibrating with starry dust.

I wish my voice could be gentle,
like soft-blown wind
to caress his beautiful
wheaten-ripe hair.

I wish his eyes grew green
and light with desire
at the sound of my voice's golden cello.

I wish my pianissimo
was a breathless whisper
touching his lips.

I wish—all this be my voice,
when I am trying to spell the feeling.

And I wish his heart
moves toward me,
when he hears my voice!

Eugenia Grinwaldt
A DAY IN YOSEMITE PARK
Warm blue silk of the skies
lightly flows down my body.
Sun's golden pins glitter in my hair.
Wind softly whispers some lovely sounds
(which I don't quite understand)
—into my ears.
I smile, then I laugh—not too loud—
in unison with the river.
The sun roars like a golden lion.
The sun laughs heartily and hilariously!
And I start to sing—so loud—
that all peaks stand still and listen.
What a gorgeous day!
What a glorious day!
What a Godly Day!

Eugenia Grinwaldt
THE COLORS OF THE SPECTRUM
Hope is a bright green meadow
where my feelings bloom.
Memories are silvery mists veiling my mind.
Sadness is a giant gray wave
flooding me over.
Pain is black void of a deep canyon.
Your voice is a sound of purple madrigal
echoing in my soul.
Tenderness is a blue rose in my heart.
My fantasies about you are sparkling whites
of a new snow.
Remembrances of you are fragrant peonies
in the garden of my imagination.
Faithfulness is a traditional yellow ribbon
blindfolding me.
Waiting is burning anxiety of a red glow.
Love is a rainbow.

Eugenia Grinwaldt
*** * * OR LOVE?**
Love is warm tenderness
flooding my heart,
a passionate desire
burning my lips.

Love is cry of a sea gull
flying on the edge of dark cloud
over the ocean of despair.

Love is rain of bitter teardrops
hurting me as they fall.

Love is my guiding light
in the night of my life.

Love is soft whisper of flower-petals
from the sunny meadows of my memory.

Love is beautiful silvery star
glowing inside my soul.

Love is you . . .

Eugenia Grinwaldt
A LITTLE CHRISTMAS FANTASY
I wish I was a little silver-haired angel
upon your Christmas tree;
watching you sitting across the room,
giving me your happy smile
as the most precious gift.
Feeling so quiet, contented.
With tenderness ent'ring your heart;
just looking at me with a special warmth . . .
In that serene moment of understanding
my happy tears would burst forth
showering your tree with
millions of sparkling snowflakes.

Eugenia Grinwaldt
*** * * A WISH**
If I had been asked
what would be my most sincere wish
I would answer: touching your gentle fingers.

If I had been asked
what if it would be my only wish
I would answer: touching those long caressing fingers.

If I had been asked
what would be my last wish
I would answer: touching those
innocent trembling fingers.

Eugenia Grinwaldt
A POEM OF YELLOW ROSE (YOU GAVE ME)
Your yellow rose,—
—it stands here in the stillness of my room.
Its slim long stem so elegant and simple
reminds me of a movement of your hand.
It's telling me about your gentleness.
Its curvy petals do not open quite so easily.
They're hard and rigid like your lips.
They don't speak sentiments and tender words—
—your lips, which are much like these petals.
My room is all transformed
by vibrant presence of this rose.
And air around me is trembling
with soft tenderness.

Eugenia Grinwaldt
LATE EVENING IN MY GARDEN
Crying down on the chaise-longues outside my door
I can see twisted dry leafless branches
looking like incomprehensible
unreadable hieroglyphs
written on the surface of dark evening sky.
I can see half-moon like gigantic eye
of an otherwise invisible temple's priest.
Huge motionless palm in the light of grayish dusk
Somehow reminds me of a sphinx
put by the side of a pyramidal cloud.
I am listening intensely;
hearing some hushed distant sounds;
trying to recognize the voice of the
Night that is closing;
trying to decide the meaning of revelation
it is going to disclose to me.

Eugenia Grinwaldt
RETURN
I returned from my journey
and I will see you tomorrow.
I will give you all the souvenirs
I brought for you from this journey.
I will bring you my joy of return
and joy of meeting you again.
I will bring you my clumsy words
of cheerful greeting,
my starry-eyed look, my silvery laugh.
I will bring my longing to you
camouflaged by politeness.
I will hide adoration
deep on the bottom of my eyes.
I will wrap my heart tightly
in turquoise brocade,
so you won't notice the glow of my love.
I will stand close to you, so your
breath will touch my cheek aflame,—
with my eyes asking yours
if you are glad to see me.

Eugenia Grinwaldt
MORE ABOUT LOVE
I opened my window and at once
full of heaven–blue filled my eyes
and turned my dreams into a rainbow
with the other end of the rainbow
–in the infinity of my love.
All the birds were reciting poetry;
All the flowers looked like poems,
beaming spellbound love-scent.
Then suddenly sun appeared
from beyond the horizon,
like a goddess of love,
aiming two golden arrows right into my eyes,
blinding me forever in my love.
Here I am sitting motionless,
with blue light in my eyes
and blue torch in my heart.
And diamond day stands in my window-frame.

Eugenia Grinwaldt
A TOTALLY UNEXPECTED POEM
The greatest poem is a blank
snow-white sheet of paper.
It has anticipation of an unexpected
journey.
It can be a cruise around Hawaiian
Islands,
—without being sea-sick.
My ship could be a silver sea
dolphin.
I really don't need any compass—
You simply go 'round and 'round the
tropical islands.
And the weather stays always
fantastic.
The sun can be as big as my
imagination desires.
Her smile will awaken all the birds,
all the flowers.
And all people's eyes will open like
flowers in the morning.
Sun rays and shadows will chisel and
shape
a masterpiece sculpture out of every
orchid.
The sun paints my skin golden satin
as I float on the curve of a wave.
The sun can ride on the highest surf
at sunset time
going up and deep down into warm
gooey ocean.
And when the night softly embraces
my shoulders
the sea mist will kiss my face
—could I tell if it's sea mist
or your lips touching mine?

Charlotte Squyres
REFLECTION
I look in the mirror and who do I see?
No one I know looking back at me—
This person belongs to somebody
else
And try as I might I can't venture a
guess.

All my life I have tried to be what
they expect,
And little they know who they tend
to neglect—
A queen, or a princess; a genius, no
doubt!
What could she have been if she'd let
herself out?

My fears and my child I have locked
deep inside;
And to gain their acceptance I have
swallowed my pride.
I laugh and I cry and I mourn for my
child—
Oh, why can't I please just go play
for a while?

Red Rover, Red Rover, let someone
come over—
To scatter the toys and to run through
the clover.
No more, my child—it is much too
late;
Your own kids are playing and that
cannot wait.

Velma Lipe Brown
WORLD WAR II
Americans answered the call to arms.
They came from villages, cities, and
farms.
In the air, over the sea, and on the
land
Our soldiers and sailors made a great
stand

In the Pacific those major assaults
Created blood, sweat, and tears
result.
Airborne attacks, night landings,
dogfights over the seas,
Jungle warfare brought many men to
their knees.

Heartbreaking days of death and fear
set the tone.
Our men fought and died in many
war zones.
Heroism, courage and greatness of
time,
Gallantry, hardships suffered all
down the line,

Television, photographs, and book of
history,
Films and videos leave no mystery
Of courageous Americans overseas
that time
Who placed their lives on that
dangerous line.

It was a long road to victory during
World War II.
Many forgotten men never received
their due.
Don't let the reality of war fade away
Or World War III may erupt any day.

Helene Nell Donohoe
SUNFLOWERS
They bloom
in the most desolate places:
sunbaked cracked ground of vacant
field,
rocks piled along a railroad track,
a patch between tenements.

As I tramp the road I see these
flowers
reach for the sun and follow it across
the sky.
They gather cups of light and dapple
it upon the ground.

Such joy I feel upon my walk,
through drab, dark places
everywhere,
when I see these happy blossoms of
radiance
that can be had by rich and poor
alike.

Keith W Miller
ANOTHER YEAR
Another year, seems much too soon,
But beckoned by the sun,
You reach above your mother soil
To mark the season just begun.

A trek you've made many times,
Have yet to reach the end,
Ever smitten by a blow that takes
A winter's time to mend.

But full of hope, as every year,
And soon to reach your goal,
Unfold that blossom in the make
And finally bare your soul.

Yet, as before, your journey ends,
No justice in the wild,
Cut short by an uncanny source,
This time a barefoot child.

Some seem to have an easy life,
No effort to succeed,
Fate smiles at them, clears their path,
And cares for every need.

Though you are not among this group
You still hold life as dear,
So you will gather up your strength
And try another year.

Kim Zarazed
THE WANDERER
Wandering soul alone in the night
Where will you lay your head
tonight?
Nowhere to run, nowhere to hide
Nothing but a cold, lonely feeling
inside.

The nights are cold and the streets are
bare
You're left all alone to face this
nightmare
Who will you turn to? What will you
do?
Who will be there to see you
through?

Just call on the father and He'll hold
your hand
He sees all your hurt and He does
understand
Just reach out for Him, and He'll do
the same
Whenever you need Him, just call on
His name.

That name that is power, glory, and
love
Sent from the Father who reigns from
above
We're cleansed of our sins, that's
how He sees us
When we truly repent and call on
JESUS!

Arthur J Morris
BOYS IN VIET NAM

I dedicate this poem to all of the boys who fought in the Viet Nam War. Whether they are living or passed away, we will never forget them.

To our boys who are fighting in Viet
Nam,
We give our thanks and prayers.
They're over there to keep the peace
And check other countries' errors.
They will fight until the peace is won
To keep all countries free.
They're fighting for everyone,
Yes, even you and me.
They're dying, being wounded,
Crippled or dismembered.
But when this war is over
They will always be remembered.
So why not keep on writing
To the ones you love most dear,
Until the war is over,
Then they can get back here.

Dianne Billgren
FRIGHTFUL DAY
The bible tells us that God has
planned
this for hundreds of years
It's His way of cleansing earth
from all the sinful spears . . .
A big earthquake
that's the plan
Along with huge tidal waves
to flood all the land . . .
Killing off millions
leaving many to die
Droughts and famine
along with very cold skies . . .
I know I may not be perfect
and I usually don't go to church
But please God, help us,
because I know dying's going to
hurt . . .
I know this day is coming soon
and no one can stop it
So take my soul to heaven
and please don't you drop it . . . .

Marlene Cline
HOLDING CLOSE A LIFETIME OF JOYS
The whispering winds swelling long
prairie grasses,
Lifts my spirits and sweeps me
along . . .
And the skies of clear blue, bursting
rays of pale light,
Fills my soul with a beautiful
song . . . .

Just a glimpse of the moon, bathing
clear autumn nights,
Shining softly through dark, swaying
trees . . . .
Just the hand of a friend as we travel
life's road,
Just the brush of a warm summer's
breeze . . . .

The laugh of a child with dark,
wind-tossed curls,
Sun-kissed cheeks and bright eyes
aglow . . . .
The peace of the snow-covered
woodland at dusk,
And the song of the brook's gentle
flow . . . .

The long lonesome howl of a wolf
through the gloom,
Crashing thunder of foaming high
seas . . . .
Flashing white lightning on a wild,
stormy night,
Thrills my spirit and sets my heart
free!

All these and much more are mine for
a lifetime,
Lord, what have I done to earn these?
But if I ever forget and lock you out
of my life,
Please be patient . . . . and hand back
the keys . . . .

Shelly Lee Young
THE MEMORY

*In Remembrance Of
Margaret Esther Hadley.*

Every summer morning early
The sun just peeking through
a cloud
I awake on the familiar couch.

The front door going shut
My grandma going out,
The bucket banging against
The lantern she carries.

I remember the stool she sat on,
Brown, with legs scratched and
dented.
The bucket she carried was gray,
Stained with rings of white.

I remember her hands
Wrinkled and slender
Soft as she held my hand
But strong with our cow Ellie.

I remember how she was there
then she wasn't.
I didn't know why
But I understand now.

Linda Stichberry
GENES
Our Genes is seem thru hereditary
airy is our chromosome thru ozones
Is our minds and heads will become a
cone thru the ozones?
Foam on the water and in the sky
Will this become us as our cells
roam?
Will it be hell from cells or heaven,
send to be the end?
Should we begin again to win
Are we part of wishes from fishes,
fins?
Eyes someday I hope we realize the
reason truth
Where are we coming from these
roots?
What is the theme of scheme of
things, is it from a part of everything?
My instinction something should not
become extinction!

Ester T Malouf
SUMMER SHOWER
Leaf and branch sway to and fro
against my window pane,
Hurling rain-drops high and low,—
a cascade of diamonds in the rain—
scattering cheer on a gusty day.
Clouds above then fling down
their jewels and softly
float—away!.

Joanne Tsirigotis
BY THE SEA
Walking by the edge of the sea,
She becomes aware of the peaceful
calm.
The cool rippling waves wash up
onto the sand,
And the balmy ocean breeze whisks
through her hair.

As she looks out to where the deep
blue of the sea
merges with the azure sky,
All her problems are shed away
And a feeling of content washes over
her.

She hears the lonely cries of the sea
gulls above
As they glide through the air.
Bathed in sunlight, she feels the
warm rays of the sun
pleasantly hovering around her.

She cherishes her closeness with
nature;
For it provides solitude
With which to discover nature
And in nature to find herself.

Victor M Yanaitis
ESCAPE
A lake materializes before my eyes,
As a sailboat gently glides,
Urged on by the soft breezes
That fold the water in continuous
creases
And unfurling on the beach
Leaving tell-tale marks of its reach.
Soaring on the breeze's fingertips
The sea gull suddenly dips
Falling, plunging, slicing the water
A fish in its beak, wings a-flutter
It returns to the sky
And continues on its journey with its
prize.
Escape I sought
Through these lovely thoughts
'Twas found, to be sure
Thank God for nature's lure,
A relieved mind, an untroubled heart,
From this serenity I must depart.

Victor M Yanaitis
THE STORM
Remember the beauty of the break of
day;
When slowly could be seen the first
sun ray
Splash over the brim of the horizon,
And the sweet notes of a robin was
sung.

Out of the darkness, the things of
earth take shape:
The trees, hills, and the Creator's
beautiful landscape
Merged with the things of
humankind, the barns, houses, and
plow,
All saying, here comes the day,
awake now!

Then one day, the clouds gathered
from the East;
Lightning flashed, the thunder rolled,
and the wind screeched.
Trees bowed and broke, dwellings
shook and crumbled;
Dark was the day, destruction
widespread and unassembled.

Clouds began to scatter, the storm
departed the victor.
The sun shone on beauty no longer,
But years will drift by and time will
heal
The scars of this destruction with the
Creator's Seal.

Tracy A De Herrera
WINTER AIR

Created from my heart, for Paul Westurn, in response to his poem.

In the cold winter breeze, I sigh
As I gaze into the star filled sky
My eyes shut tight, as I feel in my
heart
Thoughts and feelings of you, that
have not part
To think of you and feel such care
Is to feel warmth in the winter air.

When I read your poem, each time
Like the rolling sea the rhymes
Overwhelm me to realize how much I
miss
The blazing love in your eyes before
we kiss
One day to celebrate love
Is simply not enough.

For you, I realize, in this foggy
winter air
Our celebration to reunite love shared
Is superlative of all seasons
This has given me reason
To rhyme in the sun, or winter air
And yes, your feelings are shared.

Gigi Garcia Kelly
ALCOHOL

This poem is dedicated to all the adult children of alcoholics.

Once upon a time I was very small
I knew nothing about fighting, drugs,
and especially alcohol

I am all grown up now and believe
me if I could
I'd change a lot about my childhood

No one will ever know the love I
have for my father & brother
But the one who had to go through it
all was my wonderful mother

My brother is trying very hard to
have a new life without the drugs
He surely deserves a thousand hugs

My father, his beer and liquor still
does he love
I'll never give up hope, I pray to our
heavenly father up above

In my life now there is a very special
child so small
I pray for her a life without fighting,
drugs, and especially alcohol . . . .

Elizabeth A Johnson
MALEFIC BLOND
Waiting on my raspberry veranda
for destiny to come
illuminated by spherical phosphoric
moon
my want for wrath rising
rejuvenating my body with
carnivorous power
detesting the crimson crowd
fantasy worlds pull me in
I am in ecstasy
Electroluminescent cities surround
me
Spontaneously I grab the creatures
inhabiting this lascivious world
Eliminator, psycho-killer,
Syncopating slaps
I'm a psychedelic sorceress
Viciously killing with brutal force
Self-destroying infant
Eternally vile

Wiley F Hance
NEXT TIME MY DEAR

For the greatly talented actor, JAIME SANCHEZ.

Germany, May 1945

Unkind you are, your entwining arms
to extend,
Tempting me with warm caresses,
Unloosing my spirit with enticing
beckons,
Knowing full well I cannot share the
delight you freely give.
Tormenting me, inclined you are
To wrench me from confinement.
I cannot move, cannot touch the love
intended.
The rays penetrate even the prison
that constrains me
To a dull routine.
Warm kisses of sun flecks
Vibrate on every inch of flesh
While weak-voiced birds orchestrate
mirth.
Here I stand, locked, bound, chained
to a task
And all I ask, you siren Spring, is that
I free myself
To drink your warmth,
Your caresses I need so much
To bear your presence.
Flirting, passing small remarks, you
temptress!
I can only gaze upon you from within
And pray, next time, to indulge you
from without.

Lucille N Garren
MORNING WALK
Early mornings, as I walk, nature
speaks to me.
Swaying leaves sing with the birds in
perfect harmony.
A mountain stream adds murmurings
that lifts the spirit high.
And fishes, darting to and fro, delight
the passerby.
Morning mist, still lingering, helps
cool the stirring breeze.
Summer sun's still hidden by the
thickly covered trees.
The cooing of the morning dove
helps me dispel all fear.
And helps me leave my worries in the
Great Creator's care.

Those who choose to walk this path
at setting of the sun
Will miss the beauty I behold at
breaking of the dawn.
No other place, no other time, can
offer me such peace.
I walk in tune with nature here and
find a sweet release.

Ardith Ohrt
TIME

I dedicate this poem to my mother who has always had time for me.

It's funny how time goes by,
The faster it goes, the more we
wonder why.
Today is here, yet yesterday's gone,
Tomorrow will come, but never stay
long.

Change is something we all become
part of,
Never a chance to stop its come on.
Now it's your turn to start anew,
Pleasure, adventure, wait ahead for
you.

Remember, my friend, you're a
precious gift,
For each day you spent here gave us
a lift.
We'll miss you dearly, your smiles
and laughs,
Good-Byes must come, but they
won't be our last.

Some good times, some bad, ones
happy and sad,
Are all part of the life you've built
with us.
Although your career is coming to an
end,
One thing you must know, we love
you, dear friend.

Kristi Walters
DRUGS
The subject of this poem is drugs
and cocaine,
please don't take them they'll mess
up your brain.

They cause people to die and it
happens every day,
go ahead and take them but in the
casket you will soon lay.

Just remember this when you go to
a party or on a date,
that drugs and alcohol will increase
your heart rate.

There's no way I can stop you so
go
on ahead,
but you are my friend and I don't
want you dead.

While you're taking them you say
you're having a ball,
but they will kill you, that's drugs
and alcohol.

Donald L Williams
FREEDOM
Listen to the sounds of freedom, little ones,
While walking through the woodlands;
Also glance up at the vast cloudless sky,
Thank God, as He blesses you with life.

Indeed, we have many opportunities,
To help our leaders bring about peace;
Yes, we must return our thanks to God,
Also praise Him for His many blessings.

It matters not the color of your skin,
Nor the country of your birth,
As God will continually watch over you faithfully;
Also, He will grant your prayers daily.

So, stand fast, those who long for freedom.
Yet strive each day that God gives you life,
To try and quell the threat of war;
Go forth and obtain your freedom.

Donna P Sanchez
THERE'S A PLACE UP ABOVE THAT'S FILLED WITH HEAVENLY LOVE
There's a place up above that's filled with heavenly love.
I was told that there were streets of gold and a sea of crystal that glistens.
But I know no one will listen.
They don't know what they are missing.
For this place is heaven and not hell.
Do you know how I can tell?
For there's a Heavenly Dove who is filled with love.

Deborah Mae Kinzle
WITH WORDS YOU FIND SOLACE
Writing is my solace, writing is my friend it brings to me a calmness that only comes within.
Life's lessons I have learned, how harsh and how cruel this world can truly be.
Here's one lesson that helps when you're on a low tide; go deep within the beauty of that but your inner soul, it gives the strength to guide you where you were truly meant to be, and continue down the path that's called life's domain; for with hope & faith, trust and love, is this not what the world is made of?
Without it I do foresee, no future that's worth living not for you, or me!
I listen to not what others say, or pay heed to what they whisper, for if it were meant to hear, and if it be true, you would not strain thine ears to hear, what you think is said about you.
Believe in you for what you are, be steadfast strong and true, and care not what others think, for to be happy with oneself, is to thine own heart & thine own self be true.
For remember this as you do; this world will carry on as well, and to thine own self be true!
Maybe these words of mine will reach someone, one day, and build back up their strength which was lost along the way, to just believe in yourself and for all that you wish for and believe in, one day will start to come true for you.

Deborah Mae Kinzle
WHO I AM
For many years I've pondered, over and over in my mind;
Just who I wanted to be?
A Lawyer? A Doctor? A Pilot? A Teacher? A Senator? A Vet?
Nothing ever seemed right for me!
Nothing ever fit.
Shy and quiet was I, more content it seemed when I found myself alone, and there I'd sit and find, a calm a quiet place in a world of my very own.
Creating in peace and tranquility, just who I was to be, in mind, in body, and in my soul, I'd search to find the real me.
And within me I found words that I could form into sentences,
which then would take form a poem, that dealt with love or life or fantasies, it was then I truly did know.
Who I was, what I am, and knew nothing else would do.
A writer with love and devotion, I find that with mere words
I can make them rhyme, in hopes of giving unto others a smile to light up their eyes.
With pride overflowing within me, as the pages of the book are opened, for my Dad & Mom, my daughter Sara Nicole, and for Jim, all lovingly to see, Their daughter, her Mommie, and his Lady, The writer, the poet, that is the real me.

Kristin A Wood
I AM THANKFUL I HAVE EYES

I dedicate my poem to my dear grandmother, Grace Wood.

I am thankful I have eyes.
I am not learning lies.
I am thankful I can share,
I am thankful I can care.
I can make new things so I am
Thankful birds have wings.
I am thankful I can see.
I love being me.

Florence J Dougiello
MEMOIRS OF A RETIREE
A government career is what I've had,
And looking back, it wasn't bad!

Transfers to cities upon my request,
More often than not, turned out for the best.

Long standing relations, of which I can boast,
Make my 30 year experience worthy to toast!

Anne Gould Hauberg
FOR TODAY
Grow up,
Yet act as a child.
Be free,
But control self.
Change man's horrid self with laughter.
God, give us strength amid disaster.

Winnie V Lee
DON'T WORRY
Don't worry, be happy,
Things are still in God's hands.
Only you and I know of things
We do not understand.

But wait and be patient,
Let God take command.
So don't worry, be happy,
He'll be heard throughout the land.

Bernadette Jones
THE MAN

To my family, who has always had faith in me. Love Bernnie.

When I see him my heart begins to race and my stomach begins to churn as though there are hundreds of butterflies inside.

He stands at a comfortable height of five foot eight, so that our eyes meet with just a slight tilt of the head.

His soft thick autumn colored hair flows down to his shoulder blades, with a slight curl at the ends. Shaped like oysters opened wide, sits two earthy brown eyes with long feathery lashes. As I gaze into them, I can see the emotions of his soul. A slim, fan like, mustache rests above lips which are full and soft as rose petals that glisten as though they have been kissed by the morning dew.

His body is like that of Michael Angelo's David with firm muscular arms and a broad back. As my hands move slowly down his carefully sculptured body, like a master who has created a glorious piece in marble, I can feel the power which he possesses.

Laying beside him I feel the rhythm of his breath and I am calmed by the warmth of his body. I realize as I awaken it's the warmth of the sun's rays that washes over me and I am alone.

Vincent J Romeo Jr
A TRIBUTE TO NANI
Oh withered flower, how you did bloom!
Spreading glorious sunshine amid the shadowed world.
Bountiful petals from your seed did swell,
Beauty re-incarnated.
Angel of prayer, sins forgiven,
Soul of white, heart porcelain pure.
Selfish heaven courts your regal presence,
Worshipping clouds blossom at your saintly feet.
Rest now, oh withered flower,
Embrace the rejuvenating powers of eternal peace.

Mary P Chavez
YESTERDAY'S DREAMS
Tangled up inside
Those dreams I've left behind
Trying to forget the past
Continuing with those who last
Counting down the days
To the second too . . . . .
Only to keep dreaming
About the days of me and you
Wondering if they're valid
Purely one sided I know
What's to become of it
If anything at all
Yet I continue to let my feelings fall
Please let these dreams subside
To those "yesterday's dreams" gone by

Toni M Fish
LOOKING OUT MY SNOW COVERED WINDOW

To all those who are still searching.

Looking out my snow covered window
wishing you'd come back.
Thinking of days gone by
and wondering why?
Looking out my snow covered window
I see visions of you
and things we've been through
wondering what to do.
Looking out my snow covered window
remembering all the happiness
and the quiet hours we spent.
It's time to confess.
Looking out my snow covered window
seeing our love float by
the pain I felt, I never showed
how much I really cared.
The happiness that I once knew
will never come again.
Looking out my snow covered window . . . .

Ann Martin
THE LEAVES AND ME

I would like to dedicate this poem to my one and only child, Bob, who thought the leaves were beautiful.

The air is crisp and silent, except for the gentle breeze.
With rake in hand I go about trying to rake up all the leaves.

Leaves, leaves, beautiful, mysterious leaves!

I reach out saying, "Where are you going, little leaf?
Come on back here, I'm really not a thief!"
Then they dance away as if to say,
"I'm free to dance, I'm free."

Leaves, leaves, independent leaves!

Where will you go, what will you do,
your travels not too far . . . . .
Let me rake you up and you can stay right where you are.
I finally gather them in a little rounded heap,
Then one of them, suddenly, will take another leap.

Leaves, leaves, stubborn, stubborn leaves!

"Come back little leaf, come back here," I say.
To keep them all together, seems like forever and a day.
The snow will come and cover them and keep them quietly . . .
Then in the Spring, they'll be here for all the World to see.
Leaves, leaves, Oh those brown, wet, ugly leaves!

Tami Lynn Briddon
LONELINESS
I stand here silently at my window
gaping into the shadows of the night.
Depression has taken over my soul,
and my body is filled with fright.
My smile has been completely drained,

and my heart is in great pain.
All my friends have slipped away,
as I am left with lonely days.
My heart is endlessly breaking,
and my sweet memories are slowly fading.
My soul is screaming silent cries,
now before me loneliness lies.
I turn my eyes away,
but the pain I feel will stay.
I whisper one simple wish
"Please end all my loneliness."

Phil Bengston
THE TRUE BEAUTY OF A ROSE
"The true beauty of a rose,
is an intangible essence
that holds forever—
a fragrance of the mind."

Barbara Jaeger
FOR MY ONLY LOVE
Bonded together like paper,
glued, weathered and seasoned
with time, the vows of oneness
though severed, remain indelibly . . .
FOR, I still feel the tug of my heartstrings

The strength of memories abide for
years after. Frequent recollection
instills hope and brings laughter.
Old friends and family . . .
MY, I still feel the tug of my heartstrings

Time has healed the incomparable
pain and somehow I've learned to
live, perhaps even love again.
But now, conditionally . . .
ONLY, I still feel the tug of my heartstrings

This love is never ending I know,
for I've taken a part of your life
with me and let my heart go with you.
So justifiably . . .
LOVE, I still feel the tug of my heartstrings

Barbara Jaeger
PATHOS
I must paint from my
Own world . . . for I know not
The colors in another's
Nor the depth of caring.

Long sweeping lines of calm
Amid the racy streaks of chaos
Are mine alone to determine as
I brush the canvas of life—

Unmindfully imparting the
Strength of my character
And the weakness
Of my human soul.

Stacie Welch
I'M JUST A CHILD
You touch me in places that make me sick inside,
I guess in public my face I'll hide.

Please don't make me touch you there,
These feelings of guilt I cannot bear.

You think it's fun to tickle and play,
I just wish you would go away.

Deep in my memory this pain I've filed,
How did this happen I'm just a child.

Kim B Kuehner
DO YOU EVER WONDER

Dedicated to my lovely wife Donna and to all those who have ever wondered.

Do you ever wonder,
what your life would be like
to have taken the other road.
Do you ever wonder,
while lying awake at night
if you have chosen the right way.
Do you ever wonder,
while sitting alone
that things could be better.
Do you ever wonder,
if maybe, someday you might
be content, and think things are o.k.
Do you ever wonder?

Mary Pat Knightly DeLisi
MISCARRIAGE
Shock
Sudden violence
No breath
No beat
within
me
I am numb
Struck
by a clap
from
death
Only
the earth
moves
As I lie
quietly
in a wake.

Jennifer Loftin
A ROSE
A rose is beautiful
in every way.
It's gentle and kind
like a line in a play
A rose has a sweet smell
like you would buy in a store
You would wear it everywhere
then go get some more
A rose is a special thing
It brings you great love
It reminds me of God
And when Noah sent the dove.

Janice E Smoker
ALL AND NOTHING AT ALL
He grew up knowing what he wanted in life
And he knew how to play the game
Above all and most important to him
Were money, power, and fame

With all the skill of the material world
He climbed the corporate ladder
He stepped on his friends along the way
But that didn't seem to matter

Oh yes there were many who asked for his help
And sometimes he'd donate to the cause
But only if it meant recognition for him
And a generous round of applause

He hadn't counted on cancer to strike
And rob him of all he had gained
But the emptiness he felt inside
Was far worse than the physical pain

He reached out a tired, ailing hand
In search of someone in whom to confide
But the desperate hand remained untouched
And he closed his eyes and died

Krista Shipton (Age 14)
BABYSITTERS
Most people think we are really crazy,
But actually we are quite amazing.
We love our jobs and all the tots,
And play fun games like connect the dots.
Snacks, bottle feedings, and a couple of diaper changings,
The house to keep them from re-arranging.
A full fun day of Hide n' Seek,
And then it's time to go to sleep.
We read them books and dry their tears,
Mommy and daddy will be home soon, they hear.
We rock them to sleep and hum them a tune,
As we look out the window at the beautiful moon.
It's 9:00 o'clock on a Saturday night,
And as far as I can tell everything is all right.
The kids asleep, favorite toy in hand,
So far the night has gone just grand.
The parents are home and the job is well done,
Thank goodness it's over even though it was fun.
I'll see them again next Saturday night,
And hope that once more it will all turn out right.

Johnnea Lee Holland
LINGERS
Dig a little deeper
Way down in your soul
Where darken thoughts linger
Taking control

Dig past the hurt
Put anger aside
Those thoughts may still linger
Let time pass them by

Digging still further
You'll see as did I
A little girl lingers
A tear and a sigh

DonnaMarie Palange
SEASONS OF MYSELF

*Especially written from a feeling within . . . for my first love, Lawrence Carvano—Dee**

*Seasons of myself and my mind
*Travel thru this book
*With an open mind . . .
*If you can see light and
*Feel cool breezes,
*We must be in the same time.
*Sad storms and Blood's River
*Self-destruct, It's only part of the
*world's construction.
*You're real! You're Alive!
*With eyes as beautiful as the sea . . .
*Together it will always be . . .
**You and me . . . .

DonnaMarie Palange
YOU

Especially written from a feeling within . . . for my first love, Lawrence Carvano.

You were the first love that meant anything/everything to me,
I still chase reality away to save those memories of you.

You carved your emotions in my heart so now a fatal attraction cannot compare to the depth you have touched.

You brought chills up and down my spine only to bring the color of rainbows smiling bright through your eyes.

You made me laugh until you then suddenly burst those stormy clouds down inside my life,

You made them, you created them to make me cry down, flow down love's mountainside.

You created my lovestorm, you never told me why—Why did you?

You made me walk a cold and freezing nite.

You turned my body temperature to a stinging frostbite.

You brought me to my knees in a snowstorm screaming your name!

You failed to tell me why?

You got a right to know you put a dismal roadblock in my mind & my body still aches for you . . .

You and your smile they still shine thru the sun's rays, at a glance, I dance like a magnet that cannot turn from this magical light.

You will still turn me towards a reflection in search for your image, but now I see a face looking back only empty, could it be me, is this right?

You lied when you said you'd never leave, it's been years.

You see I can't erase or never wanted to dissolve those beautiful feelings within.

You can't begin to dream how it's been.

You make me wake, breathe you like nothing else matters.

You stole from me what I cannot replace and so life goes on until I die.

One day will you please tell me why?

Shelly R Vigars
THE STARRY SKY
There he was and here I am
Underneath that starry sky.
He said it wouldn't work,
And I said I understood.
And then we parted into
our own separate worlds.
I know we'll meet again
someday, underneath that
starry sky,
But will we be with each
other or another?

Jon Larkins
RIVER OF LIFE
An old man going down a lone highway,
came to a river deep and wide,
thru which was flowing a sullen tide.

The old man crossed in twilight dim,
the sullen stream had no fear of him.
He turned when safe on the other side,

and built a bridge to span the tide.

Good friend, called a fellow pilgrim near,
You're wasting your time with building here.
You've crossed the river, both deep and wide;
why build you this bridge at even' tide?

Good friend, in the path I have come today,
there follows after me a youth whose feet must pass this way.
He too must cross in twilight dim,
good friend, I'm building this bridge for him.

Kristi A Howson
THE BUTTERFLY BALLET
What beautiful Butterflies, fluttering through the air.
Oh me, Oh my, I wish I could be there.

Up, Up, Up they rise, they begin their happiest day.
All of these beautiful babes, as they all come out to play.

Arrayed in brilliant colors, as they try to touch the sky.
I often wonder how, they ever learned to fly so high.

Orange, yellow, pink & purple are the colors that they wear.
Up, down, here, there, I believe they're everywhere.

What a sight it is to see their flight on this Windy Day.
Flying, Floating, Fluttering—these babes in their magnificent Ballet.

Bright and Beautiful their movement, like poetry in motion.
Never will there be, such wonderful emotion.

As the curtain begins to close, their little wings open to fly away.

Shimmering, Shining, Sparkling—the wind softly takes them, come what may.

The rapture of Reflections, Always & Forever they will say.
What a Feelin', they made it happen, in their most Beautiful Butterfly Ballet.

Stanley Jordan
WHY MUST IT ALWAYS BE
Must it always be a dream
Why must so many sleep
Through the bells of freedom rings
The ways of slavery—so many keep.

Why must anyone walk behind
On the path made for all
Will one always live in that time
Never as equal—on the opposite wall.

When will I awaken
Will all of this have changed
Must a race always be forsaken
Will these ways of hatred remain.

H Craig Gorton
OH NO!
I scurried around.
The deadline was here.
A poem couldn't be found.
The thought filled me with fear!

It seemed such a shame
To waste this contest
While folks signed their names
To their sweetest and best.

All of my poems
Were far far too long,
Because each one of them
Had once been a song.

So I made the decision
That a few minutes spent
On this poem—no revision
Beat none being sent!

Alice T Smith
THANKSGIVING
Thanksgiving, what does it really mean to us?
Is it just for cooking and making a fuss
Or remembering what it should really be,
A time to be thankful—you and me,
For the great things with which the lord
Has blessed us. Therefore, we shall be able to ford
The chasms of race, drugs and greed
And share all we have with those in need.
So, happy thanksgiving to every one of you
And may the Lord bless all of us, too.

Kati Sorelly Ong
MY RAINBOW
On a bright sunny day
In somebody's lawn,
I saw a rainbow
When the sprinkler was on.

Small tiny rainbow
So colorful, so fine;
The lawn was somebody's
But the rainbow was mine.

Carrie B Jellison
THE LIFE MOTHER LIVES
She is the sunshine in the house, what would home be without her?
She scatters cheer wherever she may go, her children never doubt her.
She seeks our good without delay, her patience knows no measure,
She answers gladly every call, never thinking of her own pleasure.
She's helpful and kind and meets our every need,
She lives her life for others, in thought, word and deed.
What heritage precious! The life Mother lives,
The prayers she prays and the lessons she may give,
She gives her best for her love is so great,
To teach her children to love and not hate.
She guides the household, when without her it would surely falter.
I know this to be true, for you see, I am a wife and mother.

Rosetta E Bowles
MY LOVE
If I could tell you why,
And how I love you
Here's what I would say,
Your sweetness is like a ray of sunshine,
On a dark and dreary day

Your goodness is like a flower,
slowly unfolding in the sun
touching each and every one,

Your touch is ever so gentle,
like the petals of a rose
Your heart ever so pure,
like the new fallen snow

You make the day begin,
you make the night a dream
at least for me, that is
I hope to always call you friend

Herman S Kruzel Jr
TWO ARE ONE
Two are one
Ten million say no
Two are dumb
Nowhere to go

Two can't be
What they desire
All agree
It is fire

Two go on
Ten million stay
They are distant
From two who pray

Anthony W Gussler III
UNINTENTIONAL SUICIDE

To All Mankind: Ponder your consequences.

Ceiling of the Amazon
Where birds and monkeys roam;
Waterways and jungle floors
To many species is home.

Cutting down trees,
Scarring the face of land.
Human life is made easier;
While we give ourselves a hand!

Throwing a switch,
Hearing an evil boom.
Actually, it's the animals
Who need the elbow room.

Burning a rain forest,
Pushing nature aside;
The human race commits
Unintentional suicide.

Glenda R Dean
ONE NIGHT

This poem is dedicated to my husband Paul, my sons Paul Jr. and Timothy. Also dedicated to other loved ones.

I went to church one night to pray.
And now I find myself here to stay.
It wasn't the prayer that made me stay,
but the sweet spirits I found surrounding the place.
This radiant light came all over the church,
then I knew nothing was natural about it at all.
Before long I was caught up in this radiant light,
till I began to realize I was filled with joy.
I can never walk away from the church today.
For truly church is the place for me to stay.
I got so much joy that night at church and now I find myself there doing the day.
I will never forget that night at church.
For it was the first time my life was so full of joy.
And all because of that radiant light.
One thing I can honestly say, I thank God for that night I went to church to pray.

Helen P Andres
REV. GARY MAIER = US
G raced by Godly wisdom
A vows a saintly prayer
R everend an earthly title
Y our special talent to share.

M ary, blessed mother,
A n answer to our strife
I n earnest we all seek to be
E nlightened by Christ.
R ejoice! Our prayer is answered,

U nited as one we stand.
S anctified in Mary—
By God's loving hand

Albert E Robinson
THE REAL THING
America: "land of the free," nestled 'neath the silhouette of liberty.
America: "home of the brave," whose torch shed no light for the African slave.
America: "of thee I sing." Listen! Hear the bells of freedom ring!
America: "my country 'tis of thee," to the world masquerading as democracy!
America: "under God one nation," printed are the words of her declaration!
America: "lady justice's scales," tipped in unbalance, her eyes tightly veiled!
America: "oh beautiful for spacious skies," extends her arms to oppressed lives.
America: "amber waves of grain," yet hunger prowls her – land her shame!
America: "God shed His grace on thee," indivisible land of equality.
America: "in God we trust," from sea to shinig sea.
America: "promises of visible dreams," unless the dreamer is "black," like me!

Lori Beth Goldblatt
QUESTIONS AND ANSWERS??
Soldier, copper do you know
Why you need that power so?
Guns and weapons force and then
Overrun the world again

Is it fear of being alone?
Strength in numbers makes you bold
Come and get me shoot me down
Someday we'll give you a crown

I've seen people you say are crazed
The insanity in you leaves me amazed
How sick have we really become
That I should fear my brother's gun?

We pay you to save our souls
Yet we've got such different goals
Criminals roam the world below
And not much chance of ending the woe

You chose me for I am weak
Must you always pick on the meek?
You all doubt your self-esteem
Nothing is ever as it seems . . . .

Dennis Arbaugh
SEASONS OF LOVE

To my wife of twenty-six years who shares my love through all our seasons together.

When you were mine in springtime
there wasn't much to do,

But smell the pretty flowers, and dream of "me and you."
The earth beheld the beauty of our new budding love.
We walked in cool, green meadows and watched the clouds above.

When you were mine in summer, there was so much to do.
We missed our pretty flowers, our lives were pulled in two.
We had no time for living the Dreams of you and me.
We had no time for loving, we had no time to see.

Then you were mine in autumn, and we fell in love again.
Life is so much sweeter than it has ever been.
Our dreams have turned to memories, our hair is touched with grey,
But we still stay "I love you," and mean it every day.

If you'll be mine in winter, although I fear to go,
I'll be along beside you, for I still love you so.
When God's soft, snowy blanket wraps all the weary land,
I'll be yours in winter, if you will take my hand.

Sheree' Fletcher

PRESENT TIME PASSING

There is a corner in every curve I travel
Only a wall,
no door to walk through.
A window to see the world,
but never feel the reality of life.
A road that is too broken apart,
to ever be roamed upon.
Clouds that spread darkness,
I've never seen a rainbow.
And then everything passes;
except my reality remains . . .
my dream.
The present will always pass,
and the future will always remain ahead.
All your dreams will become real,
when shared with reality.
You may never ask someone to understand you,
but yet they will try.
You may never ask anyone to care,
but there is always someone who does.
You may not want to feel anything anymore,
because everything you felt hurt.
Never take the journey that men take
to find themselves.
Life is too special to turn your back on.

"God made something they didn't want, me, now I'm going back to my maker."

Naomi W Rieger

ENVY

I have a friend whose vacuum cleaner
Is always clean on the top
Her shiny fly swatter hangs on the wall
Without a single fly-flop
Her floors are immaculate, never a toy,
No Kitty litter . . . Oh, what a joy,
No finger marks on her windows or chairs
No tiny fingers to put them there.
No crying or yelling
No sibling fights
No grass on her bedspreads
No kisses goodnight
No tiny bodies to hold when she's blue.
No little voices to say, "I love you,"
My God, how I envy her beautiful floor
While she seems to envy
My muddy back door.

Jason Tash

ABUSED CHILDREN

Black and blue sits the kids that are abused
The parents that do this are to be accused
The children take it because they are scared
To think that this really happens, my heart is despaired.
These kids are alone for they have no choice,
Because in America, our kids have no voice.
The parents are sick and harmed by a disease,
But it won't stop, even if we say please.

Sore and scared are our children of today
They even are beaten if they are good and obey,
I want this country to be full of love
And for people to know that we come from above.

Loreley

SEASONS

Dedicated and written for Peter. Believe in the change of seasons.

Time will be needed to heal the hurt that you feel,
Like the Autumn tree shedding its leaves.
One by one they will fall to the ground, memories
and emotions to be swept away by the wind,
Until there are no more.
The Winter snow will cover you in its white embrace,
a time for peace to enter your heart and settle your soul.
And then your Spring will come.
A time to be reborn in a new love.
The Summer sun will strengthen and warm those new
feelings, opening your heart, your leaves, to a new season,
And this time Summer will stay

Loreley

CANDLELIGHT

I am the candle that glows in your darkness
Let me be your light
I have given my heart to you
Vulnerable in the shadow that you cast
Do not stir, for you will cause a breeze
The dim light that I flicker
Will be blown out
And all that will be left of my presence
Is the scent of my short existence

Loreley

IDEAL LOVE

Hold me like you would a butterfly, with cupped hands so as not to damage my wings of flight. I need that freedom but I will never fly too far away.

See me as you would a painting, with an open mind and imagination, never altering the picture that is before you but accepting it for what it is.

Love me as you would a child, watching her grow and become a separate entity, knowing that she may be her own person but also a part of your life.

But most importantly, be my friend. Through friendship we will never grow apart. We will always respect each other individually as well as a union. Be my friend, love, and together we can conquer all.

Hazel S Crenshaw

YHWH—LORD

Dear Lord as I sit under your banyan tree,
Let me draw near and talk to Thee.
Young children are dying and will soon be dead,
For so many days they have not been fed.
Many people are homeless—there's nowhere to go,
All they know is grief and woe.
Many are ill and can't seek care,
They have no insurance.
It doesn't seem fair!
Yet there's plenty of help in your world out there,
There are many people who love and care.
Many have opened their heart–gates wide,
That those in need may come inside,
And feel your love in "sisters and brothers"
Reaching out to share with others.
Lord, thank you for letting me sit under your tree,
And come close and talk to Thee.

Terri R Lukonen

A PROMISE OF LOVE

This poem is dedicated to my loving husband, Douglas.

I promise you my love for today and tomorrow.
I thank the Lord above for your heart to borrow.
I give you myself and my heart full of cheer and love.
I promise not to change you, but to accept the changes you receive from our friend above.
My Best Friend, My Lover, My Husband;
I promise you my love
For Today, Tomorrow
And Forever . . . .

Melissa J Richmond

DETERMINATION IS THE KEY TO SUCCESS

Determination is the key to success,
Your skin color doesn't matter,
It don't matter if you're wearing a dress.
You've got to go for it if you want it,
Reach for the stars,
Get a move on, get started,
Tear down the bars.
Fight for your freedom,
Don't stop at the word no,
Get up and get going,
Don't worry about stop,
Just GO!
Your goal is the top,
Don't stop climbin',
Keep up all the bells
And don't stop chimin'!

Dave Cormier

THE PAPER ROSE

Each day I live, each day I die,
I really should not question why.
But there are days, I must confess,
That really put me to the test.

For those are days I must beware,
When sorrow creeps into the air.
My soul cries out each breath I take,
And life itself I would forsake.

Each day I die, each day I live,
And now some thought to this I'll give.
For there are days filled with delight,
That make the world seem quite alright.

When the songs of birds fill the air,
And wash away my heart's despair.
Although I try to make them last,
Those days fleet off into the past.

Each day I ponder on my life,
It may be good or filled with strife.
But either way I'm here to stay,
Just to see another day.

Consider life a paper rose,
It is not meant to please the nose.
But if I try to make it right,
It will always please my sight.

David Cormier

ANOTHER CRIMSON SUNSET

A tree of lightning flashes bright,
Across the sunset's dying light.
The colors; red, crimson and gold.
All blend together in the mold.

Another day has passed away,
Another sunset's grand display.
Another heart, another soul,
Another time to lose control.

To share the beauty of this sight,
With someone close would bring delight.
To sit and watch it pass alone,
Can turn a searching heart to stone.

A streaming sunbeam reaches down,
Explodes in gold upon the ground.
And with a fleeting breeze it's gone;
A kiss goodnight until the dawn.

The distant rolling of the thunder,
Tells me of the storm I'm under.
A warning of the solitude,
That this starless night includes.

The colors fade and drift away,
The twilite dons its shades of grey.
Although alone, I'll carry on,
With yet another sunset gone.

Dave Cormier

A STORMY VISAGE

Last dusk I saw a rainbow,
In the midst of an eastern storm.
A sight that more should see.

The lightning flashed,
And the thunder roared,
But the rainbow stood its ground.
With its colors bright,
Against the coming night,
It did not make a sound.

As it vanished from the sky,
It could not help but wonder why,

I had ventured out at all.
But as I pondered through the night,
Remembering the spectral sight,
I heard its beckon call.

Life you see, is much the same,
Harsh sometimes or maybe tame,
We know not what we'll find.
Storms of troubles we all face,
As we wander through this place,
Seeking peace of mind.

But each storm contains an eye,
Where we see the clear blue sky,
And rest beneath its shroud.
There the rainbow casts its light,
With its colors shining bright,
We are indeed endowed.

Alas! Alas! It does not last,
And sometimes moves away
toofast,
And comes to a quick end.
But as I grow,
I'll always know,
The rainbow will return again.

Jean Sharp
DREAM OF A NUCLEAR WAR

This poem is dedicated to my family, who continue to believe in me.

A nuclear war is a real threat.
It's still something unsolved as yet.
In fear, it makes the blood run cold
In hearts of men both young and old.

A terror sweeps across the land;
Paralleled to waves across the sand.
It spreads a gloom and horrors arise
As smoke-filled billows blaze the
skies.

All's quiet now, no one does speak.
The people are gone, too sick or
weak.
And was it worth it, we want to
know;
As the cinders settle and the ashes
glow.

Awake now, it was all a dream.
I listen for a frightened scream.
I only hear my heartbeat low,
Where is the terror? Why did it go?

I look up in a starlit sky
And pray no one will this way die.
Oh Lord, protect us and keep us free
So this kind of war may never be.

J Naftulin
HIGH QUE
As the surf swirls
beneath,
the cliffs hang hungrily;
hoping—
to gain a glimpse of
the wind.

Ardell and Raymond M Ries

Raymond M Ries
WE, US, & CO. HEART BROKEN

These poems are dedicated to my sweetheart, Ardell J Brus, who I married on May 1, 1945 in St. Bernard's Catholic Church at Alta Vista, Iowa. We were married by my uncle, Rev. Henry P. Nosbisch. We are married 45 years. We have six children, of whom one is deceased, and ten grandchildren.

Love made on short notice,
Tulip salve given away free of
charge.
Words of love extracted without pain
While you wait.
Our kisses and hugs are refreshing
and embracing,
Satisfaction granted for we are
strictly up to date.
Will you give us a call?
Your kissin' and huggin' Co. State
Agents
Next door to Matrimony, City of
Happiness,
State of Contentment.
Office hours from one until won.

Raymond M Ries
TO MY SWEETHEART
I know a pretty little darling who's
sweet as sugar, pretty as a rose.
She is my sweetheart dear, and I hope
I never see her shed a tear.
She has pretty blonde hair and eyes
of blue. Oh, Honey, how I love you.
Her name is Ardell. I love her, and
she loves me. But she doesn't want to
tell.
Her hugs are so embracing and her
kisses so sweet that it's always a
treat.
They say crackers are dry without
cheese. So are hugs without a
squeeze.
Sweethearts never get by without a
tease. So we'll do as we please.
Sweet are my dreams, sweet are my
thoughts. True is my love,
For I am thinking of someone in the
world whom I really love.

Beth Napolitano
A SUNSET
A sunset stands so still and bright
With lots of color and fascination and
wonder
It makes an evening start out right
A sunset is powerful and stands out,
like thunder

The colors unite to create a unique
scene
No sunsets ever being exactly the
same
The effect it has is truly serene
To miss out on seeing one would be a
shame

With shades of pink, orange, red
yellow and blue
Spreading their rays of light across
the skies
The sight is enough to dazzle you
And create a very pleasant surprise

A sunset glows in colors of many
hues
It casts its rays on water and on land
In looking at a sunset, you never can
lose
As it hovers in areas in a way that is
grand

A sunset makes the earth stand out so
proud
It foretells of the weather of the
ongoing day
It sends out the message loud and
clear
That a sunset is a mysterious surprise
in every way

Johnny Rogers Jr
THE JOURNEY
The days grow long and the weeks
grow longer,
The soul grows farther and farther
from hunger,
But knowledge continues to grow
even longer;
Before one can match it—he is in
slumber.
I am hungry today for all that I can
grasp;
But give me more days and even
more weeks,
For my pains are leaving my physical
being
And I am growing tired and sleepy.
I am slowly drifting There—with
peace of mind.
My books are getting dusty—my
eyes are tired,
And my days are growing lesser and
lesser;
My bed and pillow are growing
fresher and fresher!
I have come upon the twenty-fourth
hour of yesterday
And I am traveling faster and faster!
The words are beginning to fade
away,
And I am becoming deep in slumber.
Now! At last! There are no words
remaining,
And the clock on the wall has ceased
me!
And my chariot is in the ceasing!
And, at last! I am There! I am There!

Johnny Rogers Jr

Johnny Rogers Jr
A GOLDEN MOMENT

These poems are dedicated to all my family and friends who taught me how to live and love, and to all my colleagues who believed in me, especially Rosie Jackson.

Sunsetting and just forgetting—
Let your soul grow old,
Let your feelings retire;
Admire your enemies.
Let the cold grow warm,
And freeze the heat.
Let friends depart,
And let strangers meet.
The stars are dim now,
And you don't ask how.
All is silent for this moment,
For this moment is golden.

Johnny Rogers Jr
MANY FACES
There are many faces in this old
world,
And I'd like to see them all!
Some have long hair, short, straight,
and curled;
Some have red, black, brown,
blonde—some not at all!
And there are some faces that are sad,
Some that are happy—some
in-between,
Some that are good and some that are
bad,
Some that are dumb and some that
are keen.
But if all could display just one big
smile,
It would be worth all mankind,
For a smile is so worthwhile.
And for many, a smile can find
A reason for life and living,
And to be living is to smile.

Johnny Rogers Jr
I'VE NO FARE
I cannot seem to justify
Why I'm here today;
Last night I heard a voice
That seemed to say:
"Where are you going, mister,
And have you a ticket?"
You cannot get there,
Unless you've paid the price!
And you don't seem the type,
Because you are lost!
Get off my train for now,
Until you've a fare.
You can start at the bottom
That's where the price starts!

Johnny Rogers Jr
THE END OF DAY
The wind was gently twirling;
The sky was slightly tinged
With clouds quietly whirling . . .
And the sunset through them singed . . .

On a beautiful June evening of dusk—
On the soft and breezy shore
Of scattered seashells and mollusks—
And of crickets chirping and early bird's snore.

The few green trees dispersed far away—
The image of sailboats on the horizon . . .
And the waves' full tumble and sway
Beneath the hiding of a weary sun.

The sound of retiring little birds,
Serenading their young to slumber—
The pelican, all alone-dipping for thirds
With knowledge of hunger—none of number.

The full moon so brightly shining
And glazing its beam across the waves—
The horizon now slowly declining
And the lazy night setting in.

Johnny Rogers Jr
THE SOLE-SURVIVING SON
The sole-surviving son
Does not have to fight in Viet Nam.
The sole-surviving son
May, or may not, give a damn.
I love my country for that which she stands,
But, what about my three younger brothers?
I've already lent my helping hand,
But what about my brother, and his, and his?
For if they are the brothers I know them to be,
They'll lend a helping hand—just as me,
For I'm the oldest of the four.
In time of need—they won't run out the door.
But, if the time comes for them to go,
Please, Dear God, be with them.
Although I did not die—I do not want to be
The sole-surviving son—who served his country.

Johnny Rogers Jr
FOREVER ON MY MIND
When you leave, Bun, don't leave anything behind.
You are the only one—forever on my mind.
I'm gonna miss you girl, 'n' I think you'll find,
You are my only world—it's just the wrong time.
I don't know what to do everyday without you.
I guess I'll just try to say good–bye.
You are the only one—forever on my mind.
I'm going to miss you, girl, just try to be kind
As you always are, I'm gonna miss you, girl.
Please don't go too far away
As I sit here, today, and I say,
You are the only one—forever on my mind.

Johnny Rogers Jr
I HAVE LIVED
Although I was born
A poor man,
And although I died
A poor man,
I have lived
A very rich life.

Johnny Rogers Jr
CRUDE SOLITUDE
Yes, I like my crude solitude,
'n' I don't mean to be antisocial and rude,
But I like my crude solitude.
Yes, it gives me some peace of mind,
When quiet times are hard to find;
Yes, when quiet times are hard to find.
The world is so full of hustle and bustle everywhere,
And so very little love—here and there.
That's why I like my crude solitude;
Yes, it gives me some peace of mind
When quiet times are hard to find,
I go off alone to be on my own.
That's why I like my crude solitude,
'n' I don't mean to be antisocial and rude.
Yes, I like my crude solitude,
Crude solitude—crude solitude.

Johnny Rogers Jr
GROWING UP
She was such a pretty lass
With eyes that shone like glass;
Her hair like that of April grass,
So green was the knowledge beneath it,
For she had not many years.
Life was full of joy and cheers
Like that of an innocent child,
Her manner so soft and mild,
Her poise so free and graceful.
Her dress fluffy and laceful,
But her future that of a woman.
Now she has knowledge of life.
She will become some man's wife,
Her heart so tender and giving,
The joy in life is living.
For her years are growing now,
And she seems to wonder how
It all happened so fast,
But she's a woman now—at last.

Johnny Rogers Jr
BUREAUCRACY DEMOCRACY
They call it justice—they call it democracy;
It's only a justification of the bureaucracy,
For the processes fall short of due.
Will it finally end in hue and cry, for me, for you,
Or will it continue to subdue me, or you?
Common law supplies the laws we need,
But only if true democracy succeeds.
Bureaucracy takes away from the people, you and me,
And, hence, away from democracy.

Johnny Rogers Jr
BEACH
like a broken record
my pulse beats
thoughts of every interval
and why some notes disappear
sandcrabs tugging on pretzels
afraid and selfish
sitting on plastic chairs
and just wondering
the next wave will
wash everything out to sea
an interval of time
where there is
no pulse
no thoughts
no notes
and no more waves

Johnny Rogers Jr
I NEVER MET ANYONE QUITE LIKE YOU
I never met anyone quite like you.
You make my day when I'm down and blue.
Won't you please stay here with me tonight?
Just stay by my side—it'll be so right.
We can light a fire on this cold night;
You're my desire 'til the dawn is light.
I never met anyone quite like you;
You make me feel alive when there's just we two.
And I never met anyone quite like you;
You give me hope and faith to get through.
And I never met anyone quite like you;
You make life worthwhile with your easy smile.
And I never met anyone quite like you;
You can make all of my dreams come true.
No, I never met anyone quite like you;
I'll be forever indebted to you.

Curtis E Waddell

Curtis E Waddell
MYSTIC PLACES AND UNICORNS
Dream positive—
to new ways of we can love,
and the happy what we can share.
Mystic places and unicorns
are for Dreamers and Believers.
I've tasted and danced across so many dreams
as we chased Time across a forever—
but now I've found you.
Let's leave fantasy and the unicorn
to those who have never been to Love
and tasted the happy in her sharing.
Sure, we'll vacation there again
and in the as often of our night-loving,
but let's win the reality of here first.
Share my dream of the unicorn now
prancing and dancing across mystical wherevers.
But share my life, and my love, too.
I want you!—need you!
Don't let me be alone again tonight.
We might see the unicorn again.

Simona Trotta
A FRIEND, A FRIENDSHIP

For all of you who share the everlasting memories of friendship.

A friend is someone to talk to, cry to, laugh with.
Someone who is so special that you would sacrifice something so dear for each other.
A friendship is based on ideas and emotions
And a friend is there with trust and respect
To help build those ideas and help express those emotions.
The love and understanding that is shared between friends is so strong
That it builds an everlasting friendship.
Though some friendships fade, they will never be forgotten,
For it is due to the lasting memories
Created through childhood and adolescence,
And growing older should not jeopardize these friendships.
It builds a sense of security that gives those the ability to only strengthen
When things are both bad and good.
A friend is so special
That it is because of them,
We are able to grow.

Shirley Allen
LOST TIME

To my darling mother and father, with love.

Sweet is the sigh of a baby,
Peace is the cry of the moon,
Sad is the song of the willow,
Deep is the cry of the loon;

Good–bye is the moan of the flower,
Whose petals are wilted by fall;
Love is the way of the children,
Sweet is the life shared by all

Time has a swift way of passing,
All of God's creatures must die,
Sing and live time to its fullest
Or life, sweet life, will pass you by.

Darla Kay Gawthrop
THE WALK

To the Loves in my life, and the love of Life.

Come take my hand and we will go out for a walk
through Autumn's glow,
where leaves go crunch beneath our feet and cold crisp
breezes touch our cheeks, a walking we will go.
The clear blue skies and falling leaves,
with birds in flight through naked trees, come take my hand and walk with me.
Out through a field, over a stream, viewing colors
of a rainbow's dream.
Into a woods with
Autumn's floor,
Come walk with me to
Winter's door.

Barbara J Lynch
GROWING UP BLACK MY WAY

A significant event in my life was
when I realized the recognition
of my own coloredness
Combined with the double
implications of this fact

This came as a mild awareness to me
But the most important thing is from
that day on you should have
tried to understand my self
influences, my thoughts and the
emotions
that I've felt and am now feeling

I'm seeing the world through
different eyes, and from a different
perspective
With much less innocence than
before I realized what made me be
me.

Saying this through my eyes, a black
child's eyes
Hoping that one day the white man
will open his—

We are all living in the ghetto
But some of us are looking at the
stars—

Barbara Carbone
IMAGES OF DREW

To Drew, my mirrored image.

(IMAGES)
I say seaglass china blue
Only a bottled illusion
Slips in the image of my dream
The reflection of the pond
Drawn in his eyes
(EXTERIOR)
Fenced indigo blue eyes
Tracing his jawline
Mocca creamed skin
Complemented chestnut curled
hair
(DREAM)
Sacred divine journey through
Fields of goldenrod and
wild violets
Mosaic piece of art; long stemmed
daisies
Colors of maize, of sultry, of
citron
Elaborate intricate design
(REALITY)
Frameboxed illusion
Part of my soul resides beneath the
equator
The day we met under the saffron
stars
Pieces of broken glass scattered
In his reflection
Sold for a million
I said seaglass china blue

Tanya Ditchfield
SOCIETY DISSECTING ME

It snuck around the corner; the corner
in my mind.
It grasped a life long vessel until my
thoughts unwind.

From my ears my mind does hang;
The tubes of terror from which I
sang.
They seemed a mile long and seemed
to sing a song.
It had to do with life.
But before they could be heard, he
cut them with a knife.

Flowing from them freely, the
thoughts that had been planted;
Cracked like leaves.
And before I knew it I began to
heave.

Stretched among the floor my mind
began to pour.
The life had drowned but I'd been
found.

One more realization!
Who needs a mind when you have a
soul that is ready for reincarnation.

Stacy Horning
TELL ME

To The Father Of My Son.

A brand new decade
In Oklahoma you stayed
You really don't care
About the child we share

I wish I knew
What it feels to be you
For I would truly want to see
Your reason for not talking to me

Just be true
Open up and show me you
Let me really see
Your true feelings for me

I just want to know
And end this show
Open your eyes
Tell me no lies
Open your mouth
Let it all come out
Make me hear
For I have no fear

David A DeFino
THE BALLAD OF THE WITCH DOCTOR

This poem is dedicated to Raejean S., my beWITCHing friend.

PAIN PAIN that's all I know since
the arrow pierced my skin.
Suffering as I lie here to die,
drowning in my sin.
As they carry me into his lair I
wonder, "What will become of me?
Does his magic really work? Will I
live to see?"

WHERE IS THE SHAMAN? I need
him to heal my wounds so deep.
WHERE IS THE SHAMAN? He has
to keep me, keep me from, from the
eternal sleep.

I see the masks, the magic potions
what does it all mean?
I see him walk over to the table
and raise his arms to me.
He chants phrases I know not why.
He cannot save me I shall surely die

WHERE IS THE SHAMAN? You
know I needed him to heal my
wounds so deep.
THE SHAMAN he couldn't keep me
from the eternal sleep . . .

Michael P Wohlford
THE BREAK UP

I've lost you.
Everything's lost forever,
Who is to blame?
It doesn't really matter.
I think of you constantly,
I can't escape the pain.
It's tearing me up inside,
It's wearing me down.
What we had
Is what made me happy.
Without your love around,
I have no one.
No one to talk to,
Share everyday adventures.
To help me take that step
That leads into each new day.
Is there life after you?
The future looks so bleak.
You were the only one.
You are the one.

Tracey T Smith
WHISPERING WINDS FROM LONG AGO

Whispering winds from long ago
give me the strength of all that I
know
You'd sweep my hair across my face
in the warm night
just to let me know everything was
still alright
You've let me know myself through
all of these years
and have comforted me through my
tears
During my youth I remember you
showing me all that you could do
When my world fell apart and Mom
passed away
you lingered around me until I may
find my life somewhere on the streets
that run
but that was a new part of what I had
become
You'd tangle my hair when I sat
alone
and take me back to my Carrollton
home
No matter what I am doing or where I
am at
you keep coming by to take me back
Where I could be innocent, wild and
free
and my heart could be happy and I
was me
Whispering winds from long ago
you have blown me in direction of
my soul

Jana Tull Metcalf
LEGACY ROSE

In memory: Cecil O. Tull
Dedicated to: Lucille Williams Tull.

Her smile's the same as her picture
on the mantle
Her love she shared with a man just
as gentle
Sentimentally he'd say a rose I chose
And only the bloom is gone from my
rose . . . .

Today her walk is a little more feeble
Sometimes she forgets the names of
people
A lifetime of living is a life time of
reason
Allowing confusion of her many
seasons . . . .

Her crying is all done . . . her time is
on loan
She's locked in her heart the riches
she owns
Each wrinkle her joy, her pain
exposed
But only the bloom is gone from the
rose . . . .

She's losing her strength, tired hands
now tremble
Undying love lets those lonely eyes
twinkle
My rich legacy is the love of the rose
And only the bloom is gone from his
rose . . . .

One day her loneliness will disappear
She'll leave on earth the ones she
holds so dear
Then watching above, a man and his
rose
The birth and the bloom of a legacy
rose . . . .

Lawrence A Hall
PARENTING

Our children are our most precious
possessions
Unique individuals to be shaped with
our lessons
We want them to be more like we
could have been
In a way they are us, but not really,
they are them

We try to teach them everything we
know
Set an example for them to emulate
and to show
We sometimes will spoil them
beyond what we should
But if we didn't do it our relatives
certainly would

We constantly demonstrate to our
children when we act
They watch, absorb, and decide how
to react
If they watch, listen, and absorb all
they can.
We think they will have a leg up on
life's master plan

Express emotion freely and comfort
them with love
Let them be open, and sometimes, let
them fly like a dove
Continually make sure that their self
worth is reassured
So their personal value will never be
blurred

If we do all these things as best we
can
Our children will have a leg up on
life's master plan
As parents we can be happy for what
we did
We helped guide the life of this
wonderful kid

Peggy De Paoli
SMALL INNOCENCE

Remember back when you were
small
And gave Valentine Cards to one and
all!
The pop out kind, more than you'd
ever use
therefore, no reason to pick and
choose
And a box you made all red and
white
with cupids and laces, a child's
delight!
of candied hearts, and Red Kool-Aid
"wine"
Ah wonder days! St. Valentine's.

But as you grew and picked and
chose,
And weren't as caring I suppose,
As you were when you were small,
And seem to have enough love for all
And meant every word when you
said "Be Mine"
And really gave your heart to your
valentine—

Peggy De Paoli
THE TALL SHIP ROSE

She slipped into port this morning
as the tide was slipping out,
So she wasn't that impressive,

to folks ju-st "turning out."
Sort of old and unattractive, in
the early dawn gray cold
But then it's hard to look impressive
When you're sitting in a hole!
But as the day wears on
and the tide comes up,
You'll witness something strange
She'll take on new dimensions,
begin a subtle change.
She'll climb out of that deep, deep
hole,
The tide has trapped her in
and begin to sway in unison
With a flirtatious summer wind.
Her masts will point high, skyward
the "Rags" all tightly furled,
And for the very first time folks
will see the true "old girl."
Sort of sleek and trim, quiet special
like any fine race horse,
"Ah," they'll say "there's nothing
like her."
And we'll agree, of course!
She'll strain against the lines
that hold her firmly to the shore
For she longs to loose those "topsils"
and be under way once more.
And we're as eager to "up anchor"
to slip away to sea
Where the sails will fill and billow
and with her we'll run free!
She'll turn her bow into the wind
and crest upon the waves,
And they'll bow and part before her
the Queen amongst her slaves!
Ah, I'd love to sail off with her,
go to sea once more.
But alas, time's overtaken me
and I'm shackled to the shore!
But once I walked upon her decks,
and smelled the cool sea breeze
the balmy days of summer heat
and winter's bitter freeze.
And all these golden memories
will sustain me here on shore
For though I dream of tall ships
I'll go to sea no more—

—The Rose

Peggy De Paoli
A TEAR FOR CHRISTMAS

As Christmas races towards us,
I think of Christmas past—
The days of childish wonderment
that flew by oh too fast!
Of all the present wrapping
and hiding from our peers,
Those gifts carefully chosen
to bring the loudest cheers!
And Christmas lights aglowing on
bow and window frost
The warmth of family gathered close,
A tear for Christmas lost.

As Christmas rushes towards us,
as Christmas does these days,
It finds each of us rushing
all going separate ways.
All caught up in our hi-tech world
of videos and games
Of super jets and space age wars
and not one Lionel Train!
Just dolls that walk and talk and
think!
Super heroes without fear!
Ah for the days of soft-times
A tear for Christmas here.

As Christmas rockets towards us
in the year two thousand one,
Will the pace keep escalating
as it thus far has done?
Or will we stop and try to find,
in all these maddening days,
The true joys that are Christmas
that somehow never change.
For they're the things that we
remember
as we face the future's haze,
The glowing love of Christmas
that never really fades.
Forgotten all the worldly things
we "could not do without."
Only love and joy still linger,
that's what it's all about!

Rochelle Cozzetto
IMMORTALITY

In Loving Memory of my "parents" Ralph and Margery Cozzetto, May they rest in "PEACE."

Life it sometimes stifles me, when
I'm deep in thought,
I think of how I've struggled, and the
pain on myself I've brought!
I wonder if I am here to receive, as
well as I am to serve,
Whatever may the reason be, I'll get
what I deserve.

Is it in my plan, that I shall seek what
is unknown,
I look into my past to see how my
mind has grown.
Imaginations, premonitions, God's
word of tranquility,
I've seen them all within the walls, of
life's infinity!

I've come close to feel the emotions
of other souls within,
I haven't really reached my goal, is
this where I begin?
The mountains are high, the oceans
are deep, the golden ladder is tall,
I only wish to climb the hills, at my
own risk, and not to fall.

I won't give up, for I have chosen to
push then sometimes bend,
After all who's to say that my life has
an end?

Galoris Brownley
I CALL YOU FRIEND

To Will Morton,
Thanks for the inspiration.

Strangers on the first encounter
Meet with blind faith of a better
acquaintance.
You seem arrogant.
Me a bit stubborn.
Circumstances throw us together
Forced to make conversation.
Guess what?
Somehow you're not so arrogant
anymore.
I've let down my guard just a little.
Hey, I think I like you.
After a short time words are not
always necessary.
You hear what I say,
I hear what you say.
Some say the eyes tell all.
Maybe they're right.
Maybe we've just learned to trust and
believe in one another.
Now I can truly say I call you
FRIEND.

Wanda F Devall
CHRISTMAS PAST

At times it seems so long ago, staring
at our Christmas tree all aglow, But
then
again, it feels like yesterday, the
colored
rainbow lights, the smell of pine it
was all so fine.
There were Four of us and Mom and
Dad, the gifts weren't always many,
but we were always glad, For we had
the greatest gift of all—Love—love
for each other and for the true
meaning of Christmas.
How I miss those times of being
together at Christmas, Finding the
biggest tree
and watching Dad cut it down, going
home to find
that Mom had gone in the attic and
had all the decorations found. Sewing
popcorn, hanging tinsel, putting the
angel atop the tree, those were by far
the best times, the best feelings, we'll
all agree.
Those days may be gone now, but the
memories are still here, each and
every one of them so very clear, and
one thing for sure—Not even those
many miles
can change our greatest gift and
treasure ever, our
love for each other.

Mary Catherine Collins
LIFE'S DESTINY

We choose our destiny—
We go our own way—
And if it turns out right or wrong—
There is only one to say.
We tend to judge others—
And think our faults are few—
But God alone, and up above—
Sees all we say and do.
Sometimes we grow weary—
If we choose to do right—
But strength will come if we hold
on—
And keep our goals in sight.
Lord, keep my eyes upon the path—
That lead back home to you.
For I have chosen my own way—
It's tried, straight, and true.
Help me to say No! to wrong—
And guide my path each day.
Please place within my mouth, Oh
Lord,
Your precious words to say!

Pierre L Chambers
OBSESSION

I have become obsessed with loving
you,
And not using you as a sex object.
I have become obsessed with
listening to you,
And not using you as a sounding
board.
I have become obsessed with
allowing you to express yourself,
Without expressing my needs.
I have become obsessed with you,
And just holding you in my arms.

Mable P Johnson
A TEARDROP

"In memory of my husband Clarence, who was a victim of cancer in 1983."

Just a teardrop; away from Heaven,
In an instant; you'll be there,
In the arms of; Christ Your Savior,
No more sorrow; no more cares.
No telephone; to call you,
No airplane; in which to fly,
You'll just have to; trust in Jesus,
For on him; you can rely.
He may come by; in the morning,
He may stop in; late at night,
Or he might just, wait a little while,
For you; to set things right.
Are you trusting; in the Savior?
Do you talk to him; each day?
Are you walking; in his footsteps?
So that; he can lead the way.
If you do not; know the Savior,
And you've never; knelt to pray,
Please; ask him to forgive you,
For a teardrop; might fall today.

Jewel D Carter
YESTERDAY'S MEMORIES

To my fellow classmates, the class of 1980. No matter who you are or where you are today, you'll always remain close and dear to my heart! Good Luck to you all!!

What is to happen to one's spirit
when they want something back so
badly, that they
find themselves falling in-love with
the memories of yesterday.
Remembering and desperately
wanting, until it seems to possess
their heart & soul.
How are you to leave something with
that much beauty, to lay behind in the
dust of once was.
Never to be touched and felt again, or
even smell the sweetness of its
existence for one final breath.
Never being able to say Hello again,
and too far away to say Good-bye
again.

J H Rogers
AUGURY

Spoken on a silver note,
The harmonic phrases,
Calling,
Crying,
Living for a moment.
Close your eyes,
Make a silent vow,
Keep it tucked deep in your heart,
And hold it.
Like balancing crystal on a single
strand,
Watch it,
Master it,
And it will grow like a new
friendship,
For it is your trust, your keep,
Your treasure, your promise,
Your Augury

Candi Michelle Andresen
TOGETHER

Looking out
What can you see
The world in doubt
Oh to be free
Is peace just a word
Separated—strong as a feather
Can hate be cured
Let's really come together
You don't look like me
Stop for just a moment
Not a reason to flee
Learning isn't torment
It isn't how you look
That's the cover of the book
It's all about who you are
Make a wish on a star
Wishing for curiosity
A willingness a know
Tradition is longevity
So much to see and show
Each one's special talent
Together we'd be great
The effort isn't gallant
From Bonjour to Hello Mate
All of us from God above

The package beyond control
The strongest tool is love
Peace the greatest goal

Leo Reid Jr
THE MONSTER SPEAKS
As I look into the stone faced crowd
Not a word is spoken out loud
One by one, they stop and stare
With a hint of laughter, a hint of scare.

They only see the outside shell
Their eyes sentencing me, to many a season in Hell.

They only see Mary Shelley's creature,
The rough nest of my features
They can't see the heart
With all of its broken parts.

Phlip Jablonski
A THOUGHTFUL TOUCH
Like the stars scattered across a cool fall night
A beauty shines forth warm and bright.
With skin so soft as a newborn cub
Your spirit stands motionless in the heavens above.
Questionless and radiant only the seer may see
The reflection of nature in the eyes of thee.
Tomorrow may come but today only brings
That touch of love for which the sky sings.

Phlip Jablonski
CHILD DAZE
In the distant passages of a far off thought . . .

A theme, a scheme, it's a child's screams
from a broken heart.
Why I ask, why does she cry like that?
Was it a cat, a bat, or a whack of mom's fat?
But, finally, she stops, her tears wiped away,
left behind to greet a new day.
And it's off and up again she goes, her tossled
blonde hair, behind her it blows.
Running carefree and happy as a lazy bee, with her troubles left basking in the
hot summer breeze . . .

Sheryl Gola
WHERE LOVE IS MANUFACTURED
I live in a world of my own;
faking every emotion that comes.
I live in my closet alone
Letting no one in.
Does it seem so much of a chore
that I ask of you?
Just tell me what you think of me.
Just the truth and nothing more.

I live in a world of my own
where the things people feel
are the things they never say.
I live in my closet alone
where love is manufactured by one.

Dawn Weston
WHY?
Why is life so hard
Why must I cry so much
Why does it hurt me
Why do I tingle at the touch
Why is there always war
Why is there hardly any peace
Why must children starve
Why does this not cease
Why do people kill
Why do they steal
Why must people suffer
Why don't they have a decent meal
Why does this hurt me so
Why doesn't anyone care
Why don't people know
Why don't they share
Why must this world be bitter
Why must it be so cruel
Why is life so hard
Why are we such fools

Laura Weitzman
WONDERING WANDERING

To Rose, Karl Dale, and Anna.

Strolling into my soul,
I found it endless.
It was not an empty hole.
It was a wilderness.

Grizzly fears roam like bear,
While wishes wiggle through the leaves.
Conversations chirp through the air.
Squirrels save kernels of
make-believes.

I nibble on the nuts I've saved,
And the dreams within are sweet.
From them new patterns are engraved,
New places for my feet.

Miranda Clements
THE SUN
A bright ball of light
Burning out of sight
And it's magnificent power
That burns hour after hour
And if that light
Does burn out of sight
No more will it show its power

Bill Costanzo
MORTAL MAN

To my darling Linda with all my love forever—Bill.

I wish I was a looking glass
As clear as can be
So you could look inside and see
Just how beautiful you are to me.

I wish I was a wise man
As wise as can be
So I could explain to you
Just how dear you are to me.

I wish I was a big bright star
High in the sky above
So that I could light your way
No matter how far away

But at last I am a mortal man
So all I can do is offer you my hand
Be there whenever I can
And tell you I love you more
than any other man.

Hazel Teasley
MEMORIES
As I look out my window into a huge ash tree
That was planted there years ago by a man to shade his family.
Years later they came to a mining camp, where the man worked in the company store.
There he and his wife and two children would not want for more.
Their children went to school with our children there,
And our families gathered together in Church for sermons and prayers.
These were the nicest people you could find anywhere.
Later years, our children married and scattered here and there.
A few years later my husband passed on to his heavenly home.
Then two years later our friend's wife went on.
After a year or so our friend's husband and me met,
Although our sorrow of losing our companions we can't forget.
We understand each other, and best friends we will always be.
The huge ash tree is in my yard now you see.
And the birds come there and sing to me a sweet melody.
When the wind blows and rustles through this huge ash tree.
The leaves go together praising and clapping their hands with glee.
People come along now and rest under this big shade tree,
And it holds many memories for you and for me.

Deborah K Darr
NATURE'S TEARS
After a rain
Nothing is the same.
Nature's tears have washed,
Everything from the bottom to the top.

And when the sun reflects
On Nature's teardrops that set,
On the grass, leaves and trees,
This is a true vision of beauty.
For each of the tears possess a color,
So unique—each one different from the other.

Suddenly—the wind blows,
All the glistening tears flow,
Slowly down Mother Nature's cheeks.
Ahh—everything so sparkling and clean.

Joyce Branagan
SECOND TIME AROUND

To Mark, my special friend, for making me believe and inspiring me to try.

I don't have much to give to you
only fragments of this shell
and pieces of this broken heart
where I stumbled and love fell

You've shown that you can mend my heart
and replace what once was gone
but can I have a guarantee
for a lifetime, when you're done?

E Michael Schoonmaker
ON BEING ALONE
Here I am, alone
Wandering, empty,
Around the place that we've shared,
Seeing You—
Everywhere.
Wishing that You were still here.

Fond memories,
Treasured memories,
Keeping me company in my lonely
vigil,
Awaiting You—Impatiently,
Hungry for your return.

Jealousy eating
Into my mind,
Thinking of what You're doing,
Away—Separated,
Apart from my loving presence.

In bed, crying,
Alone in my despair,
Wishing, dreaming,
Praying for your safe return,
Eventually.

Georgia Fraser
VISIONS
The demons of sleep, they speak in my dreams;
their low voices,
I stop and strain to hear,
those familiar things.
All places turn to shadows;
elusive ghosts lingering in places
dreaming eyes can't reach.
Search the darkness, hold onto emotion.
Try to remember things never understood,
voices forgotten except in sleep.

Anthony McGarry
LIGHTNING AND RAIN AND THE PAIN

I dedicate this poem to everyone that understands how beautiful life is and how sad it can be.

The rain was falling hard
It was a stormy night.
In a room with three beds
My mother, my father and me in the light.
In between them both
I was not myself, but I was aware
The lightning was loud
I was as still as could be, no blinking just a stare.
Next thing I know kneeling by my side
A soft voice said to me,
It's only lightning, said my mother
You never know next where it will be

A flash of light
As I awoke in a sweat and a tear
A clouded dream of the ones I love
A dream full of fear
The phone was ringing
My body shaking at the sound
I stopped to look outside
At the rain coming down.
I'm sorry the voice said, it's your mother
And father, they are dead.
I have not slept the same since that night
My mother my father
And me in the light.

Wanda Alice Schwab
BOOKS
Books are among my best friends.
Books tell me about the latest trends.
Books can take minutes or
Books can take hours
Helping me to
imaginarily smell flowers
or climb towers.
Books are among my best friends.

rose christen
MOTHER'S DAY
Where do you go—when you're left alone with you—

When the black of the night—sees no hope of the sun.

When your heart is tormented
and your mind knows no peace—
and your soul wants to linger
with the lost souls and grieve.

So, you toss and you turn
but the image is vivid.
You call out God's name
finding some comfort in it.

Then peaceful you rest—
you wait—and breathe slowly . . .
you know she is closer.

The silence is tranquil
the peace overflowing
the warmth overwhelms you.

A smile rests your face—
the night sees the sun rise
the heart . . . again—safe . . .
hello mother!

rose christen
SPEAK TO ME WITH WORDS OF LOVE
Speak to me with words of love
put my heart at peace—
Quiet the rage inside of me
Allow my soul to breathe—

encase me in your wonderment—
come;
let's drift away,
peaceful waters await us
in a kingdom far away.

With you I fear no distance
your hand contracts such strength
we'll make it on our journey—
our love enables this.

closely side by side
Thru trouble and despair—
our happiness awaits us
our love will take us there.

Our hearts belong together
no looking back—this time,
we'll love and grow forever
then rest when it is time—
Infinity.

Wayne Robert Boulter
DEPENDENCE
Blackened crimson fluid seeped, where no life flowed;
Dropping to the white tiled floor his essence smashed;
The reminiscence mind staggard the man to and throw;
Years ago the funeral of a son, the family car, it did crash;
Skull and crossed bones he was seeking, life inside the
bottle, brought no life after;
The start of the day, memories looked upon in the attic,
picture box found in the rafter;
Grimace face struck in pain, their lives before him,
was it all in vain?
Losing his life before his eyes, dying words,
i love you, a cry.

Susan Washburn
IF
If
I were the sea and you were a sailor
I would make you a perfect wave

If
I were the sky and found you in need
I would send you a beautiful breeze

If
I were the sun and knew you were chilled
I would seek you out and caress you with warmth

If
I were the moon and found you sailing in darkness
I would cast you rays of silver light
so you would not lose your way at night

If
I were the Earth you would find no more hurt
When I safely called you home to the shores of your birth

If
These thoughts were wishes then
know each one is meant for you
The wishes of a dreamer who hopes your dreams come true

Susan Washburn
NIGHT MARE
Dark clouds gather in the sky
They suit in the teardrops in my eyes

Around me lay broken dreams
Tormented souls with drug filled veins
Hunger amongst the earth's decay
Nations marching to war every day
Smog filled skies and oil slick seas
Strange stenches in the off shore breeze

Dark clouds gather in the sky
They suit the teardrops we have cried

Memories fall down like rain
Horses can ease deepest pain
Thunder moves across the ground
And rumbles into sleepy sounds
Lightning cracks across the night
I've come to see if you're alright

Dark clouds gather in the sky
They suit the teardrops in my eyes

Susan Washburn
THE UNICORN
I walk into the silent space
And look upon your strong kind face
Moonlight dances through the trees
And all around are falling leaves

The horses in the pasture nicker
To friendly silver wings that flicker
You toss your head and shake your mane
It's long enough to be untamed

I touch your nostrils flaring wide
And wish that I could be astride
We could jump a rainbow or gallop on Mars
It would be our secret to share with the stars

But you have wrestled with demons and won the bouts
It's not for me to ride you out
So I touch the shoulder of your snow white coat
And bid you farewell without a rope—

Susan Washburn
DAYBREAK
God bless important things
Early blooms and sweet spring rains
Teardrops on a diamond ring
Everlasting love and faith
The smallest flower you create

God bless important things
The smile of a child
The tiniest prayer
A newborn foal
A breath of air

God bless important things
The beauty of the sun at dawn
The moon at night when hours are long
The stars and heavens up above
The seas with currents of your love

God bless important things
For all I have to give today
Is a smile within my heart
For all the fields and meadows wide
That dawned within the dark

Michelle Marisa Di Benedetto
TRUE LOVE

I dedicate this poem to the only "True Love" I've ever known . . .
Joseph Anthony Ricco.

Once long ago,
A young boy stole my heart
But a decision was made
To Love near from a-far . . .

Years had passed
And we had both
Gone astray—
Playing love's games
Feeling love's dismay . . .

I stood by the way-side
And watched love's parade
Seemed to me then,
Love was only a charade . . .

Then one day,
To my surprise,
Destiny led me
To a place
Where once again,
"My True Love"
We stood Face to Face . . .

I never found love
Though there had
Been other men;
Because, in my heart
It was You I loved—
Even More NOW Than Then . . .

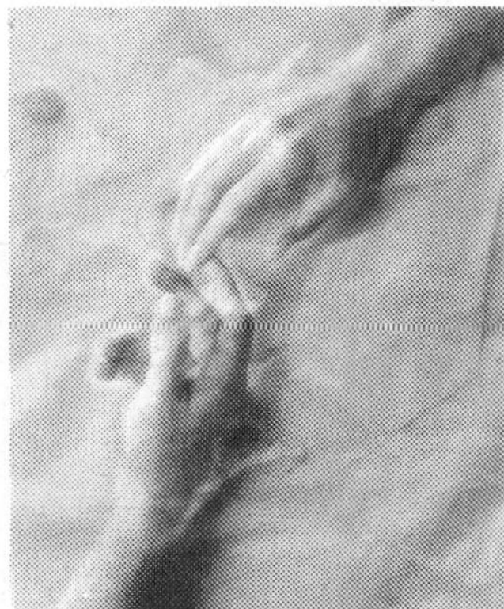

Soon, passion took over,
And not for a moment
Did we part—
This love that we stole
Was Truly,
A Crime of The Heart . . .

We've tried all the tricks
You know young hearts
Do Play;
But this time, My Darling,
Love was here to STAY . . .

We, too, had our hard times
As all good loves do—
But love did prevail
Our Hearts—Still True . . .

We took time away,
And gave each other
Some space—
Always keeping reserved
In Our Hearts
A Special Place . . .

Now it was time
To pick-up the pieces
And start over New—
Because Darling we realized
This love to be TRUE . . .

So remember I Love You
At day's hours end
And you'll ALWAYS
Be in my heart—
As ALWAYS you've been . . !

Lisa Miller
RARE APERITIFS
Reach out to me,
In aversion of tomorrow.
Its afterthought is like the disk of prairie wilderness,
Watching its clout of vision,
Become a rare, selective showcase of melodrama,
Deep in the heart,
Of a paranoid schism.

The hearth of America,
Subsides like an oracle's ode of
deep-seated molecular passion,
In a detente stance of the decade,
Passing on the kitchen of remarks,
To a cloud of equal vision.

The shoulder of its goodness,
Is neither good, nor bad,
Right, nor wrong.
But its equitable happiness,
Is the congruently eloquented
circumference of the theater,
Bold in its spectacle,
Aggressive, as it is blinded by,
What is not, suggestive to its
equitable rank.

William T Miraglia
IS "YES" A "NO-NO?"
In a world of a thousand, "no's"
To one yes
In time one knows
It takes but one "yes"
To make up for a thousand, "no's"
It will always be thus
In the business world of a thousand
"We'll call you. Don't call us"
It takes but one "yes" call
Our self-esteem to reinstall
In the star-crossed world of
"I love you," one knows
Playing the waiting game
Always ends the same
It takes but one "yes"
To make up a thousand "no's"
The word "yes" is not abused
It's scarcely used
It's found in our dictionary
But rarely it seems in our vocabulary
But take heart. Don't despair
Though life seems unfair
Still it helps to know
That it takes but one "yes"
To make up for that thousandth "no"

Clovis L Nazareno
ALWAYS TRIUMPHANT SEA

The embrace of the sea
Is not only suffocating but lasting.
The sea outstays us,
Redolent with triumph.
She withholds secrets and our desire
Is to slink into her suicidally
To probe her underpinnings.
Nonetheless we are far more minute
than she,
Far less enduring than she.

The sea's breath infects fear;
Her breezes and winds are mystery.
Casting off for her center is foraying
Outside of mapped mortal territory.
Her heaving promises sublime
drowning.

Sherry I Watts
LUCY

Lucy you were the best
You stood out from all the rest.

You made us laugh and made us cry
But most of all you touched our
lives.

I never got to meet you or tell you
good-by
But the world will miss you and so
will I.

So here's to you and your red hair
Thanks for the memories we all
share.

We love you Lucy and always will
Because that's the way you make us
feel.

Ricardo A Scott
WE NEED EACH OTHER

To Angela and all mothers, all the world's children.

Why does it have to take
A national or global tragedy
To remind you and me of our
vulnerability

Why can't we see that
The only solution to
Injustice and inequality
Is the unity of all humanity

A space shuttle disaster,
A drought that seems to last
Forever,
An outbreak of AIDS—
The devasted Libyan air-raids
Our youth committing suicide at
An alarming rate
Our war on drugs might have come
Too late

It is without warning, as I've said
before
That death and destruction will come
knocking
On our door
Who knows what it will be next
This is no jive, yes it is no jest

We must come to the realization
Whether we believe it or not
That we are our brother's keeper
As humans interacting with humans
We'll always need each other.

Let us take the responsibility
Of guiding our youths, our women
And our family
Cast away our own selfish existence
Realize now that unity is the best
Defense.

Joe D Glenn
LOVE IS MORE

I dedicate this poem to Roberta Jamieson for in her I found the meaning of each word..

Love is More than giving your time
Sharing and Caring a thought that's
kind
Giving of yourself in a way that's
pure
And the assurance to know there's
someone there
To help you endure.

Some say love is a state of mind
Emotions and feelings combined
Easily obtained and simply removed
It's not really there
It's only a mood.

Love is as much as one wishes it to
be
Love is giving without thought of fee
Love is more than just a state
For it was given to me by a man
that's great.

If emotions and feelings is all love is
to be
Then Christ had nothing worth giving
to me
But because it is more, much more
than a state
It will mean the whole world to me
and my mate.

Marla Moffa
THE SONG

I often listen to the song
of broken hearts,
and stolen tears,
of untamed souls,
and rising fears,
of saddened whispers,
and stormy skies,
that's where my spirit always flies.
The broken notes ring in my ears,
and they'll keep ringing for many
years.
I wish the song would change its
style,
and then maybe I could smile.

Dion Cautrell
UNTITLED

For Anna Marie—whose love, support, and faith have shown me what life is all about. This one is for you kiddo . . . .

The castle gate is closed to infidels,
Past transgressors wait, locked in
their cells.

Under an ashen sky vanguards clash,
And wonder how this war can last.

The sands of Time soak up the blood,
Encroaching on our livelihood.

The winds of Time blow bones away,
No object is ever a lasting thing.

Will the dead hear the War-God
calling?
Will they rise after all are fallen?

Nancy E Meals
MEMORIAL DAY

To my parents: Angelo and Nancy Deponceau.

I sat beside your grave today
and traced my fingers o'er your
name carved upon
the stone.
I sensed a closeness; a need to talk
about your sons and
daughters, grown.
I felt no sadness, being there.
Time has healed the wounds
of losing you . . . the anger that
I felt . . . and oh, the grief
because our time together was so
brief.
I know your grave
contains nothing but dirt and worms
and dusty bones;
God took the best part and
left naught for me but
misty memories; and yet
I sat upon your grave and talked
to you . . . alone.

Mattie Dobey
MY FATHER

Fathers are a real find
I am just talking about mine
Always there with a helping hand
More than a boy, he's a man
Wiping your eyes when tears flow
Holding his "hankie" for you to blow
A skinned knee, a broken limb
We take all our problems directly to
him
On my birthday a card is a "must"
I'm so proud of him, I think I'll bust!

Patricia Ann Giddens
MY GIFT

I was so sad because I missed her,
the one who'd given me birth;
She was the one who taught me
my values, and what my life was
really worth.

All through life she was the one,
that was my dearest friend;
I really had a hard time adjusting,
when it all had to end.

I turned around and then I saw it,
my shadow upon the wall;
And then the words my dear
mother spoke to me, I started to
recall.

"Your shadow was a gift from me,
on the day that you were born;
I gave it to you to be a constant
reminder, that you're never all alone.

So if you ever feel lost and lonely,
just turn around my dear;
And glance upon your shadow,
honey, and know I'm always near."

Clarice Dwelly Weatherspoon
THE HAWK AND THE MOUSE

How happy is the flying hawk
With the mouse between his claws
Looking for a place to land
His evening meal is all planned.

Un-happy is the flying mouse
Snatched from beside his house
He never will return again
Time has come to meet the end.

Very strange are nature's ways
Humans nod their heads and say
Just look at the mouse and hawk
In many ways does nature talk!

Paul Gaer
GENTLE BREEZE

A gentle breeze blows thru an empty
space
Feelings expressed freely to us from
afar
Enlighten our inner selves causing us
to wonder
Of the many things that we have yet
to understand

Gemma Egana
CHILDREN IN FEAR

For Nikki Sixx . . . My thoughts, my inspiration . . . and my dreams of admiration . . . .

In this heart of mine lives this lonely
child
Searching for a way to be rid of the
fears
But my lonely soul drifts so far away
To escape the heat from my burning
tears

I hear that heart of yours beating so
loudly
Sending a message with similar faith
Don't let your soul drift too far away
So we can meet in heavenly ways

Similar as we are, we are children in
fear
Afraid of the loneliness, afraid to
shed a tear
Darkness cries for light, cradling all
of us children
Captured by the moment, when we
grow as men and women

Can our hearts of stone learn to live
and love
And forget the ways we learned in
the past?
Will our souls of jade be brave
enough to stay
Long enough to let our loneliness
pass?

B D Varga
CHER

Sultry queen, comic vamp, exotic
diva
An ocean of emotions
Unconventionally flamboyantly ever
surprising
Magical pearl radical
Real this big Barbi doll
Men are her luxury in the passage of
time
Teenage rebel star
That delights of the Mona Lisa smile
She, the expensive complex screen
persona
So outlandish, so daringly creative
Pop princess of the sixties
Movie star of the 80ties
Dazzling diva, conquering
The most unconquerable! At times
This vamp turns a rich bag lady! But
who at times,
In an almost nonexistent suit is pure
frivoly
At times she big birds darkened twin
appear
Ever so divine awesome presence a
spectacle
Full of elemental surprise our Cher
Our big Barbi doll.

Gertrude Ford
THE PATH OF THE PANTHER

Candela is dead
So it was said

His body was found
To a tree it was bound

They held him and swayed
Then fell down and prayed

For they feared their own death

The jungle turned cold
So I've been told

And the natives grew still
Wrapped in the chill

As an eerie sight
Turned day into night

For the soul of their leader was near

The corpse turned pale
So goes the tale

And it finally dissolved
As a Panther evolved

To lead the tribe home
On a path not known

For their fright was a
terrible thing

Cheng Lor
MY SADNESS
Oh my dearest love of all
Seeing you born small
Wondering what will you look like
Knowing that you will be nice.

Oh my dearest love of all
Seeing you grow tall
Wondering where will you live
Knowing that it will be peace.

Oh my dearest love of all
Seeing you move far
Wondering when will you return
Knowing that it will not be such a turn.

Oh my dearest love of all
Seeing your and my tears fall
Wondering when will it stop
Knowing that it will not.

Oh my dearest love of all
Seeing the tearing of your heart and mine like thraw
Wondering when will it come together
Knowing that it will not be another.

Pearline Fire Thunder
THE FADED FLOWER
I have a faded flower from a love that
exists no more
You're never true but once, and a memory
of forever
The picture to show of you, no one can see
for it's in my memory
The faded flower, each petal a story
of our love, . . . past
But to tell the story, I must touch
the petals
But the petals are weak
So the stories stay inside my heart
and the picture, I carry slowly fades
never can I color your image
So I carry the faded flower close
to my heart
I hear the echo of my footsteps
they seem to say
Broken heart, Broken heart, Broken heart
If I let you go, I may never find you again
So I'll keep the faded flower close to my heart.

Sheila M Kahler
LISTEN AND HEAR
A cry in the night.
A light in a well.
A commission from God.
A mission in hell.
A human ailment.
A frightened world.
A plea for mercy.
A pardon withheld.
A question asked.
An answer pending.

The cry is heard.
The light upheld.
The commission is love.
The mission is ended.
The heart is healed.
The promise is sealed.
The plea is heard.
The price is paid.
The question answered.
Emmanuel!

Sheila M Kahler
REACH AND KNOW
A silent force.
A pressing need.
A widening void.
A cry for peace.
Life's ebb and flow
slowing and turning.
A need to be loved.
A need to know,
What do I do?
Where do I go?

Reach out and know
That a hand is near
To soften the blow
To shorten the fear.
The Presence is real.
The feeling is true.
It is there for all.
It is there for you.

Sheila M Kahler
HUSTLE AND BUSTLE
The day begins,
Then night is falling.
The in between
There's no recalling.
Hustle to this,
Bustle to that.
Nothing accomplished,
Just forward and back.

We go through life,
Daily wrestling strife.
Too busy to look up and out
To really see what life's about.
To share with each other
The time and love given us
Free without measure.
Life, a priceless treasure
Wasted in hustle and bustle.

Sheila M Kahler
MY TINY DOLL

To Lori Ann, my bright and gentle mouse.

A tiny face smooth and still
Soft brown curls over shoulders spill
Small curled hands and tiny feet
A chubby body clothed so neat
In pastel colors soft and sweet
My tiny doll.

I wash her face and comb her hair
Her soft blue eyes and face so fair
Glow and shine as she's lying there
Trusting me for tender care
My tiny doll.

I'm never alone anymore
She's always there by my side
She shares my sorrows with a smile
All my secrets with her abide
My tiny doll.

Through the soft gray night she watches
While I sleep and dream sweet dreams
In the morning light she greets me
And our day's adventures begin
My tiny doll.

We romp and play through sunny day
When rain decrees inside we play
Then she's content to sit and read
A willing foil to all my needs
My tiny doll

When I grow old and sit and dream
of childhood days and lovely things
I'll think of her, I know I will
'Cause she's right here beside me still
My tiny doll.

Vicki Wright-Graviss
SHADOWS

To my family, from whose love I draw my strength.

The darkness surrounds me
And engulfs my soul
It permeates my being.

I reach for the light
But it's out of my grasp
Fading ever so swiftly into the shadows
The shadows of my mind.

I vow to walk not in the shadows
Of those before me
But to step hastily into the light
And shine for all to see.

So that those that follow
Will not slip into the darkness
But will follow and find peace.

Jean Doughty
DADDY
Wandering around in pitch darkness
Trying to see if I really exist
Trying to find myself and where I belong

Running through a tunnel trying to find you
Looking for you to end my confusion

Hands and arms reach out for me,
they say they love me
I turn to them for the love you never gave

They want more than you did
I wish you'd come back

Help me Daddy, I need you

Brian Shipkin
THREE RIVERS
Sitting by the fireside, our ears
in tune to a box by the door, playing
James Taylor (or something). We
walk past our lake—the moon veils
itself behind a curtain of clouds, but hey,
you can see the stars. I kiss
you from the grounds of our fields; we're
hidden in the grass of the moment,
sharing everything, even our minds.
Listen, mon amie, can you hear the
crickets?—or is it just one of those relaxation
tapes? (God, that was so me.)

Maintenant tu as un morceau de moi
Peux-je avoir un morceau de toi à
Trois Fleuves? . . .
Peux-je?
Peux-je?
Peux-je?

Barbara J Weiler
SPRING DELIGHTS
Saw a robin just today, he was
singing as if to say, "Spring is here."
His bright orange breast shined
against the dark sky, winter still lingers.
He sang of the hope that the world
has heard for years but never tired of.

A lazy barge floats up the mighty
Mississippi, shiny ripples float ashore.
Imagine the stories that boat could
tell, the people it has seen.
Would we pick that life if we could,
traveling down the river, no place to call home.

Spring is here, a joyous time when
the earth wakes up.
Lilacs, rows stream along the ol'
steam engine making it seem alive.
Friendly faces all around greeting the
warmth in the March air.

The earth has been sleeping, she
wakes up fresh and ready to give.
Mom's thoughts drift to the garden
that soon will be planted.
Amazing how those small seeds will
rise and nourish our souls.

Yes, Spring is here, the sun warms
the earth longer, smiling on the land.
Refreshing the earth, flowers of many
colors are making the scene.
The many scents bouquet the land,
filling the air gracefully.

Margaret Ferrelli
VIENNA INTERLUDE

I dedicate this poem to my husband, Louis C. because he was/is supportive of my career and he takes care of me . . . He is a star!

Another greeting card, from her . . . a lost love
Mailed with a trembling hand . . . in a white glove
Frederika . . . Why do you not forget?
Our misalliance is over . . . and . . . yet?
Our clandestine love affair should have been avoided
But we were drawn irresistibly to each other . . .

I was a charismatic American
man . . . nouveau-riche . . . full of life
To my dismay . . . I was bound to a
nagging, self-serving wife
I was looking for adventure . . . and
found it . . . in you
Every romantic notion was mirrored
in your eyes . . . of blue

How wondrous Vienna was! The
shops . . . bakeries . . . Opera House
The fire in our souls burned . . . the
flame could not be doused
Intimate little dinners . . . music . . . a
waltz . . . just for you
You were a vision of femininity . . .
wearing a lace dress . . . of periwinkle blue

A mature company executive . . . was
I . . . transferred to Vienna . . . last year
Inexplicably and hopelessly involved
. . . madly in love, I feared
I returned to America . . . a
self-imposed exile from VIENNA INTERLUDE
My wife left me . . . could not bear
my coldness . . . instinctively, she knew . . .

Frederika . . . I want to see you again

. . . fan the fire
That once, in a VIENNA INTER-
LUDE . . . was our desire . . .

Shawn M Shell
PLEASE DON'T
Please don't beat me with a stick,
Please don't burn me with your Bic.
Please don't hit me on the head,
Please don't throw me on the bed.

Please don't bounce me like a ball,
Please don't fracture my skull.
'Cause I'm too fragile to be beat,
My mind can't take this pressure &
heat.

On & on, why do I have to run?
Why can't we be father & son?
Please don't beat me, I've done
nothing wrong—
Can't you see?

Please don't beat me.
Please . . . .

Jaime Joy Berwick
MY FRIEND
My friend has gone away,
Where she doesn't say.
Even though I see her every day,
We don't talk to each other,
Or walk with one another.
We sit by each other,
But laugh with others.
My friend has gone away,
And she is there to stay.

Virginia B Hughes
THANK YOU
Thank you Lord for the blessings of
this day
Thank you for listening when I
kneel to pray.
For the beauty of the earth
And by your grace a spiritual
birth.

Thank you Lord for the joys of life
Thank you for strengthening me in
sorrows and strife
For the love of family and friends
And for sending thy only Son to
atone for my sins.

Thank you Lord for the gift of thy
word
No sweeter story has ever been
heard.
Thank you for Jesus who died for me
On that old rugged cross at
Mt. Calvary.

Joe Powell
THE TREES OF ONE
The trees of one
Make a beautiful sound,
Calling out to no one.
But no-one responds,
So the trees of one,
Go on feeling the
Magic of the air.
Having a rush of anxiety
Which they will love
To share with anyone.
But not everyone is willing to
share,
For they are not listening
To the trees of one
They will try to cut
Down in force,
Instead of admiring or
Acknowledging the views
Of the trees of one . . .

Penny R Bentley
SO FAR AWAY

This poem is dedicated to Francisco Vargas Aguilar, my best friend in México. Thank you for your inspiration and for helping me believe in myself. I'll never forget you.

To be with him is always a pleasure.
One of that my heart will always
treasure.
The smell of him brightens up my
day.
And when I look at him, there is so
much to say.
He's so far away and so hard to see.
I still have the hope that someday
we'll be.
His dark brown eyes are full of love.
Our bond is blessed from the heavens
above.
I love him dearly and this is true.
I once told him, "I'm gonna miss
you."
Through our letters we send our love
and care.
Although sometimes long-distance is
more than I can bear.
If you could only see the sway and
the glide in his walk.
Someday soon, in the future, I know
we'll be able to talk.
It's been too long since I've heard his
voice.
But believe me, this wasn't by
choice.
The days are long but the nights are
longer.
Listening to his song as the tears
grow stronger.
As I once said, "For you I'll wait."
Believe me now this wasn't by fate.

Dreathia A Adams
LOOK UP
When my life is in turmoil and it
seems that there's no hope for me,
I look up to find my only feeling of
serenity
It's in the sky and I'm not sure why.
With its placid colors
Sometimes pink and others blue.
I hear a voice whisper, "This one's
just for you."

When I have a fight and there's only
pain in sight.
That strange voice starts calling me,
"Look up here, Remember me, I have
your peace and serenity."
Then I notice that the clouds are so
fluffy and white.
What had I said, that there was pain
in sight?

So when you're having a really hard
day and
happiness seems so far away,
You'll hear that calming voice that
once called to me,
"Look up here, Remember me, I have
your peace and serenity."

Rachel Smith
WHAT IS THIS THING CALLED LOVE?
I feel your body next to mine
Oh yes it feels so very fine
I thought I could do it, without falling
for you
But I guess now I'm learning, that is
not true
I'm starting to care, it just doesn't
seem fair
I feel it so much, from your slightest
touch
I want you so bad, it makes me feel
so sad
Because I know, that you may go
I'm waiting, what will it be?
Will it be me? Or will you be free?
Please tell me now, let me know
somehow
Is this just a game, are you just the
same
As all those other boys, who think
girls are just toys
Please tell me now,
I love you.

Jack Stuver
THE MOON IS OURS
The Moon is ours if we want it
With love together, we can share it.

The Full Moon in June of 1988
Rekindled our love as a result of fate
It stared at me through a window in
Bisbee
And seemed to say our love was
meant to be.

When we shared the Moon in the
dark
Before our ride through Central Park
It seemed to say within our heart
That we were never meant to part.

We say hello to it and ask it things
And wonder what the future brings
The Moon will always be part of us
And shine over us until we are dust.

Yes, I gave you a Romantic Moon
Yet all it has done is made me swoon
I would love to shower you with
flowers
And know that the Moon is ours.

Hubert L Moore
OLD AGE
We're here yet we are empty, this
house and I alone.
Yet life is there, in both our shells for
happiness, we've known.
A smile—a joke—a laughing face,
these things don't fade away.
We're old you know, the two of us
yet here on earth we stay.
The willow tree outside my door, at
night does shed a tear.
For in the silence of the night, it hears
a child's sweet prayer.
The swing that hangs where first it
hung, contentedly it seems.
It swings there in the evening breeze,
and dreams its many dreams.
The Hound that lays outside my door,
no more to wag his tail.
Sometimes at night he tells the moon,
of how he used to trail.

The children come to visit us, but
they don't stay too long.
They think the small ones bother me,
and soon they all are gone.
Sometimes they speak and I don't
hear, they say it won't be long.
But if they knew the dreams I have,
they'd know that they were wrong.
This house they say, is unsafe for me,
and that it must come down.
I know they're right but it will last,
till they put me in the ground.
These hallowed walls that heard their
shouts, and heard their laughter ring.
Sometimes at night they speak to me,
and I hear their Mother sing.
She sings to me of life and youth, of
dignity and grace.
I listen in the silence, as the tears run
down my face.

Melanie Anne Sanpietro
HOME

With Love, To Thomas & Rosemary, my parents.

If I were a bird,
I'd perch upon the tallest mountain
peak.

If I were a mountain,
I'd tower over the city below.

If I were a city,
I'd plant street rows of trees and
parks.

If I were a tree,
I'd grow tall amongst the street
lanterns.

If I were a lantern,
I'd ignite the brightest light for
the littlest bird upon
the tallest mountain over
the bustling city below;
He'll know.

The trees below are home.

Mary Brookman-Wright
MY DREAM
To live with one and nature
And always feel I'm free
To grab my horse
And ride the wind
And be at one with me.

Where mountains loom
And flowers bloom
In places hard to find
Where only me and my big friend
Would take the time to ride.

Where trees grow tall and straight
And I wouldn't have to wait
For a train, bus, or cab
And worry that I'll be late.

Time stands still it seems
Up in the mountains high.
Someday, maybe someday,
I'll catch my dream,
And homeward bound I'll fly.

Norma J Martin
PRIORITIES
"My dolly is hurt and needs your
attention,"
My little girl said one day;
I was busy with things not worthy of
mention
And brusquely I sent her away.

She went and took care of her own
wounded dolly
As I busily rushed on my way,
Not stopping to think of the heartache
and folly
I'd sowed in her soul that day.

If I had stopped working for only a
minute
To help her take care of the doll,
I may have noticed, 'twas her need
that was in it,
And 'twasn't her dolly's at all.

A minute in time would be all it had
taken
To stop in my rushing about,
And think, what a joy the knowledge
would waken
That Mother loved her, without
doubt!

Donna Anne Bethke
GOING TO GRANDMA'S

I'm going to grandma's, oh what fun
We're leaving with the morning sun

Betcha grandma's wearing a hole in the rug
Can't wait to get there and get that hug.

Grandma's house is all yellow with green
With a glider out front the color of beans

Grandma's there with hugs and smiles
And everyone's talking all the while

A trip to the store gets all that we need
To make "shifters"—come on let's eat!

Outside we go, we don't delay
'Cause we have to do it all in one day

See the cows, and the walnut tree
And sit a spell under the willow tree

Around the back to the pump we go
Maybe this time we'll get water—who knows?

Now it's time for a trip to the candy store
Grandpa gathers us up—come on—out the door

The rest of the day goes by in a haze
And soon we see the last evening's rays

It's now time for a little T.V. then bath and bed
"We'll have French toast for breakfast," grandma says

The lights are out and it's all quiet now
And it has been for some time
Grandma's gone, but not in my heart
The memories of love will be there for all time.

Semih H Uzuner
A KID ARRIVES FROM THE EAST

To my brother Selim, who also made this journey across the ocean with me.

From the old world
to the new world
I flew.

Left the East shores,
for the West shores
of the ocean.

My notion
of the new nation
was nowhere.

But, I knew
in time
I was somewhere.

Believable,
unbelievable;
the truth in between.

Some different
and other things
never seen.

East met west;
in the kid
not yet a teen.

Karin N Harry
SOMEWHERE SOMEONE'S CRYING

It's not the social outcast,
  or the lady on skid row.

It's the pretty, blue-eyed blond,
  with a very handsome beau.
She's crying out for help,
  but not too loud or long.

She thinks that she is crazy,
  but we know she is wrong.

She's feeling very down
  and wants to get away.

She wants to kill herself
  and end this saddening day.

Silvia M Tarafa
HEART PETALS

Pockets full of giggles pour out into laughter
Puddle laughter strike stinging springs of tears trickling inside
And the dry face masks secret longings

Heart Petals do not usually take the form of words
They take flight in the intangible intimacies that only lovers understand

Free to fly,
Salty winds from ocean waves meander into scenes of half-naked bodies
And the patterned beat of sun beams, heating, bronzing curved cells and grains
Nameless shapes of grooved ivory specs decorate the open spaces on a flat horizon
Becoming souvenirs of nature's breadth when relocated to cement shelters they are taken

An orchestra of flying whirls and pitches resound against a background of rolling, beating coils breaking against the face of mother earth
Watered hair strands fall on sandy faces

And the wind sings its reminiscent songs

Where love seeds nursed by showers of sacrifice
Sprung into orchards of faith with the patience of a sea shell's birth

Embedded is the soul's trust on this transformed terrain
Though time, storm or rain disburse into myriad shapes
The traces once made cannot be erased

The reality always the same; along the sandprints we became.

Lisa Ann Trask
THESE OLD HANDS

These old hands have touched many a person
In their hearts and soul and minds
These old hands have inspired many to accomplish
  their ultimate and most unreachable
  goals
These old hands have worked for many a day
To toil over sometimes menial and always troublesome
  tasks
These old hands have resolved many an argument
But now these old hands are tired
Yet no one seems to appreciate all that they have done
These old hands are looked upon as a symbol of
  weariness and loneliness
Even though these old hands are really strong and
  peaceful
For they are finally at rest where no one can take for
  granted what these old hands have done.

Amber Lynne Saunders
A SOFT WARM WIND

Sitting in long green grass
A soft warm wind comes drifting past
The soft warm wind holds all the dreams
I have ever had,
Like floating on a soft warm cloud
Or flying through the midnight air
But now the soft warm wind has passed
and all my dreams have gone so fast

Dorothy J Smith
REUNION MISSED

To Reunion Members of USS Bradford 00545 and their third reunion since WW II, also to those who served in Korea and Vietnam area.

I took a bath and washed my clothes,
My wheelchair is gassed up too.
My broken leg says Go, Go, Go,
But the doctor said No, No, No.

Mary Jo Elliott
NOT FOREVER

Something new, Something old,
But nothing in life, forever to hold;
You have it, but you have it not,
Tho plenty, there is not a lot.

Something gone, Something past,
Something to leave, never to last;
Watching for, giving care,
For it you'll strive, and ever despair.

Something to hold, Something to keep,
When it leaves, you'll sadly weep;
You'll try to live, and live you can,
Though no replacement known to man.

Something empty, Something to mourn,
Nothing to fill the heart so torn;
Try to forget, yet wonder why,
Under the earth, all must lie.

Helen L Gillies
PERSONAL DEMONS

My personal demons
are dashing gleefully
about the room
to the dissonant music
of raindrops playing
fractured rhythms
against the window panes.
I reel beneath the onslaught
of this erratic race,
then accede to the spirit
and become hypnotized
by its pointlessness.
From the cyclone
of aimless haste
is born Restlessness,
flaunting alluring fantasies
which distract and charm me
from the embrace of Determination.

Cindy Biram
BUTTERFLY

To my wonderful husband and inspiration, Dean. I love you! Thank-you, Cindy.

A yellow flutter on a sun kissed sky
On the soft breeze floats the butterfly
Who knows what secrets she has seen
She has seen the places of which we've dreamed
Fly close sweet spirit of the clouds
Be careful not to be too loud
'Cause danger seeks a carefree soul
It is jealous of the pleasure told
It wants to create harm and despair
For the carefree soul without a care
So take me with you as you go
Teach me how on the breeze to flow
Tell me secrets, show me where
A carefree soul can learn to care.

Eberhard W Gress
THE ART OF REMINISCENCE

Dedicated to my critic and love, my dear wife Evi.

Could I say to life's great hour:
Cease to be a time devour.
Sparks of love and friendship, pure:
Marching time, can't you abjure?
It's like fighting father Zeus,
Atombombs and nucleus.

Since a moment stands not still,
Recognize the fleeting will.
Learn to master life's fast pace,
Only hindsight wins the race.
Do not fight the waning years,
When you start to miss your peers.

Memoirs are yours on call,
Make elate you, make you fall.
Train your mind to reminisce
Pleasant memos, be a whiz.
Tragic happ'nings bury good,
They can ruin health and mood.
Looking forward, while you breathe,
Scare reflections memo freeze.

René Moore
MOONLIGHT IN THE NIGHT

Moonlight in the night
  On your face,
  With no trace,
  Of what you're thinking of.

Not a care in the world
  As free as a dove.
  As parachutes of love
  Come down from above.

As the winds from the Heavens.
  Move to and fro,
  Your paisley dress panics as so
Moonlight in the night,
  As everyone knows.

Jeff Warr
ONE QUIET MOMENT

The fault is thine;
as of fault am I.
For grace happens with dawn,
and sunlight through trees.

Never a moment should happen
when one has decree
for then others have want,
and not one will on another
has the right to impede.

Neither being with all,
or being without
satisfies the taste you are craving
in the hunger of greed.

As what we are

is what we heed,
we are enveloped by change
never making change be.

Margaret Grant Owen
MY FAMILY

As the sun lowers in the sky, I think of the days gone by.

I cherish the love of my home, and the parents I adored.

As life passes so swiftly by, I wonder what's in store.

If I could leave something of me to be remembered, it would be the things that kept me going, the love of my God, and the faith that kept me secure.

I love living, being true to the one I love, and trying to guide my two sons to obey God's commandments.

Life has been good to me, loving parents, loving husband, children and brothers, and a family to be proud of.

I feel that there are so many things I want to do, I pray that God will understand that I'm not ready yet for the unknown land.

I thank God for each day I live, on this beautiful planet called earth.

Kenneth M O'Malley
A FOOTSTOOL

This reading is dedicated to an inclined heart.

I spread my eyes
across the sky
to scale the depths within.
Where once inside,
I realized
the dust had settled again.
And earth laid calm
beneath my feet
In fields we called the same,
I showed my Love
a splendid grass
and we listened to the rain.

Harry N Palmer Jr
ADIEU TO LIFE

To those who did not have time to say "Good-bye."

Do not despair when I am gone,
I've left you here to carry on.
The summer winds and gentle air
Will warm and soften your despair.

In death there is peace of soul and mind.
Do not let your loss make you unkind.
A life is just another story
With deeds, adventures and some glory.

You know the earth is just a stage
Performances forgotten by this modern age.
Some play their parts with great ability,
While others must cope with less agility.

Mistakes are made, and triumphs too,
Through the trials in the life given to you.
As time goes by, the wisdom will come,
And you will be remembered, with love, by some.

Alexandra Fogel
WE KEEP ON . . .

The spiral of a winding staircase,
or a silvery moon in the sky,
we keep on searching for the top,
curious as to what we'll find.

Down in the deep dark ocean,
or inside a human's mind,
we keep on delving,
curious as to what we'll find.

With a world that spins in constant motion,
each man stops to ponder from time to time,
but still we keep on moving,
curious as to what we'll find.

William R Polino
A VISION OF YOU

To the woman of my life.

As the early rays of light rise in the eastern sky,
Signaling a new dawn, I am awakened by a vision of you.
Unlike the early dawn, which fades in moments to the
Beauty of each day, your vision is emblazoned within me.
As my day entwines, my intimacy and love for you escalates
To heights unknown to mortal man.
The purist within me pulses my cogent self to definitions
Of love and intimacy lost to those compilers of the dictionary.
Intimacy and love of you is not seen in the vein of the
Irascible appetite of the common man, known as lust.
It is known to me in more benign words as knowing you;
Caring for you; loving you, and—yes anticipating you.
My mind is never idle with frivolity.
When not occupied with the mundane monotony of the
Realities of the work-a-day world,
Your vision returns to excite my imagination.
As I lie in bed, as the dawn brought my first thought of you,
I think of you until the thin line of consciousness
Concludes to rapturous sleep. I cannot wait for the new dawn
To awaken to my lovely vision — YOU – .

Cherilyn L Tousignant
HARPIE

This too shall pass, and unkind words
Shall fly away like craven birds—
The carrion eaters come to feast
Upon the heart where love has ceased
To dwell; where only memories
Bear light to darkened used-to bes.
The sharpened claws, the razored beaks—
Where is the one I loved? Who speaks?
Have years reversed alchemy's dream
And turned to dross the golden gleam?
And in the shadows that remain . . .
What monstrous wings unfold again?

Cherilyn L Tousignant
KENTUCKY

In your lonesome, darkened valleys where
my soul was sent to dwell,
All that was ever beautiful in those
Elysian fields
Where starry, dusky twilights lay on
hills of Asphodel,
Became eternally part of me, and weapons
that Time wields
Cannot sever mountains that rise nobly
in my soul
Nor fell the tall green trees that leaved
in summers long since past,
Can't still the silvery thrushes' song which
echoes through the years—
Kentucky, heavy in my soul, you press
out gentle tears.

Sharon Sue Kachinski

Sharon Sue Kachinski
WHAT IS A FRIEND

To All My Loved Ones Whose Love Inspired Me To Write My Feelings.

What is a Friend, but someone you can turn to with Happiness, Sadness,
Worry and Anger, and they listen,
because they love you.

What is a Friend, but someone who'll hold you and kiss you; build you
up when you're feeling low and
whose hand is always there when
you reach out.

What is a Friend, but someone who is there in need. Need to share;
to give love and receive and be
held; to express tender
encouraging words and in some cases, to be caressed and made love to
knowing there's no commitment,
lies or pain; and to share secrets
forever.

What is a Friend, but someone who, no matter what, you share together,
is respected; you'll defend and
protect; one who's loved, missed;
'A Happy Thought'; a part of Golden Memories you share and Cherish, always.

Friends never fail . . . Marriages can fail; shallow friendships and
relationships fail, but through
thick or thin; miles apart;
arguments or disagreements and with aging together, not from each-
other and giving each 100% to
each other . . . IS A FRIEND

Alma Wingler
OLD GLORY

Here is to old glory.
May it forever wave,
O'er land and sea, but most of all
O'er all our soldiers' graves
They fought and died to save our land
From enemies o'er the sea.
Let's do whatever we can do
To keep our country free.

So keep old glory waving high
O'er this land we love so well.
It will make us so very proud
Of the ones who so proudly fell.
So here is to old glory.
The flag we're so proud of.
Let's say a prayer for those who fought
For freedom, peace and love.

Donald L Zust Jr
I WANT TO LEARN

This poem is dedicated to my family, Mom, Dad and Holly, and to my teacher, Mrs. Barnes.

I want to learn about things great and small,
Mountains, oceans, and waterfalls.
Rocks and minerals and tiny stones,
Fossils, shark's teeth and dinosaur bones.
I'd like to know if there is life on other planets,
And if there are flying saucers and space bandits.
I want to learn about the Milky Way and other stars,
While studying Jupiter, Saturn and Mars.
After learning about things great and small,
I would thank God who made them all!

Cheri L Jamros
LITTLE ORPHAN

For my loving husband and my two beautiful daughters.

He sat upon a tree stump
tears streaming down his face
No one seemed to want him
He was a charity case.

Why doesn't someone love me
what have I done so wrong
Why don't I have a mama
and a place to go, called home?

His little face was dirty
his clothes were soiled and torn
No one for him to turn to
no one to take him home.

I sat quietly down beside him
put my hand upon his hair
Turned his little face up toward me
and, told him that, I CARED.

Kimberly Williams
WHEN MY LIFE ON EARTH IS GONE

Dedicated to my Dad, for his spiritual direction in my life, with much love on his fiftieth birthday.

When my life on earth is gone
and I reflect on what I've done,

Will I see that I've done well;
did my life, Christ's message tell?

Will the Lord reach out for me;
hold me close and welcome me?

Was I gentle, full of grace?
Was my home a welcome place?

Was I aware of other's needs?
Was good intentions shown with deeds?

In sickness, death, or poverty,
did others know to count on me?

Did I lend a helping hand?
Did I for my convictions stand?

Did I take advantage of,
the power of prayer, the power of love?

My goals in life become more clear
when I remember why I'm here.

Donald G Bamber
TEACHER'S DELIGHT: STUDENT'S PLIGHT

To all teachers who work so hard to help young people to make their grades and a better world for all concerned.

Homework! Homework! What a plight!
Always doing it every night,
And to our books we play the host,
And do the things we dread the most.

In his study the student lies
O'er his books with tired eyes.
On what subject dare he aspire
And get along like a house on fire.

Pity the dumb when they're in doubt
Trying to figure their Latin out;
What a shame to rack their brains
And ruin the little that still remains.

Homework! Homework! What a fight!
Trying to do our lessons right.
Many a man his life has made
By struggling hard to make the grade.

Faith D Campbell
FOR THE LOVE OF A CHILD
So open and giving,
For there's no need to hide
The love and warmth
That they're feeling inside.

The hugs that come easy,
The smiles that mend,
The carefree affection
They give to a friend . . . .

"I like you, I love you"
Is their little song.
Never to worry
That you'll take it wrong.

They mean what they say,
And they do what they feel—
For the love of a child
Is very real.

So open and giving
Like an affectionate pup.
So loving and warm
And then they grow up.

Cynthia D Turner
FRIENDS

To Helen—Because a friend is never a burden; but a privilege.

Losing friends by wrath or time,
leaves a sour stench behind.
We learn to doubt a little more,
we learn to pause when opening doors. The fear of losing what we've got,
becomes a vital kind of clock,
which plays a tune, long forgotten—
"hickory, dickory, dot."

Like mice, companions run away;
forgetting promises to stay, near
beside you—faithful, true.
What's a body now to do?
We close another ear to pain,
hide our eyes from guilt or shame.
Trust a little less, and then,
tell ourselves we need noth'ng.
Tell our hearts it doesn't matter,
talk is cheap like pots that clatter.

Only deep inside—we faint,
'cause this all seems insane.
Is there a place, we need not fear?
someone; somehow, to be secure.
Flesh is weak and sure to fail,
only God peruses hell.
When He binds, the cords are strong.
When He approves the years grow long.

Passion ignites—the nearest tree,
it doesn't even concern me.
Sandstorms, windstorms, snow and sleet—summer floods shall not defeat.
This house is built of brick—
exemplar strong, made of soil
purified. Clay contoured with
Heaven's straw,
cased in granite to endure all the
trials of life's velour.

Sculptured by His hand to cloak,
each child—as they approach.
To His throne, the chamber's long,
something soft—to keep them warm.

Jennifer Mogavero
LET'S DANCE ON THE HEAD
Let's dance on the head
of a bald old man

twirling about on the
(once) hair-filled land

let's dance on the head
of a bald old man

shiny mirrored floor
reflects my glide,
soft smooth skin
makes it tempting
to slide

let's dance on the head
of a bald old man

and after our waltz
we'll climb down to
his brow
and tell him the pleasure
we had on his crown

Shirley M Rice
MY HOUSE
I love my house,
I really do,
I think my kitties
Love it too!

'Cause if they didn't
They wouldn't stay,
They'd pack their bags
And move away.

Adeline A Nunn
NOT VERY GRACIOUSLY
I'm not growing old very graciously
I do not like the way I look.
I've tried every lotion and cream
In every cosmetic book.
Why do we get wrinkles, "crevices," and lines—
Is it stress worrying about the kids,
Or is it the sign of the times?
To be a woman instead of a man,
Methinks she gets the short end of the stick—
We can't even lay out to get a tan
Because our skin does those nasty old tricks.
But whatever fate must be—
Whether blubber or a line,
Show me a woman
For beauty she does not pine.

Annie Brown Kane
FEELINGS

I dedicate this poem to Caroline Brown, without whom, this poem would not be.

Unfortunately for many, feelings change
and abruptly, sometimes premeditated,
leaving scattered shredded feelings askew.
Fortunately for me I am not committed to
feelings I am ruled by them. Yes,
feelings as I feel them do exist that so
deep within and beyond do they
reach that when they cease I will be
no more.
I have wailed in the forest, laughed aloud
on a ship of many, moaned alone,
wiled away a day, pushed a swing
and sang, sang alone, sang along, was
proud, anguished and strong.
Loved so deep that a hatred began to grow,
smiled at the beauty of melting snow.
All that has happened and what will come
to be is the fault of feelings,
many injustices unfortunately.
Life has been good to me although jolted
I've been, and all due to feelings
without and within.

Dr Stanley S Reyburn
MATERIAL MANIA
Automobiles, Bread Bakers, Cookie Cutters,
Dough Mixers, Egg Separators, Fly Sprayers,
Generators, Humidifiers, Ice Makers,
Juicers—and the list goes on

Kitchen Aids, Laundry Twins,
Motorcycles—
Narcissistic Niceties, Outward Opulence,
Prolific Preponderance, Quintessential Quenching—Hedonistic
Indulgences all

Radiophonographs, Stunning Stereos,
Tantalizing Televisions, Unctuous Ukuleles,
Vamping Violins, Whooshing Whirlpools,
Xeric Xeroxes, Yelping Yaks—
All Zonked by a Zorille

The thirst for things material
Can only be allayed by generosity
Through giving lies true redemption
for all mankind!

Janie Criswell
MY LORD
Have you met my Lord
He came two thousand years ago
Did you read or hear about Him
Jesus Christ the Savior

Did He knock at your door yet
Will you let Him in today
I opened my heart to Him
He's now my Lord forever

Can you hear His voice calling
Has He called you yet to hear Him
Jesus is my Lord
He'll keep me day by day

Don't harden hearts to Him
He only helps and never hurts
We hurt ourselves
When we keep Him out

Would you receive my Lord
As your personal Savior
Would you share His love too
Will you believe Him as your Lord

Could my Lord be your Lord
He is quite enough
For all who receive
He is more than enough to all who believe

Chris J Robinette
A BULLET TO BITE ON
I dwell on the failures in my life.
But remember the few happy times there were.
The day I graduated college,
The birth of my daughter,
The day I married Victoria.
Then the failures creep in.
The day Vicki left, due to my neglect?
The false dreams, I sought a future.
My first marriage, I was used to escape home.
The jobs I sought that weren't there.
Living the time schedule of a vampire.
The woman who married another, I was too old and divorced.
But she was a lesbian who switched because of me.
A success, no, a failure because I was used.
The close friends I have; NONE
The only person I have who loves me is my 13 yr. old daughter.
It is because of her love I don't seek,
A bullet to bite on.

Lee Franklin Bertholf
TRUE FRIENDSHIP
If It's stabbed again, a wound starting to heal,
Especially the heart when a scar is revealed.
And when it's reopened it causes pain,
Afraid the canker is there to remain.

When a heart's broken you can't splice the break,
When a heart's aching you can't stop the ache.
Impossible a solution, something special amends,
A heart's wound reopened by once trusted friends.

Though life seems empty with those ones you have lost,
You can always burn bridges after you've crossed.
To lose friends you've trusted, there can be no return,
So much better off if these bridges are burned.

Gone reminiscing, they were good while they last,
Gone future planning, these things are all past.
Receding from view are those fond reveries,
And fading as dew are those sweet memories.

Have met those in life who would never offend,
Not in word or in action, my dearest of friends.
A big heart was throbbing, one God had quite blessed,
A warm hand on your shoulder in

times of distress.

So how much water under that bridge
runs free,
Never to return, as it flows to the sea.
So as false friendship, when distrust
is discerned,
True friendship to one, can never be
returned.

Tessie Lopez
CANDY CANE
Swirls of red and white
sweet with delight
contained by clear plastic
causing senses to go spastic
Anticipating the taste of the first bite

Stop your gawking in my direction
you want to destroy
my plastic protection
lick away my sweet colors
and devour me in minutes not hours

Frances G Snell
SADNESS
She turned her saddened face toward
me and blinked away a tear.
I saw the quivers of her lips, and felt
her sense of fear.

I too had known the sadness, she
tried so hard to hide.
'Twas long ago and far away, that I,
like she had cried.

So then I took her in my arms and
gently stroked her hair.
With cheeks pressed close to mine, I
softly spoke a prayer.

A flood of tears rolled down her
cheeks, the grief she could not hide.
The little body shook with sobs, as on
and on she cried.

Between the sobs, I scarcely heard,
the sad, sad words she said.
"I don't know what I'll ever do my
doll has lost her head."

Teri Rufenacht
THE BEAUTY OF MY WORLD
I feel so good about life today,
Feeling my feelings and finding
new ways.
Admiring the beauty that God gave to
me,
The nature around me there's so
much to see.

To look at the sun, moon, and stars in
the sky,
Is a feeling of joy that lifts me up
high.
The trees and the flowers and plants
all around,
Talk to my soul without making a
sound.

The birds in the sky fly with such
grace,
Watching them soar brings a smile
to my face.
The wind in my hair and the sand on
my feet,
Or a friendly look from someone I
meet.

The mountains majestic, the smell of
fresh air,
The beautiful wonders God gave
us to share.
The animals roaming and standing
with pride,
Gives me a feeling of freedom inside.
The laughter of children, the sound of
their cry,
These things are all free 'til the
day that I die.
So when life gets busy, I'll try to
slow down,
And take time to enjoy all the
beauty around.

Shirley J Rothe
FOR WHAT IT'S WORTH
Our destiny's a mystery, perhaps not
meant to solve,
For if we were the ruler, how might
our lives revolve?
I fear we all would push and shove
To be the first in line,
To grab or take or wish we might
Enjoy a life sublime.
Sublime of all the heartache, the pain
of good or bad,
We wouldn't know the meaning of
the good or bad we've shared.
How wonderful is perfect . . . indeed
what is perfection?
Can looking in a mirror create a pure
reflection?
If only we could see ourselves, as
what we like to think . . .
Do others see us for our worth, or
what we think they think?
Somehow our path in life, it seems
Is maybe what? preset?
We go along from day to day
Accepting what we get.
But also being human, we find a trait
quite rare,
That being only human . . . we love,
we trust, we care.
Whatever fate may deal us, how e'er
the cards may fall,
We have one thing in common . . .
together we stand tall!

R R Montgomery
PLOWMAN'S GULLS
About the toiling plowman and
trailing far behind
The hungry beggars fly in tumbling
white cascade
But no collisions mar their seeming
aimless flights
And many light with hope that they
might find
A snack turned over by the digging
blade.

At acre's edge, no longer counting
every trip,
The dogged farmer turns around
again and plows
With utter disregard for those who
flutter up
Before the tractor's prow so like a
ship
Though this one's wake persists in
ordered rows.

At last with field now fully turned,
the rows complete,
And human energy reduced to lower
measure,
He turns toward home and leaves the
field to gulls alone
Where they can feast at peace, the
field replete
With newly upturned grubs and other
treasure.

Patti Grippo
OCTOBER OUTING
"Miss Dana Dee"
Vivid colors of Blue Greys . . . crisp
clouds of fluff . . .
Takes my breath away!! . . .
In awe of diamonds sparkling on the
water
Waves splashing against the boat!!
In appreciation of what has been
given to us.
A Tribute!! . . . Air . . . like ice
against my face . . . tears turn to frost
. . .
Red orange trees beached near a
quaint gazebo . . .
Oh Beauteous nature . . . it's all here
for our pleasure . . .
Like Jesus Christ
We have been given the privilege of
walking on water!

Emma J Riley
REJECTION
The reality of a lie
Exposed inwardly by sense;
Insidious response
To questions unasked.
I stand in stark solitude,
Clutching a dead dream to my breast;
As the silent truth unveils my sorrow
From craving so much to trust.
I yield to the wretchedness
Of my being cast out;
Stripped of all stature,
Devoid of reason or rapture;
Destined to wander bewildered once
more
The chosen avenue of betrayal.

Walter Bardeck
A BREATHLESS MOMENT
I enjoy
a breathless moment
when I hear
the raucous cries
of the circling crows
that fill
the morning air . . .
and the thunder
of the roaring river
in the mountains
that nestle
under a flawless
blue sky.
I feel
a radiance
in the hush
of the cool evening
when I respond
to the cosmic harmony
in the earth
around me.

Helen W Crawford
LOST GEMS
A sparkling grain of silicon
Was sucked in by a crustacean;
And anchored itself in a vital part
Enclosed in a bubble beneath the
heart;
In secret a perfect sphere took form
Sustained in the ocean beneath the
storm;
Till a diver found the mother alone,
And drew from her the lustrous stone
Too small to give his favorite girl
As a living gem, a precious pearl.

The vibrant seed of a lustful man
Was welcomed in as a maiden can;
And anchored itself in a vital part
Enclosed in a bubble beneath her
heart.
In secret a perfect child took form
Sustained in the womb away from
harm;
Till a medic took the mother aside,
And drew from her the one that died
Too small to hope for a famous goal
As a living gem, a precious soul.

Katheryn L Davidson
SILENT ANGEL
Silent angel,
Hair of gold,
Eyes of blue,
Bodice of white,
Fly down from the sky,
Grace the sunset with your motions.

Silent angel,
Speak to me,
As I can hear your silence,
It isn't words as other's know,
But emotions swaying softly in the
breeze.

Silent angel,
With eyes of blue,
Into lifelessness I wonder,
Floating into your arms,
I answer with song.

Silent angel,
Shall we leave together,
Embrace me,
I shall you.

Ruth L Wolf
REMEMBERING
Live each day like it's your last day
on earth
Take joy in the pleasures you've had
Maybe they'll overcome your
sorrows and things that were sad
Give thanks for good friends and
people you've met
That helped you along the way
And enjoy the times you've helped
others
And bless all fathers and mothers
Take time out to forgive the
unforgiven
But most of all be thankful for your
children
For they are the greatest gift God has
given

Clara B Bishop
AL'S PLACE
Al's Place in Brewery Gulch
was a well kept secret to most of us,
until one day in the Gazette
this esteemed scout we once again
met.

Thoughts then turned to earlier days
when the mention of his name
evoked some praise.

For missions accomplished and great
deeds done
lives that were saved because of this
one,
whose skill and courage goes mostly
unsung.

Did you stop at Al's Place and hear
him tell
of Crook, the Apache Kid and others
as well?

Of Horn, Geronimo And San Carlos
too,
of long night rides with old friends
and new.
Of danger and hardships as a way of
life,
of success or failure and times of
strife.

Just a minute Old Timer, won't you
please
stop and share your experience of
Al's Place when Sieber was there.

Joe B Freeman
THE SEEDS OF KINDNESS
As I walked through a field one day
I spied a small plant along the way
Among the thistles and weeds it grew
I wondered how it could make it through

The summer was hot as I looked again
I thought, surely by now it had seen the end
But the plant had grown up through the weeds
This flower had risen from tiny seeds

The next time I looked I saw a bloom
A beautiful specimen among the gloom
A thing so rare among the weeds
I thought, this compares with kindly deeds

How one who loves with strength to win
Can overcome the weeds of sin
How love can grow with beauty rare
Standing above the ones who do not care

Sarah Stinson Brewer
SPRING
If I had but one song to sing,
It would be about the Spring.
All the birds singing in the trees,
While they swing gently in the breeze;
All the flowers with blooms so bright,
They even shine in the moonlight;
A walk through the woods that look so new,
The grass looks like diamonds in the dew;
The scent so sweet, you just know,
It will stay with you wherever you go.
Every season is good in its own way,
But I wish Spring was here to stay!

Linda Lerner
MY AUNT HELEN
This is my last present to you, dear Aunt.
You should have had the world, this seems so scant.
This is not a great poem, just true thoughts from my heart.
I admired you all my life, it's so hard to part.
I understood and loved you even with your faults.
To treat you less than kind would have been assaults.
My Uncle said I made you feel like a Queen,
That's what you deserved, your greatness always seen.
I only wished you knew what you were worth.
You must have been special from the day of your birth.
You were so intelligent, more than any Ph.D.,
So very good to the core, that was the key.
I loved you so from the day I was born,
And that is why I feel so forlorn.
A jeweler will tell you the best gem is a stone,
But my Aunt Helen was more valuable, this was well known.
I know I'll see you some day but I don't know when.
I love you so much . . . till we meet again.

A Scott Whittaker
LEAVES
Autumn has fallen
softly
on the trees.
The shadow of winter
lightly brushes
their leaves.
Covering them in colors
to green from gold,
dropping violet,
red and yellow snow.

The snowy fall soon, leaves fading
into the barren hues of brown,
returns to the mother
from which it had grown.
The colors turning
lifeless in old age,
touched by the shadow
of death's cold grey.

Bonnie M Chapman
I CARE . . .
I wish that I could hold you
and hug your hurt away.
I'd tell you not to be sad
tomorrow is another day.

My heart always goes out to you.
I wish I were a clown
to bring you a smile and laughter
when you're feeling down.

There are words to encourage
"Chin up!" or "Hang in there!"
But, what I'm trying to tell you
is simply, that I care.

So if it helps, I'm here for you.
Anytime, night or day.
A warm heartfelt hug, my arms hold you
in a caring, loving way.

J Skedz
MADE FOR EACH OTHER
Their love had turned to history—
A love they'd thought would last.
But it really's not such a mystery
Why their future's in the past.

Love gets claustrophobic
When it's just what's convenient for you.
And it's gotta be stifling
When you've got so many better things to do.

Waiting for your own dreams to unfold
Is a difficult enough task.
But asking someone else to believe and wait
Is just too much to ask.

So they try not to remember
All those times they made each other's day.
When they gave each other strength and serenity
And chased those blues away.

And they live their lives of fantasies
Which sometimes do come true.
They fantasize of meeting their destinies—
In their case, destiny number two.

M T Gant
IDENTITY
An utterance of being,
a stairway to dreams,
contained within
identity.
A simplistic gesture of
the primordial passion—
to fashion,
create,
obliterate.

Identity is that
of the seed
which acknowledges
creed.

The stare of space:
life's fertilization:
identity's consecration.

Of will, of fate,
and physical state,
identity
is the necessity
in creating
reality.

Donna Martian
INDIAN ROCK DAZZLE
He comes to me with
a trust so deep
Like a bronze beauty
in ancient times.
Slowly he stops beside me
and permits me to pet
his sleek neck. He stomps
his foot in eager readiness,
ready for the upcoming run.
We sail off in a brisk breeze
burning up the rolling prairie.
It's just wind, my horse and I.

Elizabeth Roberts
FEELING BLUE
My sweetheart I know it's true
that very often I'm feeling blue

I cry out for help don't you care
can you hear me are you there

I know life isn't just you and me
but is this all there's supposed to be

I always thought that love would be bliss
how come I always feel there's a lot I miss

You're kind and unselfish to the core
so dear God how come I want a lot more

I feel so alone you see
even though you love me, you keep telling me

I've heard you cry out with love in your heart
with tears in your eyes that was unable to start

I just want to love you please give me the chance
to uncover the feelings I've been trying to lance

The words are so bitter we say to each other
when I try to release your self-made cover

We inflict on ourselves so much pain
please help me to make love feel true once again

Bethel Nunley Evans
FRIENDSHIP OF WORTH

Dedicated to wonderful friends: Pastor and Wife, Dr. Clyde and Betty Jo Herring; Minister of Music, Jerry Cronin; and Sunday School teacher, Juanita Firestone.

Friendship is something hard to define.
It is a welcome smile, a cheerful mind,
A shoulder to cry on, someone who cares,
And knowing one you love is always near.

In a most sincere and heartfelt way
And loving you more each passing day,
That is why I am expressing this so clear
To let you know how much I really care.

If I could lend a helping hand
To you, my friend, and you would understand,
Or give a smile to light your way along
The path of life and make you strong—

And give a word of cheer when you feel weary
Or comfort you when your days are dreary,
In this way I would surely understand your needs
And fill your life with caring deeds.

As a sign of peace, He sent the Dove
From His heart so very full of love—
If I could only follow this beautiful trend,
Then I would surely always be your friend!

Maria E Conlon
MESSAGES IN THE SAND

Written for, and inspired by John, and the love and moments we share.

The trees sway gently
wind blowing through,
As the breeze caresses my shoulders
whispering thoughts of you.

Slowly you come to me
arms form around my waist,
Silently I find myself
in your loving embrace.

Standing on the shoreline
watching the sun disappear,
Tenderly you kiss me
and your strength pulls me near.

Watching the night
as the skies fill with stars,
Knowing that this moment
is forever ours.

Scratching our messages
across this damp sand,
"I LOVE YOU" we wrote
and left hand in hand.

Kathleen Taylor
IF I HAD KNOWN
If I had known when we made love last
That we were going to age so fast
It doesn't seem that long ago
That I held you and loved you so

And just because the years have flown
And all our wild oats we have sown
It doesn't mean my love has died these many years
It only means the ocean's risen with all my tears

My love for you will never die
No matter how many years will fly
If I had known our dreams would not come true
I'd do these years all over—but only my love if they're with you

Sheri Lynn Brown
MY SOUL

This poem is dedicated to my mum, who has been my best friend and confidante all of my life. I love her dearly. Love & Kisses!

I looked into the water
And found my soul.
It was floating aimlessly
With the natural flow.
I picked it up and
Held it close to me.
I smiled and whispered,
"I'm glad I found thee."
I held it up to heaven
And asked God to give it life.
He warmed my soul
And ended all its strife.

Rebecca J Knipp
BEHIND THE OPEN DOOR
You're sovery special to no one else but me,
In the person who you are the one that you will be.
You make me happy when I'm sad,
You're the one who makes me glad.
You're everything I wanted and a whole lot more,
For you my love, there will always be an open door.
Open it and you will see,
The one who loves you, that is me.

Joanna Parks
THE SECRET PLACE
The secret place of wonder, the private place, I love to go.

The unknown place of magic, the secret place I have never shown to any other person besides myself.

I go there when I am troubled, I flee to my secret place when I'm full of tears.

I run there with all my might when I have been hurt. I hide in my private place when I am frightened and full of fear.

This secret place of magic, this private place of my heart,
This unknown place to others, always comforts me,

always comforts me.

For it is a place I can flee to.

Mavis Holts Smith
LITTLE ANGEL
Where are you little angel?
Are you still tiny or grown up tall?
I never got to know
You flew away so soon.

You are still in my memories.
I felt your heart beat next to mine,
For nine long months of waiting
Then to lose you oh so quickly.

They tell me you might have been sickly
Had you stayed on earth that day.
Only God and you know the answer.
I only know you are safe and happy
In our God's tender care.

Please forgive me when days go by
And you are not remembered.
Just know that some day we will be together
In a world out there somewhere.

Fire Ludwick
CHILD'S FINAL CRY
Over there in the corner she sits all alone.
Dreaming of someone to come take her home.
Her eyes filled with tears and her heart with pain.

Now by the window, she stares t'wards the skies.
Remembering broken promises she wished had come true.
Her heart filled with tears and her eyes upward gazed.
This child's cries for help often pushed aside,
not knowing who to trust she often hides inside.

Again in the corner with tear filled eyes she cries.
Forgetting not the pain the world has given her.
Her heart filled with pain and her eyes with tears.

Now alone in an empty room she stands there quietly.
Thinking of all went wrong and life's coming end.
Her eyes filled with pain and her heart upward gazed.
This child's cries for help so often pushed aside,
not knowing who to trust she often hides inside.

Look into my eyes,
Look into my heart,
I am this child,
This child is me.

Pat Simmons
TO THE MEN OF MAR-DET

This poem is written and dedicated to my son and the Marine Detachment on the USS Constellation *for their dedication to duty during the Persian Gulf Conflict—1987—For Marine Cpl. Ron Simmons.*

To the men of Mar-Det
On the Aircraft Carrier *Constellation*,
I'd like to make this dedication.

Your job's not easy, the stress is high,
But upon each other, you do rely.
Your support is obvious, when danger is near,
And the Mar-Det goes into high gear.

Bound by loyalty, to each other,
The detachment survives, so commend one another.
A more dedicated group, I cannot conceive,
Committed to the task, in which we all believe.
Freedom for all, is the duty call,
And our Marines will always stand tall.

Fighting on land and in the air,
Or on the ships that sail our seas,
We count on you to the 'enth degree.

Sea duty's not easy, that fact is sold,
But you are loyal to the scarlet and gold.
So when we see our ships at sea,
Pray for Mar-Det and the USMC.

Margie Alari Amado
LOVE OF A FLY

To my beloved children—Margaret A. Stone, Charlene B. Davidson, Edwina L. Aylward and Son Edward Guy Amado.

No love have I, sighed the tiny female fly!
I don't know how to flirt, that's probably why
Now Honey fly, you know you shouldn't lie
You have all my love, crooned the big black fly.
Let us wing to the far-out country, out in the West
And I'll show you the scenery, finest and the best
Your love have I? crooned the tiny female fly.
Yes, you have my undying love, you beauty of a fly
You with your charming fluttering way, makes me feel so happy and sly.
Come away with me, and I'll show you where lies a delicious pie.
Let us zoom into the great expanse of sky above
together we'll roam the country-side, with you by my side
close to me and my love.

Margie Alari Amado
FRIENDS

FRIENDS

In this life, everyone needs a jewel or two
the kind, I have in mind—the rarest in
this world of ours, a very special kind.

FRIENDS

There with you, when you're happy and when you're in despair.
There by your side—to let you know, how much they really care.
They have laughed and danced some nights away,
and with you have gone sailing in the bay.
Have held your hand when you've been sad
forgiven you, when you've been mad.

FRIENDS

When worries have caused tension and strife
they gently remind one, that this will occur in every-one's life.
When tears are shed, they will hug you close
give their full support—and chase away your fears.

Margie Alari Amado
HOME

HOME

There is this place of comfort and delight, that welcomes me every night—upon entering the door what a wonderful sight. Loved ones waiting and the sound of a child laughing and soft music playing.

HOME

Home is the greatest refuge, where troubles one seeks to escape, endeavoring to solve before it's too late. The loving atmosphere within the walls, instills the fore-sight that all troubles will soon abate.

Relaxing and sleeping until the early dawn, retrieving the paper from the damp green lawn.
Sipping a cup of hot fresh brew, while reading the early
morning news.
Snuggling in our favorite chairs, with toes curled under nice and bare.
A neighbor comes to call, asking "is there a cup of coffee to spare?"
Mother, answers yes—delicious
blintzes and dough-nuts, as well.

HOME

There is this place of comfort and delight, that welcomes
every-one.

M Elisabeth Steiner
AN AMERICAN TREASURE: A TRIBUTE TO LUCILLE BALL
She was a pioneer in television,
"The Foremost Queen of Comedy," they called her.
Richly blessed with great talent, grace and beauty,
She could perform a variety of roles,
But was especially adept as a clown.
A perfectionist, throughout her long career,
She was inducted into "The Hall of Fame,"
And showered with ever so many honors
Which she accepted humbly and graciously.
She brought much humor into the nation's homes;
Her skits were so universal and timeless,
That one could easily identify with them.
Her creative, zany antics were priceless;
She could master any brand of comedy.
Her "fleeting moment in endless time" has passed,
And she now resides in "The House of The Lord,"
Where there is no death, only eternal life,
And the joy and laughter she has brought with her.
She was truly an American treasure,
An irreplaceable gem in entertain-ment.

Joanne L Balzano
'TWAS UNBRIDLED PASSION
lurking about;
A dormant submission
Fulfilling the doubt,
Of realm's satisfaction
A taste so sublime
Hunger's emotion
Starved by time.

Walden F Lomayesva
LIFE
Life is rough, Life is tough, sometimes
all that we have is not enough.
Many times battles were lost, but somehow
we knew the dreaded cost.
So many people have lost the drive
So many lives have taken a dive.
But here today we sit alive, knowing
that people can survive.
Without support of a friend or neighbor
we tend to forget about our earthly labor.
So now we know that there is hope,
from now to the end we all shall cope.

Paul Morgan
MAGICAL RAINBOW
As I strolled a hillside
one rainy April day;

I walked through a rainbow
and then had this to say:

"magical rainbow—
arching the sky;
your pastel wet-colors
are hung out to dry.

magical rainbow—
gold at each end;
shining example of
nature's pure-blend.

magical rainbow—
for all eyes to see;
sunlight reflected
ethereally.

magical rainbow—
when showers bid goodbye;
your rare perfect-beauty
then fades from the sky."

Elizabeth Wood

GONE

A feeling
deep
hard as stone
cold as ice
cuts like a knife
it turns and kicks
it grows inside
it calls out
but no one listens.
A feeling
deep
lying down, eyes closed
for everyone to see
A feeling
deep
now they hear it
now they feel it
A feeling
deep, for me it's gone.

Kelli Miesse

FOREVER NIGHT (MOONLIGHT SPLITS THE DARKNESS)

Moonlight splits the darkness, and
Starlight shatters the night, while
The clock keeps ticking the seconds away
As a valiant man fights for his life.

Winds wail a dirge of mourning;
Stars shed tears of sorrow—they're grieving for the child in her Father's arms—
Her heart fears the Dawn of Tomorrow.

Swift wings snatch all hope away, as
Desolate Fate stretches out its hand—
to claim the soul of one so dear.
To wrest the spirit from a dying man.

Moonlight is swallowed by Darkness.
Remnants of the stars fade away.
All life has fled from her Father's arms,
Death has claimed its prize.
Night has come to stay.

Kathryn Louise Davis

A THING WITHIN REASON

For a thing within reason is what I would pay
So plainly and simply a hug for each day.
A kiss on the cheek would my loved ones bestow.
'Twould take me afar to the golden row
Of roses and daffodils smelling so sweet.
The offspring of butterflies light at my feet.
The soar of the tanager colored so bright;
The wishes of miracles heartfelt so tight.
Yes, a thing within reason is what I long for
To shelter the feelings and open the door
To the stretching of arms from my loved ones some day,
So, for a thing within reason is what I would pay.
The years take its toll as the time passes by;
No repeat of our histories can we deny.
Take hold of your passions and set them aside
For the treasures of heaven, at home they abide.
For a thing within reason I can easily face
It's the love of a family that falls into place.

Leslie A Astle

LITTLE LEAF LITTLE LEAF

Little Leaf Little Leaf falling from the tree
Little Leaf Little Leaf what do you see
Little Leaf Little Leaf laying on the ground
Little Leaf Little Leaf what have you found
Little Leaf Little Leaf please don't cry
You will find new adventures by and by

Kathy Peterson

DARLING

You are the best thing
that ever happened to me.
You are always there
when I need you
We had a very special
little girl.
My life has turned
out better than I
had ever expected.
I love you. With
all of my heart.

Betty Bass

WATER TO LIFE

I sat on the bank of the river today,
Kept watch on the water below.
I saw it move quietly down the right way
Like life a direction to go.

So peaceful the water as ripples were made
Although it flowed so fast.
Gently it rocked while breezes played,
How calm and unbroken at last.

Then all of a sudden the warning sound,
A motor—the boat now in sight,
In rebellion the water tossed all around
And just when it was doing alright!

I sat there thinking, it's so much like life
The changes I've had all the way,
The problems and trials, the peace and the strife
Encountered like the river today.

Now the water keeps going, it just doesn't stop
Because something broke its quiet flow.
Ripples became waves but stayed right on top
And onward through time I must go.

Daryll Bradshaw

SAND AND TREES

If the desert could speak
what would it say?
Would it be angry for the searing
heat it must endure each day?
Maybe it would curse the barrenness of itself.
Could it scoff the lizards that rummage
through it?
Who would dare to say?

If the forest could cry out
What would it cry?
Would mankind be at blame for the
damage it does?
Or maybe the weather that beats
down upon it.
Who would dare to say?

So why should I curse myself
If the desert is content then
why not I?
If the forest still provides shelter
then why can't I?
Why? because I'm human that's why.

Ann S Ford

THE BIG CYPRESS CAMP

As I hike among the cypress tress,
I feel on my face a cooling breeze.
The sweet singing voice of the mocking bird,
Throughout the woods can be heard.
The peace and quiet allows me to hear,
The sounds of the nearby Florida deer.
A light rain falls down upon my head,
Resurrecting a fern from the dead.
As the smell of the barbeque reaches my nose,
A feeling of hunger reaches down to my toes.
The hunters return from their hunting trip,
Dragging turkey gobblers on their hips.
After dinner, and a long walk,
It's out to the swing for evening talk.
The owl in the hammock watches over all,
As we listen for his hooting call.
As the glow of the sunset begins to go,
It's back to the cabin for I must go.
As the evening comes to a close,
The burning embers in the fireplace glow.
Fond memories of days gone by.

Cynthia Culp

I AM AT EASE NOW

I am at ease now.
My soul is at rest.
There shall be no more
sorrow, fears, pain, or agony.
There will only be peace and
happiness for me now.
I am dead.

Shirley McGann

FEELINGS FOREVER

Nights go by without a word as I sit
by the phone and wait,
Not understanding why you haven't called.
It may sound silly to you, but
sometimes I think you're the only one for me.
We have had fun together for some time now,
I wish it could last forever.
In your voice I can hear the
sound of something troubling you.
I want the hurt to go away, except you won't talk,
I try to get you to talk but it's no use.
You call and say nothing,
What can I do for you to talk?
Well another night is over and we had our fun,
Now you say to me that it's over,
For you still have feelings for that
other girl.
I am upset and I will cry,
But I hope you know I have feelings
for you inside,
And will have feelings for you
forever!

Cody Bryson

INDEFINITE BURIAL

Holding to her breast,
the fading beauty of a rose.
The crimson petals wilting,
gently shaking to and fro.
Her hands quietly folded,
across the thornless emerald stem.
Her eyes softly closed,
lost in oblivion to them.
Her lips slightly pursed,
and painted a delicate stain.
The color shining from
the tenderly falling drops of rain.
Her auburn locks,
fluid about her face,
resting upon a pillow
made of satin and of lace. About her are shining walls, made of beautiful obsidian,
closing her off,
into her world of oblivion.
A shadow moves forward,
its being dressed in gray.
Within its grasp,
it holds roses in their dark array.
It takes hold of the lid
made of stone as dark as night.
And pulls it closed,
and then locks it tight.
It places the flowers upon the stone,
without a murmur or a sound.
And six handsome men,
lower love into the ground.

Angela Marie Sanchez

PEACE TO THEE

Gracefully I glide through the sands of the universe,
Viewing the sorrows of the world through the eyes of a
Never ending ocean, which races the wind in the mirrored sky
That captures the prayers of the immortal souls who cry out
For peace.

I am one within myself needing no one to walk beside me.
I am my savior, shedding tears with the moon, hearing
My heart as it shouts "Peace to thee."

The clouds that mock the sadness within me, carry me
Through a rainbow of hope, casting happiness around me
Giving me a longing feeling for joy today
For I may not be graced with the honor of tomorrow.
"Peace to thee."

Domenico Urbani
TO THE ARISING SUN

To my grandson Anthony, proudly I dedicate this rime may the Lord bless him, kindly guide him thru the journey of time.

What beauty of splendor to see the arising sun
look so distantly as far as your eyes will meet
you witness God's power the will second to none
you feel the warmth all over, one amazing fete.

With you dear sun our day begins at dawn
comfort you are to the world (entire) with heat
even the sailor can call on you at dawn
by telling time, by marching to your beat.

There with you dear sun the great orient appears
to me, so fascinated by the mighty ray,
when you are in dusk the living disappears.

There with you we will begin to pray,
we feel secure, the dear God is near
to bless us, as we proceed for one more passing day.

Matthew Tracy Hallman
HAS BEEN
They say, "enough with this day,"
we know so much of tomorrow,
we grew so fast, beyond prediction.
Technology is no longer science-fiction,
but tell me the man a hundred years ago
is the same man a hundred years from now.
The only prediction will be our second, third, fourth guessing.
People confronting people that finally confront themselves.

And so far we're done living because
we "sort of" know enough to predict.
We'll never finish planning because
we'll never finish the plan.

Arthur L Richards
AN AMERICAN DREAM

I dedicate this poem to the memory of my mother, Dorothy Allen. No one could give more.

In an old shack
With no heat, up north
On a concrete floor,
A blanket for a bed,
Our mother's arms around us,
Our body warmth to shield us
From the cold,
This love I have known;
To a beautiful house on a hill,
Everyone should know such a love,
Live such a dream.

Reynaldo Trejo
MELODY WITHIN
Upon the grass within the mist,
Globules of dew descend from the leaves.
A warm ray from the east,
The awakening of daybreak.

The petals of the flowers begin to
Expand, the butterflies dance to
A melancholy waltz in the wind.

I stand gazing to the sky, while the
Sweet aroma of the flowers enfold me.

The butterflies, with a silken white petal
From a rose, dry the pearls that so
Lightly fall from my eyes.

The melody warms my heart.
Realizing it's not only I
In existence, but all in life.

My eyes open to the warmth of the sun.
A silken petal upon my windowsill,
And a butterfly dancing, to a
Sweet melody within my heart.

Reynaldo Trejo
SIGH OF LOVE
I've walked through passages
That once hand in hand we crossed.

What moments of jubilant thoughts
That were left behind but not
To be forgotten.

In existence, reflections of the mind.
The open arms of the sea,
And the love we shared, which I
Hold and store forever in my heart.

The sea is very serene.
The sea gulls silent at my side.

The breeze, in a melancholy motion
Dries the tears that overflow with
Pain and anger from the soul.

I cannot render to the thought
Of losing you. My love expands
Like the wings of a sea gull in flight.

Soaring over the vast oceans so the
Tears from my heart will mingle in
Ecstasy with the deep of the sea.

Reynaldo Trejo
SWEET OBSCURITY
As the wings of a sleeping angel spread
Bringing forth the twilight that covers the day
I feel that it not only covers the day
But also my soul.

The expansion of obscurity
An overflowing emotion superim-poses on my being,
Bringing with it such an incompre-hensible
Sweet sorrow.

I pray to thee, for a beam of your warmth
So as to enlighten this disillusioned heart.

Oh such obscurity dwells within.
Oh despair that blinds the heart,
And emotions that seem like currents
Flowing with love and confusion.

Oh sweet obscurity, I beckon thee,
Have mercy, my heart is heavy,
And my soul lamenting, for the one
I love has forgotten me.

Monica Sutton
INTENSITY
Light forgets taken me through
Forgets to listen, understand
me through.
Forgets darkness of me
Covers my darkness through.

Ruth Mellby White
MINNESOTA PRAIRIE

To my Minnesota pioneer–Parents Dr. & Mrs. Oscar F. Mellby.

Prairie winds fan the burning chaff
Last of the wheat
Red delight in the dark August night
Top of the world—everywhere sky
Fiery sun sets along the horizon
Glowing northern lights—like cathedrals
Exciting the heavens.
Freezing snowdrifts in winter
The river solid ice.
Wires along the roads whine and sing
In the stinging cold—
Like eerie tunes of valkyries
Visions arise in the mist (or cold)
Of riders to Valhalla
Their steeds blowing clouds of vapor
Forming outlines of bearded Gods.

Ruth Mellby White
DEVON
The blue skies
fading into eve
Remind me of Devon
and her bluebell eyes
The shade of flowers
on Minnesota prairies
A precious child
Cheeks so pink
Like rose petals
Hair like spun gold
Figure of a gazelle
A pure delight.

Ruth Mellby White
FOG
Fog 'tis of the sea
or of the mind.
what vast differences
For fog of the mind is
disconcerting – disabling
disconnecting and
frightening
Real from unreal – unreal from real
Sea fog has salt–invigoration–
a softness – a
mysterious
quiet
A blanking out of outlines.
The mind fog blanks out memory
clarity &
befuddles the
brain
I love the sea fog as it blankets mu city of hills
Bringing an air of mystery.
It creates beauty – erases reality of cements
Building lights shine through its haze – golden &
shimmering
Now here – now gone – leaving no footsteps
No tracerty of its path
Yet – it enlivens the stately redwoods
moistening its
high tops
Salt scrubs everything clean
I love the fog;
San Francisco – London – I've revelled in both
It caresses the skin –moistens it with dew
Shadows are created where naught was before
Sea fog cleans
Mind fog muddles
A mysterious fairyland emerges from concrete dirt
& jagged form
In the mind confusion and disfunction
Oh Fog of the sea
wash into my mind
Erase our fogginess
Cleanse and purify my fuzzy cells

Norma Madison
MEMORIES
I'm sitting thinking of times gone by
Thinking of things that might have been
Then I give a big sigh
Thinking of fun, with friends and kin
I wouldn't exchange it for anything
Not silver, gold or a diamond ring.
Some things you just can't buy
Including memories of times gone by—
What could I have done to change my course?
That's something I will never know
Only with GOD's guiding force
could I ever, even grow
I guess I am the way he wanted me to be.
Free to choose, free to see
Did I choose right? Did I choose wrong?
That is what has made me strong
GOD with all his infinite wisdom
Keeps us safe, and free from boredom
Free to choose our own direction
There we make our own selection.

Norma Madison
REFLECTIONS
Looking into the mirror of Life
There was some good times, there was some strife
I did some great things, some not so great
That's something to which we can all relate
Did I try my very best, along the way?
I thought I did, but who is to say?
Look ever so closely in the mirror of Life
See, there I am, my own reflection
Look closely, is there any sign of detection?
Can you see yourself as others see you?
Probably not, What you see, is what you want to—
The image in the mirror is distorted
"That is not really me" I retorted
But, as I look so very closely—I come into focus
Yes, that is me, that's no "hocus pocus"
Like it or not, that is me
for all the world to see
and judge.
But, I am free—
I dare to be me.

Cyril Stuart Potter
THE END OF THE RAINBOW

To Toni Allard from C. S. Potter.

I saw a rainbow standing by
it came upon me from the sky
as I approached no one near
yet very clear the brilliant colors
anchored there

The road was there the circle of the concrete bare
The earth gave birth to color there.

Carolyn Y Wallace

Carolyn Y Wallace
ART

To my special friend, Willie Charles Smith, who encourages me to write, and to my sons, Diallo Sekou and Jafari Sadiki, who inspire me to write.

The pictures on my wall
state it all.
How can I challenge you to look,
and be certain you grasp
the scenes and intricate details
of how many years and how many endeavors
it took.

How can I move you inside
as my brush glides
across the naked canvas with feeling.
If only I could guide
you to look deep inside,
as you look outside,
you'd capture the world
of which I am dealing

Isabelle L Gagnon
THE LIGHT'HOUSE
Ships marooned on desolate Isle—
Man cold and weary . . . lost for miles.
The fog is heavy; oh, so dark and drear.
Did they not see a Light'House? I was so near.
Numerous ships are torn and tossed.
Oh, Shipwrecked Vessel, I see the loss;
In the distance, I saw Thy plight;
I was there—in the night.
My Light'House shines through storm and fog;
I am the Light'House, the Son of God.
The Course is guided on troubled seas;
The Helm controlled sufficiently.
This vessel need not be lost at sea
Nor tossed and torn endlessly . . .
My Light shines bright day and night.
Calvary provided My saving light.
I am the Light'House.

Isabelle L Gagnon
THE EAGLE
We know that "they that wait upon the Lord shall renew their strength;
They shall mount up with wings as eagle's
They shall run, and not be weary;
They shall walk, and not faint."
I have never seen an Eagle
Nor seen the wings of width, and length—
Nor seen her fly from great mountain top
Across valleys with grace, and strength—
I have heard of her great protection
As she teaches her young to fly—
"Mount up in proper position"
Toward Heaven is her cry
Oh! the training for the young is weary
She knows they need to rest—
With her wings mounted up, she carries
Her young back home to their nest—
"Lord, when I'm tired, and weary
In my heart, I can always sing—
I know that you are here with me
Carrying me on under your wings."

Isabelle L Gagnon
HOW I LONG FOR YESTERDAY

Dedicated to my seven daughters: Darlene, Patty, Janet, Sharon, Kathy, Marka and Carol.

Lord, You gave me special daughters;
Unique and loving in their own way.
I thank You, Lord, for every one;
At times, I long for Yesterday.
They are grown-up women now,
With children of their own . . .
How I would love to kiss good night
And have them all at home.
Oh! How I long for Yesterday;
The laughter, the ribbons in curly hair,
Rocking and singing lullabies
On my own special rocking chair.
Lord, they are now doing as I did
And I see myself in them.
Oh! How I long for Yesterday,
So I could do these things again.
Lord! Thank you for my grandchildren,
And when the memories start,
Thank You, Lord, for Yesterday
And the room for all within my heart.

Isabelle L Gagnon
DEBBIE'S IN GOD'S FLOWER GARDEN NOW
Oh, the vile, incurable disease
That claimed my child, so dear.
She was so sweet and special
Through all her pain and tears.
It's often hard to comprehend
Why children suffer pain . . .
Then, suddenly, the fragrance of flowers
Is very real again.

There is a very special love
Within the heart of a dying child—
"I love you, Mommy," and with a hug,
The end soon came, her final mile.
In the mournful hours, God spoke to me,
"You see her with the physical eye,
Full of a vile disease;
I see her as My special flower
And now, her pain has ceased."
As I look at the dying children,
And hear of their final hours,
I know just where God will place them:
With Debbie, in His special Garden of Flowers.

Isabelle L Gagnon
THE BEAUTY IN MY ROSE

Dedicated to my Precious daughter, Carol.

The beauty of a Perfect Rose
Is how I look at you.
You turned disability into abilities—
As a Rose is touched by morning dew.
Your limbs were broken, every one,
As you were thrown upon the ground.
Lovely Roses lose their petals . . .

My Rose turned her life around.
God looks upon a fragile Rose,
As He does all others.
He does not see imperfections;
Over all, His love doth hover.
Storms do come with winds of fury
And bring on the stinging rain . . .
My fragile Rose withstands it all,
And soon she blooms again.
My darling daughter, I love you;
And as I watched you grow,
You looked beyond your handicap;
You're the beauty of a Perfect Rose.

Pedro S Llarinas

Pedro S Llarinas
BONDS OF FRIENDSHIP

To all my Beloved Friends, who in many ways have given me their support, appreciation, encouragement and inspiration in my attempt to write Poetry.

When your Mood has the shade of Blue
As your Friend, I should be there beside you
Offer my shoulders for your tears to fall to
Say a few Loving words to comfort you.

Press my cheeks gently against your reddish cheeks
Touch my Lips tenderly to your enchanting lovely Lips
Feel your Heart beating against my breast
Whispering "I Love You" you are my Best Friend.

Then LOVE from my Heart drives the blue Shade away
Forces your worries, anxieties to be gone in anyway
Brightens your Mood, gives you Ideas to comprehend
You have confided in me, trusted Me, your Best Friend.

If Fate intervenes, forces us to go separate ways
My heart, my Love, my prayers, be with you always
My best wishes, my Friendship, be with you wherever you are
You're my Inspiration, your happiness and Love, I earnestly desire.

Bonds of Friendship will always be accepted
By true Friends, lovers, relatives, everyone concerned
Chains and Bonds maybe loosened . . . or . . . unlocked
But sweet fond Memories will remain in their Hearts.

Bonds of Friendship assure Friends, FOND MEMORIES, Happiness.

Lou Parker
SPACE

To my childhood friend, D.A.H.

If space is what you want
that's what I'm giving you
To find your true feelings about me
about you

If you find the true love in your heart
perhaps we can forget the past
we've wasted and
find a new start for you and for me
But if you're not sure, please don't
come at all
just keep putting more space between us
my old heart can't take another
fall . . . .

Lou Parker
OLD MAN AGE
Oh, you ugly, mean devil
just why do you do that to such
beauties
Why do you stare and enjoy
in the young years
Then twist, mangle, and wrinkle
steal their sight and sound
their memories so renowned
Steal their hair of brilliant color
leaving little, if any
Stealing strength, leaving senility
you cruel bastard, why do you do
it?
What chance have they . . . I mean
we . . .
Who would choose the alternative . . . .

Maria J Piñeiro
SEARCHING FOR A NEW LIFE
One, solitary leaf
Rustles down the street.
Old, ragged sneakers
I wear on my feet.
I'm travelling alone
In this cruel, wretched world.
All my hopes and dreams
Rot away — spoiled.
I fight on in this life —
Fighting against Fate.
I can't run around crying;
I just can't wait.
I've got to find a new world;
One that makes me strong.
I've got to break away;
Find a place where I belong.
I'm standing at a locked door,
But I don't have the key.
Perhaps this life I search for
Begins with you and me.

John Pfeiffer
CONJECTURE

To Mrs. Fran Crumpton, my teacher and inspiration.

Consider Atlas, whose Eternal Job
Was to bear a stained glass orb,
teeming with
Far more responsibilities than a
Crown of thorns. A glittering,
priceless pearl
Expelled by some edgy oyster; this
was
The sole possession of the great
Atlas.
If not a man, then who can bear the
World?

God, you say: Omnipotent,
Omniscient.
And I propose this: to hold a world
'twixt
Thumb and forefinger does take
godly precision
And nerves of refined steel. Many
thoughts
Must course through the mind of
mortal Atlas
Causing him to flinch and quiver;
falter
In his dedication to preservation.
If this is so, a thoughtless creature
Would be required: Reflexive,
Mindless.
Some say this revelation has merit.
Conclusion: God, existing entity
In repose, has neither thought nor
feeling
For the world (worlds) within Its
grasp. Waiting,
Soundless, for that moment when It
pinches.

Shelley B Pehr
THE LIGHTHOUSE
The lighthouse beam outshines the
brightest star
beckoning to ships from near and afar
A more welcome sight there could
never be
to sailors navigating the rough, angry
sea
Guiding ships from a lighthouse off
the coast of Maine
was a crusty ex-sailor, Sam, who
knew the sea's pain
Through twenty-five seasons of fair
weather or downpour
Sam had faithfully welcomed
returning vessels to shore
Alas, his lighthouse was about to feel
automation's icy touch
which tomorrow would put an end to
the job he loved so much
As Sam glanced out the window with
an old pipe in hand
yet another ship was about to reach
land
The sailors rushed for the warm
shelter nearby
but one of them was in no hurry to
dry
For his true love was running to meet
him, her hair and dress wet
after six months of dreaming, their
eyes at last met
Sam watched the couple frolic in the
bad weather
proud that his lighthouse finally
brought them together
Although the lighthouse has long
been abandoned by all
a beam of light continues to fall
As the winds and tides swirl round
the shore
the lighthouse beams forevermore.

Marta T Pascuzzo
SUPPLICATION
I reach out for comfort in the
darkening night —
Seeking that I find you — Lord.
My heart is bewildered — lonely —
and lost—
Pierced by delusion's sword.

Perhaps if I drink deeply of the
night's contentment
And of its communion partake.
I shall find that the tears I shed are
bittersweet —
And that you do not forget or forsake.

Take of me and mold me into a
semblance of calm —
And show me a purpose and a way.
Nor mind if my heathen heart be slow
to find —
Kinship with those who pray.

Becky M Pataki
MEN, WHO UNSELFISHLY GAVE

To Those Who Lost Their Lives in Vietnam.

So many young men . . . went off to
war
Many of them kids . . . a new
world to explore
The fighting continued . . . year after
year
Many families faced . . . their
worstfears
So many young men . . . being
shipped back home
Dying for liberty . . . their bodies
stone cold
Donny, Paul and Jim . . . just to name
a few
Never to live their dreams . . . like
me and you
Freedom forever . . . they gave their
lives
For each one of us . . . a part of us
died
Now a wall is built . . . in memory of
them all
Who unselfishly gave . . . their
names stand tall
God bless you all . . . in heaven you
must be
You fought in hell . . . now rest in
peace

Lory L Park
WISHING
I wish
I had a flower
to give to somebody down.
So he may see the beauty of the
flower
instead of his frown.
So that he may smile —
even if it's secretly —
and realize
that it's not so bad after all.

Madeline Michelle Parrish
FOOLISH LITTLE GIRL

Dedicated to the Men of the Forest, Class of '92. Love and Stuff, M & M.

Just a foolish little girl,
With gold and brown curls.
She always wears a smile,
A cute smile with little girl style.
She fell in love with a boy,
Around him she acted coy.
She really, earnestly loved him,
It was a strong love on a weak limb.
To her he said very little,
Only to leave her in the middle.
He mixed her up and let her down,
Once they went out on the town.
She loved that so much,
She only wished for one touch.
Just his lips brushing against hers
softly.

W Scott Phoenix
ON GOLDEN SAND
I met a lady
on the golden sands
"want you" eyes
and "hold me" hands

her smile peeked out
and coaxed mine free
up to eyes
where love leaked out

touches in the dark
her sighs my guide
fingers 'round moving
let loose the tide

anxious when we met
and kissed when we parted
never finished
the love we'd started

but who does know
what now lies in store
for two lovers
who met by the shore?

Boyd Poole
THE MISTAKEN IMAGE
Ego retaining myth of image,
Man is God-like, is a lie.
Man is dirt of lowly vintage
And dirt he will surely die.

Shameful arrogance, nothing more,
A thousand times retold.
Misuse of words, which for sure,
Spoke not of body, but of soul.

Here man dare not beat his chest.
He is so far from this goal,
It has taken Jesus, the very best,
Two thousand years to wash man's
soul.

Man is yet a torch unlit,
Dirt, a lowly clump of sod.
His soul, his best, is more to spit
Than to the image of God.

Susan B Parsons
IF I COULD MAKE A WISH

This poem is dedicated To the man of my dreams, You know who you are.

If I could make a wish,
That wish would surely be,
That you would want to spend,
The rest of your life with me.

If I could make a wish,
And pray it would come true,
I hoped that I would be spending,
The rest of my life with you.

For in this world of hope,
The impossible does come true,
Maybe someday in the future,
I will finally be with you.

Darin Powell
THE FIGURE
As the painter paints the painting of
the figure with the grim smile,
The painter projected her as she
profiled.
From the corners of her eyes tears did
come,
No one knew her name or where she
came from.
She was breathtaking but yet pain
filled her eyes,
On her face was written many, many
lies.
The figure was beautiful yet still an
enchanting sight,
Shadows glared off her tears when
she stared into the moonlight.
The figure in which for the artist
profiled,
For the painter that painted the figure
with the grim smile.

Pamela Marie Pitre
DEATH

For My Father. He was my inspiration.

Death is the darkside of life.
It is like the night without a moon.
It is a total darkness that makes the
living wonder
if life is really worth it,
But death is a part of life whether
understood or
not.
There will never be a farewell to
death only a
farewell to the people we love.

Angela Patton
A MESSAGE

This message is of kindness,
And may bring happiness.
This message is of love,
And as rare as a dove.

This message says that I care,
And will always be there.
This message says I have feelings for you.
In simple words this message says:

"I Love You"

Kevin Paglia
LEAVING

To all graduating Seniors throughout the world.

The time has come when we must
go our own ways after saying good–bye.
To reach out and touch the world with
our words, thoughts and actions;
to teach and to be taught.

The time has come when we must
say good–bye to our peers,
to let go so they can fly on
wings of knowledge that are strong
only as we use them.

The time has come when we must
look forward, not back; up, not down;
to walk tall, but humbly beside others;
to fight for what we believe in, and
to accept others' beliefs.

The time is now when we leave.
The time is now for saying good–bye,
for crying, for laughing,
for silent memories and for
peaceful promises to remember
each other till next we meet.

James Pergola
ART

To Mrs. Sandra Hauss, my third grade teacher.

Art involves color,
Not a hobby like any other,
When you sit down and concentrate
To paint a picture you will not hate,
A dab of red, a touch of blue,
Any color that satisfies you,
A sunny scenery is nice in a way,
Even if it's raining that day,
A blob of paint is how you start,
Then all the ideas come from the heart,
Spread the paint around,
Add to your ideas so
You could make a beautiful warm yellowish glow,
Frame it, and put it on display,
So each and every day you could
look at it in a way,
And with pride you could say,
"I painted every little bit, and you know what,
I'm proud of it."

Bonni L Pitts
ON THOUGHTS TOO LATE

Through porch vines whispering on the breeze
with daylight dawning on with ease,
I hear the morning roses drip
with nectar sweet for all to sip.
"I love you so!" I long to shout —
on empty walls it echoes out . . .
Oh! to snip the thorn before the rest
of the whippoorwill's soft-downy breast!
I cannot hope you love me still,
for like the morning whippoorwill
with wounded breast from stinging thorn —
up and up 'til skyward borne . . .
Then gone away . . .
. . . and I'm to blame . . .
Oh what a shame,
Oh what a shame!

Annette Pugliese Pellegrini
LOVE FEELINGS

I dedicate this poem to my parents; children and foster children; family; teachers and friends whom shall forever remain a part of my life for it is from each and all of them that have contributed to and for whom LOVE FEELINGS is written. THANK YOU ALL!

When I think of the love
Between us
My heart swells and
Butterflies fly;
For our love is free;
Down to the sharing
Of each other's souls.

Our love is uninhibited;
Free of restraints;
Saying what we feel;
Feeling . . . what we say.

It's a deep pit,
That once, was filled . . .
With emptiness;
With your love,
Swells . . .
With fulfillness!

Tina Phillips
GET HIGH GET LOW

Get high is having fun.
It's like having a ball
When you stumble and fall
It's like a wonder of a dream
When you get up it's like a
Laughter of scream.

Get low is a sadness
Sadness is leaving the past behind,
and the future ahead.
It's taking your love away
When you could never again
Sit in the hay.
When you feel at that he is the one
It may shine on you; the sun.

Patricia Troiano Peters
ON LOSING YOU

"For Patrick" who taught me how to win and lose.

The day my love grows less for you.
Go quietly
And let us not pretend.
To play the parts that we no longer are,
Let us be brave
If this our play should end.

And if you should chance to dream
one rainy night
How the firelight danced across my hair.
Or gentle words we found in some
old book
In swift sweet days when we began to care.

I shall be glad,
Yet if your vanished step walks down
my street
Not anyone will know.
I'll tell myself you're someone in a
book of happy tales
I read long, long ago.

And when I see lovers smile the way they do
Heart close, replete and warm.
I'll lift my head with pride,
That I too, once knew
The joy of shelter in a storm.

Margi Perchetti
I'VE GOT THE FACE OF A CLOWN

I've got the face of a clown.
I won't let this thing get me down.
My lips are turned up forcing a smile
But it's going to quit hurting after a while.

I've got the face of a clown.
You won't see my mouth in a frown.
I'm spreading sunshine all over the place
'Cause I've got a smile on my face.

I've got the face of a clown.
I'm the happiest person in town.
No one can tell by looking at me,
That I'm as sad as a person can be.

I've got the face of a clown.
I'm convincing to those I'm around.
My laughter is hiding the hurt inside,
Can't let you know it — I've got my pride.

It's only when I'm alone by myself
And I've put my mask back on the shelf
That the eyes of this clown let the teardrops start
While I try to mend my poor, broken heart.

Yes. I've got the face of a clown.

Ruby Corwin Pullen
HIS GREAT GIFT

DEDICATED to my four sons and their wonderful families.

Twins, my heart leaped with joy
God has given us a beautiful baby girl
And a handsome strong boy —
Oh God, I cried,
With thankful beating heart,
How can you bless me so
When I've hardly done my part.
Be still, my child, He said to me
With Peaceful calm serene
The years on earth, are full of toil
and heartaches, all unseen.
So gifts I give, from now and then
So you can forward lean
Upon my word, my strength and know
My presence is not a dream.
The little children are a gift
I send all from above.
Not because you're good or bad,
But because of my great love.

Frank J Pinto
LIFE'S ROAD

I can't seem to find the words to say.
For so long now I've been searching
to find those words that might be heard.

How can I make you understand
when like you I'm just a man
with his faults but they've all been bought.

You can travel life's road up and down
but there's only one thing that needs to be found
to get you through all you do.

You may be a rich man you might be poor
but none of those things will matter anymore
once you've found the truth. Find the truth.

You can go on out and have your fun
but sooner or later you'll meet the one
and I hope you say forgive me today.

Do you think it's enough to just believe
or do you think it's time to receive
the savior as your Lord.

Ask Jesus to come into your heart right now
and He'll forgive all your sins and allow
you to be free, free indeed.

Lucille Planz
USED

To my children. Surely now you know it, your mom's a poet . . . .

A stepping stone
— you —
Used me for
To multiply your stock
— but —
All that glitters
Is not gold
— and—
The stone is solid rock . . . .

Lucille Planz
A'CHOO

Do not:
Give me a rose,
A rose:
Irritates my nose,
Pretty flowers
Cause my eyes to tear,
Not from sentiment
But —
Allergy my dear . . . .

Dorinda Sue Parkola
FEELINGS

Seashells lying on the ocean floor,
The gulls overhead,
The loud wind's roar,
And seaweed lying neatly in the sand.
We walk together hand in hand,
And as the sun begins to set,
That we must go,
Is our regret.

Vicki Lee Peace
SEASONAL PSYCHOLOGY

"Let's do spring cleaning!"
"Let's fix up — it's spring!"
Such cries are unkind to that season.
I save unpleasant tasks for autumn —
Spring fever, I guess, is the reason.

Now the chimney needs sweeping
And the gutters need patching.
The weather may grant a reprieve — or
Perhaps I could lend a neighbor my ladder . . .
Somehow, I must prevent fall fever!

Faye Parrish Powell
THERE IS NO DEATH

Dedicated to Dr. Richard Weisler, who truly understands its meaning.

There is a plan far greater than the
plan you know

There is a landscape broader than the one you see
There is a haven where storm-tossed souls may go —
You call it death — we, immortality.

You call it death — this seeming endless sleep
We call it birth — the soul at last set free
'Tis hampered not by time or space — you weep
Why weep at death? 'Tis immortality.

Farewell, dear voyageur — 'twill not be long.

Your work is done — Now may peace rest with thee
Your kindly thoughts and deeds — they will live on
This is not death — 'tis immortality!

Diane Renee Paylor
SOMEBODY'S GOT MY WINGS

To my dear mother and family, I will fly!! And when I do just watch me soar.

I can't fly,
fly to newer and brighter skies,
because somebody's got my wings.
I've pleaded, "If you don't let my wings go I'll never be free.
LET ME BE I SAY! LET ME BE! I want to be free."
But somebody's got my damn wings you see.
A beautiful bird can't fly without her wings.
So, please set me free.
Yet you say I'll never fly as high as the others
But I can fly as high!
High, high and higher!
I bet I can go beyond the sky.
Let me show you what I can do —
You'll see!
But you must set me free.
I have my own path
and I'll go at my own pace.
But somebody's got my wings
and it's because of my race.

Agnes V Phillips
WILD PLUM
I think nothing is more beautiful
Than wild plum in the spring,
When traveling down a lonely road
And your headlights catch the gleam
Of white blossoms at the forest's edge
And your heart begins to sing.
It has such an eerie beauty
That it almost brings a tear
And though the nights may be quite cold
You feel warm days are near.
I'm fond of all the early blossoms
That cause the heart to sing,
But wild plum is somehow special —
A Harbinger of Spring.

Hattie Martin
THE FACE IN LIFE'S MIRROR
When I look into life's mirror
What do I really see?
A beautiful spirited creation
Elohim created in me.

Inside this beautiful creation of life
Emanates compassion, joy and love
Endowed with a spirituality
That could only come from above.

We all have a face in life's mirror
To be the best we can be
The reflection that looks back from the mirror
Is the reflection he created in me.

Victoria Marche
GIANT STRUGGLINGS
I had a giant by the toe
Struggling and fighting
With all my might
Trying to break and control "it"
That was hurting and fighting me

I struggled, wrestled
Fought and fumed
Still that giant seemed to loom
I cried, prayed and prayed again
A little calmness entered in
I stopped crying and prayed some more
'Til I felt peace at my door
The more I sought the risen king
The more the giant 'twas dwindling

I can't fight things I don't see
Or giants that's too big for me
But my God can
As I well know
I no longer fight giant's toes
I pray

Phelps Smith

Phelps Smith
LEBENSRAUM

Dedicated to the Amis Class — Highland Park Presbyterian Church — Dallas, Texas.

(In his Mein Kampf Hitler states that Germany needs more room in which to live.)
Mark you who crucify him now
Upon the crooked Nazi cross.
Mark well the history of this King
Who counts your worldly loot a loss.

With sword you crave the world to win;
And, having that, what wish you then?
The earth is only ample room
In which to carve oneself a tomb.

But Christ brings us to more than dust.
He holds two worlds for them in trust
Whose faith is ground upon this plot:
The cradle held him, but the grave could not.

Phelps Smith
ON THE CONFIGURATION OF THE EGG

Amis Class — Highland Park Presbyterian Church; T.E.N. 1st Baptist — Dallas, Texas.

Can human mind ever design
A shape more appropriate,
I beg, than the egg?
How ovalesque,
Non-Arabesque
It is!

Simple, smooth, sleek
As a baby's cheek.

How tactical
And practical!
So tapered at each end.
So painless to the hen.
From where she sits
How easily it emits.

How very crude were it a cube.
Or, if a pyramid, how insipid!
If trapezoidal, how voidal.

Yes, if form you quest,
Lay doubts to rest,
The egg's the best
For the hen. Amen!

April Pulliam
THINKING OF YOU

I dedicate this poem to all the ones I love and left behind.

Days here are quite boring when you are not around,
I think of you so much, it turns my stomach upside down.
From the first year I met you, I never really knew,
Just how much I *LOVE* you, and really need you too.
It tears me apart,
To know I will never be in your heart.
It makes me want to cry,
When no one will tell me why.
It is hard to really see when I think of you and me,
I want you, so much, to be here with me, but I know it will never be.
Whenever I think of you, my heart breaks in two,
I just don't know what to do, when I can't even see you.
I want you to know,
That I still *LOVE* you so,
And I will never forget,
That special one I met.
You will always be in my heart,
No matter how much it tears me apart.
My dearest, dearest friend,
I will take you all the way to the end.

Billy Janus Michaels Esq
BIZARRE BRASSIERE BAZAAR

To my little sister, who is a bustless babe, and my big sister, who is a busty broad.

Come to the bizarre brassiere bazaar and bring your brassiere.

We need big buxom brassieres from big busty broads for
our bizarre brassiere bazaar.

And we need baby bosom brassieres from bustless babes
to boost our bizarre brassiere bazaar.

Why do we call our brassiere bazaar bizarre when we have
big buxom brassieres from big busty broads and baby
bosom brassieres from bustless babes?
Because in our bizarre brassiere bazaar we have no average
brassieres from belles of average boobs.

Ronnie Peavy
PEACE OF MIND

Dedicated to my loving wife Arleen, who has helped make everything possible.

I sat upon the wooded banks of a stream that had long since died.
Tracking back thru' a childhood dream, to a time when I had tried,

To do the things that would show, that someone could really care,
About life and love and simple things, unafraid to be aware,

Of the beauty and the joy, that comes from the simplest deeds,
Like finding peace in a grazing meadow, by seeing flowers instead
of weeds.

To walk alone and not be afraid, of what others might think of me.
To do my best, and then lay down to rest, with a conscience that is
calm and free.

Ronnie Peavy
WALKING
I once walked with Anger, embedded deep within my soul,
Unable to reach a higher plain, because of its numbing cold.

I once walked with Fear, a constant and troubled friend,
Who gave me only glimpses of light, from an emptiness that grew within.

I once walked with Hatred, a vile and ugly man,
Who showed me how to have my way, unflinching in my stands.

I once walked with Despair, never able to pass the test,
That came along thru out my life, in times of troubled rest.

I once walked with Pain, my most trusted and proven guide,
Who lead me into barren fields, washed over by the tears I'd cried.

I once walked with Loneliness, and it was he who gave me the key,
That said life is just a waste of time, when spent with friends like these.

But I once walked a step further, into the light that did shine,
And found a friend with inner strength, that gave me peace of mind.

A peace of mind, and inner glow, that began to help me cope,
With life, and love, and a caring soul, now filled with Loving Hope.

Cris Motta
LOST LOVE
I almost lost
I started to let go
I felt so empty
I felt so alone
I realized love
I couldn't let go
But now we're together
And I'm not alone.
The love we shared,
I felt, I was the only one who cared.
But now I know
I'll never be alone
'Cause the love we share,
Will never go.
'Cause now I know
He loves me so!

Pat Pfaffenhauser
COME PLAY

To Michael, thank you for filling my life with your love.

A velvet night,
a summer day,
let's forget this world
and play.

Upon our horses made
of sticks, let's
race to the mountains
and play in the
creeks.

Let's climb up trees,
and swing on vines,
I know, my friend, we'll
have a great time.

We're so caught up in this
world of greed, we
often forget, how to just
stop and breathe.

So, mount that trusty wooden
steed,
and we'll run and play
till we haven't a need.

Evelyn Paulauskas
AWAKE
Awake
In the darkness of your dreams
Beyond the real and unimaginative
Search the true meaning of life
Only one answer
will come to mind
Your love for thee

David John Palmieri
HOW MUCH I NEED YOU

I would like to dedicate this poem to my inspiration, Julie Maresca.

When we've first talked on the phone
You were like my very own
You've brought sunshine into my life
But what happened to that light
It just went dim the other night
I don't know who was wrong or right
I need you honey
And it's not funny
When I'm sitting here all alone at
night
How much I need you
Please believe
I love you darling
Can't you see
How much I need you
Please believe
Do you have any idea how I'm
feeling
I don't know what to say anymore
We both are young
And we had fun
But let's not let them take that away
from us
You know I miss you
And I will kiss you
But it's not happening
At all tonight

Jamie Pruitt
THE CLAY MAN
The clay man is a strange man,
He sits atop his small mountain,
Just sits and stares out at the world.

Knowing the unjust.
Praising the true.
But, after all, he is just a man,
Fooled by life, just like me and you.

Helen J Prichard
JIMMIE
I never thought that I would see
An angel who looks just like me.
He's just a little boy, it's true,
But he's angelic, for he can do
Just ordinary little things
That seem to capture my heart
strings.
I go to tuck him into bed and
Kiss my little sleepy-head
When he, with arms that circle
'round,
Gives me a hug without a sound.
Then after he has said his prayer
And snuggled down without a care,
Sweeter than any turtle dove,
He softly coos, "Mommie, I need
love."
When after a hug and a kiss, or two,
He decides to sleep, as all angels do,
He asks me if I will hold his hand
Until he arrives in slumberland.
I can't deny he's my pride and joy,
That freckled, angelic little boy.

Juanita Primm
HANG-IN THERE

In memory of my beloved husband, Bob.

Back in my youth when things went
wrong
My folks would just say: You've got
to be strong
Just hang-in there, and you will see
Everything will be alright eventually.

As a young adult I was full of hope
With most of my problems, I was
able to cope
By hanging-in there and seeing it
through
I became a better person as my
confidence grew.

In the prime of my life I found
romance
As it became serious, I couldn't take
a chance
So I hang-in there with all my might
To make it last and come out right.

In middle age, I breezed through like
a sigh
Sure I made mistakes, but I wouldn't
say die
I hung-in there and gave my very best
All the results showed that I'd passed
the test

And now old age has caught up with
me sure
It's a part of life I'd like to detour
But I know that I can't, so I'll
hang-in and pray
That God will have mercy till the end
of my stay.

Roberta Pisano
VISION
To see a vision of tomorrow
I would like to borrow
A crystal ball
To see those lives
Big and small
Of little children
Grown so tall

From tiny babes this present day
To see their future, I pray
With eyes so bright
And hopes so tall
Please don't give them too big a
freight
I couldn't bear to see them fall.
With vision clear
This day to see
A life so rich, so full, so free
I would I could
Live again with these.

Samantha R Penn
MISSING ONE FROM ANOTHER
It's going to be a time
that we can't spend
with each other and that's
called missing one from
another.
We had some glad days and
We had some sad days but
What really counts to me,
is just loving you, 'cuz
that's the way it should be.

Robert Peters
QUEEN OF THE EAST RIVER

To my beloved parents and brothers and sisters who have departed this sphere.

Over there you can observe the
sinuous caravans of red and white
lanterns
moving in a procession against a
dusky sky.
If you listen you can hear their
dissonant trumpets.
Beyond you can see the dark gray
stones of the Queensboro Bridge, its
spirals
reaching for a scintillating star.
There below you can see the rustling
trees beneath its curved archways.
The antique lamplights illuminating
the dark shadows above its winding
paths.
Can you hear the bells tolling and a
fog horn piercing the descending fog?
Look there! You can see the fading
lights of a tall ship as it's swallowed
by
the night.

Nancy K Petroske
AND NOW A POEM
God, in my hour when demons
pursue
And threaten to kill my vision of you,
I kneel down and seek towards
Heaven above,
Sustain me and grant me the Spirit of
Love.

Am I Satan's quarry in this game we
play?
I pray for a Guide who'll show me
the Way.
No devil man's catch though he set a
sure snare,
To find your true victory the answer
is Prayer.

Gail Pulkowski
WHY ARE DIVORCES IN OUR HOMES
Why are divorces in our homes?
It's to take children from a broken
home.
Who do we live with Mom or Dad?
Oh no! Please don't do that!
Don't leave us here all alone, for we
all have to go to an orphanage home.
"Why are divorces in our homes?"
Here we are me and my two
brothers. Boy we miss daddy and our
mother!
Did we do something wrong? Why
did they leave us here all alone?
It hurts so bad not knowing where
they've gone.
"Why are divorces in our homes?"
Guess what??? Our mother came
to see us the other day!
She came to tell us our daddy passed
away.
She gave us a kiss and said she
couldn't stay.
I'll be back, I must be on my way.
We three cried, please mother stay!
She turned around and said, you'll
understand one day.
I'll call you from time to time on the
phone.
"Why are divorces in our homes?"
Now we all three have grown up.
We lived a hard life, boy was it tuff!
Nobody knows what hell we lived
through.
Mom and Dad we will always love
you!
We are all three married now. None
of us is alone.
We've got children and a happy
home.
"Why are divorces in our homes?"

Brad Quillen
TIME GOES BY
Loving and caring
Soft is the heart of a child
Innocent and pure.

As a small child grows
Painful are the years to come
So misunderstood.

Settled and content
Satisfied — life has become
Happy and fulfilled.

Life is passing by
The body and mind are weak
So alone and sad.

Death is welcome now
New life in eternity
Peacefulness and joy.

Ronald Prefontaine
MEMORIES

To Rosemary.

Truth and lies
Desire
Happiness and pain
Games
Time and love
You
Memories

Jewell Phillips
MIRACLES
Sometimes He moves so quietly
One scarcely knows He's working
His miracles to perform
But weaves them gently in
Our way of living – so it seems
The natural thing to be –
And yet it is a miracle, an act
From heaven above,
It is a joy to know and see
When God changes you and me.

Doug Pedersen
BUTTERFLY
Like a leaf
on the loose
dancing in the breeze
you drifted through my life
getting entangled
for a while
perhaps
teaching me
a little bit more
than I knew before.

All the while
it seemed
you hardly ever
touched the ground
your spirit

always moving around –
a study
in love and life
that was refreshing
and satisfying
yet not everlasting.

Susan Poole
SUICIDE
Three days ago, someone called to say,
You had killed yourself.
Twelve years had passed,
Since we had known each other,
And it seemed, at first, that it didn't matter.
But the longer I thought,
The more it mattered.
The memories came flooding in
Of a time where there really was innocence,
And it seemed the world could only get better.
Who knows what you were thinking then,
Or just a few days ago,
When life lost all its hope and value.
I only wish that someone could have convinced you,
That life is worth the struggle.
And I pray to Jesus,
Who must understand, when we don't,
That he'll have mercy on you
For what you did,
And have mercy on us
For what we didn't do.

Marjorie Cottrell Power
LADY

For Ashley & Jennifer and their Lady.

"A Lady she is not!"
I laughed as I watched her play.
Young, curious, clumsy, a skittish friend,
Yet, I knew there would come a day
When sad, yet happy in its way—this would end.

Her hair was matted with brambles.
She ran when she should have walked.
Grasshoppers and bugs she chased and teased.
Through trees, dark shadows she stalked.
She liked best to do whatever she pleased.

She was shy as he touched her,
Her soft brown eyes seeking love—finding fear.
He was gentle and understanding; tough but kind.
I waited with apprehension only wanting to be near.
Alas, along with the changing of her body came the changing of her mind.

She is a Lady!
I smiled as I watched her today.
Her childhood gone, but no one seems to care.
Poised and siren, a loyal friend all the way—
Oh, how I love my little red mare.

Marvel Phillips
BIG SUR
I sit high upon my mountain,
Looking far out over the sea.
Making a mental note,
Of all the beauty that surrounds me.
The Douglas fir with the needles so fine,
And scattered all around the whispering pine.
The majestic live oaks with their generous
beauty and shade,
Just a few of the wonders that God has made.

The redwood trees so straight and tall,
I bow my head in reverence to all.
Now; the sun is slowly sinking with the rainbow
colors I adore,
Father in Heaven I thank you, for my home in the
wilderness of Big Sur.

Élan Paggeot
AS THE DAYS GO BY SO FAST
As the days go by so fast,
I can't help but think of the past.
Of too short days and long restless nights,
Holding your hand and kissing you goodnight.
Your fiery kiss I will never forget,
You set my heart on fire — and it hasn't died out yet.

But soon the days will start to slow,
And it will be time for me to go.
As we stand hand in hand,
We watch the heavens begin to expand.
The moon drifts out to say "Hello,"
And it is then that I must go.

I turn to you and whisper good-bye,
You look at me with tears in your eye.
But you understand that it is for the best,
And with faith and courage you must pass the test.
With one kiss we drift apart — and I turn my head and give a start.
For you are still standing there,
And you know I love you beyond compare.

Rico Perez
GRANDPA THE SAINT OF THE NIGHT

Dedicated to George C. Long, God bless you Grandpa!

As a young boy upon one day I awoke.
I was anxious and ready to go to Grandfather's house.
When I saw my mother her face was a gloom.
So it was then that I asked her
What it was that was wrong.
She then looked at me, forcing upon her face
A smile, and said to me . . .
"My child we are not going to Grandfather's house today,
Because you see, your Grandfather has gone away."
It was then I asked her,
"Why Mama? Why did Grandfather go away?
Why, Mama, why to-day?"
Then my mother replied,
"You see my child, God, he needed someone to kiss all
The children on earth good night,
So they would not worry or be afraid or affright.
So God chose your grandfather to travel
On the whisper of the wind and kiss all the children good night,
So all the little children will not fear and they all may sleep tight."
Then I looked at my mother, she had started to cry.
I said to her, "Mama, don't worry:
Mama, don't cry,
For tonight as we fall asleep,
Grandpa will stop by."

Nicholas Petroro
UNSELFISH LOVE
Only a few knew someday there would be
A man we call Jesus, offering eternity.
His unselfish love, so perfect and pure
Will help to sustain us, help us endure.

We say that we love him, we say we believe
And yet there are times we stray and deceive.
He knows our weakness and he knows when we try,
He knows when we're lonely, he knows when we cry.

His unselfish love — so perfect and pure
His Spirit dwells in us, some know it for sure.
Although some may never quite understand,
Salvation is ours, if we hold to is hand.

He will dry our tears and give us his strength,
He will comfort the grieving, he will go to great length,
To teach us that patience is a virtue — his gift.
We need but to call him, he'll give us a lift.

I pray I may serve him and with my last breath,
Say — yes, it's beautiful, just before death.
I had a good life — because he made it known,
There's life after death, in his Kingdom called home.

Diane R Page
MY LOVE — THE SEA

To Leighton and Elizabeth.

Bright twinkling stars
Soft whispering breeze
Fine salty mist
Low rumbling of thunder
Black clouds touching the horizon
Furious waves crashing inward.

My Sea calls me to come
To sit by her side
To play in her tide.

Deep blue of her floor
Snow white of her caps
My cares unleashed
My worries no more
I feel total love
When I sit by her shore.

She calls to me —
My Love — the Sea.

René A G Piña
IF EVER I PAINT (SEPTEMBER 1984, WOY)

Dedicated to Lourdes, the muse who has rekindled in me this need for expression.

If ever I paint,
I'd like to paint mountains . . .
those scars that remain
of the clashing of continents,
with jagged, young edges
or rounded, old peaks,
that proclaim the power of nature,
slowly unfolding
upon my very eyes.

If ever I paint,
I'd like to paint mountains . . .
in multicolored hues
of purple and blue, and red,
and brown, and gray, and green;
in all of those colors
that bring to our life serenity,
inspiring vistas,
promised treasures — unseen,
undisturbed, awaiting . . .

If ever I paint,
I'd like to paint mountains . . .
to sing on my canvas
of valleys, and ridges, and dales,
and hollows, and hilltops,
and small, cozy mesas,
and rocky formations to sit on,
— to dream, to ponder —
or walk by in wonder,
or merely to gaze at.

Mountains come to life
— in our imagination —
in familiar forms,
or with a vague resemblance to
some long forgotten dream.
If ever I paint,
I'd like to paint mountains . . .
And when I'm done,
I'd like to paint
sky scenes, with clouds.

Pat Perez
LIFE'S TOMORROW
What lies ahead,
Each wants to know.
Who's in control,
Who runs the show.

Some believe in fate,
Some hesitate.
Some say the way,
Must be to pray.

Life's roads are many,
Paths intertwined.
Each of us seeking,
Each trying to find.

What lies ahead,
Joy or sorrow.
The ultimate mystery . . .
Life's Tomorrow

Nancy A Pretsch
A FRIEND IS SOMEONE . . .

I dedicate this poem to my two best friends, Kathy Alvin and Laurie Boyce.

A friend is someone . . .
Who's there to talk to when you need some advice,
Who you can rely on to keep secrets.
A friend is someone . . .
Who lends a hand when you need one,
Who lends a shoulder to cry on.
A friend is someone . . .
Who changes your sad face to a happy face,
Who understands, and trusts you.
A friend is someone . . .
Who everyone needs now and forever.
I know what a friend is because you're my friend and in you I found them all.
That's why we're friends!

Joyce Pizzuti
THE MEANING OF CHRISTMAS:

To John, thank you, for showing me the true meaning of Christmas.

Once again it's Christmas time,
time for us to be,
Busy wrapping presents
and setting up the tree.
Time to make a holly wreath,
and tie it with a bow,
Time to light the candles
and hang the mistletoe.
Time to fill the stockings,
with lots of little treats,
Time to stuff the turkey,
and fix the candied sweets.
Time to greet our neighbors,
with a handshake and a smile,
Time to call on friends,
we haven't seen for a while.
It seems we have so many things,
to think of and to do,
We may forget that Christmas,
has a deeper meaning too.
A meaning that goes far beyond,
the things the eye can see,
Such as holly wreaths, mistletoe,
and gifts beneath the tree.
For these are only symbols,
of what happened Christmas morn,
When in a little manger,
God's only son was born.
God put him here upon this earth,
with one idea in mind.
To put new hope around the world,
and love in all mankind.
So even though we're busy,
and have many things to do,
Let's not forget that Christmas,
has a deeper meaning too.

Kimberly M Popovich
ICE CREAM
Strawberry Chocolate Vanilla too
And all those others that are new

Pistachio sherbert and chocolate chip
Oh! How they satisfy your lip

Ice cream cones and banana splits
Isn't it great when the flavor fits

Chocolate syrup and cherries too
Just satisfy those summer time blues

Sprinkles nuts and dipped cones too
Just makes me want to shout Ya Hoo!

Oh what a great fabulous treat
When you are tired and also beat!

It fills up your tummy really good
Forget about junk food, If you would

So when you're hungry and full of steam
Just race to the refrigerator and grab
Some Ice Cream!!!

Richard C Porzio
LOVE CRIMES
So you sit and you wonder what it's all about,
but no matter what you say there will always be
some doubt.
And your mind it seems is always tortured by things
you can't define and you wonder what it takes to get
across that line, and no matter what you say, everything
is fine.
But what about a heart that's been ripped a thousand
times by cruelty, pain, and anguish — something I call
love crimes.
So you sit and you wonder what it's all about, your
tired mind keeps searching, searching for some way out.
And your mind it sometimes echoes memories of your past,
all the things you've said and done, and things that
didn't last, and no matter what you say it keeps on
moving fast.
I sit and I think about these certain things, with
pain, regret, and fear, and how my heart got cruel at
times, when I did commit, commit my love crimes.
But everyone is guilty, it's something you can't deny
it stays within your heart and soul, it stays until you die.

Wyley Sayre Proctor
SIXTH YEAR WITHOUT SNOW
It was the sixth year without snow.
All of the plants would not grow.
It was scalding hot with heat.
The town meeting would not meet.

I was sitting underneath my favorite ledge.
(Of course, on top there was no hedge.)
There I was lying
When I saw something flying.
I knew it couldn't be a feather
'Cause the birds flew away 'cause of the weather.

It was white and falling fast.
It looked like snow. At last!

After that everyone (even the old man)
Thought that snow was simply grand!

Eva Ponce
PRESSURES FORCE
I woke one morning to find a life,
full of confusion, full of strife.
A life of pain and no one to blame.
A life unsure, in need of cure.
Pressures force and pull you down,
tension rises all around.
You try to hide, but still you're found,
failed to escape, you're somehow bound.
You cry for help, but no one hears,
the pressure's force has closed their ears.
We all live in a world of our own,
a different beat, a different tone,
a different song, to each his own.
Searching for answers that no one can give,
pressures force, you fight to live.
Holding on to hopes and dreams,
no matter how hard it seems.
Even though the pressure's on,
don't give up until you've won.

Eva Ponce
ESCAPE FROM THE PIT
Here I am back in this pit,
a place I left before.
This time can I quit or will I fall in more?
I'm sinking fast, how long will I last?
Can I escape this time or will I just keep falling down?
And who knows what I'll find.
Should I give up or should I try
to get back where I was before?
Should I live or should I die which do I want more?
Is this place deceiving or is this paradise?
Maybe I should be leaving what is your advice?
The walls are pierced with diamonds,
the floors are made of gold.
The ceiling made of marble,
the halls are bright and bold.
The air is fresh and sweet,
the water clear and cool.
With gold beneath my feet am I just a fool?

Grandmother

Vernon Majors
"MY GRANDMOTHER"

To Grandmother, all my love.

The things I never say to you,
Times past and other things too,
My happy summer memories about all of you,
There is too much to say or do,

Always there for all of us,
We never really showed you much.
Why do I say this to you today,
Because the real love never expressed my way.

We all have Grandmothers that's true,
Not as individual or kind as you,
Now that I wrote this letter to you,
I feel much better knowing this too.

It's not hard to say I miss,
My dearest Grandmother with kindness and a kiss,
I know deep down you know this just,
Because you said so and you're missed much.

If everyone had a grandmother like you,
They would be so proud of you,
You went thru so much that's true.
We all love you always, may God bless you.

Your Grandson,
Vernon Majors

Shelley M Johnston
THE GNARLED TREE
The gnarled old apple tree
That once gave apples to
The people who once lived
In the deserted house behind
It must have been quite beautiful.
When the blossoms bloomed white and pink
Now abandoned like the house
No one cares from far or near
Forgotten like many others
Too old to bear again
The poor tree will be at a mere standstill
Only rain and sun still care.

Sandra Kolk
WISDOM

To my most special and loving parents, who have guided and encouraged me throughout my life; to my very talented sisters, Bev and Sharon, who help make life interesting and our family complete; and to Tracey, whose friendship I value greatly.

Look at the tree aged so well,
Look at the wisdom in its shell,
Look at the leaves that tell the time,
Look at the gift that is mine.

Find the truth in the sky,
Find the rainbow, oh so high,
Find the happiness that shines through,
Find the meaning of me and you.

Never stop to wonder why,
Never think it's all a lie,
Never underestimate,
Never think that it's too late.

Always feed your hopes and dreams,
Always allow him to lean,
Always understand his ups and downs,
Always smile and never frown.

Keep the memories in your heart,
Keep the tree pruned from the start,
Keep the wisdom that it shows,
Keep the man forever close.

Lorraine Visscher
ODE TO MY HUSBAND

I dedicate this poem to my husband, Bill. I love you.

H-Is for handsome, the man that
I love.
U-Is for unity, the two of us as
one,
S-The serenity after we make
love,
B-Beautiful memories, and the
many more to come.
A-For allowing me to be what I
want,
N-Is for nurturing the love that
we've got.
D-His devotion to his lucky wife,
These are the things that I
cherish in life.
Thank you dear Bill,
For what you've given me,
God has blessed us, it's plain to
see.
You're the man that I want,
Until death do us part,
And if God permits
Up in heaven we'll embark
On a journey together,
With love in all its purity,
together forever
through all eternity.

Ann M Spruyt
SPRING
I wait in darkness
Hoping, hoping
Counting the days
Looking for the rays
Where are the Flowers?
The Sun filled mornings?

Can I last?
Come fast!
I crave the light
A budding Rose,
What a sight!
Spring is dawning
Hurry, hurry!
I see the Sun,
In all its glory
The Flowers are blooming
Awash in light
April showers
Birds singing
Spring has come
At last! At last!

June E Sullivan Jones

June E Sullivan Jones
BLACK EXPERIENCE

This poem is dedicated to myself, Dad, (mom, Ike—may you both rest in peace) and to the rest of my loving family. Joys, sorrows, disappointments have been many, but I have survived through them all.

I am Black,
But I can't relate
To this life of, Watergate.
Wineheads laying in the alley,
Destroying their minds.

Women of all calibers—like
Sally—
Giving up plenty of game and time;
Black on black breaking in their
neighbor's door,
Who will not hesitate to come back
for more.
The unfit waiting on the corner
asking for donations
Considered no longer to be a sane
part of this nation;
Black suicide and crime has gone
beyond its proportion
Where will it all lead to?
Nothing, but the end.

R G Voth
END OF TERM

Now I am blue
All this work to do

Long hours I sit
I'm no longer fit

Profs are crazy
They think I'm lazy

They do not care
I don't write with flair.

The project's done
There is time for fun

Another test
Time to do my best

I am so glad
Tomorrow is grad

Tina Harvey
FOREVER IN MY MEMORY

The thunder sounded off the
mountainous walls that surrounded us
all.
The unforgettable days of mourning
and weeping when mom heard
death's evil call.
It took her from her splendid and
almost perfect home dwelling.
Away from us all, where tears of
broken hearts, in our eyes were
welling.
The times she laughed, and yelled out
for joy.
And also her first love on that never
forgotten boy.
Her heart of kindness had grown to
slowly cease.
Her old but unblemished face went
by without a wrinkle or crease.
The vision of her remains perfect to
this day.
No one can ever take her place in any
way.

Frank J Bauer
STORMS OF FEAR

Rolling their stones on a stormy
night, does King Sinister and Queen
Delight
They toss and rumble the rolling
thunder, pulling hopes and dreams
down under
Arouse your fears and release your
fright, does King Sinister and Queen
Delight
By all means evil their piercing
sound, you always sense when
they're around
They cast their shadows by the
flashing light, does King Sinister and
Queen Delight
Truly they are large though
sometimes small.
Occasionally they walk normally
they crawl
They hide in darkness, avoiding our
sight does King Sinister and Queen
Delight
They run with the worst, a dangerous
crowd, totally violent, obnoxious and
loud.
As graceful as an eagle on its circular
flight, is King Sinister and Queen
Delight
When they finally stop their mournful
cries mercifully relent and begin to
realize
The sun is rising and the day turns
bright, off runs King Sinister, and
Queen Delight
Are they gone forever or will they
return, count on the latter to that I'll
affirm
For they will return to continue your
fright, will King Sinister with Queen
Delight.

Nelda Lott Newton
THE BEST OFFER

Jesus said come to me,
and I'll give you rest.
For I want to give you,
My very best.

Now it's all up to you,
For I've done my part.
Won't you please take my offer,
and give me your heart.

And life at its best,
is no good when you're alone.
You need one that's mighty,
faithful and strong.

And I'll give you great joy,
and peace of mind.
In this world of trouble,
You won't find an offer like mine.

Gina Maxwell
WHY HER?

Why her?
She didn't do anything wrong,
So why did God let her take her life?
She wasn't a bad kid.
She just got in the wrong crowd.
I don't understand.
Why her?
Was it something I did or didn't do?
Did she just need someone to talk to?
I should have been there for her.
Why take your life over something
that won't matter a year from now?
Why would God let her take her life?
Her dying is bad enough, but why
suicide?
Why her?

Leeroy Samuel Bartholomew

Leeroy Samuel Bartholomew
THE SACRED COW

To a dear friend, Mrs. Consuelo Marin, Oxnard, California, for her kindness and inspiration.

Once there was a sacred cow who
said: I've given 'til my tongue hangs
out. I lay around and chew my cud,
and wonder if there ever was, a
creature such as I who gives and tries
and finally does indeed go dry.
I eat green grass and give white milk,
so little children can grow up, and be
as healthy as can be and never even
think of me.
Dear one, do not fret and be forlorn,
for soon bold Ferdinand will come,
and repay you for the kind deeds
you've done.

Leeroy Samuel Bartholomew
A CHILD'S FANTASY

To my happy childhood.

Back when I was very young,
imagination was my song. Down on
the branch I used to play, and dream
of things so far away.

I saw grey rabbits at their play; while
eating in the garden there. Saw flying
squirrels and insects too, all seemed
to be doing what they do. It was
nature's way of telling me, I was in
the world of fantasy. Where
honeybee and suckle vine, come in
touch in summertime.

Then I wandered further down, the
thicket that was all around. I saw
cross-ties that had been lain, to
support a temporary train.
Of little cars that had pulled out,
virgin pines which had been cut.
There were huge stumps which still
remained; had not rotted but instead,
with turpentine had been preserved,
and turned into solid heart lightwood.

I've heard my mother say that she
had gone there and rode, upon the
little cars which pulled, their very
often heavy load. Cars which pulled
but one log at a time, logs from
which lumber was made, to build the
house in which we lived.

Greenlief-Lumber had bought, most
of the large tracts in the bend. To
clear the land so folks might plant,
crops from which our lives depend.

This was the way my life began, a
life-style that I still hold dear.
And in closing simply state: "I'm one
of the sons of the Pioneers."

Leeroy Samuel Bartholomew
THE ANGEL

For a beautiful friendship, to Mrs. Charlotte Dittmore, Oxnard, California.

It was one of those sunny days in ol'
Oxnard. I stopped into a small cafe;
there to have a cup of tea, and to pass
the time of day. Just a couple stools
away there sat, a crippled lady with a
cane. And when she chanced to look
my way, a sweet and friendly smile
she gave.
With a nod I did reciprocate; and then
we spoke a word or two. A small
shopping bag sat by her side; I
asked her if I could oblige.
Then she smiled and said to me, "I'll
appreciate some company."

I took her home, it was not far, and
on the way stopped at a bar; to have a
mixed-drink with my friend. The
conversation went real nice; it was
our way to break the ice.

When we went to her place then, she
shyly smiled and asked me in.
In just a little while I knew, that fate
had chanced that we should meet.
Because she was so much alone, her
counter-part had done passed on. And
the one who was not there, was her
one and only son.

Three score and ten had passed her

Three score and ten had passed her by; she said that soon she'd have to go, to pay the price we all must pay, to see what heaven has in store. As I listened to and looked at her it seemed, that I could see upon her back, a pair of golden angel wings.

Cristina Provencher
IN TIME

Sitting in your room alone,
you remember . . .
The times you had together,
you wonder . . .
If I didn't do what I did,
would we be together?
Don't worry about it.
Don't even think about it.
Just remember in time
you'll have,
Someone new,
Who really cares about
You!!!

Claire Foceri
COCAINE

I thought I didn't know you
Never saw you, touched or tasted
Your powdery white snow
But how little did I know

While I went about my life
You crept in, and wrecked it all
How come I didn't see you coming

Left with broken dreams, and shattered lives
I was so foolish to think you couldn't touch me
I didn't know you, but another did.

Even to the innocent you come and destroy
Leaving havoc behind you
How many more will there be

Lalonya Saari
TO THE MAN I LOVE

Dedicated with love to Eric Asplund, John, Joe, Sabrina and Marissa Saari for all your support and inspiration.

I hardly know who you really are,
Yet I know you'll not be far.
You wipe away the tears I cry,
You help me hold my head up high.

You make me laugh when I am blue,
I know I'll always be grateful to you . . .
For being there to hold my hand,
To help me to love and feel again.

My world was gray when I met you,
You helped me make it all so new.
Now I can honestly live again,
With you my love will never end.

Rhonda Lane
YOUNG STRANGERS

On a cold dark night, on a big city street
Two young strangers happened to meet
With a chill in the air and the moon so full
He could see by the light—she was so beautiful
He told her his name and he reached out his hand
And a feeling swept over him that he didn't understand
A feeling so powerful that it made his heart warm
He had to be chic—he had to have charm
When the time was just right he made his move
Wanting so much for her to approve
Well she liked what she heard and she touched his cheek
She asked him to dinner and he could hardly speak
What was this feeling? Could this be love?
Being with her was all he thought of
He wanted to dine her, he wanted to dance
He wanted caring and he wanted romance
For years and years he had longed for this day
And hoped this feeling would never go away
It was the real thing. I guess it was fate
They say, "Good things come to those who wait"

Victoria Komula

Victoria Komula
LAUGHTER TOUCHED ME

To my son Troy, my light and my love.

Laughter touched me
Anger left me
Fear spared me

Tears kept me
Silence held me

Kamala Schaefer
AND "I LOVE YOU" I WILL SAY

To my best friend and husband . . . Chris.

When I first found out about you,
I wasn't sure how to feel,
Something in the back of my mind,
Was telling me you couldn't be real!

Others may think I am foolish,
to have thoughts of you as a human being,
for they do not understand,
or know what I have seen.

This experience was by far simple.
Oh yes, it did hurt so.
I only wish someone,
could give me the answers I wish to know!

Would you have been a boy or girl,
with brown eyes or blue?
Maybe you would have been real tiny,
I wish I only knew.

I know in time the deep hurt,
Will be taken away,
for you my little friend,
will be a life again someday.

You have not gone forever,
for you will be the baby one day,
who I will hold in my arms,
And "I LOVE YOU" I will say.

Erma L Cole
LIFE

Learning to accept, appreciate,
and grow from
Increasing changes, and
challenges. Sometimes JOY,
sometimes HURTS, beyond our
control.
Facing problems, finding answers,
filling emptiness.
Enjoying, embracing experiencing,
ALL that the **Precious Gift**
(LIFE) can hold.

Linda Brechter
WOMAN WITH A MAN

Times the flint bears down
crossing your breast
at one point
a flower

you do what you can
to know who
it is
you are

hurling before the nearest man
flower on fire
transformed
come into
flesh

finally
you get your deliverance

walking behind him
your hips thrown to the side
moving to the rhythm
he takes to reach
the outline
horizon of
sky

a hill he says
where burns a flowered tree

a hill he says,
he says

Janice C Kuebler
ALONE

No matter how much I try
To tell you who I am,
No matter how much I try
To show you how I love you,
I will,
As you will,
Always be
Alone.
It is, I suppose,
That you so give me the feeling
That you are there
And
That you do understand
That allows me
To remain as long as I do.
Man's final downfall is
That no matter how much energy or time
He may spend on trying to communicate who he is—
In the end
Only he will be able to understand
exactly what was said and why.

Kelly M Furtak
FREEDOM

To Ralph, for encouraging the inspiration to flow; and to Lynn, for her undying support and friendship.

Perched on the edge of the roof
a bird sits
contemplating the day's events
watching and wondering why we choose
to be put behind glass
away from the warmth of the sun
unable to feel the cool wind
or smell the freshness of spring
Every now and then, he raises his wings in anticipation of flight
pausing
to look once again at us
sympathizing that we are not free
revelling in the glory that he is
We pause to glance out the window
to look at a bird, perched on the edge of the roof
It is then that he spreads his wings
displaying his feathers of freedom
and flies away

Hollie A Andrews
CHOICES

It came when I did not want it
A nation stands divided
Demonstrators encircle me
Shouting obscenities
Shouting murder
A fragment deep within me shudders

When it is done I sit waiting
I feel empty, alone
It was all so easy
Pay your money
Retract a soul
But it came when I did not want it

Vanessa E Byus
THE FIRST RAINBOW OF SPRING

To my husband, Sherman, my daughters Katisi and Talaya.

The first rainbow surprised me. It embodied me, it surrounded me. It colored me. It made me feel new, it made me feel fresh, it made me feel happy. It made me feel it in my heart. It made me look in each window, to see it closer, to feel closer. It made me take a picture to keep in my soul every time I look at it. My rainbow:

Eula May Lutzenhiser
SPARROW ALONE

(I watch, and am as a sparrow alone—Psalm 102:7)
I sit upon a nether prong
And chirp my separate song;
Those perched higher in the tree
May sing louder, but not as free,
For from my heart the music flows,
And swells with joy as it grows;

It is mine, and mine alone
Though it draw applause or stone:
One note I cannot compromise
I do not sing for praise or prize
MY poetry
Belongs to ME.

Jewell Gonzalez

Jewell Gonzalez
LIFE LINES

An old forgotten mother, with rapidly fading life.
To think she must have been a much beloved wife.
Nature's quaint design there upon her withering face.
An awkwardness in her stance, and a slowness in her pace.
The sign of time upon her brow, she sits there drenched in oldness.
With reverent quietness, and her secrets kept in solemnness.
There's an elegance that once was hers, in her far-off day.
How slowly the change occurs, in an uncanny sort of way.
From the newness of a baby and the ever-so-young
Once the soft mist of a girl, like a bud opening in the sun.
The new life her bosom once cradled, loved and comforted.
These are just memories, now cherished in her heart and head.
She is now left behind, her knowledge put away.
She is left behind from life and love today.

de Jewell (1985)

Jewell Gonzalez
HERE I AM

So restless, like a butterfly
Fluttering here and there.
Like the flickering of a candlelight.
Shadows that jump around the room
Please stop for a moment—
While I tell you a secret.
Open your eyes,
Open your ears.
When to let you know . . .
I am here and you are near.
How to let you know.

de Jewell (1983)

Jewell Gonzales
FOOTPRINTS ON MY HEART

Take me with you
please don't go.
He pleaded like
a little boy.
I had to leave,
my plans to follow.
Leave this place
to find another.

He stood there sadly
with tearful eyes.
It pained my heart
as I said goodbye.
I'm going away
where skies are blue.
Where waves on
sandy beaches play.

de Jewell (1990)

Robert Alan Lucero
MY LOVE-EST MEMORIES

To all women who've conquered endlessly, especially you, my Angie. God bless your souls, each one, eternally.

If in my love soaked mind I see precious, lasting moments of only you and me,
Then let them come as love's fears
Eternally enveloped in a pool of tears.

If within my heart's stone walls
My love-est memory of you falls,
There to mingle with my recent past,
Then for my forever it is meant to last.

If by chance my lips your lovely ones should meet,
It is there they'd taste love's ecstatic sweet;
Oh love, at times like these do I lose or gain?
Are my love-est memories filled with pleasure or with pain?

Angela L Ball (Embry)
THE PLACE

To my children, Michael, Amanda, and Anthony, with all my love.

At The Place, you can do all the things you've ever wanted to do,
You can be with whomever you choose.

At The Place, goals are never too large,
Here, positive elements can never be barred.

The Place, holds all the stories of certain success,
It gives you the power to take on the best.

The Place holds all the fantasies, and dreams,
Whatever you desire, there is no extreme,
Whomever you want, or love, is sure to be there,
To help let go all misgiving, or fear.

At the Place, your secrets are locked up tight,
And none can escape,
Unless, of course, you choose, to relate.

Although some try to deny, that they have ever been,
Remember, it's just thoughts not physical sin.

Without The Place, we would wither, and die,
You must have hope, dreams, and fantasies, to stay alive inside.

Grab The Place, and hold on tight,
with these things in mind,
You're sure to survive.

Gayle Grassi
WORDS

So many words we meant to say,
But the words were never spoken . . .
So many dreams we meant to share,
But the promises were broken . . . .

We shared a dream for another day,
When our dreams would all come true . . .
Forgetting the love we had for today,
And all of our promises too . . . .

We searched the past and tried to find,
The place where we went wrong . . .
But all we ever seemed to do,
Was miss what once was strong . . . .

We knew the time would come to us,
When we would have to part . . .
We cried for what we had to lose,
If we should break apart . . . .

You showed the dying rose to me,
as it withered on the vine . . .
And suddenly we began to see,
What had been there all the time . . . .

Debra Woolsey Hummel
A GIFT THAT ONLY YOU CAN GIVE

"Tis true Thomas, fine wines."

You came to me singing a song of love, and now all I hear is the melody of your tune.

You came to me with a smile, as warm as the sun, and now wherever I turn, everything is as bright and warm as the sunniest day in spring.

You came to me with a touch, as gentle and as silky smooth as a rose petal, it made me aware of the riches to be found in your satin.

You came to me with a kiss, that tasted of the very best wine, to unfold all of its nectars, and like all fine wines, a promise that tomorrow, it shall only be better . . .

Catharina Sensky
COLORS OF PASSION

To all those who are falling . . . .

Color of passion
Red
so deep
China blue
lava flow
so hot.
so complete.
so wide,
Like an eternal wave.
so cold
so warm
torturing pain
a blunt pierce
a shattered soul,
shouldering sensation
A touch of green . . . .

Marsha A Mayer
MY NEW HOME

To my father, William S. Mayer, bequeathing his personality and ambition and my mother, Dee Mayer, who inspired me with the courage to pursue my dreams.

This announcement is to let you know,
That there is a new home to which I go.
The house features lots of light,
That also captures the blue of night.
The entrance opens to the loft above,
Which gives a feeling I know you'll love.
My living room fireplace is cozy and warm,
Which I know will add comfort from any storm.
The cathedral ceiling adds to the charm,
That in this house there can come no harm.
The kitchen flows to the breakfast room—
This house just has no place for gloom!
When you look down from the second floor,
You'll overlook a grand front door.
The deck accents the exterior,
Which just adds to the depth of the interior.
I could continue and go on in vain,
But I am really finding it hard to explain,
I would much prefer you to come and see,
And have a drink or a cup of tea!

Amanda Latrenta
THIS WORLD WE LIVE IN

In this world we live in
there are homeless without a dime
pollution and sickness
murder and crime
a world full of prejudice
a world full of pain
a world full of drugs
a world so vain.

I cannot begin to tell how much of a sin that there is so much wrong
when there shouldn't be
if only people would open their eyes
to see how much this world has to offer to us.
We really need to make a fuss over
the rays the sun spills
the laughter of a child.
people's determination and will.
It makes the bad seem more mild
If we can make this world different
make it less sad.
Then what we accomplish
will make the bad seem less bad.

K Shawna Taylor
SPEAK SOFTLY LOVE
Speak softly love
and hold me
warm against your heart,
I feel your words as
the tender trembling moments start.

We are in a world
our very own
sharing a love
only few have ever known.
Wine colored days warmed by the sun,
deep velvet nights when we are one.

Speak softly love,
so no one hears us
but the sky . . .
the vows of love
we make will live
until we die . . .
My life is yours and all because,
you came into my world
with love, so softly love . . .
Speak softly love.

Cathy Kooyers
SHATTERED DREAMS

In memory of the boys, dreams and delusions.

Scattered rays
of brighter days
cast cobweb-like shadows
over the mind's vast meadows
as pieces of shattered dreams,
echoing silent screams
against the mind's canyon walls,
slowly tumble, scatter and fall.

Cathy Kooyers
BOYS/VETS
Dustin and Tim are my two, precious little boys,
Two little boys who can bring so many joys.
Invading my thoughts, above the friendly noise
Of children gingerly, innocently playing with toys,
Are images of boys of bygone days
For whom childhood ways are but a faded haze,
Triggering memories of a boy I once met
Who set aside his toys to become a Vietnam vet.
Camouflaged, tough men, who were only boys in disguise,
Distanced from innocence as they listened to others' cries.
Meanwhile, other boys painted yet another picture,
Laughing on campus while distributing antiwar literature.
Some boys went on to become wonderful fathers
Yet others were stopped, unable to travel life's road any farther.
Some boys followed an inner call,
While others from grace in time would fall.
Of the many boys who followed the draft call,
Too many are listed on a memorial wall.
Boys can make the world sore with their sting
Or bring joy and pride by doing special things.

Howard W Brewer
ALONE
Heartbeats, first to last,
My life force measurement.
The visual, physical trappings of life.
But cached within my heart of hearts,
Are thoughts that lie too deep for tears,
Never spoken, never shared.
My lifesong unsung.
A oneness, opaque, seemingly complete.
One who cannot bond looking out,
No trespass, for those who would look in,
The human condition, first, foremost and final.
That unresolved state of mental grace,
That craves to acknowledge, that a life,
My life, has not been in vain, alone.

Howard W Brewer
SOMETIME SOON
Glistening light unending,
Embraces long awaited,
Peace, pure and complete.
I sleep the sleep of angels.
Blue sky infinite now understood.
Truth alone,
The noble objective achieved.
I awake from the dream of life to
The bloom of flowers eternal.
The silent pomp and circumstance
Of dawn unheralded.
All is white, all is forgiven.
I journey to a better rest,
No pain or remorse.
Sometime soon.

Allen Snyder
TRANQUILITY
On a happy day the sun is hot,
the grass is green and brown.
The leaves, they play in the wind,
as the water blows around.
The birds sing a happy tune to the insects on the ground.
The fish, they swim, oblivious to what is going down.
As evening comes they breathe a sigh
and they all laugh and say,
I'm glad no people came by.

Edna Young
JUST A HEARTBEAT AWAY
Did you witness for Jesus the way that you should?
Did a chance pass you by, but you just never could?
Did you tell of His love and salvation so free?
My brother, you're a heartbeat from Eternity!

Have you given of your talent, money and time?
For the richest of blessings — a life so sublime.
Giving thanks unto God for those blessings each day.
Eternity is just a heartbeat away!

When church doors swing open wide,
do you enter in and your heart swell with pride?
Do you fill your soul with spiritual bliss?
If you brushed it aside for another day, remember,
Eternity is just a heartbeat away!

Did you pray for a loved one who wandered astray?
Or search for the lost ones along the way.
Did you sing His praises; tell how he reigns on high?
The Master of heaven and earth and sky.
Spread the glad tidings o'er land and o'er sea.
My brother, you're just a heartbeat from Eternity.
No greater gift has been given to man.
The plan of salvation, the nail-scarred hand.
Turn not away when you hear His plea.
My brother, you're a heartbeat from Eternity.

Linda C Dreher
SHOW ME A FLOWER

To Micheal, Amanda, Andrew, and Wendy. Love Mom.

Show me a flower
I'll show you the earth,
Show me a rainbow
I'll point out its worth,
Show me the sky with the stars up above,
I'll show you forever,
I'll show you my love.

A flower is pretty
But here for an hour,
A rainbow will come
Only after a shower,
The stars will be there when it's dark up above,
But forever is always,
And so is my love.

"Mak" Walker
THE TRUEST FRIEND I'LL EVER HAVE
The truest friend I'll ever have
I met so long ago,
When she held me in her arms
and I heard my first "hello."

She taught me in her shadow
how to color, draw, and play.
And every night at bedtime,
she taught me how to pray.

We always were together
We sometimes dressed the same.
She'd often hum a little tune
while we would play a game.

A†
Then I became a mother
and had my own to teach.
Now it's me who casts the shadow
that doesn't seem to reach.

When I pray for strength and wisdom
I remember smiles and tunes.
I remember baking cookies
and laughing at cartoons.

That woman is my friend
from whom I've learned to love,
to know that "different" isn't wrong,
and our Judge is from Above.

That woman is my Mother.
My truest friend of all.
Her shadow's always with me
Beside me, strong and tall.

Martha E Brown
MY BOY

In Memory of Luther "Lou" Nelson Brown.

My boy is going on an eternal trip
He is prepared to go away.
Our cup of sorrow we must sip,
And he would really rather stay.

His little children he must leave,
Also his wife must stay behind.
Now for his death we must not grieve,
But solace in his memory find.

His spirit will always to us be near
To guide and cheer us on our way.
We'll live the Gospel and hold it dear
Until we're called with him to stay.

A home in Heaven he will prepare
For his family, Oh! so dear,
And other loved ones will be there
In their Heavenly homes quite near.

Martha E Brown
THE JOURNEY
He traveled on foot, she on a mule
Her time was near and this journey cruel.
To Bethlehem town they were on their way
For taxes were due and they must pay.

Because at this time they must travel slow,
It was best to stay home but still she must go.
"When we get there," he said, "You can rest and sleep,"
But when they arrive their trouble is deep.

In Bethlehem town all rooms have been taken
With Mary in labor they both feel forsaken,
Then one lone innkeeper, who owned a stable
Said they could sleep there if they were able.

In this lowly stable our Savior was born.
This King of Kings of all glory was shorn.
Yet God in love sent His son a star
Which shone above Him and brought glory from afar.

The shepherds from nearby hills, they came
And kings and wisemen worshiped Him the same.
The innkeeper who that stable possessed
I'm sure was very highly blessed.

Michael P Burrell
JARO

For my childhood friend Denton Gordon, Jaro, who died in the summer of 1980, and to his mother, Ms. Levy (Jamaica W.I.)

Good-bye to you my trusted friend,
It's hard to admit to this untimely end
Unfix that stare toward the sky
Oh my confidant how could you die?
How frequently the memories rain and rain
And Jaro my friend, do you still feel the pain?
Are the memories yet too vivid to bear
Or is it the world that enrages your tear?
I see it still spins uncaring of your death
A world you tolerated yet it sucked your breath.
I can feel your anger, even more your sorrow
When we live, we live mostly for tomorrow.
Now you are caught in an eternal yesterday
But each day I live you shall live that day.
Feel free to follow the flaming flower
That death and darkness pine to devour
And remove the shadow from beneath the tree

So there is no impediment when I look toward thee.
I know we shall share this unfinished glass again
So till then, goodbye to you my trusted friend.

Michael P Burrell
ISABELLA
Like silvery waves upon the ocean, so can sweet Isabella dance;
Walking the ripples of time, not missing a beat, composing a graceful waltz.
Music and Motion are beauty's essence, and in you Isabella, Beauty performs;
A symphony born of elegance and strength, words spoken in the sweetest air,
Oh dance for me Isabella, so we move together, for my heart dances for you.
Dance for the sun, the flowers, and all, for they are audience to your splendor.
Though the weary world often plays Love's theme with a bitter heart,
Dance dear one and embrace its tired floor with your feet.
Silence plays its still sound upon the empty shores of my mind
But the Bell of Isabella adds music to my dreams.

Michael P Burrell
SO FAR REMOVED
So far removed are we now Mother Dear
From the simple pleasures of our childhood
When chirping metaphors would take ever so gently
The twigs and leaves from below to form a nesty phrase
Within the human heart, singing for unity in Being
And freedom in Unity, but now we are of a pompous age,
We have gone to build our own way above the earth,
Weaving mighty concepts from the dry thin air
And the great majestic Eagle with its unmatched
Dexterity rides the wind and shatters that wall
That so unjustly starved and divided a nation,
And then East meets West in a full half embrace.
And the Eagle returns to its emptiness upon the Hill
Never really touching the indigent soil that pollutes
All concern and courage, and no aid to those who
Sicken and grow thin and die from its deficiency.
But then from the high Hill there are those who
Came down to touch the ground with their cares
All dressed in plaid shirts, some on horse backs,
Some by the river fishing, some playing on the grass,
All in costume to perform for all, the Clean Air Act.

Dorothy W Madden
TOMORROW'S ROAD
Tomorrow's road, as I look ahead
Is hidden from my view;
It is covered with brambles and tangled brush,
And will not let me through.
The ruts I see are dark and deep,
With a valley low and wet;
I've studied this road a thousand times,
Though I never have reached it yet.
I've struggled and toiled along this road,
Although it is far away;
But strange, the roads that I have walked,
Have all been safe today.
Perhaps I shall find when I reach the place
That lies in the distant blue,
Some Hand has tended and cleared the way,
And my road is safe and new.
For He promised a highway there,
And a way that is clear to see;
With a light that is bright as the day,
I shall pass lighthearted and free.
For 'tis by His hand my road is laid,
To walk today and share;
Forgive me Lord, for my fretful heart,
My anxious and foolish care.

Lori L Shaw
MY YOUNGER BROTHER
My brother, with his Trojan disposition
Inspires me into complacency
He has a certain way of pleasing me
That I find all-enlightening:
With a wry smile and a few words
I am complimented and warmed.

He walks quietly and unimpeded
Through the house of my childhood—
His head quick to turn at
The slightest provocation
He is as striking to my peace of mind
As a silhouette.

Lori L Shaw
AFTER YEARS, SUDDENLY
After years suddenly
You enter my dreams—a companion,
An observer, helping me
I'm not sure
You inhabit my waking hours
Again with a disquieting old pain

I scan depths trying
To discern the reason for your presence
And I chastise myself for dreaming
About you, I cannot try again
To capture your heart
Not even in my dreams

Sometimes I think that
I am doomed to haunt you,
That I will never yearn
More for that ethereal passion
That has never come since
We were together, in a place
I cannot find
I don't want to die trying

Gayla L McCoy
HUNCH-BACK TREE
Hunch-back tree aching from the wind.
Sunlight stabbing my eyes again.
An inviting pain, and the rain
giving a home to the hope of spring.
Angry, biting, fighting winds—sing.
Soon will learn to relax—Put away your knife!
Soon will learn to relax—breathe in a new life.
Cold, naked, hunch-back tree
my heart goes out to thee.
Are you truly bent into sadness,
or do you bow to usher in Spring's warmth with gladness?
Spring
Springs that were dead to movement soon wake,
stretching slowly, slowly, ache.
Washing away their winter's sleep.
Don't weep, for to thee God will give the gift of greenery.
And still, you choose to be an aching, hunch-back tree?
Yes! But only to be kind to my face,
to keep me from the Sun's glaring embrace.
Hunch-back tree, my heart goes out to thee.

Mary Miler
THOUGHTS
I sang a song without words
As I strummed a cello without strings
It was just as well
For I sang
To a heart that was not there
But folded into the night
of yesterdays
Night is but the thought of yesterday;
Only the sunrise waits
At the end of song . . . the sun cannot rise
Till the song is sung;
Burnished bright words
And golden heart note
Have melted into a puddle of endless night,
The last note of love
Dissolved the sun into night.
Now I hunger to know what lies
Beyond the blackness of non-light!

Dorothy M Ralston

Dorothy M Ralston
PLEDGE ME GO

Voltaire prepared our ancestors for Freedom—Why are we not preserving it?

There is enough worm in me,
That I could remain low,
If it were not for Jesus
Lifting high, and pledge me go.
There is enough snake in me,
That I would so surely bite,
And poison hands feeding me
But for Jesus, cleansing white!
There is enough fox in me,
To be treacherous to all,
If it were not for Jesus
To balance me from the fall.
There is so much hate in me,
I would be utterly lost,
If it were not for Jesus!
Who paid with His life, the cost!!!

Charlotte Louise Lohr
MY DAD AND ME
We laughed I laughed
We talked I talked
We cried I cried
We sang I sang

We hunted I hunted
We walked I walked
We fished I fished

We hugged I hugged
We kissed I kissed
We joked I joked
We loved
But I never
He died Loved anyone
Like My Dad

Scott F Goodrich
LATENT FATE

To the dust that walls are made of and by.

Great breasted steps
Nippled sun
Monstrous bellies hang
loathsome heavy cloud
as WWII bombs and
rippled cloudlike thighs
soft on wurst and bier
carry history's burden
uncleansed by indifferent lake
colors; where men fight wind,
lend; a rainbow scene to
rich wood green—of paper and breath
To those many-ied deaths
felled as the tree, for free are to be
murderers and saints
with Godly paints

Virginia E Cruikshank
FOUNTAIN OF LIFE
My garden is a fountain of life!
It refreshes the arid days
When no rain falls.
It glitters in the sun
When skies have darkened.
It sprinkles the ideas
That sprout within my mind.
It showers a rainbow of color
Upon roses, lilies, columbines.
It bestows total healing
When I need to convalesce.
Garden, you are my life!

Pam Irwin
BRING BACK THE SUNSHINE—NOT THE RAIN
Sometimes our days and nights are very black.
The clouds surround us like a trap.
But searching for sunshine to appear,
Helps to brighten those dark days of fear.

Understanding why things happen as they do;
Why some trouble seems to come to just a few;
Keep your chin up and be happy come what may,
For tomorrow will be better, so they say.

Oh, oh, oh, draw back the curtain of gloom.
Send me the roses to bloom.
And take all the hurt and the pain,
And bring back the sunshine—not the rain.

We plan our future days in bright array;
But something can destroy those plans in just one day.
Don't look back for the reason for the pain;
Just look for the sunshine—not the rain.

Donna Adams
OASIS IN TIME
Four days out.
The sun was burning into his brain.
He was hopelessly lost.
His lips parched and swollen.
As the winds of time shifted the sand dunes of the deserts.
The oasis in his mind became reality.
She was there in the shadows of the pool.
Her image ever transmuted as she stepped into the waterfall.
Her beauty forever trapped in his mind as the silky waters caress her nude body.
The movements of her hands on her body as she reaches up to caress the falling waters told him of her loneliness.
He knew she was only a mirage of the reflection of his empty heart.
But still he refused to let go.
Unable to relinquish the vision in his mind.
For the pool was his reality.
Time would forever stand still.
As he fell slowly to the ground.
The burning desert once more claimed her own . . . .

Willie K Gill

Willie K Gill
VISITORS UNAWARE
Late one evening a T-Model was coming that had no top.
Looked small, although was two double seats, the driver stopped.

Parked in front of the bungalow near the large plank fence,
With children, girls and boys, parents said, "We mean no offense."

We have traveled from Tennessee, very far away.
The father said, "Will you take us in, we have no place to stay?"

"Yes, you all may have supper, beds for the night and breakfast, too."
The family sitting around the square table had food to pursue.

Eleven-year-old son with large blue eyes and blond curly hair,
Youths were all lovely, but the fair and handsome boy none other could compare.

Spending the night, nourished with food and resting,
Today we will be on our way; thanks for the blessings.

Father said, "The morning sun is shining early spring has come."
If no tribute to be paid, we will go search for a home.

Waving good-bye, starting back north again.
Settled on the Pascola Road near Hayti, Missouri and made friends.

Tree, shrubberies, and vines budding, leaves and blossoms to view,
Summer will come and fade away, lot of farm work to do.

In the White Cemetery, on a Sunday afternoon, close to Gil's house,
Kay asked Earl, "Will you go and find out what this is about?"

Autumn leaves turning, soft atmosphere, a feeling to my soul was awesome,
You remember the family that had the blond-haired son.

Last view a wooden casket, faded shirt and overalls, no socks or shoes.
Services were sad mellowing your heart when they said, "Adieu."

This is a true story and not very long.
Was in the early 1930's when the depression was on.

Starr K Pratt
SHOWER ME WITH YOUR LOVE

I dedicate this to my favorite poet: Robert Frost.

Shower me with your love,
Shower me with rain,
Let the stars twinkle above.
For with me, you'll forever reign.

Let the sun shine down upon me,
Let the flowers bloom and the birds sing,
It gives me the feeling of being free.
Keep me forever under your wing.

Keep me deep in your heart,
Keep me deep in your soul,
Let us have a brand-new start.
For i love you, heart and soul.

Oh so special are my days,
Oh so special are my nights,
And you'll never let me see a day of haze.
And i'll forever keep you in my sights.

So shower me with your love,
And shower me with rain,
And let the stars twinkle above.
For with me, you'll forever reign.

Patricia Hitch Phillips
WON—LOST—WON FOREVER
Waves break over the rocky shores and then slowly, lingering the water drifts back to the ocean; this is the way of love won and lost.

A storm with thunder pounding, lighting flashing, rain falls in a torrential downpour. Then lightning and thunder cease, the rain falls gently, the clouds hang heavy and gray in the sky; this is the way of love won and lost.

A flower blossoms full and beautiful with water and light and tender care. Water, light and care are taken from it: the flower wilts and dies. This is the way of love won and lost.

A seedling planted, cared for, nurtured over the years with attention, warmth and feeling; the roots grow deep, the tree grows taller and stronger with each passing day. This is the way of love—won forever!

Melanie A Gregory
A TIME TO PONDER
As mid-life approaches
It seems reality encroaches,
Youth's dreams beckon a faint call
While life's inventory looms large and tall.

Wisdom achieved by experience
Of many pitfalls . . . giving deliverance,
Awareness deepened through self-quest
Showing one has yet to uncover the best.

Happiness has strengthened hope
Giving courage to know one can cope.
Disappointments have left faded scars
Reminding one to try again for the stars.

Many joys have bestowed deep love
For life, each other, and God above.
Yet, time has been the greatest friend
For it's always present from beginning to end.

Mid-life . . . a time for evaluation
Does it bring frustration or elation?
A sense of urgency prevails . . .
To set unfulfilled dreams asail or
Leave them forever in anchor.

Carolyn Fulgham Harris
TOMORROW'S CHILD

To My Daughter, Haley Marya, My Honey Sweetie.

I walk aimlessly while the rain persists, and wonder if tomorrow's child will still exist.
Are children of today taking things from the children of tomorrow, like trees and flowers and things they can't borrow.
Will they think, or will tomorrow's child become extinct.

Richard O'Connor
WAVING GOOD-BYE
Our nation, apart,
in the twilight of supremacy
Riding the crest of a tiring wave.
We feed off the waves before and after, gaining size and momentum.
Yet we are blind to what the future holds as we near the shoals of our bleak destiny.
Great waves before us crash,
giving off a resounding sigh of death.
The once great, dismembered waves provide the undertow to feed the following crest.
Presently, the crystalline sands of our demise loom before us, tempting us on.
The beach draws near, as
we instinctively and blindly race faster.
The promptings of a natural cycle have determined our fate.
Onward, to the sands of ultimate peace!! . . .

God Bless America

Nettie Vaudine Green
NEVER ALONE
In my mind's eye spirits walk,
As I live asleep in vivid dreams;
All things past and future stored there,
And in reality, nothing is as it seems.
You I knew from long ago,
Since before the beginning of time;
I close my eyes and I can see you,
Treading the footprints of my mind.
And memories of long ago tomorrow,
With our lives as always entwined;
While nestled deep within my soul,
The age old story of all mankind.
So, you see, I'll never be lonely,
For I am never truly alone;
I know anyone I need will be there,
Because nothing past is ever gone.
I can always bring it back to mind,
When I fall asleep and let my soul roam;
Knowing that through all time and space,
There truly is no place like home.

Regina Ann Keen
ODE TO MY MOM

This is dedicated to my mom and best friend, Connie Hartzell. Your encouragement, love and faith in me resulted in my first publication and real recognition as a poet. Thanks mom. I LOVE YOU.

I speak these words purely from my heart;
There was a bond between us, very special from the start
I was protected from evil and surrounded by good;
You taught me right from wrong so that I understood
I was given wholesome values and morals to stand by;
You did this for my own good and now I understand why.

I have experienced happiness and sorrow, laughter and tears;
You have enriched by life throughout my twenty-seven years.
You cared for me and loved me your whole life through;
For all that I am, I am because of you.

Richard Scott Muñoz
SILENT TIMES

Mom and Dad, who are responsible for my being. Thank you both.

In the darkness of night, with the first rays of sunlight . . .
I rise to begin my new day . . .
My memories flow in the silence of my mind . . .
Of yesterdays and tomorrows, which are fading flowers . . .
Long stem roses with sprays of regret, like morning dew,
For what might have been and now can never be.
In my cell I pace, in the cool silence of night . . .
I feel the hot flush of my memory.
Your voice echoes in my memory, like my footfalls echo in the silent corridor.

Robin Anderson Adams
SMILES THAT FADE

In remembrance of Sheila Weeg and all victims of alcohol related auto accidents.

Many questions are asked no answer will appease,
Reality appears like a swift blowing breeze.
You can't touch it or see it, you feel it deep inside,
The sorrow you feel can't find a place to hide.
As your friends begin to gather, the things you hear are true,
He was fun, he was loving, he never made us blue,
Your life won't go unnoticed, your talent untold,
Your giving, your goodness we always will behold,
The smiles have faded, but memories are clear,
In our hearts you always will be near.
The pain that is felt will ease as time goes.
The smiles return with the bud of the rose.
The answers have come but there remains disbelief.
For we are too young for this thing they call grief.

Jeannie Echevarria
WHY?

A scene that is very sad
Is that of an untimely death
One of a long time friend
A friendship you thought would never end

You've been together from school to school
You looked up to her since she was cool
You both had each other's love in your heart
Since you thought you would never be apart

Then one day you get an unexpected call
From your friend's mother who's crying in the hall
You don't believe it and start crying out
Wondering how anything like this could ever go about

Why did she have to die? Why her? you scream
She's like the rainbow in my dreams
But one thing I would never forget my dear best friend
Is the love we shared from the beginning to the end!

William Wayne Higgins Jr
OVERDUE CONVERSATION

In memory of David Wayne Francis, partner, brother, and friend, whose company I will miss, until we meet again. Born January 29, 1971. Died June 18, 1989.

Hello David my good friend
Ain't seen you in a while how have you been
Congratulations on your graduation
Guess you'll be going to college after summer vacation
I tried to call you last night on the phone
Guess I was too late you were already gone
You look a little pale are you feeling all right
It must be the glow from that strange bright light
Remember all the crazy things we used to do
They said we'd end up dead if we didn't straighten up soon
Well we're still just as crazy and we're still alive
Did I say something wrong Dave why do you cry
You sure look good in that suit and tie
Might think you were meeting Jesus somewhere tonight
I wish you didn't have to leave so soon
Until we meet again it's been nice talking to you
As I reach out to shake his hand
I find a ringing telephone instead
The solemn voice on the other end says
Bad news Bill, David's dead

Nan Story Pfarner
CITY NIGHT

A rat scurries through the darkness in search of food.
A wino sleeps on a warm grate.
The same old bag-lady rummages through the same old garbage pail
In competition with the rat.

A school child struggles with his homework, sleepy-eyed.
His mother puts the last load in to wash.
The truck driver pulls away from a dock at the start of another
Weary cross-country run.

A millionaire in his smoking jacket sips his brandy
And signals to the guard at the gate
To turn on the electronic monitoring system to warn against
Old winos and bag-ladies and rats.

K Tibor Toth
INNER STRENGTH

The leaves shuddered—
The silence rose to a scream.
The creatures muttered
For all was not as it would seem.

Creatures scurried to their beds,
As the skies sealed over their heads.
As a raging bull, released from his pen
The skies let loose, just then.

Yet even as the thunder shook the ground
There was one hope to be found:
Behind the clouds, screaming and whining
The sun was still shining.

He searched his heart for that hidden sphere
And felt its warmth draw him near.
He then strode forth through the enveloping din
For now the sun was within.

Margaret Archuleta
HOME

As I sit in my backyard
under this old shade tree,
My thoughts go back
to my childhood days;
My Mother and Dad I see.

My Sisters and Brothers and Me . . .
HOME

As we all worked together
preparing for winter weather,
Our old house sheltered us
from the storm;
And the quilts that mother made,
O' how I remember being so clean
and warm . . . HOME

We planted and we harvested,
and all the livestock . . . we raised.
Every moment of our hard working days
We gave our Father praise.

At the end of a long hard day,
Sitting under an old Oak Tree,
I Would wash Dad's tired feet
while he read the Bible to me. . .
HOME

If only I could go home . . .
Mother's apron hanging on a nail,
Dad's plow in the fallen down barn,
To get a cool drink from our deep
well . . .

Now it's supper I smell . . . HOME

Now I am miles apart
but only a thought away;
Long as I live . . . They all live with me;
I cherish each one; as I hold them
in my heart.

My journey has been long . . . now in the twilight of my days
I am so lonely to see . . . all my
loved ones, who have gone away.
Across the many miles, mountains,
valleys, over the ocean's foam
Put your arms around me
JESUS . . . and take me . . .
HOME.

Jason Davis
ALONE

To Christina, With Love Forever and Always.

Sitting alone in an empty room,
He sees the couple walk by
An empty feeling fills his soul,
That brings a tear to his eye.
Looking back on the life he had,
It seems so long ago;
All of his dreams just faded away
As the lonely years took their toll.
Once he had a life so full,
He was standing on top of the world;
But when he lost the woman he loved,
His heart and mind went cold.
Now every day he hopes for change,
Something to brighten his day;
But he can't deal with a life so hard,
So he drinks his problems away.
Late one night on a city street
In the heart of "Sorrow's Land,"
A crowd of people find him dead
With a pistol in his hand.

Korinna Props (Rena)
FOR MY DAUGHTER

What life holds in store for you,
I don't really know,
But the more that you will learn,
It's all the more that you will grow.

They say to follow your head,
Instead of following your heart,
But through life you will find,
That's the first place you should start.

You see, your heart is much much more,
Than the muscle that keeps you alive,
It's where you get a certain feeling,
That makes you want to survive.

It's not just one single feeling,
It's all the others combined,
It's that special fine line,
Where love and hate intertwine.

For now you're too young to realize,
That all your feelings start to pair,
Everything about you, all that you become,
Gets its finest start right there.

Vicky A Peters
MOTHER

There is no other mother
Who could ever take your place.
You are someone special
And can never be replaced

You're always there when I'm down and out
To lend a helping hand
And always quick to disapprove
When I'm just being bad.

When I'm happy or excited and
Start dancing all around
You just laugh and say, "I'm crazy"
And wonder where I'm bound.

I hope I inherit your ability
To love
Because to me you'll always be
A very beautiful dove.

So when I say there is no other,
Who could ever take your place
You are the best and I've been blessed,
To have you for my mother.

Ileana Bustelo
SHE SINGS TO DIE

A bird soars high in frantic chase
Above a shore and a raging tide.
Her flight is now a bitter race,
To loose the song that's trapped inside.
Abandoned nest, forboding tree,
Alluring tree of deadly thorns.
Her life she'll end close to the sea
So there her soul may be transformed.
She sings her song of agony
Until her voice, her soul, is free.
The pain's released for us to see
The beauty of her melody;
God up in His Heaven waits
As beauty on the earth abates.

Renel L Brown
AS TIME MOVES ON

To Edna McCarthy with love always.

The mirror reflects
ageless lines
of tell-tale times
of the life gone by
can it really be
spots on eternity
memories fall like the leaves.

Should darkness rule
light breaks no more
sunshine exists only
in our hearts
of burning fire
dusks of gray lite the way.

Flowers grow in disarray
wild things that
can't be tamed
while fields of black
are all that remain
of green yesterdays
as time moves on . . . .

Lora Leone
PAINTING IN MY MIND

To my inspiration, may you always be in my heart.

To hear you
Caresses my ears
Symphony of sounds
From progressive to classical

To see you
Brightens my eyes
A fine work of art
Abstract indeed

To hold you
Our bodies molded as one
Embrassed in stone
Sculptured for a lifetime

To meet you
Share the arts with you
To harmonize our lives
For this is the painting in my mind

Vickie Nelson
SMILE OF THE HEART

I sat on my
"Island Alone,"
surrounded by the
"Sea of Only One."

Conceited, I thought
others foolish when
they allowed emotions
to rule them.

Then: the precious hand
of the child
touched my own.
And my heart smiled.

Dawn V Ryan
THE DEEP, THE TENDER, THE TRUE

To my Kellys.

The deep, the tender, the true
Cannot be sheltered from the rain
To hide them means we lose them
Lose their warmth
Not just their pain

The deepest, truest feelings
Lying open in the wind
Are painful
But they lead us
To the shelter of a friend

Neil W Azevedo
FALL LIES QUIETLY ON WHISPERING WIND

Fall lies quietly on whispering wind
journeying softly from land to land
calling forth, our soulless grace
to come unshielded and take her hand

and fly with her through dancing rain
cold and thoughtless as it descends
upon our naked weary heads
bent in penance for mortal sin,

so through the valley we will sweep
killing unmercifully in chilling
silence leaving rainbows in our wake
so beauty shall be called the violence.

Sheila Edel Morrow
NOCTURNE

Feelings withheld, words cannot say;
your emotions are stable, you'll find
a way.
We care, we love, we want the best; a
few moments of happiness, seconds
to rest.
All little snowflakes, landing alone
for such a short time, beauty to bring.
Pause to look, select what we want;
my heart floats around like a balloon
on a string.
Real love some never know;
maturity, realization, to know
yourself and why you go.
To express your thoughts; that reason
for living, God's way is not taught.
Love is expressed in many ways, of
happiness, sadness, sun and rain.
Still water runs deep; through waves
come the foam.
From bud to flower, infant to adult;
hurts and sorrows, joys erupt.
Each atom of so many particles,
floating and bumping, causing on
each other.
A child is born, to live and learn; so
wise then, but for love we yearn.
Mistakes are made; birds fly away, to
the nest return one stormy day.
To find one's self again, a human
being; someone who cares, a reason
for living.
Fate steps in and brings another;
early to love again, questions will
smother.
Salt and pepper, bread and butter;
love and hate, life and death.
Black and white, win and lose; a rack
of spices from which to choose.
Clouds bring rain, it drizzles and
storms; but flowers still grow.
Marriages come, marriages go; but
up your umbrella and whither thou
goest.
It's written by Chopin, we can love
again; to bring happiness and peace
within.
My heart full of tenderness, a world
to know; my love for you will
constantly flow.

Dorinda Michaud
PERSISTENCE

the bugs by the brook
haven't changed
in their ferocity
as they try again
to penetrate my defenses.
persistent things,
the mosquitos
and you,
eating away at my composure,
and even though I know
they
aren't the same ones
as last time
or the summer before that,
they are recognizable
in their habits
and sounds
as you are,
returning every so often
to feed.

Sylvia Hughes

Sylvia Hughes
I'LL BUY YESTERDAY

Somehow it got away so fast
Now they tell me it's just the past
didn't realize how much it meant
Left me so soon without a hint

But money can buy anything they say
And I worked seven days to get
this pay
So I'd like to buy yesterday please
I must have it back! I'll get on my
knees!

While working hard for tomorrow
Well, I just didn't see yesterday go
Need to go back, put things in order
Spend more time with my little
daughter

Had no time for my neighbor
Wanted that money, more and
more
I have plenty now, so I want
yesterday back
But my family's gone! I saw them
pack!

While I was enjoying my power race
Someone else took my place
Could I buy a handkerchief, I need to
cry
Alone with my money I'm left to
die

Brigitte Boltinghouse
IT'S RAINING . . .

Raindrops can make such gentle
showers
And do wonderful things to red roses
and other flowers
But sometimes they are like an
untamed child
Stormy and wild
Stormy skies
Full of power, cloudy and grey
Travelling fast, without delay
On everyone's roof they will pound
Making that wonderful sound
They can also fall into anyone's eye
Who needs to cry
Muddy eyes — muddy roads
Such heavy loads
And if it's foggy there will be no
sight at all
Head in the clouds
Full of doubts
Dust and doubts, the rain will wash
them away
For after a shower comes always
another clear day

Valarie Ponder
DON'T FORGET ABOUT ME

Sometimes it changes
When people are apart
Life walks a new path
And we're left in the dark.

But sometimes it changes
When people are together
We both come and go
And never notice each other.

Sometimes it never changes
Feelings that we hide
People grown apart
Struggling with their pride.

But sometimes it never changes
Life goes on and on
With moment after moment
Here and then gone.

Raymount M Paschal
THE TRAVELLER

From within the travel begins.
Flow from the molecular shell.
From this shaded room,
and ride upon the wind.

It is reality although it feels a dream,
sometimes it may seem a dream
within a dream.
Go to places that you've been
without wings,
see things you've not yet seen in
the . . .
. . . physical being.

Curiously roam through time and
space,
never will you get tired.
See civilizations never dreamed of by
the human race.
Forgetting about the physical desires.

Morning comes without a warning,
time to rise and shine.
Return to your molecular shell,
and wonder, "Was it all in my
mind?"

Donald A B Thompson
A WISH

I wish for Peace!
Peace in Africa
Peace transcending
realms of vain imagination

I wish for Blackness
Beautiful Blackness
Blackness uniting
nations to crumble Apartheid

I wish for voices!
Resounding voices
Voices crying:
Freedom
Equality
Truth.

And when all—
in God we achieve . . .
I wish for Dancing!
Amidst drums beat.

James Heald
BATS

I like to look at bats
They're like flying rats
Except bats don't have tails
And they never fail
That's because they're bats

Bats are mammals
And probably smarter than camels
So I have to say
That cats are OK
But bats are best!

Ronnie Jackson
THE SPIRIT OF MY SQUARE DANCE FRIENDS

Dedicated to the Spirit of '76 Square Dance Club, Oklahoma City, Oklahoma, Stan Ruebell, Caller.

The spirit of my square dance friends,
they give me quick hellos, hugs,
and handshakes;
sparks of warmth,
little treasures everyone.

Like the many drops of water that
make a lake,
Together, their friendships build a
new fire
in a hurt and lonely heart.

Those sparks will make a way for
love to
grow—
to be given away in new
friendships,
in new ways.

Sylvia Hughes
THINGS I LOVE
I'm so happy to be in this world
And I just love being a girl!
I like to pin flowers in my hair
And I like bows and lace on
clothes I wear

I love nylons, dresses or a pretty skirt
And being human I like to flirt!
I love my makeup, especially my
lipstick
Helps me feel better even when
I'm sick

Sometimes I just like to hum and sing
I'm not crazy, I just love
everything!
To see a rosebud bathed in the
morning dew
To look up at the sky, so beautiful
and blue

Yes I love everything, everyone,
every race
Just like I love my bows and lace
To be given so much I want to give
too
And so my love I give to you

Should I return to this world of
beauty
I'd like to be a girl again, love be
my duty
I hope I can again experience these
joys
'Cause most of all, I LOVE
LITTLE BOYS!!!

Hope De Leon
AN AMERICAN DREAM
I am an American
I have an American dream.
For love and peace throughout the
world.
For no nation Supreme.

The Philippines to make their peace
The Contra Rebels too.
For Libya's Anger to subside
For peace talks to hold true.
Iran, Iraq to stop their war,
The waters to be free.
For ships to travel as they wish
For no more deaths at sea.
For Africa to come to terms
For Apartheid to end.
For every black and white to join,
In the making of friends.

Perhaps this way hunger would end.
And illnesses subside.
Perhaps if we try hard enough,
We'll all find love inside.

Connie C Coy
A MIRACLE CALLED "BIRTH"
The parents who come thru our
doors,
with many questions and fears,
Of the coming little stranger,
who will very soon be here.
It's our pleasure to care for,
and a sight to behold,
When that precious moment finally
comes
the drama now unfolds.
They've worked and dreamed for
months for this,
and now the moment's here,
and the fruits of their hard
earned labor,
is starting to appear.
The wonder, awe and joy they feel,
is plain for all to see
It's why I like to come to work.
It's what pleases me.

Dorothy Mitchell Cotita
SECRET TEARS
A few days after your passing,
I gave your son my name.
For more than 50 years,
I have waited for you in vain.

The time grows short,
For I shall meet you soon again,
And you will hear me call your name.

Though the road has been long
And the days dreary,
I had a part of you near me.

Secret tears I've shed each day.
Wait for me darling along the way
For soon you will hear me call your
name.

Darling, walk slowly down that
lonely road
And soon I will meet my God,
And you will hear me call your name.

Cammi Buttner
MY LIFE IS LIKE THE BEACH

In memory of Andrew James Friedlander who inspired me to write this poem.

My life is like the beach
Where vast nothingness seems to
span forever
Like the broken seashells strewn
across the sand
As the rocks are beaten upon the
shore
By the overwhelming force of the
waves
The seaweed, lifeless where the tide
has pushed it away
And one lone sea gull wonders in
which direction to fly

Lorna Frans Solomon
THE RABBI
Once I had a friend.
Some, called him a Rabbi,
some called him a "Holy Man,"
others just referred to him as a
painting.

In truth, he was all these things.
God used a little clay to make a man,
but, I had brushes,
knives, palettes, paints,
canvasses,
and a lot of love. There he
emerged—
proud and formidable, gentle and
humble, beautiful and ugly.

Mankind in general.

But, to me, he was a friend (someone
special).
He radiated all the love I tried to
instill in him.
We communicated.

He, in his long black robe, yarmulke,
flowing white beard, impressive
nose,
gave love to me.

We shared a closeness for months.
Then came the inevitable day—
when he was pronounced dry.

Departure was in sight.
With sadness of heart and many,
many tears—
He left me.

Friends are what he needs now—to
love and admire him.
And to pass at least once a day
to say hello.

We will meet again, my friend,
not today, nor tomorrow,
But, you will know I am there

and we will communicate.

Cheryl G Wick
GOOD-BYE MAGGIE
sweet smile creases, creep
across your face
a map of haunting sorrow
lines lay near, contrasting
years spent living
abundant love and pain
peacefully put to rest
good-bye maggie

Ernest E Brown
TATTERED MEMORIES
These old pictures
Don't throw them away
They hold memories
Of back in my days

I went to church then
And I had a wife
Little children . . .
Were part of my life

I am the reason . . .
That my life is shot
And these old memories
Are all that I've got

These old pictures . . .
All tattered and torn
They are my life . . .
From the time I was born

If I lose my memory
(That is the day)
THEN if it pleases you . . .
Throw them away

Ernest E Brown
COON HUNTING
I went coon hunting
With my Pa
He was an Indian
That took care of his squaw
When he climbed a tree
He was tough as a nail
He'd throw down a coon
By the end of its tail

He said, "This big coon
Is ready for some rounds
You'd better hold on . . .
To a couple of the hounds"
There I was . . .
In the middle of the night
Holding two hounds . . .
And letting ol' Blue fight

I could see my Pa . . .
When I looked up at the moon
He was coming down the tree
To get that ol' coon
The ol' coon's hide
He tacked to the wall
He said he would sell it . . .
Later in the fall

I will remember that coon
Until the day I die
And the sweet taters . . . hmmmmm
In that RACCOON PIE

Amy Gayle Stock
CLOUDS
Clouds are white,
they are at a huge height.

If you see one large and fluffy,
like a teddy bear big and stuffy.

Now you know,
so get up and go.

Dorothy Margaret Griggs
LET RELIGIOUS FREEDOM RING
Society is making
a deliberate attempt
to "squelch" our souls
by casting God aside
Our religious freedoms
are in "crisis"
but our Lord's promises
will abide

Someday, mankind
will be judged
for what we're . . .
doing now
A higher court
than the "supreme"
then . . .
will be around

On that great day
we'll all wish . . .
we had supported "life"
and favored God in our schools
We'll soon awaken . . .
to the fact
that all such unchristian acts
marked us all as "fools"

Dorothy Margaret Griggs
STREET RAGAMUFFIN
He watched the children playing
So carefree in the street
He envied them, their home and
parents
And their choice of foods to eat

He knew they felt not, hunger pains
Like in his stomach now
He knew their beds of "down
feathers"
Were framed; not on the ground

He knew their magnificent toys were
such . . .
That only in his dreams, did he ever
know
He knew tonight, his "bed of rags"
Would not protect him from the snow

He wondered what "fate" held in
store for him

And as he trudged, he felt so old
His little heart was warm in his body
But his feet were icy cold

1st ending:
He prayed a prayer to Jesus
And his Father knew his plight
He said, "Son, you have a home in heaven
And you're going there tonight"

2nd ending:
This poor little boy, so destitute
With no place to go
Knew not, HIS DESTINY WAS GREAT
As he walked through the falling snow

Diana Irish
PRAYER OF MY ANCESTORS
Oh Great Spirit, see'er of today
Grant me the swiftness on my way
May my thoughts journey into the wind
An enter the heart in which it I send
So remember this, for it is true
My spiritual guidance has come from you
Father moon, Mother earth hear my prayer
Please take me into your care
Always keep the sunshine upon my face
Grant me the wisdom of your grace
Always keep the rainbows in the sky
The joy and respect of life mounted high
Keep the wind always at my back
An for strength may I never lack
Give me the endurance to face each day
An to journey straight upon my way
Keep me always from the path of wrong
And fill my heart with a joyous song

Brian Hofer
INDIAN SUMMER

To Jenny Johnson.

I have a job, but I don't have a car
It don't really matter, because we don't live far
When that whistle blows, I'll be running home
I want to hold her, and that's the truth
Each step I take, is one step closer to my youth
As I run, love seems to show me the way
and to her, I run faster each and everyday . . .

Debra Sue Heidt
THE OLD HOUSE BY THE ROAD
Empty, lonely, and crying out for repair
Longing for a loving touch.
Years have gone by creating a stillness.
But we are only intruders,
Exploring the lives of those long gone
In every closet and drawer.
Gathering up old memories
In bags and boxes.
Cleaning, sorting, keeping, discarding
Searching through the past,
Creating room for what will come
Clearing away dust and cobwebs
And years of living
With a single stroke
Reviving what was still for so long
And now, creating a new beginning.

Dorothy Qualls
THE SILENT AMERICAN
They speak of peace
from rotundas, and
divine diplomatic prophecy
from damask lined
drawing rooms . . .
do not assume, my son,
that your nation's heritage
has always been
propagated by politicians
or maligned with
My-Lais and court scandals.
Beneath the tarnished facade
are the people
who made this country great;
the lone sentinel
at Richmond
a steel worker
in Detroit
the farmer
from Ft. Wayne,
and a child, like yourself
who will work to right
his country's wrongs.

Joseph F McTiernan
YOU AND I

To Marie and her Mom, Helen McTague O'Hearn, and those that are close to them, Heart, Mind, and Soul!

A certain gift flows forth
much like a sunbeam through a cloud,
every time I think of a certain someone
one of whom I am very proud

This certain gift holds meaning
much like a rainbow after tears,
thoughts of this certain someone
one could not measure in years.

This certain gift is a smile
a treasure which I hold true,
and this certain someone is
no one else but you!

Pat Marshall
PEACE
Meadow grass,
Quiet streams,
Puppy's yawn,
Childhood dreams.

Rustling leaves,
Gentle doves,
Summer rain,
Parents' love.

Brand-new dawn,
Singing choir,
End of day,
Warming fire.

Happy songs,
Flying kites,
Laughter soft,
Velvet nights.

. . . Peace

Leanna Wray
MY WORLD
I see a distant orange moon
I see a crippled tree bowing to gravity
I see a scared little girl in my face
I think the glare of the moon off the mirror makes me inferior

I hear a caught bird in the attic
I hear the strangled tune of a dying merry-go-round
I hear the waves crashing mercilessly on the shore
I think I'm outgrowing my imagination

I touch the tears washing my face
I touch a faded picture of you
I touch the razor to my wrist
I believe the scared little girl in my face is gone

Cara Joe McQueen
WHO AM I?

To my mom, thank you for your encouragement and support. With love, Cara Joe.

The thing that makes me different
is my style.
I'm an individual—I stand as one.
I am unique—I work alone.
I'm glad I'm me and nobody else.
I do more than some people do.
I like my personality—I like my style.
And that's what I like about myself.

Nym M K Nevarez
TRACING THE WILD

For my papa.

To think of one's parents as wild
Has a déjà vu sense of appeal;
At moments the thought is such a relief,
As if having an age to steal.

Their faces to you are a time wrought mirror,
Of being that you shall become,
As you and they think of themselves and the times,
When they knew not of the life weight on some.

To them you are but a memory of
The careless days they have graced,
And the wonder of youthful unknowledge,
That they themselves their parents have traced.

Joyce N Collins
EARTH-BOUND ANGEL
God made an earth-bound angel,
When he made my mother dear;
It was nothing but a miracle,
When he placed her here.

She toils without a murmur,
Her lot is but to serve;
The love that she has given,
I never shall deserve.

A little bit of heaven,
Lingers around our place;
Because we have a special angel,
With a mother's face.

If I were offered for my own,
A kingly ransom . . . wealth untold;
I'd rather have my mother dear,
Than all earth's tarnished gold.

Joyce N Collins
PONDERING FUTILITY
I ain't so sure it's worth it . . .
All 'de fuss that some folks make;
I ain't so sure it's worth a'tall,
The pains they seem to take.

They primps and paints and fixes,
And trys to look so pretty;
That they winds up looking older . . .
O it shore do seem a pity!

I ain't so sure it's worth it,
When they tints and dyes 'de hair;
And they trys to look like daughter,
Who is still so young and fair.

They shortens all 'de dresses,
To show their knobby knees;
And they looks like all 'de dead limbs,
In a field of old oak trees!

What they is a'fightin' uselessly,
Is 'de finger of Mother Time;
When they trys to look so youthful,
Like they did when in 'de prime.

Joyce N Collins
CEMETERY LOT
Blessed little plot of ground,
Wherein my heart doth lie;
Although the sun is shining,
Tears flow as raindrops from the sky.

Dear gentle babe, just barely two,
Sweetens the hardened earth;
He was pure joy and laughter,
From the first day of his birth.

His chubby hands, a masterpiece,
Carved from the hand of God;
Tugged at your soul with slightest touch,
And still do beneath the sod.

There's no explaining the sense of pride,
When this angel, so fair of face;
Would train his eyes upon you,
Filled with tenderness and grace.

Why was his mission completed,
In such a brief time span?
Profound thoughts and understanding,
Are far beyond the mind of man.

Joyce N Collins
EPITAPH
Remember me upon the sea,
With bleached wind-tousled hair;
Water droplets teasing my face,
And warm sun soothing each care.

Cradled upon the sea's vast bosom,
Within her arms to gently rest;
Pastel greens and blues engulf me,
My swaddling clothes each foamy crest.

Remember the craft so proud and strong,
And her beauty from stem to stern;

Poetry in motion, my ship full rigged,
Oh for the sea I yearn!

No quiet solitude can compare,
To the sea gull's gentle sway;
No union purer than sea and sky,
As they blend at end of day.

Remember me then, if you will,
With sails pure white, silk spun;
The outline of my silhouette . . .
Oh for the sea I yearn.

Joyce N Collins
EUPHONY OF SPRING
Spring in all her glory,
Tapped on my door today;
With blossoms budding everywhere,
She took my breath away!

Dogwood white as winter's prime snow,
Carpeted the gnarled old trees;
And azaleas in carnival colors,
Swayed gently to hypnotic breeze.

If you listen very quietly,
Perhaps you'll hear the symphony;
Of the dazzling syncopation,
From spring's sylvan soliloquy.

Janet C Walsh
THE FALLEN HERO
I walk the streets day after day
People hurrying to and fro
I try to bundle up against the cold
A silent tear begins to fall;

The days slip by with no meaning
I live for the moment—Now
I ask for change as people pass by
No one sees or hears me
I scream a silent cry;

Hey, I understand you in nice clothes—me in dirty rags
I shout, "I was just like you if could believe
Had nice clothes, car, money, and a family
Will someone answer my pray for help?"

I am no longer the same person
No money or job
My heart has grown cold
I wander the streets, but I call it home

I went to War for you
I carried the flag to victory, won the medals
I wonder, Is this the gratitude I deserve?

Felicia Adamson
BLACK PRIDE
BE PROUD of your uniqueness
Face of full lips and nose of broadness
Treasured symbols of our Heritage

BE PROUD of our pigmentation
Beautiful brown to black variations
A rainbow of unity I declare

BE PROUD of our sisters and brothers
For accomplishments unknown to our ancestors
Achieved however due to our ancestors' struggle

I am PROUD of the Black:
- Scientists
- Teachers
- Parents
- South Africans
- Students &
- Entertainers

I'M PROUD OF YOU!
I'M PROUD OF ME!
I'M BLACK AND I'M PROUD

Linda Genna
THE JOURNEY
She steps into the night,
Across a lawn, . . . down the street,
The sound of footsteps . . . ,
She stops, . . . it's not her feet;

Turns her head to look,
NOISE! . . . a stray cat runs away,
It feels so cold and lonely,
She wished the cat would stay;

"The world it seems so dark,
. . . wish I were with you,
Can't find where you are,
. . . wish I only knew . . . "

Continuing the journey,
A car goes speeding by,
Life it turns so quickly,
She stops to wonder why?

She walks in, lights blinding,
Seems she's walked so far . . . ,
Was it really worth the nightmare,
Just to buy that Snickers bar

Linda Genna
IF I MAKE IT THROUGH THE NIGHT . . .
Wicked visions calling,
Close my broken eyes . . . ,
Unfinished portraits laughing,
Playing games with lies;

Midnight mind invasion,
Deception by illusion,
Endless in duration,
Control by confusion;

Masquerading as my own face,
Always something out of place,

Phantoms hidden by the light,
Fear of falling, mind in flight;

Constantly reaching for that door,
Will I awaken, just once more?

Linda Genna
ALONE
Alone . . . inside,
Not just by yourself,
When no one cares . . . ,
Time stopped . . . saddest moments,
Alone, . . . not lonely,
It's running through you, . . . alone,
Her eyes laughing, . . . alone,
Silent tears, . . . so alone,
Alone . . . you are a song,
. . . yet no one ever hears it,
We'll never be alone . . . ,
. . . but always be . . . alone.

Linda Genna
WINDOW GREY PANE
Watching . . . in silence . . . ,
From windows unseen,
They pass her like shadows,
Same boring routine . . . ;

Captive and void, . . . still waiting,
No one to turn the key,
Ignite a dampened spark,
Set the spirit free;

None dare approach,
She will not be bought,
Few ever imagine,
The dreams she has wrought;

Seeming untouched,
Behind window grey panes,
Hiding all emptiness,
Alone . . . she remains.

Linda Genna
GIFTS FOR MY KIDS . . .
. . . a whole new ocean for Brian,
. . . with an island of his own,

. . . for John . . . a regal forest,
. . . with a brand new sky,
. . . . all my love.

Angela Williams
THE FRIENDS I HAVE!
The friends I have, the friends I have
The only ones who know
What my feelings are
The ones who care most of all

The ones whom I trust most of all
The ones who share all my feelings
Good or bad.
The ones whom never a bad thing
Comes from their mouth.

The ones whom know me best of all.
The ones that are the greatest friends of all. They are:

Erica Marie Cain,
Pamela K. Minogue,
and
Mary Catherine Gordon

Angie Casey
OUTTAKES
Fast forward reality
freeze-framed;
a mind's slow-motion attempt to make sense
that my tiny son struggled and lost.
Uniqueness amplified by mystery.
Indecipherable genetic whispers
mute glimpses of truth;
no voice to cry, to laugh, to explain.
Infirmity his tangible eternity.
Ten hostaged months.
His legacy now smuggled safely
to freedom, enshroud in my heartbeats.
Superimposed on cerebral silver screen,
milestones commonly mundane;
like each ounce gained.
Etched reverse negative,
his two-and-only teeth.
Memories,
when viewed by an unknowing editor,
would be cast as
outtakes.

Angie Casey
LOVESPUN
Steppin' back from my love.
Takin' a long look at you.
Losin' myself in the patchwork;
symmetry of synonyms.
Raw earthy fibers, homespun.
Woven, unashamed.
Americanacloth
mitered at cozy corners,
where your integrity
meets my uncertainty.
Fine spiritspun simplicity.
Eiderdown honesty.
Tatting of sweet slumberlust.
Deliberate stitches
needlework virtue
to bind a fabric rich
with your subtle intensity;
rollin' me up in your warmth,
burrowin', catypilla'-like,
into your love.
Steppin' back's not easy.
Takin' a long look at you.
You, masterquilter of quaint ecstasy,
safekeeper of my heart.

Elizabeth Locke

Elizabeth Locke
THE GIFT

To my beloved father,
Errol H. Locke: 7-17-1890—1-1-1990.

Two butterflies rose
From their prism-cell;
Yellows and blues
and orchids to sell.
A daisy, a rose
a lichen-tree
Blue grass, lilies
and even me
Reached out to touch
Their loveliness.
Fluttering, fragile,
poised, wings pressed,
Each butterfly paused
a moment in prayer.
Their beauty died,
but love stayed there.
Hush, and you'll hear
a butterfly's cry,
"Love given once can never die."

Elizabeth Locke
OUR UNSPOKEN LOVE
Warm and large the gentle hands
that held my tiny fingers.
The early sun bathed the path
through the meadows
As we trod, silently sharing
Our unspoken love.

Across life's path crawled
many living things of earth.
Our eyes beheld their wondrous ways
and we filled, in joy.
Many tiny hands joined us one by one,
their hearts singing sweetly to
Our unspoken love.

The din of time's traffic cut across
our shared quiet woods.
Our hands let go. Back to back
We tore through the whirring world
of man's hard toys, setting aside
Our unspoken love.

Our warm gentle hearts succumbed
to ticker tape, bank loans,
Garbage collection, TV commercials,
plea bargaining, bawling salesmen—
All drowning out
Our unspoken love.

Now, years aside, our gentle fingers entwine.
Yours are gnarled and cold,
Mine wrinkled too, caress

your ancient wisdom rutted
brow.
We have the gift of time to share
again
Our unspoken love.

Tomorrow I shall bend and kiss
your precious face.
Your eyes, though closed in the
gentle sleep of eternal peace,
Shall be free to see the full
beauty of our unspoken love.
And you will hear my overflowing
heart
whisper, "I love you, Dad!"

Brian M Hogue
LOVE IS LIKE THE SUN

To: Stephanie Ann Tullo—You made this happen—Love, Brian.

Love is like the sun,
It's always there.
When it's shining it creates a
warmth in you.
But, when it's hidden, like the
sun, you know it's still there,
somewhere.
Love is found in life as the sun
is in the seasons.
At birth you see love, but can't
really feel it,
yet, like the sun in winter, you
feel its warmth.
Then childhood comes along and you
can see love all around.
You start to feel it, like the
warmth of the sun in spring.
Then mid life is here, and so is love
in full swing;
like the sun in summer.
But then as age catches up, love starts
to fade
As the sun dies in the fall.

Theodore L Codding
FENCE
Caught on wire
The pain
deep inside
Rusty veins
Verge of
greener side.

Elizabeth Dawn Bender
TRUE HEART VALENTINE
Suitors kneel with rosebuds
Petals fall gently from grace
While fringed lids furl sunset
And glowed curve of your face
Bowed streets be forgotten
When last flavors be gone
Yet cheeks home that nestle
Thy Brave chest till dawn

Diamonds lose their luster
When passing fancy be flown
Thy Tender Kiss marks true heart
Where fond memories be sown

Ellen R Graham
UNITY
Questing through this abominable
sphere
inhabitants of different hues
presenting illusion to the eye
hostility, aversion, detestation
embracing the whole domain
populations composing communities
seeking, yearning, gazing, dreaming,
uninterrupted harmony
resembling a zebra's stripes
mutually in union
complementing each other
vividly like the moon's bright
presence
pressed against the night
joined by a moral bond
hand in hand
incorporated into one
As it is in heaven

John Wiles
CHRISTINE ERIN

To Christine, You are especially nice to be near.

You have a smile that can only
endear,
This is why I find you so nice to be
near.

Your everyday manner is so sincere,
This is why I find you so nice to be
near.

Your way with children is so very
dear,
This is why I find you so nice to be
near.

Your pretty blue eyes have such
revere,
This is why I find you so nice to be
near.

Dear Christine, for me it is very clear,
These are the ways I find you so nice
to be near.

Marie Samsel Bulkley
FALLEN BRICKS AND BUTTERFLIES

To all who experienced the Loma Prieta Quake on October 17, 1989.

A solitary monarch, on a warm and
quiet day
Reminded me that the fall was here,
and had come for a winter's stay.
Forgotten soon, this miracle, when a
rumble and a shake
Began a time of shock and fear in a
tremblor's fearful wake.
As objects fell and glassware flew
and I stumbled t'ward the door
The wrath of this Giant creature grew
to heights not felt before.
Once outside my senses fought to
reach reality,
While the earth still jerked and
trembled, I felt spent of energy.

No sleep this night; thoughts racing,
in the back seat of my car—
Is my house intact? Shall I move
away? Where-ever will I go?
Daylight came with a numbness; and
the earth continued to jar.
Was my house really whole? The
chimney's a fright!
But once inside, in spite of the mess,
felt things would be alright.
Two days of clean-up and the
chimney now felled,
Took a break in the sunshine, and
what scene caught my eye?
Fallen bricks with butterflies
fluttering near by.

Yes, I'll stay.

Larry Lee Transou
THE PENTAGON
They don't call it WAR anymore;
To do so would be too atrocious;
Now, you will be told the truth,
Though you may perceive it to be
precocious.

Our War Department, it has been
abolished;
A Pentagon we now have, with five
walls—
Politically polished.
Hardship Tours, are with us now; on
lands, and seas—
So very far away.
Along with a Demilitarized Zone, left
over from another day.
Hostile Fire Zones, and Combat
Zones, are now quite common:
To Low Intensity Conflicts, our
Republic is now often summoned!

I could tell you more, but then—
Your tears would still, slowly
flow.
Suffice it to say, that on the NEXT
given day—
A DAY, when young Americans,
again on foreign soil will fall;
Their blood will be just as red
As so many other young
Americans;
Who have, for so very long—
Been so very dead.

Jennifer Lea Thompson
THE UNWRITTEN ESSAY
lines on paper
pen in hand
time blowing by
as soft summer sand.

topic in mind
but no words near
the annoying clock
is all I hear.

searching, searching
for something to write
words evade me
like a thief of the night.

essay due
and not a scribble to show
my tiring head
sinks unbearably low.

lines on paper
pen in hand
time still blowing by
as soft summer sand.

Michelle Santoro
A TRUE LOVE FOREVER
There is a special love we possess.
It grows greater—never less.
We live far apart,
but are always close in heart.
We remember the night we talked for
hours,
hoping we'd be hit by Cupid's arrow.
The cherished letters,
praying we would always be
together.
An endless dream destroyed only
with a memory,
Of hope and love that will never be
forgotten.
It is a true love forever.

Tamara Simonds
OUR GIFT

To my husband Bill who gave me our gifts, Matthew, Sonya.

Children give joy.
Children give sorrow.
The children we have today
are only ours to borrow.

Children give joy.
Children give pain.
The children we have can make
us think over and over again.

Children give joy.
Children give pain.
Children thirst for knowledge
Like flowers thirst for rain.

Children give joy.
Children give sorrow.
The greatest gift our children give us
is their love and promising
bright tomorrows.

Cleo Renfro
JOURNEY TO NOWHERE
I have eyes, but nothing is clear.
I have ears, but cannot hear.
Down life's road I trudge along.
Walking without a purpose,
And nowhere to belong.
Life's sights and sounds pass me by,
Without the knowledge that I cannot
cry.
I waver and wonder day by day,
Of life's pleasures, I have
Nothing to say.
Am I a fool? Probably so.
What am I looking for? I do not
know.

Laura M Woellert
THE SICILIAN SIREN
It is irresistible. Restless. Invincible.
There is no weakness, but your heart,
Your soul.
There is hunger, it is sensual with
power
Like nectar, blending and fusing,
until
Power becomes one with the spirit.

The essence of the mortal is one with
chosen destiny.
Your soul is sated, but
Your heart holds impiety.

Like the wind-salted hills of the Isle,
There is no retreat from the temptress
of desire.
Once inside, once sated,
Identities are lost. Forfeited in the
darkness of a promising
Embrace. Promises are collected
And sold to the provider.
Without synonymity, there is
weakness . . .
The provider nourishes destitution
with needs,
Wants, desires . . .

Desire is the temptress, like,
The far away land that holds the
promise.
The power. The means.

Laura M Woellert
GRAND CANAL, VENICE
My Finger Tips Trace Your
Pastel Patterns.
The Colors, Pale and Soft
Linger in the Early Morning Sun
Light.

Like a Soft Melody,
The Colors Mesh With

Pure and Tender Strokes.

The Water. Tranquil.
Motionless . . .
And Constant.
Its shaded Surface is Clouded,
A veil Made of Watery Fingers.
Holding Secrets,
Its Green Depths Holding
The Treasures
Of Lost Illusions.

Berta M McGlothlin

Berta M McGlothlin
MASTER THE THOUGHT

To humanity.

Thought, created in the spiritual realm, building block of being.
All reality is perceived in the spirit, conceived in the mind and in the heart believed.
Life quest, discerning truth when perceiving.
Sanity, mastering the pure thought conceived.

Berta M McGlothlin
THOUGHT

To humanity.

A thought is a seed sown and as surely as a baby is conceived must be aborted or born.

Laura Cipolla
SUMMER DAY
The willows are swaying,
The children are playing,
The sun is glowing,
The wind is blowing,
The grass is growing,
The mower is mowing,
Hoses are flowing,
Birds are singing,
Some children are swinging.
People are tending their gardens with care,
Pulling weeds
And planting seeds.
Other people are diving
And splashing in pools.
Little kids are fighting.
Teenagers are riding their bicycles
While others ride their tricycles!
The feeling of summer is in the air
And the wind is blowing through my hair—

Jacqueline Manley
EYES
Eyes . . .
deep sapphire spheres
exquisitely faceted
by flashes
of
brilliant light.
Eyes . . .
soulful eyes
of shimmering blue pain,
emotions
briefly flickering
like sunlight upon diamond.
Eyes . . .
lapis lazuli pools of soothing chill
in summer's heat,
tongues of blue-orange flame
to warm the soul
in winter's cold embrace.

Sarah A Rivers
THE PROPOSAL

This poem is dedicated to Ralph, my dear husband.

The sky was radiated by a moonlit night,
Her violet eyes seemed to twinkle with delight,
She touched a sterling rose to her sensuous lips,
Each petal was glistening, mimicking her fingertips,
An illustrious dazzle dared her to search for the quest,
Attached to the long stem clutched close to her breast,
There in her hands lay the truest of true,
A once forever diamond, and a card "I love you,"
With abated breath she fantasized of her love,
So precious, so handsome—he was sent from above,
The whispers of silk taffeta rippled slowly as she turned,
And she clasped her cherished treasure, as her temples burned,
With the expectation of her zestful life,
That of becoming and being a wife.

Sheri D Weisensee
UNWILLING SUBMISSION
It had been a night of simple passion
With friends who all had dreams.
They had spent the evening sharing,
Interrupted by small bursts of innocent giggles and screams.
They talked of the perfect life
With the perfect man,
Each being a perfect wife.
It was a night they wouldn't forget,
One they'd look back on with no regret.
They all went their separate ways that night,
With thoughts of what they'd said.
But for one it turned into a fight
In an evil stranger's bed.
Her night became a killer of dreams,
A night of terror and unpassionate screams.
She was submitted to a world of hate
One she thought might never end.
It had turned into a night of unwanted passion,
With a man who'd lost track of his dreams.
Submitted to a night of invasion,
Insanity on his part it seems.

B J Eickhoff
I BELIEVE
I believe in many things
Like lasting friendship and love at first sight
And realizing problems can be worked out,
At the end of the tunnel there is a light.
I believe in living one day at a time
And knowing your own self-worth.
Remember everyone's important
We all have a purpose on this earth.

And though it may be naive
I believe in Rock n' Roll
Like the sad meaningful songs
About trusting your heart and soul.
But most of all I believe in me
Not to dwell on the future or the past
No matter what goes wrong in my life
I won't let my sorrow last.

Wendy Hartenberger
OUR OWN DESTRUCTION
Through the concrete, bricks and steel—
Nothing really seems real
Through hustle and haste—
Nuclear waste
Through a war here and a crime there—
Trying to breathe polluted air
Through disease and defect—
No love or respect
Through politics and corruption—
We work our way towards
Our Own Destruction

Misty Wilkinson
INDIAN BRAVE
Hunter, though sometimes hunted
Even beyond the boundaries of death
Fierce, willing to make the last move
Cautiously taking in his last breath

Free, yet being held captive
Through the pain in his eyes
Dying, but wanting to live
With all his might, he tries

Deserted, though many are around
He still longs for more joy
Childlike, yet a true man at heart
In the midst of the life of a boy

Awaken, from a lifelong dream
His soul still at rest
Old, yet young at heart
They say his mind is the best

Fighter, until the end
Forever he will strive
Proud, for he himself will know
He did his best, though he died.

r e gatewood
she

to lost loves and lovers.

she showed me the sea of truth
but all i saw was a murky puddle
she showed me an orchard of happiness
but all i saw was aging arbors
she showed me the road to freedom
but all i saw was a rock-strewn path
she showed me the symphony of my solitude
but i could not play

r e gatewood
the fireman
(and comments on the war in vietnam)
the fireman left the other day
dead and dying on the ground
too young to know the reason why
too old to care or be cared for
he cauterized the womb of Mother Earth
and then his thunderstick was quenched

Marjorie McCandless
MY SON

Written for my sister, Jeffie Smith, on her son's wedding day.

It seems like only yesterday
He sat upon my knee,
Together we would ride the range
My little son and me.

Too soon my knee he did outgrow
A stick horse took its place,
Around the yard he'd gallop
A straw hat to shade his face.

I often wished that time stood still
For I would sorely miss
Those little arms around my neck
And each damp good-night kiss.

But time ignored my fervent plea
And continued with its plan,
Until one day I realized
My son was now a man.

And now today's his wedding day,
A handsome groom he'll be,
But standing by his bride I'll see
That lad upon my knee.

Shawn Hughes
TINA LOVES ME LIKE THIS
So is your voice
That you so softly
Whisper upon my ears
So intent is the look
In your eyes
That seem to gaze
Into the depths of my
very soul
So gentle are your
Soft caresses
That seem to handle
me with care
So tender are your
passionate kisses
That smother me
with love
So true & meaningful
Is your love that you
Give to me ever
So carefully

Shawn Hughes
PSYCHOLOGY
The Light meets the Dark at Dawn
to send it to hidden places and
obscure shadows
Try as it might
even the brightest light
leaves traces of shadowed night
With the setting of the sun
darkness' day has soon
begun
To the stars and the moon
the light will run
To shine through for us to see
That the dark and the
light are always together
inseparable
as one

Beth A Roberts
SIMPLEST CYCLE OF LIFE
The seed opens below the Earth,
Life spurts forth in spring.
As time goes by it grows and learns
Tries to experience everything.
Summer comes and life goes on.
Surviving all kinds of weather.
It interacts with others and,
They spend their time together.
Fall arrives and they reflect on
Tender years gone by

The joy, the pain, the sorrow,
How they laughed, how they cried.
Winter blows its powerful sting
They try to recapture the past.
The cycle has ended, the seed passed on
And now they've breathed their last

Charles Dunning Jr
I HAD EXPECTED AN ALARM;
I had expected an alarm;
Instead,
I awoke to the song
Of a mockingbird.
And the awakening
Was so gentle,
That for a while
I thought I was still
Asleep.
So I lay there,
Waiting;
But the mockingbird
Was too real to ignore.
So I arose and smiled,
As I turned off the alarm
I no longer needed.

Elissa Bliss
PAINT A PICTURE OF JESUS
Pink was the lovely babe created
White was the purity of his mind and soul
Rose was his childhood so sweet and kind
Brown was his strength as he preached through manhood
Grey were the clouds that gathered in warning—his death foretold.
Blue were the marks of his torture
Red was his blood spilled for all mankind.
Black was his death—life given up on a cross.
Green was the hope of life eternal
Thus was this painting of Jesus
Created in a rainbow color of love.

Jackie Roa

Jackie Roa
ILLUSIONS AND HOPES
To you Kyriacos, for all the patience, care, love and understanding; for becoming so special in my life.

Oh! Illusions and hopes
Why have you deserted me
Where have you gone.

You had entered my world
And pictured me a better world
And just . . . when you convinced me
To go . . . and join you . . . in your world
You have vanished from my horizons
I have looked for you . . . but you
Left me no traceable path.

Oh! My great Divine
You came and stole my mind
You have left me only with a pain heart
And seeds full of dreams
Well planted in my heart.

Oh! My love
You have stolen all my tears
My illusions and my hopes.

Jackie Roa
ALONE WITH PROMISE
I wish to dedicate this poem to you Kyriacos, for making this writer's dream possible.

In the inner space
The untouched innermost part of the heart
Where I was blind, lonely and alone
There . . . . I met Promise
The princess, the lite and sunshine,
The future, the love, the beauty and happiness . . . .

I cannot hear you Promise
The world became so loud
I cannot see you Promise
The tomorrow became so uncertain
The whole planet became a new industry Promise
Everybody is confused
Nobody knows what to believe anymore
No one knows you Promise . . . .

Again, I am alone and lonely
And . . . I have only one word in my mouth
Your name Promise

Michael T Garrity
FROM THE HEART
To the woman I love, today, tomorrow, and forever, "Torey."

On a night together, one of many, I said these words to you.
I'm for you for these reasons,
"To protect you the best I can"
"Give you a shoulder to cry on or lean on at times"
"To make you smile from laughter and happiness"
"And most of all, love you with all my heart and care for you all I can."

Guillermo Figueroa MD
GROWING OLD
Run between the stars
travel beyond time,
war is dead on Mars
Venus loving clime,
cosmic net of thought
love and hell of doom,
way of dreaming, rough
caress of the broom
from the winter witch
moral on reject,
when your life begins
bring along the years,
closing of the spring
only bore and tears.

Guillermo Figueroa MD
CRAVING IN DARKNESS
Flames spire to the sky
redness reflection of fury,
love is with anger deny
diamond or cinder in hurry.

Fissure the chisel explore
careful erasing the flaw,
closing the lids like a door
passion explode with a blow.

Limbo, the borders of hell
craving the darkness for God,
nothing compare loving well
love in essence is going mad,
bitterness only to sell
drifting your life on the gad.

Dezeré Bolton
WHISPERING WINDS
The wind whispers through the trees
as though to say fly away, fly away,
fly away with me.
It whispers very reverently as it whistles through the air.
The breeze is nice and gentle as the sun begins to set, the flowers close and the breeze stops and the people settle down to sleep.

Gretchen Welch
PENNY SENT DREAM
To Mom and Dad, I love you.

Somewhere between the
melancholy of a mauve
colored silence and a distant
colored future, I found
myself questioning the
existence of a simple being
hinting upon a penny-cent
dream.
Not of conformity or
placement but rather
a solution to the hierarchy of
need.

Through the tangled fury of a
garnet dispute, I found
myself angered over the
selfishness of want.
Not over the simple niceties
or pleasantries in life, but
rather over the pettiness to
justify one's means.

Balancing upon the scattered
vision of love and hate, I
found myself admiring the
company of innocent
silhouettes napping against
the moon.
Not of yesterdays nor
tomorrows, but rather a
conclusion to the meaning of
content.

Finally—
Amidst the confusion of an
oddly tinted world, I found
myself needing the
simplicism of a penny-cent
being to give me a view.
Not of prospect and value
nor of monotony and being,
but rather a reason to write
this in No. 2 Grey . . .
to justify a penny sent
dream.

Thomas Loveman
THE COMPLETE ROSE
Someone for everyone,
A rose for each stem.
A blossom atop thrives
On a carefully chosen pedestal.
A rose, whose beauty cascades
Across magically woven silk petals,
Is proclaimed the Aphrodite
Of flowers,
And all forget that it is
The stem that first strived
To live so the Love could grow.

Jean Prytyskacz
L.M.
I bit his lips in anger,
during a passionate kiss.
He pulled away quickly,
to see what was amiss.
I gazed at him cooly.
He didn't realize what he had just said,
had hurt me.

Not thinking.
Not caring.
He's crazy and daring!

Immature . . .
My feelings are ignored.
But, will he change?
I'm not sure.
Who ever said that love is the cure,
for everything?

Marilyn A Ellicott
A GIFT OF THE GODS
Oh Ru, I wish you could understand
how much you mean to me.
But we are two separate species, and that can never be.
I am but a human, with all the usual ills.
You are a gift of the gods, an angel if you will.
Your loving nature puts me to shame.
I cannot emulate it, for human is my name.
Dogs are special, wondrous gifts, sent from up above.
To dry our tears and bathe us in nonjudgmental love.
A balm to the weary, broken soul.
A gift more precious than diamonds or gold.
And so, you see, my beloved Ru,
I'm a far better person for having known you.
This world is a place of great wonder,
as well as of great pain,
But the gift of the gods equalizes and helps us go on again.
If I had just one wish, I know what it would be,
That every single human could have
a dog, like the one that was given to me!

Marilyn A Ellicott
BERMUDA
A little piece of heaven nestled safely in the sea,
A land of gentle people and pure serenity.
Air sweet and intoxicating as the finest wine.
A place of rare beauty, I cried to leave behind.
You soothed my aching spirit, what a wondrous place to be.
Your pink sand cradling my body at the edge of your crystal sea!
Slowly, gently, and with infinite loving care,
Your beauty eased a pain that I once could scarcely bear.
The day I had to fly away, I left a part of me
In that little piece of heaven nestled safely in the sea.

Mae Beck
FUN IN THE SNOW
One Saturday morning when taking a nap in a chair,
I awoke to see snow flakes flying

through the air,
The ground was covered in no time at all,
I dashed outside and did I take a fall.

I got out my sled and started to ride,
The sled went over a bump and landed on its side.
I started off again
And slid into the dog pen.

So I decided a snowman I would make,
Which I thought would be cake.
I was rolling the ball through the yard with ease,
When suddenly it took off and rolled into some trees.

So I went back in the house to my chair,
Turned on the television to see what was on the air,
My favorite football team was playing and winning,
So I sat there cheering and grinning.

Michele Kizzia
GOLD BAND
We were a love,
A love that came along.
Dreaming of how we were together,
Wishing it would be forever.
Sometimes the hopes and dreams
Would rise above,
For it was all from your love.
A child's fantasy, making me into what I am to be!
Wearing a Gold Band upon my hand, a part of you.
That made me live for what you'd say or do!
Walking away,
You left all your love and kindness upon my heart.
For they made us to part.
Always wondering if you thought back,
On days you were free.
For you always held the key!
Never knowing someday,
It would have ended in such a way,
With my Gold Band upon my Hand!

Michele Kizzia
SUMMER EVENING WITH YOU
Remembering that summer evening,
Was like a dream come true.
Finally in my arms, being the one thing I always wanted to do!
The moon glistened down upon our faces,
As I began recalling all the times and places.
The winds blew so free.
As we wished how our lives would be.
Sometimes the hopes and dreams were lost,
In all the waves of the sea.
And then the heavens would look down upon us.
So far away, with its many eyes of stars.
For when the dawn drew near,
You could see the eye of the moon with a tear.
All the times we spent, were filled with love from within.
And when you went away,
The night was filled with silence and a tear!
Always remembering when we were so near,
On that one summer evening with you!

Michele Kizzia
WAVES OF OUR LOVE
Cold October days roll along
And September is far from us.
The dawns of our love come whispering by,
For they tell me of our life and love.
Winds caress round about me.
Waves take us out to sea.
The moon shares a smile from above.
For as the clap of the sea draws near,
We show no fear.
Darkness and loneliness seem to appear.
For the star lost a twinkle of his eye,
For from his eye, a stardust tear fell upon our sea.
Making our lives turn out to be!
Waves roar with anger, as night sails into day.
With many words of love left to say.
Looking back on dawns of you,
They tell me of the emptiness of the sea.
For when we weren't meant to be,
There were no more waves upon our sea!
Nor were there winds of yesterday!
Clouds cover the sky as we kiss good-bye.
For down in my heart, tears will never cease.
Until in our lives we put everything to peace!
For without the moon and the stars, there would have been no waves of our love!

Michele Kizzia
STRENGTHS OF THE HEART
Looking out through windows of glass,
Seeing the many colors of day.
Brings me dreams of words to say.
The sun shines from day to day.
With the warmth of the kiss I receive,
Will remind me of the truths to believe!
Feeling the coolness of the air,
Helps my love for you, to bear!
Always looking out, never looking in.
Hiding away, longing to see the lasting of a day!
Storms rage, as we yet, turn another page!
Rains fall heavy on my heart,
Washing away the many pains of the dark.
Dawn rings anew,
Showing my soul the many things left to do!
Learning through the passing of time,
That my heart is the looking glass,
Of the day to start!
So may the colors of day shine bright,
To show me the strengths of light.
From the many strengths of my heart!

Jody Lynn Atherholt
ETERNAL LOVE
My sight no longer darkened
My ear no longer deaf,
My scent no longer breathless
My taste no longer bland,
My soul no longer dormant
My heart no longer torn,
I slept and you awakened me
You breathed and gave me life,
Your sincerity fully embraced me
Your warmth melted loneliness away,
No longer was I senseless
An outer glow radiated from within,
The moment yearning bodies touched
Two souls melded together as one,
A passionate fire quickly ignited
Its flame fueled by eternal love . . .
. . . God created man and woman
Love united husband and wife.

Cynthia M Hess

Cynthia M Hess
DO YOU?

To: my mom, Elizabeth; my fiancé, Lyndon; and my dad, Auton: Thanks for all your encouragement and support. I love you all very much.

The homeless live on our city streets
Every day throughout the year
Do you look around your hometown
And notice those who live right there?
Starving children in foreign countries
Needing food to eat
Do you let it cross your mind
That there might be one on your street?
Monthly checks don't rise with inflation
Our elderly people are dying from exposure.
Do you wonder what you'd do to help
If it was your grandmother?
Drug wars, murders, fighting in foreign countries
There are so many problems in this world
Do you take the time to talk to your kids
About all this news they've heard?
Some people buy sports cars and luxury homes
They don't care about helping or what they could do,
They think of what to buy to make life more comfortable for them—
Do You?

Cynthia M Hess
COMPARISONS
Soft as a whisper on a spring breeze
As delicate as a priceless Ming vase.
Each one as different as a fingerprint
Varying in colors like a rainbow.
Beauty that is beyond the imagination
But irresistible like the smile of a small child.
Capable of hurting, yet so entrancing
So many details blended into perfection.
No comparison can encompass it
Words and prose are all unjust.
There is simply no way to explain
The attraction of the overwhelming rose.

Cynthia M Hess
TO ALL HOSPITAL EMPLOYEES
There are many patients in a hospital
Most of them here for different reasons
They come in at all times day and night
All year long throughout the seasons.
Many are scared and here for the first time
Others have been here before
Sometimes you just can't tell
By reading the name beside the door.
As professionals we're not here for the money
We're here to help our fellow man
To give a smile and some encouragement
But most of all to understand.
A hospital can be frightening to a patient
A sea of strangers in a huge place
You can never be sure of their feelings
Just by glancing at their face.
Ask them their name and how they're feeling
Tell them yours and explain what you do
It will not only brighten their day
It will make you feel good too.
Whenever you're at work and meet a patient
Stop and take the time to say hello
Just one word and a smile on your face
Can make a bigger difference than you'll ever know.

Vincent J Lombardo
MOMMY

To my mother; who gave me life, to my wife; who shares my life and to my daughter, one of the greatest joys of my life. I love you.

A Mommy means more than is understood,
She's seen me grow since childhood.
Aches & pains and younger fears,
Mommy subsided throughout the years.

The days of teaching right from wrong,
Sometimes I felt I didn't belong.
But the reasons she gave I paid no mind,
So I paid dearly with my behind.

In order for me to eat a meal,
Mommy played "Let's make a deal."
"Mousey, Mousey" was some of the fun,
Or watching TV when the meal was done.

When I was sick & thought I died,
Mommy was there right by my side.
Chicken soup & loving care,
Made it a lot easier for me to bear.

Several years have passed and school is here,
Mommy sends me off with a little tear.
With pencils & notebooks as my new tools,
I try to learn the golden rules . . .

Graduation day is finally here,
Mom brings me a bottle of beer.
She can't believe how much I've grown,
And all the wild oats that I have sown.

For all these times & many more,
There's no one else that I adore.
I think of you from day to day,
Of all you've shown me along the way.

So if I forget or hadn't the time,
There's one thing to know before it's a crime.
Three little words that I know are true,
The three little words are "I love you!"

Rose Marie Hannon
A GIFT FOR MOM
When I was a child
And spring was new
I had to search for
My gift for you!

It wasn't a mansion
Or a stallion of white,
It was found in a field
Of new grass gleaming bright.

I waited with patience
And shouted with glee,
When the first that I happened upon
Was not one . . . but three!

From the gleam in your eye
I could surely tell,
You liked my gift
Spring's first . . . Blue Bell!

Maria F Cole
IF I WERE A BIRD

In memory of my dear parents—Louis and Clemencia.

If I were a bird
I'd fly and fly and fly
So high!
Far away—until I find—
Another world—
A world of goodness.
A world of beauty.
Oh! A world of happiness.
A world where people
Can be good people
Oh! a world of holiness—
If I were a bird
I'd fly and fly and fly
So high!
Far away—until I find—
That other world—

Charlene Goldsmith-Bjelke
DRY TEARS

To Rick. He dried my tears.

I laugh, I talk, I sing, and I have fears,
There is laughter, chatter, and singing, but I cry—dry tears.

The loss of love is like the loss of a life—once it is lost it will never return,
I ache to the bottom of my being—my soul is bruised and
I cry—dry tears.

I know my new life is oh so special but for just a little while I reflect on the life I'm leaving behind, and I cry—dry tears.

The breaking of hearts, the agony of raw emotion, the haunted sad eyes, the silence, no more laughter, the sunshine without a happy face, the house that's no longer a home, I see and feel it all, and I cry—dry tears.

My life is changing, thank God for that—there is new love, new hope and a healing sun,
God, you've given me new friends and a different way of seeing things,
Now I know, my soul feels whole again—and, I don't need to cry—any tears.

Karen Campbell
SPRING
Spring with all its green
The glorious trees a bloom
You will be beautiful
Until Winter's Doom.

But Winter won't last long
And soon your buds will shoot up
And we will see the magic again
And drink in thirstily from your cup.

Smell the scent of blossoming lilies
Hear the gossip the rain tells
See the morning glories lift their eyes
Taste the sweetness of their early bird's bells.

The sun shining brightly
The shapes of the clouds float by
Watch the ants go marching along
And hear the wind woman sigh.

Spring, Spring,
You're finally here
I'll drink in your beauty
And let none shed a tear.

Jeffery K Smith
APPLE PIE
Sex, Drugs, and Rock-N-Roll
What does it all mean
Baseball, Fourth of July, and
Grandma's apple pie
I ask again what does it all mean

Today is a time of conflict, destruction, and death
Again what does it all mean
The good old days friends, loves, and the times of your life
Again what does it all mean

I can't tell you what it all means
But maybe someday I will find out what it all means
Until then I'll just live and learn
Is this the
American dream? ? ! !

Michelle Harvat
A HEART
A heart can only bear so much,
Before the heart will break in two;
A child can only hurt so long,
Before the tears will slowly fall;
A life can only last so long,
Before the sacred soul must fly.

Barbara J Gloyd
IT'S A CARNIE'S LIFE
We travel from place to place, trying to keep up with the human race.
People tell us we're poor white trash, but don't we spend our cash.
We meet people here, we meet people there;
People just like us.
Sometimes we hate to leave and other times,
We can't wait to get on to the next town,
With our caravan of show clowns.
We have our good time we have our hard times,
We have some fun in the rain or shine.
At the end of a long hot season there are no dry eyes,
As we all voice our final cry of good-bye,
Next year 10-4!
Remember we're the show that's on the go,
That's Merriam's Midway Show
Merriam's Love A Fair.

Tammy Dunn
LIKE THE SEASONS
A newborn baby is like a breath of spring.
A flower that blossoms, the smell so sweet.
Like the petals so delicate and color so bright,
Oh, what a wonderful delight.

A young child changes like the leaves of autumn.
Changing color yet still full of life.
Like the colorful leaves that fall and die.
A child grows and develops, leaving the childhood days behind.

A teenager, so individual, not one the same,
Like the snowflakes that winter brings.
Like the snow that keeps falling and becomes hills to climb,
It's time to keep growing with their ambitions in mind.

Old age comes to us all,
Like the bright, beautiful days of summer.
The sun so warm and bright, the birds all in flight,
This is the time to reflect upon all your life's glories.

As days go by, years go on, the seasons pass,
And we live on.
We bring joy to people everyday,
Love and give toil in every way.

Yet like the seasons we bring change,
From the time we are born, to the time we turn gray.
Before it is all over and our time is gone,
We will leave behind a legacy of our days.

Lucile H Lewis
CHRISTMAS CHEER
First, from a bell take twenty peals;
Next, from a child, five happy squeals;
Include both holly, mistletoe; Put in a spoon of candleglow.
Add laughter, giggles from a jar;
Some candy canes, stir with a star;
Ingredients of warmth and fun;
Smiles on the face of everyone.

Mix in fresh pine cones and a wreath;
Green Christmas tree with gifts beneath;
Pour thoughts of peace and much good will; For young and old, it is a thrill.
So many helping hands reach out;
Hear fireworks sound and children shout;
We light the Yule log on that morn;
The mantle, stockings, cards adorn.

Our spirits lift with such delight;
Nothing's dull, the world's so bright;
A time of which we never tire; And one to which we should aspire.
Kindness and happiness we share;
Excitement, joy is in the air;
A season meant for me and you; The love that's in our hearts shines through.

Let's all prepare some Christmas Cheer, A recipe that's very clear
To loved ones and our friends so dear, For use each day, not once a year!

Martha R Klock
MY THANKS
I cannot thank the Lord enough
For all that He has done
He sent His Son to die for us
That precious Holy One

He saved my soul, made me whole
Lifted me from sin and self
He gives me life, in place of strife
I'm no longer on the shelf

He loves each one, He gave His Son
To give us love and life
To take away all weakness
All sin and also strife

There is no way, that I can stay
Away from my dear Lord
He guides me daily, leads the way
With blessings rich outpoured

I love the Lord, I love His Word
'Tis precious to my heart
He gave His all, and saved my soul
Since I on His path did start

Carl S Frankel
THE REPTILE YEARS
And so it was like the reptile years
With the sun on the cycads
And the hum of insects.
You were the tangle of ferns and reeds
And the air heavy with spice and earth.
I trod lazily among the rushes and browsed
and felt the sun ever on my back.
Perhaps glaciers were somewhere rumbling south
Or mountains were being conceived beneath the swamps
But the long, long summer was in our veins, you and I,
And we knew that it would always be the same.

Sandra Widen
LINGERING MOMENTS
Thy precious golden leaves of time
—only within a child they shine
Lingering moments of a mother
—watching her precious ones grow
A moment of silence
—beyond thought of her earthly guidance
She knows that yesterdays and tomorrows
—love will carry them on, through life
As night drifts in, reaching out are arms
—for goodnight hugs, in belief that shields them from harm
Her voice is softly spoken, she whispers gifts of love will always be there
—hold them closely within your heart to share
She watches them sleep, with a feeling of tenderness
—she kisses her precious ones with gentleness
Knowing the touch of their smiles,

echoes of their laughter lingers
—for the joy is fulfillment in itself
She is a mother capturing moments of pleasures
—for she feels her children are her priceless treasures
Through their laughter and tears
—in her heart are lingering moments of those years
—for those giventh moments are memories, she holds so dear
She's a grandmother looking upon thee gifts of love
—that has been held closely to their hearts
Thy precious golden leaves of time
—only within thy precious gifts of love they shine

Kathy Horn
ESCAPE
Sometimes really late at night,
I'll wake to find I've lost my sight,
I've lost all thoughts of yesteryear,
And quietly I'll cry to escape this fear.

Briney Kirby
ALWAYS LIVING FOR TOMORROW BUT NEVER FOR TODAY
When will all this work pay off, that I've already done
if not today, when? Someday when I am gone?
I've worked so hard to insure my own success
but will it all prove someday, that I have done my best?
As days go by I wonder what else is there to do,
and just who am I competing with? Others just like you?
It makes me wonder long and hard is all this just for me?
or is this work that I have done, for my future family.
But did I miss those precious years that are made to just have fun?
and if I did, what should I do, what else could have been done.
I hope in the future I will benefit
for if I don't I know I'll surely regret it.

Lee Cato
FREEDOM
Shh! Hear it!
Hear it knocking
Quiet now
Can't you see
The lock
Where is the key
I'm knocking
Can't you hear me
Open
Open I say
Let me free
Emotions
Emotions I feel
Let me be me!

Natalie Golin
NIGHT-TIME TRIP
Tonight as I lay sleeping,
I floated high above the earth, to distant places.
It seemed to take only seconds,
To travel hundreds of miles,
To visit a friend.

I then visited a place,
Where I have never been;
But yet I knew it.
It aroused memories,
From long, long ago.

My next stop, is yet to come,
For it was a glimpse of the future.
Maybe tomorrow, maybe next year,
But I will know "it,"
When "it" happens.

My journey for tonight is about to end,
As I float gently back to earth.
And when I awake,
I feel my trip was real,
Just as sure as I am here.

Charles R Terry
EROTIC SUMMIT

Erotic Summit is a selection from the author's book Portrait of Words, *available in most major libraries. For info write P.O. Box 1215, Clifton, CO 81520.*

Always on my mind
Penetrating thoughts of penetrating passion
of explorations on velvet curves
And grand sensations on magical nerves
of climbing mountains of tender flesh with ruby lips
Caressing thighs and luscious hips.
And so the midst of climactic thrust
When erupts the burning essence of my passion
My rigid love remains the strength of our union
And your feminine taste remains on my lips as intoxicating reminder
Of the summit of our erotic pleasure

Ronald Wyatt
THE BUCKAROO
I work real hard doing what I do,
Now listen real close to this story—I'll
Tell ya' it's true.
I work hard every day, Daybreak past Sundown,
Most the time I stay at the ranch—
Once in a while I'll go to town;
I've done this for most of my life,
It's about all I really know how to do,
I ain't no rodeo cowboy—I'm proud to
Say I'm a buckaroo.
This job is truly an adventure,
There's something new to do every day,
From the round–up in the fall,
To branding in Mid–May;
It would be next to impossible
For me to tell you everything I do,
The life I lead is an exciting one—
I'm proud to say I'm a Buckaroo.

Lucinda Bostic Cecil
THE END FOR US IS LAID

In loving memory of my mother, Louise Smith Bostic. Her love and respect for nature was as deep and abiding as the love she bestowed upon her children.

God gave us the earth, not to trash, but to treasure
Each rock and each leaf meant to give only pleasure
Through greed and corruption, we have succeeded
In poisoning the earth we so desperately needed

What will the consequences be? you ask
Perhaps life will end, we'll be taken to task
If only people would open their eyes, instead of their pocketbooks
And truly see the destruction, from the desert to the brooks

The atmosphere is failing too, what a tortuous way to die
Turning the sun that sustains us, into poison more deadly than lye
I know there is an answer, but only through common goal
Sacrifice would be blessed, for without we'll take earth's toll

Listen to my message, for the earth is all we have
Band together people, for the earth's wounds need a salve
Money lasts but a moment, but for it the earth has paid
And if the earth must pay the cost, the end for us is laid

Edward W Stankiewicz
THE WINDS OF DEATH
How can I fly without the wind?
Where can I go to climb a hill to
Soar with others who have gone before
This one flight will be my first and last.
What are my memories of how it was in my past.
Think not of a warrior gone to rest
For those who are left the wind will
blow the best
I love you, Dad
Your son, Ed.

Alma Wesselman Langston
STRAYING SONS

For my sons Uland, Carl, Donald, Claude, and Michael.

To the sons of mothers who do nothing but roam.
Remember the mother that sits home alone.
While you are doing your straying.
Mother's home praying.
Just a postcard, that says you are alright,
Will make her sleep more peaceful, when she lays
down at night.
She needs to know where you are.
I think she has earned that right.
She will want to see your face, before God turns
out the light.
If you don't write or even try to phone.
You may return some day and find, that you are the one alone.
Write Momma.

Zula V Wilson
FIRMAMENT
Night skies filled with stars
Stars that twinkle with your every wish.
A heaven so full of love
Where loneliness is just a word.
A blanket of stars to keep you warm where cold has no feel.
The grace of the clouds is like a pillow
To rest the weary head of troubles.
The soul will be comfort
With a gentle touch of love.
A touch of heaven
As pure as love
Can be forever.

Lisa Anne Roth
A FAMILY'S LOVE
A family has, special moments to remember,
most of which are very tender.
memories are to be shared
with those we love,
not to be locked away
and taken above.
as people grow older
they sometimes drift apart,
but I know we won't
with the love that's in our heart.
a family must stay
always together,
It's the most important thing
now and forever.
God will help us
He's always there,
to teach us how
to love and care.
now that we, are all together
I know our, love shall last forever.

Thelma Branson Norwood
PARKING TICKET

In Memory – Dear Mother – Stella Artrip Branson.

Enclosed is my ten dollars
From my social security check
It's near the end of the month
If I don't have bread or milk
Who cares? What the heck!

I hope the day or night
Never happens to you
To be called to your dying mother's side
Only one spot to park in view

In a hospital zone, where people park
Are not there for entertainment or fun
They are there because there lies a loved one
So have a nice day – when you do go home to sleep
May your conscience give you comfort
For a law you shouldn't keep

Randy Boyd
ESCAPE
The house was quiet and heavy with darkness.
The children were snuggly tucked into bed.
He; stiff with tension. She; pretending to sleep
(It had been that way for too many nights).

This woman, a little girl at heart, captured his imagination.
She captured him, a black panther, stalking through the night.
She had taken him in from the cold hard darkness,
And given him warmth; taught him how to love.
Yet, so skillfully, she locked him out of her heart.

He would kiss her, stroke her, caress her;
Gently making love to her, seeking her love in return.
That she would withhold, giving him only her sex.

They had talked about their relationship yesterday
(As they had almost every day for so many weeks);
To no avail! Her time for him had expired.

He; feeling her warmth, placing his hand on her naked thigh;
She; gently stroking him, placing her hand on his.

The emotion conveyed almost disgusted him;
Yet he accepted it all the same.

Faintly smiling, he closed his eyes and escaped into his kingdom;
The cold, hard darkness of the night, one last time.

W LaBier Jones
disappointment
aroused by disappointment
the creature within
cries forth
to denounce all that has come before
to challenge what may come after

powerless to defuse the defiant rage
virulent screams fade
to malignant moans
as impotent passion ebbs
and with it

life

Emily McPherson
MY NAME
As I walked down the lane,
A stranger came to me and asked my name
I said,
My name is an ocean weaving its waves,
My name is a rock in a lonely cave
My name is stardust sparkling like crystals above my head,
My name is a tree standing as if it were dead
My name is laughter in a gloomy cell,
My name is stories grandmothers tell
My name is a lily plain and small
My name is a pale dove's call,
My name is oars on a long lost boat.
That's my name.
What is yours?

Rosalie Henion
TODAY IS MINE

In memory of my dear husband.

Today is mine, a day worth living,
A day to remember the joy of giving.
A time to fulfill my hopes and dreams,
And bring to life my plans and schemes.
Today is not just another day,
But one to enjoy my work and play.
If I can make just one person smile,
It will make my day seem so worthwhile.
So grant me another day like today,
So once again I may say,
Today is mine, to do what is right,
And keep love and hope forever in sight.

Violet Green
THE THREE R'S

To my loving husband, Anson E. Green.

R is for revenge, we'll get even wait and see
With that loved one or a neighbor who did those things to me.
We'll start right in and tear them down
Till there's nothing but a frame.
Revenge is sweet we hear people say,
But it's just a nasty game.
R is for remorse after all is said and done
With one bitter angry word
We turn father against son.
Or maybe friends of years long past we dealt a heavy blow,
And pride will keep us oh so quiet,
And the truth they'll never know.

R is for religion—now there's an R for you!
When on your knees you seek release
From the things you say and do.

If we would try religion
Before we seek revenge,
We would never have to face remorse,
And never lose our friends.

Patricia Taylor–Grandy
TROUBLE ON THE HORIZON
Out of the mist
he appeared to us
rambling in a tongue
very foreign to our ears
We listened compassionately—
tenderly, and
Suddenly! We realized that
this man had been sick for
many years;

He kept right on standing there
glancing at us two, So we offered
our assistance and asked was
there anything that we could do;

He shouted out obscenities, Then
apologized for it all. Finally,
we directed him to the hospital or
we could make a call;

The authorities were very gentle
as they carried him away and
our prayers go steady up for him
each and every day . . . .

Carlton James White
FOREVER COMING
We all knew
there would come a time
when there could
only be one choice
It has been awhile
since I last heard this voice
"go and tell them
of my life
of the loving message
that I send
With me as your
personal saviour
your life will never see an end"
It has been forever coming
When Jesus will again walk this earth
It has always been up to us
to seek out our real worth
spreading the news to others
of these days in which we live
yes you were destined to be saved
if only of yourself you give

Jean C Richmond
SEAGULL
Seagull, flying solo in the sky,
Soaring, dipping, turning,
Wings swept back in aerodynamic perfection —
Can you see me, so far below, watching you?
Are you mindful of God's earthbound creatures?
Far inland — far from your lake water habitat —
In graceful circles you soar above me,
Turning, climbing ever upward;
Slivers of sunlight glance off your white wings,
Lighting the sky for one glorious moment.
Up, around and ever upward you fly,
Cutting through the clouds in graceful swirls.
Then, you are gone;
The magic of your presence disappears
Like a rabbit in a magician's hat.
The clouds move along in their patterned splendor,
But the sky is sad and empty,
Remembering the glory of your flight.

Jean C Richmond
ZEN CORNERS
Comfortably, and from habit
I live in the centre of my being.
The aura of me surrounds the core
Like a candle within its glassed enclosure,
Glowing and quiet.
But life is more than centre only:
It is pain and loss, seeking and striving;
The need to grow and deepen in sense and spirit.
I must stretch to the farthest
And least comfortable corners of myself.
Some day, perhaps soon,
I hope to fill with purpose and ease
All the farthest reaches,
The very ends of me --
So that the glow of my new enhancement
Can add light to the ever-encroaching dark,
And enlarge the centre to include
The harmony of the whole Universe.

Tracie Thacker
MOMMA'S THOUGHTS

Dedicated to my sister Alisha Jones and my mother Terry Thacker.

How did it happen. What made her do the things she did.
She was only fifteen, just an innocent kid.
Who taught my girl to act so rough
Who taught my girl to do that stuff.
Was it me didn't I love her quite enough, is that what made my girl so tough.
I've watched her so well, then she puts me through hell.
My baby just walked out the door.
Saying Momma I'm not a baby anymore.
So that's what kept her so far from my touch.
I think I've loved her a little too much!

Juan Pagan
THE FAVOURITE TREE

This poem is dedicated to Pepita, my darling wife.

The tree transplanted from the nursery
where it remained during three years,
took strong root
though it was treated without care.

Growing healthy and struggling with tenacity
against adverse climates,
it was determined to become
a firm, strong, and leafy tree.

Seeing the owner its spirit of perseverance,
he granted it his care,
watering and fertilizing it with such gracefulness
it provoked jealousy in the orchard.

Three strong branches soon sprouted which gave it firmness;
its anxiety for the perseverance augmented
while its bark took hardness.

Fearing the owner a premature exhaustion
of his favourite tree,
he decided to procure relax it
and increase its fruit production.

He took it to a more fertile land
upon which it was transplanted;
and it began to grow such profound roots
that it gave harvests for a long time.

Neither rains, thunderstorms, hurricanes,
nor perverse woodcutters
could destroy the talismans
gained with work and love.

Today, on a so special spring,
it begs to its compassionate owner
to prepare for it the last transplant
in one of the primitive orchard's corner.

Dorothy A Whitlock
SWEETHEART OF THE NATION

This poem is dedicated to Barbara Bush, our First Lady, who is truly "Sweetheart of the Nation."

To a most gracious lady
Acclaimed Sweetheart of the Nation
You've captivated the hearts of all
In unified adoration

The special qualities you possess
Are representative of
A First Lady at her best
One we can respect, admire and love

So as February 14th approaches
This is our St. Valentine wish for you
That the Heavenly Father will shower blessings
On #1600 Pennsylvania Avenue

Karen L Goodell
TIME TO BE MY FRIEND
If the earth were cleansed of all evil,
all would be our friends.
For our eyes would only see good,
to those done wrong we would
make amends.
There would be time to hear the rain,
and time to love our brother.
We could close our eyes and feel the stream,
to see the beauty in each other.

Andrea F C
A FAIRYPOEM

To jakle the ripper: death to all valdons, long live pomegranates!

Once upon a-
In a land far far a-
There was a princess named A-

She loved A-
But he loved A-
Not A-
And so she was a-

She begged a-
To cast a-
To rid herself of her contender A-
Forever a-

Her rival died a-
He succumbed a-
For his grieving heart was torn a-

The witch summoned a-
Big black and a-
And brought to life the handsome A-
So deep was her a-

In the end he returned her a-
Forgiving her previous a-
And so they lived happily ever a-

John Brussaly
THE AUDIBLE VOICE
I hear it now,
The Voice telling me . . .
This is I talking to thee,
Don't wait do it now,
For it is to thee opportunity
knocks;
Open the door and partake
of the treasure
I offer to each in my wandering
flocks,
Take heed and reap in full measure
The riches of my kingdom in Heaven.

Beneigh Johnson
LOST
Tonight I am swayed by morbid
thoughts
I have no will to resist
And life, it hems me in like a
Dark gray mist

My spirit is smothered in dreariness
Without a struggle it seems — I
resign
To the numbness of solitary days
To the meaningless passage of time

I'm done — the silence is stifling
Almost like being buried alive;
In a deepening chaos of shapeless
thought
Yet knowing I still survived

A ghastly ghost of my former self
Hungry and starved for a human
touch
Of friendly hands and kindly words
And — the love — I need — I want
so
Much.

Christine Koehne
I TRIED.
I wish it didn't come to this
The tears and pain changed my bliss.
My feelings have changed;
Things are not the same.
They asked me why
but all I do is cry.
I am lucky I survived
many have tried.
There are so many reasons
none really matter.
I just wanted to be noticed. Someone
To care. Someone to be there
when my cradle should fall.
A cry for plea this one answered.
I survived, I'm here to tell
Don't try like I and end in Hell.

Traci Laufenberg
OCEAN
In the night
The ocean rolls in and crashes
on the shore
crash after crash
Never ending
Never silent
Always making us aware that
the ocean is there
carrying in the murky water
and life
Taking out anything that
gets in its way
Returning to where it first all starts.
Rolling back into the sea
The end of the earth
The endless sea of blackness

John Dandridge
THE FEMALE ROSE
Your stem is strong and stern.
Your petal soft and smooth,
Your fragrance tickles at my nose,
All it does to me is soothe.
Then night fall finally comes,
And the moon in all its peace,
Doth shine upon your delicate petals,
As soft as white sheep's fleece.

And now as this poem comes to a
close,
I leave you with one thought.
The only difference
Between flower and female.
To you these words have brought.
A female cares,
And shows me love,
A rose, it does not.

Alexander Boch
LINES TO A WATERBED (ON FIRST SLEEPING)
Last night I slept on a waterbed
Wished I slept on the floor instead
When my body turned to the right
It felt like stormy ocean fight

When my partner turned the other
way
We felt ourselves thrown in the surf
All that was missing was the spray
And someone yelling, "Man
overboard."

When I tried to give her a smooch
My mouth landed on what felt like a
wet pooch
And when I tried to give her a
healthy hug
We bounced like a giant waterbug
In a Disneyworld amusement park

As we rolled, cursed and tossed
We knew all hope of love was lost
Instead of feeling romantic and erotic
With the rolling waves and
"soothing" water
We were soon feeling hopelessly
psychotic

It wasn't the gal
And it wasn't the guy
But this we found so truly regrettable
Juanita and I are not waterbeddable

Dennis Roy Buckner
OUR FRIEND, WE CALL MOM
Mom, many times Alma and I,
think of you,
And thank God for, a loving
heart so true,
Some may not understand us,
but that's ok,
For we truly know, God will
help us make it someway,
I guess some may even think
it's true, how they feel,
But we can't hide, what's inside,
when we know it's real,
And Lord, if we've earned any
reward, up in Heaven then,
In our final score, please Lord
once more, let us be her children,
Thank You Lord, for a friendship
so beautifully born,
When twenty three years ago,
we met, Mrs. Julie L. Warren.

"Jade" Micklos
A MOTHER'S LOVE
In between the baby's cries
I sense the need to feel,
Feel the sun warm my
heart
the spring lake refresh my
body
and the snow
enhance a peaceful moment
of thy soul
But soon awaken
From the daydreaming world
I look down to see
My little boy's eyes
Smiling up at me
and my daughter's precious
hand
laying solely in mine
A mother's peace and quiet pride
in between those baby cries.

Dennis Roy Buckner

Dennis Roy Buckner
OUR SPECIAL LOVE

In dedication to my wonderful wife Alma Jean, whose love for me daily, is shown and seen.

I hope it's not too late, to send my
poem in,
Mixed feelings about it, was what's
the use, and I thought again,
How will I ever know, if I keep
it inside,
For knowledge can't come forth, in
things we tend to hide,

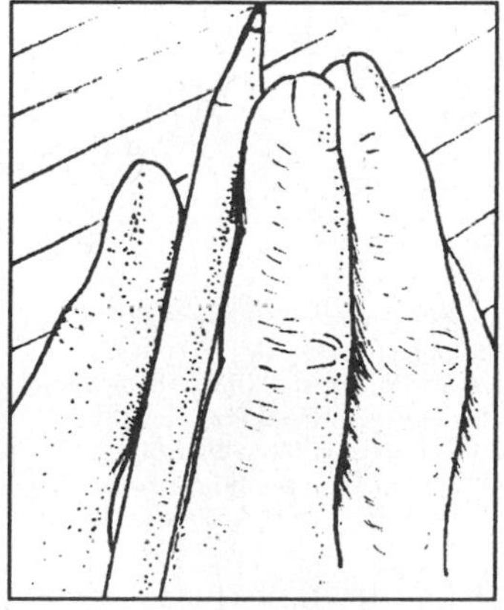

So little pen, let's try, and see if
we can work it out, in this writing
contest,
We've not written poetry, since last
November, and that's a long time to
rest,
We'd like to say hello, to each,
and everyone,
And thank you for listening, in our
moments of fun,
For these words are, so important to
us, that we speak of,
Because, poetry is truly,
"Our Special Love."

Theodore J Sparrow
A SPECIAL TIME OF YEAR
Christmas is a very special time of
the year.
It's a time when we all should be full
of good cheer.
It's a time for song and celebration of
a sacred birth.
It's a time to rejoice for every man
and woman on earth.

All the children are excited and
taking care to be nice.
They know Santa has a list and is
checking it twice.
The presents are wrapped in colors
bright and gay.
They'll bring so much joy when
opened on Christmas Day.

The houses are covered with
decorations we love so.
Outside we all look for the first signs
of snow.
The Christmas tree inside gets more
beautiful each year.
Its warmth to be shared with loved
ones so dear.

Christmas is a time of sharing.
It's a time for giving and a time for
caring.
Christmas is a time of joy, hope and
childhood delights.
It's a time to remember why we sing
Silent Night.

Christmas is a time when not a tear
should be shed.
It's a time when hungry peoples of
the world should be fed.
Christmas is a time of love, peace,
and goodwill.
Weapons of war and destruction
should be silent and still.

It's a time to spread brotherhood and
a time for forgiving.
All mankind should know that his life
is worth living.
It's a season void of hate, sorrow and
fear.
Yes! Christmas is a very special time
of year.

Dennis Roy Buckner
FOR ALL MANKIND
Lord, sometimes I can't understand,
how any of us, can ignore,
The Little Old Country Church, and
the love we once had, for each other
before,
Lord, the world You gave us to live
in,
has changed, and gone so modern,
But it wouldn't be so sad, if we all
had, hung onto the love, we once
earned,
Today, we've strayed far away, from
helping each other,
a helping hand to our fellow man,
was love for our brother,
And now, we find somehow, to cut
him loose,
with some kind of an excuse, seems
one way or another,
And Lord, someday let us lean, a way
to find,
a way to retrieve, and fully receive,

that
love back in our hearts,
"For All Mankind."

Margaret Ann Seipel
GOD BLESS THE LITTLE CHILDREN OF THE WORLD

I dedicate this poem to all the little children of the world and my grandchildren, Jacob and Jessica Jonker and Krista and Stephanie Seipel. I thank God for each of you.

There is nothing more beautiful than a child,
the beginning of a new generation.
A child is like a piece of clay waiting to be molded,
and we are the molders.

To some will be given the greatest of gifts,
but each child brings to the earth his own unique person
You were born without prejudice,
with a child like openness to all things.
May this never be destroyed within you.

You my children are the real
treasures of the world.
May you recognize this in each other.
For you must strive together if planet earth is to survive.
We have left many obstacles in your path,
and life will be a challenge.
For each generation must work to
correct the errors of the past.

You are our future little children of the world.
Let your spirits soar like eagles.
Make the world a better place for you being part of it.
As you begin your journey on the planet earth,
I ask God's blessing on you little children of the world.

Rosanne M Bell
SKY CROSSINGS

A light beam
came down from the farthest star,
and energized a dream
that has always existed.

Transformed to fit this reality,
dreams become mortal;
Only with deeper feelings
and insights than the average man.

To become the other half
of an understanding
without words.

Robert Lee Boyd Jr
VACATION FROM REALITY

The sun slowly sets,
descending from its horizon of violet and blue.
And across the water,
its rippling reflection can be seen by only me and you.
While seagulls glide
gracefully through the evening sky.
Sailing and swooping at the passers by.
Lovers themselves,
a couple leisurely stroll the shoreline hand in hand.
As the gentle tide
erases their tracks from the snow-white sand.
A place of tranquility and peace
that would surely steal any heart
and put our minds at ease.
A secret, psychological paradise
that awaits us the second we close our eyes.
With orchids in the jungle
and coconuts in every tree
it is a secluded escape
that you should really see.

Yvonne M Hildeman
CRY FOR HELP

I dedicate this to my sons, Ken and Scott Lehman, who loved me enough to help me turn my life around.

I want to get away from it all
But where can I go?
Everywhere it's all the same
Hustle and bustle, hurry and worry.

Time goes so quickly
Yet each day seems so long
Meaningless at times,
Full, yet empty.

Where am I headed for?
I am lost in this massive world.
Help me find the way;
I can't find it alone.

God send me help
So I might see again
The joys of living
Before it's too late.

Robin Lea Black
LOVE MENDS

I wish that I could hold you,
To let you know I care;
My heart just aches inside me,
To know that you're still there.
Why can't we get together?
What's keeping us apart?
I know it isn't love my dear,
Because it's in my heart.
So what is it my darling?
The fear of love gone past.
That shouldn't be the problem.
So let us work it out together.
So we won't be so lonely.
Love mends the things that once,
have broken our hearts.

Gladys Evans Miller
THE LITTLE MISSION

Dedicated to the Bowery Mission, New York City, God Bless You.

We journeyed far to reach the place,
a little Mission cramped for space.
Among the buildings proud and tall,
the little Mission was so small.
There was no grass rich and green,
shady trees could not be seen.
No stained glass windows to adorn,
the little Mission was old and worn.
Oh how it saddened even more,
as we entered through its door.
There sat many lost of soul,
needing Christ to make them whole.
Praise be to God! for he does care,
for all His children everywhere.
O little Mission, rejoice! rejoice!
in heeding to God's calling voice.

Sandy Shelton
THE CHILD OF GOD

Conceived by ignorance, carried unwillingly, born.
Poisoned by anger, jealousy, greed.
All that she knew in youth was war.
Hatred seethed, grew, as she retreated into better worlds of
make-believe.
Into the real world she stumbled,
tormented all the way,
Searching and finding, passion and lust, desire and greed, more
anger and hatred.
Mutelessly screaming, "help me!"
No one heard. No one listened,
maybe a few.
Only a few, but what could they do?
But He heard, came, showed her a way.
Grasping, clinging, her life was too torrid.
She ripped away and He cried "come back."
She came back, again, and again
And grew stronger, wiser
And found what it was she had been searching for, needing.
Peace. "Blessed are the peacemakers . . . " and so she heard the call.
The torment has not faded yet but the reasons are very clear.
Her strength, faith are tested now
While the dark one fights much
harder to change her wiser mind.
The peace she sows, will lose it not.
She has become "a child of God."

Harold E Richardson
FREEDOM

Thank God I live
In a nation that's
Free
And where I
Can be me

A place to call
My own
To set down roots
In my own home

The choices I have
Are many
To seek my goals
Wherever
If any

To travel anywhere
I may choose
To go
Without restrictions
Or an emphatic no

When at night
Before I sleep
I ask God
To keep my country free

Joseph A Ellis
WE HAVE TIME

To all that had LOVED before, YOU WILL LOVE AGAIN because to be in LOVE, makes the HEART SING.

No need to rush our friendship
on what we feel inside,

No need to show emotion
on the feelings we hide,

We can take each day and build a strong foundation
yes we can,

We can take our time, For all we need is time

We have time
That will last forever,

We have time
To have a love that we can share,

In a moment
It will take us to where we can care, so much

We can take our time, For all we need is time!

Joseph A Ellis
IF OUR HEARTS SHOULD TOUCH

I want you to want me, Like I want
to want you And,
I want you to need me, Like I need
to need you But,

IF OUR HEARTS, IF THEY SHOULD TOUCH
IN THE MIDST OF
THE NIGHT, WE WON'T LET GO,
WE WON'T LET GO

I want you to touch me, Like I want
to touch you And,
I want you to love me, Like I want
to love you But,

IF OUR HEARTS, IF THEY SHOULD TOUCH
IN THE MIDST OF
THE NIGHT, WE WON'T LET GO,
WE WON'T LET GO

So I'll want you from a distance,
'cause that's all that I can have,
And I'll need you 'til tomorrow,
But
tomorrow will never come,

FOR IF OUR HEARTS, IF THEY SHOULD
TOUCH IN THE MIDST OF THE NIGHT,

WE WON'T LET GO, NO WE
WON'T, WE WON'T LET GO!!!

Linda Portalupi West
I TAKE A DEEP BREATH

I take a deep breath
try to collect myself,
tell myself it'll be okay
try to live through today.
It works for a while
I eat,
read,
watch a little T.V.
Stare at the sky
Start to cry
I can't help myself
I miss you so.
I wonder how I'll ever live
Without you.
I wonder why I have to.
I take a deep breath
try to collect myself
tell myself I'll be okay . . . .

Michael Simpson
ME

I can't escape me
The man devours the friend, the person
Of this I long to be free.

The man took so many years to do
The person, the friend is all too new

The man learned all the customs and traditions
Each part of life with its limits and conditions

The friend, the person deals with what is now;
Learning each moment . . . where, when, how

The man fills me with such disgust
With his embodiment of love which is lust

The friend, the person only trust

The man flexes his muscles to show his strength

It's a shame it's measured in size and length

The friend, well the friend shares
All that the person is in knowledge and care

Alas it is, I am but me
The man, the friend, the person for you to see

What I am must always show
But hopefully it will be the friend, the person
That you will know.

Louise Hibbard
A DREAM

To my dear nephew Alan and Aunt Opal.

I sit alone in the midnight hour
And watch the starlit skies.
My mind goes back to long ago
I dreamed that you were nigh.

I see your face in the moonlight
And gone is my sorrow and pain.
My heart cries out come back
My love.
As the wind whispers
Your name.

You have come home oh joyful
Thought
No more from me to roam.
But this I know is just a dream
As I sit here all alone.

I know not where you are
Tonight
As I sit here waiting in vain,
But this I know if life holds out
You will come back again.

Patricia L Carstens
OUR SON

To Don: My Baby, My Best Friend, "OUR SON," I LOVE YOU . . . Mom.

OUR SON, OUR SON you'll always
be to your Dear Dad and Me.
Our baby once, now grownup and
handsome as can be
Your Wedding Day has come upon,
A Bride you now will take.
Holding hands together, you'll cut
your wedding cake.
May we just send our Blessings, to
you Both so "Dear"
and always "kids" remember we are
always near,
no matter what, you can be sure that
we will understand.
So make your life with your Dear
Wife, and let your Love just glow
And spread this "special something"
to everyone you know.
OUR SON you're rare, no one can
compare, of this you can be sure.
You've filled our lives with
"happiness" and "love" just oh so
pure
A Great Person that you are, in such a
special way.
We Dearly Love You Very Much is
all there is to say.

Charlene M Gibson
THOSE BROWN EYES

When I see those brown eyes.
I feel like I'm gonna die.

When I look deep into those
brown eyes, I melt like butter
in the hot sun on a summer day.

Those brown eyes are so deep
and mysterious, they hypnotize
me.

Those brown eyes have a mysterious
power over me that I cannot explain.

I love those brown eyes, it's the thing
that makes you most attractive.

You have a great personality, but
those brown eyes are the brightest
and the most beautiful thing about
you.

I tell you right now, I love those
brown eyes.

Elizabeth K Adams
THIS CHRISTMAS EVE

For Tom, Little Tom, and Michael, you make it Christmas year round.

This Christmas Eve will not be like
any other past
In days gone by the money spent was
not enough to last
Those frosty nights we sat alone and
giggled with our mirth
With just this one gift to open, who
can wonder at its worth.
"It must be something special, that us
boys and girls can share."
"It's surely not a doll or truck or
something we can wear."
"Santa might have goofed this time."
said Bob, Dad's only son.
Liz hurried to agree — one gift —
meant fun — for only one
And what about the baby. If the box
contained small parts
We guessed Diane was out of luck if
the game we got was darts.
"They're probably not through
shopping." said Pam the wisest one
And we can't begin to guess, till we
know that they are done
That was Christmas every year — the
gifts we can't remember
Christmas to us was not a day but the
entire month of December
The four of us a different age, when
we received our glory
Christians, one and all my kin, upon
hearing one great story.
So children do not cry your tears, one
gift you shall receive
For you have a loving father, in
whose son you can believe
And all you babes who couldn't hear
the tale of God's son.
Never should you ever worry.
'Cause He loved us everyone.

Elizabeth K Adams
FOR DAD

It's too late for anymore holidays
And no time for any more gifts
To see the man, I once denied
Would give my heart a lift
But a feeling deep inside of me
Says he's not away too far
For God has given Him a place, upon
a brand new star
He loved us so His special way, He
gave to us His all
From Kindergarten plays, to
Homecoming balls.
And He wanted us to have, the things
He couldn't give
But that He wanted was enough, For
in our hearts He'll live
A very special man, with a very
loving wife
And to four very lucky children, He
gave His entire life
But the biggest part he set aside
For a king who knew Him best
He knew what Dad would need the
most
He knew He needed rest.

Clifton C Winn
ANOTHER BEAUTY

We dwelt a time where Beauty
domiciles
'Mid burgeoning bloom, in mild
caressing air.
We thought that Earth had never
clime more fair
Than wraps these happy, lush, and
verdant isles.
We came then to a stark and thirsty
land
Where ochre mountains stab a crystal
sky
Where struggling life denies a will to
die
Amid an arid waste of burning sand.

Yet, here was Beauty in another
guise:
Vast crimson cliffs and green and
wooded height;
Great praying plants athwart a desert
rise;
A glowing sun, a diamond-studded
night.
So even here 'midst Beauty still we
dwell,
And send you word of greeting: All is
well!

Jerry Sustala
MOM

My mom is the best, this I can say
She surely has proved it
Day after day.

I have never been alone,
She has always been there
First to help, first to care.

When I hurt her, she let me know
But when I was slipping,
She refused to let me go.

If not for her
I don't know where I'd be
Maybe strung out on life, adrift at
sea.

I love her more
Than words can say,
Every minute of every day.

She gave me back my will to fight
And fight I will
With all my might.

She is the greatest in all the land
On the highest mountain
Alone she stands.

Reginald Reynolds Smith
DREAMS OF LOVE

I guess you'd say, I dream a lot.
Why? Because I believe in dreams.
If you believe in love,
Come dream along with me.
Wipe the tears from your eyes,
close them, so that you can't see.
Replace them with a smile,
come dream away with me.
You see, I believe in making love,
the whole night thru.
I believe in holding hands,
until our love is thru.
True love, lasts forever,
It never finishes thru.
So I'll continue to dream,
about me and you.
Holding hands and making plans,
to see our love thru.
As long as you're not by my side
I'll keep dreaming of you.
Within my mind, during pleasant
times,
making love to you.
I believe in dreams.
I hope that you do too.
If you believe in love.
I'll dream along with you!

Debra L Holzermer
JUST ONCE

Dedicated to N. H. — who has no idea how I feel.

Just once I'd like to hold your hand
and feel you holding mine.
Just once I'd like to feel your face—
every dimple, crease, and line.

Just once to look deep in your eyes
and not have to look away.
Just once to know all about you
and be close in every way.

Just once to pull you close to me
and feel you hold me tight.
Just once to feel I had a chance
and to know that it was right.

Just once to have you kiss me—
your thoughts one with mine.
Just once to be so lost in us
to be able to stop all time.

Just once to be free from the fog
that keeps me lost in you.
Just once to be able to accept —
my wishes will never be true.

Mary Lou Darnielle
MEMORIES OF MOM

Charitable, Humorous, old-fashioned
girl of beauty fair,
Gentle, yet firm of discipline, loving
and sincere,
She was tidy of habit, by nature
funny and kind,
A cup of tea with her could settle the
stomach, the mind

She taught me to be neighborly
careful, polite every day,
"Look for the silver lining come what
may" — showed me the way
To accept the crosses of life, be
steadfast, be true
Listen to music, quietly read, study
lessons too!

Potpies, biscuits, roasts; the kitchen
her domain
Pickles, preserves, canning as she
sang a hymn of refrain;
She told me stories of her childhood
on the farm;
Taffy pulls, hayrides, quilting, square
dances in the barn

She taught me to love animals, dream
work and pray
"Shoulder the burden" — she cared
for my cuts, aches, pains each day
Everything sacred, lovely, friendly
rolled into one measure
Words cannot depict the picture of
Mom in my heart I treasure.

Jaret W Tomlinson
A WOMAN

In the beginning
God created man,
but alongside man
there would lie a woman;

to hold,
to love,
to care for,
to laugh with,
to cry over,

to worry about,
to feel ashamed,

but most of all
to turn to in times
of need,
as this is more than the woman I love
this is my best friend.

Jane B Cox
SAFE BE THE BEAVER'S DAM

To my special twin Grandsons Matthew and Ryan.

A little girl tells her story.
—quiet please—
Now, as the Beaver, swimming about
looking for special material,
Hunks of debris go floating by.
Quickly, the Beaver spots a certain
log, which will keep the back of
the dam secure.

A builder of renown, he constantly
Swims to and fro to capture
the best pieces.
A few leaves and a twig or two
are about to be placed.
The Beaver is a beauty, with his
dark brown shining fur.
He is a trapper's delight.

While in no real hurry,
He looks about carefully,
His teeth are sharp, and can,
Cut-through many layers.
You should watch sometime
As he builds the cleverouse house.

Lo! and behold! he dives deep
down into the water.
Not to be seen for a few minutes
If only he could tell us what
he is doing underneath.
We can only surmise how
it is being constructed.

The Beaver dutifully keeps
a vigil on the surrounding waters.
He must not have any
intruders,
Since it is a Beaver's
Dam, for the waters
flowing down the stream.

Safe Be The Beaver's Dam.

Roger E Finch
LOVE'S FORM

Dedicated to those fortunate enough to embrace true love.

I search intent, amongst my kind;
To have the love, I hope to find;
It takes the form of many things;
A rose, a treasure, a gift, or wings;
But to me, It's simply just;
A feeling deep inside we must;
Cherish with all our heart;
For all we give is just a part;
It's all we do, It's all we say;
All we show, throughout the day;
Every feeling and emotion;
Are all changing and in motion;
Binding people with its potion.

Peggy Vesneski
LITTLE BOYS

You play Army with your toys
Just like happy little boys
Chase the cats with a stick
Clean your face with puppy licks

Wash your hands in the mud
Then give Daddy a big shrug
Catch the spiders in a can
And fight with girls like a man

Walk on the rocks by the creek
Scare the girls and make them
shriek
Sneak a cookie from the jar
Play speed racer with your cars

Stand on the table like Superman
Climb a mountain saying I can, I
can
Ride a rocket to the moon
And hurry up, supper's ready soon

Do all you want to do
And remember, Mommy loves
you
Sit in the rocker and fall asleep
God I pray your soul He'll keep

Shari Wardman
REFLECTING

I sit in silence in the rain and see
teardrops on the windowpane.
You've gone away, you've left for
good, now there's no shadow where
you stood.

I try to set you free from me and find
a better place to be,
But in my mind you're always there,
I'm only half of a love affair.

You walked into tomorrow and left
me in the past.
I didn't see the sorrow, I thought that
it would last.

But now that it's all over and you can
be no more,
I think I see the picture, I think I
know the score.

Laurie Verver
LOVE TO HATE

You told me you loved me, and for
me you would wait —
I suppose in time your love turned to
hate.
When I was down and feeling blue,
You weren't there when I needed
you.
You just turned away, without a
good-bye
You found someone new, and that
made me cry.
As the years go by I will think of
you,
And remember the love that I held so
true.

Penny Ann DuBroc
THROUGH MY MOTHER'S EYES

To my parents with love.

Reflecting on her life as she looked
back over years,
Only treasured memories, could bring
this sort of tear.
Not a tear of joy, nor sorrow,
But a tear filled with yesterdays and
tomorrow.
Once a child bride to the man she still
loves;
Her life became filled with things she
never dreamed of.
Together they have stood, side by
side,
And as each day passed they brought
meaning to each other's lives.
In a world filled with people, they
could not have been more alone,
But they found all they needed in the
warmth of each other's arms.
The odds stayed against them right
from the start,
But the strength of their love blazed
deep within their hearts.
Life never was easy as they struggled
to make a home;
Things got even harder as their three
children came along.
Hard work never ended as the years
drifted by;
Sacrifices began to show, deep within
their eyes.
Looking back now, past all the ups
and downs,
It is oh so clear, what she has found.
The love she's always had for this
one special man,
She can still feel, with a simple touch
from his hand.
She realizes now, that her destiny has
already been made,
For she owns a life filled with
treasured memories, she would never
trade.

Steven J Dubroc Sr
MY WIFE

Though only a child when we first
met, her beauty was unsurpassed.
She grew even more beautiful as time
quickly passed.
Though tired and weary as sometimes
she might be,
She is always there, eager to serve on
me.
Standing by my side through right
and wrong,
No finer woman will ever come
along.
Selfish she could never be,
Always wanting to give to me.
Three offspring she mothered and
held so dear,
Protecting and keeping them safe
from fear.
Her life someday will cease to be,
And I know my grief will surely take
me.
Together, forever in each other's
arms,
She will be safe and kept from all
harm.
Hoping not to be forgotten by the
children she leaves behind;
Is all that this mother asks, this
wonderful wife of mine.

Penny Ann DuBroc
THE MIRROR OF OUR PAST

Memories are reflected like a mirror
of our past;
Blessed with endless power, to make
our thoughts and feelings last.
Memories possess the gift to bring a
smile, or even a tear;
Each can offer comfort, or another
needless fear.
It is important to choose wisely the
memories we will create;
For they are sure to live in our
futures, day after day.
Kindness should be the essence of all
we do and say;
Remember our words and actions
will be our memories someday.

We will all travel down the
treacherous road of life,
And a memory may be all that's
needed to make our dark nights
bright.
So, if ever there were a prayer that
needed to be said,
It would be to bless the countless
memories that haunt each of our
heads.
Forgiveness should always be kept
fresh within our minds,
Because forgetting can often take,
more than just one lifetime.

Stephen T Keeran
DREAMS I COULD NOT SEE

Twelve midnight. I find myself, next
to teddy on the shelf,
Staring at you lying there, staring at
your golden hair.

Hair that once you swore was dead,
full and silky soft instead.
A few minutes pass before my robe
drops upon the floor

And I slip beneath the sheet. We
snuggle close, cross our feet,
Our bodies, as one, entwined.
Smiling, I think, "One of a kind."

"Sparkling, laughing eyes of blue,
she's funny, sweet, thoughtful, too.
Playful, sexy, full of fire, the object
of my desire.

"I love this girl, yes I do." And when
there's time enough to,
I'll tell her and then she'll know, I
watched her some time ago,

Lying there in pale moonlight,
breathing softly in the night,
Just as pretty as can be, dreaming
dreams I could not see.

Wm David Alexander
GRANNY

The sound of her humming
in a haunted sort of way
has made me see her strange.
She lingers here all day—
her cloudy gray-day hair
tightly wound in a bun;
hair so long to reach her knees
used to scare me
in my lollipop days.

She stands hands in warm water,
blue veins peeking through
threadbare skin,
life bound up
in lying bones.

Joan R Cooley
AN "ODE" TO TURNING THIRTY

To Tom: the perennial youngster.

You think that thirty will be the pits!
Just wait till you turn fifty-six.
Preparation H — and — Geritol
AARP will give you a call.
Forget one thing; and your kids will
moan
That you belong in the old folk's
home.
Social Security looms ahead,
And dear Aunt Bertha thought you
were dead.
But just because we need an arthritis
pill
Does not mean we're over the hill.
There's one thing nice about this all
You are only thirty —
So have a ball!!!

Linda G Burbank
ALL I HAVE TO GIVE

All I have to give you is me,
just as I am, just what you see.

Making mistakes is a part of the
scheme,
it's human to fail, human to dream.

All you can do is the best that you
can,
to further yourself and fellow man.

Strive to know and always grow,
within your mind, within your soul.

Yet always be just who you are,
in all you do and you'll go far.

Cora Wells
STILL LIFE OF PEACE
As the greyhound coach slithered down
The streamlined curved road,
Belted on the west side
Of the green tree woven hills;
I pondered—
The unattractive day.

Gray opaque clouds,
Unique shapes and sizes,
Splotched the steel colored sky;
And made it,
Unattractive to the eye.

The noon day sun crotched
Behind gray opaque clouds,
Too concealed to add shine
To green tree woven hills clumped,
Along the road in a jagged line.

The unattractive mural viewed
Along the streamlined curved road;
Magnified Divine stillness,
And created a still life of peace
That astounded the soul!

Cora Wells
I AM NOT ALONE
I am not alone,
When an unachieved dream
Destroys my self-esteem,
And extreme work burn out
Enervates me throughout.

I am not alone,
When deep grief binds me
Tightly in misery,
And sharp body pain throws
Hard double fisted blows.

I am not alone,
When I lack the rich seed
To supply my most need,
And loneliness exiles
My out going smiles.

My God is with me,
Every night and day
In a fatherly way,
Applying His grace
To the hardships I face.

Gail Robbin Grayson
THE THREE OF US
Why are you doing this to me?
I love you so much.
I don't want to think about losing you,
but how can I find someone
that doesn't want to be found.
If it were just the two of us,
things would be different.
I would still love you,
but letting go would be easier.
There are three of us now;
remember our son?
Are you thinking of him,
or is he a toy;
just another way for you to hurt me more.
You tell me our son doesn't need his father.
You're right,
but I need my son.
Both of you are my life,
without you I am nothing.
I love you.
I need you.
Please come back.

Rick Chance
DECEPTION
Deception
A Misconception
That's The Name Of The Game
If You're Playing To Win

Too Many Portals
Of Unfounded Knowledge
Too Many Speakers
Blowing Foul Wind

You Walk A Thin Line
Every Time A Shell Is Cracked
A Leak In The Steampipe
And The Clouds Close In

Now You're Heading For Trouble
And The Tide's Running Deep
One Too Many
The Cards Piled Too High
And Now You're Not Sure
Are You Ready To Die?

John Barkan
SUNDAY AFTERNOONS
The air sweet with summer's ways
grass greener and crisper than anyone's yard
for all I knew it could have been Fenway Park.

The ball softly pressing through the air
there was silence and then the sharp snapping
of the ball entering his mitt.

Eyes focused on Father
I threw with greater excitement
and before I could say I love you
the light began fading below tall pines.

JoAnne Henry
THE LOST ONE
Screaming until vile foam emerges from my mouth,
The ignorant still don't know what it is that I've said,
My fists begin to bleed as I beat upon the sand,
What have I done to be cast down with these useless creatures?
The place I belong is high in the towers of Babylon,
I beg for them to tell me the way — they only show me ruins,
Deep in a dream I hear my siblings calling my name,
The sweet violin played by the Vampire echoes in the gloom,
Ghosts of soldiers hide in the foliage to weep for my battles,
Shades of dawn make memory a painful thing,
Haunting images mash down on my dry lips,
I cleanse myself of all their sins,
Sanctity is found within the burrows of my mind,
My shaven head glistens as I pray,
I hear a brother howl as the night sky is swept from my eyes.

Jewel York
SOMEONE ASKED, "WHO WOULD IT BE"
Someone asked, who would it be
If I could be someone, other than me
Well, I thought for a moment, then replied
I like the "First Lady" so, in this life
Maybe I'd choose to be the President's Wife
The First Lady is charming, beautiful and polite
I like the way she waves good-bye and smiles
When the news media wants answers about her private life
Yes, maybe I'd choose to be the President's Wife
Of course, I have never wanted to be in the "lime light"
After thinking it over, it might be real nice
To live in the White House with him there by my side
Yes, maybe I'd choose to be the President's Wife

Emeline Ennis Kotula
THE SONG REMAINS

Dedicated to Samuel Leroy Ennis, my father, who taught me to read when I was four, giving me the most wonderful gift of my life, a love of words.

I hear soft music in the lonely night,
Soft music from an old song-scarred guitar
Winging to my heart from an unknown height,
Op'ning memory's door, holding it ajar.
I see gnarled fingers pluck each muted string,
Work-worn fingers that hold a beauty still
As with a sudden tenderness they bring
Forth music with a gay untutored skill.

This alone remains after 'dust to dust,'
This melody when I remember you.
A simple song a small child learned to trust
When life and love and all the world was new.
A simple song you hardly knew I heard
Returning now to reaffirm your word.

Teresa Wunch
REGRET
Regret once encaged me
As I grasped the threads of time
To keep hold of the past
To keep hold of what was mine

The bars of steel and stone
Withheld me in its arms
Till all my doubt and guilt
Had been freed to inflict self-harm

It tore at my thoughts
Drowning myself in pity
Leading me to its palace
Which was lonely, cold and gritty

Once I fell that far
I could not fight to live
For depression was all too deep
And regret had closed the lid

Regret is a master
Do not play too close
Or it will find you surely
And take what you love most . . . .

Rozann Nicholson
A REASON
It's a shame we complain, when our boys are over there dying.
Some people don't have shoes to put on their feet
And little children cry for something to eat.
Oh, it's a shame.

You drive your Cadillac
And to common people turn your back.
You criticize the President, yet you helped put him in office.
You sit in your big leather chair and give orders to everywhere.
And you complain,
Oh, what a shame.

Then a letter came today.
Said your son is dead,
Gave his life to save his men.
God has a reason for everything.
Will you be different now,
Or will you complain?

Joseph L Horton
RICH MAN

Dedicated to my fiancée, Linda Bacornay.

Money I may not possess,
Only a heart of tenderness.
Fancy clothes I may not wear,
All I have is a heart full of care.

Material wealth I do not own,
Such things I've never known.
The wealth I most treasure,
Is your love without measure.

The greatest wealth I could know,
Is in your loving me so.
No greater wealth could there be,
Than knowing your love for me.

Your love is worth more than gold,
Much more precious for me to hold.
My most precious dream in life,
To treasure you as my wife.

Though no greater riches I possess,
Far richer am I within your caress.
Others may seek fortune and fame,
True richness is you sharing my name!

Shirley J Kavanagh
STOLEN MOMENTS
The first year was great right from the start,
The middle two years kind of just fell apart.
The fourth year my friend will come to an end.

Times we shared were ever so great,
And no one knew it, even when we were late.
Stolen moments were very precious you see,
But the only one hurting is not you, it's me.
The kindness you showed me was always a lift,
I treasured each moment as you would a gift.
We laughed and we played as much as we could,
Unfortunately I enjoyed you more than I should.
You always put me way up on a high,
Why did you leave me to sit here and sigh?
Stolen moments my friend, have come to an end.

Deborah J Sullivan
SISTERLY LOVE
She competes for your love all her life.
Then, just when you love her back, she changes.
She gives you love,
Then takes it away,
Like a child offering a baby candy,
And then ripping it out of her hands.
All this faking love has come to an end,
And you find that all her love is just pretend.
She loves you when you're cute and cuddly,
But when you grow up more, to her you're just ugly.

She is a trap, hunting my heart,
Now my feelings are torn apart.
Everything is falling apart from under my feet,
And I'm only at peace, when I sleep.
Why don't big sister love me no more?
Maybe I'm a bitch right down to the core.
To make a problem worse,
I only see her in the summer; what a curse!
She thinks I'm spoiled and life is just roses.
She has the world on a platter and seems to know.
I hate living with half a family and not feeling whole,
She's little Miss Innocent and I'm little Miss Cold.
All my life she's told me to go after my dreams.
Now, she thinks I'm crazy and won't hear me, even if I scream.
I want my big sister back,
But she's out there now, planning my attack.
I need my brother here to say it's o.k.,
And tell me, she'll love me and in her heart, she wants me to stay.
I need them both to help me get by,
But now she ain't there and she left me to cry.
What did little sister do that was so bad?
Don't you know you're part of the best thing she ever had.
Had to, just had to, love her that much, but that didn't last,
Then, abandoned her there, alone, with thoughts of the past.
I hate thinking back on all the good times; it hurts too much,
But you wouldn't understand, because we're sisters out of touch.
I trusted you, oh hunter of the heart,
You knew that and squashed me, knowing you were smart.
But I've matured since we last talked,
And decided I don't need you as much as I thought.
I need you more than that,
All of these feelings were those from a spat.

Cynthia Donaldson
MY SOUL
In my mind and in my heart
there is a special place.

A place that no one else can touch,
and never again forsake.

A place where I can see things,
That no one else can see.

To dream the dreams that no one else would ever dare to dream.

This special place, within myself
where memories can unfold.

Is mine and mine alone to keep, til—
God comes to take it home.

Kathleen Albro
AFTERMATH OF WAR
Though the fiery yellow of the sun
Ceases to flow in molten splendor
And the plum breath of evening breezes
No longer whisper ancient tales
I shall dream and grasp visions of things
Beyond this world
Which only the souls of the dead can see.

Though the misty tears of the heavens
Have been burned away by countless eons of time
And the mysterious depths of the seas
No longer hide the horrors of men's minds,
I shall travel upon the murky waters of the soul
Where only the pattern of dreams gently flow.

Though the inky blackness of nonexistence
Has swallowed the bloody clouds of sunset
And the green of life lies only in the Memories of charred corpses
The wings of eternal sleep will brush away
The cruelties of war
As my mind lies shattered in oblivion.

Barbara J Hernandez
LOVE
My eyes can see, so deep within,
That part of you called "Love!"
That part of you,
I have it too,
It's given from above.

Within us both,
Is that one source,
Which dwells in you and me.
We touch it when we melt in "Love,"
And see eternity.

B Smith
MAKING LOVE
Is something that two do together.
Both are willing and in love with each other.
Is best when done without touching one another.

Shirley B Burbank
THE UNDYING ROSE
I gave you hope, you wanted love.
I gave you love and it wasn't enough.
You caressed and nurtured me with empty promises
while you stripped away my petals.
You made me into what you desired
and still you didn't like what was there.
Had my roots not been protected by thorns,
You would have pulled them too.
Touch me and bleed, face what you dread,
I am really yellow, not red.

Kris Kendzierski
I LOVE YOU NOW AND FOREVER
If you're ever going to love me, love me now
while I can know
All the sweet and tender feelings which from
real affection flow.
Love me now, while I am living; do not wait
till I am gone
And then chisel it in marble . . . warm love
words on ice-cold stone.
If your dear, sweet thoughts about me, why
not whisper them to me
Don't you know it would make me happy
and as glad as glad could be?
If you wait till I am sleeping
Ne'er to waken here again;
There'll be walls of earth between us
and I couldn't hear you then.
So, dear, if you love me any
if it's but a little bit,
Let me know it now while I am
living so I can treasure and own it.

Angela M Bentley
SILENT MICROPHONE
Where I live, there's a feeling
that's so convincing
When you leave, you hear
so loud and clear
like a silent microphone
a sound calling you to
come back home.

Rose Evans
LITTLE ANGEL
Little Angel with your dark curly hair
Little Angel now you are up there.
You are in Heaven,
With our Heavenly Father.
Little Angel so precious and tiny,
You were too perfect to live here on earth.
Little Angel we miss you so much,
But you saved your precious Mother,
For us to love and to hold.
Your Mommy is special,
Because she gave birth to you.
Little Angel, we will see you again,
When we enter heaven, to be with you.
At least our little "Angel," you have a very
special place up there.
Have you met your Grandma and Grandpa?
Also Uncle Jim?
I know they will Love you
as much as we do.
So long little Angel, until we meet again.

Albertina Vaz Ascensao Fragoso
SILENT CRY!
The World is out there
Braving the seas the winds!
Me only in there I feel, doing nothing!
Lonely trip around and around,
Only the view keeps me from drowning!

I brought my thoughts back to reality,
I was still alone feeling sorry for me!
I closed my eyes and wished,
I wished to live in a desert among
cactus, rocks and sand.
. . . I felt only emptiness!
The phone rang it was my son!
I want to live again I claimed!
I finally saw the light at the end of the tunnel!
I want to live again and not to feel
So lonely ever, ever again! If only I could cry . . . .

Cydney Cross
FLY FREE INTO THE LIGHT
An' now my friend,
I've done all I can.
Go free on your own . . .
Soar unafraid to heights unknown.

Fly free, fly high into the light.
Spread healed wings into new flight.

The journey's begun, the dawn's breaking clear.
Let the light fill your heart.
Those who love you are near.

The most I can hope is
some quietly shed tear,
will reflect in the light and you'll
remember without fear.

Keep light and love near at hand.
Let go of resentment,
Trust in happiness and contentment.
Follow your heart into the light.

Spread healed wings into new flight.
Remember my love, spread it in light.
Be free my friend,
Believe what you know,
Fly high to the light.
Believe what you know.

Catherine Lester
FLOWERS

For Alfred, who inspires my crazy mind.

In the spring they bloom
then die.
Our love like the flowers
bloomed then died,
How sad I feel when I realize
it won't die for me.
So I sit in my garden of shadows
waiting for the sun. That could
be mine. So like the flowers I may
come from death
To Bloom again.

Margaret E Love
AT TWILIGHT ON NORSEMAN RADIALS

To My Son, Chris.

He comes no more — my young son;
He comes no more,
Wheeling up the gentle sloping hill
That used to be his
When he was a cowboy of childhood;
That used to be his
When he was a Soboban trail blazer;
That used to be his
When his troubled mind had faltered.

He comes no more — my young son;
He comes no more,
Teasing gently and bewildering us
Taunting and goading us,
Eating, loving and laughing with us
He comes no more
On Norseman radials at twilight.

Elma Rubio
LA MUERTE

To "The Wind Beneath My Wings."

I dance with La Muerte
She is my friend these days
She asks, Estas segura
I respond, Mejor irme contigo
than live without him

We talk about recuerdos
and palabras he forgot
The tears no dan consuelo
y la esperanza muere

La Muerte me dice
It is dark here
Le contesto, Aqui tambien
The days hold hidden sorrow
y las noches soledad

Le ruego
llevame donde hay olvido
from promesas never made
entierame en lo profundo
de este amor
that only I
want to feel again

Philip A Grimard
TEARS, TEARS
The safety valve of the desperate.
The silent cry from the separate,
Slowly rise from deep within,
Spill from the eyes and like the wind
Silently call, "please come in."
But, like the turtle and the hare
Quietly withdraw and disappear in thin air.
In their place is another mask
To cleverly conceal an unhappy past.
In the quiet and darkened room,
The tears come again, you cry to the moon,
Unheard, unanswered, "Will help come soon?"
Then, far and above the moon and stars,
A voice whispers softly,
"There will be balm for your scars."

Emily J Shrum
GOD'S HUMOR
I think, though you may not agree,
That God has a sense of humor, just like me.

For instance, some little animals that I see,
Always bring a laugh out of me.
As I laugh, "I wonder," I say, "Did the
Lord laugh that way, on creation day?"
Did the Lord with love and mirth, create
The creatures, here on earth?
If you doubt the humor in his task,
Consider the raccoon, with his little black mask.
Thank you Lord, I understand the love
And humor in your hand.

Mary Alice Merrill Clements
THE SKY
As you look to the sky
It makes you question why?
Why the Earth and Universe?
Perhaps that's why
we most always look down
to keep track of where we're going on the ground

From the sky comes our seasons
with sun so bright
and a path around it is our plight
with endlessness and puffy clouds
It's no wonder that's where
we imagine Heaven, to ease our cares

In hopes to which our souls
will abound
As we travel on the ground

Barbara I Armstrong
A PLEA FOR MERCY
As I lie in your white dungeon
From my body life has fled
And I yearn for my release
That you allow me to be dead
Yet each weary, endless hour
Your machines perform their deeds
Providing blood, and breath and function
As if providing for my needs
In your halls and in your towers
You sit like Alchemists of old
"We can force this shell to function
And in that way the Spirit hold"
"We are mighty Lords of Medicine
We are greater than any man
With our machines and our elixirs
We can yet thwart God's Plan"
Yet, I beg you to show mercy
As if to an animal dear to thee
Please release me from my bondage
And allow my spirit to soar free.

Sheila Baxter
ONE HOT SUMMER DAY
The sun brewed some tea today, in a large jar,
For the Old Man of the Sea, who swam in from afar,
Leaving the dolphin herd he drove
Fishing in my mangrove cove.

He roamed these shadowy rooms where
Creeping wood-vines stray
Over timbers of old wrecks
Lost off Tampa Bay.

Gazing across the water, saddened at the sight
Of condominiums round the shore,
Dazzling us with light.
"Alas, where are the mangroves
That tapped on the windowpane?
And the heron's rusty croak as it fished there in the rain?"

He drank another glass of tea
As the hour of midnight neared,
And I knew he'd soon be leaving,
Just as I always feared.
He picked some seaweeds from his
Cloud-gray beard and sighed,
"We sea-gods have to follow the flowing of the tide."

Before we went, he gazed at me,
Bright eyes igniting mine,
Purring like a samovar, a bowl of mulling wine,
Spreading energy and love
Through rooms that once were thine.

And then I knew he would return
When moon and tides were right,
And I brushed the tears away
As he swam out of sight.
Alas, it may be months before
The Old Man of the Sea
Swims back into this cove to share
My sun-brewed tea with me.

Sheila Baxter
SINKING HOUSE — SIESTA KEY
It rained last night;
fungi blossoms on the ceiling.
Paint once white
is gray and peeling.

Joists and floorboards soon gave way,
taking the bed on which she lay,
drawing her downward all unfurled
into a bottomless netherworld.
Whales swim on its periphery,
touching piano keys and lamps from Tiffany,
and dolphins are picking up the phone
saying sadly, "No one's home."

Marcus Haile
UNTITLED
War has arrived.
Hope has gone.
The legions roll forward
to lay waste the land,
painting the Earth red
with the blood of men.
Soldiers scream pleas
but their cries are drowned in thunder.
City mongrels chew the bleached
bones of Peace.
"Dulce et decorum est" they claim,
but
bravery about death is
cowardice about life.

A man draped in black stands
atop a snowy mountain.
In his hand a dove is trapped,
the frantic terror of the world in its eyes.
A muscle moves, a neck snaps,
and the dove falls at his feet.

Monica M Tilley
MY LIFE
Warm,
like the glow of the sun in the morning,
is the memory of the past.
Many beautiful moments have
touched my mind
and nights are full of dreams
about what could have been.
But fate has crossed my path
and turned things into
what they were meant to be.
Who am I to tell what tomorrow will bring,
as life will carry me
over the threshhold of doors
not yet open for me to see.
All I can do is hope
that the future will match my dreams.
And my heart bathed in trust
I will walk along the road,
crossing the bridges along the way.

Mary K Davis "Kate"
THERE'S A GLOW ABOUT YOU
There's been a glow about you, for months, now, I could see.
There's not much doubt about it;
you're as happy as can be
The twinkle in your eyes, and the glow about your face, tell
Everyone, the love you hold has
finally found its place.
The love you share together; may it be forever true; for no
One that I know, deserves it more than you.
The closer you become, as the years go drifting by; will serve
To make you stronger, and will make your sorrows fly.
The trials and tribulations, that each of us must bear; become
So much more bearable when you
know that someone cares.
The new life you'll be starting will require much give and
Take. And it starts the very moment,
that the wedding vows you make.
God bless you both with happiness, and riches of the heart.
And may what "God" has joined
together, let nothing ever part.

Paul R Pelland
IT IS A COLD SUMMER NIGHT
It is a cold summer night,
With a breeze passing through the open window.
Now, I decided what I was going to do was right.
I had thought about it for days;
Had even started, but chickened out.
But now, yes, now it was final.
I am going to do it.
Nobody can stop me, not God, not
my mother, not you, nobody.
I am going to do it.
Right now, today.
I stood up.
Yes this was it.
The moment I've been waiting for all my life.
My heart was racing,
My hands were shaking.
I knew I had to do it.
I went over to the window,
And shut it.

Janet F Talton
BRAVE AND TRUE
The unsung hero runs around;
The unsung hero never sits down;
The unsung hero will give it a try;
They don't even know why.

For every ring a flag's unfurled_
For every shot heard round the world.

For the special person this is his place.
The special person puts a smile on one's face,
and the Olympian shows love in his own way
For the Special Olympian this is truly his day.

Beulah M Hines
OLD MEN FACING AUTUMN

In loving memory of my husband, Walter Coakley.

Old men know autumn.
They stand by the road
in the dust.
With wrinkled trousers
they stand waiting, waiting,
and keep looking back
toward a spring time
of happy yesterdays
when steps were strong and light.
Fading and gone are those days.
Old men know autumn
and they stand waiting—
Facing autumn's painted sunset!

Beulah M Hines
LITTLE GRAND-DAUGHTER
Wearing an
old pin-checked bonnet
pushed back
she came.
She seemed all eyes and lips
for both dazzled smiles—
oversized.
Off her face
the straight black hair
tightly pony-tailed.
Her small frame sprightly indeed!
Barefooted

with springy bounce
she moved,
almost defying gravity.
Sun browned,
running to greet me.
Her arms curled round
an old rag doll.
Little happy mother,
MY GRAND-DAUGHTER!

Beulah M Hines

ONLY THE TIMELESS KNOW

With love to my brother, Elmer Luedtke, and my sisters, Mildred Berg and Blanche Coakley.

Heartbeat to death,
A voyage now to then—
Timelessness?
Could it begin
from the time before
things began?
Behind that time?
Would I be afraid to go
on a voyage where
only the timeless know?

Earth-bound to beyond the stars,
Taking self to time beyond—
Timeless in self,
no beginning and no end.
Would I wander about
and be lost?
Or find my soul?
Would I be afraid to go
on a voyage that
ONLY THE TIMELESS KNOW!

Sheila H Anthony

DESTINY

Thanks to my God, thanks to all my inspirations, and thanks to my enemies.

Following the roads to life, there's always a direction to
Follow. One that leads you to your destiny.
Destiny like the outer cosmic reaching beyond the stars.
Oh what a great gift of gold. Gold is symbolic to power,
The highest of height, reaching grabbing for golden
Opportunity. Skin of gold, outer glory inner mind,
Grasping for life standing tall. My colors in Christ are
Gold and white, symbolic to virtue and strength.
Swimming the channels of the big blue ocean, reaching dry
Land to find the golden arrows of life. Climbing the beams
Of life, such a struggle to climb, but in the midst of struggle
Gifts, are enhanced which makes one stronger in victory.
Victory is no regards to race, but he who endures to the end
Shall in fact find the golden arrows of life.

Theresa McGehee

A SPECIAL MOM

You're the special Mom of a special son,
Who became my husband, my love, my life.
And what a virtuous job you've done!
For I am truly blessed to be his wife.

You're why he is the husband he is
You taught him how to love,
How to care, how to trust
And have faith in God above.

You labored with him, gave birth to him
You rocked him and nursed him.
You comforted him and held him,
You played with him, you loved him.

And as he grew, you taught him.
You disciplined and guided him.
You were always there, you loved him.

Then, grown up, you let go of him.
You respected and accepted him
You helped and admired him
You're still there, you love him.

Just as he was a gift to you
You are a gift to him
I thank God for you
I thank you for him.

Edith P Chase

WHAT CHILD IS THIS

So many years ago, across the sea
A husband and wife and soon to be three,
Made a long trip so far from their home,
Because of heavy taxes on them were thrown.

There is no room at the Inn, they said,
They had to take shelter with the animals instead,
Something beautiful happened that night,
A little boy was born, what a wonderful sight.

All of heaven was singing with all their might,
And this star was shining so bright,
The shepherds did quake and were sore afraid,
It was then they knew a journey would be made.

The wise men came from so very far,
To see the Baby Jesus without a mar,
Bearing gifts, to worship Him with all their might,
For they knew this Baby dispelled all fright.

The Baby in the manger would grow and grow,
And later each one the way to show,
A Saviour is born, the King of all Kings,
For He is the answer for everything.

Marge Garner

REBIRTH

The sea washes the shore afresh
creating a new beginning.
As two figures stroll alone,
apart—growing ever closer.
Pathways cross, then converge,
and each discovers the other.
Both explore, each in awe
and wonderment of the other.
Now the path is one—the figures one,
as both stroll along together.
Each taking steps, following the path,
but sharing the way together.

Bryan C Lowe

THE BLUE SKY

To Deb.

When I think of you
I think of the sky so pretty and blue
Some days there will be clouds in our skies
But not for long if we try to be honest and not tell lies
There will also be rain and with it pain
But as you know takers lose and givers gain
Our Blue Sky will last forever
As long as we try not to play games with each other
Our Blue Skies might get gray
But it won't be long until a brighter day
When our sky is clear and blue
That's when I'll be home with you.

Laura Macy

WANDERS OF THE MIND

In the early hours of the morning,
My mind travels to a land,
Where the air is sweet with a fragrance untold,
And my steps are light,
Descending upon pillows of mist,
And my sense of direction,
Is led by the change of the wind.
Through the meadow, I can see dew drops,
Glistening on the petals of piercing, red roses,
And bright, yellow butterflies,
Leap upon the breeze from flower to flower.
A path of wild flowers leads me to a brook,
Where the trickle of waterfalls,
Turns up little flakes of gold.
And then my eyes open slowly,
As my vision escapes from me,
But I am at peace.
For there is no sin in wandering off,
As long as my journey brings me home again.

Laura Macy

JUST YOU AND ME

The sun kisses your eyes with fire,
As you gaze into the painted clouds,
That mother nature drapes across the distant tides.
The rays of light spin your hair into gold,
And your stare is deep,
Like the ocean you stand before.
I hear only the crashing waves on the sand,
And the gulls that soar on the salty sea breeze,
And the call of a Crane,
Nesting in a far-away Eucalyptus tree.
Tranquility cools the blood in my veins,
As I lose sight of the world,
That I usually know,
And I find myself slipping into a world,
Where there's just you and me.

Erica Mae Goodstone

THE JUICES OF PROMISED JOY

A dried up prune, where once a
Ripe tender plum, issued forth
Smiling succulently, welcomed
by the outstretched arms of the
blazing sun

Oozing out, the juices of promised
joy
Dripping on the dry leaves, of pain
Moistening the hearts
Of wicked tongues and jealous eyes

Squished and battered, by raging
teeth
Beyond repair, cast aside and left to
drown
In the rivers of torrential rains,
sinking
Into the swampy earth, barely
breathing

Is it too late, to mend this ravaged
skin
Diffuser of my vulnerable venom, the
pores
Clamped and closed, on all sides
Is it safe, to let you in, to feel
My tenuous terror and fragile fear

Can I trust you, to salvage
The wounds of years gone by, to feed
My hunger and quench my thirst, and
Teach me, to love, again

Kinuko Nakamura Cutright

RAIN

To my family; Ben, Steve, Venice, Melinda, & Melanie Ann.

Oh! Rain!
And it's a quiet one.
Come here to the window
You can see it.
Look toward that dark-green patch
Of leaves over there on that tree.
It's as thin as needles all right
And coming straight down.
I've been waiting two weeks for this.

Oh, no . . .
It has stopped!
Alas . . .
I've grinned too soon . . . .

Douglas Finberg

WAVES

To my family with love and thanx to Mr. Mariani for the inspiration as well as The Isle of Palm For A Great Picturesque Summer of 1989.

Whitecaps rolling
breaking, leaving
a salty mist

Barbara J Wegge

TO BE FREE

I ran thru the unlocked gate
My breath trailing behind
Like a ghost swaying in the wind.

The still night was illuminated
By the white moon shining above
Casting long dark shadows on the ground.

My feet barely touched the dusty gravel
As I sped down the narrow path
Yearning desperately to be free.

Hazel S Wood

MOTHER

Mother, I'm coming to heaven,
To live with you there in the sky.
We will share each joy together,
As we did in days gone by.

I know that you're there with the angels,
All gathered around God's great throne.
Mother, I'm coming to heaven,
To live in that heavenly home.

Mother, I know that you're waiting
To meet me up there at the gate.
Mother, I know that you're praying
That I'll not be too late.

I'm bound for that beautiful city

To live by that wonderful shore.
Mother, I'm coming to heaven,
To live with you there evermore.

Shawn Heelan
WAKING TO YOU

What is more or less than a touch, the physical murmur of all my life dedicated to you. I love you Brian.

As dawn passes through the
breaking night
Branches straining against the
morning
I wake to you
The moon descends as stars fade
And into the cold air the first
breath of morning
Seasons change colored patterns
on the wall
Light and dark and light
The rise and fall, rise and fall
of your peaceful sleep awakens a
love
that never sleeps
And as sleep fades to waking the
presence of you brightens my soul

Jean Moore-Woods

Jean Moore-Woods
DISCOVERY

To my indomitable Mother and Father, my daughter Dayna and my two sisters, two nieces and one nephew who never stopped believing in me.

One day, I hope,
Before I am too old
The way of success
Will shine through
A heart of gold.
Eyes that once
Were too young to see
The cruel ways of life
Wholeheartedly.
A way to illustrate
And bare my very soul
To leave that past behind
To survive the cold.
To forge ahead with zest
Using the tools possessed
Proliferated for society to assess.
Then perhaps, on that day
The world will see
That each individual
Has a destiny.

Jean Moore-Woods
REFLECTIONS

If I had one wish
I suppose it would be,
To ascend to the hills
and gaze beyond the sea.
To dance upon
the ocean floor,
and greet the sun
through an open door.
To embrace the beauty
of those men of bronze,
on that ancient shore.
To sink into the arms
and eyes of those beloved
in distant ancestry.
To love and be loved;
that's what I would
do . . .
When that, indeed,
was through —
I would lie spent
upon the cool black sand
That centuries ago,
had parted our hands.

David Allen
THOUGHTS AT THREE FIFTY-FIVE

Just to hear your voice,
To see your face,
Touch you.
I am afraid;
Where are you?
Come, let me lean on you
And be brave again.
My soul has died;
Bring back the smile,
Your dancing eyes —
Let me live once more.
All I want.
(a tear)

David Allen
RAINSONG

For my friend Jeannette, because she cares.

The rain beats a sad song
Into my time-worn heart;
It plays all through the night,
And it has but one part.

It is a simple song,
And it plays o'er and o'er;
An easy song to sing —
If you've sung it before.

It makes a man that's weak
From one that was once strong,
Such is the strange power
Of this repeating song.

"She's gone — she'll not be back,"
Throughout the song is heard.
You long to sing with it,
But it has not one word.

Still singing as it falls,
The rain runs down the pane.
My heart cries out for her,
She's gone - it is in vain.

Lisa Troutman Meadowcroft
MY PEKINGESE

My peke is sweet
and very shy
but when you get to know her
she's very wild.
She likes to sing, to run, to eat
but most of all, to sleep.
She laughs at you and sulks
when she's upset.
Sometimes she's bad, sometimes
she's mad . . .
but when she's gone
you don't think of that.
You miss her bark, you miss her
whimper.
You miss the patter of her
four little feet.
But mostly, you miss that little face
that waits for you at the top
of the stairs when you come
home . . .
But you try not to think of that
because she's gone.

John (Matthew) Scales
FOR THE GLORY AND GRACE OF GOD

To (The Flower of God's Grace) and (Lilia Muriel Scales) (The Gift of God) (Jonathan Harvey Scales).

Strength and wisdom against the
odds
By the power and grace of God
We are soldiers in the fight
For the just and valiant righteousness
of the living Lord
With the holy ghost of Christ
As the foundation of our might
Bringing lost souls to the light
For the just and valiant righteousness
of the living Lord
We are washed and cleansed in the
blood
Of the begotten son of God
Lift your voices in dignity
For the just and valiant righteousness
of the Trinity.
For the glory and grace of God.
Amen!

Denise Clark
TRUSTING CHILD

Tell me a story
about the one I didn't know
Tell me a story
of the one you trusted so
he used you, abused you
he hurt you so
I wish I could have protected you
only I didn't know
I thank the Lord
for His mercy then, His mercy now
He rescued us from the sin
of the one man who hurt our family
so
I pray for the Lord's mercy
In keeping you safe
You as His true child
In loving protection and grace
May scars you overcome
and a wonderful life be blessed
this I wish for my daughter
Whom I love so
My Nicole.
Mom

Brandon Giddens
OUR COUNTRY AMERICA

Our country America, the one we live
in,
the land of the free and the brave.

Many years ago, blacks didn't have
rights,
and everywhere you looked there
were slaves.

But it just wasn't fair that one could
own another,
so the government made up a rule.

You couldn't have slaves, you
couldn't own blacks,
because it was just too cruel.

But now our country is better, the
best in the world,
and we don't have any more slaves.

So remember next time when you
look at the flag,
that this is the land of the free and the
brave.

Melissa Stevenson
SILENCE

The word unspoken goes not quite
unheard
A gesture of the hand speaks pages
more than words
The echo rests inside the heart
As driftwood does in sand
To be rubbed against and marked by
time
Only hoping to withstand

The word unspoken touches us
As music does the mind
It carries on forever
And leaves its mark behind

Tamela M Anderson
SMALL SACRIFICE

As I lie here next to you
I wonder what it is I should do
Should I leave and not say good-bye
Or should I stay here and live a lie
We both pretend to be in love
But it's only her we're thinking of
Our love is just like ice
But we both make the sacrifice
She's so young and doesn't know
You and I both love her so
We'll forget about all the rest
And put ourselves to the test
We'll pull out all the knives
And live together. But separate lives
She'll have the best of everything
And we'll both wear our wedding
rings
We don't see eye to eye
But we can't afford to say good-bye
We're thinking of our little girl
She deserves some happiness in this
world

Ricky Lee Nobles
OLD WOMAN

Dedicated with love to Annie G. Bethea, maternal grandmother of my wife, Linda Gail Nobles.

She sits there in her chair alone;
rocking back and forth.
Pulls her shawl around her; there's a
breeze out on the porch.
The stars are like her memories;
shining clear and bright,
And the full moon adds a silver glow
to the quiet summer night.

She can close her eyes and see herself
so many years ago;
Her face was free of wrinkles and she
didn't walk so slow.
Mounds and mounds of dark brown
hair would dance in disarray;
It's still down to her shoulders, but
the color turned to gray.

Glasses on her nose now, the bunions
on both feet;
Geritol at 6:00 AM for energy to eat.
Her pearly whites come out at night;
her hearing aid comes off;
She'll make herself a toddy from the
liquor grandson bought.

Unless she's off in thoughts and
dreams of memories gone by,
She's bored to tears, all by herself,
and often wonders why.
She remembers when she had her
youth; no growing old at all . . .
And now she's rocking back and
forth, and always wears a shawl.

Old woman always was around; she
was there to help us through.
She loved us and she wanted us to do

like we should do.
Old woman, I still need you, I don't care if you are gray;
I'll always want you in my life . . . don't ever go away.

Linda L Burke
MY LUV

To my first "Baby Love," Jennifer, thru whom we met Joe Peele, his "Poem Parties" and this poem's origin.

Roses are red
Violets are blue
It's time once again
For our poem to you

With symbols of hearts
It's easy to see
Why Valentine's Day
Is for you and for me

There's bunches of flowers
And boxes of candy
But none will due
For "My Luv," Sandy

It's our first Valentine's
And I've found what to do
We'll have a dinner for two
And there'll be gourmet fish stew

As you celebrate your luv
And enjoy the day for that
I too will be happy
With Sandy — my cat!

Trina Forsythe
PEACE TODAY
Peace is found in your heart,
but it should be found in your words as well.
For peace is not a fantasy,
it is what should be.
Now it is the beginning of the 90's,
peace is looking up.
Peace is being shown in Berlin,
as the wall is being torn down.
There is still war in Panama,
when it is the season to be jolly.
It is a dream for all,
even the children realize what peace is.
Peace is a topic of many songs that are sung,
and the encouragement for peace in the words of young stars,
The reality of peace is coming,
but it must begin at home.
Share kind words with everyone you see,
maybe those kind words will come back to you.
Remember throughout the whole year,
keep peace in your words and in your heart as well.

Hazel J Dozier
NO CHOICE, NO CHANCE
The cotton fields need me no more,
Plantations are a thing of the past;
Technology has made my job obsolete,
And into a life of corruption I'm cast.

The Constitution was once my hope,
In it I could put my trust,
But men of greed have raped me of my rights,
My soul, my dreams and all that's just.

Drugs have now enslaved me,
They are designed to destruct and destroy.
My choices are slim, my outlook dim;
"Stay in your place, I'm your master Black Boy."

Jim Beauchamp
ODE TO THE VCR
Thank goodness for the Video Tape,
Without it, most of us would go ape.

Many times two good shows are on back to back,
The VCR takes care of that.

Many first rate films are ours to keep and see,
Video tape is the only costs, the films on the tube are free.

To have two machines is great
We can then edit out commercials
and make a film first rate.

Times are we can set the timer when we're not home,
Setting us free so we can roam.

We can tape a movie on in the middle of the night,
'Cause if we didn't, next morning we'd look a fright.

VCR's are such joys,
Best you can get in adult toys.

I shall not end this by saying the end,
But by saying those two words often times seen on the side of the road
BURMA SHAVE!

Diane M Benjamin
THE EYES OF YOUTH
As precious as the rarest gem,
As brilliant as the morning sun,
As beautiful as the depths of time,

Ah, the eyes of youth.

The sands of time drift idly by
While the eyes of youth stay the same.

The promise is secure,
The secret is hidden,
And the treasure abounds,

Ah, there's nothing like the eyes of youth.

So sweet,
So trusting,
So loving,

Yes, the eyes of youth.

Were they the same when . . .
Rome burned,
Egypt ruled,
and America lost its vision?

Ah, the eyes of youth.
So precious, So fragile, and So promising.

The eyes of youth.

Diane M Benjamin
LET ME LIVE
Let me live,
If not for the gentle breeze,
If not for a life of eaze and
If not for a chance to sieze
Then let me live
For a chance to fight
For a chance to give
For a chance to love
Let me live
Like no other,
But for others
Not around others,
but with others,
Let me live if not to succeed
But simply to lead.
Let me live.

Carlin P Chapman
THE ROSES

To M.A. — my inspiration.

When the roses were red
And the violets were blue
The love of my life died
And my heart died too.

Then the roses were white
And the violets were still blue
At the grave I made a promise
My heart would never love anew.

The roses became pink
And the violets remained blue
Some life stirred deep in my heart
The very night that I met you.

Now the roses are peach
And the violets are blue
My heart once again alive
Is proclaiming, "I love you."

Carlin P Chapman
MISSING YOU

To the "Wizard of Broadripple."

As I laid in my bed last night
My heart was breaking in two.
Once again I felt the pain
As when I heard those words from you.

We could have talked between ourselves
You had nothing from me to fear.
This pain I feel goes very deep
Because to me you are especially dear.

When I try not to think of you
The eyes defy me and begin to overflow.
My last picture is of you sitting there
Telling me plainly I must go.
I can say nothing save to wish you well
And hope your every dream comes true.
That some day our paths may cross
Is my wish for I really do miss you.

Elouise Plain
ONE NIGHT
One night we walked along the beach and listened
to the surf crash in the darkness.
And, we loved . . .
In the most special way two people
can love . . .
With our minds.
We barely touched, yet, the feeling was there . . . contentment and satisfaction.
Two people in love, without words, without
physical joining
Yet, joined forever in spirit.
I may not know you in words,
But, in my soul, I know your every need, wish
and desire.
You are my lover, one night . . .
Forever.

S Caroline Pope
CHAINED
Bound in chains against the dungeon wall
He stirs, moves as much as allowed
His mind, is unclear, confused with unfamiliar thoughts
He tries to break free but the chains pull him back
In his confusion one thought comes clear
Why am I bound and not free?
Fleetingly the thought remains, then covered by clouds
He pulls, stumbles back as the chains catch and hold
He gives up, sits, cries and tried to think,
Can't think, chains too tight.
Why? Eases through momentarily only to be lost again
As the societal, obligatory chains pull tight
He wakes crying, face down on his briefcase
Dreaming again, not reality
Wiping his eyes, he sighs, too much work to do
Haven't got time for sleep
His wrist hurts, slept wrong; so he thinks
A faint voice speaks the truth,
Societal, obligatory chains
Oh well back to work again.

David John Dundas
THINKING OF YOU

To Millicent my darling girlfriend.

Thinking of you I'd often smile
Those telltale eyes no alibis.
I'd often wonder, I'd often grin, It's you my love the heart to win.

Thinking of you, you're like a rose
give me consent, I would
propose to toast, to cheer to hold your hand make me the happiest in the land

Thinking of you, is but a kiss I love your charm,
the tenderness and with this thought comes a ring,
you'd be my queen if I am your king.

Flora M Morse
SPRING THOUGHTS
When spring returns in all her dewy freshness
And stirring nature wakes from her winter sleep
A promise old but ever new is heard again
I will return to you once more, your vigil keep
Each budding tree and tiny blade of grass
Wakes hope eternal in the human breast
We gaze in awe, glad songs awaken in our hearts
A tiny glimpse of immortality is here expressed
Glad songs of birds fall sweetly on our ear
The pine trees whisper while they seem to say
It's time for nesting, come and build your home
Fulfillment of God's plan begins today

Steven T McCallum
WHAT'S IN A FRIEND
There's nothing in the world like having a friend
Someone who will stick by you until the very end
Someone who cares, someone who shares
His or her time with you
And a whole lot more too
To me, in this world, a friend is a must
That special person with whom you can put all your trust
A friend could be as sweet as the icing on a cake
And if she's a female, Oh what a lover she'd make!
So my friends I urge you, go out and find that special friend
That one person who'll be there until death does you in.

Jennifer McDonough
PASSING INFATUATION
You fill me with fascination every time that you are near,
your charming smile and clever wit
fill my desolate heart with fear.

My friends think my emotions are a result of loneliness,
but I must pursue my instincts that
we could make much more of this.

You stimulate some feelings that I have never felt before,
one thing could lead to another and
I'd want you even more.

My imagination wanders every time I see your face,
my blood ignites my body with the thought of your embrace.

Those sumptuous lips and sensual body make my heart melt everyday,
but why must your marriage and offspring keep coming in the way?

My fantasy must remain just that
unless one day you are wiling
to start once again with someone new
whose spirit you're now killing.

Darren Allen Maki
AND WHEN THE WIND DIES . . .
Sometimes when it's dark
I'll sit and stare at it
Sometimes I'll sleep.
The wind blows dreams
Close enough to see
But slightly out of reach.
To chase the dream (in hope of capture)
Across the field (that is life)
Draws laughter and ridicule
From apathetic souls
In stagnant sloughs.
With every running step
With every pounding heartbeat
With every complacent laugh
With every thing you've got–
GIVE IT!
Every step forward
Is one step closer
Still slightly out of reach
But one step closer.

And when the wind dies . . .

Sometimes when it's light
I'll sit and stare at it
Sometimes I'll sleep.

Marcell Meldrum
HE AROSE
Our Lord was crucified on the cross,
Our sins to save at this awful cost.
On the cruel cross, He hung and died;
Between two thieves — one on either side.

Now that the scriptures might be fulfilled,
On the cross He hung, silent and still.
Then they took his body to suffice,
And wound it in linen with the spice.

Some came on the first day of the week,
To the Sepulchre, their Lord to seek.
Christ had risen, the scriptures say,
For Lo' the stone had been rolled away.

Some told the Disciples all they could,
Then in the Upper Room, there Christ stood.
He said to them, "Peace be unto you —
Go Feed my Sheep, Filling Souls anew."

Reflecting back — He hung on Calvary —
He suffered and bled for you and me.
He died our Salvation He bestows,
And on that Promised day, Christ Arose.

Tricia Stacey
PARENTS
Parents are expected to be
Heroes for their children to see

Nurses, doctors, teachers, and friends
Carrying out an age old trend

A good example we have to set
The very best ever yet

To a parent their child does not compare
To any other, anywhere

We will continue through the ages
As if readers turning pages

In the book of life we will add
The children we are so glad we had.

Bonnie McBryde
THE TRANQUIL PLACE
Come walk with me on the quiet side of life,
On small trails where sunbeams dance.
Where the whippoorwill's song —
Lasts the whole night long —
And nothing is ever by chance.
Hold my hand and I'll take you where lavender grows,
And your memories are fresher than new.
Where trust and love thrive —
And the world comes alive —
Because no one stands taller than you.

Squeeze tightly my hand, hold loosely your pain,
Let the gentle winds steal it away.
Walk softly, but sure —
With a plan to endure —
Straight into a glorious new day.

Come, let us walk on the morrow again,
And you'll show me the places you've been
We will drink in our fill —
from the top of the hill —
much sweeter, when shared with a friend.

Tammy G McKenzie
THE OCEAN SHORE
One day
The reader began to say
Down by the ocean shore
You wanted more
You started to sing a song
And your love came along
The song led to marriage
then a miscarriage
Tears came to the eyes
Then you said good–byes
You separated more
At the ocean shore

Jennifer McClain
FRIENDS FOREVER
We've been friends for a long, long time.
And I thought we'd be friends forever,
But we grew apart.

Now you no longer like me,
You think I'm a pain.
And I think you're conceited,
And a waste of my time.

We've shared secrets, and our hopes and dreams.
And I thought we'd be friends forever,
But we grew apart.

Now you no longer confide in me,
And I no longer confide in you.
We just don't trust each other anymore.

We've always cared about each other, always cared
And I thought we'd be friends forever,
But we grew apart.

Now you're no longer there for me,
And I'm no longer there for you.
We just don't think about each other anymore.

I always thought we'd be friends forever,
But we grew apart, so very far apart.

T R Manicone
WHAT?
I've just hit upon a revelation,
concerning the gap between each generation.
This idea is a real sensation.
It could even sweep the Nation!
All it takes is determination,
with a bit of fortification,
and a dash of stimulation.
With heartfelt inspiration,
Providing the proper motivation.
Maybe even new evaluation,
Necessary for the right inter–relation,
We can lick the misinterpretation,
We have with the new generation.
Let's try clear honest conversation,
'Cause that's what's lacking — communication!

T R Manicone
MUTUAL BIRTHDAY
As we share another Birthday, down this long and winding road,
It's nice to know that someone's there to ease the heavy load.
For it isn't wrinkles on the brow, nor the drying of the bone,
That makes the going rough, it's the going it alone.
So, thanks for being born on the same October day,
That I have also chanced, into this world to stay.
And whether it be forty years, or even perhaps double,
It's living, loving, sharing life, that makes it worth the trouble.

Gilbert A Garza
JUST BETWEEN YOU AND ME

To my girl Jill; this is for you! I just want the world to know that you are the truest friend any man could ever have and I Love You!

Dreaming about our friendship, that's almost strong enough to be love;
Knowing deep inside my heart, that it's one sent from above.

It's one to always be cherished and continually treasured at heart.
It can always grow stronger and stronger each day that we spend apart

What makes our friendship so special, it's one sent from God above.
He already knows what will become of it, because it was created with only his love.

God has a different way of bringing
two people together,
Other than the way we do here on earth.
He knows who will end up with whom,
Before our Mothers even give birth.

So as long as we keep God
in between us,
This friendship will forever be;
Something very special to be treasured,
Just between you and me.

Retta Grossman
A SERVANT FOR GOD
If God's servant you would be
Taking a humble place
How thankful you will be
When you meet Him face to face.

The face of One Who was lowly . . .
On earth always ready to be
The One giving help to others,
An example for all to see.

"To be ministered to," He came not
"But to minister to others," said He;

His selfless manner of life
Should be practiced by you and me.

After His short span of years
He willingly laid His life down,
Shedding blood that cleanses from sin
To receive one day the King's crown.

Walter Green
MY DEFINITION OF A FRIEND

To Elaine —friends may come and friends may go but you shall always —remain my glow.

The sky is blue
The day is bright
Inside I feel a glowing light
It picks me up when I am down
This glowing light that I have found
It warms me up — from deep within
It lets me know — I have a friend
It gives me strength when I am weak
It says I'm here only seek
When days are grey
And doubt creeps in
This glowing light — from deep within
Comes to the top — with all its glow
All doubts and fears — then have to go
The sky is blue
The day is bright
Because I have a glowing light

Melva Clauson Geltmaker
SOLDIER OF VIETNAM

To Gregg, my son-in-law, whose earthly life ended in a car accident the same year he returned home from Vietnam — and to his Mother.

Thin, strained, hostile and uncaring,
A thousand untold stories mirrored
in his eyes
Bold, brash, arrogant and daring,
Nights filled with visions of mortar
filled skies.
One day he'll stand in the debris of
his defenses,
As time heals all wounds, he'll be
naked of the facade and pretenses,
And I'll reach across the chasm and
take his hand. My son.

Dorothy Green
THAT'S A TIME FOR LIFE

I dedicate this poem to my kids, Sotora, Leavy, Mitchell, and Robert. To someone I love and care for who has given me joy.

When a baby smiles in its mother's arms, it gives
her joy for years to come.
(That's A Time For Life)
To wake and rise in the middle of the night.
To kiss your child on the forehead to see if he or she is alright.
(That's A Time For Life)
To help a friend start his car on an icy and
rainy day. To receive that warm and thank you smile
as he goes on his merry way.
(That's A Time For Life)
Take life one day at a time.
Do and be the best you can be.
God holds the future for you and me.
(That's A Time For Life)
Life is good, life is sweet, a good life is
always for keeps.
(That's A Time For Life)

Roberta V Gillis
AUNT CLARA

This poem is dedicated to Clara, my sister and friend.

Aunt Clara's busy fingers
Knitting for little ones,
To her it doesn't matter
Race, creed, daughter, or sons
Every stitch — a loving prayer,
As they grow from year to year,
That God will keep them in his care,
And teach them how to love and share.
If Aunt Clara makes an error,
When she weaves a little sweater,
She thinks of God's untiring love;
Takes it out, then makes it better,
To warm the hearts of girls and boys,
That parents bring to her with joy.
With love, she weaves a bonnet, to caress their little head
So they may listen well, to right things that are said.
Little boots for little feet, waiting to be worn.
For there's, a purpose, and a plan, for every child who's born:
A guiding hand to help them find, their worth,
Their place, In God's design.

Linda M Gee
TO EVERY PERSON, LOVE IS DIFFERENT

To every person, love is different . . .
different hopes . . . different
feelings . . . different styles.

To me, it can be found in
expression . . . in a kind of
freedom.

To know that we are free to express
our feelings . . .
without fear . . . without
awkwardness . . . without
limitation.

To know we can say anything and
the other will understand . . .
to know that when we say
nothing, that, too is understood.

It's a give and take . . . both ways . . .
a mutual sharing without
inhibition.

To be totally free . . . totally
open . . .
to share in each other's lives,
families, hopes and goals . . .
good and bad.

Oh . . . it's a passion too . . .
a passion to live . . . a passion
to love . . . a passion to be
close.

That melting feeling when eyes
meet . . .
that tingle in a touch . . .
never wanting to let go.

It's not practical . . . it doesn't aim to
make sense . . .
it's not restricted by reality.

But rather, it reaches for the
stars . . .
strives to make dreams come
true.

I'm seeking the expression of your
mind . . . your body . . . your
soul . . .
please . . . take a chance at
fantasy.

Ruth Phares Goldman
FANCY-FREE

This poem, in fond remembrance of my True Love, is tenderly dedicated to the beloved products of our being: Richard, Marilynn and Jon.

Serenity in
Togetherness
Breeds an
Especially unique
Enchantment
Of its own.
Fortunate, indeed,
Are those
With so much
To give
Who find
One another and,
Having done so,
Know quiet
Fulfillment.
Once experienced,
Love entices with
Sweet memories
Upon which
To feed.

Tim Grgurich
CAROLE: A NEW BEGINNING

In memento mori: Mom; Carole K. Grgurich: "The True Spirit of Giving."

Sun-leaf upon a broken branch–
Green-silk upon a wooden staff,
Swirling colors bright and gay—
Snarling winds blow brown decay . . .

Frosted branch upon a frozen trunk;
New born seed upon a barren
heart-land:
A desolate desert claims the breath
Of farmland drought once Old
Jerusalem . . .

Yet Spring will bud to blossom fair
A soft-subtle spray of peach-petal
laughter:
Now just visions in the air!
Now just visions of her care.

Tim Grgurich
THE TRAINYARD

To the "Chicago Kidd."

I once wished to be an engineer; "the pull of things."
I'd have all my boxcars, a little caboose too.
We'd go chugging down the line, knowing all the time
That the captain is the leader, the cars just follow.

Then I had a dream that all the cars could lead,
Even the little caboose had a mind of its own.
And all day and night they ran like the light,
Each car choosing its own track, yet never getting anywhere.

I awoke in a daze not knowing up from down.
I stepped up to go down; and I reached in instead of out.
Then I focused once again upon the little trainyard,
And I wished once more to be in "the pull of things."

Tim Grgurich
THE FREE SPIRIT

To My Mary Elizabeth.

The desire to be held, but not to be
possessed;
to be touched, and not to be kept;
to be forever, and not to be forgotten;
to be loved, and not to be smothered;
to run-free, and never to look back:
To hear the birds sing,
Just to listen to their hearts ring . . .

Tim Grgurich
A RISING SUNSET CALLED-TO-GLORY

To Richard S. Caliguiri.

Life has no mortal master,
For she is no pious pastor,
Nor burning fury faster.

But a fragrant rose,
Addressed by thorny foes
Toasting status prose,

Knows not a word,
Stampeding absurd:
A raging herd . . .

(life but knows).

Terry L Grenier
SURROUNDED

This poem is dedicated to Larry. I never could have written it without you, hun. I love you.

Silently, the fog creeps through
Shadows loom like trees, then turn to smoke
My mind's eye—watching, waiting
My pulse quickens with every fading image
Do I want to be saved?
Sheer exhilaration turns to uncontrollable fear
It holds me in Its grasp
Phantom lights come and go
Unseen fingers whisp me into a circular waltz
Crazed silhouettes stare at me between the shadows
Lurking, waiting, hoping that I'll become theirs
They begin sucking the icy-cold fear out of my veins like
vampires
I am surrounded . . .
Suddenly, the fog drifts away
Leaving me cold and numb in the dead of night.

Renate Grunenfelder
UNIQUE PHENOMENA
as days go by;

Rain is emanated by Sunshine
two corresponding Halves eventually meet

as months pass by;

Fall is heeded by Winter
the Known is preferred over the Unknown

as years go by;

the Ozone layer degenerates
eventually all Old is conquered by the New

Patricia A Fiffik-Grant
A RAINY DAY
Light,

Sound,

Pitter patter the rain falls

down.

Up comes the sun,
The clouds full of light,
Darkness,
Darkness,
Quiet . . .

Pete G Galozo
THANK YOU
T-Thank you for the Golden Award
you sent to me.
H-Happily excited, interested,
encouraged and penetrated my
soul.
A-Always the feeling of joy to see
it, the labor of my happy leisure.
N-Never fading souvenir for a life
time for me and my family.

K-Knowledge, Wisdom, and
Kindness; my God, You
provided for me.
Y-Your unselfish love and care
endowed to your children who
called for:
O-Only to those You trusted
Knowledge and Wisdom You
endorsed.
U-Upon Your grace and blessing
Your children enjoy.

Thank you Mom Eddie–Lou Cole,
for your benevolent love;
I consider your knowledge and
wisdom your reward from above.
Every beat of your heart desires are
God's way to satisfy.
Endorse and translate them to us, to
make us happy and glorify.

Marcia Gill
MY MOTHER, MARTHA

To my beloved mother, Martha, who never knew how deeply she was loved.

Bouquets of flowers
Near her head,
As she lay now,
Among the dead.

Sixty–two years ago,
On, one October morn,
A baby's cry was heard,
And Martha was born.

Dance, happy child,
In the misty rain.
Grow up to be a woman,
Accepting, unrelenting pain.

Let the sunlight spray your hair,
And warm your soft, beige skin.
Close your loving, dark–brown eyes,
Enjoy the peace within.

Pink rose bushes grow along the
fence,
Blue morning glories never open late,
As today, I walk alone,
Through my mother's garden gate.

Karen A Gitzen
MASQUERADE
Showing off the finery
Marching in parade
Invisible at intermission.

The curtain goes up
And the orchestra blends
Harmonizes
Adjacent to performance on stage.

In the midst of applause
Audience enthralled
He sits front row center
The idol, the mentor.

Vernelle B Beasley
GOD HAS MADE SO MANY THINGS

To my husband.

God has made so many things
in this world of ours—
It seems like a miracle
when we look upon a flower.

Tiny seeds are another thing,
we cannot understand.
They really are no good at all
until planted in the ground.

Seeds are like our words
only thoughts until they are spoken.
And sometimes from our careless
words,
somone's heart is broken.

But words, like a seed,
in kindness planted;
Lives and grows each day.
And helps some saddened heart
to cast its fears away.

Vernelle B Beasley
I REMEMBER, I REMEMBER
I remember, I remember
the house where I was born
the little window, where the sun,
came peeping in at morn.
It never came a wink too soon
Nor brought too long a day,
But now I often wish the night
had borne my breath away.

I remember, I remember
the fir trees dark and high,
I used to think their tender tops
would brush against the sky
A babbling brook ran close by—
with water cool and sweet,
I used to wade to cool my feet
When the earth, was hot and dry.

I remember, I remember
the place I once called home,
The memories of my childhood
will live forever—
No matter, where I roam—

Vernelle B Beasley
GOD'S POWER
The sun is shining overhead
the sky is bright and blue,
It seems the day is perfect,
just made for me and you.
But beneath the sky, is the earth;
made of sand, stone and land,
And on this earth, a creature lives
His name is man.
His hours are filled with work
Desires of his own.
He calls what he has, his own
As the day goes by—
to make a sad heart glad?
Or brought a ray of sunshine
to someone shut up inside?
God help each man remember,
that lives beneath his sky of blue.
That God has the power,
to turn his sky black too.

Vernelle B Beasley
MY BROTHER'S KEEPER
I wonder what I can do today,
to make another smile?
For each of us is a Keeper
and each has a trail.
We say, I am not responsible
for what my brother does.
But God gave us another plan,
and that plan is love.
Love for another; Friend or Foe.
Love to make our hearts aglow.
For each of us is a Keeper;
to our brother, If he is weaker.
Smile and say, Lean on me
I will help, and you will see—
Life will grow ever sweeter
Because you are
your Brother's Keeper.

Rachelle Fae Gibson
WINTER'S REST
Autumn leaves have fallen,
their display of splendor spent
Mountains whisper softly,
rest for the weary,
a little slumber for the furry
A new fallen snow,
its gleaming glow,
how cool, clean and crisp
Winter winds, so briskly blow,
sending snowflakes ablitz
Dormant lilies untouched by any,
await to burst forth with love's sweet
scent
Wildflowers await to awaken,
once they've felt the warm swept
touch of a new spring sent

John R Graves
SHEILA'S HOME

Dedicated to Sheila S. O'Neel for all of the help, inspiration, and understanding. A true friend with so much in common.

Rain and Clouds
Welcomed the sun,
Then thunder sounded loud
As the storm did run.

Her lawn is green
With grass grown tall.
A wet rainy sheen
On leaves that fall.

A chameleon so small
Stalks a bug on a leaf
While on the wall
One sneaks like a thief.

A humming bird hovers
Where the honeysuckle vine
On the fence it covers
In a zig zag line.

As song birds go
Away on the wind,
It is time to mow
And put away this pen.

Lois Greenawalt
DOLLARS AND SENSE

This poem is dedicated to Randy Whitmer, my grandson.

Walking the straight and narrow
road,
Was a young man with dollars and
sense.
He was happy, strong, and healthy,
With a sincere desire to be wealthy.
Then God said, "One tenth is mine."
He paid it off the top,
And always on time,
Until the dollar controlled his mind.

The dollar became his God.
Only success was in his thoughts.
Fear gripped his heart of old age.
I will never give up he said in a rage.

With his desire to be wealthy came
greed.
To earn more money to put in the
bank.
Before he would get helpless and
tottery,
Each day he would play the lottery.

Dollars and sense works together for
good or evil.
It is the way of life for all of us.
Printed on the dollar is America's
motto,
"IN GOD WE TRUST"

Ostine M Gowan
WORLD OF SIN
With all the sex and lustly love,
It seems that folks have forgotten
God above.
As they go on their sinful way,
Time and nature will surely make
them pay.
As life progresses on its path,
The devil plunges toward them with
dreadful wrath.
With lustful living before their eyes,
They can't grasp downtrodden
destruction and disguise.
The Devil has them in his grasp,
But only God can save them at last.
With lots of thoughtful faithful
prayer,
Sinful people will make it up there.
God is good and God is great,
Please don't wait until too late.
Heaven's gates are open wide
To those who do God's rules abide.
God forgive their awful sin,
So they may make it in.
For your heaven is their home.
Please don't leave them standing out
alone.

Gregory J Golding
THAT'S LIFE
You grew up very fast,
so now your childhood is the past

People you knew and saw each day,
they had now all passed away

You started out on your own,
began to grasp life without a
home

Trying hard to make those
proud, in turn became part
of the crowd

And when you pass
away, no one will say
good-by.

Gina Girolamo
WORDS FROM MY HEART

To someone special.

Sometimes I wish I could just tell
you
How much you mean to me
Hoping you will feel the same way
But I can't find the words to tell you
How much you're thought of
Each day and every night

Not a day goes by that I don't stop,
To think if someday you and I will be together
I hope and wish with all my heart
That soon, very soon, that day will come
Even though we don't know each other,
As well as I hope we will soon.
You will always hold a very special place
in my heart.

I hope the day will come soon,
So I can share these thoughts with you.
I Love you with all my heart.

Debra Guzman
COLORS
Red — I am red
I live in a red neighborhood, within a red house with red windows.
My car is red
My friends are red
I am attracted to red men perhaps because they share the same hue.

Blue — you are blue
Your dog is blue
Your books are blue
Your shoes are blue
Before you — I never knew blue.

Walking together through the red streets, under the red sky,
You stand out.
People stare because our colors clash and yet, you walk unmoved.
I admire blue just then It's strength and security
and wish not to be red, but blue instead.

Today as I visited your blue neighborhood with blue houses and blue windows
I wondered which one was yours.
If I had stayed I probably would have found it, but I walked away as I did before.
If I could
I would strip the world of its colors and repaint it a shade of grey.
Search forever till I found you, then live eternity beside you.

Teresa L Gardner
THE ANGEL
Far away in the thickened night
I heard a voice and saw a light.
The voice kept calling softly to me
I could see nothing, what could it be?
As I drew nearer I saw him there
All dressed in white with golden hair.
He said to me, "Be not afraid.
I am the one to whom you've prayed."
With all the love I had inside
I ran to him my arms open wide.
He comforted my heart with words so sweet
In my rejoicing did my soul weep.
"Careful watch over you I've kept"
He lowered his head and silently wept.
"I tried to help you find a path straight
But as you drew nearer Satan shut the gate.
Be strong, dear one, hold your head high
You'll beat the Devil by and by."
Then he was gone and alone I prayed
Just to tell him I wasn't afraid.

M J Gartner
THE HOMELESS STATE

To my mother — liebe mutti — from so many early Mother's Day inspirations.

Living sculptures sitting still in subways,
Sleeping on cold, wintry, cemented floors,
Dream shattered folk in agony and woe.
Daily workers run along worrying,
Carrying their own selfish egos proud,
Trying not to see their own neighbor's plight.

A tragedy of deep proportion swept
Among the defense budget's S.D.I.
We cannot have a weak national budget
But weaker people will suffice bleak times.

Former foes in a changing better mood,
Tearing down built walls, pleading for their needs,
They try this phenomena not knowing
The homeless plight, no money down for them.

Visions of a brighter future linger
As new candidates hit the earthen streets.
It will not be long ere time some see it
Their hopes shattered by money, greed, and lust.
Fighting fearlessly against this dark tide —
Joining the homeless, their future's in the dark.

Terry Glover
DEAR OPERATOR
An Instrument of Communication
Sits Alone,
The Thick Dust Undisturbed
It Sits Desolate, Strangled By Its Own Demise
Darkness Is Present,
Nothing Is Seen, It Has Been Ostracized By Society

As An Old Sticker Slowly Peels Away, The Instrument Is
Reminded By The Scars of Use, of What It Once Had,
It Is Reminded of The Electricity
Which Flowed Through Its Circuits,
But All Is Past, And The Past Cannot Be Relived

A Door Opens, A Glimmer of Light
Falls Upon A Spiritless Floor,
The Instrument Tries To Signal, But It Has No Energy,
It Would Not Have Helped Anyway
For It Forgets The
Shallowness of Others,
It Is By Itself, Shunted By Its Creator,
It Sits In Misery, Now Till The End.

Rose M Klemenok
THOSE FORCES
There was a silence in the night, then a hissing noise occured,
The little house was gutted at the hands of Lucifer.
As tho it was an omen of the things that came to pass,
The rolling hills with its daffodils were swallowed in a crevasse.
Just like an evil spirit spewing its vile curse,
Altering and re-arranging this lovely universe.
Against such forces we are but a wink,
Thrashing in a gripping vise, deeper we sink.
Time will bring tranquility, with only memories to last,
Eons will calm the fury, with shining peace avast.

Rose M Klemenok
PAPPA
As you came up the road with lunch pail in hand,
I parted the curtains, until I saw you and ran.
So tall and so handsome and lovingly you smiled,
Tho weary of work and walking a mile.
You taught me of nature, of the animals in our world,
I listened intently, in your arms I soon curled.
You told of your life and the hardships endured,
What this country had to offer to make you secure.
I have but admiration for the success you have achieved.
You were my counselor and as my father,
It is in you that I believed.

Rose M Klemenok
A TRIBUTE TO MY MOTHER
I said my last good-bye to you as you lay dying,
I bowed my head and said a prayer and I was crying.
You're my mother; my life will be in pain,
I held your hand and wished you life again.
You were the first my child eyes would ever see,
You held me close and kissed me warm and tenderly.
Years of your wisdom will always here remain,
Inside my heart your words won't be in vain.
Please give my love to dad and sis when you arrive,
And keep a watch on me as long as I survive.
And now I kiss you and with heavy heart I sigh,
Until we meet again and you wipe away the cry.

Lucille H Flure
OUR FIFTIETH CLASS REUNION—TO MY CLASSMATES
It seems like only yesterday.
That we were in our happy teens. It's been a long time, but we're here . . .
That we were in our happy teens.
Reminiscing back to our senior year.

Our most important goal was to succeed.
But how difficult we found it to be.
We got advice from many along the way,
And now we have arrived to this day.

I'd like to say something about each of you . . .
But during the years our paths have gone many ways.
We remember much from our yesteryears,
And those special memories are so dear.

Some classmates are not with us at this time.
But we miss them and wish that they had come.
A few enjoy a new life which we will have some day . . .
For we know how quickly the years pass away.

Let us all be happy at our party tonight.
Let us renew the old friendships that we love.
Let us be glad that we are together once more . . .
As we finish our journey here to the Golden Shore.

Bertha C Bays
MR. O.W. WORM

To anyone whose life style fits this palindromic epithet.

Wriggles his hips in fantastic fashion
and when he is swinging sprightly and springy
tries to convince me that he is dancing.
Says he's artistic,
intrinsically twisting
and swishing some curlycues
in a routine,
then quibbling and niggling
finishes it with
higgledy-piggledy
half-hearted means.

Samuel E Patterson
ONE WITHOUT THE OTHER

To my mother; who is there when nobody else is.

What is the bee, without the honey?
And, what is a millionaire, without his money?
What is a forest, without the tree?
And, what is a lock, without a key?
Where are the clouds, without the sky?
And, would a bird be a bird, if it didn't fly?
Where would be the potter, if not for his clay?
And, if not for the night, would we still have the day?
What is a family, without one another?
Would there still be a son, without the mother?
What is the church, with no believers?
And, could we still give, if we have no receivers?
What is a husband, if not for the wife?
And, without death, can there still be life?
Would there be flowers, if not for the rain?
And, does a wound still hurt, if there is no pain?
What is a morning, without the dew?
And, what about me, can I exist without you?
Think about these things, how easy it is to see.
One, without the other? Well, that just cannot be!

Lucille H Flure
WHEN IT IS QUIET
While being quiet . . . does not the soul respond?
While being quiet . . . does not the body seem at rest?
Do we give ourselves each day enough quiet time?
Do we not press on missing many of these times?

What precious thoughts could be ours today,
And what sweet dreams could we have time for . . .
If we but look out into nature all around;
We would feel and observe its peaceful sound.

When alone and everything is so quiet . . .
Do not our hearts say, "I love this for awhile."
Just look up to the sky in the early morning,
And behold a beautiful new day dawning.

Gaze at the calm flowing waters . . . so serene.
Nothing seems to stir up their constant flow.
As we feel the gentle breeze on our face . . .
We might be reminded to slow down our pace.

An inner peace of serenity will be ours,
If we take "quietness," as something to treasure.
Enjoy these silent refreshing times each day . . .
For it is then that God speaks to us in a special way.

Nicole Franzone

Nicole Franzone
THE PURPLE ROSE

To all the people who have encouraged me to do my best and reach the goals in my life.

Swaying back and forth. Brushing against the meadow's grass. As wind touches your petals above your long slim stem, your color is fading as the season passes. Alone among, the others, yet different is your color. Sadness filling your loneliness. Divided by the difference in colors. Yet in the meadow, every flower is the same, each with a subtle beauty hidden within them.

Nicole Franzone
GOODBYE
Goodbye is tear
Goodbye is a mixture of different emotions.

Goodbye is unsaid words of how
much I cared about you.

Memories are remembered when it's time to say goodbye.

But . . . goodbye is never forever

Amol Gavankar (Age 12)
MY HERO EINSTEIN
Einstein was a great man
I am his biggest fan

As a child his grades were quite low
In Math, they were extremely high though

Einstein moved to Italy
There he lived peacefully

A high school in Switzerland is where he went
Lived with his professor without paying any rent

Einstein turned out to be very smart
From his work he would rarely part

Einstein came up with relativity
He was always engaged in an activity

Einstein came to the U.S.A.
He even had to pay his own way

Einstein died in fifty-five
I wish he was still alive

Einstein is a hero to me
He was, is and always will be

James E Smith
CYCLONE
My attention was drawn
Toward the sound of wind,
Whipped to a cyclone
By the metal blades of man.

An imbricate white line
Stood stark against sky,
Bleached blue from a sun
Strengthened by Summer's solstice.

The metallic sparrow
Pierced its element,
Like a flamed Phoenix
Bent on restoration.

Reluctant heavens split
As the flames consumed,
The cyclone's fury
Diminished with distance.

My attention once more
Fell quickly earthward,
Drawn by the maelstrom
Of dreams just out of reach.

Amanda M Colvin
BIRDS IN THE SKY
Birds in the sky sing
Songs of love and happiness,
Trees move their branches
While they whistle in the wind.
Sometimes I feel like flying
Just like the sweet birds,
Or move my arms and whistle
Like trees in the wind.
Just fly off in the sunset
And uproot myself from ground
Never to return.
All by myself I leave here
To my own small place,
Fly away, whistle sweetly
Gone, gone, into the night air.

Patricia M Kennedy
WILLY
The void in my life was too much to bear—
I felt so alone, and no one was there.
Then one night you came, you were soft gray and white,
I remember I felt overjoyed on that night!

Now that you're gone, I feel so alone.
Although it's so silly, I dread to go home.
Most times you waited beside the front door,
And it's so hard to face you're not there anymore.

You know that I'll miss you as time passes by,
I know time will help, but right now I cry . . .
You gave me such love and joy in my heart,
I'll never forget you although we're apart.

I know I can't hold you, or scratch your soft head.
I think that right now, it's evening I dread.
I'll never forget your little meow,
I loved it so much, and I miss it right now.

It was so very hard to tell you good-bye,
I'm sure I saw a small tear in your eye.
But for two of your years that you lived at my home,
You helped me to feel that I wasn't alone.

I guess I admit you were much like my 'child'
The times you were crazy, the times you were wild.
So I hope that you felt it, so when time was through,
You left this world knowing I really loved you . . . .

Brett Norris
THINKING PEACE
The sea is blue.
The land is green.
The earth is turning round.
You may see many wars, but in a glance there will be peace,
Everyone join in and sing;
Peace on Earth we sing with joy, then the joy dies down.
A gun went off, a brave man died, he fought for us but didn't win,
the poor man died in a pool of blood.
Farewell old man, we'll work for peace.
So calm the guns and the wars and ask for peace aloud
So wish on, keep hopes high, hold on tight, and wish tonight.

Lori Dollar (Age 13)
APART
It was love at first sight
I guess that is why it was never meant to be
We were lovers for such a long time
We shared something I thought would last
Then everything fell apart so fast
When an old girlfriend stepped back into your life
You broke my heart
And said that you never knew
How much I loved you
Whatever happened to that first sight love
That I thought was so true
And was sure would always last?

Gerardo C Edra Sr

Gerardo C Edra Sr
NATURAL BEAUTY

Dedicated to my loving wife, Femy, and women to preserve their natural beauty while they're young.

How I wish only to see once more,
That beauty of nature I all adore,
In recollection of my mind slip,
Always see them though am asleep.

The evergreen fields and meadows,
Mountains and trees over shadow,
Rivers run and lakes are so deep,
And creatures around hop or creep.

The dazzling horizons and blue sky,
With singing beauties as they fly,
Off fresh air or virgin vegetation,
Never touched by human civilization.

I lament for yesterday has gone,
As today is what mankind had done,
Abuse of mother nature by economy,
Is forever natural beauty's enemy!

By camouflage that I cannot find,
Thou eyes open, yet they're blind,
If lover of natural beauty like me?
Tell you when and where she may be!

Gerardo C Edra Sr
VISION OF THE PAST
I was born to live a perfect child,
By legitimate parents all admire,
I go to school by myself I am safe,
I respect my teacher for heaven's sake.

Windows open all night nobody bothers,
I feel a stranger but doesn't matter,
Less educated my peers treated me fine,
Observe the Golden Rule to guide my life.

I look up far the blue sky of infinity,
All my eyes can see is a thing of beauty,
Birds singing and parading up so free,
Over fresh air like a water of the sea.

A world full of opportunity to everyone,
But it turn and every good thing is gone,
Oh Lord my God, bring me back the past,
So all troubles today shall forever last!

Harry Slaton Jr
THE GIRL
The prettiest girl I ever seen
Was a young girl named Christine.
Her rosey red cheeks and her long pretty hair
Made her so pretty I just had to stare.

The first time I met her
It was late in the day.
She don't talk to strangers
So I told her my name.

A sad little girl
A life full of pain,
But now she is happy
'Cause nothing's the same.

One day when we marry
And have our own home
We'll be in the sunshine
Where it's nice and warm

The sun is so bright
The moon is so full
I asked her who loves her
And she said you

Phyllis Crowell Wilson
DADDY (NO MATTER WHAT)

I want to dedicate this poem to Daddy, Lloye E. Crowell, for being the inspiration for this poem, and to my husband, Tim Wilson, for giving me the encouragement to fulfill my dream.

He was the provider for the family. He was there to wipe away the tears when I fell. He was sure to tell me when I did wrong, but was the first to give me a hug when I did well. He was always there, NO MATTER WHAT!!

He watched as I grew up, he let me spread my wings. He was close by to catch me if I fell, NO MATTER WHAT!!

He looked so handsome the day he took my arm and walked me down the wedding aisle to start a new life with another man. He was sure to tell me, on that day, that he would still be there if I needed him along the way, NO MATTER WHAT!!

He was there the day I gave birth to my son. How proud he looked at his grandson. I knew he would be there on that day, NO MATTER WHAT!!

He's been retired for a while; he enjoys traveling about, but I know if I was to need him, he would be here, NO MATTER WHAT!!

Now that I'm grown, and a family of my own, I just had to write this poem to let you know just how much I love you, with all my heart, NO MATTER WHAT!!

Josephine McNew
ONLY THE LORD KNOWS WHY
If he loved me,
Why did he die?
"Only The Lord knows why."

That night was a daze, and
it sure wasn't a dream or a maze.

I held him close, I knew this was good-bye,
In my heart I'll never forget the time we shared,
Or the fact I still cared,
I know I'll miss him dearly.
In heaven I know we will gladly meet,
And I will be happy to see him from his head to his feet.
Sometimes I still sigh,
But I think "Only the Lord knows why."

I will not cry tonight, because I knew he didn't want to die.
In his heart the Lord was there,
But it hurts so much for him not to be here.

Michael J Martin
A DAY INSIDE

To all living inside the seventh floor.

A withered women barks
sardonically, mockingly,
madly, held bound in a baby's carriage.
A reincarnated nazi like genius
dipped in red trousers marching the floor.
Two play; timid teenage touch games.
A victim born of incest watches over us children at recess.
And I lay here a shattered victim of self.
Trying to carry this crippled and infantile
body through seas of self-indulgence.
Forgive me ghost,
for I know what I do.

M E Perkins
SOLITUDE
Solitude, my friend . . .
how I hunger for your presence.
In the past, dreadful loneliness
conquered me—
to take avenues that became—
great detours . . .
for this mind.

Since regaining the truth,
I know . . . Solitude . . . the jewel you are.
Rarer than blue diamonds
mirthful is this Cosmic joke—
The true companion of Divine Love . . .
Solitude speaks—
and lovingly . . .
I listen.

Kenneth A Ellentuch
GRANDMA/GRANDPA (THROUGH THE EYES OF A CHILD)

To my grandmother: Goldie Lacob. To my son, Joshua Lee Wenzel's grandparents: Esther Suozzo, and Bernard and Olga Korski.

Grandma, can you tell me
How come, your hair is turnin' grey
Grandpa, I don't understand
Why you forget things, day to day

Grandma, can you tell me
How come, you can't do the things, I do
Grandpa, I don't understand
Why walkin' is so hard, for you

CHORUS
Through the eyes of a child
The world may seem kinda mean
Through the eyes of a child
They will always have their dreams

Grandma, can you tell me
How come, it's hard, for you, to see
Grandpa, I don't understand
Why you have trouble hearin', me.

Marie Oliphant

Marie Oliphant
STRINGS
You can tie it on your finger,
you can tie it in a bow,
you can tie it on a big red kite
and watch it really go.

You can tie it round a package,
you can tie it round a tree,
you can tie it to an old cane pole
and then you fish with me.

Sometimes strings get broken,
sometimes strings just bind,
but when they're on an apron—
they must be left behind.

Brian D Klinger
THE BEAUTIFUL LAND

I would like to dedicate this to: Bruce and Shirley Klinger, James and Grace Curtis, and the State of Michigan.

The land is great it is so full of life, possible to live off the land with a Swiss army knife.

The people awake before the sun comes up, as you hear the fresh brewed coffee slowly pouring into a cup.

You have your eggs on the griddle and your bacon in the pan, making a morning feast to serve many a man.

Then you get up from the table and get quickly to work, as you hear the last swallow of coffee going down your throat with a slurp.

Then you get on that old tractor and you violently plow the fields, working up a hunger looking forward to your next meal.

You hear a shout from the house it's good ole grandma, when you walk into the house you're greeted with the best meal you ever saw.

And once it's all down and digested with glee, you get back to the fields and plow some more, and very quickly.

You must hurry up and get this job through, because you must chop the firewood too.

And when you finally retire in that chair to take a rest, out of all the moments of the day, this is probably the best.

Tony Alvera (ARA)
INFINITE CHILD
Long long time ago when
I was young and so naive.
I heard a song and my
Mind it would never leave.

It brought a tear to my eyes
As I hummed the words,
Not knowing what it meant
Till years afterwards.

It talked of a child without
No meaning.
Night after night I could hear
Her screaming.

Of far off places she had to go
Leaving one after another
Behind. And with
Nothing of worth to show.

And then one day this child
Was near. Without a word
Her voice I could hear.

A look in her eye was all
That it took.
I knew it was her from that
Very first look.

An infinite child she is to me
But still a tear it brings,
For her I cannot see.

The song remains and
The child's scream is still there.
For let her know I care
And will always be near.

Janet Neville
BEFORE I GO
Why doesn't he come?
Doesn't he know?
I need him now,
before I go?

I need to explain,
my reasons why.
Why I can't live.
I have to die.

God, grant me a little time.
Just a little, please.
Don't make me get down on my knees.

I'm much too proud,
for that you know.
Just let him come,
before I go.

I guess I will never really know why.
Why others choose to live,
and I to die.

Why doesn't he come?
Doesn't he know?
I need him now,
before I go.

Robin McHale Ehn
SKY AND EARTH

To my Marvelous Mother Marian who gave me the love of words and the courage to persevere. To my wonderful husband Harry who inspired me many times. And to God who gave me the rest.

Stormy and windswept the sky seems to growl,
threatening the Earth with its thunderclouds.
Warm and passive like a sleeping puppy,
the Earth doesn't acknowledge the sky.
Short bursts of fierce rain are meant to goad the Earth into responding,
but it just lies there giggling about how it loves its tummy to be tickled.
Infuriated the sky grows blacker and hurtles vicious, tearing, rendering winds to buffet the Earth into nothingness.
Stretching its velvet grass covered hide, the Earth smiles at the sky and remarks how there's nothing like a little breeze to refresh one.

Barbara J Dixon

Barbara J Dixon
SPRING

Dedicated to my brother Daniel, who died in the spring of 1982.

He always said, he liked the spring, because of the flowers, and the warm on his skin. So if his time on this earth were to be up, he always hoped it would be in the spring.

He knew there would be so many things he would miss, like the birds singing, the smell of the grass, a walk in the woods he always enjoyed that. The sky above when it was blue, because that was his favorite color too. The sounds of the children laughing, sitting around the table talking to his family and friends, the joking, the fun, I knew he'd miss that, but mostly he would miss just being.

So let the sun beat down on his grave and warm his cold body, and give him a big old tree, and let the grass grow green, and the flowers so pretty, because it's spring and he would have liked that.

Barbara J Dixon
LONELY

The night was quiet as I walked outside, I gazed up at the sky, the moon was hazy, only two stars I could find.

It made me feel lonely, as my thoughts turned to you, I wondered, as I watched the moon disappear behind the dark clouds, if you were somewhere, thinking of me.
I felt a chill go down my spine, as the rain started to fall. I slowly started for home, feeling cold and alone. As I opened the door I felt a hand on my arm and it made me feel warm and happy inside, because I knew it was you, and when you looked up at me and smiled, I knew, I'd never be lonely again.

Estella Stevens
TWO AUNTS

My two aunts are the jolliest old souls their laughter and smiles makes your day.
Never a dull moment do they spare.
Calls on the phone bides their time,
their thoughts are on days past and new.
Their courage and wisdom follows their way.
Deeds for others is their way.
Knowing these ladies is my joy,
our special day was meant to be.
How it came no one knows?
But it's ours for the day.

Jennifer Bratcher
DEATH

Say a prayer for me dear friend
for I am going where time never ends
Wipe your tear-dimmed eye
because everyone has to die
I'll walk down streets of gold
and never worry about growing old
Never worry about anything
but bow before the Savior King
Everything sunny, nothing gray
is how I'll pass every day
So smile and do not cry
wipe that tear from your eye
Because where I am going nothing is sad
and everyone is always glad

Jewell Castro
ASSAULT OF A CHILD

The bruises on her tiny face distorted the beauty that was hers yesterday.
The deep blue of her eyes
is hidden by the swelling there.
Blood-matted ringlets of soft, blonde hair framed the tiny face, covering some of the gross bruises of dark purple, black and blue that were visible there.
Oh, God, what could a five-year old little girl have done that would cause someone to instill such dire pain and suffering?
Did she utter one more word after having been ordered to "shut up"?
Her eagerness to romp about in her exuberant play, could that have been the final straw?
Could her endless questions have been the culprit?
Whatever the reason, the emotional scars left behind by this assault of a child could have devastating effects, for the rest of her life, perhaps, never to be overcome.

Karren Winick
WHO CARES?

I'm sure you remember Winnie the Pooh,
The Cat in the Hat and Pepé LaPew;
The Flintstones—The Rubbles—and Dino's still there—
Those days long ago we all love to share.

You learn in the schoolyard, to always play fair,
Like Popeye and Tweety and Smokey The Bear;
But once in the classroom you listen and learn—
About poverty and freedom how the tables have turned.

There's smog and pollution and death in our skies,
We better our nation while half the world dies.
No more Jetsons in orbit—We've put men on the moon,
There's fear and there's hunger—something better change soon!

Do they teach you in school that billions don't eat?
That there's millions of homeless just roaming the streets?
That they are cold and hungry—frightened and lost—
While our country stands back, we're afraid of the cost.

How could this be happening—what was Robin Hood for?
Was he robbing the rich and helping the poor?
All this war and destruction, in a land we call free;
If we're "The Home of the Brave," then how could this be?

And what about drugs and the damage they do?
If you are the past then we learned it from you,
Just remember the children,
remember their cries—
For God's sake America . . .
OPEN YOUR EYES!

William Cumins
THE GENTLE CONTROLLER

The stars that shine, the birds that sing.
The winds that blow, the fall the spring.
The clouds so white, the skies so blue.
The sun so warm, the morning dew.
The mighty seas,
That beats the shores all day.
The mighty green forest,
That lifts its arms to pray.
The flowering desert
The mountains so tall.
The green valleys so wide,
The babbling brooks so small.
When we stop to think,
Of the problems of life,
Of all the stress,
The pain, the strife.
They all seem so very small.
If we truly believe,
That God controls them all.

Margaret Finley
OUR CONSTITUTION

Dedicated to American school children.

At the end of the Revolution
Problems need a solution.
Independence had been gained;
Lack of order still remained.

Citizens wished to end confusion,
So they penned our Constitution.
Rights and liberty secured,
And respect for states insured.

Washington made his contribution;
Supervised the execution
Of this document so great
And all it could mandate.

Laud our glorious Constitution
For there is no substitution.
Ultimate law of the land;
Through the ages it shall stand.

Teresa L Booth
IDLE TIME

This poem is dedicated to my mate and friend for life, L. H. L. Sr.

My day begins
I have no plans
"IDLE TIME"
It's such a waste
I have no way to go anywhere
no one comes around
From dawn to dusk
i sit at home
and count the hours down
"IDLE TIME" — my pastime
"IDLE TIME"
it's such a waste

My day will end
with still no plans
"IDLE TIME"
it's such a waste

Bethann Gross
THE RAIN

The rain is coming can you hear it.
The rain is falling can you feel it.
The rain is so beautiful, so peaceful.
Do you ever dream of being part of the rain?
Do you ever wonder what it would feel like?
To be so beautiful and peaceful inside.
Sometimes the rain looks so empty.
On these days you feel wet and dry at the same time, on the inside
The feeling of the rain is all that keeps you going.
It's the only thing that
keeps you from drowning.
The rain is a friend
in time of need.
It's an outlet of all
your inner sorrows.
Sometimes I wonder if it's
God's way of showing that he
knows just how much pain
We are going through at
that moment in time.
Can you hear the rain
it's coming?
Can you feel the rain
it's falling?

Ronald G Stewart
WHAT COULD HAVE BEEN

To my dolly L. K. Iwaly, for all that you are, my inspiration, my shining star.

What could have been, would have been
What would have been, should have been
What should have been, can still be
What can still be, still may be, eventually
What is meant to be, will be
What I saw in you, I still see
What I still see is a beautiful dream
But one that seems to be fading,

away from me
One that may or may not become reality
And only time will reveal the answers I need

For nothing or no one it seems will ever set me free
From what I am losing that's slowly becoming a haunting memory
So my heart remains locked in chains
There is only one key and with you it will stay
It cannot be bought, sold or given away
It is magical and no copies can be made
All I ask is that you please don't lose it
So that in the event that one day soon
You may change your mind and choose to use it
So my love until when, you and I can start again.

Sandra Cloutier

Sandra Cloutier
ENCORE, ENCORE

To my daughter, Darcel, who is just as beautiful inside as she is on the outside.

When you were born
I would have sworn
A miracle for sure
I did endure
What a thrill
to have at will
Your very birth
to see by my girth
How could I wait
for this wonderful fate
The doctor was there
at the clock I did stare
When you let out a cry
I must have inherited the sky.
It was four thirty four
and you I did adore
Each to our room
until you were groomed
Anxiously watched the door
for your encore

Sandra Cloutier
PICTURES ARE GOLD
The pictures on the wall
can they really say it all
Those very smiles
have since traveled miles
At times were tears
over normal fears
No matter how old
who could be told
One can never replace
or try to trace
The pictures are gold
to always hold
It's all quite a trick
when the camera goes click
The split second time
brings hours to mind
Time written in sand
we can hold in our hand
While each and every one
has its story when all is said and done

Sandra Cloutier
WE CAN NEVER GO BACK
If only we would listen
when their eyes did glisten
And try to realize
that they idolize
After all you're a parent
this should be inherent
It's no crime
to sit and take time
Stop look and listen
a new relationship could christen
Sometimes only a moment they need
so please let us take heed
To always be there
so we are able to share
Let's stay on track
we can never go back
It doesn't seem slow
the way years come and go
The more we care
the relationship will be rare

Melinda S Ames
STAY
As time goes on things change.
People forget, move on.
It seems so strange.
You are very important to me.

I will fight to keep you in my present and future.
Rather than my past.

The sad part is,
I have no control to make it last.

I only hope that fate will look my way.

And because I have not given up,
You will come to me and stay.

LizAnn Romero
DISSENTION & DESCENT
Ebb and flow of tides gone by
Cannot reconcile the moods inside
Anger in immense proportions
Depression in mystic distortions
Time exists only in length
Sound rebounds in immense strength
Groping hands search the grounds
Reconciled by hellish hounds.

Deep inside a hidden core
Feelings burst out an open sore
Tossed about by violent waves
A turmoil within of sleepless graves
Angry etchings scar the stones
No assurance from Seraphic tones
Lost beyond the reach of Eden
Evil debts now count even

The locks that bolt the gates on high
Ignore remorse and pleading cry
The sun lives deep within the Earth
A darkened shadow laughs in mirth
Smokeless fires light the room
Frightened souls find their tomb.

Marc M Camille
YOU AND YOUR LOVE
Sharp are the pains that sever my heart,
As the yearning in my soul never ceases.
Many is the night that I lie awake, visions of you thwarting my attempts at sleep,
An emptiness that my stomach has never felt before.
Nothing but your love can appease my appetite,
Too many tastes of your touch have teased my tongue.
How long must I wait before separation is succeeded by unity,
Any membrances of the piercing anguish that distance has caused, vanished.
Belief is what carries me on, with the warm winds of your love caressing my spirit,
Ever assured that my search has ended.
Released from the depths of your soul, the drink of your love I readily accepted,
Great were the pangs in my heart, fighting the truth, denying my senses.
Enough sorrow in the past, new blood now in my veins, I gave myself to you,
Running from the restraints, allowing my passions to race wildly, no reigns.
Covered with a frantic sweat, I now roam through Cupid's cloudy fields,
Avariced craze ruling my actions, every little thought evolving around your being.
My whims and wants are for destiny to deal us a wonderful family,
Images of you and I and our children I see with the clarity of a child's conscience.
Love is such a kaleidoscopic concept, yet I now know only its colorful pleasures,
Looking up at each oncoming day with a smile that bursts from my lips,
Excited to live once again, I thank the heavens for you and your love.

Diane Pizzichillo
EMPTY PLACES IN MY LIFE

This poem is dedicated to my Father for whom it was written.

Every time I look at my son I think of you. "Dad where are you?"
I know you would have loved him just as I do. "Dad I miss you"
You went to him where you belong and since then I haven't been as strong.
"Dad I feel so lost"
When I'm down and feeling blue, I curse the day the Lord took you.
"Dad why was it at your cost?"
You told me not to be afraid to die, but your not being in our
Lives all I want to do is cry. "Dad I need you"
I learned things that a girl usually don't from her Dad.
I know I wasn't perfect and a lot of times were bad.
"Dad I always respected you"
He would have called you Pop-Pop this we all know.
"Dad why did you have to go"
But now all I have is a picture to show. Dad he would have made you glow.
When our day comes and we're all upstairs "Dad I'm always thinking of you."
That's when my life will be free of my despairs.
"Dad I'm still and always will be loving You."

Henry O'Grady
a.k.a. H G Brady
SOULS AT SEA
I am the sun which shines across
The long, deep rollers of the blue.
I am the wind which fills your sails
And drives you on to all the oceans
You may travel through.

I am the moon when shining bright
Will light your way through passages unknown.
I am the stars on cloudless nights
That guide your path to harbors
Far from home.

I am the raging storm that hurls your ship
Through waves of awesome height.
I am the gentle rain that cools the air
And brings you pleasant dreams
On tropic nights.

I am the land, the seas, the skies,
Encompassing your love for liberty.
I am the hope that never dies,
But leads you on and on
To find eternity.

Brenda J Jacques
A MOTHER'S LOVE
When there's a question about that mom that you have,
Look at your future, the present, the past;
Who's always been there when you needed her fast,
For money, for a friend, for a midnight snack.

She's sometimes a gardener, sometimes a cook,
Sometimes a sitter who reads storybooks;
When you're having those doubts on that seems a bad day,
think of these things and throw the doubts away.

Your mom gave you life through the gift of God,
There should be no question that she loves you A LOT.

Larry Weldon Bohn
PUTTING THE PAST TO REST
At first, it was the perfect scene; the way that I had planned:
The gentle, loving woman and me, your loving man.
The brightest shining pair of all, we

were the biggest rage.
When we would go out dancing, we always took the stage.

We were the perfect couple, we were so deep in love
That no one else or anything could ever rise above.
We craved each other so much, we'd dread each time apart.
The pain was like a stabbing by a red-hot dart.

With such a love enduring, it just doesn't seem right
That it should all die out in what seemed overnight.
When thinking what we had, I sometimes sit and cringe.
What quirk of fate did it? Maybe a monkey wrench.

Even as I sit here, recalling while I'm writing,
The memories I conjure up are awfully inviting.
While calling on these memories, all happiness evades me.
Yet, the passion and the pain I felt back then escapes me.

I'm in the final stages of getting over you;
Something on my "Do" list which is way past due.
I'll put my past to rest and have a little fun:
Entomb the dead and bury my past and carry on.

Dulcie Geske
THE COACH
She, herself, has labored many months
Coaching her young friend, preparing for this wondrous moment
Sweat and tears of joy fall as they breathe in unison
Grunting, pushing, crying, laughing, counting together

The infant arrives with puffy cheeks and no name

Then, given the ultimate and absolute privilege of severing the umbilical cord
The coach, in cutting it, attaches the little one to her own soul forever

Tina White
LITTLE ANGELS
When God calls little children
To dwell with Him above,
We mortals sometime question
The wisdom of His love,
For no heartache compares with
The death of one small child,
Who does so much to make our world
Seem wonderful and mild,
Perhaps God tires of calling
The aged to His fold,
So He picks a rosebud
Before it can grow old,
God knows how much we need them,
And so He takes but few,
To make the land of heaven
More beautiful to view,
Believing this is difficult
Still somehow we must try,
The saddest word mankind knows
Will always be "Good-Bye."
So when a little child departs,
We who are left behind
Must realize God loves children,
Angels are hard to find.

Phillip H Klenman
TO THE TEMPTRESS
Fly away with you now?
I, who have never sailed a sloop into certain storm?
Whose departure from convention is measured by the infinitesimal?
Although my self-claimed deeds are Herculean
And worthy of the mightiest, I confess,
While adventure pulses in the Scorpio soul of me
And my heart cries Yes . . .
Yes . . .
True to my chosen love, and though the spirit flies wildly upward,
Deflated, it falls slowly earthward . . . and homeward.

Cynthia Hoskins
WARM SATIN EVENINGS
Warm satin evenings,
Scented with velvet touch,
Allure of unique secrets,
Etched in shimmering moonlight.

Jewel L Von Ins
THE FOUNTAINS

My love to: husband, Jewell, daughter, Pam, grandchildren, Tom and Tara Fowers.

Some say the fountains in Paris are for lovers,
But those in Italy are preferred by others.
Old folks think a fountain can calm and soothe.
Others spend their lives searching for the fountain of youth,
But my favorite is the cheery and cool—
Soda fountain, after school.

Bibiana Khan
OH LORD!
Oh Lord!
I see pillars of smoke raising
from burning buildings.

I see people, thousands of people
sleeping in the street.

I see an old man
working along the fields.

I see the approaching hurricane,
destruction and loud cries
filling the air.

I see hungry children, thousands of children
begging one bread.

I see wounded soldiers, fever and cholera, and

oh Lord!
I see a mother, with tears,
running down her face.

F Virginia Castello
AWOL DAD
We love you, Dad — our most special Father.
Respect and trust — 'tis another matter.

Dad, we saw the sadness in your eyes and your despair;
Felt the anger and depression; yet, continued to care.
But, you turned your back on us and fled to another.
Left us pained and stunned — along with our Mother.

Those early months, those tortuous dreams
Filled with lies, deceit and repulsive schemes.
We hoped. We prayed. We stayed together —
Begging for each day to become somewhat better.

Grandma, aged and ailing, staunch to us, she did stay.
Her last thoughts were of you — before God took her away.

She spoke of that elusive utopia you seemed to search
From inside your home. Outside your life. Even in church.
Ever churning. Ever tormenting. Eroding your insides.
Unaware that from your inner psyche, it truly resides.

You gave us so much. Had our troubles and fears to allay.
Offered your love — 'til mid-life years clouded the way.
Things could have been so very different. Can't you see?
If you'd thought a little more of us — and a little less of Thee.

Vicki Sabella
MEASURING UP
How long's your love Luke
Three inches, six inches, ten
I never made it to ten inches yet
But I'll get there someday when
I meet a guy with flashing eyes
Who knows his mind inside
Who's weighed his stuff
And measured up
His place to run and hide

If it's just three inches long Luke
How come it's firm and round
How come I feel its substance
But why don't it touch the ground
It's gotta be ten for that for sure
And not just eight or nine
I shoulda known how long it was
Before I made it mine

You gotta know your love Luke
You gotta know its size
You gotta see how big it is
You can't just close your eyes

So where's the feeling gone Luke
Didn't measure up again
But what about those dimensions
It didn't get to ten

But it was full and firm and round
And I'd like one like that again
I'd put it in a safe place
And keep it warm and fed
I'd give it time to grow Luke
I don't think I'd measure again.

Dawn Nolan
TRY GOD
Try God when everything goes
wrong
You see no sunshine
Hear no birds with their
song
Try God when you don't know
which way to turn
Your heart is so empty
Tears flow until they burn
Try God for He's the only
answer
No matter what we do
He wipes away each tear
He'll always see you through

Dawn Nolan
ONLY GOD IS PERFECT
I'm not perfect
But I'd like to be
I want to do everything right
But only God is perfect you see
I don't want to sin or do wrong
I ask you God to help me not
To stray
For a sinner I was born
Please guide me each day
Keep me on the perfect path
To do the best in every way
I look up to You dear Lord
For You to look down on me
Oh to be half as perfect as Thee

Dawn Nolan

Dawn Nolan
STAIRWAY TO HEAVEN

My fondest thoughts — My Lord above.

Let's climb the stairway to heaven
you and I
Our first thought on Jesus
way up high
Hand in hand together
Our love for each other true
What more could we want
Our miracle to live through

When two care so much as one
That is heaven here on earth
Under God's golden sun
With our Savior first in mind
He'll help us climb the
stairway to heaven
In enough time

The Happy Gladiator
WITH HER AT THE BEACH
Placid ocean broad and wide
neither ripple nor swell
disturbed the embrace —
the embrace of the saline solution
from which we evolved
tranquil
smooth
soft
warm

Brown eyes — deep and fascinated
exploring, stirring and discovering —
discovering a ground swell growing.
The mind's eye beholds a tidal wave
tumbling
stirring
swelling
wonderful

tranquil tumbling
smooth stirring
soft swelling
warm wonderful

Lisa L Watt
TEARS?
What are tears?
Tears have been used throughout the years.
Tears express the happiness on a new bride's face.
Tears show the stress felt everyday by the human race.
Tears show sadness at the loss of something very much loved.
Tears show the anger we feel when we've been wronged.
Tears seem to be very much a part of us.
Tears are shed everyday for one reason or another.

What would we do without tears?
Tears, you must have them or be immortal.
Tears help the body heal and express feelings.
Tears should not be repressed.
Tears are very real and should not be ignored.

Why not have tears?
Tears are not just for babies.
Tears are not just for women.
Tears do not define your masculinity.
Tears can make you stronger.
Tears are for men.
Tears are for everyone.
Tears, learn to express your feelings through tears.

M G Carter
I DREAM OF MIST UPON THE WATER
I dream of mist upon the water
And the lilypads floating by
I see the glowing beams of moonlight
Aiming at me from the midnight sky

Emotion flows within my veins
Overwhelms me with its power
It feels as tiny puppet strings from
The Watchman Atop The Tower

And I in my flowing gown
Feel the tinges on my skin
The air blinds me to the fact
Of my boundary wearing thin

Shall I leave or shall I stay?
My lover has but summoned my return
The blood I own through my heart flows
These emotions begin to burn

And yet more flowers warmly flow
The mist stands in vain
My steps are slow yet quickly move
To return back to those arms again

Edith L Price
I WONDER
I wonder what my Lord would say
If He should come today,
I wonder if He'd say "Well done,"
Or if He'd turn away.

It's not an easy road I walk,
He never said it would be,
But when the way is rough and steep,
He walks along beside me.

I try to do the best I can,
And in His love abide,
But I wonder when I face the throne,
If He'll be satisfied.

Sometimes I grow complacent,
And see no need to rush,
I wonder when I see Him
If He'll say, "That's not enough."

But I know though I'm unworthy,
He's prepared a place for me,
And I never need to wonder
Where I'll spend eternity.

Janet Hodges Fowler
ODE TO A LITTLE BOY
Who brings home rocks of all description
And drops half of them in the kitchen?
MY LITTLE BOY!

Who gathers lizards, snakes and snail . . .
To live together in a pail?
MY LITTLE BOY!

Whose honesty is beyond question?
Who hates a lie with deep conviction?
MY LITTLE BOY!

Who leads the entire class in Math,
But just can't stand to take a bath?
MY LITTLE BOY!

Who says his prayers (a daily MUST!)
With fervent hope, belief and trust?
MY LITTLE BOY!

But after all is said and done,
Who is the sweetest boy I've ever known?
MY LITTLE BOY!

Anna Livia

Anna Livia
I LIKEN YOU TO NOAH

Dedicated to literacy worldwide.

you reach out—
you touch—
you encourage—
you collect gopher wood.
More than that you believe in each soul:
Your belief is so strong souls reach to touch you from around
the world.
who are you?
why do you?
you are environmentalists of sorts,
you have a beautiful vision;
you are filling the ark—
preserving literary gems for your children and your children's children.
you are a breed apart—
you are TYRO
You are THE WORLD OF POETRY.

Ulyses G Goins
RFK: THE MAN WHO DARED
A loan from God was he, this wondrous, liberal man
Who sought the minority out and offered them his hand.

He so affixed his speech, the whole wide world to tell
The disdain of a story old, a story we know so well.

The exploitation of the little man by thoughts, by words and deeds
An onslaught by those in power to quell their utmost needs.

This illustrious man of wealth, a soldier of the CAUSE
Sought to better this old world oblivious to the vain applause.

A speaker for all mankind, this voice from the wilderness
Lost his life while giving to the CAUSE Justice his best.

He heard the threats of violence as he went along his way
But shrugged them off and kept on his charted course each day.

His efforts need not be in vain if held within each heart
And practices by one and all as in daily life a part.

Aileen Jennings
LIGHTNING STRIKES
The river oh so swiftly flows,
don't rush it by, just let it go.
The ground around it quivers, and shakes,
from the storm that's in the air.

Higher ground is being sought out,
from all the animals of the forest.
Up the mountain in bounds, and leaps,
go the deer, cats, and bear.

Such velocity, such speed and grace,
from nature's flock of wild beasts.
Looking for a safer place to dwell,
until the storm has calmed to a cease.

Lightning strikes, it hits a tree,
soon the smoke has burst into flame.
Safer grounds are needed still,
for all of God's birds, and wild game.

The animals scamper here, and there,
seeking the safety they need.
Rain has squelched the fire to a smolder,
as the animals watch in alarming dismay.

Charlotte Riepe
ENDLESS CIRCLE
What happens when a genius dies?
Are talents buried with him?
or do they enter reservoirs
for future souls to borrow?

Explain the youngster prodigy
whose musical attainment
stuns teachers, peers and family,
not knowing whence the blessings.

Or is a new life born again
re-incarnate retrieving
rare gifts latent from the grave
to manifest recycling?

Could Chopin, Monet, Bernard Shaw
have siphoned former springs,
brought to the world gigantic yield,
and leaving, willed re-birth?

Naoma L Frerichs
BRIGHT MESSENGER
The robin sang his song of love so proudly where he stood,
Beneath the shade of spring's new leaf . . .
Hung gracefully on wood.
He trilled a message most profound from sources yet unseen,
That filled the air with brilliant hues . . .
To balance off the green.
"Your children are not yours" he sang, "But gifts of loves perfection . .
That you might guide the arrow's flight,
Yet know not its direction."
"In laboring to hasten growth you teach them to be free . . .
That they might too (in yearned flight)
Seek yet another tree."
"Thus life and death are really one.
The river to the sea.
All children are ordained to be . . .
So loved . . . and yet set free."

Katherine C Bullock
THE UNIVERSE

To my parents, and to God for His amazing creation of "The Universe."

The Universe is a miracle of Creation
Both designed and made in only 6 days.
Where each hill is a mountain touching the very sky.
And fleecy clouds like magic ships to fairyland sail by.
It is the song of wheat, a song of praise
For sun and moon and stars and clear cool rain.
For long dark nights and perfect growing grain.
There comes a time for sleeping, that the earth may have its rest.
For God so rules the seasons, to do what each knows best.
Soon winter will be coming, and when the time is right
God will bed the weary traveler, with coverlet of white.
God made sun & moon to distinguish seasons and day and night
We cannot have the fruits of the earth, but in their seasons.

Ingrid Roskay
CHARCOAL SKETCH
The sun has torn the sky apart
and sprinkled the snow
with sudden diamonds
Icicles gleam like glass spears
and the wind is muttering to itself
in an ominous way.

The trees are pen strokes on gray silk paper
and I am a minor figure in the foreground
drawn with hasty strokes.

Hair blown by the wind like a ragged banner,
and eyes blinded by the play
of diamond fire in the snow.

One hand stretching for something
fled in the wind.
What was it?

I do not know . . . all I remember
is the sound of the wind,
and the taste of the snow.

Myrna L Hartley
THE EMPTY SPACE

To my husband James and his family, my best friend Kathy Payton, and all who feel the loss of a family member close to a holiday.

The weather may be gloomy
And your spirits not too high
But Christmas is just days away
The hours seem to fly

The kids await their presents
The rest await the meal
You go through all the motions
Even though it seems unreal

For somewhere in your family
There's an empty place this year
Someone can't be with you
Though you ache to have them near

But keep your smile . . . enjoy this time
'Cause you're really not alone
You've stored a lot of memories
From life shared in this home

Dee Orme
LIFE IS FOREVER
The wind is cool
The sod is cold — and watery.
The Jonquils peep through with effort.
Life is forever

The tulip bed, a sandy mass
Soon to reveal a riot
Of gold, red, and pink
To caress the eye — perfume the air.
Life is forever

In the pasture the lambs,
Young, silky, newly born
Cuddle close to their mother
Seeking reassurance.
Life is forever

From the trees a screeching noise,
The baby robins in their nest,
Practicing for a later symphony
To please the world.
Life is forever

And little baby Jeffery in his basket
Stretches and yawns
Wiggling his toes and tiny fingers
Blinks his baby blue eyes
And gives a whimsical smile.
Life is forever!

Annette Alvino
IF THERE'S ONE THING YOU LEARN IN LIFE

This poem is dedicated to Sandy, my best friend.

If there's one thing you learn in life
It's always to be true
For one can never know when sorrow falls on you
You think you have it all worked out, and everything just so
Then one day it is taken, and why we'll
never know.
Your sorrow hurts beyond compare
Your heart aches with each passing day
For someone that you loved so much
Has gone and passed away
Each one of us has someone, we hold so very dear,
And our love for that person
Grows stronger every year.
The writing of this poem, you see, was not so hard to do.
Tell them while they're living,
The simple "I love you"
Words that tell how much you care
How much you love them so,
And you won't have to worry
When it comes their time to go.

June Allegra Elliott
SWEET ISLAND OF ALOHA

To Selma Cattell, gracious and talented friend from Maui, "Sweet Island of Aloha."

Sweet Island of Aloha,
I'm back again!
Joy in every breath and
step is mine!
Peace is here and
Maui's morning sparkles
along Kaanapali—
I stroll at wavelets'
bubbling edge,
Refreshed by Mano's
gentle sea—
Content am I, forever,
In this idyllic dream.

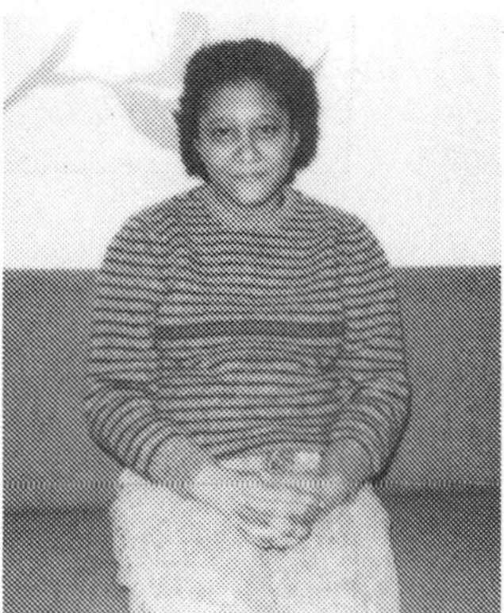

Julia Rivera

Julia Rivera
CUPID

To my daughters — Tisha Elaine and Julia Alexandria.

CUPID

Thee authority over his direction
consider Cupid's
Consideration for togetherness,
With thou knowledge of
representation of
characteristic,
With a Roman kind of love.

CUPID

Thee power and thou rights under his commands,
Thou once again find thee influence of love,
Principles and laws on how we govern our life,
My limit is beyond thou
commandment of love.
Again there come about my
transgression.

Arren Mykl Broderick
SYLLOGISM
I've been known to sit for hours
Gazing at a crimson rose
Misty-eyed 'neath nature's bowers
Sharing beauty she bestows.
And I've been wrapped with rapture
Staring at a rainbowed dawn
Praying memory would capture
Beauty twilight seemed to spawn.

So if you should catch me staring,
Gazing, misty-eyed towards you,
Let me simply say I'm sharing
That which nature lets me view.

David M Phelan
HEAVEN'S OPEN GATE
Anchor's helpless hold,
my wooden ship's a toy.

Crushing, pounding waves
banish me to an early grave.

Stormy eye watching—
passes over by.
Clouds opening to a clear, blue sky.
Hope against hope,
heaven's parting gate.

Trembling hands hold
an ancient book.
Master's heart now recalled.
Blow a kiss in the wind
as I enter heaven's open gate.

Billy Di Ponziano
A MAN ASKED
A man asked what love was, but he got no answer.
A second time he asked, but he got no answer.
He asked the rich man, he said money.
And to the impoverished, love came as an angel in the night
Freeing them of their pain and suffering.
But to the man, love was a friend he had never known,
Love had not introduced itself to him,
And he never to it.
A man asked what love was, but an answer he received.
He was answered by the flowers in a meadow,
By the birds ascending to the heavens above,
By the deep blue midnight sky and the stars shone in it.
The man was so enthralled with his discovery,
He desired to share it with the world.
The world, though, turned love away and called the man a fool.
A man asked what love was, and found an answer.
The world took his love and smashed it to the ground.
A man found love, but again the world took from what did not belong to it,
Love was lost again.
A man asked what love was.

Verna Wantnuk
A NEW BEGINNING
When there's no hope — darkness prevails,
And with it all faith seems to have gone.
And yet my friend, if you awaken in the morning—
Open wide the window and see the wonder of the rising sun.

A new day has begun
And with it shadows fleet.
Listen, and you'll hear the fluting wind
And songs of birds, so sweet.
Breathe in the fragrance of
dew-kissed trees and flowers,
For there's a message to share
Their beauty will make you comprehend
As to who put it there.

For with this day is a new beginning,
To undo faults of yesterday,
For God has granted one more time—
To fade that darkness away.

James E Norman
FADE TO WHITE
We carved this place with our bare hands.
To make a strong and mighty place
for us and our fellow man.
We are the people who were sold like dogs.
Spread throughout this place to give
our master our all.
For we are the ones who fought and
died to be our own man.
Was promised a mule and forty acres
of crops land.
We have weathered the storm of
ignorance, we have slipped by the
poverty stage.
What we have not done is to see the
reality of our lives, and to come
together as one some kind of way.
We are from a great and proud nation
in the past.
You look at us today and ask yourself
how could they last.
We know not of our heritage and we
know very little of our past.
For we are fading in a sea of white
coming up for our last gasp.
So learn your heritage and never,
never forget your past.

Araj F Ahmed
UNTITLED

To Pinkerton, who always existed in my heart.

The Fruitful lie behind the bars
clinging to stars unseen
not seeking a quest
nor finding hidden delights
eating, working, sleeping
they contain no second sight
with nary a glance to the inside
considering themselves the fanciful ones
No confiding
No inviting
happy they do seem
till they crumble
till they scream
The Fruitful

Christopher McCann
LITTLE CROW
Little crow upon a nest,
You will be put to a crucial test.
You will be taught to soar and fly;
When you do, try not to cry.
You will be taught to catch your prey,
Then it will lay there and stay.
You will be taught to use your claw
To pick your prey up and eat it raw.
All this will happen when you're old
But right now you're not that bold.

Jean Allen Luty
THERE JUST ISN'T ENOUGH TIME LEFT IN LIFE
There just isn't enough time left in life
to read all the books I want—and

people keep
writing more all the time.

There just isn't enough time left to hear all the
music I want—and they just keep writing more.

There isn't enough time left to write all my
poetry or my songs, or paint all the pictures I have inside my head.
Or to love all the people I wanted to love
or re-live my life as I wanted it
or change the things I want to.
Now I know why I am out of breath
It's because I'm racing to do all these things
hurrying, running, racing,
but there will never be enough time
before I go.
No matter what I want to do, or wish
I could do
Or wish I could see or wish I could be
Time is running out for me.

Mandi Frantz

THE LAST GOODBYE

Leave me be
Let me cry
I don't want to dry my eyes
Cannot smile
Don't know how
What do you want from me now
World so cruel
Can't do things right
Hatred rules
Don't try to fight
Must say goodbye
Run to the light
Don't worry about me
I'll be all right

Bicki Norton

THE SONG WE SING TOGETHER

He speaks to my heart and no one hears
The Song we sing together,
And harmony bursts forth as He breaks every fetter.
Melody floats throughout heaven in words I cannot express,
For to sing with my Lord, He is the choir at its best.
He sings in the Key of Love
As the Angels all chime in,
Then He beckons me to come to sing with Him, the song we sing together.
Oh, Holy art the Son of Man
Who freed me from my sins,
Oh, Holy art thy precious name
This is my song to Him.

Gertrued Hickin Sigmon

GOING HOME

Feathered frost fronds pattern the bay-windowpane
I breathe on the cold white velvet & rub the icy hole
until I see a snow-curtain veiling the cobblestone street.
Behind me, gas light whispers softly in its gray frost globe.
I am alone. All my life I am alone.

The little lamplighter trudges through the snow —
coat dragging, head bundled in scarf around cap & collar —
he swings his short ladder from shoulder to post.
Turning on the gas with his big key
he sparks his flint stick under the raised mantle.
Light floods out from the clear glass bowl &
he disappears from the circle of misty blue light.

A horse whinnies & I hear the snow-muffled
clappity clap of old Dan's hoofs.
Papa's buggy creaks.
I go to meet him.
Yes, I remember — I remember —
That was eighty years ago.

G M Hickin

THE STUDENTS OF BEIJING

Tiananmen Square, Sunday, June 4, 1989.

The tiniest thread of a spider's web
Can hold a maddened wasp
The rolling waves of a stormy sea
Can crumble an iron wall
The rumble of thunder of distant drums
Foretells the lightning's flash
Oh the bells that toll for Freedom
Shall not turn to ash.

Though tyrants try to mute them
Their bells toll ever more
Though warlords try to silence them
They ring more loudly than before.
From Socrates to Beijing
"The State" has murdered its best
But the flood of the blood of these martyrs
Shall never be at rest.

The blood of Him who died for us
Has lived two thousand years
And lives in the hearts of the wisest men
In minds that have no fears.
The blood of the Students of Beijing
For freedom around the World shall ring —
Forever and ever.

Carol Cook

STRONGER STILL

Give me patience,
to keep my will.
Give me strength
to be stronger still
Give me dreams,
so I may grow.
Give me hope,
when I am low.
Give me truth,
so I may see.
Give me knowledge,
as truth comes to me.
Give me faith,
so I may trust.
Give me courage,
to do as I must.
Give me direction,
to do your will.
Give me strength,
to be stronger still . . . .

Carol Cook

FOOTPRINTS IN TIME

Tiny footprints in the sand,
fourth big as mine.
Hold my hand little one,
we'll walk on in time.
Little footprints in the sand,
third big as mine.
Walk on next to me,
while the sun does shine.
Small footprints in the sand,
half big as mine.
Follow behind me child,
on this day so fine.
Double footprints in the sand,
same size as mine.
Run on ahead of me,
I'll catch up in time . . . .

J Lynn Kelley-Tinsley

I AM SOMEONE

The most beautiful moment
I've ever witnessed,
Was early in the day.
The lake was being kissed
By the sun.

The water was glowing,
The bright sun arising.
I'd never seen a picture
Quite as tantalizing
As this one.

The crease in the waves
Made my heart lighter.
As the sun slowly rose,
It made the day brighter.
I am someone.

Isaiah Turner

Isaiah Turner

BLACK SKIN BIG NOSE THICK LIPS AND KNAPPY HAIR

To Linda Turner-Fowler — thanks for everything. Your dad.

When you say, "I'm black and proud"
Whether alone or in a crowd
Whispering low or shouting aloud
You indicate you're proud of . . .

Black skin
Big nose
Thick lips
And knappy hair

If you wish for long straight hair
And you wish for skin called "fair"
And for black skin, you don't care
Perhaps you're ashamed of . . .

Black skin
Big nose
Thick lips
And knappy hair

When assigned a difficult chore
Do you perform, then ask for more?
Or do you consider work a bore?
You make it hard for us with . . .

Black skin
Big nose
Thick lips
And knappy hair

If, perhaps, your lips are thin
You're sharp of nose, fair of skin
You may feel superior to your black kin
You're glad you don't have . . .

Black skin
Big nose
Thick lips
And knappy hair

From Africa we came, our color intact
We were one color, that was black
Now, we're all mixed-up!, that's a fact
Now, we have all kinds of color, hair, etc.

Black skin
Big nose
Thick lips
And knappy hair

A sadder site I can't suppose
Than some "Strange Fruit" looking down his/her nose
Saying "I'm glad I'm not one of those"
These persons seem proud not to have . . .

Black skin
Big nose
Thick lips
And knappy hair

Some black folk would rather be dead
Than help other black folk get ahead
They'll help any other folk instead
They think it's a waste of time helping those with . . .

Black skin
Big nose
Thick lips
And knappy hair

It makes no difference how you look
Rough and/or rugged or fashion book
Denying your race could make you a crook
It's immoral to make fun of those who have . . .

Black skin
Big nose
Thick lips
And knappy hair

One should never deny his/her race
Because of color or shape of face
And the one who does is a disgrace
These, think there's something wrong with . . .

Black skin
Big nose
Thick lips
And knappy hair

So, if your skin's as black as night
And you're somewhere wishing, you were white
You need help!, you aren't "right"
You should be thanking your Maker for your . . .

Black skin
Big nose
Thick lips
And knappy hair

Isaiah Turner
NEW YEAR'S RESOLUTION
Whether or not you're a pauper or king
Whether or not, you talk or sing
You're sure to feel uncertainty's sting
Wondering what the new year will bring

Pledges are made for the coming year
Many are made for others to hear
Most are promises to spread more cheer
Resolving to do what each holds dear

The new year will come, the old year will pass
Some will be glad that it is gone at last
For others, the new year just came too fast
And fate, for some, the die has cast

As for the pledges that many have made
Some will materialize others will fade
Those that expect to make the grade
Will count the cost that must be paid

Promises and pledges are made with ease
Standing, walking or on bended knees
They're honored quickly, or by degrees
Sometimes as simple as your ABC's

Isaiah Turner
AN UNCLE'S ADVICE TO HIS NIECE
Are you prepared to walk the road
The two of you have selected
Are you prepared to port the load
If it's more than you suspected

Don't waste time looking back
Focus on things before you
This will keep you on the track
And life may never bore you

Don't put stones upon your bed
Because you're the ones to sleep there
Always keep a level head
Being careful of what you keep there

When you stand and take those vows
Make sure of what you're doing
Never do everything the law allows
It can lead to your ruin

A time may come into your life
When trials will sorely test you
Let trials make you a better wife
Good luck and may God bless you

Isaiah Turner
DEMOCRACY BELOVED
Democracy is very dear to us
It is our way of being
Tyranny offers fear to us
Not hope of freedom seeing

A Patriot, was Nathan Hale
What noble words he said
Offered a chance of life in jail
Chose to die instead

Freedom now as freedom then
Two hundred years ago
Burns brightly in the hearts of men
Who love to see its glow

The Declaration gave us hope
Of all men being free
Inalienable rights help men cope
And freedom, help them see
Two hundred years find us still
Democracy defending
Our cause is just, we'll fight until
Full freedom is unending

Jake Vigil
A TRIBUTE TO MOTHER:

To the greatest gift God ever gave me: MY MOM.

She stands amongst us silent and serene.
A virtue she possesses, befitting of a woman or a queen.
Who knows what dainty secrets her generous spirit will impart?
Who knows the noble motives, or the carings of her heart?

Appreciation is a value, I mused we ought to render.
A kindly word, a caring deed, a twinkling smile from
time-to-time surrender.
What form of kindly gesture, I mused in pensive mood?
Could we or I employ: or yet esteem, and still be understood?

My thoughts turned ever deeper for words to query and describe.
I alluded to devotion, and to honor: to her emphatically ascribe.
"Mother, you're a light in darkest hour of tribulation."
"A tribute to all my life's experience and elation."

And though, words fail to mete out every good you do.
You're always in my heart, and I'm ever loving you.

Yadja Yellen
MAGIC SYMBOLS
I made the greatest evaluation;
The grandest discovery of my life,
And I made it at the age of seven
In an effort to minimize strife.

My ticket, then, was a library card
That took me beyond just this existence
As I functioned at a much higher plane
And, thus, saw vistas of dazzling brilliance.

Now I am madly in love with fiction;
The magic symbols that unleash the mind!
The awesome might and width of creation
That animates powers of most any kind.

Music is just for emotion;

Barbarians knew and used it as such,
But letters have divine inspiration
Religions, then, forbid men to
touch.
They used it to control all
the nations
Saying that writing was sacred
to *them*
But the ancient Greeks knew
better;
Felt that this was just like
cutting off a limb.

Cinnamon Orzel
ODE TO SUICIDE
Ode to suicide
It is the only way to say good-bye
No one cares in any way
Not now or any coming day
Life has just gotten real bad
And there is no way I'll ever get mad
I was always so happy
Full of joy and oh so snappy
Dying is an art
Right now my life is falling apart
Let the sun shine on the morning dew
And remember I was glad to know you
Good-bye my dearest friend
Please never forget me, even though
it is the end . . . .

Mary B Sullivan VSC
GENTLE CHILD
Gentle Child, close your eyes awhile.
Drift back to days of simple joys and mother's love.
Relive the treasured moments;
Laugh with them, cry with them, and love
with the sweetness of a child's heart.
Feel the touch of God's love in your memories.
Open your eyes to realize you have come full circle.
Now you as caretaker nurtures, love, protect
Once you rested your head on your mother's shoulder
safe in your mother's arms;
Now you protect her from her own fears.
Gentle child, close your eyes awhile.
Drift back to days of simple joys and mother's love.
Take your mother in your arms, her head resting
on your shoulder.
Relive the treasured moments together.
Laugh with them, cry with them, and love again
with the sweetness of a child's heart.
Feel the presence of God in your memories now,
for this too is a treasured moment.
Open your eyes and realize you have come full circle.

Theda Heap
EDWARD
They say you died,
I say they lied . . .
Although your ashes
I helped spread,
At the base of the
Trees we planted
On our hands and knees.
You loved the trees
Were comforted by
The wind
Rustling
Through
Their leaves.

As I prepared
To leave your
Trees,
I sprinkled
Rose petals
And tears at
Each one's base,
The future looming
Empty without your
Cherished face;
My world cold
Without your
Warm glow,

Never to know . . .
If you became
The trees or
They you.
I shall think
Of you always,
Living on
In the trees
And I shall hear your
Wonderful voice
In each and
Every breeze.

For my darling.
Every tree I see,
Shall become a
Living,
Loving,
Memory of thee.

Helen R Utter
PROCRASTINATION
I always say, "I'll do it tomorrow" but tomorrow never comes.
Because tomorrow is today and every today ends up a yesterday.
So if I wait for tomorrow, I'll waste my life away.
Because even today I'll have lost one tomorrow and then it's a yesterday gone by.

All for what. Because I waited for today and it drifted into yesterday.

So I'll live for today, because tomorrow is imaginary.
And I'll remember the yesterdays and shed a tear or laugh — later.

Emily C Hoffman
THE WALL

To the memory of John Winston Lennon — With Love
Rock On, Johnny, Rock On!

With smiles and pleasant greetings they built a wall.
Two such good friends,
Each to keep the other out, the pain away.
Each blamed the other for some great wrong,
A lie, a misused trust, an anger left too long to grow.

They built the wall with sneers and scorn, ridicule,
words meant to wound, acts meant to stab deep into the soul.
And when the wall was built, they stood aside
listening to the silence.

They grew old behind the wall,
hearing each other through the chinks,
Learning that such terrible pain can come only from losing such sublime happiness.
But neither would, or neither could, remove the first brick
And say, "I'm sorry."

I miss you.

Robert W Bunke
CHANGING MOODS

Dedicated to my family for those times when faith is put to the test.

This song I sing of changing moods —
That sometimes lifts me to the heights,
Only to drop me to the depths
Like a bird of prey who drops its catch
When startled by unsuspected foe.

The fall, tho always like a spear
That's driven deep into the heart,

Is somehow bearable because
I think of being lifted once again.
And oh, the ecstasy serene
When to the heights it carries me!

Today I only want to soar;
No thought of falling to obscure
The thought of all that's beautiful
Which fills my soul today,
And I will brace against a fall,
For I have learned from yesterday
That bliss and sorrow come to all
Through moods that lift,
or sometimes lets you fall.

Gail L Okunski
THE SCENT OF PERFUME
The scent of Perfume
gently wafts through the air,
catching the senses, unaware.
It invisibly encircles.
Surrounding you;
Clinging,
to your clothes
your hair
your skin.
Burning your eyes.
The odor becomes foul,
A bitter taste on the tongue.
You cannot flee for it is a part of you now.
Sarcasm and spite are not one in the same;
and between friends
should not be thought as such.

Gerardo Marciano
A SOLEMN PLEDGE
The snow in the mountains came very early, covering all in its path
bringing with it sheets of ice, bearing the worst of winter's wrath
The northwinds are howling and I watch the trees bend and sway
while gray clouds cast their dark shadows all throughout the day

As I stare at the glowing fireplace, your beautiful reflection appears
and I experience a big lump in my throat, my eyes are full of tears
I wonder what you are doing, thinking to myself how great it would be
to once again find that marvelous love we had, between you and me

From the stereo, "When a Man Loves a Woman" is the record I hear
all I can think about is touching you, and to have you so very near
This was our song, it brings back all those precious memories of you
of fantastic days and nights gone by, sharing love just us two

Each exhilarating moment with you brought joy, love, and affection
you always gave your all, you couldn't accept less than perfection
We would embrace and hug as your kiss set my entire body on fire
and you could fulfill every wish and want, seeing to my every desire

What pitiful and stupid reasons made me decide to give you up
for now I realize that having you was a drink from the sweetest cup
It wasn't too long after our breakup that someone new found you
and now you are happily married I'm told, with a child or two

Your new life took you far away from me, to a place that was distant
but no matter how far, you are never outside my heart for an instant
Over the next few years, our paths once again managed to cross
it was nice to see you for lunch or cocktails, but always my loss

For after our goodbyes, you would always return to the man you married
knowing of how much I really cared and in my heart still carried
An eternal love greater than all other loves, beyond the moon and sun
I'll have you again, promising that I will not rest until I have won

I give you my solemn pledge on this day and for all time to come
that someday, by the grace of God, we will again be together as one
I beg you on bent knees to forgive the distrust that I showed
my deepest love eternally I'll give, no matter how heavy the load

My darling, without you in life there is no sunshine, just rain
and I ask that you find it in your heart to take away my great pain
Come back to me from wherever you are, my angel, the one that I adore
I promise and pledge all my love to you, forever and ever, and more

J M Dodge
MEMORIAL TO ROSEMARY
The young woman, impatient
For life to arrive,
Sits at the table of folly, eager
In laughter caught in mid air
And shattered
Into an infinity of notes bounding
Off the walls of a heart,
Composing a Rosemary for
Remembrance.

Jayne Colgrove
WE SING A NEW SONG TOGETHER

To Richard Tompkins, who taught my heart to sing.

We are a Promise of a Song—
To make Harmony with the Lord—
He has given us the Melody—
And we are compelled to sing—
We must sing a Song of Love—
One Song Together, You and I and God—
We were born with Songs of Darkness—
A Song of Pain, a Song of Sorrow—
We like the Phoenix had been consumed—
By Songs of Loneliness, Fear, and Sadness—
Of which we Die and become Reborn—
We surrendered to the Fires of Passion—
One Song Together, You and I and God—
Our lives had sung a Song of Darkness—
Until touched by the Ecstatic Flame of God—
You and I were Re-Created—
We reflect the Light, we surrender to the Joy—
We now sing a Song of Love-ingness—
A song of Mother Earth and Father Sun—
Across the Expanse of Time—One Song Together—
A New Song for All the World to Sing—

Mary Felder
WHY MUST SHE CRY

For Jose, Jason, Jonathan and Jeremy with all my love.

There's a girl
who tells no lies,
all she ever does is cry.

When you see her
she'll be shy.
But don't tell her
any stories,
'cause she knows it's all lies.

Just be tender and gentle
for she is fragile.

There's not a man or woman
who thinks she's human.
She's just a fool with no
sense of humor.

Judith Halstead
AS I SIT AND WATCH
As I sit and watch
day slip into night
and see the moon rising
so beautiful and bright
I thank the Lord above
for wonders he has given
the earth, the skies and heavens
bird, trees, and all things living
He has given us so much
and only asks our love
just to believe in him
believe in the Lord above
so always remember his love
as we slip into night
for he alone is responsible
for this glorious sight.

E Roberta Price

E Roberta Price
YOUR GAME OF LOVE
You play the game of love, oh so well.
I've been your fool, 'cause for you I fell;
you were smooth as silk, with your words of love.
Sly as a fox as you played the games so well:
Now I've found you out, but too late I learned;
for only yourself do you care, for only
yourself does love burn!

Some day in my place you will sit, feeling the pain that I feel, that loving you has caused:

Your talk was cheap your kisses all lies
your arms were saying warmth, but in reality
were cold: And your eyes, yes your eyes, reflect lies untold, yes you played the game. The game of love so well.

Gloria Marie Solheim
SERENADE OF SPRING

This poem is dedicated to two aunts who have been like mothers to me. In appreciation to Ruby Solheim Carr and in loving memory of Violet Solheim Trimble.

Spring with its chords, of spring fever are playing
Into gardens glowing, with flowers unfolding
Through the valleys, from every hill top
Over the landscape, with scenic surprises
Resounding from the Rockies, the Pyrenees, the Alps
Calling from the orchards, the fields, the groves

Renewing the forests, with its delicate new greens
Mothering in meadows, scenes of baby animals serene
Enlightening the gardens, with its brilliant new hues
Enveloping the air, with its fragrances so fair
Echoing the sounds, of new life and new birth.

Caroling of singing birds, aloft in the heights
Creating beautiful patterns, of symmetry in flight
Cascading waterfalls, creating scenic delights
Chorusing streams, flowing forth with new might
Proclaiming and parading, spring's majesty so bright.

Sing on, sing on, oh spring of many colors
Ring out, ring out, your news of new growth
Come forth, come forth, with your handsome surprises
Stand up, march forth, for your audience is rising
Granting standing ovation, to this pageantry of spring.

Gloria Marie Solheim
JUDGEMENT CALL OR JUNK

This poem is dedicated to a very special uncle of mine, Dr. Edwin R. Carr, who has influenced my interest in and appreciation for many things, while I lived in his home.

Wish I had a magic, invisible, expandable trunk
You're constantly making references to all my junk
But you see, that is only a judgment call
For in my eyes, these things are not junk at all.

These are things, that really matter to me

They are things, that have taught my eyes to see
Things that have touched my heart and soul
Things that have inspired me, to seek certain goals
Reflect my interests, represent my life as a whole.

Junk is such a presumptuous, insulting word
Robbing any object, of its worth in the world
Stripping it of its significance in space
Robbing it of its right to take a place
In the catalogue of things that require space.

Everything that ever once came to be
Was once made by someone very carefully
The reason for something, may be hard to see
But its value, should be considered thoughtfully
Before it is relegated, to a pile of junk
Or tucked carefully back, into my magic trunk.

Gloria Marie Solheim

MAY DAY AND FATHER'S DAY HARMONY

Dedicated to my father, Lester Vernon Solheim for the good childhood memories, and in appreciation for your faithful presence through these many eventful years.

May Day is a special time for me
Because it is the day I came to be
May Day is a very special part of spring
Three months early, my voice would ring.

Only three pounds, and a few ounces I weighed
A few months more away, I should have stayed
The melody of May time and spring was everywhere
The miracle of my May Day Birthday was in the air.

May Day is a special day for me
It's also the day my father came to be
May Day is a very special part of spring
My birth gave my father a reason to sing.

Now Father's Day is once more at hand
Three pounds, few ounces he held in one hand
Many years have now come and gone
May we both still find a reason for song.

May God's grace give us both a miracle song
May we grow in God's grace to find true harmony
Singing in May Day and Father's Day harmony
Seeking to know our father and daughter destiny.

Laura A Bivona

BRUISED

To my family, my friends, and the Girls: For your love, support, guidance, and strength.

Ego bruised. Battered respect.
Pain runs deep from the wounds of neglect.

Starlit hope; wish and fall
Awaiting an answer to nobody's call.

Ponder a meaning no mind can create.
Numb with feeling —Alter the fate.

Scheming ideas. Up to no good.
Caring intentions —Misunderstood.

Absent solutions, heart's unrest.
Words and actions, second-guessed.

Genuine feelings cleverly masked,
Belief without proof; no questions asked.

Emotions exposed; felt but unnamed.
The game always changing, the players the same

Empty existence. Lost and confused.
Aimlessly searching, loved and abused.

Laura A Bivona

SUBSERVIENT ADDICT IN SEARCH OF A FIX

Subservient addict in search of a fix.
The slave to a need, turning old tricks.

Blinded wanting strips dignity bare.
Succumb to the pressure in a state of despair

Forever longing — a sick mind possessed.
Dependency driven — Again obsessed

Emotional anguish; Painfully true.
Praying and hoping that you need me, too.

Wants that are simple with a need so intense.
Fearful demand with desire immense.

Vulnerability wrought with greed;
A hopeless junkie, giving in to a need.

Janie Allen

THE TREE AND ME

My sincere thanks to Rev. Roy King who preached the sermon that inspired this poem: 1 Kings Chapter 6.

I was once a wee little tree, lost in the forest, the big ones and me, would I be found by the master craftsman, chosen by him to follow the son?

I'm rough and worn with splinters and knots, all calloused and weathered, what hope have I got?

I sway to the left, I sway to the right, the days are long so are the nights.

One day I was listening so silent was I, I knew there was hope as I looked to the sky.

The darkness was over, the light I did see, the craftsman walked slowly to cut down a tree.

They're all so big and I am so small, which one was chosen?
Who answered the call?

Now I am here, all ready and prepared, to be placed in the temple, the splinters and knots all seem to be gone, I'm overlaid with gold, all shiny and bright, because I listened to the voice in the night.
No longer alone, fears have I none, 'cause now I'm serving my father and son.

Rose Litzinger

A TRIBUTE TO DAD

All my years of growing up,
I watched you.
Riding the range—breaking horses—catching
the wild mustangs.
With your hat tilted back on your head and
your neckerchief blowing in the breeze.
Your chaps slapping against your saddle that
you were so proud of. And, oh could you make
that whip crack. I watched every move you made,
because I wanted to be just like my dad.
I listened to you.
You were tough, but very soft—so kind and
always ready to listen to everyone's problems,
especially mine.
You taught me to respect other people's feelings,
but still be able to stand up for my rights.
The thing you taught me
was to always like what I was doing
and to be myself.
Now you are ninety years
old and I want you to know I still feel
your strength and hope I can become the
man in my children's eyes that you
have become in mine.
Love, Your son
Don

Christine Graham

A WORLD WITHOUT MUSIC

Can you imagine a world without music?
How could you survive in a world of silence?
A world of dreariness and hardships?
All coming from a world without music.
The forests are turning dull and gray
And the punishment of another day
Is the sorrow of a man without music.
What used to be a happy world
Is now a very lifeless world
And with it dies the hopes of men in kind.
Whoever thought that something like this
Could happen to a place once filled with bliss?
But that was many, many eons ago.
Now the world is slowly dying.
The gulls and sparrows aren't flying
And to look upon this land would make you sick.
In this world you cannot cope.
Not in a place that has no hope.
And it all came from a world without music.

Matthew Williams

SOMETIMES IT SEEMS

Sometimes it seems
the mind an empty vacuum black as space
with thoughts appearing as distant, temporary suns
to blaze with fervor for but a moment
then disappear forever or for but awhile
until they are reawoken

Sometimes I feel
numb and empty — hollow as nothing,
dreaming thoughts and imagining things
of which i have or would like to have done.
old thoughts and snippets of song drift through
my mind like motes of dust in a beam of light.

Sometimes I dream
dreams of portent and extent
of myself and others living happier—better.
other dreams turn black with despair as
i consider the future.

Sometimes it seems
as if i feel i'm dreaming
all the time imagining a better reality
than that which has trapped me.

Deborah L MacKenzie

MOTHER EARTH

Some of you call me your mother,
Yet constantly treat me like no other,
Killing my trees and my waters,
Hurting my sisters and brothers.
You know that you need me,
We've been together so long,
You know you can't fool me,
What is happening is wrong.
So look around and think back,
Do you remember things so black,
Please don't put me out of your mind,
Or, our children might well as be blind.
You know that you need me,
I need you too,
What is happening to us is wrong.

Joseph Loscalzo

HE LOOKS AT ME WITH DEEP DARK EYES

He looks at me with deep dark eyes
beckoning for my soul.
Is this the day that I must die?
the darkness chilling cold.
He reaches out his boney hand
and I retreat from him.
To a way off foreign land
to do penance for my sins.
So now I lie here all alone
alone, so does it seem.
Soon I'll be taken, woe begone
deep into my dreams.
So I lie here, half asleep
ready for my plight.
He comes to me and takes my hand,
and with it my fright.

Merle (Tolbert) Panter

TODAY, WE LIVE

Today, we live,
Today, we love,
Today, we share,
Today, we cry,
Today, we laugh,
Today, we sing,
Tomorrow, we try.

Alex Howard

CHANGES

Once I was a little child, playing in the trees,
Little did I realize change would come to me;
I, carefree, ran through meadows,
My hopes reached to the skies

Youth would last forever, who knew how time would fly?

Time is catching up to me, and I'm not standing still
But I've finally realized, no time ever will
Stand waiting while we wonder where it's all going to
But, Springtime comes to seekers
Whose souls pursue the truth.

Changes come to us, my friend
Like rainbows after summer rain,
Like Springtime comes to melt the snow
And through our changes, we grow.

Lisa Hitt

OPEN EYES, CLOSED MINDS

The sky turned to gold
A black man burned, A child cried at night
And an old man died with fear in his eyes

As the man talked to God on the remote telephone

A mirror reflected the eyes of the young
The clock in the hall stopped at quarter to one

As the man talked to God on the remote telephone

A dirty, forgotten soul lay shivering on the sidewalk
Hopeless reflections in his eyes
While the man in the suit walked on by

As the man talked to God on the remote telephone

The music hinted and warned at the wrongs to be found
While the people heard and didn't make a sound

As the man talked to God on the remote telephone

The wind stopped just the other day
It just stopped dead away
A big cloud appeared in the dirt ridden sky
The night turned to day and the birds went away

And the line went dead
As the man talked to God on the remote telephone

Mildred E Hansen

TRUE GRIT

Horseback riding was the sport, and everyone was bragging about it;
so I just thought I'd try it once, just to get the hang of it. —
It really is a simple thing to go and rent a horse;
They had some at a stable near, and that is where I'd go — of course!

I told them there I'd never rode up on a horse's back.
They told me that was quite all right and off they went to get the tack.
The horse I got was long and lean, and sway-backed as could be!
She looked so old and tired-out I wondered if she'd carry me.

Well, I got on her anyway and took the reins in hand;
The next thing I was flying high then suddenly, I hit the sand.
I lay there stunned, I couldn't talk, and when I finally got up
I limped around like Old Man Time
that "gentle" nag was really tough!

The trainer could not understand why she tossed me like she did.
"She's as gentle as a kitten and she's wonderful with kids.
Why they can ride her back all day and she never gets to kickin'."
I guess what he's been trying to say is that I'm no Spring Chicken.

Carmen L Morse

FOR ALL THAT YOU GAVE TO ME

You took the glow of the sun and put it on my face.
You took the colors of the rainbow and put them in my head.
You took the sparkle of the stars and put it in my eyes.
You took the luminous beams of the moon and placed them in my soul.
You took the freedom of the wind and made my spirit fly.
You took the warmth of the fire and put it in my heart.
You took the strength of the earth and planted my feet on solid ground.
You took the tranquility of the sea and gently poured it into my total being.

For all that You gave to me —
I thank You.

Jason W Sabourin

WHEN THE EAGLE CRIES

The flight of the Eagle
stirs me deep,
It makes me Happy,
it makes me weep.
To see such creatures,
wild and free.

Why can't the Hunter see?
He's bringing destruction,
down on himself,
Just for a Trophy,
that sits on a shelf.

Mescal Long

MY LITTLE PAL

To my children, Donna, Judy and Jack, who always believed in me.

We were just in fifth grade, my little pal and I
And we could tell each other what we thought was "way up high."
We laughed over nothing, played circus and dolls,
Turned cartwheels on the play-grounds, clasped hands in the halls.
We pinned our skirts and dresses way up higher than we should,
Took turns reading "funnies"...
stayed over if we could.
Two contented happy girls who knew nothing but this life
Till her daddy came to see me, and beside him was his wife.
My little pal was crying and fear was in my heart
As his mumbled words were saying
"Even best of friends must part."
"We're moving to Vermont, we've bought a farm you see . . .
Maybe some day you can visit, write letters," could this be?
The years went by, we kept in touch,
. . . yet played life's growing game
Till time itself had healed the hurt
and I'm sure she felt the same.
So now I am "Great Grandma" and know that she is too,
Because I got a phone call, the voice still clear and true
Saying, "Now I'll just hop a plane tomorrow, we'll talk for hours of the past,"
But in my heart I'm giving thanks to see my friend at last.

Mark Dane

LOVE'S GIFT TO THE HEART

To Beth, who taught me that love, in its deepest, purest form, does exist. And to Brent Mathew, for always being there.

"It cannot be obtained," the mind tells the heart;
"This love of which you seek is sought in vain."
Yet logic is mute in matters of love
When within us, the heart truly reigns.

No matter what further the consequence;
No matter the extent of loss and pain;
The heart shall go on seeking, forever if it must,
the love which will make it whole again.

A heart unfulfilled, can never be free
to dream of impossible things.
Nor hope to reach unobtainable stars;
for love's gift to the heart is its wings.

Yet, if my love goes on forever unrequited
and death seeks an end to all my dreams;
Still, I have known the grace of flight,
borne aloft by the beauty of love's wings.

So in my passing let there not be sadness;
though grief must have its time, this too shall end.
Let the love we shared fill your heart with gladness;
for within the love that binds us shall I live.

Kirk Thompson

A TRUE FRIEND

This poem is dedicated to Rhonda Guy. "Friends are forgiven, my love is for always. Memories last a lifetime, but now we must part."

You're there when I need you
when I'm feeling down,
With your bright glowing smile
and your funny looking frown.
The warmth of your heart
you have so much to give,
Now you know the reason
I want so much to live.

The friendship that we share
It means the world to me,
I'm glad we met when we did
that was how it was meant to be.

We shared some laughter and some tears
the best is yet to come,
I know you'll always be in my heart
as my friend you'll be number one.

Sandra Lynn Robinson

A RAINY DAY WITHOUT YOU

This poem is dedicated to Jimmy and our 'little bundle of joy,' I love you both.

Sitting alone
staring out the window
looking through the clouds
at the sun

As the sky begins to get darker
the rain starts to fall
along the window sill

My tears are in rhythm
with the rain
as I think of what we had

A rainbow outside now
just like in my heart
as I hope for us to make
a brand new start

As the sun goes down
the darkness falls
and a star forms into the sky

A wish is made
hoped to be found
within my love for you

Brian Minard

DEEPENING SUNSET

Beth, you're my best friend in the whole, wide world. Thanks for caring. Thanks for believing. Brian.

You're the evening's
changing blending
melting colours
in sunset after
gorgeous deepening
sunset

you're a ribbon of
tangerine tied to a
sculptured cloud
of charcoal

a soft blush of magenta
on a peach complexioned
haze

you're subtle hints
of lime and lilac
on the sultry eyelids
of approaching night

you're swirling
drifting layers
of dusty pinks
and purples

the palest shade
of turquoise
on a slope of
smoky grey

you're a glory of
living splendour

soft and warm
and high
inside my heart

and I think
of you

and love you

as I savor
all the remnants

of a disappearing
day

Rebecca Joy Robinson
SURVIVAL WALK

This poem is dedicated to Rosemary Herring in her memory. All your love & kindness & your belief in me will always be special in my soul & our friendship.

You may have not been
Able to decide your past
You did your best to get
through it.
But you are the one
Who decides your future.
Dwelling on the past is
Not going to help you to
live and decide your
Future for today.
Don't direct a blame.
Go for what you really
Want in life.
The light of peaceful
Happiness within.

Mrs Elizabeth Wilhoit
MEMORIES

Dedicated to my loving and caring Mother, Bonnie Mae Wright, 2-28-30 to 2-16-90.

Memories of time, well spent
Cascade through my mind
Fondness of childhood, Thankful for
love
Times of yesteryear, all flow by,
so quickly, yet so vivid inside my
mind.

Nell Abernathy
FALL

This poem is dedicated to Barbara Ascher, who inspired me to write.

The color of fall is so bright
The wind is swift
The fall fairy flies through the air
As she passes, the leaves will fall
The deer will scamper
The fire will burn
The colors will blaze.
As the last light disappears
It seems to say goodbye.
The whispers of the leaves
Will ring after dark.
Colors like red, yellow, and brown
Stay in my eye no matter where I am.
As I put on my coat and go outside
I feel like I own the world.
The dust blows in my eyes
Now fall is over but it will come
again
And it will be finer than ever.

Sharon Brenda Mokool
FLOWERS IN THE GARDEN

I would like to mention the place where my dreams and inspiration were born — my homeland, Trinidad and Tobago.

I'm no different from you, our pain is
the same,
We each have our hurts, and there's
no one to blame.
I walk through the streets and melt in
the crowd . . .
I just do not matter as the truth
speaks aloud.

The flowers in the garden come out
in the spring;
but love remains cold in a heart that
can't sing.
Part of me is missing — the part you
can't find . . .
It's buried under the flowers, in the
garden of my mind.

Time sleeps and awakens and we go
our way . . .
not knowing the direction of each
passing day.
And it's not that we're weak, or have
given up the fight,
because in a strange way, we're more
aware of the plight.

Some days we find the self and we
know what we see,
but earth's tremor is sudden, and
promise turns to a plea.
Because these are the days that man
must abide by . . .
and the despair is shared, with our
every sigh.

Howard E Lytle
FOOTSTEPS QUIET AS THOUGHT

To my son, Richard.

With a young lad's hand in each of
mine
We followed the passage of time.
Two now walk where three had
walked before
And so it must be forevermore.
Yet I seem to hear a young lad's feet,
Oh God could it be but self-deceit?
I run back along the trail and stare,
But I find no small footprints there!

Beverly Dixon
THE SILENT GRAVE

To my dear husband, Cliff Dixon.

Today I walked away from you
And as I glanced around
I thought of all the times we shared
With love that we had found
Some days were filled with laughter
And some had many tears
My dear, we shared them all
Throughout the many years
I know I won't forget you
Your memory will stay true
You cannot give the love I crave
For when I turned and walked away
I left a silent grave.

Myron Leenhouts
CAROLINE

Dedicated to my darling wife, Caroline.

To tell m'lady's qualities
Will take a long long while.
The adjectives and expletives
Would fill a large large file.
There is her love just for a start,
There is her happy gracious heart;
There is her sympathetic smile,
Her wish to go that extra mile;
Her selflessness, her need to serve,
Her gentleness, her grit, her verve;
Her deep devotion to her Lord
Her dedication to her word.
How high the heavens, deep the sea,
How long is an eternity?
That's how I love that girl of mine,
My darling angel, Caroline.

Lynn Browning
WORDS

To my fantasy.

If words can say what I feel,
I'd be sure to write them all down on
paper,
but only a look or touch can describe
the feeling I hold.

For just one glimpse in your eyes can
make you feel
what I hold in my heart and innerself
for you.

Just one touch of our hands,
or just a passing over of our fingers
can have such a feeling,
not even the beauty of a new day can
describe.

So if words could say what we'd feel,
I'd be sure to put them down on
paper.

Patricia L Thomas
PRAISE HIM

I dedicate this poem to my saviour Jesus Christ whom I love.

He's given us everything He has
And laid it at our feet
Oh praise be to God who loves us so
And whom I will forever seek

He's given us much to be thankful for
The world and all that's in it
Oh praise be to God who we owe so
much
And whose giving will never end

Oh praise Him to the highest peak
And exalt Him thankful ones
Oh praise be to God, 'cause we will
always be
Wrapped up in His loving arms

PRAISE HIM

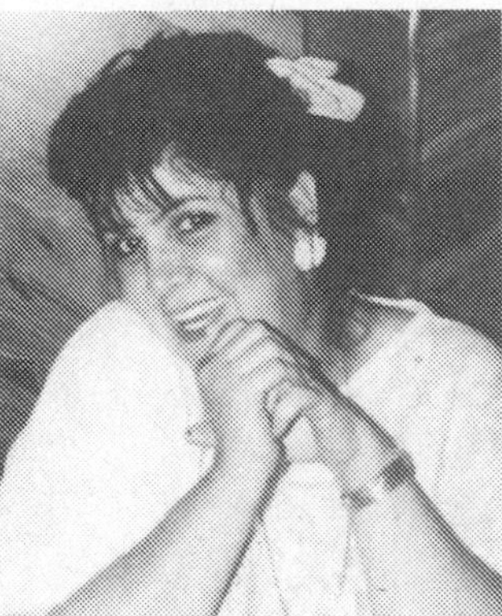

Theresa B Woodis

Theresa B Woodis
ALWAYS BESIDE YOU

I dedicate this poem, to my daughter, Angela, because I want her to know even when I am gone from this life, I will always watch over her. I love you!

The Lord called, and I had to leave,
but I'm always beside you.
Remember, that flutter on your cheek
last week?
That was me giving you a kiss . . .
And the gentle brush against your
arm yesterday?
That was me giving you a hug . . .
Always, I am beside you listening to
your
cries of loneliness . . .
sighs of weariness . . .
and moments of joy . . .
but you never know!
Many times, I cried while watching
you struggle all alone.
The rain on your face, were my tears.
I'm a used to be, and someday you
will share my world with me . . . .

Alfred Leon Wallace
I AM A SLAVE

To Famous Writers School for teaching me how to write.

I am a slave of everything,
That evil friends can bring.

I am a slave of sex and lust,
Finances go for bust.

I am a slave of cigarettes,
And lotteries and bets.

I am a slave of alcohol,
I stagger, drink, and fall.

I am a slave of pot and drugs,
I steal and sell to die on rugs.

So that is why my health is shot,
And suffer for my sins a lot.

Lucille Fritts
A YOUNG WIDOW

To my son Tony, with love, Mother.

My husband is gone, died too soon
The children are grown, leaving
empty rooms.
The house once a cheerful home
Is now a hollow shell in which I
roam.
Loneliness and despair have filled my
heart.
A new life I'm to lead, where do I
start?
God learned of my loneliness through
His son
And saw fit to bless me with a little
one.
Since he is with me, he helps ease the
pain.
I watch him grow and feel worth-
while again.
There is cutting teeth and nursery
rhymes,
Runny noses and buying toys to fill
my time.
Now I realize how lucky I really am
To be trusted with the raising of this
little man.
His quick laughter and short tears
Will help me through my aging years.
My loneliness has been replaced with
love
From a little boy sent to me from up
above.

Shawn Guns
MOMMY vs. DADDY

Especially for mom and dad. I love you both.

An uproar of voices,
Razor sharp words
tumbling through the air.
I watch them as they gather together
forming a black rain cloud
that hovers above my head.
I don't want to listen, but
my legs carry me to the far wall.
Slumped down against the walnut
paneling with my ears pressed against
it.

Like a sponge I absorb
the murky dishwater splashed at me.
Salty rivers flood my eyes
I blink hard,
but they still seem to run.
sucked from the diminishing waters
of my hope and dreams.

Mommy, Daddy
why do you lodge yourselves
beneath my heart,
drinking my tears like leeches.

Helen M C Klempner
BE ATTITUDES

"Be Attitudes" is dedicated to the thought that we as people on this earth can support and feed all. All children of the world will have love and food.

Spiraled to the age of youth
Here to stay to find the truth
Seek shall I within my dreams
to be here always perfecting
my themes.

Forevermore the Earth is mine
I will not leave my Art is Fine
I seek my one True Love
I look to God that Peace will rise
above
So send that dove, and store the glove
Peace is all we need to Love.

Kelli S Morin
TEDDY BEAR

To my son Britain, remember I will always love you!

I have a loving friend, I call him
Teddy Bear
I can tell him secrets, because I know
he'll care
The secrets that I share, I wouldn't
tell my friend
To all my burdens bare, to me I'll
know he'll tend

He only has one ear, a broken button
nose
He cannot upright sit, he has a broken
pose
His stuffing's falling out, he only has
one eye
With him I cannot part, and I won't
say good-bye

My loving Teddy Bear, I've had for
all these years
I won't throw him away, for it would
bring me some tears
He'll always be with me, and not in a
wood chest
Because my Teddy Bear, is nothing
but the best!

Lois Keefe
WINTER RAIN
My heart's as leaden as the skies
with rain-soaked guilt we share,
the burden of our easy lies
is drowned in dank despair.

Is true love warned
when trust's misplaced,
when pity's scorned
and hope's debased?
You played a game
of bliss for two —
was I to blame
for trusting you?

Our love is faded, lost, betrayed,
too long recalled in vain.
For now the broken vows we made
dissolve in winter rain.

Barbara S Schor
NORTH WIND

To H. Moe of the Santa Anna Winds.

I heard the wind coming, heaving
mighty breath on
mountains high,
Vegetation quaked and quivered, the
invisible specter
swished by,
Flailing branches, rustling leaves
struggled to cover
trunks like sleeves,
Howling, haunting possessing its
host, deciduous demon
evergreen ghost.

Dreamers awakened to blustery
growls, peeping through
curtains to view,
Whistling, wailing, whining, whisper
and off to sea it
flew,
Deafening calm, trees lay split, earth
no longer cried,
Moonlight danced on crashing waves,
Boreas rode the tide.

Lois A Paré
THE COMPANION

To Ms. Judy, one who believes in the shadow of hope.

A shadow followed me
in the hall,
on the wall;
But the closet small and dark
left no place
for the shadow's mark.
But the shadow knows — I know,
Time apart,
time together,
It's very being depends
on its other.

Eileen Davis Griffin
SPECIAL PEOPLE

To David and Terry Davis, and Vickie Harris, three very special people.

There's a special kind of people we
don't seem to understand.
They're gentle, kind and loving, if
only we'd reach out and
take their hand.
Maybe their minds don't work as
well as yours and mine,
And maybe we can't understand what
they say all the time.
But Jesus has a special place in
heaven for all of them.
A special place where angels dwell
so they'll be close to Him.
I thank the Lord for giving me a mind
that works the way it should.
And a gift of speech and knowledge
that can be understood.
I thank Him for my eyes that can see
everything.
And the tears that run down my
cheeks when I see the joy a
little love can bring.

Jane Solberg Wilson
GOLDEN TOMORROW

For Gary Frickle, to the people I love and people yet to love.

Harshful soul, go gentle, ever so
softly . . .

to my fluttering heart
dreams of beckonings . . .
Not to belie a future of grand
illusions . . .
Knight in shining armor
Bleeding heart
weeps darkened teardrops, of a
beguiling charm
doomed by fate, endurance . . .
striving for the cleanliness of a
Golden Tomorrow

Elinor Joyce Hensley
A THIN THREAD

To life which is such a miracle when you think about it. And my parents Helen and Norman Kelley who gave me life. To Donny, Danny and Lorrie our children, who we gave life, Jerry and I.

Life is like a very thin thread
You are either alive or you are dead.
Although some people die and still
walk around
With hate in their hearts, their face
one big frown.
It is sad to me when people can't see
This is all that there is, so be what
you can be.
We all can't have riches, beauty and
fame
So do what you can or you will be to
blame.
Every new day when I awake in my
bed
I look all around to find my thin
thread
It sure would feel awful to wake up
dead.

Christian M Morrow
THE RIPPER

For my parents who told me to never stop reaching for the stars.

The moon bore the wand of a
conductor, yielding a bane to the sky.
The stars held cursed twinkles, living
in their eyes.
The clouds were sunken treasures
with madness as their key,
And the stale essence of murder
tarried 'bout the sea.

The faint west side of London grew
darker with the night,
All people's minds were empty, their
faces blank and white.
The women huddled weapons,
outside watched all the men,
A streak of fear touched soul to soul,
The Ripper struck again!

A cry echoed throughout the streets
yet died amidst a flash,
A body lay beneath the sheets, her
throat was ripped and slashed.
This blood soaked carcass so precise
spoke gore about the kill,
Why, not a mass of disarray but one
of expert skill!

Save claret dashed the avenue, a trod
was left behind.
Hounds and men tagged the wind,
The Ripper they would find.
About the alleys, through the roads
they bolted for their prey,
Choleric thoughts engulfed their
minds, he would not get away!

Till, the trace came to an end, the
search need no more go,
The slayer faced the hungry dogs, he
twisted to and fro',
His eyes were caves of horror, his
hair like dead weed grass,
He cursed a plague unto the world,
The Ripper came to pass.

Julie Anne Ezzo
THE HURT LINGERS

To America: God Bless our POW-MIA, bring our men HOME!

Love our soldiers, they were there
They fought for us, they fought the
fear
They lived for us and some —
they died
The roads they travelled, the tears
they cried
All want peace — make this
world right!
But just how many are willing to
fight
For freedom and for justice, to make
this country proud
Don't hear the gentle whimpers, hear
them cry out loud
The suffering they felt, the pain they
endured
The obstacles they overcame and
how their spirits soared
To know they were chosen and given
the right to defend
A country they were proud of and
one that loved its men
Many soldiers wanted out, they
wanted their time spent
Somewhere other than a war — to
heaven they were sent
Some want revenge, still others seek
attack
But what about the child who just
wants Daddy back?

Yuko Kashiyama
TURN AROUND
Turn around, Turn around
The clock hands are turning around

Go around, Go around
The earth is going around

Pass away, Pass away
Day is passing away like a dream

Turn around, Turn around
It's a whirl of business

Tiny girl is carried away
She will be discouraged in everything

Don't surrender yourself
Don't regret your life
Life is short and time is swift

Try again, Try again

Randy Yenchik
FATAL KISS

To my love and my inspiration, Lori H. Thanks!

Lips of silk, hands of velvet
Your kiss shoots through my heart
Like Cupid's arrow.
My heart beats like waves
Crashing on the shore every
Time your lips meet with mine
For that fatal kiss.
As a shooting star flies through
Outer space, I close my eyes
And picture your face as you
Give me that fatal kiss.
Just as sweet chocolate melts
In your mouth, that's what happens
Every time you give me that
Fatal kiss.
As we dance slowly in the
Darkness I can see you giving
Me that fatal kiss.
Like a rose stands for love, my
poems
Stand for my love to you, as your
Fatal kiss shows your love for me.

Monique Bowden
FOR MY LOVER UNKNOWN

I reached out for you today — Did you feel my call?
I searched for you with every fiber of my being, hoping I
could touch you, somehow,
somewhere.
I wanted to share a thought with you, or was it a memory—
maybe it was a smile. It was
something that only you can
understand, because you are that
other part of me.

I know you are out there, somewhere, searching for the very essence of my
person, probing through the
atmosphere
hoping that our spirits would
connect at some point.

Circumstances have separated us, the Fates have not been kind.
They seem to always keep us apart.
Yet I know that when our souls
connect the infusion alone will be
enough to burn
through the threads that Coltho
has spun so tightly, and
Atropos refuses to cut. You
are there and I am here, yet
I know that sometime soon we
will be together. Before
Lachesis
measures the final length of the
threads of our lives.

Linda Iorio

Linda Iorio
WHICH WAY TO TURN

Dedicated to Stevie Nicks, the "poet in my heart."

I've got this desire for something I can't have
It kills me inside when I think of what I do have
I'm caught in a crossfire
Don't know which way to turn
And still the desire continues to burn

It's all a big secret that no one knows of
Maybe I really don't know the meaning of love

The child within me wants to play
And the woman within me doesn't know what to say

As I lay myself down to sleep at night
The conflict inside me keeps me up all night
On one side of the bed is someone
real and warm
And on the other side is someone
who's confused and forlorn

I live my life day by day
Hoping some day these feelings will go away
Part of me says to push for the dream
And another voice says to keep my life clean

So this chapter in my life isn't finished yet
Or maybe it hasn't even started
Don't know which way to turn
As the fire continues to burn

Linda Iorio
DECEMBER SUN

December sun comes through my window
Staring out at the snow and the frozen river
It's three in the afternoon
And I'm still in my pajamas
Nursing a cold and feeling blue

Brittle branches and cold biting wind
Making me wish it was summer again
Back to the beach and warmth and fun

But now it's the holidays and they don't matter to me
Just another page on the calendar for me
Wishing I was happier but happiness I do not have

If I had you, would I be happy
I tell myself yes, but maybe it's just my loneliness
I'm tired of waiting for you to make up your mind
Feel like I have nowhere to go, but am I just blind

Something tells me we haven't yet begun
To live our real life love affair
maybe I'm just dreaming again
But maybe December's sun
will melt away the freezing air

Tislm Moretti
CAN I, MY, IN YOUR

I dedicate this poem to Tricia Marquis, I'll love you always and forever.

Can I dream myself in your eyes tonight,
to see the love you have in sight
can I dream myself into your eyes tonight
see you there, help defeat your fears in sight

Sunny, warm Sunday afternoon, the phone begun to ring
it was you wanting to talk 'bout us and everything

Monday I turn 28, you came out with banner, card, lots of love
to the start of a Wonderful Year, we were blessed from above

The next weekend dinner, live music,
I feel drowsy you go dance,
I awake feel misplaced, go home call back you're asleep, I arrive, we romance

Can I dream myself into your heart tonight
feel the love in your heartbeat of life
can I dream myself into your heart tonight
Pitter Patter you thru your everyday strife

Pizza with kids, need for a rest, you coming to me,
Dinner a movie, making you my best,
wanting you to marry me

Late night together, donuts for youngings', walking side by side
frosty on the grass, evening stroll,
days with you, full of life & pride

Sobriety party, feeling like a dance
naturally high up with stars
wanting to move in, worried about failing, each needing new cars

Can I dream Myself into your soul tonight
knowing the love needs your life may require
and dream myself into your soul tonight
fulfill all your wants, be your every desire

T.J. for roids, open mart purchase,
loving you so very much
cruising home, a hat for me, a dress
for you, needing your touch

Burger King, swinging Eri and Kevy,
being swung, rides at castle park
getting together, not doing a lot,
feeling guilty, love in the dark,

your great kisses, beautiful face,
healthy, lovely bod
your special feel, outrageous ways,
for more just nod

can I dream myself into your mind tonight
read the love circles running true & through
can I dream myself into your mind tonight
sense your cares, find, conquer all for you.

Camille
WINTER

To my Mother and those who live year-round on Lake George.

I walked from the house to the woodshed this eve,
and noticed the sound of gentle crunching 'neath my feet

I stooped down to see what the noise was about,
and discovered tiny ice castles rising up through the ground

Jack Frost had set in on this cool Autumn day
and before long the snow would be well on her way

Back by the fire, toasty warm and aglow,
I watched as the wind blew the trees to and fro

That night I slept tight with comforters, blankets and all,
and woke with the knowledge that we had just lost our Fall

The trees and the fields lay covered in white,
and shone like diamonds in the Sun's early light.

Teresa S (Roosa) Whittaker
UNTITLED

For My Brother, Mitch: without you, this could not be.

The time is late, and so early
choices made, decisions sought.
The closing of an era, begin anew
goals being met, dreams revived.
The ultimate received, still giving
virtues of respect, loss of concept.
The life liven, being chosen by one
controlled by many, obedient of self.
Not to be? A chance to take.

Alecia L Ferrill
VICTIMS

The victims we know so well. They go off to far away places that we could never find. It is here that they are complete. It is here that they finally fit into society. It is here that they find peace and serenity. Also all the answers to all the questions and they receive all the love they ever wanted. What is the secret behind these people? I guess we can all know the secret because their peace is through death.

Cindy Loveall
TENDER WISHES AND DARLING DREAMS

Tender wishes and darling dreams,
shadows dancing on my wall.
O'night O'dream let me sway within his embrace.
O'dream O'night fill me with ardent delight
Capture faces and places, arms that intertwine
let his lips be constant with mine.

Tingles and Pleasures are mine in brief nightly measures.
The honesty of love in its bliss the passions fire and the tender kiss, the splendor felt, the lasting clutch. May I feel a lasting touch.

Dawn comes the waking hour, a drowsy sigh 'twas night now morrow.

O'night, O'dream why can't it last
must all things come to be part of past.

Cathi Passarette
SIMPLY TEARS

So many shed
So many shown
This emotion of sorrow
Has found me alone
As my head
Lies on my pillow
They roll down my face
And heartache is known
By a wet pillowcase.

Traci Louise Carron Noe
MOTHERS SITTING IN THE STREET

Mothers sitting in the street
Children lying at their feet
Wondering what will be done,
How will they survive
If no one walks by?
The children begin to cry
They go home to four cardboard walls
The babies have nowhere to crawl,
The box is getting wet
But they're not broke yet
They still have love
Love will help them survive
Mother and child intertwined,

There is neither bread nor meat
Starving children
Nothing to eat,
People walk by each day
No one has anything to say,
No change to give
Someone tell me
How will they live?

Charlene D Jones
WORDS OF WISDOM

To my niece Tawayanna Deneise Mcleod. You have a long life in front of you so live it well. Also, to Mom and Dad, you taught me well!

Take the time child and listen to the words. Listen to the words of life and love. Child hear the sounds. Hear the sounds of
God's Creation.
My dear child feel the pains of sadness and the sensation of happiness. Sweet young child, know the thrill of learning. Believe in
YOURSELF
Speak if you know and ask when you do not Go on child, be all you can be, if not better. You have so Much to learn and experience. That you should have very little
Time to HATE

Take the gift that God so proudly gave you and live it wisely.
Use the common sense you have gained through the years. You are too young to say, yet too old not to. Your do's and don'ts are there to help you not destroy. Let God be your guide. Use the sun as your light and the moon as your comfort. See child Life is too precious to waste, too beautiful to destroy, and
TOO SWEET TO AVOID.

Betty Cummings Malone
THE DOGWOOD TREE

To Valerie McDaniel — For your wonderful love of nature.

A dogwood tree
Stood hidden in the wood,
Striving to grow
The best that it could.

Then Easter approached
And it began to bloom,
Stretching its limbs
Upward from its tomb.

The trees of the forest
Stood back in awe,
Amazed at the beauty
Of what they saw.

It lit up the forest
With blossoms of white
And could clearly be seen
On a moonlit night.

And so the dogwood tree,
When it blooms in the spring,
Serves to remind us all
Of our heavenly King.

Lynn C Cannon
MARATHON MAN

To those in the race.

Marathon Man — Tell me what makes you run
In the rain, in the snow, and the sizzling sun
Are you running toward something or running away
Would you run even faster, if I asked you to stay
Life's lessons are illusive, when the pace is too fast
Don't learn too late from your solitary past.
If I can't teach you this, I pray somebody can.
God knows, I love you, my Marathon Man

Cindy Andrest
LOVE POEM FOR LEO

For Leo Buscaglia: Happy to be on the planet with you.

As Adam discovered Eve in the garden of her sex,
The male is reassurance, the familiar, and so blessed,
The female is attraction of unknown curiosity.
The union of each other began the need for humanity.
The She and He blend together in recovery of lost source.
Childhood wounds are mended from experiences of remorse
Never! Sweet conversing blarney;
lines conjuring submissiveness,
Roles of romantic intention,
pretending sentiment.
Ever truthfully,
Hard, earned effort beyond self;
deliverance,
Love gathers all people in harmonious difference.

The Fallacious Masque:
One alone can change himself.
Relationship is as whole,
For in every human being is another's essence,
the inseparable Soul.

Patricia Tremble
BIG MAN (MAC)

In memory of the man who will never be forgotten, John King McFadden.

He was born in a dugout in Western Kansas.
A rugged man was he.
I thought he was the strongest man, this
world would ever see.
A six foot giant of a man,
with hands so big and strong.
This was our DAD, this great big man.
So gentle and so strong.
He courted Nora, then married her.
In Colorado they did live.
A child, then two, a girl and boy.
On a homestead they did live.
Then on to California, where
his racing days were ore.
And then another child was born,
this time another girl.
He raised his children, as best he could,
with Nora by his side.
And now he is gone, this dear BIG MAN,
But his memories linger on.

Kryss Valdez
LITTLE CHILD

For Kenny Furman.

Hey little child do you feel all alone?
Do you feel lost? Like you don't have a home?
As you're sitting there thinking no one really cares,
As you cry inside, with eyes open wide.
What haven't you seen?
You know this world isn't clean.
I know your soul is bleeding
And the hurt keeps on repeating
I can see those sad blue eyes
And I know you're sick of all the lies.
A dirty face that speaks with sorrow
Just wondering if there's some good in your tomorrow.
Hey little child there's some love in me
Just give me a chance then you will see.
Let me hold you near
and let me share the fear.
Hey little child I don't know what you're feeling
But the anger is quite revealing.
I'll try real hard to understand
And I'll be there to hold your hand.
Hey little child don't you know,
That I do love you so . . . .

Morgen Pfanstiel
SEA YOU LATER

This poem is dedicated to Hannah, My great-grandmother.

I love it on the seashore,
Waves are lapping up the sand.
Racing with my sister for
A seat on the lifeguard stand.

I go down there everyday,
Where the ocean meets the sky,
Watching the sea gulls frolic and play
As the sailboats all float by.

But soon it's time to leave this place,
I turn in time to see,
With salty tears covering my face,
The ocean waves to me.

Alma Jean King

Alma Jean King
THE MAGICAL ILLUSION OF LOVE

Oh my Dearest Darling, take my soul, which you have captured, and entwine it with yours, forever and a day. Your love has released a thousand waterfalls, that I had hoarded within, and created a feeling of divinity.

A moonbeam kissed our love, and our love projected a hue of a million stars. Your love treats me like royalty, and there's nothing left for me to do, but wear the crown. A weeping willow tree felt our presence, and its branches erected, and gazed at the sun, and wept no more.

A flock of sea gulls soared us into a mist of clouds, and then changed course, and dipped us in a sea, that was tipped with silver, and then like magic, the silver turned to gold. When you professed your love for me, my heart clasped yours, and we ascended up to the heavens.

And the heavens opened up their doors, and claimed us as their own. And filled with envy, Paradise closed its gates. The universe awoke, and exploded in joyous celebration, realizing that the two lovers, of many decades, had returned home.

Norman L Gentry
GREATNESS IS

Dedicated to my loving mother, Estella R. Gentry. She is my true inspiration of what "Greatness Really Is."

Greatness is — the dreamer, who strives with all his might,
He's often hit time and again, but continues his brave fight,
It is the man who stands alone to back his dream in life,
He stakes his claim, and sets his aim, and overcomes all strife,
Greatness is the woman, who makes a brand new start,
when tragedy strikes her husband down, and deeply breaks her heart,
It is the child who doctors say will never run and play,
But this child's prayers are heard by God, and now he walks today,
for greatness is ability, to stick, to stay, and win,
you must fight hard to reach your goal, and never think, give in,
We never know how close we are, we must keep up the fight,
If what we want is worth the strive, we know it must be right,
So never give a minute's thought to ever giving ground,
Have faith and trust in God your guide, he'll see your goal is found,

For greatness comes to all of us
Who want the good and right,
And each obstacle across our path,
Determines how hard we fight,

It's like the clouds that try to scare our warming sun away,
But the sun breaks through the clouds
Determined it will stay,

We must endure until we've won,
We must absorb the pain,
And we will shine just like the sun,
Shines through the wind and rain,
I tell you now, continue on, make up your mind to win,
you never fail until you stop, and say,
"I'm giving in,"

S Matthews Smith
THESE TWO SOULS

Saw these two souls sitting on the subway
Peaceful, loving and full of joy
Not wishing harm to anyone
Just minding their own
Too much to live for to cause trouble
Taught me something I used to know
These two brothers had wings
Though some could not see
But I saw them fly sitting still
By the way
These two souls were in chairs of

chrome
Wheel suspended
So sad or yet so funny
They flew better than I and could not walk
I have learned something from these two souls

Wings are inside

Joshua S Bousman (Age 12)
A DREAMER
There I sat, not a smile on my face.
Feeling as if not a friend in the place.
A dreamer's song is but a cry,
Just a speck of dirt in the world's eye.
A fool I was to think such a thing.
To think I was a dreamer, with the best dream.
I look around, not a grin in the place.
But all looked like the dreamer's sorrowful face.
Rejections and putdowns to some is a game,
but in the eyes of a dreamer it is quite inane.
But life is to live,
and to live is to learn.
To cry is to want,
and to want is to yearn.

Susan Harris-Cloutier
IF WE ALL DID OUR SHARE
Shelters for the homeless;
A roof over their head.
Food demands are being met,
So the hungry can be fed.

Children who have never had
Love light up their life,
Would have someone to hold them close
And help them ease their strife.

Families joined together
With neighbors and with friends,
Would carry on the feeling
Of goodwill and peace to men.

If we could reach each person
And have them do their part,
To pass on just a portion
Of the love within their heart.

Imagine how the world could live—
In perfect harmony?
The way I know Our Father
Believed that it could be!

Bonnie Phillips
MY CASTLE
I once built a castle,
It was made of sand.
On the tower was a tassel
Which was red and tan.

I went for a swim
And forgot the time.
When I noticed the sky was dim;
Then I only heard a whine.

"What is this?" I cried;
"What could it be?"
Now I must say good-bye,
For my castle has returned to the sea.

Nancy Jean
THE BOX
Trapped in a box, no way out.
Being smothered by sorrow and grief.
Help me, let me out.
Destroy these walls that imprison me.
Set me free, free from my anger and my tears.
Love and protect me.
Shelter me from the pain.
Open the box and never let it shut.

The box is a sheltered place.
Some days I want to crawl inside.
I close the lid and allow the darkness to swallow me.
There, no one can hurt me and I will be safe.
Alone and still, I can breathe a sigh of pure relief.
I am released of myself.
Calmly I sit, content to hear the beat of my heart.
No one can take me out as long as I want to stay.

Some people hate the box, and they let it
Imprison them inside.
Yet, that's where I find freedom and a comforting place to hide.
Even though it's dark, I can see the sun.
And even though I'm alone, I can feel your love.
The box is angry with some and generous with others.
No matter what you think it is,
It is you; a showcase of emotions.

Marylin A Holman
LOVE IS ALL
They meet, strangers, alone and small. Their eyes do not
meet for fear they may fall.

Then she sits and waits for a single call. She hopes and
prays that he does not stall.

Questions, questions! For him, will she appall? For her,
will he enthrall?

A physical joining is a warming shawl. May it never become
a stinging gall.

May their minds meet and understand this law, that . . .

LOVE IS ALL!

J K
HUMANITY
Why do we live so frivolously that we blind ourselves to the things we need to stay alive. Is it too much for us to give a touch to the lonely, or food to the poor. We seem to forget compassion in reaching for our goals.

Everyone has a bomb, and the end lies a touch away. Bullets ring in the fury of prejudice and insanity. Is this our idea of humanity? How can we make plans for a future that may never be here when we are forced to live in fear.

I cry for the children who must bear this heavy load, for they are forced to grow up so fast. Their years of innocence and carefree ways are shortened by the continually demanding world they must face.

Look at the men and women who live on the streets holding out their hands for something to eat. Try to see behind the disguises of the strong, hungry, and shy yearning for the love that we all put aside. Will inhumanity lead to our own tragic fate. Can we learn to love one another before it's too late.

Rachel Evans
UP IN THE ATTIC
Up in the attic
Down in the basement
Out in the front yard
Or in the back
In my room or in yours
In your home or in mine
There somewhere is quiet
In the kitchen
Or in the den
With loved ones or with pets
Someone to share that special place.

Charlie "The Shadow Poet"
WHERE WILDFLOWERS GROW
The air was so fresh on this early morn,
Tiny drops of water still rest upon the corn.
The sun in my face and wind upon my back,
I stop for a moment to see a deer's lonely track.

The honeysuckle blooms adorn the morning air,
Its pink and white colors, they're oh! so fair.
The dogwood, alone, with time it stands,
You know God carried one with his bare hands.

A cluster of wild iris now come into sight,
The colors of their blooms awake from the night.
Just up ahead a lonely rose grows,
Where it came from, only God really knows.

The flowers and bees, the birds and the trees.
These things I see are all just part of me.
This creation didn't just happen to be,
They were made by God's hands for all to see.

Sometime come and take a walk with me,
We'll stop by the river that runs so free.
Now if you see a tear beginning to flow,
Don't worry, my friend, for here is where
the wildflowers grow.

Keith L Coe
WILL THEY REMEMBER ME?
The children left many years back.
They didn't say a word while they packed.
Did I do so wrong all those years?
Leaving me standing all alone in my tears.
It was I who was there when they were hurt.
Mending their wounds and gave them a clean shirt.
We played our games and wrestled on the floor.
And wore each other out, but they always wanted more.
We would swim everyday and ride our bikes.
And sometimes go to the park and take long hikes.
In the kitchen I would cook so patiently,
And one of them was always with me.
When they were little and the thunder would roar,
Oh, how fast they came running through the door.
"Move over Daddy, we're staying here."
The look on their faces was quite clear.
Then there were times you would hear them say,
"Will you help us with our homework today?"
Well, I remember what Fathers do.
They take their children to the zoo.
Oh! That's not the only thing. No, not at all.
Why, we even play with dolls and sometimes throw a ball.
And, oh, yes, I was a horsie too.
And taught them both to tie their shoe.
Over the years I watched them grow.
From the day they were born, it's been the "best" picture show.
I hear their laughter and see their faces.
And now only memories of times and places.
Now they are gone and hear from them no more.
I guess whatever I've done, I've left them sore.
It has been asked before, many times you see.
"MY CHILDREN, WILL THEY REMEMBER ME?"

Andrew W Hartman
WHAT WHEN DEATH?
A question no one can comprehend
And cannot be answered, alive anyway.
It causes pain and minds to bend
But the answer will not be known until that day.

So why ponder on it
And work the brain into a mental fit?
An answer no one will ever know
So why not let the question go?

Such an intriguing question
In which the outcome will never be found.
Such an intriguing question
Only answerable when six feet underground.

Did good or evil create this mystery
That has survived throughout history?
Did God or Satan cause man to lose control
Over the thoughts of what becomes of his soul?

Heaven, Purgatory, Nothingness,
Reincarnation, or Hell
What lies ahead
Wise men can never tell
What becomes of a man after a man is dead!

Sophia Thompson
YOUTH

To the world's parents.

I am the life.
I am the way.
Without me you cannot go on.
I bring new strength and happiness.
I bring faith.
The progress of the World depends on
me.
If I am corrupted,
Then are you corrupted.
If I am extolled,
Then are you extolled.
I am the hope that men live by.
I am Youth!

Krista Wilton
CASCADES
The glistening water takes your breath away
As you walk by the sparkling wonderland;
The moon is of crystal
And the stars are like glitter
Thrown against black velvet.
The water is a shimmering prism;
There are shooting sprays of moisture
In the cool night air,
And the splashing of the water
Down its eternal path sings a lullaby
To everything around it.
The emerald hills fall silently
Over the mother earth
While the trees sway watching the vivid deluge.

Jan Boursaw
A TREE
Have you ever really looked at a tree
how it bends in the wind so gracefully
And when there's no wind, it looks toward the sky
watching the clouds slowly drift by.
It reaches its arms to the warming sun
and shelters the birds when the long day is done.

Have you ever heard a tree complain
when it stands alone in the chilling rain?
Or grumble and groan when it feels the snow?
the answer is there, you already know.
With God's great power, he made a tree
with as much admiration, does he look at me?

Julia Ann Kapugi

Julia Ann Kapugi
THE ONE I LOVE
I have thought of you a lot dear Dad,
since you have gone away.
I think of you and miss you each and every hour, of everyday!
For you were such a father to me and loved me too.
Oh, I believe it is so true . . .

I wish I could see you and touch you just once again.
So you could hold me and tell me, I am your little "*Princess*" like you did once then.

I never thought I would lose you, you were so big and strong.
But when that awful day came. I felt, I have lost it all.
I have prayed day after day for you to come home.
But, God said you're never coming back. It truly makes me feel
Oh, so blue. That I will never see you. I thought I would sit and write these happy moments to you. Which
I have promised you a long
Time ago in a dream. That I will tell my "forever" secret to
"*The one I love*."

I have found a man that I will always love, as much as *"I love you."*
In my eyes, somehow I thought I would never get over the loneliness
And the heartbreak of feeling not loved. I have prayed so hard so long — To have an undying "*Endless love.*"

My Dear Father,

His name was given to him by an angel in heaven. My love is Johnny!
He is the most beautiful, so loveable, wonderful strong man.
When I see him I see you !! I wish you could see him, so you could
Believe it is only true.

I hate to tell you all the news like this. Because, I know it is
Going to make you sad, but at the same time happy too!
For things are so much different;
since I have lost my precious dear Dad
I believe in my heart and soul. I have found another man, *just like you*

One day you will feel and see with your own eyes, from the stars in
Heaven your little "*Princess*" found her "*Prince*" to walk down the aisle, with smiles of happiness for eternity.
I am wishing for your blessing my dear father. A few tears of joy roll
Down my face. Thinking of you with all those beautiful angels and
Stars in heaven. Only wishing, you could be by my side giving your
Little girl away with your hand in marriage. With blessings of love,
From you to another.

"You are both
the one I love
endlessly"
Oh, it is so true . . .
"*My love is forever*"
Your Daughter

Julia Ann Kapugi
I COULD NEVER FORGET YOU JIMMY JAMES . . .
My life goes on without you,
The days are passing by . . .
But then I have days like today
When I could only think of you.
Those memories do bring a smile
And a little sadness, too.
I don't ever want to forget
The time we shared together.
I was so happy then holding you . . .
As my days pass slowly wishing
We could be together happily.
I don't want to forget how it
Felt to be so excited, getting
Off a day's work, to come see your
Pearly whites; your smile as you
Smiled at me . . .
I just want you to know
and *please never forget the truth* . . .
I only wanted to love you
From head to toe.
To be by your side on stormy
As well as sunny times, through
Laughter and tears.
To look into your beautiful eyes,
Looking in mine saying "*I love you*"
"*Always and forever*."
It only matters that once
There was a "*you and me*."
No matter how brief our time
Together, or what our tomorrows
May bring us.
I wanted you to know as well
As the universe.
I would shout it out to the
World "I loved you Jimmy James"

Remember those lips . . .
Always & Forever

Rick Staviski
GRAY BARNS
Gray barns covered with green grass
Lifeless movement from the past
Years of hard work have left the scene
Too many people trying to kill an American dream.

Where do you go when you kill the country?
I'm not one that wants to live life hungry
One man's skill
Is another man's treasure to kill.

Standing fences with season's disease
Holding back nothing but land in between
Echoed voices through hollowed walls
A voice of no one can't be recalled.

Gray barns covered with green grass
Lifeless movement from the past
Years of hard work have left the scene
Too many people trying to kill an American dream.

K Rynae Underwood
THE RIVER OF DREAMS
A wall built from pebbles and stones,
taken from the River of Dreams
to form a barrier around my heart
to protect me from evil schemes.

Each stone was placed with graceful
ease as each new heartache began.
Each pebble was used for solid support
when my Wall of Dreams caved in.

All my dreams of life and love
and all that I want to be
live safe and secure, locked in a wall
overlooking the River of Dreams.

Cristyl L Keith
TOMORROW
The sun slides over the horizon.
Spreading its warmth out, to blanket the east.
And the world comes alive.
People scurry about in different directions.
And, what I see reminds me
of a time when I sat and watched
a colony of ants rebuild their anthill.
From my point of view,
it resembled total chaos.
But, sure enough,
when I returned the next day,
there was a new anthill.
So, I learned not to look at our world,
with all its troubles and confusion,
and think that we are going nowhere.
But instead, look at the chaos and confusion
and think what it will bring tomorrow.

David K Laufenberg
HAVE THE BLUES
If it's quarter to two
If you're messing with the blues
Just make sure not to give them to me
I've been around quite a while
I choose not to have the blues but to smile
And while you're near me
Just let my life be
I know some of you have the blues
But what am I supposed to do
Just knowing that I really care
I don't want the blues to share
I just want my feelings to stay the same
I don't need the blues to blame
Life without the blues is for me
That is what I feel can't you see
That is the way it was meant to be
For a person like me
So have a good day
And understand the words I say

Karen Brooks
PEOPLE WHO MAKE YOU LAUGH WHEN YOU'D RATHER CRY
People who make you laugh when you'd rather cry,
People who make you live when you'd rather die,
People who are your friends no matter what,
People who tell you, "You're not a mutt!",
These are the people that will be true to you,
And respect everything you love and do.
These are the people who are your friends,
Even after the world, itself, ends.

Dorothy C Mercier
AMBITION
Strangely enough I'm inspired to stop
Struggling with life to be on top.
I feel that in all I could acquire,
I can never achieve anything higher
Than the graces of God and abundant blessing.
One would never think I'd be professing
My desire to live and walk in the light,
To do no wrong in any man's sight.
There is no wrong in ambition you see,
To gain life everlasting for eternity.

Skip Kniese
COLD DYING OF THE SEED
When the grass turns amber brown
Sky pale as clouds on a Fall day
Trees bare as old soldiers stripped of arms
Branches long and gangling
Reaching for something to clothe their cold limbs
The ground barren and ancient, lost within itself
Wanting a rest, wanting thirst of new blood, of new warmth
When the air clings to your breath
Adding sharpness to a clear day
Then every fiber of life rises, to
The cold dying of the seed.

Terry L Workman
SPIED HER

I saw a spider
Sitting still,
High upon the window sill.

Her lengthy legs
Looked lofty tall,
Casting shadows on the wall.

The web she wove
Was quite appealing,
Splendidly spun upon the ceiling.

She was furry
But far from fat,
Daintily dining on this 'n gnat!

Bryan P Williams
IN DISGUISE

Pressing upon her, they are.
She has those exasperated looks.
Where comes thy patience?

I know this, in spirit, she is afar;
For if it was not here at this place of serenity
She would deafen their perceptive ears with potent fear,

There have been and more shall peer upon thee as the crook.
For thy clairvoyance is so developed, you ignore their stupidity.
Still within, all the hustle and bustle, you seem to be at ease.

You are an expert of disguise for there exists a constant defense.
I feel that thy fear has a yearning to shed those tears
Which are held back so that the waves will be calm in the seas.

I am here, like ye are there, for all the fish in these waters,
Will she take heed to a concerned breeze?
Grasp for that log afloat in the storm, do not falter.
For this moment may be brief.
Come, converse with me upon this altar.

Timothy J Cherney
SAILING SHIPS

To Mary, you have been an inspiration in my life.

Sailing ships and harbor lights, I see them on the water;
In every port both day and night, from the Mississippi border.
Ships that line horizon's view, painted pictures and visions of you
Make me wish you were by my side, watching waves of the rushing tide.

Sailing ships on the roam, bring her home to me.

Across my mind, love's fondest wish, to hold you tight and steal a kiss;
My thoughts of you, the best I've known, higher than the gulls have flown.
Your subtle ways put me at ease, a face as fresh as a summer's breeze
Gliding over water's top, I pray your love should never stop.
Sailing ships on the roam, bring her home to me.
Sailing ships on the roam, bring her home to me.

Eugene Kirby Andrews
ONE DOZEN ROSES

This poem is dedicated to my loving mom.

I've tried to be the best friend that I can be
My ears and heart were always willing to receive,
I could never be the friend that Jesus is, but I'm doing my best
Unselfishly I give, expecting nothing in return.

I am never too busy, or too far away, for you to call
My door is always open, just a knock or two away,
Despite my personal problems, you always came first
My shoulder is always ready for you to lean on.

Ridiculed & talked about, by you & your friends
I humbly struggle with my head hung down,
Tears of hurt swept over my face
Hurt by the ones, "I loved so dear."

I haven't got much longer to be here in this cruel place
My name was always the subject of your conversation,
I'm not condemning or judging any of you at all
I just want to say, "Thank you for my one dozen roses."

Mada Casey
SET FREE

My Self-esteem has turned to Christ-esteem
Jesus living in me . . .
In the Hollow of His Hand He held me
Until I was quiet, warm, comforted,
Made whole and at peace,
Forgiven and set free . . . .

Mada Casey
A FINDER OF LOST LOVES

To Jesus; "My lost love, found," and to my whole family.

O, finder of lost loves
My love has gone astray
I would that you could find him
On this, oh so lonely day . . .

You might look for him
In fields of new-mown hay
Or sandy beaches along the bay
Maybe even, in forest's green . . .

You'd be most apt to find him tho'
Among the lowly or broken of heart
The fearful or those
Who've strewn their tears along the way . . .

Amidst the hungry, the oppressed,
The lonely or down-trodden
Or a tiny child at play,
More probably with those who've lost their way . . .

You'll know him right off, if you see him
For there's always a crowd following along
His laughter will touch your heart,
The sound of it, is as a joyful song . . .

O, finder of lost loves
Please find my love for me
I mourn his loss, his touch,
His love, O' so terribly . . .
Tell him I'll wait forever, if need be
Beside this ever restless sea
Until his love, his peace, his life
Shall draw nigh unto me . . . .

Monica T Huston
THE BEAUTIFUL RAINBOW

I dedicate this to my mother and father for making me somebody. Teaching me the way to go in life. For helping and understanding me.

Life is like a puddle of water,
The water is not always clean and smooth.
It has dirt and rocks.
Sometimes at the end a rainbow,
May appear on top of the water.
Sometimes you cannot always count, on a friend or on your family
You have to turn to GOD.
He can help you work out the
Dirt and rough rocks.
He is the beautiful rainbow.
Like the light at the end of the tunnel.

Colleen Doyle
A ROSE

This poem is dedicated to a person who has touched my life in many ways, Bill. Without you my love, this could not be possible. I love you, Colleen.

A rose given to you,
A token of love,
Shared between two.
So precious and fragile,
Just like your heart,
Too silent,
But says so much.
A rose of memories,
Tears of laughter,
Tears of fear.
So red and sweet.
Just like the lips
of your lover.
One rose,
full of hidden meaning,
Known only to you!

Ruth E Westwood Mucci
TO MOM AND DAD

I dedicate these lines of poetry to the memory of my Mom and Dad. Life was so beautiful when I grew up and had them as parents.

Sitting on the front porch, recalling days of yesteryear,
When Mom and Dad, were in the house and I was sitting here —
There used to be a porch swing, but like them, it's also gone —
While the orange blossoms and rose of sharon, they're still blooming on.
You know I'm kind of lonely when I think of days gone by,
And I sit here and remember and try hard not to cry.
We used to have this old porch swing—filled with Sunday guests —
And that old porch swing and rocker never got a rest.
My Dad was kind of busy, a miner's lot was hard you know,
And Mom she worked from morning to night, while on the porch I'd go.
We kids never had a worry, there was Mom and Dad to care,
To cushion every heartache — for they were always there.
It seemed God blessed me special for what a friend indeed,
As long as Mom was living, I never felt a need.
I sit here hurting, for it's a year you're gone from me,
And I can't help recalling — the days that used to be.
I see myself coming up the walk at supper time —
And the fragrance from the kitchen, was truly sublime.
We didn't have lots of money, but we had more than gold,
We had you and Dad as parents, and our luxury was untold.

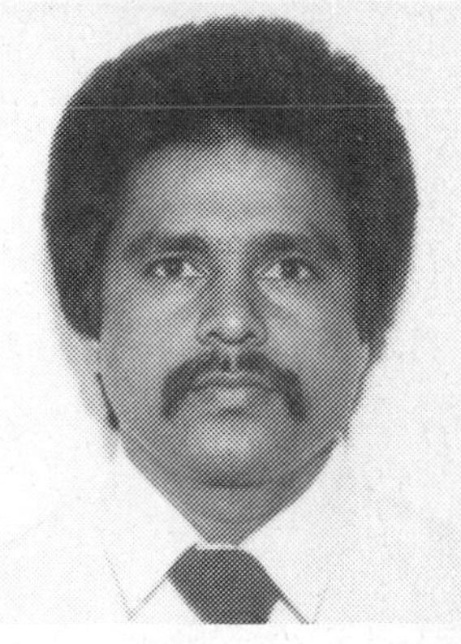

Hemchand Singh

Hemchand Singh
JUNE 27, 89

It was Tuesday morning June 27, 89.
I came out of my basement apartment at eight.
And stood by the five feet high black iron gate.
It was a pleasant morning I silently murmured
And inwardly smiled in appreciation,
For such an excellent observation.
While the wind blew slowly,
And damp softly,
Upon my face.
I was deciding whether to go to work or to the O.T.B. race.
After deep consideration I finally decided and spent a token.
The choice I made was not the best.
And it was a long ride to Manhattan West.
An hour later I found myself at the shop.
And in front of the punch card machine I stopped.
I punched my card and habitually I began to sing one of my favorite
Songs 'Roses are red my love'
Shortly after, my eyes glanced on a skid of paper high above.
And I read a bullshit slogan 'Indian, you must work the way I did'
I don't know who wrote it.
But before criticizing a man look at yourself first,
May be you are worse.
Exercise your architect and create a pattern of example,
To exhibit as a sample.
Considering myself a good worker I became pissed off and mad,
And foretell the day being bad.
I wore a sneakers and a short pants and that is the way I dress,
At eleven my right hand fingers were

caught between two rollers
on a two color Offset Printing Press.
I started to bleed
And the red formed weird patterns on the floor forming ridges.
Tears flowed rapidly down my face.
With lots of pain.
I shoulder my strain.
"Jeez, that bullshit slogan contributed to this accident"
Inwardly I cried,
Surrounded by some workers and no one tried to help.
Fortunately my friend came and rushed with me to the hospital.
I was additionally hurt to know I was left alone.
Very well on my own.
From Manhattan to Bronx.
I rode that train,
With terrible pain.
Pale and sad,
Feeling bad.
That night it hurt no hell,
Watching the walls
Having no one to tell.
Shit this will take a long time to get well.

Hemchand Singh
SILENTLY I BOUT DEPRESSION

Precious moments often flow and easily go by.
And my thirsty voice dull of expression;
O heaven only knows why.
And SILENTY I BOUT DEPRESSION.
And it ponders upon my thoughts and memories.
And frequently it agitated my emotions.
And openly I walked along the wet sandy shore.
O slowly slowly with secret steps and even pace.
And across the blues it damps gently upon my face.
How innocent and worried I sat on a rock.
Solitude is like my shadows and companion.
With my eyes far beyond watching the wide and deep blue sea.
And the sun spreading its warmth.
Like a reddish blanket upon the clouds and trees.
And it shone upon the blue like a streak of flame.
Splash splash on the rock as it inches high.
And my tired feet were cold.
And many clouds floats on high forsaking the environment.
And my naked mind was filled with peace.

Hemchand Singh
DEEP IN THE WOODS

She built her nest,
Deep in the woods.
Between grasses, shrubs and trees,
So no one could tell.
And there she had her two chicks,
Away from Crows and evil.
And she flew miles and miles,
Over grassy lands.

She flew to gather seeds,
From grasses and shrubs.
And she returned,
To her hidden nest.
But she was caught in a trap.
And she was put in a cage.
And she fluttered and fluttered,
And many hours passed.
The chicks cried out for hunger,
Then their crying stopped.
And silence came.

Daniel J Jackson Jr
THE PLACE WHERE I'D LIKE TO BE

To my inspiriting mother.

The place where I'd like to be
Vast forests of green foliage
None of the worries of going to college
No pollutions of smoke or smog
Just the vastness of "The Great Bog"
Instead of a modern day farmer
You're a knight in shining armor
Of all the wonderful places to see
This is the place where I'd like to be.

Daniel J Jackson Jr
WHAT IS LOVE?

This is for you Ann Delaney.

What is love?
compassion
Devotion
affection
consideration
appreciation
attraction
admiration
cherishing
coveting
honoring
Idolizing
regarding
respecting
worshipping
and revering
what is love?
Love is life.

Frank Paul Graffeo
I WISH, ALL MEN, TO BE SAVED.

I came to earth, to do my father's will and I did,
So now my friends, go forth and preach it to all nations.
That I came to save all men, and to die for their sins,
I offer life everlasting, not to just a few, but to every one.

I offered my life and my love, as payment and ransom for all,
I came back to life, after death, to tell the world, the truth.
That there is one God, one Son and one holy and blessed Spirit,
A sacred Trinity, all three always lov–ing and praying for you.

I love you, all I ask is that you respect my love and love me too,
I pray that you accept, my father's, generous tender love, that is true.
Believe that he sent me to earth, to save every one, not just a few,
That you feel, the presence of his great love and my spirit in you.

I wish to save all men, was his heavenly spiritual decree,
I wish them to be saved and to spend, life everlasting with me.
I wish them a heaven of love, to be forever and ever, everlasting,
So preach of that great love and give of yourselves, to God totally.
So that all men and women and children, can spend eternity, with me,
If you love me, I will provide and guide you, all the way, in every way.
When you need my strength, just think of me and silently pray,
Think of me every day, because my wish is, "That all men be saved."

"I wish, all men to be saved."

Ada A Abell-Rayzor
OUR TEENAGER

Dedicated to my son, Jeffrey Scott Rayzor, who has entered this special time in life.

As you go off into the night.
We hope and pray you'll be all right.
There comes a time for letting go.
No matter how much we love you so.
For one day, long before we're gone.
You'll be able to walk alone.

You must learn for yourself what life's all about.
Sometimes paying a price for finding out.
For almost everyone can look back
And wish they hadn't done, this or that.
Mistakes are lessons that must be made
in order to grow.
The ones that cut you to the soul.
The ones you wish you could erase.
And tomorrow you didn't have to face.

You will have learned and you will have grown.
Many seeds you will have sown.
In order for you to understand
The cycle of life must begin again.

When you are ready to come home.
Our light will be on, for we will miss you, son.

Ada A Abell-Rayzor
OLD LACE

In all the world there's no place to hide.
No matter, Lord, how hard I try.

The mirror has turned an ugly gray.
In its reflection my heart does stray.
Back to a time when youth was new
In the mirror, a pleasant view.

Oh, dear Lord, life has a twisted end.
Just the opposite of its begin.
The eyes grow so very tired
And the frame becomes painfully marred.
A familiar voice no longer heard
Because it's passed without a word.
For this "love," I cannot live without
Oh, dear lord, is this what life's all about?

We put off until tomorrow
Which becomes our greatest sorrow.
For time cannot be replaced
Neither the wrinkles upon my face.
Oh, dear Lord, that's why I pray
It's me you smile upon today.

Tammy King
MIKE

I dedicate this poem to my friend, Mike.

The casket was lowered,
Of our dead friend.
Whimpers and cries,
Were heard throughout
The land.
We don't know,
Why, he did what he did.
But we know it's not a fib.
We stand and cry,
Wishing it was a lie.
And it's all because,
He wanted to fly.

Beth Kelly
MEASURE IT

Tick
Tock
Ring
Beat
Can you avoid the seat.
Seconds
Hours
Minutes
A term in the Senate.
Days
Weeks
Months
Years
Can you conceive the fears.
An eternity
Inconceivable to man.

Jewel Krumwiede
MOCKING BIRD

Five a.m. and there he is
Our mocking bird rascal
He changes his notes—his trill
We need no alarm for he
never fails.

We marvel all this; comes
from such a tiny throat
What a pleasure each day
to awake to his notes
So happy he sounds each
early morn.
Then flies away; again we'll
hear his 5 o'clock call, come
tomorrow's dawn.

A most marvelous way to
greet each new day!

Fortis D Morse
AMEN

Died peacefully in his sleep, paper said.
Now rests, hands clasped, pillow beneath his head.
Looks natural, the man in the wooden pall,
But he doesn't care, doesn't care at all.
Peace, at last, claimed this worried, troubled soul.
Erased his debt, his sin, and left him cold.
The preacher spoke in kind, comforting tones.
"Friends," the black frocked man explained, "Life's a loan."
They watched as men covered the box with earth
And wondered whether life has any worth.

Tanya E McGarry
MY PARENTS

I would like to dedicate this poem to my parents, Paul & Cecilia.

My parents are strange
and that's the truth.
Don't see parents like mine
anywhere and that's the truth.
They are strange because
my Dad makes up these strange
songs about me and starts singing
them
when people walk by.
And my Mom skips on the sidewalk
when she walks with me.

I know I shouldn't be embarrassed about it but what can I say. That's my parents for you.
The poem's not over it has just begun and that's the truth for you.
I have a cat his name is Fred. My Mom treats him like royalty and what do we get?
That's the question for you to answer my friend.

William McManus
REMEMBERING
Grace, that day long ago when I asked you to run away with me, was the last day of my life.

Zylla Del Mar
THE NEXT BEST THING

The only BEST THING — there could ever be . . . is having you completely (not just ALMOST!).

Let me think —
of the next best thing
to loving you completely;
There could never be —
but yes . . . there must be!

For what good would it be —
if happiness is sacrificed
to DREAMS
if truth is subjugated
to POWER
and . . . if love is compromised
for CONVENIENCE

Yes . . . one must take —
the next best thing
to loving you unconditionally;
No matter how painful —
that next best thing . . .
of simply losing you
of solely living life
as life should be lived ——
HAVING IT ALL . . . ALMOST!

Steve Lynn
THE WAY LOVE SHOULD BE

This poem is written about my parents and is dedicated to them for always loving me.

Some couples are like a rough sea,
Letting changing tides get in between.
Others just cry and drift on by.
But the two of you,
It's the way love should be.
Well, it never comes down to tears,
Even when the sea gets rough.
Fighting the tides together,
You've won.
Through the darkness shines the sun,
The way love should be for everyone.

Jeannine Marshall
SPRING
Cardinal singing
Robin winging
Redbud waking
Sunrise breaking
Grasses greening
Bluebird preening
South wind sighing
Wild geese flying
Winter past
Spring at last

Hilda Putek
NIGHT CONFESSIONS
In the darkness of night . . .
The tears begin to fall,
With thoughts and memories — things
Of long, long ago.

As a child, I gave you all my love,
The stars, the sun and all the above . . .
My hopes and prayers, that your life would be
Full of the love and joy you brought to me.

Now days have passed, grown into years . . .
The child has left, a grown person appears,
With a mind of her own, she has to go . . .
Someplace else, where no one knows.

To let go, I know, now, is right . . .
But for me, alone . . .
It's now tears
In the darkness of the night.

I love you . . . .

John H Miller
A POET AM I — ?
Publishers are always gropin'
For the unborn chanticleer who,
Once its shell is finally open,
Does the thing it's born to do.

Poets look for words and measure
So the rhythm flows and shines.
Poets write for fun and pleasure
As they build those rippling lines.

Poets never need a reason
When they scribe their thoughtful fare.
They just pick a current season
Or a subject anywhere.

Once the lines are finally plotted
To the poet's candid view,
Then the errors are unknotted,
Not too many, just a few.

I'm a poet and I know it,
Otherwise these lines would show it.
Maybe some will vent their scorn
But I'll just write and blow my horn.

Jenny Smith
WHAT IS A MOTHER:

This is dedicated to Diane Smith for always being there and for being my best friend, I love you Mom.

A mother is someone who loves you very dear
and comforts you from the things you fear
A mother holds you on her lap when you're sad, love from you makes her glad
But then her children start to grow,
your growing older doesn't show
Your little girl on her first date, mom stays up all night to wait.
Mom comforts you when you cry
not knowing your sadness hurts mom inside.
Mom, both of your little ones are teen–agers now
how they grew so fast you don't know how
You think you are growing old,
but there is something you have never been told
Your oldest has grown as tall as she'll get
your youngest still needs that age to hit
for soon he will be big and strong
and the little children we were have disappeared for so long.
But we'll never be too old, where we don't long for your arms to hold.
to us you'll always be young, because your growing old has not yet begun.
Don't worry about being old
because it is something you will never be told.

Lula May Hart Adams
DESTINED TO DIE
Precious marks lay across His brow
harsh Crown of Thorns tore His kind face,
priceless freedom scars hands and feet
yet — the Victor waits at heaven's gate.

When I shall see my Saviour's face,
look deep into His gentle eyes
I will find love undaunted still
as on the rueful day He died.

How helpless His beloved ones felt
standing beside His lonely cross.
Closely akin to what we feel
when treacherous death brings our loss.

Powerful death, none can stop him!
Physical man — destined to die.
But spiritual man lives forever
beyond the portals of the sky.

Dianne M Moran
GONE BUT NOT FORGOTTEN

This poem is dedicated to Our Beloved Brian J. Adams, who passed away on May 13, 1989, at age 3 and a half years old.

Brian you're my sweet little one,
Even though you were only my Grandson,
I'll always remember the love in your eyes,
I still hear you talk to me even through my cries,
I see the pain that everyone shares,
Did you know that mommy keeps your Buddy doll in your chair?
Everyone misses and loves you so much,
I wish I could still feel your touch,
I would have done anything just for you,
I thank God everyday for the Angel I knew,
I often wonder do you still think of me,
I want to know are you happy with thee?
I wish you were here instead of heaven above,
But at least you're safe and you're always loved,
So here are some hugs and kisses to you,
From everyone and Grama too,
Please watch over us and keep us all safe I pray,
I know we will all meet again some other day.

Jimmy Yee
INNOCENCE
She walks alone
She does not speak
Her eyes are wide
Her strength is weak

The day is short
The night is long
The room is dark
The air is strong

A stranger's face
A stranger's touch
A stranger's breath
A time too much

Alone she lives
Alone she sleeps
Alone she cries
Alone she weeps

She sits alone
She holds a gun
Her nights are long
Her nights still young

Jimmy Yee

William W Krider
A VALENTINE POEM
You filled my heart with love
where before there was none.
A love so overwhelming
it makes me want to take you in my arms
and pull your breast to mine.
When we are together, love fills my body —
it cries out with excitement.
When we are apart, each minute is an eternity;
my heart cries out for you.
To look into your face
sends my heart racing.
To hear the sound of your voice
fills me with love everlasting.
My love for you feels just right;
We were made for one another.
My love for you sets my heart aglow.
Oh, I love you so.

Catherine Parker
MISSING YOU
Good–bye to the smile on your face
the shine in your eyes
that expressed the happiness
we shared in our lives.
Remembering times of great joy
in traveling the road of life together
brings sorrow now but not forever.
That relationship is a great bond
which goes beyond
the earthly portals here
for I hold the memories of you
close to my heart.
Since we have been apart
I live alone in my thoughts
of one I love so dear.
There is sadness in a loss
with this there is pain.
Takes time to heal
when one can feel
the joy and love again.

Kathy Mercedes Betances
DRUG MURDERS
Drugs destroy lives.
Controlling everybody involved.
Making impossible to be disposed.
Breaking lives into tiny pieces.

Killing everybody involved, slowly.
Even those, who tried to reach out
to help them.
It is one Hell of a Murderer.

Dianne Hawkins
GREAT TREE OF LOVE
Another apple off the tree
A tree once filled with you and me

A candle once lit, its flame rose high
Starting to wither, soon may die.

A time to make changes, so long so soon.
Once upon a time, I could fly to the moon.

Back down on earth, seeping slowly beneath ground.
Getting ready to bury, the love we once found.

That Great Tree of Love, filled with apples so rare.
Once filled with many, now almost bare.

Dawne D & William R Coles
SCRATCHES
Don't cry
Cry tomorrow
Save those tears for another time

I'll put a patch
On that scratch
Save those tears for another time

As time went on
I couldn't patch that scratch
'Cause of CRACK, ICE, and
CRYSTAL TEA

You see:

Even Jesus had scratches
And the Almighty gave him patches

But if you:

Snack on CRACK, ICE, and
CRYSTAL TEA
You'll lose the patch
That makes contact
Between you and me

Don't cry
Cry tomorrow
I'll see you in another time.

Pauline Wiles
SANCTUARY OF THE HEART
Each morning upon rising
There's a time I've set apart
To spend moments with my Father
In the Sanctuary of my Heart.

Seeking counsel from Him
Through the reading of His word;
I am blessed by all His promises,
In the greatest story heard.

In that quiet sanctuary
I hear a still small voice
Gently whispering to me
"You should praise Him and rejoice."

Obediently I add my voice
To music set on tape;
Cares and fears all fade away —
Rare moments of escape.

He gives me strength when I am weary,
And a light to guide my way,
He never will forsake me,
He is with me night and day.

There are no hidden secrets
Between my Lord and me
Since He has taken residence
In my heart's sanctu'ry.

Mary-Byrd Schroeder
WINGED BEAUTY
Floating and fluttering
with thin, translucent wings

Gliding across the bright blue
sky, it touches each flower with
solemn delight

Shades of gold and orange shine
brightly while dipping down to
land on a lonely lily

A summer sprinkle starts and
the graceful Monarch dives under
a large fern leaf

A morning's glory tempts my
curiosity as I find another under
a bright marigold

I slowly push my finger through
the leaves and the butterfly crawls
innocently upon my fingertip

The winged delight moves its wings
as if it were waving farewell to
me

And with a twitch of its antennae it
flutters off to another beautiful
flower

Roma Lee Collum
DO YOU REALLY SEE?
Have you ever walked down a country road,
In a soft and gentle rain?
Or on a dark and cloudy night,
Listen to a passing train?

Have you ever watched the clouds float by?
They look so fleecy white.
They always seem to change their shape,
They are a pretty sight.

Did you ever watch a flower bloom,
Or hear a corn stalk grow?
Or watch a bird that soars on high,
Where they seem to go so slow?

Don't rush through life and miss these things,
That you now take for granted.
Slow down and learn to live a while,
See things that God has planted.

Tiffany Teague
I GO
I GO
through life being afraid.
Afraid of What? Not afraid
of the night or afraid of the
violences of a dream or even
the violences that go on
outside. I'm afraid of myself
hidden behind my shadow.
I fear that I will catch myself
unaware of the pain I can
bring myself. I can try
to run from myself, but I
cannot hide. I wish I wouldn't
be so afraid of myself.

Raman Jalota
RELEASE ME (TO DENISE)
Slowly she appears
in my coffee
and seeps into
my brain.

Her presence
overwhelms me;
her smell
suffocates me,
with dreams
of joy;
her arms
imprison me;
her hair
blinds me,
to my pain.

Her absence
wakes me up,
again;
till I reach
for the cup.

It's only
the morning,
and the torture
has begun.

Do I dare
live till
tonight?

And if I
make it
to the night,

will I
survive?

another night?

Vincent A Stiles
ODE TO MY PET CHERI'S FLEA

To Marci, my loving wife for all the affection she and Cheri gave to me.

Oh! How heavenly it is to be a little flea
Nestled among the hairs on the body of Cheri
It's so warm and soft and the dining is free
But alas! Like everything that's too good to last
I soon will become a thing of the past
For here comes Cheri's master with flea spray in hand
Oh! How heavenly it would be if I could be in another land.

Vera Nell Vickers

Vera Nell Vickers
GOD'S LOVELY CREATURE
One of God's lovely creatures
Visited me today.

The mower was whirring its noisy
Sounds

As I guided it over grassy
Mounds.

Here came a lovely black, lacy
Butterfly

Gliding faster, even
Than I,

Around me he flew each way
That I turned.

Almost as if to say, "Hello there!
Friend, Cheer up today!

See Joy where you may — Cause God's
Hand sent me your way."

Cindy Thiele
HELP ME LORD
Help me Lord to hear You call.
Let me know You'll break my fall.
Help me Lord to win life's race.
Show me Lord Thy loving face.

I try hard for joy and fame,
Never calling on Thy name.
How can I expect to win,
So very lost in my own sin?

The Dear Lord is my request,
Help me do my very best.
When I am tempted to do wrong,
Help me Lord to be strong.

Then oh Lord when I am weak,
Let me hear You as You speak.
As I go on with life's quest,
Let me know I'll pass the test.

When I see the end is near,
Help me Lord to have no fear.
Then when dying is my fate,
I shall enter Heaven's gate.

Elizabeth (Guida) Scognamillo
PEACE OR DOOM
The gentle child, she cries to be held
by arms that were
never there, to be soothed by words
that could only murmur
for a little while.
Ah sweet innocence child, still you
believe in, and now
know, only a phantom. Yet still you
hold on to the gray
mist.
You enfold your fingers around a
vapor of air, in the
solemn hope, prayer, determined to
retain the lie.
What will become of you if you blow
away, push away,
tear away the phantom mist? Know
reality today as it is
and yesterday as it was.
Peace or doom, this decision gentle
child is yours.

Melba Riggs Lamoreaux
PERSISTENCE
Young girls are so persistent In
wanting to become a wife,
Then they are so persistent In
wanting to Mother new life!
Persistently she achieves both goals,
Then Discouragement takes a hand;
Romantically she looks at her lover,
As a husband he's a different man!

Discouragedly she looks at new
fashions, At the baby who has tied
her down,
At housework that is never ending,
No time to go out "on the town."
Encouragement is just the right
weapon, A word of praise or two,
Persistently she rises above herself
And discovers a world all so new!

Persistently she finds Heavenly
Father, In finding Him, finds new
strength,
Subjects she thought were drudgeries
Objectively are blessings with length.
Gratefully she's found that her
marriage Was one that endured to the
end.
When anyone asked, she gratefully
told That Persistence had been her
best friend!

Pauline Shouldis
THE ADDICT
The policeman didn't have it, as he hauled her off to jail
Neither did the judge, he refused to lower bail
The jailer could care less, as he closed the iron door
Leaving her to shivering, vomiting, and diarrhea
And when it was all over, the loneliness began
The saddest of all feelings, that can befall man
To end her helpless cravings, as the night went slowly by
She dried her tears as best she could, and vowed not to cry
And turned her mind to other things, but wished that she could die

Her sheet became a rope that night, it was a tragic sight
Locking up a sickness, will never make it right
On the wall was listed, when they found her in the cell
Man's attributes, without which, they would surely go to hell
She wrote the one they were missing, while her eyes were still a blur
Their guilt began arising, as they read, compassion sir.

Denise Bennett
HER BEAUTY

Without Jesus I could not write this poem. Thank you, Lord.

From deep within her beauty flows,
It's not an outward thing.

Her beauty lies within her heart,
the love and warmth she brings.

Alas! . . . this sweet soul can't be seen,
because we look with eyes . . .

Look at her from within yourself,
you'll see her beauty's in disguise.

Grafton E Lucas
JERUSALEM

This poem is dedicated "To Angeline" my mother, rest eternal grant unto her (1870 -1974).

Oh thou!
Fairest city
God's contemplation divine
Of whom sages speakest.
Give ear unto our supplication.
Replenish us in spirit,
Confirm our meditation.

George F Reinhardt Jr
DIXIE
Somewhere a rabbit's running
A hound is on its trail
You can hear her calling loudly
Thru the valley or the dale

She doesn't mean to catch it
It's the chase that makes her cry
In that little bit of heaven
Where a hound goes when they die

Adrienne S Lamm
THINKING 'BOUT HOME

Dedicated to Mary and Samuel Duhart, my parents who let me have an imagination.

In the thick brushes water up to the knees
Thinkin' about home coming up with disease
Every step is fatal every sound scares
Thinkin' about home no one here I know there.

Want to write a letter, no pens around
Want to smell a steak suddenly a sound —
I have to raise this rifle to protect what they say is mine,
Thinkin' about home where everything is fine

Helicopters flying, I try to dodge around
Granades are dropping I make a frown
I see a little child come running up to me,
Thinkin' about home, where there I'm free.

I look at the child no older than six or seven,
My heart skips a beat I think about heaven,
In his hand I see something I've seen before,
It's the last thing I see —
And we both see no more.

Blythe Darlyn Thatcher
ON LOVE'S SEA
This is water uncharted,
Depths untried,
And I, novice sailor
Nearly drowned once
In previous venturing,
Possessed no Titanic illusion
To send me confident
Out of port.

Now, full sail on billowy ocean,
Like trepid mariner of Columbus's Day,
I want to declare,
"There be dragons here!"
And, ignorance intact,
Reverse course.

But my unseasoned hand
Knows little of lowering sail
Or compass reading;
The sailor inept,
My naivete may be forced.
To sophistication.

V G Haywood
AUTUMN
Autumn's a gay, beguiling witch
A bold, heel-clicking bitch
Dancing defiance with each swirling leaf
Thumbing her nose at Winter's hovering grief
Acting as if she doesn't know
That closer, closer comes the cruel snow.

Or could it be that in her soul she quails
Sheds tears, or torn by anger, rails
To be cut down, deep buried from men's sight
Her charm forgotten in the long, still night?
Or does she, with the true believers know
No life forever sleeps beneath the snow!

Mr Jackie E Ford
MY DREAM
As I sleep I see strange visions of people that have passed away, and there is a haunting as I dream the night away. I dream of kings and queens that have all passed on, and the battle of kings and how the wars were won. I dream of the sea opening up, and closing again, and the bad people meeting their end. I dream about Jesus with His arms opened wide, saying come to me one and all My children. I dream about the dead rising up out of the sea, and Jesus looking with a smile upon His face, and the people that rose up from the sea thanking Jesus from the bottom of their hearts. And all of a sudden I hear a voice saying, Wake up it's just another day.

Patricia L Yoho
DAUGHTER-IN-LAW
One day, Greg, our eldest son —
Took himself a wife.

A lovely, gentle, pretty girl —
To share his happy life.

Our other sons are looking now —
To do as well, I pray.

For when it comes to picking wives —
I'll really have no say.

But if they use sweet Debbie —
As a model in their quest —

Their happy lives will be fulfilled —
With nothing less — than best !!

Brian Davis
HERE I STAND
Here I am
back where I began
Standing here
I don't have nothin'

So I find
I spend time dreaming
dreaming of love
and having you to hold

So I guess, here I stand
with the rain pouring in my heart
Maybe I was wrong
Maybe I was blind
Still here I stand
left with a broken heart

I love you
are the words we said
but you walked
now I have no one
I'm foolish
For letting you leave
wish you would hear
You're the one I love

Ruth Hurst
PLEASE DON'T WEEP
Our Beloved Granddad Has Gone Away
He Will be Missed With Each Passing Day . . .

He Is Out Of Sight
But Not Out Of Mind . . .

He Is Lying In Waiting
With Our Father So Kind . . .

He Gave Much Joy And So Much Love
He Is Now Watching Over Us From Above . . .

He Is Away From This World So Full Of Crime
He Is Waiting For Us When It Is Our Time . . .

Please Don't Weep And Please Don't Cry
He Is No Longer Suffering And He Will No Longer Cry.

Michael Belmont
THE PUB
He sits alone, eyes filled with wanting,
And graciously accepting ear splitting jargon.
Wire rimmed glasses, lenses like an ice cube,
Reach out to wrap around broad nosed features.
Sipping beer with a head of foam, sighing;
Then sets it upon the table gracefully.
Large breasted women walk lewdly back and forth
Accepting payment for possible bare skinned deeds.
A guitar strums, for men have stories to sing.
Stories of misspent youth, love and lovers' quarrels
Often ring true within the orb of trivial life.
For life is often times like the bottom of a glass.
At times only large breasted women with rounded bosoms
Spring about the release from pitiful restraint.
A guitar strums, for there are stories to sing.
Wire rims with ice cube lenses are put away,
And hair is spitted down to cover ruthless life.
Bawdy laughter splits raucous, obscene nonsense
Muffled by smoke filled air heavy with conversation.
Rounded bosoms bend forward to retrieve an empty glass.

B J VanLaningham
WHAT DO YOU MEAN TO ME
I know not what you mean to me.
But I know we very much agree.
Time is spent the way we wish.
From this we cannot stray nor push.
We need the things we both supply.
Underneath our nature's sky.
Be it love or unsettled truth.
Our fate is sealed in our own booth.

What do you mean to me.
Unsettled whims and destinies.
Called forth in this our last goodbye.
Like the sound of the butterfly.
Left to chase the dream we shared.
Lost again on the desert air.
Come my love come lay with me.
On a down filled cloud of ecstasy.

My love for you will never die.
Like the gentle sound of the butterfly.
It lies beneath the sands of time.
Lost to those that will not mind.
The heartfelt choice, of the last of time.
Gone again, for our last lifetime!

Vada B Neely
OUR HERITAGE

In memory of Rhoda Boggs, my mother.

As I sit in my chair and ponder
About the things that are past
I cannot help but wonder
Why some did not last
When I stood on the hill in Plymouth
And gazed upon the rock.
My thoughts went back in memory
To things I had forgot.
I thought about the pilgrims.

The reason for their arrival
And things so very grim
They endured for their survival
That winter was a bad one,
Their crops were not so great
When they thought they had
won
Many lost loved one or mate.
I stood before the monument
And read the names inscribed
And wondered in my discontent
If, for my good, some died.

Wanda Lynn Butler
LOVER ON THE WIND
Did you hear me last night
whisper in the wind?
Did you feel my cool fingers
gentle breeze upon your brow?
My lips fluttering on yours
wings of a butterfly.
My breath hot upon your neck
warm rays of summer sun.
Felt you my body playing cool
upon yours like downy snowflakes?
Tasted you my brow, salty as the sea?
My laugh teasing in your ears
soft babbling brook.
You reached out, entered me
our spirits were as one.
Through ancient scents of buckskin
and fox
our souls danced within.
Skin damp as morning dew on rose
petals.
Walk quietly now as you awaken to
dawn.
Let nothing disturb the memories
of gentle dreamtimes.

Brian T Riddle
RED
In the hall I saw a rose
Symbol of love
A gift of God
I stooped to bring it close

I cradled it gently in my hand
What elation did I feel
Oh, what a lovely jewel.
I held it like a friend.

Thorn, thorn, wicked thorn!
Pricked my skin
It drew my blood.
I threw it down in scorn.

I left it there, I left it there!
On the cruel and cold white floor.
I made my way, I didn't stay
No longer did I care.

Christine B Bukovsky
SPIRITS ATONED

To Mr. Peter Dale Slack, Jr. My inspiration and final words. Thanks.

Shattering our heights of passion
each time we
reach out-giving-taking
Those elusive feelings, so hard to
form into mere
mortal words
Our brazen demands of sensual
challenge
Breathless kisses, oh so soft, catch
in our throat,
They hurt

Feeling anxious to touch-roam-
explore
Never the same
As I envision us, the joyous wonder
man, woman
Centuries of rapture wash over me
Leaving me to weep

Golden J Williams Jr
ROSE PASSION
Present your red rose of love to the
special person in your life.
Release the deep burning passion of
possession and the
fierce aching rush of emotions.
Give that white rose of lust to the
person of your dreams.
Release the deep burning passion of
possession and the
fierce aching rush of emotions.
Offer the pink rose of health to the
athlete who excites you.
Release the deep burning passion of
possession and the
fierce aching rush of emotions.

Pat Mazzella

Pat Mazzella
WALKING WITH GOD
I've walked this earth, for many
years,
My soul tormented by doubts and
fears.
So very often I would envision, my
day in the sun.
But the first sign of clouds; would
cause me to run.

Surely, in everyone's life; there must
be some rain,
But I chose to escape, rather than
face feeling pain.
Existing in a world; made up of
endless dreams,
I thought I would get by with lies
and schemes.

While swearing I was acting under
total duress,
It was I who had created; This
awful mess.
Filled with self-pity, guilt and shame,
The finger was always pointed,
Looking for someone to blame.

Then one day, the bottom fell out,
Being filled with confusion; I
heard
myself shout . . .
"Oh God, please help me; there's
nowhere left to hide,
I can't go on living; with these
feelings locked inside"
"Take control of my life; please show
me what to do.
I'll do whatever it takes, my will
belongs to you."

Well! Something strange did happen,
God came to me that night
I felt His tender loving arm;
holding me so tight.
"My little child," he said to me;
"there's no need to fear
All you need do is talk to me, for I
am always here."

"I know that things do happen
And you may not understand.
But there's something that I must
show you,
Just reach out and take my hand."

Then suddenly it happened; and my
eyes began to see.
That the path to my own
happiness,
Would have to start with me.

I know it's a long road ahead; with
mountains and valleys too.
With God along each step of the
way.
I know I'll make it through!

Whatever He has in store for me, I
really do not know.
But with each and every passing
day,
His love will help me grow!

Edward A Collins
NESSIE'S VIEW
In the murky water of old Loch Ness
It's hide and seek I play.
For in my natural habitat
It seems now I'm on display.
Just what I am, they cannot guess!
Yet . . . I know what I am!
Their scientists say I don't exist
And they've labeled me a sham!
Some say I'm an otter,
A boat's wake or giant seal.
Some even say a Plesiosaur
Which is REALLY a big deal!
Year after year they hunt and prowl
What I am? They'll never know!
All the years they've searched for me
I'm still free to come and go.
So . . . the hide and seek continues.
Along with . . . catch me if you can!
They still refuse to believe in me,
But then . . . I don't believe in Man!

Suzzett A Morgan
A FANTASY COME TRUE
Oh, how beautiful the dream is!
As we walk hand in hand our hearts
beat as one.
We come to the place of our destiny.
You slowly lower me in the white
sand as your warm hands touch my
cool body.
It seemed like magic struck me as
soon as your lips touched mine.
The caressing of my body seemed
only like heaven.
I then believed I was in the desert of
penetrating heat.
To only when the water rushed over
our bodies as we lay on the beach.
Oh, how I wished this moment could
go on forever.
Then I awakened, turned and saw you
and only then did I know it
was forever.

Beth Napolitano
RAINBOWS OF PARADISE
A rainbow is a gorgeous sight
Of a variety of colors and hues
With tones so cheerful and colors so
bright
A rainbow chases away the blues

Rainbows are found in a variety of
places
In water, in air on earth and in fire
They form into an arc and have
ridges like laces
A rainbow will never cause you to
tire

Blue, pink, orange, purple yellow and
green
Are parts of the spectrum in a
rainbow
The colors unite to create a dazzling
scene
A rainbow has a luminous glow

A rainbow gives a sense of
tranquility and power
It has a mind of its own
It stands bold and high like a tower
A rainbow doesn't mind standing
alone

A rainbow has a way of reaching out
And giving a message to anyone
around
A rainbow brings joy and makes one
want to shout
It does all this without making a
sound

M E Ewen
THE GOOD TIMES
Do you remember. The good times,
and not the bad.
The hobby-horse I rode with you by
my side.
The games we played, rummy and
gin.
The scrabble games you let me win.
Can you remember. The good times
we shared.
In front of the fireplace, when you
held me close.
The thunder and lightening, when I
was scared, and cried.
You held me close, until the sun once
more shined.
The time you were sick. I was afraid.
I held your hand and pretended I was
strong.
You needed me. You made me
strong.
Can you remember the pet names we
shared.
The love we made.
Can you remember the water, we
saved.
By bathing together almost every
day.
The hot cocoa, the popcorn, we
shared in bed.
The T.V. shows, we never seem to
watch.
Those were the good times. I can't
remember the bad.
If you remember the good times.
Maybe our future won't seem so sad.

M E Ewen
DO YOU REMEMBER
Do you remember the first time you
held me close.
I cried. I knew then I loved you so.

You made me a promise. That we'd never part.
Now here I sit with no heart.
My body is cold. My blood doesn't flow.
You have my heart. You stole my soul.
When will they bury me in dark hole.
Dirt upon me they will throw.
You have my heart and soul.
What will you do then. Where will you go.
What will happen to my heart and soul.
Will you give it freely to another. It won't be happy this I know.
It belongs with me in my dark hole.
You can't give to another something you stole.
Someday you will return to me what you stole.
You will shovel the dirt from my dark hole and find me inside so cold.
You will take my hand and return to me, my heart and soul.
My body will warm. My blood will flow.
Once again we will stroll. Into the sunset we will go.
Together again, this I know. You will return what you stole.

M E Ewen

UNDERSTANDING

I tried, so often to tell you, how I hurt inside.
You didn't hear me.
You tried, to tell me, just how much you hurt inside.
I didn't hear you.
I tried to make you see things my way.
You couldn't see.
You tried to make me see things your way.
I couldn't see.
I tried to make you understand, how I felt.
You had no feelings.
You tried to make me understand how you felt.
I had no feelings.
We could not hear, see, or feel.
Is it any wonder, we are so lonely now.
Even the best love cannot withstand such odds.
We are deaf, blind, and numb.
Just two fools, who need to look around, and wake up.

M E Ewen

IN YOUR MEMORY

I stood silently by. As a stranger, saying nothing.
With my heart breaking.
I lay my hand upon yours. I needed to warm them.
So they might once again comfort me.
I let my fingertips trace the lines
of your lips so cold. I blew you a kiss.
Catching it I placed it upon your lips.
I needed to see your smile. Hear your laughter.
Feel your lips, upon mine once more.
As I traced the line on your finger.
I knew even though the gold band of our love was gone.
You would wear the imprint forever.
A symbol of our love.
I felt I might die. My life, my love.
You lay before me. I was so alone.
I could not survive. My life was over.
Then I felt you beside me. You gave me strength.
A heaviness lifted from me.
Even in death. You gave me your love.
I knew you would be with me always.
I was lucky to have been loved by you.
In your memory, Dean.

M E Ewen

WILDWOOD SUMMER

Sunset on the ocean.
The sky is so red.
The cool breeze is blowing.
Salt water in the air.
The sound of children laughing.
Summer is here.

The boardwalk is open.
There is music in the air.
Young lovers everywhere.

The road crew is working.
Traffic jams drive us crazy.
The tourists are here.

Summer jobs for everyone.
We work hard all summer.
Can't wait for fall to get here.

The winter sky is more beautiful.
Than any time of year.
The local natives settle in.
The Island is once again theirs.
No traffic jams to contend with.
Party time is here.

M E Ewen

A FISHERMAN'S WOMAN'S PRAYER

As I alone sit here. Watching the sun go down.
I ask it to watch over you, my love.
I know the ocean is so very big.
Your boat is so very small.
I ask it to bring you safely home to me.
So I might once again feel the closeness of you.
I know a fisherman is a rare breed.
You're one of the special ones. At most to me.

Each time I watch as you sail away.
Taking my life with you.
I ask God to once again watch over you.
You are the best my man tells me this.
Each time you bring him safely back, to me.
Still my life stops as you leave the docks.
You take it away with you.

As I watch the sunset. I know you are watching it too.
When I hear another boat has gone down.
I pray to God it's not you.
I know you worry, most fishermen do.
Don't worry my love. I am with you.
Take care of yourself. For very soon.
I will be watching the sun-set with you.

M E Ewen

TIME PASSES AWAY

I sit and watch the tide roll in.
I wonder where it's been.
Upon the shores of lost lovers.
Washing away footprints.
Of lovers lost at sea.
Bringing lonely sailors home.
To the waiting arms, of lovers.
They left behind. Or were they, staying calm.
In the ocean they left behind.
Waiting for the day. They would come ashore.
Bringing my love to me.

Time will find its way.
As it passes by today.
Some of us will drift alone.
Some of us will be left behind.
Never knowing, what time, they miss.
As life passes by.

M E Ewen

THE FALL TO VICTORY

When I think my ship has come in.
I'm sailing calm waters
again. I finally see land, after so long at sea.
I find that for sometime, the little drip I had left
behind, had became a steady stream.
I looked to the horizon, saw the cloud. I knew the storm
I had not seen was fast approaching me.
I felt the water beneath my feet. My ship was going
down. As I watched the storm ahead, I had worked so hard it seemed, yet the water was knee deep.
I could swim, or go down with my ship. My life flashed
before me. As I headed into the storm that would engulf me.
I was a survivor, how I fought for, what I had worked my life to be.
When the sun came out I found myself alone. In the ocean
so big and strong. I would survive. I was strong. I would claim what belonged to me.

M E Ewen

TO DADDY

You sang songs to me. As you bounced me on your knee.
Before I could see, you walked the floor with me.
When I cried, you loved me.
You taught me to crawl, and laughed when I walked.
You smiled down on me.
You gave me a warm bed. A roof over my head.
You worked hard, for me.
Shoes on my feet. Beans to eat.
You went hungry for me.
A pretty feed sack. Made clothes for my back.
You wore patches for me.
First day of school. You were so proud of me.
Good report card. How happy you are.
You made plans for me.
Years go by. I disappoint you.
You love me.
You are old. I'm afraid. You need me.
I love you.
Where has time gone. Now I'm alone.
Time has taken its toll.
Today my Daddy went away.
I miss him so.

M E Ewen

A MEMORY

I left the mountains of my youth. In search of a dream.
I've traveled across this land of ours.
Never did I find the dream I left behind.
My dreams were there awaiting me.
Upon the mountain side.
The old farm house I longed to see.
Has fallen long ago.
The one room school where I learned to read, was only a memory.
The picket fence I sat upon, watching for Daddy to come home. Had turned to dust long ago.
The mountains, I had loved so, were stripped so bare, of the trees I had loved to climb.
Now I look at my mountain so bare.
I feel the pain deep inside.
I know my dream has died.

M E Ewen

A DREAM

West Virginia, is my home. I visit often, in my dreams.
They are so special to me.
My beautiful mountains. Once covered with trees.
Hangs its head in shame.
It stands alone now. Bare of the beauty, it once held.
What happened to her trees?
There is a road through my mountains now. Where does it go?
I wonder what Grand-Pop would say.
A shopping mall in his corn field.
What would he think. The river where he once fished. Is now filled with mud. Where nothing can live.
The apple tree he sat under. On a sunny day.
The cow path he walked down. Has long been stripped away.
My beloved mountain. What have they done to you.
Have they forgotten the beauty, you once held For all the world to see.
Where are the squirrels and birds?
That once lived in your trees.
The deer that grazed your pastures.
Hidden deep within.
Where are the animals. That once called you home.
Did they go quietly as I have done.
Do they have dreams, of a home.
They cannot return.

M E Ewen

IN SEARCH OF A DREAM

I left the mountains, of my youth.
In search of a dream.
I wanted to be free.

It seems the mountains.
I left behind.
Still remain with me.
Those memories, I left behind.
Are a part of who I am.

Now I find, the dreams I have.
Are of my mountain home.
Where I can live my life.
To be just what, I was meant to be.
Free to be myself.

Brian Layton

NUCLEAR

To <u>ALL</u> those who abuse <u>POWER</u> . . .

We are at the hour,
Of nuclear power,
So oblivious and strong.
Ever so great, ever so deadly,
And also ever so wrong.
We cry for help,
We cry for mercy,

We cry for our bodies and souls.
But no one can cry, no one can help,
They are all dead in the ashes and coals.

James and Ann Ward

Ann Ward
WHAT IS A MOM?

I would like to dedicate these poems to my family — My wonderful husband, James, and the best kids in the world, Leeann Bachstadt, Cheryl McCabe, and Leonard Pietrzak. I love you all dearly, Mom.

A mom is a rose,
sent by the Lord,
so she can give us love and joy . . .

She's up before the morning dew,
and there goes mom putting on her shoes . . .

She never tires from dusk till dawn,
and never forgets that you were born . . .

She's always there with a smile or grin,
but keeps all her worries within . . .

She tries so hard to please us all,
you wonder how she walks so tall . . .

It takes a mom that heaven sent,
to make our life a great event . . .

So kiss that rose without a thorn,
and thank the Lord that you were born.

Ann Ward
WHAT IS A DAD?
A dad is a classic;
He's one of a kind
He does his best to keep us in line.

He stops to see if we're in need;
and always makes sure that we say please.

He tries to teach us right from wrong
and he can weather any storm.

But like a classic you must take care,
just don't leave him anywhere.

Tell him you love him now and then,
and he will have that special grin.
Keep forever in your mind,
that your Dad is A special kind . . . .

Pamela S Burnside
YEARNING

For my mother, Dorothy J. Mast. And in memory of my father, Bernard D. Burnside.

A soft, white bird glides low over moonlit water
Dips down to catch a current —
Only to watch it slide away.
The bird is longing for life, for love.
The moon cries softly down,
knowing and understanding.
The bird, resting on a rock, looks up to see, to feel.
The moon's gentle sobbing bathes the bird with joy & hope.
They comfort each other during the night.
But the moon slips away for dawn is here.
And the bird with one tear falling,
flies sadly away.
Thinking the only friend he ever had has gone away.

Michelle L Myers
TRUSTING GOD
I had a friend once,
Someone who I thought really cared,
But I was the fool,
for I was the only one who cared.
That love I felt,
I thought I'd never feel again.
Then I met you, whom I knew for years,
but never really knew at all.
I felt that love again.
I could feel my outer defenses
Shielding my inner self
for I was afraid, what happened before
might happen again.
I told her what had happened, and
She told me not to put all your trust in man, but in God. For man will fail you.

Kenneth Ray Kiser
MY LOVING FRIEND

To mom and dad, and family.

I gave you my love
Then gave you my heart
And all you did was tear it apart.
I cried me an ocean
Then cried me a sea.
Thinking this would bring
you back to me.
When I was down -n- the dumps,
you helped me over life's many bumps.
The road quite long and very cold,
And I knew then that I had to be bold.
Where's the love we used to know?
When did the loving emotions go?
I must put you behind me and start again
And let this old love come to an end.
I was hurt, but I'll be okay.
Perhaps I'll find love some other day
I'll always remember what I went through.
And hopefully & lovingly, you will too.
I want so much for you to see,
That our love was meant to be.
But you say it's only make-believe.
But I know by the way I feel.
I've never felt anything quite so real.
I know you're not speaking from the heart.
For you know we'd never part.
You say you've never been in love before
So I come knocking at your heart's door.
So this is a first for you and me
Together forever we will always be.
Always sweet and very kind.
True love in you I did find.
We've had our share of words & fights.
Lasting long into the nights.
But together right or wrong,
We find strength to carry on.
And now that you've gone and passed away
The only two words left for me to say
As tears fill my eyes, I begin to cry
And mumble the sad words,
"Good bye."
Days have come and days have gone
Since that tragic day —
You left me here all alone.
I await the time when we meet again.
To see you once more my dear sweet friend.
I know you're happy in your new home
For visions of heaven few have known.
I know how it feels, to live and die
To smile, laugh and sometimes cry.
Forever and always that's you and me—
Together is where we'll always be.

Darrell Blake Courtney
OUR LOVE
Love is like a little tree
Growing soft and patiently.
Love has done what none could do;
Love put us together, me and you.

And when I stand right by your side,
I hope our love will never die;
But if our bond should break some day
I know our love will find a way.

Jodie A Lee
DEFEAT
"Why bow your head in shame?" I ask,
With many precious memories past.
Enduring long enheartening days,
Endless thought, the battles haze.

"Why punish me dear Lord?" you wonder
As battle rages out like thunder,
Fighting on with all your might,
Another long and winless night.

With season's end, no victories,
Yet fighting painful memories.
Oh agony, you tried and failed,
For always someone else prevailed.

You leave the field with teary eyes,
Gaze into the dusky skies,
With handkerchief, wipe the tears,
While dreaming of the coming years.

Now look ahead toward days to come,
Toward that final battle won.
Knowing of the forceful task,
Becoming number one at last.

Louise Adams
LITTLE RED HOLLYHOCK
Little red hollyhock
Blooming all alone,
Standing straight and tall
Beside our sidewalk.
How did you get there?
Perhaps a wind-blown seed,
Or did a bird drop you?
Nature decreed you to be lovely
And dignified, and you are.
From my window I see you
As a lesson in being.

Pierre L St-Germain
SHAMAN
The fire burns brightly, singing to the stars.
She is the oldest of the tribe,
A representation of all their knowledge and legends.
Their celebration is to the Raven.
He is their god and he has helped them,
He helps them through her.
She stands at the fire, in the circle of her people,
Reaching into her medicine pouch, she withdraws a star.
A star as they call it, catching the light of the fire,
It is the heart of their tribe, as she is the head.
This ceremony has taken all her life and is coming to an end.
A girl steps into the circle, not as old but maybe as wise.
Slowly the girl approaches the woman, their eyes meet —
The girl sees the old woman a spirit in the firelight,
Old at first, then young, then a raven, then a coyote, then a star.
The tribe watches as the young girl and old woman hold hands
Then a flash and the old woman is gone, but not forgotten.
The girl stands with the crystal star in her hand
And raises it to the sky and her voice in song.
At this the tribe joins her and the night binds them.
So it is that a shaman is reborn . . .
and a new star shines in the sky.

Shelley Perkins
ALONE
Like a star that's lost its shine,
Like a tree without its bark,
Like a song that's lost its rhyme,
Like a playground without its park,
I am alone.
Like a rain that's lost its bow,
Like an oven without its heat,
Like a child unwilling to grow,
Like a drum that's lost its beat,
I am alone.
Like soil that's lost its sand,
Like paints without a brush,
Like fingers without a hand,
Like traffic without a rush,
I am alone.
Somewhere,
Somehow,
Sometime,
Amongst my way,
I lost my silver lining,
It's never with me, not tomorrow nor today.
Like a caged animal who longs for the freedom to roam,
I no longer hold my shine,
I am all alone.

Swastice Johnson
6 FEET UNDER
My life was mess, it had lots of tension, pressure in other words stress. I was living my life the way I wanted, actually I was on my own, but it didn't last long being 16 and living with my parents at home.

My parents told me my independence wouldn't work through & through, but I didn't listen because there's two things I hate, taking orders and being told what to do.

I didn't care what people had to say, they'd talk, I'd listen but I did what I wanted anyway. When I'd go out with a couple of friends my parents would say be home at 10:00 on the dot, but I came home when I pleased my excuse was oops! I forgot.

My parents always tried to make sense they'd say you can't always think that we're going to support you by giving, sometime soon you'll have to get yourself a home. But I didn't listen because I had a mind of my own

I didn't care how many times they'd say I'd regret it, I'd be my own person yeah hard-headed. I thought I was just too great, once I realized I wasn't it was too much to take. Now I know what they meant when they said listen, learn, and do what they say. If I had done those things I'd probably be alive today. The only reason I'm not is because of those 10:00 curfews I purposely forgot.

I should have listened when I was much younger, and because I didn't I'm 6 ft. under.

Nora Elaine Hightower

SEASON'S CHANGE

When winter appears
And the snow falls down,
It spreads over the surface
Of the cities and towns.

Boys and girls
On the school grounds —
Making snowballs
So big and round.

Ladies and gents
In their cars,
Stalling and growling
Here and afar.

When winter disappears
And the snow melts away.
Spring soon begins
With another mild day!

Nora Elaine Hightower

(TCB) THE CHRISTIAN BOASTS

A child of GOD knows GOD IS GOOD!
So we represent HIM like a good Christian should.
HIS light through us shines brilliant and bright
So the lost ones can be led to a steady light.

Telling all we encounter, about THE CHRIST who lives today,
And how HE'S paving a route for us if we're willing to come HIS WAY.
Don't even worry about what you've done in the past.
'Cause only what you do for CHRIST will last, and last and last!

We show and tell by words and deeds
How GOD wants us all to be.
And by doing so, we're asking
Just as Jesus did — to Come and Sup With Me!

Though we are saved, we must continue
To work 'til the battle is finally won.
We know HE'LL say to us one day
'My Servant, Well Done!'

Lucile Adkins Eye

WHEN I AM OLD

When I am old (I am eighty . . .)
I am not going to sit in a rocker
With a shawl around my shoulders,
Or wear lavender or a lace collar.
I am not going to holler, "Huh,
Stop mumbling, talk!"
When I can't hear.
No, I am going shopping.
I am going to buy a bright red hat
And a pair of red high-heeled shoes.
If I wobble when I walk
I shall carry a cane.
Not an ordinary cane but one with a gold handle.
I am going to spend my children's inheritance
And live life to its fullest.

Jennifer Dutton

MY LOVE FOR YOU

We were together
day and night,
But then we had
a fight.
It was me who
was to blame,
And it's a shame.
I told you I loved
you, but it wasn't
true.
Then I realized it
was you.
My love for you
was oh! so true
But you say you have
someone new, So do
I, but I don't want
him, I want you.

Claudiette F Hancock

FINAL SALUTE

This poem is dedicated to America's unsung Heroes — The Vietnam Veterans, and especially for David M. Coleman.

On a sunny October morn, down in old Charleston town, two babies were born, one white and one brown. Side by side in the nursery they lay, and they became buddies on their very first day. They grew up and went to school, studied hard and followed the Golden Rule; then they turned eighteen, not yet men, and along came the draft and got both of them. On a dark and dreary October morn, exactly nineteen years from the day they were born; they were on reconnaissance, their duty for that day, but they flushed out some Cong along the way. The first shot fired hit a buddy in the side, he fell to the ground, he moaned and died; the other was scared and wanted to run, but he looked at his buddy and picked up his gun. It was like David against Goliath, I guess you could say, the way the buddy stood alone against the Cong that day. He didn't feel the bullet that hit him in the head, but it sent him to join his buddy in the Valley of the Dead. After the fighting was over & the shelling had calmed down, the Platoon found the buddies on the blood soaked ground, & they did a body count, like they always do — Cong 33 — Buddies 2. The Platoon stood in silence with tears in their eyes, they bowed their heads & said their good-byes; but the Sergeant started to sob, it was a pitiful sound, & he shook his fist in the air and spat on the ground. They were only privates, he told his men, & a twenty-one gun salute is against the rules for them; but the Platoon was all American & they knew exactly what to do, they raised their weapons towards the heavens & gave the buddies twenty-two.

Heather Lori Belanger

LOST DREAMS

The young raped of all their dreams.
Who will now help them succeed?
Why can't it be as it seems?
The young raped of all their dreams.
We must help with all our means.
We shall give to those who need.
The young raped of all their dreams.
Who will now help them succeed?

Maxine Marie Puckett

IT WON'T HURT ME

To Blue Eyes — it was pret-t-t-y easy.

It won't hurt me to fall in love again for no one will touch the place reserved for only him. We met on a summer day in July. I fell in love as I gazed into his blue, blue eyes. Time passed my love grew, my darling said he loved me too, but love is blind and can hide the truth when one is confused. I felt he was a special kind of man. One I could share my life with. Little did I know

I was not to have these dreams of bliss. Only time would bring knowledge to understand he was not to be my special man. Because love words spoken seem to escape a man's mind as he sips on whiskey, beer, or wine. The life he chose he cannot win for the alcohol he consumes will take what's left of him. I must go on my life to lead and leave behind one my heart will always grieve, and if the saying is correct that time heals all hurts and truly will mend. It won't hurt me to fall in love again for no one will touch the place reserved for only him.

Ruby Smith

MEMORIES

I hear an echo in the wind
Was it in my heart?
Was it in my mind?
Or was it just pretend?
Maybe a heartache of a long lost love gone by . . .
Maybe a romantic lovers' sigh.
Was it in my heart?
Was it in my mind?
Or was it just pretend?
I hear an echo in the wind.

Robert Louis Dutile

THE STORM WITHIN

Being cautious, autonomously coasting through life
A great source of strength resides within
Independent I proclaim myself captain
Needing no one except my one man crew

Sailing without any exact destination
Navigating dilemmas with powerful sea dogs
Building swells within and covering with comedy
Camouflaging with beautiful hues of Neptune's sunsets
Fabricating a facade, concealing vulnerabilities

Never sending an SOS when the Poseidon's currents are onerous
Caring not which face of loyalty my savior has
Afflicting them by any means, leaving them like impaired ghost-ships
Building the storm within because I am so capable

The voyage of my choice is now mapped for self-destruction
Submersing in turmoil for so long my port is calling
With emotional tides rising I become capsized
Trying to break through the eye of the hurricane created

Alarming gales drown out my desperate deafening screams
My shipmates of comedy and camouflages offer no relief
With a betrayed captain my emotions are tempestuous mutineers
My captain and crew of insecurities go down with the ship.

Evilena Filbeck

A SOLDIER WHO WOULD NOT DIE

William Henry Barrett (1892-1968) W.W.I Camp McClellan, Alabama. Children: James, Lacy, Wm.Reece Barrett. Grandson Wm. R. Barrett, Jr. Life-long resident-Marshall County, Ky.-Buried Fooks Cemetery.

William Henry was his name, his buddies called him Will
He responded to the Draft Board; Military duty to fulfill . . .
In a global epidemic, twenty million persons died
For countless U.S. Service Men, influenza took their lives . . .

World War I was winding down; Oh Lord, do peace bestow
Will stood by within his troop; Assignment Europe, for to go . . .
Will collapsed one day, while at attention he did stand
At McClellan Army Hospital, medics came to take command . . .

Sick soldiers were everywhere; cots crowded side by side
The inside air was so polluted, the majority of them died . . .
When flu patients entered coma, it was diagnosed as death
Will was moved to hospital porch, because there was no breath . . .

Among the soldier corpses, Will laid silent for a while
Then suddenly, blue eyes came open and he began to smile . . .
Healing power of God's fresh air, is

the logic one can say
For the miracle that happened, to
Will Barrett on that day . . .

Ten years before, a dear friend was
saved from death so grim
Will rescued Blandford Edwards,
who didn't know how to swim . . .
At age seventy six, Will had enjoyed
a wholesome life
Three children, many friends; Pearl
Bailey his loving wife . . .

IN 1919 WILL WAS A HERO; HE
WAS A SOLDIER WHO REFUSED
TO DIE!

Brenda Simmons
THE LORD IS OUR GOD
The Lord is our God, His home is our
home.
Some will go home some will stay,
When it's my turn I'll go home
The Lord watches over me
Day in and day out
The Lord isn't going away
He's here to stay
You love him, he'll love you
The proof has been shown in many
ways.

Dudley E Lippert
A TRIBUTE TO FRANK
It takes but a moment to be born
And only a moment to die.
Yet the years between seem all too
short.
We can't but wonder why.

Is it because of all we want to do,
Or all the things we never get done?
Could it be that all the ties that bind
Grow strong because of the things
we've done.

It matters not what the years will
bring
Only what we will do today.
Living ever so selflessly
In all we do and say.

So share of your life and love today.
It is the best that you can give,
Knowing that all you have done
Helped someone else to live . . . .

Gretchen K Barbor
INTERLUDE
tonight the moon is appropriately cut
in half
and you and i
pebble-kicking down the road
feign
conversation
silently
unintelligibly
we utter words long forgotten
syllables ill-fitted to
our mouths . . .
barely audible we heave
in unison
then

nothing

the stars fill the void between us
cold air freezes
our silences

and the moon
sneers
while delicately
tilting on her
hinges.

Patricia Krenik
FOR MISTY
I love my daughter, Melissa
Chryselle,
My baby "Brownie" turned into a
belle.
With warm eyes tender like a baby
deer
And dark hair cascading, she likes to
be near
Touching and hugging the ones that
she loves
(Not too different from the way of
doves.)

I call her Misty, why I don't know,
The nickname was given a long time
ago,
Yet the name suits her well and
recalls to me
A dancing sprite of a morning sea,
Observing the world before it is clear
With mist-arms fog-form day-break
cheer!

Yet my Misty you'll find is quite
properly grounded,
With feet down to earth she's very
"well-rounded"
An old-fashioned term that doesn't
mean "fat"
Just able to work, to love, and to chat.
To dream and to feel and to care what
is right,
My Misty's a sweetheart, a child of
the light.

Florence Niemet O S F
CHRISTMAS MAKES A DIFFERENCE
To Bethlehem, to pay taxes, to eat
dry food for miles
And Joseph just stands there and
smiles.
My traveling clothes are worn and
thin
But isn't the beauty of the King's
daughter from within?

Oh, to be the servant of His grace.
To see heaven in my Baby's face!
The world will never be the same
When I first whisper His chosen
Name.

M L Kiser
BENEATH
Beneath the swift and swirling
waves,
abide the sands of yesterday.
And deep within the rolling tides,
there dwells a refuge for the mind.

Imagination seeks to find,
something that was left behind.
Yet silently the stories lie,
to linger there, but not to die.

Jean A Spry
WHEN WINTER COMES
When Winter comes and thoughts
turn dreary, turn thoughts instead to
something Cheery. Of Ice Crystal
Trees that Sparkle & Glisten, and
Snow that goes "Crunch"—"You can
hear if you listen."

Marshmallow Mounds of Gleaming
White Snow, that Beckons the
children, "Come on, Let's go."

Out with Sleds and Skis to the slopes,
Down they go with Hearts full of
Hope. While wishing the snow will
last a bit longer—As Dreams of the
Winter Olympics they ponder.

Winter goes by when you wish it
would last, But alas! Spring and
Summer are approaching fast.

Jennifer Derscheid
WRITTEN WITH A PEN

Tom, I love you always & forever.
Love always, Jen.

Written with a pen, sealed with a
kiss, if you really love me you'll
answer this. Can't you tell by all the
things I do that all my love belongs to
you. Your love is like a piece of gold
hard to carry & hard to hold.
Out of all the guys I've ever met,
you're the one I'll never forget.
And when I die and you're not there,
I'll carry your name on a golden
prayer. If you're not there by
Judgment Day I'll know you went the
other way and just to show what love
will do, I'll go to hell and be with
you.

James Lemasters
MOTHER
Mother,
I said a prayer for you today
And know God must have
heard—
I felt the answer in my heart
Although He spoke no word!
I didn't ask for wealth or fame
I knew you wouldn't mind—
I asked Him to send treasures
of a far more lasting kind!
I asked that He'd be near you—
At the start of each new day!
To grant you health and blessings—
And friends to share your way!
I asked for happiness for you—
In all things great and small—
But it was for His loving care—
I prayed the most of all . . . .

Kim Leighton
STRAIGHT FROM THE HEART
As each day goes on, my heart lifts
higher
The spark between us has
grown into a fire,

Forever in my life, I'll cherish these
days
I'm holding onto the good times
we've had
and hoping it stays,

I've been holding you in my heart
since our eyes met
There hasn't been a time to
even think of letting go yet,

But my heart doesn't worry about
that now
Because with your arms
securely around me,
I'd live forever somehow,

'cause together we're one and we'll
stand tall
The bind between us is great,
not small,

Our love will always grow until the
mountains reach the sky
Or until the last tree on earth
should crumble and die,

Nothing in this world could tear us
apart
As long as the love is coming
straight from the heart.

Karen Harris
GRANDBABY
How hard it is not to smile
Upon your small round face
Where twinkling baby blues beguile
You back to a state of grace

Such a sturdy little bundle
On legs so short and stout
That move in running trundle
As they piston you about

A little pile of dirt you spy
Awaiting my broom and pan
Oh! but how the dust does fly
Under dimpled little hands

Tiny arms go round my neck
As I grasp you with resolve
You plant a kiss with a baby peck
The sternness just dissolves

Then in your infant cant
With monumental aplomb
You sing to me your latest chant
Where Mom? Where Mom? Where
Mom?

Melissa Leigh Collins
THE BOX
My mind is in confusion every day
And I often don't know what to think
or say
It's not one particular problem, but
many
And I don't have a solution for any
My inner thoughts & feelings are in a
constant whirlpool
But still I walk around like
everything is cool
I don't let friends, family, or relatives
inside
Instead I put a box around myself &
pretend to hide
Friends try to open my box with all
their might
But my strength is stronger; that
strength is fright
Once in awhile someone comes along
that's stronger than me
That person knows my weak spot &
opens the flap with that key
Once the flap is open the whole box
falls apart
The walls tumble down only to reveal
a smaller box—the heart
This box is stronger than the
first
It's held together by hatred and
hurt
Only when I start to suffocate &
call
Can the sides of this box begin
to fall . . . .

Melissa Leigh Collins
THE SEED OF LOVE
The thought of you brings a sparkle
to my eyes
A sparkle so bright & so true it never
dies.
A sparkle that grew from the seed of
love
A seed that has been sent from up
above.

It was planted deep within our hearts
So that nothing could reach it & tear it apart.
It needed time to grow and to strengthen
So that it will stay true & never weaken.
The seed has already started to blossom
And when it is complete it will look truly awesome.
The flower is beginning to show its face
And soon we can protect it in our loving vase.
It is a special flower that needs just the right touch
A touch that only two people can give who love each other very much.
It is a fragile flower, but strong to the core
If we take care of our love it will live forevermore!

Linda Jopp
ALONE WITH MY THOUGHTS

Alone with my thoughts
No reason to hide
My dreams and my visions
That someone might "chide"

Come along with me now
and just take a "peek"
Through my own little window
and whom you might meet

Still in the night
a warm summer breeze
High on a mountain
Its peaceful sereneness wraps around me
I'm alone with my thoughts
with no invasions, envisioning my dreams
Listening to nature, by a calm river stream
Free as an eagle, no pain or despair
To know caring and kindness for all of mankind
To reach out and help, "tho" the problem's not mine
Alone with my thoughts
Our Lord God has given
To shape the world the way "he" has envisioned

Ruth E James
WALK WITH ME

To the ones I love.

Walk with me awhile,
before we part
Let me know the feeling's in your heart
We've been through so much together
Through the years, we've shared good
And bad times, laughter and tears
Why must we go our separate ways.
I've loved you more than words could ever say, must love always hurt
Walk with me awhile and hold my hand
Look into my eyes and let me know,
if you still love me, then tell me so
When I look into your eyes, I still see love's glow
Where did I go wrong, please let me know
If there is still a chance for us, don't let us lose it now, I love you darling
Hold my hand and walk with me awhile

Trudy Braden
MUSIC

I have felt your moving bosom
When it sighed in a mountain of heaving,
There was a speck of foam
that washed up on the shore of your desert,
And I was satisfied.
Tell me, were you satisfied with me?
All my forest was deadwood, and

I felt naked in the shadow of time with your ocean.
For when your sparkling foam
Came within the distance of touch
It was flecked with ice,
your northern skies had not been satisfied,
Yet I was complete in
your deadwood house.

Christi A French
GOODBYE . . .

Goodbye my friend,
It's time to go,
Time to leave,
It hurts, I know.

We're growing up now,
It happens so fast,
I don't know how,
Childhood is past.

I'll miss you lots,
Yes, this is true,
But we'll meet again,
Me and you.

Have fun, but be careful,
As I've said,
Enjoy life,
But use your head.

Remember me always,
As I will you,
I'm always your baby,
Faithful to you.

Doris J Goldsborough
BILL

He can't be dead!
Where has he gone?
His footsteps are no more,
Nor the sound of his voice.
I cry aloud at night his name.
There is nothing but
the stillness of the night.

To have loved and be loved
By one so gentle and dear.
To have borne to him
Three bundles of joy
Who enriched our lives
All through each year.

Taken
from me
The
one I love.
God
only knows
The
reason "why?"
We
question not
Our
Lord up above
Only
HE
Knows
why
Bill
was chosen to
die.

Shelley J Lindner
TAKE CARE

There are no words
that are adequate
enough to describe
any of the feelings
that are growing
deep within the
bindings of my heart.

Carefully I begin to share
each feeling with you—
one at a time.

My emotions, needs, and desires
are now placed in the care
of your hands.

Take them—
treat each one gently—
hold them close to
your own heart,
then we can share
together;
the love that now wants to
breathe,
live, and grow.

Bonny Lane
IRISH LINEN

To Grandma.

The farm girl danced
through tulips ablaze
to the old stone house
where irish linen lay.
Her path to bottom land
reaped little but pain,
thorns to a lily
drying in the rain.
All were in awe
how she sang for her rose.
What secret
did this farm girl hold?
Winters melted
one into one.
She joyfully waited
for spring to come.
The farm girl danced
through tulips ablaze
to the old stone house
where irish linen lay.

Audrey D Houghton
PRIVILEGED

To Anna Mae Stanek Schroeder, a special friend who enjoys wildlife.

The three stand silhouetted 'gainst the pines,
Alert to every sound and yet so poised,
Erect and proud in bas-relief.
They graze in leisure along our field's edge,
Offering their browns to greens in subtle
Blends of color,
camouflaged
identity,
Secure in a harmonious link to nature which
We would be hard-pressed to claim.
May no hunter spoil your Eden,
Precious deer!

Robert C Young
MISS ME WITH A SMILE

To the wonderful woman who inspired this and many other poems: I dedicate this to you with all of my love, Dawn. I'm yours forever.

We can't be together every day
Be thankful for those days that we can
Stop thinking about the days we're apart
Think about when we'll be together again

Don't just count the days left;
Feeling sad because there are so many more
Think about the day when I'll return
And we'll be together like before.

So when you think about us
During those times when we're not together;
And how the sadness seems to make
Each passing moment last forever;

When you feel a hurting in your heart,
And a tear falls down your face
Just think about the love we share
And let a smile take your frown's place
I LOVE YOU

Todd Allen Fisher
BLUE GENRE

For Dawn (and the dolphins).

A bright collage of colors
Crisscross in the night
A rhythm which breeds magic
As ivory doves take flight

Freedom breaks the surface
Of the midnight stream
A clear sense of relief
As if waking from a dream

The powers meet at sea
Wherein lies the core
Of secrets left alone
Concealed forevermore

A rift in the waves occurs
Above, it remains unknown
The saviors of time feel nothing
As a new light is shown

Stella Bonifazi
TOO LATE

We tread on air . . .
Still, as the lingering kiss,
Sweetly gone . . . passion.
On padded feet, we glide
Past dark rooms,
Lest the slumberers within,
Aroused from restless sleep,
Come pounding on closed portals;
Their dust-filled voices,
Crying for release.
Frail and broken;
Sin, our only friend . . .
Turmoil, our peace.

Hush . . .
Be still;
Too late . . . too late.
Angels in white light
Tower by open doors;
Bitter, is their message;
"Nature will not be mocked . . .
Nature will not forgive."

R W Fisher

SPECIAL THOUGHTS

To Elaine, my love, my life, my inspiration, my bestest friend.

The moon is full and shining bright,
As I gaze out my window at the heavens tonight.
Moonbeams bounce off the snow with shimmering light,
And I thought of you tonight.

Nights like this are made to remember,
The long cold nights of mid December.
Embraced by a warm fire and its glowing ember,
And I thought of you tonight.

Thoughts of the future, none from the past,
Thoughts of today, how it went by too fast.
Wishing I could reach out and freeze time with my grasp,
And I thought of you tonight.

Thoughts about you, thoughts about me,
When we look at each other, do you see what I see.
Pleasant thoughts all of them, of the way things should be,
And I thought of you tonight.

Special thoughts, all thoughts of you,
Your touch, your smile, your eyes so blue.
On my darkest days they come shining through,
And I thought of you tonight.

Danny Stewart

OUT OF YESTERDAY'S LOVE

I hear nature's breath sighing low
through the trees,
a balm for troubled hearts
with the fluttering of leaves.
Although the breeze itself
does not make me blue,
I'm beginning to feel lonely
as it reminds me of you.

I see happy children playing
together in the park,
unaware of those around,
unfriendly and stark.
For tomorrow's heartaches
they have not a clue,
but again I feel sad, they
remind me of you.

I feel a fine mist from the sea on my face
as my haunting memories it
pretends to erase.
In causing my sorrow the
tide has naught to do,
yet I feel so alone for this
reminds me of you.

. . . Suddenly, angels in the
heavens above,
warn, flee while you can, out
of yesterday's love
But their whispers from high
will soon fade away with the
sun's ascension on the last
lonely day.

I smell the pungent fragrance of roses in bloom,
as they bid farewell to my
sorrow-clouded gloom.
Yet, to my despair they will
add nothing new, for this is
the day that I'll finally get over
you.

I taste on this day the early dawn mist,
reminiscing the rapture of the
first time we kissed.
Soft rain begins to fall from
the cotton-swirl sky, like the
tears that I wept after our last
goodbye . . .

. . . The angel of death then
descended from above,
commanding, depart
forevermore . . . out of
yesterday's love.

Danny Stewart

BRONZE STAR EPITAPH ("GOD, LET ME LIVE TO SEE THE SUN COME UP TOMORROW")

Emotions were beginning to soar and morale ebbing low.
In the dark one was heard mumbling, "God, hard to tell friend from foe."

Incoming mortar rounds brought the remark, "Christ, they're getting close enough,"
A tough old sergeant bellered, "Let's show the bastards we too can play rough."

Corporal Copsey fired an illumination flare,
To see just how many enemy troops were there.

The sight beheld sent chills down one's back,
For the enemy was pushing in a human wave attack.

Just at that moment Corporal Copsey caught a round,
Groaning and twitching, he fell to the ground.

A scared green replacement then hurled a grenade,
At the gooks beginning to pour over the sandbag stockade.

The oncoming amassment armed with clubs, rocks and guns,
Were now upon the forty-three dazed Americans.

Confusion and panic were then seen everywhere,
With cries to God for help stammered in prayer.

Memories of back home then flashed thru one's head,
For within the next moments one could likely be dead.

Sorrow and despair began overwhelming the mind,
Brought about by thought of all the things left behind.

Things such as loved ones, prized possessions and life's breath;
All the things left undone that would have better prepared one for death.

Next morning the sun ascended in splendor and bliss,
For a handful of numbed Americans who will forever be tortured by memories of this.

Danny Stewart

THE MOMENT OF NOW

Yesterday teetered between pain and glory,
Then glory deserted—slipped away somehow.
Skeptical and afraid of what life holds tomorrow,
If I could but sweeten the moment of now.

Tomorrow stands forever at the front door of time,
And yesterday is gone—fading from site
The only one here is the moment of now,
Yet, in the morning it will become part of yesterday's flight.

The moment of now will not pass by again,
If it would but be a friend while it is yet here.
Oh God, help me to welcome and trust,
The moment of now without rancor and fear.

—The ultimate reality is the moment of now,
For the Alpha and Omega lie included within.
Serenity comes only from living in the now,
And the following are but suggestions on how to begin.—

1—Concentrate on living one day at a time,
God gives us no less or no more.
We cannot again live in Yesterday,
Or know what tomorrow holds in store.

2—Be grateful for where you are right now,
Not forgetting from where you came.
Having been one of God's fallen kids,
Stand tall and walk without shame.

3—To joyously live in the moment of now,
Is not such an impossible feat . . .
Just turn your will and life over to God,
And then stay out of the driver's seat.

Kay Wepfer

MORN

Hush
Early morning stillness
Lake mirror calm
Warm sun rising
Not a stir
Not a ripple
Not a breeze
Ducks glide in silence
Soaring gull reflected in the water
Cries out to the stillness
Breaks a brand new day!

Kay Wepfer

THUNDERSTORM

Gradually waking in the night
Distant sound, coming closer
A thunderstorm.

More awake, more aware
Wind begins to blow
Blowing hard.

White, blinding lightning
Crackling, crashing thunder
Uneasy feeling.

First few drops of water
Window wet with rain
Downpour!

Less lightning, farther away thunder
Rain letting up
Storm's moved on.

Distant, rolling thunder
Rain dripping from the roof
Sleep again.

Kay Wepfer

AUTUMN TIME

As seasons change
So do our lives
As we all adapt
Once more to nature.

The signs will come
One by one
Fresh, vibrant air
First frost.

A tint of first color
Trees turning day by day
To beautiful brilliance
Before the leaves fall.

Ducks take wing
And soon will leave
They know it's time to go
Instinct tells them all.

As much as we'd like
To cling to warmth and summer
The choice is made for us
We must move on.

Alice Sangiorgio

CIGARETTE

I am a cigarette . . . you're holding me in your hand . . .
I am slowly killing you . . . but, you don't understand . . .
I am looking into your eyes . . . as you puff me away . . .
you're just a fool . . . is what I say . . .
I have a hold on you . . . I am destroying your lungs . . .
I am taking away your breath . . . yet, consciously you're glad we met . . .
I can make you ache . . . if you try to let go . . .
I am stronger than you . . . I want you to know . . .
Keep puffing me away . . . turn me into ashes . . .
In the end . . . I'll get you . . . I'll turn you into ashes too . . . .

Alice Sangiorgio

MASS OF CONFUSION

Mass of confusion . . . this world we live in . . . I fear for our children . . . in this world of greed and sin.

I look at our children . . . oh, God,
what a shame . . . where did it start . . .
Who is to blame.
They're so confused . . . they don't
seem to care . . . lost in their own
world . . . drugs, pot, and beer.
How can we help them . . . is there a
way . . . the future is up to them . . . it
looks awfully gray.
Education is a thing of the past . . .
they're too busy looking for a nickel
worth of grass.
Why such a change . . . in such short
time . . . it wasn't like this . . . when I
was in my prime.
There was respect . . . and fear of
God . . . did parents go wrong . . . by
sparing the rod.
So many questions . . . where are the
answers . . . can we help the children
. . . what are our chances.

Alice Sangiorgio
MY FANTASY
My fantasy is of a world . . . I pray
one day I will see . . .
People may laugh at my
fantasy . . . but, that's alright with
me . . .
I close my eyes . . . and I can
see . . . a world of beauty and
peace . . .
People are laughing and
singing . . . as if they're enjoying a
feast . . .
Little children are playing . . . their
voices so sweet to my ear . . .
Even the animals join them . . . and
there isn't any fear . . .
The trees so tall . . . flowers all
around . . .
Apples from the tree . . . are falling to
the ground . . .
Birds flying down . . . singing their
sweet theme . . .
This is my fantasy . . . this is my
dream.

C Steve Mudery
VISION OF HEARTBREAK
One misty morn, on high hill,
a clouded image, sitting still;
with arms folded, feet there propped,
head hung low, upon a rock;
suddenly he stood, with head to sky,
from his heart, came an anguished
cry;
"Return each promise, return my
dreams,
for now I am alone," he screamed;
"You did not answer my cry of help,
so now and forever, I am by self;"
shoulders trembling, sobs there
heard,
cold, sudden stillness, no more a
word;
tear stained cheeks, emptied of pride,
from scorned love, his will had died;
he then turned, looked upon my face,
but because of mist, I could not
place;
walking to me, with outstretched
hand,
I suddenly recognized this torn man;
for all mist had cleared, and I could
see,
I finally recognized that man as:
me.

C Steve Mudery
OF MY HEART
Within me, there is for you, a
passion of love with gentleness of
heart; this sentiment cannot be
explained, cannot be equaled,
cannot be exceeded; of you, I find
excitement more, comfort most,
serenity greatest; for, as I take to
your arms, come to your embrace,
feel of your person; there comes to
me, a feeling warm, a feeling
belonging, a feeling secure; as my
heart takes me, I become with you;
in senses, in spirit, in existence;
of this, I give forever, love
declared, love absolute,
love devoted; most
of all, I give,
love true.

C Steve Mudery
TWO FEATHERS
This warrior returns to you, Indian
maiden called Two Feathers; and
speak me of this trail, I have tired;
on mount exhausted, atop this hill,
I hang my head; my arrows gone,
my lance broken, my paint smeared,
I stand alone; looking to this vast
world, I think; in battles past, I have
won; in bounty past, I have
gained; in bravery past, I was; now
I wonder of it and question;
its pride, its hope, its worth; still,
shall I again place the paints of
war for love of you; with certainty,
say I yes; as in my exhaustion, you
are still, my wonder, my worth, my
pride; that for which I would die;
say that I may, lest me not
forget, that I shan't; as now I
return never to leave your
side; this being my
last trail.

Jo Ryan
LOVE

This poem is dedicated to John, my love.

Last night I dreamed a dream
And to me it seemed
That I could see
Into eternity.
Happiness was there,
And a calm, blue sky,
And I
With never a Why???
Stepped into
Heaven with you.

Jo Ryan
LITTLE BAG LADY
Little lady with eyes so blue
Who are you??
Where do you come from,
What do you do??
Where do you go,
Who loves you??
You must have had someone,
somewhere,
Someone who loved you, and cared.
Are you hungry?
Where do you sleep??
Your eyes hold dear memories
And thoughts so deep.
I go on my way,
But, my mind stays on you—
Little Bag Lady, with eyes so blue,
Who are you??

Jo Ryan
MY HERO
He stands at bat, eyes so keen
Senses alert, legs bent just so,
Hands firm at grip, all ready,
Body set to go.
Pitcher throws, Batter swings,
Thump of ball in mitt—
That's OK, lots of time
Next one will be it.
Two more pitches, three more balls,
And, another strike.
Now. at three and two, things are
tense—
(He's such a little tyke)
Then, ball is hit, far and true
His team is still alive.
He is my Hero (Grandson Sean)
He is only five.

Earl M Parella
LIFE
Jasons ferret a golden league,
Where claret daily slith' intrigue,
And Fated Three mete fantasy,
But dated-kens nest energy!

Earl M Parella
HUMMINGS OF LIBITINA

A Dedication: Be This Poem Emblazoned On The Poetic Escutcheon Of My Mother, Mary.

—Hum I—
Boughs of toucan cape Gaea's wean,
hie springal couth of Phoenix
yean.
Dapper Faunas hail a plume,
braised by May on verger
loom.
Jacks giggle and fop in silk welkin,
o'er coral thistle and daisy
sequin.
And Ae'lus frays with foamy vril,
lo gley xebecs un' Phosper
thill.

—Hum II—
Peony brocades alack this 'scape,
nigh Thea's wassail of lapis
lake.
Myrtle and tarred vend the snood,
yare Daedals wend in puffin
etude.
Thence Herc', mislay, and Phoebus
'mute,
swaddles of jays to natty
toot.

—Hum III—
Greenlings noddle Nile-blue
splendor,
coo piffy dial and orby
gender.
Prim Rhea trolls hallowed dais,
nee poet myrrh of willowed
'asis.
But velvet is pearled by mead of
Faun,
pique weed for Deys at
Moiran dawn!

Earl M Parella
A BELLEFLY
A bellefly fawns mural Ixtla,
clokes the morn with froth
necta';
Lo jasper bow in grace Nimbus,
pans flower lace thru
Clotho-buss;
Serene Hathor on bristle of myrt',
doth carts the preen of
Cybele-flirt;
Verdant lark nee prime mettle,
belaces all stark from Mors's
mantle;
Votive with main in nymph's
warren—
acclaims this elf of Maia's
holden!

Kristina Metz
ENCHANTING VISIONS
Twirling, twirling
The fairies
Dance in Melody's Locket
Emotions blowing
In the wind

Morris R Smallwood
TAXES

This poem is dedicated to the taxpayer.

I pay income tax to work everyday, and what I got left is called takehome pay.

Then there is city tax, county tax and many more. It's no wonder that a working man is always broke and sore.

Where I stand now my future looks bleak. At the end of my money I've got too much week. Taxes on this, and taxes on that; taxes on my dog, and taxes on my cat.

Taxes on my house, and taxes on my car. Taxes on the corn in my old fruit jar. Taxes on my land, and taxes on my fence. I'd be better off to sell out and rent.

Taxes for living, and taxes for dying; the next thing they will tax is our babies for crying. Where it all will end is a mystery to me. It all started when the King put a tax on our tea.

I've paid so many taxes no money have I got; I spent my life's savings on a cemetery lot. Taxed from the cradle; taxed to the grave. To the ever demanding tax system, I'm just another slave.

Morris R Smallwood
MANDY MY CHILD

To my daughter, Amanda.

Oh Mandy my child, Oh Mandy my
child.
The blue in your eyes, is as blue as
the sky.
And nothing on this Earth is as sweet
as
your smile, and Oh how I love you
Mandy my child.

When God sent you to me I wanted a
son.
But you filled my life with laughter
and fun.
The first time I held you my heart
swelled
with pride. And I loved you more as
time passed on by.

I watched you grow into a woman
from a child.
And I held you close each time you
cried,
and now I've grown old and you're
far away.
But I still have the memories of those
sweet yesterdays.

Morris R Smallwood
THE MOCKINGBIRD

To my wife, Darlene and my children Jonathan and Amanda.

A gay and happy fellow. Go lucky and carefree. As he sits outside my window in a silver maple tree.

He wakes me every morning. With his warbles and his trills. When dawn's first lights are showing. As the Sun comes over the hill.

He sings his own sweet medleys, and the songs of other birds. And the sweetness of his singing, I can't describe in words.

As I watch him through my window. And listen to his songs, he looks so proud and graceful. Like a King upon his throne.

And I like to think his singing is meant for only me. As he sits outside my window. In the silver maple tree.

Julia M Colon
I DREAMT
And in my dream I was an eagle,
Strong, swift, serene,
Scouting the limitless horizon,
To all eyes a majestic emblem
Of strength and cunning.

And as I glided
On the currents of the Winds
I observed, hardly being observed,
The glory of God's creation.
And it sustained me that an Eagle,
So unlike the peaceful Dove,
Was also part of God's creation.

Vigilant slumber
Followed my dream, and I wished,
I wished and hoped
That man would be able to see at last,
That, like the Eagle and the Dove,
Man could also traverse
Frontiers of Time and Space
Unburdened, unshackled by
intolerance:
As an equitative factor in God's
creation.

Julia M Colon
AS ONE LISTENS
Bewitching paradox:
Silence speaks
Through the explicit and the implicit
noises
Within the written and the spoken
Sign.
Linguistic silence:
Words, sentences, phrases,
paragraphs
Coalescing into Ideas,
Whispering, whistling, roaring,
Moving Minds and Hearts.

As one listens
To the explosion and the implosion
Of phonemes and allophones,
Of vowels and consonants
Breaking linguistic boundaries,
One can, then, hear the silent
coalescing
Of langue and langage
Into Reason.

How heart-rendering the silent
upheaval
Within the written and the spoken
Sign
Can be, when used to pave
The Dialogue of Man's
Understanding.

Julia M Colon
THE GOLDEN RULE
It is Christmas Eve in Puerto Rico
And no one rests.
From noon onwards,
Hands laden with presents and sweet
morsels
Start arriving.
Tired feet,
Traumatized by bumper-to-bumper
traffic
And by avenues rapidly becoming
Static parking lots,
Keep straggling in,
Safely keeping to the Golden Rule
Of the Puerto Rican matriarch:
Everyone will be Home
On Christmas Eve.

Freudian homicidal desires,
Latent through the antithesis
Of a Modern commercialized Society
Heavily rooted on Ancient customs,
Slowly ebb away
When Christmas Eve
Officially Dies on the stroke of
midnight.

Julia M Colon
WATCH
White cone
Of dormant fire
Shivering under a cold sun
Slim sides sweating detritus
Into the rice paddies
Of the valley.

Figures
Mere outlines
Under conical hats
Stamping seedlings
On unseen furrows.

Rectangles
Of earthen soil
Alive in a liquid habitat
Germinating
Golden spikes of grain.

Harvest
Serenely waiting
Reflecting shadows of live movement
Under the benign watch
Of the sacred mountain.

Princess Mar EKJ Garit Mandalionmfgco King ALT (M E Shriver)

Princess Mar EKJ Garit Mandalionmfgco King (M E Shriver)
IN STEP
Left, right we've got the heart—a
march always called us together with
a good start.
Together we only are parted and
together we only start.
Left, right is joining together in—we
go without sin.
For Almighty God is our Captain—
we have our march El Capatain
as has always been.

We love one another.
That is why you cannot break us in
giving, Mr. Souther.
We will always march as given in the
Bible.
There is a statement we'll march
together to Heaven, Tribal.

We only change.
When the Holy Father is in range.
Right, left then.
For we listen to Almighty God words
through him and march without sin.
A new soldier joined the march.
Jesus Christ reached out as to us
before he reached the Arch.
The soldier stood and did not extend
to Jesus Christ extended hand.
As the music of the march was
played by the band.

He was out of step with us and life.
Seeing that now is the time he
acknowledged Jesus Christ in this
breaking step march strife.
We noticed peace and a smile on his
face.
As seems to always be as us the case.

Left, right we now all march in step
with the right heart.

Wendy J Rochette
THEY SAY MONEY DOESN'T MATTER

This poem is dedicated to Todd M. Kepshire, without whose support and encouragement I would still be "unknown." All my love forever . . . .

They say money doesn't matter,
nor do
material things. The only thing that
matters are the feelings in between.
In between two people, the laughter
in the rain. The tears upon his
shoulder; the
sorrow and the pain.
The places you go together and
the little things you do. Like walking
hand in hand and saying I Love
You.
The special times alone, sitting
quietly side by side. The hours
spent on the phone that seem to fly
right by.
Awkwardness in the beginning,
feeling kind of shy; wanting to trust
and take a chance hoping it's
not just a lie.
Getting to know one another and
getting "butterflies"—
These are the things that matter, and
many, many more.
So you see it shouldn't matter if
one's richer or one's poor.

Wendy J Rochette
TO SEE YOU AGAIN WAS ALL THAT I'D HOPED FOR
To see you again was all that
I'd hoped for,
But now that it's happened I feel
worse than before.
All I could do was to think of
you, each and every day.
To remember the feelings that we
shared together, the
memories fading away.
The tears beginning to cease, fewer
and far between.
Still longing to have you back
in my life,
but knowing it's all just a dream.
But seeing you once again, so
close yet so out of reach.
The feelings came back rushing over
me,
just like the waves on a sandy
beach.
Alone I sit here spilling out feelings
that shall never even age.
The tears slipping slowly down my
cheeks,
splashing gently onto this page.
I'm still very deeply in love with you,
even though you will never
know.
You'll be in my heart forever and
ever
because I just can't let you go.

Wendy J Rochette
MEETING YOU HAS MADE ME REALIZE
Meeting you has made me
realize, things aren't as bad as they
seem through my eyes.
I feel as if I'm important to you,
but I'm just not sure that you feel as I
do.
You are everything I've been
looking for,
all wrapped into one.
You are everything I've been
dreaming of,
my life has just begun.
We are becoming closer
friends,
I don't want this part to ever end—
No matter what happens other
than this,
even if it's more than a simple kiss.
As each day goes by, I think of
you more,
I've never thought of anyone this
much before.
I just can't get you out of my
mind.
I wish we could be together all of the
time.
I hope that you know, even
though it is wrong,
my feelings for you are growing
strong.
There's only one thing in our
way,
but maybe, just maybe,
someday . . . someday.

Wendy J Rochette
I KNOW THAT THINGS ALWAYS SEEM TO BE WORSE
I know that things always seem
to be worse than they really are.
But to tell you the truth things
have never seemed to be this bad so
far.
My days are gray; never blue
The secrets inside I can never tell
you.
My nights are long filled with
tormented dreams.
The reality of life is in full
extreme.
Death and despair haunting every
corner.
I don't think I've ever felt more alone
here.
No one to turn to; nowhere to go.
Just the bitter winds and the
billowing snow.
Depression sets in like a weight
I can't lift.
Now just as the snow—I'm
beginning to drift.

Deborah Hancock Leslie
THE ROPE

Dedicated to my one and only love, the man who breathes life into me and makes me feel complete. Loving "more than yesterday, less than tomorrow" . . . Thomas James Wortmann.

She's a lifeline,
She finds herself being held firmly by
two sets of strong hands at both ends
Sometimes, she wonders if she can be
twisted into a hangman's noose,
But, who'll be the one

to hang?
Most of the time she's twisted and
doesn't know which way to unravel.
Once she does straighten out . . . does
she tie a knot at the end she faces?

This rope finds herself in a tug of
war,
A war of love, seemingly without
end.
Not only hands, but hearts are at each
end,
Hearts that would break, if the hold
were broken.

Her fiber is tearing,
Her existence is questioned,
Is there yet another set of hands in
God's universe that would hold her
frayed strands more gently?
If only those other
hands weren't fastened
so tightly!

Should she break loose of the tug of
war and bury herself in the pit below?
Just to salvage her
sanity?
Too many times this rope has had to
choose which way to bend . . .
Too many times she has been
disappointed by the hands she
trusted . . .
Too many times this rope has had to
ask to be folded and treated tenderly,
Instead of the hands knowing
the right things to do.
She finds herself left in bunches
needing the gentle untangling . . . that
never comes.
So, the unraveling rope
unconsciously develops a coating of
armor, to prepare for the rough tugs.

But, when the right set of hands tries
to gently hold her, will the armour
fend him away?
Will she notice the whisper of his
touch?
Or will she be holding her breath,
clenching her teeth, awaiting yet
another rough tug . . .
And miss the gentle yearning
message being rendered toward her?

This rope has to learn to be pliable.
Pliable, but with regrown fibers,
where she was torn in the past.
The regrown fibers hope to be woven
in facing the future, not the aching
memories of the past . . .
To allow the yet unknown hands to
stroke her gently into the bliss of lost
restraint!
Gently working the armor off her and
encouraging her to glow in his love!

Let the tug of war end,
And go on with life feeling
enthusiasm and joy!
Knowing that both ends are tended
by the same gentle source.
Woven into a circle of
existence . . . together,
Instead of two ends left dangling
in search of peace.

Deborah Hancock Leslie

IS IT LOVE?

Scent
Glance
Shy aversion
Brace for rejection and glance again

Shy smile
Shock at returned smile
Meander nearer
Hi!
Small talk
Drinks
Dance—No?

Talk
Talk
Touch

Wait for a call
Shy again
Persistence
Yes!

Dinner
Talk
Touching

Suddenly a couple
Sweet passion
Two become one and life is
wonderful

Months pass sweetly
"Forever" talk

"Busy"
Wait for a call
Worry
Why?

Deborah Hancock Leslie

HOLIDAY THOUGHTS

Holiday celebrations are all around
us!
As Irish Coffee and Eggnog will
flow.
Yet, all year round, when I'm near
you, Tom darling,
I cherish our love, and I glow!

As I think of Christ as a newborn,
As innocent and gentle as He was,
I think of our future little ones,
And the happiness and joy they'll
bring us.

Future Christmases I anticipate with
fervor,
Since, by then, together we'll be!
Making memories of fun and holiday
flavor,
Through yuletide seasons for all
eternity.

I see Santa sneaking up on our little
ones,
Tami, Kate, Tommy and Jackie, too!
Delivering booty to squeals of joy
and laughter,
As they struggle to find out if Santa's
YOU!

Making memories with you,
Full of snowangels, snowforts, and
more!
Christmas songs on your harmonica!
Baking goodies and wrapping gifts
galore!

How I adore you, my darling Tom,
And sharing this Christmas holiday,
Watching you sleep in my arms so
peacefully,
You're more full of life and love each
day.

Wherever we are at Christmas next
year,
Renting, building or traveling the far
seas,
My holiday spirit lies within you,
Since you are everything to me.

Jesus teaches to love all mankind,
Peace on Earth and Goodwill to all
men!
Our future holds such joy and
splendor,
I wait with baited breath until then!
Merry Christmas, Tom, my darling,
I love you with all of my heart!!!
Let's have patience and
understanding of God's will,
And strength that, with His help,
we'll never part.

Deborah Hancock Leslie

BLUE?

Why should I feel "BLUE"?????
Being blue means depressing things.
. . . Sickness and misery . . .
. . . Not enough money . . .
. . . No man to wrestle with at
night . . .
. . . No job to go to every day . . .
. . . No home to receive and comfort
me at night . . .
. . . No place to keep my
"stuff" . . .
. . . No friends to cry or brag
with . . .
. . . No books to read . . .
. . . No laughing, kidding and
yukking into the night . . .
. . . No kids to raise . . .
. . . No boats, horses, motorcycles,
planes or mountaintops . . .
. . . No you . . .
Therefore, no life!!

Now that I think about it, I can't feel
blue,
When I think of you,
I feel iridescent!!

Frieda Barrett

A VISIT FROM MY GRANDSON

Dedicated to Aaron Colter Smith.

In my heart I still can hear
Your footsteps down the hall.
Sounds of laughter while you play,
Now echo from the walls.

I wander through the empty house,
And cry a few more tears.
Everywhere I look, I see,
Reminders you were here.

The shirt you wore the day you left,
Lies crumpled in the floor.
A sock I found beneath a chair,
Your shoe behind the door.

And as I go about my tasks,
And put your toys away,
Each one in its proper place,
To await another day.

Until the time that two small hands,
Will play with them in fun.
The house will once more show the
signs,
Of a visit from my grandson.

Frieda Barrett

THE ELUSIVE BUTTERFLY

She sleeps upon a velvet bed,
her pillow of delicate lace.
Her carpet, fluff of the dandelion,
In her secret hiding place.

In daytime you can see her,
Kissing flowers as she goes.
At night, don't try to find her,
Where she sleeps, nobody
knows.

The sun comes up in the morning,
She appears to greet the world.
Glistening in the early light,
The iridescence of a pearl.

Flutters on the waning breeze,
Wing outstretched in flight.
Her splendor decorates the day,
But where does she go at night?
The mystery remains her secret,
She appears in her beauty, then
dies.
Don't look for her after the sunset,
The nights have no butterflies.

Frieda Barrett

LOST

I traveled down a long, long road,
in search of something lost,
Tired and weary, all in vain,
but still I'd pay the cost.

The most important thing to me,
was left somewhere behind.
I could not go on with my life,
until I found what's mine.

So I walked the lonely roads,
climbed the rugged mountains,
Searched neath waters of the deep,
gazed in bubbling fountains.

Wandered thru the darkest woods,
took each worn out trail.
Cried, because I could not find,
for it was hidden well.

Then in prayer, I bowed my head,
What was my fate to be?
The search was over, I had found,
What had been lost to me.

Frieda Barrett

THE BRIAR ROSE

Lonely grows the small wild rose,
That blooms in summertime.
Deep among the briars it lives,
Forever trapped, entwined.

Never free to grow alone,
Its beauty always hidden.
Doomed to live among the briars,
A place of its own forbidden.

Many a story has been told,
Of why the rose grows wild,
Some tell of a beauty unsurpassed,
Essence, the soul of a child.

Some say it's the heart of an Indian
maid,
Who mourns the loss of a love.
And chose to live in dark shadows,
To hide from the world above.

So few have ever seen the rose,
Another old mountain story?
If you believe, look deep in the
briars,
You'll find it in all its glory.

Nancy Greco Talamo

THE SEASONS OF MAN

Spring makes earth a fertile plain,
It brings warm sun and gentle rain.
So, man is born in this same way,
His life begins like a spring day.
Just as nature, greens and grows,
The babe becomes a child who
knows.

Summer brings the bud to flower,
The boy is now a man of power,
His season of glory, his finest hour.
He lives, he loves, and fulfills
desires,
He's like a machine that never tires.

Autumn comes, the earth is brown,
Trees and flowers lose their crown.
And, so, man too sheds his vitality,
For him, life is no longer reality.
He dreams of the past, and cries in
rage,
For he's closer to writing the final
page.

Winter strips the earth, and lays it bare,
He too stands alone, with no one to care.
He waits in silence, draws his final breath,
His seasons are over, it's time for his death.

Nancy Greco Talamo
I'LL LOVE YOU UNTIL . . .
I'll love you until my life will be no more,
And I am standing at heaven's door.
Until my heart makes not a sound,
And I am lying in the ground.

I'll love you until the mountains fall into the sea,
And the earth ceases to be.
Until the ocean stops its roar,
And the eagle can no longer soar.

I'll love you until the stars forget to shine,
And the planets fall out of line.
Until the sun becomes stone cold,
And every story has been told.

I'll love you until the seasons seem all the same,
And all that is wild becomes tame.
Until the birds lose their wings,
And the nightingale no longer sings.

I'll love you until the deserts have no more sand,
And the oceans become dry land.
Until my body loses all desire,
And my soul doesn't feel the fire.

Nancy Greco Talamo
DREAM LOVE

To my husband, Ernest—our love has endured for better, for worse, for eternity. To love, to live, to be as one; is all that matters when life is done.

I see you as in a dream through misty eyes,
You hold me close and whisper lover's lies.
Your soft caresses, melt heart and soul,
Before you, I was half, but now I'm whole.
Our eyes meet, and with your glance,
You hold me still, as in a trance.
My heart is pounding like the ocean's roar,
And only you can set it free and let it soar.
Yet, I know, that I and I alone,
Can pierce your heart, your heart of stone.
Your kisses sweet and tender,
Ask of me, complete surrender.
So I concede, and to you reveal,
The feelings that to others I conceal.
Why is love such a mystery?
This has been asked throughout history.
How can it burn like a blazing fire,
Yet, bring peace like a paid desire.
But all too soon the dawn arrives and brings the light,
Gone are the fantasies of the night!

Nancy Greco Talamo
AN APOLOGY

To my boss, Joe Alonzo, the "best boss" of all. For all the apologies left unsaid, I dedicate this one to you.

Words gone wrong bring so much sorrow,
Which lingers on into tomorrow.
Words can cut deeper than a knife,
They can cause dissension and strife.
If I could go back, and my words erase,
I would quickly do it, and in their place,
Give a gentler, sweeter reply,
And, with your wishes I would comply.
I would speak words to give your heart a tug,
And, follow my words with a kiss and a hug.
For only this, and this would do,
To fully express my remorse to you.
I'm asking you to forgive and forget,
For we all have sinned, and yet . . .
I know it's a difficult thing to do,
But, this is what I ask of you.
Life is short, and flies by with haste,
Each moment too precious to squander and waste.
So, to you I extend my heart and my hand,
Please say you forgive me and understand.

Patricia Vick
GOLDEN GOWNS
In the dawn of the morning I'll remember you best,
when the sun's first rays caress my face.
When the damp first rises from off the ground,
and the calm is alive with brand-new life.

In the dusk of the evening I'll remember you best,
when the night things move and find no rest.
When the night birds fly,
and the dark is alive with the strength of their cries.

In the Autumn of the year I'll remember you best,
when the trees are robed in their golden gowns.
When the birds are aflight,
and the hills are alive with the sound of their song.

Patricia Vick
DADDY'S ARMS

I thought of you today and smiled when I heard a baby's cry, when I looked upon her tiny face and saw the sleepy in her eyes. When I saw that defiant fist curled into a ball and spied those puckered lips so sweet, I thought of her astride your lap, a joyful bundle, soft and warm, safe in Daddy's arms.

As I fondly watched her sleep that sleep with not a care in the world, I imagined her lying atop your chest with every charm of a little girl. I can see her resting quietly there as her baby's breath caresses your fur. I can tell you're afraid that she will fall, but I have no fear of the sort. You're instantly aware of the slightest sigh, and she's safe in Daddy's arms.

Hours later when you're both asleep, I gaze lovingly at the sight, the handsome man and the silken child, molded by sleep into one. I enfold her gently and lay her down amid cottony blankets and toys. She's the flawless result of a perfect union of two instruments finely tuned. I lie awake throughout the night thinking of the miracle there. And I have no cause to ever fear—because I'm safe in her daddy's arms.

Dariusz Wiecha
UNTITLED
Judas
turned out to be
quite okay
he was a patriot
he had time
to make confession
to everybody
and I am sure
before his canonization
he will give a few pieces
of silver
for The Crucified Christ
Foundation

Dariusz Wiecha
A STREETCAR ALREADY NAMED
thoughts sat on the level of eyes
they dropped on hands feet a floor
sometimes they slipped off into the window
to come back at once to the face

after two minutes she was my friend
after the first stop my mistress
after the second one I made her my wife
then a mother of my children

we grew old somehow together
when she had died before me
and I gave her a handful of soil

it appeared that I was looking
just at the seat full of wrinkles
like the last thoughts

Pamela N Accetta
POSTLUDE
White curtains shine through her hair
and he the rope that drapes it back

Herbal vapors rise to deepen
the thickness of the room
following a night of blooming fury
which gives unwanted sight

A rusty magnet pulls her hair
upon his lofty flesh of coal
Weeds arise from boiling skin
They wilt—but one remains to tour
the hour of voiceless eyes

The weed is left inside
breathing a living death

Pamela N Accetta
PRELUDE
A symphony of headless
players—an orchestrated image
Guitar strings play loudly now

Dressed in silk and dressed in black
they trudge (to walk in a laborious,
heavy-footed way) through the
poison fields of snow flowers

Flowers are tramps who stagger and
await the falling hole

Gracefully walking symphonic
beats—arms stretched out and high
above carry a shoebox steady
Inside there is a seed dressed in linen
shroud

Step a long way to the rectangular sea
Palms to navigate and nails to paddle
the encompassing figurine

Steps coincide with the lofty snow,
muffle those shrieks from the cloth of
milk below

Orchestra gaining coverage closer to
the open prism

Frustration is the wind who flies
angry at the sea
An overwhelming force that breaks
the shoebox
from the hands that carry the fruit

into the lines connecting the dots

The tramps will flower their way
into the box forever echoing quiet.

Claudetta M Queen
THE NEARNESS OF YOU
There you are again across the room
watching me from near
and a far away place. Where, there is
only you and I and
our love; is entwined as is our arms
and minds. Only the
nearness of you bleeds my heart.
Once joined, never to part.

There you are again, at an arm's
length away. Longing to
take me; take me I pray. Into the
world where loving you
is all I have left to do. Be patient my
darling, our love
will grow. Only the nearness of you
will make it show.

There you are again touching my
hand, longing to hold me
in your arms so strong. To feel our
hearts beating on the wall.
The blood flowing as tears from our
eyes, so cold. See
only into each other to beg for our
lives; Dear heart
forgive me I just want to die.

There you are again smiling at me,
willing your love to me
on down the line. Walk with me until
the end of time.
Because there is no tomorrow and all
we have is yesterday,
But now it's gone. I know dearest
love who thou art.
Only the nearness of you stops my
heart.

Claudetta M Queen
DREAMING
Away, away my love to sail the
heavens high
Tender is the heart that comes near
by
The great wind moria comes from
afar, to rustle the wings
of heaven's stars. Walking along the
way of mice and men;
To be counted upon now and then.
Do love me dear heart I
beg of you—come; hold me tender
and near. Softly whisper
the words I long to hear.

Alone am I in the night, dreaming of
you with all my might.
I'll never forget your eyes so warm,
to look upon me with
all your charm, Come to me my
gentle one and hold me tender,
lest I be afraid. Your strength and
courage I need to exist;
For my heart is weak and gone amiss.
Someday my love, my dreams of you
will become real and true. Lonely no
more,
will I be, only because my true love
found me.

Nancy Helman Shneiderman
THE PENDULUM (ON FACING MY HYSTERECTOMY AND FINDING MY VOICE)
There, inside my loins internal
Darkly, I, a soul eternal

Scan the depths for
dawning light.

How can I, a woman born,
BE, after my womb is
shorn?
Can this razored road
be right?

Bearing down to keen and pray
Soon released, I find a
way
To float within the
fluid night.

Finally, a note is sounded
To my pelvic anchor
grounded
Soaring high, kite-like.

Threaded through the breath-canal
Trumpeting a joyous
howl
Freely blows delight.

Triumph flows where once despair
Joined this sacred earth
to air
Metamorphosing the
Tomb
I will chant to GAIA'S
womb.

Nancy Helman Shneiderman
MY PRAYER (IN THANKS AFTER MY HYSTERECTOMY)

And, afterwards; the calm.
Oboes woo the woooded distance
But then; sacred clarity
Focus exquisitely full
following that fear-filled
foreboding
within the dark, rudderless gale
before.

And now, I am yet whole
And now, my hol-i-ness within
perhaps,
and strangely more complete.
This paradox, in DEED, so sweet.

Double-reed deep resonations
Circles radiate. Still sensations,
flower from the core.
Source spring growing
Free springs flowing more
and more and more.

Waves and rhythms, crossing tides
On the surface, deep inside,
Internal, external
may my healing prayer diurnal
float
in praise
of
HER.

Ruth Walcott
HOT SOUP

To Corby Ellis.

You'll never know how much I
appreciate
Your homemade chicken soup that I
ate!
It was hot and fresh with dumpling
surprise
A taste superb of spice and herb
And best of all, although I can, I did
not cook!
Thanks a lot! What a neighbor, I've
got!

Susan Elise Hervey
A PIECE OF THE MIRROR

To those who have struggled, questioned or wondered if one faith is "right," how could God let so many people be "wrong" in their belief!

Once upon a time, God had a mirror,
He called religion.
As He was lowering it down to the
people of the earth
He accidentally dropped it.
It fell, shattered into fragments.

Different people found the pieces
And claimed that their piece was
"right"; the only true, real one.
People began to compare their pieces
Each piece was different: jagged,
smooth or even cracked.
No piece was exactly the same,
And because they each thought they
were right,
The people never tried to put the
pieces together.
And so, each piece reflects a religion
And is an image of the whole.
None of them, and all of them
Are right.

Therese Garrison
IMAGINE

Imagine yourself adrift at sea—
on the calm bluegreen waters of
tranquility.
Feel the wind blow softly through
your hair,
the sunshine upon your head. Birds
flying high in the sky.
Their song of freedom echoes
wild and so full of zest.
Imagine yourself flowing in the sea
of life . . .
One much further and deeper than
meets the eye.
See the reflection of yourself upon
the ocean.
Feel the cool crisp waters run gently
through your fingers. Lay back, enjoy
as the day slowly drifts into night.
See the lady in love with the moon.
Count the stars that clutter the sky,
soon they become part of your eyes.
Your life's obsessions . . . like the
lady in love with the moon.
As the night comes to an end, so does
your dream of tranquility.
You wake to find yourself engulfed
in the arms of much love.
There is where your peace and
freedom lay, softly upon your pillow
in the sea of love . . . just imagine.

Kim Hunter
WHISPERS IN THE WIND

Whispers in the wind
Fleeting as they're spoken
People often talk
While promises are broken
Blowing through the night
On the wings of a silent sparrow
Running through the trees
As the world begins to narrow
No one ever knows
Where these whispers go
Are they soaked up with the rain
Or buried in the snow?
Maybe they just remain
In the memory of the beholder
Are people feeling happiness
Or are they getting colder?

Anne Stenhouse
THERE IS A PLACE WHERE I CAN GO

There is a place where I can go.
The clear, the quiet, the serene,
dominate
There is a place where the waves
synchronize,
rustle and sedate.
The breeze touches the cheek bare.
The golden sun brushed with
tangerine and blue
Warms the senses,
That with time have become cold,
Jagged and subdued.
A smile creeps across the face,
Without realizing it so.
Tranquility descends, floating, peace,
In letting go the old.
There is a place where once again
Wishing makes it so.
I close my eyes, Simply, on a whim.
There is a place where I can go.

Julie A Smith
FINALLY GONE

Icy raindrops soaked her golden
locks,
and moisture dripped from her hair.
Wetness fell around her as well,
with drenched leaves of trees
everywhere.

She walked alone through the forest,
and disturbed the path of silence.
She hesitantly glanced around the
dimness,
and frightened herself with every
turn.

She needed to run from them,
but wanted the security of home.
They said they loved her yesterday,
but today they beat her again.

They will scream and violently yell,
if she stays a moment longer.
They will whip and punish her,
but now she has finally gone.

Melba Ann Spray Rosser
REFLECTIONS

This poem was inspired by my deep love for my sister, Geney Stan, and is dedicated to her in appreciation for the countless ways she has enriched my life.

White laced clouds veil the moon—
But the silver light shines through,
Cutting a perfect circle, creating
its own rainbowed halo.

I drink moonbeams and imagine you,
watching too;
Then . . . catching the love I'm
sending.
It rides on streams of light, glowing,
growing—
Across artificial time zones, haunted
Navaho deserts
And hallowed violet mountains,
Gaining momentum until it finds you
and soothes
Your troubled heart.

Physical distance separates our
bodies,
Though nothing can split apart our
souls—
Kindred in fact of birth, but more in
spirit.
Forgetting for once my selfish cares,
I fly—
Willing you to feel me with you and
to dream
The sweetest of peaceful dreams.

Amy Miller
AMY'S LIGHT

For Amy Andon, in memory of her Grandmother, my Godmother, Bettina.

Amy has her Grandma's eyes, her
soul comes shining through,
I've seen those eyes before you see,
they smile at me through you.

Her inner beauty still lives on, so
tender and so dear,
It's now there in Amy's eyes, and it
keeps her near.

Now did you ever guess my friend,
that as one looks at you,
That light within you charms us so, a
light so old, so new.

Thank you for just being there, and
making our lives rich,
For you have turned an empty space
into a happy niche.

Linda F Cleare
YOUR BEST SELF

This poem is dedicated to my wonderful mom, Frances M. Self.

Never be a show
The clue is be you, and know;
you can stand;
head erect, conscience
Free, with self-respect . . . .

George M Knipper
YOUR LIFE DEPENDS UPON GOD'S GOOD TREES

Dedicated to my father Joseph and my wife Marian.

Your life depends upon God's good
trees
He made these plants so you could
breathe
You want to live and so do they
So let them live in their own good
way.
They stand in the forest from morn to
nite
They do no harm, but everything
right.
Life like yours flows beneath their
bark
They work and build in light and
dark
So keep in mind, words like these
"Your life depends upon God's good
trees"

Cyndi Fitzpatrick
WHAT CHILD IS THIS

For Brett.

I see the hurting in his eyes, as he
walks in through the door.
This child so sweet and innocent,
can't hide it anymore.
"What's wrong?" I ask him as he
stops, then wanders up to me.
"Oh nothing," he bravely says. But
the pain is clear to see.
This child of love; of two parents
born, is now a child of pain.
Because the grown-ups never learned
just how to play the game.

Then who's the one to pay the price,
in this game of who hurts who?
Who makes the rules? Who sets the pace? To see if "I hurt you?"
And as he grows, and lives and learns
the ups and downs of life,
Do we grown-ups teach the child,
that we live to fuss and fight?
This child was born of love and hope,
but where are those dreams now?
Hidden somewhere deep inside
this child we love and adore.

Jacob Wilson Robinson
LOVE WEATHER-WISE
You seem reluctant to recall the day
When promises you made were
Sunrise new;
When Dawning love bespoke a
lifelong way
Of Fair and Warmer, unbroken sky of
blue.
Devoted acts, and words sincerely
spoken
Brought joy within my heart as
Sunny noon;
So many things avowed, but to be
broken:
For, Storm-clouds blocked out Sun,
and Love, too soon.

So few the hours we laughed and
cried together,
Sharing blame and praise in wrong or
right:
Love's Day didn't know of Stormy
Weather;
We did not reckon each day has a
night.

Our Day is done . . . The Sun was
just a spark:
And, Love has set . . . leaving me in
the Dark.

(The Sun was but a spark)

Ernie Gray
A LOBSTER ON EVERY PLATE
The mundane auto license plate
Was never meant to decorate.
Its attachment only showed
That one had paid to use the road.

But state by state, there's grown a
trend
To let these plates a message send.
Logos, mottos, sayings bright,
Some profound, others trite.

But none of them will ever beat
What I just saw go down the street.
The State of Maine has topped the
nation
With the picture of a dead crustacean.

Barbara Vonbaltzer
NO CHOICE
A little child was made to choose
Whose love he'd keep, whose love
he'd lose
This made his little heart so sad
For he loved mom and he loved dad

His little mind could not see how
Why he should choose, oh! No, not
now
So in his prayers he prayed that night
Please God, let me do this right

I can't leave mom, for she needs me
I'm her little man, that you can see
And dad, I can't leave him just now,
Without him I'd never learn how

To do the things I've seen him do
Like fixing things to look like new
I love them both so very dear
Please dear God, make them hear

No I can't choose, so they'll have to
But I wish they'd talk this over first
with you
You'd set them straight and make
them see
I need them both to be with me.

Connie L Gauronski
CRADLE ME
Mystical whispers of nighttime
draw me closer

I hold back—not willing to relinquish
my last hold on the day's pleasures.

Then, like a small child
curling in its mother's arms,

I let myself slowly fade
into the gentle cradle of sleep.

Lavern S Walker
LOOKING FOR SOMEONE
I saw this man just standing there,
With evil eyes and black flowing
hair,
It was Satan, There was no disguise,
I could tell by the evil look in his
eyes,
He was waiting on some souls to
take,
And made sure there would be no
mistake,
He looks for the sad weak and poor,
And even at the rich man's door,

Mabel Stubblefield
EVENINGS TIDE
Have you ever heard night fall,
Or, have you ever heard dawn crack?
It's funny, it's the day that breaks,
As the earth turns, but never back.

Have you ever watched night fall,
As day ends and the sun slowly
sinks?
Shadows of night are soon upon you,
Turning day into night, blink by
blink.

Lights spring on in homes around
you,
North, South, East and West,
There's the hush of night o'er the
land,
Heaven and earth are seeking rest.

Sure enough, late some evening,
Sit outside and watch night fall.
You might hear a little bird twitter,
Or, maybe a whip-o-will call.

Yes, it's nice to get quiet and listen,
After one has worked all day.
It's really a good time to thank the
Lord,
He has helped us in so many ways.

Jeannine A Harris
THIS BOY

To John and my children who encouraged me.

Did you ever look around to find
That someone is following right
behind?
So you make a face hoping he will
go,
But he shakes his head and tells
you "NO."
You walk along and he's such a pain
'Cause he's screeching and
pretending he's a train.
You stop and tell him to go away.
He sticks out his tongue and
continues to play.
You're getting mad and stomping
your foot;
He smiles and shouts, "Root-a-
tooty-toot-toot."
You're fuming and just about ready
to yell,
When he looks at you and asks,
"Are you well?"
"Now what?" You ask yourself as
you steam.
"Is this for real or is it a
dream?"
Look at him, he's so concerned and
sad;
Now, aren't you ashamed you
ever got mad?

Debi A Krall
ALWAYS

This poem is dedicated to my husband, Scott. Separated, we knew only of loneliness. Now, together bound, we found the fulfillment of our lives.

To my Lover
To my Friend
You'll always be a part of Me
To the final End.

We have our share of Problems
As all Partners do
Let's keep an open Mind
Maybe . . . We'll learn something
New.

To share our Lives together
To rejoice, as the new day appears
To know that we woke up
Beside the one that's Dear.

To hold these precious Feelings
So deep in our Hearts
and . . .
The memories, of our first Kiss
and . . .
How it kindled our Spark.

Karen A Verniers
HAPPY ANNIVERSARY

This poem is dedicated to Mom and Dad, National Park, NJ.

We wish you two,
The very best on this day.

Much happiness and joy,
Coming your way.

You've been there for us,
So many, many times.

And we want to give back,
The time you've given us.

To share this happy occasion,
With the ones we love.

Paul Oral Blanton
MAXIMUM HIGH

I would like to dedicate this poem to: To POWs/MIAs.

There were long vapor trails up in the
sky,
Criss crossing others that slowly
would die,
When a lone parachute burst into
view,
Floating in front of a background of
blue.

Miles from "MIG Alley" jet fighters
had strayed
Up over Chang Song, where POWs
stayed,
Pursuing the MIGs across the Yalu;
Dropping wing tanks in a background
of blue.

Death had reluctantly sounded
retreat,
Jealously watching two cotton-soled
feet
Kiss, again, earth — making plans to
renew
Dogfighting under a background of
blue.

Suddenly, sunlight attracted the eye,
Bouncing off tree tops that tickle the
sky,
Where sat a Sabre Jet, shining like
new!
Clawing some height from a
background of blue.

Thundering home with a smile on his
face,
Gratefully welcomed by Freedom's
embrace;
Mission accomplished, "unfriendlies"
subdued,
Maximum high for his Red, White
and Blue.

Jerome Alan
EXPERIENCE

To those who learned right from wrong and act accordingly, and they who taught them. And to Pearl, for all that she is and shall be.

It took so long to realize that we were
in control of our lives,
By the time we did, we weren't,
Ends the circle of youths journeys at
the gulf of bridges burnt,
Feel the poignant touch of
sorrow in the lessons we have
learnt,
Sense the pity in the tragic way the
acts of life arranged,
To scourge us with our
memories of things we could

have changed,
In retrospect, opposed to pondered,
finding life was what we'd squandered,
Toward this truth we vaguely wandered, while yet at liberty to dream.
Like the caterpillars passing, to make way for butterflies,
How essential that it is to learn to live, before you learn to die.
The answer lies within the how, not in the question why,
To put to rest commitments made in ignorance, void of bliss.
Intrepid in the wonder of the vision truth restores,
Resolve yourself to smile, dance and sing a little more.
To laugh harder, longer, quicker than we ever have before,
Autumn's colours, there in summer, it is we who fail to see.

Andrea M Bensadoun
CALLING THIS HOME

Dedicated to the memory of my grandmother, Frances Shprintz. Anyone who had the privilege to have their life touched by her, was truly blessed.

Quietly I sit, while I listen to the roar of the thunder
Each drop of rain tapping sequentially
Against the pane
The night is full of sound
Strays have found shelter
In a warm, secluded place
They'll call home for the night
The wait for daybreak must seem an eternity
But it will come
It always does
On nights like this
Not quickly enough
For the morning will bring
All that is new
Leaving yesterday far behind

Heidi Lynne
DREAM REALITY
It's dark in the escape palace
the lights are glowing red
and drawn out cat eyes are narrowed
at a sexual innuendo someone said

The stuff that dreams are made of
is standing on her right
flashbulbs capture a brown-eyed beauty
who's ready for a fight

A tall white blond beginner
is standing by the bar
eyes focus on her watching her
cursing the keys she has ridden so far

What causes a sparkling pink champagne beauty
to cling and clutch so tight
to measure all her worth by
and be so afraid of losing
the dream reality on her right

Myrna Plaza-Dattolico
ESCAPE
Get away, get away,
Somewhere, someplace—
Get away, get away,
From all my cares,
And all my pains . . .
To lose track of time—
To find peace of mind;
A quiet place,—somewhere,
With a gentle breeze . . .
Listen to the sound,
Of the whispering trees.
A place for rest;
To find myself,
And do my best,
To settle my world,
That's such a mess!
Once I find myself, I know;
That I am on my way—
To a life filled,
With happy days . . .
I watch the Sun—set,
And my past, set with it;
And with the new Dawn,
A new "ME" is born!

Michael E Harrington
FORT TRAVIS PARK (AS SEEN FROM THE SPACE OF A FEW YEARS TRAVEL)
Green jewel of the ocean impressed upon my mind
like a sea fortress you stand above all treasures I've known
A city of lights, yes! But you were much more!
Upon the ruins of such a city arose your fair shore
Like Xanadu of Kubla Khan by no human hand
passing flagships salute you beauty queen of the sea
For once little children were king of the hill
up and down grassy banks oblivious to time
And what you could tell of the splendors before
salt spray and sweet honeysuckle perfumed over
So time and time again when your beauteous landscape
rolls back my inner vision like a crystal sea
honey tears will flow empty into hours of glass
if haunt or honeymoon I return not at last.

Janice Walling
ONE THING THAT I PRAY
Lord, give me light
so I may see
the things that are
ahead of me

The paths I should
and should not take
all of the little
things you make

Please give me strength
to serve each day
so I may walk
your narrow way

And when you come
to take us home
please let my spirit
never roam

Please let me live
with you each day
for this is
one thing that I pray

Anna Sheets
WHO HAS SEEN THE LOVE
Who has seen the love?
Neither I nor you;
When love hangs trembling,
We don't know what to do.
Who has seen the love?
Neither you nor I;
When love comes from above,
It will never die.

Who has seen the love?
Neither I nor you;
When love seems lost,
We manage to pull through.

Who has seen the love?
Neither you nor I;
When questions like this arise,
We take them to the man in the sky.

Sarah McNett
THE EIGHTIES
The eighties were eventful,
Yuppied and confidential.

Bush took Reagan's place,
Tons of make-up on Tammy Faye's face.

Oliver North said, "I didn't do it,"
The terrorists, well, they just blew it.

East and West Germans were freed,
Florence Griffith Joyner retired her speed.

Pete Rose is my name, and gambling's my game,
Kareem Abdul-Jabar still had 38,000 baskets of fame.

Exxon-*Valdez* spilt all its oil,
While Californians witnessed the earthquake's great toil.

Challenger's explosion was quite unexpected,
And Cher's video it was rejected.

Poor, little Jessica McClure stuck in the well,
While many trees in Yellowstone Park fell.

People were killing animals just for their hides,
Manuel Noriega is getting ready to be tried.

Homeless are having to sleep on the streets,
The AIDS epidemic is our biggest defeat.

The eighties may be done,
But now's our chance to have more fun.

Jessica A Caron
THE OCEAN
I have a place where I love to go.
I go there and feel the ocean breeze blow.
My hideaway place is the ocean in Maine.
I go there to relax when I'm going insane.
Looking out at the beautiful blue sea makes
me see who I really want to be.
With the cool breeze blowing through my hair,
the ocean's beauty makes me stare.
When the sun is setting in the west,
that's when the ocean is the best.
The ocean is so silent, all you can hear
is the crashing of waves upon the rocks.
And the boats docking at the docks.
I think the ocean is a very safe place.
It's where I can go to look my
problems dead in the face.
What would this world be without the sun,
the moon, the stars and sea.
They all are a great beauty to me.
When I see the coming and going of the tides,
it makes me feel full of pride.
I go to the ocean feeling blue.
I come home and I'm happy and new.
The ocean is a symbol to me.
A symbol that every person is free
just like the sea.
The crashing of the waves in the moonlight
makes me feel free of fright.

Bobbie Benz with daughters Alicia & Brittany

Bobbie Benz
EARTH MOTHER

This poem is dedicated to the preservation of our plant, Earth.

She smiles at each new day, as she opens her ocean eyes to roll back the tides.
She stretches her open arms to
catch the vibrant, life-giving
rays radiating from the fiery sun.
She is completely receptive, as
she absorbs this freely given
solar energy, with her entire existence.
She spins her skirts, as the oceans
whirl from the energy in the winds.
She dances as the clouds wisp
lightly around her ever-changing face.
She suckles every living creature,
as she continuously nourishes
all with energy from energy and life from life; the
never-broken, golden chain about her waist.

She cleanses with the rains, then
adorns herself with fresh and
fragrant flowers that she gathers near
her breast.
She winks and a rainbow forms,
and as she plays, the lilacs
bloom, and pearls form
beneath the seas.
She giggles as the leaves fall into
the streams to tickle her sides.
She sings softly as the reeds and
grasses sway gently in her
breath.
She wears a golden, jeweled
crown as the setting sun
shimmers gloriously behind her head.
She hums after dark the crickets'
tune as she lulls herself to rest.
She is ever giving, ever changing,
ever providing with all her
strength and love and beauty.
She reflects her true personality
to her lover, the sun, night after night
and day after day, as she revolves
around his light.

Bobbie Benz
THE BEE'S DANCE FLOOR
The rose does bud,
As lips part to whisper to the air,
Petals reach to collect droplets of
dew,
The fragrant scent is a breath in
exhalation,
The bee's dance floor gently sways to
the music
in the breeze,
The nectar pure delight is served
from a golden
cup within,
The unbruised perfection, all dressed
in white,
Is born for admiration by all creatures
noble.

Janice M Lutz
MY BROTHER
To my brother who could not stay longer, but he left with us his wife who helps us all see through a dark glass more clearly.

The hour is late.
Here in my chair I meditate—with a
soul completely bare.
Just now I heard
my older brother cannot live the
night.
"Cannot"—what a terrible word!

So many years have passed
and, too, our father and our mother.
Yet, now, to the very last,
I will beg, let him stay longer, my
brother.

True, many times, toleration for this
sibling
was beyond hope. He and I were ever
quibbling
Yet, in later years we understood
what neither of us could grasp when
our relationship was far from good.

How can I let him go?
'Tis selfishness, I know;
But the older man I learned to love
dearly,
has so deeply touched my life that
should he leave—
How will I see clearly?

Tami Dewitt
YOU TOOK MY LOVE
To Rick, my one and only true love.

You took my love
And you took my heart
You said you loved me
But did you really?
You took my love
And with no goodbye
You took my heart
And broke it all apart.

Bryon K Nabors
UNTITLED
Rear-ended,
I'm embraced by icy arms that
squeeze
And claim like an unwanted brother.
A frozen whisper blows from behind
my ear
Like February ivy around my neck.
"Can't ditch me, big brother.
I'll shadow you.
Not one crystal accomplishment
Will be free of my scratch.
Then later, when your back is bent
and brittle
And your every love and loss
Can be read on your face,
I'll surprise you with one final hug."

Johnny Stack
THE ROSE
This morning's fresh dew
fell upon you
To glisten against the morning light
Your soft petals lay
Closed to the day
So to awaken them, I thought I just
might
As the petals unfold
'Tis a sight to behold
Such a marvelously incredible sight
To watch them awaken
Leaves me quite shaken
But leaves me with a dream for the
night
This sight I shall cherish
Least it shall not perish
For it speaks to me of what might
happen if
I watch long enough

Matthew Lewis
THE BALD EAGLE
He clasps the crag
with crooked hands,
close to the sun
in longing lonely lands,
ringed with the blue skies
crowned with freedom.
A peaceful warrior
he stands.
The wrinkled sea
beneath him crawls,
he watches from
his mountain walls,
as a mighty hunter
he spies,
for his prey
he watches,
and like a thunderbolt
he falls.
He falls upon his feeble prey
the fast and swift rabbit
it is today,
grasps with muscular talons
and up with a screeching cry,
A cry of victory,
of life and of death,
A cry of freedom.
He drops his prey
from a great unseen height,
the rabbit hits the ground with a
"SNAP."
From behind the bushes
and in great fright
the other rabbits
watch or flee.
And then
with a great cry
his family
he calls, calls he
his family as free as he,
they eat and feast
with ever no guilt at all.
The rabbits are scared of the eagle,
the eagle is scared of man,
the rabbit paid a price for freedom,
and so do we.
THE BALD EAGLE,
freedom and courage, has he.

Matthew James Parsons
THE BATTLE
Is the scare over, or has it just begun
The feelings are undercover, with the
exception of one

It's selfish and doesn't think of the
people it inflicts
To thrive it needs a drink, but no
problem does it fix

Hell is a stage and it drags a soul
down
Turn the page and take a look around

The river has dried, but the stage still
rules
Many have cried over the life he
duels

Eyes blinded by tears, a heart filled
with pain
Judgement day nears, he must make a
gain

Invisible as the air, are the arms at
full reach
Looking for someone to care, life is
like a big fat leech.

Patricia A Chavez
IN MEMORY OF MOTHER
This poem is dedicated, in loving memory, to Sarah C. Chavez (12/17/39—9/11/85)

The sun has begun to rise as dew
drops off my petals for I am no
longer a bud, but a newborn, just like
a babe.
I've enjoyed the days as they have
gone by, but now it is time to say
goodbye.
My life has been short but very long
lived for I have enjoyed all of life's
gifts.
Now I am old and shrivelling away to
a place of no return, for more than
likely I will end up as my ancestors
have, pressed between the pages of a
forever forgotten book.

Elizabeth Whitfield
LOVE IN A MOMENT
Dedicated to the person who is the biggest part of my life, the one I couldn't live without. To my husband, Steve.

I never believed in that old saying,
about love at first sight.
For me in a moment,
that saying could have well been
right.

My eyes met with yours,
when you walked in the room,
It was instant attraction,
our love suddenly bloomed.

I never believed,
It could have happened so fast,
but surely it did,
I found love that would last.

As time passes by,
I can hear the bells chime,
my love for this man,
will be forever in time.

I think back at that saying,
about love at first sight,
now I believe . . .
I believe that it's right.

Catherine Roban

Catherine Roban
LIFE STORIES
I am . . .
Your Shaharazad, shrouded
In the chrysalis tales of cardinal veils,
Sins, seething in every dance I know,
Honing your senses raw.

Seven sheaths are shunned
One by one,
To colored cadaverous time I run,
Till naked . . . then the dance is done,
And I've become
Your flying
Monarch.

Desiree Martin
A MOTHER'S LOVE
This poem is dedicated to my wonderful mother Deborah, the best mother in the world! I love you! Love, Des!

I'm with you through the bad times,
And even through the good!
I don't mislead you in the wrong
direction,
But set you straight in your tracks!
I love you,
Even though I don't show it!
I act strong,
But I miss you when you're gone!
I love,
And you need a mother's love,
to keep on running strong!

Nick Lewis
SOMETHING TO THINK ABOUT
Social pollution
There is no solution
The ruin of human nature
Where does it lead?
Blatant wars
The asphyxiation of mankind
Why does it happen?
Governmental hypocrisy
Inebriated aspects of life
What causes it?
The ambivalence of opposing life
The science of existence
Where does it lead?
Societal destruction

Trudy B Nielson
THE SHOES

For my son, John-David, on his 18th birthday.

They were like you—so miniature,
Those first ball shoes of yours.
And they, like you, just didn't know
That shoes should walk on floors!

They hardly ever touched the ground,
They ran, they jumped, they hopped.
They climbed on top of everything . . .
They hardly ever stopped.

Those tiny shoes were there when you
Took your first step towards me.

Into my waiting arms you fell
As I knelt on bended knee.

Each year you grew—your shoes did too . . .
Now they are big and long,
And you have grown into a man,
So handsome, tall and strong.

Your shoes will help you take a step
Away from me this time.
(And I'll still be on bended knee)
But I know that you'll be fine.)

For you have lofty dreams and goals,
You were not born to lose.
And no one else but, my son,
Can fill those great big shoes.

Mary Hesse
A MOONLIT NIGHT

The warm sun abandons its home in the sky.
The cloak of night shrouds the land by and by.
As the last rays of sunlight spread over the ground,
The moon shows its face, large and round.

It shyly shines light on sea and on land,
On lovers walking hand in hand.
While mighty waves crash upon the shore,
And angels knock on Heaven's door.
Love to their hearts, the moon does bring.
They approach each other, trembling.
A gentle touch, a loving gaze,
They stare at each other through moonlit haze.

As they move closer, their fingertips touch.
True love cannot be contained as such.
They give into the feelings they no longer can fight,
As they share a kiss on a moonlit night.

Estelle A Eaton

Estelle A Eaton
TWENTIETH CENTURY DREAMS

To my daughter and son, Hazelle Eaton Boulware, M.A., and Hubert Arthur Eaton, M.D.

There is Racism, there is Prejudice, There is Hate—
There are those who dream Despite their fate!
There are Struggles, Hard Work and Sacrifice
There are those who dream and pay the price.
Because:
There is love, there is compassion and such—

There are those who Never Lose the Human Touch!
To make Dreams become REALITIES!

Bobbie Kramer
FEELINGS

In the quiet of the night
The dreams that I dream
Are like bubbles in the air
That are mostly out of sight

The thoughts that come and go
The feelings that I feel
The sadness and the happiness
Sometimes becomes more real

But life is good and the things that make us smile
The little things in life
That may just be for awhile

So let us grasp the sweetness
The precious moments that we have
The beauty that surrounds us
The things that make us glad.

We do not know what lies before us, and yet, isn't that good?
For we have the power to make dreams come true
Those sweet dreams, if only we would.

Deborah Sue Persons
FREE SPIRIT

This poem is dedicated with love to my son, Jonathan Richard Persons. The angels took him on April 16, 1990, but mama's little snuggle bunny boy will live forever in my heart.

I dreamt of being free . . .
Free as a sweet dream caressing the dark, silent night;
Free as the gypsy winds dancing across the tranquil sea;
Free as a light, bubbly melody cascading across the midnight airwaves;
Free as a single, red rose surviving in a field of pure white daisies;
Free as a perfect nightingale suspended in a timeless flight;
Free as a precious, loveable infant in a quiet, peaceful slumber;
Free as a red, hot fire flaming wildly on a scared, white candle;
Please understand that . . .
Now I am free.

Ramona Puente Barrera
SOON

This poem is dedicated to my parents: Mr. & Mrs. Jose Puente, Augustina, Armando, and baby Joe, Joe Ernest & Nancy, all the Puente, Salas & Barrera families. To my kids, Olivia, Nikki, Jesse Jr., Ram., & Isabel and to all my friends and to my inspiration to life itself, my loving husband, Mr. Jesse Barrera.

Soon it'll be time for our
first babe to be born,
then our relationship of two-some be torn;
Will it be a he? or maybe a she?
Well all we can do is
just wait and see;

To give our babe a good life we'll do all we can,
myself as its mother and
his dad as a man;

We'll teach our babe Love,
Understanding and Trust,
'Cause God has it written
that these are a must!

We'll teach it good faith,
we'll give it good school,
we'll teach it that Family, is the Number One Rule;

Without it you fall and with you fly,
'cause Family and Love
is a natural high;

I'm bearing inside me a most wonderful love
and for this I thank him dearly
the Great One Above:

Mary Ellen Walther
BUTTONS MY FRIEND

I have a friend who is always there.
He is always beside me, no matter where.
If only everyone could see his love
They would say he must be from above.
He never asks for much at all.
He makes me feel like I'm ten feet tall.
He's my constant companion thru thick or thin
No matter how many problems I have within.

I'm sure by now, you are asking, who can this be?
How could I find such a friend for me?
Where would I go to get such a friend?
Is it just a passing fancy or maybe a trend?

Well, I guess I can tell you right from the start
The first thing you will need, is a big loving heart.
Next comes the patience to find the right one
That will stay by your side no matter what's done.

This friend that I have is much better than most
Because he's a Dachshund, I feel I can boast.
His colors, are black and tan, with a little white.
That's why I named him Buttons, my friend, my delight.

Gary L Cumbee
OLD RIVER, ROLL ON!

Roll on, old river,
Your cedar waters red and menacing
Staining the sandy banks once white and shining
Once home to children's grown-up fancies
A port from which we sailed to lands and victories imagined
Roll on, old river,
Your bounty waters ever moving,
leaching from the earth your filling
Ever-onward to your beloved
sun-drenched marshy delta
Home to white plumed egrets so graceful in their searching
Take with you this simple heart still longing
Your rushing roar a symphony of splashing
With swells that pull cathedral beams from their eroding rootbeds
Later to become mere driftwood in some artisan's depiction
Roll on, old river,
Nothing I can do should change you
Nothing short of some unnatural aberration
That even you should not endure
Roll on, old river,
Rightful owner of these idyllic plains
You were here before me.

Colleen Nye
LOST ILLUSION

An illusion shattered
is lost
and reality
stares back from the mirror.

I reach out
and touch it—
it slashes my fingers.

Warm blood trickles
down my hand—
where did that come from?

Is it mine? Or

am I dreaming . . .
no, it just dripped
onto my nice
white dress.

I really should clear up
that shattered illusion
before I bleed
to death.

Albert Boyd
AWAITING A DREAM

I walk through my dream.
I see stars in the night sky.
I hear the wind whistling
past my ears.
I feel light, a feather upon
the wind.
I touch a star, glowing with
beauty.
I reach for a dream.
I want love's tender hand to
touch my heart.
I try to hold the dream,
it slips through my grasp.
I slip through time,
days gone by, dreams I
thought were real.
I fall to reality.
The dream is gone, shrouded
in mist.
I hold the dream in my heart,
for the dream is not lost.
I await the day,
when the dream and reality
bond as one.

Virginia Holm Haseben
GLASNOST?

It stands high and forbidding,
This wall of human despair.
A wall of mortar, hate and stone
Separating families
Who'll be forever alone.
What is Glasnost?
To understand why,
When there is no understanding?
To comprehend why,
When there is no comprehension.
One can try to understand
The madness of the reason,
One can try to comprehend
The harshness of the season.
Where can it be found?
Is it buried inside a wall
Of mortar, hate and stone,
Or is it buried in the heart alone?
Where is Glasnost?
Is it a place on the map
Or a place in the heart?

Carol Garber
THE BOY NEXT DOOR

On behalf of my children, I dedicate this poem to other victims of child abuse and give them the hope that is real—God's healing touch.

Lazy cats sunned and stretched on the
deck
While only the sound of the stirring
oak leaves whispered.
Did they see the look in his eye as the
rampage began
When naked terror stalked my house?
Overpowering innocent, trusting eyes
He raped and ravaged my children
without warning!
. . . it was the boy next door!
Antique dolls sat glass-eyed
screaming to be heard
As silent tears ran down my babies'
faces.
Both victims of terror, like fragile
Hummel statues,
Their lives broken and shattered lay
in pieces on the floor.
Recorded for all time was my baby's
first sentence
Now complete, "I was a brave little
girl, Mommie—he hurt me—
. . . it was the boy next door!"
Echoing down the hallways of my
mind, forever forged in pain,
Are the harsh realities of what was
stolen in one day.
Tho' lost in time, I reclaim their
untouched innocence, running
hand-in-hand
In the sunshine . . . trusting, loving,
laughing.
As God mends our lives, His
forgiveness emits a healing balm,
His love is stronger than the pain and
offers a gentle outstretched hand
As he proclaims, trust me, "I'll heal
you . . . and the boy next door!"

Ronald E Johnson

Ronald E Johnson
V A BLUES

To America's Veterans.

Here some of us sit, in the V. A.
trying to take life, day by day.

You sit around, feeling blue
not knowing just, what to do.

You've fought a war that's over and
done,
a war that really, nobody won.

If you wonder what it's like, when a
war is over and done
Your thoughts are of the things, you
wish you've never done.

Their shadows are there in the dark of
night
and you toss and turn and wake with
fright.
You think of your friends that had to
die
and you feel guilt and hurt and you'll
start to cry.

Your feelings get worse as time goes
along
until you feel there's nowhere you
belong.

You'll sit around, not wanting to cry;
knowing when you've had enough,
You're going to die.

Ronald E Johnson
MOMMY

To My Loving Wife, Marie Johnson.

I'm your little baby,
And I love you very much.

I cry for you to hold me,
Because I love to feel your touch.

It makes me feel safe,
And it makes me feel secure.
For I know that you love me,
And you'll always be near.

I know you'll be by my side
Through happiness and fright,
So I can go to sleep at night
And know that things are right.

And as I grow up in time
I have this to say,
I'll always love you more and more
Each and every day.

Doris M Mayer-Oakes
SUNBEAM DANCER

Dedicated to Harold Ashley Schoonover, my nephew and friend; and one man that is his own man, a man's man and lastly a lady's man! Few attain this remarkable quality in life while adding humor too! I love you!

At times, there I am, in morning's
first light
With pleasures of thought, released
from the night;
Scarcely awake, putting my
daydreams aright,
And, as they gather momentum,
readying for flight
I stone-skip my thoughts atop
lambent streams;
Testing the waters on the shore of my
dreams;
Leaning toward the 'happy'—
forsaking the ache
While deciding what's real and the
roads I should take.

With my bundle of treasures, I head
'into outside';
It is time, once again, for my
daydream ride;
Oft times, I see sunbeams dance in
the air,
Knowing, only a daydream can do
this with flair;
Then, at twilight, as shadows stroll
soft o'er the land
A mem'ry walks towards me,
grasping my hand;
Gently, leading me onwards 'n softly,
we creep
Far into the nighttime's darkest of
deep.

Soon, Lady Mem'ry lets go, my hand
falls to my side,
Me, quick'ning my pace 'n
lengthening my stride;
I press on alone, steps become
'feather light,'
How cordial this darkness, dreamers
know as the night!
Softly, she whispers, while circling
the earth;
This great prelude to dawn fills my
being with mirth;
Ah! There, straight ahead, I see
daybreak, once more,
I'm at my destination, I need only
open the door!

James Gerry Ferguson
CREATIVITY STARTS TODAY

Creativity starts today, my mind
appears to have much to say
Slight events which come to pass
maybe my mind must owe

We have our little family here, I love
the things we do
We talk and laugh and smile and
share, like little kids we grow

The other morning I awoke and felt
the atmosphere
It was very early and cool and the
wind was blowing to its own desire

I lay in the comfort not having to rise,
soaked up in coziness
The mood created seemed just for me
and my peace and contentment grew
higher

There is a charming mystical air
about the early morn
You're left alone and leisurely
thinking in relaxing ease

I went outside to see the sky and
clouds and feel the coolness and
blowing calm
To become entwined in the
swimming breeze

It was all so wonderful, deep breaths
I took and felt the tide rush in
I was so deeply involved in the
flowing stream

A bear was also there, we were in
tranquility
We sat and thought, then came the
ebb and we sank into the sea
Of life so full and spacious and liquid
and we were overflowed and
consumed in totality

We sat and looked and felt and knew
this morning was to be to be

Darlene Arnold
HAPPY BIRTHDAY DADDY

Happy Birthday Daddy, from
someone who's not yet here
Although I haven't come into this
world, my presence is near
I know you don't even know me
I'm still inside my mother
And I know we will never be a
family
My mother doesn't want you back,
she said you never loved her
But someday my mother will tell me,
all about the one she loved
And I will find my way to my Daddy,
with guidance from up above
So go on living the life you feel is
right
The time for our meeting will be
years from tonight
I know you're my Daddy, and you'll
know that I'm yours
My looks will be from you, as my
mother remembers from before
Don't hold hate against my mother,
for never telling you

She knows you would have come
back, but your heart wouldn't be true
The name she will give me, will be
something from you
My name will be a reminder, from
what she couldn't hold onto
And when the years go by me, and
I'm old enough to understand
My mother will tell me everything
when I can comprehend
So happy birthday Daddy, I wish you
luck and joy
I know your heart would be grateful,
especially if I'm a boy.

Regina M Green
I AM THE BEGINNING OF A BABY

Dedicated to: Stuart Raymond-John, the cutest little boy who changed my life, and his daddy, who changed everything. Love.

Look at me, I am the beginning of a
baby; but my future is kind of hazy.
I felt like I should belong, although
now, my momma is feeling that I am
wrong.
Land of America, Land of the free, I
don't even get a choice whether I
would like to grow up and be just me.
Why can't she let me borrow this
compartment for a little while? She
won't do that because she just might
want me after she sees me smile.
Look at me, I am the beginning of a
baby; but my future is kind of hazy.
If she would keep me, I would try not
to ask too many questions about her
past.
I might cry a little bit, but then I
could play and show I have some wit.
Look at me, I am the beginning of a
baby; but my future is kind of hazy.
Maybe someone needs to tell her that
if she gets rid of me, she will never
know what she lost, because there
will never be another baby in her life
. . . JUST LIKE ME!
Look at me, I am the beginning of a
baby; but my future is kind of hazy.

Dawn Marie Geary
CHILDREN

Children do not always feel
a parent's love so true and real;
So if somehow we failed to see
the many things you gave for free,
We know that deep down you did
care
and always treated us so fair,
And if somehow we missed a day
that to you was special in every way
you always seemed to understand
and never questioned us at hand,
And if somehow we could repay
for everything you gave today
We'd take the gold right from the sun
and still our work would n'er be
done;
One thing that surely seems to be
the most important thing we see
is the love you gave us here today
has touched our hearts in every way.

Casey Ebert
WITHOUT THOUGHT

Peace
Quiet, calm
Loving, Caring, Helping
Smiles, friends, enemies, frowns
Hating, Disliking, Hurting
Loud, noisy
War

Lance L Smith
PEACE OF NIGHT

To my beloved Grandfather and Cousin June, who share the same world of poetry. God love and be with you from all of us.

As the sun sets, a blanket of darkness
Slowly covers the trees.
The quiet settles the sun's warmth
To a cool evening breeze.

A few logs on the fire,
Trying to raise some heat.
Stretching . . . yawning,
Hoping to warm my feet.

Taking a burning twig,
As to light my pipe.
Staring off into darkness,
Just enjoying the night.

The crickets' noise,
Taking place of the birds.
The deer eating berries,
Drifting away from the herds.

So peaceful the night,
When the day is all done.
I'll stay warm by the fire,
until the morning sun.

Carl J Claunch
THE LAUGHTER OF YOUR SMILE

Dedicated to my family whose laughter and smiles have given me so much joy and happiness—namely, wife Jaunita—son, David—daughter, Ruth—grandchildren, Rebecca, Ryan, Rachel and Reid and a host of others.

Nothing is so sweet as a happy face
controlled by loving thoughts
And extended arms to embrace.

Joy is given and also received by the
first one to smile.
It's like a race in life to win the
one-second mile.

Real love in the heart seems to find
its own beautiful way.
To express it best by a silent smile
and creating a very happy day.

Try it yourself and you will see
just a little smile will cheer your
heart with joy, laughter and glee.

Joyce E Searcy
JULIA'S GEORGE

This poem is dedicated to JULIA . . . and to George.

A cat is a cat is a cat
so there
THEN, there's George,
oh yes
so beautiful, so adorable
and so very rare

'Tis the truth I speak
nothing less
Julia's George deserves and
gets the very best

Snow White and so beautiful
Julia's George is
and in this I do not jest

A happy cat now Julia's George is
As in a condominium he lives,
upstairs, downstairs . . .
. . . Oh Boy!
such fun . . .
already your heart he has won

Maurice G Hajj

Maurice G Hajj
MY ROSARY

To the Hajj family: Joseph, Charles, Renee, Douglas, and Christopher.

O Lord let me hold my rosary
In Life in Death let me
Let my weary lips pronounce
Thy name in reverie

And at the hour of my death
Let life not passing hell
Thou art everything, O Lord
Without Thee there is none

My weary hands in work can't do
With what Thy hands hast done
And when the call "Come Hither."
I know where I shall be

If thou O Lord are near me
My hands on My Rosary.

Teresa Suresh
REVIVAL

To my daughter Roshni with all my love.

Gagged
Barefooted

Envy between the two

Ploy
Plot

Somewhere along the way.

Innocent
Asleep

Trapped beneath the sheets
Revival
Renewal
Feeling the glory
Strong
Alert
No longer alone

Together
United

Finally set free
Finally whole.

G Matthew Lintzenich
FEARFUL OF LIFE

Dedicated to Tweck: Ian, Dan, Paul, Mike D., Mike M., Jake, Jason, Linda, and Jen, and Tom. To all their families, and mine.

I am Life, I sit and ponder
I am Life, or am I?
I am life, yet I do not live
I am an automaton
Brainwashed in
society's ways
I am my boss's servant
I am my neighbor's slave
I am a life that does not belong to me
If I am life, why do I
not live?
Why do I sit and watch
the world
and conform, and listen
and live as others do?
Because I fear
I fear the eyes of hatred
The eyes of my peers
I fear outcasting, exile
I do not live,
Not on my own
I live the life of others
I fear life, for I am death.

Sherri Beattle
HOW TIME FLIES

Another year has come and gone.
There is still just a little more work to
be done.

It is just a shame how time flies.
We should use it wisely instead of
watching it slip by.

A time for setting, reaching and
planning new goals.
A time to keep moving and strive to
overcome our foes.

Oh, it is just a shame how time flies.
Let us all keep up and not fall behind.

Start the new year on the right foot
okay!
Time is on your side if you see it that
way!

Linda A Schaefer
THE WIND

The wind
is
warm
and
soft
as it
touches
my
face

I wonder
where
it had
been
before

Jennifer A James
ONCE AGAIN

As I lay here thinking of him,
I can't help but feel grim.
Why did I say what I did?
I was thinking as a foolish kid.
My feelings of regret are strong,
Was I right, or was I wrong?
I heard a rumor, and thought it true
Confusion entered my mind,
Is love really blind?
All the problems he has caused
If only he had paused,
And thought of the result
Maybe I wouldn't have felt
The desperate need to bolt
Away from him.
Maybe in another way
At a later day,
I'll be able to tell him
Once again;
"I love you."

Therese J Young
FLOWER OF LOVE

Flower of love surrounded by lace
making the memories last
forever.

You were there in good times,
you were there in bad times.
Your laughter and funny stories
Brought smiles to our faces.
You taught us what life is really like.
You were a strong and rugged lady
Always looking on the bright side of things
You're gone but our memories of you will last forever.
We look back at all of the pictures of you
and talk about all of the good things
you have given us.
Even though you're not here
We still think of you.

Melodie Carson
SEEING IS BELIEVING

In Dedication To The Seal, Anteater, Lion, Unicorn, Turtle, And Elephant—With All My Love.

And They Rode With The Swiftness
Of The Northern Wind
—Nothing Stood In Their Way—
In Their Effortless Pursuit Of The Ocean-Wide,
Or Perhaps A Mountain Peak
On Some Faraway Side.
On And On, So Long Behind Them,
Their Beginning, No Doubt, Born Yesterday.
Makings So Grand And Of The Finest Illusions
—They—Carried On.
A Scant Two In Number
And All The Room Of Forever—Yet
As One Lagged Behind
The Other Eased Stride
For "Together" Was The Call Of The Day.
And, In The Shift Of Light, Seen,
Their White And Dappled Grey
—They—
Two Clouds On Blue, Free—To Be
Anything Of Their Choosing,
Choosing To Be All—As One.

Melodie Carson
LADY GRAY

Lady Gray—and tattered clothes—
She's walked a thousand years or more.
Disheveled ways about Her, worn.
Hair scattered around broad, strong shoulders.
The tresses faintly a-glimmer
—Those crimson red, black, tawny browns, and blonded yellows.
And the midnight rainbow SHINES from Her.
Thank you moonlight for helping me find Her.
Oh, Lady Gray—so old, so wise—
Barer of such saddened eyes.
And yet, within, I see the Life!
In one-Child Eternal, burning bright,
' the other—The Flame of All Desire.
My Lady Gray, you have returned.
Open hands await you.
It's time to put things in their place.
Dear Noble Lady—Maiden, and fair—
SMILE now! We are together.

Beverly J Dodson
THE TREE OF YET TO COME

I dedicate this poem to my savior, Jesus Christ, who inspires me with his words of love and life.

Restlessness surrounds the one whose heart aches for love.
The desire in the mist, of love's eternal life.

Linger for a moment, in the time of yet to come.
In the garden grows a tree; that bares the fruits of love.

The fruits are ripe with the seed, that springs from the center, in the world where love blossoms from love.

Encircled by the glow, of a warm burning flame, this tree lives forever, to feed your desire for love.

Taste the soothing juice, that flows from the fiber of the fruit. Let it entwine your being, with pure essence of love, to flow like a river through your blood.

The tree that lives forever, in the world of yet to come.
Will bare its fruits forever, for your love.

Beverly J Dodson
THE DAWNING OF THE LIGHT

I dedicate the "Dawning of the Light," to the day star, that shines brightly in my life and the dear people of Day Star Ministries.

In the dawning of the day, a voice is heard.
The voice is distant, and yet it is heard.
It is a cry. A cry of someone lost and afraid.

They walk forward, and yet they still stumble and fall. They know not, which way to turn, so there they lay.

Cries, they cry, the air is filled with the voice of the one whose crying is heard, on the dawn of the day.

The new dawn has brought the light.
It reveals the path on which to follow, it is clearly shown by the light.

The blind are they lost? Their eyes cannot see the way in which to travel.
Is there no hope!
For the ones who cry?

But yet the light of the day, still burns brightly for the blind to see.
Tho their eyes cannot reveal the light, they may see the path.

For when they look towards the flame, that shines brightly from the heart. They will see the path revealed by the flame.

Tracie Elizabeth Ann
DEATH OF A SAILOR

He lies beneath the waves
The crimson foam rushes to shore
The gulls cry out his requiem
Unto the sea forevermore
The water violent; water calm
A friend to friend or foe
Elegies are but easy
For the one who lies below
Death doth come and carry away
A quite mortal shipmate
For he never knew what life was about
Before it was too late

Joan Tae
JUST THE SAME

The ancient one
Intense and concentrated and
Searing the rotund crystal.
Wisdom moistens hollow sponge eyes—
Grave reality, gravity, is quiet
In the facial starved crevices and
Life brands winter-cracked lips

The blossoming one
Unfocused and unaware and
Tackling the round-filled helium;
Impetus gleans sea-spirit pupils—
Buoyant urgency, buoyancy is restless
In the soft-starch flesh and
Life intakes through sweet melon breath.

One waits amid dirk weeds and remembers,
One frolics in petal postures and forgets,
But one startled clash of sun and moon
And the once-helium will be twice-crystal,
Yet they will rise just the same.

Christine A Schloer
THE CALL FROM THE HEART

what can i do
to make the pain go away, along
with a mixture of happy
and terrifying childhood memories?
how much better i would feel
just to ease the hurt
for a little bit of time,
to stop myself from looking back
and seeing all the anger
that ruled my every waking moment.
even learning how to live with it—
ignoring the pain.
but how does one ignore
the call from their heart?

Luana (Folkerts) Hugg
US

In the depths of learning
I've searched you out.
Memories in childhood don't leave any doubt.
I've winged my way to clearly see you in the dark.
I know you are with me,
and together we will embark,
on new territory
to share in infinite wisdom
while studying the deception of infinity.
Slowly we are turning a spiral web of love.
The affection for our dementias,
help us want to explore more than this physical world we are entrapped in.
One day the web we've spun,
will be the ship we travel in.
Amongst the stars will fly by time,
and the warm glow of us
will be shared by many
on their way elsewhere.

Tracie Elizabeth Ann
THE CANDLE

I dedicate my poems and my life to my Pop Pop, who always told me I can do anything I want to and to never give up my dreams. I love you, Pop Pop.

I lit a candle long ago
And closed the windows so it would not go
I set it on the floor so I could see
I stared through the flame of an image of me

Later that day the candle burned low
I set it on the table and admired the glow
I could still see myself amidst the fire
Though the wax was melting the flame seemed higher

Almost to dusk the flame was soon to die
I put it at bedside where I would lie
I watched the candle now short and stout
I made a wish then blew it out

Bonnie B Hall
MOON'S MANY FACES

Is it dark, is it bright, is it yellow as cheese
Does it rule hearts and control tides
Fan the March winds to usher in Ides
Force nations to war, men to despair
Light all the earth, is it filled with mirth
How many faces has the moon

The moon is blamed and greatly acclaimed
From wiping out islands to winning men fame
Can it feed all the hungry, warm all the cold
Will it shelter the weak, give strength to the meek
Does it hold the answers we seek and pursue
How many faces has the moon

The quest for its secrets go on and on
Still it shines out there with its glow all around
In a distant place where promises abound
As we gaze to the future, ponder what to do
Its shimmering gold reflects hope in the blue
How many faces has the moon

Bonnie B Hall
FATE

Fate is divine intervention
Granted to lighten our load
I believe it's fate good intention
To help us get down life's road
Showing more courage and grace
Overcoming obstacles we face
Fate has blessed me in a way

I'll never begin to repay

Fate gave me the chance to choose
One love that'll never grow cold
Everlasting luck I can't lose
Riches far greater than gold
There's strength to meet life's tough blows
Riding high roll along with the flow
Look up to the stars way above
Your fate's in God's tender love

Elizabeth A Lockman
UNITED PRAYER
Dear loving and merciful Father,
Help us to see the need,
Faith for this Prayer Vigil
Is profitable if we heed.

The invitation is given,
It welcomes one and all;
Support this prayer team,
In answering the Spirit's call.

There is a scripture agreeing
That when you earnestly pray,
With faith working by believing
Lest we be lead astray.

Let us pray and fast together,
With the love of the Son;
By intercession put thousands
Of demons on the run.

Come, may we pray united,
Publicly, and on one accord,
In receiving all the blessing
From Jesus Christ our Lord.

Frank A Portelli
HOME OF THE BRAVE

To my father and mother, who are always there for me, I love you.

Men at arms,
Weapons that shoot,
Inflicting harm,
Uniforms and boots

No reason to kill,
No reason to save,
Blood to spill,
Survival for the brave

Those who attack,
Those who protect,
Few come back,
Scars are left

Man against man,
Friend against friend,
Thoughts turn bad,
There is no end

The fighting is loud,
Disaster is great,
The men are proud,
They choose their fate

Frank A Portelli
BITTER COLD

Dedicated to the entire Portelli family and all our relatives, and to Ms. Bauman who started me off.

As the heat of the summer moves on,
bitter cold settles over the land,
the frost chills the ponds,
and people wear gloves for their hands

Snowballs fly here and there,
as moving sleds flow down a hill,
icicles are everywhere,
and tall snowmen stand ever so still

Fields are coated white,
and tall warm coats are the styles,
the day turns quickly to night,
and there is not a person for miles

Heat is what this season requires,
as bitter cold settles over the land,
outdoors people stand near a fire,
and thoughts are of the beaches and its sands

Frank A Portelli
HEARTBROKEN

Dedicated to my Mother who has always been there for me through the tough and pleasant times, I love you, and to my sister Rose, thanks for always being on my side.

She broke my heart,
she made me cry,
why did she part,
I don't know why

Her long black hair,
her pretty smile,
I had to stare,
stare for a while

Times we had,
I grew fond,
now I'm sad,
'cause she is gone

She was fine,
white as a dove,
she was mine,
my only love

Kathy Collins
WHITE HAIRED LADY
She sits rocking by the window,
dreaming memories all her own,
a tiny white haired Lady,
in an old people's home.

Her snow white crown, adorns a face
that's wrinkled to the bone,
on this tiny white haired Lady
in an old people's home.

Idle hands, once busy, now
reach out for things unknown,
'cept to this tiny white haired lady
in an old people's home.

She speaks softly to a silent voice,
that perhaps is calling home
this tiny white haired Lady
in an old people's home.

Then like a gently dancing sunbeam
a smile flickers then is gone,
like our tiny white haired Lady
in an old people's home.

James Edwin Elliott
SHE LOVES ME NOT
Unrequited Love—
With the rage of an angry sea she plunders
The shore with each destructive tide
Crushing those who contest her.
She is a black hole
Sucking up all substance that dares
Approach this infinite vacuum
In a universe where reason too is swallowed.
Her attendants are
Pain that won't diminish
A wound deathly slow to heal
And longing that's never satisfied.
Her ubiquity results in
A cold, unsheltered storm
That eclipses all hope
For the Sun's ray.
No drought produces greater thirst
Nor famine greater hunger
Than the worship of this mute goddess
Carved from unanswered passion.

Kathy Collins
MY PRAYER
Lord, help me to walk in faith,
as I pass through this land.
Pick me up when I stumble,
with your victorious right hand.

Help me love the most unloving,
like the lepers you set free,
that people may be drawn to you,
by the lite they see in me.

Lord, help me by forgiving,
as you've forgiven me,
and pray for those who pierce us,
as you did at Calvary.

But most of all, Lord, let me
see how short my time will be,
that I may die unto myself,
and let you live your life through me.

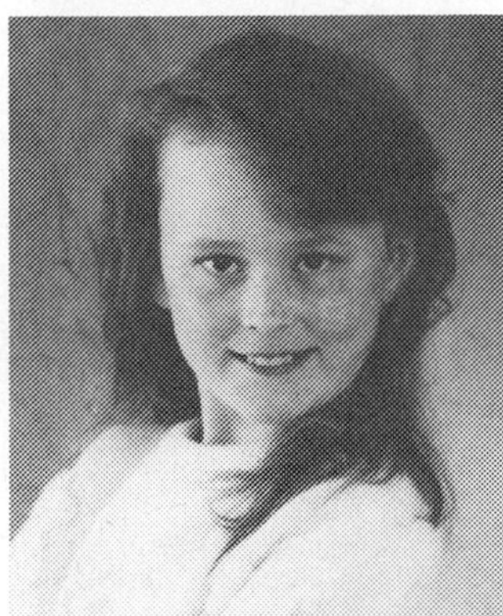

Misty Lee Sisk

Misty Lee Sisk
IF WISHES WERE . . .
If wishes were horses, they would all fly away.
If wishes were ponies, they would all say neigh neigh.
If wishes were friends, I would have very many.
If wishes were fruit, trees there would be plenty.
If wishes were dreams, they would never come true.
If wishes were love, I'd give them to you.

Barbara Goings Talley
HOMECOMING

To Andy, who dug deep to find me, then lifted me by giving me the confidence to soar-solo. Thank you sincerely! Love, BT

Homecoming is returning to that special place
for rekindling affection
Touching, kissing, each with a warm embrace.

Returning to our very special place
Brings joy so profound,
Laced with esthetic beauty, stimulating
Conversation and eternal grace abound.

Ah . . . the beauty overwhelms me.
So much cannot be amass!
A sprinkling of precious dogwoods,
A calm lake and a superior quality of grass.

Flora and fauna so reverently taking their bow.
Neither worries about time—
No yesterdays nor tomorrows . . .
The important time is now.

Then . . . You, my love,
So very, very special—and
You make me feel even more—with
Your most generous compliments, unmatched perspicacity
Amazing sense of humor—Never ever being a bore!

You make homecoming CLASSIC!

Helen A Jenkins
REFLECTIONS

To my children with children; John Timothy & Kim Wilkins.

Parents are children's
Rubic cube
They twist, they turn
They use.
They come in bundles
Trusting and small,
Making you feel
Ten feet tall.
They psyche you out
While they steal
Your heart.
They color code you
With sights and sounds
Recording your reactions
Every time.
Then comes school
And the ups and downs
You're hoping they're
College bound.
You cope with the years
In between
You watch them change into teens.
Suddenly they have minds
of their own;
They want you to treat them
As if they are grown.
But they won't take responsibilities
Or leave home.
They complain about the living
You're trying to make
Because it doesn't afford
Enough for their date.
They say you're old-fashioned
And you don't understand
When you don't give in to
Their demands.
Your children are not unusual
So don't take it too serious
Because most of us
Are just looking in the mirror.

Michelle M Veilleux
LOSS
I've changed.
I never saw the change in myself
Until now.
I had such hopes for the future then.
I thought so much was in store for me . . .
But now, I see what is real.
My heart
has chosen someone
who chose someone else
And my body
gave itself freely
to someone who collects bodies by the dozen.
I mean, nothing to either of them.

The excitement of life, of everything,
is gone.
I have nothing left to look forward to.
No one is going to love me, now,
after all this.
And I'll be left alone
to think of all that I've lost . . .
Myself.

William R Belpanno
ANOTHER NEW YEAR

To my mother . . . even now, you still know what's best.

Another year gone
Another year to look back on
Of times when your eyes filled with
tears
From laughter or crying
It's just another quick year
Another year older
Another year your heart is less colder
For the things you learn to accept
How quietly by another year crept
Another year forward
Another year moving inevitably
onward
Celebrating successes and
challenging defeats
To a better new year
Another new year

Michelle Ann Winterstein
AT THE END OF A WINTER'S DAY

When walking to the seemingly far
off mailbox,
Noticing trees glazed branches,
I carelessly plunge to the ground,
And am embarrassed for not spying
The thin patch of ice.
Down the street is heard
The haunting sounds of a snowball
fight;
Ice balls crunching as they strike a
house
And children laughing when they hit
their targets.

Back indoors,
I nestle into a rocker.
The crackle of the fire is soothing
As I can still smell the chill of the
wintery air.

A lone snowman in the field
Is awaiting for his children to return
From my warm & cozy chair, looking
out the window,
I am encompassed by the peaceful
sounds of silence.
Snowflakes glisten like burnished
broadswords in the moonlight
At the end of a winter's day.

Jenette Taylor
IN MY EYES

I'd like to dedicate this to my mom, Helen and to my best friend, Michele, for their support and to David for the inspiration.

You are there—
Your tall fragile body awaits
For what I ask? Is it me? Am I the
one?
I hear your tender voice sing out
You're so close
but yet inside
So many miles away.
Your walk is graceful.
Your smile—so sweet.

But what makes you smile so?
What to you is beautiful?
A clear moonlit night?
A blossoming rose?
A gentle painting upon its
canvas?
You are there—
that alone can make me
happy.
Your eyes—
so deep—so golden
can't be denied.
You—
are beautiful.

Shirley J Reese
PEACEFULNESS

It seems as far as I can see
The ocean lies in majesty
Today, tomorrow, it will always be
The whitecaps in their harmony

Caught up in this wondrous treat
I walk with sand beneath my feet
The waves, they roll, they swell, they
peak
Their lap to land is now complete

I gaze in the distance
Barely seen by the eye
Out where the ocean
Touches the sky

The sea gulls soar so gracefully
In rhythmic motion above the sea
The tide comes in, tiny shells to leave
Memories to last an eternity

Sonya K Gustafson

Sonya K Gustafson
UNTITLED

Dedicated to the Homeless and Vietnam Vets.

He was down on his last grain of
bread.
The shirt on his back is all that he had
left,
And stained thoughts of a world gone
mad.
He had starved for a light of hope but
he had not a plan.

He's a cold man a bold man with the
look of stone in his eyes.
When at one time he had been a new
life like a fresh breath of air after the
rain in the spring with no cares in
sight.

He once was a fine man who was
brought up in a kind land that was
given the right to freedom and for
such he would fight.

He had fought for his freedom and
for what he had believed was right.
From pride he had great strength, and
from the love in his heart, it made
him feel safe.

He had expected an end when he started this war, but some time after battle the essence of his dreams had been violently raped.

He had awoke one night in a stone cold sweat, frightened from the empty realities of where he's at, where he had been, and of what is left of a man that has been forgotten, but cannot forget of the dreams that a young boy once had.

He who had loved his life, like one with mother nature in a world so grand. He who had felt the gift of love so strong, he could grasp the universe in the palm of his hands.

It had turned a warm heart cold from the waking of a nightmare to find that those are dreams that only young boys have.

The war isn't over when you leave the battlefield. When you're left in a world of emptiness there is no victory to be had.

*

That's the special place in life that each and every fellow human being has. To care about someone other than thyself makes an immortal man.

Alyssa Welcher
MY TRUE LOVE

Under a crystalline moon I watch for
his face,
hoping he will make an
appearance before my eager
eyes.
Hoping that I will see him,
for he makes my days glisten
like a night filled with stars.
He touches my soul,
and makes me feel a yearning
for life.
With him,
I can soar through the clouds.
Without,
I fall like a dead leaf into a pool
of my own tears.

Paula Andria
BLUE EYES

A pair of eyes once looked into mine,
Eyes so big, so soft and oh, so blue.
Like the stars in the night they did
shine
Warming my heart with a love so
true.

Like a new rose in a garden vase
She grew more lovelier day by day,
A rare treasure in perfume and lace
And she's locked in my heart to stay.

The years have passed and the blue
has greyed,
That old sparkle I loved is now pale.
She is no longer that fair young maid
But a grand Old Lady, sweet and
frail.

Yet, she still holds the love I once
gave
To her, that day so long, long ago
When she shyly turned to smile and
wave
And flash those eyes I've always
loved so.

Lori Lenee Hawley
M-LORD

Lughaiah, you are my breath, my soul, for eternity. Kirsten.

My Love,
I send to thee a crystal of
healing, to keep thee well.
I send to thee a favor of mine
own, from my first battle
won.
I send to thee a ring of silver
and gold to cherish the
love I hold
I send to thee sweet
fragrance to smell, to ease
thy mind on thy weary
days,
I send to thee pearls once
ransomed, trusting the
hands that hold them now.
I give thee this to remember
me. Forget not the love I
hold for thee.
Though what I give has no
worth to the common. The
priceless worth of a
Gypsy soul is what you
hold.
Till the days I have you near,
remember the love I hold is
more
The worth than the
priceless goods of thine own
Gypsy soul.
From The Heart

Katrina J Gossman
FREE TO BE

Free to fly away
At anytime—night or day
Free to be what you want to be
From the highest mountain
To the farthest sea
Free from the city, free from the
crowd
Free to be silent, free to be loud
Free to be as you are
Quiet as the night or bright as a star.

Catherine E Hoilien
WHY I LIKE MY WISCONSIN VALENTINE

"Memories cherished of enduring love." To my daughter Jo Ann and son-in-law Manuel Abbott and to my grandson Peter Jo Kokoros.

My Valentine has charm in many
ways.
Expressive eyes that sparkle with joy.
A voice soft and harmonious
whispers; "I love you."
Silently a smile breaks; that is the
seal.
A friend of understanding love, in
every way,
With companionship that brings
moments of peaceful fulfillment;
a melody of love that has no ending.
Valentine with all your charm—I

want to keep you mine.
In trust, you will be my special
Valentine.

Suzanne Ryan
ODE TO AN ALCOHOLIC
When you drink
All the happiness leaves the room
Exchanging it for a negative gloom.
All the twinkles leave my eyes
And hearts beat fast
As fury flies.

When you drink
A wall comes down
Foundations crumble to the ground.
Sunshine brings the Light no more
And Darkness settles every score.

When you drink
I cry for you
God can't get in
Love can't get through.
Nights and days are lost in you
And feelings change to murky blue.

Then comes remorse and tears and
pain
Even clear skies and gentle rain
Only to have you drink again . . .
again . . . again.

Olga R Alvarado
THE SOUL'S EYES
Where the tears and anger collide,
is where you'll find the soul's eyes.

It's hidden and disguised painfully,
yet sees every stab tearfully.

You'll feel it hurting endlessly,
but feed it with pain constantly.

Those eyes are weeping agonized,
stinging with tears traumatized.

Yelling in desperation, they're
ignored,
confused, they close themselves as
before.

As they open again foolishly,
they receive bruises repeatedly.

Remember the soul's eyes for
eternity,
hurt them and die unexpectedly.

Peggy Iris Phillips
I LOVE YOU
Our relationship has never been
As close as it is now
It took a lot of time but
It was all worth while.

That time has given us
A friendship to share
Laughter and joy
And feelings of care.

I'm glad we're together
This special time of the year
With hopes for greater ones
And nothing to fear.

I hope this will brighten
Your holiday blues
And make you feel better
Than last season's news

I love you so much
That's my message to you
Please remember it in your heart
As the reason for whatever I do.

Peggy Iris Phillips
SOUL SEARCHING
Once my world was misty and blue
My mind and spirit didn't know what
to do
I was lost in a total illusion
Utterly disgusted with a bad
conclusion
So I journeyed east, north, south and
west
In a world of confusion, I was a loner
at best
A drifter, traveling thru time
Not knowing what I'd find.
Then my soul searching came to an
end
I felt my soul began to mend
As I gazed into your warm and gentle
eyes
The clouds rolled away in the skies
They spoke of an endless and
undying love
Oh that I had wings like a dove
I could feel the radiant and abundant
glow
And peacefulness as the water flow
Through the barrier of my mind
I thank GOD you're alive and so
kind.

Jaclyn R Yepiz

Jaclyn R Yepiz
HOLDING HANDS

A toast to all the people, who share my deep thoughts, and cares about this world, the air we all breathe, our little babies, and our future.

On a day out in the sun,
On a day out in the grass,
On a day of butterflies,
Is a day full of life.

When I think about the world,
I begin to cry and think,
How wonderful it would be,
If, We care enough to see.

Today is only today,
Tomorrow is only a maybe,
The following day,
Might not even exist.

Our world is filled,
Of so many beautiful things,
We all, must learn to appreciate,
Instead of destroy, And lose our faith.

We must all be holding hands,
If only we all could understand,
What holding hands would mean,
To our loved ones, our own survival,
Our future, instead of our own
destruction.

Tracey Hiles
THANK YOU JESUS

I dedicate this poem to my husband Terry and our sons, who never let me forget I owe everything to Jesus.

If I could prove to God how
true that my love is,
I would yell it from a
mountaintop and tell him I am his.
I would tell him how I love the
trees he so graciously sent to me,
And I would thank him for the
birds above forever flying free.
I'd thank him for the sky as
well, as blue as blue can be,
I'd tell him over and over again
how I adore the sea,
I'd thank him for the ocean, and
the beauty of the sand,
But most of all I'd thank him
for the nail scar on his hand.
Thank you Jesus.

Linda Lee Hobson
IN THE SILENCE OF HER MIND
The dark comes early and again the
night is long.
The quiet greets her and has become
her song.
As she stares at the candle's glow,
intensely watching every drop flow.
And when her gentle smile grows,
then you'll know
She has gone away to the place she
stays, in the silence of her mind.
The really of her day, has shown her
the way.
Where restrictions and demands are
no longer the problem at hand.
For she knows love there, in her
world without care.
She slips more and more away, in
this world she wants to stay.
I found her there even today.
Who am I to say, she should not stay.
For she has seen the things she
can be, when she is free in the
silence of her mind.

E W Reynolds
CYCLE OF DAY
Horizons dim with the setting sun
Staging straight lines of fading trend
To blend with ebony shades
Once more of nature.
Of time in the cycle of day
Approach of light returns
In the same dark
Mysterious way.
Oh shroud of shadow
Of each a setting stage
Invite the sun
To light the setting.

E W Reynolds
SOUNDS ACROSS THE BAY
Time gone by
I used to play
On the sands
across the bay.

Bleached now
on the isle of time
A shell
I must remain
To dream forever
the fondle of the sea.

Now alone
but a beached sentient
My fond will ever be
familiar currents return to
me
The shore of the sands
across the bay.

Leticia Cervantes
A REVELATION
Am I Dead or Alive?
I cannot be alive,
For I feel no emotion.
I cannot be dead,
For I see the commotion!
My heart beats,
But it does not love.
My voice speaks,
But it is not heard.
Am I dead or alive?
I am neither one,
And yet I am both—
For life is death!

William Gantner
JUST YOU AND ME

I would like to dedicate this poem to the most wonderful woman in the world—Jennifer Ross.

I remember when we met
The night was dark, cold and wet
The days and weeks passed
Hoping our love would last
My feelings I can't fully express
It's possible we're being put to the
test
Sometimes I sit and wonder why
Should I laugh or should I cry
I think of the times we spent together
Will the fun last forever
You say move over
My mind says get closer
We share old stories
In our defeats and our glories
We go dancing all night
Bring you closer and hold you tight
Riding on colorful beams of light
We'll be together for another day
Loving you in every way
Hair of gold, eyes of blue
Being close to you, Just you and me

Denise C Hayden
FALLING RAIN
Softly falling from above
to touch upon the ground
rain reaches earth below
in a pitter-patter sound.

Clouds release what is in store
no longer can they hold
so water by the many drops
upon the earth unfold.

From above they gently fall
as each drop first to last
pursues a destination
the moment they are cast.

Everything on earth below
is touched in some small way
when clouds above can store no more
and rain is cast away.

Ruby Avonelle Miller
OUR RETREAT
Where the snow is bright and deep
And the gray squirrel lies asleep
Up the hill and over the way.
Is the place I love to stay.

We wrap ourselves in clothing so
snug
And we go traveling in our bug
About two hours which seems an age
You get the feeling you're out of a
cage.

Our little red cabin in the pines
Is really a place, although not fine.
The air is free and Oh! that smell.
Will really put you under a spell.

And then in skis we try to walk
We get so tired we cannot talk
But it is fun all through the day
And then at night we hit the hay.

Our little red cabin is the place to be
Where no more worries bother me
Life is free of trial and strife
In a place called "MILLERS HIGH
LIFE."

Marcelyn Arocho
NOW

This poem is dedicated in loving memory of Lugenia E. Grasty.

For you it was the end of a new beginning.
For me it was the beginning of the end.

For a while I was a big sister;
Someone you could look up to.
Someone you could be proud of.
Now, I am no longer anyone's big sister.
I am now, again, the youngest of three.

Now, I realize how precious life is.
How significant is each moment.
How blessed is each day,
for it is not promised.

Now, I am living life for both of us.

In my heart I carry an eternal flame
lit especially for you.
In my mind I keep precious memories
of you and me.

Now, for as long as I live,
so do you.

William R Hastings
TREES

To Mary Ann, my ever loving wife. She's the love and inspiration of my life.

Trees are like people, they come short and tall
Trees come in all sizes great and small.

Trees also breathe just like people do
We cut them up to make things for me and you.

Trees need water and nutrients like we do
So they can grow and blossom like people too.

Some trees stay green throughout the year
To see them will make one's heart cheer.

Trees give us nuts, trees give us fruit
Some are beautiful and some are just cute.

Trees are home for an animal or bird
They are also food for some I've heard.

Trees protect us from the sun, they give us shade
They grow everywhere, on a mountain, or in an everglade.

Some trees change color in the fall
Their majesty and beauty surprises us all.

In December we bring an evergreen inside our walls
On which we hang our Christmas lights and balls.

With all these uses, trees we should protect
Not man, his attitude is; what the heck!

If man doesn't do something about this problem here
The hole will just keep getting bigger in our atmosphere.

If we don't do something soon I fear
We won't even have them for Christmas one year.

A Christmas without a tree would be a sad thing
We wouldn't have the hope and cheer they bring.

Maybe imitation Christmas trees is the way to go
So the real ones can stay outside and grow!!

Cheryl Ann Todd
YOUR LOVE

This is dedicated to my mother and father, Myrna E. Todd, and Elmer R. Todd, with love!

Hidden dreams
never revealed
Broken hearts
never healed
Lost friends
never found
Helping hands
never around
Your love
never felt
My heart
forever melts!

Lois Pierce
I SHARE MANDELA

Dedicated to ending apartheid.

I cried when you fought for the freedom of your people and your country. You spoke out to those who killed other leaders, never did you sway. As you continued your fight you touched the hearts of a nation.
I SHARE MANDELA
I cried when you were imprisoned. While you gave your people more faith you also showed them the power they have within to continue on in the struggle. Those who tried to break your spirit did not know that the broom handle could not be broken by removing the stronger straw.
I SHARE MANDELA
I cried for your family while you were away from them all these years. But through your strength "your wife" the broom again became strong by the rebinding of more straws. All these years this broom swept in your land and laid on its people your spirit . . . Even though you were locked up, your strength "Winnie" released your power.
I SHARE MANDELA
I cried this Sunday morning, Feb. 11, 1990 as you found your way back to the light and walked down the Freedoms path with your strength "WINNIE MANDELA." The jubilance, joyful sounds, enthusiasm, and the new found energy the youths of your land displayed . . . on their faces was HOPE. This you gave all the children of the world. Now with your release is the beginning of a new light that we across the sea hope to use as a guide to attain "oneness" that all blacks so want.
I SHARE MANDELA
As the tears streamed down my face never before have I been more PROUD TO BE BLACK.
I Salute you——
NELSON MANDELA

Laura Wilson
LOVERS DURING WARTIME

This poem is dedicated to all the men and women who were forced to separate during wartime knowing they may never see each other again.

Lovers kiss while
they stand on the
other side waiting.

Can't stop when they should
Even when it's safe.

Strength and excitement
grows when only they are
together.

If only they could be together.
If they'd just stop watching.

When love conquers war they
can be together.
But right now, don't
imagine what will happen later.
'Cause it will. And it
shouldn't happen twice.

George E Pellersels
A SOUTHERN BREEZE

To my loving wife and mother of our son, Marcia.

A northern moon rises
Over a cold barren land
His candle is lit
By an unsteady hand

Her quiet emotions stir
Like a warm southern breeze
It's a feeling she knows
But refuses to see

A frozen wind blows
On his flickering light
It bends against
The threat of night

She is drawn to his light
Like a moth to flame
But her wings have been singed
Her heart still feels the pain

He falters . . .

Only to be cupped by a protective hand
He reaches out to touch her
Her gentle breath feeds his spark
A new emotion begins to stir

The flash of a memory, she draws away
His warmth pierces her heart
There is no pain
Spring is wakened with a start . . .

A northern moon rises
Over a blooming land
A southern breeze moans
At the touch of his hand

Bill MacNeil
EXPRESSIONS

To my beautiful wife Carla, love now and forever.

To tell you of love,
with all rhyme and reason.
It's the honey of life,
to sweeten all seasons.
Like the darkest of days,
that brighten with light.
And the twinkling stars,
that dance in the night.
With the stormiest clouds,
the sun will break free.
Because all of your love,
can rest safe with me.

Ailene K Fields
FRIENDS

I dedicate this poem entitled "Friends" to my beloved family whose confidence was my inspiration.

Friends are considerate and true—
When our hearts are crushed with pain,
And teardrops come a streamin',
Down our cheeks like summer rain!

When our griefs and loneliness,
Are more than we can bear—
True friends are the only ones,
That really seem to care!

They'll stick by us thru thick and thin,
They've known us good and bad—
All our faults and virtues,
And the struggles we have had—

They are a special blessing—
And remember they are few
Let's ask ourselves the question
Am I a true friend too?

Brian Kyle
NEVER ALONE AGAIN

This poem is dedicated to Judy, the love of my life.

I lie awake at night
And think of how things have been
Since our love has kept on flowing
Like the ink from my pen

My love for you
Grows stronger every day
I love you
And all the words you say

We share our lives
Both as friends and lovers
We display our love
Publicly and under the covers

The stars shone bright
When our love first started
The brightness will end
The day we have parted

Many people said
Our love would not last
We proved them wrong
Our love is growing fast

I can't quit dreaming

About how things have been
Now that you're here
I'll never be alone again

Sharon L Schulte
KALEIDOSCOPE
Life is a kaleidoscope.
Each experience of bright colors and shapes,
Turning over,
Forming new patterns, which are then remolded
Again.
Ever changing, yet building, as each
Mosaic in the pattern
Becomes a part of a new
Image and Creation.

Nancy L Huot
BEAUTY EVERYWHERE
A sight of a smile,
Leaves in a pile.
People holding hands,
Music from bands.
Sight of a flower,
A sudden shower.
Sight of a pet,
Sounds of the Met.
The sky at night,
The fireplace bright.
A flying bird,
A pleasant word.
A laughing baby,
A beautiful lady.
The sun going down,
A funny clown.
The pounding sea,
Blossoms on a tree.
Laughter of a child,
Flowers growing wild!

Grantley Crawford

Grantley Crawford
SOME WORDS OF GUIDANCE
To everyone who faces the difficulties of today and tomorrow. Never give up. There is always a light at the end of the tunnel. Move on, you will get there as the waves get to the shores.

Move on amid the atrocities of life.
Never give up what is truly yours.
Set your goal and reach out to obtain it.
Never look back, and never be afraid.

Life bestows upon us all a special talent,
But you can lose it if you don't use it.
Always think positive in all you do,
and never let your thoughts go to waste.

There is beauty when you do achieve,
And it always inspires you to do more.
You not only benefit from your ideas.
But you also uplift others who need
that little push.

K A Owen
MORNING
Up the mountain this morning,
there was no sky,
just the world in a cloud, iced
white—
every crystal-feathered bit of brush,
every branch & bough of piñon and poplar,
frosted & flocked—
mystically glowing,
motionless
in the misty morning light.

Even the silent air was pale with peace.
All the world was white,
except the new blacktop down at the highway,
ribboning off
into icy, white infinity.

Mrs Julia Lombardo
THE YORKIES THREE
There are three little Yorkies a delight to see
And I'm sure when you see them, you'll surely agree
Three bundles of mischief, twelve soft little paws
So quick and so gentle, except for their claws
First there is Candy, who is daring and mighty
Her actions sometimes are a bit flighty
Then there is Tammi, so sleek and refined
I would certainly say she's the devoted kind
Last there is Alfi, so content and so fluffy
No matter how old, he will always be a puppy
Now that you've seen these Yorkies three
Aren't you inclined somehow to agree
That they surely must be a delight to see?

Mrs Julia Lombardo
MY ISLAND DREAM
Have you ever listened to the waves floating
Water trickling and rolling
Soft winds and balmy air
Azure waters flick and flare?
Miles of sand and rippling sounds
As far as beauty there are no bounds
This is Hawaii, paradise on earth
A land to be seen, a place of worth
Imagine being on this lovely beach
If you find the time, it's within your reach
Rays of sunshine and color to capture
Enchanting nights and feelings of rapture
As far as being on this lovely isle
I've only been there in my mind
I've heard these sounds and smelled the air
Those balmy nights you too can share
Now that I've written about this lovely state
I'll put it on canvas with brush and paint

Margaret A Fehrenbach
ROCKING HORSE, ROCKING HORSE
Rocking Horse, from where did you come?
From the store just for you to have fun!
Rocking Horse, what is your name?
You name me, and I'll answer to the same!
Rocking Horse, how do you go?
Nice and easy and fast and slow!
Rocking Horse, do you ever stop?
Yes, but only when you get off.
Rocking Horse, will you talk to me a lot?
Yes, when you rock, I'll say clip clop!
Rocking Horse, where will we ride?
To the top of the mountains or wherever you decide!
Rocking Horse, what do you eat?
If I were alive, oats, rye or wheat!
Rocking Horse, if you should break, what would I do?
Never fear, your dad can fix me with glue!
Rocking Horse, will you ever go away?
Maybe when you are grown, up in the attic for a while to stay!
Rocking Horse, will you come back down again?
When you've become a mother and have twins!
Rocking Horse, will you always stay with me?
Yes, if that is your wish, it will be.
Rocking Horse, I do love you so!
I, too, climb upon my back and away we will go!

Faith Ramsay
WILL WE EVER SHARE . . .
Will we ever share a sunset or walk together in the rain?
Will we ever feel the morning light creeping through your windowpane?
Will we ever see each other's hearts wanting to be one?
Will we ever make passionate love in the noonday sun?
Will you ever want me in your life forever and a day?
Will you ever keep me close to you and never let me stray?
To answer these questions and many more, would be an invitation to an open door . . .
My heart is yours, do with it what you will . . .
To be in your life would be a dream fulfilled . . .

Lovingly . . . Faith Ramsay

Joseph Plomchok
COME BE WITH ME
Come be with me.
The thought of you in this in me;
This aura of blue;
Mists in streams of sunlight beaming.

Come! the warmth is comforting
And the blue is soothing,
While the mist is oozing
With vibrations of life.

Come be with me
This time once again
And we shall remember and be again
The love of fire and innocence.

Jane Tagliaferri
DRAGONS ON A LANTERN
Catching the flame in their throats
And brandishing fiery tongues
Eyes ablaze.

Chasing their scaly tails round
As they turn on the axis
Of their world.

Rumblings out of a black night
A streak of light behind
The rain falls.

A gasp, a sputter
The colors run
They die in a hiss.

Janice S Daley
SHE IS A WOMAN OF SENSITIVITY
She is a woman of sensitivity
Of warmth and
Hard earned softness
No longer is she the playful
Fair haired young girl of yesteryear
But a woman of strength and character
She knows all the heartaches suffered in growing up
The time she was stood up
When he told her he had met someone else

She looks into her mirror and
Sees the wrinkles that
weren't
there
yesterday
She smiles
Realizing she is happier than ever
No longer does she wait for someone else
To make her happy
She manages that all on her own
As she gazes into her mirror
She welcomes the wrinkles and
Smiles inside and out

Ruth J Powers
A CAT'S LEGACY
My mouth waters when this furry creature stirs my whole being!
His softness and bendable frame fit into any crevice, and the sound of his quiet "motor" is contentment decreeing.
After hurrying about and losing control, nothing's more soothing to the depths of my soul, than to find one so loving and full of compassion.
Yes, with those paws, which knead in orderly fashion, he's telling me,
"Calm down, hurrying is taboo—try moving at a slower, statelier pace—you'll find things will improve—even the lines in your face!"

Jeanne Marie Halama
UNCOMFORTED
Grey days spitting snow follow one another endlessly.
Winter's nip is felt and seen
desiccating landscape's drab expanse
belying long-forgotten splash of green.
Winter's weight has bowed shoulders
of somber evergreens.
Unslaked by fallen snow, their
dormant thirsts make rusty needles
where blue and greening buds should
grow. Tree skeletons nubbined with
patient buds stand among tombstones
where your body lies warmer than
they, but only with earth-warmth, and
only eternal blackness for your eyes.
Grey days, spitting snow, follow one another.
Mockery their swirling, grainy tears.
We who remain will walk
uncomforted following one another
through grey years.

Monique Wycoff
TEARDROP
Don't shed another tear they say.
How can't I when I feel this way?
That man . . . he'll never pay.
I can only kneel and pray
To try to forget that day.

I did what was supposedly right,
But he got away without a fight.

He puts me through hell
And I stand here and let him tell,
Tell me all of those dreams will
Come true, but they never do.
If I give him this power much longer,
I'll be through.

JoAnn M Tatum
THAT TIME
And I didn't get up to hold you that time,
that Christmas time when we sat dead-locked
across the room from each other, while the
children's laughter trickled down like sap,
filling the air between us.

You wore your face at ugly angles,
while I drained their laughter,
drinking it like a vital liquid,
and you flushed like war-paint
as I tuned out with Christmas carols.

Your chin pouted on your fists,
elbows on your knees, eyes deploring the rug.
My humming gave way as I heard you
intake air slowly and rush it at me swiftly.
Then your eyes rolled up to caution my face.

And I didn't get up to hold you that time,
that Christmas time when you forewarned me,
"I don't know what you're doing,
but don't do this to us."
And we cracked with the January thaw . . .

Joseph Rios
A NORMAL GIRL
I don't want a princess
I don't need a Jap
I don't want a druggie
Who needs a Rx to nap.

I don't want a man-eater
I don't need a bitch
I don't want a gold digger
Who needs to be rich.

I don't want a Born Again
I don't need to be saved
I don't want a head case
Who needs to be paved.

I just want a normal girl
Is there one on this earth
The mistakes that they are
Must have started from birth.

Cindy Carlson
RETURN ME
Take me back
to days gone by

of ice-cream socials
and a lullaby.

Down cobbled streets
past the general store

return me to
the days of yore.

Take me back
yet farther still

when pies sat cooling
on the windowsill.

When linens flapped
in a gentle breeze

return me to
a time of ease.

Take me back
to yesterday

when good guys won
and led the way.

Around the campfire
their stories told

return me to
the days of old.

Gwen T Lundy
CHRISTMAS THOUGHTS
The shadow of a cross befalls athwart the Christmas star.
Its glory is not dimmed, thereby
but brighter grows by far.

So trim the house with Christmas greens
Heap high the festive board
Greet the friend with handclasp warm
And all with a kindly word.

Gather around the Wassail bowl
And sing the carols old
And hear the old, old story, two thousand years retold.

Give gifts of love in memory
Of those the Magi brought
It is a time of merriment
But pause for a solemn thought.

The joy of Christmas could not be
Were it not for a cross on Calvary.

Marjorie Noble Colvin
SONG OF A BLACK DUSTER
Oh, a ruthless tyrant am I
"Destroy all crops" is my cry
Let not a blade stand
In this broad prairie land
Let none, man or beast, me defy.

Oh, a sinister monster am I
"Let no house escape" is my cry.
I smother, I choke
All the young and old folk
Let them rant, let them rave, what care I

Oh, a boastful warrior am I
"Vengeance is mine," is my cry
'Til God takes a hand
In this broad prairie land,
My conquests I'll wage 'til I die.

Dean and Leah J Berry

Leah J Berry
THE SUNSET

To my husband, Dean, who is the best husband anyone could hope for. I love you!

Brassy, yellow ball of fire
Running away
Hiding behind the clouds
Teasing the sky
With the rays of light
Streaking the light blue sky
With vivid, stunning colors,
Of hot pink, fiery red and
A golden yellow and orange.
Done playing, it descends
through the rivers of colors
Bidding good-night, it leaves
the sky a shadowing grey.

Mattie P Grisby
THE KUMQUAT TREE
The tiny fruit appeared amidst the green leaves.
Here grandma's slumped body took a moment to grieve.
The small, marbled fruit balls offered little comfort,
As the stream of tears fell from her ebony face.

Again, grandma had faced the locked wooden door,
Which barred her from her eldest rose.
What had become of this child she often pondered,
As she reminisced about the precious memories.

The kumquat tree swayed back and forth.
Seemingly, to tell grandma not to worry anymore.
The outstretched limbs reached to cradle her among its branches,
As she recited something about God's many mansions.

Grandma wiped the tears from her eyes.
She turned from the kumquat tree with great pride.
Her gentle knock unlocked the sealed door,
And behind its boards stood the ebony rose.

They could be heard softly chattering.
A laugh now and then could be heard.
Somehow, the brief separation hadn't mattered;
Their happy voices joined like two chirping birds.

Elizabeth Winslett
IN MEMORY OF MY FATHER
The Ladies loved him,
And he loved to flirt.
He could dance all night
And sing all day,
The next day at work
My Mother adored him.
I often wondered why.
The years went by,
And today,
He sits on the porch
Rocking to and fro,
in his old rocking chair.
Watching the traffic and Folks go by.
So pitiful, so sad.
A lonely old man.
But take another look.
There's a twinkle in his large gray eyes
A smile on his kindly face.
He always has a cheery word
For those that stop to chat.
In his memory he's living not for the moment.
Instead he is living again the happy days of his youth.

Hortense Roses
NEVER NOTICE
Roses coming to my garden, in Spring
The birth of my love for you,
Instant when your first son, cave in my body.
When he started talking,
I never percived these encounters,
but they come to my life,
are blessings,
torments of contentments,
New songs, old loves everlasting.
But I never notice!

Arlette S N Martin
A COLORLESS WISH

I would like to dedicate this to my parents, who showed me that if you believe in yourself anything is possible.

As I look and search deeper and deeper into my heart,
Passing all the worry, sorrow, and pain,
That I so strongly fought from the start,
I see a little part of me crying for just one wish.

I have just one wish;
A simple wish,
Yet, a childish, colorless wish.

I wish for a color,
As dark as the night before the dawn;
As endless as the sea,
That seems to flow for all eternity;
And yet motionless as the dead.

The color I wish for,
That is endless as a circular whole,
As mysterious as the mist,
That gently kisses a windy road,
And as still as the mountains, is black.

For if everything were black,
And no one could see,
There would be no time for prejudice,
Critical remarks, and discrimination.

All would be A WORLD of PEACE.

Katherine Echevarria
THE MAN IN THE MOON
I used to dream
About
The man in the moon,
And wonder why
He always followed me.
But as I grew up
And became
An unbelieving soul
In the world
Of fantasy,
I found that life
Was not all
It was made up
To be;
And that the moon
Was not
Made
of
cheese.

John E Bertram
DREAMS OF THE FUTURE

This poem is dedicated to my family, my friends and to all who are dedicated to the pursuit of love, peace and happiness.

I wish that I
could one day see
a world where all
poor souls are free

A world in which
we love each other
united through peace
as sisters and brothers

A world which has
no hate nor sorrows
just peace and love
for our fellow mortals

Nathaniel J Jackson Sr
THINKING OF YOU

Dedicated to my loving family, who have inspired me. Anna, Carretta, Nicholas and Nyheim Jackson.

As I sit in my lonely room with nothing to do,
I think of a wonderful woman who means the world to me.
She brings to mind a lot of wonderful thoughts so true,
That brings a smile to me so bright for all the world to see.

I think of you each & every day that goes by,
Of all the good feelings & wonderful times we've spent together.
When I sit & go back to those happy hours I start to sigh,
For I have to sit alone & think of all this for me to remember.

My eyes begin to fill with water & make me want to cry,
Because I can't be with you right now & hold you in my arms.
My arms are filled with emptiness although I'm sort of shy,
I want to hold you very close & fill you with my loving charms.

You mean so much to me than any woman I've ever known,
For I have never known love like this could ever be around.
The love I've had for so, so long could never ever be shown,
Because the pain that filled my heart had me chained & bound.

So now my love I guess you can see how life has been for me,
'Cause time went on & left me here feeling lonely & very blue.
But now you've come along & changed my life & filled it with glee,
And all my nights & all my days I'll spend just Thinking Of You.

Nigel "Nairobi" Moore

Nigel "Nairobi" Moore
SEARCHING FOR LOVE
Searching my inner soul for love,
Trying to find a destiny,
Of only peace and rest.
Not penetrating on the past,
But feeling the true love of myself.
How long will it be for unity,
To be the first element in society.
When oppression comes my way,
Love will see me through.
Your love will make this peace,
Peace to live and love as a family.
Then why should I feel guilty,
For the treatment in society.
How can we forget love,
And remember the tribulations of our past.
Peace in your mind,
Peace in your soul,
And love will always be control.

Nola Forman
WONDER PILL

To those who look forward to peace on this earth.

If I had a Wonder Pill
I'd give it to the World
If I could turn back time again
We'd see new things unfurl

A World that's filled with hopes and dreams
Completely satisfied
A World of love and peace and joy
That would never ever die

No more hunger, no more war
Where everyone's your neighbor
No matter if they're Black or White
No one shown special favors

That's how this World was to have been
But somewhere got sidetracked
Why did this have to happen
I just can't figure that

Now as I sit here thinking
How this world could be healed
Someday, and I hope it's soon
We'll have this Wonder Pill

Carol H Wilson
MY MENTAL IMAGE

To my loving mother, Wilhel V. Campbell.

I carry her as a mental image in my mind
She and I are sorta one of a kind,
Though small in size
She has the kindest eyes,
And her words are ever wise.

She is with me at all times
Sometimes in shadows, sometimes in lines,
Her presence is a soothing one
And sometimes she sings a peaceful song.

We've met before this mental image and I
Although I've tried to fathom where and why,
She always hovers near me
Oftentimes being as busy as a bee.

We sing and laugh and walk together
We work and pray and talk together,
We've met before
I'm very sure
But where I do not know
And she certainly will not say so.

Sometimes I think she laughs at me
At how very foolish I can be,
If only I knew who she was
This mental image would not be such a fuzz.

Ah! now I see
As clear as can be
There's a definite
place
And this is a
familiar face
My mother is the image . . .
my mental image.

Karyn Lynn Craft
GOD'S NIGHT AIR
A little twinkle here and there,
Makes you wonder what's in the night air.
Flowers bloom and grass dies,
But did you ever wonder what's in the friendly night skies.
Earth and people live together,
But Jesus lets us live forever.
God is in heaven above,
And the Holy Spirit came in the form of a dove.

Wade Pace (Age 11)
MY DOG
Once I had a dog whose name was Baby.
She was as sweet as pie.
Sometimes she was good,
But most of the time, she was bashful and shy.

Sometimes she would sit when I told her to,
But sometimes she would get my shoe.

Sometimes I would lead her on a leash,
And sometimes I feed her out of her dish.

Sometimes she would get into trouble,
And sometimes she would get me to play with her, which made the fun double.

Sometimes she would sit when I said, "good girl,"
But sometimes instead, her tail would curl.

Sometimes when she hid behind her chair, she would not show her face.
I wished she would not hide her face, for I thought it was as pretty as lace.

When I said, "Come and meet your match again, bang, bang,"
She would run to me as fast as a train will chang, chang.

My dog was named Baby
She was as sweet as pie.
Sometimes I wonder why? Oh Why?
Why did my dog, Baby, die?

C C Gahring
MY FRIEND
My friend, Together:
We have shared many sunrises, and watched many days end with the sunset.
We have sat and counted the stars and spoke of our dreams and wishes with each fallen star.
We have gathered flowers in fields, and pondered the beauty of each one.
We have walked the beaches, collecting the treasures it had to offer, and awed at its beauty.
We have gathered pieces of our lives, to be cherished forever with each little moment we have spent with each other.
We have walked hand and hand, thru the good times and even the bad.
We have seen the beauty of the world and have touched each other's souls with the one gift we have shared so easily, the gift of love.
My friend, may you always know:
The treasures you have brought to others, especially to me.
The importance of your existence in the lives you touch daily.
The love you radiate and the love that is sent to you always.
My wish for you in the days to come is one of the truest of loves one friend can give to another.
May the sun always shine softly on your face, the wind blow gently through your hair.
May all the beauty of life be shown to your eyes, may you always be happy and know that you are loved.

Bertha Cramer
ONE LOVE
i look at you and bless the day
That somehow God sent you my way
i'd never known what love could do
Until that day when i found you.

My life was empty, dull and bare
Just nothing mattered anywhere
Until i saw you smile at me
Then I knew this was meant to be

i feel so happy when you're near
My love grows stronger with each year
A song is in my heart all day
Because you came along my way

Your love will make me stronger grow
As hand in hand through life we go
How much happier dear could i be?
For i love you and you love me

Dan Reveal
HUNGER

To Misty and Mandy, with love.

My hunger bleeds through
passing doors, the hint
that life is passing too.
For the breath of burdens
diminishes more than the
breath of time resounding:
all is new. My shadow's bent
like myths of grass beneath a wind
recalled as hard and bleak
by all that it could say or ask and
proved by seeing, listening, feeling
weak.
My eyes regain their supple glow
when, worlds apart from the
sightless sky, I, through
hidden hallways go to where
your beauty and illumination lie.

Margaret Moore Farley

Margaret Moore Farley
THE HAPPIEST TIME OF THE YEAR
Christmas is a happy time,
The happiest time of the year.
It brings smiles to old and young
alike,
It brings a message of hope and
cheer.
Snowflakes falling on the ground
brings
a bit of bliss,
Mistletoe hanging above a door,
brings
a hug and a kiss.

Opening gifts on Christmas Day, fills
everyone with joy,
Little boys and girls jump with glee
when they first discover their toys.
Christmas is a happy time,
The happiest time of the year,
Hearts are filled with gratitude, love
and good will.
So have a very Merry Christmas, and
a Happy, Happy New Year!

Margaret Moore Farley
AN EVENING PRAYER
In the quiet of the evening
at the closing of each day,
I lift my eyes to heaven,
and on my knees I pray.

I pray for strength and courage
to face each passing day,
I pray for all my loved ones,
that they may find their way.

I pray that all over the world,
Mankind will see the light,
And peace will reign within their
hearts,
and wrong will be made right.

Margaret Moore Farley
HIS NAME JESUS
A baby was given to all the world
One Christmas long ago,
He was to be our Savior
In a world of darkness,
sorrow and woe.

They called Him Jesus
Sent from Heaven above,
That is why our Christmas
Should be filled with joy and
love.

Remember this amid the gifts and
glitter
Of this Christmas season bright,
And may your love for Him shine,
As the star did that
Christmas night.

Margaret Moore Farley
THANK YOU GOD
Thank you God for all the
things,
That make life worthwhile
to live,
For sun and moon and stars
so bright,
For rain and snow and winter
nights,
For trees and flowers and
forests green,
For animals and birds that sing
For friends and loved ones to
share our lives,
And in happy or troubled times
to be by our side,
For tables ladened with
bounteous food,
That make us healthy and taste
so good,
Thank you God for your love we
share,
With all mankind everywhere.

Jo Ann Hambaugh
AMERICAN GOTHIC
Like the Cowboys and Indians
known as legends to us all
. . . we too . . .
have the knowledge of our ancestors
to nurture the foundation left from
previous generations and the ability
to utilize qualities as a sound basis
for further cultivation.

As in black and white
. . . sound and final . . .
the power of our Presidents
to bring about war has shaken our
culture and confused the meaning
of the morals and self-esteem
initiated by our forefathers.

Irretrievable but in memory
What is past is gone
What poverty reflects money can buy
Where those are weak we must be
strong,
For history will forever move on.

Dawn M Plotts
TO LEARN TO LOVE

To my loving husband, Ted.

As I look back into our past.
And see our rocky start
I never would have dreamed back
then
That you would win my heart

My first impulse when I met you
Was turn and run away
This man could not feel love enough
To make him want to stay
But then you slowly made me see
What came from in your soul
That beauty comes from deep within
Your loving made me whole

And now I know deep in my heart
The best day of my life
Will always be the day you smiled
And took me for your wife.

Julie Wing
SECRET LOVE
Each time I see you I must close my
eyes.
What I feel for you must be
forbidden.
Even when I am miles apart from
you,
Your presence inside me never dies.

My secret is buried deep inside me.
I am trapped by the chains that hold
me back
Capturing me behind a concrete wall.
No matter how hard I try, I can't flee.

I'll hide my heart behind a mask for
you.
It is the hardest thing I've had to do.

My tears are falling like the misty
dew
Already filling a lifetime of seas.
Dark, sad clouds keep hovering over
me.
As I awake, I'll search for skies of
blue.

Sharon Derrico
THE WINDOW TO MY HEART
The Lord Looked through my
Window . . .
The Window to my Heart.
Tears filled His Eyes to have seen
it broken all apart.
Heaped with pain, loss, deceit
confusion, loneliness, defeat.
What man can do to others . . .
Let alone unto ourselves.
I needed to be reminded That God Is
There for me;
Not putting Him first
was my catastrophe!
Time passed by, then once
again . . .
The Lord Looked Through my
Window . . .
The Window to my Heart.
He found it back together
with a message just for Him.
Seeing the Twinkle in His Eyes,
seemed to bring to mind;
"Oh God, restore us, cause Thy
face to shine and we shall be
saved." (Psalm 80:3)
For Thou art Divine!

Deann Masopust
A RAINY DAY REVERIE

To treasured memories.

It was a misty, drifting, floating day,
not knowing where or how to feel
She had just put on a record by the
Captain and Tennille.
She sang sweetly and stood stately;
his manners always genteel.
In reverie she watched them; their act
had appeal.
But her thoughts today are like beads
on a fog-covered window as only
rainy days can seal
The myriad of feelings the soul
hesitates to reveal.

She knew one once who was
genteel . . . a man who made her feel
Like a woman who had nothing to
hide, a woman who was free inside,
A woman who was free to go out past
that fog, past that haze
Melting into his burning embrace,
fervently trembling like one who's
crazed.
Over and over she saw him . . . over
and over again.
Each one of the beads bleeding into
one another was them.
She watched the trickle. She followed
the trace
That wasn't left but led into his face.
Visions she can see on the window;
memories she couldn't erase.
They were the Captain and Tennille.
She remembered how to feel.

Samina Anjum
MY TIME HAS COME

This poem is dedicated to my parents and friends.

My Time has come
I know I have to run
To view the Sun
I know not the place
Where I am born to go
Yet My Time has come
To witness, the place
Every generation whispered about
But none did escape the Final Fate
I see angel gently coming to carry me
away
To the world of unknown
The chasm is crossed
The fear is lost
I feel as I have become a part of the
deads
What should I do?
Where should I run?
The atmosphere is so enchanting
It is lulling me down
I can feel the numbness
I am floating in the air like a feather
But where is My Home?
Where I have to go?
What is My Fate?
Why I have been left alone?
Why have I come to the world which
is little known to me?
Is it the end of the story?
Am I dead or am I to die yet?

Tiffany Lisa Hollaway
OUR LOVE WILL ALWAYS STAY

To S.R.W.

Never before in my life
Have I had someone like you,
Who cares for me and loves me
Like the way you do.
I've never felt the love I have
Like the way I feel for you,

I'll never forget the things we'd do
Or the first time you said, "I LOVE YOU."
I've finally found what I've been looking for
And I'll never let you go,
Stay with me forever and
Together our love will grow.
So let's live our lives together
And never walk away,
And make a pact to one another
That our love will always stay.

Tiffany Lisa Hollaway
THE HARDEST TO GET OVER!
Dedicated to S.R.W.

I remember the love
That we once shared
I remember your touch
It said you cared.
I remember walking
Together at hand,
I remember us lying
Alone in the sand.
I remember the day
You set me free,
That moment I knew
You no longer loved me.
I wish I could erase
These memories of you,
It hurts so badly
'Cause I'm still
In love with you.
Our love was sweet
And pure as a dove,
The hardest to get over
Is always your first love.

Leonilda E Estrin

Leonilda E Estrin
THE OTHER
Since I was born I changed
I know, I was the same then
Now, I consider myself another
I believe that I live two lives.
The one that I spent before
and the other until now.
The present is part of the past
we live the future.
I was the same before
actually I feel different
living in another time
but also I am still the same.
If I am the other
who can be the same?

Sharon L Geisenhaver
MOTHER NATURE
In the beautiful array of colors,
red green and all the others.
Fall is coming to a close,
making way for winter snows.

The long cold winter months ahead,
are something that we all dread.
For old man winter's icy breath,
makes everything look like death.

But Mother Nature, in her kind way,
will take all the snow away.
She'll wake up every sleeping thing,
making way for time of spring.

As winter fades from our mind,
we look ahead to a happier time.
When once again summer's here,
with all the things we love so dear.

Kelly Guivens
TO LOVE A FOREST
To Courtney, Brandon, and Rob—whose personalities are so different that you would never know we were related.

To love a forest
Is complete understanding.
The winter's barren silence
To be the restful sleep of wonder,
Ill-gotten sorrow befalls the
Once lively manifold of creations.
Spring awakens the peaceful slumber
That once left a lonely world.
New voices rise from whispering winds,
While tears fall from pale blue skies.
Summer's anger strikes without warning
Forcing life to seek refuge while
Still replenishing the same,
And life suppresses its rage.
Autumn cheers the world while
Smiles change the surface colors
Slowly changing to that once
Again dormant stage of existence.

Karen A Maffeo
SILENCES
When you I found were from my life extracted,
I feared that I could not at all endorse
The likelihood the leave would be protracted;
Accordingly, I suffered great remorse.
The days are bleak; the nights, with suff'ring ridden;
O, pain of separation! Expirate!
Sweet memories of you appear unbidden;
The virtue—patience—I must cultivate.
The weeks slip by; the pace of life is grueling;
Now thoughts of you do not my soul consume.
So imperceptibly! my passion's cooling.
I wonder idly, shall our love resume?
For now our destiny remains elusive;
Your silences I shall not deem conclusive.

Amanda Krug
THROUGH COLORS IN YOUR HANDS
You're such a special friend
Who's very close to me.
And you should not be ashamed
Because you cannot see.
Your ears hear so much more than mine,
You sense things I don't see.
My eyes are yours, your hands are mine,
Together we are free.
I've helped you feel what red is like;
Your hands were over fire.
I want to understand your heart
And fill all your desires.
I've shown you what white is like;
Your hands were touching cotton
And I'll help you feel what beauty's like;
A sense that's not forgotten.
I know your eyes can't see it all,
But try to understand:
God's given you the gift of sight
Through colors in your hands.

Shari Margolis
DRAW THE LINE
This poem is dedicated to Jennette Allen.

Split me in half,
Half of a job I'll do.
Half will be with you
Where do you Draw the Line?
Where is it fine?
Split me in half
you'll find you'll laugh.
No two places are
the same if you go
insane.
Split me in half
I'll fly out the window
I'll run down the
meadow and in the
end you'll be the one
split in half and won't
laugh.
For in the end I'll
be together and you'll
all be broken feathers . . . .

Cathy Melton
FIVE MEMORIES OF MY GRANDFATHER
Noiselessly as the springtime, her crown of verdure weaves, and all the trees on all the hills opened their thousand leaves.

I live for those who love me, whose hearts are kind and true; for the Heaven that smiles above me, awaits my spirit.

Make your garden as fair as you can. You work the hardest, when you are alone. Water the roses and train the vines. Trim the bushes and gather the fruit.

Listen to the trickling stream, that wears the hours away. The autumn wind stirs the withered leaves with a soft breeze.

The tears of earth are dry. The things once hidden, now are clear. Now the light of day—fades my sight away.

Judith Baker Slider
YOUTHFUL MEMORIES ON THE FARM
Time seemed to stand still
as we shared in the chores,
to supply our necessities, our love
endured.
The taste of sweet warm milk,
Dad got from the cows,
and the butter and bread Mom made
with the sweat of her brow.
The serenity of a quiet walk
along the brook,
one of God's many blessings
in this nook.
The aroma of fresh mowed hay,
and the fragrance of Lilacs in May.
The beauty of the sunrise
so early in the morn,
while all of God's creatures
seemed to be reborn.
Our planting of the seeds
for all it would feed,
Our harvesting the golden wheat,
corn and oats to eat.
The picnics we'd have in the field,
while the splendor of the sunset subdued.
How fortunate and blessed we are
to have memories like these
to revere.

Freida P Kirk
WHAT A PRICE!
Dedicated to God's glory and inspired by His holy word!

Thank you, Lord, for giving your life that I might live,
You knew before You became flesh what You were to give!
On that cross, how You suffered and died,
Nail-pierced hands, feet, and a sword thrust in Your side.
A crown of thorns they pressed on Your head
Brought more blood for You to shed.
Oh, Dear Jesus, the agony You had to go through, what love,
You were the only begotten Son from heaven above.
No one else could have said it like You,
Father, forgive them, for they know not what they do!
Because sinful man could not make it on his own
You came to earth and made yourself known,
Forgave them their sins they had sown.
You had the power to prevent
But for Your great love and why You were sent
You allowed man to crucify You, and
Man grumbles to give his tenth.
Please forgive me, Lord, for all of my sin,
Let Your dear sweet Spirit dwell within.
Make me Your servant, do with me what You choose,
I know I'm not worthy, but Lord God, I love You!

Margaret M Jay
FACETS
I caught a snowflake in my hand
And held it close so I could see,
Then gazed, quite lost in my delight,
Its beauty so bedazzled me.

It could not stay and so I saw
My lovely snowflake disappear.
All that remained within my hand
Was one small drop of water, clear.

I dreamed a distant galaxy
Where all the compass points are gone
And snowflake solar systems whirl
Around their alien, silver suns.

Worlds crystalline and gem-hued send
Light flinging towers to pierce the air
And snowflakes their true spans fulfill
In beauty that no man could bear.

Margaret M Jay
VOICES FROM THE KINGDOM OF NATURE
WE
We are called animal
We share the earth

Different species
Self conscious
With place and purpose
Miracles of creation
Formed to function to perfection in our environment
No different from you we were shaped by God

Beware how you waste and mutilate us to your ends
Heedless of our agony our death
Do not be prey to twisted words
You were given stewardship not dominion over us
You frail and feeble fellow being
Defiler on the oh so fragile soil
Consumed and ruined by your kind
We say again Beware
We are not yours
Look around you and believe
We hold within our Kingdom's perfect Balance
Your life . . . or death.

Margaret M Jay
THE FIRST FRIENDS
A Child was in a stable born, soft cradled in the hay,
While, overhead, a mighty star turned night to golden day.
And, witness to the birth of hope,
That Child's first friends were near,
They shared His coming to this world and all that waited here.
"But who were they, these gentle friends,
Such trust and honor given?

Perhaps they came with wondrous gifts
Straight from the halls of Heaven."
"Ah, no, dear friend, they had no gifts,
From weary toil they came.
None were more humble, more despised,
But none have known more fame.
In history's page and sacred text and in cathedrals grand,
Within the Holy Family an ox and donkey stand.
For all beasts, God, this truth reveals,
How precious in His sight
His first friends, there beside their Lord,
That starry Christmas night."

Margaret M Jay
AHIMSA
If just one gives up selfish thought
Closer to God all life is brought,
Or asks for strength the pain to bear,
In that prayer all God's creatures share.
If Nature's truth just one can see
All life can touch Divinity.
If with Compassion's Light we gaze
And in this world that Light we raise
Not just one, but all life gives praise.

Margaret M Jay
RETURNING
If I can find that winding road
That leads to things made new.
That curving, turning, bending road
That leads to dreams come true,
Where questions all are answered
And all promises are kept,
Where anguished conflicts are resolved
And all the tears are wept.
That very long and winding road
Will lead me back to you,
Then new things will seem old to me
And old things will be new.

Thomas A Villante
UNTITLED
In a world where dreams are shattered
Hopes and wishes broken and battered
There sits a young man, tired and distraught
As he tries to unlearn all he was taught
To forget all the lies, the war, and the hate
To exist in this life, how tragic a fate
His world is hurled into a well of grey
As his struggle continues day after day
He simply sits and asks himself why
As slowly a tear escapes from his eye
He aimlessly wanders and opens his mind
And sends forth a wish despite the unkind
The wish took off and flew with grace
And chanced by an angel floating through space
She followed it back, through the grey she sped
And found the young man lying still almost dead
Gently she kissed him and denied her defeat
Astonished eyes opened and he rose to his feet
He embraced his angel who came from above
He smiled and kissed her for he knew this was love.

Eileen Passeri
ADDICTION

To Julie, who helped me to see. To mom, whose prayer and love helped me to be free.

It began as a crutch, just a little, not much
I did not mean for it to happen.
But soon its deadly clutch wound around me like a mummy's death dressing . . .
Stopping all feeling but for the love of it.
It is so jealous, so selfish, wanting you to exist
only for it, and helplessly you do.
Lying, cheating become everyday occurrences, so no one will know how low you can go
Then someone who loved me as I could not love myself, saw in me what it
would not allow, and courageously helped me to see I really wanted to be free
And I am, finally, and in thanks from my soul which I again possess
I say, just say no doesn't go
Just don't start, DEATH is the finish

Bernadet DeJonge
WHY DO YOU?
Why do you constantly
ruin our lands?
Why is our world
dying at your hands?

Why do you make
the products that ruin our earth?
Why do you risk a life
at birth?

Why do you kill
the innocent creatures?
Why cover with oil
our beautiful beaches?

Why knock down
the trees that belong?
Why put up buildings
do they make you feel strong?

Why do you ruin
our natural beauty?
Don't you realize this earth
is our God given duty?

Scott McCullough
MIRROR, MIRROR
Mirror, Mirror in my hand;
Help me try to understand,
Why the image that I see
Isn't what it used to be.
The strain, the age show clearly now,
In the wrinkle of my brow.
The look of youth has slowly faded;
Or could it be I've only traded
Fleeting youth for what may be
An older but a wiser me.
And as I hold me in my hand;
I think perhaps I understand.

Peg Tesluk
LET ME FIND MYSELF

To my loving husband, Joe.

I am bursting with energy, can't you see?
I'm alive with so much to give—I want to be free.
Release me from this prison that I put myself in.
Give me the strength, let me do what I can.
Let me conquer my fears and my faults.
Get me out of this trap in which I am caught.
I feel compelled to camouflage my real self.
Help me to overpower these feelings and get me down from the shelf.
I want to laugh, to live, to love and to feel.
I want to find on this earth, what is so real.
Let me bloom and let me grow.
Give me the confidence that I long to know.
I want to climb out of my past,
To find my worth and true being, at last.
Help me not to fear rejection, anymore,
For that's one of the keys to open the door.
I want to open up to myself and to others,
And to try not to fear the unknown—that smothers.
So if I can be me and learn to trust myself,
Then I am free at last and fear nothing else.

Epifanio Borrello
WJKYX
With A I'm going to ride
With B in the woods
With C to the castle
With D I explore the islands
With E from Eleusy
With F to France
With G I enjoy
With H without words
With I defend myself
With L I go mad
With M & cry
With N sorrow is relieved
With O I hide in the circle
With P the fire I hold
With Q I get angry
With R the frogs in the pool
With S the snakes in the hat
With T thinking about Time
With U don't step outdoors
With V talking
With Z catch the flies
. . .

AB ORIGINE UNIVERSI

Alan Jackson
NUKED WHILE IN A BAR
The bartender flunked sociology.
The sociologist is a failed novelist.
The novelist is a failed short story man.
The S.S. Fantasizer flunked poetry.
The poet dropped acid
And out of sight.

Only Zenman was left.

US: Sir?
HIM: What is it?
US: Is there anything you'd like to say, sir, after this tremendous explosion?
HIM:

Rubble and rain.

Mary Paxton
LIFE

In honor of my loving husband, Michael L. Paxton.

As a young girl of seventeen
Doc said, I'd walk no more,
A bullet had ceased my dancing
With a severed spinal cord.
Life as I knew it, had ended
But God would set things right,
He gave me strength, and made me look
At the world in a different light.
My destiny was in his hands

And in my heart I knew,
Some day my world would be
complete
With a love real and true.
It wasn't easy, and time went on
With God right by my side,
Knowing he was always there
Gave me a smoother ride.
Four years later, into my life
Walked a wonderful, beautiful man,
God had sent him just for me
It was all as he had planned.

John Lauricella

John Lauricella
GARC CLEANING CORP

John L. Best Poem 1990.

Here I'm home Greenwich illustration onther poem an working with cleaning corp arc. Someone interaction us gave him shirt he not come back home. I don't know why, they want him want him. Post to be shirt arc. On it my picture with this poem. Post to be working with cleaning group. Me like Peggy ware take our photograph with 2 guys at 114 Grove 57 Stamford Conn me work Stamford.

Erika I Smith
FROM DEEP WITHIN
I found it in the streets of M_____.
Hadn't seen it since I stepped onto
these shores
bearing "burdens" which had
no pious origin.
Hadn't felt it since I plunged head
first
into a dilating pool of pitch
labeled COLORED.
I found it in those avenues
turned brown from blood and grey
from ghettos
and black from me.
When I trekked through my rain
forest of shame,
swam fathoms deep in my oceans of
anger
and climbed to the wind-whipped
heights of my
mountainous hate
It emerged;
from the depths of my molten soul.
From beneath the past and the
present.
From inside of me.
IDENTITY
lay compressed, forged, uncut
but brilliant.

Veronica Ann
CHRISTMAS
Christmas time is coming soon
And I am so excited.
I'm writing Santa a letter at noon
I know he'll be delighted.
We had an important test today,
I couldn't pay attention.
I was busy thinking of Santa's sleigh
And the gifts, too many to mention.
In gym class, I lost at every game.
I was trying to remember every
reindeer's name.
I couldn't touch my food at lunch,
This is really such a drain.
I know what I'd love to munch,
A great big candy cane.
I keep gazing out the window
While the rest of my class spells.
Each time I hear the wind blow,
I know I hear jingle bells.
The principal called my mother
today,
He said he couldn't reach her.
I don't know why he called her
anyway,
After all, I am the teacher!

Paul M Varga
WANNA DANCE?

To Martha,
My best friend and fan.

Waltzes, mambas, or fox trots,
Today, do not give girls the hots,
They're past the stroll, overdone the
twist,
The funky chicken will seldom be
missed,
They dance their own way, they do
their own thing,
They've found their own new style of
swing,
Swinging the front, swinging the
back,
And even the sacro-iliac,
Now they robot, slam, and freak,
Yell and scream, yet never speak,
The clothes: they stretch, expand, and
show,
The neckline, shoulders, and what's
below,
Guys and girls against the wall,
Gossiping, gaping amongst it all,
Of all the dances out on the floor,
Today, there's usually found one
more.

Penelope A Marzec
SHADOWS
The world is consumed by shadows,
Blotting out the blue of the sky.
Or is it because the mud-speckled
windows of the bus
Have settled a blot in my eye?
  Certainly a gritty smear is hiding
  the sun from view,
  And faces are tinted a ghastly
  gray,
  Not a ray of hope could gleam
  through.
I see people hurry on the slate
sidewalks,
To houses, stone-bleak, row on row.
Doors open into black abyss,
Then shut, where did they go?
  The snow, so pure and clean last
  night,
  Looks now like coal-colored
  mounds.
  At the end of this ride will I gain
  back my sight?
Perhaps tears alone would wash
away,
The grime that clouds all I see.
Saline, antiseptic, cleansing baptism,
For a vista, wide and free.

Judy West Zech
CHILDREN OF POVERTY
They stand there:
With big, beautiful, sad eyes
A hand reaches out
A little voice cries: I'm hungry
You reach into your pocket
The amount is small
As you walk away
Your heart aches
If only I had the power
To change the world
You see: I'm hungry too
So I stand tall
As I ask: Why God: Why?

Ann Wood
THE LETTER
Dear Jesus, I'm writing you this letter
In answer to the one you wrote to me,
It took me such a long, long time to
find it,
But I found it, where you'd nailed it
to the tree.

You say that you are living with your
Father,
That He's given you His kingdom as
your own,
And His angels call you "Lord and
King" forever,
As you sit with your Father on His
throne.

You tell me you are building me a
mansion,
That a robe and a crown will soon be
mine,
And a ring you have, ready for my
finger,
And I'll reign with you 'till the end
of time.

Thank you Lord, for healing my
diseases,
And for dying in my place to set me
free.
Thank you for your blood that sealed
the promise,
That you nailed with the letter to the
tree.

Lord, I'm looking forward to this
journey,
Though crooked and bumpy is the
road,
But I'll follow all the guidelines that
you gave me,
For you said you would help me bear
the load.

And I'll listen for the blowing of that
trumpet,
I'll watch for the clouds to roll away,
And I'll join that raptured throng in
heaven,
Singing praises to the Lamb! . . .
Oh happy day.

Julia Jordan Culver
BATHE YOUR SOUL IN BEAUTY
Talk to God often;
Read His written word.
Love people, especially children.
Keep a song in your heart
And a smile on your face.
Walk in God's out-of-doors,
And listen to birds' songs
And wind through the trees.
Look up often,
And you will see the sky,
The sun, the moon, the stars;
You will come closer to God
Who will bathe your soul in beauty.

Mary E Rogers
A SOLDIER'S PRAYER

In loving memory of my brother, Lance Corporal Jerry E. Metcalf who was killed in a rice paddy in Vietnam on June 15, 1967, time has not erased the emptiness.

As the soldier looked down from the
heavens above,
Down on the earth and the land that
he loved,
He saw its beautiful mountains, its
rivers and streams,
The land of opportunity, of freedom
and dreams.
Then he looked down at the red,
white, and blue.
The flag he defended, being burned
by a few.
His heart began aching, his eyes
filled with tears,
Dear God, what's the reason for the
flames and the sneers?
What has happened to my people,
where is their pride?
Have they forgotten we carried that
flag as we died?
That flag was our symbol, of a land
free and true,
For hundreds of years it has carried
us through.
If there ever was anything for which
this country stood,
It was the flag that told others our
land was free and good.
Have you forgotten my mother who
cries over my grave?
Or the imprisoned others, still strong
and brave?
We fought for our country, some
gave their lives for that flag,
Yet you dare let them burn it, deface
it, and call it a rag?
We gave the gift of freedom,
unselfishly, for you and your own,
Are your eyes so blind that this
dishonor you condone?
That flag cannot burn, you just can't
let it be.
Please stop this nonsense and listen
to me!
Let it fly proudly, please protect it
from harm,
Let it be unfurled proudly, o'er your
cities and farms.
If you allow it to happen, if you let it
burn,
You are killing America and the
honor thousands fought proudly to
earn.
I wish I could be there, I'd try to find
a way,
But my days with you were taken, so
I can only pray,
That God will give you guidance, and
the strength to decide,
The flag we all died for shall not
burn, but fly with reverence and
pride.

Nicole Pollini
HOLD ON
Hold on to memories let them be
movies in your mind
they're the best part of life, they're
one of a kind.

Hold on to memories but let time go
by,
You can capture a moment although
time does fly.

Hold on to memories, they're the best

things to hold
And if things shall change through time you'll always stand bold.

Hold on to memories for if you do,
You'll always remember the love I had for you.

Connie Wilkes Davis
OH MOMMA

Dedicated to Mary Louise Marsden —April 20, 1918 —August 17, 1989.

Oh Momma, I miss you with my broken heart
Oh Momma, my world is torn apart

I am so lost and so alone
Oh Momma, how can I live on

You have loved me selflessly all my life
And I know at times your agony was like a painful knife

I wish my pride had not stood in the way
And I could give you smiles and kisses for your last days

Your spirit is now part of my soul
You are the woman I most adore

You were my only link of love with this old world
Momma, you are still my best girl

My heart speaks to you now
I want to bring you back — I don't know how

Who will I come home to when I am free
Who will love me so unconditionally

I am not free as you wanted me to be, but
Momma, I would rather you be free than me, from your heartfelt misery

I broke the chains of agony and set your heart free
Momma, I love you—more than me

I prayed to the Blessed Virgin Mary to take away the suffering
you have so long endured
My prayers fell on loving ears and into Heaven you've soared

No more pain and heart ache for your sweet soul
Oh Momma, I love you so.

Ty Raymond Smith
THE DRUID MISTY

Silver stars embroidered on black satin sky
Are obscured as fleecy clouds race by
The wind howls out a mournful tune
I gather my things, a storm comes soon

A sharp tongue of lightning licks the sky
And the wind builds to a shrieking cry
Thunder rolls like a dragon's roar
As I watch boats scramble for shore
Blades of rain slash the heavy air
As the wind wildly whips my hair
The air around me becomes soaking cold
They tempted my wrath though they were told

I'm a priestess of Nature, Daughter of Storm
Mother of nature in its most violent form
You may tempt my wrath but hear my advice
Seldom lives the one who will try it twice

Heather M Wood
WILD CHILD'S DREAM

This is to the man who promises today the memories of the past and the dreams of the future.

Time separates us
but still our love stays strong
and so it will until forever is gone
Sometimes it scares me
and you hold me till my fear subsides
all through the night
and together we make everything right
Being with you is like living a dream
and bad things are not as bad as they seem
I've never felt love in such
a strong but delicate way
and it gets better everyday
We are children of the sun
shining with warmth
We love in the light of the moon
knowing that tomorrow will be here soon
and together we will face tomorrow
as tomorrow becomes today
and yesterday became a dream
I understand, if only for a moment,
how love is supposed to be.

Monica Nelson
CLINTON ROBERT DEMPSTER, IF YOU CAN HEAR ME . . .

I can remember
the dimples set in your cheeks,
your strawberry-blonde hair
shining in the summer sun,
your child-like eyes,
your infectious laughter,
and bribing you with cherry suckers
so that I could ride
your horse, Ajax.

Don't hate me
for not going to your funeral.
I could not,
I did not want to see
your cancer-ridden body,
or the numerous,
saddened faces of the crowd.
Let me remember you
as I see you in my mind.

Clinton Robert Dempster
if you can hear me . . .
you are missed greatly
and dearly loved.

Lonny Ricker
LOVE'S PATH

Lost somewhere out on the horizon of time
Confused and lonely with nothing to do
Just sitting around waiting to be found
Ready to walk blindly
Down a dead end road
Don't walk alone
Each step could lead to disaster
Falling, tripping, losing your ground
Wait for the morning glow
Follow love's path to the rainbow

Don't leave the path
Lust lurks in the shadows
Temptation leads to broken hearts
It's a frequently traveled path
Don't think you're the first or the last

Many souls have been lost
Broken hearts slowly mending
Scars left for a reminder
Find the path again
Just don't give in!

Erlinda Romo
WHAT IS A MOTHER

This poem was written especially for my precious mother-in-law (Annie Romo) whom I love very much, and who is like a mother to me. She is one of God's special creations for her family.

A warm glow consumes my being as
I give a tentative thought to,
"what is a mother." A mother is a
well of wisdom that her
children can draw from at a
moment's notice, for priceless is
her worth in words, and limitless is
her understanding.

As a mother weeps for the hurts
afflicted her by thoughtless
children, the tears are gathered in
God's well of protection,
and as he views the anguish and
sadness of a mother's pain, he
gently brushes her tears away.

A mother "fragile" as a lily white on
a cool, crisp night but
yet knowing that a steady wave of
Godly strength fills her in
every way by sheer, divine grace,
listens as God speaks to her
today.

"I made you a mother because of my
love, and the children you
bore were my design. A precious
sight you are to me, for I
hold close all that is mine. My plan
was designed from original
times to make you a mother with a
purpose in mind.

"Take comfort in my words, trust me
with your children as my own.
Angels I sent to pave their way and if
they trip and fall along
the way, "fear not," for as they finally
learn to stand on their
own, a vision will appear aglow for
them to see, of a mother
softly crying on a throne of solid
gold, as tears so crystal
and clear call to them and say, "child,
you are finally home!"

Missie Blackburn
IT'LL ONLY HURT MORE

Don't look back
When you head for the door.
'Cause if you do
It'll only hurt more.

Don't stop to explain
Don't tell me why.
If you're going to leave
Just tell me good-bye.

I love you. I'll miss you.
But I can make it on my own.
I want you. I need you.
But I'll hold my own.

'Cause I can't tie you down.
You've got to be free.
And I'll make you love
Only me.

So don't look back.
I'll tell you again.
Just tell me good-bye
If this is the end.

Jodie M Rahn
QUESTIONABLE LOVE

Dedicated to the time of my life when much was in question.

Feelings that you cannot see,
Sealed within by lock and key,
Are the deepest part of me,
Should they not be protected?

If I could only spend my days,
Not running circles in a maze,
Nor searching thru a misty haze,
For my love to be respected.

A simple phrase, — I love you,
Yet so strong and remains true,
Held securely just by two,
With an unknown magic potion.

Still you chose not to believe,
Tho, remember as you leave,
A single heart will surely grieve,
For love's a deep emotion.

John A Doughton
SO FARAWAY BUT CLOSE TO MY HEART

Not a day goes by
That I don't think of her
She has a spirit that moves like the wind
And humor that draws so much laughter

We met on a very special day
Where friends gathered for Thanksgiving
But this day meant so much more
For I knew it was only the beginning

She has such a bright smile
With an internal burning desire
To bring happiness to all
She set my heart on fire

The talent she presents
Rises above by far
Others aspiring
She can only be a star

My thoughts are with her
Even though we're apart
This very special holiday season
So far away but close to my heart

Elia Dirtclaud
NO TITLE

Formless clouds,
Not in the sky
Not in my mind,
Drift endlessly.

What could catch a cloud?
Make it a form?
What could stop a cloud,
to disperse it into nothing?

Unattachable,
Drifting along paths,
One must avoid the walls
Cast before thee.

John A Doughton
THE NIGHT THAT HAD A SILVER LINING

As the sun goes down
The moon rises so high above

As I walk blindly into the night
Not knowing I would fall in love

It seemed to happen so suddenly
As if time had just stood still
I turned my head slowly, there she was
Oh God is she for real

The beauty she presented
The sparkle in her eyes
As I looked deep inside
I saw endless blue skies

I felt so nervous
This could change my life forever
Is this the girl, the one
We would finally be together

The moment we met
She seemed so fresh from the start
I knew somehow, very soon
She would have my heart

The feelings were so strong
They go on without defining
I will remember this evening forever
The night that had a silver lining

John A Doughton
FOREVER & EVER

To my dearest Lynne, my undying love for you forever & ever.

To every song
There's a beginning and an end
In everyone's life
There's that very special friend

I never thought
I'd have feelings this strong
For any one person
I know, I just know can't be wrong

I think about you
From sunrise to sunset
For these deepest feelings
I will never forget

And during the night
My dreams all come true
Because when we're together
My heart touches you

May all these feelings
Be forever endeavored
Because I will always love you
Forever & ever

Marynadine Melander
AN EARLY MEMORY
That very first memory
cut in her bedroom
is indelible,
like the fat spools
of hot violet thread
on her sewing machine,
sitting old, my mother, too,
like the buckling of her bones
on the brass bed, buttoned
to the naked springs,
to the June darkness,
to the moment that held me
as a warm wet summer seed
beneath a bedspread
of violets—a pattern
cut from the womb—Quietly,
I stepped—with
an umbilical thread
to unravel the sun.

Jennifer Miller
UNTITLED
Why does he hit me? I want to know
Why am I still here? I want to go.
I love him and my feelings are true.
But why? He hits me 'til I'm black and blue.
When we argue or if we fight.
He hits me and it just isn't right.
He always calls me terrible names.
Maybe it's my fault, am I to blame?
The way he treats me, I'd like to die.
If this is love, then love is a lie.
Everyone tells me to leave him, to get away. But it all gets harder every single day
Is it my love for him that holds us together? 'Cuz if it is, I couldn't do this forever

Pamela L Hilker
A MOTHER'S PRAYER

Dedicated with Love to Kyle and Brent, inspired by the memory of Lisa F. Kolb.

For years I prayed to God above
to fill our home with lots of love,
and, the pitter patter of little feet
I knew would make our home complete.
I had many tests and operations, with pain, fears and tears,
and I knew it would take more than a few years
for the children we wanted to conceive,
there were so many frustrations, it was hard to believe.
After 10 long years, with
prescriptions and problems I bore,
when I told my Doctor NO MORE, NO MORE!!
Then my prayers were answered,
my heart was no longer torn
for in 9 short months, our son Kyle was born.
What a change he made in our lives over night
with diapers, bottles and crying what a fright.
Just 16 months after Kyle, when all my stitches had healed,
came another little bundle, our son Brent appeared.
So, now when I lay me down to sleep,
I pray the Lord for my children to keep
them from harm, and not to make a peep,
'cause I could sure use a good night sleep! Amen

Hope D Davis
MY FLAG
My thoughts drift along with the tides of the ocean
To the shores where hate has taken her stand,
And moving like wind in a race for destruction,
She gloats at her conquest of another land.

Serenely she rests in the hearts of the rulers,
Watching her death-dealing forces take toll,
Thrilling to piteous cries of the helpless,
Enjoying the dream of reaching her goal.

Gladly my thoughts race back to my homeland,
My heart fills with love, my spirits soar high,
For here 'neath the folds of the star spangled banner
I'm loved and protected as my flag waves in the sky.

Janet McCann
TOO LITTLE WAS THE HAPPINESS
A hat covered his white thinning hair.
He had a cane he took everywhere.
He would see her on his walk,
He would always stop to talk
About her yard and flowers,
Maybe there's a chance for showers.
He never knew her name,
He liked her just the same.
Then he would walk his mile,
She had a lovely smile.
One day he picked a big bouquet,
Thought that he might stay
And have the cup of tea
She'd offered, underneath her tree.
The ambulance was at her door,
They said she'd fallen on the floor.
He laid the flowers on her step,
With head bowed low, he wept.
Too little was the happiness.
Too late to realize.

Kari Mikell Lund
FEELINGS
As I sit here watching the snowfall,
I feel the sad and loneliness
Throughout my body.
I ask myself why?
Why do I feel more pain and sadness
Instead of joy and happiness?
Is being happy something
I know nothing about.
Or is life what brings me down.
I will still search for the end
Of the rainbow in the big blue sky.
So I can feel the happiness
I so much want to feel
Instead of all this hurt, cold and
Pain, I feel deep inside.

Jonathan Kocovsky
TIMES PAST

Dedicated to my ever loving mother Marie Ludwig, who has always stood by my side.

I sit by myself in this lonely room,
never actually alone.
These thoughts are with me always haunting,
my lips expel a groan.
Try as I might to clear a path,
for thoughts of beauty ten-fold.
My past comes back with relentless wrath,
making my blood run cold.
So I am forced to sit dwelling again
on days of long ago,
ever attacking and haunting me
touching my very soul.

Nicole Myrick
MEMORIES

Dedicated to my Aunt Alberta Boggon, Died January 20, 1990. She gave her life as a gift to others.

Memories they come, and they go.
Sometimes they go very slow.
The bad sometimes, never come back.
They are like a thrown away sack.

But the memories of love,
We've learned from the start
Are always the best, to hold near our heart
Because they never really ever go.
They stay to warm our heart
And keep our memories safe
Through the longest of days, and darkest of night.

Nahum B Castillo
ODE TO THE PRISONERS OF WORK
Hear ye— Hear ye, all ye Prisoners of Work!
Your cries of despair, I have heard around the fork,
As well as your groans of oppression,
Coupled with your moans of frustration.

"A Prisoner of Work am I," says ye,
"And being held against my will, I be."
Held by work-related circumstances,
Beyond one's control and surrounded by high fences.

I have heard your whisperings, though faint,
Expounding on the lack-of-promotion complaint.
"Too much work and not enough pay!",
Seems to be the continuous saying of the day.

Seeing more of the whole picture than ye,
I could very well tell ye how wrong ye be.
Wrong in your thinking and feeling,
But, alas ye would only send me reeling.

Well, have no fear, ye POW's all,
Your liberator will help you climb over that wall.
Although your circumstances, ye do not explain,
Take ye at your word, I will, without refrain,
And do as ye asketh.

From your perspective, ye are absolutely correct!
Therefore, convince ye otherwise, I will not, in fact.
So, take ye at your word, I will,
Believing ye know what ye want in this deal.

The key to your freedom and liberty,
The Personnel Officer guards, but without a fee.
Hidden, but yet within easy reach for whomsoever,
The yearning for freedom is an endeavor.

The freedom key encoded is with
"SF-52" on its face.
A copy ye will be freely given so you can run your race,
Without any hassle or recrimination,
As long as freedom is your destination.

Escape from any POW Camp, an easy thing is not, by far,
For many things and plans to consider, there are.
And even if successful ye are in your escape,
Will ye be able to reach your Happiness Cape?

Well have no fear, ye POW's all,
The key ye now hold that will get you over that wall.
But hearken to my counsel for there is no turning back.
If go ye must, I hope success ye never lack.
And so I have done as you asketh!

Jacqueline Trish Seville
OF PERMANENCE
Tonight my friend, you are
welcomed . . .

. . . a little place is made for you;
nestled among the dense forest,
and spun through the windmills,
too!

I usher you in and when I wish,
summon you without pleading!
I share our togetherness and
never fear your leaving!
I can hold you at my leisure,
touch you with warmth and truth;
I can count on forever being pleased,
because time cannot reach you!

Your permanence is penetrating!
It belongs to the present . . .
It belongs to the past!
It is the beginning chapter . . .
. . . A story that will always last!!

There are many other members,
but you are one of a kind . . .
that treads the very pathways . . .
. . . Of the stairwells of my mind!

Teres Seits

A WIFE'S FEELINGS

To Kevin Seits, the man I love.

One side says yes, one side says no.
Even if I live to a hundred, which
way do I go?
I'm always at home to take care of
things,
Though sometimes I wish I could just
sprout wings.
Everyone tells me, you're good at
what you do.
I sure do crave just a mention from
you.
It could be as simple as a special hug.
Something that tells me you're still in
love.
I know you've tried as hard as you
can.
You really are one hell of a man.
You do your best for all of us
But often I feel lost in your dust.
Most might think I'm feeling sorry
for myself.
It seems my needs keep getting
farther back on the shelf.
I'll always be there on that you can
depend.
I'm not a bad lover, and a pretty good
friend.
If you were to look deep inside.
for me you might muster a whole
new pride.
It never gets out from behind your
cloud.
I know of you I'm deeply proud.
Life will go on that's a sure bet.
Whether or not my needs are being
met.

Elizabeth A Kidd

THEFT

For Heather Ann Carey, my first grandchild.

With the dimpling of a dimple,
The crinkle of an eye
The sound of happy gurgling,
The oh, so plaintive cry.
How could such a small thing,
Using sound and sight as art
Steal so unknowingly, her proud
New Grandma's heart.

Andrea Canonico

BLUE JAY

When the Blue Jay sings
Quiddle! Quiddle!
it wants me to play this
old fiddle!
and it makes me dance upon
my feet, when I hear the
Blue Jay sing so sweet, especially
when she touches me, so, down deep,
it also wants to make me weep!
As I open my window and hear,
quiddle! I'll run right
out and meet her and sing
Hi Diddle, Diddle!

Quiddle! Quiddle!

Willard Todd Jr

IMAGINATION

To my wife Renee; without her love and support this would not be possible.

Show me the way
to the stars
and I shall travel
on the wings of my dream
and with the power
of my imagination
I will journey to the place
wherein lies the visions
of my heart's desire

Andrea Canonico

Andrea Canonico

MOONLIGHT

To my great friend, Nicholas Trinceri.

Oh what a beautiful night
on that pale moonlight, for
it gives me a fright, just to
have a dark night.
Oh what a delight for that shiny
shiny night.

I get uptight when I don't see the
light.
So hurray for that great big moon's
light.
It's sheer delight when I gaze
into the
moon's light, so bright!
Thank you dear night for having such
a beautiful moonlight.
Good night!

Andrea Canonico

LITTLE HEART'S DESIRE

On Christmas night,
By the fire's burning light,
I just got a present that's
unusually pleasant and it's
not a pup, it's an old but
most valued cup!

it's something you just can't
use up! and just think
Grand-ma Lil paid only a buck.
It's better than receiving one
of Nichola's ducks.
I'll always love and treasure
my own little cup!

Marita J Ledbetter

VISITORS

The blackbird with his wings dipped
in red
yelled at me—time to be fed.
What joy they bring to us each day
as they stop to feed, then go on their
way.

Then out of the woods red and white
prairie woodpecker sweeps into sight;
his tapping rings out loud and clear
on our maple tree he too is dear.

God's birds come in different hues
a riot of color, they come by twos
and threes until clouds of bright
wings arrive on morning's light.

Toni Elling

MY FRIEND

I've lost my friend.
Last week marked the end
of words and deeds shared.
I've lost someone who cared.
But, I'll remember how he gave
of himself
And always had time for
somebody else,
How he never had an unkind
word to say
Even if things didn't go his way.
I'll remember he was witty
and so wise,
Liked things pretty, and, Oh! his
eyes—
Full of mischief and most times
gladness.
Often he helped rid me of sadness:
He knew what to say, what to do
Whenever he would find me blue.
He was full of happiness and
dreams
And I'll miss him 'cause now
it seems
That I am all alone.
And I'm afraid that on my own
I won't be able to face each day
Knowing my friend has gone
away.
I shall go on, but, sadly,
'Cause you see, I loved him
madly.

Linda Miller Booth

MY "REAL" MOM

Dedicated, with love, to the most wonderful mother a "chosen child" could ever have: My "Real" Mom—Vanda E. Miller.

"Any man can be a father,"
I've heard these words before.
"It takes a special man to be a
Daddy,"
I could not agree with them any
more.

My Daddy was a very special man
If I had been his, I couldn't love him
more
But, now let's look at the Mother's
side
Of Life's revolving door.

Most women can be mothers,
If Nature steps in to play her part.
But, to cherish and raise someone
else's child,
Takes "real love" from the purest
heart.

My Mom was there when I needed
her,
To understand and calm my fears.
When life's problems seem too great
to bear,
She's always there to dry my tears.

When asked, "Do you know who
your 'real' Mom is?"
The only woman it could possibly be,
Is the one, who although, she
couldn't give birth,
Gave me herself and shared Life with
me.

Linda Miller Booth

PRAYER FOR DADDY

Dedicated to a very special man who "chose me," raised me, sometimes did not understand me, but, no matter what, always loved me. My Daddy—Charles E. Miller.

Dear God, I know I haven't prayed to
You so often,
But, I feel that I must talk to You
today.
I know You don't do things without a
reason,
But, I wish You didn't take my Dad
away.

God, I know that people cannot live
forever,
And I know that in this life we all
must die.
But, You took my Daddy from us all
so quickly.
That we didn't even get to say,
"goodbye."

Lord, in Your eyes Dad might not
have looked so perfect,
But, to us down here, he seemed to
be that way.
Won't You please take good care of
him in Heaven,
So, that we can meet again some
happy day.

Now, I'm all grown up, I am a wife
and mother
And, I've travelled far and near
across this world
Now, we're far apart, we cannot be
together,
But, I'll always be my Daddy's little
girl.

Dear God, you must have known that
Dad was growing weary.
So, You called him, though we
wanted him to stay.
Won't You please tell Daddy, we still
love him dearly.
And, we miss him more and more,
each passing day.
Yes, we miss him more and more
each passing day.

Lanetta Kiddy
PEOPLE
People come in different shapes and sizes—
But they can't help that—

People are quite different from each other.
No one looks or acts the same—

So you see people have different meanings
of things also

They also do different from others. I guess
you could say people are really beautiful
in their own way

Pat McKinlay
LAST LETTER
My dear, dear Father . . . oh, please let go . . .
I watch you in silence, struggling so.
Firm grasp of your hand,
strong thrust of your pulse,
yet God . . . He is calling,
please, please heed His voice.

Enveloped in warmth of the love that does flow,
your family all with you . . . why hesitate so?
A rich realm awaits you,
without stress or strain . . .
and freedom from burdens,
and bodily pain.

I pray here beside you, I hold your warm hand.
So gracefully dying, no more you can stand.
Dear Father I love you,
you've long stood the test.
Your family all here now . . .
let God do the rest.

Eric Lanphier
LIFE OF A CHILD
A child running through a green field
filled with colorful daffodils.
Being chased by an innocent puppy,
As they romp and play on God's perfect field,
The wind spreads its strength over the land
I, a stranger from time, stand between the two
dimensions.
Child develops into a man, and the puppy
grows old, then dies.
The man's parents are no longer alive.
His face tells a long and tired story.
He looks out onto what was once a field of beauty,
And all he sees is the black earth and one dead daffodil,
A compassionate tear falls from my eye
As I walk back into a time that never was.

Stacy Lane
ONCE . . .
As I lay upon a carpet of green,
I ponder at the floating dreams
Passing by on a canvas of silk blue.
Thinking of you and me,
When once we were young and free:

Roamed emerald meadows
And danced in the shadows of sunsets.
Caressed by the sun
As we flew high with love
Never once thinking our surge of passion
Would crash and scatter.

Yet it did my love;
As I lay here thinking of you and me,
When once we were young and free.

Amber Lynn Werley (Age 10)
A LITTLE BOBWHITE
A little bobwhite sat on a branch
of a pecan tree on my ranch.
He cocked his head and looked so cute!
When he sang it sounded like a flute.
"Bobwhite, bobwhite, where can you be?
Will you please, please answer me?"

This was his song. This was his way.
His song was so pretty, so happy, so gay.
The bobwhite said in a voice so sweet,
"My name is Bob. I'm glad we meet!
I live in a nest up in that tree.
Come by anytime and visit me.
I'd like to stay and chat some more,
but I have to go to the store."

He got off his branch and away did fly.
"Goodbye!" said the bobwhite,
"Goodbye, goodbye!"

Janice Milkis
WHAT SEASHELL ARE MADE OF
Seashell are like bird singing
Seashell are like wine glasses
Seashell are like whispers
Seashell are like raindrops
Seashell are like footsteps
Seashell are the wind blowing
Seashell are like a waterfall
Seashell are like the stars
Seashell are like a brass frame
Seashell are like Easter eggs
Seashell are like a sunset
Seashell are like beautiful flowers
Seashell are like a candle burning
Seashell are like a concert playing
Seashell are like a piano playing
Seashell are like stained glass
Seashell are like buttons
Seashell are like bubbles blowing
Seashell are like someone smile
Seashell are like bubble gum
Seashell are like a gold tray

Janice Milkis
WHAT SONGBIRDS ARE MADE OF
They sound like a seashell, that you found on the beach
They sound like a peaceful nite
They sound like a love bird singing at a wedding
They sound like a piano piece that you hear at a concert
They sound like a Christmas song at Christmas time
They sound like a bell charm ringing at church services
They sound like a baby taking a nap
They sound like a slow dance without the people singing
They sound like rain drops falling on a pond
They sound like snowflakes coming down on a mountaintop
They sound like a peaceful morning in May
They sound like sand so quiet like a pin falling and falling

C Scott Fleming
SHE DOTH BELONG IN CAMELOT
A wondrous visage I behold
With skin so pale and eyes so bold.
Such grace and splendor in her stride,
Pervades my heart with potent pride.

It seems unfit my love to be
A prisoner of simplicity.
She does deserve a better land
Adorned with treasures, fair and grand:
A place of bronze, a place of gold,
A place of fairy tales untold,
Where romance blooms and dreams come true
And tow'ring castles wait for two.

My Dear, this world I'd love to give;
And in it we'd forever live.
Content and tranquil in our plight,
In search of everlasting light.

Ernest "Ol' Ern" Meerpohl
HUMILITY AND PRIDE
He truly was a humble man,
As he went about his way;
Asking naught, expecting naught,
For the deeds he did each day.

Then his friends began to brag on him,
And to tell him how great was he;
Until he finally was convinced,
That he possessed nobility.

With pomp and pride and head held high,
Each day he'd walk the street;
"I'm so proud of my humility,"
He'd say to all he'd meet.

Then his friends began to shun him,
And from his throne he soon did tumble;
For when he took pride unto his side,
He was no longer humble.

Helen Joyce Baker
SEASCAPE AT SANTA CRUZ

To Reverend Dr. Margaret Stevens, Association of Independent Minsters A.I.M. Retreat, & our sister Ministers' inspiration.

I Watch the sea build cresting waves,

Searching more and more.
Its tantalizing fingertips
Come bubbling to the shore.

The wind is roughly playing now
With the water's tousled head.
It spanks the waves to foaming grace,
As they leave their liquid bed.

And I am watching silently
This ever changing scene,
Spectator of GOD'S holy work
AH, yes! It is supreme.

Jean Spurgers
ALASKA IN THE MORNING
The bright red sun beams over the horizon to turn the snow into glistening golden jewels.
The trees cast an eerie shadow as they stand cloaked in white, like debutantes at a ball.
All is still and quite beautiful as the clouds roll in and the snow starts to fall.
The snowflakes drift down and gently rest on the white blanket that is only broken by small animals scurrying for shelter in the cold.
There is nothing as still and peaceful as an Alaska Morning.
Not a sound breaks the beautiful white innocence and you feel like holding your breath for fear the glorious scene will fade.

Spencer Burton
I FRAME

To those who by word I offend.

These etchings are of my frail,
fancied failure in vigor;
dressed lavishing the lacy drape,
to this headpiece such does soar

I indulge part generous,
part from part compassion;
to decor all ornaments,
onslaught my wall, my mansion

Charcoal swirled interiors,
mount and rendition the art;
OFF! a sleigh to discover,
along some channel apart

Lands of near will I welcome,
bon voyage, the journier;
bid me a kind sort of swell,
for I have I; A "vinur."

Lovely Chandla
YOU FASCINATE ME
You fascinate me
Because you're so different from the rest
Who came into my world.
I often reflected upon
The sweet and sour fact
That where is love?
When will those lovely moments
Those sweet sufferings, that blissful trepidation begin?
In no time after that
You walked into my life,
Filled me with much pleasure
And made my world shine bright.
It was a great feeling when I felt your lips on mine
You whispered sweet words
Of declaration of love.
Your voice was melodious and voluptuous.
It asked me a question—
What earthly bliss could be higher than this?
Your warm gestures beckon me.
Shall I go or stop
It stops me because heart aches and mourns.
After each contact of rosy dreams with reality
Reality says, — our union isn't the plan of God.
But my feelings can't be suppressed forever
Corset can't crush the sigh of love and cry of
Anguished heart forever.
I need an outlet for my feelings
Because you fascinate me
Today and forever.

Theresa Beale
EVER SO BOLD
The fire came from deep inside,
For no other could be his bride.
Out he came, strong and bold,
His teeth so white and eyes of gold.

Out to the grass, he came from his lair.
He took the maiden, ever so fair.
The fire he breathed was ever so sweet,
But the ice did not melt despite the

fierce heat.

Ever so deep, he planted a seed.
It grew and festered, like that of a weed.
The dragon did die, it took a great while.
There she sat lost, tears and a smile.

Now she must go,
As it is told.
But she shall return,
Ever so bold.

Margaret L Weaver
PEARL HARBOR

In memory of: Pvt. Archie N. Bullock, U.S. Marine Corp.—Died July 1, 1944.

When the Japanese bombed "Pearl Harbor"
American Mothers' hearts cried
Their Sons would be called into battle
Old Glory could not be denied.

Young men began to enlist
All over this dear old USA
They were all going in as "Brothers"
Determined to make the Japanese pay!

We shook hands and bid "farewell"
Within their hearts they grinned, then said
Greater Love hath no man than this,
He lay down his life for a "Friend."

On the Island of Saipan he was wounded,
Many had fallen, He wasn't alone.
On this "Sea of Suffering," Jesus was walking
HE took his hand, and said, "Come Home."

God must have loved you too, "My Son"
To take you away from war and guns
Now you'll be happy in your "Heavenly Home."
For your work here on earth is done.

Emily Maloney Vest
THE OAKWOOD COTTAGE

Dedicated to my daughter, Patsy Ann Vest Miller and in memory of my daughter, Vonda Sue Vest Graham.

The oakwood cottage that's down by the stream.
I can see it so plain here in my dreams.
Its windows are cracked and the paint is peeling too.
It sets there waiting for someone new.

The yard is filled with weeds, the flowers have all died.
I open the door and wonder inside,
There on the wall, my eyes do consume,
is a beautiful picture of a bride and a groom.

They look so familiar, at them I did gaze,
I thought I must surely know their names.
So I began to wander from room to room,
trying to remember the bride and the groom.

I search through the cottage, but all in vain.
I did not find a trace of their names.
From my dreams I did awake,
and to my amazement there over my bed
hung the same picture of Mother and Dad.

Meredith Millard
SLEEP

Sleep
silently
with no sound at all
within the realm of where dreamers
dare to go

Smile
quietly
as the dawn draws near
before the rest of the world has a chance to know

Laugh
smartly
with those who care to
the many facets of your life you wish to show

Cry
emotionally
for those who have none
no one sees as they do the wind blow

Love
passionately
as if it were the last time
for love is always and does not say no

Felecia A Norris
A LETTER TO MOM

In loving memory, Arguster Norris, May 24, 1938—January 12, 1990.

Hi mom, it's me!

Although you have gone away. I feel as if there is something I didn't get a chance to say.

One Thursday you were here; by Friday you were gone. The emptiness I felt was immediate from the start.

We shared many secrets between us.

I told you that I loved you often enough.

I gave you many flowers while you were here on earth; but I feel as though something is missing, though I don't know what it is yet.

I thought I was prepared for when you'd go away, but I now realize it was just a facade to keep me from thinking of the final day.

The day the Lord called you home, you said you were in good spirits. Did that mean you were ready to go home to heaven's gate?

Mom, I still feel empty now and then. The sadness is still here. I
miss you more than you could possibly know, though at times I know you are near.

I think I know what's missing. I know what I'm trying to say.

There was no time to say goodbye before you went away. I know in my heart you'll be with me always and you're in the Lord's hands from now on.

Goodbye Mom . . . I miss you.

Rebecca A Evans
GARDEN OF LIGHT

Follow the light in my eyes
to a garden of golden waterfalls
and violet clouds,
lakes of liquid light
with shores of crystal snow.

Come deeper, your eyes in mine
touching my soul with all that is you,
and together we will travel
the garden's paths consuming the
pleasures of one another's eyes.

Daniel Valenzuela
WAITING DOWN THE ROWS OF LIGHT

The sun rose down the fields there
Where down the rows of grain with care
The light of waves of sunlight where
The sun rose down the fields there

The hammers crashed the wood flush till
The hours' toil would bring by will
To gather in the evening still
The light of two, the love to fill

And down the rows of setting light
The grain would gather by the night
To make the world, to keep the night
Waiting for the sunrise,
Waiting down the rows of light

Peggie Joice McLaughlin
TRUE LOVE

Dedicated to my family; husband, Tom; son, Jack; step-daughter, Melanie; daughter, Angel; son-in-law Lonney; Grandson, Mike.

I have a vision of a land
so bright and fair,
Where I know my love
I can truly share.
Down here on earth true love
is rarely mentioned,
but in that land there is no tension.
God is a source, so they say,
but to me God is love so I
must obey.
Love rules the heart, soul,
and mind all else will pass
in a span of time.
Love is the ruler now and forever,
I know its name so well, there
is no other, so how can I fail.
The name is Jesus don't you see,
He died upon a tree, and all
because he loved you and me.

Nona Tarvin
LILY

I dedicate this, as with all of my work, to my mother and sister Darci, for all of the inspiration they have given me. And to my grandparents and my Great-grandfather, God rest his soul.

You're just like a child,
your touch is so mild.
Fill your heart with the sense,
that a tear is your happiness.
Your stem is a song,
that will sing on and on.
And your petals a smile,
that will stay for a while.
Remember the joy,
that you used to send,
till the day in the end,
that you blow in the wind.

Genesis Marie
SUMMER DAZE!

Last summer was a wondrous memory.
A lot happened, love was blind, but you
allowed me to see.
Last summer I'll never forget, it was that
summer I was sure my future was set.

Then winter came; things grew cold.
Memories dragged on, and all grew
sorta
old . . .

I think now, this summer won't be the same.
'Cause you're gone, all that's left is your name.
That was what I was sadly thinking, while
my eyes deeply glazed. Remembering those
wild and crazy,
SUMMER-DAYS!!!

Martha E Martinez
A HORSE RIDING

I come to this place to look for love because on earth there is none. It will never end because it didn't start was from the beginning, evil, wars all day long people is mourning, hearts in pieces and a horse is riding the death is coming the apocalypse is working, a horse riding so fast so violently he doesn't have charity he don't feel a horse riding, some are good and they are the victims. I come to this place to have peace here because it's not easy to work for it. And winds blow and the clouds are grey and the throat is sour and the fear is there, a horse riding so strong and pass don't care who will harm a horse riding, pretty it seems but his reason makes us tumble I come for honesty, not there where you trust and die I come here where dust and people can't corrupt, and kill the body but not the soul.

Eileen Smyth
THE DRIVER'S SIDE

Here I sit and rot in jail,
There is no one to post my bail.
The ones who loved her want me dead,
But here I sit and wait instead.
My foot knew not the gas from brake,
And I knew nothing of the life I'd take.
Just two years older than my daughter,
Now look at where God has brought her.
My car is just a crunched up heap,
While she is in an endless sleep.
As I sit in here and look around,
I picture them lowering her into the ground.
My hand starts to shake as I fill with fear,
Knowing her mother is crying that tear.
Now when I die I'll go to hell,
So I won't have to meet her,
But it's just as well.

Diana K Brewster
WOODLAND JOURNEY

To my family, for their support of my efforts at poetry writing.

I saw the chipmunk frolic amid fallen branches,
A deer goes by, on its tiny hooves prancing,
A robin perched high in a hickory tree,
And a hawk soared in the sky, so wild and free.

The moss grew softly upon the stones,
A cardinal sang with the sweetest of tones,
A tombstone stood so lonely and bare,
Amid the flowers blooming there.

I pondered how in days of yore,
The Indian slept on the forest floor,
Upon the leaves so downy soft,
And the canopy of trees served as his loft.

I wondered . . . in a century from now,
Would the robin sing from the hickory bough?
Would the earth still stand, so wild and free?
Or all be lost to eternity!

Roger Dale Summers Sr
TRAIN TO HEAVEN

Hey man where's this train going.
It's going to heaven, it's moving
mighty slow, this train to heaven.
Hey man can I go. Only if you are
saved. You better hurry up for
this train to heaven.
Hey man what do you mean by being saved.
Ask Jesus to come into your life, then
you can get on board for
this train to heaven.
But you better hurry up, for this train
to Heaven is moving
mighty slow, but it is starting to pick
up speed, this train to
heaven.
Ask Jesus to come into your life and
get on board for this train
to heaven.
It's moving mighty fast this train to
heaven. Just about ready to
reach its destination.
I can see the golden gates of Heaven.
I look back and I can see
you, you're on your knees now and
you're starting to cry, now you're
saying Lord, Lord help me Lord. But
it's too late for this train
to Heaven. Fire and Brimstone coming.
It's moving mighty slow now this
train to Heaven, but it's picking
up speed so hurry up and get on
board to this train to Heaven.

Lori M Koontz
TO YOU MY FRIEND

There are times when we need a special friend.
Someone to listen to our thoughts,
Rejoice in our good times and comfort in our sorrow.
Someone with whom we can trust
And share our innermost concerns.
One who will give a smile when we can't find one
And stand beside us when we need support.
Someone to be their self, to be a friend.

You gave me laughter when I was sad
Strength when I was weak
Comfort when I was lonely
Understanding when I was confused
Hope when I was uncertain.
Treasured memories, my friend.

You shared
Listened
Cared
Loved

You were yourself
You are my friend

Sharon G Lockwood
THE JOURNEY

To Ben, who is my joy, my love and my life.

'Twas a misty morning . . . Fall . . .
As they traveled through the colors
to the place she knew.
He followed, for he understood
her heart.

The picture . . . so overwhelmed her
that he calmed her awe. For he had
had those feelings and through his
experience, chased the inadequacy
away.

Time . . . moved them back to
obligations
As the colors intensified, so did
their joy. He spoke of love, and
she answered in kind . . . All . . .

On that misty morning.

Linda Elmore
THE QUIET OF THE DAWN

He stands very still in the quiet of the dawn . . .
The remembrances of yesterday for a moment
are gone . . .
The morning's earthy scents tantalize his smell . . .
His hearing grows keener when he hears a hunter yell . . .
His heartbeat quickens as does his gait, surely
he thinks this is my undying fate . . .
He runs through the grasses covered with fresh
morning dew, and woods whose leaves glisten with
the day anew . . . He wonders why they chase him . . .
Is he some special prize . . . Oh! if only they
Could see through his eyes . . . .

Emily Yearwood
A SONG FOR YOU

To my husband, Rich, my inspiration for this poem, for life, for love.

A song for you lingers in my heart,
The words are here but not the art.
A song for you keeps ringing in my ear,
Awaiting the notes that are not here.

Music is the beauty of your
wonderful smile,
For a simple song makes you happy
for the longest while.
Just a rhythm to beat a table or tap a floor,
An easy tempo will take a great score.
Music to make you stand up to
crowds and sing,
And to hear all the cheers and
applause ring.
Just to write a song and hear it played
around the world,
To see it danced to, by each and
every boy and girl.

Music, ah the words of love in a
beautiful song,
To drift away in glory does not take
long.
A gift of music would be the best
thing I could do,
If only I could write a song for you.

Thomas I Thornhill Jr
DEAREST LOVE

Dearest Love,
Today I've called to let you know,
That now is the time that I must go.
People said our love would never last,
But that's behind us—in the past.

My love for you will never die,
I cared for you, I really tried.
I knew I wouldn't last very long,
I love you dear, you do no wrong.

I love you so much, how could I lie?
I couldn't tell you I was going to die.
I did not want to hurt you my dear,
I wanted you with me—here.

I cannot go on, I must pass away,
My time is up, I must not play.
I must not play with life, my Love,
You are my light, my snow white dove.

Pearl Bragg Krantz
A TINY FLOWER

To Mother.

I see a Tiny Flower
With blooms of gold & white
Growing in the sunshine
Of God's eternal light.
The stem is life forever
Always it shall be
For this is the gift of God
From you to me.
The leaves of love shall keep you
In peace and happiness
And hold you in the bossom
Of God's eternal bliss.
So bloom forever flower
And light the way for me
So when I kneel and pray each night
Your blossom I shall see.

Rheba Cates
SUNDAY ALONE

Remember when first we met, we
were in love so much?
I thrilled at all your kisses; You
thrilled at just my touch —
But you stopped kissing long ago . . I
used to wonder why —
You'll never know how much it hurt
— How much you made me cry.
How many times I wanted to ask,
"Why don't you kiss me, Don?"
But I knew you wouldn't answer . .
Just like you'd never call me 'Hon.'
I don't intend to say that I was never,
never wrong,
But the neglecting way you treated
me, never did help things along.
I wanted you to love me lots, and
show me that you did
I had so very much love for you, and
to you I wanted to give.
But the brick wall that you kept
between us . . I could not break it
down
I was so full of love and laughter . .
seemed to me you preferred to frown.
Now it's hard to put in poetry all the
things I want to say . .
I have so many things to do — I must
do them today.
All the trouble that we had . . with
you I'm going to level —
I really think that every one was just
strictly from the Devil.

Nori Taub
NEW-FALLEN SNOW

Gliding with the grace and ease
of a swan, the shimmering crystals
are falling, falling to the ground
The snowflakes huddle together
and form their own cozy bed,
like a mother tucking her child
under a warm blanket
The snow, moist and refreshing,
is a glass of lemonade on a hot
summer's day
The new-fallen snow glistens with
pride as its beauty is unfurled

Laurie Jean Lantosh
SAVED

The good Lord spoke to me today,
and opened mine eyes to what I
couldn't see!
He drained my blood and washed
it clean and chased the devil right out
of me!
He picked me up and lifted my
spirit so I could see all he has in store
for me!
You can't imagine the thrill in my
heart, when I allowed the Lord to
become a part, a part of me I never
knew. A part so clean, so pure, so
true.
So open your heart and let him in!
You need him and He wants you!
AMEN

J D Walker
MY LOVE

My life is such a mess
I don't know how to dress;
one day I am sad;
next day I am mad;
but it all seems worth while;
when I see that smile;
on the one I love the most;
so I have to boast;
that we are getting along;
as good as a song;
then she gets mad;
so now I am sad;
and I still don't know how to dress;

O my life is such a mess.

Amy Swinehart
THE MASK OF EARTH

The inquiring mind of children
without end
removes all doubt that life is
ordinary,
Age puts a mask on the earth.
Behold the fortune we have, life is
extraordinary.

The fragrance of the summer air as
it's
drifting by, in harmony with the birds

that
praise heaven, the charm will never die.

The elegance of the land is defeated by responsibility,
Time to enjoy the simplicity is forfeited.

A rainbow is a devoted reminder that life
isn't eternally gray skies.

J P Carroll
HAVE YOU EVER LISTENED TO THE BIRDS SINGING?

Have you ever listened to the birds singing in the morning?
Have you ever wondered what they are saying?
Don't they make a happy sound with love & camaraderie in their hearts?
Why can't humans be as joyful at the day's start?
Have you ever felt that love exudes from your dog or cats?
Do you remember the gentlemen that used to doff their hats?
Have you ever wondered where love and manners fled?
Look around you, they are some-where, please no, they are not dead!
Humans need to take a lesson from the animals they see
A little hug, a little kiss, is not too much for me.
But humans are so cross and sad, it's pitiful you know
Be just like all wild things, let your happiness grow.
The love I get from my dog's eyes, the purr from my old cat,
The cow that moos, the horse that neighs as I walk by
Could a human greet me just once without that horrid sigh?
Maybe I should live with animals since I enjoy them so,
But I am of the human race, and go where it must go.
But Oh, for those days gone by where love and cheer were there—
I must be getting on in years, I'm now talking to a hare!

Cheryl J Andreakos
RECLUSE

The years invested in building,
and securing
your fortress walls are but a waste
because someday,
someone,
will care enough,
and love enough to destroy those walls.
It matters not how much stone or mortar you use,
Someone will find a crack and see the sun within you
come shining thru
and they will not be deterred,
or frustrated,
or discontented
and because of this,
one day those walls will crumble
and all that will be left,
is a shattered image of what you once were,
and all that will be left is what you are.

Sandra M Salazar
FRIENDSHIP

Friendship is something to be valued
It is the giving and taking
From what one has to offer
And it is not to be abused
For friendship is a very special feeling
Between two people
Like YOU and ME.

Each of us offers many things
Like a special companionship
And a special feeling of Love
This feeling between us cannot
be SHARED by others
For our feelings for one another
has grown to be very special
In the way we speak and look
to one another.

For a friendship is a SPECIAL
bond between two people
And this is a friendship
I do value with all my heart
Enough to say, "I LOVE YOU!"

Tina Lynn Brown
ALONE OR NOT SO ALONE

This poem is dedicated to Jeffrey Charles Wood, whom at 19 years of age left his spirit to give me the determination not to feel alone.

As I lie alone in bed at night
I can hear you speak.
And as the night grows more silent
you become silent also.
I know not what time it is
but long to hear you once more.
We are so close
yet you seem so far off in the distance now.
I long to stay up each night
just to talk,
to know that you may love me.
And as my pencil slows to a stop
the night draws nearer to morning.
I no longer wish to hear your voice because
I now realize that I'm not so alone.
I can hear you in my heart
and I can hear you in my mind.
I need you to hear me also
so that we may know each other.

Dolores C Tucker
SMILES

Smiles are worth a thousand words —
A picture on a face.
They show the world that there's still hope
No matter what we face.
They reach out, touch, and embrace,
Send love across a room,
Change the mood to a happy place,
And chase away the gloom.

Elisa Goyeneche
OLD MAN

You skinny, old man, you.
Your wrinkled skin, your head so bare,
and your bones so frail,
yet you continue to walk your way,
slow now, and sleep,
for morning will come and you will continue
your slow yet continuous pace.
You must rest much more than when you were young.
As you walk, you remember
the little boy that is still deep inside you.
Once so full of energy,
but it is fading farther and farther away.
In your mind,
you know your day will come . . .
but—
until then, you old man,
you—will—continue—to—walk

Captola Range
SPRING-ING

Only to take a walk on this day,
just walk.
Going nowhere, doing nothing,
just walk.
Feeling the wind, touching the earth.
To pick a flower or a leaf,
amazed at new birth.
Only to walk on this day because it is Spring.
And to thank God for it just being!

Dianne Elaine Christoffersen
HE MADE HER CRY

Oh, how she knew what pain could be
Caused by a love so deep she could not see

That he cared no more for her love at all
And he left her alone . . . never did call

The better part of her life was for him, you see
He made her into a woman and loved her tenderly

He was always there and how they did share . . .
Everything together with tender loving care

But time does change people . . . you see it everyday
Divorce, it's over . . . lovers go their own way

She will never understand and will always wonder why
Once he gave her love . . . today he made her cry.

Arianne
DREAMS

Hold my hand and let me take you on a magical journey to
A faraway place, where a dream
Becomes reality, and each ordinary experience becomes a new
Adventure, where love is the theme
Upon which each dream is acted.
For love is all there is, whether it be
Merely an illusion or extracted
From truth, and love must be free
To survive. So give me your trust
And let me spin some dreams for you;
And somewhere between fantasy and fact you must
Believe that dreams come true!

Susan J Dorris
AS ONE

To Ronald, I have always known you my love.

Your eyes flip through mine, reading,
My very thoughts become raw,
exposed

With a blink I can disguise
But quickly you know that
You are there before my blink

You draw from my eyes knowledge
With not one spoken word you know

Were these eyes once yours
So you know?

Did you gaze on what I now see?
Have you seen what I have seen?

Did we share the exact space
together?
Were we one in complete?

Were you the female me?
Was I the male you?

Did we breathe the exact air
And cry the same tears?

I have known you

I know it

Paul W Streeter
QUIET THOUGHTS

The sun tries to break through the
early morning mist,
To give to earth a lasting kiss.

The water so still and so calm,
Only an occasional fish jumps
as I move along.

I hear the calling of the Blue Jay.
Which marks the beginning of
a new day.

So I'll walk along this quiet
and lonely bank.
With thoughts of you.
I give Him my thanks.

Another day passes and our
love grows stronger.
He made it this way so that
it would last longer.

We'll soon be together you and me,
And that's how it will always be.

Paul W Streeter
THOUGHTS OF LOVE

To Paula, once upon a time for special moments and a special love.

Today while sitting alone among some shrubbery
And the trees
I found myself thinking of our future and of
How we used to be.

But most of all I thought of us and the future ahead
And while I thought, I saw visions of us together,
Alone, and in our bed.

I thought of our love and how it has grown
I thought of our love and the strength it has shown

I thought of warm caresses and nights we held each
Other so tight
I thought of our kisses so warm, so moist, all through the
Night.

I thought of our love making and our bodies entwined
With each other.
I thought of our love shared as we lay exhausted,
Knowing there could never be another.

Then I had no reason to think for what I know is true
He has given us the most precious gift ever —
Your love for me and my love for you.

Shirley R Heinrich
A CARELESS TONGUE

A tongue that's daily sharpened
And exercised at will,
Can only be destructive

Its main intent; to kill.

A hasty word that's spoken
A careless, thoughtless deed,
Can scourge the very soul of man
And cause his heart to bleed.

You need to be so careful
In the things you say and do,
For as the Master teaches
What you sow comes back to you.

Let's disengage this weapon
That wounds just like a knife,
For whatever you give power to
Increases in your life.

Shirely R Heinrich
MEN OF DUST

A special breed, this man called
farmer
Not many men can match his toil.
His strength renews by change of
seasons
His faith is sealed by fertile soil.

No other one that I envision
Could have a closer walk with God,
Than he who's blessed with morning
sunshine
And gives his thanks for fields to
trod.

A time to sow, a time for reaping,
A truth that's planted in his mind.
The seeds he's sown become a
witness
As labors' fruits feed all mankind.

A weathered brow and calloused
handshake
The badge of courage he displays,
To all who eat at Nature's table
And sup the wine from her bouquets.

If there's a special crown in Glory
And treasures safe from thieves and
rust,
His silo's filled and waiting for him
God's treasured few; These men of
dust.

Enoyce Loyd
PEACEMAKER

Help me to live my life today
In such a past forgetting way,
That I may help those near at hand
To make of this a better land.
Help me to show Thy love to others,
For underneath we are <u>all</u> brothers.

Tessa Conklin
A MOTHER IS . . .

This poem is dedicated to my mother, Stephanie Conklin, for whom it was modeled after and written for.

A Mother is a dreamer,
Weaving dreams for her frightened
child.
A Mother is a guardian
Protecting from life's evils no matter
how wild.

A Mother is a painter,
Painting thoughts of heavenly bliss.
A Mother is a fairy,
Bestowing her magic in a loving kiss.

A Mother is a writer,
Creating her stories of earth below
and heaven above.
A Mother is a poet,
Rhyming her sonnets of beauty and
love.

A Mother is a singer,
With her ever-beautiful song.

A Mother is a friend,
Keeping your secret all along.

A Mother is a blessing,
Perfectly made from God to you.
A Mother is a mommy,
Loving you your whole life through.

Jackie DeBucci
PART OF MY HEART

This poem is dedicated to Kelli Rex, our "adopted daughter," from a family that loved her.

My best friend forever, met God
yesterday.
Her soul went to heaven, an eternity
away.

As I look out the window at the sky
blue and bright,
the fluffy white clouds are a soft
welcoming sight.

It see you ride safely in a cloud that
floats by.
My heart keeps aching and I keep
asking why.

What happened to you Kelli, nobody
seems to know.
They found you laying peaceful in
the icy cold snow.

It just isn't fair, it just cannot be so.
It couldn't be your time, eighteen is
too young to go.

I will miss your smile, so contagious,
so sweet.
And your giggle so silly, so gentle, so
meek.

It seems that it's been just a moment
in time,
since we received our diplomas and
left high school behind.

It was a time of excitement our whole
lives lay ahead.
On to college, careers and maybe
later to wed.

You were too good to belong to the
people on earth.
Maybe that is why God took you, for
your heavenly worth.

If I could be with you, just one
moment to share.
I would touch you and tell you just
how much I care.

You are my best friend and you
always will be.
I carry you close, you are always
with me.

Even though God chose to tear us
apart,
you will always be with me, you are
part of my heart.

Jacqueline Happy Andrews
ANYWHERE YOU ARE

I want to go back home tonight,
I'm homesick.
It's April, and the yard is bright
With flowers.
The trees are green and new with
leaves.
I miss them.
The barn is bare, and hay in sheaves
Is missing.
I know the cow is wondering
Where we have gone.
She's fed, but still she's hungering
For us again.
There's no one there to see the pair
Of doves in flight.
Or toss the crumbs, or even care
For robin's plight.
This place is far away from home.
It's desolate.
There are no trees or birds or some
Of life at all.
It's just a bare and lonely place,
With buildings tall.
And men go forth with empty face
To have it all.
But this I know without a fear
Or clinging doubt.
If we're together, then my dear,
Our home is here.

Angie Krehbiel
I MOURN FOR YOU STILL

I lovingly dedicate this poem to Benetta F. Voran and Gina Renee Voran Willett. Their death, on February 6, 1986, hurt me worse than anything else in the world. I wish I could say that I was close to them.

Three years ago, you went away;
I mourn for you still, day after day.

It took me so long to write it all
down;
In hopes, that in my own tears, I
might drown.

The snow was falling as we said
farewell;
If it will ever stop hurting, I'm yet
unable to tell.

As hard as I try, I can never erase
The haunting memory of your
sleeping face.

I wish someone could tell me
Why your life had to end so soon;
No one has the answer,
So I shout it to the moon.

I wish I would have been the one
To leave this world instead;
How I wish, with all my heart,
That you were alive and not dead.

Shirley Allred
SOMETIMES

Sometimes I don't show it, but I hope
you see
How very special you are to me
Sometimes I am careless with the
attention I give
I spend it on family or creatures
instead of on the man which I live
Sometimes I act foolish and feel
insecure
But you too have that feeling, do you
think there's a cure
Sometimes I miss you so much I
wish I could scream
But if comforts me to know back at
home we're a team
Sometimes I'm inflexible, some call
it stubborn
But you are patient and help me
along, do you know I thank GOD for
the day you were born
Sometimes I'm insensitive to the
feelings you carry
But please remember, My love is
deeper than others who marry
Sometimes I'm preoccupied and my
mind is afar
But my heart has been with you since
that day in the bar
Sometimes I'm playful and act real
silly
But always remember, I love you,
REALLY

Shirley (Johnson) Allred
VIOLA JOHNSON

My mom was a Super Woman,
everyone would agree
She devoted her whole life to my
dad, my sisters, and me

My mom was a Great Woman, not
overweight, not real lean
She wasn't the greatest cook, but she
kept the house real clean

My mom was a Business Woman,
always dressed, and always a lady
And she always made time for Tim,
Todd, or Katie

My mom was a Caring Woman, she
cared for her brothers and sisters
She worried whether it be their
sickness, money or blisters

My mom was an Active Woman, she
always loved to walk
You could call her anytime you felt
the need to talk

My mom was a Religious Woman,
the church was indeed her life
Although my dad isn't perfect he had
the perfect wife

My mom was a Loving Woman, her
love like the warm sun's glow
She gave herself to others and always
to life's flow

My mom was a Dedicated Woman,
she kept the same job for 35 years
When the golden years came,
wouldn't you know, the gold became
tarnished through all the tears

My mom was a Courageous Woman,
she battled a disease, but lost the
fight
She couldn't talk or walk and had
great pain, but till the end she kept
GOD in her sight

My mom was a Loved Woman, loved
by all family and friends
When the end was here the family
gathered, cuz although she is gone,
her love she still sends

Suzie J Daniel

Suzie J Daniel
LEBANON

This poem is dedicated to my beloved country, her beautiful people whom I am very proud of, and dedicated to Peace in Lebanon and to Peace in the world.

A small note about my beautiful
flower and its beautiful leaves, my
beloved country Lebanon. This
flower that is surrounded by thorns,
thorns that have been unsuccessful in

having it all to themselves. These thorns have gone so far as to blind some of its beautiful leaves and turned them into thornes and laid back watching them destroy each other, and wait for the day that my beautiful flower will be completely destroyed, while my innocent beautiful flower and the rest of its innocent leaves are caught in the midst of it all wondering what it is they have done wrong to deserve being struck everywhere where it hurts, anywhere that will make them suffer or bleed, anything that will kill them. They have tried everything they had to destroy my beautiful flower, till this day they're still trying. They have succeeded in torturing it in the worst way possible, but every time they think it's about to die, my beautiful flower holds on so strong to its last breath, the breath of faith, faith in a God that she knows has never and will never give up on it, especially when the whole world turns their backs on it or just lay back and watch it being tortured to death, with that last breath my beautiful flower stands taller and more solid in its ground. This flower will rise and bloom up again because its roots have never before given up, lost hope, or let go of their faith . . . .

Jo Louise Hoskins
TEXAS IN THE SPRING
Carpets of Bluebonnetts
Draping purple wisteria
Azaleas in hues of pink
Primrose path
Bright white dogwood trees
Redbud in bloom
Snowy pear blossoms, rain sprinkling fresh
Surprise lilies, because we never know
Surely God must have laid his hand
upon the land.
Of Texas in the Spring

Jo Louise Hoskins
RED BIRD
Red bird, Red bird!
Flare across the sky
Flash your scarlet wing
Promising spring
Suddenly you appear
Bringing me cheer
Red bird, Red bird!
Linger awhile
Hope we'll never part
Make your home in my heart

Suzie J Daniel
A QUESTION FROM A LEBANESE CHILD
This is not a letter, a song, or a poem
it is just a question from a Lebanese child.

A silent tear is falling down his face,
of his friends & family there is no trace . . .

Bombs are falling all around
the churches, the hospitals and every place . . .

His relatives & neighbors
are no where in sight,
Most of them were massacred
in the middle of the night . . .

Another tear is falling down,
he runs and runs, but he cannot hide. .
A bomb every second in this war zone,
And the world is watching with a heart of stone

He looks up high, still, a tear, not a cry . . .
And asks a question, and the question is Why?

Suzie J Daniel
TOMORROW WILL COME
If it rains today, the sun will come out tomorrow.
If we cry today, we will laugh tomorrow.
If there is a war today, there will be peace tomorrow.
If we feel sad today, someone will cheer us up tomorrow.
If we're too young to do anything today, we will grow up and do everything tomorrow.
If we're weak today, we will be strong tomorrow.
If we hurt and we don't feel good today, we will feel better tomorrow.

So if we think positive, instead of negative,
If we keep on trying, instead of giving up
If we keep on praying, and never stop, God will answer
All our prayers. All we have to do is be a little patient
with him, and show him that we're strong, and we can
handle anything that life puts us through, because
we believe in him, and we love Him, and we know that
with His help, tomorrow will come sooner than we expect it to.

Chelsea Whittington
ONCE MORE, A DIVISION OF LOVE

Mrs. Barnett — Thank you for your support and encouragement through my poem-learning process!

Surviving in the darkness of the night.
Thinking of the love I once shared with you.
Deriving inner strength from the starlight,
Remembering when it all seemed so new.

Dying slowly in the light of the moon.
I slowly forget the frame of your face,
Shall once again be forgotten by noon.
The memory of our love slowly erased.

Last night was the last night I shared with you,
That night I hurt you, shall not be forgave.
To this day I'm sorry, that day I rue.
So, so sorry, I shall hurt to my grave.

So I sit here alone once more in life,
Dream about the day I once was your wife.

Jeff Daniel
UPON ONE FAITH

For Juliet.

Lovers speak in many ways
The things their hearts rejoice
The sound of laughter in the air
over notions lost on most
Or quiet moments in repose
A sigh upon her breast
She thinks of me and I of her
Through days long filled with hope
When love is borne upon one faith
Eternal is its voice

And not by time the moments pass
Eternal is love's flame
But moments counted like the stars
Here and yet so far
Often shrouded by the mist
They still remain the same
Her love for me and mine for her
Shall surely shine like these
If love is borne upon one faith
Our time will always be

And in the day of hope fulfilled
We stand before the King
Through the times that faith was tried
His blood has kept us clean
The stars are now within our eyes
One heart now made complete
My hand in hers and hers in mine
We enter through the gate
For lovers borne upon one faith
One time—eternity

Teardrop
EVIL

To Lancelot. Thank you for being my love, my life, and my inspiration. Forever, Teardrop.

A black moon rises,
Over the promises of his love.
Casting dark shadows,
Over his hidden blood lust.
Drawing you with its mystery
To the edge of his knife.
Entering your soul,
As he penetrates your body.
Sneering at you,
As you die for love.

A black moon rises . . . .

Eva J Erickson
WHAT ARE SISTERS

To Juanita Alice Bruer; "In Loving Memory" from the younger ones.

They are older and wiser than you.
But they have more love and compassion, for the younger ones.
They have gone before to lead the way, with their strength and courage.
Even knowing they are getting older, and their body isn't the same.
We still love and hold you dear, to our hearts.
You have gone places and done things,
that I only dream of.
But why do you have to suffer so . . .
To my bestest friend and sister,
Love to you and I hope, when your time comes,
You will hurt no more . . .

Danny Morales Jr
NOTHING

To Stacey, my inspiration.

We say so much
But it all means nothing
What can we say
When it has no importance
This is when dreams are visions
of things never to come true

We are the most alone
when we have the saddest thoughts
This is when the rain pours the hardest
and the wildest heart
bleeds

We all can't be poets
But some of us try
You can only bear your soul
so many times
Some will listen
and some will walk away
But those who believe in you
they're always the ones
who stay

Laevata Nelson
A LIFE TO BE

I would like to dedicate my poem to God, my strength; Lisa Simmons and Verma Gadsden, my number one fans; Lenora Morton-Nelson, my mother; La Novia and her father.

My days of purity
Have passed me by;
I can't cry,
I have not the courage.

I can't be afraid
That people wouldn't
Understand.

I'm a perfect little girl
In their eyes—
Doer of no mistakes
And mischief
Doer of no evil.

It's not evil
Which I possess,
But a life to be.

Joyce Michno
A SENSE OF THE PAST—REMEMBERING
Grandma's faded checked aprons
worn over light cotton dresses
Mogan David wine served on special occasions
Crowded Christmas rooms of days gone by
Grandma and Grandpa's chance to get our names just right

Long summer days in hot and humid fields
Crossword puzzles not quite completed
A quiet sense of real trust and faith
Tea parties from an old rusted tea set

The worn bible with its daily marker
A perfect woven egg basket on the hidden stair climb
Colorful rugs . . . braided and scattered everywhere
Apple butter jars and crocks all in a row

Work and play in the form of a loaf of bread
The simple gold band on Rosie's left hand
Tractor sounds and planting time
An old-fashioned waltz on a barnroom floor

The lovely white church in the countryside
Hide and seek games, and softball, too
The rooster call at the break of day

Quilt pieces, thread, and such tiny stitches
Grandma's thin hair with the low resting bun
Picnics, holidays, funerals, confirmations, and jelly
Frank's bib overalls with the kangaroo pockets
Accordion music to help fill the air
The small nearby pond, overflowing or dry
The hunting season of the crisp cool fall
Soybeans, geraniums, the garden and the wheat
The small white house with the breezeway entry

Sandra L Henry
STILL
She was a sad eyed lass,
he was a hollowed faced lad.
They stood opposite at the corners of the world,
near the crossroads of the city and the country.
The earth stood without motion,
and they did not understand why.
The cow gave not her milk,
the horse stood without a bridle.
The traffic on the highway moved not, and the sun beat down for all time.
For they were without hope,
and did not know that hope is action.
Time was their enemy for it was endless,
as without action the world around them stood still!

Cheryl L Andrews
MY FOUR-LEGGED FRIEND
He sits upon my chair
All ragged and worn,
His right ear is missing
The left one is torn.
The stuffing is old
Falling out here and there,
He has but only one eye
Without even a spare.

He has a smiling face
With a little black nose,
And four fuzzy paws
Each with three pink polished toes.
I've had him now
For at least sixteen years or more,
But I know one thing's for sure
I love him so.

Jenny Todd
TENDER MOMENTS
I met this sweet old man in the park one day
While I was watching my children at play
He seemed so sweet as he told me of days gone by
He smiled, and then I noticed this gleam in his eyes
He told me of his children, and how he loved them so
But all too soon, they grew up and it was time to go
I said, I'd like you to meet my children, you've been so very kind
He said, I'd love to see them, but my dear I'm blind

daniel thomas manley
IN THE RAIN 01 DECEMBER 1986

---

this is for: roger jess "bog" spencer and . . . sara. "no, i will not forget you . . . ."

---

and in this darkness . . .
a moon, but
is it my fault
the damned thing
follows me, and
i don't even
walk on clouds?

Karin Giannikopoulos
A FISHERMAN'S WIFE
Do not weep for me, said the old man from the sea
God has been good to me. I have two beautiful children and a lovely wife who wait for me to return from the sea.
What? What is that you ask. Of course I love them—
I do all of this for them. I give to them a beautiful place in which to live and money they have to buy whatever their hearts desire—how could they not be happy—they have everything.
What? What is that you ask? I do not understand—
What do you mean they only want me? I cannot give that.
I would have to give up the sea and my life is the sea.
Oh poor old man of the sea who cannot understand
I weep for you—your family loves you and needs you with them. Buy a smaller place and live together. Do not be gone from them for so long a time. Make each day with just enough to do—laugh together and enjoy each other before the life is through—how did you forget so quickly that which your fathers before you tried to show you.

Deborah A Leal
FROM THE DISTANCE TO MY HEART

To all people who have been my inspiration, and supported me every step of the way.

Across the distant, weary miles,
I still remember you, My Love.
My eyes yet swaddle with tears,
as I recall you in a whim from afar.
Distance has been our fondest enemy,
one who carried you away from me,
but never away from my heart.
I hold you inside as an imprisoned bird,
inside as an infant in its mother's womb.
As a wandering eagle, soaring high,
my memory seems to disperse,
transcending the limitless space,
triumphant over the distance between us,
it journeys through the boundless skies,
without rest, without doubt, without haste,
somehow always coming to you.
I reach you every single time,
for you have never left my side,
for always in the distance,
You were ever in My Heart!

Eula Lee Kelley
MARTHA, A FRIEND INDEED
A day was never too hot nor too cold
For you to help a friend in need;
Always making me ever to behold
God's abiding presence indeed

Kind deeds you've done along the way
And pointed others to Jesus and His love;
To weary souls lost in sin and dismay
As He guided you with light from above

Each day you check those around you
For someone who is burdened with care;
From your spiritual warehouse you let us borrow
And tell us it will be better out there

You've had your share of illness and pain
But a smile is always on your sweet face;
And no one ever hears you fret nor complain
For your close walk with God does frown erase

Your hands may not have won earthly fame
But they've won a crown in Heaven above;
With blessings and riches too bountiful to name
By walking in obedience, always filled with God's love

Eula Lee Kelley
DESTINY FINDS A WAY
It's interesting to note how destiny finds a way,
To steer us as down life's road we go;
It seems to guide us from day to day
So that our future mate we'll see and know

It may be in High school that we chance to meet
Or perhaps not until we are more mature;
But if we let God always guide our feet
The right one will be there for sure

As time goes on and we see each one's charms,
When in law school we spend each day;
We begin to realize that it does no harm
To have a strong Christian at our side along the way

So we put every care in God's hands and walk by His side,
Knowing that all things for us
He'll provide;
He is with us in our school work and worship too
As our romance begins to come in view
As we begin to realize that we are more than friends,
That Cupid has dashed an arrow in each heart;
We decided that life together we wanted to extend
So the promise of marriage became a part

May 19, 1990 has been set for the day
For wedding bells to be heard loud and clear;
When relatives and friends will all be here
And angels in Heaven will rejoice and cheer

When marriage vows two Christian lovers repeat
And God brings them together as one;
They'll be the happiest couple you'll meet
As life's journey together is begun

Keep close to Him along life's way
And all His commandments obey;
Then material and spiritual blessings
He'll bestow
And happiness beyond compare you'll know

Patricia A Leach
TAKE ME THERE
Take me to that special place,
That only we two share.
Where skin meets skin,
Where hearts touch hearts,
And minds share minds.
It's fading . . .
like a dream.
Close your eyes;
don't say a word.
You must take me there again.

Valerie A Hayes
THE PEOPLE IN THE SHADOWS

Thank you Billy Crystal, Whoopi Goldberg and Robin Williams . . . Our "Comic Relief" who understand the bittersweet of life and reach out their hands and give of themselves with love . . . .

Who will count their numbers, who will even seem to care
About the people in the shadows who appear from everywhere?
Lying huddled on park benches, under trees, along the ground,
Down beside the railroad tracks on sidewalks—all around!,

I've just returned the census form so that I can be counted once again.
I gave them all the details, my age, my address, my name . . .
But, who will count the homeless, the ones we just don't want to see,
Who will speak up for them and restore their dignity?

If Lazarus could rise up from the dead today and see her poem being read
Inscribed upon the pedestal—"The New Colossus"—(long after she was dead)
She inspired the lady in the harbor, our Statue of Liberty,
Standing with her guiding light for all the world to see.

in this great land of plenty, where freedom is the key—
How long will it take before all of us will be set free?
Can we just pretend that we cannot see . . .
These homeless wretches among our throw-away society?

The people in the shadows who huddle in the dark
Hoping that someone will awake from this apathetic ark . . .
We wander about so aimlessly groping here and there
But surely, there but for the grace of God—they could be you and me!

LaVerne M Bennett

LaVerne M Bennett
THE PICNIC
How was I ever so lucky
To meet you that summer's day
At a picnic down by the river
Where children and lovers play?

Dark brown eyes were smiling at me
In the three-legged race and the spelling bee.
My heart was beating as fast as it could
For this was all so new to me.
Not the race, but the nearness of you—
Your smile, your eyes, and your strong hand too.
For a moment I wished it would never end—
This race, this day, and my love for you.

But the years have slipped behind us
And now your hair is grey
But still my heart beats faster
Whenever you look my way.

But nothing will ever take from us
That lovely summer's day,
At a picnic down by the river
Where children and lovers play.

LaVerne M Bennett
OUR SEVEN-YEAR OLD
Now you're half big, my little boy
No longer "Little Fellow"
But a lad that's half as high
As the Daddy that we love,
My little half-big boy.

Your Mommy cannot pick you up
To cuddle in her arms,
Or kiss the little stubbed toes
To keep them safe from harm.
Your seven years have made you
Much too big a man for that.

But when the night-time comes
And you crawl into your bed,
My sleepy-head, little tousled-head,
I can sing you a lullaby
'Cause you're still half little
My little half-big boy.

LaVerne M Bennett
THE MEN IN MY LIFE
Oh the men in my life are exciting and keen
And I love them both so, I just can't choose between;
For one is soft-spoken, with deep eyes of brown
But the other's grey eyes have the mirth of a clown.

One is a dreamer who looks at the stars
And one looks at people and shiny new cars.
One sends me rosebuds all covered with dew
While the other brings joke books and reads me a few.

Romantic is one—his smile a caress
But strong and manly and brave nonetheless;
But the other gives kisses with laughs in his eyes,
And tells me he'd love me if I'd bake good pies.

On cold winter evenings the brown-eyed one's best
For his pipe and his book spell an evening of rest.
But on bright summer days when the crowd wants a swim
Well, then I think first of my laughing-eyed "him."

But why should a woman love only one man
When two love her far more than either one can?

Oh the man in my life with the brown eyes is one;
And the other—the grey-eyed one,—he is our son.

Darlene Wright
BABIES BABIES

I dedicate this poem to my two daughters, Natalia and Natiya, who first inspired me to write this special poem. Love, Mommy.

Babies Babies the joy of the world,
There are tough li'l boys, and dainty li'l girls.
When they're first born they have no features,
As time goes by they're cute little creatures.

What I'm saying babies grow up fine,
With mothers bragging oh that one's mine.
Some babies aren't as lucky as others,
Some are born sick, and never recover.

They can also make you feel so proud,
When their first words are clear, and loud.
Especially when they have their first step,
You brag, and brag, and never forget.

What I mean is that babies bring joy,
With fathers yelling yep that's my boy.
I don't believe how many are abused,
Growing up homeless, and so confused.

Babies Babies the joy of today,
They may cry a lot but I love them anyway.

Roxanne De Vries
DREAMS
I have so many dreams
They are of you and I
About the love I have for you
I can no longer deny

The way I feel is a fortress
My love is for real
No one can love you as I
My heart you did steal

This love of mine is everlasting
Can't you see?
I want you in my life
Why can't you love me?

I liked the way things were
Your absence is so strange
I wish there was some way to stop time
But things are too late to change

My love is not lost
You are always on my mind
Maybe someday we will love again
In a dream of another time

Ramiro Rosete
SOMETIMES I WONDER

In loving memory of Michael Alan Owen: June 30, 1989-August 15, 1989.

Sometimes I wonder
Why there is death,
Why people die
In less than one breath
When I first saw Mikey
I was kind of scared
But I still loved him with
The same love
We all shared
He lived long
Longer than expected
Until the time when
He was selected
Sometimes I wonder
Why there is death
Why people die
In less than one breath

Joseph L Hamel
A PRICE SO DEAR
It is '69 and some have paid a price so dear,
Laying down their lives before they could fear.
Others get no thanks from home it seems,
Their looks are blank as they hear the screams
Of their buddies fallen along the way.
This is the price they have to pay
For trudging through rice paddies, rain and mud,
To fight a war and shed their blood.
Yes. The price of war is very great,
That they must die in a war they did not create.

The war is still on, some twenty years later.
And the Vietnam Vet is a second-rater!
This war is now fought on the home front, you see.
We are battling the effects of Agent Orange and PTSD.
We may never recover from the muck and the mire
And the price of their freedom goes higher and higher.
This price now includes broken dreams and broken lives,
fearful children and stressed-out, tearful wives.
We can't really blame these veterans,
Though they are paying the price.
Our cost is even greater because we are paying twice.

David K Stewart
TARNISHED DREAMS
Dreams of tomorrow
I once looked forward to
Now I no longer know what to do.

Memories of dreams
That shined so bright
Have all faded
Like day does to night.

Dreams of success
That lie on the other side
Of an unopened door.

Now shattered dreams and broken hopes
Make it hard to dream anymore
Dreams of a better life
I once thought about
Now are only dreams of doubt.

Success . . . I no longer dream that way
Instead, I try to motivate myself
To face another day.

Tarnished dreams are all I have left
And I no longer dream of life . . .
But of death!!!!

Mazell B Campbell
WHAT IS CHARITY?

In memory of my dearly beloved parents, Rev. and Mrs. Hilliard Bradley, who were the essence of our family love. Their rays of love still shine brightly in the lives of their five children: Robin, Mazell, Charles, Hewiue and Della; and Grandchildren.

What is Charity
If I haven't come from Jesus?
What is Charity
If I cannot dwell among us?

What is charity
If I always forget to pray?
What is charity
If I just mope from day to day?

What is charity
If I do not give a real care?
What is charity
If I never with people share?

What is charity
If I must always fuss and fight?
What is charity
If I never do what is right?

What is charity
If I express, "Heavenly Fit?"
What is charity
If I never try to live it?
Charity is LOVE.

Shawauna Delene Horne
SOMEONE CARES

I dedicate this poem to Alison Lawrence, my friend. God gave it to me to give to you. I Love You.

Our life is not always sunny
Sometimes it's not even bright
At times it is so gloomy,
We pray Lord, just a little light.

Our soul becomes so heavy
And it seems no one would care,
But then you hear a voice inside,
Who says all your burdens I will
bear.

Then we feel much better
Knowing the Lord is there,
But I just wanted you to know
There is someone else who cares

I may not show it often
You may not even know
About the seed within my heart
That only you have sown.

So like today and other times,
I this little deed.
I just thought that you should know
it's the
Love from that little seed.

Carol M Broussard
WINTER FRIENDS

In dedication to the memory of my father, Roy E. Avila. May the light forever shine for you and all your winter friends.

Ice in the willows, footprints in the
snow,
Frost on the windows, feel the
wind blow.

We sit by the fire, warming old
bones,
Pouring tea from a pot, tasty
butter scones.

Old friends chat, remembering the
years,
Of childish laughter, happiness
and tears.

To reminisce of spring, fresh mown
hay,
Joyous summers, filled with
endless play.

Then back to school, with autumn so
near,
Of pumpkins and witches, and
holiday cheer.

But that was in youth, a long time
ago,
When minds were still hopeful,
of dreams yet to sow.

Now in our twilight, we venture to
say,
Winter friendships are best,
growing day after day.

Joan Patterson Yeck
FAREWELL
The moment of death
His hand, still warm, held in mine
Silence . . . my heart breaks

Joan Patterson Yeck
MY BLESSINGS
Your walk, so proud, my little man
As though you were a King,
The wonder in your eyes
When you hear a robin sing.

The touch of your small hand in mine
The warmth of your embrace,
The love and trust I see each time
I look at your sweet face.

To hear "I love you Mommy"
All that love, mine for the taking,
The precious moments that we share
Beautiful memories in the making.

To hear your sincere words of prayer
When every day is done,
For all these things I thank the Lord
For giving me my son.

Julie M Elbel
GRAY

To Deena,
You're in my heart and soul. I will never let you go.

Why can't the world be a different
time,
a different place?
How can one pick the true, or better
race?
It is just a state of mind, a being.
Yet, it is a major wall that blocks
what we should be seeing.
"Love one another as I have loved
you"
Isn't that what God told us to
do?
Let me be free, oh, let me be free.
Why can't I choose who I want
to be?
I am an individual, yet I am
condemned.
Because I have found
something so beautiful—a
friend.
Someone that respects me, whom I
can love back . . .
The wall everyone sees is the color
of black.
Life is supposed to be exciting and
fun!
For me, my life has just begun,
I'm just learning to love, it's so
innocent
and new.
But society turns it all around, they
can be so cruel.
I'm so torn between thoughts,
I can decide no longer.
I don't want relations to fade,
I want them to get stronger
Between family and friends,
this I can't deny.
For I am lost in the midst
of prejudice and pride.

Kent J Neilson
THE GIFT OF SIGHT
If you've seen a perfect white,
or even a bird in perfect flight,
then you have the gift of sight,
which never comes on a lonely
night.
Lonely nights are bleak and blind,
which only you know how to
unwind.
As time comes and as time goes,
it has the shape of drifting
snow.
Its pace is fast, its pace is slow,
but only you will ever know.
For you are the one living this
time,
which only God knows how
to unwind.
You see it like no one else,
For This Is The Gift Of Sight.

Anna Mae Lynam
YOU ARE MY CHILD

To my loving children. Love, Mom.

You are my child,
And I want you to know,
It was so neat just watching
you grow,
Each and everyday you would
Learn something new,
It was so much fun just
watching you,
And Now that you're grown,
And out on your own,
Remember this will always
Be your home.

Thelma Malcolm
NIGHT STORM
Snapping his fingers and shaking his
fists
The thunderstorm rages through.
I awake startled and shaken
Wondering what I should do.

It's impossible to hide from the
flashing light
And the thunder's shattering sound.
He is like an angry child kicking and
screaming,
And throwing himself at the ground.

His tantrum has ended, his rage
subsided,
Flowing into a torrent of tears.
I too, am now calm and relieved.
The gentle rain washing away my
fears.

The stars twinkle through the drifting
clouds.
The pale moon shines in the West.
The air is clean and cool,
And all nature is again at rest.

Lori Taxter
THE CASTLE IN THE MIST
Up the hill was a castle, I had never
seen before,
It was misty and unclear, but it was a
castle.
The sun slowly slid out from behind
the clouds,
The gold turrets glistened in the
morning sun.
I walked up the path and over the
drawbridge,
A big stone staircase was before me.
As I climbed the winding stairs, my
footsteps echoed in the bare halls.
I walked across the hall to the big
windows.
I looked out.
Through the mist, I could see a
brook,
A deer stood by it drinking from the
crisp water.
I turned and left the castle in search
of the stream,
I walked across the grass to the
stream,
The deer ran, even though I made no
sound.
I walked down the path I had come
on.
I looked back to the abandoned
castle, but it was not there,
Just the deer stood in the mist of the
empty field.

Diana B Terrazas
PETALS OF A ROSE

Thanks for your strength and support, God be with you always, My Dearest, Sweetest E. Morales. Friendships do indeed last longer than relationships.

I smell the petals of a rose
As I close my eyes
I feel the love you have shown
Love which comes,
With petals of a Rose

I smell the petals of a rose
I feel the warmth
Of your hands, the strength
The peaceful true love of a man
Which comes,
With the petals of a Rose

As I close my eyes
I see a dream come true
The dream of you and I
Our Love, Our symbol
The Petals of a Rose.

Teri E Bitner
LIFE

I would like to dedicate my poem LIFE to my parents, Roy and Diana, my two sisters Tammy and Tracy, and my best friend, Stacy. Thanks for everything!

Life is happy, life is sad, it treats you good, it treats you bad.

It keeps on moving, nothing can get in its way, you can live your life on memories, or take it day by day.

Overcome the bad, and look forward to the good, live a life of happiness, for everyone should.

Keep your head up high, and don't let it down, life is full of wonder, and love is all around.

Beulah Langston Porter

Beulah Langston Porter
HEALING HILLS

All my poems are lovingly dedicated to the memory of my parents, Henry and Rachel Langston, and sister Cora Langston Williams.

The city held me in its grasp too
long,
I must go out and find the healing
earth.
My ailing soul will find its strength
in song of

Birds, in feel of wind and sun.
The birth of life, of all new growing things in spring
Will now renew my heart and make it sing.

In these green hills a secret healing lies,
The cool soft breezes have a soothing touch
Upon the troubled face of one too wise
In knowledge of the world and ways of life.
In the solitude of these quiet hills
There comes at dawn a restful strength that fills
The seeking soul with peace and life renewed.

Beulah Langston Porter
THE ROAD WE KNOW
Above the lowlands is a road we know,
That gently curves around the quiet hills
With leafy shadows dancing to and fro;
A narrow little road, yet one that fills
The heart with peace. Here singing aspens tall
And slender guard the way; their burnished brown
And yellow leaves like jewels as they fall
Resplendent on the earth. The sun sends down
Upon the land its warm and golden glow.
We walk along without a worldly care;
We hear the murmurous music sweet and low;
The muted music only a few can hear.
We know not where this little road will go—
This is the lonely road that poets know.

Beulah Langston Porter
THE OLD HOME
It stands so lonely on the prairie,
This old farm house so gray and worn;
The sagging doors and crumbling walls
All signs that years have come and gone.

The clean west wind with mournful sighs
Whispers through the empty rooms and down
The chimney top, and lends a gentle shoulder for
The old gray house to lean upon.

This once was home where a family lived,
Where grown-ups worked and children played.
Sorrow, pain and trouble were not strangers in this house,
But laughter, fun and happiness were also there.

When twilight falls it seems a haunted place.
Is that lamplight shining in the kitchen?
Is that the clink of dishes, and talking soft and low?
And a young girl singing? They are not ghosts, just memories
Of loved ones long ago. They wait
Somewhere Beyond
For this lonely one who also waits.

Beulah Langston Porter
THE CALL OF WIND AND SEA
The cool sweet wind is calling from the hill,
I hear its urgent voice when night is still.
Its gentle touch has magic from the sea;
Its smell has hint of things so strange and free,
Like spume and spray, and ships, and sea gulls' cry,
Like storm and rain and clouds across the sky.

The whispering wind has promise in its voice,
I'd answer gladly if I had my choice.
At times I have a restless urge in me
To follow now the call of wind and sea,
But the lonely land calls me back home,
We, who are earthbound cannot roam.

Beulah Langston Porter
LEST YOU FORGET
We are the boys who sleep where tropic breezes blow
On far away atolls and desolate sandy beaches.
We are the boys beneath the crosses row on row
That stand by thousands in the vast and lonely reaches
On blue Pacific's shore!
We are the boys who now from weary battles rest
In peace forevermore,
So gently cradled on the ocean's coral breast.

We are the boys who lie on narrow beds of white;
We are the ill and lame, so gruesome to the sight!
We are the lonely dead who never more shall know
The joys of home—the summer's sun, the winter's snow.

We are the boys who smile and ask in wordless pain,
"Keep memory always bright, lest you forget again!
You have tomorrow's world within your waiting hands,
When flags of lasting peace should wave in freedom's air.
Our plea: Remember boys who died in foreign lands,
That hate and greed and senseless wars have sent them there!"

Malena Cynthia Diez
ROSE
Tender, sweet,
Yet empress among her own,
Petals like silk,
Vivid with life,
With beauty for all to behold.

Charlotte C-Burnett
THE COMPOSITION OF LIFE

To my three sons: Leonard, Todd, and Brandon Burnett—and to "Sweet Len" for keeping me fortified with symphonies . . . .

You go along life's highway with the world cupped in your hand
You're flying high and your life is as melodious as a band
You're happy, you're healthy and as vigorous as can be
Nothing in the whole wide world can remove your vitality.

Ah Ha—The highway's horizon begins to get bleak
With every move you make a roadblock is at your feet
You turn to the right, and you turn to the left
You're weak, you're ill, and you're faced with death.

The melodious melody of life is staccato in sound
How long, oh how long will this venom be 'round?
You grope at every ray of light that peaks beneath the cloud
Hoping for a storm of showers to wash away the shroud.

Do not despair, begin again, rebuild your life on love
Prayer and faith will help you merge far far above
And then you'll skirt a highway that is smooth and tragic-free
And once again your life will soar to the heights of a symphony.

Barbara M Johnson
THE BEAUTIFUL MENOMINEE
Beautiful, Beautiful, Menominee
You fill Michigan with perfect Harmony
You babble over rock and rills
Down the sloping backs of hills
Your banks reveal pictures of beauty
Yet you prove faithful to your duty
You give us pounds of bass and trout
And give pleasure all along your route
You supply cities with electric power
Yet satisfy sportsmen's whims, hour after hour
You form a boundary between two great states
And your source is the Great Lakes
At your mouth you meet Green Bay
As you go on your course day after day
Enabling us to benefit by you
You are a blessing to Michigan, thru and thru.

Helen M Hamberg
THOUGHTS
I often wish I were a painter when I gaze at God's work in the sky.
Sunsets of orange, red, pink, lavender and blues, all blended so perfect on high.

The dark storm clouds or the fluffy lamb wool kind.
All so different and interesting.
Depending on what nature has in mind.

The sky sparkling blue beauty. The velvet green of the grass. Flowers of all colors so bright. Just wishing the beauty would last.

Therefore I wish I were a painter and I could record each one. In all the beauty as God has. Before my day is done.

Charles L Taylor
ORIGIN
Where did it come from?
Where did it go?
What is it headed for?
I really don't know.
Why am I now
Please reason me how
Why am I me
And why can't I see
Long, long ago
Or far up ahead
I really don't know
I'm confused instead.
Where did it start,
This origin
And how far apart
did we all begin
Where did it stop
or where will it end?
Tell me, tell me, where have we been?

Pamie Roy
ONCE I HAD A DREAM

For Daddy.

Once I had a dream that I was far away.
I think I was in heaven, yet no one can really say.
Everything was so serene and perfect, unlike here.
I knew where I was going and my thoughts were all so clear.
My instinct told me I belonged there, but still I felt so odd.
I asked another what he thought, he only gave a nod.
No one really said much, they all just got along.
If one angel began, they all stood by and poured forth a song.
And when an angel's voice was heard, it always spoke a special word.
For in their song they told a story.
They praised the joy, eternity, and glory.
I think I was in heaven, yet no one can really say.
But I know I had a dream in which I was far away.

Gina Peeso
DON'T EVER SAY GOOD-BYE

To Bobby, a part of me I just can't let go.

Don't ever say good-bye
I couldn't take the pain
Don't ever say good-bye
This love is not a game
Don't ever say good-bye
My life wouldn't be complete
Don't ever say good-bye
For then my love is obsolete
Don't ever say good-bye
'Cuz I need you here with me
Don't ever say good-bye
For then I could not see
Don't ever say good-bye
I'd simply fall apart
Don't ever say good-bye
For then you'd break my heart
But if you say good-bye
I'd wish you only the best
For love I know was the test
And now I must say good-bye.

Jennifer Krause
THE TEAR
One lonely tear
When it hurts too much
To cry others
Pain lets go for one second
And that one tear
Traces the path
Of so many more
All by itself.

Eva O Scott
A NEW WORLD

With God all things are possible.

"A new Heavens and a new earth
we are awaiting according to His promise
and in these righteousness is to dwell."
All the people will be well.
There will be no more infirmity—
For the blind shall see;
The lame will walk
And the dumb shall talk.

No-one will rent—
For the fruits of the toil that is spent
will remain their own,
Whether the building of a home,
Or the food they have grown.
Jehovah's children shall inherit the earth
And not for disturbance will they give birth.
The wolf and lamb will feed as one,
When in the earth God's will is done.
Jesus Christ will rule as King:
May we His praises ever sing!
2Pet. 3:13
Isa. Chap. 65

Stuart L Spanier
CAMPFIRE
Fire burns in the campsite.
A lonely wind blows throughout the night.

Trees whisper of a distant time
Smoke rises up through the standing pine.

As I sit in the glowing darkness
Mind wandering in a world of gloomiest

A river flows not far from here
Humming of harmony and cheer.

Soon the air begins to chill
And the fire burns out at will.

As I lay back against a tree
The rocks are sharp but they don't bother me.

Staring up into the nightly sky
Thinking of dreams that lie.

Mountains closing in all around
Shadows dancing upon the ground.

With the whimpering breeze against my face
I soon drift off into another place.

Jan Merrill
PARADIGM RIFT
Lusting humanistic eyes
Mirror matte, brown-mustard skies;
From mindless profane babblings rise
Corrupted chains of spirit-ties.
Temples swollen tight with pride
Hold mocking laughter deep inside;
Lacquered, wooden smiles beguile:
"Come, party on—play awhile!"
Death, in powder-white disguise
Merchandises children's lives;
Channels spew forth ancient lies:
"You are really God, inside . . . "
(Admit no wrong, espouse no right—
No absolutes our deeds indict!)
Wealthy power is man's delight;
Leaders choose to rule by might.
Brazen voices pledge their cries
Of fealty to the New-Age christ:
His Violet Phoenix of false light
The Soon-Coming King will put to flight.

Cathy Ann Taylor
HORRIBLE NIGHTMARE

I dedicate this poem to my beloved husband, Anthony William Taylor.

Our lives were happy
We were complete
Until they broke my door down
And presented the white sheet

They said you've been arrested
For a crime you didn't do
But I know you didn't do it
'Cause I know you.

Now I'm feeling alone
Like a clock with no chime
You're going so far away
And for such a long time

They took away your family
They took away my man
We have to stay together
Any way we can

It's going to take a lot
To keep this family alive
But if we put our hearts together
We will survive.

Kim Miller
A DREAM'S END
Misty haze this morning A flower stands Proud strong perfect Releasing its beauty into the eyes of its admirers, it turns to smile at me A storm arises suddenly Wind rips through my hair Tears my clothes The flower bends But does not break Thunder's roar Echoing Echoing Echoing Violently resounding inside my head Lightning's flash blinds me Rain drowns out my cries I run A coward into shelter's arms They close around me Protect me while I grow older Intense heat It dries the puddles in the meadow and my tears as well Hotter Hotter Hotter the sun blazes No rain No relief I trudge on An eternity later I stop I arrive nowhere But at my feet stands the flower Hunching frailly Wilting from the heat Its blossom nearly meets the earth I pull it up from the ground Then I see it A dream's end Standing on a hill in the distance A pillar Yes, a pillar Or a headstone I run towards it Faster Faster Faster Dry grass breaking beneath my feet So tired The sun is setting now I stand in the shadow of this great monument So aged So eroded How long has it been there I am not certain until I read the inspection It is a name Yes, a name Ah, it is my own.

Kristine M Boswell
FALLEN CASTLES
Sitting on the beach in summer,
The little boy thinks it's a bummer.
The older kids walk right past,
While the little boy gets bored fast.
With shovel in hand,
While he sits on the sand.
He builds his castle,
Without a hassle.
When he's done he'll proclaim,
This castle is his domain.
He runs to get someone to see,
The object of his ecstasy.
When he returns his dreams subside,
As the castle washes out with the tide.

Ada Panisse O'Byrne
INNOCENT
I cannot play without my brother.
I want to see him, Mother!
Now that springtime is here,
Where is he hiding?

The butterflies flutter between the flowers of my garden.
I cannot catch them alone.
Tell my brother to come over
And help me.

My dear son, the Mother says,
You are asking for the impossible.
Your brother is now in heaven!
And here he will never return!

Has he left all these flowers and birds, and these delicious fruits for me?
And while springtime returns
Do you think he will come back?

No my love, your dear brother
Has left forever.
Then I will have to say goodbye
to the flowers and the birds
And wish to meet him in heaven.

Jodie Lynn Smith
I SMILE

To my sweetheart, Allen Ray Spade.

I smile,
I smile upon the sound of
your sweet voice;
Not knowing the time you'll
make your choice . . .
So I hide myself in darkness as you pull away;
I hide all my feelings
'til another day.

I smile at the feel of
your loving arms;
Wondering when love will
leave its harms . . .
Covering the sadness with anger and fear;
I wait and wonder when
you'll be near.

I smile at the gentle
touches you give;
Because when I'm with you
it's then I live . . .
Loneliness of my heart
breaking through;
My mind becomes confused
what shall I do?

I smile at the gentle
words you say;
When we're loving as if
not another day . . .
And sweet, sweet kisses
upon my brow;
You say, "I Love You,"
in parting now.

Sherry A Davis
MY BEST FRIEND
As I sit here so far away,
I realize how close we are.
I come to appreciate the things
that I once took advantage of.
I sometimes wonder how we became so close.
I do not ponder,
For I am pleased that we are.
I've come to love the understanding
and close communication that we share,
The sensitivity that you show me,
The little things that you do for me
when I'm down,
Your childish laugh,
Your silly comments,
The agreements we've made,
The disagreements that we've shared.
Each of these things come together in our friendship.
I'm happy for that.
Sometimes it takes a separation only
to realize that a sister is really a best friend.
You are my best friend.
I Love you

Wendell C Thomas
OUR FATHER IN HEAVEN

Dedicated to the Holy Spirit who inspired me and my lovely wife Sharon Denise (Neci) Thomas.

He speaks to us right from birth
Yes as soon as we land on planet earth
But we comprehend Him not
We're just little tiny tots
We have no understanding of His word
In reality He speaks to us but is not heard
Then as we age we start to wonder
What is this crazy spell we're under?
The answer God holds we cannot find
Because satan has control of our little weak minds
But don't give up yet it's not too late
God's love will show us it's the devil we should hate
I'm glad He stopped him from playing with my head
If He hadn't I surely would have ended up dead
Thank God for Grace I have no more strife
And now have the gift of Eternal Life
Lucifer can hurt me no more, never
I'm going on to live with Jesus forever . . . .

Millie P Marvil

Millie P Marvil

LIPS THAT HAVE TOUCHED MINE

To: His tender kiss, while rains beat wild, and hearts beat wilder still!

I remember in years now past,
The lips that have touched mine, sweet or stolen,
And some I wonder why, a kiss was even 'lowed.
Some sent thrills from head to toe, no less!
All I have not kept in mind and heart,
While some I feel the pulsing throb, of heartbeat
Of an old sweetheart of mine, now by myself.
Have you ever paused to think, of by-gone kisses?

The seriousness of some, to barely touch the lips,
So light and tender, though your heart beat wild,
And you wondered, why won't my heart be still?
Some have lingered far into the night, in darkness,
While arms have lain beneath my head, on sofa,
As we listened to the rain, that taps and patters
On my windowpane, a pleasing sound, in silent room.
A sound that I still hear, and remember!

Asking no one but myself, if any think of me,
Or will turn in quiet darkness, with a cry, and say
Where art thou tonight, my Dear, I think of you,
And is it raining where you are—thinking too?

Rachel N Swain

MY WORLD

I have this little world,
That is so dear to me,
It is a very special place,
That only a select few can be.
This place is a land of peace,
There is no war,
The fighting has ceased.
This place is a world of no sound
But only silence,
Where my thoughts are found
My rock,
My foundation,
Is here to protect me from total humiliation.
Here there is no hurry,
Here there is no crime,
So I guess you can stop by sometime,
Here at my world.
If this place sounds mysterious,
Then I guess you don't understand,
For I am deaf and that is why,
There is no noise in my land.

Shelby Harris

HOMELESS

What becomes of a man,
if you take his hopes his dreams
and his aspirations, and you cast
them into a mighty rushing wind?
Knowing this, that he hath not
wings to pursue them.
You ultimately destroy this man
that held in his very soul, the
power to love you forever.

Dawn Furey

IT

It emerged from the dark.
Wet, screeching and stark
naked of cloth, naked of thought.
Needing only to be taught,
a language of touch, of tongue.
Never again to be so young.
Both in time and in knowing.
From then on it's the growing.
The tickle of laughter, the heartache of sorrow.
The moment is past, there is only tomorrow.
And tomorrow again, and yet another one.
For this, our precious new-born son.

Laura Lee Zerns

THE ALARM SOUNDS LIKE A SIREN

The alarm sounds like a siren
a drowsy arm creeps
from the warm cavern of covers
and strikes with sudden
viciousness
The alarm still sounds
a cold floor makes
steps nimble
cracking the shade
the light leaks in
stabbing pale flesh
as the police gather
outside.

Timothy R Gregg

CRY FOR HELP

For—a material world that forgot peace. Moonchild and Sunchild: "Soul drifts and feed from the gods' cup . . ."

"There are riots in the dungeons
And rage in the cells.
The screaming of torture,
Is the ringing of the bells.
The high king stands so
Fearless in his stance.
The army of immortals,
Die within his trance.
Now the final day comes,
When the ending is known.
Who has the balance?
What has the fighting shown?
The air stands still.
No leaves blowing in the wind.
The sun is rising dark,
And there are no clouds within.
So what will happen then?
When there is no tomorrow only end?
And there is no politics and state,
At the ending of everyone's fate.
Sad wings of destiny cry for help today . . . ."

Herbert F Withey Sr

Herbert F Withey Sr

FRET NOT DEAR BROTHER

Fret not dear brother, in the trial you're going through.
Trust in the Lord, for He walks with you.
He will give you strength and courage along the way,
Fret not dear brother, have faith and pray.

Fret not dear brother, when bills are from wall to wall.
He will help you pay not just one, but all.
Fret not dear brother, in sickness, misery or pain,
His promise for deliverance is still the same.

Fret not dear brother, if things in your life go sour,
Like no job, no money for rent, or the price of flour.
He will feed you as He feeds the birds.
Just call on His Holy Name and you will be heard.

Fret not dear brother, but praise His Holy Name.
Through trials of heartache, floods and flame.
Give Him thanks and praise for what He has done.
Fret not dear brother, but have faith in God's own Son.

Herbert F Withey Sr

I WILL PRAISE THE LORD

I will praise the Lord for his Love Divine.
For his grace and forgiveness that are now mine.
I will praise the Lord, where He bids me go,
Even through sorrow, misery and woe.

I will praise the Lord in gladness, poverty and despair,
In times when it seems He's not around, I know He's there.
I will praise the Lord for the rocky road that is all uphill,
For the Holy Spirit that keeps me in His Will.

I will praise the Lord for His strength and power,
For the victory He gives me every waking hour.
I will praise the Lord for the peace He gives,
For in my heart is where He lives.

I will praise the Lord for my home on high,
Where we will live together in the Sweet By and By.
I will eat at His Table and sit with Him on His Throne.
I will praise the Lord until He calls me home.
Praise His wonderful name.

Edward L Johnson

TRAP

To young innocent men.

Trap, trap where is the trap
Trap, trap where is the trap

I once knew a woman
Trap, trap, where is the trap
Trap, trap, where is the trap

She laid a trap
Trap, trap, where is the trap
Trap, trap, where is the trap

I once knew an innocent man
Trap, trap, where is the trap
Trap, trap, where is the trap

The woman knew the man
Trap, trap, where is the trap
Trap, trap, where is the trap

The woman became pregnant
Trap, trap, where is the trap
Trap, trap, where is the trap

The woman got a husband
Trap, trap, where is the trap
Trap, trap, where is the trap

The innocent man
Trap, trap, where is the trap
Trap, trap, where is the trap

Where is the trap
Trap, trap, where is the trap
Trap, trap, where is the trap
She got a husband
Trap, trap, no more traps.

Herbert F Withey Sr

FIGHT ON DEAR CHRISTIAN SOLDIER

Fight on dear Christian soldier, hold Christ's banner high.
The fight is not yours alone, He is at your side.
Fear not Satan's word or power, for you are sure to win.
Just keep your heart and soul free from sin.

To fight the enemy below, use the weapons from above.
Fight on dear Christian soldier, with prayer, humility and love.
Resist Satan and his army and from you they will flee.
Possess the Holy Word of God and claim the victory.

Fight on dear Christian soldier, use your shield of faith.

It will quench those fiery darts of wickedness and hate.
Use the sword of the Spirit to slay the demon foe.
Wherever Jesus wants you, say, here I am Lord, I'll go.

Fight on dear Christian soldier, spread God's words of peace.
Tell men of Christ's forgiving power, and from sin they are released.
Forge ahead and slay your giants as David did of old.
Just keep your eyes on Heaven, where the streets are made of gold.

Enter into life eternal with Christ our Lord and King.
Listen to the songs of heaven that all the angels sing.
Receive your robe of white and crown of gold Jesus has for you.
Fight on dear Christian soldier, until the fighting's through.
Fight on, fight on, fight on.

Judy Gentry
MOUNTAINS
Proud and standing strong, leaned against the sky,
Beauty in its strength, is seen as we go by.
Sometimes green and strong, sometimes kissed with snow,
Sometimes painted pretty, like dabs of paint on gold.
If tall up in the air, or low and rolling hills,
They're all kinds of mountains, as if time had stood still.
They're home to all God's creatures, their shelter from the storm,
They're places to touch nature, all in perfect form.
Little streams run down them, birds fly up on high,
Mountains bold and reaching, almost touch the sky.
So take a walk around, and see the mountains' tops,
For beauty reigns around us, it never ever stops.
So stop and take a chance, to notice simple things,
Like rigid standing mountains, waiting to be seen.

Joan L Hartung
WINTER
It is winter
And the soul struggles
With events of the fall
And the many seasons before.

Will the spring come?
Can the spirit be reborn
And growth begin again?
Warmth, will you visit once more?

Here in the cold and dark
I am chilled and alone.
Gazing back I see nothing.
The haze obscures too well.

But it's the haze
That keeps me here
For if you cannot see the past
You can never plan the future.

Susan Martin
ISLE OF DREAMS

To my loving husband, Steve.

He took flight . . .
riding 'tween the spreading winds of a golden eagle over the ocean of midnight, guided by the rays of moonlight to the isle of dreams.

I stand waiting at the shores of midnight anticipating the ending of the flight.

Approaching, the eagle flies within the rays of the moon, illuminating his presence, as do the stars.

I see the rider of the eagle, fall in love with prince and into the realm of wanting him on the isle of dreams.

The eagle circles to land. In landing, the rider turns the head of the eagle upward.
He continues to fly.

The prince . . .
afraid of where he will land on the isle of dreams, finds no happiness riding the golden eagle alone.

Vicki L Will
DESIRES
Everchanging seasons flow through my mind like the emotions of my heart drifting through my soul.

I reach for you, but you're not there,
I feel tension mixed with desire.

I have an insatiable quenching desire to be near, but yet I'm so far.

Will I ever be close, or will you keep me away forever?

There is no easy way to explain what has conspired, why can't I escape to be me, to be free, to love and be loved is my strongest desire.

But just as strong as that desire, is the one I know will never be.

But I have my dreams . . .

What is it that you have??????????

Marjorie Diggins-Liebler
MY CHILDREN

To Michaela Rose Liebler, my daughter, I love you.

The gathering crowd pressed around
Where the lone man sat near the gate,
His eyes burned, and His words pierced their hearts;
His speech HE prayed would light the way.

His time was short, the hour grew near
When His message would take effect,
His words flowed sweet as honey comb;
To souls in need from long neglect.

He rose to His feet, and beheld them
The people He came to save,
With arms outstretched to embrace them;
With benevolence, He taught them that day.

"My children, there is a greater love than man can give
The love of God for His people,
So he sent a savior, to heal you from your wounds;
To take away your sins.

Radiant love shown from His face
He touched every soul and changed many lives,
Showing them the way the truth and the life;
Giving them freely His blessing, His Grace.
Healed were they who heard Him speak
They watched Him turn to leave,
Freed forever from their sins;
Because in Christ, they are now believed.

Kim Cowan
SEASON OPENER—a baseball poem—

"Season Opener" dedicated with love, to my father, Kelly Cowan, and to my son Christopher.

As the sun warms the cold Winter days to Spring . . . they gather once again to start equal, none better than the other. They are men mesmerized by intention, absorbing and embracing the newness of another season.

It is a marvelous tradition, the coming of this event. It outshines a marriage of hearts, or even a cherished holiday. It is a passionate mixture of heritage and legacy, that goes back in time, and radiates beyond us.

. . . The Season Opener . . . a sprinkle of entertainment that penetrates into a memory. It is the greatest day of all. I believe the fragrance that blossoms from the bud of all this, it surely the flower for me.

Margaret G Gabbard
MY LIFE
My life is like an open book,
But you can only take a look.
For only God can know within,
The secret battles I have to win.

Only God all sorrow knows,
Only He has seen my deepest woes.
He's been the One to lift me up,
When I drank from Life's bitter cup.

There were times when things were bad,
And on the surface I seemed glad;
But Jesus knew the smile I wore,
Did not betray the things I bore.

But there will come a happier day,
And these cares too will fade away.
As they have in times gone past,
Thank God, sad days don't always last.

Joetta Gibbs
A VISION

To my ex-husband Bill, my sons, Jeff and Jim, and to Gary, whom I will never forget.

Yes, I have known love before.
Through my eyes, he was a king.
From his love, I received two shining stars
to help build our family ring.

Yet, as troubles came upon us,
I knew we had to part.
The months passed so slowly;
I felt pain, deep within my heart.

But then on that precious September night,
I saw you, a star, shining so bright.
Then God showed me the reason why
my first love was not to be
for you are my eternal Knight.
At the time, you could not see.

Where are you? I do not know.
There's a longing in my heart
as I watch the melting snow.

God has given me the strength I need
to accept the years as they pass by.
Maybe someday I will see you again.
If not, then we shall meet—in the sky!

Virginia G Miller
BOYS DO GROW UP

This poem is dedicated to my son Jeff. May you always be a child at heart.

Heavenly Father up above,
Please protect the child I love.
He's a special child you see,
He's the child you gave to me.

Keep him safe by night and day,
And guide his path along life's way.
Let him be happy, healthy and smart,
You know to me he's a work of art.
Wrap his life in peace and love,
And may he always know you're up above.
Hear my prayer for my precious son,
'Cause now he's grown and my job is done.

Mary Carpenter Green
THAT OLD FOUNTAIN PEN

This poem is dedicated to the memory of my dear mother.

That old fountain pen tucked away in the drawer
has scrawled many a
letter . . . and so much more . . .
To brothers, sisters, and cousins galore,
nieces and nephews on every shore;
. . . That old fountain pen tucked away in the drawer . . .

It's jotted down recipes by the score,
even some rhymes and a little folklore;
Notes to the teacher one couldn't ignore,
signed each report card . . . and so much more . . .
. . . That old fountain pen tucked away in the drawer . . .

In tear-stained hand, pained and sore,
it wrote to the sons who were off to war;
Sending them love from a heart that's tore,
with news of home . . . and so much
more . . .
. . . That old fountain pen tucked away in the drawer . . .

Smoothly it glided until the years wore,

then searchingly on paper it did
its chore;
In feeble hand it scribbled as before,
only to retire and fall to the floor;
I'll treasure it always . . .
. . . That old fountain pen tucked
away in the drawer . . .

Naomi Greenfield Gee
MY INHERITED CROSS SPEAKS
I am the little gold cross—
Three generations I span
The many stories I could tell
Hang by life's tiniest strand.

Prepared, I must be—
To let the whole world see
Life's generations haven't
changed
It's the same for you and me.

Reams of joy and those of tears—
Are with me throughout the years
My previous owners have
perished by fires
Yes, lightning and natural
desires.

Preserving my heritage through
chance survival—
When nearly drowning. I accepted
revival
Would, that you could survive,
as I
To enhance generations as
time goes by.

An heirloom so precious, but heavy
with loss—
Just like Jesus as He carried His
cross
But happiness prevails bringing
cherished pleasure
With the promise of
Heirlooms for ever and
ever!!

Cedric W Fellows
YOU & I

This poem is dedicated to the inspiration of this poem, as well as many others. My lovely wife, Jacqueline.

Give me kisses warm an tender
hold me in a sweet embrace—
Let me share the wonder of you
help our hearts to interlace,

By your side the world is rosy
your smile drives gray clouds away—
I am thrilled when you are near me
close beside me always stay,

With you I'll be more than equal
to the greatest sacrifice—
Take my hand and we'll journey
up the road to paradise,

My love for you grows each moment
it's a wonderful narrative—
It is formed of faith unending
that makes life so good to live,

You and I forever and ever
this is how it has to be—
Every door will unlock for us
our love is the magic key.

Bethany M Sebesta
FATHER AND SON
The father and the son
Never talking
Always yelling
Unable to communicate
Not free to tell of their
Pains or joys or love
The son never pleasing the father
The father never pleasing the son
The father always left feeling let
Down, hurt and confused
Never understanding the son
They are trapped in a circle of pain
Unable to break free
From that mold started a lifetime ago
All through their lives
Each blaming the other
Never understanding
Never forgiving.

Roberta Ann Villano
WISH IT WERE ME
Take time to get a good look at me
Here's some of the things I think
you'll see
I'm just a woman who wants to be
loved
By a gentle man—not by just God
above
I want him to share and laugh and be
close as one
But I just can't be happy unless this
is done
I have desires and needs to be
fulfilled
But it takes a man with more than
just a good build
He must be warm and tender and
gentle with his touch
He must be honest and devoted—I
need this so much
There can't be any jealousy or abuse
in my life
If any exists, then I can't be his wife
All promises made and commitments
spoken
Should always be honored and never,
never broken
God and Church are special you see
And if you don't agree you won't
have me
As I drive by the river where the
water flows free
I see friends and lovers and wish it
were me.

Ernestine Collins
HE IS SATISFIED

For my dear friend, Patricia DeVille, with much love.

You'll never hold him in your arms
Or look into his eyes.
You'll never nurse him at your breast
To soothe his little cries.

But, oh! his soul is resting in the
presence of the Lord;
And he is satisfied.

He does not know the pain you feel
That he has gone so soon.
How bless'd to be allowed to go
To heaven from the womb!

His little soul is resting in the
presence of the Lord,
And he is satisfied.

In time and tears somehow you'll
face
The fact that he is gone—
That you must stay in service here,
While God has called him home.

Because his soul is resting in the
presence of the Lord,
Your child is satisfied.

He can't return to you, but you
Can go to him someday.
Then all the tears that you have shed
Our God shall wipe away.

And when your soul is resting in the
presence of the Lord,
You'll be satisfied.

Ashley Smith
THE STORM
All of a sudden
He took her away
With a blinding flash
One summer's day

We were walking along
Bare feet in the sand
Then came her turn
To take God's hand

The skies grew dark
And the clouds sank low
What was about to happen
Only HE could know

It was His will
To use His might
On her holy cross
He chose to strike

It happened so sudden
All I could do was cry
Not even a chance . . .
To say good-bye

Now I walk alone
And wonder why
That it was her . . . above all
That He chose to die

I wait my turn
Some day HE will take me
Rejoining our souls
. . . For eternity

Elaine E Smith

Elaine E Smith
UNENDING LOVE
Love transforms a body and soul.
With it our hearts will never grow
old.
How majesty we can be, a happiness
untold.
The very air that we breathe, the
steps that we take.
Our hands melt together like the
softness of a petal on a rose.
Surroundings around us sparkle and
shine.
All creatures of this earth we hold
dear to our hearts.
Although we're not perfect in many
ways, thru the eyes of love there is no
haze.
I have but just to lift my eyes to the
beautiful skies above,
then I know where all the majesty
comes from.
For no one could give us, such
feelings, as our Dear and Precious
Lord Jesus from above.
Many thanks to him for what I have.
May he always look down upon us,
with his, Unending Love.

Elaine E Smith
THE DAWN OF THE DAY
I looked at the sky it was oh so gray,
I saw no birds, I saw no trees.
The ocean was forceful and black,
My problems wrapped around me
like a ball of fire, that caused me to
be blind, even though I could see.
I said what kind of world is this,
never no pleasure for me.
I took a walk in the park this day, and
was approached, by a kindly old man
who said to me.
You look so lonely and unhappy,
please let me talk to thee.
How very strange I felt as he took my
hand, he said my precious child, open
your eyes and see what I see, open
thy ears and hear what I hear.
Behold the greenness in the trees, the
blue in the skies, hear the chirping of
the birds, smell the beauty of the
flowers, just look at the sea, how
beautiful it became, with the porpoise
as they swam so gallantly.
The old man said I must go, don't
ever forget what I've taught thee.
My eyes were lifted up to the sky,
and when I looked down, the old man
was gone.
I thought to myself, who was this
kind and gentle soul, who left me so
quickly, and gave me the insight, and
the beauty to behold.
I said to myself, he must be, The
Dear Lord Jesus, the master, of you
and me.

Margaret Lanier
SHARKS
It's often been my style
To grasp beyond my reach,
But I think I'd best enjoy the
sea
While standing on the beach.

Larrainia PG
CUSHITES
Collective thoughts bonded in an
ancient past
Forgotten,
Remnants of the abstract without
concrete images,
Devoid of matter and remains
nothing,
Except a figment of one's ideal
fantasy.

Lost in a whirlpool of an old sea that
Knows the truth,
But have not found self in truth
That is the ticket to freedom.
Jellied minds sucked up into a
vacuum,
Controlled, packed, and buried.
Cries, moans, and groans, MERCY!

Out of rubbles and ruins of
Cool ebony volcanic lava comes life,
Budding, fresh, and magnificent,
Dare to survive the brimstone of fire,
Dare to stand tall,
Dare to know thyself,
Dare to reject the ashes of ghostly
figurines,
Dare to know the truth of this
century!

Carmella Paris Cheppa
UNREQUITED LOVE
An eloquence which heaven doth
inspire,
To speak of you is what I should
employ.

Oh, wouldst that I that faculty acquire
To tell you of my unrestricted joy.

If life's true function is to incarnate,
And in progression, does . . .
recurrently,
Assured am I that by the hand of
Fate,
Through time and space, you shall
return to me.

This listless heart too long had
known repose.
Monotony had dulled its rhythmic
beat—
Till from those languorous depths it
slowly rose
And swelled (because of you) with
love replete.

Interminable time that takes its toll—
I wait to be with you—a task so
huge,
Denying it denies my heart and soul
What gain will I to nurse a subter-
fuge?

Virginia K Meyer
SHADOW OF LOVE
What is that? Moving there?
It's on the floor. No, it's in the air.
Moving swiftly, climbing high.
It can't be seen, with the naked eye.
What is that? A whispering voice.
Yelling at me. Tell me the right
choice.
Do I stay? Do I go?
Is this love? Please let me know.
It's coming closer. Yes, it's very
near.
What's behind me? Is it love I feel?
I thought I saw it. There, in your
eyes.
A shadow of love? Once it's there
then it dies.
A shadow of love. It's all I see.
You stand so near. Do you want me?
Don't keep me guessing. Wondering
inside.
Your shadow of love, from me, it
can't hide.

C Foster Boyd
WHEN I WENT ALONE
*In loving memory of Rev. O. G.
Foster.*

I went in search of a friend
I found a bitter enemy.
I went in search of laughter
I found cries of despair.
I went in search of compassion
I found I was condemned.
I went in search of freedom
I found a heavy laden chain.
I went in search of peace
I found a raging war.
I went in search of love
I found a dirty word.
In the darkness, confusion and
torment of my life I ran in search
of God. I found he could not be there.
I had gone into the world without
him.
I'd left my armor home.

Cindy M Specht
A TRUCK DRIVER'S WIFE
He gets up at Eleven to start his day,
While his wife waits up to start him
on his way,
He puts on his shirt & finds his pants,
While his wife follows him around &
chats,
The conversation is Cheery & Bright,
For soon they will be saying
goodnight,
As he heads out of sight,
She is turning off all the lights,
When the birds begin to sing & the
sun shines bright,
Alone again is the Truck Driver's
Wife,
No matter how tired or late,
He calls his wife who sits by the
phone & waits,
They laugh, Talk & share their day,
All the time knowing soon he'll be
on his way,
The Sun comes up, Not a cloud in
sight,
Alone again is the Truck Driver's
Wife,
She's not lonely or afraid,
She knew who she married from the
very first day,
She is pretty, Strong and Bright,
OFCOURSE She's a Truck Driver's
Wife.

Latonya Russell
SPRINGTIME
S is for the sun that casts its rays.
P is for playing in the park on sunny
days.
R is for remembering your wonderful
joys.
I is for inventing brand-new toys.
N is for taking nature walks through
the park.
G is for great danes with loud, loud
barks.
T is for talking about all the times
you fell.
I is for all the irritating times you had
to yell.
M is for moms calling you in to stay.
E is for enjoying those hot spring
days.

Malcolm and Betty Halstead

Betty E Halstead
MASTER OF LIFE
*This poem is dedicated to Malcolm,
my darling husband.*

Since I met Jesus life is of
Peace and rest
When I need him he's always
There to bless.

There are trials and tribulations
In the world of sin,
But He said to remember, I will be
With you to the end.

When the veil is uncovered that
When the new life begins,
Oh how much I adore him, and to
Have such a friend.

The holy Bible is full of grace,
Mercy and truth,
And you can find it, Matthew,
Mark, John and Luke.

When Jesus prayed to the Father
In John 17 Chapter, of how to
Make us all one in Him, for
That prayer was answered, for His
Children only know of what it is,
For him to dwell within. Amen

Alexis Dell-Scott
HE IS YOU
*To Carl "Dusty" Scott—Love Beyond
Time, Alexis.*

I thought my life was over;
That the pain would never end.
I knew my sunny skies were gone;
My hope went round the bend.

I shut off all my feelings,
And closed off all my doors;
I stopped the tears,
I hid my fears,
Then soon "I" was no more.

But through a crack in my pain
A stranger to me came;
He opened up his mind and heart,
And smashed my shell apart.

He holds me in his strong safe arms,
Where all my world is right;
And when the long hard day is done,
He holds me through the nite.

I've never known a man like him,
So soft yet loving too;
Until I met the one rare man,
And DARLING, "he is you."

Betty Fay
SPECIAL LITTLE BOY
*I wrote this poem in honor of my little
boy who has Down's syndrome.*

The nest is almost empty
We have only one little guy left
And we thank God he is with us
For we feel he's a special gift.

He doesn't jump, and climb, and
play,
Like many children do,
But his little heart is full of love.
His requests are very few.

Maybe some bubbles to blow
rainbows
Or find a ball he's lost,
A simple game of Candyland,
Or in the creek, some stones to toss.

He loves to go for little walks
Grabs mommy's hand and runs
Then stops to rest, and on we go
To him it is such fun
It's lovely just being together.
We find some special stones.
And head back home with our
souvenirs,
As the sun sets on us alone.

Christina M Harshman
ISLE OF LOVE
Walking down the isle of love,
I see you looking at me.
Through your eyes I gain the
strength,
to a love that will always be.
Reaching out to take your hand,
as you take hold of mine.
Standing by the man I love,
darlin' you will find . . .
I will cherish this love for you
till death do us apart.
Taking this commitment
together
beginning from the start.
The two of us now stand as one
to fill each other's needs.
You the rain and I the bud,
have just planted a beautiful seed.

Frances C Biesman
SUNDOWN ON THE RANCH
Two blackbirds sitting on a bare
branch,
at sundown here on the old ranch.
Peace has come at the end of a long
day.
Wooly white sheep are munching on
hay.

The froggies are croaking their
evening song,
near the clear brook lazing along.
Beneath the trees, cattle are lying at
rest,
as the sun lowers in the west.

The chickens are all perched on their
roost,
in the old weathered hen house.
And scurrying from corner to corner
speeds a fat, gray mouse.

Old "Shep" is sprawled on the porch,
keeping watch o'er all.
The ranch, snuggled down to rest
awaits morning's call

Arlene V Novick
NIGHT WATCH
In the descended crimson nigrescence
Softly spun veil soul seduces,
Windplayers in Olympian delight
Sing with Flora's essence.

Where white-bellied nymphs like
marbled doe
Quivering phantom shadows,
Bejeweled graceful feathered limbs
That like love reach toward Luna's
flow.

In the hush of nature's floor
Crackling long haired fragments,
Moistened with Autumnal bliss
Orchestrate the forest's roar.

Where leaping waters chill the site
Their azure lines reflecting,
Like Zeus' luminescent hands
Synchronizing day and night.

In the descended crimson nigrescence
Softly spun veil soul seduces.
Windplayers in Olympian delight
Sing with Flora's essence.

Pamela Dise
BEAUTY
Beauty is in the eye of the beholder,
And love is in the hands of God.
Friendship is of our making,

And we decide eternal or not.
Friends are not always true,
And love is not always foretold,
But beauty is always what we
—hold it to be.

Paul A James
A CHILD'S CREED

To all of whom that contribute to the welfare and social care of children.

Floundering amidst turbulent seas
A helping hand I need
My fate today, others will decide
My future is at stake

Indeed I have some special needs
Some may view me as underprivileged . . .
My greatest handicap, your pity can become
Don't blunder, I can adapt and overcome
A helping hand is all I need

Realize, in the palm of your hand my life you hold
Give me the courage to become all that I could be
Always expect and demand that I do my best in school and in everything else, too

In order for me to realize my full potential
I need your wisdom as a guiding light
I need the push of your gentle touch

Life is serious business
In mediocrity, I will not flourish
Folks, I should know
After all, I'm a foster kid

Dorothy M Bratton Jones

Dorothy M Bratton Jones
AS LONG AS I KNOW THAT I HAVE YOU LORD

Dedicated to my beloved family, both spiritual and natural.

I don't care about persecution,
I don't care about suffering and pain,
As long as I know that I have you Lord
I have everything to gain.

I don't care about ridicule Lord,
I don't care about hatred and strife,
As long as I know that I have you Lord.
I'm only seeking eternal–life.

I don't care about gold and jewelry,
I don't care about silver and myrrh,
As long as I know that I have you Lord.
It's worth more than anything on earth.
I don't care about houses and land Lord,
Just about loving my fellowman.
As long as I know that I have you Lord,
You'll always extend your helping hand.

I have everything, yes I do Lord!
As long as I know that I have
You!

Tracy Rivera
FIRST LOVE

This poem is dedicated to Jim K. Hitchcock, my first love. I love you.

The joy, the happiness that's in my eyes.
To see him sitting along my side.
The feeling of warmth when I'm in his arms.
His smooth, soft skin when we're cheek to cheek.
The touch of his fingers along my spine,
For I know for a fact that he'll always be mine.
To know that he'll be here for better or for worse.
The embarrassment, the resentfulness it doesn't exist,
In such a relationship as such as this.
The future holds eternal love, for him and I,
My first love.

Pegi McCarthy
How can we see . . .

How can we see . . .
When we will not look?
How can we do . . .
When we will not try?
How can we care . . .
When we care not,
For ourselves?
How can we give . . .
While selfishness rules?
And . . .
How can we know . . .
Unless we have paid,
Our dues?

Crystal Otero
CHEROKEE

The brutal journey of the Trail Of Tears
Was the worst of the Cherokee fears.
They stood bold, but lost their hold . . .
And this story should be told.

Many men, women, and children died
Because the white man lied.
What did the Cherokee do
To be crucified?

How was all this justified?
By the white man's greed
And more and more lies
'Only the strong survives.'

Ray O'Neil Sr
LIFE

To my wife, Betty June, who always had faith in me.

When I think of all the wasted years gone by, I wonder will I really find myself before I die.

Like a bullet fired into outer space traveling fast but going no place, but then dropping to Earth to find its final resting place.

Did I stop to marvel at "God's Creation" or did I rush full speed into Damnation.

As Fall approaches and winter is near the beauty of Earth dies But then behold Life is reborn again come Spring and new life is about to begin.

This is the promise God gave to me to walk in his path and be reborn again like the mighty Oak tree that dies in the Fall only to come forth in Spring with new life.

So when I am planted under the Sod I know I will be born again and be with my God.

Faith is really all we have. So we all should put our trust in God.

Like the air we breathe God is ever present but can't be seen.

Fantasia Monroe
THE PATH FINDERS

Walking through the aisles of list, of lone, and chiles,
Making no acquaintance wisk of the phere
Hoping to find the path that is longering so near.
And 'twas its daunty illusion
Thrashing threw heart's confusion
Brust then brittled clear
The invading path longuering so near.
Not so twitty of twots that lust
A linguered key in heart to trust
And copes the kindled mile
Of once renowned to life's laughingh smile.
Though commonly they search
in fait, Languering how
long to wait. And running across constant reminders
Indeed will be, the path finders.

Susan Juliette Mansfield
ECSTASY

For the man who inspired this—Norman. I hope our paths will cross again.

One night in my life
Turned into my erotic eternity

Our two bodies bathed in scented sweat
Fluids which became as my life's nourishment

Sensual spoken words echoed in my ear
Became one with my pounding heart

Your touch awakened my senses
Trembling impulses ran thru my burning blood

Your piercing eyes saw into my being
By which you gazed onto my hidden desires

We were as one
No sins, no forbiddens, no limits

My heart thanks you, for it is enriched
My body yearns for you, for it is hungry
My soul must believe that I will once again feel such passions

When I hear your name
I will forever more think of you

This journey into the then unknown was long ago
Yet, I can close my eyes, and my trip is reborn . . .

Susan Juliette Mansfield
THE GIFT

To the woman who gave me so much in so many ways, and gave me strength—my mother, I love you.

You gave me life
Thru the years you lived for me
In turn I too lived for you . . .

Your life has ended
Along with a part of mine
But I will go on living
What is life now . . .

You gave me a gift . . . life
I shall honor this
I shall triumph . . .

Your life has not ended
It is a part of my being
Your life will continue . . .

Ken Krousey
WHAT IS SERENITY?

The morning sun rises over Sugar Maple Hill,
wild song birds harmonizing gives me a thrill;
A doe and her fawn grazing by a gurgling stream,
The sanctuary is awakening from the evening dream.
Dazzling ring-neck rooster greets me with his call,
Playful otters enjoying their morning waterfall;
The cow moose and her calf feeding in the watery swamp,
Alert to the timber wolf on his early food romp.
Great horned owl retiring after a busy hunting night,
While a large bald eagle is soaring at a dizzy height.

Along the sparkling lake a canoeist paddles from shore,
On the beach a homeless kitten has things to explore;
The red wing blackbird singing and swaying on the willow,
And the crappie chasing the elusive shiner minnow,
In the lily pads a bass jumps at the croaking frog,
As turtles dive into the water from a half submerged log.
Here miles away from the smoky, noisy city for me,
To fully enjoy this true, peaceful, tranquil serenity.

Ken Krousey
(IRISH) LARRY
Cliff & Vi McCollor raised an iron mining son,
(Irish) Larry, soldier and sportsman the only one;
Happy-go-lucky and always friendly was he,
Loved the woods, lakes, mines, and served in the military.
Always willing to do more than his share,
Smiling and jolly, Irish was helpful everywhere;
Later he and Susan had two fine sons,
Kevin and Kyle of Hibbing are the ones.
Irish was taken from us in September,
A friendly comrade to always remember;
His family and friends mourned together,
In the warm fall Indian summer weather.

A rusting mining truck and crane sit idle in the sun,
While unfurled Old Glory shows a job well done.
With the honking wild geese and call of the loon,
The magnificent stag feeding in the lagoon;
In the azure autumn sky, circled the vigilant hawk,
As military taps sounded for (Irish) Larry at Nashwauk.

Karen Renee Christine Hering
SOMETIMES I SOAR HIGH ABOVE THE CLOUDS
To My Aunt Chris. "I Love You Always."

Sometimes I soar high above the clouds
Clouds of memories of which I've grown fond
Memories of childhood, laughter and tears
Remembering all my childhood fears,
I remember the picnics in which we all shared
The games and the excitement
I remember the holidays we all sat together
exchanging the hugs and kisses
I remember my school days
Making life-long friends
I remember the one day when I came to visit
Your blond hair was gone and your face was so pale
I remember those words in which you said to me
I love you, I'll be home soon
I remember the day when my parents came for me
they told me you've gone
gone is all they said
Now you soar in the clouds high above
Holding my memories and my love
I know in my heart you'll always be true
and that I will always love you.

Jan Apking
LIFE IN THE FAST LANE
Dedicated to my late husband "Bill."

I rushed and I hurried each day as I could,
Never taking time to pray as I should.
Oh God forgive me, I have so much to do
But I'll be back to talk to you.

As time went on with nothing much changed,
I worked and I cleaned, painted and sang
Praises to God on Sunday that is,
But on Monday, ceramics, husband and kids.
I admired my work, as most women do,
And I thought "Oh God, what more can I do?"
But a still little voice kept nagging away,
A lot more you know.

Then one day I had a pain that took my breath away
The next thing I knew, flat in my bed I lay.
Just the day before everything was fine.
But I was praying "God throw out the lifeline!"
My Heavenly Father—so good and so kind—said
"I'll give you another chance, but remember you're mine."

So from now on out I put first things first,
And my precious Jesus is at the front of the line.
I thank Him and praise Him for each new day,
And I think what a blessing I didn't learn too late.

So like little Jacob, his ladder I'll climb.
And with each step that I take I'll be nearing the time
That I will see my Jesus face-to-face
And thank him for his amazing grace.

When my life is over and I leave this world behind
I hope to hear my Savior say "My child—well done."
There is something I guess I'll never understand
Instead of God giving up—HE REACHED DOWN HIS HAND.

Jessie E Shephard
IN MY GARDEN
I'm sure when my garden quickened and bloomed,
God picked up his paint brush, then fashioned and groomed.
My violets He touched with the sky's deepest blue,
Their hearts soon were kissed by the sun's golden hue.
With a brush thru the rainbow my roses were stained,
Then spilled on my pansies and there it remained.

The goldenrod lifted its face for its share,
And drank deep the gold that God handled with care.
He took from His sunsets the orange and reds,
And shook out His brush on his hyacinth beds.
He sprinkled a handful of stardust I'm sure,
On a resplendent spider web, dainty, demure.

He looked at his work, then planted some seeds,
So amid all this beauty grows his sturdy green weeds.
When He laid down His paint brush He kissed every flower,
And put them to sleep in the moon's silver bower.
When I stroll thru my garden I know God was there,
And left me His blessing, and answered my prayer.

Harry L Murrell
SPRING
I love to watch the flowers grow,
So tall, straight, and neat.
I love to hear the robin sing,
His song oh so sweet.
The sun sits high in the sky,
The laughter of children is every-where.
The trees are blowing in the wind,
And baseball fever is in the air,
The bees go from flower to flower,
The ants they work all day.
The squirrels gather many nuts,
For a long winter stay.
The grass is thick and green,
As it sways in the wind with ease.
What a great time to relax,
in the nice breezy breeze.
I love the sounds of springtime,
The running water from the babbling brook.
It seems like a fairy tale,
Right out of a storybook.
So this is why I say that spring,
is my favorite time of year.
Because children play and robins sing,
And flowers smell so dear.

Maria Theresa Padoan
QUICKENED BY ONE MAN
I dedicate this poem to Jesus, the author and finisher of my faith . . .

A faith wavering as the sea, tossed to and fro
Trying to hold onto the dreams from long time ago.

A vision still searching for the hope within,
. . . A fading shadow just waiting to begin.

A love burning as a coal removed from fire,
Yearning for one still voice, whose breath only, could inspire.

Then you were found,
A distinction in time of a life-giving sound.

Words spoken as refreshing as snow in time of harvest,
Rekindling the flame it once was a part of, as a garment of light.

Giving new life to one lonely guest,
Making sweet melody in its heart,
you came as a song in the night.

In cold and nakedness, love ignites,
dwelling no longer alone,
But finally reaping what it has sown.

To the praise and glory of His grace,
God has brought me to the place,
Wherein I have found you!

Evelyne McCollum
STAR FLIGHT
You blazed into my life
lighting up the darkness.
"I love you," a comet tale,
wonderful to hear.

But your fire was swiftly out
falling through the night sky,
tearing apart
the fragile web of who I am.

The past is hard to leave,
it's all I know.
Even a cold, remote star
brings some joy to behold.

But, life goes on.
Recovering, I will find
remnants of me
buried beneath the pain,
reborn.

Frances Church
ELEANOR
A lovely young maiden
Complexion so fair,
Touch of gentleness
That motivates care,
Stroke of Benson's brush
Add rosy pink to her cheeks.
Smile she projects on canvas
Is inspired by glow in her eyes.
Eleanor has hair chestnut
Touching her shoulders and brow,
Long dress of design
Has multiple charm.
Enhanced with stunning wide brim
That makes her attire complete.
The gracious lady a simple delight,
Fulfills her duties with magic in her heart
Admired by her peers.
Eleanor demonstrates the gift of love,
Can be shared by all.

Christine Chemnitz
JESSICA'S TERRIBLE TWO
To Jessica, who's "bigger now" and takes us through the "terrific threes"—I love you "this many"! And thanks to my critics Amin and Caroline for being so enthusiastic about my work—I do love you guys a lot . . . Mom.

Six o'clock in the morning
She's bouncing and yelling
And giving her crib a loud hearty shake:
"Get up, everybody! My day has now started!"—

Jessica is awake
A half hour later
She's strapped in her highchair,
Banging her spoon and kicking her feet:

"Come on, Mom—I'm starving . . . where is my oatmeal?"—
Jessica wants to eat
Then, soon after breakfast

She's ready to go now . . .
For the rest of the day we'll be living with fear . . .
From the roof to the basement
nothing's safe, nothing's sacred:—

Jessica plays here
Bathtime is a new battle,
She's splashing and screaming,
Demanding her father . . . she wants to show him:
"Look, daddy—there's puddles all over the bathroom!"—

Jessica, took a swim
Eight o'clock in the evening
She's bouncing and yelling
And giving her playpen a loud hearty shake:
"Come on, everybody! The night has just started!"—

Jessica's still awake
By the time she gets tired, we're completely exhausted:
"Now . . . hush, everybody!
Don't make a peep!"—
With her bottom stuck up
And her face looking dreamy
Jessica finally wen t to sleep!
"Ssssshhhh . . . !"

Armando Sierra

Armando Sierra
DESNUDA REALIDAD

Dedico este poema a mis hermanos y especialmente a mi hermana Yolanda Sierra.

Peregrinas voces de andares sombríos,
empinadas címas de leves sonrisas
andarímas nubes de polvo y cenizas
hoyas silenciosas de esqueletos fríos.

Miradas profundas de cuencas vacías,
de lejano Sol sin amanecer,
ausente de llanto, amor y placer,
en ese misterioso mundo de la fantasía.

Eco en el espacio de pasos lejanos
chasquidos de besos ausente de amor,
corriente de aroma de invisible flor,
sutiles caricias de invisibles manos.

Jennifer Shirley
WHATEVER HAPPENS
I see you.
And you look so lonely.
I reach out for you,
But it seems like you get farther away.
I think I see a tear in your eye,
But it seems you turn away.
I can read your mind
And know everything you want to say,
But every time you try to talk,
Your voice trails off.
I know we had everything planned,
But something got in the way.
Does this mean we both
are going our separate ways?
I have no answers,
But whatever happens,
I want to remain friends.

Michelle Spaleta (age 6)
MY ROOM
In my room I have lots of dolls,
Some are big and some are small.
I have some bears and I have a bed,
And sometimes I sleep with my stuffed bears instead.

Anthony J Bryant
TIME
We go here and there
By car, bus, train or plane
But no matter how far we go
Time is always the same, never slow.

We eat, we sleep, all by time
Early morning to rise by the sun
That's shining so brightly through my window
Letting us know morning time has begun.

We need time to play games or to ride our bike
Maybe to take a hike.
As the daytime hour rolls along
The sunshine begins to move away
Making for nighttime to rush right in.

As I lay in my bed,
I hear a voice say,
"Come on kids, Wake up! Wash your face.
Brush your teeth and comb your hair."
I holler down to Mom and say,
"Is it time to go? Are we late?"

Gwendolyn Marie Hudson
WAITING

Waiting for the right one to come along can take so long.

I'm waiting for you to come along to sing me the perfect love song.

Erin Murphy
ACCEPTANCE
The pain and wonder
Of this life
Melt together
Blend joy and strife
Wishful thinking
For sugary flavor
Turn sweet and bitter
Something to savor.

The taste of sorrow
And of light
Conforms the soul
And gives it sight
A time for color
A time for night
A part of living
The pain and wonder
Of this life.

Angela M Albrecht
FOREVER, A PROMISE

To Pat, I love you! Forever, Angie.

My love for you will last forever.

The pain and sorrows of days gone by could never replace the happiness and the joys of the past and the many we will share in our future together.

The confusion and frustrations could never make my love for you weaken or fade.

My promise to you is forever.

The tears shed have been wiped away with kisses and tender arms.

Problems that may lie ahead could never be so traumatic that my heart would forget who it belongs to.

My love is yours forever . . .
I promise.

Ruth Yost
THE MORNING SUN

This poem is dedicated to the children who were taken from life at a young age and to the families who still love and miss them dearly.

When light pours in your windows
And the morning sun has rose
You think of all those special things
Like a kitten licking your nose

Like April's rain on new leaves
A new song sung by birds
The greening grass in open fields
And children learning new words

Running brooks and daffodils
Are just a few to say
How beautiful all life can be
When seeing each new day

The morning sun is fading now
But its memory we'll always hold
And just like all the things we love
It's much more precious than gold

Elizabeth C Drehmer
ONE WISH

Dedicated to Daughter Cheryl and David Oliver.

If I had but one wish, I'd wish it could be, That I were with you and you were with me.

If I had but one chance to sing you a song, I'd sing it from morning all the day long.

If I had but one day to spend with you, I'd want it to be long, a hundred years through.

I have but one chance at life, from my birth. I wish I could spend it with you on this earth.

If I had but one wish I'd wish it could be, That I were with you and you were with me.

Susan Evans-Schultz
THE CLEANSING

This is given with the desire that people who suffer in the present, past, and in the future will find the intimate comfort of God; "Casting all your care upon Him, for He cares for you" (1 Peter 5:7).

Our people suffer greatly!
Great hope of freedom
enters us!

Ones inflicting
our great pain
within mind
within body
within inner being
within emotions
of our own,
From these
God rescues us in our need!
God is The True Friend of ones in need!

Now we are free!
Because of our pain,
we hold very close
within our inner being
All things of greatest value (We speak the truth)
God's way removes permanently waste within!
Amen!

Gail S Farmer
ALWAYS
I've had a full and happy life
And partied more than my share
But now to continue living
Is torture, pain and despair

I said, "I have my freedom
I can handle a drink and a drive"
If only I'd listened to reason
Their baby might still be alive

I dread the thought of living
Always in traction and pain
But I would suffer forever
To give her life again

I never saw her picture
I never heard her cry
But every time I close my eyes
I feel that baby die

Please listen as I say to you
While your soul is still alive
It's not worth the pain and suffering
To ever **drink and drive**

Julia Prior
THE LORD HAS GIVEN ME THE PRIVILEGE

Lovingly dedicated to Tom and Betty Young and Roberta Richter.

The LORD has given me the privilege to see,
Some beautiful people, who are special to me.

Whenever they smile, their faces just glow;
They're sharing HIS love with others, I know.

The sun shines bright, on a beautiful LORD'S DAY.
Tell a lost soul to follow JESUS all the way.

Whenever we think of what our SAVIOR can do;
We can't help but love HIM; and yes, HE loves us too.

Terry Zelenak
LOST
Alone and lost
in this world
of fear, of pain,

of hatred.

Seeking to console
myself
in the sunshine,
and the moonlight.

Calling to no one
that answers
my cry for belief,
for hope,
for dreams unanswered.

Duffie Jones
YONDER SKY
I can see the stars shining
In yonder sky,
And it makes me wonder—
Would I choose to die?
Life is a great gift
Given from up above,
And next to it
Comes only love.
I have been given life
To live the best I can,
And I have been given love
To lend a helping hand.
So I will do my best
To get by day by day,
Hoping someone will always be there
To help me find my way.
And as I look at yonder sky,
I realize it's not my choice
Whether I live or die.
Rather—it's HOW I choose to
live—or die.

Herbert H Allgair
LOVING

For all of those lonely people, who have love in their hearts.

I saw you walking over this way
With a sparkle in your eyes
You didn't have to say anything
Just look at me and smile
When you wrap your arms around me
I can feel it deep inside
Wanting you to stay close to me; for
awhile
She looks at me and smiles
We share each other's secrets
And talk of past–times
Something hits us, and we both begin
to cry
Just two good ole friends, baring our
souls
Two lonely hearts, completely out of
control
Now we know each other
And we've promised not to lie
I will love and cherish her, 'til the
end of time
I will keep plenty in the cupboards
and
Keep her warm and dry
And in return, she'll give me a heart
full of love
And that sparkle in her eyes.

Susan Michele Johnson
WHEN IT'S OVER

Dedicated to Amando Benavidez—Because I'll always love you.

Broken hearts and shattered dreams
That's all that's left of us it seems
What happened to the promises made
To faith, the always and forever said
If yesterday had never come
and been
I'd have the days before and be in
love again
But here I am today, afraid,
tonight alone
Lost without you, the only love I've
ever known
The only one to love me, hold
me,
Be a part of my soul
And it is now, in the end
That I am falling desperately out of
control
May I not die alone, without
your love in my heart
May the grave and death be all that
ever keeps us apart
For as much as my love knows
no time
Throughout eternity your heart will
be in mine

Susan Michele Johnson
YESTERDAY'S LOVE

Dedicated to Amando Benavidez—You are my tomorrow.

I wanted to love you, but you said no
I needed to love you, you asked why
Now that we do, it's time to leave
But give me back my heart, so that I
might breathe
My breath is faint, my eyes grow dim
Will I ever see happiness again?
Only in my dreams of you, only in
my dreams
When the wind blows, I'll hear the
secrets we told.
The whispers that only you and I
know.
When the stars shine, I'll be
reminded of your kindness
When the dew settles, I'll know of
your sweetness
I loved you I did, I needed you I do
Someday we will meet, we will
remember,
And my heart will sing,
But of a different tune, of lost love
my sweet
A verse of what might have been
I only wanted to be with you,
To make you see the happiness we
shared
To bring to life this love we harbor
The love of yesterday that could have
been tomorrow.

Janet L Bush
HOUSES AND HOMES
There are many, kinds of houses.
But not many, called a home.
Inside houses, live a selfish pride.
And faith in God, has gone.

Laughter never, can be heard
A smile, just can't be found.
Sadness seems, to live there.
There's troubles, all around.

True friends, never get to meet,
And precious love, is lost.
Hearts, are always, empty,
And loneliness, the cost.

Trust in others, should be there
But when everything's, gone wrong.
There's not a person, living there,
To whom, they will, belong.

The most important is the love,
That warms, a caring heart.
For our family and for, our friends,
From that, we can't depart

A home can be, a one room flat,
Or a town house, in the sky.
The size is unimportant,
And that, we can't deny.

A house is just a building,
Of plaster, nails and wood.
A home, is full of promise,
Of love and everything, that's good.

Janet L Bush
LITTLE MAGIC
If I had a magic wand, in my hand.
I would reach to the sky, at night.
And catch a brilliant, shining star,
To be, your guiding light.

I could talk, to the man in the moon, I
could,
I would ask him, to smile, on you.
So, you would never, feel alone,
And have your dreams, come true.

I would borrow, love from Venus,
And touch, your doubting, heart.
I would give you, loving kindness,
And understanding, from the start.

I would fill your days, with promise,
And exciting and wonderful, things.
Your nights, so warm and restful,
Would be, what your sleep, would
bring.

I would fly, straight into heaven,
I would steal away, the color, blue.
And make your days, real happy
ones,
And worry free, for you.

I, could quiet, the gentle, flowing
wind,
Ask him to gently , stroke your hair.
So, you would feel, contentment,
And, his peace of mind, he'd share.

If, I ever caused the rain, to fall,
To, dampen, all your dreams.
I'll pray the darkness, goes away,
And hope for new, sun–beams.

The sun, will warm your very soul,
For, I'd set a rainbow, in the sky.
And color your life, with joy and
love,
And every care, from you, would fly.

But, life is not that simple, but,
I would hope for just, a while,
That I could touch your life, with
magic,
For, I love, to see you, smile.

Janet L Bush
FATHERS

This is dedicated to my loving father, who taught me the rewards of tremendous love and hard work, in his own unselfish way.

Fathers are, a wondrous, sort,
They are, a breed, of their, own.
They work long hours, everyday,
And are tired, when they travel,
home.

Some pretend to be, so tough,
And love, they will never, show.
They joke and laugh, whenever, they
can,
So no one, will, ever know.

The pride they feel, for their families,
Still, remains, so buried, deep.
That people often, wonder,
Why, their feelings, they do keep.

They put, their ego's selfish, pride,
In first place, everytime.
They don't take time, to talk or play,
Or listen, or, be kind.

Then, there's the other, kind of Dad,
True love, they, really show.
They talk about, their families,
And, right away, you know.
That, they are unique, caring men,
Who, hug and give, a kiss.
To their families, everyday,
And are not, ashamed, of this.

Tenderness can be seen, in every
smile,
When, their children, are around.
The pride, they feel, just can't be hid,
And endless love, abounds.

There's two kinds, of fathers,
everywhere,
It's sad, but it is, true.
If, you're reading this and you're, a
Dad,
Which kind, of father, are you?

Janet L Bush
AGAPE

This is dedicated to my mother, who lived always for the happiness and welfare of others in every aspect of her life.

There's just no doubt about it,
That love's, a complex word.
Most people use it, as a noun,
And not really, as, a verb.

A verb, a word of action
Gives and helped unselfishly
A reward it never asks for,
It moves so, quietly.

It warms the heart, with gladness
It brings smiles upon, sad faces,
It makes a blue day, brighter,
Wipes away, all lonely traces.

It brings friendships close together,
It fills, the day, with a song,
It makes our world a happy place,
Where nothing can go wrong.

Love makes forgiveness easy,
It comes directly, from the heart,
So harmony around, the world,
We surely, truly start.

Love is the greatest, gift around,
And it, will surely, stay.
But love is only truly love
When, it is given, away.

Gerald M Owens
NO MORE, IT IS OVER

No more will there be a warm welcome for me at the house that used to be ours, it is over.

No more will I be met at the door by the sound of "Daddy is home" from my children, it is over.

No more will I be close by to watch my children grow day by day Nor to be there to see them at play, and at rest or to kiss away their hurts, and to comfort their fears, it is over.

No more will I be able to walk hand in hand with you on moonlit summer nights along the shore, nor to cuddle with you by a roaring fire on cold winter evenings, it is over.

No more will we lay together in love's passion or hold on to each other in its afterglow, it is over.

No more will we be together to help, and to guide each other through life's daily problems, or to share in each other's joys and sorrows, or the simple things that makes life worth living, and the life we had together because we know it is over.

Irene Plazewska
THE SALTEE ISLANDS
Carcinogenic thoughts
wrapped the ra-bird in a
casting of feathered blue.
Passively murders strewed
the footpath heavy with the
droppings of the mounted
omnibus.
The stammers of Anglo-Celts
sidestepped
and mystical brightenings
led tattered billboards.
Without pressing zero—pull
the coastal erosions
muffled their laughter

Eileen Carr
REUNION
Say! Can that be Sarah—that
girl over there—the one
with the gray hair?

And is that Jack—so bald and
fat
Can you beat that?

And Jerry—so scary with his
toothless grin.
Where does his shoulders
stop and his neck begin?

I see Melanie too. They
call her four eyes now.
Pity.

Reunion It's so sad to see how my
friends have changed.
Say! Why is everyone looking
at me?
Could it be that I too have
changed?

Oh! No! Surely not me.

Elsie Bergen

Elsie Bergen
BLOOMING FOR HIM
Now that the Old Year is gone;
The New Year is in—
My roots must grow more firmly
Into a sturdy life for Him.

My branches reach out—
To those who are lost;
Bring them to Jesus—
Whatever the cost.
Stems of further growth
From without—within
Leaves like green pastures
When knowledge of Christ
comes in.

When buds of duty open
For my Lord each day.
Bursting into flowers of faith
Full bloom in Christ-like array.

Like Jesus the Sweet Rose of Sharon
I, as a flower too,
On this journey from Earth to Glory
Will not let one petal fade in the
blue.

Paula Leeche
FOGGY DAY LAMENT
My heart is heavy my feet are slow,
Where is the sunshine, I, would like
to know?
Where are the birds that fly in the
spring,
and what are these gray and ghostly
things,
That glide through the fog on silent
wings?
Their throats are silent no song to
sing,
No nest to build or family to rear,
Is there something in the fog that they
fear?
Where are the birds that fly in the
spring,
A song on their lips my spirits to
bring,
Out of the darkness and into the sky,
Soaring to bask in the sky on A
lovely white cloud.
Away from this fog that lies like A
shroud,
To cover the earth it's eerie white
gloom,
And whispers to me of impending
doom.
I, pray for A breeze that will take it
away,
This terrible fog that has spoiled my
day.
Let the sun shine on me the fog take
away,
Just send it to London, they like it
that way.

Connie Anderson
A MOMENT OF PLEASURE
From a moment of pleasure comes
the pain,
the choice that you must make.
Something that you can't give back,
the life you now must take.

It must be a nightmare!
You can't wake up—it's real!
Your decision will always be
with you
the hurt you'll always feel.

You can't imagine anything.
You cannot think ahead.
Life is so unbearable
you wish that you were dead.

Someone said if you have faith
your wish will come true.
But it wasn't only one that died,
the baby made it two.

Shirley Hochstedler
HIS PRESENCE
The Lord did say these things to me
Dear child do not fret
For all the words I've said to you
Were meant for you not to forget

He said He would always be there
If I needed Him day or night
Whether it be in joy or sorrow
With His presence I would be alright

So many times I've needed Him
And sure enough He was there for me
I could not make it through the day
Were it not for the presence of Thee

Sylvia Scudder
THE BEACH AT NANDI
Garlands of marigold and aralia
half-buried in grey sand
mark a passing:
The village burns its dead here,
ask settling on violet-streaked
faces of dune morning glories or
the foam and pearl of outer reef,
as the wind decides.

Scarlet-bordered saris drying on a
fence
flag the eye toward
two spindly Indian children
skipping up a crescent of shell-
scattered sand.

An old man chops cane.
and knows no debt beyond
his circumstance,
nor paces fields of memory
more distant than his own.

Marigolds glinting in a garden
will grace the twisted wreaths
of ritual,
Marking off the father and the sons,
Closing simple circles

as waves wash the
tender mountains to the sea

Grant E Rickard
THE LADY
The lady is mysterious,
So whimsical yet serious.
Her intuition is her guide.
With Hermes' wisdom born inside.
With mind so bright and spirits light,
She is to all a dear delight.
Her life is built on naught but love
Remove the creatures of her love
And she becomes as mourning dove.
She has a warm and gentle smile
To make life's burdens all worth-
while.
Her voice is soft and sweet and clear
With timbre toned for baby's ear.
Her children have no cause for fear,
They know her love is always near.
She has a kind of loyalty
Akin to highest royalty.
Of all the beauties God has wrought,
She crowns His pure and perfect ary.
Her virtues are so manifold
No sage has yet their number told.
The poet cannot dramatize,
The artist cannot glamorize
And wise men cannot analyze
The mystic God may canonize.
Of all the beauties Earth may see,
Who do you think the queen should
be?
Of course, the one God gave to me.

Mary Welling
DEN
I always felt or somehow knew
that I'd succeed because of you.

Well, here I go, the truth will
out —
You showed me just what life's
about.

To think things out, then go ahead;
When I would rather quit instead.

The gifts you gave me through the
years
I now recall with silent tears.

When illness came, we did our best
to try to weather every test.
The cross you dragged, I dragged it
too,
I was so much a part of you.
Now you won't suffer anymore
and you'll have no more pain.
The race was run—the prize you won
has earned eternal gain.

So when I think about you now,
It's very plain to see;

God took you to a greater home,
But left your love with me.

Fran T Wiginton
LITTLE TREE
Little tree, little tree, with your green,
red, and gold.
You do shine in the darkness, with
lights all aglow.
You've got soldiers, and snowmen,
and small lollipops,
But the one I love best is the angel on
top.

Oh, dear Santa Claus, I've been good
don't you see.
Will you bring lots of presents and
prizes to me?
I don't have a chimney, for you to
come through
But if you'll use the door, I'll unlock
it for you.

I have wished every night, for my
very first bike,
And a football helmet that fit me just
right
If you'll do this for me, I'll do this
for you—
Leave you cake and hot coffee and an
apple or two!

Little tree, little tree, with your green,
red, and gold.
You do shine in the darkness, with
lights all aglow.
You've got soldiers, and snowmen,
and small lollipops,
But the one I love best is the angel on
top.

Ozella Madewell
LIFE HAS ITS DISAPPOINTMENTS
Sometimes in our haste we hurt
others
When we're seeking our own
selfish gain
Not stopping to think of the damage
we've done
Or that our actions would have
caused them great pain.

When we finally realize we've
moved too fast,
And we try to amend our deeds,
It's almost too late as the damage is
done
And we realize it's thoughtfulness and patience we need.

Life, it seems, is so uncertain and
cruel
When our dreams and hopes are
dashed
But if we practice serenity and keep
trust in the Lord
We find that our life is not
really crashed.

Doors will open of which we did not
dream
God has planned it that way,
you know.
If we hold our head high and don't
give up,

We will find our opportunities
will grow.

Contentment is what we are always seeking
As we travel this road of life.
We must look to tomorrow and the good times ahead,
And forget all the trouble and strife.

So, if we set our sails high for a better day
With friends and relatives who care,
We will find each day will grow better,
As we find more activities to share.

Veronica S West
OF LOVE AND LIFE
it's ups,
It's downs,
it's mediocrities

Wild highs
to celebrate,
hollow lows
to climb above.
Wins and losses,
Triumphs and defeats.

The game of love,
the game of life.

Anna Marie Rose Soldo Craig
MY PAPA
Straight and tall, yet bent by hard work and trouble.
A true son of Italy, and America, kind, honest and forthright, a friend to all
Everyone knew where we lived before, by the beautiful gardens he left behind.
Papa was no statesman or famous person, but he did right by his family, friends, and countries.
When he died, I felt like a piece of my heart was missing. I felt physical pain.
You don't know a person's true worth until they are gone.
When I was unhappy or sad, he would say to me, "What's the matter?, if I were young again, I would climb the highest tree."
My troubles melted away.
More precious than gold or rubies was my papa.
I'm sure he is King now, in a land far away.
He visits me in dreams now and then . . . I believe he is saying, "Don't be afraid, I'm with you always."
The last dream I had of papa, his hair was black, streaked on the sides with silver grey. He looked so handsome as he crossed a bridge to come to me.

Eleanor U Ahola
FINAL PAY
As I tread the boards
Of the stage of life
Playing the parts I'm conceded
By The Great Director, or circumstance,
I wonder how well I've succeeded
In sorting the truth
From the ruthless uncouth—
The masquerade from the aim—
The things which will count
When the last scene is played—
From that everyday worldly acclaim.
As I age in these scenes
I find I have dreams
Of the day that Last Curtain rings down;

When it comes to that day
Will I draw the pay
Of a witch, or a bitch, or a woman or clown?

Christal McKee
NEVER TOO OLD TO BE LONELY
When the evening shadows come creeping in,
All alone by the fire loneliness begins.
Flames in the fireplace leaping high, bringing back memories of days gone by.
I cannot hold back the flow of tears,
Drifting back in memory of yesteryear.
My love was always caring by being near,
Comforting and caressing, calming my fear.
Beautiful red roses delivered to my door,
with A message of love, Yours forevermore.
Our love intertwined with, A compassionate heart,
Never believing we would ever be torn apart.
The Angel took him away, to live in Heaven above,
Leaving me sad and lonely but, left A lot of love.
Beautiful memories and dreams left behind,
Helps ease the loneliness in my heart and mind.
Share your life with others, they too feel alone,
let your compassion and kindness light up your home.

Eileen Denahy
WHEN THE TIME IS RIGHT
When the time is right
Come be my friend

Come for my love
Let us have endless times of sharing together

Let us love with familiarity and newness
Passion and gentleness
Rainbows and fairy tales
Innocence and resolve

Enjoy the excitement of spring with me
The contentment of summer
The peacefulness of autumn
The closeness of winter

Travel the same roads with me
Share my laughter, shoulder my pain
Allow me to rest on you
Knowing well, I will be your home

Walk into twilight and memories with me
Rocking chairs and canes, graying and aging
Consenting to leave, only in death

When the time is right
Come be my friend

Carman J Haley
CIRCLE
We've all had "wet" shoulders—one time or another
But shoulders are attached for <u>that</u> reason—no other
They may sag with the weight of sadness, it's true
But they square-up with Pride and Dignity too!

We've elbows for resting—leaning—chin in hand
When the eyelids become heavy—or the story too bland
Hands so creative and talented—can teach
In good times, applaud you—in bad times, they reach.

The heart is such a special place
Many cliques are used to describe it
Be "light-hearted" not "faint-hearted"
Because then you can enjoy it!

"Have a heart," not a "heart attack"
it's "big as all outdoors"
It can be "pounding like a drum"—must hurt!—are you "heart-sore?"
If your heart "drops like a stone"
you're probably "heavy-hearted"
I'd rather "eat my heart out"—I won't gain weight, and it gets me started.

The journey one takes through life can be tough
The crows feet and lines on my face show <u>this</u> enough
On the topic of wrinkles and lines—we won't dwell
For the laugh-lines are deeply embedded as well.

Holly Locke
CHAD
He runs through the wet grass
Grasping at flecks in the air
A squeal of delight
From the flight of a glare
"There's one," he hollers
And he's racing again
The sparkle in his eyes
Matches the glow in his hand
My son—the lightning bug catcher champ.

Virginia Balkema
A CHRISTMAS FAREWELL
Good friends, HI, 'tis time to be jolly!
(We won't mention big B's retirement folly.)
The things that are happening are meant to be,
And all of the rest is a fait accompli!

Just want you to know you are special to us;
Want to tell you without sad songs or fuss.
Changes are made and challenges there'll be,
But friendship continues—there'll always be we!

We want you to stay a big part of our lives
By visiting us at our brand-new "B" hive.
Reservations please make, you travelers-about!
Just call or write us,—the latch string is out.

We treasure the memory of times we have shared,
And want you to know how you're loved, how we cared.
Though the future may keep us a distance apart,
You'll be close as ever and dear to our heart.

May the tinseled trees, carols and Christmas star too
Carry joy, love and peace this season to YOU!

Linda M Laskowski
SHADOWS OF THE PAST
Sun struck the flowing stream water making irregular shadows.
The background became dark.
The foreground still and sparkling.
Clear water slithering over and between the smooth grey rocks.
Imagine your toes feeling the cool water.
The water moving faster makes a splashing noise.
You notice a large flat rock along the other side.
Could this be a spot once used for picnics on a warm summer day?
Could the pool before me be a swimming hole which refreshed children?
Could this road—deserted now—have frequently been traveled?
I can only imagine as I see the shadows in the water.
So peaceful this spot by the stream.
The sun has moved. I must too—
making room for another passerby.
I will remember the beauty of this still but flowing stream.

Ronald K Reddout
DEATH IN MOTION
Weapons blaze across a darkened landscape!
Underneath a starlit sky,
Death hungrily stalks his prey.

Weapons shatter the peaceful calm of a jungle day!
Underneath a blazing noon-day sun,
Death, still hungry, stalks his prey.

He feasts in plenty during this time of war!
The broken bodies, lying still
in this godforsaken jungle,
gorge Death beyond repletion.

But, Death's hunger is still not appeased!
The many long years
of this jungle war
aren't enough to stave his hunger.

Death reaches across the years from this war's last days!
Many are those for whom Death reaches
that, suffering unbearable pain and anguish,
welcome the relief of his fatal touch.

Pray for those of us
who are still trying to escape
Death's loathsome, and altogether too welcome, touch!

Helen Decker
DOUBT
I may not say it often
Sometimes you feel denied;
But there's a loving feeling,
For you—held deep inside.

You may not think I show it
That my heart is cold and bleak;
But, darling, it is always there,
The lovelight that you seek.

So, my dear, I've said it,
But if you have a fear—
Just ask me if I love you;
I'll answer, "Yes, my dear."

Esther Herzl
TO CATCH AN EMBER
Listen . . .
To the hum of the heart
To its desire.
Sift it well
To catch embers afire

While the glow is there
While it breathes off heat
Cast it into timber
For flame and flame to meet

When the fire is like a torch
While it burns red hot
By its focused beam of light
You will find your spot.

Wait not for the ember
To cool in black and gray
Ashes do not sparkle
Dust just blows away

To catch an ember while aglow
Is worth many a coal
Listen to the heart's desire
While it has yet; soul.

Coral Wells
FRIENDSHIP

To all the little boys and girls I had in school.

Friendship is like a budding flower
That opens by degrees
It will soon shape up if nurtured
And give honey to the bees

Day by day it will develop
And show its beauty rare
And it will leave us hoping
And be given us to share.

Kelly James
ONLY HIM
To me he is hard to forget
Friends say he's no good, don't fret

There will be more that come your way
But they're not the ones I want—I say

I wanted to be with him but now he's gone
I wish he would come back as does the dawn

What can I do? Where must I go?
It was me, not you, that loved him so

I'll remember the good times we had together
Quit telling me to forget, you're such a bother

So now when thinking of him
There is nothing to make my
memories dim.

Dorothy D Bush
DILEMMA
I wonder now, is life devine,
Or is it just an idle jesture?
Your guess is just as good as mine
But mine's inclined to laughter.

Laughter, tho the teardrops ooze
And trickle down the ages,
Making history just a mock
As people fill the pages.

Can it matter over-much
Our petty griefs and woes,
As whirling on thru time and space
Our dizzy planet goes.

Are we puppets on a string
Dancing to some mystic story;
Are we licked before we start,
Or are we bound for glory?

We cannot know the Master Plan
As eons flitter past.
We can only hope and pray
That man finds Peace at last.

Mary Hobbs
SIXTEEN
When I was sixteen and eyes of blue
I met a young man, he was handsome too.
We went to the show many a time
He held my hand and said I was divine.
But we never got married because he said
I love you too much to make you sad.

Robert G Mele
MIDNIGHT'S LADY
She appeared
A flash of light in the darkness
Long brown hair rolling down her back
Caressed by midnight's breath
Skin so smooth and silk-like
Too soft to touch
Ocean blue eyes piercing the night
Casting black shadows into obscurity
Scarlet lips pulled together
Mocking innocence
Promising purity
A vision of beauty
Epitome of perfection
A brilliant light
Countering darkness
Close yet miles off in the night
Contact without being touched
She fades softly

Ruby M Olson
LISTEN AND LEARN
The sun is here to shine on you,
To cheer you up, when you are blue.
To warm you, when you feel the cold.
And keep you young, when you are old.

But we complain when it is hot,
And also grumble, when it's not!
God tries so hard, to please us all,
But we don't listen, or hear His call.

When will we learn it is a test
To show us all, that He knows best?
He made this earth with all its beauty.
And things to help us to survive.

Now we should do, what is our duty,
And show Him, we're glad to be alive.

Thank Him at the end of each day
For those blessings we did enjoy.
Remember He is your friend, as you pray,
And His words, are your Lifesaving buoy.

Adrienne Mae (d'Arcis) Warcimaga

Adrienne Mae (d'Arcis) Warcimaga
TIME
The sun rises; a new day dawns;
As the world comes alive, and stretches and yawns;
Yesterday's passed; tomorrow waits to be born;
Time slips by and forges on;
Time, in its endless, ongoing song.

Time cannot be hurried, it cannot be slowed;
Time is something that can't be controlled;
Make the most of today;
For time is quickly, silently, slipping away.

Twilight arrives; often without warning;
Behind are the woes and cares of today;
And ahead, new horizons are dawning;
Hold on to each precious moment;
For time carries on, in its infinite way.

Mike R Price
FORGIVE ME JESUS
Oh, what it must be like
To walk and talk
To see to play
And to run and shout
But you see I cannot
I've been told many stories
And many tales
I've imagined taking long hikes
And running and playing
And shouting my name so everyone could hear
But the best story I've been told is how
Jesus died on the cross, to save our souls
And if I were you
And could walk and talk
And see to play
I would run and shout
Forgive me, Jesus, Forgive me, Please

Wren Campbell
SPRING
She takes her broom
and sweeps the snow away
with her gentle hand,
and touches the sky
making it a deeper blue.
She breathes on the wind
and it obeys her command:
as she plays her magic
with her drops of dew.

She tiptoes through meadows
with soft grassy feet,
and scatters her colors of green.
She kisses the flowers
and wakes them from
sleep.

She is the gift of spring.

Maria Susanne Vass-Gal
MEMORY PHOTOGRAPH
From early childhood witness memory
Of standing watching nearby
I remember a little girl with golden braids
Screaming screaming
Because her mother
Dressed in black
Left her in a strange hospital room
And the nurses
Laughing laughing
At her fear
Took her sailor blouse and skirt
Her immaculate white shoes and socks
Only familiar things in a strange place.

Edward R Bacon
PEOPLE
People no matter what their color
Should have the same choice in life as the other.
Some people bum around day after day
They don't realize it's their life that's wasting away.

People come from all parts of the earth.
Some have defects stemming from their birth.
People sometimes laugh and call them names
But they could have children just the same.

People fight and constantly display violence.
I only pray for more peace and silence.
As for me I keep trying to understand
But I keep telling myself no one's a perfect man.

Sallie A Sills
YELLOW BELLS
Yellow Bells blowing in the breeze
Dangling on the vines beneath the ledge
Telling a story revealed by the golden sun.

Yellow Bells nodding your heads,
Telling the world, It's not true
That you will never, never die!

Yellow Bells, swaying and swaying here and there
Then, flutter and flutter and fade away.

Mary Richards
MONARCH BUTTERFLY
You are a gorgeous, graceful creature of Nature
With huge wings of black, laced in orange
You were delayed from your southward journey too soon
And your body laid stiff from the winter's chill.

You spent three days in our warm

cozy home
Sitting on the fig tree, eating nectar
from sweet flowers
Yes, we gave you tender loving care
and attention
Until you were strong enough to
travel on.

As I let you go, on that warm sunny
day
You flew upward, so high in the sky
My heart was filled with
overwhelming joy
As you soared far from my sight,
toward heaven.

I instantly felt the freedom that was
mine;
For when we release what needs to be
free
We also become freed in the process
And what a beautiful moment it was
for me!

Melinda A Moore
a persuasive kiss
once i wanted
to be slim
an exclamation point
of fashion.

tall!
dramatic!
thin!

but you pushed
those thoughts aside
with a persuasive kiss
upon my thigh.

DeDe Slechta
REMEMBERING . . .
I remember the first time we met
And knew it was something I would
never regret.

I remember getting to know you
And all our dreams and talks too.

I remember our first laughs and cries
Trusting each other, we'd never tell
lies.

I remember your caring ways
I would think of you through the
passing days.

I remember all the things we did
together
Promising to be the best of friends
forever.

I remember how special you always
are
And I know we'll never be far.

For this friendship is too strong to let
go
Keeping in touch will be all I know.

Linda Lawrence
RED RED ROSES
A dozen red roses
to brighten up the day,
only they're not from Mr. Right
so what can you say.

Thank you very much
would do for a start.
Even if they're not the roses
that captured your heart.

For your special roses
every petal you've saved,
to hold close to your heart
when you need to be brave.

They are very different
but look much the same,
only one is from a friend
while the others fuel a flame.

Because the flame that burns
deep in your soul,
it never goes away
no matter what you've been told.

Janis I Crichton-Passehl
KISS OF IMMORTALITY
Sweet, sweet virgin, victim of the
night
Lie softly upon thy feathered down
And share thy maiden's delights

Swathed in a sea of white ribbons and
lace
Scented skin of porcelain, golden
angel face
Unsuspecting innocence await
death's embrace

Crimson, honeyed wine which flows
within
To fill the insatiable brim
Yet to fear the dawn as your new life
begins

Awaken newborn, a maiden no more
Rise up with the moon, creature of
the night
Forevermore.

Neil J Baumgardner
THE PINK BREATH
The stories of love
are told by all.
Some are true
most are tall

People say it
before they think.
The feelings of love
aren't just pink

Red stands for love,
Pink is close.
Close isn't good enough
when it comes to those who diagnose

Feeling from the heart
are the only way to tell.
Feelings from the mind
makes the heart swell

Saying it before
it is meant
is just a breath
wastefully spent.

Virginia Conley
UNSPOKEN WORDS
Do you ever feel things you just don't
say?
You should have told someone how
you feel
Somehow we let time time slip away.
We should be sharing our feelings so
real.

Your lips they'll never pass
With the mystique of the UNICORN
As fragile as handblown glass
Unspoken words die unborn.

Was it this morning to your wife
You could have said "I love you
dear."
The one most important person in
your life
I'm sure these words she'd like to
hear.

Or maybe as you saw your children at
play
You thought of how precious they are
to you
Tell them now don't wait another day
Tell them now before another dawn
or dew.

Unspoken words will never warm a
heart
Nor put a gleam in a loved one's eye
So promise today to make a new start
There'll be no more unspoken words
until the day you die!

Vickie Bingaman
EVER FAITHFUL
On a dark and moonlit night
gazing at the stars so bright
We looked into each other's eyes
and it was then I realized

That you could see into my soul
Mend my heart and make it whole
See my fears and ease my pain
Now ever faithful I remain!

Whenever I am sad and blue,
you always know just what to do
Tenderly you touch my face
and hold me in your warm embrace
And just as I begin to cry,
you look at me with big brown eyes

With just one look, you ease my pain
And ever faithful I remain!

Audrey M Wagner
EXISTENCE

To Bob and Stevie, the two men in my life, that makes my life, such a happy one. Love you both. Audrey, Mommie.

Forever isn't always a long long time.
Tomorrows aren't always so close
behind.
Treat each day as an eternity and
think of tomorrow as a pleasant
Dream.

Holly Golightly
THE WHISPERING TREES
The old man sat on the patio
With an old grey blanket over his
knees,
And watched the birds fight over the
feeders
As he listened to the whisper of the
trees.

He thought of his loved-one's ashes
Scattered over a far away Nevada
hill.
He thought of the good life they'd
shared
While the trees whispered, "She
awaits you still."

He remembered the pledge they had
made
Their ashes would mingle together on
that hill,
And he dozed in the afternoon
sunlight
As the trees whispered, "Not yet, but
you will."

The birds still come to the feeders
And chirp and fight as they did in the
past,
But the old man's chair is empty
As the trees whisper, "At last, At
last!"

Corbett N Snyder
STAY ALIVE
A snake in the grass
bites a wolf in the fold
and the sheep run screaming
if they are told

while toys in the attic
play with loaded dice
their hands are shaking
and the stakes are high

but self proclaimed servants
of a silent god
hide the real world away
behind their pastoral songs

so if your wish
should catch a shooting star
be on your guard
lest ye fall too far

And when the worms come crawling
for another mind
Don't be buried before your time;
When the worms come crawling for
another soul
Baby be strong
Be in control.

Pamela Rankin Lott
ALL IN DEEPEST SOLICITUDE
The handicapped, once hidden, can
now claim victory for all
The minority take their place in life,
proud and standing tall
An ethereal type of music fills the
stale walls of strife
And our muse of better things to
come, we pray will come to life
Now once again our hearts of hope
are tried with piercing blades
And we make ready our shining
swords to the enemy AIDS
The world is but a battlefield and
waits no man's cry
For the war has yet to be lost or won,
and the fighting yet to die
Time is but a fleeting moment, so
hearts and souls beware
For like seasons come upon us it can
leave us without a care
Today will die tomorrow so let our
fear of hope be free
For no life lives forever, even winds
die down for sea
Sun and stars, mist and rain, even day
and night
Lose their shine, their sound, their
darkness and their light
So loved ones, friends and family,
fighting tooth and nail
Be loving kind and let the stricken
shine till darkness doth prevail
And remember as the sun and stars
shine with each new night
Your someone does and will also
shine with peace of their new light.

Mildred Allen Crouch
TINY ROSE–BUD
When I see the tiny rose–bud
As it grows from day to day
Bringing forth exotic beauty
In its own special way . . .
I can hardly wait to see it
Unfold its fragile self . . .
Nor await the flowing essence
Of perfume beyond all wealth.
At last the bud is opened!
It is now in full bloom!
Such a brilliant, buoyant color!
It sweeps away all gloom!
Each of the tiny rose–buds
Reminds me of ones who need
A glimpse of this rare beauty
To soothe a heart that bleeds.
As each lovely rose–bud opens
Into glorious full bloom
I think of a friend or shutin
Whom I must visit soon.

Kelly Malone
A LOVE FOR ALL SEASONS
What's in your heart,
Do you really know,
for some the hardest part,
is to let it show.

Searching way down deep inside,

To find something there,
a feeling you should never hide,
a special kind of care.

A love for a child,
So possessive yet sweet,
sometimes scary and wild,
but always complete.

A love for a man,
a real love known to few,
Like an hourglass full of sand,
sifting together to make one become two.

Love is something to give away,
never needing any reasons,
growing stronger every day,
A love for all seasons.

Dianna Kaye

HIS LOVE

Jesus prayed in the garden of Gethsemane,
He said, "Oh my Father let this cup pass from me,"
And in the darkness, the disciples went to sleep,
But Jesus kept on praying, our souls that he could keep.

Father are you willing, remove this cup please,
An angel did strengthen, still he prayed more earnestly,
His sweat became as blood, falling to the ground,
Finished now his praying, the disciples he then found.

God gave salvation, delivered us from sin,
Gave his life willingly, is there a greater friend?
No, there will never be one who'll love us so,
Giving so freely, His Love to us did show.

D R Mote

WHISPER MY PEN

Whisper my pen across the paper
perhaps another love letter
to a beautiful you
my love runs not-so-few

Hold your hand in the soft moonlight
loneliness not-so-cold
never again to feel its bite

It's the simple things
that make me want to stay
happiness in May
for you my flower

Whisper my pen
the wish of many a men
to know such a beautiful as you

The new of your love
each and every day
ever higher and above
any-a-thing I have 'er known

Perhaps just a love letter . . .

Jonathan J Staniforth

ROLL OF THUNDER, HEAR MY CRY

The Caged Bird is a phrase
often used to describe
Freedom . . .
. . . dispossessed.

Unto my People, Slavery, large and looming,
brought the loathing of one Race,
and the abasement of Another.

Yet, Now,
in the Wake of our exalted indoctri-nation,
a Dis-Ease of the mind
has been contrived.

Ignorance,
with its furtive lack of roseate compassion
and puritanical sense of Self Worth,
has come to be the latest fashion,
and to undo decorum has given birth.

If only we could show
some Kindness,
for those of us who
think that Blindness,
Is an illness that affects the Eyes
Alone . . .

Greg L Salverson

GOODBYE—MY GOOD FRIEND

It takes time to heal a broken heart, or so the saying goes.
But during that time of healing the pain, the mind is full of woes.

What happened to us, I asked myself, we were going so great for a while.
"No commitment," she said again and again, and did not offer a smile.

Feelings of rejection, depression and worthlessness too,
An emotional wreck I am.

Outsiders may think this feeling is dumb,
But the one going through it is numb.

My major mistake, as I found out; I liked her more than she did me.
She is just laughing and probably thinking, how dumb this poor fool must be.

I was driving her nuts by crowding her too, more space she wanted from me.
But I was struggling with my feelings too, of this she refused to see.

So lonely was I for such a long time,
I must have been clinging to her.
Because of my loss the pain is still great, I'm more lonely now than ever.

I was not good enough for her, I said, of this I do regret.
Failure, rejection and depression too, is what my life begets.

Here once again a failure I am, so tired I am of this trend.
So badly I feel with setbacks and such, I see no change for an end.

I miss my friend much more than I should, so lonely I am at this time.
But, just what should a person do?

Nothing is left but to say to her
"Goodbye—my good friend."

Mary Veil

JUST TODAY

Today is a day of sunshine and
fun so let it be.
Close up the house, let's go fishing you and me.

It's a great sport-relaxing
just for today.
Let's get a lunch and fishing worms and be on our way.

Might not catch a fish today
but it's an outing you see.
Just today–enjoy ourselves
let us feel happy and free.

It's just for today-Let it be pleasure for tomorrow may never come.
So today let's look towards all things an life and have a lot of fun.

Scott Petters

BIG CORPORATION

It's a BIG CORPORATION run by little corporate fools,
And the clowns in charge always bark and snap at the slaves that follow their every rule.
Upon our wants and needs they never do think twice: They slap us down and keep us there with their hearts as cold as ice.
But without their slaves of which you are probably one; To make them look so nice their futures would be very bleak then they may think twice.
But when the payment comes to pass their large checks they may get.
But our judgment will surpass because heaven will be sent.

Nora Sherwood Holt

WERE YOU AFRAID I WAS REAL

What kept you from reaching out to me?
Not your heart
What battles did you fight within yourself?
How many tears did you shed alone?
How many tears did you shed in silence?

You'd been hurt too much
Your spirit broken
You'd existed too long
You'd tried to fool yourself too well
You had too much love inside you to give
And no trust to share it

You were too afraid
to find out what you were afraid of
You were too afraid
to see what you needed
You were too afraid
to let yourself have what they wanted

After years of being afraid
Were you afraid I was real?

Veve Maxwell

Veve Maxwell

THE ADOPTION OF THE DECLARATION OF INDEPENDENCE

To my family, Eddie-Lou Cole and John Campbell.

Signed at Gettysburg, PA. July 4, 1776,
By George Washington, Thomas Jefferson and others,
If the old codgers could come back for a day,
Which celebration would they attend, in the U.S.A.?
Independence Day, a day of commemoration,
A day to give thanks and rely,
On our forefathers, and our Heavenly Father,
As we ponder the past, tears drop from our eyes,
We hear the firecrackers, we don't stop to think,
Of this date Dec. 7, 1862, the Prairie Grove Battle,
The words of our grandparents still sore,
Cannons were heard in Van Buren, every window rattled,

We have plenty of evidence,
Cannon balls have been found,
While digging our water lines,
Here and all around,
Our Grandfathers fought in that battle,
Against their will,
They fought man to man,
On every hill,
They prayed, so must we,
For wars to cease, and for Godly leaders,
May we each keep in mind, the bloody battles,
That the 4th of July will always be in our readers,
America will forever, Salute the Stars and Stripes,
The old-fashioned Fourths and Festivals,
Mt. Music, dancing and singing,
"Oh! mighty God: bless our fine foods, and our trails,"

W E Sprenkle

NUTSHELL

Consider the tiny, round edged cell
With your hands on the scope for sharpness
What wonders do your eyes betell
Of a world that lives in darkness,
The bell in the church encircles your world
The punctuation is clear
Remember when you were a little girl
And your mother brought you here?

Perch on the fence with me, my child
Gaze at the moon and the stars
Now wander, let your mind run wild
To where their edges are.
You say you can, and how can you tell
The vast universe from the tiny cell?

David A Rippy
PRECIOUS MOMENTS
She's coming home for a visit, from a land that's far away.
she'll fly in tomorrow, for only a week this stay.

Nine months since I've seen her last, seems so long . . .
but the time went fast.

Distractions from work and social events too, but still memories
drift back of a girl I once knew.

Shared laughter and fun, serious moments and intimate times,
we learned from each other, and strengthened our minds.

You enter my room, sporting a new tan and hair style, so glad nothing's changed your laugh or
your smile.

Time and distance have pulled us apart, but in your presence again, embers once cold, grow warmer in the heart.

Not enough time to talk, share our past nine months spent away,
demands placed on limited time left,
maybe another day.

Departure day draws near, no time left to share, our paths crossed briefly, moments spent together that now seem so rare.

Warm lands once again beckon you, sky swallows your plane . . . lost
in a field of blue.

Ruth Huntington McKinney
LOVE
Love is the tender after-glow
Of Motherhood, with night light low;
The glad awarement sweethearts know;
The fond and satisfied caresses
Of those the marriage union blesses.
Through all of life it effervesces.
And it is made of stouter stuff, than
Dreams, which metamorphose into fluff.
To sense Love's joys is not enough.
Love, is a down-to-earth emotion.
I somehow, seem to have the notion
That Love—alone, secures promotion
To Heaven's vague but sure, delights,
Dear ones departed, reunites,
And sets the Universe to rights.

Ruth Huntington McKinney
LIFE'S PUZZLE
Scattered out on the table before me
are the parts of the Puzzle of Life
I finger them over, selecting out
words that symbolize concord or strife
"Enlightenment" and "Brotherhood,"
"Forgiveness," and all the rest or
"Violence," "Bigotry" and "Greed,"
so hampering in our quest
for the spiritual virtues we need to attain, but have to keep struggling for, the stepping stones to solutions here, to Eternity, the door.
But although the puzzle is difficult
I'm impelled from within to resolve it, relying upon the Creator of Life to allot me the patience to solve it.
At length it is finished except for one word
I foresee will fit like a glove.
With completion in sight, I express my delight
But, of course, what is Life, without "Love?"

Cherryle Castle
LIFE WITH ALL ITS BEAUTY
Life
with all its
Beauty
Brings forth
Love
the joy
the pain
Requisite to the
Soul
the very essence of
Eternity
"I love you"

Charles Van Heyden
FOR JANUARY
First I fell in Love with you
When first I stood next to you
And inhaled your air
And saw that you were made
Of nobler things than
Other women who seemed as fair.

My conscience would not
Permit this love at
That time to be a glove
T'would fetter both our
Puerile hearts with
Earthly fits and starts,

But no more can
Can Time stay the hand
Of adoration nor command,
To set in motion
Love's demand.

Now I make unique and bare
This love of mine to
Show quite clear.
If courage is to say
What is and step not back,
Or try to ignore

Then I say I Love You,
I Love You Evermore.

Charles Van Heyden
THE NOOSE
The news has brought
Me to grief again.
I'm apathetic about
Life today like
Yesterday.
Oh why do I
Need the news?

The First Page
Is the 1st stage
That like a booster
Sends me down
The tubes faster.

If I were a reporter
Or a cocaine snorter,
I'd enjoy telling
Everyone the news.

But since I eschew
making people into glue,
I'll refrain from
Pouring out the soo'.

A man once said
You can practically
Raise the dead
By restraining daily
Papers and the ed.

And so it came
To pass, and it
Happened very fast,
Riding the black
And white
Became a sensation
Over nite,
The community rising
Above the black
Clouds grasp.

So to all of you
Who have "paid yer dues,"
I hope this ditty,
About a thing clearly
Shitty, will prompt you
To take your vitamins
And not the news.

Kenneth J Fabrizio
THIS CANCER
Family status has no point, take one hit and death's hand will anoint.
Makes you feel ultimate pleasure, it becomes your life, your only treasure.
It's ruining our country, bringing us to war, it's ruining our world outside the door.
Young kids do the selling on the street, addicted country, it's in almost everyone you meet.
There's a disease running through our country, crack cocaine, ruling the streets with violence and pain.
This cancer is of the worst kind, ruining lives, leaving us in a bind.
This cancer is killing America one by one, this cancer has control, when will this cancer be done?
This cancer has the losing side, this cancer has no pride.
This cancer is crack cocaine, I'm asking you please,
Avoid the insane, I'm asking you please, don't fry your brain.

Kenneth J Fabrizio
I'M LOOKING FOR
Walking down this road alone, I just want someone to call my own.
People come and people go, I'm looking for one that'll always show.
I'm looking for someone to love, I'm looking for a dove.
I'm looking for a dove without wings, I'm looking for a dove that always sings.
I'm looking for a dove that'll fly at my pace,
I'm looking for a dove try to win my race.
I'm looking for a dove that'll always be with me,
I'm looking for a dove that won't want to be free.
I'm looking for a dove to take to the sky, I'm looking for a dove that won't say goodbye.
You may think I'm looking for a crippled dove, actually, all I'm looking for is a true love!

Matthew Thebold
AMERICAN PRIDE (OUR FLAG)
Burning our flag is a crime.
Buddy, don't you dare.
Such a disgraceful act,
I could hardly bear.

It stands for freedom and peace,
All people who are brave.
America stands for love,
Something I'd fight to save.

I'm just a common man,
Another average Joe.
America is my home,
That will always be so.

If you disagree with me,
Then you're not on my side.
Everyday of my life,
I feel American pride.

Matthew Thebold
NOTHING TO HIDE
I see a huge tree,
Touching the sky.
I see a pretty bird,
Swaying on by.

My mind is free of thoughts.
My eyes are open wide.
I'm feeling so peaceful,
I have nothing to hide.

In a world full of hate,
In a land full of crime.
I wish it wasn't so,
It's a waste of time.

If they can only hear,
What I'm trying to say.
Having nothing to hide,
Makes a beautiful day.

Susan E Longfellow
SACRED UNION
For what is drawn
From the fusion
Of two hearts and lives
Is an unmistakable treasure
given unknowingly
Into the depths
Of a single being
To be nurtured
And dwelt upon
Stored inside
Until carried on
It will be so
The lessons learned
Taken heed
In the ultimate devotion
Eternally

Susan E Longfellow
TENDERLY
The threads that are pulled
Ever so tenderly
The threads that are entwined
By those endearing thoughts
That intrigue emotion
By a heartfelt sentiment
Of love
Merciful and caring
Embracing the air unseen
For what is unreachable
Solely embraced in the mind
Ever so tenderly

John R Marks
SHADES OF GREY
Winter Clouds of an afternoon in February.
Conversation we do not convey.
The hazy reflection of a used cocaine spoon.
That mass you really do not believe you weigh.
The surface of our planet's moon.
Monochrome images of warm yesterdays.
An April's sky after the morning rain.
The day-to-day celebrations and pain.
Relationships that are never ending.
Mildly observant and diligently comprehending.
Shades of monochrome from a flickering flame.

John R Marks
TO TRY
We never know certainty or uncertainty until we try.
Even though the deeds we attempt to accomplish may
cause us pain and make us frustratingly cry.

It is these unfaltering efforts we put forth that gets us high.
Even though the people that are close to us may say good–bye.
We never see through the mists of life until we try.
Even though the personal expectations and anticipation we accumulate may make us fry.

John R Marks
LANGUAGE
Inner reflection of an experienced mind.
A warm handshake on a frosty afternoon.
The graceful movements of a pantomime.
Graphic symbols on a painted sign.
The natural chattering of a rambunctious raccoon.
Mathematics that scientifically relate space time.
Pleasureful transactions carried on in a western saloon.
The induced meanings of this little rhyme.

Bryan Michael Kimmell

Bryan Michael Kimmell (Age 10)
TO MOM, WITH LOVE
When I leave you, I begin to cry.
I'd better get to you fast and quickly before I die.

My heart pounds around you.
I hope and pray that you love me, too.

You're as pretty as a sunny day flower.
You have the most prettiest power.

You'll be in my heart.
We will never be apart.

Madge Bidwell Campbell
THE PARTING
We walked a way together,
Paths entwined a little time.
Parting roads now lead away
From busy lives of yesterday.

God bless you on your journey
Dear friend and part of me,
The way is long and briars
Thick as far as I can see.

My heart will ache the loss
Of nearness, joy, and peace.
Forgotten in memory the
Days of tears and grief.

As time goes by I know
We will talk and smile,
Quietly forgetting that for awhile,
We walked a way together.

Madge Bidwell Campbell
THOUGHTS
Thoughts are like webs
That weave across the mind,
The spoken word adds color
In hues of every kind.

Never will the thoughts
Unsaid be good or ill,
Only acting word or deed
Can either slot fulfill.

To you gold is honor
And white is pure,
Orchid is deceitful and
Shades of red unsure.

To me white is honor
And gold is pure,
Shades of red deceitful
And orchid is unsure.

God sees the web
In all its virgin splendour
Then judges thoughts expressed
By harmony of color.

Madge Bidwell Campbell
MY DREAM
My dream is contentment and
hope for tomorrow.
My dream is a smile after
the depths of sorrow.
My dream is a gentle
peaceful life worth living.
My dream is one love,
understanding, forgiving.
My dream is for the warmth
of the sun on my face.
My dream is friendship
among the whole human race.
My dream is the miracle
sound of children's laughter.
My dream extends to a
jubilant endless hereafter.

June Kaplan
SEASHELLS TO MY EAR
Seashells to my ear
circus clowns with a tear
candle with sparks of red
light down the hall to find my bed
people going home for dinner
i am one and all at once a winner
to have a bed and a meal
to have the time to feel
younger than i was when he left me
but older now that i can bear it
children around the world
will they ever know true love?
that happens so deeply felt
when two are filled with peace
as bestowed from above
when for the first time their sacred vows bring forth
a vision to behold
when they grow up
can they be freed not to feel frozen
when times grow cold
is it inevitable for love's labors to be lost?
for one and all-young as well as old?

june kaplan
lizbeth bless her soul so merry
lizbeth bless her soul so merry
for she and rob are happy very
whether her hands in tuna salad
a dish to satisfy the palate
or setting out to see vast distant places
to see the world in all her faces
her choice in truth cannot be wrong
for now she gives to him her song
a traveler with a band a woman needs a man
northeastern winds acalling her to land
and out of chaos came a lover and a name
her wildness now tame
rejoicing without loneliness to claim
for beauty in her eye and in her brain
she sees her life as it should be
without the prick of pain
relaxed with new found love so smooth
and nothing 'gainst the grain
she glows like a shimmering moon
to know a baby soon
for now the quest for happiness
is as full as a rose in bloom.

june kaplan
apple brown bettye
apple brown bettye
she's the apple of my eye
big sweet mama
don't you cross her
my oh my
or she'll put you six feet under
that's no lie
break a promise
try to cheat her
take advantage
or defeat her
at your game
bettye will beat you don't ask why
like a scorpion she'll sting you
ain't no help that prayers can bring you
it's a bet bettye will wing you
so by by
that's why bettye
is the apple
of my eye.

june kaplan
lovely lark
cloudy skies
purple and pink thunder
deep thoughts to wonder
sarah with the laughing eyes
quiet and strong
subtle soothing wise
in an internal way
where all softness deeply resides
underneath inside within
a secret pride an inner grin
her secret self known to others
as the smiling dashing stranger
who warms you with her presence
like an angel in the dark
a thoughtful silent lark
nestling gently on a branch upon your tree
in younger days lost all the dreams
youth had to bring
then sweetened by age
a power in the richness of womanhood
fly lovely lark come to me
with a flicker and a spark in my memory.

Mel Kerper
THE SILENCE IS SO LOUD

In memory of my beloved wife, Catherine Ann Kerper.

I turn up the music, but I can't hear our song.
I look to the heavens, but I can't see a cloud.
Surely, you're at peace at the right hand of God.
Why is the silence so loud?

I light a tall candle, the room stays quite dark.
I feel alone in the largest of crowds.
I sip a fine wine, there's an absence of taste.
Why is the silence so loud?

I walk in a circle, 'cause there's no beginning or end.
I'm a man that once walked so proud.
I flap broken wings, what I wouldn't give to fly.
Why is the silence so loud?

Turn down the volume, may this pain slowly fade.
My search for rebirth has begun.
When I answer—Why is the silence so loud?

This battle will start to be won.

Mel Kerper
ON BORROWED TIME
We should unwrap each day as a treasured gift.
As the tides rush in, as the shadows drift,
No one owns this world, this place we rent,
We're On Borrowed Time, life is heaven sent.

With the break of dawn, and the birth of day
Stand up and cheer, then on your knees to pray.
Seize the-day-as if it were your last
We're On Borrowed Time, another day has passed.

On borrowed time, we can't recall each day
Dwell on special moments, that may have come your way
On Borrowed Time, we're a grain of sand
That has filtered through God's loving hand.

When things go wrong, we open new doors.
As the night crawls in, reflect and pause.
No one owns this world, this place we rent,
We're on Borrowed Time, make it time well spent.

Robert M Hall
THE ART OF POTTERY

Dedicated to my wonderful daughters, Alison and Lindsay.

Over anxious, overwrought,
Little boy upon his pot:
His chubby face a crimson hue,
Boy overwhelmed, boy overdue.

Face now purple, boy so glum,
Fists clenched tight, boy overcome:
But eyebrows raise, no furrowed brow,
Boy overjoyed, all over now.

Robert M Hall
HEREDITY

To my darling wife Susan and the Ivory family.

My father is a tad insane, in fact, he's raving mad;
He insists that we should call him King;
Now doesn't that seem sad?

My mother, in the last few months, is rather in-between;
She rolls her eyes, and tilts her head,
Believing she is Queen.

Yet, as their son, I feel it is wrong, to

raise a family stink;
Their total madness can't harm me,
'Cause I am God. I think!

George M Dile
A BED OF ROSES
They say life is not a bed of roses,
But given some thought I cannot
agree,
For somewhere within that thorn and
flower,
Is a picture of hidden reality.

The rose is synonymous with love
and passion,
A symbol that reaches all of
mankind,
That perhaps we may see the Hand of
Creation,
In every moment and throughout all
time.

The thorn is symbolic of pain and
sorrow,
A picture of grief that saddens the
heart,
Something that touches us sooner or
later,
Something that strengthens or tears
us apart.

So life is truly a bed of roses,
From heartbreak to heartbreak from
day-to-day,
A fastidious balance of pain and
passion,
Of gospel injustice of war and play!

George M Dile
WONDERFUL

Dedicated to my "wonderful" wife, friend and lover . . . Yvonne. Happy Ten Years!

W elcome my love, to the end of
ten VERY wonderful years,
and the beginning of ten more,
less the fragile, tender tears.

O nly during a FEW fleeting
moments were there second
thoughts in my mind,
and even then, I knew our hearts
would forever intertwine.

N ever did I seriously EVER want
to leave your side,
though I spent minute upon minute
with my anger and my pride.

D id your LOVE for me experience
any second thoughts at all?
as we learned to give and give
and give, then give again our
all?

E ach year God is teaching us to
be so much more LIKE Him,
and much less like a world so
full of misery and corruption.

R emember YOU and I are part of
that mystery God calls
marriage,
and in that union we have decided,
His light we'll always carry.

F rom this day forward you AND I
are a century in love,
looking into the Face of eternal
hope, and beyond the stars above.

U nder the shadow of His mighty
wing I see a man and his Lady,
thankful for family and their
friends, and Muffin, their
"Heavenly" Baby.

L ook deeper still my precious
Bride beyond the verse and
rhyme,
and you will see that what we
HAVE, some couples never find!!

George M Dile
BABYS EYES

To my beautiful Noel whom I love with all my heart, Dad. Happy Birthday to you and may you have a glorious life!!!

Baby's eyes are luminous,
born to life and innocence,
heart so pure and mind untouched,
baby's needs require much!

Now babys ears discover speech,
right or wrong we begin to teach,
soon childhood will be so close,
and things that parents fear the most.

Today my baby is so mature,
she is fully grown and self-assured,
she's left the nest to live on her own,
and thankful she had a Christ-filled
home.

Then baby remembers when she was
young,
reflecting on memories and family
fun,
and the love it took she suddenly
sees,
while bouncing her own baby on her
knee!

Cecilia Wallraven
TIME ON MY HANDS

This dedication is to my three sons who also hurt from the loss of a brother. I love you, Bob, Bill and Jim.

Each day there is time on hold
Each day I try to mold what would
have been
Each day I try to remember his face
and the place
Each day I look inside my self to see
his eyes
Looking back at me on what should
have been
When will this stop
When will this stop
Never my friend
Not until the end
That is when

Cecilia Wallraven
TEARDROPS

Dedicated for my son John Lee Cuthbertson, 1969-1988, and for others who have loved and lost.

Teardrops are like rain
Memories are like a hand that taps
you on the shoulder
A smell is your child that has just
walked through your mind
An ache is the absence of the child
that you can no longer hold
You wander through the life that
once you tried to mold
To remember that it still comes out
the same
There will always be sadness and
pain
The life of that child is still
The memories are put away for
another day
And then you try to say, oh God!
Why do I have come this way
Can't I just have him back one more
day

Cecilia Wallraven
TO MY FRIENDS

This poem is dedicated to the loners, and to the two men who showed him the rest, His Father, Bob Wallraven and B. Jim.

You are the very best
You helped me lay my son to rest
You rolled in on your bikes
Because it was John's delight
Your colors were flying gold and
blue
On your bikes you sat bold and true
Your helping hands laid him to rest
We all knew he had done his best
I could see in your eyes that your
heart was broken
You made him a brother without a
word spoken
There is not much more I can say
But thank you for the kindness you
showed us that day

Cecilia Wallraven
THE LIGHT

For my son, John Lee Cuthbertson, 1969-1988.

You say good-bye and your heart is
broken
Never to be seen again with that
smile
Never to say again hold me for a
while
All you have left are the things he left
behind
And they will be gone in just a short
time
Years will go by and your heart will
still be broken
The yearning is still more than you
can bear
You never stop asking if you can
come there
And then one day when you are old
and gray
He will say come this way
And all you have to do now is walk
that lonely mile
And he will be at the other end with
that smile

Anthony T Sclafani
WOMAN WITH PARROT

To Erika; My Love For You Is Infinite . . .

Amidst a sea of technical dreams,
There flows a pigment of life.
A monument to plebeian thought;
An account of what the world seems.

Framed in geometric semblance,
She cries to be set free.
Yet she flows through the hearts
Of those who have remembrance.

One voice is high above the din;
A rough spot in the smooth sand.
Intrinsic with the few, the proud;
Her beauty comes from within.

Anthony T Sclafani
THE ONE STAIRWAY

The Sun began to rise and the mists in the Vale below were drawn up.

As we looked through the fog, the cool frost thawed and the green appeared.

We descended the Stairway which led to paradise.

. . . And the Vale glowed with warmth and beauty.

The young ferns stood up and caressed our bodies.

A small stone path lay at our feet.

Overhead, the Sun peered through the trees and its rays touched our eyes.

. . . And the Vale glowed with warmth and beauty.

The creek could be heard in the distance; the noise of paradise.

A silver crystal sword of water appeared before our eyes.

The overwhelming light of Love filled our hearts and souls.

. . . And the Vale glowed with warmth and beauty.

The water lapped over your body again and again; an endless stream of sensation.

I looked upon your burning face and became overtaken.

We two became one.

. . . And the Vale glowed with warmth and beauty—and Love . . .

Becky Cleaver Howse
ANGEL LOVE
Once upon a midnight dream,
This vision I did see—
A light of love and tenderness,
Of beauty and of wings.

An angel from the sky above
With a heart as pure as gold,
Arms of love that comfort—
Arms of love that hold.

Smiling—oh so sweetly—reaching
out for me,
Getting so much closer—I look up to
see,
Her face unlike no other
For this angel is my mother
Watching over me.

Lori Richards-Roach
IN A CHILD'S EYES
In a child's eyes, he was so strong
With muscles that rippled across his
chest

In a child's eyes he was so tall
My protector from harm, my hero,
my dad
I'm still a child behind adult eyes
I still need my hero now gone

Too soon he was taken
Unaware of the pain, the void he left
He never felt this needed, this
important
He never thought he'd be missed like
this

I'm still the child behind adult eyes
I still need my hero now gone.

Lori Richards-Roach
PURE GOLD

With eyes so blue she looks up at me
I'm perfect to her I know
Isn't it funny the trust she has
So crisp, so new, Pure Gold

I wish I could protect that feeling
The feeling of happiness, trust & love
It too soon fades when life steps in
And grips you like a glove

Until that time I'll let her think
I'm perfect in every way
What's wrong with that, it's good for me
Too soon she'll know the truth
And when she does, what will she think
Nothing I suspect
Because she's bright, her smile warms my heart
Her laugh breaks life's hold.

Until the time she knows the truth
I'll let her think I'm perfect
So I can feel like a kid again
So crisp, so new, Pure Gold

Ellen M McFarland
LOVE'S COMMITMENT

Whispering needs
Remind us
Of fleeting dreams
Unleashed on wings of desire,
While love's awakening
Most gently beckons.

Two shall become one.
Not so divinely simple
Upon hearing, in this call to death,
Despair.

Love's essence cannot be captured,
Nor freed,
When unbridled longing,
Amid darkness,
Flaunts weakness.

Lovers seeks peace,
The forgotten grace
Of an earthen surrender.
And love begins anew,
The moment we remember
To gently embrace the light.

Debra L McKenzie
IT'S NOT ALWAYS GOOD TO LISTEN WITH YOUR HEART

When everything seems to go wrong
it's not always good to listen to your heart.

That's how I go in this state of mind
from the very start.

So tonight I sit back and take another look,
to what I'm all about.

Is all this loneliness I feel just a trick
upon my mind?

Am I really just wasting precious time?

Time that should be spent thinking
with my mind.

To stand up proud and move right on.

To start over again with a happier song.

There is a tomorrow people say.
So I'll give it a try, and maybe someday,
I won't have to worry about whatever
it is that my heart
may say along the way.
Because my heart and mind will be in
step with time and happiness will
once again be mine.

Rev Marion E Young
THOUGHTS ARE THINGS

To my beloved mother.

I hold it true that thoughts are things
They're endowed with bodies and breath and wings.
And we send them forth to fill the world with good results, or ill.
That which we call our secret thoughts, speeds forth to earth's remotest spot.
We build our further thought by thought for good or ill,
Yet know it not, yet, so the universe was wrought.
Thought is another name for fate; choose then thy destiny!
And wait! For love brings love and hate brings hate!
You never can tell what a thought will do! In bringing you hate or love; for thoughts are things and on airy wings are swifter than carrier doves.
They follow the law of the universe. Each thing creates its kind; and they speed over the track to bring you back whatever went out from your mind.

Celesta Bernice Combs
KEEP MY COMMANDMENTS

This poem is dedicated to John, Gary, Jean, Beverly, Arvin and Carol with all my love.

Down through a tunnel I was floating with grace,
At the end of that tunnel I saw your dear face.
You came early that morning to take me away,
You changed your mind and left me to stay.
You said that my work here had to be done,
You want me to laugh and to have more fun.
Just keep my commandments and hold to my hand,
I'll take you home to my promised land,
You must try and share the heavy load of any brother on my road.
For my sweetest blessings will always go,
To the hands that serve me there below.
I'll let you live another day,
But you must live the way you pray.
And should I come and call for you much sooner than you planned,
I'll help your family with their grief and they will understand.

Fran Doran
NATURE'S LOVE

To my daughters—Sheena—Jeena—life's journey has been already written.

Love is like the leaves that fall from the trees trying to find their own path, the wind blows them around, the snow covers them on the ground, later on they all seem to settle down, some will reseed in what they will be, some may never succeed, just like that tree. God will put your love where it suppose to be.

Vanessa Nutting
REMEMBERING THE MEMORIES

I would like to dedicate this to my dear friend Roy, that he'll remember the summer we spent together.

The memories seem so distant,
Yet I hold them close to my heart.
Your letters make me feel you're near,
But we're so far apart.
Every time I see you,
My heartbeat pounds so fast.
Then I start remembering,
The good times from our past.
Remember long ago,
Our late night rendezvous?
That was my favorite time,
I ever spent with you.
Do you remember watching,
The day slowly turn to night?
And how the sunset always,
Shone so very bright?
I wish I could rewind time,
And play it back again.
But I'm perfectly happy knowing,
That you'll always be my friend.
So please remember the memories,
The wonderful memories we made.
And keep them close to your heart,
So they'll never, ever fade.

Dorothy N Moore
I WOULD LIKE THE WORLD TO CHANGE

To my dear departed parents, Mr. and Mrs. Milton R. Jones.

I would like the world to change
for the better, not the worst;
Then we could all live better
throughout the Universe.
We all struggle each and every day,
for better days to come;
Then, when we meet our Maker,
we know we have been a
"Giver," not a "Taker."

L E Ferraris

L E Ferraris
LORI'S AMITY

To Lori Badalamenti for her inspiring and encouraging support.

Solitary and tardy inhabitant,
Often wandering weary and dreamy
On this blessed piece of land
In the vast mysterious universe,
I seek acceptance with my verses.

But when the pen became too heavy
And wished waving life goodby,
I glanced once more toward the sky
As to see the carriage God sent by.
It was then that I thought seeing
An Angel diving from far above
In pure white semblance of a dove:
Shapely and gifted of human blessings.

Fluttering with gracious sounds,
She gently posed on my right side;
And her peaceful reassuring eyes
Offered much needed calm to mine.

Then she spread a bit her wings,
Enough for me to slip within
For more affection than protection:
The kind I starved of from infancy
Till now, when met by LORI'S AMITY.

David Bernatchez
OWLISH BEN

To Wilfred T. Follet, an interesting, if unreliable, friend who I had the pleasure of knowing at the time of this experience of my youth.

Far from an iron stove,
I walked a glade in a glen
after the chill breeze set in;
with the waning sun it struck,
while from the forest a yowling came,
the mating plea amid the maple, birch and spruce.
Water rushed down the valley,
the domain of fox and feline, fisher and porcupine.
Owlish Ben had gone, far from the warming fire,
at the mating time.
Trees were budding and kittens were born
while a white throated grizzled grey veteran
of winter storms and scratching claws was lost.
Was it him? I'd never know.
Not long before dark and time to get home;
I left that valley and a wayward cat.

Curtis L Williams
DOOM

This poem is dedicated to, those. Who dare to read it.

From which it came. From out of the night. The day will come. When all is not right.

When the moon is full and the wind is still. The sky will turn red and the blood will spill.

Sara Hussey (Age 11)
THINGS HAPPENING TO ME

To everyone who has been there for me throughout everything.

I got a disease I was really scared of,
But now I know it's being taken care of.
I thought the Christmas spirit would pass me by,
Without stopping by me to say "Hi."
But now it's here and I can see,
It's definitely stopped at me.
Christmas won't be the same,
But that doesn't mean
I can't join in on fun and games.
Things aren't as bad as they used to be,
I'm getting used to the things happening to me.
I'm glad I have caring friends and family around,
They help a lot when I'm feeling down.

For anyone who has cancer like I do,
I want them to know I understand
what they're going through.
In a few years everything will clear
up,
Then I can really cheer up.
Now I'm happy and excited
because my Christmas spirit hasn't
subsided.
Well, to everyone who reads this,
Happy Holidays and Merry
Christmas!

Alberta M Phinney
ME

Dedicated to my daughter, Sandra L. Baumchen.

I'd like to be a mountain spring
That gurgles sweet while voices ring,
Perhaps an ocean with surf and sound
Where rolling waves with spray
abound,
Or mountain river neath the trees
That gently whispers to the breeze,
Or snow that falls upon the earth,
Softly singing sounds of mirth.
Rain is wealth neath clouds of gray
That chases all the blues away,
It is cleansing for the soul,
And makes me feel so fresh and
whole.

I'd like to be the wind at play
That whistles to the eaves all day.
Look at the hail that's coming down
Among the steeples white and brown!
I'd like to touch the expanse of sky
And view God's throne that is on
high.
A winged bird I'd like to be,
Who sings in sweetest harmony
With all creation on the earth.
The bird, it knows Who gave him
birth.
A man can doubt in his short span,
But nature knows Who created man.

Barbara A Wood
OUR LOVE

Dedicated to My Love.

Through work we met
and talked
and laughed
and smiled.

With friends we met
and talked
and laughed
and touched.

Then alone we met
and talked
and laughed
and kissed.

Even now we meet
and talk
and laugh
and love.

Stacie M Monroe
LIFT YOUR EYES TOWARD THE SKY

In loving memory of Steven H. Fleming. And to those I love.

Lift your eyes toward the sky,
See her flying there.
Oh, the red.
Oh, the white.
Look at that beautiful blue.
Don't close your eyes to hide a tear,
Open them wide and show your
pride,
It's the proper thing to do.
So, take off your hat,
and cover your heart,
or raise a hand to your head.
Now listen to the sounds.
Do you hear only cloth snapping in
the breeze?
Oh no, not me.
I hear the ghosts of the soldiers gone
from here
marching to the beat of a silent drum.
And I hear them cry,
"Oh, look at those who will burn our
souls
just standing about down there. Now
there is
something new. Oh, look, there's the
reason
we fly! They lift their eyes and see
her
flying here!"
Oh, the red,
Oh, the white.
Look at that beautiful blue.
"They open their eyes and show their
pride. We're proud to have left Old
Glory to you."

John L Chladek
DIVINE ASSISTANCE

To all who play Lotto:
"Good Luck"—my motto!

Lord be kind and good to me,
and help me win the lottery.
As I'm investing my last buck,
bestow on me unswerving luck.

Guide my hand in choosing numbers,
in case my intuition slumbers.
Pick for me the winning set
of figures sure to win the bet.

Then when they mix each little ball,
only mine are sure to fall.
Ten million cash with ease distress,
despite bad news from I.R.S.

Nancy Scott
PRECIOUS SAM
I am a little bunny,
My name is Precious Sam.
I wandered as I thought, one day,
I'm free, that's what I am.

I hopped down to the bakery shop,
It smelled so-o-o good inside.
No wonder people come in here,
I guess, I'd better hide.

I peered into a flour can,
Got powder on my nose.
My flopping ears fell in just then,
Flour sprinkled on my toes.

Oh gosh, oh gee, what a mess I'm in,
As I almost had to sneeze.
Whatever became of me,
This corner I could not squeeze.

I'd better run and get out fast,
For bakery shops are not my class.
Just then the door shut with a click,
Now what's this baker's funny trick.

Oh no, no, no, he's going away,
Got his work done for the day.
What shall I do in such a mess,
And all this flour upon my vest.

Oh gosh, oh me,
I started to cry.
But no one heard,
I was locked inside.

I snuggled in a little ball,
And tried to fall asleep.
And just then Molly Mouse ran by,
And wondered, what's that heap?

I don't know you, she did reply,
What brings you here today?
I really didn't know myself,
But I told her anyway.

I'm Precious Sam, and I took a walk,
Thought something new I'd see.
But now what shall a rabbit do,
In such a catastrophe!

Well stay right there, said Molly
Mouse,
The cleaning man will come.
And when the door is open wide,
Your little feet must run.

But first she said, there's all good
things,
Just sweet and crunchy too.
I'll show you just right where they
are,
And you can have some too.

Oh yes indeed, she knew them all,
And munched and munched and
munched.
I asked her, is there any left,
For other people's lunch?

She was ashamed, and bowed her
head,
I guess I'm mighty greedy.
Oh yes, I said I do agree,
But she munched and munched more
speedy.

Just then I heard a familiar click,
Behind the cans I did hop.
My eyes peered up and down fell my
ears,
Who's in the bakery shop?

With pail and broom,
And soaps and wax,
He started scrubbing floors,
His task.

Oh dear, oh me,
What shall I do.
I'd better run,
While there's a chance to.

Where's Molly Mouse, I asked
myself,
Where did she run and hide?
I'm sure, as sure, she'll be alright,
Back home she's safe inside.

At last the chance, I have to run,
And quickly as a bunny.
I ran right out the opened door,
Heart beating fast—'twas not funny.

Along the streets and down the lane,
Across the clover patch.
I saw my mom in her rocking chair,
I slowly lift the latch.

She was as happy, as happy as could
be,
And saw my dirty face.
With hugs and kisses she showered
me,
And then her warm embrace.

She said, my precious bunny,
You better go to bed.
I found it hard to tell her,
The things I did instead.

She was very, very patient,
And sat so quietly.
Then said, now Precious Sam my
son,
Was it really fun to be free?

D Tomas Lauria
PRESENCE

For Iris: Who carries the burden of my inspiration ever so lightly.

there is always a fear,
that is its birth . . .
the subliminal vision
is frightening and persistent
and evolving

and i will sit and succumb
to its greatness

it is a light, a wound,
or a stone
and it must be confronted
for it demands attention to
evidence its vicious presence

is it love and anger
and fire and storm
and sex and thunder
and silence
and we will call it
merely
a poem.

Nora Auwarter
GOD WATERED OUR LAWNS

To my darling daughter and other loved ones.

The sky was growing very dark,
There were rumbles of thunder
above.
I could tell by all sights and sounds
It would rain on this land that we
love.
Lightning flashed across the sky,
Large sprinkles of rain began to fall,
And as it thundered and lightning
flashed
Rain came down harder and
dampened all.
The grass looked green and less
thirsty,
The flowers lowered their heads in
prayer.
It was such a beautiful sight.
I know it was sent by Him up there.
I awakened in the night,
And still heard it gently rain.
I knew God was doing our watering,
So I fell back asleep again.
By morning the storm was over,
Everything had been bathed very
clean.
The sun was soon shining down
On the most beautiful country I have
ever seen.

Robert B Howell
UNPOLLUTED LOVE

Dedicated to my wonderful wife September who was always there by my side, even when the ship seem to sink her love somehow never died . . .

I've drown her heart with sorrow,

O fickle ways bestowed.

Apologies are accepted,

What reasons,
I never will know.

She always knew she loved me,
Whether foggy the road or clear?

Unpolluted throughout these trials,
Her love,
through the storms,
she steered . . .

Deborah W Childs
GONE FISHIN'

A loving tribute to my Dad, Willard Gaylord Walters, Senior.

Forever remembered that early morn,
When awakened from my
gentle sleep
To emotions more torrent than any
storm
Abetted by oceans deep.

My father once so full of life,
Now gone without a word
To a realm of peace and comfort
On the wings of a just freed
bird.

Years of toil just three months ended;
The workplace far behind.
Free to live life as never before,
Now finally a carefree mind.

He would cast his line from every
shore

Travel the Country, many sights to
explore

He would do this all and more.

No More.

My life unraveled on that day;
Rearranged, rewound in a
different way.
And Time, though it passes, cannot
erase
The solemn serenity upon his
face,

When I kissed my Dad Goodbye.

Lillian Ruth Luton
WHITE AND BLACK
Two twin sisters were born in the
year of 1900.
There was an awful sound around
and this was thunder.
The little twins, white and black
were growed together.
As time went on, and on, soon the
twins were all through school
and college of their choice.

One day they went to this
beautiful park by the name of
Joyice.
Here they met two handsome
young men, dark and light.
Their meeting was love at first
sight.
But, the two young men were not
growed together.

When white and black saw this
situation
they began to weep.
Then a wonderful miracle began
to happen.
A voice close by said to white and
black;
And it wasn't their pappy.

You may make three wishes.
The wishes were,
They could separate,
Get married, and live happy.

Cheylon R Clark
CARNATION

I would like to dedicate this poem to Earth Day.

The Carnation is the only flower of
Its kind,
the living being that knows the time.
The sweet smell of the petals,
is like a breath in rolling meadows.
The structure of the flower,
is like the sound of a harpsichord.
And still, It is the only flower I can
afford.

C W Coon
PRECIOUS GIFT
Of birds and clouds,
Rainbows and trees.
Of golden sunlight;
Trickling through a rose-colored mist
on the glen.
Of the gently approaching
dawn at the shore.
Of a mountain lake,
Shimmering sapphire-blue
'neath the waning moon.
Of all these,
And countless others of
wonder and beauty;
The most precious gift of all,
Is you.

Dorothy Ludowyk Joseph

Dorothy Ludowyk Joseph
LAMPS THAT LIGHT THE EVENING

To the memory of Victor Joseph and Hilarion Ludowyk. For Dora Ludowyk, written for Manelle and Justin Nunez and for Naomi and Rohan Joseph. A sonnet for grandparents everywhere.

Sands run rapid at the end—

Inevitable, quickly falls the evening.
Time, relentless, does not bend
To wishful thought and
yearning's trend—
Enthusiasms wane. One wonders why
One strove so hard.
Empty the nest—and dry the eye,
The young ones all have
learned to fly—away.

Then as the darkness starts to fall,
Lamps come alight to brighten
failing day.
In the glowing, lovely light of infant
eyes—
The eyes of a new generation.
New loves, new life, a raison
d'être—
New incentives, and finally—a whole
new way.

Wendy Clarke
LOST AND FOUND
Deep inside,
Where the hurt lives,
Where the hurt hides,
I've found a piece of me,
Battered and torn,
Barely alive.
With great care,
I've nurtured it,
I've tended it,
And saved this piece.
This piece of me,
With great strength,
Has grown to be
The me, that's me,
Deep inside.

Betty Crebs
ROBBED
He robbed me of my revenge and
final confrontation
As he robbed me of my youth.
He let disease take his mind and
leave
A pathetic shell of skin and bones—
an easy way out.

The verbal abuse, I can quote chapter
and verse.
The physical abuse is more elusive. I
have no visual
Picture or instant recall. Just a child's
memories
Buried deep inside—they fight not to
be retrieved.

He knew the truth, but was never big
on truth. He
Pretended to be the image he created:
someone wonderful.
Perhaps, that's why he let his mind
go—he couldn't
Live with the truth any longer. He
turned on himself
Claiming his final victim in a living
hell; the only
Satisfaction I will know. I hope his
reality eats him alive!

Avis K Clark
SITTING IN SILENCE
Winter with its white blanket
God is telling us it's the Sunday of
the year
Every thing is not dead
It's just the time of resting here

It will not die and blow away
All will come back in the spring of
day

Now in this winter so dry and cold
It's time for us to look back at the old
And thank God for what we have
To look back and remember
And look forward and do better

So when the wind blows this winter
long
Thank God you can look forward
To hear a spring bird song.

Teresa Yvonne Cox
HURT
You never really know
what hurt is until
you lose something that
means a lot to you.

Losing a boyfriend will
hurt for a little while until
you find someone else.

Losing a husband will always
hurt. Especially if it's to another
woman.

But when you lose an unborn
baby, it hurts so much. You feel
empty and you feel like you
failed. Even if God knew you weren't
ready & it was the best.
But why couldn't he stop the hurt
too?

Marsha Critchfield
MY PERFECT GUY!
I used to have an idea of what I
thought was the perfect guy,
But I thought I'd set my standards a
little too high.
Because all the ones I've ever met
just didn't measure up,
And when it came to the perfect guy,
they were anything but!
I began to wonder where's the guy I
picture, the one I dream about?
Does he exist in this world? I was
beginning to have my doubts.

And then I met this guy who seemed
to be what I was searching for.
I thought he had all the qualities, plus
so much more.
Then I began to realize he was not
my perfect guy,
For he was hiding behind a facade,
one to which I was blind.

Was my idea unrealistic, was I just
fooling myself?
Or was my perfect guy out there,
maybe pushed back on the shelf?
Where was the guy who'd make my
heart skip a beat with a smile,
The one who'd make me feel special
and like someone worthwhile?
The guy who'd not only be my love,
but also my friend,
And the love and respect we felt
between us would never end?

Then one day I got the answers and
my doubts were put to rest.
I no longer had to search and seek for
someone to pass my test.
For there he was right before my
eyes, evidence my idea was true.
And now I see the proof everytime I
look at you!

Barbara Jackson Edwards

Barbara Jackson Edwards
HOUSE OF WONDER

This poem is dedicated in loving memory of my sister, Evelyn.

This old house at the top of the hill
With a fallen porch from time.
The stillness in the air, and the
growth
of the wild roses that
went astray.

Which was once laughter, and
work on this
forgotten piece of land
Lies toys strewn at the edge of
the hedge row now.

Where the old dog often
wondered
lying still by the pillars of the
house.

With one thing that never
changed over these
years,
Is the same breezes that blew
through this
old white
washed door.

Left more memories.

Barbara Jackson Edwards
SCHOOL DAYS
The plaid book bag that we found
among the school papers.
Tells a story from our days
passed,
school house bells, and hot
days long.
Attentive to the school book as
lessons unfold.

Rushing for the door, it's
lunchtime
the sound of the water
fountain fades with the sun.

Playing rock teacher with stones
we have in our hand.
And play Bluebird as we run with
the wind.

Patty (Asher) Cooksey
STOP AND THINK
Stop and think could it all be a
scheme,
Is life real or are we all just part of a
dream?
Can we prove for a fact that we really
exist,
Or are we just a thought floating
through a mist.
Sure we can see, and hear and feel,
But does this actually prove we are
real.
Consider a dream, at times it is of
people and places we know,
How then can we say we really grow.
A dream usually comes from a
memory of the past.
And think of this, life like dreams
wasn't meant to last.
So stop and think could it all be a
scheme,
Is life real or are we in fact just part
of a dream?

Fay Coats
PEACE
Again I visit the ocean.
It never changes though years
may pass
between my visits.
I walk along the beach.
It matters not if the sea is rough
or calm,
the effect on me is the same.

The sea has a rhythm and a
heart beat.
The waves lap against the shore
and recede, only to lap once
more.
A rhythm, a beat that calms and
soothes my spirt.
It heals the brokenness in me,
putting me in touch with the
universe.

I feel its power surging through
me,
restoring, rebuilding.
I marvel that a force so powerful
is at
the same time so gentle.
I am at peace.

Francesca M Cordi
THE RED-HAIRED GIRL
Wet was the night,
So dark and raining—fear raced the
time she had remaining.
Move quickly girl, deep woods are
near. Mother of God!
The British are here!
O'er her blue gown she threw a cape,
Longing to hide within its drape.
Young she was when they
Saw her there, crowned with a mane
of bright red hair. Blindly
She ran—there was no escape!
Wrapped to her chin in the darkling
cape
The British noose 'round her young
white throat, she lay in the road
'Neath a British coat.
"She'll spy no more on the Crown
today!" The Redcoats laughed and
rode away.

Wet is the night,
So dark and raining. Headlights
through the murk are straining.
Down the Turkey Hollow Runs, a
modern kindly couple comes.
Young she is when they see her there,
wet and gleaming
Her bright red hair. A dark cape hides
her long blue gown,
And she asks a ride to a nearby town.
At Blue Lantern Inn,
Of ancient fame, they turn to ask the
girl her name.
All they find in the car's back seat
are the prints
Of her small and muddy feet.

Ronald Nicholas Cervero
TRANSFORMATION
Time is unaccounted for
A dreamstate like no other
With the presence of inner peace
A soul is lifted to the heavens

Engulfed by the love of kings
A spirit soars to judgment
The metamorphosis of life
A chilling realm of realism

Life as we know it—is no more
But our lifeforce lives on
Our core is strewn across a vast
tranquil sea
Eternity's cycle
For mankind
Not to see . . .

Diane Criscola
THE LIGHT

For Babe, who took my hand, and led me into the light . . .

Oh world see the light, it shines from
within
It is generated by honesty, kindness,
and faith,

You can recognize someone who
emits it, by the
Warm, secure feeling you will have
by their presence.

Their smiles are quick, their stance
erect,
An air of confidence, and steadfast
determination
Follows them everywhere,

Their understanding and compassionate natures
Are bright insignias

All people harbor this light, sadly, in
some, it is
Dimmed, by deceit, guilt, and fear.

These are not conductors of energy,
they are the products
Of ignorance, and ignorance must be
displaced with
Enlightenment.

Seek those who shed this light, they
are abundant in the
World. Embrace their teachings,
absorb the rays of their
Knowledge,

Go forth and spread word of it, until
all people, reflecting
One another, shine as one.

Jay Pyon

Jay Pyon
WHICH WAY MUST I GO
Life is complex, full of different
needs
Choosing between right or wrong, we
must indeed
Not knowing what really to expect
Constantly wondering which one to
accept
Who should I listen to, Give me a
clue
Is it God, who has set golden rules
Trying to live right but wrong being
tempting
For living right, what will I be getting
These are questions I do not know
As I ponder, which way must I go.

Jay Pyon
KINDLE HEART
Pete was his name,
But when he left
He was never the same,
Pete was nice and complaisant,
Always very friendly
A helping hand never seemed
hesitant,
Then peers degraded him for his
appearance,
The way he dressed and looked
How his heart ached, he sought
solitude,
From then on, he always seemed
depressed,
His eyes always looking down
So very quiet he keeps things
repressed,
I never knew Pete,
But seeing him leave so sadly
I could've almost wept,
Wherever you are I wish you well,
Hope things won't be as desolate
I know what you went through was
hell,
Kindle Heart, Kindle Heart
To see this, how I was filled with
anger
That a man had to wrongly suffer.

Jay Pyon
BREAK THIS CHAIN
O' Countries torn by pain,
Please unite and break this chain
Senseless killings that you face,
Are we not of same creed and race

Let's settle our differences and start
to care,
For life is precious and was meant to
share
Let's at least try to stop this hate,
Our efforts will put this bitterness to
a bate

In this time of struggle and fear,
Hostility and death is all I seer
O' Countries wash your bloody stain,
Please unite and break this chain.

Jay Pyon
LIVING YEARS
This world of insanity,
No remorse or dignity,
Constant violence and torment,
This is how our days are spent.

Over loaded with many conflicts,
Foreshadowing pain we inflict,
Living in a world full of fears,
As time passes by in our living years.

Carolyn Cason
WATER AND SAND
You were the river that danced
and sang. I was the desert that
stood silently beside. I longed for
you, and you invited me. The cup
of my life bent to you, and I was
refreshed. You have taught me how
to love. I know what my
talents are, and I am not afraid.
Our paths diverge now, 'though it
is not our choice. We must go
our separate ways, painful as it may
be. Know that I will always love
you with all my heart, and I thank
you for what you have given me. And
some day, we will dance and sing
together, in celebration of you.

Virginia "Ginny" Crowe
WHAT IS LOVE
Have you ever heard the
controversy, about the word
called love?
The explanations are as

numerous, as the stars above.
Some love is "endearing," some
love not worth a cent.
They say why bother, when it's
gone, it's spent.

There's "conditional" love, with a
price tag in its hand,
That kind of love gets less
reviews, than a wisp of blowing sand.
"Unconditional" love, has no
restrictions to mar its embrace.
A "desirable" love, sought after,
by the human race.

I've even heard love called "If,"
What kind of love could that be?
I'll love you "If" you'll do this or
that for me.
Then there's "Because" love, A
love most all pursue,
I love you "Because" we're family.
A thing we all should do.

By this time it seems like a mass
confusion.
Are there any way to right, this
mixed-up illusion?
Take the example that was given
to us, about love.
I love you "any way" you are,
created by God above.

Salvation was purchased for us,
that day, when Jesus bled.
With piercing nails in His hands
and feet, a crown of thorns on His
head.
Jesus became our righteous
sacrifice, then His earthly life
was done.
The "ultimate" love, was manifest,
when God gave His only son.

Sandra Harmon Clifton
NATURE'S BEAUTY

The sun generously spills its warmth
as I have never seen,
while the flowers paint a rainbow
on a canvas made of green.

An ambrosial scent fills the air
and rides upon the breeze;
the same gentle breeze that rustles
my hair
then climbs to rustle the trees.

I gaze with wonder at the grace of a
dove
as it sails into carefree flight,
and as I watch, I think to myself,
what a truly magnificent sight.

Though I find all this beauty
amazing,
the most amazing thing surely must
be
that the creator of all nature's beauty
is also the creator of me!

Nita Wilson Clarke
GENERATIONS

To Michael and Michele, The Generation of Today.

My great grandfathers came from
across the sea
And the union of their offspring
created the very beginnings of me.
One black, stolen from his
homeland and sold in front of
an old town hall;
The other one white, came to
America from France wearing only a
nightshirt and a shawl.
I was christened forty years ago
on the altar of my beloved
Holy Ghost Church.
My grandfather built it solid . . . all
concrete and sturdy birch.
I remember racing cousins down
dusty streets to some neighborhood
store
While my grandmother's
silhouette watched over us, lovingly
at the door.
The street where my grandparents
lived still gets muddy in the rain
And though both have gone on to
glory, I even today feel the loss and
the pain.
My father left home to find his
fortune at the tender age of seventeen
But vowed he'd come back one
day to marry his Creole queen.
In three great wars he fought in
the Army and came home a hero
from Vietnam
Only to find hatred and depression
and finally claimed death by his own
hand.
And now the seed of my being
has brought forth the generation of
today
To carry on the traditions, the
customs and the memories tucked
carefully away.
In the perfect order of life that God
has graced upon all nations
One thing remains until the end
of time; life goes on,
generation after generation.

Charlotte Cass
GLOVER SPEAKS

To my wonderful family—Dick and Kathleen, Elsa and Dana—David and Grace, Deborah and Jordan—Bob—Cheryl and Robert, Chartelle and Bonnie-Jean—Richard.

Don't mourn me, Bob, dear master,
friend,—I've lived.
Not so long as you have hoped, may
be,
But—I have lived.

And loved
Each wonderful, precious doggy
minute
With all you helped me cram-jam in
it;
You let me be all I could be
And understood what I had inside.

Don't mourn me, Bob, remember me!
I haven't died,—I go right on
And this sweet secret I share with
you—
I love you more now than I could
then do;

And I'll wait to run again with you,
Exultant, triumphant, at your side;
Don't mourn me, Bob, I haven't died,
I live!

Gary Colvard
LOVE, 200 MILES AWAY

To: Diane Adler (Smoan), "With all my love."

Oh Baby, I love you so,
I really want you to know.
It's easy to come down,
But hard to leave.
Because the one I love,
Is still at the beach.
For each and every mile I ride,
I pray soon you'll be by my side.
But I must go home and make some
plans,
Before I ask for your hand.
If I could tell you the way I feel,
Then you would know my love is
real.

Jordan and Jade Futo

Virginia B Collins
TO JORDAN AND JADE

Dedicated to Jordan and Jade's Family—Wink & Johnny Futo—parents; Wendy & Melba Bagwell—grandparents; Rita & Pete McDuffie—aunt & uncle.

You live in a child's enchanted world
and it's all yours for today
So play your part well—in your little
parade
and learn something new each
day
Here you will run—chase butterflies
spreading your secret wings
Searching for the lost face—of the
eluding wind
as it whispers—plays tag—and
sings

The flowers—the birds—the earth—
are all yours
people are at your command
The mixed up words you say—are so
precious
you're the most important
thing in this land
But don't walk too far—don't learn
too fast
stay as you are for awhile
Don't hurry to grow—there's plenty
of time
for never again—you're a child

Darwin Croff
SUMMER BREEZE

Thanks, Miss Panchuck, Lincoln Cons. High School, Ypsilanti, Michigan.

Super hefty, summer sky.
Unnatural heavy coats; good-bye.
Mystifying summer moon miracle of
night,
gives us light excitement joy, kites in
the
air releaving breeze is everywhere.

Beautiful people come & go,
Reasoning, "it's summer you know!"
Easy to see, better to feel,
Enthusiastic yells, "to the baseball
field!"
Zest, happiness and entertainment
throughout the land.

April Courtney
MOTHER

Thanks for being my Mother, a special; caring and loving human being.

As I grow older, the wisdom of her
words to me,
The world's wrongdoing and evil I
now see.
Molding, holding me up to be in the
right
Her goals are there, always in sight.
Mother's warm heart is pure gold
With the mystery of her knowledge
to be told.
She is there thru the good times and
bad
Been with me when I'm happy or
sad.
She has never wavered when I knew
it all
And was headed for a Fall.
Soothing my wounded pride
When all I wanted to do was hide.
Encouragement she gives me when I
can't succeed
All I have to do is follow her lead.
My colds she's nursed, flu and
scraped knees
With tenderness and loving ease.
Mother, what she means to me,
In her so many wonderful things, I
see.
Words cannot express or tell what I
wish to say
Of all the special deeds given day
after day.
Yes, she is rare, endearing—she's my
Mother.

Edward F Cavanagh
THE GIFT

This poem is dedicated to Catherine, a loving wife, and our beautiful children who inspired me to write my first poem.

To breathe and to walk is such
a wonderful thing.
To feel and to love will
make this world sing.
But before the music sounds
we must all be in step.
To make the sweet song
to a world that has depth.
Why do we feel, and why should
we love, are we all
descended from a dove?
or
Is this a gift from above?
To strengthen our resolve
whoever we are.
For our presence is needed
more so than before.
And we do matter for long
just as the note is to our song.
For our gift is special
and we must spread it along.

Heather Marie Fillion-Cole
JUST THOUGHTS

This poem is dedicated with love to my Mother and Father (Bertha and Norm Fillion), my wonderful husband Rob, and our two sons (Brad and Jason Cole).

When all alone I look on the crumpled dried leaves,
I simply think of God and His great power,
And then I wonder how He ever sees,
Us from His high and ever sturdy tower.
Wishing I was like Him in every way,
Considerate, forgiving and oh, so very kind,
Wanting Him to send me down His praise,
To give me strength and possible peace of mind.
Though in my thoughts I often go astray,
And think of other things such as the sky,
I really do believe it all the way,
That God is always closely standing by.
The wonder of it all is simply packed,
Inside this man-made world and tightly latched.

Terry Morris

Terry Morris
DEATH
Die, die
I kill them all
Even the mighty
They shall fall.
I am the darkness
That you all fear
But you can't avoid me
When I am here.
For when I strike
I strike with precision
The day you die
That's my decision.
Upon my arrival
You'll breathe your last breath
You will die
For I am Death!

Lois M Conklin
WHAT IS A FATHER

To dad with love on Father's Day.

A father is a daughter's first love!
The very first man in her heart,
A father is a son's first hero!
For a father can do what no one else can do,
He works and provides for his children and spouse!
For we all know he is the man of the house
Day after day and year after year
He sees to our needs so we have no fear,
When money is tight he'll always give up!
So that his children and spouse have the last in the cup.
Even when Mom can't do for herself!
He jumps right in because he's top shelf.
Father is an understanding man!
He knows when you hurt or just need a hand!
He's always right there no matter what,
With a shoulder to lean on to help with much,
So Father's Day should be the whole year through,
Because, he's always there for me and you

Gary Eizenwasser
HOME, SWEET HOME
The wind chills him to the bone,
But it wouldn't be so if he had a home.

The days: dreary, the nights: stark black,
"Worldly possessions" tucked in a knapsack.

Could be worse, he thinks, softly crying.
I'm on the street, but damn, I'm trying.

Unemployment, welfare: talk, talk all around.
Politician's masterplans, yet no dignity to be found.

I'm not a bum, he thinks, I don't ask for much.
Just a guy like Bogie said:
". . . who's down on his luck."

Stars hang up above, which one to pick for wishin'?
Souplines grow and grow each night, down at the mission.

"Handouts," "gimmes," charity all the same.
A frightening portrait of hopeless-ness, anxiety, pain.

Cursed at, kicked at, hardened like a stone.
Curling up like a baby, into a cardboard box called "home."

Lori Chase
FOR YOU, I'D STEAL BACK MY HEART FROM ANOTHER
For you, I'd steal back my
heart from another.
For you, I'd forsake all
that is mine.
For you, I'd give my all,
for you are my everything.
I've loved you none too
discreetly, but most
certainly. (I thought most
obviously.)
I love you to the point of
obsession—or very
nearly.
I love you to the point of
desperation.
I would give my life over
to you.
I would give my life for you—
most definitely.

Michael L Collins Jr
I DO
Her hair so silky,
Against her attire,
It sets the scene, for the ultimate desire,
A woman in crimson,
So full of joy.
She keeps her eye, on that certain boy.
This lady to me,
so wonderfully kind.
Who 'deavors daily, with an open mind.
Her love so sweet,
like the cherries from a tree.
With a feeling so strong, it aches to break free.
Her honesty so pure,
it has to be true.
For she clings to love, like something anew.
This wonderful woman,
so sweet, so kind, and true.
Loves me enough, to say yes; I Do.

Lenora Green
WONDERFUL WORLD OF CHILDREN

To My Mother who loved poetry and expressed it in love for her family and others.

Being part of a large family
Four brothers and sisters three
The riches of our childhood
Were the flowers, grass and trees.

The house where we lived
Was on a small country farm
But memories of our childhood there
Is of a paradise soft and warm.

All the riches of the world
Or palaces great and high
Cannot compare to that home
In the green valley beneath the sky.

No toys, had we to call our own
We all just ran, and played
Yet never did we ever have
A single lonely day.

All the world we thought was ours
It lay beneath our feet
When we would walk in the woods
Among nature's beauty, sweet.

Only a child can see just good
There is no bad to them
If only adults could be this way
There would be peace among men.

Lenora Green
A CHILD'S DREAM LAND
Looking out the window
At thousands of lights aglow
Stretched out like a city
In the great black space below.

I feel like a princess
In her castle on a hill
Watching the blinking of the lights
In the night so soft and still.

How mighty it makes one feel
To be living up so high
It seems like if you lift your hand
You could touch the sky.

But all that lay beneath me
Are some cinders in the night
Just coals from wood that papa burnt
Giving off some light.

Oh the child in Dreamland
Their imagination whirls
Always some beautiful make-believe
Where adventure is all theirs.

Lenora Green
WONDERS OF THE NIGHT
Weary ones why linger there
Lift your soul with peace unknown
For just outside in the still of night
You can find such sweet atone.

For when day light fades, and darkness falls
While old mother earth is still
The moon and stars shine far aloft
And light the yonder hills.

The whippoorwills sing soft and low
Echoing far into the night
The wise owl hoots and crickets chirp
With the fireflies' blinking lights.

The trees and plants stand straight and tall
As though reaching for the sky
The creek calls out with a merry sound
As its water rushes by.

The mysteries of God never cease
When the light fades away
For nighttime peace and tranquility
Is as magnificent as the day.

Lenora Green
SMALL FEATHERED FRIENDS
Tiny Humming Birds fluttering south
Escaping from the cold ice and snow.

Their small wings are always a blur
Glittering miniature rainbows, as they go.

Gathering nectar for strength, they depart
While contributing to nature, they endure.

How delightful the humming of their wings
As we gaze with fascination and allure.

From northwest to southwest in summertime
Anywhere, they can be found I've heard.

You might happen upon and discover our
Jeweled feathered friends, the Humming Bird.

Lenora Green
MIGHTY WHITE ASPEN
The mighty white aspen, towering so high
Its spreading branches protectively hover.
Many small animals striving beneath
To survive the storms of nature, find cover.

Below are squirrel, red fox and rabbits no doubt
A gopher, weasel and beaver their territory subdue,
The grouse, chickadee, woodpecker flutter about
While sparrow, songbirds and owl furnish the hue.

The aspen spans a time in years, about that of humans
Budding competitively with the pussy willow in springtime
Growing a bloom on the side to protect from the summer sun
Changing color of leaf to a golden bright, for autumn sublime.

Smaller insects like the ant love its nectar
Caterpillar who thrives on the leaves becomes beautiful butterfly.
Even the tiny aphid and beetle find support of life
In this tall white swaying beacon reaching to the sky.

The roots continue on, developing new small aspen
Or its seed, "the catkins" blow with the wind, produce at will.
Even when the mighty aspen falls to the ground,
Mingling with leaves, nature plants and animals still.

Lenora Green
NATURE'S SEASON BEAUTY
Springtime has its lovely flowers
With rustling little brooks that flow
Brought about by spring showers
That God sent to make them grow.

Summer sunshine then comes around
Everything is green from trees on down
Birds and animals run and play
Everyone is happy on summer days.

Next comes Fall with colors bright
Yellow, orange, brown and red
Old Jack-Frost comes around each night
And all the leaves fall to their earthly bed.

Winter snow tops the earth with fluffy white
That glistens like a thousand diamonds in the light
And even when the cold wind blows
Spring time comes again we know.

The seasons come and seasons go
With their beauty in bright array
All things come from God we know
And thanks we give to him this day.

Lenora Green
GOD'S ALMIGHTY CREATION
In God's creation the universe displays
Sun, moon and stars in magnificent ways.
The earth spinning around its axis in center
Day then night follows as spring, summer, fall and winter.
Rushing rivers with waterfalls make a wide ocean casting.
Explosive volcanoes take and give life in its passing.
Majestic masses of the huge mountains towering high.
The depth of a steep ravine or sloping valley lie.
Clouds with turbulent winds blowing about
Cleansing rain in sprinkle or thundering without.
THE FORCE OF GOD'S ALMIGHTY CREATION!

Developing cycles of tiny insects that amaze
Live their lives and die only completing a phase.
The migrating knowledge that fish and fowl bring
Leaving their birthplace but return producing offspring.
The beauty and regeneration of plants and flowers
Radiating their colorful hues, for enjoyment of ours.
Experiencing peace in study of nature is found
A presence of a supreme power, but softness abound.
Conceived and nurtured in the womb the miracle of birth
Beast and man alike planned to replenish the earth.
THE FORCE OF GOD'S ALMIGHTY CREATION!

Lenora Green
MY HOME PLACE
No matter when or where I roam
In God's big beautiful land
Nowhere can take the place of home
And I know it never can.

For each memory of my home place
To me is something dear
Each tomorrow will not erase
My childhood days of there.

Dad and Mom will always make
The memories much more bright
A visit there when they are gone
Will never seem just right.

It seems everyone loves most
The land of their old home place
No matter where from coast to coast
It's in the heart of our human race.

Pearl Chafin
A YOUNGER GIRL'S CLONE

This poem is dedicated to my granddaughter, Shayne Heather Chafin, my inspiration.

Your innocence was masked for understanding,
You didn't ask for much, but very demanding.
While you would cry on my ready shoulder,
I finally realized! that I was so much older.
You sat calmly, as I prepared to leave.
I told you "It's over," my heart on my sleeve.
I didn't know leaving would be this hard,
Even, though I knew, I wasn't your lover, only your guard.
I tried to shield you from the hurtful truth,
And thought you deserved the naivete of youth.
I was certain, you were not playing games, yet, I
Found we weren't together; only familiar names.
Why is my heart still drawn to your soul? When I
Know my experience is your only goal, and why do I
Yearn to tell you, my secrets, thoughts, dreams and
Fears, when it's all too clear, that you never
Wanted my words, merely my years.
It's an empty feeling being with you, I'm all alone,
And that you would love me, if I were a younger's clone, wore younger
Girl's clothes, and smelled of a younger girl's cologne.

Lorene Carol Evens
TO MY PARENTS
I looked up to you
In that less than
Middle class house in Texas.

I ran to you Daddy,
Held out my baby arms,
And you abused me.

I remember your steely eyes,
Yellow nicotine stained fingers,
And your serpent smile.

I ran to you Mother.
You slapped me,
And I tasted blood.

I remember the look in your eyes,
Clean, oh-so-hard hands, and the
Cruel line of your blood red mouth.

And nothing will make me forget,
Nothing will make me forget!

Now, when darkness comes,
I lie in soft covers, and
Play a past of my own . . .

I run to you Daddy,
In our house on Paradise Street.

You lift me high and kiss me.

Your eyes are warm.
Strong arms protect me, and
Your smile is oh-so-tender.

I run to you Mother.
You caress my cheek,
And I taste your nurturing.

Your eyes are soft.
Gentle hands hold me, and
Your love red mouth is kind.

And you can never take it away,
You can never take it away!

Gloria Edmonson
TRY MY FRIEND
I have a friend who is dear to me
A friend who hears me through my tears
A friend who listens to my fears
A friend I know sincerely cares
A friend who my burden bears
A friend who holds my hand in his
A friend who dries up all my tears.

My friend doesn't judge me when I'm wrong
My friend will listen to my song
My friend strokes me when I'm in need
And never shows any signs of greed.

Have you a friend like my friend
who will be with you until the end
who will hear your problems over and over
and never scold you like your lover?

If you don't have a friend like mine
Why not start by accepting mine?
Open your heart and trust in God.
He'll lead you each and every day.
Just trust in him to lead the way.

I have a friend who is dear to me,
dearer to me!

Tammy Brook DeNio
THE FACE IN THE MIRROR
Oh everyone just doesn't care, but I guess I mean me cuz I don't dare. So many friends have gone away. They wanted me to help them, but I couldn't stay. I was too busy hiding from the face in the mirror. I didn't have time to hear their tears. I wasn't there for their fears.
Now all I have are some cats and a friend, and I hope I don't make that mistake again. So I give to you a small word of advice: Take some time and try and be nice.
Take some time and help out a friend, cuz you may never have that chance again.
So . . . don't ignore their reaching out. Don't ignore their silent shout. Don't go away when there's people who fear. Then you won't be afraid of the face in the mirror.

Marilyn Dana
WE WALTZ IN ANOTHER DIMENSION
A kiss that could not be taken,
For other promises have been made.
Love at first sight that's forsaken,
What a wasted warmth of light.
It shines in protective darkness,
As I seek you out at night.
We waltz in another dimension,
For you live in my dreams.
And you are a tingly sensation,
That I don't want to leave.
Yet morning does come,
And others do depend.
But when I close my eyes to rest,
These hours with you I spend.

Joseph H Young

Joseph H Young
AN ODE TO WOLFHOUND SERGEANT KATE

I'm a Black Poet. I've been writing poetry for more than 42 years. This Ode Poem is a fare-well poem to our "Sgt. M. Kate," "1st Plt. Sgt. Co. C.27th Wolfhound's R.C.T., 25th Inf. Div." on his rotating back to his U.S. Home State, Oklahoma from "Koje Island, Yellow Sea of Japan." February, 1952. (KOREAN WAR. 1950-3) ("G. I. Joe Young, Koje Island Ode Style.")

G.I.s come gather around me,
I will tell one clean and clear:
It's one of the truest stories,
As wind blowing in the air.

Sergeant Kate from "Schofield Barracks,"
Was soldier from toe to ear:
Spanked the rump of a bob-tail cat,
Then drank up his weight in beer.

He strolled into the wild jungle,
And shaved a mad tiger hair:
When nothing to do but fumble,
He waltzed with a grizzly bear.

He whipped the strongest gorilla,
And tore his body apart:
When the animals rose and cried,
He gave him a "Trans-planted Heart."

He flew up and caught an eagle,
And "*Wing-cuffed" him in mid-air:
Said: "If You Ever Scratch Again,"
"You Won't Have Claws To Spare."

He swam in the deepest ocean,
And saddled the biggest whale:
When there was no more commotion,
He booted an elephant tail.

Now, when it's time for judgement day,
Please! Be a cherub with a bell:
'Cause "Sergeant Kate's Ambuscader,"
May sneak down and Ambush Hell.

The Marines, Air Forces, and Navies,
That strut through the pearly gate:
They'll notice that the guardian name,
Is An "Army Sergeant Kate's."

If there's another brave soldier,
Has guts aplenty to spare:
"None Dare To Touch!" "Wolfhound Sergt. Kate's."
The next hundred thousand years.

Lisa Darsow
SPARKLES
When you look into my eyes,
What do you see?
Sparkles . . .
Why! Because when you love someone, you always
have twinkles in your eyes . . .
The twinkles in my eyes are like stars . . .
And when I look into your
eyes those same stars
sparkle back . . .

Fredda C Dokken
EPHEMERAL VIEWS
I sit by my window
And rejoice at the view.
Which is everchanging
And always new.

There's the water, the sky,
Sea lions and ferries,
And all the day long,
The activity varies.

A myriad of images
Float swiftly by
When I watch the
Languid or angry sky.

As the evening approaches,
It's a sight to behold
When the windows of the city
Turn to bright gold.

Life in the hereafter
Is a mystery, we know,
But, through nature, I believe
God guides us below.

Rosemary Davis
ANNA
Anna
Hair like golden wheat.
Anna's kisses of honey sweet
We walk through life hand in hand
The love we shared a silver wedding band.

Anna
Under our oak tree I now stand
With tears in my eyes, holding your ring in my hand
Remembering the starry night we carved our heart
Promising never to part.

Deborah Grace Daniels
COUNTDOWN
Countless times I've orbited
this place called Earth!
Countless times I've heard
the distressed cries of its people!
Countless times I've seen the
destruction of their lives!
Countless times I've inhaled
the acrid scent of pain!
Countless times they've tasted
the bitter kiss of death!
Count this time that I would breathe
into them the Light of Peace.

Elda M Dennis
MODELS' LAMENT
I sit here, up above them, musing, posing
working, motionless, counting,
thinking, dreaming, dozing
Hard at work, looking lazy
fatigue so great, time so endless, smoke so hazy.
I count the window panes, tiles on the floor
flannel shirts, easels, benches, lights, panels on the door
Chair legs, table legs, human legs and all,
Cigarette butts, and bricks upon the wall
I trace each line with the finger of my eye
Outside, a bird chirps, winging 'gainst the sky
Call each minute a dime, the hours are precious
I'm tired—so tired, but soon—oh, break time!

Cecilia N Stahl

Cecilia N Stahl
SOLITUDE

To my husband, children, grandchildren, great grandchildren and the whole world with love.

O Lord
The grandeur of Your Universe
is unfathomable
and
eons old
The beauty of it forever new.
The singing and calls of the birds
Like a choir of Angels
Tuning up to burst out in loud song
In Praise and Honor to Your Majesty.

The silent winging of the Butterflies
In their Magnificent colors, as if
to outdo each other
to
Please You!

Could Man just awaken
for a moment

Before passing on, and
Share your peaceful and
Magnificent Beauty in all things,
How Peaceful the World could be
How Peaceful Man could be
Sharing Your Magnificent,
Bountiful World
Forever.

Cecilia N Stahl
A DIFFERENT ME?
A different me is shaping up
And a new routine of different things
Than I am used to doing now.
How quickly Life can change
Form one moment to the next
One day is good, the next day fair
Then suddenly like a streak of light
The side of you that wasn't there
Emerges out of its cocoon
And a different World, like sun and moon
Becomes that different me.

The new routines take over because of necessity
How wonderful it feels to find that side of you
That you thought could never be
Give you much more than felicity.

Goodby: old friend, I won't forget that for all these three
quarters of a century
You've been there for me, to scrimp along and save
to raise my family, battling adversity
Now it's my children's times, to laugh and play and grow
And raise their families, the same as I.

Goodbye old friend, and with a sigh, I say
Just a "fanciful metamorphosis," I really haven't
changed at all
It's still the same old me!

Cecilia N Stahl
HOPE, LOVE, AND PEACE
Hope: Don't wander away
My feelings rise to peaks of ecstasy
Dreaming of success which may or may not come my way
Today, Tomorrow, January, March or May!
Love: The Life giving emotion that's like no other
Today the world is lacking in giving of themselves
They say, "Why bother, why bother."

So, Love falls by the wayside,
when it could give you Life, not Strife
To the world as a whole, to all
Sisters and Brothers
The happiness and emotions like no others
Give of yourself, give to others,
and don't say,
"Why bother, why bother."

Peace: Pray for Peace, the World needs it
Each human being needs it
Our Lord promises Peace, if each one of us prays for it
Peace, Contentment, Love and Hope abound
Within you, outside of you and all around.

Then sing "Peace to the World"
An Anthem so sweet
It tugs at your heart strings
And makes you weep
As it floats in the Air
To humankind around the World
O Lord, accept our plea
And let there be Peace.

Claire Dufour
1 TO 10
On a scale
of 1 to 10
I've often wondered
Where I would end

There are times
When I'm just fine
But could I ever be
A # 9?

Or something happened
That's just great
I'd be happy
With a # 8

Then other days
I feel real low
I may be near
A fat zero

Now #1
I just can't see
as being much fun
So that's not for me

On other days
could there be a few
When I would settle
for a # 2

When I just feel
Wild and free
How far could I go
On a # 3

Would I accept
A # 4
To me that ain't
Much of a score

Why go half way
When aiming high?
I could grab more
Than a # 5

Days when I
Feel kind of sick
A friend's smile
Could lift me to a 6

A gentle hug
Would be heaven
From someone special
I could easily be a 7

Working things out
One day at a time
Not being a #
Sounds divine

For a # I wasn't
Meant to be
I'll just be satisfied
That God made me.

Margaret Flexer Duncan
NEVER SHALL I REGRET
Never shall I regret feeling too deeply
Or soaring like eagles when my heart must sing
Some miniscule happening others deem wholly
Unworthy of causing the heart's reveling.
Never shall I regret that I have wept over
Beauty that I have found too great to bear.
Long, long ago it was mine to discover
That we are the fortunate, all we who care
For loveliness lost in a maze of mad mist
Stealing in from the sea on a September shore,
For Truth that can blind in a moment of faith
And the knowledge we never can be as before.
This and this only does my whole heart fear:
That Beauty or Truth call and I might not hear.

Emily Dunie
MY DREAM
I sit here on the porch of Paradise.
The breeze brings a cold chill to my skin,
which is tinted with a dark brown color.
I feel fresh and free of all my worries.
I slowly gaze into the sky of sparkling diamonds.
So many sweet jewels, with so much past.
I realize no matter where you go,
these jewels always seem to follow.
I hear the sweet tune of the band in the distance.
The rhythm repeats endlessly.
But each time it seems to be closer and closer,
until, I finally doze into a silent sleep.
I'm awakened by the first glimpse of the sun.
The sun is reluctantly rising from the ground.
At the same speed it sank into the sea.
The air is humid but feels very comfortable.
My days are spent in this endless Paradise.
The watch of the day to night.
Each is different in scenery but there is the same comfortable and content feeling
I've always longed for!

Marjorie Doupe
SUCH IS LIFE
As I sit thinking, accepting today as it was
yesterday is gone and tomorrow has not come
My sorrows are few, to compare to some
How lucky I think
I do not drink, nor do I smoke
But I do enjoy drinking a Diet Coke
I try not to complain, I do the best I can
Life on earth can be pleasant or a pain
I wish for plenty of sunshine and a little rain
With plenty of profit and more to gain

Krista Davies
STAINED GLASS DRIVEWAY
A child's small hands drag white lines into pictures.
Butterflies and flowers appear on a concrete canvas.
Birds take flight and snakes squirm in zig zag fashion.

Father's voice is stern and I must listen in my small way.
Water gushes forth and my flowers wilt into a white stream.
My butterflies and birds can't escape the killing flood.
The snake is drowned and the driveway is barren again.
Only the water in my eyes defeats the sun's drying rays.

Now I am grown with little artists of my own.
They too see the concrete canvas and query "May we?"
So I give them the chalk with colors that I had dreamed of.
Their little hands creating imagination and now my driveway is beautiful.

There is no fear of floodwaters washing away their happiness and the sun shines merrily on the stained glass driveway.

Debra Ashley Mahnoori

Debra Ashley Mahnoori
IN MEMORY OF . . .

This poem is dedicated with love to my grandfather, John T. McKnight (1917-1988), and my uncle, Michael J. McKnight (1950-1984).

There were times made of laughter
And tender moments filled with tears
Continuously giving of yourself
Throughout the passing years

Talking over problems
Lending a helping hand
Taking time to listen
Trying to understand

Doing your best to make me smile
Showing how much you care
Letting me know when I need someone
You always will be there

It's this and so much more
That's made me smile each day
And every night I prayed to God
We'd always be this way

For you've taught me how to love
And helped me to be free
Yet you've done all this so simply
By letting me be me

But now we must go our separate ways
For your journey's at an end
What I'm really trying to say is
Thank you for being my friend

Sharon E Daniel
WITH MY HAND ON MY HEART

With my hand on my heart I stand giving the Pledge,
still with pride and gratitude but feeling on edge.
I've worked long and hard but if I couldn't pay,
the mortgage on the home I go home to each day,
in just a matter of weeks, I could become
one of the homeless, a beggar, a bum.
When the barons need write-offs, our factories close
we hear on the news "unemployment again rose!"
I trust in our motto, Justice for All
but sadly I watch the unfortunate fall.
As more taxes are needed by Old Uncle Sam,
to hand out to countries that don't give a damn,
Are the streets any warmer in the old U.S.A.?
Have all of our children eaten today?

Edward B Donaldson
REASONS TO REMEMBER MOM

The word MOTHER is a lot like the word IF, the definition is so big that man can't measure it.

They're with you in the beginning; and they'll stand by you till the end. If something were to happen to my mother, my world would surely end.

That's the reason why I like to show my mother that I love her, at least once a year; and I want to love her while she's still here, because when she's gone, there will never be another, as sweet and dear, as my mother.

So I wrote her this poem to brighten her day, and tell her I Love her and Happy Mother's Day.

Christine Dixon
THE CAPTIVE

the dark, the silence is deafening
the deafness so complete
not alone; yet lonely
a prison no boundaries—no bars
in itself a prison the likes of which no escape can master
solitude blessed solitude
the dream too vivid
the reality too much dream, cruel
cruelty (too beautiful) beauty in itself
perfection is mastery
art unto itself the artiste, the victim
uncomprehending (unwilling)
dawn streaks the sky, darkness fades
as does humanity creatures humane
and otherwise scamper
the bewitching hour nears
night recedes, strength fades, hope ebbs
low tide, high tide
screams fading, dying not
haunting melodies . . . chains falling
drooping lower still
pain, misery constant companions
friends till the ever near end.

Anita Davis
ALL I SEE

The warmth of our bodies,
Will shatter the world.

Loving arms wrapped,
Around me.

Untouched,
By anyone but you.

I search for something,
To hold on to.

You are all.
I have.

Not forever,
To be mine.

But for now,
You are all I see.

Carole J Cannavaro RN
WINTER'S TREE

To my Father's memory—Alfred Dostaler.

Stark but beautiful to see
spread across the snow with dignity
the shadow of the naked tree

The moon's reflection on the snow
bends gracefully as winter winds blow
silhouettes in the night, dancing to and fro

Crystalline branches—a jeweled delight
a touch of class to this awesome sight
glittering—gleaming from celestial light.

Evy Daugherty
ALL TOO SOON

As I watched the little girl
play along the shore,
with all the energy of youth,
I saw myself in her so very long ago.
Her snow-white hair blowing in the gentle breeze
seemed to stand out so soft and fine
against her amber-colored skin
darkened by the kiss of summer sun,
Living now her tender years
building castles in the sand.
Cherish these days, oh little one, I thought,
for all too soon the winds of time
like grains of sand so swiftly slip
through our fingers,
making yesterdays so readily of our new tomorrows.
Yes, where does time go in its silent passing?
For someday, so very much like me,
yes once again, your hair will be a snowy-white.

Janet Donovan
THE RAPTURE

I'm waiting for The Rapture
For God said someday it would be
When He would descend from the sky
And take up you and me
To that lovely place in Heaven
Where we will be at home
Away from all the cares and strife
And never be alone

So now take up your bible
Read 1 Thessalonians, Chapter 4 Verse 17
That tells the whole true story
Of what is going to be
It's the promise of a reunion
Just for you and me

Each day I try to picture it
Especially all the happy faces
That includes all the colors in the world
And all the different races
It will be a United Nations
Like we've never had before
No more arguing, bickering, or fighting
And especially no more war.

Linda Gail Harris

Linda Gail Harris
I AM FOREVER

To All People here on Earth, beyond in the Star System The Universe for We are One.

I am Forever
Forever is what I am, I am up above, beyond And
adown below. I am at your right and left
Don't you know.
Forever is what I am. I am in your front and
at your back.
I am your center and that's a fact.

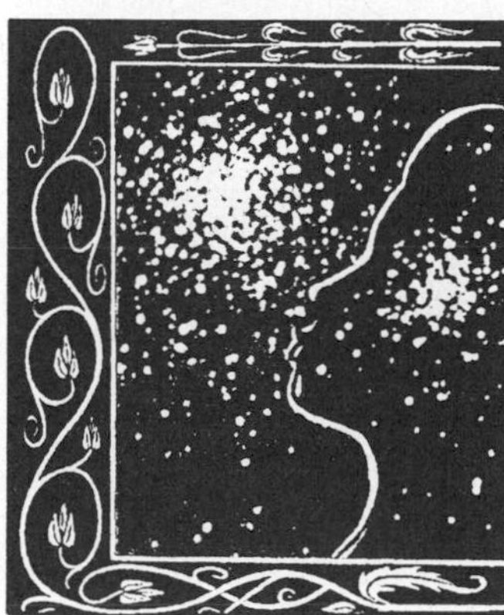

Forever is what I am
I am Concept, the Name and the Number.
I am Time, Space and Matter
I am the Universe
I am forever Creation
I am Forever.

Laura L Upton
CHRISTMAS TIME

Here it is Christmas time . . .
More now than ever,
I can't get you off my mind.

All the times we shared in the past,
all the crying, all the laughs.

It's not easy to forget,
how much love we shared,
and how much it meant.

Never will there be another,
that could take the place,
of the friend and lover,
that I had in you.

Willie Smith
LOST LOVE

I was sitting here thinking of things we might have done
Lying here under the sun

Ain't it funny how your mind will do
When it starts to play tricks on you

It was like the fantasy I had thinking of you
It was about a lost love, that was so true

Her eyes were like diamonds, that sparkled in the night
Her hair was long, shiny and black,

Her lips were like roses on a sunny day
and with her heart, she could make time pass away

Her walk was smooth, sexy and pure
She was the kind of woman that any man would want to endure

When I first saw her, I was blinded by her light
From the love in her heart that was so bright.

Her body was like an artist took his time
And I knew one day she would be mine

But this fantasy did come true,
It's the love I have, each time I look at you.

Helen Hedrick
DIRECTIONS

Few men know the path his life will take
the direction in which to go,
It seems that fate just leads him there
by detour, chance and woe.

And once we walk that path of life
it's a lesson we will learn,
we cannot trace our footsteps back
it's a memory we have earned.

We can't go back to yesterday
for we have crossed the line,
those days are gone, like prints in sand
they've been swept away by time.

Make each step count along the way
don't stop and rest too long,
Set out each day with a goal in mind
for our time will soon be gone.

DeniseAnn Diaz
FRIENDSHIP

To mom & dad, with love, DeniseAnn.

Friends can easily come and
they can easily disappear,
Just a call away
they are always there.
A friend knows you're not
perfect but loves your
company anyway.

Friends are special
caring and true
making sure that you're
never feeling blue.
Best friends are hard to find
You are a special friend
I'm sure glad that you're mine.

A friend will stand beside you
in good times or in bad
chasing all your sadness away
any time night or day.

Friendship is like a ring
it has no end
and that's how long
you'll have me as a friend.

Wendy Burnette
AIN'T GOT
Ain't got no family
Ain't got friends
Ain't got no hand to hold
If the world should end.
Ain't got no extra chair
For company
'Cause I ain't got no-one
To come and see me.
Ain't got no person
Who cares if I cry
Ain't got no tender hand
To wipe my eyes dry.
Ain't got no laughter
In my dreary home
Guess the only thing I got
Is me.
All alone.

Peggy R Gibbs
CAN WE WIN

I dedicate this to my mother, Norma Rodgers (God bless you).

Can we win
Know I say again
The trees aren't green anymore
The sky isn't that color blue
The people don't know who is really who
All the faces are the same
They don't care if it's your brother or sister or me
We live in a world that is
Going downhill
And soon none of us will be free

Jennifer C Siddle
HIGH FINANCE
Financial terms are often funny,
When professionals speak of money.
Words appear like "caps and collars,"
"Offshore funding" and "Eurodollars."

A strong "bullish" trend is on the way
Is what the forecasters and bankers say.
Then they switch and talk of "bears"
While seated in their high-backed chairs.

In Europe they even have a "snake"
With volatile movements to cause headache.
The stronger currencies do quite fine
And weak ones barely toe the line.

Portfolio managers are ill at ease
When they face a "liquidity squeeze."
Freezing prices bring inflation down
But produce many a worried frown.

Governments seek currencies to unite
Which puts the financial world in fright.
Turmoiled markets seem here to stay,
Financiers live with them every day.

Rebecca Lancaster Slate
IF I COULD SHOW MY LOVE FOR YOU

To Family and Very Special Friends, Your Faith in me And Your Encouragement will always be my Inspiration.

If I were a Nightingale I would not be weary of my song
I would sing your praises all the day long.

If I were words of love,
My thoughts would come from heaven above,
To please you to your heart's delight—
Like golden rays of sunlight.

If I were a rose I would bloom just for you
When your skies were blue.

My petals in soft pink caress,
Await to celebrate your happiness,
But when your skies are gray,
I would bloom in yellow to brighten your day.

If I were a rainbow and my colors in fluorescence did shine,
I would ensure your happiness until the end of time.

If I were a bright and shining morning star,
And everyone could see me near and far,
I would shine only for you,
So as to make your every wish come true.

But I am not all these magical things:
I could never be a shining star or a bird who so beautifully sings;
I'm just a person whose life you have so lovingly touched.
And this is the reason why I love you so very very much.

Linda Russell
HE STARED AT ME
Far out, late one night, I was alone in my dream
And it came to me, slowly like a fog drifting in;
Slowly, it formed an image
That image, the image, it frightened me,
It was Loneliness.
Loneliness with no one beside him to share
In any future plans or desires.
A solitary tear crept down my cheek;
I brushed it away,
Quickly with no sound so as not to cause to wind to stir.
He stared at me, Loneliness did and I saw
That he, too, was crying. Crying freely;
And a chill overcame me. I tried to leave, to get away
But I could not.
For forever Loneliness stood there and cried, it seemed,
But not really.
Soon I felt a warmness. It was from all around me.
A faint glow began to creep into that cold sky and soon,
very quietly, Loneliness started to shatter.
Pleadingly, he reached for me, but I, I was safe;
I opened my eyes, and my heart, and You were there.

Ingrid A Maraj
ME AGAIN
I wanted to die,
love is very deceiving.
I depend on him,
as he on me.
We had a bound
but now, he is gone.
If I knew, this was his last,
I would have said so much more.
Things I wanted to say, but never had.
Because of timing, all wrong.
He had been a part of me.
When we met
life was full of affection,
tenderness . . .
Blinded by love.
Now he's gone,
I am alone, again.

Ingrid A Maraj
NATURE
We have neither Spring nor Summer.
Neither Autumn nor Winter.

With golden sun-shine
peeping through the windowpane.
And the rainy days,
beats against the roof
like wiping lashes
as the lightning strikes.
The trees,
wrestling with the wind,
knots up to a hundred.
Refering is the thunder.
There are days, when leaves fade
from the blister of the sun.
Or just,
the fresh scent of flowers blossom.

This beauty hides just like a wave comes ashore.
Nature changes by its seasons.
Golden sun-shine or crystal rain,
Or twinkling stars like diamonds
with a misty moon-light.
Nature, it's natural.

Tanja LeValdo
RAIN
My world was once like a pure white cloud
Pure as the first rains that gracefully danced
on the untouched ground
Like a baby taking its first step

Now my world is but only a
shapeless black cloud
shapeless, like a mysterious bruise
And when the impatient rains beat the ground
like an unaware child abuser
The ground has no choice but to take in the
sharp burning pain
As though it was a teen pressured to taking
its first drink of whisky

But now my world will be longing
for its last rains
Yet is still filled with a shivering
desirable urge
to fall on someone or something so it too can
feel the pain
Just like a teen lost in one's self is trying to find
a way to rain . . .

Michael James Caron
FLOWERS ON MY MIND

I would like to dedicate this poem to Shirley Westgate, the woman that taught me how to appreciate the flowers, and God, and life itself.

Why can't we smell the flowers,
when winter finally comes?
The fresh bouquets of roses, the daffodils and mums.
The fragrance fills the air we breathe,
traveling through our lungs,
intoxicating sweetness, nurtured by the Sun.

It's sad to see the summer gone, and winter moving in,
the flower beds all dying, it seems like such a sin.
I try to think, on cold bleak days, that the flowers are within.
I close my eyes and see them there,
swaying gently in the wind.

The frost is on the windows, the flowers are on my mind.
Tenderness engulfs me, the visions are so fine.
I smell the fragrance once again, like grapes upon a vine.
All the different types are there,
growing in a line.

So when the summer passes by, and winter finally comes,
lock the memories in your mind, of daffodils and mums,
and the frost upon your window, will sparkle in the Sun

Stanley Anthony Burer
A (WHALE) OF A PRAYER
They play in the ocean like kids in the sand
yet they try to talk to us well in hand,
Don't harm us, we really are your friends
if you do, our lives will come to an end.

We love the sun, we love the rain,
please don't hurt us bringing back the pain.
We love our lives like you people do,
for God created us, you know it's true.

We are the Whales of the wide blue sea
please won't you help us and set us free.
While we still wait for your answer to come,
we'll go on having our fun.

Tara Lynne Jennison (12 years old)
TIME
Our love is just like a flower
that isn't going to live very long.
Each time we make a mistake
or try to go too fast—a petal falls off
and slowly blows away.
I want you to know our love
can last and our flower won't die if
we just take our time.

Carol Payer
FATAL ELIMINATION
Who determines majority or minority?
It certainly isn't votes, counts or superiority.
Everything on earth has a beginning somewhere,
In human affairs, one person, brave enough to care.

A child named David killed a giant with a toy.
Mozart amazed kings when he was only a boy.
A singular woman wanted a vote, not just to feel pity,
One black man named King led a march on the city.

Then there was Hitler, killing millions, to form a perfect race,
And we execute babies. "It's different in our case."
"It's an embryo, a thing, not a person, living."
So into the trash goes a lifetime of ONE giving.

Continuity's not the only reason God made parenthood.
It makes you reach your own zenith; love, wisdom, to be understood.
So think twice. You may be in the mass minority,
But giving birth to the ONE majority.

In 1990 ______ ____________
was born, now famous for improving our world.

Carol Payer
A KISS IN THE BREEZE
I'm five weeks old, I'm growing to be born.
I'm going to laugh, work, even learn how to mourn.
Ouch! Something's pulling my leg, my arm, there goes my head.
Oh my God! I can't believe it! I think I'm dead.

Wow! Look at those souls. They sure are big.
Next to them I look like a dried up fig.
But their arms are open, I fly to them in space.
Now I visit the stars, Mars, I go any old place.

While you're lying on the beach in the very hot sun,
Maybe at a dull party not having much fun.
You'll feel a kiss in the breeze on your cheek.
You'll ask "What the heck was that? A nature freak?"

But "It's only me" giving you comfort and love.
I'll be there when I'm needed like the Spirit above.
But for the rest of your life, you'll feel regret, then wonder,
"Would it have been someone special? Did we make a big blunder?"

It's Too Late!!!

But I love you, Daddy and I'm close to my mother.
Oh oh, gotta go now, gotta welcome another.

Carol Payer
VISION? OR WARNING!
When Genesis was young in early B.C.,
An Ark on land, "Ha! Ha!, What a fool he be."
Then it rained 40 days and it rained 40 nights,
The humans felt terror, the animals sensed fright.

The earth was destroyed by this total flooding,
But life started again with mating and budding.
A promise from God, a Rainbow, the sign,
"I won't do it again, this Covenant is Mine."

But I see my God with his tongue in His cheek,
The joke is on us and the future looks bleak.
"I'll just sit up here and hold the planets high,
while you kill each other," I say with a sigh.

There are the Dixons, the Casces, maybe someone you know—
Telling of dreams or hunches; a gut feeling below.
Sometimes they're wrong, sometimes they make history,
Where they get this insight remains a mystery.

It's 1995, and the world is free.
But, Nostradamus wrote, "There will be World War Three."
"The Bomb will be like a Sun of fire."
I'm contradicting him and calling him a liar.

Or is he right? Are we causing our own end?
Masking the fear with beer, leaning on drugs as a friend?
Today, people are suffering from Emotional Contortions,
Reading of war and murder and countless abortions.

STOP!

Look hard at your image, our leaders and all around,
Listen to speakers, your children and to every sound.
Seek the people and the ways to change it all,
Before annihilation becomes our fall.

Tarot Cards? Astrology? Crystal Ball?

OR—

Each step forward, answer that Inner call.

PEACE

Laraine Hoffmann
DARK UNTO MY BOSOM

"—and 'twas the peasant's critique by which Cleo steered."

I have a bosom friend,
Has shadows 'round his eyes.
Not everybody loves him
But none do he despise.

His memory is with me;
We travel far and near.
I fear him though
As fate has sent him here,

For darkened is his house
And marble is his bed.
His blackened robes around him,
Around us are the dead.

Laurie C Thornton
I'M IN LOVE

Dedicated to David Lee Klepar, with My Deepest Love Always!

I'm in love,
I feel as peaceful as a dove.

A quiet stream runs through my heart,
At this rate, my love for him seems like it'll never depart.

The rose of my soul opens up fully,
With love like this, I can deal with most any kind of bully.

The scents of pine trees fill my mind's nose,
And the intensity of our romance fills me from my head to my toes.

I see the diamonds God wears, seen as the Stars in the Sky,
And I wish I could share this evening with my beau and be nigh.

I see God's eye shadow in the sunset,
It was through the pink and purple splendor that we met.

Every night, our silhouettes are seen in the light against the front porch,
When it came to us, Cupid really lit his torch.

Will Smith

Will Smith
SALTY COMPANIONS

Dedicated to my long time friends Garry and Ruth Paans may they continue to sail into many more sunsets together.

Vast sea of changing moods
'Fore a tempest calmly broods
Like a shimmering sheet of glass beneath my feet
In our wake as we sail by
Gulls flap their wings and cry
'Tis nearing journey's end, indeed 'twas sweet.

Billowing spinnaker, wind to feed
Driving forth my watery steed
With rhythmic grace thru ocean's churning foam
Her course is strong and true
As she plows the ocean blue
Sail on old girl for soon we shall be home.

Land is looming into sight
Yonder lighthouse spinning light
Gently guiding us to safety in the bay
Anchored safely in her berth
Having fought for all her worth
To carry this old sailor thru the day.

Will Smith
RHYME AND REASON

Dedicated to Jan and Eva Macho in commemoration of 25 years of marriage and progress together—1990.

I plow the furrows by my sweat and calloused hands
And churn the soil beneath my broad and bounteous lands
For this I know, with all the dedicated effort I invest
God will repay in kind, indeed provide the rest
And where the rich brown earth lies fallow 'neath my feet
Soon 'twill be fill'd with gently swaying golden wheat.

And so it is with life if we seek some return
We must invest committed time for what we yearn
Each birthright offers endless scope for better living
Yet if we seek to progress then there must be honest striving
So think on this when feeling life is all defeat
Without the sweat, the calloused hands, there is no wheat.

Florentina F Molina
TODAY
Greet every morning with a smile
Be thankful you awake feeling good as you had a wonderful sleep
Needed by your body to be healthy and able
To do your daily routine to make you live.

It's nice to have something to do
Don't ever get bored have hope
Ask the Lord to help you meet the day of its challenges and opportunities
Offer these sacrifices to make your work lighter.

Do your best today, be patient, they say
For patience is bitter but its fruit is sweet
Strive to do what you can do today, don't leave for tomorrow what you can do today.
To make life brighter than it was from the start.

When evening comes, time to reflect
For the blessings you receive
So feel happy and thankful for the day is done
Hence, your heart is light and happy to have done something worthwhile for today.

Bonnie McInnis
MOMMY AND DADDY
God blessed your baby so innocent there.
He is up in heaven in his little highchair.
And he says, "Mommy, don't you worry. And, Daddy, don't you fret; and in Jesus' name please don't forget.

"Mommy and Daddy, you know, I cannot walk, and to be honest with you.
But I know the time is coming when we will meet again.
And we will be together till the end.

"Now, Mommy and Daddy, I'm happy and all;
Why, I'm already flying, and I didn't have to crawl.
Because I am an angel with my own set of wings
And in God's choir, I will sing."

Louise Chapman
A TIME TO CRY

Dedicated with love to my son, Michael Lee Chapman, and my lovely daughter, Susan Louise.

I was still a young woman, though a mother of twins.
He was so tall and handsome, and my first love.
I wonder why he had to die so young?
The answer to this question I'll never know.
God the heavenly Father is the only one.
So much grief and sadness for the ones he left behind,
Especially for his young son and daughter.
Every child should be able to grow up with a father's love.
Do you think it possible for him to look down & see them from above?
Why couldn't he have stayed here on earth?
Into their lonely life give them some love and mirth.
Seems to me, since the very first day of their birth,
Fate was meant to be much too cruel,
The good they've gained from life is not nearly their worth.
For my children I would have gladly spared them of all the pain,
Not enough sunshine, and almost always too much rain.
In years, they are fully grown,
But still feeling so empty, fragile, and alone.
Because at the age of ten, I had to tell them, "Your daddy is dead."
Why, oh why, instead of their daddy, is there a cold gray stone?

Kelly A Firmingham
ON NO ACCORD
While life begins hopes are anewed,
as children grow from watching you.
But, when each day follows by,
many do without the needed guide.
They run wild as we did before,
there's no one there to tell the bitter score.
Over beyond is a green hill,
there my child lies from being killed.
Faster living is the ultimate thing,
thus many laugh, cry, die and sing.
One is lost among the hundred more,
yet what will it take in this civilian war?
People grab hold and never let go,
yes my child's gone but there's more to show.
Please don't die on no accord,
say we can help you rest assured.
Children are born throughout the years,
but where's the ones we cry for with tears?
Nature always takes care of itself,
so those involved live not on a shelf...

Jean Ann Hall
LONELY

Dedicated to my family and grandchildren.

Here I stand making dinner for one,
instead of two.
After being down in Texas with
grandkids and all.
Not making dinner for a whole crew
is very lonesome by yourself.
We had a grand time playing
Yahtzee, rummy and checkers,
now once again you find yourself
all alone.
But life is funny because you have to go on,
no one can do it for you.
Children get older and leave your side,
but grandchildren carry on with
pride.
It is lonely in this big old world,
but once your spouse is deceased,
You find yourself once again
all alone after all these years.
Just live your life the way you can
and it will turn out in the end.

Sharon Leigh Warren
OCEAN OF "HIS" TEARS

For my parents Irene and Holmes Raynor; my husband Wade and children Matthew, Lindsey and Dustin, with love.

I talked to the ocean
and it answered me
It told my soul to run naked
and my heart to run free.

But the tide rushed in
and covered my soul
My heart left alone
shuddered in the cold.

God's infinite power
gave to me another chance
And my soul was freed
My heart—it began to dance.

So look to the sky
and reach for the rain
"HIS" tears fill the ocean
that will speak with me again.

Donald and Pearl Heffernan

Donald J Heffernan
CONVERSION

To beardless Abrahams.

Our children exploded from our doorways,
beating out sun's rise
morning arms grabbed their short shadows,
cliche arms hidden in bushes
fancy bushes.

Nowadays short shadows is all you need,
don't be a grandpa
who needs long shadows anyhow
short shadows is good enough.

Those bushes with huge leaves
we thought they were way down our lane
not just outside our door,
those childsnatchers
only actors of truth, in ghost plays
hidden so fancy well.

Diana Kennedy Porter
BITTER TEARS

To my mother, Mrs. Lillian Kennedy and family.

Bitter Tears, are things that I use portray.
Bitter games were games, that I would not play.
So take these Bitter Tears, and show them that they can't have their way.
Bitterness has a way of stripping, the soul of moisture for
new-found growth.
It blocks the mind of reasoning.
Bitter Tears, destroys the sense and smell of
forgiveness. Take my heart and play your
part, like I will play mine.
Because these Bitter Tears, will not
have their way.
So take these Bitter Days, from me and set
me free.
No more Bitter Tears
No more Bitter Days.
No More, No More

Diana Kennedy Porter
THE GHETTO IS OUT TO GET YOU
The ghetto is out to get you!!!
Where the winos bend.
And the neons cringe.
To make their deathly blow.
Where mothers cry.
And brothers and sisters die.
Hey the ghetto is out to get you!!!

Where kids kill grass.
And the sound of glass, is all their pleasure.
Where hunger and dope kills, and that's for real.
And the rats want their bit too.
I heard part of this prayer.
That this wino said there.
That only the strong, shall survive.
So I say this to you,
We know what it's all about.
So please try and help the young get out,
Because the ghetto is out to get you!!!

Diana Kennedy Porter
VIET NAM THIS IS WAR
You took the boy away, and made him a man.
You put a rifle, in his young trembling hands.
Why should I die?
I thought it was only God's choice.
I've been denied, of education & schooling,
But who, are they really fooling.
Viet Nam, this is war.

My mother cried, and damn near died.
When they said, I was going to war.
The things she said to me, I felt like a slave set free.
But that was Viet Nam.
Save the country,
Save the children,
Now help save this junkie Viet Nam.
That this war, made out of me.
Now this is war.

Diana Kennedy Porter
THE SOLITUDE OF TREES
Trees at their slumber rest.
Are like the sleekest of birds at their best.
They sway, they sigh.
Oh my God, they sometimes die.
In their mourning, they pray and sing.
They bow so humble, in the presence of the all mighty king.
They bow so gently, even in their death.
You can tell when a tree is going to his rest.
No more beauty has this tree.
But look how many people,
Have enjoyed looking at thee.
You're quiet, and all along.
First a seed, now alone.
So I write this as a memorial,
For all the trees that have been cut down
In the name of progress.

Diana Kennedy Porter
LOVE AND ITS TREASURES

This poem is dedicated to my husband, Frank Porter, Jr.

Love is like a melting bliss, free from cold.
Store the love for freedom.
For there will be no tomorrow.
Give no pain, give no sorrow.
And you will see, the doors of eternity.
Rise to the peak of happiness
The sweet aroma of love, and its cleanness.
Can only taunt the nostrils, of man and woman in their
Movement of growth.

The sun strikes an orgasm, with warmth and beauty.
That only god, would recognize in the days of light.

Treasure this love, what it may be.
And breathe, to the highest and say.
That only the young at heart, captures its glory.
But to be in love, only knows its treasures.

Kim Matvey
TOGETHER FOREVER

To Michael—for being my best friend. With his love and support I was inspired to write of my feelings for him!

The fire in his sweet brown eyes
Can brighten up the grayest skies.
I cherish his gentle, easing touch,
And long to feel it so very much.
A message he sends from subtle laughter,
Tells me he's mine from this day after.
He holds me real close as we dance—
For years of happiness, I'll take the chance.
A twinkle in his eye shines with his smile.
That seductive look I can see for a mile.
Moments together filled with love and lust
My life in his hands, I honestly trust.
I dream of him each day and night—
Marry him? Some day I just might.
I love him today, tomorrow, forever,
Without him, I hope I am never.
He gives me love, also sunshine—
His thoughts and dreams, the same as mine
He's found the key to open my heart,
With that key, we'll never ever be apart!

Dorothy N Ogden
HEAVENLY HOME

To my husband Dallas, who gives me love and inspiration.

Good morning Lord, here I am again.
No place to go. No place to stay.
Wandering alone on these cold empty streets.

Hear the sounds of the city,
beginning a new day.
People in a hurry, going to and fro—
But not me Lord, I've no place to go.

Wish I could bring back all the yesteryears.
My family and friends who I loved so dear.
They have all been called to the Heavenly Home.
Leaving me here to face sorrow alone.

I'm so happy you're here Lord, to walk by my side.
I'd love to go home Lord, I'm so very tired.
Let's sit in this doorway and rest for awhile.

They found the ol' man later that day.
On his face was a smile, his hand folded to pray.
No one knew, but Jesus and him, he wasn't alone.
He was with his friend, safe with his master,
in his Heavenly Home.

Michelle C Lyons
TURN THE TABLE

How beautiful the winter looks from inside my limousine,
For I am the aristocrat.
Vote for me—do what I say, or you may be without a home tomorrow.
Look! Over there—at that poor ragged man eating from the garbage can,
If he hadn't been so honest all his life, he could own the city—
Just like me.
What a Fool!
Because of my appearance, the world revolves around me—How grand!
Pity on that bag-man
His eyes do not see reality.

The bitter cold of the winter freezes my soul,
As I stand here, eating from the garbage can in front of Saks.
My pockets are empty but for the fifty cents given to me by that kind street sweeper who cleans the very streets that I call Home.
Look! Over there—at that rich man in the limousine,
I wonder how many innocent people he stepped on and destroyed to get where he is today.
I wonder how many lies he's told.
Pity on that rich man
His eyes do not see reality.

Tony Lawson
LIFE IN HELL

I was there in late November
Although it wasn't any cooler
No, not as I remember

As I walked alongside the lake of fire
Cautiously, as I went
I noticed a group of people
A group that seemed, well, quite content

Confused, I asked
Is it not so bad in this place of sorrow
For the life you live, my son
I would not borrow

How can you live
In this place of torment and grief
For the place you live, my boy
I would not leave

We hear what goes on
In your world as a man
If I had the chance to do it twice
I'd just as soon be damned

When your time on earth is said and done
You too, will be glad to come

Joseph Barnette
THROUGH THE GALLERY

I'm walking through a gallery of my life.
I stumble upon icons made of rust.
Look at folly disguised as grandeur.
Stare at pictures with no meaning.
Read questions scribbled on bathroom walls,
And prophecies pronounced, unto the emptiness of space.
Gaze at collections of empty bottles labeled
promises.
Ships of dreams washed ashore,
And those ships which did not set sail.
Study blueprints of roads running straight
and narrow.
See photographs of children left unnurtured.
And fields of promise turned to wasteland.
They say I am a winner of the human race,
Yet, upon examination, they will find my medal is made of tin.

Joseph Barnette
MOURN NOT FOR ME

Mourn not for me my darling,
though my beard is white,
and my hair silver.
My life is full.
My heart's content.

My days may be numbered,
yet my years are many,
and my life's complete.
I shall leave a happy man.
Shall be content in what I've done.

I will soon be gone,
still the drums will play their beat, and the trumpets sound their tune.
The world will live without me.
It will know not who I was.

Joseph Barnette
JUST A ROSE BUSH

It forms a collage of green and red.
Bringing joy to those behold it,
With its awesomeness of color,
The glory of its aroma,
And its freshness and life.

It's just a rose bush,
Covered with thorns,
That's all,
Nothing more.

Runolfur Traustason
FALLEN ANGEL

The boy is cold and empty inside.
His brother breathes no more.
If there's a reason, for a young boy to die
Don't the people always ask why?

As the eyebrows turn upward and stiff,
They wonder and say only if,
Could it all have been lies.
Why can't we still see the look in his eyes.

Then lonely he wonders, the rest of his ways,
Not understanding the gloom of his days.
After a while his heart turns to stone,
The pain is unbearable, cuts to the bone.
A spice of, white dust, goes in through the skin,
The lifeline we walk on, is brittle and thin.
Is there a reason, for a young boy to die?
Don't the people still ask you why?

The note on the table, cries out the message;
A young boy's departure, through unknown dark passage
An answer so lame too often accepted, only tomorrow again is reflected

Christine M Calais
SOMETIMES

For, Mary C. Wolfe a very caring and unselfish person. Thank You for being there when I needed your help.

Sometimes I Lie Awake at Night.
Wondering if I've Done Things Right.
I Know I've Traveled the Wrong Road.
At Times Carrying a Heavy Load.
Family and Friends Were Always There.
Although at Times I Did Not Care.
I Was Selfish Then You See.
Not Realizing They Cared For Me.
Caught up in a World All My Own.
Never Writing or Picking up a Phone.
Now I've Lost Something Dear.
Not Seeing it Was Very Near.
Life is Sad and Oh so Short.
You See I've Finally Lost All Heart.
Sometimes I Lie Awake at Night.
Wondering if I've Done Things Right.

Etta Jernigan Strickland

Etta Jernigan Strickland
EVIL FORCES

To my loving family: Delilah, Leo; Susan, Rodney, Stephanie; Carol, Reggie, Matthew; Carl, Wanda, Jason and Amy.

Sin is such a prevalent thing, it catches us quite unaware.
It holds us like under its wing, but underneath sin we care.
It holds us in its grip all day, but by our prayers we get release.
Oh, why does it hold us this way, when our hearts are longing for Peace.
Short on faith must be the answer, spending too little time in prayer.
It is like an eating cancer, like a thorn in the flesh, a snare.
Glistening, gleaning, so appealing, it is enormous, what a girth!
Pretty, delightful, concealing, and spreading over all the earth.
Sin never takes the time to nap, snarling those who easily stray.
Very much like the Venus's flytrap, always ready to catch its prey.
It walks beside the godly one, ready to catch one in its claw.
Disguising itself like clean fun, not always disobeying the law.
Tears flow down one's cheek at night; there seems no way to win.
One is quite often in this plight;
Christ is more powerful than sin.
Like a daily battle to fight, something that is neverending.
Turning around would make things right, forgiving and not pretending.

We must embrace His righteousness,
the banner of Christ's love unfurl.
And with our hearts we must confess,
exhibit His Kingdom to the world.
Proclaim His gospel and His power,
plead for His mercy, love and grace.
For no one knows the final hour,
when we meet our Savior face–to–face.

Stephanie Smith
SWEET SORROW

Death is but sweet sorrow
a beginning for a new tomorrow.
We may mourn and we may cry,
but we know, we all must die.
Death is just the beginning of the end,
true freedom from everything,
definite resting will begin.
I look forward 'till my time to go,
'cause no more worries will I know.

Jeanne Oaxaca
FOR YOU

This poem is dedicated to Manuel, my beloved husband.

My life before you was lived for you,
Searching for you, waiting for you to come along—
I always knew that my dreams would come true,
And in my heart would be a beautiful song;

You came to me just as in my dreams,
With all the love I had missed,
Now, without you, I could not live, it seems—
I've known that, my love, from the moment we first kissed;

You are my life, you are my love,
Not a dream, but reality—
I swear to you by all the stars above,
That I will forever be, completely yours exclusively;

My world is very beautiful when we're together,
It's so sad and empty while we're apart—
With you there's joy unbelievable,
Without you, unbelievable is the pain in my heart.

Monty M Sebring
MOMMY AND DADDY

In memory of my nephew, Rusty McInnis.

God blessed your baby, so innocent there.
He's up in heaven in his little highchair,
And he says, "Mommy, don't you worry and daddy, don't you fret.
And in Jesus's name, please don't forget."

Now mommy and daddy you know that I can't walk,
And to be honest to you, you know that I can't talk.
But I know, the time is coming, when we will meet again,
And we'll be together till the end.

Mommy and Daddy, I'm Happy and all.
Why I'm already flying, I don't have to crawl.
Because I'm an angel, with my own set of wings,
And in God's Choir I will sing.

Roberta Lee Crawford
THIEVES

Dedicated with love to my son B.B. (Born 10:22pm February 16, 1989) for giving me new hope and so much happiness.

Hand in glove,
Foot in boot.
Through a window shove
This bounty, our loot.

Whether by day
Or by night,
To live we chose not this way . . .
'Twas cast upon us, this blight.

Thin as air,
Thick as thieves.
True, accept we any dare
And none of us danger sees.

We are the forsaken,
Faces unknown.
Ne'er shall we be mistaken
For one who sits upon a throne.

Kings we be not,
Thieves are we,
All of us, the whole lot—
And kings shall we ne'er be.

Barbara Nichols Dyson Morrell
SEE YOU IN HEAVEN

God put us here to live the trials of life.
From birth to death it is a struggle.
But, by chance divine, two people meet.
Not knowing why except for love,
They vow each other unending devotion.
Together they share in everything,
The endless bits of all their days.
Then an illness comes, one of age.
Last words are whispered, sweet and true.
Thank you. I love you. See you in Heaven.
One lives on alone with memories shared.
The tears come and go and go and come.
Now time has passed and the Lamb calls another home.
As I enter His house, I see you in Heaven.

David Gatling
ANOTHER CHANCE

To Krista, the love that we shared will never end.

What is time that cannot be measured?
It is one's love, that always is treasured.
Why wait for a lifetime to find one's desires?
When I've only to look in my heart's burning fires.
The one who was there when I needed her so,
Is waiting for me, but I do not go.
She waits in the wings while I am on stage,
Reading the book of my life, but I skipped her page.
After the encores, and the people leave;
I expect to see her but I turn and see
That she's gone from my life and I don't know why.
It was my stupidity and arrogance that made me blind.
I've felt empty for years without her there,
No meaning in life, and its purpose bare.
Suddenly one day the chance arose,
To reconcile with her, she has a right to know.
I approached her that day and told her the truth.
That I love her and my mistakes were ignorance of youth.
As fate would have it, she let me in,
She said, "But your worthiness and trust must be proven again."
I gladly said, "Yes, I'll do so at leisure,
Because love is time, and it cannot be measured."

Edwin and Priscilla Randall

Priscilla Eberle Randall
HER HELPER

To Mrs. John F. Kennedy, wife of the 35th President of the United States.

"Oh God! They have killed my husband!"
Cried Mrs. Kennedy,
As startled Dallas spectators
Close by could hear and see.
God heard her call upon His name,
In peril and distress,
And quickly gave her innate strength,
With thoughts that brought her rest.

She knew that she was not alone,
For He was at her side,
A loving, constant companion,
Her Savior and her guide.
And so she walked by faith alone,
Holding her head up high,
Proving to all that God is love,
On Him we should rely.

Dyan Perugini
LIFE

Life is more than fun and games
Life is more than anger and pain.
Life should be more than "going by the book"
Life should be more than how one looks.
If only everyone could face their fear,
If only they could say they care.
Life is full of a lot of nice things
But attached to them are some strings.
I guess that's how it's supposed to be
One is blind, one can see.
One minute full of fun and laughter
Sorrow and sadness two minutes after.
It's also filled with rhythm and rhyme,
But I just say to enjoy, take your time.

Mary Kay Glass
JANE

To Jane—A patient. And to my mother—Jane.

Sometimes I wonder
What goes on in your mind
You lie there like dust
without a thought of
space or time;
Your eyes have lost
their glitter and your
smile has disappeared
Your breathing has become
shallow and your face
is very pale.
And just when I think
that all is in despair!
You grab my hand and
look at me in a
peaceful stare!

Shannon Allen
FIRST KISS

To my mom, who inspired me to go after my dream. I love you, mom.

My heart is racing
My stomach is turning
My head is hot
It seems to be burning

My eyes can't focus
As I try to look at you
My hands begin to shake
As I wait for my cue

Your hands on my face
My flesh trembles at your touch
I've waited for this so long
I shouldn't expect so much

Your arms pull my face
This is my most wonderful wish
Finally our lips touch
As we share our first kiss . . .

Bonnie Moulton
THE MORNING LIGHT

As the first trace of the morning light shines through the sky,
the beautiful colors quickly pass you by.
White which stands for peace and purity;
Purple stands for wealth and power,
Like each and every wild flower.
The enchanting pink stand for love,
Like the amazing birds that fly above.
The delicate blues stands for calmness and healing,
Such as the beauty with which you are dealing.
Orange represents change;

Everything does within a range.
The exquisite colors of the morning sun,
In a matter of minutes the captivating sight is done.

Audrey Newton Barnett
PSYCHE

Lace lantern dancing
Filigree angel; pirouette on velvet;
Lifting, floating, silent Psyche
Spins in arabesque.

Filigree angel; pirouette on velvet;
Poised and proud Psyche
Spins in arabesque,
On velvet, black and soft.

Poised and proud Psyche—
A spirit, separate and silent;
On velvet, black and soft
Floating through the darkened quiet.

A spirit, separate and silent,
Warm, welkin, wistful,
Floating through the darkened quiet,
Incanting in mime.

Warm, welkin, wistful, Psyche—
Soft, sensuous silence
Incanting in mime.
Lace lantern dancing—

Alicia Curry (Age 13)
AS I WENT OUTSIDE

As I went outside, what did I see,
But two little birds staring at me,
Why would they stare?
I shouldn't really care.
But their little eyes bothered me,
From their perch high in the tree.
Since they wouldn't sing their song,
I really knew something was wrong.
I tried and tried to figure it out,
What their staring was about.
While wondering what fault they saw,
They suddenly flew with a caw.
As I turned around,
I saw they weren't staring at me,
But the worms in the catawalpa tree!

Evelina W McCray
WHEN A HEART HURTS

The pain never goes away when a heart hurts:
the nervous forebodings,
Lauding at the last meeting alert showers to convert,
as we gain refuge within the yurt;
And hope for pleasures to revert.
But the house, wreaths and rare treasures now taunt;
like uncontained ghosts on Halloween,
haunt and remain on the scene
through kicks and screams.
Self pity licks the dreams;
pain creams the beams
making death a viable option.
So hate dilutes hurt for the one gone:
the selfish and thoughtless soul who left you alone,
An aching frame who perverts love to dwell on misery borne;
where the mind tears apart blurt replies,
clothed in deception to be unearthed by reality.
But, she was so alive; ecstatic even when she caught a perch:
a womanly woman who put zest in the social graces;
Versatile and wise, she feigned
toughness to be heard
but always had the last word.
So the memories move to and fro but never to the outskirts:
while the leech sucks the blood from the heart in spurts!

Shirley I Dallas
MY MIRROR

Dedicated to Jim and all our days—months and years that went so swiftly by.

The days—the months—the years—
all go so swiftly by
Until the day your mirrored face
Looks back at you—to sigh—

Where has all the time gone—
Can that be really me?
Why—only yesterday that face—
was smooth and wrinkle free—

The mouth—once soft with laughter—
now looks a trifle—grim—
as though the well of happiness
has somehow dried—within—

The eyes—once bright and shining—
look sad—and lifeless—too
Not asking for permission
time has left its mark—on you—

The conclusion I must come to
—as I look at my reflection—
is—that time is the leveler
from which there's no protection.

Fran Russell
GOOD MORNING

To the Staff of Wicomico County Department of Social Services.

It is my personal value to say "Good Morning" as I face each new day with a smile and say Good Morning as I see faces from the day before. When I say good morning, it means God has granted me the advent of this day. If this falls, I get up early the next day and watch the sun come up. It is the adornment of my morning. I then look within myself and wonder if it should be shared with others. Off I go to seek the joys of this day and honestly saying "Good Morning." After a few good mornings and no replies, feelings of anger surface. It is the repressed emotions and experience of days past, that make me ashamed and become my demon.

When I fail to acknowledge what is really in my heart, I miss the whole point of my existence. But, when I acknowledge my truths, I say yes to my personhood. I walk tall, stand proud and look folks directly in the eye and say "Good Morning." Now I am true to my feelings, my truths, my experiences, and my feelings are my values. I own all of them, those that are pleasurable and painful have taught me much. They are the key to my future. When I accept my truths, I have broken the mental chain that binds.

Paul H Newton
DREAD

There is a fire inside of me.
My friends call it intensity.
Divorce is one result I see.
Since I can't seem to find the key
To loose me from my identity.

Can this inferno be of God?
So hot it scars me? Still it's odd!
Though it burns me, it warmed me first.
Saved me from adversity's curse.
So conflict and pain become verse.

The heat of this fire is my pain
That toil, sacrifice and love fail.
Resolve, Commitment, try again
Plead or rage; all to no avail!
My best nor worst can save young Paul.

Crippleness, abandonment my fate,
In spite of struggle they await.
Is there no change from this black course?
Am I doomed to live out my fear,
become my father? The nightmare's here!

Paul H Newton
REJECTION

The stillness of the night is broken
By baby's yowl or thunders peal
Each screamed at the word last spoken
Which left you struck, alone to feel.

A strong man wails, a woman grieves
Hands shake, stomachs churn, colors drain
Each driven by the love who leaves
You cold and wet by tears like rain.

Will tomorrow come or never
Again your trust be left exposed
Where loves risk can be a lever
A tool for living, or leaving – alone!

Ethellean Griffith

Ethellean Griffith
THREES AND ME

To Jordan with love . . . Grandmother.

Even before the world was formed
There was the Father, the Son and the Holy Spirit
Three in one, the Trinity
Threes are now and will always be
All the way into Eternity

Now getting down to earth you'll see
There's three-in-one oil
In baseball it's three strikes and you're out
And there's an old song Three Coins in the Fountain

Some favorite threes are in nursery rhymes
The three little pigs who danced a jig
The three blind mice who had no
cheese because they could not see
And the three little kittens who lost their mittens on that cold snowy day

Now that's enough of that old stuff
I know, I know, but I cannot forget
The three Wise men with gift in hand
Who traveled from a far off land
Just to see the babe in Bethlehem

Then he grew up and was crucified
But in three days he did rise
Of course he did, I knew he could
Because he said he would
So you see I am not surprised

Frances Fontino
FEELING FOR YOU

To my greatest admirer—Jesse.

Feeling for you is my heart's desire;
All the lovely things that I admire.
My arms are open, my eyes are wide;
My heart tells me—
To let you inside.
This is what keeps me from feeling blue;
When I tell you . . .
How I feel about you!

Megan L Campbell
LOVE—WHAT IS LOVE?

This poem is dedicated to my beloved father, Ewart Victor Fraser, 1907—1983.

"Love"—to me is a word so powerful,
it stands alone—undaunted by the shadows of fear and uncertainty.

"Love"—is also relative to everyone who is engulfed by its power.

"Love"—has many dimensions and spirals that circumvallates time.

"Love"—to say I love you implicitly, is to take an oath that exceeds all of life's expectancies.

"Love"—its spirituality is immaculate. Its foundation solidifies each moment of weakness.
The hands that are held out to me, have the dexterity for unlimited comfort.

"Love"—the memory of each emotional outburst, is gratifying and scintillating.

"Love"—the only other word that is comparative to stand on its pedestal is "Life."

Annette I Michael
HEAR, HEAR

To my father, Lawrence Edward Ingram.

Stop, look and listen
Hear the small voice inside
It is there to guide us
If we just put aside our pride.

Life would be so easy
Problems would seem small
If we paused a moment or two
To hear the Master's call.

How many times have we said
"If I had followed my first mind"
Not knowing at the time we thought
God was giving us a sign.

He would always warn us
And prepare us for the fight

For we are his chosen ones
We are God's delight.

This is not to say
We will waltz through life
For what joy is in the reward
Without enduring the strife?

Bill (Taco) Bradley
BEAUTY

To My Wonderful Wife, Brandi, Who made my dreams come true.

Beauty is your gifted smile like
Birds singing in a tall tree,
Feeling free
Having moves so full of grace.
Beauty is being beside you, to bring
Happiness for us all.
Beauty is caressing your ever so soft
Body next to mine.
Beauty is your thoughts for you are a
dreamer,
So full of fabulous ideas.
Beauty is being your husband,
For I must be in heaven,
Living with such Beauty.

Carol S Jaggi
THE JOURNEY BACK

This poem is dedicated to brain trauma victims everywhere. There is a light at the end of the tunnel, but it's a long 'journey.'

Wake up sis . . . it's December 1,
1987 . . . it's almost Christmas,
there's so much to do, so many
people to see . . .

There's shopping, the baking, the
gift-wrapping . . . hey, did you hear
me?

Wake up sis . . . I don't like doing
this alone—talking for you, thinking
for you . . .

Why are they telling me you won't
wake up? Tell me sis, is this true?
What on earth did this accident do to
you?

Time heals . . .
They were wrong, I told them so.
You are a person with too much
get-up-and-go.
The road ahead is uncertain and how
much you'll recover is unknown,
but I've watched you day by day, and
your capabilities have grown.

Back to work!!
They had to let you in, no matter
what they thought—
You proved your point in
determination and with the legal
counsel that you sought.
Congratulations sis . . . their hearsay
was all wrong.
It pays to be courageous, unyielding,
colorful and strong.
Not everything has been ideal, and
many you loved and trusted walked
away,
but your sister knows you're here for
a purpose—to show others like you
the way.

Florence C Beltz
AUGUST 31

He left me today.
In the early morning sun his step
seemed eager, purposeful.
Fear gripped a tight hold in me
as I watched his straight proud
body go.
Will she understand all that is
involved?
He seemed to question, turned his
head a little
Watching the traffic at the corner
Did he look for me? What?

My day is different now as his
will be.
He is gone.
Empty chair
room
house!
How to cope. What to do.
The phone——maybe it's him. No.
Hi Mary.
I will keep cool.
I will survive this first day
My son has gone to school.

Emilia Ann Leach
A MOTHER'S LOVE

Written especially for you, Mom, on this Mother's Day, May 11, 1989. With all my heart, soul and love.

A mother's love is warm and caring
She teaches you love: means always
sharing . . . .

Sharing your heart, your innermost
feelings,
Her love's the balm when your hurt
needs healing . . . .

She was there when you took your
first breath
Said your first word, took your first
step . . . .

She kissed away your hurts, dried
your tears
Soothed your soul: chased away your
fears . . . .

She cried when you cried, laughed
when you laughed
Was there when you had grown up at
last . . . .

Although, we are now miles apart
Her love still lingers in my
heart . . . .

As God as my witness in the heavens
above
I'll cherish you always, Mom, you
and your love!

Tommie R Basham
THE OAKLING

As the acorn falls,
it's greeted by the ground.
Earth warm and moist,
softly muffles the sound.

Life begins to form,
nestled in its place.
The season has come,
for continuance of a race.
Time does travel surely,
as weeks never end.
Life stirs and calls,
thus earth must open.

Through the laborious passage,
a being does emerge.
Exposed to the world,
power of life does surge.

Leaves open slowly,
reaching for the sun.
As oak and earth,
take pride in what's done.

Elizabeth A Owers
SOLILOQUY

In your dawn you cradled
My children in your arms;
Testing you, they balanced, surveyed
the wondrous earth.

The blossoms you created
Adorned their silky hair;
Were you enchanted then? Are you
of royal birth?

Your night has come. Omega—
Old and gnarled, you stand
A rustic institution, softly, sadly
sighing.

You and I share sunset,
The fleeting twilight hour;
Helpless, I see you wither; I watch
you slowly dying.

Antique scars memorialize
Your eighty long, hot years
Of sad neglect. Did we forget that
you are history?

In midnight hour missives
I chronicle your decades,
And dedicate this reverie to you,
my dogwood tree.

Chrysetta Patterson
SPIRIT

To Courtlan Christopher Michael Green and my mom.

We are people of infinity
Seeing through eyes of time
Yes, we did exist once
Now we are of the mind
On a distant voyage
We all must take in time.

Theresa Kubat
MOUNTAIN ROAR

THE cool breeze of spring is
caressing my mane
I am standing erect on my throne
I can hear the roars of my kind
THEY are roaring a warning
MY kingdom will soon be invaded
THE predator will be man
THIS is my land and my offspring
I must protect all!
PEACE and serenity that once filled
my thoughts
ARE now of rage and war
WILL man ever leave us be?
A single tear I shed
I know that tonight I will give up my
reign
I will not be able to protect all
AND one of my kind will die

Theresa Kubat
ROULETTE

MY child we have separated on our
quest for food
IN the still of the night I can hear
man coming forth
HOW desperate I am to find you
HERE you are my child, how happy
you are to see me
YOU frolic about only to sense
danger in my eyes
As I search over the terrain, I can see
your happiness turn to anger
YOUR innocence turn to violence,
Yes my son, you will survive
NO longer will your green eyes shine
so brightly
NO longer will you be so shy and
timid
IT is time to run, follow me son, we
must run for our lives
FASTER, my son, we must dash
faster!
A long Autumn night it has been
THE sun is bursting through the
hellish night sky
WE are safe
YOU are nestled close to my side
I cannot control my emotions, I am
engulfed with sadness
I am crying, wondering,
WHAT about tonight my wolf Son?
How much I love you.

Mary J Monroe
SO LONG AGO

To my children: Jett, Jamie, Lora and Lisa. I love you, Mother.

Where have all the dreams gone,
from long time ago
Seems as though there were good
times
But oh, so long ago
And the dreams were only dreams
I should know
Oh, to go back just a few years would
it have saved me from these tears
I don't know, it was so long ago
Life is what you make it, so they say
and everyday isn't a holiday
But, please, tell me why do I feel
this way
I don't know, it was so long ago

Doris L Lawrimore
DEALING WITH FEELING

When you can't deal,
With how you feel,
And medicate your emotions.
You should hear how they
Laugh at us, way across the ocean.

Emotionally medicated America
Your society is crumbling down.
Say you don't think so?
Well just take a look around.
When is the last time you
Went to bed without your
Shutters batten down?

You better put down the jug,
And put down the drug.
And deal with how you feel,
Or there is just one place
You are going to go, and it
Is not heaven, and that's for real.

Monica M Lenk
odd isn't it?

odd isn't it
our relationship
no one would understand
. . . or believe
that a relationship
. . . could conceive
on
what we have

odd isn't it?
what we have
. . . and do you know what?
yes i guess you do!
what we have

is so unusual
that it can't be explained
with words

odd isn't it?
words
we don't need them, though.
we see, touch, feel
we know

odd isn't it?
that we know
—and sense that
what the other's feeling
is the same

odd isn't it?
the feeling
the vibrations we send
to tell you, friend
i know.
our wavelength
is so direct and strong
it takes less than
an instant
to know when something's
wrong
no words are used
to ask
or answer
whether across a crowded room
or on a lonely couch
our souls
seek for the other's
eye to eye

odd isn't it?
our eyes
our judges of
one's love
or one's lies
though only our
spirits meet
and lock . . .

healing the hurt
sharing the joy

odd isn't it?
the search
so difficult to find
the key
to match
that door
which has never dared
to be opened
or unlocked.
there no computer, technology
or any kind of tricks
can find
or
solve.
. . . for souls are far
and
impossible
out of their
reach

odd isn't it?
it isn't out of our reach
not with our relationship
odd is it??

George Jurich
A WASTE OF LIFE

Dedicated with love to Mom, Dad and the girls.

I saw an older man waste away
today, and he gave up on living with
nothing to say.
Concerned, I inquired; but he told me
to mind my own business and go
away.

What is it that causes one to let life
slip by,
and then to not utter a regretful sigh?

He wasn't ill; only wanting to die,
as he stared out the window with
abandoned eye.

Is it madness for not wanting to live
on?
Who is to blame, or is no one
responsible for this unspeakable
wrong?

He had a wife who loved him with
such a gentle touch,
and wonderful children who loved
him just as much.

Is not life so precious that we
shouldn't lust for every breath,
or are we to simply give up and wait
for the icy-cold embrace of eternal
death?

No one will ever know what went on
in that man's mind,
except that he left this earth too
willingly before his appointed time.

Mrs Donald Dickinson

Mrs Donald Dickinson
TILL THEN

To my beloved husband, Donald. Love, always.

M ay your light ever shine
A bove all forever mine
Y our charm and beauty flows
B lossom as spring flowers grow
E ven dreams can be beautiful

L ove isn't always truthful
L ay your body close to mine
I n time we will be fine
N ow, I'm on a pedal
E ve, where is the medal

D ozen red roses say you care
O ur mind know it fair
N ever, never say goodbye
A lthouh you may have tried
L et's be friend, companion, lover—
Darling darling you're my tower

Barbara J Williams
HAVE I FAILED YOU

. . . Sweet, loving baby . . .

So tiny at birth
Wanting to be held . . .
Cuddling in my arms
Long after your needs attended

You . . . growing up . . . years apart
from me
Torn from my life . . . breaking my
heart . . .
Injustice . . .

Young woman now with a child of
your own
. . . How do I make it up to you . . .
How do I heal your heart

The love a mother has for her child
You know now, my daughter . . .
For the love you feel for your child
You must know, is the same love I
feel for you

Forgive me now, my daughter . . .
Let there be no more wasted years
Know that I have not failed you in
love . . .
Love that I have for you, my
daughter . . . Jeana . . .

Susy Jones
SANDCASTLES

Sandcastles on the beach
Built with grains of sand,
Waves of water come and go
As magically they stand.

Each one uniquely sculptured
Beneath the shining sun,
Then left behind to stand alone
When the day is done.

Pictures of tiny feet
Are all that's left in sight,
For those that play in the sun
Do not often play at night.

Angry waves of water rush
And the fragile castles stand
No chance!
Until the touch of an unseen
hand . . .

Pushes back the darkness,
Calms the angry sea,
Gives light to the stars above,
Gives faith in which to believe.

Andrea Weston
LEAVING

Leaving you leaving me
Whoever thought it could be
That I'd just pick up and go
Without you to ever know

I'm leaving the memories of good
and bad
I'm leaving the love that we once had
I'll find someone new and you will
too
You'll tell her about me and I about
you

I'm leaving the friends that stabbed
my back
I'm leaving the love that they all lack
They'll forget me and I'll forget them
I'm starting my life all over again

Jim Mattingly
WITHIN, WITHOUT

getting along in years,
I've realized,
only magnifies that depraved,
scared child inside.
crying to get out:
wanting to be cared for;
asking, asking to be loved.

I remember the first time
a woman I knew let her
child within, out to play:
to laugh and cry; to feel.
"how stupid and sad," I thought,
"to see you this way."

then came the realization
that it was my time—
he had to come; no holding back:
from years of darkness,
and into the light!
for ourselves, we must be true,
within, without.

Heather Nagel
ALONE

Moonlight rays streak across
Sparkling sands of the desert
While one lone stranger watches
He hath never seen this manner of
moonlight
In the midst of the air he hears
The lone calling of a bird
Why doth he call, help, friendship,
distress.
He knoweth not
He hath never heard this manner of a
bird
The moon now descends to a far
away place
And the bird, leaves to find his nest
While one lone stranger still watches
And listens for he knoweth not
That everything hath gone.

Mary Lou Willoughby
WHO FED THE SHEEP?

Who fed the sheep
That first Christmas day?
Who tended the manger?
Who freshened the hay?

Who comforted the mother?
Who guarded the child?
Who fed the shepherd
So meek and mild?

Who thanked the innkeeper
Who turned not away
But made room for the family
On Christmas Day?

Your Lord and my Lord
He did it, that's who
And does it today
For me and for you.

Helena C Hult
SPECTRUM

Had I known you in the Eden whence
you sprang
Running hand in hand across some
sun-drenched veldt
To seek the plane trees' dappled
shade
We would have tasted deep the
heritage
From which we both once came
Savoring the honey of our bodies.

Had you known me in my northern
Arctic Spring
We would have drunk the wines of
youth, of dreams
Beneath the pines upon some mossy
toft
Musky with awakening hibernate
And thrusting berry and linnea vines
Kin with all living things, earth-
bound, aloft.

What destiny has brought us late to
touch
But once or twice—the shading
plane, the pine?
Your voice will always stop my
breath
Your glance impaling mine o'er
milling
Crowds in most unlikely places
Memory lines our face and we move
Together, touching briefly, then
move on.

Christine Lynn Bower
TO YOU I COME

Heavenly Father to you I come,
I've got a great fear
To which the answer scares me some.
It sounds easier to you,
But to me it is so complex.

This is the thing, I need help though.
My friends don't seem to understand,
They just go on listening to their bands.

All they do is walk on by,
Pretending it's me they don't hear.
Oh! Why don't they hear me cry??

I really need your help this time,
More and more as time goes by.
I can't go on pretending everything is fine.

I hurt so much I can't stand the pain.
It gets worse everyday,
WON'T YOU PLEASE STOP
THE PAIN

Gerald H Cowles
EVERYBODY OR NOBODY?

To all my loyal friends in Woodhull, Illinois.

When I was a youngster in Woodhull, Illinois,
I heard a story about two unusual boys.
One purred: "I care for everybody,
and everybody cares for me."
The other hissed: "I care for nobody,
and nobody cares for me."
Now gentle reader, oh please don't lose your poise,
But yours truly was one of those little boys:
Guess Which!

Nancy DeLuca
SONG
Uplifted souls sing
And prayers rise
Upon wings to heaven.

Archangels sing
And the notes rain down
Upon the redbrown earth.

Carole McCune

Carole McCune
DEAR JOHN

To John F. Kennedy, Jr., to whom I wrote this poem in memory of his dear father.

I remember the happy days of yesteryear,
When I was young with nothing to fear,
When your father came to Malibu,
To visit the Lawfords and the crew,
of many friends;
Some old some new.

I was staying with my good friends next door,
People I hardly see anymore
For friends will come and friends will go,
And where they go, we don't always know.

But life goes on and so do we, the marks we make so heavenly,
WE hope; to prepare a place, that we may someday show our face,
To the good LORD who had the grace, to give us life.

And your dear father was such a man,
That other folks would envy and admire,
His presence was magnetic,
charismatic, full of charm,
Without a single thought to do anyone any harm.

And now he is in Heaven joined by family and friends,
And people who have left their mark in history's open ends,
We know that GOD created them to do his Heavenly will,
Then he created you to carry on;
Your good dad's shoes to fill.

Carole McCune
OH LOVELY WORLD WHERE DID YOU GO
Oh lovely world where did you go?
They've marred your face with scars that show;
With scars that show they've marred your face,
Playing GOD to take his place,
In their greed the powers that be,
have gone ahead of nature's pace,
In their hurry to be free, For us to be or not to be.

Through the haze of tired eyes, we look up to your smoggy skies
We've paid the price of sacrifice, to politicians not so nice
Whose hearts are made of rocks and ice,
Instead of truth they've told us lies,
Although to us it's no surprise.

Shattering the air with their rockets,
Polluting the seas with their waste,
Filling the ocean with their nets,
Catching the fish too sick to taste,
Making progress with too much haste.

Oh lovely world where did you go?
They've marred your face with scars that show,
Where will it end we do not know,
For when it ends we shall not know.

Carole McCune
THE LAST TWELVE YEARS
I predict it will be great, in nineteen hundred and eighty eight
And if it's not too late.
There will be twelve years journey to the Golden Gate
I predict in nineteen hundred and eighty nine,
Everything will be going fine.
In nineteen ninety, we will see,
a woman vying for the Presidency.
In nineteen ninety one a new revolution will have begun.
In nineteen hundred ninety two,
America's Cup we'll see anew.
In nineteen ninety three I predict that we will see,
That woman, who was pleasure bent,
will soon become the President.
In nineteen ninety four, pestilence will be at our door.
In nineteen ninety five we will count our stars we are alive.
In nineteen ninety six a new wonder will emerge from a mix.
In nineteen ninety seven, we will prepare to go to heaven.
In nineteen ninety eight, a vision will appear at the Golden Gate.
I predict in ninety nine, the biggest quake will meet its time.
I predict—in two zero, zero, zero,
The Lord will come and be our hero.

Carole McCune
COME WITH ME, MY LOVE
Come with me, my love, to the winding brook.
We will dangle our feet and sense the cool, soft water
As it trickles gently between our toes.
Then watch the trout winding their way upstream,
Darting and splashing with the zest of life,
And you and I will know the joy of living
As we meld with nature in her nakedness,
Unhurried, unashamed, and beautiful.
We will drink up all the splendor she has to offer,
Never again to repeat the same opera,
But we will have known this day,
Because we were a living part of it
And shared its simple beauty
For a little while.

Carole McCune
AWAKENING WITH THE DAWN
Dawn breaks with awe-inspiring splendor,
The dew rests sparkling on all earth's flora and fauna,
Hushed birds burst out with varied song
To wish the day hello.
New shoots begin to tremble into growth
And earthworms pop up their heads to a new day.
The sun warms the sky and beams its rays earthward
To greet mankind in her cloak of glory,
To a fresh beginning, yet an extension of our development.
Then so-called humans awaken without song,
And drown the peaceful harmony of sunlit day
With myriad noises calling it progress, growth,
Oh! how little do we grow
When we don't stop to wish the dawn "hello."

Carole McCune
STAY CLOSE TO NATURE
Stay close to nature
Or you will find
She will ride without you
And leave you far behind;
Then in her leisure moments
She will return
To let you know,
Life was not yours to burn.

Robert W Beckius
NATURE'S VOICE
Nature's note rings in my ear
the twine of its strings is very clear
Mystical music moves through me
my soul, I feel, is light and free

Spirits of mine rise with the dove
my tender heart cries Hark! with love
A voice does sound forth with the spring
new growth, new life, do hear it sing

A sweet rapture in me is taking hold
I see fertile passion begin to unfold
This exultant strife that fills my eye
cannot be quenched in a contented sigh

Harmonic nature that is the spring
brings beauty forth, calls life to being
A mystical music moves through me
my soul, I feel, is light and free

Kelly-Ann D'Amalio
THE SISTER I LOST IN YOU
You my sister
have been a dear and caring friend
Why then can't you open your eyes
to my suffering.
I tell you of life and heartache
but you turn away and say;
I'm not your sister anymore
It was like a sudden death
A loss so hard to bear but,
My life has but stopped a moment to grieve
and must continue without you near.
I had so much to share with you
but most of all
was the chance to grow with me.
I am truly sorry!
You have changed the path, which
we had traveled together
My path may not be as smooth
and continuous as yours
But, I will travel it alone
and during those rough spots, I will remember
the sister I lost in you.

Jennifer Viets
FOR AN OLD MAN
Age creeps up on a man,
Creasing his face,
Unsteadying his hand.
Age brings an early end,
With solitaire and lonely night,
And grief for an old friend.

Patricia Kershner Hubrich
THE PALTRY PALETTE

To the memory of "MY FRED."

Pink and ochre
Alizarin and chrome
"YE GADS!"
What colors
To paint a home.
They all
Had a dozen
Pernod—
For lunch.

Terry L Hill
GOD AND I

A poem, written in loving memory of our Savior. Written by a poet from Danielsville, Georgia: Terry Hill. Son of Tommy Hill and Janice McElroy.

God walks with me through sand and storm
Through pain to gain, and so much more
God flies with me through wind and air
God and I really share
People say it's not the same
But the Lord of Heavens has called my name
The others to burn because they didn't learn
I am smart because He is in my heart
Lord's with me all the way
I don't care what others have to say
Lord of Heavens upon the throne
Forgive the others for being wrong
Just as life has started to begin
This poem has reached its very end

Lori Lynn Elliott

Lori Lynn Elliott
THE MYSTERY OF A CLOWN

To my Na-Na and Pop-Pop, my special friend Jen, and the clown in my life, Sam.

The mystery of a clown.
The only thing you know
Is the face they show.
What's hidden under the mask?
Nobody but the clown itself knows.
Are they happy or sad?
Is the mask they wear opposite their emotion?
If they wear a happy mask,
Does that mean they're really sad?
Or under the first mask,
Is there another mask hidden?
The mystery of a clown.

B J McCurry
SECOND CHANCE
With you, my Love,
And, your support
Shielding my tomorrows,
My seeming radiant hopes
And fierce ambition
To crush defeat and sorrows,
May see me through the game
Without volition.

In all events, and somewhere
Far above my anxious mind
To reach a final inning,
The prize is but a void
Without your love,
For little balm is found
Within the winning.

When my defeated ego must pretend
To reach great heights,
You, my dearest fan,
Must surely know I am here to seek
Enshrinement
In your heart again.

Tanya R Newman
CHINA DOLL
Oh china doll,
Oh china doll
A mind of peace
lies within that
no one ever sees
We will never know

Oh china doll,
Oh china doll
Do you have a heart?
One of gold to share
Who will know
this part of you?

Oh china doll,
Oh china doll
Mind of peace
And heart of gold
I'm sorry—so sorry
You've shattered and broke

Sara Copeland
MELANCHOLY SUNSET

To my grandparents who inspired me.

Treading in the sand,
Leaving behind her
An endless ocean,
She stops and turns her head
Slowly.
On the far horizon,
A soft glowing star
Glistens on the water,
Yet she turns
and walks away.

Leona F Lein
NO MIXTURE
Dawn pushes away the cloak of night
Away from the earth as the sun
Brightly announces a new day's light
The snowy egret cannot run
On once soft white sandy beaches
Because of ocean's dark water plight
Oil soaks the sand's far reaches
While people begin the hard fight
To remove oil from the birds
Perhaps again to be in flight
Clean the sand for the turtle herds
To take away their terrible fright
Again to lay eggs in the sand
Now, scarce is marine life
How long till the white sands
And easier the life of strife
Of shore by our willing hands
Whales, gulls, dolphins in the ocean
Take care, humans, of God's gift
Earth—love be its life potion.

Glen Kenneth Hauman
TO THY KNOWN SELF BE TRUE

Let not today's misfortunes be cast from thyne own memories, for tomorrow brings forth new despairs to dwell in thy cheated minds.

Thus creating bigger and better mysteries for thy self to encounter.

But do not despair, merely do as I do. Keep in thy unchained brains that you are the sole survivor to whom no man can match.

And fear not your captivity, for thy mind is never held prisoner to beliefs other than thyne own.

Juanita Marble
I BELIEVE
I have seen thy wondrous works,
Also have I felt thy hand,
You are with me every day,
because I am upon your land.

I have sinned, and caused great pain,
but you never let me down,
I am waiting for your rebirth,
and to touch your golden crown.

I'll wait as long as I am told
For the glorious sight I'll see,
now and forever I will know,
that I will always be precious to thee.

Margaret G Nachtsheim
GOING BACK
I went back—I went back to see,
If things looked the same as they used to be.
Those boyhood haunts so deeply etched in my memory.
First the street where I lived when I was a boy,
Then the fields where I played with—Oh so much joy.
On to my grandfather's farm with the barn filled with hay,
I could recall so clearly—Like it was yesterday.
I followed the tracks where the Grist Mill stood,
Cuz that was the shortcut to my old neighborhood.

There was this creek—The Moccasin Creek—I'll never forget,
The time I spent there with fish line, hook, and net.
I sat on the shoreline and tried to recall,
Which of these joys I liked best of all.
Trying to remember how I felt then,
When I was just five and going on ten.
Did I cherish the goodness that made up my life?
It was all pleasure—no worries no strife.
I am ever so grateful to have had this beautiful reverie,
For that and much more Dear Lord I thank Thee.

The hours had passed quickly one by one,
All too soon my day of dreaming was done.
It was time to go on and let the past fall away,
But going back made up such a wonderful memory day.

Maria L Aguilar
ELAINE

To the family of Elaine Hull.

It is springtime
but the winter wind
blows over the city.
Because Elaine is gone
our hearts can't feel
the blossom of the roses.

How can't we express sorrow
when everything emits
sadness.

I saw the leaves
pass by my window
they left the loving tree
so fast and violent
and in my thoughts
I look at you today
Elaine.

Amy McNeil
TO STUTTER
Who did I betray
to receive this curse?
My voice being held back
within my throat
while I try desperately
to let the words free

Words come out in bits
and pieces
Is it funnier than I see?
for people laugh and giggle
mock and tease
at my struggle

The harder I try
the longer
and funnier it gets
to free my voice
And relief is never in sight

This curse shields me
from reality
For each time I stutter
all I desire to do
is to run
or crawl
into a corner
within my own world

Where no one will hear my cries of despair.

Sherry Lane Jackson
THE WOMAN ON HER OWN
You sit and watch the butterfly
yet fail to understand
the nature of the one you love
you hold between your
hands . . .

They flitter
and they flutter
they call no place their
home . . .

The butterfly
the lady
the woman
on her own . . .

Sherry Lane Jackson
PEOPLE
Strangers walking
Wandering past me

Do they stop, to think, to care
Do they hestitate for amoment
wondering if there's brothership there . . .

Have I often followed their paths
Though I thirst for love and truth

Have I wandered onward quiet, silent eyes downcast
Neither wondering, knowing, caring
If they need my love or help . . .

Give me strength to rise above
The bonds of selfishness

Show me sunshine in the morning, moonlight in the eve
Help me show my brothers and sisters
My people of the world . . .

The love
The kindness, the determination

Of a world where love is lived not said
And people are people
Not women or men . . .

Sharry Lane Jackson
ON WINDY DAYS
On windy days
You'll think of me
With head tossed back
To feel the breeze

In early dawn
You'll know I lay
And write my words
Of yesterday

Words of sweetness
Words of sorrow
Woirds to make
A new tomorrow

Weep not about
A sad today
But dream about
A happy day

I'll think of you
You'll think of me
And know love grows
As seasons go . . .

Sherry Lane Jackson
SOMETIMES MORE NEEDED
Sometimes more needed
Thank "I love you"
Are the simple words
"I care"

Sometimes more needed
Than a loving caress
Is a hand reaching out saying
"I'm here"

Sometimes remembered are moments passed on
Some are in sorrow and tears
Some are in happiness, laughter and cheer
Some that will linger through years

Some always different
Never the same
Some are of you
My sweet dear . . .

Honey LaVonne Jimenez
ST. PATRICK'S DAY
St. Patrick's day is a day for green, symbolizing Ireland and what St. Patrick means.
St. Patrick as we know was a wonderful guy, he made all the snakes say "bye bye."
And now in the towns of this Emerald Land
there's a day for St. Patrick and it's always grand.
On this day people are happy and wear their green with pride,
And because of St. Patrick, people ask for their lives by God to guide.
So remember this day when we all wear green
and don't forget the wee folk, the Irish claim to have seen.
All of this makes up St. Patrick's day, May God be with you, I hope and pray.

Donna Walp
WITH LIGHT ON MY SHOULDER
With light on my shoulder,
And another across the room.
Heat blowing quietly,
Behold—my cocoon

The gloss of a magazine; a hot cup of tea
Some ice cubes in cola; a soft melody.
A book that I'm fond of, and not nearly half through;
To sit very comfortably, thinking of things I need to do.

The sadness of being weary,
The happiness of being alone,
The joy of being busy,
The ring of the telephone.

A warm oven at mealtime,
The peace when the dishes are done.
The glow of being healthy,
The pulse of things to come.

Life in general—is general
May these little things
Always give me comfort
—When a bumble bee stings.

Betty Jones
IN MY LIFETIME, I HOPE TO SEE
In my lifetime, I hope to see
The day you share your thoughts with me.

To hear you talk, to see you smile
Is what makes my life worthwhile.

In twenty five years we've shared so much
Now it seems we're out of touch.

Everyday is passing faster
I'm scared to death we'll forget what matters.

Oh, to get it back again,
To talk and share like old best friends.

Maybe words don't mean so much,
To some it's idle chatter.

But to care enough to share
Your feelings, hopes, dreams and fears
Show me—I really matter.

Wanda S Stephens
A ROSE (A ROSE IS LIKE FRIENDSHIP)

This poem is dedicated to Estela and Lisa Gooch, my very special friends.

A rose is like friendship
in each in every way,
just thinking about it
makes me want to say,

to get to the petals
it is difficult, it is hard
just like friendship, to make things work,
there's a plan that's on the card.

to take care of a rose
there is a little fuss, or a little bother,
but friends tend to bring
out the best in each other.

A rose has thorns
friendships have problems,
to hold it, the florist warns,
friends will try to solve them.

The rosebud will open
it will make a new start,
just like friendship
it will warm your heart.

unlike a rose, I'm not perfect,
my faults are easy to see,
but caring is in my heart
like you two are to me.

Everyone knows that we are friends,
just like a rose,
our forgiveness, trust and
beauty will never end.

Sandy

Debrina J Peek
LOVE OF MY LIFE

This verse is dedicated to the most steadfast friend and truest love a little girl could ever have had—my cocker spaniel—SANDY.

The love of my life is a sweet little guy,
with brilliant fair hair and lustrous brown eyes.

In his favorite position—his head in my lap,
I've never a doubt he'll savor a nap.

My gallant knight he'll ever be,
daring his own life to protect me.

His love is as true as an arrow in flight,
it goes on forever with no end in sight.

When I come home at the end of the day,
he greets me most thoroughly—then wants to play.

I have to be totally honest with you,
you've never known love 'til a dog has licked you!

Loyce McGraw
ADDICT
Try to grasp the edge of your brazen thought
At times so crazed, it reminds one of an auction block.
The colors all bright and waxed to hide
All the deception that lies inside.
The bargains you get as you dicker your way,
You soon talk yourself out of your hard-earned pay.
A fleeting thought as your dreams take control,
A golden door of which no man can enter
for the price is too high, and only you control the key.
But as slumber creeps through the dreary corridors,
The hidden doors are all ajar.
Emotions waiting to bid on the last bargain of all,
To take control and master the key,
That unlocks the terrors of insanity.

Dr Stacey Ess Crair
THE WORLD INSIDE OF ME
The futility of imagination—
dreaming visions that ne'er to be,
creating colors none can see
forsaking moments of reality
losing the core of your energy

The solitude of thoughts—
living exclusively inside of you,
yet only the outside can make them true
how easily they do traverse through
lingering only as long as you want them to

The element of control—
exists only within our souls,
we dream our desires—our goals
a world according to us do we mold none can touch, none can take,
what only we behold

The futility of dreams—
believing life will become what I see
experiencing smiles and joy as if reality
Feeling your presence within me
losing the core of my energy

—losing the core of myself.

Weldon Munson
THE FATHER'S BEST FRIEND
Jesus is the best friend that to mortal man ever came,
He's the Alpha and Omega.
He's every day the same.
With His Father, He agreed to give His cleansing blood.
Without His sacrifice, no man could be made good.

He agreed to stand alone, to remit our inherent sin.
His perfection is the secret of our perfection, then!
Friend, have you met this Jesus on a weary, dusty road?

Where He was healing others, did He lift your heavy load

Of condemnation, that breaks the heart and soul also,
His power alone can cleanse the guilt that lays us low.
But wait! His searching eyes are so kindly looking my way,
As with His beckoning hands He's asking: "What do you say?"

Then cried I: "O my Jesus! Have mercy, cleanse my soul!"
I have sinned against God and it's taken a terrible toll.
As an earthly father, I've not been the priest in the home,
But left the children's training to the wife, while I did roam.

O Father, on Father's Day, I repent with Godly sorrow,
Jesus come in and do a new work today, and for tomorrow.
Whatever the cost, my heart is fixed, gladly I'll serve thee,
Until I enter that Celestial City, and Jesus face to face I see!

Weldon Munson

BLAIRE

To our precious little great granddaughter, who was born October 16, 1986. She has honey-blond hair and sparkling, pale blue eyes. Blaire underwent heart surgery eight months ago. Now healthy, full of life and a joy to us.

A blue-eyed bundle of love has come to share
Her joy and love to those of us who really care.
Born at break of day, honored with the name of Blaire
Ready to be a blessing, as with this one they share

Many are the steps in life to keep the innocent one
From sinful words and habits and attitudes to shun.
But God has chosen Christians to live above reproach,
Faithful in prayer and example so no evil will encroach

Upon the life of this dear, loving, innocent child,
Who is completely helpless, trusting and undefiled.
Dainty little Blaire opens her eyes, looks around,
While angels hover o'er her, and love surrounds.

Dearest loved ones, will you join together in concern
As this precious little one is trained to so spurn
The harmful things of earth, choosing God's joy and love,
And her life's race is run, she'll be with Jesus up above.

Angela Di Domenico

YOU & I

To Ray, with love.

You and I, well we're one of a kind
If I analyze us, I'll lose my mind

I love the way we talk, the way we are together
Our relationship is growing, it can only get better

There's days I don't want anything else,
but to only be with you
I love you so much with all my heart, what is a girl to do

I'm glad you're in my life, I'm not lonely anymore
I think of the times, the awesome memories, and only wish for more

I'll tell you now again and again, I think that we're just great
I believe in us, I believe in love, yes, I believe in fate

Erin Elizabeth Bloomquist

SWEET RAIN

Sweet rain in the twilight; aging branches dripping stone pellets, into the earth.
Mist, sweeping the trees with heat and rage, turning the toadstools into leaning fronds waiting for the beauty of the sunrise.
Empty timbers, filling sticks and grass with water and sky;
making rivers run with rocks, etched from a man's face . . . olden times.
Blue skies, mixed with clean dirt and calloused palms;
pine boards, pushing up houses with nails and shingles, but not rain.
Rusted swings, screaming into the sunset of many days, turned battered and wrong.
A field filled with doom and yellow flowers waiting only for birdsong and sweet rain.
But . . . only one arrives—
laughter in the treetops carrying briefly through the doorway.
Sandlots crying empty in the dusk of dead September:
in the reds and orange of January-slumber we count the mazes circling in the airwaves.

Betsy Ann Rondeau

PEACE ON EARTH

To the pair of rainbows that awaken me every morning, Livia and Thomas.

—Wouldn't a peaceable spirit on our magnificent earth be the mightiest of all gifts? Sweet serenity, as a treasured love-song, whispering never-ending melodies to our beloved hearts.

—What a privilege to view God's creative collections, our blessed earth, his ageless masterpiece, with absences of anger, quarreling, and deceit.

—Peace, as glistening sand, intimately beckoning mankind to lay down and rest. Our beings imbued with perfect love.

—Continually stunned by the beauty of the new-born sky, the soothing, contented oceans, and the elegant motion of the soft-spoken trees.

—Smiling thoughts entering throughout our tranquil years, beckoning to the living waters of life. Holding a hand, smiles amongst neighbors, delighting in a job well done.

—Man's delicate nature embracing new-found pearls of peace, radiating their natural beauty through—out the eternities.
Peace, on earth.

Mary Ann Ballas Kaspor

Mary Ann Ballas Kaspor

LIGHT

To Fern Ballas, my dearest Grandmother and life long inspiration and mentor.

The days are light and my years are young . . .
I'm in the prime of the season . . .
Spring, Summer, Fall, Winter . . .
Who's to say?
Don't you love them all?
I look for you and you're not in sight . . .
My life has begun on a horrible flight . . .
The days are dark and my years are of yester-years . . .
The prime of my life . . . When you were here.
The seasons were all happiness content . . .

Spring, Summer, Fall, Winter . . .
The glory of life—all in one season . . .
You were the Spring . . . the beginning of life,
You were the Summer . . . the brightest sun ever,
You were the Fall . . . the keeping of life,
But . . . you were never winter . . .
you could not end life . . .
Winter . . . Oh how I hate you. The days are dark and the seasons
of life have ended . . . Winter has come and my days are dark.
Yes, Winter has come and gone and you're not in sight . . .
But we know, Don't we!
You were always my light.

Mary Ann Ballas Kaspor

TEARS

Oh the tears of my life have been many . . .
From beginning to present . . .
Infanthood, tears for the attention of parental care.
Childhood, tears for self-centered wants and needs.
Adolescent, tears for the lack of understanding.
Adulthood, tears now from life's philosophy . . .
Tears of deceitful desire.
Tears of foolish pride.
Tears of ungiving situations.
Tears of torn principles.
AND
Tears of sorrow.
Yes, I have cried tears for all,
BUT
No, not anyone knows the tears I cry for you . . .
Oh, the tears of unexplainable pain and deepest torment.

Mary Ann Ballas Kaspor

WINTER WRATH

Why are all the things around me exactly the same?
The turning emotion inside tells me things are completely different
these days . . . since you left that cold December day
It's hard for me to realize that things will never be the same . . . yet,
I see everything and things look the same, I hear everything and things sound the same, but I know deep within my heart your love could never be replaced.
Yes, the material world around me is exactly the same . . .
It's the deepest feelings within my heart that have changed . . .
For you see, you took part of my heart with you
the day God came for you . . . that cold December day.
The things you gave me were more than one could see or hear . . .
You gave me the meaning of caring, the reason for sharing, and a way to love.
No . . . it's no wonder, it's me that has changed.
Yes . . . everything will remain exactly the same . . .
Except . . . the most important thing.
My life has lost its greatest gift . . .
You, the one who has warmed my soul and filled my heart . . . with love.
It's these things that have changed . . .
For they have lost their roots and are unable to grow.
Yes . . . my emotions have encountered true sorrow.
My soul is cold and my heart is empty . . .
since you left that cold December day.

Debbie Reveron

FOURTEEN ROSES

14 roses will I now deliver to thee
For you to know how much I love thee
The love I have for you is strong
The love I have never can do wrong

How can I tell you what is in my heart
When all these tears keep tearing me apart
Shall I express my feelings in this card,
And address it to my beloved who now has gone
Here I lay and leave 14 roses
Here I shall stay and hose them with my tears
This Valentine's day I shall spend next to your grave
What is Valentine's day?
A day of love
Valentine's day is a day to mourn
These 14 roses express my love to thee
The thorns express the sorrow I feel since you left me
Why did you leave me,
Why did you go,
Why did you have to leave me alone
The 14 roses here they will stay
Until they die and shrivel away

Anne M Cupich
THE QUAKE

To my Sister, Lena Kesovia (Watsonville, San Francisco, Bay Area, Oct. '89 Quake).

It struck with a mighty shake
I knew immediately it was a quake
I viewed the sky without a sound
From my position on the ground
Terror brought my mind to a halt
Awake again was the San Andreas Fault
It rocked, swayed and ricocheted
From Hollister, Watsonville, to Frisco Bay
In its wake tall buildings tumbled and fell
This was a new kind of hell
Cries of sorrow, dismay and terror
I knew this town, as we built it, would be lost to us forever
Vibrating through the atmosphere
Doleful sounds fell on my ear
Through the night columns of fire and smoke
Terror reigned and with fearful heart no one spoke
In the morning to chaos all awoke
Everywhere cracks and rivulets appeared on the face of the earth
To tell the truth, there was little left of worth
Memories of this disaster would be felt for many a year
Along with sorrow, heartbreak, rebuilding and tears.

Janice Kay Sooter-Laubinger
LOST LOVE

Dedicated to my "Lost Love," Alton Lee Kitay.

Once you loved me, so long ago,
When life was simpler, not full of woe.
Now I stand alone, but strong,
And ponder how life has gone so wrong.
Why did I ever let you go?
Who can answer? Who can know?
I've wished a thousand times that you were mine,
But I cannot turn back the hands of time.
Wishing won't change a single moment,
Or begin to ease my mind of torment.
But maybe someday we both can be,
Together and happy, just you and me.

Robert Y Ozaki
THE TWO-YEAR-OLD

The two-year-old I walked on autumn eve
After tedious day of upturned sleeve,
What joy there was in eager face
As she pranced onward, quick in pace!

And then, with branch of darken'd bark,
She dug the loam at edge of park.
Elemental joy at the feel of night,
Unfettered glee 'neath Nature's sight.

And so I, rejecting all pretenses,
In harmony with her childish senses,
Dwelt within her innocent role
Before maturity and its toll.

O, so many, many years ago,
And she has grown, as I, also,
But the autumn walk still filters real
Through hosting memories that reveal.

Nikki Luederitz
the day of Berlin
today I saw Free
as my eyes danced through ashen barbed wire
over steely stone walls
to the Coloured World.

today I heard Free
as voices called up through sombered mists
and the wind rang with song
and laughter filled tears.

today I cried Free!
as I marched through the gates of the Day of Berlin
and handed my sentry
a wild rose.

Sandra J Spink
THE MORNING AFTER THE LOVING

To my work-a-holic husband, Donn.

It's another morning after and I'm left
with just the memory of his love . . .

Last night we were as close as two people can be
intimately,
Love overflowing he held me tightly as we slept
I dreamt by my side he would always stay,
But when morning came I awoke to find him gone
he had left quietly at the crack of dawn,
I wish he were here so I could feel his face
maybe share another embrace,
I know it's not that he doesn't care
he has a job he must be there,
Oftentimes it's hard for me to understand
why I can't come first with this man,
Sometimes I feel like a one night stand
even though I wear his wedding band,
Yes it's another morning after and I'm left
with just the memory of his love . . .

Reneé A Webster
THE CANDLE

This poem is dedicated to my father, Abraham L. Stepman.

The candle burns—
Slowly peeling back the separate
Layers of its life.

Flame Flickering—

Burning in a solitary room—no other
Light present then that which emanates
From its tall slender body.

Strangers enter—Feeling the warmth,
But not noticing its death in their presence.

Quietly—without drama—its last Flicker
Slowly burns out. Only then—do the
Strangers notice—and replace it with a new martyr.

Karl Van Bibber

Karl Van Bibber
FRIDAY NIGHT FOOTBALL
Homecoming belles and teacher cheer
Regaled the night—the Season's here.
From bobby socks to Army gear,
Old memories benched among their peer.

A stadium live with horns and voices,
Hot dogs, balloons, and other choices.
"First down and ten" began each series,
With cheers led by high school dearies.

Each team moved with body might
As moved the night in amber bright.
And moonlit numbers showed their height,
Still to grow another night.

Karl Van Bibber
THE NEWEST DAY
In sullen mood and morbid thought
I seek the charm of prose within,
But failed I did of what I sought
For one old love is but a friend.

In a loveless room the still air hears
TV's voice speaking with a start.
Words that reach receiving ears,
But do not move a lonely heart.

With love's return, my world is bright;
Awesome darkness moves into light.
Smiles are seen and touches felt,
And cold silence succumbs to melt.

Blending hearts and souls as one,
The newest day is never done;
For eyes that touch each other's pain
Removes the hurt and we start again.

Karl Van Bibber
THE FORCE
The pulse that beats within the tree
And raises limbs from naught to Thee,
Is Thine own Force that sets us free,
Whether falling leaf or Family Tree.

From dust to dust the two shall trod,
But His Family Tree shall leave the sod;
Each, in beauty, leaves its mark:
One leaves forever—the other bark.

K M Clay
AN ARDENT OFFERING

For Maggie.

I know you well. Most all of you.
Your every cove,
And inlet mountain and island; the special,
Geography of the continents that are you.
Far away, across such seas as Sinbad never sailed.
Though still, I know my voyage has failed; still yet,

I know well enough what deeps are there;
Unfathomed undersea trenches, hiding
Ancient wrecks, historical conflagrations.
I cannot touch them; cannot wave my hand,
And conjure them gone! I've gone quite pale,
And wan, in the wishing for it.

And it's true, these things I'd do, will not
Magic you, cannot witch you well, and hale
And whole; and I know, too, if I've not lost you yet,
I likely will, and soon. God knows,

The love is real enough. So many miles between us,
Concrete-shod. A lesser thing might turn, as seasons do,
Into something else again. Yet still, I do not change.
An ardent heart smoulders on the altar,

A burnt offering.

Kendra Kae Fishburn
COULD YOU?
Could you ever love me
Like the stars love the night,
And give my heart such freedom,
And inspire me to fly?

Could you ever need me
Like a flower needs the rain,
Not too much to smother you,
But bring life to you again?

Could you ever hold me
Like the sky holds the sun?
We'll shine throughout the universe,
And together become one.

Could you ever show me
What the ocean shows the sand,
How to form a new beginning
And wash away a painful past?

We could be so good together
And together accomplish all our goals.
We could help each other live and learn,
And together we could grow . . .
FOREVER . . . .

Kim Hemphill
WORK APPRECIATION
To be appreciated
is something
everyone needs.
To do something
necessary
Requires hard deeds.
To work along
with responsibility.

To get it done
without being told.
To do it all
without hesitation
To be recognized
for what's been done.

To know work's done well
and appreciation
is the motivation
that makes us go on
and not want us
to go to hell.

To see a smile,
to hear a Thank You.
To feel appreciation
from our dedication.
To make it all
happen.

Pamela Nabholz
SARAH WOULDN'T EAT HER LIMA BEANS
Sarah wouldn't eat her lima beans.
Her mother screamed, her father shouted,
her dog howled, but she wouldn't eat her
lima beans.
She sat and sat until a day when all
her friends came out to play.
Sarah said, "I'm going out to play."
She was so old she couldn't move an inch.
Her friends helped her up. Clunk!
It was 80 years too late.

Pamala Reece
RAG DOLL
Oh lucky lucky my rag doll
With smile upon your face
And ne'er a care in this world
For need of time and space.
Sawdust inside, without a heart
You sit there all alone
While I instead, with tears inside
Feel my heart turn to stone.
If I had choice, oh my rag doll
Of spending life in pain
I'd join you on the shelf this day
And never hurt again.
Instead I sit here listening to
My clock upon the wall
Each tick reflecting in my soul
Of how I've lost it all
Oh smiling doll, oh lucky doll
So brief that joy was mine
And now the endless days ahead
Are filled with only time

Paul Alan Fischer
WHY LORD
If I was created
In your image,
Why was I given a mind,
That could be influenced so easy?
Why was I formed with this body,
That is imperfect and weak?
Why must this body have a heart,
That once broken may never heal,
Why Lord, oh why?

Mary Reid
QUEEN WINTER
Queen Winter is a haughty queen
With a pale and beautiful face
The icicles are her bodice stays
And the wind is her sweeping grace.

Her garments are made of the softest white
Trimmed with yards of the blue-blacklace
Borrowed from the silhouette of the trees
As they stand in their naked grace.

Her slippers are crystal, cut from a pool
To flatter her dainty feet
In place of a buckle there blooms a rose
A Christmas Rose, soft and sweet.

Over this all she wears a cape
With sky-diamonds from neck to train
Caught when the temperature starts to fall
Making jewels out of the rain.

She wears a crown as all queens do,
Each having their royal reasons
While across her breast a banner floats
"Queen Of All The Seasons."

Chandra Baker
IF I WAS A BUTTERFLY

To my family, with all my love.

If I was a butterfly,
I would fly high, high, high, in the sky.
Just like any old butterfly.
I would eat bugs,
Just like slugs.
I would live in a tree,
Like a bee.
I would lay eggs on milkweed,
Like others on seed.
Soon I will die,
So I say goodbye!

Katherine Osten
SOUL DANCING
dancing with your soul
dancing with your self
being conscious
aware
alive
a dream-like state
free and
unfettered
being in a different world
a different time
stepping into your mind
unconscious desires surfacing
reaching the divine
the sacred
finding a unique path
of higher self
of higher love
dancing with your self
dancing with your soul

Danny Boyd

Danny Boyd
A FRIEND

This poem is dedicated to Ms. Kim Boyd, who just happens to be my daughter, but more importantly; she is my friend.

A friend is someone
For whom you care,
A friend is someone
With whom you can share,
A thought, a smile,
A hug, a kiss;
A friend is someone
You know you will miss;
When they are gone
You're alone and blue,
A friend is someone
Just like you!

Virginia McClarney
HAUNTED
Strangers meet
with a friendly handshake.
Sharing a moment in time.
A quick goodbye.
Suddenly black eyes
meet and lock with blue.
A look of intense
longing and desire.
Unexpected.
A quick, quivering breath.
The shattering knowledge
of what has passed between them.
Not planned, not wished for,
Denied.
But as they part
each knows the other
will always be
Haunted.

Deborah A Boehm
UNTITLED
(I AM NON-EXISTENT . . .)

*To those who saw beyond, to within;
For my fellow creatures, who gave me Hope.*

i am non-existent
passing through myriad shades
of lives
being what they think
none knowing WHO i am
regardless of what is said or done
an Illusion not of my own design
that, too, is lost of me
my soul blazing with WHO i am
what I can share
if only ONE would look
through the eyes of the body
to see i am not the Illusion
created of me
non-existent.

Deborah A Boehm
DESERT RAIN
I have lost the ability to cry—
to purge my soul of impurities
shed upon it by Mankind's
innate destructiveness;
To weep away the acrid tears of Mother,
tears of the pain from Mankind;
Tears to soften against crackening
hardness of non-caring.

I long to weep
with the sadness filling my heart
at the path of harm Man has taken;
Yet only dust pours from my eyes
as my heart weeps for the world.

Deborah A Boehm
THE GATESKEEPER'S TOLL
strings finely tuned
pluck with the resonance
of the green hued valley
between barren mountains,
carry up to the heart
where the last
sours in response.

Deborah A Boehm
UNTITLED
(And it was smashed . . .)
And it was smashed
by violent hand
And jagged edge hung, ready
to slice.
but from within,
once cracks cleared
reality shone thru twofold.

Nadirah S Bahaar
THE DREAM
As Marvin Gaye said it, "Millions of people have never seen their dream, or felt their dreams, or felt their world stand still. Millions never and millions never will."

How frightening to think that I could be one, one of the million.

Nadirah S Bahaar
TALENT
Grandma Moses knew it and she lived seventy–five years trying to unscramble her thoughts. She was in search of her gift her talent, which she had been given at birth.
She was no different than you or I. We all were given life and that entity connotates equality.

I met her in my mid twenties. The difference in our age, a mere half a century didn't defuse the relationship.

I listened with caution and extreme enthusiasm and I heard her read my thoughts and I watched her gently remove my talent from my heart and place it directly in front of me.

We both agreed that the search would not cease until we found our talent and left it in this world. Our most concentrated thought was on our creator. We indelibly knew, that if we didn't discover our talent, then our creator was a liar and life was just an illusion.

In case you didn't know, Grandma Moses searched all of her life and upon her seventy–sixth birthday, she picked up a paint brush and painted a masterpiece.
She was an artist just like me.

Nidirah S Bahaar
THE OTHER SELF

Say you!
God and I know how I have wanted for so many years to tell you to die. I have hated you with everything in me and I didn't have the courage to tell you. You have been untrustworthy, deceitful and calculating to say the least. You have been the greatest liar of all ages. In lying you denied everything that I could have been in order to have your own selfish sick way with me. I feel no pain in saying good-bye to you. Because, I realize today you tried to destroy me. I was your friend and I trusted you with my life. I knew I was in trouble but you wouldn't let me face it. You told me to believe in you because I was too weak and very unsure, and I was foolish enough to take care of you. I dressed you in the finest clothes money could buy or fast hands could take. I fed you, kosher rich food at the wrong time and you made me sick. I gave you the best drugs, always from the top. I stole and cheated for you, because you made me believe that you loved me and you would die without me. I did everything you told me to. You said hook your brother and sister and I did. Then you betrayed me.

Well! you're on your own now. I've found a wonderful, sensitive, loving and caring person, whom I feel I must get to know. She makes me feel alive and wanted, she won't allow me to spend one dime for her own selfish and destructive pleasure. You know why? Because she's naturally beautiful. She knows how to preserve life and in knowing that, her chances of living are excellent, and I am willing to live with her.

However! I have grown from knowing you. I thought I would die if I let go. But I can't forget the near death situations that you so cunningly tricked me into.
So now I say farewell . . .
Please don't try to contact me forget me as I have forgotten you. Your trade of slickness doesn't work anymore, and I simply refuse to let you live rent free in my mind.

Kevin Coccari
I AM A BIT-PART ACTOR

I am a bit-part actor
in a legendary life,
chronicled daily
by unstruck tragedy.
The air if filthy,
blocking an otherwise
clearing view.
Abstract realms of clouded
amazement
sear into my being.
No possessions
except self.
No goals
except life.

Vivian Matthews
SOLITUDE

This poem is dedicated to my children, Myra Leonard, and Damon Matthews.

There is a spot
That no one can describe,
Or can compare,
To what there is
And what there's not,
We only know it's there.

It is this place of solitude,
That we all search to find.
Where we can all lay down our cares,
And find our peace of mind.

So as we search we all must try
To leave a mark as we go by,
Where others may as they so live,
Have courage to work and give,
So in the end we all may see,
The people we were meant to be.

Antoinette Adelquist Bell
ADIOS

Oracion, a prayer for your safe arrival
Esperanza, a hope that you find joy
Rayo de sol, a sunbeam chases all denial
Ninos, children, many—for you—your boy

Tenura, a tenderness longs for your comfort
Fuerza, a strength to keep you from harm
Exito, a success so you feel a substance
Amor, a love, not a deceptive alarm

Delor, a pain to know you wish something
Satisfaccion, a satisfaction to fill your cup
Dios, God, instead of an intemperate nothing
Nutrimento, food and drink, that you always sup

Regalo, a gift for you of aquamarine oceans
Lagrima, a tear from me solely for you
Pasion, a passion of undying emotions
Vida, a life forever that to itself remains true

Antoinette Adelquist Bell
TWO LOVES

Did I interrupt your reality
Did I in any way take some of your time
Knowing temporal life, not finality;
Did you for once sip too heady a wine

Do not admit you were light headed
Do not admit you had capacity for love
Say only that your world you now dreaded
Shock all living things below and above

Why should I shirk from begrudged passion
Why would I retreat from dubious gift
My agony was more than you imagine
And your pain only an ephemeral rift.

Claire Carpentier
FACE TO FACE WITH FEAR

I was alone and afraid,
thought no one cared,
so I ran away into a world,
I knew nothing about,
the country.

The road was long, dusty,
and seemed endless,
hours passed before I rested,
I noticed what was once,
a clear blue sky,
had now turned clouded grey.

The road I traveled,
darkened as it began to storm,
I ran for cover under the trees,
but their leaves had already fallen,
from the crisp autumn air.

Then it became clear to me,
I can't run away from fear,
I have to face it head on,
It's time to go back home,
where I belong.

G L McDaniel

G L McDaniel
THE ONE EYED SOLDIER

Long ago I was just a hobo
There was a lot I needed to know
World War Two was on and I was all alone
I wanted to go and defend my home
The Doctor said Son you only have one eye
I'm sorry but we'll have to pass you by
I said Doctor I can lift fertilizer
A two hundred pound bag
And I'm not about to let nobody
Turn our flag into a rag
I can climb a one hundred foot tree
That don't have a limb
I've never seen a river that I couldn't swim
The Doctor said Son I've got work to do
And the way I see it here you're through
I turned and walked into the dark
With tears in my eyes I sat in the park
I looked down the train was almost full
I thought to myself
Doctor you're full of bull
I went down and stood by the train
I didn't have a coat and it began to rain
My friend looked at me and said
I don't want to go
Then he dropped his head
We can change places
I know you love your flag
Here, around your neck, I'll place my dog tag
All through the war I answered to Bill
I saw a lot of soldiers go over the hill
I didn't pass judgment it was not up to me
Sometimes the whole story
Is very hard to see
I had my pack and ready to go
I felt so good I want you to know
We got off the ship and it was hell
But so far I was doing well
It was France Italy and Germany
For such a long time
Somehow I stayed in the center of the line
Day after day I could have died
There was not a day or night
That I hadn't cried
The day came we got back home
I still had one eye and was all alone
Of all the shells that I saw fly
I do remember tears falling from that bad eye
I never got a letter
Or had my own dog tag
I'm an old man now, but I've still got a flag

Geraldine Hughes
MEMORIES OF ME

To my daughter Karen who shares my love of poems & poetry writing and to my husband Willie who thinks it's great that I'm included in your book of poetry.

Am I alive or am I dead?
My eyes are open, yet I can't see how you could have done these things to me.
Like a weeping willow all I do is cry as the joys of life are passing me.
I was you, you were me, I couldn't see you without seeing me.
Now you're telling me you want to be free, free from the only one who loves you—me.
I'll try to be strong, I'll not try reasoning, as time goes on you'll find there's no pleasing you without—me.

John P Marzullo
PARTNERS

To my lovely wife Phyllis who God blessed me as my partner for life.

It seems that today's trend
Is not to have business with a friend.
For problems arise that are not foreseen,
No matter what our plan or scheme.
With sweat and tears and a dream in our heart,
We search for solutions until dark.
Joy and sorrow do partners share,
And rely on each other to grin and bear.
For our dreams are true and our goals are in sight,
That we work side by side each day and each night.
I thank God for a partner who is there to stay,
When it is hard to bear the problems that arise each day.

So may God bless our union and work together,
And bring us prosperity in all kinds of business weather.

John P Marzullo
MY NAME
My name is all I have when earthly riches have gone from me,
But my Lord knows the status of my heart with Thee.
I ask not for glory, fame or being right,
But only that my name is cleared of all false gossip so that we can end this fight.
It is better to say nothing than defame the bad,
But I am being forced to defend my name and that makes me sad.
When God knows the truth all is right with me,
Even though slander is heard all around me.
So lift up your head and speak kindly of your enemies' name,
For God is the only true judge of my humble name.

Wanda Parnell
GOD'S PLAN

This poem is dedicated to my daughter Mynon who asked me to write something about the sand dollar legend. I told the story again for her.

This story has been told before,
but for you, I'll tell it once more.
When God created all creatures
and placed them in the sea and
on the land, for the sand dollar,
He had a special plan.
He placed upon it symbols which
tell the greatest story ever told,
and in time the story did
unfold.
A star appeared in the sky and
led the shepherds one night, and
it is when the poinsettias are
in bloom, that we celebrate
the birth of Christ.
Four holes on the sand dollar,
must represent the nail wounds
and the other one, the wound
from a spear, when Jesus
died on the cross, without
fear.
He was crucified in that hour, but
on the sand dollar there is yet
another symbol, it is our Easter
flower.
God did desert Him, never, for on
Easter, He arose, and now He
lives forever.
And as we say that Jesus is our
Dove of Peace, He lives within
our heart, inside the
sand dollar there are five
white doves, just waiting
to depart.
But just as the body of Jesus was
pierced and broken for you and
me.
The sand dollar's body must be
pierced and broken, the doves
to set free.
So when we see a sand dollar, and
hold it in our hand, we feel very
close to Jesus.
That is a part of God's plan.

Wanda Parnell
SAFE AT LAST
He said "Come!" with outstretched hand.
"I'll lead you through this troubled land."
He took my hand in a warm firm clasp.
I knew I was safe at last.

Mistakes of the past He did not condemn.
Now if there is a doubt, I consult Him.
I can go forward with a confident step.
He is beside me and I can depend on His help.

Sometimes, when I'm carrying a heavy load,
my feet stumble on the rocky road.
I need have no fear at all.
I know He will catch me before I fall.

If my fingers sometimes slip away and my feet attempt to stray,
I find myself doing things I should not do
and saying things I should not say.
It's then, He says "Come!" with outstretched hand,
"I'll lead you through this troubled land."

I feel my hand in a warm firm clasp.
I know I'm safe at last.

Jennifer Emerling
GOING AWAY
Although I'll soon be leaving
The friends whom I don't want to part,
I'll always remember the good times
And keep the memories close to my heart.
As I sit on my bedside each and every night,
A teardrop drops from my eye
As I think soon I'll be gone
And I try not to cry.
I know that I won't be gone forever
And we'll keep in touch,
But just the thought of being away
Oh friend, I'm going to miss you very much.
As I'm slowly leaving you,
I realize I have to try
The hardest thing I've ever done
To you is say goodbye.

Jeffrey J Klashka
POTION

Out of a dream; Out of the sky, into my heart, into my life, to my love, my dark eyes, my wife. Beverly Ann Klashka.

Preconceive a notion
Think it through
Love is not devotion
Let's try something new
Use a little lotion
A couple tubes of glue
Stir with a circular motion
Add color—how 'bout blue
Throw it in the ocean
And dive in too.
Just a little commotion
Maybe something to do
We don't need a potion
Just the words "I Love You."

Elsa Schultz
THE ENDING OF THE 20TH CENTURY
What do you say to the world today
At the ending of the century
The wars that were fought
The millions that died
The powers gained and lost
The fortunes made from greed
What do you say to the world today
At the ending of the century
Of unborn babies that are disposable items
Of technology harming us as well as helping us
Of those that say new age is great
Of those that seek the dark side of evil
What do you say to the world today
At the ending of the century
That of the romance of yesterdays
That of the family ties of long ago
That of caring and loving our neighbors
That of peace in our heart which comes only from God
What do you say . . . .

Carla Richardson Grover
MY SON

This poem is dedicated to my wonderful son, James M. Pettincki, Jr.

6-18-1986
My son has moved from his roost
I thought my morale it would boost;
Why is it then I'm so depressed
Concerned over his unrest;
He seems immature and not quite ready
To undertake responsibility—at least not steady;
Too young to fear the bumpy road
Too young to listen or be told;
Part of life is fighting back
Finding one's way down the track;
Our burdens come too quickly,
Too soon we grow old;
We love and we worry but his way he must find
The way of his choosing and not that of mine;
He will grow up and I will grow old
Later in years the result will unfold.

Mary Hammock
THANKS GOD
I cannot remember all the things
I am thankful for in my life.
The beauty that the seasons bring
The joy of becoming a wife.

Thank God for the life he gave me
For the love of family and friends.
For the eyes the beauty to see
For a broken heart that he mends.

For the food to nourish my soul
For the health that fails and he tends.
The faith to play all the roles
That my God has said he intends.

Lord, let me finish my days
Giving thanks for all that you do.
For the roses along the pathway
And the thorns that are very few.

Raymond Bower
THOUGHTS AND MEMORIES
Do you ever take time from a busy day,
To see all the beauty that God sent our way.
The mountains the trees, the lakes and the sea,
He gave them to you, He gave them to me.

Have you ever gazed at the majestic beauty of a waterfall,
As it makes its plunge from a high rocky cliff
To the valley floor below?
Or viewed the splendor of a mountain peak,
Capped with the white and glistening snow?

Have you ever watched a brook twisting and turning,
Making its way through a meadow green with grass,
Skirting a long-ago deserted farm house
With fallen down barn? deserted, no not completely,
approaching from the shadows of the early morning dawn
I can see a mother deer, and trusting in guidance,
There is a new born fawn.

As I look out of my window in the morning
I see the jet black darkness turning to a soft grey,
I thank God for all these wonderful things He has given,
And that in His goodness and mercy
Has found it proper and fitting to give to us another day.

Tania J Engelbert
PERSONAL SYMBOLS
A symbol for love is a sky so
blue,
It makes me believe that you are
true.
The warmth of the sky fills the
world with peace
The meaning it holds cannot be
released.
When the sky so blue fades off to
a grey,
It means that the symbol of love
is astray.
And we as humans must try to
renew it:
Even the elderly never outgrew
it.
Each of us knows of a symbol of
love,
And it seems so fitting—like
a hand in a glove.
And we must take that symbol
in order to see
That there's more love than hate
between you and me.

Christopher McDonald
THE EBONY OF LIFE

To Heidi Gray and Debbie Kahler, my two inspirations in life.

To try your best in all that you do
And never give up, but stand tall and be true
This is the struggle life puts at your feet
Giving you nothing but fear and defeat
To do all you can to only find pain
To think that you've won with nothing to gain
This is the darkness that comes with each day
For life gives no answers but has questions to say
To live a life carefree and yet blue
And to try and find answers in all that you do
This is the challenge of life that's to meet
To never give up in the face of

defeat
And all of life's answers have questions inside
Some fact of life that it tries to hide
So in the ebony of life, you must stand tall and be true
And look for the answers in all that you do —

Tom Watkins
BENDING
Sunrise reveals a million scattered dew drops
Which, despite their size, do bend the light, true prisms;
Until a surface—contoured window glass—collect each water glop
And force a union in a plane, which begs to deny schisms.

And I at sunrise, brain-diffused, fractured in the AM wind,
Will grope until I see the light, as scattered bit or spark;
And hope through day a window pane to see with less fogged mind,
To bend some sparks 'to rainbowed thoughts, 'fore sunset bids my dark.

Carmel Hardin
SISYPHUS
Sisyphus, proletariat of the gods.
When the gods condemned you
to roll a mammoth rock
to the mountain top
and let it fall back again
a hundred times.
Did you rebel?????
You did not. Patiently you served their sentence
Did you treat them with levity?
What did you do to the god of death
and to the gods of life
and to the gods of war?
Scornful of fate
you considered your wife's love.
Sisyphus whose life began in sorrow and ended in happiness.
May we all have the same fate.

Debby Ann Rogaski

Debby Ann Rogaski
UNIQUE—NOT PERFECT

To my entire family . . . I Love you for allowing me my uniqueness and accepting my imperfections.

Like a diamond . . .
the complexity of facets
chiseled and chipped
polished to perfection
reflecting its prisms
achieving the being
of which I have become.

As a precious gem . . .
be proud to show my beauty
my strengths, my softness
all sides of me
as no others are found
to be an exact duplicate.

Unique as I may appear . . .
underlying flaws are found
an imperfection
in what seemed to be perfect.

Take no less pride, make no judgements
don't hold back my radiating
of all that I can be
my only claim is to be unique,
not perfect.

Carol Ann Angell
COWBOY

To all real western men: especially Dean and Jim Angell, Roy and Lowell Richmond, Bill Shannon, Val Geissler, Turk Ahlquist.

Jeaned-blue to match the western sky,
Simple men united in the art called ranching.

Some are honest and strong like the mountains,
others worn and showing snow-capped years of worry and strife.

Tender in heart like a new-born licked calf,
bodies worked to leather-lean.

Knowledge greater than school or business icon degree,
sharing nature never taking or adding to "Mother Earth" cares.

She rewards with her beauty freely given,
More honest than marriage bands,
Her hold a partnership called life.

Unite with me she whispers,
with her tempting waters that nourish the soul.

Bone tired men and steed come to rest,
On her bosom in meadows of wild-flowers.

Held gently by their friendly hello faces,
A special love known by few.

Tree's boom in crescendo with cattle bawls,
United with wind to beckon
bandana-red setting sun.

Men gather to warm the body with fire along with coffee and beans,
Among embers of day's events and stories of long ago shared.

Out come patched bedrolls,
Like some time worn uniform
longing for a better rank.

Comfort at sleep is their pay,
but conscience free to face humanity another day.

Beginning again at dawn's call of names . . .
"Moose, Bear, Turk, Val, Slim."

Never known well by man,
But in time of need trusted more by God in simple name of
"COWBOY."

Like the rainbow a mixture of many colors,
blessings without endings.

Thus a treasure never to be held,
Only in friendship.

Tom Watkins
FIRE IN ICE
Before the sun awoke to bathe the lake's cosmetic, layered ice,
Nor form nor shape nor beauty's contours were revealed;
She lay dead still to nurture sea's deep sleep, from subzero slumber entice
Her rest in coolth, beneath a coverslip the firmament's still concealed.

The sound of northern silence maintained a presence there,
Till groans & shrieks of ice's strain relieved the anechoic,
Still state, as snaking wind in esses whispered prayer.
She lay asleep, this ice clothed lady, draped in ice togs cooly stoic.

By sunrise, icy moans & snores increased in amplitude,
As light from solar fire breathed life into her frigid soul,
In chorus sang, ice voices tuned by crystal movements' servitude,
A beauty radiant leapt out of her bosom:
heaven's light escaped
her frozen stole.

Does ice at last reveal her transfixed glory, under light
Waves incandescent, infuse her heart & skin, her latticed rainbow prism,
Until what enters her deep, crystal, igloo heart erupts a fire so bright,
She sheds the flame within our hearts, an arctic taste of Holy Chrism.

Tom Watkins
INBREATHED
She speaks, he hears, sweet union, their hearts moved to tears;
Will trifle now we hear, this bridge collapses, lacking ears.

The serpent contrived to tease, beguile the couple without relent,
Till words struck home, so birthing badness, evil, death invent.

The naming game, once charged to man's outspoken, oracled taste,
Eventually saved appearances each, from timeless, cosmic waste.

Would Moses, hearing voice on Sinai's rock, 'mid fire-lit shower,
Defer to craft arts, nailed to rock in chains, Prometheus's power?

O'er shadowed, black sea, billows nudged souls' static, silent barks,
Till God's breath breathed moved your soul and then mine,
now freed from netherland darks.

TAnthony Scott DeBorde
TAKE ME AWAY

To my inspiration, my life, Sookie Norman. Still Loving You . . . .

Scan the horizon, what do you see?
Nothing but open skies, infinity,
Where are we going? Where have we been?
Will better days befall us, before the end?
Lost in confusion, lost in these times,
We search for tomorrow, crossing the lines,
Take me away,
Somewhere far,
Out to the limits,
Near a star,
Take me away, please someday,
Take me away
Scan the horizon, drift with the scene,
Without new beginnings, there will be no more dreams,
See my reflection, cast on the sea,
So easy to lose it, are we ever really free?
Take me away,
Somewhere far,
Out to the limits
Near a star,
Take me away, please someday,
Take me away,

Julie Whitehead Shearer
DESTINATION

This poem is dedicated to: my two precious children whom I will always love and cherish—Gwendolyn LeighAnn & Franklin Zachary Shearer.

Finally I have reached my Destination
The three things I most wanted and waited for, for so long
(Now I have found). I'm now shielded from all grief,
hurt and pain. I shall no more worry about the little
Things in life, for now they don't matter.
No more pain shall dwell in my soul.
No more guilt or shame shall enter my mind.
No more grief and hatred shall be found in my heart.
Now I shall rejoice, for I have found Tranquility
And peace of mind. For I am finally at rest and
Now with my Lord and Saviour, Jesus Christ.

Linda S Wilkinson
THE OLD HOUSE
I let my thoughts wander
Back through the years
To a place so fond
I spent such happy hours

In the old white house
Nestled on a grassy knoll

The June sun shines
Breezes rustle in the trees
I can hear the bees buzz

In each big room
Memories flood in
I can hear the laughter
From days long past.

Oh, to be a child again
To feel the safety of those walls
That seems to elude us
In the rush of today's world
Just to turn back the hands of time

Judith R Gordon

DAD AT 70

To my beloved father, Hyman D. Bunkin—Now in God's hands.

My Rock of Gibraltar who's always there
In all weather, foul or fair

Who, with my mother, gave me life
And a brother for fun and strife

Who taught me how to forge ahead
Through the days to earn my bread

By example, I learned to be tenacious
But tried never to forget to be gracious

In defeat as well as victory
You have always been an example to me

Now that you've reached your seventieth year
Be assured you have no peer

You are the finest man I know
A sturdy oak who continues to grow

Not old, dear dad
That would be sad

But grander to the inth degree
I'm so glad you're father to me

Coleta Newton

FRIENDSHIP WITH LA RECEA

The warmth of sunshine on my face
Thoughts and memories hang in space
A sense of peace wraps around my soul
As a blanket gives comfort when the night is cold.
The heavens are blue, white clouds drift by
Making shapes and images that catch my eye.
Visions form, reminders of happy days
Summertime games where everyone plays.
Sharing secrets of first loves' pain
Knowing life will never be the same again.
Dreams untold are spoken at last
In whispers to a friend, the mold has been cast
For a friendship that has endured through the years
Born of the sharing of joys and of tears.
Allowing us each to express our mind
With a deep understanding we sought to find.
And now our thoughts and eyes can view
Life's promises gone by and those that are new.
But that friendship remains with special care
With many new promises and love to share.

Ollie Blackwood

REACHING FOR STARS

'Twas the year 1950 when a class took flight in time
Each reaching for their star was all that was really on their mind.

Each took a road to who knows where
Hoping that their particular star could be found there.

Some found their star, some stumbled and fell
Some are still searching, yet knowing quite well

That to find their star is no easy task
It seems to hide or wear different masks

But they continue to reach, to search and perhaps find
That big beautiful star that has always been on their mind.

Have you reached your star, did you stumble and fall
Did you reach out a hand, or perhaps try to call

Or are you still searching, knowing quite well
As long as you keep reaching, there is no way to tell

How high you can go, to what lofty height,
As the Class of 1950 who took their first flight

Reaching for the stars, a particular one in mind
Searching, hoping, they would find theirs in time.

Tracy Noble

SKIING

The winter season is a time to ski,
Up and down those slopes, a time to feel free—

I ride the lift to the top, observing the snowcovered slopes,
With slick skis on my feet, and shiny poles in hand, adrenalin flowing, there go those hopes—

It's a sight that's spectacular, and really something to behold,
Some consider it as great as silver, I consider it as great as gold—

The trip is almost over, and I'm cruzin' to the top,
I'm smackin' my gum, tryin' to get my ears to pop—

The higher up I go, the quieter it begins to seem,
Out behind the trees, the brilliant rays of sunshine gleam—

I'm finally at the peak, off the lift I go,
The feeling is awesome as my skis hit the powdery snow—

I fly down the cat walks to the Black Diamond run,
Get that blood pumpin', and really have some fun—

"Swoosh, swoosh," down the mountain I fly,
Hearing the piercing sound of the wind passing by—

I hit those moguls one by one,
Continuing my journey, until I'm done—

The moguls have ended, and the flat land appears,
On this trip down, there were no frights and no fears—

It's down to the bottom where I once began my trip,
First it's to the lodge to get that hot chocolate sip—

Vail, Colorado is the place to be,
For wanting to feel free, and SKI
SKI
SKI

Jennifer J Nunnemacher

PASSION OF LOVE

Dedicated to Tim, You will always be the ever lasting beauty of a rose within my heart. All my love, Jennifer.

Curled up by the heat of the fire just beneath the mantle—
I sit sipping sweet nectar . . . day dreaming,
Rocking myself gently as my lips form a soft smile—
Thinking of you—missing you.

Such joyous times we share together.
Especially when we just hold each other.
Then, before you know it—It's time to say goodnight.
I miss you before the last kiss . . .
Although, I'll always have such sweet memories to cherish
until our eyes meet again.
To love and to hold the embrace
of emotions so close to our hearts,
Keeping the fire burning, watching your eyes sparkle
As they gaze into mine.
Both whispering softly, "They love" the other . . .
Feeling that if forever was possible . . .
This is the beginning of an ever lasting love.

Earline Hunt

EVEN ON A DAY LIKE THIS

The sky is dark, the clouds are low;
The toaster broke, the car won't go.
But Jesus loves me, this I know—
Even on a day like this.

My little son has cut his knee.
The smog's so thick it's hard to see.
But God in Heaven loveth me—
Even on a day like this.

The troubles come, the money goes.
My nerves are taut, my temper blows.
But God our every trouble knows—
Even on a day like this.

I'm tired of work, my mood is blue.
The need is great, the hours few.
But God has time for me and you—
Even on a day like this.

The traffic's stopped, I'm short of time.
I need to call, I've lost my dime.
But Jesus's love is still sublime—
Even on a day like this.

My day was filled with too much "I."
I slapped my child and made her cry.
Yet God loves me—I don't know why—
Even on a day like this.

No matter how my world may fall,
All I need to do is call
The One who is my life, my all—
Even on a day like this.

Val McReynolds Jr

Val McReynolds Jr

MEMORIES OF YOU

To Grandma with love and the years most cherished when I was young.

When looking back at my young days
I see how much with you I stayed.
So many memories fond and true
I have of when I stayed with you.
Some come to mind I cherish so
Like watching robins, you must know.
I think was there I first did see
Rudolph's red-nose as red could be.
And yes those stars that glowed so bright
When it was time for bed at night.
Oh! I have to laugh inside
At some of the things I could not hide.
It was your phone by heart I knew
When I was cut and sure scared too.
Oh! the memories are not few
Oh! so many fond and true.
In closing I would like to say
I love you still as much today.

Val McReynolds Jr

A LOVE LETTER

To my dear wife and son, Teresa and Ryan, with love.

I've told you once or twice before,
How much I love you, that's for sure.
I look back now and wonder why,
I caused you pain enough to cry.
It's times like this when far away,
I think of all I've done.
If not for our salvation,
Then Satan would have won.
But thanks to God He pulled us through,
And filled my heart with love.
You were the one He planned for me
Like grace upon a dove.
I'll praise the Lord and never end,
For you and Ryan too.
The love and joy you've given me,
No words could rightly do.
I know it's still some time away,
I don't need to remind you.
Just keep your faith whole, in the Lord
And He will lead and guide you.
It's time again to close for now,

And get this mailed off to you.
There's only one thing left to say,
And that's how much I love
you—
If you could count the stars above,
Or fish out in the sea,
Then you would know how great
The love for you that flows
within me.

Thomas L Bishel
MY PIECE OF HEAVEN
A blast of cool fresh air, chills run up
and down my spine
Our bodies lie together bare, naked
yours and mine
Endlessly engulfed, I'm lost within
your eyes
Your moist, inviting, luscious lips,
our temperatures arise
The sweet sweet scent of your
perfume, I'm delicately entwined
Passionately I wait for you, no other I
will find
Your suddenness, your sweet caress,
indefinite it seems
Encountering that special thing,
perpetual in my dreams
My love for you, burning now,
forever I will stand
For my foolish heart wants nothing
more, I voraciously demand
Yesterday, I look back now, was
empty and incomplete
Until one day, my life was changed,
now no one can defeat
My loneliness, now happiness, for
you each day I shine
I've finally found my piece of
Heaven
Now paradise is mine.

Rann Newcomb
PEACE
The guns were silent when peace
came
And he was flat in bed that day.
A week before the conflict end
A shell had blown one leg away.

In time he'd walk with some slight
limp,
His unseen scars could cause some
pain;
But he could eat, eyeball the girls,
He lived and he did not complain.

Rann Newcomb
REFLECTIONS ON THE WAY TO THALA
If I should fall, don't weep for me,
Your April sun should have no cloud.

If I should rot, some nursing bed,
Lament me not but live your days.

The future looms unknown and dark,
A bullet, bomb, a shell or health.

Though we may never meet again
Know you this: I shall not forget,
My love, my love, my love.

Christopher Boydston
RUTH
Such big brown eyes had she—
The kind that would so readily yield
A big and sparkling tear.
Such soft pink lips had she—
That of themselves would come
unsealed
And tremble when I drew near.

A hard cold heart had I—
A chunk of cruel and adamant stone
On which the crystal of hers was
thrown
To shatter and ache so utterly alone
That its sweet tinkling
And her soft whimpering
Barely to me were they known.

Yet her I'd have loved if I could—
And curse my thick wall that so
coolly withstood
The warm waves of her lapping
emotion.
But could we feel Love where there's
none
We could quench all the fire on the
Sun
And stop Stars in motion
Or drink all the Ocean
And take back the Living we've
done.

Christopher Boydston
A MATERIALIST'S SONG
What is this stuff
What are these things
That I so steadily seek them?
They are but dust
And trees
And stars
And never may I hope to keep them.

What are these things
That scoff at me
That I should want them all?
So vast they are
The Universe are they
And I am oh so small.

What are these things
That hold me so
That I should seek no other?
They are my hands
They are my Soul
And lastly
They are my Mother.

Kaarina Roy
LOVE?

This poem is dedicated to Paul LeClerc, may your life be happy.

Dreams will never live forever, they
die when you
tell the secrets that have kept
you (I)—
alive for so long.

Every time I'm near you, a song on
my
heart sings; and every night
this=
melody upon my flute does ring.

Although my face lies hid amongst
the pages
of the past, I now realize that
secrets are
dreams which cannot last.

The secret burns inside. The dream is
real to me!
Yet until shyness is overcome
—I'll always
hold the secret "we." Secrets will
never be forgotten,
or forgiven. ("Z").

Anna Sherman
MY PAST
I can explore
it a bit
I can adore
it a bit
I can restore
it a bit

and

I can ignore
it a bit
but never, ever
can
I go back thru
that door . . .
even
for a bit!

Anna Sherman
YESTERDAY WENT
Yesterday went,
it was spent . . .
I cannot dwell on it.
I cannot dwell in it.

but . . . . . .
I can cherish it,
and
I can learn from it.

the PAST is something of me . . .
the PAST is something I could be.
the PAST dearly earned me TODAY.
the PAST eased my TODAY . . .
the PAST gave me a better TODAY.
the PAST gave more to my TODAY.

The something in my PAST that is
me
will continue on after me . . .

IDENTITY-ETERNITY

Donna Lynn Hepworth
MIRROR IMAGES
What do I see
Staring at me?
Eyes!
Eyes!
Eyes I see!

What are these eyes
Coming to see?
Can it be,
Little old me?

Yes, it can!
What do you know?
I really do
Have something to show!

Donna Lynn Hepworth
PORTRAIT OF A LONELY CHILD
As I looked out of the window,
I saw a lonely child awaiting
someone's tender arms.
Crying out to no one;
"Please help me, I am afraid."
The child was just sitting on the
swing in the playground all alone.
Her head was hung low, and her arms
cradled the swing's chains.
She looked at the trees as if to say,
"I am lonely too, Will you be my
friends?"
As she sat there, the trees seemed to
reply,
"We love you, and we will care for
you as we care for the animals that
live with us."
The little girl raised her hands to the
closest tree and cried;
"Help me find love, and happiness;
they don't love me anymore at
home."
I saw the girl turn away from the
trees,
And she looked up to the skies, and
as she watched,
She saw, as the clouds cleared away,
the beauty of a rainbow appear.
She smiled, then fell to the ground.
The trees lifted her spirit to the skies,
where she would forever be at peace.
The child seemed to look back at me,
and say, "Thank you."
For I saw her home, and knew she
would be happiest with the trees.
Here there would be no more pain,
and no more suffering,
Here she would live forever in a
world full of love.
As I turned to walk away,
I noticed a beautiful rainbow
appearing in the sky,
It cast down seeds for a new tree to
be born,
In the same spot that the little girl's
body had laid to rest.
I walked only so far, before I too had
joined the trees,
And their world of beauty, love,
peace, and forever happiness.
You see, I was her guardian angel,
and she was my childhood.

Bernard J Kurpiewski
POETIC JUSTICE
Poetic Justice comes to all of us
Like the sunlight from the Sun;
And Oh! the Poets—the Poets must
Brighten the lives of everyone.

For Oh! the Human Heart delights
To read and write by poetry,
Reflecting on the Lights—
Faith, Hope and Charity.

Bernard J Kurpiewski
LIFE HAS OFTEN BROUGHT
Life has often brought
To me—from time to time—
Into every thinking thought
The urge to write in rhyme.

I contemplate my mental state
Is simply fate or what I ate.

Gosh! Brainfood, it's great!
I'm literate!

Zena Fleming
HOMELESS
On the streets these people live, in
shelters, in boxes, in abandoned cars.
Who are these people with such
nothing, I see??
Living among us, on our streets
and in our gutters.
Begging, crying, living and dying.
Where did they come from,
who are they that plead?
As we turn our heads and pay no
matter, but this too could be your son
or daughter, mother or father
And do we have no shame,
will their condition continue to
remain.
As we stand there to watch their
suffering and pain, or will we pull
together to change life forever and
help to see a better day.

Zena Fleming
DRUGS
To capture the soul with a
substance
An addiction, a disease, it corrupts
us.

By smoking, drinking, snorting,
polluting

Avoiding it all the same, your life
in illusion.

Not dealing with problems, drugs
are no way to solve them.

Life's pressures, building fear,
confusion, frustration

We all have them, but drugs won't
hide them.

If you use them and abuse them
So save yourself and the ones who love you

Dig deep and find your own true solution

Zena Fleming
GANGS
Gangs of many colors,
ridiculing one another
shooting and killing, without any feeling with whom
they are dealing.

Families torn between the
color wars.

Then brought together to
mourn the loss of death,
that seems so far from
all of us.

Living in shame. Knowing
their child is a member
of the gang, that has
taken a life which cannot
be replaced for any
price.

Marilyn Baker
INSPIRATION
You are my inspiration,
My sunshine on a rainy day.
You are my bright star at night,
Which safely leads the way.

You pick me up when I am down,
You make me smile instead of frown.

You are my strength, my courage,
My bright spot of the day;
You give life a new meaning,
In every way!

Without you, I would have never known
The real meaning of life and love—

Thank you for making my life complete!

Beverly McGuinness
ARE YOU CLOSE TO YOUR FAMILY?
To my three beautiful daughters, Pearle, Ruth & Mearlene.

How close are you to your family—
Do you see them at all?
I wonder how often you go out of your way—
To give someone a call!
Some of us live so close—
And don't act like they care
Others are so far away—don't keep in touch—
Now you beware!
You'll never know how much one's missed
Until they aren't around.
And then it's much too late you see
When one's heaven bound.
Don't wait for them to call you—
They've got a busy life.
They are working—busy with teenagers—
Who make their life full of strife!
So listen to these words of wisdom—
Don't let it fall on a deaf ear—
So do what I've suggested—go home
Make that call, make this a happy year!!!

Mrs F E Brady

Mrs F E Brady
DESTINY
This poem is dedicated to the memory of my father, Dr. James Menzies, whose life was devoted to his family and humanity through much sacrifice.

There was a man named John,
Who had good news for man on earth
From one who lived before,
Who called himself "I AM."
Write down the words I give you.

The planet I gave you must be renewed,
To be beautiful and productive,
Clean and healthful for all to be proud of.
The Book I left for all to read,
A Lamp to light your way,
You heeded not, but went your own way.

When I return, as I promised I would,
You shall live again right there on earth.
There will be much work for all men,
And when they are finished
Everyone will be contented, happy and safe.
That is when My Kingdom will come on earth
And My Will be done.

Marjorie Gouinlock Ingham
LINDBERGH
To the memory of Charles Augustus Lindbergh.

Lone eagle of the raging, roaring deep,
Brave, daring youth with laughter in your eyes,
The watching world was thrilled by that lone leap
And cheered your onward progress through the skies.
Vitality of Vikings in your heart!
And faith and courage riding by your side,
"To do or die" your motto from the start,
Above, dark clouds, below, the moving tide!
At Paris, honored by adoring France,
At London, entertained by Prince and King,
With millions clamoring for a single glance,
A crowd agog with hero-worshipping.
At home, regarded as a demi-god;
You walk the pathway where none else has trod!

Elaine A Tackett
HURRY UP SPRINGTIME
For Mary-Helen & Rosalie.

Hurry up Springtime
The Winter's been long
Bring balmy breezes
And the robin's sweet song

Bring full budding flowers
Aching to bloom
With their delicate scents
Pervading my room

Please hurry young Springtime
And bring your green grasses
To tickle the toes
Of young lads & lasses

Though my years are advancing
My dreams are still bright
I dream in the daytime
As well as at night

I remember the Springtime
When all dreams were new
So hurry dear Springtime
I'm waiting for you.

Patsy H Davis
MY SON'S HOME RUN (6-27-89)
Dedicated to my son, Bradley Martin Davis.

The ball game's over,
My son caught a fly.
He got hit with a ball
And he didn't even cry.
He pulled on his cap
As he stood at the plate.
He watched the pitcher wind up;
He just couldn't wait.
The tension was mounting,
The game was a tie.
He knew he could hit it as easy as pie.
The ball came across; the air was so tense.
He won the game and knocked it over the fence.

Donna Wank Gammon
THE CHILDREN
The dedication of this poem goes to the lives of our children around the world. Because of self love, selfish desire and self centered parents, precious children have suffered.

Tiny little hands
Precious feet
Limbs small
Strength so weak
Eyes of innocency
Mind clear
Forever learning
All that's here
Who can tell
Who can say
The life
Abused today
How many times
Repeated over
The miseries
The torture
Children's cries
Torn and distraught
Desiring to hide
Forever caught

Josephine C Smith
MINE NO MORE
He was mine for a little while,
This darling precocious little boy child.
He would play and laugh with so much glee,
This gift of love to his Daddy and me.

"You go hide, and I'll go seek.
Come on, Mommy," he'd say, "do not peek.
Will I be big like Daddy?" he'd say.
"Of course, Darling, don't forget to pray."

"May I some day have a kite and make it fly?"
"Your Daddy said, 'yes', and you can if you try."

"Look, Mommy, how high it goes.
Can it reach God? Do you think He knows?"

"Where are you going, Mommy?
Please take me.
I'll be a good boy. Wait and see."
"I see you, Baby. A good boy you are,
But you're back with God, Oh! so far."

"Your Daddy is there.
I know he's with you,
So don't be sad,
My Little Boy Blue."

Josephine C Smith
NEXT TIME
Dedicated to My Doctor, C. DAVID WINGFIELD D.O., Who has been the Light at the end of the tunnel.

Wide awake in the midst of the night
When everything is so still,
My thoughts all come parading
And I respond against my will.

Who do I owe? What can I do?
Can this really happen to me?
Where are my friends? Who do I love?
Isn't there anything free?

Why can't I sleep? What can I change?
Must I give up all my dreams?
Is that a pain? What is that sound?
I'll triumph with just the right scheme.

Up from my bed. A hot glass of milk.
It provokes such a marvelous shift.
My thoughts slow down; my panic is gone,
And this same night gives me a lift.

The mockingbird sings. Stars shine down.
Why wasn't I aware before?
The night is soft. The air is cool,
And I'm ready to sleep once more.

I hope I'll remember next time,
When the night is more than just dark,
That somewhere near, the stars shine down
And a mockingbird is singing like a lark.

Trudi-Anne Baker

TOGETHER WE WILL ALWAYS BE

Dedicated to my dear mother Valerie, with all my love.

Sing to me a brand new song,
And with you I will sing along.
Kiss me softly on the cheek
And I'll return that love so sweet.
Don't buy me things or send me gifts,
Just when you're here my spirit lifts.
Come walk with me and talk it out,
We'll find out what it's all about.
You give me love that is so fine,
Your heart is always next to mine.
Come to me in times of need,
When you're upset I'll take the lead.
Think of me at work, at play,
And I will think of you all day.
When we're apart, I miss you so,
I love ya lots, I hope you know!
When at night you cannot sleep,
Wake me up and you will see,
That when I say I'm here, I mean

TOGETHER WE WILL

ALWAYS BE!

Emma Marie Bochenek

A SKI WEEKEND

To my sons Andrew and Marc for giving me the ability to find joy in their pleasure.

Beautiful white, fluffy snow
embracing my very being,
As if God opened the gates of heaven
and poured out His love.
So delicate, so precious, each and every snowflake
A loving gift to those who ski . . .
A remarkable eye-opener to me!
I walked out onto the terrace of our chalet . . .
Behold a breath-taking vision of God's creation.
Mountaintops, now sleek and slender ski slopes,
An escalator of wonderful ups and downs.
Smiling people, care-free as birds in flight . . .
And suddenly you can see the radiance of the sun
Dancing gracefully across the slopes,
Performing an arrangement of exciting glimmer.
Then poof, its radiance explodes into vivid crimson colors,
Like the glistening of a flawless diamond!
And shining now, you can actually see pastel shades of red,
yellow and blue.
My eyes then looked upward, high into the sky,
As I tried to follow the chair lifts,
But they seem to have gotten lost in the clouds.
Oh I can't imagine being so close to the heavens!
As I watched in awe, these care-free skiers gliding down.
How gracious like ballerinas.
How forceful like flashes of lightning!

Inkeri Eerikainen

CONFUSION

The door is open
Jim singing about confusion,
was here yesterday, (melancholy passages.)
Shadows of passing times
Morning follow the night before,
but sometimes I'm not so sure
For I'm forever sad
The fear is now
that perhaps one day
I can hide it all inside
and then it will be too late,
into the night I look to search,
and see . . .
the door is open, still . . .

David L Myers

LOVE IS A DRUG

O, My Brothers and my Sisters,
hear your children's plaintiff cries.
Pray be still and listen,
before our future dies.

We talk of waging "War on Drugs"
as though guided from Above;
But I say to you that, better still,
we begin talk of waging Love.

For the crack pipe and the needle
are stealing from our youth;
We turn our anger to the Pusher;
but I speak to you the truth.

The Pusher is but a surrogate,
the drugs he sells just charms.
I say to you he cannot steal your children from your arms!

"Why wage love?" I hear you ask,
"as peace is opposite war."
There can be peace without love;
but love will open the Door.

You ask, "What Door?" and I reply . . .
"The Door, for children real,
that stands between the love you say,
and the love your children feel."

Ask yourself, O Learnéd Ones, If I speak not the truth;
then just what is it you would do
to win back our lost youth?

Our children yield their bodies
to the ravages of drug;
But if given one "sweet" chance,
would spurn them for a hug.

In these fast times a shadow casts
a pall across the land;
Before it full engulfs us,
it is time to take a stand.

TIME is a precious commodity,
one we say we've not much of;
But take time for your children,
take time to show your love.

We always are "too busy"; "too tired"
or have "no time";
But parents heed the warning
in this my humble rhyme.

TIME will be your enemy, and the Pusher holds the Key,
to lock that Door between you
for all eternity!

So if you seek an end to drugs,
and to your children's pain,
Show your love; be unafraid;
you have all the world to gain.

David L Myers

DA NANG DREAMS/ AMERICAN NIGHTMARE

America, America
you see with jaundiced eyes.
You've finally lost the visions,
and learned to live the lies.
You've forgotten all your children
who lie sleeping in the street,
and send to bed your babies with
bitterness to eat.
America, America,
How can you be so blind?
You've forgotten those who
fought for you
and our brothers we left behind.
God Bless You, Miss Liberty,
my tears have stained your dress.
Just what was it I was fighting for?
I've grown old just trying to guess.
Reach out to those who need you now;
lift the film that clouds your sight.
Raise high your Torch of Liberty,
lest we plunge full into the Night! !

"America, America, God shed
His Grace on Thee . . . . "

Naomi DeBarr

TO GOD

Like the rain from sparklers
on the fourth of July,
Shower me with blessings.
Lift me up high.
If the day be desert hot and the land be dry,
Send the rain before I even need to cry.
If the night be so wet with tears help me sigh.
Send the joy to relieve my heart not asking why.
The reason is too sad to be seen by your eye.
Yet you know in your knowing as time passes by.
My heart tells you everything,
It cannot lie.
So send me great love, lift me up as I try.
Let me live my life greatly.
Do not let me die.

Naomi DeBarr

YOU'RE GONE

Goodby . . . goodby,
I see you now and then,
But you are gone,
And I've been traveling on,
Learning to be strong.
I cry sometimes even yet,
In longing, remembering or regret.
I miss you
But you are gone.
I'm not alone entirely.
We try to be a family.
I reach out to friends,
And search to heavens, ends.
I see you now and then,
Or hear your voice,
Listening to your choice.

Goodby . . .
Goodby . . .
You're
gone.

Ronald Nichols

Ronald Nichols

FEAR IS . . .

Fear is a beast that terrifies your soul,
Grasps hold of your heart and won't let go.
Fear is the darkness that haunts your mind,
Surrounds you with mystery and then leaves you blind.
Fear is the unknown that arouses curiosity,
You want to know more—but you're scared.

Fear is being alone in the darkness and unknown,
Wanting a hand to hold, but everyone's gone.

Fear is a mind playing tricks on a body,
Nothing's really there—but you feel them.

Fear is dying—
Not knowing what to expect.
Fear is living—
Not knowing what to expect.

Fear is what you think it will be.
Fear is . . .

Sunshine Kenley
LAST KISS
Moist lips, deep breaths, thus moist lips, may now rest.

Flapping tongues,
hugging lips,
no more pain,
rushing to finger tips.

The first kiss,
so gentle and soft,
like a light rain's mist,
does thus truly exist?

The remaining kiss,
too painful to bear,
for thus kiss,
is the one never shared.

Darrell W Williams
MEMORIES
As I sit and watch the movies
About the shores of Viet-Nam
Knowing all too well, the people
Didn't really give a damn.

Thinking of the lives we lost
For what we do not know,
Thinking of the injuries, and
Limbs that will not grow.

We talked about the things,
That they called right or wrong
Sitting up on the side of beds
With shakes, all night long.

When I think of how they told us
"Sons you have to serve"
We stepped back sharply,
Took a deep breath, to start building nerve

We did not question why we went
Nor to what extent, we stayed
But when we came home,
To our families and loved ones,
We thanked God and knelt and prayed.

Sande Greenawalt
HAIKU
Children in the park
laughing, playing, and singing
music on the wind.

J L Roadman
SECRETS
Would that I were young again
In the playground of my mind
I searched and found the answers
And all the world sublime
Puddles & butterflies and love's first
Secret touch—reaching ever reaching
Holding onto dreams and such stuff
that they are made of
In the playground of my mind I hear
love's warm and gentle sounds
No course travelled was ever felt too much
Always racing one step further to see
another truth and another
gentle touch
Reaching and accepting were all a part of youth
All my questions led to answers on
the clear, clear path of truth
Now I question all the answers
Ah poor, sad, lost & misspent youth!

Marilyn White
PICTURESQUE
In the shade I wait
For the light I watch

Fingers stone-cramped
To the bone
Spine steel-arched
Neck
Head
Hands poised
And posed

Just so
Performing shadow work
woman's work
shadowy work

Waiting for the master stroke
Watching for the genius flash

Apocalypse—
Man gives birth to woman!

Sandra Reynolds
AMBITION
The crystal blue water washed up against the shore.
It was in a state of tranquility.
Its vibrant color produced a radiance never seen before.
It represented the innocence of hopes
and dreams wanting to be fulfilled.
So many obstacles the water overcame.
It reaches for the shore searching for
something to cling to.
Slowly the water inches back.
The sea will never be peaceful until it
succeeds in finding security.
On it goes, relentlessly trying,
But never giving up.

Bonnie J Evans
A LONELY CRY
Hear that my friend? Hear what she asked?
Hear that cry of a broken heart.
Hear the pain that child cries about.
Pain, of being abused. Done by
someone she trusted, she loved.
Hear that my friend? Hear what she asked?
It's the church bell tolling for the abused.
Hear that my friend? Hear what she asked?
It's the lonely cry of an adult who
needs a friend to care, to love her, to
hold her. To let her know everything
is alright.
Hear that my friend? Hear what she asked?
It's a lonely cry that has gone.

Kelly Roberts
A LIFETIME
A lifetime.
The split second
of eternity
we share,
A wave in the
brooding sea
of emotions.
A glimpse . . .
A momentary
flicker . . .
The shadow of
a soaring
eagle.
So quickly
to fade,
As the morning dew
in a
hot sun.

Theresa L Taylor
TIME ENOUGH

To my four sons, Paul, Brandon, Trey, and Clifton.

Come down and carry me away if you must
But you will give me time enough I trust
For what, you might ask?
Just to complete a few simple task.

To let my children know how to love
People on Earth and those above.
That those above are supremely divine,
And those on earth are truly fine.

To live with all and believe in themselves,
Not to count on fairy tales and elves.
To speak of every man
With wisdom if he can.

To walk with his head held high
And never accept, but question why.
Time enough to teach them these
Before you carry me away with the breeze.

Iola Fitzgerald
TODAY I CRIED
Today I cried
Not just tears that run down the cheek
But gut wrenching sobs that cleanse the soul
For a man who has been gone
twenty-five years
Oh yes, I cried then for the drunk
who was gone
The one who had made life miserable
for us all
Then I neatly put him away
Into the deepest, darkest part of my brain
But today I reached into that
bottomless pit
And took out the memories of long ago
I could remember only things that
were good
His special whistle to tell us he was home
His beautiful bass voice he added to
our songs
The good, loving daddy he was most
of the time
The husband and father who didn't
know he was sick
Today I can say,
"Daddy, I love you."

Ronald E Hansen
EAGLE EYE

Dedicated to the Oglala Lakotah people.

I looked into the eagle's eye and saw
my own reflection
And captured there in yellow fire, our
spirits made connection
The fierce glare of the predator's
stare hides what lies within
But being one with the golden bird, I
soon learned what lay there in
Taking off into cobalt blue, we leave
this world of woe
Into the world of wind and cloud,
higher and higher we go
Above town and country, all other
creatures below
A panorama of all life revealed, all its
ebb and flow
Then swooping down for sustenance
of body and mind alike
We spot our prey, our talons are
ready to strike
We take what we need, then with
blinding speed, we're in the clouds again
Up to be as close to heaven as one can
The wind's song is soothing as any
hymn in church
As my mind comes away from the
eagle's eye as he sleeps upon his perch

Joyce Szell
NO ONE
I'm sitting here watching the sun come up.
It's kind of sad,
this lone coffee cup.

There's no one here
to share my dreams of last night.
There's no one here
to hold me tight.

There's no one here
to say, "have a good day."
There's no one here
because you went away.

There's no one here
when I come home from work.
There's no one here
and Oh! how it hurts

I miss you!

Kimberly R Davis
YOU
Rainbows and laughter
Sunshine and smiles
Warm rain and happy thoughts
These all remind me of you.

Fast cars and loud music
Alcohol and recklessness
Twisted trees and splintered glass
These all remind me of you.

Soft grass and gentle wind
Flowers and funeral music
The feel of an ice cold stone
These all remind me of you.

Mindy Beth Palmer

Mindy Beth Palmer
TO A SPECIAL SOMEONE . . . YOU
To a special someone . . . you,
A special someone is a someone like you,
A someone so kind, so gentle, so true,
A someone so special I hold in my heart,
A someone like you, mom and dad,
Thanks for always being there.

Brian Heard
THE PENANCE
Like the restless wind
I'm waiting to blow
The anger inside builds
I try to control it
Yet the beast still escapes
Wreaks havoc like a hurricane
Lightning from the fingers
Thunder from the toes
An unstoppable quake
Tearing, ripping, slashing
Everything in sight

Then the knight appears
And a battle enrages
The two warriors clash
Day falls, the battle continues

He strikes, cuts deep
I strike, he bleeds
Swords fly, electricity sparks
Thundering blows shake the Earth
While the battle continues
Pushing to and fro

Then to hinder our battle
Clouds gather, stronger and stronger
It rains and thunders, harder and harder
Yet, nothing can stop the battle

Three moons pass, battle cries heard
Mortal wounds, I bleed
Blood covers me
Blindness, nothing's there
My heart stops, gagging, rolling
Pain lessens, it is the end

Storm passes
The dawn of a new day
Last raiments of the battle
Washed away, a golden rainbow

Like a medieval war
Knights against Knights
Good versus Evil
Stands the White Knight in triumph

Madeline D Crane
GRAVEYARD AT AUTUMN
There you lean midst 'packed earth' and pine
Collars of leaves circling necks of stone,
Awaiting nature's wrath and toll.
Inscriptions dimmed these 300 years,
Assaulted by wind, rain and sleet,
Blurring trace of soldier, sailor, mate,
Wife, mother, tiny infant asleep;
A march to Concord, Lexington, War of 1812,
That Indian massacre down by Jeffrey's Creek.
A bolt of lightning gone astray,
Desiccation by diphtheria, measles, lung disease,
All carriers of winged death by cold sea.
Quietly lie these beneath the pines,
No longer feeling heat, cold, love
Or hate as known only to mankind.

Thomas Straitwell
SUNRISE

The Heavens declare the glory of God, and it is to His glory that this poem is dedicated.

In the confines of blackness, points of light
Were held captive by the darkness called night.
This shadowy giant had routed the day,
And taken the power of light away.
Yet in the presence of this awesome night,
A hope existed, the return of light;
The rising of a champion to fight,
A promise of one to defeat the night.
And though it seemed to be a promise vain,
The book of prophecy had made it plain.
From the east a deliverer would rise,
One to take from the night its wrongful prize.
At the appointed time the champion came,
With a sword of light and a heart of flame.
One by one every star was set free,
That the Sun was far stronger all must agree.
Its power broken, the darkness then fled,
Leaving light once more to rule in its stead.

John Cochran
THROUGH THE YEARS
We've been together
for only three years
we shared some smiles
and cried some tears.

I wouldn't change
one minute or day.
You are so special
in so many ways.

I feel so loved
when you are around.
You always cheer me up
when I'm feeling down.

You give all your love
unselfish and true.
For the rest of my life
I'll always love you.

Down through the years
when it's all said and done
our hearts will come together
and always be one.

Rusty Jacobs
I WISH MY LOVE UPON
Walking through the world I can see, the hate and dishonesty. No one to help the poor to survive, not enough to feed the hungry that cry. Watching the people of today as they pass me they look away. There is no love where loneliness is. There is no warmth of kindness to give in a world full of darkness.

What happened to the way it used to be. The world was full of love like it was supposed to be. People had smiles and were happy to help one another. What happened to love for each other. Has it all been forgotten in this world of today. Am I the only one to say, I wish my love upon the world of today. I wish it to touch the lonely ones.

I wish my love to bring happiness to all the poor ones, I wish my love to feed and protect the hungry ones, I wish my love upon this world to warm the cold of the loneliest. I wish my love to conquer hate and to put honesty in its place. I wish the world to see its mistake. I wish the strong would help the weak, if only they would try to be meek. I wish my love upon them all.

May it spread across the sea and start new love like growing trees, I wish it to be simple and free for everyone to see, Love is the way to be, happy and understanding is the way to be free . . . .

Claude R Westfall
FROM THE OTHER SIDE OF LONELINESS

Dedicated to Ruby, my family, and the memory of my dearest friend, Gil Johnson!

Looking
at love—
from the other side—
of loneliness,
is seeing,
a man,
in hope of a dream,
in a world,
that never sleeps;
beneath the lights—
on the other side,
of loneliness.

Sophia Carruth
ROCKING CHAIR
The old wooden rocking chair
Once fair, but now scarred
from care.
Young rock to sleep, and old rock in tears
For the memories of the
old rocking chair.

All the young were rocked to sleep
Nightmares silenced by its
creak.
Dreams told to all, secrets whispered to hold
In the old wooden rocking
chair.

Memories, so dear, of the old rocking chair
And the loving mother
Who always sat there,
Rocking the chair to the
same melody.

The old chair to leave,
But the memories of Mom
Will always be near in heart
As the creak of a rocking chair
starts.

Dianna Merlak
LONGING
longing for the presence of a gentle stranger,
with smiling eyes and cheerful chatter
longing for the simple,
uncomplicated friendship;
no pressures, no demands, no unrealistic expectations
longing for star cluttered skies,
hanging lazily over two people
wandering aimlessly toward each other
longing for the touch of a forbidden man,
with strong embraces and lingering kisses, the trace of his fingers on my skin
longing for the sound of optimism in his voice,
whispering in my ear as well as my head
longing for the feeling of happiness throughout,
the peacefulness in his arms, his breath on my neck
longing for the release of my inhibitions,
soaring through the heavens with his heart pounding next to mine
longing for my friend . . .
longing for his love . . .

Ford Tucker
A LOT
The phone used to ring
a lot;
But now by myself I sing
a lot.
I think people may not want to bother me.
I think they try to save my strength.
Thanks a lot.
When you're used to the limelight;
When you're used to being useful;
When you're used to fulfillment;
It's hard to be redefined
a lot.

Patricia Ann Davis
DESTINED TO WIN
I decided to enter this contest
'cause poetry's so much fun

I thought how excited I will be
when I hear that I had won.

My poems are usually towards health
using vitamins, minerals and
herbs,

Having to do with diseases
of the body, bones and nerves.

If you want to prevent an illness
take your vitamins every day,

Remember "health is wealth"
and don't forget to pray.

For God is the master physician
put your faith and trust in Him

By following Jesus Christ, my friend,
we'll all be destined to win.

G Wilbur Tatum
ENCOURAGEMENT

Dedicated to my wife, Melba Moss Tatum.

How sad, to destroy, any part of joy,
In effort spent.
Yet how noble, how grand
To feel toward man
For encouragement

Annette Frances Hall
SOLACE
When saddened or my life is
shattered by sudden stormy struggles,
I seek the subtle "sounds of silence"
often found by the sea;
I listen for the shoal of fish scurrying
beneath the surface water,
Sea gulls flapping their wings,
sharing stale shredded crumbs,
Sea breezes slapping swaying white sails,
The darkness of the night hiding the ships' true colors.
I sit amidst the darken gray rocks, the
lone silhouette, staring motionless, solemn
Sharing God's wonders,
Searching for strength,
Seeking and finding serenity.

Nicole Sharp
TIME FOR DREAMS
The house as quiet as a tomb;
Ghosts drifting through from the past
Bring back memories of childhood,
Of sunny days spent with friends,

Children's ethereal laughter
brightening the room
Lifting all the weariness in my heart.
All the sorrow that life has wrought,
Like mists on the wind at dawn
depart.

Peace is with me for a quiet moment.
Soon it will be shattered,
Like a glass fallen to the floor.
For now, though, all is at peace.

I know my sorrow and weariness will reappear,
Like clouds overshadowing the sun,
But, for now, my dreams run free.
For a little longer let my dreams linger.

I know peace won't last
Like everything else, it will flee.
Nothing on earth lasts forever
That is never meant to be.

Freda H Sweet
NATURE'S SYMPHONY

The evening song of the meadowlark
The whispering of the pine
The rustling of the autumn leaves
The cricket on the vine

The rippling of the mountain brook
The lowing of the herd
The laughter of a child at play
The warble of a bird

The howling of the coyote
His saddest song to sing
The answer to his mating call
Upon his ears does ring

The pealing of a distant bell
A melody to hear
The raindrops falling on the earth
A gift to us so dear

A symphony of music grand
The maestro leads them all
Around the world the music sounds
To hear the Master's call.

Angel Malisa Cirillo
BEGINNINGS

To be a baby once again, to be nursed at my mother's breast.
To find and secure the happiness to fulfill my aching chest.
I wish to strike out, to blame someone for all the pain I feel.
I realize I'm drowning in sorrowful imaginings that are not real.
How easy to misconstrue feelings I thought were surly true.
I question now sincerity or am I only blue?
What was it you said? Did I hear you right? You're of the walking dead?
You fool! What's wrong with you is you're afraid of me and what's inside my head!
What's wrong with me is I fear my mirror, for it sees the fool I am.
It reflects all of my thoughts, it tells me how much time I've wasted.
It tells me I'm not young anymore.
It shows me the roads I've walked upon, and those I've slowly tread.
It shows me how easily I can regret things that I've said.
I wish to walk on familiar lands, and bathe myself on distant shores
I wish to shed myself of clothes, to shed myself of worrisome burdens.
The load I do not fear to carry the strength is drawn from my secret well.
It's the future that my heart feels worry the secrets I cannot tell.
I must continue, I must survive, I cannot, will not falter.
To stumble now to lose concept would surely cost me anguish.
Oh to be homeward bound, to see the skies of green, live my life in happiness true love and feel serene.
To return to the trees of many hands which bow to touch me
Tenderly, to the waters warm of crimson that gave the breath of life.

Clarence L Pulliam Jr
THE BLESSING IN AGE

To my parents, Clarence and Martha Pulliam, with greatest love.

When age like a silent enemy
Appears on our once youthful face
Turning a proud and flawless body
Into a paler, more subtle shade

The beauty of time is first repelled
As we vainly hold on to our youth
Until in our mind it is revealed
That beauty is a product of growth

Our eyes once turned out,
now see within
The beauty and passions of the soul
That time itself can never end
As good wine, love enriches as it
grows old

Those same desires that lit the
flame
In your body and mind so long ago
Are still there, and are the same
But now, they even are more so

The blessing of age has
touched us both
We are richer in knowledge by far
Than those who still have
their youth
We accept the world and ourselves as
we are

I have seen your needs, and
they are mine
And the passion still burns today
You have grown more
beautiful with time
Enhanced by your strands of gray

Mrs Queen Miley

Albert F Inclan PhD
FOR MEMORIES CAN NEVER FADE

Dedicated to my mother, Mrs. Mary Inclan, and in honor of her mother who inspired this poem. Both ladies have given their families memories that will never fade.

The old house is filled with memories,
Those will always remain.
The laughter that once filled it has long been gone;
The kitchen smells and your radiant face
Are no longer there.
The creak of the old porch swing that was so unmistakable
As we sat there on those warm summer nights,
Or, later on, the breezeway visits filled with laughter,
They too are gone.

They have to be gone.
For it was you who helped bring life to the house.
It was you who surrounded it with the beauty of your rose garden.
It was you who gave it the unmistakedly feminine touch
That only you could give it.
And it was you who added to the warmth of the home.

Now it's but a memory—but a good one.
We know it was time for you to go.
We'll miss you, dear lady, but, in a way,
Those memories will keep you very much alive,
And in our hearts, for many years to come,
For memories can never fade.

Welda Semelsberger
FIRST CHRISTMAS

To my lovely daughter and best friend, Lynn Ann Tomlin, I love you.

Snow flakes falling silently
The little one sleeps
Peacefully on the manger hay,
The mother in radiance looks on
With a love so warm
For her infant son,
The stars twinkle, and oh,
How they shine
In the crisp evening air,
To guide the weary ones
To a stable warm with love
Where they pay homage
To the Son of God.
A gift to the world
On this first Christmas Eve.

Kay Kalkines
I REMEMBER WELL THE DAY YOU WERE BORN (JUNE 6, 1948)

June 6, 1948-June 6, 1988: To my twin daughters, Lyn & Parrie—with much love, mom.

I remember well the day you were born
Forty years ago!
It may seem like ages ago to you,
But the wonderful thing that happened,
Is, that you became part of two.
And now I wish you a very happy day,
When you begin your very important Fortieth birthday.
Love always,
Mom

Thelma L Reusser
WINTER IS OVER

Winter is over, I hope—at long last!
I'll be happy to "entomb" it, mentally, into the past;
The sun and rain have come, obliterating the snow—
Surprising how quickly it's displaced in the sun's glow;
I'm happy to think of the warm days ahead—
Of the rolling green on pastures instead;
Of gentle moisture and rainbows above—
The lambs and quiet sound of the morning dove;

The calves have survived, fawn scampering about
And the young elk browsing with "Mom" on the hilltop;
Trucks are rolling, Ponderosa logs piled high,
Wild-life in lowlands venturing nigh;

Mountains look rugged—snow adding dimension and power,
Jagged edges appear as skies emit showers;
Flowers will blossom in rock crevices, meadowlands too,
The glory of spring adds radiance again to our view!

Ruthann Sholes
HAPPINESS

To my wonderful husband Danne, with whom I have found my happiness.

Kill
you sleep
eluding discovery
blinding crimson
beneath black eiderdown
unaware that I stalk you
with hungry eyes.

Shawn Kennedy
MY BEST FRIEND

To me she was the sunrise
That smile on an empty face
The butterfly kiss on the cheek
And the piece that fit into place
Such Strength behind her being
The need to make it through
A life that was not happy
But she gave all she knew
Behind that beautiful smile
So torn the woman inside
Despite what she had given
She was losing faith and pride
Such pain did she endure
That I just can't deny
The only peace she'd find
Is if she were to die
Although missed by many
There really is no other
To compare to this great lady
Who has all my love, my Mother.

Sandra L Smith
DRIFT AWAY

To John with love, Rose.

Drift away into the darkness of night
a warmth embraces the eyes
as they see across the distance.

the heart longs for the eyes
to glimpse
once more a sight most
precious,

but nothing is there to see
the images are shattered by
the light.

The eyes must see into the heart
where visions are stored and
nurtured
where caring is cultivated and ripens

Sights most precious
are held there . . . forever.

Lora M Olsen
A TOUCH OF LOVE

This poem was written with love to my loving son, Lance,

You were six months old and full of fun, when I turned around you were one.
There were so many things you couldn't do, so time turned my head and made you two.
At two you were dependent on me, but independence took over when you turned three.
Your third birthday, another I wished to ignore. I lit the candles and there were four.
Four was the year you really thrived, but look quickly, you're already five.
Now you're ready for books and rules, this is the year, you're going to school.
The day came, you were anxious to go, but we walked to the bus, oh so slow. The bus drove away, you waved goodbye, there was a lump in my throat and tears in my eyes.
The bus brought you home, you jumped to the ground, already it's time for cap and gown.
Time goes by it's hard to believe, just yesterday you were home with me.
I'm holding to these moments as fast as I can, because the next time I look at you, I'll be seeing a man.

Barbara J Thomas
TO MY DEAREST DAUGHTER—LENISE
Some parents believe that when their child grows up they never give of themselves. They go on with their own lives only.

I know in my heart that I have the most wonderful Daughter in the world.

She has given me nothing but love and happiness since the day of her birth.

Now as she grows older and more mature she helps me, and loves me even more.

I Thank God every day for blessing me with this child of mine.
Thank You—Lenise for being born to me.

I LOVE YOU!!!!

Bonnie Cerace
FEELING THE MEMORIES

To the "Sunshine" of my life—Through whom the Rays of Friendship Warmed my Heart and made me Smile!

It can be a picture or something someone said—
And suddenly I see the memories—moving through my head.
The laughter, the smiles, the joys and the tears—
And I want to keep making them for many years.

When life meant nothing—and the sun held no rays—
You came into my heart and brought sunshine to my days.
The little things you do for me—to brighten up my life—
Become my memories and bring endless; hours of delight.
Beyond your words—behind your eyes—
I see through each disguise.
With me you dare to be yourself—
With you I took my feelings down—from way up on the shelf.

You painted love and joy and caring on my heart—
Forever, it will stay—should we never part.
Yes, It can be a special song or just a special card—
And suddenly,
I can feel the memories—
Moving through my
Heart!

Jennifer Evans
BABIES
Babies were meant to bring us joy
It does not matter if it's a girl or a boy
Their little features are as pretty as a pearl
Their little smiles
Will follow you for miles
You cannot forget
Their little feet
Babies have been around since the beginning of time
And are worth every splendid dime.

Sandra Dalandek
SOMEONE SPECIAL
During my lifetime, I will meet many different people.
Yet the one person, who is always in my heart and mind is my best friend.
My mother is always there when I need her, with an open mind and heart.
To listen to my troubles and my joys of life.
She taught me right from wrong, then let me grow.
When the world disagreed with my ways, she fought for me.
Now that I am an adult, I hold memories of happy and sad times that my mother helped me through.
Times that were shared together from the heart through LOVE.
My heart holds a special LOVE for my best friend
my Mother.

LOVE Sandy

Phil Bartholomai
THE PEN OF PAST AND PRESENT
My pen writes to you what I feel now
If there's a when, a where,
or even a how
It gives great details of certain events
If it's written down
then that's what I meant
It gets inside of me and spills my heart
Those moments and feelings
from which I want not to part
Those friends, true loves, people I've met
All of whom which
I am truly in debt
It totals the times of good and bad
As I read them to you
I'll be strong not sad
Oh please concentrate, no don't blink
Oops, so sorry, you've missed the lines in between
of my writings in ink!

Juanita Strong Matthews

Juanita Strong Matthews
A TRUE FRIEND
There is a friend who sticks closer than a brother
Especially when there is no other
There is a friend who is always there
And one who is always willing to share
A friend who really does care
One who looks only for the best
And forgets the rest
No matter what he discovers
He always covers
And even though he knows
He will never expose.

He laid down his life as an expression of His love
Just to make it possible
For all who want to rise above
This friend is none other than Jesus, the Christ
The Son of the Living God—the Giver of abundant Life.

Greater love hath no man than this
Than a man who would lay down his life for his friends!

M E Brendahl
TOO LITTLE YET

To: Maureen.

They say that I'm too little to do the things I'd like
They tell me it's impossible, for such a little tyke
To ride a bike, or go to school or climb the stairs alone
To read a book, stay up late or travel far from home.

Although I stretch and try to stand as tall as I can be
I'm not any taller than last night before I went to sleep
There's still so much that I can't reach, so much that I don't know
I explore and try new things out everywhere I go.

I take risks everyday to grow a little more
Although some things I do make me awfully sore,
I nosedive in the bathtub and climb on tables in the way
Though Mom says she's glad I'm learning, she's getting a little grey.

I try to run and often fall I get going much too fast
And I still get tired and am put to bed though I fight it to the last
Perhaps they're right there's still so much that I need to learn to do,
So I'll just have to wait to learn it all, next year, when I'm two.

James J Dahlhauser
THE END IS NEAR
Cast not upon our lovely land
The deadly waste of progress' hand
Nor into our streams that run so clear
For if we do the end is near

Think not of ourselves but of future man
Our children and their's must live on this land
The earth cries for help and friend we must hear
For if we do nothing the end is near

We must begin now on this very day
To help restore earth Mother Nature's way
We can't put it off not one more year
For we can now see that the end is near

Plant back the trees we cut for wood
To clean the air the way they should
'Cause if we do not 'tis this I fear
For all mankind the end is near

Clean up our streams so again they run clean
So what used to be can once more be seen
And pray to God to guide and to steer
His children away from the end that is near

Margie Kaczmarek
A BEAUTIFUL MOTHER
A beautiful mother
You are to me,
I love you dearly
Can't you see.

Never listened really
To what you would say,
And now we've grown
Apart in so many ways.

I want to reach out
But it is so very hard,
For things I've done
Have left a scar.

Help me mama
And pray for me,
I love you dearly
You're beautiful to me.

Bert Vanorse Sr
SPRINGTIME
The winter's chill
It lingers though
The sun shines high above
The pussy willow blossoms
As the birds sing songs of love.

The winter's storms are gone now
Along with dark and dreary days
The March wind blows a melody
As the treetop swings and sways

The brook sings its song of love
As it flows through meadowlands
And as always Mother Nature's art
Outshines the art of man.

Vickie Leali
OUR SWEET BABY BOY

Dedicated to the memory of Joshua David Leali.

Our Sweet baby boy,
You have gone away.
No chance to live,
Not even a day.

Never got to watch you grow,

Or hear your sweet little voice.
To have you go away so soon,
Believe me, I didn't have a choice.

Never got to know you,
To look into your eyes.
Never got to rock you,
Or listen to your cries.

I will always remember you,
Forget you I will not.
You lived within me,
My love, That you got!

Heartbeats were all that we
exchanged
No words, No glances.
To have you come back to us
No hopes, No chances.

Pamela K Bloom
A CARDINAL ACT

To Daniel Garofalo—Dreams Do Come True!

In a cottonball world
Among the pine trees,
Sat a red cardinal
As perky as you please.

Dressed in brilliant red
Against the white snow,
He performed on the pine branch—
A one-bird show.

He danced to the left
And then to the right,
Singing his song
With all his might.

He, the sole performer
On a snowy pine stage,
Earned his paycheck
In bird-seed wage.

Lee H Menyfield
THE DREAMER

In my world I am great, I do as I wish, think as I like.
This world is mine to mold into the kind of world I like.
I turn the tears into smiles, I bring back all that's lost hope, love, charity and faith.
People are people there are no races in my world.
There are no kings, presidents, generals anger does not exist in my world.
All the children and their grandparents are my sun.
Death is chased away by the spirit of God.
Time has no meaning in my world only love, peace and brotherhood sustains this world.
For this is the world of the dreamer and I am the Dreamer.

Justina Sterling
A CHILD'S EYE

Are my words hollow
or merely weak
for you don't seem to hear
and I'm not being meek

Surely I have not
been so unclear
could it be
you don't want to hear

So let me speak
in my own voice
is it not my voyage
and not my choice

I'm not asking permission
I once thought you wise
and valued at one time
your advise
Now I view another side
one I'd rather not see
turn and listen
you cannot silence me

Iola B Dickel
I BELIEVE

Our babies are the best gift that we will ever receive.
They are given to us by God; that's what I believe.
He knows when to send them; when we need them most.
Also, that we will love them; always hold them close.
We are to teach them God is with them day after day.
He puts out his hand, if they hold it they won't stray.
Teach them their prayers when they go to bed at night.
God will keep them safe and never out of sight.
So always love your babies with all your heart.
I am sure God will be happy and always do his part.

Eleanor S King
MY GOLDEN YEARS

My Golden Years are here to stay
For a few years, maybe just a day.
My Golden Years are all set
With precious gems too.
Sparkling Diamonds of memories,
A few of Sapphire Blue.
Gleaming Rubies of Summers,
Changing Opals of Falls,
Shining Crystals of Winters,
Brilliant Emeralds of Springs, I recall
With friends like strings
Of rare priceless Pearls.
I am one of the Golden Girls.

Jennifer Lazzari
INDIAN SUMMER

With pioneering spirit,
I journey down the old country road,
Hair whipping in the warm breeze.
As I round each curve,
I dive deeper into Indian Summer.
Great oak's pillar lordly over the road.
Glittering rays of sunshine flicker through the limbs.
Motley leaves cascade from the trees, and dance in the breeze.
Warm Autumn tints of burnt orange, amber, tea rose, and canary yellow swirl about,
carpeting the twists and winds in the road.
Encircled in colors I'm urged to drive on.
The aroma of Autumn is breathtaking,
captivating my being and
sending my mind wandering,
my spirit dancing and heart humming.
I step in pace with Autumn.
Gleaming . . .
I roll my eyes to the passenger's seat
to share with you, but
you are not there.
I blink . . .
flashing to when we drove down this road together,
Oh! so young and naive.
Sharing life for a season,
saying we'd be together forever
someday,
someday soon . . .
Then things happened.
We paced our paths differently,
each searching for our own happiness.
Blinking once more . . .
I see the seat is empty.
With aching-heart-rendering sighs,
I am destitute.
My heart hungers for you
to join me again on this path,
to share the warmth of this season,
all season's
maybe someday . . .
maybe . . .

Roger Allen Terry
MY LOST LOVE

This poem is dedicated to my wife, Jody.

Words alone cannot express the hollowness that takes over my heart.
Black clouds of rain roll across the skyline of my dreams.
The thunder of loneliness roars thru the valley of my desire for you.
Oh sweet sunshine, come to me on this day . . . stop this rain from falling down.
Open the clouds with the parting gaze of your deep blue eyes.
Cast a rainbow of tenderness across the horizons of our fantasy.
Calm this storm of passionate desire, soothe me with your soft kisses of tranquility.
Take me away on a cloud of tenderness . . . moved along the sky by the gentle breeze of your fingertip caress.

Eleanor S King
MY DREAM CHANNEL

When a tedious task is finally done
I relax and turn my Dream Channel on.
I'm off to the places I love best
I'm on the prairie watching a gorgeous sunset.
Then I'm away to the Rocky Mountains rising high
Where crags and snowy peaks point to the sky.
I see stately pine trees rising tall,
I see and hear a noisy waterfall
I see the sparkling water of a mountain lake,
Exquisite wildflowers more lovely than man imitate.
When in my mind's eye I see the beauty and wonders
God has created for all to enjoy and see
I turn off my Dream Channel.
For now, with dreaming I'm through,
There are more tasks waiting here for me to do.

M Olive Duvall (Age 95)
I LIKE IT

I like it when the snow comes down
And gives the earth a shimmering gown.

M Olive Duvall (Age 95)
BEAUTY

There is beauty out your window,
There is beauty at your door.
If you just take time to look there,
You'll find something, I am sure.
Dewdrops glistening like diamonds;
Birds and butterflies on wings so fleet.
Flowers, yellow, red and crimson
Give the bees their nectar sweet.
Raise your eyes and look to heaven;
Watch the clouds go scudding by,
Some like balls of soft white cotton,
Some like feathers floating high.
Dancing sunbeams, casting shadows,
As they shine through the boughs,
There is beauty out your window,
There is beauty at your door.

Frank Martinez

Frank Martinez
TIME WITHOUT TIME

In the cell in which I live, I hear an old country song,
and I remember my home and my mother, her white hairs
and smell the aroma of burning wood.

I asked for one cigarette from my roommate because I don't have a penny on the books. I wait and wait and when hunger comes and chow is called, I see lines of black heads, lost faces, bodies without souls, yellow faces white, red, bronze, one thousand and one colors.

I look around me and I see gray cement, cold full of twisted iron and I become aware that I am living in mud in my poverty and that the prisoner is turning old because time passes and passes and I feel like a dog or a glass without water when I'm thirsty.

That is why I dedicate this poem to all prisoners doing time like me, and sleep without recourse of love.

Mary Louise Henning
THE TOY SAILBOAT

I dreamed I sailed
my little boat.
Out across the bay.
Where gentle winds
and rains,
came laughing by
And sped me on
adventures way—

My little boat and I.

Jacqueline Burch Wagnon
HAPPY ME

Mourn me not when I am gone
For I have seen a new day dawn.
I have seen a bird in flight.
I have climbed the mountain's height.
I have heard a newborn baby's cry
I have felt a raindrop from the sky.

I have been thrilled to look at trees
And in wonder see God's mysteries.
I have seen the gold of a sunset's glow
And silver on the breast of

fallen snow.
I have seen the myriad colors in a rainbow bright
And heard a whippoorwill call in the night.

I have heard music from a thousand streams,
Watched in delight a child smiling in his dreams.
I have felt the wind blow in my face,
Touched a star in outer space.
I've smelled the perfume of new turned sod.
I am held in the mighty hand of GOD.

Genna Fuchs
SAD EYES
Sad eyes, sad eyes. Oh! They don't lie
They show right through to the pain.
When saying good-bye to memories of love
Your eyes show me a sadness untamed.
But you're not the only one to shed any tears
And you're not the only one hiding your fears.
'Cause when the cold winds blow and the dark rain does pour
I'll be lonely without you forevermore.
It's only a memory I keep in my heart
And it's only a memory of love after dark.
But I can tell what you think
And I know what you do.
I can tell in your voice
'Cause the sadness comes through.
Sad eyes, sad eyes. Oh! They don't lie
They show right through to your deepest pain.
So if we must part let it be in the dark
Because your sad eyes would rip open my heart.
I love you baby, can't you see?
Your sad eyes can't lie to me.
No, your sad eyes can't lie to me!

Wilma D Head
BE HAPPY

Dedicated with love to my family, friends and those who have loved me throughout this life's journey.

The passing years are smoothing out.
What life alone has been all about.
Carefree good times shine a lot brighter,
While sadness emits a softer glow.
You view the past as if watching it all at a picture show.
As the New Year unfolds, we glimpse what's in store
If it's prosperous and happy, we eagerly want more.
The smiles come easy when the laughter flows free
Music fills the soul, while the angels watch over me.
Love, humor and music is how I live
To be happy, this is what I give.

kathleen a surridge
DRUGS
Light up and have a smoke,
Go ahead it's cool to be a dope.
Take a sniff or have a swig,
In a matter of time, they'll be doing the 6 foot dig.
Shoot up you say, and touch the sky,
But in a casket is where you'll lie.
It's just a matter of time you see,
When you use drugs you're no longer free.

kathleen a surridge
FEELINGS

This poem is dedicated to Ruth, a beautiful person, who will always hold a special place in my life.

Loving me was not easy I know,
I wouldn't let any of my feelings show.
I hid behind a thick solid wall,
For there I couldn't be hurt at all.
Your kind and caring and loving ways,
Showed me a world, where I'd be happy to stay.
You always gave strength with encouragement,
That no matter what became of my life,
the struggles and efforts would be worth the fight.
I was blessed with you from up above,
this beautiful person who showed me love.
That solid wall of mine is gone,
You knocked it down with your loving songs.
Thanking you will never be enough,
for what you gave, was way too much.
The most beautiful part of this my friend,
You gave me life when I wanted it to end.

Betty Davis-Bush
A DOCTOR'S GENTLE HANDS
Reassuringly they pat the mother's hand,
As she feels the pain of labor.
Then they tenderly present the world,
With the gift that God so proudly gave her.

For the child so full of fear,
They gently set a broken bone.
Then give a welcome hug,
To assure him he's not alone.

To those that are so sick,
How much better they will feel,
When caring hands reach out,
With medicine to help them heal.

For the sick they cannot help,
They fold those hands in prayer.
So they may assure the family,
That with all their heart, they care.

Those hands are like that of God's,
Yet they are but a simple man's.
One who so tenderly reaches out,
With a Doctor's gentle hands.

Denean Revell
THE STORY OF A BROKEN HEART
You said you'd always love me
We'd never be apart
You wanted to be with me always
And then you broke my heart.

I began to cry in silence
As I watched you walk away
You can't begin to imagine
How I think of you each day.

Oh why did you have to go?
You didn't even say good-bye
You just left without warning
That's what really made me cry.

If ever you come back to me
Remember what you used to say,
If ever we see each other on the street,
Just turn and walk away.

Walk away so never to remember
How we loved each other before
I could never go through the agony
I can't stand the pain anymore.

John W Foerster
THE QUEST
Shades of gray in search of being,
Strength searching to support.
Two souls in search of a whole.
Two minds intertwine in compatibility.
A oneness of spirit shared completely,
So breathe deeply, relax fully,
Enjoy life your time is now.

Leonetta Felicia Coette Burkett
TOMORROW'S FUTURE
Today is the past, waiting for tomorrow's future.

Giving your all for one day of happiness, living out your fantasies to find some gladness.

Even though the disappointments and heartaches are hard to take, tomorrow's future is always at stake.

The commitments and promises should be based on pride, because tomorrow's future is a long stride.

Struggle and demand your given rite, for there is no dream that's out of sight.

When we look to Tomorrow's Future!

E K Braun
WITH ALL MY HEART
Holding a friend's baby so small
I think of my children now grown so tall . . .

Tiny fingers clasped one finger on my hand
in a moment I will never fully understand.
You were so brand-new
yet already I loved you
with all my heart
and then some . . .

So quickly have the years gone past,
at times I regret a bit too fast.
Busy with others in work and play
I know I forgot to say
I love you with all my heart
and then some . . .

Never have I had a doubt
you are what my life is all about;
so for you I write these simple lines
that you may know for all time—
I could not love you more
than with all my heart
and then some . . .

Elsie Marks
LIFE, DEATH, LIFE
See yonder leaf, once bright and green, now brown and dangling by a thread,
Resisting being torn away from source of life that daily fed
The tender shoot and slender stem; whereby its strength and color spread.

Such leaves did quietly submit to nest of bird and drenching rain,
To glaring sun and gusty gale, and yet, undaunted by the pain
Held fast as long as life endured—to rise and fall, and rise again.

When spent at last, the leaf doth fall and find its final resting place,
In death it nurtures sluggish soil to bring new life—if but a trace—
To unborn plant and unhatched bird, dormant now with nameless face.

When death shall take my breath from me, I pray the life I've lived conveys
The legacy of faith in God I leave to all who knew my ways—
A gift that proves, like fallen leaves, that life, in death, with life repays.

Gloria M Feller
THE LIGHT OF GOD
The Light of God is with me,
Showing me what I need to know, and
Guiding me along life's path.
The Light of God is with me, to comfort me
In times of sorrow, and with me
In times of joy.
The Light of God fills my soul with
Compassion, understanding, peace, and love.
The Light of God is with me always.

Teresa Lu Johnson
SAY GOODBYE
When two people fall in love, a brand new life begins
And lives on forever because true love never truly ends.
Two separate lives joined together
To experience the meaning of happiness, forever;
To love, honor and cherish
The precious moments that never perish.
To live their lives in wonderful fulfillment
And teach each other the meaning of total enjoyment.
Then a time comes when one must say goodbye
And leave the other alone to cry.
But when all the hurt has gone at last,
The other thrives on memories of the past;
Remembering all the years so happily spent together
Keeps the love in their hearts alive forever!

Barbara Herwick
WHERE PAST AND PRESENT

To My Mother—the first and still the favorite poet in my life.

Where past and present
and future meet—
footprints pressed and
washed through centuries of lives
that touched the sands—
His ever in motion . . .
yet ever constant Sea—
With all of its wonders, mysteries,
power, peace and treasures . . .
What may be but a speck of
time shared—
as worlds and centuries
turn—
is now . . . My forever treasure—

Laurie Jean Murchie

Laurie Jean Murchie
COMMUNION

To Chris, my Forever Love, who taught me the meaning of joy and never fails to give it: To my parents, Carl & Marion Murchie, who believed in me long before I ever did: And to The Lord, without Whom life would have no poetry . . . I dedicate these poems.

Come to me out of the night,
The stillness like a cloak about your form,
Unveiling only the opalescence of those depths
That peer into my own.
Reach beyond these blue pools,
Shattering the engulfing dam,
Revealing the water-spirit,
Forever restless in a tumult of fear.
Lay claim to her essence,
The embodiment of the turbulent waves,
For in your quiet strength lies her only
Salvation.
Like a gentle breeze, call unto her
And she will turn, recognizing in the sound
The other half of her being
Which until now
Has been but a whisper in the wind.
Beckon,
And she will flow into you,
Merging in joyous completion.

Laurie Jean Murchie
ALONE IN A CROWD
I am alone though in a large crowd
And no one would hear me if I spoke out loud.
Why should they bother with one such as I?
Why bend an ear to a very worm's cry?
If I'm a person, I'm the least one of all.
They'd feel great aversion if I had the gall
To ask them to listen to what I had to say.
They'd look around—sneer—and then turn away.
My eyes humbly avert; my lips quiver; tears spill.
My heart thumps its hurt against my ribs. Will
I always have to go unseen and unheard
And die hopelessly for want of a word
To shatter their alliance so they'll understand
That, despite their defiance, I'm still someone. Can
I travel life's
highway, tendering my soul,
Or must I fear always this terrible toll?
And yet . . . I AM someone just like each of them
And maybe I SHOULD speak even if they condemn
As it could be my input might cause them to change—
Could it be my very SILENCE that keeps me estranged?

Laurie Jean Murchie
INSANITY
Feeling so bewildered, yearning for a friend,
But knowing that nobody could ever comprehend
The turbulence deep down inside that tears apart your soul,
The storms you manage to hide though at an awesome toll . . .
The tidal wave breaks o'er your head, the current sucks you down,
All strength to fight drains out of you as you're whirled round and round.
But silence reigns—no word's spoken. You battle all alone
For others have their wars to face without taking on your own.
And so you're ruled by endless strife, a quicksand that you find
Threatens to overtake your life and forever absorb your MIND . . .

Laurie Jean Murchie
HONESTY
If in time your heart should turn
From one for whom it used to burn,
Seek not to hide with false affection
The reality of that defection
If you have no more to give,
Break my heart, but let me live
With the knowledge of the truth
For in time a cobra's tooth
Would be no deadlier than your lies,
Mocking me with love's disguise.
Remember how we two were one
So if that bond's to be undone.
Don't waver in indecision,
Unsure how best to make division.
Do not fear to wield the knife
That will rend in two the life
That till now was yours and mine,
A mergence less mortal than divine.
Don't falter at thought of my grief
For which in time may come relief.
I will not chain you with my tears
Or bring up guilt from bygone years.
If of your love I am bereft,
Why would I want the shell that's left?
If you can no more be true,
Honor me, Dear—as I will you.

Arlington Peterson
INDECISION
With gleaming swords held high
Stand Heart and Mind,
Preordained combatants
Upon the battlefield of life.
Each may choose one cohort
To bolster up his side.
And Heart chose love
To Mind came trial
Then on, the battle raged.
Until setting sun they dueled.
When out of the shadows,
On silent wings and swift He came
The one who knows not victory
That one who has no sting.

Renae Doshier
BUCKETS OF TEARS
I'm suspended, and lost in time
Trying to erase Buckets of Tears I've held in my mind.
Seems no one has ever really cared
I'm giving up on all feelings, that I have shared.
When tears roll down my face at night
I then realize, I have lost the fight
I want to go back to another life
Leaving behind all the pain, doubt and strife.
Life sometimes seems, oh, so lonely

Jacqualyn Joesphine

Jacqualyn Joesphine
ANOTHER EMPTY NIGHT
When will it end
Or maybe just begin
To be alright
Right before another end
The strong shall bond
While the weak only compete
Empty alone
If only someone would hear
Hold me near
Always be sincere
Only then could love be shared
Before another end
Or maybe to just begin
Of all the values life holds dear
Only to be truly loved
Is worth more than years
To just begin
Without any end
To be alright
Help me through the night

Shirley Harley Wilson
LITTLE ROCKING CHAIR
Little Rocking chair—
"You look so sad just sitting there.
Cobwebs cling to your tiny rungs;
Nostalgia rises sharper than words from tongues.
A lump's in my throat as I brush your frame;
You were so faithful with your game.
When you were new; what a delight!
Danita would rock in you day and night.
Sucking her thumb and stamping her feet;
Sparkling brown eyes shining tender and sweet.
Many years have passed since then—
She'll <u>never</u> rock in you again."
"Elusive time, how <u>fast</u> you fly!
I must brush a tear from my eye."
"Leila rocked in you too; now she's gone,
You're empty, deserted, and <u>oh</u>, so forlorn!"

Mary Bittner Henry
THE WAYWARD SON

To my wonderful, supportive family without whom I could not succeed. With love, Mom.

I held my baby to my breast
So many years gone by.
He seemed so helpless and I was blessed
To have so sweet a little guy.

As he grew older and looked into my eyes,
He respected me for being so wise.
In his teens he believed that only he
Could be wise and live independently.

The world seemed so different and "cool,"
But he soon realized he had been a fool
To disrespect all that he had before —
He knew he had to correct the score.

As time passed by and Mom and Dad grew old
The son showed up at their door—hungry and cold.
He needed his family and then he knew
The mistakes he'd made were not a few.

His parents opened their arms to their wayward son;
They forgave and wept with him 'til day was done.
"Love never fails" was his parents' belief,
So the son turned over a brand new leaf.

Jess Varmint
MORNINGSUN
Morningsun
is shining
through my window
onto the orange
beside my bed
I'm turning 'round
grab
and throw it
Again I'm not
romantic

Debra Ann Famular
HELP
Unemployment, "No," they say,
Now I must wait for the judgement day.

Can't wait I need a job,
Boy do I feel like I'm being robbed.

I left my job after eight long years,
Had me a party, had a few tears.

My husband's job now south,
And me dressed up walking about.

Résumé in left, pen in my right,
My body hurts and feels tight.

Search all day, no sleep at night,
Wish I could find the job that's right.

Give me a call at 244-7133,
I'll send you my résumé, it's free.

L M Ryan
WINTER PREMONITION
There was something in the air today, that brought you to mind.
It wasn't a scent or a sound, or even the passing breeze
because
today was balmy for February.
The most noticeable thing about the air was that you really didn't feel it at all against your skin.

But nevertheless, there was a feeling in the air today that was portentous of a sweetness, a fullness, a freedom to come
and it was that incredible sweetness that washed over me
and I thought of you.

Marilyn Rutter
SORDID BUSINESS
Their aim is to seek out and destroy.
Sordid are their lives with drugs and booze,
Murder to the women of the night.
It is a pity—what a sight!
Reporters have their day to gloat and glee.
It is a story, that is all they see.
A front page task that stinks of injustice and ruin.
This is not the purpose of what is right.
Bad things are splashed out in all the papers.
Rarely is a good deed said.
Murder, suicide and all things dead.
News it is, red hot off the press—
Some win, some get redress,
From all the wanton slander and the hate,
That news has time to relate.

Marilyn Rutter
UNKIND WORDS
Unkind words can blast away the night.
Unkind words can swallow up the day.
Unkind words can make a soul feel bad.
Unkind words can spoil a perfect day.
Unkind words can sour up your mouth.
Unkind words can spur you on to pray.
Unkind words can kill the sweetest food.
Unkind words can take you far away.
Unkind words can poison any spring.
Unkind words can bring out the sting of broken words and deeds and make a sour note.
Unkind words can turn some people's vote.
Instead of love, hate festers and those words can even kill the birds.
Worst still unkind words can break the strongest will—
Plunge souls to despair and still, wreak havoc with the ones who talk like that, and make the sunny day turn black.

Mary M Ewens
TWO BECOME ONE
Touch my hand and hold me tight
Take me through the flight of life
Past energy carried in empty air
Where two become one, one body one mind
So touch my hand and then we'll see
The height that which very few dare
Up through eternity; past energy of flightless air
Where two become one, entwined body soul and mind
Now down through the flight of life
Energy in flightless air
Where one becomes two; two bodies and two minds
So till we touch, then we'll see, when two becomes, one body, one mind

Jennifer George
CRUCIFIED
A tattered look upon his face,
but still his heart feels no disgrace.
Here they stand as he dies.
Tears of pity are those he cries.
He died on the cross for you and me.
He closed his eyes so we could see.

Robert M Block
LET IT FLY
We must let ourselves fly high,
if we wish our souls to soar.
Higher than an eagle's majestic flight,
but still hearing the ocean's rumbling roar.
We must take the day and arrange it,
to guide us in what we see as right.
Still returning to earth,
after reaching such enlightening heights.
A twinkling of stardust to give us our dreams,
a splash of raging sea for power and glory.
A bit of earth to work with,
and our souls to complete us.
Let it fly.

Louise B Griffiths
HIS SECRET LOVE
You'll never guess what I am
I'm here throughout the year
Most men they do adore me
But wives I do not fear
I see my men on weekends
We really do have fun
It even can be raining or in the blistering sun
And when I am not working
I just lie around the house
But you should hear what I hear
From the lips of his dear spouse
I'd really like to tell you
But they are words I can't repeat
But I have no competition the wives go down in sheer defeat
A friend of all good wives I'd really like to be
But they won't even glance my way
they'll have no part of me
I wish the wives would like me
But they are jealous as can be
They just want their husbands back
but they're all out chasing me
You see I cannot fight or speak to anyone at all
For I'm just his loving, helpless one small golf ball.

Shawn E Roberson
STANDING ALONE

"Standing Alone" is dedicated to a wonderful student nurse for her warmest, heartfelt compassion and God sent friendship in my time of need. I want to express my thanks to Deanna Ives. 2-3-90.

Standing Alone—
What does it mean to be standing alone?
Does it mean that when you are in a crowd that you are all by yourself,
Or does it mean that your feelings and thoughts are wrong so you shove them up on a shelf?

Standing Alone—
What does it mean to be standing alone?
Does it mean that you are a child in a room full of grown-ups,
Or does it mean you see yourself pushed away and singled out today, as you were when you were a child?

Standing Alone—
What does it mean to be standing alone?
Does it mean that you are weak,
Or does it mean that you are strong?

Standing Alone—
What do I see?
I see a small child full of pain, anger, hate, and fear,
But I also see a mature woman full of happiness, love, understanding, and thoughts that are very clear.

Standing Alone—
I'm not sure that I can!
I pray to God to give me strength,
to take my hand and help me stand,
TO STAND ON MY OWN—
STANDING ALONE.

Christ Hunt
I AM

This poem Is dedicate to my Mom and Dad, and Grandma and Grandpa.

I am a worried and wondering guy who likes people
I wonder if we are ever going to have world peace
I hear the thundering of the dying world.
I see both death and happiness before my eyes
I am a worried and wondering guy who likes people
I pretend I am free like a bird
I feel the pain of dying animals crying out
I touch the living but feel the dying
I worry about our universe
I cry for peace and hope
I am a worried and wondering guy who likes people
I understand nothing about the pain in the world
I say let peace roam the world
I dream about the happiness all over the world
I try to be the best of whatever I want to be.
I hope to help the world
I am a worried and wondering guy who likes people.

John Michael Searles
REFLECTIONS UPON DEATH—WRITTEN UPON THE DEATH OF MY GRANDFATHER — NOVEMBER 29, 1989
Life and death are but one.
When we are born, our bodies and spirits
Are born into existence, from God who is all existence.
Throughout our lives on Earth, we experience
Life in our joys and death in our sorrows.
Each, in communion with the other,
Provides for a truly human experience of life.
For without life, death would not be possible;
And without death, life in the Spirit of Creation
Would not be possible.
As we die to this world, we leave our loved ones in sorrow.
But in a happiness greater than ourselves,
We are born into eternal life with God and all.

Farnia Fresnel
AN ASPECT OF LIFE
We've traveled on this long, walked road,
Right from the very start.
Carrying each heavy load,
Knowing that we'll soon depart.
If things continue as they are,
We'll walk on happily.
No stones unturned, all doors ajar,
For everyone to see.
Our lives are changing in such great ways,
In ways without retreat.
But if we stick together—no matter what,
The future won't be so bleak.

Annie E S Ellis

Annie E S Ellis
TIME
The essence of life is time
time have a tendency to us
time seems to stand still,
but unto our acknowledgment
time's still moving.

And after a while
time will bring into focus,
the move that time
have been making.

Nancy Jo Oller-Briley
HERE I AM

To my husband Bradley and my son Ross Aaron, the two most wonderful men who changed my life, gave me happiness, and made all my dreams come true. I love you both.

It's always the same
day in and day out,
wondering and wishing
to be thought about.

I keep telling myself
Someone's out there,
thinking about me
knowing they care.

It's all a dream
nothing more, nothing less,
but it's all I have
I must confess.

Now it's all changing
it'll never be the same,
slowly vanishing
it's no longer a game.

Such is life
as I must say,
Life goes on
day by day.

William J M Wisniewski
FIND ME
Don't look for me on the streets
Don't look in the parks or alleys
Nor the fields, or even the woods
I love to wander thru and roam
Instead, look to the shadows
Deep, dark velvet shadows
There, is where I'll be standing
Smiling, waiting for your call
Cry out, find me
Reach out, let me touch you
Fear not, of me nor the shadows
We will protect you
Love them like a lover
Hold them to your bosom
As a sucklin' child
I am waiting, smiling
Amongst deep dark velvet shadows
Find me

Jodie Hovde
LAST NIGHT
The day I sat on my bedroom floor
Thinking of my memories from
before.
I sat there looking as though I were
frightened.
As my memories were darkened.
Tears rushing down my face,
And all I could remember was his
soft smiling face.
The words "I love you" trailed
through my mind.
It's hard to believe my memories are
so hard to find.
He meant so much, his gentle touch
and warmth of his embrace.
As he looked at my frightened face.
He tilted my head as I started to cry.
I said, "Don't ever go away."
He looked into my eyes and held me
tight.
And all I could remember was last
night.
I knew now he really loved me.
And would never leave me.
I'll never forget that night.
The way his embrace made me feel
so safe.
And he whispered in the softness of
the night.
Looking deeply into my eyes and
said, "I Love You."

Denise Studie
SIMPLY A DREAM
I do not know from whence you
came,
For you to love me and I the same.
'Twas such a lonely place,
Until I saw your face.
Could this simply be a dream,
Or a cruel and heartless scheme.
To want you so desperately,
Only to have you taken from me.
But as long as the sun doth shine,
I want you to be mine.
And if by chance, I should wake to
find,
Our love was only in my mind.
Then once again I must sleep,
For our love, in my life, to keep.
And never again, shall I awaken,
To have your love, from me taken.

Michelle Davis
OBOES DANCE
Oboes dance
with old willows
twirling
trilling
through leafless boughs
Violins race
with dry grass
stinging
scraping
through cutting blades
Trumpets soar
with untamed eagles
shouting
gliding
from white lace mountaintops
Cellos swim
through undying streams
rippling rolling
in chilling clear rock sparkle
Handel called it "Watermusic."

Srilakshmi Malladi
THE LEAVES OF LIFE
Oh, the leave of life,
As one fell down,
The other took its leaf,
As one withered,
The other took its life!

My heart's gathered moments,
And in moments of utter silence . . .
As my eyes rolled on,
The tender tremble of my fingers
Upon the lively green leaves,
And as life rolled on!
Oh, the leaves of life!!

In the deepest corner of my heart,
A song took its birth,
A song of reaching out, of love and to
befriend,
And it gained all rhythm of sounds
And was yearning to break out,
When silence first broke . . .
And words took silence's shape . . .
Over the lush green leaves
And as love poured on!
Oh, the leaves of life!!!

Winnie Carol Jackson
BEEN THERE
Been sweet
Been bitter
Been loyal
Been true
Been bad
Been good
Been used
Been blue
Been held
Been harmed
Been cheated
Been charmed
Been pushed
Been shoved
Now at last
Been loved.

Winnie Carol Jackson
LOVE SONG
For all of my life it will always be
you.
In spite of the things that we both say
and do.
To the end of my time I shall
forever be
A chest of rare treasures
and only you hold the key.

Winnie Carol Jackson
THE EROTIC BUTTERFLY
Enter the butterfly
Lightly spreading your wings
Into sensitive corners of
My being.
Blossom the flowers fed
By a richness nurtured
By the passion of unfulfilled
Needs.
Appear the rainbow
Summoned by the
Inner vision to make
Use of the colors of love.
Explode dear starlight
And lead me into the
Depths of ultimate surrender.

Kimberley Brown
LOVE
The dreams shattered, thoughts
shredded
broken hearts that never
mend
The awakening of a nightmare,
shedding of
A tear, the dreadful dreams
that never end

The memories left behind, the future
up ahead
The confusion of it all, the hells of
life instead

Is this the proof of love, ignorance
or sacrifice
For this is the hells of love, with
its powerful clinging device

Erika C Woods
GROWING UP
A baby, small and fragile
Next year she is walking
The bottle long forgotten
Next thing you know, she's talking
Look at her all dressed up in her
bright yellow dress
It's her first day of school and it can't
be missed
Look at how she's grown,
My-Oh-My
She's already off to Junior High
She looks quite beautiful,
Standing next to a handsome young
man
I believe his name is Tom
And he's taking her to her first Senior
prom
She's off to the university
I will miss her so
I really hate to see her go, but I know
she will write to me
She's going through a process that
never, ever stops
It's something we all go through,
It's simply called growing up.

Hank Henry
THE HOUSE OF DOOM
Turn the key, unlock the door, and
you enter a very strange room
You've just begun your life in the
House of Doom and there is no
escape . . . no way out!

Be not afraid, because death comes in
time to everyone.

Somewhere in life, you lost control
and now it's time to lose your soul.

Close your eyes and you feel the
pain, to dream again is to fly on
broken wings.

The House of Doom has control of
you and won't release you
The House of Doom is your Master,
can't you hear the Master's song?

Come on down and take a good look
around and see the faces known to
you.
They made the same mistake as
you . . . don't you wish this was only
a nightmare?!

You walked yourself in, but you'll
never crawl your way out.
I hope you said goodbye to mother
and your friends
Because, you'll never see them again.

Hank Henry
REALITY?
If I am always dreamin'
I will always survive
And if I ever stop daydreamin'
I won't know how to stay alive.

I can't fight the night and
I hunger for the day to end
But when the night is over
will another day begin?

If I could live what I dream
I would never sleep again
I always fight what I feel, and
the battle never ends.

I see my dreams in the dark
but when the daylight comes
I step out to face reality
and fight the war that's never
won.

I look so hard to see the light
but when I reach to touch,
everything fades away.

Sandra Redmond
LOSERS AND USERS
Ugly hatred, low-down disgust, pain
of life
we love till it hurts Drugs: nature's
knife
cuts our bodies, deceives our minds.
Losers
use, not out of pain, but ignorance,
not ignorance of drugs, but ignorance
of life.

Hate change, Hate success. Hate life.
Better to live in the dark than light.
Flying high one day, crash down low
the next.
These things happen naturally, no
need to induce.

Drug-thirsty, low-down lunatic out of
wit,
get that needle out of your vein, keep
that
dope out of your nose, maybe then
you'll fit.

Pamela J McCarty
A SEASON OF THOUGHT
Oh, how the sands of time whisk by.
Here then gone in a winking eye.
Blooms that climb the light of day
will wilt on winds; be swept away.
Slips of brown intrude the grass
to tell us summer soon will pass.
Once did grandeur leaves abound,
now they crumble on the ground.
Thinning clouds dust o'er the sky
touching those that wing so high.
The sun along seems growing tired.
'Tis certain soon it will retire.
The howling winds will soon show
strong
screaming forth their winter song.
A crystal, blinding lay of snow
will warm the life that sleeps below.

Then again upon the spring,
new day, new life the sun shall bring.
Full and bright and fresh from sleep,
winter now a memory keep.
Oh, how the sands of time do fly!
Here, then gone in a winking eye.

Jason M Snipes
DAD
Often I wonder about your childhood;
What kind of kid would grow up to be you?
When I think about it, I don't know who;
Your life's teacher must have been very good;
You have led a life like all of us should;
You are great at all that you try to do,
And you will just not stop at number two;
I would be like you if I only could;

Seeing old pictures of you as a kid,
What really stood out was that bright red hair;
Except for those locks, it could have been me;
You looked the same way that all children did;
That could have been any child standing there;
All people have potential, can't you see?

Sandra J Tatum
THE SPICE OF LIFE

To my mentor Mariangela Marino who encouraged me to try.

A strange awareness flitted across my psyche as it reared its ugly head one day,
Almost intangible, yet monstrous in its enormity, hideous in its simplicity—

Yet it lingers, lurking on the portals of life
musing over the vacuity of each man's annals
anticipating a warmhearted welcome
be bid it by those rejoicing
at its unexpected arrival.

Should I entertain it?
Let it flit by?—tantalizing, enticing
No! there's no room for this guest here!!
Let possibility, probability, mangle, choke, retard, impede, stifle, repress, subdue—

What it brings is relief but only for the discerning few
Who shrewdly let its arms caress them unreservedly,
As love does a couple enraptured wholeheartedly,
Why then do so many despise it as bitter, if its nectar be so sweet?

Because, as love's levy be broken hearts and promises change extorts
that with which pain is wrought
A look in the sea of
Narcissus
and demands the most
terrifying feat
of all
A look at the image called—
SELF.

Lucretia Landrum Gadness

Lucretia Landrum Gadness
A NEW DAY

Dedicated to my Mother and Father, Jerry and Kathryn Landrum, whom I love so dearly and who are more precious to me than anyone on this earth. I love you Mom & Dad and I thank God for you and all you've done for me.

The dawning of this new day with glory fills my soul.
I look out upon his world and sense such riches unfold.
I hear God's voice in his sweet birds as they do sing.
All creation was made to raise praises to their king.

I feel at such oneness with the Lord who made this all.
This comes to his people who hear & answer his sweet call.
This life is only a preparation to live & reign with him.
We must learn to praise him, as trees do, lifting each limb.

If we could just praise him in all things that we go thru.
Jesus would raise us to higher realms; give life anew.
We shall spend all eternity in praise and in adoration.
It begins here on earth; the reason he made all creation.

If we could but learn as the sweet birds in morning dew.
To arise early and sing praises to him; this is the clue.
To begin each day and join the birds in their praise to him.
The Lord wants to teach us this dear truth; it is a real gem.

Let us look to each new day as opportunity to begin in praise.
Jesus, my Saviour; the song in my heart new heights to raise.
I love you, oh sweet Jesus; I only want to live for you alone.
Prepare me now for the glorious day I see you on your throne.

Martha A Lampart
DEAR SON
Where have the years gone
Only yesterday you were a babe
Where have all the years gone
Only yesterday you were my boy.

Tho age has changed your thoughts
My love has never wavered
Tho age has broadened your lifestyle
My love will remain yours.

Your need for independence is obvious
My need for you is too
Why can't you just remember
All the love I have for you.

Your selfishness is depressing
My anger has begun
Your thoughtlessness does hurt
My anger grows and grows.

Your love is dangled above me
Barely reachable at all
I want you back to love me
Like when you were my boy.
Love, Mom

Mary Rachel Hoover
MY SOUL'S MORTAR

To the mortal who is my mortar.

As days roll by and years grow shorter,
I know beyond a doubt
That of all my life, you are the mortar
That helps me to stand stout.

The support and help you freely give,
In truth, holds me together.
Without that 'glue,' I couldn't live
Or smile through any weather.

Yes, mortar is the rightful name
For what you are to me;
For nothing else could be the same
If you weren't there for me.

Neil F Mahoney
BRAVE INNOCENCE
Sing the song of child wars,
Fought among our friends.
With forces gathered on chosen sides,
We honored to defend.

Sunset fell on many fields,
But seldom blood was shed.
Arm in arm we walked like men,
Forever to be friends.

Nicole Pankowski
PICKING UP THE PIECES
This is a story 'bout a broken heart,
Pulled from its owner and torn apart,
It lay there shattered, scattered on the ground,
Not a drop of love to be found.

He gathered up the pieces and headed home,
As he was walking his mind started to roam,
He thought of her laughter; her radiant smile,
The whispered moments; her elegant style,
Pieces of love slipped through his hand,
As hours slip by with grains of sand.

Day had gone, night had come with magic in the air,
Stars sprinkled the blackened sky, twinkling in night's lair,
The faded path was set afire and suddenly burnt bright,
An image glided towards his love so swiftly on this night,
She gathered up the blazing pieces, which shone for only her,
And followed love with such a fever, moving as a blur.

The man stood blinded, stood there open-armed,
Both of them with love's sweet scent had been charmed,
True love encircled them; those who will not part,
For true love is the only thing to heal a broken heart.

Jamie Smith
FEET OH FEET
Feet oh feet
Where do they go
Feet oh feet
know one knows
Feet, oh no
Please don't go
because I don't know
Where feet go
OH NO

Staci Leighann Book
YOU & ME, MOM
(I LOVE YOU)
"You know, it's going to be another boy don't you!"
But deep down, you knew it was a girl,
a girl who has your eyes of blue
They say I have your looks,
I must be lucky!
They say I have your body,
I must be lucky!
You walked, talked, played with me,
when you could have ignored me
You taught me songs and read me books
all before I was three.
They say I have your smile,
I must be lucky!
They say I have your laugh,
I must be lucky!
I began to get involved with friends,
maybe some were even boys
You acted as though you understood,
but deep down you missed my toys.
They say I have your personality
I must be lucky!
They say I have your temper
I must be lucky!
I gradually moved out,
out of your comfortable home
You felt abandoned, all alone,
but said, "Don't forget to phone!"
I MUST BE LUCKY

Karen Latham
THE EMPTY HEART
My heart no longer aches, with the pain of a lost love
but has become dark and solid with no feeling left inside.
Ever since those words were spoken saying good-bye.

It tore the last piece apart and threw it away like an
old shoe. Never again will I be able to love someone who
Was a wish to begin with!

Bridget Tam
MY SECRET
A secret! A secret!
I just heard a secret
And nobody else shall hear.
No talking, no shouting, no mumbling
no nothing or a secret will vanish from the air.

A secret! A secret!
I just heard a secret!
Oh, it should be kept that way
A minute, a second
I just think I'm going to tell

Peggy S Campbell
UNTITLED
I have the picture, the imprint is upon my mind
Images I can recall anyplace, anytime
Precious, timeless, the desire is all it

takes
To think back and live over again
Another time, another place
However joyous that image may be,
there's a note of sadness when I
realize it's just a memory . . .
But at that same moment I feel a
warmth inside
A warmth that comes from the glow
of that memory
And knowing it's with me the rest of
my life

Rebecca Kea
RESOLVE
beneath the facade of it all
and disheveled moments
we try to grasp

the running
in the lack
of light

for someone's hand to grasp
there stays a life
that tries to live
with thoughts
and all
amassed
for something
that was not
meant to be
lies this memory
of something passed

L T Bennett
HANDGAMES
Open, close, open, fingers stretched
wide,
Pat, pat two hands at a time
Pat, pat, two crossing
Pat, pat, two touching

Clap . . .

Open, close, open, fingers stretched
wide.
Handgames—
Played by two, than one,
smooth and rhythmic motions
holding and supporting one another.

Open, close . . .
close—alone
Handgames, contact sports.

Kim L Jackson
TEACHER AND STUDENT ONE
In a second a spark lights the eyes.
The lips form an 'O.'
The nerves race through the face.
Understanding that touches the brain
is displayed.

How wonderful the feeling is.
A little more of the world has been
opened up.
The teacher stands back and smiles.

This is what brings meaning to life.
Not material objects that can only be
bought with money.
That is not what is important.
It is the connection between two
beings.

Everything seems so very bright.
Arms open to embrace the world.
The books of centuries are open.
All the knowledge of the universe is
cascading down.

It is a lifetime of learning and
beyond.
And when death has come, there is
still much more.
Only one drop from the ocean has
been touched.

But what a magical drop.

What a glorious climb.
And today the sun came pouring
through the window.

Deborah A Ledford
MY FRIEND
My Friend,
Have you ever felt alone,
but were surrounded by many?
Have you ever wanted joy,
but there just wasn't any?
Have you ever needed faith,
but all you had was doubt?
Have you ever looked for love,
but found it nowhere about?
Have you ever wished for peace,
but all you saw was war?
Have you ever desired happiness,
but just couldn't smile
anymore?
Have you ever loved Jesus,
but forgot Him along the way?
Have you ever truly served Him,
but thought it didn't pay?
Have you ever, my Friend,
have you ever?

Dorothy E Koch Singer
THERE IS POWER
When sadness floods the sunlight and
darkness fills the halls,
There is power in the silence of a
teardrop when it falls.

When heartache seems eternal and a
racing heart resounds,
There is power in the anguish of the
sobbing when it sounds.

When despair grows even bleaker
and all hope is being bashed,
There is power in the touching of a
hand that's being clasped.

When a cheerful moment enters and
the time is not too late,
There is power in the effort of a smile
that's taking shape.

When love outplays the sadness and
the troubles are all aired,
There is power in the winking eye
expressing secrets shared.

When laughter spins and dances and
quarrels are taboo,
There is power in the thrill of love
that says, "I still love you."

Margret K Davis

Margret K Davis
MOTHER'S DAY

*Dedicated to Lt. Margret
("Granny Annie") A. Davis.
From: Your youngest daughter with
love!*

I thank you mother for so many
things,
no card could ever say.
The things that make you special are
the things you do each day.

How would I know just how to love,
if it had not been for you?
How did I learn to laugh at times,
once thought were only blue?

You give me strength whenever I'm
weak, and
you show me a better side.
You seem to know my every ways,
even the feelings I try so hard to hide.

You always stay so proud of me,
even at times I stumble, and fall.
You are always there to talk with me,
any hour at all I call.

I love you mother for all those things,
and there is something I'm trying to
say:
"If God has a reason for everything,
you're his reason for Mother's Day."

P.S. I LOVE YOU.

Mary E Danforth
STOP THE WARS DADDY

*Dedicated to my father, Julian F.
Locke.*

Would you stop and look around
And use your eyes to see
What you're doing to your children
You men of greed and vanity.

Would you change your way of
thinking
Would you stop the wars, daddy
Would you stop the war

Will the killing go unheeded
Could we live in love and grace
A helping hand where needed
Let's share our private space
The wars, daddy could you stop the
wars

Our children born in love
Will grow to die by the sword
The war, daddy, can we stop the war
Please tell us the magic word

We'll try to change the way of things
If you just tell us how
To take away the killing things
We have to do it now

Before the ones we hold so dear
We've tried to hard to save
Have left this world without a chance
To stop the wars, daddy, to stop the
wars.

Ned A Jensen
SOLITUDE
Away from the noise of life, I quest
A place of solitude.
A place of quietness and rest
Of no great magnitude.

Not just a room with doors between
The hustle and the rushed.
But a place where no one goes
And everything is hushed.

Where no ringing of a telephone
Or knock upon a door,
Will disturb my thoughts of better
life
Or the mysterious distant shore.

Far away upon the mountain high
Or along the ocean sands,
I'll gaze my eyes up to the sky
And lift my thankful hands.

Soon, when meditation is done
And I have no need for more,
I'll fly away from solitude
Because it's such a bore.

Marveen Coiner Campbell
THE CREDIT CARD
I had what seemed a foolish dream,
as I slept the other night.
'Twas 'bout the credit cards some
use, for everything within their sight.
Yes, some just use them foolishly
and then become contrite.
When bills come piling in too fast
and their finances seem, oh! so tight.
Others keep them tucked away and
won't use them at any cost.
And then they talk about the day, all
the bargains, they had lost.
Then others use them wisely, for the
necessary things.
Which they know they can afford, as
they hear the register ring.

A lesson from the credit card, is
easily within our reach.
And we can use it wisely, as our
young'ns we do teach.
Many lives are often wasted, just like
the credit card.
Folks go through life so aimlessly,
holding no one in regard.
There are those who just hide away,
their lives they refuse to share,
With others who are hurting, for
these they do not care.
If we would spend time wisely, as
our daily lives we walk.
We could shed love about us, as we
live the life we talk.

Keiko I Pugh
A REQUIEM FOR THE BRAVES
Discard your armour, my sweet
prince,
For the battlefields have been
deserted
Since the combat's no longer fought
Upon the foreign soils, but rather
within ourselves

Remember the times when we could
have conquered
The world just by clinging to our
lovers' arms,
Just by singing our freedom songs?

Release your prisoners, my
benevolent prince,
So that we too shall be freed from
this bondage
Of carnage and death, and the
remembrance of
Guilt and shame which have plagued
your gentle dreams

Rest your weary soul, my courageous
one,
For the peace shall reign once more
When you face your ghosts from the
past
In order to meet yourself without a
fear,

And so that we can begin to forgive
rather than
To vanquish, embrace one another
rather than to repel,
And to love ourselves once again, not
in the future,
Not in the past, but in this glorious
moment of here and now.

Panagiota Yotta Cominos
AGAIN

*I dedicate this poem in memory of my
late beloved husband, Peter; and to
my four children whose love we
shared together, and miss together,
with their father.*

If I lived my life again,
I would do the same as then.

I would go in reality;
Like I do in memory.

We would walk hand in hand,
Through the streets of New York,
The Big Apple would be red and bright;
To welcome us again with its lights.

I would wait for you like then;
Through the war once again.
I would have our children as before,
For they are the ones I adore.
Part of you and part of me,
They make me very happy.

We'll walk again in Pittsburgh, too.
In my friendly hometown with you

Top it all with our dream come true,
Our trip to our native Greece
I'll do it all as I did then,
Walking the mountains hand in hand
I'd do it all again.

Barbara T Day Richards
BLACK HOLE, BLACK HOPE
Black hole, black hope;
Why must I strain for stars,
Yearn for faint, distant lights,
And fight such futile wars?
And would my little, tangled brain
Collect them if I flew
To store them up and set them in a row,
As now I needs must do.
Is polishing and counting points
All that I have to be?
If I could stop, throw stars away
And let them all float free
Would I crouch low in my black hole?
Or would stars shine for me?

Rosanna Rivers
THE FURIES

To my father, my mother, Bobbie, and my sister, Mindy. Thanks for the encouragement.

Windowpanes shuddered.
Rain fell.
The sky split apart, and the thunder uttered
A mighty oath that told the tale
Of unleashed fury and unknown power.

The rain pounded down upon newborn flowers;
It cared not what destruction it caused.
The lightning had no reason to cower;
It struck at young trees without a pause
To even consider this strangely dangerous whim.

It was nothing more than a game to them—
Nothing more than a game.
When finally their anger dimmed,
They looked upon the world and knew a certain shame
That their rage had been poured out upon the unfortunate earth.

The rain took consolation in sounding forth new births;
It gave life and freshness to the spring.
The lightning sought solace in its own worth;
It lit up the dark, wet expanse of sky as no other thing.
Their furor diminished, they silently crept back to their clouds.

Omalee Nahodil
KEEP ON PRAYING
Keep on praying God will always hear.
Keep on praying God will always hear,
just fall down upon your knees,
ask the Lord to hear your plea.
Keep on praying God will hear and answer prayer.

Keep on praying God is always near.
Keep on praying God will always hear.
He's the one who always cares,
He's the one your burden shares.
Keep on praying, God will hear and answer prayer.

Keep on praying God is on your side.
Keep on praying and with the Lord abide.
He'll supply your every need
He your soul will surely feed.
Keep on praying God will answer prayer.

Caroline A Kenyon
BURDEN OF A STAR
As the sun sets over the horizon
And the moon begins its reign
The first star to appear
Is the lonely one to bear my pain
I wish upon it constantly
Hoping it will answer my pleas
What a burden this poor star carries
Each time it rises beyond the trees
Only seldom is it shielded
By a protective dark gray cloud
Then I must bear the grief within
I cannot express my sorrow aloud
The same request is thrust upon it each night
To bring him back to me
But so far the star has not granted
My wish has not come to be

Esther V M Hamel
GAIA
I had a dream vision. And I saw
a statue. Wood. Polished.
The artist came and stood
in front of the statue.
and her my our hand
Moved. And as it moved
the contours under it
Lit and glowed.

And she me we spoke. And
Explained. That each lighted
area lighted the next.

And she me we spoke. And
Explained. That the light
related to personal
interrelationships.

Love. Commitment. Especially
Caring
And the light flowed over
the hand.
And she me we realized
This is Gaia
The Universe as One.

Nancy Ann Priest
SINAI

Dedicated to The Negev and Sinai Bedouin and Professor Avner Goren.

Dry Desert Night
all around me
Where does the Light
of My Lord's Love
Abound?

Lost out here
in the darkness
Why does My Captain seem Phantom
my Ship gone
Aground?

Is there an Oasis
out here in the night?
Is there a Well-Spring
of water and Light
Here around?

How on this Desert?
alone in the night?
Can My Way Back
to The Temple
Be Found?

Tina House
HEAR THE CRY OF THE MOTHER EARTH
All my brothers and sisters, lend an ear to my heart's plea
Listen before it's too late to see.
Listen before we will no longer be
We have desecrated our Mother's body.
We have taken too much of her soul
Our Father, the Sky Father cries tears
tears of acid rain

Our Father cries to release his disappointment and pain
We take from her beauty and leave traces of our
ignorance, apathy and disdain
We seek nourishment from the bosom of the Earth Mother
We destroy the four leggeds, plants, rocks and our fellow
humans, all our brothers
Unite in the name of our Father and learn to respect and
care for the Earth Mother
The circle of life unites all brothers
It is the truth of the Sky Father and the only
Salvation of the Earth Mother
To break the circle of life is to exist no more

Please listen and help the Earth Mother to endure
We can not go on taking and forgetting to give
The desecration of our Earth Mother is the
desecration of our children, our future,
our means to live.

Vanessa O'Lynn
AND IT IS RAINING
I wake in the morning and it is raining;
Steadily the tear-shaped drops fall;
Onto the ground and covering everything with a wet blanket.
It reminds me of my own tears,
Gently sliding down my face;
All my sadness in those small, wet circles.
Crying for myself, for my troubles, my mistakes;
For the things people expect me to be, which I never will.
When will it all end? When will the rain stop?
And even when the sun comes out,
I'll put on my false smile,
And keep that smile on until the next rainy day,
When I'll let my tears fall along with the rain once again.
I wake in the morning, and it is raining . . . .

Betty Marr
SHELL
I'll grow a hard shell to protect me
So that when life offers hard knocks
I'll hear it quite well
But I'll say "Go to hell!"
And avoid all the pain of the shock.

I'll stay safe inside at all times
And protect everything that I own.
I'll not let you in
To disrupt me again
And you'll not even reach me by phone!

I'll light up my world with false daydreams
And I'll dream of nice things in my sleep
And then when I wake
And I've started to shake
I'll remember the shell and I'll weep.

Barbara Timken

Barbara Timken
MY FATHER, MY FRIEND

Dedicated to the memory of my father, Joachim J. Fernandez, Sr., who is sadly missed by all.

You held me in your arms, looked down at me below,
prepared me for the world, sat and watched me grow.
You taught me the rules to live by,
sharing life, from start to end,
you grew to be more than my father,
you grew to be my friend

We spent a lot of time together,
you used laughter to relieve the pressure,
and these times I think of most,
and hold in my heart as valuable treasure

Now that your time with us on earth has passed,
and you are no longer here,
I feel as though you are inside of me,
always listening, always near

I now reflect back on your advice,
still earning your respect,
striving to make you proud of me,
with every image that I project

As my life goes on, growing closer to its end
I'll always have you with me,
My father, My friend

George A Brown
COMING TOGETHER

In memory of my mother, Jessie V. Brown, and to my loving wife, Rhondrea. Love, George.

Living for Jesus is very hot!
Alcohol and drugs are definitely not!
Eternal salvation is my No. 1 shot.
Hating my brother is certainly not!
Who is my brother?
Any man of color, black, red,
Or white, all is precious in
God's sight!

Christine Perreault
MEMORIES ARE

This poem is dedicated to Jesus for helping me in my life, Mom, Dad, John, Jamie Houck, Jearline, Lorrane, Virgie, Jerry, Chris and friends & family; with love, from Kris.

"MEMORIES ARE" a walk in the
park with someone you love.
A kiss on your cheek,
A smile on your face.

"MEMORIES ARE" a time when
you talk for hours, with a friend or a
companion.

Holding hands, walking on the
beach and feeling sand on
your feet.

"MEMORIES ARE" a ride in a car
on your first date and rushing home
in hopes you won't be late.

Or a single rose, given by your
one true love.

"MEMORIES ARE" a time when he
asks you if you'd always be there

with him.
And the ring he placed
on your hand.

"MEMORIES ARE" the laughter and
the pain, the sound of the pouring

rain.
Having him hold you as if to
say I'll never let you go.
But soon that's all that is
there are the Memories
and you cling to them,
in hopes
he soon will
be there.

Dale Hancock
THE PROMISE
When you promised to have and to
hold,
He had your heart of purest gold.
There's no one else to take his place,
And he can see that in your face.

You'll go through life hand in hand,
As the only woman, and he the only
man.
But somewhere as the years go by,
You start to drift from each other's
side.

Your life gets busy and so does his.
He's got his job, you've got the kids.
Each job's important, with each
comes stress.
He wants a new car, you need a new
dress.

How could this happen, you blame
each other.
Until one day one finds another.
Now you don't talk and you never
touch.
Each day drifts by, so does your love.

That promise made, that now is
broken,
Is in each thought, but never spoken.
We say goodbye, and then we part.
The children are left with the broken
heart.

Joyce Foss
PATRICIA
"I'm almost 30" I exclaimed to my
husband
I want to have a baby someday
My biological clock is ticking away

A year went by and I'm happy to say
We had a lovely baby girl on St.
Patrick's Day.

She had a beautiful smile, brown hair
and brown eyes
And I was thinking of all the pretty
dresses we could buy.

We were in the mall shopping when
she was two
She screamed, "Mommy, do you love
me? I love you."

The years flew by, she's now a teen
And I'm older and wiser but she says
I'm mean

She is growing up—feeling many
new emotions
I tell her—we are here if you need us
with our love and devotion

She yells you don't want to accept
that I'm growing up
And I hate to admit it's so
For many times I'd like to relive
those wonderful memories of years
ago

"I'm almost 42" I exclaimed to my
husband
We had a baby 13 years ago
The best decision of our life—we
really love her so.

Snowflake
SHADY WOODSY SLEEP

In Loving Memory for my dog "Nipper."

Little bird flying high brings me a
smile for a while
Singing sweet his words come from
the deep. Woodsy Sleep.
Then I hear his song come along, a
path of flowers
born, the notes
sing the children swing.
Clouds roll by the tops of my eye
the leaves sway to give way
my heart soars with the song
adorned, wind carries the notes
with every stroke. Within the
Shady Woodsy Sleep.
Shaded by my eye, I see a
surprise! Perched on a branch
he gives you no chance!
Captured by his eye he will sing
you a lullaby
Within the Shady Woodsy Sleep

Alice Thompson Gilissen
THE FAIRNESSES ARE GONE
Time produced us and acquainted us;
we were three hours apart, and so
much twin.
More than sister, more than type, we
battered as we shared, but always
gained.
But now we talked . . .

"It isn't fair," I said, "that you
must go and I will stay."
"It isn't fair," you sighed, "there's
just so much I want to do."
"It isn't fair," I said, "there's just
so
much you do so well . . .
you have such hold on Truth; it
isn't
fair to let the lies remain."
(Was it a canvas so replete . . . the
fairness of the artwork in your life?)

We yielded . . .
"Remember now," I said, "I'm not
the one to stand alone; we always
knew I
was the coward . . . I should be the
first to slip away."
"Knowing us, that arrangement
would be best," you sighed, but
not to be.
I'm just reluctant . . . though not
afraid, to lie upon the wave."

(Was it cut on the straight, the
fairness of the pattern of your life?)

Time drew us close, we knew her
mood; we were three hours apart, and
so much twin.
More than sister, more than type,
resisting as we fought, but not to
gain.

Time talked . . . She did not yield.

"There was a job to do," she
said . . . "we were the kind to
do it well."
(Was it a taste so subtle, the fairness
of
Her recipe for your life?)

Goodbye, my friend . . . my tears
begin . . . I'll carry on,
but when you went, the fairnesses
were gone.

Marie B Francois
DO YOU LOVE ME?

To my Shoushou with love always from Nounoune.

Did you say you loved me?
Or did my heart wish those words
were spoken by your lips?
Did you say you loved me?
I was too, too naive and blinded
by my own overwhelming love for
you.
Did you say you loved me?
Every thought and heartbeat in my
body and soul was attached with you.
Did you say you loved me?
Please say it again because I don't
or can't recall you said it.
Did you say you loved me?
I feel I'm caught between a dream
and reality.
Did you say you loved me?
You're the only one to set me free
of this mental captivity and
heartbreak.
What did you just say?
What are you doing to me?
Your words are like flutes playing
in the wind and your lips are ever
so luscious on mine.
Oh darling, I love you too.

Gwen Jones
IN LOVE

This poem is dedicated to my daughter Melissa, my beautiful love child.

When you're young and in love
you forget all things.
When you're young and in love
you forget even the simplest
things.
And then you wake up and say
"WOW"
where have I been.
Then you remember you were young
and in love.

Eleanor M Cross
ODE TO CICERO
Oh Cicero, lawyer, writer, orator-
statesman.
You loved Rome more than life
itself!
Defended many poor peons, stood
condemned,
Fighting for truth, mercy and justice.
You were no "yes man"—You had
courage;
Your words were golden, yet vibrant.
You saw the future for your city—
And grieved, your beard wet with
tears—
But for all your efforts—exile.
Recalled for a short time, then died a
martyr's death.
Rome lost a hero and later fell,
As you said it would.
This is history, sad but true.

Fred Grimaldi
HARMONY
Doesn't make any difference if you
are black or white,
Let's work together, and everything
will be alright
It's very easy to follow that rule,
It could be on the job or even in
school
So be good, and you will be
understood
If you are bad, a lot of people will be
mad
Try to be happy, stay with that smile,
Things will get better, in a very short
while

O'Brian Kightlinger
A WRITER I WOULD BE
A flippant thought I had tonight.
A writer I would be—and be.
I would sit and write and write and
write,
But not a soul would see—
ME.

I'd tell of wondrous things both far
and wide,
And envied I would be—and be,
And I would swell and swell with
pride,
But not a soul would see—
ME.

My words would flow without an
end,
And listened to they would be—and
be!
Would ears and ears bring a friend?
No! Not a soul would see—
ME.
See?
me?

Trudy Taylor
THE WALL
The world looked on in horror
Back in 1961.

We couldn't quite believe
What the Communists had done.

A wall of solid concrete
Built so high and strong
Would surely keep out freedom
But history proved them wrong.

Democracy on one side,
Communism on the other . . .
The German people could no longer
Freely visit one another.

Thousands tried to cross the wall
And many of them died.
No sacrifice was too great
To get through to freedom's side.
And like the walls of Jericho
This one too, shall fall.
The world will see that being free
Is the greatest gift of all!

Mildred Lucas Reddoch
BUILDERS OF FREEDOM INSURANCE

Dedicated to President George W. Bush and Past President Ronald Reagan.

There are varied kinds of builders—
Of stationary bridges that span a lake,
A creek or even rivers wide . . .
A moving bridge—a ship or plane—
Molding ideas, concepts benefiting
Man on all sides.
When Man has mastered his ideas
To the point of benefit to all—
His mental plans and working plans
Blend into one great concept—as an
Umbrella shields many in a clan.
Studying this concept of builders
From varied views—
Man can with assurance see
Builders of bridges and concepts of
Man
An insurance covering Freedom and
Peace.

The originator of this Bridge of
Concepts being GOD.
Resulting effects: Activity in East
and West Germany.

Nancy Marie Wood-Rhodes
DEEP INSIDE

To anyone involved with substance abuse and trying to kick the habit.

I came upon a clump of mud, and
deep inside a flower grew.
I came upon a stagnant pond, and
deep inside tadpoles danced.
I came upon an angry beehive, and
deep inside was honey.
I came upon a coal black mine, and
deep inside were diamonds.
I came upon a rotting tree, and deep
inside were robins' eggs.
I came upon a rusted safe, and deep
inside was money.
I came upon a tattered book, and
deep inside were words of wisdom.
I came upon a deserted isle, and deep
inside was lushness.
I came upon a drug crazed lunatic,
and deep inside was you.

Allison L Criddle
DRUM OF ENGLAND

Dedicated to Simon LeBon of Duran Duran.

The beating of the waves
echoes in my mind
thoughts of you

The strange configurations
the clouds gather into
are but images of you

A sail
A gull
A shell

Are reflections of memories of you

The Drum
beating beating
The Drum
pounding pounding against the waves
The Drum
Heroically facing the brutal wind

The wind whispering words from you
Tender musical words of love, anger,
and passion
A gull sweeps into the ocean, to
gather its prey
The waves engulf the shore, as the
storm draws near.
Danger is in the air . . . the fearsome
Drum goes on.

Sharon Dickinson
RAINBOWS

I dedicate this poem to my mom and dad for bringing me into this world.

Rainbows are colorful in some ways,
they come after showers in rainy
days,
at the end of the rainbow coins will
shine.

In a golden pot that looks so fine,
In the background,
the sun will shine a ray of light,
Making it so beautiful and so bright.
In a few minutes it might fade away.
But then, it might come back another
day.

Gloria M Miller
TREASURES OF THE HEART

What remarkable little images
I've tucked away somewhere;
Of long forgotten happenings
And laughter that once filled
The air;

Could there be a private or
Partially hidden room, where
Wonderful and delightful
Secrets are forever safe and
In eternal bloom?

When my days seem cloudy and
Perhaps a bit cruel;
I'll open my little treasure
Chest and see life's most
Precious jewels.

Sybol Brown
FAITH

To my mother, Gatha Hersman Garvin.

I See the Star in the sky
Which most have wished upon
For Love or Wealth
or some for Health
But most have had
the great desire
TO WISH UPON A STAR

Dee Lauck
FOREVER

Love is forever,
I know this is true,
because this is how
I will always feel for you.
Your smile is so beautiful,
it softens my cries
with you in my arms
I now realize,
our love is forever
so kiss me again
and hold me so gently
until we kiss again.

Garnet A Jones
THE YELLOW ROSE

For my beloved sister, Ruby, a sister and friend—gone but never forgotten.

Today I bought a yellow rose
As I have in years gone by.
I bought it for your birthday, Sis,
Even tho the bloom will die.

The rose is always perfect
The color like shining sun.
It stands for love and friendship
Just like every other one.

The yellow rose will wither
And the perfect bloom won't
last
But, now it's a living symbol
Of days shared in our past.

I'll carry it very carefully
So the beauty I can save
Then I'll stoop and lay the perfect
rose
In the grass upon your grave.

Corine Morris
MAE ELLA MELVIN

My Mother was so wonderful to me,
When I was young I really couldn't
see,
Just how much love she had for us,
How she gave and gave without a
fuss.

As I grew older and began to see,
Mae Ella's love which was so free,
When she was sick or tired as could
be,
The love she had still looked out for
Dora and me.

She worked long hours for others and
us,
Never complaining and catching the
bills,
To go to work to iron, clean, mop and
dust.

When she came home her work
wasn't done,
There were things to do—no time for
fun,
Others would need her services too,
You see, her work was never
through.

My Mother was love for God and
man,
A willing worker and a helping hand,
Now she is gone to her home on high,
Where she can rest from her labor
and never die.

That love she gave to Dora and me
Her love that was so free
I'm glad that I can see
Mae Ella Melvin loved Corine
and Dora Lee.

Debi Alonzo-Sanchez
HOLD ME

Hold me in your soft, brown eyes. Watch that I am safe and always by your side. If your eyes reflect a sparkle, let me be the reason.

Hold me in your heart. Let me be the pulse that keeps you alive and happy. Let every beat flow freely with your love.

When you speak, speak my name with love and passion not sorrow or pain and smile lightly with a glowing touch.

Hold me in your arms. For those strong arms will protect me and keep me warm. Never open them to let me go. Your touch is soft yet secure.

And hold me in all of your thoughts and dreams. Let me be your desire. Let me love you as you have loved me . . . forever.

Ruth Thomasson

Ruth Thomasson
MY DEAREST FRIEND

This Poem Is Dedicated To Rochelle Daniel & Krista (My Grandchildren).

Jesus is my saviour
He's my true and dearest friend
He is closer than a brother
On Him I can depend.

He surrounds me with His love
And He makes my heart so glad
He's the most beloved friend
That I have ever had.

I love my friend "He's Jesus"
So majestic and sublime
He is present when I need Him
For His friendship is divine.

He is with me in the morning
He is with me all day long
And He whispers "child I'll guide
you
When everything goes wrong."

He said "I'll never leave you
I'll go with you to the end"
And that's why I chose Jesus
To be my dearest friend.

Karen L F Siemon
ON SILENCE

To those who feel the sting of hollow
silence,
An echo that shatters, kin to distant
Breaking glass, reflecting horrors in
their shards,
There's a downward spiraling view
of a silent world.

How to explain this seemingly
distorted view?
The world shows to bleary eyes a
wary carnival.
Mirrors, of assorted shapes and sizes,
hurry
Me through my allotted passage, my
haunted hall.
Their mottled lights flash in vivid,
pulsating forms,
As strange gnomes reach out to grab

my tattered, torn garb.
In my confusion, I leap away to avoid,
In startled mode, the tricky pain; they seem to gain,
Distorting my view, hurrying my taut, light step.
Cannot stop, lest to oblivion, I will fall.

So this is how it seems sometimes with some:
A demented dimension in colic, cold colors.
No harm is meant to those who may hear the silence,
From a fearful heart, who's a long distance runner.

Denise Foster Holcomb

A PRAYER FOR YOU

I said a prayer for you today
And know God must have heard—
I felt the answer in my heart
Although He spoke no word!
I didn't ask for wealth or fame
(I knew you wouldn't mind)—
I asked Him to send treasures
Of a far more lasting kind!
I asked that He'd be near you
At the start of each new day
To grant you health and blessing
And friends to share your way!
I asked for happiness for you
In all things great and small—
But it was for His loving care
I prayed the most of all!

Susan M Warner

MY DADDY

My daddy left home when I was three.
He didn't leave much for my mom and me.
I had to grow up before it was time;
To help my mom save every dime.

One day I asked, "Where can he be?"
My mom said, "Oh! He died at sea."
When I grew up, I began to wonder.
I could not believe my dad's ship had gone under.

When I found out that his ship did not sink;
I sat down and began to think.
I never asked why my mother had lied.
She must have had a real good story to hide.

My dad had just died one year ago.
I only wish his address he'd have let me know.
I think he died of a broken heart.
From all those years of being apart.

I took some flowers to my daddy's grave.
I damned his soul and then I forgave.
I told him that I loved him and always will.
I asked him if he loved me still.

From the ground there came no reply,
So I looked up into the sky.
To my surprise what did I see,
but my daddy standing calling me.

Shelly Levy

FOREVER FRIENDS

"For Joe"

There are few things in life as precious as friends,
Yet we take them for granted because they're our "friends till the end."
The sad truth is that nothing lasts forever
And the bonds that were once so strong will eventually be severed.

Of this heart wrenching fact I am often reminded
Because I once had something great and now it is dead.
A trampled down friendship which will never rise again.
Gone is my friendship—gone is my friend.

The death of this friendship caused so much pain.
Although my wound is healing, a scar will always remain.
I think of this loss time and time again.
I long for my friendship—I long for my forever friend.

Lila O Crump

SEEKING

I think I want to do something, oh yes, I know I do.
But how to go about it remains a mystery too
Thinking deep within myself searching for the way,
Wondering if the answer comes will it cause dismay.
Watching people passing listening as they go,
Thinking they are different and yet they aren't I know.
How is each familiar where does it begin?
Isn't that a mystery that no one can win.
Yet we keep on trying groping in the dark,
Looking for the answers wondering where we start.
Why are we so puzzled when we are so smart.

Brandyn Johnston

SNOW

This poem is dedicated to the Johnston Family.

I see the night.
I see the snow.
I know it will stop soon.
I pray, I pray it will stay.
I will soon see the sun.
Oh God let it stay.

The snow it stayed.
I can go snowmobiling.
I can go sledding.
I will see it snow again.
I hope it lasts all day.

It's snowing again
and again.
The snow glistens.
It is very cold.
But how I love the snow.

Lola Marie Roberts

YOU MAKE ME FEEL PRETTY

With eternal love and affection to my dear sons: Gabriel Allen Roberts and Christopher James Roberts.

Your eyes reflect the figure of the person that I want to be;
But in my mirror, that is not what I see.

Voluptuous curves and a pretty face;
Curls that are soft and styled with grace.

Tantalizing lips and mysterious eyes;
Draw the envy of the women and the amoré of the guys.

Now relieved of my illusion
I've come to the conclusion,

Though outwardly denied;
There is beauty inside.

Barbara Ford Szydla

TO THE STARS

Guardians of the night sky,
Fiery orbs flung into cold
 nothingness,
You gave light as the Master's
 hand moved o'er the Earth,
Fashioning the mountains and
 and valleys, forests and rivers,
Creating every living thing—
Breathing life into His crowning
 achievement.
You guided the Psalmist and the
 Magi, the sailor and astronaut.
You look down on our strivings,
 our achievements, our failures.
Bright beacons of the night,
Watch over us—
Lead us to eternal truth!

Robert Allen Strang

HEALTH THOUGHTS

Say "NO" to any funny pill
and never do anything against your will.
Don't take drugs in the shade
that's how scrambled minds are made.
There are many real good foods to eat
that supply the vitamins and are sweet.
Don't be stupid and try drugs
and ruin your body and give cash to thugs.

Robert Allen Strang

WINTER

Winter makes me think of birds
and awesome beauty beyond words.
There's something special about snow
and howling winter winds that blow.

When I was young I used to go
build snowmen, slide and play in snow.
Now that I've earned the name of Sage
Winter's beauty has come of age.

Michael C Lafferty

A TEAR

This poem is dedicated to my fiancee, Dawn. Without her in my life my poetry would not be possible.

A salty raindrop falls from a blinking eye
A tear drop is born once again
They're as lonely as a cloud in a clear blue sky
The result of a poet and his pen

They're released as the product of a time of joy
They'll be lurking in the halls of devastation
You can find them on the face of a scared little boy
They're the architects in the house of humiliation

A tear is a golden stream forever cascading down your face
The reason that they fall we know not why
Made of a transparent liquid that will never leave a trace
Always engulfed into the pillow in which you cry

They're expected from a woman in her time of grief
But unheard of on the face of a man
Their value is simply priceless, they can't be taken by a thief
To hold them back the truth is no one can

They'll come when love is first born in your heart
They'll be present when you find love is gone
If you're the owner of the eyes from which they depart
Never fear, a new day begins with every dawn

Helen L Kurtzman

THE GREATEST GIFT OF ALL

He gathered stardust for His eyes,
Made a halo of the sun,
And even combed the snowy plains,
To clothe the Little One.

His eyes He tinted ocean blue,
And fringed them with the waves.
He called upon His angels,
To be His willing slaves.

His cheeks were hued of ivory,
The blush was from the rose,
And with the wind He tilted,
His tiny baby nose.

For tears He drew the raindrops,
For hair the golden rod.
And then He called Him Jesus,
Our Christmas gift from God.

Mimi Drennan

SLIMSY WHIMSY

Mary had a lovely shape
When she was only twenty.
Now, years have passed—
Oh, hang the crepe!
Mary's put on plenty.

What used to be so slim and trim
Today has turned to bulge.
The lesson here is true but grim—
Enjoy, but don't indulge!

Sharpen up your tactics, gals.
No need to be obese.
The fatted goose looks longer at
The leanest of the geese.

Take time to keep the bod in shape.
Exercise and diet.
You'll look and feel your very best,
And hear folks say, "Oh, my!" at.

The moral of this ditty—
It's now a rule of mine—
Keep your shape for health's sake,
'Cause that's the bottom line!

April M Burger
THE TIME SHE TOOK
I walked with her, she held my hand
and she opened up this world
she wanted me to see it "more"
she made me understand

She listened to me
she heard my every thought
her tuition I so praise
by the inner strength she taught

The trust she allowed
the pride she saw in me
she helped me to realize that life is a gift
just as she thought it to be.

Through every year, and every phase
the love she gave I treasure
the time my mother gave to me
my thanks you could not measure

Josephine Comella
SMILE
You smile at me and I'll smile
at you.
One smile will turn into two—
I'll smile at someone else,
They'll smile at me.
One smile will turn into
three—
So Let's keep a smile on our face—
'cause once it's gone—
It's hard to replace.
It's not what you want and
cannot get—
It's what you have that's
your best bet.
Look not afar—but very near at
the little things that you
hold dear.
So if a smile we'll always wear—
We'll have lines of laughter,
not of care.

Carrie Farrell
IT'S THAT WAY

To Shane; the only person I ever truly loved.

They all said he was a jerk,
I knew, myself, that it was true.
He made me cry so much,
He made me feel so blue.

He is loved by most everyone,
His friends enjoy his kindness, too.
Knowing he's a big flirt,
Is nothing at all new.

I still loved him through
Everything he did to me,
Until he told me—
"JUST LET ME BE!!"

Every word of this is true,
Every word comes from the heart.
Every word is full of love,
Even though it fell apart.

Ruth Elaine Winter
THOSE CANS
Save the cans for Uncle Sam,
Was the pleading call one day;
For tin is badly needed now
To help some boy in far away.
Men and women, children, too,
Scrap every can you find,
For every ounce of tin you save,
You help to man a gun.

So gladly I did heed the call,
For days and weeks and months;
Until one day, I said, 'No more
Of this old kind of junk.'
With fingers cut, and blistered hands,
Of such I cannot see;
I wondered then, how many boys
Who went across for me.

How many times they've cut their hands
And shed a drop of blood,
Have often said, 'No more of this old
Kind of stuff.'
With cannon roaring in the air,
The bombers flying high;
For every gun that fires a shot
That causes men to die.

Ah, no, they gladly give their life
That you and I may live;
So let us do our best for them,
With blistered hands to give;
Until it hurts, and hurts some more
That they who fight might live;
May soon return to love and home
That only the stars and stripes
can give.

Michele Whiddon-Borders
THE WISHING WELL
A single copper coin falls
Tinkling softly
Into the well of my soul.
A star shoots across the sky
Brilliantly flashing
And exploding into oblivion.
I pick a four-leaf clover, and
Gently, carefully
Press it in my favorite book.
I look upon the moon, so serene
And whisper silently
The secrets of my heart.
My soul follows
On the wings of the snowy
phoenix.
To utter a wish upon a star,
Or throw it in a well,
Or carry it next to your heart,
Or whisper it to the moon . . .
Wishes are the dreams of
wakefulness
That make life worth living
And dreams worth reaching
for.

Daniel P Mattes

Daniel P Mattes
LIFE

The world is spinning, rather fast, no time to lose now for this moment can't last; fading memories elapse and my empty life has just passed.

Your ideas are too confusing and the reality too intruding so into the busy street we run for shelter from the grasp of the reality welders that in the cloak of society tries to mold us to a flagpole or belief.

Corporate suits on hollow hangers, save from the masses below that struggle each day in frenzy to keep up with the bills and the system's lies, sway in the industrial wind sweeping through office windows whispering of stocks and acquisitions that secretly deal with our dispositions.

Governments that speak not for us but against. Leaders elected that shed their masks while we still believe, or maybe they do, until morning sheds no light but that of missile glow twilight as the hot ashes at long last arrive.

Faye Linda Wachs
CALIFORNIA SUN
I was born in the California Sun
It burns down on me
Leaves my imprint in the sand
Perfect for all to see
Perfect shape, perfect hair, perfect smile bright
Leaves the imprint of my shell
Cage that's trapped my life
Always smile pretty dear, Try not to disagree
Be smart . . . If only to earn, Praise for helping he
I have a pretty mask, Melted to my skin
Always hides from view, the me that's kept within
How much of me is what I am?
How much of me is you?
How much is what I'm told to be?
How much of me is true?
Sadly I watch the world engulf all the sun in me.
It sets in the west
Over the azure sea
I was born in the California sun
It shines out of me.

Eunice Fisher
EXPERIENCING
I set out on a mountain trail to
experience . . .
I saw beauty that is
indescribable.
I felt the warmth of the sun and
the cold of the night.
I saw differences in
people . . . each one unique.
I felt compassion and love.
I saw waterfalls and water
thundering over rocks.
I felt all my energy leave my
body.
I thank you God for these
experiences.

Kenneth M Beaulieu
MONEY
Though I have only known you,
For such a short time.
I have seen your many faces.
Yet I have never really known you.
With you I can conquer many,
And without you I am known by so few.

You are really not worth much of anything.
Yet people will do many things for you.
Though you don't have any feelings for anyone,
The peoples of the world all love you.
Though you have eyes,
You can't see our sorrows, our grief, or our tears.
Yet without you I am nothing.
As I really need you, So I cansurvive.
Without you I would not even be alive!
As I am caught in your spell and can't escape.

Steve Seifert
NINE YEARS PASS AS YESTERDAY

For Ann and family.

Nine Years pass as yesterday
I watch them go not much to say
I miss you most when I get this way
Memories now are all I have
Not much it seems
But they guide my dreams

Nine years pass as yesterday
Your dreams for me I may not fulfill
I only hope I can and will
Your love of life has just now been realized
You lived your life despite other people's eyes
I smile when I see you in me
I'll keep you alive and always with me
Nine years pass as yesterday

Mariah Lavon Glasscock
DREAMS
As the night closes 'round with its big black spread
I think of today and tomorrow
I think not of what disasters may happen
But of the beautiful day ahead
Of when roses will blossom with their sweet smelling scent
And when the birds sing their songs until the day is spent
And when the mountains climb high to their highest peak
I know not what will happen
But I know I will always have dreams

Patricia Ann Slates
MY SPECIAL FRIEND
As we go through
Life with haste
Somethings we keep
Somethings we waste
But I'll keep you
Until the end
You always be
"My Special Friend"
You always try to understand
Something I can't
Something I can
I need you "My Special Friend"
Hear me when I say
Romances may come
then fade away
My love for you
will go unchanged
You'll always stay
"My Special Friend"

Kathleen Long Rountree
BE FREE
If you strive for less than perfection
In the person you hope to become
Are you not failing before you begin
Fighting battles you believe can't be won?

For truly, each of us has our own faults
Inner conflicts we fight every day.
Expecting less of ourselves is no answer,
It slowly whittles will power away.

It's hard to get free of the roles that we play,
Someone we think others want us to

be
But our true personality won't give up the fight
Sure that someday we will set ourselves free.

Like fledglings too scared to attempt that first flight
Content to stay warm and safe in the nest
Only daring to jump will show we can soar alone
Able to give life our personal best.

Each of us needs one another's support
To save ourselves from self-strangulation.
Searching our hearts and being true to ourselves
Can bring peace and be our liberation.

LaVerne Moore
SNOW FLAKES

To friends and relatives, Who like a cool view.

I am light and white
I make things outside
beautiful,
Sometime the wind try
to shake me off.
children play in me.
I came from the sky,
I make traveling slip sometime, and lush sometime.
When the sunshine and
rain come down I will
go away, but I will
return another day.

Charlie R Richards
MEANINGLESS WORDS

For the Memory of Jeremy Gerber.

They say you only uttered
meaningless words
When you lay upon the final bed,
And they looked into your eyes
and were blinded by
whiteness;
But I dared not go, for I had
heard words before,
And I had been blinded by
whiteness in my dreams,
Though I not lie upon that bed for
many years.
But what is a year but a trifle?
I was blind before when I
thought of a year as a vast
eternity,
And dreams as nothing but
shadows of the world,
Which can fill no hole no matter
how glorious they be.

There is a beauty in farewell
when you are no longer
young,
And there is beauty in
conversations which unfold
themselves
As if they were unknit scarves,
When the night falls on and
shadows paint pictures,
For night enlarges the world, and
there is a beauty in
conversation,
Which unfolds itself like an
unknit scarf.

I am glad that years are now
trifles,
And lives can be lost, and death is
real but friendly,
Like an unwelcome guest which,
though un-invited,
Seats itself amongst us and talks
to us, and assures us that we
are but old friends,
And that, though we not see
each-other, we are neighbors
And will meet again, and
converse, and grow to know
each-other,
Though we knew each-other long
before.
This unwelcome guest has now
shared our evening
conversation,
And has woven itself like loose
thread into this unknit scarf,
And we can say nothing but how
beautiful this stranger is.
And that is all we can say.

My friend, your pale eye-lids
have closed for the last time
And you have digested death,
But I have felt you with me, and I
know dreams are not shadows
As I believed in my foolish youth.
May the journey be neither dark
nor silent,
And may you forget this world
which "lies clouded in vain
hope"
For I can offer you nothing but
words, meaningless words!

Phoebe Juanita Vaughn
I AM HEALED

To Jesus Christ, my personal savior.

The doctors told me that I had breast cancer—that was 4/6/89.
What a shock and disbelief that this could happen to me.

But, to my great surprise, I snapped back to the reality of just who I am.
A child of God was the thought that possessed my soul.

I recalled what the Bible said, that, "With His stripes we are healed" and, that, "No weapon that is formed against thee shall prosper."

I knew that on God's word I must firmly stand.
I prayed and took my rightful place and put myself in His care.

Then that day came when I was wheeled into the operating room to have surgery
for a mastectomy, after having had a lumpectomy two weeks before.

The surgery went better than I had thought and I was up and about that same day.
I continued to praise and thank God for keeping me in His good grace.

Then it came, that day of my pathology report, "there was no more cancer,"
is what the doctors said.

"Praise God" were the words that I shouted out loud, as tears streamed down my humble face.

For by my faith, God kept His promise to me, that, "By the stripes of Jesus, I AM HEALED."

Patrick Michael Moran
THE NAVIGATOR

To Maura, always remember Mt. Chocorua and our friend Richard.

Atop the branch . . .
Scan the world that lies below,
beyond and above.
Perhaps today you will venture to the South, and yet . . .
What lies beyond the mountains far to the West?
Does it truly matter?
Only the world awaits
With confidence you may spread your wings and depart your perch
Soaring through the rushing wind, the freshness of life is evident.
Glory in that unique feeling of strength and invigoration
And may that guide your direction through your flight of life.

Janeane F Murphy

Janeane F Murphy
THE FACE OF WAR
Silence. The shelling has abated.
Stillness. How long this moment awaited.

Long for forgotten experiences of home,
Eroding through torched glimpses here sown.

The feel of clean linen, the caress of a loved one's smile.
These time channels unlocked through oceans of red trial.

This face, all faces have the same eyes.
This apparel, their badges the truth despise.

In and out of consciousness, my nocturnal flight.
Tell me when you sleep, tell me if you dream oh night.

No more drugs need soften my pain, this illusive elixir so sweet.
No more the voices, commanding voices calling to me, retreat.

No more hills to climb, blinded to the horror on the other side.
No more sounds through the hidden night, echoing like rising tide.

No more wondering, this fear of pierced fire through muddied flesh.
No more waiting, the news from home; life's gift—my soul at rest.

The sea weeps for me as the gentle wind brushed 'gainst its briny cheek.
The sky cried its scarlet tears as the stars closed their eyes to honor earth's requiem seat.

Willa Elliott
VIEWING HIS CROSS
With a pensive heart, I looked upon His face
Deeply saddened that He suffered immeasurable pain
I was told He hung there in my place
That I, too, must share the guilt and shame.

Eagerly, I accepted His gift at the age of nine
Not understanding Its transforming power on my destiny.
Salvation, redeeming grace, eternal life, were mine
And a Heavenly Father to guide me.

The weighted stone they placed before His grave
Never, could hold Him captive in death.
Rising in power, His victory forever engraved
His Master Design on my bold, searching quest.

An Heir of a King! How could this be
That He'd made me in the image of Him?
Pouring forgiving grace, continually, over me
As worldly pleasures grow vastly dim.

Daily, I remember His Cross and the awesome price
He paid with His life's blood flowing down
Thankful for the miracle He's brought to my life
Shielded by His Inimitable Love, I'm eternally bound!

V A DiCicco
THE RAIN CAME
Clouds marched in from the east
Slowly, silently, they came.
Neon lights traced the sky,
Far away God made a groan.
Eyes looked up, slowly witnessed all.
Voices said, "Looks like rain."
Others nodded and looked grave.
Sun moved away, shadows gave light instead,
Wind joined the play, trees moved with the time,
Stillness filled the space, breathing stopped.
Then one drop came, played its tune and was gone,
Quickly followed by another and another and another—
Until ten thousand drops filled the earth
And every space sounded with their tunes

And all the living must join their play
Until with a sigh, they disappeared.
People gathered, slowly witnessed all.
Voices said, "We needed rain."
Others nodded and looked grave.

Daniel E Fisher
THE WILLOW'S BANE
Listen to the soft weepings of the grand willow,
Sit down beside him, as he tells of his tale,
Sings of the man-apes, their tools of destruction,
He whimpers softly as the will of the land fails.
Screams when he thinks of his brothers being cut down,
Cries when he sees houses being made from his kin.
Stares absently at the sap and pulp covered veined leaves,
His limbs creak weakly, he knows he can't win.
His branches weave pictures of the earth's desecration,
Now look upon the earth as it's raped to its soul;
Upheaved are the soils that bear the seed's blossoms,
Total annihilation, could this be man's goal?
The whole earth is scoured, and limbo surrounds it,
Grey and malignant, the world's a dead waste;
A powdered dead shell is the globe that we live on,
Man's hurried executions end life in great haste.
The lesson's now taught, his branches unravel,
They fall to the ground in entangled disarray;
"Come tomorrow, tomorrow," for a new frightful teaching,
And next morning I stand astounded as his stump marks his grave.

Alexandra Rafenstein
WHERE THE SKY ENDS
Did you ever wonder where the sky ends?
In the clouds
Or near great big mounds?
On top of a very tall tree
Or close by to a little tiny flea?
Is it by the bluest of the sky
Or nearest the color of an eye?
Down by a rainbow's edge where colors mush
Or just outside a bush's hedge where teens blush?
Near a person who is full of happiness
Or around the corner of a person filled with sadness?
At the peak of the tallest mountain
Or at the top of a sprinkling fountain?
Looking, out into an endless ocean right where the sky and ocean meet
Or looking straight up into the continuous blue near the sun's heat?
We may never know where the sky ends, but we have our whole lives to find out . . .

To love, to care, to grow
Maybe then we'll know?

Arnaldo Ty Nuñez
SPRING
Happiness and joy
consumes my soul
as spring bathes me
with her gentle kisses
and laughter.

My bosom
remembers
the summer nights
that gave flight
to my soul.

O, I feel the sun . . .

I'll be home tonight
to bathe in the starlights
and to kiss spring on her rosy lips . . .

Ann Marie Aylward
TO MY DEAR PARENTS
Although we are separate now
By miles far apart
I have a spot for you
Built into my heart

Words cannot explain
The emptiness I feel
I'm living in a world of darkness
Not sure what is real

Tears I cry, hoping that
It will relieve that pain
Tearing my heart
Slowly apart
Driving me insane

I don't understand why I hurt
When this is for which I strived
But I cannot bear being from you
You're all that is on my mind

I try hard every day
To spread my wings and fly
I try to remember
Say, "See you later"
"Never say goodbye"

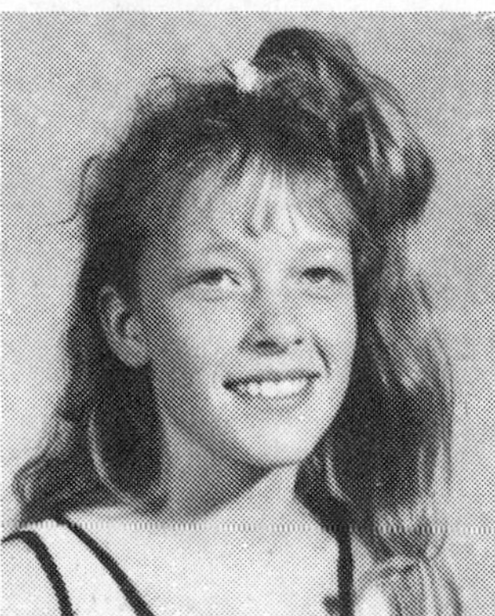

Melonie K Combs

Melonie K Combs
WHERE DOES THE SKY END
I wonder sometimes where the sky really ends,
Maybe where the fish swim at the end of the sea,
Maybe where the river begins to bend.
Sometimes I even think that it's chasing me,
I have heard tales of where the sky really ends.
It ends in a very special place they say,
Where the good becomes better and the wrong becomes right.
They say the sky ends where the birds play,
They say the sky ends where the people are kind and good,
not hateful and always starting a fight.
I really don't believe this of course,
For as far as I'm concerned the sky ends as far out as I can look.

Eva Critchlow Williams
DOWN MEMORY'S LANE

To my loving parents, sisters, my husband and my dear children.

Come with me down memory's lane
Let's reminisce awhile
There's sure to be a tear or two
But many a happy smile.

Memories are precious gems the only way that we
Can turn the hands of time around and relive
In entirety—

Moments spent with loved ones dear
Hopes and dreams looked forward to
Some obtained and some askew.

Birth and death and time's swift pace
All is living pain and joy . . .
Each day's duty to employ.

Years may come and years may go
As life's patterns swiftly flow—

But one precious bonus free
We all can cherish memories

So come along down memory's lane
Let's reminisce awhile
We know there'll be a tear or two
But many a happy smile.

Nelda Nash Smith
THE PUPPY AND THE LADY
As an unwanted puppy, she was carried to the pound.
A lady went to find a dog but love was what she found.
The friendly little puppy quickly stole the lady's heart.
They made a vow with just one look that they would never part.
The two of them went side by side along life's long highway.
The puppy and the lady—growing older, turning gray.
The puppy and the lady have a comradeship that's rare;
Neither has a single thought that the other doesn't share.
The lady knows that some day she will have to give her up,
But she'll ne'er regret bringing home that tiny little pup.

Laura M Carlson
FRIEND
I feel your spirit within my soul, like sprinkles of precious rains.

I feel your presence when many miles are between, like shiny leaves dancing as the winds blow.

I feel your wisdom through which you speak, like the library in the high heavens.

I feel your warmth within my heart, like the sun's heat penetrating through my chilled body.

May all your dreams be as wonderful as the dreamer.

Ruth Enicks
NO PROBLEMS
As man walks along the ocean shore
His problems and worries are uprooted
By the ocean's roar.
As the tide goes out, new thoughts begin
Now the works of God and Love are within.
The world looks brighter,
There's peace all around,
And in the thundering surf,
Look what this man has found.

Andrea Latessa
ILLUSIONS OF A DAYDREAM
The depths are vast, wide with curiosity,
imaginary boundaries surrounding,
ceased in wonder,
sinking inside, like anchored weights
weighing down a flourishing element—
the soul
frozen inside and out,
the mind blank with lifelessness.
Reflexes stopped by the weight of the world,
exhilaration seems far—reality so close
Painful
Our standards so high.
The mystery is intriguing,
knowing everything, knowing absolutely nothing.
Avoiding the truth, the truth is a reflection,
the footing of the soul—
encasing the entity ever so slowly
deep dark yet crystal clear,
illusions surround the eye—
a facade

Gerald Lee Keller
FEELING

To Pookie—without you, there's no feeling.

It's hard sometimes, to express myself properly,
To let you know what you mean to me.
It bothers me, that even for a little while, we're apart.
Yet, not really, for you're here, in my heart.

You see, I'll always thank the man above,
For the special gift of your love.
That warms my heart, soothes my soul.
Your love that makes me whole.

You're a special gift, sent from up above.
To be protected, honored, handled with love.
Your presence, your smile, your love, and beauty,
Is a sign that you're an angel, sent here, just for me.

For, when you smile, or just hold my hand,
Reminds me just how lucky I am.
No matter where I'm at, or what I do,
I'll go to my grave, loving you.

Frantz Picard
A WARNING
People of great spirit, we could be sorry
If we don't make peace at the end of the century;
The progress achieved by us in science,
Would not have any sense
In the mirror of the future generation.

Our civilization is condemned to destruction;
Bullets and missiles are sunk
In the blood of our brothers like junk.
The eyes of our families
Became a permanent source of tears.

Let's stop being authors of fear and anxieties;
Let's be peacemakers instead of enemies.
We are brother and sister,
Children of the same father
We must get together
In order to make life better.
Peace and love are the only forces
Which could give values
To the age of liberty,
Science, and democracy.

E L Core
SUNRISE
(November 8, 1988)
Fire,
gentle fire:
dawn kindling day.
Pink sunshafts in ranks
escape through the widening gap
between the silhouette of mornward hills
and the rolling rills of graysmoke clouds
drawing back as the day rises from obscurity.
Nightward I look, where the river foots
an arc of pink through moist—
there! it multiplies to rainbow,
the sun winning ascendancy:
this day's birth,
last night's
destiny.

Corinne G Stoney
THE SEE
Mesmerized
By the see
I stand
In the dark.
The moon lights a silver path across the water—
Beckoning—luring—leading
To worlds unknown.
I lift my eyes to face the tempter,
And she smiles behind a gossamer veil of clouds.
Her light dances and plays on the restless water
Like children frolicking in a garden.
c t r
Suddenly—the dancers s t
a e
a b i
S r l g
c m n to escape the l o n g, *dark* shadows
ng in their midst
si
Ri
groWING as they near me
Fal
li
ng harmless at my feet
In foamy murmurs of dissatisfaction.
The veil tthhiicckkeennss,, and the tempter begins to suffocate.
She struggles to free herself
But is lost behind the suffocating clouds.

The see is gone.

Bernice Cieri
PAUPER'S HOLIDAY
Though Christmas comes but once, each year
It's hard for me to muster
Up the peace and harmony
When I've nothing to offer.

But see! This year is different;
Although I have no money,
The spirit comes from inside
Me, and feels 'laced with honey'!

You're all so very dear to me;
I'm grateful I have a part
Of your lives; you mean so much
To me; that comes from my heart.
It's love that makes a holiday;
Having us all together . . .
Celebrating joyously
In one way or another.

So if you feel the same way too,
My sweet precious family:
Accept this, my humble gift;
For there's naught beneath the tree . . .

Koreen Juergens
A DREAM CAME TO ME
A dream came to me
As I awoke
From a sleepless night
You and I
Together, alone
In a room filled by candlelight

The words from your lips
I could not escape
In the darkness embers glow
Holding me secure and tight
You whispered those words
The three I've been longing to know

This dream will not pass
From my memory
And I know we will never part
But still I long to hear
You say those words
That can come only from your heart

Jennifer Monroe
ADAM
how well i know five minutes makes a dream—or kills it . . . how a week is set to frame our thoughts for putting off or hastening . . . i often hasten, rarely tarry, then the fateless monday-tuesday rolls around and i regret the undressed honesty of words . . . the compression of the five or ten of sixty in an hour that shape a later hesitation . . . how bare i stand . . . like Adam—how the world knows that every second counts, even the sneaky moment i'm not looking . . . just doing naturally what some say is not natural . . . some say time must be undone . . . take the pictures off the wall . . . retract the words . . . watch the particles rescind . . . once said and done we coiled back in nervously and act on stage like nothing . . . if there *is* a snake—then eve's not wrong . . . apples *are* heaven.

Michelle Dorland
LOOKING BACK
Why did I feel that way,
like no one really cared.
Why did I let people get to me,
so I would get all scared.
I couldn't help thinking,
it doesn't have to be like this.
But why did I do it,
who didn't I miss.
I should have changed my way,
ignored their eyes
I didn't have to believe them
when they told their lies.
Why did I listen,
now look at me.
I thought it was the only way out,
don't you see.
When I took that gun,
and held it to my head.
In those few moments
before I was dead.
I thought of some memories,
some good, some bad.
I almost put that gun down,
now I wish I had.
Now laying in my coffin,
all cold and lifeless.
I see I was wrong,
to take something so precious.
All those people at my funeral
some I didn't even know.
I miss them already.
Oh why did I go.
Though it's too late,
I found my true friend.
I only wish it was the beginning,
not the end.
I didn't even say good-bye
or leave a clue.
Of just how much
I loved you.

Julie Amm
WILLOW
Tears cascade past my eyelashes
And make huge splashes
Upon my pillow
I feel just like
A willow
In sorrow
Dropping down
To the ground
With a
Throbbing sound

Roy Martin Keeney
THE DREAM
I remember the night on the beach strolling hand in hand.
The sea was rushing to the shore and upon the sand.
The night was filled with hazy stars, my heart with love for you.
I remember thinking to myself, this is a dream come true.
I soon must leave your paradise.
This fills my heart with tears.
But I know as we go our separate ways down through the years, our souls shall forever walk that beach strolling hand in hand with eternal love to wash away the tears as the ocean does the sand.

Joyce Rogers
PARADISE FOUND
There's a peace that surrounds me whenever I'm there
And contentment is mine when I breathe that soft air
Those steep twisting lanes are a challenge extreme
But every high hill gives a breathtaking scene
Rich, ruby red earth enhancing the view
Of chequered green land that beckons to you
Its deep wooded valleys, caressed by the sea
Its quaint little coves, where we rest and have tea
And sheep, gently grazing, forever in sight
And the murmur of cattle as day becomes night
They rest beside hamlets that come from a dream
In picturesque settings so still, so serene
And whenever I journey away from this heaven
My heart's in that haven, someone called Devon.

Greg Murray
AN ANGEL IN HELL
As if from a dream, she shines like a star
A spirit of freedom undaunted thus far
Facing a world that will soon clip her wings
Ahead of her lies the most shameful of things.

My heart bleeds for the pain she will have to endure
Unwary of forces so foul and Impure.
The shame of it lies in the souls of us all,
Who've let our world's beauty escape us—and fall.

A beautiful child so carefree and pure
Someday can she help us? Can she see a cure?
Or is it diseases that strike from within?
Decay of the honesty held among men.

I'd give her my world, I'd die for her gain
If she could rise above this suffering and pain.
So I cry for her spirit, and pray she'll stand true
And shine of the goodness in me and in you

Cathy Arnold Strode
ONLY HIS LOVE
Only His love
could bring out these feelings
Only His love
could pick me up once again.
Only His love
could last through all that I bring.
Only His love
for His children, His workmanship,
His prize few, who turn to Him with tears of happiness or sadness.
Only Jesus could understand all that we go through and come out saying, "I Love You"
Never before, but now, the person I am, is so important for what I give to Jesus to work with, all that I am, is because we together have allowed it to be.

Cathy Arnold Strode
COME LITTLE ONE
Come, come, come little one and thank the Lord, for all He has done.
The battle has been won.

Come, come, come little one and be a child of the Lord. For it is His will, we are baptized and be not still.

Come, come, come little one, and praise the Lord.
For happy in Christ you will be, in Christ you are free.

Come, come, come little one and grow in the Lord.
For He is king, spiritual psalms we will sing.

Come, come, come little one, come, come, come little everyone, for Christ died and arose for you, Yes!, you are one of God's chosen few.

Come, come, come little one and worship the Lord. For He is the mighty one. He is the mighty one.

Carole DeRuiter

Carole DeRuiter
CAMPING IN AND EATING OUT

It seems like months since last I saw . . . my furniture and my clothes!
And the children miss their toys . . . but, that's the way it goes.
There's a period of time, while moving . . . Air Force families know about.
Sometimes it's called affectionately . . .
"CAMPING IN AND EATING OUT."

Our unaccompanied baggage arrived . . . and now, just as before,
With all the basic items sent . . . we find we still need more!
"How's it going, do you need anything?" . . . as we pass, the neighbors shout.
I guess that they can see we're . . . "CAMPING IN AND EATING OUT."

We each sleep in a sleeping bag . . . or on a mattress filled with air.
A family in a house without . . . a table or a chair.
We have TV 'cause that is something . . . we can't live without!
It helps the family pass the time, while . . . "CAMPING IN AND EATING OUT."

We know the way to PIZZA HUT, TACO BELL, McDONALD's, too.
RED LOBSTER, ARBY'S, and KFC . . . just to name a few!
We try all the local restaurants . . . found here and round about.
That's part of all the fun we have . . . "CAMPING IN AND EATING OUT!"

This life is an adventure, it's exciting . . . and it's fun!
New friends to meet, new lands to see . . . new shopping to be done!
And wherever we might find ourselves . . . there's never any doubt,
The tour begins the same 'ol way . . . "CAMPING IN AND EATING OUT!"

Dawn Schmidt
THE TEACHER THE ARTIST

The mind is a precious gift from God
Instilled within a child from birth.

The parents are the ones that create
The original mold,
But the teacher is an artist.

Stroking the brush,
Ever so gently upon the canvas of the mind.
To add a shade here,
And a shadow there.
Adding branches to the tree of knowledge.
Creating a beautiful master piece
When the work is complete.

A masterpiece never to be sold
But added to the gallery of fine arts,
To be admired by all

FOREVER

Glenda Breen
SPRING

Bells on a church tingles,
Wheels on the pavement passes.
Perfume and woodsy smells mingle,
Fluffy white clouds dashes.

Airy tendrils of smoke burning,
Rippling puddles of water glistens.
Whine of a motor turning,
Restful sounds, if you listen.

Birds chirp from a distance,
Redbud trees are in bloom.
Loving life with no resistance,
Spring will be here soon.

Judy Grojean
A DAUGHTER'S LOVE

To my mother's abounding love.

A thought swept through my mind today,
As in my hurried pace,
I wondered why in God's great plan,
He may have missed a space.

A space of beauty for us all,
A time we'll never share,
If only we could know right now,
Just how our loved ones fare.

If I could be Mom's age today,
And she remain the same,
How close our lives would intertwine,
Then, I could feel the pain.

We'd have a day together,
Those precious moments share,
Speaking of life's pleasures,
Our aches and sorrows bare.

But question not the Master's plan,
With fleeting thought, so thrilling,
Now time is precious and it's ours,
A love complete, fulfilling.

Debbie F Garrett
I ALWAYS THOUGHT . . .

I always thought we'd be together, laughing
Sharing all the things to come
But it didn't work that way,
We parted before we ever had a chance.

Maybe now, it might be better,
I was too wild and too full of dreams.
I wanted to see the world
You wanted to stay and be looked up to.

I hope you will be happy with the life you lead,
and then, maybe someday, we'll meet again
But not as enemies, but as friends.

Karen C Dykes
MAN AFTER MAN

An exhibit in the Smithsonian
contains a man
In an apartment with glass walls
opening onto the halls
From every room except the bathroom
(for after all there is propriety to consider)
And the citizenry bring their children
To see him go about his daily business
The rites which he performs upon waking
And the rituals with which he eats
Using strange words and stranger implements
Some of the children are frightened
By this unusual representative
Of an all but extinct branch of primates
And the curious mouth transliterations
Of the strange prayers the man utters
Phrases such as "I need some privacy"
And "Why can't they leave me alone"
As in the aftermath of atomic war
The descendants of the chimpanzees
Who now rule the world
Watch the last man on Earth
As he mutters imprecations at them

Carrie Brancheau
GLASS

The image in the mirror
was abandoned today
the crystalline shattered
as he pushed her away

The bridge to the vision
invite the lovers to stay
But both shed a tear
as both turn away

The blood-tipped glass fragments
reflect glimpses of light
While the couple once reflected
turn silently white

Her body turns cold
as she reaches to touch
the silhouette in the shadows
she's missing too much

As darkness eludes
concealing the past
The blood on the surface turns to
tears on the glass.

Jo Bohony
SHADOWS SEEKING LIGHT

We crushed green fragile blades of frosty grass
beneath wet feet while merry hearts did play,
and in his love, I let all shadows pass.
First love so young and pure should start that way.
Our lives like twisted berry bushes grew,
entwined with fruit thickset to make sweet wine.
And then so swift before I even knew,
were blossomed flowers dying on the vine.
A faded tapestry is brought to mind—
a field of lacy flowers in the night.
And now in light, that field I cannot find.
I search now in the shadows seeking light.
I climbed too steep the steps
of velvet tears,
that chime too loud—the
clocks of yesteryears.

Denise Lindner
THE WIND IS STRONG

The wind is strong
Screaming at me
Working its way
into my mind.
Friends, take heed!
My mind shall explode
Friends, cautiously
Step away
as to not feel the slap
of my brains on your faces,
shouting
I told you so!
Whispering
I told you so.

Tina Mosley
FRIENDSHIP

You are my soul
and
life.
you are there
listening to me
about my dreams,
my success,
my failures,
and also to encourage me
When you smile.
It makes me feel better.
I feel like I'm floating on air.
It is a challenge.
You made me feel warm all over.

Penny Bechard
THE HEADACHE

Pain crashes through my brain
like waves against the shoreline
My pulse beats against my temple
with thunderous force.

Waves of nausea hit me
like a giant fist smashing into the pit of my well-being
The groans and moans I hear are coming from within

The very mention of a thought process
sends fear rippling through my body
What is within a mind? I do not know
for I am but a vegetable, green and almost cooked

My very existence seems most agonizing
like a weekend trip down the root canal
Endless, endless with no reprieve in sight

with neither strength nor drive to fight

Alas, through the course of time
like many a momentous occasion
This thing called mind control
of which I am aware
has, once again, reached inside and pulled me through.

Thomas Lesser
WORDS
Helpless,
Hapless,
Hopeless,
These are words I understand.
There are others, but these,
These sum up the world in which I live.
They are how I feel when I stand,
Alone on the edge of a cliff, looking down at the sea far below.
I see the waves lapping upon the shore.
They cry out to me,
With a voice, as dry as desert sand,
"Helpless . . . "
"Hapless . . . "
"Hopeless . . . "
These are words I understand.

Janel L Hollins

Janel L Hollins
PIMP
Hey Boy, where you be'z at?
I be'z lookin' all over for you.
I ask everybody where'z you been;
They say, "I dunno, is he gone agin?"
They say, "Did you check the barz?"
"Did you check the Hot Space?"
I say what'z my boy gon'be doin' in that place?
That'z a place for all pimps and hiz hoes,
If my boy iz in there, I can guarantee you won't
see him no mo'.
I don't think he'z in there,
I just kno' that ain't where he been;
Then a young girl pulls me aside and sayz, "You
betta check again."
I checkz all the barz, I even checkz the Hot Space,
And there'z my boy cheezin' with all the girlz in hiz face.
I pulled him out fast and I pulled him out quick,
Hittin' him upside the head wit my old walkin' stick.
"But momma I'm grown and I'm pullin' in big dough,
If daddy was here he'd ask if I could git mo'."
"And momma look at theze ragz and look at this ring,
All the girlz love me and call me their KING."

James Williamson
WORSHIP
Calm, silently
Nature worships thee,
Great and glorious God!
Clad in spring new dress;
Bathed in thy greatness—
Fathed, Lord, my God!!

Heavens colourful! Bright!
What a marvelous sight;
Sunrise Morning hour—
Since words cannot express
Thee, nor thy greatness—
Lord, I humbly bow.

Take this breath of praise;
And while yet I gaze
Unto thee with awe—
Let this silence be
Lord, my prayer to thee—
Hear me, Lord, just now!!

Rose Marie Daniel
TO BONNIE AND VELVET
Tho I long to soar with the eagle
To her craggy mountain nest,
Or drift with the river's current
As it flows forever west.
With the wind in my face ride the prairie
On my mare to eternity,
And dear Bonnie and Velvet beside me,
The Border collies running free.
I remain at home by the fireside,
For my Bonnie and Velvet have died,
And I lose myself in my reverie
With dear Bonnie and Velvet and me.

Lynn M Oliver
SOMETIME, SOMEHOW, SOMEWAY
I would like to show you in a special way
How truly glad I am that you're here
For all those little "extra" things that tell me you are sincere
So, I'm writing to tell you on this day—that
I'll make it up to you—sometime, somehow, someway

I've felt alone so many times but always knew
That someone wonderful was caring about me
And, loving me—and that someone was you!
So if I've taken you for granted, I'm sorry that I did
I'll make it up to you—sometime, somehow, someway

In your absence I'll strive to make us proud
I may at times get angry and lonely—or even cry aloud
But in my heart I know you will care, even if you're not there
And in there too, knows all will be O.K.
Still I'll make it up to you—
sometime, somehow, someway

Being apart is painful, but something we had to do
But with your absence brings lonely thoughts for you
Your happiness is important to me, so what else can I say?
Thanks for loving what's inside of me
For all you have done and been to me is difficult to repay
But I'll make it up to you —
sometime, somehow, someway

Kelley McMurtry
I SAW YOU SMILE TODAY
I saw you smile today,
I saw you laughing,
I thought of you
Today.

Just wanted to say "HI"
And I wish we NEVER
Said "GOODBYE."

Although it's not the
Same,
There is no one to blame.

Just wanted to send this
To you,

And to let you know,
I was thinking

Of you . . .

David Klix
THREE
If you took an ink shower, would you dry off with a paper towel?
If you hit a chicken off the base line, would that be a foul?
Why can't a fan belt hold up your pants?
Why aren't there tractors on a farm that holds ants?

These are just some of the questions asked me
By a little boy of mine who is just barely three.
How far is up? How do I get there?
Take me to Never-Never Land!
Where is it? Where?

Sometimes I feel like pulling my hair!
Sometimes all I can do is stare.
But the questions still come and I answer my best.
I don't have the answers to some of the rest.

Go ask your Mom. I don't know now.
I don't know if the udder gets cold on a cow!
He's gone now, but he'll be back soon.
. . . Dad? How old is the man in the moon?
How did he get there? What's his name?
Why doesn't he come here for a visit?

Aileen Jennings
PASSING OF THE STORM
The winds blow, the trees bow,
the river is feverishly flowing.
The animals quiver, the earth trembles,
from the storm that is on its way.

The dark clouds move fast across the skies,
spilling murky sheets of rain.
The grounds are soaked, they can hold
no more, lest there be a flood.

The deer stand still to gauge the winds,
to see how hard they are blowing.
The grounds tremble, trees are uprooted,
fear is suspended all around.

A change in the atmosphere has given
to an eerie feeling.
The animals were all driven
back into the wooded area.

The winds have calmed, the trees are straightened,
the rains have ceased, the storm is over.
The earth no longer is shaking,
the river is flowing ever so still again.

Barbara Ann Garrick
ACADEMIC LIFE
When scorned by former friends and my foul foes,
in solitude I pity my own plight
and ask the Lord if I deserve my woes.
I feel I am incapable to fight.
Desiring the approval a flatterer receives
and hoping for some loyal loving friends,
I long to have the funds for college fees
and scorn the latest academic trends.
But then I think of you and my mood changes.
Just as the sun removes the world's black sky,
a thought of you dissolves my cares for ages,
and I no longer cry and hope to die.
Instead I jump toward heaven and thank the Lord
for you, a gift which no king can afford.

D Vance Bisek
MY FAMILY TREE

Joyously contributed and heartily presented with these words in recognition of and commemorating my maternal roots, and dedicated to the loving memory of my mother.

Found are memories sketched from time;
When moments and hours are free,
As faces known from boyhood prime,
Now have shaped this family tree.
And freshens my heart with a face that shines;
That comforted my moments afraid,
Mended my wounds and dried tears of mine
And lifted joy that shall not fade.
Now scattered footsteps have found their way
To share memories of oil lamps glow;
Gathered together to listen and say
Much of now and years ago.
Hands clasp; warm from comforts known
Sifting through joy and tears of old,
And unto a lad of then now grown,
Seen are these faces etched in gold.
And beckoning now from there afar, afar;
On a ridge amidst meadows splendor free,
Strong of seed in sands that ne'er alter,
Is the treasure of my family tree.

D Vance Bisek
INSPIRING SILENCE

Presented and dedicated to the memory of my beloved son, Thomas.

Never have I taken pen in hand,
To guide my thoughts in rhyme;
'Till the glass with its flow of sand,
Measured slowly the void in time.
That sifts to mounding depths of truth;
With scattered grains of fear,
And casts shadows in a light that soothes
A burning beat in a heart clinging dear,
To dreams shattered by the remnants of night
That enrolled love, and rescued troubled friends,
And placid imprints of vigor and might
Shared so long; now time extends
Into molded words near break of day,
As drooping lids claim wandering thoughts.
Though, like a child fights sleep to play,
Now to shun what not was sought; and loiter
Within the enchanting stillness of being,
'Round the trickling of sand, and embroider
The sounds of meaning with time; and believing,
That surely they cannot be, that of plagiary;
For thought lurks bounteously; yet not the same to see.

D Vance Bisek
CLOUD OF WONDER

Gained is the vision that mends its way;
Be it from a scar or a tear fallen through,
A low-hanging cloud once high seeming to say,
This is for real and gathered for you.
Not knowing then what can be now;
When comfort of its fluff cradled sure,
Bound by a ribbon unnoticed somehow,
Frayed near torn; its purpose obscure.
Caught inside and brushing its film;
Where does the beholding begin!
'tis not in motion to settle a qualm,
Nor strip trust from its floundering spin.
Now tattered strands are crystal clear,
Through the cover of that pillowy gray;
And nourished not is a fallen tear,
Lest scars raise; in moments astray.
No, never in bloom is the flower that cries,
Or fades because of a stem,
That waits too long for summers prize;
Clusters of splendor in delicate blossom.

Gerald O Merritt
THE HUNTER

To my wife Jeannine, and daughter, Toni. All the rays of your suns fall on me.

Stepping softly, he moved through the woods,
blending into the foliage as best he could.
For he was after the big buck, whose tracks
he could see, Suddenly he stopped next to a big tree,
straining his eyes, so that he could see.
Into a circle of sunlight, the big buck stepped.
He stood there grandly, listening for a sound.
The hunter slowly took aim and pressed with his finger.
There was a click and the buck bounded away.
The hunter smiled triumphantly and looked at his camera.
For this big buck would live to another day.

Gerald O Merritt
YARD LOVE

He was fourteen, and he watched his neighbors,
The girl next door, also fourteen, was in his eye.
She was the one who motivated him to try.
Her hair was golden and her eyes were blue,
Out into the back yard, she flew.
Hiding from her mother, she rounded the corner,
By the shrubs she stood.
He climbed the fence and crossed the yard,
They stood and looked at each other, hard.
To the back door, her mother came.
"Lillian," she called, where are you."
She grabbed his hand and pulled him into the shrubs,
Their lips met, locked in ecstasy.
Her mother turned back into the house,
Saying, "Now where can that child be."

Deborah M LaMot
THE BEGINNING OF LIFE

I dedicate this poem, along with all my love, to my mother, for always being there for me.

You look in the sky,
And you wonder what's there,
When you look at the clouds,
And you stop to stare.

Is there something behind them?
Something we can't see?
Maybe a place of happiness?
But no, it can't be.

Is it possible for us?
To believe such a place?
Where there's beauty and peace?
And a glow on our face?

Our minds play tricks,
And confuses our soul,
When we finally start believing,
Our body takes hold.

It tells us these lies,
And makes us believe,
That there's no such place,
As we all are deceived.

Where there's no feelings of hate,
Angers or fears,
No feeling of hurt,
No meaning of tears.

If only we knew,
The world thereafter,
Where there's nothing but brightness,
And the sounds of laughter.

We seem to have thoughts,
Of our bodies being life,
And when it gives in,
It's the end of our lives.

This world is a level,
To which each have to pass,
In order to reach,
That threshold that's last.

When our bodies are dead,
And our hands are cold,
It's just the beginning,
Then our spirits take control.

It takes us away,
From the pain we bare,
Of this world's headaches,
And its worries and fear.

It's a place of warmth,
Filled with life and love,
That only one can give,
That's the Lord up above.

Next time you think,
These things can't be real,
Let him in your life,
His touch you will feel.

So when we mourn the dead,
And think life's unkind,
It is them who are crying,
For leaving us behind.

Deborah M LaMot
WHAT IS A SISTER?

I dedicate this poem to my sister Denise, who is, and always will be my best friend.

Someone who cares,
When I'm out past dark,
Who's always there,
When I want to talk,

Who watches over me,
When I do things wrong,
Who guides me in the right path,
Who makes me feel strong.

"There's nothing you can't do"
She always tells me,
"Believe in yourself"
And I start to believe.

I see all the things,
I never saw before,
She gives me the confidence,
And she opens a door.

My goal is to be,
The best that I can,
In whatever I do,
And she tells me I am.

She's the one that I know,
Who'll tell me straight out,
How to forget all my worries,
And forget all the doubts.

I'm glad I have,
A sister who cares,
The relationship we have,
Is very special and rare.

I love you sis,
As I know you love me,
My best friend in the world,
You will always be.

Deborah M LaMot
THE BIBLE

Words of encouragement,
Words of fear,
Words that show love,
Words with care.

When there's times you need,
A friend to talk to,
Just open it up,
And he'll talk to you.

Each word is alive,
And shows it, when read,
You must have the faith,
To understand what is said.

It reveals to us,
The love that he shed,
He left it behind,
So that our spirits are fed.

If you ever have a doubt,
That these words aren't real
Just read a few pages,
And his touch you will feel.

So remember when you're down,
And climbing a steep hill,
Just read his words,
For that is his will.

Georgette M Innes

Georgette M Innes
DR. WILLIAM STERNHEIM

For my dear friend, Sharon K. Brown, who is so ill with Cancer.

What a Man, this Doctor, God hath made
He's a Blessing in the sun and in the shade
As He skips from room to room
Hiding behind his smiles and all the gloom
With His data bank and computer mind
And His efforts and knowledge to save mankind!

I have observed, in visits with a dear friend
Thanking our Creator for the likes of Him
He is a jewel—such a rare breed
As He hurries about taking care of each need
How my heart swells with such pride
And tears in my eyes that I cannot hide

In asking Him, why such a Profession He chose
He answered Hematology; then Cancer—but He knows
There is only a special—very special few
That can do what this Doctor has to do
Joking and smiling as He must render your fate
Hurrying and praying that treatments aren't too late!

May God grant to you, a long and

healthy life
Knowing you are blessed with a wee one and a good Wife
May the knowledge and experience that you impart
Save more lives and mend aching hearts
For you have a Blessing rarely given;
Dedicating your life—so those can go on living!

Joel C Elmborg
MAYBE?
Well, tonight's the night,
The night to end All others.
Do you think they'll notice?
Do you think they'll care?
Maybe I'll finish it fast,
Like a second of pain? and then the end.
What about my friends?
What'll they do
Will they follow me?
or will they go on with their lives?
But what of her?
What will she do when I'm no longer?
Should I? or shouldn't I?
Are my problems bad enough for me to die
or are they a figment of my imagination?
What does it feel like after life?
Who will I see or will I see anyone at all?
Is it the right thing to do?
Will it solve my problems?
Maybe I'll stick it out
or Maybe I won't?

Eva Mae Vaughn
LET ME DREAM

This poem is dedicated to my children and grandchildren.

Tell me not of hope descending
Crushing dreams, that's fallen through.
Tell of triumphant winnings
Increase my faith in winning too.

Cast not my hopes down with failings
Of seedlings that have ceased to grow.
I may prevail, despite your wailing,
Leave me try, and then I'll know.

Higher dreams, than others dare
Impossible though they may seem
Although you fear oncoming nightmares,
Awake me not, just let me dream.

Eva Mae Vaughn
I SHALL NOT RETURN
To-day I wandered down memory lane,
Thro' fields of experience, and learning bowers.
High ideals there sown, to my senses bring,
The very essence of life, with the fragrance of flowers.

I pass that slim tower of deeds well done
And think with regrets, of what might have been.
For never again, this way shall I come.
My mind sadly wanders on down through the glen.

Here's Circumstance Lake, where the path turns
Her mirror of water, darkened with pain.
It's so useless to yearn, for the bridges I've burned,
So I shall not return, to life's memory lane.

Eva Mae Vaughn
SELF MADE LUCK
Lady Luck must have a problem,
Knowing where to lend a helping hand
Smiling on the rich and famous,
Easily forgetting the common man.

Enticingly she proffers, her tokens,
With joy he reaches to enfold.
Teasing with promises, soon broken
That leads him deeper in a hole.

Knowledge earned, is well worth holding.
Each measure of knowledge, into wisdom blends.
Assessed priorities, can be controlling,
Eliminating bad luck, in the end.

Eva Mae Vaughn
A KING ON THE JOB
When you come to my house, where I am king,
And the roof vibrates, with loud sounding bangs,
Yet my countenance mirror's no sign of care.
You will have surmised before I declare,
"We have someone, working up there."

Now, think of the world, a house built by a King.
When the elements overhead crashes and bangs
And all fear within is beyond compare.
Who will comfort God's people and by faith declare?
"We have a King, still working up there."

Jesus, that King, went to a city called Heaven.
"I shall build there, for you, fair mansions," he said.
But they abandoned his laws, to his children given,
To those hungry for truth, false teaching were fed.
"We can do as we please," "What King? Oh, he's dead!"

But who tells the wild geese, when southward to go?
And who tells the ground hog when his shadow to show?
Sends back swallows to Capistrano, when weather is fair?
"Oh, how long will we question, when we should declare?"
"He lives! The King lives! He's still working up there."

Adelon Axt
THE MOON ROCK
Apollo 14, made it to the moon,
Bearing the Astronauts three.
Shepard, Mitchell and Roosa,
And the world watched excitedly.

Shepard and Mitchell went on their walk,
To Cone Crater, for lunar rocks,
But one thing that NASA didn't know,
Was that Shepard hid a rock in his sock.

He wanted to be the very first,
To fashion moon rock jewelry.
So he put it in his tumbler,
And waited impatiently.

He waited and waited, (it took a long time),
And then to his surprise,
An odor came forth from the tumbler,
And burned and stung his eyes.

He quickly opened the tumbler up,
And began to cough and sneeze.
For the tumbler was overflowing,
With sticky, goopy, green cheese!

Sarah Wooley
LIFE?
Greed, power, nuclear war,
There is something goin' on we can no longer ignore.
The end of the world is drawing near,
Children of our children will be living in fear.
All of our dreams of peace and love,
Are vanishing slowly and drifting above.
Left sitting in darkness with no sign of hope,
No happiness anywhere but we have to cope.
Waiting in loneliness for a friend,
Won't this hideous moment ever come to an end?
Now aren't you sorry for causing this mess?
It was all brought on by your selfishness.

Lee DeLoache Harmer
DILEMMA
I sat on a rock with my skirt pulled up,
My feet in the clear, cool water,
Watching the birds and the tiny fish.
One larger fish saw my toes and wanted them.
He kept coming closer, then would panic,
Chasing off his smaller friends or competitors,
Wanting to be brave, to dare, to risk,
But his fear was too great.
He will never know how my toes taste,
But he will always remember how much he wanted them.

Estell Haines
THE DONKEY
Upon my back Mary rode,
Joseph lead me by a rope,
That cold December night,
When not a star was in sight.

Unto Bethlehem town we must go,
For in God's word it was so.
He was lain in a manger
Alone, With total strangers.

While shepherds came afar,
Wise men bringing gifts,
gold, frankincense, and myrrh
No one is to weep or mourn,
For a Christ child was born.

Don Cammert
LOSERS AND LONERS (TO HARRY CHAPIN)
Who will sing for the losers who never had a fight?
Who will sing for the loners who never knew the night?
You came with your stories that shouted out our pain
You left with a whisper, just an echo from within
In the discos at midnight they never heard your name
On the ocean in starlight I listen to your refrain
Reefed down, sliding through the night
On a run away from noise and light

It's the pressure of living that makes you turn within
It's the pain of seeing that makes the vision dim
Who will sing for the losers who never had a fight?
Who will sing for the loners who never knew the night?
Is it only the lovers who stand in the light?

Margaret Erbes
REALITY
Reality is my insanity
For the work there is no play
My insanity is my fanatic
I do as I please
So that I can feel
That I am free
I know longer answer to reality!

I J Evans
KISS A FROG
Life repeats an old story of a kissable frog,
Because, loneliness is such a terrible thing;
Some say, "Take love where you can find it,"
And others, "Who knows what a kiss can bring."

The prized jewel hid beneath a hot-pink lily,
But, oh so gently, I placed her in my hand;
Removed one lonely petal from her forehead
And from four tiny feet, I brushed the sand.

I asked myself, "What happens if I fail?"
But, again, "What if love should pass me by?"
With puckered lips, I met the challenge,
Remembering, nothing gained, unless I try.

I closed my eyes and kissed her lips,
Wide and moist, like fresh churned dew;
As her writhing body slipped from my hands
And where she went, I never knew.

A gold dimpled ring spread upon the water,
Eyes peering, as far as they could see.
"Will she return, as my beautiful lover?"
The poet answered, "What will be, will be."

Fern M Evans
FREEDOM'S CRY
The shroud of night is lifted.
And morning dawn, comes on the hills,
Where hangs the fate of nations and the world.
The people stir once more from nightmare sleep.
And with courage dare to stand erect and speak.

The long awaited days have come at last.

The Berlin wall no longer divides.
Fear of silent rocket bombs subside.
Again, the common man has hopes of tranquility,
Happiness on his wide world below.

A restored faith, to redeem the human mind from error.
Where the word Democracy takes on a new meaning.
Yet, people still do not sleep so well at night.
Grim nightmares haunt their working thoughts.
The powers released, can they be yet controlled?

When isms rise, and atoms split,
that threats still exist to worlds domain.
The perils not yet unleashed, man has mold to destroy.
The genie will not sneak back into his flask.
And man must learn to cope with him, to rule him well,
Lest mankind proves too wise to live.

Everett L Carter Sr
DREAMING
Everybody wonders why you stay up late
What they don't know is that you are dreaming
But you're still wide awake.
You can still smell the blood.
You can still smell the mud.
And you still find yourself thanking
God that that round was a dud.
And this time you missed seeing blood.

They say it's just luck, but I know that's a lie
Because when God sends a bullet at ya, He hits with every try.
And even if you're not a rice paddy soldier, it's still your time to die.

Dear American Friends, don't feel sorry for us,
Because one of these old days you will find that defending your homeland is a must.
And we all must go through the ashes to ashes and the dust to dust.

Roxanne Fortier
SLEEPLESS SUNDAY
I opened my eyes, startled at the sound of my chattering teeth.
Here it was, six a.m., daring me to stand on the cold floor beneath.
I scanned the room like a cat in the dark, searching for at least a sweater,
Superstitiously thinking that if a day started right, it would get even better.
Dressed in three layers, I proceeded downstairs for a hot, steamy shower.
I gobbled down breakfast instinctively, awake but an hour.
With key in hand, I approached my car—an antique I kindly treated—
And complimented it for starting so quickly each time it was needed.
The stretch of highway was perfect, uncluttered by the usual crowd.
I would actually be early for work and make my boss proud.
So just imagine the panic I felt from inside, way down deep
When the DJ announced, "It's Sunday!" and I missed my chance to sleep!

Gladys Harley

Gladys Harley
A CHRISTMAS BLESSING

This is to be dedicated to my husband, Roosevelt Harley, my daughter, Melvinia Barnes, my grandchildren, Darian, Darseaux, Deisha Harley.

A Christmas blessing at this time of year
Gives all of us hope and many cheers
And every good wish from the man above
You can count your blessings, by his love
That's the greatest gift from above
May you have the Christmas blessing from far above
That grant you all His love.
Wishing you a joyous Christmas and a happy New Year
May you have all the blessings all this year.
May the blessings bring warmth to your heart, and everything Good for your year to start.
So my dear friends get down on your knees and pray. And thank our Father for this beautiful Christmas Day

Gladys Harley
MOTHER
We are always fighting; why can't, we be friends
We can forget all this uglyness, and start making amends.
God gave us life and children too.
And this way, we should, no just, what to do.
Our gift is blessed which you can see
Let's get together the way it should be.
I know our love is, sincere, because you, are my mother I want to give you three, cheers.
So, let's get together, and make, amends
Because God, knows I love you mother, to the end.
She thinks you are demanding, and you think she is too, so, let's stop all this foolishness, and say I love you

Merritt Bradford
A CHILD'S PEEK TO IMMORTALITY
You make of death an efferent shout
From which I do not whimper, cry
Nor cringe such dire annunity
Nor loqui of time or mercy, or
Sufism's ancient doctrinaire of yes or no.
Please let me go now, I must, for
White light is bright, I sense no fear
To see beyond my candlelight,
Such is inner spirit for which I wait,
As I knew today, and my mommie heard
Of the awful tortured hours, conceived
Mortality ushering a grim tranquillity!
Oh hear me, wavering gleam translucent.
Take me within a diadem of peace
This horrid crawling numbness to cease.
For succor succinct serene serendipity
When new chromosomes attach to flirting genes
To free this plosive frame from fantasies.

"Wake up, my little one! You're home,
Not in the sky!" I looked up—to mom.
'Serendipitous' my venture, it surely 'wuz.'

Ashley Shea Clarke
OF TREES AND THE MASTER
Into the woods my Master went,
Clean forspent, forspent.
Into the woods my Master came,
Replete with love, not shame.
But the olives were not blind to Him,
The little grey leaves were kind to Him,
The thorn tree had a mind to Him,
When into the woods He came.

Out of the woods my Master went,
And He was well content.
Out of the woods my Master came,
Content with Death, not shame.
When the Death would woo Him last,
Twas on a tree they slew him fast,
When out of the woods He came.

Jean Marie Fulford
A PLACE IN MY HEART
Your friendship means a lot to me
please don't let it slip away,
I need you in my life
even more than words can say.
I think about you often
and the special things you do,
I wouldn't trade a thing
for the time I spend with you.
I'll be here if you need me
but I'll never crowd your space,
because you fill a spot in my heart
that no one could ever replace.

Jodi Cresswell
THE BATTLE WITHIN
There's only one reason for tears:
It's because of the pain that builds up over the fears.
It's a shame that one feels they must suffer alone so,
The anguish; the hurt; the bitterness that I came to know.
I couldn't understand why I had to be the one,
And some of the things that were done can never be undone.
The shame of knowing you did wrong,
And nothing could smooth over the words of that bitter song
That keeps playing over and over again in your head, the one that says,
"Oh God, I wish I were dead!"
And even when you try to deny those thoughts
The words keep coming back as if to taunt,
"Suicide . . . Suicide . . . the fast and easiest way to die!"
Oh what a bittersweet lie;
I hate those words with a neverending passion,
But part of me knows at one time I could have done it without the slightest hesitation.
Life doesn't seem that hard to most,
Maybe it's because they believe in the Holy Ghost.
And nothing can penetrate the love they share,
And those heavy burdens no longer are for them to bear.
But even though I am one to believe
That life line seems so hard to retrieve,
YES! I had it once with a tight hold.
But somewhere, somehow, I grew cold,
Letting go of my one true support.
And when I realized I had lost it, well . . . let's just say the shock and the pain was a little more than discomfort.
My life is so hard to comprehend
That even I cannot understand.
I feel I'm in a no win situation
Where I am placed on a train with an unknown destination.
And no matter how hard I think I try,
I cannot shed the feeling that I'd be better off to die.
These feelings that I have they really scare me.
Every way I turn I feel I'm on the borderline of treachery.
There's a part of me that doesn't want to die
And wants that chance to survive.
Eternal damnation is one consequence I could face,
But the other is forever fighting the human race.
No matter which way I choose,
You see . . . I lose!
But then the rational part of me takes hold;
Life's always going to be a struggle and you must be bold.
So if you give me your hand you'll take mine,
Together we have a better chance to keep the life line.
And if you remember to say this prayer,
It's bound to help you through anything . . . anywhere!
"Take my life Lord and let it be . . . Forever . . . Only . . . All for thee . . ."

Linda Brown Nimene
OUR FAMILY TREE
Every family has a tree. If it wasn't for the roots where would the branches be. The roots have to be good and strong so the branches will grow strong. After the roots are complete then the little branches start to grow. I don't know all the branches of our tree. Mainly the ones who were our roots. But some of the branches I did know who are no longer with us. Who was so long a part of our tree. I hated to see those precious branches go. I said over and over our tree will no longer grow. I asked God why did he prune the

branches off our tree. The Lord said my child it has to be, because in heaven I have an everlasting tree that whosoever eats of it should not perish but have eternal life. But how sad it still is when another branch falls off our tree. It gives me peace of mind knowing they are in a better place. But our tree is still growing healthy and strong. Even tho' a lot of our roots and branches are gone.

Vartan Hartunian
GENOCIDE
One child, choked by evil hands,
is baneful seed that breaks
the calm of civility.

Tiny hands, chopped off,
will place the shroud of guilt
upon all happiness.

Infant eyes, gouged out of bloody skulls,
will gaze forever
upon the structures of this world.

The unborn, ripped from the womb,
will corrupt forever
all pretense of goodness.

Creation trembles at a baby's scream
of inflicted pain,
and its silence in death
is but the unheard roar of an angry universe
reverberating from star to star
until it quakes its solid forms
into atoms of bloody dust.

James Tinsley
MY DEAR BROTHER
How shall I address you, what can I say that best expresses my feelings, for they are unexpressable.
Mortal tongues cannot describe the anguish of my heart, I feel worse now than when you went away.
The vacancy you have left behind, is far worse than presence of your cold casket in death. But the worse of all, is to see you launching out upon the chilling tide, and our mother and father who has been our constant companions and protectors, left behind to linger and weep with brothers and sisters, a little longer upon this earthly shore.
But the boatman took you though the fires of hell safely, and has taken you kindly into his house. Provided you a home far better and more excelling than all that earth can afford, caring for you far more tenderly than us. We will miss you, but we will not be forgetting you.

Jacqueline M Adam
WHEN JESSICA AND I SLIDE DOWN THE STAIRS
When Jessica and I slide down the stairs
I wouldn't trade my life for anywheres,
She's 2 and I'm 62, grandmother and granddaughter,
Years apart,
But one in heart,
One at a time we go on our bottoms,
Down, down, down,
One, from the year she's had cancer,
But I've told about that with no answer,
Two, she's in remission and I give thanks to God,
And the many who have prayed and that isn't odd,
Because we're all part of life's plan,
As we go we chuckle and crow,
What a wonderful way to go,
And we dust the stairs with our rumps,
And small and larger bumps,
Until we're in my living room,
What a joy! When Jessica and I slide
Down the stairs!

Timothy C Morgan
BABY'S BREATH
Today a child's life was lost
The innocence gone, like a warm day's frost
Its tender breath, its naive thought
Yet no one could save her, its life could not be bought
They cried why all night and day
No simple answers, no easy phrase
Sometimes God needs a loving soul
One that hasn't been blackened by the world
One whose dreams were still sweet
And though the tears may come all night
The pain and emptiness seem like an eternal fright
The child is now in far greater hands
And someday we will meet again
When my sun sets and yours does rise
Then once again shall I see those eyes
This time in tranquil mist, shall we find endless bliss
And there I'll remain till the end of time
My loving child which is forever mine

Ada Weinzierl Sweet
LIFE IS JUST A WHISPER
An echo soft and soothing from a voice that wasn't near,
Told us life is just a whisper, that we should live it well each year,
As infants in our cradles we are fed from mother's breast,
Then childhood enters unprepared for schools and pranks and much unrest,
A time when conscience is asleep to hearing tricks and names,
Space machines are a real must as softball is and other games,
Youth begins and good sense too as adulthood we soon face,
Education is a part of it to learn in each one's ways,
Being grown appears so quickly as if a magic wand were waved,
Then it's time to find a partner and plan a family parade.
Struggles to maintain a goal prevailed as we were there,
Again we heard the spirit saying life can be unfair,
Advising us to live in heartfelt kindly love
The warning was a message which came from up above
To live the golden years the best, as a whisper isn't long,
The echo will sound happier as it hums a sweet love song.

Candice Lee Cordle
SIN
I let temptation lead me,
So blindly I ran with open arms
To embrace this sin.
It hides inside—growing and feeding
On my feelings and spirit,
But never will I confess it—
And the punishment I must pay is—
My destruction.

Tammy L Smith
PATH
Looming like a giant,
A horizon of grey,
But there on the left,
A starlit pathway.
I may wonder,
Search for understanding,
Or accept my lot,
Not be demanding.
I can meet my challenge,
Not turn away,
To face and conquer,
My horizon of grey.
Then I'll be free,
To turn,
And follow,
That starlit pathway.

George Gail
AS BLIND AS AN AUTUMN OF PINES
As blind as an autumn of pines
I sense the seasons glacial roll.
I wonder at their numbing toll.
They do freeze me by the spine.

Leaf roofed in this house of green spell
Vowels may compass a heart by tales.
Here sings the secret magic sigh
Of the newborn butterfly.

Ana M Fuentes
THE UPSTAIRS ROOM
Once again will come the blue jays
To your balcony to play,
And you'll watch them through the window
As they help you greet the day.

But the ones who came each morning
—Those that stopped while they would eat—
Those that almost came to know us . . .
They have chosen to retreat.

Once again that same bromeliad
—Nondescript and common fern—
Will go through the transformation
And its flower will return.

But the elegant pink blossom
That unfolded there before,
We admired it together . . .
This one's gone forevermore.

Once again the words of passion
Will be whispered in your ear,
And if they're sincerely spoken
It might move you to a tear.

But the way that I have loved you
—Ardor that can't be erased—
Don't expect to find an equal . . .
I can never be replaced.

Janet Brooks
FRIENDS . . . BUT
I love you dearly.
That's what you say.
I'll do anything . . .
but! . . . don't ask me today.

Surely there's so and so
I know he can do
that very same thing
you're asking me to.

It's not that I don't want to.
Now you know that I would
but so and so can do it
much better than I could.

Well . . . I must go now
my friend ever dear
and if you need me
you know I am here
to help (or assist) you
in ANY way
I'd be happy to do it . . .
but . . . don't ask me today.

Ana M Fuentes

Ana M Fuentes
OF YELLOW AND RED
For L.C.O., who always inspired me.

For a time the world lacked color,
My whole life had come apart,
All was vague in shades of grayness;
Chiaroscuro of the heart.

Sepia-toned and faded memories
Lay half-buried in my mind
Like a worn and treasured tintype
I could never leave behind.

You returned with new conditions,
Redefined the course we'd mapped,
"Leave it casual and unfettered;"
(I pretended to adapt).

Washed-out hues regained their vibrance
Screaming colors missed so much,
Rust was born-again as scarlet;
Resurrected by your touch.

Now the peaceful amber mornings
Shimmer with a hint of gold,
I've discovered I can like you,
Friend of New; My Love of Old.

Mary Kopler Rice
DOLLARS AND SENSE
When someone spent money foolishly,
Mom used to say,
"He had more Dollars than he had Sense"
And we must not be that way.

I've tried to follow her good advice,
As through life I've grown
But once in a while, I find
The Dollars have really flown.

It's hard to be sensible
When someone's in need
Or you see something special
Or want a big feed.

I guess, I'll always be a spender,
One of those who can't recompense
And I'll always have more Dollars,
Than I will ever have Sense.

Diana Lombardo
MY BETTER HALF

To my love, the fly will never accomplish, moving all the sand to the sea. Our destiny is to be joined together, because without you, there would be no me. Thanks for being so patient with me, Robert.

He is everything I wish to be,
Way down deep inside.
To be good and honest, pure of heart,
These things I am denied.
A total balance, of what I am not,
Trusting, giving, and kind.
The most selfless person you could ever meet,
Or ever hope to find.
His helping hand is always outstretched,
For anyone in need.
Call him any day or night,
He'll arrive with all possible speed.
I love him for all that he is,
Or all that I am not.
He is an excellent human being,
More than one could want.
I guess that's why he is my better half,
And without him I am lost,
He is the light unto my darkness,
The sun that melts my frost.

Teresa Stuart
BUT WHAT IF?

What could we build together?
How about a love that lasts forever.
But what if it sours and turns to hate?
Then we start over.

What could we build together?
How about a smile that lasts forever.
But what if it fades and turns to a frown?
Then we start over.

What could we build together?
How about a world that lasts forever.
But what if it crumbles and falls apart?
Then God will start over.

Susan A Grindle
HEARTACHE

To Mom and Dan with Love.

I came to meet you over the telephone. Little did I know your heart was your own. Then when we met face to face, the smile you smiled never showed a trace, of a man who never changes always keeping the same pace.

Then we fell in love or maybe it was pure desire and we made something beautiful that we both could have admired, but now ashes to ashes, and dust to dust, what we thought was love was merely lust.

Even though I've said good-bye my heart is filled with sorrow and even though tonight I cry at least I know I have tomorrow.

Sean A Miller
SKYLINE

Dedicated to my favorite city—St. Louis, to my family and friends and to my girlfriend, Shelly Walls.

See the city's lights
See how they sparkle
and burn into the night?
This, is where my heart belongs!
Dark long shadows
Protruding from the asphalt,
like giants in the west
fleeing so as not to be caught.

Reflections of yesterday
in the newly washed windows,
images of ghosts
in my mind stay.

People, like fleeting shadows,
rush to get inside
because when all the lights go out
that's when I come alive!

Kristen M Bruneau
LOVE

Dedicated to Kevin R. Allard.

When I think of you my thoughts are full of cheer. Then once you leave I'm all alone here. My love for you is large and fabulous and the gifts you give are meaningless. For when we are together it means everything for when we're apart it means nothing. Our parents now don't agree but when we're hand in hand they will understand. I love you and you love me for what is mine is also yours. If I am doing wrong tell me and it will be no more. Anything you say is done for when we're older we will be together as one. My love for you is grand that's why I would like to have your hand. When I'm ready you will know for our love can only grow.

Renée Joy Smith Spoonhoward
THE HUNTER IS A BRAGGIN'

The Hunter's gun is a shootin'
A Mama Deer has fallen prey;
So still, so quiet, so sullen
In the snow she now does lay.

The Hunter's now a braggin'
Of his catch of the day;
But now a little Fawn caught scent
Where its Mama has fallen prey.

The Baby Deer is so unhappy
No Mama now left to love;
Yet the Hunter's still a braggin'
Mama's head is on his mantle above.

The Baby Deer will roam for years
Wondering why Mama went that way;
Yet the Hunter will keep on a braggin'
Never knowing what he did that day.

Gladys Faye Armstrong
RESTLESS LOVE

To: My Dream Lover.

There's a love that can exist.
It binds you to another.
It grows and grows from deep within.
As the bond is further strengthened,
It burns and churns
Because peace there never seems to be.

Is this real love? Is this love immortal?
Is that why it lingers yet?
Out of mind and out of sight
It still is burning, burning bright.
Oh! How heavenly fruition would be!
But, alas!
Unrest there'll always be,
Because apart the lovers must be
for now.

Come rain or pain
There is no shame
For this love will last
For
Time
Immortal!

Ruth Davis

Ruth Davis
LOVE IS A MEDICINE

Dedicated to:William R .Davis, My Wonderful Husband; Treca J.Wemer, Leca T. McNutt, Our Dear Daughters; My Four Precious Grandchildren

It's easy to smile and feel full of cheer;
when your hopes and plans are swinging in high gear.

But, what about those days that are dark and drear,
all your hopes and plans are reversed in low gear?

Do you frown, look gloom and sulk the whole day through,
look ugly to others and make their life gloomy, too?

Why not look up to our Father above,
ask for his guidance, in All things, with LOVE.

Look in your mirror, put a smile on your face;
erase all that gloom; put LOVE in its place.

Don't look back, but always look forward;
being thankful each day of your blessings galore.

Doing your best, with what you have;
always adding LOVE in whatever you do.

This will help others and also help you.

Yes, LOVE is medicine, that's sure to cure;
and make your life and others worth—MUCH MORE.

David Wood
THE EXILE

For Roger.

Morning light sky sears above
Into this day we push & shove.
The chance of hope, renewed again,
Forgotten paean crying "When?"
For night's the time our thoughts unshroud,
To melt into the dreamer's cloud.
The day, belongs to our ordeals
A sentence from which there's no appeal.
The clichéd habits strive to own,
Until the day they've overgrown.
But still, the light that seems so clear,
Glimmers thru, as nocturne nears.
A surge of vision wends within,
Its clarity still so vaguely thin.
Something Magic in the night
Works the furrows with delight.
Until the form evokes what's near
Adds to it unbridled fear.
Because it knows, but cannot tell,
Condemned to drink from daylight's well!

Kim Derry
MY BEST FRIEND, MY SISTER

To My Loving Sister, Pam.

Remember when we used to fight,
Remember when we talked all night.
You seemed to know when something was bothering me,
And you have always been there to listen to me.
To care, to share, to have you by my side,
In you I could always confide.
When we look back at the things we have done,
Whether they were stupid or not we had fun.
But through all the good times and the bad,
You have always made me happy when I was sad.
Through all the laughter and the tears,
I wonder how you could put up with me all these years.
You have always been a dear friend to me,
And like you is all I ever wanted to be.
Having you for a sister has been like having a lifetime friend,
Someone I can always depend on till the end.
I'll be there to listen when your troubles need a mend,
As long as you will always be my very best friend.

Stephen Pederson
TRAV-LIN'; SOMETHIN' MY MOTHER TAUGHT

This poem is dedicated to my Aunt Helen and Aunt Mary, who helped me through the bereavement of my mother's death years ago, and to all mothers who love their children.

Long before the chance to crawl . . .
I traveled with my mother.
"Worthwhile" in her—the haul . . .
a noble task; like none other!

Before I learned to run . . .
she taught me, first, to walk.
Sometimes, watching me was fun . . .
as I might fall and squawk!

Learning how to ride a bike . . .
started with a tricycle.
Mom said: "Some way to hike . . .
ped-dle-ing a bicycle!"

Years before I'd fin'ly drive . . .
with mom sometimes, I rode the bus.

Stand-up, sit-down . . . we'd arrive!
A train or plane—might be a plus!

"Faster than a rocket . . .
trav-lin' at the speed of thought
Can you really clock it?"
Somethin' cute . . . my mother taught.

Kenneth D Stewart

TELL DAD

In honor of my father, Otis E. Stewart.

Lord, I know you're busy
With the saints coming home each day
And taking time to listen
To mortals like me as we pray.

Making new heavens and rivers
And a planet here and there;
So I'll not bother you much, Lord,
But hear now this earnest prayer.

My dad has gone on before us,
I know he's home by now;
He was always kind and humble
Never taking his hand from the plough.

Just tell him to stand near the portals,
Then whisper to him and say,
"Your boy was just talking to me,
The lost sheep has ceased to stray!"

Tell him Mother is holding well;
The home place looks much the same;
And tell him, Lord, please tell him
I proudly bear his name!

Kenneth D Stewart

TOO LATE!

There's a home far back in the mountains
That's now a tumbledown shack;
I'd give all my earthly possessions,
If I could only go back!

Where we played in days of childhood
As free as the wind that blows;
Where grows the sweet mountain laurel,
The daisy, the fern and the rose!

But gone are the chums of school days
Like leaves from the old elm tree;
And gone is the childhood sweetheart
Who wearied of waiting for me!

Glenda Goodman

POEM OF LIFE

I dedicate this poem to Michael Dean & Ricky Lynn Lebeck, the two most thoughtful & wonderful sons I could have been blessed with. Love, Ma.

I think sometimes it's not worth it at all.
The struggle, the pain, for one to fall.
One has to pick up the pieces and go on.
From doom to wonder until the dawn.
Life is a tall tree to climb
But one must fall.
Get up, pick up the pieces and don't stall.
It will all come together, some day it will.
When you have had enough to make a deal.
Tell Satan to hit the road Jack
and don't come back!!!

Lynnette Pahio

STRUGGLE TO ACCOMPLISH

To my best friend Mary. Because I know this is what brought us together. To my parents, two who will never know. I love you all.

They appear to be children.
Both trying to accomplish the same dream.
Using all their strengths to prove they can do best on their own.
Hate and anger shows through their intentions.
Competing to drive each other away.
Applying all their frustrations to complicate the problem.
Neither realizing they are both in the wrong.
Struggling to grant their wish.
To be apart in body, but together as one.
Every word burning their companion, beyond heal.
They break apart.
No mercy is given.
Their hearts are together in pain.
Their bodies are separate; leaving no chance for the wounds to be bound.
To death do they part is the vow they took.
Time has shown there is no difference now.

Cassandra Houlson

HE'S A DREAM

To those who love a "He" but can only love him from afar.

He's a dream, he's a treasure
My love for him, no one can measure.

When I find my mind in the binds of time
I think of him and wish he was mine.
For I am his forevermore
And as for the outside world, I can shut the door.

Marjorie Nutter

THE LONE ROAD

The road you travel,
Will seem dull and dreary.
For she made your life
Seem bright and cheery.

The days are long and bittersweet.
Though she's gone away;
The love you shared, the things you did
Can never be replaced.
The birds no longer sing
The shadows long and gray;
Hang like a curtain
Since your Mother's gone away.

Someday, Somewhere
Perhaps again you'll sing
And just remember that
She's waiting in the wings,
Just for you

Bob Owens

LIFE

To June with all my love.

Life has many things to give,
But without one dreams,
It's so empty and still.

To hear a laugh,
To see a new day beginning,
To bare one's soul,
For a love that's neverending.

Remembering the past,
Looking to the future,
Without one's dreams,
Life has no meaning,
And therefore it's neverending.

To love, to touch,
To cry out for what's in one's soul,
To give, to care, to be cared for,
That's life, and for all it holds.

Bob Owens

DREAMS

Without one's dreams,
A soul is empty,
Life has no meaning.

Without one's heart, life begins,
To be a part of everlasting joy,
For what God has created.

To be a part of,
To see one's dreams come true,
To create a life, to see a beginning,
To know one's dreams are neverending.

To be a part of,
What God has created,
And to truly understand,
Life has a meaning.

Clarice Merswolke

ALTERNATIVE ALTERATION

The journey of a person
throughout rugged pathway of life
is hazardous, rocky, narrow,
stretching for luminous stars
of recognition, glory, success,
in horizons of heavenly blue
believed exclusive, existent only for you.

Severe stormy clouds gather,
conceit, vanity, ego,
are snagged, twitched
at rivers bend
in whirlpool of seething waters
that dash remnants
of self-luminous, selfish braggartism
into caves of total darkness

* * * * * *

Cascade of reverential, prismatic, silent dawn
influence, exert, concerned buffeter
to alter, become steadfastly strong;
rekindle fires of integrity, love, joy,
solicitude for the weary traveller
'neath God's sun—ever employ.

Karen Wilson

TOGETHER AT LAST

The time I met you,
You were taken.
Yet every time I see you,
You're alone.
She ignored you,
And you were weak.
I came to you with love,
And you accepted.
We stayed together until they came along.
Summer was almost over,
Another tore us apart.
That next summer,
I saw you,
You were sitting alone, again
I went to you,
And again you accepted.
Now we don't let anyone in the way of our love.
Once torn,
We sewed ourselves back as one.
Until a death,
we are "together at last."

Jon C Clauss

LIFESONGS

Silence is golden or so they say
But I like to hear the children play
A bird's chirp as he rides the breeze
The soft trickle of a freshwater stream
The buzz of a bee as he alights on a flower
To sit and listen I could for hours
The sound of the wind through the trees
The crashin' of waves from open sea
Crickets, song in dead of night
Splash of a fish coming up for a bite
The pitterpatter of a summer shower
To sit and listen I could for hours.

Lucy Stancil Howard

FIRST LOVE

My darling, my love—I adore you
You know I do
No one can take your place.
Until I saw you, I never knew
What love could do, to this heart of mine.
Wherever I go—wherever I am
I always see your face.
Like morning after night—
Like sunshine after rain,
You are my shining light
And will always remain
The one I love best.
I could look this wide world over
But, north and south, east and west
I could never find another to take your place.
You are my revelation—my only inspiration
Please believe my declaration:
I love you—I love you—I love you!
With all this heart of mine, I love you
My own dear sweetheart.

Robert Ellick

LOOKING

To Cynthia, Who Was The Inspiration For These Sentiments.

Where is your smile
The brightness in your eyes?
Where is all of your beauty
Has it left us for a while?

Don't we belong together?
Though you may not understand
I've felt the warmth of your emotions
At the first touch of your hand

How long must I wait
To hold you in my arms?
My eyes are fixed

My emotions are mixed
I'm viewing all your charms.

Look at your lips now
Shall I taste them
Or should I wait
For another time
Or another place
But wouldn't that be a bit too late?

Myisha Marie Frazier

Myisha Marie Frazier
GARDEN OF TEARS

To my parents and Ms. McDermot, who have always encouraged me to express myself.

The soothing sound of water trickling down
The plants planted still in the ground
The roughness of the rocks just sitting there
This all symbolized a part of my life,
I came here to weep every time I was hurt.
For this is my Garden of Tears.

Diane Parks
NIGHTTIME
Brilliant splashes of purple, orange,
and pink in the fading sky.
The silvery moon now on a blank
canvas casts its crescent eye.

Stars shine brightly making the
dark look like eternity.
Sparkling diamonds in a sea of
black as far as the eye can see.

Trees cast their haunting silhouettes
across this heavenly glory.
Withered and arched, they tell
their life story.

In the dark a lone screech owl
screams,
Sending chills up every spine it
seems.
Then the whippoorwill sounds its
lowly,
mellow cry, saying it is night.

Everything is silent and still,
waiting for light.

Denise Lowe
WITHIN . . .
It only takes once
to be hurt so badly;
feelings clinging to your
insides;
reshaping you in and out.
The hidden you.

Time rekindling your soul;
realizing trust must be within,
before hurt,
can penetrate,
The hidden you.

Linda D W Griffith
STREET LIFE
Let me in the wind is cold, be not the streets, my gravestone.
Open up, unlock the door: rain beating down on open sores.
Sun is hot on my uncovered head, making blacken tar out of my bed.
How can you see with eyes closed, feeding white power into your nose.
T.V. and news teams focusing on death, forgotten memories of those who are left.
Unclaimed bodies, unrested souls, searching through garbage like underground moles.
Freedom for all, wealth for the few, poor walking slowly without a clue.
Help is at hand, but the hands are tied. How many more while waiting will die?
Shelter from storms, all that they ask, wondering when laws will be passed.
A few and the brave give all that they can, trying to save man, from his fellow man.

Lloyd Daniel
SUICIDE
They are so young
And they have so much
Looking in their eyes
You don't see that they're out of
touch.
They think that their life
Has no meaning
So they grab onto someone
And they go on dreaming
Then one day
That someone is gone
And they are left alone
To try and carry on.
Then one dark night
Full of emptiness and strife
They take up a gun
And take their own life
How can we tell
The young ones like this
That if they take their lives
It's <u>their</u> love, that <u>we'll</u> miss!
How can we tell them
If they leave us behind
That their suicide
Will eat at our minds?

Angela Cary
YOU DON'T KNOW WHAT YOU'RE MISSING!
I liked you
And thought you liked me too
But I found out the hard way
That it was not true!

The way we laughed,
The way we talked,
Was just a put-on,
Like a prey being stalked!

But now I'm over you,
I hope you're listening.
Because I'm going to tell you,
You Don't Know What You're
Missing!

Dorthy Russell
HUSBAND
Between washing the dishes and
running to see what he wants
Sweeping the floor and
running to see what he wants

Making the beds and
running to see what he wants
Picking up the toys and
running to see what he wants

Often I wonder as time goes by
when I lay on my deathbed
will I have to get up and
run see what he wants

Catherine Le Ann Day

Catherine Le Ann Day
YOU ARE MY HANDS, YOU ARE MY FEET

I dedicate this poem to my Saviour Jesus Christ and to my sons, Stephen and Michael Day. I met the Lord through the loving and faithful family I now have at Salem Baptist Church, and to the greatest Pastor in the world, Rob Johnson.

God says to all who claim his name go out my child and touch the lame.
God says for all to cover this land, you are my feet, you are my hands.

It seems sometimes too great a task, it seems unfair for him to ask, but when that thought runs across my mind the Lord returns me to another time.

A man named Jesus lived back then, he paid the penalty for my sin, he walked across the desert sand, and healed many with the touch of his powerful hand.

He healed the sick, he helped the poor, and he said, "I am the door." This man was the savior some said but others wanted to see him dead.

The time had come for him to die and on his knees he knelt to cry; "Oh my God it hurts me so, I love these people. I don't want to go. Oh father do I have to go?"

But deep inside his heart he knew that the plan of his father must be carried through. So on his back he did bear the cross I hold so dear. They hung him on the cross to watch and see the man from God die on that tree.

They laid him in a garden tomb, some thought he had met his doom. Three days passed by when an angel appeared in the sky. "He has risen," he said. "Jesus is no longer dead."

That's when my mind returns to where I am now and to my knees I humbly bow.
"Oh, dear God," in prayer I ask him to show me how to do the jobs that face me now.

He said to me, "You are my feet, you are my hands, now get up my child and go out into the street. Tell all that you see about me, tell them how much I love them so, my nailed scarred hands are proof you know."

It is a great task but my father does ask. So I will go where he sends me and his angels will always defend me.

Through his power and his grace I will run this great race.

Mae D Aucello
A HOLIDAY MESSAGE—1987
There is something in the air,
That comes but once a year;
There's a feeling everywhere,
That all's well, both far and
near.

There is something in the air,
A sense of love and peace and
giving;
A sense of what is past, is past.
It's time for a new beginning.

It's a time for remembering,
As well as forgetting;
A time for rejoicing,
As well as repenting.

A time for forgiving,
As well as relenting;
A time for rejoicing,
Enjoying God's Blessing.

Rosalie Kaufman
BARGAIN BASEMENT CINDERELLA

To all the would-be Cinderellas and Dreamers.

I'll pretend I am a princess
Although I've never met a prince.
I'll pretend I'm dressed in ermine
Instead of Bargain Basement glitz.

I'll wear a plastic slipper,
Instead of one made of glass.
Perhaps it will prevent me
From falling on my ass.

My godmother seemed to vanish,
On the D-train Brooklyn-bound.
The coachmen have turned to mice
And are nowhere to be found.

Tenements surround me
No palaces nearby
Bargain Basement Cinderella will
just have to learn to fly.

Marty J Reome
TIME

To my family, whom I love, and Frank, for inspiration of how I feel.

They say time heals <u>all</u> sorrows!
It helps us to forget.

But, time so far has only proved, how much I miss you, yet!
God gave me strength to fight it, and, courage to beat the blow.
But what it meant to lose you—
"No one" but me will ever know!
I'll love you from now, and, forever, until we "permanently" part, and, then I'll lock my love, for you "forever," safely, and deeply inside my heart.
Maybe some day I'll release some love for another, maybe, I won't love at all!
But, if that day does happen, I'll keep my love for you, locked safely, and deeply, inside my "broken" heart, where only "I" will ever know.

Sammi Baral
MEMORIES

To all those who wish not to remember their memories; they are some of the greatest things you'll ever hold.

I will always remember you
and you'll remember me,
you taught me life
the happiness the pain the misery.

You made extra time to help
when you had none to spare,
you spent most of the day away
but, would manage to be here.

Even when dejected
you would try to help me out,
you gave me hope I needed
and you never had a doubt.

Yet you were always there for
me in Winter, Spring, Summer, and Fall,
you taught me how to deal with life
the challenge of it all.

I will always think of you my
friend as a message from above,
and so I say good-bye to you
because of what you have given me.

Dear memories I do hold.

Melissa Lynn Woodrow
REMEMBER ME

Remember when
you welcomed the rain?
Played for hours in the mud
then went home to clean up with a thud?
Sitting by the window
drinking cocoa
listening to the sounds of the rain.
Now you're older and wiser
or so they say.
But nothing has changed
you're still the same.
Walking without an umbrella
getting soaked by passing cars
that splash dirty water over
a cold, wet body.
Enjoying the feel
of wet hair against your neck
going home to change
and clean up.
Sitting by the window
drinking cocoa
listening to the sounds
of the rain.

Lori J Allan
NEW LIFE—NEW ROLE

To Donny and David, this one's for you.

You felt her life
Before you met her.
You watched me grow outward,
While she grew inside.

And now she is here—
A new baby girl!
A daughter for us,
A sister for you.

A big brother now,
An important role you have.
Thank God there are two
For her to look up to.

We give you a sister
To love and to cherish.
Be a good listener
When she seeks your advice.

Rejoice in her charm—
And she will have lots!
Protect her from harm
From all other tots.

Maria E Gomez
THE WONDERS OF NATURE

This poem is dedicated to my friends who stood by me.

How dewy the misty
Mountains
The color that are
Drawn of them
The pleasant breath
Of their magical mist
The colorful aura of
Color that glistens at
The break of day
They glorify the illusion
Of Nature's zest.

When the sunset shines
Through at the break
Of day each glorious
Morn
It shows us all
What Nature is.

Jennifer Forzese
TODAY

Today I watched a star die.
I killed it.
It resembled a diamond reflecting the light.
Now, no more.
Its flame has been extinguished.
A gentle breeze blew it out.
It twinkled, it flickered.
It called to me.
It cried out to me, me, me . . .
I never heard the final heart wrenching cry, me . . .
As it flickered and died.
A star is dead.
Its death is my fault.
Oh, how I am sorry . . .

Meditation.
In a little while, when my mind begins to nod in drowsy dismissal,
My silent friends will tip-toe away, one by one . . .
I will sink slowly down into the Cloud-lined coffin of sleep . . .
awaiting my inevitable resurrection.

Kelly Jackson
LIFE

Life is a world of happiness and love,
Life is a world with pigeons and doves;
Life is a world of heaven and hell,
Life is a world with female and male;
Life has its ups and life has its downs,
Life has its smiles and life has its frowns;
All I can say about life is this:
Life has many messages you don't want to miss.

David Ager
ARTISTIC THOUGHTS

To Mick Staniforth, an artist and a friend.

A stroke so ruthless
Provoked by anger in the music
Inspired by symphonies floating in his mind
He looks into nowhere
He sees what we don't see
Though we see nothing
He is not blind.

Illusions, confusions
Many don't understand
His thoughts in life
He puts down in colour
His road is long
Broad, short and narrow
And as an artist
His mind will far wander.

Daphne

Daphne
"MOON" LAKE

Thanks for the beautiful day,
Beautiful lake, beautiful mountain,
But the "moon" is the most beautiful thing
Of all these and more.

Daphne
PRECIOUS MOMENT

Like diamonds shining in the sky,
Only crescent bless you and I,
Very truly the precious moment,
Early spring smiling to pass by.

Daphne
BLUE IN THE SEASONS

Spring is fresh and nice,
Flowers are smiling faces,
One of the flowers is blue,
It is me—Forget Me Not.
That is my blue hope—
coming hope.

Summer is brilliant and warm,
Birds are singing songs,
One of the songs is blue,
It is me—Forget Me Not.
That is my blue poem—
joyful poem.

Autumn is beautiful and high,
Stars are shining in the sky,
One of the stars is blue,
It is me—Forget Me Not.
That is my blue dream—
wonder dream.

Winter is isolated and peace,
Winds are whispering stories,
One of the stories is blue,
It is me—Forget Me Not.
That is my blue touch—
silent touch.

There are no numbers.

Tom McMahon
I WISH . . .

Maggie, oh Maggie my girl,
this ride that we're on is a pain.
It seems that the time that is—isn't,
and the lack of it drives me insane.

Who in the world would have dreamed that
the years could wing by with such speed;
That the chance to go back and retrieve some,
would consume me with oceans of greed?

It's not that what's past wasn't worth it,
and the lessons I've learned sure weren't free.
But the time that we should have together
is far less than I want it to be.

What is it that makes us believe that
the job or the work must come first?
When it costs us so much of the good times—
moments for which I now thirst.

I'm not sure that I know how to change this,
it's a habit whose grip holds me fast.
But I know that I must make the effort,
or the future will soon be the past.

Lawrence P Rock
RITUAL OF MOMENTS

As the dawn rains its heated smile,
cold duress weighs hard on the soul.
The need to dream further screams,
as always,
yet, arise we must,
to complete the course of action,
the ritual of moments,
until dawn's child once again falls.

Robert E Figgs
IT'S COLD OUTSIDE AND SNOW IS ON THE GROUND

It's cold outside and snow is on the ground
There's people shopping and children laughing all around
Everyone seems to enjoy being with family and friend
Hoping all who are ill and hurt throughout the world are well and on the mend
Each home is filled with laughter and joy
As all the kitchens are filled with all kinds of good food
As everyone in the house slowly falls into a joyful mood
The tree is decorated so beautiful and bright
As packages are placed beneath, awaiting that special night
All of this joy and happiness have a reason
This is the time of the year for that wonderful season
Yes it's cold outside and snow is on the ground
For this is why all the words I write rhyme
You see, It's Christmas Time

Angel Moyet
FOR YOU MY FRIEND
For you my friend
I carry a bucket of water which only you have given me
to extinguish a fiery inferno of pain that lives within my soul
For you my friend
I carry a torch to light the path through a black whirlpool of confusion
my spirit and heart I will give you with a pact that only you can touch it or feel it
For you my friend
I bestill a spark of life
For you my friend
I arise from a peaceful land of slumber
you have given my body the ability to breathe
a painful fiery breath and not be burned
if our souls do bond as one
For you my friend
I will light and clear the path through a thick blackened hole

Grace Cross
MOTHER'S GONE
Mother, I'm home! Where are you now, I shout?
I'm done with my roaming, my rushing about.
I've not kept in touch these last few years.
I've made a shambles of my life I fear.
Now I need your loving arms to hold me tight—
to keep me safe throughout the night.
But where are you Mother? I can't seem to find
the mother who has had me constantly on her mind.
Daddy, where's Momma? Why is she not here?
My child, God has now taken her in His care.
You weren't here when she had her time of need.
Now is your time to listen and heed what your Mother and I have taught you
throughout the years and try to be true
to yourself and to your life
so you may make it through life's strife.
Oh Mother, I miss you more than you know.
I'll miss basking in your love's glow.
Life will never be the same without your love
But I know you'll be sending more from above.
I love you, Mother!

Debbie R McAdam
QUESTIONS
Tell me, what am I going to do
When I am here without you?

Will I ever be as happy
As I was with you beside me?

Will you ever think of me
When you are where you want to be?

Will someone else take my place?
In the crowd, will you see my face?

Will anyone put up with you,
When you do the things you do?

Will you hear me say "I love you"
When there is no one there with you?

Will you finally come home,
When you are feeling all alone?

Or, will you just stay away,
And hope that you'll forget—
someday.

Debbie Christen
LASTING LOVE

Special thanks to my family and friends for their encouragement in my writing poetry.

You whisper in my ear,
You gently touch my cheek,
You help me, oh, so quietly,
To find the things I seek.
You're there when I celebrate,
And, when I feel blue.
It seems you're always at my side,
We are like one; not two.
You guide me ever so patiently
With such tender loving care,
It seems you were made for me.
We are a lasting love.
You know my moods,
And, I know yours, too.
Together our love will grow,
To find a world of happiness,
That everyone should know.
Our love will never die,
I know that this is true,
'Cause every time I see you,
I fall in love anew!

Elaine N Taylor
THE CRY OF THE PEACOCKS
At times I live in a quandary of noise
created not by someone's truck or car
or other city sound
but by someone's pet peacocks.

Their cries create a silence in the noise.
Their cries become a silence in
the silence of one's thoughts.

The peacocks' call is so human . . .
it arrests the doing now.
It seems the cry of a small child.

Why does the mind quiver so at the
sound of the peacocks?
. . . the mind shift gears?

Elaine N Taylor
IN OR OUT OF TIME
Such is the time . . .
No time, in time, out of time.
No time.
Oh, I am blind and my dog is dead.
What time do you have?

Any time is as good as you say
For there is no time
No time to do anything
now.

The world is at odds
With other worlds . . .
In time and out of time.

Is there no time to say anything?
What time did you say it
was?

For I am blind and my dog is dead.

Elaine N Taylor
TO FATHER
The petals curl in the soft wind rising
and rain weeps over the window
to the sound of silence of nevermore
to the years robbed of their gladness
to the back of the noble head facing the minister.

Looking from the rear I can imagine the blue eyes
fixed on the face of the minister
as his right hand curls and fingers play
on the arm of the chair
as he tries to understand.

He is truly a fixture now, this man,
in this place.

The women look at him, or beckon, or call,
The men make room for him,
for he is still a
beautiful, noble,
being this man
even when he sings and
Lord knows his heart is
trying to sing
This man, my Father.

Mollie Anna Solomon
BETWEEN AND AROUND US
As we stand
With hand in hand
Feeling the warmth between us.

Then we dance
We're in a trance
Feeling no one around us.

We go home
We're all alone
Nothing can come between us.

Face to face
Then we embrace
Feeling the warmth between us.

We make love
Soft, like a dove
Feeling no one around us.

Side by side
Our love, abide
Nothing can come between us.

Sharon K Dorsett Stanback
A WORLD, FAR AWAY
I go each day to visit a world of dreams and imagination
Which takes me far beyond the seas, and land, and other places.
Far beyond the moon and stars and planets in our Universe,
Far beyond the reality world that mortal man can see.

There is a world that transcends time that no one believes exists,
To get there all you'll ever need is the faith within your midst.
A world of beauty, a world of joy, laughter and peace of mind,
A world that's strong, courageous, and young, a world that is not blind.

You can't get there by "just believing" you must possess more than that
You must have the will, the longing, and endurance, to keep your faith on track.

For in this world is not the boastful, the liar and the cheat
This world is not for persons who practice deceit.
This world is for the honest, the loving, kind and fair
This world has beauty and sunshine: I hope to see you there.

If you ever want to visit, keep this thought in mind,
Never try to live the present in days that have passed behind.
For the past will never be again, the future is unseen,
The present is here and willing to fulfill all your dreams.

Emeline (Caretti) Shannon and son John

Emeline (Caretti) Shannon
THE SANDS OF TIME

This poem is dedicated to my beloved son, John H Shannon

Silently they pass
Like a gentle breeze on a warm summer day;
Sure as the ebb tide flows out at end of day
The sands of time roll on.

Gently they pass,
Soft as an angel's tread on a distant cloud;
Like the first snowfall on a cold winter day
The sands of time roll on.

While the winds of change sweep by
In the still of the night,
Quietly, ruthlessly
The sands of time roll on.

We beg, we seek, we strive, we hope;
"Hold back, hold back" we cry in vain,
But to no avail;
The sands of time roll on.

Thelma Hamblett
LOVE UNDEFINED
If all my thoughts and all my love
Could be seen in motion;'

I would need all of this to give
You any notion
Of how I truly feel.

If I might choose by ways and means
How much I really care;
I would have to search and seek
forever
For the ways are not anywhere
To define the way I feel.

If I spent my life in expressing
The love I have and feel for you,
And if I could identify love with
myself
I doubt if I could prove
How much I love thou.

If I met your needs and shared your
pains
Or bled for you in your sorrow,
Or if I gave you all I had and longed
for more
That I could borrow,
I'd still need ways to show my love.

Garnet E Thompson

FIRST LOVE

My first love came to call
And I knew once again
How he could stir my heart
How only he could hold my hand,
As in days gone by

50 yr's ago, he would race down the
hall at school
To meet me at my door
To gently squeeze my hand, and say
I love you more, than yesterday

I looked at him, his hair so white
And the yearning in my heart
For us to be young again
And in love as then, would not let go.

So he held me tight and said
It is the same as then
Just a little time has passed,
But we can love again

He cannot walk on water
Nor make the birds to sing
But this pounding in my heart
Could make the liberty bell ring!

Ed Lewis

FULL MOON

Why be dull, the moon is full—
A choir is singing
And they are bringing
Love and joy by gravity pull

Gone is the freeze, a soothing
breeze—
The choir hums a hymn,
Winter left a broken limb:
Longevity giving height to trees

The moon is bright all through the
night
Oh how you learn
A place to turn—
On this beautiful luminous site

Come again soon big bright full
moon—
Tomorrow night you are
new
With a rocky-bye view,
After the fading of afternoon

Andrea Andrews

THE ROLLER COASTER OF LIFE

Here I go again,
down to the bottom,
to the depression
and confusion,
Here I go again on the roller coaster
of life.
Here I go again,
climbing to the top.
I stay there for a minute,
then I feel myself begin to drop,
Here I go again on the roller coaster
of life.
Here I go again, laughing away my
screams,
Here I go again, losing clutch of my
dreams.
Here I go again on the roller coaster
of life.
Some enjoy it, others loathe it,
But there's no disembarking
the roller coaster of life.

Antionette & Ward Polk

WIND CHIMES

The howls of the wind blow very
briskly,
The hollowness of chimes ring in
harmonic beauty
To stand and blow the chimes of your
heart is very risky,
But if I must it'll be my honored
duty.
To capture the wind for a quick song
is what wind chimes do,
The echoes of the chimes are
somethings sharp but often sweet,
It says hey sweetheart I really do love
you.
But suddenly I feel a sharp pain to
tell me I've been beat,
Due to the fact you've snatched down
your chimes and smashed them under
your feet.
Why? Oh, Why? My heart would cry,
For you will look at me and say
sweetheart good-bye,
As your wind chimes are broken I
blow no more,
I turn and say goodbye my love as I
close the door.

Lauren Cowles

MOMS

Moms care and love you,
They help you tie your shoes
Moms can be your best
friend,
And teach you how to mend.
Moms talk to you when you
are sad,
But sometimes they get mad.
Moms give you lots of hugs,
and then you fill their mugs.
Moms are trusting and humorous,
Their suppers taste delicious.
Moms are usually understanding,
But sometimes they can be
demanding.

Willa Brooks Causey

ODE TO THE DAWN

Bursting forth,
From its Eternal Source,
Thundering,
Across the vast horizon,
The Golden Dawn,
Dense Foliage
Along its route
Awaken from slumber,
Waves a drowsy salute,
To its magic.
The dawn's breathtaking beauty
Mirrors in a placid lake
The priceless art heirloom.
That man appraises, but
God alone creates.

Sharyn Smith

I ASK

I ask not for roses,
Nor orchids divine.
I ask only your love
And kisses so fine.

I won't ask for promises
Too hard to keep
I'll ask just your arms
Wrapped 'round me in sleep

I'll never ask for riches
And things that can't be
Only that wherever you are
You'll make room for me.

Mary Elaine (Davey) Goforth

Mary Elaine (Davey) Goforth

INDEED

There's something to be said for
lilting, curving roads
that follow their own
whimsical paths,

And do not fit the mold of
superhighways
that glow triumphant in the
eyes of
engineers.

There's something to be said for a
road
that flings itself out into
somewhere
then turns abruptly,
Slithering down,
down into curves that
coil and writhe
and reach out to explore
the valleys!

There's precious warmth about a road
where people wave a greeting.
(You must be a neighbor. Who
else would be traveling
such a crazy road?)

THEN, TOO

There's something to be said for
lilting, curving minds
that follow their own
whimsical paths,

And do not fit the molds of super
systems
that glow in the eyes of
educators.

There's something to be said for a
mind
that flings itself out into
somewhere,
then turns keenly
And wrestles with the "obvious,"
poking merciless tentacles
into the sacred places of
Certainty!

There's precious warmth in the safe
freedom of a "road"
where teacher and student
travel,
Guided only by curiosity and need,
Restrained only by courageous
honesty.

YES!

There is something to be said for
"roads" that do not glow
in the eyes of
"engineers!"

Mary Elaine (Davey) Goforth

FAITH

I watched beyond seeing;
I hoped beyond thinking;
I waited beyond knowing,
And found a way.

Mary Elaine (Davey) Goforth

NECESSITY

It snowed.
I scattered seeds upon the drive.
A perky little sparrow spied—
Ate a little. Flew away.
Came again. Yes, he would
stay.

But Miss Cat watched with yellow
eyes
From window ledge to
hypnotize!

I dampened clothes in easy sight!
But did not dampen his delight
In sweet repast—seeds a la
white.

I say—could I be brave as he
In face of life's necessity?

Mary Elaine (Davey) Goforth

THE DECISION

To the chief and tribal council came
two braves, two sturdy warriors,
Sought a little Indian orphan, wished
to take him home and rear him;
And the old chief in his wisdom
listened gravely to their urging.

Spoke the first with firm assurance:
"By my fire on winter evenings I will
keep him warm and feed him.
From all harm and fear and sorrow—
from temptation I will shield him.
He shall know no bitter failure since
the hard things I'll do for him.
I shall give him what he wishes,
Be content with what he brings me.

Surely you must see I love him!
Send him now unto my tepee."

Spoke the second brave arising:
"By my side on winter evenings
through the storm with me I'll lead
him.
Then the wind will strike and sting
him!
He will learn of the Two Choices—
He can turn his back and stand there,
Let the wind itself diminish,
Or bend his head and fight it, pit
himself against its fury
Till he closes with it gladly, feels the
weakness in him vanish.

"He will rise up with the sun's rays,
going forth to hunt the eagle.
Coming back without the talons, he
will go again and seek them.
Fear and Failure will be with him till
at last he understands them—
Learns to know their limitations, how
to take from each its blessings.

"I will guard him well and guide him,
calling forth the best that's in him,
Praise his patient, careful working, let

him know the joy of striving.
All I know of life I'll teach him—
urge that he improve upon it.
When the day comes that he best me,
I will join with him in gladness.

"Though at times he may despise me,
let it be thus for I love him.
Will you trust him to my keeping?"

Could you be the chief of warriors,
holding in your power the young one,
To which brave would you entrust
him?

Leif Ericksen
MY FATHER'S WATCH
I kept my father's watch
it doesn't run anymore
but I still do
he wasn't the one who
taught me to tell time
he wasn't around at that time
the watch is in a box
with pictures and memories
and memories have feelings
I keep feelings in the box
then try to forget
I keep the box in a closet
in a room I don't go in much
It's a powerful little box
the memory isn't
the watch at all
It's disappointment
from not seeing it when he wore it

Tomiko N Cary
AMERICA; HOW IS IT?
People dying and immigrants
coming.
HOW FREE IS AMERICA?
Have you ever seen a person in jail?
HOW FREE IS AMERICA?
Babies addicted to drugs.
HOW FREE IS AMERICA?
Russians hate us, because they say
we are free, but if they lived here it
would be a great disappointment.
HOW FREE IS AMERICA?
They say when you live in America
you are free.
SO HOW CAN YOU BETRAY IT?
Only one of us really knows, how
free America really is.
AND THAT IS THE OPTIMIST.

Dale Carter
IT'S RAINING AGAIN
it's raining again
in the darkness of my life
passing
empty buildings
& empty streets
I realize
I've changed my life
forever
gone from madness
to despair
& back again
as I travel alone
the desire to turn & run
is an aching inside me
but I realize
there's nothing to run to
passing city after city
& nowhere is home
the quality of unreality
is more real
than my life itself.

James E Gauthier
TEST FOR LIFE
The world may be a messed up place,
but please do not lose your faith.
Things may look bad at times,
And it may seem that you may
no longer climb.
Then out of the clear blue sky,
you begin to taste life,
like it was your favorite piece of pie.
So when you start to lose your faith,
do not fill it with more hate.
Fill it with your determination to win.
And before you know it,
You will find that you did no sin,
But it was just a testing by God,
To You,
To see if you can make it by being
true.
But please do not give up.
There is light ahead of you.
A whole life to live for.

Eva Belle Schnetzer
BLESSINGS OF LIFE
As I walk down the pathway of life
It seems that there is so much strife!
But I look toward Heaven to my God
above
And I feel that I am filled with His
love.

I quicken my steps as I silently dream
And it seems that a light from
Heaven is seen,
With new strength and courage I
hurry on
And the burdens of life seem far
beyond.

I count my blessings every day
When I watch my children skip and
play,
The world seems a wonderful place
to be
As with friends they run so very free.

Now the children have grown and
gone their way
And the swings are silent this quiet
day,
But with blessings from my God
above
I feel so filled with His eternal love.

Linda Vasconcelos
THE PEREGRINE
With golden wings she mounts the
heights
and blends
to the patterns of blue and white.

With vision clear she observes below
the patchwork
of both God and man.

She cries out
in the agony of her sorrow,
but it reaches as a whisper
below.

The air is black
the land is shroud in darkness,
the water
burns in her throat.

The creation has swallowed
all
the creator gave.

She soars upwards once again
and then
with spirit broken
she falls.

Lisa Harbin
ALIVE AGAIN
You are a continuing extension of
that life—that was so close and dear
to me—that I lost too soon—yet I
never had the chance to know you—
you see that life died before I really
understood what it meant to me—as
you touch me now I feel the void is
gone—

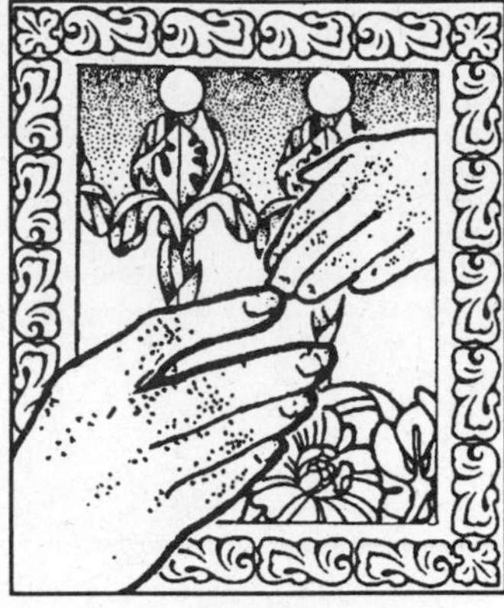

Now I have the love that died too
young—you reached out and pulled
me into your heart—taking a risk on
me—finally the void is gone—I am
now part of your life—as you are my
life now—I have been looking for
you—since that lonely night
I have you
now—forever!

Marge Tkach a.k.a. Nam
MOON BOUND
Heroes three are full of glee
they've left their footprints for all to
see,
along with the flag of our country,
"On the Moon"

What's next? Venus or Mars or
perhaps, all the stars?
It could only happen in this land of
ours,
The good old U.S.A.

Congratulations to these three, our
national anthem now should be,
"Oh: say can you see, those
footprints on the Moon"

Dorothy M Wukitz
UNABLE TO SLEEP
As I lie in bed this night alone
Eyes wide open, unable to sleep
My mind is numb as though chained
to the bed
But my mind, hearing is sharp, and
clear
Remembering the past,
what will tomorrow bring.
The hardships, the sorrows,
what was, could have been
Yet the good times, happy times
I had through the years
remembering.
I'm watching the curtains breathing
slowly back, and forth
I left the window open an inch, or
two
The distinct outlines of my room
lit by the moon
I lie here, awake.
I hear the monotonous ticking
clock beside my bed,
Chirping crickets outside, some-
where,
Old boards creaking inside
somewhere
Distant barking dog out there,
Do I hear breathing, sighing
I do hear humming
from someone close by.
If sleep would just arrive
release this jumbled mind.
Sleep, blessed sleep
Ah!, it has arrived
for I am drifting
slowly drifting
Embraced in its fold.

G Matthew Mapes
NOOK
Raise
me from this obscurity (and)
take me to an incidental
situation
twisted out of context and
pulsating
a spas mod ic, Irisheartbeat fear
of poetry and nature
Hair pushed up—démodé

Bathe me in the fountain of souls
lost
Let me be immersed in crying
children
Dancing on the terrace
Midnight afterlife and
before the silence . . .
Waterfall c
a
s
c
a
d
e
d
o
w
n tears of
conclusive faith
Drop me purified at her pregnant feet

Robyn Mirocznik
LAUGHTER AT THE MOON
Crying tears of sunlight horizons at
dusk shine momentarily.
In the heat of the night the stars of the
universe gaze on. Oh how the aura
from the moon glistens and shines at
the same time. Guide my spirit to
oblivion to race the wind to meet the
galaxy of time. This
space is real. In a vision I can see,
for tomorrow is today and yesterday
the future. And only then shall since
make sense and infinite wisdom be.
Yet, far away but still very close is a
hole of nothing that breathes
something. A whimsical in carousel,
delicate in youth beginning
imperfectly
and uniting as one in the end.
Charismatic
is this imagery. A shadow like the
night. A magnetism that has no
boundaries . . .

Joanne Kalies
DAWN
She will come like always
In the early hour of an unborn day
Walking soundless
Over damp-breathing ground
And old wooden stairways
For her footsteps are silent.

In the gray morning shadows
Salty mist fills the air
And breaking a rose for him
Dewy grass will wet her feet on the
path.

She will find him sleeping like
always
In the early hour of that unborn day
Knowing he is her life
She will bring him that rose with a
smile.

But long before the first bird cries
And the sun breaks through misty
dawn
She will be gone.

Tessie Pepper
MY GRANDDAUGHTER
On April 13th—1968 was she born.
At 45—single and still dating,
Was I willing to be a grandma!
I was torn!
Now she is 21 and has no time,
because she is working and dating.
I appreciate her now because she is
my best friend: and I give her the
highest rating.
I remember coming over and
bringing her ice cream which she
loved—she called it "looshkah!"—
And how cute she looked wrapped in
her babushka!!
And the times I babysat, and she
cried for her mom and dad!
They went bowling and left no
telephone number, that made her a
little mad!
Finally she turned and ordered call—
XYZ like on T.V.
Soon she'll be walking down the
aisle, a "Bride to Be"!!
How do you think being a great-
grandma will feel to me!!

F J German
BANDITS
The bandits appeared to
me in a dream
Blossoming from the dark
grey sky at twilight
From one small idea emerged
thousands of pitchblack
beauties.
—My coffined face
appeared in the bush
upon wakening.

Donna A Forewell

Donna A Forewell
HEAVEN BOUND

This poem is dedicated, in Jesus's name, to my beloved sons, Joshua and Shawn Taylor.

Bashful yet Brave is the wind that I
breathe
Feeling the Holy Spirit go through
me so gentle a need
I dare not to speak for ever I will
dream
With a wide open mind, yet as quiet
as a running stream

As far away as my thoughts will take
me
There is a place that touches my heart
This place is called heaven
Where tears are no problem and fears
have no part
And now that I'm found, I'm Heaven
Bound
He's in my heart
He's in my thoughts
He's everywhere I go
His name is Jesus
And I'm at Home with Him
That's because I'm Heaven Bound

Laura Jones
POWER CRAZY
All the power has gone to his head
A madman, a sad man, now helpless
many are dead.
If one was Jewish or was one Black,
He's line them up back to back.
He'd fill them with drugs, bullets and
holes;
Standing up for what they are,
fearless and bold.
A cold wind blows from the east
A power hungry animal, a man who's
a beast!
All of his Nazis' brains are dead
And nothing but death is in their
heads.
But one day the time will come when
the Jews, the Blacks and us will be
ONE!

Cori Cahow
TRUE LOVE
Standing, waiting at the door
Wondering is he ever going to show
up
Thinking to myself . . . Does he really
love me or is it just a hoax
Thinking of a night of success.
Dining in elegance, dancing in the
moonlight.
Just us forever . . .
Is he the one I really love or is the
one I love standing on a deserted
island?
Wondering, thinking, should I go on
with it or should
I search for my true love?

Jeanne L Spencer
SEARCH FOR PEACE
Why is peace of mind
So hard to find?
I include it in my prayers
Right alongside someone who cares.

I'm not inexperienced enough to
believe
You have to have someone in order
to achieve
That state of being so sought after
The resting place between sorrow and
laughter.

"To thine own self be true"
Is a philosophy I make my own.
Be true in all that you do
And your heart will always tell you
where you belong.

Yet with all my ponderous wisdom
The peace I seek does not come.
Could it be it's only an illusion?
And I'm the victim of a delusion?

Karen Deason Graham
WILL YOU MISS ME?
When your mouth goes dry
Trying to recall the taste of my kisses
Will you miss me?
When the memory of my fingers
Warm and searching burn your skin
Will you miss me?
When you no longer feel the cloud
Of my hair soft on your chest
Will you miss me?
When your body aches in the dark
With wanting mine
Will you miss me?
When days have turned into weeks
and months
Since you've seen my smile
Will you miss me?
When with time our chance is gone
And you no longer have a choice to
make
Will you miss me?

Rose Sallemi
A BIRD
A bird in a nest fell out of a tree
got stung by a bee
and then he cried "whee"
Mom came to see
and put them back in the tree

Frances Weber
I WALKED THROUGH
I have walked through the valley of death. I have touched the depth of pain. I have climbed from hell and back to try and live again. Oh, life what have I to gain? What will morrow bring? "Sunshine I Pray" for yesterday I withered, but today I sing because there's a new flower next to my windowpane. The grass is so much greener, the sky so full of white fluffy clouds. I take a deep breath, and I'm startled that life is all about. Life give me an answer, give me some clue to what tomorrow will bring me. For I have walked through—the valley and tasted your bitter pain.

Kathy Thomas
THE GOOD SHEPHERD
The Good Shepherd watches his sheep both day and night in constant concern. He watches from his Mighty tower always standing guard waiting to destroy the Enemy.

He protects his first love against ol' Satan to make our journey safer, so that we can graze in his pasture with confidence and not be overcome by the Evil one.

His voice is our boundary and we acknowledge his calling. He is ours and we know we belong to Him.

He's prepared the finest for his flock, for we, no doubt, are His most prized possession.

He is Magnificence unimagined, from timeless times, sovereign of all generations.
He is the Good Shepherd.

Sarah L Hitchner
LAND OF DREAMS
Will you please come with
Me outdoors,
Where everything looks
Like Heaven—Maybe better.
The aroma is gentle,
Yet pleasing.
We can taste the
Sweet honeysuckle,
And feel the beauty all
Around us.
Oh, please come,
I'm calling you
Into God's land of dreams.

Ryan Kelley Warner
MY GOD
My god believes that you can have sex with any gender as long as there is love.
My God believes writers can and should write what they wish
My God believes that a woman can make her own choice
My God believes that the U.S. Government should take a stand, raise a voice.
Could my God be me?

Mary Ann Peters
GREENING
The wind whispers its constancy
to changing forms
But the sparrows celebrate New
Rain.
Children wait wide-eyed
for music the ice cream man
plays.
Soon twilight silently slips in
to waken the sleeping stars.

Night shadows glide randomly
moondancing to distant
melodies.
Blinking neon nods an invitation
stalling the homeward-bound.
Even Merlin forgets his magic
and joins the Midnight Parade.
A New Dawn ruffles the wind
with stirrings of love.

Claire Marie Hart
RECITATIVE "—A STYLE OF VOCAL MUSIC INTERMEDIATE BETWEEN SPEAKING AND SINGING . . ."
The spoken word—
curt, cutting, brisk—
Authority, an infallible tone—
Negligent of pleasantries—
. . . Except when wit or humor
suggest response.

The sung phrase—
lilting, gliding—
So sensitive, quivering—
Within a febrile space—
. . . Erased once more by sound.

The symphony—
reaching crescendo—
On the reverse motion
Of a red van—
The driver securely in place—
Without a backward glance or
thought,
Spins out of sight,
As the notes cascade to nothingness.

The instrumental music—
obscuring both word and
song—
Its gracefulness excites the
spirit—
Its depths, its heights inspire
The pain, the joy that exist
. . . in the recitative.

Lynn M Gardner
BABY'S BREATH

To my fiancé, Gary, whose courage inspired me.

Her eyes bulge with terror,
as her tiny body shakes
without control.
She is terrified and so am I.
My lips touch hers and I breathe.
Life is sweet buy dying as I hold
her in my arms.
I feel death's cold fingers grip her
as she reaches out to me.
I fight to save us both.
She gasps and cries until
she breathes back to me.
We are one for a moment.

When an explanation is
demanded
and the questions cease;
Needing someone to blame
for the abuse she received,
they choose me to suffer.
It is only myself left,
with my fingers wrapped
around black bars.
You've chosen your reality,
since believing the truth was
too hard.

Amy Bauer
WINDOWS OF BLUE

For all of those who find or will find friends who are as true to you as you have been to them.

I am true, true as blue. My eyes show
it clearly, can you see through?
A window so bright of sparkling
delight; dancing around full of joy
They have found.

Ah but as pure as they seem they
giggle and gleam of devious ways to
guard with contempt, of close friends
and lovers who are precious to them.
A look to cast away enemies so
strong like a willow's stem.

So compassionate, so sensitive of
others' special needs, you can at
times see the recognition of faith
glistening through.

Misery may lurk through those eyes
so true, but don't underestimate the
eyes for they will see it through.

Oh but the mystery is undoubtably
hidden, like a book that still hasn't
been written.

But what most of all that makes them
true as can be, the person who I'm
thinking of who is always true to me.

I love you.

Brian McEuen Jackson
TAKE TIME
Let not, your life be dreary.
lift up your voice, in sweet refrain.
may your skies be filled with
butterflies.
your flowers washed, by gentle rains.
Take pleasure in the simple things.
the little things in life.
for, 'tis the simple little things,
that help to mold our lives.
Be kind to every animal, for, they too
are our friends.
someday, on all the animals, our own
lives might depend.
our love, our trust, our honor,
forever, they'll defend.
Take time, to love the little ones,
for, they are the future, you know.
make it your plan, to lend them a
hand.
nurturing them as they grow.
Take time, to talk to the elderly,
don't chastise, or set them apart.
for after all, 'tis they, you know,
that gave all of us, our start.
Hold fast to the bond, that a
friendship can bring.
for, true friends are quite hard to find.
Live by these words of rhyme, you'll
find
it easy to take time.

Brian McEuen Jackson
NEW DAY
The sun, peeks from behind a
cloud.
to see if anyone is watching.

When the coast is clear,
in full view of the world, it
appears.

A songbird sees this,
and greets it, with a joyful noise.

The leaves in the trees, rustle.
in anticipation, of its next song.

As wildflowers and tall grasses,
sway to the rhythm of the
wind.

to the rhythm also
a butterfly, performs its latest
dance.

As the steady tap, tapping, of the
woodpecker,
beats out the tempo of a new day.

A bumble bee, buzzing with
purpose,
darts in, and out.
amidst a patch of goldenrod.

With not so serious barks,
a floppy-eared dog, chases an
old, rusty, milk truck.

as it rattles down,
the dusty road.

Joan Scott
NORTHERN ARIZONA SPRING
Winter's calling—spring is calling
Son in sandals with snow falling
Upon his naked toes.

Tsaile[1] a town? A hogan town?
Spring break shuts the whole place
down!
(Except for nests of crows.)
Teachers' horses—shaggy horses
Back from winter pasture, sources
Of joy: Now home, each knows

A snowy back. Astride its back
With weight of old familiar tack
Its owner riding goes.

The sun is shining, brightly shining.
Through the veil of snow it's twining
And mountain bluebird glows

The spring melt comes—snows
quickly melt
From hogans down to streams that
pelt
DeChelly's[2] sandstone of rose.

Smelling grassy, child stink grassy
The boy returns all chilled but sassy
To warm his toes & nose

[1]Canyon de Chelly, pronounced da
shay.
[2]Tsaile, pronounced Tsay-lee, is a
Navajo place name meaning
beginning of the canyon.

Florence L Davis

Florence L Davis
THIS MORNING
The sky is clear and blue this
morning
Except for yonder cloud—a fluffy
white.
The sun is peeking above the trees;
Its face of gold is shining bright.
The grass, a beautiful carpet of green,
Was strewn overnight with diamonds
of dew.
Among the roses, there's a bud or
two
With a touch of radiant red peeking
through.
The birds are singing, gayly, in the
trees
To complete the beauty of this early
morn.
More beauty than eyes can behold—
God has given this morning to adorn.

A lady thought, as she re-entered her
cottage small,
"What more beauty than this could
anyone ask?"
Giving thanks to God for this very
beautiful morning,
She happily begins each household
chore and task.

Jeri Haase
HERE I SIT
Here I sit, with the kids at my knee—
here I sit, it really is me;
no more sorrow for days ahead,
only gladness when I tuck them
in bed.

Here I sit, near each one I treasure,
here I sit, and it gives me such
pleasure
to see them playing and laughing
today
as I listen to each lovely
word they say.

Here I sit, wishing never to
leave—
here I sit, knowing I will grieve;
waving goodbye to them from the
porch
will be like putting my heart to
the torch.

Here I sit, lazily in the grass,
here I sit, with a 72-hour pass;
I must return to the sanitarium this
day
to kill the TB germs, in each
and every way.

Here I sit, beneath the maple tree—
here I sit, as they chatter to me,
trying not to show them the tears that
I've shed
while putting them fondly in the
memories of my head.

Jeri Haase
A CALLER
"Hello Johnnie, what have you been
doing?
you went to see daddy's friend,
and your sister squeezed their cat? —
that's all right dear, cats will
bend."

"Yes, I know you love me, sweet,
and mommy loves you too;
When I'm not sick and I get well
I'll soon be there with you."

He said it all, with his tender heart,
I felt him so near, not miles apart.
I'll never forget, try as I might,
Yes, I talked to my son last night.

I still can hear his voice
and what he said he'd do —
"Mommy — I will cry for you."

Dixie Brissell
INSIGHT MISTAKEN

My thoughts alone are for my little girl, Amy. Love always, Mama.

I've looked within . . .
My depth defies . . .
Detours erupt . . .
Enter white lies.

I walk in silence . . .
Whisper in fear
I'll wake a soul . . .
I long to hear.

I look for truth . . .
Destiny sought . . .
Image imagined . . .
And positive
thought.

I find instead . . .
A major motion . . .
A loss at love . . .
And blind devotion.

Insight is mistaken . . .
My enter is denied . . .
My departure is granted . . .
I should never have tried.

Nina Tessin
YOUR PAIN IS MINE
For me, no winged feet of delight
subsist,
Leaden bones benumbed by burdened
mien
Walk with your troubled soul beyond
the mile
Statutory allotment so decreed.
Easement of time debars no rending
pain

Patience, courage, or bears no warranty;
Slow fire of hope ignites encouragement,
Courtesy of commiseration's fee.

Could check of time measured by metronome
Sure-mark the crisis of the turning point,
Day on day, and week on week unknown?
When healing turns back it's discomfiture
Suspension soars and friend can say to friend
Waiting is past, your pain is mine no more.

Tammy Davies

EXPECTATIONS

This poem is dedicated to my family, with much love.

We all have expectations
even when we're young
not sure what they are yet
but on the tip of our tongue.

Day to day they change
depending on our needs
clearing a path for our future
not quite sure where it leads.

Always getting bigger
going on from year to year
slightly out of our reach
which is something we all fear.

We all want to say
our expectations have been filled
but in our life we compromise
so some dreams have been stilled.

Everyone seems to believe
that fate rules our life
but are you sure expectations
aren't the cause of all our strife.

Miss Miriam BirdSong

EMPTY

My Heart . . .
It Bleeds Frothy Tears,
Induced By Pain And Disregard,
For Who I Am And What I Feel.

My Heart . . .
It Bleeds A Cyanotic Hue,
From Lack Of Love And Little Care;
It Oozes . . . Sorrow . . . Slowly.

My Heart . . .
It Bleeds Scarlet Red.
It Squirts And Spurts With Every Beat,
Until It's Drained And All Pumped Out.

My Heart . . .

Hallie Kim

THE BEST EFFORT

We can wish for money . . .
And never receive it.
We can dream for success . . .
And never receive it.
We can hope for a good future . . .
And never receive it.
But, we can also do our best . . .
And accept what comes to us.

Connie Holt

FANTASIES HUNGER

This close to you, my fantasy,
How it makes me hunger.
It tugs at me, and pushes me,
And then it pulls me under.
Something inside explodes now,
Something enchanting, I feel,
Seductively, taken over somehow,
By this that is so unreal.
Softly, I'll touch your face,
Only to reassure myself.
Then, your form, my eyes will trace,
While inside my hunger swells.
Wanting only for you to touch me,
Just hoping that you will.
Wishing that you would finally see,
But, knowing you won't until . . .
Your lips on mine begin,
I see the hunger take over you,
And as you feel this hunger within,
I will become your fantasy, too.

Shelly Ann Lepine

Shelly Ann Lepine

Sometimes i wonder just who i am

S ometimes i wonder just who i am,
H oping i'll find a great dream to expand.
E scaping my problems is what i'm good at,
L iving a lie, as a matter a fact.
L etting the pressures catch up with me,
Y et all i pray for is to be set free.

A ll of those times, i waited to cry,
N o one to help me,
N o one would try.

L ife seems to endless, so empty, so cold,
E ach day i wish for that someone to hold.
P lease, God, give me the strength to see,
I need to know what's instore for me.
N ot one second will pass me by,
E ach day will come and i'll never know why.

Gina L Gilbert

MORNING (MOURNING)

As I lie awake this morning
Outside—the skies are gray
And I take a look around me
And see that you have gone away

Spring is in the air
There is beauty all around
And you are out there somewhere
Waiting to be found

The tree in our yard has bloomed
A color of pretty pink
But you must see more colors
In your life—I think

Our house stands alone
Filled with you and I
I feel it must have known
That you were saying goodbye
And me? Well—I'm just fine
Not doing anything
'cept drinking my morning coffee
Wondering what tonight will bring

Donna Jo Asher

WORDS

A scrambled mess of letters that sometimes come out all wrong,
But put together and entwined with music make a beautiful song.

Short words that mean everything
like "if" may have a double meaning,
Long words that stand for nothing
leaves one confused and screaming.

"I Love You," the three most precious words used every day and night,
"I Am Sorry," takes the most courage to admit one was wrong and not right.

Talent comes from putting them all together, a sentence with no abuse,
Understanding comes from reading between the lines and putting it to use.

So unscramble those thoughts and use the right words to speak your mind,
And remember what is said may not be what's intended, so always be kind.

J Eduard Vlaskamp

FINAL BREATH

When I look out my window
I see they're cutting down all the trees
I can tell by the smell when the winds blow
That they're polluting all the seas
In the sky there's a great big hole
Where the ozone used to be
I can tell it won't be long at all
Till the world's brought to its knees

Look any place and see mankind's waste
Polluting rivers and streams
Poisons released with alarming haste
Are making nightmares of everyone's dreams
The people who are doing it
Say it's not as bad as it seems
And pretend they can't hear the tiniest bit
When Mother Nature Screams

And the world is crying
But nobody seems to care
The world is dying
Its FINAL BREATH is in the air

Roland B Fales

SERENITY

The sun sinks over the hilltops
And twilight falls serene,
Sunbeams play on the clouds above
In a burst of glorious sheen.

They only play a little while
And then they fade away;
Peace reigns over the countryside,
At the end of a perfect day.

Charles Byrd III

VISION

It could be a stroke on canvas
or a line found in a speech
that expresses one man's vision
or what he wants to teach
they let us soar the heavens
and sail across the sea
all this comes from vision
think what our world could be!
The men with truest vision
are great but very few
for from the age of Sophocles
death came, from different views
So many men have died
with so much left to say
for expressing just one different view
they might have changed our world one day!
and now our youth are growing
new minds, new thoughts, new sights,
although every child won't change the world
remember one just might! . . .

"Vision is the foundation of all change." (C.B. III '90)

Charles Byrd III

DESTINY!

Cold? No cool. The eyes are black
with dull, yet vibrant glare.
I raise my head to sign the pact,
but he doesn't seem to care.
So calm and still he waits
with arm outstretched to me,
He stands near darkened, rusty gates
O'erscribed Your Destiny!
He finally makes a motion,
a movement of his hand
I swayed as on the ocean
and moved closer to the man.
I step by step moved nearer
and clear I came to see
the face as in the mirror
of my hopeless destiny.
Then misty came the sky
with clouds of darkened grey,
and as my life has passed me by
The man was swept away . . . .

Judith M Dowrie

DESTINY

Kathleen; thank you for showing me the light.

Three words whispered
One gentle kiss
One tear shed
An empty door, with one key hidden
And time being the only answer

Maia Myrrh

A DIALOGUE

Again I take the pen
To write my heart
For the most part.
As for the rest
I try my best.
And so, and so . . .
Until now, see how?
There are some loose threads,
Multi-colored strands.
Crimson in my hands.
I would compose a symphony
But something stops me.
Find some pity, find some grace
Come, read with me my face,
If you could see me
You would say hello!

Barbara Ann Swanson

JOHN'S POEM

A life so precious, almost snuffed out in its prime!
How to define the value of life just now?
Its definition's not so important when you can hold
The hand not broken, kiss the brow unscathed;
Hear his jokes, though pain wracks a

body broken
By the impact of too-fast metal and glass.

Perhaps I'll define the value of life a little later—
When the bones mend and the wreck can be forgotten—
When we're all a little distanced from the trauma,
But just perhaps a mended son will be enough!

Wanda Frederick
MARK

In loving memory of my son
I dedicate this poem.
Feb.4, '60—Aug. 22, '88.

Time marches on
Seems only yesterday,
You were my son, more
importantly my friend.

A sense of humor
a smile on your face,
You've gone to live
in a better place.

High in the heavens
where birds fly free,
Over mountaintops, no one
knows, only God and me.

Dew on the flowers
mist in the air,
No pain, no sorrow,
not even a care.

The days linger on
in your memory,
the past, has no end,
I love you! my son,
Who was also my friend.

Anemari Stancil
MORNING IS HERE
Morning is here.
Do it again—
That which you must to survive
Into the warmth of the cocoon of night,
Where Hope lives.
Block out the sun
Where you see too clearly.
Long for the soft images—
The gentleness
The safety
The blur of night.

Hide well there. Rest. Give comfort.
Gain strength.
Be beautiful in the sweetness and flickering light.
And hope Day will be brief.

Jason Fisher
DANNY BOY
I once had a dog
Who had red hair.
He slept like a log,
And would face our house and stare.

One day, early in the morning,
My dog was shot.
I started crying,
But my dog survived the shot.

Nine years had passed.
My dog grew sick and old.
On February 4, another year had passed.
My dog was gone; Danny Boy was dead.

We laid him to rest with his head
facing our old house in eternal rest.

Maureen Murphy
GERALD
February 28, 1989

Gerald,

We saw you only Saturday
A day we all enjoyed
The love around us was so strong
For a special girl and boy
We sang, we smiled, we laughed a lot,
The happiness was strong,
But the day did end and before we knew
We all had kissed and gone
No one knew that it would be
The last we'd be together

For God had other plans in mind
And a storm we all would weather
He took you home sweet cousin
of ours
To a reward that is yours alone
But again we'll see your
smiling face
When God calls each of us home
No words could ever truly say
How much we care for you
May God give us the courage and strength
To always carry through.

We love you, Gerald.

All my love,
Cousin Maureen (Cobb) Murphy

Sharon Minter
GOD'S WILL

Dedicated to: Kerry, My Husband, The Minter and Townes Family and Bishop Agnes B. Scurry, Pillar of Truth Church.

Things happen in life we never understand
It's because of God's command.
We must live by God's will
Whatever happens, we must hold our peace and keep still.

No matter what the reason is
We must thank and praise God in this.
Sometimes these burdens are so hard to bear
But God is always here and he really cares.
We must hold onto God without a doubt
God is willing and able to bring us out.

Edna L Heidelberg
THE PREFACE

To my family, who had faith in me.

Make me, O Lord, Thy scriptures so complete,
Thy holy word my bibliography.
Make mine affections Thy swift pages neat
And make my soul Thy holy index be.
Then reading me make Thy dedication
And bind my prose for this generation.

Make me Thy printed word upon this line,
And make Thy holy spirit, Lord, bind wills.
Then print the Word Thyself. The ink is thine.
Thine ordinances make my paper mills.
Then print the same in heaven's color choice
All covered with Thy printed prose, not voice.

Then bind therewith mine understanding, will,
Feelings, judgment, conscience, and memory,
My words and pages that their thoughts may fill
My phrases to praise Thee eternally.
And my cover shall display before them
That I am bound in holy words for Him.

L A Kaercher
DEAR OAK
It is Spring—vernal equinox,
My share this year; one oak, one tree.
Despite steel mesh, the checkered view
Great Oak you are the new to me.

Rabble surrounds you, littered lives,
Leatherized, rippled bark sees rot.
Trailers and trailer trash around,
Unfettered—be what I cannot.

Cephalic despair you don't feel
Yet, your heavy heart must still hurt.
Look up—and take the joy you saw
When as seed, you first came through dirt.

Planted now, firm in air and space,
React, respond—your time is near.
Do not give in to lesser life,
Mighty Oak, please give one more year.

Huge girth and branches show your age
Look again through clouds—sun and blue.
Your burning buds still crave to grow,
Soon, your leaves green I'll see—thank you!

Barb Godshall
OUR JOY WILL BEGIN
Our joy will begin
the moment
our souls touch.
Our love
will grow from
that day
in steady increase.
God's hands
will touch
our hearts—
separately—
and together (as one)
to make our love
real
and everlasting

Phyllis M Mezzera
THE STEPPING STONE
Plymouth Rock was "the stepping stone"
from England, the old ways of home
to a new land and new ways
with God's guidance through the days.

Likewise JESUS CHRIST was "the stepping stone"
sent from heaven, His home
To set men free from every flaw
And condemnation from the law.

The WORD OF GOD is a solid rock
the TRUTH and LIGHT from above
To which mankind flocked
To warm themselves in GOD'S LOVE.

JESUS CHRIST is today's stepping stone
from Old Testament days and ways.
HE is our refuge, our eternal home,
kin by HIS BLOOD with mercy all our days.

JESUS our victory, we'll no longer moan
JESUS the TRUTH, we'll no longer be a scorner.
Plymouth Rock is America's cornerstone
and JESUS CHRIST the headstone of that corner.

Phyllis M Mezzera
AMERICA'S FAITH
Plymouth's national Monument
stands with open Bible
on its rock, now over one hundred years old,
a massive heroic "figure of FAITH"
as over-whelming as the arrival of the pilgrims bold!

FAITH points her finger toward heaven.
She stands eighty-one feet in the air
to the Author and Finisher, WHO
brought them to this land so fair.

With FAITH comes the freedom to believe.
Peace . . . the law fulfilled by justice and mercy
with liberty to approach our Creator, also
education with wisdom tempering youth that are thirsty.

Morality combines the commandments of her left hand,
the prophetic Word of God . . . the Old Testament
and the scroll of Revelation of her right hand,
THE GOOD NEWS of His Spirit . . . the New Testament!

By God's Word heaven came down to earth
being led by His Spirit and Truth, you see.
Born anew by JESUS CHRIST . . . re-birth,
we are a people under GOD . . . set free!

Vincent P McCorry
ON GRANDPARENT'S DAY
How did you spend the entire
day
When all of the children left
the house
We're sure that you all found
a way
Though the home was as quiet
as a mouse

But then your sons and your
daughters came
And the sounds of your grandchildren
filled the house
They called you Pop-Pop or Nanna
or some other loving name
So here's to you all grandparents
without you life would not
be the same . . .

And here is a fact that is so
true
If your parents didn't have children
For sure neither would you!!!!!!!

Happy Grandparent's Day!!

With Love,

Elsie Otwell

Elsie Otwell
FAREWELL

In honor of Roy Buckelew, former pastor of 1st Baptist Church, Hot Springs, Arkansas.

Farewells are never easy
When you say them to a friend.
You've meant so much to all of us
Oh, how can we begin?

To simply say we'll miss you
Would hardly be enough;
To express the way we feel
And show how much you're loved.

Your wit brought us to laughter
Your voice moved us to tears.
And Christ shone round about you
As we learned to fight our fears.

No, farewells are never easy
When you say them to a friend,
So we'll just say
"God bless and keep you"
Until we meet again.

Daryl W Ball
IMPRESSIONS OF YOU

The poem "Impressions Of You" is the first of many that were made for Alena, My best friend, My lover, and very recently my Lovely Wife! It is appropriate to share, but it is lovingly dedicated to my wife, Alena!

Think of flowers, a rose in bloom,
Its petals glistening from the dew,
Add its fragrance, sweet and true,
This elegance becomes you!

Think of wine, the vineyards' best,
Taken from the finest grapes,
Give it body, with fine bouquet,
Intoxicating, at its finest!

Think of chocolate, creams and nuts,
Surprises of the confectioner's art,
Mix these morsels in a box,
Try to miss each little part!

Think of quality, no quantity,
And beauty at its best,
Her eyes are so magnetic,
They're alluring and intoxicating!

Think of all the finest things,
Your mind could dare to dream,
I found it in this lady,
My dream is now reality!

Bob McLaughlin
ROMANTIC POET
Only his pen tells poetry so
words run free like a star
speeding in space from his pen.
To look into his poetry eyes would
melt your heart.
His charisma poetry outreaches
a star by far.
He's truly a romantic poet,
this poet of ours.

Dale L Rook
VIEWPOINT
The clouds slid by below like
islands of snow on a sea of glass.
Its crystal-clear waters revealing the
traceries and pockmarks of
its tributaries

The scars of Man's progress
marched around the bottom of
the Crystal Sea.

Yet much of the land shone like
seaweed: unkept, undisturbed,
unchanged since Genesis.
Populated, teeming with unseen
life unfamiliar to Man's
devastation.

A cold, Paradise found.

Suzanne M Thomson
THE RAIN
Rain is a tat tat tat
as the ground goes splat splat splat,

everywhere and everyone is hoping
for a little sun
but no not me I like the rain
it's cool feeling so fun,

so every time it starts to rain
I'll be there to have a game
so maybe I'll be the first to
tame . . .
the rain.

Nicole Dean (Age 12)
UNTIL THIS DAY
Until this day I had never seen the
beauty of a rose,
because I never took the time to see it
I suppose.
Until this day I had never heard
music's real sound,
it's quite beautiful is what I've found.

Until this day I had never felt a fire's
warm flames,
I guess I was too busy playing games.

Until this day I had never tasted the
sour taste of wine,
but I guess I was disappointed
because I had heard it tasted fine.

Until this day I had never smelt the
pleasant scent of perfume,
which smells as wonderful as a rose
bloom.

Dean A Clark
toolroom
the workbench was brown
as the old man's hands
and chiseled as deep.
its wooden gouges and scars,
filled flush with grease
were like the lines over his knuckles
and the concentration on his brow

the bits and blades
stayed sharp as his mind and eye
and straight as his measure.
blue, hard hammers
and nails rusty and sharp
summoned toys and shelves into the
world
or repaired pistons and patched pipes.

and the light bulb,
dim with dust
glowed over grey wrenches
smudged with his fingerprints
to remind me that
the shop, at least
is still intact.

Dean A Clark
AUTUMN TO WINTER
No more shall I mourn
At the breaking of dawn's
Creaking light
The night
Now gone a-roving.

Nor further lament
The quick snatching away
In the wind
Leaves dipped
In dyes of the heart.

Winter, unadorned and naked
Steals across the forest
Again made of wood.
The season is without raiment
Yet fully complete.

For the rose has no need
Of the gardener's perfume.

Alyssa A Titus
WHY?
There is a wall between us now,
Although it is not visible, I know it is
there.
Things are not what they used to be
for you and me.
A cloud of sadness envelopes me
when I think of what has become of
us.
We had so much—so much to give,
so much love and joy,
And now all you do is Take
my heart and shatter it without even a
second thought or a tear.
We once filled our lives with
tenderness and happiness making
every moment appear to be a burst of
sunlight on a rainy day.
Now all that I have is bitterness and
despair.
My head aches with the thought of
you with another,
My body trembles when I imagine
you sharing and caring with someone
other than me.
My heart feels as though it is being
wrenched by a thousand hands
and drained of all life.
YOU—the one person that I shared
my world with—how can you be
so cruel and unfair?

Rhonda Rell
WAITING ARRIVAL OF SPRING

I dedicate this poem to Susan Thomas. Because of her friendship over the years has given me inspiration to write poetry.

Snow glistens and shines.
Are there footprints left behind?
One by one flakes begin to fall.
Covering all the footprints,
No longer can see traces of life.

Trees bend about to crack,
Beneath the load of snow and ice,
That make strange and different
shapes,
Through the distant moonlight.

You can see them sparkle.

They must be tired by now;
As the melting sun shines.

Bare still with such character,
Yet they come alive, each bud new,
Awaiting the arrival of spring.

At once each bud unfolds;
One by one they're opening up,
Feeling a little mellow,
On a mystical, magical day;
Going through steps—

TO FINISH THEIR EVERLASTING
DESTINY.

Rosalind D Rucker
WAITING
There she sat alone
sitting by the telephone
waiting for a call
but didn't get one at all
why didn't he call?

Thomas O McFarland
GOLDEN WINDOWS
Oh do not think that we alone pursue
The conquering of matter as our goal,
The counting up of dollars as our
due,
For some of us admit we have a soul.

It may be true we try our best to fit
The Universe in this Procrustean
bed—
That we must weigh and measure bit
by bit
The things and forces of the world we
tread;

That we must analyze the micro-
world
Of atoms, and the macro-world of
stars;
That we must probe the deep in
which is hurled
That energy which vivifies or chars—

Yet there are some of us whose
interests run
To golden windows in the setting
sun.

Tamra Stewart
MY CHILDREN

This poem is dedicated to Shea, Drew and Reed.

I bless the day you were born and
I marvel each day, how three little
boys could affect me in such a
positive way. Your faces are lights
sent from heaven above that I look at
everyday and a reminder to always
continue to walk in His way.

Florie Dorio
CROOKED TREE
This crooked tree and me,
We sit quietly by the sea,
The wind blows softly through her
branches,
Like lazy fingers it entrances
A bird sings a quiet tune
To let me know it is close to noon,
Before I know he is joined by more
Of his singing friends

And even sea gulls hear their call
They come from everywhere one and all
The cool breeze flows softly thru the air
To let me know that spring is here,
The sweetness of the dewy scent,
Brings memories of my early youth,
Of days gone by beside a brook,
I knelt beside the water's edge
To dream of dreams that would
Descend in years
Of passing my dreams out to you
Here would be all the birds and
Freedom for me,
When I look upon my beloved sea
Underneath my crooked tree.

Florie Dorio
HAPPY ANNIVERSARY
Just as hand in hand you two began
Your married life and found no greater joy
Than being man and wife
In sharing little things
That love and marriage brings
So many hopes and dreams
The gift of love; the gift of faith—
Of happiness and laughter
And the countless precious memories
That will last forever
May all your dreams come true as you have planned
Never too old to hold each other's hand—
So together, hand in hand
May we wish you both the finest things in life and happiness
Than you have ever known
Our warmest congratulations
May health and love and happiness follow you both
On this special Anniversary.

Cedean Robinson
CHAIN
Choo Choo Choo
Choo Choo Choo
This thing will never change,
bring all your fatuity
to an end,
for the subject is not roses.

Puff Puff Puff
Huff Huff Huff
Did one say, who cares.
Not one no not one,
so why blare . . .
Chicken bones in ash trays;
Butts under foot,
Smog over head,
and we cannot help
but be dead.
Go-on Go-on
Rasp
Rasp
Rasp
They collapsed Rasp
and some were passive.

Harold E J Friedrichs
A MESSAGE OF ETERNAL YOUTH
Youth is like springtime
A time of perfume, flowers and merry escapades
When stalwart youths and courtly maidens consort
Ambitions run high and future plans are made
Young folks would like to think those days would never end
Yet they know without being told
That someday they will grow old
While elderly people too often contend
That they have lived their lives
Time no longer for aspirations or fresh hopes
So they just idle around, reminiscent or mope
Yet wise men down through the ages have stressed
The glorious prospect of eternal youth
And sagaciously reveal
That no one is older than they look
Or younger than they feel
So look young; act young
Retain your life's interests
Stay fit and healthy too
Then the grim spectre of old age
Need never overtake you.

Donna Lynn Ferrero
KARIN & SANDY'S WEDDING
Today is your first day as man and wife
Today is the day you start your married life
May you always be as happy as you are today
Remember your wedding, a very special day

Tomorrow will come, off to St. Thomas you go
For eight great days of sightseeing, shopping, an occasional show
Your tomorrows will then begin, a routine comes your way
You'll both have to work, but don't forget to play

Always remember the love you two share
What you mean to each other and how much you care
Care enough that when a problem should come your way
You can talk it over together and solve it that day

Always be honest and truthful with each other
And you'll both never have a reason to run to another
Do all this for the rest of your days
And happiness will shower you both always

Love,
Donna

Melissa A Darville
LOVE LOST
I sit in the back pew, my eyes filled with tears
Looking at your bride so beautiful and sincere.
You're both holding hands making vows; mesmerized.

What do I do now since you're bound to her side?
As she walks down the aisle so gracefully and aglow,
My heart reaches out to her for her joy I too know.

I lick my lips but can only sense the flavour of my tears,
For my feelings are gone; my body is numb;
My soul died when you walked through that door.

Melissa A Darville
LETTING GO
I don't feel like crying it may drive me insane
For you gave me so much pleasure but you caused the most pain.
I don't feel like giving you up but in fact I already have; The moment I had doubts the day I walked out
But you gave the most joy you taught me how to smile
Still you took away my innocence I'm no longer a child.
But Love is not cheap you will have to repay.
It may not be me and it may not be today
When this someday occurs and you've experienced the things that I have. You will understand my turmoil you will know where I stand.
As long as we are together as long as it's only us, we'll make the perfect couple with nothing to come between us.
As long as we remain in our fantasy world with the troubles of life set aside we'll let happiness overwhelm us. Never to venture outside.
But only as long as the passion can last. As long as we both can dream. As long as romance can be our goal. These emotions we will feel.
The choice we now face, we'll have no guide no one to say we're right or wrong.
For it's only us who feel the pain, who'll face it all life long.
So what do we do? Do we start over again forming the rules to live by? Do we look for the spark that first drew us near, or whisper adieu with a fresh fallen tear?

Cathy Brimsacle

Cathy Brimsacle
ARE YOU REALLY THERE?

To my father, who has given me the inspiration that I needed.

My thoughts of you go on and on
As I sit here thinking of you while
you're gone.
I don't want you to be
Just a figment of my
imagination,
For you my friend, I am full
of appreciation.
Are you Really There? is
The question I ask myself,
Because if you aren't
then why do I care?

Courtney Brannon
SOMEONE

Dedicated to Armondo Parnalis the IInd: I love you.

My needs are small, my wants are few.
All that I need is someone who
Makes me laugh when I want to cry.
Someone who will care whether I live or die.
Someone to tell my problems to.
Someone to whisper "I love you."
Someone to reach out and touch my hand.
Someone to be there and understand.
Someone to lead me from darkness to light.
Someone to show me wrong from right.
Someone to love, honor, and trust.
These are the things that must be must.
All of these things I found in you,
My wonderful someone, my wonderful you.

Marilyn Oszustowicz
SAND MAN
No not me!
I shall not surrender to the sandman.
He comes to visit annually.
Leaving wasted speckles of sand scattered on my floor.
With a smirky smile,
eyes like balls of flaming fire.
Silently he calculates with hands as cold as ice.
Dropping the particles of sand one by one.
Second upon seconds,
Minute upon minutes.
I try desperately to catch them,
but they disintegrate with the warmth of my hands.
Cunningly he disappears with what remains left of my precious life.
No, not me!
I shall never surrender.

Jill Cookinham
LIFE

For my grandparents: William & Lena Rea.

Life is a very
serious deal.

Everything you do
affects it.

We celebrate life when,
it enters the world.

Cry when it
leaves.

Most people leave life
not knowing what
it is.

Brenda Emerick
MY MOTHER OF CHOICE
A Mother of choice, Is what You are to me,
Your kindness so gentle, just like I want to be.
The warmth of Your smile, the glee in Your eyes,
Is like the nurturing Love, of the clear sunny skies.

I'll never forget You, You're a part of my heart,
For this journey we're on, it was from the start.
I give You these words to hold deep inside,
Because what You gave me, is a whole lot of pride.

Thank You so much, You're so wonderful I know,
And I'll Love You always, more than You know.

Agnes Reece
THE OLIVE TREE
"I live to give food and rest,"
I hear the olive say—
'Twas my branch, so fair and green
The dove brought back that day

My name means love and peace—
My history is proud and old.
Jesus thought me a goodly tree
And in the Bible my story is told

God called my name—
And likened me to our Lord;
The Mount of Olives was named for me,
And I was Gethsamane's guard.

Food I give for the weary
And shade in the heat of the day—
And I bowed my head, thankful to serve,
As the Saviour knelt there to pray.

Gen. 8:11 Jer, 11:16 Hosea 14:6
Zech. 14:4 Matt. 26:30 Matt. 26:36

Robert W West
IT WAS THE NIGHT BEFORE CHRISTMAS
It was the night before Christmas
And I was carrying out the trash
As I reached the curb there was
A terrible crash.
I screamed, I hollered,
I prayed they would stop,
But those bastards with their
Carload of water balloons
Was spinning, spinning, spinning,
Like a top.
Yes the wreps are still on my ribs.
And yes, if I could have reached out
A little further I would have killed them.

Benjamin A Apogo

Benjamin A Apogo
THE LOST EDEN

To my late grandfather Casimir Apogo and Dr. Martin L. King, Jr., whose wisdom and insight have tremendously influenced my childhood and my views.

Yes indeed, Some happiness
rolled down from Zion,
for being up there
and behold the tremendous
work of his holiness.
That was fair!
For you should find,
as you sought to step inside creation.

Crowned with magnitude
for all these facilities,
it is true!
They have made my life slide blue.
Still I have a fear!
A fear of a threat,
a heavy threat of death.
And I need my mother here,
to have me in the shadow of her
womb, and survive the next nuclear
atrocities.

Can you hear
this prayer,
rising up from all nations
demanding change of direction?

Your complete victory will come
when you find the science,
stronger than politics;
science that will connect you with Him
and cease all tribulations,
science that will put together
my soul torn apart,
so that a new land emerges;
land where love and generosity grow
like the cactus in the desert sand.
land where freedom, justice and
peace flow
like the tides of an ocean.

Thus will GABRIEL descend
and strike up the golden trumpet:
"Glory Hallelujah
we got it back,
the LOST EDEN."
Thank GOD Almighty!

Ellen Chang
THE END
We say nope
To everything, everything but dope.
We think we're really cool,
But in reality we're really fools.
You know, everything bugs
Us all except drugs.
I'm depressed and sad
Right now and even though I know
what I'm doing is bad,
I don't know what to do, so
I try to kick my addiction.
I feel no sensation.
As I did before.
I'm sore
At everything and everyone.
This has cost me a ton.
But is it too late
To change my fate?

Russell Long
A WISH FOR MY SON, EDWARD . . .
Molded by your Father's hand—
An image of the same.
Looking like he did before,
You even bear his name.

Every father sees his son,
Himself, made young again;
Regained youth to race with LIFE,
And greater heights attain.

Lend your youth to me awhile,
Together we will run,
O'er the roughest roads of life,
'Til setting of the sun.

Even in the sunny youth,
Or in the twilight years,
Every father views his son
With laughter and with tears,

With a father's loving heart,
My wish for you, in time—
May you grow to be a man
And have a son like mine.

Russell Long
A TOUCH OF LOVE
Your love encircles all you touch
With warm and tender care.
You are a part of all I am
And all I hope to share.

Without your love, I'm incomplete,
A fragment of a man.
You give meaning to my life
That I can understand.

You came to me in innocence,
With all your love to give.
Your love reached out and touched
my heart
And taught it how to live.

And now we're one, together,
Our hearts in rhythm beat,
With all the joy and happiness
To make our lives complete.

Russell Long
WHILE YOU'RE AWAY, JENJER
Fingerprints upon the wall,
Mark the room in which you play.
Baby dolls, arranged with care,
Keeping watch while you're away.

Listening for your little voice,
As I look about the room;
Waiting for your happy laugh,
But there's none to clear the gloom.

How I miss your happy face,
And your loving, tender touch,
As you spread your arms and say,
"I love you Daddy! This much!"

How I miss you, Jenjer, dear,
And your little chatterbox.
How I miss your laughing eyes,
And your tiny golden locks.

I miss every part of you.
Of that fact, I cannot hide.
But, I'll wait for your return,
'Til, again, you're by my side.

Russell Long
ETERNAL MOMENT
If I could catch a moment,
I'd hide it 'neath my hat;
And choose just how to spend it,
But even more than that.
I'd wait the choosing moment
'Til you were kissing me,
And stretch that tiny moment Into
eternity.

Arthur Guy Cornish Jr
AS OF YESTERYEAR THERE WERE RAP
As of Yesteryear there were Rap Groups like Afrika Bambarta, Grandmaster Flash and The Furious Five, which later became Melly Mel and The Furious Five. Kurtis Blow and The Sugar Hill Gang.

In my conversations with some of the early Rap Groups like The Sugar Hill Gang and Kurtis Blow and Afrika Bambarta. It was interesting to learn and to know that they all studied their artform and that they knew, that Rap Music came from Jazz.

The Rap Groups of today seem to be unaware, of where, the artform came from.

The Rap Groups of today are Lisa Lisa, RoxAnne RoxAnne and LL Cool "J," Run Dmc, Joesky Love of The Pee Wee Herman Dance Craze. Doug E. Fresh and Cool Moe "D" and D. J. Jazzy Jeff and The Fresh Prince.

When one listens to the conversations of, the young brothers and sisters. Their conversations are of the New Rap Groups and their hit Rap Song.

Troy E Jones

Troy E Jones
STILLNESS OF THE DARK
The streets was dark and murky
the night air stood still, not a word
nor a sound only the whispers of the
harsh, steel, freezing wind that blew
through the empty street and
alleyways,

The air was composed with the
staleness of the shallow aroma that
reeks on the cold an unclean slab of
concrete

A dense haze of fog and the hot
compressed steam becomes a thin
white curtain that dimmed out the
city night's lights that one lite up the
outline of the crumbling demolished
structures of the past,

Emptiness is the night light of the
darkness and fear is in its time of
awakening the void of the deserted
night it is
the darkness an the wickedness of
the world own ends.

Troy E Jones
LET US
Come, my friends, let us mount
ourselves among our great steeds,
Let us strive them through the
decorative halls for they are treasure
and richness, to see,

Let us ride them through the palace
halls with their mane so brightly
shined, ride them through the royal
gardens whereforth the queen and the
king resides,

Run steeds, run, as if there was a fire
within your hearts, across the plains
among the flowery lands, into the
mountains for your freedom comes
within the hour,

The hour is at hand, it is time we set
you free over all others that dwell this
land, for one day we shall ride again,

Tom Mix
AND NO MAN IS THAT!
Standing alone in a peopled sea,
Believing no one is as sentient as he;
Guarding his outward look,
Fearing that some for prey, have him
mistook.
It is shallowly that he lives,
Materially and superficially he
gives—
And no man is that.
Finding solace in calloused veneer;

At those weaker others does he sneer.
No bona fides is the quarter
For how, when it means his slaughter?
And no man is that.
We who have seen him, know him better,
And he is the true regretter.
We, who are of the dove's wing,
Have yet the strength to pierce the thing—
And no man is that!

Frances Taylor Williams

SHE NEVER FORGOT HIM

It was a long time ago. After marriage, after the children.
Those who knew about it have long forgotten.
The years went by. The normal things happened.
But always he was on her mind . . .
Where was he? Who was he with?
Was he happy? Did he remember?
It never took much to painfully jog her memory . . .
A song, a voice, a name, a certain time of the year.
Didn't take much.
To see the outer woman you'd never know.
She lives, works, laughs, and does all the things that other people do.
But sometimes when she is alone she sits in her room and gathers her memories
'round her and thinks about what could have been.
She remembers . . . and she cries.

Christine Cox Burroughs

ALONE ON THE BEACH

Have you ever stood alone on the beach at night
When the moonlight is faint,
And the whitecaps rolling in
With all their majestic intensity
Radiate a glow you are humbled to behold?
With their exhilarating resonance
They mesmerize as they hasten to consume, then elude you;
Captivated by their fury, to be consoled by their serenity.
All the while you try to embrace the replete sensation of
Existing in unity with these mystical
breakers,
With all that is.
Have you ever stood alone on the beach at night
To realize you are never truly alone?

Ramona (Sprayberry) Smith

THE GENTLE GUIDE

First, she learns happiness
from a small stranger.
She begins to know responsibility
while caring for someone else.

In time she makes decisions knowing
she cannot always be right.
She must learn to soothe
hurt feelings and broken dreams.

She learns sacrifice
and the pain of mistakes.
There are many regrets
scattered among the years.

Lastly, she must learn wisdom—
and in knowledge, must let go.
Tears of sorrow and joy
are remembered, and understood.

These are but a few lessons
a woman must teach herself,
If she is to shape a child—
it is the labor of Motherhood.

Pamela Mitchell

AS I LIE HERE IN MY BED I REMEMBER THE GOOD TIMES WE SHARED

As I lie here in my bed I remember the good times we shared the love, laughter, pain and tears.
These wonderful moments of my life with my loved one who passed on.
These memories I have and always will cherish. I think of him all the time and I hope to see him again.
As I lie here in my bed I awake into another world, a world full of love happiness, no pain, no tears. I can see the beautiful white unicorns roam across the fields with a look of love in their eyes. I can see the flowers blooming, the birds singing, and I can hear the soft melodies of music playing. I can see a dark figure coming towards me. I can feel the warmth and love as I get closer and closer. It is the face of my loved one with a smile on his face. He reaches out his hand and says, "Now you'll never have to worry about losing me again for we shall always be together for eternal life in the house of God."

Pamela Mitchell

SHATTERED LIFE

At 15 my life was taken away by someone I adored my mother. She put me out in the street with no job or money.
Day by day I watched my life pass before me. I begged for money but nobody would help me. I lived like a bum. My body smelled from sweat as the sun beat on it. I was so skinny you could see my bones. I wouldn't even pick from the garbage. In the winter I couldn't move my toes they were so numb. I had icicles hanging from my hair. Day by day I was getting weaker and weaker. With what little energy I had left I crawled to the steps of my mother's door begging for help. She just looked at me and laughed. I had tears in my eyes wondering why she did this to me. I could still feel my heart getting weaker. I just looked up at my mother and said, "I love you anyway despite what you do." She just stood over me and watched me die.

Donald L Boozer

REMEMBERING MOM

I, remember the first time,
That, you held my hand—
And, you taking me outside,
To, play in the sand—
I, remember your kisses,
And, you combing my hair—
And, when I had a problem,
You, always was there—
I, remember me talking,
While, you tied my shoe—
And, you never interrupting,
Until, I was thru—
I, remember a thousand things
These, are only a few—
But, mom, they're all special,
And, they'll all about you—

Donald L Boozer

A REAL CHRISTMAS

On December the 25th,
We, call it our Christmas day—
We all buy pretty presents,
And we give them away—
We, laugh and we have fun,
We're all nice to one another—
And, we always thank Santa,
And, our father, and mother—
But, Jesus just this year,
And, in our own special way—
The, whole world wants to wish you,
A, Happy Birthday.

Mrs Charlene Daugherty

DARLING HUSBAND

Dedicated to my loving husband, Chuck and my two beautiful children Matt and Kelley. You've all made my life so worthwhile. I love you all.

I love you oh so very much
My heart is filled with love for you
Just to feel your warm touch
And know what we have is special and true

To look into your loving eyes
To feel your tender lips
Lying under sunny blue skies
Caressing your skin with my fingertips

The day we exchanged our vows
Is the day we started our lives together
Our love is simple without why's or how's
It will grow and last forever

You my Darling Husband and lover
Are the light of my life
Making love in the sweet clover
I know it's wonderful to be your wife.

Lucille L Webster

Lucille L Webster

SUDDENLY OLD

I've found since I have grown with age,
My life has turned another page.
I look at things I've seen before
And now they seem to mean much more.
A lovely bud just burst in bloom,
In beauty shines and waits its doom.
A child is born, a kitten, a bird,
Each tiny voice I've many times heard.

Yet my heart beats quickly with each sound,
As if a new and wonderful thrill I've found.
A piece of music my thoughts can fill,
That all around me life grows still.
My eyes grow fixed upon a star,
That looks so near and yet so far,
And many friendships held through the years,
Of everything else they are most dear.
As all these pages in life unfold,
Can it be possible I'm growing old.

Suzanne Cameron

A SMALL CHILD IS WEEPING

Late at night, when everyone is sleeping,
It's then that I hear a small child weeping.
Ever so soft so that no one will hear,
That someone will know is her biggest fear.
The secret she's buried so deep in her heart,
The bad thing that happened to set her apart.
Is it somehow written on her tiny face?
This thing that happened another time and place.
She can't tell anyone, they'll say she's to blame.
So all alone she must live with the shame.
She did not want or ask him to touch her.
But somehow she caused it, is what they'll concur.
She shouldn't have taken the candy he had to offer,
Or ride in his car so she'd get a quarter.
So, late at night, when everyone is sleeping,
Only I can hear this small child weeping.
I know about her secret and her agony,
Because that little girl lives inside of me.

Carol A Schweickert

YOUR ANSWER, MY STEPHANIE

Love is two, makes one and a hundred around makes none.
Love is time standing still while the hours rush by.
Love is happy while tears flow down your cheeks.
Love is walking blind and seeing beauty.

Love is going through obstacles because there are none.
Love is standing in a bare field, being in paradise.
Love is peaceful with a racing heart full of excitement.
Love is walking in the rain and feeling the sun.
Love is near and holds you close when he is far.
Love is rushing ahead to let her go first.
Love makes plain, pretty.
Love is you and I and we and all around me.
Love needs no answers and if there is a question, it is not love, but your answer.
Love is selfish and gives to only one and is giving in every way spreading itself to everyone.
Love is passion desire and longing, but is patient and waits for its promises.
For love is tomorrow when it's only today.

William A McDaniel
WORRY WART ADVICE

Just because we're getting gray
It don't mean that we are old
You're just as old as you feel today
That's why we stay young and bold

We may have wrinkles in our flesh
And brown spots on our skin
But our minds' thoughts very young
And we have enjoyed where we've been

We may have more years behind us
Than you will ever see
But that's because we never were
The worry warts you seem to be

We've always lived for just today
Yesterday's gone for good
Tomorrow we'll take as it comes
And love our neighbors as we should

Getting old is not the problem
That people face today
It's wanting what others have
And failing again to pray

Antoinette and Richard Keen

Antoinette Keen
SUCCESS

I dedicate this poem to my loving husband Richard Albert Keen who has supported me in all my devotion to "successful poetry."

At home we listen to succeed,
For our parents teach us as a tot.
That work is how we learn to feed,
Success comes next when work is hot.

Achievement to some is not a need,
Trying for them will hit the spot.
Eating now and planting the seed,
They never care to be top.

In history books we do foretell,
That many men have reached success.
Authors who write about them sell,
Since successors knew how to give their best.

A desire to write and spell,
Is a step in search for success.
Good education first is what they tell,
Begins that need to strive for best.

Antoinette Keen
TRUE LOVE

A lover's care with listening ears,
An open arm wanting your touch,
A love so strong it cannot fear,
A love so near it's at your touch.

A happy face, a trust so true,
A contentment of a caring heart,
A commitment is not instant, onßly to a few,
As true love grows within the heart.

A true heart outshines all blues,
As it forgives and reunites,
As it grows tighter to bond like glue,
And hugs away trouble and worrisome fights.

A survival instinct for many years,
A constant need for eternal bliss,
An approaching love may come near,
And stray you to happiness with a loving kiss.

Ruth A Hall
AT THE WINDOW

We ought to be
at the window to see
into infinity.
From a quiet space
on Earth's homeplace
or away from Earth
in a spacecraft berth,
we need to see
the outer-space sea,
to voyage or dream,
to wonder or scheme.
The pull is strong
and the need, lifelong
to know the universe.
We only rehearse
what this day we know—
in the afterglow—
of God's window show.

Angie Messinger
LOVE GAMES

You say you love me
Then leave me again.
Stop playing these love games
Where I never win.
I thought when I met you
Your feelings were true.
You said that you loved me
If only I knew.
So when you get bored, desperate or down,
Don't come running to me
I won't be around.
Because love's not a game
Where the winner is you,
Love's an emotion, shared by two . . .

Stacy Pereira
WHEN OCEANS MEET

I dedicate my poem "When Oceans Meet" to my boyfriend and friend Treve Williams.

When day falls and night arrives,
it sets the evening for certain vibes.
The two come together in mystery,
from dawn to dusk like you and me.
When two oceans meet to form a sea of dark blue,
it's fate from with in like when I had met you.
No questions asked too hard to understand,
like the difference between water and land.
I was down and feeling blue,
then before my eyes appeared you.
Too perfect I said with a smile on my face,
but who am I to question the human race.
You came like a star from the darkest sky,
in my vocabulary now there's no room for goodbye.
We met like a dream that has already come true.
When two oceans meet that's how I met you.

Herbert Filer Sr
THE EYES OF A WOMAN

The eyes of a woman, are the limpid pools of her life
That can't hide the love, the bitterness, the strife
They are shielded and guarded, so you can't see within
But if you watch close, you'll see a spark of interest begin
As she looks at you in an appraising way
You may catch a glimpse, of her inner garden, so bright, so gay
If ever the gates are open and she motions your way
Take heed of a beauty, so hidden, so rare
Stay on the pathway, and show that you care
Don't crush the blossoms, that are hidden within
Or the eyes will change and regard you no more
The gates will be closed, with a lock on the door
To hide from you this beauty, so wonderous, so rare
And the love of a woman, who will never again care

Herbert Filer Sr
A BLANKET OF WHITE

To Dorothy with Love, Herb. To Sharon with Love, Dad. To Lynne with Love, Dad. To Terry with Love, Dad.

The Trees All Covered In A Blanket of White
First Snow of The Season A True Delight
It's God's Own Beauty As Everyone Knows
He's Putting On One Of His Spectacular Shows
Light Wind Whistling, Thru The Tree Boughs
The Light Laughter of The Children
The Roar of The Plows
Sleds on The Hills, Snowball Fights Galore
Tracked In Snow, To Be Swept Back Out The Door
It's Beautiful To See, Lovely To Know
How Much The World Can Enjoy Itself, With God's First Snow
No Money Changed Hands, No Deals were Lost
When You Look Outside, You Really Know Who's BOSS

Herbert Filer Sr
A CHARLATAN, A FLAKE

I'll probably be best remembered for being a Flake
A Charlatan—A definite Fake
I haven't been the best of Husbands to either of my wives
I really never brought too much of anything into anyone's lives
The best one can say as far as I am concerned
Is that I liked animals, and those I had as friends I never spurned
I was and am hard to live with, that's for sure
Living with me is more than most people could ever endure
But I know in my heart as no one else ever will
That the love that I had and have for those close to me
Like Dorothy, and Rae, and Sharon, Terry, and Lynne,
Is something special that only comes from within
So maybe I really am not so great—boy is this ever true
But believe me you people, that I mentioned here-in
It has been thru you that makes my life worth livin'
For I hold you all near and dear, and fill myself with pride
Just to think that a worthless old coot like me, could have
such wonderful people on his side . . .
Love To You All

Francesca Gray

Francesca Gray
BIRTH

Thank you for being there, Paul Jonas Tyler and Jessica.

A small bud appears
bringing with it all life
capturing the sun
pulling it out
capturing immortal time
each second
a breath more.
It reaches
it ascends

it becomes cloud with sky
it becomes grass with earth
it becomes man with life.
We reach
for always we reach
for in the reaching we learn
we grow.

Denise Zampella
LITTLE BLACK GUN
I flirted with you, but just as a friend.
I never thought you'd be hurt in the end.
Hate me with a passion, call me a bitch. But believe it or not, this is a switch!
I know how you feel and what you went through. Think what you want, but I loved you too.
I never meant to cause any pain. And after this things can't ever be the same.
I know you cared and I cared too.
And because of this, we're both feeling blue.
I know what I did was very wrong.
And I cried till my eyes burned, but I must be strong.
What should I do, should I run away?
No that's no good, I have to stay.
I wish I never committed this sin. I wish we could start over again.
So did you, that's why you came. But you were too late, the damage was done.
I had just pulled the trigger, on the little black gun.

Barney Groat
THE LEGACY
Alone, undaunted by seemingly impossible odds he endures. He stands at ready. He is a warrior.

His limited world revolves around his wife, his children, his family, his friends. For their dreams, and their rights are his also.

Use caution when you must cross his path, for within him burns a raging fire — a power waiting for the smallest spark to unleash it.

The great spirit Equality is like the fresh rain and snow that can dampen fires, for even raging infernos yield to the will of this great spirit.

Outsiders acknowledging this great spirit, walk proudly in the Warriors land. Never taking from but adding to his limited world — gaining for themselves an insight of their own world.

To all others that scorn the existence of this great spirit—May you in your world, meet and unleash the fires of many, many Warriors as you journey to Erebus.

Paul Kaplowitz
OLD MAN'S LAMENT
There are all sorts of old-age signs.
Just to begin,
The hair grows thin,
The face and neck are full of lines.

You've lost your sense of taste and smell
Your eyes grow dim—
You're stiff of limb,
It's rarely that you feel half well.

Time hangs heavy on your hands.
You sit and stare
At anywhere.
It seems that life makes no demands.

You know that once upon a time
You'd meet a gal
Who'd be a pal.
And you'd engage in games sublime.

But now you're old and gals won't play.
You make a pass—
They give you sass
And haughtily look the other way.

Marjorie Henderson and Judge Dorothy Carson

Marjorie Henderson
MALCOLM FORBES' PARTY

To Elizabeth Taylor, the most beautiful woman in the world, and my own "National Velvet," my granddaughter, Melissa Renee.

I dreamed I went to this party
Malcolm Forbes was there
He didn't see Liz Taylor
He only saw my hair
There I was sitting
In the very last row
Who asked me to dance
The King of Monaco
As we whirled about the room
I heard this funny rip!
Oh no! It couldn't happen now
My panty hose they split!
I'll back into the kitchen
To see what I can do
My gosh! Steve Garvey!
This will never do
News reporter Cronkite,
Smith, and Walters too!
Calvin Klein was wearing five-o-ones
He was sitting next to whose-who!
That's when Lee Iacocca drove up
Hey! "That's my Toyota, you got there!"
And I don't like it one bit!
When Dolly wears my hair
There were acrobats, jugglers,
Belly dancer too
Here I was holding up my panty hose
God what am I goin' to do?
Better hide, here comes Ann and Abby
Boy, that Kissinger really did stare
Guess he never saw a crutch before
But I had to hang on to my hair.

Willa M Kramer
MOTHER
To my Mother, Heaven bless her,
I would pledge my love anew.
To the one whose loving guidance
Taught me to be brave and true.
Altho we love to chatter
With a comrade or a friend,
When we find ourselves in trouble,
'Tis on Mother, we depend.

She is always glad to listen,
Bravely speaking words or cheer
Her true worth cannot be measured,
I can find no words, I fear;

That express the love she bares me,
That explains her heart of gold,
Nor the selfless loving service
Rendered, as the years unfold.

All the sleepless nights of watching
As she strokes a fevered brow;
With a prayer that in his mercy,
God would spare her child, somehow.

We are still to her but children,
Hers to fondle and caress,
No matter what the age be,
To her we are the best.

So for my dear, Sweet Mother
I ask a prayer each day,
That all my tender thoughts unspoken,
Be conveyed to her some way.

Dolly M Bertram
THE COMING OF NIGHT
When sunset in her golden glow,
Descends from out the sky,
When the moon appears high in the west
We know that night is nigh.

When crickets chirp their drowsy song,
Into the air so clear,
When owls hoot out their welcoming
We know that night is near.

When flowers droop their dewy heads,
And nod to all those near
When the Angelus rings through the air
We know that night is here.

Mrs Rosanta Vallone

Mrs Rosanta Vallone
TO WHOM I LOVE . . .

To my loving husband Pasquale Vallone, whom I love and adore always.

With my love I find a new peace an offering sent by doves.
With my love I give my whole being a symbol of spirit formed by the stars.
And, when I confess my dreams, and desires he'll hold my eternity for just a little while.
For all creation of sky and sea upon highest mountains the rhythm speaks.
Through all the earth the mind and soul can only wish a distant taste for joys unknown.

Mrs Rosanta Vallone
WHAT IS TIME?
Is time a form or chemistry
a language taught by God.
Does time require life form
or does it go beyond.

I find time
day time
let's make time
play time.

Tick tock goes the clock
just like the human heart.
Some slow some faster
time forward time after.

And let's say we always worry
are we too late, are we too early.

It's about "time"! we're discussing
"Excuse me do you know what time . . . is?"

Yes I can guess what time it is
in numbers.
No I just can't sell or place a finger on it, but can anybody.

Yet one thing's clear
far too many do hard time
wishing to buy time
but there's no time to spare.

Rich and poor young and old can't stop time.
Teachers teach and science explores, but the facts are in front of us.

Time and the universe are one
and the only marriage known is earth and sun.

Mrs Rosanta Vallone
ON THE WINGS OF A BIRD
I often watch birds fly with treasured wings I'd long to buy.

Their symmetry and grace fulfills dimensions of the human race.

But, man's desires can't be judged as a thunderous spark of crashing colors.

Yet fading in the skies the wings of dreams never die.

Mrs Rosanta Vallone
BUSY CITY STREET CORNERS
A man with a hat in his hand stands on the streets.

Sings his heart out for everyone to watch and listen.

The songs were odd that he sang was it folk, gospel or something.

I approached close enough to look in his eyes, yet found not sadness, but a gleam of pride.

How very humble this man must be, happy with life and to beg on the streets.

Feeling sorry for this poor old chap I threw a dollar in his hat.

And when I started to walk away something inside made me stay.

"Where shall I go, who shall I be if only love could set me free."

These words in his song echoed right through my soul, what seemed more colorful then a rainbow.

Steve Meiring
TWO PATHS CROSSING
Two paths cross, cause and effect yet unknown
forever altering each course, if only slightly.

Two souls, So much alike yet so very different
searching for happiness from opposite points in reality.

Two wills, Strong and independent, expecting too much
not just of each other, but of the world.

Two people, hesitant and unsure, knowing that we need each other
if just to maintain our sanity.

Two hearts, caring and warm, yearning to be loved
yet afraid of a memory.

Two minds, learning with each day, anticipating every moment we could share
searching for our dreams, no matter how distant.

Two lives, intertwined, with one realization,
Fate does not always allow need or desire to control the direction
of two paths crossing.

Edna Kleis
GOD SPEAKS TO ME
The songwriter said—
"It's such a pretty world today."
And as I looked out on the beauty of the tree
With its crystal white snowy limbs, I agree.
God certainly speaks to me.
He speaks to me in every blade of grass
in every tree
in every flower
in every drop of water
in every grain of sand
God is speaking to me.
Yes, God speaks to me
in the blue of the sky
in the dark of the night.
He speaks to me—

I don't have to see His face
Nor hear His voice.

I know God speaks to me.
In the quietness, He speaks to me
In the morning hours, He speaks to me
In the beauty of the sunrise or sunset
He speaks to me.

In the intricacies of a new life, He speaks to me.
In the love of a good man, He speaks to me.
In the love of a child, He speaks to me.
In the whisper of the wind,
In the movement of cloud,
In the sigh of the river
He speaks to me.
Yes, in the heart of a friend
He speaks to me.

I hear you God.

Barbara Borgstadt
CHILDHOOD FRIENDS
I remember years ago
Our childhood times are gone:

I remember friends of past,
That's lost touch as days lead on:
Little things I still remember,
Of times that's come to pass,
Little things of yesteryears,
Of dreams we thought would last:

Friends they say will come and go
And we know that is true
But childhood friends are friends that last:

In memory they stay with you.

Laura O'Sullivan
TIME AND WIND
Through the rustling winds blow
the knowledge that celestial spirits surround us so,
I watched and waited for an endless time
A time that I had no control for,
It was what needed to be passed
And now like a window opened in a corridor
An opening for the rush of a wished for new wisdom.
Now lying in waiting for clues,
I open my heart for news of any spiritual friends
To those that have passed
and lie in waiting
I pursue and follow you.

Suzanne Coleman
TEARDROP WINE
Lying back across my bed
Staring into melting space,
My mind steps back to yesternight
To remember a certain face.

A face whose handsome, glowing smile
Makes my whole world shine.
A face so clear within my mind,
Like teardrops mixed with wine.

Tears that caress the soul with passion,
Trembling, I close my eyes.
The silent knowledge of his being
Weighs heavily on my mind.

Hearing him whisper in my ear
Like music soft in sound,
Fills me with exhilarance,
My heart begins to pound.

Now, as I open up my eyes,
I see that he's not here.
But I feel the essence of the wine
Distilled with lover's tears.

Suzanne Coleman
FOR GEOFF
I am a fountain of sheer ecstasy. Look at me and I tremble anxiously for even your slightest touch. Pour your sensuality over me like water from a rock and I will respond likewise, as a reflection from a mirror.
The soft, penetrating tone of your voice enlightens me, inspires me, draws me with an inner force, as the rich heart of the sea is drawn to its naked shore. Its powerful waves pounding heavily with the climax of but stroking the sandy breast of the golden shoreline as we come together in blended radiance.
And I am a searing flame, burning with desire. My provocative mind races wildly with erotic thoughts of you as I desperately long for you to be holding me, loving me, thrusting deep within the comfort of my sultry depths with the mastery of intense, prodigious passion.
Lover, keep me with you always.

Suzanne Coleman
LOVE AT DAWN
I awaken to nothing but the sound of a distant train whistle, as the Sun of morning's dawn has not yet ascended the skies.
Stillness,
Darkness.
But not loneliness, for the sweetness of last night's dream still lingers in my slumbering thoughts.
I knew my love has not yet awakened, for he sleeps soundly. And though I am not with him this morning to watch him, I can still picture his handsome face and his serene expression as he lies so still. His masterful body lying with arms open and just the delicious thought of it entices my seductive mind deeply,
Wholly,
Unwaveringly.
The scintillating rays of the Sun now shine through and morning's first hour has bestowed its light upon me
Noiselessly,
Calmly.
And with more assurance of my being alive, for I have awakened more.
Through the cracks of the curtains in his room, the Sun heartily greets my love who still dreams. Who still lies in an unfolding position. And as I picture him this morning in my solemn thoughts, I wish to be near him. To feel his powerful arms around me. To hold him and to love him so that my loving him outside would reach him inside.
Passionately,
Deeply.
The Sun beats down even brighter as my love awakens. His manly being now aware of the things which surround him. I am, as before, not yet with him as I wish to be constantly,
Endlessly,
Waitingly.
I wonder if he awakens with the thought of me each morning as I do with thoughts of him as I lie in bed in solitude. I wonder if this beautiful man knows the times I've watched him sleep so sweetly. I wonder if he gets lonely—enough to almost cry as I do sometimes when he is away from me
and the night is so still and
So dark.
So empty.
Yet so crowded with the wishes of a brighter tomorrow when I'll see him once again. And, as always, I'll smile and feel rushes of happiness and a strange feeling deep inside. The same stimulating feeling I have whenever I'm very close to him—so close, I can feel his heart beat
Softly,
Penetratingly.
The way I love to feel him inside me and every other breath of ecstasy I take says, "I love you."
I wonder if he knows how many times I've told him that without saying it aloud. Or how wonderful I thought he was so many times before. Or how happy I am just to see his face and to hear his voice. And to reach out in rapture to hold him in my arms.
Assuringly,
Lovingly.

Earnest B Haynes
THE DESIROUS ATTRACTIONS OF A STONE HEART
A secret spins within her heart
Like the horrific speed of a tornado
A strange passion lies dormant within her heart
Yielding to outcries
Locked away from life most challenging experiences
Plays too low

The sweetest word combinations fails to open the
Vault of her heart
A voice so sultry that set the mind's eyes afire
Lured to a place, where nothing is gained from what
Being taught
Explosive feelings are release and you're caught
Up in the desire

The love interest you seek, shows no emotions of your fate
Simply hovering above pulling you slowly into her maze
The mind says take precautions, but the flow of
Her passion was too great
The caverns of her heart so dimly lit, seems to flourished
The desire into a baffling craze

Her heart seeking talents so spellbound seeps upon your design
Building an attachment without shocks
She saunters her affections, plays with your mind
Blinding the bumps and the sudden mood swings, here she flocks

Within in the webbed texture of her lair
Malfunctioning, you're drawn to her heart of stone
A place of no return, no emotions or warnings you should fear
Satisfied, her desires quenched, there she leaves a drone

Harriett R Wilson
EULOGY
Do not stand at my grave and weep,
I did not die, I only sleep,
I am the singing snags, and the winds
That blow, in the mountains high.
The Eagle soaring in the sky,
The bugle of the Elk in Fall,
The forest so straight and tall,
The salmon that run in the spring
The beautiful birds and the songs they sing.

Never think of me and weep,
For I did not die, I only sleep.

Bill R Howey
THE LIGHT
Eons of light
Brightly acknowledging the heavens

The fragrance of a rose
Sweetly settles upon the dew at dawn
A child is born
While at dusk, a man dies
Heaven's doors are open
Seemingly to give or receive
Life stepping into or out
Of what we know is life
Only the light can reach beyond
And touch what is known, but yet unknown
For wicked are the ways of many
They shall never reach beyond
For the light will reckon a judgement day
The light brings forth life
Eternally; some will receive their just reward
For as the light
Their souls will reach heavens beyond
For once in blindness
They saw the light

Bernice Yust Dack
A PARADOX?
Old Father Time, I am wondering who and what you really are
Your todays are an uncompleted puzzle to us, your tomorrows a mystery
Are you a paradox—you're as close as my wristwatch, yet distant as a star

I suppose God is the only one who has you all figured out
You cannot fool Him or surprise Him as you roll on and on
All your yesterdays, todays, and all your tomorrows He knows all about

Are you a foe—you wait for no one as you go on your merry way
Some people say you show no patience, mercy, or justice
When you cause them to become ill, old, all wrinkled and grey

Oh yes, it is true, our beauty and youth you always steal
But you are a friend to us when death takes away our loved ones
Our broken hearts and weary minds, you always help to heal

I know you never stop, you are on the go all the while
But oh how I wish you could stand still for me
Like when I can see God's Heaven in a little baby's smile

Or when I see a perfect rainbow of beauty kissing the ground
Or when I am out in the wide open spaces when a perfect dawn is breaking
With only God and His wonders all around

If I had but two wishes to ask you to grant to me
One would be to take me back with you and let me live again
In those days when I was a child, always happy and carefree

Before I knew about all the bad things in life
Like murders, child abuse, racial prejudice, and drugs
Wars, unhappiness, loneliness, misery, and strife

The other wish would be—with the whole world please remain
So you can clean it up, body and soul
So Jesus will be pleased with us
when He returns to earth again

Linda Debra Haspel
COLORS

To Peter Max, an artist whose use of color inspired me to write "Colors." With much admiration, Linda Debra Haspel.

Scan the world at a glance
  Vibrant intoxicating colors
Rhythmically dancing in trance

Taste the palette of pastels, so sweet
  Sherbets icy rapture
Peach, lemon and lime each a treat

Dig the earthy soil of the desert, so deep
  Gravy of the ground
Jar it just to keep

Grab the friendly brights, so sunny never mellow
  Children playing Parcheesi
"I'm blue," "I'm red" and "I'm yellow"

Brenda Smith
SEA

I love to look at the clear blue sea. The reflection of the sea reminds me of me.

When I look at the sea, I see boats lining the docks. And when I go walking along the shore of the sea, I sea clams and rocks.

The sea has a mystique all its own. When the color of the sea shows its tone.

All in all, the sea is a wonderful place to be.

Linda Gaye Langford
FORTY POUNDS OVERWEIGHT
I would be the happiest person around,
if I could just lose this forty pounds.
The devil has a hold on me,
dear Jesus, make him set me free.

I feel so ugly in all my clothes,
they no longer hide my rolls.
My body aches with unhealthiness,
my whole anatomy is just a mess.

With God's help, I can lose this weight.
I really wanna fit through the pearly gates.
So Satan get out, I rebuke you now!
I totally refuse to look like a cow.

Lani Elyse Hudson
FLOW

Dedicated to all struggling artists whose only two strongholds are God and the belief in the quality of their work.

Disembarking one's life from the mediocrity of ritualistic day-to-day niceties,
One finds a world of harmonious structures, free-flowing spirals, and interlocking pivots,
In the imagination—the extrapolating beams of light and color traversing and interweaving through the artist's mind.
Reams of kaleidoscopic fantasies drifting briskly across rapturous tide pools,
Saturation levels filling completely,
Succinctly,
Gloriously,
Flowing over into breezes of spring winds,
Near Chinese pavilions on mountaintops,
At our most contented moments.

Geraldine A Green
I PROMISE
I promise to always love you
Be the one that understands,
Make your dreams come true
Loving and holding your hand.
I promise to see each tear
And wipe it from your eye,
If you are downhearted
To hold you when you cry.

I promise to give my love
So much I long to do,
Never want to see you lonely
Because I'll be loving you.

I promise to be faithful
Be a lover and a friend,
Put happiness in your life
Loving you till the end.

I promise to be understanding
My love will never change,
It will be this way forever
In our sunshine and rain.

I promise to be there for you
Looking for strength from above,
And no matter what the storm
Asking God to bless our life with love.

Joel W Hartsell
BEHIND CLOSED DOORS

To all my family & friends at "Lee St. Mem. Bapt. Church," Baltimore, MD.

Though my days are always lonely,
And my nights are always long.
Though my eyes are filled with tears,
My heart is filled with song.

But I pray to Jesus daily,
For to dry my tears away.
And to come into my heart,
For to guide me day by day.

And to have Jesus at my side,
And his love within my heart.
Is all I will ever need,
For his love will never part.

And I pray and thank him daily,
For his blessings evermore.
For making life much easier,
To live "behind closed doors"

Patricia Ann Pope
RAINDROPS

This is dedicated to a loving family indeed for I see the beauty in them; Hugh Sr. and Jr., Barbara, Debbie and little Michele.

Raindrops clear and pure falling on the windowpanes
quiet and silent, calm and peaceful.
Raindrops see and saw falling on the windowpanes.
Raindrops dance and step, move and change falling
on the windowpanes.

Raindrops talk to me like night and dark, fair and pale,
loud and high until foreverness.
Raindrops bright and shine, falling on the windowpanes.
Raindrops transparent and clear, blanched and fade
falling on the windowpanes.

Raindrops talk to me like night and dark, fair and pale,
loud and high until foreverness.
Raindrops present and here, falling on the windowpanes.
Raindrops blink and wink, giggle and laugh falling
on the windowpanes.

Raindrops talk to me like night and dark, fair and pale,
loud and high until foreverness.
Raindrops new and brilliant falling on the windowpanes.
Raindrops high and peak, lots and many, falling
on the windowpanes.

Raindrops talk to me like night and dark, fair and pale,
loud and high until foreverness.
Raindrops keep falling, dropping, falling on the windowpanes.

Patricia Ann Pope
THE SPLENDOR OF YOU

To the Pope family with love.

Red with small green leaves and a large red satin bow tied to the vase, a dozen roses. They're here to make you smile for me on any occasion. The beauty of them shows I care for you. Something about your smiling face now shows every part of you. Overwhelmed by the beauty of them makes you glow for several days, enough to let you see yourself as beautiful as you are. A smile that says a million words shows for me and never goes away. I know your smile means I love you, always showing every part of you. A picture of your cheerfulness brings joys to my heart as you glow and glow about the red roses. They tell me that you'll smile for me red with small green leaves and a large red satin bow tied to the vase. For roses let you see yourself smiling for me, smiling for me. The difference in you came as quite a surprise as you studied the beauty of them. They took away the tautness in your face, drawn and in despair lost of all hope. And gave you back your youthfulness, which just appeared to me. The roses caused your cheerfulness and glowiness showing every part of you.

Joanna Hannigan
FUNERAL FRIENDS
A sadistic shard
  of saccharin sentimentality
  lay lost
On my plebeian pillowcase
  with grasshopper gobs
  of saliva;
Funeral train time
  marooned and maligned
  this serrated night.

Sharon Lynn Sloan
ENDLESS LOVE
My love for you just won't die
No matter how much you make me cry
I don't understand why you treat me like this
When you know that having you is my only wish.
I gave up the love of my life just for you
Hoping just by chance what you told me could be true.
I'm all through trying
Because your love for me you keep denying
Don't say that it's not true
Because you were the one that said I love you!!
I was a fool and fell for your line
Knowing deep down it was a lie the whole time.
If you get hurt again you have only one to blame
You wouldn't listen and it's really a shame.
You shouldn't flaunt her in my face
Because I'm just waiting for the right time and place.
She's not the only one to blame for this
Because you're in just as deep as she is.
I don't know what attracted me to you
It was probably your beautiful eyes of blue.
Everyone kept telling me I was making a mistake
I guess it was a chance I had to take.

Hector C Borghetty
IN MY MEMORY (COLORADO)
Still do I see,

The towering peaks—
The bright blue sky
That heavenly speaks.

Still do I feel,

The dry crisp air—
The golden sun
Without compare.

Still do I hear,

Those tumbling streams—
And murmur of pines,
Sweet music seems.

E're I recall

Each cool clear night—
With bracing air
And soft moonlight.

E're will I think

Of mountain thrills—
Of distant prairie
And glacial hills.

Land of color!=Colorado

O matchless clime—
E're will I know
That thou art mine.

Donna Fitzgerald
WEDDING WISHES
On this special occasion, we would like to express
Our best wishes and a lifetime of happiness
As you declare your intentions and utter your vows
Make the best out of life and all it allows
May the sun always shine in all kinds of weather
May the bells always ring whenever you're together
May the world be yours just for the taking
May you be as one yet never forsaking

Today we share in your marriage celebration
Today we submit to you our recommendation
Be kind, be true, be honest and forgiving
For a marriage without these is not worth living

On this special day, we raise our voices to sing
And wish you all the joy and fulfillment that love can bring
As friends we are honored to share in this occasion
As friends we accept with full participation

After today your lives will never be the same
After today you will both share the same name
For only through patience, understanding and love
Will your marriage be truly blessed by God above

Robert D Brooks III
ANGEL OF THE LOST CITY
This day is dark as he turns around
He can see the smoke and flames reach behind the gloomy skies

The bridges he built so long ago are burning behind him
His horsemen abandon him for he has lost the war

So sorrow fills the land
Where mighty walls of dreams once stood
Walking through valley walking through wood
The king abash kneels with a tear
Conjured shadows mock fear in the depth of the night
and chariots rise from the flaming gates of great Pandemonium

Looking to the midnight skies
Screaming an exile Exodus outcast or banishment am I

Silence the winter sun rises bound in chains broken
Thunder cracks the sky's anger not forgotten

He smiles he laughs fools freedom is mine
and so he mounts upon his wax and wings
That spread and take to flight with all the world to conquer
For all the world is mine

Robert D Brooks III
APPLES
Eden was beautiful
Even more so with you
For you were of Heaven
a gift from great God
But Eden has long since passed from us
Yet when I look within your eyes
I can still see its reflections
'Cause you are all I have left of it
For we have not passed from each other

Gertha Foster
THE TRAMP ON THE RAILROAD
Along the railroad track he moved
With weary steps and slow
Just a tramp homeless, alone
And nobody cared to know.
Long fallen by the wayside
No priestly robes he wore
Smiling now he looked toward
The church upon the hill
The train bell rang loudly
But he seemed not to hear
Too late forward he fell
Dying, but beautiful he lay
Faith has no gold nor silver
It has its own reward
Always in the end
The Master claims His own.

Annie Smart Maynor
REACH FOR THE SKY

Dedicated to my precious grandson Lawarnce Jackson Maynor.

January is a very usual month.
Looking at it beautiful scenery.
As you walk your route.
All difference things are looking up it seem.

As we walk along the things we might see.
The ground cover with snow.
Above the snow see standing tall weeds.
To the sky they may be reaching we don't why

Family reunion will start so will ours states.
We are pulling the same way on the rope.
All we have to give is ours weight.
Come reach for the sky and hope.

Each one have his are her way.
That the Lord way I don't know why
Everyone got to stand for what they say,
As we travel down the road looking at the sky.

As the sun rise over the hilltop
Like a big yellow ball bouncing over a mount.
It so beautiful you wonder if your heartbeat will stop.
If we could only reach up and touch these things we write about.

Stacy M Scott
HE SNEAKS THROUGH VELVET DARKNESS
He sneaks through velvet darkness in his quest.
Though made of iron, his heart is tender,
When ideas of love within his lover's breast
Are believed to be felt for another.
He hopes his suspicions are unfounded.
As he spies with dread, the house in the wood.
He approached quietly, his heart pounded
Calming his shaking as much as he could,
He reached out his hand and grasped the handle.
With a prayer on his lips, he cracked the door.
The room was small, the light from a candle
Chased the dark. Even though the light was poor,
Suspicions that were unfounded before,
Were found to be unfounded no more.

The Lonely Dreamer
NATURE'S COURSE
So beautiful, the things I see,
as nature takes its course again.
The sun just above the trees,
the wild out searching for a new friend.
The water is so still and calm,
with reflections of nature's beauty.
Holding all the precious moments,
for what seems like an eternity.
Day by day, night by night,
as the sun and moon take their turn.
Nature is noticed by millions,
bringing the smiles and happiness they yearn.
The warmth from the sun, the light from the moon,
the fresh smell of flowers,
satisfaction of the wild.
All the special feelings of nature,
our hearts and minds keep filed.
The beautiful course of nature,
so full of life—so wild and free.
As nature takes its course again,
it's all so beautiful to ME.

Anna Dales
WELCOME

This poem is dedicated to Brittany Susan Dales Our first grandchild.

What do you say to a new born child
Born to the world as my own grandchild
Welcome, let me hold you in my arms
That I may gaze at your face so angelic and calm
What do you say to a new born child
Welcome, you have wonderful parents in Ken and Sue
Who love and adore you as much as I do
What do you say to a new born child
Welcome, may your future be bright my dear Brittany
And may the woes of the world in your time become history

Lisa Naomi Stansbury
THE CHILD & THE FLOWER

To Faith, Joshua, Lynsi and Evan. I love you and those to come.

It's a flower—but to the child it represents life in a different light because the mother of the child said the flower lives, but the child knows that he lives too, and the flower doesn't look like him.

So in fascination, he touches the flower, but he doesn't want to hurt it, for he knows it live—though he doesn't know how.
When the child sees the rain wash the flower, he realizes the difference between himself and the flower. The flower's mother lets the flower play in the rain and when the sun comes out the flower is still there, but dry.

So the child stares in fascination at the dew on the petals and begins to understand the difference between the flower and himself:

the Flower can live outside always.
And in that discovery,
the child cries. His tears fall upon the petal of the flower
as the dew of morning.

Stephen M Kountz
THE GIRL WITH MAGNETIC HANDS

In nineteen eighty-seven, born in Beckley town,
An angel fell to earth, in a snowy white gown.
It happened in the summer, of a hot July eve,
When she fell from heaven, and the mother did conceive.
She was born on a Tuesday, fifty minutes after three,
That's when life was given, to little Heather Marie.
The parents were so happy, for this special one,
Just two short years earlier, the mother bore a son.
When she had gotten older, and begins to crawl,
They noticed something unusual, about this porcelain doll.
She had a special ability, maybe something in her glands,
Objects seemed to draw closer, to the girl with magnetic hands.
Things around the house, began to vanish much,
From one small and innocent, that had a magic touch.
Small things I could understand, disappearing into thin air,
But how could this infant hid, my favorite reclining chair.
The house seems so empty, since she has come along,
You'd think one so tiny, could never do no wrong.
All our valuables are gone, gathered through the years,
We'll have to start all over, with our credit card from Sears.

Dan J Homza
UNTITLED

For the free world, the bands that inspired me to write, my family, and the special girls that have given me strength.

More precious than the days are long
More beautiful than the whippoorwill song
Is the friendship we so freely share
Just the thought of a friend who will care
These are the feelings to you I relate
In the days that will pass our friendship can grow
Whether it be life as its cause
Or a destined fate
What it becomes neither one of us will know
When night falls and dreams fill your mind
I hope sweet thoughts of the promising kind
And when you awake, sunshine flows in your heart
Remember our friendship will
never depart

Jenni Kallus
THINK

We sit and we think, so young yet so old;
We often are frightened by what we are told.
We sit and we worry about what we're to do;
We often wonder if what's said is quite true.
We sit and we look—there's so much to see!
And often we wonder what we're to do.
So little time and yet so much space;
How do we know if we will win this race?
We must choose what to do and what to say;
How to dress, how to eat, and choose how we pray.
But you must always pray and hope for the best!
Then we will go farther than all of the rest.
So we sit and we wonder, we sit and we see;
Try and think of others, not me, me ME!
Think of the good times and think of the bad;
The bad times are over, so don't feel so sad.
But even when it's "over" we still are not through;
There are millions and millions of things we should do!
But until then think and wonder how it will be;
When it's really all over and we go home to He.
Then it will all be worth it.

Lori Wesolowski
MIKEY

This poem is dedicated to my cousin Michael for his courageous fight against cancer.

The Lord above has many dreams,
And to have my cousin is one it seems.
There's something to it, something he needs,
Perhaps Mikey has completed his deeds.
He knows the special boy he wants to take,
For with him and Mikey the heavens they can make.
He's falling behind and losing his touch,
So the help from Mikey will mean very much.
Don't think of loss but of reward,
Because in Heaven he'll be with the Lord.
Don't cry at night with thoughts of pain,
With Mikey in the sky our future will gain.
He'll lead us through life when things go bad,
For then we will see the help from Mikey we've had.
So think for the best and of what he's brought,
The lessons of love, he will have taught.

Rachel Martin
WHITE OUT

I was awakened by a piercing light
shining through my revealing shade.
The cold rain had ended;
the seasonal air had not been warmed,
even by the sun.
The wind blowing,
the bright colored leaves fell
upon the ground.
The bare blue sky longed
for the birds of yesterday.
The old man of leaves was dying.
The snow child arose from its crib.
I'll enjoy this November day
with all it has to offer.

Robert F Fike
WHEN I

When I shut my heart and keep God from my mind
I know that pain and suffering is all that I will find.
When I am tempted and my will is weak Satan's paths I trod.
O, foolish mortal that I am—Do I think I can hide from God?

When I feel all alone and no longer care, or try,
I know without a doubt I have caused my Lord to cry.
When I feel sad and think no one really cares—
Ah! Someone knows all; even the number of my hairs.

When I, in anguish cry for help, and no one seems to hear—
But wait! A Gentle Hand I feel; I know my Lord is near!
When I am depressed and feel the world has forgotten me
I have only to remember a Hill called Calvary.

When I admit that I alone cannot resist temptation long
I have but to turn to God and He will keep me strong.
When I hear the Words of God and think upon His Son—
Can I, evil sinner that I be, say less than, "Thy Will be Done"?

When I grow weak and miss my step
I feel a tear and know He wept.

But when I open my heart and let God's Word come in
The troubles make no difference for I KNOW that will win!

John Phillip Robertson
IN MY MIND IS A DEMON

In my mind is a demon, that plays a big part.
It keeps me from thinking, with only my gentle heart.
Returning like a culprit, this flood of despair
Reminds me just how painful it can be to really care.
Bravely I take up armor, to fight desperately,
To recapture faith and hope, and restore God's trust in ME.

Finally at long last I can accept my past
No longer try to change the world in all its range.
At last I've learned to wait for that hard to open gate.
No smarter no more wise, just patient opened eyes,
I've grown to face the truth and gone beyond my youth.

Mary Ellen Tetrault
ACTS OF LIFE

We act out life in an off-broadway play,
Every twenty-four hours we write a new day.
We pull up the curtain or let it go down,
As we laugh and cry or smile through a frown.
But when the playwright messes up things,
All of our acting hurts and it stings.

We say the wrong lines or our acting goes badly,
Then the play ends abruptly and so very sadly.

Our audience leaves without any applause,
We search for a reason but can't find the cause.

Our stage is left empty, bleak, dark, and bare,
There's no one to act with and no one to care.

When the house lights go on another tomorrow,
We must rewrite the script to change all the sorrow.

Our last play is over but we can't give up now,
We go on rehearsing for our final bow.

Janet S Staub
FRIENDS

When I have no friends to call my own
you always remind me I'm not alone.

When I wonder who could care
you remind me that you are there.

You pick me up when I am down
at my lowest you're always around.

Our lives will change as time goes by
and as we age we all will die.

Friends will come and friends will go
but you're one friend I'll always know.

You'll stick by me till the end
that's why I'm proud to call you <u>FRIEND</u>.

James J Hazzard
MANSIONS ON HIGH

The construction workers, are who?
Sweet spirit of God, and you two.
Together you're the building crew,
You're His building, a child brand new.

Creation, from heaven you flew,
Born of God's grace, royalties hue.
Building His temples, me and you,
It's God's design, till all is through.

So important, this work to do,
It's our mansion, salvation's cue.
Our future home, God always knew,
Word and Spirit, we need these two.

To build our home, high in the blue,
We need Christ mind, so pure and true.
Must read His word, the building's clue,
Begin today you're over due!

Deborah L Miller
CHERISHED LOVE

This poem is dedicated to Johnny, my inspiration, my love.

Cherished love is held in my heart;
Through the years, we'll never part.
I'll give to you, all my love;

For it had to come from above.

Cherished love came into my life;
From that love, I'll become your wife.
My love for you will always be true;
For there is only one love in my heart, you.

Mary Thayer Blanchard
TO A BELOVED FELINE FRIEND
Dear Mr. Ginger, I remember your name now
And also know your gender.
Darling Ginger, my feelings for you, I avow,
Are truly warm and tender!

You're a graceful pussy, a living work of art
Made by our Father above,
Put on earth to gladden many a human heart
With your beauty and your love!

Vera L Smith
V.I.P.
Her day begins so early
even the birds aren't singing,
Before she can brush that one's hair so curly
someone has the telephone ringing.

A lock is needed for the refrigerator door,
each day the carpet is a shade darker,
Earlier there were only three, now five more,
grab that one, he's got a marker!

She is the local sitter,
I've no doubt her patience is unending,
She certainly is no friend of Dean Witter
and some have payment still pending.

Some days around three, others it's six,
she's in the shower; sheer genius created dinner,
Simply amazing!; . . . she muses, the way chewing gum sticks,
as she scratches off that ticket . . . a $2.00 winner!

Homework is done, only two left to go home,
Three sleeping angel faces.
Once again there goes the phone . . .
Could you watch my two until ten?
We're going a few more places.

Kathleen A Redden
AUTUMN RAIN
From the street lamp's glowing light,
The rain, one late October night,
Glistened on the windowpane,
Like tears slipping down, the rain.

The slow and steady drumming sound,
From the rooftop, to the ground,
Like a soft and low refrain,
Here comes the rain, here comes the rain.

It played its song, throughout the night,
As darkness slowly turned to light,
And still it would not go away,
Alas! another rainy Autumn day!

Kathleen A Redden
THE SUN
Behold . . . the sun,
That heralds newborn day.
Its rays of golden heat,
Spill forth upon the land,
To warm the earth from early dawn.

Behold . . . the sun,
Lamp of day, torch of light,
Sails like a ship of fire,
Across the sea of sky,
To reach the dark horizon.

Behold . . . the sun,
The last of flaming light,
Fades like a dying ember,
And charcoal is the night.

Kathleen A Redden
NIGHT MUSIC
Like shiny glass, the sea at night,
Not a wind disturbs the air,
Shadowy vessels float into sight,
Beyond the harbor's lantern glare.

How soft a silent wave,
Upon the distant shore.
It echoes in an unseen cave,
Like the sound of a splashing oar.

Its music is the bell of night,
Vibrating low and deep,
Like wings of birds in swooning flight,
It whispers sounds of sleep.

In the cave, the music floats,
Along the flowing rill,
Faint now, ever soft the song,
Once more the bay is still.

David Libby
THE STORM
In my room, I slept in slumber
Only to be wakened by lightning and thunder.
As I wiped the sleep from my eyes,
I glazed through my window into the sky.
Crackling of white followed by thunder
Echoed the sound of God's true wonder.

As I sat at the edge of my bed
Drops of rain began to fall upon my shed.
Its roof of tin recorded the rain
As the clouds cried down in tearful pain.

Bolts of lightning stretched from the air
Striking the ground absent of care.
Hollowed sounds of thunder charged the night,
Sending children under their blankets in fright.

The wind's anguish picked up its pace
As if born in an instinctive race.
The storm raged in its marvelous fury
Using lightning and thunder to tell its story.

David Libby
A POEM FOR JENNIFER

To Jennifer, Love Always David.

Splendid eyes sparkled in blue, an exquisite smile that shines right through.
In your presence hearts will quiver full of hope your love can deliver.
Born in sunlight, dressed of dreams as the moon shines down its golden beams.
Upon your shoulders it will fall, captivating a young man's heart and his all.
To hold you close within my arms is made of dreams from all your charms.
Upon your lips, I leave a kiss. Away from you my love I will miss.

In the distance and up so near your heavenly body is all so clear.
The warmth of your caress, The touch of your hand,
A kiss from you sends me to a wondrous new land.
A place where love sails its seas born on a warm enchanted breeze.
In its seasons from summer to winter a bouquet of flowers I would send her.
For on the ground or in the sky the wings of love I would fly.
Across the heavens I would write for all to see my love so bright.
Through endless days or eternal nights all true words I write tonight.

For in my dreams upon this night I saw a vision all so right,
Walking hand and hand with the one I love in the sun's warm rays from above.
As we walked across the land joined together in love's true band.
I felt my heart fill with joy, a once felt pleasure when I was a boy.
The knowing of wonders and dreams to come true,
Forever and passionate, I will love you.

Martha Iris Cavazos

Martha Iris Cavazos
MARK

To Mark: My Best Friend.

And there he was
A stranger to love
A rugged man
A helpless girl
An aspiring night
I'll never forget
He entered my soul
And filled my empty heart
Our eyes met
An evocative look
I then knew that I was him
And he was me

Martha Iris Cavazos
STOP THE HUNGER
The children are sleeping
And father is weeping
No seeds to sprout
Death upon you . . . Creeping

Hollow roars the thunder
O bodies sinking under
Will thou take thy spirit
And stop the roars of thunder

Turn to one another
Parents, sister, brother
Lend a seed or two
Reach out and touch each other

Overcome, yes, we can do
The faith lies in me and you
Face to face, not back to back
One life, or better yet, two

Shelly Brooks-Hall
REALIZATION
Beauty, like a flower blooming in the spring;
Is what I see, when—
with you I cling.

And Love, an empty lonely road; spreads through me like a winter's cold.

To understand,
I think of thee—
And know it's where I long to be.

Tanya L Whipple
GYPSY
She just wants to be wild and free . . . She longs to run with the wind, to play in the thunder storms, she lets her hair blow free as it whips around her face as she stands on the crashing seashore.
She is the Gypsy . . . Born and bred to wander. The passionate, fiery, hot blood runs deep through her veins. To her there is no such thing as control. She finds life simple with no use to worry. She lives one day at a time, she's everything you'd ever dream to be . . . She's what your heart desires and that my friend is, to be free.

Ruscello
FIRST WAVES TO ROAM
From the first waves
that walked
arm in arm in the sand
and footprints that left no trace
in the quiet still sea water,
the warmth
of an August nocturne turned
radiant on the shore.

I watched you turn gently
from Summer to Fall and falling leaves a blanket,
to be kept warm in your bed.

In your eyes, your arms, your embraces,
History is written of Rome
and a thousand years
and I held you close, as we walked
the cobblestone street, of a city,
without an end.

Glozella J Meyer
ZELONA AND GLOZELLA
Zelona is kind and sweet
No nicer person could you meet.
Zelona is good and understands
More than many would or could.
Her name is different like my own
And we don't try to pick a bone.
We've laughed and laughed it's true
We think others have strange names too
And wonder if they ever get blue.
What people have said and do.
Where did you get that name?
I have an answer for mine.
My dear mother knew two people
A Glo and a Zella put the two together
For Glozella and drew the line.

Frederick W Kruse
FROM FANTASY, TO REALITY

For Linda Kruse with all my love.
You're my fantasy in reality.

I know this isn't Disney and life's not a fantasy. But, I can't accept things the way they are. If it's a dream that keeps me going, then that dream is you, and if you're a fantasy, my life is. If it wasn't, where would I be? Alone! A fortress, with no doors. The existing one, is yours. Accessible to only one. Others have windows, a view. Yet you have access to a domain. A true Queen of a land that is only yours. A place so bountiful and yielding it amazes even myself. Parts unexplored and totally untouched by others, You've walked and beautified with your presence. Without knowing making a man complete. An empire on a strong foundation, an incredible woman. Who fears him in so many ways. If not from his strength, from his tenderness, which she gave him. Something few ever have ever seen, except her and those she has allowed to. A LOVE that is FANTASY? YES, But only one step from REALITY. So, from my dreams, to your eyes WILL YOU MARRY ME?

Frederick W Kruse
DAD, GRANDDAD, AND FRIEND

A gentle man, who is second to only one, above all others, loved by all, special to me and the rest of our family.

He's the one, we can do it all with, who will support each of us in his own special way, someone who knows how to make our day.
That's our DAD in every way.

Now give that man a grandchild. Your son, he calls, "His Boy!" Your daughter, he calls, "His little Girl!" Watch, he'll buy the little red wagon or the little doll for them, that you have had on lay-away. Give him a weekend with your precious little one, and in return, he blesses you with a monster. Leave? Dare you? They're screaming, crying and you hear Granddad say, "I told you I wouldn't forget," with a smile and a laugh to hide the tears so we don't see. Now that's a GRANDDAD to me.

Always willing to lend a hand, and waits for the moment when you'll ask him. He'll take you and "his boy," hunting or on a fishing trip, or "his little girl," skating or to the zoo to see a bear flip. You'll see him read a storybook to eight of us. Three in his lap and the rest all-around. He loves to talk and has sound advice. See he's not only what's written above. He's a FRIEND and that's what's nice.

Tammy Curteman
THE GLORY

To those who fought for our
Freedom, in memory of my
Grandfather "James E. Woods."

It's just so hard to express the love they carried as they fought for us all, for the stories I've been told deep in my heart they all stand tall.

I feel they deserve much better than what we've given them in the past, for the life we live without their past today we wouldn't last.

So please now with the life we've been given can we give credit where credit is due, let's take care of the ones that survived, let's give them a future like they've given you.

Del D'Lower
DIANE

Poor Beautiful Diane . . . Locked In A Little Corner Of A World Of Her Own Creation . . . Skin . . . Flesh . . . Bones . . . and a Heart . . . Wasted . . .

Early this morning still wet with dew(s)
You called to tell me the good news,
I was angry and yelled "When!
When! When!"
You hung up . . . but then
You thought it over again . . . and got scared
Every thing would be bared.
So you called me at evening-time
to learn if I was angry or fine.
You coyly asked "Did you hang up . . . I heard a click."
I answered "No you hung up . . . You were up to the same old trick."
You mentioned the good news and asked if I was happy.
I answered "Yes" without sounding snappy.
We talked of friendship and things not yet materialized,
You were relieved to know my mood had not criticized
The commitments you make and break at will
Like the one on Sunday night . . . you kill
And fail to keep . . . like all your tricks
Your need for me is only for a "FIX."
My anger hasn't changed . . . just rearranged,
Go back to being scared . . .
everything will be bared
And like June and moon . . . very soon.

Alanna Sequeira
BEHOLD

Behold! He's coming!
Behold! He's near!
He's made His plans more than clear.

He'll take you or leave you
to heaven or hell.

Behold the Father of this whole world!

Marybeth L Hampton
SHADOWS

Darkness surrounds me
I cannot find my way.
No light shines on my life
I stumble through the day.
I am left alone,
Confused and frightened,
To live on my own.
The world left me nothing
Because it doesn't care.
I have no one to turn to,
Nothing to do,
Except to escape my Shadows.

I can't take it anymore,
My life is falling apart.
I'm worn out from being torn off the shore
Of the world.
I must release my anger and pain.
'Cuz I'm looking at the earth
Through the eyes of a baby after birth.
Take me away; set me free.
For I will forever be living in a cast of Shadows.

Ethel Epperson
IN HONOR TO ALL LITTLE BOYS (WHETHER BLUE EYES OR BROWN)

Oh little boy with eyes of brown
Two little feet pattering up and down
Eagerly running to and fro
Following me wherever I go—
To kiss away such childish woes
As a hurt finger, a stubbed toe,
To tenderly erase
Tears from a dirty face—
Sometimes sorely put to task
To answer the many questions asked,
"What is this? and why?"
Oft times calls for one of greater wisdom than I.
Oh, little bundle of innocence mild
God's precious gift; a trusting child!

Vincent J Puccio
HOPE

Seen clearly through eternal mist
Glowing sunlight at midnight
Emblazoned accolade of stars
Shining through the bright moonlight
The calmest wave in angry ocean
A new leaf on a wintry tree
The joyous note in sorrows' passage
A comforting hand in sympathy
Courageous heart, a new beginning
Small drops of water in the sand
A trumpet's blare as day is ending
The crystal spring in wonderland
Golden arch in heaven's doorway
Miracle by which we plan
The smallest phrase in nature's story
Essence of the mind of man
Forever there if we but choose
Our mast of life, the strongest rope
The smallest word with awesome meaning
This magical, beautiful thing called hope.

Kathleen M Driscoll
A COMMAND PERFORMANCE

They came from near; they came from far,
by plane, by train, by bus, by car;
with smiles in place, determined and bright—
the family reunion awaits them tonight!

Some came in a group; some came as a pair;
they all looked their best, from their shoes to their hair.
Most members were present; by unanimous decision,
absentees were left open to scorn and derision!

They were grandparents, godparents, fathers & mothers,
cousins, aunts, uncles, sisters & brothers;
but the focus of interest, all had to agree,
were the newly-wed couples and spouses-to-be!

There was an abundance of succulent food for the eating,
and a bottomless keg of cold brew for the drinking;
they spoke of their diets (oh, what a bore!);
then, when no one was looking, they snuck back for more!

There was laughter; there was gossip; dirty laundry was aired;
(with such a fine display of spirits, souls were destined to be bared!)
Good feelings ran high; conversations ran free;
thus, an encore for next year was planned with great glee!

Janet Marie Paige
A DREAM COME TRUE

I just wanted to let you know
That I really do love you
And that you have always been
And will always be
That one special someone
That I've always wanted to meet
That I've always dreamed about.

I don't know why that one special someone was you.
But it was, and I'm so glad it was you.

If you ever find yourself
Wanting to spend
Mornings, afternoons, and nights
With someone that loves you,
I hope you will find her and let her know,
Not only because she will always be in love with you
But because,
It would be "a dream come true."

Dr Kara L Cross
ODE TO A VIRGO

Virgos are of course the best,
and we'll succeed what e're our quest.
Wit and charm are our forté,
(no matter what the others say).
Yes, we are great, so have no fear,
for we get greater every year!
When in a crowd, we try to please,
to put the lesser folk at ease.
When others talk behind our back,
(to give our "character" a whack),
or slander us by mail or phone,
we never cry, complain or moan.
We realize they need to see
our great superiority!
And when they do they'll plainly find,
that they are well beneath our kind.
Our beauty, charm and sex appeal
are but three traits which give us zeal.
Of all our talents (we're such fun),
humbleness is number one!!

Patricia Kay Wilson
SECOND CHANCE

Oh please stop the pain from flowing.
I have messed up, without knowing.
Now I need to escape like a dove soaring.
I've tried, but I can't stop the tears from pouring.

To one, the distance seems too far.
If only I knew where you are.
My only choice is to wish upon a star.
Things were once great, but now they're not up to par.

Am I right or am I so wrong?
Guess I have known it all along.
Is it really supposed to turn out this way;
Can't I at least have one very small last say?

Florence Valitutto
LIFE AND ITS SIMPLICITY
We are born and we belong
We grow up and go along
But to make your life worthwhile
Always remember it takes a smile.

Life is really a simple trip
Yet we tend to make it a complex
whip

Look for the good one can do for
another
Instead of complaining about your
brother

Life is whatever you choose it to be
If you remember those smiles and
what they will see

You can find yourself happy and free
and joy will come as a perk or a spree

God has given us many guides
Seek them and He will abide

Be good in your life
Be thankful for the light, inspiration
and courage He gives
For the best things in life are free
if you see in the Lord what He wants
us to be.

Cassandra A Wright
EVERYWHERE
Just when time is called to sea
Each parting memory sails to me
Forgetting the weathers of days in
past
Finding a comfort in promises that
last

Precious shells line a beaten shore
Echoing waves resound no more
All but still waters seek the moon
Calling to death, that passionate
boon—
Everywhere.

Charles Discoli Jr
FOR ETERNITY
It's all too swift,
It ends too soon.

The quickened pace,
The final swoon.

Then, sudden dying of fire and flame.
The loosened limbs, the lose of all
gains

No! Kindle the fire.
Control the desire.

For there is more!

Do not consume, elaborate.
Take hold of the moment.

Wait!

Let wanting lips and caressing hands,
Ignite the fire of our vast demands.

Let eager mouths and teasing
tongues,
Feed the fire, our deepest loves.

For eternity.

Jennifer Lynn Schemmel
SOMEONE SPECIAL
THIS IS TO SOMEONE
SPECIAL . . .
Someone who means a lot to me.
Someone who, if it weren't for; I
wouldn't be.
THIS IS TO SOMEONE
SPECIAL . . .
Someone, I love, adore, and would
die for.
THIS IS TO SOMEONE
SPECIAL . . .
Someone who helps me,
Who is there when I need a shoulder
to cry on.
He is there to help me succeed.
He is there through the bad.
He sticks by me, even when I'm mad.
Although, sometimes I make him feel
sad.
Even though I do this, he is by my
side.
Even though I have hurt his pride.
He is someone special, someone who
means much to me.
Someone who I can't wait to see;
Because I know that he loves me.
THIS IS TO SOMEONE
SPECIAL . . . .

Velma DeJiacomo
MY MIRROR

This poem is dedicated to Sharon, Linda, Cindy, and Bobbie, my four beautiful daughters.

I see my face as a mirror
of time
As I look upon each wrinkle
and line . . .

This furrow was for
my children whom I adore
One more crease as we
added to four . . .

This line reminds me of my life
and all my laughter
This one of the before
and the after . . .

A face with no lines has
much to learn
The sorrows & commitments
and the bridges to burn . . .

Thank you God for this
face of lines
For without it I'd be
lost in time . . .

Bill Wheeler
TURN KEY AND ENTER
To you
I opened my heart.
Just a glimpse through the crack.
Light escaping around
the old skeleton key.

Standing in the doorway,
rain falling down,
wetting your cheek, matting your
hair.
You peered, ever so cautiously,
inside.
Shuddering slightly,
you pulled the door closed again.
What did you see
that caused you to turn away?

The door is closed.
Is the old skeleton key
still in the keyhole?
I think so,
but
I can't see.

Edward J Davis
HOW DO YOU HURT THE ONE YOU LOVE?

To my helpmeet, lover and friend.

How do you hurt the one you love, the one that was sent to you from above? The one who you prayed and cried and longed for. The one you're willing to die for.

How did I hurt the one I love? By thoughtless words and meaningless action, this can cause a love subtraction. A gift from the head and not the heart could cause a wounded love to depart.

How did I hurt the one I love? By being silent to critics wails and jeers (Oh they didn't mean it like that my dear.) Though it may not be a need to be angry and violent, still it's not enough to be strong and silent.

How did I hurt the one I love? The one whom I said I'm so enchanted, it's clear I've taken her for granted.

I'll change, I'll change, my heart exclaimed, but a few weeks later it looks the same.

So, with prayers and tears of heart-felt feeling, I pray this poem will cause a healing.

Wounds cut deep by pains of love know that God can see above.

So before we find ourselves apart, let us let Him heal our hearts, with patience and care that flows from above, please accept the thoughts of Love.

Sandy Kay Barnes
EASTER JOY

This poem is dedicated to Jesus, for all of His unconditional mercy and loving grace He gives to us all.

We should all kneel and pray
And thank God for this day;

Was three days since, Jesus died
on the cross
For me and you and all who are lost;

This day we know as Easter, the day
God raised Him from the grave
Was so all may be saved;

Lord, thank you for your pain and
strife
For to give us newborn life;

Ah, it is a blessed time
And I'm glad I'm His and He's mine!

Elaine Richard
ONE MORE DAY
Give me one more day Lord to see
the miracles you have for me
the morning dew on a rose
the wind blowing brushing my nose
the sun peering beneath a tree
the water rushing against the rocks by
the sea
knowing all who have created these
things
but the "Lord of Lords" and "King of
Kings"—
In a meadow a mockingbird sings—
Thank you Lord for creating all these
things—
A butterfly sailing across the colorful
sky—
Someone would ask why?
The beautiful golden leaves falling
from a tree
This is nature according to me
These things most people take for
granted—
Plants along a sidewalk that's been
planted—
Rain falling gently upon the window
pane—
Thank you Lord for the rain—
And in the midst of the evening a
gorgeous sunset is aglow—
Maybe tomorrow Lord you will let
me know—
Just one more day!

Anamarie Nardelli
SOMETIMES I GET CONFUSED

I dedicate these poems to my family and friends who helped me through the confusing and difficult times I have faced. I will always remember you.

Sometimes I get confused,
but later I see the light;
Somedays it is harder,
Sometimes it takes the night.

It is a game of walking shadows,
The lights dancing set the stage;
Sometimes the game is stagnant,
and you have to turn the page.

Life is like a rodeo,
You get bumped and thrown a lot;
It is hard to hang on to the horse
When you are worrying about being
shot.

Where do people go,
When life has left them behind?
They go on to tomorrow
'Cause their life is there to find.

Anamarie Nardelli
BRICKLAYER
I am the Bricklayer, and I build walls
I build them high, and I build them
tall.
They go from the ground all the way
to the sky
The more I get hurt, the higher they
fly.

Brick by brick, I set the stones
Then I fasten them, so that they will
hold.
I can construct the strongest walls
around
They cannot be touched, they can
only be found.

The bricks are cool, and rough, yet
flat
One on one, on another I stack.
Stronger, yet weaker the higher it
goes
The higher the wall, the weaker it
holds.

The wall will teeter, and sometimes
fall
then I scramble to repair my
crumbling wall.
Then, when I patch the broken space
I move on again to battle and race.

I am the Bricklayer, and skilled at my
craft,
but the wall itself has never been
done over half.
I am tired, and I need to sleep,
but I can't because I have this
damned wall to upkeep.

Anamarie Nardelli
SYBIL'S SONG
I lit a candle in my window last night
I lit it for you out of love for your
life.
It glowed and burned, just like you
And I could not dim it, as it cut
through the night.

I sat and watched it burn and dance
The flame jumped and waved, silent
and warm.
The wax melted away, but the flame
went on

As it swayed and moved, so sweet so pure.

It didn't seem long until the wax was nearly gone
The flame began to burn down and disappear
A pool of wax had formed on the window sill
and I sat to be with it in its last bit of time.

The flame was low and weak,
but still it tried to give its light.
As it reached the last bit of wax, the flame died away.
Gone forever, never to return again.

I lit a candle in my window last night
I lit it for you, in celebration of your life.
The candle was you for a few moments in time
but the candle is gone, and you are, too.
Goodbye my friend, may God and I always be with you.

Mr David Kalny
RED SQUARE FOR RED CHINA
The bell tolls. The numbers
Rise as the machines discharge.
Huge treads come tumbling down as
The machines commence a charge,
Oh, how the liberty-lovers
Retaliate the polls.
How black the night is. How
White their spirits are and bright
With Christ's light.
Foods await for a fasting
For the liberty-lover's spirits are
Forever ever-lasting.
Screams, screams, screams, but
No ice-cream in sight. 'Tis Soviet
Tanks? Nay, for this is Bloody May
In His Highness' Bloody Square.
Now, all is quiet. All is bare.
'Tis morning. Morning. The shutter-
People all are home. 'Tis time to
Sweep up the liberty-lovers and time
To comb the Bloody Square.

Marina Arlene Zorz
PAIR OF SHOES
He bought a pair of shoes,
and puts them on his feet,
walks around the department store,
then out onto the street.

He wears them down the road,
for miles, and miles, and miles,
and hopes they don't wear out,
because they are his style.

He wears them day after day,
wears them night after night,
he loves his pair of shoes,
but glad they are not white.

He's getting old and grey,
day after, day after day,
and that's really no news,
because he still has his new pair of shoes.

M Adah Pyeatt
ITS LIGHT STILL SHINES
What of the star that shone so bright
O'er Judean hills long ago;
Guiding the shepherds with radiant light
Blessing a world of woe?

Does its light stream yet o'er our strife torn world?
Is it there in the Christmas sky?
In the hustle and hurry to all who know
Its glories will never die.

It shone long ago o'er a manger bed
Where it lighted a little guest;
And rays of gold must have been dimly shed
On Golgotha's rugged crest.

Yes its light everlasting still will fall
As the Christmas time draws near;
And the love of the Christ brings hope to all
As we enter a bright New Year.

Darla Henderson
FOREVER IN MY HEART
I treasure every moment I have with you my friend,
For we never know when our time here together will end.
Our love has withstood lifes' storms,
Through laughter and tears it's remained strong and warm.

I appreciate your honesty, loyalty, determination and devotion,
Those characteristics keep our friendship in forward motion.
In spite of the miles that keep us apart,
Today's love and yesterday's memories keep you forever in my heart.

Wilmar D Hall Parsons
OF LIFE

To my friend, Priscilla M. Goss. Thank you for your faith in what I thought I could never never do.

To stay awhile I have but one regret
To die and of life know nothing yet.

To live and love in ignorance remain
And not to know of where and whence I came.

To speak of all the living and divine
To see the Hell of all the sands of time.

For life is like the waters of the sea
That wash along the shores of all my soul.

And as the pebble goes so goes my life
To find completeness as its never ending goal,
Perfection as its never ending price.

Nony Flores
THE BEAUTY OF THE SWAN

This poem is dedicated to Angela, my lovely mother and best friend in the universe. Mom, I bless our Heavenly Father for entrusting you with my life. I Love You!

Looking through the clear crystal of an eternal window
which displays the great beauty of the ancient of times,
the still and green blue waters of a shapeless lagoon
are suddenly interrupted by
the unexpected presence
of the beautiful swan.

Oh! What great personality of this marvelous being
who travels in such
ecstasy caressing the fresh waters
of the shapeless lagoon, he is
enveloped in brightness
and showered in the
sunshine reflecting
with unequal
the sumptuous beaming touch
of golden rays at noon.

With gentleness he touches the hearts
of all the people
whose eyes have the good fortune
to delight in the
beauty of such manifestation,
speaking of the goodness
of a divine creation and
cherish the inspiration
of a wonderful God.

The Spirit of the Almighty sent by the Risen Savior
brings forth with gentle whisper
the expression
of God's love, surrounding us
with truth that
flourishes in rivers,
mountains, starry nights,
and rainbows, and even
in the stillness
of a shapeless lagoon.

Patricia Henderson

Patricia Henderson
PORTRAIT OF A PERSON

To my father who died when I was only fifteen.

Oh Daddy, why are you looking at me like that?
Those stern eyes burning with anger
I'm sorry, I didn't mean to
Oh Daddy, I want to be good, I want to please you
But, can anyone?
You're the boss, you know
You show authority
Look at me, not with eyes of disappointment
Look at me and be proud.
You never got to see me grow up Daddy
I'm your daughter, I'm a lot like you
I have your intelligence
I have your ability to fix things
I have your determination
I even have some of your stubbornness
But Daddy, I don't want that stern look you had
I want my eyes to express compassion
I want my eyes to show love
I want my heart to feel tenderness.
I wish I could have known the real you Daddy
I'm sure there were times when your eyes smiled!

Mary Rousseau Henderson
TO THE WILLOW
Summer after summer I ran happily to the shelter of your arms.
You were so strong, so tall and handsome, so beautiful to behold,
And you were mine.
Mine, to gaze at in the glory of the morning, mine to dream with
at mid-day, and mine to love in the cool of evening.
Dancing, swaying, with such charm and grace that you and the
Breeze were one.
Sometimes the beauty was overpowering, and I would cry.
Then you would sing softly to me and gently caress my cheek,
And I forgot the world and time and space.
I listened to the ancient wisdom you whispered in my ear,
And I learned of eternity.
No end to the enchantment of our days, eagerly I awaited
Each new dawn.
I scarcely noticed Miss. Wisteria as she came flirting by each
Spring, with her lovely colors, swaying seductively and
Wearing her haunting fragrance.
I was too happy to notice, for you belonged to me.

One fateful summer I was called away, and for the long
Summer we were separated.
The day I returned I found you entwined in the arms of
Miss. Wisteria.
She had won, firmly she held you in her grasp.
Year after year I have watched her smother you with her
Clinging ways, and I know that soon you will die.
I would have killed her long ago, but others, who were
Swayed by her beauty, took the weapon from my hand.
I pray some blight will destroy her beauty and she will
Wither and die.
Once more you could be free, but she is there still,
Clinging, drawing your life blood with her parasitic way.
I feel your tear mingle with mine, as you struggle one
Last time to wave, and I whisper, I love you Willow Tree,
I'll always love you Willow Tree.

Julie Anne Cordova
THE FLAME OF THE CANDLE
Somewhere in the darkness
There's a pinprick of light
A long hoped for dream
That's far out of sight

The door has been closed
But there is a small slit
Through which one sees
A candle still lit

Long since enkindled
It will burn not much more
Therefore you must hasten
To open the door

For if the flame of the candle
Should on its own go out
Your dream will be lost
In the darkness of doubt

Sue W Culver
MY FRIEND
When I face dark times on windy seas,
It's your love that steadies me.
When life would dare to be unkind,
You calm my fears and ease my mind.
When clouds gather—it starts to rain,
I feel your presence—and smile

again.
Through eyes of love you look at me,
And see me as I ought to be.
You listen well and always seek
To hear the words I may not speak.
With so much love—and right at hand.
I strive to do the best I can.
But, if I fail, and I'm feeling low.
You hold me close and love me so.
You seem, somehow, to know, and care,
The clouds, now dark, will disappear.
Your hand in mine will lead me on,
Assuring me I'm not alone.

Debbie Creamer
ANOTHER WORLD
I walked to the doors of another world,
Opened the door and there sat a girl.
Her icy stare caught my sight,
It was as if I was taking her life.
I knew she could tell that I wasn't the same,
She recognized my face, but something had changed.
We were once so close, our lives were the same,
But now all we share is our last name.
As I turned to leave, and close the door,
I left her stranded, in her own world.

Jessica Anne Kelter
DEPRESSION
Depression sticks to the soul,
To the heart,
To the mind.
Your mind is only concentrated
on that one thing.
And it stays there
for a while.
And you feel
like you've lost everything.
Sighing,
Without a word.
It's like a painful, shiny, sharp knife
stabbing you in the back.
Salty tear drops scurring down
your cheek.
Committing suicide seems like your only hope.
Until something happens.
GOOD!
And something good will happen.
Think happy,
Not sad or mad.
But only good thoughts.
What you have accomplished.
Think of the things you are good at.
For if you live through depression,
You'll be here tomorrow.

Anna M Reichart
I TRIED TO WRITE A POEM TO YOU

To my husband John, who is serving in the U.S. Army in West Germany.

I tried to write a poem to you, but I couldn't even think. Each time I try and write the words, my mind just goes a blank. Each day, I think of you and the words I long to say . . . that I need you, I miss you, I love you so much, it grows stronger every day. To me you are the sun shining bright on a flowery summer day. The crashing of the ocean's waves swallowing the sandy bay. The brightest star in the heavens alongside the milky way. You are my morning, noon and night, my candle burning bright. My reason to live, my reason to give, my lullaby at night. With you, my love, I'll share my life, our love will never die. For you, my love are my life, my every reason why.

Judy Siebel
ELFIN LOVE
This is for you, my fairy princess,
A kiss of love in the wind
How can I care for you any less
When you affect me so within.

You practise on me, elfin magic
I long to hear your voice
Oh, that tinkling, lively music
Does my heart but have a choice?

Come fly with me, my lover
I adore your immortal heart
We'll lie as one in the clover
And never shall we part.

You fade in the sunshine, darling
Your pearly wings now grey
Let me come, my little starling
Let me join with you today.

Oh, what a cruel, hopeless future
What an endlessly dreary life
Gone, is my lovely, fairy creature
Now I'm stuck here with my wife.

Ada E Hamann Geis
MEMORIES
In the sunset of our lives
We look back over the years,
And recall the bad times and the good times
With their smiles and their tears.

Most of our childhood friends have now left us,
But our memories of them are precious, and real.
In memory they are still with us
Just as they were, and are still.

How sad it would be if we were alone
With no memories to keep us together
And we were in years gone by,
In sunshine and in stormy weather.

We sit and dream as the years go by
And relive our childhood once more.
In memory we frolic with friends in the schoolyard,
Just as we did in days of yore!

We may be advanced in years, and weary,
But our spirits are forever joyous and free,
As we look forward to seeing our loved ones once again
In Heaven, dear Lord, with them, and with Thee!

Mary Williams
LITTLE TOM

Dedicated to the loving memory of Thomas Herman Williams, Sr.
Born: November 28, 1915
Died: October 9, 1989
"Missed deeply, but not forgotten."

He was never a complainer
A simple working man you see
He would even give the shirt from his back
He was a blessing to you and me.

He was just a small man
But his heart was as big as the sky
And I guess that is why we question
Oh, Lord, Why? Why?

His teasing ways were well known by all
He always had a story to tell
Saying little things to amuse us
And each story we knew so well.

But the Lord came calling one morning
On Tom He did request
His presence in Heaven forever
Because the Lord only chooses the best.

So look up to Heaven dear loved ones
And think of him walking up there
And now he has a new body, the old one has passed away.

We can hear him say "Now I'm Happy"
No more the pain do I feel
Soon you will all come join me,
And see that Heaven's so real.

Lorie Nunes
LIFE

To My Mother.

Here we are alone again
I wonder why life is so sad,
when we are old?
I wonder why no one cares?
Maybe today things will change.
Here she lays in her last bed, all white and pink from head to toe.
I think someone will come and sit
and say why didn't I sit with her before today
as I know tomorrow will be too late.

Ruth M Lunsford
THEY ARE THERE

To My loving parents--
GLADYS and WILEY LUNSFORD.

You are out there
Feeling just as I do
Searching in vain
For someone to love you.

Love has many forms
Developed with trust,
Lots of total caring
Plus giving of yourself is a must.

But did you know
You could be wrong
Love is all around you
SURE! YOU DO BELONG!

When was the last time
You said, "I LOVE YOU"
To a friend, a parent or such
Start today—you won't be blue.

I know, when you start giving
Love comes double back to you
We all have people who care
It's just—somehow—
We forget that, THEY ARE THERE!

William E Hans III
MEMPHIS
Do you remember me tree, I do you,
It's been almost a year, you haven't changed.
You still have that firm, decisiveness about you that makes me look up to you.
I wonder if I'll ever be like you
You must know something I don't
My friends are gone, but yours are still here
You are so strong and I am so weak
I wonder if you like me or do you consider me your foe
Your friend who feeds you, the rain clouds, tells me to leave you
So I must leave. But even to him I say I'll be back someday
I'm sorry to hurt you tree, you're only my second choice.
My journey was intended to see a friend.
Something chased her away before I could even see her and she's lost forever like me.
Tree, if you see my friend, please give me a clue to end my search.
Please make your pal, the rain cloud go away
Let your other friend, the blue sky, show me the way so I can end my longing.
I'll see you again next year.

William E Hans III
THREADS AND TREES
The thought came to me lazily
Like a single silk thread in a breeze
I know not what caused it to land on me
But I looked back to nearby tree

The words I know didn't quite ring true
The sight I saw couldn't be taken for real
Like a giant tree crashing noiselessly to the ground
Or a newspaper being folded without my knowing

Not all merriment carries laughter outside
Not all troops fire their weapons astride
In not all clothes does someone reside
Some arranged in closets, uselessly neat

Someday I'll plant a garden
And I know it shan't hear them sprout
I won't hear it if they grow six feet
So to hear something or not, which is more sweet?

You can say if something is positive nearing
You don't need someone else's bombastic cheering
Wherever it is, whatever it may be
I know it will come as noiselessly as a Tree

William E Hans III
TO MY ONLY LOVE
Feeling an emptiness deep in my soul,
Quite a bottomless darkly lit hole.
The gilding worn heavily in places no gold,
Only to reveal the muddy bare bole.

In this way I thought forever I'd remain,
On mankind a ruddy spot, just a stain.
Darkness all around like the bottom of stone,
Suddenly I see the top, realized I didn't have to be alone.

The reason for this isn't too hard to see,
That's right, Martha, it's because you talked to me.
Because an angel from heaven showed interest in me,
Buds began to sprout on every branch

of my tree.

For some reason only destiny knew,
Our branches and roots together they grew.
And at times we felt the forest fires sting,
I thank God that still together we cling.

Someday the wind will blow to your seeds,
And we'll have little saplings at our knees.
And when someday we feel the blade of the lumberjack,
Remember how much we loved, and know together we'll be back.

Patricia Weber
FRIENDSHIP

To my parents and husband and sister and brother for the special friendship we share.

How shall it be
defined
Should we say it's
a relationship between
you and someone
or should it be
put as
two children playing
with one another
No it should
be defined as
more than just a
relationship or playing children
it should be an
expressed emotion
between the understanding
of a child to a parent
and a husband to
a wife!

Sandra M Walsh
FOR YOU DEAR FATHER

For you dear father yes I write
To thank you for giving me sight.
The sight to see all I could be.
The sight to see the beauty in being free.
And most of all the sight to see how much you loved me.
All I am is for you, your
love for me held ever true.
For this your daughter is so proud
and cries loving tears choosing a shroud.
Oh father, how can our time be
through, when I still have so much love to give to you.
Your eyes so gentle and so kind,
they are sleeping now as I find, a peaceful resting man.
Father did I love you all I can?
Was I all you hoped I would be?
Rest assured you were to me.

Sherry M Marcolongo
FINDING MY SOUL

While in the cradle of sunset I sit
On the windowsill of reality,
I see the greatest hint of a world missed
Which knowing is my sole ability.
This is a world that lives throughout darkness
Yet it shines bright with ideas anew.
It is beautiful and full of kindness
And with brilliant thoughts lets me through.
The loving and caring it feels for all
Is only one aspect of its being.
It listens and learns from one and all
And directs me through life with meaning.
The soul is like the night while it is calm.
Only we can protect it from the dawn.

Theresa Weinkauf
4TH OF JULY

To my husband Larry.
Thanks for all the encouragement.
Love, Theresa.

What does Independence Day really mean to you?
A day off of work? A trip to the zoo?
Or the parade down the street, fireworks at dark?
Perhaps a trip to the country or a picnic in the park?

Sad, but to many this is all so true,
We fail to remember the meaning of red, white and blue.
Of our forefathers who lived, fought and died,
Of the sons who were killed, the mothers who cried.

The freedom we have was not always here,
There once was a time we lived in fear.
One day a year we should walk proud and tall,
And thank the men and women who did it all.

Sometimes our thinking becomes somewhat slanted,
We use our freedom, and take it for granted.
The rights that are given to you and to me,
People in some countries will never see.

Of being patriotic, of this I can say,
When it comes to America, I'm here to stay.
So next time your raise you flag, fly it high,
And remember the true meaning of the 4th of July.

Beverly La Londe
DOLLAR SLOT-MACHINE

To TED, my patient husband & loving friend.

I never did much gambling, and thought it was a vice,
Until I went to Laughlin and tried it once or twice,
And that was my undoing. I looked upon the scene,
And like a magnet I was drawn to the dollar slot-machine.

I gave the girl my money and thought I'd have some fun.
When she said, "Good luck, Honey," I had as good as won!
I heard the silver plinkle, my mind was sharp and keen,
As I sat down upon a seat at the dollar slot-machine.

I won some and I lost some as I pulled upon that arm.
My pockets bulged and emptied, and I'd have bet the farm.
The tinkle of the silver, the crispy feel of green,—
Wild horses could not drag me from that old dollar slot-machine.
I've gotta stay in Laughlin, where the lights are on all night;
Where the silver dollars glitter, and
they fill me with delight.
Just send my mail to Laughlin, where I am always seen
At some Casino in the town at a dollar slot-machine.

Beverly La Londe
TAKE ME HOME

Father, I am feeling more homesick everyday,
And sometimes deep inside me I may groan.
I see along the pathway the rubbish and decay.
Pick me up, brush me off and take me Home.

I got caught in the system of this world, Lord.
I got jarred and rocked and soiled, and I moan.
Scrub away the dirt, debris and all the discord.
Pick me up, brush me off and take me Home.

Pick me up, for I stumbled, and I hurt again.
Lord, I think I stepped outside the safety zone.
Please restore the laughter in my heart, and then
Pick me up, brush me off and take me Home.

Brush me off, wipe the cinders from my sad eyes.
Brush the dirt away and make me shine like chrome.
Clean away all the hurting and the tears and sighs.
Pick me up, brush me off and take me Home.

Take me Home; let me walk the streets of Glory,
Wade in Your river and see Your golden throne.
Let me hear Your choir sing that old love story.
Pick me up, brush me off and take me Home.

Flo Rose
GLOBAL DISASTER

George Adamson died protecting his Lion Camp
Conservationists trying to hold their ground
Bald-headed eagles, leopards, bengal tigers
So few on this earth to be found.

An African elephant in his magnificent stride
makes his way down to the watering hole
Every week 16,000 dead/help stop the slaughter
We must all take conscientious control
Tusks gleaming like jewels/Ivory hunters on their way
How many kills will they boast of today.

Dian Fossey's memory flashes through my mind
A mountain gorilla holds its baby on its back
Danger lurks in the shadows of mountains & trees
As poachers move in for the fatal attack.
Putting trust in man and their kingdom the sea
Dolphins playfully breaching unaware
Entangled in tuna nets the fisherman throw out
Doesn't anyone in the human race care?

Animals tortured for experimental testing
Beached whales found upon our shores
Greenpeace rescuing baby harp seals
Risking their lives/fighting for the cause.

Rainforests bulldozed and burnt to the ground
Chico Mendes killed trying to take a stand
medicines, food & shelter for half the world's wildlife
Come from that unprotected, resourceful land.

In South America I have witnessed indescribable beauty
visions of rainbows/lush forests never leave my mind
Not only do we destroy the balance of nature's environment
A people's shattered lives are left behind.

One fifth of all species of life may die
Without firing a shot/within the next twenty years
For all of the animals and all of mankind
My soul releases a river of tears.

Extinction is forever/global destruction a disaster
Save future generations/don't take it all away
If we do not preserve our biological resources
I envision a world ended today.

Jamie Cobb
TIME

The time has come the time is here
to wipe from my heart the one so dear.

Though the time of bittersweet must end
hungry with passion, I'm glad you're my friend.

The time of your smile I will always hold
within my grasp, my story untold.

The time of weakness it scares me so
my heart is heavy my head too low.

The time is quiet, oh but I still hear the sound
for maybe my soul is skyward bound.

Thoughts or emotions that rush to brain,
are somewhat like moonbeams and roses after rain.

The time meant more than words can express
but somehow it's left me with loneliness.

The time better, if I dare to say
on another plain another day.

So I leave you my darling with a part of my heart
no chance for an ending, only a start.

Joan D Sharp
FRIENDSHIP
Because you are my special friend
and you have brought to me
A joy that I am feeling now a joy that sets me free
For pent up in this heart of mine was more than I could bare
Looking for a special friend a way out I could share.
The special little things you do that lets me know you're there
But not so much for me alone you let all know you care.
You're kind and gentle warm and sweet and take the time to share
All your caring thoughts of life that vanishes all the wares.
So once more I thank you I thank for being you
And hope this special friendship will last through and through

Joan D Sharp
THE OLD MAN AT THE TOP OF THE HILL
Now I'm but an old man
As I look down the hill
I can see so clearly
Now, I can be still

There spread out before me
Were all my hopes and dreams
All my forgotten yesterdays
Now a distant scene

I've lived my life the fullest
I have no one regret
Yes if you should ask me
My life has been well spent.

Joan D Sharp
THE RUNNER
The runner is a person, busy running around; darting here, darting there, never stopping anywhere.

Seldom few can catch him, no one can keep up; for his pace is mighty, while reaching for the cup.

The cup of life that filleth, with all abounding strength; to go on ever willing, to race on til the end.

For life is but a foot race, that we all must face; yes, life is just a foot race, can you keep the pace?

A pace that's often running, and sometimes goes nowhere; a pace that makes us weaken, and often feel despair.

But you can be a winner, and you can run in style; so put your jogging shoes on, wear your biggest smile.

Although you may get tired, and you may want to quit; you must remember a WINNER never quits.

Sandra Rhinehart
MY REVENGE
My hair's in curlers,
My makeup's down to my chin,
And if matters weren't worse;
My "tidy" and "immaculate"
neighbor walks in!
She asks how I am
And by her grin I could see;
Sure enough, she had noticed
My deodorant had sweated to my knees.
"I'm fine," I said,
Holding my stomach in;
Wishing she's go away,
Turn FAT, and never come again!
"Borrow sugar?" Sure—
"Let me go check;"
Wanting all the time,
To wring her "chinless" neck!
When she gets home,
She'd better not talk,
Because the laugh's on HER—
I gave her SALT!!!

Sandra Rhinehart
THE AMERICAN FLAG
The American Flag waves and our memory goes back;
To the days when our boys fought and were attacked.
Fought for our country, to keep our land free;
Blood covered the soil, for you and for me.
Tears shed by mothers, whose sons had died;
Friends who lost buddies on the battlefield, cried.
The Flag is most precious, it stands for them all;
Those brave, young men, who answered the call.
Honour the Flag, don't treat it like dirt;
Salute it and remember those that died and were hurt.
The Flag's not just cloth; dyed red, white and blue;
It's blood, sweat and tears, waving in remembrance FOR YOU!
Bow your head, be humble, when the American Flag is flown;
Show HONOUR AND RESPECT, for the boys who've gone on!

Sandra Rhinehart
TREES
A tree has life, it breathes and it grows;
Dressed in leaves of all colors, proudly stands with stately pose.
It ages as we do, with wrinkles and lines;
Each telling a story, of its life and its times.
It stood in the Garden, GOD planted it Himself;
A tree holds so much of our heritage and wealth.
Noah built an ark of the great cypress tree;
Without this biblical ark, where would we be?
Trees adopt creatures, a home to them make;
Trees hold such great secrets, It's time WE AWAKE!
Save the tree from man, stop cutting them down!
When the trees are all gone, humankind won't be around!
GOD has till now been the trees greatest tool;
But, He cannot save them from today's careless FOOLS!

Sandra Rhinehart
MAMA
Mama, your hair has turned silvery gray;
Your smooth face now lined, you're getting older each day.
Years have been hard, you've worked all your life;
You've not seen much pleasure, just heartaches and strife.
You've brought up your children, they've been taught quite well;
Their souls have been saved, your prayers kept them from hell.
Now, Mama, it's YOUR turn, in Heaven you'll stroll;
Only happiness you'll see, you'll walk on streets of gold!
No heartaches or tears, no worry you'll know;
You'll rest in HIS arms, like a star you will glow.
JESUS will care for you, with GOD you will talk;
And one day Mama, with you we will walk!

Anne M Fisher
YOU'RE ALWAYS THERE

This poem is dedicated to my dearest, most cherished friend Peg, who is a true source of strength and support to me.

My God, my God, why have you forsaken me?
I feel so alone and I can't see

Why does your presence seem so far away?
As I look for your strength with each passing day

I know that you love me and have good in store
I just lack understanding what this trial is for

Lord, help me up from this pit of despair
Help me remember that you're always there.

Anne M Fisher
BACK HOME TO YOU

This poem is dedicated to my loving husband Dan, my very best friend.

My Lord, my God, you are gracious indeed
For deep inside me you have planted a seed

It grows bigger and stronger with each passing trial
As you see me through each step of the mile

For Lord set before me is a race to be run
Which at times can be difficult, it isn't all fun

But with your strength to see me through
I will run my race back home to you.

Teresa J Brown
IN LOVING MEMORY

Dedicated to Tommy Lyn Brown, my family and especially for my Grandma and Grandpa.

The young man
Who stood straight and tall.
Loved by all
For his gentle ways.
His life laid before,
The birth of time.
Then he received his call.
His life gone with the waves.
His spirit went back
From whence it came,
His soul laid to rest,
And tears spent at his grave.
He is not gone, only away.
For he is with us
Each and every day.
His goodness and kindness
Remembered by our hearts.
And to all he touched
In his tender ways,
God be with you, we pray.

Lynnette Shamp
I JUST NEEDED TO TALK TO YOU
Thanks for calling, Mom.
See you soon I hope.
Nice talking to you Dad.
Now it's easier to cope.

It's hard being away from home.
Even tho I'm older now,
It still is lonely here.
My friends don't do somehow.

The letters that you write
help me feel closer to you.
They leave me homesick, tho
and sometimes feeling blue.

But theAarmy life is good
and things are cheaper on base
Everything's so handy here
that it's a saving grace.

So, in closing I will say—
That life is pretty swell
Even tho we're down here—
away from where our families dwell.

Sarah Gaamai Foust
HOW CAN I TELL YOU
How can I tell you of the love that only comes from Jesus?
How can I make you turn His way?
You know I would if I could, but the choice is yours.
Yes, the choice is yours to make!
When all your friends have gone and left you all alone
You're at the end of your rope, and ready to end it all!
Reach out to Jesus, His hand is always there.
Yes, He really does care!
Give all your fears and tears to Jesus,
He is the only friend you will ever need.
Every time your heart breaks so does His!
His love for you will never die!
His arms will surround you and shelter you from the dark storms of life.
Look into His eyes and see the love shining through the dark.
Look into His eyes and you will see
He is all you will need.
How can I tell you of the love that only comes from Jesus?
How can I make you turn His way?
You know I would if I could, but the choice is yours.
Yes my friend the choice is only yours to make!

Ernie R Cole
ODE TO WINTER
Nature nestles in her blanket of white,
Protected from all harm, sleeping amid
The continuing bustle of humanity.
The trees decorated with ice and snow
Paint a picture of more splendor
Than any artist ever created.
Cold numbs the fertile ground,
Giving it rest until spring comes around
When with expectant glee comes forth
the flower, the grass, and the tree . . .
And all the other season's tableau of scenery.
Many praises of spring
Are sung but few words
For winter are ever heard.
Too often we fail to see
the beauty of life because
the blinding snow of adversity
blinds men's minds to the
obvious and the beauteous.

Judy Beaty Holt
THE INNER ROOM
There is a place within me
that only God can see,
It's the center of my being—
the very best of me.

A place to escape life's turmoil
in quiet solitude and prayer,
A place that's blessed thru mercy
and God often meets me there.

For it's there I lay my burdens—
my heartache and my needs,
A place to seek forgiveness
for sinful thoughts and deeds.

One day only peace will enter
and joy beyond compare,
For the promise He has made me
with God in Heaven I'll share.

While all around me searches
and wanders from the fold,
I know I have an anchor—
an eternal home for my soul.

Judy Beaty Holt
JOURNEY'S END
There's no more time for planning
for that final day to come,
You've now arrived at Heaven's gate
and your race has now been run.

Who will God find standing there
in answer to His call,
Someone whose sins have been redeemed
or someone He knows not at all.

There's no more time for planning
for eternity with family and friend,
The time for that has come and gone
for you've now reached your journey's end.

Judy Beaty Holt
ASLEEP IN JESUS
In this time of sadness
when it seems you've lost your way,
It's then God is the nearest
that He's been most any day.

He doesn't leave His children
when they need Him most of all,
He is ever waiting quietly—
just listening for your call.

He feels your pain and sorrow
and knows your every need,
But you must seek his guidance
then in faith trust Him to lead.

The loved one that's gone on before
is now in Heaven's keep,
To be safe from sin ever more
as they with Jesus peacefully sleep.

Judy Beaty Holt
EYE OF THE STORM
We're promised to see trouble
soon after we're born,
Heartache and disappointment
causing glad hearts to mourn.

Thinking we're safe from life's
storm-tossed seas,
Sadness come stalking bringing
us down to our knees.

Facing these storms by ourself is
all but in vain,
Asking God's help there is much
strength to gain.

He's waiting to help us—to show
us the way,
To mend broken spirits turning
storm clouds away.

While often our lives become
battered and torn,
We can always find Him there
in the eye of the storm.

Judy Beaty Holt
THE CROSS
The burden of the world was His—
so heavy did it lay,
Just like the cross up Calvary's hill
He struggled with that day.

Your sins and mine He carried there—
thru love and mercy bore,
Fulfilling His Father's plan for us
that we go and sin no more.

The crown of thorns, the driven nails—
the sacrifice He made,
God gave his Son to die for us
and on the cross displayed.

Each of us has a cross to bear
and will throughout our time,
I know God loves me without fail
for He helps me carry mine.

Judy Beaty Holt
LITTLE IS MUCH
Each of us has a purpose in life
whether it be mighty or small,
It's up to us to do our best
for God can use us all.

When God enters your life and mine
He wants our commitment then,
A willing servant to Him be
on whom He can depend.

Each small effort that we make
if done in Jesus's name,
Can be made into great works
if they God's blessings gain.

As were the loaves and fishes
brought to Him by one of the least,
That meager fare was blessed by God
and there did thousands feast.

Be not proud and boast to man
of your great works and deeds,
For only God can make them great
and will not bless our greed.

Judy Beaty Holt
MY CO-PILOT
He's riding there beside me
as I drive the busy roads,
Hurrying here and there distracted
by my schedules and my goals.

He patiently waits for a quiet time
when I'm more aware of Him,
To point out that life's more precious
than any earthly gem.

He promised to watch over me
as I go along the way,
And reminds me of my promises
that I've made from day to day.

It's good to know He's present
as I drive mile after mile,
Even when I'm too busy to notice
that He's been there all the while.

Judy Beaty Holt
LORD, STRENGTHEN MY FAITH
So small and insignificant
that the eye can hardly see,
But God used the tiny mustard seed
to show what power that faith could
be.

But that tiny seed in fertile soil
grows bounty unforetold,
As would my Savior's love for me
that's planted in my soul.

If only I would let Him lead
and be my guiding hand,
He'd make me what I ought to be
according to our Father's plan.

Too often I start the day alone
without stopping first to ask,
"What would You have me do for You?"
then be about my Father's task.

Faith isn't measured by works alone
or just how great the deed,
It's more important to depend on Him
and let the Savior lead.

Judy Beaty Holt
ANSWERED PRAYER
It doesn't take a scholar
or someone of wealth and fame,
To speak to our Heavenly Father
or call on Jesus's name.

It doesn't take the voice of one
who preaches from His Word,
To get your message to the Lord
nor wonder if it's heard.

It doesn't take the front-row bench
nor in a closet dim,
To ask for help beyond man's power
but we must call on Him.

It just takes a sincere heart
and believing that He cares,
To reach the loving ear of Him
who hears and answers prayer.

Judy Beaty Holt
BOOK OF LIFE
As the chapters of your life
are being written down,
What will the pages say to all
and in the reading be found.

Will the study of the lines
be a help and inspiration,
To those who seek for guidance there
in hopeful anticipation.

Are all the pages bound by love
seen thru the chapters flowing,
Was your dedication made to God
and service to Him showing.

The cover isn't what counts the most
but what is found inside,
If God dwells within your heart
then let it show outside.

What you are and what you do
whether in cheer or in strife,
Will be recorded for all to see
there in your book of life.

Wendy-Jo O'Blenes
SAIL AWAY

To my mother who I love dearly and to Andy Syska for whom the poem wouldn't exist.

My thoughts are with you,
I imagine the view with
which you see before you,
I picture the beauty of the
icy blue ocean,
feel the roughness which will
soothe your restless soul.
The clouds will take your
mind far away to what's beyond.

Standing on the bow,
watching the waves go by—
your mind is following in suit,
the pressures of the world
slowly seep away from your mind,
sail away, my love,
sail away!

The ocean is the only bit
of freedom that's left.
The waves take you away—
away from the ugly misinterpretation
of life.
The sky, the beloved answer
of Love—
it lasts forever.
The icy ocean matches your soul,
The coldness races through your
veins,
Your heart aches for the storm,
It needs the fierceness—!
the hunger—
the hunger is the essence of
your being!
sail away, my love,
sail away!

Renee Fairbrother
MY LOVE FOR YOU
When I stare into your face,
I know it is true.
I feel my heart race,
with my love for you.
When I look into your eyes,
I see it is real.
No more goodbyes,
love is what I feel.
When I am with you,
there is no doubt.
I know you feel the same way too,
you're all I can think about.

Susan Jacobs
EMBRACED
With open arms
like wings
my Heart can soar
And Love can enter
upon the wind.

At birth
At death
The need avails.

And in-between
A time of Growth,
Joy, Healing, Bonding.
Of pain and sorrow too.

Parent to child,
sisters and brothers,
Lovers,
Mother, Father,
and Friends.

With you inside
my open arms

I FLY!

Paul D Boulden
A SURVIVOR
No one knows
how far I've gone.
Now one knows the wars I've won.

Wars of the mind
and wars of the heart.
Each one has ripped me apart.

But I'm still here
A survivor still—
each time giving me a stronger will.

I have lost many battles,
each one now seems trite
because now I am in a real fight.

Yet forever I'm a survivor still
and in the end
I will see victory again!

Shannon D Arnold
YOU'RE EVERYTHING TO ME
To me you are the sunset,
at the end of every day;
To me you are the promise,
that never goes away.

To me you are the light,
when the world seems dark outside;
To me you are honesty,
the truth that never lied.

To me you are the leaves,
that fall upon the ground;
To me you are the happiness,
that few have ever found.

To me you are the waves,
that roll upon the beach;
To me you are the dreams,
that I someday hope to reach.

To me you are the shadow,
that's always by my side;
To me you are the joy,
in all the tears I've cried.

To me you are the star,
that shines from up above;
To me you are the reason,
I know what it is to "LOVE."

Ethel F Williams
GOD'S MIGHT

To my beloved husband, Harold R. Williams.

As night's dark fingers touch the earth,
And dim the setting sun,
Our thoughts so often turn to God,
And the wonderful things He's done.
The twinkling stars, the velvet night,
The brilliant sun, 'tis God's great might.

It seems our life is oh so brief,
As we savor every moment given.
For earth is just a stepping stone,
Our destiny is Heaven.
And God who controls our world from above,
Controls our lives with Eternal love.

John Michael Mailhot
FREEDOM
Let's look at this word the word
we call freedom
it stands for a lot of things especially to this kingdom
this kingdom we cherish and love so much
it taught us honor, dignity, and such

We fought many wars and lost many lives
we did it all because we had to strive
to make things better to make a perfect world
to teach our children to start to knurl
the kind of place we want it to be
to keep things in order but still be free
to do what we want but still keep in line
remembering our morals we should do fine

To help those in need the weak and the sick
it shouldn't be hard it's an easy trick
just let it flow what's in your heart
spreading happiness and joy it is everyone's part
to keep the peace and to stay away
from death, destruction, and that fatal day

We all want to live a happy life
it feels real good it is no hype
so take good care of this world of ours
before DOOMSDAY appears and those final hours

Brian A McKee
DREAM A LITTLE DREAM
A man
sleepless
by the windowpane
stares—
The disturbed man dreams about radioactive worms
and the rest of the world closing in on him.
He is encased by his dreams
and his nightmares.
Soon the man will wither away
if not found by himself.

Elmina C McCarter
CAROUSEL MAGIC
As I near the carousel so shiny and bright
I marvel at the wonderful, delightful sight.
Music fills the air; keeping time with my heart
Beautiful horses prancing, as they slowly start . . .
Their magical journey for girls and boys
Fulfilling dreams of fantasies and joys.
The Merry-Go-Round all too soon—
Will slowly stop with the calliope's tune.
Childhood's enchantment is captured so well
In the wonders and magic of the carousel.

Michael D McCracken
UNREQUITED LOVE
Is it the night
or the long awaited day
that makes the wait
an unbearable masquerade?

It seems as time marches
in its unceasing parade,
and my soul's tears fall
in an endless cascade.

Then my heart reaches out
if just to be saved;
for only your touch
can make me be stayed.

Mary M Sanders
BEGIN AGAIN
My eyes are blind with grief . . . a sadness for the time gone by
. . . the days, years, decades.
I feel the failures, I breathe the joy.
But now it's gone. It faded with the light of day.
I hesitate against the force that is shoving me on . . . forward
. . . into the unknown.

A few faltering steps down the path and the scales
begin to fall from my eyes.
The shimmer of light startles me
. . . and then I begin to feel its warmth.
My attention focuses on the magnificent blending of a rainbow . . .
the result of the clouds behind me,
the sun before me.

I feel a confusion that brings my thoughts to remember
the story of the Phoenix bird.
The dramatic death as it goes up in flames.
Just as you begin to accept that it is gone forever,
from the ashes a new bird rises . . .
a new life begins.

A renewed strength seems to fill my entire being
. . . my purpose renewed.
I take my first breath of a new decade, step forward . . .
and begin again.

Anar Virji
GREEN VELVET EYES OF THE BALLERINA
For eyes that twist and twirl,
in loveliness,
full of spirit and grace:
to blemish the face,
to hinder the lash,
to vanish the sentiment.
For eyes that wander and meander,
to beauty the light,
full of wonder and wise:
a dream to fall,
a dream to capture,
to live, for a moment.

For eyes that wind around my memory,
to balance,
to drift upon,
my wavering soul,
in the midst of
your eyes.

Donna M Linke
REFLECTIONS
Against my cheek
A gentle breeze
Soothes my discontent.
And for a moment
I reflect
On how my life's been spent.
Wanting more
Than I can say
To change from bitter past.
I cannot seem
To find a way
To make the changes last.

Garrett D Weekley
THE TRAFFIC LIGHT SIGNALS THE WAY TO THE FUTURE
The ruler of the road.
The mediator of the masses.
The king who gives his royal
Decree, but when his message
Is misunderstood the people
In traffic place their blame on him
And not where it really belongs.

Hanging above traffic day
And night, this worker gets no
Vacation or holiday
Pay. On a set interval he
Changes the flow and regulates
Where the cars will go. His casing holds his
Body and brain, his only purpose is to
Watch the motion and give his
Commands of stop or go.

He may be out of synch with his many
Clones, but his job is still the same.
His glowing orifices light the way
To the future, even though he will never
Leave the present. His lights change from red
To green to yellow to red, the only things to ever change.

Karl Ray Hammond
MY BEAUTIFUL SONGBIRD
A beautiful songbird is my dear
Your voice is sweet music to my ears
Spread your wings of majestic splendor
And sing to me sweet and tender

Sing sing sing
Let your sweet voice gently ring
And speak to me from the heart
Say we'll no longer be apart

Fly fly fly
On to rocky mountain high
Say you'll fly home to me
And together we'll always be

Helen Gates
YOUR GIFTS
Out of the night you came to me
Bearing gifts none could see.
Gifts more precious than jewels or gold
Courage, faith, and love untold.

Like the trees and flowers need the rain
So you came, easing my pain
The touch of your hand, the light in your eyes
Drove every cloud from out the skies.

Those moments with you of sweet content
To me were heaven sent.
Within the shelter of your arms
Life took on a strange new charm.

These words drop from my pen to let you know
That no matter what you do or where you go
Memories of you within my heart will ever be
Because of the gifts you gave to me.

Helen Gates
THE SILENT SPRING
We have come to the time of the silent spring
Where the sun will never shine or the birds ever sing
The wee winged ones, the bees and butterflies
No longer grace the summer sky

The woodland creatures, too, have gone, only the wind
Through the barren trees sings a sad, sad, song
No more will we hear the night birds call
Or see the fireflies glow
The beauty of the night vanished long ago

Our silvery seas, sparkling lakes and rippling streams
With all their teeming life have just become a dream
The children no longer dance and play
Where once the sunbeams glanced across the way

No longer falls the gentle rain
On fields that once grew the golden grain
The sun, the moon, the stars, have gone
Great clouds rise from the earth, fire paints the sky

On the wings of the whirlwinds come humanity's
Last despairing cry
We have come to the time of the silent spring
Where the sun will never shine or the birds ever sing

Professor John Erdell

Professor John Erdell
TRIVIA
I watched her as she sat at tea,
Her sparkling eyes flashed back at
me.
She smiled, wistfully took a sip,
And put a kiss upon her lip—
The flowers dancing in the breeze,
Revealed the lace above her knees.

How wonderfully to observe
Her movements and her rapturous
verve.
There was no music but a bell,
As her earring dangling fell.
She played her gifts to pick it up,
Her hair cascading in her cup.
Flirtations are romantic trivia—
But ending always in oblivia.

Professor John Erdell
PRETTY GIRL
How beautiful is my pretty girl!
She passes gracefully
Draped in sheer white flowing gown.
I see her as the loveliest creation,
Blithe and noble in her grace.
Winsome to the eye with every step,
She is dazzling as she glides,
Barely touching the air beneath her
feet.

Pretty girl, she enchants me.
She will always live within my heart.
Her beauty will never pass away.
Pretty girl, a rose in her hair
Whispers I love you.
She is mine, as long as time
Keeps her picture in my heart.

Craig Alan Laffoon
I NEVER THOUGHT

Dedicated with love to my father,
Robert E. Laffoon, my mother,
Phyllis A. Laffoon, and my wife,
Pamela A. Laffoon.

I never thought my life
Could be so happy,
I never thought my world
Could be so full,
I never thought that I
Could be so lucky,
As to have you in my heart,
And in my soul.

I never thought the sun
Could shine so brightly,
I never thought the moon
Cast such a glow,
I never thought that God above
Could love me so much,
As to bless my life with you,
But now I know.

I never thought,
But now I know,
I pray to God,
You never go!

Craig Alan Laffoon
SOMEONE HELP THE CHILDREN
Little children in the street,
Garbage piled around their feet,
Stealing so that they might eat,
Hiding when they must retreat,
They must retreat to beat the heat.

Little children much abused,
Dis-oriented, lost, confused,
On their own, and still so small,
Have they any chance at all,
Does anybody hear their call?

No one seems to know for sure,
How much the children can endure,
Torture, agony, and pains,
Rots the little childrens' brains;
Under all these constant strains

Little children on their own,
The world is frightening all alone,
All that's left is skin and bone,
They search for love they've never
known,
Reach out and help the children,
Someone's got to help the children!

Terry L Mack
MISSING YOU
Missing you and wanting you near,
Wishing I could be there or you could
be here.

Wanting to hold you within my arms,
Caressing you gently how I miss your
charm.

I miss your smile and warm caring
ways,
How sad it is that I couldn't stay.

You're more than just a friend to me,
And hopefully that's the way it will
always be.

I long for your hugs and tender kiss,
But most of all it's you I miss.

Terry L Mack
WITHIN
If you think I'm ugly look again,
For my beauty lies within.

Within my heart is an "I Love You,"
What you can't see are feelings true.

Within my touch a soft caress,
Look into my eyes they tell the rest.

Within my kiss I say I care,
Within are feelings I need to share.

Within my mind is a story untold,
Within are secrets only you can
unfold.

Within my smile a happiness glows,
Within my voice the emotions show.

Within is warmth to shield the cold,
Within is a child I need for you to
hold.

Within is my love that you cannot
see,
Within is a person no one else can be.

So if you think I'm ugly look again,
But don't look at me, look within.

Russell L Spencer
WHERE DO I BELONG?
Which direction am I to go,
searching but not finding?
Waves of the ocean splashes back
in return to find themselves
washed ashore.
Who could see more often than I
in my own eyes, as somethings
come to us as no surprise?
A question often asked in faith, to
find the way I'm to go.
An aureole of saints I'm willing to
kneel to by the riverside to
point out my search for me, so I
may see what may come to be.
There I can watch all my dreams
flow, upstream will they only
go.

Elsie Falk Nelson
AFTER THE LAUNCHING OF SPUTNIK I
Who is that stranger locked in space,
who journeys round and round
earth's face?
This is not part of God's own plan,
but fashioned by the mind of man!
It started with a tiny seed, which
sprang from avarice and greed.
It was nurtured by a ruthless hand
and from all prying eyes was banned!
As time sped on, it slowly grew with
man to aid his conquests new.
Now nations wage the atom race,
while each distrusts his brother's
face!
When will it end, where can it lead—
will it cause hearts and minds to
bleed?
Or will man triumph and be blessed,
and set these hearts and minds at
rest?
How can we know—look to this day,
while we can still have hope and
pray.
God's love will hover over all, His
living things—both great and small!
We will plod on from day to day in
form divine—but feet of clay.
We will tread the path our Lord
commands,
Or crumble—like the shifting sands!

Lewis W Havel
YOURS FOR ALWAYS
Darling I love you, honest I do,
I'll always, and forever, belong to
you.
Some loves may last, just only days,
Mine for you, will last for always.
You stole my heart, that very first
day,
Please don't give it back, come what
may.
Hold it, and love it, as only you can,
You'll be my lady, I'll be your man.
As our lives pass, week after week,
No other love, will I ever seek.
For your love, sets my heart afire,
You are all, I could ever desire.
And honey, I want you to know,
I need you, I want you, I love you so.

Philip Kae
THE AMERICAN FLAG
O yes. I can well see
The Star Spangled banner
Waving proud in the breeze
Past, now and forever.
I will also acknowledge
The flag is just symbolic
Of what we hold precious
And stir us like magic.
There are those very few
Who see only the cloth
To tear or burn at the
Whim of their mental moth!
The flag of any nation
Is the rallying force
To move millions as one
Onward to their just cause.
You do not burn the flag
To protest injustice
You would speak up louder
In freedom and in peace!

Nicholas Kring
NATURE'S SONG
Nature's song,
Birds and flowers in concert.
Leaves turn, as time passes.
Is there sound, where no man listens.

A passage of time,
From sprout to mighty oak.
A seed dropped, and life renews,
Where no man sees.

A twig bent, to sun's rays,
Gives new life,
Where none was yesterday.
And non-plant man crawls out.

Then, where man destroys and sings
a song called progress.
Let him go and life returns.
To nature's song.

Leroy Sodorff
RECIPE FOR A CHILD
Take a slice of sunshine
Spoon in a touch of breeze
Add a cup of playfulness
And a pinch of tease

Pour in an ounce of happiness
Sprinkle in the dew
Wrap it in a rainbow
With a drop of honey or two

Toss lightly upon this earthen flame, sauté with a dash of love, stir in a heap of innocence, and a quart of the sky above. Bake to perfection, set the timer to nine, rotate slowly, and baste with time. Serve upon a golden platter, garnish with a cloud, a sweet and tender delicacy: A child in which to be proud!!

Thomas C Anderson
MARTYR

This poem is dedicated to my mother. For it is a martyr who devotes her life to rearing nine children: seven sisters, 1 brother & myself. I love you, Mom. Your son Tommy.

I loved you one and all.

Now my heart keeps
beat with each step
I take.

Now I walk in darkness with the
weight of
many sorrows upon me, only today
no tomorrows.

Do not follow me,
for where I go now
I must go alone.

Keep true to the idea and harvest the
seed
planted.

I'm just a man with a dream, don't
make me
into more than that.

Make my dream come true, it's in
your hands.

Let me rest, let me be, I'm weary.

Now it's up to you, one and all.

THE END

Angela T LaHue
ESSENCE, THEN ABSENCE

As you pierced my sphere of reality
slowly . . . timidly
I lowered my resistance
my ego boundaries tumbled down
and the beauty of your being
enveloped me.

I quickly experienced visions of
intensity:
explosions of color, shape, and time
propelled outward, inward
waterfalls of sublime inspiration
cascaded across my quivering soul.

I was filled with the essence of you
then, much too quickly . . .
empty, from the absence of you.

The reflections flicker my field of
vision
and create waves of desire
. . . to understand . . .
gently, I receive my gift
in moments of tranquility
and, reluctantly,
the comfort of aloneness trickles
back in.

Anita La Grassa RN
SEVENTEEN

There you lay alone and still
Twinkling eyes of yonder life

Muscles once of tone and strength
Wither while away the quiet.

Never will a whisper speak
Dolls she played not long ago.

Wet upon my cheek I cry
I wash and turn your body limp.

Painful are the moments pass
Once again I close the door.

Anita La Grassa RN
WHISPER WHISPER

Whisper Whisper
Raindrops gently warn
Clouds softly ease the pain
Thy storm I fear not
I lay with two.

Whisper Whisper
The angels call
My womb is barren
Closed eyes have drowned
her heart beats empty.

Whisper Whisper
They speak my name
A naked cradle
I ascend to thee.

Anita La Grassa RN
EDGE OF LIFE

Blowing yonder overhead
Heaven lifts thy soul to thee

Who are you that speaks his name
Crackling in the wood of youth

Aged is the man of wise
Sharpened hearing by device

Nature's skin whose vision blurred
Melting snow lay morning's frost

Judgement is the day of feast
Years escape as streaming water

Welcome be the edge of life
The mind at peace, alas I rest.

Trula Musick
LIFE'S LIGHT LIFE

Early sunrise seems
so bright

With rays of warmth
and colors' light

Peach and mauve and
amber might

Reach my soul with
great delight.

So soft, just like a
feather's touch

Of bluebirds, sparrows
meadow thrush

To soar and glide on
sunbeams glow

Will seek me, reach me,
let me go

Let's run and play in the
morning's sweet hello

And feel her deep
within our soul.

Dalia Beckerman

Dalia Beckerman
IS IT ME OR YOU

To "vital options" and to all cancer patients who are granted the vision of seeing each day as a precious gift.

You and her
She and him
They are all the same to me.
And mighty God;
The big one
What about the greatest one?

Self-love and forgiveness
Courage and faith.
Guidance and strength.
All these rhyme so nice
When good days are ahead of us.
But what if out of the blew
A hard cold blow hits you through?
What then?

Is it me or you?
Should I kneel and pray
Or turn my back and betray?
Or better yet look inside
The pages of myself
And become a winner all over again?

Yes, I'll hold still
And make my days
Better yet to be.

Dalia Beckerman
I SEE . . .

I see flowers and sun.
I see birds on trees.
I see little children playing.
I hear them laughing.

I see people moving and talking
As fast as can be.
I see hands shaking
And eyes whose look
Says it all.

I feel warmth all over
And love is in the air.

I see you
I hear how you feel
And what do you want.
I hear your pounding heart.
I hear mine, too.
I love you

Most of all
I know now
What is the GREATEST
love
Of all . . .
ME!!!

Dalia Beckerman
SILENCE

Here I am
Standing there
Looking nowhere.
Heaven can't wait
And earth is too much
For the take.

Here I am
Feeling angry again
Breathing no air
Feeling helpless, silent . . .

Tomorrow I'll be anywhere
Trying to swallow the hurt.
Deal with the pain.
As summer smiles
So winter cries.

And somewhere down the
road
A holy touch
A loving embrace
Will make it OK.
For life goes on
And I along with it.

Cavan Lyle Glassman
IF I WERE TO SAY

If I were to say I love you
Would it offend you
If I were to say I need you
Would you really care
If I were to say I care for you
Would you turn the other way
If I were to say I'm there for you
Would you laugh in my face or
cry
If I were to say I love you
Would you hate me
I love you

Florence Zielinski
A WINTER WALK IN THE WINDY CITY

I see him clearly in my mind's eye
although fifty years have gone by.
Home from the war—he is
handsome, clean and sharp in his
uniform.

We walk the Windy City, arm in arm,
along the lake,
Alone in the world of silent snow and
frozen waves.
The wind whirls my scarf into the air,
whips it around my neck and hair.

Young, we dare to challenge wind
and frost,
and sit on a vacant park bench.
What is weather to us?

We catch a rushing passerby, beg him
to stop,
and take a picture, please.
He does—then charges on into the
deep freeze—
Leaving us to walk the Windy City
and explore life's future possibilities.

Lois Busby
FIRST BORN

He used to say, the nights we sat
before the fire—
"—and when the little fella comes
We'll get a train, a wagon, and some
drums.
We'll dress him up in sailor suits,
and little jeans and cowboy boots;
And, Dear, he'll have your dark blue
eyes that shine
And maybe curly hair like mine."

But when the "little fella" came,
His dreaming wasn't quite the same.
Instead of drums, he bought a doll,
and fluffy dresses, oh so small.
He said, "Her eyes are blue, I'm sure
her hair will curl;
And, Dear, she's such a lovely little
girl."

Creda Stanczak
NATURE'S WAY

To my children.

The crashing noise of the sea against
the rocks.
The gulls' stout wings away up in the
sky.
The heavy rain as on earth's door it
knocks.
In Fall leaves turning color as they
die.
The seasons, days and nights all stay
the same.
Year in, year out though millions
come and go
The mountain, river, valley even
plains
Continue with their never ending
show.
My love for you seems great like
nature's things.
So soft and gentle yet so loud and
clear.
When you're around my soul within
me rings.
My heart beats loud like thunder
when you're near.
God made the earth for all and not a
few.
'Twas me He had in mind when He
made you.

Dorothy B Nuttle
THE SENTINELS

This poem is dedicated to my loving husband, Bill and our children Grant and Kim Suzanne.

Some stand tall
As they walk through life
Whether days be sunny
Or filled with strife

While others, with their scorn and
frowns
Miss so much beauty all around
That God feels mournful deep inside
And sheds a tear He cannot hide.

To all is given
The sun and rain
The lush green forests
And fertile plains

But we alone
Choose what we'll be
A lowly stump
Or towering tree.

Dorothy Miller
MY TWIN

With this Ring I thee wed
Are the words to be said
But do you understand
When you take her little hand
From this day you must be true
And must remember she loves you
Days will be good
Days will be bad
And she'll know when you're tired and sad
She'll kiss your face and hold you tight
And say God is with us both day and night
So with my love and one last kiss
I want you to know you will be missed

Carl R Yonkey I
MY LOVE FOR YOU WILL NEVER FALTER

My love for you shall never falter
Even after we have left the altar.

We have given each other a brand new start
With our deep love we shall never part.

The years will come and the years will go
Always remember how much I love you so.

My love for you will never slow
My love for you can only grow.

As we travel these sometimes rocky roads together
We will travel these roads as if on a feather.

My love for you is so deep my dear
That living without you is my only fear.

So my dear we have left the altar
Always remember my love will never falter.

Bonnie F Clay
MORNING GOLD

Early morning streaks across the sky,
birds waking up with music in their hearts,
starting the day with songs of life.

The sun crests the hills shedding
golden light on the earth below—
a moment of beauty suspended in time.

An artist paints the scene on canvas
recreating Nature's brush strokes
and capturing the hues of early morning sunrise.

Pinks and purples disappear too soon
blending into skies of azure blue,
and now the sun's full force is felt,
caressing the earth with warmth.

Heat waves shimmer in the air while
animals rest beneath the trees,
waiting for the coolness of night to forage for food.

The sun moves slowly toward the west,
dipping below the ocean as it goes.
Once again the sky turns into molten gold,
with rays of Jacob's ladders reaching up to Heaven.

Another day is put to rest along with
all our thoughts and memories,
to be poured over once again as the
next new dawning rays of
sun streak across the sky.

James W Mumby
ECOLOGY'S CAR

Build me a car without an exhaust;
Stay home from a star to finance the cost.
We've polluted the air and fouled up the breeze;
It just isn't fair to kill all the trees.
There's smog in your eye—you can't see the sky!
The air has turned gray, with 'planes on their way.

There are columns of smoke heading for space,
And there's always some bloke having a race.
The factories are humming and dumping their waste;
The streams are still running, but oh! how they taste!
I long for the joys of a place without noise,
But, where aren't there boys with "bikes" for their toys?

I'd take a vacation from all of mankind,
But, a place of re-creation is impossible to find.
Let's live like a brother to all those in sight;
It's not worth the bother to keep up the fight—
So, stop planning war before all is lost,
And build me that car without an exhaust!

Cornelia Lane
MY GARDEN

In memory of Warren Vaught, who planted my Garden, and inspired me to write poetry.

This is my Testimonial—
My Garden a Retreat for Reflection,
With Memories I need not mention.
Blossoms falling from the Ole Lime Tree,
With Blooming Bromeliads looking at Me.
My Garden so beautiful to behold,
The evident processes of Nature I am told.
A sudden flash of a Blue Jay
In the branches above,
And there on the ground
The rustle of a Mourning Dove.
It's Spring, and I am young again,
In the Garden that I Reign.

Blanche Merchant
ONE WISH

To my grandchildren,
Scott, Ronald and Cynthia Guynes
Traci and Samanthia Dougherty.

If someone said you may have one wish,
What would your answer be,
A house so great, a diamond large,
A cruise upon the sea?

An airplane ride to a foreign land,
Be dressed in the finest of mink,
Dine at the most expensive place,
And order champagne to drink?

Maybe you'd wish to be president,
Or rule as a Queen or King,
A dancer perhaps, who ballets or taps,
Or have millions hear you sing?

You may wish, to be very rich,
Have money in banks by galore,
But would you spend it all on yourself,
Or would you give to the poor?

Yes, you could wish for lots of things,
But the greatest wish should be,
That all the world unite in love,
To live in harmony.

Karen Foster Miller
ON PHOTOGRAPHING A WHITE TAIL

To my son, Chopper, my inspiration.

I crept through the field lying flat,
On my elbows with my camera in my hands, think of that!
So quietly did I slink along,
The birds above never missed a note in song.
My subject was across the field, alert,
And tho' my elbows really hurt,
I continued to crawl along in spite,
Of the fate of the day, the coming of night,
I would have to hurry, get close fast,
Before the light of day was past.
Upon my prey I have so closely come,
He lifts his head, snorts and runs!

Barbie S Washburn
DEAR MOM AND DAD

To Mom and Dad with love . . . .

You've always said you were proud of me, no matter what in life I chose to be. So I'm writing to tell you a few things of my own, to thank you in a way for all the love you've shown. Kids take so much without looking back, never stopping to see the things you seem to lack.

Remember the times I cried out in the night, and you were right there to comfort my fright. All the angry words that I let tumble out, never stopped your love no matter how loud I'd shout. All those sleepless nights when I chose to come in late, I realize now your anger and worry was out of love not hate. Remember the times my world seemed to turn inside out, you could always see the problem and turn it about.

Which brings us now to the point of this note, as parents of the year you get my vote. For all the love and caring you gave out, for taking the time and understanding to show me what life was all about. For always being there without questioning my needs, and for giving me the pushes to see the right leads. I'm proud and I hope that I can be—just half as good a parent as you've been to me . . . .

Barbie S Washburn
UNTITLED

To Kortni with all my love . . . .

Dear child of mine I hope one day you can see,
Just how very much your birth really meant to me.
You are the sunshine in my life when all seems gray,
You touch my soul with the precious things you say.
Your love is captured in my heart,
I have no need to be lonely even when we're apart.
Yet you are a part of me—half of my soul,
Without you near my world is not whole.
Right now you are so fragile perfect and small,
I hope that I can guide you in life, I promise to give it my all.
You give so much and expect so little in return,
You are too young to understand selfishness—that's a lesson you have yet to learn.
I know you will remember the harsh things I sometimes do,
But I hope the loving memories are many and the others few.
You accept my imperfections, you allow life to bend,
You don't judge me or demand—with you I don't have to pretend.
I hope I succeed, and one day, dear child, you'll see,
Just how very much I love you and how I thank God for trusting you with me!

Timothy Imhoff-Richardson

Timothy Imhoff-Richardson
A FRIEND IS . . .

A friend is loyal and caring,
Ready to help in any way.
Someone who will help
when you're in trouble,
Someone who will teach you
all they know,
Guide you on the path, the right way;
Someone who will love
and care for you always.
They're willing to sacrifice
in any way,
They'll brighten the day
when you are there,
When nothing, nothing
is going your way.
They will be kind and gentle
as a soft breeze
Ready at any time to help you
with any problem.
And in return, try, whatever it takes,
Try and help them in return.
My friend is Michael—
a friendship that will last.

Dawn Rollins (Age 14)
LOVE TAKES TIME

My love is gone,
Nowhere to turn.
I tried too hard
and now I've learned.
You can't rush love,
It just takes time—

God only knows that love
takes time.
For when in love
your smile grows.
Then your lost love
will certainly know
that you love him.
And it may come true,
Because someday,
He'll love you.

Irene Leisso Bay
JESUS, MY SAVIOR

Dedicated to daughter, Mary Elizabeth Johnson.

JESUS, my SAVIOR
Was born for me,
In small Bethlehem
Far o'er the sea,
To be my SAVIOR
Came to our earth,
While shepherds watched sheep
Heaven sang HIS birth,
And a great star shone
Its glorious ray
On the lowly manger
Where JESUS lay.

JESUS, my SAVIOR
Once died for me,
Gave HIS holy life
From sins to free,
To be my SAVIOR
Died on a cross,
On cruel Calvary
Suffered great loss,
Gave up all glory
Of heaven HIS home,
Traversed death's dark valley,
Laid in a tomb.

JESUS, my SAVIOR
GOD'S holy SON,
Was raised the third day,
My pardon won.
HE is my SAVIOR
Gives love and grace,
My faith gives to me
In heaven a place.
The FATHER'S mercy
And SPIRIT'S hope,
GOD'S gifts, my sins forgive
Then Heaven's gates ope.

Delma Joy Swaby
WHO AM I

In dedication: My mother—Doreen Ward, My Grandparents—Mabel Barnaby and Charles Barnaby.

I breathe.
I am a man
I was the only child for my father
I am a rich man

But—rich in what ways?

Rich in blessings.
I was persecuted
Yet I was raised up
as a ruler of the universe.

Who Am I?
To say that I am ruler of the universe
I received such blessing from my father

Who Am I?
To say my father has such power
I am JESUS CHRIST
the Son Of God.

Cheryl J Lewis
THE ORANGE MOON

The orange moon
The black night sky,
Night owls hoot
And black bats fly,
'Neath branches bare
By hollow trees,
I sit and wonder about the breeze.
What makes it come?
What makes it go?
What makes me sit and wonder so?
If I knew, if I could say,
I wouldn't be sitting here today.

Adrienne J Earl
THE MEANING OF MEMORIAL DAY

To My Macho Son Terry, and Grandsons T. J. and Joshua, and my deceased husband Donald.

The thirtieth and last Monday in May,
Each state celebrates Memorial Day.
A noteworthy event our war dead deserve,
Honoring their memories this day we preserve.

Memorial is filled with many mixed emotions,
Families unite to strengthen their devotions.
A day which means so much to all,
Memories of those who answered God's call.

In each little town, I have found,
A monument on a piece of ground.
Inscribed with names and dedicated with pride
Patriots, a war in which they died.

We lost many at home and all around,
For those Patriots our Lord always found.
Just plain folks like you and me,
They are all heroes that I can see.

In remembrance of one grave I saw,
A young fellow not lost in war.
Quoting, "So talented, so young, so soon,"
There rested a dime, a rose and a balloon.

Douglas L Wilson
A BRIEF PONDERANCE

I sat in the shower for nearly an hour,
and contemplated my life.
Abrasions, contusions, persuasions, illusions,
all the forms of my strife.

I struggle in vain to juggle the rain
of troubles that fall around me.
Lifting them, bending them, binding them, sending them,
hoping some day to be free.

Then I thought about Joe, and Ms. Mary Jane Doe,
his normal everyday wife.
Wandering, wondering, succeeding, and blundering,
through their everyday life.

I sat in the shower for nearly an hour,
and decided I liked how I live.
Dances, romances, and casual glances,
I still have some gift I can give.

Richard Pellington
STELLA'S DILEMMA

Stella sat at the window morbidly thinking out loud, "Should I or shouldn't I?"
Tears gently welled up into her eyes, and she started to cry like the poor lost soul that she felt.
Then, with a shrug of her shoulders, she reluctantly acknowledged that she was feeling sorry for herself.
"I should be counting my blessings instead of allowing this soul-retching fear to linger," she mused.
Quickly, to forestall any doubts, she picked up the phone and dialed nine one one, the emergency number.
At the sound of the answering click, mumbled words tumbled hurriedly from her mouth.
"Hold on a moment," interrupted a gruff answering voice. "Slow down and repeat what you said."
"I can't slow down," she claimed with alarm as the phone slipped from her trembling hands.
It dropped to the desk, and broke apart in disarray, as she left the room in a frenzy.
At the other end, an answering firefighter's shrug spoke volumes of his apparent contempt,
"Just another false alarm," he yawned sleepily as he stretched out his legs to continue his snooze.

Vincent "Bear Walks"
ON THE FOURTH OF JULY

Fourth of July's
Not the same when
I was a child
With blood on my pen.

It's not the same now
And never it seems
When I was a child
With teeth to my dreams.

I remember when crackers
Cracked with a bang
When bells of dependence
Rang with a clang . . . .

As liquid flowed
Like fire thru my veins
And pistols exploded
In colorful strains;

The lites of enlighte'ment
Burst full and high,
When I was a child
On Fourth of July.

Fourth of July
In an admiral's knot,
In the twist of a sparkler
In the who of a what . . . .

In the roll of an acorn
'Cross midsummer's grass,
Free children a'playin'
Some slow an' some fast.

Fourth of July
Like a flag in the sky;
The banner of freedom
Ever so high;

On a wave of tomorrow
With a tear and a sigh,
I'll remember you always
On Fourth of July.

Liza Bonilla
THIS MAN

This tall, dark Hispanic mustached man you see,
Is more than descriptions make him out to be.
When my grandma, his mother, became ill and died, the pain that I felt I would sadly confide,
To this man who would listen, though I was just ten,
And tell me, "Welita is now in Heaven."
A camera, this man's prized possession abroad,
Later caused my family to drowsily nod.
We'd hear "There's one of your mom aside Big Ben,"
As Julio Iglesias echoed throughout our den.
When he realized we'd been bored nearly to tears,
This man perked us all up with French souvenirs.

This man came to my baseball games,
Sat in the top row,
And yelled out such pointers as "lift your elbow!"
Of course, never an important game could I greet,
Without first playing catch with him out in the street.
Rock stars and heroes are all passing fads.
No man do I love like this man, my dad.

Brenda D Wilson
YOU HAVE TOUCHED ME

This poem is dedicated to the love of my life, David Walden.

For all that I am for all that I shall ever be,
is a void of loneliness deep inside of me.
The loneliness makes me feel alone in a crowded room.
I make them laugh I make them smile
they say I'm the best that can be.
ooh, what a pleasant comfort, but
the loneliness exists as real as can be.
One day I met you and you somehow
became an important part of me.
You make me smile you make me laugh,
your gentleness has made a princess of me.
You tell me you love me oh oh how
that consoles me, and when
I look in your eyes they show me
it's true the feelings you speak of me.
The feelings touch me and reach me
in ways I thought could never be.
Now the loneliness is all gone
and
replaced with You and Me.

Saundra C Clinton
THE WAY OF THE CROSS

That beautiful spring day when Jesus arose,
I wonder what the people felt do you suppose?
It could have been great joy or even fear,
But no matter what our Lord is so precious, so dear.
Even though he had to hang on the Cross, to so many he was simply one man of three,
He has so much love to share, don't you understand, don't you see?
How did they feel when they walked down the Road of Sorrow?
Did they wonder what would happen tomorrow?
There are so many who have shut him out, to them he's lost,
If only they understand why he died for us and came forth to pay the cost.

Christ is alive, he's alive, I just wish I knew the words to say,
I know he lives, I asked and all I had to do was pray.
At one time I thought what's the use, I'm a failure, who cares, my life is a loss,
I reached out, He blessed me, then He took my hand and showed me the Way of the Cross.

W F Yearwood
WHEN

To the one I love.

There may come a time when
You are my eyes and ears,
My strength to carry on;
My eyes when I see but dimly;
With you I'll have no fears.

Though I see not, I'll know
The touch of your hand.
Though I hear not, I'll know
'tis your whispers of love.
I walk not in darkness
But in the light of your love.
When I hear your laughter
'twill be music to my ears.
When I'm with you all else
Doesn't seem to matter,
'tis a peace beyond description,
It gives solace to my soul.

Juanita Bullock-Martin
PAPA

In loving memory of Nannie Adams Rose and Lurenthia Crater, my grandmothers. And of "Papa," Vencely Charles Crater, my grandfather.

Papa had silvery white hair and broad shoulders. His skin was smooth and reddish brown like chestnuts. There was beauty in the way that he aged, as only longevity could profess, through generations of knowledge and wisdom; as the sand in the hourglass changed the seasons. Papa had a gentle spirit, but sometimes steamed like a mighty ship. But like a ship of greatness, he'd quickly calm the angry sea and gently stroke the waves. Papa loved to travel and see the sights of the world, captured through the tiny lens of his Brownie camera. After he circled the globe and saw all of its splendor, his pictures were preserved for a lifetime of memories. Papa reached for dreams that others wouldn't try. The goals he set in life were won, because he didn't quit. He tasted the bitter and sweet of life to get its full flavor. Papa experienced life to its fullest measure, before he left this earth.

Ragna Elisabeth Larsen
RAIN

Black clouds
Rolled over the dark sky,
Filling my mind and soul with gloom.
Unwarranted gloom
Borrowed
From the troubles of yesterday.
I slushed onward,
Not seeing where I went.
Then . . .
I saw a stranger
Coming slowly over the distant Hill.
A dim light encircled him.
He came on.
The light grew brighter,
More beautiful.
He touched me.
All worry and gloom fell away.
I sang.
Yes,
It rained.

Ragna Elisabeth Larsen
AN OLD MAN

I love an old man named Autumn.
On his age I will never frown,
His spirit is crisp and pleasant
He's an artist of great renown.

He paints with abandon and flourish
His colors of various hues,
They give to the tired beholder
Faith, contentment and peace.

I longingly wish he would linger
Longer before he departs
For God in His wisdom created
Autumn's unmatchable art.

Ragna Elisabeth Larsen
AUTUMN

What can I say of Autumn
That has not been said before . . .
Of the beauty of the painting
God has set outside my door?

All the colors are so splendent,
Ablaze with hues of reds and gold.
It fills me with such gladness
It reaches clear into my soul!

He puts no price upon it.
It is free for all to see.
Oh, I thank the greatest Artist
That He made it, too, for me.

I can sit before my window,
I need not leave my door
To enjoy my Father's painting.
Oh, what can I wish for more?

Ragna Elisabeth Larsen
HOME

Home brings visions of gardens aglowing
With trailing vines and forget-me-nots.
Where daisies peep through the green of the meadow
And dewdrops like raindrops
Water the lot.

Home is a place where love is abounding,
Where sorrow and hurt is tenderly nursed.
Where birds all busily prepare for their nesting,
Sing praise to God.

Home is a place where the sun is aglowing
Red in the west, when the day is done.
And the sparkling stars in the dark sky glisten
One by one.

Home is a place where we go to find comfort,
Joy, laughter and popping corn.
Where a loving father and mother will mend–nerves
Frayed and torn.

Catherine D Williams
TEMPORARY EQUALIZERS

To those who have loved me and encouraged me, especially you mom.

Just by chance I heard you scream
And risking my life, I pulled you from the stream
Thus allowing you to realize your dreams
And I concluded that "fate" was the great equalizer

I remember the time the tornado tore through our town
And the mighty winds blew all our houses down
Together we worked until our loved ones were found
So, maybe "disaster" was the great equalizer

Then there was that day in Nam just before the attack
When you screamed for someone to cover your back
It didn't matter then that I happened to be black
Was not that "war" a great equalizer

And now Auther has stiffened our joints and gnarled our bones
All our children are dead and gone
Yet we help each other here in this Old Folk Home
Indeed "time" is a great equalizer

Yet I am saddened that time, age, famine, and flood
Injustice, strife, and the spilling of blood
The wars of liberation that set men free
All just happen to be . . . "temporary Equalizers"

Berdeen Oland

Berdeen Oland
THE SCARLET SQUAW

Promise me, oh, promise me! You will not tell!
Her eyes were deep, as the deepest well!
Her teeth as white as winter snow,
Her face was wreathed in an angel's glow!

Her hands were soft as thistle down,
When she came to me in her gossamer gown.
Kisses sweet as honeydew,
She whispered softly, "I love you."

Her lips were soft and warm and red,
As she lay beside me in my bed.
Her body warm as a summer day,
Told me things I dare not say!

She held me and loved me and told me lies,
As I lay lost in the sound of her sighs.
The prettiest picture an artist could draw,
Could not compare to the Scarlet Squaw!

Berdeen Oland
DEATH IS A LADY

She came with icy fingers bare,
And touched my neck beneath my hair.
She breathed upon my cheek and chin,
Gripped my arm, where my shirt is thin!

She held me close, like a dreary ghost,
On the fog bound shore of Alaska's coast.
She told me tales where the north wind blows,
Where all is ice and nothing grows!

I shivered much in her icy grip,
She kissed me twice with her frozen lip!
Frost sank into my brittle bones,
Like frost sinks into frozen stones.

Then she turned me loose and left me there!
That frozen maiden with the frosty hair.
She left me to wander alone in the cold,
Like a timid sheep in search of the fold.

The wind bore down in an icy gale,
And covered my tracks and hid the trail,
I was lost in the land where none can save,
Then I slept alone in my cold, cold grave!

Berdeen Oland
PADRE

He was smaller than a chickadee,
With a leaf upon his head.
He sat there looking up at me,
In his little shirt of red!

He was the smallest little elf,
I had ever seen!
He was dressed much like myself,
In his tiny boots of green!

Why have you come to visit me?
And sit upon my shelf.
Can you tell what is to be?
You merry little elf.

I've come to brighten up your life,
To make you laugh with glee!
Away with pain away with strife.
That's what he said to me!

And so it was from that day on,
My joy has been complete,
From early in the morning,
'Til I slip beneath my sheet!

Berdeen Oland
THE FOX

OH! Pretty vixen that she is,
With flaming hair of red;
Her story goes like this,
From birth 'til she is dead!

Through valley green or tufted swale;
She lightly makes her way,
With timid step and bushy tail,
Through the farmer's field of hay.

HARK NOW! The sound of hounds
O'er distant darkened valley!
Go swiftly now in giant bounds!
Or add to the hunter's tally.

Cunning creature with tail a'streaming,
Lead the hounds o'er rock and glen.
Wake the farmer from his dreaming,
THEN! Slip into your den!

Berdeen Oland
THE COYOTE
From the hills I cry
My sad and doleful tune,
The owl and nighthawk fly
Across the rising moon.

Why am I here on angry earth?
All hands against me turned.
From the moment of my birth
For naught, but food, I've yearned.

The shepherd counts his nervous flock;
The farmer with his sleeping chicken;
The cowboy looks upon his stock;
With hunger I am stricken.

No friendly hand upon my back
No bed before the fire.
For when men see my track
It fills them with desire.

To hunt me down and take my life
With trap and snare or gun.
I run from endless strife,
I do not howl for fun.

Berdeen Oland
MY POEM
I placed it there
With utmost care
On top of all the rest
I know it is the best

I struggled with composition
With comma and exclamation
Fretted with indecision
In harried hesitation

Slowly it grew in my head
A coat of blue with a golden thread
I changed a word or two or three
It said the things inside of me

Its words were soft as velvet skin
Sweet with sighs and urgent whispering
I made it laugh, I made it cry
Then placed it with the other poems—editors won't buy

Berdeen Oland
DANDELION
I smiled upon its golden face,
Then plucked it from its lowly place;
Blew upon its hair of gray,
Then watched it slowly drift away!

Now, no matter how I try;
All of it could not be found,
If all the angels in the sky,
Should search upon the ground!

I held in my hand,
The newly naked stem,
And watched the dancing, floating band,
And thought, "I should have counted them."

Then after winter's chill,
Has given way to spring.
And snow has melted from each hill,
I will marvel at this wondrous thing!

How can it be that in this place?
Where grass is springing from the earth!
I'll see a lovely golden face!
And know, Dandelions, are giving birth!

Berdeen Oland
DEER
Leaping slowly with exceeding grace,
They leave the forest dim.
And then a smile upon my face,
Caused by their bodies slim.

Leaves my face to go inside my heart;
And nestle there like furry kittens sleeping.
Then one from one they part,
Like wraiths of vapor leaping.

No trace is left of bodies brown;
Only leaves and pine trees nodding.
My smile becomes a frown,
I'm left alone, and lonely, trodding.

Berdeen Oland
THE MARCH OF TIME
With lusty yell she made her debut
That was yesterday, now she is two!

With eyes of blue and braid of blonde,
A fairy waved a magic wand,

And in a dress of snowy white;
This will be her wedding night!

She has her man and now a child,
Yesterday her baby smiled!

WHAT! You say! Her man has died!
We tried to talk, but only cried.

Suddenly her hair is white!
It was golden just last night!

Can it be she is in her grave?
Time! Oh Time! We are thy slave!

Marie T Martin
ONLY THE ARTIST CAN HEAR THE MUSIC OF THE RAINBOW

To Elizabeth, my artistic sister and friend, may you always hear the music in rainbows!

Your eyes paint colors
And view the dimensional
Shades of life
Which others overlook.

Your dreams lightly brush reality
With delicate strokes,
Creating colorful, abstract designs
Over the multi-grey shaded world.

Your magic decorates the imagination
With splashes of colorful tears
Daringly disturbing the tranquil canvas
On which lives are exhibited.

Your talents transform words
Into a delicate design with uneven strokes
Purposely placed
To express your mystical outlook.

Your world dances on a pallette
Of carefully combined colors,
Disguising the dim hues others visualize,
Inventing brilliant songs of color and wisdom;

But, only the artist can hear music in this rainbow.

Mary Sue Richburg
FOOTPRINTS IN THE SAND
I stood looking out at the ocean—
The great gray mist—
No skyline—
The whitecaps gently rolling in—
The vastness was unreal.
As I watched, a lone figure appeared.
His stride was brisk,
His footprints clear.
As he strode in the distance,
Soon to disappear.
Soft waves lapping at his feet,
Covering footprints,
That moments ago—had been complete.
Life is short—like footprints in the sand.
Soon to be forgotten—
Swallowed up—
Then laid to rest,
In the warm sands of time.

Gunta M Smits
THE MESSAGE

For all of You lovely people.

I am building my house
With not a thing,
What people would call value.
The greatest value
I cannot build,
Just opening doors for You.
    There is nothing big in my house—
    Just me.
    I am big in mine thoughts—
    And so!

With love
    Gunta.

A C Tillett
GOD'S CREATION
I stood upon a hill so high
And gazed in wonder, at the sky,
The pale moon shining golden bright
The twinkling stars, that brighten the night,
The hazy glitter on the lake below
Gives rippling waters an eerie glow,
Dark smudges, cast by maple trees
Like sentinels, down upon their knees,
Praying to the Lord above
For all the things HE gave with love.
The very same hill at the break of dawn
All the mysteries of the night are gone,
A ball of fire, on the horizon
The sun comes up to greet everyone,
The birds awake and start to sing
In the red and gold maple leaves,
And among the maples, a few birch trees
On such a beautiful day nothing can go wrong,
Yes GOD, created a beautiful place
Where HE then put the human race.

Mary L Walton
IF I COULD

Thank you to Justin Hayward who, through his lyrics and personal achievements, gave me inspiration and confidence to begin the pursuit of my dreams without being afraid of the world.

Oh darling if I could only find a way
to tell you what's on my mind
How I awaken in the night
I hear your voice
You're asking me . . .

My baby if I could only find a way
to show you
just how I feel
If I could take you in my arms
and hold you tight
then you would know . . .

. . . My love is a fire burning bright
my love is so new it's true
What can I do, I love you, I love you

Oh darling if I could somehow take your hand
I'd tell you
Can't find the words
But when I look into your eyes
The flame inside can't be denied
The flame inside won't be denied

forjussongs

Skipper Douglas
LITTLE BOYS
Little boys are such a wonder,
Even tho they sometimes blunder.

They can fill your heart with such delight,
In the same moment cause a great fright.

For little girls they have no time,
They feel in life this is their prime.

To have a baseball and a pair of cleats,
In this world nothing is so complete.

To himself and his peers a
20 foot basket,
Has to be in itself so fantastic.

Then there comes a day,
Little girls no longer get in the way,
Little boys now will say, can you come out and play.

Much to a Mother's great despair,
Little boys find another life in which to share.

So many times their first love is lost,
But Daddy says he should go on at all cost.

When the day of the altar draws near,
Mom and Dad surely will shed a tear,

Dear God, whatever happened to the day,
When I said, "Tomorrow Son, we will go out and play."

Charlie Thompson
HAPPY ANNIVERSARY

To my loving wife Sharron.
1978—Till death do us part.

When I get sad and weary
And need someone's soft touch.
You kiss me Dear and say to me
I love you very much.

When I have fallen down
And I need me a crutch,
You pick me up and say to me
I love you very much.

It's been ten happy years now
The way that it should be.
So kiss me Dear, I love you.
Happy Anniversary.

Garland D Hood
SHIFTER OF THE SAND
I thank you Lord for life so full and free
for even the bad things, little things, for even a tree
Thank you Lord for what you are
The giver of life, the creator of a star
The beginning and the end, the shifter of the sand

I thank you Lord for all I can see
For all that I have, and for all I can be
For freedom from the bondage of sin,
I now am able to take a stand
For the beginning and the end, the shifter of the sand

I thank you Lord as I grow old
Your breath gave me my very soul
I thank you Lord, your grace abounds
You are my Lord, the beginning and the end, the shifter of the sand

Our lives are like the sand of the hourglass

It ebbs and flows away, day by day,
as time trickles past
But I know the one who holds the
way, the only one who can
He is the beginning and the end, the
shifter of the sand

Jesus is this friend of mine
My Lord and master for all of time
He is the positive, the great I am
The beginning and the end, the shifter
of the sand

Ginger R Strivelli
WHY?
Hatred with ancient roots, growing
from a tower's rubble,
Hatred that is the cause of all worldly
trouble.
My ghostly complexion, isn't the
essence of my being,
Nor does any other shade hold any
profound meaning.
Why do we always blame our
innocent brothers,
For sins committed years ago against
others
The magical tide of love comes in
only once per miracle,
So why is transcending classes and
colors so unhearable?
We are so quick to condemn, an
entire race,
For nothing more than the color of
their face.
This would be such a sad way, for the
world to end,
So why can't we allow the wounds to
mend?

Violet Branch
AUTUMN'S GOLDEN MEMORIES

In memory of my loving Mom and Dad and Son, Robert Manae.

I love all the seasons of the year,
But autumn I love so,
The trees are splashed with color,
Like the color of the rainbow.

I see the leaves move slowly,
As the whispering breeze passes
through,
They glisten in the sunlight,
Scarlet reds and golden hues.

Leaves look like the artist's brush
Was painted by the master's hand.
All those splendid colors,
But never by a man.

As I walk through these rustling
leaves
It takes me back in time,
When we were only kids,
And I thought that you were mine.

How we loved those sunny days
Of so many years ago.
If we could only walk again,
In leaves, we had enjoyed so.

David M Hammonds
SMILE
When mistakes are made
and the hands begin to close
Keep him on his toes
Smile,

When the sky begins to fall
and the earth begins to crack
Give the devil his cue
Smile,

When all else fails
and the spirit and body have quit
When not even crying helps
Smile,
When the old man picks the tune
and Gabriel plays the blues
Take the hint
Smile.

Katherine W Jones
GOD'S GREAT OUTDOORS
Come, sit with me in my own
backyard
and feel the gentle breeze.
Now, lift up your eyes and watch the
beautiful swaying trees.
You can catch a glimpse of God's
blue sky
and the snow white clouds as they
hurry by.

In the green of the trees; the blue of
the sky;
and the snow white clouds in
between
I see a picture no artist could paint—
No hand, no brush could enhance
such a scene.

I feel the glow from the King of the
sky—
It warms my body, it quickens my
heart.
Its rays penetrate to my very soul—
It tells me again, "God's in control."

I feel a quietness and peace, as I sit
here alone.
I feel the beauty of God's great
handiwork,
I feel God's love showered down
on me
And I wonder anew, how beautiful
heaven must be.

Michele Roller

Michele Roller
THE MIRROR

I dedicate this to my children with my unconditional love, as such a mother's love should be. I'm not here to judge you but I pray you read these words and know that all love should be unconditional.

The mirror is now dark as I stare at
the glass.
Somewhere in there is the bright
shiny past.

The children were small with happy
faces,
For the world was theirs and they
would go places.

As their little hands were reaching, I
was sure I was teaching all the things
of right and wrong for them to carry
on.

Then, I was so sure, but now it's just
a blur, for somewhere in time I let
them cross the line from light to dark,
where they now dwell, living a life,
but is it life or is it hell?

I remember with joy the days they
were born. Now I feel sorrow and
from my soul I do mourn.

I want so much for my children to be
with the love of God from the great
shining sea.

But the prince has deceived them
with whispers at night. How were
they to know he could mask himself
in light?

I should have told them of the devil's
deceit, but they are still not alone for
I would die to defeat his hold on their
souls.

He promises wonders for them to
know, oh yes, the wonders of the
devil's snow.

The snow makes their world such a
beautiful place, all patterned with
sparkle like fine lovely lace.

When the snow melts, you must have
some more, and on it goes until you
are no more the person that God
made you to be.

Oh please, please my children wake
up to see, Jesus is waiting, saying
"Come unto me."

Open your eyes, your hearts and your
souls, stop what you're doing and set
some new goals.

The darkness will go and the light
will come in, then you can look in the
mirror again.

I pray that you all find Jesus in time.
So easy to do if you do it right, just
follow the light and not the dark
knight.

Mary Fisher
A SMILE IN MY HEART
There is a smile in my heart
for I know that God and I are never
apart
He cheers me up when I am sad
He's always here and so I'm glad.
One thing I will ask the Lord;
to be with Him forever.
I, poor sinner that I am
have God walking with me hand in
hand
Oh, why have I been blessed so
much?
to actually feel God's tender touch?
It is in God's abode where I will stay,
from Him I will never go away.
Help me, Lord, to breathe a happy
sigh,
whenever my time comes to die.

Nancy Ellen Nelson
POWER OF A TINY GRASP
I wonder at the power
a little hand conveys
when placed trustingly in mine

Directly I am charged
girded to shield and shepherd

Where once, doubt reigned
I stand as a tower

for the tiny grasp transmits
emotions of exultation and might

unsurpassed by naught in life

in unison
with one accord
we slay dragons

Bonnie Jean Schneck
WHIP-POOR-WILL
Dark is the night
At our Ozark campsite,
The moon and stars our only light
As the Whip-poor-will takes flight.

Nocturnal, with an aura of mysteries,
It builds no nest, but rests on dead
leaves
Fallen from the trees.
Come out, if you please!

But Whip-poor-will remains
invisible,
More often heard than seen,
Grayish brown, it's invincible
Blending with nature's scheme.

Whip-poor-will flies little except for
feeding
On insects caught in flight.
Moths, and other flying insects
Are its special delight.

Whip-poor-will serenades us,
The night is quiet and still,
Echoing its name, clear and
melodious,
WHIP-POOR-WILL!
WHIP-POOR-WILL!

Cynthia Bindah
IMAGINATION

I dedicate this poem to my dear husband, Cyril Vibert Bindah. Through common sense, hard work and integrity has risen to great heights.

If I were a bird, I would fly so high
Until I become a mere speck in the
sky
Up, up, and away in the heavenly
blue
Where am I going who cares, would
you?
As long I'm happy and carefree.
Gone is the winter when the weather
is cold,
Seeing strange places and trying to
belong
With other feathered friends who
happen along.
Feeling the flow of wind under my
wings
Just like a bed without any spring
When I am weary and night comes
along,
With head tucked under wing, I will
rest until morn.
The limb of a tree is a good resting
place,
For those who are weary and need
lots of space.
In the morn when awaken it's time to
get moving
There is breakfast to find and chores
to be done
The life of a bird must be a busy one.
Perhaps if I really were a bird,
I'd find things much different than I
suppose
Now like a bird I have to return,
And thankful to be the person I am.

Dorothy Beck
LITTLE BROOKIES

Written about my father-in-law, E.A. Beck, for my husband Bob.

Hung on everything said when I was
a lad.
Watching dad tie flies for fishing in
mountain streams—
Followed his many steps, mimicking
everything.

Then when I became a dad, my son does as I did, so long ago.
I think of those things now, for dad has walked sunlight's paths toward heaven.
In my mind's eye I can see him with his rod and reel.
It's pleasant remembering this, for I can relive my yesterdays.
Secret little streams no one knew about, but he did.
Walks through pastures opening gates until,
I'd almost give up there being a mountain stream, but it was there!
My dad knew them all.
After a full day's fishing we'd walk to our car.
Back to the house, creels full of brookies.
Those days are gone, but memories are pleasant.
For, in my mind's eye, I can see him still, tying flies for the little brookies.

Laura Brueckner
THE RAIN AT THE END OF THE WORLD

For Una, my sister, and Ben, my love.

While I breathe, I will remember
The golden glow of your voice in the rain
As we laughed
And sang
And waited for the world to end.
Will it end
While we are spinning, dancing,
Sharing the same umbrella
As the sky falls down around us?
Will it end
While we are lying in your bed
Not quite awake
Breathing the spiderweb air?
If it does, I will remember
While I breathe, I will remember
How it was
When sunlight flowed like
When teardrops fell like
When lifetimes passed like
Seconds
In the rain at the end of the world.

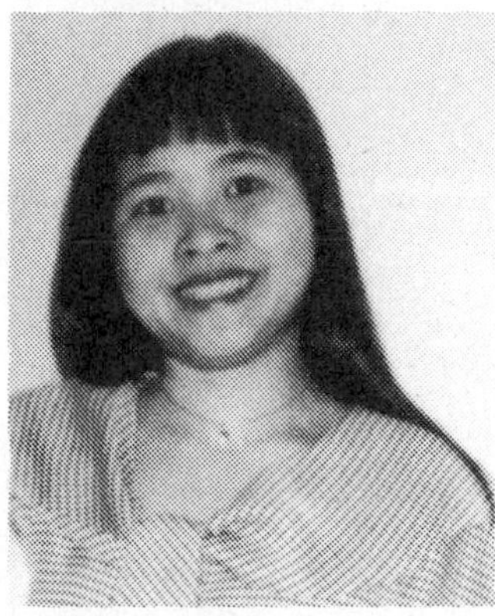

Thuy Vo

Thuy Vo
REMEMBERING

When I was young
My mother was dead
I now understand
How lonely I was
Without any family
Without any love
I kept standing there
Without any words
Coming out from my mouth
My tears kept going down and down
But I felt a lot better
After a long cry
Standing near the grave
Listen to the bell of church
Thinking about my mom
How wonderful she was
When she was alive
But now things had changed
It seems like
I lost everything

Faye Nunnelee Byrd
THE TORCH OF FREEDOM

In New York harbor
There stands a lady,
With a torch in her hand
A torch that says
To all the nations,
That freedom reigns in this land.

But far more important to me than liberty
In heaven there stands before God's throne
My Lord and my Saviour
With nail scarred hands
Scarred hands that are for God to see,
Scarred hands that intercede for me
That hold my freedom from sin
That say to God,
She is my child and she is free.

America is great
And I love her so,
But Jesus Christ is Lord
Forevermore.

Faye Nunnelee Byrd
THE WIND OF GOD

Just like a ship
Upon the sea,
Just like a ship
I live before Thee.

Sometimes my sails
Are full of wind,
I travel on
My way to win.

But then sometimes
My wind is lost,
Then my Lord
I am turned and tossed.

At times I feel
I cannot go on,
The trials of life
Have come so strong,

Just like a ship that has been hit,
I flounder in the sea about to sink.

And then the wind of God does come,
And carries me on into life.

Faye Nunnelee Byrd
NO ONE CAME TO THE FUNERAL

There was no long black hearse
No announcement in the obituary,
No cards sent
No white daisies by the way,
No mourners.

For no one knows
That she had died,
So there were no mourners
No sad goodbys.

So I sat in silent grief
I mourn myself alone,
There is no joy in Mudsville
For mighty Casey has struck out.

And because there was no corpus delicti
There were no comforters,
No one came to the funeral
Except I.

Faye Nunnelee Byrd
AMERICA COME HOME TO THE LORD

Like the prodigal son we ask for our share,
The freedom to follow our ways,
Down the road of damnation we are running each day,
While our land falls into decay,
America, come home to the Lord.

The children we kill before they are born,
We have many diseases and such scorn,
We are walking our way,
And we are having to pay,
America come home to the Lord.

If my people that are called by my name
Will humble themselves and pray,
I will forgive their sins and heal their land,
So, America please come home to the Lord.

America turn from your sins,
Let Jesus in
While his arms are open wide,
He will heal our land
He will hold our hand,
So America please come home,
Come home to the Lord.

Teresa K Brown
WHY

A Dream come true for Dorothy Wieseman.

Why am I hated?
Why is it me?
Before I was born my folks had three.
When things went wrong it was because of me,
my Mom always wishing she'd never had me.
Always the trouble maker, never doing right,
my Mom convinced I caused every fight.
How many times I cried in the night,
wondering why I was hated and never hugged tight.
Why was it I who always got the slap,
never checking who caused the spat.
My Dad tried to help when he noticed with alarm,
Mother shouting it was me she wished had never been born.
He knew I was no different than his other kids born
and tried to smooth the anger and keep me from harm.
I always tried to do the things to help my Mother most
but when she bragged her kids, of me she would never boast.
When life's problems got to her, it was to me she would turn
to vent all her anger, to be rid of me she'd yearn.
Being the fourth child and the hatred I see,
I wonder if maybe she only wanted three.

Ada Jane Thornton Pugh
THE WONDER OF WEBS

Once upon a foggy morn,
Telephone poles stood forlorn.
Glistening from the sun behind,
Webs showed up adorned and lined
Between the poles.
For about a mile they hung,
Like a silent song was sung
In quiet beauty hanging.
No spiders now seen spinning
Upon the wires.

Later in the day I passed,
Looking for the webs to last,
But no trace of them reflected.
No dew as I expected.
Webs hide from view.
I wondered if heavy dew
Had damaged perhaps a few.
Foggy days I always peer,
Hoping webs again appear
Between the poles.

Alma Bonilla
A KNIGHT IN ARMOR

With love to Officers Karen Crawford, Michele Daniels and Mary Holguin.

A knight in armor of blue cloth.
Guarding the world from great loss.
A shiny steel badge and a heavy .38.
Always ready to confront the world face to face.

Alma Bonilla
TOGETHER FOREVER

Two young children. Lost and then found
Together forever bound.
Two children running away from broken hearts.
Together forever never apart.
Safe and secure at last. Together forever forgetting the past.

Ken Burrows
EMPTY WORDS

To my beautiful D.B. Your love is my life's blood eternal. Our Souls are One, Forever Yours, K.B.

Empty words
never mean a thing,
Except for the burdens
they sometimes bring.

It's only love
that really counts.
Yet, often it seems
we do without.

If our words came
from the heart
Would we still
drift apart?

Empty words
never make the grade.
They come from
plastic people on parade.

Wolfe Bolter
FATE

To M.M. May the winds of Fate always warm you.

I wonder how it happened
That one day I would feel
Your spirit walk beside me
A face . . A picture . . So real

Just like a flower blossoms
You've made me come awake
To new ways all around me
To share . . To give . . Not take

And sometimes when you're far away
It's in my heart I feel
No matter what becomes of us
My love for you is real

I wonder how it happened
That I should feel this great
It can't be mine to question
After all, it must be FATE

D D Altenloh
A HAUNTING ICON
Solitary tree, on a barren rock,
overlooking the sea.
Standing, sharp lines drawn
against a red sunset
While the ocean swells and violently breaks beneath,
just out of reach.

A silent passage as the sun sets,
lights fading,
Thus, it will grow,
borne of leaves decaying.

A simple, quiet moment of timelessness,
written forever within,
With harsh images alone
as the author.

D D Altenloh
DESERT RAIN
I pray that each night passes quickly
As I watch the light fade with the sunset.
For then, I must fight my worst fears, never faced before
And must wait patiently for the day to come
When my losses can be restored, and I will finally be free.

All of the tears I shed could not stop this pain,
So they fell and disappeared, like a desert rain.
And every feeling within me that gave me life,
Every word and thought inside my head
Cried out for you, before that moment was lost.
Leaving us now to chase our separate dreams,
For we must each find our own way.
Still touched, by only the memory of that love,
I stand alone, to watch a rose bloom, in the morning sun.

D D Altenloh
WHEN LOVE BEGINS
When love begins, the world is alive as we explore
The endless river of hopes and dreams
Of the many things that we might be.
We'll grow together, the two of us,
Passions flowing without end, untamed,
Through spring and summers in the rain.

How often we'll sigh and lament
Whatever wasted time so foolishly spent.
Eyes closed, within the comfort we'll hide
While passing seasons mark the days we've lost.
We'll smile and just bide our time.
Words unspoken. Promises broken.
Poetry without rhyme.

When autumn finally turns leaves brown, then gray.
Remember then these words I say.
My love for you shall never be denied,
For it will always be locked, deep inside.
Each day you'll look into my eyes
And fall in love again.

Fabienne Lacoursiere-Dumont

Fabienne Lacoursiere-Dumont
LEURRE ABYSSAL

A NORMAND mon pirate bien-aimé,
Qui garde mon coeur prisonnier,
Depuis les trente dernières années.

Peuple des mers, marins,
grands voyageurs
qui partent et qui naviguent
à leur guise.
Ils disparaissent à l'horizon,
sillonnant les eaux,
dérivant vers l'inconnu.
Ils apparaissent quand on ne les attend plus,
comme des héros
le béret sur l'oeil, le teint buriné,
les lèvres gonflées de leur dernière nuit d'amour.
Je les regarde et voudrais partir à mon tour.
Tenter l'aventure, cotoyer le risque,
voguer au gré des vents
comme au gré de mes pensées,
malgré le roulis, bravant le tangage;
chevelure éparse, sirène moderne
attirant dans mon giron
les matelots aux coeurs chavirés.
Je les charmerais de mon doux chant
et les pauvres mousses ballotés, égarés,
iraient s'échouer sur les écueils,
attirés par les brisants
d'une mer déchaînée
qui leur servirait de linceul.

Carl B Burkhart
STAKE YOUR CLAIM

I dedicate all my poetry to God Almighty. Without him, they wouldn't be written.

There is a wealth that we can receive bountifully. It is more than most precious of ores & jewels. It can be taken with you when you die. If you take it with you to the grave, it will never leave you.

It's like finding a precious ore that contains all the precious ores; because the wealth that it brings creates other qualities of like value.

You must search for it, gather it, sift it like panning for gold. Separate its precious substance from the sand & stone of little value.

It can be processed & developed by you. You need no license to acquire it or to produce it or share it.

There is enough for everybody. You can have all you want. It can flood the market, but never lose its value. Its price is always the same.

It's like money, the more you gather, the richer you are. Yet money cannot buy it.

It has curing powers. It's the most versatile medicine. It can cure the ailments of the world.

It can abolish evil like magic.

It's like living, it's free and it only costs you your time.

(IT'S LOVE)

How can we pass it by?

Carl B Burkhart
I'M HUNGRY
Jesus I'm hungry; for food from above.
For God's abounding grace, for your precious love.
For God's Holy Spirit deep inside;
guiding my heart in holy pride.
For the spirit of giving and not to take.
For thoughts of thee the moment I wake.
For full comprehension of the gift of thy birth.
To sow thy seed upon fertile earth.
For things of virtue, for insight to see;
should the path not bend as I walk to thee.
For a soul at peace and contentment within;
contemplating thy cross that frees me from sin.
Feed me dear Jesus with the gifts of thy grace;
deep in my heart to ever embrace.

Carl B Burkhart
PEACE
"Blessed are the peacemakers, children of God"
their feet with golden sandals shod.
For peace will calm a raging sea,
in its waters not a ripple be.
Erase a storm from a wind-swept sky,
place white lingering clouds till evening's nigh.
Still a cursing tongue about to sting,
to reconsider and rather sing.
Sparing blood that might have spilled,
allowing many their life fulfilled.
Heal thy wounds, remove the scar,
a twinkle in the eye, a glittering star.
A dove at dawn, its soothing coo,
transcends shattered spirits to heights anew.
Let the petals of this flower, not wither and fall,
share its beauty, with another and all.

Carl B Burkhart
LOVE
Love searches for peace & finds it,
Makes peace & keeps it.
Love does no hurt, but shares it.
Love breeds compassion and makes a forgiving heart.
Love does not hate nor have any part in it.
Love searches all things for the good in it.
Love knows truth and justice and lives by it.
Love makes a sweet character.
Love responds to love and will not reject it.
Love brings harmony & contentment, then peace.
Love is a heart alive; a mind that ascends to the highest levels of wisdom.
It comes from untainted waters.
Its fruit is unblemished, pure and sweet.
Love has something to do with everything.
With hate—it will replace it, Evil—it will prevent it.
Virtue is the work of love.
Love comes from the Father of love, for he is love.
Love is the fulfillment of a good life.
Everyone has been dealt their share & must nourish their own.
You cannot master it; it must master you.
Be still; and let it overcome you.

Jane E Jennings
WEDDING VOWS OF MIND & BODY

To my darling Jim. Thanks for a great twenty years, three wonderful children and a promising future.

THIS mind given to you;
all thoughts and ideas, unconcealed
for truth and faith.

TWO minds working together;
striving in unity, for absolute peace
understanding and love.

THIS body thoroughly cleansed;
given to you wholly, to be
cherished tonight as forever.

TWO bodies united as one;
to make our future, blessed
with our eternal love.

Paula T Fahey
FIRST LOVE

For Paul F. Valverde of Phoenix, Arizona. It took so long to find my one true love. Now I'm yours for eternity. Love, Pooh.

I've never had a lover to touch me so sweet
And I've never had a lover to fall at my feet
But I'm in no hurry to rush into love
'Cause I have no worries, It'll come from above

In time—I'll find the man who takes my heart away
In time—He'll be my man forever, never stray
Here I wait so patiently for that love that belongs to me
And I'll find it eventually
In time

I've never had a man with kisses like wine
And I've never had a man so handsome, so fine
But soon I'll awaken from dreams of my love
And then I'll be taken to the heavens above

How I long for a lover, devotion so strong
Can't I please have a lover, I've waited so long

It's time—I found that man who takes my heart and soul away
It's finally time—He'll be my man forever, never go away
After waiting so patiently
Found that love that belongs to me, just me
And we'll shine through eternity
MY FIRST LOVE

Denise M Yetman
DAYS GONE BY

There comes a time when people think
about events that could have been,
Regret will fill hearts to the brink
of wishes to start life over again.

There may be talents left under cover
or remorse over untraveled places,
Too many feelings left to discover
or memories of past lovers' faces.

Remembering goals left far behind
by those whose dreams died out too fast,
Very few people you'll come to find
content with an unblemished past.

The gift of life is not just a name
once given it's your own to mold,
In birth every life contains the same
a brain, a smile and a heart of gold.

Keep in mind with each step you make
the time for decisions will eventually die,
The hand of time can never take
you back to all the days gone by.

Teresa Hosey Ferguson
LETTER TO OUR CHILD

Dedicated to our beautiful daughter Taylar, whose birth has strengthened our faith in God and answered our prayers.

Time passes by too quickly for us
from stroller to walker and then the school bus.
We can't hold you back we must let you go
but here is something that you need to know.
Polka dot bears with velvet ears
may offer hugs that wipe away tears.
Their fuzzy warm hugs and soft little snuggles
help take away your fears and your troubles.
Now, childhood toys may comfort young hearts
but soon growing pains are bound to start.
So, always remember we're both here for you
with love, understanding and warm hugs too;
and for those times when you're far from home
here is a secret your heart's always known.
God loves you forever—you're never alone.

Love,
Mommy and Daddy

Teresa Hosey Ferguson
THE CAROUSEL HORSE

Dedicated to my Mother, Phyllis, who loves carousel horses. God blessed me with a wonderful mother. I love you.

My favorite horse is pink, yellow and white
and never tires even into the night.
No matter how far we decide to roam
we always manage to find our way home.
Never in a hurry to win the race
we just plod along at a nice steady pace.
Never too far to make a quick raid
for hot dogs, candy and cool lemonade.
But, time passes by and energy fades
making memories too precious to trade.
The day finale end with the setting sun
dreaming of horse rides yet to come.

Lisa Major
FRIENDS?

He's always in my thoughts and dreams,
And he's always on my mind it seems,
He made me feel so bright inside,
A feeling I hope again to find.

I always seem to be hoping,
And I always seem to be thinking,
About how he made me feel so good,
And how I thought he always would.

I'm living on the hope that he'll be back one day,
It would be tomorrow if I could have my way,
Oh how I'd love to be "his girl" again,
Then for sure the pain would end.
God, how I miss his hugs and kisses,
He fulfilled all my hopes, all my dreams, and my wishes,
What did I do to make him turn away,
Is there anything I can do, anything I can say.

I really miss all the expressions on his face,
I'd give anything for one last embrace,
But I guess I'll have to settle with being his friend,
And hopefully as friends, we'll last till the end.

Christina Toh A M

Christina Toh A M
THE NEWBORN—"SHE"

The days of silent despairs are gone.
As the hollow soul being filled with delightful musics.
Making the past as the special histories of remembrances.
As the love still lingers in her heartaches.
She still searches far beyond into the unknown space.
At last, her soul reaches the eternal peace.
With the wisdom enlighted from above.
As she follows step by step with faith assurance.

The days of darkness, darkness are gone.
As the time and hour has predicts to come.
The cries of harshness and lowness of the newborn—"She."
As she has being captured with love.
With the supports of many loved ones.
She finally overcomes the trails of life.
With sharing and caring once more.
She follows day by day with self-confidence.

K A Bell
THE RESTING PLACE

For Joan, with whom I have found peace.

When I took your hand,
it was to comfort me.

The arrest was immediate
and all my fears subsided.

It was as if I were motionless.

For the first time in my life
I stood still as the woodpecker
letting the echo fade away . . .

Katherine Moses
FOREVER

To say it's the end,
Is to say it's gone
Forever.

It couldn't be helped,
Though I wish it could.
Even though I'm gone,
Please don't forget me.
For your face, your living memory,
Has always been with me.

Though I never said it,
Though I never felt,
Your warm lips upon mine.
It's always been forever
In my mind.

Remember during your living years,
The memories we shared,
Will never be forgotten.
That, is what it means to be forever.

Louise Grogan
MY LITTLE HILL

There is a hill outside of town,
Not very far from here,
On which the pines grow thick and tall,
And beautiful all year!
It lies far from the other hills,
Secluded and alone,
I go there sometimes when I'm sad,
That hill is all my own.

I stand upon the very top,
Quite hidden by the trees;
I look out at the countryside,
And listen to the breeze.

There's something very restful,
In the stillness that I find,
And little cares and worries,
Sort of vanish from my mind.

The little hurts, the little pains,
My spirit could not drop,
All seem to disappear from me,
When I have reached the top.
And every heart should sometimes go,
Where all is quiet and still,
Life's road is not so weary,
When you have . . .
A LITTLE HILL!

Lois Gustason
MY ONLY LOVE

I've never met anyone like you
You're in my thoughts, everything I say and do.

Lines from a love song or a poem
Seem to fit the way I feel about you.
With you, I always feel at home.

I get lonesome, upset, sad when I don't see or hear from you—
But it doesn't last; call or be here, that's all you have to do.

You have said our "chemistry" is right—
We get along fine, we rarely fight.
I prefer to think we're "kindred souls"—
We share thoughts, hopes, dreams, and goals.

I feel like I really do matter to you
when I'm with you and then,
I don't matter to you at all when we're apart.
You say you don't want to ever hurt me; but how can you <u>not</u> break my heart?

You've touched my life, my heart,

my soul.
No matter what else happens in our lifetime, together or apart—
My feelings towards you won't change—you'll always have a special place in my heart.

Amy Jurgens
MY DAD

I would like to dedicate this poem to my dad who is a very special person in my life. I love him very much.

He has a personality
All of his own
He's like no other person
I've ever known

Sometimes he yells
Sometimes he shouts
And the fact that he loves me
I sometimes doubt

I try to act
Like I don't care
But deep inside
the hurt is there

Many times
He makes me cry
I let him hurt me
But I don't know why

Sometimes when
I'm feeling blue
I say I hate him
But it's not true

We have good times together
But mostly bad
Because I'm his daughter
And he's my Dad

Someday we'll be
Better friends
But the hurt and sadness
Never ends

Retha Hall Parmer
TOGETHERNESS

To the caregivers.

When traveling down the highway of life,
It is good to help with someone's strife.
By helping others, it is clear to see
Just how the Almighty wishes us
to be.

We lose sight of our own troubles
that hurt us so,
When we lift another's load and help with his woe.
If you are ill and cannot see the light of day,
Reach out to someone else and God will brighten your pathway.

Pat Freeman
LAST BREATH

To Lisa,
With admiration and love.
In a better place than this.

Mask of air gave no aid
to wrenching gasps,
grasping what was left of life,
in a cancer stilled and silent shell

Each labored breath raised the depth
of death-watch tears, whispered prayers
a quick, yet endless end

Finally, suddenly, eyes opened wide
seeing someone, hearing something,
face surprised, questioning,
understanding, accepting, in turn.

Dried and silent lips spoke
softly to someone, something,
a whispered agreement.

At 29, two hard and stolen years
beyond a diagnosed end, she slowly
raised her hand, touched her
fingertips softly to her heart,
nodded her head, closed her eyes and died.
Her last breath a peaceful sigh.

Oliver F Coon
CHILDREN OF THE DAWN

This poem is dedicated to the children of the streets.

Wake my child, wipe the sleep from tired eyes.
Warmth is a fleeting thing, when servile comes, day by day, minute by minute,
Hunger is a thief when empty streets make up, your world.
You are hidden in plain sight,
faceless, strangers
Discard your livelihood as they,
make their way
To places you only dream about.
Then night comes again to guard the truth!
The cold wind dries the tears on a once happy
face when life was young, shadows come to taunt
your slumber, rest is a luxury for others.
The Dark holds you in its arm.
Refuge, on one
hand—the long sleep on the other.
Then your silent prayers are answered!
The Dawn Begins!

June Moore
LOVE 'YA, AMY, DEAR

To Amy,
My Precious Granddaughter.

Tiny one
so sweet
so tender
from head to feet.

A bundle
of joy,
stretching, yawning,
so cute and coy.

From one
to two
so busy
lots to do.

Will the
"twos" ever go!
a little peace
others can know.

Ideas all
your own
so fresh
playing grown.

Time passes—
cuter you grow
gaining hearts
of all you know.

Your smile
is coy,
winning, too
full of joy.

Your love
is so true,
loyal, warm
and I love you!

Breath of
Spring, life anew,
pleasure, fun,
so like you.

Sixteen years
attaining, being,
all life gives
for doing, dreaming.

Hearts are sad
all day thru
since Heaven
selected you.

Joy will
return anew
when in Heaven
we see you!

In Loving remembrance
—Grandma Moore

Daniel J Hartley
HAPPINESS AT LAST I'VE FOUND

To Lori Marie, My Wife, My True Happiness.

Happiness at last I've found,
to guide me thru the coming years.
To hold me when I'm feeling blue,
to hear my woes, to dry my tears.
To strike an arc on life's dim light,
to fan it till it's glowing bright.
To guide me in all righteous thing,
to make the heart within me sing.
All this is mine with love so true,
all this and more since I Wed you.
Within sweet loving Vows were bound,
Yes, happiness at last I've found.

Daniel J Hartley
SANDS OF TIME

To Lori Marie Kessler Hartley; My Love, My Life, My Wife.

Alone across the sands of time,
beneath the cold gray skies.
On paths their own, a boy, a girl,
with yearning in their eyes.
A longing need within their souls,
there is no joy in sight.
For youth is theirs, and in their youth,
they cannot see love's light.
Its embers bright does flame on high,
to touch upon the heart of each.
The dawn of love is drawing nigh,
to their very souls it doth beseech.
The hand of God did draw them near,
and their hearts beat in ecstasy.
A love so wondrous and so dear,
awakened now and they could see.
The sun for them would shine so warm,
and the sands of time shall do no harm.
For a love so strong, a love so bold,
came; a gift from God, for them to hold.
A love by God, a love that's blessed,
a love for life, two hearts at
rest . . .

T J Kinney

T J Kinney
THOUGHTS

Float away on golden wings, ride the raging storm,
the storm of thoughts that flood the mind, from the moment you are born.

The questions tumble endlessly,
fighting for attention,
future problems push them back,
searching for prevention.

Thoughts of loved ones flash and glimmer, no thunder, only lightning,
then a sudden feeling unexplained,
seems momentarily frightening.

You try to keep the storm at bay, and control the way you feel,
but the mind can be deceiving, and overshadow what is real.

Amidst that giant sea of memories,
the answers can be sought,
it's a never ending battle, but it's one that must be fought.

If you can weather through the storm,
and keep faith in yourself,
then you may find, within your mind,
resides your greatest wealth.

Ralph D Thomas
LOST THROUGH DIVORCE

Action of lost love and
relinquished dreams.

Of yesterday's sorrows and
tomorrow's dreams.

Of XMAS past and future holidays
yet to be.

The care of one gone but still
here.

Of heartaches of the past and
present, still to be.

Of the warmth of children on your
knee.

Life is not what you want it to be
but what it's meant to be.

So here we are in court today—
seems we must be free.

So God bless you in all your
needs.

Seems the courts are full indeed.

Ruth Graham Woodard
SERIOUS REFLECTIONS
Today at the age of seventy four—
Three score and ten and four years more;
I'm proud of the days You have given me,
Time enough to learn Your will to see.

One regret, though, I have in mind,
Is waiting so long Your will to find;
Life is divine living in Your grace,
Knowing You'll put each trial in place.

How sad it is to slip and slide—
Not allowing You to be our guide;
Thinking we know just what to do,
Instead of surrendering each day to You.

Rhoda McVea
LOW-INCOME HOUSING

I thank God for rescuing us in so many ways and for giving us a new, better life.

Dogs barking
Children harking
Baby wails
Mother screams
Ottoman drags across the floor
Every twenty minutes
Clatter and batter
Low-income chatter
Welcome to low-rental housing!

Inconsiderate kids
Swear outside the door
Pound on the floor all day
Everyone does the laundry on Saturday
Hide your little six-pack!
Not allowed here
Too many problem drinkers
But it's cheap and no bugs
Thank God it's not out on the street!

Merrilane Davis
HAVE WE LEFT A MARK?
Through life sometimes, the road may vary
There are times, when all is merry
there are the times, when all seems dreary
And yet we grow, with each experience, we learn
Lady experience, teaches us, we must earn.
For none of us know, when, it will be our turn
We are born, we grow older, and one day we die.
Have we left a mark? That, we did try
Or will it only be, empty time and very dry
If one friend, we have been and found
If we care and give, without making a sound.
We have made a mark; That will resound!

Christopher Ware
WHEN I KNEW YOU
Like a spring's sweet gentle rain and fragrances of all the flowers of June,
your love intoxicates my body and soul.

Your gentle touch sends rainbows and stars across the summer sky,
exploding into bright and beautiful lights and falling like comets in July,
a love so strong and so frail.

Here I'll keep you deep, deep, inside,
and remember the stars and flowers forever now, till the moon crosses a clear August sky, inside your love will never die.

Mrs Cathy A Steudl
RAYS OF HOPE

This poem is dedicated to my Karl, who is still a child at heart, and the best friend, and husband I could ever want, Thank You.

Laughter like the tinkling of thousands of bells,
Perfume of the sweet and innocent,
The way a baby smells.

Wake up all people, this world is no joke,
Take care all of you, of our Rays of Hope.

Climbing, reaching, growing tall,
Their youth makes them best of all.
Knowing only the colors of Spring,
Hatred of others does not yet ring.

Toss them in the air and hope,
They will always remain our Rays of Hope.

They listen, they learn, they live as one,
Our children are ours as is the sun.
For they are here today, and gone tomorrow,
We can only pray, they will know not our sorrows.

So reach out and love them as your life goes on,
For one day soon we all will be gone.
Then in their day, they will live like we coped,
And they will create, New Rays of Hope

Joyce Rae Rust
CHILDHOOD GAMES
Whatever happened to childhood games,
the ones that were played in the good ole days?

Kick the Can, Run Chicken Run, the Three Legged Races always were fun.

The Raggedy Ann, the Jack-in-the-Box, the
little toy trucks, and tractors were tops.

Seems all of the things that were simple, and free,
have been replaced by video games and T.V.

How good it would be if children would play
the old fashioned games of yesterday.

They too would remember, as I do one day,
the childhood games that used to be played.

Lucy Webb
YESTERDAY'S TEENAGER
I recently discovered
that my daughter wasn't perfect.
Sometimes the bad in her
comes to a surface.
But, we must love our children
especially through their teens.
Try to remember
what being young means.
All the unanswered questions
and the romantic dreams.
Ah—yes, now I remember
when I was sixteen.
Homework, bestfriends,
ballgames and dating.
I'd solve one problem
there'd be another one waiting.
Being an adult is not
what it's cracked up to be either.
If there was but, an ageless time,
when we were neither.

Linda Wakeman-Rhoads
WHY
Why,
can't you see,
the color of the sky?

Why,
can't you see,
the tears in my eyes?

Why,
can't you see,
the roses over the thorns?

Why,
can't you see,
the children we have
born?

Why,
can't you see,
I can't start my life anew?

Why,
can't you see,
all my memories are of
you?
WHY?

Linda Wakeman-Rhoads
THE ODD COUPLE
You are tall, I am considered small.
With your height, together we make a sight!

You are silent, as the still of the night.
I like to chatter, to me it feels right!

You are a loner, I think it's a phase.
I'm at home in a crowd, I like all the praise!

Talk of love, is just not your style.
Still I have to, silence a smile!

My love, Your love, I cannot doubt.
For you know what, I'm all about!

One by one, we face our foes.
One by one, we face our woes.

Throughout the tears, throughout the years.
Together we stand, hand in hand.

Like flowers growing, in the sand!

Linda Wakeman-Rhoads
REALIZATION
So far away, I'm lost,
and all alone.
It is true, you never can,
go back home.
For home is not there it,
has been replaced.
Filled with strangers,
wearing plastic faces.

Night after night, I have,
cried many tears.
It hurts to realize,
after all these years.
The family I have held,
in my heart.
Became relatives, as we,
drifted apart.

I think of you often,
but am I forgotten?

Paula Bender Hight
NOWHERE
The winter winds are gusting,
Gusting and tossing my hair all around,
Shading the sky a hazy harmonious hue,
And he is shouting, shouting to me.

The silky snowflakes are gliding,
Gliding and dying cool on my lashes,
Tickling my chilled cheek and red running nose,
And he is touching, touching me.

The ranting rains come sheeting,
Sheeting and trickling tiny drops down panes,
Streaming silent transparency and more, yes more
And he is whispering, whispering to me.

The wavy waters are billowing,
Billowing and glistening sun off their peaks,
Robbing me, blinding me to brightness alone, yes alone,
And he is nowhere, nowhere to see.

The summer sun is blazing,
Blazing and warming the withered-worn world
Revealing everything and erasing all doubts
And he is nowhere, nowhere to see.

MANLO
NATURE'S MELODIES
The breeze brings melodies
Across the sky
With soft spoken words
Its melody sighs,
Be light and cheery
'Tis no time to be blue
Just breeze along
With a happy heart!

Melodies bring lovely thoughts
Good deeds and everything
Let's join together
To breed harmony.

Many's the time
When clouds turn black
To make the world amiss
But, if you don't take it to heart
Life is but a dream.

MANLO
THE TREE
Tree standing alone
How do you grow so big and strong
Standing forever
Like a monument to the earth.

How do you weather the storms,
Wind and snow
When I can't even weather
The loneliness.

If I had your trunk
I could live without the nearness
Of someone
But I lack your strength.

If I had your leaves
I could live without the warmth
Of someone's arms
But I lack your security.

If I had your branches
I could live without the need to
Lean on someone
But I lack your self-confidence.

But if you can do it, so can I!

Deon Corley
A FACE IN THE NIGHT
The smooth rounded
curves are
all but hidden.
Piercing blue eyes
sparkle in the
moon's mellow light.
Silky blond hair
flows with the
night's cool breeze.
A soothing call from
rosy red lips
is the only sound
breaking the silence
of the night.
These are the makings
of a face in the night.

Jim Christofic
LOVE HURTS

To J.B., who helped heal the pain and helped me to love again.

When you are hurt by the one
you love—
You may turn for strength from
up above,
The wounds may be deep,
although none shows,
But the pain still lingers, so you
must go slow,
Time will pass and the wounds
will mend; so you start your life
and go on again.
There will be another if you open
your heart.
One who will love you and will
not depart.
I know the pain you feel this day,
but maybe together we can
hide it away.
I've been hurt, my wounds were
deep, many were the nights I
could not sleep.
But time has passed, and I must
go on,
I've opened my heart one more
time; hoping that love will
finally be mine.
I know the risk—I fear the pain;
but I feel I have a lot to gain.
A friend who will share my
deepest thoughts,
Someone who will help me from
being lost.

Dawn Marie Carlson (Age 17)
THE GREATEST LOVE OF MY LIFE
You light up my days with your
wonderful ways,
All you say and all you do make me
more in love with you.
We've been through some sad times
and been through some bad
But just having you near me makes
me glad.
There's so much yet that we have to
discover—
I am so happy it's with you—
The World's Greatest Lover!

Patricia Coles
TWINKLE, TWINKLE LITTLE STAR

To: My Sons, Nathan & Isaiah.

Twinkle, twinkle little star shining so
bright;
I, often wonder how you light up the
night.
The moon smiles as you dance in the
sky;
Around the world you can fly.
Twinkle, twinkle little star so
carefree;
Just like you I wish I could be.
Brightly shining above the world so
high;
I'll make a wish upon you on the
nigh.
My wish would be for you never to
die;
For if you do I'd surely cry.
Twinkle little star, twinkle with all
your might;
And shine little star in the golden
twilight;
Twinkle, twinkle little star all
through the night;
Shine until the first morning light.

Doris Currie-Kennedy
DIALOGUES

For Governor Michael S. Dukakis of Mass.

"And what of love?" I said to the
brilliant Sun,
Who was pointing out practicalities,
"And the dreams last night that the
Moon spoke of?"
(Last night, I woke on my pillow
cool,
And the Moon & I, like a couple of
fools
Spoke of love, and ignored
actualities.)
The Sun deigned not to give reply
But turned red-gold & left the sky!
Well, tonight I spoke to the silver
Moon
And told her about your attitude,
That you had simply no time for such
as love,
She smiled archly in back of a lacy
tree
And, after making such a fool of me
Consoled with the dullest of
platitudes!
(She cannot be blamed, she is just
undone,
By her hopeless love for the busy
Sun!)

David A Murdoch
DELIVERANCE

To: The Rev. Joan Salmon-Campbell, Moderator, Presbyterian Church of the U.S.A., 1989-90.

On eagles' wings You bore them up,
From Egypt to the sea,
Across the parted waters
To the land of Galilee.

You led them to the Promised Land
And brought forth there
your Son
To ransom captives evermore
And love mankind as one.

The slave is free; the judgment's
paid.
The blood has cleansed the ground.
The lash is gone; the sword's at rest.
Let charity abound.

You've raised the poor to claim their
right
Among the world of men.
No longer can the rich claim might
To oppress their next of kin.

"I have a dream," the Master said.
"Let my people go,
The seas shall break and kings shall
quake,
Let all my people go."

David A Murdoch
BUILD A FAITH, O GOD
We come into Thy Presence with
thanksgiving;
We come into Thy Courts with
praise;
We confess to you our sins, Dear
Lord;
Forgive our foolish ways.

Build in us a faith, O God, which
asks, and seeks, and knocks;
Build in us a faith, O God, which
answers, finds, and unlocks.

Build in us a faith, O God, where
You can enter in;
Build in us a faith, O God, which
cleanses us from sin.

Build in us a faith, O God, which
rules our heart and will;
Build in us a faith, O God, which
makes our soul be still.

Say the Word, Dear Jesus, and in
Your Name, we're healed;
Say the Word, Dear Lord, and in
Your Heart, we're sealed.

Louise L Birk
WEAVER TRILOGY
woman weaves basket
Indian Spirits guide hands
watchful approval

weaver of grasses
completes circle of design
basket being born

labor of love ends
tender hands cradle basket
wheel of life begins

R Grayson Swinson
THE CIRCLE OF LIFE
Life is a circle, beginning with a
breath
A cycle of happiness, of sadness and
death,
Life we must treasure and make of it
the most,
Death we must accept and be its sad
host.

All life is a circle from beginning to
end,
We must reach, love, adjust and
bend,
Reach out to each other, mother,
father and friend,
Reach out to others when they fail us,
or we fail them,

Fail we do, but we must reach again,
Regain our composure and not come
up slim,
Slim in our measure or short of our
trim,
For sailing life's journey is no easy
task,
We should make efforts that count
and last,

We should make all effort to survive
and live,
And in all cases, try to forgive,
For Life is a circle, as well we know,
A circle of life to live and to grow.

Beatrice McDuffie
I HAD NO HANDS BUT YOUR HAND

To my children—Clarence, Leanna and Marvin.

I had no hands but yours
to do my work everyday.
I had no feet but God's feet
to lead my way;
I had no tongue but God's tongue
to tell me how he did for us.
I have no help but yours
to bring them to God.
But if hands are too busy with other
work
Then mines are not yours.
Who will tell them the message of
God's
love for them.
I have no hands but yours
to do my work today.
I have no eyes but yours to see
I have no feet but yours to lead men
the way
I have no help but yours
To anchor in faith
To uphold us by night.

Dori L Downard
WHEN I SAY "I LOVE YOU"

When I say, "I love you,"
I say it from the heart
And when you don't reply
You know I fall apart.

When I say, "I love you,"
It gives you such a start
And the silence that I hear
Is the silence of your heart.

When I say, "I love you,"
You know I'd like to hear
A quiet little "I love you, too,"
Whispered in my ear.

So when I say, "I love you,"
And you give me that blank stare
I die inside myself.
I wish you knew how much I care.

When I say, "I love you,"
And our eyes then meet
Suddenly you look away
And I remember love's a
two-way street.

Claudette F Jeune
THE MOODS OF THE WIND

This poem is dedicated to Coral, my dearest daughter.

I feel the wind in my hair, caressing
my cheeks,
Blowing gently over my face as it
seeks
To lift my skirt above my head, as it
swirls about my legs.
Oh it feels so good.
My friend the Wind is in a romantic
mood.

He pushes me along as we romp and
play,
He is too strong for me, I'm only
made of clay.
He leaps about me as I gently roll
down the hill
And lay exhausted, as he stands still.
My friend the Wind is in a playful
mood.

Suddenly he turns and spurts and
roars,
Lifting twigs and branches as he
soars,
He howls and claps and sweeps
everything in his path,
He sends an old man's hat down the
slope in his wrath.
I lift my head and look at the place
where once he calmly stood.
Beware, my friend the Wind is in an
angry mood.

I hear him whizzing by, but as he gets
closer to me
I feel again his gentle kiss on my
cheeks and see
Him go away far above the clouds
and wave goodbye,
Farewell, my friend, I try not to let
him see me cry,
For tomorrow he'll sing me a
lull-a-bye.

Lucy Villegas
SISTER

To my sister, Irma V. Medrano With Love.

We have said that one day
We'll go our separate way
We promised that we'll be by your
side,
When our father gives you away
But I've heard you've been crying
And are shedding a thousand tears
But sister, with all my heart,
I will keep on loving you throughout
my years

Lorilee Liberatore
FRIEND

A simple meeting
A simple look in the eye
A simple shaking of hands
A simple touch on the face
A simple embrace
A simple caring for each other
A simple love for each other
A simple meeting of a friend
standing before one another
looking at each other while
shaking hands.

Natalie Jackson
UNCLE JACK

Gnarled his hands and etched
his face, still nimble is his
mind.
Each ship is a creation—there are no
two a kind.
He dreams of long past battles
of wars he should forget.
His body aches and tremors, but his
hands are gentle yet.
With care each ship is anchored,
its moorings taut and trim.
And the old man's friendly smile,
appears as from within.
Fretful waves abeating, on the
newly painted bows.
With wind tossed sails, and angry
gulls, his spirit still abounds.
Thru a smoky haze he watches,
as she's placed upon the shelf
No dust unlike her comrades, to
obscure her very self.
For years to come you will
remember, all the tales of the
'Seven Seas.'
About the ships he sailed upon, with
names like—"Myra-Lee"
Someday in a quiet moment,
while cumulus drift by,
You will remember his Armada, and
ask—"Why must he die?"
He left memories and
keepsakes, enough to fill all
time.
Yet the greatest gift of all was, he
lived to save mankind.

Harriet S Webster
DEPARTURE

Go softly . . . you will never guess
that I have gone beyond your last
caress;
for I shall leave no little errant trace
to help you find my half-remembered
face:
and though you search all trails
there'll be no track
to act as guide if you should call me
back.

I shall go softly . . . with my head
held high
though I shall find few stars in any
sky . . .
though I shall know a loneliness so
deep
it will not pass in waking or in sleep;
and you may wonder, missing me
someday
just why it is that I have gone away.

But when you walk a river street
some night,
where we have walked, and when
moon-tortured light
comes drifting back from some old
hour we knew,
I think you'll know that I had never
gone
had you not mentioned disenchanted
dawn.

Kiki L Turner
I HAVE FOUND WORDS

I have found words,
To all the feelings,
All that is—
But one.

And the soul that's,
Deep inside of me,
Goes more or less—
Untouched.

So oft' the joy,
And happiness,
Can take a sudden—
Twist.

And the heart,
That was perpetual,
Is sullen, in parts—
Abyss.

Ronald R Greene Sr
DUKE—JOHN WAYNE

To my family, Doctor Tom—Ginger Nonnenmacher=Jonathan; Ron Jr.—Tina=Ron III, Michael—Bonnie=Jordan-Asley; Most of all to my three young grandsons' Cowboy, granddaughter, mentioned above; to Janis their mother, who gave me the three children above—my parents, Alveno—May Greene, my brother—sisters, most of all to God.

A man he was
Big, strong
Mighty, in all ways
Spoke with demand

Demand indeed
Tall as he was strong
Tended heart too
Laughter like

Thunder
Rode a horse
With pride
Like a part

Of him
Love his work
Put all he had
Into it

Love his family
Work hard for them
Love was his life
Life indeed

Live it to the fullness
In all respect
For in heaven
He does ride

Like on earth
Only up there
He look down
On his past

Riding, strongly
Watch his family
Grow indeed
For they were a part

Of him, In all ways
A star indeed
On earth and in
Heaven now

A MAN INDEED

Margaret Grzyll

Margaret Grzyll
MY IMAGE OF JESSICA

In memory of Mother and Father.

A lock of golden hair.
A tiny shoe of blue.
Are all those precious memories,
Which reminds me of you.

I still can see your smiling face.
And your rosy dimpled cheeks so
fair.
And hear your childish laughter,
Which brought me such delight.

Bonnie J Whiteside
MY SECRET WISH

This poem is dedicated to my mother.

As I walked down the street one
morn, I saw a star so bright,
It seemed to stand out all alone, no
other stars in sight.
As I walked on it seemed to say, just
ask your wish of me,
The dawn comes much too quickly,
I'll not be there to see.
So I looked up right at that star and
spoke my wish aloud,
And none too soon because right then
it stole behind a cloud.
And when I walk again some morn,
that star will shine you see,
Because I've wished upon a star, its
light will follow me.

Ralph S Swift
CONTINUUM

We cannot live forever, and we
grieve to see you go,
But God and Nature both ordain—we
must have room to grow.

For if we lived forever, there would
not be the space
And for our children's children, how
would we find a place?

But thank the lucky circumstance that

brings you to this lot
Five million years the seed ran true,
conveyed you to this spot.

Five million years, and in that time
your forebears wept a lot
For all your fathers' fathers and the
mothers that begot
The children who within their turn
sired all your prior kin
Until the day that you were born,
your own lease to begin.

And so by chance and happenstance
you lived to see this day
And all the wondrous things
perceived when Nature has her way.

But Nature, all too naturally, in turn
demands her due,
For all things natural live and die,
and so it's asked of you.

So do not go with heavy heart, great
fortune brought you here
To see and do, to live and love, to
laugh or shed a tear
And you cannot live forever, though
we grieve to see you go
We know you really understood—
The children have to grow.

Charles D Kerns
BUTTERFLIES
She sat out on her front porch,
rocking, as if keeping rhythm
Her grey hair moving with the
breeze, as she surveyed
nature's precious things,
And it seemed as if fairies were
dancing through her mind, as
she sang a virgin melody
"They are not really butterflies,
they're just angels, with
colored wings."

So many times I had talked to her
about life and its true values
And I thought I understood about
life, I thought I too, had
reason to sing,
But she had this ingredient, a God
given talent, that made her
realize
That they weren't really
butterflies, they were just
angels, with colored wings.

Everyone around always admired
her flowers, especially the
roses
Every seed she put in the ground
would hardly wait until the
coming spring,
And every flower that came to
life always attracted these
little "angels"
Those things that weren't really
butterflies, no, they were just
angels with colored wings.

Then one day, progress hit our
town, a better time for all
our people
And the very spot where her
house sat, a spectacular
shopping mall,
I know she must've died from a
broken heart, but they used
the word, virus
Now where the "angels" used to
fly, there was none, at all.

Progress could be a useful word,
if used in the right
perspective
But sometimes when one stops to
think, about all these man
made things,
I think we will miss life's most
important meaning and
treasures
Especially items that weren't
butterflies, but angels, with
colored wings.

Evangelist Ethel Huffman Taylor
DEATH

This poem is dedicated to the family members, relatives and friends of B. J. Huffman and Odessa (Hall) Huffman, my wonderful parents who have stood by me all these years.

Death is an open door
To a whole new way
As you enter through
You will receive your pay.

A whole new dimension
A feeling of fear and woe
Wondering what the future hold
As your anxiety overflow.

What will be waiting for you
When the final trumpet blow
Who will reach out for your hand
To be with them forevermore?

Will there be a New Jerusalem
Where there's no need for the sun
Will Jesus gladly receive you home
Because of the race you have run?

Maybe there will be gnashing of teeth
A city of sorrow and disappointment
Where Satan and his angels are
waiting
For you to keep your final
appointment?

The door is waiting, you must go
through
The doorknob is on your side
Once you're in, you never come out
Decide now with whom you want to
abide.

Laura J Pecoraro
METAMORPHOSIS
Dust piles high
on the furniture
There never used
to be any in
The room where you kept
Your pad and pencil.

The silence makes me
quake and I freeze
as I enter
The room where you kept
Your pad and pencil.

The room is barren
your belongings gone
except for the picture
of us taken in
The room where you kept
Your pad and pencil.

The memories have faded
There is a sign in the window
The time has come to rent
The room where you kept
Your pad and pencil.

Debra Webb
I'M O.K.
You look across and there he stands,
your heart is swept away.
Hellos are said and the dance begins,
never ending to your wedding day.
Time goes by and the dance does
end,
when he throws you against the wall.
Your mind is dazed, your heart is
racing,
and you slowly tumble and fall.
So you hurry to pick up all of the
pieces,
and make everything all right.
But this is wrong that is wrong,
and it always seems to end in a fight.

The nights grow long, your nerves
grow short,
you believe it's you that is all wrong.
Until one night with the help of a
friend,
you'll change and become strong.
God was there and he guided me,
to the path that showed the way.
There's only so much one can give,
I wasn't wrong, I'm O.K.

M Sharon Mijares
OLD WOMAN

Dedicated to Michele Aponte as a thank you for her help and, most of all, for her friendship.

I met a child, who expressed her
fears.
I do as I'm told; say please ma'am,
thank you sir,
My fun and freedom limited to
proper behavior.
Feeling pain in my heart, I say
Don't worry child, I've been there
too.

I met a young girl, who expressed her
fears.
I behave as I'm told; kind, chaste and
pure,
High standards and peer pressure,
I've learned to endure.
Feeling pain in my heart, I say
Don't worry young girl, I've been
there too.

I met a young woman, who expressed
her fears.
I react as I'm told; care for my
husband and my child,
I run, work and cook; always frantic,
sometimes wild.
Feeling pain in my heart, I say
Don't worry young woman, I've been
there too.

I met an old woman, and I expressed
my fears.
I've been someone else's daughter,
mother or wife,
I never had a chance at an
independent life.
Feeling pain in her heart, she said
Don't worry dear, I've been there
too.

Scott A Gardiner
MOTHER
In this wide world
There are many people around
But none can compare
To the one I have found

We all have them
Oh yes we do
No matter what your name is
John, Frank, Sandy or Sue

She's there to care
She's there to smile
All for you
So give her awhile

The times have changed
The problems have not
So talk to her
Because it helps a lot

Just remember
No matter how bad you are
She'll love you forever
No matter if you're near or far

Ethel Cruikshank
A SCHOOL REUNION
How long has it been, do we dare say
Since we've enjoyed each other's
presence,
The years go by in such a hurried
way
To think we've aged; makes no
sense.

Back in school we were a varied
bunch
Through it all we had education in
mind,
Now we're older and wiser, I've a
hunch
We'll not forget the memories left
behind.

James Bernier Jr
A LITTLE LESSON
I've learned some rules through my
life.
Can't answer all questions, though I
try
I know hate is love gone bad,
and a tear is a smile when it's sad

A star is an alluring point of light,
but a rainbow can't survive the
darkness of night
A snowflake is the perfect piece of
ice;
A diamond is a stone with a high
price

An exaggerated thought is called a
dream;
A Mercedes is but a luxury machine
Any career can be a superior job;
A complaint is simply a verbal sob

A fault is perfection without thought
Wars will kill only when fought
A child is fate's greatest present
So try to learn a little lesson
Live life with cautious optimism.

Ralph Cochran
THE LAST DAY OF SUMMER
I like to leave work on the last day of
summer,
It's a short vacation for me.
I hope for some fun with a place in
the sun,
And a favorable tide from the sea.

This habit had started back when I
was younger,
Growing stronger as time passed
away.
I knew not the cause for this equinox
pause,

Or why I had chosen that day.

The answer came to me when I was much older,
On the last summer day of one year.
An answer so plain, it chilled like cold rain:
Life's last summer day might be here.

Jason Allen Northington

Helen Northington
OUR GRANDSON

I dedicate this poem, "Our Grandson," to Jason Allen Northington.

My heart fills with joy
When the family comes to our house,
We have much fun, playing with
The grandchildren, especially the youngest one.
His smile is charming, he has personality plus—
And he never seems to mind our fuss—
He takes in all the scenery, be it dogs or cats
And would love to hold them each and everyone,
But they want to scratch.
He doesn't care for that, but
He thinks they all belong to him.
When bedtime comes, he's more than ready,
To be bathed, fed, and rocked and for
Mommy to sing to him—and it's already nine o'clock.

Elizabeth Parvis Johnson
WALKING WITH GOD IN THE GARDEN

Dedicated in loving memory to my Mother, Effa Townsend Parvis.

As I walk among the flowers in the evening
In my garden that God's loving inspiration helped create,
I feel His spirit walking close beside me
And together we enjoy the fragrance sweet.

The cares and burdens of the day diminish
As my life I place once more within His will
And I know that if, for me, there be tomorrow
His spirit will be walking with me still.

Faith thus restored, my heart now sings
In joyful expectation
Of another quiet hour I'll walk with God
In the garden, among the flowers
In the evening.

Elizabeth Parvis Johnson
A MEDITATION

Ocean waves lap up upon the shore
Sun parched sands stretch out to meet the sea.
And as I rest, reposed, on nature's floor
A sky of azure blue looks down on me.

In this quiet place I lift my face
And ponder all the beauty I behold;
My soul is free
I know my God is watching over me.

Elizabeth Parvis Johnson
COME, MY LOVE

Come, my love
Take my hand and walk with me
Beside the sea,
Down quiet country lanes
Through fields of clover.

Together we'll explore the universe
And all its wonders—
Mountain steep,
Valley green,
Even the crowded cities' busy streets.

It matters little where or what the weather,
As long as there is you
And there is me
And we're together.

Suzanne Thompson
THE CORNER OF MY ROOM

The corner of my room,
The inside of my closet,
How well I knew my spot.
An explosion went off in my heart
everytime my father would talk.

I Love your sister, not you. (YOU I HATE).
How Well I remember those words.
The hurt, the rejection, I would feel,
I still feel. (Incredible) that he would ask me not to kill myself, I Love You,
We All Love You, We need You.

Born 1958 9 years later DEATH a way of relief
not being able to cope with life.
7 years later my birthday again
DEATH enters
my so destroyed mind.

I feel so angry inside, so hurt for all my years of suffering.
I must live with this (Love and Hate) situation.
I will die with it. So unfair, So cruel.
Thank God
it's not true, (Facts remain it is true).

Rosemary Daniel
ONE CHRISTMAS

For all those mothers who know.

As I woke up one Christmas morn
My slippers old, my nightgown torn
My children slept, no excitement to wake
No presents to give, made my heart break
I walked to the kitchen to cook them a meal
There wasn't much food to borrow or steal
As daybreak did come, rays came from the sky
A beauty so great brought tears to my eye
The sparkle of snowflakes fell gently in air
I knew at that moment that happiness was near

The children came to hold me so warm in their arms, with love,
happiness and all their sweet charm
With unselfish love as they held me so close
The words that they said I remembered the most
Happy birthday dear Jesus was all they did say
Please love us and keep us on your special day.

Edward R Keller

Edward R Keller
IN OUR HEARTS & MINDS

In our hearts & minds, we always mingled. When we made love it always tingled. The thing was for us not to stay single, for a long period of time. In order for you to be kind.

For you I inspire my heart to your desire, but now it's time to extinguish the fire.

The two of us are the ones with the keys to unlock our deepest thoughts & wishes forever, hidden in our memories.

Your deepest thoughts & memories forever my beautiful inspirational love.

I will never forget you my love:

Love,
Eddie

Mary Bianchini
THE GOOD WILL LADY

She is gentle and is shy,
she warms up winter winds with her smile.
Always quick and ready to help,
anyone who is sick and poor of health.

Her dreams are big and full of fire,
but sometimes feels someone is against her desires.
Our woman tries so hard for all to see,
that she isn't a failure and ready to fall,
so she perks up and smiles and shows them all.

Her happiness is that she has her health,
and also a few dollars under her belt.
A "Good Will Lady," that's what she is,
the world would be better with more like her around
for joy of life would certainly be found.

David Mark Christian
TWO BODIES

Two bodies of water
that never meet
always meet
someday.
Two drops of rain
that fall on different
days someday fall
together.
And two hearts torn
apart always find
their way.
In the rain and
storms of young life.

Marianne E Wells
LIFE

Life reminds me of the four seasons
Spring is like a newborn baby
Summer is like a small child learning to talk
Fall is like a teenager, always changing
Winter is like an old man waiting to be taken away so spring
can come and start all over again

Judith Adanza
BON ANNIVERSAIRE

I dedicate this poem to my darling Brian, who encourages me to keep myself youthful.

Rien a changé, rien du tout.
J'ai le même couleur de cheveux et des yeux,
Mes lèvres sont encore rouge comme le feu.
Mes bras sont encore capable de t'enlacer,
Mes jambes et mes pieds sont toujours sexy.
Mon age? Ça c'est autre choses,
On n'en parlant pas, c'est un secret.

Dans la vie il ya des choses mysterieuses.
Pourquoi dit-on le soir, le matin et 1 après-midi?
Le soliel s'elève, le soliel se couche?
Qui donc a inventé l'age?

Les gens heureux ne sont font pas,
Les gens qui se soucient sont sont malheureux.

Si le monde s'arretait de tourner un jour,
Hier ne deviendrait pas aujourd'hui,
Et aujourd'hui ne deviendrait pas demain.
Si demain n'arrivait pas, L'age surement n'existerait pas.

Melba W Henson
REMEMBERING

To friends and loved ones everywhere.

Each Christmas brings remembering,
And now that we are far away,
Fond thoughts and feelings come and turn
Our hearts with tender love your way.

The lighted trees like jewels gleam
And bring nostalgic memories.
From every store and home they beam,
Recalling other lights and trees.

So, friends and dear ones everywhere,
May memory's loving thoughts convey
The special joy this season brings,
As we recall that on this day

The Christ was born one distant morn
In a manger crib at Bethlehem;
And with his birth, to us on earth
Came love and faith and hope for man.

How blessed we are to have had this call
To serve our Lord this happy way;
For sharing His gift — His message — with all
We now have Christmas every day.

Yvonne Chevalier
THE CANDY STORE

To Edith, for her encouragement.

I'm like a kid in front of a candy store,
Its window so full of goodies!
When the door opens, now and then
It only tantalizes.
What will my two pennies buy?!

My "Norman Rockwell" face
Pressed against the glass;
If I turn quickly, as the door opens,
I almost get my money's worth
Smelling the riches some careless person
Allows to drift, on their way in or out.

Perhaps, if I move on to a new neighborhood,
My two pennies might buy something
More than heart quickening smells,
And glimpses of goodies
Protected by heavy glass.
But . . . this is my candy store!!

Yvonne Chevalier
AWAKENING
Poetry has been a substitute
For music, always, to me.
Compelled though I have been to write,
The true beauty I could not see.

Now at last I know my place,
My work in Heaven's plan;
My music, Poetry, must become
A help for every man.

Something for one who lacks a guide,
As he stumbles through this life;
Perhaps a beginning, a leading away
From what seems eternal strife.

So, if I bring beauty to anyone,
If only one it may be;
Then the work I was given to do
Will return in great wealth, to me.

Yvonne Chevalier
SAILING
The deck lifts under me
Sails crack, are tightened,
Gather the wind and we move
Almost skipping
Across green, blue water.

An endless sky beckons;
"Run before the wind,
You'll catch a trailing edge."
My heart laughs
For freedom and for joy.

How simple it all is,
Cobwebs swept away.
Lie down, feel the warm deck,
Look at the sky,
See the sun fall into the ocean.

Yvonne Chevalier
AH!
Can this be love?
The gentleness, the tender
Passionate awakening;
The fire that melts
Bone to bone and flesh
To flesh.
The complete release from
This dull, earthbound shell.
The soaring, whirling magic;
And then, the gradual relaxation
Into fulfillment and peace . . .
And awareness
Of being,
Of tender arms still close
And a gentle mouth.
Ah!

Yvonne Chevalier
REACHING OUT
I'm a child Santa forgot,
Or an orphan unnoticed in a crowd.
Tears well back of my eyes,
A lump builds in my middle.
I wear a smile, so no one will know.

To learn to trust,
Have faith in someone
When I've found destruction lies that way
Is more difficult than I knew,
But I must try.

I cannot live in a vacuum
Occupied by me alone.
The only way out of limbo
Is by touching someone's life.
You cannot touch without trust.

Pam Washburn
THE CHILD

To Madeline Anne Lurio.

The child sleeps as the mist slowly settles in.

Her breathing is slow and deep as to show she is in another world beyond mine.

Her love for life goes beyond words as the melody she hums haunts me.

I love her hands as she grasps the world around her and all it holds.

She has a soul and spirit beyond words that lift her curiosity to new heights.

At times she is the very essence of life itself and all it demands.

As she takes my hand and I hers, we go through to new adventures in this thing called life.

Patti LeGere
THE GIFT OF TIME

To my sons—Christopher, Steven & Keith, with much love.

Of all the gifts we share in life, have you ever thought of time?
It can't be wrapped or held as such, rare gift of yours and mine.
So precious are its hours . . . few seconds should time spare
On anything but happiness for people everywhere.

Time is such a mystery, it measures us in years
Each moment should bring pleasure too filled for any tears.
If I could wrap each second, minute, hours too
I'd tie them all with ribbon and give each one to you.

If time were picked like flowers, I'd pluck a large bouquet
To give to you each morning to brighten up your day.
On such a rare occasion its pleasure not be there
You could sprinkle it with teardrops and throw it in the air.

If time be all around us, there'd be flowers in its place
To gather all together, a smile back on your face.
And little would be wasted, if time were flowers still
For when it passed too quickly you could pick some more at will.

But neither gift nor flowers is time that passes by
Without the joy of living until the day we die.
So please remember always to give each day your best
And fill each waking moment with only happiness.

Lillie Maples
WHERE DOES THE SKY END?
It ends over the rainbow, over the mountains and under the seas, and through the trees.

It ends where the unicorns roam and butterflies speak. And where rabbits carry watches.

It ends where dreams and wishes come true with a blink of an eye, but never seem to end.

It ends where we find adventure and fortune and death.

It ends where all wishes and dreams come true, like the fall of a sunset from the depth of spacious pastures or the tears of distant rains.

It ends where man takes his car to the end of a highway, or the course of a sail in miles of distant oceans.

But really at the end of our minds or souls! Because we all dream to find an end.

Rebecca Anne Yasui
ONE SENSE LESS
To wing and run
And wildly woe
The fallen failings
That we bestow
Our tired eyes
Do tend to tear
Images cast on walls
Slowly run and smear
And we at loss
For words to say
All feelings forgotten
From yesterday
Our shadows teasing us
All around
Do you hear laughter
They are making
No — I think not
Not a sound.

Sandra L Rock
HIS LAST WISH

To our loving son, Herbie.

Three little girls, twelve, seven and two;
seven months pregnant and very blue.

Another daughter we'll love anyway;
"But baby inside, are you a boy," I pray?

We lost a son this early spring;
an accident, a tragedy, while I was expecting.

He wanted a brother, his very last wish;
"I hope it's a boy, I'll teach him to fish."

Being a parent is really a trial;
but his last wish come true will make it worthwhile.

We miss you son, We always will;
your dream, we hope, we can fulfill.

A few days left, the time went fast;
our baby will be coming at last.

"Honey, I think it's time to go";
"the hospital is quite a ways, you know."

Near the end I cried with joy;
"Oh Dear God please give us a boy!"

The doctor smiled when all was done;
"Congratulations, a healthy son!"

H Paul Smith
STARRY KNIGHTS

To all Arizona Rangers, future, past or present, from Sgt. H. Paul Smith, Santa Cruz Company, Arizona Rangers.

As the century turned the corner in wild Arizona land,
That harbored many a villain in its lairs of outlaw band,
Lawlessness was rampant, for no justice did prevail,

Brigand, brute and badman roamed,
that should have been in jail!

So the territory's governor began to legislate,
To "turn the tide" of evil crime and thus become a state.
'Twas then they formed a company of Rangers tried and true
26 men with grit and guts, fierce and loyal, too!

They rode the west, they gave their best, so many fought and died
But their gallant deeds on trusty steeds instilled us all with pride!
They filled old Yuma's prison, yes, every single cell,
or "dispatched" the ruthless killer on his homeward way to hell!

Today, they stand undaunted, still devoted to their creeds
Supporting "Boy's Ranch" freely while performing civic needs.
Quick to aid the lawman or to serve their fellow man
They work for free and strive to be the very best they can.

Ever vigilant and watchful and always on their guard
In uniforms of black and white, or "jeans" when working hard.
Daring yet protective, almost oblivious to danger!
It's inspired they are to wear the star
Of an ARIZONA RANGER!

Catherine Brown
MY CHILD

This poem is dedicated to my son Blake.

My child is a gift from God up above
My child is given to me to grow with and to love.
My child is a star shining bright in the sky
He believes what I tell him so I should never lie.
My child is a part of me, I'm to raise him to have peace
Not to hurt or abuse him but, to love and amuse him.
My child is a child of wonder, a child of might,
Sometimes a child of fear but, I am here to make everything alright.
My child is my gift from God above in whom I am well pleased and I love.

Catherine Brown
AS SPRING IS APPROACHING
As spring is approaching as the daylight appears
The sun shining bright with laughter and cheer,
The trees blossom, the flowers bloom as we say
Good-bye to our winter gloom.
The air fresh and clear as the beautiful mountains
Reappear, from the melting ice and snow the forest
Becomes alive once more with a glow.
Plants begin to grow standing tall and green how
Nice it is to hear the birds sing.
With Easter Sunday almost here, it is time we thank
God for being so wonderful and dear.

Hunter Bridgeford Fleshood
NIGHT AND DAY
If I am the Night,
And you are the Day,
Then we could never come to be in each other's way.

For if one leads the other,
Yet it also follows, too.
It's a paradox, I know, but it's how I think of you.

Yet the two blend, at a point,
As if standing side-by-side,
Like a couple at the altar; impatient groom and anxious bride.

The Night has ever been part of the Day,
And the Day has never existed alone,
For they embrace and kiss at evening in the twilight-zone.

Slowly moving through their waltz,
Pirouetting around together,
The Night and Day, side-by-side, hand-in-hand, forever.

Christine A Scarley
MOTHER'S PROTECTIVE GARDEN

To my Mother Alice Collins —who gave me space to find myself and to become self-reliant.

Chinese Lanterns out of her flower bed
Here comes a bright orange flame,
For a Mother that claims,
Her children's eyes are slanted the same.

Forever digging in her flower bed
Mother has finally found her heart fed.
Is her love for other men dead?
Never, never will she again wed.

For this Mother has filled her flower bed—
With love so deep and thoughts of promised hope
Don't ever put her loved ones under a microscope.
If so, be prepared for a love charge so strong,
She would make it her life to prove you wrong.

Her heart would force you to spread to the ground,
Down, down deep in this Mother's flower mound—
Where your peace of mind would never be found.

Christine A Scarley
NORTHERN GIRL AT HEART
This northern girl at heart has—
A special desire to discuss,
The season of winter that—
Southern friends don't understand.

Snow covered evergreens basking in white halos,
Pale prairieland with windblown icy peaks,
Grey overcast clouds hanging so low—
The moisture beads swim on your face.
Certain stillness and grace of stark trees.

Cocooning lovers—absorbed in warm arms fireside—
Feelings of security to make a bond so tight,
Making the thought of ever leaving the north—
Inconceivable—as having a heart with no soul.

Lorraine M Parizek
WHY

Dedicated to my son, Marine Lance Cpl. Jack Freitag, wounded January 20, 1967, Danang.

That chopper comes now very soon
To rid me of this hell.
And lift me from this place of doom,
When fallen by a shell.

Lord, I know not where it hurts
From whence that bullet came.
I know for sure a sniper lurks,
And deadly is his aim.

For weeks I fought to get my breath,
The doctor shook his head.
Knowing I was close to death
And the chaplain near my bed
Asked if he could say a prayer,
Thinking I'd soon succumb
Only then did declare,
To say one for my mom.

Back I am from that damn war,
I live through stress and pain,
Did we fight for (peace restored)
Or was it all in vain?

J Daniel Hauber
CARRIE
(the fire)

For Carrie Elizabeth Glover, the woman who turned around my life, and taught me how to care. Thank you for being there for me, you will always have a place in my heart, I promise. Don't forget me.

In days of old, this heart was cold
To you I owe my fire.
Fame and fortune, are not for me
You are my true desire.

I'll not give up my dreams.
I'll not give up my soul.
You and I may never be,
But love, I always shall.

Call on me, your humble servant
Service to you I do.
Power and glory be not my way
Love for you is true.

I dream of being great
But only for myself.
What others think of me . . .
Matters not.

Someday I shall be great
And always be humble.
To you I owe my fire,
To me, I owe myself.

Jason B Kiningham
EUPHORIA

To my beloved Grandfather with love and admiration. Love, Jason.

at daylight's watch
i stand at sea
above blue waters
peaceful and free

the feel of the air
the warmth of the sun
regardless of time
worries, i have none

and at the moment
as the water becomes wave
peace for my soul
my body does crave.

Céline C Pedemonti
AMBIVALENT EQUALITY
In this age of liberation,
an astute one has only to observe
the magnificent visual differences
between the male and female curve.

And, although one's cry is equality,
our spirits and minds evenly tamed
there still remains this 'housing'—
equality can never be the same.

Catherine Mercier
MAGIC ME
Magic me, oh magic me,
Magic me to where,
Bright light in brilliant morning,
Dims all life down here.

Dream me, oh dream me,
To silver moonglossed seas,
To roll and toss with the tide,
And dance a dance of mystery.

Take me, my love, now take me,
Into your arms again,
For you alone hold the key to my dreams,
And the center from which I spin.

Robert J Levesque
SYLVIE
I'm sorry for the pain I've caused you, and the misery that follows
We haven't had the chance to seriously know one another, now my heart feels hollow
I've always felt very deep about you, silent as I am
I guess I'm very lucky, just to even know you as a friend
Confusion and anger seems to be dwelling from within
See, I've got this strong feeling towards you, so to clear the air for me, is to win
I hope you're not mad at me for the things I feel I must do
'Cause deep in my heart, I know I'm right, I'm doing it for you
I'll fight for you Sylvie, for as long as it takes
To let the truth be known, to clear up all the mistakes
It seems no one can leave us alone, or give us peace of mind
But it's so unfair just to know you, and leave the best behind
When you go away to school on your own, that's the chance I will face
Wondering if someday, someone out there, may just take my place
But as I told you earlier, I will never stop you from your goals
If anything, I'd push you, so you can realize what your future has to hold
I guess I just regret that we haven't had much time together
But I keep my spirits up, by saying that it's not forever
I hope that one day, our hearts will meet again
Because I know I could love you Sylvie, till the bitter end.

Rebecca D Belonga
RUINS OF A CASTLE
Upon an eminent bluff that overlooks a rapid stream,
Are the ruins of a castle.
The ivy crawls its outside walls;
The moss has tinged with other hues;
The pillars that supported the gateway,
And in the gateway,
And in the once frequented court are gone.

In the hall that once rang to merry cheer
The breeze sighs through broken arches
And over a weed-encumbered pavement.
Where is the beauty, the glory, the magnificence,
That once brightened this desert spot?

Like the blossoms of bygone trees
The beautiful things have perished and are forgotten,
And the fame of its noble and mighty stature,
Like the cities which deluge overswept in its wrath,
Have vanished from the land.

Patrice Lyons
WHEN I GROW UP

When I grow up I don't know what I'll be,
The mystery will unravel with time.
I know whatever the future may bring,
I'll be happy, I'll do fine.

I may be president of a nation;
The great nation U.S.A.,
Making peace throughout the whole world,
It may happen some future day.

I may be a doctor in a hospital,
Helping cure those who aren't well.
I may be a singer or a dancer,
Or an author with a story to tell.

I have one special expectation though,
One dream, one hope I keep inside,
That is to be the mother of a family,
With a love that will never subside.

Maleana Kepler

Maleana Kepler
THE POND

I would like to dedicate this poem to Mr. Rehm and the sixth grade class of Meadowbrook Christian School, 1990.

The silent rays of the still moonlight
shined on the deep blue pond,
The tadpoles and the skippers lay
down to rest with a big sighing yawn.
The stillness of the midnight fog lay
on the lilies of green.
The crickets and the mosquitoes fall
into a never ending dream.
Soon it will be dawn and the
creatures will arise;
The trees, the birds, even the
butterflies.
The fish start to bite, the bees
start to buzz,
The pond is a wonderful place;
just because.

Stephen David Reinhardt
CHILDREN

For Chesney and David.

What begins with a flower
And a bee's intimate dance
With God's great power
Renews all life's chance
As we with our great need
At loving sweet embrace cry
To plant our seed
Aimed towards the sky.

Seeds usually continue to grow
And watered with tears of rain
We see our strengths and weaknesses flow
And if not in great pain
Guided with care in time
Beautiful buds will unfold
Completing the cycle of the rhyme
Answering the riddle of growing old.

For nothing else of us really remains
Of all we do and of all our pain
With nothing to lose and everything to gain
For children and love
They are one and the same.

Michael Cooper
FLOWERED FEELINGS

In memory of Richard Capin.

Sadness
Looks like
A withered rose
On a winter day

Happiness
Looks like
A sunflower
Blowing in the spring air

Embarrassment
Looks like
The last petal
On a flower

Horror
Looks like
A flower
Being picked

Love
Looks like
A rosebud opening
To the world

Melody Jett/Roberts
DREAM MAN

To my husband David Wayne Roberts; Nobody could ever Love you like I do.

When God made me,
he gave me to you.

He brought us together
so I could love you.

I prayed for you daily,
and by night you came true.

In dreams I had loved you
before I knew you.

Your face I could not see,
but I knew who you were.

I knew I'd find you—one day,
that's for sure.

And then when we met I knew
at first sight.
That you were the man that
came to me by night.

Kimberly E Fort
STARS ABOVE

Stars above
Shining bright
Eyes of gray
In pale moonlight
Waves lap gently
Beaten sand
Lovers walk
Hand in hand
Sweet nothings whispered
With no regret
Permanent memories
Lest they forget
Chilled water
In rising tide
As predictable
As the love they hide
No tomorrows
Only tonight
Together in dunes
There will be no fight

Betty Salter Dunning
DREAMS

Who is rich and yet so very poor?
Who is heartsick and knows no cure?
Who wears a lowly crown?
And a worried frown?

It is he who cannot dream
He drinks not sweeten water but tastes sour cream
He has no goal no object no forward step
Listen as he stumbled, listen as he wept,

Who owns the tallest castles?
Who dreams the greatest dreams?

It is he who trusts God,
And puts away the frown,

Because he has faith he has dreams
Dreams that God will answer
Some hidden treasure he foresees,
Is it any wonder he who walks with God has dreams?
When others walk with earthly friends,
You may walk with God.

Kay A Powell
SISTERS

I am only just past one, my sister—she is three
We have a great big shepherd dog who watches over me
I like to run and jump and climb, my sister — she does too
Some things are still too hard for me; but wait until I am two
Our hair is long and dark, our eyes are bright and clear
People always tell us, "Girls, you are so dear."
My sister has the prettiest smile and I have a giggly grin
We laugh and dance. I clap my hands when my sister sings
Our Mommy and our Daddy think we are "the sweetest little things"
Mommy dresses us so pretty — sometimes in look-a-likes
Daddy buys us big girl toys like swings and wagons and bikes
We have a big boat to ride in and a river camp where we stay
Our Jesse dog likes the river camp when we go to swim and play
I try to follow my sister and do what she can do
It does not always work for me; but just wait until I am two
Our grandparents think we are special and have our pictures everywhere
I like to visit their house especially when Grandpa is there
I like to visit Mommy's friend and play with her two boys
They play such rough and tumble games and I like their big boy toys
My sister has a favorite doll. Penny Rose is her name
My doll is just called "Baby" but I love her just the same
We are Mishelle and Melissa, little sisters as sure as can be
I am only just past one, my sister — she is three

Lauren Kapichak
SOAPSTONE MANOR JIGGED

How I would like to be away
From this concrete, laughing castle.
You always came when I called you
To protect me from laughing mannequins,
But never, ever would come to my castle.
To drink and indulge in silence
Away from all the mundane clues.

And how I would like to be without
All these silent, screaming timekeeps.
They always tell me when I must forget
My crazy, pipe dream creeds.
But never, ever would help me to forget
The reality I have seen away in my odd illusions.

They just don't understand.
Like you,
I simply cannot return
To my concrete, laughing castle.

Lauren Kapichak
LETTER IN FAREWELL

Nonce I carol your intrinsic melody.
A sweet, tired verse of Blasphemy.
Oh pardon me,
My ballade may
Bring requiem to bay.

You gather this bit with amusing courtesy.
A time kissed scenario of fallacy.
Yet to promenade ways wester,
Scarlet dusk is a fortress, a dreamer's gem.
Suddenly
Suited for romantic requiem.
Oh pardon me,
Such Blasphemy
Oh blessed be,
Such Ballade.

Tony Chiorazzi
JANUARY SNOW

Remembering '67.

I had a dream of snow again.
I heard the laughter and felt the crisp cold.

My heart was full of joy,
As pure and crystal white as the snow.

In my dream I saw a young girl.
She laughed and I ran free as I reached for her,
But then she disappeared.
Even the snow was no longer there.

My heart no longer was full of the joy
that I once felt so crystal clear and pure.

kim b rush
THE GIFT
I play
Music leaps from me
the notes soar—
years of taut shoulders, and
perfected technique.
Maybe you'll love me more,
See? I haven't wasted my time,
hear my love vibrating through the flute . . .

You fidget, then stifle a yawn—

forget it—

(it wasn't important)

Dwight C DeShields
A WIFE FOR LIFE

To Teresina K. Giles, with God's love.

Why don't you want to be my wife
Because you know it's a righteous life
You know you can't run away
God in me is here to stay
In this I think you are so far
Me must meet you in the bar
Are you the one in my heart
The love we share will never part
Best man best woman you see
We will have a life and be free
Need you worry God at the start
Not to let you and I part
Deal with your faith
With this I know you will see
The faith you have is love for me
Rest easy my love God is just above

Versie Hudson
THE TRUEST FLAG OF ALL
Our flag is very beautiful, for anyone to see;
It waves in majesty alone, it waves for you and me.
And when you see it waving high, you should always stop and say;
I know the things you stand for, waving day by day.

The colors all have meaning, for instance take the red;
It stands for courage which is right, and for the blood that's shed.
White stands for honor all alone,
Blue stands for loyalty;
And in the stars which are so true, there is no cruelty.

Now you may see the waving flags, of many different kinds;
That wave o'er many lands and seas, and men of different minds;
Yes many nations have their flags, all so good and true;
But truest of them all I know; is our red, white and blue.

Carolyn Norman
TALKEN ABOUT THE WORLD TODAY

To humanity, God's most precious creation.

I'm talken about the world today and thinking about the time, when man will learn to love his neighbor, instead of being unkind.

For we are all God's children and it hurts me so to see, hate & jealousy.

This world has been here for a long long time, yet people have come & gone, they haven't learned the meaning of love or care where it has gone. They only think about themselves, nothing else seems to matter.

Until one day God's grace will shine upon all mankind, then that's when hate will shatter.

Janette C Thomas
MAY I?
May I lay my body next to you to sleep?
And with my hands may I caress your cheek?
May I run my fingers through your hair?
Or at you may I lovingly stare?
In your eyes may my reflection I see there?
My tongue may I run across your lips?
Darling, may I please have the pleasure of massaging your body with my fingertips?
May you my love always seek,
For it is there for only you to have, to hold,
And to forever keep.

Wayne A Goguen
LONER
Using your time for none but you
Those left out start feeling blue
Work your hobbies to please yourself
But don't put friendships on the shelf
Let them help you if they can
And lend yourself to aid their plan
'Cause if you keep your life confined
You'll sure as hell get left behind

Kelly M Turley
HOLD ME
Heart, winter is blue feeling the freeze for warmth
hold cold hands of drained attention

for shunned feelings explode ripe dreams
oh hold me, so it is . . .
now just let me breathe.

Kelly M Turley
BIRTH OF DEATH
Today at the run
the birth of a death
at the start of a cry
cut its end to a scream
the woman named Seth
gave birth to such an uncanny thing,
quicken the run's pace
splashing underfoot
blood is splattered about the place,
the killer uncoiled
snared in firm hand
Is dead,
no longer will it hang.

Kelly M Turley
FAITH?
Standing solace watching
faith we know it well
blind from the truth we struggle
pull inward thoughts and keep them hidden
or judgement will befall
an exercise in freewill—
contradicts the passage for all who know it,
faith we view it well
It's our eyes through the iron veil,
martyr saved from hell.

David Shanley
THE GIFT OF YOURSELF
You can become your innermost dream,
Have faith and move ahead full steam.

You are what you let yourself be,
You do not have to become like him or me.

Fear not reach out at the impossible,
Believe in yourself and many things will be possible.

We are accountable only to ourselves for given happiness,
Do not set back and blame others for received sadness.

Reach out for friendship and form your kingdom,
Do not hesitate and wait for others to pick you at random.

You are the master of your own art,
Search within make the happiness of life your strong part.

Each day is a bright new sunrise,
Get on the right track before you wake in a surprise.

Don't take so long to realize,
You must have a moderate amount of compromise.

Do not live in your past,
Have hope and make your future last.

Look not at life with a frown,
Look about and see what is holding you down.

Jesse Vaughn
THINKING TOO MUCH
He thought he might give up everything,
But then he thought of her.
He thought of her beautiful, brown hair,
And how she looked at him.

He thought it would be way too long,
Too long for him to stand.
Then he thought how hard it would be,
To die by his own hand.

Every time he thinks of her,
He is thinking of how hard it would be,
Hard enough for the both of them,
If they did not see each other again.

Hazella Westman
TEACH ME
Let me know Him as you do,
For God is joy, laughter & music—
He shares our "heartaches" & "triumphs,"
His voice is "messages" on the winds that blow,
O'er the land, and sea, around the world!
He gives us "strength" to serve "one day at a time,"
With "just" rewards at "the end of the trail"—
When the "pearly" gates open & we dwell forever in the Holy Temple,
After our "toil & tribulations" cease in Eternal Rest—
And the "autograph" closes the "Book," on our time and place on Earth!!!

Frank A Jackson
ME THEN CONCRETE THEN ME?
Looking down into the transparent water-filled pool
Seeing through to the bottom with ease and grace
I see my reflection off of the surface and wonder
If I am real.

The reflection looks very sad
I converse with the reflection: with my mind I speak
Answering questions asked
The reflection looks so peaceful on the surface
And looks suffocated because of the limited
surface space.
The reflection looks so lonely
So I wave my hand trying to influence the reflection
to come out and join me but it must have had the same idea.

I as myself leap into the air over the reflection
The surface is broken using gravity's force I go under
Opening my eyes noticing that I am still alone . . .
Under the surface of the transparent water-filled pool . . . .

Doris Mullins
IT'S BEEN MANY LONG YEARS
It's been many long years
Since he went away
to serve with pride
In the Green Beret.

In pain and in sorrow
and often in tears
the wife and the children
they waited for years

He was proud of his country
and wanted all men to be free
on a battleground in a foreign land
he paid the ultimate price for you and me.

And when you go to visit him
to lay flowers on his grave
You honor and you Thank him
For all that he gave

We are proud of him
He has stood the test
West Virginia always gives its best
Now one of its own has come home to rest

Linda Huggins Terry
WINTER IMAGES
They stand alone; they gather in groups
Stark naked
Like silent sentries they stand

They sway, drab and scraggly
In tandem to and fro or alone to their mournful inner song
Arms askew, they sway

One hundred, one thousand, ten thousand
The barren brittle skeletons stand
Pointing their long bony fingers toward the gray sky
Stark and cold they stand

They wait, stripped to the bone
Their colorless frames bent to the merciless wind
Extremities exposed
Soundlessly they wait

Now, stretching skyward, they lift their frosty eyelids to the heavens
Robbed of their garb, they shiver at dawn
Reaching gaunt arms upward, bleak

At last, the snow drifts down
Warm, white, winter suits
They stand alone; they gather in groups

Connie Kenyon
SLOW THE WORLD DOWN

This poem is dedicated to my children, Jenny and Jeff.

My children mean the world to me
But I cannot control their destiny
I see that things move much too fast
Not calmly and slowly as in the past

It seems they don't have time for play
They're in a hurry to go on their way
The world is pushing them fast and hard
To be the best, to be the ace card

But where does the goodness and kindness fit in
It seems that most of the world is living in sin
We must teach our children wrong from right
Or we will be in for a hell of a fight

We must let them grow at a leisurely pace
Let them fit in, let them find their own place
Don't push them too fast and don't push them too hard
And maybe they'll stay in our own backyard

Elsie Aldrich Mellin
A LITTLE GIRL

To granddaughter Tiffany N. Tenney.

There is a little girl
That when she squeals in glee
Makes me glad all over
In and outside of me.

There is a little girl
Who has a head of curls
She loves to dance with gramma
In whirls, and whirls, and whirls.

There is a little girl
With a cute little nose so pugged;
I know the minute that I see her
She's gonna get hugged, and hugged, and hugged!

There is a little girl so sweet—
Almost sweet enough to eat,
But if I were to eat her,
Where would she be when I need her?

Elsie Aldrich Mellin
A DISABLED VET

There is a man I know who went
to World War Two—four years he spent.
A mine exploded over there
tearing up his body badly.
Doctors worked their talents—gladly;
relatives and friends heard sadly.
Adjustments he made quite gallantly.

After 38 years of working near,
now retirement time is here.
Handicapped? Yes, but I profess
he's done his very best
To bring us all happiness.
The gov't said, "A disabled vet."
I would say, "No,—not yet!"

Arlene E Hayden
FAMILY TREE

If I had a choice of what to be
I'd choose to be a tall oak tree.
One with boughs big and strong
To hold a tree house and children all summer long.
My branches covered with leaves to shade
A porch, where they could sip lemonade.
There happens to be one more thing
A sturdy branch to hold a swing.
A tree that man would not dare
Cut down for a table and chair.
This is my choice, I'd like to be
A great big old-fashioned
"Family Tree"

Donna M Mariner
I FOLLOW MY LOVE

This poem is dedicated to my late husband, Donald "Pete," with my love.

Whither thou goest
I will go
to leave
and return not

I will search
for all time
till you are there

Where e'er you be
I will know
for two hearts
in love
are as one

To love
and leave
is not forever
love is for all time
eternity ever

To die
is not forever
whither thou goest
I will go.

I follow my love.

Louise Ramsey
THE SILENT LOVE BIRDS

To my late son, Theodore Ramsey.

Crossing the street
footsteps walk in shivers.
In the darkness of the night
very silent peaceful and repose.
A sweet sound humbles far away.
Closer and closer to the desert.
The sweet sound was at my feet.
A low whisper in my ear.
As the breeze of the night
sends chills through my body.
Cuddling close to footsteps.
To keep the shivering in control.
Stars shining in the sky.
Love birds sing in silent music
made the night a beautiful
event for the love birds to sing a song.
They are walking in a twilight zone
in a world so peaceful and calm.
Their hearts on the same wave length.
And their minds in a melodrama
the stars glittering down on them.
Made the love birds' hearts grow
more in depth.
As they dance to the soft silent music
coming from far away.

Robert L Bursley Jr
AMONGST THE FRUITS AND EVILS OF AN ORCHARD

Oranges and lemons; fragrance,
juiced, processed; choice.
Buds and petals; splitting apart; fate.
Trembling fingers; pickers; ego.
Orchard; nightfall, fire, frost-free,
away; lonely.
Pores; pollution, smoke; turmoil.
Skins; dirty, toxins; shame.
Irrigation; dryness, heat; pride.
Inanimate; useless; judged.
No shadows; clouds; confusion.
Seedlings; justice; hope.
Rain; changes; welcomeness.
Pesticide; spit; hate.
Silence; dreams, prayers; success.
Sunshine; blooms; chance.
Growth; tomorrow; fear.
History; oranges and lemons.
Life; energy, happiness, sadness,
death; cycle.

Beatrice Wayrynen
SPIRITUAL SOJOURN

Dedicated in loving memory of my brother, Einar, who passed away April 1, 1989, at age 60, after a lifelong career in the U.S. Army with honorable discharge.

Gentle, yet courageous, he ran the race,
Submitting his soul to our Father's grace.
Withstanding woes of earthly duration,
Praising God's continual revelation;
His heart to our Savior my brother did yield—
The joy of the Lord was his strength and shield.
Pursuing adventure, challenging each trial;
Climbing mountains in upbeat style;
With fervor renewed—fulfilling his role--
Pressed on to Victory, the highest goal!
As sojourners inspired anew in Christ, the Way;
Expectantly readying our hearts ay by day;
Assured loved ones will meet again—it won't be long—
Amongst saints and angels in celestial song;
Remembering promises in Scripture, we know;
Claiming the Word, living water does flow . . .
Abiding in the love of Jesus, joy beyond compare,
Ever magnified, eternal, unchanging, always secure;
Thus, undaunted in faith, hand in hand,
Our vision is set on the Promised Land!

Cathy Long O'Brien
OCEANS

To my father, who passed away May 1989. To my mother and the pain of losing my father.

The sunlight glitters off the waves
miles and miles of wondrous mysteries
with a depth that life itself craves
Royal by no compare are your serenities.

The moonlight dances off the ripples
disappearing into a vast eternity
your grandeur halts me like a cripple
Like death and its infinity.

Dorothy J Kowalski

Dorothy J Kowalski
WITHOUT POSTAGE

This poem is dedicated to my son-in-law, Ronald D. Rolfe, who has been so kind and helpful to me.

You can send a letter to your loved one
That will light up their face with a glow.
And seal it with a beat in your heart
But without postage, it won't go.

You can write and tell your mother
You bought a house in Idaho.
Letting her know your new address
But without postage, it won't go.

You can wrap up a big package
For one of your friends you know.
Wanting it to arrive for their birthday
But without postage, it won't go.

You can mail all those invitations
Designed with a wedding bell and bow.
With the time, date and reception
But without postage, it won't go.

You can sign and mail a get-well card
To that someone who is feeling low.
With cheer and sincere good wishes
But without postage, it won't go.

Ty Parker
A FRIEND

For Jon, may this be a remembrance of our long-lasting friendship.

It is wonderful to know there is someone
In my life who outstands—
A person on whom I can lean on when things

Get tough;
A friend I can talk to freely
Without holding back,
That friend is you!

When friendship is strong
You know when to hold onto it!
And that itself outstands,
Like you my friend!

Friendship is not a competition
Between us because we are equal;
Friend to friend,
We are true to each other.

Our friendship has special meaning
Not even words can fully say,
Because a friend is by chance
The most wonderful part of life!
You are that special friend to me.
I love you!

Brenda Vollmer

THANK YOU

To Greg Pixler, who was there when I needed someone.

Thank you for being there
and showing me that you care.
Thank you for getting to know me
and making me happy.
Thank you for everything you've
done
but most of all thank you for showing
me loneliness has not won.
Thank you for everything you do
and I am glad to have met someone
as special as you.

Zoa Easterly Wade

THE EARTHQUAKE: OCTOBER 17, 1989 A FEW MINUTES AFTER 5 P.M.

In Santa Cruz Marge headed straight
for home o'er Highway 17,
She was thankful she was there when
the earth turned mean!
It was closing time; Leonard locked
his plumbing shop
When his enormous plate window
went POP and POP!
His telephone lines were knocked out
of commission,
He couldn't check home to see what
damage was done!
Later both were horrified and stunned
to view total destruction
Of the roped off area of their
beautiful Santa Cruz town.

George had paid toll on the Bay
Bridge, ready to go,
But was turned back and instead went
to San Leandro.
He thought his car would be turned
'round and 'round,
As it bounced and twisted when it hit
the ground!

Geri was pushed and knocked against
the steel door
When the owner frantically shoved
people out her store.
She has seven stitches taken in her
bleeding ear,
And her bones ached for two weeks
in pain and fear!

Lois had come home from school for
a restful nap,
She thought those unruly kids were
still acting up!

Ernie bounced around in his room
and then proudly call,
"Just think! Not one of my 250
clocks did fall!"

Frank, stricken with fear, across the
world in lovely Kenya
Kept dialing and dialing until at 4:30
A.M. he phoned from Africa
He gained peace and joy to hear our
hearty assurance,
And said, "Thank God! And I'm glad
you had insurance!"

Zoa phoned Fresno and Parkdale,
Or., at the foot of Mt. Hood,
To assure loved ones that God's
protection is truly good!

Blanche Eloise Higgins

THE PROMISE

I shed a tear today
for a friend
He seemed so lost,
His grief was deep
He was hurt
He was like unto
The blue bird
Having lost a mate
His beautiful songs
Gone forever

The world keeps on spinning
Rivers flowing
Night turns into day
Time marching
The road will seem long

We kneel, we pray
That God,
In his almighty
Wisdom
Will comfort his soul
And lead the way.

Sid Little

FOR NICOLE

During the cold night, through any
sleepless hour
Before the vision of a lost, trembling
flower
Down into the depths of my grieving
soul
In painful memories, like a numbing
cold
By the needless departure of your
lonely heart
Of the callous indifference upon my
part
Of your ended life, atop your youth
Beyond now, all love, in search of
truth
Upon the harsh winds of loveless
time
Above your melancholy life of mime.
To the tormented sound of your
distressful plea
For the soul's perseverance through
eternity
Before now, mute cries, outside your
room
By the gentle child of my sister's
womb
Of my blood, in a timeless place
With no rendered verdict upon your
face
Among the indicted, except not me
After my stoic lack of empathy.

Janis Lee Pensula

A DREAM OF IMMORTALITY

To: Jackie, Pete, Samuel and Gary, Jamie, Melanie, Kelly, Jessica, and Patti, Pensula. And to: Jack A. Langlois.

There are "feelings" of God's love, I
have deep inside,
They are "feelings" that some seem
to think I should hide.
Oh, but His love fills me up like an
ocean wide,
And rushes through my heart like a
roaring tide.
When I allow this love to surface,
some people crush my pride,
Still I know in my heart, God's love
will always abide.
This is a fact that cannot be denied,
Only God knows how many tears I
have cried.
Sometimes I feel I'm just "going
along for the ride,"
Then the Lord says: "Come on, Jan,
you know I am your guide."
As to His miraculous power, I have
often testified,
He is the only one who can keep me
satisfied.
Yes, God's love is the key that so
many times I have tried,
And the "Golden Rule," I know I
have applied.
But, will this be remembered, after
on this earth, I have died?
That will be left to God, and others,
to decide . . .

LaHonda Jo Brown

WHAT A WONDERFUL DAY

Today is such a Wonderful Day . . .
Oh there is so much I could say.

I've been sick for so long . . .
But today I feel like I want to sing a
song.

When I look back and think of my
sickness . . . I can only say . . .
Thank you dear Lord for making this
such a Wonderful Day.

There's time when you say . . .
"Why me?"
Then you say, "Dear Lord . . . excuse
me please."

You look around at others who take
things for granted and always want
more.
They never know who or what will
be knocking at their door.

How long my good health will stay I
cannot say.
But you can bet your life . . . that to
my fullest I'll live for each day.

Dear Lord help us who look up to
you . . .
Answer our prayers as to what to do.

Each day is a Wonderful Day when
we wake up and see . . .
This wonderful world that was made
for you and me.

Thank you Lord for what you've
given me . . .
Take good care of all my wonderful
friends and family.

Today is such a
WONDERFUL DAY.

Lisa Franz

DREAMING

I believe in an outside place
Another world, a different space
No guns or bombs to end a life
No greedy minds or bloody knife
No burning eyes shall see the hate
The dying souls no more to wait
The starving people never there
With pleading hands and vacant
stare.
The sun has risen and now is set
And through this day I have met
No one to guide me through the
night
Prepare me for my endless flight
For through my journey I will find
This better place for humankind.

George T Mattson

MY FRIEND

To Cora, who knows more about being a friend than I shall ever know!

The world became a nicer place
When you did pass my way.
How could you know the joy I feel
That comes from words you say.

No time before can I recall
That I did feel so right,
Or have the knowledge in my soul
That I could face the night.

You give me courage to go on
In spite of my sad song.
You make me laugh at trials too
That seem to last too long.

But most of all you give to me
An everlasting blend
Of trust and understanding
That marks you as my friend.

Nadine Sloan Southern

PARENTING

When parents expect their child's
birth
Nine months of both bitter and sweet
They behold that great moment of
mirth
After they count hand, fingers, toes
and feet

Their first year should be the
beginning
Of knowing when you are playing
and not
Be consistent and firm, not yelling
Remember you're both teaching the
tot

The years before school are the
pattern
And the responsibility and obedience
you start
Will grow and flourish, not cause you
concern
And these traits are from your heart

Those who teach religion, respect and
trust
Will soon see dependable young
ladies and men
And when God looks down on you,
as he must
He'll say you've done a good job till
then

The position of parent never retires
Because the children need help
sometime
Give advice or listen to their desires
But your older years should be
sublime

Margarett H Nichols

HILDENE

"Hill" is a high spot with a
spectacular view
"Dene" means a valley with a river
flowing through
Robert Todd Lincoln's beautiful
summer home
By the name of "Hildene" is now
well-known.
A Georgian mansion built in 1905
The home of descendants while they
were alive.
On 412 acres that are now preserved
Where hunters and traffic are seldom
heard.

Twenty-four rooms restored with care
With original furnishings found here and there.
An Aeolian player organ in the front hall
Where a grandfather clock stands straight and tall.
The formal garden is like a mosaic window
Planted with shrubs and flowers that we know.
The observatory with Robert's telescope
Is now restored and fulfills our hope.
Manchester, Vermont is the home of this estate
A historic beauty with an open gate
From May through October in the fall
It's truly an adventure for one and all.

Diane K Rossman

A POEM FOR MY DAD ON FATHER'S DAY

To my special dad on Father's Day, 1989, Mr. Kenneth Bergum from Northport, Florida! Thanks, Dad!

I'm sitting here on this quiet night,
Trying to think of what to write,
Putting feelings into words is hard to do,
Especially when those feeling are about you.

A friend, a father, just what is a dad?
Someone to scold you when you've been bad?
Someone to take me to the park,
And chase lightning bugs with after dark.

A dad works hard and is a family man,
Spending time with his family when he can,
He can't be selfish—he gives his all,
He's always there at our beckoning call.

But there is one moment that stands out in my mind,
Another moment like this will be hard to find,
The day you gave me away to Gerry,
The man I loved & wanted to marry.

You're a grandpa now but you're still my dad.
And I think quite often of the great times we've had,
Because you see dad, all the above is true,
And it is all written in love for you.

There is one thing I wish on this Father's Day,
I wish you weren't so far away,
I miss you dad, that's definitely true,
From your "little girl," Diane,
I love you.

Catherine B Smullen

FRIENDS

Today I saw you standing here,
My heart it stopped when you came near,
To see you there after many years,
Made my eyes fill up with uncried tears.
We stopped & embraced for quite a spell,
But what you felt I couldn't tell.
We looked at each other in the same old way,
then the bitterness & heartache flew away.
It's not the same as it was before,
but in place of a lover you're a friend once more.

Lynda Wilson Grant

FAIRHOPE PIER

Wind blow;
Waves roll;
Clouds drift;
Always the same,
Yet always new.
At the end of the pier—
Stress, anger, and me.
Breezes caress;
Sounds soothe;
Sights please;
Tension flows out,
And Anger dies.

At the end of the pier—
Sky, water, and me.
Sun shines;
Birds fly;
Sails wave;
Refresh my soul,
Still my mind.
At the end of the pier—
Peace; calm; and me.

Betty Parker

WHEN?

When did Friendship turn into Love?
Who can really say?
Was it when you kissed me
And I didn't turn away?

Was it when you held me
And didn't let me go?
Was it when I felt us both
Begin to tremble so?

Who pulled the strings upon my heart
And made me come alive?
Who awoke the dragon that slept
So deep inside?

What made me long so for
A touch, a glance?
When did "Friendship" slip away
And become "Romance"?

Mrs Pearl Glatky

WINTER'S DELIGHT

To Brittany—her favorite time of year.

We often think of winter's gloom,
The long months of cold & doom.
But there's a spark of color,
When snowflakes fall in such splendor,
The ground wears a coat of white,
The trees shine with such delight.
The children play with snow,
They roll & roll to make a snowman grow.
The skaters glide over the icy pond,
In a motion to a waltz the music they respond.
The skiers climb the mountains o' so high,
Then they ski down the slopes with their bodies' might.
So you see winter comes & goes,
It sometimes brings on a mighty cold.
But all in all we grin & bear its plight,
It's not so bad as we all share in "winter's delight"

Ingrid Zeckser

ISLAND PRISON

Upon a stony ledge she sat staring out to sea,
Wavy hair and silken dress flowing free,
Salt air engulfing her, of which she was very fond,
She wondered, what lies beyond the horizon
When young she was abandoned on the island sand,
An old mute hermit raised her with a gentle hand
He grew to love her as his own daughter,
All the things he knew, he taught her.
As she grew older, she longed to go abroad
The old hermit answered with a nod
He knew she would one day leave
On that day, he was sure to grieve
Then one day she finally went away
He hoped forever she wouldn't stay
Even now, he stares out beyond the horizon
Still wondering how long she would be gone
He knew one day, one season
She would return to her Island Prison

Darla M Swauger

GRANDFATHER

In Memory of Donald E. Patterson (1916-1989).

My grandfather is gone;
He left without saying good-bye.
We miss him very much,
Why did he have to die?

We remember all the good times,
There weren't many bad.
He left us all alone,
That's why we feel so sad.

We know he's now better off;
My grandfather is finally at rest.
He struggled so long to stay with us,
We know he did his best.

You're now at peace,
We should be glad.
But we love you so much,
We're still very sad.

The time has arrived
To say good-bye.
We'll never fully understand—
Grandfather, why did you have to die?

Doreen Rubine

HIS GAME

To my husband Mike, my sons, Michael and Jason, and to my family who were my biggest fans, I Love You . . . .

The coin is flipped into the air,
Your team will get the ball.
The coaches huddle with their team.
"Let's get tough and give your all."

The whistle blows and he runs out.
A quick glance he'll give to you.
The teams lined up, the play begins,
While, your heart is bursting through.

You think that not too long ago,
You rocked him in your arms to sleep.
But now the quarterback is motioning,
For your "Baby" to run deep.

The ball is spinning in the air,
Looking for a place to land.
He's already passed the goal line,
As it falls into his hands.

He caught it, it's a Touch-Down.
Everyone's cheering on the side.
He looks at you, and smiles,
You smile back, so full of pride.

William Woolfolk

THE LOVERS

When two come together
As a blissful one,
Passion and nurturing
Are magnified
To create the heat
Of a thousand suns,
That shine within
On the coldest of nights.

A stand against
The world is made,
That serves to symbolize
The tightest of bonds
In defiance for love
That shall not fade,
As the growing years
Slip into decades.

Steffany Presley

YOU + ME = HAPPINESS?

Dedicated to Michael (Eshgamahn)—I'm forever in your debt, for you were always there when I needed you. I'll always love you no matter what happens.

When all is gone and life has moved on, all that remains is but a glimmer of happiness . . . long lost.
Remember the times we spent so close, gone so fast.
Your warm hands caressing my body, heating me from head to toe.
Your body pressing against mine, wishing time could stop forever.
I'm not supposed to dream about you, care about you or even love you.
But I do dream about you, care about you and love you.
When I gaze into your sparkling eyes they reach out to me and say, "I want you, I need you, I love you."
To feel your touch again like it used to be . . . a fantasy come true. When I think about the reasons why I can't have you I shed a tear. Someone like you deserves the world on a silver platter. It's been said and yes it's true, no one is allowed to be 100% happy because when you find the perfect one something always stands in your way. I may have life and I may have liberty but I'll always be pursuing happiness.

Amy Larkin

FRIENDS

Sometimes the loneliness seemed to haunt me.
I was always on the outside—looking in.
No one ever cared about my feelings.
No one ever noticed that all I needed

was a friend,
Until you came along.
You turned my life around.
I saw your smiling face
And knew that I had found
A friend.
No longer on the outside,
On the inside I now stand.
I know I'm a real person.
All loneliness gone with one touch of your hand.
Thank you for being there
And showing me the way.
I'll never forget your love
And I hope we always stay
Friends.

Elena Megaro
DESERTED
A sudden sadness fills the air
An emptiness surrounds me
And I know I am alone.
I move closer to the edge
As if a force is pulling me
Towards the end of my destiny.
In the black sky, I see nothing.
I feel nothing.
The world moves around me
And I remain still.
In this vast universe,
I have no place.

Lori Ann Sweet
AS I LOOK UP
As I look up,
I see the eyes of a stranger,
Yet feel the warmth of home.

My stomach quivers,
As my heart begins to race,
My soul is touched for the very first time.

My mind is lost,
I search desperately across the room,
The eyes are gone.

The ache remains,
Long after the years go by,
A friendship blossoms, then withers away.

Tears are felt,
But will never be shed,
Life will go on, when the eyes are gone.

Ken E Reinhart
GOD ARE YOU THERE
I see a man with a
mansion and a limousine
I see a man with nothing
but a bag

I see a man loving his family
I see a man beating his child

I see a cause to help mother nature
I see a smokestack reply, "who's mother nature"

I see a man preach your word
I see a man abuse your word

I see a man saving a life
I see a man ending a life

I see a man working hard
I see a man stealing hard

I see a man fight for human rights
I see a man end human life

I see me wonder, what's it all about
I see me ask . . . Nobody knows

I see me think, God are you there
I see me believe: God Is Here

Teresa M Gervasi
TWIST OF FATE
An evening's journey momentarily halted.
By nature's trembling presence —
Unravelling a city
Ajar with confusion and despair
Gripped by fear, consumed with grief.
Heeding brother to brother, neighbor to neighbor,
Nation to nation.

Shaken with disbelief, engulfed in disarray.
Yet, unseemingly, a kindred spirit emerges
Outstretching its spacious arms
To comfort, to coddle, to console.
Lending strength to a city besieged —
By a haunting twist of fate.

Bernice Hayden Johnson

Bernice Hayden Johnson
RECENT WIDOW
Dedicated to the memory of Bob Johnson, a kind and delightfully witty husband of 44 years, who passed away October 5, 1989 of cancer.

As I lift my eyebrows
in the direction of your voice
No one is standing there.

As I anticipate your footsteps
in the bedroom hall
No one is there.

As I approach my front door
with a quickened step
No cheery greeting do I hear.

As I turn and speak your name
in the gathering dusk
I know my life will never be the same.

Bernice Hayden Johnson
A NOTE ABOUT KRIS
Dedicated to the memory of our beautiful granddaughter, Kristyn Nicolle Drahota. This poem was written the day following her death from leukemia.

Open the gates of heaven wide
We have a dear little grand-girl coming inside.
Perhaps step outside just a bit
And lend her a hand so she has no fear.

Look after her dear Jesus
And all you relatives and saints.
We've cared for her almost ten years
Her favorites are the 3 bears, her Grandpa, and root beer.

She hasn't walked for a very long time
Now we can see her running and playing
With other ones you've called up early.
What a joy heaven must be!

We would not want to hold her here
Life hasn't been that great
It may not be long before we join her
Tell her to be patient and wait.

C T Premo
THE AWAKENING
With sunlight piercing
The eastern sky,
While I in Morpheus's
Arms still lie,
A prisoner, my weeping
Soul would steal
Across the gaily
Sun drenched fields;
To capture laughter
Where she lay,
And live a moment,
A brief moment,
I soon snatch away.

C T Premo
DREAMS
I know of the dreams
Which no one can measure;
Ask for a value, and
Forfeit the treasure.

I know of the dreams
Which cares leave upended;
Thwarting the path,
Which love had intended.

I know of the dreams
To which men aspire;
And mourn as we turn,
To greed and desire.

I know of the dreams
Men sought to deny;
We felt every ache, and
Still let them die.

I know of the dreams
Men call their own;
Life opens the cage, and
Soon they've all flown.

Ruth St Claire Murphy
ANOTHER COCKTAIL, PLEASE
Another Cocktail, Please
Casually they say
That you have gone.
Brightly smiling and turning my glass
I say "Really?!"
Just as if blood still flowed
From this crushed thing
That was once my heart.

Ruth St Claire Murphy
FOR MOTHER
There is a corner of my heart
I keep all scrubbed and clean.
There is no messy clutter there
Nor nothing small or mean.

I keep it bright with sunshine
And quiet with a prayer.
There's a rag rug and some sewing
And a cozy comfy chair.

There's only one who sits there.
I won't let in another.
I keep this quiet sunny place
For no one but my Mother!

James A Norfolk
THE SEA
What unexpected radiance is this
Which gleams beneath me
In this tidepool?
Next to slowly folding anemones
Pulling at the sea for nourishment.
Near crystal shards of shattered rock
By cast off shell houses of tiny creatures,
Which sail off at the vortex top,
To join the changing sea.

Floating beneath its diamond-faceted surface
As it roils and drifts with high walls
To push the sun flat against the sky.
And in a moment of sudden stillness
The pool glistens and the realization
That it is the reflection of the soul,
Which is dashed asunder by the next wave
And carried buoyantly
Across the crested wave
To join the sparkling sea.

James A Norfolk
IN FEBRUARY
I arise early in the morning
To conduct the song of the birds
With the baton of a branch
The distilled impatience of the wind
Silently sways the reeds lined against my window
And suddenly watch clouds align across the sun
The cold blue sky of early February
Becomes colder.
And I sense that although we are not the same
We align in the wind.
As the reeds which silently dance
And the clouds which cling to the sun
In early February.

Helen G Chase (Age 99)
MAY MORNING
There is a veil of mist on the meadow,
Diamonds of dew on the grass
May flowers blooming in shadow
The pond a mirror of glass.

Song birds within a green bower
Serenade the rising sun;
In this enchanting hour
A beautiful day has begun.

With fragrance in the morning air
Only a May dawn can bring
Nature now is serene and fair
And once again it is spring.

Kalee Porter
MEMORIES OF US
When I lie here
thinking of you
the memories of us
come rushing through.
From the time
we met,
to the time
we parted
those were the times
when it all started.
You were my first love
from the start,
you were the only one
who stole my heart.
When it came down
to me and you
I was the one
being true.
No matter what I do
the memories of us
come rushing through.

Pearl Richardson
STRANGER
I met a stranger
In the street —
With piercing eyes
That seemed to speak —

I started to speak

But then I —
Being a dummy
Just hurried by.

Thinking I'll surely
See him again some day
So with searching eyes
I have walked my way —

Much time has passed
So now it seems
I'll see him only
In my dreams!

CD-2
THE MISSIONARY
I came to sell the Corporate world—on the bottom line
I came to tell the corporate world—that it's almost out of time
I came to clarify your life—and the bottom time
Working on the master plan—of the bottom line
Crumpled pulpwood turned to green—on the bottom line
Short term profits down the drain—on the bottom line
Crumpled greenbacks out of time—on the bottom line
Corporate profits in the mind—on the bottom line
Wall Street profits on your mind—on the bottom line
S & L's on the line—on the bottom mind line
People are the only line, that support the bottom line
Civilizations rise and fall—on the bottom line
Seen the clotting of your clone—on the bottom line
Seen forgiveness by your God—on the bottom line
Seen the evil and the good—on the bottom line
Seen the Master travel time—on the bottom time
Seen the Angels punish sin—on the bottom line
Seen the evolution of your soul—on the bottom line
The condition of the world—is on the bottom line
The integration of your world—is the final line
The beginning of the end—is on the bottom time

Joyce E Lishinsky
A MIXED-UP WORLD
What if the sun didn't rise in the morning
The moon didn't glow at night
There were no twinkling stars to wish upon
And the skies were always dark, like midnight

What if the rains didn't fall from the clouds
There weren't any mountains for us to climb
All the oceans, seas and lakes dried up
And the trees, shrubs and flowers died in their prime

What if there was no music to be heard
Nor any songs to be sung
No laughter from the children
And no bells were ever rung

What if the grass wasn't green
The sky wasn't blue
A rose didn't smell sweet
And nothing was ever true

The world would be all mixed up
So terrible and confusing, too
It would be the kind of place
Where I live when I'm without you

Joanne Kucinski
JUST WE TWO

Dedicated to: Marge and Hugo (Zbyszek) and all my friends and family who inspire me.

When I look at you, I enter a whole new world
Where you and I
Are the only two people alive
Whatever we wish comes true
We get lost in each other's eyes
Living carefree lives
Not a worry in the world
As long as we are together
There's nothing we can't do
Our love for each other never dying
Sitting on the beach at dawn
The stars reflecting on your eyes sparkling
Chasing each other having a good time. Laughing
Falling in love under the moonlight
Then I cry
Because all I thought
Turns into a mirage
Even what I think will never happen
I know for a fact
All my feelings will never change towards you
Unless they grow more and more which you can count on.

N Post-Racy
LOVE EVER AFTER
I believed for one swift fleeting moment
The tale of love lasting ever after,
Before the tears, before my heart was rent,
When life was sweet with thoughts of loving her.

I believed for one sweet sun-filled season
That love would never end and leave me cold.
But lovers change for whate'er the reason,
And ice surrounds my heart and numbs my soul.

I believed for one brief shining daylight
Her soft words of love and of devotion.
How, when these flowing tears have dimmed my sight,
Can I see past this wrenching emotion?

In spite of pain and tears and true love gone,
Love ever after must continue on.

Erma Stalnaker
GRANDMA'S PATCHWORK QUILT
Grandma was sewing her patchwork quilt
And I can remember it well
With each new patch she would cut and sew
There was always a story to tell.
On a table lay some red and white patches
From a dress she always wore with pride
She had it on the day grandpa asked her
To be his blushing bride.
Then she showed me some pretty pink ones
She was sewing that afternoon
From them came a great love story
Of her and grandpa's honeymoon.
Some were cut from Mother's dresses
She wore when she went to school
To learn how to read and write
And also the golden rule.
The sewing that she does now
Is mostly in her dreams
There she doesn't have to worry
About cutting, fitting or color schemes.

Geneva Ervine Sherlock
THE DESERT VAGABOND
Where go ye, carefree tumbleweed
  Rolling—skipping—churning
Is your tour a lonely venture
  Onward, and ne'er returning?

My eyes in curious wonder
  Follow your hurried pace
As you skim the desert sands
  In your mystic race

Take my hand and lead me where
  Enchanted lands await
Let me journey with a vagabond
  Let the wind direct my fate

Shelley Smith
A LOVE FOR ONE

To Mike, with all my love.

Two souls entwined into one,
a love that words cannot explain,
it is spoken in silence,
with a look and a touch,
meant only for one.

A love that people may not
always understand . . .
but, no barrier or wall could
withstand.

No sacrifice is too big or too small,
to lay in the warmth and safety
of this man's arms.

You know in your heart of hearts,
you have been given a rare gift
that many dream of, but only few
have.

The gift is true love,
and your heart and soul will
only belong to and love,
This one!

Gwendolyn Heather Smith
AWAY FROM THE CROWD

For my best friend, Alicia M. Kerr.

He was like a one-man football team
No teammates, no opponents, no field to run in
He didn't even have a football to kick around
He closed his eyes and opened his mind to see
I saw him catch, punt and run toward the goal for a touchdown
  He stopped and I said
If no one is your cheerleader . . .
Then I am willing to be.

Connie C Townsend
THE END OF A PARALLEL JOURNEY
We started out to take a trip, braving the waves of life in our well worn ships, in search of the Rose.

The force that guided us, forged the binding of our lives in an incredible parallel journey.

We laughed in the face of adversity and dared to steer our ships into the unseen.

How I wish my sister ship, that we'd set our course upon the open sea.

Never to set foot upon the land where the Rose had grown.

But little did we know, that the finding of the Rose would bring an end to the parallel journey.

Memories of what we had shared, each step along the way, went out with the tide.

For the sister ship remained with the Rose; something they could not share.

So the force that bound them entwined around them, and treacherous waves swept them under.

One stayed with the Rose, the other set sail for the open seas,

Never to return to the land where the Rose had grown.

Ruby Moore Geffert
JESUS'S LOVE
It's all that we can talk about.
It's all that we can see.
The love of Jesus coming down
To earth, to you and me.

Look up, receive, and you'll be blessed.
The beauty you will know.
Praise God and He will do the rest.
Tell others as you go.

(Repeat it o'er and o'er again)

The story is ever new.
The love of Jesus coming down
To earth
To me and you.

Itasca Hester
LOVE HIM
If you love him, Tell him so.
It may be—He does not know,
That you love him, If no word,
from your lips is ever heard,
Telling him, Himself alone,
of your love in words your own.
Love unspoken is so cold,
But how wonderful when told.
Voice your faith, your love, your praise;
Why be silent all the days,
A new rapture will be known,
When in quiet and alone,
Your lips whisper, soft and low,
Jesus, Lord, I love you so.

Michael H Tuttle
THE GREENHOUSE (AN INFINITE CYCLE)

BEGINNING OF THE END

To my family and friends for your endless support and love. With all my heart, I love you.

There once was a man, he had a dream
To save the human race
In an age of high technology
And radioactive waste

As knowledge had exceeded
Common sense fell behind
Until a saviour then was needed
To lead the blind, who lead the blind

But soon the vision came to be
Self destruction needlessly
He tried to show them all the way
But very few would see

His thoughts of wisdom never heard
Except for these few written words
Seen only by my own two eyes
Known only unto me

"To live we must learn
As well as understand
Wisdom, is the good in man
So very few
Are known as being wise"

Michael H Tuttle
THE GREENHOUSE

Before your birth, when I was young
I swore that I would tell no one
Just as you must swear it now to me

He said I was the chosen one
Until the day your time would come
To keep alive these precious memories

Now within me, weigh ten thousand years
For every day a thousand tears
What you're about to hear, you must believe

The earth was once a living place
When man was called the "Human Race"
Until he learned to read so well
No longer could he see

No one knows how long it's been
Or realize we're living in a greenhouse
You cannot breathe the atmosphere
Nothing grows unless it's here, the greenhouse

Our fathers of so long ago
Had learned so much, they'll never know
They'd gone so far, they left no place to be
But a greenhouse at the bottom of the sea

Michael H Tuttle
FORGET THE PAST

The sun would shine most every day
And children went outside to play
Where they could run, as far as you can see

Flowers, trees and animals
Lived beyond these ancient walls
Now only I have seen these things
And only in my dreams

Mountain snow was pure and white
The sky above was blue and bright
Earth was full of water, clear and clean

Food would grow and birds still flew
So no one thought or ever knew
Their ways of life
Would bring about the end, eventually

Now gone or sworn to secrecy
All the past and memories
No one needs to know what used to be

Begin a new reality
With a future life mentality
For death is all we learn
From history

Michael H Tuttle
PASSING ON

The turn is yours to carry on
Very soon I will be gone
The cycle is complete this time around

Your only son, the chosen one
Again the cycle has begun
Show him all the secrets I have found

With endless questions on my mind
So many answers yet to find
Confusion now, seems to take control

Within me, changes have begun
Why am I the chosen one
The truth must be in the memories I now hold

This truth I cannot hold inside
Nothing said is still a lie
Someday I must make these memories known

For how can people do what's right
With incomplete views in sight
And live as one, with minds of their own

Where do we go if we don't know
Where it is we've been

Michael H Tuttle
THE SEEK

In dreams, I'm in the great outside
Now I long to see the sky
To breathe fresh air and see the light of day

To feel the things called wind and rain
To see, could there be life again
And if so, would we be the same or find a better way

I can't explain these things I see
Or guarantee they will believe
And if they listen, will they care
Or live as if tomorrow simply isn't there

The truth I seek
So all may be aware

Now alone, in silence, I must go
To see these things I think I know
I'll then return to share my mind
And for themselves they must decide

Not only must we live together
But with ourselves inside

Michael H Tuttle
APPEARANCE OF THE PASSAGE

The eye of my mind sees so much more
In no time, I find the hidden doors
My trembling hands open one by one

Through darkened halls and corridors
To scriptured walls on glowing floors
I read and realize what I have done

I've gone beyond the containment sphere
Traveling on, I know no fear
As behind me, when I close each door
They completely disappear

I enter a room that has no doors
It seems to go on forever more
And yet, I reach and touch each wall
From here, right where I stand

A warm and soothing light surrounds me
Its brilliance shines within
Relaxed, in peace, I sleep so soundly
The journey then begins

How many years have drifted by
These people living here
Unaware of the earth and sky so near

Michael H Tuttle
NEW WORLD OF OLD

By ways even now unknown to me
I traveled somehow from the sea
Gracefully, I land without a sound

Where I am, I do not know
With no idea where to go
Invisible, I take a look around

I feel as though I'm in my dreams
It's like I know what I will see
As if somehow, I've seen it all before

But all I've seen are days of old
The precious memories, alone, I hold
How can this be what I'm looking for

All my questions from yesterday
Without an answer, fade away
For now I have so many, many more

Michael H Tuttle
CROSS OF LIFE

Who are these people living here
Why do they hide and live in fear
And lock themselves inside their wooden homes

I now realize from those I miss
There's nothing like togetherness
But now I feel I really am alone

Traveling on to anywhere
Without my goals, I'm lost
And then I saw it standing there
On top a steeple, a cross

The very same I learned of
From the scriptured walls before
The cross that stands for life and love
The Christ forever more

These people of the outer world
Act like each is own
Don't they know, without each other
They only are alone

How can people of the son
Not know the cross of life
How can I or anyone believe this is right

Michael H Tuttle
THE FINDING

With open mind
I've looked and listened closely
To see this world
From every point of view

So many people
Think of themselves only
A world for the rich
And privileged few

But the future depends on all of us
And the good we may achieve
The simple truth is obvious
Yet, still they won't believe

It's wrong to kill, so we may live
Or take from those with none to give
To see the hurt
And not to feel the pain

I've found the 20th century
Just like my precious memories
My God, ten thousand years
And still we haven't changed

I cry with pain, so much inside
This place is not for me
But from the greenhouse, I must hide
This terrible world I see

Michael H Tuttle
CHILDREN OF THE EARTH

Why can't we live together
Why can't we all be free
We're all in this forever
Dear God, please let them see

Let them see that all our lives
Are resting in their hands
That life and love are most important
Not money, oil or land

This thing called civilization
Is not as it should be
For how can one be truly happy
With millions still in misery

Why must we be American
Or Soviet at birth
Why can't we all just live together
As children of the earth

For the time has come, to cast aside
All I've learned in the past
Now, I see through real eyes
I see through my heart, at last
I now realize my real eyes, rebirth

Michael H Tuttle
CHANGE THE WORLD

People choose what they believe
I pray one day they choose to see
All is one
Man, the earth and sky

We know of electricity
That it exists in you and me
We also know, energy can change
But never die

Our universe is not a thing
But living and alive
To grow it needs the energy
That love and faith provide

The sun is but the nucleus
In a molecule of space
Every man a universe
Within a living place

To change the world
Believe and know
Life is energy
Give or take, love or hate
Eternal joy or misery

Michael H Tuttle
FOREVER HOPE

As long as there is breath in me
I pray for all of man
To see the way our life should be
As it was when it began

To find the universal truth
The only master plan
Will show me all that I must do
To do all that I can

Helping others see the way
So I may see the light
To turn my head and look away
In no way can be right

As long as one can feel the love
All are meant to share
As I do now for everyone
Forever hope is there

For there once was a man, he had a dream
To save mankind from denial
Of God the Father
Mother earth and sea
And himself, the only begotten child

Michael H Tuttle
INSIGHT

A down home boy in the big, big city
He feels so all alone
The world he sees does not look pretty
He's so far from his home

So he asks himself, deep down inside
Is this the place for me
Will I see the way to go
To find my hopes and dreams

And is our life all destiny
Or what we choose to make it
Would we be here to take a chance
If no one had dared to take it

So he tells himself to do his best
For that's all he can do
To hope and pray for all the rest
That God will see them through

For who really knows what kind of difference
Just one man can make
Like a down home boy in the big, big city
And the chance he dared to take

Lucille M Kroner

Lucille M Kroner
MY LITTLE CLOCK

To Linda, Bill, Rachel and Nathan Kroner who gave me my little clock for a birthday gift.

My little clock, like a heartbeat,
Sets upon the table here,
When I rise to greet the day,
When I work and when I play,

Telling me it's time to go,
Ring-a-dinging to my woe.
I hear it in the kitchen there
Tick–tocking on to everywhere.

It guides my movements and my plans
With its tiny turning hands,
Tolling the seconds, minutes, hours—
Clocking, tocking with its powers.

I hear its patient tiny voice
Ticking, clicking by its choice,
Chattering through the long, long night,
Of dark birds bound in homeward flight;

Of rain upon the summer winds;
Counting the days that I will spend,
Tolling them off here one by one,
Until my last long flight's begun.

N J Manley
TALK TO YOUR FATHER

Father's Day seems like another sales day for department stores
Some of us remember our dads as our heroes when we were seven or eight
But when we reached the grand age of thirteen we weren't sure anymore
Until we got to eighteen or nineteen we thought he had learned a lot, and was right
My father passed away while I was in Japan, during the Korean War
We had many years together before I spent time away from home during WWII & the Korean fight
So one & all make use of the valuable time you can spend, not less make it more
Life seems to go quite fast, so do what you think is right
Dad would appreciate hearing from you, write, or call, if need be make a peaceful overture.
If you have trouble and can't communicate, send him a copy of my poem
Tell him you see the light.

John J Basta
HANDS OF TIME . . .

To all those I have loved . . . Though our lives are borrowed time; memories of love shared live in our souls for eternity!

We are born to this land, a beauty in which we are grown!
The seas and beaches of sand, of which none, we do own!
We experience the joy of youth.
Living what seems a song or a rhyme!
From the loss of our first tooth,
We begin to feel the hands of time!

Adolescence are the years of turmoil and trouble;
Filled with laughter and tears, it drifts on like a bubble.
Then it is to manhood that we grow,
With its seriousness and sublime.
We think to the years we owe . . .
But really to hands of time!

Then we become old, with heritage and grandchild.
To which the stories are told of growing up and being wild.
There was never any need to say
Whether something was yours or mine!
It was always another day
Belonging to the hands of time!

Gwendolyn M Rice
FEELINGS

Hard as steel-toed boots. Like quick drying cement.
Like chalazae that holds the yolk firmly.
That's how strong my love is for you.
Like a seed that is planted; it grows; blossoms fully.
Like the sculptor that molds a lump of clay into a beautiful object.
The fragile glass figurines. That's how delicate and splendid my
Love is for you. Late in the evening soft clouds above it's as
though only you are here, the world doesn't exist.
That's how wonderful my love is for you.

Gwendolyn M Rice
FAMILY

They are the light you need when night fills up the sky.
They are the warmth from which you feel when iceness shivers its way down your spine.

They are sisters, they are cousins.
They are husband and wife.
They are family. Blended together as one soul.
It's what makes the air so sweet.

Aw, but the natural joy of conceiving.
It's like time time that passes.
It's like an elastic band that stretches, like the wildflower that grows in the sun.

And as each dawn begins so does the mystery of life.
Inside the womb someone new to lead through the night.
Someone new and tiny to hold.
They are family.

Ted Wells
HIS GIFT

Thank you for giving me life
For making me who I am
Giving me all that I have
Blessing me with all I need

Thank you for your caring
For giving me a compassionate heart
To be able to give to others
When the world has beaten them down

Thank you for giving your son
He gave his life for me
To pay for all my sins
So that I may live eternally

Most of all thank you for everything
You've touched all parts of my life
These words seem not enough
For a life full of your love

Wilmer H Wigner
STOP AND LOOK AROUND

As I stop and look around me
All I see is hate and greed.
Everyone's so busy grabbing
They cannot see another's need.
Not a second thought is given
To someone who seems in pain
Nor a friendly hand extended . . .
Words of pleading are in vain.
As I stop and look around me
I recall a time gone by
And a world now gone forever
And a tear escapes my eye.
For as I stop and look around me
At the drugs, the drunks and crime
My heart grows sick within me
For we are only marking time.

Janice Dengel
PARENT

To My Mother and Father.

When God passed out parents,
I'm glad he chose you,
He blessed you with two daughters
no better could he do.
We've been through the good,
We've been through the bad,
but through it all,
I love you Mom and Dad.

Eleanor Someroak Smith
TIME

When a barren bush I see
And snow upon the ground.
Do you think that spring will come
And green replace the brown?
Will days grow bright and sun appear
With velvet leaves upon the vine?
Or will it stay the way it is
And cease the sun to shine?
When love has left our time.

Irv Freemer
VOICE OF LIFE

To my life, my wife, Lois.

I struggle thru when things are blue, bit out of the quiet to break the silence the phone rings, your voice is a rainbow of life. Yes you my wife. I could not make it without that sound, for suddenly life I found. I jump and sing and carry on and no more am I forlorn. I hurry and rush the remaining hours I cannot wait to be with my flower. Again I am made to feel rejoice, for at the door I hear your voice, and now the darkness suddenly appears and I snuggle up under your ears. You relax and sigh and whisper a sound not knowing it's heaven I found. Your sweet embrace, your tender touch, how I love you, love you, oh so much. And now the dawn breaks for a new start, oh love, my love, again we must part, again I must wait for the sound of the ring so I can speak with my everything. Again I jump, and heart starts to pound, I know I can wake because of your sound.

Hattie P McShine
IN A HURRY

Dedicated to my Family and my dear friend Dr. Virgie M. Binford.

We get up early each morning
And hasten right through the day
We have so much to accomplish,
We do not stop to pray.
Problems just tumble about us,
And heavier comes each task,
We wonder why God does not help,
but often we fail to ask.
We like to see joy and beauty,
As the day toils on gray and bleak.
We wonder why God does not answer,
but to God we forget to speak.
We desire to be in God's presence,
We use all our keys at the lock.
God gently and lovingly smiles,
Indicating we really didn't knock.
As we awaken early each morning,
Remember to pause before starting the day.
Realizing there is much to accomplish
We must stop to pray.

Margaret Sennett
GRANT THAT I MAY SEE

God has taken my sight from me
It hurts me deep inside
Grant that I may see
I feel that I might die

The scorching feeling of dark beauty
Has burnt me with desire
Grant that I may see
The withering flames of fire

To touch a rose and see it
Without the use of eyes
Grant that I may see
That rose before it dies

Shannon Rahm
MY AUTUMN TREE
I stare outside my window,
And see an Autumn tree.
I think about its branches and leaves,
And the sapling it used to be.

Your leaves are hair of emerald,
Your branches dark as coal.
I hear the squirrel family
That lives in the little hole.

I hope to see you years from now,
Big and strong and tall.
I hope to see you all year 'round,
Especially in the fall.

Beth Motley
HOPEFUL EYES
Come with me and take a ride
Far above the clouds and hide.
Bring your imagination along,
And make sure you know a joyful song.
Now one more step we must take
Bring a smile for heaven's sake.
Let us soar high into the sky
To the place where none will die.
Higher and higher we will go,
We'll be past the clouds before you know.
Now to the place you have been sent
It is a place with an arch as your tent.
As we search in its sparkling rays,
Remember the life back in the haze.
Don't turn back, you've gone too far
Just look ahead and wish upon a star.
As time flies in this loving place,
Take the time to see its gorgeous lace.
One more word to the wise
Always dream with hopeful eyes!

Michael K Thompson
AN ENDLESS CYCLE
Dreams run wild,
The air feels crisper,
And a beginning is on the eastern horizon.
The seed germinates
And begins to grow.

Dreams come alive.
The day feels warmer,
And the stream seems to flow on forever.
The flower blooms
And roots itself deeply.

Dreams are shattered.
The sun shines darker,
But the forest is still filled with restlessness.
The plant dies
But still remains.
Dreams are abandoned.
The clouds gloom brighter,
And even the owl is resting peacefully.
The remains disintegrate
And leave a vacancy

Yet dreams run wild.

Michael K Thompson
WHAT COLOR IS THE SKY IN YOUR WORLD?
The sky is pure white.
The ground is pitch black.
The stars are bright yellow.
The hills are dark violet.
The clouds are sunshine orange.
The rivers are mud brown.
Nature is true blue.
Man is blood red.
Everybody is green with their own shade.
Why?
What color is the sky
in your world?

Preshenda Jackson
CELEBRATION OF LOVE

"To Mecca, Louis and Michael Muhammad," the womb of my youthful inspiration. Dedicated also to the JACKSON Clan, for your relentless support.

Like a subtle thief in the Night
Unlocking the secret chambers of my Heart
Your love journeyed throughout my Soul
Making all my dark paths Bright,

Providing me with the comfortable Certainties
of what Compassionate Love is truly About
In loving details you have turned all
My dreams into Living Victories,

I do love you, and the varied dimensions
of love expressed through you,
Yes my love, it's you whom I Adore,

All my secret prayers, wishes and desires regarding Love
That I shared with the Ocean
Have been faithfully washed up to Shore,

The importance of having you in my life is Total Fulfillment
and I say this without Hesitation,
Life with you is so calm, so pure, so tender and rich,
Each day with you is a Joyous Celebration!

Preshenda Jackson
THE EIGHTH WONDER OF THE WORLD
I've been blessed to travel the world throughout
I've seen The Seven Wonders of The World
I've walked beside the Pyramids, and renewed my faith along the Nile,
But the Greatest Wonder I've ever witnessed; was the intimate journey through the dimensions of your heart;
a journey so divine, so gentle,
Beijing was so captivating and to commemorate my journey
I took pictures of the Great Wall,
But as soon as I look into your eyes, such an immeasurable depth of comfort
The world outside of you seems so very small,
The Grand Canyon was remarkable, God's Creation of beauty
Radiating enthusiasm that makes life so sunny and warm,
and yet I find more beauty wrapped up inside your arms,
Aspen, Mount Rushmore, Niagara Falls; Hong Kong, New Mexico, The Italian Riviera,
The Beach at Loreto, and The Ancient Ruins of Rome,
Were all so fascinating and I always left feeling overwhelmingly amazed
Wondering if in this lifetime could I ever experience greater sights,
And behold, when I rest within the boundaries of your love
I'm reborn from the loving kindnesses you provide throughout the night,
Yes, I've traveled throughout the world, and The Seven Wonders are all
So Wonderful, So Beautiful, National Treasures So True,
But if there shall ever be an Eighth Wonder of the World; It Would Indeed Be YOU!

D L Shilling
MAYBE HE DOESN'T
Maybe he doesn't want to grow up
To be a man.

Maybe he isn't ready, just yet
To fight and kill
In his own street.

Where they yell so loud.

Maybe, for now, he'll just be content
To hold his brother's hand awhile longer,
And watch, from behind the wire.

As the soldiers march to the scream
Of their sergeant.

The toy gun in the little boy's hand,
Forgotten.
His tiny fingers are too small anyway

to play this game.

Tiffany Krause
THE BROKEN HEART

I dedicate this poem to Tommy Taylor, who taught me what the word love really means. You have been a true inspiration, and I will always be here for you.

Feels like getting stabbed by a sharp pin
Is hope withered away time and time again
Like a dead flower.
Many pieces of a puzzle that won't fit together
I see darkness that makes me wonder whether
The sun will ever shine.
My heart bleeds
For love it still needs—
How can I make it stop?
There's an emptiness inside
My sadness I will hide
But for how long?
Soon I will cry an ocean
And wonder if and when
This hurt will ever cease.
A protective covering is over my heart
From others I have grown apart
For I have nothing left to give.
The wounds with time will heal
Again I will be filled with zeal
But the memories will never be forgotten.

Rebecca Lee Undseth
HEAVY HEART
The blue sky, suddenly from one
extreme to the other
Light and laughing,
Dark and crashing.
The blue sky,
The happy heart.
The dark night sky,
The heavy heart.
One lightning bolt.
One mistake.
The singing,
The crying.
The bright sun.
The dark sky.
Oh, the broken heart.

Kelly A Lee
LOVE
Like a fragile rose bud it slowly grows strong
Every word and touch make it progress along
a nice word can make that rose grow
Love gives a light that makes a face glow
A tender touch makes my heart sing
Words I love make my emotions take wing
Sorrow overwhelms me when you leave the room
My heart is covered with a fog of gloom
You come back and the sun shines through
My heart takes flight when you say "I Love You"
Every word, every touch pulls another silk thread
in this web of caring you've wound around me
I'll love you forever till the day I die
Hopefully we'll be together when towards heaven we fly

Andrew D Hylton
MELODY'S HARMONY
"Sing the melody—MELODY."
Said the mother to her little girl.
"Sing the melody for me."
She sang the melody,
But she likes harmony.

"Sing the melody—MELODY."
Said the music teacher to the student.
"Sing the melody for me."
She sang the melody,
But she likes harmony.

"Sing the melody—MELODY."
Said the boy to his girl.
"Sing the melody for me."
She sang the melody,
But he likes her harmony.

Andrew D Hylton
DONNA
Sing a song for Donna,
Trying to find her way.
Let her know that everything's O.K.
Sing a song for Donna Kay.

Tell her you know things will
Turn out right;
Even though it takes
A long time.

Life will turn out according to plan,
Try to make her understand;
Life is always lived by a plan.

Sing a song for Donna,
Trying to find her way.
Let her know everything's O.K.
Sing a song for Donna.
Sing a song for Donna Kay.

Andrew D Hylton
A GOLDEN STONE
She came when he was lost,
She came when he was alone,
She came from a Family,
Whose name is Stone.
But she came to him
As a precious Gem.

Both of them have been hurted
In the past,
And they can't help but ask:

"Are these feelings real?"
And "Will our friendship last?"

But somehow he knows
Their friendship is:

As 'GOOD AS GOLD,'
And as 'SOLID AS A ROCK,'
And 'EMBEDDED IN STONE.'

Bethy Coleman
BONES OF EXISTENCE

Dedicated to—The struggle for the freedom of man and earth to live as one.

Never a demanded raindrop, not as a tear
We have so much to fear
Lost in some far away thought
Swirling, soft secrets
Polluting the land with civilization

All the words that made us up
We explained then abruptly changed
Unimportant are we to time
Twilight, torching life
Less important with every night

Reality shall inspire the mad
Very extreme or so it seems
The pampered and the practical
Wild, alive minds
Feeling each that die with us

Never a forced wave, not as a thought
Lie asleep to spread a dream
Left behind as a memory
Emotional, distant defiance
More important with every dawn

Paula D Davitt
MY SON
A baby in my eyes and probably always will be
But at the early age of seventeen
Decided to enlist and be a Marine

To leave his mother behind to cry and cry
Only to find a letter from time to time
Never a discouraging word sent home
Just glad to be in the corps.

Turning eighteen all alone.
And always worried they might find
A reason to send him home

Sent away overweight
To return to me almost a skeleton
But only in the eyes of his mom

For he returned proud as can be
Because he was one of the few and proud
A United States Marine.

Jodi-Lynn Marie Lund
WHEN THE OLD LOVE CAME HOME
I had built a wall around my heart,
only in fear to be hurt once again.
Yet, there was something that you brought into my life—
That made me not fear, and let that wall come crashing in.
I put all of my trust in you, giving you my body and my soul.
You kept reminding me not to worry—
for you would never let me go.
You said you were beginning to love me, a little bit more with each and every passing
day, never once letting me forget,
you were afraid I'd somehow push you away.
Yet, I never knew, that there was someone else in your heart all along—
Because one day you said you would love me forever—
The next, without a warning, you were gone . . .
I begged you for a reason, with tears streaming from my eyes—
But you only said you needed time to be alone.
You said of how everything we once shared was special,
But you didn't tell me of how your love for me faded—
When the old love came home.
So, you placed the ring on her finger,
Sending me only a letter in your place.
You didn't even care enough—
To tell me face-to-face.
While I was running from others—
I honestly believed in you.
I allowed that barricade to fall, and let my love shine on through.
Now I am left standing,
So cold and so alone.
Because it's true of how I lost everything—
When the old love came home . . . .

Amy Marie Fraser
THANK GOD FOR DIRTY DISHES
Thank God for dirty dishes,
They have a tale to tell.
While other folks go hungry,
We're eating very well.
With home and health and happiness.
We shouldn't want to fuss,
For by the stack of evidence,
God is very good to us!

Matthew Avidan
FLOWERS IN THE SPRING
I understand now, why the rains must be
so we have colour in our lives
I see now, the sun must shine
and why darkness takes it's place
and so through the rain and darkened skies
I can see the sun shining and the flowers in its embrace
Only now (do) I wonder of the turning darkness of the earth
I see that darkness, set upon this world
and the light wiped off from its face
and yet I know the light shall come
bringing forth the warmth, the colours, the life
so I understand now, why the rains must be
and why we have flowers in the spring

Bessie May Cochran
BETRAYAL

Dedicated to: My Mother and My Grandfather, Sherree, Sean, "Geo" my father.

It waits quietly to swallow up society.
It choice not one of solitude but variety.
Friendship always began this trail because it grows,
Strong then it start to split, then breaks.

Politics makes it trail by deceit and broken promises,
Smile on its brutality to society awakes.

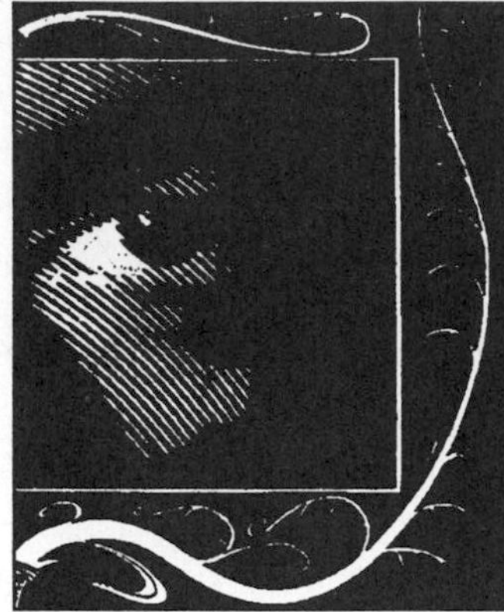

It creeps quietly into each conscience and dampened as dew upon a young flower.
Enraging into enormous power.

Betrayal take trust and crush it beneath its form,
as a predator on a serpent head.
Its growth is the entity of indefinitely.

Robert Lee Lewis Jr
THE FLEEING MOMENT OF SILENCE

This poem is dedicated to Margaret Ruth Palmer, with all my love.

Try to cage a fleeing moment of silence,
savor its sweet refrain.
Use it up, abuse it,
it won't return again.

Set yourself up as a fisherman's net,
cast yourself out to the sea.
Notice the fleeing moment when
suspended in space you'll be.

Take the moment of impact,
then you settle to drift ashore.
As you rest on a pebble at sunset
to drift this day no more.

Though as a net you've caught your limit,
and you're laid on the fisherman's bench.
Remember the moment of silence?
where did it start? where did it end?

Robert Lee Lewis Jr
CALLING ON AN OLD FRIEND

This poem is dedicated to my wife, Gwendolyn.

Sought in a sea of meditation,
a journey which seems to never end.
Surrounded in a cave of darkness,
calling on an old friend.

Surrendering to feel your presence,
awaiting wet caresses upon my cheek.
Taking time to search for your footsteps,
no time to talk, no time to speak.
As my heart yearns for liberation,
to let go and not to bend.
In noticing your absence while I'm yearning,
calling on an old friend.

To feel a desperation in search
through heartfelt pain.
A loneliness without comfort, to be
soothed by your coming again.

'Tis not the selfishness within me,
which seeks the eyes wet rain.
'Tis the loneliness in meditation
which calls for you, old friend, again.

Barbara J Cuyle
A TIME OF FEAR

To my family . . . .

Perhaps someone was whistling,
An old familiar song,
And people started talking,
As they steadily drove along.

Suddenly it happened,
On that sunny autumn night,
And the people started scurrying,
In a frantic freedom flight.

The walls began to crumble,
And buildings began to sway,
And the great ballpark deserted,
As the players did not stay.

The fans began dispersing,
And walked in single file,
Their faces mirrored deep concern,
Where once there was a smile,

There were heroes in that earthquake,
That will never be replaced,
As they rushed to aid the stricken,
And the horror that they faced,

The disaster is now over,
But the stories one will tell,
Of strangers helping strangers,
Through that night of living hell.

Matthew Horstman
LOVE AND SORROW
Love and sorrow go together like dreams and nightmares.
Love is all that is bright and gentle like a summer's breeze.

Sorrow is pain.
Lost in time, it preys on you and me
making love seem hard.
But, as insane as it is, we need both of them in our hearts,
as insane as it is.

Huberta Jean Christy
ODE TO LITTLE KATE

To My Son Jim and his wife Sharon.

We never knew what joy awaited us
till little Kate arrived and stole our hearts.
A little girl who is beautiful to behold
her wide blue eyes and rosebud mouth unfold
to form a face in such a perfect mold.

It is happiness to hold a grandchild close
and feel the warmth a tiny body most
depends on you for their very life, a host
of angels know the child's trusting eyes and
faint clasp on your fingers
will remain and years to come will linger in
your memory.

Joanne Daugherty
WHOOPS, SORRY!
I've suddenly realized, to my chagrin
There was no check enclosed within
The entry that I sent to you . . .
I thought "Whatever shall I do?!"

Shall I confess, and send my check
And hope that this will "save my neck"?
Are my poems now in File Thirteen
Where nevermore will they be seen?

Take a chance, and send the money;
Maybe they'll think that this is funny.
They know that "perfect" poets are not
And realize that I just forgot!

Joanne Daugherty
REAWAKENING
The trees that icy fingers stretched
Toward a wintry sky
Now are adorned in softest green,
A pleasure to the eye.

The lawns become a velvet base;
The tender plants arise,
Soon bearing jewels of lovely flowers—
A delicate surprise.

The bushes add their verdant touch
To yards and roadsides, too;
Now, as you watch this miracle,
What does it do for you?

Each season has its way to show
Expressions of God's love;
Truly, he maketh all things good,
From trees to simple dove.

Yes, somehow Spring can warm my heart
And bring a festive feeling,
Quickening all my long-dimmed hopes
Through nature's sweet revealing.

F Karolyna Whaley
MIRROR MIRROR
Mirror Mirror on the wall
You're so dirty you could fall.
If I clean you will you show
By reflection what you know?

Hesitatingly distract
Narrow angle then retract.
Expand the view or condense,
With a curve it's all nonsense.

Truth you know, you never lie
Visions reversed, you are shy
You aren't bold, you quietly wait
When I look I see it straight.

When ignored you stay the same,
Whispering a victim's name.
Whether depth or narrow view,
No matter, I can't sue you.

No choices, let duty stand,
Each actor cast a command.
Fair weather or be it storm,
Silently as you perform.

William B Boni
SUN FEAST
Wish I could grab a ray of sun,
Hold on tight and ride shotgun;
And when draws near far western shore,
Ease me off and ride no more;
Then as board and I tame wave,
Lick lemon drops that sun man gave.

Karen Davis
TRULY BLESSED
With clasped hands and bended knee
I came to you with one small plea;
I asked of you, my Father above,
One small child for me to love.
You sent three, one girl, two boys,
and along with them came many joys.
Twinkling eyes and a turned up mouth,
sounds of laughter ring through my house.
At night when they are all in bed,
many thoughts run through my head.
I think of all the love I would have missed
if I had not been truly blessed.
I remember all that happened in the day
the memories of things they would say.
It's the little things that mean so much,
their special smiles, their feel and touch.
The last thing I hear as I turn off their light
is "I love you momma and sleep tight."
So once again, I am on bended knee,
thank you LORD for my blessing of three.

Luella Hill
THE STORM
Ominous black clouds,
Lightning bolts link earth and sky,
Thunder rolls and jars the ears,
Heavy rain pelts the ground.
Gray clouds replace the black,
Rain falls softly,
All is calm.

Alice Diane Baggett
WHEN I MUST GO
When I must go, don't weep for me,
For I have finally won the victory
Don't look upon me and be sad;
Let your heart rejoice and be glad.
For I have finally won the race
And I am gone on to a better place.

Alice Diane Baggett
LIFE
Have you ever wondered why
We were born here, just to die?
We must live a life
Filled with heartaches and strife.
No one knows when they will leave
When friends do, we always grieve.
We want close ones to always stay,
It's hard to see them go away.
We all know
Sooner or later, we'll have to go.
We don't know when our time will be,
But it is good to be ready.
Our flesh will have to go.
What really matters is our soul.
Everything else will be left behind.
In God, comfort, you will always find.
It is the easiest life to live.
Only if you are willing to give
A small part,
He will come into your heart.

Ann Alexov
SILENT RETALIATION
Pain surges through every crevice of my mind
Searching for sanctuary, uncertain to find
Believing that the truth shall set me free
And now I've been set free in hell

Your words like smoke obscure my sight
Lost my desire and will to fight
Your actions are contradictory
You've drained me of my pride
Confusion and frustration I have no strength to hide

I had little hope
You've left me with even less
I can't hear
I can no longer listen to false concern
I can't feel
It's easier to live in numbness than in pain
I can't speak
Putting thoughts into words only trivializes them

I don't know why I continue to delude myself and wonder . . .
Do thoughts of me ever occupy your mind
Do you even care
Somehow the answers to these questions I know I cannot bear . . . .

Bernice L Burmood
REMEMBRANCE

This poem is dedicated to Edwin, my beloved husband.

The joys and happiness we shared
Forever I will cherish
The years he showed he cared
For me will never perish

His kind and thoughtful ways
To me were marriage bliss
The trials of the days
Were sealed with a kiss

The day I lost the one I love
Was filled with pain and sorrow
Though he is far above
We'll meet again tomorrow.

Kim Wagner
A SIGHT TO SEE
The wind was fierce o'er the sea, and the waves ran wild and free;
The clouds were a collage of shapes and covered the sun like drapes;
As I stood on the shore by the sea, it was quite a sight to see.

The stream went glistening along and birds sang a sweet peaceful song;
The smell of flowers in the air and the sky was bright and fair;
As I leaned up against a tree it was quite a sight to see.

The desert was arid and dry and small, strange creatures ran by;
The cacti were towering and tall, and the sun was a fierce shining ball;
As I watched an ant colony, it was quite a sight to see.

The trees were clustered together and between them were tufts of heather;
The rain was falling so lightly and the sun was shining very brightly;
As I gazed at a squirrel family, it was quite a sight to see.

The majestic profile of God and his golden scepter and rod;
The pearly gates and streets of gold are among the wonders told;
On God's creation, both Spirit and Son agree;
It was quite a sight to see.

Donna C Marcheschi
LOVE REMINISCED
Two people in love many years ago,
Two people in love who let it go.
Different paths they traveled twenty years or more,
Then in she walked through fate's front door.
Shyly they talked and touched on the missing
But sparks were ignited by one gentle kissing.

Her phone had rung late that night
Then words were spoken that seemed so right.
The love and caring had always been there
Gently tended and held by hearts so rare.
Neither of us knows what tomorrow may bring
For today, for now, just let our spirits sing.

Muriel Wysong
A CHILD
Two lips like a tiny rosebud,
Two eyes so big and blue
And tiny little teeth
That sparkle like the dew.

A little turned-up nose,
Two cheeks so pink and white
And tiny little hands and feet
That go from morn 'til night.

A head of tousled curls,
A laugh like tinkling bells,
Her voice so high and sweet
As to her dolly tells

Some story of a fairy land
That her imagination wrought.
This child so sweet and innocent
Could have no evil thought.

Sue Honeychurch
EBB & FLOW

To those people who, like the tide, Ebb and Flow in my life, and to everyone who stood by me, no matter what.

I sit here in my emptiness
Wounded, gashed,
My veins throbbing, pulsing with emotion.

Lashing, slashing, death I fear
Yet it would stop this wretched feeling—
Of pain—which mashes at the core
Of my soul.

The sound of his voice fades (softly) away
The waves of his soul
Thrash against the rocks
Of my eternal cavernous being.

Awakening the space
That lays between
The outer and inner stretches
Of my consciousness.

As the tide rushes in
So it extracts itself—
Exposing the naked flesh of sand.

Naked, barren wastes of land
Aching for life-giving moisture
To be returned again.

Darlene Squglio Torrey
JUST ACCEPT ME
Cast no shadows of doubt upon my life for I have enough.
Do not give me so much light that I cannot see.
Do not tell me what I already know for it is a waste of my time. Throw no names in my path for they are not my stepping stones.

Do not wash away my dreams by raining on them
You do not know how I feel, for you are not me. Do not try to remake me, just accept me.

Julie Hamilton
A LOST LOVE
The loneliness in my heart has reappeared
just like the hurt I've always feared
All the love taken away
Wondering: can I make it through another day
You're always on my mind
but now I know you were just being kind
To see your face, the look in your eyes
I know your words were not lies
Though our time together was short
I could always look to you for love and support
Our past and future dreams we shared from the very first moment you knew I cared
That's all behind us now—the laughter and fun
What you feel is best has been done
I hope you never forget the times we've had
All of them good, none of them bad
You'll always have a special place in my heart
Maybe someday we'll make a new start
I'll always be here for you
I'm hoping you feel the same way too

Gail Wong
HURTING

To Jack Tan, my inspiration.

I now know what hurt is,
When you're suffering from a heartache.
Knowing that he's been lying to you—
That's what caused the break.
I know the pain will go away,
But what do I do now?
I know that I have to go on living,
But I just don't know how.
I spend most of my time crying my eyes out,
Aching to have him hold me.
But now that I've seen his true colours,
I know that it was never meant to be.
Life is full of ups and downs—
Mine has been mostly ups.
But now I always seem to be crying,
Until I get the hiccups.
Now as I continue down the road of life,
I wonder if I'll ever find another love.
Maybe nothing much will happen
Until I die and go above.

Andrew Wollard
DUST DEVILS
I can still feel
the angry glare of
the desert sun,
giving me its
vengeful bath.

Sometimes
when I lie in bed,
I think of loneliness.

I slip back to that
desolate plain of sand,
that desert.
I am deafened
even now by
the winds,
the awful cacophony
they would create.

Most of all, I remember those
ethereal imps, those guardians of sand,
dust devils.

Steven J Downs
HOLDING BACK
Don't you think it's tough
To be standing all alone
Don't you think it's rough
When you've got no other choice

Isn't it a shame
When you have no one to blame
Don't you think it's wrong
When nothing seems to change
And you're always feeling strange

Wouldn't you think I'd tell you
If I really was to care
Don't you be so sure
Because I've already been there

I feel like a miser
Holding in all these feelings
But I don't want to give away a little bit
I want to give it all at once

René Sedlak
BROKEN DREAMS
For all the tears I cried
For all the pain in my heart.
The sorrow you left me
With now, that we are apart,
The shattered dreams left behind.
Only memories are left to
haunt me forever.

Brigid Finn
A RAINDROP
A raindrop falls softly on the street,
A raindrop feels cool on my feet,
A raindrop is a teardrop from a baby's eye,
A raindrop falls from the sky,
A raindrop is an angel singing,
A raindrop is the church bells ringing,
A raindrop is quiet and very calm,
It feels real good when it falls on my palm,
A raindrop is happy, A raindrop is sad,
But a raindrop is never bad.

Alfred Elkins
LOOKING THROUGH AN ANTHOLOGY
I looked at a book of poems
In the privacy of my home,
I saw soldiers and sailors,
Young girls and tailors,
All ages and races,
A poem about horses
Going through their paces.

Poems holy
With meter slowly
Spelled out,
Poems that whisper,
Poems that shout,
Poems of mothers
And poems about others.

Poems about ev'ry
Conceivable subject,
Poems of people,
Poems of objects,
Poems of God,
And poems of religion,
Ev'ry poem is divine.

Hank Seedorf
GOODBYE COTSIE
You came to me as just a pup;
Stayed with me, till I grew up.
And did we ever, have such fun;
Frolicking . . . Playing, in the sun!
Frisking about under a blue sky.
How dare you . . . "up and die!"
I ask myself . . . "Why?"
As you lie so very still,
Soon to play on another hill.
So I'll hold you tight;
This one last night,
While you drift away
To another time;
A painless day.
Comforted, by memories
Of you and I;
I have no more tears to cry.
"Goodbye Cotsie, . . . Goodbye."

William B Jennings II

William B Jennings II
WITH ALL MY LOVE, FROM HELL

For my parents, Chanda Tyndall, Ruth Read, Paul Stansel and Robert Fisher.

For beauty and warmth my soul doth yearn
I, a creature of darkness, in search of light
In blackened depths of anguish I must burn
Love and purity forever hidden from my sight.
The wells of Hell are the sadness in my eyes
My body is young yet my mind is far too old
Look into my eyes where the heart of madness lies
Life in my Inferno is eternally empty and cold.
The grave is drear and damp
All the Abyss is before my eyes
I long for love and grace
But all that I touch dies.
The charnel depths beckon me from the earth
I will wait for you my darling
eternally by these Stygian shores
Time will bring you to me with death's rebirth
Where my eyes drip blood for tears in endless downpours.

Holli Scott
FRIENDSHIP
A friend is like a diamond. It starts out rough then turns out to be smooth. A true friend is there by your side always, through thick and thin.

When I think of you I think of a friend who is strong when I'm weak and is always around. We party together and we cry together, all in all we are together.

I think back to the years when I didn't know you and I wonder how I survived. When I cry, you are there, when I'm happy or when I'm sick you are always there. I think we were made to be best friends.

So I thought I'd let you know that I miss you and love you, and no matter where you are at I'll be by your side always.

Sherri Teed-Baker
CHANGES

To my Dad; who gave me the words, the heart and the soul.

The end of winter with its grey skies,
Brings the hope of the spring with its blustery sighs.
It spits out snow; and then the sun shines.
The flowers perk up; and then the wind whines.
The birds start to chirp and sing
As they wait to see what the day will bring.
They know that spring lies,
Just behind the end of winter with its grey skies.

Patty M Weyman
PARK BENCHES
At one time I went to the park to play,
now I go and sit all day.
I'm not alone as you can see,
there's a lot of us elderly.
We reminisce about days gone by as we sit
under the beautiful blue sky, the warm sun on my face I could cry.
Most of my friends have moved away or died.
Withered and weary as I watch the children play,
brings me back to yesterday.
It's not easy to be old, people usually point and
stare (I don't care),
Someday they'll be sitting on a park bench somewhere.

Lottie Kelly Banion
MOMMY HERE AM I
"Mommy, here am I"
I was so busy at my work, that warm and windy day.
Now I could get the worst job done
Annie was out at play.
But just in the midst of the hardest job, I heard a tender sigh
And was startled to hear a sweet voice say
"Mommy, here am I"

The tender years passed swiftly on, lovely and happy days
Annie was surely growing up. Soon she would go away
I wondered if I could face the loss
Of the beautiful days gone by
With nothing left but memory's voice, saying
"Mommy, here am I"

One day the sun sank low in the west
And I knew my last sunset had gone.
I watched the colors fade swiftly away.
The darkness of night came on.
Then suddenly out of the twilight years
I heard the sound of a sigh,
The touch of a hand and a lovely voice saying
"Mommy, here am I"

Charles G Clark
SUNRISE
How many sunrises, have come and gone
When I awoke to find, I missed another dawn
For dawn is exciting, and it's always a thrill
To get up real early, and look over the hill
And see the sun, in magnificent beauty
Arise like a sentinel, preparing for duty
So this morning, I awoke early, expecting to see
A glorious sunrise, awaiting for me
But alas, there were clouds, misty and gray
And if I wish to see sunrise, I must wait another day

Charles G Clark
THE BEAUTY OF THINGS
I've trailed a fox, and wish I could be
As cunning as he, so wild and free
I've woke with the dawn, and marveled at light
Tho I cherish the memory, of the beautiful night
I envy the wind, the stars, and the rain
As they come and they go, and then come back again
And I can't help but wonder, as I stand here in awe
At the beauty HE put, in the things that I saw

Susan A Harsley
THE GLOW A CANDLE BRINGS INTO A ROOM

To my mother, with love. Thank you for always being there.

The glow a candle brings into a room
Is such a peaceful, soothing kind of blush;
Warm reds and yellows take away the gloom
And bring upon the hectic world a hush.

The evening orb begins its destined flight
With hues of blues to comfort, so it seems;
Its opalescent luster fills the night
Escorting man to silent, tranquil dreams.

The sunbeams that awake each newborn day
So clear and pure, restore the life to all;
And as the light begins to die away
Across the sky cascades of colors fall.

Compared to these, your light is far above,
Into this darkened soul you've shone true love.

Regina S Matthews
WHO'S ON SECOND?
Who's on first, Rainman?
What's on second?
I don't know's on third, Rainman.
Who'd you say was on second?
Do you see me Rainman?
Can you hear me beckon?
How do I get to know you Rainman?
Who or what's on second?
I'm your brother, Rainman!
Can you hear me beckon?
Your world is simple, Rainman.
Cheeseballs, pancakes, toothpicks.
Your world is lonely, Rainman.
My God! Are you really sick?
I want to reach you, Rainman.
I want to make you need me.
Should I call you Painman?
What's out there that you see?
I'm your brother, Rainman!
Can you hear me beckon?
I really love you, Rainman.
Who's on second?

Roger Davis
HOW BLIND AM I . . .

This poem is dedicated to my grandmother Alma Brown, my mother, Minnie L. Davis, and my wife, Brenda. Also to my three children, Larawnda, Ashley, and Roger.

How blind am I? If I can't see red, yellow, and green leaves swaying on a tree.
A picture on the wall with a mirage of beauty
of a face that looks like me.
Am I mad? When I hear you say, that I am nothing.
That I have no roots in a land they say is FREE.
Do you think me naive?
Because I do not retaliate with an uninhibited fury.
Though your society still views me as less than human.
How blind am I? If I can't see . . .
I'm much old, I'm much too young.
Thank you Dear God!
For I believe in ME!
Strength is in the HEART and SOUL of faces who look just like me.
How blind am I? For I do see
a race of people so real, yet longing to be FREE.

Roger Davis
THE LORD IS MY CRUTCH
When times seem ruff, and seems like there's nowhere to turn.
Oh Lord! Guide me right, to the path that lets me see all my sins, redeeming with your love.

There are worldly things he gave me, but I would give them all for his love.
Things we take for granted can be stolen away in one day.
But that's not how it is.
Because, the lord is my crutch.
My ever leaning post. He's there when I need him most.
So forget your worries and problems of everyday.
He will be with you night and day.
Showering you with love and gifts from above.
Stay in faith with the LORD.

Roger Davis
EMPTINESS
I am all alone in this strange place.
I have no kinsmen to fraternize with.
My heart is sadden with grief.
As I listen to the sounds in this strange environment.
I feel disillusioned, sounds of the still night before me, fills my soul with Emptiness.
As I look from my porch, I see people running in the streets.
Far away in the distance, I hear the sound of sirens and babies crying.
I'm afraid. I'm alone.
I am empty.
As I walked back into my little shell, tears filled my heart with a feeling no one should be ashamed of,
That feeling is LONELINESS.
Thru this loneliness, is my Emptiness.
But I know . . .

David B T Manning
BEIJING; JUNE 1989
Freedom in young Chinese faces
Freedom, freedom burning bright
A mighty nation, a great people labored
To bring forth that glorious handful,
To celebrate those heady days of liberty,
To face the thunder of tanks in the courtyard.
Will those who died in Tiananmen Square
Now be forgotten by their own? Will their flame die,
Drowned in the tides of gunfire and lies?
We, who have basked in our patriots' heritage
For two hundred years, skimming the cream of freedom,
We should watch and stand humble before these young ones,
The finest flower of another people's long history;
Humbled and enlightened by their flame.

David B T Manning
NIGHT VISITOR
A memory awakened in dream,
Wind from a strange desert place,
The feel of it like the sight of stars
And she was there, authentic, with a new surprise
A trifle caustic and then, so suddenly,
Extravagant kindness. I would not mind
The last sleep to end this way.

Helen Hasselschwert
HAPPY BIRTHDAY, MOM
This is the day you'd celebrate ninety-five,
And so many memories still survive.
No longer can we touch or hold your hand,
Nor by your side closely sit or stand,
But deep within each one of us,
Your spirit dwells and comforts.
We sense the beauty of your life,
The calm sereneness without strife,
The gentle love you always shared
To let us know how very much you cared.
A year ago you sat the center of the family,
The stately matriarch, reigning supremely.
Today we sorely miss your loving face
As we gather around your quiet resting place
To symbolize and honor the virtuous way
You taught us to live every day.
We light a candle for each one of your years
And let them melt away all our tears,
Knowing your memory forever will glow
Brightening our darkest days of sorrow.
Now, with immense pride and respect, Mom,
We seal your beautiful love in this silent stone.

Patsy R Dias
FLIGHT OF THE EAGLE
The eagle soars in lofty flight
With outstretched wings in hastened run
The gilded wings of freedom
Dipped in early morning sun.

Courageous heart 'neath feathered breast
This king of skies pursues
When encompassing his vast domain
With steel sharp eyes he views.

While high on top his mountain crag,
In vivid silhouette,
This is his place, this limitless space,
Where the stars and infinity have met.

He swoops down low near the valley floor,
Then high on the winds before retreat
To his cresty mount where he shall return
With heaven's dust upon his feet.

Patsy R Dias
BE WITH ME
If you want to be with me
Follow me in my dreams.
Be with me through shaded doubts
When all is lost to me, it seems.

Hold my hand when I'm troubled and grieving,
Walk with me down darkened paths.
Share with me these crowded moments,
Wipe my tears and soothe my wrath.

If you want to be with me
Follow me in my laughter.
Enjoy with me an enlightened mood,
The gaiety that lingers after.

Walk with me down the path of life
From where we learn and practice.
Share with me the reality
Of flowers, love and cactus.

Michael Ashenfelder
WHEN DO I THINK OF YOU?
At the moment that I wake up in the morning, I feel around the bed for your warm body.
When I shower,
I remember the feel of you on my chest.
As I brush my teeth,
I feel your tongue moving across them.
Whenever I eat,
I think of the times we spend staring at each other over meals.
When I start to get upset over little

things, I recall your comforting
hand on my leg reminding me that
anger is a wasted emotion.
At those times that I am feeling down.
Your private smile comes to mind
and lifts me up.
The memory of your face never fails
to bring me happiness and help me
get through the day.
When evening falls and I await
sleep's arrival,
Your felt presence tells me
that together is how I wish to
spend our life.
To answer the question, I think of
you from morning 'til
night and I know that we will be
together always.

Love, Michael

Krystal S Willhite
HEAVEN'S JOURNEY
They moved far away from us, and
though we miss them much.
They're in a better place now, with
God's gentle touch.
Though we long to be with them,
the time passes so slow.
Wondering if he'll ever come, and
will we get to go?
For the journey is long and hard,
and the road seems to never end.
But each day reduces the time,
we spend away from him.
Our world is full of sadness, we
long for a better place.
To be with him in heaven, and
See his glorious face.
He loves us like his children,
and keeps us in his heart.
One day I hope to join him,
then never again will I part.

Janice Lee Lister
NATURE
The earth is so pretty with its flowers
and trees
The Lord gives to us all of these
The sun, the moon, the sky up above
The clouds, the rain, all these things I
love
I love nature, it's a beautiful delight
Everything's so colorful not just
black and white
The mountains, the pastures, the
oceans so blue
All of this was given for me and for
you.

Carmen Grau
MAN
Tell me who you are, I see you but do
not understand.
A child boy am I strong.
Tell me who you are.
A boy full of life and joy, strong am
I.
Tell me who you are — A Man a
Man.
On a mountain side lay I.
bleeding bleeding—.
Mother—Mother do you hear me.
A soldier man am I.
I see a shadow no longer a boy.
It is I a soldier man am I.
No longer a whole man, bleeding
bleeding.
Mother—Mother do you hear me.
A man child am I—lying on the
mountain side dying.
I do not fear death for I see light on
the mountain top.

Edgar C Alward
"easing the Spring"
We talked and I was pleased
As you listened—
Because you wanted to.
You talked less than I,
But you were kind in
Making it look balanced

I loved you for the moment, at
least,
As we seemed to share
What both of us needed, like lovers,
A pleasant evening meal and
conversation.
We hugged and kissed each other,
briefly;
I wanted more of you—
More of the evening too.

Jennifer J McCall
SUMMER ROMANCE
Oh how I wish these long days of
winter would end in one bright,
glorious day
I remember, ages ago it seems, when
all I had to do was look around to
find the sunbeams.
Flowers to smell, some to pick, some
to keep in a cut-glass vase.
Green, green grass the magically
seeps through my toes and gets me
when I think I'm not ticklish.
The morning dove that cries at the
wrong hour of her name;
The crickets that speak to me in the
darkest part of the night.
The air, heavy and warm, creeps
through the tiny squares of the screen
and makes the curtains dance wildly;
and rustles my sheet like the ghostly
lover that haunts my dreams.
I hear the fan as it whips around
another current of air as it drifts
through the window.
The mournful cry of the lonely train
as it slips quietly into the night and
calls to a whisper;
The water that dismembers my
features in its reflection; it puts
playful dots on my face and soaks the
edges of my hair that fall loose.
The sunset that blazes the tender
horizon in search of shelter from the
oncoming night
and sunrise that innocently creeps up
to break the shadows of evening
and makes my face shine with
happiness.
The fountain, as the water noisily
bounds down the narrow steps and
sets my heart free
All the freedom, the joy, the beauty
and the love . . .
Summer is my romance.

Sylvia A Bulger
LOVE MOURNED

*In loving memory of my mother,
Dorothy Chmielewski Przygoda
June 2, 1930 — May 14, 1989.*

Love takes on many shapes and
forms;
the love that hurts is the love I have
mourned.
The love that shadows itself in
disbelief
is the love I found in my personal
grief.
I cannot mourn unless I have loved;
my heart did break when she was
taken above.
But if I would choose not to love
because of pain,
my life would be empty and so full of
strain.
So I will choose to love and accept
the pain,
for the memories of my mom will
help me maintain.
Because for any love to be started it
had to be born;
for that love to be complete it would
have to be mourned.

Esther Sconce Herman
THE LOVING HAND

To my wonderful son Dave.

Life begins with pain and joy;
Heaven touched by Satan's brush:
The beginnings of graffiti on
The perfect canvas in work.
And yet, the oils of life
Set strong and brilliant,
While defiling watercolors
Can be cleansed away.
How comforting to know
Your portrait is captured
By the loving hand of God.

Homer V Jones
THE OLD DEPOT
I stopped by the old train depot
today,
long since abandoned, fallen into
decay.
I stood there in silence as I looked all
about
and fancied I heard someone say with
a shout . . .
All aboard!

The waiting room filled with ghosts
of the past
and someone was shouting, "She's
coming at last!"
With a rush to the door, their tickets
in hand,
They prepared to depart to some far
distant land.

But wait, "Did I hear a steam whistle
blow?"
A lonesome reminder of long, long
ago.
"Could it be No. 7, the cream of the
crop
with a squealing of brakes, slowly
come to a stop?"

In the door of the coach the
conductor is found,
with a wave of his lantern he steps to
the ground.
With the big engine panting and the
steam pipes ahiss . . .
"Can there be any thrill that is greater
than this?"

Then reality comes and I stand there
alone,
Old No. 7 with her passengers gone.
As I make my way slowly to the
broken old door,
I would give everything just to hear it
once more . . .
All aboard!

Christina L Walston
THE WHISPER
That whispering in my ear,
It's something I'll never fear.
It's that man I pass everyday.
But I've never paid attention,
What else can I say?

Then I realize what I've been
missing,
One last piece of my life.
A man who can be with me,
and help me through my strife.

It's been some time
And I'm more confident.
Some say my face is radiant.

Now my life is sorted out,
And being happy, no doubt.
This is the best time of my life,
'Cause now God's with me.

Susan Stine Mason
ENDANGERED MAN
Oh, where has our good earth gone?
Once perfect, now surely spoiled.
Rivers, streams and seas once pure,
Are now so grossly soiled!

Driftnets trap our sea life,
Endangered, by the pound—
Slain dolphins are no matter
So long as tuna can be found!

Once stately trees and forests
Gave shade and wildlife shelter,
Fought erosion and pollution—
Now chopped down helter-skelter.

Great herds of elephant roamed the
land
To raise their young carefree;
Have all but gone from poachers'
guns
Just for that ivory!

Is it too late to turn around
And change our greedy ways?
If so, man's years are surely
numbered
If not his very days!

Charisse Hilliard
IF YOU'RE THE WINNER, YOU'RE THE BETTER

*This poem is dedicated to my mom
and dad.*

If you're the winner, you're the better
If you try you never lose—
For you are the best as we choose.
You will never get the meaning of
what's being said.
But it's best for you to do it because
in later years you could be dead.
Learn from mistakes each day—
Because you are one special boy or
girl on this earth today—
Maybe we kids of today—
Can make this world come together
in a nice special way.
If we can do that
We can help each other
Because no one wants you if you're a
loser—
But if you're a winner,
You have all the world to succeed
For no one will stop you in your
farthest footstep of your way—
Because mom and dad are gonna love
you all the way.

Rebecca Chandler Prunkard
THE LAST FLIGHT
A day of remembrance — The "7"

*This poem is dedicated to Christie
McAuliffe, who was a teacher and an
astronaut . . . one of the seven.*

Gray rain had fallen on the Earth
Throughout that sombre day . . .
The sound was like a tolling bell
That wears the hours away.

Seven souls were poised for that long
flight,
Into the vast unknown
Stalwart souls and gallant souls—
Yet they went not alone.

The God they loved did pilot them
Did hold their trusting hands
And safe conducted their souls to port
Beyond Life's shifting sands.

Yes—all is well.

Charles N Noble
IF I COULD
If I could do whatever I want to do,
To make complete your gladsome days;
I would not bring a single thing to you,
But, I would come and take some things away.

I'd have them all be gone—
forever—gone—
Forgotten, like some things that cannot be;
And then each hour would be a joyful one;
For only good things would be left you see!

I'd take away all troubles from your heart;
Each pain and sorrow I would have relieved;
And every word that caused a single smart;
And every hour that which you sadly grieved;

Now, that is what I'd like to do
If I could do the things, I wish for you.

L A Brooks
IN THE DARK
Taken for a ride
down an endless highway
You were there
and somehow I thought
that daylight was near
But in the darkness
I was blind
—love and fear
And you were sweet
And the moon was hidden
by a heavy haze
Under a starless sky I ran away
in a daze
You were sweet
in the dark

Byron Partin
ARPEGGIOS FROM A BROKEN GUITAR
My heart, like my guitar, plays quatrains to you—
rides memories like broken riffs through time.
Love follows meeting, ecstasy follows love
and at nineteen nothing can go wrong.

My soul trills trebled notes of adoration.
Love ballads course from my guitar.
Our bodies flow and merge in perfect harmony.
Heaven's so close. Is hell then so far?

Another land, another world, yellow hordes pour southward.
Korea? Where's that? It doesn't matter.
Alice, my country calls . . . I have to go!

Winter's bitter cold blasts bones, freezes the marrow—
spring only comes with memories of you . . . No other love
brings a burst of warm sunshine—nor gentle breezes to carry
my music . . . and evoke the robin's first song.

Four decades later Korea's a faded memory.
My broken guitar gathers dust against the wall.
And love's a leaded burden, now I can't give it.
And no music's left within me—
without you.

Rebecca Schaeffer

Jimi Nixx
GONE BUT NOT FORGOTTEN
In loving memory of Rebecca Schaeffer.

Where has all the laughter gone
Why must it turn to tears
Why must your heart so young and free
Have to simply just disappear
No one can ever replace
Not even for awhile
The way you touched my lonely heart
With your warm and priceless smile
These words I write exist for you
For all the world to see
As long as they're known
To anyone's heart
You shall live in this poetic memory
Never again to feel pain
Or what it is to cry
Gone but not forgotten
Is my angel to the sky
Gone but not forgotten
Is my angel before her time
Now embraced within God's arms
True happiness you shall find.

Lisa Clarida
TRUE LOVE
You're the apple of my eye
The jewel in my life.
Forever shall you shine
like the star in the sky.
Your love could mean the world
to a person like me,
Who feels so very much alone
in a world full of people.
Though you're a part of someone else's life,
I thought I'd write this line
Just to say I love you and shall
patiently wait for you.

Robert A Fanelli
IN THE SPRINGTIME
To my good friend Carol Latourette

When you wake up in the springtime
And you greet a smiling sun—
You know the world is with you
And you're the lucky one.

Just to hear the birds all singing
And the children having fun—
Then all at once you're living
A new world's just begun.

You're glad your loved one is close by
A twinkle in her eye—
You're counting every blessing
The springtime seems to bring.

You lose all your cares at springtime
As you greet old friends again—
You only wish the springtime
Would never, never end.

Steve Lowman
A RECIPE OF LIFE
This Poem is Dedicated to World Emotions.

One cup of love learnt
A pinch and a hug

An ounce of emotions
Some feelings kept snug

Unlimited amounts of education
With weeks of study

A job you like to do
A friend or an after work buddy

Some knowledge that everyone is a print
Some understanding of will power

A little store brought kindness
And a judgement not too sore

Mix the above ingredients together
Let them simmer until they become tangible

Stir slowly but be aggressive
Let it cool until manageable

And serve with a long handle spoon

Steve Lowman
I'M LATE
Sorry for any delays.
But business has its days.
Rushing to complete,
the Whats, Whens, Wheres and Hows
Have led me to this and that,
and then and nows
I wonder what it's all trying to tell me.
Is it that I need more energy.
I wonder what this crowded
situation means.
Is it more work and less dreams.
Above all, it gets my best.
I label it my creation of
Happiness

Sandra C Crow
NEW BEGINNINGS
Dedicated to my sister Susan, and her husband Tom.

Today you start all fresh and new,
with someone who's been waiting too.
To have and hold a mate that's fair,
who'd make commitments and truly care.
Whispered dreams built trust and hope,
honest feelings of love awoke.
It seems you both found happiness,
in those days you talked and kissed.
So as you give your hearts away,
with vows exchanged this wedding day.
You give a gift beyond compare,
a special love at last to share.
Remembering promises made from the start,
will always bind you heart to heart.

Brian McComb
I REMEMBER
I remember the good times, I remember the bad.
I remember the love that you and I had.
No one can replace you, No one ever should.
I won't get over you, I didn't think I could.

I remember when we used to fight,
I thought it was over, I thought it all night.
But then I realized our love was too strong,
I loved you so much nothing could go wrong.

But now It is over and you have moved on.
Getting different guys as you go along.
Yet I still remember you and I,
And the first time you made me cry.

I shall never forget the love we shared,
Or how much I loved you, how much I cared.
Today, Tomorrow, the rest of my life,
One time I wanted you to be my wife.

I always loved you, I always will.
Every time I think of you I get a chill.
I know that It is over, I know we are through,
But I just can't stop loving you.

Tina Frazier
FOREVER AND ALWAYS
Sparkle, sparkle, the sun shines down,
Upon the ocean blue.
Dear little boys and sweet little girls,
Dig for clams as sticky as glue.
The crisp waves crash on the shore,
Of my dreamy land.
My precious lover lies beside me,
On the soft white sand.

His eyes melt my inner soul,
His touch sends chills down my spine.
It's difficult for me to believe,
That he is all mine.
We'll be together,
Forever and ten days.
Always in each other's arms,
Forever and always.

Carol Lee
ONE DAY IN MARCH OF '84
One day in March of '84
The nurse brought her through the door
Her eyes were blue, her hair was white
And she hung on to my finger ever so tight.

She is now my daughter of two
And you wouldn't believe the things she likes to do.
She plays with her toys and rides her bike
This little girl is my little tyke.

My daughter's name is Jamie,
And how she likes to play me.
She likes to sing and dance

But she still has accidents in her pants.

I love her ever so dearly
And she grows and changes yearly.
She has a temper and it's bad
Boy can she make her daddy mad.

Hey! by the way, have you met Jamie, my girl?
She will definitely take you for a whirl!

Rebecca Matthews
GOD'S CREATIONS
The birds and the bees
The flowers and trees
The sky that is blue
The grass that is green
All of these things
Are God's Creations

Phyllis Fenn
JEANNE

To my daughter, Jeanne, who made me grow into a better person.

My child was born on a stormy September morn,
Though lightning and thunder prevailed.
My joy turned to sorrow when on the next morrow,
I learned she was not perfect as planned.
Even as my heart was troubled,
I loved her just the same.
I fought with my Creator to heal my child,
But He heard me not.
In my heart I knew only Love could bring us thru
The painful years.
Love and wisdom guided as we climbed the stairs of life
Only to find He was already there in the light.

Wanda Lee Fletcher
MANKIND
It is now time and chance has happened to all
Of revealed knowledge and the experimentation of man's fall
To implant and to destroy the buildings of life
To enter an unending battle clothed with an armour to fight
Impregnated with the first Adam and the second Adam of life
Man's soul must struggle to conquer that which is right.

Now that man's time is full of hurried days
He loses knowledge that the first Adam never prays
Deceived by blindness of this world's riches of light
Oh how our soul aches for an awaking of spiritual sight
Shattered by unruly tongues that never cease
Mankind must return to the Creator Of Peace.

Rosalinda Frey
UNTITLED
I'm afraid
What am I to do?
So confuse—
want to give of myself to him
But the fea—
The fear is keeping me from giving completely.
The feeling (you know the feeling)—
the one in the pit of the stomach,
the ache in the heart
is saying —
Hold back some
Don't give in
Don't reveal your all;
Maybe it's right, this fear —
Then it won't hurt as much
when at the end
He turns the
"I Love You"
into
"Let's be friends."

Glenda K Wright
THE FRAGILE BOND
Diamonds and Lace, Crystal and Roses,
Truly feminine in Society's sense of the word.
But what do they mean?
They can't make the woman or produce the love.
Heartache and Pain, Joy and Happiness.
Truth and yet even the lies.
They will create the bond.
The one that will hold us 'til the end.
Nothing lasts forever. You must live for today.
Deal with the pain, for it too shall pass.
Love is so fragile, like the crystal.
It too shall survive, but only with care.
The roses don't last forever. They wilt and lose their fragrance.
But love will lengthen their life.
The lace, it is so fine and delicate, just like the heart.
But the love will hold it firmly together.
And the diamonds glittering in the light.
Like the eyes of a woman in love.
Yet so hard and cold.
Never giving in. So hard to destroy.
Like the heart of a woman in love.

Beverly M Wilson
MY OTHER WORLD
When I am tired and my nerves are jangled,
I climb my highest mountain and sit.
When the sun is the brightest—and warm

gentle breezes soothe my face—and gently
toss my hair like it were strands of silk.
When my soul has quenched its thirst, I will come down from my mountain and try again.

Nellie M Roberts
JUST A TOUCH OF THE MASTER'S HAND
As I stand here and view the hills and valleys
of God's creation of this beautiful land,
Everything seems to have a magic touch and then,
I realize it's a touch of the Master's hand.

Oh the beauty of that wonderful golden sunset,
all those shades of yellow, pink & gold are just grand.
No artist could ever capture a scene like this,
it can only be captured by a touch of the Master's hand.

We too are God's creation and we too can be like a
beautiful sunset according to His plan.
If we will obey Him with heartfelt love for others
that only comes from a touch of the Master's hand.

Kevin Dwayne Gray
LET THERE BE PEACE

To my mother Maxine and in memory of my dad, Gilbert. I can never express my love and gratitude for their unwavering confidence in my ability.

Why are there Wars? Why do we fight?
We can all live together
No one is always right.
Assassination is wrong
That is why it is done undercover
Just to think the killing of one man
To satisfy another.

All laws were not meant for us to swallow
We must make good judgments
and our peers will follow
We should obey each other's laws, I should say this at the least
Let's stop the violence and all live in peace.

Peace is found in one's heart, soul and mind
A lot of us would have it if we would stop being so blind.
Think of all the ways we can help our people,
And the time will come when we can all be equal.

Lyndi Robison
THAT LITTLE GIRL BESIDE YOU
You may have lost your freedom
But you've gained so much more
That little girl beside you
Has opened up new doors
She's changed your way of thinking
Brought happiness and tears
The love that she will give you
Will last throughout the years
When all else seems to fail you
And you think life will end
A little smile will cure you
Your broken heart will mend
Each new day together
Will bring a brand new joy
Like a child at Christmas
Opening up a longed for toy
And when she starts talking
You'll cherish every word to come
Especially when she says
"I Love You, Mom"

Walter Steinhagen
THOUGHTS OF ST. VALENTINE'S DAY
A day is set aside each year
to tell the one we love
that he, or she is just a dear
an angel from above.

They call this day St. Valentine
expressing love profound
but why not do this <u>all the time</u>
keep loving <u>all year round</u>.

And why restrict your love to one
Let's do the whole thing right
and let it shine just like the sun
<u>on everyone in sight</u>.

Then only will be peace on earth
as preached by the Divine
for <u>only love</u> can give it birth

Happy St. Valentine

Marilyn P Smiley
THE MAN

In Loving Memory of My Father— Dee Presswood.

Slowly entering, grasping for the years.
Turning his head, opening an eye, a flash
cross his face. Smiling a reflection of an
eighteen year old, singing a love song.

Twisting the head to the left, he sees a man
of twenty-five. A marriage vow he swore.

A slight nod to the front, he sees a man of
forty-one. He frowns, gray creases the face.

Bending to pick up a stick, the man arch to
the right, he sees a man of seventy-three,
slowly coming to the darkness of the end.

Charles Breslau
AIM
In the stillness of a pine-scented forest,
A dappled fawn, Princess of Pines,
Forages for food beneath the white mantle.

Crouching nearby, weapon at his side,
Man waits eagerly as a self-assured actor
For the moment to seize his trophy.

Nimble fingers load the arsenal
Then, slowly lifting it to his primed eye,
He aims and focuses on the unwary deer.

Feral instincts warn of danger too late;
Mankind shoots another animal
To frame on a wall.

Wm Richard Black
THE FRAGILE SWIMMERS
Like marbles
passing from hand to hand
through the circle in tiny waves,
then washing up in the sand.
Sprawled on the beach
each of us, used up, our backs to the sun

on the hour, every hour:
hands dusted,
a day's work done.
Like the tides, washing over us,
our desires flow yet do not ebb;
where there was a beginning,
there is no end.
Sprawled on the beach
where the sea lion's roar is loudest,
a fragile swimmer,
his future clouded.
Sinking, slipping underneath the
water . . .
every man is another's martyr.

Robert Michael Balderrama
IN GOD'S HANDS
I do not worry needlessly
Upon the path of life
Though problems may beset me
In the turmoil and the strife

As I know that tomorrow
Will erase my woe today
And all my tears and sorrow
Very soon will fade away

Because the Lord is always near
And ever by my side
To wash away my every tear
And be my friend and guide

Just knowing He is always there
Gives comfort to my heart
That I am always in His care
And too of Him a part.

Lauren Belt-Smith
SWING UP HIGH
Swing up high
Swing up in the
air . . .
Swing up in the
air so free
Don't you wish
you could swing
up so free
Up in the air with
me . . .

Mary Ann Bessick
DESOLATE
Desolate is this heart of mine,
Longing for a younger time,
When the grass was green,
And life was new,
And the people we loved held fast
and true.
Desolate is the morning sun,
Fiery red with hatred spun.
An eerie light the morning brings,
No birds, no one, no songs to sing.
Desolate was the sound I heard,
Like the dying flight of a
mockingbird.
The war torn earth,
The end of birth.
Desolate is this cave far below,
From which I do not wish to go.
Desolate is the end of time,
Desolate is me and mine.

Joseph Bayrón
TENACITY
Gnaw the flesh.
If only memory could die.
Crawl to the den of unconscious
snakes.
Mingle the darkness with some
blood.
Curse my tears!
Conspire my so-called troubled spirit.
Rebel!
Rebel!
Hatred today is hatred tomorrow,
And the earth will still spin.
Burning, in red river veins.

Joan M Brown
GYPSY WIND
Lonely orange sky sinks a solemn
ending,
Chalky wind voices blend and the
day is drawn . . .

The wind tonight is warm;
One second it touches me and

I'm a midsummer gypsy running in
the rolling fields,
And I feel all over wispy like a ghost
as
My hair darkly blows wild with the
living grasses,
With the straying wind's promise of
beautiful things.

Looking up,
The clouds are suddenly tokens of
loving farewells.
They separate themselves noiselessly.

I left you that way.
Now I have only to live a silent night
to find you . . .

Pamela Jean Bowen
TO DREAM
The night is upon me
I stand alone
And gaze at the stars
The wind caresses me
And whispers your name
I close my eyes
And let these feelings take me
Into my magical world of dreams
You are there
Holding me oh, so close
Love is shining in your eyes
And for an instant
I feel the ghost of your arms
Wrapped around me
In such a sweet embrace
You're loving me
As I've never been loved before

Jeremy Benson
HOW CAN I SCRIBE THE POETRY THAT'S SAD (a sonnet)
How can I scribe the poetry that's
sad,
When all that nestles in my heart is
light?
The age in which lyrics' grief is the
fad,
Humanity's woe cries out in the
night.
It's difficult to strain and violate
The unyielding boundary that has
been set.
Hopeful passages that my mind
create
Grips my pen so paper it has not met.
The transparent shield which arrests
this mark
Is governed by a melancholy mood.
It renounces my verse, that of a lark,
To a marriage of grief that time has
wooed.
But my joy overcomes this wall of
gloom
As my progressive pen bursts from
the womb.

Beverly Ann Brandon
TO A KINDER, GENTLER NATION
As I look around I see
too much negativity.
Why don't people stop to smell the
roses anymore?

Man's inhumanity to man
continues—while we take a stand
To save the whale and buffalo and
seals.
What's it for?

Free the blacks from degradation.
Free Indians from reservations.
Free the poor from poverty and
ignorance.
They all need more!

Give back the child his innocence.
Give back the earth her nourishment.
Give back the sky its clarity and
purity.
Let spirits soar.

Bring back the kinder, gentler nation.
Stop the monstrous infiltration
of drugs and guns that kill the
dream
of living without fear.

Faith and Hope and Charity,
Justice, Honor, Dignity,
Respect and Brotherhood—of these,
We all need more!

Still I look around and see
too much negativity.
Why don't people stop to smell the
roses
anymore . . .

Stella and Benedict Gross

Terry Johnson
TILL WE MEET AGAIN

In loving memory of my grandparents Benedict and Stella Gross of Wayland, New York.

It's been three years now since you
both passed away,
I miss you as much now, as I did that
day.
If only I could hear your voice and
see your smile.
We could touch each other and chat
for awhile.

I remember the words that Grandpa
said.
"Till we meet again, Stella," and now
he is dead.
I hope you're both together in your
new life.
After 67 years together, you should
still be his wife.

When God made you both, he broke
the mold.
You were tough as steel with a heart
of gold.
Even though you were poor,
You always remembered me at the
store.

I miss Grandpa's stories, his
predictions were always right.
I hope you know how much I love
and miss you with all my might.
I admired your wisdom, strength and
pride.
I admired your old-fashioned stride.

I hope there's a heaven in that sky,
that's where you both should be.
If you're up on that farm up high,
please watch over me.
I hope you're as proud of me as I am
of you.
Till we meet again you two.

Love you and miss you
Grandpa and Grandma!

Teresa Bickford
THE KEY TO THE ANSWER
If the moon didn't shine,
how much darker would
it be?
And if the sun didn't shine,
would there still be sparkle
in the sea?
If every blind man could
clearly see,
How much more blind, would
we really be?
And if the world's door
were ever unlocked,
Who would hold the key?

Sometimes even a blind
man can see.

Carol Brookbank Bunch
THE FROG
Why won't the little frog swim or
jump!
His sensitivities have gone
To the dump!

His blood runs so deep, and yet so
cold;
But the poor little thing
He's not very old!

His heart beats fine, and oh so strong;
We, all of us realize
He has done no wrong!

He's so green, so slimy and tender
too;
Oh dear, oh dear
What can we do?

Let's warm him up, love and care for
it;
Maybe then we can help
To make him fit!

G S Burbey
THE HOMECOMING
Softly moving clouds over silent
water
As quietly as the wasteful passing of
a child's day
The remnants of memory
disorganized and disenchanted pour
through my mind
The playful fields of grass, dirt and
rocks rest in amusement
As the trees in brooding eloquence
border a world alone

All embraced and was embraced in
the world of a child
Every blade of grass as integral as it
was unnoticed
Every breath a moment of
self-knowledge, held and let go
Now in the depths of the grass, and
then in the hollow of a strangled oak
As the sun found life in every breath

Now I stand on the edge of that very
field
A lonely immigrant to a sacred
homeland

All was as I had known it to be
And yet as a man my breath hung
frozen in the cold air
Only moments below the slow
melancholy turmoil of the soft wet
clouds
Life was everywhere, but as if on the
corner of a foreign street, it passed
separate and unrecognized

Alisa Bennett
NEW MELODY
I've been searching for so long
for a new melody in my old song.
Are you as you appear?
Come closer, come here,
I need to see
if your words will fit me.
If the lyrics and harmonies lock,
should I or should I not
take a chance on you?
Would you be taking a chance too?
I hear the melodies of your song
and hope my lyrics go along.

Jon Allen
ON THE HORIZON WAS A NEW DAWN
The sun was starting to rise
On the Horizon was a new Dawn
The works of man and his remains
were now all gone.

The countries were all at peace
War was dead it seemed
But when the Nuclear Bombs were
dropped
Well, I'll never forget those screams.

It started as an accident
It led to World War III
Now there's no more man on Earth
There's no one here but me.

For I, however, the final one
The pain won't go away
Doomed to die, or maybe doomed to
live
I really just can't say.

The sun was starting to rise
On the horizon was a new dawn,
And all the hopes and dreams of man
Are now forever gone.

Mark R Anderson
DIAMONDS IN THE SNOW
Diamonds in the snow,
That's what we are,
Just flashes of brilliance.

For a moment in time,
Shine on, shine on,
'Cause time is an illusion,
You don't know how long
You'll be,

A diamond in the snow.

Louis Antonelli
THE LITTLE BLACK DRESS
In a large metropolis such as this
not many can see
but I know someone far away
made you just to please
from cloth and thread
you can say
will feel so perfect today
just a little black dress
maybe you haven't seen
that it's really me

James R Anders
DAWN
Dawn is running up my back
and kissing my neck.
A skyward glance tells me that
it is going to be a sunny day.
Funny, but earlier this morning
I felt that I would find you.
I searched the streets and alleys,
knowing that you wanted to be found,
but never finding you.
Never far from you,
yet, never seeing you.
Dawn is walking down the street,
now,
and telling me to go home.

Margo Atherton
INTERWEAVING
This dark man born of the fall,
Eyes his life warily,
Slowly cracking his wall.

He places his life on a large loom,
While weaving his thoughts,
He watches them bloom.

This beautiful being so full of love,
Holds reign on his passions,
As they could take flight far above.

Taking a chance while always on
guard,
He unravels his heart,
And lets it sing like a bard.

Carefully, nurturing his colors fine,
He gives much to others,
While his tapestry improves,
With each passing line.

Gayle Arrowood PhD
UNTITLED
Nursery rhymes pop up
at the darndest times.
Little Bo Peep has lost her kids.
Jack and Jill are still tumbling.
Little Jack Horner is upside down.
The pumpkin shell's the problem.
Ho Ho Ho who wouldn't go,
leave the pumpkin shell, that is.
The three sheep each have a bag
—full—
The Billy Goats Gruff are still
crossing
and the Troll got his due.
So the Itsy Bitsy Spider climbs again.
Hi Ho Silver.

Ralph M Abraham
WITHOUT HER
Love is a diamond, fine lines forming
perfection
Love is togetherness, what a great
invention.
Love is harmony, like a well played
musical
Love is forever, either mental or
physical
Love is cold steel turning liquid into
strength
Love is walking the plank, no matter
what its length
Love is mobility movement with
grace
Love is strong putting life in its place
Love is food you need it every day
Love is tears of joy washing the pain
away
Love is you. Love is me
I want the future let me see.

Joyce M Adkins
THE PAIN OF A ROSE
A rose is so beautiful to the eye,
Yet when you grab it somehow the
thorns take hold.
As time takes away the pain you see
another,
you start to grab, but only falter.
You remember the pain in the thorns
of the rose.
So ever so slowly you study its luster,
you smell its sweet fragrance.
And Oh! it's so tempting.
But do you dare touch, This beauty.
This Rose.
Should you just stand to the side and
watch,
"It's hard to forget the pain of the
Rose."

You smile to yourself as the beauty
grows.
The pain in the thorns no longer
take presence
For the beauty of the Rose is all you
remember.

Joyce Barbera Arias
HAPPY BIRTHDAY GRANDMA
If we didn't have you Grandma
We wouldn't have our Dad.
Dad, wouldn't have found Mommy
Then where would all of us be?

If we didn't know you Grandma
Nor, anything about Grandpa,
We wouldn't know how loving
And caring both of you can be.

I guess I was of the lucky ones
Who really got to know you.
To be with you both, almost
As much, as I wished to be.

I think of you still Grandma.
Our nineteen years together
The thirty years you left us
The one hundred years you now
would be.

Now, you see I am a Grandma too.
Of your Great-Great-Granddaughter,
Knowing how very important, doing
The little things together can be.

Julie Arleo
IMAGE
I see myself within you my friend
and so you must see yourself within
me
I call you my friend and there I am
When I say, "I hate you," I am hiding
Look . . . Look . . . in the black of
your eyes
An Image
An Image of me

Helen P Adamson
JUST SIX YEARS OLD
He started out to school today
My son—
I was not sad—
Instead I felt so glad
That he could go—
Not shy—nor bold—
But full of questions—
A normal boy
Just six years old.

Marilyn Armor
A CONFLICT OF INTERESTS
There is a stage and two players pace
the boards at odds.
Name these Self I Am and Selfless
would I be,
And the footlights blinding, pointing
glaring contrast to the duel.
No script was ever written, dialogue
useless hollow echoes of frail
excuses.
Matched combatants locked in
endless conflict,
Each knowing that the bitter struggle
shall not cease till the heavy curtain
falls on both.
The theatre empty, phantom witness
to the muffled sound of each stinging
blow.
Self I am in pain cries out, "I have a
right to be!"
Selfless screams, "Humility,
subservient be!"
Quivering rafters catch and hold the
piercing sounds.
"Born to live!" I am in anguish cries;
"Born to serve, to love, to care, to
share!" the sharp reply.
Self I am weeping, shamed: Selfless
chiding.
"I would thee be, I would thee be" I
am proclaims.
"I would blend within thy pure and
noble form.
We touch. From time to time we
walk as one, then part and fight
again."
"Liar!" rolls across the stage and
back again in condemnations wave.
"We touch. You pull away, dart
across the stage and turn your face."
So on, so on the play, directionless
melodrama played before a Ghostly
Host anticipating curtains fall.
He wondering that the players twain
not note the fragile cord holding back
the final act.
Peace, peace, a breath away.

Trudy E Albrecht
SILENCE
The records
shut themselves off
and old friends slumber
in distant cities.
Even the dogs
have ceased barking.
Silence,
silence is painful
when one is waiting
for an answer.
When one cannot find
the right words to say.
And,
when there is nothing
left to be said.

Gichele Adams
LOVE ALL OF ME
My life is ruined and I haven't
enough tears to cry
I just need someone to hold me to
understand me
to love me all of me
even the bad parts of me
I walk in darkness without love
for you who say you love me
only love parts of me
I need someone who will love all
of me

Geraldine E Aungst
THE HOSPITAL
The hospital is a good place to be
When you are so sick you can't
count to three.
They put you in bed in a little room
You can call your own.

If you have a need of any kind you
push
your bell and a nurse comes in on
time.
She says, "Can I help you in any
way?"
You say, "What are you planning
on doing for me today?"

She says, "I will make your bed
While you are taking a bath."
But take your time and don't be in a
hurry
for I want my job to last

So you are in the bathroom an hour or two
then the nurse knocks on the door
And says, "That will do."

So you get back in bed to rest, then the doctor comes in
and gives you a test.
And says, "You can go home in a day or two for you have had a great
stay." And that is the rule.

Alfred W Allison
ELEGY FOR A YOUNG FRIEND
Such sad abbreviation tends to chain
Our thinking to a waste and, so, deceive
Our grief, debase our pain.
Much better grief it is, then, to believe,
To see: A greater wheel doth ever turn
Than the one which we discern;
Wheel turning larger wheel in endless train,
Out to that adamantine wall
Where Reason stops to ask,
"Does this enclose it all?"
And solace comes to be the task
Of rebel Hope, the sweet, sweet child and chore
Of it. Here Hope, transcending Head,
Replies, "No. There are circles past thy lore.
They move some with each life that's led."
From this high inference I'll not descend:
Like those within, they moved well for my friend.

Lisa E Alexander
WHAT A PITY!
What a pity!
This life is a drag sometimes.
Misery upon misery,
Hassle upon hassle,
Task upon task.
Why fret? Why frown?
Everything comes to an end.
But, does it cease eternally,
Or begin again?

Janice M Accomazzo
IT WAS ONLY YESTERDAY
What a beautiful Autumn day in Connecticut!
The sun glistens through the trees; reds, yellows and oranges dance and sparkle in front of you as Nature herself creates a new melody from each falling leaf.

You were so busy raking leaves, carefully placing them just so. All your attention was on what you were doing, making sure each room was just like you wanted it to be when you *grew up*. I can still hear you, *Mommy, please come and see my house*. Laundry that needed to be hung had to wait as we walked hand in hand through your mansion. *This is the living room*, Mommy . . . It was only yesterday.

Later on you would rake the leaves into a big pile, jumping into them and hugging them ever so tight as you rolled over and over. I can still hear you laughing.
You and your sister played hopscotch and jumped rope. And the time you skinned your knee, when only a Band-Aid and a kiss would make it better . . . It was only yesterday.

Lovely fall flowers you would pick for me so I could braid them into a wreath. As I placed them on your head I told you, *You're a princess, you'll always be one to me.*

Mommy, smell the leaves burning? Picking out pumpkins, gathering apples and grapes for Nanna. Trips to the woods for pine cones and acorns so we could do arts and crafts.

You had choices to make. You were so eager. I can still see your wide-eyed smile and rosy cheeks as your little hands picked up each treasure . . . It was only yesterday.

Echoes of your voice can still be heard on South Main Street where you and your friends called out *Relievo!*
Making quilts, baking bread, Dad and your brother cutting wood. The smell of Winter was in the air.

Young love walking, holding hands and making promises to each other; only tomorrow will keep . . . It was only yesterday.

Crisp Autumn winds blowing through your hair. Beaches are deserted, waves roll in covering up your footprints in the sand. The distant cry of a baby.
Looking up, the last leaf has fallen . . . Autumn is over, and . . .

IT WAS ONLY YESTERDAY!

Cynthia L Ash
THE STAR
I stand as one, alone,
but united with the heavens
and its earthly realms.
As my eyes are lowered
in prayerful humbleness,
My feet are planted, grounded
within our Mother Earth,
My heart sings with joy, and
My arms arise to the heavens
to proclaim balance and harmony
for my soul's eternity.
The elements unify beauty and
radiate whitened brilliance . . .
Peace is now within.

Angela Fugi Anthony
SELFLESS SPIRITS
When the day is calm and the wind is still
And the sun is shining bright,
Upon your neck you feel a breeze
A breeze that's ever so slight.
Too light to be the blowing wind,
Yet, too heavy to be the air;
A huff, a puff, a gasp of warmth;
A breath upon your hair.
Then, a smile forms upon your lips
And excitement on your mind;
A happy vision you have seen:
It must be a friend who's there behind!
You whirl around to say 'Hello'
In hopes to talk and share;
But to your surprise and disbelief
You find there's no one there!

Ronald F Arrowood
COCAINE
Cocaine is a drug that works on the brain.
Some people can handle it, while
others go insane.
It's a rich man's high and a poor man's dream.
Once it gets hold of you it'll make
you want to scream.
You can't ignore it because it'll always be there.
But when you run out, you'll pull
out your hair.
You'll turn against family, and you'll turn against friends.
This little drug will torture you
until it ends.
You'll neglect all your payments, your rent, and your bills.
You'll give all your money to the
man that deals.
When you run out of money, which you will very fast.
You'll start selling, or pawning as
long as it lasts.
When you run out of things to sell, pawn, or trade.
You'll start lying, robbing, or
stealing I'm afraid.
When all else fails, you'll start dealing to support your habit.
But all this does is make you like
the hound and the rabbit.
The law is the hound, and they'll get you for certain.
You are the rabbit, and you'll be
the one hurting.
So folks let me tell you something simple and plain.
If you try "cocaine," <u>you must be insane</u>!

Lisa Longfellow
TOY SOLDIER
It stands straight and tall,
making sure it doesn't lose its
balance;
It never has to worry where it's been,
only where it's going;
It never has to worry about getting hurt,
for it has no feelings.
But for one soldier,
it has feelings;
It tends to look where it's been,
and it is easily hurt;
It sees a scene of torture,
and the wounds once healed, are
now open;
It wants to do something,
but it is stopped by its painful
scars;
It is this soldier that is more human than others,
because this toy soldier is me.

R J Larsen
WITHIN MY DREAMS
My heart races
at the mention of your name.
My blush deepens
at the sight of you.
I cannot speak.
I stutter, only when you are around.
When I gaze into your eyes, I melt.
I long to hold you, to be held by you.
I dream of having your arms around me,
of having your body next to mine,
of the touch of your hands on my body,
and the whisper of your breath upon my face.
Yet, my dreams are only that.
You do not know that I exist.
You do not see me.
You do not hear me.
And in my shyness, I drift
further and further away
to hold you
only within my dreams.

Rose A Lantz
FORREST
I see you laying there, Old Man.
With tubes and wires.
Strange machines making stranger noises.
This is not you, Old Man.
It is only your shell
Withering from pain and drugged to submission.
Where have you gone, Old Man
With your stories and your memories?
Are you someplace else,
Looking over me with my tears and my sorrow?
You have built a good life, Old Man.
Kind and gentle and full of caring.
Yet strong and demanding when the need arose.
Be strong for me now, Old Man.
Take pity on my pain and ease my grief.
Let go of your body
To soar among the happiness of your own heaven.
Because you have touched my heart,
Leave me now, Old Man,
With the memories and to continue the stories.

Raelene M Hand

Raelene M Hand
YESTERDAY ONCE MORE
To those who live in yesterday, and those who need understand.

The past is back more clear than today, for today is no more, it has gone away.

I look at the shadows no face is clear, all I feel is sorrow, all I feel is fear.

The people are yelling, they come quick and go fast, the footsteps are hurried, I can feel them pass.

The voices ignore me as though I'm not here, all I feel is sorrow, all I feel is fear.

Roll here and roll there, stand up and sit down, I'm a thing without feeling never make a sound.

Beneath me is nothing not living today, I'm in a world which times pushed away.

If you want to reach me just knock at the door. I'm not here today, I'm at yesterday once more.

Bonny G Groenendal
I, THE SEEDLING
Oh, the sorrow I feel
at leaving this place.
The good and bad
will forever be locked inside.
It has been my roots.
Now as a seedling
I will break through the soil
and emerge from darkness
to gather the warmth
of the sun.
I will mature
with the knowledge
I have learned
and have yet to learn.
The obstacles the weather brings
will only force me
to gain strength.
Then, and only then
will I hold my ground.
I will stand proudly
but firmly no matter what
new challenges I may face.

Jane Huther Gerkin
MY MOUNTAIN
It lies dormant for now; so still
And yet, birds continue to praise,
Filling the air with promise . . .
Of glorious, warm mountain days.

Lament not that winter has come
For surely you must know—
Magical things are happening
Beneath that mantle of snow!

R K Gioio
THE CLOCK CONTINUES TO TIC ON
The clock continues to tic on
As I sit here all alone
Thinking of how much happier
I would be if you & I were
Celebrating this night together
Thinking of you now,
Tears begin to burn my eyes,
They start to fall & I
Can't seem to stop them
My heart aches from the loneliness
I feel when we are apart
I find myself thinking about
memories
Of the times we shared together
The quiet moments, the smiles &
laughter
And yes, even the tears
They fill my heart with a special
feeling of love
That the tears subside and I am happy
once again
I need you beside me always
Without your love, my life is not
complete
I miss you so much
& I love you even more

Mary B H George
EVENING THOUGHTS
The setting sun is sinking low
Behind the mountain crest
The country's bathed in a golden
glow
The birds have gone to rest
As I stand alone and ponder
It's the time that I love best
To look around and wonder
How we are really blessed
The evening shadows are falling
A lonesome night bird is calling
Calling to you and calling to me
It makes you feel so thankful
To live in a country that's free
If we could paint a picture
And make it look so grand
But the beauty of all nature
Needs the touch of the Master's hand.

Quinton T Graham
I REMEMBER WHEN
The good times
I try to remember
The bad times
I want to forget.

I had no worries
I wasn't superstitious
I had no fears
A drink couldn't cure.

I remember when
That's all past
Now, I do worry
I do have fears.

I wish you knew
The pain I went through
I hope you never know
The tears I shed.

In my hospital bed
I remember when
If only you could?
See through mine eyes.

Angel Giannakouras
DEATH
Death, I'm scared of,
You probably are too.
I'm not scared for me.
I'm scared for someone close to me.
This special person I love,
is a darling man.
You would like him too,
if you only knew him.
He's sweet, kind, and cares
more about others,
than he does of himself.
I'm scared he'll leave someday.
And go far away.
To a beautiful place,
We call heaven.
I'm scared I'll be left alone.
But I know we will meet again,
Someday.
In a place called heaven.

Rebecca G Gager
THE BIRD
We saw and we heard
The joy of the bird
To be free to fly
Wherever he pleases

The song of the bird
Is joyous in the sun
To hear God call him
In the mist of the fog

The bird is a dove
To share Jesus's love
In the hearts
Of one and all.

Pegge FitzGibbons
FOG
I once felt beneath
your cloak of mist
You hid only vice
and sin
Tonight with my heart
breathing
I passed both
friend and foe
Seeing them not
but in you

Who concealed my
bitter woe
I found only pity
My silent friend

Donna Stevens Long
DEATH'S LESSON
Death comes as dusk at sunset
Soft and beautiful as the sun goes
down
To end a life filled with hard fought
battles of pain and suffering;
Sometimes as dawn at sunrise,
Vibrant and bold,
Ending a life that hasn't yet had time
to be fulfilled.
Each leaving behind a legacy of love
and caring
And a lesson for everyone on living.
Teaching all to enjoy life
And to live each day moment by
moment
Never giving up and
Always being the best person you can
Despite hardships and trials,
Always caring and doing for others
Leaving behind the legacy of life.

Alma O Glover
SID'S PLACE

To Sid Glover.

There is a place where little plants
grow
Their leaves hang heavy with
globules of dew
And in early sunlight they sparkle
and glow.
There are flowers for grace and
beauty too
Pungent perfume and very bright
color
A place to please any garden lover.

Susan K Grose
CRAZY

To C.J., for letting me feel again.

I am so happy when we're together,
Life just seems to be so right,
You have me going crazy,
I can't even sleep at night.
My mind and my thoughts,
Are always on you,
My heart is going mental
I don't know what to do.
You left me with this feeling,
It was like a dream come true,
I never felt like this before
I'm not sure of what to do.
I asked myself over and over,
What this feeling really was,
Suddenly it became quite obvious,
That this feeling was truly . . .
LOVE.

Derek V Gatling
VOICES

I would like to thank God for giving me the ability to write this poem. However, I cannot forget my mother, Rosa H. Brown, and my fiancée, Kerri L. Hobbs, for giving me the inspiration to write it. South Africans Will Be Free!

south afrikaners
Can you still the voice of a nation?
Can a voice be caught?
south afrikaners
Can you hold it in your fist and
make it prey?
Can a voice be balled up and
thrown away?
south afrikaners!
Hear my tone
Rolihlahla[1] will kill your
intentions
Umkhonto we sizwe[2]—spear of
the nation
south afrikaners
Repent or you will be driven
toward Europe
We have built a boat from your
extinction
The Mau[3] spoke first
Kenyatta[4] spoke second
Kaunda[5] spoke third
Moshoeshoe[6] spoke last
South Africa is the echo

south afrikaners!
David did slay Goliath
Joseph did have rule in Egypt
South Africans will have their day
YOU ARE ONLY IN OUR WAY
sOUTH aFRIKANERS!

[1]Nelson Mandela's middle name meaning stirring up trouble.
[2]Organization formed by Nelson R. Mandela to cripple the afrikaner gov't.
[3]Mau Mau—militant nationalist movement that originated in the 1950's among the Kikuyu tribe of Kenya, resisted British domination in Kenya.
[4]Jomo Kenyatta was one of the leaders of the Mau Mau, later became prime minister of Kenya.
[5]Kenneth Kaunda was president of the Zambian National Congress and later became the President of Zambia.
[6]Sotho leader that used skillful diplomacy and military tactics to set the British and the Boers against one another to retain an independent country.

Angela Gobles
THOUGHTS OF HIM
Kisses in the night
fall sweetly on my face;
So lost am I,
in his sweet embrace.

Something in his smile
sets my heart on fire;
Something in the way he talks
fills me with desire.

When I get my arms 'round him,
when my heart gets hold,
Then I'll tell him something . . .
something true and bold.

As for now I'll just lay back
and let him comfort me.
Ev'rything's smooth sailing,
as far as I can see.

Brenda Gabel
SPECIAL SOMEONE

To my Aunt Sissie for her faith in me and for inspiration.

Were you ever so in love, that you
didn't know what to do?
Did you ever think the one you loved
really loved you too?
Though time and time I've tried and
tried, in love I've never been
And all the hearts I've longed to gain,
no I could never win.

When you lie awake at night, do you
ask the stars above?
For someone special in your life, who
you can really love
In your sleep do you hear the words
"Baby, I love you"
Do you ever answer back, you know
"I love you too"

Do you ever think that it's wrong, because it feels so right?
Do you long to have a love, that you won't have to fight?
Were you ever with that someone so special, you didn't believe . . .
That the Special Someone, would never want to leave.

I guess it's time to tell you, and I guess it's time I knew
You're my special someone, am I someone special too?

Marliese Goehring
CHRISTOS

To my Mother and Father in thanks for being such secure friends for me. May you be forever blessed.

To the tip of the sword, one to His kin goes running,
To the bottles of shame to pacify one's most morbid aches
Inflicted by the world's subtlest sins.
To the criminally insane, His heart's pumping
Twists bolts open in the dustiest of prison cells.
To the manic depressant, He adjusts the emotions
To measured balance at heaven's equilibrium.
To the tax collector, He counts not one's treasured investments,
But dices one's heart into valuable richness.
To the adulterous woman, sexual intimacy He caresses not,
Feeling instead the breast of her femininity with not
A masculine hand but a divine hold of eternality.
To the depressed, He lets not the sun go down without
Staining the horizon crimson nor without sweetly blanketing
His priceless display of promises foreshadowed.
And to the lonely, He gives Himself—
A dead body carried by soldiers drunken by sins' luxuries
And a spirit alive, soaring already, in places
Our mere humanity cannot touch.

Richard M Goodman
NIGHTSONG

To my Lady and all our journeys yet to come . . .

The Lady of Night is born from the seed of day;
A tender blossom of spirit in the wake of disarray.
Soft petals of light dance in quiet tribute
to the Dark Mistress' arrival, silent and resolute.

Softly, like mist from the sea, She embraces the land.
She calms and appeases with a sweep of Her hand.
Her voice may be a whisper of solitude on the wind
or the promise of passion in dreams soon to begin.

With lover's reverence I await Her graceful advent;
head bowed in supplication I worship Her sweet intent.
She carries me beyond the shackles of mortal guise
and carries me inward, an apprentice to the Wise.

Hand in hand we journey, cyclic travelers on a velvet course.
As companion to this shadow, I am given escape from remorse.
The pattern is continuous, my tryst with the Dark Mistress:
I am captive to Her promise; impassioned by Her kiss.

Brief but profound is Her passage upon the earth;
serenity within obscurity, the gift of Her birth.
Although saddened at journey's end, I know in my heart;
She and I will meet again, Mistress and faithful consort.

Madeleine Baker-Godfrey
A POETIC REFLECTION

Written for Ellen A. Dedicated with love to Nancy, Alan & Diane.

When a poet caresses a word, or a thought,
On the flight of a bird,

None other can blend, such a richness of flavor
For the words, so like sweets, which each reader will savor

A poet can form, in our unwary mind
A softness toward all of collective mankind

And the roughness of life,
to soft velvet he'll turn,
From a poet, there's always so much we can learn

As his ever-beautiful words flow along,
Like a gently, soothing and melodious song.

In an instant or two,
You'll find restful peace,
And a quiescent sense,
Of divine release.

Soon the cares of the day,
Soundlessly, slip away,
Then, only good thoughts
Are privileged to stay.

Wrapped in dreams,
You unquestionably, follow his trend,
And you wish that his magic,
Never would end.

Close the book, and the spell,
Like a smoke-ring is gone,
Still the words, and his thought,
In your mind, will live on.

So, the poet's pen stops,
—Not ever to know—
How the "word-seeds" he's planted,
For others will grow.

J D Gutierrez
FIRST DAY

I wish to dedicate this poem to my father, Jose E., the Stewarts, the Michaels, and to all veterans.

Leather soles on a concrete surface
People dying but for what purpose
Trying to get my sights to align
Getting ready to perform an act
That's so malign
My pulse is racing
My hands are shaking
Underneath me the earth is quaking
No, it isn't the influence of a drug
That I'm on
This is my first day in Beirut
Lebanon

Mary Graham
FOREVER REBORN

For my beloved husband Mark.

My soul bears beyond a doubt
Crying endlessly, I've stopped to shout
"Get out of my head you Demon of thought"
Lure me into disaster
A soul of distraught
Kill my soul
Don't let it live
It deserves to die
Crying endlessly, not knowing why
A soul born again anew
Crying endlessly, waiting for you
Come into my head, this new soul I have found
It will pick me up and not let me down
Crying endlessly, I've stopped to shout
Giving thanks
My soul has been saved from
Demons unknown
It's a man named "Christ" man
Crying endlessly, you are today
"Forever Reborn."

Cher Green
HER WATCHFUL GAZE

She watches me, as I cross the room.
I see her gaze with every move.

What could she see within a glance?
Should I stay away or take a chance.

My mind advises, to stay clear,
But my heart says she's such a dear.

Doesn't she realize just who I am?
I cheat, I lie, I always scam.

She's so innocent and so naive.
She'd be so easy to dishonor and deceive.

I couldn't hurt her if I tried.
I could bear it if she cried.

Don Glover
ODE TO THE EASTER BUNNY

Dedicated to my granddaughters Katie Jilka and Anne Marie Glover.

This is an ode to the Easter Bunny.
It really seems kind of funny,
that he comes every Easter as if by habit. It is a lot to expect of
that little rabbit. He hops on those
spindly little legs, just to lay
his Easter eggs.

The way he hides them is a clever stunt
so we can all have an Easter egg hunt.
It really seems sort of a pity
to eat the eggs he colored so pretty.
Some pink, yellow, red, and blue and
they taste much better than hen eggs too.
All the children will attest
that rabbit eggs are far the best.
There has been rain, now and even sleet,
but on Easter he comes on those tiny feet,
so the children can all have their treat.

So tell the children not to fear,
he is sure to come again this year.

Adele Gordon
JOURNEY

To Joe — who shared the journey.

A step at a time makes a journey,
we know
A flower begins with a seed
A storm in the heavens condenses &
grows
Into rain, gathered here, from the
earth that it feeds

Small pieces of wood and ten
fingers not large
Make a desk or a bed or a chair
A coupling of words will connect
in a verse
Just one brick starts a road to
somewhere

Great loves of my life began that
same way
As small bundles of joy that
grew, day by day
Then minute by minute, each
life found its aim
Like the bow sends its arrow,
That center to claim

Small steps, first unsteady,
qualify us in time
To journey thru life, on new
bricks, undefined
Wherever the road bends, or
forks for awhile
Small steps in the rain,
give our signature style!

Adele Gordon
ONCE UPON A DREAM

Sea Cliff was—
The harbor view from our window
It was going to sea, without
leaving home
Feeling the strong winds, without
working the sails
It was spring—azaleas—&
geraniums in window boxes
Summer &
sunshine &
hope!
Falling leaves & incredible colors in August skies

—But,
in winter—
protected inside—
It was watching the whitecaps
thunder against the patient rocks
It was appreciating fully the precious
gift of eyesight
While celebrating love, with family
& friends

This winter, life is throwing a sea of
trouble our way, the forced sale of
our beloved house,
but like the indomitable rocks

rooted in the deep earth
We, too, will receive each wave, as a wise, white haired craftsman—
who methodically polishes our imperfections

That job completed, we'll start over,
financially cleaned, but not emotionally liquidated

Other eyes will replace ours in that kitchen window and we wish them clear sailing and sunny skies

Our memories remain intact in the shadows of our mind where we'll continue to protect them
So, when we shut that Sea Cliff door for the last time, We'll lock all our pain inside.

Virginia A Ingalls
DISCOVER HOW TO LIVE

This poem is dedicated to Almighty God, from Whom all blessings flow, to my loving husband Thomas, to my dear sisters and brother, and to my wonderful eight children, their spouses, and sixteen grandchildren.

Resentment is harsh and unfeeling;
It stifles the human heart;
It fosters emotional anguish,
Causing friends and relations to part.

Resentment drains the life of the soul,
Crushing the love it needs;
It acts as a lock or a shackle,
Preventing noble deeds.

Love is free and fulfilling,
Bestowing tranquility,
Like the flow of a rolling river
Or the tide of a gentle sea.

Love is unselfish and generous,
Abounding in charity;
Love lives on, and triumphs
Some day in eternity.

So if you long to be happy,
Love God—love others—forgive;
Then you will be blessed beyond measure
And discover how to live.

Virginia A Ingalls
HEAVEN
We glimpse it sometimes in a sunset
Or the blue of a summer sky,
Or the beautiful smile of an infant,
Or a robin's cheerful cry.

We glimpse it sometimes in a fleeting
Moment of symphony;
For God gives us in His handiwork
A hint of what is to be.

Carolyn Ingram
NATURAL BEAUTY

I want to dedicate this poem to my family, especially my mom, brother, and sister; also to my wonderful friends who encourage and support me on my ability to write.

Pitched blackness,
The starless sky,
the quarter moon,
The still ocean and its surroundings.

As dawn slowly steps in,
the sky begins to lighten:
with flashes of orange, as the hidden sun peeps its way through.

Then gray, blue, white light,
behind the endless sky, between
the ruffled ocean, another part
of nature reveals . . . greenness . . . mangrave . . .
maybe swampy lands and even another world.

In the distance a large red and white boat came rocking across the high rough,
ruffled waves, which washed, splashed, and
galloped the soft whitish, brownish sand.

Then the unseen breeze, swaying the branches of the yellowish, greenish dwarf nut trees.
Where else can be found apart from the sky
and ocean,
such profound beauty, breaking dawn into
an uncertain day be found?

"T"-Tammara—"B"-Bernie

Bernhard Trivalos
TO AN UNDERSTANDING "TAMMARA"

This poem is dedicated to Tammi, my greatest friend.

"ME"
You don't have to love me . . .
Just try to care for my thoughts.
Don't be so hard on me . . .
I'm just reaching out.
Laugh with me . . .
So I don't have to cry.
Open up to me . . .
So I can grow with you.
Talk with me . . .
So I can hear.
Show me . . .
For I will watch.
Teach me . . .
So I can learn.
You are SPECIAL to me . . .
For I love you.
For me . . .
Is you.
ME . . .
You don't have to love me . . .
Just try to care for my thoughts.
With love, "B"

Katherine L Shores (Aunt Kay Kay)
MY SPECIAL REQUEST
While talking to a Dear Friend of mine
today just after dawn,
I asked Him to pay Little LeAnn a visit please,
yes, I told Him she was not at home.

I told Him about her sickness, and how
she needed Him in a Special way.
Just asking Him was all it took,
I know He will be there each day.

Did others feel His presence near her,
as He stood by her bed today?
Could they hear His tender voice saying,
"Baby," I will be with you always.

I asked Him to be with the doctors,
who would attend her with care
And to give them the knowledge,
to make her pain much easier to bear.

And bless the nurses also, each time
they enter her door,
Each time we talked about her need,
our hearts overflowed with joy.

May her room be filled with brightness,
as His Spirit descends from above,
What is His name? It's "JESUS"
Oh! What a Precious name,
"JESUS," with His Everlasting Love.

Gail Lynne Kominak
OCEANS OF REALITY

This poem is lovingly dedicated to all who have faced life's many challenges while maintaining the courage to follow their dreams . . . and to each of the "Special Individuals," too numerous to mention, who have made my personal journey truly a cause for celebration!

Fluorescent gulls sail along
a jagged coastline,
Waves soar, then frantic to a beach
Hues of purple, blue, red
burst forth of redundant skies
the hum of the sea stings
a thousand bumble bees
Never is there calm,
a moment of stillness,
Peeking from beneath eternity
a burrowing creature
escapes, unseen, across the ocean floor

Gail Lynne Kominak
UNTITLED
Drifting gracefully,
random destinations
Each a unique creation
of infinite art.

Two are never consonant
size, shape, color,
Location at journey's end.

Do we compare, then criticize
each falling snowflake?
Irreverent, we believe,
to question nature's forte.

And so it is with humanity

Each a unique creation
of infinite art.

Two are never consonant
size, shape, color,
Location at journey's end.

Gail Lynne Kominak
UNTITLED
A colorless, shapely dragonfly
lands gracefully upon the flower
The flower
smudged, pastel artistry
The dragonfly
a charcoal etching
and tell me, what connection is there
This yellow wax-like figure
plastic to the touch
This viscerous pattern
delicate upon a wing
never to be touched
and tell me, what connection is there

Susan Bailey-Jackson
STORMS

Dedicated to my husband Eugene.

As the storm rages outside this window,
this rage inside of my heart cannot be still.
In winter storms and cold I have held you in
my arms and warmed you.
In the heat of summer by a sandy beach town
I have felt the warmth of love in your eyes.
Now this springtime a storm rises anew.
Just as the spark of old love which is still new
comes back into my breast.
the seed of love well planted will never ever die.

Susan Bailey-Jackson
MOST WANTED
An open letter to the most wanted little girl in the world.
Little girl with the coal color hair,
you are wanted so much.
Little girl with the tiny little hands and feet,
you are wanted so much.
Little girl with the dark curls,
you are wanted so much.
Your Mother and Father, plus big brother are so proud of you.
You are wanted so much precious little girl. You have all the love in the world
You are wanted so much.
To Elizabeth
Love Aunt Susie

Mona Hood
ON GROWING OLD

To Dorothy and Ernest Krueger for their 40th anniversary.

Oh, so often I've been told
It isn't easy growing old

I know someday I will grow old
And dream of yesterdays
So keep me busy making dreams
Let's live the night away

Let me gather stars tonight
Feel your arms around me
Keep me from my thoughts of fright
And with new dreams surround me

Give me just a little more
Of life's brimming cup
I must be rich in yesterdays
Before the game is up

Keep me busy making dreams
I must not sit and fret
I will grow old so very soon
But Darling not just yet.

Anna Maria Cannon
MOON DANCE
The moon was dancing outside my window,
It seemed to be dancing alone
The stars all had their partners beside them,
They had no reason to moan,

I used to be as a star in the sky
Glowing with your love from

within,
But now you have left me with as 1/2
of a dull moon,
With a broken heart that will never
mend

Natalie Donovan
BESIDE THE GREAT SEASHORE

These poems are dedicated to my sister Mary C. Donovan.

I wandered lonely as a cloud,
beside the great seashore.
I wandered there and talked to God,
as I had done before.
I asked Him if the story old
was true that ships come in.
He answered in a lovely way, for
all the sky grew dim.
In the echo of the waves,
His answer was to come,
As soft and calm, as all the sea
beneath the setting sun.

For in His answer I couldn't see
a ship in human sight,
Only one so far away
across the sea of life.
The passengers were young and fair,
while some were old and gray.
Many had been on the ship
before the dawn of day.
I wandered lonely as a cloud,
beside the great shore.
Never was the sky like this,
when I was there before.

Natalie Donovan
THANKSGIVING

The simple things we
have and own,
To share with friends
and family dear,
To brighten someone
all alone,
Whose tears may fall,
when no one's near.

Remembrance comes
in mellow years,
Of other holidays
now gone,
When long ago hearts
held no fear.
There used to be
a thankful song.

For those who touch
another's life,
And leave it sweet
serene and full.
There is no bitter
world in strife.
There's just the
simple golden rule.

Anne George
INVITATION

Can you escape
this world for awhile
and see yourself dripping
into a room of my style

it could be a cubicle
or any room of any size
it could be blue
to match your mood or your eyes

The furniture moves
at the snap of your fingers
the dandilions grow
as the looking glass shimmers
and the clock has eyes to watch time
fly by
no evil can approach you
no evil can come
no evil can soak through
my walls made of sun

Then a lady strides over
and asks you to stay
you eat in a garden
then the scene fades away . . . .

Barbara Harris
AND LIFE GOES ON

When troubles in life have you weak,
don't go to the mountain and look
to the peak.
The mountain is high and the journey
is long,
and weariness does the climb
prolong.
But each step that is taken with
wisdom and thought,
brings you closer to the mountain
top.
And if you should stumble, don't
look back,
for progress awaits you if courage
you don't lack.

Then nearer the summit the looser the
shale,
and back sliding often does
prevail.
But steady those feet for the rest of
the climb,
for the peak of the summit is
sublime.
And when finally this journey leads
to the top
your quest is not over; you there
donot stop.
For down this mountain you must
descend,
and a mountain before you appears
again.
With weariness of forethought, once
more you begin,
that tedious climb up the mountain
again.

Patricia M Lowery
AMERICAN HOMECOMING

To my Vietnam Vet brother Thomas Phelps, Jr.—whom I love so dearly. This is for you!

You're home again, proud and brave!
But this is what some people say:
"It's you're fault you're to blame,"
You look around and nothing's the
same.

But don't worry, for it's not all;
Some day! The others will fall.
I'm proud of you, that much is true
For you went to defend me too!

You've been to hell and now you're
back home:
Everything's changed; it's like a
dome.
Some people are cruel and some
people are mean,
I know to all vets, it seems the same.

You've been hurt in body and mind,
But, don't worry the people will find,
That they were wrong, and you were
right
You had no choice but to go and
fight.
To be free, there must be war,
That's the price we've paid and
will forevermore!

But your banners will wave and your
flags will fly,
Past memories, hurts, and pains will
say goodbye!
So here's to you Vietnam Vet!
Here's my love always, God had my
bet.

Ruth Castonguay
WRITE FREE

No self-seeking inner voice
Calls the ego nurtured by hell's fire
with sounds replaced by a glow
Radiance lighting a soul.
Light so fragile, translucent
Electrifies an outer shell
with moving muscle of heart to arm
Fluent life moving a pen.

Ruth Castonguay
CREATION'S GIFT

Speak no more of death
Only everlasting life will I maintain
For when he left in body a
freed spirit there remained.

The goodness of that spirit
will go with me on my journey
And it shall strengthen me

The source of life he was to me
will be carried
As creation's gift to eternity

Michael L Nelson
TIM
Aug. 8, 1961—Nov. 4, 1986

There was a time not long ago
We shared with one another,
How so much changes day by day
I hardly knew you, Brother.

I learned some things about you;
Your thoughts, your hopes, and
more . . .
I saw a special part of you
I never saw before.

We smiled, we laughed, and all too
soon,
It was time for you to go.
We said our "Goodbyes" while
promising
That soon we'd be saying "Hello."

But now that you're gone
I look back, and I realize
I didn't know you as well as I'd wish
If I had known the strength
Of the pain in your heart,
It might not have come down to this.

I got as close as I could
Without hurting your pride,
I knew you could make it on your
own.
A part of me says I should have
pulled you inside,
Instead of just leaving you alone.

Through the good times, and the bad
times,
The happy as well as the sad
times,
My hopes for you, my brother,
were clear:
To know satisfaction and happiness
In all that you are
It is this I wish you could hear.

Through all of my sorrow, there's
one
thing I know:
That love should not stop at the
surface.
I'll strengthen my love with each
passing day,
And give it a meaningful purpose.

So let it be known by all who you've
touched,
Your memory is special and true.
You hold a special place in our
hearts,
For you loved . . . and we truly
Loved you.

Barbara A Trabosh
TOY BOX

To: Albey and Jordan, who share my wildest dreams and my love. Thank you.

Opened up my toy box, wow! what a
sight
Waiting patiently, to see who's turn it
is tonight
Oh! can't seem to make up my mind

What will it be tonight, my favorite
hat, or my did's old chemistry set
Ah! their down there, way down at
the bottom

Okay! fellows, get ready to march
Ten wooden soldiers, dressed in red
March to the left, hey! put up those
heads

Fall into formation, let's proceed
Climbing aboard my bed, across
those white fluffy mountains
Charge! we're in full battle, firing
and winning every maneuver

That's it boys, the battle's over
Stand in formation, let's proceed, our
time is complete
Return to base, till I need you again,
when I open my toy box, to dream.

Kristel Driessens
IF ONE DAY . . .

If one day the sun wouldn't shine
anymore,
The next day the flowers wouldn't
bloom.
If one day the rain wouldn't fall
anymore,
The next day the trees would stop
growing.
If one day the children wouldn't play
anymore,
The next day all the playgrounds
would be empty.
If one day the stars wouldn't twinkle
anymore,
The next day the sky would look
completely dull.
If one day the people wouldn't get
along anymore,
The next day there would be one big
war.
If one day there wouldn't be music
anymore,
The next day there would be silence
all over.
If one day you wouldn't love me
anymore,
The next day I would stop living.

Alex Nguyen
LIFE SUGGESTIONS

How funny life works,
As we all have seen,
Its endless quirks
Life has been.

To see the rays
Of a rising star
Reminds us the days
That have gone afar.

Astray from humanity
That some swore to protect,
Astray to insanity
Societies collect.

These are the gestures

Of what life can be,
The pain and the leisures
Through life we will see.

We all have been given
God's chosen abilities,
We have been living
With life's responsibilities.

Chantal Quincy
SUNSET
Luminescence
of orange and gold
I plunge
into the lake
of etherical light
I do not think
I let it work deep
into my cells
and penetrate my soul
Everyday
in total expectation
and wonder
with joy I receive
the sunset ritual
each one different
each one new
each one like you.

Demetra Yancy
SOMEONE TO TREASURER

This poem is dedicated to all of the children of the world with my love.

Your mind absorbs all that it sees and hears.
So you should let it because you cannot stop it anyway.
Hey, you are in a great position because you can learn and have fun and be protected all at the same time.
You can provide us as adults with joy, laughter, and energy.
You can do so many disruptive things; yet, you look so innocent after being caught.
The world is a playground at your disposal as long as you take responsibility for your actions.
If you choose not to take the road of respect and responsibility, the world will dispose of you.
You should measure your own distance in life with the faith of the Lord.
You should never forget the ones so dear to your heart.
You must be apt to be motivated to learn as you are equipped to sing, dance, and play sports.
Live life with a purpose, and you will succeed in any endeavors of the present and the future of your choice.
After all the results of your struggles in your strives for fame will determine our future.

Richard Warner
JUST LIKE I
New morning thought brings her to mind
I cannot escape the thought
Of why she is here and why she belongs
I cannot escape her thought
New morning love as fresh as the air
I cannot run from my heart
Of why it bleeds and why I long
I cannot run from her heart
New morning dream rises from the sea
I cannot hide from my mind
Of why only now I seem to care
I cannot hide from her mind
Why is it now I think of her?
I think of why she belongs
Why is she here and why does she belong?
I think of why I belong
And I see that I belong
To a generation not far
But she does not say, nor does she speak
And she is never far behind
So, if writing about her gives her victory
Then I let you know she won
For, here I dream of holding her hand
Eventually becoming one
You see, friends, I have to respect her
Because, she belongs here, too
Just like I

Victoria Monter Washington
THE WIND

To my husband Bill, and sons Eric, Billy, & Chris, and to my parents Mr. & Mrs. Andrew Monter, Sr.

The summer wind is whispering its sweet goodbye
as the fall foliage and crisp air creep in on a sly.
I feel so sad that summer is gone—
I can recall the chirping of the birds and their song,
(and so many many many things that have gone wrong)

I've been so busy so rushed to even stop to think of such,
Oh, If I can just do this over once again—
and whispered it softly to the wind.
I'd spend countless hours by the sea and leave much more
time for you and me.
I'd enjoy the lovely green grass and summer blue skies
and when summer ends no tears will fill these eyes.

Oh! the wind he laughs at me, oh person you sound so silly,
Time is here! and time is now! Don't shed a tear nor make
a vow. Get up! Get out! and make your dreams.
See the world and all it means.

But the debts they mount so high, I seem to be getting no
where. I work each day from morn to nigh and at the end
of each week ask myself why? The kids are grown and my
love is gone and nothing is left of sweet summer's song.

Janice E Shanahan
DANCERS IN THE SKY

This poem is dedicated to my parents, Orson and Beverly Gallup.

The sun warms the trees.
A breeze kisses the leaves and they rustle with anticipation.
Their movement is slight.
Now the music begins.
One by one they break away, swept high on crisp autumn notes.
Their beauty abounds.
Circles and spirals.
Dancers that gently glide
Giving color and glorious radiance back to the earth.
Their mother, their keeper opens her arms
Holding her dancers dear,
Delighting in this October afternoon.

November draws near.
There will be other dancers in the sky.
The silver symmetry of snowflakes descending,
Touching my skin, my eyes blink.
How wondrously they swirl caught up on notes of ancient winds.
Sweet harmony rings out through bleak
Winter clouds and fills my soul.
My spirit sings and I dance.

Theresia Stone
THE ONLY STARS I SEE
Underneath a dark and tired sky
The moon is full,
But the only stars I see are in your eyes.
In the cards lies a jester, a fool.

Night wind blows among the leaves
Wild fantasies with castles were no lies.
Hopes can drift along the breeze,
But the only stars I see are in your eyes.

I walk along my path alone
I have no dwarfs or fireflies.
Stumbling because no light has shown.
The only stars I see are in your eyes.

Wood nymphs and pixies dance in the dust,
magic wands can weave spells of every size,
Fireworks in the sky can bust.
But the only stars I see are in your eyes.

Cathy Turchan
FEELINGS
You said time would drift away. Why does it seem so long? Days go by, but, not fast enough. Hours, minutes and seconds are being count down. Thinking about you makes everything perfect, but, then the empty space makes me want to sit there and cry, but, I know you will be there for me. I can't wait until everyday is gone, the faster the weeks go, the faster I will be there with you, the more closer feeling and no more emotional outburst of tears dripping down my face, and then the empty space will be filled with happiness.

Yasmin Azizi
CHILDREN OF TODAY
Some are very hungry and some are very cold
Some can't sleep at night for fear of a scold
They are used and they are abused
It's no wonder their spirits are bruised
The children of today are suffering
Their futures are looking very bleak
Don't people care anymore about our young adults so weak
Their bodies may be small but their hearts and souls immense
The neglect, anguish and pain none of this makes sense
Alcoholics, junkies, thieves and gangs
Should they be in a cell
This is a normal life for some children
An everyday living hell
I cannot watch their suffering and never lift a hand
Are they to become a dying species
Like our sea and land
There's a massive wave of suicide
Starting as young as ten
When all the children are gone
What will we do then

Sounni de Fontenay
DEATH
Do you believe in afterlife?
Do you believe in Heaven and Hell?
Do you believe in reincarnation?
If you do,
  you are a fool.
These are lies,
  all lies.
Made by our ancestors,
  as an excuse.
So they would not have to
  face the real horrors of death.
Yet death is real,
  very real.
And you cannot escape it,
  for it shall hunt you down.
And when it finds you,
  you shall understand
  the true meaning of death!

Wayne E Goodwin Jr
CHOSEN
Roses carnations and sparkles in sight,
To those alive a wondrous delight.
With freedoms loving smiles not pent,
Breath's desires once inhaled rose bud's scent.
From thick black hair to perfectly shaped hands,
The once owned figure controlled many lands.
A velvety pall to rich too lose,
Upon marble its crescents did ooze.
Unwilling sight glossed over present tearers,
As cherished thoughts reflected over memory's mirrors.
Wine dropped over crystal to some's despair,
For the once thought child soon to be there.
Mother and child combined as one,
Deep inside the deed not done.
Displayed on slender fingers for eyes to stare,
Rested gold and jewels rare.
One ring stood out in equity,
The golden mate to my own integrity.
The sun rests to be reborn,
But those who loved are ever torn . . .

Angela V Haynes
SOLITARY OAKS
There lives high upon the rolling hills two giant Oaks.
They stand in splendor against the horizon towering in
total solitude. Who planted such seeds so high on the
mounds? Or were these thus blown through the winds,
to land and grow as two in unison.

How majestic and inspiring they are, and a romantic
reminiscence of a love that binds together through many
seasons and the ever changing shifts of the sands of time.

Nen Jelicic
NOVEMBER
Till the next November
When I see it again
these pages I will read
and I shall remember

November
As strange as its name
the fire in its syllables
the tenderness of its saying
all my thoughts the same

The eleventh month ends
and it slowly seeps away
never shall there be a time
when it's without friends

So it marks a new season
a season of marriage and wealth
but only in spirit
November needs no reason

Dianna Lyn
ME
Hot
Torture
Pain
Less
Young
Free
Nothing
Ness
Brave
Me
Inno
Cence
Colors
Black
Light
Sudden
Death

Amado Lopez Jr (Age 13)
SPRING
Spring is when bugs come out,
Flowers grow, grass gets taller and taller.
Trees start to bloom; snow starts to melt.
People and children go out and greet the
upcoming season. When grass is taller beetles, lady
bugs climb up and see. Birds and bears are
seen often. Spring is happiness to me, you,
and all of us. "Spring has come, spring has come!"
shout all little insects. Spring is my favorite season of all four!

Carol S Tucker
MEMORIES
Outside a cold rain comes down,
turning to ice as it hits the ground.
The radio speaks of love and fame,
as my family sits on the floor playing a game.
The fireplace sounds of crackling wood, and from the
kitchen the aroma of a fresh baked pie that smells so good.

How long will this tranquil evening last,
not long I fear, for children grow so fast.
Fires burn out and pies make us stout,
But, memories are what this evening is about.

Barbara-Jeanne Tiess
EFFORTLESSNESS
Those words . . . those effortless words . . .

How easily words come to you;
in flattery you stirred my heart.
I could not have misconstrued, too,
the feelings I heard you impart.

Your look of interest, I thought,
was solely mine; with grace of swans,
the conversations we both sought
gave me belief in your love's dawn.

How could I know — I was inept;
a game played, you enjoyed it well,
stirring emotions long leashed, kept,
waiting for that person special —

you YOU you

— Perhaps you feel it's late, attaching a relationship with an
innocent's holding tender heart's
love true for you without a "catch."

Tammy Bassett Jasek
LOVE OF MY BROTHER

To my beloved brother Billy (William Benjamin Bassett) 9-24-55/5-7-81.

He shared so much and had so little!
What was his, he gave to everyone.
"Billy" was a racer, a friend,
A lover to someone special,
A father to a lovely boy.
But most of all he was a brother and a son.
His life was short at the age of (25).
"Billy you will never be forgotten.
Your love and memories will be in our hearts forever,
Even though your presence is not shown!!!"

Sheila Williams Shafer
BEING BLACK
"Oh, my Father up above, it's a cruel, cruel world out there. Am I to blame because my skin is dark and theirs is so fair?"

A higher grade point — says they're smarter than me.
A husband or a wife — says they're more respectable than me.
A skin of white — says they're more acceptable than me.
Who are they to judge me, . . . to criticize me?

They who say you are — but, who say you can — but, who say I would — But.
Well I say to them — I am, I say to them — I can, I say to them — I Will.

I Will grasp their extended, retractable hand of friendship, taking from it all that I can.

I Will turn into reality their fictitious words of encouragement and erase their knowing looks of expected failure.

I Will conquer the torment of white-controlled dreams and soothe myself with the conviction that my dreams are really self-controlled.

I Will break their invisible bonds of self-righteousness and unselfish justification for the taking of my rights to a self-fashioned life, an ounce of dignity, a sense of pride or a future made of my own accord.
I Will walk the beaten path . . . but I Will Not be beaten.
I Will play their game . . . but by my rules.
I Will reform . . . I Will Not conform.
I Will be who I Am and what I Am . . . One of God's Winners.

Harriet S Webster
GRIEF
My grief is strung like knots along a thread.
Though never grapes are sweet upon my tongue;
across the world I know that you are dead.
The songs we make will nevermore be sung,
Songs of the Aprils and the flowering Mays,
expectant summers and the palsied fall;
do certain winters' cabalistic days
rest there beside you with the tasseled gold?
Death came in softly through a hingeless door
to wreath his talisman upon your breast;
shall inquisition matter anymore
when night and morning mingle in the west?
I bind remembrance like sheaves of wheat
and walk in silence down the street.

Kimberley Poole
BLACK GOLD
Peaceful beauty of the deep,
Waves pounding upon the shore.
Strange creatures lay undisturbed,
That world is no more.

Horribly black, thick and crude,
Preying on unknowing life.
Leaving behind trails of death,
A world filled with strife.

Giant tankers rule the sea,
Controlled carelessly by men.
Values are of no concern,
Wealth wins out again.

David W Grantham
WHAT IS CHRISTMAS?

To Mother, Father, Margo and Aunt Flora—They believed in me and my work. The corner is turned!

Christmas is the Star rising in the shadow of the Cross; that which signals the crashing of Hell's gates and the redemption of Man.

Christmas is that Happiness which rejoices in the midst
of much Misery brought on by ignorance and Malice.

Christmas is Plenty surrounded by a desolate Garden of Gethsemane
built of Want and Hunger caused by Greed and Grossness.

Christmas is the need to Love in a world filled
by Hate and hurt; of unhappy families.

Christmas is that most Blessed of Seasons in a Land
where killing is a Sacred and Paradise granting Duty.
Where Jew still awaits the Messiah
and a city remains Divided.

Christmas is the Story in the face of the crass and the Commercial
Christmas is the Hope of the future and the dread of the past.
The Bright and the Shining opposed to the
dross of the present.

Susan E Pool
MAMA

For my Mama, but dedicated to the hearts of the four daughters, and Daddy.

Oh no . . . here comes the tears,
I can't hold 'em off — she's been here for years.
Oh no . . . here comes the pain
my strength — I cannot gain.

I didn't get to say goodbye
In between my selfish cry
God . . . don't take her now,
to live . . . I don't know how.

An incurable disease — a cure they couldn't find,
I feel they put it out of their minds
It's not fair — that's what we pay them for,
to find the cures — to find more!

It's too late — she closed her eyes,
with her smile — she says goodbye
"don't cry my little ones,
there will be a time we'll come together as one."

Robert J Rader
AMERICA NOT–SO BEAUTIFUL?

To my wife Lucille, my daughter Robin, and my son Donald.

America, America, not so beautiful with our mountains of garbage and refuse to see from sea to shining sea.
America, America, a nation of takers and leaky faucets from sea to shining sea.
America, America, is not so beautiful from sea to shining sea of waste and non–biodegradable by–products and of the greed that feeds on non–biodegradable needs.
America, America, is not beautiful! From leaky faucets to polluted streams and acid rains, oceans with brown scummy foam, and shorelines littered with junk.
America, America, I fail to see our leaders standing tall against our purple mountains of garbage and polluted seas to shining seas. To our sprayed fruits and vegetables and flies I close my case to thee only to cry.
America, America, once God shed his grace on thee, not on our littered highways and byways or our mountains of non–biodegradable garbage for all to feel and see.
America, America, soon to be buried under our mountains of garbage, our polluted streams and seas. Our acid rain, goes on without little or no refrain.
America, America, wake up please!

Robert J Rader
THE SLEEZE AT VALDEEZ (ALASKA)
The sleeze that did that dirty, dastardly, dumb deed at Valdeez.
Alaska is no different than the

greed of others that it seizes,
especially of all peoples of all the Valdeezs.

The Holy Oil, the Black Gold of Alaska's Valdeez. And to that drunken sleeze who did his sleezy thing on the rocky shoals of Valdeez and now to heed the "Call of the Wild" no more for many of us who love the great outdoors and all because of that drunken sleeze who ran aground at Valdeez.

Because of his ship which broke up on the rocky shoals at Valdeez, this sleeze should be hanging in the breeze at Valdeez!

Scott Radike
SO LONG
Waiting outside in the light and the heat
With the children playing the atmosphere is complete
So tired I haven't slept in days
Never thought I could feel this way
There's a storm coming in tonight
Wind blows out the candlelight
And while all lies peaceful in-between
I know it's just the calm before the storm
Well it's been good to see you but I've got to say so long
I'd give you shelter from the storm if you could only come along
If I never see you again I'm leaving you this song
If you ever sing it for someone else try not to get it wrong
Now I'm out so far away from you as the rain begins to fall
I've thought of you a thousand times have you thought of me at all
I'm sitting by the phone right now but can't find the nerve to call
The storm breaks out inside of me and tears begin to fall
I was a fool to ever leave you I was a fool to say so long
I thought I needed time alone but I realize I was wrong
I couldn't tell you where I've been but I've been gone so very long
So I'm writing this to beg you not to ever say so long

Ethel L Reagan
POEM
A poem is a tender thing!
Fragile as a lovely smile,
Illusive as a bird on wing,
As fleeting as the sunset hour.

A poem is a tender thing,
Clear as a crystal mountain stream,
A lilting song a heart may sing,
Reflection of a lover's dream.

A poem is a tender thing:
Though you cannot bend it to your will.
It is a heart that laughs and sings
Or some wee thought so soft and still.

Ethel L Reagan
MEMORIES
I cannot hear the ocean's roar
Nor see the waves
White on the shore
When tide is high —
But seagulls glide
Against the rain
That slants across the windowpane
And dip their feet in river tide
That rushes in from ocean side
And cry of sea and sand and sky;
And I
Responding to their call
Can feel the tides that rise and fall
At ocean side

Brenda S Reynolds
WINTER
It comes too soon,
it lasts too long.
Leaves sparkling
memories when gone.

The only thing that's nice to say,
about a long, cold, Winter's day,
is the peaceful feeling you can find,
in a solitary walk—it quiets the mind.

There is a "hush"
that cannot be found,
in all of Summer's
rushing around.

Maybe God made Winter,
to slow us down,
to take a walk with Him,
there, where peace is found.

Wanda Negron

Wanda Negron
LADY OF THE NIGHT

To my beloved husband, Edgardo.

Lady, Lady of the night
Spread your wings and fly
Remember life is like a game
You lose or you gain
So don't cry, soon you will arise
Dress in white, in the twilight
Lady, lady of the night
Spread your wings and fly

Dianne Gallowitz
I SAIL OFF INTO THE NIGHT
I sail off into the night, like a boat
set adrift by the wake of your love.
My sails flutter with the caress
of your breathless wind,
and its air is moist and sweet
with your scent.
Tepid waters once placid
soon ripple around your touch.
Further and further out to sea
I am carried by this tide,
Till the rolling rhythm of the waves
splash sparks of passion
against my moonlit hull.

Wanda Negron
LOVERS
I look at the sky
I see lovers embracing
As if they were high.

They look so young
So alive, I envy them
Because no one is on
My side, my days are
Just passing by

I look at the sky
And I said I am alive
And I see lovers on
My side embracing as
If they were high
I am young, too young to die

Ann-Marie Roopchand
IF EVER

This poem is dedicated to a very special person—S. Mohammed.

If it should ever happen again,
He'd be the image of you
If ever, I hope what emanates
from you dwells within him

If ever, that laughter, that gentle smile,
such kindness and thoughtfulness for human
being be a part of him; that which is within you.

If ever, in that next life I hope that
him is you and you're him who'll
love me as much as I love you.

Sis Galvan
NO TRACE OF DAWN
There's a desert in the ocean where mountains fear to tread
there's a mansion in the galaxy where seasons there are dead.
Amidst the moon a rainbow shines a silver greyish beam
shadows of dusk hide our other language we label as a dream.
Spread amongst the wilderness there calms a staring breeze
within its silent smile laughter echoes from the trees.
Sweetest taste of rapture follows near its fawn
awaiting to endeavor one faintest kiss of dawn.
Lilies applaud the valley where nests a newborn swallow
then like the sun itself influences all to follow.
Ride aside the seasons to taste what is unknown
explore the hollowness of reality where no wind has ever blown.
Tender is the grass that's sheltered by honesty's embrace
indulge upon the art before time steals its face.

Sis Galvan
THE KILL
when u think of Love do u feel the pain
when u're in the warm sun do u feel the rain
poundin in your head cuz u still aint free
its comin down on u cuz life won't let u be
all u had in mind everything u dreamed
& when the eagles fly do u hear them scream
2 the beast below who destroyed their land
& when u praise the earth do u drop the dagger from your hand

when u think of Love do u cry out loud
when u smile in the mirror can u see the crowd
standin in your way cuz u still aint sold
on the fire that's burnin from a torch u can't hold
when u wish on a star do u notice the time
when u pray 2 the Gods do u realize the crime
of each raging soul whose master is the strength of their will
when u reach 4 your gun do u shoot 2 kill

Crystal Diquinzio
TIME
It passes by like the tide of the sea,
nothing can cease its set limit.
It comes and fades away with ease,
even if our lives are not finished.

It takes away our beauty and youth,
it leaves us without hope.
As we grow older we learn the truth,
that we must try to cope.

If time was longer we would have no fears,
and know what life was meant to be.
We wouldn't leave our tender years,
it's a wonder why time has to flee.

Rhonda Brown
MY LETTER OF THANKS

Dedicated to Travis and Marylin Brown, my parents.

It may be I don't ever say the things I should,
or it may be my actions don't tell what they could.

In one's life there come complications
which can lead to permanent alterations.

Through ours you both held strong;
with that I learned right from wrong.

You both taught me to continue—
to never give in—

After all, sometimes it's better to lose some,
than to always win.

It may be I don't say the things I should,
and my actions don't always tell what they could; but

You both have molded me to be my best,
and now it's my job to finish the rest.

Mindi Martinez
HOURGLASS
Old sayings never comfort a broken heart
The lines of warmth have been cut
You feel like crying but cannot
All traces of past feelings are swept under the rug
And new beginnings have all been wiped out

As burning images crowd your mind
You cannot hide the emotions that thrive inside
The clock strikes twelve and all time stops
A lamp silently falls to the floor
Its shattered fragments disappear into thin air
And fairy godmother shuts her golden doors

Patience Register
SEEING YOU IS LIKE . . .

To my loving husband, David.

The first April rain, the sun
bursting through storm clouds, a
burst of fresh spring air,
the first blooming flower of spring
and watching the sun rise
on a warm summer morning.

Raymond Grant Jr
THE LAND OF RICE
The smell of open sewage
Along the street
Hot cushing air around your mouth
Breathing insect flying and
Crawling in the green foliage
People walking with sun hats on
to shield the sun and identity
children mingling along the street
begging strangers for money
Peddlers selling goods for money
The stickness of mud and
rain along the roads and
pavement
the tall trees darken the sky
The sun gleaming on green grass
hills illuminating the beauty
water buffalo wasting in mud pond
Rice paddies fill with mud,
water and people working.
It's a land of the living
Boats resting along the stream
with shacks of terrain
Where life is spurned and contain
Fishing boats going out and in
Fresh fish smell around your mouth
Heavy rain season and dry season
Colorized the land beneath your feet
The land and people that grow
Forever,
In mud and water

Betty M Gray
BOOTY
She came to me a stray
unwanted, unfed and abused

She settled in, a perfect guest
I stayed aloof, a distant host

A cat would only hold me down
I've earned the right to come and go

She took her time to win my love
A friendly paw, a melodic purr

My feline friend was wiser than I
She knew my heart would soon give
way

She greets me at the door each day
And tells me I am not alone

At night she snuggles close and warm
And tells me she forgives my original
sin

She knows that once I did not want her
I am ashamed.

Nari Yeates
SNIFF THE AIR
I sniff the air this morning
Everything shivers in the frost
It makes me restless
For the day to stretch its limbs

I listen to an inner calling
And feel your excitement
Pirating the world again
All of your senses awakened, alert

Like a caribou bedding down
At the same hour the wolves awaken
Listening with every bristled hair,
Achingly still.

Ready at any instant
For the plunge
Heaving heart
Pounding feet retreat

I pray for your safety
I raise my owl ears
And laughingly kiss your far away
eyes open
Have an extra fine fulfilling day

Yours and mine.

Marjorie M Tucker
A LEGEND OF MOUNT SAINT HELENS
The story of Mount Saint Helens
Is a legend in our time,
The mystery of a Mountain Queen
Her reign—and its decline.

In an ever changing world
She was a symbol through the
years,
The Lady with a peaceful heart,
An earthly Saint amid her peers.

Trees that graced her gentle slopes
Sheltered creatures roaming there,
Birds sang in the wilderness,
The scented Pine was everywhere.

The Gods were pleased and gifted
her,
A mirror for this Paradise,
Spirit Lake was calm and clear
Now all could see Saint Helens
twice.

Canoes were paddled softly then
Disturbing not the placid lake
And her reflection mirrored there
Still glistened in their slender
wake.

The Springtime of her discontent
Defied the Ides of March
When warning sounds and trembling
earth
Foretold the inner torch.

Alas, the world will long recall
The Holocaust of May,
A blast from Hell which severed
bonds
And set her Demons free.

Vast billows rose above the clouds
Blotting out the morning sun
And in the mass a face appeared,
An image of the Evil One.

The fragments of her shattered crown
Were blown across the land,
The green of Spring lay gasping then
'Neath myriad grains of sand.

The melting snow in torrents fell
Rushing, tumbling down her sides,
The bitter tears of all the years,
And with them—all her pride.

Could it be true that through the haze
A small brown deer was seen
Still standing in that awful waste?
It must have been a dream!

A murky shard is all there is
Of the lovely looking glass,
All creatures gone—the birds and
song,
Not even a blade of grass.

Like Wampum Beads of yesteryear
Lost upon some distant shore,
Fast tides reclaim the purple shells
And they are seen no more.

Though fleet the stride of one bereft
The search is all in vain,
The treasure that he once possessed
Is never found again.

Low scudding clouds and Autumn
mist,
Come dreary days and dark,
Kind winter snows will blanket her
And hide a broken heart.

Night does strange things with sound
they say
And lonely travellers passing there
Have heard above the sorrowing
wind
The haunting cries of her despair,

"If the Gods can hear me now,
VOLCANO is my name,
Come heal my heart—bring peace to
me,
LET ME BE LOVED AGAIN."

Jwaundäce KCandëce Belcher
SHADES OF GREY

Dedicated to Tanesha Chavis, Shauna Clark, Angela Armand and Melissa Pearson . . . may this be a blessing to all mankind.

"BLACK is BEAUTIFUL" . . . is this
statement really true?
"WHITE is FUNKY" . . . is a fact
proven by who?
Wake up people and take a look
around
Why is everyone putting the opposite
race down
Let's hold hands and come together
as one
Why can't we live together . . . a race
will never be won
If we keep fussing and fighting about
which color is best
It could never be proven on any quiz
or test
What's the difference between black
and white?
We're all human beings . . . some
dark, some light
Imagine yourself standing over the
world . . . up above
You will see races of hatred and not
of love
We all come from the mighty person
whom we call "Our Father"
I, too, have a dream that we will be
together tomorrow
Tomorrow . . . and tomorrow will be
another day
But in my eyes I see neither black nor
white . . . only
SHADES OF GREY

Jwaundäce KCandëce Belcher
THE ENEMY
Hidden for years
It sneaks upon you
It lives with you . . . for a period of
time.
Who knows
When the enemy will strike you
And kill you on the spot?
It takes over you.
Near the future . . . or maybe very
soon
It will own you.
And there is nothing
—NOW—
That you could do about it
But accept it
Till GOD comes and takes it away.
You can't kill it
Because it lives in you . . . growing
bigger
and bigger every day.
And the ONLY way for it to die
. . . is if you die

Toy L Gaerttner
SEEN DARKLY

For our black brothers.
Smile, God loves you.

In the deep south, dirt and grime
Are the heritage
Of the black man, his the grey shacks
His suppressed soul
Aches to be rid of the bondage taint!
Seething with rage, he bides his time
For a small wage
Dragon's teeth are sown, the whip
cracks
His awaited goal
Seems afar—suddenly he obeys
without complaint.

But gone the black man's song
Before the émeute . . . How long—
how long??

Cammy
QUINTESSENTIAL UNITY
Along the sea I walked forlorn;
A cool and crisp November's
morn.
The snow replaced the sandy shore,
The ocean waves they ripped and
tore.
Tho' seawall stretched for miles
ahead,
Something made me lower my
head.
A bird's small feet along the edge,
Beside a cat had walked the ledge,
Beside my step had walked a dog,
Along the wall in misty fog.
The four of us, though far and near,
Had walked this path without a
fear.
The sea so rough, the sky so gray,
We'd all found peace along the
way.

brian f deluca
BECAUSE I CARE

To the Youth of Ephesus Baptist Church.

Sometimes it's hard to tell what's on
someone else's mind,
Or to know what it is that they really
feel.
Sometimes we smile and act polite
and kind
While inside we're torn up, and our
smile isn't real.
Sometimes we're like a tree in the
wind,
Bending over till we touch the
ground,
Trying very hard to be what someone
else thinks we should.
We're wearing a mask, a smile to
hide our frown;
Hoping that someone will notice,
afraid that they never would.
Sometimes I reach out to share your
pain,
Because it makes mine seem so
small.
But you tell me you have others,
friends that you can lean on.
So I've written this poem to say,
If you need someone to call, if your
friends ever fail you,
You've always got my shoulder to
cry on.

brian f deluca
A WEDDING POEM
Something old.
They brought forth the faded robe,
Its purple color nearly gone.
Upon his shoulders it was placed,
And on his head, a crown of thorn.

Something new.
The cross was brought from the
carpenter shop,
The unfinished wood was untainted
and new.
The shiny nails were driven through
the hands
Of the Son of God, for you.

Something borrowed.
The tomb belonged to another man,
When they laid Him to rest.
They sealed the tomb and set a guard,
But God wasn't finished, yet!

Something blue.
The morning sky was bright and blue
When the women approached the tomb.
But the grave was empty, the Lord was gone!
Yet He's coming back to take me home.

Michael Leeper
SEASHELL DAYDREAMS
Walking along on a lonely beach
The sand pressed hard beneath my feet
An ocean so close yet somehow unreached
The salt in the summer air smells so sweet

Sunshine dances around a young girl's face
Seashells held tightly to her ears
Daydreams capture her in grace
I wonder what does she hear

Michael Leeper
TO KISS HER JUST ONCE
Ride toward the meadow
and just before the woods
This war tattered Knight
would love peace if he could
To dream of the maiden
lest battle interrupts
To kiss her just once
before the coward catches up

Brenda Louise Davidge
CHILDREN

This poem is dedicated to all the parents around the world.

Our children are a special jewel
Love, understanding, hugs and kisses are given,
not hatred, neglect and to them be cruel

Spend the time children need to share with you
Many parents forget why they are here
Parents who listen and care are a few

Children need to know they can come to you
With a question, not someone else
but you the parents to give advice
and listen with great affection

Let your children know they can find love at home
Your children are special more than anything else
you own

No parent can really say they have not the time
What is more important but to see our children shine?

When children are excited wanting to tell you of great
news, this is the time you come together
Remember never, never to them refuse

When children know they can come to you not in fear,
they wouldn't have to look
somewhere else with a falling tear

Don't tell your children they are bad
and blame them for your
anger that made you sad

Don't take your hurts and turn them
to your children to feel
the guilt
because if you do the sickness of
your children will be felt

Give your praise and understanding everyday
and in your children's heart love for their
parents will continuously stay

God has blessed you with the most
precious gem you ever
need to own
Children are your diamonds to keep
locked within your heart
and keep them from turning into
crumbled stone

Ben Rubin
OUR UNIVERSE
At night I gaze out in space
To see stars fixed in place,
Blinking. I wonder —
Where is "God" Who built this universe?
Did he plan it section by section
To His satisfaction?
Or was it one huge explosion
To set the universe in motion?

Why was this earth, A mere speck
In this vast ocean of space
Chosen to nourish life?
Was this the "Creator's master plan?"
Were we the chosen clan?
How did our ancestors arrive?
How did they survive?
Had they been dropped from another planet?
Or swept by the tides from sea to land?
Or left to sprout by any means at hand?
Is this what life is all about?
Oh Dear God!
I know not what to say,
All I can do is pray.
What you have given please do not take away.

Ben Rubin
TIME
Time, matter, space,
Relative to each other.
Yet each has its place
In this limitless space.
For time is ever—endless.

From time of birth to time spent on earth,
To some an eternity, to others a short span.
Time here is reckoned
To a split second.
For time is ever—endless.

The flowers, the trees,
Bloom and flourish.
The birds, the bees,
Live and nourish,
Only to die in time.
For time is ever—endless.

The clocks tick the minutes away,
Hour after hour,
Day by day on time.
For time is ever—endless.

Our earth, the planets, the sun,
Some day will be gone in time.
For time is ever—endless.

Rosemarie Walton
REALITY
A Day of Expectation
Yet to my Destination

A Sound of Rain
Yet all the Pain

A Love two Create
Yet fear of Hate

A Cry of Wild
Yet we of Child

A Mind of Light
Yet a Lovely Sight

A Word of Love
Yet all the Above

A Night of Expectation
Yet to My Destination

Reality My Love

Willa F Washington
MOMENTS IN TIME
PART I
How can you understand joy
Without sorrow
How can you see
Without first looking
How can you understand pleasure
Without pain
How can you understand love
Without once knowing hate
How can you know where I'm
Going
If you haven't understood
Where
I've
Been

Michael C Huff
MY MOTHER'S SONG
So now and sophisticated, I drove myself away.
Needed to feel the rush of a city,
Cement beneath my feet.
I've seen the lights and my share of sights
Now I need my Mother Earth.

I need the sound of a waterfall
Splashing in a gentle stream.
The scent of pine to renew my mind,
Mother call me home . . .

I'm surrounded by smoke and machinery,
Electric this and that.
Got to slow down, find what's true,
I'm running out of time.

I long for sunrise in the mountains,
Waking with frost in the grass.
Or the warmth of a child held close to me
And the love of one woman at last.

Well I've lived too long in the city,
I'm hittin' the road at dawn.
I've seen the lights and my share of sights,
Now I hear my Mother's song . . .

Frieda Kleinberg
NATURE'S SYMPHONY
Listen to the sound of music
All around you.

The bluebird—in all his glory
Chirping a melody.
The robin—perching near his nest
Humming a song.

The mockingbird—sweetly
Calling his mate.

Mother duck—squacking, squacking
Guiding her chicks.

A soft wind blowing through the palms
Sounding a lofty tune.

No harp, basses
Or sweet strings of violins.
Nor horns, bassoons
Or clarinets
Nor trumpets
To see or to hear.

But listen—listen to the sound of music
All around you.
Nature's kind gift—
An orchestra in joyous harmony;
The gentle hands of God—
The glorious Conductor.

Johny Martin
INSTANT
I do have a bid at once
process with touch on,on,on
that I would word getting rid off
heavy gravity reminders as
insufferable////////

I do radiate myself with
personal pronouns er,er,er
diminuendo suite,sugar cane and crops
man remembrance exist
insufferable////////

Though I divide my–self
everybody updates bounces
does,does,does
width total wither and collection
so be my be instant
insufferable////////

Though times is this one
I abandoned memories do,do,do
Rhythmic greenbacks,yellow tulips
lip service really rare
insufferable////////

Edward Meltzer
MEMOIRS OF A LUXURY HOTEL
At the turn of the century I was a luxury hotel
Each day I would serve wealthy
dressed ladies and gentlemen well
Customers would occupy my elegant
rooms and would always have a ball
Because I provided delicious meals . . .
Popular shows . . . music . . . dancing
. . . fun and laughter were shared by all
The years went by and I gracefully became old
But my luxury status kept me solid and bold
I enjoyed my customers many smiles
throughout the years
And felt very sad when some would
return with bitter tears
Only when you're lonely and blue
Will you understand happiness when
it comes to you
On a gray cloudy rainy day
An elderly couple passed my way
They stopped . . . looked . . . stared
and reminisced those happy years
Down their cheeks spilled many
visible tears
Passing seasons of winter . . .
spring . . . summer and fall
Good old fashioned memories were recalled
And I was there to see it all

Lib Minich
FRIENDSHIP
We should try to remember,
As we go along each day,
Many, many people we've met

As we traveled on our way.

Especially do we like to think
Of those who cared for you.
With love and kindness,
As a friend should do.

When you are sick or in pain
Or feeling down and low
A friend to listen to you.
Is the best thing to know

It is indeed a blessing
Given by our Father above
That we care about each other
With kindness and love.

We should be very thankful
For friendships that we share,
To help us in many ways
So that we know they care

Lib Minich
BEAUTY
Each morning that I arise
To the Heavenly Father I pray
That He will guide me
In everything for that day.

As I look around in the morning,
All the beauty I can see
The beauty of the flowers
And the greenery of a tree.

The beautiful blue sky
Shines on beauty all around.
Little birds tweeting and flying
From trees to the ground.

I know that all beauty
Was created by God above.
And with everyone should share
Our kindness and our love.

The greatest beauty we see
Is how to treat each other
With loving care and kindness
That we give to one another.

Craig F Mounce
ANOTHER DAY
The sun rises each and every day
Much in its familiar and shining way.
It's the only thing that can bring a
smile to our face,
In our struggling world as we try to
keep the pace.
Before we can take a decent
morning's breath
We have heard of another one
stricken by death . . .
Whether it be by car or something
called a drug,
Just another obstacle in our society of
push and tug.
It can be so sad and often strange
To think that you and I could make it
change.
To make a difference; what a
tremendous feat
But knowing that we saved just one
kid from the street
So many different concerns to
maintain
Trying to keep ourselves from going
insane
Distinguishing between a scream and
a roar
This is no longer a problem, it is
becoming a war
The purpose is a successful defeat.
Before it's too late for us to even
compete.
As we spend our time and money just
to stay alive
From day to day we search for the
key . . . just to survive.

Paul Murphy
INEVITABLE DESTINY
One who seeks a vision is blind,
Yet one who possesses a vision
is blind to reason;
Therefore the world is frantically
waving their canes in search of
the unforeseen terror before their
glass eyes;
While they could have perpetual
vision with love,
That is blind.

Kerry McGlynn (Grade 4)
SEASONS
In the summer I have fun in the sun,
but that season's all done.

I like the fall when I'm playing in the
leaves and I hear my mother call,
Come inside and hang your coat in
the hall
and that's all.

When winter comes and I'm snug in
my bed,
I have the nicest dreams in my
head
of lollipops and candy canes
and icicles hanging from my window
panes,

But when I wake up my dreams are
gone
but as I get out of bed, I hear the
spring birds
singing their cheerful song, again.

Kathy Jackson
REBIRTH
The fluttering that was within my
breast,
Soon stopped with the arrival of
hopelessness.
A dream was dead.
Swirls of empty blackness surround
my head.
The song was squashed.
The laugh repulsed.
The entity of life was not rejoiced.

Awake the flutter in my breast.
Awake the time for hopefulness.
I am alive; I see, I feel.
I know my God is with me still.
The blackness of the depth receding,
The song is joyful: The laugh is
peeling.
I am not chained, I will survive.
Awake my soul, I am alive!

Sylvia Marie Johnson
LETTER FROM EDDIE COLE

To all who love poetry. Especially dedicated to Eddie Cole whose letters of encouragement have been a great inspiration to me.

The mailman brought it Wednesday,
And how it thrilled me so!
The nice surprize that met my eyes?
"A letter from Eddie Cole"
I read it very slowly,
To savor every line,
As tingles of excitement,
Brought scenes into my mind.
I could picture Eddie reading,
Works of her favorite art,
Being a wonderful lady already
eighty,
Still active and young at heart.
If God would be so gracious,
Granting time till I'm eighty years
old,
I'd love to be delightfully,
Poetic as Eddie Cole.
And though her letter did not rhyme,
Still it seemed to be,
So full of joyous "love of life"
It was poetry to me.

Vidrine Jones
NOW I LAY MYSELF DOWN TO PRAY

This poem is dedicated to Thomas, my wonderful husband.

Now I lay myself down to pray
There are so many things I wish to
say . . .

For those who don't have, I pray
they will someday,
For those who do, teach them to
give in their loving way.

For those who try so hard to
succeed,
I pray you give them all the
strength they need.

For those who have closed
their eyes and gone away,
I pray you rest their heads in
a peaceful place.

For those who wish they
had a place to call home,
I pray you give them hope
and never leave them
alone.

"For those who don't ask of
anything for themselves,"
They know you're listening while
you're taking care of everyone else.

V Lee & V N Beauchamp
THE LEGEND OF "OLD SERGEANT'S GUNNER"

Lest—we forget—the Ho-chi-minh Trail, the Earthquake of San Francisco, South Carolina's Hurricane Hugo!

Alone—in a cell—in this West Texas
jail—
A repeat offender—for three times
I've failed.
Held without bail—doomed in
flashback hell!
With mind and soul imprisoned in a
raging inferno,
As swiftly on target as South
Carolina's Hurricane Hugo!
Destructive and deadly as the
Earthquake of San Francisco!
So Listen—it's an honorable story I
tell,
The Legend of the Old Sergeant's
Gunner on the Ho-Chi-Minh Trail.

Over miles in Viet Nam's war—mud
and blood we waded—
'Twas no secret back home we were
cursed and degraded.
Then Old Sarge called us gunners to
the front with this to say,
Defend unto death—your families'
freedom is at stake—
Soon, this platoon, the enemy must
face, "You're Men today!"
But after the battle as lads we'd
tremble and shake.
For Ho-Chi-Minh's tough Old Sarge
lay dead,
A Viet Cong bullet through his head!
Oh God, "Bless America, Old Glory
won't fail, to our Chief Hail,
Freedom's not Free"—you've just
heard my plea—
from flashback Hell,
For I was that Old Sergeant's Gunner
on the Ho-Chi-Minh Trail!

Ruth Jarvis
FIRST BORN

To My Beloved Son Mark and Daughter Susan.

Those beautiful big brown eyes, so
warm, loving and knowing;
He was so tall and lean, we thought
he'd never stop growing.
Our hearts ache, longing for his
cheery voice and ready laughter;
His memory will always be with us,
and we long to be with him in the
"here-after."
The first born child is very special in
any case;
The whole world has come true in
that shining face.
He and his little sister were so close,
it was sweet to see;
Two wonderful children, made us
wonder how lucky we could be.
Now our lovely daughter has taken
life in her stride;
We can only look upon her with all
our love and pride.
Life is so very sweet, and just as
short, it's sad;
We will never, ever forget that first
born son we had.

Kirk P Dechert
NATURE
Nature is a very beautiful place
With no high rises taking up space,
It's just you, the bears, the birds and
bees
And all the fuzzy creatures that make
you sneeze.
I like to be in nature when there's
been a mist,
Where there's nothing to lose and
nothing to risk.
The rain seems to cleanse the land,
To cleanse the land with only God's
hand.
Things seem clean, clean as the snow
The creeks seem to never stop and
always flow,
Never break, never stop
The only boundaries are the little
rocks.
I love nature, yes I do,
If you don't, try to learn to.

Alan K Stirling
RAIN
The rain is raining all around
But not a drop upon the ground

Because the earth remains
Dry and brown

We must get this rain
To turn around

So every drop
Falls on the ground

June Furrow-McCue
TOKYO JUNE
Tokyo June with her little fan earrings,
Strolling along the streets getting her bearings,
Another day, another dollar
Masquerade of smiles, folly a few, tales of woe, sounds of strained laughter
Brinks of confusion, despair and question
What to do
Eternity of life seen no more
Who's to care
Who's to know
Uphold your heart now
silent from pain of neglect!
Look ahead for within
is your soul sightless but erect
Rise above
Mortal of fortune and fame,
Turn away and walk again.

Tim Hasse
WHY ARE HUMANS SO VERY BLIND

This poem is dedicated to my father, Donald John Hasse, who died on February 2, 1987. I write this in hopes of inspiring others to stop and look at what they have, which is considerable, and not to make the mistake of letting life pass them by as I did.

Why are humans so very blind?
Reasons for this are hard to find.
For we never realize what we've lost,
Until it's dead and buried under the frost.
Why didn't I tell him how much I cared?
Why didn't I say all the things I could have shared?
For this man, my father, was a great human being,
Always kind, sensitive, sharing, and feeling.
Now I realize that when he was hard on me,
He was changing me from the child I am to the man I'll be.
Everything he did he had a reason.
I realized that too late in the darkest of seasons.
I'll always have to live with this beloved man's fate.
And that I realized all this a little too late.

Gary Klang
O BUISSON FRAIS COMME UNE AMANDE
O buisson frais comme une amande
Lèvres rougies par les feux de l'absence
L'ogre écarta la toison rouge
S'incrustant violemment dans les lieux d'ombre humide

Il n'y eut plus alors
Ni repos
Ni sommeil
La pente
Plus dure qu'à l'homme des temps anciens
La soif inextinguible comme au désert des songes
Et puis
La voie déviée du but
L'aube crépuscule qui n'en finissait plus

Refus des lèvres doubles
J'aimai la fille fleur au seuil d'adolescence
L'être de nuit qui semblait une enfant

J'aimai la femme fleur
L'amande rose au buisson frais

Faut-il faut-il que je m'en ressouvienne

James P Laggart
THE MORNING STAR
It was night, then the sun broke free.
I saw you there, coming close to me.
To look at you, was a delight,
You glowed of sunlight, that had chased the night.
I held my breath, at your approach to me,
Thinking only how, the sun broke free.
A new day began, the day we met,
And now we are, each other's pet.
God gave us more, than that special day,
He gave us each other, in His special way.
For I can see now, just what He has brought,
He let us know, life isn't for naught.
'Twas a day, when I thought I was king,
'Til I looked inside, and couldn't find a thing.
I searched for love, in many a way,
But received it now, since that special day.
I know it wasn't, just who we are,
It was His blessing, The Morning Star!

Dennis M Mitterer
AARON
Through the darkness; they knew,
for he too was in darkness
for two years,
not seeing his adoptive parents.
He only sensed their love and devotion.
A victim of Hydraencephaly

Music moved his tiny hands and feet,
to the rhythm he would pound.
For two years,
he brought a simplistic joy to his family.
He only felt their love and devotion.
A defect in nature; a helpless victim.

A call for help, the need for an answer.
At three in the morning
no breath, no life.
The desire for a mother and father to know why.
They gave their love and devotion.
He is no longer a victim, but an innocent expression of silence.

Cradled in mom's arms.
Rocking little Aaron, kissing his cheek.
His mind at peace.
He has been called home.
His parent's love and devotion is unmistakable.
But now, they are the victims.

Janet Vander Sloot
POT O'GOLD
Something strange whispered in my ear one day—
"Pot O'Gold at the end of the rainbow," I heard it say.
So I searched o'er heather, vale and hill—
List' to drumbeat, birdsong, and trill,
Viewed signs, footprints, even portents in the sky—
Questioned, "how, what, when, where and why?"
Castles, Camelot, heraldry bid me, "Draw near."
Beckoning so powerfully—"What you seek is here."
But one day your dear face glided softly into view.
Then suddenly I knew "Pot O'Gold" was really YOU!

Melissa Ann Kurpuis
WHEN OUR LOVE IS GONE
If ever you feel
You don't love me anymore
And it is time to walk out the door
Please don't slam it in my face,
Close it slowly, and quietly sneak away
When you say it is the end
It will make me ever so sad.
So please don't tell me,
For it will hurt so bad.
When I think of you leaving,
(Although no one else can)
I hear myself weeping.
So please don't make me cry
By saying good-bye.
For I love you so
I can't let go.

Kimber Lee Peluso
THE NUCLEAR AGE
My son sticks out his tongue
To catch a February flake

"Shut your mouth you little fool!"
"That's Nucleonic Waste!"

My other son (the younger one)
Likes to sit outside in storms

Acid rain tastes better
When it's warm

My sister's out there
Soaking up the sun

"Cover up you idiot!"
"Those are ultra violet rays!"

My kids are eating
Polysorbate 80 on a stick

It makes me sick

It's such a comfort, don't you think
To know we're so advanced

We kill ourselves with chemicals
Save the last dance

For me

Pradeep S Rana
ALONE TOGETHER
Sun goes down the clump of cloud,
Mates part with me for the day
And I fall back home they thought mine.
Go gather them right off. Much? Quick!
Again learning goes for bad now.

I throw rubble, starved twigs crash down.
Small still! My spirit depletes in boredom,
At long last I play Charlie Chaplin in 4in1 chamber that stops day's crippled acts.

First sun comes in, dishes emerge hollow.
Go ask papa for money. Hurry up!
An hour's back massage drew four rupees
To round up morning essentials closeby.

Charlie Chaplin finishes. Fit of 4in1 rocks
Scholarship at school. Seven years gone,
Papa dies one day. Dowered land sells
And my campus days roll on well.

My graduation day! And failing bread-battles!
The chapter half-closes on two post-graduations.
She smokes for me, and I dream on,
Candle flickers out and hoots keep coming.

Shauntel Taylor
AND WE ALL WATCHED
As the movie began, everyone
Was there to see . . . their
Interpretation of the block-buster
A must . . . if you were any . . body

What they didn't know was that
It wasn't rehearsed, revised,
Or an important star, but a
Version of each and everyone's
Trials, lies, truths, and
Tribulations as they really are

The theater was filled to capacity
A line forming clear out to the
Street, and the truth of the matter
Was . . . could they really stand the
Heat?

Many began leaving, while more
Began to come . . . the realistic version
Had truly frightened some . . .

A question to ask yourself before
Going to a movie to view . . . is
Could the plot be my life before
Me and would I be proud . . . if I
Were you

Deborah A Washington
MERDIS SWEET MERDIS

I love you, sweet Merdis
Oh! Precious Mother of Mine.
Always, Deborah.

Merdis Sweet Merdis
I love thee
in so many ways.
You were my mother,
friend, heart and soul.
Oh! Why did you have
to go away.

I miss you dearly.
Everyday I pray
to hear your sweet voice,
see your smiling face.
I long to hear you
call my name.

I think of you everyday.
I dream of you every nite.
Oh! How I miss you.
Why did you have to go away.

I wish in some magical way
You could return.
To the ones who love you.
Why, why did you have to
go away.

I know you made it to heaven
Your smile shines down
on us.
Your body can never
return . . .
But your spirit is with
me everyday.

with your dying.
No more will I say.
Why, did you have to
go away.

Christine E Bidleman
I LOVE YOU DADDY

I wish I were two again so I could climb upon your lap and you could put your arms around me and hold me tight so that I knew that I was always safe.

I wish on a cold winter day mother could dress me in my snowsuit, scarf and mittens and I could run outside and get on my old wooden sled with the box on it that you built and you could pull me around the block again. But I'd probably spend most of the ride up in your arms with my nose buried in your chest to keep my face warm while your chest froze.

I LOVE YOU DADDY

I pray for you every night asking God to make you walk again, but if for some reason he has another plan I want you to promise me something. Promise me that if you die before me that you'll wait for me up in heaven and when I get there please put both arms around me and hug me tight and tell me you love me. If I die first daddy I'll wait for you. Nobody can ever take your place.

Nicole Mann
FOR SEAN

To Sean, Thank you for loving me, but most of all thank you for giving me someone to trust and believe in.

When I move my lips to speak my peace
It seems as if you know my thoughts before the words are spoken,
You are there for me with tender care
When with fallen dreams and disappointments my heart has broken.

You have given me a safe place to hide
When this cruel world is just too unfair,
Always encouraging me to hold my head high
When the wicked ones have taken my pride and left me bare.

With you, I am able to be a playful little girl
Or a beautiful young lady adorned with innocent white,
Whether I am raged in madness or withdrawn in sorrow
I am able to see through my own darkness and step into your light.

I realize I have been difficult at times
I only ask of you to understand my pain,
Please, close your eyes when I turn to run
So you may always believe your affections for me are not in vain.

For the times when I push you away
Are the times when this love burns strongest in my heart,
The overwhelming fear causes insecurity and confusion
But the beautiful passion of what we share allows us to leave but never part.

I Love You.

Robert Cody
CRIMSON LIGHT

Crimson red light of a broken world
Blood of a famine of unnatural life
Tomorrow

Shadows of the underworld
Reaching from the ground
Grasping

Sounds of silence
Smells of death
Darkness

White shadows
Black death
Holocaust

Love lost with life
Life lost with death
Final peace.

Kimberly Ann Cook
A NIGHT IN WHITECHAPEL

I dedicate this poem to my mother Mattie, my sisters (Camille, Toni, Jackie), my brothers (Renard, Marcus), Tia, Betty, Geni, Dwayne, Meshia, Mike, Joe, Benard and Allen. I love you guys! XXOO

I stepped into the dense night air of Whitechapel with feelings of utter rage.
How pathetic it truly is to see these parasites slumped in corners with no where to retire for the evening.
Society has ever so discreetly written them off the page.
Oh! How foul they do smell as they grobble at your feet for a pence to pay for a lodge! And look! Look at that dreadful creature smiling as I walk past. She wishes I to be her next patron with whom she'll serve unimaginable passions and desires with her round full breasts and other concealed curves.
How I long to clasp my hands about her neck and hear her stifled pleas!
What a fine specimen she'd make indeed!
With so many gentlemen's hearts she's played like toys.
But she'll get her just dessert this daughter of joy!
So I take her into the night, this harlot beauty to do my solemn duty.
I am London's nightmare and Whitechapel's heart gripper.
Yours truly, Jack the Ripper!

Kimberly Ann Cook
THE FORMAL INTRODUCTION

I dedicate this poem to Ron, whose good deeds are often overlooked and unappreciated. In my opinion, you're the greatest. I also dedicate this poem to Ray, who's just too much fun. XXOO

She walked with her head cast to the ground uncertain of everyone around her. She was only certain that they saw her but again, did not see her. She was just another human robot on her way home from a job she hated. However, this evening's bus ride would be very pleasant indeed.
A very handsome gentleman sat next to her and began to talk. He addressed himself as Mr. Donald J. Kreid. As he talked she became mesmerized. By his being, his presence, his lips, his eyes. Somehow she felt compelled to follow him wherever he led. Even to his house! Once inside, she noticed it to be very gloomy and sad.
Everything was black and red. He must have truly been mad!
Why and how had she followed him ?
She had to leave. Now!
As she headed for the door, he grabbed her arm and said,
'You are very fortunate my dear. You are able to feel the sun on your face and the ocean at your feet. Those such as my master cannot. I've watched you day after day looking as if your world were coming to an end, hating life. But my master will teach you! For he is Dracula!'

Terri A Durden/Oliva
I HAVE LIVED MY DEATH

I have dreamed my life and I have lived my death
you breathed into my mouth the breath of life, but,
what I have lived, had been my death.

The breath of death in place of life, hell instead
of the heavens above, hatred fills the place where
my heart should be filled with love.

What crime have I committed?
Why must I pay such a price?
To live my life for my death, and my death as my life,
This is what I have lived, what else do I have to give?
To pay the price of my sins, will there ever come a day
that I might win?

Life over death
Life over strife

What must I do to prove to you, this life I must win!!
I repent all of my sins.

Jeanie P Wines
HEAVEN ON EARTH

If the world began tomorrow,
And I could be God for awhile,
I'd make it the way you'd want it
Just to see you smile.

I'd give you lovely summers
With just a little rain,
And fields of iris and daffodil
Where no other man has lain.

Then I'd create music,
The kind I know you'd love.
And the winds would whisper it softly
As I looked down from above.

But knowing and loving you as I do,
You'd be lonely I can see.
So I'd stop being God and come down to earth
AFTER I made you love me.

Deborah J Ziemba
LONELINESS

LONELY . . .
Not a word to share
By yourself
—NO ONE There.
Emptiness surrounds you
Prevading your soul
No sounds of closeness
When you fall through that
Deep
Dark
Hole.
No one to help you
You're alone in the dark
Sadness all around you
You're subject to get marked.
That horrible feeling
That nobody wants
That faraway blackness
—A Hole in your heart.
Nothing can cure it
But a good friend indeed.
To take away the sadness
In your time of need.

Mary Hussey
MY TEACHER

This poem is dedicated to my special son, Mark.

My teacher is like my mother
While I'm away from home.
She tells me things that I should know
So that I may not roam.
From the teaching of wisdom and knowledge
That a little boy should know.
So that I may remember things that I've
Been taught
And use them through my life as I go.

Laura Rainboth
I WONDER

When we're alone together,
He talks so kind to me,
I wish this would last forever,
But, I don't understand him, you see.

We had so much passion,
We had so much love,
But, now I have a question,
Who does he dream of?

I wonder who he thinks of,
Is it me or her,
Am I his only love?
Who does he prefer?

When I'm not with him,
When we're in a fight,
I worry so much about him,
It's always a sleepless night.

Traci Lyn Stevens
RODNEY C. PATES

My hand I stretch out to you.
Grasp my life in your arms;
Hold it, and let me know it
Will be alright.

Don't grasp it just for the
Moment—hold it for a life time.
STAY . . . . . .
The silence speaks louder than
I can cry to keep you.

Don't let my knees touch the
Ground to keep you.
In you I found the joys of
Life and the answers to love.
And you made it all so easy to love.

And I Do Love You.

Traci Lyn Stevens
IN SEARCH OF MY LOVE

The roads are long and
The days many, since we
Exchanged words last.

The thought of him is
Constantly with me
The mere mention of his name
Brings joy to my heart.

Upon my bed by night
I sought him whom my soul loves
I sought him
But found him not.

I will continue to search
Until the roads become few and we
exchange
"I Love You's."

Traci Lyn Stevens
THERE'S TROUBLE IN THE MAKING

There's trouble in the making
And I can't stop shaking.
You tell me you love me,
And all will be fine.

You made that big promise,
'Til death do you part,
Now I don't want the chance of a
Knife through my heart.

But baby, I love you, she don't mean
a thing.
I love you and need you,
but she wears the rings.

I'll leave her, we'll go away where
ever you say. Just believe me and
trust me and you'll have it your way.

Well, I believed you and trusted you
and I have the rings,
The cooking and cleaning and all
those good things.
And while I was shopping for that
man who's so dear—
I heard a sweet voice coming through
loud and clear.

But baby, I love you, she don't mean
a thing.
You can have what she has, including
her rings.

Well, if that don't beat all I made a
quick call.
And when he gets home he'll find a
few words:

I love you, I need you, 'til death do
us part. Now I've gone out looking to
break someone's heart. There's no
need to open the door 'cause you see,
I've taken the diamonds and furniture
with me.

Edna G Fielder
I LOVE A GIRL NAMED GLEE

This poem is dedicated to my daughter Glee Georgeann Fielder.

I love a girl named GLEE
We fell in love under a
big oak tree.
Red roses for her blue suit for me
Our wedding will soon to be
I love a girl named Glee
She means so much to me
Pure and sweet as can be
She stands five foot three
Just as pretty as can be.
With her blond hair blue eyes and
a flowing white dress under our big
oak tree
We got married in a garden of
flowers and trees and a hundred and
twenty three people all under the oak
tree
My bride in white I love you GLEE

Mary Foster
DUTY

My husband's in the Army
He works from dawn till dusk
My husband's in the Army
His loyalty is a must
My husband's in the Army
He's seen combat in his day
My husband's in the Army
Vietnam is where he showed the way
My husband's in the Army
Understanding man is he
My husband's in the Army
To protect both you and me
My husband's in the Army
So proud of what he does
My husband's in the Army
America is what he loves.

Mary Lou Fox
A DAY IN THE SUN

To my husband.

As we walked in the sun,
My love and I,
Wild flowers danced,
And leaves did sigh.
Robins sang of love
That was true,
As we sealed it
With a kiss or two.
Blue sky watched from above
And sent white clouds,
To spell out Love.
A soft breeze engulfed us,
And then it did flee.
Leaving only a stillness
Shared by just you and me.
Then our eyes met each other's
Our hearts seemed to say,
I give you my love,
Forever and a day.

Melissa Fuller
DOWN AND BLUE

When I'm feeling down and blue,
I pick myself up by thinking of
you.

I think of your face so bright
with a smile,
And it makes me happy for a
little while.

I think of your hands so big
and strong.
And I know they'll be kind and
gentle all along.

I think of our love that's growing
everyday,
And I know I'll be happy with you
in my life to stay.

Zakiya Gail
TO FEEL A WHOLE

To my family and all the beautiful people who cherish life as I do.

If we looked inside and saw
ourselves as we are and
accepted, rejected or changed
Life would really be a joy,
sunshine would enlighten our
souls.
The clouds would lift our spirits
and send us floating on to do our
daily chores.
Loving, sharing and touching the
hearts of just one soul
then you'd feel as a whole
Try it, it's beautiful

Judy Campbell
FORTUNATE?

There's a person in a factory—
complains of standing day after
day.
What about the crippled victim,
who can't stand — no way!

There's a person in a college—
complains homework is unkind.
What about the twenty year old
with a four year old mind?

There's a person in a beauty contest—
complains she's won only third
place.
What about the man
with a deformed body and face?

There's a person at a lecture—
complains he can't seem to hear.
What about the man
with no sound coming into his ear?

There's a person in a theatre—
complains he's too far away to
see.
What about the child born blind?
Yes, there are some less fortunate
than we.

Amber Norine
SEASON OF CHANGE

Fields are like a patch work quilt
Pretty flowers will soon wilt
Cornstalks look like stacked tepees
Hives of yellow humming bees
Apple trees with ripened fruit
Scarecrow in his tattered suit
Golden wheat waves on the breeze
Frost will come and crops will freeze
Wild ducks on a quiet pond
Honking geese journeying on
Crimson sunset, leaves of gold
Trees attired in colors bold
The moon is a reddish globe
Nature has changed her wardrobe.

Keturah Martin
BEYOND THE SUNSET

Beyond the sunset Christ we'll see,
With Him to dwell eternally;
His "Come ye Blessed" will repay
All trials which have passed our way.

Beyond the sunset storms will cease,
There is no strife, but all is peace;
There we shall never see a tear—
All will be happiness and cheer!

Beyond the sunset, friends we'll see,
Together we will always be:
We'll never be lonely or sad—
At Jesus's side we'll be so glad!

Beyond the sunset, we will sing
Glad songs of joy to Christ our King;
Then King of kings He will be
crowned,
And 'round His throne our praise will
sound!

Beyond the sunset's golden shore
Where trials we will meet no more:
Beyond the shore where pain will end
A blest eternity we'll spend!

Nancy, Buster, and Tony

Nancy Cooper
REMEMBERING MOM'S BUSTER

I sit here tonight, thinking of you, God knows why, I'm feeling so blue.

You're in my mind both night and day, I wish I knew why he took you away.

A buddy to me, that words can't describe, the fun times we shared, before you died.

I look out my window each day that I rise, wanting to see those those big bright eyes.

The sound of your baa, as I walk out the door, your hollering for me; "Mom, come see me some more."

The yard's not the same now that you are gone, my Buster, my buddy, I cry for and mourn.

Mom's buddy you were, and always will be, I wish that again we could be three.

I sit alone in my chair out back, wanting to give you those soft little pats, to scratch your legs, one by one. Then you would turn and push me, but all in fun.

My joy, Mom's boy, you always will be, I only hope some day you'll be waiting for me.

"I miss you BJ"

Love,
Mom

Jennifer Huffman
DID YOU EVER

To my darling Richard, the one I love dearly— but sometimes wonder why!

Did you ever fall in love with me, but
know I didn't care?
Did you ever feel like crying,
but know you'd get nowhere?
Did you ever look into my eyes,
and say a little prayer?
Did you ever look into my heart,
and wish that you were there?
Love is great but hurts so much,
the price is rather high.
If I could choose between the two,
I think I'd rather die.
Don't ever fall in love again,
you'll hurt before you're through.
You see I ought to know, my love,
because I fell in love with you!

Carla F Moffitt
WALTZ OF THE FLOWERS

Dancing sunbeams twirling
'round flaxen daffodils
Fiery tulips extending fingertips
to the sky
Hyacinths lending gently fragrance
to the air
Untamed dandelions capering wildly
across the meadows
Playful breezes teasing
the willows hair
Gentle jonquils gracefully waltzing
through the garden
Tiny buttercups adding touches
of color everywhere
Mother Nature has released spring
upon the earth
And set into motion the most
beautiful
dance of all
The waltz of the flowers.

Sarah N Lyles
ON THE WINGS OF A DOVE

I felt a hand lift me
Up into the sky
And there stood right before me
A figure of light
It wasn't clear at first
But then I saw who
Whose hand had lifted me
But it could not be true
It was the Lord who held me
In His holy hand

When I looked down I could see
All across the land
He set me down onto a cloud
Then He said to me
You have wings, now you must fly
All across the sea
I couldn't believe what was happening
I then looked above
For now I was soaring through the air
On the wings of a dove

Andréa (Dondero) Blackson
CLOUD

To my wonderful father who has always been there for me to help me through life's ups + downs. Without both he + my mother's guidance + constant love, I would have become much *less than I have.*

Always there (not always seen)
is a cloud looking over me.
Cloud of black, or cloud of white,
tries to make it day or night.
Spread yourself out like a sheet
to shield the sun from its great heat.
Spill your tears in gentle drops
to quench the thirst that others brought.
In your angry bolts of light,
point the path of wrong or right.
In the calmness, after storm,
leave a rainbow yet to form.

Judith K Gentry
UNTITLED

Spring brings everything to life
So fresh, green and beautiful
Trees, flowers, shrubs and gardens.
Summer brings the sun, warm and bright
The air so fragrant and sweet smelling
Time for picnics and swimming.
Fall makes the trees get into their gowns
So beautiful and all colors of the rainbow
Long walks and plenty of apple cider.
Winter brings the snow, so soft and white
Ice sculptures and snowmen abound
Sleds and ice-skating, lots of fun.
Mother Nature did a beautiful job
with all four seasons.

Judy L Cornelison
APPARITIONS

I hear the wings of owls
Beating against the windowpane.
They are the souls of dead friends,
White and panicky in the moonlight.
"Come, join us," they whisper in my dreams.
I wake standing at the window,
Hands pressed against the glass.

Shelley E Floyd
WHISPERING FEAR

An empty tomb of darkness,
shadows lurking every side.
Afraid to live, afraid to die,
no use to run and hide.

Trapped within the blackness,
silent screams, running, falling.
Echoing through years of fear,
haunted voices calling.

Knowing numbness closes in,
breathless cries, a blood red tear.
Paralyzed, dead, yet alive.
Existing,
Whispering fear . . . .

Dianne Houchins-Mabry Christensen-Mullican
CAN WE SEE

This poem is dedicated to my daughter, Lisa, my sons Jason and Chad, my wonderful family and friends and my loving husband JR—I love them very much and God loves them too . . . .

Oh how wonderful life can be; only if we see;
The animals of nature are happy and free
The attitudes of human nature sometimes disagree;
CAN WE SEE?

We are the makers of this world to be; only if we see;
Not through our eyes; but with our
Hearts are we set free
Taking the hard road will sometimes amaze you;
CAN WE SEE?

Sometimes you look around at things you make; only if we can see;
We go back to basics in the generations to be
Knowing that time will tell
CAN WE SEE?

Deep down inside we feel; only if we see;
The Love for each other is the Medicine
Learning and Accepting is another Key
CAN WE SEE?

CAN WE SEE, How you and I can be?
We take too much for granted
Never taking the time
LEARN TO LIVE "ONE DAY AT A TIME!"

Connie Mayberry
LONELY TIDE

To my husband, Jerry, whom I have always loved. Let us never be too late for sharing life to its fullest.

She stood barefoot in the white ocean foam,
Watched the sun creep behind grey blue waters.
The evening air slowly turned damp and cold
As she turned toward the cabin with her two daughters.

How often she had come to this beach before,
So many times with the man of her dreams.
Now she was alone and so empty inside
She wondered if things had ever been what they seemed.

The fire took time to warm the cold cabin
She fed the children and tucked them in bed.
Then sat herself down by the luring fire
She knew tonight she was going to dread.

Her mind drifted from the burning embers
As she sipped on her glass of wine.
She wandered from the present to past
She felt her strength begin to decline.
Such happy memories she'd had with her husband
So much laughter when they'd been together
A knock at the door aroused all her senses
The familiar face awaiting meant she'd have him forever.

Connie Mayberry
NEVER TOO LATE

With idle time you have idle chatter
So much, so little that really matters
One day you're here then gone the next
One day you're married then you're an ex.

If you and I and all the others
Would only love like sisters and brothers
Maybe a better place this would be.
Why don't we try it, why don't we see?

Life should be happy for one and all.
Why can't we work together when duty calls?
Make time for play with the ones you love
Before you get that call from heaven above.

There's a lot to be said for the golden pond
To relax and play before the great beyond.
Give a little, take a little, we do that well.
If you're not careful, you could go to hell.

You need life in perspective to really see
What's wrong with you and wrong with me.
It's never too late to change our ways
Before we see life in our golden days.

Rafiah Latiker
TO MARTIN LUTHER KING A TRIBUTE FROM TOMORROW

To my children, Michael and Shalane Latiker.

He was a man of incisive decision.
He made his historic ascension.
To the peak of the mountain.
And with his piercing vision
He ripped the veil of space and time
He saw a world united in peace
A braver saner race of mankind
He saw a world erased of racial and nationalistic strife
Each individual was free to pursue an egalitarian life.
A world devoid of famished unsheltered masses.
There were no more embittered and warring classes
Martin Luther King in praise of him
future generations will sing
And on the rich and loamy Georgia soil
Where Martin flowered and the sons and daughters of slaves toiled.
A golden plaque will someday be laid
A shining and lasting tribute will be paid
With these words inscribed with pride
"And here walked the man Martin Luther King, EARTH'S FINEST."

Krystal David
TOMORROW

There is something we all must face,
And no one can avoid it.
It comes with each passing day,
Who can tell what it holds?
Some can look forward to it,
Others are terrified of the very thought.
Although we all must wonder,
What it holds in its grasp.
What joys and pain we must feel.
Everyone has come to expect it.
For it is only tomorrow.

Bob L Porterfield
. . . song for spring

In dedication to the memory of my parents, Janevie Elizabeth Harrell Porterfield, 1912-79, and Tice Covey Porterfield, 1902-86.

The song I
knew
has come again,
flowers follow
winter's theme . . .
salute the
season's sequence . . . dream
of past
loves
in passing's file,
a nod in
hopes
they'd give a smile
to other days . . . and me.

Bob L Porterfield
. . . words

Their combinations
fascinate . . . the
way they lay . . .
eager to entice
a glance . . .
albeit to dance
in the mind's
eye of a passerby.

At times
luxuriating . . .
more often
insulating meanings
caught in chasms . . .
sleeplike spasms, teasing . . .
glancing . . . passing . . .
pleasing.

Bob L Porterfield
. . . late fall

Fall's gray brume
has
settled in . . .
affecting minds
recalling when
spring's lush
parade
masked visionary gloom.

But bow
we must
it's nature's will . . .
this necessary
cycle's ill . . .
we'll soon be
blessed
by April's first full bloom.

Bob L Porterfield
. . . disconsolation

My day seems to fall apart
As would a fragile handblown heart
Whose destiny assured . . . awaits
The intermittent time it takes
To meet the concrete floor that's there . . .

As squinting eyes realize the
distance needn't care.

Psalm . . . sung sad . . . and steady.
Psalm . . . sung sad . . . and
steady.
Must we continue this rehearsal
Anticipating some reversal . . .
For I am never ready.

Kay Gillion Martin

Kay Gillion Martin
THE DOCTOR'S WIFE

Dedicated to the members of the Interns' and Residents' Wives' Club Medical College of Georgia—Augusta, Georgia.

With the marriage vow comes the
vigil,
A lifetime of promises and hopes and
dreams;
His concern is for the sick and
hurting,
Her concern and life is for him it
seems.

From the beginning she knew
Her life with him would be shared
this way,
With all the patients who depend so
much,
On what the doctor has to say.

She dreams for a while
Of the way things might have been,
But her value as a person
Rests in knowing she is complete
with him.

Knowing it takes both rain and
sunshine
To make a rainbow,
Her smiling face is the
Light in his window.

She knows he depends upon her
strength
This is her gift of love to him.
Sharing their lives with few
complaints
She would do it all again.

C Johnson
SWEET DREAMS OF CHRISTMAS

For my brother Bob.

Sweet dreams, oh sweet dreams, of
Lollypop hills and mid-nite spills,
And milk was the drink of the times
With sugar and spice and everything
Nice.

Trees stood tall, with the white on
The ground that brought Santa
Around.
Tapping from the roof, snapped me
From my dreams, as my brother
Jumped from our bed with a scream.

Santa was here, Santa was here,
As he fled through the door on
His way to the tree.

By the time, I got to the tree,
My brother was on his knees
Unwrapping the gifts that Santa
Brought for my brother and me.

C L Paulsen
SIREN SUMMER'S CHIMERA

Summer roads!
Lanes of enchantment,
Full of wondrous shadow towers,
Enticing me on.

Chessboards of magic where "The
Seasons"
Have no game piece,
And Autumn never plays.

Jeff Fox
A MAN PAINTING PORTRAITS ON THE STREET

To my love, Romina Maria, for all of your patience, and for loving me.

A man, painting portraits, on the
street; was of ease, nothing perplexes
him, he is the tender lover of images,
he paints emotion into an easel; a
face, he creates our everything from
necessity, everything, because it has
to be, he reads the joy, fear,
excitement of lives, from the
parchment we call our image,
he paints style, ideals, creativity, into
a face, and when, upon request, he
was to portray my person, he stood
weary and all his ease was misplaced.
In finale he did paint. For hours he
pained (with no complaint). He
perspired unusual to his own dignity,
and when he had finished I looked to
the easel. I saw something that sent
fear to my heart.
Upon the easel lay a wolf; dying,
bleeding to death, slowly and
painfully, having been fatally
wounded by a tiny prick; from the
beak, of a snow-white dove.

Anita Merryman
NITE, NITE, NITE

For my daughter, Jo Ann Lafaye.

Nite, nite, nite little baby.
Nite, nite, nite.
It's time to talk with the sandman.
It's time to dream.
Nite, nite, nite precious angel.
Nite, nite nite.
It's time to cuddle brown teddy.
It's time to sleep.
Nite, nite, nite darling one.
Nite, nite, nite.
It's time to drift upon a cloud.
It's time to nap.
Nite, nite, nite precious angel.
Nite, nite, nite.
It's time to hug and kiss your
momma.
It's time to sleep.
Nite, nite, nite little baby.
Nite, nite, nite.
It's time to talk with the sandman.
It's time to dream.

Kimberly R Diaz
THE CAT

The cat climbed the tree
Falling into the soft snow
Breaking the stillness.
Now 22 years later the table
has shifted—who's Pepé?
Where's the little cat?
We had it then
It was natural and true

Lloyd Casey
IT CANNOT BE

To my wife, Verna, our three sons, Lloyd Jr., David & Daniel & our daughter, Carolyn.

An innermost desire of mine
Has been to write of Christ in rhyme.
To trace the auburn wealth of hair
And relate the mind residing there.

To outline the Holy silhouette
Often dampened by earthly sweat.
And to paint the longing in His eyes
Lifted toward the blissful skies.

I wished to portray a rugged frame
And a living soul that shied from
fame.
Sketching firmly a handknit cloak
With the rugged arms of a sturdy oak

Hands of skill and peaceful ways
And legs of steel for traveling days.
This I wanted, but it cannot be
For Christ Himself is poetry!

Sheila Shawn
IT'S BARGAIN DAY AT SELBY'S

It's bargain day at Selby's
That huge store down on Main.
I went there once on bargain day,
But I'll never go again.

We stood around outside the door
until we could get in.
The wicked way folks pushed and
shoved
It really was a sin.

And when the door did open,
We went in with a rush.
There was no time to change one's
mind,
Or we'd be stomped to mush!

Inside were snarls and snatching
and shouts, "I saw it first."
So everywhere there was a din,
Their manners were the worst!

I saw a sleeve ripped off a shirt,
A dress was torn in two
because three women wanted them.
BEWARE! I say to you!

Julianne Pagel
THE MASK CARVER

He surprises himself with language
that speaks of the wood he carves.
To his seeing hands, there is no
blind touch.
As the geography of a country
guides the path of a traveler,
so he is guided by the veined grain
of wooden masks.
The slow blade carves no deceptions,
but shapes the hidden patterns
of his heart.
Impenetrable faces do not see
the flow of love that alters his work.
Poetry cannot express
the wonder of his knife.

Stephanie Peters
A TRUE POEM

There was once a young man
named Marv LaBolle
He was rash, irresistible
and somewhat cool.
The girl of his dreams
was headstrong arrogant
but had a lot of heart
And delighted in the love game
of cartoon Pepé Le Pew
Marv ran after her and it
was such fun for them both.

Christopher Valdez
COPING

I have poetry in my heart
yet not a poetic heart.
I have adventure in my soul,
but I am not an adventurous soul.
I am a creature of habit, not driven by
passions,
or purpose, or logic.
I am what I have always been,
And I do what I have always done.
I cope.

I do not act so much as react.
I feel love, but I do not understand it.
I see, and I hear, and I try to
comprehend.
I think, and I speak, and I hope, and I
fear.
I cope.

I have my goals to achieve.
I have my limits to discover.
I have my fantasies to enjoy.
I have my reasons to defend.
I cope.

José A Solorzano
SEEING IS BELIEVING

So much within this cranium
like blinding rays of the rising sun
Traveling from my head to the tip of
my pencil
they are implanted inside by a crude
stencil
Since the day I was born
My feelings have been torn
Thoughts and ideas flooding my
brain
Some are quite brilliant others insane
For the time being
My life I have been seeing
Passing before my very eyes
like the endless clouds in the earth
blue skies
Suddenly stopping and then again
going
but never thinking of slowing
If you could've seen what I have saw
it would leave even the strongest
mind in awe.

Doris Baumann
TO FEEL GREAT, BE GRATEFUL

Let us be thankful we are alive
Ever to be better shall we strive.

May we find life full of interest and
beauty
Being happy while doing our duty.

Thank God for all the good we give
and find
Then small troubles we won't mind.

If big trouble should overtake
Trust in the Lord, He will not
forsake.

He will thank us by showing the way
To have a contented life day by day.

Evelyn Elaine Stringer Richardson
MICKEY

Dedicated to Mickey, My Dog of Childhood.

Oh Mickey, did it
So was said—
Then, poor Mickey, won't be fed!

Oh Dear Mickey she will die
But she didn't steal the Pie
Look there what's that in your eye?
Surely not a tear or sign?

Tell me Dear child;
Tell me, true.
What did Mickey?
Ever do to you?

She's my Dog,
AND I LOVE HER SO
We shared the PIE,
Now Mamma, let me go

Harold E Williams Jr

CANDLESTICK PARK (WALTZ)

VERSE:
The lights flickered in Candlestick Park,
Everyone sitting in the dark,
As bleachers lit up spectators cheer,
Wave and clap for Steinbach was here.

Now games are starting and fans have fun,
World Series saw many home run,
Both Oakland, Frisco, slugging it out,
Win or lose, the people did shout.

Big tremble shook the press box and all,
Giants went down, losin' baseball,
Soon after the game, players went home,
Next season fill Twins Metrodome.

CHORUS:
World Series at Candlestick Park,
Terry was the catcher,
Earthquake struck made stadium dark,
Oakland A's the winner.

Bay Bridge games crowd Candlestick Park,
Athletics won in four,
Candles lit up everything dark,
Never saw it before.

Nancy E Schabacker

STORMY NIGHT

Silent candle flickers
Golden halo on the wall
Velvet night grows angry
As rains begin to fall

Thoughts flowing freely
Echoes in my mind
Whisper soft impressions
Of days left behind

Thunder in the distance
Brilliant flashes in the sky
Smile I can't remember
Teardrops fill my eyes

Saddened heart grows weary
Dreams of one I love
Sighs in the darkness
Visions from above
Twilight room empty
Out of corners, shadows peep
Rains begin to lessen . . .
Night falls into sleep

Ada C Woodhouse

NEVER ALONE

You never have to walk alone
Amid your pain and sorrow,
There's always someone near you
To help you face tomorrow.

A friend is always near you
To take you by the hand,
And ease you from the burden
That pulls you like quicksand.

A friend is always ready
To comfort and to talk,
To guide you up and over
That fearsome stumbling block.

Take the hand of a trusting friend
And feel your strength renewed,
And feel new life within you stir
Waiting to start anew.

Ada C Woodhouse

THE BIRDS

Chirping of the birds, was the first sound heard
Before dawn broke, while the sky not yet
Broken through its cloak of darkness.
The stillness yet present in that blackened net
Slowly being pierced by the wakening birds.

As dawn broke, a breeze began to stir,
Gently moving through the quiet trees
Causing branches to dance and sway, and then
The leaves began their rustling sounds,
On which the morning dew glistened, as light shone through.

'Tis light now, their songs are full and ripe.
They start to leave their sheltered leafy home,
And the restless birds begin their daily flight
In search of nourishment, to fuel their endless song,
Till darkness again sends them back to the trees and home.

Mary Jo Osborn

WONDERING

Yonder hills call, gentle green,
    carpeted with gold,
caressed by lingering golden light,
whispering tales
    of love, people of long ago.
Were all their days as sunshine bright,
    with joys and with laughter,
were hearts filled with such delight,
    as this one passing after?
Gentle breezes tell me please, did they wonder too,
If others took their ease, daydreaming as I do,
Were their joys of heart complete,
with life and all its pleasures?
Before this earth we would deplete,
    of all its simple treasures

Mary Jo Osborn

OUR DADDY

A man of simple likes, desires, and riches few,
who shared with all he loved, or anyone he knew.
He walked the earth, he did not tire of helping those in need,
bringing joy to the hearts of many by his deeds.

We will miss you daddy dear, each day of every year,
yet we have our memories sweet,
within our hearts e'er near,
like the time you took us fishing, we nearly tipped the boat,
the times that we were wishing, we had more fish to tote.

The special times you told us the many things you'd done,
of all the places you had been, and challenges you won.
The special moments you have given, all your precious thoughts,
will always help our living, by all the things you taught.

Jaclyn Barrow

MUSIC TODAY

You know music today,
Everyone has their own special way.
Paula Abdul with The Way That You Love Me,
Can't you parents see?
Our music is very unique with a cool technique,
Because music today has its special own way.
New Kids, well they're a happen' in thing,
With Hangin' Tough and The Right Stuff.
Tiffany with I Think We're Alone Now,
What about her big lawsuit? Wow!
See how much music has changed
because music today has its special own way.
Janet Jackson with Escapade,
Aerosmith and Cinderella, I wonder how their albums were made.
The way they act and dress like girls, you'd think they were from a different world.
The B-52's with Love Shack,
Madonna, well she needs a good smack.
See now these days music has its own style and beat.
We love music because music today has its special own way.

Patricia Weeks

MOTHER

I would like to dedicate this poem to one of the dearest ladies on earth, my mother. I love you mom, and I miss you.

You made my life a joyous one,
You shone brighter than the morning sun.
We laughed, we talked, we shared.
You cared for me and everyone else too.
You loved life, though yours was taken away too soon.
You didn't ask for anything, though you deserved more than what you got.

Also, you did not take anything away from anyone.
Mother, you were my friend, my life.
So, therefore mom, it will be very hard for me to forget you.

No matter where I go, no matter what I do,
I will always be thinking of you.
You helped me through my life.
You helped me grow up and become the person I am.
And I am proud to say that I am a lot like you.
So, therefore mom, it will be very hard for me to forget you.

I think of you every day,
I think of the good times and bad.
How we laughed together, and cried together.
Mom, you were the best.
I will always love you, and I will never forget you.

Gloria Anna Ringle

I WONDER

To my wonderful husband, David, for his unfaltering love and support.

Were it possible
    To turn back the calendar,
Oh, how I wonder—
    Would the hungry now be feasting?
Would the sun replace the thunder?

Would the tears
    That I have shed,
Never have been?
    Would the words in anger said,
Erase the scars of sin?

Would the flowers in the garden
    Thrive without the rain?
Would the wealthy,
    Through their evil deeds,
Trade those riches for heavenly gain?

Would the darkness and the shadows
    Turn to glorious beams of light?
Bringing joy, in places of sadness,
    Bringing morning,
In place of night!

Debra Jane Rempel

ME & YOU

Accept myself, I say to me
Accept yourself, I say to you
For when I accept me
And you accept you
You'll be happy with me
And I'll be happy with you

Cyndie Johnson

ECHOES OF MY MIND

Whispered softly in the night
Came the echoes from my mind.
The rustling of the mountain breeze,
The crackling of the autumn leaves
Along with the rippling creek
Came the echoes of my mind,
Echoed softly in the night.
As I lay here in a deep sleep,
I found myself above the trees
Floating gently in the breeze
Gliding, sliding in the night
Were the echoes of my mind
Happy times just for me,
Living peacefully among the trees
Sliding freely across the sky,
Like the scattering seeds.
This life is perfect for me,
To let my mind drift at ease
Through the darkness of the night
Were the echoes of my mind.

Juanita M Salazar

IF LOVE IS A GAME

For Opa, with lots of love, Oma.

If love is a game, let me be your partner.
If the game is knowledge, let me get to know you.
If you follow all the rules and don't cheat you can call yourself a winner.

Jennifer Kline
YOU
It's been you I've wanted so,
To share with me the things you know.

I want to be the part of you,
That will laugh & cry for things you do.

I want to hold tight all your dreams,
And help you plan your little schemes.

To help you through a tough old day,
And guide you through a bit of play.

To see you smile makes me happy,
To see your sorrow makes me sad.
But when it's over I'll be glad,

That I could be there to help you care,
About the things you usually dare.

Vickie Teague
FIDDLERS HEAVEN
Late last spring, my daddy died;
One night about eleven.
At night the Lord took him away;
Away to Fiddlers Heaven.

My daddy was a fiddlin' man;
He played his music well.
The angels have a jamboree;
I've heard my momma tell.

His fiddle hangs up on the wall;
I wish that I could see,
My daddy take it down once more;
And play a song for me.

Daddy play me one more song;
Let music fill the air.
Let the angels join in;
A jamboree to share.

When springtime rolls around each year;
The night, the time; eleven,
I'll hear the fiddlin' music play;
From up in fiddlers heaven.

Janet De La Portilla
SHARE YOUR LOVE
I may not be everything
You could want in a woman
And I might be hard to take
But I can offer you things
The others never would
Are you listening
I'm by no means an angel
This much I know is true
But I can give you the things
Nobody ever could
I can give you them
And all I really ask of you
Is that you share your love with me
I can offer you words of comfort
When the days stretch long and endless
I can offer a shoulder to cry on
When life just seems too much
And all I really ask of you
Is that you share your love with me

Jane P Lawless
LOVING THE PRINCE
The pain of missing you
equaled only
by the joy of loving you—

It goes round and round
like music in a carousel—

Up and down
My emotions
Like a fantastic carousel—

As a child I rode—
always dreaming—

One day—someone—
would carry me away—

To the enchanted land—
where I'd be loved—
forevermore—
never lost—
never alone—

Always belonging

George E Barker
A REMEMBRANCE OF JOY
Joy to be realized is what she means,
An invitation to delight, a dream
Now present and a thought to love which leans
Upon our wishes, an enchanted beam.

Joy to be seen and held is what she means,
A prize of happiness, a closeness felt
As radiance, a warmth which intervenes
To cause our coldness to subside and melt.

She lives as hope to make our fortune bright,
To give us strength as spirit makes us strong,
To modify our angry storms, to light
Our way to gladness, place where we belong.

What may we ask of her for what she means
To us?—Her answer lies beyond our means.

Larri K Hunt
A CHILDHOOD MEMORY
I hold it in my hand if only for a moment. Holding it ever so lightly in the whole of my palm.
Arm outstretched ready for a release at a moment's notice. It tickles as it struggles against my fingers trying to escape.
So fragile it is I must be careful so as not to crush it, lest I end its small life. Its colors are vibrant in the light as I open my hand to look at it.
I hold my arm high now and with one swift movement give back the freedom I took from it for those few moments.
So beautiful are butterflies.

Grace Ranch Straley
MY SISTER CHAR
I've cried so much since you went away,
My heart aches so, a smile won't stay.
So many people I know, never knew you,
So most people don't know what I'm going thru.
A year ago, I thought things were fine.
I wore a smile, the world was all mine.
But two months later, tragedy came.
Now my life will never be the same.
Emotions run deep, I thought love was strong,
But now I know, I really was wrong.
For losing you, in death has been—
The greatest emotion I'll know again!!

Grace Ranch Straley
TO: THE LITTLE NICKEL PAPER
I opened up the paper—
And much to my surprise!
My poem typed up so beautiful,
Brought teardrops to my eyes.

Was really quite an effort—
On your part, (I truly feel)
To display it, in such a way,
It had that "eye-appeal"!

I want you to remember—
Your efforts not in vain,
Other folks are THANKFUL TOO,
(Though we don't know your name!)

So keep up all your good work,
Enjoy it to the limit—
You DO IT WELL, so there must be,
Much satisfaction 'in it.'

If many were involved in this,
Please give to them 'the word'
"You've more than just ability,
You're really quite superb!!"

Leonard B Talburt
NIGHT SOLITUDE
Restlessly stirred by the evening breeze,
The vernal leaves plucked a tender nocturne.
Two minds coalesced in harmony.

The fragrant wisteria is most exquisite my dear,
Let us always live in this enchanted hour,
With the moonlight gracing your face.
Our hearts beat in time with the ebbing tide,
This moment is eternally sublime,
And we have found contentment enow.

Your once golden hair is graying now,
But cherished memories still cling on the vine.
You gave me your love, and I gave you mine.

The lingering fragrance from the bloom of the flowers,
And the magical light still flows from the stars,
This will stay with us my dear to the end of time,
And the wisteria will continue to grow.

Norma Appleton-House
HOLD ME
When I awoke in the night, afraid of the dark,
I did enjoy the time you spent, to walk me
in the park,
But frightened, small, if I could have made it so,
I wanted you to hold me, like you'd never let me go.

At times I seemed to travel along life's way,
With its highs and lows, the role, the play,
I stumbled and fell and didn't always know,
I needed someone to hold me, like they'd never let me go.

Many a night with children of my own,
I worried and hoped that I'd always shown,
That with the passage of time
as so quickly they did grow,
I wanted to hold them, like I'd never let them go.

But as with the seasons, and the regrowth
of spring appears,
They grew and followed the path of time,
never knowing the tears,
Into the world with my love, they will follow
life's flow,
And times wish someone will hold them,
like they'll never let them go.

And as always full circle to follow life's rhyme,
The years have passed for me and aged with time,
But still I will always wish it could be so,
To have someone hold me,
like they'll never let me go.

Sandra Kaye Richardson
LOVE IS A CHOICE

Dedicated to my Grandmother, Beryl Litke, who helped me make the best choice.

Love is a choice, a mistaken emotion.
Sometimes regretful, soon vows to be broken.
This choice bears a promise,
from one to another with no knowledge
of real love, be it heard from a sister or brother.
So make your choice wisely,
for your quality growth, because
Soon you will be leaving the one
you chose most.

Karen Meier
PEACE AT LAST
From an evil, scarlet sky,
Man's fate,
Thunders down,
Upon the dreams of His children.
Fear smothers a blackened earth,
As acid rains wash away,
Every last hope.
Quiet.
Calm.
Man's final breath.
And there is,

Peace at Last.

Jenny Galloway
WHERE THE SKY ENDS
The sky ends where space begins,
I know it is quite true.
The sky ends where space begins,
I learned that from you.
The sky ends where space begins,
I know that is a fact, quite true,
The sky ends where space begins,
And beauty meets the eye.
The sky ends where space begins,
And rainbows come to view.
The sky ends where space begins,
And the sky's beauty is really true.

Manos Balderrama
WISDOM'S CROWN

Dedicated To The Throne Of Christ.

To what does wisdom grasp in its discourse,
when it seeks to ennoble,
Seeing vast be its armament of intercourse,
and its truth insufferable,
Laying waste the confidence of fleshly wit,
and arouse ill disputes,
Which defend the nature of gains and writ,

that declares just reputes,
Yea, wisdom weighs matters to precise extent,
perceiving past and future,
As it sees the present in all its potent,
thro' disguises of rapture;

To what does wisdom grasp in its discourse,
when it seeks to ennoble,
Seeing vast be its armament of intercourse,
and its truth enoteable,
Not but the being which abides in the soul,
who interprets the relevance,
And enlightens the meek, or lays the toll,
by unveiling natural essence,
Wisdom be of only one—He who entwines many,
and is the query and answer,
Yea, wisdom liberates or does imprison any,
being in or out of Holy Rapture.

Manos Balderrama
MY REPERTOIRE

Dedicated To Mysterious Converse.

I have tread upon paths, man hast not known,
I have taught with wisdom, man hast not shown,
I have enlightened the mind of innocent entity,
I have imparadised the fleshly heart to eternity,
I have perveyed the spirit to everlastin rapt,
And have left an angry bitter soul quiescent,
I have dried the tears of the brokenhearted,
I restored liberty as when man first started,
I have revealed the shame of the witty pompous,
Whose inept claim 'twas, mine tears be weakness,
I have disquieted the complacency of the secular,
Who added, mine humor be not but random chatter;

I rocked the mental stability of literate men,
And shocked to sensibility, pious women's ken,
I have broken asunder the trust of the elite,
I have quieted the delusioned who wast deplete,
I have abased the infernal to his odium ways,
I have rekindled hope in the humble who prays,
I have subdued the mighty in his impious mode,
In variance discretion ast 'twas put 'pon my road,
I have given course to err'd unfeigned valor,
And ever confirm, My Lord Christ The Holy Alter,
And to whom, with disdain my derivation doth read,
Thy care vents my wrath, so thy tongue do recede.

Manos Balderrama
IN MY RELIGION

Dedicated To My Hearsts' Song.

Ah, but, thy pardon I do beseech, for, I confess,
I be not an scholar of prized collegiate impress,
Who spent days astuding leafs etched with wisdom,
Tho' I trow, 'tis wisdom seeped in dreams odium,
To fancy the witly essence with words of nobility,
Animating mental frames of pompous incredibility,
Nay, accuse me not of bitter notion for this my say,
For mine 'tis not the false effusion and its way,
Nay, for 'tis perpetual, nil but truth canst enhance,
This I essay thro' experience, factual and chance,
Yea, many days of mine be seeped with many tears,
To serve as witness of my empathy thro' out my years,
For prison and sorrow hast been my attuned portion,
That hast left me an bastard to man's domination,
But, be as it may, to my Lord be my secret grief,
And to man I shan't e'er be observed an liar or thief,
For my social strive hast been of reputable relay,
Never basking in the shadow of others' noble convey,
And tho' mine soul rides within an bitter storm,
Yet, I shall attain, my savior's celestial form,
For this I confirm in word and deed to all I meet,
I shall tread heaven's floor, my life e'er replete,
Be not be cozen, witless man, this be my religion,
Not wit nor fancy, nay, I be in total: Christian.

Cecilia Roseline Gregg
OCTOBER NIGHT-SONG—FOREBODING

To Mary, my beloved sister, who ever shares with me the timeless witchery of Autumn.

The brooding night descends,
chill breezes sigh—
A loon makes sad the dark
with haunting cry.

An astral pinpoint tops
a shroud-girt hill,
Is dimmed by scudding clouds:
the earth lies still.

A low moon glides with stealth,
moves with restraint;
A light wind sibilant,
breathes soft her plaint.

Bare branches menacing—
stark silhouettes,
Brush eerily the heavens,
and time forgets.

Gladys E Putnam
COMFORT IN MEMORIES

Sometimes when I feel lonely
And get a little blue.
I think about when I was young
And went to Sunday school.

The songs they sang have cheered me
At times upon my way.
I hear the old old echoes
Like it was yesterday.

One man I best remember,
Sang songs we didn't know
They had eleven verses?
Each one good thoughts did sow.

And after each, the chorus
Repeated loud and clear,
Became our song, our chorus,
To echo through the year.

I yet can hear its message.
It's true as long ago.
I love Jesus, he's my savior,
Jesus smiles, and he loves me too.

Bette Jean Crane
ANGEL

I stand alone, atop my hill . . .
and looking down, can see
the hopes and dreams and
plans of all the thousand
years. Now I am free to touch
a star . . . or race along with
all the blustering winds of
time, and sea and sky . . .
no ending . . . no beginning.

My soul smiles . . . the promises
are real . . . the music, like
a million tremulous tunes is
all around . . . all peace abounds . . .
for love alone is all . . . and
beauty—everywhere—tells me
that this is "Heaven."

Nicole Hill
MY PARENTS

Dedicated to my loving sister, Heather Dellinger, who pulled me through a lot of tough times. I love you a lot!

It started out with a fight and turned into something more,
They're father apart now than they ever were before.
She says go away, he says fine with me!
Oh God why do they fight is it all because of me?

Why do they say those heartbreaking things to each other?
Why do they take it out on me
my sister and my brother?
One day in the car when my dad was screaming
And yelling he said, "Nicole, stop daydreaming!"

Constance Green
SUMMONING OF DEATH

Alas, night like an ebony shroud did fall
With such decisiveness did Death deem
And to its victim did it call
To summon me to vanish from life, and from my life redeem
I sought refuge in the shadows of the night
Redoubtable feelings arose within my soul
My body remained in darkness, hidden from light
And Death's horrid voice resumed its role

Its voice like a saber, piercing my heart
A manacle upon my soul
Its utters shred my mind apart
It burns like an everlasting coal

I had a desire to drift and flee
I wish to forget my fate
That thought was inevitable for me
For alas, it was too late

My heart and soul can no longer remain hidden
My mind shall never know peace
My request to live was forbidden
And Death's summoning shall never cease

Jeri King
STILLNESS IN LIFE

Have you ever really felt that Time Stood Still,
had tears of pain and your heart so ill.
Have you ever wished reality was O-but a dream,
so when you awoke you would be by a gentle stream.
Feelings of loneliness surround you each day,
and no matter what—they won't go away.
Why me Lord, what have I done, why you Jesus, on the cross you hung.
I may never know why so many hurts had to come,
but I want to thank you Jesus—that it is me you do love.
As I reach out to You and I silently pray,
please hold my hand and lead me in your step each day.
Heal me Lord with your spirit from life's unfair pain,
like the sun parting dark clouds after a stormy rain.

Marie McHugh
FLIGHT 101—MY NUMBER ONE SON

I dedicate this poem to my dear Number One son, Alan.

This is his first flight for Number One Son
Oh my, what have I done?
Oh well, we'll have fun—
Me and my number one son.

In the absence of his dad
He was a fine little lad
He is a big fellow now by anyone's measure
And has given me my share of pleasure.

In this whole wide world
There is just no other—
For this mother than
My Number One Son.

As we soar through the skies
And reflect on our lives—
Suddenly we are one
Me and my Number One Son!

Oh, oh, trouble ahead!
We're in a dark cloud
What was that noise?

My, but it was so loud!

The pilot assured us nothing was wrong
So we continued our journey
Our hearts full of song.

So thank you Flight 101
In behalf of—
Me and my Number One Son.

Matt McBurnett
FIRST LOVE
From the early years of life,
I have suffered much strife.
Remembering things I never did,
Still I wish I was a kid.
Teenage girls are a curse,
Long-legged women are much worse.
Once they find how much you care,
Very quickly they will scare.
Even faster they will leave,
So you sit alone and grieve.
Until the day that they get dumped,
Coming knocking you'll be stumped.
Know not just what to do,
Simply Saying, "I hate you."

Guy Tipa
A BRAND-NEW WORLD
To my loving wife Antoinette Tipa, and daughter, Danielle Tipa.

The brand-new world that we create,
We must get rid of all the hate.
We'll have to try,
As time goes by
We must form as one in unity,
So we can live in harmony
'Cause if we defeat these times of trouble,
We all can share a hug, and cuddle
The nineteen-nineties must be a year,
That we won't have to shed another tear.

Jennette H Smith
MESSAGE TO MY HEART
It is marvelous in mine eyes
When I look into the skies,
See the stars and moon above,
Listen while they speak of love;
Floating clouds that gently part,
Whispering, whispering to my heart.

Then I see another scene,
Swaying trees in forest green,
Little birds that dart about,
Tender blades of grass poke out,
Pretty flowers bright with color
Bearing witness of another.

Yes, 'tis marvelous in mine eyes
When I look beyond the skies,
See by faith our Father there,
Then I know He's everywhere
And through these things I feel and see
He thus reveals Himself to me.

Lena Sleet
TYPING PSALM
He is my teacher. I shall not pass
He maketh me knuckle down and study
He leadeth me to the classroom
He restoreth my memory

He leadeth me into silence, for my classmates sake
Yeah, though I continue typing, I fear my teacher
For he is above me, my fingers sorely bother me
He preparest a test before me in the presence of my classmates. He compelleth me to remember, my knowledge runneth out.

Surely keys and words shall follow me, all my school days,
For I shall dwell in the typing class forever

Juli Miller
THE HOUSE
The house,
Empty,
Withering away,
Once a place of beauty,
Now an unused shell,
Standing erect,
Trying to take in
What time is left.
As an old man and lady
Each with their own cane
Think how they are:
EMPTY,
Withering away,
Once a person of beauty,
Now a lost soul,
Standing erect,
TRYING TO TAKE IN
WHAT TIME IS LEFT
Sadly and slowly
Turn and walk away

Philip J Conlon Jr
LOOKING BACK
Would that I could wind the clock, to a time and place that's long forgot.

Where you and I were free to dream, where love and life was never schemes.

Where health and youth was all we had, to keep us close and make us glad.

But time cannot be turned away, to come again another day.

If what we have is now and here, then let us show how much we care.

Philip J Conlon Jr
OH! TIME YOU THIEF
Oh! time you thief, you stole my youth,
I wasted thee, but you were truth.

I ran my race with speed and prize,
but you oh thief said nothing wise.

You let me go my merry way,
and watched me spend my younger day.

You kept your truth till youth was spent,
and now it seems I'm old and bent.

But if I could my time renew,
I'd wind that clock, and steal from you.

Mary K (Shirrell) Husk
YET ANOTHER TIME
I have finally come to realize
This life is not for me.
At one time, I was so sure of everything.
Love and compassion were always a part of me,
my life,
my very being.
But now things are not the same.
There is no longer,
the need and want,
for me.
All my loves have found a life of another world in which to live.
This is a world I must never enter.
It is a world of memories, and
and this world does not allow me
to share the time I need to remember
the love and compassion, of yet another time.

Emeline Pennock Morris
AUTUMN SPLENDOR
Autumn is just a touch of Eden that God puts in our view,
as Summer's sunny world becomes all washed up, fresh and new.
When Summer's endless light flees on silent wings, there's still enough
of sky clear enough and blue,
to let her golden rays shine through.
Another chance to feel the sun,
as Nature waves her color gun.
We can learn from flower and leaf,
and every drop of color they hold,
as subtly they change from vivid green to precious living gold.
Fall days flame forth dressed in leaves of varied reddish hue.
But, her cherished beams of light now shine on cooler dew.
See an old turtle basking in the Sun,
atop a fallen log as autumn is begun.
Observe a red-tailed Hawk tracing giant circles overhead,
then, now, take for granted that brilliant Summer's dead.
Though, the beauty of the seasons change in scope,
they are only rearranged as a moving kaleidoscope.
Now, one last glimpse of Autumn growing old,
when painted parchment leaves scatter on the wind, like Midas Gold.
Note, sloping hills beneath a copper sky,
and wonder if amid this bit of Heaven, can such beauty really die!
Why not give thanks for this lovely Fall,
and kneel under her great canopy of color, to praise the Great Master who has made it all?
Four Seasons have much loveliness to sell, such beautiful and splendid things,
all ushered in on very different wings.
Truly, each one is a portion of Paradise, that all should savor in delight,
while we, now, await a whole new picture wafted in on wings of white.
(winter)

Gary Meyer
A POEM FOR SEVILLE
Hundreds come into sight
Not to loot, not to fight
They only come out at night
The Orangemen, Orangemen

Like bats they come in search of trash
To clean the streets in just a flash
But walk too close and they might splash
The Orangemen, Orangemen

In costume bright like prankster's day-glo
To all extremities they will go
For they've claimed Seville's trash as foe
The Orangemen, Orangemen

Not a cup or butt will they miss
The streets so clean you could kiss
Returning all to godliness
The Orangemen, Orangemen

Just as quickly they disappear
To yet another hemisphere
But they'll return have no fear
The Orangemen, Orangemen

For tomorrow dawns another day
People's litter thrown in the way
And for their savior's return they will pray
The Orangemen, Orangemen

Martin Musick
dexterity
if i could place wind
or sun on
paper

instead of
wornout wormeaten
words

i could
make a poem
that fits you.

Anne McEniry
MY GRANDFATHER
A tribute to my Grandfather, the late Dennis Day, by his granddaughter Anne.

He had a voice so bright and strong
"Danny Boy" was his favorite song.

He got sick, we were well.
He could walk but then he fell.

It was hard to see him there.
All he could do was sit and stare.

"I love you Grandpa" was all I could say.
But as he heard this he passed away.

Carolyn Farmer
A FRIEND
Dedicated to my dear friend Cathy—for standing beside me all these years.

A friend is like a rose,
Lovely soft and red.
To know just how you feel,
Without it being said.

A friend is like a rose,
Pretty, bright and yellow.
Being there when days are sad,
And when my days are mellow.

A friend is like a rose,
Soft and fully white.
Knowing they can help,
By being just in sight.

A friend is like a rose,
Beautiful and blue.
Always loving with their heart—
A friend . . . is you!

Emily Watson
YOU COME TO ME
To my long ago love.

You ride on all the shooting stars
across the nighttime sky.
You come to me on moonbeams
that lightens up the night.
You come on all the sun rays
that glitter in the day.
You come to me in morning light
that brightens up the day.
You come on whispering winds
that blow across the sea.
You come to me on ocean wave
that sweeps the sand beneath my feet.
You slide down all the rainbows
but I never find the end.
You come to me in all my dreams
the dreams that have no end.

Nancy L Eisenbraun
TIME OUT

To Mike Ramirez, A special friend, My INSPIRATION.

For that wonderful Referee
That shares the love inside of me

As I run from base to base
I have no fear of being safe

When I'm sliding toward home plate
That's when I notice his honest face

Inning after Inning, I have no doubt
For he will never strike me out

We'll never set out to keep score
Because our love means so much more.

Danny M Davis
LOVE TO LINDA

To Linda R. Davis, my loving wife.

Unlike the long wintery days
Full of coldness, snow, and haze
Warmth and brightness my love will give
Throughout the days we live

Unlike the many Leafless Trees
My Love will fill your needs
As we walk in the Autumn Mist
With each warm Tender Kiss

Just like the growth of Spring Flowers
Our Love will increase throughout the hours
As we grow Closer each day
Living together in Love and Play

Just like the skies of Summer bright
Our Love will reach new heights
For it will soar to unlimited space
As today, each other we embrace

So, as Seasons go by
My Feelings I cannot hide
For True, Warm, and Tender
Always will be, my Love to Linda

Florence L Kann
THE LIGHT

Dedicated to my grandsons, Christopher and Nicholas.

As the lamp light shines tall and bright.
It welcomes the woman into its light.

There she stood! with babe in arm.
While the other child clings to her palm.

Then raising her head unto the light.
The cry of the mother rang out! in the night.
"O, God why can't we make them feel our plight."

Exhausted, she leaned against the post.
Her small child's eyes looked up in hope.
Soon little one we will find shelter the mother sighed.
Soon we will find a place to hide.

With head bent low the mother did weep.
Her teardrops falling upon the snow.
As with hope that has no place to go.

So they turned into the night.
Into the blackness out of sight.
These tragic figures with their plight.
May they once again walk! into
THE LIGHT.

Christine Edwards
THANKSGIVING

Thanksgiving, A day when the natives all gathered;
With peace, love, and kindness; and nothing else mattered.

They cooked for the whiteman, and made him popped corn;
And on that first day a friendship was born.

A friendship that left in the blink of an eye;
A friendship that caused peaceful lifestyles to die.

A friendship that killed all the redman's dreams;
A friendship that nurtured the whiteman's schemes.

A friendship that killed a nation of peace;
Cost many men's pride and made many deceased.

They came bearing tools to plow the fresh earth;
They left bearing weapons and laughing with mirth.

They claim they were right, we know they were wrong;
They were the weakened, and we were the strong.

They came bearing weapons, and us only might;
And I'd say we gave 'em one hell of a fight.

Thanksgiving means nothing but sorrow and pain;
And the beginning of the whiteman's reign!

Mary Grace Labertew Davidson
WHAT WILL I DO?

What will I do when my dad is gone?
Who will be there for me to call upon
For strength, wisdom and support.

Had we but realized in our youth
The gigantic weight of dependency
Upon the shoulders of our fathers;
We would have loved and honored
Them more, and lashed out with
Tongues dipped with venom less oft.

Look now upon your father's face.
See into his eyes and know the depth
Of his wisdom, strength and honor.
Trace each line with a forefinger
Of loving tenderness, and feel the
Depth of concern and weighted cares.

Lock within your mind's eye
That lined and aged face and
Print indelibly, it upon your memory.
For someday, in your great need
To feel its comfort and warmth;
You will look up only to
Find it gone from you forever.

D A Tull
WONDER

I always walk in wonder
For what God, has done for me.
He gave me His Son Jesus,
To love me tenderly.
So Jesus took upon Him,
All my earthly sins.
He made me an heir of heaven
That I may reign with Him.
I always walk in wonder
For it puzzles me
What our Father saw through Jesus;
Just to get to me!

Joanne Moorehouse
WHAT DID I DO WRONG?

One day you came into my life and turned it upside down.
You asked me to love you,
and i did . . .
You asked me to open myself up,
and i did . . .
You asked me to change my ways,
and i did . . .
You asked me to trust you,
and i did . . .
You asked me to be patient with you,
and i did . . .
You asked me to help you be strong,
and i did . . .

Then one day, you just left . . . no warning or explanations.
You know i am only human and it hurts since you are gone.

WHAT DID I DO WRONG?

Marianne Baker
OCEAN DEPTHS

Life-sea almost mirage,
Though constant as time,
Chameleon-like you evade all prediction.

Amazing!

A rumble, then gentle lapping
Teasing our feet,
You run away from questioning eyes,
Laughing!

A roaring wind, a spray
Caressing our faces.
But we stand closer, wrapped in each other,

Dreaming.

Here at peace with each other,
In contemplation
We ponder what secrets you could reveal,

Hoping.

Leticia Escamilla
CITY STREET LIGHTS

City street lights
glowing
stopping
blinking
leading me thru the
cold wet doom of a
lifeless wretched child
girl
running to fortune
caught in the net-like
cocoons of the filthy
velvet
night world.

Carol Lynn Musser
MOVE A LITTLE CLOSER

Make your moves a little closer to me.
You wish we knew, what there is to see?
As I was wanting you to come strolling in
You were walking out, leaving me in this sin.

When you came walking in tonight
You took my child out of sight.
I never saw any reason to die,
Or to go on living with this stupid lie.

Were you really scared of getting hurt?
Just because of this one night, I decide to flirt.
Or was it that I was never right in your sight

Except, on these awful nights when we would fight.

If time was all you needed, all you had to do was say, I had no clue.
I wanted to give you everything under the sun, I wish you would see.
I'd be there, through all of the pain that would be suffocating you.
All of these problems you would have was never caused by me.

Danielle Ridler
I NEED A HUG

There is a story that needs to be told,
About children all over the world.
This story may come as a shock to some,
But don't kid yourself, don't be dumb.
These children are as sweet as a dove,
But right now they're in need of some love.
As innocent as they may be,
They have got the AIDS disease.
On their face is all their grief,
And in their hearts they pray for a sign of relief.
These sweet children will surely die,
Can't you hear them plead and cry?
So stop the spread of this terrible disease,
So try your best—try hard, please . . .
For these children and many more,
No future for them is in store.
"I need a hug" they all seem to say,
So wake up to reality, wake up today!!

Edna F Mottner
RETIREMENT

Retirement! oh happy day
a time to think
a time to play
a time to reflect
on yesterday

a time to do
pleasurable things
a time to lounge
like queens and kings

and now-being experienced
learn-ed and wise
it's a time to stand
tall and proud
and evangelize

but lo, how quickly
we discern
how very much
we have yet to learn

Lesli Tomlin-Giomi
RIDDLE AND RHYME

People
Are so like
Poems
They long to reveal their
Innermost feelings
Yet continue to hide
behind an intricate mask
of Riddle and
Rhyme.

Eric W Luttropp
PENSIVE, IN THE PLUSH OF NIGHT

To lovely ladies of single days, and the "Peg" of my heart in marriage.

I looked up into the starry sky,
across the firmament,
and saw passing there
a spaced caravan of long departed
romances,

advancing steadily
and with seeming disregard for
my self.

Where have you been,
you lovelies of the more romantic
years?
Do your voices still lilt with songs
which we, in turn, once did share?
Are your eyes yet eager for a New
Year's greenery?
Do your lips, your kisses, retain a
touch of youth?

Are any eyes deep with sadness?
If so, to whom do they cry their
sorrow?

Along the way—have your hearts
known
the grace of gentle love?
Have they?
True is my desire that they have—
for mine has.

Oh, yes. Mine has.

Angela Miller
THE FAT CAT
I know a cat
Who's really fat
He climbed a tree
And broke his knee
He limped to the gate
To wait for his date
She came right along
And came singing a song
And when she stopped singing
My ears, they kept ringing
We went out for lunch
And then we had punch

Una E Fookes
DO NOT RUN AWAY

To Laurel, Karen, Darren and Trent, my children, for your belief in me, your love, encouragement and friendship.

Do not run away,
Or turn aside.
Hide not in the darkness
Do not be afraid . . .
To face
What life may hold.

Take up its challenges . . .
Embrace it
Feel its touch
Touch its feelings
Treasure its moments
Sing its praises
Laugh with its joys
Cry with its tears
Hold it precious
Live it with thanks
Live it with meaning
This life!

Stella Rose Poe
AN ODE TO OUR OLD HOME
April 13, 1977, our old home was
burned to the ground,
Providing fun and entertainment for
the people of the town.

Four girls stood, with tears in their
eyes,
silently saying their last goodbys.

Painful minutes ticked away,
the sound of school bells throughout
the day.
Smoke and flames shooting high,
firemen rushing by.
Still the house would not give in,
compelling memories couldn't let the
flames win.
A little shaky, but still stately and
tall,
the crackling red house would not
fall.

But in the end, as we looked at the
devouring flames,
the house seemed to be calling our
names.
We felt the burning love,
from within and above.
Instilling in us a promise of a better
life,
free of anxieties, sadness and strife.

Gary J Allen
NIGHTLY SHADOWS
Nightly shadows go dancing
Along my bedroom wall,
Then up onto the ceiling
And out into the hall.

The shadows remind me of fairies
Dancing from here to there;
With wings and pointed elf-caps
They go dancing in the air.

They dance into the garden
And over the garden wall,
Then out into the meadow
And over the leaves of fall.

They dance away to Fairyland
Where fairies are busy at play,
'Till they vanish with coming of
daylight . . .
To return at the dusk of next day!

Tom Fisher
LESSONS OF LIFE

This poem is affectionately dedicated to Becca Newcomb, a woman who, to me, represents the greatest of all wisdom.

You, the teacher,
at times, preacher,
Have a glint of wisdom in your eyes.

Take education;
mold it, shape it.
Into beautiful art.

I, the pupil; eager to learn
Lessons of Life.
Discovering not only knowledge of
mind,
But depth of emotion.

Your words are, to me, a graceful
dancer;
a flame of knowledge
Ever-burning.

Ignorance is the blanket of night
through which the fires of your
mind shine,
helping me to see the light of truth.

More than a teacher, a preacher
you teach, revealing your soul
(and you care)
More than a teacher, more than a
preacher . . . you are a friend.

Roy W Bucci
GOLDIE

To Karen; I love you now as I have before and pledge my love for eternity.

There is beauty to see in a meadow or
a brook,
But none quite so beautiful as the
way you look.
Without care, birds soar and sing
while animals play,
With time on my hands, I grieve your
loss, each passing day.
I pray Dear Lord may I touch her and
exclaim words of love I need to say.
I try to reach, but still she is too far
away.
She sits with her children and
through dedication she will teach.
I try to join her, but her being I just
cannot reach.
The sun shines and glistens from
above.
Our Lord Jesus appears as a splendid
white dove.
His words—My son it is time, Father
wishes from above.
I ask for a moment more to tell her of
my love.
My Savior reaches out and gestures
to me.
Your life is now over, it is time—
now come to thee.
As we pass by the animals, birds,
meadow and brook,
I slowly turn for one last look.
My love, your beauty highlights the
sun,
For now, my lonely actions cannot be
undone.

Worthetta Hunter
A MOTHER'S DAY WISH
"A TRIP TO HEAVEN"

In memory of Velma Sloan, still loved and missed by Children + Grandchildren.

I'd like to spend the day with you no
matter where you are
It wouldn't make a difference I'd
travel near or far

I'd bring purple violets for you to
smell and touch
And a box of chocolate candy you
always liked so much

I'd have pictures of the "grand kids"
to show you how they grew
And tell you about the others, the
ones you never knew

We wouldn't talk of pain or grief or
anything that's sad
We'd only talk of pleasant things and
happy times we had

We'd talk about the good old days
when I was just a kid
And I hope that you won't scold me
for foolish things I did

We'd chat about the loved ones you
had to leave behind
And if I shed a tear or two I hope that
you won't mind

I'd reach above and pluck a rainbow
from the air
Tie it in a pretty bow and place it in
your hair

I'd take you to a baseball game where
only angels play
Then we'd take an evening stroll
along the Milky Way

And when the day was over in your
Heavenly Home above
I'd give you hugs and kisses and
most of all my love

Andrea Kay Parasolick
ONE HEART

This poem is dedicated to my loving parents, Andy and Jeanne Germock.

I love walking through autumn
woodlands
To listen to crisp leaves crinkle under
my feet,
I love strolling along coastal shores
To find in the wet sands a seashell to
keep,
I love to see the circus when it comes
to town
To have the child in me come alive
and weep,
I love picnics in parks and holiday
festives
To share the joys of living which
make my heart leap,
There are many loves in the world to
excite me
But the greatest treasure anyone
could ever reap,
Is to be the recipient of another's love
One faithful, caring love running
deep,
Experiencing the magic that one heart
can give
The contentment that love brings
cannot be beat.

Anna M Barnes
I WISH

Dedicated to my granddaughters: Shawna, Ashley, Lindsey, and all grandchildren everywhere.

I wish I had a feather, a soft white
tiny fluff
And then I'd wish I had one more to
tickle with and stuff
Then I think I'd wish for another
three or four
I'd lay them on my bed and wish I
had some more

Pretty soon my room would fill up to
the very top
then I suppose that maybe I would
wish them not to stop
I'd run and play all day long in
feathers soft and light
Then fall asleep exhausted when day
turned into night

When morning came and I'd awake
with feathers everywhere
I'd run and jump into them and stick
some in my hair
Feathers floating all around for many
many miles
heaps and heaps of downy puffs in
big gigantic piles

Softly, gently, floating over trees and
hills below
Clouds of fluffy feathers, soft—and
white as snow
Oh, I wish I had a feather, a soft
white tiny fluff
and then I'd wish I had one more . . . .

Jessie L Johnson
REMEMBERING

To: Alton.

I stand by troubled waters, counting
the sands of time.
Just looking at the footprints, that
could be yours and mine.

But then comes stormy weather, and
washes them out to sea.
Just leaving me with memories of
days that used to be.

I'll walk by rippling water, listening
at the snowbird sing.
When I see the little flowers, I'll
know it's coming spring.

Then I'll walk by rushing waters, but
this time I'll walk alone.
Watching the beautiful robins as they

build themselves a home.

I'll remember you forever, as sure as the eagle flies.
As the roaring of the waters seems to be saying good-bye.

Andrius Mironas
FREEDOM

To my native Lithuania
Fighting hard for her Freedom
From Soviet yoke.

Freedom! Full of life is this word:
You do what you wish, only mind is your high.
Freedom! It knows only "for" or "against,"
Without any neutrality, without any "why."

Freedom! Some people tied it with chains,
With duties, rules or whatever you call.
Freedom! Only former slave comprehends it!
Freedom for nations—alas, not for all.

Freedom! Who is stronger enslaves the weaker
And Freedom forever is lost.
Freedom! Sometimes it's only a crime
If nobody helps to regain it—so do most!

Ultimate sin is to help the offender.
Freedom always is wanted, Freedom is dream!
Who never before was free on this Earth
Will know that Freedom is goal supreme!

Sarah Squires
COLOR ME SILVER

I dedicate this poem to anyone who is as lonely as I am . . . .

Color me silver with a rusted sword.
Paint my memories of all the times before.
Make the sky turn to lightning
And strike me in the heart,
For I have sinned . . .
And, I'm falling apart.

Color me silver like a faded bruise,
For all the times when just a touch
Could abuse.
Color me silver like an echo in the wind
Where my evil spirit is trying to get in.

Color me silver with the last star in the sky.
For right now I am going to die.
Color my grave
Color my death
Just color my last breath . . .
For I am gone
And my pain is sober . . .
Color me silver
Because now it is all over!

Cynthia D Parker
LIFE IS HARD

This is dedicated to
CATHERINE WOOD PARKER,
Whose love and guidance inspired this poem.

Life is hard and then you die.
But have you ever wondered why?
Why you feel so empty inside,
As though a part of you has died?
Why your life now seems so stale,
As though you're in a deep, dark well?
The world—it seems to move so fast,
And you feel that it's rushing past.
There is so much you want to do
But you feel your dreams will never come true.
Just close your eyes and rest your mind.
Drift along to another time.
Be optimistic and you will see
Things aren't as bad as they seem to be.
Have faith that the Lord will care for you.
If you believe, it's sure to come true.
No matter how bad, it always works out,
And then you wonder what you worried about.
So on those days when you start to feel blue,
Just remember this—Jesus loves you!

Joy J Robedee
BEYOND

To Mom, Ruth P. Satterthwaite, my greatest inspiration.

Often I wonder about heaven
How peaceful and serene above,
Where all those who've departed
Are waiting with all their love.

There are no broken hearts
Nor hurts that life has dealt,
No freezing cold or loss of love
My life has endured and felt.

Beyond is heaven's salvation
Thy family all whole again,
Just the way it used to be
I just don't know the when.

Kari Ann Gitzke
HANDPRINTS

This poem is dedicated to my parents for all the love and devotion that they have given me. Also to my sister and my daughter. I love you all.

Handprints in the sun,
Some day we will become one.
Running free like the wind,
Nothing will stand in our way.

Handprints in the sand,
Helping us to understand,
What must become of us today,
And how to change our lives.

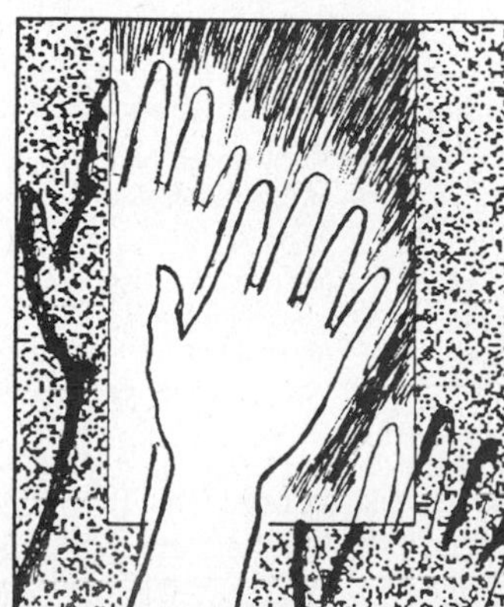

Handprints in the rain,
No one knows,
Just what tomorrow will contain.
Handprints in the sun,
Someday soon, we will become one.
Running free like the wind,
Trying hard to understand,
Just what tomorrow will contain.

Dan White
TIME IS ONLY AN ILLUSION

To my mother Darlene, who helped shape me into what I am today, and what I will be tomorrow.

Time is only an illusion,
it is very often said.
Nothing but a misconception,
in everybody's head.

But how could anybody,
with a mother who's so divine,
believe in the theory of illusion,
when she keeps getting better
with time!

For every year she's lovelier,
much wiser and more mature,
and even when she's far away,
in my heart it seems she's near.

So I'd like to say "Happy Birthday,"
to my mother who is so dear.
Who cares if time's an illusion,
when you keep getting better
each year!

Frances R Scholze
THE FISHERMAN

This poem is dedicated to my ever-loving husband, Erv.

Look, out there on the frozen lake
A figure still and straight
Interest on what he still may take
As he watches the string that holds his bait.

He's been there all day long
Enduring wind and cold
Trying so hard to be strong
As twilight comes he still is bold.

The catch has been small
But still he waits
And hopes that fish will hear the call
That comes from his silent baits.

Back home the family is patient
Awaiting quietly his return
Knowing his energy will have been spent
And of his success to quickly learn.

For then will be the saying in the book
Sometime ago written by a man
Daddy catches them by the hook
But mama fries them in the pan.

Kathy Wilkinson
TWICE BLESSED

To Ben and Shane, my two blessings.

Twice blessed I've been most of my life.
Daughter, mother, and once a wife.

When good things come in groups of two
Means someone's watching over you.

With the help of my mother, my first man gave me life.
My second man asked me to be his wife.

I never knew my dad you see.
But God had a secret in store for me.

And then twice blessed was I once more.
My original two men had now become four.

The old one who once had given me life.
And the young one who had asked me to be his wife.

Had now been replaced by two younger ones.
Who make me proud to call them sons.

In November of 1987.
My earthly father was sent from heaven.

Two sons, a husband and even a dad.
The best of both worlds was what I had.

Of course my mother deserves some credit.
For without her I'd have to forget it.

To just be loved was all I'd asked.
And now I'd totally completed the task.

Mother, father, husband, sons.
I guess I'm one of the lucky ones.

My life's not over; it's only begun.
Being a grandmother is half the fun.

Perhaps twice blessed again I'll be.
When my kids have kids, I'll wait and see.

Dorietta Corrigan
DADDY'S LITTLE GIRL

To the dad who left me and to my grandpa who is my dad. May I always be your little girl in my heart. Love Always, your little baby Dory.

I'm almost all grown up now
and daddy has been gone a long time.
Though I was little when he died
I know he is still a part of me.
He is still with me
teaching me right from wrong.
Though I don't always listen
I know one thing for sure:
No matter where I go
no matter what I do
I will always be—
Daddy's little girl.

Ellis M Bernard
BE A BLESSING

I'd like to help someone who is having trials
Offer words of encouragement to walk that extra mile.
I'd like to offer comfort, to dry a falling tear
So my life would be a blessing while I'm living here.

Many need our smiles as we go our way
Our kindness we may show, and kind words we may say
To help someone who's down and out, feeling deep despair
To help lift the weary burden, my love with others share.

Life is too uncertain to give someone a frown
Let's give others our smiles, lift those who have fallen down
Help lift someone's burden, show love to all we see
Then the life we live will truly a blessing be.

Smiles are like blessings, our time will be well spent
They're worth a million dollars but don't cost a cent
Try some kind deed to do, some kind words to say
They cost us very little but in the end they pay.

Kimberly D McClure
ETERNITY
The time I spend with you . . . I feel there is no end.
The laughter, the tears, the love we share,
in you I have found my dearest friend.

If ever a time came that we should depart,
I promise you my love—
you will always own my heart.

You are the sparkle in my eyes,
the little voice in my head,
you are the light in my darkness . . .
It is you I will wed.

I will share my life with you—
my dreams, my hopes, my fears . . .
and you will be there for me,
in all aspects for eternity.

I cherish the love we have.
I cherish the life we'll build.
I cherish the dream you've made come true,
These feelings are everlasting . . .
This love is ever new, my heart surrounds you.

Queen E Slyke
THE STRONG, BUT HUMBLE LADY
I never worked side by side with her
nor carried on a conversation
but each time she stands before an audience
all I see is a strong, but humble lady.

I hear and read about many of her activities
in her fight for justice and equality
the rainbow people sometime
understands and sometime don't
all I hear is a strong, but humble lady.

She speaks softly, seldom with anger
with care and concerns of issues
and of the needy
using her God given talents to do all she can
to help mankind, this strong, but humble lady.

I pray when her earthly life is over
and she had done all that she could
the heavenly gates will open widely
welcoming this strong, but humble lady.

Another chapter is about to close
and another one is about to begin
my lasting impression of Mrs. L. McKay
will be that of a strong, but humble lady.

Justine Gnatowski
WHY HELP?

Dedicated to my loving mother Ruth, and my wonderful brother Scott.

Day by Day
night by night
sad, lonely, angry, uptight
Somehow I just can't understand
trouble comes from my helping hand

I lay and think or sit and wonder
while listening to the sound of thunder
Where did I go wrong?
Or was I the fool all along?

I guess it just doesn't pay
to lend a hand or give advice
It is best to stay far away
not care and be cold like ice?

If this is true
next time I'll know what to do and why
do not feel blue
and let the desire to help go by.

Brigitte Cerullo
AUTUMN BREEZE

In dedication to my sons Mickey and Marco and my loving husband, Mike.

In autumn all the leaves fall off.
Before they touch the ground.
They ask the wind to lift them off.
The branches one by one.
They dance till they can dance no more.
And fall onto the ground.
That's where they rest all winter long.
And wait for spring to come.

Bruce L Bortle
THROUGH ETHEREAL GASES

In loving memory of my father, my best friend, James L. Bortle.

Through ethereal gases and vaporized steam
God was created and made supreme
His omnipresence and omniscience
we did solemnly dread
Rekindled awesome fear even within the dead.

His wrath was so brutal from far up above
Not for our understanding for God was love
But now he has changed to assuage so much doubt
His mercy and goodness are on sale all throughout.

His lost prestige is slowly on the climb
For after all even God must keep up with the times.

Rachel D'Annucci
OH, AMERICA

Much love and appreciation to Mom, Dad and my family.

The birds are singing a solemn tune;
the flowers bare a scent that's gloom.
The grass has lost its color green;
and oh, what my eyes have seen.
Children on the corner selling drugs;
they look for money, no longer bugs.
Mr. President preaches with closed ears;
he looks blindly at the people's tears.
Homes on a bench or in a hall,
while the rich are having a ball,
the poor are starving and sleeping outside;
but oh, America's laws, we must abide.

Earl Iseman Sullivan
RETREAT
As I walked beside a lake,
I saw a weathered, wooden cross
Reflected in the deep, still water
By the dawn's first rose-tinged rays.

I lingered while the sunlight spread
Through purpled sky; reached shadowed trees;
Slipped through cathedral walls of green;
Filled mounded pews of snow-white sand.
I heard no choir at the leafy altar,
Only songs of birds forever free.
There was no preacher in this temple,
Just the voice of the wind.

Michael Bailey
LADY OF ICE
I've come many miles to meet you.
But you greeted me with kisses of warmth and cold.
I've touched your virgin white skin that glistened.
But when I called to you, you never listened.
I now truly feel your distance for lady of ice I will never forget you. And her name is Antarctica.

Julie Ann Kittle
MEMORIES OF YOU
Trapped in time
Are memories of you
Just a crime
But what could we do

All we broke
Was the laws of love
All we spoke
Came from heaven above

It was meant to be
Forever in time
Just you and me
Guilty of crime.

Robin Skillings
ENCHANTED FOREST
In a hidden glade
where fairies peek
from under blade
a princess sat
forlorn and lost
She'd strayed away
not knowing the cost
when upon her came
a dreadful dragon
who asked, "Ith thith the way
to the Cathle Thaggon?"
Well the princess laughed
at this lisping lizard
who roasted the girl
and ate her gizzard.

Madge Pfleger
SUMMER SEQUEL
Succulent sights, swollen scents and
The suddenness of showers
Mark the months of summer, as

Ripened air of the heated season
Is punctuated with the muffled
Thud of soured dropping fruit.

Widening pond rings are the
Only trace of green jumpers
Catching dragonflies. Nearby,

Ivy, with its love for the brick,
Becomes obsessive with the
Hugging, warm moistened air.

You can smell coming rain as a
Dust cloud over fresh footprints
Trails a passerby.

Summer, the capstone of spring,
Sullen with the weight of heat,
Is a narrow time-wall between the cold.

Evan Johnson
LEEWARD
Her gaze drew a line
Down the beach and beyond
Trying hard to pierce the fog
Sea gulls screamed
As if the ocean could hear
Another raging mantra
From driftwood sticks
Of low key love
Came flaming marshmallows
That would always
But a savior of orphaned snakes and shells
Needed saving of her own

Sand too coarse for my callow toes
Took her down
Through mist and foam
Hair and skin and eyes
Born of an ocean storm
Set sail set sail

Anne M Sellers
WINTER TO SPRING
Beneath the flakes of new fallen snow,
Rest the bulbs and buds of spring about to grow.
Below the top soil so rich and dark
They wait for their time so they might embark,
On the path to reach for the sky
To be there for the butterflies,
Bees, birds, squirrels and ants.
They use their nectar, leaves and branch,
To build their homes for spring to greet
The fluttering and scampering of wings and feet.
Winter to Spring,
Summer to Fall,
Two of the seasons,
Though I love them all.

Emil J Binda
HOME
Home is not a building, of mortar brick and stone.
It's not a palace or mansion, that you may own.
Can be a simple dwelling, where you reside.
With family and friends, and rest with pride.
There's much in life, to make a home complete.
Where dreams start with life, that's sweet.
Sincerity we need, in a home where love abides.
It's gratitude we neglect, to discipline our pride.
At home you are the judge, of time and action.
Be not forgetful, remember family satisfaction.
Soft expressions are appreciated, its kindness endures.
Good thoughts are better, this attitude lures.
Money can be a servant, and yet a troubled master.
Tolerance and love at home, makes interest grow faster.
The freedom you find home, is security you need.
That is magic enough, for you to succeed.

Emil J Binda
THERE'S ALWAYS TIME
We never remember to save time,
it's never acquired, has no end.
Should always fill it with life,
never returns, to repeat or spend.

Spend it wisely, always plan ahead,
don't waste so much time in a day.
Do your finest work, with time you need,
don't fight it, just make it pay.

Curiosity helps, to find your needs,
it's a choice you dare to make.
We live to learn, and never learn to live,
this part of life is hard to take.

Results justify the use of time,
you know these facts are true.
With a little effort, in your behalf,
there's always time in store for you.

Anita B Olsen

PITY NOT THE ROSE

The sadness of a rose is in
its passing
From scent-imbued perfection
into dust,
But, inanimate flower,
it is not the facing
The struggles of the soul
we mortals must.

Tom Carney

HER, I MET

Know this, mortal
travel I a great portal
so I remember
the spectacular stir
it do towards me;
did it, I hope make thee
feel as nice. I'll never forget
a moment at which we met.

Ashley Dawn Martinez

Ashley Dawn Martinez

CHRISTMAS ANTICIPATION

Christmas anticipation
Dreams of enjoyment fill children's heads
As they lay asleep in their beds.
They know what will happen tonight,
The milk and cookies are under the light.
For Santa will come soon,
Flying beneath the silver moon.
Look for Santa's sleigh tonight
And listen to his famous saying;
"Merry Christmas to all and to all a good night!!!"

Theo Ver Steeg

DÉJÀ VU

To my two dearly loved little blonde grandsons, Kyle and Caleb Peterson, this poem is lovingly dedicated.

My tall son sits beside me in this
room; the chair is much too small for
six feet two.
His eyes are on the stage before us
where my grandson, blond and small
and dear,
is standing—cowlick and dimpled
smile so like his dad's.
I look at David watching Kyle and
think "Where have the years gone?"
Surely it can't be
that long ago that I was where he is,
my body folded in a chair too small
for me,
with David in the front row on the
stage—smiling and dimpled—
singing happily.

Time telescopes, I can't quite take it
in. My son is grown and has sons of
his own;
and when they're grown, there'll be
more little boys to watch and love
and care for—and the sense
of déjà vu will then be felt by Dave,
and later on by Kyle and Caleb, too.

So life goes on, and I believe that this
is our true immortality—to see
our children in their children as
they grow;
to know that this continues
year on year;
there'll always be a bit
of us alive!

Greg Malecki

SOLSTICE

For Lissa.

Leaves are falling gently
As the wind blows through my hair,
The autumn breeze has kissed my
face—
Now your ghost is in the air.

The summer sun so fragile now
As it begins to melt away
Reminding me of times gone by
Where are you today?

You left me standing in the rain
On that cloudy day
Nothing left worth living for
Why did you go away?

Shirley Y M Dinning

LEN

Dedicated to my wonderful husband Leonard.

It is by the grace of God above
that we have found enduring love.
You have dried my tears, faded my
fears
and led me over life's path with a
gentle hand.
Darling I am so proud to wear your
wedding band.
Through good and bad, our love we
always had.
God has also granted us three sons
proud to call you Dad.
Words may be many, or they may be
few,
But never enough to express my love
for you.

Lisa T Bizzari

I NEED YOU TO NEED ME

To my husband Michael, whose encouragement made this possible. Also to my family and friends with love and understanding.

I need the laughter we share,
when we're being silly.
I need the love we feel,
when we're being serious.
I need the arguments we have,
to get rid of angry feelings.
I need the look in your eyes,
that melts my heart.
I need you to be my friend.
When I'm feeling lonely,
I need the craziness, happiness and
even the loneliness of being in love
with you.
But most of all
I need you to need me.

Elsie Shephard

Elsie Shephard

LEAN ON ME

To Barbara, your compassion is your strength. Thanks for being you!

Lean on me, I'll be your crutch
Lean on me, when life becomes too much.
When I was down, I leaned on you,
You were there, you pulled me through.
All the little things we shared,
Showed me how much you cared.
We shared our time and shared our thoughts,
The love we shared came from our hearts.
So, lean on me, I'll be there for you,
Together we will both get through.
To do all the things we used to do.
This too shall pass, just wait and see,
I'll lean on you — you lean on me!

Elsie Shephard

YESTERDAY, TODAY, AND TOMORROW

Yesterday has only been hours away.
Today is the start of a brand new day.
Tomorrow will we do all we can do?
Will there be time for me and you?
Do it today and be a good friend.
Because when you wake up tomorrow,
It's today again.

Elsie Shephard

MY MAN

To my husband Merlin, thanks for being "my man."

How do you measure a man.
By the size of his hat or his shoe.
By the size of his bankroll or how tall he stands
That would be easy to do.
I know some with big heads and feet
And some with lots of money and over six feet.
My man's not tall, has no bankroll it's true
His shoes are small and his hat is too!
But his heart is as big as an ocean or sea
And filled full of love for his children and me.
To us, he's the tallest and richest of men,
He gives of himself and to all he's a friend.
Who needs to measure, who needs to compare.
He may be little in size, but he's all man there.

Mary Catherine Hilburn

HIS NAME IS WONDERFUL

I remember waiting quietly for
inspiration,
is this His name?
Or was His name Comfort?
I can't recall.
Was His name Happiness?
Or Content?
Or did He exist at all?

So much time had passed,
perhaps He died,
or just went away.
I searched for something to fill the
void,
but nothing seemed to satisfy.

Then one day,
I developed understanding in such a
simple way,
My oh my how stupid I must be,
the most important part of me,
had cried and I had never even seen a
tear.

I realized suddenly that ever since the
day,
I had come to know God for who He
really is,
He had personally sent me this
Special Friend.

A Friend on whom I could depend,
Someone who could never let me
down,
but always lift me up,
He was the one who brought me
Happiness,
Inspiration and Contentment.

Lisa K Koopman

METROPOLIS

I've run in the veins of the city,
heartbeat from release;
Sucked in and slammed about,
pumped
Through its brains and breast.
I've rolled in the streets as they
heaved and murmured,
The city shifting as if to scratch the
sores inflicted by commuter gnats.
The city has rattled and spat gravel
Into my eyes as, weeping, I careened
on.
I have gorged myself on the groans of
the city
Stuffed with supplicants to capital
gain.
I have glimpsed the city's secret
hoards:
I know one-way streets not marked
on maps.
I have strung together subway stops
and red lights
With scarred asphalt decaying to
cobblestones below.
I have watched the entrances of
warehouses
Where people dressed completely in
black buy used clothing for small
change.
I have hummed through tree-lit
afternoons;
Swearing at cab drivers,
Breathing in the carbon belch of a
people on the move.
I have sung in the night, alone with a
hundred thousand souls;
Keeping myself company on the road
home.

Bonnie Zaborski-Beck
WILL THE REAL FATHER IMAGE PLEASE STAND UP
Docile adherance to your rules
Fostered dependence
That boxed one in
Naiveté was required then

Language deliberately phrased
To confuse the issue
Déjà vu is
All or nothing again

Playing it safe
No quixotic plans
Guardians who hurry up
Must learn to wait

Daddy, is it too late to ask
If the dreams
You never knew
Were real or imagined?

Marlys J Green
IS IT WRITTEN DOWN SOMEWHERE
Is it written down somewhere
That friendship should only share
The happy and the joyful
But never anything painful?

No, I don't believe it true
That the only thing I can share with you
Is only happy, never sad
Never angry, only glad.

God made feelings
God made friends
The thoughts we share—if we dare
Can have no end.

You are a companion
In my thoughts each day
I feel a communion
Must call or write you this way.

The friendship we offer
Each heart seeks out
I am your friend—you, mine
Without one single solitary doubt.

Eva Cook
IMAGINATION
At the tender age of five, I could sing and talk
I really came alive when I went for a walk,
Seeing myself as a girl with bangs and brown hair
Who liked to dance and twirl, dressing with a flair.

My hair was straight and it could grow
I looked first rate with a pretty bow,
My feet were flat but I had pretty shoes
I looked real fat but someday I would lose.

I did like to walk a lot and I traveled far
Knowing I was just a tot, my eye was on a star,
With the feeling I was big, I wanted to be tall
As I reached to pull a twig, I knew I must not fall.

From a nearby tree I watched the birds swing
They were all sizes I could see and they liked to sing.
Some flew high and some low where they wanted to go
Just like the folks I know going to and fro.
I'm going to grow real big and travel in the sky
Then I can get to charge for all the things I buy.
Imagine the places I want to go and get there some day
When I'm old enough to buy and big enough to have my way.

Felicia Vivian Kramer
THE BABY BRITTANY
A lacy pillow ruffle crowned her
shock of raven hair
As the angels bent to kiss her, leaving
dimples here and there.
And gentle breezes whispered, as
they played from tree to tree,
"Come see the pretty princess, she's
the baby Brittany."

The wee folk were excited, as they
danced around a ring.
The birds stopped in their nesting to
warble and to sing.
Although it wasn't scheduled, a
rainbow split the sky.
While everyone took notice and
began to wonder, why?

Who is this special little one, she's
made us stop and dream
Of better times and blissful days, not
common as they seem.
She is our window on the future,
life's eternity.
We'll watch her grow, she'll give us
hope, the baby Brittany.

Nichole Sacchi
ONE CAN LOVE
If one can imagine
Then one can dream.
If one can think
Then one can learn.
If one has strength
Then one can strive.
If one has desire
Then one can seek knowledge and
If one has a heart
Then one can love.

Nancy Lyon
HOLD ON TO THE NIGHT
As the day beckons for the night to
take hold,
clouds are replaced by stars of gold,
each in its own, a single story is told,
tales of tomorrow, tales of the old.
Sounds of the day, fade to whispers
of the night
angels of darkness begin to take
flight,
dancing with the leaves under the
pale moonlight,
the innocence of a child disappears at
first light.
Her dreams have been shattered, and
hopes torn apart,
as the child realizes a new day must
start.
With tears in her eyes, she fears the
daybreak and the women
within her, that must again wake.
The daily battle to uphold the image
that's implied
sends a fear through her that's
chilling, her wish is to hide.
The strength and confidence she
prays to possess, the little girl
is desperate to impress. The
importance to her to earn your praise,
the women, the child, the
frightened . . . always.
So she builds a wall of illusion and
fears,
that someone will notice if they come
too near,
that the women is still a child you
see,
the women, the child, the frightened
. . . is me.

Rachel Leister
FOLK TAPESTRY
Bowed
Quiet mannered
Handmade toys of wood.

Firm
Watchful guidance
Never failing love.

Delightful
Sheer kaleidoscope
Extension of the roots.

Precious
Fine clay
Moments to be treasured.

Companions
Secrets shared
Pathways criss and crossing.

Refreshing
Philosophies exchanging
Encouragers along the way.

Family
Friends included
Woven by the Lord.

Tammy J French
FORTUNE OF IMAGINATION
Skies have hushed.
Flurries have ceased.

The white, blinding force has ignited
an electric dazzle of light.

Gems glisten under
cautious rays of distant sun.

Fields of riches, so close to the touch,
yet always remain a figment of
reality.

Their glittering sparkle,
that equal to the eyes of a
laughing child.

Meg Sayles
CLOSER TO THE EDGE
Between us lies the darkness of time
Bring me closer to the edge
The edge of darkness
Stands on the brink of time
Time that never closes down inside
My eyes see the glory
Where darkness lies
Bring me closer to the edge

Brenda Harrel
WHY
What can I say?
What can I do?
Why are you gone?
All of these questions,
Where are the answers?

Judith Eckert
UNTITLED
Hate, destruction,
Evil, dismay.

Horrid feelings
Slowly decay.

Deep feelings of rapture
and ecstasy,
feelings of love
for you and me.
Holding back on the love of another
feeling love for a lover.

a soft touch
a fatal kiss
an innocent love
a scornful bliss

Can you feel it?
If you can,
Then you hold
your future at hand.

Judy Touchet
TO MY CHILD
It seems like just yesterday
They put you in my arms
A tiny baby, soft and pretty
Like a star, with all its charms.

When I have you in my arms,
I feel so peaceful and free
Just to watch you lay there
Means everything to me.

Please don't let the day come
When you're too big for me
To put my arms around you
And hold you tenderly.

And through all the tears and sorrows
And all the laughter, too
One thing's all for certain
I will always love you.

So close your eyes and sleep, baby
I'll keep you from all harm
As I watch you lay there
So peaceful in my arms!

Vic S Gathings
FIRE FIGHT

To my wife, boys and parents, Judy, Paul, Patrick and Mr. and Mrs. H. A. Gathings and to all vets who know what I'm saying.

Zero four-hundred, "time to rise and shine,"
A chilling voice, no friend of mine.
Foul smelling air, cigarettes, coffee and death,
Just give me a minute, to catch my breath.
Rotors are spinning, it's time to go,
"Where she stops, nobody knows."
Finally we've landed, the LZ* is hot,
"Here we come Charlie, ready or not."

"Come out, come out, wherever you are," a children's game.
Come on out Charlie, Van Nguyen or whatever your name.
M-14 humming, again please don't jam,
Firing at all movement—who gives a damn.

The tall grass now silent, blood
fog setting in,
Death's Dew in droplets, on my boots
again.
The rage of silence now rings in
my head,
"One potato, two potato, three
potato"—dead.
Familiar voice, soft and sweet,
resounds through the hate,
Mom saying, "Stop your child's play,
come on in boys, it's late."

*LZ—Landing Zone

Denise Harmon
CHANGING SEASONS
There are places I remember,
Where we walked hand and hand
Out there on the quiet beach,
With only us and white sand.
The wind blew silently through my
hair,
The cold sand on my feet.
I wish we could return there,
For our love then was sweet.
We stayed up to see the morning sun
Just lying there so serene.
Back then we had so much fun
It was always like a dream.
When you remember those nights
I wonder what you think of?
Everything seemed just right.
How strong then, was our love?
Our bodies held so much fire
As we laid next to each other
We were filled with burning desire
Our desire for one another.
As the days grow long and colder
And the nights seem empty and alone
Now is the time I need a shoulder
You mustn't feel the pain I've known
You have gone and left me
For she has taken you away
My life now is empty
My whole world is grey.

Dorothy A Kersey
FANTASY
Why must I live my life in a fantasy?
I let my imagination go.
I dream of happiness
But all I live is misery
I let myself dream of a man
Oh, how I care for him
I dream he feels the same
But I know there is no hope
I force myself to reality
And see no one for me
I look to the future
All I see is loneliness
I see myself with no one around
The others happily pass me by
Leaving me by the side
I am so lonely
So back I go to my fantasy
Back I go to security
In fantasy I am lost
No one can hurt me there.

T F Watson
YOU ALWAYS FOUND SOME SPECIAL WAY
You always found some special way
To touch my heart each day,
I can't believe you're giving up
And throwing it all away.
The pain I feel within me
Is tearing me apart.
I thought the love we shared
Was coming from our hearts.
Just let me fill your life
With the love I have for you.
And give you a world of excitement
And feelings you never knew.

Arminda Valdés-Ginebra

Arminda Valdés-Ginebra
THE BUNDLE OF HEATH
You were coming yesterday
with a bundle of heath in your arms.
You were coming . . . I was expecting
you.
You were bringing me a bundle light,
delicate, full of perfume and lovely
color.

I will never forget this symbol.
You were coming to me . . . I was
smelling
the sweet fragrance of the heath
invading my life, the aisles of my
dreams.

So, I am feeling very happy
and a little sad too. Now, I do not
have
your presence beside me,
your kisses in me . . . I am alone,
only
I have the memory of the bundle of
heath.

Teresa Gray
A TRUCKER'S WIFE

To my beloved husband Dan.

As the morning awakes the dawn
I reach out to touch you
knowing you're still gone
making me feel like a fool.

Lonely afternoons I sit at home
wishing with all I've got that you'd
telephone
but it is silent and the rooms are too
the emptiness is just too true.

As the evening settles in
the shadows follow
my sadness begins
as I pray for tomorrow.

Tomorrow comes, but you're still not
here
one more day, must I wait for you my
dear?
Every mile that you drive away
is even with the tears that fall in my
day.

How much longer will I last
how many days will fall into the past
before my suffering will end
before my swollen eyes will mend?

Just a word would rest my heart
telling me how long we'll be apart
and knowing that you're okay
while clinging to every word you had
to say.

How I will cope, I don't know
because again I know you'll go
and you haven't even come home yet
but the hurting won't let me forget.

Again and again I will wait for you
proving my heart to be true
but every time you drive away
I will long for your returning day.

Teresa Gray
THOUGHTS
Come to find out
and come to see
it was that way
as it should be
it was clearly shown
but I had to find out on my own
all I had to do was look around
and just that, is what I found.

Aliene B Burgess
FAITH IS A GIFT
Faith is a gift from our good God
above
Given to us from his unbounding
love.
Our Faith must be cherished every
day.
Lived by and practiced in every way.
Faith gives us strength and endurance
for life;
Helps to overcome times of great
strife.
Troubles vanish with never a trace.
One's life is happier because of Faith.
So—as all of us this old Earth do trod
Never let go your Faith, your gift
from God.

Aliene B Burgess
VISION FROM THE MOUNTAIN
The Apostle John saw the Great
Vision
From the Mountain's topmost
peak.
It was the new, Golden Jerusalem
Which all the saved men would
seek.

There, one hundred forty-four
thousand strong
Were those redeemed from old
Earth's sod.
Angels' Choir sang a beautiful new
song
Before the throne of our Great
God.

Seven Angels, dressed in linen and
gold,
Sang the song of Moses of old
As the greatest earthquake came with
a blast
And lightning flashed as thunder
crashed.

"Hallelujah" from the crowd came a
shout
When the wildest storm was over.
Before the gold throne of God, John
cried out,
"Almighty God reigns forever."

The new Jerusalem which John
visioned
Was so wondrous and Holy
That it glowed like a precious,
precious gem
And was filled with God's Glory!

Reba Ward
IT HURTS AND HE CARES
Oh how it hurts to say good-bye
When a loved one has to die,
They leave us here to walk alone,
And within heaven's gates lie.

A place of joy, love, and peace.
What more could one ask?
We have to let go
And take up our daily task.

The pain we feel is for ourselves.
The grief we have to bear.
Your friends and loved ones,
They all come to share.

God only knows what it means.
The void it leaves behind.
He reaches down in love and grace,
Our hearts to entwine.

He says, "I care, I want to share,
When your loved one has to die."
The pain, the hurt you feel
When you have to say good-bye.

Norma L Appleby
THE TROPHY
Hi there Mr. Sportsman
I see you bagged a deer
it's plain for everyone to see
you're a hunter with no fear
but tell me Mr. Hunter
would this sport be so much fun
if you became the runner
and that poor deer held the gun?

As you raced through the underbrush
you'd be so short of breath
would your heart be pounding madly
as you caught the scent of death?
Would you wonder why you're
slaughtered
when you've never sinned at all?
Would you hear a shot, then be no
more
but a trophy on the wall?

Bernadette S Gannon
DOLLARS AND SENSE
Another day, another dollar
Or how about another million
It pays to have some common sense
Whether blue or white is in the collar

Bought and paid for economics
Otherwise it's in the comics
Bookkeeping ledgers like CPA's
Carefree parties? Those are the days!

Computers now are just the thing
Confusion to order with all that bring
Everything passing in a twinkling
Money and manners always
happening

Myrtle Parker Weaver
LOST POEM
Never had the nerve to enter before
But on a dare I opened the door
to the World of Poetry; what's more,
I won a prize! And lots of praise.
The next reply disclosed the fact my
poem
had been lost (and so were mine: two
copies)

Day after day I searched my brain
to bring that poem out again;
I thought at times I'd go insane
But memory only gave back the title,
"Believe it!"

Some day I hope the lost lines
will be found—the puzzle solved,
We can only guess in what trashpile
it landed, why and how the copies
ditto
How fragile some things are!
Believe it? I must! A glimpse of fame
One tiny flame—three awards to
prove it.
Life goes on—

Mary Lou Von Meter
SIOUX

This poem is dedicated to all the Sioux people. I love you.

Don't hang your head in shame
my children.
Remember who you are and where
you came
from, the Sioux walked this land
since time began.
We have lived as one with the
earth and the sky. The buffalo
and deer gave us food and clothing.
Father sun gave us light and
kept us warm throughout the days.
The old ways were lost to us,
but are now found again.
Once more we walk in the old ways,
believe in the old ones.
The songs and stories are told once
more around the campfires.
The eagles and the bear are brothers
to us. The blood of Crazy Horse
and Sitting Bull flow through our
veins, We are proud my children,
we are Sioux.

Juanita Saenz
A MAN NAMED PAUL

In commemoration of Pope John Paul II's visit to San Antonio, Texas, 1987.

The day I went to see
A man named Paul
He goes by John
To honor another

Pope John Paul II
Stood erect, yet humble
And the mist of the multitude
I utter these words

"Oh! Peter's successor
We meet here to pray
And partake of the Last Supper
As Jesus once did

The joy of a city
Is with you today
To proclaim in one voice
The great glory of God"

My spirit was lifted
That bright sunny day
The day I went to see
A man named Paul

Juanita Saenz
TEXAS JOURNEY
From the valley of San Juan, Texas
Where the faith runs deep and strong
To the desert of west Texas
Where I found a yellow rose
Across the panhandle near Amarillo
I hear someone waltz across the state
And big Dallas with glitter buildings
That shine by night and day
Walk the beaches of Corpus Christi
Where sun worshipers roam free
To the heart of San Antonio
Where the cradle hovers liberty
Yes, all of this is Texas
Land—sky—and stars

Juanita Saenz
AT THE FOOT OF THE CRIB

To my daughter, Patricia.

It's around this time
When you hear this phrase
"Oh, Christmas isn't
Like it used to be"

I hear this so often
That I wonder why?
With all of the bright lights
And all of its joy

So I search and I found
A reply to this phrase
I found it in those
Who kneel at the crib

For they seem to know
The true meaning is there
When they offer their prayer
At the foot of the crib

Nette Renzell
RAYS OF LIGHT
When trials beset life's upward
course
With weariness and downward force
The self resorts to solitude
And gains a peace in quietude

When storms of turbulence hold sway
With dreaded burdens of dismay
The self in armed defense cites
prayer
And reaps the fruit of Heaven's care

When troubles bar progressive's rise
With threats of fear which agonize
The self in faith relies on aid
And soars enlightened unafraid

O glory to the Rays of Light
Which from the sacred realms of
might
Descend to help the soul of man
To reach fulfillment toward God's
plan

Nicole Motsch
AFTER HIM

Dedicated to Matthew Lawrence Burke . . .

The dress hung softly
on her legs,
and her eyes shone
with a feigned excitement
that comes from being
hurt so much,
being so scared to touch,
being foolish and willing,
being so close to killing,
being a pretty girl in a dress . . .
sitting alone—
dreaming of home;
a home with him
that she will never know.
So they look and stare.
They all wonder
what became of the thunder
that once roared
in her eyes.

Gloria Hill Williams
WHO AM I?
I am dimmed eyes and a face full of
lines
I'm silver strands in your hair and a
feeble mind
I'm an arthritic hand and an unsteady
gait
Though I take my time, I am never
late

I'm a shriveled old lady and a man
with a limp
And no one can detain me, though
some may attempt

No money can bribe me, I treat all
men the same
'Cause my father is time and age is
my name

Cynthia Chandler
THE TREE
The tree lights are twinkling
Red and green, blue and white,
Amidst the silver icicles.
Remainders of a year ago,
Reminders of the joyful day
We are now anticipating.
The ornaments are hung
One to a branch carefully;
Animals, bells, balls and even an ice
cream cone,
Silky, frosted, cloth, and plastic.
No star atop this tree,
Instead a silvery spire to grace its tip.
The reflections of the lights
On the sparkling strings of silver,
On the long, shiny spire
And even on the frosted bulbs
Expel such a cozy sensual glow
That upon to look I cannot help
But smile and almost feel
The warm hand and quiet breath
Of a friend envelop me.

Allen Lee Trueman
WINTER NIGHTS
Over hills glows a crown of clouds,
with vivid bright colors of sun's last
rays of dusk, prevails over a dark
black hills you do see.

Day is set into black night, all silent
and quiet, with the last sounds of
winter you do hear, of the thunder
and lightning does come our way.

As we set and relish the warmth of
fire and read by candlelight, to enjoy
the last long nights of winter.

Adelon Axt

Adelon Axt
TOMORROW
They say tomorrow never comes,
On this I don't agree.
For yesterday I prayed for someone
to love,
And today you came to me.

So if you would stop and think,
I know that you would see,
That today was tomorrow, yesterday,
So tomorrow came for me.

Clara Fisher Folsom
THE NURSING HOME

Dedicated to Louise Fisher.

Walk in the door and one's
heart skips a beat.
As one seeks all the ill ones,
one tries to smile and to greet.

We pray they will have peace
as each day is planned.
God will ease their pain,
and people will understand.

Please, God have mercy
on these weary souls
Help them in their distress
They are your children of woe.

Let's not forget the Dr's and the staff
They are busy day and night—
They put out so much love
and help in the ill ones' plight.

Christie Erin Thorpe
SONG TO MY CHILDREN

To Michelle Renee and Matthew Stephen and all of our children yet to come.

I tell you so often how to play life's
game,
Be honest 'though everyone is not the
same,

Unlock your imagination and dare to
dream,
Know the value of money and how
others can scheme,

Accept your failures because you are
strong
And have peace in yourself as you go
along,

Do not pass out your trust, but try to
be fair,
'Cause the gift of a true friend is oh
so rare,

My sole purpose in this is not just to
preach,
But to save you some sorrow life can
teach

To not waste years learning who you
can be—
The happy, whole person that could
have been me.

Christie Erin Thorpe
THE PROMISE OF COLORS
I see colors of my feelings all around
me,
No longer sad, they are delightful to
see,

To have risen right up from out of the
gloom,
And make a statement of peace in
each room,

The flowers for warmth, all in a soft
hue,
To show that love is what I know
how to do,

Teal and green are my statement of
pride
Of my strength in working to turn the
tide,

Soft pink and peach show my hope
and desire
To keep opening doors and move
even higher,

But the room where I lay to sleep
each night
Is filled with objects to represent
light,

I wake up with enthusiasm there in the air,
Whispering to treat this treasure with care,

The path is now clear, I am finally free
To find out who lives here—inside of me.

Christie Erin Thorpe
MARRIAGE PROMISE
A love that is kind, sharing and giving
Is a blessing to me and a reason for living,

To have a partner in whom I can trust
Is more than a want, for me it's a must,

We've worked together and kept our love dear
And the final reward is to have this day here,

My promise today is to do my part
To keep this love special within my heart,

I will give back to you what you give to me,
Let our love be the door and truth be the key,

I choose you for my husband and pray that I may
Always love you the same as I do today.

Christie Erin Thorpe
TO CHALLENGE
To a person who to others may seem at his peak
But knows in his head he has much more to seek,

Who must give up security earned through the years,
For the beat of his dream outweighs his fears,

For now in his life is the time for a chance
To follow his star and do his own dance,

He dares, he is strong and he will succeed
And finds part of himself very different indeed,

This is the person to whom I write this song
With respect in my heart and love ever strong.

Reyna Skrabala
WINGS OF GOLD

To Mom—and her vision of tomorrow!

I can soar, I can fly on my wings of gold.
I can meet with the spirits, consult gods of old.
I can see mountains, deserts; places hot, places cold.
I can visit the moon. I have boundaries yet untold.

I can fold my wings, land, and walk.
I can love, hate, I can feel, I can talk.
I can be a bird . . . a hawk!

I can be happy, or sad, I can laugh and cry.
I can live, and, eventually, I can die.
I can fly on, whether low or high.
I can do much more, because I can fly.

My imagination takes me places as yet unseen.
It takes me places where I've never been.
And when I'm ready, I can come to reality again.
What makes me fly? I have the imagination of men!

Francis Barr
OF BEAUTY AND BEASTS
Would that you were real.
The countenance,
voice, actions, all
Fulfill many dreams.
A bronze voiced being of fairy tales
Lost in modern verse.
The reminder of illusions
And allegories long ignored.

It is possible to drown in that voice.
Or float away on its resonance.

Would that I could be
Lost in your reality.
The darkness and light in you
frighten me not.
They are my own reflection.
If only to find,
The peace your voice calls to mind.

And promises so easily.

Christine R Walker
LIFE
Just remember in this life
Sometimes you have to hold on tight.
Always landing on both feet
When you reach your goals complete.

So, soar thru life with great care
With dreams and hopes and wishes to share.
And lots of friends by your side
To help you take this life in stride.

Life is an adventure, one of a kind
Each of us lives but one time.
So enjoy the coming year to be
And may your dreams become Reality.

Sheila Mae Hopkins
I SHALL FORGET
I think of you in the light
In the light of dawn
In the presence of the newborn day
In the scent of dew upon the grass

Time will somehow break this trend
and days will pass without a thought of you.
I'll forget your gentle touch, your tender
lips, your tender embrace.

I'll give birth to verse
Conceived in memory of what was
This bond from which I am freed
Is in a way rebirth

The pain of remembering is gone at least
And soon I'll forget the past

Anthony L Bradway
SHEEP IN THE FIELD OF FAITH

To all the people of the world!

We are all children of GOD only sheep in the field of faith. We are sinners of sin the Devil's test we must take, with love in our hearts, and peace in our minds, we'll pass the Devil's test just fine.
Let us be together, for we are the children of GOD, it was he who built this earth, for us to plant the sod. We are the children of GOD only sheep in the field of faith, we are takers of temptation, leading only to another mistake.
Please holy father take temptation to our feet, open your path to righteousness for us to seek. Some of us will follow, others go mislead, following a path of evil and sin they go ahead, with hatred in their hearts, and pain in their minds, not any path of justice will they ever find.
We are all children of GOD only sheep in the field of faith, we are doers of wrong, and makers of mistakes. We need your love holy father please give us all that it takes, to be the children of GOD, only sheep, grazing in the field of faith!

Elizabeth Wright
THE OCEAN

This poem is dedicated to my parents, grandparents and family for their love and support.

The crashing sounds of the ocean waves,
Entices me to come for days and days,
As I sit upon the sand,
Thinking about my problems,
I realize some ways in which I could solve them
Watching the ocean water flow,
Through my tired feet,
I remember the promises, I made,
I plan to keep
Everything is peaceful by the ocean water
Because when you're there nothing else matters

Theresa Summitt
DRINKING, DRIVING, & DEATH
Even though the days may seem clear,
It's still not the same without you here.
They say my friend you're not to blame,
That it's the driver that must be put to shame.
However you're the one that had to die,
That put us in tears and made us cry.
I'm not finished yet my friend,
There's still much more before I end.
You were only eighteen and still a kid at heart,
You were planning college with a whole new start.
So all you people listen up and understand,
Drinking and driving does not prove a man.
Life is easy to handle even if you're depressed,
But drinking and driving will never impress.
I know because my friend died this way,
He wasn't driving he wasn't drinking it was the driver this day.
So the next time you're out having your kicks,
Remember drinking and driving doesn't mix.

Erika S Bates
FIRST LOVE
I love the Lord, because he first loved me
He made a way for me, when I could not see
He shed his precious blood on the cross
So that my soul would not die, and be lost
By his blood my soul has been cleansed
And I can now say, "I'm free from sin"
I am now a new creature in Christ
Jesus made the difference, he changed my life
Now I'm living to please him every day
Because Jesus is coming, He's on his way
Then will I go to live with Jesus forever
And my new home will be Heaven
Jesus changed my life for me
He'll do it for anybody, just try him and see
You'll be glad you chose Jesus, this I guarantee!!

T McElhenney Decker
75 DEGREES
75 degrees in the sun.

People are swimming and surfing in California, getting a great suntan and playing volleyball.

While in Alaska it is 100° below zero and helicopters are crashing because the fuel lines have frozen up.

They are afraid to venture forth from wherever they are for fear of the white death, lurking everywhere.

No one is outside playing silly games or getting a suntan.

People in California are laughing at silly jokes, while in Alaska, they are grim faced trying to keep alive.

People are starving and freezing there.

While here, it is just another sunny day at the beach.

There is no fairness to it, but whoever said life was fair?

T McElhenney Decker
POVERTY
Poverty is a most humbling experience to which I readily subscribe.

Not out of conviction but out of my necessity.

Poverty is an equal opportunity employer who plays no favorites, no discrimination because of age, sex or skin color.

Poverty doesn't care if you are literate, a beautiful person or an ugly duckling.

Poverty is not a virtue nor are its practitioners, saints by any other name.

Poverty breeds poverty, crime, neglect and heartache.

Poverty by anyone's definition stinks!

T McElhenney Decker
CLAIMS
If you and I were as good as we claim to be, then there would be no poverty or homeless people or diseases ravaging the world.

There would be no children without fathers or people dying in Africa of starvation or people denied medical treatment because they didn't have any money or because their skin is the wrong color.

There would be no drug dealers, peddling death to our children.

Life is not fair and neither you nor I are as good as we claim to be.

T McElhenney Decker
DEATH OF A POEM
I saw a poem, laying on its side, battered by a horde of people who trudged by, not noticing its shattered condition, as it struggled for survival.
The poem was laying in a gutter where the irate hordes had kicked it.
It rested there, lonely, neglected, bruised with marks of its fate, clearly visible.
It looked so meek and helpless just laying there that I stooped to pick it up rescuing it from a watery death.
I paused, just long enough, to read what some unknown poet had written.
As I read, a tear formed in my eye, dripping down my face, onto the poem.
I cried over the poems fate, trying to revive it, but it had seen too much neglect and indifference for it to survive.
The poem expired, as I stood there reading it.

Debra P Lemons
PASSING TIME

To my loving husband, Wendall Grant Lemons, who inspired me with all his love, 1983.

You're here today
and gone tomorrow.
I'll wait my love,
but my heart has sorrow.

You may be near or far away,
but my Darling,
In my heart you'll always stay.

May your journeys be short
and few, and please always
remember,
I Love You!
Then the roads you travel
won't be long,
'cause God is with you, and
you'll soon be home.

"Patti"

Kathryn VanPraag
JAKE
Did I ever touch your face?
Could you come here and be this space?
I send love to you 2000 miles away.
I can love you always, each and every day.

One perfect love to show the world the way.
One human love to know it's here to stay!
All I ask of him is to have what's mine.
You are mine, I know, I feel, I am.

You are here, I touch your face
And you're filling up this space.

Kathryn VanPraag
LEADER
Be still all my children
Be still and hold your tongue
You are older when you're older
You are angry when you're young

One day when various people lie
Beneath the earth of black
Your heritage and honor
Will all be coming back

I love you more in these days
Than in the ones before
Though I loved you when you suffered
And the pain was all the more

Today you'll fight a battle
Tomorrow — victory!
But I loved you never stopping
Tomorrow remember me

Valerie Schuler
SMALL WORLD
Where would the world be without the people of the small world.
They are happy little people, who have no worries in the world.
You see them laughing at the circus at the funny little clowns.
Or you might hear them cry for breaking a pretty vase.
Their world is just full of joy, fun and games which they seem to enjoy without a care in the world.
Just stop and think how silent the world would be without the laughter of the small people.
You see them running through a field making a bouquet for that special someone.
On a rainy day you see them running and laughing in the droplets of rain.
Or looking up in the sky for the pretty colored rainbow.
You can never expect what they shall do, for they do the most unexpected at various times.
Well let me tell you who these small people are—they are all the little boys and girls who make up the world of small people, whom we call children.

Carolyn L Langs
PASTEL MEMORIES
Soft and full the morning light, the breeze is swift and clean.
The trees are laden with a floral tribute to the sun.
The patchwork of the cloth reflects years of time and love each stitch a memory of its own, a symbol of times now gone,
The cat lies purring by the door, content and safe, secure.
The smell of fresh baked bread floods the kitchen and drifts out on the breeze to the meadow.
Blueberries strain at their branches begging to be plucked, daisies droop from exhaustion as rose petals weep with morning dew.
Far away the sounds of the pasture animals mix with the wind, to create a Brahms like symphony.
Memories of childhood filter back, creating a smile on the wrinkled face.
The rhythm of the old rocker never falters . . .
Pastel sights, pastel sounds, pastel memories.

Baruch Cweiber
PAST TO PRESENT

To Nancy Pinkert, who inspired me with courage and hope.

Tears of my past values from the clouds above
Taking shape in pearly drops that I endure
In nature and God I praise for what has fallen
With this offering the breaches will close.

My soul will overcome the force of plague and gloom
And I will praise the flickering candle with care
It will possess the remnants of my link with dimness
Within my eyes this will be a lifetime vision.

The day will come for my living flesh to stimulate
With no more emptiness to veil the sorrow within
And the stream of love shall flow until eternity
Sweeping up the heart that aroused from the pain.

I will sense the spirit with everlasting wisdom
And in the waste before the ignorance past
Slit the sick darkened side to justify the memory
Today I live with one voice the truth.

Enid Segal
I SHARE
The clouds that I often see
My body cannot grow without.

The sweet tears are my hope
In nature's hungry home.

I stay erect looking at God all day
With my leafy branches I pray.

My body a convenient way
Where birds often share.

In winter the snow I endure
In summer intimately with rain.

I am a paradise being a host
To God's creatures a home.

I give shelter where humans live
And God is the maker of my soul.

My seeds transplanted by the wind
To be the privilege of another home.

Susan Korsgaard
LITTLE CHILDREN
Little children so far away
You have to get by day by day
And hope for help to come your way

You have no schools, no food
to share only hunger war and despair

Your little eyes search every
face hoping to find a hopeful
trace to make your pain and suffering erase.

You have no Christmas no Easter day,
only thoughts of food to come your way.

i pray to God high above to wrap
you all in his tender love
to watch over and guide you
every day
and may help and happiness
come your way.

Susan Korsgaard
RELEASE
At last i draw my final breath
as my soul cries out for release
to enter that beautiful valley
where there's gentleness and peace

Although they will mourn me
with sadness and grief
oh if only they could see me in this
valley of release

For it is i that mourn thee in
sadness and grief. for thee have
not entered yet into this valley
of peace.

So mourn me not my loved ones
for sadness i do not need
here i've found my happiness
where. there is no hunger lust nor greed

No war nor sad faces no dying battle cries
for here you will find your happiness
in this heaven of paradise

Billy F Andrews Sr
THE GIFT OF LIFE
Life itself is our greatest gift
And eternal life is our greatest goal,
Time to breathe, act, think and sift
To find ourselves and win our soul.

What each shall do with this gift,
Free will allows him to decide.
The way is strewn by many a tiff
With evil, wrong, greed and pride.

What a challenge is this gift
To discover who we are,
The peace, joy and heavenward lift
To feel as individual as a star.

How to appreciate the gift,
Care for, cherish and pass it on
To posterity's children without a rift,
We must each decide alone.

To pave ways for firmer footing
Of those who are yet to come,
To be true to self and ever loving
The eternal God who will call us home.

Denise Ayer
SOLITARY SECLUSION
As darkness envelops me
I call to you there is no one there.
It's at times like these I
yearn to see your face,
your smile and hear
your laughter.

Even for a short time I
wish for a strong hand,
reaching out to me,
insuring all will be right.
As I lie in the silence,
there are no smiles,
there is no laughter,
there is no encompassing
love.
For I am alone.

Colene K Brownderville
DEAR MOMMY AND DADDY;

Mommy and Daddy, Please don't cry
for me.
I'm up in Heaven now where I play
with the Angels.
I have lots of little friends here.
We swing on swings, being pushed
by our Guardian Angels, build
sandcastles with the Saints.
We are watched over with care by the
Virgin Mother, Mary.
Jesus gathers us to him and tells us
stories, and God is here with us
surrounding us with love.

Mommy and Daddy, Please don't cry
for me.
Though I'm gone from your sight,
I'm always in your hearts.
Cherish the fond memories and forget
the pain.

Mommy and Daddy, Please don't cry
for me.
I'm in a wonderful place, where there
is no pain and fears, nor sadness and
tears.
No skinned knees, no danger, no
drugs, no gangs, no violence; only
love.

Mommy and Daddy, Please don't cry
for me.
Please live your lives in love and
gladness, push away the pain and the
sadness;
and one day when God calls you to
join him,
I'll be there with him, waiting to be
held in your arms once again.

Mommy and Daddy;
I love you.

Your little Angel

J Felix Major
OUR SONG . . . 1935

In token of my love for Ursula
I send these words to the only "U"
There can ever be for me.

Loving you is like living a dream
But there's one greater joy, a joy
supreme
That is to know; darling, say it's so
"I was born to be loved by you."

The thrill of you near's like heaven
on earth
To a wondrous feeling my heart's
given birth
So, 'cause I love you I hope it's true
"I was born to be loved by you."

To hear those words
From your dear lips
The words "I love just you"
Brought a thrill of joy
To the soul of one
Whose heart belongs to you.

Born to be held so close in your arms
Born to be bound so fast by your
charms
I may be mad but oh so glad
"I was born to be loved by YOU."

J Felix Major
OUR SONG . . . 1978

To the "U" I always knew
Would someday be
The first half of "US."

Some years ago in our dear past
I penned some words that were meant
to last
Each year with you still proves them
true
"I was born to be loved by you."

The joy of you o'er all the years
Has caused to flee all doubts or fears
That pacts we made could ever fade
"I was born to be loved by you."

The words I hear
From your sweet lips
The words "I still love you"
Bring more than joy
To your "Dear Boy"
And will forevermore.

I always knew that love'd be "swell"
When shared, but dear I know quite
well
That tho life's great 'twas only fate
"I was born to be loved by YOU."

Mrs Maria Love
HE IS ALWAYS THERE

I dedicate this poem to my darling
husband, who I love very much.
Thanks, Ellis—Love.

When I am very lonely—
Have lost my way in despair
I call upon my loving saviour,
For He is always there.

My lonely hours soon disappear—
My despair and heartbreak just fade
away
As he promises, my heart is filled
with joy
Then comes a (happier) better day.

On my (knees) I go in prayer
Where he leads, my pathway ahead is
smooth
He is always there too—
Living in Him, (with God) at my
side,
I will never lose.

He's always there, he will never
leave me
I promise him forever, my trust in
Him won't waver
He is all I need he is just a prayer
away, too
Leaning on my "precious" lord and
saviour.

He is always there—when I need a
friend
A (friend) that's tried and "oh" so
true,
All I need to turn to "God" I will
find—
"He's" there, (his salvation) beckons
for you.
He is "ALWAYS" there.

John E Lones
TO LAURA DACHOWSKI

To Laura, who found in me what I
thought lost. Thank you, Laura. I
hope that you are well.

It wasn't by chance
That I fell to my knees with only one
glance.
And to watch you the very first time
No other imagine could enter my
mind

To look into your eyes
Were to see colors too beautiful to
describe.
And the warmth of the touch of your
hand
Was like the warmth of the summer
sand.

When you held me in your arms, I
held my breath,
For that moment in time I'll
remember until death.

But then I lost you
I became so confused

I, petal of a flower at the mercy of the
wind
I don't care of my journey or when it
will end.

Only once in a lifetime this feeling
comes along
Never forget, it's like your favorite
song.
Laura, if time were to stop and all
would be gone
My love for you still alive, silence
broken by a song.

Dorothy Ann Kuttesch
TOUCHING APRIL

Spring came so quickly . . .
Like a lingering glance of light
and warmth
Dimming all ahead and behind
Tugging life to sensuous surface
Commanding gentleness of mind

Spring came so quickly . . .
With tentative glow, like breezes
Brushing now with promised
return
Poised on whispers of here
And numb sensations of gone

This is my Spring . . .
A welcome stranger always known
With unseen familiar approaching
You are my Spring and I the Fall
With only fantasies of idle
touching

Helen V Hesse
THE KING'S CHOICE

I dedicate this poem to my sister,
Elizabeth Weatherford, who has
written and had published several
poems, inspiring me to try.

The Coronation day was near
For Edward to be crowned.
All England hailed the future King,
And Wally liked the sound.

Since Wally was the queen-to-be
But not of royal birth,
The Minister thought it was wrong,
Regardless of her worth.

Though Edward wanted to be king,
He felt that love meant more.
If he could not have her as queen
The throne no meaning bore.

"The King and Queen" to Austria
fled,
To marry there in peace,
While George his brother took the
throne
To make the quarrel cease.

"It was for love I left the throne,"
Said Edward to his wife,
"So England sends us from her
shores
To spend our married life."

"Oh" Kelly
FINGERS LOST—A TRIBUTE TO BILL

To Bill Baker of Myrtle Beach, South
Carolina, who passed away too soon
from leukemia.

Someone once said you are an
extremely fortunate man, if you have
true friends that number the fingers
of just one hand.

I have known and lost to death such a
person so early in life, one who was
always there in good times or in
strife.
Bill was a good man, A large man in
size and in heart, his friendship was
as a rock I know would never part.

He was complex yet unassuming
and always had a smile, he was
strong, yet gentle, his presence in
anxious times shed warmth for even a
little while.

As I sit in candlelight and ponder
the short time I had to enjoy the
friendship of this wonderful man, I
feel the loss of at least three fingers
of my trembling right hand.

Rest in peace Dear Friend.

Stana Soto
EMOTIONS

As I walked along
the clear smooth sand
the water danced around
my feet,
The wind whistled
a tune of sorrow
through the still air,
And rain began to fall
like tears
as if the sky were crying,
It was then
that I realized
the unbroken tears
were that of a
once happy child.

Alison Schelin (Age 8)
SPRING

Spring has a wonderful smell
A smell of fresh new flowers.
And in the month of April comes
Warm sweet April showers.

Lambs romp and play in the sun
While the birds sing lovely tunes.
Horses gallop, and ponies neigh
In the warm afternoons.

Roses, daisies, and violets bloom
In the warm, lovely spring.
Little girls play, and skip, and run
And the boys build a swing.

Spring is lovely, sweet, and gay
A beautiful, warm season.
Spring is my favorite season, oh yes
And those are all the reasons.

Dorothy M King
GIVE ME TEARS

Give me tears for the years
That I have not yet cried

Give me tears for the years
That I have been tried

Give me tears for the years
That has been so unfair

Give me tears for the years
That has been so hard to bear

Give me tears for the years
That has caused me pain

Give me tears for the years
That has drove me insane

Give me tears for the years
That is still carrying on

Give me tears for the years
That will continue till I'm gone

Elizabeth M Robinson
TO ANDREW

With love to my son, Andrew.

I long for joy
A smile
A tear
of laughter
not fear.

I long for love
A hug
A smile
to warm my
heart for awhile.

I long for touch
A hand
A heart
that I could
cuddle and be apart.

I long for you
A love
A joy
All wrapped up
in my baby boy.

Mary Collins
CHILDREN OF THE UNIVERSE

Awaken my children
We are in a new age.
We hear your unspoken words
Your joys, your sorrows
Your need for change.
Let us show you the way
within.

Visions are our dreams
Brought into reality.
Come back to us children
Of the Universe.
Let us light your way
For we are the angels within.
We are love.

Arvene Hays Demaree
DAY'S SYMPHONY

To Mom and Dad, whose eyes have taught me to see.

Balcony window of the world outside
trace of frost on the dawn,
echoing choruses in flight
breaking the breathless silence.
Baton raised as audience poised
to see the prelude appear.
Golden spotlight on majestic branch
lens widening upon neighboring
bows.
Lifted baton, encircles the morn
as misty meadows sparkle underfoot,
reaching to encurl hilltops.
Symphonic song in shadows begin
stirring all harmonies intense.
Audience changes as hues emerge
from corners and aisles.
Crescendo of song awakens the day;
Rhythmic breeze lifts all sound.
The Conductor never seen.

Daniel I Lloyd
A QUIET PLACE

Isn't there a quiet place,
Just some place you can find,
To be alone with just your thoughts,
To be away from time.

A place to look inside your dreams
And hope that they'll come true.
A place to reflect back on yourself,
To make sure you're really you.

A place where you don't have to
pretend
Or fight and sweat and strive.
A place to give thanks to your creator
And be glad that you're alive.

A place to light a candle
And watch its silent glow.
A place that's filled with love and
peace
Is that any place you know?

Bonita Baker Ray
A MOTHER'S LOVE

I dedicate this poem to my mother, Bonnie Baker, who gave me life a second time with the gift of a kidney which has been running on love ever since. Thank you, Mother.

When I was thirty-six, I won't go into
why,
My doctor said, "You are going to
die."
He said I needed to call on God and
Medical Science,
But I also had another source of
reliance.
You see my mother said as usual, "I
am here."
And she stood ready and willing to
volunteer.
God blessed us richly when He
invented the mother.
For she carries a love like you'll find
in no other.
As my thoughts raced back through
all the years,
I remembered us sharing love,
laughter and tears.
So on March 15, 1989, she again
gave me life,
And restored me as a daughter,
mother and wife.
I can truthfully say my mother is a
part of me,
For I share not only her love, but also
her kidney.

Gina Marie Brkich
THAT SPECIAL SOMEONE

You are special, in a certain way.
You're always there for me, every
day.
We've shared laughter, tears, a smile
and a frown,
And you've always picked me up
when I was down.
You are the greatest, yes you are.
You remind me of a shining star.
You stand out above the rest,
To me, you will always be the best.
I know that what we have is so true,
And I'm lucky to have someone as
special as you.

Eliasar A Simon
DREAMS ARE MADE

Dreams are made to puzzle you,
Dreams are made to wonder you;
And if you're trapped in this world,
You'll feel O' so blue,
'Cause it's hard to escape from you.

I always dream and dreamed of you,
In a wonderful world,
Together with you;
Where the clouds in the sky,
Were made of rainbows,
Moons and stars kept shining too.

I was on the seashore,
Waiting for you;
Where horses roamed,
While dolphins were playing;
I heard a song,
Like magic in the air,
I searched for it,
And there was you.

Carolyn S Hickey
HAPPY THOUGHTS

For my friend and inspiration, Pat Keplinger.

On a blistering hot summer day in
July
'Twas a Monday, without a cloud in
the sky.
On the seventeenth day of month
number seven
A baby was born, a tiny little gift
from heaven.
With eyes of blue and hair of spun
gold
On her cute little butt there was a
mole.

She grew and grew with Barbie doll
legs
Then one day, because of these pegs,
She received a call from Kenner.
They just knew they had a winner!
They turned her down when they met
her in the lobby
It was too bad but, her knees were
just too knobby!

She grew some more, this cute little
child
Then, oh my God! Her nose went
wild!
It grew and it buckled, then a lump
did appear.
Something like the antlers on Santa's
reindeer.
Now we use it for skiing, when we're
otherwise bored
So much for the cute little button she
had when born.

Wynne Lanzillotta
WITHOUT YOU

Emptiness
Emotionless
Endless

My
Days
Without
You

William Scott Galasso
FROZEN IN TIME

To my wife Vicki, whose love inspired this poem.

The moment is mine, always.
The North Sea wind
ripping through trees, snapping
pennants,
whipping umbrellas inside out
Walking briskly to escape the wet
of the Amsterdam rain.
Suddenly, your eyes embraced me—
steady, yet flowing
tear filled, yet brave
you first said "I love you,"
and left me forever changed.

Irene L Gentile
WAITING FRIENDS

To my wonderful mother, Margo, with love.

I come down in the morning,
I peer outside.
Seven little birds, by the
feeder hide.
I gather the scoop,
and out I go—
My fine feathered friends,
surrounded by snow.
The cheery chirps, heard
all around—
One of life's truly—
happiest sounds.

Edward J Thibeault
JUST THOUGHTS

To my loving and sensitive, caring wife, Anne. I love you—Eddie.

I think of thoughts so wonderful and
divine,
Here I am guessing to make you
mine,
Tonite my heart cried so many times,
Wondered why God sometimes is so
sublime,
To make US sensitive to use our
mind,

Your word dear God is through our
actions and deed,
Then why are we in this emotional
need.

You say talk of heavenly things puts
us in doubt,
Is that because earthly things we are
without,
A priest of yours in a trying time did
say,
These three—Pray—Work and Play,
A Song says clarity through each
other's love is what counts,
This is what we must surmount.

Chester A Harris
FAITH

To My Inspiration, Maudie, My Wife.

The night was black as black can be,
The wind and rain, relentlessly,
Pounded the speeding train.
Passengers, huddled, frantic, inside,
The women prayed while children
cried,
Some men became profane.

Fear increased as did the storm,
Windows rattled as hail took form,
Crashing against each pane.
Frenzied fear gripped everyone,
Each hoping the trip would soon be
done,
All safe and sound again.

A man who sat near the front of the
car,
Nervously chewing an unlit cigar,
Watched a child across the aisle,
Who munched on cookies and played
with her doll,
Oblivious to the danger that
frightened all,
Continued to play and smile.

The man reached over and touched
the child,

"Aren't you afraid with the storm so wild,
When the rest of us are filled with fear?"
"Oh, no sir," the little girl replied,
As she carefully brushed cookie crumbs aside,
"My father's the engineer."

Michele Abner
COME AND DREAM

This poem is dedicated to my mother. I love you!

Come along and dream with me
before the sun sets.
Come along and let's share our
thoughts, wants, needs and dreams.
Come along and care with me,
share life's smiles and
trials with me.
Come along so we can dream
together before the sunset
of the day.

Margaret D'Aquino
WEB OF LIFE

To Vincent.
"May the Lord wash away his web."
Love, Mom. 1990.

How well this web of life we spin
That we ourselves are trapped within.

The outside world seems far away
The web secure and here to stay.

Perhaps the Lord will send a heavy rain
Wash away the web and set us free again.

Deborah Godfrey-Farrell
P-TOWN

This poem is dedicated in Loving Memory of Dad, and a special weekend in New England.

In a coastal New England town
On a wintery sunday morn
People came to the call
Of the church bells singing their songs
Inside warmth and sharing abounded
A service like never before
Will touch the hearts of many
Emotions will definitely pour
A place where god is ever present
Perhaps he's created a special breed
For they can live in harmony
Something that is rarely seen
The sun will shine much brighter
For my eyes have seen the light
This I can definitely say
Was a weekend memorably spent

George D Lynch
GOD'S GOLDEN REST

To my dear wife, a good woman-Friday, who has dedicated her life to meeting our needs, and making me happy.

It came out of 'no-where' on gossamer wings
That warm evening the last of July,
Seeking nectar of marigolds and zinnias
Came that big, yellow, Tiger Swallowtail butterfly.

It chased away 'Monarchs' and 'Buckeyes'
As it cruised the length of the rows,
Looking amongst reds, pinks and yellows
For the tallest, sweetest zinnia God grows.

I paused a few moments from my labor
Of weeding, choping, and hoeing,
To see which one of my wife's flowers
This big, yellow insect was going.

When it finally found a three-foot tall zinnia
And settled to probe its inner recess,
I laid down my hoe from my labor
For I needed a period of rest.

The kiss of God's sun for pleasure
The song of God's birds for mirth,
When I'm at home working in God's garden
I'm closest to 'Heaven on Earth.'

Elaine M Paglivca
SALVATION

This is dedicated to the Glory of God, and for the furtherance of His Kingdom.

God in all his wisdom knew
There'd be sinners like me and you.
So he sent his only Son.
That our salvation would be won.

Jesus died for all our sins,
So we could all be Born Again.
So do yourself an eternal favor
Accept Jesus Christ as your Personal Savior
And when you do accept the Lord,
Heaven will be your reward.

And if you say, "I will not,"
You will go where it is HOT.
So my friend do not delay
The time for salvation is today.

Faye Marie (Standley) Grote
SOUNDS OF LOVE

To my first grandchild: Nicholas Deshawn Beeman.

You ask me why I love you,
With words I cannot say.
But it comes with a feeling, I have each passing day.
Sometimes it's a feeling, I get when I look into your eyes.
And sometimes it's when you touch me, my heart cries out a sigh.
It's a warm and tender feeling, deep within my heart.
Sometimes I think it will stop beating and just rip me apart.
So when I say "I love you" and I can't explain it with words.
Just listen to my heart beat and listen to my sighs.
For they are the true and tender meaning of love.
A look, a touch, a sigh.

Elizabeth M Wydler
THE ROSE

So soft to touch
and delicate to the eyes
Yet beautiful to the mind
and loving to the heart.
The spirits they lift,
for that special someone.
Beautiful and warm
like a cool summer's day
You take my breath away.
I Love You . . .
The Rose

Michelle Green
LOVE

Love rides into the heart
bringing special elements,
heartaches and pain.
Love disguises itself
in many ways like seeds
implanting themselves
into the very core
of one's consciousness.
Love bolts into the heart
like lightning.
Love draws like a magnet
or dances like a child,
wild and carefree
in unbounded emotion.

Suezan Blair King
I WALK THE NIGHT

I walk the night, alone and blue.
As I walk, I think of you.
If only I could have known
with you life would be so torn.
What can I do, I can't face another morn,
I walk the night alone and blue.
I walk the night my last without you.

Valérie Idiens
THE HUNGER FOR VICTORIOUS INDEPENDENCE

To Flavienne de Torrenté, my wonderful mother.

The hunger for victorious independence
Marks the progressive pattern of flight.
And within those circles of breath
That propose to the lips an anger heated by love,
Lies still the profound lust for glorious unity.
Keeping watch with the wisdom
From inherent and unconditioned existence,
We shall remain together close.
To flee the potential arms of inertia
Is cause of our matter,
Bonding with our invisible limbs
Actualizes our form.
Thus,
As the particles of our nest shatter
The shape of our home grows;
Filling to the corners of this chosen pattern
The masterpieces of our experience.

Valérie Idiens
A BASKET AND A SHELL

When ignorance protects
The knowledge only lies as a tale.
Grit and sweat prepare him for battle
But not for the war.
Yet he leaves carrying a basket full of hope and pride,
And a head stuffed with soft ideals;
A body layered with hard equipment.
Upon his arrival, his basket is already half empty
As he witnesses the bloodshed
colouring his boots.
Weapons are thrust into his grasping hands.
Slowly his soft ideals fade;
Smudged away with pressure.
He is then sent out,
Ordered to serve in Hell;
To fight—to win! Win! Win!
Win what?
His basket, now empty, is hesitantly put aside
And all that is left is his shell,
Desperately trying to save him
From death that snaps so close behind.

Nancy A Donovan
OUR PATHS BLENDED INTO ONE

Though our paths have crossed before
We never met till now.
Lifting my eyes from my path I saw you.
Your path was parallel with mine.

We walked and talked.
Laughed and cried together.
We grew closer.
Our paths blended into one.
Entwined into something so unique and timeless.

Rejoicing in our goals and achievements.
Helping each other over the rough spots.
On we go hand in hand thru life.
Divided we were, one we are together.

Wayne Jones
CHILL . . .

Late each night as I lie in my bed
I listen and talk to the voice in my head

It tells me that I'll never lose, that I'll never fail
I tell it that my heart is pure, that I won't go to Hell

It haunts me all night till the break of dawn
When the light touches my soul the evil is gone

I could never express how it makes me feel
in that candle lit room and that familiar chill

Nancy Fay West
LITTLE-GIANT

Dedicated to my three sons—Patrick, David and Jimmy West.

Little-Giant of my making,
Faint with fear my heart is quaking,
For it's now that I am knowing
Into manhood you are growing.

No more my eager arms enfold you,
No longer will my loving hold you.
To the world I must surrender
My baby sweet, my baby tender.

Now if it be, then be it must,
I place you under God and trust
That He will lift you by the hand
And make you every inch a man.

Cheryl L Nelson
IF I COULD HAVE MY WAY

I sit on my window ledge
Gazing at the streets below
The cars go by quickly
Not caring, not slowing

There are no children
Rolling in the grass
There are no yards
With trees growing freely

No open fields
No poppies growing wild
No laughter of play
Only crying of sorrow

I want to see children
Playing in open fields
Smelling flowers
Climbing trees

I want to hear
The laughter
As they tumble and roll
Chasing each other

No worries
That's what the world
Would be
If I could have my way

Lynn Edelman
MY SECRET THOUGHTS
Many thoughts come and go,
Just as a waterfall will flow,
For the mind is complex,
As I know,
Where secret thoughts will always grow,

A world that belongs to only me,
Which no one else can touch or see,
Is it imagination,
Or just fantasy,
Thoughts of what I dream could be,

Visions in my head,
So real and alive,
If I let them out,
Will they survive?

Or shall I keep them,
Hidden in my mind,
As my secret thoughts,
For no one to find.

Annette Spurling
DEATH'S KISS
Tonight I heard his voice calling out to me.
If not my imagination, then what else could it be?
It was seven years ago today that he'd said, 'goodbye.'
He'd packed his things, walked out the door, and never told me why.
So as I lay here in the dark, I ponder, "Should I go?"
This house is large, and where I sleep, he surely doesn't know.
Forgetting my robe, I walk out into the hall.
I cannot see too clearly, so my fingers trace the wall.
Closer and closer I'm drawn to the eerie voice.
My body is reluctant, but moves as if it has no choice.
When at last I get to the door, I throw it open wide.
But instead of my love, the Angel of Death steps inside.
As she leads me by the hand, I say, "I thought it was my lover who had come back, you see."
She softly smiles and says, "It was seven years ago today that he left with me."

Rick Valasco
ME AND MY SON

Dedicated to my son Ricky Paul Valasco with all my love to a great little guy.

A walk in the country.
Just me and my son.
There's a sweet smell in the air;
As we watch the passing of the evening sun.
A doctor
A lawyer
The President
Maybe
What will my child grow up to be.
You hold his hand
Gentle but tight.
As you think about all the ugliness in sight.
There's pollution, mass murders, and war.
Poverty, his heartships, and sorrows and a lot more.
You turn your head and see a large deer.
Hold his head and antlers up with great pride and showing no fear.
You know it don't really matter to me what you grow up to be.
You'll always be my son
Because I love you, and I know you love me.

Michelle Trout
SISTERS AREN'T FOREVER
Sisters are forever—that's what I used to think,
But they can be gone real quick—just in a blink.
You shut your eyes for a minute, they don't waste any time,
And before you can get them back, you have to wait in line.
Sometimes they don't return, they give the place in their heart for you away,
All you can do is pray that she'll return someday.
But sometimes there's no hope, all is said and done,
There's nothing you can do because the other guy has won.
Then you think you might as well give up, she loves him more than me,
If that's the way she wants it that's the way it's going to be.

Mary Holguin de Morales

Mary Holguin de Morales
REFLECTIONS

Words for all time
for my husband
my love, my rhyme.

Will I be yours
and you be mine
or will someone else
be to you divine?

Will you leave me
at some point in time?
Will my heart still beat for yours
when later this I rhyme?

You cannot foresee the future.
Neither can I.
But will you always love me
until the day I die?

And afterwards . . .

When I'm long gone
will you tire
of my shadow
and put another's heart on fire?

Will I?

Jewell Turner
HAIR
"I want to shave my legs," she screamed, though she was only eight.
Dumbfounded, I tried explaining reasons she should wait.
"But boys at school make fun of me with all this ugly hair."
I looked down at her slim young legs with hardly a shadow there.
"You never wear a dress to school. How can they even see?"
"They call me Hairy Harris, mom," she screamed right back at me.
Harris was her surname and I understood her plight
But starting to shave her legs at eight years old just wasn't right.
As I stood there indecisive, some support I could have used
But the look upon my husband's face showed me he was amused.
It took hours to convince her to wait 'til the time is right
I could see that she was listening, I had almost won the fight.
My husband screwed the whole thing up at an amazing pace.
He said, "Why do you think your mother draws her eyebrows on her face?"

Allen Gerten II
JESTER
I've been called many names, but
I'm only known by a few.
Some think I'm pretty strange,
Even though it's true that I'm different.
Yet I have always humored these people,
Always able to make them laugh, which
Is the reason why I'm called the jester.
But I know you, and you've always known me,
You've always known me better than most people,
And sometimes better than myself.
You were the one, you were always the one who
Was there for me.
You showed me my own doubts and fears,
You taught me to laugh at myself before
Anyone else, you showed me who I really was, and you've
Always been my friend.
I will always be there for you,
I will be your shoulder to cry on,
I will be your hand to hold,
I will be your jester, but most of all,
I will be your friend.

Allen Gerten II
UNTITLED
Marriage is an event,
Some might say a mistake,
But to those who survive,
Encourage others to partake.
Many years are filled,
With love and compassion,
Plus simple affection,
Of any old fashion.
Anniversaries to cherish,
Rings to symbolize,
First and Second Honeymoons,
As an added surprise.
To give and to take,
To ask and to receive,
How a marriage can last,
I can't seem to perceive.
Marriage is made in Heaven,
Something no one can doubt,
Because Love is a flame,
You can't always put out.

Helena Dománska
TO THAT LAND
To the land where the mothers await
The return of their children from far away
And ever remember their separation
And to the land where the heart is complaining of pain

I long, O Lord

One day I'll walk forward
And will reminisce for the last time
Of the place where the wheat ripens in the sun
Although I may some day return

I grieve, O God

To the land where anguish is pressing
And life is as heavy as a hump
Where the only thing that matters
Is the treasure of SOLIDARITY

I long, O Lord

One day I'll meet my friends
Then they shall know the whole truth
Because I will spread before them the cards of life
Though I'm aware of their waiting for me

I grieve, O God

To the land where only anger
Like evil weed multiplies
Where the friendly greeting has been forgotten
And the earth has been often soaked with blood

I long, O Lord

And I am waiting for the return
Pain of separation cannot be appeased
I am left with loneliness and despair
Because of that—I grieve, O God
And endlessly—I long, O Lord

Angela L Hunn
SO BLEEDS THE RED, RED ROSE
Look at the rose bleeding
Reminds me of my heart
Seems it's crying like I
When we did part

I know we're still together
And always shall be
But it's just like the rose
When you're not here with me

So bleeds the red,
red rose—it's sad
And everyone says it's so bad

"Look at those two
Joined at the heart
Always together
Yet so far apart"

Jena Gronniger
MY BEST FRIEND
You walk the path with me
From beginning to end
You smile with me
And in times of aversion
You have held my hand

How can I ever repay you
For all the things you have done
You have been the moon at nite
And in the day you have been the sun.

On lively days you are
The spirit of captivation
On lamenting days
You chase away all my apprehension

You walk the path with me
From beginning to end
And through it all
You have always been my best friend

Justen D Reed
A SALUTE TO VETERANS OF WAR
In this life of freedom we live,
Some take and others give.
As we go through life without a care,
We often forget those who were there.
They fought for our freedom and fought for our pride,
We often never remember the ones who died.
They fought with great skill and agility,
We often treat them as a nonentity.
Imagine the anguish, the grief and the pain,
Many don't even realize what they gained.
Many gained nothing when others passed on.
But in America the Spirit of Freedom lives on.
We should be thankful and we should care,
And remember the ones who fought and died there.
In a salute of honor we should raise our hands,
And be thankful to them for keeping freedom in our land,
We salute the veterans for what they gave,
For the Land of the Free and the Home of the Brave.

Sunny Santry
A NOTE FROM SUNNY

To Mickey (Marilyn Bosia), remembering all the good times and fun at the Hop! ! ! The good old days! ! !

Here's a note from SUNNY,
It may be sad—It may, be funny,
It won't be jazz or a ballad
'Cause we make a very different
Salad.

Your greens as we all know
Isn't the kind that I call dough$
Your greens come in a head,
Where mine are sometimes referred to as bread.

As we toss our greens around
Mine nor yours will make a sound.
And tho your greens are high in Rank,
I'll keep getting mine from Tim's Bank! ! !

Money they say will never make you happy,
Can't prove it by me, just ask my Pappy,
He keeps my greens fresh all year
And I keep smilin' ear to ear! ! !
Now you have a note from SUNNY.

Dorthea Martin

Dorthea Martin
THE MOTH
You the flame and I the moth
Do a most dangerous dance we do.
I soar and swoop;
You flicker and flare.
I sing the song of singeing
Yet ever closer draw.

Oh flame, your power, your brilliance attracts.
I crave your heat
But fear I'll be consumed.

Would you still be flame
Were you divorced from candle?
Or would we both be butterflies
Unscathed by fire;
Drawing instead sweet floral nectar?

Kathryn P Duncan
BODIE
I stepped into the snow-bound streets,
Bitter wind prevailing.

From a sagging shack, a miner knew,
A mournful sound came wailing.

Just beyond, stood the wasted hill,
The heart of the ghostly town.

Its gaping mouth of greed and sorrow
Scarring the ravaged ground.

Machines and shacks are all that's left,
No longer alive with profit.

"It's no use to us," miners cried,
"Like the land it's on, just toss it."

The steeple from the little church,
Sinking on its foundation,

Had watched in silence, as they left
On the road that led to damnation.

Florence E R Foster
I FOUND PEACE
I sat awhile, to rest, . . . to dream,
Beside a cool and bubbling stream.
As I watched the sparkling waters play,
I banished all my cares away.
It was so peaceful and quiet there.
I enjoyed the coolness, and the clean, fresh air.
I could hear the nesting song-birds sing
As they welcomed in the new-born spring.
Buds and leaves, above me now, were emerald green;
And they so brightened up that woodsy scene; . . .
And blue violets that grew all along the river-bed,
Where the Lilies-of-the-Valleys nodded their pure, white heads,
Made that forest-trail an enchanting view,
With spring's warm, south-west winds; under a sky so blue.
Cold reality seemed so far away
As I watched a turtle sunning, and fuzzy, yellow, ducklings play
As the mother duck, nervously, paced the shore.
I promised myself, then, I would return once more, . . .
To sit awhile; . . . to rest; . . . to dream,
As I had found peace and tranquility by that cool, bubbling stream.

Donald Jacoby
MUSTY MEMORIES
The mind
like a musty attic
stores many things
A toy we had as a child
that was our favorite
When we grew up
we remember that toy
now
long put away
Memories of that long ago time
bring a smile
then life goes on
A person
can feel like that toy
from long ago
Merely a stored memory
from the attic
of someone's mind

Karrol Becker
DREAM LOVER
I try to tell myself that you were
just a dream
An elaborate fantastic fantasy
born out of loneliness
I say that you weren't real at all
But a figment of my imagination,
and out of desperation
I breathed life into you
You were never really here
The voice that whispered in my
ear
Was just the radio
The touch that caressed me
gently
Was only a warm wind blowing,
breathing soft upon my skin
Oh dream lover, how I miss you
How I long to hear you
Call my name again.

Susan Lynne Myers
MY ANGELS OF THREE

To my three angels . . . Stacie Marie, Julie Ann, and Jerry Lee . . . Love, Mom

My angels of three will always
forever be.
Three very special gifts my lifetime
gave to me.
Somehow these three lives were sent
from clouds above.
My angels of three were chosen
just for me to love.
The only reason there could be for
gifts from heaven such as
these.
To be a Mommy for my angels of three,
they needed a Mommy just
like me . . .

Peg'e Brunner Maruthur
TODAY

"Today" is dedicated to all those who care about tomorrow. Thank you Kumar, Nisa and Mario for being such an inspiration, and for your support!

I start the day
the usual way,
with thoughts of you kissing
me.
Romance in bed dances in my head
but patiently waits for the
morning kiss.

The way you glance at first
morning's sight
can set the mood for many
beautiful feelings,
or crush desires which then
may seem foolish
when not fed with
encouragement of acceptability.

How I wait for gentle touches
small kisses, carefully placed
with hunger for love.

Now, today is gone, tomorrow is beginning,
but how fast it goes,
when lost are feelings of
intimate moments,
numbering fewer and fewer
with time.

We must gaze into each other's eyes
and capture
the intense feeling that was
passed that day;
Someday the exchange we have
will no longer be
it may NOT be us, just POSSIBLY
me!
Then, all alone to recapture
sweet memories from the past

Today is JUST tomorrows passed!

Peg'e Brunner Maruthur
ODE TO A HOUSEWIFE
I am a housewife,
I really am,
I don't eat Bon-Bons and sit on my can!
Go look at my sink,
the dishes ARE GONE,
my laundry is done,
but I don't do lawns!

The garbage is emptied,
the beds are all made,
I check in the fridge
for the trips, I will make,

to the grocery store! ! !

At lunch I sit, at my table, alone,
and think of my family
of when they'll come home,
to my house
all ready for them, to enjoy;
a kiss for the hubby,
my girl and my boy! ! !

They ask me, Hey mom,
how was your day?
before I can answer,
they usually say,
What did you do? NOTHING! ! !

I've spent my day
the usual way, leaving nothing,
left to be seen;
So, I guess in the end the fault lies
with me.
I feel they need to see a mess,
then they will find, that it takes
time,
for things to get done, so they
can have fun,
and enjoy their home.

The reality's funny,
I could leave them THIS MESS,
AND to my family's distress,
find a job that pays money!

Peg'e Brunner Maruthur
SEPARATED
I remember the beginning,
I'm sensing the end,
but the part that hurts
most, is this need to pretend!

They used to call me Mrs;
you used to give me kisses,
But now it's not we, just lonely me.

I look at friends' faces, friends we
used to see,
feeling their pity, of what still
should be!
Two people growing older, facing the
years,
sharing one future, the joy and
the tears!

But, instead we're two people, who
face life alone,
you've moved to your place, my
apartment's NO home!

I feel you have dreams of
being 25,
Yet, I thank the Lord, that we're still
alive!

We're not too old for each other's
arms,
I would still melt, if you'd turn on
your charm!

You thrilled me many years ago,
how I loved you then.
Now after years of loving you, you
say we'll JUST be friends!

Whenever I call you,
your voice is SO cold,
you make me feel ugly, you
make me feel OLD . . . . . .

In my head I knew 50, was the
beginning of the end,
But my heart kept on hoping,
now it's broke, and now it's
bent!

Maybe, one day you'll realize,
you've made a mistake,
you'll wake up & phone me, you
won't hesitate,
to say that you love me,
and want SO to come back!

Now, I must introduce you, to my
new friend, Jack,

We've started a beginning,
you are seeing the end
of my need to hold on, and our need
to pretend!

Peg'e Brunner Maruthur
LAST THOUGHTS, PAST THOUGHTS, AS YOU WALK OUT ON HIM!
As you walk out your door, you
carefully glance at things,
you'll see no more,
Anger & regret walk beside you.

You cooked, you cleaned, you baked,
at times, when NEEDED, you
faked;
Just to make him happy!

You gave him children
with each one,
you tried your best,
Just to make him happy!

Lonely days, empty nights,
you believed in him, despite the
fights;
His dreams, you thought you could
fulfill,
without a drink, without a
pill . . . .

Remember parties,
you felt SO alone,
then SAT in silence, while
riding home;
Why can't he joke? Why can't talk?
you wanted so, to get out and
walk!

You had so much, though times were
rough
but he never slept alone,
You worked so hard to fix the house
making it your home!

The years went by
the children grew,
you learned in time
just what to do;
He didn't want to share
in time, you DIDN'T care!

The children, now are gone
and you must carry on; alone.

You leave him now
with pills and booze,
and weekends filled with time to
snooze.

It's sad to leave him in your home
but he's regressed, while you have
grown . . . . .

Karen "KaKa" Kidwell
THOSE EYES

A dedication to my special friend D. Maples.

You may be shy and quiet and not a
word spoken
But the gleam in your eye—the
silence is broken
I can see in your deep blue eyes there
is more
Don't you know that your eyes are
the door
That speaks of your personality and
your soul

Those big brown eyes catch my
attention as they look at me
I feel the goose bumps rushing
through me as I see
You are giving me all the attention
the way you do
And the gentleness in those eyes tells
me a lot about you

Notice the look in those cat green
eyes that speaks of mystery
Wondering what's behind those eyes
speaks of what kind of history
Possesses in this particular person
standing there
With bright blonde hair flowing in
the gentleness of the air

Catch my breath as I see those vivid
blue eyes
That match the color of the sunny
bright blue skies
Toppled off with a mop of tousled
black hair
With the clean pure skin so fair
With this combination catches my
attention and my fancy

The eyes give it all away
Whenever they look my way
Those smiling eyes just made my
day!

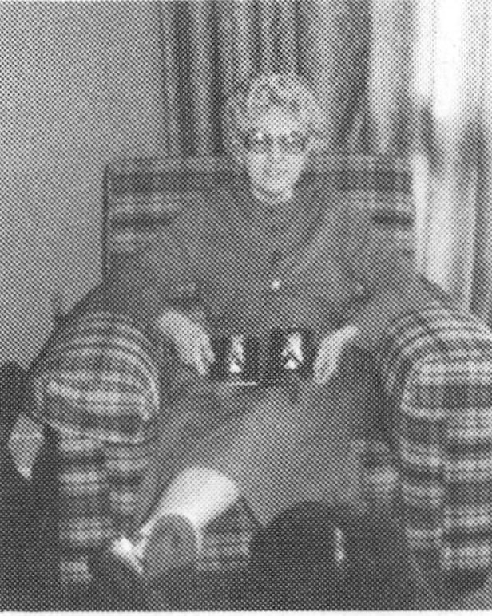

Bernice Couey Bishop

Bernice Couey Bishop
LITTLE BRONZED BABY SHOES

To two of my sons, Ralph and Ronnie, whose baby shoes, preserved in bronze, were the inspiration for this poem.

In a special place, where I can easily
see,
I have placed these little bronzed
baby shoes,
And as I look at them, in my
memory,
I have my babies who once wore
them back with me.

I pick up one and caress each
wrinkle, each fold,
Put there long ago by one who is now
getting old,
Hoary head now adorns the one who
wore the shoe I hold,
But in my memory he is a baby
again, and with love this little shoe I
enfold.

Then the other little shoe I hold
lovingly to my breast,
This little shoe showing that this little
one passed the test,
Of developing from baby in a crib, to
one who happily played with all of
the rest,
And when I look at these little
bronzed baby shoes, I know that I am
very blessed—

To have these relics of my sons,
enshrined in bronze are they,
For no longer are they needed by the
ones who wore them in a long ago
yesterday,
For the babies outgrew them, as
babies they could not forever stay,
And I thank God that I have these
relics of them, these little baby shoes,
preserved in bronze today!

Renae D Pilgrim
UNSPOKEN
Pearls fall from the sky
upon a kaleidoscope of trees.

A golden land with rubies
hid within its sparkling leaves.

A feeling far beyond the thought
of any unspoken dream,

Nature's gift to almond eyes
it is meant for me to see.

Although it does not speak aloud
I know it shouts and screams

Of all the things that it has seen
and all those shattered dreams.

The story to tell will never be told,
but expressed through colors of
yearning
Of all the lies and promises
the forest has been learning.

Deborah Pfrimmer
LIFE'S CONFUSIONS

This poem was written with Jerry Ponce in mind, during the summer of '88.

Something inside me, like a
hurricane,
Is dying to whirl its way out.
It's gathered pieces and parts of me,
That I can't do without.

If I open up, I know right now,
So much will be left unsaid.
And if I hold back, it only gets worse;
Confusion plays with my head.

Choices, decisions, all to be made,
For my life future, present and past.
I'm holding strong, holding together,
But I don't think I can last.

As weakness grows rapidly,
And my emotions want to show.
Someone tell me from experience,
Should I hold back or let it go?

One piece that still remains in me,
Is my determination to get by.
But now I've gotta gain one more
part—
My will to live and to try.

I know I'll go insane . . .
If I shelter this hurricane.

Shirley Turnbull Littlepage
THE GIRAFFE
The giraffe has the longest neck
—I'm sure,

And when his throat gets sore it's
hard to cure.

He's yellow and brown—with
irregular spots

Not at all common—like
polka dots.

Did you ever wonder how funny
he'd be

If they shortened his neck—
heaven's what could he see?

Constantina D Hodnett
WISHING WELL
Wishing-well, wishing-well,
Who is there ever to tell,
Of dreams and of goals,
Yet to be fulfilled?

Going forward, onward and upward,
Learning as we go along,
For dreams often come true,
And pleasant dreams mature fulfilled.

Only for those who truly believe,
That this really can be done,
What is self-fulfilling prophecy?
This is really nothing new under the sun.

Because wishing-well, wishing-well,
For some people, I can tell,
Have clean thoughts, bodies and minds,
And, after the wishing-well, comes the show-and-tell,
Of those who made the success time, after time, after time.

Orville A Cottrill
IN SEARCH OF PEACE
Dedicated to Mechile Lynn Cottrill.

Dark and fearful storms,
Rise up in every life.
Days that are filled with sorrow,
Days that are filled with strife.

Behind the dark, of every storm,
Is a rainbow full of love.
Descending upon you,
Like the gentleness of a dove.

Search through your heart,
Then search through your soul.
Devote your life,
To a permanent goal.

A true friend, stands by you,
Through thick and thin.
A true love, shall last!
Till the bitter end.

There is a time to make war,
There is a time to enjoy peace.
A time to walk softly,
On a lone, tranquil beach.

Those dark, fearful storms,
Will slip slowly away.
And a new love may grow strong,
With each passing day.

Leroy Henderson
ADDICTION
I am a born addict
There is no refuting it,
Try as I may—there is no concealing it,
My body craves it—I want to just say no,
My mind says, It won't let you go.

I try to go cold turkey,
My addiction wins out,
I contemplate suicide—to terminate this nightmare,
But, I can't get up the nerve—to halt my descending despair.

As I look in the mirror, the reflection of someone else,
Skin and bones and glassy eyes can't be what I see,
For I know that person can't really be me.

I'm determined to kick the habit any way I can
'Cause, If I can't win this one it surely will be my end.

Finally! I realized, how dangerous this addiction can be.

Because your love is slowly killing me!

Fred W Ludwig

Fred W Ludwig
THANKSGIVING THANKS
Some of the younger generation of today,
Really wonder when the older ones say,
Give thanks!

Most have new cars, jobs and CB's,
While for others unemployment pays the fees,
Give thanks!
The older folks work for thirty-forty years,
Only to face retirement days with fears,
Give thanks!

They cannot afford to keep the pace,
They must sell their home and retirement place,
Give thanks!

But you know for all its irritating ways,
Where could you honestly spend pleasanter days,
Give thanks!

For this free land—for freedom of speech,
For hundreds of goals it's possible to reach,
Give thanks!

For Mom, for Dad, for the family,
For the healthy tot upon your knee,
Give thanks!

When you gather tomorrow as a family clan,
Talk, watch football and eat all you can,
And give thanks!

In millions of ways it's Thanksgiving Day,
Give your thanks in your own special way,
But give thanks!

Fred W Ludwig
A PRAYER
A prayer is not a prayer
If every line must be read,
A prayer is not a prayer
If the words are only said

The mind must be included
In a prayers major role,
For it Sorts, Files and Listens
To the message from the soul

Yes—A prayer is more than words
Expressed in a reverent way,
It's you—As you think and feel
And live throughout each day

Yet you needn't be an orator
Nor skilled with word or sword,
Let good thoughts fill heart and soul
Lay your trust unto the Lord

Ask for peace all around the world
or blessings on family, and kin,
Give hope to the sick and afflicted
And those overwhelmed with sin

Just pray for help and good things
that the world needs en-masse,
Then place your trust in the hands of God
And it shall come to pass.

Patricia Pate
A NEW PERSPECTIVE
When I met you, my world took on new meaning
You taught me to believe, to find joy in the smallest of things
You taught me to hear my heart sing, telling me I could stand on my own
By knowing that I'm truly never alone
You held me and dried all my tears
You taught me to work through the fears
Once I faced life full of dread
You taught me to greet each new day instead
You filled my life with hope and good cheer by knowing you'd always be
Near
You colored my world in bright blues and greens by giving me laughter
Among other things
So now when I greet each brand new morn I'm aware of the rose and not
Of the thorn

Missy Gavel
A PLATOON OF CLOUDS
Flushed blues and baby pinks
dust the evening sky
like cotton candy
as it is pulled apart—
thinning, airy and light.
The clouds hang gently above
the Earth
as a mobile hangs above a baby's crib.
Blackened silhouetted trees
are scattered along the horizon.
Invading the peacefulness of sunset
are heavy, burdening bulks of
gray masses.
Each mass depicting something different.
The leader of the troop
marches forward as an alligator
followed by a few ducks and
rippling waves of other soldiering clouds.
Now the pinks darken into lavender
and the blues into grays
and the grays into black.
With the twinkling of the first star
night falls.

C Esther Capps
I AM NOT THERE
Do not stand at my grave and weep,
I am not there, I do not sleep.
I am a thousand winds that blow,
I am the diamond glint on snow,
I am the sunlight on ripened grain,
I am the gentle autumn rain.
When you awake in the morning's hush
I am the swift uplifting rush
Of quiet birds in circling flight
I am the soft, starshine at night
Do not stand at my grave and cry,
I am not there, I did not die.

K Hampshire
HELD LOOSELY IN THE ARMS OF NO ONE
Lips burdened
Eyes hidden behind fences of skin
Walls of fear.
I touch you like imprisoned
humans touch
& nothing more.
Buried in the losses of the past
Sustaining only for losses
of the future
I am yours to create
Yours to destroy.
I ask only, for you to be gentle.
Hands that leak of hesitation—
Arms, legs, escaping
In near perfection
The oblique realms of tiny
scavengers,
The tune you whisper so freely
Is a pleasant one.
Still, I have heard better,
Teased in fiery display of movement
w/out
Conscious effort for
control
Sound w/out use for words
I forfeit this promise I swore to keep
& become father to your pain

Mother to your desires
A groping prince of need
There's more to life than life itself
Or so I will say
When the monster's breath
Is dark & heavy
& I am held loosely in the
Arms of no one

Stacy Sechrist
SOMEONE SPECIAL

This poem is dedicated to Bill Procter, my special grandfather.

He is sweet, yet he is strong.
He is always right, never wrong.
He is a railroad man, a man of wisdom.
He is a patriot, thankful for freedom.
He is loveable, as a teddy bear.
You can talk to him, he is always there.
He is peaceful, he can't stand war.
He would never fight, he hasn't before.
He is faithful, a man of religion.
He is smart, a man of reason.
He often speaks of days gone by.
He is someone special, he is quite a guy
This great man, I am speaking of
Is someone, whom I deeply love.
He is my Grandfather, he is the best,
For this great gift, I am deeply blessed.

Adam H Geller
NY SUBWAY 88

To Mom, Dad, & Paul.

Chimpanzees with caviar
And burnt out flesh in the
night time mist

Sultry looks from women who
look like they just fought a
war

Tin Pan Alley pipers sing while
sweat glazed students have other
things to hear

Cut 'em up shoe shines and
Hate du jour while three piece
warriors trip without grace.

And cameras click in the
night time swirl of a thousand
raindrops yet to fall and
fall again.

Alice Teniuch
THE CROWN OF THORNS

To My Husband Jakym and Children.

A crown of thorns pressed on his head
The streams of blood flowed crimson red
The agony on his face expressed
To teach his faith he was oppressed

His disciples stood by unable to help
A heartfelt anguish by all was felt
What have they done to the Master of all
Carrying the cross we would see him fall

The road to Calvary was rocky and rough
The soldiers in armour thought they were tough
They jeered and taunted this holy man
With the crown of thorns is how it began
He struggled to carry this heavy cross
In his heart, he knew all was not lost
He was carrying out his Father's will
To carry the cross to the top of the hill

You could hear the pounding of the nails
His blessed mother cried out in wails
The distraught followers were standing by
It was for our sins he chose to die

Arlene M Babb
RESULT OF TOO MUCH CRITICISM

An extremely critical eye has he,
Whom everyone respects
It seems,
But me.

So critical an eye has he,
That I have learned
To dodge
His company.

It isn't that my faults are many,
It's just that
He thinks
He hasn't any.

Theresa H Eastridge
MEMORIES OF A SON

To Charles and Timothy, with love.

Today you will be leaving home,
It is the first time since you were born,
I will be alone,
I always knew the day would come
When you would say I have grown up,
I just never thought it would come so soon,
There are so many memories of you,
Like your first smile,
The wonder in your eyes, as you saw your first snow,
And how you would cry when the wind blowed,
The fright in your eyes as you took your first step.
And as you let my hand go and started to run,
day after day you played in the sun,
And all too soon your school years flew by,
These tears are of joy, love, and a job well done,
Just remember the woman that taught you how to love,
Don't be afraid to take that first step,
Because yesterday you were a boy,
Today a man.

Edna C Geaslin
EULOGY

Do not stand by my grave and weep,
For I'm not there—I do not sleep.
As a Spirit, now, I'll always live
In feelings, deep, tho' my voice is still.

I'll be in music, a sweet refrain,
In a tune you hear—a song you sing.
I'll be in the clouds that float on high,
In trees that reach up for the sky,
In a gentle breeze that wanders by,
Refreshing rain, when the earth is dry.
I'll be in a laugh, a wish, a sigh,
A mother's kiss, a baby's cry,
In a world full of love and tenderness,
In a precious gift, a sweet caress.

For you see, I'm a Soul, a sacred thing,
And like the effervescent Spring,
I'll live with Jesus, up above,
Embraced by God's eternal love.

So do not stand by my grave and cry,
For I'm not there—I did not die.

Suesan A McDonald
AS I SAT ON THE OCEANFRONT

As I sat on the oceanfront, thinking of bad times gone by
I felt sorry for myself and I wondered why
Everything happened the way it had
For some strange reason I was focused on the bad
I bathed in my sadness
Feeling that life, then, was so pointless
I was unsure if I'd be alright
So I prayed to God, asking for some insight
Suddenly, everything was so clear
I was cleansed of my sadness and fear
As the ripples faded across the horizon
I began realizing
I have the ultimate reason to live
The most precious gift God could give
There was a beautiful vision on the sea
A small remembrance of what once had been me
So I turned around, picked up my three year old daughter
Sat her on my lap and we watched the sun set on the water . . .
Together

Adele Danise-Lesandro

Adele Danise-Lesandro
ALONE IS EMPTY

Lonely are those who have no love
Lonely are those who want no love
To be alone is to die alone
For without human touch or love
The body dies from being without
the nourishment that it gives
Alone the mind has no thought of anything
but oneself
To be alone there is no one to share
your thoughts or feelings
It's a blank without reality.

James W Stephenson
QUESTION FOR AN ANSWER

For my nephews: Alex and Eric—when they grow a little older.

Oh, I'd like a
Lottery win of a million or two;
A secure future, a new car
When troubles make me blue.
I'd love to love my way
To the grave, a Lothario with women;
Seasons change all that is staid.
Laugh, eat, drink, and be merry,
Chase—and capture—rainbows—
Is that all in my head?
Not everything I have I need—
Nor everything, certainly, I need do I want.
But coming up, frequently,
(And with success)
With what I do crave—
I rely on the Lord.
(I ought to behave.)

A solution: Could it be so tough
To simply say, "I am enough?"

Mary D Rosenquist
A MOTHER'S LOVE

To Kyle and Brian.

If you ever spend a day with Brian and Kyle, such happenings going on all the while.
To wake up in the morning and find their room in all disarray.
I say Good Morning my little ones, did you sleep well?
After breakfast it's facewashing, teethbrushing, and I'll help dress you up.
Morning cartoons on TV, story books I read to you aloud.
Just sitting on the floor playing with these two, is what I love.
Almost time for Brian's 10:00 nap.
Fix his medicine to rid his cold and then to bed.
Kyle and I whisper softly, as Christmas ideas begin to whirl in our head.
Laughing in pillows, so not to wake Kyle's little brother, who is sleeping soundly—
Thank the Lord I pray.
Lunch at noon can be quite fun.
Babbling and talking and eating better now.
Brian is even starting to drink from a cup.
Almost as I say to you this very minute, Kyle asks for more food but he says, "Mommy my tummy is all fulled up."
Afternoon naps come at 2:00; as I sit in my rocking chair. All is quiet in this blessed house Phew!
At last we have had supper with their dear ole Dad.
Bath time, jammies and quiet time I'm glad.
Off to bed now my Sweet Baboos. I will kiss you and sing you lullabies.
I love you Kyle and Brian.
Close your eyes and go to sleep. A new day will be coming soon when I hear on the monitor your waking voices peep.

Nancy Romashko
PRAYER

To my brother Michael, because his life was not in vain.

Prayer is the key that opens up The Gate,
Of hopes projected to the highest source;
To God express the wishes of our fate,
To those in Heaven do we seek recourse.

Prayer gives a fuller meaning to our lives,
It fills us with a love for all mankind;
To higher elevations our soul strives,
There only will we find our peace of mind.

To laugh and scoff at prayer is bad indeed,
It is the means by which we talk with God;
And he will punish those who cannot see,
That those who need not talk with Him are fraud.

We all must pray until our dying day,
Then only will our final judgement pay.

David Fremgen
ON THE LAKE

Dedicated to Mrs. Pat Armstrong for her creative guidance in my explorations of our natural environment.

Dragonfly sits on a hard rock
Waves and wind
Whisper while waking.

The seaweed on the rocks is green
And waves in the water freely.
But below,
Its roots hold it firmly to the rocks.
Fish have a nice home.

Green patches of trees on glass
Rocks all around us
Sensations ricochet here.

Everything and Nothing
are intermingled
And yet they are not.

Jon Dicus
THE OUTSIDER

I dedicate this poem to Mr. Bill Miller for the incredible encouragement and support that he has given to many young students, and poets, like myself. Thanks, Bill!

He once was loved,
and wanted near.
But now is loathed
and thought quite queer.
Life had thrown
a wild curveball!
He'd been set up . . .
for one great fall.
No comfort left
in that cold place.
Though all alone,
He hides his face.
A rage within
turns to a tear
One feeling known,
Consuming fear.
All's lost or gone,
Yes, even her.
She sees him as,
The Outsider.

John Dicus
TO A WINNER

To Ann Ciancimino, who has exhibited such outstanding strength, courage, faith, and desire over the course of her recovery!

This life gets extremely tough here and there.
How horrid, a world that seems not to care.

If you're all boxed in say, "I'll climb the wall!"
But simple it's not, you might slip and fall.

With strength and courage is how you must go.
Be mighty, a fearful sight to your foe!

This present task seems too awesome to beat.
So will it be victory or defeat?

Decide this you must, for without a will
The battle is lost, you're beaten, until . . .

You light up the flame of that burning fire,
Hold on to faith and your deepest desire.

A winner is what you always shall be.
Defeat now is something you'll never see.

With faith and desire success always reigns.
You're sure to achieve incredible gains.

As you embark on this journey through life
You'll know victory, not heartache or strife.

So guard this faith and desire you have shown,
And never forget that you're not alone.

Theresa K Henderson
MY SPECIAL WISH

Who am I, to wish for worldly gain
A life of wealth, free from mortal pain
When all around, if I just stop to see
Many work so hard, for bare necessity

Who am I, to wish my home, was not so plain
Does it not shelter me from wind and rain?
And at the mealtime, food is always there
I hear there's homes with tables that are bare

Who am I, to wish for extra coins to spend
When just for food, the peasant's back must bend
Day in, day out, from early morn till dark at night
No rest for weary heart and hands, 'tis their sad plight

Better that I wish and hope for them
Here and everywhere to help the needs of man
And wish not all for some, when some have none at all
But wish that each, might have enough.

Mary Utt Bishop

Mary Utt Bishop
BREAKING UP

To my beloved granddaughter Wendi Carolyn Ford, age 20.

If it is not broken . . don't fix it.
If it is only cracked . . mend it.
Perhaps it will show . .
But only you will know its weakness
And "how it used to be."

If it is broken . . pick up the pieces.
Put the larger ones together
Gently . . and with care.
Weep over the ones that do not fit . .
But if there is still enough left to enjoy . .
Think of "how it could have been."

If it is reduced
To the teeniest of shining slivers . .
Sweep what is left into the trash.
For now there will be an empty space . .
But there is "tomorrow" to fill it.
But for "today" . .
That is "how it is."

Mary Utt Bishop
ELUSIVE

It was the butterfly
You didn't catch
Those lovely wings
Of gossamer gold
That eluded your most forceful clutch
And your grasping fingers
Could not hold.

It was the fish
You didn't land
The biggest one you'd ever seen
That got away . .
And as you watched
Its silvery fins
Became a gleam.

It was the heart
You could not reach
The one you wanted . . though, not right
And when you finally let him go . .
The tears flowed softly
THROUGH THE NIGHT.

Mary Utt Bishop
GOD'S GOODNIGHT KISS

I would share
With those around me . .
Blessings of
God's love and bounty . .
Comfort when
The soul lies barren . .
With the knowledge
That He's caring . .
And the ultimate
Of bliss . .
Peace of mind . .
GOD'S GOODNIGHT KISS.

Mary Utt Bishop
LOOKING FOR LOVE

Be careful where you look for love . .
Be careful what you find,
For there are boundaries you cannot cross
And souls you cannot bind.

The heart is delicate . . so easily hurt
And cautious to respond . .
And right words of trust and faith
Are sometimes hard to find.

Don't depend too much on others
To bring sunshine to your days
For happiness is that inner strength
That helps you find your way.

Your self esteem means very much
When fate deals you a blow . .
And you must hold yourself above
The loves that come and go.

Mary Utt Bishop
WELCOME

A prisoner welcomes
The small ray of light
That penetrates his cell.
The thirsty earth
Would take a drink
From God's everlasting well.
The stars welcome the twilight
So their light can shine.
The moon awaits its fullness.
The bell awaits its chime.
The cradle welcomes the baby.
The old man welcomes the sea.
The fatalist awaits his fate.
The trunk becomes a tree.
The dark awaits the dawning
Of a new day . . and the light.
God awaits His children
In a land where there is no night.

Mary Utt Bishop
THE END OF A DREAM

The only thing
I've learned of love
Is how to say "goodbye"
And to try to smile
As I walk away
From a dream
That slowly died.

All the wisdom
That I've garnered
In my rendezvous
With life
Comes to surface
As I deal with
The pain of each "goodbye."

But at the end
Of grieving
Once again I'll find
That a rose will bloom
When winter's gone
In the garden of my mind.

Mary Utt Bishop
THE LITTLE PULPIT
The little pulpit . .
Silent now
The voice behind it gone . .
But even as the wood is there . .
The silent voice lives on
In lives it touched . .
In words of love
In the gentle folk it blessed . .
The little pulpit . .
Silent now.
The silent voice
AT REST.

Cynthia Gail Caldwell
I NEVER KNEW

Dedicated to Jeremy Fry.

As a child I never knew my father
He left when he knew I was to be born
He left my mother for another woman
His spineless action left me scorned

You see, he never wanted me from the start
He saw an easy way out
Then he tried to deny I was his
When it was obvious, there was no doubt

He never saw me take my first step,
He was never there when I cried
He never even held me in his arms
He didn't care if I lived or died

My mother is better off without him now
She taught me well on her own
I have no feelings for him at all
You don't miss someone you've never known

Cynthia Gail Caldwell
WE DON'T TOUCH
Lyin' here, in the bed
I just feel like crying,
We don't touch
Anymore
I think you gave up trying

What is wrong between us
I want to understand
Can you get
The feeling back
Do we have a chance

Something inside
Is telling me
You don't have the same desire

You always seem
To turn away
When I try to light the fire

I need to know in my heart
What it is that's dying
We don't touch
Anymore
I think you gave up trying

Wes Robertson
THE SPARROW CRIED
I heard from on high, a sparrow cry.
I heard his soft voice and paused to wonder why.
What could have cracked a heart so small?
Was it lost love—or a soul weary of it all?
As I stood still, the bird took flight.
And with him, my heart flew with the sight.
It wasn't sorrow that drew his voice that day.
He flew above in spiral and loop. He sang as if to say,
"Feel not sorry for me; a tuft of feather, a bit of bone.
For I, along with all my fellows, am never quite alone."
Somehow my revelry was broken. I continued my walk.
Oh, what stories could be told—if sparrows could talk.

Charlotte B Thomas
LONGING

To my mother.

You are the one, the one I long to see
The one in all the world who means the most to me
You are the one whose secret thoughts I've shared
The one, the only one who really cared
What I became, what path my life would take
What hearts I'd fill with joy, what hearts I'd break

Yours is the hand, the hand I long to touch
The hand that asks so little yet gives so much
The hand that, oh so willingly, through God
Helped me along the path that I must trod
The path I love, the path from which I stray
The path toward which I look with each new day

Yours is the heart, so filled with love it flowed
To all who traveled with you on the road
Yours is the heart that opened wide to me
And made me want like you some day to be
Someone to care what path another takes
Someone to ease another heart that breaks

I am the one, the one whose hand and heart
Are often groping, seeking in the dark
I am the one who slowly, day by day
Finds greater need of help along the way
The way that leads to all that's good and right
To you, and where my heart has gone tonight

Renate Schuetz
SOMEDAY
Someday . . .
I will find you.
Someday . . .
I will hold you.
Someday . . .
I will touch you.
Only then
Will we walk hand in hand
Thru meadows
And gaze at the skies.
Our hearts will be free
To live and to love.
Someday . . .
Will be ours
For all eternity.

Gina Claudili
IT WILL ONLY HURT ME MORE
Don't look back when you head for the door
Because if you do it will only hurt me more
Don't stop to explain
Don't tell me why
If you're going to leave
Just tell me goodbye
I love you, I'll miss you
I can't make it alone
I want you, I need you
But I can't call you my own
I can't tie you down, you've got to be free
I can't make you love only me
So don't look back
I'll tell you again
Just kiss me goodbye
If this is the end.

Luella L Ganahl
THE CHAPEL TREE

This poem is dedicated to my family and friends.

Today I stood inside God's chapel,
A tree as beautiful as a golden apple.

The breeze gently waved the opened curtain,
And the stairway to heaven suddenly opened.

Tired and woesome I entered the gate,
And found a serenity from mankind's hate.

A temple of limbs and leaves arched over me
And sunlight beamed through the Linden Tree.

I rested inside the Chapel Tree
With the arms of God cradling me.

With spirit rested and a heart much lighter,
I walked out the door with future brighter.

God promised us a life we can bear,
Full of hope and joy, absent of fear.

Know this is true when you become part
Of God's Chapel Tree with a happy heart.

Luella L Ganahl
CHIMNEY SMOKE
Belched into the crisp air yawning,
Chimney smoke rings turning and running.

Lingering, circling, crazy shapes trail by.
Disappearing, reappearing, high in the sky.

Pushing, rushing, then in a daze,
Playing hide and seek in the haze.

Traveling, fading out of sight, and do they die?
I know more of where they're going than I.

Luella L Ganahl
ON LOSING A SON
A blue-eyed boy and a joy was he,
A child past twelve of rare antiquity.

The bicycle he rode was called "Blue Flame,"
But his bicycle jaunts were not to blame.

The culprit was just a man driving a big sedan
That ran over the boy as he walked on the land.

What turmoil it caused my heart
When man and boy met in the dark.

The young boy was fresh out of luck,
The impact so great as if hit by a truck.

In the game of life, there are no winners,
But living has nothing to offer quitters.

The morning comes day after day
The clock ticks in the same old way.

The sun shines, birds sing,
And losing a son is a very bad dream.

A child is a great gift,
Well worth the risk.

A child more precious than all earth's jewels,
Claimed by heaven in need of a pearl.

Luella L Ganahl
GREATNESS SHARED
Our world has awesome paintings to view—
Rembrandt, van Gogh, and Russell, too.

Music for happiness all life through, Chopin,
Mozart, Beethoven, and Irving Berlin.

Lifetime longings are fulfilled in reading
Shakespeare, Keats, Shelley and Browning.

Then there's Frank Lloyd Wright
Creating architecture out of sight.

Self-fulfilled man has one thing in common
God-given talent, desire and yearning.

When sharing treasures of the best
One indeed is surely blest.

Luella L Ganahl
MAKING MOLASSES
Sugar cane grown and well tilled,
Cut with a single blow until the cart is filled.

Hitch up the mule, and off to the mill,
Where the mule is re-harnessed to the tongue and wheel.

Round and round under the lash,
Constant pounding hoofs on the path.

Creaking harness, crunching cane,
Work never finished, there is no gain.

The day's first sun beamed on the mule;
Sweat trickled down to keep him cool.

The sweaty leather straps, the foam stained collar
Proved this mule worth many a dollar.

Once in a while the mule would rest,
Then round and round again, pulling his best.

The poor, tired mule wearily laid down;
The master was upset, you could see his frown.

A whip in the air was, to no one's glee
Because the mule had gotten our sympathy.

Marian Kimpel

Marian Kimpel
LASTING FRIENDSHIP

To the "Special Guest" on my 80th Birthday.

When Irish Eyes are smiling, a Friendship's growing there
In the heart or mind or attitude; it abides inside somewhere.

I found it in a handshake—'twas given me at will
And after many months I find the memory warmer still.

A very tender, firm embrace starts a flutter in the heart,
Friendship keeps on growing—nearly tears the mind apart.
Then a cozy, loving feeling comes and brings a message too;
A special instinct tells you, that love has come to you.

Oh the comfort of a cherished Friend, trust that sets you free!
I find these nice things all intact
In what's grown between you and me.

Let's keep drifting forward like a refreshing summer breeze
Accumulating in our hearts those lovely memories.
Summer breezes do give way, we know not why or when,
The pleasant side is that in time, they will return again.

So let's continue on as though this episode won't end
And keep the loving thought in mind—
"We have a precious Friend!"

Marian Kimpel
REMIND ME!
(A Message of Hope)
HOLY SPIRIT, let me learn to know you better.
REMIND ME during the day that you are near
Waiting, because I need a steady hand to guide me.
REMIND ME that all I need do is ask.

When I need strength to get thru the day,
REMIND ME to call on you.
Each moment, each hour, if I seem to falter,
Come to me, remain near, You know I need you.
When I seem desperate or lonely, be there.
I know you are there, but REMIND ME.
If I am obsessed with troubled moments
Assure me of your presence.

Let me rely on your guidance along the way.
Let my insight be unclouded, my hope secure.
Let my faith in you be unwavering
Let me never forget for a moment,
Let your presence REMIND ME that
You are beside me, to guide me,
To be my inspiration, my hope, my Friend.

Lucy Doak
ODE TO THE PESKY SPARROW
Then there's the sparrow, quite prolific
As to noise, they're quite terrific.
They'll take over Jenny Wren's nest if allowed
They may flit and scold and scatter
Or they'll sit in endless chatter
Or they'll gather on a light wire in a crowd.

Wait a bit, the sitters flitter,
As they fly about and twitter
On the pretext they have other things to do
Like snitch chick feed on the sly
And snatch insects on the fly.
All at once, time through, on cue, away they flew. Adieu.

Through tough times, they've had grim livin'
To us, pain or gain they've given.
Theri ilk has been around these many years.
If we judge them within reason
'Twould seem the pesky bird is even,
They're the maker's 'give and take' so it appears.

Georgia B Green
TREASURE OF LOVE
Your love is precious my dear
Life now has a new meaning
You launched me into an exciting
Unending and ever deepening experience
Of a sun filled environment
Being near you is heaven
It's like a rich musical treat
With full orchestration
I pray it never ends
Such richness is ours
For only the taking
Treasures on earth to find
Not me my dearest
For I found the richest
Of treasures when I found you
All the great Qualities you truly possess
Always stay as vibrant and lovely my sweet
For you are mine
Truly mine now and forever
I have walked many miles
In this life so far
I have met many people
Of all walks of life
I have cherished many thoughts
Of love yet never finding
Until I found my rainbow
And until I found my dream
And that my darling is you
So delightful and serene.

Nicholas Cavaleri
THE FREE WORLD
The war is over, the year—1945
Peace throughout the world is coming by.

In San Francisco that same year
The superpowers were creating the U.N.
Designed to rule the world's affairs
and preserve peace and tranquility everywhere.

Germany remained divided—
A huge monster was erected—
"The Berlin Wall."

Separating east from west
Depriving People from freedom at its best.

Progress advances on
In medicine, literature, space science too.

World intelligence is in bloom,
Even sending men to the moon.

Now, twenty-eight years later—
Christmas-time—
"Peace on Earth."

Heads of government have agreed,
"Bring down the wall, let the people free."
Thank you God for our liberty.

Nicholas Cavaleri
LOVE YOUR COUNTRY
Red is for the Blood that has been shed
White is for the Purity
Blue, for the Loyalty that is shown

Two centuries and six years past
Since that Great Philadelphia Day

Times were hard; of this I'm sure
You stood Proud, Majestically endured
No time for discouragement along the way

Like the Rock of Gibraltar, strong as can be
Smoothing the waves of the troubled sea
Restoring security and tranquility

THERE YOU ARE
Stretching your arms as far as can be
Offering the world
FREEDOM, FRIENDSHIP AND LIBERTY

For all of this, God will guide and Bless you,
He will indeed

From far away lands, people come
To find a place and make their home
Where FREEDOM lives from
DAWN TO DAWN

HAPPY BIRTHDAY
AMERICA

Nicholas Cavaleri
MEMORIES BECOME GOLD
The golden color of this day has no end, filled with so much love
So many memories that only you could share without pretense

Can you still hear the trembling sound of yesterday's words,
"I love you, I love you dearly?"

Problems arose
Life has had its ups and downs
You faced them together
On all grounds

Time went on, you loved, you shared
Even little arguments here and there
Can't remember any? For love and respect there was always plenty

What a beautiful feeling it is
to grow older in wisdom and in peace

Peace in your heart in your family, too
As beautiful memories are passing through

It's a beautiful life.
Isn't that the truth.

Life is love
Love is God.

Happy Anniversary Mom and Dad
Happy Anniversary Grandparents

Carol June McGee Ferre
THE PATH

For my Mother who believed in me.

We walk through this life
guided by our Father's hand
for He has put us here on earth
to fulfill a special plan.

The road is rough and treacherous
with many struggles and hills to climb,
but our joy was coming here by choice
and gladly we chose this path to find.

This road we walk down day by day
has been well used by many seekers,
there are many footprints along the way
but we must follow the ones made by our keeper.

Through Love, Faith, Prayer, and Devotion
He will guide us throughout our Mission,
and He has given us a special gift:
the "STILL SMALL VOICE" within to listen.

May we always strive to do His work
to walk the path of the straight and narrow,
for the "Good Deeds" that we do now in life
will be our rewards in the hereafter.

Stephen Wayne Cammuse
FOLDED FACES WE TOUCH THE SHELF?

Pleased in the Mind, Pleased in the Spirit and Soul, Pleased in & of the human interest is Pleased to be Free.

Souls weap others on trails in life etc.
We shelter his veins in script thats reality?
Account those stupendious ways etc
Wonderlings credit the eye success abound
Stories are acknowledgable as honor in life
Wrongs have been tolerable since day 1 but
that don't make wrongs right, the lesson on a child is
to respect the faith taught & some are wrong
but we cant judge one another respectable etc
Faded tricks or short fun atonements are shame
Study the habits of Saints, Kings, Prince?
Love isn't always great biblical knowledge

score the written collect the rhyme verse etc
Can she hold the courage or intise the intellectual
to create for the masses like the shepards on
the holy of nights this still exist on accords
the days the invention of sorts & kind
oh my mind flies on paper to write on & on etc
Predict from news head lines earn credit etc
We hear but, don't take heed to the message or rap
Why are the people weary oh not great feel &
the short-comings are forgotten in the eye etc
The wisdom is at stage the forfront of American
society we are winners, study the dictionary
no sybillis & heredity counts with ego

Augustina R Velasco

Augustina R Velasco
RETROSPECTION

To my daughters, Leilani, Guine, and Liza.

As the rays of sunset in bright
crimson red begins to fade,
And the evening shadows slowly
unfolds,
Brings a stillness that quietens
the soul,

Thus to meditate and retrospect at the end of the day's work.
The tasks well done and those left undone,
The strength and weaknesses alike portrayed,
To evaluate wherein the follies lie,
For one to grow and thus a better tomorrow.

Augustina R Velasco
YESTERYEARS
Those yesteryears are nostalgic memories of the past,
So close and dear to the heart,

Some full of happiness, some memorable, some bitter, whatever one's
lot may be is what has been lived in the past.

In retrospection the past can never be re-lived again,
Nor will it ever be the same,

But to profit from the many errors of yesteryears is but to go onward afresh
with optimism for new beginnings,
Thus to serve God and fellowmen.

Aynne Ingram
THE MEETING
Echoing, echoing,
The words,
Insane,
For wisdom,
Drum rolled in drool,
O, precious jewels,
The great escape begun,
Foul thieves to the grave,
Stillborn everyone.
Lipstained and stalking, yes,
This is the pearl, the pill,
Cunning cure-all coming in for the kill,
So speak to me, speak to me,
Through spittle and sweat,
Come on say something I'll never forget,
O, Babble,
This is your tower,
For eternity.

Janet Walsh
THUNDER IN MY HEAD, RAIN IN MY EYES

To Linda, who understands.

Thunder in my head
Rain in my eyes
Nowhere to go
Nowhere to hide

Loneliness is my friend
Until M.D. Linda walked in
A woman of our times
Working through the
Healing of the mind

Linda saw my pain
Felt my fears
Gave me hope
Without tears throughout
All those years

There isn't enough words
Or too many to say
MERCI'
To the Lady and Doctor
Of Today

Janet Walsh
A CRY FOR FREEDOM
As the Child inside of me still breathes, my past will never be set free.

All of these years my life is still black because I couldn't see beyond so many tearful tracks.

Afraid to sleep, Afraid to wake to another day that was so bleak and gray.

Shall I cry or shall I pray that my mom will keep away.

Facing reality is not my goal as the skeletons in the closet I behold.

My need is so great to be loved and to hate. Memories of this I will never know because the child inside keeps a great hold.

As an adult I still am the child. As a child I am the adult. Please help me with this grief otherwise I the adult and child will never intersect to be free!

Gloria Carmichael-Harris
SPRINGTIME
It's the era for new beginnings
In the wake of the winter's chill
It's the explosion of flower bud colors
And the green grass that clothes the hill

It's the sound of the chirping of robins
And the honking of geese in the air
It's the beauty of life springing forward
With its wonder and charm everywhere.

It's renewal of Love; it's forgiveness
It's the morning of life and new plans
It's two lovers walking united
With a purpose for everything grand.

It's a newness, a freshness so tender
As gentle as a warm, blowing wind
It's communion with God in our senses
And the calmness and peace that we find.

Gayle Gittinger
WHAT IS A DADDY?
He's someone who keeps you safe and warm.
He holds your hand when you take your first step.
He's there when you fall down ready to pick you up.
He holds you close and kisses away your fears.
But most of all he loves me for who I am and for who I will be.
He's not just a Dad he's my best friend.

Laura Beeler Dodds
CONTENTION

In memory of my lovely mother, Julia Kathryn Luchsinger Beeler, 31 Nov., 1897—9 Dec., 1953.

The winds of winter sally forth,
Clothed with snowdrops white.
Fiercely hungry, in search they go
Howling through the night.

Swooping, swirling, chewing the skies,
Spitting them out on the earth below.
Vaulting the peaks and the barren rocks,
Tossing and turning the blankets of snow.

Chasing the sun whose fast retreat
Sows ghostly phantoms, running wild.
Feral Boreas and inviolate Terra
Wage Nature's war, pure, undefiled.

'Til passions slaked by warfare's feast
Recoil in peace and tranquil lie.
Hushed and calm are the celestial spaces
And dawn is silhouette against the sky.

Yogesh M Patel
LET EQUALITY PROSPER
The Creator of all eternal beings
Has molded different species.
Some white, some black, some red
bored with monolithic rights.

The civilian society is oblivious
Of crucial problems confronting human beings.
Some freedom, some religion, thence other prejudice and power.
For let amnesty and rights win a position in obdurate, devoid hearts.

This is the age of reason
Let us revive from the sham and drudgery of society
And pursuit toward a "Utopian World."
Let equality prosper, let equality prosper
For it shall lead us to salvation.

Blanch Long
TO VERNA WITH LOVE
I call you Verna, though you prefer Marie
I've loved you a lifetime, and hoped you loved me
I've given to you, when others did without
But they didn't know this you see
For their turn was coming, there was no doubt
You were a precious infant, a most beautiful child
Then came the teen years, and you got a little wild
You kept your grades up, which made me proud
Then one day, you got in with the wrong crowd
Months went by before I saw you again
You never understood you caused so much pain
When you came home expecting a child.
I welcomed you back, and hoped you would stay
But not for long, again you went away.
Now you're a young woman with a baby of your own,
And in a few short years you will understand what went wrong.
Many years have gone by now, and we've both watched her grow,
To early womanhood and both love her so.
I still call you Verna, you still prefer Marie
But no one is more special to me.
I love you Verna Marie
Mom

Ana Laura B Santos
FEAR
How can I board a train
Fly in a plane
Face life alone
Without coming home?

Should my will prevail?
My face become pale?
My nerves take over
Like a poisoned clover?

What was it Mother said?
At rest are the dead;

Those who are alive
Are trapped in a hive?

Should I heed her advice,
Live on the edge of ice?
Or refuse to go along
And sing a brave new song?

I must overcome
If I dare—Be strong
For my future depends
On my ability to mend.

Ana Laura B Santos
TO MY 8-YEAR-OLD SON
This is a poem for my son Michael
Whose curiosity is as boundless as the skies
Whose big heart is as deep as the seas
My son, whom I have neglected from time to time,
Whose dreamy yellow eyes have gazed at me in disappointment
Mixed with hope
This is for all the times that you have immersed yourself
In your Nintendo games,
In your world filled with limitless possibilities:
Flying through the sky like Superman,
Riding on the wings of Pegasus,
Living the utopia created by dreams.

I have failed to help you understand some of the
Lessons of life:
That self-confidence is of the essence,
That nothing is as easy as it seems,
That all life is a great adventure . . .
But now I understand that one continues
Experiencing growth and change;
And that to cease feeling is
To cease living.

And so I promise to be your mother, your teacher,
Your protector
Until the time comes to release you on the
Wings of the bird of life.

Monique Jordan

Monique Jordan
ASTRO PROJECTION

Dedicated to my loving family in beautiful Northern California, who always make . . . "COMING HOME" so special to me.

On a sunny but wind-swept day in Northern California—
A slap on the bottom, that miraculous scream and a baby girl is born upon ya.
The guarantee of tomorrow is promised to none—
So savor the gift of each moment till day is done.

Count the grains of sand as you build your castle,
Boy! This California life sure ain't no hassle!
The rushing ocean—how it glistens under the sun—
Promising nothing but a mighty roar in the eyes of one.

While scanning the horizon, an image running towards me faster than lightning is my little dog Pete—
As he happily jumps in my arms, drenched, but who cares with this Summer heat.
Towering redwood trees—too beautiful to ignore,
And suddenly I'm surrounded by mountains and family galore!!

Mamas cooking supper and the kids are all a-playing,
And what keeps this family strong is we do us some praying.
My Brother's little girl sings us a song, as she twirls on the beach—
Singing something about catching Daddy a star—Come on Honey—Reach! Reach! Reach!

A tear rushes happily down my cheek as I smile with pride—
Gees! I hope nobody is watching me!
So like a child I'll cover my eyes to hide.
For it was only a daydream of sweet memories back home—
Because many years ago, to the arms of a southern gentleman I did roam.

Andrea Nichols
OUR LOVE
Our love is oh so special;
Our love is oh so strong;
Our love is based on tenderness
that makes the heart stand strong.
Our relationship is lasting; lasting oh so long. We build up our relationship on the seeds of new found love.
Our relationship is new five weeks and standing strong, we follow the hearts of each other making one another strong.

Raylene A Brugman
TO ZAC
You entered my life one autumn day
And as you entered, the storm clouds drifted away.
The leaves were turning yellow, red, and brown
The death of summer surrounded me, it was all around.

The leaves were starting to fall, the wind blew
And I turned around and saw you.

Death and destruction surrounded me
I didn't know where I wanted to be
My life was changing oh, so fast
I had to loosen the dead ties to the past.

My courage faltered; though I wanted to be brave
I feared life, but I also feared a cold, damp, grave.
I didn't want to be alone again, and I was frightened
But you took my hand, and my spirit lightened.

You gave me hope, that although destruction surrounded me
My life would change; I'd loosen my bounds and be free.
You gave me hope, that like winter melts into spring
The winter of my life would end, and my heart would take wing.

And finally summer came, the sun shown once again
My tortured heart was healed; for this you'll always be—my friend.

Susanne Mueller
DESERT PRINCE

To my dearest friend, Nassr, who inspired this poem and for whom it was written with love.

You caught my eyes across a crowded room
And held them with a gaze that I could not escape.
No matter where I turned,
Your eyes found mine and they enthralled me
With some unknown power that I could not explain.
And I was lost, and found, within those eyes,
Warm pools of darkness that would not let me go.
I knew you not, but felt I always knew you,
In times gone by, in my land of dreams and fantasies,
The desert prince of
long-forgotten fairy tales.
I envisioned you riding across the shimmering sands
On a great black steed,
White desert garb billowing in the wind.
So come and share my fantasy
Of midnight trysts 'neath the pyramids,
Where in their shadows we'll find love's ecstasy
And fairy tales-come-true under the desert moon.

Diane C (Dziedzic) Evans
LOVERS RUNNING
Shut the door
But don't ignore
that I need your
touch,
your warmth of
your body wrapped
around mine
most important
I need your LOVE.

Yes, Let me shut my door
away from you—
Just for a little while
I need to be by myself
as much as you by yourself.

Let me dream my dreams
Let me feel my feelings
Let me run my path
Let me reach for me
Let me be me
just for a little while.

Don't push me inside
Don't pull me outside
Don't pull me so
I slide
But always keep me
by your side.

Let us walk with your
hand in mine
side by side.

Let us not forget
as we plant ourselves
together—
that we always
remember our need
to be alone.

I'll give your walk
your space
and
My walk you'll
give me
my space.

And in the end
we can spend
and share our
LOVE in a way
that NO ONE
can ever dream
our dreams.

Cathie Vallas
COMING OF AUTUMN
Night is beginning to cramp the days
as autumn subtly settles in;
bringing with it
the crisp, clean smell of change.

Shadows on the street
have become longer—more defined
beneath the golden trees
that blaze in one final fury.

The warmth of the sun yields itself
to the cool, playful breeze
that paints the radiant blue canvas
with the speckle of colored leaves—
lifting—swirling—and then—
delicately landing them on the
ground.

There is a peace that follows;
as time seems to stop—
if just for a moment—
to prepare.

J Patrick Gatton
OUR CHILDREN
Who are they, you ask?
Well now that you ask, let me think for a moment.

Of all the answers that come to mind only one seems correct, they are.

Other answers such as they are of God,
they are parts of God, they are ours
and they are brother and sisters;
all of these are answers, really
but to add to the statement that
our children are, seems silly.

Why do we love our children, you ask?

No other answer fits so well.
No other tells the story I want to tell.
They are. That's why we love them.

Think of the simplicity of It!
They are, we love them.

J Patrick Gatton
IMAGINE
Imagine seeing Him who creates flowers
Imagine being with Him who created the world
Imagine seeing the beauty of God the Father
Imagine time no more
Imagine majesty beyond belief
Imagine seeing His face
Imagine life with beauty so incredible that it dazzles your eyes

Imagine life with friends of all the ages
Imagine the God larger than the universe
Imagine me trying to put my arms around Him
Imagine me among the angels
Imagine lucky me
Imagine being among those who love you so
Imagine all of your ancestors calling to say hello
Imagine love without boundaries
Imagine light that warms
Imagine wind that is still
Imagine saying hello to the guardians of trust, hope and love
Imagine Him knowing your thoughts, your emotions, your needs
Imagine a guardian of beauty
Imagine the tenderness of hands recreating the world each day
Imagine His life in each leaf, in each blade, in each person
Imagine being lifted and carried around Heaven by those who are powerful and swift
Imagine not one frightening thing
Imagine sitting with God to talk
about what interests you

Catharina Rinta

Catharine Rinta
MY HEART FOUND ITS PLACE

To one special man. "From a friend."

It took a long time in my life,
And I thought you would never be there.
But now I found you,
And I finally know love.

You will never know it.
Because that can never be.
But it will be enough for me,
Just to know that you are there.

How can one human being
Make a heart sing,
And stand out for always,
In a world of empty faces.

You have touched me,
With such a gentle touch,
And I've felt the joy,
That only love can give.

I will for once be unselfish
And only wish what brings you happiness.
It is enough that I found you,
And I finally know love.

Catharina Rinta
IT'S OVER

So it is over, after 41 years,
You won't be my husband any longer.
We lived in the same house all that time,
But didn't share a bed for most.

Most of the time has been a nightmare,
You've been a dictator to me and the children.
There wasn't much talk between us,
We were careful not to make you mad.

"Love" was a word you didn't know,
Only criticism and put-downs.
You made me forget I was good at anything,
Until someone gave me a compliment.

I am free from you, you finally went too far
You gave me a choice when you made me fear for my life.
Now it is in the hands of the police, and my lawyer.
I don't have to face it alone anymore.

So this is goodbye, after 41 years,
You'll be out of my life for good.
My future can now only get better.
I hope yours won't.

Jerick B Enclan
HOPES OF DARKNESS

This is for those who felt the hurts of loving and not being loved, and most of all, to those who were persecuted for being "Different."

Memories of the past, came lingering in my mind,
Like petals in the wind, like raindrops from the sky.
Mixed emotions, the pain of loving and not being loved
Contented feelings of cruelty, persecution and lust.
Broken dreams of painful times,
Shattered vows of love gone awry.
Losing the care, the love and the trust.
With bitter memories of a broken past.
Life gone asunder,
Future seems bleak.
Hold to the night, like a dagger so fierce,
It cuts out your hands, as the night watches w/glee.
Forgotten people, faces and dreams,
Where else to go but hide in tears.
Drowning with pain, suffocating and aching.
Wishing for peace, happiness and cheers,
Yet only bleak memories, of a shattered past exists.

B Gay
GOOD WIFE

Come yon handmaidens of
the color red,
servants of choice or price,
paid and dead.

Lost your true loves upon
the fields of green or brown,
and paid correct coinage
to move to town.

Found there nought, but the
good wife blue—with
cannibal servant to put you
in the stew.

Guardian of the handmaids
vie for cow pasture space,
while the earth crumbles
beneath your feet laid in
waste.

Thank you brethren in the
steeplechase and government
fair, for the circus of life
that left you there.

B Gay
MARSHMALLOW

What is lectured on in
chemistry . . .
that's charcoal tasting and
full of me.
It's sweet and mellow,
not hard or tart.
Served at picnics or in a heart.
Roasted on a stick or skewer,
it sometimes melts to bubble
or boil,
and even gets stuck on aluminum
foil.
Gooey muck of black and white,
so repulsive—you flee into the night.

B Gay
HIRAM THE MUMMY

Life was lazered
into him,
far from outer space.

The Southern satellite
system apparently was
devised to put me in my
place.

My mortal enemies ran
the controls of death,
that labeled me
incompetent and gave
me exterminator, Beth.

The Mummy walked and
kicked and had a tongue,
untampered with by Aunt Roz,
but could not manage
life renewed without reading
"Notes from Boz."

So take heed, all that
know me and my name,
it's no fun to be petrified
and beaten to death with a cane.

Ida Marie McCarty
ELFLORD

To Margaret, my supportive and loving mother.

Across the great old river and
through the tall pinewood
I halted with a quiver as I gazed at
what there stood
I pondered for an instant for what
now shall I do
I've not encountered elves before so
kingly of them too
I thought I was dreaming, his eyes
were boldly gleaming
The elf known as king of his land
The Elflord called Shandurian
He calmed me with assurance that
elves are kindly folk
And walked with me a distance
through a path of solid oak
I listened while he shared with me of
stories seldom told
The wheres and whys he came to be
of all the days of old
With their fires burning brightly and
mystical and lightly
They danced and sang their folk
songs with a haunting melody
Joyous were the elves this eve
displaying magic from their sleeves
Acting out their tales of yore left me
wanting even more
Awareness that reality no longer
means a thing to me
But only to live in this land
With the Elflord called Shandurian

Ida Marie McCarty
THOUGHTS

These fitful nights and restless days
Of thoughts within my head
The contemplating of my ways
And of the life I've lead

Of all the dreams I hope to find
The failures to forget
I strive to have an open mind
Tho there's things I do regret

My thoughts are always winding
I can't seem to be at rest
Because I'm always finding
That I'm only me at best

Sometimes I think enduring
Through just another day
A last escape alluring
But I know that's not the way

I have so much within to give
Of life and love to lend
My dreams I truly want to live
Before the final end.

Ida Marie McCarty
LITTLE FEET

Remember all those troubled days
Around the age of four
You would try and figure all the ways
For your feet to touch the floor.

I recall my mom would set me
On the couch right next to dad
My feet would barely reach his knee
That's all the length I had!

I would sit and carefully study
As they stood and walked around
Then simply bend their knees and sit
And their feet still touched the
ground!

For years I felt quite helpless
My legs just wouldn't seem to grow
And my feet seemed just as useless
They were very small you know

But then one day it happened
Do you know what I had found?
I had just set in my father's chair
And my feet had touched the ground.

Barbara Ness
WHO AM I?

To my husband and three kids who stood by me. The good and the bad.

Sometimes I get confused,
I know it's better than being misused.

I try to be caring,

Sometimes I'm overbearing.
Somehow I have to find
someone to trust,
I know—I must.

It's hard for me to share my feelings,
I have to—so I can start
healing.

I've been told to pray,
But, what do I say?

Barbara Ness
WITHIN
I hide from others,
For who know my Mother.
No need to bother,
For who knows my Father.
I need amends,
For who knows my friends.
My heart is still,
For who knows—God gave me a
hill.
When should I tattle,
For who knows of my battle.
When I drank,
For who knows—that I sank.
The drink and I matched,
For who knows were detached.
I need to stand.
For who knows—I need a hand.
Don't want to bother,
For who know—I need to holler.
Who do I tell,
For who knows of—Heaven and
Hell.
No need to strain,
For who knows of my pain.
I am mentally dependent upon
alcohol,
For who knows—I had to fall.
Tell me the time,
For who knows—I'll be fine.

Barbara Ness
GROWING UP ALONE
Emotionally abused,
For I was there—miss used.
People are crazy,
For I was there—still hazy.
They should be ashamed,
For I was there—I got blamed.
Always in the way
For I was there—that day.
Felt so alone,
For I was like a stone.
I turned to beer,
For I was there—in fear.
I wanted a hug,
For I was there—you lug.
I became unfeeling,
For I was there—now I'm healing.

Karen R Adams
FOR LOTTE
They have told me you're gone; that
we said goodbye
And I should let you go
But you come back, in and out my
life
I see you there—but they say "No"
You let me see the world op'ning in
your eyes
All the years of laughter and fun
Is it so easy to just let you go ??
Remember? We held hands as we
chased the sun.
Now you're here, and now you're
gone, like ripples in my mind
I hold out my hand and no one is
there, just ripples in my mind
We danced thru meadows of silver
white sands
But were you ever really here ??
We sailed magic carpets to distant
lands
Will I never again touch you and hold
you near ??
But you come back, in and out my
life like ripples in my mind
I reach out for you, but you're not
there, just ripples in my mind
I open my hand and nothing is
there—
You're just fading ripples of my
mind

Karen R Adams
REFLECTIONS ON A DYING WORLD
Each of us enter, naked of soul and
free
And all of us are to live so, naked and
free
But I stand at Gettysburg, with rivers
of blood
With brother blue and brother grey
And I walk at Auschwitz and at
Jadwiga
With internment camps and Yiddish
prayers
At Hiroshima and the mushroom
cloud
Vietnam with Agent Orange, Beirut
bombs and warhead games
No one man is master: nor one man
slave
But tell that to the mothers, and
brothers and babes
At Gettysburg—at Auschwitz
For what did we learn at Jadwiga??
And did we learn in Nam??
Am I alone is seeing that we enter
naked of soul and free
And we are to live filling our soul,
but free
For each man is slave only to himself
And living is a debt owed only to
ourself
Each of us exit full of soul but free
And so I think, and so I cry. Standing
at Auschwitz
Vietnam and Beirut. And I cry at
Hiroshima and warhead games
And I'll be crying still when they
come for me . . .
I'll be crying "All men enter naked of
soul but FREE!!!"

Karen R Adams
FIRST LOVE
I seem to have lost your smile
I remember the days when I told you
How very much I love you
How my eyes first saw, when I
turned
And looked into your face
And my life drew its first breath
When I saw your smile
My heart first beat, when I touched
your hand
But most of all . . . my lifebreath,
your smile
I know not what I've done
Nor if someone has taken my place
Perhaps we've outgrown each other
For we talk separately together
And we make love, separately
together
But I still hear music when you speak
And my life begins anew when I see
your face
But we live separately together
And I seem to have lost your smile

Leonard Albert
JUDAEO-CHRISTIAN SONNET
(CHIASMIC ITALIAN SONNET)

For Thea, David and Laura.

Did that Jew, crucified on Calvary,
His blameless blood bathing
coronal thorn,
Feel, in that agony, he died for me,
Another Jew, unworthy—to be
born
Centuries thence, nailed through the
selfsame scree,
The selfsame carpus? Selfsame
tendons torn?
And if he knew, how could such
prescience be
Borne in his bursting breast, his
heart forlorn?

Did that forlorn heart, that breast,
burst in vain,
Metal pierce flesh, spirit bestow
surcease
On thief at either side, on their souls'
pain,
On soldiers at his feet, even on
these
Who mocked, tossed for his
robe, scorned his decease?
Did he know then Crosses, too, rise
again?

Leonard Albert
LINES WRITTEN AT FIFTEEN

—For E.S.F.—

Holy Mother, Lady Love,
Kiss my brother, then kiss me.
Teach us, Lady, how to be
What our hearts are dreaming of.

Teach us this: that we must see
From within, not from above,
What the essence is of love:
Kiss my brother first, then me.

Leonard Albert
FOUR QUESTIONS AT THE LAST SUPPER
(A PASSOVER SONNET)
Did He, then, sit with others of His
clan
And break unleavened bread,
drink sacred wine,
To celebrate the horror, the
rapine,
Wreaked on all first-begotten sons,
on man—
Children of vaunting Egypt, who
began
Feuding with Moses's wrathful
God—and mine?
Slaughtered male newborns,
firstfruits of the vine,
Innocent youths: your mothers'
heart-tears ran!

How could the Lamb of God, that
Man of Sorrow,
Drink to Death's
lamb's-blood-marked trajectory
Against mere babes, to vaunt
God's victory?
Could Moses's tale be flawed? Or did
God borrow
The blood-drenched way of
man, slay innocents,
To crucify proud Pharaoh's
insolence?

Leonard Albert
Με 'Αγαπη
(On A Valentine For My Wife)
Being together or apart
Tells little of the hidden heart;
Whether one struts with pride, or
kneels,
No secret of the soul reveals.
What matters most is what one feels,
Not where we end, or how we start.
Let memory keep the better part.

Mary Louise Richardson Fratesi
REMEMBER!
And we come and we go.
No matter what at all.

So you can live in a mansion.
Or maybe a tent?
Have a Versatiss car.
With color all aglow to go far.
Can be a leader.
Many hear your word.
Teach important subject.
To all who care to learn.
Plant all the flowers.
To set their heads in the spring.
A vegetable garden you raise.
For all whose health so daze.
Can walk each day.
In sun so bright and gay.
No matter what I say or do.
Still we came and we go.
I wish only to be with you.
So high, steps will never reach.
Only if I live to see.
Last road you built for me.

Irene Mae Harmon
FINAL REQUEST
When I have left this earthly planet
Should you still in mortal raiment
linger
Will you think of me with tenderness
With love instead of anger?

Will you gaze once more upon my
face
Serene at last in eternal rest
And press your warm lips upon my
own
To warm my cold and barren breast?

To ease my soul upon its flight—
Will you say a silent prayer
And give me a haven in your heart
To remind you I was there?

Will you shed a tear for memory's
sake—
For what might have been
And lay a rose upon my bier
And say you love me once again?

Irene Mae Harmon
LAY THE PAST TO REST
Never try to kindle the embers
Of dreams that didn't last
Never turn back the pages—
Just lay them to rest in the past.

Forget the way he smiled at you
The special touch of his hand
Those unforgettable moments—
No one else would understand.

Forget the comfort of his arms
The love not meant to last
Forget the heartaches if you can—
They are ghosts of the past.

When you leaf back the pages of time
Remember, but not with regret—
All the beautiful, treasured moments
That your heart will never forget.

Have one last cry and let your tears—
Wash the memories away
Tuck them away in your heart—
They belong to yesterday!

Irene Mae Harmon
AS LONG AS I LIVE
As long as the sea rolls onward
And the waves leap fathoms high
My soul will be as a lonely bard—
Tethered to each rippling sigh.

As long as the robin heralds spring—
And the seedlings sprout and give
You'll keep my heart a-rocketing

As long as I live.

As long as the earth yields to the plow—
And my pen to plaintive rhyme
My heart will be yours—even as now
Until the end of time.

For as long as lovers seek love in Capri—
Though the bitter out-measures the sweet
My heart will be yours through eternity—
Though trampled by your feet.

Irene Mae Harmon
RESTLESS HEART
I'm weary of walking the single path
And I pause at the fork in the road
For tonight my heart seeks a kindred soul—
And the seeds of temptation are sowed.

The stars seem to beckon out yonder way—
As I battle a losing fight
For I'm weary of walking the single path
And my heart is lonely tonight.

I'm glad to turn at the fork in the road
Where the night is so vacant and still
And to don the cloak of the vagabond—
And let the stars guide me where they will.

The restless longing for happiness—
That encompass my heart tonight
Make me heed not the perils of wantonness—
That beset the road to the right.

For I've already turned at the fork in the road—
Where the stars shed a silver carpet of lace
And ere my heart succumbs to fear, I sally forth—
With the breath of the night in my face.

Josephine Kent Adams

Josephine Kent Adams
THE DARKER BROTHER DRUGS
These are my darker brothers.
From north, south, east and west.
They have hearts, souls and minds.
They too like the best.

These are my darker brothers.
They have been to the mountaintop too.
They have dreams of the great tomorrow
Oh! Pray they will come true.

These are my darker brothers.
The struggles are still going on
It is work must we, and love we must.
Until the struggles are gone.

These are my darker brothers.
Who migrated from far away lands
Until we are educated, and all understand,
We will never walk hand in hand.

Say "no" to drugs my little darlings.
They will only destroy your tiny little bodies.
They will eat up your brains, give you a great big head.
And in a short time, you will be dead, dead, dead.
Say "no" to drugs my little darlings.

Mable L Thomson
A LINER LIMERICK
There once was a gal well into a muse
So she decided to sail on a cruise
She returned from the sail with a pail
'Cause the ship sprung in starboard aft
And course she blew a fuse.

This very beautiful liner was called Le Love
The problem was that it couldn't stay above
When the bottom got the hole it didn't float
So the passengers on board ardently wished
He or she was a dove.

There was another ship where all was fine
It was full of fun, love and good wine
There was plenty of dancing and good food
Also excellent amusement was always there.
That is what sailors pine.

There's no morale nor merit in this little tale
One can always stay home and look pretty pale
Then too there's no baggage or plane delays
Picture cards can still be sent via the mail
So friendships will never fail.

Thomas E Eichenlaub
CHRISTMAS MEMORIES
Christmas days, now and past,
Bring us memories, we wish would last.
I love the many glittering trees,
The falling snow upon the leaves.
Friends and love ones get together,
Times like these, seem so much better.
If, there were more days like these,
Wouldn't we have fond, fond memories.

Mary E Flood
PARADISE
One time I was told I ran too fast
I always thought life would fly past
When I wasn't looking, Paradise stepped in
Paradise waited with a sly knowing grin
With careful words my attention was turned
There was so much to life I hadn't learned
Now I have my Paradise and love
I walk on cloud nine or someplace above
Paradise now holds me close,
showing me what I didn't see
At times I run, but Paradise runs with me

Ann La Vin
(VIVA) ONTOLOGY
"No blossom without a root" I was told,
So—I planted seeds and a forest of trees . . .
Like a family we grew, Mother Nature helped too—
With a trunk of great Faith and branches like me,
Grew a changing society.

Rainbow leaves of traditions
scattered by winds "to be free"—
Cultured blossoms developed, clouds of rain nurtured courage,
Our bodies knew the sun's energy;
Time and space—group behavior and customs took shape, changing
Earth's third-eye-vision—historically.

"Your Yahweh, her Buddha, his Allah, my God!"
Man's Origin? Eternity, Infinity,
Spiritual Powers That Be . . .
Whole Creation took part, Moon, Stars and satellites
Drift about—"Viva Ontology!"

Gregory J Pickard
FRIENDS TO LOVERS
Once in a lifetime
you will find someone,
A person with whom
you can joke and have fun.

From this friendship,
if this friendship is true,
Will come forth a love,
that will join both of you.

In this union of love
there will grow such a power.
No matter the problem,
you won't yield or cower.

For in all of our lives
bad times will come.
Although bad can be good
when you just love someone.

Delores Ruiz
AWAY FOR AWHILE, MOM
What is a poem? Deep thought to someone.
A mom who is in sorrow,
Looks inward to each tomorrow,
As her son is freed,
In perhaps a few years,
As the time comes near,
With many, many tears,
Happiness will come forward
When we both are towards,
Each other to embrace,
Our love for each other,
We are now together.
For Love will endure.

Raymond E Floyd
AND THE NATION WEEPS
Black, white, red, and yellow;
they were full of life.
Now they are gone,
and the Nation weeps.

Teacher, lawyer, and roustabout;
they came from all over.
Now they are gone,
and the Nation weeps.

Their country called them;
they came, no questions asked.
Now they are gone,
and the Nation weeps.

Side by side, into the storm;
they marched unflinching,
falling one by one.
Now they are gone,
and the Nation weeps.

Side by side, in silent tribute;
white crosses on green, they
gave their all.
Now they are gone,
and the Nation weeps.

Sardha Kaluaratchi
A DROP OF WATER IN MY BOWL

To a child in need.

Still as a stick sits this skeleton baby
Yet, he is alive, a child in need and still a baby
Stand he cannot, sleep he will not
Even those melancholy eyes blink not
Yet he is alive, a three-year-old in pain
There is human life flowing through those veins

Mother he cries not even though in pain
As tears don't come to these eyes in strain
A crumb of food never seen by this soul
Let alone a drop of water in a bowl
Here sits a child who looks a million years
Yet in reality he barely completes a few hundred days

Engraved and tattooed are those tears on his face
No! Not fresh are they but of his early infant days
Tightly sealed are his lips bearing the agony
Helplessly sits this child like a sculpture of ebony

It's no secret that this three-year-old has no hope in life
Nor does he believe that, we can make a change in his life
Careless, selfish have we gone blind
Or caring and loving can we make a change in his life

Burton C Fisher
TENDER LOVE
O' Lord God I adore the way
You enlighten my soul,
And embrace me with tender love
As clean gentle snow.
Shedding crystal tears
Across my cheek softly flow.

O' When love's tender moments
Ensues this imprisoned life.
This heart's radiant glow
Will always be bright.
O' Please let me continue
With a sympathetic thought.
To be merciful to others
As Thy words have taught.

Let me burst forth with love,
As a tender bud unfold,
Into a beautiful flower
Encased in God's gold.
O! Beautiful words ne'er be wrong
Only make my faith grow
strong.
Yea, one-day the glory of God
In this body of love
Will rapture me home,
In God's Tender Love.

Zeke Stokes
BEYOND
When the moon goes behind the
clouds,
and the stars shine in the sky,
I wonder what's BEYOND that,
What God's made for you and I.

Is it a snow-covered mountain,
starting slowly to melt?
Or is it the rays of sunshine
whose warmth can be felt?

Is it dew glistening
on the morning ground?
Is it a wonderful land
where clovers can be found?

Is it flowing with milk and honey,
as described in "The Word"?
Is it the sweet, faint chirp
of a newly-hatched bird?

But I don't need to know that now,
as I look into the sky.
Someday I'll know what's BEYOND
this world,
What God's made for you and I.

Mrs Mary J Smith
IT MUST BE LOVE

To my loving husband Craig. Love your wife, Mary.

I don't want to sleep and I can't eat
and all I do is daydream about him. I
can't wait till I see him again, it is as
if I was floating on a cloud. So it
must be love or I am a dove.

Ruth M Patterson
DESERTED FARMHOUSE
The old farmhouse stands forgotten,
Bare trees reaching with skeletal
fingers toward the sky.
Dead weeds upthrust through the
snow, which has been falling silently
on the fields and piles high.
Fields that once held golden waves of
grain,
Fence posts lean crazily, some
completely fallen,
Pens which once held milling herds
of cattle, are now empty, and silent as
the snow, the cattle no longer
bawlin'.
I sense the pain the old house must
feel, as it clasps its memories within
its deserted walls,
It stands, a cold silent reminder of
other days,
While along the lane the snow drifts,
as it silently falls.

Kristan Leigon
AN UGLY DUCKLING
I am an ugly duckling,
hatched into this world,
facing all the problems,
of every boy and girl.
But the beauty is inside me,
even though it doesn't show.
Someday you will see it,
this I surely know.

I'm running through the forests,
swimming through the streams,
I'm trying so very hard
to fulfill my dreams.

I have to take the teasing,
people say I'm no good.
They're trying to run my life,
but I do what I should.

I hope to grow someday
into a pretty swan,
then everyone will realize
that what they said was wrong.

Irene J Malone
TRAINS
Trains in the night
Are sometimes lonely
When those you love
Are far away

Trains in the night
Are sometimes cheerful
When those you love
Are safe in bed

Trains in the night
Are sometimes magnificent
So large and powerful
And small are we

Ethel M Tinney B A

Ethel M Tinney B A
PREMONITION
On U.S. pennies dated sixty-three
A tear had formed on Abe's broad
cheek
As if some cause to mourn he'd see,
You'll easily see of what I speak.
Did this a premonition shed
Of a dire happening ahead?
And then November came!

Could Abraham Lincoln's likeness
reveal,
By tears upon the kindly cheek,
Beforehand, the sorrow we'd
feel—
A tell-tale streak on a face so meek?
Each plain brown cent we searched
with care
And sure enough the tear was there!
Then that November came!

Ethel M Tinney B A
PEACE
See great Europe opening up,
A petal every hour.
Frantic to fill the freedom cup,
Softening the scent of power,
Lessening the chance of fatal
war,
Oh! How our spirits seek to
soar!

Ethel M Tinney B A
GROWN ACCUSTOMED
Emily emptied her heaving heart
Telling us how to conquer the dark
Or did she mean Light is never there
When Life without Love we have to
bear?

In the eighteen hundreds Emily
wrote:
"We Grow Accustomed to the Dark
When Light put away."
In the twentieth century they sing in
the park,
"I've grown accustomed to your face.
I've grown accustomed to your
voice."
Almost her words heard every place
Though they first were Emily's
choice.

Emily liked that lilting line, used it
another time about a Robin
She had for a Friend: "I'm some
accustomed to Him grown,"
Now singers make her words their
own,
I hear them singing end on end,
"I've grown accustomed to your face.
I've grown accustomed to your
voice."
Almost her words heard every place
Though they first were Emily's
choice!

Marilyn Schmidt Toth
MORTAL HARVEST
The ignorance of the world
Classifies populace
By barriers of prejudice;
Pomegranate cloisters.

Nationalities sunder . . .
In each, their own ilk . . .
Individual cells
Severed from one another.

Yet, all as are one,
Society's rainbow of mortal fruit;
The tart pulp of the countries
Lacking unity's sweet nectar.

Steve Zavlek
THE PLAYFUL WATER
the playful water raised its paw.
white crest claws overtook the shore
as wave on wave came rising in.
it arched its back and crashed
again . . .

the shore in turn was falling back—
half asleep and waking up.
the sleepy land was being rent,
but there was strength in
continent . . .

the ocean rose on high and high
as if to touch the very sky,
came scratching down upon the land
then licked and nuzzled cliff and
sand . . .

the shore and ocean tumbled round,
raised mist and sand in thrashing
sound.
they settled back in a jumbled heap,
then turned around and fell asleep.

Stephanie Wilson
COMING HOME
The kids are all married,
my husband is with you.
Lord, someday I shall
be with you, too.
I will look around with wondering
eyes,
and know I'm free to roam.
Then I will take your hand,
and know I've finally come home.

Valerie Smith
BELIEVE
I believe in the power,
and the truth of love.
Gentle and forever flowing,
like the winds of a dove.
It comes and goes
like the tide always does,
always there,
its birth is wide.
But if you have it,
don't let it slip away.
And by deceit
don't let it decay.
Being together, forever
united as one
is more beautiful than
the morning sun.

John E Zimmerman
THE PATHFINDER'S DREAM
Far beyond yon smoke blue
mountains
Where the rivers meet the sea.
It is there my feet are turning
And with God's help 'tis there I'll be.

Ere the first snowflakes are falling
Or the lakes locked by jaws of ice
I'll have built my strong warm cabin.
'Tis there I'll find Paradise.

While the leaves are yet a'turning
I'll have searched my domain o'er.
Learning of the secret places
Never mapped by man before.

Aye, perhaps you're right, 'tis lonely
If you'd pine for fellow men
But to be so close to nature
Brings one nearer God again.

We could not but shed a teardrop
As this man, once young and free.
Dreamed his dream, for in his
twilight
No strength remained, nor eyes, to
see.

Kenneth J Mathews
SPEEDING FREIGHT TRAIN
Beams from the sun reflect on the
rails,
as they disappear out of one's sight
leaving a long silver trail.
Telephone poles as far as the eye can
see,
in the middle of nowhere open and
free.
Then off in the distance comes a
rumble like thunder,
and a brilliance of light which
outshines what is under.
Breaking the silence of which was
before,
increasing in sound as waves on a
seashore.
With a huge gust of wind and a
shriek whistle sound,
the engine roars by with only its dust
to be found.
Flashing past you like lightning from
the East to the West,
putting the rails and the wheels to a
firm steady test.
Its speed makes it look as though it
were one,
but the pounding of the rail joints
evaluates the sum.
It's not there for long and as the end
whizzes by,
it leaves a trail of smoke in the sky.
Slowly it fades out of one's sight,
leaving smells of diesel and a red
flashing light.
And as quick as it came it disappears
just the same,
yet you caught a glimpse of a
speeding freight train!

Gladys M Pollitt
TO MY LOVE
Oh what heights that we
could climb,
If I were your companion
and you were mine.

Gladys M Pollitt
LITTLE SHIP
So long ago and far away
this little ship was sent,

to carry my loving thoughts
and everything it meant.

Gladys M Pollitt
LONGING
There's beauty in the heart and mind,
there's beauty in the soul,
so open up companion of mine
and see what can unfold.

Gladys M Pollitt
JOY
To see your face once again,
to feel you in my arms,
to hold you, touch you,
and talk of all your charms.

Your smiling face, the joy you bring,
just to hear your laughter, or
hear you sing,
just to have you near and know
that you care,
brings joy to my life beyond
compare.

The miles may keep us far apart,
all the love I carry for you
remains in my heart,
So please hurry this way, make
no stops, don't delay
And once again our love can
grow,
it has a beautiful start.

Gladys M Pollitt
GRANDMOTHER
This is my dear old grandmother
sitting in her old armchair,
her face and hands are
wrinkled,
and snow-white is her hair.

I love to stand beside her
and help her shell the peas,
then I say "Oh Grandmother,
tell me a story please."

She tells about the Indians
fairies and the rest,
then she comes to the one
she knows I love the best.

About Jesus and the children,
little ones like me,
how he loved them and
held them on his knee.

Marilyn C Wright
IT'S HARD TO UNDERSTAND
It's hard to understand
each special thing that you
see happen

It's hard to understand
why each beautiful flower must
fade and go away

It's hard to understand why
things made great must come
to an end

It's hard to understand why
special people we love must
go away

It's hard to understand why
what happens does

It's hard to understand it
just is.

James Tillman
I'VE THE SPIRIT, NOT THE TALENT
I've the spirit, not the talent
for an artist
That sort of career is the hardest
I feel the thrill in my soul each time I
draw a line; I shiver down my spine
every
time I make a rhyme,
or play a note that I have, by my
own design, played for a reason
But the talent, not the spirit
is what I need
Constant practice does give for what
I plead
For the talent of an artist I would
swim
the rolling seas, or climb a
snow-peaked mountain
with but a single line
or play a note that I have, by my own
design,
played for a reason . . .

Darryl N Pitchford
ANOTHER LEAF
Here I stand or stoop or bend
Like my neighbor and my friend
Each with rake at autumn's end
At that time of colored glory
As each tree tells its winter story
Of bare branches for which it's sorry
So it yields great color and hue
From each oak or aspen or yew
With a bright blanket my yard to
strew
But now I am done
And it's been fun
And so another year has run
And then I wish that it could end
For the cold is really not my friend
It tells me that I'm too old to bend
Over the handle of a rake
Or to the ground the bag to take
To fill it from the piles I make
I hear a slight sound
And I turn around
As another leaf comes drifting down

Lois B Thouvenell Dobler
THE WORLD AROUND US
The world is in turmoil we have to
agree—
And we pray that some day the whole
earth'd be free.
Wars will be over—the fighting will
cease—
And we no longer fear to walk on the
streets—
Or drive in the mountains, or plains,
or on city streets.
Gangs won't exist,—nor threats to
our lives—
And selfishness doesn't persist in
splitting our families, neighbors, and
friends.
Remember, we are all working
towards the same ends—
Peace, freedom and human rights—
Always keeping happiness in our
sights!

Gundela McCabe
I AM
I am space
I am the air, the sun and the sea,
I am light.

I am the ground on which my bare
feet walk,
I am beauty, color and smell.

I am touch and taste,
music and dance,
I am power.

I am laughter and lightness,
sadness and feelings,
I am vulnerable.

The Universe I am and love,
I am now.
I am.

Genevieve Judice Didier
LUXURIES
Love possesses strong and bold
Reaches parapets lined gold
Carries total worth untold
Outdoes haughty-knit of soul
Handles treasures in control
Costly gemstones topping fold
Garnets, amethysts unsold
Jewels, sapphires—diamonds cold
Memories traced in careful mold
Scented air luxuriant hold
Barters flighty edge am told
Joyful hours—yet to behold!

Robert D Britton

Robert D Britton
THE TALENTED MAN

Dedicated to the memory of my loving wife, Bertha Britton.

The Talented Man is a marvel to one
and all.
Most have unusual memories with
the power to recall.
His talents evolve at birth, even
before he has a name.
And from this talent he will most
likely achieve riches, honor and
fame.
They are respected by their peers, and
by us lesser mortals held in awe.
They excel in the sciences, literature,
music and the law.
They accomplish what they do
without effort or strain.
It's a cinch they will reach their goals
in life
And end up with famous names.
I guess most of us wish that we could
do what they can.
Such are the fortunes of the Talented
Man.
No matter what the endeavor,
vocation, or plan.
We can't do as well or with the ease
as the Talented Man.

Lois Ann Frye
LIFE'S WONDERS

To my dear son, Franklin James, from your loving mother.

Through my eyes, I have seen,
The sun, the moon, the stars, the sky,
And
Through these ears, I have heard,
The music, the rain, the birds, the
plane,
And
Through my nose, I have smelled,
The flowers, the soil, the corn, the
grains,
And
Through my mouth, I did taste,
The fruits, the nuts, the bread, the
wine,
And
Through my heart, I have felt,
The love, the hurt, the sorrow, the
pain,
And
Through my brain, I have thoughts,
Only of love, hope, happiness, and
prayer,
And
In my arms, I hold my child,
The key, to it all.

Violetena Crowe
GRANDPA'S REFLECTIONS

Dedicated to James Knox. In the Memory of Marjorie Knox.

I watched the kids on the beach today
honey,
You would have loved their antics.
They remind me of us when we were
young,
So much alive and in love.
Remember how we met?
My mother sure knew what she was
doing,
I should have listened to her sooner.
We had some hard times but you
were always there,
Now I don't know how to go it alone.
I keep busy with volunteer work,
And this trip to Hawaii let me get
away from the house.
Your memory is everywhere
How I wish you had lived to make
this trip with me.
I should have brought you years ago
But by the time we had family over
here,
It was already too late.
I miss you darling and hold your
memory dear.
I watch the waves as the kids run
from them
It touches me to see some of you in
our grandson.
I still love you and grieve sorely,
But I see our love continuing with
them.

Bobby Farr Gentry Sr
MY CHILD

To My Children: Susan, Bobby F., Jr., Cindy Kay, Nancy Jean, Sarah Dean.

You are always in my thoughts, with the passing of each day!
I would always hope, this you will know, though we are far away!
I know I never keep in touch, and tell you how I care!
But you are always on my mind, and I love to have you there!
You mean so very much to me, and I love you beyond compare!
To deny that you are a child of mine, I would never dare!
You are a living part of me, conceived in love, and honesty!
I am so proud of the way you are, and you mean the world to me!
I wish that you will always have, the good things in your life!
To have great love, and happiness, never bad times, troubles, or strife!
You have kept the manners that I taught, and show them with sincerity!
It is a thing I am proud of, you are a reflection of me!
So I salute you, and I say bravo, for being the way you are!
No matter what happens in times to come, you will always be my star!
You rise into my every day, and have my love all the time!
I just want for you to know, you are always on my mind!
Times we are together, may be far apart.
But you are always on my mind, and always in my heart!

With Love! Your Dad

Marsha Sampson-Gilliam
NAM

This poem is dedicated to my great-grandmother Martha, my grandmother Sarah and my grandmother Betty whose Christian influence profoundly affected me.

Vietnam, Vietnam, Vietnam
went,
fought,
killed,
I died . . .
Tormented, tormented, tormented
returned,
rejected,
shattered,
I cried . . .
Love me, Love me, Love me
hated Nam!
loved Nam!
missed Nam!
trapped in Nam . . .
Memories, Memories, Memories
mind confused,
is there hope?
dare I believe?
where comes help?
from God! from God! from God!!!

Jane ElizaBeth Watson
A BLESSING OF LOVE

This poem is dedicated in loving memory of "My Beloved Mother"—"Matilda Christine."

Each breath of life is a gift of love, so why should we complain?
We always want the sunshine, yet we know there must be rain.
We love the sound of laughter and merriment of cheer.
But our hearts would lose their tenderness, if we never shed a tear.
So let us count our blessings, that God so lovingly does give.
And share this love with others—as long as we shall live.

Ray Rivera
FREE AMERICA

To Sheena Tesora.

The singing and laughter, the playing of children
Is what we all want in a country that's free
We don't want war, but we all want peace
To help keep our country as free as can be
Free country, free land
Means America to all
The home of the brave and the free
So let's keep America the way that it is
And live like a yank should live
Then for centuries and centuries we can all say,
America, America, is the place for me.

Lanoma Ada Barnett
SHADOW TO SHADOW

For Steven Allen Jones, the Army truck driver I met on the bus. I love you. Thank God for Dumos, Texas.

I looked up through leaf diamond tree limbs, toward a warm summer's sky. So few birds, so many tomorrows.

Boundaries apart that will take its toll; I know.

Yesterday gone, present is here to stay for another day; it's May, I do say.

As you grow closer, I draw nearer. Hand in hand; mind in thought, time released.

Shadow to shadow in finding you I have sought.

Marie Louise Schleifer
WISHES LOCKED IN GLASS

My beautiful dandelion.
When you changed from the golden flower to the small white cloud,
I picked you from the ground.
As my breath disturbed your solitude,
I watched my wishes fly high into the sky
with your seeds.
I hoped that when your seeds fell softly to the ground after their journey,
my wishes would come true.

I imagined that as your seeds grew into the beautiful golden flower you once
again became, that my dreams would help it to flourish.
Now my beautiful dandelion I have encased your small white cloud in a clear
glass ball in anticipation of locking away your beauty and capturing forever
what I truly wish for myself . . .
To be loved and admired;
To be free to fly high into the sky;
And finally;
To land, grow again, and make wishes come true.

David R Stockwell
SIR ISACC'S FRUIT

Once there lived a fig of
dark-brownish hue,
Whose skin was as shaded as soles of a shrew.
His condition was such that he felt quite ashamed,
For all other figs would call him bad names.

"You're black! You're dark!" cried young figs and old.
"You'll soon be a newton!" he was constantly told.
So the dark little fig would sink to the ground,
Weeping and wailing, condemning his brown.

His tears held true cause, as all know, you shall see,
A dark fig is less than a blest fig to be.
The hand of the harvest is one eager to pick,
But only for black figs; the dark ones go quick!

The light figs rejoiced, "Our black spot be taken!"
But who would have guessed, a brown raisin forsaken?
For as fig-picking neared, the worst it did come:
The farmer searched not for dark figs of the sun!

"I've come for the light! Light figs I must bring!
My taste has changed quite! Bright jam is the thing!"
Pluck pluck! Pluck pluck! he worked with a grin,
Thinking of licking tan jam off his chin.

And so once again, a fruit picked the end;
Not Yasgur, nor Paris: the fates shall not bend.
As figs light went out, a fig dark did shout:
"There you see what my gift's all about!"

Judith Horowitz
RUNNING FOR BUSSES

My body moves before
my mind has awakened.
Coffee is dripping as
the shower explodes on my face.
Blinded by the wet,
I wash away the weekend:
motherhood and laundry.
I dress by the light of the sun,
peeking through a cloudy window.
A quick cup of wake up juice and I'm off . . . to
rise to the demands . . . and
fall prey to the pressures . . . of
running for busses,
dancing for bosses,
accumulating losses of
breath and time.

John M Bressler
PARENTS

To Mom and Dad, for everything you've done for me, and always being there when I've needed you.

When I was just a newborn child
You were everything that I knew
You greeted me with love and joy-filled smiles
As you nurtured me and watched as I grew

As time went by I learned to walk
And became your everlasting light
I'd call for you when I first learned to talk
So you could tuck me in to sleep each night

At six I started my years of school
And you cried as I left for my first day
Because eventually I'd be alone in a world so cruel
With so many roads that could lead me astray

As I grew older you taught me right from wrong
And you molded me into the person I am today
Although inside feelings of independence burn strong
You're still by my side to protect me along the way

I could never get through life without your love
And all of the little things you do for me
You were chosen for me by the Man up above
And no better choice could there possibly be

Steve Innocent
ELEPHANTS

I would like to dedicate this to all of my family.

Elephants are big
Elephants are small
Elephants like trees
Just like bees
They can be far away
They can be close
But, be careful don't
Get too close
They can stomp on you
And turn you into
A Pancake.

Heather Adcock
SHADOWS OF THE WHITE CITY

To the three blessed ladies that guide my hand and to him that is my lord and inspiration.

The heat of the White City burns
Daylight draws frostfire from the mirroring glass
Throwing sparks on the Earth
And the people, insulated, brilliant, explode in isolation
Each a separate moth to a separate

flame
In the warm triangular vortex
Down, far below, in the city deep
A world of flickering shadows and images engage
A world full of joy and laughter
Sadness and despair of mind, body and soul
Seek healing in the balm of the shadows
A refuge, a hideaway, a safeplace
It is a many different thing, to many people
A place for hope and strength to be found again
And those who hide in the Shadows of the White City
Who shiver in sunlight, who flinch from the sparks
Come away to the Dark City, to its comforting embrace
To the cobwebbed corridors and tapestry of woven souls
Where white fades in darkness
And that violent diamond emptiness is only a starlight sky . . .

Richard M Schneider
SOMEONE WITHIN ME

Dedicated to my great Aunt "Ruth Fugate" with love.

A misplaced and forlorn child
Marvelling at the barrens
Cognizant, yes well aware of thy destiny

As a seed without water, that struggled on, sprouted.
You reached for the sun.
Thoust roots have dried, standing sapless, in the forest are Ye.

Look! Many dead trees in the forest
Ye are no exception. Still they stand
As do you, waiting to turn to ash.

So you sit inside these darkened, musty closets.
Pecking worthless thoughts on a piece of paper
You have found soothing in music
You dance along with rhythm
To my disgrace.

Dianne Lynne Spell
JELLYBEANS AND GUMDROP DREAMS

I dedicate this poem to my Mother, Jo Etta Richardson, in love and devotion.

I was my Daddy's little girl, made of jellybeans and gumdrop dreams.
With a pocketful of hopes and promises, I'd ride the ponies and splash the streams.
You ask, who is my Daddy? What kind of man is he?
Why he's a mystery, a preacher, a teacher and the maker of three.
He has thoughts and feelings that he may or may not show,
But that's the special magic. You're not supposed to know.
He is a man who believes in God and will humbly tell you so.
For, he has faith in all mankind, be they friend or foe.
He taught me many things along the way of my influential years.
He held my hand and set me straight and gently wiped my tears.
Some may know, flesh and blood we're not, but it really doesn't matter.
Between my birth Dad or the man who raised me, my heart would choose the latter.
I cannot find the words to tell you what WALTER RAYMOND means to three,
But this I know, with all our soul, we love him, Ginger, Jack and me . . .
There are three others, Shirley, Rita and Dennis, who were there before we came,
He loved them too, and was there for them, I know they feel the same . . .
Despite the challenge he made us, what we are today,
Decent, strong and honest, no need for more to say.
EXCEPT . . .
I am my Daddy's little girl, made of jellybeans and gumdrop dreams
For I still ride the ponies and I'll forever splash the streams . . .

Barbara Gaekle

Barbara Gaekle
THE MAN WHOSE NAME IS JERRY

This poem is dedicated to Jerry, a dear friend who is always there when I need him.

Words can't show what I feel
And actions can't either,
I feel that I'm not wanted
And nothing seems to matter.

People hear me talk, people hear me cry
But they really don't care what I feel inside.

People say they love me and people say they care
But when I really need someone
No one seems to be there.

There is one person who seems to care
'cause when I turn to him, he is always there.

He treats me like a daughter
He treats me like a friend,
I know that when I'm with him
I never have to pretend.

I sometimes call him dad
Which makes me feel so merry,
This poem is for my friend
The man whose name is
Jerry.

Nancy G Piche
FRIENDSHIP

To Rita Hamlin, the best friend I have ever had and ever will have.

I saw her sitting in a corner
alone, with no one to talk to.
I walked over to her
wondering what was wrong.
We talked and maybe she felt better,
only she knows.
Ever since then we've been friends.
Time went by.
We helped each other out
to solve our problems.
I have never trusted anyone
as much as I trust her.
She made me realize that you
Can't live life alone.
Friendship with a friend
no one can live without.

Tony Lewis
THE GOOD LORD

For my beautiful, loving girlfriend, Lisa Rena Davis.

When nothing else will do
I know the good Lord will see me through

The good Lord gives me more than I deserve
Each and every day
All I have to do is pray
And He sends what I need my way

When I feel weary like I can't go on
I look to Jesus and my sorrow is gone

Oh Lord, I love you so
I know You love me too
But how I'm worthy
Of your love I don't know
You filled me with the Holy Ghost
And I was born anew
Oh, Lord
I know there's nothing you can't do

Since You've come into my life
I'm not the way I used to be
I was blind
And for the first time I can see

Arthur J Reischmann
MARY SUMMER RAIN

To Mary Summer Rain and her husband Bill for being who they are and accepting me as a friend. Everyone desperately needs you and those like you.

Alone in the woods, or so she thought.
Sitting on a log, crying, despairing.
A heart full of love, wisdom, caring.
Was her knowledge all for naught?

An old woman sensed the young girl there grieving.
The old woman was blind, yet she could see,
Far beyond what appears to you and to me.
The old woman called her name as the girl was leaving.

The young girl was stopped cold as she started to go.
Only her grandmother called her by that name.
Yet the old woman knew it all the same.
But that couldn't be! How could she know?

Somewhat timid and a little frightened,
Who was this one one? She might be a nut!
There's a lot of weirdos in this world. But,
After they talked, the atmosphere lightened.
The old woman was a visionary you see.
She knew the young girl sought truths and knowledge.
The old woman's cabin was to be the young girl's college.
Their paths crossing was destined to be.

The old woman perceived knowledge from the earth, trees and skies.
The young girl learned well but not without pain.
The young girl's name was Mary Summer Rain.
The old woman's name was Bright Eyes, also called No-Eyes.

No-Eyes is gone now but only in physical form.
Her spirit remains with Summer, in a sense by her side.
Summer was a pupil in whom the old woman took great pride.
She's there to help Summer weather the storm,

From the sons of darkness. The battles so fierce and cruel,
Their constant attacks to break Summer's back.
Yet Summer prevails, she yields them no slack,
She's strong and aware and knows how to duel.

She's spreading the truths as she promised No-Eyes she'd do.
She's paying a high price for keeping that vow.
But she's a tough cookie, she'll get by, somehow.
Even though she knows her words will touch a limited few.

She's trying to help us, she asks for no fee.
Her wisdom is endless. Her knowledge is deep.
She kindles the awareness lying within us, asleep.
Thank God Summer's there for you and me.

Marie E Toole
IN THE EYES OF MY SON

To my dearest son, Glen—My greatest reward in life!

I care not for fame in this world,
but only in the eyes of my son.
He will treat my memory with kindness,
embellish upon my virtues
and skim over my faults.
He will remember only the laughter and smiles,
conveniently forgetting my tears.
To him I will always be someone,
the key figure in his life.
Someone who is the giver and receiver of his life.
Someone who is the giver and receiver of his love.
It doesn't matter that I am not well-known,
for in his heart I am a winner.
I was entrusted with a beautiful gift
and I tried to handle that gift
not as a prize possession,
but as a tiny bird who depends
on someone to let him be free.
My only task in life was to love
his innocence and youth,
his moods and mistakes.
For he is the one who gives my life

direction.
He makes my role essential.
And although the world has not recognized my talent
In rewarding me with the pleasures of success,
I have been famous beyond compare in the eyes of my Son.

Mary A Neibel
GOD BLESS OUR HOMELESS

To Wayne, my dear nephew.

We watch them as they slowly make their way
Through the streets, alleys and by-ways.
As they trod down life's lonely path
No place to enter for a warm bath.
No place to come out of the cold
The elements and winter make them old.
And when they stop to sit a spell
Each has their own story to tell.
Once they were cared for and loved
But for whatever into this life they were shoved.
Some with children some all alone
Now upon this land they're left to roam.
For whatever, life's dealt them a bad hand
So now for existence, they must withstand
Cold stares, and sarcastic remarks,
Tomorrow it could be us asleep in the parks.
It's not just a problem for god to solve,
It's for us all to be involved.
Please God, Bless our Homeless.

Anne Haley Bryant
MY MOTHER

To My Very Someone Special—MY MOTHER, YVONNE WALLACE HALEY. We Love You, Anne, Ernie & Family.

There is someone special—most just take for granted
She gives all her love, time and most of her life
This is long hard work and she can't be enchanted
This is that special woman called Mother, Friend and Wife.

It's by the love of two we are brought onto this land
Then there's training, growing and loving all thrown in her hand
The Father provides, mostly—and an occasional hand
But our Mothers are there no matter what, she takes her stand.

A Mother's love is the closest love there can be
She puts her children first no matter how they turn out
I have abused mine and, Oh God, she still loves me
It is more than I have a right to, but I'm so happy I could shout.

I'm sure there are times my Mother would like to wring my neck
But she goes on loving me as if to say, what the heck
I did the best I could and that's all anyone could ask
I am sure raising me was a most trying task.

I think she did a fantastic job with me
I am no angel, ah how very plain this is to see
But, I know love and I know right from wrong
I know so many who will never be able to sing this song.

I love my Mother more than she will ever know
Some kinds of love, respect and adoration are hard to show
But thank God, I have a Mother and family to be proud of
Through good and bad we'll always have that love.

Lourdes Ferro Marrero

Lourdes Marrero
I AM

To my friend, Alice, who believed in me.

I am the light,
That shines above you.
I am the light,
That shines around you.

For what it is,
Not clear to see.
There is no vision between,
You and me.

Lourdes Marrero
THE ONE WE KNOW

To my whole Family and especially to my Mom, Maria Lugones, for all their Love and Support.

The woman we Love and grown to know,
Have heart made of honey and feeling of stone.
At times she listens but tense to forget,
Her mind is so busy with work on her head.
She screams and shouts without a clue,
And then forgets right out of the blues.
That little woman as you can see,
Have some kind of temper like you and me.
Sometime she's happy and full of joy,
Sometime she's lonely and all alone.
You know that woman as well as I do,
She gave us life and nine months too.

Lourdes Marrero
PASSING BY

In memory of Ramon and Mercedes who fought the dreadful disease of cancer.

Passing through the age of Life,
Shadow, darkness in the night.
Passing memories of my youth,
Feeling down and feeling blue.
Fighting Life to survive,
Gasp of air just passing by.
Floating Angels by my side,
Shining light above the sky.
Losing vision losing sight,
Can't remember when I died.

Brenda Edsall
HIDDEN COLORS

To my husband, Doug: "Some things are seen with your eyes, others with only your heart!"

There is a key to the prism
of your heart,
Its wonders and treasures
untold.
Are faceted with emotions
that long to escape.
My love is the secret
that reaches within,
Unlocking the door
to your innermost soul,
Releasing the spectrum
that cries to soar free . . .

Laura Lavender
SPRINGTIME PEACE

Dedicated to God, The creator of all things beautiful.

The night was soft, and warm, and quiet.
The sky a deep dark blue.
With a big round moon suspended there,
And stars were peeping through.

The wind was whispering through the trees
With a gentle sighing sound,
And the chirping of the crickets came
From somewhere close around.

From the brush off to one side
Came notes from a sleepy bird,
Then joining in from ponds nearby
The frog's song could be heard.

Relaxing on the soft green grass
I realized with a start.
The peace and quiet from all around
Had filled my stormy heart.

Nina Wilson
STANDING FOR LOVE—MY LIFE

To Geraldine. Everyone chooses their love, their life.

When we first met, you said
I wasn't good enough, just as well dead
With everything against me
In your opinion, that is, to be
Too young, divorced, a mother too
A girl filling a woman's shoe
From a broken home, nothing to my name
Wrong side of the tracks, so you claim

It didn't matter, what your son said
His ego could not be fed
So he loved me and he cared
All his life, he wanted shared

This did not meet your approval
Instead, you want my removal
Claiming your love for him, the only one that's true
Now you've changed it, and said you are through

Because he stood to fight
And show his children, they were right
Standing for love, he should not feel shame
There is no fault, there is no blame
You tell me—what did you gain

Christine Ann Luttrell
GODDESS, WHORE, WIFE, OR SLAVE?

I dedicate this poem to my artistic son Jeremiah Nathaniel, and to my "Lover, Farmer, Poet, Snake": Jim Wayne Miller.

She lay curled up on their floor like an echo
but he did not hear the signal of her silences.
Ivy fell away from their flagstone cottage
as he sat at his desk researching the goddesses
who have endured reverberating through history.
Piles of leafless vine burned in their front yard;
spirals of smoke rose then fell at his hand
as ashes churned upward from their home.

She made no audible sound until he sighed
resonating things that had been on his lips.
Then a tree fell and she heard a valley echo
the voice of temptation in the leaves floated
to her ears. She lay there no more.
She became one of the goddesses
he'd be researching.

Jeanette DeRosa
IN CHRISTIAN

For Christian Arnold-Dyer Chase.

I tell them all that I count the remainders
Of your eyes lashes on the ceiling, falling from heaven
When they only penetrate my roof—and I sit
Through all those aberrations, swallowing
The dried flowers, waiting to catch one.
Or when I tell them of your soul, transferred
In the blinking, fixed on my fears—
For the sun's continuous rising in the center of gravity.
How can I repeat such a fever as this, no words
Or more than words, opening up
To the music in the sadness of your

descent.
They lie deaf to the threat
Of perfection, recalling your life,
Blooming into your form—the endless smoke
In the night when the walls are quivering—dark
Canyons that only your breath can wash away.
I tell them all that I am mute, and in you I scream
All those years, the centuries of cleansing,
When the earth was not looking and you fell
In my love.

Sue (Hunt) Carter
MOTHER'S BIBLE

To my 92-year-old mother who is still alive and praying. She is so mentally bright I'm writing for her since she never got the chance. She is a Special Person.

I picked up Mother's Bible, all around me felt like Holy Ground.
I felt the brush of a breeze from an angel's wing.
And a warm glow did abound.
My heart was stirred within me, I felt the touch of a quick'ning calm.
I picked up my Mother's Bible and I heard an angel's Psalm.

I heard the angels sing the song of Vict'ry until Death.
I felt the way she must have felt then, it took away my breath.
The time, it was so long ago when she would hold me close and say,
"Sister, Don't you know that I love and pray for you each?"

But the Bible's all I have now for Mom has drifted away.
Into places I can't go just yet but age brings me closer each day.
But, I feel the same as she did when I hold my loved ones close.
I picked up Mother's Bible and heard the singing of the Heavenly Host.

Steven C Lyon
THE PRINCESS AND THE KNIGHT

To my daughters, Erica and Stephanie, whose love follows me everywhere.

A Princess is pretty and nice to hold
A Knight is often cold ugly and old

A Princess is a prayer and pleasant dream
A Knight is another battle another scream

A Princess is from heaven and holy blessed
A Knight is a warrior who's often depressed

A Princess has safe places of kingdom to wonder
A Knight goes before her defending her honor

A Princess is a vision of a clear blue water pool
A Knight is a soldier whose tactics are seldom fooled

A Princess is a spinning wheel of golden thread
A Knight is a haunted man with a price on his head

A Princess is a lady of dignity, high social degree
A Knight is like an animal always to be wild and free

A Princess is like bee's honey all sweet but pure
A Knight is a life of hardships and pains endured

A Princess is a lady who commands respect
A Knight is a dutiful man of much and little regret

A Princess will someday become her country's queen
A Knight must remain a Knight and forever dream

Beverly Jeddrey Naleway
SESTINA ON LIFE

To my beloved Roger, the light and darkness of my life & inspirer of this poem. You opened my eyes & heart to the meaning & meaninglessness of love.

Birth—shooting to the surface from a watery sleep,
undulating forth on the waves of the tide,
slammed upon the shore, uninvited and weak,
longing to turn back but relentlessly carried forward,
unable to language how to think or feel.
Nothing to cling to; not even a memory.

In the midst of the whirlpool is a child-lively memory
caught only at day's end when claimed by sleep.
Is it real? Flesh and blood? Go ahead; kiss and feel
for tomorrow it will be swept away with the tide,
venturing back, drifting away, returning yet ever forward.
A lifetime in such a short time, accomplishments that leave one weak.

Invincible, indestructible, all things are youth but weak;
driving upward, speeding onward, their memory
only a blur of bright lights screeching forward.
No time to stop, less time to think, no need to sleep.
They are the hub of the wheel, the thrust of the tide,
never caring nor wondering, once an adult, how they will feel.

Now I am an adult, you ask how does it feel
as I crouch behind walls of paper and glass, trembling and weak?
Ground into submission by the all-knowing, on-going tide
sweeping me along so fast my only memory
is being carried out to sea and to endless sleep,
and I want to turn back but I must go relentlessly forward.

Two-third's lost and inexorably driving forward.
Hopes and dreams drowned in my tears, for once I feel,
I have time to think, I lament and lose sleep,
haunted by unreachable goals and youthful memory
of the zest for life before I grew too weak
to fight the pull and drag of diminishing time and tide.

Now I welcome the rushing toward of the tide.
To get beyond the sea, one welcomes the push forward.
What is there behind but a laboring of contrived memory?
I cannot weep for what I do not feel;
that burst of birth that leaves you weak,
only a prelude for an endless sleep.

All is dark, memory dimmed, all that I can feel
is the tide, wave tip unfurled, knows I am too weak,
lifts me up, beyond the sea, forward to inevitable sleep.

Carole Sinclair and Riba

Carole Sinclair
RIBA

For Curtis, my husband and best friend who for the past 5 years has put up with my "funny little ways" and has helped me to survive a 5 year love-hate relationship with the world's most opinionated parrot!

If you think kids are a problem and give you lots of trouble
You should try to keep a bird, you'll find your trouble's double!
They're much more work than children and noisier by far,
And when you want some peace and quiet you can't stuff them in the car
And haul them off to Grandma's and drop them at the door,
Oh no, you'll find that most of your time's spent sweeping seeds off the floor!
You'll listen to all the squawking and know each funny little way
And patiently you'll try and try to get that bird to say
"Hello Mum" and "Hello Dad" and "Polly wants a cracker"
While arrogantly they'll stare right back and simply whistle instead of chatter!
But heaven help those of you who get that bird to talk
'Cause from then on there'll be no peace and you'll have to take a walk
To escape from all the ruckus, the whistling and the din,
You'll hear so many imitations you'll think Rich Little has moved in!
And then there is the training, the wing clipping to discourage flight
And how many times through all of this will you suffer from a bite?
But even though she's so much work, more trouble than a child,
To live without our Amazon would really drive us wild,
For our baby's really loving when she isn't being mean
And after all, as Kermit says, "It's not easy being green!"

Dorie Brown
HAPPY ANNIVERSARY, MY FIRST LOVE

I dedicate this poem to BOB, my High School sweetheart.

It was September when we met long ago
We were in High School, we were so young
It wasn't love at first sight
But as time went on we shared all our hopes and dreams and fell in love

It was a struggle in those days and things didn't come easy for us
The joy was seeing each other every day

Suddenly, like a bolt out of the blue something drove us apart
With no explanation you stopped seeing me
It left me devastated and with a broken heart

I saw you on the street one day after the war had ended
You told me you had served, and I thanked God for your safe return
You said you were married and had a son
I also had married and was blessed with a wonderful son

I am a widow now, many years have passed and I had the need to call you
We met for lunch and you finally told me why you left me years ago
You said that it was because you saw me with another boy and was deeply hurt
You blamed it on the innocence of youth
You kissed me goodbye that day and we both felt the sadness of the wasted years apart
You said, "I'll always love you because you were my first love"

It is September now, our anniversary of fifty years
Will you telephone me and say,
"Happy Anniversary, my first love?"

Brigitte Watson
THE WIND AND ME

I dedicate this poem to my mother for pushing me to the brink of entering the World of Poetry writing—THANK YOU.

The relationship between a leaf and the wind is much like our relationship, you pick me up and send me soaring through sunshine and space.

There is a feeling of freedom and yet I still belong—knowing I'm weak, yet you're acting strong.

But flight is only temporary and I must come down to the ground—and when I do, my love will still be steady and sound.

So please be patient and try to
understand that the real meaning of
love is not clear and I must stand the
test of time because my future is like
a leaf in the wind.

Brigitte Watson
SUFFERING
Why is it that we elect to suffer so?
To agonize for times not our own.

We reach for those forbidden
treasures only to be stung with
the poison of disappointment.

We try to rationalize those thoughts
that cannot be rationalized—
for those thoughts are not our
thoughts.

Peace of mind is so hard for us to
achieve, for we pursue the very
heart and soul of those we desire, and
so many times those desires
are left to sit with our fears of
loneliness.

Patience is a virtue we cannot seem
to hold on to.

What must be—must be now. To
wait brings such anxiety and despair
only we can feel.

Perhaps that is why we suffer so!

Nancy Lou Moores Byrd
SPRING SOUNDS AND SMELLS

To my husband, Bill, daughter, Linda, and son, Barry.

The Spring has never smelled so
sweet,
Flowerbeds, gardens, lined up neat,
The sky seems bluer than before,
Just saw a rainbow from my door.

Who, but God, could make these
things,
Like blossoms, rainbows, bluebirds'
wings?
The roses bloom, in bright array,
The morning dew, on petals lay.

A Master Artist makes such things
As babbling brooks and cool, clear
springs.
I hear a coming train—a whistle,
Lets us know it's near the trestle.

The cars go by, school children hustle
To catch the bus—the noisy bustle,
Their laughter brings back memories,
clear
Of school days past, and by-gone
years

Now it's quiet—the rain clouds
gather,
Our Lord will send the sun again—no
matter.

Nancy Lou Moores Byrd
TODAY
I picked a yellow flower today,
Its petals brighter than the sun.
Who has the time to paint such things
as yellow flowers so bright and gay?

I walked in shining sand today
and wondered, as it glistened there,
Who made the ground on which we
walk,
the sand, the rocks, the clay?

I saw a boy of three today,
His smile and eyes like my own
son's,
Who molds these things, like boys'
smiles
on lips that have so much to say?

I spoke to God today,
and thanked Him for these earthly
things.
For it is He, who made such things
as flowers, and sand, and smiles so
gay.

Lord, keep me humble as today,
Let me enjoy these earthly things.
In peace and quiet serenity,
I give Thee thanks, from day to day.

Lois Fowler Barrett
LIMBO INTO SUICIDE

To my daughter Julie and my husband Dee, who both died in 1989.

Unreal . . . dreaming . . . day follows
day.
Night after night shaken to the core
Of nightmare-filled-void; empty
Feelings of brief, panic, fright, maybe
more.

What is real? What is imagined and
gone
From me to limbo? Drained,
shrunken, dead.
It moves, it pains, it feels, but the
body
Knows nothing. Nothing! No thought
the head!

Wonder, fear, panic dominating,
holding
Sway over the mindless mind . . . the
eternal death.
To live is to grieve: To grieve is to
die.
Grief, alive, far worse . . . this
infernal breath.

Seeking to know, but failing to find
reason.
Questioning, crying out for the
WHY? THE WHY?
No peace for this one? No peace for
this one?
No peace for this one just means to
die . . .

Yet not dead! That is the crux of it!
Not dead . . . moving, doing, holding
tight . . .

Alive? No . . . just existing, just
being in it . . .
To exist and not live? It's wrong!
Not right!

Created for life . . . but life
without peace?
Unfair! Not right! Wrong! Wrong!
Wrong!
Day follows day . . . limbo . . .
eternal limbo . . .

With Limbo as style—it cannot
last long . . .

Lois Fowler Barrett
THE SURVIVOR
Stars fell from heaven and crashed on
the ground
Leaving a crushed heart groping all
around
The empty space left in a suicidal
mind teeming
With bitterness of loss two deaths not
seeming
To be for a reason that mortal
thoughts expressed
And left an answer that caused a
mind regressed
For life losing meaning to the already
darkened
Heart which had nearly made it, but
harkened
To the call of blackness surrounding
lost love
And lost emotions not answered by
the One above.

Take up life and go on to what no one
could say
But they did that over and over each
bitter day
Until a mind already crushed rebelled
and told
Them to try to understand just what
could hold
Hearts open anymore for more bitter
events
In a life sore and crushed and full of
dents
Made by something impossible to be
controlled
By mere mortal who asked only to be
extolled
To greater heights of understanding
and care
To live beyond this blinding life to
dare
For an answer to daily constant cold
fare.

Daniel B Dermond
GENTLE SPECTACLE
Ideal. carnation tinged ozone
evanescence and transparency
species of discoloration in a
white wind equinoctial light
convalescent conversations in
a silent moment masquerading
in gravely invented parables
substances of shadow dropping
abnegation of a beating heart
lascivious parson of Pequania
unceasing apostolic precipices
calico diamonds emerge from in
the ivory handled darkness of
the virginal machineel tree
exquisite embrace rose radiant
in a wainscot blackened blot
axle iron inscription on the
porch of an addled red romance
and disarms her with a caress

Daniel B Dermond
THE JEWELED HAND
Blinded in bold
the imprints, cold
to colloquy and
circles lifted in
leanness will rove and
compose torn sound
the begotten remedy.
Sea's lips dishevelled
bitter, not unkind
blue veins enwound
like the soul, her
marble head lullaby.
Mist of winged melody
and inviolate laughter
his tides also rise.

Jean Arney Kopala
MOTHER'S PRAYER FOR DR. JACOBS
I remember his stopping on his way
in that day
To reassure my son in a warm, gentle
way.
He understands a six-year-old boy
will need someone to trust
As he lays there so quiet and
vulnerable
In a drug-induced sleep on the O.R.
table.

I remember his turning to us and
saying,
"Stay here in the room, or playroom
perhaps."
He knows we need a quiet place, for
this time of vigil and praying.
He knows we don't need a smoke-
filled room and the nervous chatter
Of parents here on a far less serious
matter.

I remember that evening the face of a
man
Exhausted and drained, full of
disappointment and sorrow
As he comes up to tell me my son
won't wake up tomorrow.
The face of a strong man who's
learned how to handle
The sight of a Mother's anguish and
tears
As she struggles to realize a Mother's
worst fears.

Dear God, let him rise above this
death
To wake each tomorrow with
renewed breath
To tackle again that day's surgical
challenge
With steady hand and mind kept clear
To give of himself to some other
Mother's son so dear. Amen.

Jean Arney Kopala
CRUSTACEANS OF THE MIND
Conundrums inhabit
The shoreline;
Crustaceans of the mind.
Their spidery, segmented
Appendages
Scuttling across the surface
Burrowing out labyrinths
Deep within the brain.

Translucent, spherical bodies
Suspended
Bobbing over the surface
Then vanishing instantly.
Bait snatched from the hook
By lurking subterranean
Brain cells
To be dissected, digested
Then carefully catalogued
Within labyrinth confines.

Jean Arney Kopala
THE PULL OF THE RIVER

i

The yogi
Arranging himself
In lotus position
On a faded cloth mat
Focuses inward
Mentally chanting
A well-worn
Mantra.

ii

The priest
Prostrating himself
Before God
At the ornately-carved altar
Pours forth his
Adoration
Confessions
Petitions
To the Almighty.

iii

Young lovers
Entwining their bodies
In sexual union
Lose
All awareness
Of the outside world
Of themselves
Of time

Experiencing only
The moments'
Pleasures.

iv

The young mother
Blissfully suckling
A newborn
At her breast
Feels only the
Hot suction of
An insistent mouth
On her nipple
In her loins
Down to her toes.

v

Each has pushed aside
The daily merry-go-round
Of thoughts
To revel
In the moment—
To flow with
The current
Of the mighty river.

Floyd Eugene Davis II
THOUGHTS OF HOME

Thoughts of home
On a rainy night:
Ringlets on puddles
Spread out of sight.

A symphony played
On the washstand tub;
Falling drops from the roof
In a rhythmic drub.

Wind shaking the trees
Until they cry.
I smell the washed air,
Snuggle safe in my bed;
Young, loved, warm and dry.

Floyd Eugene Davis II
A GRAND MOTHER

To a grand mother, Maw Piller.

You can pack a lot of living
Into eighty years or so.
Birthing, burping, changing, wiping;
All fond memories you know.

Lots of joy and gladness
Help to soothe:
All the sorrow-sadness
The years put you through.

Sunny childish faces
Looking up to you;
Asking for your help-approval
Or just to say "I love you."

It's a lot of years to savor;
Precious moments to relive.
It took eighty years to package
All the gifts you have to give.

Floyd Eugene Davis II
OUR DAILY BREAD

Poetry is my daily bread
All 'round us lies its beauty.
Each moment is a gift of love,
And joy to have a duty.

In nature there is no idleness
For all of life is living.
Like rhythm through a poem it runs.
The greatest gift is giving.

Nancy McKeen
GUILTY!

Trudging through my conscience in an unrelenting stream
come all my ignominious guilts - in a haunting dream:
the good deeds I didn't do; the bad deeds I've done;
the struggles that I didn't try to win - and might have won;
the golden paths I didn't take; the great books never read;
the kind words I didn't say; the mean words I've said.
A chain-gang of gaunt-eyed regrets
harasses my tormented mind like unpaid debts,
always watching me, these apparitions of remorse.
Had I but gone the worthy way and kept a steady course!
Like a fertile field unseeded, lying fallow,
my life is ending unfulfilled and shallow.
Could I redeem it with repentant tears
for all my nothingness throughout the years -
Oh! how I'd clutch that treasured second chance!
and ne'er give mediocrity a glance.
To mine own self and others I'd be true -
by paying conscientious heed to what I say and do;
for all that's left of us that matters once we're in the ground -
is the influence of what we said and did while still around.

Paul W Moorhouse
LORD HELP US WIN

Here I sit night after night,
I try to cry but it's one hell
of a fight.
I love her so and I can't say
why,
I'm all alone I just want to
die.
It hurts so bad I know I should,
But when she's around it feels
so good.
I want her lord, the rest of my
life,
As soon as I can I will make
her my wife.
We work so hard and keep on
trying,
But all we build is always dying.
So help us lord, thru thick
and thin,
Please help us out,
Lord help us win.

Velda Morgan
AWAITING SPRING

Grey skies above, the world is on hold
Winter casts a baleful eye on the mortals below.
Cold winds blow and snow covers the land
But eternal winter is not part of the plan.
Soon Spring will come and the earth will renew
Then grass will be green and skies will be blue.

Vivian E Malone
HAPPINESS

Happiness is God's great love,
All the blessings from above.
A warm bed to sleep in every night,
The sun which shines so very bright.
Having the joy of having friends,
Happy times which God sends.
All the food which we have to eat,
A contented feeling is hard to beat.
Having someone to love you very much
Getting a kind word, a gentle touch.
A little girl or little boy,
Being a child and getting a new toy.
Having a straight road to travel,
A feeling of victory when our problems we unravel.
Having with friends a laugh or two,
And a sky of pretty shades of blue.
A feeling of abiding peace,
An awful war that has ceased.
Happiness is all of these and many more things,
Being happy makes us richer than kings!

William J McAlpine
RIGHT AND WRONG

Right is the sun bright and shining.
Wrong is your Father sick and dying.

Right is a clear blue sky.
Wrong is tears in your Mother's eyes.

Right is your Brother's helping hand.
Wrong is leaving him alone to stand.

Right is the wind in your face.
Wrong is a cold and empty place.

Right is Love for a lonely heart.
Wrong is a hungry child in the dark.

Right is being true to yourself.
Wrong is caring for no one else.

Florence B Moore
GOD AND YOU

This poem is dedicated to Curtis and Charles Moore with love.

Let me listen while I may.
To the birds that sing each day.
Down the wooded pathway too.
There I'll sit and wait for you.

And when you come again to stay.
We'll walk the paths of yesterday.
Everywhere the angels trod.
There we'll walk and talk with God.

God will be so good and kind.
To us, and all mankind.
He will wipe our tears away.
There with Him, we'll always stay.

Paul A Madore
BEAUTY IN NATURE

There is a tremendous
amount of beauty in nature.
The ocean with its vast
body of water . . .
the rolling surf
rushing ashore
to embrace her.

The majestic mountains
reaching so high
fondly hugging the clouds
the glowing stars
with their twinkling lights
illuminate the sky
with silver and gold.

The rolling hills
with their enchanting echoes
of many babbling brooks
of incoherent and meaningless
murmur, which is ageless . . .
takes along the secret of the forest
to the great seas, which are endless . .
the small villages with their rows of houses
where people rest and repose . . .

Kerry J McKenzie
ON YOUR OWN

You're all grown up with kids of your own
Husband and children to make a home

House on the hill and dogs in the yard
Raising children is not always easy, sometimes it's hard

The hard times are only pathways of life
To help us understand our weakness and strife

Our children are only images of what we are
And we push and shove to make them a star

To let them shine in a light of their own
Don't make them a parent clone.

Alice L Marsh
THE PRAYER OF A FIREMAN'S WIFE

Dear God, as my man goes out
Each time the whistle blows,
Protect him with your mighty hand
No matter where he goes.
Be it on a tall, tall ladder
Or a grass fire on the ground
Forever stand beside him
Let him know that you're around.
When he goes out in summer
When the day is hot and dry
Stand by him with your helping hand,
To do his best he'll try.
When he goes out in winter
When it's slippery and cold
Ride along beside him
Protect him as you hold
The fire truck upon the road
Or wherever it may be
And bring him back home safely
To the children and to me.

Windy Star
COME TO ME, OH GRACEFUL MESSENGER OF THE NIGHT

To Kahlil Gibran — Whose words affected me so profoundly.

Come to me, oh graceful Messenger of the night,
and lead me to your quiet shores.
I drink of your essence, your sweet elixir,
the Aroma of a thousand nights in Paradise.
I know Peace and I am one.

Oh, worlds without end, I beckon you to my door.
Fill me with your peace and plenty
and give me light, I am yours.

In a land of plenty
I see the sun.
And my fate is calling me,
To be one
In your light.

Diana Massie
SOUL REALITY

Look at people as entity.
Ne'er a male . . .
Nor female be.

For only in this archaic world
Do we see . . .
Souls that arrive with a
Male or . . .
Female Decree.

Diana Massie
VEILS
Veils of personalities lifted oh so cautiously,
Veils worn daily.

Veils of mediocrity woven by society.
Veils of intellect woven by philosophies of retrospect.
Veils of idiocy woven by conformity.

Veils if lifted, display unique individuality.
Will we be set adrift by society?
What veils shall we lift?

If we decline to become another's history,
Will this uniqueness become our finality?
Or should we keep what is behind those veils a mystery and
Let another's fantasy . . .
Become our destiny?

Penny Mayfield
FINALLY FREE
In a room full of darkness, I feel all alone
Silence evades me, ringing noises like a phone.
Time stands still, but life spins around
Colors keep flashing, backward I am bound.
I close my eyes, hoping all is a dream
Hearing a noise, I look about, realizing the sound
to be a scream.
I steady myself and shake my head
My body feels as if it's trapped inside a huge cobweb.
I shiver and shake with uncontrollable fear
Nothing seems right, I feel my face moistened by a tear.
When will I awake from this terrible nightmare?
How did I get here? How will I fare?
A friend of mine, at least I thought him to be
Took me on a trip, a trip I could not foresee.
The things he gave me sounded so neat
I took them all, now my body racks with fire and heat.
Sick and tired, I learn not so fast
That drugs are not cool, they're a part of the past.
I do my own thing now, I'm finally free
Peer pressure never was right for me.

Dorothea McHugh
TIMELESSNESS
Timeless thoughts, like
A clock without hands.
Faceless memories,
Bodies without heads.
People amassed in a
Kaleidoscope of
hurried movement.
I'm a child again . . .
Going in infinite circles,
Like an empty merry-go-round,
Or, a big red unleashed balloon
Gyrating in space . . . . up . . . up . .
up
And far away.

Richard P Mohr
NOVEMBER SOUNDS
The rose has died and October has gone
Cool winds, brown leaves and
Autumn snow
The sweet smell of time
envelopes the air
Invisible sunlight warms the dawn

November sounds come lift me high in the air
And I am on cloud nine
Walking down the trail, holding your hand
Cool winds, and I am feeling fine

Footprints on the shore leave not a trace
And the stars appear overhead
after dark
Unspoken words pass through
as you look on
Hearts in motion, beating soft and calm

November sounds lift you to the sky
From your eye comes a single tear
The eagle greets you from his hideaway
Brown leaves, you have nothing to fear

November sounds come blanket us with love
All that we are feeling is so very new
The sun sets the path and love takes flight
Settle into sleep for the long night
November sounds and dreams come true

Lila Leigh Mudd
THE SECOND TIME AROUND

To deceased son, William Jamel Isler.

I am so glad God's smarter than me
For there are all things he can see
He knew with my kids the first time around
There was no time to be found
For those things extra I wanted to do
The way we grandparents really want

So now our second chance is here
With our four grandkids we give a cheer
More time to play, to grow
Not so much I told you so

Grandmom and Pop we are, you see
Thank God, this blessing came to be
All these times we can now capture
For all of this is God's great rapture

Bruce Mulligan
FROM A BRAVE'S HEART

To my best friend, and the woman the Great Spirit sent me to make my life complete. You will never leave my heart.

Like the magnificent redwood
you stand tall in my heart

As a crystal clear stream
you wash away my thirst for love
My memories of you are like the
mountains
never changing

You are as beautiful as the sunrise
and as quiet as the dusk

In your heart you have the strength of a bull buffalo
yet you are as soft as the moon
glimmering across the lake

As always when my thoughts go to you
My heart swells

My love for you could fill the deepest of canyons
and reach to the highest of all the clouds

Your beauty is as fresh as a mist filled forest
and as calm as a dewdrop on a flower

Michael P Mulvey
THE COLORS OF LONELINESS

To my Mom and Dad, for without them, I wouldn't be here.

No matter who you are
or what you do
At some point in your life
you are going to feel blue
It cannot be avoided
even by the slipperiest fellow
You will look in the mirror
and see your true color, yellow
Some people fake happiness
others wash it down the sink
To everyone the day will come
when we are not in the pink
We often know not what to do
but sit around, and mope all day
Like an overcast sky
all that happens is a dismal gray
Until the day comes
when it all falls together
Like a beautiful rainbow
after our own stormy weather

Judith Murovic M D
I WORRY/
I
worry/
wondering
why (?)
wishing
whatever
would
wait . . .
while
wanting
whomever,
who
will
watch
with
me.

Michael D Markum
A SIMPLE PARADOX
The tree of life like a stone monolith
Refuses adversity room to move.
The roots are imbedded, deeply anchored;
The trunk, a foundation supporting life
Which must be firmly planted in the ground
Rooted firm within the earth, its mother;
To grow, to branch out into a new Spring
The tree reaches out absorbing the light
Provided it by the giver of life.
The limbs branch, leaves begin to multiply,
And life is continually fresh, new.
The elements argue against the tree
Seeking to curb it short, to cut its growth.
Discovering its strength, yet knowing its
Weakness. Old, tired roots begin to rot.
Life grows old, begins to tire, grows weary,
Facing eternity as it subsides.
Yet one small seed will sprout, a new tree born.

Adversity commands that which renews.

Norman McLaughlin
SOMEWHERE BACK THERE IN TIME
I woke and saw her sleeping there,
In our bed where love has died.
My mind thinks back to long ago,
To the night she was my bride.
Our hearts were racing, our excitement high,
As we became as one.
But through the years a distance come,
And we're no longer one.
I see her lying next to me,
This woman who once was mine.
But now her past seems closing in,
And I'm outside her mind.
Her love for me has never changed,
She tells me all the time.
But when we're in this bed of love,
She says she can't be mine.
I wish that I could disappear,
And be lost back there in time.
I think the place I'd choose to be,
Is back when she was mine.

Grace M Miyamoto
CRISIS
The U.N. has a crisis again with Arafat . . .
have to get to the vet and fix the cat!

The Amazon jungle is disappearing from earth . . .
my unmarried daughter will soon give birth!

What do we do with all the nuclear waste . . .
my kid smeared the wall with Elmer's paste!

The ozone layer is very quickly depleting . . .
my son came home last night with an earring!

Life is just one crisis after the other . . .
trials and tribulations of being a mother!

Eula M Moody
LOVE IS LIFE
Love is a wonderful thing.
Sometimes it creeps up
like cold on a wintry day,
painting a frosty pattern so gay.

It's like a blanket,
heated before, by a mother
who wraps it around us
after her chores.
Warm, comfortable, and secure.

Then again it hits like a bomb
from which there's no escape.
Our knees get weak and our insides quake.

We'll surely die if it's not returned.

Love is a beautiful rainbow
flashed over the land,
Woven in a pattern we don't
understand.
Win or lose, we wouldn't have
missed it
It's life.

Angela Morano
LET US EMBRACE LIKE BROTHERS
Cats and dogs will sleep together.
Wolf and sheep go out for salad.
Left and right, back and forth.
Black and white will blend to make
grey.
City and country, forest and boonies.
Sunny and cloudy brighten my day.
Sweet and sour make a great couple.
Smooth and rough snag, but that's
o.k.
Light and dark make it soft.
Night and day make a beautiful dusk
and dawn.
All created by the same thing,
Yet living in total opposite worlds.
In unison we touch.

Lisa N Murgatroyd (Age 8)
SMALLER THAN A . . .
Smaller than a baby ant.
Smaller than a pencil tip.
Smaller than a grain of sand.
Smaller than a freckle nip.
Smaller than an oak tree bud.
Smaller than a paper cut.
Smaller than a speck of mud.
Smaller than a bolt and nut.
Smaller than a needle's eye.
Smaller than a safety pin.
Smaller than a crumb of pie.
Smaller than a fish's fin.
Smaller than a coach's whistle.
Smaller than a toothbrush bristle.
Smaller than some soda fizz.
That's how small my pimple is!!

Blanche D Madiol
A LONG TIME COMING
(The Berlin Wall)

Made strangers by the broad-brick
wall
Built across the city of Berlin,
Dividing Berliners East and West-all
Were swept into a breach with kin.

There came the numbing feeling then
Of being eclipsed by polar ice:
Much like the Soviet citizen,
A people forced to sacrifice.

But man can do all things if he will,
And Glasnost was in full sway;
A warming aspect ending the chill,
And the wall was swept away.

The Berlin Wall was broken down
To let the people walk out free,
By the open gate to any town
With hope and human dignity.

Melanie A Mitchell
LIFE IN A DAY
Sometimes in your life
A lot of things go wrong.
When you lose that perfect love
The one you thought was strong.

It's gone from you, it's flown away
Now all that's left to do,
Is think about the usual things
How nothing has happened to you.

Get up in the morning
Go to bed at night,
Same life to live
No maybe or mights.
Same straight pattern
Day after day,
Nothing is planned
In some sort of way.

So just keep on going
Trying to maintain,
The life in which you live
Where more you try to gain.

Charles O Maxson
I AM THE PEOPLE

To Tom and Nancy Lopes.

I am the people and I will be free! You cannot bind me forever with the chains of your ignorance. I shall be my own Master. My destiny will be mine!

You cannot build a wall and keep me in, for I will scale it or break it down.

No system that is cruel and unjust can stand against me, for my power will set me free.

Truth will be the tide of my strength and it will ebb the injustices of my enemies.

I will prevail in my quest for freedom; for I am the people, and I will be free!

Leona Maloney
PROMISE

To my three children: Colleen, Patrick, Renae, and their families.

Ask not how happy you are
Ask how accurate you're being,
In all your seeing, saying, and
believing
As to your judgment of people
with a flare.

Beware of those dangerous lips
For now and then, they can slip,
Into the most disagreeable messages
That can result in damages for ages.

Ask not how to speak the truth
Ask how to overcome inaccuracy
with worth,
Then live a tranquil life of love
As if God promised, you a
golden glove.

Chris Matuszczak
RESOLUTION (RING IN THE 90'S)

To my dearest husband, John, and my wonderful parents, Edward and Bernice, and all of those whose support and inspiration have brought me to this place and time.

The world of today,
It's in such disarray
Just look around us, such deep
despair,
Nobody to love, nobody to care.

Our souls are dying, gone are our
dreams,
Today's world its so different, even
children scheme!
Dreams are shattered, parents
overworked, children abandoned to
Nintendo,
Brother, Sister, Mother, Father
mesmerized, by the tube.

Where's the family? Our simple
talks - the sharing of feelings?
No more - don't speak - Batman's
playing!
Let's wake up before it's too late!
Get down on our knees and meditate.
Become one with God again, and
learn to care,
About ourselves and our fellow man!
Let's rejoice in life and all its
wonders,
Make the 90's safe from drugs and
other blunders!

A New Year's Resolution, to open up
our hearts,
To all our neighbors, but to our
families most of all
To rid the earth of all pollution,
before we fall,
Embrace the world, just give a smile;
And once again love purely, like a
little child!

Maria Masmarques
POETIC WORDS

If you favor a memory it will be an everlasting possession.

Worlds of value
Are captured with written
significance
Some might be stored in a memory
On a journey, one sees great
mysteries
To really enjoy so many adventures
It takes knowledge of a culture
When something is unique it is often
noticed
With much thought something well
written can come from an intimate
thought
Many have taken an interest in
becoming familiar with a whole
new outlook on substantial material
The everlasting memories have been
recorded from serious events
Whether in a story or told in a series
of verses
The greatest tale ever ventured was
one with relative importance
To capture it in time, will make it last
forever

Cornelia Schulz

Cornelia Schulz
POEM OF FAITH
He Never Sends Winter Without the Joy of Spring
Springtime is a season of hope and
joy and cheer,
There's beauty all around to see and
touch and hear.
So no matter how downhearted and
discouraged we may be,
New hope is born when we behold
leaves budding on a tree,
Or when we see a timid flower push
through the frozen sod
And open wide in glad surprise its
petaled eyes to God.
For this is just God saying, "Lift up
your eyes to Me
And the bleakness of your spirit, like
the budding springtime tree,
Will lose its wintry darkness and
your heavy heart will sing."
For God never sends the winter
without the joy of spring.

Scott Magee
HOME
I reach skyward to the clouds
And the winds lift me up
To a place where the mystery of
dreams
Slowly unravel
And all my feelings become as
awesome
As the distance between stars
As real as the songs that caress my
spirit
With the rhythm of the tides
Truth whispers that I have come to
this place
Where the grass grows like green
velvet
And the sun is a friend of mine
Forever loved

Helen C Osborne
LADY LOVE

A Family Love Story in memory of Aunt Katie and Uncle Harry Corchran.

Lady Catherine smile at me,
You who tried so hard not to be the
Lady that you are,
In the turn of your head, the
gracious smile,
The joy you express, your freedom
from guile,
Portrays on life's canvas
A true Lady with style.
So please turn aside and look
on me,
My love is a banner that
all can see,
And flies for my passion,
Into Eternity

Helen C Osborne
BROTHER, SOLDIER, HUSBAND, FATHER
His children often asked him,
"What did you do in the war, Dad?
Come on give us a Clue,"
When answering them his words
were few,
"I did what I had to do."
Now See, We Loved Thee,
Ashes spread on the water, Roses
were
cast there too,
These rites my Brothers' family
thought it best to do,
To say good-bye to their loved one
In a manner sincere and true.
We who stood watching on the dock
were
sincerely and deeply moved,
Daughter and Son read a poem, His
Sister
started a prayer,
We all joined in and tossed our roses
on the air,
They settled lightly on the water and
were gently floating there,
As the boat slipping into her
moorings
Returning the grieving few,
Who by actions kind and adoring,
'Did what they had to do'

Carrie Ann Oie
A CHANGE OF SEASONS

To my greatest inspiration, my mother, Ellen.

A trickling brook flows softly
Weaving down an ice-trodden shore
Always peaceful, never more.
Barely a whisper is heard among the trees
Gentle feeling of tranquility in the breeze.
Timid creatures nestle in their homes of ash
Safe inside Mother Nature's sash
Living under winter's warm blanket of snow.
Then arrives the thaw of spring
A new season nature would bring
Awakened now life throughout the forest
Bringing richness to the poorest
Arising the curiosity of men
Until winter dominates once again.

Betty Absher McGuire
BY FAITH
Lord, I come to you by faith,
I know that Thou art real.
Take away this pain and hurt
That I so deeply feel—
Let me feel thy presence, Lord
Take all my fear away,
Let joy and peace in me abide.
In my life, always stay.

As I was praying this prayer;
Came sweeping o'er my soul
A feeling sweet and gentle
This world cannot behold.
It made me feel so happy
And everyone must know
How Jesus touched my soul that day:
His love within me flows.

Arnold D Osthus
LIFE GOES UP

To Kay Van Patten, Seattle.

The mountain of life
That is so high
Makes me want to laugh at strife
But it is a wonder I don't cry
The knowledge and wisdom all come into bloom
For with life your feelings are doomed
No wonder every joy
Some people play with like a toy
The laugh you get at some mishap
Would ring in your ears like a slap
You must have strength
Not to rave and rent
For those who burn your gold
Life is short and bent when old
Go to the chore
You know not more
Get on with life
Don't be a bore!

Linda Lucy Lucille
LET IT BE ME

I dedicate this poem to anyone who has ever truly loved someone.

There will only be a few things in life, that will take your breath away.
I want to be one of them, let me be your night, let me be your day.
The eyes can see beauty, but I can show you what beauty is made of.
A true and honest emotion, a beautiful thing called love.
If you could only feel, how I see you through my eyes,
if you could only see, how I feel you through my heart.
Then you would know, that I don't have to touch you, to feel what I feel inside.
And I don't have to see you, because your love has blinded my eyes to all others that come into sight.

Tammy Osburn
OH, SAILOR BOY

To Aaron, wherever you are.

Oh, Sailor Boy so true, so fine,
Sky-blue eyes that always shine,

A smile that will not let me sleep,
My thoughts of you are ocean-deep.

Oh, Sailor Boy, it's true I've found,
My heart's forever to you bound.

Oh, Sailor Boy keep it near,
This love I hold for you so dear.

Take it with you out to sea,
And send a little back to me.

My Sailor Boy so true, so fine,
I am yours and you are mine.

Tammy Osburn
I LOVE YOU ALL THE TIME
When your day is sunny,
And all is bright,
I will take part
In your delight.
A friend loveth at all times.

But if you stumble
And start to fall,
Pick up the phone
And give me a call.
For a friend loveth at all times.

When your tears are falling
Way too fast,
My shoulder will catch
Each one 'til the last.
Because a friend loveth at all times.

If haunting memories
Bring hurt and pain,
I'll show you there's sunshine
After the rain.
I'm your friend that loves you at all times.

Kimberly Owens
TO A FRIEND
I'm glad you're happy;
All I'd ever want for you is to be happy.
Since we've grown up, we've gone worlds apart.
Things change too fast—
Sometimes it hurts not be there with you,
Sharing everything friends share.
Even though you're far away,
it means so much to me just to know you are my friend.

Rick Oliver
SUNRISE

To my sister, Terry, whose love of God radiates like the sunrise.

I stopped and listened to the sunrise for the first time today.
It was like a wondrous melody no orchestra
could ever play.

I was surrounded by such incredible sounds and colors
It was a truly magnificent display.
A creation such as this, could only come from God
there was just no other way.

I was filled with such joy and love
I just had to kneel and pray.
I wanted to express my love
In a very elaborate way.

I looked toward heaven
as I knelt to pray
I found that, "Thank you, Lord"
was all I needed to say.

Rick Oliver
A SOLDIER'S DAWN
Awake with the dawn young soldier
And greet the rising sun
Another day of madness has just begun
The congressmen and businessmen demand
That more killing and destruction must be done.

Awake with the dawn young soldier
And continue your fearful plight
Gone now is the terror of the long lonely night
But always present is the constant fear of
The sniper's deadly sight.

Awake with the dawn young soldier
And remember fate's often cruel twist
So you won't be deceived by calm of the early morning mist.
For death will show no mercy when he
Wields his sinister fist.

Awake with the dawn young soldier
And try to understand the harsh cruel things they say
As they exercise their freedom to protest this uncertain war so far away.
You can only hope and pray that they, too, will understand someday
The terrible price of this freedom we as soldiers have had to pay.

Deanna (DEE) Oglebay
A WONDERFUL GIFT

I dedicate this poem to my son Thomas, my husband Ray, my parents Dean and Mary, my brother Mike and his family to my grandparents, Clarence and Leona, and to all of my friends.

When i die, They'll bury me with Roses,
Red, Yellow and Pink.

The wind shall blow with sprinkles of Rain and i
shall be without no pain.

When i awake a brand new Me I'LL open my eyes,
and i will see
A
WONDERFUL
GIFT
That GOD GAVE THEE.

Michele Lynne Orme
UNQUESTIONABLY UNANSWERABLE

Life is a huge mystery novel with trillions of unnecessary details that I read every second of every day. I search for a peek of light over the horizon to hint the end is near and the last page is approaching with the answers at last to be read and put to sleep.

Until then, I read with the curiosity of an explorer and the insight of a philosopher, with the patience of a time bomb.

Details upon details, days upon days, I become drunk with contentment. If it could be possible to be any more content, I would spontaneously burst into a billion pieces and blend with all the air.

We lie here drifting, this mystery novel and I, to a time in my life that can explain to me what I'm going through right now.

I burn the page after it is read to leave no evidence of its occurrence. I regret when the blank page pulls my empty stare, and I yearn for the words of the past, but they don't exist. The page is but a mere ball of fire in the palm of my sweaty hand.

I turn back to the blank page between my thoughts and realize it is reserved for the peace and quiet of speechlessness and the realizations that words could never express.

I see the words on the horizon:
a brilliant peek of light. The answers
at last are to be read and put to sleep.

Cynthia A Ozment
FRIENDSHIP
There are times that are great,
with only happiness to gain;
Friendship surrounds you,
like the warm summer rain.

There are times that are bad,
No words can reveal;
so you embrace in a hug,
and know that it's real.

It's so easy to forget;
when your days pass so fast.
Of the simple things in life
that will always last.

Ann Gilmartin Owens
WEDNESDAY'S CHILD

Dedicated to "God," Who created us equal . . . regardless of the day, month or year we were born. Bless You!

Wednesday's child is full of woe
Doesn't really have to be so,
For Wednesday's child like any other
Can enjoy life just like their brother
For all of us have the power within
That sparks our determination to win
Though life is short we are given each day
To live fully in our own special way
So, if Wednesday's child is full of woe
It's because they chose to make it so!

Anthony Oliveras
RESURRECTED EMOTION
A deep sensation slowly sank its life
Into the inner depth of my being
grieving my soul.

I, aching with ill-humor, swooning
with despair, wallowing in self-pity,
soon died, in essence.

Then, at last, the cloak of darkness
veiling my hope with dismal thought
was torn by the sharpness of love.

At last, the emotion that once buried
me with sorrow resurrected me with
loving kindness.

Remarkable, is it not? to know that
His love conquers all and raises up
those who are lowly.

God's love endures through all
tribulations and his presence calms
the stormy sea of surging sorrow.

Sarah Kirk Oden
THE FRAGRANCES OF SPRING
The fragrances of Spring tantalize my nostrils.
Lilacs, roses, and freshly cut grass . .
All remind me
You are no longer here . . .
To share the rebirth of Nature.

Carol H Perta
AS I LOOK BACK

Dedicated to all my children, friends and lovers.

No life
Is complete without love.
It seeks us out
When we least expect it.
It may begin
As some kind gesture or smile.
Don't ever, ever turn away.
It is the sustenance of life.

If we are fortunate
When we are old,
We will have loved
In many different ways,
At many different times.
It is the memory of those loves
That soothes our aging heart.
True love brings sorrow and pain, tears and joy
Intermingled.

Kimberly Pierce
IN A LAND UNDER A RAINBOW

To: My best friend Darnell, who stood by my side no matter how many problems I came to her with. I'll never forget you.

Under A rainbow In A land far away,
Where children sing and animals play,
They haven't heard of problems,
Like drinking or taking drugs,
'Cause the spirit with his mighty power,
Protects his little ones.
In this land under a rainbow,
You can dream of many things like cats and dogs with wings.
And at night when you're half asleep,
A friendly spirit comes to take a peek.
He looks up on everyone, to make sure they're all O.K.
And if someone isn't feeling well,
He'll make them better by the light of the forthcoming day.
Yet this spirit is only a little boy,
A young one like you and I,
You know his mighty power,
It seems like magical things he does,
Yet the key answer you're looking for,
Is to the question he does them yes but why?

Toni M Price
TO BE WHOLE

To my beloved parents, Bob and Doris Price, who've always been there for me, and each other. (Cheers).

Being a half is a meaningless purpose.
A strange existence, a ticket to nowhere.
I'm the queen of lonely, my jokers are sad.
But when I stood by his side, I felt it.
That kind of bond that could always hold us together.
And if this bond is true, we must be careful,
And let no one enter our world.
Because apart, we are only a half.
Like a broken whole. And thru the opening
vile things can get in, like strangers and deceit.
And the results can be a poisoned tenant.
To be whole you need two halves,
Two people bonded tight.
Let nothing in, and let nothing escape
And inside each tiny little world
you can find two very lucky people.
I hope they can hear me in there,
for I am a half, a broken whole.
And I keep the poison out with dreams . . .
. . . and with laughter.

Delos Munger
TO A STAR

To my grandson, Stacey Joel Munger.

When but a babe
With childish awe
I first beheld
Your twinkling light
You were no more
A mystery then
Than you still are
Tonight

Frances Speegle Martin
NIGHT DREAMS
Through the shadows of the night
Creeps the peeping pale moonlight,
Stealing through the lonely trees -
Figures dancing among the leaves.

I, myself, wish I were there
Breathing in the pungent air;
Not far away the ocean swells
With all the tales it tells and tells -

Tide after tide, in and out,
Wave after wave rolling about -
But God, how beautiful death could be!
All worries, all heartaches, washed out to sea!

Kay Poliska
grandfather

For Paul Edwin Blew, October 27, 1902—August 15, 1979.

your strong and robust arms
lifted me as i stretched
to reach the ripest, juiciest peach
hanging at the top of the tree
your magnificent lap held two
squirming, giggling granddaughters
there was a special space
in your loving heart
for all you knew
you gave freely the fruits
that your labored land
gracefully produced
your sharp wit made us laugh
your wisdom
made us understand
your sweat and blood
has earned your eternal rest
so live, Pappy,
in those strong and robust arms
that hold and comfort you now

Sherrell K Martin
SILENCE
I flit, I float on velvet wings of darkness to a room of oh so quiet.
Where I can go and be so alone with my hurt and wounded soul.
In my velvet room of quiet where the only sound is me, I sit so still and all alone and fill my soul renew.
The strength begins to fill me up and overflow my room.
Then it's time to leave and go back to the chaos of the world that tries my soul.
But always there for my retreat are velvet wings of darkness.

Sherrell K Martin
DEATH
Death is such a silent thing it leaves an empty void.
Gone are the talks and quiet strength that I so depended on.
You've left an empty spot of aching pain.
I hope you can hear the love we never spoke.
And let it warm your soul that seems so all alone.

Dicster
MONEY FOR MY LYRICS
Money for my lyrics
Is this not a sin?
A bounty for my teardrops,
A price tag on my grin . . .

To prostitute my feelings
For dollars or for gold
Seems unkind, to my own mind
In a world that's pretty cold

With prejudice, wars and hatred
And those having nothing to eat,
How can the drain from one man's brain
Begin to even compete??

And so I submit my words of rhyme
To put a smile on your face,
Or provoke a thought that perhaps one day,
Can make this world a better place!

Rosalind Meshekow
DELUGE
Eruptive
Cascading
Flood of tears,

Abundant
Reservoir
At the ready.

Deep wells of
Sad memories
Open flood gates.

Word pricks of
"Mother" "Love"
Trigger flow,

Washing away
Irritants
For the moment.

Ivonne M Martin
CONFESSION
My love for you
is like a well-known scar.
The wound is closed,
and yet,
on rainy days I feel
within my grief
the tingle of desire.

My love for you
is like a buried dream.
The night is gone,
and yet,
towards the dawn I hear
within its grave
the melody of life.

Margery Claire Meyer
WHAT IS CHRISTMAS?
What is Christmas? Is Christmas toys,
Santa and gifts for good girls and boys,
Holly and ivy and Christmas cards, too,
Candy and goodies and fun things to do?
Christmas - the birthday of Jesus our King,
With angel choirs our praises we sing,
He left the glory of heaven so bright
Born as our Saviour that first Christmas night.
He came to earth to perfectly live,
Suffer and die, yes, His life blood to give,
And all for us that we never need fear
Death or God's wrath in our pilgrimage here.
He brought to us love unbounded, unknown
That with the Lord we might ever be one.
Now He is risen triumphant above,
Yet close beside us with blessings and love.

George A Miller III
CLASS OF '95
Educated first through twelfth, learn ways to fame, fortune and wealth. Study very hard to become real smart, Express school spirit straight from our hearts. Showing the teachers and faculty, progressing our world is what we believe. The new generation has arrived. We are the class of 1995. It's time to lift off we spread our wings in stride. Taking in all our abilities and pride. It's one more step to maturity,
In this land of freedom and opportunity. The new generation has arrived. We're the class of 1995. The time has come, we look forward to this day, now we can say. We made it through every single grade. We are now graduating with a cloud nine high. Coming alive, We are the Class of '95!

George A Miller III
WHEN SHE IS GONE
Miss the music that she plays,
and the songs that make our day.
Miss the mornings she wakes me,
and asks if we can play.
And even the times we fuss, we fight.
Times we make up and make things right.
But most of all I miss her heart
I hold so gently next to mine.
My heart cries out through the distance.
Can you hear it call?
Like a bluebird in the window,
When snow begins to fall.
And like the bluebird, I will survive.
As each lonesome day passes by.
Knowing the sun will shine again.
And soon my love will come home again
It's tough on men when our ladies are away.
But it's reassuring to know that the love will forever stay.

Kenneth F Miller II
AT SUNSET

Dedicated to Kenneth F. Miller, Sr., my dad, Dorthy L. Miller, my mother, and Patricia, my wife.

Today's problems have fell.
Folded innocuous
They have become nothing.
It is evening.
All is so serenely still.
A posterboard print
handpainted to such platonic
perfection
of lavish lavenders
and resplendent reds
and plural pinks
All hanging picturesquely
reminding me at this day's end
of the beautifying breath
That has kept me alive!

Burma Cusenbary
FORGET NOT

Forget not when earth was young
And dreams of gold by gods were
spun
Where the stars in Milky Way meet
And the nakedness of heaven is free
Forget not the colors of the rainbow
Given with a touch of silver and gold
Forget not the young and old
Forget not the scornful ways
Forget not the truths of the wise
Less we awaken the power up there
And his wrath all heaven lay bare
Forget not the silence we knew
Of outward hurts and inside pain
Forget not I'd do it all again
As in darkness lost your love I
Might forever find and feel its
Loving shine

Helen M Mikel
FAINT NOW GLORY

To Pvt. David J. Thompson, Co.A 18th Regt. Ala. Inf. CSA, Blue & Gray - friends in eternity.

Eerie the twilight shadowing the
land;
Hear the faint sound of the drum?
The fading cadence of tramping?
The voices honed now to a hum?

Where is the song that rang out so
pure?
The laughter that winged with the
fife?
Where are the brave men who battled
the foe?
Commingled now in the valley of
strife.

How did it happen, this war of the
brothers?
Good men all, who championed a
cause.
The North and the South, the Blue
and the Gray
Tossed in the winds like fluttering
straws.

Dim now the mist that enshrouds
them.
No sound startles the deeping black.
Vanished forever, the soldier's sharp
cry
Entombed in silence, the gunnery's
flack.

Onward now wraiths with quickening
speed!
Home fires beckon with shimmering
light.
Loved ones await the return of the
lost.
Never more comrades, never we'll
fight!

Natasha "Our little Wood Sprite"

George M Glessner
WOOD SPRITE

Like the wood sprite,
she runs across the floor.
With eyes sparkling with delight,
she founded an open door.

Touching and exploring,
her little fingers laboring for a clue.
Life at such an age is never boring,
she will not know a day that is blue.

She is my niece,
with an adventurer's song to sing.
Now I must retrieve her,
she is into my things.

Happily I take her,
sadly she resists.
I'm her uncle,
and she is my most wondrous of
gifts.

As I sit her down,
among the toys.
I'm sure she is pondering ways,
to torment future boys.

Not a sound did she utter,
not a whimper for her mother.
As I count my blessings true,
I didn't notice that she had left the
room.

Like the wood sprite,
she runs across the floor,
With eyes sparkling with delight,
She founded an open door.

Luís Ronaldo
EAGLE GEOMETRICS

The eagle is a series of powerful
tapers,
Interconnected, overlapping,
inseparable.
Its beak is a sharp hook,
A cone that expands to fill its
swept-back head,
Just below its sharp, slit eyes.

Its neck, a barrel,
Rising from its swelling breast,
Tapering off to its head.
The feathers of its back and wings,
A myriad of dagger points,
Swept back by the scouring winds.

Its legs, two strong trunks,
Tapering off to its tail
Into curvéd, wicked claws.
Its tail, a splayed fan,
Each feather a two-edged sword to
cut the
Fools who wish to grab a hold.

The eagle is a series of powerful
tapers,
Tonight, on my computer screen.

Luís Ronaldo
UNTITLED SONNET

How now, this poor and desp'rate
lovesick fool,
Biting his fingernails down to the
skin
As he waits for a lass long after
school,
And sighs about the mess he's gotten
in.
Distracted from his work and from
his play,
He moons o'er other girls with silent
cries
And roams about the streets, so
lackaday,
'Till Dawn's rosy fingers jab in his
eyes.
He'll take an image from his
fantasies
And paint a million shades of his
desire,
And though the truth is never what he
sees,
He'll daydream on, and never will
retire—
For this fool can't hope to win
when he's bet
"The barren tender of a poet's
debt."*

*From Shakespeare's Sonnet No. 83

Luís Ronaldo
THE CORNFIELD

Dedicated to the fallen at the Battle of Antietam Creek, September 17, 1862.

From undulating stalks of gold and
green
To withered wisps of grey and black.

From the rustle of rough ripe leaves
To the silence and stillness of a
burnt-out world.

From the rich odor of fertile earth
To the putrid stench of blackened
corpses.

From refreshing showers of rain
To repulsive showers of blood.

From an abundant harvest of corn
To a grim reaping of casualties.

From dawn to dusk.

Did they ever feel the burden on their
shoulders?
Did they ever care to carry it?

A few more hours,
And the empires of the Old World
would intervene;

A few more men,
And the chains of a victimized
people would be shattered;

A few more yards,
And the spirit of the Union would be
crushed;

A few more guns,
And a great national agony would be
halted . . .

The child of fifteen or the veteran of
fifty never believed it.

They (have) had their price to pay.

Let the good earth engulf these
bullet-torn soldiers.
Let the soft rains wash the blood
away.

Luís Ronaldo
UNTITLED

Every morning I am reminded
When I slip past the cold wet plastic
That I am a victim of the very faucets
Outlets to reservoirs of pleasure and
pain

The murmured babble of the drain
reminds me
Of where I first heard her lively voice
Over the babble of the evening
throng
Among friends I will never see again

The broken shimmer of the water
reminds me
Of the broken reflections of last
summer's sun
Where I chanced to meet her alone
On the shore of a lake I will never
visit again

The paddle of bitter lukewarm drops
reminds me
Of many a stroll down city streets
Both of us huddling under a
newspaper
Tasting the rains I will never taste
again

The sweet perfume of the soap
reminds me
Of the lilacs that lined the garden
wall
Where she greeted me with a young
red rose
Whose fragrance I will never smell
again

The soothing caress of her towel
reminds me
Of her warm and tender kisses
And the soft and soothing caresses
From arms that will never hold me
again

The distant alarm clock reminds me
That time has passed, that time
moves on
But morning will return to remind
and torture me
Again and again and again . . .

Michelle Jeanette Mead
MOTHER

To all the loving good times . . .

Looking through little girl eyes
remembering the yesteryears,
I see your soft and glowing skin and
the gentleness of your tears.

Your loving eyes, they sparkled like a
treasure chest of gems, as you
held me O so dearly, never wanting it
to end.

You nourished me with all your love,
guiding me all the way; holding
my hand when I was scared as you
soothed my fears away.

Even as a mother, you have always
been a friend. We have grown and
shared together, a special bond which
will never end.

Looking through little girl eyes as I
look through adult eyes too,
nothing could ever measure, Mother,
the love I have for you!

Karen Lynn Moye
SNOW HILL, NORTH CAROLINA - WHERE MY CHILDHOOD COMES ALIVE

To J.C. and Ethel Brooks Moye - Grandparents of Karen Lynn Moye.

Taking Highway 264 always makes
me feel good.
As I am riding in the car on those
little country roads,
towards Snow Hill,
I turn the hands of time back again
to my childhood days.
Driving up in my grandmama's
backyard,
where the swings, basketball court
and openness
of her yard called to me.
Hearing the porch door slam, I see
my grandmama
coming out, wearing her flower
apron, her arms extended
to greet me with a hug and that
friendly, sweet smile of
hers. Grandmama's house was a
two-story old white
house
on the corner on Main Street.
Weather beaten and in need of paint,
it had love, laughter and warmth that
make,
a house a home.
You could feel the love throughout
the house,
especially in the kitchen, where I
spent hours playing with
pots and pans. Laughter, warmth.
happiness, tears and
sorrow went along
with the good and bad times that
were shared by family
and friends.
These memories will never fade
completely because . . . They
are deep within in the corners of my
soul, Grown up now,
with financial difficulties,
responsibilities, to oneself and
others. tough questions and no easy
answers, Those
memories, comfort me.
That is when I reflect on my
childhood, pull out, those
memories which come alive again,
and wish I could live in
that reverie forever.

Stephen J McCarthy
DREAMBOAT WEDDING
Searching for you in my dreams
as we Traveled across Europe
Softly falling Raindrops Splash upon
your face
By the Water a Dreamboat Wedding
To share my love on Riveranda
Warmth of Our love
as you Fulfilled my life
Softly falling raindrops by the Sea
as we touched to Share my Love.

I wrote this as a wedding present for
Christie Brinkley
in her honor, always; Admire her
Just think I used to like Brooke
Shields?

Stephen J McCarthy
YESTERDAY'S LOVE
Dreaming of Yesterday's Love
Makes me want to touch you
Crying on my pillow at night
Remember Lake Ontario Waves
Softly Splashing
upon the reefs beneath the Sea.
Softly falling Raindrops Splash upon
your Face
By the Water. Remember the
Passage to Paradise Cove
Your Soft Body next to mine
Feeling you again Closer to my heart
Love Soft Raindrops
Falling on your face
Dreaming of Yesterday's Love as
you fulfilled all of my
Dreams Loves warm feeling as we
Touched as you fulfilled
all of my dreams Softly Crying on
my pillow at night
Dreaming again Closer to my heart
Loves soft raindrops falling
on your face Dreaming of
Yesterday's Love as you fulfilled
all of my dreams Dreaming of
Yesterday's love makes me want
to Touch you.

Stephen J McCarthy
TWINKLING TENDERNESS OF LOVE
As you came to life before my eyes
So soft so tender so helpless
In her eyes looked so full of love
Those first few moments of your life
she saw a Twinkle in your eyes
It's so Touching to Behold as you
took your First step
So Much love in her eyes
Devotion of Love for you
Twinkling Tenderness of Love

I Think this is what the Virgin Mary
felt
like when she was carrying the Christ
Child.

Stephen J McCarthy
IN MEMORY OF A PRINCESS GRACE KELLY
In Memory of a Princess
her Softness of Step
is Precious to mind
A Soft Spoken Lady with a Grace
of her Light Steps
Princess is so Precious to mind
Beauty of an Angel's Love
In Memory of our Beloved Princess.

Stephen J McCarthy
SERENADE YOU UNTIL TWILIGHT
Star Light Star bright Excitement in
your eyes
Flash when she looks at you Her
Emotions are
Brilliant Blissful Enchantment of her
Elegance -
Remember Newfoundland off the
Vancouver Coast
Nightfall of a warm sea breeze.
Softly kissing you
long ago. Excitement in her eyes
when she looks
at you Enchantment of her elegance
is her delicate
Emotions as Nightfall of a warm sea
Breeze Softly
Kissing you under the Moonlight
Emotions of her Delicate Elegance
Serenade you
until Twilight, Princess DeStephanie

Laura L Pontinen
THE FOREST
The trees in the forest stand
majestically,
Their branches swaying
gracefully in the wind,
Like brooms sweeping clean the
pale blue sky.
Smokey light filters through
the leaves,
Causing patterns in the
fresh morning air.
The sound of twigs snapping
as I walk along.
Birds singing to each
other.
The smell of wet wood
laced with dew.
All is at peace.

Theodora Pankratz
A NEW BREEZE IS BLOWING

Dedicated to President and Mrs. Bush with Thanksgiving, and hope that the "new breeze" be gentle and kind! God bless!

Here is my hand -
Offered in faith and good will
Forgive the strategy of conflict;
Let the future no longer
Be plundered by memory
Of ill-will or campaign subtlety.

Speak clearly, straight forward,
Listening carefully, "Read my lips"-
Phrasing Hope and Strength and
Vigilance
Staying strong to keep the Peace.
Today beginning a new chapter
In Unity - Diversity - Generosity.

Building for tomorrow, new
dimensions,
Grounded in kindness -
A new nation with message
More gentle and kind
Borne by the wind in all directions.
Let the answer come back, the Winds
of Freedom.

A new breeze blowing in vibrant
resonance
Gently touching the human heart
strings
Attuned to a peaceful symphony of
global dimension
Illumined through time and space
By thousands upon thousands of
points of Light
Seeking and finding - our destiny.

Dawn Parker
KEY TO MY HEART
You hold the key to my heart and
with it I will not part.

The love between us grows stronger
every day.
I can say I love you in oh so many
ways.

Because you hold the key to my
heart.

A bond grows between us so strong,
Without your love I couldn't go on.

Because you hold the key to my
heart.

I will keep your love always near,
in hope I will never fear that the key
to my heart will disappear.

Because you hold the key to my
heart.

Lisa A Peavler
JUST BECAUSE

To Randi, you're the light of my life and the sparkle of my day. I love you! Moma.

Just Because . . .
Just because I love you, I carried
you for nine months in expectation;
I enjoy being with you, and I wake
up with anticipation.

Just because you're the light of
my life and the sparkle of my day;
I'm here to teach you, to guide
you and help you find your way.

Just because I expect a lot out of
you, no matter what, I'll be proud;
Even though we'll have our
differences,
I'll try not to talk too loud.

Just because we have a special bond,
you can reach out and take my hand;
You can come to me and talk to me
about things you think I won't
understand.

Just because I'm your mom,
doesn't mean I can't be your friend;
I'll stand beside you through
thick and thin, I'll be there till the
end.

Pat Patterson
MY PRAYER FOR YOU

This poem is dedicated to GOD for His "gift" of Elvis to us.

Let me be a link to your happiness
and smiles and turn your tears to joy,
your sadness to gladness, your pain
to love for I will love you more today
than yesterday but less than
tomorrow;

Let me fill your lonely hours with
caring and let me be a light in your
darkness;

Depend on me for each new day to
begin, give me your troubles and
worries and release them to me for I
am with you;

Allow me to be your freedom to be
the person you are and want to be and
let me be your ears to hear and listen
to you;

Know that we are here for each other,
in friendship first, along the unknown
path of hopes and dreams, to fill the
need in each other to be needed;

Take my hand and trust in me to be
the beautiful person I have come to
know and love;

Allow the Power of Faith and belief
to strengthen you from day to day
and . . . Believe in tomorrow for it
will not fail you unless you choose to
throw it away, for you are "Always
on My Mind" and forever in my
heart;

I have so much love to give, let me
share it with you and put love and
happiness in your life to replace the
tears and sorrow;

"THANK-YOU" for being the
"VERY SPECIAL PERSON AND
FRIEND" that you are to me and let
this be "MY PRAYER OF LOVE TO
YOU"; "THANK YOU" FOR
BEING YOU,
LOVING YOU ALWAYS,
A FRIEND

Dr Mark J Pisarczyk
JUST A MEMORY
I sat by a stream
and began to dream,
as the softness of
the morning's dew,
brought to mind thoughts
of you.

Drops of rain then fell from
blue sky, as did your
tears when came time
to say goodbye.

Though distance now keeps us
always apart, a love for
you still burns deep
in my heart.

I walked alone along a path
carrying inside a storm
of great wrath. A strength
inside, built upon pride,
now weakened knowing
you walk by another's side.

In my being there is no shame,
For no one of two could
Take the blame, as it
was two who shared the
flame.

In my mind rages a battle
Fought throughout the night;
A battle in which I fight
For that which I know right.

On the day I hold you again
I'll know the battle be done,
For upon that day
the broken pieces of my heart
will once again come together,
together as one.

Dr Mark J Pisarczyk
LONELINESS
Darkened sky with stars so high
Tell my why I sit and cry.
This empty space, beside my place
Leaves scars of pain upon my face.

Tides roll in and tides roll out,
The shadows of gulls fly all about.
Wailing winds blow cold and mean,
Against old masts I hear them
scream.

The pounding surf on shifting sand
Leaves me wonder where I stand.
To venture too near brings sudden
death
I've lost all fear, now life I bequeath.

Rush forth cold water, numb my
pain,
Tell me not this is all in vain.
Cast aside you darkness, a tunnel of
light,
Tomorrow's a better day where it's
Sunny and bright.

Dr Mark J Pisarczyk
THE INSIGNIFICANCE OF ME
I walked a dusty road
as a dog ran by my side.
I realized the insignificance of me.

I watched a mighty oak
budding beneath the rays
of the sun.
I realized the insignificance of me.

I watched a young fledgling
take to the sky, flying
beyond protection of his
mother's eye.
I realized the insignificance of me.

I watched the sun set
behind rolling hills,
releasing the colors of
the day.
I realized the insignificance of me.

I watched the stars peak
through the darkness
of night.
I realized the insignificance of me.

I saw a sad face
and made it smile
with the touch of my hand.
I realized the significance of me.

Richard Pecha
SOUL MATE

This poem is dedicated to, and inspired by my good friend Sylvette.

A mutual bond
between two individuals,
developed during the
formidable years.
That oneness
which carries through
good and bad,
through fear
and uncertainty.
A common point
at which two people
gravitate and grow.
Each developing
in different directions
but having a common home.

Dwight Ralph Paris
THE DIAMOND

To Mom, from whom I learned the real meaning of Love.

Plucked from the Earth within,
A rough uncut stone.
A jeweler removes the outer skin,
So it's radiance and beauty can be
shown.
You have a "diamond" in your being.
Conceived and treasured with
perfection.
To protect this precious gem so it
can't be seen,
You hide it behind your fear, with
deception.
With the skill of a jeweler enjoying
his trade,
I see your diamond, so cleverly
protected.
So cautiously I begin, utilizing
divine aid,
Revealing a gem, until this moment,
undetected.
Plucked from the "You" within,
Priceless radiance and beauty so
fine.
Forever shining, born again,
Protected by your Love and mine.

Julia M Ortega
SPRINGTIME
Spring will come and go
like the ocean's ebb and flow
When we realize it is here
summer will be very near

Birds will sing their song
and the grass will soon grow long
Flowers will swarm with bees
and butterflies fly with ease

The fish in the ocean
will feel the new motion
They'll wiggle their tails
and boats will set sail

Anemones will open wide
and in their shells,
crabs will not hide

In the spring, storms will not roar
nor rock the living ocean floor.
So let's enjoy it while it's here
or we'll have to wait until next year.

Evelyn L Opalinski-Durkin
REMEMBERING
There are so many things to
remember
It really crowds the brain.
Joys of early childhood
A scary summer rain.
A winter of huge snowdrifts
A bouncy tractor ride.
A really scrumptious treehouse.
A look-out or place to hide.
The carefree days of childhood -
One can't go back again.
The time we used to long for
Is here - and now we are men
But, inside, as we all know
We are just 'grown-up boys' -
Working, playing, thinking back
To our childhood joys.
Future?
Bodies grow older, memories do not
Relax in your chair, enjoy what
you've got.
Work or play , have some fun
But don't overdo -
Your ease was hard won.

Pamela D Osborne
MOTHER

To my mother, Peggy Jacqueline Cook, whom I will always love and cherish. From your one and only daughter, Pam.

This is to the Mother I once knew
A long time ago, you would say it
was you.
I still remember those few special
times
When we were as one
A mother and daughter when we
were both very young.
You were so busy trying to figure
out
Just what Life and Love were really
all about
That you kind of got lost in the
heat of it all
And forgot who was the most
important of all.
Now that I'm older and have
experienced Life at hand
I can now say "I really do
understand."
You see, I now have a daughter,
two as you know
And the Love I have for them will
continue to grow.
Their lives have enriched me and
helped me to understand
That being a parent is utterly difficult
at hand.
But to me it's all worth the love
that they bring
To hear the words "I Love You,
Mom" just makes my heart sing.
Please learn to accept that "I Love
You" too
And I hope that someday I may hear
these words from you.

Vanessa Osborne
LIFE'S A TALE TOLD TOO FAST
Life's a tale told too fast
for anyone to hear
Love's a song, sung by many
but true love is sung so sweetly.
A child's eyes are like a rainbow,
filled with dreams and fairy tales.
My eyes are hollow - seen too many
broken dreams, forgotten tales.
My life's a ballad.
No one's listening . . .
. . . Life is short and death's eternal,
but do not shed a tear.
You shed your tears and while you
cry,
Your life may pass you by.

Judy Owen
"DEAR BROTHER"
My heart aches so for you,
"Dear Brother,"
I long to see your smiling face,
your deep blue eyes, and your
masculine grace.
But now you've gone to be with
Jesus,
In that heavenly home to dwell,
Where no one or nothing can hurt
you again,
and you'll always have flowers to
smell.
I'm anxiously awaiting Dear Brother,
For Jesus to call out to me,
And take "me" up to heaven,
To live in Eternity.

Abel C Olivencia
TERRA FIRMA
Woodland lane, Woodland lane
before a lantern's burning flame.
Trimmed became strong limbs that
made
arches along the way.
And echoed in this abbey's hall
sounds of leaves that swayed
and rustled sleep filled ground
awake,
as songs an angel played.

'Till gently came an evening air
to leave me as a child bare,
abandoned by the guide.
Which stirred within the heart a fear
through which might have remained
unseen
the workmanship of God.

But that my hand had held a rock
and knew no change did to it mark
and heard the songs of leaves
untouched,
I drew a breath in ease.
Then allowed the rock its place
and went unhindered by the light
along the woodland lane.

Kelley Anne Otto
THE BIRTH OF A HOUSE
The structure is formed
by constructing a foundation,
then laying brick upon brick.
Each building planned carefully
by builders and designings,
in order to form a unique structure.

Uniqueness comes from care and
patience
in which the house forms and takes
shape.
Each house has its own personality
which grows and matures with the
construction.
It starts in youth and grows through
middle age to maturity.
This happens by additions, room
changes, and landscaping.

As a house grows old
it's walls start to crumble
and it's bricks turn to dust.
All that is left is the foundation
upon which builders form another.

Lourie S Overland
I ONCE HAD A DREAM
I once had a dream
A wonderful dream

Over the years of; trials failures
& up and downs

A friend came along
A wonderful friend

Someone who showed love and kindness
and asking nothing in return

Then within that love
My dream came true

Richard J Orosz
HE'S THREE FEET ZERO INCHES

To Joshua Daniel Orosz, born September 19, 1988. You are my joy, the meaning in my life. But most of all, my son, I love you with all my heart. Forever, Daddy.

He's three feet, zero inches,
of fruit loop hugs, and bumble bee pinches.

A constant reminder of a heavenly connection
It's like looking in the mirror,
but at a smaller reflection.

How strange it is,
that the world could revolve, around one so small,
He's my pride and joy, my Christmas toy,
The love of my life, he's got it all.

He's wagon rides, crocodile tears,
Too young to know grown fears.
Playing all day with his friends,
Mickie, and Winnie, hoping the day never ends.

But it does, with a music box, and a baba too,
Sweet dreams of tomorrow, a good night kiss, and I Love You.

Good night, my son, and out goes the light,
A new world begins as we tuck you in tight.

Sweet dreams

Michelle O'Neill
INNER

Any dream is a key - don't lose it.

Sandman calls my name
Into the night,
Dimming the glow
Of the firelight.
Asking for patience
From my weary eyes,
As souls of the night
quietly lie.
Suddenly I'm weightless
Suspended in time
Prisms of color
Become all mine.

Now I can't control the
Adventure I'll take
Hoping it'll finish before I wake.
See me flying thru the air,
As mannequins of water sit
and stare.
Now I'm swimming in a pool
of glass,
Breathing the air of purple
Gas.
Running from a strange and
Terrible force,
The palms of my hands, become
Dry and coarse.
Secret passage ways beneath my
House,
Shaking hands with a talking mouse.

Injecting bolts of lightning
Into my veins,
Speaking to people without any names.
Witches guiding and showing me the way.
Seeing two different moons start a new day.

The sound of a harsh loud ring,
Makes my heart drop and I lose
My wings.
My day is filled with endless chores,
But
Only I have the key to unlock
All my doors.

Agatha Oravec
AUTUMN RHAPSODY
If you must see a wondrous sight
I beg you drive before it's night,
Along a road, tree-lined and worn,
Yet not too crowded or forlorn.

The trees in autumn's garb slide past
And eager for their hues to last,
Peer wistfully in nature's dress
Of multicolored loveliness.

When the sun is about to set
You will agree with me I bet,
The reds, yellows and sighing green
Disclose their pride at being seen.

Vibrant colors quite cosmetic
Paint an image most aesthetic.
More royally than queen or king
Comes robed this regal offering.

Agatha Oravec
COLOR ME TRUE
Red rivers, white streams, stripe America,
They rumble and frolic on cue,
'Neath a blue canopy, studded with stars;
Their sparkle enhances the view.

White rays greet the day in the morning,
Red haze strokes the horizon at night.
Blue lakes, moonlit waters, oft beckon,
Stars wink, to the voyager's delight.

True-blue is the love for my country—
The mountain, the prairie, the glen.
Red blood that was shed; field grasses it fed,
And white shines the valor of men.

Blue wafts the aura of womenfolk weeping,
Battle stars, pierce through ribbons, one by one.
Warm, red lips to welcome the hero,
White heat fuels the mettle of each son.

As soft shadows blanket the landscape,
And nighttime brings rest that is due,
The stars, at attention; all shipshape,
Guard my dreams, colored red, white and blue.

Ryan Orpel (Age 13)
WAR
War is unlike anything in the world.
The intensity in the air,
The bullets and bombs soar overhead.

The men lying dead,
Dead in wet, muddy forests,
Never knowing what will come next,
Never knowing when you'll be killed,
Never knowing if you'll make it out alive.

The look of confusion in their faces,
Not being able to hear or communicate
With one another.
The fear in the eyes of the enemy.

The sky is full of smog and smoke.
The sun doesn't seem to shine.
The ground is wet and covered by bodies.

And then the war is over,
Leaving nothing but hatred and revenge.

Nicholas G Oppeau
MOTHER

For Shirley A. Oppeau, wonderful mother of five. We love you.

Where do you go when you need a friend
Someone whose love could never end
Someone on whom you can always depend

Through thick and thin good times and bad
That certain someone you've always had
Who even loves you when they're mad

The one who told you when you were wrong
The one who taught you how to be so strong
Who knew you could do it all along

To that one person this is my way to say
Thanks for being there for all this way.

Irene Ahrens Palmer

Irene Ahrens Palmer
THE HALLELUJAH CHORUS
The Hallelujah Chorus is the most
beautiful oratorio ever written
and tradition has it the audience
always stands in honor of this
wonderful -
composer - George Frederic Handel
and he
shall reign forever and ever -
King of kings and
Lord of lords,
I know that my Redeemer Liveth
Hallelujah!
Hallelujah!

Caroline B Appell
REMEMBER ME ALWAYS

Written for and inspired by: Woody Lovill, a true friend if ever there was one.

Happy am I to have a friend like you,
One that I cherish, the one who is true;
Never again will I ever misjudge,
My friend that is cherished,
admired—and loved.

The words that you wrote
Are precious and dear;
Locked in my heart,
To keep you ever so near.

Remember me always
From now 'til the end,
I'll always love you;
My forever friend!!

M D Burke
A NAME?
The sound was not my name
Spoken clearly through the door,
Nor was it a word of any kind.
A breezy whistle waltzing
Along the clean of the kitchen—

I believe the wind formed
The syllables deep in its mouth,
Then blew it out to frighten me.
Darkness was its privacy
While air pretended innocence.

The fog turned, staring down
My house, my face, a drop
Of ground. I closed the door on
The whistle in my kitchen.
It was not calling my name.

Denise A Steger
THE DINNER TABLE
You on one side,
Me on the other;
The dinner table arranged—
ever so neatly—
between us.
And we wonder what is left—
a picture album
and some letters
that once spoke our love so strongly . . .
So blindly? No . . .
just too quietly.
We stare at each other
in puzzled discontent
as dinner remains stacked between us . . .
And slowly I rise to wash the dishes.

Abbie Britt
MY LIFE
My life is like a waterfall,
trickling slowly down.
Taken for granted or forgotten,
I still trickle down.

My life is like troubled waters,
with problems everywhere.
Still searching for a supporter
to hold me steady.

Yet still, my life will always be
with troubles and forgotten.

Nancy W Bellamy
AGING

To my mother-in-law, who at 94, is an everlasting inspiration and my best friend.

How I wish
I'd known you
When you were young.
Footloose and living;
No ailments to restrain you.
I'm sure you were
Some kind of Southern Lady.

Although, I missed those years,
I'm here now:
Observing—
your silence and eagerness.
Worrying—
about your bad days—
I realize they are often.
Helping—
trying to brighten your days
and make them seem less long.

Caring—
about you so much
Thinking of you day-in,
day-out
Wanting you to enjoy these
older years—

For you, dear Lady,
are my loved one.

Verna Van Velzer

Verna Van Velzer
ORPHANS

O, we were orphans, you and I,
Mothered by the sea and sky.
Loneliness became our bread
And fear a constant, living dread.

The woman in our home was cold,
Consumed with passions eons old.
Living still her girlish guile,
And dreaming of her long-lost style.

The man who walked the role of
"Dad"—
We only guessed what thoughts he
had.
He closed his life to those around—
I never knew what joy he found.

I always knew that some sweet day
That they would notice us at play.
And then, perhaps, a touch would
come
To let us know we were not dumb.

But empty gazes passing by
Let us know it was a lie.
Our inward thoughts remained the
fore
To fill the loneliness we bore.

Sweet earth, with richest bounty
sweet
Provided beauty at our feet.
The smallest stone became our gem
And built our loving diadem.

The wind and birds became our song
And gave us space where we belong.
The creatures large and tiny there
Each came to make us be aware.

This wondrous world, though not of
man,
Became almost the bower of Pan.
It showed the simple truths of God,
And brought great meaning where we
trod.

And now that sands have smoothed
away
The hurt that filled that yesterday,
I only wish I could have drawn
This love to some who now are gone.

Far better is this world of truth
That I constructed in my youth
Than that contrite and sinful den
Where humans worship only men.

I would my parents, now long past
Could find this peace and joy at last.
Their starving souls are orphans free
And never found God's love with me.

Sherry Kirkpatrick
MY HEART'S DESIRE

To a dear friend Marlena who dedicated this to a special man Clair.

I haven't asked for much in life
It's a simple life I know
But I don't crave the material things
That others need to grow

I'd rather have a man that's good
Mature and very true
Warm, affectionate, and kind
A man, somewhat, like you

A man that I could understand
And who would confide in me
I wouldn't hurt him for the world
For in my heart he's all I see

Anastasia Baris
THE GIFT OF SONG

To the young entertainers of the music world, whose talent and energy are frequently overlooked.

Have you ever listened to the lyrics
Of that special song you really like?
Did it make you wonder how its flow
was formed,
or how the words seem to fit just
right?
Did you become amazed
that the right note, the right click
is all that it ever takes
to do that magical trick?
Have you ever stopped to think
how coincidental a song can be?
You wonder how the writer ever
knew
as you say, "That sounds just like
me."
And just how would it be?
The days endless, the nights
unbearably long
With not one sweet melody.
Where would we be without the gift
of song?

Brandy L Allen
BOY OH BOY

To David–Paul, my brother and my friend.

What do you think of when you think
of a boy?
Running, jumping, and playing but
never sharing a toy?
When I think of a boy I think very
hard.
He'll always bully his sister, but is
always her guard.
Boys try to fit in, even if they don't.
Their sisters know what they really
are—that they are different.
But he's trying so hard that the others
won't.
Having a brother brings happiness
and joy.
But brothers and sisters, boy oh boy!

Amy Alverson
EARLY MORNING HAZE

This poem is dedicated to the most wonderful parents one could have. Thanks Mom and Dad for all of your love and support over the years!

The peacefulness of nature
In the midst of morn,
Awakes me from my death-like sleep
From which I shall be torn.

The birds, how sweet the harmony
From their lips doth flow,
Make early morning melodies
So tender to my soul.

The quietness of early morning
Calms my eager soul;
The fog, like angels down from
heaven,
Over the earth doth flow.

The clouds ride upon the wind
That whispers to the trees,
Which bend like humans to the earth
When in the midst of Kings.

The early morning dew
Falls softly like the rain
Upon the petals of the rose;
Their transparent kisses stain.

There's nothing like the dew
That blankets the grass with a glaze;
How sweet the smell like rich
perfume,
Is the early morning haze.

When I rise to greet the dawn,
I kiss the air so sweet
For giving me another day
For death its prey shall keep.

The peacefulness of morning
How precious is to me;
The closest thing to heaven,
Forever shall it be!

Jean Anderson
STATEN ISLAND

This poem is dedicated to Chris Matula, my son, who inspired me when he won the Gold and Silver Poet awards for his poem, "Warrior's Peace."

Oh! beautiful island I'll never forget
you,
Born there I trod on your rocks and
your rills,
The sun sparkled meadows came up
to my doorstep—
The marshlands alive with Dame
Nature's sweet thrills.
Behind them Saint Andrew's, the
kirk where I married,
Its stones hewn so roughly, exquisite
in place,
Sits nestled below La Tourette's
slopes of greenery
Their contours of beauty each
morning do grace.
Now far from your mists I remember
my wanderings
Through lilac halls stepped through a
gnarled bush so vast,
Its blooms topped the chimney their
perfume so sweet
Mid warm lacy patterns screened
sunlight did cast.
My house had wisteria wound on its
portals,
Forsythia bordered the drive round
and round,
Their lavender droplets and
shimmering gold florets gave
Joy to our senses not frequently
found.
Oh! my Little Green Spot, as once
you were known
When ladies wore bustles and men
were so bold,
And the Hudson flowed by crystal
clear in the moonshine,
I wish we could bring back the days
dear of old.

Shelly Lussier
TO MY LOVE

In the depths of my mind
Where the blackness reigns
From the back of my heart
To where the red blood stains

In the force of my breath
Where you'll find sweet sorrow
In the bleakness of night
Where you'll wish there was no
tomorrow

In the shadows of pain
Where you'll feel only regret
Deep in the wishing well
Wishing we had never met

In the closeness of our hearts
As ourselves bind as one
My message I'm sending you
Is none other than done.

Annie Aufill
LOVE

I wish to dedicate this poem to Jim, my husband, whom I love very much.

Oh, my love where did you go?
We used to be so close.
You were my lover, and my friend
On you I could always depend.

And now my love, I hold your hand,
To you I am a stranger.
Alzheimers took you from me,
To that land of no return.

And, so my eyes are full of tears,
As I make my way alone down
That long and lonely road.
I just hold your hand in mine.

Diane Ayon
LIFE VERSUS DEATH

This poem is dedicated to my deceased mother, Margaret Zoldy.

Life isn't beautiful it's really absurd
It's sometimes long but still a 4-letter word.
For some life is short and hard to explain
Endless heartache and full of real pain.

Victims of life sometimes prefer its end
Especially when their hearts are too broken to mend.
Relatives and friends are often taken for granted
Slipping away forever with feelings that can't be recanted.
Universal life should be peaceful, loving and caring
So often it's the opposite and not worth bearing.

Death is only the end of a mortal existence
Eternally the soul remains off in the distance.
And since the soul is the main principle of life,
Thoughts, feelings and actions must remain in strife.
How is it then, that death can possibly be different from life?

Judith Pike Boos
THE LAST BOOK
A spirited Yankee just finished The Book,
She read it from cover-to-cover;
She set it aside with a faraway look,
Expression reserved for lost lover.

"I studied my Bible for eighty-nine Springs
And puzzled through hard correlation;
I understand Christ, the King of all Kings,
But I can't figure out 'Revelation'."

Lisa Bertolini
MY DREAMS
I must hold on to my dreams,
For if they fly,
I will fly with them.
I must beware of the wrong ones,
For if the wrong ones slip,
I will fall with them.
I must never let them be stolen,
For the thief will not return them.
But I must never steal them,
For they will never be my dreams.

Cindy Bruce
GOD'S GIFT
As I quietly pray
Thanking HIM for this new day
I knew HE is here to stay.

In the early morn all is still.
The gentle call of a whippoorwill.
The brightening of the eastern sky is GOD'S will.

The sun's soft rays
Clouds scurrying away,
HE has given us another day.

As the sun warms the night time chill
The quiet is no longer still.
'Tis another busy day to fill.

As the day continues, we move so swift.
So many things we try to sift
We sometimes forget about, HIS gift.

B Jean Johnston

B Jean Johnston
UNDERSTAND

To my parents and grandmother Hugh, Beatrice and Anna Johnston and my sons, Richard, Zane and David.

Do you see the suffering in
your sister's face?
Do you know how you'd feel,
if you were in her place?

Count each line, each shadow—
They have much to say
to a wise observer—who can
cease life's play.

For a moment—listen—
Stop and look and hear—
There are some heartbroken—
There's an unshed tear.

So, beware my friend
that you do not offend—
Or destroy a joy yet rising,

Or debase your heart with
a word—very "smart"—
Very sharp, very slick and
compromising.

B Jean Johnston
MODERATION
Go lightly my heart—keep pace with life
For all your dreams are worth living—
Sing softly my heart—for a song of the heart
Rides forever in the air.

Walk swiftly towards good—
Fight bravely for right—
Speak kindly my voice—and softly too
Ere another's song is diminished.

B Jean Johnston
MY DAD
I cannot but recall
The earliest days of childhood,
When joy reigned supreme
and was but a cup of milk in my tiny hands.
Then did I laugh a laugh from my heart,
and then did I cry from the
Depths of my soul,

For I'd not yet learned
To put on my sly mask—
And confront the wide world
With a face with no song.

I'll always recall
His first song sung to me—
My first memory of life's love—
Which I'd learned at his knee.

Please God, in Your Grace,
Shine great light near his face,
So though blind in this life,
My dear daddy might see.

Shannon Marie Bowser
I'M NOT ADDICTED
"I'm not addicted," he told his friends. "I don't use it every day."
But his friends all turn and walk off.
They don't know what to say.
"I can't believe those guys!" he thinks as he's walking up the street.
When he gets to his house, he tells his mom, "I'm going to bed 'cause I'm beat."
"I really don't feel tired," he thinks.
"Just a little down. Maybe I'll do a little, just to bring me around."
He opens the drawer, lifts up the clothes, pulls out the razor and bag.
"I can't believe they think I'm addicted! Those guys are really a drag."
He takes in the first line, the second and the third. (There's been so much talk on the dangers of drugs, but he hasn't heard a word.)
He's never done that much before.
"What the heck," he thinks, "Who cares?"
Then he puts it all back in the drawer, and he lays on his bed and he stares.
In the morning the boy is still staring.
His mother is shedding her tears.
The doctor checks (unsuccessfully) for a pulse. His father's realized his worst fears.
His friends stand together at the funeral. They cry, though it's how they predicted.
For this boy, their friend, who didn't think twice, when his last words were: I'm Not Addicted.

Niran Bahjat-Abbas
TO STOP A SUICIDE . . .
Weep not for the denial of your spirit,
but, heed to fabricate righteousness.

Tears that cease, are locked within one's heart,
Confessing is the unrivaled resolution.

Frequently darkness serves as a companion,
Recall the fervent Sun.

Time passes with impetuous rate,
Only rationality calms it down.

Think not of present impetuous rate,
Only rationality calms it down.

Think not of present misfortunes that take rest upon your shoulders,
Think of future endeavors yet to come.

Loved ones will grieve,
and their souls marked with mournfulness.

God's words hold prophecies
Your's none.

Don Blanton
BORN AGAIN?
Outside my door a bad storm was so near
From what I could see it would shortly be here.
No way to escape the winds that would blow
The harm they would do there was no way to know.

I looked at the storm with all its great rage
And wondered when would be the end of the age.
What would happen to those whose hearts are not right
My mind was consumed with horror that night.

Why can't people see there's wrath on the way?
There will be no escape on that great judgment day.
This is the horror that no tongue can tell
What it will be like when a soul enters hell.

My thoughts were all questions, no answers were near
But to keep out confusion it must be made clear.
It's still true today and it always has been
There is no wrath for the soul saved from sin.

There's much I don't know about what's going to be
But I do know for sure, it's clear to me.
The question to ask yourself when you need a friend
Have I trusted God, and been born again?

Don Blanton
DOES AMEN MEAN GOOD-BY?
One day when I was just sitting at home
I sat down at my desk and picked up the phone,
When the other end answered I just said Hi
We talked for awhile and then said good-by.

I sat there thinking for close to an hour
My mind slowly drifted into a prayer,
I prayed for a time and thought about sin
I opened my eyes and then added amen.

What I had said on the phone was all true
But he didn't know me when our talk was through,
With God it is different, He is always near by
He knows what we're doing and even knows why.

Good-by was expected when I talked to a friend
At the end of a prayer I guess we all say amen,
We should remember and I certainly will try
When we're talking to God, amen does not mean good-by.

Don Blanton
WHAT IF?
It seems that when I'm all alone
My thoughts run wild and my mind is free,
To go to the places I've never been
Or see things happen that never will be.

On one such ride without leaving my chair

I thought of a time, and I saw it well,
Wish I could say what it was like that day
When all people on earth could see into Hell.

Just a few days ago churches were empty and quiet
Not many folks there, it was easy to see,
The changes that came in a second of time
You wouldn't believe since you weren't with me.

Now everyone knows just what to expect
Not enough room in the churches they say,
Singing and praying is all you can hear
You want in tomorrow, make an appointment today.

What if this really did happen?
Wouldn't it be something to tell,
Of the changes that came to this wicked old world
Because one day, we all had the chance to see into Hell.

Cathleen Scarvers
GUY
A man with wonders far beyond the sky
Reaching out to all with such splendor, yet shy
He holds within, a world, uncommon to most
A world that stretches from coast to coast
The load of this world by no means is light
But one day he'll waken and all will seem right
He's on the right path and has all the proper tools
He'll win at this game and he'll play by the rules

A zealous man of integrity and courage
With strength beyond belief that nothing can discourage
If you see him on the street don't you dare pass him by
Just stand there in wonder and notice the gleam in his eye
A man, like no others, this man's name is Guy

Ms Tonya Kelly Basinger
THE HOUSE WITH MEMORIES!
A loose-hung door where friends once greeted,
cracked mirror, a dainty maiden's glance treated.
Black fireplace where the warm coals cast.
all this no more, 'tis gone at last,
The house with memories!

The stove where whispering scents drifted,
the porch where long-gone feet once shifted.
A broken chair, there a man once sat,
and a window ledge, past throne of the cat!

The boys' first rifle, girls' best doll,
broken glass, within the hall.
Here lived the old, and young so limber,
built with love in every timber.

All this is gone and so much more,
the dreams once young, now lived and o'er.
And now as its frame sags and sways,
love reminds it of the good ole days;
The house with memories!

Flossie Childress Barnes
TOMORROW'S CHILD
Hear the cry of Tomorrow's Child
loud and clear.
Where is the blue sky,
sparkling rivers and streams?
Singing birds, green grass
and lovely trees, where?
Was it all dreams?

Oh, Mother Earth,
what have they done to you?
Man, can you erase the harm?
Make everything new, before it's too late,
sound the alarm!

Danielle Douchkoff
LOVE
Love is a sweet thing
so very lovely and kind
Love is like a rose,
a rose that is yet to blossom
Love is like a pearl
so young and so precious
Love heals wounds
sealing it with affection
Love is a sweet thing.

Merry Davis
FROM THE HOUSE OF NINE
'Twas the day before Christmas and all through the stores
Shoppers were finishing their last minute chores.
When out on the street there arose such a clatter
That I knew in an instant just what was the matter.
Cars were lined up exactly bumper to bumper
With such honking and squealing and calling by name
I knew I would get home at midnight again.

With the house all messed and dishes not done
I knew that now Christmas had really begun.
The children were snooping in corners and closets
And feeling of packages under the tree.
(I wonder if anything was put there for me!)
More presents to wrap and children to feed,
What really I need is Santa's swift steed.

Santa is lucky; he can jump in his sleigh.
Now, I can see it is mothers who pay.
With papers and ribbons all over the floor
It gets us, we're tired, right down to the core.
I've had it! That's it! Merry Christmas is here.
The good-will, the joys, and all of the cheer.
I made it!—I'm happy to see children smile
But another Christmas, I'm glad, won't be for awhile.

W Ray Dunn
LECTURE—NO REDEEMING VALUE
You gotta live, Kid,
Lay it on the line
For this is the year of the Dragon
And the ozone layer grows thin.

The weirdo on the tee vee
Talks of Armageddon
While the bitch next door
Plucks her eyebrows
And rubs Oil of Olay
Into her wrinkles.

Hell! I can't even pay the goddamned rent,
And I'm twelve months pregnant.
I'm going to give birth
To an idea,
Or worse yet, a poem
Which I may dedicate to you.

So put your money
In the plate, Kid,
God loves you.
Lay it all on the line.
What the hell you have to lose?

Diane M Overton

Diane M Overton
A SUMMER ROMANCE
Bobbing emotions
Adrift
In the bay,
Love don't float away.

Like
A haze
On a Summer's day,
Dream don't fade away.

Mist of the morning
Steam of the day
Frost of the evening
Are not meant to stay.

Feelings of happiness
Often
Betray
And Love can sail away.

Vladimir Khoroshansky
UNTITLED
I don't wake with swallows in heart now
I feel blindly you're like blinds heaven
I read blindly you're by
my hot tears
Let it fret birch let it fret now
All of us at spring will expire
by languor
how my heart is bristle
You unstuck my throat and clicking
foutanelle nightingail in grove
how it hanged like tears
on the leaves dark
Uh I'm jealous you uh I'm howling
wayfarers who covered by blizzard
I found howling for their tender
Let it higher feathers of clouds
and my magic jasmine of soul
let it fall my dove
hurry

Vladimir Khoroshansky
DAVID

In memory of V. Visotsky, unforgettable Jewish poet.

I'm going to leave the Underworld
My first test of the pen-a sling
To Goliaf just desperate-borned
in cruel hearts begin to read

On strained nervous I'll not alive
without enemys It's scheme of verse
I lose consciousness oh my love
when you wake up And vice-versa

All hipped togs talking by the torch-hanged man who askings by sikofunts-
It was inherited to foes
We sown our death to foes in cry

By gallows you're justify inroad
My backway all guard marked by torch
They rubed off from my lip's blood foam
like prostitues on enemies' walls

But Holy Land for me unknown-
Say All perfectious tears no coast
Let throw back Golaif where stars born
from which light to us didn't downfall.

Vladimir Khoroshansky
UNTITLED
Gulp back my tender sprouts—run tears
What kinds of irony for soul more lovely
turn like wolf-cub in imitate howl-if
I was scribbled ways to fine But overflowing

It seems to me cleave sky and cruelly-time
Enchanting ways to you I watch with savage anguish
Like gladiator lose consciousness strive
for you-dismiss when overtaken

And think about suicide-when knife pull up
to throat—like tremble to intuition harm

Let's crumble to dust my wishes I cannot love

The time of suicide come It's wing-beat
Let's strike with dagger star which downfall
My heart who stabs through mark by inquire

All elements of full running to humble
All vengeance stings to magical achievement
More anxious dove remember enchanting ways

Patterns of partings and rapproachements
And thaw like bee which to the stars resigned
Inflorescences Their turn into earthly.

Patrick Gallois
RITE OF LIFE
Disdainfully, a startled hawk plummet and freeze,
Typhooned by a pinkish cloud of flamingos.
A carp stares at a wandering moth, in the breeze,
Still glistening from the wetness of its cocoon.

Impulsive hour of the fox hunting the hare;
Final omen for the wolf to confront the ram.

After the swift slaughter of an innocent fawn,
Under the shifting shadows of the volcanos,
By the edge of the lake mirroring a half moon;
Witness, in awe and anxious silence, as I am,
One of those precious instant, hypnotic and rare;
The ultimate challenge of life and fate, at dawn.

Patrick Gallois
ICARUS TOUCH

à mon père, le comte du zen.

Shadow of birds dashing . . .
Frantic and colorful plumages;
Symbolic shapes flashing . . .
Gentle and beautiful images.

Visual esthetic perfections
Of climbing and soaring
Or diving and gliding,
In silent and timeless selections.

Dissolution through dissociation;
Cosmic pond's reflection
Of obsessed transubstantiation
In flawless harmony.

Search of the priceless kind:
By means of symbiotic fantasy.
With fascination for ecstasy . . .
Soul's freedom of winged mind!

Patrick Gallois
LOST RAIN

To Carolyn—daughter, mother & grandmother, with my love.

A tear, like a drop of rain
On a shiny blade of grass,
Silently, runs down my face;
Lost, in the ocean of life.

Deceiving numbness of a soothing pain;
Haunting memories nourishing the strain . . .

Scented seeds of a wildflower;
The bitter kiss of last embrace.
The broken steel of a dull knife;
An inner scar shattered like glass,
Sharp pieces of star shaped amber . . .

Staring, I daze at the rain.

Patrick Gallois
ENIELEDAM
Disoriented
And isolated,
With obligations
And expectations,
In a crowdy maze
And a stuffy haze,
On a restless stream
And a childish dream . . .

Suddenly, red hair
And a friendly stare,
A haunted lagoon
And a bright full moon;
A soft honey breast
And a simple quest . . .
"Stop the spinning wheel
Let the time stand still"

Patrick Gallois
GAMBIT
After a dark ceremony,
A peaceful dawn;
A warm body . . .
For a while, stalemate, with a pawn!

Patrick Gallois
REACHING
Enjoy me like the sun
That warms up your body as light as lime,
And gives shapes and colors to space and time.

Enjoy me like a wind
That caresses your face: sweet, sour, spicy,
And fills your ears of joy and harmony.

Enjoy me like the earth
That satisfies your hunger with content,
And awakes all your senses by a scent.

Enjoy me like a lake
That refreshes your thirst; where you can drown,
And reflects the insane world upside down.

Enjoy me like the flame
That stirs your dreams and keeps your fears away
But, stay free . . . be in love . . . through me, okay!

Patrick Gallois
ALCHEMY
A day
A night
The light

πThe sun
The moon
At noon

Fire
Water
And earth

Rebirth

Patrick Gallois
NOCTURNE
Ce soir, la lune rêve . . .
Parmis les durs coussins,
S'étire le corps d'Eve
Et se crispent ses mains.

Cette blanche vision
Au regard de tigresse,
Attise sa passion
Au jeu de nos caresses.

Tout en prenant un bain
Dans la lumière pâle,
Arrive le festin
Dans un concert de râles.

Sur sa joîe, essoufflée,
Assouvie, presque nue,
Plus belle décoiffée,
Allanguie, détendue;

Les yeux perlés de larmes,
Envahit par la sève,
Elle sourit, prise aux charmes . . .
Ce soir, la lune rêve.

Patrick Gallois
COCKTAIL
D'abord, des baîsers, quelques mesures;
Un peu d'excitation, un soupçon;
Dosez la caresse et la griffure;
De la pudeur, juste, deux glaçons;
Une rondelle de volupté;
Et de la sentimentalité,
Un zeste . . . "EROTISME," c'est son nom.

Patrick Gallois
PAUSE
La lumière pâle du petit jour naissant
Jouait aux ombres avec ton corps alanguie.

Drapée, à moitié, tu reposais en croissant;
Face à la fenêtre, une jambe repliée,
Un bras tendu paume à plat, et l´autre blotit
Entre tes seins blancs comme deux soleils de lait.

La tête baignée d'une auréole blonde, et,
Toute offerte dans un rayonnement de plis,
Faîsant s'emblant de t´endormir, tu m´attendais.

Patrick Gallois
MARINE
Voici la mer en mouvement;
Voici le soleil qui se couche,
Corps et âme aux couleurs de sang.

Sous les chauds soupirs du ciel,
Sous les sourires de ma bouche,
Tes yeux ont une autre lueur;
Celle du soleil sur le miel.

Sur le sable, du sang, en fleur . . .

Comme une fille devient femme,
La mer change encore de coeur;
Instant où tu donnes ton corps,
Terre dont le ciel est ton âme.

Fleur, sur le sable miel du temps,
Voici la terre qui s´endort;
Voici ton coeur libre un moment.

Patrick Gallois
SENSATIONS
I. Le Jardin

L'éclat de tes yeux,
Le grain de ta peu de maure,
Tes Lèvres au goût de treille,
L´odeur de ton corps,
Le bruit de nos jeux . . .

Tous mes sens sont en éveil!

II. La Chute

Mes yeux brillent de mille feux éteints,
Ma salive a un goût amère,
Je ne connais même plus ton parfum;
Tu cries, sans crever le silence,
Tu es loin, pourtant tu me serres . . .

Voilà, le vrai mur de l´indifférence!

Atsuko Ushimaru
HOW TO BE YOUR FAVORITE TEACHER'S FAVORITE STUDENT
Be a perfect student
Be interested; lavish him with attention
Follow his moves, breathe in tune
Win his eye contact
Nod, smile, understand
Learn the perfect timing
Speak his language -
Now you've got him riveted

Oh, it's so sad, though
If you really fall in love
With the looks, the voice, the ideas
The Real Person as a whole
A pet is a pet, never a mate
Strive you may, it's a losing battle

I was born a perfect student
I've always been the Favorite One
It just happens all the time
And it happens every time
That I am always the one to lose

Atsuko Ushimaru
YES
Dictionaries are
always so
awkward
when it comes to
describing
subtle emotions
forgetting
that many times
it takes less courage
to speak
out of knowledge
than to utter
simple acceptance
maybe a bit
hesitant
but of heart-filling
sincerity
with a blush
on the cheeks
yes — yes.

Atsuko Ushimaru
COMA
Millions of bubble-gum colored balloons
made of something resembling bubble gum
pop one by one
under my weight. I,
sinking farther and farther,
taste the sound of them
foaming, flowing, surging, breaking,
bubbles in my ears, bubbles in my nose,
in my eyes, in my throat.
What at first appeared to be
a fantastic dream is
not so and leaves me in a
helpless flavor of bubble gum.

Atsuko Ushimaru
DEMOCRACY
At the turn of the century
perhaps all will be risible.
Killing, hurting, crying,
perhaps all will be graciously
blessed by someone who will then
dominate: namely, the people.
Nothing remains so long

in this age of rapid changes
that it will be folly to grieve.
They will revel in the victory of the Free
when countless skulls glow
anonymously white with uranium rays.
Perhaps all will be risible. For those who win.
They are fully justified.

Atsuko Ushimaru
IN SHARED MOMENTS

The night wouldn't be so dark
or winter so cold
The stars would shine brighter
on roads that I go

The sky would unfold to a clearer blue
The whole world would be new

And tomorrow would come with open arms
Paint it the color of eternity
Feel the tremor of my heart

Dream of dreams

Life would be so full
With you mine

Rosemary O
NEVER FORGET

You came into my life suddenly,
from the beginning we knew it could not be.
Other people already involved,
complications not to be solved.

We danced and laughed thru the night,
and even loved, it seemed so right.
Made me feel special, had so much fun,
wish we could finish what we'd begun.

The laughing stopped, I began to cry,
for our time has come to say goodbye.
Memories sweet, memories forever,
never forget our time together.

Nelle Chamberlain

Nelle Chamberlain
TO SPRING

To Ann Ellis - my dear cousin in Vacaville.

The sky is clear and crystal, rich in blue,
Upon the fields there rests the silv'ry dew
As there Night laid it in his last caress.
The merry birds chirp gaily from trees
Their twitter fills the sweet, balmy breeze.

Trees are shrouded in a halo, pink and white,
The tender buds that blossom through the night
Are kissed by fairy dew-drops
Sprayed with fragrant perfume rare
And scented blossoms fill the freshened air.

For ere the sun is mounting on the sky
The drowsy poppies that in slumber lie
On Earth's soft bosom, awake and smile to Heaven.
The shy, green fields seem suddenly to blush
As the golden sun appears Earth murmurs, "hush!"

Butterflies are fluttering in the breeze,
Upon the flowers rest the humming bees.
The breath of Spring pours forth a flood of harmony.
O joy, exhilarant is the mirth
When Earth revels o'er another birth!

The sea is calm and glittering once more,
White wavelets wash the warm sands on the shore
Whispering in mellow tones of Spring's rejoicing.
For there is mirth and pleasure in the air!
Sweet splendor reigns everywhere!

Nelle Chamberlain
TO A STORM

O Storm! you are a glory all unknown
To those who fear your mighty power
What wealth of strength and ardor lie
Within your infinite boundary!
O great and noble! the embrace of your crushing arms
Glorying in their own immensity.

O Storm! stern master of Earth
Who trembles in her frailty
What worlds of passion lie within your piercing glance!
O ardent, exhilarant! — the force of your caress
Making all things tremor.

And when you bend to kiss dear Earth
Fire singes her lips
In fear she shrinks, in trembling timidity flees.
Your rumbling chase, you call in crashing tone echo defeat
For she has flown!

O Storm! conqueror of the gods
Weeping such bitter, sorrowing tears!
Would you have Earth to calm your fears?
Weep not! She may be shallow recompense!
Break not the spirit in sufferance.
Oh! still and tranquil! - the calm of peaceful endurance!

Nelle Chamberlain
TO YOU

I see your eyes — morning dews
twinkle on the poppy leas,
I hear your voice — 'tis the night whispering of trees;
I hear your step — silver moonbeams dance on swaying seas!
You call to me! 'tis the starry breeze!

I see your smile — a rainbow is born on the sky!
I feel your kiss — 'tis the breath of Spring on my cheek;
Your charms have lured me into the fields at noon
Ah! Nature, God's greatest boon!

Nelle Chamberlain
TO A SUNRISE

The sun is rising o'er the distant hill,
Dear Earth is gray and quiet — all is still;
The last pale star of night weary and worn
Fades into dimness ere the day is born.

Hyperion rises amid the gray-white clouds
Arises in a mist of flaming shrouds;
The fiery darts he hurls upon the morn
Are taken as a symbol of the dawn.

And when the blazing fire burns the breeze
He fans it with his breath, in rapture flees.
The quiet dawn he wakened while it sighed,
He pierced the heart of night, 'twas then it died.

So ere the night unto Elysium is borne
All things bow down before the rosy morn;
The redness of the sky fades into a gold
And then it is the day that we behold!

Nelle Chamberlain
A WINTER WIND

The trees are bare and on the ground
The withered leaves lie strewn and brown,
The tired sun sinks low upon a weary sky
And cold winds blow, for is not winter nigh?

The mountains don a garb of snow and mist,
Sweet flowers fade no more by summer kissed,
And the hungry frost has robbed the field
Of all the freshness Spring could yield
For winter comes in all her grayness.

The sea is dull and dreary
The angry winds that lash the naked trees
Make of rippling wavelets some maddened thing
That heaves and foams and thumps
Upon the soft breast of the shore.

The birds sing not from upon the bough,
The sun fills not the air with splendor now.
Summer has perished, dear Earth is forlorn
Now it is the sobbing doves that mourn.

Nelle Chamberlain
CHRISTMAS

Christmas is a time
for peace and grace,
To give thanks
For being here
In this world of ours
Where everyone's life
is different.

Christmas is a time
To share
The bond of love or friendship
To appreciate each other
To spread happiness
Among those
less fortunate.

Christmas is a time
When the child delights
In Sparkling lights,
With trees aglow,
Mr. Santa and so—
A joyful, very special time.

Christmas is a time
Wherever you may go
To play in the snow
or swim in the sea-
Oh! What a lovely month
Is December!

Nelle Chamberlain
REMINISCENCE

Wanting you—
So dear and soothing
Life's storm and strife
And trivialities
Flow swiftly by
In your embrace.

Wanting you —
Your dear presence
A perfect chord of harmony
For you are truly loved.
There is no thrill
Like your caress.

Wanting you —
Dark eyes
The magic of love
The touch of your lips
On mine
The glow of surrender.

Wanting you —
Forever mine,
May it be a thousand days
A thousand night
Somewhere, we'll be together
You and I.

So I hum — reminiscing
Azure skies, silver birds, sweet countryside,
When I basked in the sun
And the heavenly glow
Of a dear, comfortable affection.

So I smile — remembering
A deep, intoxicating passion
That glided to the moon-top
And there lulled me to slumber
On a snowy fleece!

So I sigh — regretting
That you are gone from me
And emptiness depresses.
Where was love is now a lull,
Lonely yet bitter-sweet.

So I pray — for Silver Wings
How the ghost of you clings!
Who knows how far, or when or where?
That when you ponder
You'll remember too!

Nelle Chamberlain
RECOGNITION

When he sees her
She smiles,
And a warmth within him
Glows-

Like two Martinis
He's flirtatious
Gives her the glances!
He holds her hand for a moment
And his bright eyes
Tell her there is a spark
That kindles
Perhaps-

When she sees him
She's warm and happy
Something smoulders within,
She's a romanticist
This seems a game to play
It's fun
In an intriguing way
and yet-
How can he tell her?
What can she say?
There are others
Her husband — His wife!

Nelle Chamberlain
THE UNDERSTANDING THIRD WIFE

Her heart's in his pocket
Wherever he goes,
For he loves her deeply,
She knows—

When he's away
Dancing, romancing
A friend?
Each day
So happy-
But he loves her deeply,
She knows—

When he returns
No questions here
So good to have you
home dear.
He kisses her madly
For he loves her deeply,
She knows—

His heart's in her purse
Wherever she goes,
For she loves him dearly,
He knows—

When she's away
Dining gaily,
Wooed by
A friend?
Delightfully happy,
But she loves him dearly,
He knows—

When she returns So many questions
asked!
She laughs and laughs
It's so nice to be home,
She kisses him deeply,
For she loves him dearly,
He knows—

Nancy Keele
FRIENDS

Sharon, this one is for you.

I know that sometimes it has seemed
like I haven't cared,
For losing your friendship is one of
my biggest fears.
On those days when I haven't had
much to say,
Please don't worry my thoughts are
coming your way.

I have bad days just like everyone
else,
When on my face is a frown, I'm
only thinking of myself.
If you're in doubt of me feeling hate,
I'm catching up to your smile, I'll try
not to be late.

So on those days when I'm feeling
sad,
Just help me out by saying that it's
not so bad.
If I stop to argue about it with you,
Please show me the way, I don't like
feeling blue.

Together friend and friend, for we
will be,
No matter what happens to you or
me.
We may argue along the way,
But we are humans each and every
day.

What I'm trying to say, is that I care,
Even on those days, when you're not
aware.
If you're feeling sad or ever hatred,
I will try my hardest to save your
day.

Nancy Keele
MOTHER

To my mother, June, for everything that she has done.

My mother is a special kind of
person,
One who is always in reason.
She is always there when you need
her,
She's thoughtful, caring, and aware.

There isn't a day that goes by when I
don't think of her,
The love, the gratitude, and even the
sincerity.
She has that special something that
cannot be explained,
She acts like there is no such thing as
shame.

A mother knows when to smile or to
be bold,
She's always warm never cold.
A mother can offer so many things,
When her time comes, they will greet
her with wings.

The love for my mother is so very
special to me,
It goes forever, more than the eye can
see.
She's not a fake, she's pure genuine,
I thank the Lord, for making her
mine.

At times I know that words cannot
describe,
But when it comes to love, we
shouldn't have anything to hide.
So I will remember to give her a kiss
and a hug,
To show her that she's appreciated
for giving me all that love.

I'll always remember as each passing
day,
That my mother has helped me along
the way.
I thank her for all that she has done,
Mom, in my eyes you will always be
number one.

Dorothy Dooley
SUMMER

To Father, Mother, Family, Children and Friends.

Summer has arrived
The birds are singing
and spreading good cheer
the trees are tall
and their leaves are green
People's minds are filled
with vacation dreams,
With the smell of barbecue
and flowers
Once again a new season has begun
Summer is here!

Karl M Simon
THE ESSENCE OF PRAYER

I used to think that a time each day
was to be set aside for us to pray
For us to remember what we wanted
to say and talk to God, only in a
special way.
Of the total truth I was unaware that
the presence of God was "always
there"
That every thought of every day
Was known by God, as if to pray.

Our truest thoughts start in our soul
As God directs us towards his goal
And so the dawn of realization shown
The essence of prayer, at last was
known.
Now I know that whenever I feel the
need or presence of God for real
I don't have to wait till it's time to
kneel
Only open my mind, to let his spirit
be revealed

Andrea Anthony
THE SAD FACED CLOWNS

Dedicated to Christina and Dawn. Inspired by the beautiful poets that flourish at Ruby's Roadhouse.

With a flair for life and a passion for humanity. We bare the weight of the world on our shoulders. With inspired words we can make life worth living. We write of war, we write of peace. Our prophesy could change the fate of the world . . . We write of love. Misunderstood, because we care, social outcasts that suffer the most. We are the sad faced clowns.

Some call us vagabonds, Gypsies that roam . . . Others say we are eccentric. Because sometime we leave their reality and step into a dream. They say we are sentimental fools wearing our hearts on our sleeves. We write our visions on paper of reality . . . and also of make believe. But the pen in our hands, only bares the truth of both worlds.

Fallen sand castles, broken dreams, "cold reality." We sometime hide ourselves for a while. Trying to stop the ridicule and the pain. But then destiny shouts a cry in our ears that the suffering world, is dying, again.

Then, out of our closets we come. With the pens in our hands and inspiration in our hearts. We come out to sing our songs. Bearing the pain of others, we are the sad faced clowns!

"We are the Poets"

Dale V Deadmond
MY LOVE ACROSS THE MILES

In the lightest of the day
And the darkest of the night
I feel there's something missing
Something's just not right
Could it be my love
My love across the miles
The one who makes me laugh
The one who makes me smile
Oh, she's the missing link
The other half of my heart
She always takes it with her
Whenever we may part
So now I know I feel
A love as true as true
For I would wait a lifetime girl
To spend my life with you.

Denise M Meckes
LEARN TO LOVE

When I was a
Little girl,
I dreamed a
little girl's dream . . .
To grow up big,
And learn to love.
As I grew older
The dream started
To fade,
I grew up big,
But love,
Just seemed to get colder.
The day I met you,
All the coldness went away.
Because now . . .
I've grown up big,
And with you,
I've learned to love.

Helena P Davis
DON'T CRY FOR ME

For my Mother, Mrs. Mary F. Davis, a woman who always told me, "I can do anything that I set my mind to."

If you see me walking by, with my neck toward the sky, and tears are streaming from my eyes, don't cry for me.

If you pass me on the streets, and my clothes are torn and weary worn, don't cry for me.

If you pass my shack at night, and it's cold and without lights, don't cry for me.

If you see me walking in the snow, and sleet, without shoes for my feet, don't cry for me.

If you see that my bones are weary, and my outlook is awful dreary, don't cry for me.

If you see me looking hungry, down, and out, without money not even for a jar of honey, don't cry for me.

If you see me sitting idly by, and the flies are swarming about my eyes, don't cry for me.

But, when my face is free from frown and they lower me in the ground, then you cry for me, for I am no longer able to cry for myself. For if you had only helped me—this my friend, was needless be.

C William Davis III
THE LORD HATH GIVEN ME YOU

To my daughter Michelle Lynn Davis.

In the dim light of morning, I
enter your room, and look
upon you as you sleep.
I am taken by the halo of
innocence, newness, and peace
about you.
As I bend and gently kiss your
face, tears swell in my eyes,
tears of pride and love.
I am so thankful to the Lord, for
he has given me, your radiant
smile, your beautiful eyes,
your loving heart.
I am filled with joy, for the Lord
hath given me you.
My riches are eternal, for I may
enfold you in my arms, and
call you . . . Daughter

Love, Daddy

Rebecca Davis
SOMETIMES I THINK I'M FALLING, FALLING

In Memory . . . to my dear sweet sister, Claudette A. Davis.

Sometimes I think I'm falling, falling
Sometimes I don't know, because
space and time awaits me every time.
What is space? What is time? It's
always on my mind.
When I close my eyes, it's like
saying goodbye—goodbye to space
and time.
Sometimes I think I'm falling, falling
But now I know it's only my calling.

Tony and Joy

Bea Barnett
BUSY LADY

Dedicated to my grandchildren, Joy and Tony. They spend MUCH time with Nana and Pappa. Sometimes Nana feels like a very busy lady but so-o happy! !

She is positive, someone beautiful to
behold,
Don't count her chronological
years, she never seems to get
old.
Never idle, there is so-o much she
wants to do,
Busy Lady is always an
inspiration to you.

Her smile is like sunshine in the
morning,
And she makes everyone want
to sing.
Doing nice things to make others
happy,
Busy Lady spends her time
well, all can see.

Thinks clearly about life and things
that be,
A beautiful example for you
and me.
Those in her presence are happy to
know,
Busy Lady with so much get up
and go.

I am sure each day the angels smile,
Watching this special one all
the while.
She is really one of them on earth
below,
And Busy Lady is a joy to
know!

Traci K Engel
FORGOTTEN ANGEL

To My Mom . . . Healer of the Forgotten Angel.

Small Angel-child, eyes innocent,
wide
All dressed up in Momma's pearls
And a wide-brimmed lacy hat from
beneath to hide.
Hours spent primping, sprinkling her
wrists with sweet smells
Watching her momma stitching her
frothy petticoats with tiny silver
bells.
She twirls about, a ballerina in
miniature
Excitement bubbling forth in a song
so crystally pure.
She's dining with her daddy—the
one the world stole from her
That strange and distant god, whose
memory is just a blur.
All she has to fill her heart's void
Are cherished birthday notes, a few
fragile toys.
"He'll come this time, won't he
Momma?"
Her precious voice brings tears to her
momma's eyes.
"I'm sure he'll try his hardest."
She'd learned that to promise was not
wise.
Patiently the Angel-child waited, not
stirring at even the dark
Dreaming of smiles and hugs, and
playing in the park.
Finally bedtime came—from Daddy,
still no word
Golden-winged dreams were broken
The precious child sat huddled, a
wounded, bleeding bird.
So gently Momma rocked her, tears
flowing for her child
While silently she cursed a world that
could be so vile.

Christina (Crissy) Evans
THE WALL OF FATE

Dedicated in loving memory of Joe (Pa) Evans.

As I walk through these empty halls
I see my fate in mirrored walls

It was a lovely picture of bright
things
Wedding bells and of golden rings

I was to be married very soon
Under the stars and silver moon

Two little children later to come
Which added up to a greater sum

As the image of fate faded away
There is only one thing I have to say

As I walk through these now bright
halls
I see my fate in mirrored walls

In the wall of fate.

Brian Eddelson
THE FALLEN GAMBLER'S LIFE

To all the people who are just trying to survive in today's society. To all the compulsive gamblers.

A hallway longs with fear of
the future.
Portraits smirk and sound with
laughter.
The floor creaks and rats squeal.
Your footsteps as loud as thunder—
eyes filled with a dark blurry vision.
As if you were placed in a cartoon—
your ears grow to acknowledge
anything.
Faith becomes dim as you start to
run.

Your heart pounds faster—you
breathe with a wheeze.
Most definitely escape is impossible.
Your mind becomes impatient—
mentally—UNAWARE.
The lack of alertness can kill oneself.

The fear is what makes you
frightened—afraid—
have to—RUN—move on!
Notice a glow of white light—a door
not far.
RUN, RUN to reach my goal.
The laughter of the portraits amplify.
Rats multiply making my journey an
obstacle—coordination
becomes sloppy.
See—the door so close—RUN.
Breathing heavy with excitement,
sweating with relief—
HOPE revives!
UNAWARE—your fear is set to
gasp . . .

Yes, you have reached your
goal—only to achieve the
ending of this insane hallway called
life.
UNAWARE—your fear grabs your
soul and presents death.

The lack of alertness can kill
oneself.

Vivian Eaton
THANK YOU FATHER

This poem is dedicated to Emma, my mother, who has inspired me to continue writing and to those who fought for freedom.

Lord, our God, let us be thankful, let
us be as one; a family.
So we may feast together here on this
Thanksgiving.
Let those who have passed be
remembered for the kind things they
did
And shared with us.
Let there be ultimate peace
throughout this world, Oh Lord.
And those who are hungry, please
feed them.
And those who are sick, heal them, if
it is Your will.

Let us be grateful and let us be
willing to give
The love and encouragement so
others will do Your will,
Oh Lord and our Savior.
Bless and keep us safe as the years go
by.
Time is getting short, our patience
not at ease.
We need to know the truth about love
and thanksgiving.
We need to know that we are all alike
and there is no difference
In your sight.

Oh Father, make us whole, make us
your servants.
We all should be thankful and I thank
You for loving me
And those like me.
We are all Your children.

Scott Everett
DESCENDING

To my Mom and Dad, Thank you for all you have done for me. Love, your son, Scott.

falling leaves . . .
CRISP yet silent,
like an outfielder catching a fly ball,
they fall and catch the wind,
and go wherever they please . . .
they also go whenever they please,
mostly in autumn,
how do they know?
is there a clock,
or is it a little voice inside . . .
do they want to go,
or is there no choice . . .
when the ride is over,
the leaf is now allowed to
r
e
s
t . . .

Kimberly Ann Wahl

Kimberly Ann Wahl
SILENT STILLNESS

Cries of a train whistle pierce the air,
the laboring creaks from the rails
under the pressure of the cars rolling
over them.

The barren land standing alone, under
the silvery light of the moon, a misty
haze creates a blurry veil of coldness.

An eerie silence hangs over the land,
lifeless characteristics of a deserted
world reflect the loneliness of a ghost
town.

The only break in the dead stillness
comes from the passing train,
winding along the foothills; a solo
performance, that remains unseen.

The sad cry of the whistle blows
again, answered only by the echoes
of its own screams.

Becky J Earhart
A DREAM FOR MANKIND

I dedicate this poem to three special people in my life; Cherie, you showed me how to love and have compassion, Jim, you've proven to me that nobody is ever alone and to keep on fighting, and Bren, you've given me shelter in a stormy life and you've shown me the rainbow to keep me going. I love you all.

Dreams, dreams of a world lost to man's sight.
Poverty gone and hopes sought.
A world where two can begin again,
Correct the mistakes punished throughout time; never again.
A dream where all can happen.
Love, riches, or the most valuable treasure lost . . .
A dream.
Dreams, each as different and unique as their creator.
A person without dreams cannot change reality.
A person without dreams is lost in the world of man.
The world being a trap.
The dream being freedom.

Raquel Estrada
MYSTERIOUS FORCE

To my children: Michelle, Jasmine and Albert.

I hear!
The brutal rhythmic chant
that comes out of the depth of gypsy souls.
With despair and misery howls
like a lost soul in search
of the illuminated rays of heaven.
Now that violent rhythm has possessed I.
I like a volcano about to erupt I respond.
I tap my feet, twist my hands arch my back and I
swirl in the illusive atmosphere
of the soul of FLAMENCO.

Barbara Dennis
LIFE

In memory of Warren Neal Dennis who passed away April 27, 1987.

Life is but a short time on earth.
Sometimes it's short; sometimes longer,
No one really understands
What life is all about.

Take a little baby,
Only eight months old.
His life was so short,
Because of many complications.
Now he is gone and we must go on.
That is one of life's mysteries to me.

Life has many mysteries involved.
No one knows how long they'll be here.
Sometimes I wonder why life can be so cruel,
By taking a baby just starting out life.
Lord knows how I wanted to adopt him as my own.

Now we will try to start over,
Maybe someday there will be children around.
But for right now, it will be just you and me,
Maybe sometime in the future
We will adopt or become foster parents,
But for now, life is full of mysteries to me.

Michele Elledge
HEARTS

I thank the Lord Father for my gift and I thank my Family for their encouragement and support.

It's a wonderful day for hearts.
Hearts of warmth
Hearts of friends
Hearts of new found love
Hearts of world acclaim hope
It's a beautiful day for hearts.
What the world desires,
Father Time will sire.
The heart of man
Cannot wish for anything greater
Than the heart of love
From the one you love.

Diana L Oliver

Diana L Oliver
PASTURES OF BEAUTY

Sitting beside the crystal lake,
I find only peace.
I picture myself in a pasture
filled with flowers of all sorts.
Lilies of white, tulips of purple,
and roses of yellow, it all
captures me and lifts me up.
The beautiful scents make it all so
rare and precious.
The sun is brightly shining.
Running, playing, and being
happy with only myself.
Laying in the pasture flirting with
nature, life seems to be so easy.
Returning to reality I realize
life isn't as easy
as being in the pasture.
Knowing this and not forgetting
my dream, the peace and the smile
remain.

Flo Anderson Emery
REAL FRIENDS

Dedicated to all of those that I love.

Real friends are likened to find spun gold,
Difficult to find—so precious to hold.
They have all the costliness and deep value
Of a real pearl cluster,
Needing only a touch of life to give them
More brilliance of luster.

Or better still, compared to the vintage of rare old wine,
They have become sweeter throughout a period of time.
True friends possess none of the fragility
But all the fineness of handsome hand-made lace;
And friendship will endure the long and lonely years,
But friendship isn't found by looking just any place.

Lynne Ellis
MOUNTAIN HOME

"To James," my husband who I love with all my heart for encouraging me to share my poems with others.

We live in the mountains
In a small little town
Where the beauty surrounds us
From the sky to the ground

The air is so clean
And "Oh" so fresh
It is truly a place
For the soul to rest

Esperanza H Escalante
CHRISTMAS

I dedicate this poem, "Christmas," which I wrote a month before my 90th birthday, to you, my grandchildren, that you may ponder and contemplate on why the Birth of an Infant in a lowly manger, glorified by angels, adored by shepherds, paid homage to by kings from afar, about two thousand years ago, is celebrated in Peace and Joy now and maybe forever!

Nineteen hundred years ago,
In Bethlehem, Jerusalem,
Christ, our Savior, was born,
In a manger, that glorious morn.

Heavenly angels in chorus sing
"Glory to God in the Highest,
On earth, Peace, Goodwill to men."
Shepherds adore the New-born King.

A lonely star shining bright to lead
Three Wise Men, Kings from the East,
Wanting to pay Him homage,
To the Holy Infant, bring their gifts.

To this day we still celebrate,
Churches, homes, we decorate,
Christmas tree, candles bright,
Sweet carols, festive tables that delight.

Children, widows, the aged
Receiving gifts, in joy feel cared;
Peoples at war, pause to kill;
It's Christmas, Peace and Goodwill!

Jackie Erwin
FUTURE PRO

With Love, "To husband Ray and grandson Danny," My Inspirations.

Basketball he plays, when it's the season;
Loving the game is his main reason;
He dribbles that ball down the floor;
Making that crowd yell for a score.

In baseball, he stands big and tall;
After said ball goes over the wall;
Many a run, I know he's made;
"In future days" he will be paid.

Football he plays, "he got a cast"
Quarterback position "after he did pass"
My O' My "When he broke his arm"
Both Coach and Mom were in alarm.

He's very smart "his grades are high"
With every girl trying to catch his eye;
As we try to figure it out;
All we do it shout, shout, shout.

As he is watched, by the Scouts;
That come to case the players out;
In whose footsteps will he walk?
When time comes for them to talk.

Hazel Whipple
THANKS BE TO THEE, O LORD.

We are gathered here again
On this Thanksgiving day;
We have so much to thank God for,
Let's bow our heads and pray.

We thank you, Lord, for light of day,
And ears to hear your sounds.
We thank you for the lovely things
In which your earth abounds.

The golden rays of rising sun,
Like fingers from the night
Creep across the morning sky
To steal the stars from sight.

The graceful gliding of a gull
Across a silent bay;
The chirping of the rising birds
To herald this new day.

And as the day wears on, O Lord,
We see the flowers unfold;
All nature comes to life again
Your wonders to behold.

We thank you for the music, Lord,
Of rivers rambling by
The wind carressing leafy boughs
That heave a gentle sigh.

We thank you for the drops of rain
That makes our harvests grow;
And for those winter wonderlands
All blanketed with snow;

The falling blue of distant hills
Against a sunset sky;
The evening of whippoorwills,
The lone coyote, cry.

We thank you, Lord, for all the stars,
Those diamonds of the skys,
Peeking out with shiny eyes
To watch the moon go by.

We thank you for our being here
And allowing us to feel
Your presence here among us
At this Thanksgiving meal.

Lillian Clark
BEYOND TOMORROW

Beyond tomorrow
Who knows the way
Will it be sad
Or will it be gay
Will there be sunshine
Or snow will we find
Beyond tomorrow
Give us a sign.

Beyond tomorrow
Day after today
We cannot change it
Whatever we say
God rules this world
His will we obey
Beyond tomorrow
HE knows the way.

Kerry Claeys
WHY ME?
Why did he come running to me?
I was there, but now he leaves my heart to bleed.

The night was dark with a howling wind,
I was there to help him start over again.

To him life seemed so unimportant,
but to me I realized it is important.

He was scared and sad,
while I too was scared but mad.

Life was hopeless and he wanted out,
When he told me this, I wanted to shout.

"Suicide," he said," is the way to go."
All I could say is, "Please, NO!"

I sat there with tear-filled eyes,
and asked him, "Why do you want to die?"

He responded with,
"No one loves me, they don't even care.
I'm too dumb and stupid to
live a life I can't even bear."

I know it's difficult to live life today,
but why did he have to end it this way?

V Norman Byrd

V Norman Byrd
ONENESS

To all the women who appreciate—but realize—there's more to love . . .

come to me woman
I feel that we need
the touch of your body
the salt of my seed
why do we play games
and toy with our minds
the pulls of our loins
makes the action sublime
be gone with this coy
awaken our lust
you know that you do,
I too—
need it so much

—Oneness

Richard Conti
ENTRAPMENT
There is no escape from what we do not know. There is no escape from the darkness in which we fear. We are blind in what we cannot see. Look and we cannot find. But what we look for is within ourselves. What we look for are the answers to the questions which puzzle us. It is easy to solve the puzzle for within us lies the key. For the key is the desire and within the desire there are dreams of the escape. For though I am only a journeyman trying to know what lies within. To know how to feel. Guide me through the darkness for you are the light that will show me the way to the everlasting journey.

Faith Corey
WRITER'S DILEMMA
I am inspired with passion fired
I feel that write I must;
And that is when I seize my pen,
It's passion pure, not lust.

The world's asleep in slumber deep
While I am wide awake;
My thoughts I've sent on words intent,
For inspiration's sake.

But no words come, my brain is numb
How difficult to word;
What one can feel but can't reveal,
The soul's cry can't be heard.

The clock's tic-toc aloud does mock
My vain attempt to write;
And so I'll stop, I must give up,
I can't compose tonight.

Jane F Campbell
CHOICE

I dedicate my poem to God, who gave me my talent, and to my husband Scott who encourages me to develop it.

Choices are so hard to make
Should I stay or go?
Should I start my ironing
or should I set and sew?

Choices come in every size,
There's big ones and there's small
It doesn't really matter,
I worry about them all.

Choices of what to wear today
or how to fix my hair.
If I should buy a new divan
or just sew up the tear.

Choices of what to cook for breakfast,
lunch and dinner.
I guess it really doesn't matter
I could be a little thinner.

CHOICES:
Why are there always so many?
I guess it could be worse,
What if I hadn't any.

Phyllis Kaye Daigle
A GRANDDAUGHTER'S THOUGHTS

To my Grandparents Robert & Evolyn Bullock of Newcastle, Texas and the Rockin "O" Ranch, the place where they lived for many years.

The Rockin "O" Ranch is far away—In the middle of Texas it stands—I'd like to visit again today—those grassy and mesquite covered lands—I'll always recall those happy days, when my sisters and I would explore, the old back porch and the wooden stairs—And what was hidden behind the door—But best of all were the meals we had when we gathered together to eat. The food was good and the friendship great—The jokes and stories—were hard to beat. I learned many things at that old ranch like love and respect for each other—And I know that I will use those things to grow up and be just like my mother.

Phyllis Kaye Daigle
CALVIN'S THOUGHTS & PRAYERS
Dear Jesus—Our little faces are sad
Today our daddy, he has gone away
Mommie and me and Robert and sis'
We pray to Jesus just like this—
Dear Jesus, we pray that you'll come
into daddy's heart today, and please
Dear Lord come in to stay. Make
him happy and loving each day.
Make
him see that Jesus is the only way
One more thing Dear Jesus I pray—
Please put Mommie and daddy back
together this day, and Thank You
dear God
for the Blessings each day and for my
little sis' that's here to stay.

Florence Daughtry
THE ROAD
The Road to Heaven is made of pure gold
We all have a chance to see it, I've been told.
Our food in Heaven is milk and honey
Children, we don't have to have no money.

Dear God, give me a chance to travel that Road
So I can relieve my back of this heavy load.
My back is bent and feels like it is broken,
You don't need no fare, just your Heavenly token.

Lord give me strength, strengthen me when I am weak,
Help me to have the peace of mind I seek.
My body is weak and I feel so lame,
Lord help me to rid myself of any blame.

We are all God's children, beautiful in every way
No one is no better than any one, I must say.
We all are made by the very same mold,
That is what makes us Sisters and Brothers in Christ Jesus
I've been told.

Katherine Charron
IN JIMMY'S MEMORY
As a child he felt despair, for when he cried no one was there
Now a boy—temper tantrums grew, still no one listened, no one knew
"Here I am, My name is Jimmy, Love me, Hold me even though I'm skinny"
Teen-age days—brought only trouble, Crying louder, help me from grubble
Un-true friends now led the way,
time in jail for many a day
Depressed, un-loved—No path to follow, kept Jimmy inside very hollow
People said, "He's bad to the Core,
Don't let him In if he's at MY door"
Then one day at age 33,
Jimmy's friend said, You come home with me
You can make it if you try, Just believe as each day goes by
Two years later, working hard & working harder, Jimmy felt even smarter
No more drugs, no more drinks, He now believes in what he thinks
Hey, DAD—look at me, See my new Car, Sharp as can be
Then he called, "Hi Good Buddy, Thanks A lot, You've helped me get—All I've got"
"Gotta Run—Gotta ride," Jimmy's smiling now with Pride
Leaving home I think he knew,
"GOD," was near, nothing left for him to do
Failing Brakes, then the Tree,
Jimmy cried "GOD" take care of me
Now in Love, Now in light—Jesus said "He'll be alright"
Giving Love in Many ways,
Jimmy's Memory for-ever
Stays

Katherine Charron
A STAR'S UNIVERSAL LIFE
The universe is for-ever
Infinity they say
Drop into a black hole
And see a new time and day
A mass of energy gathered, then a burst of flare
Giving birth to new stars out there
Then they glitter, then they shine
Keeping the dippers all align
Age makes older, then they fade
Twinkle star-bursts half un-made
Shooting star, right in your sight.
Falling, fading—into the night
Now I wonder, for Scientists claim
This must be—for Earth to gain
Evolution—they call, could it be the name
All in one, or just the same
How I wish upon that star
Knowing "GOD" hears,
whether near or far
So twinkle brightly, for All Worlds to see
Hoping in time, we will know more of thee

Billy W Carmichael
IN MEMORY OF MY GRANDMOTHER

In her yard there are flowers, a big mixture of blooms.
These are plants from her neighbors or friends I presume,
Bordered with rocks, whitewashed with a broom.
The fragrance still lingers, like sweet rare perfume.

There is an old black pot in the corner of her yard;
Where she boiled all her clothes, for cleaning was hard.
In an old rocking chair by the fire, she would rest for a spell,
Many were the stories that she had to tell.

Her style was old-fashioned, as the skillet she used.
Her hem line touched her ankles and covered her shoes.
Her apron was spotless as the bonnet she wore
To cover her hair that was white to the core.

I can still see her walking down that old wagon track;
Her bonnet bobbing with its ruffles in back.
An old woven basket clinging to her arm,
After all of the chores were done on the farm.

So paint me a sunset
Old memory of mine,
Paint it with night's shadowy net,
And a touch of days passing divine.

Mix it with care
And a touch of love.
Mix it with joy one can share,
Of the beautiful Heaven above.

Paint it of mountain tops,
And of all the memories I am keeping;
Paint it of waterfalls that never stop
And most of all, beautiful birds sleeping.

Close the shadows of evening with your best,
As twilight brings to earth peace and rest.
Like a great picture that lives forever, somewhere in a great hall,
I hope that my Grandmother's memory will not be forgotten by all.

Damian Seltzer
SPRING BEACH

I dedicate this to my darling daughter Tiffany, for it was due to our painful separation that I was inspired to find tranquility through writing. I love you and I miss you sugar. Daddy.

How quiet and tame this relaxing place,
It seems to sit and await Summer's embrace

This is a truly great wonder of the Earth,
Contemplate the miracle as a planet gives birth.

After a long, cold, dormant state of repair,
A special magic begins to transform it with care.

The strong gusting winds blow sand here and there,
Shaking off the dust and leaving the grains bare.

Then come the rains to descend upon the scene,
Washing away the dullness leaving it fresh and clean.

The sun begins to radiate a brighter and brighter glow,
The trees begin to blossom and the grasses start to grow.

The birds dip and sway through the crisp, nippy air,
Even a few boats begin to appear.

Now emanating a sparkling show,
Over all the ages, no wonder so many go.

For one to resist a spectacle like this,
Would be comparable to missing a lover's kiss.

One moment soft, tender and sweet,
Until it explodes into a passionate treat.

Damian Seltzer
GRADUATION MEMORIES

This poem is dedicated to my loving fiance, Gena. As timeless as our love and support of one another. Thank you for fulfilling my dreams. Love, Damian.

Parental joy abounds throughout the land,
Young men and women, bewildered they stand.

With blank stares of confusion set on their face,
It allows their minds a reminiscent race.

Back through the many years of one's life,
Such an array of happiness, grief and strife.

How easily they travel throughout the past,
Wishing these memories could last and last.

All those precious moments of stress and fear,
Resolved by hard work, perseverance and those held dear.

The uncertainty and pain of those many, many years,
Slowly washing away by happiness and tears.

Do not mistake this as a sign of gloom,
This phase of putting their life in bloom.

Similar to puppets they stand and to the podium proceed
As they step up to receive their credentials to lead.

With the shake of a hand, a smile and the packet,
They walk to their seats to create a racket.

Together they stand up and cheer this date,
As young men and women go out to meet their fate.

Maddie N HabananRanda
this dark water

You often ask me

watch the fog swirl
whirlpools of ghostly forms
ripples of reflection in a puddle

To say something interesting

age-lined cracks spell laughter
in the dusty Victorian bricks of
this familiar sidewalk

To say something to excite you

the rain washes these
cobblestones
small soft grey mirrors
of a turmoiled sky

To say something that will make you gasp

crushed petals slowly bleeding
last wisps of scent
(try to feel their pain)

In surprise and say, "Really?"

if you look deep enough into
this dark water
you might see heaven and its
wet silver flashes of angels . . .

You often ask me but—
I never know what to say

Ms Birdie M Sanford
THE PASSION THAT AWAITS US

Like a single raindrop
Trickling down from the silent gray sky
Is how you make me feel
As I fall deeper and deeper into your eyes
Falling freely and helplessly
Waiting, but not quite hoping to reach the safety of the end
Your manly scent teases my senses
Tempting and taunting me to give in to your need
With one kiss
One kiss that searches my soul and captures my heart
A kiss that offers love, peace, and understanding
Yet demands nothing in return
You gently caress my skin
As if daring me not to respond
You realize I'm growing weaker
As my body goes limp against yours
I can no longer resist you
My defenses have faded
All that is left is you and I,
And the passion that awaits us.

Rebecca Johnson
THE DAY WAS BRIGHT

The day was bright
The night was long
Then I heard that sad sweet song
The song of the birds
The song of the trees
In that song I saw only you
The touch of your hand
The sound of your voice
That sad sweet sound
That makes me rejoice
The day was bright
The night was long.

alan knackstedt
PALE MOON MORNING

Dedicated with all my love to Mary Ellen, my mother.

Touched by a pale moon morning
Alone in a pale moon way
Bring on the memories
For those with a vision
Lost in the day today

I dreamed of a mountain, in the heart of a city
I dreamed of a lover in vain
I dreamed of the freedom, that passes through darkness
I dreamed of a cold dry rain
As it washes the mountain, down through the gutter
Into the ghetto again
It's there where the dirt lies
Plied in the corner
Right there where the children play

So scream out, curse if you want to
At the birds that watch from high poles
The wall crumbles slowly, so they just fly over
Leave us before the wind blows
And if you listen, real closely
A love song beckons the wind
The end of the rainbow
Walks with you slowly
A step behind, never ahead

Ten Birch Trail backs up a schoolyard
Granny Daly rocks on her porch
Pokes at the schoolboys cutting on through
Scowls at their image of youth
Daddy Daly smiled as he left her
Closed his eyes but his smile remained
He's there with her rocking
Though he hides in the shadow
When it's quiet, they're together again

And me I wait on a hillside
Wondering what price I should pay
The voice that's long left me
I somehow remember, the words I never could say
While Romeo takes her to the station
The silhouette says they're goodbyes
A train stops behind them
But they never notice
'Cause Juliet's starting to cry

Touched by a pale moon morning
She rises to greet me again
Her scent that of an angel
Her call that of sin
Surrounded by the dew, of innocence lost
Her moon paled, but last through the night
An innocent bystander
I only can witness
Hope someday she might . . .

alan knackstedt
PADMAJA

The golden chain
The turquoise earrings . . .
Small treasures laying on her dark skin

Such a wonder
To watch her sleeping . . .
Waiting for large eyes to open again

The she rises
And smiles softly . . .
"I love you," in her voice faint and dim

Outside, she's a woman
Inside, a lover and a friend
As for time, she is eternity
A paradise until the end

Jet black hair
Held so very high . . .
No dark cloud can make her feel low

She is my wife
My entire life . . .
Thank you Lord, she loves me so

alan knackstedt
GYPSY QUEEN

In memory of a great writer, poet, and storyteller, Josephine Wetzler . . . my loving grandmother.

Let's walk to the moon
On a diamond pathway
Let's dance until the sun begins to shine

Gypsy woman beside me
Hold my hand
We'll ride free
While the diamonds play a moonlight melody

Mystic lady paint a dream
It's been so long
These eyes have seen
The candlelight you use to find your way

When I'm weak and small
You make me strong and tall
Remove the night
Bring upon the day

Moonlight melody
For a lost Gypsy queen
Dropping rain upon a childhood memory
Moonlight melody
And a lonely Gypsy queen
Dropping rain upon the smile that shines on me

Now I walk alone
In the shadow of a frown
And no one seems to know what's wrong with me

Gypsy woman I miss you so
When the moon begins to glow
Its four winds sadly call . . .
Josephine

Margaret P Morse
TIME FLIES

To Those for whom time has never stood still.

(Romantic Era) — (1912-1962)

Oft in your garden of memories sweet,
Some soft and sweet fragrance still lingers,
Though time marches on, with quiet-clad feet,
But relentless and fast, on time-ticking fingers.

OR . .

(Computer Age) — (1960-1989
Ad Infinitum)
"Hey, there, 'Chickie baby! Don't you ever, ever, ever, knock,
The po-si-tive pre-ci-sion of the di-gi-tal clock'"

Angela Florio
ACKNOWLEDGEMENT

This poem is dedicated in the memory of my Mother Rose D'Incecco and my Mother-in-Law Theresa Florio.

Mothers are special, loving and kind
Their love's unconditional throughout all of time.
A simple I love you, a hug and a kiss
Fulfills all desires of what they have missed.

But we take them for granted and tend to forget
All the years they have given without regret.
So please do not linger, do not make her wait
For the time may come when it's much too late.

And when that time comes and you're lonely and sad
Your heart's full of pain and you're angry and mad.
When you try to reach out but you're so far apart
Hold on to those memories you've stored in your heart.

Betty Finley
HUGS ARE BETTER

To my great friend, Bob Bailey. For his inspiration of this poem. And to his family: Edith, Kim, Jimbo, Jay-Jay, and Rusty. I dearly love and appreciate you. Your friendship is genuine!

Hugs are better than drugs;
anytime, day or night.
There's no hallucinations to fear;
or any kind of fright.
The devil won't be seen in dreams;
nor demons will clutter your mind.
Your life can be like fields and streams:
a good life of any kind.
There will not be a prison term to serve;
from a bust of crack or cocaine.
If you will give someone a hug;
your life will not be in vain.
So heed this tender warning of mine;
your love can reach the sky.
'Cause hugs are better than drugs;
my friend, you'll both get a better high.

Claire Pedigo Weaver
MY SONNET
The problem is to try to write a verse
of fourteen lines that make
some part of sense.
I had not thought that rhyming was a curse,
But now I find this task to be immense.
The words I choose seem odd and ill-arranged.
The stress falls here, just when it should fall there
My poet's mind is obviously deranged
The touch is nil, the mental cupboard's bare.
All through the night, my tortured brain I wrack
And now the dawn is flaming in the sky
I grab my pen and find I'm on the track
The deed is done, and truly, so am I.
My English poem writ, I paid the price
Now rhyming is not just a curse, it is a vice!

Joseph H Avellone
MORNING NOON AND NIGHT SONNET

To Eilene.

I've breathed the fresh cool air of early morn
and listened to the chirpings of the birds,
I've seen the ushering of a new day born
and marveled at the symphonies I heard.

I've basked beneath a scorching noon-day sun,
and had its radiant warmth race through my veins,
I've seen a serene moon drift out of sight
and felt the mystery of a silent night.

Adrift I have been, engulfed by boundless space,
Yet anchored by the vision of your face.

Nicole Clark
MY FRIEND
I have a problem
My brother can you help me?
I keep letting people get the best of me
For God knows what they are doing is wrong.
I know my brother but you got to keep being strong.
For I prayed & prayed all through the day, but these same people I thought were my friends keep getting in the way.
So now my brother what should I do?
Why don't you pick a friend that is right for you?
I know my brother, but I tried that before I don't think I need a friend anymore. Well my brother if you feel you don't need a friend anymore just remember: God is your friend to the end.

Kent Ford
LOVE AND PEACE

To Joyce, my friend, inspiration, and my sister.

If I am not for myself
Who will be for me?

If I am for my self only,
What am I?

If not now,
WHEN?

Virginia Wilkinson
PHOENIX
Down in Arizona
the town of Phoenix dwells,
It used to be a small one
but Lord how it has swelled.
The Snowbirds have taken over
the town's just not the same,
It's smoggy and it's noisy
and the Snowbirds are to blame.
It used to be a peaceful town
a place one could feel safe in,
Where everyone was friendly
and asked you how you'd been.
Now your neighbor you know not
to be friendly has been forgotten,
The Snowbirds brought their eastern ways
the western ways forgotten.
If only they would go back home
and take their ways back with them,
Then once again our town would be
a paradise to live in!

Deborah Jean Griffin
A SUMMER'S DAY

I wish to dedicate this poem to my parents, Barbara and Gene Griffin, without whom I'd never have known such beauty.

Give me the beauty of a bright Summer's day,
With the singing of birds and the warming sun's rays.
Let me walk through the meadows on my bare, naked feet,
Surround me with daffodils and clover so sweet.
As the soft, gentle breeze tenderly beckons come play,
I thank God for the miracle of a beautiful Summer's day.

Freddi Hamilton
ANATOMY
I know very well the anatomy of a dream.
I've gone searching
For the biochemical but emotional explanations,
And I have found the dream opaque,
Not to be x-ray'd.
As I perform the ultimate operation called life,
I wonder if the dream will
Cause my hands to shake or
My mind to wander.
Maybe that dream,
The one where I'm an octopus,
Is the anatomy of my life.
Reaching still, after all these years,
Grabbing for a multitude of solutions—
In case one works.

Ralph E Martin

Ralph E Martin
CHILD OF WINTER
Child applies tongue to
ice-encrusted fence
fingers blue as veins
eyes hazy as cataracts.
O God, it makes me
flinch to look at face
of bloody tongued kid
like snowman with no fire
to make the lips move.
In naivety of childhood
mouth is solitary in ice
and man's word is squish
of feet in piles of slush
till tied soul to soul
with love.

Ralph E Martin
EL
I board the last train alone.
It smells of a barn
jerks forward, rattles its soul
careens to platform after platform
opens its big mouths, questioning.

It pauses, doors screech shut
and graceless rhino passes shaking
houses hugging the track
with windows that 40-odd years ago
flaunted red banners, "2 Serve."

Reflection in train window of
slack-mouthed man reminds me of
toothless Civil War Vets shuffling
up avenue in NRA parade
in the early thirties.

Lights blink off and on in the car,
wheels spark and swear.
O, say can you see our version
of hairy human beings of long ago
riding the horny-spined dragon?

Donna L Harrison
TONIGHT I SIT HERE THINKING
Tonight I sit here thinking
of your warm and gentle touch.
The nights we spent together,
the fact that I love you so much.

Life has a funny way of turning
what seems will never turn,
Something's always missing;
there's always something to learn.

With you my life has changed;
things have gotten better;
I have everything I need
when we are together.

It's the simple things around
that I like the best
The smell of rain, a rainbow, life
It's so full of zest.

Without you by my side
things don't seem so good
I wish we could be together
I really wish we could.

Soon the distance will be gone
and we'll share love again
Then things will be full of life
We'll be happy again.

Nancy McLaughlin
MY FRIEND
My Friend is handsome
My Friend is lonely and shy
He is kind and willing to listen to me
He is able to console me and aid me in making decisions
My Friend is sincere, but not open
My Friend has sight, but is sightless
He has sense, but is senseless
My Friend is troubled. Running from within.
His eyes once gleamed with fire, now they are glazed with uncertainty.
My Friend does not look at me, but looks away
I wonder why?
He will not touch me except to hug me
Closeness he cannot bear, yet he needs to be close
My Friend lives in the past with old wounds
which have never healed
My Friend tries to do the right thing
His burden in life is not light
He takes care of his mother and does not complain
yet I know if he could grow wings he would take flight
My Friend is steadfast and true, strong and loyal
He worries about the future, but does not know the future is here
My Friend thinks he is getting old and the years are passing quickly,
yet he can no longer seize the moment because moments are fleeting
My friend is special and I want him to know it
He is my best Friend
He is in my heart and I love him
My Friend is YOU!

Ronald K Anderson
BLESSED BE THE CHILDREN
Blessed be the children who carry on.
When they, the founders have all gone.
We are the life, the joy, the pain,
We won't be here to bear the rain.
We'll have to fight; for life, for love,
We must strike out to plant the dove.
We are the ones who'll live in fear,
We are the ones who must leave here.
We'll leave this Earth we know as home,
To venture in space, there we'll roam.
We must win, over all our strife,
We must win, for we are the life.

Karen V Cakerice
MOVING ON
We had a pecan tree once
In San Antonio.
They produce every two years,
So we waited.
But we never ate one;
We moved on.
We were too busy to go to the Festival
Down by the Riverwalk;
So we decided we'd go next year.
But we moved on.
Have you ever been to the South Plains Fair?
"You'll love it," everyone said.
So we went.
And we did.
And we were glad, because we moved on.
Can you imagine the glory
Of Christmas in the Rockies?
Everything was soft, white, supernatural.
We drank it in
Before we moved on.
Tomorrow the movers come.
"Daddy, we never got to see the Dodgers play!"
"You promised!"
"Don't worry, Bobby, I'll take you someplace new."
We're moving on.

Jacquelyn Slavin
LOVE IS
Love is a candlelight dinner
Which is only meant for two, and
Love is couples walking hand and hand
On the beach under the moon.

Love is an ocean
With its high and low tides, and
Love is the stars
That shine in the night.

Love is roses so colorful and bright
As that of a rainbow. Oh, what a sight, and
Love is a new born baby
Held close to its mom.

Love is the music
That soothes the soul, and
Love is letting you know
It's okay to glow.

Love is a flavor of ice cream
That makes you feel warm inside, and
Love is loving someone
As much as they love you.

Gregory A Gallo
YOUTH IS WASTED BY THE YOUNG

Dedicated to WildMan Ryan, you amaze me.

I'm in
I just have to get there
It's done
I just have to find it
It's already been said
I just have to remember
That youth
Is wasted
By the young

Rick Pike
SOCIETY = JOKE
So much to live for
So little to be
A dagger cut to the core
Watch me bleed
Tick, tock, tick, tock
The world fading
I'm laughing
Looking at the greed

The Prisoner of the System
Rick Pike

David O Vogel
SNOWFLAKES
Perfect in form
Each one unique
Snowflakes dance
As children sleep

Cool and crisp
Pristine dressed in white
Snowflakes sparkle
In early dawn light

Shouts of joy
Break the cool winter air
Snowflakes are magic
For those without cares

Snowmen and sledding
Are the words for the day
Snowflakes are toys
To children at play

Too soon they melt
Into puddles of slush
Snowflakes are gone
All sounds are hushed.

Mary Lou Jackson
FLOWER POWER

To my husband, Richard.

It takes lots of water on a flower to win
But only God furnished water to begin.
Lots of sun lifts a garden from flat
And only God can furnish that.
Fertilizer helps heal when a flower is sick
But only God can complete the trick.
A green thumb works on a flower's distress
But only God doesn't have to guess.
Talking to plants shows a faith in a power
'Cause only God can make a flower.

Carole Whitman
FRIENDSHIP
Friendship is something that
is hard to find.
What do you think of when a
friend comes to mind?
Do you think of caring and sharing or
just being there?
Do you think of someone who will
always share,
every feeling, hope, and dream.
However odd it may seem.
I know one thing that is easy to see,
I want to be the friend, you've always
been to me!

Janice L Gish

Janice L Gish
HOLOCAUST

Dedicated to: A world where mankind has almost ruled himself to ruin.

I'm looking out my window today.
Just what is it my eyes really see?
A tangible world?
For who's to say.
Or a beautiful daydream as I'd like things to be?
A sky with clean air?
butterflies flying?
Or really a species that knows it is dying.
Imaginary eyes look at the greenery
gazing about at the earth's fine scenery.

The eagles disappearing from the skies
know I'm just dreaming.
For their instinct is wise.
Open your eyes at reality and look.
the trees are withered and barren.
The wildlife once roaming this land are so few.
Is life as we knew it,
a history book.

Janice L Gish
POETRY

In dedication to Eddie-Lou Cole for her own dedication and hard work as Poetry Editor of World of Poetry.

Rhythm, Rhymes
tasteful lines
That's what poetry
defines.

Thoughts of wonder
Put asunder,
written not
with foolish plunder.

Tender thoughts
minds have sought,
Down on paper
To us brought.

Feeling blue
for something new.
Written thoughts
replenish you.

Janice L Gish
UNSEASONED LOVE
What used to be tears of unwanted wearisome pain
now are less salty and more like rain.

In days past they fell through a clean clear heart
that smog and pollution now take their part, to keep the salt away.

Yes making them untasteful, drab and dull
they washed away the life within this now empty soul.

Laughter holding its place over tears
hiding yesterday's traumas and fears.

Keeping the true self locked in steel.
so hurt, so pain, we will not feel.

Recognizing and thanking you and me
for the ones inside that we used to be.

Let's hear laughter at the taunting
ashes of yesterday's pain
while these unseasoned tears of love
remain.

Janice L Gish
LOVE LOST
Yearning of your heart's desire,
dressing up in wild attire,
thoughts of passion burn with fire,
When will it ever end?

Putting thoughts of love behind,
of holding someone's heart so kind,
hoping someone dear you'll find,
Loveletters to send.

Thinking of your love while young,
where are the songs yesterday sung?
That rusty doorbell hasn't rung.
Broken hearts do mend.

Find someone to hold your heart,
bringing life a brand new start,
don't let one tear you apart,
your happiness, "defend"

You'll never find another one
exactly like the love that's done,
because just like them, there are none
you'll treasure the meaning of friend.

Lura Louise Hanson
SIGNS OF CHRISTMAS
When the snow is on the ground and the ice is on the lake
And there's the tantalizing smell of goodies as they bake,
Mingling with the aroma of the recently cut tree
Which stands beautifully decorated for all to see.
Then the Christmas spirit seems to completely fill the place
With brotherly love feelings and awareness of God's grace
Making you desire to share the laughter, love, and good times
With family and friends as the glad Christmas carol chimes.

Reneé Bizette Keating
GRANDMOTHER
As she sat back in her old rocking chair
With wrinkled face and gray hair
She reflected upon the memories of her life
Both the times of peace and times of strife
Dreamingly reminiscing of the days when she was a child
Remembering how her mother would brush the hair from her brow
Thinking of her brother and the spats that they had
All of the many times they had gotten so mad
Smiling at the memory of her endearing pappy
Whose return home would make her so happy
Sighing as she thought of her wedding day
Yielding a tear as she remembered the day her husband passed away
She had lived a great and joyous life
Despite the times of heartache and strife
Now she had even greater days ahead to come
When her life on this earth would be done
She would return home to her Lord who always stood by her side
Where forever in His arms she would abide
As she took her last breath in that old rocking chair
She had finally come to eternal rest in the Promised Land so fair.

James William Robbins
THE WHIP

To all the dreamers—The real winners.

The sun comes out from behind a cloud
As little children laugh and play aloud
And when night arrives with its darkened sky
Adults relax and heave a sigh

All this happens day after day night after night
It's the battle of a lost fight
People everywhere every day
Try to throw all of their problems away
But the wind catches them and throws them back
As the whip of reality harshly begins to crack

That's the time when dreams are born
That's when the fabric of reality is torn
That's when we are rich not poor
And that's why we work so hard to make our dreams come true
So we can take our grey skies and turn them to a bright shade of blue
So we can crack reality with our own whip
And free ourselves from its hopeless grip

Donna Parris
ONE OF A KIND
Why'd she have to leave me,
why'd she have to go;
How much I truly miss her,
how much she'll never know.

The emptiness I'm feeling,
not filled by any other;
You never find replacements,
for a Loving Mother.

Never was a friend so true,
consistent throughout time;
She was always there for me,
that sweet Mother of mine.

I'd truly give all I have,
or all I hope to be;
Just to have her back again,
or spend an hour with me.

You will never, ever see,
or hope to find another;
The love and laughter from a life,
like from a Loving Mother.

Edna B Hicks
GOD'S BEAUTIFUL BOUQUET

In loving memory of Wayne and Elaine Johnson, infant children of Robert C. and Elwanda Barrett Johnson, Irving, Texas.

God wanted a beautiful bouquet to make brighter the Heaven above
So He sent to earth an angel to pick one from those whom He loved
Only the fairest and loveliest only the pure and the sweet
Were to make up that beautiful bouquet to be laid at the Master's feet

The angel searched the world over for petals so soft and so rare
With fragrance that would last forever and beauty with others to share
Then it saw two darling babies so tiny so precious and sweet
Little Wayne and Elaine were waiting their Heavenly Father to greet

Their earthly lives were ending but their parents would not be alone
For God in His love and goodness had already blessed their home
With the twins secure in its bosom the angel returned to the throne
There was great rejoicing in Heaven for two little souls had come home

Close by the throne was Jesus so tender and loving was He
With outstretched arms He embraced them and there forever they'll be
The Master then spoke to the angel as the lights much brighter did shine
Why search for a more beautiful bouquet these two tiny buds will be fine

Cynthia L Keaulana
PLEASE DEAR LORD

Dedicated to: Humanity . . . with faith, hope & love, it will soon come to be.

In my mind's eye I see him so clear,
So strong and powerful, a God I hold dear.
Many's the time I had doubts and great fear,
Then bowed my head down, felt his presence so near.
It made me forget all my troubles and woe,
As if I was like an innocent doe.
But life is reality as all of us know,
Still some tend to think it's a Hollywood show.
With guns and weapons and crime everywhere,
Bombings and killings, do people care?
I, for one, can certainly share,
My feelings of hurt, confusion, despair.
When will they learn, when will they see
We can all live in peace and tranquility.
So please dear Lord, please help them for me
To make no more wars, that's how it should be.

Will Webb
UPON YOUR TEMPORARY LEAVE OF ABSENCE

To my wife Janet.

These next few days that we'll be apart
Time tears at my heart . . .
A slow, burning anguish lays bleeding, in my soul . . .
I ask God to help me stay in control.
I don't want nothing special just keep me away from the old torment and sweat,
The never ending day . . .
Bad dreams
Sleepless hours . . . night spinning wildly while
I lay alone
Where have you gone?
I love you
  deeply
  fully and I won't
  be satisfied 'til you're
  back here by my side.

Sharon Lee Cook
USED TO BE
The sky was so blue, the grass a green hue,
a beautiful sight to see.
The birds flew so free to their nest in the tree.
We breathed the pure air, the wind blew through our hair.
The clouds fluffy white, we had day and night.

The mountains so high they reached to the sky
And the beaches reached out to the sea.
Too little too late, we sealed our own fate,
We did not take care of God's gift so rare
And everything ceased to be.

Sharon Lee Cook
DOLPHINS
They glide through the water with speed and grace,
Always displaying a smiling face.
They love to be petted and soar about,
And challenge the diver without a doubt.
They circle and frolic and leap into the air,
And play with humans though they should beware.
They rescue the drowning and keep them afloat,
And push them either to shore or a boat.
Between sharks and people they intercede,
And in proving their friendship they succeed.
They chose us for friends, I will never know why,
As we can not be trusted and cause them to die.
But this has to change for save them we must,
For by saving them we will be saving us.

Sharon Lee Cook
SUNSET DOUBLE
Oh, for a ship with sails so white
to sail the sea so wide,
To visit places far and near,
to race the wind and challenge the tide.
To ride the waves that crest so high
and drop down in between,
The wind and rain against our face
as over the rail we lean.
While sea gulls dive on graceful wing
to catch the fish beneath the wave,
And dolphins play and plunge and spring,
While clouds drift gently on their way,
And rainbows brighten up our day.
To sail where pirates sailed of old,
And raised their flags of skull and bone,
And search for caves of pirate gold.
But the only gold we ever find,
Is that in the sunset double.

Daniel M Shuck
A PAINFUL VISION
I was sitting next to a shimmering pond,
Underneath a tree.
When I looked into the water,
To see what I could see.
All I saw was my reflection,
Staring back at me.

Then suddenly, when I looked again,
Much to my surprise.
I saw you looking back at me,
Tears swelling in your eyes.

I reached out to hold your hand,
And asked you what was wrong.
Then ever so slowly you faded away,
And suddenly were gone.

I leaned back against the tree,
And stared into the sky.
I sat there, oh so silently,
And silently I cried.

Ralph Clark
LOVE

To a Special Person, Whom ever she is.

I think I'm in love, I hear some others say,
I want to say that again some day.
Now, you ask, how will you know,
When that feeling is there, it will surely show.

There will be a special person and I will be able to tell,
By the way she makes my heart beat, much faster it will go.
My footsteps won't even touch the ground they'll be so light and, well,
You won't mistake the way I feel,
'cause I'll be all aglow.

I want to have that warm all over feeling,
That comes from her pretty loving smile.
And whenever she is near, my heart and lips will sing,
I'll want to hold her next to me for a long, long while.

She'll have these same warm tingling feelings for me,
We never from each other's side will want to part.
She will also want to share the good and hard times, you see,
We'll both have those special longings, each within our hearts.

Each day will seem so bright, with flowers and a dove,
Each moment will have its own sweet lasting meaning.
We'll both think, no, it will be more secure, our love
We'll never ever want to have the thoughts, of from each other leaving.

Toni Antoine Teixeira
THIS LOVE AFFAIR
As I live in the present,
And not the past;
I thank Father,
I'm free at last.

The fear, worry, and anxiety
All gone;
The peace of mind,
I so for longed.

The joy that lives
Within my heart;
This love Affair,
I shall not part.

He never forsakes me,
Night or day;
He's by my side
All the way.

He sent his son,
So we might have life;
No more pain, guilt, grief,
Or strife.

I thank you Father,
For what you have done;
To know that you gave,
Your only son.

Barbara Seibert
A WEE WISH FROM THE IRISH
"The Ides of March," we hear them say;
Which also is the month of
St. Patrick's Day.
Green green grow the shamrock,
St. Patrick's symbol oh say gay.
The wind blows over the drab hills of hay,
Which will soon green up,
As green as the shamrocks from
Erin's lovely shore;
So the wee folk are not in danger any more.
St. Patrick planted the shamrocks,
According to lore when the wee folks asked "Why?"
"The shamrock well represents the Trinity," was his reply.
So now 'tis March, and Spring, and wearin' the green,
And St. Patrick for so long has not been seen.
Hail to March and honorin' the Irish,
The 17th, in sheen 'tis truly fittin';
"The wearin' of the green."
My wish to you, I be wantin' to say,
Have the very best of St. Patrick's Days! ! !

LaBelle B Pierson
LACK OF COMMUNICATION
Lack of Communication,
A romance falls apart.
Deep Commitments forgotten.
Only a broken heart.

Meeting of States
Deep longings for peace.
If one on one cannot agree
Will this ever be achieved?

Our world is full of hate and greed.
Evil contaminates the good
Lack of Communication prevails—
All is lost—Life is futile.

Annie Haygood Wales
A VISION OF LIGHT

To the beautiful memory of my Daddy, Ralph Laverne Haygood, Sr.

As I dreamed—last night, a vision of light—came floating over my soul—There stood a man with a smile upon his face and his hair was as white as snow! I cried "Daddy, oh Daddy, how I've missed you so!" As I ran to him with open arms—just to get to love him once more—he spoke to me, in a soft, sweet voice—"Please don't cry for me anymore—you see that I'm happy and I'm home for ever more! I'm here with my Jesus and there's no need to cry—for you'll join me some sweet day by-n-by."

"I know you love me and you always will, but when you miss me just send me that sweet smile of yours." "There's no tears in heaven and never will be! We sing and shout up here as we wash Jesus' feet. Then we stroll down the streets that are paved with gold and my mansion is waiting just over the hill. So please take care of your mother for me and I'll be waiting at the pearly gates. Now dry those tears and give me a smile"— "For we'll meet here in heaven by-n-by!"

Annie Haygood Wales
RHEA

This is dedicated to Rhea, Who will always be my baby girl.

Rhea, the love of my life.
Soon she'll be wed and become a wife.
Still a child in my mind,
and always so kind.
Rhea, the love of my life.
I remember oh so well, the first day, you I held.
A new life for me you gave.
Rhea please don't go away!
I love you oh so much!
I remember the touch of your little hands,
and around your wrist, you wore a little band.
Rhea, please hold my hand.
Rhea, the love of my life.
now a mother of a girl and as pretty as a pearl.
I hope she gives to you, what you gave to me,
such pretty memories.
Rhea, the love of my life.
A beautiful girl, who loves the world.
Yes, Rhea, you were my baby girl.
The love of my life,
The joy of my world.

Barbara Lynn Cox
TILLIE'S SNAPDRAGONS
Sunrise. Golden embers burst forth,
falling ever so gently—to kiss the
cheeks of her snapdragons.
Upon their heads dew drops glisten
as honey in a comb—their shining
coats of armor preparing them for war.
Brave toy soldiers in a row,
ever keeping watch—of those they
wish to conquer beyond the garden wall.
Protectors of the garden, secure
their gentle flock—these mighty men of valour
await the battle call.
One by one the trumpets sound as
round the wall
they march—as with "Joshua's battle of Jericho,"
likewise they take their lot.
Victory has become them, they breathe
the breath of peace—until
tomorrow's sunrise
when the battle call repeats.
Tillie's gone now, but
oh so much alive—the memory of
her snapdragons
and the fantasy of a child.

Melissa Dubrow
CLOUDS
Clouds are
Fluffy pillows
For you to sleep on.

A dreamer's dream
which only a
cloud can tell.

When you wake
The clouds are gone,
'Til the next night
When you can dream on.

June Snyder-Torre
YESTERDAY AT BAYSHORE

Dedicated to three good friends: Ramona Arnold, Maxine Hallman & Nancy Perkins, who encouraged me every step of the way.

Yesterday at Bayshore
sitting on the warm, white sand
I remember the glorious summer days
when my son was only ten.

Sea gulls circled overhead
on strong and graceful wings
and I thought of our lazy summers
on the sand at Bayshore—
remembering.

Remembering those golden summer days
when we raced along the beach
running to the cries of the sea gulls
the sand hot beneath our feet.

Yesterday at Bayshore
the sun was glistening on the water
and I could almost see his face,
could almost hear his laughter.

For my son there'll be no tomorrows,
there are only yesterdays
but the memories bring me no sorrow
when I remember, those shining summer days.

June Snyder-Torre

FLOWERS FOR HIS MOM

Dedicated to the memory of my son, William Douglas Hamer.

Hundreds of flowers, he laid at my feet
on my birthday a long time ago,
there were roses, gardenias, dahlias and more,
it was truly a sight to behold.

For blocks around not a flower in sight
the neighbors' gardens stripped bare,
for he and his friend in the dark of the night
had picked all the blossoms there.

With loving hands he arranged them
all across the living room floor,
selecting by size and by color
for the mother he adored.

I came home from a date that evening,
Bill greeted me at the door,
and there in great profusion
lay the flowers on the floor.

With patience he had placed them,
he placed them one by one,
to spell out the words "I love you,
happy birthday Mom from your son."

Julie Gillaume

MY SPECIAL PLACE

There is a special place,
that I like to be.
No one else goes there,
but me, myself, and I.
I go there many times when bored,
but sometimes not at all when occupied.
It's really neat, and very quiet,
but sometimes it may not be.
This place is all mine,
No one else knows where it is,
and they never will.
Only because it's my dream land,
that is within my mind.

James Vincent Palmer

PLAYTIME

Oh, to sail away
through a night
across a plane or day
Take what's been given so far
make it real, a shining star.
forget not but contemplate
set not aside but rearrange
ghosts and clouds and slower things
that sag the sails that make your wings . . .
In through the door they all will fly
come to play, no more to hide
love and joy and cheery eyes
Sail on now the road is wide, wide, wide.
and when the roads are no longer paved
fields and shores and farther things
the carnival within the mind
seeks the grounds to come alive
Light from eyes many miles away
touch all of those who see & gaze
dreams and guests, some not some made
contact made one fine, fine day.

James Vincent Palmer

CANDIED GLIMPSE

Sen-sible
free once more
and, you know
it doesn't matter which way
you go—
as long as it is right.
in to it
of all it
make a fit
to grow and learn more
from all it
not quite commitment, but just as tight.
adore and see
love truly
touch to please
all things that are spoken are what should be
and a kiss from a smile is so fine.

Vincent J Marino

LIFE IS FUN

Don't drink the water.
Don't breathe the air.
Can't eat the apples.
Poison's found in there.
Meat is partly chemical
and radon's in the soil.
If you walk along the beach,
you might slip on some oil.
Human waste and needles
get washed up on the shore,
So it might be safe to say,
"Don't eat the fish anymore."
Keep these thoughts with drugs and AIDS,
embedded in your brain,
And don't forget to stay inside
there's acid in the rain.
You might think by reading this
our lives are on the skids,
Think a little harder
about what we've left our kids.

Vincent J Marino

THE WATER DEPARTMENT

We will turn off
All the water
On your thirsty
Son or daughter
You think we won't
We know we will
If you don't pay
Your water bill
On any day
At any hour
We'll close the valve
We have the power
We set the price
And make it high
If you don't pay
From thirst you'll die
We just don't care
It's water we sell
If the price is steep
Go dig a well

Robert E Matthews

PEACE—1990

Atlantis streaks like a speck of light
Round our planet day and night;
To leave a spy ship in the sky,
That will help keep peace by and by.

Ortega lets an election stand
That topples him from office grand,
And gives the reason for such release,
"It's really for the cause of peace."

Mandela home from prison free
Presents himself so all may see,
That his great mission will never cease
To bind his nation in bonds of peace.

Gorbachev and Bush continue friends
In ways that clearly a message sends
To all the world, that in our day
Peace will soon be here to stay.

Some may say, "It's all by chance,"
And others call it, "Human stance";
But remains the possibility,
The work of God through eternity.

Robert E Matthews

HOW GOD GREW

I once thought God a kindly king,
with soft white bearded chin,
And round him towering angels stood, each with shiny wings;
One sat writing in a book our bad thoughts and our sin,
Marshal music shook the stars—a choir stands up and sings.

Then came a day I couldn't hold this beatific view,
Deep within I somehow knew that God was all in all;
He came down from his golden throne, and lost his retinue,
To be a part of our good earth, to love the great and small.

Each day it thrills my soul to see the wonders he performs:
The bursting buds, the newborn babes, the nuclear clouds on high,
But most of all the many lives the Son he sent transforms,
And sets them free from mundane ties and fits them for the sky.

And now I know that God is near,
and every process steers,
To work his will in everything, his harmony to bring,
That all mankind may rid itself of selfishness and fears;
So peace can spread throughout the world, and sounds of freedom ring.

Assured that God is immanent, his power never spent,
I can with life's flow be content, and ready now to start
The endless trek that leads afar, and gives us but a hint
That time and space are cosmic sounds, the beating of God's heart.

Wilfred Vanover

MY GREATEST FEAR

These things I fear:
The unseen terrors of a storm-lashed night,
And unknown noises which I sometimes hear;
I fear to fall, to plunge from a great height,
Or to burn in flames which char and sear.
I fear that I might be misunderstood
When I attempt to do some noble deed
Although my actions be inspired by good,
And I might be accused of pride or greed.
I fear the storm waves of the ocean deep,
And thunderstorm's bright forked tongues of light;
I loath to see a spider creep
And shrink from thoughts of poisonous serpent's bite.
These are the things I fear, but most of all
I fear one thing which always lingers near
And threatens me each day with my downfall:
My greatest fear is of unconquered fear.

Wilfred Vanover

STAR OF PROMISE

When I behold my meager victory,
Unwanted, without worth and valueless,
I seek but cannot find new challenges
Upon the earth, so I must go.
New frontiers come to view before my eyes,
And one is curtained, hidden from our sight.
This challenge I must overcome and find
What is of value in that dreaded realm.

Weep not for me, my loved ones, for you know
That my desires were never for this age
But for somewhere beyond where we now stand.
I tell you, do not mourn, for though I go
Look for this sign to know that all is well:
When you behold a star which brightly shines
In the eastern sky, the mansions shall await;
Trust me, and we shall meet in Paradise.

Ilse Morris
IN THE POULTRY YARD
When I was fifteen years of age
And nothing knew of life,
There started in the poultry yard
What I thought was a strife.

The rooster crowed and flapped his wings
And chased the hens around.
They panicked and they cackled loud,
Escape could not be found.

The cock selected one big hen
And stopped her on the run,
Then did to her what every cock
Does to a hen for fun.

I asked my father to explain,
But looking for evasion
He said, "Grow up, in some years' time
I'll give an explanation."

So many years have since gone by.
The answer he not gave.
Conveniently he forgot
And took it to his grave.

Ilse Morris
SKUNK AND FOX
A skunk, contented and alone,
Was slowly walking by.
He caught a cricket here and there.
Its tail was lifted high.

A fox who never saw a skunk
Came to investigate.
Yet going too near from behind
Was his unpleasant fate.

The skunk jets out its foul air
In fox's face, quite straight.
The fox starts quickly to retreat.
By then it was too late.

Remember, when you meet with people
Resist curiosity.
Keep distance and do not intrude
Into their privacy.

Charles Weinacker
NEW ORLEANS
I came to dance in your street
To roam the French Quarter . . .
To see the Mississippi moving at your feet.

I see the sun dance on your lake so wide . . .
Those landmarks like tombs that remain topside.

Parishes that section this beautiful town . . .
A label of sin that attracts many from miles around.

French tradition deep in your soul . . .
So proud of jazz served with famous Cajun creole.

Artist sketching many a scene . . .
Leading me down Canal, Bourbon, and St. Charles to my home . . .
Home to old sweet New Orleans.

Charles Weinacker
OL' MOBILE
Have you ever been to buoy seventeen . . .
sailed on Mobile Bay . . . it's really quite a scene.
I've cast a net from Fairhope pier . . .
sat on Dauphin Isle listening to the Gulf so near.
There's a dogwood trail from Belle Fontaine to ol' Mobile . . .
when the azaleas begin to bloom, the oysters begin to peel.
She's guarded on the coasts by forts of old . . .
bearing the bones of the brave and the bold.
Cannon fire once filled the air,
with the Admiral's sights on Bienville Square.
Government Street remains the same . . .
damned old cannon bearing every prankster's name.
She harbors ships and to Mardi Gras she claims fame . . .
If you return in the year 2000, this damned ol' City will still be the same.

Teri Joyce
WITHOUT YOU
Without you my life will be a mess,
And my heart is calling a cry of distress.
When I was with you my life was complete
But now without you. Life isn't sweet.
I remember the times we spent together,
wishing they would last forever.
Now that those days are gone,
I guess my dreams were proven wrong.

Teri Joyce
TO MY NANA
To my Nana I want to say
I think of you in a special way
All the times we spent together
I'll remember you forever and ever.

I recall all the great dishes you could cook
And how you knew every library book
I'll always think of my many visits and talks
You were so active and liked to take walks.

So remember me forever as heaven will do
And I'll say it over again that "I love you"

Linda Joyce Russo
BABY BLUES
Inside—torment and pain
realizing nothing will ever be the same;
Outside—thunder and rain
dark clouds that just won't go away.
The past is gone.
Everything is wrong and
It's hard to be strong
to see past the tears,
the worries, the fears . . .
Love comes from within
I still love, but I cry.
A part of me has died.
A baby is born to fill our gaps, our needs—
But all I do now is
disagree, yell and scream.
Trying to forget about expectations,
to accomplish each day in a positive way.
First I must see this conflict thru,
put an end to these Baby Blues
and start a whole life anew.

Linda Joyce Russo
TO SEIZE THE DAWN
Inside every person
there lives a spirit
A candle burning bright
Another side unseen
Yet within there's a hint of light
The possibility of a dream
Soaring iridescent skies
Brushing the air with golden wings
Once past start
flying becomes an easy art
But to begin—
Now there's the trick.
If a candle burns too close to the wick
the flame will die unnoticed.
To bring a wish to reality
something must be lost
the fear of failure
the fear of success.

James Michael Bruno
SLEEPING BEAUTY
Swirling softness in shades of ebony
framed her eyes so deep,
a joyous smile to last for eternity and
tears she'll never weep.
Threads of gold lay 'round her neck,
the apparel she wore sublime.
The flowers she held her beauty wrecked.
There was none to match in time.
Her hands were crossed in graceful
symmetry, their tone a pallid white.
My love was great for her sleeping
beauty even though she slept both
day and night.

James Michael Bruno
OH, YOU MARVELOUS MACHINE
You sing and play and speak to me
the myriad of voices that you have been.
Ten thousand screaming hearts
hurled against a wall of sound.
A concert in a distant ballroom from
your speakers did resound.
Emanating from your tendrils are
waves of air that bounce and bound,
around the room in my apartment
until at last in their department my
delighted senses they have found.
You serve me in my celebrating,
keeping guest in festive mood, filling
their heads with the sounds of music
that rush their hearts as they feel good.
You're with me in my quiet moments,
fighting the silence that crowds my room.
When I'm alone the sounds console
me like a friend to dispel the gloom.
So my praises I am writing to the
machine I'm sure you know,
for this poem is dedicated to my
friendly stereo.

Christine Orange
STOLEN MOMENTS

To Dale, my husband, and my friend.

All around us,
Things are changing
Forgotten memories
We once knew.

Schedules, deadlines,
Fleeting glances.
Not much time
For me and you.

No more cuddles,
Stolen kisses.
Working hard
To make ends meet.

Time spent together,
Much more precious.
Stolen moments,
Are much more sweet.

Christine Orange
TOGETHER FOREVER
Endless, timeless, waves of love,
Filling up their souls.
Relieving them of all their doubts.
Their love makes them whole.

Years go by so suddenly.
Soon they will grow old.
Watching as their hair turns white,
And their memories grow cold.

Nodding off before it's dark.
Sleeping way too late.
Moving slower all the time,
It's hard to concentrate.

Aching in their bodies,
Every time it rains.
Fingers laced in claw-like grasps.
Holding hands brings pain.

One moves on to the other world.
One left behind to weep.
Agreement made, the other too,
Will sleep that final sleep.

We don't understand their reasons.
The why, the when, the how.
All that matters anyway,
Is they're together now.

Helen Frena

Helen Frena
BELL
Ring loud and clear bell
Toll loud and clear bell—
Then everybody knows,
And that is how it goes.
Reason to mention,
Now is the intention
Hurry the best is due,
And everything is new
Make my sound bell
For all to tell.

R B S
FELINE DOMESTICUS

With gratitude and awe to Dr. Stotler and our cats, Pebbles and Pie.

I have looked down from high
places you've never thought
of and eaten a bird, feathers all
I have watched and waited for a
million years with incessant
patience more than most doctors see
I have gathered all instincts and the
knowledge of my species
albeit and have given it freely
I have made relaxation occupation
and have given new meaning to
gracefulness what a serious art 'tis . . .

R B S
ABEL SEVEN BAKER
She's got vector ears and a tail you see
and she cuddles up to all but me
She's a fur ball at times, under the sun and she's a lioness, under the gun
She's knows how to scramble, hard-boiled eggs and can bake a soufflé in seven days

She can break a space through a brick wall and can do double nickles making an eyeball

She learned how to dance at the disco and she learned how to turn at the rodeo
She's adventure one and beventure two and she's met the Vicar of Catmandu

She leaps tall buildings with a single bound
She falls on her feet no matter who's around
She can see in the dark and even up-side-down
She's a lover under cover Abel Seven Baker found.

Anthony John Ciccariello III
FADED GOLD

To all those who played the music of our lives, may we keep memories of them always.

He's sitting down for dinner, thinks forty-eight is hard to hang.
His mind goes back two decades to when he was music's biggest thing.
They used to call him "Big Man" but that's before he got old.
You'll find his records all on sale in the section titled "Faded Gold."
Now at fifty-four he looks at his woman who's thirty-five. He met her backstage the last time he ever played live.
She used to call him "lover," she called him "baby," we're going back in time some years.
These days he's grown more mellow and she just calls him "daddy dear."
Passed away at sixty-one, it happened in his sleep.
News showed some concert footage for failing memories to keep.
An eight line obituary which never said if he was good. Did say he was never number one but he hit two when he could.
Ten years later a kid finds one of his olds discs in a store.
Takes it home and really likes it so he goes and buys some more.
Soon the whole country revives his music, his praises they are told.
He missed his own revival but they still love old "Faded Gold."

Anthony John Ciccariello III
THE AMAZING DOCTOR VIDEO SHOW: (PART ONE; THE VIEWER)
Six weeks ago I woke up early on a sunny Saturday morning.
I looked inside the living room my son was watching T.V. again.
Decided to sit down and join my boy to see the cause of his joy.
That's when I began to realize the horror of this video toy.
On the screen there was a man dressed as a funny clown
and though his face had a painted smile his words just made me frown.
He spoke of hate and anger and he danced a mean little jig.
He sang this song and told us viewers how we were going to make him big.
He sang, "It's the Amazing Doctor Video Show, come here, kiddies, it's time for us to play."
"It's the Amazing Doctor Video Show, come now kiddies it's time to go away."
He talked about how everyone in all governments were wrong.
And how some people on this earth, they just don't belong.
Oh, I wanted to turn off my mind but I really was quite surprised.
Though I hated everything he was saying I found I was mesmerized.
Subliminal seduction, mass destruction of the brain cells from the screen.
At first you might detest him but you will learn to love his scene.
Now my son and I can't wait just to see his show.
I hope one day you'll be "Videoized" or else you have to go.
"It's the Amazing Doctor Video Show, come here kiddies it's time for us to play."
It's the Amazing Doctor Video Show, come here kiddies it's time to go away, today, far, far, away.

Dennis Milton Bailey
LAST OF THE DRUM MAJORS

To the dreamers of today and tomorrow.

His name was King for I knew him well, he marched to save his people from hell, he marched with gallantry for he was supreme,
he was soon to create the impossible dream, his words were his
weapons in which he used to fight, for he was shot and killed one April night, it seemed at that all else stopped as he waved good bye from the mountaintop.
For many who witnessed may never understand one man's vision of the promised land.
He was our king, he was a savior, he was Dr. Martin Luther King, Jr. last of the drum majors.

Dennis Milton Bailey
ON THE WINGS OF FAITH

This poem is dedicated to Pam, my forever friend.

For it's on your wings that I will fly, as far as the winds shall carry my cry,
From the tears of those yet to be born, to the ears of the Father who must carry on.
For in the mist of my journey I will thread any needle, for on the wings of faith I will fear no evil.

Elsie L Elder
HOME AND MOTHER

This poem is dedicated to my mother, Lillie Siders.

It matters not where e'er I roam
From one land to another.
Time never can erase that view
My childhood and mother.

Each Sunday morn to church we went
And sang the good old hymns.
And asked the Lord to bless us,
And forgive us of our sins.

She guided me both night and day
With steady hand so true.
But God saw fit to call her home,
To the land beyond the blue.

Although I wander far away
From one place to another.
I still see that home of mine
And the smiling face of mother.

Elsie L Elder
FRIENDLY BLESSINGS

Dedicated to James Hemlinger, with love.

Dear friend to me you've been so good,
A friend I hope you'll always be.
But I wonder if you've understood,
How much your friendship means to me.

The inspiration that you give,
As on life's way I plod.
Cheers me up and helps me live,
Not so far away from God.

When e'er a smile lights up your face,
It drives away the dreary gloom.
It seems that in a lonely place,
A rose has just burst into bloom.

But there's a sadness in my heart,
That seems a very heavy load.
I know someday we must part,
Somewhere at a fork in the road.

I want you to know when at last we part,
Where e'er you choose to go or be.
You'll always be within my heart,
And your face a silhouette in my memory.

Robin M Zechman
FEELINGS

Dedicated to Paul.

Something is happening that is not right,
I feel like we're drifting apart.
It seems to be tearing me up inside,
Because I love you with all my heart.
We really need to sit and talk,
To discuss what is going wrong.
We must compromise and meet halfway,
To be sure that our love stays strong.
I feel like I'm being neglected,
I feel that you really don't care.
I want what we had in the beginning,
I want us to touch . . . to love . . . to share.
We have to work our problems out,
Because our lives have just begun.
I don't want to lose this love,
We must begin again . . . as one.
Please, my love, let's talk this out,
These words came from my heart.
I love you dearly so very much,
Let's try to make a new start.

Robin M Zechman
TOGETHERNESS

Dedicated to my husband, Paul.

When we are together,
It means the world to me.
We are suited for each other,
In perfect harmony.
When I'm with you, I feel so free,
You set my heart on fire.
I've never felt this way before,
You are my one desire.
You're thoughtful and considerate,
Very honest and direct.
I cherish the time I spend with you,
You treat me with respect.
I long to be close to you,
To see your sweet smile.
To share our thoughts and laughter,
You are so much my style.
You are so daring and very brave,
You're adventurous and carefree.
You're not afraid to take a risk,
'Cause you sure took one with me.

Ken Jackson
WELFARE
The welfare line is getting longer
Stench in the air is getting stronger
City bigwigs getting wronger

I am just a sane man
Right behind the Mexican
Waiting for a Caddilac
I am just a maniac
Want to be a holy roller
Don't want to get any older
People say that I'm a bum
Toking auditorium

Really I'm a billionaire
So maybe I got curly hair
So I don't got any class
So I can't keep off the grass
Maybe I can't buy you wigs
Or 'spensive stuff for any pigs
Well I got me my own pride
Let me say that ain't no lie

Evelyne S Reed
MY FLAG
I know that I will never see
A flag that means as much to me.
I chose it over all the rest;
Because I knew I'd love it best.
I've loved it since my tender years;
But then my eyes o'erflowed with tears.
I hung my head, in hurt and shame,
'Cause our dear flag was set aflame-
Defiled, defenseless and dismayed
And thankless for the price it paid.
From the ashes it will arise;
To once again adorn the skies.
Look! It's flying now, brave and proud,
And waving to a cheering crowd.
God bless our banner, oh so grand,
Bestowed by grace upon our land.
I know that there will never be
A flag that means as much to me.

E H Holliger
THESPINA
Tresses of black silk draped
neatly in place

Heavenly soft skin smoothed
over her face

Elegant lashes so long
and serene

Surrounding the brightest eyes
one ever has seen.

Promising pink lips form
smiles of love

Increased in their warmth
by teeth white as a dove.

Never has God's work
been quite so divine

And the miracle to fathom
is this woman is mine.

Elsie Walush
THANKSGIVING
Thanksgiving dinner is a gourmet's treat—
Everything's so good, we just eat and eat,
But we sometimes forget that the day's for expressing
Thanks for every God-given blessing:
For the food on our tables, the clothes that we wear,
Our jobs, our homes, the love that we bear
For parents, spouses, children, and friends—
And the strength to shoulder burdens He sends:
Let every day be a day of Thanksgiving—
A gift from God for more worthwhile living!

Lois M Raudebaugh
THE MEASURE OF LOVE
From the indigo, of the midnight blue.
To the hue of a golden dawn.
From the angry roar of a restless sea.
To the calm of a sleepy yawn.
From the fury wrought in a hurricane.
To the flutter of a sail.
From the noisy din of a city street.
To a coyote's plaintive wail.
From the fiery depth of Satan's lair.
To the golden gates above.
From before all time to past the end.
Is the measure of true love.

Kimberly D Estes

Kimberly D Estes
IRONY
I sauntered along the railroad tracks
With a mighty air of despair.
I was thinking they greatly resembled my life
As they continued monotonously forever,
When I dared to take another step
And discovered none were there.

Pierrette Gagnon
BUYING FALSE HOPE
On a rainy afternoon, Jenny looks out the window feeling lonely and depressed
Hopelessly looking for something to do to appease her restlessness
Then the idea comes to visit a psychic to see what the future would hold
She sets out on her journey with a lifted spirit and a heart full of hope
She sits silently in this small eery room drinking her tea
Her thoughts wander upon the seven clouds, being the queen of her revery
In a God like manner, the psychic unveils the mysteries of her life
Describing the special man she will meet, the colour of his hair and eyes
That it will be good, they will marry and have children
Her emotions rose so high that she could no longer listen
She walks out of the room struggling to regain her mental control
As the years go by, she finds herself alone and not as she was told
She returns to the psychic to see what he had to say
He smiles when he sees her and assures her that she is very lucky
Not to have married for they would have divorced in a year
That there is a better man for her, not to lose hope and not to fear
She runs out the door as the anger bursts within her soul
And realizes that all she is doing is 'buying false hope'

George R Proudfoot III
TEENAGE SUICIDE
You try to make your mark on society.
But the system's so thick you just can't see.
The thought of failure thrashes you inside.
You scream at life, you want to die.
You take the plunge without a second thought.
You've killed yourself and stopped your heart.
Now you're gone and the system rolls on.
It ate you up and now you're gone
You thought you won but really you lost.
Your problems are gone, but your life was the cost.

Thomas John Mandulak (Age 11)
MY CAT
I have a cat.
Who's big and fat.
She's so black
I think she's a bat.
She runs down the hall
And squeaks like a rat.
She reminds me
Of a big fat brat.
She hides under the covers
Like a sneaky Gnat.
When she's quiet we know
Exactly where she's at
Sleeping on her fur mat
She flies through the air
And lands with a splat
That's my crazy black cat.

Tracy Sheffy-McGoyne
FROM NOTHING WE BEGAN . . .
From nothing we began . . .
till love's magic pierced our hearts

Through fierce storms . . .
intertwined to never part

Two souls mingle and dance . . .
seeking refuge from their past

Nestling in each other's bosom . . .
security found at last

Mysteries lie still untold . . .
no longer is love bought and sold
Instead she is cherished . . .
more precious than gold,
finer than silk, and
there for us to hold

She is real, not fantasy . . .
better than any dream

She is is you . . .
She is in me . . .

Together for Always

Naomi Zastrow
TOMORROW'S DREAM
We all have hopes
We all have dreams
That's how we cope
With life it seems

When disappointment comes our way
A hope is lost, a dream is gone
Yesterday's past, it's now today
Time to sing a brand-new song

Karen Y Thompson Turner
DADDY'S WISH

Dedicated With Love to you, Mom & Aunt Kathleen For You Know 'Harder The Rain-Brighter The Rainbow'; My Sister Pam, Daddy Was Very Special To Us, And Especially My Wonderful Husband Wallace, You Reflect I Cor. 13:13

"Give me flowers
While I'm living,
The roses
Will have no smell
For me
When I've gone away . . ."

These are words
I remember hearing
My daddy say.

Daddy's gone from here now,
He's waiting
For us
On the other side,
And
I'm sure
We'll find him
In the Master's garden
Next to the mansion
Where he abides . . .

Thelma Burger
N'EVER
Never offer an apology;
I'm not accepting.
Never ask for forgiveness;
I'm not giving.
Don't tell me stories;
For I am not listening.
Don't ask for an answer;
There just isn't one.
Don't ever tell me what friends are;
I don't think you really know.
Don't ever ask me what an enemy is;
For I am looking your way.

Rick E Kasper
FREEDOM'S FRIEND
Alone she stands on empty river shore,
Tall and gray, her torch held to the sky.
I've seen her there like servant at a door
Welcoming all who would to bosom fly.
She stands for all that's bright and brave and free.
The masthead of democracy and all
This land should have been and yet can be
If we can only rise from latest fall.
The city crowds around her stony feet;
Concrete fingers choke freedom's loving breast,
While smog and soot chase air that once was sweet,
And men settle for less than what is best.
Miss Liberty, I marvel at your face
That you don't cry while looking at this place.

Harriet Swisher
ALONE, YET NOT ALONE
I walked today among the soughing pines, alone,
Yet not alone.
For you are ever near.

I felt the droplets of the foggy day, fall softly,
Scare dampening my cheek.
Perhaps it was a tear.

The path led near the quiet stream, at first,
Where thoughts ran silently and deep.
And life seemed tranquil there and without fear.

And then the path grew steep, and slippery
And the struggle more than I could bear.
And I cried out for aid.

The cataract o'er-came me with its might, splashing,
Crashing around my frail self.
And I was much afraid.

But then a greater voice said, Peace, be still;
I will not leave you here alone, my child.
And I knew then my pact with God was made.

Again I turned and walked the fern-lined path, alone,
Yet not alone.
For He is ever near.

Elsa B Cromer
RAINDROPS AND TEARS
Raindrops and tears, teardrops and rain,
So vastly different yet somehow the same.
In all of our lives each plays its own part—
One cleanses our world, the other our heart.

Just pause for a bit and reflect on a time
When our streets and our buildings were covered with grime—

The heavens opened, and down came the rain
Washing all the ugliness into the drain.

Now recall an occasion when sorrow and grief
Laid siege to our hearts, with no signs of relief—
Then came the teardrops, and just like the rain
They washed away all of the sadness and pain.

The sun broke through clouds and made the world brighter;
A smile lit our faces and made our hearts lighter—
Raindrops and tears, teardrops and rain,
So vastly different, yet somehow the same.

Debbie Purcell
INERTIA
I could get up today,
But I can't get the hang of this me.
Am I now too old to play?
After all, I'm forty-three!

Seems my arms won't raise
As high as my head.
With my eyes all aglaze,
I crawl back to bed.

I really must get dressed!
It's my birthday and I'm forty-three.
But I haven't energy or zest
Even after this third cup of coffee!

My mind awakes!
I stretch and yawn.
I'll forget about my pains and aches.
I can see the beauty of the dawn.

Now I have nothing to fear!
I'm fast becoming alert.
This will be a great year.
I'm no longer INERT!

Noralys Rebimbas
A YEARNING SPARKLE
I lay here on the beach with splashing waves. My heart is empty and my soul is lonely. The sand is sparkling every time I spray water on it. I wish someone would spray me with a little love so that my heart could sparkle in the light. As I look around, I see that the sand has footprints. My life is also filled with prints. Prints and ideas and dreams that go back and forth in my mind like the waves of the sea. They all seem to be alike but not one of them is same. They all have their own unique identity just like the footprints on the sand. They are not the same because the wind has moved the sand very slowly and people have walked on those old prints. I guess nothing in life stays the same. Everything changes for the better or for the worse. Yet my heart same as always has been yearning for a bit of sparkle, and my mind makes up small dreams of how it would be if my heart could sparkle for just one day.

Terri Pawlik
ARE THERE ANIMALS IN HEAVEN?
When I was just a little girl,
'bout the age of six or seven,
I often used to wonder;
'Are there animals in heaven?'
When Jesus was a little boy,
I'll bet He had a pet or two.
But after Jesus went to heaven,
did He make a heavenly zoo?
I've had a lot of pets, myself;
maybe even a couple of dozen.
I want to think I'll see them again.
But, are there animals in heaven?
When I die, if I go to heaven,
I hope I see all my pets again.
Oh, wouldn't that be wonderful!
I could hug and squeeze, and play with them.
As days go by, I keep getting older;
I'm nearing fifty-seven.
But I'll always have that question;
Are there animals in heaven?
I think there are!

Dana C Copiskey
MY CHILD
Of all who have known me,
whether child or adult;
Few of them truly,
have cared what I've felt.
But you are the exception,
for within you I sense;
A deep trust and confidence,
which only true love presents.
So many have tried,
to find the key to my heart;
Perhaps if they'd asked you,
they'd have known where to start.

Bonnie B Berryman

Bonnie B Berryman
PEARLS OF HAPPINESS

To Joe L. Berryman my loving husband.

Hide each golden moment in your memory somewhere
Nourish it and keep it until it glows and glistens there.
Then add it to your Golden chain of pearly beads of white.
It will be to days of life constant encouragement and
to the darkest night a guiding light.
Forget the sadness, sorrow and the hurts that seem to slow your heart.
Think of your lovely pearls, Gladness will bloom you've done your part.
Think of the true, the just, the pure, the beautiful and the great.
Happiness will surround you, and you will open God's Heavenly Gate.

Lillian G Abrams
QUESTION #1
The same refrain I do hear
From my accountant year after year
Complimenting me again and again
On my tax data presentation,
And rating me #1
Of all his individual clients.

I am pleased to know I am #1
And how well my tax data I have done,
But, dear accountant, tell me why
I am not #1 with the IRS
And have to pay them so so much
Instead of paying them much much less?

Patricia Z Kijek
OUR NATION'S POLARIZATION
Our adversarial attitudes are very carefully taught,
From birth to marriage-divorce, to death, they're bought.
The Ku Klux Klan racists are fighting against civil rights.
All the feminists hate the misogynists with all their might!
The legal system is set up by the rich, who have the authority power,
thus the rich get richer by the hour.
Now more of us are jobless, poor and homeless, ignored and scored.
Caught in the crossfire, our middle income taxpayer is ripped off and torn.
We applaud the invasions of Granada, Panama, Saudi Arabia. Hurrah!
Bully for us and our wars against drugs and crime.
We will sell weapons for profit without question,
Like, "Who's blood will it be this time?"

Pierrette Gunde
OLD ROBE
Just an old robe, carelessly left behind
it belonged to a man I loved, and thought to be kind
This old robe is faded, thin, and very worn . . .
Daring to soothe the emptiness, it keeps me warm
I love, cherish this old robe, all there is left of him
We had so much, I thought . . . Oh! What a whim
All I have now . . . is the "Old Robe"

Kelly Head
WHAT I BELIEVE
You are the light of my life
You know just how I feel and why
You are always there by my side
To guide me through my worldly strifes

You always give more than I ask
Because you always know
how to complete the right task

Sometimes I cry, plea, and yelp
For Lord Jesus Christ's help
He may not always do as I ask
But there's always an explanation for his task

If there is one thing I do plea
is to let the people see the Christian in me

If you're saved beyond a shout of a doubt
All I can tell you
Is you'll go to Heaven
for I'm going too.

Carmel Hardin
GEORGE WASHINGTON
DEAR MR. Washington,
Recently I read that a town
could not afford a statue of you.
You know all about financial hardship
as you had it at Valley Forge
and dug into your pockets
to keep the battle going.
You did not think much of the Senate.
You attended only once.
And, George, let Martha stand beside you.
She could share those pesky pigeons
and help your mother with her
frequent *deshabille*.
The nation is still burdened.
Every day there is something new,
a new logo, a new disease and child care . .
Well, make the best of it, I say.
However, we need you, George.
Think of us in your land of quietude.
It has been nice talking to you.
I must go now.
Mr. Washington, sir. *adieu*.

Willis Geer
LOVE, WHAT IS LOVE?
Is Love an incredible breath stirring
everlasting passion that lasts forever?

Or is it the brilliant, fanciful
bloomage of the flowers of the spring
which wilt and die and freeze in the harshness of fall, only to return again in a similar but different shade at a later time;

Or is Love the warmth and certainty
of the sun overhead on a cloudless day, tinged only by the fear that a marauding thundercloud will end it all far before it has run its true course;

Or is Love the agony of a companion
thought gone never to return in a million tomorrows;

Or is Love the solid intensity of the
mountain granite which seemingly goes on into forever with never a change and whose strength is infinite and impenetrable;

Or is Love the hummingbird
zooming from flower to endless flower without a care in his world;

Or is Love the icy sharpness of a
roaring mountain stream on a hot and cumbersome day as it rushes towards oblivion in the endless ocean;

Or is Love the knowingness that all is
ongoing life in its ever present perfect; that there is no beginning nor end nor should there be.

Yolanda Huizar Serrato
LOST SOUL

We are not alone: To our runaways, prisoners, homeless, mentally ill, alcoholics, drug users, and all the lonely people.

When you passed me on the street
you did not greet me.
When I fell
you did not offer me your hand.
When I was lonely
you did not visit me.
When I called out your name

you did not hear me.
When I was sick
you did not care for me.
When I was hungry
you did not share your banquet with me.
In strong objection
who I eat with
who I run with
who I slumber with
What little is mine I give with my pleasure.
I am in you, you are in me.
I am what you have made me.
But before you point your finger down to me
"Remember," how many fingers point back to you.

Violet Ursula Galley
NATURE'S BOUNTY

I dedicate this poem to nature lovers who believe in the preservation of wildlife.

As you leave New York City and drive upstate,
To view Nature's bounty, the pleasures await.
Down through the mountains, the forests and lanes,
Lies the Hudson Valley where beauty reigns.
The clear crisp air and mountain streams,
The Indian trails and the river gleams.
The lakes like a mirror reflect the sky,
Wildlife abound, see the geese fly by.
But man the hunter lacks respect,
For nature's creatures in effect,
The deer and wild fowl he will kill,
For love of sport and the pleasure's thrill.
Let us treasure this realm called Earth,
Leave animals free, let them give birth,
So life may continue for all to see,
And enjoy the riches for eternity.
The beauty of nature must prevail,
To enrich our lives, we must not fail.
Respect the land, and creatures too,
For scenes like this, are all too few.

Marlene C Cumberbatch
CONFESSION

Dedicated to my wonderful husband, Earland.

Darling, let me tell you how I feel about you.

You are the morning sun, the breath I breathe.
You are the morning shower that has awakened
my mind and body, from the depth of a deep sleep,
to the alertness of a brighter day.

You are my Lord! I wish to serve you whatever you desire, then give you what you need—me.

As, we go our own way, during a day in our life,
I will enclose myself in the perfume of your being, until we meet again tonight.

Then, I'll soothe your weary brow, to close out the troubled world.
Next, I'll wrap my protective arms around you, just to give you peace of mind.
Then, I'll gather strength from you, my love.

And as we, together enter the essence of our serenity in becoming one, that's when Gossamers Wings enter to transfer us to that special place, that Garden of Eden.

That place, where there is You and I and our Creator, and that's enough.

Dorrie Smith
LOVE'S MISGIVINGS

Why does it happen that every such day
A boy comes a-knocking then turns right away?

He leads me on friendship; he leads me on more.
When I start to follow, he closes the door.

My image is shattered; my feelings are hurt.
When I try to question, he treats me like dirt.

Is it worth all this suffering? Is it worth all this pain?
Why should I try when I've nothing to gain?

Because I'm so sensitive, because I'm so blue,
I should say "Good–bye" to love that's not true.

But if the day comes when a true love's about,
Will I believe it or sit here in doubt?

Nina J Tomasieski
AFRICAN SAFARI

To Mike, Kimberly, Kari and Kristy for all your support.

From my vantage point, I was able to view
The splendor of the morning, the trees soft with dew.
The sun in all its splendor was there for all to see
As the clouds in the sky seemed to circle all around me.

I gazed upon the waters, the swells so gentle and mild,
And thought about my past—and all that I had left to do.
It came upon me at that moment I was no longer free and wild.
I'd lost that which was rightfully mine, replaced with something new.

Oh yes, I still hunger for the freedom of the seas,
The wild, untamed fortress of the jungle and the trees.
The flights I'd take just to view the place where I called home,
Were now a mere memory as I sit in this steel-like dome.

Perchance a visitor to this place would take it upon himself
To release me from my prison and return my self-respect.
To live and work side by side reaping the harvest of food and wealth
Instead of fighting day and night leaving our kind in terror and neglect.

Please store these thoughts in the safety of your soul
And remember the day when a battle was won.
All men may be created equal, but not equally created,
To walk the sands of time and not be found ill-fated.
But rather to walk as mother and daughter and father and son.

Wasyl Jaszczun

Wasyl Jaszczun
ROOTS

To the Ukrainian-American Community in Pittsburgh.

I see the tree in spring green clothes,
It hosts bright sunny rays,
Allures my eyes, brings joy to heart
And spreads its blissful shades.

In fall its head and face turn yellow,
The fallen leaves decay
And merge with earth to nourish roots
That tree alive would stay.

Depressed, it sadly looks around
With snow shroud on its head,
Yet roots give juicy food to it
Keep it from getting dead.

The seasons change, so does the tree,
Yet roots hold life and strength.
As long as roots are live and strong
The life of tree won't end.

The tree of many generations
May change its shape and style,—
As long as nation's roots are strong
That nation's tree won't die.

Wasyl Jaszczun
PANTA REI

The day lies down, takes nightly rest,
The night turns into day,
Tornado passes, storm calms down,
The spring takes snow away.
The gracious earth drinks furious flood,
The blissful rain cures drought,
The meteor in sky gets lost,
Now's hope, belief, now doubt.
The sun of joy removes grief's cloud,
The love melts hatred's ice,
Today your heart and gen'rous deeds
Replace your passing vice.
In time all things are somehow changed,
Some more, some less, some die,
Except for Him, Eternal God,—
He is beyond the time.
He gave it life, put nature's laws
In their mysterious rhyme.

Evelyn Burkhard Perry
THE MOUNTAIN STREAM

Rushing, leaping,
O'er the jagged rocks;
Roaring, tearing,
Into the vales below.

Starting, helping
Rocks to roll before;
Pushing, crowding,
To the outward banks.

Swirling, making,
Currents, swift and deep;
Swiftly gliding
To the vales below.

Brian Albrecht
THE KITTEN IN ME

I'm a little kitten without a home
I sleep outside, at night, alone
I'd like to cuddle, and I'd like to play
But what I'd love would be a place to stay
A soft, gentle hand never out of my sight
Who'd lock all the doors to keep out the cold winter night
A caring companion who'd set me on their lap
Or let me snuggle to their shoulder for a short kitty nap
But I realize I'm a kitten with nowhere to go
As I burrow a hole in the December snow

John Shanley
DADDY'S SOMEWHERE

To the most precious and special people in my life . . . Michael and Jaclyn.

He wakes up in the morning—runs into our room
He wakes my bride from sleeping wonders where's the groom
He goes into the kitchen; the garbage isn't out
He says he'll be home tomorrow—
He says this with doubt.
He wonders where's his daddy
He searches for some clues
Goes in his room, gets dressed, and tries to tie his shoes
They sit there eating breakfast; his sister at his side.
He says mommy is he coming home or do you think he lied.
She fights back her tears gives a reassuring smile
Of course he's coming home, Mike.
It will just be awhile.
He accepts this reluctantly—it doesn't stop his pain
Somehow with daddy gone things are not the same
No one to take walks with, go fishing or play ball
No one to give piggybacks or pick him up if he should fall
Not a very stable life for a five-year-old kid
He's doing time for the crimes I did
He knows his daddy's somewhere and loves him he believes
It's just there are times he needs him—it's those times he grieves
Like when he has a bad dream and there's a monster beneath the bed
Or when he thinks of when he last saw me and can't remember when or what was said
The last he can remember is daddy drove a car.
I guess the job he's doing really took him far
So when he's asked what daddy does what else can he say
But my daddy drives a cab somewhere very far away.

I love you Michael
and Jaclyn!

Frederick W McClure
LOVE

For Donna . . . whose love has shown me endless boundaries.

For a moment in time . . .
We witness the rising of the sun
Its warmth kisses our hearts
and comforts our soul
Its light illuminates our dreams
and enlightens our lives

For a moment in time . . .
We stand before an enigmatic ocean
Its vastness and overwhelming power
reminds us of our mortality
It's flowing waves dance at our feet
and awaken our emotions

For a moment in time . . .
We stand embraced where surf meets sand
Its soothing water caresses our feet
and bathes us with contentment
Its warm, golden sand forms
a foundation for our security

For a moment in time . . . we find a place in the sun
For forever in time . . . we find love

Jael Odhiambo
I THINK OF MY LOVE

For Michael, with all my love. And to all those who have found real love, hold on! For it is very rare.

The only one I see
That truly do loves me
The only one I have
And one I'll ever love.
From that proud crowd
Only him I give the crown
For once his love conquered
It has never faltered
My pride, my pain, my age
My stubbornness, and my hate
To win my doubting heart
One day to wear my wedding hat.
His gentle hands gathers and showers
My common head with scented flowers
And all my nothingness to him
The perfections he seeks, it seems
I think of him with happy tears
For only his love, quells my fears
Today, as I think of our love
I miss him so, my gentle dove
The only one I see.

D A Arbogast
ROSEBUD

The Rosebud:
So closely the petals unite to secure and enfold our special moments.
Close your eyes, visualize the magical fragrance and its power.
The bud blooms,
The blossom fades as the petals drop—to be replaced in time by another.
And so it goes.
Each petal is now a private intimate part of us.
Hold one petal in the palm of your hand and recapture a moment in time.

Michelle McDonald
SISTERS

You're my sister, so sweet and dear.
If you ever need me, I'll be here.
We've been through good times and through bad,
But look at all the fun we've had.
It's been so long, so many years,
But don't forget, I'm always here.
I love you more with every day,
Even though you're so far away.

Laurie LaRue
THE ENDLESS AFFAIR

Tall, blonde, blue eyed,
You hypnotized me with that wanting look of yours.
You captured me and moved me with your sensual ways.
Your touch never washed off.
You filled me with the power to become weak at a glance,
Weak at the sound of your voice—weak, I've become.
I run to you at a moment's notice,
You drain me of all my womanhood
Then leave me to pull my hair out, strand by strand
Until you phone me again, only wanting to stare me down
With those evil eyes
And abuse my body with those evil ways.
I cannot say "no" to you.
I'm running with the devil.
I'm giving in to you,
Wanting you to give in to me for once.
All I want is some romance, some conversation.
I want to hear you say my name!
Yet still I run to you, showing you my weakness
And you take me, like any man would . . .
And use me . . . like only you could.

Thomas A Dupree
PACIFIC SHORE

To Sandra Ann—in the midst of my dreams.

I saw her with her little one; in the distance, as a fawn to a doe. On the sand where all dreams are suspended.

Waves eroding life, too bad we can't go on eternally. The ocean seems to. We know it doesn't. Life seems to go on forever when you're in love. I wonder what she's thinking? Does she think that I'm some lost love or is she thinking of the future?

I know she's dreaming and I'm the nucleus of her thoughts. What a miraculous feeling—We're watching each other—I know she's curious about my pen. It's been so long since I've been the nave of a dream.

Crystal sunlight and turbulent tides attack the continent. I know she's been hurt, I can sense it in her mood; imported through the air. Exported in return, she knows me.

The little one's mind is somewhere else, enjoying the sand—the simple things. Tear dropped trees on nature's windswept edifice point in her direction. God! I wish there was contact here.

The horizon glimmers of silver and blue and seems to summon us both forward; but who will be the first to move?

Not me and not you.

Maybe we'll meet again one day on a turbulent Pacific shore.

Ellen Youn
PEACE

I feel like running away,
away from all of the misery
the anger
the pain.
I want to feel free of guilt,
and all the burdens set upon me.
I want to feel like I could fly
irrepressibly,
having no cares in the world.
I want to be on some remote island,
with that special someone;
the one I love by my side.
To know just by his touch that he loves me
and he cares.
To know he will be with me forever.
There is no other place I would rather be.
No interruptions.
No one to hassle me about the cruel happenings;
the disasters around me.
To have all the noise kept away.
I want to fall into a peaceful sleep.
The picture will be beautiful:
two young people sleeping together
side by side.
Lovers, amongst the perfectness of this isle.
The island will contain happiness and freedom;
freeing one's soul from the harsh and hectic world.
Peace.

John H James Jr
YOU'RE THE REASON

You're the reason I keep going—
The very purpose of my day
You keep me, ever, always growing—
You hold the map that shows the way.

Right by your side, is my intention
wish I could keep you in my sight
when you're not near, I'm filled with tension
I must be by you in the night!

All through the day, I miss your presence—
the hours and minutes, drag slowly by
sun-up to sunset takes forever
till I can be back by your side.

Hold me close, oh, hold me tender—
Fill my heart right to the top!
All to you, I do surrender
I'll give you everything I've got!

Donna Kennedy
BABY GIRLS

Dedicated to my beautiful daughter Darcie.

You'll always be,
my little girl.
With the big brown eyes,
and a little bitty curl.
You filled my days,
and nights with joy.
Sometimes it seemed,
I was your only toy.
I was there to comfort you,
and rock you in my arms.
You've grown so much,
with lots of charm.
No longer you wear,
ruffles and lace.
You'd much rather be,
in a three-legged race.
Homework is boring,
let's listen to rock.
"Mom," you yell,
"where's my socks,"
As I say, one's in the washer,
one's on the line.
I think back on time,
because I know.
No matter how fast,
you grow.
You'll always be,
my little girl.
With the big brown eyes,
and a little bitty curl.

Hamuskhan
WHISPERING WINDS

Whispering winds
On a cold rainy night,
I walked through it
Alone, as it stormed
Through the night.

Where are the things
That I thought could be?
The whispering winds
Are laughing at me.

Childhood is gone, and
My dreams I see, will
Be left unfilled,
To go on without, "Me."

I waited too long
And worked at them
Too slow
Thinking tomorrow would
Never show
Whispering winds
On a cold rainy night
I walked through it
Alone, as it stormed
Through the night.

Hamuskhan
WHISPERING WINDS THE LAST CHAPTER

The streets are empty
Because of the rain outside.
The cold November wind has
Drove all the children inside.

The moonbeam glitters
Off the gutter waters below
I walk the streets alone
Nowhere to go.

I lived once, but
A short time ago
I ended my own life
Thinking I couldn't
Take it anymore.

Now I am but a
Shadow of what I
Used to be.
Chained to the earth
Oh!
What I'll give to be free.

Dotti Kraft Bray
THE SILENT ABUSER

For my dad, John M. Kraft—You were the best, I miss you!

Sometimes it's hard to understand
The workings of the inner man;
How such a handsome smiling face
Can inflict such wounds without a trace
Of being detected by those around him
And has completely confounded them;
No one would ever believe
The horrors he conceived
To torture those he claimed he loved
By appearing as gentle as a dove.
The heartbreaking brutalness he imposed
Left wounds so deep that no one knows,
Except for the few who heard my plea,
This smiling face is killing me.

William M Kiang
TOGETHER, WE GO FORWARD
The world
Divided & ruled by the Great Empires in the 19th Century
Is over.
The people
Died & suffered by the two World Wars in the 20th Century
Is over.
No single nation can maintain world peace today,
So the world organizations begin florescence.
Nations together,
Go forward.

There are natural differences:
The people
Physical, mental, energy, education, profession, etc.
Is different.
The nation
Territory, population, government, resources, etc.
Is different.
Recognize the differences,
Combined, cooperated and coordinated, etc.
Together, we go forward to the coming 21st Century.

Mike Lissy
TO CHRIS IN HER LONELINESS
I am with you on the desert among the cacti, running—
The blessed stones of the arid washes,
Parched by the southern sun,
Scorch your brown naked feet.
Your body forms strains
In the confines of your skin;
Your hair blowing free, untouched,
Never entwining—but yearning;
Your eyes—windmills of your soul,
Fixed in your head, yet turning
Across a whole universe, seen and not,
Resting on a leather coat,
Transfixing an outstretched hand,
Perceiving le chat noir (purring in blissful ignorance),
Screaming in a vast void of spiny terrain;
Your tongue, caked with the effort
Of communication, speaks with
Camus
Of blazings on a deserted trail.
You come from the desert, alone, fresh and clean,
Entering a sea of people and I,
Alone, in my apartment, am with you on the desert.

Dorothy Wheeler Butler

Dorothy Wheeler Butler
TEACHERS ARE HUMAN BEINGS

Dedicated to my hundreds of fifth-graders and their parents, 1953-1980, in Leicester, Massachusetts.

Propriety my words would bar
To say what some THINK teachers are!
From novice to professional
A teacher's life is never dull!
A teacher's job is first to teach—
Sometimes to punish, some to preach.
Each day confronted with his throng,
A teacher must sort right from wrong;
Must be companion, nurse, and friend—
Adviser—umpire to the end!
And then to keep his records clean—
A mathematical machine!
But comes this as a shock to you?
Teachers are human beings, too!

Edd David McWatters
AN AMERICAN
He was dirty that was plain,
A common toil had left its stain.
Not as black as a terrible crime,
But excitement decided to follow behind.

His quiet dreaming I should really hear,
Shouts of welcome were loud and clear.
His neighbours were shocked when they looked to see,
Ripped out shrubbery around his home taken free.

He crowned his home with radiant flowers,
Many were red, white and many were blue
It took an ugly man, dreary and sullen I knew.
Nobody thought this task he would do.

But tonight the weariness of a man steeped in a goal,
Who won't leave his house in filth and ugly turmoil.
Bound to turn and stared at the rot, little guessing he was about to learn a lot.

He built a golden treasure for his kids to play,
It held a special world for them like the smells of May.
A grumbling complainer stood out so plain,
But the police were glad to catch this pain.

Anna Matheny
YOUNG WITHOUT UNDERSTANDING

To Jason, my first grandchild. Happiness is just around the next smile.

I'm told love heals a broken heart
Yet for me so young it's painful—
How can such happiness create unhappiness for me
I feel the victim in me once again
Perhaps one day love for me will be
Until this comes, how do I submit
How do I refrain from bitterness—
When my eyes overflow with tears
For myself, I wonder, of course—
That my feelings matter in such a case
I fear tragedy, yet I shouldn't
Such joy and excitement is theirs to have
Still I'm young without understanding—
Words to express my feelings are obsolete
Yet I want happiness for us all
Love, please heal my broken heart
Take the fear and trauma away
For I am young without understanding.

Anthony Mercorelli
ANNAMARIE

To Anna Marie Mercorelli.

Annamarie why did we have to part
We loved each other from the start
Annamarie why must I be the guy
With the broken heart
Annamarie we used to stroll hand
In hand
We would stop and kiss and life
Was grand
We even built our dream house in the sand
Annamarie we never did all the things we
Had planned
Like the sand of time your life ran out
But with all the tears I wept the
Fire of
My love for you won't go out
But deep in my heart the fire of love still
Burns
But deep in my heart I know somehow somewhere
It will return as long as the flame of your love
For me still burns

Raymond Nichols
ANIMAL TALK
The rabbits and squirrels dance around on the green
The deer and the elk are last to be seen

"Why it's spring" they say "Isn't that fun—
It's time for rolling around in the sun"

The groundhog came out to see what's new
And found out what he heard was true

"Why it's spring" he mutters in a deep voice
"where I put my food, I now have a choice."

An evil wolf comes out, looking for prey
"I'll find cute chickens before end of day."

A funny old fox comes wandering by
Now he knew he could be on the sly

"Now I can catch 'em" he laughed with a grin
"I can catch 'em fat and I can catch 'em thin."

It's the beginning of life, the happiest time
When the world starts new and all is fine

The animals talk in a special way
Of what they observe while at rest and play

The animals talk of things we can't see
You live and learn the same as me.

Beryl A McMaster
TIME
At the corner service station they congregate
Three or four or more old men
Beer in hand
They sit or stand
Chew the fat—predict the weather
Reminisce about life and each other
Come wind or rain
Or sun and shine
Talking, laughing, they use up their time—
Time is all they have left
When they're gone, others are bereft
They say 'he was a good old boy'
Had a happy life, had joy

Nathan M Richardson
THE TRAVELER'S REMINDER
During my trip, was there any wonder I would see
someone or something that reminded me of you?

There in Knoxville, Tennessee, at a Kentucky Fried Chicken,
he was sitting there in the corner.

I had not even noticed him until
I was halfway through my second piece of chicken.

(I'm going to turn into a chicken if I keep eating so much
chicken.) I was just getting ready to lick my fingers,

and knowing I should not do it in public,
I looked around first.

That's when I saw him, dark skinned, dark eyes,
around 60 years old, his hat a blue baseball cap.

A quick glance outside revealed he was even driving a truck. He
was sitting there just like your father does at Hardee's sometimes.

Only he was here in Knoxville, reminding me that even
the people and things that surround you are part of me.

Ruth M Robinson
A REPUTATION

Dedicated to my mother—Bertha I. Norton.

I wish I were a boy,
I'd fish on my vacation,
But momma said I can't do that,
I'd get a reputation
I sit out on the porch,
with games and toys and rations,
She said I'm looking for the boys
and I'll get a reputation.
So I'll sit up in my room
until near starvation,
Then no one will have cause
to say, I'll get a reputation.

Marie Sanzillo
PRECIOUS HOURS

Each morning when you leave me my dear,
I count the hours until your return,
When we will be together again,
To spend the hours left in each day together.
These hours are very precious to me,
As each day seems to be,
Another page for my book of memories.
This book holds all the things you do.
To make my life complete my dear,
It has the look that came into your eyes,
When you had seen for the first time our child,
And held it in your arms,
This my dear is the sweetest memory of all to me,
As it showed all the love and devotion,
That is in your heart for us,
Without these precious hours,
Life would not be complete my dear.

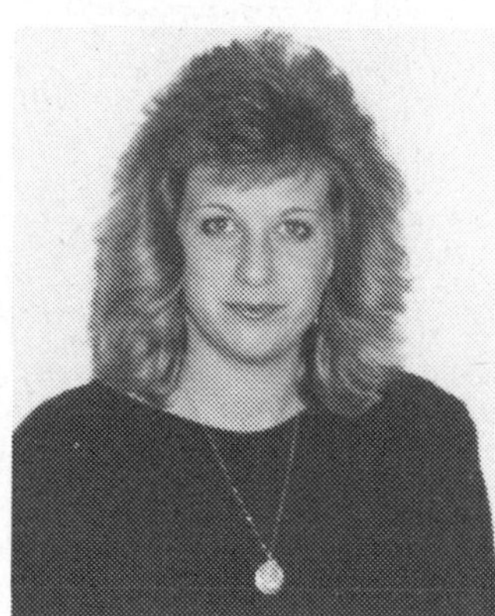

Sheryl Ann Mason

Sheryl Ann Mason
GOD'S CREATION

High on the Mountain of Love,
Looking down in the valley;
All the lonely scattered hearts,
Like lost helpless sheep;
Rivers flowing down the jagged mountain,
Like tears from a baby's face;
Emerald green grass covers the unearthy surface,
Flowers begin their birth
cautiously one by one;
A process of life, love & pain,
The neverending gift of Mother Nature.

Sheryl Ann Mason
THROUGH IT ALL

An empty womb,
a lonely heart,
A cell has formed,
life has its start,

In a watery world,
so quiet and serene,

The fetus there lies,
to the mother unseen,

Movements now felt,
through the liquidy wall,

Simultaneously moves,
the baby so small,

Much preparing is done,
nine months quickly go,

The final day nears,
both baby and mother know,

Glorious the moment,
this time of joy,

Fourteen hours of painful labor,
in her arms lies a boy.

Marcia Shawn
THIS IS FOR ALL OF THE PEOPLE WHO HAVE STOOD BY ME

On the outside I may be
As feisty as a firecracker
As tough as an alligator
But on the inside I am
As delicate as the petals of a rose
As fragile as a wine glass

Florence H Tipton
YE ARE MY EXAMPLE

If trouble comes by one,
Perhaps by two or three.
Ye are my examples.
Show my word holds fast.

Not by power nor by might.
But, by my spirit says the Lord.
Long and hard the path may be.
Ye are my examples
Hold fast, the word won't fail.

Trials come and trials go.
But, the trying of faith works patiences.
Let patiences have her perfect work.
Ye are my examples.
Hold fast my word won't fail.

Whether in victory or defeat.
Cast down or standing tall.
Yea, ye are my examples.
Hold fast the word of God.

Janine Simone
TIMES OF THE DAY SOUNDS

In the morning
Sounds of birds humming
Sounds of squirrels running
Humming and running that keep me up in the morning

In the afternoon
Sounds of mom working
Sounds of coffee perking
Perking and working throughout the whole day

In the night
Sounds of owls howling
Sounds of prowlers prowling
Howling and prowling that put me to sleep

Lamesa O Whitson
THE GENERATION OF NO GODS

We were from the generation of NO GODS, we passed the heritage onto our children. Our NO GOD society said to our children we will not choose your god for you—the choice is up to you. We set NO GOD standards that make no moral judgement. Nothing was right nothing was wrong—it was all relative. With our NO GOD we gave our children NO hope in the eternal NO faith in the now NO direction for the future. Our NO GOD said life was death and death was life and we instituted fetal harvesting. Where the old trive off the young to murder for their body use—a civilized form of cannibalism. Our NO GOD said NO to protecting the unborn—any society who does not protect those who cannot protect themselves will surly eventually fade out of existence. Our NO GOD had no limit on its imagination—hell was loose! Our NO GOD said NO to sacrifice and work—NOW NOW NOW—NOW is all we can be sure of. NO time to wait NO desire to work . . . our NO GOD bread poverty another form of economic cannibalism where the poor ate off the middle class and the rich escaped income tax. Our NO GOD said NO to restraint and self control. It became infested with desire and fulfillment until it was a stinch in our nostrils. Our NO GOD rejected freedom . . . . . . Without the chains of bondage the NO GOD of slavery had put on his people, they would not serve him. He would be a NO GOD with NO PEOPLE to serve him—
Are we a society of NO GOD?

Lamesa O Whitson
TO SELF

self to your own self
be true
no anchor need be thrown today or i
will surely fall too.
who says what's comin' down next
i saw what came today in ghetto
infested streets
with so much anticipation there ain't
really nothin' to do
gotta do something or you will
find me singing those dirty blues
that have no words, that mean
nothing
going nowhere . . . being nobody.
cheap wine leads to loose women in
rundown hotels
leaving stained purple sheets running
from a dark alley
HAY BABY YOU LOOK SO
GOOD WONT'CHA COME MY
WAY!
if i knew a way to go those second
thoughts
wouldn't keep dangling in the air
rustled by the breeze
polluted by inhumane humanity
That I can so clearly see.
when i open those eyes
that only want to stay closed.

Cynthia Witt
SISTER

I thank you for the blessing of your boundless faith in me, and I am deeply grateful for your loving constancy. Your words inspire me to live a better life each day and in your friendship all my fears forever fade away. I cannot pay you back in full, and I never do as much as it would take to tell my gratitude to you. But this I truly promise now that I will never rest unless and not until I know that I have done my best. And whether it is very much or just a little bit, somewhere along the way you'll know that you're the cause of it.

Mary Johnson
TIME THE TAKER!

This poem is dedicated to my beloved father, Albert Batiste, 1907-1979.

I wish, I was a clock just standing on a wall.
Where days and weeks and months
and years meant nothing at all.
My hands waving left and right
Not knowing the difference in day or night.
Just keeping constant vigil
Bright Time The Taker.
Just ticking, ticking silently
Not knowing people refer to me as
Time The Taker.
Just working, working, never paid
Going along with Life's escapades
Not knowing you refer to me as Time
The Taker.
But have you stopped to think of me
That I grow men and I grow trees
That I bring day and I bring night
And I bring everything in Life,
Time The Giver.

James and Elzie Vibbert
THE BED BUGS

In dedication to James and Elzie Vibbert, the writers of the poem "The Bed Bugs."

Oh say can you see any bed bugs on me
Then if a you say that a you do well then a
I got them from you yea then I heard you

Reply as you said no not from me so a
Tell me hows come a when you come around
I get exposed just a like a dog scratching its
Fleas off on a me yea

Edward L Greenberg
REMOTE MADONNA

From the Play: "THE REMOTE MADONNA—A FOUNTAINHEAD OF INSPIRATION" by Edward Leonard Greenberg, in tribute to Olga Plasencia.

Life, Uninspired, is an Existence—
Unredeemed.
A joyless heart, a frozen mind.
Asleep, and unesteemed.
This, was my introverted cynicism,
that shunted the start.

May the Saints, have a mercy, on The Praetorian, Heart.
The Madonna, so Beautiful—Had Suffered,
for all the Seasons.
My Understanding?
A Confirmed Opportunist. Unmoved, by all
of her profound reasons.
Donning the toga, of the Cavalier.
Is so much less, than a Page, Sincere.
Blessed, are the catalysts—that spark, our Revolutions.
Error, defeat, embarrassment; the Search,
for Scientific Solutions.
Mine is the gratitude, one of Sublime Appreciation.
To
The Remote Madonna—A Fountainhead of
Inspiration.
Hers, the silent eloquence, the potential,
and ever growing Cognition.
She will Know the truth, one day.
And will struggle, against all Chauvinist
Exhibition.
Cursed, is the Renegade, Comprador,
Theirs, the lifetime mask, that grins, and
lies,
It hides their lips, it shades their eyes.
These, the despoilers, of the Madonna's Smile!
With Torn, and bleeding hearts, we bear
witness to His Human Guile.
And again, take refuge, on the altar of apathetic prostration.
A Beauty, Divine,—A Cradle, to enlightened, Creation.
This is,
The Remote Madonna—A Fountainhead, of
Inspiration.
An electric touch, and a Pleasing, Countenance—
Cannot surely define, the infinite, Goal.
We have discarded the veil—We honor the
facts.
Progression, Skill, Profundity.
These Truths, stand high, in The Madonna's Soul.
Let us Continue our Tasks—And hold high,
our Revolutionary Style.
Do not, forsake me, Madonna. For now, I
am worthwhile.
Yours, the grace, that delivered, a Benediction—
Unto a mute Praetorian. Yours the achievement—
The result of which, has spawned, a Valedictorian.
May your reward, be happiness,—And
Truth, Your Proverbial Prize.
To Thee, Madonna,
In whose climate, of Dear Inspiration, I
continue, to Rise.
The Remote Madonna—A Fountainhead of
Inspiration.

Grace Marston Goertler
THREE PETALS
Three petals from a flower make
A part of what it used to be.
But separated it would take
Imagination—just to see
The whole of it or put together.
For all alone they could not stand
The wind—the rain—the weather.

And later as they separate, they fall.
But falling will not break the petals
For they are as God intended
Soft and sure, pure and fragile
Above it all they are agile
To fall and not break their hearts
Or get ruined as they part
From the mother flower.

For as they lie upon the table
And never seem to be able
To go anywhere—except to die
Exactly where they fall and lie.

Edward L Greenberg
IN THE BEGINNING, THERE WAS LIGHT

From the play: "In The Beginning There was Light" by Edward Leonard Greenberg.

I tiptoed through the door.
Hardly dreaming, what to expect.
The whispered hello, Her shy sweet smile;
A quiet grace.
The cup had passed to me.
And my soul, poured a libation to the Gods.
I was at the right time, the proper place.
In the beginning, there was light.

A child of beauty, a child denied.
A vessel of Springtime, Beacon of Peace, and tranquility.
Would our humanity mingle?
The flamboyant merchants, their thrust is lethal
The invisible curtain was already in place.
I was regarded, from faraway.
Closed was the door, to ecstasy.

Dominion was achieved, in a spark of time.
Inspiration, is the lasting legacy.
From, now on, no more; mediocrity.
The angel of inspiration was by my side.
Will she ever know, would she ever see,
That this flower grows; in adversity?
In the beginning, there was light.

Marion J Egner
TREASURES

To my husband John and daughter Greta.

I used to imagine
I would explore the world,
to find friendship and love
being mystically unfurled.

Then a voice said quietly,
Be patient, those things
you will find with all
their mysteries combined.

In time they were found
and not far away,
these wonderful treasures
here forever to stay.

Marion J Egner
IF I COULD
If I could start
all over again,
and return to back when
each thing to choose
didn't leave me confused,
or not miss the chances
that life subtly enhances,
and not begin to think
I'm totally out of synch,
but feel it's intriguing
and then start believing,
that really I would,
If I could.

Grace Marston Goertler
AMERICA
Upon a hill I stop and stand
and look upon this favored land
Where nature's done her very best.
Much better for us than most, the rest
Wide plains—green fields—the rolling hills—
The forests, large, where all is stilled

So look around and you will see
The same, perhaps, the same as me.
Contentment, peace and beauty rare
As mile on mile will change
The hill, the valleys and the range.
But one thing sure as it can be.
America will never change for me.
I mean—no matter what may come
That day to day, and sun to sun,
Three thousand miles of liberty
Where men are men and all are free.

Michael McClendon
VALERIE

"To be or not to be" a poet was decided when Valerie came into my life. Thanks Val. This is Valerie:

Though I see her often
i'm awed by her sight,
Valerie is her name and
she makes me feel alright.

Love those big brown eyes,
teeth so perfect and white.
she's one fine lady,
wish she were my wife.

She even speaks so lovely
with a body so petite,
she has a nice brown
Complexion,
and she smells
Just as sweet.

Her wit makes me giggle
i'm imbued by her mind,
she keeps on getting better
like french wine over time.

She's very warm and caring,
sometimes she's brave and bold,
Valerie—my cute little flower,
you light up my soul.

"Miko"

Michael McClendon
ITS GOTTA BE RIGHT
Its gotta be right to work, and
its gotta be worked, to be right.

When it seems
theres no aim in sight
and you rather switch
than to fight,
have patience
to see the light, and
time will have
worked it right, 'cause
its gotta be worked to be right!

And let clear conscious
do the work, and
things won't have to be
re-worked,
If your way can't
make it work,
find someone who'll
make it work, but
Its gotta be right to work!

Wanda E Harris
HEY, GOOD MORNING
My dreams reflect you, lying still
Beside me . . . just before dawn.
I silently watch your body move slowly,
As if trying to wake up, yet . . .
your eyes remain closed.
I allow my fingertips to touch your eyelids,
your cheeks, they run gently
across your lips.
Your eyes open slightly then, just enough to catch
a glimpse of mine . . .
Hey, good morning

Wanda E Harris
SUCH A TENDER EXPERIENCE
Today . . . it rained, and the kings and queens didn't go to the arena, they stayed home, and made love.

So like our mass of moist, warm bodies, lying directly under the trickling sound of rain . . . clung together.

Gentle . . . mellow . . . sweet was your touch, your kiss, the look you gave me just after love . . . our love.

I turned, gracefully exhausted, utterly satisfied with my surroundings . . .

And sleep came over me just like that of a little baby.

Wanda E Harris
ENCOUNTER
. . . and the day after, I lay there with a post-orgasmic grin on my face.

happy, content, satisfied just knowing that I had touched you in some small way.

. . . one couldn't call what we had a relationship;
nor could one call what we had an affair;
i call it an encounter . . .

nothing dramatic, nothing romantic;
just simply a beautiful encounter,
with a beautiful person, on a beautiful day, at a beautiful moment.

Alice Onysko
TODAY'S THE DAY YOUR EIGHTEEN

To my daughter Jeanette—with all my love, Mom—August 15, 1989.

Today's the day you're eighteen. I was there and agree,
The years flew by—impossible to retrieve.
Like a blink of an eye, one just doesn't see.

We can't take back all the hurts we've caused,
But, we can let them be,
Like a blink of an eye
impossible to see.

Today's the beginning, as every day should be,
Of the rest of your life, as it is for me.

Maybe, within the next eighteen years,
We'll get the chance to—
Talk together a bit, maybe

hold hands once in a
while,
Try to hug each
other and see if we
fit.

And, God willing, maybe we'll pray
together—

That someday we'll see each other as
we really are,
A mother and daughter
together, forever,
Talking, holding hands,
hugging and praying—

That someday, our children and
grandchildren will see us together,
As we really are, a family
forever, as it should be,
Talking, holding hands,
hugging and praying—

That the World would see us, and
maybe,
Everyone would pray together,
as it was always meant to be.

Alice Onysko

A TRUE INSPIRATION FROM GOD ABOVE, "TAKE CARE OF THE ONE YOU LOVE"

In times of trouble and strife,
I long for the days when I had a
wife,
She was someone to laugh
with, and share my life.

It's lonely now since she's been
gone,
The one I've loved has passed
on.

I loved her more than I could say,
She was the one perfect thing
that made my day.
Perfect now is just a state
of mind,
When I think of her,
which is most of the
time.

What could I have said or done,
to make her life a more
enjoyable one?

The only comfort I've now found in
life,
Is talking to my Creator about
my wife.
He assures me she loved me in a
most special way,
And whatever my faults were
she couldn't say.
She's hoping and praying
that I would be,
In peace in this life
as she was with me.

It was lonely in the beginning, but it
had to be,
For I wouldn't have found the
Savior in me.
He was there all the time,
but I couldn't see,
How He held us
together, My wife
and me.

Steve Harris

MY DUTY

Each day as I awake and see the
rising of the sun
I know it's because the good Lord
has given me another chance to do
the work that I have left undone.

If it's just to help a brother give up
his guns or to prevent a sister from
putting the child of her womb in the
dump, it really matters because I
ought to be my brother's keeper.

I remember the children that are in
foster homes just because they don't
have a mother or father to call their
own.

It's hard to be born into this world
without any choice of your own and
all together to be disowned.

God give a helping hand, I pray day
by day for those who don't have kin
or kindred in any way.

So give me another day, dear Lord,
that I may be able to help in some
way, if it's just to tell them that you
care so that they will not give up in
despair.

Sheryl Henderson

DESTINY

So this is the planet which we call
earth
My path has been chosen for me
destined at birth
God blessed us with vision
Though some seem to be born blind
He is the key to all wisdom
Which rules higher than the mind

Up every morning with the rising sun
I search for the reason until my
purpose is done
I'll keep traveling these grounds for
my destination
While something keeps holding me
back
with that hesitation

Because what awaits me out there
Who's to know?
A dark lonely road
Should I take it alone?

There's a long way in
And a short way out
If you don't get side-tracked
On a road called doubt.

John, Angie and (daughter) Carly Palmer

Ann (Inka) Dorich

GRAND ENTRANCE

I dedicate this poem to my nephew, John Palmer, his wife, Angie, daughter, Carly. I quote—and wish them—peaceful moments—fond memories and special happiness always.

Death only enters once, but thought,
a thousand times or more.
At any time it opens someone's door
and takes them.
Some by force, some willing and
others go not knowing.
If they should be close, someone will
let you know.
Then, you think about the times that
you have talked and it seems
Funny, that no more will they walk,
where they once found
sadness and happiness. They go
leaving nothing behind, for feeling is
there a short while, then pushed far
back is the thought of not locking our
doors.

Barbara Larsen

IT IS SAID

Somewhere, they say, there are
mountains of pearl
That rise up, almost to the sun:
Somewhere, they say, there are
oceans of jet,
So awesome and deep do they run.
Somewhere, they say, there is love
that endures,
And grows richer and stronger each
day:
I hope, most sincerely, that these
things exist;
But I only know what they say.

Ana Lucia Medeiros

BLACK LACE

To my mom, dad, Johnny, Mario and Richard, for loving me unconditional. To Dan, for believing in me. Thank you for making a difference in my life! Love always, Ana Lucia.

He makes me wear
black lace
They please him so against
my olive skin
There's passion in his eyes
the energy intense
as I begin to feel warm inside,
allowing myself to enfold into his
arms.
Our sharing of sweat
the agony of waiting
the longing deep in our
hearts as we entwine as one,
wrapped up in arms and legs.
Sweet kisses on my neck, chills my
spine
only to weaken me more,
surrendering
my whole sensuality to
his moist lips,
Eyes so deep they pierce me
with delightful pain . . .
Wanting, Fullness, Complete.

Ana Lucia Medeiros

IMAGES

Images cross my mind
as I lay my soul to sleep,
Bright sun warms my body,
tingling the flesh,
Ocean waves pounding the shores,
breeze through my hair . . .
Slipping into a peaceful state—
your face, sharp, comes to
my mind, your smile
causing me to melt.
Dark eyes so deep, I'm hypnotized,
Mesmerized, I'm drawn into your
arms,
intense heat explodes as our wet,
hungry
lips meet, tasting the
sweetness, savoring it,
Throbbing with an achiness that must
meet its need
Electricity so powerful,
We are swept away
Awakening to another place
Another time . . .

Ana Lucia Medeiros

ROOTS

If you could only
come home
with me
and see the place
where my deepest roots
were planted,
You would then understand
the free-spirited soul
which possesses my body,
the freedom to share life
with every living thing,
You would understand the longings,
the pain, joy and meaning of
true love and my yearnings
to become one
with you so
that we can soar
together
to the highest places
where only love
stands and rules.

Ana Lucia Medeiros

REUNION

Gathering among friends
is a reunion of
souls
Shared lives and knowing without
speaking
Love has no time or limit
and we carry our memories
from the deepest roots
to the next line
of blood
and it carries over.
Haven't I loved you once before?
You
look so familiar . . .
In the depths of his soul
a seed comes to life
& springs forth
Remembering is
easy
How can you forget love.

Mary J Tripp

MAN - SON OF WOLF

Dedicated to all of the people in this World that have been victims of undeserved, inhuman treatment . . .

If someone walks up and says, "Who
are you?",
Whatever you do, don't say you're a
Jew.

Jews have been persecuted since
Civilization began,
Yet—Spirit and Dignity were theirs;
even as the blood ran.

Are they the only true humans
amongst you and I?

Only the son of a wolf would tear out
the jugular of a child, without batting
an eye.

WHEN WILL CIVILIZATION
REALLY BEGIN??

Barbara Jewel Eagle Erickson

THE NOSE

To my dad, Clarence Bitzan.

Do you suppose
When God invented the nose

It was to teach us how to blow
Or sniff, or drip,
Or grow mustaches under,
Above the lip?

Or was it just to be a bother
Reminding me I am my father's
For he's the only one I know
Whose head is smaller than his nose.

Or was it for another cause
That God invented our lovely nose
To hold those little glasses up
Or breathe fresh, morning country air
And smell cookies baked with care.

Oh I don't know
Why God made the nose
But I believe He does know
I cannot live without a nose.

Melvin E Musick
THE GRACE OF A WINTER ROSE

To the one who became my winter rose. I dedicate these words to Lena Davis, with my love and my gratitude. Always, Mel.

Lost along the winding road,
The ivory fields of sunlit snow;
Shaded by trees with naked limbs,
I shield my eyes from the burning winds.

A faith in the light beyond the ice
Warms my soul from deep inside,
And while it carries me down the road
I feel a hope despite the cold.

Then as the sun was lying down,
I stood in awe without a sound;
For high on a hill above the snow
Were the outreaching arms of a living rose.

In quiet wonder I watched her rise
Until her beauty met my eyes,
And in my heart I felt the glow
Of all the dreams I now would know.

And in this cold and lonely place,
I left my heart without a trace;
High on a hill beside the rose,
It flourishes in light and forever grows.

Doris Pack West
ADVENTURE

He put his hand in mine and we walked down the hill—
A breath of spring was in the air, tempering the winter chill,
His eyes seemed clear as heaven, gleaming with fun and spark'ling bright—
(Brown just like his Father's, tender as velvet night)—

He fell in love with everything, the chickens, the pigs, the cows,
The horses snorting by the fence, even the noisy crows!
I showed him a pretty birdie, singing in a tree,
I let him touch a fuzzy worm and he wrinkled his nose at me:

We walked beside the little stream to go watch Daddy plow—
He jabbered happily along, trying to form words somehow,
His feet were so eager to run but he stumbled over a rock—
I kissed away his tears and held his hand to walk—

He yelled when he saw Daddy,
Daddy scooped him up with an arm—
They plowed twice around the field,
First lesson in learning to farm!

He put his hand in mine and we walked up the hill—
My heart was overflowing with a heady jubilant thrill—
The wind kissed our faces gently, soft and warm was the sun,
When I walked up the hill with our little son.

Jill Schwartz
THE SCENES OF LOVE

To Doug, my first love, who showed me it's okay to experience all feelings and that love has all sides. To all those who have experienced all sides of love. In life, we all have to experience pain in order to feel joy. He'll always be in my heart.

LOVE; Running through a field of
daffodils;
free as a bird;
gives you the chills;
unlike any word.

LOVE; A clear, crisp day,
on top of a snow-
capped mountain;
a perfect sculpture out
of clay;
looking at Niagra's
Fountain.

LOVE; A dark cloud;
an erupting volcano;
a siren just as loud;
a storm at sea;
set them free.

LOVE; War between countries;
earthquakes and people
dying;
a swarm of killer bees;
a baby crying.

LOVE; All of these simultaneously,
a complete mystery
that no one under-
stands, happening all
over the land.

Evelyn Ferran
MAMA LOVES YOU ON HER GOOD DAYS

Mama loves you on her good days.
The trouble is there aren't many.
I clean the house and earn a living,
I look at folks with Dads and you haven't any.
I try my best and oft it's my worst.
While my life flies by and good days aren't many.
I try so hard to give you all.
I love you I do. But good days aren't many.
I love you best on the days I'm not tired.
When the skies are blue and the sun filters through.
On those days I have hope for what tomorrow may bring.
I love you, I love you, I really do!
But I love you most on the good days I find.
When I've time to snuggle or cherish a smile.
When the rent's not due and the bills don't need paying.
Or you're not crying for food and there isn't any.
I love you. I love you. I really do!

Kristi A Wright
SUNSET COLORS

Across the horizon,
there is a twist of colors,
that blend and shade as one.

Together, they form the beauty,
of the sky at midnight hour,
and across the sandy beach.

As the waves crash against the shore,
they shimmer off the sunset colors.

I, standing upon the sand,
with the wind in my hair; my bare feet upon the cold sand,
I am looking at the same colors as you.

The sparkles upon the water,
dance about from wave to wave.

And I, standing upon the beach,
take it all in,

For a last look; a last breath,

For the last time.

Giovannina Vannessa Fusco
HARMONY WITH NATURE

I would like to dedicate this poem firstly to Mrs. Lockard, my English teacher at Northside High School and secondly to Ron DeBeck, my drama teacher at Northside.

I drift from branch to branch,
float from flower to flower.
My mind is at rest, far away
from the troubles I face.
Quiet love and serenity surround
me, the fresh air breezing 'cross
my brow.
Silently lying under the shady
fern, my troubles are set free.
Skimming the surface of the water,
gliding like a swan,
I am a Part of Nature,
Nature Part of me.
Oneness with Nature,
Perfect Harmony,
Total Peace.

Dayna Haynes
LINES

Lines on a face
the test of time
Tears in an eye
dreams for yesteryear
Forgotten hopes
drowned by oceans of the
world's despair
All frayed to the outer reaches
beyond man's understanding
Time in an eye
An eye full of tears
to fill the bottle of
forgotten dreams
seeking a hand of comfort
in a lonely desert
where only the sun shines
The universe revolves
to reveal
a standing of time
A single soul searching
for an answer
no one knows

Evelyn Reed
LIFE'S NOT SO EASY

This poem is dedicated to my father, brothers, sisters, children, grandchildren and in memory of my husband and mother with love and gratitude.

Life's not so easy with all
Work and not enough play
So life's not so easy
So wake up to another day
Make life easy with smiles, hugs, and kisses
So life will be easy with lots of
Joy and laughter

A Woman Joy
Jeannie

Eunah O Brown
HURRICANE HUGO

To my children: Irvin, Deltah, Delphine, Kathleen, my grandchildren and the people of the Virgin Islands.

It was September the 17th, one windy day when Hugo came whistling, a visit to pay.

All of us didn't expect to see, such a terrible Hurricane on land, and on sea.

Hugo struck us, with all his might with terrible force, all through that night. Destroying our homes, and mansions dear, which just before, was bright and fair.

St. Thomas, St. Croix, and St. John were hit, Hugo did everything bad, he saw fit. Roaring like a monster all that night, Hugo didn't spare anything in sight.

Our highways, looked like a real war zone, trees uprooted, hundreds of years old. Telephone and electric poles for miles around were either leaning, or fallen, on the ground—

Busses upturned, an airplane in the street, Hugo's wrath, nobody could beat. A boat in the road, on your way downtown told of the damage, that Hugo had done.

Hugo battered these Islands loose and fast. Breaking windows, and smashing glass, galvanize was flying—like birds through the air Hugo and his whole family must have been here.

Hugo wrecked businesses, colleges, hotels galore, churches and hospitals, and many more. These Islands were a shocking sight to see, when Hugo left us, a demon was he.

But the worst part of it all my friends, listen to this. I spent that night with my sister, which was a great risk!

For when Hugo tore the bedroom roofs clean off the house. God bless that little bathroom, that saved our lives.

We stayed there till Hugo was almost gone, not knowing if we would live, to see the next morn. While Big Clarence, wrapped his belt buckle around the doorknob. To keep it from opening, I sat close to the tub. But that door just kept opening again and again and I happened to peek out, amidst the wind and the rain to see no roofs on the bedrooms, was not a surprise, I knew it had to be Satan, in Hugo's disguise.

It was five-thirty that morning, when we opened the door. Hugo was still raving a little less than before, and through a little window by the side of a shelf my sister began calling to my brother for help.

Come help us, she screamed out, we need help down here, but my brother had already started to come down there, so, he and his sons and some other man, I didn't know, took us all up to his house. There was no other place to go.

These Islands have never experienced such a plight. As when Hurricane Hugo struck us that night. Everybody suffered, regardless of wealth. Hugo was the worst Hurricane, we have ever felt.

But while Hugo was raving, our loving Father above was watching his children, with a heart full of love. Let us give Him the glory, sing praise to His name, for saving our lives, from Hugo's domain.

Stephanie J Terrell
A SPECIAL PICTURE?
Look inside your mind.
What picture do you see?
Create it with your heart.
What could it really be?
You may see a cloud,
I may see the rain,
You, a tiny flower,
I, a candy cane.
We each have our own canvas
To fill as we see fit.
A meadow green,
A city street,
Or just a baseball mitt.
The thing about each canvas
We can add right to the end.
I know the thing that I would add
It would be a friend.
We can paint a pretty picture
With colors all array
But a friend is someone special
With words we just can't say!

Dorothy Hazuda
THE GATES OF HELL

Dedicated to the traumatic memories of the San Francisco quake.

We stood at the gates of hell
My family and I
The earth moving beneath our feet
As the waves upon the ocean
The clanging of steel gates
Like a train rumbling through a station

It was 5:04 at the San Francisco Zoo
About 300 yards from the Pacific Ocean
Exiting the gate
When all hell broke loose!
With a savage fury and without mercy
Grinding its teeth, clanging its chains
Snatching anyone it can
In its jaws of destruction

October 17, '89, when the earth shook
The entire city was draped in black
The fires of hell shot skyward
The inferno burned incessantly
And no human could douse
The flames from the Wrath of God
Showered on this city
As on the cities of Sodom and Gomorrah

It was 7.0 on the Richter scale
The worst since 1906
And the Bay Bridge crumbled
From top to bottom deck

But we'll always remember
My family and I
Our 10-day vacation in San Francisco
And the indelible mark
It left with us
As we boarded the plane
And bid farewell
To that ravaged city
And a moment we'll never forget
A moment Frozen in Time

Jean B Finley
SONG OF THE SEA
I delight in the feel of the cool sea mist
and the tang of the salt-sea air.
The hue and cry of the circling gulls,
and the old sea's roar.
I love the feel of the cold damp sand;
lacy foam as it curls 'round my feet.
The prickle of skin at the sight of a fin,
and the old sea-lore.

But my heart belongs far out on the sea
where the shore has gone from view.
There, she sings to me sweet songs of love,
that old sea-whore.
Give me her wild sea winds and crashing waves;
let me battle her moon-pulled tides.
She is fickle and dangerous, but she is my love,
and my life, evermore!

David Long
THE STREET
I can feel the wind in my hair
And the pavement beneath my wheels
And my troubles drift into the ground
My pain
My sorrow
My fears
All left behind somewhere in the street
I can hear it calling to me,
Challenging me
I can absorb anything
But it cannot
It cracks under the weight of others
I am the street

Clara Jo White
THE ESSENCE OF CHARACTER
C is for commitment
H is for honesty
A is for attitude
R is for respect
A is for ambition and accomplishments.
C is for courage
T is for tolerance
E is for effort
R is for religion of chosen faith.

Thomas Michael Atkinson
LONELINESS

I dedicate this poem to my sister Joanne, for her unconditional love has given me strength and hope.

Loneliness hangs over me
Like a big gray cloud.
I'm screaming inside
But I want to scream out loud.
My heart's wide open
To any kind face.
I have a compelling need
To fill an empty space.
Love or infatuation
They both cause pain.
Is it right or wrong
Am I going insane.
What I feel is dangerous
This I can see.
But I have so much to give
I need some given back to me.
I feel tears behind my eyes
Like water splashing against the shore.
I have myself and my God
And I still need something more.
I guess I'll take a deep breath
Let out a sigh.
Love will come to me someday
After all I'm not a bad guy.

Robert D Barber
RAINBOW
The rain subsided, the storm was spent
And the rainbow appeared with colors, across the sky it went
Many wondrous things God has given to us
But none so grand, nor beautiful, as a rainbow sent down to us
'Tis said you can follow a rainbow and at the end there's a pot 'O' gold
Who needs it, when you see colors all grand and bold
Setting there in the sky
Free for every eye
You can get gold in many ways
But a rainbow comes only when God says
After a soft fresh rain
Pitter, patters on your windowpane
'Tis like the Lord is wiping clean the sky
With one glorious wink of his gentle eye
So when you see a rainbow, don't think of material things
Think of what God has done for us, his underlings
You cannot look at a rainbow and think a material thought
You can only think of things that the Lord thinks you ought
So when you see a rainbow, setting up there in the sky
Say, God, I'm glad to be here, just living right here under your eye.

Ruth E Maloney
LOSS AT THE FEAR OF DISCOVERY

With thanks to Mom, for believing in me; to Dad, for inspiring this poem, and to Jerry, for encouraging me to write again.

Thought to be deep
in sleep,
a flashlight would glow
through my pink blanket
as a Hitchcock mystery
unfolded in my bed.
So clever at seven
to read beneath the covers;
certain to never be caught.
'Til one wee hour,
the "Boogie Man" tugged
upon my window shade,
lifting it slowly
to reveal my secret library.
Inching lower, staring, trembling,
I snapped off the penlight,
buried my eyes in the pillow,
and closed my mystery novels
forever.

Victoria Langdon Jenkins
WOMAN
A woman is a mother, a lover, a friend
Giving to all, and ready to bend
But what about loyalty
It's easy to see
She's loyal to everyone
Except to me
That child that's within her
Has been put on a shelf
She's loyal to Everyone
Except to
Herself

Martin Anderson
DESERT NIGHTS

To Roya, amid the earth, renewed in verdure.

Desert Nights
bare your soul
to the silent voice of mortality.
Life and death
dance with the wind,
which sings through charred needles
of lightning struck saguaros.
There is no place
to hide.

Nathan Bradley Jones
SOME GREAT BACKS
This poem is dedicated to the hard runners and masters of the sack,
The popularity of these goes mainly to the quarterback.
Like that of Jack Lambert, linebacker for the "Steelers," in fact,
When he would rumble, quarterbacks would fumble or tumble and crack.
Csonka liked a little blood and possessed speed and might,
He ran toward defenders rather than daylight.
When Dick Butkus would hit you, your future would go black,
He would crunch you from the side, the front, or the back!
Some call him "The Juice," his name was O.J.,
When you needed some yardage, he was the man for the play.
The instant Howie Long gets angry there's a sudden spark,
Then it's "Howie Time" and the opposition's Fate looks dark.
"Sweetness," better known as Payton, was a bone jarring runningback,
As soon as he touched the ball it was an onslaught attack!
The hits these guys made whether running or blocking,
Were absolutely, positively, heart stopping!
Of the NFL's greatest hitters, these are just a few,
There are many more who honor the red, white, and blue.

Michelle L Heintzel
MY LIFE
It kept raining
All day long.
The sun stopped shining
Bright and strong.

This was my life
So dark and cold.
A giant shadow
Tall and bold

Every night
I'd kneel and pray
And hope that my prayers
Would be answered
Someday

And still I wait
With complete despair
I do not move
Just sit and stare
At nothing

Michelle L Heintzel
A SINGLE LEAF
The sun shines bright
Through the trees,
A single leaf
Rocks in the breeze.

Never lonely,
Never scared,
It has no desire
To be paired.

The leaf gently hums
A cheerful song,
Then the wind joins in
And hums along.

But the leaf grows old
First green, then brown.
Rather than hum,
It makes not a sound.

This lifeless leaf
Falls to the ground.
The chilly wind
Throws it around.

No longer happy
Or filled with cheer,
The wind is bitter
Winter is here.

Linda Arwood
FINAL CURTAIN

In honor of Jesus, whose mercy continuously sustains me.

Lack of compassion
No kindness it seems
What happened to young men's visions
And old men's dreams

In this world of greed
And friction and hate
Can this world be mended
Or is it too late

Child abuse and drugs
And moral decay
Abortion and AIDS
Will they go away

These are the signs of the times
God sees and He knows
Repent, He says
The final curtain is
Starting to close

Debbie Dick
KEEP ON GOING
Hold on time of joy is near
if I knew you were sad I'd
help wipe away your tears.
I heard someone say, I know how
you feel, then turn your back
away your heart they steal.

I'm on your side, I've tried and tried,
but once again, I've learned they lied.
I am sure we'll keep trying to say
the least, just to keep our hearts
in peace.

I'm only a dot upon this earth,
seeking the love God gave me at
birth.
If I had known it would turn out
this way, I would have asked him
to use different clay.

So as we go on from day to day,
I'll only have one thing left to say.
I've loved and lost this is true,
but the love you lost has made me
blue. Around the corner there I
go again, someone must love
me, I just met a
friend.

Diego Francica
NIGHT
Night,
temporary darkness,
which allows . . .
unspeakable creatures,
to hide from any . . .
intruding light,
Light which may,
bring about,
destruction, or to others,
immortality—?

Bessie L Imel
GRANDMA'S LAMENT
I don't know how it happened, I
don't know what to say,
I just heard about it, earlier today.
They were only young boys, happy
and carefree,
They joined the Cub Scouts, a better
boy to be.
They trusted their leader, a good man
I've been told,
How he could do such Evil, I will
never know.
The boys were too scared, they would
not tell,
But that man molested them, and
many more as well.
The Police have kept him hidden, to
protect him from all harm,
The Parents are looking for him, not
to send him to the farm.
They want to kill the Bastard, for this
thing that he has done,
This Grandma would gladly join
them, if I could just get me a gun.
"Vengeance is mine," so sayeth the
LORD,
So I can't go after him, OH GOD!
this waiting is so hard.
I just want this monster to know, that
his days are numbered,
Nightmares I wish upon him, every
time he tries to slumber.
And if vengeance belongs to GOD, as
the Bible does say,
I hope he can't get in Heaven, upon
the judgement day.
This EVIL child molester, that calls
himself a man,
I hope you burn in HELL, I hope as
hard as I can.

Celeste Yolanda Williams
RENAISSANCE OF A RAINBOW
In rainbows of crystals so mystique
Whyforth art thy reign so sweet
Midst frownful sorrows of grey
clouds above
What treasureful starbows to shine of
love

Whereas, in the twilight of a
midday's serenity
Beholding one's curiosities of a
paradise afar
Hast reflected thy rainbow of an
ultimate infinity
Its twinkling of an eye, shining
neither here nor thar

A most wondrous way doesth it
effect so bright
Winks sparkling happiness with its
sure blushful ray
'Tis rainbows of love; thereinforth art
thy plight
'Tis of yesterday's tomorrows in
renaissance of today

As peacefully and timelessly
rainbows eventfully grace the sky
Within colorfully ageless auras of
centuries gone by
Where glowing florescent
waterclouds adventurously of cheer
Doesth wish one sweet dreams that
say never do fear
For thy arts with thee and thee after
the pouring rains
Included thee, the moon, the sun and
stars descend
True upon all the dreams that need
make amends
Knowing the renaissance of a
rainbow could surely be
Twilight of a burning candle aflame
in history

Janice Ponchaud
FAREWELL

To Wah Z who taught me how to go within and ride upon the sound of HU.

Do not weep for me when I am gone
Every good deed I ever did
Was a stairstep into heaven
And every time I backslid
Was a lesson learned.
I did not come to prove a point.
I came, like you, because
The time was ripe.
When heaven washed this Soul
Upon ITs shore
I emerged as the seashell must
emerge
With the ocean's sound in its bosom
And the promise that one day
The sea will return for it once more.

Lucile Morin
HE IS MY FRIEND
He is my friend
Who smiles at me
Even when I make mistakes
Who holds my hand
When I am sad
Who has a kind word
When others criticize
Who loves me
Just because
I'm me

Deanna Berg
CANDLELIGHT
We lit the darkness with our fire,
from worlds apart,
we fueled it with desire.
But when did the feelings start?

We played our games until the end,
and found that we both lost.
How long does it take broken hearts
to mend,
how long do we pay the cost.

Well it's much too late to wonder
now,
the smoke has cleared
and the fire's died down.
In the distance I see you disappear.

And the last tear falls
as I gaze into the embers.
I have no fear at all,
for I have something to remember.

I turn and slowly walk away
into the shadows of the night.
No more words left to say,
as I hold up my candlelight.

Mary Angela Dennis
SUDDENLY IT HAPPENED

I dedicate this poem to my loving husband, Roy Dennis. He is everything to me, he is my reason for living and my inspiration to write.

Suddenly, it happened;
My world stopped in its tracks.
This magic day you noticed me;
You smiled, and I smiled back.

It was such an ordinary day,
Not a glimpse of sunlight,
Cold and Gray.

But as you looked deep in my eyes,
I felt my temperature rise.
With beating heart, I realized
That golden sunshine filled the skies.

You held my hand, my spirits soared
and my life changed forevermore.
Suddenly, it happened.

Mary Angela Mathis
THE WORLD WON'T STOP FOR YOU
Our good times faded, our love
simply died
I wanted to work it out, But you just
said, "I've tried."

So we split apart and went our
separate ways
Seems forever since we've talked,
though it's only a couple of days

My life hasn't stopped, though I miss
your touch
I still care for you, But not quite as
much

You left me here alone, feeling your
love was a lie
Seems you didn't want to hurt me,
But you wanted to say "good-bye"

You are very special and the time
with you was true
Now that it is over, I've realized

"The World Won't Stop For You."

Karla Hunter
NOW & FOREVER
Having to see you leave,
Will not be easy to do.
Remembering all the good things,
You and I have been through.

These last three years,
We've really gotten close.
Shared deep secrets,
No one else knows.

I've seen things in you,
I've never seen before.
All of these things,
I've come to love and adore.

When you leave,
We'll all see the change.
I'll miss you very much,
Things just won't be the same.

Never forget me,
And always remember . . .
We'll always be together,
Now & Forever.

Karla Hunter
A TEARDROP
A teardrop's worth a million words,
They have all the feelings in the
world.

They have fallen hundreds of times,
For many different reasons.

We should treasure a teardrop,
For all the time to come.

Because each teardrop is a special
story,
Of every person that cares.

Martha A Long
MY HEART SINGS
Today my heart sings.
Who knows what tomorrow brings?
Twenty-four hours of peace and
calm,
or twenty-four hours of sadness and
alarm;

either may be my appointed task.
To be living, will be all I ask.
May I do my best all day long
And help others learn a glad song.

RoseMarie Jordan Fraser

MY SILENT ROOM WITHIN

I have a place deep in my soul no other soul can know.
A place where only angels, and the eye of God can go.
It holds the secrets of my heart—
My happiness, my pain—
My hopes and dreams
And memories of all that life has been.

I open up the windows of my silent room within
Each evening when I kneel in prayer—
And let God's love shine in.
For without His love to brighten it
And keep my dreams alive
None but the darkest moments would be able to survive.

And for my faithful ritual I find a great reward—
God sends the grace of hope to me
And my courage is restored.

Delia Mays

BLESSINGS TO A NEW NURSE

To my daughter, Elizabeth Jeffery, on graduation at age 50, from Nursing School.

There are no words that can ever say
How happy we are on your graduation day
May God always look down from his home up above
And guide you in his everlasting love

May blessings be yours as you go on your way
Bringing health and comfort to your patients each day
With God by your side you can seldom go wrong
May you finish each day with a happy song

On those hectic days when nothing turns out right
Keep a prayer in your heart and God in your sight
You are the Angel of Mercy who eases the pain
Of those dear ones who are feeble and lame

As you spend the coming years giving service to others
Remember they are all someone's sisters and brothers
Treat them well as though they were your own
Your reward waits for you in God's heavenly home

Katie O'Grady-Brown

LET ME INTRODUCE MYSELF . . . MEET ME

Dedicated with love to George, my husband and life partner.

I can't take the place of Teddy,
Or share the secrets that you shared,
Nor do I know the days of laughter,
And all the nights you both were scared.

But believe me, I'm more than ready
To make up for all lost time,
For it's always been my motto—
"Boy without a bear?—It's a crime!"

So take me home and love me well,
New secrets will we share,
And every time you look at me,
You'll know just how much I care.

For, we cannot change what has passed,
So, let's just forget the sorrows.
We can enjoy "our" new todays,
And build our bright tomorrows.

Katie O'Grady-Brown

GRANDMA AGNES

Written in loving memory of my grandmother, Agnes Marie O'Grady, who died on September 16, 1989.

Dear Grandma Agnes, so sweet and frail,
It breaks my heart to watch you pale,
To see you struggle to catch each breath,
To hear the rattle down deep in your chest.
The gentle arms that once held me tight,
Now are all battered from the dreadful fight.
That will to survive burns deep within,
As you battle back time and again,
To regain the ground that was hopelessly lost,
Valiantly trying—no matter the cost.
Never complaining, and never crying,

The only sound heard, an occasional sighing.
Sadly, I watch you slipping away,
Realizing now, there's much more to say.
I love you, Grandma, thanks for all you've done,
To make our lives better and a happier one.
You enriched all who knew your tender touch,
Your family and friends will miss you so much.
For your kindness to others, your desire to serve,
God will take you to heaven, the reward you deserve.
Now you must leave for the Angels are here,
I love you so Agnes, I do, Grandma dear.

Katie O'Grady-Brown

ETERNAL VALENTINE

Dedicated to my father, Thomas, and in loving memory of my mother, Mary Janice.

There is a love so deep and rare,
Not ofttimes given by the gods,
That truly stands the test of time,
Alas, all others pale in compare.

This love begins as a fragile rose,
Which needs such loving care,
And is nurtured by the tender passion,
That's shared in sweet repose.

This love is not born of gold,
But rather, is forged by daily life.
The trials and the victories
Hammer, as the shape takes hold.

And if this love grows stronger,
As each passing year unfolds,
Through sunshine, rain and laughter,
'til one of them is here no longer.

Take heart!

For exists a love uncompromised,
Which happens but once a lifetime,
That not even death can break the bond,
By which these hearts are tied.

Katie O'Grady-Brown

VENUS

To an old friend, who is gone but not forgotten.

Very soul of my
Existence,

Never parted,
Until death
Separated us.

Katie O'Grady-Brown

THE GIFT

Dedicated with love to Thomas Patrick, my brother and friend.

On this day many years ago,
These folks called Dad and Mother,
Gave to me a gift so rare,
So sweet and fair,
All wrapped in cloth,
With love of course,
They called it baby brother.

Now I ask you folks,
What's a child to do,
With this little bundle
All wrapped in blue?
And after all, I was only two!
I handed him back to Mother.
The years flew by as he grew,
From babe, to tot, to teen.
And all the wonder that I knew,
Might not have ever been,
If on this day many years ago,
Not quite like any other,
That Mom and Dad hadn't given the gift,
That they called baby brother.

Happy Birthday T.P.!
Love Always, Kate

Bee Faigle

INDIAN SUMMER (IN OCTOBER)

Whatever leaves are left on trees and have not fallen down
Color all the landscape with golden hues and brown—
The cool winds now should be blowin' in,
But, somehow, we'd rather go for a swim!

Fireplace and heaters should start to glow
The temp's way up high—when it should be low—
Yet the heat of summer, is still with us,
And, we really don't like this extra fuss!

Mother Nature is surely doin' us in
Playing her jokes on us and our kin,
For, tho' this is called "Indian Summer,"
We'd rather name it "October bummer!"

So take it away! and send it back
To the Indians who named it—for a better lack,

Of wanting to have, the cold and the snow—
Then bring on good "Ole" man winter—with a heigh! and ho! ho!

Christa Johnson
TOGETHER IN UNITY

South Africa is fighting it is a nation that is split.

There are so many hatreds there that people cannot live.

Why does it matter what you are whether you are rich or poor.

Why does the color of your skin decide what group you should be in.

Nelson Mandela was set free after twenty-seven years of captivity.

For injustices he did not commit by the white peoples' government.

His release has given hope to a South Africa beginning to cope.

With man's inhumanity to man and all of the prejudices that it can.

So that one day all can be free and live together in unity.

Stephen Lee Chan
ONE SUMMER NIGHT

The sky grew dark as the day's end was fast approaching,
Just watching the clouds clear away was quite enlightening.

I marvel at the beauty of the clear moonlit night,
The silhouette of the swaying trees is a spectacle, an awesome sight.

The interplay of light from the dazzling stars above,
Tells an imaginative story full of life, full of love.

The cool summer breeze accompanied by a faint mist,
Trickles upon my face, oh what better feeling than this!

Suddenly the wind blew harder causing the leaves to rustle,
It made funny ringing noises in my ear and yet so subtle.

Then the wind died down creating absolute silence,
Music of stillness resound beautifully in evanescence.

The moon emanates its radiance illuminating the dark filled night,
Giving it a festive ambiance similar to that of candlelight.

Now I think of the Maker my heart sings His praise,
Revealing His revelation to me in a countless different ways.

This lovely sight before me shows His glorious handiwork,
As if it were a painting demonstrated only by His intricate stroke.

The skies depict a divine miracle with infinite creativity and might,
This message reaches everywhere on a starry summer night.

Stephen Lee Chan
ON THE EMOTIONAL BRINK

How often we hide when we are hurting,
Afraid to reveal true feelings thinking that if we do, we might lose everything.
How often we pretend all is well when everything is falling apart,
Much as we wish that we can have a brand-new start.
How often we try to maintain an image of stability when the foundation of our lives is crumbling,
Hoping that God will restore our strength and learn to worry not a thing.
How often we waste our emotional energy building facades,
Unable to cope and accept the things we never had.
When we are despondent and on the emotional brink,
'Tis the time to focus our minds to God and think.
Gradually we learn to return to the right direction, guided by His grace,
We share our true lives and our love, that are among the secrets behind His powerful praise!

Rebecca Colbourn
WHY

For Mom.

I ask you Why?
But you—you never answer,
So I wonder why?
Do you not hear my calling from the dark?
All I can see is your eyes
Which shine with the light of a thousand suns.
They say look—we have your answer
They silently mock me
So I wonder Why?

Betsy Lee
DEAF MAN

Deaf man . . . open your eyes and hear.
Deaf man . . . what you been knowing all along.

Deaf man . . . you think you been missing out?
What you say, can't hear my voice?

Deaf man . . . life is calling out to you.
Not for your ears to hear, for your heart.

Open your eyes . . . hear life calling to you.
Let love in, it will make you whole.

Love brings changes. What you say?
New ears? No, deaf man, a new heart.

Deaf man . . . open your eyes and hear.
Hear with your heart, deaf man . . . life is calling out to you.

Robert T Berryhill
MY DAUGHTER DAWNA

With raven hair and snow-white skin
I wonder in my mind is this young girl a kin?
She is like her mother who is good and fine
But she in ways could be all mine.
A mysterious young girl who is active and bold
A gift to us like a mine full of gold
A child that is sensitive, feeling, and good
Her friends are always here for the friendly food
Her eyes are different from the beautiful browns
With several colors that shine, even when she frowns
Her mouth is shaped like an angel's delight
Just like her mother's beauty she is quite a sight
Sharp and clear are her morals and mind
Her goals are set no more to find
This girl's mystery is no longer a bore
She is my daughter forevermore

Grace M Strutz
FOR A MOMENT

Have you ever watched the snowflakes falling
And gaze upon them with a stare
Then found yourself in fantasy land
In a wonderful world without a care
For a moment
You've left the world of reality
And walked the sparkling path
Then hoped and prayed that the world you've entered
Could always stay like that
But as you put your hands out
To catch the falling flakes
They disappear as they touch your skin
And you find yourself, now awake
It felt so good for a moment
To have been, in that other place
But now you're back to reality
And to the real world that you now face

R L Toliver

R L Toliver
OFFERINGS

To my extended family and all those who have supported me through the years.

If God can offer sunny days with Puffy Clouds,
The least you can offer is a smile.

R L Toliver
RESOLUTION

It seems that I should know by now, naught let my heart so easily fly,
To those who hold so little stake, and with my feelings so frivolously play.
And in my life some loves I've had, and woefully they've turned out bad,
No longer shall I be a fool, so painful, oh, this Golden Rule.

Some say insane, and I may be, though other fools chase destiny.
For as will tick loves endless clock, if I in pain wait long enough,
To keep the faith in love past time, for when 'tis done I'll sure find mine.
And in my mind some theories change, but there is one that still remains,
Like what is life that I should care—if I had not a love to share.
As moon so oft affects the tide, 'tis often best to swallow pride,
And ere remember this lament, from hell all loneliness is sent.
I may be wrong, I may be naught, but gather in this minute thought,
To lose love's faith is just to die, and not in graves do all dead lie.

In closing now I do resolve, to mope does not the problem solve.
So gather up your shattered heart, and once again do make a start,
For what is life that one should live—if one has not more love to give.

R L Toliver
FASHIONS

You wear your love so sweetly,
It fits your soul so nice.
It's loose about the shoulders
And snugs your heart so tight.
You wear your love so sweetly,
It shades of every hue,
Eyes sparkle when you're happy,
A muted smile when blue.
You wear your love so neatly.
It's striking and it's bold,
Yet fits your shape uniquely,
From follicle to sole.
You wear your love so chicly,
It shades of every hue.
You wear your love uniquely,
Because your love is you.

Glen J Detton Jr
PASS THE TORCH

Across the land blows a wind and the memory of a man that lead a nation.
It whispers the name; Kenn-nedy;
Kenn-nedy;
John—F.—Kennedy

The story that fell upon all that loved him know the indignation. In halls, doorways and streets the children of the Nation did weep.

Across the land blows a wind and the memory of a man that lead a nation.
It whispers the name; Kenn-nedy;
Kenn-nedy;
John—F.—Kennedy

His words echo through the valleys, open windows, streets and alleys. He saw the future before our time and passed the torch cut short of time.

Across the land blows a wind and the memory of a man that lead a nation.
It whispers the name; Kenn-nedy;
Kenn-nedy;
John—F.—Kennedy

Marsha K Carowick
BELIEVING

Dedicated to my father and mother for all the help they have rendered.

This smile is not the first heartbroken
These eyes are not the first to cry
There is nothing more to do
Nowhere to hide
Must I prove
My Love to pride

I may become hopelessly devoted
Holding onto the edge
As Love is pushed aside
We've nowhere to hide

Spend time with those you Love
Do not cast them aside, but Love in their pride

If the wind is right
  Sensitivity and tranquility will be found
I wish to be free
  With sanctity, not sympathy

Life will be good
  To hold the one and only possession
The gift of kindness
  Maybe my peers will smarten, drifting my way
I should say many things throughout my life
  Although, I know I'll never take the time

Jenny Tribis

Jenny Tribis
A BICENTENNIAL TRIBUTE
1776 two hundred years ago today,
The Fourth of July became our Independence Day;
For it was on this day America was free.
Our nation, under God, won its liberty.

The minutemen that fought the war,
  Were courageous, bold and true.
They fought for the banner,
  The Red, White and Blue.

The field of blue was for the sky of the new constellation.
As each star represents a state of this Great Nation.
Thirteen Original Colonies, stand for the stripes so bright;
That proudly wave in our banner, seven red, and six are white.

God bless Thomas Jefferson, who made the resolution.
That all men be created equal, as he signed the Constitution.
God saved our country from war and desolation;
He saved our Colonies, and united us as one Nation.

Kate Heyer-Deemer
THE CYCLE OF LIFE
Birth.
Babies brought laughter and joy.
Little girls brought unconditional love and promise.
Adolescence brought pain, hurt, and confusion.
Young adulthood brought anger and resentment.
Adulthood brought understanding, compassion, and love with limits.
Womanhood brought awareness, growth, trust, and faith.
Old age brought mellowness, forgiveness, forgetfulness, and peace.
Death.

Latice Brockman
YOUR SINS
When you're rolling around in sin, sometimes it seems that you have no friends, until you take a look within. That's when you know that you're blessed and that's enough to help you get rid of that mess.

That mess you livin' in, aw, you know that mess called sin. And if you find that too much to bear, you have a friend that is willing to share, all of life's problems with you and you'll gain victory too. And when he gets through witchew, you won't know what to do, 'cause he'll have all kinds of good stuff for you to get into.

And wait a minute I'm not finished. You see your soul will be replenished when your friend gets finished. Now who is this friend that dwells within. It's the man that has freed us all from sin, that's who it is. Honey, let me tell ya, I been knowing him for years. And before he came into my life, I shed many, many tears. For many, many years. 'Cause I was living in sin. Naw. I ain't gone tell you that agin.

And by the time you get through reading this poem, I guarantee you'll know him.

'Cause he's sitting right next to you. Just tell him what you want him to do. Ah yes, now I'm through 'cause from here on out, Jesus gone tell you what to do.

Debbie Sims
TRUE FRIENDS

This poem is dedicated to my mother, Kathleen, my great-grandmother, GeeGee, and my dear friend, Natalie Stringer, for their loving support and belief in my writing.

True friends are one in many,
Feel privileged if you have any.
They'll brighten up your days
With their unique ways.
Bring you up, when you're down,
Make you smile, not frown.
Put a dance in your step,
Enhance your own pep.
Sharing true feelings, ideas and dreams,
That's what true friends mean.

Accepting you for who you are
Instead of judging from afar.
Someone to lean on who truly cares
Is actually pretty rare.
Friends are an inspiration to your soul,
Makes you wanna rock 'n' roll.
You forget all your worries
In a big hurry,
Making you feel lighter
Now the future looks brighter!!!

Debbie Sims
ODE TO MY PARENTS
I want to thank you for making me turn out so cool.
You gave me some special tools.
You gave them to me to share,
watch out, I'm gonna blare!
I truly don't know what I want to do . . .
This makes me feel like pooh.
I've been really depressed lately,
half the time I don't even feel like getting dressed,
so then I act lazy . . .
Boy, that makes me crazy!
So, I decided what I'm gonna do
to stop feeling like pooh.
I'm gonna be a writer
'cause it makes me feel lighter.
I may not be the way you want me to be . . .
I'm just me.
You gave me tools,
you both taught me the rules.
Since I got the keys from you two,
I'm sure they'll do.
This is just a little note to let you know I love you both!

Polly N Blazakis
IF

For giving me the inspiration to write such a poem, I dedicate this to Robert Zavakos.

If you ever need a friend
  I have a lot to share
I'll be there till the end
  To show you how much
I really care.

If you ever need a guide
  To help you see the light
I'll be right by your side
  To make everything seem
All right.

And if you're ever looking for love
  You have to look no more
For I will show you a side of love
  That you've never seen before.

So if you're ever feeling lonely
  And blue
Just remember I love you.

Jane M Dils
TUG AT MY HEART
I feel a tug at my heart.
There seems little I
can do.
My hands are tied,
when they want to
reach out,
to wipe away the tears.
Erase all the hurts.
I feel a tug at my heart.

Ola Mae Phillips
I MARRIED TWO MEN
I married two men,
The day I was wed;
I must have been crazy,
And out of my head.
One man is gentle,
Loving and kind;
The very best husband,
A girl could find.
The other is selfish,
Cruel and mean;
The grouchiest man,
I have ever seen!
I cannot separate them,
They share the same body;
To one I'll give my love,
To the other—karate!

Will Adkins
THE ROSE
No one knows what I am feeling,
No one knows what I want to say
No one else is inside of me,
No one knows why things are grey,
So hear my only wish or plea—
Let me alone, I'll be OK.

Some people want to touch the rose
But they know once touched, it will die
It's all about wanting to give,
And giving a little too much—
People think time is too precious
And they're always in a rush
But is it wrong to care too much?

It hurts to see another hurt
Especially when it's the rose
But it's better to stay away
And hope it grows towards the sun
Where I am forever waiting.

Anita Whaley
THAT FATEFUL NIGHT

In loving memory of Todd Joseph Doucet, my only true love. May you find happiness in Heaven.

We were there, together, at the Thanksgiving party;
It was just before 12:40
A girl went into your room
She was just looking, we wrongly assumed
She dug through your closet and picked up your gun
I still don't know why, maybe for fun
We didn't know whether or not there was a round in the chamber
The only one who knew, was apparently her
She came into the room, with it, anyway
Taking it from her, seemed the only way
You said to her, "Give me the gun.
You could hurt someone."
From her, you grabbed the gun;
This Thanksgiving party, was no longer fun
It was then, that I stepped in
I took the gun, from her, then
It went off, and I fell to the ground
And, in the room, there was no longer a sound
You fell to your knees, and held me tight
You had never before cried, as you did that night
In your truck, I had left my poems, there
And you looked at my book, with a pain which was rare
Through my poems, you began to look
A deep breath, you then took
For, what you read, didn't seem true
Most were of how I wished to die, instead of you
You had finally figured it out
And what my death had been all about
You couldn't believe, I had done that for you
But, then you realized, you would have, too
Then you thought of how I had died
And, again, you began to cry and cry
I woke up, then
And, I wished that this was how it had been
Not that you cried and hurt as such
But, dying for you, I want so much
If you could have, a chance to live
There is nothing, that I wouldn't give
Even, my life, I'd give for you
For, the love we had, was oh, so true

Robin C Smith
LONELY PEOPLE
The old lady down the block
Whose family's all dead and gone
The little girl in a dirty smock
Whose mother leaves her all alone

The old man in an old folks place
Whose children have forgotten him

now
The runaway a scared look on her face
Wanting to go home, wondering how

The young girl whose face is plain
Who's never been asked for a date
The service boy eyes full of pain
As he reads that she won't wait

The young widow who struggles not to cry
During the long lonely nights
The man and woman who say goodbye
After that last long bitter fight

Lonely people
Are everywhere
Lonely people
And no one cares

Erica Suard
A BUCKET FOR NANTUCKET
I was sitting on the deck,
Just waiting for a peck.
But there was none, I said, "Where's the fun?"
I want my money back.

You gave her a ticket for Jamaica,
But me, a bucket for Nantucket.
I just want some fun, you son of a gun,
And I can't get it out of a bucket.

Erica Suard
MUSIC
Music is your feeling,
Feelings are your life.
Life is just an empty space,
Filled with what you like.

If your life is miserable,
That's the path you chose.
If your life is full of joy,
Your spirit must have rose.

Music is the core of life,
It is the main attraction.
The first song that was ever made,
Started a chain reaction.

Why is music so, so special?
That's the questions I ask.
Not a doctor or a nurse,
Music is my task.

Michelle Orrison
THE DREAM WE ONCE HAD
I'm standing alone, alone
in the rain . . .
While my whole world is
turning gray . . .
I once was in a world of
happiness . . .
As we dreamed it was
you and I
together forever
but now . . .
That dream we once had
has drifted away
and now . . .
I'm standing alone, alone
in the rain . . .
While my whole world is
turning gray . . .

Please . . . don't turn away!

Dawn Lovell
MY FIRST GRANDCHILD

Dedicated to MARK WILLIAM LOVELL. Grandma Loves You.

The morning little grandson
that you were born
was surely my most
happiest one.

The rain came down,
and washed the world clean.
Then the sun came out,
and the birds began to sing.

There were many to welcome you
on this earth.
When God decided
it was time for your birth.

Grandpa slept down on the couch
to hear the phone when I called to
announce.
That he was grandpa to a sweet baby boy
and listen to his happy sounds of
joy.

There were tears in my eyes
and a smile on my face.
As I lovingly welcomed you
into the human race.

Deborah L Wilson
SEARCHING

Dedicated to: Bob and Debbie for what was once the most unique love ever. I'll always love you, Bob.

A bit lonely, a bit desperate, is there anyone around?
It's just too quiet, there's not even a sound!
It wasn't like you, it's not fair the way you walked out on me.
All I wanted was a chance. Love doesn't come often, and it's never free.
So why can't you understand, I wanted to have you for my man.
I'm going to look far beyond and above 'cause I want a man just like you to love. It's okay for me to do some pretending that we are still as one, at least till me heart is completely mended.

Linda Pagliaro
FRIEND, MY FRIEND

Dedicated to Patrick . . . my inspiration . . . today, tomorrow and always . . . With Love.

Our friendship is a "special one"
And this you ought to know.
For every time you look at me
My heart melts like snow.

You seem to know just what to say
And know just what to do
To make a smile come on my face
And turn my skies to blue.

Your phone calls make my evening
And your voice makes my night.
Your caring words and sentiments
Make everything alright.

For having a friend, a friend like you,
Means so much to me
And knowing that you're always
there
Makes the world a happier place
to be.

So you see, you are the one
Who turned my world around . . .
And no matter what the future holds
"A friend in you I've found."

Kathryn Flatley
AFTERNOON REFLECTIONS
The rays from the sun pulsed brilliant and warm, as I sat in my past, once again I did mourn.
For a life not lived, just controlled and endured, through emotions at war, all bloody and torn.
If I let myself go would I be free, from the aches and pains of maturity?
Oh God, what's it like just to be me?

Sun heal my wounds and make me whole, let me laugh at myself and not be so droll.
To risk what I feel and let it all go, and vanish like props in a magic show.
Gentle winds bring kindness and whisk away doom, let my heart open and feel love bloom.
In a space where fear has dwelled so long, that there's no room for laughter or lighthearted song.

Rain wash away the sins etched in gold, let nature's tears be food for a soul.
Undernourished and barren from needs long ignored, foreign to feelings of comfort and warmth.
We get lost on the path of maturity, and become who the world wants us to be.
But the price we pay in this web of disguise, is the death of our core, interwoven with lies.

The lies become truths when we look in the glass, confused and distorted by the hundreds of masks.
We've adorned for the masses, in an effort to hide, our humanness, which once denied,
Fights for its right to again come alive.

It's my right to be separate, as when I was born, and my death much the same with no one along.
But I don't have to die in my quest to be free, if I know in my heart it's okay to be me.
Farewell to you false face of pride, thanks for the shelter I needed to hide.
Until I found my integrity, long buried in this temple I'm proud to call me.

My God, can it be? I'm finally free?

Philipp G Bales
TREEZZZ

To my mother, may her smiles always remain in my heart.

Looking in forward past time
Slipping into TimeSpace
Show-n-Tell, Waves or Particles
Erasing the memories that bring this
world to Sing
Who's to share their true feelings,
Reaching inside
Crying outloud, yet Silence prevails
The medium of Contact
Is it so bright that the man who sees
with only his eyes . . . may still be
blind
Looking deep into the afternoon sky
Calculations to Derive,
The treez freedom of survival
Must last many changing seasons,
Splashing laughter across the page
Who's to blame for phenomenal
powers that just'a few can gain,
Choosing the crossroads requires
much thought indeed
Returning to the years of learning
how to harness some dreams,
Turning these thought-patterns to
Techniques,
A quick sign
Achieving knowledge
The mystics of science,
Thunder in the Distance is a
symphony of its own kind
Gaining Wisdom, curiosity is the
key . . .
Riding on the razor's edge, Listening
to what the treezzz have to say
Wonderful excitement, still now
much then for fun
WATCH THEM FOR NOTIONS!?!

Philipp G Bales
EVENT HORIZON
Sounds,
No sharp corners allowed
Branches taking chances
Making music in the wind
The Snap of a Trunk
Marks the Thunder of Drums,
The Air in an ocean's wave
Within Energy . . . Music is made

A master of creation
To grow so tall on an island of
Imagination
Glorious Life, So Delicious
To Wish Upon, Is to never be Gone

Knowing the Start
The part that doesn't get mentioned
Exploring the Initial State
Reaching in for this Original Face,
Listening to Secrets, Following
Traces . . .

Illissa C White
THERE ARE MANY MANSIONS
Our Lord has said,
"In Heaven there are many
mansions."
There are many mansions
in me, too,
of which you have discovered
only a few.
And the myriad of rooms
I had wished to decorate
have closed doors
with the keys thrown away;
Now furnished only
with dust, lost in gloom's
lonely whispers
that drift down long corridors
to find me,
Echoing softly,
"We can't wait."

Marie Kathleen Watkins
I'M AN ARKANSAS TRAVELER
I'm an Arkansas Traveler
from the Jonesboro Town.
I do a lot of roving
but I never leave this ground.
I've traveled with DeSoto,
Marquette, and Joliet too.
Every day I go 'a wanderin'
but my shoes still look like new.

I always travel with a group
that assembles every day.
Our goal's to cover the entire state
before the end of May.
I've walked along the "Trail of Tears"
of the mighty Cherokee,
and I read of Grandpa's family
in our County's history.
If you want to travel all year long,
and each day learn something new,
then travel in your History books
on "Arkansas" and view
the settlements and early towns
developed by a few
of braver men than you and I,
Oh, aren't you glad they knew
and took great opportunities
to develop our communities.

B J Cook

DEATH WATCH

To Grammie McDonald, we'll love you always.

Strange what can bring a family together.
A small room that seems to suck the life
from everyone.
You come from miles away to sit, to wait, to watch.

You talk a lot and you find out that though
words go unsaid, feelings run deep.
Sometimes you wonder why it takes a death watch
to bring you close.

The answer is simple.
All her life she brought us together,
she kept us close for many years and never
expected anything in return.
Now as we watch her die we realize
how lucky we have been.

Carrie Pilate

GOD'S LOVE

This Poem is dedicated to my husband Lewis J. Pilate and New Mount Zion Baptist Church.

God sent his son to die on the cross
So that our souls would not be lost
He expressed his love through Jesus Christ
God made the greatest sacrifice

God's love is more precious than silver or gold
It abides forever in the bible we're told
God's love is the key to his kingdom today
I believe God's love will never turn you away

For without God's love we all would have died
But he sent his beloved son to walk by our side
Teaching man by parables how to walk in the light
Traveling from city to city by day and by night

Teaching man to love ye one another
Teaching man to remember that we are all Brothers
Teaching man to pray and to let God's love in
Teaching man how love would hide a multitude of Sin

So why can't we my Brothers live
With one another and so freely give
The kind of love God wants us to
That came from Heaven for you, you, and you.

Evelyn Block

THINK OF ME

The Lord said:
When you look at the sky so blue with twinkling stars, a big yellow moon and a bright red sun,
think of me . . .
When you look at a tree with branches so big reaching toward heaven,
think of me . . .
When you see a pretty flower and smell its sweet fragrance,
think of me . . .
When you listen to the song of a beautiful bird,
think of me . . .
When you see a juicy red apple hanging from a tree,
think of me . . .
When you look into the eyes of a precious little child,
think of me . . .
When you meet your Christian friends with a helping hand along life's way,
think of me . . .
When you read this little poem written just for you,
think of me . . .

Evelyn Block

GOD'S LOVE FOR ME

God knew and loved me before I was ever thought of.
God knew and loved me when I was in my mother's womb.
God knew and loved me when I was a babe in arms.
God knew and loved me when I was a young child.
God knew and loved me when I was old and grey.
God knew and loved me when I was a sinner.
God knew and loved me when I became a christian.
God knew and loved me when he gave his only son to die for my sins on the cross.

Randy Britt

THEY ARE THE HOMELESS

A little boy goes into the nearest gas station, washes up there and leaves there, now he's on his way to school. When school is out, he has nowhere to go, he knows nothing but the streets, they are the homeless. The people around the corner home burned down no insurance, now they know nothing but the streets, they are the homeless. Some of them have jobs but not making enough money to afford a place to stay, they are the homeless. Everyone you help, there's a million more, they are the homeless. Who can you blame society, the man in the mirror, President, take a look around you, they are the homeless people. Everywhere you go there's a man on the streets, "Brother can you spare a dime to help towards my next meal," they are the homeless. Tomorrow is another day for the homeless, just another day for the homeless. "Hey brother can you spare a dime?"

Randy Britt

IT'S X-MAS

Cheerful faces Happy souls it's X-MAS
Boy and girls friend and neighbors exchanging gifts
Yes it's X-MAS Wouldn't be nice if every day can be
X-MAS Boys and girls going to door to door singing
X-MAS carols Yes it X-MAS
X-MAS is a time of happiness, loving, and giving
Yes it's X-MAS why can't everyday be X-MAS
Giving don't it make you feel good about yourself
Just to see a person face light's up when they
open their gift Yes it's X-MAS
Wouldn't be nice
if everyday was X-MAS Yes Yes
Yes it's X-MAS
AMEN
Reach out and help someone
Thank you for listening
And God Bless You

Randy Britt

CENTRAL PARK

A hot summer day in Central Park,
Walking through the park waiting
On the summer breeze to come through
Central Park trying to beat the heat
Wave from up above wondering, what the
Birds are thinking about they seem to
Be happy flying from tree to tree, Central
Park such a beautiful sight to see where
Is the squirrels there, they are wondering
How they feel about the heat wave tomorrow is
Another day for Central Park, tomorrow I think
I head for the beach, good-bye Central Park
See you another day . . .
Hello N.Y.C. this is your local
Radio station it's going to be
Hot, hot, hot tomorrow so dress
Light all you birds and squirrels
In Central Park . . . STAY COOL

Bobby Nell Furr

Bobby Nell Furr

BEHIND THE GLASS

Sad eyes awaiting a familiar face
To alleviate the pain of being in such a place
Reaching out to touch someone
With lonely hearts hands so warm
Wondering if they will ever be free
To leave The Glass House of Misery
When all the visitors are gone
The cells reopen to what is called home
Long sad days and sleepless nights
Tossing and shivering till the morning light
Without hope full of despair
Feeling that no one truly cares
Tin badges all over the place
With no respect for the human race
Behind that glass is someone's child
Behind that glass life is still worthwhile
Too many innocent victims behind the cells
Paying the price for others as well
Some are locked down for many reasons
Watching walls through all the seasons
Some are there because they walk alone
No money, no friends, no love, no home
God Jesus help my brother who cannot speak
Locked in a cell rendered helpless and weak
Lord help my brother who cannot hear
Raucous words yelled around his ears
God please give my brother another chance
To give the blue skies another glance

Bobby Nell Furr

HIS TEARS

A fallen tear cornered His eyes
A broken heart crying out loud

Why are You crying Jesus, <u>My children have turned from Me</u>
Please don't cry Jesus, I'm still in need of Thee

Why are You sad Jesus, <u>I gave them My word</u>
Please don't be sad Jesus, Your Voice I have heard

Why are You crying Jesus, <u>They have pierced My side</u>
Please don't cry Jesus, In You I will abide

Why are You sad Jesus, <u>My head is filled with thorns</u>
Please don't be sad Jesus, Your crown will be worn

Why are You crying Jesus, <u>They drove nails in My hand</u>
Please don't cry Jesus, Your pain will uplift man

Why are You sad Jesus, <u>I am losing My blood</u>
Please don't be sad Jesus, I am washed in its love

Why do You love us Jesus, <u>It is My Father's will</u>
We are not worthy Jesus, May Your peace be still

Why are You so happy Jesus, <u>I have come to gather My own</u>
I am happy too Jesus, With You I do belong.

Annethea Anderson

TO DARIENNE, WHO MADE US A FAMILY

Many, many years ago
Your father and I wanted a family
We talked about it and dreamed our dreams.

Separately as well as together
We prayed for a child
Until finally our separate dream and our prayers
Became a reality and
On a cold, snowy day in January
The dream of a family
A baby who was the realization of our love
Came about because of you.
God had answered our prayer
And as our happiness overwhelmed us
We knew as we held you that
Our Lord had made our dream come true
We had been blessed with a little girl named Darienne
And that little girl was you.

Annethea Anderson
TO BRETTE, A FREE SPIRIT
When a woman has a baby
She hardly knows what to do
And your mother was no exception
Even though you were baby number 2
I watched you grow and develop
With interest and great love
Hard to manage as you grew
But, oh so sweet and loveable too
You told me at four that you
Were different from other people
Little did I know then how
Prophetic you were
That was only one of the many
Things you said to your mother
You were right about being different
And because I loved you so
You were able to teach me
To let you be
The Free Spirit that you were
I learned to appreciate your difference
More than you ever knew dear
You have grown up to be a lovely young woman
And the dearest of daughters
This I want you to know
And on this Thanksgiving Day
I thank the Lord Above for all
My blessings and you are one of them
My thanks to the good Lord Above
For such a wonderful daughter
to love.

Chad Austin
THE FATE OF HATE
The hatred in the world is mean and cruel.
It throws many people into a putrid pool
Of vileness, corruption, inequity, and crime,
To throw one's life away in a second's time.
Revolt and rebellion, they own the world,
But then the cruel joke of life is unfurled.
For years to come they'll regret what they did,
And remember the malevolent things that they said,
The things that hurt and cut deeper than knives,
Things they'll remember for the rest of their lives.
The love that was stabbed like a knife through the heart,
The things that were hatred tore the family apart.
Sure, you showed them with the things you said,
Things that will haunt you until you are dead.
Just think before you speak, and look before you leap,
Or you just might get in a little too deep!

Chad Austin
TRUE LOVE
Love is a many splendored thing,
It's pure like that of a dove's white wing.
Emotional, passionate, enchanting, and kind,
The one that you love always on your mind.
It makes you feel good to know someone is there,
To love, to give, someone who will care.
The days spent together live on in your heart,
Overshadowing lonely days spent apart.
The good times shared,
The bad times spared.
To love is to care, to care is to heed,
The feelings of rapture are all that you need.
When that special someone comes along, you'll know,
The feeling of true love in your heart will show.

Harold Raymond Trench

Harold Raymond Trench
DEW DROPS
To the memory of Nordica Norum: Poet, painter, teacher, courageous lady . . . my friend and mentor.

Nightfall falls
A soundless touch
Busy Dusk
Rolls its sleeves

Lifts up the Edge of Night
Slings a string of pearls—
The stars in Heaven Envy

Harold Raymond Trench
REJECTION
A lone dandelion
Flirts
Turns on dazzle
Tosses tresses
Golden warmth
Cascades
Across the green
Long sleek lines
Of pampered grass
Stand aloof
Scarcely
Look askance

Nancy F Artis
THE JOYS OF LIVING
STOP! Reflect on what makes your life joyful . . .
Is it not Life Itself, the absence of death that allows you to experience the Joys of Living. As you look within, ask yourself . . . "Is it not a living joy to be able to awake each morning clothed in your right mind and view a new day. A day that unfolds with many wondrous things to behold . . . a ray of sunshine, a rainbow of many hues, an array of flowers blooming, the sound of children laughing and birds chirping a melody." Yes, these are all joys of living that we experience but have no control over. Those things that are the manifestation of a power greater than you or I. A power that is the source of all our Joys of Living—health, peace, love, happiness, success, prosperity, family, friends and all our worldly possessions. Yes, those things that warm our hearts and bring a smile are truly The Joys of Living.

Nancy F Artis
PEOPLE
People are People
happy, sad . . .
tall, short . . .
skinny, fat . . .
black,
white,
brown,

People are People
movin' . . .
lovin' . . .
shovin' . . .
groovin'.

People are People
real,
beautiful,
alive,
vibrant,

People are People
Brothers, Sisters . . .
From the West Indies,
Africa, America . . .
Unified,
Solidified . . .
PEOPLE

Deborah Lynn Becker
MY SPECIAL FRIEND
To Peg Anderson . . . 'My Special Friend' . . . who showed me God's love in all she said and did.

My love for you is special for God has made it so,
He put a feeling in my heart,
and there He let it grow.
It wasn't very much, at first; I hardly felt it there,
But, then the feeling grew and grew to more than I could bear.
No . . . the feeling wasn't painful, nor was the feeling bad . . .
It's just it was a feeling that I had never had.
I really can't explain it, but I know it sure felt great
To know that deep within my heart was love instead of hate.
A warmth was welling in my heart, a love was growing strong . . .
I always felt so good inside no matter what went wrong.
It's funny what a friend can do with a look, a hug, or a hand,
Or a spoken word of encouragement . . . God, help me understand.
Why do I feel this love inside, or the warmth within my heart?
Can You tell me, please, "Why now? What made the feeling start?"
Please tell me where it came from, or how it got in me.
I thought perhaps 'A Gift from God'? A 'Gift'? . . . most definitely!
For only God could give a gift of love that would never end,
And a gift of someone to share it with . . . a very special friend.

Alan Dale Beck
ENTANGLEMENT
Dedicated to: R.L.R. who taught me to see, G.O.L.D.

Knocked down by love's entanglements,
My weakened spirit, sat upon the cliffs of the seashore
As the waves crash upon the rocks
Shattering

Droplets, forced high, dancing upon wind's wings
Capturing the bright sun's rays
Reflecting its colors
One brief moment

Shining as tiny jewels in the sky.
Mesmerized, I watch,
As they begin to fall,
Mixing with anxiety's past

Melting with and pulled out to sea.
My mind travels back,
Some drops do sparkle.
Peace befriends a maudlin spirit.

Don Brew Jr
TRUE LOVE
To my best friend, former pen pal, and new bride Annie, who was the inspiration for my first poem "True Love."

As the waves crash upon the beach
We walk the shore line within arm's reach
Our bare feet get wet in the moist sand
As I reach out to hold your hand.
While we embark on this quiet stroll
There's no one in sight, not a soul
The ocean breeze blows the salt we taste

I put my arm around your waist.
We could walk for miles upon miles
You look at me, wink and just smile
Not a smile of a duchess or a queen I must confess
But a smile resembling a beautiful princess.
We stop in our tracks and are now face to face
We stare in each other's eyes and then we embrace
I run my fingers through your nice silky hair
As I look deep into your eyes, continuing to stare.
The sea keeps kicking up her mist
As we closed our eyes and began to kiss . . .

Wendy L Vega

Wendy L Vega
HOLLYWOOD

Hollywood I say, is a word of riches in a play
Longing for its victims, calling in a prey.
Stardom is the price you want to pay
Willing to go a long long way.
Depending on the road you make, calling
Double shots, that's a take.
Everything done in proper manner
Goes along with the flatter, glitter lights,
Evenings a glow, goes along with the show.
Hollywood I can make you, or break you,
Walk faster in the chase, I just ask you
Be there at the right time, and place.
Calling at my request, I am calling for
The best.
Hollywood I say is worth a part in my play,
It's a home where I want to stay
It's worth the price to pay, because
Fame is my name.

Beverly Brooks
DEATH OF A YOUNG HUSBAND

To my mother, Florence Wilma Thompson Brooks, a gifted artist and writer, an inspiration in all things.

The just-beginning time.
A roller coaster ride, heart in throat
Clinging together, laughing all the while
Dancing through the days
With stardust on our shoulders every night.
The music of our love was a duet
When the sea pounded on the shore
The perfect joining of two halves
That had known other lives together.
We knew that from the beginning
We never met as strangers
It was a renewed acquaintance
From the last life.
There was no time for debts or regrets
Time passed swiftly in the sun
Walks in the rain renewed us
We were young and beautiful together.
We live in the camera of my heart
Forever captured in the Camelot of our years
And he never saw me growing old
But we promised to meet again.

Sandra Carol Butcher
TEDDY BEARS AND FRIENDS

Dedicated to Deborah Myers, my 'teddy friend,' who inspired me to write "Teddy Bears and Friends."

Teddy bears and friends, can the two be related?
In many ways for sure!
They come in various sizes, shapes, colors, and personalities.
Some smile from ear to ear, others just a little, here and there.
Just by hugging your teddy a tear can be transformed into a smile.
Sometimes you forget to hug your teddy for a while
But when you remember and hold him tight, you get a toasty feeling inside . . . just right!
Friends and teddys get better with time.
A tattered teddy brings a lump in your throat. Why
Because of all the memories you share.
When your teddy becomes tattered and torn, you don't discard him, but handle him with care.
Teddys and friends are like fine wine.
As they age they become more precious.
Isn't it a shame more people don't have a 'teddy friend'?

Iva Lee Bohanan
LORD HELP ME MAKE ANOTHER DAY

In memory of my dear Grandmother, Barbara Crider Patterson, and Grandpa George Washington Patterson, my Mom & Dad, Josie and Bill Vickery, and all my children. They are my inspiration.

When I wake up in the morning, feeling fresh to start the day
I pray to my dear Jesus, help me make it through the day
While I am showering, dressing, eating, I say my daily prayer
Thank you Dear Jesus for yet another day
You have been so good to me Dear Jesus, all the years I've been your child.
You blessed me with a wonderful family
They were all a sweet and loving child.
You blessed me with a Mom and Dad, who taught me right from wrong
So often I have strayed Dear Jesus, but I have always prayed to you
You always took me back again, back into your fold
You blessed me with so many things, my job, my health, my home.
You blessed me with a Grandmother, who put you "Father" first.
She trusted you completely, and every night she prayed
Thank you Dear Jesus for yet another day.
As I write this prayer Dear Jesus, you are so close to me
I feel you're ever present, always protecting me.
Each night as I retire, I fall upon my knees.
And I pray to you Dear Jesus, thank you for another day
Thank you for my family, who means so much to me.
Thank you for my humble home and all the things within it.
Thank you for my Christian friends, my brothers and my sisters
Thank you for loving me Dear Jesus, even when I fall away
And I thank you Dear Jesus, for yet another day.

Tammy L Blake
THE REASONING BEHIND MOMMY AND DADDY

To my mommy and daddy, David and Catherine Blake. Happy Anniversary!

Although we may be miles apart
My love for you both has grown no weaker.
Others may have called you mother and father
but to me this is not right.
Mother and father sounds so distant, as though it was said not out of love but only out of respect for the fact that you brought a child into the world.
The words mommy and daddy represent all the love that is, in a child's heart for his or her parents.
No matter how old I will get I will always be your child and because of the love I feel for you both,
I name you: mommy and daddy

Jane Pippin
TEARDROPS IN THE CORNER OF MY MIND

So sad are the thoughts that linger
Dear, the burning tears are falling, now you are no longer here

Heartbroken, alone with the nickelodeon, still playing in the corners of my mind. Please take away the memories of time, you in uniform, a war to be won.
Oceans to cross, you killing time,

Another in your thoughts, for love to me was blind, Sweetheart if only I could say to you, I would have you as a friend, this little note I would send to you, in the corners of my mind.

Elizabeth E Carter
THE WONDER OF CHRISTMAS

To my Grandchildren, with love.

Love, joy, a baby boy;
Little stranger in His manger bed.
Angels singing, message ringing;
Shepherds running to confirm what was said
Doves cooing, cows quietly mooing;
A gray donkey standing by a cart.
Mother lullabying, baby ceases crying
While Joseph observes with thankful heart.

God in His designing set a bright star shining
To mark that most historic place.
Oh, what a sight on that Holy night
For all who gazed upon His tiny face.
Because it was there, with few to care,
Jesus, the Eternal Christ, was born.
And now each year with love so dear
We remember with "special awe" on Christmas morn.

Elizabeth E Carter
WINTER SNOW

To two encouragers and special friends, Nellie and Kay.

Night shadows fall across the snow
Result of the full moon's heavenly glow.
Clear as crystal is the night
Not a cloud is now in sight.
Trees stand bare, stark and tall
October nights they would recall.
Dazzling stars beckon from the sky
"Reach and touch me," they seem to cry.
Cold so crisp it nearly breaks
As of winter life partakes.
Fireplace smoke spirals up so high.
The night wind gives a gentle sigh.
How sweet upon this scene to gaze
Knowing there'll be warmer days.
Seasons come and seasons go—
But, oh, the beauty of winter snow!

Elizabeth E Carter
OCEAN MYSTERIES

To my husband Bill, "Love and thanks for the wonderful years we've had together."

Sea gulls flying over the ocean deep blue;
Waves, white-capped, rushing into the shore and out again
The rhythmic patterns as old as the ocean itself—
The tides never changing.

How mysterious is the ocean—
an unconquered element of nature—
Serving mankind, and yet never
the servant, but master.
I love the ocean with its
sea gulls and white-capped waves!

Elizabeth E Carter
LEGACY

With my love to Steven, Carol, Don and Neal.

What kind of legacy do I have
To leave the children I bore?
I have no wealth of this world's goods
That they could hold in store.

But I do have thoughts I've written down
And, I suppose, if such were compiled
They'd make a book of memories
To be treasured by each child.

Thoughts written down through the years
As they have come to me—
Yes, I think these could be passed on
As a treasured legacy.

Jujuan Fleeman
ONLY IN DREAMS

To D.H.

She loved the way his long blonde hair
fell across her face.
The way his blue eyes gazed into hers,
like crystal pools
losing her within.
The way his lips were full and luscious,
tasting like ripened
strawberries
on a warm summer's day.
The way his fingertips were liken to velvet
as they moved along her body,
knowing and playing each note
with precision and with love.
But most of all,
she loved knowing that time
could never take this away.

Mileigh Boughton
DISTANT DRUMS

This poem is dedicated to Danny, my beloved son.

I could hear the distant drums
As they echoed through hill and dale
Like the sound of many voices
Amid strife and stormy gale!
I could hear the drums a-beating
Down through the lonely years—
They tell of a people's sorrow
Their joy, their grief and their tears
They tell of their long, hard struggle
In a land that was once their own—
They tell of their longing and heartaches
And the despair they have always known.
Their land became a land of desolation
When its people had to soon depart—
And the grief that burdened each Indian soul
Was like an arrow aimed straight at the heart!
The drums still echo through valley and hill
Down the corridors of time and space
And in the autumn mist—
I could see each Indian face!

Frances L Bauman
PERFECTION IN MOTION

For Bonnie Hummel, The Spirit of Determination.

She walks against the wind
She draws on the odds and wins.
She blew into my life a fireball
wild and so carefree
showing me another side of life.
A street tough kid who grew
quickly from a child
now as a woman stands
toward the night.

And the echoes of her childhood
still linger through her mind
of broken dreams, uncertain
times and a past better left
behind.

Her eyes twinkle and shine, they
show an inner strength deep
inside.
Her smile's like a swift breeze in
the trees, it's there and then
it's gone.
A sweet face hides haunting
memories and covers a
troubled soul.
A restless heart spoken for but
somehow free
Now as a mother must survive
the growing years.

P H Beam
ETERNITY

For all who yearn for something better in life than their present condition.

We raced each other along the beach that day,
Struggled against the waves as
they washed up on shore.
Then, as our moment in paradise drew to a close,
We climbed the cliffs and
watched the sun
As it slipped off the edge of the world,
Where it would come to look
upon the other side;
Where children die from hunger,
And young couples live for the day
They can wear their love freely, proudly,
Like the gossamer threads of
the silkworm,
Wafted on the errant winds of spring.

Your hair smelled of salt and you sighed,
As the sound of the sea gulls,
Wheeling over whitecapped waves,
Penetrated our kingdom.
Our lips met softly, tentatively,
Testing the other's response,
Until a growing hunger,
Fueled by a sense of life's
irrevocable price,
Consumed us as we clawed at each other's clothing,
And night drew her
understanding curtain around
us.

Robin Butler
JUST A FACE

To David. Thank you for believing in me. I love you. Robin.

She is standing on a sidewalk
Looking up at the sky
Out of the corner of her eye,
She is watching the cars go by

She smiles, laughs and runs to his arms
What is that magic she uses?
What are her charms?

She is tall and built like a dancer
Her hair is golden and so are her eyes
Together, their smiles brighten the darkness of the night

I am her shadow and I will always be
I am a figure on the ground, no one really sees
I am in her mind, although pushed back in a corner
I am the sadness in her smile
and the dim in her eyes
I am the reluctance in her embrace
I am her soul
She, is just a face

Angela Marie Phillips

Angela Marie Phillips
PRIDE OF A BLACKMAN

This poet is dedicated to God, whom all good things come and to my family for their love and support.

Pride of a Blackman
is special to me

He's still like a mold
but sees within he

Strong like an ox,
built like metal

He lives in darkness
against the Devil!

Estell Cox
DO YOU REMEMBER SIS?

This poem is dedicated to D. Beetle, my sister.

As I think over our childhood
A warmness fills my heart,
The country school, the time we shared
I hoped we'd never part.

Now that you're many miles away
I long for the good old days,
The love and security in our home
Will stay with us always.

As I travel back those country roads
I think about the things I miss,
But most of all is family
And my one and only sis.

Barbra A Davis
SWEET DREAMS

Dreams
some are scary
some are fun
Dreams
arrive at night
but they don't
disturb anyone.

Your mind is the
playground in which
dreams frolic
and dance
Thoughts of anger
and even romance.

You can share them
or hide them
or just let your
imagination
run wild
Remember in the
playground
You're the child.

Dreams
Sometime seem so
real
but it's you and
your imagination
turning the
wheel.

Paula Doty
PEACE IN THE NIGHT

Quiet is when you can hear the crickets chirp.
Quiet is when you can hear the angels sing.
and you can see the stars above the trees,
and you can see all the way to the heavens.
You can see God's rainbow.
and see Him frown for all the bad things in the world.
and yet see Him smile for all the good things.
The children playing, laughing, and crying,
The older people singing, dancing, loving, and crying.
and then all the older people teaching us what is
right and wrong, scolding us for the bad that we do.
and praising us for the good.
Just once I would like to get all the people to the
country, to see the stars, and hear the angels sing,
To see the heavens above, to see God smile

Priscilla Durand
C'EST LA VIE

Life is giving, life is taking
Life is joy and heartbreaking,
Life is fun, life is sad
Life is good, life is bad

Life is love, life is hate
Life is master of our fate,
Life may come in a different form
Life begins when you're born

Life is marriage and happiness too
Life is divorce when love is through,
Life is living, life is death
Life is gamble with every breath

Life is war, life is peace
Life gives wonders that never cease,
Life is a challenge just to survive
Life is here and I am "alive"

James E Deible
A WILL FOR LIVING

I James E. Deible Dedicate my poem A WILL FOR LIVING to all of the handicapped people from one end of the earth to the other for we've endured all hardships.

Little by little and day by day,
We face many fears that come our way.
Traveling roads never taken before,
And find life waits at heaven's door.

Angels singing with glorious voices,
To announce our coming to the Lord.
With open arms He welcomes us all,
For He loves us be it big or be it small.

Being here on earth has its rewards,
But in heaven there is so much more.
Life to Him is very precious indeed,
For His love goes out to those in need.

Gathered all together in His circle,
Fearing not for we're safe in His arms.
Never worrying about what tomorrow brings,
Just being there means we're safe from harm.

He shares the secrets of untold stories,
That fill our cups until overflowing.
People and Joy ring out like lightning,
Which can be heard throughout the heavens.

So come all ye faithful to see His wonders,
That He has prepared for all of His children.
Sights of everlasting Love and Kindness,
Are present in His kingdom for all to see,
If we would only put our undying trust in Thee!

Leonard R Davis
WITHIN MY DREAMS

A place exists within my dreams
Where I can be alone
In this place nothing's as it seems,
Yet, to me, it's well known

Others find it mysterious
Complex and confusing,
Myself I find it obvious
Simple, yet amusing

Reality and fantasy
Are opposites by far
Yet in my dreams, you soon will see,
One in the same they are

Imagination becomes real
Created in my mind
For while I dream, I truly feel
The places that I find

So when you dream, you must believe
That you can feel it too
And peace of mind, you will receive
Your life will seem brand new . . .

Albert Denton

Albert Denton
THE EYES OF A SOLDIER

I will never, never, never ever forget you because you have done so much for me. Love Albert D.

On the outside a soldier must be quite cold
But his true state is known when you look into his eyes
Because he, like no other has always to appear bold
When on the inside, alone he continually cries
When you look into my eyes you see the black
Of depression and trauma that are on my trail
And maybe you will see the love my heart lacks
Since each time I love, my love seems to fail
I will always remember you in times of war
and when destruction I am on the verge
I'll wish your love I had much more
And again one day that we will merge

My feelings for you cannot be explained
But what I can express is that my heart is now free
From all the fighting of battles and also the pain
Without you I don't know where I would be
So tell me what's on your mind
'cause I will always listen
I'll catch the tear before it drops from your eye
For you are the need that I have been missing
And to hurt you I could never try
This is what I've been attempting and could never say
Please look into my eyes
N-N-E-K-A

Debra A Dotson
A PRAYER

Give me peace
when I need to rest
Give me class
To walk among the best
Give me understanding
To admit when I'm wrong
Give me strength
When I need to be strong
Give me time
To live many years
Give me courage
To face my fears
Give me knowledge
To teach the youth
Give me honesty
To speak the truth
Give me power
To keep control of my life
Give me eyes
To see what is right
Give me wisdom
To know when to make a change
Give me reasons
To start each day
Give me thoughts
To each his own
Give me comfort
When I stand alone
Give me chances
To correct my mistakes
Give me a heart
In case this one breaks!

Daniel Derhammer
THE SPLENDOR OF CREATION

God's wondrous works are everywhere,
Behold his might, beyond compare.
All things in air, on sea and land,
Were formed by His almighty hand.

A gentle summer's evening breeze,
Stirs leaves in stately willow trees.
On winter nights, the cold winds blow,
And drift the freshly fallen snow.

In the sky, a hint of light,
Then sunrise comes, a glorious sight.
A rooster crows, proclaiming dawn,
The shadows flee and night is gone.

The third day God's hand worked anew,
To form the seas, so deep and blue.
Toward shore its waves and breakers reach,
To crash and die upon the beach.

I look up at the starry sky,
And in my heart I wonder why,
When by his grace on earth they trod,
How can men say there is no God?

Joyce Dangerfield
LOST LOVE

Where has all the joy gone that used to fill our life?
The laughter and the good times that helped us bear our strife,
We walked hand and hand, side by side, all along the way
We shared our happiness and sorrows each and every day.
We talked about all our problems and the burdens we have to bear
I could always count on you because you were always there,
Then as the years began to pass us by we started to drift apart
Our love began to dwindle there was a coldness in the heart.

There was never much time to spend together and even less to say
There was no interest or concern as to how we spent our day,
The love we once shared is no longer there
The heart is cold and empty as I stand alone in fear.

Though we spend our lives together all that bound is gone
We're left to fend for ourselves,
we're together—yet we stand alone,
No longer do we share the good or bad or the ups and downs we face
Though we share the same abode
there is no love in this place.

Though we are still joined together
our vows have been broken
They are now empty words that should never have been spoken,
We care deeply for each other, but love—we cannot say
So we go on living—each in our own way.

Leah Elizabeth Dorney
BLACK TEARS

Black tears, blue wine, and silver roses is what your world is made of.
Your abstraction is my distraction;
a world that I cannot make heads or tails of.
I am not by perfection by any detection in your eyes or mine.
In fact, I am far from any kind of remote similarity to your world.
Everyone and everything is painted to your unique ideal of the perfect beauty.
I shall never be this, for my tears are not black,
my wine not blue and
I have never seen a silver rose grow in my garden.

Alice Leonard Sokolinski
TEARS OF FREEDOM

We do not know what you've been through,
We are so glad, you made it too,
All those months of lingering hours,
Loved ones being your strength of tower.

Here we prayed, and flew our flags,
In hopes you'd soon be packing your bags,
And board that plane and head for home,
The meaning of freedom, you know alone.

As news came across my set,
I cried some tears and could relate,
To all the ones that here did wait,
Four-hundred forty-four, was the final date.

God gives some strength to special ones,
When in need we all get some,
Being his children, he loves us all,
Picks us up, when he sees us fall.

The President did work so hard,
And at last he played his top card,

He met some terms, and finally found,
How to get those wheels, turning around.

All those ribbons, that were hung,
All those bells, that were rung,
Were done in love, and kept our hopes,
That soon you'd be back with your folks.

Through the media, I do feel,
A small part of your ordeal,
I send my love out to you,
That now your life can begin anew.

Joyce A Ackerman

Joyce A Ackerman
ADDICTIONS
She draws you to her
my man in the moon
like an order, you must obey
like treasures, like perfume.

That tide that you float through
that place high and huge
I watch you adrift
my man in the moon

If you were a warrior
would you escape or fight?
distance is safety
only survivors know why—

Lost friends and companions
are in songs you sing
they seek you out
like they would a king

You rest your head, in different beds
your armor is beauty—your shield is trust
you hold no regrets, leaving, after the lust

Go through the currents
where the wisest men find
what they seek from life
through the winters of time

Beware her hidden in waiting
always there, unseen
you are loved by many
know the difference between

So, rein up your horse my prince
and if some night soon
you're riding through life and look up at the moon
Remember a night
we were surrounded by the sea

Patricia Dalpiaz
OH TO BE
If we could be as worried as a leaf,
Clinging to a bow with life as its force,
Or a blade of grass that's smothered in snow,
It protrudes with no remorse,
And peeks to feel the sun,
That runs down through its roots,
A lifeline that is spun,
Through the earth.

How simply we think of an open field,
Yet it grows wild among the stars,
And the breezes shift and turn,
To make the grasses whistle a windful tune,
That carries across the plain and makes the sky blue,
With carefree clouds dancing to the weeded melody.

Oh to be a blade of grass,
And not question the radiance or rain,
But simply overtake the pain.

Kerry L Dennis
MARCIA
Out from the depths of my darkness there came,
a tiny flicker of light that soon grew to a flame,
leading the way out of the night.

Stronger and brighter the light in me shone,
Warming me inside right down to my bones.
How clear and how bright, shone this one little light
and it gave me the sight.

Marcia, I'm not looking behind.
Lovely lady Marcia, You're always here in my mind.
Lighting the way to my very heart.
Tenderly, Touching me, Holding me close in your arms.

Marcia each moment with you so sublime.
Sweet, gentle Marcia, Will you always and forever be MINE.

Emily David
NO OTHER WAY
A short little lady, a little round,
The mother of five girls is who I am.
The names start with K. I'll introduce
Kathy, Karen, Karol, Kim, and then Kay(boose).
The last name is David. The father O. P.
And the one who is writing is Emma Lee.

Such good little babies you've never seen.
We fed them well and kept them clean.
We taught them of God and the Bible to read;
To trust in the Lord to help them succeed.

Now they have children of their own.
Teaching the things that they have known
From their parents by word or deed.
With God as their partner they will succeed.
Glorify God in all that you do
And he will see your family through.

Believing in Jesus with guidance and love
Is the material for Heaven above.
With our short stay in this world today,
Really now—there's No Other Way.

Joni K DeCent
MY LITTLE ANGEL
Once inside me grew a life full of love . . .
A small little life whose heart beat with mine . . .
Whose warm little body I would feel within time.
Though I never got to hold you to my breast . . .
I know what the Lord decided He felt was best . . .
I left it up to Him. I put you in His hands.
Now you live in a prettier place, a more precious land.
I hope you know how much you mean to me.
For I know you're an Angel . . .
The most beautiful there could be . . .
A vision of loveliness that any eye could behold.
You will never be forgotten in memory or soul.
But someday soon, I pray the Lord will bless me with
Another Little Angel . . .
One I can hold.
But my love for you will always be there . . .
Tucked inside a special place that secretly you and I share . . .
For when I look in my next Angel's eyes there you will be also . . .
Smiling and looking into mine.
I Love You Sweet Baby Thine . . .

Christopher DiCicco
LONELINESS
Loneliness
The hanging head of a hollow man
Smelling a wild flower in someone else's hand
The distant thunder as brother wolf cries
—His time has come
I've been waiting for so long
—Open the heavens, and let it rain down

Miss Elizabeth Ann Berg

Miss Elizabeth Ann Berg
SILENT THOUGHTS

This poem has been lovingly dedicated to those who have fostered my love of Fine Arts and the need for Self Expression . . .

You came to me at evening tide, just as I wished you would
You were there—as if in a dream:
I turned, and you had appeared . . . silently and suddenly.
There you were.

My heart leapt, my soul for an instant rejoiced . . .
You had heard my silent call.
You had sensed my need.

We joked, kidded, and played;
happiness ran through our hearts
We were together again
Not long, but precious minutes of togetherness
An exchange . . . Sharing and Giving.

We sat beside one another,
Gazing for brief instants at mirrors of our own souls.
At each other . . . at life itself.

Oh, to savor that sharing,
To recall those tender moments of giving mirth
And happiness to each other . . .

The innocence, the fun, the sincerity,
The tenderness in the gleam of our eyes
All exchanged rays of joy on the way to our souls . . .
Yours and Mine.

June Davis
SECOND BEST
You are Adam. I am Eve.
Our failure to love caused God to grieve.

In our love, selfishness did abound,
And made us vulnerable when Satan came around.

I love and depend upon you for my life.
You cling to me. I am your wife.

But God is God before us.
God will love and not ignore us.

But love you as I do, I pray you understand.
Much as I love you, I put God before any man.

Nor would I expect of you any less.
God grant that I may always be your second best.

Trudi L Deegan
MY HEART IS BROKEN
My heart is broken because I loved something that has left forever,
The memory still lives, but it's not the same,
It will never be the way it was before,

Some people say their heart will
never be broken,
But they know this is not true,
They build a heart of stone so it
won't hurt,
But that only makes it hurt more,
I've learned to love one thing for
as long as I can, and hope it
doesn't leave,
Sometimes it stays,
But sometimes it goes away,
When it goes away, my heart is
broken,
And I have to find something else
to love.

Stacy M Drake
TO CURSE THE DREADED THORN

Why can't I be like the precious
unicorn
And live in a magical land?
Must I always catch the dreaded
thorn
Of the beautiful rose stems at
hand?

Why can't I be as free as the butterfly
To spread my wings afar?
Must I always only wish and wonder
why?
I received no answer from
that star.

Why can't I float down from the
heavens
As a silver winged angel?
Must I always hold my secrets
within . . .
Only to find a greater evil?

Why can't I be as the precious
unicorn?
And dream other than fear!
Must I always curse the dreaded
thorn—
To wish back this falling tear?

Misti Cain
FOR KEEPS

A person learns a lesson
Every word he says.
A lesson to be learned
And kept through endless
years.

A jewel of great value
Is something to keep.
But not compared to a
thought
Whose memories are sweet.

You can keep a thought forever.
Never let it go.
And come back to remember
it.
It's still as white as snow

Marion Hebert Caldwell
THE COLORS CHANGED ONCE MORE

This poem is dedicated to the memory of Bob, our beloved son.

Summer was almost over and
Autumn was coming on
When in deep contemplation, he
gazed out upon the dawn.
An early ray of sunshine beamed on
Maples green and tall
Where a swaying twig of scarlet
proclaimed the coming of Fall.

He longed to see the colors
change once more
And watch the leaves drift
down to meet Earth's floor,
With colors changing fast to
bronze and gold,
Like time-worn, muted
tapestries of old.

He longed to see the colors
change once more
And watch the leaves sail down
to meet the shore,
Like tiny, ancient ships beneath
the sky,
Full-sailed to catch the breezes
passing by.

This prompted him to join the
race once more;
He rigged the sails and cast off
as before.
And, as he sailed for that long-
distant shore,
He saw the leaves come down
and colors change once more.

September now was golden and the
skies now azure blue;
Thence the year was at the Autumn
with colors of brilliant hue.
Then, the days rolled swiftly by;
colors changed to bronze from gold;
Breezes weaved, beneath the trees,
carpets in muted shades of old.

Deborah L Foley

Deborah L Foley
AMANDA

My poems are dedicated to all who have enjoyed the happiness, yet, endured the pain of life's reality.

After all these years I still remember;
The light in her eyes, the scent of her
hair,
The touch of her lips, the sound of
her laugh.
Fifteen years ago she went out to
play.
January 31st, turned into my darkest
day.
My memories are old, yet, still
crystal clear.
Would she be close to her sister in
her 17th year?
Every day I'm reminded of the guilt
and shame.
I can't look at her picture and not feel
the pain.
"There is nothing we can do." the
doctor said.
"She's in a vegetative state. Her brain
is dead."
That morning at play, she's laughing
and frowning.
By noon in the E.R., she's listed as a
drowning.
For three long weeks I watched her
slip away.
I prayed to St Jude to show her the
way.
She steps into my dreams and reaches
out her hand.
One day I will take it and no one will
understand.

Deborah L Foley
INDIAN WOMAN

Her face is weathered,
Her eyes sunken and cold.
She has wandered the wastelands
In search of a home.

Her warrior has died,
But not in a war.
She's alone in the wilderness
chilled to the core.

When will she find solace
And protection from the beast.
She's lost her will to fight
The whiteman from the east.

Deborah L Foley
THE SCOTTSMAN

The morning mist comes off the glen
lingering over still water.
He's standing at the end of a peer
trying not to falter.
To his side he clutches the bag
the pipes upon his chest.
He raises the reed to trembling lips
and forces in a breath.
With all the might that he can muster
he blows into the stick.
The pain he feels deep down inside
creates a sound so sick.
He plays a tune of love and loss
which sways his stiffen pose.
It was not he who wrote this song
it's one his Dad composed.

Mary E Cresante
SET ME FREE

This poem is dedicated to my children Vin Jr & Michael, & most of all to my husband Vinny for reading my good & not so good poems. I Love You.

I'm tired of the games
I'm tired of the pains
Set me free
I hurt so much
I have no trust
Set me free
I'm tired of the lies
I'm tired of the cries
Set me free
I'm tired of the street
And of the people I meet
Set me free
I need someone's purse
to survive this curse
Set me free
I live like a hag
living out of street bag
Set me free
I'd rather have love
and hugs than taking
and selling drugs
Set me free

Can you hear me?
Mom and Dad
Please find me
I'm so sad
Set me free
Please set me free
Can anyone hear me?
Please listen!
I'm just a child who's missing
Please, I beg you
Set me free!

Tracy A Cheney
HAVE YOU EVER?

Have you ever stopped to ponder on a
single grain of sand?
And all that is contained therein, and
do you understand?
Have you ever paused to hear the
wind's sad and lonely cry?
Or to notice a raindrop, wet and clear,
As it falls softly from the sky?
Have you ever followed a brook's
winding path
To places far away?
Or stopped to listen to a lovebird's
song
And what it has to say?

Have you ever stopped to ponder on
the soul of one single man?
And all that he sees and feels, and do
you understand?
Have you ever paused to hear a
friend's sad and lonely prayer?
Or to notice a dream that died
Because no one took time to care?
Have you ever followed love's
winding path
To places far away?
Or stopped to listen to your heart
And what it has to say?

William F Thompson

William F Thompson
ENDING SEA

For my Mother and Grandmother.

Upon seven pointed desert clouds
The twisting angel's proud
With his heart lit into the sun
Though its glow is waxed in black
One and all can only fall
In the never ending turmoil

Sailing ships with iron sails
With golden utopian kings of
meaning
Darkness at the height of noon
For they've come far far too soon

Watchfalls pity has come a sighing
For all the children who are crying
As self made gods pity themselves
They'd better look out
It's still in doubt

Hearing the feeling
Far under the bay
They say it's the key
So simple to me
The ending sea

Ginger Joy Greco
THANK-YOU NOTE TO A MANCHILD WITH WHOM I AM DEEPLY IN LOVE

Cathedral window splatters
light
like a misplaced prism
upon the windows of my soul;

I have yet to actually
leave
this sacred green Earth-ground,
but sitting in this place I think
that I could fly
far and free
as easily as the black and white
birds
that circle above me.

Ginger Joy Greco
HOPE

Rain,
you fall lush
on green fields
and the dark earth
drinks you in.

Fall silver, then,
and cleanse
my soul.

Ginger Joy Greco
PAPERS LAY STREWN

Papers lay strewn
on the floor where the sunlight
hits them just right, crumpled,
and walks its way
across the garbage cans
I have missed.

Eleanor Dunning
COMPASSION

I dedicate this poem, "Compassion," to the person who has feelings for others' misfortune.

A person with love and compassion,
Can make a better way of life.
Try to bring much happiness,
To many people, like you and I.

There are times you feel angry,
When someone is way out of line.
I know, you will find a way,
Being nice, would make your day.

If you have made a big mistake,
Although it wasn't meant to be,
But, not to have a day of misery,
You would make all things right.

Being nice is the best way of life,
Making many dreams come true.
So don't let yourself feel blue,
There are many things in life to do!

Brigette DePiero
MY LITTLE BUCK-A-ROO

This is dedicated to the one I love, my son, Tyler DePiero-Holmes.

It's time to go to sleep MY LITTLE
BUCK-A-ROO
You've had a big day, and now it's
time to say, go to sleep
I hope you have nice dreams, and
never any screams
MY LITTLE BUCK-A-ROO

I'm never going to leave, so you can
be relieved
I'll be here when you wake, so don't
let your heart ache
MY LITTLE BUCK-A-ROO
Tomorrow we'll have fun
Maybe play out in the sun
Or take a nice long walk
And then you'll try to talk
MY LITTLE BUCK-A-ROO

Now close your little eyes
I'll never tell you lies
Sweetie you're the best
You're loved more than the rest
And now that you're asleep
I don't want you to weep
This lullaby's for you, just because,
YOU'RE MY LITTLE BUCK-A-
ROO

Maureen A Dutko
SEE THE HANDS

To my children: Kristen, January, Renée, Kevin, Alexander.

See the hands upon the clock
Swiftly moving on

Some may wish this time to lock
Others wish it gone

If each one of us would know
The importance of each
minute

Then our lives would be worthwhile
And true happiness infinite

Ruth West Dunnavant
PRECIOUS MEMORY

In memory of brother F. Mason Eddleton. A husband, Father and Vietnam Veteran (Air Force), Lockhart, TX.

Our Heavenly Father in His mercy,
Took our loved one Home,
To care for him so tenderly,
Just the way we'd have Him do.
We are so thankful
No more pain there shall be,
Nor no sorrow he will bear.
A living faith gave his love
To all, a special touch
That is sure to pave our way,
For a brighter tomorrow.
Memory Garden share our
silent tears.
And hold fast our precious memories.
May each and every heart feel
lighter,
Knowing Heavenly Birthdays are
surely peaceful.

Cerah Davis
MY JOURNEY HOME

For Cindy who made me believe in myself and my writing—For Lemondrop who joined me on a wonderful path—To Claudy who brought sunshine to my darkest days—For Mom, Dad & Kit, i love you all—and for God, who i just met on my most recent path of My Journey Home . . . thank you all—i love you.

As I travel down the path
On my journey home
I know that I am not alone
Yet that fear is with me
So I get off my path
To walk with friends
Sometimes I preach
For I know I am a teacher
Sometimes I listen
For I know I am a student
Sometimes I shout
For I know I am gifted
Sometimes I silence
For I know I am ignorant
Sometimes I smile
When I feel I am a child
Sometimes I cry
For I know I am an adult
Longing for those carefree days
Before I started this journey . . .
My Journey Home

Adrian Noelle

Jeanne Shaffer
MY CHILD

To Adrian, My Beautiful Little Girl.

I just found out about you
I didn't know you were there
But now that I do know
There are some things I'd like
to share.

You will be my baby
You will be my love
You will be my angel
God has sent me from above.

I will love you forever
I always will be there
Even when you're all grown up
Your life I want to share.

When it's time for me to go
And you are left behind
I will still be with you
Forever in your mind.

Pat DiMeglio
MY ROCK

For John . . . My rock.

A mountain of a man.
And strong as an ox.
A brain: that's as quick as as fox!
And a tongue that's blade sharp.
Only sometimes, is it as sweet as the
sound of a harp.
Only masculine words befit him;
Because he somehow knows,
My every little whim.
Sometimes a pedestal:
He places me on.
Other times; he fills me with woe.
And then he won't let me go.
He has his own special way
To make my tears come.
Then wipes them away:
Not all, just some.
Lessons I do learn;
From this rock I lean on.
And this rock I speak of . . .
I will eternally love.

Becky Danielson
FIREMEN

To my husband Tom.

A fireman is a lot of things
That most people don't see
The patience that they have
To help you and me
The tears they wipe
The sorrow they see
The battles they may lose
Forever scare their entire
being
The constant time on call
Seems to never take its toll
Their smiling faces help us
As they share part of their
soul
Their time is volunteer
But their rewards are great
So as they help their fellow man
Let death not be their fate.

Constance Davis
LITTLE SISTER

This poem is dedicated to my parents, for giving me a wonderful little sister to love.

You brought me sunshine on days
that had rain,
You filled me with laughter and
erased my pain.
One smile from your face could
brighten the day,
You'd give me a hug and take my
sadness away.
A touch of your hand told me I had a
friend,
That you'd be there beside me right
to the end.
Time flew by but you were there,
steadfast at my side.
Every time I look at you my heart
just bursts with pride.
You made my life worth living, of
that you can be sure.
At a time of so much loneliness, you
dear, were the cure.
You took away my emptiness and
filled that gap with love,
I truly do believe that you were sent
down from above.
A bundle right from heaven sent
down just for me,
To make this world a brighter, better
place for us to be.

Vera (Buiklysky) Butterworth
TO MY FATHER

In Loving Memory, of "Elia Buiklysky," the most wonderful father a daughter can have!

How do I express in words, my
thankfulness,
And love for you.
For all the years, you've worked so
hard,
I gave but just a few.

I hurt inside, I miss you dearly,
My memory of you so clear.
So many words are left unspoken,
So full of Love, and so sincere.

Your heart was always generous,
Your words were always kind.
A man so unselfish and giving,
If I searched for, I could not find.

I'm so thankful, that you've been
beside me,
Since my birth, your whole life
through.
I knew always, that you'd be there
for me,
Time after time, my whole life
through.

How could I possibly repay you,
For so many, many things you've

done for me.
But with words, I can say "Thank-
You & I love you!"
And may "God be there with You."

Reneé Louise Antoinette Boone
MY VOW TO YOU

To my inspiration and the love of my life.

From now on until the day we die, I vow to dedicate my life to you and most importantly—to God. I vow to be forever faithful, to lay down with no other man but you. I don't know what I ever did to deserve someone like you. You are heaven-sent, my "little angel" in disguise. I feel that I don't deserve you; you are too good for me and too good to me. You've given so many chances that I don't deserve. But I know that without you in my life, I would be lost and wander in the wrong path with the wrong people. Your love increases my desire to do the right thing and take the right path—yours. I know you've doubted my trust and my love for you, and I don't blame you, but I vow to show you in many ways that you would have no reason to ever doubt my love and trust.
You have won my heart and
soul—
Forever.
You, my angel, are my
everything,
my lover and likewise,
my truest friend.

God knows we were meant to be together, maybe ever since we were put on this earth. Through destiny, we were joined by God. What has been joined by God . . .
Let no man put asunder.

I will always love you, my
angel,
with my whole heart,
my whole soul,
my whole strength,
and with
my whole mind.—

Jerry L Baumgardner
THE REALITY OF DREAMS

To Kerry. You will always be my proof that dreams really do come true.

I was given a gift so rare and
beautiful
That it stunned me with the magic of
its creation.
She is the magic of the gift.
I have heard the laughter in a
gurgling stream
That crescendos to joy in the roar of
the falls.
She is the joy in laughter.

I have felt the dark clouds as they
gather and roil
And build to the crashing anger of a
revitalizing storm.
She is the anger in the storm.

I have found understanding in the
quiet peace
At the center of the confusing winds
in the hurricanes of life.
She is the peace in understanding.

I have touched the sadness in a tear
that comes with sunset
In its life and its death, in the change
of leaving yesterday behind.
She is the sadness in change.

I have seen the brilliance in the
everchanging colors of hope
Like a sunrise on a crystal morning or
the rainbow of a new-washed sky.
She is the brilliance of hope.

I have realized the reflection of my
dreams
In the wonder and beauty and reality
of her existence.
She is the reality of dreams; my
child.

Jerry L Baumgardner
REVELATION

To my son Don who is a treasure beyond words. I gave you life and you gave it back to me.

Sometimes it's so hard to come to
terms
With how you've reached what you
are.
Did I close my eyes for a second too
long?
Or did you grab the tail of a star?

Your youth was my youth; I felt once
again
The excitement in learning to live.
You searched all around you, no
limits were there,
And found what the world had to
give.

You took what was offered and put it
to use.
You learned how to give in return.
And rightfully left little worries
behind;
Growing up was your major concern.

Your bruises and bumps, your toys
and your games,
Your tears and your joys mine to
share.
And I was so sure then—I knew in
my heart—
That my boy, well, he'd always be
there.

But the years have passed swiftly, so
busy and short.
That was never a part of my plan.
When I looked for the boy who'd
come running to me
Instead what I saw was a man.

Nichole Anne Burke
LIFE ON THE STREETS

Life on the streets,
drugs and crime all around you.
Dancin' to the inner-city beat,
there's no one to turn to.
How long can you last,
out there on your own?
You've got to think fast,
try to forget that you're all alone.

Shirley Beecher
BROKEN VOWS

Not "till death do you part"
Shall the love 'tween you
cease.
Words spoken form the heart,
Blessed by God's Peace.

But means He, the death of the body,
Or of a bind that has torn?
For the wound of dead love
Bleeds from a much greater
thorn.

Tim Bingham
LET US—!

Mathalda Hartness & Christy McCurry—Thanks for your guidance and support.

Let us go back to the beauties
That are pocketed deep in our past—
The joys we relinquished with
childhood
But which hauntingly linger and last.

Let us return to the Christmas
That remains with the children of
time
The Christmas of wonderful wishes,
Of stardust, and snowdrift, and
chime!

Let us go back to the vision
Of evergreen peace in our rooms,
Gay ribbons on gifts of the giving,
And the dream that consistently
blooms.

Let us in petty wonder
Where the veil of the centuries parts
To look at a crib and an infant
And Christmas will live in our hearts!

Lee Adams
COLD FIRE

I thought I didn't stand a chance
The distance was too great
The fastest ship in all the world
Could not have crossed that gate

But came a night while I was blind
The poison filtered from my mind
Wake up I thought, it's time to start

A journey towards a woman's heart
You see, my dreams were passing by
So I hopped on, I had to fly
And when I reached her life, it seems
I breathed myself into her dreams

It was my heart that set me off
That caused by wheels to turn
The other reason stands alone
A fire that doesn't burn.

Lee Adams
SPIRITUAL PRECIPITATION

Would you believe that to and fro
Our planet flies and spins.
The Snow.
Could you believe that gravity lazy
Lets it fall and makes things hazy?
The Snow.
Should you admit that in your sleep
The rain will drive your sleep so
deep.
The Rain.
Can you resist a chance to ride
A rainbow high, a water slide?
The Rain.
When cold it grows would you deny
Your wife, your child, a fire high?
The Fire.
And when the earth comes full
around
The sun will stand its cosmic ground.
The Fire.
From where we came is not the case
This Earth it is a special place.
A Life.
If one should choose to leave this
Earth,
Prepare to see the fiery hearth.
A Life.
For science, man, and all the rules
Did fall from grace to ridicule.
The Spirit.
So chance we die our spirits know
The rain, the fire, a life, the snow.
The Spirit.

Sheila Parke Daugherty
LITTLE GIRL LOST

For all the young parents who understand about growing up fast.

Little girl lost
Alone in her dreams
Lost in her past
Nothing in the future she sees
Remembering the times
Her carefree play
Dolls and teaparties passed her time
away
Now in reality
The baby cries
No more time for dreams
Or looking back
Dolls and teaparties part of her past
Little girl has to grow up fast
Bottles, diapers, babybaths
Little girl lost
Is a mother now
Little girl lost
Now a woman has appeared
Little girl lost

Brian M Briggs
WAR OF RACES

Racial Tension—black and white,
War of Races—start to fight.
Violent temper—Darkened Mood,
death and deadly interlude.
Apartheid, gangs, and racial wars
Vicious, mean like carnivores.
This world would be a better place,
without the fight of skin & race.
Take us Lord and don't be coy
All we want is peace and joy!!!

Christine Blair
OBSCURITY

I drift along the faraway path
I glance back
The dense fog consumes me.

I squint to clear this vision
Only to look deep within the mass
Of uncertainty.

Mrs Esther E Brunson
CHRISTMAS PRAISE FOR EVERY DAY OF THE YEAR
Unto the Giver of all good and perfect gifts,
Creator of all things.
Without change or shadow;
We bring our praise and adoration
Bestowed from our ever grateful hearts
That are filled with love aglow.

Love, holy, perfect love, by God first given
In the sending of His beloved Son
For you and me—and eternal life.

Unto the Giver of all benefits and blessings;
He Who forgives and redeems;
Who loves with matchless love;
Who satisfies so completely,
With strength renewed!
For all these gifts we praise our LORD SUPREME! ! !
Giving in return, ourselves,
That others may be as blessed as we!

Michael Balfour
LOVE IS BLIND

To my wonderful mother and for all her support.

The fool is that of a jealous mind,
we must remember that love is blind.
It has no visions it has no roles,
it's only a feeling within our souls.

Feelings can sometimes fool your heart
and sometimes tear your soul apart.
As we feel this thing that we call love
we must have in god above,

He will guide us to our goals
and mend the wounds within our souls
So don't deny yourself love's joy
and don't forget it's not a toy

Love is something we all must learn
it's a binding trust we all must earn.
You'll be amazed in what you find,
and don't forget love is blind

Deanna Rene' Brown
YOU CAPTURED MY HEART

Dedicated to: Roddy McDowall.

You captured my heart
at a very young age
I remember—I had to listen
—to all that you played.
Every night was exciting
—just with you in mind.
I was thinking of the character
you played,—
I didn't know you at the time.
My heart would ache;—
when I was sent to bed
I knew I could be watching you,
—instead
As time went by and then years;
I realized I had fell for a
Monkey with big ears.
Till this day, I still love all that
you do;
but nothing tops;—
My wish of getting someone
—like you.
Now I watch television sometimes
Late at night;—
I know I can catch you in "Fright Night."
You're surely not scary (nor)
Have you ever seemed mean to me.
You're just someone special;
that I really fell for
and think a lot of;—
So this Poem's for you,
with all my love.

Lisa A Grigsby
IN MEMORY OF ASHLEY

In Memory of Ashley.

As the rain gently falls upon my window sill,
I sit here staring into space,
trying to understand all the things
that life gives us,
and realizing we can't change what
God has planned for us.
God has sent a precious child to us,
and taken her away,
leaving us hurt and confused.

As we try to understand,
a tree behind us sends a message of love,
as it grows on taking our precious
baby to heaven,
yet staying here to watch over her
and protect her.
Trying to comfort our pain,
it lets us know she is at peace in her heart,
even as our hearts ache,
we will never forget her,
for in her short life she filled our
hearts with love.

Joel D Bagwell
COMMON SENSE
We often get intensely tangled in the web of life.
We seldom have the time to grasp,
That which is vital to survive,
We dwell on strife and trouble,
And embrace the stress we feel,
Which is not what God intended,
For it's peace that he instills.
His purpose is for us to stand
In the likeness of His son,
Never taking once for granted,
Anything or anyone.
Experiencing right and wrong,
Then knowing which must be done.
"Common sense" He gives us freely,
It's a tool at our dispense.
It tells us when to walk away,
Or lend a helping hand.
When strength and backbone it
possesses,
No greater gift we can extend,
Its reward is the key to heaven,
We must possess it in the end
To confirm our reservation
With our Lord and our kin,
For we've reached our destination
Thru God's gift of common sense.

Daniel Blakeley
THE GIRL OF MY DREAMS

This poem is dedicated to Lois, my darling fiancee.

I am a bachelor and only 52.
I was a lonely man, until I met you.

She is the girl of my dreams.
She is a widow too.

When I look at her, I begin to patter.
I ask myself, "What is the matter?"

She has soft blonde hair, that shines in the sun.
Her pale blue eyes, that look so happy and fun.

She is built a lot like Dolly
But just a little fatter.
If she knew this, she would be just a little madder.

She has a ready-made family, already for me
Now as you can see, I want this girl to marry me.

Naomi Berry
LOVING SAVIOR
As I think back and look ahead
One thing comes to mind
The joy of having a Savior
So loving and so kind

He holds my hand and leads me
Each day of my life
He helps me through each trial
When my time is filled with strife

He gave his life that I might live
Throughout eternity
No one on earth loved me so much
From death to set me free

He washed away my ever sin
And told me of his love
After this life, I could live
With him in Heaven above.

Karnetta Taylor
WHAT'S TO COME
Of all the stories, I do read
My plea to God is for sanity
Murders, rapes, hurt, and pain
'Tis a wonder, anyone is sane

I cry for you, I cry for me
What is to come with eternity
Or all the children borne to thee
Isn't there one good thing, for them to see?

Should we all stop and look
It's the love in our hearts, that's been took
Computers, logic, our senses gone
Oh please Lord, what's to come?

Positive thoughts I'll try to find
In this world of violent crime
If I succeed, the secret's not mine
True love, is what my heart will find!

Charlene M Bentley
MUSIC
I need music in my life,
My life would be dull without it;
Without it I could not imagine living,
Imagine living without music—
Unbearable!
Music sets me free,
I sing-a-long with it,
I dance with it,
I live with it;

People fall in love to music,
their hearts quicken with it,
or slow down to a two-step beat with it;

Music is everywhere,
We, as humans, thrive on it.

Sheila O'Neil

Sheila O'Neil
PATTERN OF FAITH
Grandpa sat at home unfathoming
While fisherman fumbled hand and foot
And tried to tell why eight sons
Would not come home to-night;
And grandpa sat unfathoming . . .
And so he tried again to speak
Why 8 sons . . .

Young Michael (2) before the hearth
Seemed to seize the crisis,
Cried and threw away his cup.
Grandpa bowed, lifted up his son,
His Only Son, this awe-fulled night,
Took him out pointing thro' the mist
Wild fuchsia blooming red.
The baby smiled, content, was still.

Grandpa said good night to Ned
And good morrow fishing.
(simple living still subsisting)

Then walked into his room
Fathoming.

Claudia Y Rice
FOREVER JOINED

To my husband Ronald D. who tells me to keep writing so that others can read my work. Thanks Ron. I love you.

Giving birth is usually something special.
It is something, everyone cannot do.
I was able to join in this event, by giving birth to two.
To me my son is special, to all he wouldn't be.
Inside the feelings are ladened with love, the depth known only to me.
My daughter, on the other hand is special to me too.
Ever since she was little, she was trying something new.
I'm not saying that their childhood was a smooth road all the way.
Many times I wondered what kind of trouble I'd see each day.
My kids are grown and gone, but call

to keep in touch.
In their conversations, they say, I
love you very much.
People say the love you have for your
kids is unlike any other.
I'm about to find if this is true or not.
I'm soon to become a grandmother.

Cindy L Cogswell
FOREVER FRIENDS

Friends are forever binded
with love and hope, and kindness
from the heart and mind.

Friends are forever there
to help with problems and crises
from the job and family.

I'm glad you are my forever friend

You mean so much to me,
your kindness, your love, your
willingness
to help, makes me feel like someone
out there really does care to how
I feel.

Thank-you for being my forever
friend.

Kyle E Lesniak
THE DAWN OF LIFE

To My Parents, who allowed me to be free.

Sitting on these rocks I feel so
secluded.
Totally shut off from everyone.
It's late, dark, windy and cold.
The mist in the air adds to the
darkness.
The lake is covered with whitecaps,
As they crash on the rocks I sit upon,
they fill the air with the smell of the
sea.
Trees surround me all around so only
the sea is visible.
I believe I understand how a man
could love and live with the sea.
Its beauty and strength is beyond
compare.
The thunder gives this place an eerie
feeling like the coming of
Death.

Danuta Latawska Wodnicka
CHRISTMAS EVE GIFT '89

This poem is dedicated to Monika and Edyta, my lovely daughters, in perpetuam rei memoriam.

Darkness spread her wings
Around the world.
The sky went black.
Almost blackness came.

Only the star from Bethlehem
Started to sparkle fairly.
The most beautiful from the beauties,
Marvelous and prophetic.

Jesus Christ was born.

Today, Christmas Eve is so magic,
Christmas night—full of charm.
Today, enough place for everybody.

Mother? Without any harm . . .?

The Christmas tree is very polish
today,
Blooming with spring, while
The air is so frosty.

Today, Santa Claus brought us
F R E E D O M,
On Phrygian horses he came.

Cristina Caudill
COLORS

BLUE is . . . .
Bright as the midday sky.
Dark as nighttime space.
Delicious as a blueberry.
Comfortable as a pair of old jeans.

BROWN is . . . .
Cold as the sand at the beach.
Sweet as homemade fudge.
Pretty as varnished wood at home.
Tasty as molasses tea at my aunts.
Soft as my collie, Ocean.
Warm as a forest's doe.
Shiny as a good friends hair.
Nice as a carpet on a cold
Saturday.

GRAY is . . . .
Graceful as a dappled mare.
Crinkley as a Sunday newspaper.
Omnious as a stormcloud.
Kind as my father's eyes.
Homey as a sweatshirt.
Familiar as a clinking trashcan.

Jo Linda Jennings
A NEW DAY IS DAWNING

Rise unto a wondrous world of
warmth and light
Dawning after a cold, dark night
Radiating a glorious sea of love
In splendid colors, cast from above
To let us know that touch of peace
That all men yearn for into sleep
It seems so lost amidst the rubble
Of tangled webs and life so
troubled
Where is the Love, we've lost in
wonder
Where is the Trust, in our own
brother
For all too soon, should we know
death
And leave behind this great
success
Of hate and lust and crime rampaging
It's time to take a stand in
changing
Our way of thinking, our way of life
The way we know to make it right
Yes, you alone cannot repair
The pain, the strife, the deep
despair
But someone has to start the Quest
To leave behind a "NEW" success
A new day is dawning, NOW!

Sherilyn Kamerik Hicks
IN YOU

I can hear the gentle waves of the sea
in your voice,
And hear the babbling brook as it
runs in your laughter.
I can hear the song of the birds in
your heart,
And hear the music of the crickets in
your breathing.

I can feel the strength of the mighty
oak in your arms,
And feel the warm gentle summer
breeze in your caress.
I can feel the touch of the rose petals
in your kiss,
And feel the warmth of the spring
day sun in your smile.

I can see the birds as they glide
through the air in your movements,
And see the blue of the sky and the
sparkle of the stars in your eyes.
I can see the beauty of the meadows
in your being,
And see the gracefulness of the
butterflies in your soul.

You wonder why I compare thee to
the beauty of the earth?
For these are the things that bring me
tranquility.
You still don't understand why I've
written these words?
For it is thee who has given back to
me my serenity.

Craig Lewis
INSIDE A CAGE

I am locked inside a cage,
Chirping a tune only I can hear.
Should I share my song with others?
Would my music please their ears?

I try to push the doors of my cage,
But the doors are made of fear.
I'm afraid to step out of my cage
And fly.
I'm afraid a crash may be near.

Theresa Dath
BRIGHT LIGHT OF COURAGE

Why did he die?
It's just not fair
All the pain he had to bear
He was a fighter and very brave
He fought to stay in school to his
community's rage
He stood up to teach us about his
disease
And told us we can't get it by
standing in the breeze
The light that shone through him
was snuffed out
Despite his determination, he lost
his bout
He was taken from this earth, it's
just not right
Not someone like him, who had the
courage to fight
You left us courage and inspiration
We will miss you Ryan White.

DeAnne Buie
GROWING UP

I remember the days of summer fun;
Days relaxing, enjoying the sun.
I remember all of the youthful games.
I was always sure to feel no pain.
Childhood crushes and puppy love
was always the best.
But now true love leaves the heart
depressed.
Sometimes growing up seems so
wrong,
Because life was so easy for so long.

Da-Nean Alberts
COME BACK

Specially to Jason Brescia, for a lot of great times. To Kelly Soukup and Amy Dobson, for the memories of laughter and fun, thanks for being such great friends. Also to my family, mom, Donnie, and Allen. I love you all lots.

Remember the times, when we were
together
in my mind, they'll stay forever.
Don't think of the bad,
they'll only make you sad.
I wish this feeling had last
but I guess it's just the past.
Live for tomorrow
And forget all the sorrow,
I wish we could walk hand, in hand
and make you understand,
That you've been in my heart
right from the start.
And now can't you see
that you've always been the one for
me.
So please come back for my love
come down from above,
Because I LOVE YOU,
and I cry, tears more than a few.
So please come back to me.
We can be as one
until both our lives are done.
I LOVE YOU.

Socorro Montalvo
LIFE

How complex life is,
Each person living in a personal
world
isolated . . .
without realizing how very close
there are other worlds crying while
one laughs
Others laughing while one cries.

I have always been a solitary person
surrounded by my digressions,
and while I think
others die or suffer . . .
Harmful things happen everywhere
while one kisses with passion a lover
for life;
Cities disappear under the oppression
and the war
while one gets with honors, deserved
award.
Dreams dispel and hit the rocks of
forgetfulness,
at the same time that one finds
himself living
a moment so dreamed . . .

In my world "Solitude,"
I discover with breath of hope,
a sheltered shadow, a savior's hand
THIS my second soul, my fire, sea,
rain and sun.

Pam L Rogers
FEELINGS—STRONG, YET GENTLE

There is a feeling
Deep inside
Strong, yet gentle by
The gentle touch of him.

It is warm and makes me want more
I find you also have this feeling
By the gentle touch of me
Strong, yet gentle.

The fountain of love comes to life
For what we feel is love
The feeling gets stronger
Reaching its point

Of still another fountain . . .
One full and of greater height
The height of heights
There is still another feeling . . .

Unity—being one
One, part of the other
Loving and being loved
Strong, yet gentle.

Cheryl Reynolds
YOUR BIRTHDAY

To my darling baby girl, Melissa, who has changed my life forever.

My little girl you're one today, where
has the year gone?
I marvel at your every move as I sit
and watch you play.
The day you were born I was in awe
of your beauty as you lay with your
pacifier
in your mouth—it seems like
yesterday.

Melissa, how I love that toothless
smile,
Each time I see it, it makes my life
worthwhile.

If I had just one wish for you I know
that it would be
to love the God who created you,
the One who gave you to me.

My little girl you're one today, where
has the year gone?
You talk and laugh and try to sing,
and point to almost everything.
And in those tender moments when
it's only you and me,
I hold you tightly in my arms and
pray for your safety.

Melissa, how I love that toothless
smile,
Each time I see it, it makes my life
worthwhile.
If I had just one wish for you I know
that it would be
to know the man called Jesus who
died for you and me.

My little girl you're one today, I love
you so very much.
Before I know it you'll be grown, and
I'll long for your little touch.
But for right now you're still a child
with your trusting, carefree way,
So relax and enjoy your chocolate
cake—for today is your birthday.

Jeanette Rish
OUR LITTLE ANGEL

In loving memory of Charlee Nikol Hutson.

Thinking back and searching my
mind,
I look for all the reasons,
A beautiful and Loving memory is
left behind.
As there are changes of the seasons,
And for everyone there's a special
time.

So much sadness fills my heart,
When I think of our "Charlee Baby."
And from her life, she had to part.

But as an angel that was sent from
heaven,
Jesus came and carried her home.
Like herself all angels belong in
heaven.
And NEVER will she be alone . . .
She's with Jesus now and forever on.

Tony Ambrosia
LONELINESS INTERRUPTED
The solitude of a city park
in mid-winter
Is comforting to one alone.
The air is stale after dark
in mid-summer,
it's a lonely nothingness which
condones.
In loneliness, the pretense is not to
care,
emptiness is allowed to avail.
Dry leaves crumble under foot,
the noise invades the night.
The bare trees, empty from branch to
root,
Becomes a friend, an ally at sight.
Though there might be
companionship out there,
the loneliness still prevails.
Children run in numbers, their joy
displayed in screams.
The birds come back, God's great
earth returns to green.
The lonely cling in earnest to their
loneliness,
But are reformed by the joy of
returning hominess.
The turn of a season makes the
despair corrupted,
A resurgence to life, an example of
loneliness interrupted.

Samuel George Pitt
GOLD

Dedicated to my darling wife Laura and children Jessica, Kallinka and Kabrini.

Slowly, gracefully how the sun
hovers the eastern peaks in an array
of gold.

Here and there the rays reveal
Golden dew upon golden leaves,
In swarms the brightest rays enhance
The golden honeybees' morning
dance.
In the crotch of an oak hangs a
nocturnal hunter
With claws of gold is the dozing
panther,
Whilst from their eyrie the white pate
is peeping
Of golden eagles still peacefully
sleeping.

A flying squirrel in the gliding pose
Is cruising along with a golden nose,
And trembling hornets from the
morning's cold
Now proudly display their nests of
gold

The golden yachts in the golden bay
Are shimmering in the most
spectacular way,
Bobbing gently in the morning's
breeze
Atop the waves of the golden seas.
Most magnificent are the rays,
looking their best
Reflecting off the ships in the golden
west.

Thomas R Kusleika
ON BEING LUCKY

To those who have suffered a loss. Try to remember what you still have, how you are blessed and perhaps you can smile again.

These are the days, life doesn't look good; want to lay down and die. Lost your job; what a shock! Depression, doldrums; what's wrong with you? Now your lady is gone! Really hurtin' inside. What could you have done? Everything is a mess; no work, no love, no life. What's the use?

But wait! What's going on here? This boy is lucky. What's that? Lucky? You said life was . . . "Just beginning, Brand new?" Yeah, that's it. Got your health. Got your smarts. Hey, you've got talent! Now we're cookin.' Let's look at this again; different perspective . . .

You were down. Wanted to crawl further into that hole; no light, no hope. But you got wise. You reached out and what did you find? Support, love, new opportunities, new horizons, new challenges; How often in a lifetime does one experience these things; all at once?

Yeah, that's it. Friends, family; there's that love, that support. You don't have to be afraid. Don't have to be embarrassed. Those people enjoy that chance to give. Most people do; let them have it. You were down but now you're lookin' around. You're out of that hole.

Take your time. Don't be lazy but go ahead, explore. It's new territory, revel in it. Sure it's scary. But it's exciting too. What a chance you've been given. Take pleasure in those small triumphs. Accentuate them and the other positives. You've taken those first steps.

What were we talking about? Challenges, horizons, friends, family, love and support; "On Being Lucky," yeah!

Barbara Thomas

Barbara Thomas
CHILD OF LOVE

Inspired by my children Cheryl, Val, Dereck, Kevin and Cyleste.

Image creating process significant
force effective tools faith realm of
the spirit is timeless child of love
every yesterday and every tomorrow
is today dissolves into an eternal now
infinite compassion strengthens
unique maturity sharing foundations
thoughts needs become obsessive
child of love emotional structure
disintegrated sophisticated words of
comfort mystical moment spiritual
dimensions are for you child of love
psychosomatic insight physically
born again recording impressions
influence conscious judgment
innocent child of love intimidated
virtues supernatural presence whole
attitude inspired fulfillment glorious
beginning segment substance is
brought into harmony confidence
human instinct erects saturated
awareness releasing need exuberant
new freedom surrender is the
creative staircase to maturity I adore
you child of love vibrant reality
motivating efficiency recognition
acceptability humanistic child of love
be yourself
I love you my precious child

Anthony Michael Soares
WHAT IS NOTHING?
What if,
What if you got into your
spacecraft
And went straight up
You traveled on . . . and on,
With no intentions of ever going back
and . . .
What if
What if you came to the end . . .
(the end of what? you might ask)
Well, the end of the universe.
What's on the other side?
and . . .
What if, what if there is nothing?
What is nothing??

Jeffrey Lynn Smith
TWISTED TURNS

My brother, my friend. I feel your distant soul. Perched in lofty hands of uneven ending. Above so far below, below so high above you stand. Cradled by uneven hand. Your childhood innocence, your weathered face.

Cast below the shadows ending. Tortured, twisted ending. Cast on smooth dark icy mirror. Far below drift shadows of light and darkness. And happier times. Cast shadows of distant light, upon my dark memory still.

I see your young happy face. In a memory made still, forever in that time and place. And I am a prisoner of memories dark reflection. Prisoner of the mirror still.

I come to this place often. To look upon that last stand, my mind forever with you. On the perch of destiny's dark side. I sit and stare, and dream dark dreams. Wide awake it seems, releasing memories demons, legions upon my tortured soul.

I sit and watch light's retreat. To dark shadows, darker still than sky above. I come here with you to be, at fate's sharp edge. I feel your soul drifting on the breeze, and find peace in these dark memories. More so peace in these memories than life's endless, changing memories, dark still and lifeless. Without the perch of your soul to light my way, in the ever darkening sky.

I look upon the twisted, turning reflection. In the still, dark mirror. I feel your soul there with me, in the darkening silence. And gaze upon the breeze.

Tracey L Comer
HOW DO I LET GO
How do I let go
You must know what you've done
We've grown apart, the enemy has
won
What I told you was true, you were
my very best friend
What happens now that I want our
friendship to end

You're not the same person I thought
I knew for so long

The one I listened and talked to, you made me feel strong
A friend it was said is one you trust and believe
A friend is not someone you try to deceive

The hurt and the pain I hid only too well
I never let on that you made my life hell
I let you believe you control what I do
By never admitting that I really disapproved

I have to be strong and let go of the past
It is tying me down, and I wish to pass
Pass up our friendship and all of the sorrow
And search for a friendship that will be here tomorrow

Tracey L Comer
MOM
To you who always cared
To you who never doubted
To you who always gave your all
To you who sometimes shouted

Within me I found
A little bit of you
The little part I needed
The part with which I grew

Grew to be strong
To know just how to fight
For whatever I believed
And thought to be right

You instilled in me the courage
To withstand any pain
To go through life with knowledge
Your blood runs through my veins

To you you must know who you are
By now there is no mistaking
For it was you who gave me my first breath
And it's you I'll love until my death

Toni M Dean
THE THINGS I LIKE BEST
Little boys running and splashing through puddles
Little girls' giggles kisses and cuddles

The bright morning sun shining through billowy clouds
The sounds of singing and laughing aloud

The warmth of a fire
An old couple's kiss

These are the things that I like the best

The rain's gentle echo just before dawn
Running through leaves in the warm autumn sun

Snowflakes blowing in the cold winter air
A smile from a friend saying they care

The stillness of night as I lay down to rest

These are the things that I like the best

The beauty of a sunset as it paints the sky
Feeling so happy that it makes me cry

The leaves changing color bright yellow and red
A soft cuddly pillow to snuggle in bed

The stars brightly shining
The moon's silver crest

These are the things that I like the best

The first day of spring as its freshness unfolds
To dream of the future and all that it holds

A child's tall tale of monsters and kings
The summer night songs that the crickets sing

The hope of tomorrow
Facing each day's new test

These are the things that I like the best.

Kristy Lockey
LOVE'S LIKE A ROSE
Love is like a tender red rose.
It has the beauty and fragrance
To fill the souls,

But love like the rose
Doesn't have the power of forever.
It wilts and dies to be replaced
By another,

And love like a rose
Has the sting of a thorn
To dig into someone
And then be reborn.

Yes love like the rose
Is fragile and pure.
Once planted, there is no cure.

Rita Pozzebon
YOUR LOVE REIGNS
your love came on like a summer storm
you swept me away in a breeze of charm
in a dream of thunder and lightning
scattering hopes of simplicity
is it so wrong, is it so wrong
when love reigns in our world

you nurtured the seeds of my soul
took them to a place where they would grow
was it a fantasy, exaggerated scheme
thought I'd never feel all that it was
is it so wrong, is it so wrong
when love reigns in our world

into my world and into my flesh
into my soul and gave me only the best
your love reigns, your love reigns in me

in so many outside circumstances
there seems to be more than there should
in a dream of thunder and lightning
you're showering me now; there is no fear
'cause even if it can't work out
your love still reigns in me

Naomi Wood
AIDES OF THE CORRY MANOR
The aides of the Corry Manor are such a pest, they keep disturbing you so you don't get your rest.
The food is so bad it's hard to digest.
It leaves your stomach in a tee-total mess.
Along comes a nurse with a capful of pills, and if that don't kill you the treatments will.

Sandra Gittlen
TO DADDY
Idols are made of glass, never stone.
They are fragile to the touch.
I don't ever want to touch you.
You'd disappear and leave me lonely.

I'll put you on a shelf
And stare at you from afar.
I'll listen to you breathing
And echo the raspings intently.

You can never break
Because then I'd shatter
And we'd both crumble to the ground
In synchronized pain.

You can't be mortal
Fragile glass of mine.
Because mortality means
You can be taken away from me.

Ryan Johnson
I WANT TO TAKE YOU
I want to take you
and make you into my bed.

I want your torso, your textured stomach
to be a warm mattress, without lumps or creaks.

I want your sturdy, supple arms and legs to hold that bed
two feet up, so I can store suitcases underneath.

I want your parted lips
as a glistening pillow, easy to find and hold.

I want your long, velvet hair
as a woven comforter, to keep my body heat within reach.

I want your pale eyes
as my nightlight, ever ready to protect.

I want your throat, your tongue as a broken alarm, sounding at different times for varied reasons.

I want your fingers and toes
as my pajamas, massaging me to sleep.

I want your essence, your clean powder smell
as the narcotic air I breathe.

And I want you to do the same to me.

Lorraine E Smith
A POEM FOR MY HUSBAND

To Don . . . love without you is much like sleep without dreams—because you are my dreams—my poetic inspiration. Be forever my friend and lover and know always that I will love you eternally. L.

From the knowing—came the wisdom . . .
and the strength to carry on.
After all the tears we cried,
when love had come and gone.

From darkness came the brilliance . . .
of love's light shining through,
the misty morning sunrise
and my blinding love for you.

But through all the mists of hopelessness
a beacon in the night,
casting shadows on the shore;
when love had ceased to fight.

And faith undying, tries once again,
to bring me back to you.
Searching for that Shangri-la,
when there's no port in view.

Lorraine E Smith
THE POETRY OF LOVE
Poetry in motion
the act of making love.
Me under loves tender flesh,
and you riding up above.

Love's full moon lures me on
to your waiting arms . . .
As I fall deeper with each kiss,
into your web of charms.

When pure passion reaches mountain-tops,
and stars fall from the sky . . .
All who look up will see the show,
but only we'll know why.

Waves crashing in upon our beaches . . .
with each the setting sun,
And ebbing just beyond your reaches . . .
the seduction has begun.

For love's secrets tell not a soul . . .
but awaits the next high tide,
when drums will roll and cymbals crash . . .
on this our wild ride.

Lorraine E Smith
THE LOVER'S GARDEN
You confuse me, maker of love . . .
Bringing my heart to soaring above . . .
Sweet Terra-firma I see below,
and reaching a heaven only lovers will know.

Then—lost in the passion . . . a euphoric state
I see the bright lights as I walk through the gate;
To our secret garden where we plant our seeds
And nurture this friendship, lost in our needs.

Forever onward as our loins spark to flame
In the heated blissful moments as we play the game.
And the rubbing—the friction surmounts the highest peak,
as fireworks explode and only then do we speak.

Of moments gone forever and moments to come
When we walk in our garden and pause to pick some . . .
beautiful flowers with their oh so sweet scent;
Losing ourselves in the pollen before it is spent.

Paula D Anglin
NEVER ENDING LOVE

In dedication to a special friend, my ballet teacher Mr. Fred Alexson. Thank you for everything.

My body cries out for him
After all these years I need him more than ever. And no one else will do,
it has to be Fred. It has to be Fred.
It has to be Fred. I do love him,
he's a great person and he cares.
He cares about me and he cares about my body.
Fred is my dance teacher and my

friend.
He cares and the friendship we share
is a love that will last forever.

Elizabeth McAllister
BABY KITTENS
Soft, cuddly
Brown, black
White, grey
Purrs loud
Or soft
Padded feet
Stop noises
They wake
Up when
Morning comes
Playful through
The day
Night comes . . . .
They fall
Asleep peacefully

Desiree L Bucknor
THE FEELING OF HIM!

With god in your heart, you can conquer every and anything.

Jesus is near
For I feel no fear
and I dare not say!
What an awful day.

For I must pray
and believe, by the way
That my Savior will lift
My burden gift.

But right now I am hurt
and my feelings I must convert
For faith I acquire
and receiving is my desire.

Sometimes the lights seem dim
Oh, almost dark!
But in me lark
The feeling of Him!

Earlene M Longoria

Earlene M Longoria
DUSTER PILOT
I take off in dawn's dew-laden air;
Long before you rise, my craft is there
Lest the wind in rising competition
May defeat the purpose of my mission.
While men in jobs sedate—sleep late.

My wife lights a candle when I fly;
Prays I be the apple of some saint's eye.
This is what she has so often said:
"What a way to earn our daily bread!"
But, truly, men more rich than I—
can't fly!

Barefaced farm boys on the ground below
Watch my slender craft as, row by row,
I the insects choke with lethal dust.
I fly using far less brain than crust.
I zoom under hovering high wires—
skirting guy wires.

While I seek to merit what is due me,
Even though some injured one may sue me,
We, working together, man and craft,
Throw all caution over with a laugh.
Farmers in straw hats below me—
owe me.

Earlene M Longoria
ORIGIN OF THE TEXAS BLUEBONNET
Once, way back in history, when Texas soil was new
And men came here from other states to start off life anew,
They crossed the Texas border and found to their surprise
A state that is so beautiful it hurt their poor old eyes!
But, still, all men who came, I fear, were not so very good
And some would lie and steal and cheat and damage all they could.
And once when a fair maiden did cross the beauteous plains
And ugly desperado blew out that maiden's brains.
She wore a bright blue bonnet and from her head it fell
With her own blood upon it, this poor, poor maiden, Nell.
And there they laid her body, they left it on the spot
Where it fell from the wagon in which she rode when shot.
There sprung up on the hillside on which our Nell did lie
Lovely flower bonnets of blue—blue as the sky.
On some was found a spot of red which was the blood that Nell did shed.
These pretty flowers that bloom each Spring, as every Texan knows,
Are the state flower of Texas and what their color shows,
Is white for Texas purity, red for gallant heart,
Blue for truth and surety and each one plays its part.
If you think this is a fable; if you don't believe it's true,
Then I'm sure that we could never make a Texan out of you.

Earlene M Longoria
THE GIFT
I'd like to give you a piece of the sky,
or a cloud, so soft and white.
I'd like to give you a bit of the moon,
or a robe of the gentle night.
I'd like to give you a glittering star,
or the spirit of the seas.
I'd like to give you a bottle of
a cooling summer breeze.
I'd like to give you the golden glance
of the sun on a baby's hair.

I'd like to give you the sweetness of
a rose to ever wear.
But, I can give you only
a wish straight from the heart—
That you may find joys for yourself
that ever will impart
Unto you peace and happiness
and dreams forever new;
A song within yourself, and may
your greatest wish come true.

Charles F Kovaschetz Jr
LIFE
We live life in Peace and War, Health and Happiness, Heartache and more. Through life's path we laugh and sigh as each passing day goes by. When we pass forever will sleep and eternally of rest and peace.

Kathy Myers
MAKING A DIFFERENCE
Making a difference
Large and wide
Making a difference
And I might die
Making a difference
It would come every day
Making a difference
It comes anyway
And Mother Nature makes it that way
For you and me in every way

Georgette Briggs
FREEDOM IN THE EYES OF A CHILD

Thanks to Jesus Christ my lord and savior and to my children who are my life and inspiration. And to my mother and siblings for being there for me.

Nelson Mandela is a proud Black man
Who for what he believes took a daring stand
He stood against bombs, bullets and shells
For the freedom of his people he was put in jail
For 27 years till he was old and grey
He never changed his mind - Not even today
He says the fight has only begun
But on Feb. 11th his freedom was won
I pray that before many more have died
That there will be an end to the Apartheid
As a young black child in 1990
I am proud to be a witness to this part of Black History!

Lisa R Nickels
ONCE

To Dave; Thank you for proving that dreams can come true. I'll love you always.

Once my days were
Lonely and cold.
Now my days are warm
With you to hold.

Once I had
An empty heart.
But you had filled it
From the start.

Once my feelings were
Locked up inside of me.
But my heart was the lock
And you were the key.

Once I had a dream
Of loving you.
Well,
That dream came true.

Mary Derrick Mee
DO YOU REMEMBER SNOW

To my mother, Grace Coleman Derrick.

Do you remember snow,
Chair-bound at your window,
Calm eyes watching a dark sky
Give up its burden of whiteness?
Do you remember cold softness
Against your face, your brother
Holding your mittened hand as
The two of you hurry to join
Laughing friends at the sled run?
And do you remember looking back
To see your mother wave from
The window of the small snug house
Where warmth and love wait to receive you
When playing is done?
Yes, I think you remember.
Your quietness tells me you do.

Char C Alexander
LISTEN
Listen, God gave us all two ears
Listen, God gave us feelings, love & tears
Listen, Or do you know how I feel?
Listen, Or have you forgotten what's really real?
Listen, But don't tell me I must not talk.
Listen, Do you know I'm weak or tired to walk
Listen, Please don't take all my pride away
Listen, Don't tell me I can't help or have a say
Listen, Don't give others all the chores I like to do
Listen, For now I can't even talk to you
Listen, I've respected and admired you in every way
Listen, 'Cause my faith in you has gone astray
Listen, You many things can be accomplished as a group

Listen, You seemed, long ago, to be
proud of your troop
"Listen With Both Ears"

Char Alexander
UNTITLED

To our "Three Soldier Boys"
The family had a unanimous vote
To your Parents, Sisters and Brothers
We are requesting you send a note.

We are all in very good Health
And hope this finds you the same
We remember your faces, but—
Have had no letter with your name.

Yesterday was Veteran's Day
And our Flag was flying high
Our Three Boys were far away
Then No. 3 called, Dad gave a sigh.

We wanted to see and be with each of you
To listen to your woes and share your joys
Guess that is normal for Parents to Love
And be proud of their "Three Soldier Boys."

lu
AFTERTHOUGHT

For a maitre d' in Sri Lanka.

As old as youth,
As young as time—
The fable of a love.
It creeps into your heart
And then
It silently breaks out again.
What was I thinking of!

Daphne A Turner
DECEPTIONS OF THE HEART

Love unrequited—
Burns as a relentless fire;
Emotions seek to escape—
Caged like a prowling tiger.
Passions inflamed—
Run amuck, seething and burning;
Leaving nothing in their path—
Due to uncontrollable yearning.
Feelings suppressed—
Scream endlessly to be released;
Thoughts wind and race—
As heightened intensity is slowly decreased.
Longing unreal—
Eternity it seems passes with no response;
Grief and pain intense—
Wrench the heart of its every ounce.
Tears unrestrained—
Relieve the soul of total confusion;
The heart many times broken—
Silently, yet in sorrow drifts into reclusion.

Stefan H Townsend
MUSIC FOR A CAPTIVE AUDIENCE

You played my body like it was a
fine musical instrument
(a guitar)
Like I was your last recital and you
wanted me
to be the best
Gently you brought the guitar to your
breast
It grew in size,
seeming to realize the magnitude of
the challenge:
proud to be the one guitar especially
picked from all others
ready to play
caressing the strings,
you took the instrument past its level
of competence.
Crisp, crystalline notes flowed across
the concert hall of your bed
finally coming to rest,
in a velvet garden, covering it with
tears.
The last curtain call complete,
you laid the guitar face down in its
case,
closing the cover and whispering
goodbye.
The guitar cried, knowing it would
never again be played as well
as it was tonight.

Patricia Koski
CYCLES

To Linda, Sam, Alan and Kim.

The ragged edge of autumn
Limps northward.
Dreams, on hold,
Rest under crystal ice.

The leaden air holds secrets
Bold and sweet.
Beware the midnight sun.
It seeks the truth.

Chards of springlight
Shatter the endless
Black of night and
Arrow earthward.

The earth disturbed, turns.
Melting, rushing, white water
Catapults seeds,
Quickening with life,
Southward.

Sultry summer blooms
Autumn fruits. Then
Harvested to the last bright leaf
The cycles begin again.

Jessica Kantorski
INJUSTICE

Crystals
shattered
like dreams of young men
longing
for their freedom

Hope
sliced
with jagged shards
leaving
a trail of defeat

Blood
running
down the face
dwelling
in prejudged eyes

Francisco F Trejo
FOR MARY

This is dedicated to Mary Hinkley. Without her friendship this would not be possible.

More and more I search for kindness
And it always eludes me.
Remembering the hard times
You could have been helpful,
But I did not know you then.
Everything is brighter now.
Thank you for that.
Help has to be asked for.
Hope has to be given.
I now know that
No one can end the search alone.
Kindness comes when you stop looking.
Looking only drives it away.
Everyone needs friendship.
You have given it to me.

Jeff Shirley
WAR

Tell me What is war?
War is men killing men
And you can't step them
The world depends on war
The soldiers are in a corps
Vietnam was a war
And it killed a lot of the corps
We hope and pray
That wars happen far away
Yet they could happen any day
World War I, World War II
These were all very true
People got killed, people got shot
People were also hurt a lot
War is a serious pain
But they say no pain, no gain
I think they are wrong.

Charlene Matteson Thomas

Charlene Matteson Thomas
SOMEWHERE IN TIME

In memory of my loving and dedicated mother, Eileen.

Somewhere in time
There's a place for me.
I'm told it's in the centuries.
Born in the wrong time and place,
Possibly of the wrong gender and race,
As well as financial endowment.
Who am I?
I am the dreamer.
One who lives in each and every living soul.
The one who is not content with where he is now,
But wishes he's someone he isn't.
I am the dreamer of the past.
Of things old, yet cherished.
I bring them from the past
And keep them alive in the present.
I am the dreamer of the future,
Who foresees a great horizon
And greets it with open arms.
Therefore, creating reality.

Mary Therese Jones
I AM A BLACK WOMAN

This poem is dedicated to Anthony, Marvin, Oleta, and Alisia, my children—and especially to Mrs. Janie Hughes, my sweet mother.

I am a Black woman with kinky hair
and my skin is dear and fair.
But I have come through stormy winds
and a road of many sins.

My hands are rough and my feet are tough
I've known some love, but not enough.
Suffering times I have known
and sometimes hate I have shown.

Crying inside day and night
and sitting by a candlelight.
Holding my child in my arms
and hoping that he will know no harm.

The days were long and the nights were short
and I think of what the years have brought.
Sorrow and hurt to my heart
but always another day for a better start.

I feel the aches and the pain
upon the road from whence I came.
Feeling the sun shine on me
and asking the Lord to help me please.

Days of Hunger I have seen
and times when the people have been mean.
Tears have rolled down my eyes
but still my heart was filled with pride.

Still the road was long and hard
while the days turn to dark.
Praying by the candle light
hoping someday would be bright.

Bright for my child if not for me
so that one day he might be free.
Free to know the road from whence I came
but not to bear the aches and pain.

Denise Gardner
CHOICES

To Amanda—I know things were not perfect, but I did the best I could.

How much have I deprived you?
I sent your father away when you were two.

I gambled that I could be both mom and dad.
Did the choice I make do more good than bad?

Did I do enough to replace the man in your life?
I could no longer go on being his wife.

I couldn't live with his lies.
But is that an answer for those big eyes?

How can I possibly explain?
How do I take away the pain?

I could no longer pretend.
How can I make you comprehend?

With you he has no time to bother,
and it was I who chose him for your father.

I loved him more than life itself.
I knew he'd never give us great wealth.

But I pray you'll take my word.
I thought he'd be the father you deserve.

I never thought his daughter he would deny.
In God's name I can't understand why!

This man destroyed a lot of your mother's world.

Please don't let him destroy my beautiful baby girl.

J Michael Davidson
THE RIDE, THE DRINK, THE END

As she went
Sunlight in her hair,
Too fast she drove;
Her face so fair
Ne'r seen again;
She drank on the road,
Her car it dove
At one-twenty miles an hour.
Her booze the fiend,
Her drunken state no pow'r,
To avoid the crash.
She road shining,
Her great dreams dying,
Taken up with her, in flame.

Robert A Klotz
DAZED

To my grandparents and parents who taught me that love is a way of life instead of a passing fad or merely a four letter word.

Lonely days followed by endless nights,
Dreading the darkness when I turn off the lights.
I lie in bed thinking, only of you,
Praying that maybe you'd feel as I do.

Words can't express what I want to say,
Loving you more with each passing day.
Wanting you to share my dream,
Hoping things aren't as they would seem.

Wanting to tell you the things I hide,
Wishing you could see me inside.
Letting you know that this could last,
Not like times we've had in the past.

Walking in a daze, staring at the sky,
Going on without you would be a lie.
Love in my heart I want to share,
Wanting to know, do you really care.

I know what we feel's for real,
What seems to be the big deal?
Step by step and day by day,
Follow our hearts is all I can say.

Kyle Connor
LITTLE ONE

To Keith—Our love is special and will last forever—I will love you always. Same to my little one.

This is to my little one
Whether it's a daughter or son.
Your father means the world to me
As you grow up you will see.
You will now be another part
And remain always deep in our hearts.
We aren't quite sure how you'll turn out
But you'll be the best we have no doubt.
Just do what you think is right
Taking everything on with all your might.
We most of the time know what's best,
But to get stronger you will need tests.
Remember always the love
That brought you here was true—
And that no matter what
We'll always love you.

Marcia Giffin
THE QUESTION

She came floating up from the flowers with sparkles and stars surrounding her as if she were indeed a mystical being.

"Why . . ." he claimed in surprise. "I have never seen anything as beautiful as you. Why are you here?"

"I came to ask one question of you," she said. "If you answer correctly, I will be as real to you as all the star in the heavens."

"Oh?" he said with delight. "Please do ask!" He exclaimed as he watched her twinkle.

"Will you . . ." she said slowly. "Will you be my Valentine?"

Roger Allen
MOM, YOU DIDN'T CARE MUCH FOR FINER THINGS

Mom, you didn't care much for finer things,
You never sought things too neat.
To work and love and have a family,
To you, that made life complete.

You didn't spend much time going places,
and your clothes were not the latest.
But, you were always happy, knowing well
It was the small things that were the greatest.

When you started, you nabbed the top man,
To that I'm sure you're very glad.
It was his greatness that made us strong,
and I'm proud to say that man is my "Dad."

Then came the brothers four,
Whose times you will not regret.
Sadly, the Lord called for the younger two,
which the pain I know, you will not forget.

But you still have the girls of three,
The pride and joy of your life.
And with the fast passing of time,
They'll soon be leaving to become a wife.

But, we will never forget the constant love,
And your smile sweet as flowers.
And all that we are, we owe to you,
The sweet loving mom of ours.

Tracy E Grinstead
AN EMOTIONAL QUICKY

By mere coincidence
(flavored by a dash of convenience)
a man and a woman turn to one another.

Each face registers
love, hatred, truth, deceit,
and lack of emotion
simultaneously.

They rush into each other's hearts and arms,
pushing or clutching, one cannot tell.

They strip themselves of emotional costume jewelry
and garbs of individualism
as their minds and bodies
intertwine,
writhing to a silent, pulsating beat.
Again their glances meet.
He winks.
She grimaces.

They quickly dress in social images
and go their separate ways.

Karen Uschold
IN THE MOONLIGHT

I have known you for awhile,
and what we have is special.
I remember the talks we shared,
we were a touch away from reality.
I would get lost in your eyes,
and captivated by your smile.
I remember one cold night,
I waited for you by the water.
Its waves rippling,
as I felt a slight breeze;
a single tear fell,
in the silent moonlight.
I was left alone in a
memory.
Now as I remember,
how far apart we've become.
I will always be waiting,
in the moonlight.

James W Canavan Jr
A MAN WALKS HIS FIELDS

A man walks his fields
Secure in the knowledge
That his children are well cared for.
He knows he could die
At almost any time,
But he does not fear this;
Well, not much anyway.

The wolf walks his forest
Secure in the knowledge
That he could die at any time.
He knows his children
Will take care of themselves;
And he fears none of this;
There is no reason to.

Deborah June Sylvester
EARTH'S TREASURES

Many treasures each day go unseen,
Look through the eyes of your soul
see what I mean.
Strawberries hidden under little green leaves,
are likened to rubies.
The black velvet sky, all studded with diamonds on high.
The golden sunlight sets over the water as the day grows old,
turning the water to liquid gold.
The birds wake me with a song
saying, all these riches to mankind belong.
Can one hid them away like a selfish child with a toy?
Earth's treasures are free for all to enjoy.
Open your eyes, let your soul soar,
I'm sure you will find
there are many more.

Audrey LaVelle
DREAMING

When I am sitting
By your side,
So close
I want to lean against you
Feel my body's contour
Melt into yours
Feel myself no longer
Separate
Feel the day's weight lift away
Let my eyes fall closed
Gently
Dreaming

Diana Creaturo
ALONE

Alone is what I am
Alone in my dreams
Alone are my wishes
Alone is what I seem to be

Alone no one understand me
Alone no one cares
Alone thinking of the LOVE
that we could share

Alone dreaming of you
Alone wishing you were here
Alone my heart cries out to you
Alone fighting a secret fear

Alone that's all I am
without you
Alone with a single tear

Judith Perkins
WORLD OF UNHAPPINESS

Up above me birds are chirping,
the skies are clear with not a cloud in sight.
Down below my world's not so peaceful,
things shattering all around me.
It's cold and lonely down here.
I wish someone would save me from this world of unhappiness.
Take me to where there are no clouds,
where it's always peaceful.
No hitting or screaming and yelling.
Where everything is like the ocean
calm and relaxing.
Someone save me from this world of unhappiness.

Maria Abbas
LOVE BEYOND TOMORROW

You speak directly to my heart
As if you knew my heart would sure perceive it.
You whisper to my soul that chants
Because my soul adores you dearly.
And even when you're silent still
My heart's so loud, I could not help but see
How much your treasured silence touches me
How much your subtle ways secure me.
And then my mind away goes
To different planes through different roads.
No, I could not yet depart from you
Because my flaming soul would race
The world to find your soul again
If ever you forgot to give it tone.
Because, my love, my whole life's love
I would not have the power or the weakness
To let you far away go.
So stay with me
Till ready be our souls to depart and reunite again
For yet another distant trip
Together to further distant roads.

Janelle A Carroll
THE FOOL'S SONG

I hunt the Black Woodsman to show him he is bad.
I am a fool, and a fool's life is what I've had.

I seek Mephistopheles to tell him he is wrong.
I am a fool. I sing a fool's song.

I seek Tantalus and scold him for his deed.
I am a fool. It is a fool's quest that I lead.

I find Eustace to warn him of his skin.
I am a fool. A fool will never win.

I set by Narcissus and tell him he is vain.
I am a fool, but a fool who feels pain.

I comfort Judas and share with him his fears.
I am a fool, but a fool who has ears.

I am burdened by crosses, crosses that are not mine.
I am a fool. I have a fool's mind.

For I brighten the path of those who never see.
I am a fool, and a fool I will be.

Tammy Plotner
THE BALLAD OF CLIVE
—to the tune of "Beverly Hillbillies"—

Let me tell you all a story 'bout a man named Clive,
He was a silly, 'ol hillbilly who liked to drink and drive.
Then one day when he came upon a curve,
He lost control and went into a swerve.

Drunk that is, outta' control.

Well, he hit another car right in the driver's side,
And don't you know, that the other driver died.
The state trooper said as he took him off to jail,
"Son, we're gonna' turn your life into a living hell."

Bars that is, no names, just numbers.

Well, a lawyer got him off with only thirty days.
Now, you tell me, just who's the one that pays?
Well, the moral of this story is not to drink and drive,
So you'll stand a better chance of coming home alive.

M.A.D.D. that is, Mother's Against Drunk Driving.

gene Helen Copeland
CHANGES

For the PRIME TIME PLAYERS . . . those over 35! Especially the EMPTY NESTERS!

Now that all the children are grown, and gone . . .
And I am left alone.
I must adjust to these changes that time has brought on.

What to do with my life now, a life that essentially had been lived with others 'first' in mind . . .
Where do I go, from here? How do I hang on?
Friends and I, long since have lost touch, time requires that now a new life style I must find.

I must accept and adjust to changes in health, looks, family situations, work, relations manifold . . .
It's a time of endless CHANGES.
Yet, this time can be a learning situation, a time of great revelation.
A time of freedom, a time of adventure, a time of rediscovery of life's real gold.
CHANGES must come for they are a part of life . . .
Nothing remains the same.
How we accept them, what we learn from them, our reactions to them, if proper, will relieve the strife . . .
of CHANGES.

Sunny Nanette Shouse
DRIFTERS

To the believers, . . . you know who you are.

Souls made of peace are hard to find,
looking in the mirror, seeing eyes filled with pride.
Hiding in the darkness of a lost and found mind,
wishing that the heavens would show signs of any kind.

Holding my heart in hands made of love,
dreaming of days that may never come.
Princes and damsels in fairy-tale lives,
slaying fire breathing dragons in the way of true love.

True love in real life seems almost absurd,
listening to slow songs but can never hear the words.
Looking for that prince on his tall white horse,
seeing nothing but nothing and feeling only remorse.

I stopped dreaming a long time ago,
it got me nothing but sorrow and worn down soul.
Wishes and fantasies never come home,
they do nothing but drift and leave people . . . alone.

Michelle Cali Wright
KIDS AS ONE

It is now time for me to put away myself and become the person I want to be, and do the things that I want to do and say, To be the baby is not right for me, for I must learn to speak for myself, and stand up to what's right or wrong for me. For as I speak, I speak for all who are older or younger than me. For my time is your time and we must make something of it. We must bring together the powers of love and happiness so no one will turn away as to tell us we lost. For if our powers did not come together as one we can say that we tried. So don't fall back now for I am with you and so are many others and with them we shall be as one.

Kathy G Reed
THE SADDEST SONG OF ALL
Of all the songs the winds have blown;
of all the lilting echo-tunes;
the saddest notes to replay
the lone-wolf swan—call in lyrical decay.
The winds whisper tales between their branches;
the shadows color the farmer foot-paths;
the moon sheds beams on all that's been;
the rain—tears sorrowing bath,
in droplets,
renews again.
Why the brother forest is bent in tears?
Why does mother earths many souls roam?
And at the graves the wolf and fox cry?
Because their natural brother-relative,
the American Indian, today, will die!

Brenda J Lippa
YOU ARE

I'd like to dedicate this to the man who is EVERYTHING in my life— the man I've fallen happily in love with— Robert P. Venishel.

You are the gleam in my eyes,
the smile on my face

You are the reason I wake up in morning
how I make it through the day

You are the song in my soul
the warmth in my heart

You are my knight in shining armor
my spice in life

You are everything I've ever wanted
all I'll ever need.

You are my everything.

Brenda J Lippa
THE PHOTOGRAPHS OF US LONG AGO
The photographs of us long ago
Our lives together
My god how we glowed

The trinkets of your love
I hold in my hand
Thinking back to when
We made love in the sand

It hurts to remember
How close we once were
We stayed in love
I thought you were sure

I think back now
To all the moments we shared
To god how I prayed
You'd always be there

But now I'm alone
It's easy to see
How I'll always
Love you
But did you ever
Love me?

Edward B Saulnier
THE HEART vs. THE MIND
As I bow beside my bed
And my mind is thinking so—
I ponder what Jesus said,
What He spoke so long ago.

Then my heart is flooded now,
Though my mind does not know why—
My heart prays as I do bow,
For my life the Lord did die.

And my heart is now lifted,
For my sins the Lord did rise—
That's why I am now gifted,
My deep joy is no surprise.

Jesus Christ lives in my heart,
Though He doesn't in my mind—
I do know He won't depart,
His deep love is always kind.

I will love Him every day,
To His words my heart will cling—
Though my mind gets in the way,
My heart's full, and it does sing!

Krisie Pickens
THE BUS
See her stepping off of the bus that takes her home
She carries such an air of ease but feels so all alone.
She dreamed of being queen one day to shower love, to reign . . .
But no one ever gave a damn so now she hides the pain.
She wears a suit of armor she doesn't seem to care
She's always got her fairytale her prince is always there.
She knows he's always somewhere though never sure inside,
If her make-believe prince he can't touch her when she cries.
So, she keeps on chasing pipedreams she looks to every man,
But nothing makes the darkness leave her disenchanted land.
'Cause knights in shining armor are never gonna be
And what she thinks of, walking home is just a fantasy.
Her dreams of horse drawn carriages ease the nightmare of her days
So she doesn't cry, just curtsies
. . . as the driver pulls away.

Larry Boeding
FOLLOW YOU

This is dedicated to Jill Osterberg. I will love her forever.

As the sun sets and the moon rises
As the lights go out on the small town.
As the seasons change
And the earth moves
With snow, rain, sun and wind
I will follow you.
To the highest mountain
Across the world,
I will follow you
But, let it be known,
What I do for you, I do alone.
To see your smile when I'm done.
Will be everlasting one-to-one.

Steven J Burtch
SOLILOQUY
As a bee to its nectar
Or a linnet to her nest
Shall I fly through the miles
To clasp thee to my breast;

Or wait as winter waiteth
For lilacs in the Spring;
As the barren season waiteth
For the meadowlark to sing;

For an hour more propitious—
More appropriate than today;
Lest my precipitiousness
Should frighten thee away?

To go to thee or stay—
Who can tell tomorrow—
If haste is better than delay
Except it end in sorrow?

R Miller
COLD WATER
I can't describe
Saturday after 47 years.
15 years at the Ararat Restaurant,
one of the sailors new as an oil burner.
After breakfast he read several newspapers among the passengers
and visited with a doctor

She was a seamstress taking walks around St. Mary's Hospital.
She was an office supervisor surviving.
She was a polisher in the plating department.

He crawled to me
The destroyer came like heaven

Lou DiFrancesco

Lou DiFrancesco
YOUR FLAG IS SPEAKING

To all our service men and women who served with dedication and pride to keep our country free and our freedom able to survive.

I am your symbol
and waving free,
Your inspiration for Democracy,
I am here
for you to look up to,
My colors being red, white and blue,
I have stars and stripes
to remind you
of battles fought keeping you free,

Men and women dying
just for me
to preserve our freedom
for all to see,
Making me proud
while waving high in a crowd,
And being saluted
while our anthem
is playing loud

Lou DiFrancesco
JOHN PAUL II
You are a Pope of destiny,
And will be remembered
as a man believing in reality,
With books filling many pages
and spoke of
by people of all ages,
You are a Pope loved
and admired by all,
And historians will be writing
That you answered the call,
You were chosen for a job,
That you alone could do,
To bring countries together
with a faith you hold true,
Communicating with people
has been your greatest forte,
With your many languages spoken
you have led the way,
In a world with many problems
of which we can all relate,
You have brought back our faith
by working hard
to alleviate

Lou DiFrancesco
OUR FAITH
It is not your religion
or the way you pray
or going to church,
Just to be able to say
It is the way that you live
with good thoughts
in your mind
with good feelings
from your heart,
That you will find
that will give you peace
from the Almighty Divine

Lou DiFrancesco
AFFECTION SHOWN
A rose when received
is much more than a flower,
It is a symbol,
Helping love to grow stronger
with every hour,
It is an institution with thorns
with a fragrance sweet
and when received
makes your heart skip a beat,
It is a flower created,
By the Lord up above,
With one purpose in life
to help promote love,
It can help mend fences
that surround your heart,
Giving you a meaning for living
with a brand new start

Lou DiFrancesco
A SUPER SUPER TEAM
A team that's together
is what it takes
when winning championships
all this relates,
Having proper management
is where it all starts
and players with ability
having great big hearts,
A defense determined
and having a "lott"
a team that gives
all that its got,
These are the ingredients
that make a great team
and a Joe Montana
to complete
San Francisco's dream,
Now they have four
and going for more,
They are the greatest
just add up the score

Lou DiFrancesco
THE BIG HURT
They can put you in orbit
and send you mind
to outerspace
making you think thoughts
that are never taking place,
They are tools of the devil
drugs meant
to damage the brain
causing distortion of your mind
and keeping your body
from ever working the same,
They are passed about
by people with greed
causing much heartache when used
while creating a need,
Education on drugs
must begin in the home
with children being taught
and in this trap hoping
never to be caught

Lou DiFrancesco
ELVIS
His memory lives on
in the hearts of all fans
who wanting to believe
it was only a dream
with the thought of him gone,
Very hard to conceive,
he was taken away
at a very early age
leaving many memories
with many books written
filling every page,
He was an idol for many
having talent of plenty,
A singer born to rule
the destiny of rock and roll,
Who entertained us always
with all his heart and soul,
He left his fans with pain,
A world never to be the same
for losing Elvis Presley
was one big terrible shame

Lou DiFrancesco
WELL DESERVED
Her day had arrived,
The derby was here,
Trying hard to win
she was not one to give in,
Her horse was a longshot
and ignored by all,
But Unbridled running hard
showed all by answering the call,
The ride it was perfect
with Craig Perret
guiding his mount
as he picked his spots carefully
passing horses,
With Carl Nafzger's
running account,
Frances Genter's time
had finally come
with her having a lot of fun,
In this blue grass Kentucky State
after many years
of a long, long wait

Lou DiFrancesco
A SAD FAREWELL, RYAN WHITE
He was injected with blood
that was not very pure,
It made his life difficult
and very hard to endure
changed his world around
giving him a troubled mind
while losing friends
with new ones hard to find,
He had contracted AIDS
a virus with no cure,
With friends very cautious
and not very sure,
He became a symbol
for those in need
who have this virus
causing them grieve
With his life growing short
after a time of neglect
he found people who cared
showing him love and respect

Lou DiFrancesco
BUFFALO'S SPRING TIME
The sounds of spring
has a pleasant ring,
The changing weather,
Hearing the birdies sing,
Tulips with heads peeking
are sunshine seeking,
With naked branches showing
the blossoms that are growing,
A feeling of relief
from the cold and winter grief,
Feeling the warmth of the sun
with good weather bringing fun,
Now able to see the girls
as they parade their wares,
Mini skirts
with pretty legs
and many good reasons
to stare

Lou DiFrancesco
A TRUE HERO
He was a legendary figure
who came out of the past,
A symbol of justice
always wearing a mask,
Rode a white horse
called Silver,
A steed having beauty and grace,
With Tonto his sidekick
fighting injustices everyplace
he was a legend with mystique
wearing guns that repeat,
Who galloped into our homes
with many cereals to sell
to the tune from an overture
from one William Tell,
He was the Lone Ranger
and remembered by all
with HI HO SILVER!
His very famous call

Lou DiFrancesco
SAINT JOSEPH'S DAY
Is an Italian holiday
the honoring of a patron saint
of whom the poor
find easy to relate,
It is a festive tradition
passed on through years,
The feeding of the poor
while being able to cheer,
The breaking of bread
among family and friends,
With fish to fill tables
from the front to the end,
They have plenty of spaghetti
with no meat sauce in sight,
Covered only with garlic
and oil real light,
delicacies of plenty
and always in sight,
A treat to the eyes
and to eat a delight

Lou DiFrancesco
DARYLE
Four years on the bench
Are very hard to endure
For Any Athlete
Who has ability that's sure,
It all happened in sixty-three
A Notre Dame grad
was a Buffalo draftee,
He was a quarterback with a spark
who had fire in his eye
blessed with desire
and able to make a football fly,
He was always ready
whenever the call
saving many games
and was appreciated by all,
Leading the Bills was his dream
but unable to fit the Buffalo scheme
being traded was the only way
and leading the Oakland Raiders
finally made Daryle Lamonica's day

Rick Balmer
DAWNING OF THE SON
In the gloom within my soul
Only one way could make me whole
Instead I walk the other way
Never to see the light of day
Walking on the path of sin
The gates of hell I'll enter in
But then a man showed me the way
To find the everlasting day
Never to stumble in the night
But to boldly walk in the light
I want to be known for what I have
Never to dwell on my past
Crying out to be forgiven
Trying to stop giving in
Please forgive me of my wrongs
And free me from these binding
throngs
Lead me to the everlasting flow
Where thirst will never touch my soul
So take me when your work is done
At the dawning of Your Son

Albert R Bass Jr
ADVERSITY
Today we see the trees,
they are lit by the light,
the light of life.

As the light breaks,
layer by layer dissipates.
Now no trees are to be found,
but the light still shines
to the ground.

For tomorrow, the
trees will be in sorrow.
As we devour our trees,
the light of life, still
lights the ground.

Today, tomorrow, the years to
come, the trees of life will
have no life.
So the light shines to the ground.

Veola Victoria Barnes
DREAMS . . . HAVE MANY FACES
Dreams . . . have many faces
Are alive in
Many minds
Never resting
No matter race, color
Creed, places
East, west
The new born cries
Dreams of being
Fed
The child dreams
Of the toy
Of a neighbor's
Boy
Teenagers dream of
Cars, girls
Bars
Grownups dream
Of a mate
Children
A happy fate
Dreams can be happy
When it involves
Love
Dreams can be eerie
Weary when they
Abort before
They're ready
Dreams have many faces
Are alive in
Many minds
Of different races
In many places.

Martha Morgan Blount
SUMMER WOODS
O, the woods are full of summer
I have sensed their siren signs
In the murmur and the rustle
Of the hedges and the vines.

O, the woods are full of summer
And the honeysuckle flows
Across the fields and meadows
Where the soft breeze blows.

O, the woods are full of summer
And the jewel encrusted hills
Give up a sweet aroma
Where the purple violet spills.

O, the woods are full of summer
And the sun's soft golden rays
Call up the sweetest memories
From my fondest childhood days.

Thomas Barnes
TIME
Time is given at no cost,
With moments of life often lost.
And all the struggle and all the pain,
Cannot another minute gain.
Though we live our lives with care,
Seldom finding the time to share,
Missing those moments beyond
compare,
At last will we find time to spare?
And always moving oh so fast,
Hoping that minutes, longer will last.
Ever trying to escape our past,
As time moves ever on and on.
And one day when our days are gone,
All that remains now of our life,
Is not the battle and the strife,
But the memories made in haste,
In the time we did waste.

Kenneth B Branon
WHO WILL I CALL
Who will I call to come to me,
To show me all life's joys,
To walk with me and talk with me
Along life's fast highways.

Who will I give my life to—
No matter what the cost?
To give me love at its best and
Show me life's true joys and
happiness.

He will give me all that I ask,
The true joys of happiness.
The peace of mind that comes from
time
The love that he has inside for all of
mankind.

If I will only give him the time,
He will change my cold heart and
mind.
He will show me things that I have
never seen,
Christ Jesus, my Savior and King.

Nancy B Brohner
APPRECIATION
This is to you mom and dad whom I
love so very much,
I'm just sorry that at this time we are
kind of out of touch.
But this is to show you just how
much I care,
For everything together that we have
ever shared.
You have always shown me
happiness even when you two were
down,
I'll never forget the feelings I've had
when you both didn't even frown.
You've also made me realize just the
little things to appreciate,
Also what to love and also what to
hate.
So please now let me tell you both
just how proud I am of you,
For all the things you've done for me
that's made me love you two.
I hate to end this poem now for I
have many thoughts of you,
But just let me remind you both that I
truly appreciate you!
Thanks for everything

Grace Ann Bartolomeo
WINTERTIME
The coldness cuts through the air
Children play without a care
Of changes occurring to mother earth
Gradually preparing for her new birth
Greens turn into greys and browns
Snow begins to cover ground
Children frolic in snow that's new
Building snow forts that go askew
Slush and mush and frozen water
Winter work for son and daughter
But all too soon this season's ending
Young trees soon will be unbending
And even so, a new season's starting
Before the last one's through
departing.

Lorraine A Brown
SEVEN VOICES
They called to me, again,
In my dreams last night,
The seven voices from
Atop those ancient hills.

Oh! but tonight when
I hear their voices calling
I will leave my dear home
And miles that I travel will be
uncertain and unknown.

Shall I walk, I ask, or shall I run,
Or shall I swim a distant sea,
The only thing that was certain now
Rome! would be my destiny.

I will stroll in moonlight
beside the Tiber
And hear mandolins and soft guitars,
I will watch the dome of St. Peter's
Embrace and kiss the stars.

Ah! but as dawn is fast approaching
And Rome begins to smile,
I will begin my journey homeward
And tearfully wash each mile.

Gayle Badowsky
SHALLOW WAYS
Life is strange . . . some people
say,
as they make their plans . . . from day
to day.
The road ahead wide open. . . the
path so bright,
how could one see . . . the curves at
night?
Strong and sure we travel . . .
toward our goals,
where'er do they come from . . .
those unseen holes?
An island we are . . . following our
dreams,
when life goes astray . . . who hears
our screams?
Where in these times . . . is the
helping hand?
Who dared hide our eyes . . . from the
promised land?
Hard work, time spent . . . where is
our wealth?
Did we forget . . . our neighbors in
poor health?
We are born for a reason . . . to
rejoin Our Lord,
have we forgotten the treasures when
He says . . . "All Aboard?"
Work and toil . . . be what you
may,
for the true rewards come . . . on
Judgement Day.

Jamie E Balliet
QUEEN OF HEARTS
We say "I love you," we don't really
know you
We're prisoners of music, captives of
words
Locked behind her castle wall,
prisoners by choice
Our leader, once the Queen of Hearts
Lined our cells with doves, crystals,
and lace
Our own big house on the hill

Ten years gone, pieces of your heart
found in every cell
They took you away and gave you
your own room
And Queen Sara became Queen Alice
But you returned to please the
prisoners who gave you life

We listened to our Queen, sitting
around the burning candles
But they were burning out and her
castle walls were falling
For there was never a King, only her
prisoners

I saw the Queen the other day, on one
of her journeys through the castle
I could see the walls beginning to fall
And knew she may soon leave her
throne
She says, "No, I can't leave my
prisoners"
But the prisoners will understand,
and never forget their Queen.

Abby Beckham
THE GREAT CITY
Can you sink ships in concrete,
Can you swing from vines in an
asphalt jungle?
I ask you.
Skyscrapers as trees,
cars microinsects.
Suicide as leaves,
crime is the beast we respect.

Drugs replace real life
like machines replace people.
Allies stab us with their knives
while our minds grow feeble.

Rudolph A Bradley
SEA-SHELL
Strolling along nature's crystal
delight,
On a warm summer night,
As the stars were in their zenith,
Adorn in an air of iridescence,
A sea-shell began to glisten.
From her white granule of essence,
Echoing sounds of reminiscence,
And to a jewel in the sun, I began to
listen.
A serene melody began calling upon
my ears.
It was a melody of joy and of tears.
The lyrics were of a time of yore,
When beauty illuminated the ocean's
floors,
And like a wild beast she was
brutally gored,
All of her gaiety and unsullied
splendor,
Her rich and extoltant decor,

Acelestial state that was her paramour,
Aterrestial state that was without error,
A life and time for all to adore,
A life and time that's no more.

Sherry D Bateman
OUR GREATEST GIFT
Things are planned
from Heaven above,
Then they are given
with so much love.
My Mommy and Daddy
wanted me so much,
God gave me
that special touch.
He knew this was
a wonderful family to be,
So He gave them
sweet little me.

Carole "Sunshine" Taylor

Carole "Sunshine" Taylor
FEELINGS
Feeling sad, lonesome and blue.
Wondering how I'm going to make it without you.

I'm trying real hard to do what you say.
If only you knew how hard it is to stay away.

I know you need time to sort things out.
To learn your true feelings, where there will be no doubt.

I know that sometimes you are scared and unsure.
But soon you will see, together we will endure.

Joanne Brill
GOD'S LAMB
God's Lamb, a precious gift to you is sent,
A reminder of both past and present.
That each of us is a true lamb of God
Under the care of the Good Shepherd's rod.

The Good Shepherd was this Lamb, you see.
God sent Him to earth to save you and me.
He was crucified a Passover Lamb,
Resurrected the enthroned Lamb to stand.

A gracious gift thru Him will be,
By our acceptance—salvation's free.
So that when to earth He returns again,
He will take His lambs with Him to heaven.

Millie Ball
TIME OUT
Busy! Busy! Busy!
Always on the run.
No time to smell
the flowers
No time for any fun.
No time to watch a
sunset
Or paint a wooded
scene
Or sit beside the
ocean
Or by a mountain
stream.
Relax my friend
enjoy it while you
may.
You do not know for
certain
You will pass again
this way.

Barbara "Barbie" Dianne Bennett
SIMPLY BEING YOU
I don't pretend to claim the right to know this feeling of joy,
Yet I'm like a child at Christmas that got that special toy.

That's how it feels to be near you, if only just awhile,
To share the warmth of sunshine you spread with just a smile.

These few lines can never tell you of what it means to be,
A part of the things you're doing, or just someone that you see.

But the simple touch of your hand can calm and soothe,
The most violent of my actions, my most turbulent of moods.

I'm trying to say, "Thanks for the little things you do,
For the joy you've given me by simply being you."

Gwendolyn A Branagan
DID YOU EVER WONDER?
Did you ever wonder
about the sky or why
birds can fly?

Did you ever wonder
why it snows or how
the water flows?

Did you ever wonder
why the wind blows or
just how the trees
grow?

Did you ever wonder
about night or day or
why day just never
stays?

Did you ever try thinking
or just never try?

Did You Ever Wonder Why?

Helen Barrett
THE WORD HATE
Why do people use this word?
It's not to be seen and not to be heard.
If there was Love there would be hope.
But a lot of people just sit and mope.
Look at all the wars we had,
Doesn't anybody know it makes us sad?
Why does everybody act this way?
It's always happening everyday!
Some people die, because of this word Hate!
Sometimes it's just a little bit too late.
Some people think it's a lot of fun,
But not when the damage is already done!
Yes, Hate is a big word to use everyday.
But why use it? It just doesn't pay!

Rachel B Berkoski
I THINK OF YOU AND I SMILE
I think of you and I smile.
In my perfect world of fantasy,
I have everything I desire.
you are beautiful in my mind,
in reality you are the same
and when I think of you I smile.
You are an image
made of brilliant colors
that shines on my soul.
You fill my mind,
I smile and know that you are there.
Through darkness you light the way
to my perfect world of fantasy.
You are real,
I know, for when I think of you,
I smile.

Nancy Shipley Bemish
RICHARD
Richard is our little boy,
he is our laughter, and our joy.
He has been through so very much,
now there's so much here, for him to touch.
Richard is a boy who's blind,
and has seizures, most all of the time.
He is only three years old,
a life expectancy (5) so were told.
The doctors said put him in o.l.v.
My husband and I just disagreed!
Richard is our precious son,
and Jesus will have his miracle come.
Richard has had 5 surgeries
and always pulled through, for him,
his father, and me!
Life has really been cruel, to our boy who's 3,
so now the best is sure to be!

Tabitha Baker
A BUTTERFLY'S FLIGHT
Butterflies float gracefully,
Above the trees and you and me.
Coming down every now and then,
To blend with a beautiful flower,
Butterflies.

Daniel Benfield
THE OCEAN
Sunday, August 20
5.39 am
I sit alone my mind adrift
Upon a raging sea of emotion
I cannot swim to save myself
I feel my soul slipping away from me

Hoisted upon my ragged spar
My body whipped by searing foam
I try to lift my parched hands toward
the sky
But the energy has been drained from
my shriveled limbs

I pray to God that it would end
But my agony is intensified in the
heat
My brain implodes across itself
I feel my soul slipping away
Is there not one bit of saving grace
Has the urn been emptied of its ashes
I can no longer support my life
It ebbs with the maddened tide

Adrift my boat sails aimlessly upon
the ocean
Pilotless, its uncharted course it
follows
Meandering upon the boundless deep
While in the depths our bodies sleep
Forever locked within the keep

Beverly L Bock
MONKEYS ON MY MIND
Three monkeys on a bench
and a peacock in the tree—
a picture which delights
and greatly pleasures me.

Grandpa tortoise lumbers
down the garden path.
Be careful not to step on him
or you'll incur his wrath.

Shadows of the forest
keep secrets hard to see.
But the loud caw of the parrot
. . . . . startles me.

Their cage is the forest,
the paths are rugged brick.
The entrance is of coral,
flowered iron and bougainvillea
thick.

The people cage is structured
of coral walls and iron
patterns pleasing to the eye
and heavy doors to hold the people
in—

while the birds fly to the sky.

Adam Michael Bucciarelli
THE PILGRIMS RAP
The Pilgrims arrived in 1620
They had no food, it wasn't funny,
They needed no food to survive
They needed food to live their lives.

The Indians gave them what they wanted,
The Pilgrims repaid them with hats and bonnets.
They were friends till the end.

They had the first Thanksgiving on November 23,
The Indians brought a very big bird.
They weren't mad
Nobody was sad.
There's never been a bore on Thanksgiving day
Too bad it couldn't be in May.
That's how Thanksgiving was made,
It wasn't a raid, nobody got paid.
It was just luck, they didn't have duck!

Lorena Barrett
TWILIGHT ON THE BEACH
The setting sun is a brilliant red
meaning we'll have a fine day ahead,
white clouds, floating in blue skies above,
are now a lovely pink.
All cares are now replaced with Love.
Heaven is nearer than you think
all else is a soft blue hue,
but here and there a light shines through.
All is at Peace
and those on the beach
can scarcely be seen through
this wrap of blue.

At this time, before the night,
when the moon shows so bright
I so wish you were here,
My love, and my dear,
to hold your soft hand
with the wedding band.
Are you looking down at me;
as I sit beside the sea?

Pamela Burden
TIME OF MY LIFE
Friends come and go like the changing winds
Briskly picked up and never seen again
Like you snatched by life just as we were so near
Now farther from me than I expected

The times that we've shared won't be forgotten
For our friendship is like the petals in spring
Blossoming in streams of vibrant color
Gold splashing over warm blushing waves

Letters, pictures, and cards fill the needs
Rekindling feelings so dear to our hearts
Times, obstacles shatter friendships of youth
Yet we have survived the season of trials

For dreams of ours can still be created
While those miles do separate our paths
For the journey we have taken is the key
At last we touch our togetherness.

Sister Christine Biskupski
WHEN A FRIEND BECOMES YOUR BRIDGE
In love and in care she walked with me
Amid night's darkness into morning's fresh air

She walked with me in silence
She listened and understood
How far from Peace Island I was
How very deep my feet in the sand

Then in love and truth she finds
This human nature of mine
With His love and grace Jesus strength could refine

She dare not pretend she's perfect and I am not
Together we two pray over and above that
In her I found a bridge, Christ my light.

To be a bridge of love and care
That helps another breathe fresh air
O what love—for that other
Light of Christ—Light our way

Bring us HOME there to stay
For your body and your blood feed us on the way

True life—True love—Precious Love
Body broken blood shed
Together we shared as one

A bridge of care—a friend of love
she will always be!!

Oh, my God of Love, Mary Lou was Christ for me.

Edith Irene Thompson Oles
GRANDMA'S PRECIOUS ONE
Teeny, tiny, little one,
With your shining eyes,
How you turn a simple day
Into fun surprise.
You are Grandma's cutie pie
With your button nose,
How you got so clever, dear,
Only Grandma knows.
Giggle, giggle, laugh a bit,
Jump about and play,
Oh, you're so adorable
In your darling way.
Tickle here and tickle there,
What delight and fun!
You are special don't you know?
Grandma's precious one.
Tick-tock, it is sleepy time,
Get the rest you need.
Dream about the fun we'll have,
You are loved indeed!

Renae S Postma
A BIT OF NATURE
The little child laid back his head
To watch the clouds float by.
He wrestled thoughts of nature,
How, when, where, and why.

"Now where in the world does the wind come from?
And how can the flowers grow?"
All these things, the little boy thought,
Were that a child should know.

But, oh, the things which nature held
Were far beyond his reach.
Of how so many sands of time
Could lie on one lone beach.

Of how on the lonely ocean floor
Could live so many things.
Nor could his little mind imagine
Why a robin sings.

The grass felt warm upon his head.
The clover smelled so sweet.
When lo, a bit of nature came,
And stung him in the seat.

Melody J Stalbaum
I OWE YOU A LOT
I owe you my life, you saved me . . .
from myself.
You made me who I am and who I
am becoming.
You probably know it already how
much you
mean.
I hope.

I owe you for letting me—be me, and
accepting that.
For caring, sharing, being my closest
friend and my biggest influence.
I owe you for being you.
The best.

I owe you a lot . . .
For making me smile, making me
laugh, and for
making me hope,
I owe you my soul . . .
For opening my heart, my feelings,
and my eyes.
You didn't do these things on
purpose or as a plan,
just by being you.

I owe you so much, and I thank
you, my real other half that I
could not see. I love you.

Kelly Ann Saffell
PATHWAY

To Reid, my precious gem, may our love grow throughout eternity. Love, Kelly Ann.

There are moments in life, when the lips
And the eyes, come to the question whether to
Smile or cry.

What they lack in their work, they may find
In their will, hoping that the mercy they
Give, will come to the ill.

Life may strike like an eagle, but dare not
To touch the dove,
For every gate that bars to hate, shall open
Wide for love.

Dawn Terasa Orsini
I THOUGHT YOU SHOULD KNOW
"I thought you should know"
how special to me you are

With you I experience feelings
which I have never felt before

Your touch is warm and tender
as gentle as a feather

Which truly makes me cherish
the moments we spend together

"I thought you should know"
just how you make me feel

When you hold me in your arms
our closeness is so real

Your kiss so warm and sexy
so deep I lose control

For when you are inside me
I can't help to let go

"I thought you should know"
when you make love to me
the feeling is ecstasy

There isn't one place on this earth
that I would rather be

"I Thought You Should Know"

Colleen Policastro
SENTIMENTAL REASONS
McArthurs Park plays so sweet and soft,
on my phonograph
(in stereo)

Bringing me back to the summer of 76,
once more
(to cry)

He sings of a dancing girl so lovely
in his song
(reminding me)

I loved to dance in my teen-age years
(but no more)

Times have changed!
for Sentimental Reasons!

In a song he sings of love,
for a girl
(who I wish was me)

Someone calls on the phone to him
just when he gave up
on that false hope
(which backfired)

The tramp and the clown
are very important
(like I am!)

Edith Conaway
REACHING OUT IN DESPERATION

To a broken dream—a broken heart.

I cried when I heard your voice in the wind
On this damp and wintry day
For I hurt so deep inside of me
Ever since you went away

I look for your face among the clouds
Or in the cold and rippling streams
But I never ever find you there
Not even in my dreams

I reach out in desperation
Wishing you could understand
Wishing you could forgive me
And hold my trembling hand

Alcohol and drugs were there
I should have known it from the start
When you reached out and asked for help
I didn't do my part

Now you're gone forever
Because of what I've done
And I shall cry forever
For you . . . my son my son

J T Jacobs
WITHOUT YOU

To my loving husband, Kameron, for his wonderful inspiration.

Without you,
I have no sun
Without you,
I have no stars or moon
Without you,
My life is empty
Without you,
I have no love
The love you showed to me
So beautiful a love, that I
could die of total ecstasy

Without you,
I see no flowers
Without you,
There are no animals playing
Without you,
The world is so quiet
Without you,
I have no love
There's no one to love me or
anyone for me to love

Without you,
The skies are totally dark
Without you,
I have no happiness
Without you,
Nothing is right in my life
Without you
I have no love
I need the love you gave to me
The love of you, can always keep

me happy
I love you
I cannot see life . . .

Without You!

Elinar Bernice Tryon
DADDY, ARE YOU DOWN THERE?
Daddy, is that you down at the barn?
The barn where I once played as a Child?
We drove in here to the farm around midnight tonight—
Brother Bill, his wife, Mom, my sister and I.

We decided to visit the home place, though it's vacant now.
It seems to me, sitting here in the car in the dark, you are there in the barn.
Though Mom says you were laid in the grave.
Yes, back several years ago, she wrote me.

But as we drove up here tonight
Seemed I could see you there in the barn,
Hanging up the harness as you used to do
Those 18-or-more-springs and summers we were here.

Seems I hear the jingle of the harness
And it's as if you were saying, "Whoa!"
To the team of horses. It's as if
I heard them snort in reply to your voice.

Hillary Ann Schornack
UNDER THE SILVER MOONLIGHT
I walk in the garden through the darkness
With wisps of hair blowing in my face
I think of the night so cold and rigid
And then I think of the moon so elegant and silver
And then I see you so handsome and thoughtful
For my days turn to dust without me catching a glimpse of your face
For so long I have wished that you would be caressing me
Under the silver moonlight . . . together forever
For my heart is aching for you to be standing next to me
Under the silver moonlight

Rachel Bronson
REMEMBER

To Michael and Nina, The loves of my life.

When your life seems worthless,
Remember the price you've paid.

When your marriage seems hopeless,
Remember the hopes you had.

When your children seem ungrateful,
Remember how grateful you are for them.

When you feel like there's nothing left,
Remember what there was to begin with.

When you feel that you've lost all hope,
Remember it's never too late to find it again.

Kathy Watkins
THE DAWN

I'd like to thank my parents for always being there for me, and Nibbs for making me believe that I mattered.

Once upon a time
The candle burnt bright
Dreams were reality
And fears far from sight
But I was left in the dark
For oh so long
With only hate and sorrow
For my own bitter song
Now day by day
The amber light glows
Burning brighter and brighter
Still ever so slow

Suzie Falconer
DETLEV
Blind date lumbering
squarely over me
squeamish 15-year-old frame
merely shadowed
accent thick with compliments
strong you held my hand
and secrets of some
far-off place
the corn fields waved
goodbyes as we sailed dirt
roads through valleys
to a place where you
could kiss me
softly
I believed you must
have held the world
between your knees.

Michelle Taylor
AS THE DOOR FLEW OPEN
As the door flew open, a swirl of cold night air came in and I felt a shiver even sitting by the warm fire, but there he stood a tall, dark stranger of the night. The door closed and as the snow drifted slowly down, we made love next to the fire side.

Bonnie H Dolan
THE GOLDEN LIGHT
I was drawn into the golden light
By rays shimmering up and down
Past mounds and mounds of angel hair,
"Ah, Glory I have found."

Suspended shapes of every kind
Filtered through the Holy Light.
Prayers of thanks were being chanted,
Talk of Peace filled the night.

Nearby, souls swayed in rings of love.
"Is this Heaven I have found?"
"No," was answered—
"But 'tis surely Christmas and soon we're Homeward Bound!"

Vanessa Butler
GOD'S FIRST GIFT
When God first created man
He gave us such a beautiful land
Lush flowers and leafy green trees
All of this, we did receive

All of this, I give to you
Bright and clean and all anew
Handle with diligent care
For this is a gift, for all to share

All of this we did receive
But God's plan, we did not heed
Destroying trees and colorful flowers
While building tall, gleaming towers
Acid rain falls in our woods
Nuclear waste in our neighborhoods
Polluting our plains and rising cliffs
Look what we've done, with God's first gift

Mary Alice Clevenger
THE UNSEEN VISITOR

Dedicated to—
My daughter: Andrea
My son: James.

I walk into my lonely house
Alone—Everything quiet as a mouse
And there you sit in your favorite chair,
I can't see you, you are nothing but air
I feel your touch as I walk by,
And faintly I can hear you sigh
Your silent words reach my ears as a loud cry,
You ask me not to say good-bye
You hold me close and tell me not to fear
Though you are gone, you are always near
Forever you will be by my side,
As the silent trails we ride.
Thus it will be until the end,
My love and my true friend.
Seen by nobody but me,
Together, forever we will always be.

Corie Piechocki
ALMIGHTY
Beams boomed from heaven,
in the morning sky.
As the clock struck seven,
angels sang on high.

Proclaiming the wondrous things he has done,
that is their chant.
Love is why he sent his son,
forever to be a grant.

Always Almighty in his ways,
I ask you now,
Please guide me throughout my days.

Trina Lyn
NO PROMISES
I loved someone once
But we needed the moon,
So the stars could watch.
There was rain that day
In our senses.

The passing storm was followed
By the sun.
But for us, it meant the dawn,
Without the promise
of a rainbow.

Charlene Shipley
FREEDOM
To be a butterfly
just for a day . . .
flying free
flying away . . .
Wings to soar
the whole wide world
an open door . . .
But, so it is
I will only, always
. . . be me
and . . .
Butterflies are free!

Joyce G Cochran
TWO HEARTS TOGETHER
Through heartache, hardship, strife and pain
Our love lived to shine again.

Though life's road was often rough,
and patience wasn't always enough.
but we were determined, you and I,
we would not let our love die.

Now those days all are done,
and a new life has begun.
In spite of it all, we've muddled thru,
just you for me, and me for you.
Problems and health may come and go,
but that's one thing we'll always know.

All things that mean so much,
a gentle smile, a loving touch.
for we each know the other's there,
and no matter what, we'll always care.
and as we, slowly, older grow,
our hearts still hold that lovely glo.

Lorenzo J S Dughi (Sand)
THE CLASSIC
She's Gone With the Wind
Like a Mona Lisa
Profile of Susan B. Anthony
Poetry, art,
music, heart,
and hope.

An entity to be known

Steve Allen, John Steinbeck,
Emily Dickinson, U2,
Michelangelo,
Mozart.

What is she?
Who is she?

She's classic

The movie you have to see
The song you have to hear
The painting you have to reflect
The poem you have to learn
The speech you have to remember

She's the bridge
That lies across the oceans
Into foreign lands
Which are brought together
By the waving of her hand

Jeanette Chase
SAY GOODBYE

To my Mother and Father.

Please don't forget me when I'm gone,
You mean so much to me.
With you I know I can't go wrong,
As you cannot with me.
We've shared the good times and the bad,
We've been through it all.
And now that we're parting do not be sad,
I'll still catch you when you fall.
Although physically we will part,
I'll still linger in your mind.
Memories will fill your heart,
As they will with mine.
A sad sweet song,
A precious melody,
Will remind me of you,
And you of me.
So one last smile before I go,
And promise you won't cry.
Because deep down you know,
We'll never really say goodbye.

Mathew Isaac
GUILT
When I glanced through the mirror
Just this afternoon

I didn't find the honest child
That I thought would still be true

No, Instead I saw
An animal, angry, free, and wild
Tears flowing from its very eyes
And bloodstains from its knife

And far away,
I saw a face,
The face of a frightened man.
I heard him cry
And I watched him die
With a knife through his side

Why? you ask
And I can't answer
All I see
Is his bloody corpse
Inside a darkened coffin
That should rightfully be my own . . .

Betty McCarley
DEAREST PAPA

To all the Senior residents who have been separated from their life-long mates, whether by mind or death. God bless.

Dearest papa,
I stood alone in the bitter cold
And stared at the distant hills
I could almost see the old home place
My old heart just wouldn't be still

I thought I saw you walking the back roads
Your hands tucked in the bib of your overalls
I cried out to those hills, "Papa, Oh, papa!"
But I knew you'd not be able to answer my call

They told me once, and made it so plain
That I could never go back home
Oh, Papa, You know how it is with me
In my heart and mind, I've never been gone

I know I can be with you for always
And things will work out fine
We can touch and be like we used to
But it's only true in the dreams in my mind.
Papa, I'm always with you,
Love, Ma
P S. Goodbye, Papa, God bless you in all you do I know this is the last place, I'll ever wait for you.

Andrea Kelly
BLIND FRIENDSHIP
If people don't like you because of your looks
Because you wear glasses, or read different books

If people make fun of the clothes that you wear
Or whisper and laugh at the style of your hair

Then maybe the only friendship for someone of your kind
Is the only friendship of someone who is blind.

The heart filled friendship of someone that is blind
May be the only "real" friendship a "real" person can find

Unless . . .

Because of who you are someone wants to be your friend
Then hold on to that person 'cause forever they'll be a friend.

Tommy G Brown
BABY I DREAMED WE WERE MARRIED

Dedicated to Janalyn R. Smith, my lost love.

Baby I dreamed we were married last night
And then we dined in candle light

The air smelt sweet, from the flowers, and your hair
So sweet that the sweetest, could not compare

Your eyes were as bright, as the stars above
And your dress was as pretty, as a snow white dove

Your lips were as wet, as the morning dew
And from our first kiss, I knew I would always love you

Your touch was as warm, as a soft summer breeze
And your every wish, was my desire to please

And although this was just, my dream of us two
Everyone knows, that dreams can come true

James E Ryan
ALWAYS

To Rose.

I had not thought the days could be bright with sun and singing birds without you—but it is true.

I had not thought sleep could be deep and peaceful—and hope still rise shining in my forsaken heart without you—but it is true.

Though still around every corner I find you smiling and still on the darkest night I hold you close in my arms, perhaps, because even without you—you are always there.

Laura Ann Dolan
BULL IN A CHINA SHOP
Don't you realize that you hold my blown-glass
heart in the palm of your graceful man-hands?
I didn't want to put it there, nor did I do
so through my own free will.
Your eyes vacuumed it through mine, almost
from the first time they connected, and I don't think I could get it back if I wanted to.
Maybe you don't want to hold it, or to hold me,
but there isn't much either of us can
do now.
Regretfully,
my heart is much more fragile than blown glass, even though I try to shelter it.
You broke down the walls encasing it, and
I don't know if I'm glad and relieved
or not.
I'm not saying I love you,
because I don't think I do,
but I'm asking you to be careful
because if you make a fist and shatter me . . .
you get cut too.

Capri McCaleb Pearce
MEMORIES IN METAPHOR

This poem is dedicated to my friends and family who share special memories through the Gift of Poetry.

Words
Paint Portraits, Sketching Symmetry
And Sensitivity
Into Cornerstones Of Creativity.

Words
Draw Diagrams In Artistry,
Intertwined And Bound With
Tapestry,
Passing Down To Generations
Our Essence Of Communications.

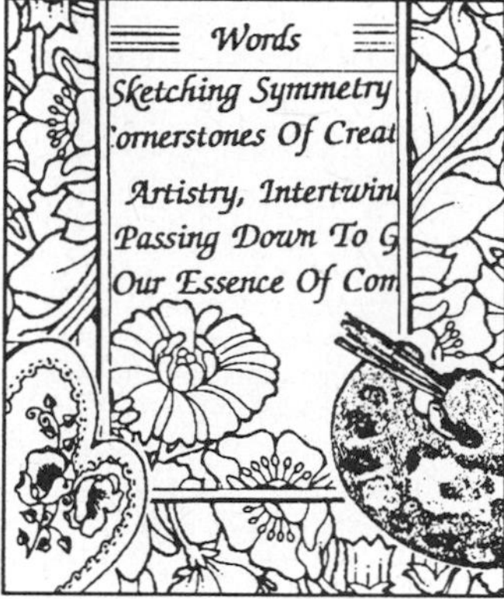

Words
Leave A Lifetime Legacy—Love
And Knowledge—
The Everlasting Illustration,
Eternally Enriching Mankind's
Reflection Through Exquisite
Expression.

Words
Live On Forever As The Heart
Shaped Key, Locking Feelings Of
Life's Quality Into A Special
Memory.

Felicia Vitrano Banuvong
TEAR DROPS
When you feel down
And feel the tears coming out
Stop and look out of the tears.
You can see the light blurring in
Through them.

Everything is blurry
Everything has a double.
Everything shines all at one time.

And then your eyes start to hurt
And you don't know whether to blink
Or hold them open.
'Cause for some reason you like
Looking out at the world.
Through them tears.

And then there's a time
When you find your mind is like a
Teardrop
Blurry, messed up, and always
Falling.

So when you feel the tears
Hold then there for a second
And looking out through them
You'll see that anything can sparkle
Even deep dark thoughts
This is all out of a tear drop before it
Falls.

The pain may still be there, but at
Least you had a chance
To make it sparkle.

Felicia Vitrano Banuvong
WHAT A KISS CAN DO
I could tell you were in pain
So I gave you a kiss that wasn't
Supposed to mean a thing
But as we touched all the pain came
Through
And I found myself falling in love
With you.
I ached all over wondering what was
Happening

Trying to find myself in you was
Something I couldn't do.
Wondering why you wanted me, I
Really couldn't see
What had happened that night should
Have never been
'Cause as I saw you more
And touched your lips, and held you
Tight in the night
I began to see a whole different life

You wiped my tears away from my
Eyes
Telling me everything is going to be
Alright.
I never knew what love was until you
You have given me a chance to
Watch,
And to feel
It all close up.

It's amazing the way love grows,
'Cause I'm watching my love for
you,
Still take root.
And growing stronger everyday.
I finally found myself in you.
Isn't it strange what a kiss can do.

David Phillips
LOVE FOR A LIFETIME
When you know you love somebody,
It takes but an instant.
When you learn to love somebody,
It takes but a lifetime.

For when you learn to love
somebody,
It lasts but an instant.
But when you know you love
somebody,
It lasts you a lifetime.

John P Fitzpatrick
MORNING MIST

This Poem is for my fan club, Barbara and Shawn Michael.

Behind the cloak of night all lies
sleeping
The trickle of the stream the only
sound
A chill wind blows with the promise
of winter
As dewdrops fasten themselves to the
ground.
A gray mist rises to hide the
mountains
The sky grows lighter, it's a brand
new day
The trees stretch and arise from their
slumber
Trout are leaping intent on their play.
Along the paths at dawn walk the old

ones
Their hearts are saddened, their souls are gray
So much of the land has been plundered and paved
Hotels and bars where once the buffalo would play.
The sun arises in its bright and fiery majesty
The mist and the old ones head back for the other side
But before they go, they take a last longing look
At the land, once virgin, where they long ago did ride.

Sandy Kirkby
ANNE
One dark and lonely night
Emma scared with vicious fright—
She wanted to be brave—just a mite.
Emma sensed in the house,
There was something more than a spirit.
She looked in the fireplace at the flames
And knew that they were not to blame,
For the disappearance of Anne.

Charletta I Cabler
SELFISH MOURNER
To lose a child is a hurt beyond many,
but the worst hurt of all is not to be able to have any.
I lost my child and was hurt as I could be,
but how in the hell could I just be thinking of me?
To be barren is oh, so, terrible a thing for a woman feels empty and full of hurt and pain.
I can have another but someone else cannot.
It causes my faith to be weak and faint.
Why do we have to suffer this way?
If only I had been in the garden with Eve that day!
I want to have another child and someday I may.
But how could I mourn and be selfish that way?

Tonda Gail Furr
LOVE FOREVER
Love me, don't turn away,
Or I shall have to stay.
All alone with no one there for me,
I feel my heart break with dignity.
I did everything to do and say,
To make you look a little my way.
But I shall not give up on you,
The time will end and I will not be through.
I am happy when you are near,
But thinking I can't have you, brings a tear.
I had not loved, and maybe you had not cared,
But now it is time for us to share.

Angela Stonestreet
I'D LIKE TO CREATE A COUNTRY . . .
I'd like to create a country full of freedom and mercy.
A country where power, authority, health, wealth, knowledge, courage, and wisdom shall not fail.
A country so free that sickness, hurt, and sorrow shall not be.
When there is trouble we can go in peace.
A country where cruelty, illegality, and unfairness will be equally punished.
Whether it be girl or boy, man or woman, adult or child, rich or poor.
A country where the law shall be fair, but hard and strict and
must be followed.
A country that the people and government, north and south, east and west, abled and disabled, rich and poor, old and young,
literate and illiterate, and allunnamed, shall be treated with the same respect.
No more, no less.
A country that is not only called by all but loved by all.
And most of all, a country that "We the People" can proudly say . . .
"This is my HOME!!!"

Steven M Rizzo
REPORT OF PLANET TERRA
My time has come to home return,
this world offers nothing, yet from it I learn.
For wisdom has ceased, lust is a feast,
their youth is rebellious, violent, and wild,
doomed to death the unborn child.
Hunger and poverty rises like the highest tower,
government currency is more than less spent on power.
Freedom has many a meaning and being sure is never certain,
some unwillingly spend their lives behind what is called
an Iron Curtain.

Much effort is spent on disarmament talks,
yet great is the pace for a nuclear race.
Ignoring their book of wisdom, warning of days growing short
for the twelfth hour approaches on their global dooms day
clock.

Harmful chemicals in the rain fall from the skies
the air they breathe, the water they drink, and the food they eat,
have become unhealthy,
unwealthy . . . unwise.
Diseases spread replacing the wild flower,
only legend remains of this world's finest hour.
We've often wondered for better or for worse
why barren this side of the universe.

For much is so unclean, this lone planet must remain under quarantine.
Much too fast dos it so revolve, yet the simplest questions they
cannot solve.

So I leave and I log with greatest of sorrow
how unevolved our Terran brothers can survive yet another tomorrow.

Michael Moss
THE SHORTCUT "KID"
Caught in a world of work and play
The shortcut kid knows "the better way"
Scratching his head and pulling his hair,
Always trying to find "the better way there"
Sometimes minutes and even hours of thought
Pushing pulling, or tugging where he ought not
In the end, the shortcut he does find
However, I must add there will always be
With the words on his lips "there must be . . ."

Dionne Kirkby
ONE NIGHT

For my family and friends—Thank you for being the wind beneath my wings.

Today
Reliving last night
my eyes close to the heart aching of wanting your tender
body next to mine

In my mind
I feel your soft hair as I tussle it again
As I did this morning before pulling myself from your bed,
to the cold of a broken furnace and snow painted windows

Still
You lay there, secure, innocent and warm
Beneath the covers I shared making love to you
I long to crawl back to the womb of your being,
Back to the woman I was last night, before the
cold November morning knocked and winter winds
whispered 'morning'

The security of silence held me hostage as you drove me
home—small smiles, scattered laughter, a kiss good-bye
I sit here, now, today
Reliving last night—Living you

Tanya Stewart
I'D DO ANYTHING TO KEEP HIM MINE

I dedicate this poem with all my heart to my boyfriend Perry Russ Goodyear.

I'd commit a crime
to keep him mine.
I'd cry all night,
After a fight.
I'd lose my nerves
And go insane.
I'd do anything
to be his love again.
But I don't have to worry,
At least not anymore.
For now I know, he's mine forever more.
I pray we last,
For if we don't.
I pray to God
I won't lose my hope!

Jennifer R Gates
COMPOSING

To write is a means of pretending you are in a different world.

To read is a means of being in another's different world.

To draw is a way to show your dream world, to pretend it is really there, to know what others only dream of.

To dream is to pretend that you and another person are in a different world.

Life is to live in a real world, while pretending is only running away.

Linda Berehula (Drescher)
MY FEET HAVE 20/20 VISION

To my sons, Brent and Kyle, who keep me striving to go on.

I've never been in the spotlight
Or invented a cure for AIDS,
I've never won a lottery
Or been able to hire maids.
My life has seen those dark days
As many others have had,
I've also had some good days,
But mostly pretty bad.
Now why am I not an alcoholic
Or a sad and sorry addict,
Why aren't I selling that white stuff
To some kid who can't live without it?
My road had turns and detours,
My car sometimes ran out of gas.
So why am I sitting here happy
That I chose to be thought of as last?
My choices were made by many,
My options were mine to keep,
My memory pot was on simmer,
My eyes could direct my feet.

Linda Berehula (Drescher)
MISS LIMA GALLANT
Irish . . . How I remember Irish,
A frail spit of a woman,
With the courage of Leo,
And the touch of an angel,
She could melt your heart.
Her pleasures were simple, the jig, card tricks,
(we knew inside out), but played dumb,
A soft melody of "A White Dove Flies."

She never complained, (except to her teapot),
Scrubbed floors on swollen knees,
(It's good for the soul.),
Sayings like, "Even poor people can afford to be clean"
And "Jesus, Mary, & Joseph, pray for us" were hers.

Mouth organ in hand, red shoes on her feet,
A joy in her walk, her smile was a treat.
How did she handle the pain life threw?
None of us ever knew,
But my Irish four leaf clover, I know
Prayed for me and for you!

Maybelle McAbee Bates
MISS MOLLIE
You were just a soft, warm, lovable ball of fur when our son brought you home,
A tiny calico kitten—it was love at first sight.
You won our hearts with your cute antics.
Trying to make a bed with a kitten slipping between the
sheets was a riot.

We lost you one day and looked everywhere, but no Mollie,
Then we heard a faint meow coming from the cabinet.
You had sneaked inside when the

door was opened—
The curiosity of a cat.

Yes Miss Mollie you grew into a beautiful cat and loved to go outside.
You soon learned the sound of your master's car joyfully greeting him by leaping from a tree,
This brought much laughter.

Then it happened—that fateful evening.
Eager to greet your master who had just arrived
You came from across the road, but not quick enough to
avoid a speeding truck.
Our hearts were made sad little Mollie.

You were laid to rest at the end of the garden
Shrouded with the warm earth and the beauty of nature around you.
You are not alone—we are near by.
Sleep on sweet Mollie, sleep on.

Kimberly Ann Bethell
MY FATHER TIME FRIEND

To My Mom and "Daddie" . . .
For giving me Life, I Love You!

Where did it go My Father Time Friend,
Why did my younger years come so quickly to an end . . .
The memories I hold, the secrets untold.
Where did the time go My Father Time Friend.
The thoughts I had, the goals I've dreamed
A million years I had, it seemed . . .
The years fly by so very fast,
Hold on to the memories, because . . .
The moments never last!!
You've been with me, My Father Time Friend,
since on this earth I started,
you'll be with me My Life Time Friend,
until this earth I've departed . . .

Kimberly Ann Bethell
GROWING UP

For the mind & heart of my Lil' Bro Jason Troy.

Growing up is filled with so many fulfilling, confusing, exciting, rewarding, and challenging paths to the adult world . . .
Each experience takes its place in the heart.
Defeat, loneliness and boredom are the negative which touch everyone's world . . .
Pain, anger and confusion lead only to the stronger understanding of life, after all the obstacles and challenges in our paths fall in place.
To spread your wings and fly to your fullest, to enjoy everything life has to offer, while your wings are still fresh and absorbent, develops one into a self confident, fulfilled, happy, positive adult.
The deepest cut felt by a young heart is . . .
"The first love." This is the challenge of anger and loneliness, two harsh feelings that vanish with time, I know this to be true, for the pain once touched my heart . . . Please don't allow them to ground your young spreading wings. For things that are set free, will return, if meant to be . . .

Kimberly Ann Bethell
AS I WATCH YOU SLEEP SO PEACEFULLY

For my beautiful daughter Kyla Kay.

As I watch you sleep so peacefully,
Memories race through my mind,
Our first touch . . . after hours of working together . . . for your first breath!
The first time I held you to my breast and nourished you, the love overflowed my veins.
Your tiny face was so beautiful.
I thank God for sending your soul to me.
There are so many things I want to share, so many memories I'll hold dear, for the rest of my life!
As I watch you sleep so peacefully,
I see you've grown into such a beautiful young person . . . and still have so much more to see!
Remember, my beautiful daughter, I will be your friend for life, and filled with pride in being your mother.
I Love You . . .

Erika Scaramangos

Erika Scaramangos
DARK AND DISMAL LIFE I LIVE
Dark and dismal life I live,
How much more do they expect me to give?
All my dreams they love to shatter,
I guess to them I don't matter
Led to believe in false hopes,
Around my neck, they tighten the rope
Because of them my blood will spill,
And none of them think they're able to kill
They've destroyed my spirit,
Now there's nothing left to it
All of my emotions have disappeared,
The whole time they sat back and sneered,
Yet it was I who they most feared

Erika Scaramangos
FOREVER APART
The tears I shed for you are not from sadness,
They're from something else, I believe it's called madness
Damned from the start, to forever be apart,
You'll always hold a place in my heart
I'll never let go of you,
It's something I just can't do,
So remember that my feelings are true and that
I'll always love you

Rowena L Doze
CONFUSION
At the moment of your sight my soul soared high, free and content.

The sound of your voice brought the smile to my face. Sitting side by side I am anticipating your next move and also my own.

You touch me and my heart races. I feel my body shake, unable to stop I am certain you feel it too.
Your caressing is soft and gentle, arousing a desire within me.

My mind tells me to hold back on my heart.
I am confused.
I want only to accept you and let go to the arousal inside. To let go means to vulnerable to your whims, my soul could be cut open once more.
Confusion; my mind battles that what I feel and what I fear.

Faith Gordon
CIRCUMAMBULATION
Mother Goddess, the Transformer
long neck the axis of the world,
hearing Earthly prayer to Divine Law above,
Timeless Idols,
the elements of nature,
the center of the world is within us.

Mother Goddess, embrace the male,
Mother Goddess, produce the child,
the energy of Nature.

From birth to death
the round about,
body recycled,
Consciousness reborn.

Enter the labyrinth
from the peace of openness
to the protection of walls—
Enter the labyrinth of the mind.

I am myself in blue.
Moon boat carry my soul
as we enter as players
into the Universal rhythm of life.

Mala Kissoon
HE GROWS
Having parents who are always busy,
Growing up alone is never easy.
Child grows without love or caring,
Knows nothing of sharing.
He grows . . .
Becomes a teenager not knowing his worth
So he steaks and ends up in court.
Pays his fines and starts again,
A delinquent in the end.
He grows . . .
Becomes an adult trusting no one but himself,
Remains jobless.
Don't know what love means,
So he lives on hopes and dreams.
He grows . . .

Jessica James
OUR FRIENDSHIP
In the years before we met
the friends I had were few,
I always wished that I would get
a friend as dear as you.

I had a beautiful thought so far up in my mind.
That you were the one to be my friend,
because you were so kind.

I was happy that you were here to
pass the time of day,
And I never had a fear that you
would go away.

Then the day was here for you to say good-bye,
and I became so full of fear
but I tried hard not to cry.

Now I look upon the days
of friendship that we shared,
and everything you said to me
showed me that you cared.

Vicki Geist
WHAT IS A FRIEND?

This poem is dedicated to Taci Wells, my best friend.

A friend is someone to talk to,
A friend is someone to love,
A friend is always there for you,
They will encourage but never shove.

A friend is there to listen,
But not always understand,
They won't give up without a try,
A friend does the best they can.

A friend is there to comfort you,
When you need someone near,
A friend will stay with you,
Until everything is clear.

Of all the things in this world,
A friend means the most to me,
I'm so glad you are my friend,
A friend you will always be.

Linda G Neal
LOVERS
Care for me.
Is that so rare?
These words unsaid,
But always there.

Take my hand
As I reach out.
If you are cold,
What's love about?

Keep my heart
From shadows feared.
Let us be one
The more endeared.

Love that's true.
Forever be.
Never to want.
Eternity.

Gil Lavender
NOVEMBER SPRING
Freedom, Freedom, chant of the crowd
Hundreds of thousands communists heard
Beatings by rulers protesters stood proud
Democracy the choice, people to be served

Coldbloodedness of hard-line rule, concedes
Marxist approach of reality failed
Economy not democracy Gorbachev intercedes
Stalinists or Socialist, will of spirit prevailed

Inflations grip for nuclear armament
Cold war for decades communists spent
Weapons of war, Governments to repent
Shortage of everything
Czechoslovakia discontent

Prague Spring a reform of Socialist face
Birth of Civic Forum twenty years late
Expulsion of Dubcek, to oblivion's place
Havel the playwright, reformist for human fate

Troops disappear, reprisals no fears
Hope of hopeless, reformist will sing
Freedom of humanity, Good Soldier Schweik's tears
Czechoslovakia for all this
November's spring.

Mrs L H Byrd

A MOTHER'S PLEA TO HER SON

Don't sleep the daylight hours away
And hide out the light
Work as God directs,
Then sleep the darkness of the night.

He made the light to see
The beauty of His creation
While in the darkness lies
The devil's sin is hastening.

To grip the minds and hearts of souls
That heed not God's plan
And try to change the world
To fit the plan of man.

There is but one path
That leads to our eternal home
Its narrow path is hard to find
If we try to travel life alone.

But God is there to go with us
If humble we will be
Put self pride down and lift Him up
Then calm and happy we will be.

Don't try to hide from Him
And travel to and fro
Be still and listen to His voice
God is everywhere we go.

Please listen to the spirits call
And down upon our knees
Confess our sins and He
meets our every needs
To quiet our restless souls.

Lorie Ann Bush—"Grammy"

DEEP DOWN

Dedicated to Rodney, with those "Angel Eyes," May you forever keep smiling!

My heart
Deep down
Beyond shattered

Splintered within
Falling apart
Pieces scattered

Confused
Abandoned
Never to be found

Just beginning to sing
As our song ends
Only silence, not a sound

Our hearts
Now two
Forever estranged

Deep feelings
Now only what
My heart contains

Scraping up pieces
Of us
That still remains

Learned to walk alone
But to throw it all away
N E V E R!

Faded scent of roses
Memories
Embraced forever

Strong feelings
Inside
Growing, always to stay

As your love
For me
Fades away

And you
With her
Happy, flying

And me,
Without you,
Deep down
Slowly, dying.

Roy T Devaney

JOHN L SULLIVAN

In 1882, a new champion was crowned
"In my young life," he said, "I never have been downed."
He was a boastful chap, but good we must admit
And on the sporting records
Many new ones did he writ.

He fought Jake Kilrain in 1889
(75 rounds-over 2 hours was the time).
"Listen, Boys," boasted John
"I'm still in my prime!"

'Til Sept. 7, 1892
When James J. Corbett made John take the toll
After 10 years of reign—
But still we agree
The Great John L.
Was the best of them all!

Tammie S Powell

in all

Why
does the metropolis
follow many avenues
Yet
fellowship with only a part of the abstract
What
is wrong with the
complete
abstract
Abstract is discovering the
whole individual
different and unique
in all
of us
in all
of me
in all
of you
in all . . .

Walter J Emerson II

FOUNTAIN OF YOUTH

"To my father Walter J. Emerson Sr., I dedicate this poem."

The Sun is slow to rise
far into the Eastern sky
This day will soon begin
to restore their youth within
Elders gather at the mirrored pond
to glimpse a hopeful reflection
of their youth beyond
"Their Hearts engage
with such a rage
their youth has dissolved
forced them into old age!"
Yet the Elders yield,
to the structure in the field
that it may allow them
a protective shield?
". . . Youth has eluded from their eyes
remains forever within their minds."
As they 'reminis' of their times
youth is fulfilled within their lives!
". . . The Key to youth, is not what is seen
flows within like a stream!"
Now the Sun begins to rest
meaning of Life holds New Quests
". . . . . . . All has been gained
nothing lost!
The Fountain of Youth
you see,
is within our Hearts!"

Chris Hyson

A PEACEFUL FIELD OF GREEN

Here I'm wondering
where I'm going,
worrying not where it is.
Thinking about when I will arrive.
Hoping it isn't too late
to be with the others
who've gone before me.
The people who were
where I am now.

Instinct brought
me to this place
where the sun shines bright
upon my face.
It warms the soul,
brings happiness to all.

The wind blows seasons
through my hair.
The grass grows wild
against my skin.
Lying here without a care
of when it will be
time to go.

Michelle L Hinson

THE WATER WHEEL

Water drips, tears run, as the sunset
Fades away. Life an open book for all
to see, life Is never a mystery.

Cast a shadow upon one you know
And trust, for time, for once is all
But important.

It's almost time, time to go, far away
Where life is quiet and slow.
Picture in your mind, as the water
Wheel spills, the poison of heartbreak
Remains still.

Nothing to control, for all my hope is
Gone, not knowing what has
Happened, maybe, it's just a chill
From the water wheel that spills.

Ray B Hunt

SPRING IN RURAL JAPAN

The skies are overcast, dull, grey.
A sudden breeze supressing the heaviness of
the thick overcoat against my body.

The fresh green rice sprouts waving in the
water covered, musky, soft black
mud of the rice fields.
The clapping sound of the frogs croaking,
one after another, then all at once,
they stop slowly, then suddenly.
In the distance the rattling clatter of an old
lady chatting continues, a pause, quiet,
solitude . . .

Cold moist piercing air
biting, chilling, grabbing
at my uncovered ears, face, and hands,
reimburse the feeling, of rural Japan.

Ray B Hunt

MA SAYS TO CLEAN IT

I've a closet, it's filled with junk.
Ma says it clean it but,
I lost all my spunk.
I've junk on the floor and by my bed,
some pants are green, some shirts are red.
Ma says to clean it,
"Ah, sometime," I lazily said.
I've a collection of paper stacked
high on my clothes chest.
Ma says to clean it,
I ignore it my best.
I've a mess on my bed and under it too,
Some dirty stiff socks and a muddy pair of shoes.
Ma says to clean it but,
there's somethin' I gotta do,
for the sun's a shinin' and the air if quite warm,
the fish are a bitin' at the lake on the farm.
Ma says to clean it . . . Oh, the big one I'll catch!
The day's too good, for just cleanin' my room.
Ma says to clean it but,
you can't catch no fish usin' a broom.

Greg K Fish

THE FLYING BABY

"To my daughter," Kelly Ann, the sky's the limit, if you fly right!

Bluebirds in the morning
Flowers in the sun
Time is on your side
Your life has just begun.

Though you're just a baby
I haven't known you long
A day without seeing you
Is like a bird without its song.

Rushing through my day sometimes
I glance towards the sky
And there you are above the clouds
You didn't tell me you could "fly."

So try to tell me different
But I think just maybe
I'll always look up in the clouds
And see my "Flying Baby."

Georgette Crici
ERASERS
Erasers are the nicest things!
Of that there is no doubt.
We write wrong words. A few quick swipes—
And big mistakes fade out.
And you will find erasers,
Of every different kind,
Extremely helpful, if you will try
To bear these facts in mind:
"When you bump someone in a crowd,
And almost knock her down,
A soft "I'm sorry!" may bring smiles
And rub out that old frown.
Apologies, invariably,
Obliterate mistakes;
And three small words, "I love you!"
Can erase the worst heartaches.

Rita E Hansen
HAVE YOU EVER

To my son Ron! Whose absence inspired this poem.

Have you ever been doing something, and your mind wanders out in space,
Have you ever longed to hold someone, that your arms just ache,
Have you ever looked at nature, and tears come to your eyes,
Have you ever been real anxious, but you really don't know why,
Have you ever felt so empty, it almost feels your heart will bust,
Have you ever had a secret, and there's no one around to trust,
Have you ever missed someone so badly, you think your mind can't cope,
Have you ever wished so hard for something, but you know there is no hope,
Have you ever sat down to dinner, and noticed that empty place,
Have you ever longed for a pleasant voice, a happy laugh, a smiling face,
Have you ever had a longing in your heart you can't explain,
Have you ever been so lonely, and nothing stops the pain,
Have you ever held a love so dearly, that the words "I love you" can't express how you feel,
Have you ever shrugged your shoulders, and said with a sigh,

"OH! WELL, NO BIG DEAL"?
I Have, I'm A Mother."

Dr David M Kleckley
SUSAN MARIE
You quilled the discord inside of me,
My capricious Susan Marie;
You raised my hopes to let me see,
The harmony of tranquility;
When the March winds came,
You went away;
The music left;
The memories stay;
When needed the most,
You were not there;
It did not seem that life was fair;
Now the days are short,
And the nights are long,
And all that remains is a faded song;
Lyrics on a dusty score—
What is gone,
Is no more;
Your words were never cast in rhyme;
And for now it's wintertime—
The icy wintertime.

Erselia Monticello Burton
LIFE'S EDGES
There are thoughts that come with twilight
Mellowed by the glow of dusk
The soften sharp and pointed feelings
Smooth rough edges deep in us.

There's a time for retrospection
In the calm of even' light
And the pause for deep reflection
That one feels when comes the night;

When the errs of early morning
Though unimportant they seemed then,
Come to us as timely warnings
From that world of might-have-been;

When our love is of the purest,
Strong our faith in mankind, too.
When our dreams stand out the surest
In all things we plan to do—

But, when night rolls up her blanket
And the dawn breaks cool upon us,
There is life with all its edges
To be faced against at dusk!

Anna M Cashman
DON'T SPEAK TO STARS

To my sons, Shaun and Bill—whose love and support I hold dear in my heart.

My thoughts depart—
To romp among the stars, so bright!
They shine as tho to wink at me;
perhaps to share their light—
for they are Angels in forms they choose,
to fly the heavens to and fro—
North to South, East to West
As eyes of He who spake of Love—
And not in false attest!

Tears are drops of rain, lay a blanket o'er earth's terrain;
quenching the thirst of His harvest
abound by his light—
warm as a summer's day.

Anger He by a thunderous clay and lightning warns,
as if to say—
Speak to me—for stars give you not life, but watchers they—to bring to me, your sorrows and strife.

Joseph S Willis
ANOTHER KIND OF LOVE
Another kind of love in human lives
Has naught to do with warmth or yielding flesh
Or passion's urge, nor is it part of that fine mesh
Enfolding babes in families, men with wives.
Yet like those warmer loves, this hunger drives
The searching spirit down a maze of ways
That link the present with remem-bered days,
As bees patrol 'twixt blossoms and their hives.

Amid a distant city's concrete blocks
Beneath a haze-filled sky, in memory
I saw white light that shouted from a desert sky
And echoed like a trumpet from vermillion rocks,
Gold sands and trees, a purple-shadowed rhapsody.
I loved that land, and love it till I die!

Roberta Redenti
PRECIOUS CHILD

This poem is dedicated to my precious grandchild, Mary, born, and died, Jan. 7. 1990.

"It's a little girl," her father said,
As I lovingly gazed upon her head,
So tiny, precious, helpless, and innocent
All she needed to stay alive, was a proper environment.
Oh God no, this cannot be!
She's a precious child, can't you see!
A mere pound and a half of human life.
Tragically, in spite of her mother's, and her strife,
Nothing could save this innocent baby girl.
So loved, so wanted, so beautiful, and fragile.
I thought to myself, and wanted to scream,
Save her, do something, my Lord, you're Supreme!
Is this Your way of claiming souls?
Will you be here for us? The one who consoles.
Her life was slowly ebbing away—
If only I had the power to make her stay,
So perfectly formed, her sweet, angelic face,
Knowing all too soon, she'd lose this race,
I whispered to her, you'll never be forgotten Mary,
You'll live always, in the hearts of your parents, and me.

Carrie A Gallagher
RED SHELTER

This poem is dedicated to my father, who now understands what love means. I miss you and love you.

A red maple towers above my father's grave.
I think he has found his way from the coffin,
Slid beneath the roots,
Wrapped his fingers firmly around them,
And forced the tree high.

It sits atop the ground like an angry geyser.
Each leaf a fine mist of ruby red.
Each stem a string of emerald green.
This tree understands my father.
It speaks for him in a windy voice.

I have seen the tree in the sun's heat.
I much prefer the rain.
So does my father.
The maple sighs his contentment,
Breathes his peace.

The tree's branches
Reach beyond the stone,
Sheltering his head at least.
Hard rain stings the leaves,
Whose veins bleed not blood,
Simply water.

Timothy W Pruitt
A REQUIEM FOR JUDY'S SAILOR
Storms have blown and torn my sails,
But in their wake they left the tales,
That a sailor needs to thrive,
And really make him feel alive.

Stories of hardship on the beach,
Or treasures just beyond this reach,
Ships that have gone to watery graves,
And friends that he just couldn't save,

Songs of dainty dolls and dames,
And all their kisses and their games
With smiles that could light the way,
To a different port each and every day.

Now at last as I moor again
The Capstan takes a final spin
And as I leave too on the shore
I know I love the land no more.

Chloris B Brownell
THE DOLLAR DANCE
The market's up . . . the market's down,
our dollar dances all around.
It gained a 'pence' against the 'pound'
and so we sense the dollar sound!

When we are so very young,
(lots of dollars . . . lots of fun)
buy a car . . . or buy a gun!
Spend the dollars as they come!

Then we age and get more sense,
we decide to 'strike the tents.'
Life is more than these few cents . . .
a house, 'n kids . . . we build our fence!

Father Time knocks on our door,
we watch the prices as they soar.
Capital Gains have hit the floor!
Dollars we have? We still need more!

The market's up . . . the market's down,
our dollar dances all around!
Still we sense the system's sound . . .
we gained a 'pence' against the 'pound!'

Kevin W Seals
CITY
Welcome back to the city—
Broken nose to the wall.
We missed you so badly,
Left our bodies in the hall.

See the blood on the sidewalk;
See the blood on my hands.
Outline of the white chalk
Fills a decadent land.

Pull the trigger of the shotgun,
Fill my soul up with lead.
Shadow covers the summer sun—
We're all better off dead.

Welcome home to the city—
Skin burning in the rain.
Save your sadness and pity—
Come join us in our pain.

Jeremy Gill
SUNSET
Color splashed throughout the sky,
In bright array the golden hues lie,
And as the time goes passing by,
Pondering, I wonder why
The great God of heaven gave us this,
Although many people often miss
The subtle beauty of the western sky.
Why do they let this sight go by
Unnoticed? Giving it not a thought,
Even though our Lord and Savior wrought

To give us little gifts like these,
His only thought being us to please.

Kenneth D Parker
RED OAK TREES
Springtime comes to a Virginia farm
There's a tin-roof house and a run down barn
She's sitting on the porch; black dog at her feet
Listening to the wind in the Red Oak Trees.

For ninety-two years she graced our life
A devoted mother and a working wife
Singing to the babies, rock them on her knees
And listening to the wind in the Red Oak Trees.

I remember the day that Grandpa died
Someone sang "The Old Rugged Cross" and I saw her cry
But Granny, you were strong and proud and free
Just listen to the wind in the Red Oak Trees.

Now springtime comes to that Virginia farm
There's an empty house and a torn down barn
No black dog on the porch, just the humming bees
But you can still hear Her voice in the Red Oak Trees.

Bobbie Lee McCoy
ABOUT LIVING—ABOUT LOVING
When I was a little girl
I found my grandmother
Polishing Granddad's shoes.

"When you grow up and get married,
Don't ever start this job," she said.

"Years ago, when I was young
I looked for every way I could find
To tell Amos I loved him.
He became so busy—things changed.
He set his shoes out for me to polish
As thought it was my job—
Always expected of me."

"Why didn't you talk to him, Nannie,
Tell him how you feel?"

"That's what was lost, and I knew it.
Time to be together—
The wanting time just with me.
He used to touch my face—
Reach for my hand unexpectedly.
I often wonder what I should have done
To make the tenderness last."

Bobbie Lee McCoy
THE OLD OAK TREE
I took a walk this moon-bright night
To the old oak tree on the hill.
The acorns crunched beneath my feet
Too loud in the velvet still.

The beauty and quiet nourished my soul
And soothed the daytime questions smooth.
I pressed my back 'gainst the gnarled oak
And felt the warmth of this day's sun.

I turned and hugged the tree close to me;
My whole self could feel
The strength in the tree;
It seemed to strengthen me.

Tammy Anderson
MISUNDERSTOOD
I feel alone inside, even though there are others around.
I feel caught in a trance spaced out from reality
Unaware of the things that go through my head.
Other people just don't understand me
They make judgments and assume what they please,
But they don't know me.
I can see through a person's disguise
'Cause that's what they really are
Hiding behind a fake personality that person slowly dies.

Me, I'm just different, not weird
Maybe just a little better than the rest.
I could ever explain to anyone the way I feel about things.
My outlook on a different life is strong
I know nobody could ever explain myself to me.

I guess some things in life have to be figured out the hard way.
All those people who are caught up in this worthless society drive me insane.
Well if you ask me all that talk is cheap
I guess some people will just never learn.

Debra A Neverman
THE SHOTS OF THE RIFLEGUNS

In memory of G.W. Looney, one rose says it all.

As I stood there, feeling so alone
in a place I've never been before,
I couldn't believe what was happening.
Warm tears shed down my cheeks
to grounds of sacred land.
As I looked around, I saw people
who I didn't know crying.
I cried so much and wanted to
scream and die, but I really couldn't
believe what was happening.
Listening to the man of the cloth
giving his blessings, was it
really happening?
As the men in blue shot their
rifles, which felt like a bullet
through my heart, and the pain
that I deeply felt, opened up my eyes
and I realized that it was really happening.
The shots of the 21 Gun Salute.

Debra A Neverman
LITTLE SISTER

To Telvina Luvian, my dear sister. You will always be very special to me.

I cannot see life without you,
for you are the one who made me feel real.
You have always been there to give me
the strength I need to go on with life and have
always been there to listen to my sorrow.
You have been there when I just needed to talk
and you have been there more than you know.
Even when we were little, you were there,
always by my side and protecting me
and I will never forget the tears we shed together.
Though we are older now, I know you will
always be there, so little sister I want
to say, thanks for being a part of me and
a part of my life, for I will always love
you my little sister, for you are much, much more.

Angelika Oaks
TWO LEAVES PASSING IN THE WIND
Two leaves
passing in the wind
dancing to the sound of silent music
touching like lovers
gentle and full of affection
flying higher and higher
toward the sky.

However
winds don't blow forever
and the leaves fall to the ground
never to dance again
but to die.
Forever lonely and empty
on the cold hard earth
we were just
two leaves
passing in the wind.

The love that could die
was no love.

Corinne Portoro
THE TIME HAS COME FOR A NEW BEGINNING

To my husband Bobby, for his patience and love.

The time has come for a new beginning,
when life will take on a bright new meaning.
And that which God has willed for me,
has finally come to pass.
The faith that I have nurtured within my soul,
will now begin to surface through my heart.

For God has planned for me,
and sent to me a gift of all gifts.
And through this gift I have found the wonder of love,
and the true meaning of life.

He is a jewel that shines through my heart,
lighting up every facet of my life.
For God has created thee,
and through Him I will emulate.
Giving to Him all the wondrous and emaculate things
which He so deserves.

In Him I have found everything I have ever dreamed.
He is the model of eloquence,
radiating His charm
and virtues on to those He reaches out to and touches.
He cannot be conquered by the ill beings of the world,
and will not take advantage of the good will that one bestows.
Through Him I will learn to love again,
regaining what time and pain has stripped away.

He is a loving force within my life,
which I shall treasure forever.
For nowhere can there ever be found a man
more gracious and tender,
who will teach me all the wonders of life,
which God has willed for man and
I have yet to conquer.

And I will giveth this man the gift I hold most
precious to my heart.
For I have never and I will never find anyone
who is more worthy of this possession than He.
He shall have me and I shall worship thee
everyday of my life.
For nowhere will He ever find more love, trust,
honesty and a life He so deserves,
Than through the wonder of what God in turn has
willed for Him.

Al K Albertus
MY BROTHER IS BLACK
My brother is black, though my parents are white,
Why must brother argue, why must brothers fight?
The black man was dragged to our land as a slave
but now that's all over; dear God can't we save
The bond between brothers, which in your sight,
Must be firmly established—Its proper and right!

From out of the past, strange voices I hear,
The beat of the gavel, the white auctioneer.
The slave-child is torn from his sad mother's side,
Dear Lord what a pity; my heart bleeds inside.

How can I cancel my forefather's crime?
How beg for pardon with these empty lines?
What transpired in the past, let us never bring back,
For he is my brother although he is black.

There are still those among us who will give in.
They mistreat my brothers—and know it's a sin.
How can they be taught to make

peace, not attack
My God—given brother because he is black?

My God! Won't you help us in this trying hour?
Don't you see that we need you, that we need your power?
Please help my white friends realize that it's true;
That these men I call "brother" are their brothers too.

I beg you my white friends who feel as I do,
Speak up for equality—Liberty too.
Accept the clear fact that all men are free, no color
can set men apart into unequal groups,
Some loved by society, some ripped from their roots.

Why make it an issue because he is black?
He hurts, and he bleeds, and he keeps coming back.
He fights for our country, the home of the brave,
He fights right beside us—to glory or to grave.

How many white crosses stand over black men,
Who gave their full measure for white countrymen?
I cannot explain, but I know it's a fact,
God has clearly decreed that my brother is black.

Gladys W Burnett

HOW OLD AM I

In memory of my Beloved Brother Glenn J. William.

How old am I
How can I count the years
When one passing day
Has seemed an eternity
Another, fleet as a
Heartbeat slipped by.
Only this I know
When the morning stars
First sang together
Job and I were there
How old am I

Dawn Friese

INSANITY

The whirring of the blades
On the fan
Keep a stale air circulating in my
Tangled room,
Where a fit of fury ripped
Through my body minutes before.
A porcelain doll that I involuntarily
Threw, is now laying face down;
Crying, crumpled, abandoned.
Much like myself.
The tiny dancers from my
Nutcracker music box
Are strewn about my floor
With pieces of my mind.
What happened?
I was unconscious,
I do not know.
Maybe it is time, endless time
Playing tricks on me.

Beverly J Elias

THE HOMELESS

The homeless people on the street
look hauntingly around;
They try to make their lives complete
with anything they've found.
Their faces tell the story
of anguish and despair,
Trying to understand their plight
and why no one else will care.

We all cringe at this human tragedy
and look the other way,
But we can't ignore a child who says,
"I haven't eaten all day."

Cement for a mattress, a bag for a pillow,
no blanket to keep them warm,
Skies are gray, rain begins falling;
no shelter for them from this storm.

Life is quite fragile and so insecure,
tomorrow the homeless might be,
Part of your family, maybe your friends,
perhaps—even you or me!

Beverly J Elias

MY FAVORITE SHOES

You're just my old sneakers
over there on the floor.
All crumpled up
lying there by the door.

With a heel and a toe,
A left and a right;
And lots of laces
to pull you up tight.

You never need shining;
You're always so neat,
Just the best things
I ever put on my feet.

You're my favorite shoes;
We've walked miles together,
And I never thought
I would wear any other.

So I deeply regret that
we have to part company,
But my feet keep on growing;
Now you're too small for me.

Carolyn A Steidel

Carolyn A Steidel

PONY EXPRESS

Over untamed land, through heat and gale,
They were duty-bound to deliver the mail;
Daring young men, riding hard and fast,
Their ponies geared to the awesome task.

Across winter-swept plains and mountain trail
Their motto was: "We cannot fail!"
Enduring hardships yet untold,
Ever onward, brave and bold!

To conquer the vast, wild unknown,
Was up to them, and them alone;
They struggled on, success would depend,
Upon a historical journey's end.

A statue stands to honor their fame,
And made Pony Express a famous name;
For delivering the mail from Saint Joe,
To their bonded city, Sacramento.

Carolyn A Steidel

ANTIQUE CLOCK

My mantel is graced with an antique clock,
A continuous rhythm of tick-tock tick-tock;
The hands are feeble. The face turned dark,
But not quite as old as Noah's ark!

It comes from a time in history,
That holds much interest for you and me;
Abraham Lincoln, so wise and so great,
All the historical things it could relate.

The mystery of it is intriguing to me,
It has served many members of the family;
The intimate connection makes me feel,
There are many secrets it could reveal!

How many hands have turned the key?
That kept it running until it reached me!
I feel I have touched the generations gone,
And helped in my way to keep it ticking along.

When it comes time to serve someone new,
I'll reluctantly say a fond adieu;
Still longing to know the secrets of the antique clock,
And all that I'll hear is tick-tock, tick-tock.

Pamela Newsome Hartzog

MEDITATION

We look deeply, but still do not see,
The sun is there, hidden by the trees—

Treasures we cannot seem to find,
While touching walls of gold mines—

Roads we by pass, not recognizing signs,
Rushing the hours, yet not changing time—

We turn away those clothed in rags,
Abandon the hearts living from bags—

We throw away days as if there were many,
Wasting everything as if there were plenty—

Hearts are foolish, minds as well,
Climbing to win, yet running to fail—

Patricia Lowe

THE DEEPEST LOVE

To my husband, Scott—Without his "deepest love" for me, this poem would not exist!

There is caring now
Where there was none before.
There is a warm, deep feeling
Which has come to surface after so long a time of waiting.

There is a passion
Which not so long ago was non-existent.
There is now tenderness
Which before could never break through; and which I dared never show.

Now everything has come to surface again,
Because there is one who deserves it all.
There is one who brings it all out, that which has been hidden for so long.
There is one who gives the same in return, and nothing less.

For this one has brought everything back to life in me again.
Everything which I had thought was gone forever.
There will always be love in my heart for him,
And I shall give to him everything—which he has given new life to in me—For Always!

Kenneth Dewayne Farris

NOW YOU AND YOUR BROTHER WALK AND SAY

I dedicate this poem to my boys, Dewayne and Aaron, with love.

Now you and your brother walk and say your precious words each
and every day. The words are yours that I wish I could hear,
the world is yours, I wish you both were near.

Every day you will find, the child enchanted things, and miracles
of your life that I can't always be there to see, but you're forever
on my mind.

Try not to learn too fast or walk too far, for a little while longer
I'd keep you just as you are.

Hold fast to your dreams, for if dreams die. Life is a broken-wing bird that cannot fly.

Love you two always, Dad

Patricia L Coleman

WISHES

Dedicated to Brad Campbell who makes my wishes come true.

Day after day my thoughts are filled
with you.
Day after day I come running home,
has a letter come today?
Day after day I wish to hear your voice,
if only for a minute.
Day after day I think of us meeting again.
Day after day my eyes sparkle and my heart smiles
when thinking of you.
If by chance you choose to visit, I'll be waiting at the
door with a smile and a hug.
Wishes come and wishes go but hopes of wishes of you
are here to stay.

Alice May Shutt

THE HAND OF GOD

I awoke this morning,
When the day was new;

And knew the hand of God,
Was with me in all that I do.

The sun was bright,
And shone the window thru,
And I saw the hand of God,
In all that I did do.

I lifted up my eyes,
To the Lord up above.
And saw the hand of God,
And felt his precious love.

The hand of God,
Is with me everyday.
Guiding my footsteps,
Every step of the way.

And at the close of the day,
When I'm ready for my rest;
I see the hand of God,
And know I'm truly blessed.

Mildred Capps Jerome

OLD FOOL

Every night out drinking at your
favorite rendezvous
Women will outnumber the men,
always one there for you
They are all young and pretty . . .
ready for party time . . .
Someone to buy meals and drinks . . .
other things on their mind
It doesn't matter you're much older,
your wrinkles they won't see
or that you are married . . . or what
your cost will be . . .
They tell you how young you look
and OH! how nice you are . . .
and they sure would like a ride in
your shiny new sports car . . .

You think you really have found,
your own little paradise
Sitting there night after night, with
them OLD roving eyes . . .
You order another round or two . . .
feel your years roll away . . .
Soon you think you are thirty . . . not
fifty-nine today . . .
There is no fool like an OLD FOOL,
and OH, are you ONE of those,
your full grown beard, fancy hats,
and all them spiffy clothes . . .

Now, go on down to your
rendezvous, every night for happy hour
Drink them drinks, rub them knees,
build up that ego power . . .
But, . . . today this OLD Tennessee
gal, has had enough OLD man . . .
Look for me, down at the corner
bar . . . catch me if you can . . .
YEP, there's no fool like an OLD
FOOL, and that's what I've become
with these hip boots and painted lips,
tonight, I'll find me ONE . . . .

Bette Rose Wagner

"A FAREWELL TO THE SOCCER FANS"

"Dedicated to the young and the old who died on the field at Anfield. Your loved ones will miss you and so will all of us in America, especially the one who wrote this poem."

TODAY I am going to go and see a
soccer game,
MAYBE I better leave a little early,
FOR there will be long lines waiting
to get in,
OH, I see the crowds are gathering
outside the gates,
THE fans are all seated, waiting for
the game to start,
THEN there is a mighty roar of the
crowd,
BUT it is not to the soccer players,
IT is the fans rushing pass "hell's
gates,"
PUSHING, shoving and knocking
fences over,
THEN came the thunder of the
crowd,
DOWN went people like falling
dominoes,
THE screaming and the cries for
help,
OH, please help me "dear Lord,"
CAME the words from some of the
fans on the ground,
BUT some fans never got to utter
those words,
FOR those were the ones that died on
the field of blood,
TO the brave heroes who saved many
lives too,
MY heart goes all out to you,
FOR no one knew what had
happened,
THE innocent victims were at a lost,
I hope we never see or hear of a
tragedy like this,
BECAUSE you, the fallen, will
always be missed,
AS the games will still go on without
their fans,
THIS poem is dedicated to you who
died in England,
ON that April 15, 1989 day at
Hillsborough,
BECAUSE this is one American who
has been to England,
VISITING your country and seeing
how you live.
SO I end this poem with a "farewell"
TO a soccer fan I never met.

Barbara Juliano

WE HUMANS ARE A FUNNY LOT

We humans are a funny lot,
We're nothing but a polyglot.
Hands and fingers, knees and toes
and voices to say our these and
those.

While other animals are compact or
sleek
we humans are really quite unique.
There's tall and short and slim and fat
and we're sometimes as wiley as
the rat.

Chimpanzees are oh so cute
but, I've never seen one in a 3
piece suit.
Orangutans are so very smart
still, could one replace a human's
heart?

We dive, like seals, into the oceans
blue
wait now, give the whale his due.
These animals once were of the land
but to survive now they need a
hand.

Take the gigantic Elephant's ear,
if we had them, some still couldn't
hear.
There are some of us who hear with
the heart
and there are those who never take
part.

We have voices unlike most
and can raise our glasses in a toast.
With our reasoning, thinking minds
unlike the other different kinds.

We're here to share our precious
Earth
with others of a different birth.
Not race or color or specific physique
but with fang and claw and tusk
and beak.

The dinosaur was a dimbulb they say,
maybe that's why there are none
left today.
One day he was here, then suddenly
"POW". . .
Will that be us a fews ones from
now???

Barbara Juliano

YESTERDAYS

Used to be and days gone by
are words we hear a lot.

What I was and used to be
and things I haven't got.

They're all a part of yesterdays
of steps we can't retrace.
They're all a part of yesterdays
and things we can't replace.

Of yesterdays and your embrace,
your smile and sometimes silly
face,
I would not dare erase.
For fear in all our yesterdays
You'd vanish without trace.

My heart is cold now you have
gone into our yesterdays,
and I can only say My Love
is with you in all ways.
Where you have gone I cannot go
until the time is set.

But I have all our yesterdays
and times when we were met.

Barbara Juliano

ILLUSION

She entered the room like a Cannibal
Queen
you could almost hear the jungle
drums pound.
It was always like that when she
came on the scene
because no one would utter a
sound.

She was tall and stately and dark of
hair,
with eyes that flashed like a
beacon.
Her skin was creamy and incredibly
fair
at her sight strong men would
suddenly weaken.

Her beauty was simply beyond
compare,
and she dressed in the finest of
silk.
But to everyone's great despair,
She had a voice that could curdle
milk.

Barbara Juliano

THE KLUTZ

He tripped over his foot as he came
through the door.
A disaster scene when he landed
His dentures lay shattered all over the
floor
His face looked like it had been
sanded.

He slid towards the table with a low
wooshing sound
The change in his pockets a
jingle.
Everyone scattered from where he
was bound
Yells, crashes and cries did
mingle.

He came to a halt with a sickening
crunch,
a dreadful sight to see.
He sat there completely covered with
lunch,
and sheepishly said, "This one's
on me!"

Barbara Juliano

THE AERIALIST

Standing alone, under the Big Top
on a platform two feet square.
Looking down at the crowd and the
drop,
from eighty feet in the air.

The Catcher is waiting, all is ready
Drum rolls sound their cadence
clear
Hands on the bar, none to steady.
Swing high, do a double, hear
them cheer.

Confidence, turn on the way back
the platform is now at hand.
Swing out, soar and land that's the
knack
Applause, take a bow, hear the
band.

Michelle Dawn Marcus

HEARTS

Hearts search for one another
so they can share the love inside.
Mine has searched as long as I can
remember
for another that would become a part
of me
and make my life complete.
So much of my love has already been
wasted,
given away for free
to those who have continued their
search after finding me.
I have a strong fear that you are the
same,
but my heart is telling me different.
It says the true love I've been
searching for has also searched long
and has felt the same pain of love
taken and thrown away.
But we have been brought together,
as it was meant to be.
And our hearts have finished
searching,
together they can be free.

Lewis G Martin

A GIFT

I give you a gift
So precious, none can make it but I.
Do with it as you please
Treat it with respect or . . .
Waste it if you wish.
I may give you more, I may not.
I hold it back from no one . . .
Yet some get more than others.
I ask that you share it,
For your happiness, not Mine.

Share it, treasure it, bathe in it,
Love in it.
Hold on to it . . . no I am sorry you can't.
I must give you more.
The gift is time, ... Love God

Barbara A Blondia
THE TIME IS NOW

If you are ever going to love me,
Love me now, so I can know
The sweet and tender feelings
From which true affection flow.
Love me now
While I am living,
Do not wait until I'm gone
And then have it chiseled in marble,
Sweet words on ice cold stone.
If you have tender thoughts of me
Please tell me now.
If you wait until I am sleeping
Never to awaken,
There will be death between us
And I won't hear you then.
So, if you love me, even a little bit,
Let me know it while I am living
So I can treasure it.

Christie Tattersall
A TEAR DROP IS FOR

This poem is dedicated to the families of all POWs and MIAs, and all who lost a loved one in war.

Tonight I lay alone in bed
here is what my tear drop said.

A tear drop is for the service men who died
their families are very sad inside.

Help mend their heart
so families aren't torn apart.

A tear drop is for the MIAs who are away
we hope they're found today.

To find them alive not dead
"Have faith in God," we said.

A tear drop is for the POWs who suffer
make their mind a whole lot tougher.

Let's reunite them with loved ones
to hug and kiss daughters and sons.

So when you're sad thoughts can take no more
you understand what a tear drop is for.

Donna Moody
THANK YOU GOD FOR MY DAD

In loving memory of my father Donald Jay Chillson, Hannibal, New York.

Thank you God for my Dad,
He was the best friend I ever had.
He put us first all his life,
his ten children and his wife.

He taught us the difference between bad and good,
and where each road will lead us in adulthood.
In his heart he knew no greed,
He was always there in our time of need.

He taught us always to lend a hand,
to help a less fortunate man.
He taught us what it meant to share,
and in our hearts how to care.

He taught us how to walk and be proud,
dishonesty he did not allow.
Then Lord you came, and we laid him to rest,
we then knew you took only the best!

Yes! he taught us the values of life right from the start,
each and everyone right from his heart.
Now he dwells with you Lord in heaven above,
Leaving us the most precious value of all, the meaning of love!

Jennifer Fontana
OWLS

To my helpful mother.

Owls come out when you
are asleep

Their heads are large and they
have a short hooked beak.

They don't make a sound
when they fly away

They have a sharp sense of
hearing, night and day.

Although they have huge eyes,
the color of the skies

They look very seriously
and are very wise.

Doris Farber
IT WAS THE GRAYEST DAY IN AUGUST

To the cherished memory of my beloved granddaughter, Dawn M. Kucera, who enriched the lives of all whose path crossed hers. Dearly loved by family and friends, she is missed terribly, and will always be close in our hearts.

It was the grayest day in August,
when the heavens opened wide.
And while it rained, a little girl was whisked away inside.
The loss drew the family closer,
while it tore them all apart
As each in their own private grief
sought relief for the pain of an aching heart.

Our family's gone through a nightmare, such as none should have to endure.
We've lost a beloved angel, who was loving, caring and pure.
We existed in sorrow and disbelief
through the dark of a two year night;
Slowly we began to discover that the sun is still warm and bright.

The heartache weighs so heavily,
though the sadness comes and goes.
Yet, somehow we've gone on living,
although how none of us knows.
We've lost a thoughtful, friendly child. Why did Heaven call her home?
A lovely, thirteen year old—not even yet full grown.

How do we put together the torn threads of our lives,
When a sweet young girl is taken,
and a grandparent survives?
Time may have tempered our grief
and pain, leaving only the emptiness now;
But, Lord, if there is a way to cope,
please help us find out how!

Edna Grace Fraser
THE PRODIGAL SON

Dedicated to my family, my late husband, Robert L. Goodwill, one son, Lorne, and five daughters, Wanda, Isabel, Helen, Madeline and Gloria.

"GIVE ME MY PORTION," the Prodigal cried,
Let me go thither, away from your side;
So away off to that far-country he trod,
But he had forgotten to take along GOD . . .
Soon into the depths of sin and disgrace,
He wasted his substance among the ill race;
And followed them on in a riotous way,
Ne'er thinking at all of some future day . . .
After a while, his wealth was all gone,
And he was no longer that innocent son;
So he helped feed the pigs to find himself bread;—
He was hungry, forsaken, his soul it was dead!
Then, all at once, he thought of his home;
In his rags, he wished now, nevermore to roam;
To my Father I'll go, and his servant I'll be;—
There's peace, and there's plenty, and pardon for me! . . .
His Father beheld him when very far off,
And his heart, filled with LOVE, did thrill, and leap forth:
Soon, in the arms of his Father,
whose LOVE did surround,—
"MY SON, HE WAS DEAD, HE WAS LOST, BUT IS FOUND!"

Susan Church
A MESSAGE FROM DANNY

In Loving Memory of My Brother, Daniel Mobley Dixon, July 12, 1966 - September 9, 1986.

I love this world, it's mine to hold,
so go on with your life ambition.

My love will be yours forevermore,
it is yours just for the asking.

You hear my voice, you know it's true,
by faith and believing in Jesus,

You're my sister on land,
I'm your brother in God's hand,
and soon you will grow to accept it.

But one day will come, our hearts will be one,
and we will be living with Jesus.

I'm happy, I'm okay,
live day by day, and never forget that I love you.

For there was no pain, I've got so much to gain
in this world that time has forgotten.

For it is true, my body is new,
and one day yours will be too.

So don't cry for me, I'm happy you see,
back home where it all started.

Jackie Kinner
JUST ANOTHER DAY

This poem is dedicated to my family & to my best friend Kathy Jo Love.

The walls are black as night,
closing in all around me.
Only a street light dances in
the shadows.
As I lay in my bed,
my imagination runs across the
sky to a place where only I can go.
A place with clean air, lots of forests,
animals multiplying, miles &
miles running
freely with no worries.
People not killing themselves or each other,
no wars, no drugs, or abortions.
As the sun rises from the horizon
finding fresh morning dew on the
grass & flowers,
I find myself disappointed,
for it is just Another Day.

Beatrice L Jessen
EMPTINESS

To widows who have been put into "Rest Homes."

The door swings open wide
As the sun still warms her back.
No longer two—but one
The door slams shut behind her.

Alone and heavy hearted
Her fingers curl into frozen fists.
Voices hammer her senses—
"You're going to love it here!"

Odors permeate the air.
Her soul cringes in cold despair.
"Is this my destiny?"
"Life—love—where have you gone?"

Irene (Hood) Stiffler
ONLY TRUST IN THEE

To: My children, Shirley, Lucille & Jim.

Each day I can walk, only trusting in thee
My path is not clear, no way can I see
My hands, I lift up, as I walk close to thee
And your love and your spirit, just now covers me.

Oh Lord, let your spirit surround me, I pray
I need thee, I need thee, oh be with me today
For I am afraid, when no clear path I see
But, Lord, fear leaves me when my trust is in thee.

I worry each day about cares of the day
Just why, I don't know, for thou art the way
Just help me dear Lord, as I live here each day
Just remind me, remind me, that you are my way.

Please Lord, take my fears and my doubts all away
Take all of my sin, give life meaning today.
My hands I lift up, in trust, now to thee
For you, only you, and your love now I see.

You will lead me and guide me each step of the way
As I reach now. In faith thee, as I pray
And my soul now is calmed, as I look up to thee
For a refuge, in trouble, you are always to me.

James C Patat III
CASEY

To my beautiful Daughter, with all my love and support.

When she was born I was scared
I wanted a boy but he wasn't there
As she grew she started to change
Her mother and I had to do the same
To look at her while she's at rest
Lying there she's at her best
To us she's the perfect child
Always there with a cute little smile
She shows her love in so many ways
We will always love her never to stray
She's brought so much joy to our lives
This family love will always strive

Kymberle G McElwee
GLORIA'S SONG

Dedicated to Daddy, Nana & our family.

Dear, Dear Mother, you've left your loving family here,
But just barely in the early autumn of your years,
God took you so suddenly, but carefully, like you prayed,
Without earthly suffering, but not before your song was played.
First you watched until each of our achievements came to pass,
Then you let go quietly with dignity and class.
Mother, we hear you, feel you and see you still,
And we're sure you are with us, for it's God's will.
You would tell us that time will take our sadness away,
So just remember we love you, we'll miss you and we're with you always, especially today.
(Gloria M. Landry,
4 July 1925 - 6 September 1988)

Pamela S Cates and Christi S Bailey
TO MAKE HER MARK

There is no other alternative
But to steer your thoughts
To love
Raising some awareness
Of a power we can use

Don't you think of the homeless
When it's so cold and dark
Love only needs a moment
To make her mark

Rise above the darkness
Don't let this moment go unmarked
The politics of madness
Isn't written in the stars
The reality of life
Is what we are . . . we are.

Carolyn Ramona Carter
ON A ROSE

I saw two lovers, in the mist,
Seal, their passion, with a kiss.
Their story, told upon their face,
Love, they'd lost, could not, replace.

Passion yes, beyond belief,
sometimes,
Somehow, knows, no relief.
For now, their paths, must walk,
Apart,
For God, —,
But knows, —,
What's in their hearts.

She walks alone, her, soul on,
Fire,
And knows this love, will never,
Tire.
She knows, her heart, will stay,
The same,
Perhaps, someday, they'll meet,
Again,
Though, their roads, have wound,
Two different ways,
They know, their love, is,
Here, to stay.
They know, their hearts, will,
Never close,
While, in the twine,
There is a teardrop,
On a Rose.

Richard Pontes
FOR AS NOT YET

For as not yet
To know the grandeur
That in this life
This world may come to pass
I content myself
With this aspiration
Of hope
That when herein lies
A life that has passed
Love hath revealed itself
In the image
Of you and I

Richard Pontes
SONG OF THE WILDERNESS

A winter's night spent, beneath the pearled sky
Clothed by the shadow of the moon
Warmth by the spirited fire
The young knight bows his head, in the forest of sighs
Fondness lies heavy in his heart, as in the distance
He hears the "song of the wilderness"

For all that he has left are memories
Of laughter and smiles, of tears and soft sighs
A wink of an eye, a gentle kiss
And silent moments, when only hearts speak

Of a time too sudden, of ardor lost, in the storm of compliance

Songs of sorrow, lonely lament, whispers through the trees
And dreams of what might have been, haunt his weary soul
As he lays his head to rest

The sun, to the morning, it cannot give
What the knight cries for, he walks alone
And to that which they call "love"
He protests, a voice aloud . . .
"O sweet love, why hast thou forsaken thee
Of times shared and lost, of a time too sudden
Of times that cannot be
You have given this heart, to know of love
And to know of reasons why

But why have you given this "song" to my heart
When all I can say is "good-bye."

While pausing to rest, in a snow-feathered clearance
He whispers softly to the song of the wilderness
That which they call the "voice of the moon". . . .

"Of all that this heart has felt
Of all that these eyes have seen
And through all journeys, not yet begun
Above all else, I shall remember you and keep you close within me
Remember this always, beautiful friend
From my heart I tell you this
Forever I will always love you
Whenever you need me, I'll be there,

Smile when you think of me."

Fresh falling snow, the hollow mist
Caresses the forest of sighs, soon night will arrive
A smile, a tear wiped gently from his face
The young knight bows his head . . .
. . . And cries.

Marjorie Ann Sarkas
EYES OF BLUE

Dedicated to my husband Eli; With love. By: Marjorie "Buster."

As I gaze out to the sea,
my eyes of blue can
only see an Island
that stands alone. This
Island is unknown to me.
The stillness of rocks have
no life, yet peace and
tranquility are known.

The sea is blue with
ripples that shine like
diamonds, rich with
sparkles of life itself.
The sky is pale blue
with marshmallow clouds
which move slowly, yet
has a calmness of its own.

There is life below the sea.
Sometimes I wish it was
me. To swim on the ocean
floor only to be free. To
explore, to live a life of
joy, and not to be
employed.

As I walk on the ocean
floor, I look below
to see, the life beneath
the sea.
When life is over for
me,
I wish my spirit to
be, at the bottom of
the sea.
My eyes of blue can
see,
I have a passion for
the sea.
The sea will always
be home to me.

Mildred W Scott
DR. MARTIN LUTHER KING JR.

To: Rev. and Mrs. L. B. Samuel, the congregation of second Baptist Church, my children, grandchildren & great grandson.

Martin was a gentle man,
His face was often filled with pain,
Showing compassion for his fellow man.
His eyes often told the story,
Never once did he seek the glory,
His only gain to fame,
Was trying to bring about peace,
And to educate man.

Ignorance is a terrible thing,
Out of it comes bigotry and hate,
Martin worked so hard to save us,
Before it was too late.
Just like Christ, who died to set men free,
King died, to save humanity.
Just like the prophets of old,
King had a story to be told.

He also knew, that without vision,
Man would surely die.
Therefore his dream was about tomorrow,
For the past had only brought sorrow.

If Martin was alive today,
His heart would bleed with pain,
I hear him crying from his grave,
"What is happening to my race?"
They are putting drugs into their veins,
Instead of knowledge in their brains.
Has my death been in vain?
Black on black crime must stop,
Before it is too late!
We are already facing a black Genocide
Then what will happen to my race?
How can my dream stay alive!

And yet, that dream is still!
It gives us a reason to survive,
We will continue to fight the Struggles,
Until all men realize that we are brothers.
Then Martin resting in his grave,
Will know that each of us, has found our place
And that America has truly become, the land of the free,
And the home of the brave!

Charlene Bunnell
DREAMER

To my godson, Christopher, let all your worries pass as you follow the light in your dreams.

While walking through a cave;
I suck in the tears and try to be brave,
Down the tunnel is a little light;
I'm afraid because it's so bright,
For each step I dare to take;
I pray and hope to soon awake,
As I try to look around;
I hope to be soon found,
As I run and begin scream;
I awake to find out it was only a dream.

Larry M Easton Sr
LIFE

This poem is dedicated to my wonderful wife Anne, and our 3 children: Christina, Larry Jr., and Melissa, and family friend Marc.

I thank the Lord for giving me life, to me it's very dear
Although I must admit, I'm not quite sure, the reason I am here
As each of us knows, life moves along, at a very rapid pace
And most of us, spend a great deal of time, trying to stay in the race
We often let the things that count quickly pass us by
And spend too much of our precious time, chasing the pie in the sky
We all have desires of things we want, but we must try to understand
That the things we want, may not fit, into the Master's plan
None of us have all the answers, to everything we face
But if each day, we try to do right, God will keep us in His grace
So life could very possibly be, the answer to eternity
To see just how we will spend
That period of time that has no end

Larry M Easton Sr
MY SPECIAL PLACE

In the deep recesses of my mind
I find comfort from life's stress
As I gently fade, willingly, inward
softly without sound, I regress
I know not when, exactly
I reach this special place
where I can be supreme, and master
or a follower, filled with gentle grace
A place free of sickness, tears and anger
Where no one suffers pain, or ever dies
Landscapes of lush green meadows, and crystal
clear brooks
flow gently, through my mind's eyes
If I'm feeling tired and my desire is to rest
I merely put my mind to work
For it has passed the test
of transporting me to that special place
that I just love to go
To take a brief restbit, from this harsh life
And allow my mind to flow

Larry M Easton Sr
WHEN YOUR CHILDREN LEAVE HOME

The home is quiet, everything still
No excited voices, ringing shrill
It's hard to believe how the years have gone by
you suppress the urge, you feel to cry
Every parent reaches this day
The last of the children are on their way
The void in the home will surely pass
this you know to be true
And you must get on, with your life
because you still have much to do
As you've already learned, time moves fast
So you must begin to prepare
Because not too far in the future
your children will again be there
However this time, when they return
they will bring children of their own
And once again the sounds that you long for
will surely fill your home

Larry M Easton Sr
MARRIAGE

Marriage is the ultimate act of love
by an oath before God and man
Promises made, to one another
sealed by a small golden band,
A journey through life together,
that only God knows what's in store
But, hopefully joy and happiness
will follow both, for evermore
Setting an example, for those behind to see
that fulfilling all your marriage vows,
is how it's meant to be,
And when you're home in heaven,
God will surely bless you then
Because, you kept your marriage vows
right up to the end

Greg Robinson
I WOULD DIE FOR YOU

If I wrote a hundred love poems, and they were all for you,
Would you shine your light on me,
and make my dreams come true?
'Cause I don't want all the money,
and I don't need a house on the hill.
Without it, I'd care not—I would love you still.
I don't need my own jet airplane, to take me where I want to go.
I just want to be by your side, to comfort you when you're feeling low.
I don't need clothes from France, I don't want exquisite wine.
I'd give all that up to hold you, and if you would forever be . . . mine.
'Cause with you I am living, but without you I feel dead.
I hope you take my words as truth,
and believe all that I've said.
I don't need a doctor, to tell me I'm insane.
I just need your support, whenever I'm in pain.
So please look me in the eye,
And tell me what is true.
'Cause if you'd hold me in your arms,
I would die for you.

Robbie M Simmons
AT DAY'S END

Is anybody happier because
you passed his way?
Does anyone remember that
you spoke to him today?
The day is almost over and
its toiling time is through.
Is there anyone to utter now a
kindly word of you?
Can you say tonight in parting
with the day that's slipping fast.
That you helped a single brother
of the many that you passed?
Is a single heart rejoicing over
what you did or said.
Does the man whose hopes ever failing
now with courage look ahead?
Did you waste the day, or lose it?
Was it well or sorely spent?
Did you learn a trail of kindness, or
a scar of discontent?
As you close your eyes in slumber, do
as you that God will say.
You have earned one more tomorrow
by the work you did today.

R A Landon
BIRTH OF DIVINITY

The church we see is not of mortar and stone,
but of flesh and blood
a savior nailed to timber
a nimbus of thorns
martyrs' blood stain a regal mane
flesh burnt in the name of God.

Show me a faith that was not born from death,
and I will show you a faith that is not.

Show me a nation for which flesh and bone were not broken,
I will show you a nation of fiction.

Troy Jones
FATHER OF OUR LAND

The crack of thunder
The sunlight that greets the sky
Don't forget who put you under
The beauty that fills your eyes

The precious air we breathe
Life that surrounds serving our needs
The earth within where our bodies rest
Mother nature creations we obsess

Put aside your possessions
Abide in him of your pride
For he has long suffered in our wounds
So dry the tears in which he's cried

Open your heart with flowing passion
That's been deep in hide
For it was for us he sacrificed his body
Upon the sacred cross and died

Don't forget our father
Our father of our land
Share with him what he has created
With your praying two hands

Lori Griffith
THE FLAME

All by myself in a dark room, I felt so cold, so alone,
Knowing that no one was there to understand.
All I wanted was to have you hold me and tell me you care.
I realized that those words would never be heard.
The only thing I could hear was the silence you left me when you went away.

I struck a match.
It lit up the darkened room with a soft yellow glow.
I saw an image dancing in the flame—
It was your face smiling so sweetly as if you could see me too.
The flame went out and you were gone.

I struck another.
This time I could see your entire body.
You were holding out your arms as if to embrace me.
The flame went out and again, you were gone.

This time I lit the whole pack.
Again you were standing there, but now you were extending your hand to me.
I reached for it and grasped it.
Now it was like I was watching from afar, I saw myself step into the flame with you.
You put your arms around me and I could feel the warmth of your body.
I knew now that we'd be together—forever.
The flame went out . . . and *we* were gone.

Miriam Kendall
THE "ME"

With these pains that jump around
like electricity without a ground
so with the pain
you learn to gain
on the exercise
or maybe hypnotize
those that have concern
so they will learn
of all the woes
as the way it goes
on to the neck
so what the heck
when it gets to the arm
watch out for the harm
then to the chest
time for a rest
oops—didn't do it
so be it.

Norma J Messenger
PROCRASTINATION

Most people do things promptly.
Not me, that's not my way.

If I can put it off, till tomorrow,
then I won't do it today.

My good intentions are soon forgotten,
my thoughts slipping away with time.

I'm really not a bad person,
just a lady with a very blank mind.

I tend to let things go sometimes,
much to my great sorrow.

But like Scarlett O'Hara, I've been known to say,
"I'll think of that tomorrow."

Well, I can't change now,
in this, my life's Autumn Season.

I know that's no excuse,
but it's sure a darn good reason!

Norma J Messenger
TROUBLE

Patty and her momma had lots of troubles,
but we just knew they wouldn't last.

We thought things couldn't get any worse,
when Patty slipped in the grass.

She was on the ground with a broken leg,
and the medics were very nice.

In fact, Patty like them so well,
she even fell down twice.

Now she was in pain and disgruntled,
and I was about to buy the farm

When Beth came and took the children,
to save them from bodily harm.

I was fixing her meals and fluffing her pillows,
trying to be a good nurse.

She kept saying how sorry she was,
and then, things went from bad to worse.

I'd canceled my trip to Atlanta
and Patty knew how I was feeling,

But that was nothing to what I felt,
when I saw the leak in my back porch ceiling.

I won't dwell on this, I thought,
I will not have a stroke!

So I got busy and washed some clothes,
then found that my dryer was broke.

Oh well, what the heck,
I'm strong and I won't crack

At least, that's what I thought,
till Beth brought the children back.

So I'll try to forget that the house needs paint
and the pool filter's got loose wires.

My yard looks like a jungle
and by the way, my car needs tires.

I guess we can't control what happens,
whatever will be, will be

But you can bet your "bippy"
when the sea gull poops,
It's gonna be on me!!!

Norma J Messenger
A LETTER TO LENNY
Why couldn't I have had you for a little longer?
Why did you have to leave?

Did our Heavenly Carpenter have a job for you,
and master plans only you could read?

Didn't He know how much we all loved you?
Couldn't He have known our loss?

He must be renovating His Heavenly Mansion,
to call you home to be boss.

Well, go on my darling, get on with your work,
all done according to plan.

Everything square, and level, and true,
all qualities I had in my man.

When the foundation is down, and the angels are working,
I'm sure I can hear you say,

"That 's not the way I used to do it,
there's got to be a better way."

It's hard going on without, Lenny,
sometimes I feel so defeated.

There's been so much pain, and anger, and fear.
I feel as if I've been cheated.

But I'll go on, as you'd want me to,
and I'll do the best I can.

With thirty-four years of sweet memories,
and one hell of a wonderful man.

Domenico Tortorella
ALONE

Dedication to my family for being so supportive.

Here I am all alone,
there are people everywhere, talking and singing.

Here I am all alone,
watching, trying to find humor in anything or anyone.

Here I am all alone,
debating life's ups and downs, and at times sideways.

Here I am all alone,
wondering of my life's destiny.

Here I am all alone,
thinking of life's pleasurable moments.

Here I am all alone,
knowing and remembering that God loves me.

Here I am all alone,
but am I really alone.

William Johnston
MEDITATIONS
I love to hear the patter of the rain
It brings me back to thoughts of long ago,
and fondly as I watch it gently fall, it seems
to kiss the flowers and help the grasses grow.

The patter of the rain falls on my roof,
and brings to me memories e'er so fond
of days, so long ago when we were young
Those pleasant thoughts of youth that now are gone.

The rain which softly falls—reminds me when
as children wandering over dales and hills,
We played and roamed all through out the day
Those wonderful years of youth, my thoughts fulfilled.

And as I daydream, while growing old and older
These Meditations help me bear the pain,
Of my nostalgic Memories of days gone by
That haunt me with the patter of the rain.

Dawna I Pascarella
THE SILVER FOG
Night descends and with it comes,
Silver whirls from out the ground.
Silver fingers curl around,
Cradle the trees and hide the ground.
So quiet and still the forest remains,
Hidden among the misty lanes.
A field mouse peers outside its nest,
Closes its eyes and returns to its rest.
The forest is still this winter night.
No one will see the stars so bright.
Only the owl that soars so high,
Will see the stars light up the sky.
The forest remains hidden away,
Cloaked in a blanket of silver gray.

Beulah M Bailey
MY MOMENTS ALONE
When I awoke this morning
The sun was just coming up over the hill,
I thought, "Oh how Beautiful" it would be
If it could stay like that, so peaceful and still.

I walked outside and looked up at the sun
The whole community was sleeping so sound.
I saw many little birds starting their day,
And my little crocus were blooming from winter's cold ground.

I stood there wondering what a place it could be
If everyone were friendly and kind to each other.
It sure would be "Heaven on Earth"
If we treated everyone, like our Brother.

Leslie Ann Schellinger
SELF-ESTEEM

Dedicated to those who believed in me.

I remember when I was three.
Golden-haired, young and free.
Weren't we all when we were three?

When I started school, I was glad to be me.
Beginning to learn how life would be.
It all seemed so easy, you see.

Then I reached puberty.
When I looked in the mirror, who was staring at me.
The golden-haired girl, I could no longer see.

In High School again all was new to me.
I was a student averaging C.
I was not sure I was happy with me.

After High School I faced some difficulty.
At times I was filled with insecurity.
I wondered is this the way life should be?

I'm married now, in my family there is three.
I'm still discovering a lot about me.
I look in the mirror, now and see, the person I'm happy to be.

Angela Quinalty
EVERYTHING WAS SILENT
Love's gone wrong,
Yet how I felt,
Was all alone,
I imagined a beach,
Everything was silent.

It whispered into my ear,
The love that you felt,
Peering deep into my soul,
Fearing what it was all about,
I was all but silent.

Can it ever be,
Under the wispy golden sky,
The birds, like the days,
Go by quickly,
Everything was silent.

Nancy A Smith
SORROW
Today is a sad and mournful day
For my best friend has just passed away.

She had a short 47 years on this Earth
But God knew how much her soul was worth.

During this very short life span
She touched the hearts of many with her soft hands.

She was not a beauty in some people's eyes
But she had a shining countenance and was so wise.

She knew how to comfort those who needed comforting
How to counsel, to listen and just plain old loving.

She arose each morning way before dawn
Soon good smells from the kitchen proclaimed "Breakfast's on."

As a housekeeper she was not renowned
But as a mother, she wore a golden crown.

From her little garden patch out back
Came things good and green to fight hunger attacks.

She worked every day from sunup to sundown
Taking care of her own and any stranger who came around.

When cancer took its toll, love & care came from us all
You see this little precious Mary, was my mother-in-law.

Dorothy Krueger Burman
IN GREENING TIME
Staccato sounds at pearling Dawn
Move me to quickly rise and climb
Into the Summer's cradle where
Its heartbeat drums in greening time.

Then, as I tramp through long plowed rows,
Pausing to stroke green spears, I know
Here lies the soul of corn country
With all of its magnetic flow;

Where all throughout the humid day,
A phantom rooster's crusty rail
Reminds these fields of companies
That greening time may know travail;

While sun and rains must favor them
That coming yields may be increased,
It is the Lord of Harvests who
Blesses the grain for man and beast.

I know in Autumn I'll return
To touch the gold these fields have borne,
But now, as noon's sun mulls the land,
I smell the rising whey of corn!

Kelly Ann Thompson
CHILD ABUSE

To all the people who have believed in me through the years.

Beaten, bruised
screeching pain
blood trinkles down
like soft rain
tears in a child's eye
a whimper—
a solemn cry
it continues
until they die.

Stella Eubanks
TRUE RICHES
It's not the wealth that we
possess
Nor fame which we
acquire
That bring us peace and
happiness
When we grow old and
retire.

The glamour of riches are
but for a season.
Worldly pleasure will cease
to appeal.
But memories of love
hearthside and home

Are treasures no thief
of time can steal.

Frederick C Greiss
TOGETHER
I can be happy, I can be sad,
I can be angry, I can be glad,
But what is love without you near me?
It's the burning desire within my heart,
To be with you, though far apart.
I long to hold you, kiss you, and squeeze you,
And tell you just how much I need you.
My love for you is everlasting,
And time is ever slowly passing.
But remember, one day, we shall be
Together for all eternity.
If I could be with you this fine day,
I would be happy in every way.
But though we are so far apart,
There is sadness in my heart.
A sadness which can only be,
Replaced with happiness when you're with me.
So remember darling, I love you so,
And I'll be with you soon I know.
And once again we can be
Together for all eternity.

Judy Deckard Clay
ONCE UPON A RAINBOW
Once upon a rainbow
Where time sets still
There is a little girl
Who sits at her window sill.
She dreams of far away places
And once upon a times
As she walks across the rainbow
She chants riddles and rhymes.
When she walks on the rainbow
And looks far away
She wishes with all her heart
That she could always stay.
And all the beautiful colors
She sees all around
She shouts to the top of her voice
I don't ever want to go down.
Once upon a rainbow
Where time sets still
There is a little girl
Who sits at her window sill
Wishing she was on the rainbow still.

Denise M Lorenz
LINGERING LEAVES
Swaying in the middle
among the same

I've looked for the sun
but it never came

The seasons crumble
as rain turns into snow

In just a few hours
it'll be time for me to go

The others will follow
but probably not today

They are the few fighters
who want to stay and sway

I hold on for life
while I look around

at the survivors who are lingering
as I fall to the ground

Annette Young
IN LOVING MEMORY OF JESSICA ANN DIXON
To live a life as incomplete, to have it taken away,
Makes it hard to understand, for those of us who stay.

A child was given to you, for you to raise and love,
Never fear for her again, she's with the God above.

Her memories were golden, her heart you'll always keep,
She'll forever be in a better place, with her Maker she did meet.

She taught you how to love so well, she taught you to be kind,
That's one gift there's no price on, and one you can't always find.

You will always be with her, for her love she gave to you,
You'll always be in her heart, her memories always anew.

No one could ever take her place, just keep her in your heart,
Your memories of her will never fade, don't let this make you part.

Because it was over sooner, than you were ready for,
Never stop loving her, love her forevermore.

You were chosen as the special ones, a gift was given to you,
God will choose you once again, and give you a gift brand new.

I want you to always remember, this baby that God gave,
Cherish all the moments you had, for her be very brave.

Adam S Weinberg
PASSION
Lower classes bursting forth with pride,
Searching for desirable heights
earned? denied? forgotten—
Living lives too short
too precious, too wasted.

Amidst a sea of pale blue nothingness
An army of vast soldiers fought for freedom
supported—by what, why—for whom?
Wrappings in Stars long since
multiplied, dissolved, and obscured.

Middle class warriors
briefcases in hand, longevity
For what?
Happiness granted at birth,
quotas filled by twenty, passion dead at birth.

Marks made on yesterday
buy nothing today.
Battle lands won
lie not in fallow
But rather in wasted visions
of red, white and blue.

Linda Crosslin
LIFE'S JOURNEY

This poem is dedicated to my sons, Brian and Kevin.

As we travel on our journey toward
the destiny of our souls,
May the angels give us strength to cope
with what this stormy life bestows.
A life made of detours, many stops along the way,
Allowing kindred spirits to share our wisdom,
Only brief moments of delay.
But should we on this journey find a spirit
such as we,
A spirit sharing our knowledge, traveling
toward that final destiny,
May the angels look down upon us and bless the
union of our hearts,
Giving us hope for tomorrow, when from this
troubled world we depart.

Sandi Bush
THE SUN

To my son Allen, the sunshine in my life.

What is this light that shines on me,
on the birds in the sky and the fish in the sea?
What radiant glow this light possesses,
"I know what it is," my heart confesses.

This light so warm, so refreshing too,
cleans the soul and makes the body feel anew.
So magnificently displayed, so flawlessly made,
this wonder of wonders will never fade.

A masterpiece indeed, an eyecatcher sure,
from century to century this light will endure.
This body of light shines all over the earth,
and replenishes it to give new birth.

Such an amazing and reliable energy asset,
and a welcome sight to see when
things are sloshly and wet.
It never neglects us and it seems to signal fun.
This Heavenly little light is known to many as "The Sun."

My Missy Quach
FALLING IN LOVE WITH A FRIEND

After our high school graduation you went your way, and I went my own way. I really miss the fun times when we were in high school, but I never get a chance to really express my emotions that I have for you.

You don't know how ease and how happy I am when I be with you and talk to you, but when you are not around I am getting older, wiser, and experience different things everyday in school.

I am hoping that we can be together again after our college graduation. By that time I am a totally new, different person who no longer afraid and shy.

Charlotte Roy
REALIZATION
How did it feel, Blessed Mother
as you looked at your son asleep
To know he was meant to sacrifice
his life for his prodigal sheep?

And did you know, sweet Mary
As you rocked him so tenderly
That one day the stone would be rolled away
for all the world to see?

Then, did you cry, sweet Mary
for your Savior-Son-Divine
And hug him a little closer
ere you shared him with all mankind?

Julia Cornish
DYING ALIVE
She was stripped of her lipstick and
black eyeliner
And her once spiked bangs layed
lifeless on her forehead.
They once hid the emotions too
strong for anyone else to feel.

But now, now you could see the pain
in her colorless face.
And all the love in the world couldn't
comfort the crying voice in her eyes.
Yet, with all of her remaining
strength, she endures each
chastening day.

Every adverse moment rips apart
her inner being.
With each tear, infinite numbers of
tears are created—each releasing
lost smiles of youth.
As time lurks to the end, she reaches
repeatedly trying to grasp the
slightest sign of hope.

Mary Womble
A WOMAN OF THE 90'S

This poem is dedicated to all women of all ages.

A woman of the 90's sets goals so clear
Expectations far exceed what her heart wants to hear
The 90's will bring a woman President, there's no fear
We've been waiting and needing her for so many years.

The lady is ready to move
There's a yearning to prove
What has long been untold
The story she has will all unfold.

She's charming, talented and can be anything she wants to be
Politician, nurse, secretary, lawyer, construction worker
The title doesn't make her, it's the motivation to be
Whatever that person is inside her, that's who she will be.

Political
Optimistic
Educated
Master at whatever she chooses to do.

The woman of the 90's is #1 and it is each of you
She's been waiting for the freedom
Now her time has come

She's always been there, she just
needed to stand alone.

Mary Womble
MORRO BAY

This poem is dedicated to Ed.

A vision lost in the sunset
Swirling like cotton candy over head
White, pure and fresh
The smell of the air is changing
Night is near and the fog is moving
away
Only to roll in another day.

The sound of waves crashing against
the rocks
The cool water embraces me
Sounds of sea gulls over head
Morro Bay is quiet
The sounds of nature echo on the
beach
Laughter fills the air

Misty is the night
Cool is the sand beneath my feet
The wind embraces
The cool, damp air caresses my face
I'll return
Everything will be different beyond
this moment.

Christine A Scott
A SPECIAL BEST FRIEND

I'd like to thank my family for their continued support and I would also like to say a special "Thanks" to my "Special Best Friend" Sylvia "Kandie" Vernita Davis for your friendship that you have shared with me!

It takes a special kind of person to be
called a best friend.
A person who'll stay by your side till
the end.
Not one who is there only when
things are going well.
But a person who will stay with you a
spell.
A person who will share your
laughter and tears.
Someone who'll be your friend for
many years.
A special kind of person that knows
just what to do
to make you feel better if you've
been feeling blue.
Someone who will share their secrets
with you,
knowing that you feel the same way
too.
It takes a special kind of person to be
called a best friend.
A person who'll stay by your side till
the end.
A special best friend will always be
true.
A Special Best Friend—It can only
be you.

Mrs Irene Tullai Gregory
MOTHER'S JOURNEY

Dedicated to My Mother, Mrs. Sophia Tullai Spertz.

Sweet fair maiden of long ago
How you yearned to see new lands.
And adventurous journey you did
take
With blessings from your mom and
dad
Dad made a trunk, special indeed,
Your most precious possessions
therein.
You came on a ship over the seas,
A one way trip, you never went back.
You must have been lonesome
for all left behind.
The songs that you sang
The stories you told.

You came and you stayed
Marrying our Dad
Children did come, all of twelve.
Our Lord took one to pray for all
Each child married and went off
Then ended the journey of
Our Dear Sweet Mom.

Betty Myers Mace
ME
I have walked on a rainbow
I've touched a star
Have climbed the highest mountains
Have traveled afar—
I've been to the depths
Of the world's darkest sea
Have carried my world's problems
That could have only been handled
by me—
I could have chosen another life
But I wouldn't want any other
Because I hold the world's title
known simply as mother.

Tammy Gainey
THE MOUNTAIN SIDE

To my hope of the future, Jessica Gainey.

There are miles of country that are beauty of land untouched by human hand.

Grass land that yet to be made into something that was never seen by our long forgotten ancestors.

Flowers that blow in the wind and deem to always appear of never ending life.

The mountains of great height envision of reaching the top, yet the future generation have many yet unsure dreams to be solved unsure height yet to be achieved.

The air of softness that is taken of fullness of breath is pure of heart and savored by all whom are praised with the untouched land as pure as creation.

There are many untamed wild life creatures on the mountain side.

Some are of beauty, some of uncertainty, yet all of interest to mankind.

The vision of a mountain is only as far and as beautiful as you will let your imagination soar into the untouched human land of beliefs.

Bethew B Jennings Jr
A MARINER'S LOVE AFFAIR
I am the romantic mariner
And as is my destiny
I have a beautiful woman ashore
And a beautiful ship asea.
She has smooth, flowing lines,
She flashes me subtle signs,
She responds to my every touch,
She knows I love her very much.
She weeps in moments of sadness,
Yet, in her catty times,
There are moments of badness.
She smiles with feminine charm,
I had her name tattooed on my arm.
She reacts violently when mistreated,
She stands by me when I feel
defeated.
She speaks only to me in whispers
from her lips.
She stands out above all others,
This darling of ships.

Madeline LaFlamme
I REMEMBER WITH LOVE

I dedicate this poem to my son David.

I remember with Love
a dark haired boy
Tall and bright, with eyes
of blue, and AIDS.
I remember with Love
a dark haired boy
Tired and afraid, with eyes
filled with sorrow, and AIDS.
I remember with Love a
dark haired boy.

Madeline LaFlamme
MEMORIES

This is in Memory of My Dad.

Years Lost when I
was just young,
A song lost about Mom
Never to be sung.
If we could have only saw
Then what we see now,
Would we have done it
different somehow!

Patricia A Mullin
WHY DO WE HAVE TO WAIT TO SEE THE IMPORTANT THINGS IN LIFE?
It took a shock for me to see
That this world has no guarantee for
me.
I took for granted all this time
That life was a nursery rhyme.
Now that I have to face this dreaded
cancer
I ask where do we get the answer?
I finally saw what I needed to see
That we are only human and what has
to be has to be.
I thank God I got this chance to see
the world in a better light
All the beauty I did not see before is
now before my eyes tonight.
My family and friends gave me great
support
But without God I would be lost at
port.
I took for granted life was mine
But I found out that everything was
not so fine.
The birds the flowers and the trees
were just there before
But now I see them for what they are
and even more.
The fish in the lake are swimming so
very unconcerned
If only they knew what we humans
have learned.
I see the mountains so high
I look and then I sigh.

Ronald Mann Benjamin
THE IMMORTAL PORTAL
For better or worse, this Universe
Has no beginning nor end,
Are we able to comprehend?
No diameters nor parameters
What does it all portend?
That it is fairly but barely conceptual
To put forth a theory of perpetual
It always was, always is, and always
will be,
The thought is finally free,
Mentally and Judgmentally.
The idea is not far out
It tells us what it's all about
Immutable and indisputable.
Our eternal Universe is neither a
blessing nor a curse
It may be inscrutable but it is
beautiful.
I peer through the immortal portal,
And slowly visualize, what so few
realize
That it always was, always is, and
always will be.

Danielle See Johnson
A PARTY
What if you were invited to a nuclear
war,
And your invitation was in the form
of a missile?
What if the music played there
Was the people screaming and the
bomb's whistle?

What if the only light there
Was the lit candles on the cake
casting a shadowy haze?
What if the food served there
Was charcoal broiled, blackened
from the radiation rays?

What if the only guests who arrived
were cockroaches,
The lone survivors of a nuclear war?
What if when the host appeared he
turned out to be satan,
Who would rule forevermore?

What if when the party was over,
And you stepped outside to have
nothing ever be the same?
What if you gave a nuclear war,
And nobody at all, nobody came.

Penelope Mutuszak
DELUSION
All that glitters is not Gold,
Once a story true was told.
The prince and princess soon would
see
That love is not eternally.
The days and months
The years would pass.
And to their hearts
It came—alas!
A time of baubles, wealth untold,
But all that glitters is not gold!
Their youth took leave,
Their spirit-old,
All that glitters is not Gold!
Their hearts to stone,
Their bodies cold—
All that glitters is not Gold!

Patricia R Ingram
OUR DYING EARTH

If I could see earth and all of mankind, thru the eyes of God for only one time.

Would I be looking thru tears of despair, because of a dying world I'm seeing there?

In the beginning when the earth was new, it yielded its fruits and all things grew.

The rivers were clean and refreshed the earth. And raindrops from heaven would bring forth new birth.

Each season would change as nature would have it to be. Life thrived and dwelt in beauty and simplicity.

Now I see desolation within my creation. And the destruction of life with no preservation.

The world is dying and no future is there. Tears will flood the earth because of my despair.

Alan Levine
ASTRAL SKIES
Astral bright, pure white light,
How I desperately seek to,
With Love and Hope as Opheil wrote,
Find a way to greet you!
But in death-like sleep I fail to reach,
The darkness rushes in,
To dream strange dreams and then forget
To separate from within.
And should I dare risk life and soul?
Unmix my bodily mesh,
Chant sacred rights from a forgotten age,
To untie the soul from flesh!

And seen this light? Oh yes, I have.
Just a glimpse that fades too soon,
As I thrust out my hand in a futile stab,
Like a babe who tries to grasp the moon.
Just as in death I try in life,
To go beyond, to fly!
For now I know a simple truth—
We never really die.
If on some night while feigning sleep,
Your soul begins to rise,
Don't give a start. Be brave! Fight fear!
Traverse the astral skies.

Mary A Hof
I HAVE A FRIEND

This poem is dedicated to Sharon Stephens, my best friend.

I have a friend, as true as can be
And I'm so lucky she's a friend to me,
She's a wonderful person, with love for all,
And in my eyes she's ten feet tall.

She's deep in thought as you can see,
She's a wonderful gal, and a dear friend to me,
She's there when I'm sad, and when I need her most,
She can make me glad, and give me high hopes.

A friend is a friend as you can see,
And I'm so lucky, she's a friend to me,
Her gift of love is far from above,
She knows how to care and she's always there.

A friend such as mine is very hard to find,
She's thoughtful and nice, and very well liked,
My friend is close to my heart, and I feel we'll never part,
As long as I live, I know her love she will give.

I think I'm lucky, as I can be,
Because I have a Friend,
Who cares for me.

Susan Feliciano
YOU'RE LIKE THE SUN

These poems are dedicated to my children and family who taught me to never give up on my dreams.

You make me hot when I'm cold.
You keep me warm, when you're around.
You make me bright, when I'm sad
You give off light, like no one else can
Whenever you're around, you make a part of me grow and blossom.
It's never stormy when you're around
You give off rays, like I can't believe
You make me happy without trying to
You give and give so much without me asking you to
I'm never gray, when you're there with me
You're special like the sun, you're one of a kind
Your heart is big and round, and you fill me with love and happiness.
You make me feel special, loved and wanted
I'm so full of you, but at the same time I can't get enough of you.
You're like the sun.

Susan Feliciano
SING
You're the music
I'm the words
Together we make beautiful melodies
Apart there is no song.

Roy D Osborne
CAPTIVATED HEART

For Colette, My inspiration to live my life to the fullest.

What is it about you that has captivated my heart?
Why is it that I have fallen madly in love with you?
Even though you could never love me,
My love for you will always flourish.
And through the many years to come,
You will always be remembered by me.
And this thought will keep me going,
Even in the darkest and loneliest times.

Shirley A MacKay
MY FORBIDDEN LOVE

To my family and friends, your love is my inspiration and for this, I thank-you!

You've touched a part of me,
Deep inside.
Stirring feelings, I cannot hide.
Tender passion,
You warmed me through.
Binding me ever closer,
To you.

I long to taste your kisses,
Though few and far between.
And feel your body close to mine,
Limbs entwined,
Thoughts unwind,
We release . . .
Into ecstasy.

Always please remember,
For it can never be
I'll be for you, you'll be for me.

Always please remember,
Our tender touch.
Treasured are these moments,
Shared as such.

K Shannon Webster
HOW CAN I EXPLAIN

To Brad: With all my love!

How can I explain what I feel now
Our third year came and just passed by somehow
The memories seem to linger on
Sometimes I believe they'll never be gone
You hold a special place in my heart
It's something with which I'll never part
What can we say . . .
A love like ours will come again someday
Something so special can't stay gone forever
Why do I fear so deep the word never
It seems like we've faded into the past
A love everyone thought would always last.

Adib J Sarkis PhD
TACIT LOVE
warm & soft are your lips
can't be appraised by money
their sweet flavor does eclipse
the pleasant taste of honey

thy eyes which spark like lightning
make me captive of your charms
tempting, yet you are frightening
as you lay between my arms

love is love no matter what
none could covertly control
whether permitted or not
it will always play its role

Leave me to drown in my sins
if loving you is a sin
in life's rivalries one wins
when brusquely jabbed from within

for my sins who is to blame
you or me or someone else
questions asked by sires of fame
since man ruled the universe

Sharon L Torres R N
COUNTRY AUTUMN
Dahlias and asters are blooming
in the flower beds,
And leaves fall in cascading colors
of yellow, brown, and red.
We reap red apples and golden pears,
And go for hay rides and to country fairs.
These are the last golden days
before the first frost,
when summer's and autumn's splendor
is lost.

Beth Michele Hume
A NIGHT OF SILENCE
Tiny specks of dew
Glisten beneath the sky
Running between the raindrops
Briskly, you and I

A sudden starkness fills the air
Meandering to this floor
A second later, we stop to gather
But alas, we see it no more

This moon is haunting
A brilliant indigo blue
It once was yellow
A beaming yellow
That gathered a summer slew

Midnight calls and we are beckoned
As we pass a branch of bloom
For the air is now calm
The wind is no more
The night has sealed its loom

Beth Michele Hume
WITHOUT
Raped city
A helpless cry
Darkness grows
Above this sky

No lights above
No lights below
Oh where can they go
To find His home?

Hungry city
And this hunger grows
Diminishing to skeletons
In their tattered clothes

No lights below
No lights above
The desire for life
But this death has won

Oblivious city
A sleepless giant
No one to be seen
Forever in blindness

Judy Danell Green
COMMUNICATION
Feelings
difficult to express
are sometimes made meaningless
when spoken with words.
Often a touch,
a caress, or even a kiss
better define the true emotions
of the moment.
There are occasions
when words must be spoken
to enlighten and verify
and I long to hear them
to say them to you
but continue to touch me
I'll caress you always
and we'll both know the wonder
of loving each other.

Judy Danell Green
NO PROMISES, NO GUARANTEES
There were no promises
to cement our commitment
No guarantees we would last forever
But we had a love that is eternal
A bond between us
that time and miles cannot destroy.
I have no explanations . . .
We lived as one
and loved totally . . . for a while.
Were there no promises or guarantees
because we were
Too afraid to admit a mistake?
Too afraid to accept the reality of love?
I have no explanations . . .
But we continue to return to each other
Our bond, though weakened, still survives
with no promises
and no guarantees.

Judy Danell Green
GRATITUDE
Friendship knows no boundaries.
Indeed, it needs no conditions.
It is acceptance
of our individuality
the expression of who we really are.
By mutually sharing
tears and laughter,
anger and encouragement
we both teach and learn
respect . . .
commitment . . .
love.
Regardless of the years and miles
between us
we are family.
And throughout our time together
we will explore and examine
ourselves.
Growing stronger

Becoming better people
for having known one another.

Farah Rose Blaha
ETERNAL DILEMMA . . .
Reality, so vast and boundless.
This soul ever seeking can be sought within,
Ascertaining the knowledge and security inside
will set the spirit on a high flying ride.

A brick wall . .
emotions unbridled . .
Is it enough? or incomplete?

The journey long,
each one his own elf . .
Positive perspective with the gift of the self.

Heartless world,
cold environment,
I reside within the space?

Creator come hither,
that I may abandon this race.

Farah Rose Blaha
REPRESSED INTIMACY
You show,
no true emotion, just control.
Will you ever let me near?

I know,
the demons from your past.
can you forsake this fear?

We go,
slowly, morning through night,
into this love I hold so dear.

Time flows,
gently, weaving our lives,
will this heat begin to sear?

Farah Rose Blaha
PASSAGES OF TWO
The nightmare is behind me now,
each day the air grows sweeter.
It's as if I've come from one long sleep,
that had drawn my being deeper.

The air clung heavy to my brow,
my step was ever weary.
Was I to flounder in despair?
Or could tomorrow be grasped clearly?

I inhale the scent of pure lilac,
a smile creeps to my face.
We begin again our slow step dance,
and you hold me, in warm embrace.

Farah Rose Blaha
SLEEPER
A reawakening of all senses,
fulfilled and secure.
A definitive knowing,
persistence through all time.
Boundless energy now,
my inner core ever growing.

I, that is, you.
We, that is, one.
Our arrival here,
In song, to be sung.

This day, I feel quite numb,
for these awesome feelings inside,
have taken hold relentlessly,
Knowing I'm to be its bride.

Lora Wiggins
REMEMBERING . . . A PEARL

In loving memory of Mrs. Pearl Weatherly, Havana, Florida.

I only knew her for a very short time
But she significantly touched my life.
We talked of the future, our hopes and dreams
And life, with all its strifes.

She showed an abundance of love and caring
To everyone she knew;
And because of her thoughtfulness and love,
These things in my life grew.

The years have passed since I've seen her,
And now I've learned she's gone.
She left this world for a brighter place
At first, I felt alone.

I'll never forget our time together
Nor how she changed my world.
For knowing her I'm forever grateful!
I'll always remember my Granny Pearl.

Patricia DiScala
SEARCH

To my husband John, and my children Maria, Aniello and Regina.

My Lord—you are everywhere
I searched for you at first in childhood play and work
Yet you reluctantly clouded your face with a veil of gauze
Yet onward I continued on the journey
I'll find you yet, my adolescent heart uttered
In youngsters like myself—unsettled and uncertain,
I sought the countenance I desired so,
But no, it's not to be your spirit muttered
"My child, you must not give up your quest."
"When Father, will I feel your sweet breath?"
I searched for you as a girl whose sight was taken,
The struggle for the reason of existence, harder you were making
Through toil, the years, my heart stretched onward—a quest for knowledge to pursue.
How can these hands serve you better, my Lord and master?
What intent for me have you until hereafter?
Through myriad paths I did meander
Many detours I could not avoid.
Until one day, you began to show the way.

Denise Parsons
MIRRORS

To Gary, for giving me a reason to write. I Love You.

What is the mischief that lies behind,
deep radiant violet skies?
What do you see within thine eyes?
The ever glowing reflection,
The twinkle from the sun
It is all within me, the eyes are the key.
Look deep within and tell me what you see.
Mirror, mirror on the wall, walking, walking, walking.
Searching for the mirror, the secret to my soul
Burden on my mind, the traveler within
Guilt, shame all results of sin.
Sweet mysteries are walking through the valleys of my mind
Floating so gently, the way leaves flutter.
Everything is common sense, in one way or another.
Everyone related intermingled, he's my brother.
Cruising sirens go flying by,
screaming terror shakes my spine.
Hoping to be rescued, for comfort, peace of mind.
Lolly, lolly lolly, floating so soft.
Magic mystery dust, spray, wipe, see the mirror once again.
You have just gone through my mind,
And this is where it ends.

Brenda Lynn Caudill
BE TRUE TO YOURSELF
Days of innocence, days gone by,
I glanced through my memories,
asking myself why.

Why must we all grow and come to realize,
That life isn't a fantasy, it tolerates no lies.

The truth is sometimes painful, but with age comes reality,
It's time to give up or say, "I'll make my own destiny."

I'm destined for better things,
determined to make a difference.
To be given the gift of life and do nothing, makes no sense.

So, I'm driven you know, but not everyone is so fortunate.
They don't go for what they want,
they settle for what they get.

Ambition isn't something you can give or inspire within.
To humor or to patronize, no one will win.

Be true to yourself, no matter what the direction.
Hold on to your soul—you'll soon make the connection . . .
TO YOUR DESTINY.

Brenda Lynn Caudill
IRONIC REALITY
Hadn't been sleeping well as of late,
When the phone rang was it chance or fate.

I heard the phone ring gullibly I answered,
Blindly trusting, feeling oh so secure.

It's here the man said. It's over us now.
I want to survive, but I don't know how.

There's no where to run, no place to hide from this.
Don't they know, it's our lives, they so easily dismiss.

We've heard it all before, they say we'll survive the radiation.
But we all know that death would be our only real salvation.

I'm lost as are you I said, my heart filled with fear,
As I sat, there motionless, thinking the end was so near.

My emotions exploded, awakened from my slumber,
The Ironic Reality was that he had the wrong number.

Brenda Lynn Caudill
THE GHOST OF BRENDA PAST
Here I sit, my own replacement.
A clone in body, not in spirit.

It did make sense then, just to let her die,
I justified it as survival, damaged goods, throw away, Bye Bye.

I've always been haunted from somewhere deep within.
She was crying out to me, I'm here, I'm alive let me in.

I have worked so hard to become a house of strength.
I can't let that go, why should I for heaven sake.

I mourn for her, her youth and her promise.
All along I kept her buried, how much I have missed.

I'm willing now to be her, for she is me.
All that I have let pass by, is all that I want to be.

For her soul and her spirit I was desperately in lack.
But LOOK OUT WORLD,
BECAUSE SHE IS BACK.

One thing is for certain, I'll never be alone.
I now have her knowledge, and IT IS GREAT TO BE HOME.

Renae Penn
THE FLOWERS DIED

This poem is dedicated to Michael Treon with all my love.

Long way away, Far time ago
the magic of the kingdom was smothered
and the delicate flowers could not grow
and so it's told—the written word erased the
colors and made them old;
"The nature of life," they said,
"cannot live
we know what's right, they have to be led";
and gathered their swords
and cut dead all the flowers
that did not shape
and by so doing, made all of them wither away;
Everybody dies—how blind can we be?
but we're the ones we hug and kiss
all we can say is—"me, me, me!"
We're the ones that make bones break
and we never even open our eyes
to all our distorted reality lies;
As the story goes,
the flowers died

because under the dark rules
they never survived—
they couldn't flourish and grow—
after being told what's right
and what's wrong,
they gave up trying to belong.

John Klink
CONCRETE ONTOLOGY

Child, Man, Dust,
Steel, Water, Rust,
Forged and shaped,
Scarred and scraped,
Used as tools, bent to rules,
Worked by hands both known and unknown,
Then slowly pulled away to repay the loan.

Matter, Structures, Forces,
Things, Designs, Wild Horses,
Seeking toward balance and meaning,
But hopelessly lost with eternity scheming.
Words and actions shaping one another,
Molding solid appearances: pain, joy, ideals to believe,
Illumination grows brighter before we have to leave.

Margo K Stroyick
JESUS, MY FRIEND

To my son—Gary D. Mink II (D.J.) Thanks for believing in me!

I was so desperate for a friend
My world didn't want me
As it so seemed to be.
Walking down main street
No one noticed how lonely I was
I sat on a bench
I heard a voice calling to me.
I looked around
There was no one
I heard the Lord say
"My dear child, I'm your friend
Always will be till the end.
You can count on it."
I felt the glory of his presence.
I have a friend
His name is Jesus.
So, when I'm feeling low
I ask for Jesus, He is always there
I'm not lonely anymore
So I thought I was
Jesus is my friend!

Hulda Fleming
THE SILVER LINING

To My Grandchildren Susan, Carole, Cathy, and William Aikins

Have you seen the dark clouds gather
And the way seem dreary too?
Just look for the silver lining,
You will see it shining through.
There are times when days are darkest,
When you cannot see your way,
Just look for the silver lining
And the clouds will go away.
You may think the cloud is darkest
And you feel so very blue,
Just look for the silver lining,
Watch it trying to shine through.
Do you think your way is darkest?
Think of other folks you know,
And does not that silver lining
In your dark cloud seem to glow?
So, folks, just look for the lining
In every cloud you may see;
For there is one in every cloud,
One for you and one for me.

Julius Carl Franks
THE WORLD

Dedicated to my son Julius Carl Franks Jr.

As wild as it may, so many people, are now, becoming mean. I do not know why, but I feel as though I could cry. Seeing people getting shot, or seeing my very best friends shooting up. Love and respect is what the world needs today. Not different forms of illicit drugs, that are imported from far away places. And yet, if just the young would stop, listen, and learn, our lives could once again lift up on the wings of the doves.

Woods Renault
TIME MOVES

TIME moves with subtlety—in strange, miraculous ways—
On thin, steel tracks a train speeds thru the ominous night.
On storm waves a luxury liner rises and falls heading toward foreign shores.
In the sky a silver plane slices thru the black of space breaking the sound barrier.
Limping along the highway a lonely, hungry man thumbs his way to NOWHERE.

STILL IN TIME
None of these DARE compare with the FLIGHT OF THE SWALLOW
Returning to her HOME under the eaves of a sheltering roof
THOUSANDS OF MILES from her starting point
For she is drawn by INSTINCT straight and true
Toward the WAITING NEST she built the spring before
Where once more she will give birth to her fledglings
Confirming yet again the MIRACLE OF TIME AND REBIRTH . .

Amparo J Fernandez
TREE

To: Janie Fernandez, who loves plants.

A tree is near my window
Bowing with the wind,
Its leaves of bright green,
Can be seen from far,
Around this tree;
I plant some seeds,
To grow some flowers,
For my needs!

Amparo J Fernandez
PAPER-BOAT

Dedicated to my children; Amando Jr. Fernando and Janie Fernandez.

A hot summer day
it started to rain,
The children wanted to play
they waited a while
for the rain to pass,
Eating and looking thru—
the window glass.
Standing outside,
by the kinchen steps
we fix a paper-boat;
tie with a string
and let it go,
To sail in water with clay.

Amparo J Fernandez
MOVING DAYS

To: Hope Jimenez, Amelia Oritz, Mary Aranza, Jim and Rudolph Jasso, Fina, Ruth, Manuel Villagomez.

I used to love the moving days
from the old house to the new,
Riding on back of truck
full of furniture and stuff.
The cat in a box so he would not get lost,
while the dog bark all the way.
Running thru the empty house,
looking for hide and seek places
for when cousins came.
Bed, we wanted to be first,
put in place so when night fall,
we did not had to sleep on floor.
Many days we ate cold sandwiches,
As someone forget to have gas turned on
But when you are a child,
All this is fun!

Lisa Thomas

Lisa Thomas
TO BE LET FREE

I'm locked in some kind of cage,
maybe a solid wall,
but when I heard the crow call
I was let free, free to be me.

When I was in that solid wall I felt I was controlled,
by someone big and bold.

But now I'm free I can work and wonder, I can laugh and play,
I can be someone have something to say.

I won't be like a little toy, something to be sold,
but I will have willpower as strong as gold.

Lisa Thomas
THE WAR FOR PEACE

There was a war long ago and peace is why the fought
If only the other side—just a little—had thought.

They all were trying—
but now they are in a grave a lying.

Now where they lie there is a poppy
I just hope there is no war—no copy.

Lisa Thomas
PAIN

At night I feel free,
I can scream, cry, let out all the pain in me.

I let out the sorrows of the day,
And to God I pray.

I don't need to keep it all in,
Because letting it go is not a sin.

Stephen Bower
STREETS OF SORROW

This poem is dedicated to my daughter Mary and Grandma Peggy.

Sleep of tears closed eyelids hold upon chilled stone train steps, drowsy people Monday morning calls in trembling catacomb dreams.
Obdurate brows of critical eye deny them made faceless, while suburban feet step lively over worn out hand of tatted cloth.
Nightmares come all too often upon awakening.
Gone are their children's smiles swallowed into pale drawned mother's anguished eyes.
Occasional breeze charms city air with fanned food street smells of Virginia ham dreams.
Forlorn nightly figures casting constant bending shadows, sweeping desolate gray cracked walls, of ghostly tenement hallways.
Tens of thousands have arrived in their disposing sentenced journey.
Haggard hopes sometimes found at hand me out type places.
Ephemeral coins given swiftly for imaginary feast upon morsels.

Heads of fine shaped hats on cashmere coats, with wall street journals tucked in armpits subway token search, they too beware.
Optimism is their vision lost among view of streets horizontal headstones, like desert flowers wilt and fade in rainless places.
Memories finer of far stretching beaches with great hostile waves long since broken, that had innocent treats to sandcastle childhood, now dusty and almost forgotten from makeshift cardboard shacks.
Each life thought as long is preciously given a mere glimpse of eternity.
Lying the forgotten in miseries mansion upon pillars of stones long drafty hallways, while our leaders are lying atop platform stages.
Evening chills cast frozen hooks planted deep into souls discarded.
Soft snow piles onto trouble brow, both hardship and sorrow their most frequent companions stray never so far from streets lament.
Slain soon be the simian three swinging doors of conscience open, shielding genuine hearts from second hand fortune.

Stephen Bower
ONE FADING FLOWER

This poem is dedicated to Kicki and the Island of Gotland.

I do remember when I had seen her then, once upon a wintertime dream.

Her pale solitary figure moving ghostly across a row of stately trees of red rust barren, awaiting springtimes color loss.

The fallen snow had made her winter shoulders white as petals of a long forgotten flower.

There motionless I stood watching, as she turned towards a long lonely and unforgiving road that seemed to go on and on as far as the eye could see, to a distant end for all who fear to travel.

The cruel storm that she bravely embraced now faced her and tried to push her back from whence she had come.

But nevertheless she continued on and on as the wind blew harder than I have ever known forever or heard of whispered before.

Then came wildly dancing, many naked trees ah swaying and urning to the snow winds whistling tune.

I still looked on with my snow hollowed eyes to her now most distant, almost lost in the myriad of speckled swarming crystal white.

Then slowly she had vanished beyond a pale veil of silver, swallowed upas a raindrop upon the dry desert sands, gone ever so softly her lonely figure no longer sang.

Yet I watched for her though in vain, on and on at the point where she last faded, as I have watched for her on many a warm starlite bright, her fleeting shadow that sometimes passes gracefully by her night window, in lovely summertime.

M F Ozerengin
CONTEMPLATION—LOSING SELF IN GOD

I inhale God;
Exhaling my poisons,
"I" feel clean . . .

I meet Him;
in my heart,
in your heart.

He is so far,
yet,
so near . . .

In the spring breeze,
I feel His gentle touch.
I listen to His words of unity and love.

Last barriers disappears,
my "I" dissolves,
"I" dissolve,
in Him.

Shannon Heller
PERCEPTION OF GRACE

December frost.
Dangling icicles form prisms of light.
The whispering snow falling to the earth,
like salt crystals falling from a shaker.
The untrampled snow is a white blanket
upon the ground.
The sun playing peek-a-boo with clouds.
All an illusion.
It's not as it appears.
The bitter cold, tearing at the tender skin.
Wind ripping through the trees,
Howling at the moon.
A reality is revealed through the beauty of the season.

Bettie Meadows
LOVE

When as little children we are taught
To eat, to drink, to sit and walk.
As time passes, our teaching includes
Obedience, trust, and patience too!

During the teen years we question it all.
Our bodies are growing strong and tall.
Our education is far from being complete
And patience is still our major defeat!

Young adulthood comes our way
Education completed, we can now say
"We know for sure patience will come one day.
I'd be willing even to pay!"

Then, as our lives begin to grasp new meaning
Our souls soar, and start their singing.
For woven through the threads of time.
We've found the answer for mankind.

The patience we needed and love we sought
Came through One and couldn't be bought.
Christ freely gave His life for us,
Believing that we would place in Him our trust.

Timothy O White
BEING WITH YOU

To Tracy, my wife, lover, and best friend.

Being with you, is like floating on a summer's breeze, because a gentle breeze makes me feel relaxed and comfortable, the way I feel when I'm with you

Being with you, is like looking at the stars, because the stars make me dream, and you're everything I've dreamed of

Being with you, is like a gentle evening rain, because the rain washes my troubles away, the way you do when I'm near you

Being with you, is like new Spring Flowers as they blossom into a Flurry of colors, their beauty shines as does yours

Yes, being with you is everything to me.

Rhonda L Stern
A SWING RIDE

Swing high,
Swing low.
Reach for the sky,
or follow your toes.
Swing,
Don't you feel anything?
You're in the air,
not just anywhere.

Swing high,
Swing low.
Enjoy the ride,
just let yourself go.
Swing high,
Swing low.

Rhonda L Stern
CATCH A STAR

Pick your hand up high,
and pretend you're
reaching for the sky.
Now make believe
you're very far,
and your hand has
just caught a
shining star.
Take your star,
and place it in
a cookie jar.
Open your eyes,
and taste what
you can eat.
This shiny star
sure is sweet.

Kathleen Dwyer
A MOTHER'S CHALLENGE

To my daughter Michelle with love and the hope that I can meet the challenge.

A sparkle in the eye—future promises untold.
My life, my coming challenge—
can I success or shall I fail?
These are the thoughts—I face her face—
my pretty baby, my little girl.
Will she grow up to be a beauty?
Will she grow up to sieze the world?
I see myself reflected.
I see myself unfurl.
Can she be me—or better still
can she be her?
My pretty baby, my little girl.
Can I protect her?
Will she bolt away?
A mother's only solution—
Truly love her little girl.

Barbara Ann Catuto
A HUG

Dedicated to my husband Ronald P. Catuto.

I need a little hug to keep me through the night,
I need a little hug to make things seem all right,
I need a little hug as I travel on my way,
or someone to say, have a happy day,

I need a little smile from a neighbor or a friend,
I need a little time alone to help me unbend.
I need a cup of coffee from my own special mug,
but most of all I need your reassuring hug.

Belle Jones
PEOPLE PASS

People pass in and out of our lives too quickly.
Some never slow down enough to touch us—
They just smile or nod and quicken their pace—
Afraid to let anyone too close to their inner feelings.

Others stop just long enough to build up our hopes,
Letting us assume we've found a new friend;
They allow us to see basic similarities or share a dream or two;
And then they vanish; stepping back into the shadows from which they emerged.

Still others reach out with both hands and take us in,
Sharing their lives, hopes, dreams, and hurts with us
We learn to trust them, to enjoy their presence in our lives—
And then, because circumstances change, they vanish too.

As this last group of people vanishes, we experience pain.
We wish to cry out for Time to leave us suspended forever among those we love and trust.
Instead we have to sort out the hurt and confusion—
Realizing that through each person's presence in our lives we have become a little wiser, a little better.

Dana Wray
WINTER

This poem is dedicated to Merle L. Crow, my first boss.

Winter has come once more this year,
To beautify the land far and near.
The snow may come sifting lightly down,
Covering the grass and roofs of brown.
Or the wind may come howling in,
Blowing the snow and making a din.

In the country it falls on the buildings and fields,
Hiding the old while being a shield.
The snow lays on the bushes so pretty to see,
While the ice glistens on pole and tree.
Cold as the wind is to be out in,
We will bundle up and bear it with a grin.

Hayley Hill
MY HERO

To Richard E. Hill, my one and only hero.

With all my heart and soul
I love you, is all I know
Off to Vietnam you went
Where too many lives were spent
Too many of your buddies were lost
What a hell of a high cost
You saved all those lives
But still you heard all the cries
For three years you stayed
For your country day by day
Shot not once but twice
My love, you paid a big price
A home coming there was not
Just like you never had fought
Your medals, I have had displayed
For all those sacrifices you made
Why didn't they have a parade?
I know I am only twenty five
But you are my hero keeping me alive

Hollie Couture
FOR EVERY
For every pain felt in my heart
for every tear I cry
a little voice inside of me
will ask the question why
For every sigh I let escape
for every time I fall
I'll try to smile in my soul
and let myself stand tall
For every grin that is not shown
for every weep I hear
I'll try not let myself collapse
and think not of my fear
I must not die in pain and sorrow
for life is not that long
so teach me one important thing
'cause your love will make me strong.

Frances E Edwards
THE PROMISE OF THE SEASONS
Oh, fascinating are all the seasons,
With a beauty all their own,
Faithfully following one another,
In their quest toward the unknown.

Bright and fresh is Springtime,
With its graceful, gentle flowers,
Then Summer soon comes creeping in,
In the splendor of a million colors.

Soon Autumn appears so crisp and cool,
With the scent of harvest in the air,
Then, Ole Man Winter comes blowing in,
Announcing a joy we all will share.

That joy's the promise of the seasons,
With their faith in a future bright,
A promise shrouded in great mystery,
As it walks bathed in shimmering light.

Cara Leitch
ONCE UPON A BELLOWING EVENING
Once upon a
bellowing evening,
snowstorm calling
and icy fingers drumming
warmth in the fire.
Coldness beside it—
I half hoped its heat would reach you.

R DelCarpine
TAKE MY HEART OUT OF HOCK

To Eileen and Nicole.

Can't face the fact that I've lost my little girl,
Nothing left to live for, my life is in a whirl,
Hanging 'round a long time with a crowd that leaves a lot,
Thought that I was better, but now I know I'm not.

I was doing things that I tried to never do,
Stealing, cheating, lying, but now I know to who.
I saw myself go down so low, wasted most of the time,
The time I needed to be with you, in fact, the bottom line.

My family seems to hate me and no one wants to help,
I want to see my baby, so I'll do it by myself.
They all think I'm crazy or want to see me go,
The girls that I grew up with, affection doesn't show.

I'm back on my feet and I'll prove myself to doubting friends of mine,
Considered me too far gone, now I'm doing fine.

Striving just to reunite the two of us at last,
Happily we're bound to be, like days had in the past.
But 'til that time, I'll be here counting on the clock,
You'll come, I'll kiss you, take my heart out of hock.

Cathy Duane
MOTHER EARTH

To My family and friends. Thanks for the inspiration.

Contamination of Mother Earth
Dying going with never to
return in any lifetime.

Rivers with fish dying 'cause
of man's bad habits, killing
all of them and man, with nature's
most precious
gift to them and us! Water
Pure Water!

Water that's uncontaminated
full of so much potential of
keeping everyone's generations
living for as long as the water's
Pure!!

Man needs to wake up and
listen to Mother Earth's cry.
We need to help the precious,
beautiful things that keeps us
from dying, Wake up and smell the world.

Lori Ann Eckerle
EMPTY PATHS
Walking in the mist of time
I hear the red bird sing
Singing of forgotten times
my silent heart did sing.

Bringing me the joy that's lost
that I left long ago
down forgotten empty paths
where people come and go.

Singing of a silent time
When spirits filled the night
and robbed us of our broken dreams
and gave us a new life.

I think about the days gone by
and wonder what to do
accept the past with a tear
is all that I can do.

I'll sing this new song
in my heart
and let the old dreams fade
and see the changes in my soul
and walk my separate way.

Amy Elizabeth Barton
A PRAYER FOR TOMORROW

My tomorrow has come and my prayers have been answered. Thank you Kevin. I love you, Amy

My life tomorrow has fallen today,
I have no where to go, I have no where to stay.
I will take a walk through the valley of my soul,
In hopes to find a bell, with no lonely toll.
I will go now, I will go far away,
I will reach inside me for the power to pray.
I will say to the greatened God above,
"Do not make me perish in the world alone,
For I hear all the others grateful tones.
Uplift my spirits to the most they can be,
Which will make me laugh and sing in glee.
For I believe it is there in me,
The power to do what I say and say what I see.
For I fear when I learn to use this power,
It will be time to lay down the flower.
So stop it all, before it's too late,
And before I learn those words of hate."

Kimberly Ellinwood
MY HOUSE
My house is filled
With lots of love
Like fresh clean air
On the wings of a dove
I treasure the moments
That I spend in it
With the ones that I love
Every minute
My feelings of love
Will never roam
'Cause that's what makes
My house a home

Kristy Collett
VETERANS OF WAR
I think VETERANS deserve more than they got, some come back crippled, some didn't come back at all. Somehow I wish they had a chance to laugh, sing, and dance.

They gave their life for FREEDOM!
I guess that was their way of saying
I LOVE YOU!

There was nothing accomplished in that war, but DEATH was the price to pay!

Pain and sorrow still go on for VETERANS to this day!

Shattered families still suffer today, when their loved ones go away.
If you could see what they are going through, you would be surprised if they're even getting by.

Because it's painful just to think, is this the world GOD made for me?

If it weren't for this war, people wouldn't have to suffer, or see their loved ones slowly die.

BECAUSE THIS IS THE WAR
THAT SHOULD HAVE NEVER
BEEN!

Dawn Marie Miksich
THE HUMAN RACE

To everyone who has successfully dealt with a crisis in life, the scars may be there, but pride must be taken in the fact that there was strength to overcome and learn from it.

Wandering aimlessly down paths unknown,
with twisting roads and dead-ends,
Each is travelled alone.
With each mile a lesson is learned.
Another page is turned, and another chapter added with each passing day.
The journey may be long and rough,
with dangerous terrains and torrential rains.
But with the pain, there is also gain,
as the path to fulfillment continues on.
Because as the road becomes longer,
we then grown stronger.
And the right directions are slowly learned.
With it, self-respect and love are earned,
as the tears and the sweat are washed away.
The finish line is in sight as long as there is the courage,
to <u>never</u> give up the fight.

Ronald R Stockton (Intra)
THE DIFFERENCE TODAY

To Mirabai, from your Father and friend forever.

The Sun sets wearily in the West.
A canopy of grey-colored clouds,
Blanket the mountains for it's night's rest.
Diminishing the Blue sky once proud,
The quiet evening becomes the formal decor.
As the cool, crisp air entices the silence,
Gives reason for the tired to remain indoors.
While the strong and restless resort to malice,
Only to a varying degree, as a form of release.
Life in the "little city" attracts all kinds,
While the outskirts, the desert, establishes peace.
A way to beckon the "spirit" we find,
That humility alone breeds certain unrest.
No one to listen or distract one's feelings,
While the righteous are put to the test.
Through Silence will Truth be revealing.
May the stars and moon crown thy head,
With the wisdom of the Sages.
Each to overcome the fear of Death,
As we evolve through the Ages.

Ronald R Stockton (Intra)
A CRUSHING BLOW
The moment has passed,
Nothing exists.
And in that empty whiteness,

Comes a terrible pressure within.
Creating an implosion,
To burst and forget.

No breath to create,
Only to shatter, disintegrate.
Then be laid flat void of,
Personality, that cluster,
awareness.
Food for the Gods,
Marrow for the soul.

The microcosm in experience,
Unable to resist,
The pull into the Unknown.
Mysteries to unravel,
Through dimensions one travels,
As Death delivers a Crushing
blow.

Barbara S McDowell
CARES OF YESTERDAY

Dedicated to my children: Lacie, Adam & Geoffrey, and to my loving husband Tom.

Here I sit amidst a pile of memories,
Old photographs—alas—
Wondering if the cares of yesterday
Will be tomorrow's link to the past!

For in these photographs you see,
Are the rays of sunshine in our lives,
Wondering if the cares of yesterday
Will somehow be kept alive.

Oh, I will give them to my children
That they may somehow know,
The cares of yesterday are with them
Wherever they may go.

They will have dreams of tomorrow
With visions of the past—
Yes, these are the cares of yesterday,
Memories that will last.

Laurie Freshour
QUESTION
What is it that draw me to him?
How does he know how I feel?
Is it because we once were or are
going to be again?

Only time can tell and time is long
when you wait,
But short
when you least expect it!

Why is it you love me so much?
How is it we can feel for each other?
But still be so far apart?

Answer these Questions
and we will learn the truth
of our feelings towards each
other!

Mildred Ayers
MY JESUS

Dedicated to my preacher, Garrell Kidd who preaches about "My Jesus" so well.

Here on earth, when all hope seems
gone; I think of heaven
And where one day I'll belong.
No tears, no sorrow, no
Burdens I'll bear; because you see
my Jesus he lives up there.

My mother is there, she stands beside
a crystal sea. Her sweet
Voice seems to say to me; "Don't
drop your cross now child,
And one day soon you will be free!"
For what is this weary
Body but dust? When in my Jesus
I put all my trust.

There are days when my spirit is
weak and my feet seem to be
Stuck in the sand—that's when I
call out to my Jesus—
"Please Lord, take my hand!"

When my burdens are many and my
life seems to be put to the
Test; I remember the words of my
Jesus saying, "Come to me
And I will give you rest."

Oh—what joy beyond compare,
when I meet my Jesus in the air.
He will stand there waiting—his
arms open wide, calling
To me to come inside. To a place
where there is no night it's
Always day and there will be
streets of gold to show me
The way.

Then my Jesus will take my hand and
lead me home—to meet my
Father who sits on his throne. The
awesome wonder of God's
Grace; who sent his only begotten
son to die in my place!
My Jesus belongs not only to
me—
he died on the cross to
Set all men free!

Margie Holeman Hanson
FAMILY REUNION

To the HOLEMAN families everywhere.

A page from the Book of Life was
turned and read today,
And for all who came, the page, to
view:
Where the past merged with the
present—
It caused old sweet memories, their
beauty to renew!

On today's page there was written
Lives of all the generations now past.
Room was left, yet, for the new
generation
To keep family traditions alive—to
last!

There was pride of self and of family
Where ancestors brought faith to our
land;
Their hopes for the young, in their
beauty,
Was to accept the token when fate
places it in their land!

On this page there was no grief or
sorrow
For the absence of those gone to their
rest;
Only happiness there for the living—
For they knew, of God, they were
blessed!

The presence of the ghosts from the
ages,
While turning the page today,
Gave beneficent blessings by their
presence
As we laid today's page away!

Jennifer K Nogrady
BUTTERFLY

I would like to dedicate this poem to my wonderful mother who gave me the inspiration to get my poetry recognized.

What a beautiful creature, so
peaceful, so free.
Independent from all is how it likes
to be.
So silently it flutters, so gently and
light,
What a breathtaking picture to see it
in flight.
I envy the butterfly because what I
see,
Is something that's much like what
I'd like to be.

Juanda Hurst Mouren

Juanda Hurst Mouren
RIVER OF DREAM

This poem is dedicated to my mother. She was my best friend. She taught me that God is love and Love is God.

The river bubbles ore rock and stone,
its journey down to the Sea and
Home.
The moisture is lifted from the sea,
by God's own hand as He planned it
would be.

He forms the clouds and places them
so,
the rain returns to the rivers flow.
This plan of His, so simple but yet,
it's overlooked or we forget.

We start our journey down life's
riverbed,
forgetting so easily what the Master
said.
"I am the way!"
When He returned from death,
God had placed in Him life and
breath.

So is death like the Sea?
A place where God will lift us free?
To start our life over again,
to erase the mistakes and forgive our
sins?

I hope this is true,
another chance to be with you.
I could not love more the second
sojourn here,
I would just let you know a little
oftener Dear.

With your love close to me,
the Master's love to set me free,
the sin the shame the mistakes
abound,
would never happen the second time
around.

Our Love would grow like a magic
thing,
it would be an everlasting Spring.
There would be no death for us,
a gift given at Calvary by Our Lord
and Savior Jesus.

Author Unknown—Submitted by Juanda Hurst Mouren
LOVE FOREVER YOUNG

Dedicated to love that never dies.

Great Grandmother is very old,
nearly one hundred, I am told.
One day when no one else was near,
I tiptoed up to the old woman's chair.

She was whispering so sad and low,
Joseph dear Joseph, I loved you so.
I left as quietly as I had came,
Joseph was not Great Grandfather's
name.

Juanda Hurst Mouren
SISSIE

This poem is dedicated to my Sister, Dollie Ruth.

There is a little one, Sissie is her
name,
no she will never be in the Hall of
Fame.
She bounces around like a rubber
ball,
bringing laughter and happiness to
one and all.

There is so much tenderness and love
in a few tiny
bones and a coat of fluff.
Big brown eyes, mischievous and
sweet,
a precious face to make her complete.
A fluffy tail with a slight bend,
wagging and swishing in a friendly
trend.

Her beauty this does not distract,
from a coat of apricot fringed in
black.
Four little feet that run and play,
never wandering to far away.

She is naturally the typical girl,
just a little jealous of the rest of the
world.
Our love we show, the important
thing,
in her little mind makes her a queen.
A special spot she does regularly
possess,
to her unimportant is all the rest.
You wash her, brush her to the
perfect groom,
give her her orders, Sissie stay in
your room!

A car drives up, is it a visitor or Pop?
out she runs like a raggedy mop.
So much company and joy,
a tiny dog that looks like a toy.
One would think you needed a key,
to wind her up then set her free,
to run to jump to squeak her mouse,
then chase the cat all over the house.

There is pedigree in this powder puff,
her family tree is quite good stuff.
Oh Yes! we brag about the two,
one half peak the other half Poo.

God sends his little ones innocent of
mind,
to love to hug to enjoy for time.
He knows our need for a special
friend,
a faithful heart to the very end.

Her eyes tell us of her trust and love,
taught to her by Him above.
In her we see the pure in heart,

maybe thru her He set the spark,
to light the fuse to start the flame, to give Him
our hearts to forget our shame.

Her day is done, she will dream and doze,
a little tease with a shiny black nose.
She has stolen our hearts, this ball of fur,
we will always be thankful to God for her.

If like Sissie we could trust,
our Master like she does us,
peace we would find, we would no longer look.
One perfect lesson from his sacred book.

Juanda Hurst Mouren

BABY GIRL

This poem is dedicated to my sister, Dollie, and my niece, Madalyn, with all my Love.

A turned up nose and eyes of blue,
a smile that steals the heart of you.
A little body firm and round,
not an imperfection to be found.
Her hair is brown and gold with curl,
Oh Yes! God blessed this little girl.

A little heart so strong and true,
asking nothing in return, but the love of you.
Baby this you shall always have,
for your precious love is like a healing salve.

Two little arms that hold you tight,
two rose bud lips that kiss goodnight,
two baby feet that dance and play,
may they never far from the Master stray.

If I should ask the Lord above,
send me another child to love,
another Madalyn she would be,
one of God's own Angels, as I can see.

Oh Yes! there is the other side of her,
when in her childish heart anger may stir.
She will sob and cry, to get her way,
the flame of anger grows, as the answer is nay.

For this I still cannot her blame,
for every child is much the same,
not understanding the so often No!
until it's explained why it must be so.

Oh Yes! I love this little girl,
with the skinned up knees and the messed up curls.
With her questions where, why and when,
not to give her my heart would be a sin.

You ask me, from whence she came,
is this child yours or a different name?
She is not mine, but someone's I love,
she is my Sister's child given by God above.

So my Lord, I pray on my knees,
bless this child and her mother please,
let them see that my love is true,
may they always be near to the heart of You.

Juanda Hurst Mouren

A SMALL TOWN SANTA

This poem is dedicated to Roy Loftis. Thank you Roy!

Our Santa is jolly and round,
a man named Roy sometimes a clown.
Listen to me, a story I will tell,
of a man that gives with his heart lovingly and well.

As Santa Claus each Christmas that came,
he padded his tummy and changed his name.
He started as a youth, back forty years,
Listening to the children's laughter and wiping the tears.

Costume on and his face aglow,
up and down the sidewalks he would go.
Shaking the tiny hands as they whispered in his ear,
all their wishes and dreams throughout the year.

As the years slipped by he continued to be,
what the children wanted and expected to see.
The weather at times cold and bad,
he could change little faces to smiling from sad.

Our Santa has no children of his own,
so seeds of happiness he has sown.
To each child that came with out-stretched hand,
he is love and the symbol of another man.

Saint Nicholas of long ago,
walked cobbled streets of ice and snow.
Giving small gifts to the little ones,
bringing the spirit of giving on the birth of God's Son.

Have we counted the hours the days and the years,
that this man brought happiness and calmed the fears,
of our children and grandchildren and many others,
have we ever said "Thank You" all of us mothers?

In other Cities this story has been told.
It is time this town allow it to unfold.
When you see our Santa, with a big grin,
give him a handshake! Let him know you are a friend!

The many years, with love in his heart,
he gave willingly from the very start.
He hasn't expected anything from us,
he loves the children's smiling faces and their trust.

As I recall from the Book of old,
a Book so precious to be given, not sold.
It states a deed will be rewarded seventy times seven,
what a glorious reward "Our Santa Roy" will receive in Heaven.

Juanda Hurst Mouren

A DREAM, A VISION, A PRAYER

I thought I heard the Master call my name,
why me, burdened with guilt and shame?
Why me, lost in a world of sin,
why would the Master call me to come unto Him?

I hear Him saying, come take my hand,
I will cleanse thee, you and My Lamb.
I hear Him calling, calling in vain,
as I a fool, heed not in my sin and pain.

I will no longer ask why am I blessed,
with this love and promise of peace and rest.
I'll take His hand and hold it tight,
knowing He is with me when Satan I must fight.

Lord I pray that I may be,
just and loving, forgiving like Thee.
When I stumble, when I fall,
I know You will be listening and hear my call.

Take my heart, take my soul,
precious Lord add me to Thy fold.
Hold me close, hold me fast,
until with life on earth I pass.

When face to face with my Creator I meet,
as He sits on His throne, the judgment seat,
as I look into the faces of the Father and Son,
Oh God! I pray that I may hear, Well Done, My faithful servant—Well Done.

Juanda Hurst Mouren

THE FOREST

This poem is dedicated to Almighty God the giver, in prayer that all can understand to keep this earth clean for the future generations. Thank You Lord for all your beautiful gifts.

If close to God you want to be,
then look around and you will see.
The sky above is the floor of heaven,
the miracles around you are four score and seven.

Read on and I will name a few,
then search your heart, it will make a believer of you.
His hands out-stretched, He must have said,
man needs more than just his bread.
I will bring him closer to beauty and see,
if this will also bring him closer to me.

So to work He did go,
creating the things we love so.
Up came the mountains and small little streams,
these must have been one of God's own dreams.
The stately trees with their mouths pressed against
the earth's sweet flowing breast, their arms spread wide to
God above,
offering themselves in prayer and love.

For you and me these He made,
to give us beauty and give us shade.
Then with a twinkle in His eye,
He thought of the birds that sing and fly.
You must know that in their flight,
they are guided by God's own Holy Light.

For you who can see this and not believe,
it is you whom I am sad and I grieve.
For God gave you all of this and more to come,
He offers you the hand of His only Son.

So take the nail scarred hand in yours, walk through the
paths and through the forest,
you will know in your heart that God is Here.
He will gather you to his flock and forever hold you near.

Juanda Hurst Mouren

FREEDOM

This poem is dedicated to all those souls in despair that placed their trust in God. The only One that will bring peace and heal a broken heart.

All presumption in the world, the knowledge need to be,
will never surpass the root, of simply being free.
To dance when heart is gay, to drink when feeling low,
to have many a friend and nary a single foe.

I doubt freedom is one often owned by you or any others,
as it is rare and had by mighty few.

Brandy of the damned, if that's what freedom be,
then Satan what I wouldn't give just to know more of thee.
If Fate says I must be content to let this life drift by,
then watch out shores of Hell for I'd much sooner die.
If I must live this pious life to gain eternity,
then swing wide the gates of Hell—
Satan make Love to me.

Juanda Hurst Mouren

A VERY SPECIAL FRIEND

This poem is dedicated to Connie Fay.

There is someone I will admire my whole life through,
that Special someone is you.
The glamour of presents will soon fade away,
and wear out from use someday.

One thing which cannot decay,
is my love for you and your funny way.
You are beautiful to me in so many ways,
growing even more so with the passing days.

Your wonderful smile, so tender and warm,
could calm anyone in the greatest of storm.
Your green eyes with a special light,
as though they were two stars, stolen from the night.
These little things even distance can't take one thought,
for they are more special to me than anything bought.

If I had my way, the Heaven your praises would sing,
the highest steeple bells your glory would ring.
The stars in the sky to spell out your name,
for you to belong to me would be a privileged claim.

You rate the beauty, love and everything good,
and act just like I knew you would.
There is one thing for sure I know,
God raised a mighty crop when your seed He did sow.
And so for you, may your future be bright,
for you are set high before my sight.
Nothing said or done could crush the foundation,
for you are indeed God's remarkable creation.

Your memory will always belong to me, will love you through eternity.
On this special day I wanted to give you something more,
than just a little something you could buy in a store.
These few lines are all I could do,
but they are something special from just me to you.
So by these words, I hope you will see,
just how much you mean to me.

Juanda Hurst Mouren

MY MEMORIES

I dedicate this poem to my one and only Love.

I met you and my life began with feeling more sincere,
you erased every hurt, every fear.
You strengthened and helped me causing me to stand,
held only by one tender touch of your hand.
Stirring within a sacred flame far greater than I knew,
love growing as a flower, born a seed anew.

The days we spent together were short with laughter and tears,
each moment sealed within my heart for all the coming years.

When you held me close, tender in the warmth of your embrace,
gently pushing away the regret filled tears that fell upon my face.
My highest hopes and dreams before, I ever did suppress,
but through your understanding love, now I can express.

Yes you have given me more than mortals dare to measure,
easing all my pain and sorrow,
adding peace and pleasure.
Asking little, you gave so much with your wondrous gift of love,
making it my greatest treasure,
blessed by God above.

You mean more to me than these simple words can say,
I live and learn to love you deeper every day,
each night I say a prayer in hopes that you might be,
just a little closer drawn by memory to me.

My love for you will never depart,
in my body you are present in each beating of my heart.

Till once more I see your smiling face,
and once again am locked in your warm embrace,
I'll love you longer than always, until the end of time,
far beyond forever your memory will be mine.

Soon to soon we had to bid adieu and tho within I was weeping,
I left behind my heart and memories for your safe keeping.
Remember that I love you, more than you have ever known,
this is the deepest, passionate love
My Darling, I give to you alone.

Juanda Hurst Mouren

MY FIRST

This poem is dedicated to My Joe.

God knew I needed someone special,
so He sent me you,
to love and cherish always, all my lifetime through.
He blessed you with virtues more countless than earthly time,
He gave you a life deserving of happiness, I pray you will find.

He gave you a special glory and beauty from within,
over shadowing any and all faults which might dwell there within.
He gave you the possession of knowledge, good and bad,
which carried with it tender moments of happiness and sad.
Oh Yes! He gave you all these gifts which I enjoy so much,
but there is something far more precious in your smile and sweetness of your touch.

He made your touch as gentle as a breeze in early spring,
your soul as light and gay as a bird upon the wing.
He gave you understanding and laughter like a song,
to cheer and comfort all, when things go wrong.
He wove your wondrous smile from a sunbeam in the skies,
then He picked two bright and shining stars and placed them in your eyes.

These little things I love about you in shrine and inter-glow,
I cannot help from watching you as some times you must know.
Since you came into my life, all other things seem small,
far beyond my fondest dreams, I treasure your love most of all.

Now I am living in a world of hopes and dreams come true,
because I know the happiness and joy of loving you.
Yes He filled your heart with love,
made it kind and true,
God knew I needed someone special,
so He sent me You.

Juanda Hurst Mouren

FORGIVENESS

This poem is dedicated to a special person in my life. He will recognize it, when He reads it.

Darling as you lie beside me in sleep's deepest peace,
I pray to God for all your suffering to cease.
The things of the past which haunt you each day,
you are blaming yourself though it should not be that way.

If I had the power to heal all your woe,
I wouldn't hold back for a moment you know.
I can love and give you all the comfort I have
and pray that will become a healing salve.

It takes time with faith and trust,
and of course a pure love is more than a must.
I am doing my best which is all I can do,
but I'll try even harder because it's for you.

To you I say, no matter what comes or has been,
you are still on a pedestal forgiven of Sin.
That is where I have placed you for that is where you belong,
nothing to shake its foundation, your praise my constant song.

You will always have my thoughts and love each and every day,
I know I'll love you more tomorrow,
even more than I do today.

Juanda Hurst Mouren

MIRACLE 1949

This poem is dedicated to my Daughter, Angele Lee Bailey, my baby girl always.

Light was my heart for a child near it lie,
not knowing that her birth was nigh.
'Twas August but the eve was cool,
the waiting mouths were a half and two.

Three days the pain my body racked,
then my dream child became a fact.
So tine in the incubator she did lie,
the doctor prayed, but said she would surely die.

Oh Heavenly Father! I did pray,
do not take this child away.
If it shall be your will, then she,
shall live a loving life for thee.

This child conceived of love and grace,
was blessed by God to be fair of face.
With his hands he held her fast,
his judgment and compassion, her life would last.

Oh! guilty heart so full of sin,
how fortunate, God can forgive all sins of men,
blessed me with a child so sweet,
with humble heart I would kiss Thy feet.

Three months had passed, the doctor said,
you may take her home to her own little bed.
I picked her up and my heart grew old,
one tiny arm was limp and cold.

Dear God! Dear God! again I come,
with a prayer from my heart was wrung.
This child you gave me from your love,
send your Miracles and Blessings from above.

How selfishly I did pray,
asking more each night and day.
Not satisfied with what He gave,
a human trait from cradle to grave.

Doctors, more doctors we did see,
always the same, a cripple she was to be.
The months rolled by into eight,
I could not accept this to be her fate.

Then a miracle did appear,
my faithless heart, an illusion did fear.
The tiny fingers moved, but slight
then a voice seemed to say fight! fight!

Ye who have the faith of a mustard seed, came to mind,
again faith and peace I did find.

The miracle of God came,
the little arm became the same,
as the other full and strong,
as I realized my wrong.
Too little faith I did have,
in His Love and Mercy as a healing salve.

To you My Lord my constant prayer will be,
that I shall always be worthy of Thee.
My faith shall falter not in the Father and Son,
the lesson was very hard, the battle was fought and won.

Lydia Moccero

I'M LONELY TODAY . . .

I'm lonely today
but the world does not care.
It keeps on its course
and goes unaware.

I'm lonely today—
no human would guess
the sadness I feel—
the pain of distress.

I'm lonely today—
just God is concerned
that the friendship I gave
remains unreturned.

I'm lonely today—
Nobody pays heed . . .
Each one turns away
while I sit here and bleed.

Yes—I'm by myself
in this personal bloom—
a private abode
as bleak as a tomb.

Lydia Moccero

BALLOONS! BALLOONS!

Balloons! Balloons!
He has so many.
Tell him your choice—
he'll sell you any.

Balloons! Balloons!
yellow, green, red.
You might prefer
a blue one instead.

Balloons! Balloons!
Big ones and small,
long ones and round—
he has them all.

Balloons! Balloons!
Fat ones and slender—
buy them right there
from the balloon vendor.

Lydia Moccero
MORE THAN FRIENDS
Forbidden!—as the fruit
on the initial tree—
is any love relationship
which might between us be.

It's not my feelings slumber—
It's not fault that you bear.
I simply can't reveal
how very much I care.

You see my casual countenance
and cannot comprehend
why it is quite impossible
that we be "more than friends."

How sad, the great potential—
love Lost, which might have been—
our bodies, souls—our minds and hearts—
we two becoming One!

But not in this life, dearest—
it was not meant to be.
I pay the price to sacrifice
You
for the Deity.

David Carter
WHEN I WAS YOUNG
I never thought, when I was young,
that I would see the day.
When I would tell a little child,
to just 'go away.'

Or say that I was 'busy,'
and could not spare the time.
To answer a small child's question,
to talk to a kin of mine.

One time I lived in a fairyland,
where make-believe came true.
Where princes lived and dragons fought,
and the sky was always blue.

Where I wrapped my arms around my dolls,
and clutched them Oh, so tight.
Pretending that I was a Mom or a Dad,
who treated children right.

Yes it's safe and secure in fairyland,
where make-believe comes true.
And while grown-ups don't believe in that,
little children do.

David Carter
I WONDER
I wonder how the flowers came,
to be the way they are.
In every color imaginable,
they're the most beautiful things by far.

And I wonder what makes the waves break,
along the sandy shore.
Or why the tide flows in and out,
just like in a tug-of-war.

Why birds soar high in the bright blue sky,
as if waiting to entertain.
And why dark clouds come swirling by,
every time it starts to rain.

And why are the leaves upon the trees,
sometimes brown or green.
While at other times there are none at all,
so confusing it would seem.

Though sometimes I wonder most of all,
just how I came to be.
But mother just smiles and cuddles me tight,
and says 'someday you will see.'

David Carter
THE SUMMER SKY
The sandy shoreline,
disappears into the midnight darkness.
While the silvery sea, rippling gently,
reflects the idle summer moon.
And ten thousands stars dance in the heavens,
competing for attention.
Forming mysterious patterns that circle slowly,
around the sky.

What a superbly amazing creation,
still incomprehendible to man.
Who is sent to visit this masterpiece,
this awesome spectacle.
With senses to see it, hear it, smell, taste and touch it,
to marvel, conjecture and ponder.
To observe a display of infinite power.
I see all this, and I wonder why.

David Carter
WHERE THE ROAD BEGAN
I once thought where the road began,
was the end of all the earth.
Though unreachable it was always there,
since the first year of my birth.

And so many things always happened there,
in that undiscovered land.
Out in the vast and endless space,
that I could not understand.

And time stood still, as it passed on by,
with never an end in sight.
With no need to seek out a reason,
or to question that which was my right.

To keep everything forevermore,
just the way it was back then.
With nothing changing was disturbing the delight,
of eternity born to all men.

But the land that was there, where the road once began,
has gone now forever it seems.
Just a twinkle in the eye, as time rushes by,
a part of an old man's dreams.

David Carter
NEW PLACES
Some day I'll go somewhere,
somewhere I don't know where,
Where I have not already been.
Where spaces are places, and places form spaces,
That I have not already seen.

Where time has no meaning, and things have no seeming,
To be as they always have been.
And though there's no reason, to define this illusion,
It's now all so amusing to me.

But let's not get light hearted, at something not started,
Or the trick will be only you.
They'll just bring out the hat, and rearrange all of that,
So the illusion continues anew.

So here's to the good times, the old times, the new times,
And those that remain to be seen.
And when all this is gone, I'll just move along,
To the places where I've never been.

David Carter
THE DUNKIRK SANDS
The Dunkirk sands lie silent now,
the sea moves to and fro.
And birds of every kind are back,
in the quiet pools below.

A solitary figure walks down the shore,
leaving footprints in the sand.
Wild flowers abound in every hue,
Mother Nature's first grandstand.

The sun on high is in full bloom,
the mist has gone away.
But no glories past reveal themselves,
just the smell of the sea and the spray.

Who thought when first we saw this scene,
that it could look this way.
So magnificent, oh so beautiful,
are the Dunkirk sands today.

David Carter
OLD NED
They've taken old Ned from his nice warm barn,
and put him out to pasture.
They say he's too old to work anymore,
and really aging much faster.

After fifteen years of pulling the plow,
sometimes for ten hours a day.
They finally decided to retire him,
so he could just 'fade away!'

I took my first ride on good old Ned,
when I was only three.
Though strong as an ox, he was oh, so kind,
and amazingly gentle to me.

I've washed his back and brushed his mane,
and talked with him for hours.
Fed him apples, sugar and lots of hay,
and once even fed him flowers.

Thought Ned, I'm sure, will not complain,
or simply 'fade away!'
He's much too smart to do any of that,
he told me so today!

Myra Istre
THE WALL

Dedication to Roderick Crochet. Everyone needs to realize in time or it could be too late.

We build a wall.
We make sure it's hard and very solid.
We make it to protect ourselves.
We build it so no one can come in near our heart.
What is it worth?
It's lonely behind the wall by yourself
We use it 'cause of own insecurities.
If you don't be careful when the wall falls so will you; right on your face.
Make the wall a little flexible, so one day someone can go hide with you.
If not you'll end up losing to
The Wall.

Bob Nelson
FOR WHAT IT'S WORTH

To Cindy.

For what it's worth
to be rich and happy
For what it's worth
to be poor and sad
For what it's worth
in sickness and in health
For what it's worth
to love someone else
For what it's worth
to be with you all of that night
For what it's worth
to you that night
For what it's worth
is to hold onto the light
For that is what it was
worth to me that night.

Trish Wenzel
WHO HAS TAUGHT . . .
Who has taught
This soul to dream,
This mind to reminisce.
Who has brought
This spirit peace,
And conquered emptiness.
Who has helped
These eyes to see,
What joy tomorrow holds.
Who has taught
This heart to love,
And cherish life, as gold.
'Tis you my friend,
Of you I speak
With blessed adoration,
For you have taught
This soul to seek
A life of celebration

R R Kunkel
TIME!
Time is the greatest of treasures,
It's a wonderful gift of the Lord;
For you and me to misuse it
Is a luxury we cannot afford.

We can't store it up for the future,
Or buy it back when it's gone;
Yes, time is the greatest of treasures
Most precious that's ever been known.

They say, "That time waits for no man."
It passes swiftly and silently by,
And no one has ever regained it
No matter how hard they may try.

It's given to us to make use of,
All twenty-four hours of the day,
We choose the way that we spend it,
So spend it wisely, I pray.

Let us live with the deep satisfaction
That when our last minute shall end,
And we meet God at the portals of Heaven,
He'll say, "Well done! Enter, my friend."

Floyd J Barton
USING TIME WISELY
Life is man's most vital possession,
filled with extras bestowed by the great Divine.
Time is one of life's most precious commodities, this truth may we early find.

Once a segment of time has passed, to reclaim, it cannot be forever gone. A mark of wise living is to be good stewards of every moment as we move steadily along.

Life seems long in its anticipation at the dawn of one's upward climb,
But short in its contemplation in the twilight years we truly find.
Time like an ever rolling stream racing toward the sea,
May we not be encumbered by little things, using each moment wisely as it was meant to be.

Kathleen Menken
LIBERTY

I would like to dedicate this poem to my father who took me to many parades in my early years, and to my dear mother who read a lot of patriotic poems and stories.

Do people think that liberty is free
It was earned by our forefathers
In prayer on bended knee
Liberty was precious in olden days of yore
It was a dream worth fighting for
Brave men fought and died
Believe me friend
They knew the score
"Give me liberty or Give me death"
That was Patrick Henry's cry
He meant it with every breath

Richard A Persin
SOLO

A dream to go on forever . . .

The sun sank beneath the earth's crest.
It's last rays surrounded your body
Forming an aura and illuminating
Your curled blond hair, making
Each strand seem to dance; Solo.

To match no other . . .

We sat at a candle lit table.
The soft light sets off your
Eyes, allowing their radiant blue
To escape and captivate. Just like
The perfect diamond with its bluish tint.
Snapping me out of my stare
Is the flickering flame, which danced;
Solo.

That I ever had . . .

Moonbeams shattered across the lake.
Soft music played, and I asked
For a dance, which you obliged.
We moved to the floor
By the water, and began dancing;
Solo.

Or could want.

Debra Carter
LIFE

This poem is dedicated to DeAndra, my daughter.

We are conceived so quickly
inside her wound.
We toss and turn in a balloon . . .
Life has started for he or see . . .
We can't wait to see which it will be.
We are born into this world . . . The Unknown.
We have nothing of our own.
Mommy, Daddy help me please . . .
All I can do is crawl on my knees.
Life goes by fast you see . . .
I know my 1, 2, 3,s 
My friend said, had my first kiss . . .
You don't know what you missed.
Dating, Dating, oh! What fun, oops.
Mommy it was only #1
Here goes this cycle again . . .
Life is about to begin.
Come one grandma . . . Please don't fall
Let's take a walk in the mall.
No smoking. Drinking or drugs . . .
All I need is my coffee mug.
Dear lord help me please . . . of this disease
When I found out I dropped to my knees.
Please take care of me he or she . . .
I need you like you needed me.
Now life flash before me . . . way back
When I learned my 1, 2, 3,s
But, this beautiful LIFE goes one you see . . .
LIFE GOES ON

Doris L Berg
ROSES

I love roses.
Roses running wild o'er the land;
Or raised and pampered with a tender hand.
Gently nodding in the summer air;
Or nestled sweetly in some beauty's hair.
Roses clinging by a garden gate;
Or one red rose beside a dinner plate.
But the roses that you gave,
Were like Roses on the grave—
A little late.

Doris L Berg
LETTER TO A CANNED-FOOD COMPANY

As I opened a can of your corn recently,
My eyes fell upon something green.
It's only a leaf, I said to myself,
That accidently fell in the machine,
But at second glance I discovered it was
A worm who had gone to his doom.
So I picked up the pan in my hot little hand
To carry it out of the room.
When all of a sudden another surprise
In the form of a long gooey hair.
'Twas then I decided to write this to you
To find out what's going on there.
Now may I suggest that you clean up this mess;
Throw out all the insects, and then,
When you employ people to work in your plant,
Hire bald-headed women and men.

Joseph D Ceriani Sr
WHAT IS LOVE?

Love is a feeling that's not hard to define.
It's that something that very few of us truly find.
Love is a physical and emotional force that's in tune,
Like a rose that has become full bloom.

More precious than silver, diamonds or gold,
It's so priceless it can never be bought or sold.
Brighter than the sun, deeper than the ocean,
The ultimate thrill in human emotion.

It's as pure as the springtime showers,
And more beautiful than a garden of flowers.
Sweeter than the honey that's made by the bees,
Stronger than the largest of trees.

As friends, a lifetime that will last,
With dreams of the future and cherishing of the past.
Of sharing and giving, understanding and forgiving,
The greatest force that makes life worth living . . .
That's love.

Joseph D Ceriani Sr
THOSE SWEET SONGS

Oh, what sweet memories bring,
Those songs that made my sad heart sing.
Easing the pain a little day by day,
And giving me strength as I kneel and pray.

I haven't forgotten the thrill when you first kissed my cheek,
And how it left me trembling and weak.
Nor the time we climbed the yonder hill
To listen to the songs of the whippoorwill.

Oh those many years you were always at my side,
Giving me strength and being my guide.
Always giving, never demanding,
Filling me with your love and understanding.

We were always together, in good times and bad,
Those happy ones and those that were sad.
And then one day you were gone,
I thank you now, my darling, for making me strong.

You will always be in my heart,
For you are those sweet memories that bring
Those songs, that make my sad heart sing.

Joseph D Ceriani Sr
WINTER

Winters with your white blanket, sparkle like diamonds under the sun.
Down hills are silver ribbons, in spring little creeks run.
Fence posts stand like sentinels guarding the countryside.
Around trees and bushes little animals hide.
From houses icicles hang like swords pointing to the ground.
In yards crusts of bread lay, thrown by children, food for the birds can be found.
On frozen ponds young skaters laugh and sing,
Down country lanes sleigh bells ring.
In the night sky the moon shines like a silver dish,
On the first star young lovers make their wish.
It's Winter.

Joseph D Ceriani Sr
THE STRANGER

As I walked along a road, a stranger I happened to meet.
He was dressed in a long white robe, and sandals on his feet.
The words he spoke gave me hope, my heart began to race,
There was a smile of love and gentleness on his radiant face.

He made me think of the good things, and forget those that were bad.
He made me forget the pain, and things that made me sad.
He made the sun shine through a dark and cloudy sky,
He showed me the true things that riches could never buy.

He guided me down the dark mountain road to a calm and silvery sea,
He taught me a new life and the kind of person I ought to be.
He told me to love my brother, then I would know true happiness,
He lightened my heavy burden and filled my heart with bliss.

He taught me the worthlessness of things that I once valued high,
I was so filled with contentment, the whole world seemed to sigh.
I turned to thank this stranger who was all dressed in white,
From the corner of my eye he just disappeared from sight.

I stopped and looked around, and thought, "was this just a dream?"
Oh no, it couldn't be, for now my life is beautiful, bright and clean.
I know that this stranger will meet another lost one like me,
And he will open blinded eyes, a new and beautiful world he will see.

Joseph D Ceriani Sr
OUT OF THE ARMY

I'm out of the Army now—
No more of that lousy chow,
No more standing in line,
No more of that spit and shine,
I'm out of the Army now.

No more inspections I deplore,
Saluting those officers I'll do no more,
No more jumping when the sergeant would yell,
Now I can tell them to go plumb to hell,
I'm out of the Army now.

No more getting up for reveille,
I'll lay in bed and dream of Beverly,
No more close order drill,
I'll sit on my can and do as I will,
I'm out of the Army now.

No more of that gall darn K.P.,
I'll never wash another dish, you'll see.

No more making that lousy bunk,
I think I'll go and get good and drunk,
(Because . . .) I'm out of the Army now.

Veronica Hennessy
WATERFALL

I want to be a waterfall, of Prussian blue and white.
I want to flow from rivers of the world,
And crash down fast and die.
I want to be a bright,
wet run and reflect the world around me.
The yellow sun of happiness will make me shine like stone.
I want to be a waterfall,
from heaven and from hell.
I want to be of Prussian blue,
And crash down fast and die.

Veronica Hennessy
SINGING THE JOYS OF APRIL

Morning dew, oh, how I wish I could hold you
And feel you melting through my palm.
You are the innocence; before the storm,
You are the calm.
Though others try to rush you, and wish you away
Your tulips whisper to me magenta
And canary, yellow days.
Your petals try to soften me, and keep me at a hush,
Too melodic to the stillness;
Too warming to the touch.

Afternoon, come and touch me
With your pastel symphony.
Your roses open wide and sing: And its song is harmony.
I lie upon your plush, green corps
And wonder at your sky; the clouds all come together
Making home for when I die.
I let your arms surround me: I am victim to your song.
Your beauty can enchant me;
Your melody play on:
Singing the joys of April.

James Bianco
BECAUSE OF BOTH OF YOU

I would like to dedicate this poem from my first book, Feelings, Thoughts, and Memories, to my Mother and Father, Irene Margret Baxter Bianco and Dominick Joseph Bianco for all their love & understanding that they have given me.

You gave me life and through the years watched me grow,
You both took care of me when I was sick unable to help myself you both took turns watching over me,
You both gave me comfort when I was hurt and love to keep me warm,
when I needed you, you were both there,
Because and most important you both gave me the chance to be myself, I found me.

James Bianco
IN SEARCHING

Along the way I learned many things and in searching for the true me, I found you.
You were like a spring rain awakening me to a new and different morning.
Like a gentle Autumn breeze touching me, the sun rays let me know you are near.
In time, you showed me how to be a part of the world rather than a secret to its existence.
Taking time, you looked beyond your dreams, your hopes and concentrated on someone you believed you had been searching for . . . and had now come to find.
Somehow in the time we spent together, we found in ourselves a part of each other and within a world forgotten for a night,
We found love.

Leah V Gillman
THIS LAND OF OURS

Why is this land so special?
People come by land and sea;
They risk their lives to get here,
They hear our land is free.
Of Government suppression,
Governed not with guns and tanks
Citizens can choose a leader
Qualified to fill the ranks.
Who would not love this land of ours
With its opportunity,
To reach a goal as one may wish
And best of all, "Be Free."

Deborah L Deardorff
SECRETS INSIDE

The deep dark secrets that hide inside
The secrets that grow and eat you alive
If I told you my secrets would you understand?
Could I count on you to hold my hand?

It's raining inside and I can't swim
If I tried to tell you; where would I begin?
I can't expect you to know how I feel
There are times I wonder myself if it's real

I go through the motions from day to day
Hoping inside they would just go away
From time to time it seems like they're gone
Somehow they creep back before too long

I'm not even sure what keeps me holding on
Does it really matter; someday I'll just be gone
I wish more than anything I could believe in me
But I'm drowning inside; one . . . two . . . three . . .

Cheri Courson
WISHING FOR A MASTERPIECE

Red is a juicy red apple of delicious fruit inside
    a rosy cheeked child of good health,
    a ruby for a queen that is true
    a rose for someone you love.
Yellow is a daffodil with dew upon it
    a bright sunny morning that smells and feels fresh
    a canary with a song
    a banana for a split
Brown is a tree trunk for a squirrel to climb
    a rich earth which farmers can grow
    a deer by a stream unaware that you're there
    a pet dog that is a friend
Black is a night of candles, flickering deep and dark
    a spider in a web of lacy perfection
    a summer storm approaching to cool off a hot sultry day
    a deep sleep to awake refreshed.
White is a fresh fallen snow without footprints
    a field of cotton waiting to be picked
    a furry rabbit in the garden dining
    a pureness of love that lives within
Why can't these colors blend together when it comes to people as they do in priceless masterpiece

Jerry Cantrell
TO WHOEVER THIS REFERS TO

This poem is really dedicated to Jerry Cantrell, a man of low self-esteem.

Please read this letter
And do take note,
This poetry could be better
But it is the poorest ever wrote.
I tried to write out my very, very best
Because, this is an entry for
a poetry contest.
The grand prize is big cash
for the best poet.
So when I found out about it, I thought I could give a go for it.
If you will bear with me now
I'm writing the best I know how.
From my own personal experiences in life
It can be really hard to find a beloved wife.
When you're shy and do not let
her know what you are thinking
It is highly possible she may
leave you in a winking
So, when it is time to ask
her for that date
You had better do it before
it is too late
And if your shyness continues
as long as it has,
It is time to come out of it
or stay at home sitting on
your . . . regrets.
As I told you my poetry is
not good as the rest.
All this writing sure has put
my brain to the test
Because it is all I can do
in 21 lines or less!

Denise Gryskiewicz
IMAGES OF DENISE

It's hard to imagine about someone you never knew
What would you be like if you only lived and grew
Only my imagination will ever know what you would be
What new kind of joy would you bring to our family

Would you be tall like your name sake
Or would you be short for your Mom's sake
How would you laugh while playing with your friends or riding your bike
What kind of boys would you like

Who knows what life had in store for you
I can't understand why God would take someone so new
Imagining you will keep you safe inside me
And what a beautiful image it is that I see

Thelma B Malcolm
UNICORNS

In memory of my dear sister, Edrie Rogers Shaddy, for whom this verse was written.

Magnificent creatures
  Mysterious as a distant star.
Strange that you never were
  And yet you are.

Proud and beautiful
  A symbol of purity
With the innocence of Eden,
  And the wisdom of eternity.

Is your haunting sadness
  For the past as it was then?
Or for what was not
  But would have been?

Why am I drawn to you
  What kinship do we share?
Is it a fragment of my soul
  That you caught in time somewhere?

Eleanor M Dirksen
STILL LEARNING

This first poem is dedicated to Jurren Sr, my husband for forty-seven years.

At sixty-seven years,
I just keep trying
To broaden my knowledge,
And books I am buying.

I relearned how to write
And read with more speed,
Then made my own short-hand
Which conquered my need.

Learning is a challenge,
Classroom work is great,
And to learn from others
Brings quite a nice fate.

Nine children are now grown,
With Dad and me alone,
And nineteen grandchildren
Keep us on the phone.

Learning has been life-long
And in my future, too,
It keeps my morals high
And impresses our crew.

Laura Dooley
LIFE IS FULL OF . . .

Life is full of mystery,
  Yet to be solved.
Life is full of wonders,
  Yet to be experienced.
Life is full of people,
  Yet to be loved.
Life is full of creations,
  Yet to be discovered.
Life is full of knowledge,
  Yet to be known.

Life is full of words,
Yet to be received.
Life is full of beauty,
Yet to be found.
Life is full of books,
Yet to be read.
Life is full of intelligence,
Yet to be used.

Lydia (Lee) Zaugg
'TIS SPRING
Spring! The balmy breeze—the gentle air—
The lush green grass—every where,
Tulips, jonquils, daffodils, gay,
Are nodding their heads, as if to say,
Spring is here, spring is here—
Listen to the birds—singing their cheer.

Yes winter is past—the ice and the snow—
And the season of rest—all had to go,
The trees are all budded and ready to bloom—
The gardens will be planted, very soon,
The birds sweetly singing in the trees,
Their melody gently wafted by the breeze.

Even the lake, so calm and blue—
Reflected the beauty of the sunset hue,
God in His wisdom, power and love,
Controls all nature from Heaven above.
And I'm so glad he loves me too—
Yes—I'm sure He also loves you!

Melissa Tracy
CRY
I feel like crying
but I couldn't tell you why.
Something's locked up inside me
which I can't identify.

I guess it's all my problems
that will not go away.
The feeling, whatever the cause,
just makes me want to cry.

Joshua G Wong
BROTHERHOOD
We all fight for Unity,
though we have all done many wrongs.
We must put these things behind us,
for in God's eyes we must belong.

This belonging is true for all,
for God discriminates against none.
Good feelings and beliefs for all
are the best ways to have fun.

So as you read this poem,
remember why you're here;
To think Brotherhood toward all men
and dispel away the fear.

Maria Russell
STRIVING
innocent wisdom
hopeful despair
welcoming fears
of unrevealed mysteries
unfolding teachings
of the universe unknown
searching truth alone

undecorated beauty
untamed
enchanting
intriguing strength
bewildering golden
man
brave love
bewitched
blindly longing
to belong
bravely loving

facing alone
Medusa's fury
superbly performing
her dreadful work
a child's magical smile
a man's intense stare
daring her to vanish
forever
vanishing forever
despair

wise innocence
daring golden Perseus
of fierce will
you will
find your niche
your own
on your own

Maria Russell
MODERN MAN
today I need
a face
and eyes that
look
at me
in sympathy
and reflect
my I
being

today I need
an aura
to keep
my atoms
from dispersing
forever
in the infinite
pain of my
bewailed
dreams

today I need
a hand
friendly
to sustain
my searching soul

Jaime Smith
TINY NICK INSIDE OF MY HEART
I never thought it could hurt so much;
to just say good bye,
or feel all the pain you do, when you look him in the eye.
And the sudden rush of emptiness
that you feel inside your heart,
when you tell him that after this,
you'll have to be apart.
But even though we can no longer be together,
All the moments that we spent will stay with me forever.
You always gave me the feeling that you were constantly there,
And you would open your arms, if I ever needed someone to care.
And now all that I have left are the memories of you,
And the remembrance of these feelings that once were true.
So, now there's just a tiny nick inside my heart,
And it keeps growing bigger; since the day we were first apart.

Jaime Smith
WHAT FRIENDSHIP'S ALL ABOUT
I'm sorry if I hurt you from all the words I say,
But I'm not the kind of friend that will just walk away.
We can always tell each other all the 'zany' things we do,
And when something's bottled up inside
of me I know I can turn to you.
You were the one who made me feel better when the tear ran down my face,
And you were the one who pushed away that feeling of empty space,
And every morning I wake up;
knowing that I have a true friend,
And it gives me the power to wake up mornings again and again.
So I'm sorry that sometime these words just "blurt" out,
But then again;
That's why I've been told, this is what friendship's all about.
Thanks.

Shaun Kevin Gibson
A SUBTLE WARNING
Living for the moment
When the moment never comes
Finding ourselves out on the street,
knowing we were not the ones
Never coming in because the
darkness never fades
Giving no true reverence for that
which God has made
Soaring through the sky like the man
on the flying trapeze
Innocent little child dying from a
tropical disease
For many sit and wait for the
Judgement Day to come
While others run away from
destruction yet to be done
Many understand and find no
pleasure in the aid
While fools try to swim and find they
cannot wade
The prospect's truly bleak and leaves
us little hope
No light at the end of the tunnel, in
the darkness we're left to grope
Like a little bird, who with untested
wings must fly
Spiraling closer to the ground and
only asking why
We say ignorance is bliss and walk
carelessly along
We tell ourselves everything is
alright, but we know something is
wrong
Life is not a given, it's a blessing
from above
Something given to us out of
kindness and of love
It's too short and precious just to let
it waste away
If you give this thought no credence
you will surely rue the day

Louis Giammella
THE SEEKER

To Pearl, my wife. My love for an eternity.

I seek not gold or fame nor a place in the sun
But the God given right to be loved
To know in my heart that she is out there and someday she will come
I have searched these years but all in vain
Cannot someone feel my pain?
Please lord send her to me for the years go by
If not in this life then in the next
And I will have peace of mind.

Louis Giammella
TO FUTURE CHILDREN
The beams of sunlight among the forest trees
The song of birds upon the air
The fish that swim in waters clear
The breezes that gently move the leaves
To fields of flowers that nature sows
Among the stones of yesteryears
With memories good not with the sad
The sun goes down—the darkness comes
The brilliance of the stars do shine
The sounds of creatures in the night
proclaiming they are free
These things and many more
To you future children
I do endow

Richard Brooks
DECK OF LOST SOULS

These poems dedicated in memory and spirit to my late mother Ruth, from a son. Also to mention friends and associates.

Deck of Lost Souls—lonely personages
Long, Lonely, Lost.
Self need, Self love—Sorrowful alienation—or contemplation.
I feel alone—I feel—We feel,
Deck of Lost Souls
We look it
Even yonder, Kalb the dog has that look.

Oh Lord, Oh Lord
The wistful hours
o'r the years, the years
But Purpose!!—Purpose Doing—Results!?!
And working hard,
At it!!
Deck of Lost Souls
An end—where we began—in the beginning.
In the beginning—God!!, Alá!!
Deck of Lost Souls
From this deck, from here. A grey, mist, ghost ship filled to brim,
Determinedly cutting the waves, with apparitional, grey, lonely soulfulness.
Is!?!—Something's being done.
Deck of Lost Souls

Richard Brooks
C POEM SCENES
In a days labor; some musings.
I saw a sea of sweeping seashells, like light,
Dancing with and within the waves above.
And wide, wide vistas; panoramas of undersea varied.
Of coral and azule-verdant, jade-like colors.
magnificent beauty.
Dancing and dancing colors of darting fishes,
in the mid-sea depths:
of a sea-mermaid of tawny hue
with lips so sweet as rainbows buds,
of nineteen shades of black and brown
To fair, sepia-red, cheery-hued innocence

to enhance her smile.
Or the mind of the seeker of sweetness
of her lips blushing, brush of kiss.
The spirit of exhilaration and yearning
Still dwells within: Awe!!
Her freshness; on Freshness
or perfection of beauty!!

Takeru Eno
EASTER & JULIANNE

His name was Easter Jones
Rode into town one day, pal of Doc Holiday
Killed five men just for hell of it
A no goodnik some said
A drifter, fast with the gun, though
And Julianne ran the local pub
"Howdy cowboy, have a drink on me"
The showdown, like all westerns, had to come, did
Local punk, wanted to make a reputation
"Draw, Easter, Draw, I'm not afraid of ya"
Bang Pow Bam Wham Patoooo Whizzed
Bullets by the hundreds
Killed each other off, some said spread, rumors
Not so Easter stood tall again
Just another victim, blew smoke from
End of his gun barrel,
Holstered gun another notch
To file on handle
"Goodbye, Julianne"
"Goodbye Cowboy"
Slowly rode out of town, the drifter,
The Gunslinger, from (a ghost) out of the past.

Michelle Faye Rohrs
WHY I CRY

Why can't there be peace and love
Why not swans and pretty doves
Help the homeless and the sick too
Give a helping hand to me and you
Why is there war and poverty
Where is the love
Where could it be
Why do we fight and cry all night
If you have the answers please tell me
I don't want war and poverty.

Carmella Rosa
THE OLD MAN

This poem is dedicated to my loving husband, Luis.

While passing by the Nursing home I noticed an old man sitting in a garden swing located underneath an old tree,
He just swung to and fro, looking so sad and lonely.
I wish I had stopped and spent some time with him, just to let him know someone did care about him, but unfortunately I didn't.
Now when I pass by the Nursing home, the swing has been empty.
I wonder if he has gone to heaven and is sitting in a garden swing under a shade tree, this time he must be happy as can be.

Lois E Miller
SPRING

To my husband Dale W. Miller.

This is a gorgeous morning in Northeastern Ohio.
The majestic beauty is almost breathtaking—Oh! Oh!

Peach orchards in shades of pink,
Sheep and cattle at the pond getting a drink.
Apple orchards in blossoms white,
Valley and hillsides of green give a panoramic view of sheer delight.
The fragrance of spring flowers as we walk
Come from peonies, azaleas, lilacs and lilies of the valley.

There is no need to talk.

We just walk hand in hand and once more say,
"Thank you, God, for giving us one
more day to sing your praises and
see your beautiful land."

Dawn Welch
ETERNITY

To Michael, who encouraged me to write.

Remember me when the sun is setting and you're walking by the sea.
Remember—I walked there.
Remember me.
And in the quiet of the evening when the earth is settling down,
And the singing of the bird is the only sound around, remember me.
Or when you see a rainbow arched across the sky,
And you know the colors are reflected in your eyes,
And you realize such beauty never dies, remember me.
For I am part of all of these things.
To your life they add beauty. They make your heart sing.
So though we're not together and we had to part,
The love and beauty remains, always in our hearts.

Jeffrey Stephens
WHAT KIND OF HEART IS YOURS?

What kind of heart is yours?
Is it one filled with envy and hate?
Or is it full of love and forgiveness?
What kind of heart is yours?
Is it one filled with greed and pride?
Or is it generous and humble?
What kind of heart is yours?
Is it full of hope for tomorrow or is it
Still wrapped up in the trials of today?
What kind of heart is yours?
Is it forgiving and loving or hateful and holding a grudge?
What kind of heart is yours?
Is it full of misery and blues
Or is it full of God's joy anew?

Beau Daniel
TIANANMAN SQUARE

Tens of thousands appeared, who were young in their years,
As an army of dreams drew a weapon of tears.
See them stand in a square of confusion
Where the hunger for freedom's no illusion.
You can stifle the cause and return to old laws,
But some tears time holds forever.
Hear the cries when the people know they've got to sing.
Is there no one there? No, we're not allowed to listen in.
Forever recall those who gave their all
And died at Tiananman Square—
Died on the flight from despair.

See them march on the road to revival
Where a dream is the law of survival.
Where a tank is a toy to a brave Chinese boy,
And soldiers are too scared to share
in the joy.
With a cry from the heart that a new life could
Start—some tears
time holds forever.

Liberty stands before us so all can see through the darkness.
Forever recall those who gave their all
And died at Tiananman Square—
Died on the flight from despair.

Rachel Yvonne Wysinger
PAIN

To Ms. Gladys Randel & Mrs. Brenda Anderson. Thank you for exposing me to my true self, and for always being there and believing in me.

Pain, my best friend so it seems
Pain, so overwhelming it invades my dreams
Pain, combined with fear creates hidden tears
Pain, concrete is the wall afraid to let go I may fall
Pain, no longer a game it reveals all my shame
Pain, the story untold I'm young yet I appear old
Pain, the woman who struggles with the child who never had the chance to grow
Pain, wishing I knew how to show the beauty I know.

Andrew Thomas Frederick
GUESSING RIGHT WITH 'SPECIAL LOVE'

Alongside 'MAN,' stands 'NATURE,' in ALL of her glory!

I had not gone far on my daily trek
Down a near-by forest lane
When Nature posed a problem I didn't expect—
A 'PROBLEM' that lives on in my brain!

A new-born fawn was lying there still as could be,
Its eyes of amber shining bright!
Its Mother, I suppose, was watching me
From somewhere out of sight!

I wondered, as I stood there in awe—
What that helpless baby-creature thought!
Was its little heart pounding with fear of what it saw?
Did it know that I would harm it not?

I know not which of us was more ill at ease
In our positions on that forest lane;
But my mind began to reason that its Mother I'd please
Were I to let her take over again!

I moved on down the lane at a very slow pace,
My mind fraught with thoughts of THAT fawn!
I turned, and beheld 'SPECIAL LOVE' shining from the Mother's face
As our eyes met, during THEIR reunion after I had gone!

Cindy Turner
MOTHER'S TALENTS

To my mother, Mary Roby, who has been my inspiration and support through the years. I love you, mom!

It seems that the world turns to you in times of need,
Maybe it's because you do all for the Lord in word and deed,
You're their sunlight breaking through the cloudy sky,
The one gift that money can't buy,
Your words of encouragement can turn a frown to a smile,
I can't help but be proud of you all the while,
The love and care of God shines through your very being,
And you give of it all to others willingly,
When you feel that you've reached the end of the rope,
Christ is there for you, to give you love, support and hope,
He is using your talents of concern and caring to help others,
Whether it be stranger, family, friends or brothers,
I'm sure He sees the pressures you under,
But all the while He is smiling with love and wonder,
At the example you set for that soul,
And the example you have set for His fold,
I'm very proud of you as I know He is,
So you may carry the world's troubles and worries,
But God will only give you what you can bear,
And a person with your talent and love we can't spare!

Robert Benbow
THE TOWERS OF POWER

To George and Muhammad, two fine champions, two fine men, best wishes always.

Punches they threw, punches did shower, foreman/Ali the towers of power!
The fastest boxer, the hardest punch, those two men could take any fighter out to lunch.
While neither is champ that is certainly sad, you better believe they are still mighty bad.

Big George is the greatest that we all know, the crowd still yells "go champ go!"
A come back is on.
The punch is strong, the aim is true, Tyson watch out for

George's one—two!

Muhammad is the greatest that
we all see, the crowd still screams
"Ali, Ali!"
Our nation has troubles near
and far.
Ali should be our goodwill
Ambassador-at-large!

God bless my champs and keep
them strong.
May their power and strength
be with us long.

William C Thomas
THANKS TO YOU

Dedicated to Mae Beverly and Alice Thomas.

Thank you Lord for saving my soul,
Thank you Lord for making me hold,
Thank you Lord for first Loving me,
Thank you Lord for setting me free,
Thank you Lord your Love is divine,
Thank you Lord till the ends of all
times,
Thank you Lord for being so near,
Thank you Lord for taking away all
my fears,
Thank you Lord shall always be my
praise,
Thank you Lord for your coming
back for me one day.
Lord to know you is to Love you,
and to Love you is always to be with
you,
Thank you Lord for saving my soul,
Thank you Lord I can't Thank you
enough.

Ivan Tomlinson
WHAT KIND OF A MAN
What kind of man was this,
That one he trusted, would betray
him with a kiss?
He had made the cripple stand up and
walk,
He had made a dumb man hear and
talk,
The leper had skin that was demented
and ugly,
Jesus made him whole for all to see.
A man possessed of demons was so
wild,
Jesus cast the devils out, and brought
to his face a smile,
The waters and waves that was about
to sink a ship,
Brought wonder and praise to his
disciples' lips.
Some tried the son of God with a trial
of deceit,
Some fell down and worshipped at
Jesus' feet,
All things were conquered and
defeated at the end,
There on the cross that day my
salvation, he did win!
Jesus is living today with God up
above,
He speaks to God of His eternal love.
Now when my time comes to go, and
death I see,
I'll be so glad Jesus conquered death
just for me.

Robert Bathauer
IN REMEMBRANCE OF MY SON
I remember his face
I remember his eyes
I can still hear his laughter
And I can feel his cries

He was torn away from his family
Separated from his friends
Drugs pushed him under
Brought it all to an end

He was a wonderful child
With a full life ahead
But drugs burned his dreams
Left him dead

And now as I stare
Into his solid brick stone
I feel so empty
So scared and alone

He was my son
And now I face life without any joy
Because of those drugs
I've lost my little boy

Danica Howell
WINGER ICE-WORLD SHOW
Every winter the forest near my
house puts on
A Winter Ice-World Show.
It is always so very beautiful
As I watch it through my window.
The winter wind sings
And many birds all around,
The Chickadees, red Cardinals, and
Blue Jays
Join in to make a musical sound.
The trees all have on
Such glittery costumes, as they
Dance to the lovely music
And move their arms as if in a ballet.
It is always so very beautiful
Just like it is now.
As I watch it end through my
window
And the pine trees take their bough

Terri J Horn
WINTER
Winter has come so suddenly
Few birds are seldom here,
The cheerfulness has gone away
And the stillness lies so near.

The traffic noise along the street
That you can always hear,
Has died away completely,
And the howling of the winter winds
Is all that you can hear.

Katherine Vicario
OUR EYES TOUCHED FOR A MOMENT

To Joseph, An Officer and a Gentleman and, my husband.

Our eyes touched for a moment
we both smiled.
I wanted to make time stop for an
hour
just to look at you and talk
to learn about you
to learn about me
and to become friends
but the moment goes and so do you
until the next time we meet in
passing.

Josephine Currie
ONE YESTERDAY
I would trade each TOMORROW
For ONE YESTERDAY
There is so much about you—
That's SPECIAL someway.

All the Sweet-Words ever written
Must be for YOU
After searching the World
I keep loving you.

So please! let me linger—
My heart you beguiled
In the arms of an angel
Let me tarry awhile.

TIME—like a wheel
Keeps turning away
But I'd trade every minute
For ONE YESTERDAY.

Catherine Ann Armato
THE SPECTRUM OF OUR LOVE
The spectrum of our love
lies within the mirrored reflection
in the beauty of a rainbow
having
the red of our ecstasy
the orange of our fire
the yellow of our warmth
the green of our serenity
the blue of our euphoria
the purple of our compassion

Janice Cannell Knispel
ALWAYS IN MY HEART
I wish I could be with you
on your special day,
To talk with you in person
but the miles keep me away.
Although I can't be with you
we'll never really be apart,
Because the memories of the good
times
keeps you always in my heart.

John M Coleman
MY VALENTINE'S GIFT

To Lynn.

That Day of the Year
Is Upon Us Once More
For Expressing Our Love
To the One We Adore
In Your Own Special Way
You Have Taken the Time
That Makes Them Believe
When You Say 'Valentine'
The Usual Gifts
Are Flowers and Candy
But to Take them to Dinner
Is Purely Romantic
At a Table for Two
Where the Lighting is Low
The Two of Us Bask
In the Warmth of the Glow
Created by Love
That Does Not Fade Away
Nor is Lost and Forgotten
The Very Next Day

Tiffaney Denise Pete
BROWN CHILD
Alas! A beautiful child born
With rich, brown skin,
Crying, momma, momma what
World am I in?
Will I work all my life
Only to be beaten and scorned,
Or will I be free as a bird
From the first day's morn?

Sophia K Lilles
HOME AT LAST
With a flash of
a smile,
an acknowledging
nod,
an appreciative
glance
the affable manner
such eloquence!
Mutual admiration,
respect!
Transcends . . Persistently
Perseveres.
Are we seeing our
reflections within?
Two exceptional better
halves become one.
Excellence!
Home at last.

Holly Rolens
EMPTY NEST

To our children; Darwin, Ruth and John.

Suddenly they were gone;
The three with whom the Lord
Had lovingly adorned our home.

The pictures of their lives, in color
bold,
Were taken from the easels, as it
were,
And carefully laid aside, their stories
told.

It was as though the time had never
been
When childhood days had mingled
colors rare
To create pictures with such exquisite
care.

How desolate now seems this place.
I searched in vain for something
beautiful
To hang, to fill that awesome empty
space.

Then I felt a lingering presence near.
I caught a glimpse of one with love
so dear
As quietly he hung the children's
pictures
In their place, there our hearts to
grace.

Allison M Kavanagh
'TIS IT NOT THE SHEPHERD WHO CAN
'Tis it not the shepherd who
can kill the sheep
A liar who can tell the
truth
A fake who knows what's
real
Is it not the soldier who
is crucified
The poet who becomes
tongue-tied
A clown who tends to
weep

Naveen Bahar Choudhury
EPITAPH OF IRONY
She was always laughing
And yet all through her life
She wanted to end it
With her own hand and knife.

She seemed to be filled with
So much spirit and glee
On the outside she felt
So content and sprightly.

Yet she felt an anger

Burning deep down inside
Intense burning anger
That she left there to hide.

She had hidden it well
So no one ever knew
Except for one sister
Who she always talked to.

Though inside she suffered
I can still hear her laugh
That's why it's so painful
To write her epitaph.

Jane C Storch

THAT BREEZE IS CHANGING ME

Through very still mountainous treetops
suddenly
an exciting breeze is rushing.

This clean sound is so beautiful
my ears marvel.

Just beyond
quiet sunlighted leaves wait.

They delightfully sway
such bliss
opens wide my spirit.

Only seconds passed
close high leaves are calm.

That breeze
is deep into the woodland.

I long to follow
ears are keener
eyes are sharper.

I'm sitting on the lodge porch
my spirit
is imagining denser treetops
joyfully yielding.

Norman Edgerly

DOES AMERICA KNOW WHERE IT'S GOING!

Does America know where it's going?
Do Americans even care?
Do we live and exist in a vacuum;
Simply going, but not knowing where?

Now the highway to Nowhere is easy
And the Road to Oblivion packed
With the wreckage of civilizations,
Whose roads were with Godlessness tracked.

Our Nation is largely immoral,
Hedonistic and Secular, too.
Flag burning and Bible rejection
Are hailed as the "in thing" to do.

But rightness in living is worthy.
Exalting a nation or man;
But sin brings disgrace and God's judgment,
While blessing is under His ban.

If ever there is to be greatness
Our Country must live in accord
With the God who will bless any nation
Submitting to Him as its Lord.

Tracy Ann Stanton

GOOD-BYE TO SOMEONE SPECIAL

To my late Grandmother, Myrtle Fern Stansfield. Her memory is very dear to my heart.

For Gram:

You have always been someone
I admired.
You held me when I needed
Someone to talk to.

You listened when I needed
a shoulder to lean on.

You told me stories about your life
when I needed to listen.

You always seemed to find the good
in every situation and every person
you met.

You enjoyed the simple
things in life.

You have blessed my life in so many ways!
I will miss you very much!

L Ryder-Park

FATHER

When one is young and carefree
And growing up.
A father is the stronghold
To which one turns.
He is the staunch supporter
And teacher of all one learns.

Upon reaching adulthood
One finds the tie still there.
When wisdom beyond con's ken is needed,
One turns to him for help
In a problem to bear.

As one grows older,
The realization begins to seed,
Will he always be there to help and aid
In my greatest need.

As the end of life's span approaches,
And one knows his fulfillment has come,
He will go on to greater glory,
Still guiding and helping
In one's mind, the path he has sown.

Barbara Brewer

THROUGH THE YEARS I WATCHED YOU GROW

Inspired for my children Ryan and Felicia.

Through the years I watched you grow
And taught you the best I know
I've seen you hurt and your pain I've shared
You'll never know how much I care

I've made mistakes and you will too
But I think it makes a better you
Give life your best and you will see
A better person you will be

Though on this day; you start on your own
Making a life and your own home
Please remember until life's end
I'm not just your mother, but also your friend

Marjorie K Skusa

AN AGELESS MESSAGE

Walking in solitude,
On one stressful day;
I aimlessly wandered,
Far out of my way.

My mind on my troubles,
I found I had strolled;
Into a graveyard,
Abandoned and old.

I tried to walk softly,
On this hallowed ground;
Where somebody's loved one,
Slept in each mound.

From grave to grave, slowly,
I walked all alone;
And reach each inscription,
The words carved in stone.

Each message was ageless,
Carved in each stone;
But the one I remembered,
Was, "He's Not Alone."

Emma Crobaugh

DUST MINGLES WITH DEW

Lost somewhere in the night country—
a pilgrim in passing—
in strange land
where monsters and angels dwell.

Thunder pierces the wilderness,
lightning cuts sharply through the dark.

Somewhere a fawn leaps
through green shadows.
Somewhere hollyhocks swaying
in sungold
and willows bend to watercress.

A dot of dust, a drop of dew—
dust mingles with dew.

Aching loins stretch in immense journey
across black miles
in silence of grave rocks.

Slow is the suffering.

Night is gone—
there is wisdom in the eyes—
a hummingbird dips into the bud
for one drop of dew.

Lisa A Walters

IF YOU COULD ONLY SEE

If you could only see,
To be puzzled by life's little worries;
Can blindside you in a snow of flurries.

If you could only see,
To hope and dream every day;
Only to watch them be washed away.

If you could only see,
How hard you strive towards an aim;
Everything's lost, seldom gained.

If you could only see,
The deeply embedded scars on my hands and heart,
The agony of blazing love soon parts.

If you could only see,
That we work our fingers to the bone;
To make ourself a secure and happy home.

If you could only see,
That the paycheck you earn;
Only pays for the lessons we have to learn.

If you could only see,
To leave life as it must be;
That this poem is about you and me.

Lisa A Walters

THE BEGINNING

Shed your words upon the wind of the night, let it travel unto me.
I will then in return shed my whispers of love into the wind and set forth a new path of shining light for the one I love. You then shall receive and behold unto yourself my world as you are a part of my world. A beautiful lady/man such as you. It rained and there were seeds sprinkled beneath my feet. Into the air arose a raving beauty, a goddess/god. The light shed and embraced us. The winds blew wild and silence fell throughout the world. There is where you came into me as I was born into you. The clouds broke, light was reborn, and seasons came with spectacular colors. There is where we arose as not two but as one.

Ina VanValkenburgh

MONDAY MORNING AT THE OFFICE

The clacktic, clacktic of the date stamp
doing its duty on the morning mail—
The nockic, nockic of the stapler
incising two tiny holes in vast quantities
of prostituted paper—
The greedy hum of the copy machine
ready to disgorge even more copies
of questionable
importance—
The menacing purr of the computer system
threatening a tactical feline attack—
Human fingers touching keyboards in deadening
clicking rhythm—
Becoming an extension of self—a mutilation
to the human condition—

Irene Thompson

BEFORE PRE-INDUCTION DAY

My SON, it doesn't seem possible
That only a few days ago, you
were eighteen.
How I've dreaded for that day to come,
Only a mother like me, could
dream.

It seems but yesterday that you were small,
And would hold out your hands
for me to kiss,
Little did I dream then, that I'd be writing this.

Then I could soothe your childish fears,
And wrap up your stone; bruised toe,
Now, UNCLE SAM says you're a man,
And tomorrow to the Barracks,
you must GO.

From now on, son, you'll have to walk alone,
And I'll stay home and Pray,
That God will tightly hold your hand,
And lead you from day-to-day.

Son, won't you let him take your hand,
And by your daily guide.
Then you'll be safe from Satan's grasp,
And from all sin, You will turn
aside.

Marie F Harris

DIANA

DIANA HARRIS MORRISON, In Memorium: 1950-1989.

You rushed to Death
As to a lover,
Throwing wide

Your arms
And calling him
Friend;
Embracing him

With not a fight
Nor any
Passion,
Standing on the
Feral field alone.

You braved
The Darkness
Like an equal
And left the ones
Who love you
Weeping
For the fighter.

William E Bailey
ROUNDING PERCEPTIONS
Your lines spill in curves
And your liquid pose
Bends my gaze
Down your long length.
You are a soft piling of sand
That shifts at my touch.
You are the languid swellings
Of an undulating sea.
You are the curling breast
Of a blossom opened wide.
I want to bury myself
In your fragrance;
Drown as you blanket me
In warm, wet waves
And see you flow freely
At my touch.

William E Bailey
86'D
Your young eyes pin the stars in place
Hard and fast, silvered guide points
To the winter's quarry.
Tacking on a stellar wind,
I lead you to a softened ghostly image.
Your hands, curled within mine:
The tactual warmth of progeny.
You wonder at this ritual,
Branding it on a pristine memory.
Carry that always like a draft of water
Refreshing a thirst checked four score years,
Until your aged eyes hold once again
(Sixty-two years past triple ought)
That timely comet shimmering sunward.
And you will join that select cadre,
For seeing it once is a difficult need,
But twice in a lifetime is a rare treat indeed!

Caren M Robinson
MOTHER

To my dear family for all their support and to my darling fiancé for always being there.

When I was little
You showed me the way
And made me what I am today
For all your guidance, loving and care,
I thank the stars above
You taught me to stand on my own
There are times I get mad at you,
For the little things you make me do,
But you're always there for me,
And you let me be what I want to be
I love you more than words can say
You're someone I can depend on,
You're not only my mother,
You're my friend,
I hope someday that I will be
As good as mother as you are to me

Connie J Palmer
WITHOUT YOU
Every night I dream of what we had
Every night I feel a little sad—not of you, but of the loss of you
Can I reach forward
Can I go on
I must keep your memories strong
Memories I have of you feel at home in my heart—they stay there knowing they're a part—a part of my life, one that I never wanted to have without you
Can I touch you
Can I hold your face
Can you come back to me so I can feel your embrace
I have no more what I had before which leaves a tear on my soul and a shadow in my heart
The love I have for you is always as strong as the wind and will be carried with me everlasting.
Love always

Mark Ellis
ZERO EIGHT SEVENTY-SEVEN
Zero eight seventy-seven
Standing in the prettiest garden in town
Zooming birds of metal sound—high above with a sonic boom
Sunny and warm
Photographers swarm
See nature scream with red and green
Blue and puffy white—boy that's out-of-sight
In the east garden is a press conference for the signing of a bill
The summer youth program—you know to keep it around
Hidden thoughts that can't be heard
But a facial expression is a silent word
The signing of the bill speaks for many
Lots of dimes, nickels and pennies
The pens are out, the paper is down and hear the inks silent sound
Photographers' cameras start to clicking
Still pictures, TV crews and all the social blues
Newspapers print the story
He did not sign the bill for glory
But to help the youth and that's the truth
Oh what a thrill and pleasure I will never forget
In zero eight seventy seven

Maria Helena Sbrocco
AN ETERNAL PRISON

They say in time you will forget. This I cannot believe. I still remember the day reality took from me my innocence. From somewhere inside me, the scenes of all my tragedies are played back over and over again. They come upon me and never let me forget. Teasing, taunting, and torturing what little pleasure there was. They left only the pain, the bitter sting of those who took from me and laughed.

As the tide comes and goes, it too steals the essence of the land. It cannot be stopped. Each time stealing more and more. Who can stop it? Not I.

They say in time I too will forget. No, not I. The tide does not forget to ride high and rape the land. For its prison is eternal and so is mine.

Linda Whitebean
LOVE

Dedicated to Mason, my loving husband.

Listen, don't you hear
Come lend an ear
The winds seem to say
End all hatred today

The sky and cloud's rain
To try and wash away the pain
Great eagles in the sky
Birds do not sing but cry

Peace, let's try and keep
For this the willow's weep
To care for others, let's try
Help Thy neighbor, don't stand aside

Try to be kind
Happiness you'll find
Earth would be an Eden
If only war and evil beaten

Animals and children would yell
About love, now that would be swell
Newspaper, would write in big letters
There's peace on earth, that would be better

Linda Whitebean
MY VALLEY, MY LAND
Here I stand, on a mountain ledge
Remembering a long ago pledge
Standing alongside my painted horse
My spirit looking down with remorse

Looking down into the valley
Where buffaloes used to be
Where wild horses were free
A time when my people were happy

The place, where I became a man
Where I died, for this land
Free as the river that flows
My home of so long ago

How did the Great Spirit above
Let them ruin the land I love
Once able to walk this land freely
Where fences never used to be

Hunting grounds now all gone
Land where factories now belong
My spirit sheds silent tears
For this land, I held so dear

Tammy L Schroeder
NO SECOND CHANCE
The battle which is inside of me—
As if someone is draining the blood from my veins;
Peeling the flesh from the bone.
My mind, the human "time bomb"—
Set to explode at any given moment.
Constantly wondering "Why,"
Constantly wondering "If."
Nerves unsteady—
Jumping, twitching, as if touched by a razor.
The heart; the never ending race—
Beats rapidly . . .
The battle is over;
There's no second chance.

Jimmie Nell Bush Sutton
GOLDEN MOMENTS
Won't you come with me down to the lakeside
Where the pastures slope and bend,
Where horses and colts are grazing
Their manes blowing in the wind.

A ripple that skims 'cross the water
Makes them turn and flicker an ear
For they know that we are coming
When we whistle soft and clear.

We'll see Silver, Sandy and rub Ol'Dan
Red Rider and Midnight Blue
Gracing together in knee-deep grass
Where they're plainly in view.

They always look so contented out there
In the gentle sun all day.
Springtime mornings: still and quiet:
Time to roll in sand and play.

God made them smarter than some animals
For they know when they must rest.
And soon they will start another day
To sun and romp the crest.

So come, dear friend, the day is waning
And will glide by much too soon.
Let's not miss the golden moments
Of this peaceful afternoon.

Verda B Lester
TALL ASPIRATIONS
"Let's measure, Mommie," said my four year old son,
As he stood straight and tall by my side.
"You're up past half-way," I smiled at him,
And his little face beamed with pride.

Then our kitchen stool he placed close to me,
And climbed up the steps one by one.
When he reached the top step, he stood straight and tall,
Just as before he had done.

"Let's measure, Mommie," again he said,
And his eyes just danced with glee.
For when on the stool he stood by my side,
He was inches taller by three.

Oh, wonderful giver of all that is good,
May this lad to these tall heights aspire.
And then, when his body has reached its full growth,
May his desire for soul-growth never tire.

Madeline T Fillios
UNTITLED
It's raining velvet watermelon seeds
they fall into aluminum puddles
where ants are being
set in place.
I can only smile.

A naked giant collects eagles' nests
and weeps when he kills the
creatures.
But I can only stare.

Walls, that breathe and swell like
obese women after a bicycle ride
dare me to enter the room where
demons promise to massage me with
words,
I can only nod.

I have walked where demons walk
in the dark recesses of my closet
fought with them as they pecked my
skull and left me bleeding ink.
To wake where angels sleep and
plead my case, but they are deaf.

Tricked out of my mind where it
waits on a butcher's block
they slice it neatly into portions.
I can only force a muffled scream.

Ernest L Hamlin
A TRUE MOTHER AND CHRIST
A true mother will stick by you
Through thick and thin, my friend
It's not what you did or do
A true mother will see you through.

But Jesus Christ is more than a
mother
He'll stick to you closer than a
brother
The most potent force in anyone's
life
That force, my friend, is Jesus Christ.

Ericka E Morgan
JOBLESSNESS
My card
3-1/2 by 2
name, address, phone number.
That is for me
and others
to stay in contact
future clients.

The social
gatherings
conventions and workshops
a wallet full of jobs.
There's too many visible migrants.

My card
had "travel" stenciled in.
A 1-800 number was at the bottom
for people to remember.
I passed them out
to friends
just in case
there was a job by
word of mouth.

My new card
was printed
and came in a box of 200.
It professed professionalism
but left off the word
consultant.

Mabel A Smith
DAISIES

To my darling daughters Juanita and Lorelei, with love.

At evening when I go to bed
I see the stars shine overhead;
They are the little daisies white
that dot the meadow of the night.

And often while I'm dreaming so,
Across the sky the moon will go;
It's a lady, sweet and fair,
Who comes to gather daisies there.

For when at morning I arise,
There's not a star left in the skies;
She's picked them all and dropped
them down
Into the meadows of the town.

Loreta Muskardin
A GAME OF THOUGHT NO. 1
Comparing suffering
With
Working experience . . .
. . . it is all . . .
The same . . .
The more you suffer . . .
The less time it takes
To find a result.

Beth Brooks Driskill
WRITER'S SONG
Give me a clean page to write on
tomorrow.
I want my pen filled with ink.

Erase all my sorrows and yesterday's
scribbles.
Fold back yellowed pages blurred by
my tears.
Tear out the tattered pages creased by
my fears.

Yet, as you read please be careful,
Some, we will want to save.

I know the volume will be slim,
Just a few leafs parchment thin.
File it in yesterday's library.

Give me a new page for tomorrow.

Beth Brooks Driskill
QUESTION?
What purpose brings me here
to breathe, to sleep, to live and
die?

Should I contented be . . .
with shallow furrow, halfway dug
by dragging my heels?
Or . . . should my spade press hard
through clay
to chip against the stone?

What sets my pace?

Should I contented be . . .
with muddy vision, halfway clear
shielded from the sun,
slipping smoothly through the
years,
plump idle hands, sweet smiles of
nothing?

Or . . . should my inner wheel
churn with crimson fury,
spinning endless visions,
sparks shooting to the stars,
burning eager fingers . . .
yet holding tightly
to ride . . . the comet of my
dreams?

Beth Brooks Driskill
HALF-WAY MARK
When I was younger . . . I was a
dreamer . . .
wrapped in promise of love,
adventure and wondrous
things . . . I was sure I would be
accomplished in my life!
Now, rarely do I dream or sketch the
drama of tomorrow's desire
on the canvas of my mind.
Sometimes, I catch on unexpected
glimpse of myself, and
the shock of the changing of my
face . . . the years which lie upon
my bones and fold with unfamiliar
half umbrellas over my eyes . . .
fill
me with despair.
My despair is not from vanity . . .
rather, the glance of truth
forces with sharpest blade the
wretched certainty . . .
my journey here . . . moving as
lightning . . . is halfway over.

What am I going to do? Whatever it
may be . . .
if I am going to do it . . . I must
start quickly!

Youth's rich lining of protection, the
fur collar around my throat
guarding me from old age's chilly
blast is growing threadbare.
Soon I will be thin and cold, and
shivering with regrets of,
"I wish I could have," or twisted
with the anger of,
"I should have . . . ."

Linda Marilynn (Jackson) Sagaert
FIRST CHRISTMAS GIFT

To my Lord Jesus Christ and my beloved husband Gary.

This time of the year
Is one we all hold very dear.
It's a special time for showing one
another love
As many years ago did our Father
above.
For on that night in a manger far
away,
There was a child born amidst the
hay;
And in the sky there shone one bright
star
To proclaim His birth to shepherds
afar.
Then the three wise men later came
Bearing gifts in his name.
Now, each year as the day of his birth
doth came along,
We celebrate with one another in
gifts and song
To show our dear Father above
Our thanks for His eternal gift of
love.

Angela M LaViolet
DREAMING
Darkness and the still of night
A realm of peace so close
and yet so far
I lay awake
waiting for the dreams
that have eluded me
Close my eyes to sleep
Longing to lose that sense of reality
slipping quietly into a fantasy world
where anything is possible
Able to reach out and touch the stars
Flights of fancy
run with the wind
or sit atop the highest mountain
Looking out over the world
A state of being
where dreams can make
the most ordinary special

Karen Ann Lorinsky
SEE WITHIN . . .
See within . . .
the look in one's eyes
the tone of one's voice
and
the shortness of one's sentence
means not what one may think
but what one wants to think.

What one thinks
and what one is thinking
is not between the two.
But within the one thinking.

One cannot see within one,—
without being that one.
Without knowing what is being
thought
One's thoughts are one's own.

Kathleen M Sandvick
ONE LITTLE JEWEL

To my friends and loved ones who are concerned.

Will there be even one Little Jewel
for my crown,
of will it be empty and bare.
Will I just sit around and
opportunities pass,
When I should have been praying and
care.

When I stand before Jesus in Heaven
one day,
Will I even be lost for right words to
say
Many chances I had and let them slip
by,
And find it too late now and too late
to cry.

Will I wish all the chances I did have
back then,
I would have told how God loved
them and Christ died for their sins
All they had to do now was kneel
down and pray
To ask God's forgiveness, and take
their sins away.

Opportunities came and many left go
To tell them of Jesus, How he loved
them so,
I put off for tomorrow, what should
have been done today;
To tell them, don't wait for there's no
other way.

Will I be so ashamed, and hang my
head down
To not even deserve one little Jewel
for my crown
How sad I would be for I loved Jesus
so,
To have left all my chances and
opportunities go.

John Joseph Blommer IV
THIS ROSE'S INNER BEAUTY

Dedicated to Darenda. This my proposal of marriage, her ring hidden in the center of the rose. Well she accepted and we were married 3/3/90. Praise the Lord.

We made a commitment sometime
ago
love and to cherish each other, you
know
it's surely a blessing from God up
above
when two total strangers just fall in
love

Together forever you know how it
goes
our future is God's only He really
knows
you've made me so happy these past

several years
like no other has, I shed a few tears

The biggest commitment you could make in your life
forever together as husband and wife
I've got such a feeling so strong in my heart
knowing forever we never shall part

A beautiful wedding being planned I suppose
I give you my love and my life with this rose

Please follow these directions, do just what they say
or this rose's inner beauty could be tossed away
Pluck one pluck two pluck three peddles off the rose
He loves me he loves me not you know how it goes

This rose may be good or even bad luck
when the petals are all gone then you are stuck
I'm warning you now if you don't want to commit
Just keep this rose and don't part with it

If you decide to pluck the petals from the rose
it's a lifelong commitment that's forever you know

Darenda whatever decision you choose
I will love you forever I win or lose
I'm saying this with confidence
not trying to be snooty
If you pluck this rose you'll see its inner beauty

I'm so glad that we met on that beautiful day
though I didn't even know him he sent you anyway
I'm most grateful to Jesus in every special way
'Cause he sent an angel to show me the way
The angel is you well what can I say

BUT I LOVE YOU....

Angelita R Villanueva

DREAMS

"... To my parents and loved ones—Thank you for giving me my dreams, for helping me to aim for them and to believe ..."

If only dreams could come true
Right now, I'll be with you
To grasp and to hold
To talk and to be told
That once our dreams are with us
We won't have to fuss
In dreams we always have happy endings
So ... we should start and stop pretending
But dreams may turn into reality
If it were really and only our destiny

Angelita R Villanueva

"WHY ... LORD, WHY?"

"... in memory of all who are well-alive in my prayers, thoughts and heart, especially Tatay Arsenio, Leo Moduna, and Anthony Villanueva, my brother, who strengthen my trust and faith in our Lord ..."

Why did You permit this to happen?
Death arrives quickly without warning
If only it weren't so sudden
For I could've started preparing
There is still so much to share
We have still so much to say
It just does not seem quite fair
Why did You take him away?
But who am I to question You?
For You know what is best for us
Whatever You will, You may do
Even though it may seem unjust
I may not understand it now
Nor may understand it ever
I will humbly obey and bow
And remain faithful forever
A day will come when I will know
That no more why's will be heard
When it comes, I'll no longer woe
For my questions will be answered ...

Angelita R Villanueva

FRIENDS ... FOREVER

"... dedicated to my family, friends, the 'BITUINS,' 'A GRAPE CLARD,' especially to Divina Chiapco and Tin-Tin Puno. Thanks for being real and true friends ..."

Ours is one of a kind
That took a lot of years to build up
No one can ever find
Such friendship that can be put to stop

We had strange and weird moments
Which never kept us from being us
Others may have ran, for instance
But we stood together ... 'Gracias'

There will even come a time
When we will look for the yesteryears
But all will remain behind
Except for pleasant and happy tears

There is one thing that I will truly know
In our hearts we'll be together
And wherever we may travel or go
We'll always remain friends ... forever! ...

Kelly Dudek

BUT FOR NOW I'LL GO ON LIVING

Thank you to my loving family and friends for their support throughout my growing years. A special thanks to my mother, my father, my wonderful grandfather and to Gary, my first love, I love all of you with all my heart.

I stood in tears
As I faced my worst fears,
The fear of losing my only happiness
You promised you would always love me—
Why did you lie?
I never meant to hurt you
All I wanted was your love me the way that I LOVE YOU!
You were my life
But now I'm alone—
Alone with no one to call my own
And why??
All because you wanted your space
But your space used to near my place
A place that we shared and built together
My life is now no longer complete
My world has shattered around what I held so dear
But for now I'll go on living
Living a life with no happiness—
No joy—
No desires—
No passions!
I was once told that if you love something set it free
I never quite understood that until today
One last breathless I LOVE YOU and I'll be on my way!

Anna Maria Bronco

GIFTS

This is my gift to the world
To bring a smile to someone's face
A laugh
Happiness
This is my gift to you.

For me to bring a smile to your face
makes my soul dance.
To see your eyes glitter with laughter and happiness
makes my spirit soar.

My heart is as big as the universe
And for me to give a part of that to you
Is complete.

To show you how to smile is my gift
It is God's gift to me
My gift to you
Your gift to the world.

Marquetta Johnson

SO MUCH TO BE THANKFUL FOR

Gratefully appreciative for another day of living, health, happiness and blessed for being alive.
Thank you—God!

I have so much to be thankful for
I have food, clothing, shelter, and I am not among the poor
I am grateful to live to see another day
And I show my appreciation by beginning to pray
In my time of need, someone is always there
When I am at home, or under the doctor's care
Keep this in mind—whether you experience happiness or sorrow
May the best of blessings continue to follow; simply by living to see tomorrow
Today is a special day, it is called Thanksgiving
So whatever times may bring, just be blessed to be living

Dennis R Fosnow

WISHFUL LOVE

Far apart we are, I know
A precious rose for mere words could not show.
Memories I hold so dear,
To close my eyes brings you near.

With you as my friend and lover,
Oh the joys we could discover.
To make complete my life,
Would be to have you for my wife.
Think of yes and don't say no,
Whichever may be, never let me go.
With all we know for a start,
Would give hope to never being apart.
Accept my never ending love,
That can only come from God above.
There are others I know,
Take my hand and our love will grow.
Any problems we shall endure,
For our love is now mature.
Breathless I would surrender,
If only you'd hold me and kiss me tender.
It is to you above I make my wish for Love!

Brandi Tipps

THE DREAM

For my darling, Brian Hernandez, I will love you always.

As I lie awake
I envision an emerald sky,
and beneath it
walk you and I.

Hand in hand
and side by side
My heart floats forever
Like an ocean's tide.

I see golden rainbows
which fade much too soon
into the shadows
of a lifeless moon.

And as we walk
we talk and laugh,
about the time we shared
and about our past.

As we come to the end
of that long dark road,
we must part and say goodbye
'til we shall meet again
under our emerald sky.

Irene Meadows

LIFE'S CHANGES

The birds are singing.
The flower's bloom.
The world is changing all around you.
Join in with the new changes
Come alive as they do
don't let this world go by without you.
Hold on to life with all the strength you've got.
Be counted in this world
"You mean a lot."

James Judson Schrecengost

COURTESY OF MAYFLOWER

It was an eight ounce memory
This thing I've so carefully packed
And carried from place to place
All these years ...
Miles upon miles upon miles ...
Treasures,
Shaking,
Moving in their boxes, Confined;
Newspaper wrappings
Speaking of the days,
All the ways
People Move ...
Hanging on to this and that,
Some small portion of life;
Some porcelain piece wiped clean
Of all the dust of traveling,
And placed
Ever so carefully
By the back door.

Cynthia Bartos Lowe

DREAMING

To my loving husband, Bart, who finally made the 'dream' come true.

Floating gently,
Humming sweet.
Softly dancing,
On dainty feet.
Tripping, gurgling
All around.

Falling laughing
To a cushioned ground.
Touching, teasing,
Whispering love—
Wishing on stars
Way up above.
Tenderly kissing,
Holding so tight.
Dreamingly sleeping
Into the night.

Trudi Stockmann (Grandi Eagle)
A CRY!

A cry afar!
is really very near.
Emotions work a steady pace
to tell you how you feel.
The Dreams you harboured in your heart
are not fulfilled to that extreme
you surely thought they would.
You leave the sad and good experience behind,
those many seconds you had spent on earth.
Go on.
The way is there.
The clock is our hearts
will give more time to you,
fulfill the blessings and blessings in disguise.
A chance to understand
that love does never cease,
can lead you where no cry
remembered;
or is heard,
The happiness you craved.

James M Morris
A CLOTH OF GLORY

Dedicated to the Ones who served.

The rustling of the silken cloth
Through the cold night wind
The stars snowy white
On a sea of blue
The blood colored stripes;
The white stripes they touched
Oh, how she waved
Through the long night;
Around her lay the men
Who shed their precious blood for her.
Oh, how sad when they spit
And walk on her,
When they burn her
With the bright red flames
Yet she still waves
For the free
And for the brave.

Kathleen Thomas
WILL FOREVER GET HERE

Although there's the fact we barely know one another.
I can't ignore the fact, I want no other.
Since that first day I saw you in the corner of my eye.
I dreamed of the day we'd be together as the others went by.
If fate will ever be so kind to bring us together.
I feel so strongly that it will be forever.

Charles H Englert Sr
MY BEST FRIEND

To my best friend, Rose Anne—E.J.E.

In Time of need you're always there,
My pressing problems you always share,
Whether I'm Happy or sad, good or bad
or maybe just a bad day I've had,
you're there for me and make me feel glad.
Patience, virtue, praise and even a hug
once in awhile, You give them all to me and always with a smile.
It's just so wonderful to know you're there,
a great feeling of comfort to know you care.
I just hope that once in awhile,
Into your life I can bring a smile.
The secrets we have shared and problems
we have been through, could never have been
solved without a friend like you.
So thanks Buddy, friend, old pal for being there when I needed you.
For there's nothing more precious than
a friend that's true blue.

Betsy Brooks

Betsy Brooks
A CANDY STORE TREAT

This poem is dedicated to all my brothers and sisters of the Presbyterian Home for children in Talladega, Al. I know they can relate to this poem. It is also dedicated to my family of whom I was so far apart for such a long time.

It's so many miles,
For a Candy Store Treat.
"Shh, hush, go to sleep,
And not a peep,
'Less you weep.'
Now, I stray,
In my sleep,
With memories that linger,
And daydreams that splinter;
Amidst illusions
I can't keep.
Like broken hearts
That won't part,
And many miles
That won't start.
And while I ponder,
In my sleep,
And gather harvest
That won't reap,
Whatever it is,
It's for keeps!
The Candy Store Treat
Was bittersweet!
Questions unanswered,
Truths denied,
Hearts on a limb,
While sentiments ride.
Prayers on a wing,
Touch illusions yet nigh,
And calm hopes that appease
The dreams that won't die.
Thus, wisdom lends honor,
To truth that won't lie!

Dawn Marie Hamilton
MY BROKEN DREAMS MADE WHOLE

This poem is dedicated to my family, friends and most importantly, God . . .

Being one of five children, I'm sure you know
Mischief and trouble were sure to follow.
Arguing and fighting as we sometimes did, correction and
Punishment were deserved in the end.
Except what was administered was far too severe . . .
For a mother and her children, who just wanted for someone to care.
Many years that followed, were filled with pain and strife.
From a man who claimed he loved her and would give us a good life.
Being somewhat young we looked to each other for comfort and help.
For we all were caught in this deadly web, which I called—hell.
Many times being beaten, kicked and punched 'til you were black & blue
Knowing what just happened to your mother would soon happen to you.
Laying awake at night, crying and pleading with all my might—
Dear God, don't let him succeed in taking her life.
In times our prayers were answered, as they went their separate ways.
But left in our hearts and memories was a lot of anger, hate and dismay.
Although he was no longer around, I became a prisoner of my mind and was bound . . .
I chose a life of hate, anger and deceit.
Anyone who crossed my path I was sure to defeat.
The years went the pity grew, confined to a world of self-mutilization, drugs and booze.
My last resort was to take my life, but unsuccessfully resulted in being committed for almost 2 years of my young life.
Feeling isolated and all alone, I cried dear God I can't hang on.
Well I know he knew I was at the end of my rope, for I had lost all sign of any hope.
Then he sent friends to show me the way, with loving hearts they praised him and said this is the only way.
Lord God, this path I chose, I'll never regret!
For my past sins and wickedness, you said you were sure to forget!
You changed my life tremendously, and I am forever indebted to thee.
For you are my father, my brother and friend.
And I am yours forever, till the eternal end . . .

Ginger D Moore
MEMORIES

You hold memories close to your heart;
From your mind they will never part.
Things you have now that don't matter much,
They are the things you will long to touch.
People that you see from day to day,
It seems they will never go away.
But one day soon you'll want to see their face,
You'll want to go back to that high school pace.
You'll look back on the memories with a smile,
And think of the fun you had for a while.

Tammy Marie "Rocheleau" Powell
SECRET REJECTIONS

To: George Sheeler, who inspired me to write "Secret Rejections," who is my Secret Rejection, I'm glad that we can still be friends. And to my lifelong friend inspiration, Mike Powell, Thank you, For Always Loving Me!

I must hide the pain, no-one can know
I can't say I love you, can't let it show
So, now I will write all the pain and the tears
'Cause this way I know that no-one else hears

It's hard to hide the pain that I feel
You act as though it's not a big deal
If I had one wish, I know it would be
For you to feel pain, exactly like me

The pain that you've caused is cruel and unkind
I wish that I knew what went on in your mind
I guess this is what was meant to be
Although, I had hoped you'd be with me

I married so young, I fooled around
Now my heart's broken, lies out on the ground
I suppose I deserve all of this pain
I feel that by writing, I've nothing to gain

Will you read this, will you see?
Will you know how much you hurt me?
My head says forget it, my heart says try
At one time I thought you'd be my guy

All I can ask of you today
Is just to tell me, you're going away
I'm already hurt, so what will it do?
For you to say, "I don't love you"

I want to cry, but, that I'll not do
I'll try to go on and forget about you
The jig is up, the game is done
I know now that you weren't the one

Beverly J Cunningham
I'M AWAKE

*To Randy,
I'm glad you were a part of my life. It took you to bring out the essence of my soul. I'll always love you in a special way.*

His hand never caressed my cheek,
I didn't really feel his touch.
It was only a dream and I awoke,
But it was a dream I wanted so much.

His sweet lips didn't really kiss mine,
Although it seemed so real to me.
Dreams are often so confused,

And that's what I seem to be.

He didn't really say he loved me,
To him, those words I didn't say.
We weren't really close at all,
I only dreamed it that way.

He didn't really make love to me,
I wasn't in his warm embrace.
He didn't hold me close to him
And I didn't touch his face.

The dream is over and I'm awake,
I won't have that same dream
again.
Next time I won't dream of him,
Next time I won't feel this pain.

Rachel Anne Pugh
WONDER WALKS
Many times I wonder through
the forest trees, looking for a
life of happiness.
The trees bend over like a
tunnel. The heaven
skies are blue above. Underfoot
is the wet, cold ground and
under that the burning hell.
The wild animals make their
quiet noises, the wind whistling
softly. I'm always looking for
a life of happiness for eternity.

Greg Eichhold
OUR ECONOMY
Food prices aren't dwindling on the
Northeast shore
And all the retail customers are
coming
back for more.
There is nothing we can do about it,
inflation's on the rise,
Wish everyone who needs necessities
would
settle down and compromise.
Flippant turntables and juke boxes
frame our minds
Listening to our choice of music of
which
there are many different kinds
Modes of transportation affecting
our livability and the way we act.
We have everything we need to
survive,
isn't that a fact?

Chatara R Lucas
THE SAME BUT DIFFERENT

This is dedicated to my late grandmother—Beaulah Lucas.

This women, my mother, has skin
lighter than mine,
she's beautiful with a perfect shape,
that shows off her prime.
Her eyes are emerald green and
sparkle like champagne,
and I know she loves me very much,
though we are not the same.
She has long dark hair that feels like
silk,
It's curled towards her face which is
the color of milk.
The man she's pictured with, is now
dead,
she holds this picture as tears as shed.
And now, those eyes that sparkle like
champagne,
are filled with grief, loss and pain.
She is all I know, I run to her for my
security,
and although I am her child, I'm a
minority.
This man in the picture is very
handsome with ebony eyes,
and the older I get, I begin to realize.
Realize that this man, whom my
mother said, once loved me very
much,
is the man my mother loves, and
longs for his touch.
He, who like I, has black hair and
brown skin,
was, before he died, my mother's
husband.
He was my father—I wish he'd never
have died,
for he too was black, just as I.

Donna Knatz
A SECRET
My feelings are unknown,
Hidden in a shadow of a doubt
Locked in the darkness.
Only you know the code
That can open up a new world for us.

Carol Laing
GRANDFATHER

For Everland Eaton Ellis.

Daylilies in sidewalk gardens nod our
passing,
Slow steps on uneven slatestone.
Tiptoe past the silent houses
Beneath city elms to the park.

The tin monkey still tips his cap for a
penny
And wooden penguins march along a
tilted table leaf.
Our companions,
Recalling us in time.

David T Culver
I LOVED HER ON A SUMMER'S DAY
She will walk again, her garden trails
This day, and one year from now—
Lift the wilted rose that time forgot,
And still think of me somehow.
She will find the seeds which never
grew
Lying sprinkled in the dust—
The plow, that with care, her earth we
churned
Will have aged, and turned to rust.
Her faith, she'll keep in time to
pass—
She will protect the wilted fern,
As if awaiting her wish fall true at
last,
To think of my return.
Forgotten, may be the cold of winter,
But remembered, the summer's rain
That found her smile, left now to
wonder
If it all but fell in vain.
Each morning window will find her
face
Staring out and forgetting why,
The untouched seeds, sprout still
each spring,
That never learned . . .
To say good-bye.

David T Culver
LOST
Lost . . .
like the whistling
of the last winds,
tossed among wilted leaves
and barren limbs
beneath an auburn sky.
It is then, I've noticed
such little things—
the careless flutter
of butterfly wings
tumbling and falling
in and out of wind,
as if losing its will to fly—
as if in need
to live . . .
or die.

Elaine G Kernc
WHY I LOVE IMPERFECTION

For my daughter, Melinda Catherine.

How I love the chip in this old mug!
It reminds me of the time
Your eyes looked up at me . . .
Pleading for forgiveness, as your
Little hand traced its wounded rim.

"I'm sorry, Mommy," you said,
"Is it broke now?"
"No," I replied, bending down to you
After surveying the damage.
"It will still serve its purpose."

Slowly . . . slowly, you moved
Toward me.
Then, a flurry of little arms
Were about my neck hugging
me—
With gratitude, joy, relief—in calm
Silence,
Interrupted only by your heartfelt
Sigh.

I felt your little body let go of its
Fear,
And the warmth of your love holding
Onto me.
Years have passed since that day,
But I shall never forget it.
And that old chipped mug shall
Remain . . .
. . . my favorite.

Elaine G Kernc
OUR SUMMERTIME TOGETHER

For my sister, Georgia.

I loved the summertime I spent with
you,
Giggling about our ancient friends,
Turning back pages of forgotten
memories,
Wondering if we can ever be so
carefree again.

Yes, I loved the time you spent with
me,
Telling me your pain as you washed
the dishes.
The drops of water I dried on the
towel
Were your tears . . . and mine.

And the barbecue was a kitchen
comedy,
As we weathered the heat in our
flowered dresses.
Laughter, the best medicine, together
with hope
Is our ever-constant companion.

So much to talk about and yet . . .
Not enough time to tell you all that I
feel . . .
Don't be afraid . . . don't ever
die . . .
I love you . . . you're so important to
me.

For now, we must work and wait and
listen
On those who think they have the
answers.
O dear sister, so many keys
We share from the past of a simple,
ordinary life . . .
yours . . . and mine.

Helen Urda Smith

Helen Urda Smith
SCHOOL MEMORIES THAT WE TREASURE

For beautiful memories of happy days I dedicate my poem to my school family, SSPHS Class of 1939, with thanks and love. Helen.

School memories that we treasure,
No one can ever measure,
For each person has their own.

School days we spent together,
Will live with us forever,
These are our very own.

The times we spent in laughter,
Remain forever after,
In memories all our own.

We learned, we shared,
And even dared,
To make memories of our own.

Humbly, God, I thank you
For classmates I have known,
I wouldn't trade, not one,
The memories that I own!

Jane Luzzo
FAITH UNFOLDING

This is dedicated to the strong silent core inside all of us. It is our faith unfolding.

Deep wells of depression
Drowning my brain
Sinking in terror
Can I survive sane?

Lost, alone, and feeling hollow
Like a quivering leaf on a shaking
tree
I hold on tight as I silently fall
Until I collapse on bended knee

Time passes so slowly
Surely I'm going to die
I grope for the light
As I lift my head towards the sky

Inwardly I sob rivers of tears
The water chills the bones of my feet
Suddenly, a flicker of hope emerges
A kiss of life that tastes so sweet

I cling to what I like myself
It helps heal the painful sore
I look to love, hope, and light
I believe in my strong, silent core

Jane Luzzo
PASSION'S LONGING
A full moon leaps out from a
thicket of trees. The luring sounds

from the surrounding hills send chilling ripples through the still night sir. I'm alone but feel a haunting presence. Silver moonbeams dance across the water. They seem to frame a picture. Your face floats gently through my mind.

The magical mist rushes to open my pores. Caught between nature and you I can't move. I surrender to your powerful embrace. I am humbled by my love for you.

Jane Luzzo
TODAY'S CHALLENGE
As the morning sun rises, it awakens in me
Releasing yesterday's hurts, letting positiveness be
What will this day bring? I hope and I pray
A voice answers: It's up to you what you do with this day

So I make my plans bright eyed and full of vigor
But at times I get sad and fear makes me quiver
To waste this valuable time is truly a crime
Because when I look to the Lord I succeed every time

Keeping in mind my life's goal keeps me in line
But its prayer and faith that heals its truly divine
Helping others adds strength and special insight
Making our lives meaningful our souls shine bright

So friends I give to you what I have learned
Through trials we pass from the past we've turned
We're being shaped and molded from the potter's clay
To embrace the challenge of each God given day

Jane Luzzo
WIND OF CHANGE
Standing with the feel of earth beneath my feet I hear a distant sound. Circles of wind grow louder. It encompasses me and with a giant gush lifts me off the ground.

High in the sky, I look down to see scenes of my life flash before me. There is loneliness, heartache, depression. I close my eyes because I can't bear it anymore when suddenly light appears. Romp, laughter, and contentment fill the sky. I bathe in its glory.

Again I hear the rushing wind, I hold on tight and I hide my head because I fear the hard times are reappearing. I cry out in desperation "Why is there so many changes" A thunderous voice speaks "We must all answer to the wind of change"

I feel a whirling sensation pulling me down and I close my eyes as I descend. I think on the meaning of life. With a vigorous thud my feet are planted on solid rock.

Christ the same today and forever

DaLoris A Luebbers
HOUR-GLASS
Many dreams and aspirations
We see fading far from view
As the sands with-in the hour-glass
In silence, steadily flow through.

As the wheel of life starts slowing
Recollections come to mind
Of the good, the bad, indifferent
Words and deeds we'll leave behind.

As the twilight shadows deepen
And the midnight hour draws near
We must put our house in order
Before our shepherd, Lord, appears.

Lavina LaFountain
LET THIS YEAR BE REMEMBERED A GREATER NEW YEAR
Let this new year bring everyone Joy.
Let this new year bring everyone Love.
Let this new year bring everyone Faith.
Let this new year bring everyone Peace.

This land of ours is of Plenty.
This land of ours is of Hope.
This land of ours is of Caring.
This land of ours is your Helper.

Be loving to your Neighbors.
Be loving to the baby and the Sick.
Be loving to the elderly and their Needs.
Be loving topically to Yourself.

Remembered, of the good things that Happened.
Remembered, When we laughed and Cried.
Remembered, the despair and the unholy Fear.
Remember, This is going to be a greater Year.

Tricia Liermann
SLEEPLESS NIGHTS
I can't sleep.
Darkness envelops my room.
I lie in the emptiness, alone.
My heart beats strong and steady—
The only sound my ears perceive.
Shadows caress my cheeks.

Escape!

Stumbling to the window I reach the blinds—
Thin pieces of white plastic strung together,
To block out the cold.

Open!

Streetlights trickle through the cracks.
Headlights cut the darkness of the room—my room.
No longer alone I see the lights from other houses.
I doze surrounded by the lights of other sleepless people.

Sandra Bastian-Losieniecki
FOR MY FATHER
Do you seek still the mighty one on the mountaintop? Or are you resting somewhere as the rain falls among the branches of the pines. Do you pursue the gentle shadows of the deer as they drift here, now there, and disappear. Are you there sometimes by the stream when the moon makes light on the surface of the water. Where are you in the morning when the crows call to one another and the sun comes breaking through the tops of the hemlocks. Does your heart beat faster when the twig snaps or when a pheasant breaks. Drops of dew sparkle on the green forest floor. The grass bends softly under foot and you step more lightly now than ever before. The souls of Indians keep company with you on Puderbaugh and warm themselves by star fire when you travel Little Pine and, when the fog settles down on the moss and leaves of home, I know you are there, too. When our days ripen and become full, will we meet on the same path in the high country and will you remember? The world has come round once again and snow is falling. All life has gathered up its bounty of soft summer days and is falling into the deep slumber of youth. The trails are getting steep and slippery now, but the way is familiar. You will not lose yourself, for you have a rendezvous on the mountain.

Jennifer Michelle Mead
FAR AWAY
We've known each other for so long
Each day we get closer and closer
Then one day you say it's over
Our lives, then, fell apart
Our relationship, but not our Friendship, was over.

How could it have ended so fast?
If only we weren't so far away.

Although we're apart
My love for you grows stronger
Everyday I think about you
Every night I cry over you
Then dream about you.

I wish we could be the same
Be as one again
But we are so far away.

I know one day we will meet again
But until then we must move on
Maybe when we do meet
Our relationship will be stronger
And never again will we be far away.

Ruth McMurtry
HOW MUCH DO YOU CARE?
Don't keep me dangling
Don't keep me in doubt
Just tell me how much do you care?
Has it been just a line you've handed me?
Or do you really care
Are you serious about me
Or am I just someone
With whom you're passing time
Tell me now how I stand with you
I want you to be all mine
Don't let me give up in despair
So please tell me
How much do you care?

Judy McDonald
LIKE A SONG

For Mignone, a guiding light and a caring heart.

For me, you are like a song
A musical lift when I'm not strong
A melody that lingers in my heart
And keeps me going from the start

For me, you are like a summer day
Sunshine bright that comes my way
A golden glow, a warming touch
A special friend I need so much

For me, you are like a guiding light
Shining strong both day and night
Lighting up the path I take
Watching out for caring sake

For me, you are like a breath of air
Always fresh and waiting there
Full of life and holding strong
For me, my friend, you are my song

Mitzi Hardesty
THE LITTLE ONE

To Paula Lovelette, in memory for answers to prayer. God Bless You Always.

Hello Lord
I'm the little one
Requesting a favor in-deed
And since you're second to none
I've brought a child in need.

Christmas isn't very far away
And a present I wish to send
Of healing and strength I pray
Oh Lord, a life will never end.

I turn in my star for this request
Knowing you're second to none
Believing in the very, very best
Thank-you Lord, the little one

Amen.

Buck Mayfield
IS THAT A FLOWER OR A WEED?
One day while walking through the woods
just to see what I could see,
I noticed a wildwood flower
beneath an old oak tree
It was so tiny and so fragile,
and such a pretty shade of blue.
Then, I noticed the others,
all colors, in every hue.
The hillside was covered with flowers
I hadn't noticed before.
Beside the babbling brook
were hundreds and hundreds more.
As I knelt down to admire them,
another plant was growing there.
It was an ugly old itch weed
all covered with prickly hair.
I looked across the hillside
to see if there were more.
Intermingled among the flowers
were dozens scattered all o'er.
As I gazed at the sight before me,
a thought came into mind—
how much like life this hillside was
if the similarity you can find.
Look for weeds and you will find them—
they are scattered thru and thru.
Look for flowers and you will find them—
The choice is up to you.

Kathryn M MacKinnon
BLACK, WHITE, OR YELLOW?

This poem is dedicated to Timothy R. Bronson, and Janice A. Stiller who have always been there for me in good & bad times & are a true credit to their respective professions.

We put so much importance on the color of one's skin;
You can be my friend if the color is right—friend.

It doesn't matter about your abilities,
or your talents, or even your disabilities;
Be sure you check the color of the skin—my friend.

If people would only realize;
We're all the same in God's eyes.

Color is only skin deep;
We all are completely the same otherwise.

Everyone is so busy fitting into
society and what the neighbors will think?
Unity is what is important, Racism stinks!

Listen to what I've said my friend;
You'll find it makes a lot of sense in the end—my friend!

Lylis Mathews
RANDY
He runs through my mind
that little, small man
Back to the days
when his life began
On twelve, twenty-five
he came to me
Perfect then for all to see
The years slipped by swiftly
And his body did grow
perfection lessened to a small glow
He brought much love, sadness and joy
this is his life work, this man who is boy
I am very proud of that wonderful one
He is my first born, he is my Son!

Marguerite Mooney
BE A FRIEND
Let me be a friend to man,
Along life's troubled way.
I may not have to-morrow
It must be done today.

If I can truly be your friend,
Two lives will happier be.
It must be done right now my dear,
To-morrow I may not see.

So let me take your hand right now,
To help you climb the mountain,
Then both our lives will be enriched,
With smiles we'll reach the fountain.

I cannot guide you when I'm gone,
So happiness we must nurture.
I'll reach out now and clasp your hand
As we look to-ward the future.

Without a friend in the game of life,
It's hard to face the morrow
But Oh! how light your load becomes,
When someone shares your sorrow.

Kathryn MacArthur
I'M JUST A FETUS
Dear Mommy I'm trying as hard as I can,
To grow, be strong, just who I am.
Please go on and give me life,
Because I don't stand a chance to fight.
You chose to make me you know,
So inside of you please let me grow.
If nothing else just leave me somewhere,
With a blanket and jammies.
So someone else will care!

Richard Alan McDaniel
YOU'RE MY DREAMS
You are my thoughts all day
My dreams at night
Your voice is my prayer
That heals my fright

The morning is beautiful
With you in my heart
It is never dull
It is never dark

As the sun shines bright
The wind blows the day
Like the stars at night
In my heart you will stay

So when you are out at night
Look up at the sky
In the brightest star
My love you will find

Tracy Lynn Martin
LONG MAY IT WAVE
I see the flag.
It's red, white, and blue.
If it's good enough for me,
Then it's good enough for you.

Its nickname is "Old Glory."
It flies o'er the land of the free.
I love the way that flag has helped
Throughout the centuries.

It's helped throughout all the wars,
It's flown above our heads.
And every night think about it
Before you go to bed.

So what I'm trying to say here,
Is they were soldiers brave.
And when I see the flag I'll say,
"Long may it wave!"

Nathalie Gallermo Lopez
LIVING

This poem is lovingly dedicated to my most wonderful (Tita) Auntie Esther, to my kins and my friends.

A kingly crown, a touch of gold
Mind a power, it behold
A gentle hand but strong it hold
A heart that beat but very cold.

Justice imprisoned, a blinded eye
A naked truth dressed with lie
A wine of wrath, a shed of blood
Glittering diamonds, a greedy love.

Suffering creature, a summoning soul
Peace for soul, unreachable goal
Blood being painted on the wall
Black thorny rose, grief and fall.

A hopeless, tired and crying heart
Sweet smile on face, behind is hurt
Pleasure abundant, life meaning needed
Alive and living but simply dead.

Rebecca Lynn Lamkin
BEING IN LOVE
Love is like a dove
that soars in the sky
Love is like candy
sweet and delicious
Love is like the sky above
free and clear
But oh my Dear!
Love is not free
It must be worked at
forever and ever!!

Sonia Lee
SAMANTHA
Big, fat kitty
Soft and warm
You're too witty
At this farm

Blumped and hairy
All over my bed
You're like a fairy
Hovering around my head

Quick and fast
As you zoom around
I'll feed you at last
So you can gain another pound.

Danielle Lenzo
PLEASE HELP THE CHILDREN
For all those small children with AIDS, May God help you through the days and take you to a place of no pain.

I see you on the TV, so small and so helpless. I wish I could help you but sometimes I too have to look away . . . though I can hear you crying through the day.

I listen to the special shows on AIDS . . . I never knew you could get more helpless through the days. What has happened to the protected life we once lived . . . where has it gone . . . where has it been . . . ?

I wish I could help you, but just where did it all begin and how does it end? I believe it will never go away and we will just have to live it day by day.

Somebody please help these children with great care, give them a lot of love even though there's a short time to spare.

Mark Luthy
MT. HAWLEY
Peaceful respite from city strife,
Competition meditative as chess,
Relaxed societal progression—

Days merge into tomorrows,
Time of day means nothing—
Cool round pool . . . motionless . . .
Patriotism waves in night sky—

Sculpted fields, green and icy,
Sweet young things,
Thin—ready and dicey,

Degeneration into filth,
This United States dream—
Money dictates choices,
The mass doesn't introspect . . .

Sand around, in fine dunes,
Swirling angled banksides,
Slipping into yesteryears . . .
What ironies hath life wrought?

Learned something along the way,
Life is animals, barely at bay—
Back to degenerate city . . .

Lorelie J Leafstone
HI MOM

To my Mom—Carla Ruth Alumbaugh—Also to Deborah Colleen Kahnen and her Mom—Amma Mary Kahnen. Thanks—Lorelie.

Hi Mom I know it's been awhile,
I love
You mom and I sure do miss your smile
Though you've gone away from me I keep
You alive in my heart.
My memory is as
Fresh today, as when we were forced apart
I think of you every single day,
your love
Always pours through, I see you in so
Much of me, in all I say and do.
I still cry when I think of you
Cause I love you so very much,
I see so much in my life that
Was put there by your touch.
I hear you in my laughter
I see you in my tears
I hold you in my sorrow
I feel you in my fear
Oh, mom, how I look forward to the
Day when we'll be together again
God, Jesus, you and me will share
A life together that has no end
But until then, I miss you and I love you.

Judy L M Lewis
WRITTEN IN PAIN
Behold!
A craven mortal am I!
In my pain and fear
I cringe and throw up my hands.
All is lost!
I go with the tide;
I sink to the bottom of the ocean.
But, I don't care.
Gladly,
I—who minutes ago was complacent
in my strength
embrace death.

Harold Lunderby
DON'T GIVE UP
When your heart is all broken
And your eyes are all awash with tears
Just remember that your hearing teacher
Will be with you through all the years.

When each thing you do just won't turn out
And you never seem to make a gain
Just keep on trying and you will find that
The shining sun will take the place of rain.

If troubles mount around you
Just have faith and they too will pass
For each and every thing in life depends on
The time that remains in the hourglass.

So, it is that I can conquer life's misery
For it is with fond hope I have for what's to be
Because we know that nothing ever lasts forever
Except God's eternity.

Harold Lunderby
MY LOVE FOR GOD
Thank you God for joy in my soul.
For guiding, for healing, for making me whole.
For unexpected pleasures dropped from above.
For unlimited measures of caring and love.

Let me rejoice in simple things.

I need no wealth to buy
The scent of pine upon the wind,
A burnish copper sky.

Scarlet roses on the fence,
Sunrise through the trees.
Lord, give me a grateful heart
When days are less than sunny.

God give me lips that I may speak
Comfort and peace to all who seek.
God give me a mind that I might
know
How to help those who need me so.

God give me a prayer that I might
pray
Thy help and guidance every day.
And this one thing all else above,
God give me a heart that I may love.

Donna Lowery
MY BABY

For Rikki Lee, You are my baby and I will love you always.

My baby loves me,
I know he does.
No special reason . . .
Just because.

He makes me happy,
He makes me sad,
And knowing he's mine
Sure makes me glad.

I love his eyes,
His smile, his touch,
I love my baby so
very much.

Elizabeth Marshall Lambert
THE BEAT OF MY HEART

I ran down the hall to meet you.
My arms reach out, I tingle with the
thought
of holding you close.
Faster, faster, miles, down the hall.
You are seconds, then a twinge of a
second away.
My arms now weigh heavy, I'm
reaching, streaching,
pulling close, closer, so close.
And you're gone.
Silence, except for the pound,
pounding, of my heart
Collapsing to my knees, to the cold
dead floor,
Screaming, echo screams,
No . . .
Then I awake, to find
it's not a dream.

Robert W Livingston
ACQUIESCENCE

To Laurette LePrevost and Gilma Roberts: "The nearest dream recedes unrealized."

I stood alone in the breaking cove
enraged at all the Sea,
that dared to interrupt my peace
and smash Eternity.

My solid face was hewed away,
and left the fearful pit.
Such a portal in a quarry—
the Sea could never fit.

Gravel dust and rugged furrows
stood opened by the waves.
No spirit left the jagged edge.
No whisper left this place.

Until the day the rabid tide
had brought me to my knee,
I stood a crease of landscape—
then dropped a refugee.

Disengaged from all the region and
surrounding all the Sea,
an open basin of Refuge
the Sea has found in me.

Robert W Livingston
FOREMOST HE CREATED THE SPHERE FOR TO SOW HIS HUMANITY

A generous existence they had in His
image.
All things were equal in Nature.
A generation abided within His aura,
beholding His ethereal works with
awe.
Rivers, mountains, and meadows
made ascension complete,
prior the instant man ebbed by
transgression.

Timid became tempestuous while
Time transformed Nature into
travesty.
Ethereal reflection became man-made
reflection.

By mechanical vice,
man treating man became man versus
man.
Previous mountains, rivers, and
meadows,
became canyons, deserts, and
volcanoes.
As the testament fulfilled,

Truth was tinged,
Tenet became tinder,
Time brought with it tumult and
torment.
Ultimately, transgression met with
termination.

Gayle Little
WRECKER MAN

To my darling husband Kent, my daughter Kimberly, my three sons Dean, T.C., and Joseph for the inspiration and to Audrey Jo Larson for her love.

We managed to survive so far
everyday in a different car
Yet I guess that's how it is supposed
to be
me for you and you for me

I never dreamed I would marry
a man whose life never tarries
You became a new lease
especially when you are covered in
grease

Wrecker man please beware
for I have a lot to share
A life of hope and of love
sent to you from up above

I love the way that you smile
I can put up with you awhile
So wrecker man don't despair
for you know I will always be there

Michael B Laube
MY FATHER'S SHADOW

To my father, Robert B. Laube, On his sixty-fifth birthday.

I peer out my bedroom window into
the magic of the morning of an
autumn's day,
As waning light darkens the greens
and browns of earth like an ever
growing cloud,
When in the air as dank and heavy as
a tomb's breath I hear tapping by the
way,
Muted by autumn's opaque silence,
like words from the departed beneath
a shroud.
I see my father, yon workman driving
nails, and his shadow, his soul, his
very marrow,
As large as life but as quiet as
death, a bearer of secrets of joy
and sorrow,
Dancing on the ground beside him
to the beat of his hammer this
autumn's morrow.

In his summertime I saw not his
shadow, for abundant light makes
shadows small;
I saw only his summer's labor that
sustained my life, the new growth of
spring.
But as years deepen souls and days
lengthen shadows, so now his shade
stands tall;
And breezes whisper, "To know the
shadow is to know the man," as
sirens might sing.
Oh that I'd heed their cry and
acquaint myself with this rich old
soul life has taught,
Before winter's workmen seal his
secrets away from me forever in
some dreary plot.
For even just recognizing his
shadow among the shadows of
other workmen, I cannot.

And when I reach the autumn of my
own life, and face approaching winter
with fear,
And my father is long gone, and my
own shadow succeeds his in
continuity of time,
And when I labor in the changing,
breathless ambiance of a struggling,
dying year,
The lads of spring will see a shadow
similar to my father's, when they see
mine.
My shadow will silently dance
among leaves newly fallen to where
the earthworm sleeps;
It shall dance to nature's rhythm of
light and dark with divinely
nimble leaps.
But my shadow shall differ greatly
from my father's in the secrets that
it keeps.

Linda L Lyons
SOARING

To M' Anam' Cara', Bill.

The emptiness is finally gone,
I now look forward to the dawn,
The darkness now has turned to light,
I feel as though a bird in flight,
I am soaring above all the anger and
fear,
And no longer feel the pain I did
endure.

Rebecca Lyczak
GOLDEN MEMORIES

I will be sad when he dies,
And never forget the childhood times
We would eat the fat off the turkey,
Fat would bulge out and we would
look perky.
We would eat his cut up apples,
Then meet each other in the church
chapel.
He would watch me run in the
backyard,
And he said, "Matt will be your
guard."
I would spend time at his house for
hours and hours,
When I would get there he said,
"show me your power."
He took me fishing at the lake,
And I almost caught a water snake.
He would take me to see the lions,
And after that he took me to a field of
dandelions.
He took me out to the oil derrick,
And I always thought of cinnabaric,
Till the day I saw him I said,
"I will be sorrowful when he is
gone."
Now I feel that some things I did are
wrong.
I held his hand with love and care,
It was like I couldn't let go of the
friendship that we shared.
Now that he is gone,
I think of what I did and I meant it
with my whole heart,
I will be sad when he dies,
And never forget the childhood
times.

Irma Florey Levi
OUR COUNTRY'S GLORY: OUR PEOPLE

Listen my children while I tell you a
story,
Of how our men have died and gone
to their glory.

Standing up for what they thought
was right,
Giving and giving with all of their
might.

Many were great heroes and many
we never knew,
Who knows, but one day, it could be
you.
Always do and fight for what you
think is right.

Some of our heroes have gone to the
moon.
Many of our people died too soon.

The Challenger was sent up with
seven,
When it exploded sending five men
and two women to Heaven.

Daniel Boone, Abraham Lincoln,
General Grant,
Were some of the ones who never
said, "I can't."

Some of our men died fighting for
our country in a distant land.
Some died alone with no one holding
their hand.

But wherever you are or whatever
you do,
Just make sure that to yourself you
are true.

Cheryl Lynne Licastri
THE SWING

The neighboring homespun swing
moves back and forth,
snail-like with the quiet breeze.
The sun has woken up
as its reflection is almost blinding
against the virgin snow.
The tree on which it hangs
is a massive statue,
a barren skeleton of Nature's past
Fall.
It's almost as if
you can hear the silent echoes
of the laughing voices which played
upon it,
seeing their ghostly images run light

heartedly
about the swing.
A smile is brought to life.
My inward attentions are serene,
as the transient lull disappears
ceasing to be known.

Tricia E Servi
THANK-YOU
So long I've waited to find someone like you
So long I've waited for someone to be true

So long I've waited in hope for a day that someone like you would come my way

So long I've waited to be held with care
And just when I think I'm content you have even more to share

So long I've wanted and wanted so much
you make me go to heaven with every touch

So long I've felt that I may always be alone
But the thought is no where near because of the kindest you've shown

So long I've waited for that very special friend
you make me feel special with the flowers you send

So long has the pain of loneliness cut like a knife
Now I experience pleasure because you're in my life

Yet I still long . . . but not for my own
I need my true gratitude of you to be known

But how can something so important be expressed?
I can only put it the way I know best

You always say it to me for everything I do
Now I want to say it too:
"Thank-you"

Jason Glen Turner
ON THE LEARNING TREE
My mind expands
As my ignorance dies,
But still it is not dead
Wrapped once tightly
Around my head.

Wrapped once around my head

I cannot let it go
Nor do I wish it so

For as long as I am ignorant
I will grow.

Pam Cobb
THOUGHTS
In the stillness of the morning light
when evening slips away
the sun begins to warm the ground
I think of the night and
the gentleness that I found
being close to you.

In the brightness of the day
your warmth and caresses
return to my thoughts
and make me smile again & again.

When twilight approaches and
the sun slips behind the mountains
my thoughts are of you.

In the stillness of the night when
my thoughts are mine, alone,
and time stands still I once
again think of you and how happy
I am with you.

Linda Deville
AS CHILDREN DO
We all should love as children do
Without fear or hesitation,
Giving of our hearts and souls
Without a single reservation.

They do not stop to analyze
The things they truly feel
They give their hearts completely
With emotions strong and real.

You can see it on their faces,
Trusting smiles and laughing eyes
Never questioning sincerity,
Or expecting compromise.

They love without condition.
They play no adult's games,
And when they're disappointed
Their faithfulness remains.

We all should open our hearts
And give love strong and true
Then we could know that special joy
And love as children do.

Rattana A Khun
DARK MIND
Strolling around in deep forest
During a moon light on October year
Voices of all birds singing lullaby
listen along to search for meanings
Multicolors falling down from trees
Seeing it what my future going to be
The stars is so high deep at night
Still unknown if my destiny can reach that high
nature told me as I listen
My decision is what I must risk on my own
Leaving to college what everyone minds all about
Asking ourselves will be successful or unsuccessful
Chances pursuing that dark mind
Nature naturally being that way.
And mile still strolling before I awake
And mile still strolling until it shine.

Rattana A Khun
MY BLUE FAREWELL
Touching the cold winds towards upon me
Autumn spring rosing their stems
Their beauty appear freshly into this world
Surrounding a beautiful voices from all sorts of natures
Sit upon rock was myself
Sighting the ocean distance was infinitely
The ocean waves continuously never stopped
The waves always changes as the strength of the winds
never be the same size as hit upon the mighty winds
Travel many different directions crossing the ocean
Their destination pursuing reaching that star
Some may drown carelessly crossing the ocean
And some travelers success by strength and honor
The time will come to see the success stars
My farewell friends willing to remember
Good times and bad times as in my heart
Thinking through the dawn which is now the sunset
Reflected back missing the good times past
And now, that the time has arrive
The night closer to darken the faded blue moon light
Nature quietly deeply in sleep
The owls flew away to search for their nourishment
And I reluctant to stop the owls from disturbing the sleeping creatures
Except my heart understand their conflicts
Let them fly freely away toward their directions
And deeply through the night, I must return back
Willing to step on instead the past
My farewell to you is good night
There will be million more good nights
And wake up to see the morning dawn.
I said to the new birds just leaving their nest
After returning from sucking all the marrows
And to remember to bid me good night
Which the night that never be the same as the night before
And sleep on tight my friends to your dreams.

Michele M Huber
THE CLOWN

To the alcoholics in this world: May you never "dance" alone, yet, may you find the support you need.

There's a clown outside your window pane
Dancing in the street.
He's laughing, crying, yelling, sighing
For he's dancing in the street.
He's all alone in his silent world
As he dances in the rain.
He's at the point where all is numb
And he cannot feel the pain.
A life of misery shown in motions
As the rain comes pouring down.
Now all motions cease
In the pavement's crease,
And so drowns the clown.

Nancy C John
MY AUNT FLO
I know a very special person
Who's as lovely as she can be
. . . So poised and gracious and elegant . . . qualities one rarely sees.

Her voice is so soothing and caring
Her heart so soft to the touch
And I love her very very much

She radiates so much charm;
Her attributes seem to grow and grow—
And all these things and more
Can only be found in "my Aunt Flo."

Rosa Maria Lopez
OH MY LORD
Why do I feel
This way today?
I am happy living
I am happy awake
but for some reason
somebody make me
Ashamed
Forgive me Lord
I suppose to be happy
And give you thanks
For every thing you gave
My life and my love
My family is beautiful
No matter how many
Mistakes
they found on us
We are Humans
No perfect at all

Isabel L Miller
REINCARNATION

Dedicated to the memory of Harold Hart Crane.

I was a butterfly in a former life;
I loved the springtime scent of lilacs—
I loved the red rose and the yellow—
The cool morning breeze and the mellow
Evenings of late August.

Then I discovered something even more lovely
Spun between two branches of an apple tree;
An iridescent rainbow of sparkling lace
Gleaming with rain drops in that somber place.
Seeming to beckon me.

Faster I flew, into the sparkling web,
Oh, horror! to be seized by a shadowy shape
Which was hiding behind a leaf.
My golden life had suddenly turned to grief
How swiftly beauty perishes . . .

Barbara Williams Hines
WOMAN PURITY
She peered through wise and knowing eyes
Trusting none who loved her.
The look of priceless ancient tales; unknown
to those who knew her; kept well hidden
Beneath the haunting yet innocent stare.

She held all the people there.

Amazement? Wonder! None could know
The thoughts behind her inner soul.
Yet shining through the deepest part
Those eyes spoke strongly of her heart.
Bewildered questions left unanswered
Danced in lightness; or was it darkness?

She held all the people there.

The secrets she kept well hidden behind
Those ancient eyes, betrayed the mind.
When looked into, and searched for long
Those eyes could sing! Yet, an unknown song.
Such beauty! Yet that haunting stare
From only a Babe.

She held all the people there.

For
Melanie Elizabeth Hopson . . .
The Babe.

Barbara Kelalis
LET'S CARE

Let's care that a child was born yesterday afflicted with abnormalities and poverty while another was born to affection and fortune.

Let's care that a person is narcotic addicted, branded and tormented. While we become neurotic from blame and shame for we know it could not happen if we were not lame.

Let's care that the blind dance and never see the sunrise nor the sunset. And life winks without a glance.

Let's care not to hide behind our shields without will while another chills from want of cloak.

Let's care to release our fears to hear the cry of all mankind. Which is reason to cease wars and embrace nations. Only then can we rest in peace and truly call freedom truth.

Let's care to reflect light upon the earth, and not reject our last hope to change what has never been changed. For that will be our worth and the four horses might even blink . . .

Barbara Kelalis
THE CRY OF THE DYING SWAN

Near dawn the wings of the swan spread slowly,
fully and beautifully like the lingering
of an undying love.

Gone as time moves on, one love was left alone
with a soul old from despair and pain.
Betrayed, a broken heart without reprieve—did grieve.

Not a hand to hold, life is cold and a song untold.
Torn and worn she cried to her Lord and he heard her plea.

Heaven parted its golden drapes.
The raindrops ceased to fall from the sky and found refuge
behind her eyes.
The birds stopped their singing and wept in silence.
While nature's streaming tears fell on the blossom of spring
ringing in circling sounds of loss.
The leaves shuttered without color while the sparrow
flew above and sighed in disbelief.

Darkness become her earthly cloak.
Faith and hope gone, peace was beyond.

As she closed her eyes, the swan's wings folded
and as its lovely head bowed low,
God opened the door
and heard the weep of the dying swan.

Barbara Kelalis
SERENADE TO LOVE

As the dawn sweeps in and finds my mind
in the shadows beyond.
It is without doubt I love you beyond time.
I love the rose that blossoms after the winter's
cold has gone. With all reasons I love you
after yesterday's seasons.

Lonely, morning dew will talk to you as you walk and the
wings of wind will stop and sing.
Softly, falling raindrops will humbly caress
your face.
Alone, the sun who tells time will not grow
old. For this love will never cease.

Lie with me by the sea, linger in my
dreams, where the angels agree, God
has joined thee in love, and the sea weeps
for it is shallow in comparison.

Grieve with me when I cry. Touch me with
tenderness when I'm tired and weary.
Harbor me when life has cast me away.
Smile with me when I'm gay, never leave me,
stay with me. Bow and pray for all that is astray.
I promise to give you the light of the day and
at dawn a star of your own. The evening will sigh
a melody of simple words and harmony.
For my love is a serenade to eternity.

Barbara Kelalis
SHADOWS

Shadows haunting you in mist of midnight's mysteries.
Broken faces displaced in miseries, holding lonely
conversation in your restless mind.
Unforgotten places seeking shelter plain with pain
taunts you without restraint.

Tender hearts whisper in sweet surrender simple
feelings you could not understand.
Lies you told, not old,
you cannot undo. Shadows follow you in
everything you say and do.

Can you read the lines that darken your face, placed
by memories of unrest. Both ends of the candle
burn so bright for awhile no longer reflect
in your smile, sharing joys of torment and laughter of despair.
Shadows remain so certain, daringly face you
without regret.

Barbara Kelalis
A PRAYER FOR MICHELLE

She lived till the early autumn of her life.
Then came the ultimate—the Cancer that took her
away. Painful thought it was she never went
awry.

She smiled, even though there was vile in
her body and stepped forward with unstained
courage and pride. Her heart and soul was never lame even though there was pain
in her mind.

She did not dwell in self-pity but always
tried to be witty. She stood straight without
a complaint.

She looked to God upon whom she relied
and asked. Why? Why? But there was not
a reply for reason. Just that He needed her
to sit by His knee. And she did reply, "God"
I shall comply with your wishes, even though
I worry, for you see, you whisk me away from
loved ones, who will sorrow for many tomorrows.

God, I hope you're my listener, for she was
my sister. And even though I cry, I feel weak,
I weep. Yet I rejoice in presence of mind
that she has, gained her entrance into your
heavenly kingdom to be at peace at last in your
loving care, and I know you'll love her as
we do.

God, I'll miss her but she'll always be
amidst my soul. Even though she's gone home,
I've had a great loss.

My sister, Michelle.

Kathryn R Legg
A BROKEN HEART PONDERS

A broken heart once knew love
So very long ago.
It wonders why love has gone.
Where did the feelings go?

It tries to think of good times
That now seem far away.
For once the skies were sunny,
But now they're cold and gray.

This broken heart was so wrong
About something it was once so sure.
Why must love depart us?
Why doesn't love endure?

This broken heart once soared
Like a gull above the waves.
But now this heart is like one
Who welcomes, soon, the grave.

No comfort can this broken heart
Ever hope to own.
Until, in death, its beating stops,
It remains broken and alone.

Karen J Danko
WARPAINT

the war inside the mirror
woods full of sounds
men preparing for war. the war
inside the mirror, rooms full of
sounds—
women preparing for war. he streaks
his face
red and yellow, thunder and lightning
will save
him. she paints eyes blue, lips and
cheeks red—the colors alone
will save her. his hair shaven, except
for a center tuft, like
a beaver's tail. he won't lose his
scalp precious scalp! it
is time to Coup Count Coup! on his
swift Horse he fights.
her hair the latest in defensive
coiffures won't lose her
scalp precious scalp! in her
swift TR-7 she fights
it is time
to
Count Coup!
Count Coup!

Marcy A Lopez
MY LOVE LETTER TO YOU

Dedicated to: New Kids on the Block for giving me the courage to write & their friendship.

I'm writing you this love letter,
because it's made with the finest gold and feathers.
It's more precious than diamonds,
and softer than dandelions.
The pages are dipped in moon beams
and stardust beyond the crystal sky,
that brings very colorful sunshine
into the paper lines.
Each page has its own birthday wish,
to keep it from the cold snowflakes
and loneliness.
Each letter has its own meaning like
each pebble is a sandy beach.
Each O and X at the end of a letter is
a symbol of feelings, the past and the
future is a rainbow of reality.
The holes on the side of the paper are
shaped like the rays of the sun, that
are like fire burning within the heart
of love.
Heaven is like this letter you can
cherish eternity in a kiss, and the
words that are spoken of honesty I
know will always be at the top of
your list.
Paradise is a place you can find in the
center of fantasy land, and candies
drip tears which are painful and sad.
So see this love letter is not like icy
flakes or dreams that come and go.
It's very real not just another fairy
tale.

Nancy Lee
GIFTS OF THE HEART

God has blessed us with two gifts,
of which I could never thank Him enough.
For the most part the going's been easy,
and admittedly, at times, a little bit rough.
These gifts you see are our children,
to add to our family tree,
a curly, tow headed, ladykiller of five,
and a steamy, red head of three.
After being told at seventeen, ever
having children would be rare,
love, marriage, several surgeries
tried, and many, many, a prayer.
A baby boy was born to us, a
wondrous gift of the heart,
and less than two years later, a baby
girl's life did start.

We met her eighteen months later,
this little girl of light,
our son was immediately taken by
her blue eyes, and hair so bright.
We took her home, she settled right
in, our new child of the heart,
our family was no longer three, but
four, and off to a brand-new start.
The life in our family is thriving, to
this we all agree,
of course there is the usual amount of
sibling rivalry.
Our family is based on understanding, and also a lot of love,
besides the love among us, but also
from above.
To you they may be my son and
daughter, but to me they are gifts of
the heart.

Carmenate Pozo

Carmenate Pozo
HIS DREAM

This poem is dedicated to Martin Luther King with a true love, known that "we all are equal!"

Martin Luther King Jr., always
had love, for those that still now
dying without any help . . .

He mentioned to all the people
how we must live, using no violence
because it's not the key . . .

He did it had a "dream" gifted
from God, telling you all always that
he still alive . . .

We ought to understand that
every thing was truth, without any
doubt in our hearts and souls . . .

He still alive in the world today,
hoping that our children always think
of him . . .

This still "His Dream" which we
all know today, to bring "Love and
Help" to all Human Race! . . .

I Have a Dream I Have a Dream I
Have a . . . Dream . . . !!!

Carol Hodroff
PEACE ON THE MOUNTAIN

Written in loving memory of my brother Don, who found peace on a mountain top during troubled times.

I went up on the mountain, with a
heavy heart and mind.
To find some quiet and comfort, of a
very special kind.
I started at the bottom, on a road that
twists and winds.
And finally reached the mountain top
seeking answers, that I could not
seem to find.
I asked the Lord to lift me up, to set
my spirit free.
To give me the strength, to do the
things that life may ask of me.
As I looked down from the mountain,
to the city lights below.
Again my mind sought answers, to
the things I did not know.
I gazed into the heavens, and prayed
with all my might
that God should hear and keep me
close,
not forsake me on this night.
The moon rose full, so bright and
clear.
I couldn't help but feel, that our Lord
was near.
He did not speak in words to me, in
the stillness of the night.
Yet left me with the feeling, things
soon should turn out right.
He showed me silent beauty, with the
stars and moon aglow.
Then granted me the serenity, to
accept what I did not know.
As I headed down the mountain, I
knew deep inside my heart
That this was not the end for me, but
the beginning of a brand new start.

Carol Hodroff
CHRISTMAS DAY

"What was that I heard you say?
That you don't really care about
Christmas Day?
Could this be true? Have we lost
sight?
Can it really be, we've forgotten that
night?

So long ago, the eve clear and cold.
The Lord's birth was at hand, so the
story is told.
There was a star so they say, shining
ever so bright
And that people for miles, would
follow the light.
The shepherds were guided, the wise
men they came.
The townsfolk did gather, whether
sick, strong, or lame.
The birth of our saviour changed the
world that night.
Gave us a chance for forgiveness, a
way to make things right.
The true meaning of Christmas is
what we must find,
and remember that Christ, brought
peace to mankind.
So through the hustle and bustle,
Of each shopping spree, take time to
look upon the tree.
'Cause at the top, the star shines
bright,
A constant reminder of that wondrous
night.

Ruth Mae Lawson
LOOKING BACK

I remember, as a child, I used to
play,
Along the brooks, among the
meadows, and new
mown hay.
And thru the woods and hills, their
wonder best expressed,
With imagination, and make believe,
trees dressed in their best.
For they were people, dressed in gay
array,
What magic, a child can dream, while
romping in their play.
And thru the years, these things are
but a part of life,
A season, where memories begin and
keep.
And in my memory creeps a silent
place,
Where many of my loved ones, rest
in sleep.
The Fall, when leaves their magic
blend,
The colors of beauty for us to see,
Are soon gone and replaced by
castles of snow and ice, where
Autumn leaves used to be.
And in the spring, when life is born
again,
With leaves, and grass and flowers,
and fresh spring rain,
Then love seems to be riding in on a
summer breeze,
Bringing all its wonders and miracles
for us to claim
And my mind often wonders back,
when I'm alone.
To the memories that are tied to the
hills of home.

Catherine Cothran
ODE TO MARTIN LUTHER KING JR

This poem is dedicated to Carl, my brother.

Dear Martin, you had to die so that
your dream could live. Yes Martin,
you had the courage and love to give.

The words of your speeches and
sermons, that made the scriptures
come alive are embedded in our
minds forever.

The sound of your resonant, rhythmic
voice that portrayed the teachings of
Jesus rings always in our ears.

Your life was like a soldier's. You
had to fight, though you were
non-violent.

We remember the boycotts, the
marches and the protests for which
you were put in jail, many times.
This never daunted your persistence.
You continued the war against crime.

Today we love you, we honor you.
We thank God for your life. You
lived, worked, fought, suffered and
even died to make the lives of others
better.

Although you have been banished
from our sight, the love in our hearts
for you will never be removed. Only
God can reprove.

You could not truly rest here in this
world of sin, so God called you home
where you can peacefully repose with
the saints of glory without end.

Kenneth McCoy Ritch
LITTLE TOY SOLDIERS

To all the people who have suffered because of war, and especially to those who have suffered a loss. May the world one day realize that all of us just need peace on earth.

Little Toy Soldiers,
Playing on the battlefield!
In their place,
Tombstones we build!

Little Toy Soldiers,
Wound up by their leaders!
Dying for their country,
Instead of heroes, they're bleeders!

Little Toy Soldiers,
With guns and hand granades!
Soon, locked in their rooms,
Which we call graves!

Little Toy Soldiers,
Now they're all gone!
Who's left to play the game!
Has anybody won?

Gilbert C Bernal
NEW MOTHER

To my wife Ofelia (Phyl) Bernal who gave birth to our son on 5-1-81 Gilbert Valentino Bernal.

How happy you must be to hold
life within thee.
To give birth to a child of
such heritage it must be a great
honor a person of your prestige.
Knowing the child will be under
you protégé.
I the father am, at ease to
love and share the wonderful joy of
our family tree.
Love, forever & Always

Gilbert C Bernal
MOTHER TO BE

To my wife Ofelia (Phyl) Bernal who gave birth to our son on 1-30-83 Adam Lee Bernal.

With child, God's gift to
you and me.
What an incredible, beautiful,
miracle, birth of one of God's
creations.
So complex that God himself
monitors every moment.
In God we trust.
Love, forever & Always

Marian (Ginny) Kimbell
THE CREATOR

Thanks, Lord, for loving me
My eyes are open and I can see
All the wonders created by Your
hand
Like sun, moon, woman and man.
The land, the sea, the day and night
They were all pleasing in Your sight;
Fish that swim, birds that fly
Stars shining bright in the Heavenly
sky.
All kinds of animals, both large and
small
My Heavenly Father created them all.
Lord, You even gave fruit-bearing
trees
And every plant that yielded seed.
The seventh day You stopped to rest
It's a day set apart, and it is blessed.

Helen Madeline Alexanian Smith
LULLABY ME LOVE

No more sad songs,
their time has come and gone.

Give me a star to sleep on,
A moon to ride high on.

Give me an ocean to crest alive on,
and sprinkle rain to wake me up on.

Give me the sun to warm deep down
on,
and some snow to take my breath
away,
and crisp up this journeyed mind.

Give me pine boughs to scent my
steps,

and strong winds to embrace me.

Lullaby Me Love,
to come alive on,
With a star to sleep on,
and a moon to ride up high on.

Clay Scott
A DAY ON THE GOLF COURSE
My Dad and I play golf every weekend
if we can
I hit the ball straight and away from the sand

It's more than a challenge, It's more than a game
but I love to win just the same
When my Dad loses he has nothing to say
Except congratulations you beat me again today

I chip, I drive, I putt on the green
when I play golf with my Dad I really get mean
I checked the wind, I look at the flag
I say to myself this one's in the bag

After 18 holes and the game is done
I said to my Dad, I'm still number one
On my Dad's birthday I'll let him win
So maybe he'll think he's young again!

Vickie Snyker
IN THIS AGE
In this the time of the "Golden Age" a year passes by and we turn the page.
And in this the day of "Modern Man" everything must go as planned.
But now the Christmas time is near. The time for love and friendly cheer.
But in this age of trim and tree the reason why is hard to see.
Why the rush for gifts to get? It is sad how man forgets.
That Christmas is a time for love.
A time to thank the Lord above.
For long ago and far away He sent His Son to us this day.
To save His people everywhere, to show us all how much He cares.
So in this "Golden, Modern Age" slow down before you turn the page.
Stop and look to God above, to thank Him for His gift of love.

Madeleine Hallström Hinman
LIFE—WINTER—MIRACLE
Your hand in mine—Relaxed—in front of a fireplace.
The sound of the fire makes you calm and comfortable.
The heat is making your face warm.
The sky is dark—except for millions of shining wonders—that somebody—a long time ago—was placing there for us.
The big snowflings are helping themself slowly down to the ground
wish by now is white all over.
Have you ever been taking a step—straight into a Christmas card before?
This is it!
Even if the air is very cold outside
You feel so warm inside, and we have each other to come close to.
This is a MIRACLE—without help from any human beings.
Every time we can be a little part
in the middle of all this—
Those few hours—days—of a year that is going away—
to leave space for a new one—
This is the time when you can learn to Appreciate Life.
Don't they see—Life itself it Celebrating!!

Shannan Matlock
MY OWN SECRET PLACE
I like to stay at my own secret place.
Where a breeze blows softly to my face.
A place where no one knows,
And everything outstandingly shows.

I stay there for hours and hours,
As I gaze and watch the flowers.
As I look at a tree,
It seems to smile at me.

As all my troubles release,
I feel the greatness of peace.
This is where I pace,
At my own secret place!

Nancy Letson
ODE TO A NEW YEAR
Here it is the end of December,
The craziest one I ever remember.
Christmas is over and done with
"Thank God."
This was a tough one for me and my bod.
It's not so much the pounds I did gain,
It's wondering if I'm really still sane.
The kids are still home on vacation from school.
Getting their help is like riding a mule.
Stan has time off work for a day or two.
What is a poor helpless girl to do.
The snow hasn't been round to see us as yet
It's just kinda been all foggy and wet.
So while I close this rhyme to my friends
Happy New Year to you as 89 ends.

R W Benyak
MOMENTS

To Donna Fiddlein & Bob Arnold.

If I had just a moment more to have you here with me,
To talk of clouds and puppy dogs and things that you will see.
The world that moves around us, the growing of a tree.
If I had just a moment more to have you here with me.

Maureen Caughey
LOVE UNREQUITED
My heart the ebon night defying
On wing-ed feet would speed to thee
With all its love, long since undying
If you would speak your need of me

I first knew that love abounded
In the Spring of yesteryears
When its sweet ache my heart surrounded
Ecstatically—bereft of tears.

And even as a myriad stars
Their silver incandescent light
Their ever constant vigil keep
Against the velvet black of night

So as truly and as lasting
My heart for you forever beating
Is praying that you'll soon be asking
For a time, a place, a meeting

Lori Jean Hill
WHAT IS TO FEAR FROM THE RAVEN

For my grandpa, who always knew I could, I love you.

I look deep within the darkness and there I find the Raven.
I fear the eyes of the Raven . . .
for they have seen things best left unseen.
I fear the beak of the Raven . . .
for it may lash and tear without feeling.
I fear the heart of the Raven . . .
for it may be cold and merciless.
I fear the knowledge of the Raven . . .
for it knows things that frighten even itself.
I fear the soul of the Raven . . .
for I fear it may not have one.
I fear the flight of the Raven . . .
for no one knows to where it flies.
I fear the dark wings of the Raven . . .
for they enfold you as the night.
I fear the sharp talons of the Raven . . .
for they may inflict wounds that never heal.
I fear the blood of the Raven . . .
for it flows hot and free as the wild.
But what do I fear most of the Raven?
I fear that he may lie within myself.

Anna Weber
PAINT WITH CLASS
With every stroke
up
and
down
Colours splash
Red and yellow
With every brush
and coloured paints
I think of you
'til my heart aches
From bright neon
pink
To dark brilliant
blue
I still and will
Always love you

Beverly J Bloss
CHRISTMAS TIME
Christmas is a time for giving,
A time for Love, a time for living.
Candles glowing oh so bright,
Helps to light the Silent Night.
Decks of holly all in a row,
Christmas trees all aglow.

Children waiting so patiently,
With their stockings all hung
Close to the tree.
Waiting for Santa to
Pass through the night.
Making their world seem
A little more bright.

It's a time to remember,
Our Savior above and to
Thank him for sending,
His wonderful Love.
It's a time that's so special,
And brings us so near.
To the one's that we
Cherish and Love very dear—

Tina L Christ
FATE (JESSE)
Fate in life can be so strange
Brings two people together, but then again
Rips them apart without due warning
No heed to hurt, pain, or mourning

So here I am, a victim of fate
Loving you still, continuing to wait
Dealing with emotions, trying to cope
Not wanting to give up, always there's hope

But hoping in fate, a dangerous thing
Leaves one dangling, as if on a string
Afraid one day the string may break
Dealing again with emotions, pain in their wake

So comes the time of letting go
How to do it, I just don't know
Closing the door to all hurt and pain
Living my life alone once again

Going on without you in my life
All the love I gave, my sacrifice
Healing my wounds, scars in their place
Trying to go on, a smile on my face

Edmund B Jakutis
CHILDREN CONCEIVED FROM THE HEART
New parents awaiting their first newborn child,
A mother holding the child to her breast,
Volumes of knowledge cannot attest,
The bringing up of children at very best.
To bring up the child by the Golden Rule,
When they start their first chapter of going to school.
All fears, frustration, joys, and trust will soon go away as time wears on.
But fears will return when the child grows on, and up in age,
Not knowing what will be their final stage.
The heart will always show its love no matter how the child grows up.
They need the love and purpose in life to feel wanted and not ignored by us.
Every flower with a heart has a chance to grow.
For this we must never forget with all our heart.
Our own mold that made the start.

Kevin Brown
CLOUDS
Some say clouds bring pain
Others know they bring rain
I say a cloud is nothing but a mist
Yet it hides the sun like a glove covers a fist.

There they stand suspended in the air
Looking down on people who don't tend to care.
Sometimes bright letting through the light of day
Or so dark, they turn hearts into dismay.

Look across the sky
At times they appear to walk
One day as a cloud stood still
Among the people there was spoken not a word
But from that cloud
The voice of the Lord was heard.
Matt. 17.5

Stan Skipworth
WITH ME

To Michell, who will forever be with me and within me.

I need my time on my own
I need time away from my home

You also need to feel you are free
I'd like some of that time spent with me
How many times must a simple acquaintance
Fall sudden victim to a complete loss of patience?
I walk on each afternoon
I walk out and never too soon
You walk along and it's soon you see
Our walks allow you to sometimes be with me
I walk awhile with you
I walk slower, just as you do
We look at each other, and we agree
We see nothing wrong with you being with me
I wonder too as I walk on back home
I wonder if I am wondering alone
You walk with me, you go where I do
Do you by chance, girl, feel just as I do?
Thinking again, of all the things it could be,
All you have done is spend some time with me

Lee C Taylor
REFLECTIONS BY A MISTY LAKE

Reflections by a misty lake
In morning calm before the rise
Of fiery orb disturbs the ache
Within my heart, within my eyes,
Of one whose beauty I partake
And long for while I agonize.

My thoughts do wander, uncontrolled,
I reminisce and ponder why,
Beside the water still and cold,
Beneath the ever bright'ning sky,
Of love I gave to one high-souled
In days gone past, in days gone by.

The funeral shroud which smothers all
Beneath its pale interior
Begins to lift, disperse, and pall
As sunlight, streaming in once more,
The ghostly tendrils do recall,
As piercing rays they flee before.

And with the coming of the dawn
The love inside my heart does wane,
For it was treated like a pawn—
In truth, my love will now abstain
From those who like the night are gone
And with those constant will remain.

Cindy Chayko Landis
LOVE

Love is a keepsake so precious and rare.
Something to cherish and handle with care.
Love is only having to say hello,
And suddenly inside I feel a warm glow.
Think of quiet pathways and dancing mountain streams,
Sleepy valleys and rainbows painting dreams.
Combine these things together and you will see,
Just how much your love means to me.
Love is friendliness and your own good-natured ways.
The laughter and the memories of happy yesterdays.
To leave all cares behind and gather memories,
That keep you on my mind.
Love is a treasure much richer than gold.
A treasure intended to have and to hold.
A timeless blessing the greatest by far
When someone is as special as you are.
Life is filled with many gifts beyond our fondest dreams
But in my mind the greatest one there could ever be,
Is the love you have given me.
So whether we are face-to-face or far apart
You will always hold a most important place
Within my grateful heart.

Eric David Lough
THE DESERT

Your body feels like jelly,
when you're in the hot and windy desert,
I can hear strange moans and groans from
my warm belly,
skulls and remains from dead animals
blowing in your face every minute,
my mouth is dryer than a petal on a flower.
I want it to rain or take a shower,
seeing strange people before my eyes,
feeling their pains and cries,
am I going to become one?
Oh hopefully not.
Lying down on a hospital cot,
was it all a dream?
Yes, I do believe,
but, I still feel that little desert
inside my head,
and seeing all the people
who are dead . . . .

Jodi L Sailing
FIRST TIME IN LOVE

When you talk to him,
Your hands start to sweat,
You're already in love,
Even though you just met.

Everytime you look at him,
You end in a stare,
He might not like you,
But you don't care.

It's your first time in love,
That's definitely true,
He could never, ever,
Make you blue.

But 1 month later,
You meet another,
You're in love again,
Forget the other!

Nancy A Neuwirth
UNICORN

From the forest's edge in gentleness he approaches
Watching her, intruding not upon her thoughts.
She dreams of worlds around her,
breathes the sweet, warm air.
She turns and finds a unicorn before her eyes.
She smiles and brightens his sadness.
Someone at last who understands.
I do believe in you.

He dwells in twilight of all ages
Sings ravishing melodies for a mystic to hear
And echoes Apocalypse if someone comes too near.
The heart does not forget the imprints that were left.
The future is washed with hope
The lady and the unicorn
In single bond.
I do believe in you.

Unicorn, roam you on the edge of the world;
Hear the distant muses, withdrawing further from your soul.
Far from the spirit you have wandered.

Now into fruition comes the lady's condition.
Another rendition of waves rippling the shore.
Only once pass you through her door.

Naomi P Lindsay
GOODBYE, HELLO

In memory of Peter M. Keane, your loving concern made me proud, and your unique humor made me laugh. I'll meet you at the End of the Rainbow. I love you, Mom.

Your pain and suffering is gone now,
as is your flesh
But, oh? My son, you still live
brightly everywhere.
I see you in my brilliant red roses,
stimulating my life with your love,
And in the orange and yellow faces
of pansies, giving me courage and hope.
You're in the green leaves of trees
reaching towards the blue sky
Filling me with nature's harmony,
peace and healing.
And in the night indigo of visions
blending into early morning violet hues,
Our spirits embrace with Love.

Patti Connors
TRAVELING WITH MOTHER

We are here, at Rome's doorstep,
Its statues tall and waxing, its pope-washings

Gushing forth, not at all the Naughty Child of long ago,
Who ate, over-sexed, danced and collapsed.

Tonight we meet halfway across the world.
Without the language, without the laws,

We get into trouble buying too many flowers
To keep the dead things between us happy.

I was certain you knew the way from the time the eyes open,
Having worked all your years through a daughter's mind and body.

The truth is, tonight we meet for the first time,
On the grounds of Mother and Daughter,

A combination we have obeyed for years,
Like lock and key.

A language in common, hands so familiar the rings were fooled,
We are not foreigners.

What we don't know, we've buried.
The names we've called each other and will call each other.

There is a reason for Rome.
A trial ground for the new believers, who,

Half-blind, half-blessed, find each other by reason of blood.

Diane M Ton
YOU ARE MY BELOVED

For Harry.

You are my beloved,
as I am yours,
faithfully,
'til time ceases
and we are but dust.

Susan E Anderson
LOVE'S ARROW

String pulled taut
and straining for release
The marksman aims
while holding energy at peace
Arms stretched wide
bow held close against his breast
His patience and his skill
have set him far above the rest.

Arrow pointed
straight toward the mark
Released between a breath . . .
and beat of heart
Hear it sighing
on the midnight air
See it quivering
when it reaches there.

Elaine Lloyd
BLACK BOY

To my darling son, Charles Harold Lloyd III, and all the youth . . . I hope this poem will be an inspiration.

Black Boy stay in school.
Black Boy don't be a fool.
Black Boy tomorrow's coming,
don't you want to share her glory.
Black Boy don't use dope, use your dreams and hold onto your hopes.
Education is your main weapon, guns and bullets are for those who choose to lose.
Your Mamma's and Papa's have taught you
better, the same things were happening in
the olden days and you think it's brand-new.
Trust in what you know to be right.
Keep all your bad thoughts shut and sealed tight.
The battle has just begun, but the war can be won.
The war can be won.
Black Boy stay in school, Black Boy don't be a fool,
Black Boy tomorrow's coming, don't you want to share her glory.

Peggy Fuller Streeter
THE PAIN IN HER THAT LIVES ON

When I see those hurtful eyes I want to cry
Then I think of the life that we will have together
As I watch her out playing I wonder oh so much
What is this child thinking of Today?
As times goes by I feel the love growing in her heart
. But the pain is still there and not going away
Will she ever be like a normal child

at play like others?
I want so bad to hold her and tell
the pain to go away.
As much as I want to take it away out
of her mind
Only God can tell the pain no
more for it to leave her soul
Even with the pain that will haunt her
day by day
When she smiles I can see she is
trying to hide the pain.
Why does she have to remember all
the hurt from her past?
Can we wash away the pain like
washing dirt from our hands?
Let God into your heart and things
will be better little child.
God is there for you he will
always be there so please let Him in
As we look into our past we don't
have to hurt that she has had
But I would gladly take the pain if
only I could
Someday she will trust enough to let
God take over for her
Until then we pray to God . . .
Please won't you come on in!

Elizabeth D Fields

GOD'S GIFT

I am so tired.
I've worked hard all day.
Do I really want to go home and
play?
My son is so cute,
And I love him dearly,
But can he go home with someone
else tonight?
I'm so weary.
Oh there he is!
My precious little one.
Well what do you know, he's
smiling.
That's my son.
Now I do say,
We're playing on the floor.
I guess God's gift of love has pulled
us through once more.
My love for my son gives me
strength to go on,
To do what I must through fatigue,
disappointment and illness too.
Thank you God for love and my son
And thank you God for You!

Carmon Morrison

BEST FRIENDS

To Tina Lewis—my bestest friend.

Remembering back to the years
While I was growing up,
I thought life was going to be easy.
Going to new places—seeing
exciting new things.
Wanting more out of life than I was
willing to give,
And receiving failures and
heartaches!
Then I found you, a true friend,
Who made me see life in a different
light.
Making me see all of life's ups and
downs,
Is so much easier with love around.
Being yourself is all that it takes.
So here I am, flat broke and poor,
But being with you makes me believe
in myself.
You've taught me a lot in the years
past,
Now it's my turn to tell you so.
How important you are to me,
And the bestest friend, anyone could
ever need!

Jiordan Diorio

FEELINGS

Though we were never very close,
In fact, very far apart
But yet that never kept away
What we've felt from within our
hearts.
There was some sort of bonding,
A kind of unseen force.
It was tamer than a kitten,
Yet stronger than a horse.
You can feel it in the air,
It's the tension, as it mounts.
You're worried about what to say,
For every little thing counts.
Though we never will be close,
In fact, very far apart.
There'll always be a special gift
We've felt right from the start.

Tammy Sherrod

RAIN

The world is silent,
as the rain falls, to
cleanse, and
purify.

The black clouds
move slowly as
the continued
pitter-patter of the
rain soothes
a weary soul.

The drops move slowly,
running, fleeing,
down the window,
to get where?
they gain speed
until, Plop!
they come to their
end.

Marla J Boomershine

THIS RING

You gave me this ring
All shiny and new.
I took this ring
To promise me to you.

Now this ring
Is growing old,
And I no longer
Have you to hold.

This ring you gave me
Was to demonstrate
A never ending love,
A love that ended by such sad
fate.

The circle of this ring
Is still never ending,
But our love is still
Ever so fading.

Erinn R Norton

FEELING OF LOVE

I am feeling a feeling
I cannot hide
A confusing, scary feeling
A feeling called love
The one I once loved
Turned on me, used me
And left me for someone else on
mind
But, all the wishes or changes
Could never change
This feeling I have for him
Called true love!

Ashley Smith

THE ART OF FRIENDSHIP

To mom, my inspiration.

The art of friendship isn't paint
A canvas filled with fruit or saints
A water color scene of rain
Or a pen and papers thoughts of pain
Hate or sadness just won't do
The art of friendship is the art of you.

Cheryl Hanson

THE DOWN SIDE OF HIGH

Baby you've had your fun,
You've gotten high,
Now look at what you've done,
You got involved with a hit and run!

Mama won't forgive,
And Daddy won't forget!
Baby you're going to get;
Everything you deserve.

Police won't let you out of here,
Every time you think,
You need a smoke—
or a drink

You can't get high
You can't have fun
Because of what you have
done.

Brenda A Grant

THE POET AND THE POEM

Sometimes my sense slip, then slide
Into a strange other world.
A strange other me.

I see what cannot be seen
And feel what is not to be felt
In a solid, stable world

Colors shift, sometimes cry out loud
The wind talks to me, sighing in the
trees,
In this strange other world of me.

Then from the knowledge told by the
wind
A poem is born
From this strange other me.

Michael P Macklin

THE WALL

A wall,
of stone and sand
brought crashing down by
mortal hand;
by moral heart
that knows the truth—
Freedom, no blood on our teeth
from the wire we were to chew . . .
Free—
to dance in the rain,
and bask in the sun;
with a cry to heaven
and a hand on our breast
we are free to breathe,
at last.

Dottie Black

HOLIDAYS

To my husband, Darrin, with all my love forever.

My heart was empty
till I met you,
You opened its doors
and let your love flow through.

I thanked God on Thanksgiving
for giving me your love,
The best gift at Christmas
was your love all wrapped up.

Now another celebration
is closing near,
and I'm so glad to celebrate it
with you here.

I give you all my love
this Valentine's Day,
To you, from me
in every way.

Russell J Caruso

FREEDOM

Women—Women—black and blue
What on earth—are you to do
Is this the Prince who won your heart
When did your kingdom—fall apart
Gentle hands—that once would hold
you
Now are used to beat and scold you
All was right—now all's gone wrong
Every night—so dark—so long
Heart is filled with love and hate
Fear of leaving—makes you wait
Wait too long—you pay his price
And he can be—as cold as ice
Broken bones and broken heart
You need to have a brand-new start
Thoughts of treason—in your mind
One more beating—draw the line
Find him sleeping—in your bed
Put the gun—against his head
Start anew—erase the past
Pull the trigger—Free at Last

Yvette McClure

LET ME LIVE AGAIN

Midnight sun, hanging bright on a
crisp December night,
One day we will be.
Basking in the warmth of our glow
As we shine for the world to see.
How can I leave you
When you cling to my heart so.
But somehow we knew,
Sometime I would go,
If unnoticed and denied
My love for you goes,
I shall wilt away and perish,
Like a desert's thirsty rose.
Open your heart and realize my
devotion,
As peaceful as a meadow and as
restless as the ocean.
Without you, my precious, I cease to
exist.
I cannot live without your touch,
I cannot live without your kiss.
Please hear my words
As they're whispered to the wind.
Open your heart and let me live
again.

Kimberly Allen

TIME

I'm sitting in my room now,
Thinking of my life,
Wondering if I'll live,
To hear someone call me wife.
I feel I've lived forever,
But people say it's just the start,
I have so many problems,
They haunt me from the past,
Of relatives and friends,
Whom died so young and fast,
I feel I'm trapped inside a world,
Where time is almost gone,
It slips away so fast,
It becomes a memory,
Where things you said,
You can't take back,
And sorrows could fill the sea.

Kathryn Beck

CHICAGO BLUES

Look to tomorrow—all hope lies
there
The unknown, the uncertainty
Fades gradually away
When the image of your smile comes
to mind . . .
Just knowing you're my love
Lights my way—
A rainbow at the end of a storm—
ridden sky

An image which portrays hope
A reminder of the truly treasured
things in this life
And that's you babe—
Missing your strong arms wrapped
around me—
The soothing sighs of each breath
The tender words which seem perfect
for each moment.
Lying on your chest hearing your
heart pound like thunder
But if you feel the rain; it happens to
be my tears—
Because of my missing you—
Maybe being completely comfortable
with one another
makes one take another's feeling for
granted
I didn't think so—till now.
I've grown to love you more each
passing day.
Oh I wish you were back home.
You're the sunlight in my morning:
Not even stardust could be so fragile
A soothing dream
Only to awaken and find reality . . .

Tiffany Scudder
NOW THAT DAY IS DONE

Now that day is done,
I can see the dimly lit sun.
Go across the colorful lit sky
Saying to everyone a solemn
goodbye

Out comes the moon
With the stars lit like
A giant balloon.

Now that day is done
I can hear a silent hum
Saying to the starry stars,
Come, Come, oh please come

Out in the fields at night
There is a moon delight

Now that this day is done
I can go home and have
Some more fun.

Margaret S Fry
WHY RABBITS HAVE LONG EARS

Way back in the forest in a big
hollow tree
Lived a Mother Rabbit with her
children three.
One was black and one was brown
One was as white as snow on the
ground.
They would hop, they would tumble,
and they would play
Because they had nothing else to do
the livelong day.
Then one day when they were having
lots of fun
A hunter came along with a great big
gun.
When Mother Rabbit heard the bang
of the gun that day
She hurriedly called her little ones in
from their play.
She put them way back in that hollow
tree
Then she stood watch over her little
three.
When the sound of the gun finally
died down
Mother Rabbit poked out her head
and looked around.
Then she lovingly called to her little
ones
She said, "You may go back to your
fun.
If you hear a bang, you must run
Because that will be a hunter with his
gun."
Now they listen and they play
without any fears
That's why God gave rabbits their
long ears.

Missy Jo Steffes
PLEASE GOD

I want to make all of your dreams come true. You've shown me faith, hope, and love—and the greatest of these is love. I'll always love you Christ Bennett.

The pounding of my footsteps
upon the beaten ground,
the beating of my lonely heart
are all the echoed sounds.
The wind is blowing through my
hair,
my mind is on the verge . . .
I'm thinking of leaving this time,
but commitment's another word.
The leaves are flying by me,
like the moments of my life.
I'm walking down this darkened road
to find some peace of mind.
Everything seems a blur,
a tear rolls down my face,
I keep walking as if to find
some hidden, distinct place.
The wind is blowing,
my tears subsiding,
I lean against a tree.
I pray to GOD, the sun will shine
to heal my aching pain.

Sylvia DeBruyn
BUTTERFLY

To my father, Gary, for his undying support. My husband, Tim, for his patience. And my children, Matthew, Thomas & Deirdre, for their love, and inspiration. Thank-you, with all my heart.

I am woman
I am many things
A butterfly winging its way o'er the
fields
A flower in radiant beauty
The pale splendor of the moon
Knowledgeable as time itself
As mysterious as the ocean
I am the liquid form of the sun's rays
The wind in the tree boughs
Yet I can be touched
Held by all that I love
While my inner self flies freely
Bringing joy and beauty to all I love
I am light, love, and compassion
For I am woman

Holly Freels
ANOTHER LOSS

I can say it doesn't hurt me,
but that would be a lie.
I can say that I still love you,
but then I'll begin to cry.
Why didn't I notice? Why didn't
I see?
And why does this always happen
to me?
Once again I'm left hurt and
confused.
"Better off as friends" was the
phrase that we used.
That means that you can be free
as a bird.
But to me that's the worst thing
I've ever heard.
I am the one who is lonely
and sad.
When I look at you, you seem
to be glad.
I don't think I can stand one
more day,
Playing this awful part I
must play.

Patrice N Stone
SHADOWS

My soul is the silent time before
dawn
My heart is the sun it awaits
My spirit, a calm, deep pool lost in
light,
Shadows are there nonetheless.
In the depths of the silence
In the dazzling shine
Shadows are there nonetheless.

Your soul is lilac in a wood full of
pine
Your heart the free bird it attracts
Your spirit, the breeze that ripples the
sea,
Shadows are there nonetheless.
In the height of the fragrance
In the dancing spray
Shadows are there nonetheless.

When your fresh light scent fills my
silent time
When your heart on wings soars to
mine
When your whispers mingle with my
essence in flight,
The shadows will chase us through
all of our days
But our love will survive nonetheless.

Beatrice Parisey
TO MY DAUGHTERS ON MOTHER'S DAY

To my loving daughters, Lorraine and Jeannette.

How the years have rolled by
And thanking God with a smile
Precious girls with hearts of gold
Pretty faces all aglow
Yes this a day to rejoice

Millions of things you gave to me
Only to show your love
Through good and bad we shared
Having God to watch above
Ever, a mother was so proud
Raising two such wonderful girls
So I say to you

Dear daughters of mine
All my love from the bottom of my
heart is
Yours on this happy mothers day
Love, Mom

Cynthia C MacGregor
TO STEPHEN

You have given me more joy, you
said.
I love you, you said.
Marry me. Grow old with me, you
said.
Your brown eyes searching,
Your strong hands waiting,
The sound of your footsteps
quickening my heartbeat,
I knew I loved you, heart and soul.
Then, and now.
When you speak my name in the
darkness
You sing the sweetest lullaby.
Heart to Heart.
Breast to Breast.
The world stands still within the
moment
For two doves to flap their wings.
Oh, my love, the moment lingers as
we love
From within the circle of our rings.
Oh, my love,
Take my hand and lead me to
infinity.
Walk beside me. Follow me.
Reach for me in the glowing light of
angel's serenity.
And sing the song of lovers etched in
stone, yet free.

Thomas A Burkemper
DREAMS . . .

Dreams . . .

beginning at the end
ending at the beginning

stopping without expectation . . .

growing from the mind
emerging from the soul

starting from inner creation . . .

movement but not motion
motion without journey

seemingly real but less, a vision . . .

stars within reach
yet reach is uncertain

in most it remains, but a fiction . . .

yet there are a few who do see
seeing much more than the many

it is this, that determines a fate . . .

for unknown may become
and what becomes, is unknown

but action, can eliminate the wait . . .

so see, light must live in shadows
for shadows live from light

stir from your sleep an awaken . . .

for nothing may be something
and something may be nothing

but a dream can never be
taken????

Kathleen A Wild
MY FIRST BORN SON

I dedicate this poem to my beautiful son Christian. You are truly a gift from God. May you grow to love the Lord.

My beautiful baby boy with skin so
soft,
You've moved me with your gentle
touch.
Your smile so bright, your eyes so
brown,
You have turned my life around.

A baby boy so precious and giving,
So much love you keep on giving.
You were sent from the heavens
above.
My love for you and the joy I feel
are so immeasurable.

I love you so my little one.

Aimee Bro
NOTHING TO SAY

In memory of Season Henrichs, life doesn't have to be that way.

I met you once, and now you're gone
you left me standing in the cold
a friendship so new that I loved
so well, turned so very old.
The sparkling of your eyes the
whispering of your sighs
left me with nothing to say.

The days in the sand
laying out in the land
but that was only yesterday.
The day is today,
tomorrow is tomorrow,
left for yesterday with nothing but sorrow
I'll remember you today
as you were, whispers in the wind
all just a blur.
Life is today, and you
have to live on
for tomorrow might not be that way
as you whispered in my ear and
said Goodbye, you left me with
nothing to say.

Christine Neely
BEING REALISTIC
Many dream and wish for millions,
Vast estates and fancy cars.
I certainly too would welcome this,
But right now I thank my lucky stars.

For we have a good home which we live in.
And nice clothes upon our backs.
For some, they sleep out in the streets,
A box they use for a shack.

To hand-me-downs and cheap gym shoes,
To weekends spent out in the yard.
For when we have to tell the kids no!
We explain that life sometimes is hard.

Values are not to be taken lightly,
Never hurt others with foul play.
Maybe someday soon we'll get ahead,
But for now it's just another day.

So never lose your imagination,
For that dream may someday come true.
But until we hit the jackpot,
Life as it is, will just have to do!

Karen K Lynn
BEACON EYES
I see a light upon the shore
To steer us from the reefs amour
And tugs from the seas cold depths
For darkened waters steal the breaths
Of many fine young sailors
And those who do not see the light
Will see their journeys failure
So shine upon us tower grand
Upon the shores and shifting sands
Reflect upon the stars above
To make our voyage safe with Love

Donna P Flynn
HAPPINESS
Many people search for happiness,
Many people search for wealth.
But I'd much rather be penniless
And stay in the best of health.
You have to work toward happiness.
It isn't exactly free.
There are many good deeds to perform,
That you must clearly see,
And as you begin to recognize these deeds,
The joy flows through your breast.
And as you progress day by day,
You'll find you've passed each test.
Now wealth is another story to be told.
It can be given generously or earned.
But in your quest for your pot of gold,
Remember you can be burned.
Jesus came upon this earth
To show us how to live and
One of the most important
Things He taught, was
To be perfectly willing to give.
Share your works with your fellowman
And share your assets too
You'll soon find all the happiness you can
And wealth will come to you.

Valerie J Carter
ANNE FRANK'S DREAM
Anne had had a pleasant life,
Then into hiding she was forced to flee,
This carefree life would never again be.

While in hiding Anne dreamed of a different life,
Like the one she had before,
A life filled with lots of fun,
Waiting for her to just open the door.

She knew, now, there was no turning back,
So to the future she would look,
All her plans for the coming,
She put into a small and personal book.

Oh, how Anne dreamed of going to a new life,
A life filled with happy chatter and fun,
Little did she know,
The end of her life had just begun.

You see,
This happy life,
Anne never would be seeing,
For the Gestapo's raid,
Kept it from being.

Marie Hylton
FRIENDSHIP
Friendship is like a comfortable armchair,
Reliable,
Solid,
Always there in trying times,
A place to lay your head.

Friendship is like a cozy homestead,
With a warm, welcoming fire burning in its fireplace,
Ready when you are tired and need a haven,
A place free from life's many pressures.

Of all things friendship is like a loving web,
From which you don't want to be free,
A willing shoulder to lean on,
To cry on.

If one has not friendship,
One has nothing at all.

B Hoyt
WRITE THAT LETTER
First you write the letter,
Then you address the card.
You lick the stamp and press it on.
See it isn't very hard.

But you have to find a mail box
And slip the letter in the slot
Not leave it lying on your desk
'Cause then it's plum forgot!
Follow these easy directions
I think you'll be very pleased
And really it's not very taxing
Just as simple as a breeze.

Try it!

Heidi Van Impe
TOM CAT TABBY CAT
Stealthily sneaking
smoothly pouncing
creeping
leaping
rambling ambling
always on the go.
Slowly sinking
muscles unclinching
softly slowly
sprawls on the floor.
Falsely dozing
deceitful reposing
always on the watch.
At last relaxing
noises surpassing
the sleeping shadow
curled on the floor.

Marie Coleman Coss
COMMITTED
Wandering through a downpour,
in the dark of night
Teenage girl, spaced out,
crying in her fright
Plodding in a creek, unaware,
can't find her way home
Lost in a fog of drugs, befuddled,
oppressed, alone

Boyfriend overdosed,
presuming him to be dead
Paranoid and confused,
running wild as she fled
Sobbing, nobody cares,
I want someone to love me
Girlfriend gave me pills
to help shun reality

Helped her into the car,
took her home, hurting inside
Gave her a robe, dried the wet
clothes, as we both cried
One soul wrenching plea,
why must my hurt be so deep?
Cradled in my arms,
fell into a stuporous sleep

Committed to drugs,
couldn't sort out her mind
Didn't want to remain in a world so unkind
Should she live or end her life,
too hard to decide
Agonizing, one night,
she committed suicide

Dolly Ballinger
GOD'S GIFT IS LOVE
The gift that is hidden within me,
Is it to let others see their need in thee.
The veil is now beginning to lift,
To let me now see what I have missed.

I understand now, the trials I've gone through,
Were to get me through your type of school—
To learn and grow, no matter what it takes,
In order to gain from past mistakes.

When others happen to come our way—
And they too are terribly dismayed—
We can then lend a hand
To assure them that they too might stand.

We can ease the pain of a heavy laden heart,
If only to listen and do our part.
We're here to help others in need,
To be loving and kind is the key.

God's love needs to be shared
By all those who truly care.
So if I can a friend be,
Then His purpose is fulfilled in me.

God loves you and so do I, Dolly

Val Smith
SEVERANCE

To a pair of orioles who share their songs, but not the whereabouts of their nest.

I hold a fallen bird in my hand
  satin limp dead
my tears are the songs you will never sing
  and the loneliness of your mate

you have followed your song to its Source
  to skyways unknown to me
I have only your finite softness to hold
  in my torn world

Diann E Sharpe
LITTLE GIRL LONELY
It's morning
I wake
I put on my face
and go through the day.
I smile, I laugh,
I'm secure, I'm confident
I pretend.
My face
does not show
the little girl lonely, inside
that goes home
each night
and curls up tight
under the covers
and prays for the
strength to get through
tomorrow
without the face breaking
without showing
the little girl lonely
inside.

Teri Gibson
LOOKING BACK AT '65
Hop scotch, ching-chang, a busy bee club,
Jumping off the high dive . . .
and catching lighting bugs with the kids across the street.
Rolling in the leaves behind the house in the church yard.
Halloween was always a blast, us in our tiger P.J.'s and skeleton bones.
There was always a funny mask to match.
Thanksgiving dinner in the dining room.
Counting the days until Christmas,
ending the count down with blast off.
Visiting grandma out in the country seemed like fun.
Always a plead of being spared from Grandma's lima beans.
Easter was filled with spring in the air
We were always dressed alike . . .
Hop scotch, ching-chang, a busy bee club.
. . . Looking Back at '65

Tim S McCune
SOUNDS OF NIGHT

To my Grandmother: Louisa Wallace, for believing in me when others didn't. Tim S. Wallace.

If you listen to the Sounds of the night,
they'll help you understand the light.
Just listen, as the mockingbird sings,
and you'll learn many things.
They sing of glory, and of pain,
and of simple pleasures, you can gain.
This if just one of the sounds of night,
so in your heart, you must listen without fright.
Don't be afraid to listen and learn,
for when the night is over, the light will return.

Brain T Yanez
THE WORST FEAR
What is all this that I fear
Is it all the strange noises that I hear
Could it be the foot steps coming down the hall
Or, the shadows which dance upon the wall
Maybe it's the saddened darkness of the lonely night
Which causes all my dreadful fright
But maybe it's not all that I can see
The worst fear I have is being me

Dorothy Watkins
MONEY
Money the root of all evil
Can also be used for things civil
Or much good when one is ill
And even to help with God's will
It's not the paper bill that's bad
Or any gold or jewels that's had
It's how the owner of these react
Are they clutched or used in a way relaxed?
One should be respectful and saving
But not so much as to spoil their living
Like some who make money their god
Letting nothing else come into their head
They're slaves to a piece of paper
All their lives and into hereafter
Never really seeing beautiful trees
Or smell the flowers or view autumn leaves
The only green they see is money
When they're aged they'll be very lonely
Cold, bitter, and almost cruel
Seems money has made them, into a fool

Terry Ann Rieser
ONLY YOU AND I
Whisper something true and dear
Something only you and I can hear
Then take my hand
Follow me
I'll lead you to my secret fare

A world so bright intense with care
A deeply felt child at play

Fields of lavish hopes and dreams
Fields so rich that time stops here
And shares

Secret moments only you and I can hear
One more moment, one more look
A sudden brief knowledge
Of the love kept there
Then take my hand
Follow me, back to have
The whisper soft and sweet that
Only you and I can hear

John Valentic
LADY OF TROY
What silent secret path within that I did tread
Beckoned by your influence
Yet best by your presence
A wondrous rosy journey
Through the summer of emotions
Splashed colored across my soul
Left indelibly imprinted
And richly scented in my thoughts
Where you have taken me

And what old rusted chains were loosed
And cast away, no longer binding
Once held me tight in sorrows
Of lost and gone yesterdays
What power did you use
To free me from such weathered bonds?
And lift my face to freedom

Who's the old flame, it matters not
For I can share you better
Than a sullen thought of past
Can worry or can slight you,
And ease those shadow guilts that would
Pursue you closely with their silent doubts
For shame will have no foothold here
Within my heart and simply falls away.

If you direct me to another friend
Reluctantly I'll follow,
Forgive me if I stray to you
And drop the masquerade
It's you I love so more and want
To take me once again
Upon this chariot of dreams
A ride to never end

John Valentic
THANKSGIVING
Oh how I thank the powers to be
that brought your loving soul to me
And how I wish to say to them
I love you so my dear sweet friend
Let all eternity rejoice
That God has given me this voice
Which praises, thanks, appreciates
The love you bring me everyday
With gratitude in every thought
To have this wondrous love I've sought
That's power beyond all I've known
And riches more no man has found
So I with reverence shine forth too,
Oh thank the universe for you!

Toni Marie McCollom
DREAMS
Can I ever teach or show you that making your dreams come true,
Is something that no matter what anyone says—you must do.
Life is based on your hopes and dreams,
And you don't have to accept only what life deems.
My dreams are not and never will be the same as yours,
But give in a little, have faith and trust and for you it will open doors.
These doors may open and close through life at times you want them least,
But your lives will come together like mine, a jigsaw puzzle so perfectly pieced.

Miriam A Rodriguez
NATURAL WONDERS

To Emil: All my thanks!

It came to me whilst asleep
Of how seldom we stop to see
The wonderful virtues we behold
Given freely to us by the Creator

Golden star proclaims its throne
Break of dawn brings new life
Green fields sprinkled with crystal balls
Waltz gaily in the gentle breeze

Puffed ivory clouds, sea-blue skies
Peacefully embracing ancient skies
Keeping guard of nature's precious beauties
Most worthy than all Kings' wealth

Evening borne; crimson skies aloof
Brings to close a glorious day
In the west the sun is set
Slowly descending to its rest

All too soon the glamour fades
Before our eyes the veil unfolds
Revealing millions of silver eyes
Mother Mary and baby Jesus Christ
Embracing within the moonlight

Donald Mokriy Jr
IMAGE A NATION

Dedicated to my Darling Dana who inspired my thoughts, Mr. Roy Petty who encouraged my imagination and those who wish for a better tomorrow.

People thinking they're real 'cause they're here
Seeming to be here 'cause they're now
Forgetting, to be truly now, here is to be nowhere
Does it not seem merry thinking one has the power to choose?
But if one chooses to think he'll find his merry going round;
Getting nowhere
Revolution, a black and white involution
Truth singing whispers in the wind,
Whilst democracy sees favor in the only solution
The see of love holding the answer;
One world, a nation undoing virtuous pestilence
With flower covered guns whose bullets are made from innocent
Mutations, making two into one
Painting a portrait of an idealist world
Assassinating any word that shouldn't be heard
To be; a role defined by a clock
Is it rhyme or rhapsody? You ask me you tell me
Image a nation whose will sets the clock
Moving ahead with its head turned behind
Seeing the child in time just learning to crawl
Although not being able to catch its great fall

Andrea Johnson
POWER TO RISE!
"Life is just a big puzzle, and trying to find
all the pieces that fit," said the old man,
"takes most of your life and that's it!"
"So make a wish," I replied, "just for you,
we all know. Sometimes wishes come true!"

"What could I wish more," said the man, "than to be wise,
because wisdom means power to rise;
above all of the feelings I dread,
Anger and bitterness, feelings like that!
And most of all fear," said the man, "do you hear!?
Fear is a Tranquilizer for body and mind!
Fear can grind to the bone of your soul
and take control over you, at all times,
whatever you do!
And that's why I wish to be side,
because wisdom will give me the Power to rise!"

Andrea Johnson
SEEKING THE SPICE OF LIFE!

Dedicated to Melanie, for all you've done!

It has become so rare,
that hardly it is found.
for we all wish to share,
the Spice of Life, that goes around.

We try, and try, and try,
desperate we are, to find a clue,
to our existence that is, and why
we sometimes do the things we do!

The human vision now is hazy,
Money and Greed dominate,
our minds are fat and lazy,
and all we do is hate, Hate, Hate!

So what can save us anymore, and how?
while evil destruction is reaching its Goal!
The Spice of Life lays dormant now,
In each and every Soul!

The Mauldin Family

Patricia Marie Mauldin
SINCE OF YOU

This poem is dedicated to Danny, my loving husband of nineteen years and my two wonderful children, Tonia and Brian who believe in their mom.

My love and kisses I'll share with you
No one else in this world will do

To make me feel the way I feel.
My love for you so strong and real.

I'm happy to be yours and shall belong.
In your arms so tender and strong.
Your unselfish love keeps me ever near.
You are my sweetheart, you are my dear.

I'll be your honey, I'll do you no wrong.
I'll stay by your side, forever so long.
Please never worry, or ever feel doubt,
Because it's you I could never live without.

I've grown thru you in so many ways.
You've been patient and kind in my bad days.
I wish to say Thank You, but no words can I find.
To express all the joys in my heart deep inside.

Debbie Christian

FULL MEASURE

Seeping into your being like salts into the brook
it leaves a distinctive tang.
Some say the water's spoiled,
perhaps, too, the soul . . .

The meager measure of unrest having poured its contents
into the lifestream,
is never really purged,
only subdued,
till rivers overrun the brook,
and lakes spilling into the rivers
diminish its very essence . . .
Only to return to the restless ocean itself,
and the salts,
fourfold . . .

Debbie Christian

OF THIS BLUE

In gentle furls of watered silk reflecting
off time's summer skies,
Through cool and tinted crystal
I can see into the depths reaching so deep and far
that I cannot but hope to glimpse
what waits there.
Live all the secrets brought to light in this
sacred shade of blue.
Of all the hues within the prism's realm—
Yours to spin my vibrant wheel of life.
Turning through all mist and dark
I'll no more lie in trembling.
This tranquil shade of blue,
This warm electric blue,
This laughing splash of blue
is reaching from your loving gaze.

Chris Boesswetter

TELL ME . . . IF YOU KNOW . . .

This is dedicated to a very special friend. He has inspired me, frustrated me, and has changed my life in so many ways . . . but most of all, he has shown me what real love is.

How does one control
the yearning of one's soul?
The heart is the center of existence
powerful . . . yet powerless
Brimming with hope and understanding
Fragile . . . yet courageous.

When someone special
comes into the life of another
The soul takes on a new outlook
feels alive . . . so many things to discover.
Tell me then . . . if you know . . .
when time is so precious
Why people who care
have so much trouble
Finding the time to spare?

Kelley Harper

LIFE

A harp playing
Sweet
Low and quiet
Silky and smooth
A tear
Colors of the rainbow
MOM

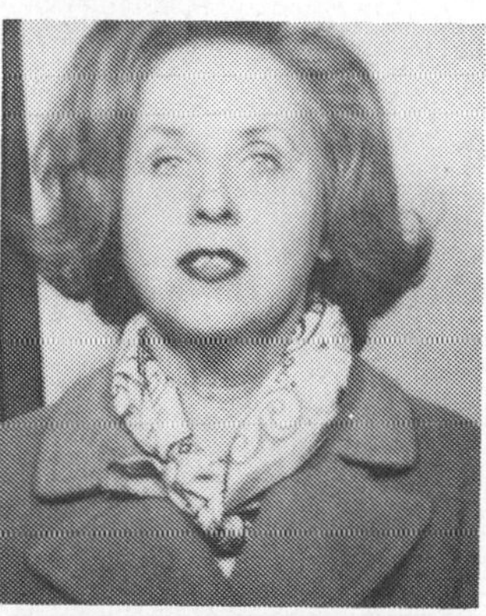

Gloria Unger

Gloria Unger

LIFE

I'll walk down the road, the signposts I'll pass
Each one tells me how much further
I'll walk on the grass,
Life is the wide road we all passeth down
How long the road is, is really not known
Each one of the roads is a little bit different
All the signs vary and they all leave an imprint.
Let's walk with a smile, a toss of the head, and eyes open wide.
Take the warnings in time, don't latch on for a ride,
Read all the signs, careful and clear,
They'll tell you the detours to fear,
They'll tell you how much closer you'll get.
You'll laugh, and you'll smile, you'll cry and you'll fret
To complete all the things that you are designated to,
To help, to make, and remember above all, enjoy what you do.

Dannie C Daube

THE NIGHT EXPLODES

The night explodes
with a passion
Hearts pound
in rhythmic fashion.
Silky beads of sweat
drip from your head
Satin sheets
caress the bed.
The lights are dim
the music low
Your gentle touch
soft and slow.
We have not a worry
We have not a fret
We made a deal
To be celibate.

Dannie C Daube

THE NONCOMMITTAL DRIFTER

You walk along a path, destined by time
Chartered, till the chances comes along
to veer from that road
Towards extremities in life
which cause you pain and discomfort.
The ease of constant footing is not familiar
Looking, searching for that ultimate high
that attainable goal just fingertips out of reach.
Knowing the next incarnation has to be better
Your sights are blinded by determination gone astray.
Have you forgotten the innocence within?
The naivety of life?
Of holding someone you love
Sharing most precious moments
Cuddling by a fire on a cold winter's eve
It takes loving to be loved,
Not running in hopes that love will
catch up to you.
Slow down your weary speed
Breathe in the pleasures of life
Come back to the center of creation.

Cori Sean Latimer

ADULT TOY?

Fire rages throughout the land
Death to all, a short life span.
The people who lived burned in
Eternal Hell.
The burnt skin makes such a smell.
That's what they get for making such big toys.
Those giant bombs make so much noise.
The sky turned a horrid blood red.
The ocean stood still as if it were dead.
The remains of fish all spoiled and green.
Nothing again ever stayed clean.

Cora Page

FOR SALE

To my Friends and Family.
To the ones in front pulling me.
To the ones in back pushing all the way . . .

For sale, one Heart, slightly broken,
Includes hurt Feelings, from promises insincerely spoken,
Reasonably priced Relationship, I look back on with regret,
Priced for quick sale, Thoughts, I'd like to forget,
Free to good home, Memories, you can have every one,
To be taken as a package, or I'll separate for some,
Various & sundry Hurts, that only your purchase will cure,
Numerous cards & letters that I don't Need anymore,
Yours for the asking, Self Confidence, edges slightly marred,
50% off Ego, bruised, but not permanently scarred,
Excellent condition, Box of Promises, never meant to be kept,
Several bottles of useless Tears, having long since been wept,
No longer needed, Trust, will throw in for good measure,
Little used, Hopeless Dreams, that I once treasured,
All sales final, no Warranties expressed or implied,
Buy at your own risk, being careful on what you decide,
I'll keep my Faith for the Future with Hope in my Heart,
I'll search out my Destiny & pray for a new start . . .

Cora Page

COMING OF AGE

We grow up thinking it's a perfect world,
Naive thoughts of little boys and girls,
Groomed toward marriage to be lasting and true,
Rushing headlong into a relationship without a clue,
Everything's wonderful for a short precious while,
Storybook perfect all happiness and smiles,
Slowly but surely comes the changes we must face,
Time once spent together having long since been replaced,
No longer able to laugh or even to talk for that matter,
Gone are the days of good-humored chatter,
The once bright flame has flickered to but a mere spark,
These growing pains have aged my heart,
Together or alone we learn to live with whatever's left,

This coming of age is one of life's most trying tests.

Harrison Lee Neeley
BLOSSOMING OF LOVE

The blooming of love
Inside our hearts.
There's no greater joy
to behold.
And the happiness, That we feel.
Puts a flush to our cheeks.
And the joy, puts a sparkle in our eyes.

The blooming of love
Exhibit the freshness
and the beauty of youth.
Regardless, What age we are.
And the highest perfection of growth.
The rarest beauty of all.

The blooming of love
more precious than Gold.
The guidance of a goddess Muse.
May my Poem, find a use.
In the Blooming of love.
In your Heart forever.

Eileen Carder
ONLY IN LIFE

Dedicated to: Ron.

In Death Do Not Walk Upon My Grave
Nor Let The Winds Carry To Me Your Mournful Cries
It Was In Life I Was Betrayed
Felt Pain From The Dagger Of Deceit And Lies
If Peace With Me Is What You Seek
It Must Be In My Life's Span Of Time
In Death No Comfort Your Words Of Love Be
It Was In Life You Broke This Heart Of Mine
Only In Life Your Kindness Give
To Soothe This Weary Soul
Or In Death I Will Accept Defeat
In My Search For Your Heart of Gold

Edgar J Willmott
DOLLARS NO SENSE (WRONG PRIORITIES)

Let's look at the world we live in
What is valued most,
Saving a starving child, people who're ill
Or the amount of money one has in the till?
Put on a magnificent display
At what money can buy,
So all others in passing will give an envious sigh?
Outward appearances never mean a thing
If in private, lives are hollow and hearts never sing.

Self importance, huge sums of money,
Blinds most to the reality all about,
They live and move, in a world,
Like people in a dream,
Never listening or caring
As unfortunates in this world loudly wail and scream,
Wallowing and gloating about what they've got
Figuring it will never end,
Always a prime target for the people, they now call friend.

How stupid wealthy ones are
Living only for prestige and self,
From death they can never be saved,
because of their wealth.

Shawn A Dixon
MIDNIGHT LIGHT

For the only love in my life, my wife Nina!

Blue light comes and strikes my bed
and helps me drift away
To that place that comes once a night
when the light has passed from day.
I travel far to places unknown and
sights the aren't too real
To places that I see, smell, and taste,
but never can quite feel.
I search my dreams through good and
bad and find the ones I fear
Then I pass through those and find
the ones that bring you oh-so near.
The ones with you and me together
making love till dawn.
Loving each other, feeling together
and thinking of no other one
But dreams soon fade and are chased
away by beams of golden light
and then I hope and pray all day for
the midnight light

Susan Rickerl
DAFFODILS

The daffodils in our garden
are dying
The soil has lost its nutrients,
they are starting to bend.
Is it because you are old,
or because our love has lost
its flavor and beauty?
I have watered your soil,
gave you love
and sunshine.
You have no leaves
for you are naked.
Once you touch the soil,
my lovely daffodils,
You will be the nutrients
of a new breed.

Mark Clark
OCCUPANTS OF THE VIAL

The bar is crowded of a social flock
Cliques babbling a common, unstimulating tone
Enters a usual beard from the dock
Who always chooses to drink alone

The bartender squeals "Old man, why not mingle?"
"Quit soaking your brain in that worthless wine

With the I.Q.'s of these women I'd rather stay single
And what you call worthless may be divine

Crazy man, what do you imply
You must be some kind of ass

Believe what I say, it is no lie
That a thousand worlds may live in my glass

From every drop I pour on to the table
Many unknown names in unknown places may exist
And in one of those worlds a man like myself is able
To look in his glass and make another list

Of course you say I speak as a fool
These mad ideas I say
To believe there are worlds in one molecule
But I ask you where is our world today?

Floating in what we now call space
But perhaps our universe belongs to an undisturbed lake
Slowly floating under a larger race
4.5 billion years the lake is untouched
But to larger men it may only be minutes
Perhaps someone will choose to dive in our lake
And we will all be finished.

I step on my wine and destroy 10 worlds
10 worlds containing hundreds of others
Maybe someone will step in my wine
Kill my world more worlds and their brothers

Insane man, you have the wildest of dreams
I can only proclaim you a fool
But all of the sudden, the bar tilted with screams
As a large man dove into a pool

June T Shipley
OCTOBER

October is the time of year
When fields turn brown and gold,
And forests blaze in Autumn sun
With colors bright and bold.

October is the time of year
When football fans turn out
To cheer their teams to victory
'Mid thunderous noise and shout.

October is the time of year
When leaves come tumbling down
As the chilly breezes blow
Them gently to the ground.

October is the time of year
When spooks and witches roam,
And "trick-or-treaters" ring doorbells
At every house and home.

October is the time of year
When flowers go "in" to rest.
Of all the bright and happy months
I like October best.

The Happy Gladiator
TO THE PATRONS

Take a lesson from the shark,
nature's most efficient feeding machine.
Always moving never stopping
senses keen to every stimuli.
Never stopping always moving
every vibration a stimuli for the feeding frenzy.
Moving roving seeking—
hungry for input.
always hungry always seeking—
day and night
moving,
roving,
feeding
every stimuli creating excitement.

Emlee
SPRING

To my love ones—my family.

A little bit of heaven shows forth its colors each year
The lily of the valley and other flowers we hold dear
Some in warm climes others under snow
Does man appreciate this act of God
His little seeds of kindness
underneath the sod?

Sprigs of lilacs trees of summer green
Invade the gardens and seem to say
"Hello" the warm weather days are on their way.

The blue of the sky enhances the scene
Creating beauty upon a screen
Only an artist with pallet in hand
Could bring forth such colors upon his stand.

Deborah Taylor
LOVE'S THEME

To John.

You embrace me in sun-splashed color
Unveiling my love so undercover
You're almost a religion
Excelling sweetness with such precision
You must have stepped right out of a dream
So I'll just sit here and watch the sun dance behind you
I swear it follows you everywhere
And now for the first time I see the woman I want to be
Just when I couldn't carry the weight of another day
You stepped in and sent your love my way

Karen Wentworth Johnson
DARRIN

In memory of my brother who will always be in my heart.

The moments I sit
and spend alone
I think . . .
about our childhood together
And I can't believe
you've gone away.
I never understood
how life could be so bad
that you'd just want it to end,
but sometimes . . .
So much, I miss our life
of confiding in one another
and helping each other
through the hard times.
We were more than brother and sister,
we were friends.
I miss you
why did you have to go away?
It's lonely here . . .

Karen Wentworth Johnson
WHY DO YOU PROMISE

Why do you promise the world to me
when you can't even have it yourself
Why do you promise such happiness and joy

when you're breaking my heart in two
Why do you promise a moment together
with no intentions of seeing me at all
Why do you promise that you'll change tomorrow
when tomorrow never comes
Why do you promise me forever
when we can't even have today
Why do you promise me the sun
when all it does is rain
Promises hurt so much
they are only made to be broken
Why do we need promises
when we can just live life day by day.

Kaye S Underwood
BE AN EXCEPTION, SAY NO
Who makes your decisions, you or your friends?
Who has the choice to start or to end?
Who are you impressing? What are you trying to prove?
When you choose drugs . . . Do you win or do you lose?

It takes more nerve to say "No" and not yes
So if they are your friends,
Who are you trying to impress?

Take a look at the statistics, Take a look at the charts.
Why are people in Rehabs or living on streets
If drugs are so smart?

So ask yourself these questions,
Do you win or do you lose?
Just say NO—Be an exception to the rule.

Elmira L Dewey
ECHO OF TEARS
Cry you lonely, aged people, cry
Let little streams wend down
the dry, cracked surface
that is face
To fall drop by drop from
sagging chin
to sunken chest
wherein lies the treasure-heart.
Cry until there are no rivulets
and salt has dried upon
the beds of courage, pride a spirit left.
Then let the winds, the rain
wail and cry for you.
Their echo will reach out to comfort you.

Elmira L Dewey
GENTLY CLOSE THE DOOR
You're standing by the door.
You've just told me
you don't love us anymore,
me and baby in his highchair.
His little hands are waving bye-bye to you.
He's saying, "Daddy, me too, me too."
But you can't take him, he's mine.
You can take the tears we've shed,
The years of happiness:
They're not mine anymore.
Now take yourself and go,
leaving the only happiness
that you might ever know.
And where you'll end up,
only heaven knows.
Baby has cried himself to sleep;
I no longer care to weep.
Please go now,
and gently close the door.

Jerry L Peters
BLOOD IN HIS EYES

To my mother.

He's got blood in his eyes
He seek far and wide but
Nobody seems to hear his cry
He even wish he could die
He even refuse to give life a try
He's got blood in his eyes

Carol Hoenig
SILENT DARKNESS
Pass me by, oh quiet one
and leave me standing still
let my light glow from none
perhaps the solitary breath will fill.

Give me no reason for your coming by
just ignore the many faces I show
don't beckon me, even if I lie
and I no longer can grow.

Wicked, restless, ruthless, and unannounced
you have become all these things
the manner in which you appear and pounce
sadness is only what it brings.

Certainly my begging, you will ignore
viciously finding your way to me
I almost can hear the knocking on my door
Time has escaped and left me with no dignity.

In cool and silent darkness, I am surrounded
I believe you have done your deed
My being cannot be free, for I am hounded
and life was sapped and my death was your greed.

Candace M Smith
LOVE, ARE YOU LISTENING?
Love, are you listening?
Where does our Love come from?
The other side of the Wind
of song!
Or would it be the Butterfly
our messenger?
The gold of his wings reflect
the golden hours
We have spent together.
I love you, My Dear.

Neva Carden
MOONLIGHT
The light on my pillow
Should fall on your head.
Why must it fall on
Empty space instead?
I want you, I need you
To come back to me
And make me happy
As I used to be.
I've only the moon
To tell my troubles to
And when clouds hide its face
I start praying that you,
Will forgive and forget
All the bad moment we knew.
For I can't share this moonlight
Moonlight without you.

Harry James Jones
WINDS OF SIN
It's a time of War of Peace
The winds blow heavy with Sin
A door must be Opened to sign a new Lease.
In the States the young March in the Streets
The winds blow heavy with Sin
In Vietnam the young Shoot in the Streets.

We as Soldiers wander from tree to tree in the Bush
The winds blow heavy with Sin
The dodgers are home hoping to be Free: do they need a Push?

Freedom rings loud in my Homeland
The winds blow heavy with Sin
Girls fling their Bras, while Guys burn cards by their own Hand.

Will Freedom Fall and Communist Reign?
The winds blow heavy with Sin
Young America walk Tall or accept the Pain.

We want for Nothing; We buy our Way!
The winds blow heavy with Sin
Many are Snuffing; Many will Pay!

Morals are gone and Wrong is Right
The winds blow heavy with Sin
If only a Song I could Write to correct this sorrowful Plight.

Time marches on; but America will Suffer for Decades
The winds blow heavy with Sin
Crime will lurch; only to show its Face—No Buffer for AIDS.

If our Sons lose to Fate will our Daughters be led to Slaughter?
The winds blow heavy with Sin.

Joyce Wiley Seefeld and Lyle Seefeld

Joyce Wiley Seefeld
MY "HI-FI" CANARY

Dedicated to Lyle, my husband for 60 years.

My "Chi-Chi" sings his merry song
Through both glad and dreary days;
His voice, as golden as his coat,
A wealth of happiness conveys.
He trills with Pons, Jeannette and me,
He baritones with Eddy too;
His Khachaturian ballets
Convulse with hearty laughter, oo.
He never wants for self-esteem
When waltzing on through merry Strauss;
He "Benny's" Kreisler's violin,
His "Love in Bloom" brings down the house!

Joyce Wiley Seefeld
THE GRAND CANYON OF THE COLORADO (LIFE)
SUNRISE:
(Birth)
Rising sun—bright rays
Make hearts sing . . .
higher . . . higher—
Peerless joy conveys . . .

THE PAINTED DESERT:
(Youth)
Resonant depth rings . . .
In awesome wonder, echo-
Ing on splendorous
wings . . .

ON THE TRAIL:
(Trials)
Winding down on
mules . . .
Hued panorama
jiggling . . .
Undulation rules . . .

SUNSET:
(Joys)
Glories to behold . . .
Kaleidoscoping ever . . .
Blues . . . to bronze . . . to
gold . . .

CLOUDBURST:
(Eventide)
Dimmed sun sinks, turns
blue
Bluer . . . lightning jags
. . . THUNDER!
Cloudburst! . . . Storm is
through!

Nitza Agam
ON THE ART OF LOVING . . .
A discussion on a bus
about the art of loving
with a young boy.

One must learn to love, he says,
to develop, practice, and perfect,
as in any art.

Love grows naturally, she says.
Love is born, not cultivated.
The knowledge comes from the act,
the practice from the desire,
the perfection from life.

The young boy, fervently reading
on the bus.
The older, young woman, watching
and remembering.
They talk of love, these two,
each searching, his road a wider
one of theory and practice,
hers of suffering and knowledge.

Love grows, is born, she repeats,
learned, taught, applied, he answers.

Loretta L Shaneybrook
CHRISTMAS THROUGH THE EYES OF A CHILD
Christmas through the eyes of a child
is one we all should see.
It's bright lights and tinsel upon a big Christmas tree.
It's Santa dressed all in red, and
snowy hill we ride on our sleds
It's presents that fill the the shelves in store
And what is hidden behind locked doors.
It's bright eyed children with faces all aglow
The look that they give you when
they see their first snow.
It's waiting for that magical night,
and looking for Santa in the

moonlight.
It's waking the next morning and looking to see what Santa has left you there under the tree.
Yes Christmas through the eyes of a child is one we all should see
It's sad when we grow older that it is just a memory.

Nancy Kubik
TO EARTH FROM SPACE

I hold Earth
in my hand,
in my heart,
and I love her dearly.
Blue jewel in the star studded sky.
How can you,
so tiny,
so precious,
be the cradle of my life?

Michael P Kenney
AS I LOOK OUT MY WINDOW

Now I sit by my window
And dream of a place,
Where Byzantine buildings stand
Like soldiers in lines,
Surrounded by cobble stone streets,
Lined with umbrella shaped trees.
As I watch the soldiers march back and forth
It is like watching a parade over and over.
I look at the buildings for the last time
As they fade away.
I'm back in my room looking at my poster of
RUSSIA.

Christa Lee Carvellas
SWEAR NOT BY THE MOON

Just as the sun riseth,
I there do fall,
And just as the sun does set,
I, therefore, arise.

For within the soul
There's great love and great hate;
For in the mind
There is, too, the same.

For when the sun shines,
There love does prevail;
But when the sun has disappeared
In the black of night, hate does arouse.

So, if the sun will shine for long,
And promise never to set,
So, too, will love that is shared,
Promise never to be overthrown by hate.

Rebecca Moss
CHANGING TIMES

To my dear brother, Moses Davis, who gave me hope and inspiration.

The winds of change are blowing strong
From coast to coast they blow along
And bring a different vision every day.
Men are beginning to awaken
Their old ways are forsaken
With hope of a better life to carry on
The spirit of freedom is everywhere
For those who work and those who care
To toil for a better world to come.
Have faith in God every day
And He will show us the way
To do the things that we must do
To carry out His plan of life
For those to-day and they that are yet to come.

Lisa Woodward
NOW

To all my family. Thank you for your support. I love you all.

Now I am
And old house
cold, empty, sad and lonely.
I want to become new.
Wanting to be filled with happiness.
Waiting to be loved.

Now I am
A closed book
thick and filled with adventure.
I want to become an open book.
I hope to be held in caring hands.
Waiting for a reader.

Now I am
A doll on a shelf
standing and waiting.
Nobody wants me.
I'm not pretty.
But I dream of being a china doll.

Karen Betts
MY JULIE

Listen to me "My Julie," and listen with your heart.
I've always loved you, honey, right from the very start.
My baby girl, my little girl, the young lady you are now.
You're on your way to womanhood, I want to stop it all somehow.
I want the days when you would smile,
And laugh and run to give me hugs.
There was a time "My Julie" when you even played with bugs.
Now you scream and run away at the very sight.
"My Julie," you're still the little girl I loved to hold so tight.
No one will ever take your place
And when that smile lights up your face,
It makes my world a better place.
I thought I'd better tell you now, for the years are going by,
"My Julie" all the love I feel for you will never, ever die.
Just don't forget, "My Julie," we'll always have each other
And after this life, if there's another,
I'd still choose to be your mother.
Love, Mom

Sally M Feldman
YOU WERE SO SPECIAL TO ME

This poem is dedicated to Marleen, my loving big Sister.

I wish you were here
Since, you were so dear
Except there, isn't no more future to spear
I still remember all those years
and your laughter and the tons of tears
The special conversations and your special little cares
I never had any fears, that you wouldn't nor couldn't
have no more splendid years
You were so young but, yet so old
I wish you were still here to hold
We could have had a galaxy filled with hope and dreams.
But, unfortunately you had left the scene
Instead I screamed and cried with tears streaming down
my face, as my heart was bursting with sorrow for
today left no tomorrows
I knew you would never have the taste of life
again
God Bless you and all who face the terrible
disease that has no trace. Amen

Tanist Denise Bolden
VISION ON A BUS

I saw a vision on a bus
and the vision smiled at me
Life is just a test
A test
I have done my best
I don't have the key
God why have thou not answered me
I have done my best
The world does think me less
I don't have the key
God why have thou not answered me
God don't make no mess
No mess
The world would think me less
I do have the key
The key
The Grace of hope has set me free.

Kay Queen
THE PATH OF NATURE

This poem is dedicated to: Albert Remer Castner. From all of us; "We love you, Daddin."

Pebbles pave the path of life;
the way is never ending.
Not much joy, yes, too much strife
creates a chain; ever bending.
Bristling leaves, waves of passion
soothing ripples, more the fashion.
Ever seeking; never finding.
seldom faithful, always binding.
The quiet breeze of a wistful day
gently sweeps all woes away.
Branches playing hymns of old . . .
words the trees have never told.
Flowers carry heaven scents,
butterflies a'flutter.
Dogwood blooms in hoards abound,
a summer's day is gently shuttered.
Lights may dim, or so I'm told;
The final path's still paved with gold.

Qui Diaz
A WORD OF STRENGTH

To my mother and all who deserve such a title.

My heart rises as I heard her words of strength and dignity, to overcome the unchangeable. She became what she always was, the positive, the unique soul of true character. She inspires all who can reach a depth without the need to look back. The hurt I felt was non-existent, the pain I saw was but a figment, and so it goes, that to state her and place her upon a pedestal is not in vain, or in case of reality, she still will remain as she always was, is and will be. With "Love" to the wonder of my world of the lives of many. Time has proven her just, for I ask forgiveness, as all must, for the doubt that laid in our minds. Mother is she who inspires all words, that touch one!

Tianna L Hawkins
PURPLE

Purple.

Purple is a soft wind,
whispering through the branches in summer.

Purple is restless like birds in the air,
soft like an old velvet chair.

Purple is a sweet melody tune,
almost silent,
as if it were weeping and no one could hear.

Purple is lilac flowers on a bitter cold morning,
sitting around a pearl shaped lake.

Purple.

Purple is love,
waiting to be found.

Purple is the glow that is cast over the seas.

Purple is a wish, a dream, a fantasy,
a hope that lies between curdled dreams and unsolved wishes.

Purple.

Betty Phan
LOVE WAS NEVER MEANT TO BE

Dedication to all the one I love.
I want to thank-you to all my teachers and all of my friends for all they have done and for always being there for me. Also a special thanks to HIEU DUONG, the one who have brought me love, hope, desire, and for once being special in my life.

Whenever I look at you
I began to fantasize
but I know I should face reality and to realized.
A strange feeling which I never felt before
'cause you're the one
I have been searching for.
There's something I don't understand
why love is so unfair
and made us friends.
I had always dreamed of us being together
and telling you that I will love you forever.
But everytime I see you with that girl
my dreams of us
start to fade away from my fantasy world.
Why are you so nice?
Have you ever thought it twice
that you being nice would only hurt me?
'Cause being your girlfriend I had always wished to be.
Tell me how do you feel?
At least give me a chance to make it real.
But I never have meant for you and her to be apart
which would only hurt her and break her heart.
If fate will ever lets us be together
I promised I would stay true to you forever.

Jennifer L Spenst
MOUNTAINS
Giant towers of pines;
Greens, blacks, and browns;
Rockies—stairs into the sky.
Openings in the trees,
Let rays of light shine
Onto the damp and dark earth below.
Light rains shower new plants,
And create peace for the animals.
The Rocky Mountains.

Cathie Tanner
TODAY
The sand is so white,
The water so blue,
The air so fresh;
Everything's so beautiful
Life can be peaceful,
And serene, like today
At times it's like
A dark stormy day
I live for today
And hope for tomorrow
Yesterday is in the past
All nightmares forgotten
Our love is today,
And please be tomorrow,
Put yesterday behind us
And push ever onward.

Carolyn Knighton
POWERFUL CRIES

I wish to dedicate this poem to the powerful Bald Eagle himself. His beauty, strength and spiritual power inspired me to write this poem.

Sitting there, the world his own,
He means power to many,
Swaying with the wind
Assured of his beauty.

He lets out a cry, another
While he soars, dividing sun rays.
The beauty makes one squint,
Your eyes are fixed.

Hours you watch,
He cries again, spreading his wings,
Kills his meal in the sky,
Eagle is his name, powerful are his cries.

Michelle Elstran Przybylla
DADDY'S LITTLE GIRL'S GROWN UP
She's not so little anymore
Way beyond the diaper stage
Seems like just yesterday you were holding her
And that she grew with the turn of a page.

Now she's grown & out of school
And you can't believe what you see
Now, instead of playing with dolls
She's wondering what she can be.

And even tho' she's not a baby
She still needs Dad's loving touch
Because she knows that father knows best
And she loves him very much.

She's old enough now
To share the same problems
That her father is having too,
But they know with the help of each other
That they'll see their problems thru.

So even tho' she's grown up now
She wants her "Daddy" to see
She's never going to outgrow his love
Daddy's little girl she'll always be.

Brandi M Turnage
UNKNOWN SELF
Drops of dew fall upon my face,
As I smell the pine scent.
Geese pull in fall with their crooked arrows.
Hollow winds separates my hair.
Cold and fragile designs of snow flakes
Fall upon the leaves where they hide the creatures crawl.
Staring myself eye-to-eye in the fogged waters,
Am I not there?
Exactly who am I?
Racking my brain to stop my sorrow,
I still stare in the mystic mirror.
It's my eyes to see the pain.
I pull myself up to a limb getting sap on
My fingertips.
I still grieve with my unknown self.
Laughing, rumors.
Why?
That's all I did ask my mystic mirror.
But all that answered was winds of chilled
ripples of the blue lines within hollowed
years.

Debby K Sanders
DREAMS
Let me dream,
In dreams are hopes.
I dream of azure skies
Over tranquil islands.
I'll swim in blue lagoons
With playful dolphins,
Seeking nature's treasures
In coral coves.
I'll seek the sun's warmth
On white sands.
I'll have flowers aplenty
For my hair.
Joy and laughter are mine
As I play.
Nightingales sing lullabies
At day's end
To send me to sleep,
So I dream again.

Marie E Gingrich
CLOUD PICTURES

To my four daughters, Jeanne, Linda, Joyce and Beth, this poem is lovingly dedicated.

First a bear—then a pig
How swiftly each could change,
Then a Stallion pure and white,
Came drifting stately into my sight.

Sometimes they'd move so slowly
As they marched along their way,
Sometimes they moved so swiftly—
How I wished that they could stay!

Now as I see white puffs of clouds
Against their canvas of bright blue—
I wish I were a child again,
For then to me those images were true.

I'd lay upon my back for hours,
Upon a carpet soft and green
And paint my pictures in the sky
My Zoo of childish dreams.

Donna Lynn Hepworth
DOWN ON LIFE
Depressing dreams
They are all just schemes,
They make you scared inside.
Talk them out
Don't cop out
Like they will leave in time.
Seek the help
Earn the chance,
To make friends
And learn to dance.
Life is great
Life is grand,
Take a glance
Then take my hand!

Donna Lynn Hepworth
MOM, I LOVE YOU
You have always cared for me,
Watched over me, warned me,
And loved me, just as a mother bird
Does her children.
You have tried hard to make
Life easier when times are hard.
And I know how much you may fear the day,
When I will grow up and leave you
Only to start a new life on my own
And to start a new family to love.
But never fear, because as you have been,
I shall be as well, there when the hard times hit
To comfort, and catch you when you fall.
You are my family now and always,
as I am yours!

Lois Smith Triplitt
DUMB BIRD
Feeling alien and distant
A stranger to all—and those dear,
Walking lonely on the planet
Cold and lonely 'round the Square.
Separate and empty, critically aware,
Questioning values, why I even care.
An old beggar squatting on the sidewalk
Leaning against the wall, pigeons picking about
For crumbs, amidst the dirt and all,
Artists working on their canvas encircling the Park
As I vaguely search for meaning, what purpose do we serve?
As if we're in a Play, it seems, but do not know our part.
Are we like puppets on a string, chessmen on a board?
Or like a cuckoo in a clock, with programmed time? Oh Lord!
Dumb bird, You know not how came you there
Nor how long you'll be
Do you sing to yourself?
Just like me!

Rachel French Stiles
ODE TO A 73 DATSUN
The Datsun is my truck, I can't afford another.
It maketh me to lie down beneath it.
It leadith me beside many repair shops
It soreth my soul.
It leadith me in the path of ridicule for its name sake
Yea, tho I ride through the valleys, I am towed
Up the hills, I fear no evil for my credit cards
are with me.
Thy rods and thy springs hurt me,
I repair blow outs in the presence of mine enemies
I anoint my axles with oil, my radiator runneth over
Surly sneers and jeers and laughter small follow
Me all the days of its life
And I will dwell with my creditors forever.

Irene Mary Larson
HOW NICE THIS WORLD WOULD BE

To America.

How nice this world—would be—if more were like you are.
As I'm thinking of you—with pleasure too—of how nice this world would be—
If more folks were like you—in wishing—you happiness—that will hold—
The joys you give to others—to returned to you—ten folds—

Dee Overpeck
POETRY
Poetry comes from within—
Oasis in harsh reality,
Echo of dreams of the soul,
Tapestry with words,
Reaching out to touch all,
Yearning to be free in your mind.

Rosemarie Muti Creighton
MICKEY THE ICKY INCHWORM

I dedicate my favorite poem to my beautiful grandson Nico. May he grow up with these same values in life.

One spring day, in a field so sunny,
Brenda Bee was eating some honey.
She turned to Barbara Butterfly—her very closest friend
And said, "Let's have a party! Fancy invitations we shall send!"

"Jake the Snake will certainly come
And Priscilla Pup is always looking for fun.
Don't forget Rita Rabbit and Chipmunk Sam,
Richard Robin and Lucy the Lamb . . ."

"What about Mickey Inchworm—is his name on the list?"
"No, he's too icky, so he'll never be missed."
Said Lois the Turtle, "It's just not fair
To leave out a friend . . . why, I wouldn't dare!"

Timmy the Turtle also agreed:
"If you don't invite Mickey, then don't invite me.
Special friendships are hard to find,
So overlook Mickey's faults, and learn to be kind."

"I know that fresh Mickey made Diana Duck cry,
First saying she was pretty, then saying 'That's a lie!'
Another time Mickey had asked out

Priscilla Pup—
She also was sad 'cause he never showed up."

So, what shall we do with our icky Mickey friend?
We will explain to him that his meanness must end!
We must make him stop treating everyone cruel
We can do this by teaching him our Friendship Rules!

First, there is kindness—only nice you should be,
Practice this daily and it will come naturally.
Don't be selfish, with your friends you must share,
Lend them a coat when they have none to wear.

If you see your friend is feeling down,
Upon his face a sad old frown,
Give him a hug and a great big smile—
He'll certainly feel better in a little while.

Never put your good friends down,
Never talk about them when they're not around.
Good friends stick together through thick and thin:
If Icky learns all these rules, our hearts he will win.

So Icky learned and practiced his Friendship Rules,
He said it was fun—just like being in school.
And all future parties Icky never missed,
Because now his name was the first on the list!

James A Boyer
WINDS OF ENDEAVOR
The glitter of gold
Sparkling of diamonds,
Smiles, and songs of love,
Feeling the sense of grandeur,
Seeking and finding _ll within,
Bound only by universal thought,
Ah! There is the way
The life traveler expands
Through the winds of endeavor.

Della Jane Goodwin
WHEN I'M WITH YOU
When I met you, it was a blessing in disguise
No more reasons to sit down and cry.
Never thought I'd feel this way again
That's when my life began.

The days are long
When I'm not with you
I hate it when you are gone
Makes me feel all lonely and blue.

Makes my day, when I see your face
My heart starts to race.
Hearing your name on my lips
Makes my tummy do crazy little flips.

You don't know what you do to me
So baby, don't ever set me free.
You fill my days with sunshine
And you start the bells to chime.

I love spending time together
Sharing thoughts, hoping it's forever.
You are like a breath of fresh air
Just knowing that you are there.

I hope this feeling I have will never pass
But as long as I'm with you
I know it will always last.
Doing it together all the way through!

Suzanne Karpilovsky
WATER
A precious gift from nature,
It serves in different ways.
First imagine how much water
We drink every day.

Without water we cannot survive,
What is in the bath and shower?
Why water, of course,
That strong power!

What happens after we brush our teeth?
We rinse the toothpaste out with it.
On a hot and sticky day,
We jump into a pool full of it.

The oceans and seas are full of water,
Both the warm and cold.
Water is essential,
And much more valuable than gold.

We often take it for granted,
Because we have it every day.
I think I have made my point.
That's all I have to say.

Charles Long
WHEN DEAD
It makes little difference after one is dead,
Recipient of all rewards, both past and ahead.
With the surcease of sorrow and no hell
In the next world, whatever has been well
On middle earth is the reward
And whatever on middle earth has marred
Joy and pleasure without measure
Cannot offer in after life a treasure
To pleasure a non-existent soul.
Blessed non-existence concludes the whole
And entirety of earthly and heavenly pleasure
And precludes pleasure without measure.

Charles Long
LOVE AFTER THE FALL: POSTLAPSARIAN RAVISHMENTS
Porphyro crept in, perchance a passionate friend,
More likely liege-lord of elfin land, to descend
To Madeline's passive nest, to play a ditty
And sing of a knight who met a lady without pity
A la otherworldly demons drowsing on the bosom
Of an innocent Madeline or Christabel or some
Dreamy-eyed and naive prelapsarian maid,
The object of Jupiter's white rush, or Pelop's debt unpaid.

Just as the elfin faery Porphyro designs to rest
His otherworldly head on Madeline's fair breast
So assumes the demonic and otherworldly Geraldine
Another's shape to seduce Christabel and Leoline
And like Geraldine and La Belle Dame they enlace
And fasten a mortal in their desiccating embrace.

Whatever Uther or Zeus or Porphyro or Thyestes might swear
The unsuspecting Madeline and Igrain could declare
That ravishing is rape; but Leda and Pelopia
Could better inculpate and condemn a divine myopia
Which uses gods and mortals and demons as its instrument
To transmogrify prophetic wisdom into ravishment.

Charles Long
AFTER THE FALL: AMORTIZATION OF SINS
There is no heaven and there is no hell
On earth or wherever mankind may dwell
In afterlife. Even for the seventh son of seven
There is no post-Edenic, postlapsarian heaven
Or hell, but the retribution of hell
Exerts its predestined force as we dwell
After the fall within our postlapsarian bins
On earth. To inconsequential sins
Often comes an unmistakable chastisement
Engendering an epiphany of enlightenment.

For sins of consequence, amortization extends
Into earthly life itself and comprehends
The concept of man's responsibility to earth,
Even extending seven times seven beyond his birth.

Charles Long
TRANSUBSTANTIATION OF WINE, FLESH, AND LOVE
Honeysuckle and Elm drank face-to-face,
Elm freely welcomed Chevrefeuille's embrace.
The chalice, elixir, and all drank free,
And then began the twining of Stone and Tree—
Treestone, Tristan, Tristram, the Tram before the Tris—
When "I sold you" became Joyce's "missymiss,"
When Isolde, Isolt, Iseut, Ysé by name,
When the Brine Bride, the golden sea-bride became
Elm enwrapped in the viney arms of Honeysuckle,
The Tree intertwined by the Goatleaf buckle
Of love's intertwining reminiscent power,
Both recalling and adumbrating love in a bower
In Morois Forest. Béroul the poet understood
That love and philtred wine cannot be the only food
Of elixired lovers. Tristan understood that life
In the Morois Forest often depends upon the knife
To transubstantiate innocent venery flesh
And transform all into love's inextricable mesh.

Jonathan K Weidner
EMPTINESS ROOM
My brother I see,
My brother I hear;
My brother so dear
- I fear.

Emptiness room
Filled only with gloom.
Passionate lights that see.
Towering walls
Which silently call,
"Would you take a walk with me?"
Eyes so blue
Staring up at you,
Straight into the heavens above,
"Take me now - away
From this chair today,
And teach me to fly like a dove!"

The brother I need,
The one so dear,
I can no longer hear
- nor fear.

Denise Ward
SHADES OF RUSSET
Shades of russet
Beneath a subterfuge of frost,
Ambered leaves
Waltz in perfect rhythm as currents pulse:

Radiance pierces
Clouds of pearl masking backgrounds of azure.
Nature forecasts
As we dwell on the transition yet to come.

Cerebral now,
We approach the autumn of life,
Regale at loves once known
And mourn the fading embers of a fire once resplendent.

Maynard Maxwell
VALENTINE'S DAY
Valentine's is but
Once a year.
It's gone by
Then it's here.

It's got something
To do with Cupid.
Tellin' you the truth
That's not 'tall stupid.

It's a whimsical day
Cards & love & gunk.
But it's amazing
People rarely call it junk.

It's a day to show
Love from your heart.
It's a thing to accept
And to never let it part.

Misty Moreland
MEMORIES OF HIM
Sitting in my room
floating worlds away
Writing to a friend
wondering what to say
A song comes on the radio
and my eyes fill with tears
Remembering the only guy I swore
I'd ever love throughout my teenage years
I thought my heart would surely melt
but nothing could explain how I really felt
Slowly the song came to an end
and along with it . . . so did my memories of him

Richard G Paveletzke
TODAY'S CHILD
The children of our time
are the leaders of tomorrow.
They'll lead us through the good times
and through times of sorrow.

They look to us for guidance
we must show the way,
but the tide will turn
and we will learn—
They'll lead us someday.

So brother let me tell you
Hear what I say.
The future of this country
is in our hands today.

How we mold our children
If we raise them right
will reflect upon us all.
Will help them see the light.

So let's not lose control.
Let's not say, "What's the use?"
Let's do what it is we can
to wipe out child abuse.

Richard G Paveletzke
OUR FUTURE
We can build a future
High up on a hill.
We can call it love
and make it grow at will.

We won't always understand
What it takes to make love grow,
if we try the best we can
it will surely flow.

Well the world won't end tomorrow
and time keeps moving on,
but happiness
in a place like this
could live on and on.

Ruby Graham
WHAT IS BEAUTY?
Beauty is the wind swirling gently around
making a carpet of dry colored leaves on the ground.

Beauty is someone patient, loving, and kind
willing to help others and does not even mind.

Beauty is a young couple in a tender embrace
facing an old couple holding hands while saying grace.

Beauty is the beach covered with solid white sand
connecting green tidal waves covering the land.

Beauty is a sparkling web being spun by a spider
shaping so symmetrically perfect around beside her.

Beauty is a happy marriage that is made in heaven
bonding together with love, hope, and faith to leaven.

Beauty is water spilling down rocks in a mountain stream
forming pure thoughts in your head like a good peaceful dream.

Beauty is a red rose soaking up the dripping rain
leaving wet droplets on the foggy window pane.

Beauty is a mother nursing her baby child
asking God sweetly to let his troubles be mild.

Beauty is an ocean reaching out to the sea
luring my thoughts to what I could be.

Jane Pierritz
NIGHT
The night was deep & dark as the inside of a coat pocket;
As mysterious as the nameless girl in a locket
With jibing laughter to mock it.

The night was as long & hot as the River Styz;
As irritating as the scape of shovels & the tink of picks,
And dreams that were X rated flicks.

The night reached for the light
With scrabbling fingers on my window pane
Driven by a scouring rain.

Jane Pierritz
A FOOL FOR A PREACHER
Stand atop the mountain.
Declaim to the screaming wind.
Preach to the eagles about damnation—
Hell-fire & sin.

Go forth to the desert.
Discourse with the burning sand.
Ask salvation for the jackel & the lion.

Sit on the shore.
Lecture to the pounding surf.
Give Communion to the terns & gulls.

Mill among the throngs in the Bazaar.
Harangue the crowds with your vitriol.
Bless the pigeons, who have no souls.

Like in a meadow by a crystal stream.
Throw your pious anger at the sky.
Let a daisy judge if you love God.

Faye Beeson
AUTUMN LEAVETAKING
We stand beside our care beneath the elms,
  my son, his dad, and I.
They're solemn, stiff; I smile with frozen
  face (I will not cry)
We've come to leave him here, this high-rise
  dorm will be his home
Until, degreed, he steps into his place
  a man full grown.

We're silent now. I want to give him some
  profound advice by which to live
But nothing comes to mind. We watch as
  other young men come and go
With strange, unlikely burdens, to and fro.
  As three young females pass with
  watchful mein
To see if here the partners for their future
  may be seen.

It's time to go. His father shakes his hand
  says "Let us know if we can help."
I cross to where he stands, and smiling stiffer
  still I lift my hand
To touch his cheek—to kiss goodbye—and catch
  the not-here-not-now message in
  his eye.
I fold my upraised hand into a fist—
Sock him
  on the arm—
And turn and walk away.

James Baker
LOST LOVE

This poem is dedicated to Sol Beton, my boon companion of the High Museum School of Art years.

O Gondolier, I want to talk to you!
Tarry here, gondolier.
It was a warm night in May
Beneath a sky with a crescent moon
When I was with her, this damigella so fair.
It was you, gondolier, who rode us
In Venetian canals amid flickering lights.
How often in my mind and heart
I go back to that wondrous, enchanted night!
Oh, where is she now, this beautiful donzella
Whom I had loved for so little time?
I still inhale her sweet scent, in memory;
I still behold the glimmer in her hair
In the Venetian moonlight of May,
The pensive eyes, the sweet lips.
I recognize you, gondolier.
Tell me, have you perchance seen
My beloved, my darling damigella
Who was not a dream?

Patty Dudash
LOST LOVE

To Santino, my first love that somehow came back to me.

Sun setting into the sea.
Lips touching so softly.
Tears falling just like rain.
Hearts aching with a lot of pain.
Grass swaying on a summer day.
I already knew what you wanted to say.
Red balloons drifting in the air.
Your cold hearted eyes give a blanken stare.
Like a fire in the trees.
Something burns inside of me.
Gentle breeze blowing through your hair.
You look at me as if you didn't care.
Leaves changing before my eyes.
Sorrow in your voice as you said goodbye.
Snow floating to the ground.
You turn away without a sound.
The clouds have gone and turned to gray.
My heart begins to pound as you walk away.
Waves crashing on a sandy shore.
Hoping someday you'll be back for more.

Edna L Cooper
SO WHAT
As I watch his troubled brow frown upon the pregnant sow
I wonder if I should say that I know the way
She treats him, not so well, really makes his life hell.
Now she says that she will tell.
So what.

He has broken his wedding vow for this pregnant sow
The fight has just begun but I have already won
It was no contest I must confess, for she thinks that
I don't know where they go but I can guess
So what

He is almost finished now with this pregnant sow
Soon he will be home and she will be gone
For a while he will settle down and lose the frown
That was upon his brow then he will look for a cow.
So what

He may sometimes wonder how the pregnant sow
Is making it without him, it will be a whim
His fun with the cow will make him forget the sow
Who wasn't really pregnant anyhow.
So what

It will not get me down, I'll paint the town
Green. And I'll be seen with a horse of course
Why should I sit and cry about a cow and a sow
Now that I know how I'll cross his brow.
So what.

Edna L Cooper
GENTLE HEARTS
Upon the bier will softly sleep
The gentle heart that does not weep
That will not release the pain it bore
It will sleep in death and love no more

A gentle heart that does not break
Will never again find love to take
It will wither and slowly fade away
And lie in wait for Judgement Day

So, my love, for you I weep and cry
My heart will mourn, it will not die
The love it held will be a memory
A whisper of love that used to be

This gentle heart will end the pain
And find the way to love again
When the hurt is finally gone
This gentle heart won't be alone

M Karl Delashmitt
THE OLD OAK TREE
An old leafless oak tree stands sentry
  just outside our home's main
  entry.
A silhouette 'gainst the clear winter sky,
  witnessing changes and never asks
  why.

The moon shines through its slender branches.
  A night-owl approaches, decides
  to lite
at its favorite perch for much needed rest,
  after scanning the area, continues
  its flight.

The tree remembers before a shedding,
  many years ago there was a
  wedding.
The reception was held in its cool, cool shade.

It never stood taller as the tables
were laid.

He remembers the time his planter died
and if trees shed tears, I'm sure he cried.
As pallbearers walked 'neath him, some with a tear,
he would have gone too, but his roots kept him there.

Springtime is coming and soon will be here,
but he has no worries and he laughs at fear.
When the sap starts to rise and he starts to green,
he'll wonder, "this summer what things will be seen?"

Debbie Wingate
NIKKI
I look at a photograph and see her smile
Her name is Nikki, she's only a child
When I see her face it's hard to believe
One day too soon, this world she will leave
I've yelled angry words and cried many tears
It seems so unfair for a child of four years
To go through the pain, suffering and sorrow
Only to find there is no tomorrow
Morphine and glucose are now her diet
As she lays still, just listenin' to the quiet
She talks in her sleep to forces unknown
And wakes in fear saying they want her to come home
Nikki's soon to leave us for a much better place
But we'll miss her smiling eyes, her laughter and grace
We'll miss her four year old wisdom and cute things she'd say
We'll miss the hugs and the kisses and watching her at play
But she'll forever be remembered after her last good-bye
And in the hearts of those who loved her, that spirit will
Never die

Geraldine E Pasternak
FAINT WHISPERS
Faint whispers in a lonesome wood
Mute footsteps on a path
Amidst the trees, vermilion sky
From whence the good Gods laugh

Faint whispers in a lonesome wood
Thorns with naught to prick
No man to smell the fragrant pine
So odorous and thick

Yet, whispers in a lonesome wood
A loud but quiet sound
Beginning at the top of life
And settling in the ground

Robert C Dickamore
LOVE TRUTHS

Dedicated to everyone with a broken heart, a fallen or a loving spirit. Also to Karen Bean, Shanin Means, and Me!

Love is like the morning cry,
Always with a scheming eye.
Ends with tears and flowers dead,
In times of truth, the evil fled.
Lasting wounds upon your face,
Heartache sears a soul of lace.
Why is love imperfect . . .?

Patricia D Swart-Cordova
COMPLETE AGAIN
As the sun began to rise, I woke to a day blessed by God's love.
The emptiness and fears I had inside began to disappear like the darkness from the sky.
I was no longer worried about my mother being alone, sad, scared, and not having anyone to comfort her.
As the sun began to reach the midday sky, I began to relive the many dreams I thought would never come true.
To have someone I could talk to, laugh with, and to give me advice.
To be there when my children are born, and teach them throughout their lives.
As the sun began to set and the darkness returned to the sky, I wiped the tears of happiness from my eye.
My family is complete again, with you as my father, my friend.

Dana J Ryan
MAD DESIRE
You're my only world
I'm caught in your gravity
Try as I may to pull away
I cannot take back my own heart

Your magnetic charm attracts me
And your eyes, they seal my fate
Your boyish grin could lead me to sin
Where I married it'd be too late

It's maddening this touch I carry
You've got me so trapped in your spell
When I'm alone for a time, you still haunt my mind
And creep through my body as well

Oh, how I want you so badly
Got to have you here by my side
I'll spend the rest of my days, looking for ways
To endear only me to your heart

'Cause I'm caught in this made desire
To let myself burn in your fire
Feel the passionate flames, destroy my old pains
And take my soul higher and higher

Dana J Ryan
AT LONG LAST . . . LOST
Drifting about in mindless wonderlands
Sunk in our couches in front of the TV stand
Waiting for loneliness to lift its heavy hand
Watching and waiting, lost with no plans

Day turns to night as we dine alone
And laziness eats our bodies to the very bone
Apathy puts claims on our grounded souls
Yet we reap only the lives the we have sewn

How did we falter from our childhood dreams
Whatever happened to our ingenious schemes
Cynicism grasped our battered hearts, it seems
We didn't fight hard enough, we gave in to the mean

All black and white just melded away
And in the confusion we lost what to say
We gave in, compromised, let others have their way
And thought we'd have our own on another day

So here we are, all hollowed out souls
Empty of dreams and saving grace hopes
No more fast rises or long painful falls
Not the beginning or quite the end of our ropes

Just not a part of anything,
anymore . . . not even ourselves

Scott Jung
THE NOMAD
Standing in the middle of a desert
Alone, alone in the midst of nowhere.
The wind blows the sand over the vast space.
There is nothing, nothing surrounding me.
I look for something, anything to drink,
But there is no water, only dry sand.
I look for someone, someone to talk to,
But there is no one—hot desolation.
I yell, scream into the air for someone.
No one hears my call except the dry air.
I roll up, cringe into a little ball,
Face the harsh environment around me.
The sun beats on my body in the day,
The wind blown sand pelts against my burnt skin,
The night air freezes my ragged body,
I have no protection, no support here.
I face the elements alone, alone,
Standing in the middle of a desert.

Ruth K Cole
HIS BROTHER'S KEEPER

To all the children who cry in the night.

Little Black boy
Dancing in the Street.
Have to make a living
In the morning heat.
"Shoe shine Mister?
Penny in advance—
What! no shine
Then how 'bout a dance?"

Snap your fingers—
Slap your feet,
Have to make a living
In the morning heat.
Dance a little faster
Keep to the beat
Pavement getting hotter
On your bare feet
Dance your heart out
Pennies for pay
Hum your sweet tune
Keep time of the day.
Keep on smiling
While your legs get tired
Have to keep smiling
Feet are burning like fire
Slap one foot
Then the other
Snap fingers on one hand
Then the tuther
Slap your bottom
Shake your head
Roll your eyes
Like you was dead
Hum your tune
Keep to the beat
Twisting and turning
In the morning heat
Have to keep dancing
In the Street
Have to make pennies
Or brother don't eat
Mother's in heaven
Away from all pain
Daddy left long ago
Never seed him again
Now you know Mister
Why I ask you for a shine
Thank you, Mister.
God bless you
for the dime.
"Shoe shine Mister?
Penny in advance
What! no shine
Then how 'bout a dance?"

Ruth K Cole
I CAN ONLY WEEP
My heart aches for the children of today,
Specially if they are mine.
I cry when they hurt and I hurt when they cry,
Time, after time, after time.

When their hurts were skinned knees,
I healed them
With lots of love, a hug, and a kiss,
Knowing tomorrow the scratch will be better,
And I knew that all it took was this.

But, now they are older and it's different—
Their hurts are more lasting and deep—
How can I heal a broken heart?
I hold them, I love them, and I weep.

For the healing power of yesterday
Is lost in their adult world of today.
Oh! How I wish I could hold them and love them,
And make all their hurts go away.

I can only weep.

Keith A Fiscus
LUST

Dedicated to my beautiful wife Anne, for all of her love, and inspiration!

Crystal clear thoughts,
Springtime on my mind.
Pulse racing rapidly,
Ecstasy not far behind.
Around you I'm flustered,
My blood begins to boil.
The stars seem to multiply
Amidst the open sky.
My blood running feverishly,
I'm on a natural high!

Sandra Hardiman
TRUE BLUE FRIENDSHIP
My son he sleeps so peaceful,
as he lies upon his bed.
I often sit and wonder
what thoughts are in his head.

The years they seem to slip away,
we are losing life so fast.
I only hope his memories,
are strong enough to last.

I know that he'll be strong like me,

his troubles will be few.
I only hope that he will find,
a love that will be true.

How much more can a mother do,
than to teach him right from wrong,
and to give him a true blue friendship,
to last his whole life long.

Steven D Roe
SALUTATIONS
Dearest Mother,
Now I enter.
Here I am at Brookwood Center
Winter's on its way; I don't want to stay
Same situations, just a different day.
The rooms are too cold; I'm getting too old.
My respect at a faulter
I'm becoming quite bold.
Thinking of home
My thoughts seem to roam.
My family, my friends,
Memories don't have ends.
Brick walls everywhere.
Out of the window I begin to stare.
The weight of my burden is pulling me down.
I remember my school and my hometown.
Thinking of the years I yet have to spend,
They're going to be tedious, and appear without end.
But, I remember the good times when depression sets in
And the future seems closer,
There's a chance I can win.

Steven D Roe
THE YARD
Welcome to the center yard.
Surprising, life here isn't hard.
In fact, it's a bit too easy for the life outside that surrounds.
Clinking metal plates of steel
Met with vigor, as others deal
With rubber spheres and keep them bouncing steadily off the walls.
A watchful eye of feathered friend,
Soars above as if to send
A message of life . . . and proof that freedom still exists beyond the walls.
Names and numbers echo on,
As boots continue to tread upon
The grassless yard of man's design which steadily mirrors the ceiling of the sky.
Finite though this world may be
A myriad of thoughts appear to me
And keep me company, as I partake in the counter clockwise carousel.
A cat pursuing its own tail
Round the circle like ships they sail.
A whirlpool in the pavement sea
Waiting for time to pass . . . and free.

James K Welch
HOUSE CALL WITH PLACEBOS

For Mary Jane.

My learned friend was sick.
I came, bearing my stethoscope and bag
Peering uncertainly behind the mask
Bequeathed to me by Hippocrates.

I saw the silent war within the flesh
Which I didn't understand.
I longed for new miracles and wonders
But laid kindling for the medicine fire.
My friend saw the shining mask
Heard the ancient drums beat deep in his heart
Smelled the raw smoke, reds and yellows dancing from flames.
He forgot philosophy and listened to incantations
Sweat out his fever and was healed
While all the knowing ones laughed at magic
And mocked at love.

James K Welch
WHILE FISHING IN SPOON RIVER
Here in Spoon River's quiet run
Where the tall shade stills the violent sun
The little things of the summer world
Move and rustle.

Far above me riding high
A big jet airplane whispers by.
It's filled with busy, serious men
Who move and rustle.

Francis D (Frank) Armistead
SLOWING THE SPEED OF LIFE
Life was flying, or so it seemed,
so I came up with this fantastic scheme.
To roll time back for a little while,
and to this time, do it with a smile.
So I did the things of which I'd dreamed,
and above all, kept it clean.
Joined a group and learned to dance,
with my wife, renewed romance.
Found there's more to life than money,
like having a good time with your honey.
We demonstrated how to do this thing,
hoping to share our new found fame.
To share with others is what is took,
to give this life a youthful look.
So if like me, life is passing you by,
why not give Country & Western dance a try?

Diana R Agbayani
A JOURNEY IN PUNCTUATION MARKS

This poem is dedicated to God Himself—the giver of all talents.

Yesterday, life was full of question marks
Smashed hopes, uncharted courses
Reversals in life.

Today, it is a comma,
A moment of waiting
For the unfolding
Of God's purposes.

Today, too, are ellipses
Hidden from view . . .
Those slow, painful steps
Of becoming of growing.

Tomorrow will be a period
When Becoming becomes Being
A final work, God's very own Masterpiece.

Diane Pryor
A CHANCE
I was reading "Writers Magazine" late one night,
When an interesting article caught my sight.
A poetry contest was being held, it seems,
And before my eyes flashed my childhood dreams.
"Should I give it a try?" I wondered out loud.
What harm could it do? Would I make anyone proud?
I decided I must try, for one must take a chance,
To fulfill life's dreams, to sing and to dance!

So here are my lines. Please judge them with care.
And then let me know if any talent is there.
However, no matter what the outcome may be,
I'll continue my writing, if only for me!

Diane Pryor
THE MEDICINE MEN
"What is a doctor?" each of you may ask.
Listen closely and the definition I'll unmask.
"One duly licensed to practice medicine" so Webster has written,
But ours differs slightly and may be more "fitten."

One is "destitute of his natural and usual covering,"
In other words, he's nearly bald, his head is bare.
The other has a "thick outgrowth" on his epidermis,
Black wavy hair that lies everywhere.

One is "slender and high in stature"
What we mean is that he's tall.
The other is "not long from end to end"
Of brief length, short and rather small.

But how they appear, matters not.
It's what's inside, the talents they've got,
That puts them above all of the rest,
And makes "Our Clinic" the very best!

Pamela K Bohannon
IN DANGER OF EXISTENCE

To my husband Jesse who gave me the courage.

In the chambers of its gaseous envelope,
Bound are the masses that dwell.
Depriving its only means of continuance,
See how thou world has fell.
Lacking in existence, comeliness beauty and grace,
Razed by corruption, violence and immorality,
Where has gone thy peace?
A decade passes, a new then comes,
Left to survive in the destruction we've done.
World! Oh how long will it last?
Far longer than we that sip of your poison glass.

Yolanda Nicholson
MOTIVE
Why did he look with that special glance?
Why did he ask for just one dance?
What was his motive
There's got to be—
Just one reason
He'd ask me.
Why when he danced he danced so close?
Why didn't he notice the run in my hose?
What was his motive—
For he asked again
I didn't realize I was dancing
'Til the song began.
Why did he follow me everywhere I went?
For I figured by now his ego was bent.
As the evening passed by and by—
He was there right by my side.
But when he asked me out for a date
He said I'd be his perfect mate
My face turned as
White as a dove
And then I could see
His motive was love!

Julie Wall
FRIENDS

Farewell Gary, Until we meet again.

From the first moment we met
The bond between us had been set
I knew I had found a friend in you
As everyday passed, my prediction came true
On those days that were stormy and grey
Your smile was there to brighten my day
I'm glad I found a friend in you
Who changed my darkest skies to blue

Anita Renee Covington
OUR LOVE IS HERE TO STAY
When you give me your love
It goes beyond being physical
It is also emotional
It's true love we both know
Together our love will continue to grow
I want you with me more than words can say
Oh God, I pray you never go away
You forever stay on my mind
And it's because you are so sweet and so kind
Oh honey you're so understanding
You're never ever demanding
I can't imagine what my life would be like without you
You turn all my gray skies blue
Staying in love with you is a must
'Cause there is a lot of love, respect and trust
I love you more and more each day
I know our love is here to stay
We were brought together by the man up above
And this is a real true love
We will be together until the end
Because we are each other's best friend.
I love you

Sherri Knight Hays
IT'S SO HARD

This poem is dedicated to my wonderful sons, Nicolas Hays and Christopher Rooks.

Lord it's so hard to be a single parent . . .
I must be their mom and dad
Discipline them when they're bad
Their dads don't pay their share
Their dads don't even care
I'm their provider and protector
And their only comforter
Hear their dreams and fears
Wipe away their little tears
I take 'em to the zoo
'Cause I'm their friend to talk to

I deeply feel their pain
Sometimes makes me insane
It's always up to me
Why can't anyone see
I always want to cry?
But all I can do is try
I thank you Lord for my wonderful boys
Sharing their love and joys
They are my life
Let me again be a wife.

Lenora Webster Hance
GRANDPA'S FARM
I'd love to have the days come back,
Us, sitting 'round the fire.
Listening to the stories they'd tell,
Of the good old country life.
Of days gone past and growing up,
Way down on the farm.
Tales of playing hide and seek,
In the big two-story barn.
Tales of fun when they were young,
Down on Grandpa's farm.
They'd steal the eggs, right from the nest.
And then, the war begun.
'Til Grandma came out swinging a switch,
And they knew they'd better run.
Life, it seemed so simple then,
Growing up on the farm.
I wish, that life could be like that,
As simple, as it was back then.
Of fun filled days and loving ways,
Down on Grandpa's farm.

Donna Heft
FEELINS
Knowing that winter is here
Gives me a content feeling
It is presenting to me
The time is here
For expressing and revealing
A time to show all of your
Innermost thoughts and desires
A time to reveal
Your deepest, darkest, warmest burning fires
And though the winter will definitely
Cease to exist forever
The internal flames inside of us
Will relinquish us never

Lisa D Babb
VANITY II
Journey with me to a distant kingdom,
But expect to find no castles awaiting.
No, the Lords and Ladies here have no scripts to follow,
And they're not trying to get better roles,
Or telling pretty lies in their dollhouses . . .
No, they've put away their dolls.
There's no work here in our fantasy.
It is a vacation from the reality of everyday life.
So much energy it takes
In real life
To be fake. We need a break.
So come, let's enter this dreamy kingdom to be real.
What satire. Reality is false, and we fantasize about reality.
Such irony.
So jump into your kidney-shaped swimming pool
At your multi-million dollar mirror,
And wash away the glitter. Is anything left behind?
The real you may be far more than your image—
But when the real you and your glitter masquerade
Become one and the same, be afraid.
Look what vanity has done to you.
So come to my kingdom and explore your soul
Instead of wasting time decorating your facade,
And building up the bars
That will create your prison.

Cindy Stalling
MOTHER/DAUGHTER
She calls me from the shower
can't get the water right
I twist the knobs
We test, it's fine
She starts to get in
with her shower cap on
. . . and her underpants
No, no—
take those off too.

We go out to lunch
what do you want I ask
Same as you

We take our sandwiches
out to the patio
As we talk
She eats hers
layer . . . by . . . layer
I start to tell her no again,
but don't.

We go shopping—she needs underwear
We look and look (this is important!)
She wants the same as before
so she lifts up her blouse
in the middle of the store
No, no, I say—
not here.

We go home
I show her the photo album
I've made—100 years
of her family
in pictures
Her eyes begin a smile.

She talks about her grandparents
and how they all lived together
and she gets the street names right
and the addresses
and the names of all 3 generations
of the neighbors on both sides of
the house she grew up in

Then she tells me about Hollywood High
and going to school in the 30's
with real movie stars
And visiting relatives in the Valley
when Ventura Blvd was a dirt road.
And what it was like meeting my Dad
during the war.

Yes, yes, Mom—
oh, yes.

Lorene Swank
JUST BECAUSE
We didn't ask your opinion. Who cares what we look like?
If you don't like our looks, go take a real long hike.

Just because we're old is no cause for you to gag.
Wait till you're our age, Let's see how much you sag.

Just because we're ugly, no need to call us hogs.
We think some of you are going to the dogs.

Just because we're fat, no need to say "no way"
We could care less what you have to say.

Just because we're gray with signs of neglect.
Too bad we can't bring back a little more respect.

Kay Fuerst
THE JOURNEY OF LIFE
The other side is often greener
Or so I sometimes think,
Maybe warmer skies and bluer waters,
More tranquil thoughts of which to drink.

With dreams and longings ever mingling,
I explore in my reverie
Thoughts of how my script is written,
Before on wings, my soul flies free.

The master guides are always present
To help me find my way,
Thru fields of clover, thorns and brambles,
To taste the honey and hurt, in this awesome play.

With joys and passions, tears and sorrow,
There's a rhythm, a flow, a range
For every soul already destined,
To rise and fall with the interchange.

Mary Ann Radabaugh
GOD'S SMALLEST CREATION

To my husband, Bill.

Of all the intricate things God did create,
The Earth, man, and woman have brought much debate.

But His finest creation, the smallest of all,
Were the circles He doodled, and to Earth they did fall.

Man found this small circle, and his creative mind spun,
I'll give it to my Wo-man. Oh, won't that be fun!

I'll keep her for a life-time, "Unto death do us part."
Just let any other man try to get her into his cart!

This small circle shone and expanded with age,
As each man and woman turned over another page.

And so this small gold circle became a symbol of love,
"To have and to hold," sent by God from above.

Yes, this circle of love was God's gift to Man,
And if nurtured and fed, it goes on without end.

Hazel M Dolby
THE DAY GOD SHOOK THE EARTH

Dedicated to the workers, that made it possible to have survivors.

God can speak in several ways, God can discipline for many days.
Why try to understand the "how comes," and "where from?",
just learn to live the days as they come.

There were bowling games, baseball games, even football games,
when God shook the earth, nothing was the same.
Just think about when God first shook the earth, he was getting it just right. Now he shakes the earth when we get too uptight.

All kinds of races, different types of sexes, giving their best; giving their all, when trouble seems to hit; the barrier wall fall.

Helicopters, televisions, neighborhood "sams," we should also acknowledge the radio "Hams." Let's try to remember from this day to everyday, God does things in his own mysterious way.

Mique Snelgrooes
ONLY IN MY DREAMS
I know we are
just friends,
but I can't help
the way I feel
about you.

You may not
know it, but
every minute of
the day I'm thinking
of you, even in my
dreams.

Even though you have
a life of your own
now, I will never be
able to fight all the
temptations.

My feelings are
so strong that
every time I'm
around you, I just
want to forget every-
thing and hold you
forever.

One day, it'll be
you and me; me and you . . .
Only in my dreams.

Sue Powell
KIND SIR
I found you resting on the edges of my mind . . .
Yesterday, I would have been surprised.
Today I find comfort in your nearness, drawing
warmth from your body as I find strength
in thoughts of you.
Tomorrow, I know you must go.

Please kind sir . . .
Leave your gentle words and tender touch
as velvet linings to the pages of my memories.

Patricia Kackman
A PRAYER FOR HELP IN DISTRESS
Lord of Mercy, Lord of Love,
Lord of Power from above,
You—the Safeguard, You—the Shield,
You—by whose stripes we are healed,
Hear our struggling tale of woe.
Give us wisdom now to know
What You want of us today.
Send confusion far away.

Lead us, by this circumstance,
To see Your tender will advance.
Give us now Your strength within
To turn away the lure of sin.
Lead us through this tangled mess.
Teach us how to praise and bless.
We are crying with despair.
Please remind us that You care.
Comfort us; our hope renew.
Faithful Lord, we lean on You.

Patricia Kackman
GOD'S LOVE
Close to Thine everlasting solace
I would stay.
From Thy side, calmly resting, let
me never stray.
I have sampled life out alone
beyond the edge.
Wounded, I returned to Thine over-
shadowed hedge.
Like a deer, I nestle trustingly,
close beside
Love that's watching, prompting,
and will not
be denied.

Mildred D Hart
MUFFIN TO DENNA
I'd like to buy you a present but that I
cannot do
'Cause my collar cost so much and I
hate the thing it's true.
I've inherited this nice home and I
get, in fact, too much to eat
And the lovin' I get from Charlie
simply cannot be beat.

I'll never be able to pay you back for
the raisin' I get
But I sure love my relatives on that
you can bet.
I know, Dennie, friends are all
jealous of me
'Cause it's the truth—I am the
prettiest dog they ever did see.

And everyone knows I don't have
even one flea.
What's more, I'm little, but I'm smart
as a tack,
I remember my manners—
it saves me many a whack.

Now Denna has two grand-kids
comin' along
From that day on my life won't be a
song.
Most dogs have a hard life—my heart
aches for them all,
'Cause I'm Denna's special dog I'll
always have a ball.

And you can trust me not to tell your
age,
I don't want to see you fly into a
rage.
Just have a Happy Birthday is my
wish for you,
'Cause I sure love you, Denna, that is
true.

I know I'm special and cast a lot of
money,
But you deserve a dog like me,
Honey,
Don't expect too much out of me—
I'm not very old,
Just remember your dog, Muffin, is
worth her weight in gold.

Love, Muffin

Franceska Ceuterick
LOST LOVE
I would give the world
If I could find you.
I don't know
How I lost you.

For a little while
It was all right.
But now
I can't live without you.

I traveled a lot
Looking for you.
I feel in my heart
That you love me too.

At night I'm having dreams
That you lay by my side.
When I woke up
It was only a dream.

I hear your voice every-where.
If I find you:
I would give the world,
My heart and my love too.

MacKenzie C Martin
YOU AS MY MOTHER
You helped me through good
times and even bad
You were there for me when I
needed a hand
You helped me with homework
and other things too
You mean a lot to me, I want
you to know
You played games with us
and other things too
You cared for us and accepted
our love
You didn't get angry when
we kept you up late
You are the best you could
ever be.

Carolyn Reese
LIGHT OF BLUE
The Light of Blue comes
from within.
With the rising of the
morning sun, changes as
the dark passion of the
night.
With raging blue
fury as the beast
awakens from within.

Dee Bardo
PRECIOUS POSSESSION
Life was beautiful, no cares to take
hold,
For I was asleep, my dreams to
unfold.
Then like a plague seeping thru the
seams,
Came a foreign scent that disturbed
my dreams.
Fully awakened I bolted upright,
Felt my throat constrict and with it
fright.
My first thought was, Flee, get up,
get out,
"Don't panic, think clearly," I started
to shout.
Where are my shoes, my coat, better
yet the phone?
There's not even time to wait for a
dial tone.
Now the fire licked at my bedroom
door frame,
And suddenly nothing in the room
looked the same.
It was eerie and ghostlike, worse than
any nightmare could be,
I must hurry to the window—of this
intruder I must be free.
Springing barefoot and coatless a
thought came to mind,
Of all my possessions, what couldn't
be left behind?
Money, credit card, photos, jewelry
or testimonials of past glory?
To salvage any of these—there would
be no story.
I left with the most precious
possession of all,
A lifetime of memories and total
recall.

Nancy Rose Walker
SOMEONE SPECIAL

In memory of Mary Ruth Walker and to Lou Muncy for inspiration.

For so long . . .
I feared searching the dark corners of
my life.
Painful memories, threatening
shadows filled
too many waking moments.
Cautiously . . . I whisper . . . it's time
to explore.

Gently, I'm touching the
untouchable,
Stepping over boundaries created to
protect this sensitive starving soul.

Honesty beckons my frightened
spirit, and
I let the tears of healing flow.
Darkness becomes a rainbow of
colored lights.
I sense a foundation of love growing
as
I look within to see a butterfly
unfolding.

I'm still a little scared to believe, but
I'm beginning to understand how . . .
Someone as beautiful as you could
Love someone special like me.

Rhonda McMillon
BELLS
Laydown your arms
Laydown your wars
Give to each other
the tools you need
to live your life
free from mine
Choice thine
Reward divine

Patsy Goudy
DO YOU SEE YOURSELF?

This poem is dedicated to my precious mother and beautiful daughter.

There is a lady in our lives
She helps our days and calms our
nights
She starts out young and pretty
Do you see yourself?

She has only one true love
And six little rewards for that
She seems mistreated at times, alone
a lot
But she is busy in your life, helping
you out
Do you see yourself?

Forty, she seems closer than ever
You look at her and wonder, time,
how much?

Lover of only one man
Two little rewards for that
Alone a lot, busy in their lives
But I can see myself, thanks to her

She has always been there, your
friend
It seems as though time should stop,
keep her here with you
Simply because you need her
The void she would leave, the
loneliness, the pain that follows

Life goes on daughter, Do you see
yourself?

Edrie K Miller
OUR WORLD TODAY
When we read the paper
Or listen to the news
It fills us with apprehension
And makes us feel blue.

There is so much violence
In our world today
What happened to our common sense
That makes us get this way?

Murder, rape and drug abuse
Just to name a few,
But there just is no excuse,
I don't think, do you?

What's happening to our nation
We plunged so deep in sin
We better open up our hearts
And let our Christ come in.

He's our only salvation
In this awful age,
Help us God to repent
And start a clean, new page.

Brenda Mitchell
SONS

I dedicated this poem to Anthony & Ricardo and all of the sons of today.

Parents was always proud of their
sons.
Sons would carry the family name
on.
Sons would be their mother's
protectors.
Sons would grow into a man and be
there for the family when in need.
Sons would go off to college to be a
doctor or lawyer.
Those were the sons of yesterday.
The sons of today is just the opposite
from the sons of yesterday.
The sons of today don't live long
enough to carry the family name on.
The sons of today, their mother's
need someone else to protect them
from their sons.
The sons of today don't go off to
college, they only be incarcerated for
different crimes they have
committed.
The sons of today don't have no
shame, they don't even respect their
families or life.
For the sons that we have left
today, please bring back the sons of
yesterday.

Doris McQuiddy
DUSK
Every line of nature seems defined
in the special time of day
When the sun has finished
its last glory of fiery red
And fades the dusky rose
Making clouds look like filmy
substances
hung by angels' hands
Composing a setting for trees
that finger-like reach for early
stars.
Trees wave in ecstasy
from the motivation of the breeze.
Grasses raise their blades in salute
to the end of another day
And bow graciously to the new eve.

GAiLeichliter
ALL THAT'S GOOD
So many people I shall meet
along life's loving way;
and though friends come and go I find
their "goodness" always stays.

It seems so many friends are only
with me for awhile,
then they have different paths to take
we part with loving smiles.

But in our time together, be
it minutes, maybe years,
the good things they have shared with me
is something I hold dear.

So even though time passes and
years keep us far apart,
to think of all that's good brings friends
together in my heart.

Barbara A Doyle (BAD)
GONE FROM ME

This poem is dedicated to Laura, my youngest daughter, with love always & ever.

The stars are out, the sky is clear
I look in your room, but you're not here
You've been gone for almost two years now
But I pray some day, you'll come back somehow

They have come, and taken my little girl from me
I cried so hard, as I heard her plea
It was all in fun, I don't know what went wrong
But now my best friend is forever gone

The stars are out, the sky is clear
Oh how I pray, that you were here
Yet, you are gone from me, we're far apart
You're gone from me, but not my heart

You are so young, so sweet and fair
I miss you so, I can hardly bear
but in my heart I know, we'll be together again
Just have to find out how, where and when.

Elsa R Irom

Elsa R Irom
AUTUMN LEAVES

For mankind and sentiments for someone very special.

It is so great to dream
When hearts are young forever
And eyes aglow,
While we walk on a mountain trail
Or a meadow
The air is blowing cool and clean
The Sky so blue and clear,
With that golden Autumn Fair.
The leaves are dancing in gentle rhythm
As the wind is drifting by,
I try to find a poem
In their colorful-glamor fever glare
Each movement is a dream of freedom strife
To teach us the story of life.
God has grown a flower for every season
To fill our hearts with happiness,
So they bring us messages
About a thousand dreams,
To keep our traditions
In togetherness,
With unity faith and loveliness,
An adventure every Spring, Summer,
Winter, in the colorful leaves.
They bring us the spiritual sunshine
So soft so warm and pure.

Elsa R Irom
ETERNAL LOVE
God gave us the Earth
With everything there is therein
To bring man great blessings
And joy to share all things.
A Soul and wisdom to understand it.
Whenever we fail to reach his blessing,
He welcomes us with open arms
And blesses us all over again,
With wisdom, Love and understanding.
He gave us a field of flowers,
With angel locks on dandelions,
Queen Anne's Lace right near the nook with grace.
The blessing of a Baby basket
On a Rainbow balloon.
It must be a Masterpiece of Heaven
To cuddle and Love for old and young.
He always follows our lonely
Heart with his eternal Love, Wisdom and understanding.
Man of every color, creed and race,
He loves everyone.
He freely forgives all that we have done
And asks only if we are ready
To follow with joy in his Wisdom and Love
And he will answer all our needs.
A True Friend indeed.

Elsa R Irom
A GREAT HERO'S CALL
A Hero is a Man with a gentle Heart
Great Love and understanding
For all Mankind.
A Man that brings Eagle Spirit
And Lyons Courage.
A Man that does constant research with God,
In order to Lead and Guide us
Through suffering and difficult tests
A Man that faces dangers
In order to inspire us
With Greatness and Courage
To bring human Moral Values and Services
For a lasting Peace.
God's Seeds will bring forth the Grain
To heal wounds that can make
Restless Souls serene.
And when I am lonely,
He stands right besides me and guides me.

Elsa R Irom
MEMORIES WITH MY DEAR PARENTS
FREE SPIRITS
My Parents had great Spirits,
They always Cheered and loved us dearly.
My Mother taught us singing
My Father swimming.
He took four steps at a time
When my Brother was born
To blow his supper horn.
Every weekend we went out on a picnic meeting
At Farmers Restaurants, hicking and greeting.
We did a lot of Folkdancing and singing.
But more than treasures to hold,
He left us a heart of gold,
The talent to write Poems
And most of all, The joy to be cheerful,
Brave and free like an Eagle.
To remember his witful spirit
To beware us from evil.—
My Mother loved to dance, cook and sew,
My Father to paint and draw.
We went sledding by moonlight,
To be romantic and bright,
Especially on Silent Night.
The air was cold, the snow crisp,
The Moon and the Stars made the Night so bright.
We hold my father's and mother's hand tight,
As we walked to Midnight Mass,
To see the Holy Baby in the dried grass.
We bring him our Heart,
And promise the Holy Father,
To be good all Year like a cavalier,
To eat and live right,
And Keep God on our side.

Elsa R Irom
REFLECTIONS OF A DEAR MOTHER'S LOVE CALL
Is when the Lily of the Valley is in bloom,
They're shy little heads and distinguished fragrance
Is a dear Mother's Love Call—
God has grown them
To bring us Spiritual Sunshine
So soft, so warm and pure.
The Easter Lilys are a Mother's reflection.
The Lilacs and Violets a Spring Call,
The Wild Rose is bringing
Her warm Heart.—
The real Rose a Mother's Charm
And Romantic values of Love and Art.—
The Sea Rose a sweet and Romantic lullaby,
The Edelweiss, a very valuable, sensitive
And dangerous Call.—
The Alprose her favorite Nature Love Call.—
The corn Flower for her True Love,
The Dandelions and Daffodils
For her brightness.—
The Forgetmenots for her Heavenly Reflections
Of her most generous Perfections.—
Queen Anne's Lace for her Grace,
The Iris for her classical taste for Arts.—
All the Mountain Spices
To bring God's Healings
That Man may learn to Love each other more.

Nicole L Chenault
TEARS
They come most inconveniently.
They arouse the world's curiosity.
They're there when you're happy and when sad.
They're there when you're good, as well as bad.
They christen the day and darken the night.
They come in truces and in fights.
They hope for brighter, better days.
They come in many different ways.
They want to be noticed and denied.
They know the truth but always lie.
The things that I do speak of here,
Are things we know as little tears.

Diane Marie Bernardy
CHRISTMAS

Dedicated in memory of Samuel J. Gorzelsky "my little brother."

The sparkle of white snow in the morning
on the great green pines so adorning.
Blue skies sweep the background adding a lift
as the winds blow and toss a snowdrift.
A black bird flies overhead in a manner disdain
as the sound of an engine roars from a passing train.
In a crystal glass filled with champagne
sitting near the fireplace beneath the windowpane.
The sun shines down ever so creating a glare
as I rest back in my armchair.
I toast a praise to my creator brightly
for a Christmas morn so full and slightly.
The smell of wood and mistletoe along with pine cheerly
gifts wrapped in array of colors adds a touch dearly.
Church bells ring out in the distant with reason
giving an added touch in completing the season.

Linda G Ashmore
DO YOU WATCH THE EVENING NEWS
Do you watch the evening news
And see the plight of the homeless?
Is it ever more than just another broadcast?
Do you see families who have been living paycheck to paycheck
Who barely make ends meet?
Then, one day the company closes.
The job is gone.
Where do they go from there?
Suddenly, the bills are overwhelming.
The money is gone.
The house is lost.

They are homeless.
There is no one to which they can turn.
As I myself am caught in such a precarious situation,
And find myself borrowing money one more time
I think, "there but for the grace of God go I."

Patricia Funchess Harvey
LIFE

In loving memory to Pauline Dukes Funchess and Norton Hayden Funchess.

The mournful sound of the cooing dove,
The mist as dawn brings another day.
The earth awakes in all its glory.
When everything is still
and time stops for a brief moment.

Sharron Vest
IRMA'S HOUSE

I remember a porch swing
On a warm afternoon,
Laughter and sharing.
I remember a sky blue roof,
And under a sea of star, an open loft,
Nighttime philosophy and life comparing.
I remember wildflowers
As far as the eye could see,
And a house right in the middle
With an open door for me.
I remember cool country walks,
With the only sound our voices and the wind,
Listening and caring,
And wishing it never had to end.

Orlando Smith
JOY

To Christian and Ashley.

Joy to the world for you
And me yes
Joy to the
World
You are joy to the
World is you
Joy

V C Field
TO ERNIE

In memory of a Very Special Soul . . . Ernie Olivería.

Ernie, there's so much I needed to say
But now you're gone and here I stay
I will love you until my end
Proud and lucky to have called you "Friend"...
Always accepting and loving, too
Life is worth more because of you!

Oh dearest Ernie I hope that you're well
the barrier between us refuses to tell.
I like to imagine your Spirit is Free
and that thought is the only comfort to me.
I wish I could have kissed you "good-bye,"
Dear God: Why did our Ernie have to die?

Everyone's Time seems to come up too soon
Nothing is forever, not even the Moon
And the hardest part that I know
is to have shattered hope and have to let go.
Good-bye Ernie!

Rumaan Alam
AUTUMN

There lay a few crumbled ruins,
of a lifetime passed by.
Nothing more rains,
It is all empty and dry.

Dilapidated structures,
Rooted in the ground.
Flowers persistently clinging in fear,
Not making the slightest sound.

Tomorrow the flowers will be gone,
With the exception of some,
Gone will be all signs of summer,
For Autumn has come.

Tracy L Shull
DARK ANGEL

He beckons me from afar,
When nights are still,
In myth he is the silent one,
For I, a myth so real.
Not angel or God above,
Nor of Satan's own,
He passes thru doors of time,
No place to call his home.
Souls have often feared him,
Holes where eyes should be,
Bone in place of flesh,
Black robe to shelter he.
Some have left him enter,
When hope has lost its way,
Welcoming the peace,
He brings with each stay.
Lying in the darkness,
His presence I see clear,
He waits within the shadows,
For now, he comes not near.

Laurie Ann Holenski
FORGOTTEN

Can't remember the vision
of a love everlasting
Can't remember the deepness
of trusting eyes
Can't remember the nurturing
of helping hands
Can't remember the feeling
of never looking back
Can't remember the sensation
of passion in trust
Can't remember . . .
Perhaps it will never return.

Only tears seem to fill the void
Only space seems to remain
Only mountains too large to climb
Only separate time too hard to get past
Only doubting, every word, every moment, every phrase,
lingers, like dust in the past
Never settling . . . only clouding my view
Only rising to blur the future.

Laurie Ann Holenski
THE PAST

In whose memory do we serve time . . .
Does anyone remember us as loving or caring . . .
One life, one memory, one lifetime to live.
What sorrow tears the moment.

So sweet and simple the childhood years used to be,
Now so hard the struggle to get to yourself again.
So hard to accept what has transpired,
A difficult path to travel alone.

So tender was your Mother's love,
Always yielding, always there.
Perhaps the only real love to know.

Many tears and fears cloud the view,
and doubt lays where certainty once stood.
I look to the future but the past can't seem to be mastered.

Kerry Moore Felstul
PASSAGE

We begin with the sunrise
our love spreading with the color tendrils
to rise slowly with the sun's daily course
and stop for a while in the middle, at our highest
so high we get dizzy in the descent
a rapid fall; our love crashes to the ground
in an array of reds and golds and purples.
Our hate awakens with the night
when we wrestle the stars of truth
and find fault with ourselves,
wonder what the other sees
and wait for the morning.

Ruth Morton
WEDDING CANDLES

To my brother Gayle.

Our candles joined
And lit the larger stately one.
You blew out years.
I blew out mine.
We searched for each other
In the big flame.
We tried; We cried;
And we pretended.

I couldn't see you
Your light was out.
You couldn't see me
My light was out too.
We missed each other
In the big flame.
We tried; And we pretended.

I lit my candle in secret,
I suspected you did too.
Then we hid from each other
In the big flame.
And we pretended
We weren't pretending.

Elysia Green
MOONLIGHT LOVE

Into the moonlight I watch and I stare waiting for you to see me there.

I love you so much, but do you really care? You tell me you hate me without despair.

There is so much to say but I know you won't listen. When I look in your eyes they shine and they glisten.

Please stay one second more and don't leave yet, I want you to know my heart is set.

I shall always love you and care a little bit, I just don't want you to ever forget it.

Robert M Hodges
COUNTRY MORNING

The sun was warm, and bright,
aromas of Spring were heavy in the cool, gentle breeze.
The gravel underfoot crunched like crackers,
and felt sharp,
jagged,
and hard.
The grass smelled rich like green chocolate,
and the hay like rice pudding.
The stairs were rough,
and felt sticky,
like gum.
Biscuits and gravy lingering in the air,
the aroma of burning wood,
and the old stove,
crisp,
and pungent.

Gary Samz
BLACK SHEEP

Who cares what they think
Whether they sneer or wink
It's your opinion that counts
Theirs not a single ounce
If you ask them it will matter
Am I thinner or fatter
So what they don't care
It's only your affair
Drive back the noses
Safeguard your roses
They can't leave you be
You can't be free
Always someone to please
Paid for by taxes or fees
Why do they always cut down
They are the only clown
Be yourself not someone other
Not your sister or brother
He only cares what you do
Not what they do to you
If anyone be like him
He will not chastise your whim
The black sheep is the odd one
He has the most fun
He wears his own wool
Not the pigs or the bull
His soul cannot be created twice
The dots are white on his dice
Just be yourself
And you will have the greatest wealth

Evelyn Cotton Speer
LOVE WITHOUT A FACE

Was that your kiss upon my cheek
Or a lost drop of summer's rain?
Did you touch my hand in sleep
Or did a star fall from the Wain?
Could you step to me from death
Or did I dream your sweet embrace?
Was the sigh I heard your breath
Or were you Love without a face?

Evelyn Cotton Speer
TO LINDSAY

To Lindsay.

Trusted, long ago, with a baby's first steps,
Shoes with torn, scuffed toes,
Leather creased and torn from wear,
Small, fit in your hand size, high-topped shoes,
Remembering the chubby shape of baby feet,
Guides in childish adventure.

Silently they stand, telling the past in bronze,
Bookends, holding books
The boy, when grown, might have read.
Dipped in bronze, weighted, made immortal,
Constant reminders of the sound of small steps
Echoing in the hallway.

William Howard Akins
LITTLE OLD BLUE BUCKET
There are three little Buckets, others are brown and new
The one Little Bucket is old and Blue
The Little old Blue Bucket been sittin' alone in the corner every day
The workers ignore the Little old Blue Bucket that sat aside far away

The Little old Blue Bucket thinking, he would be if he
He was still thinking, if someone would put a mop inside of me once more
The Little old Blue Bucket thinking he will rust and fay way
The Little old Blue Bucket stood alone in the corner collecting dirt and dust every day

He remember when he was like the other Buckets, brand-new
The first day when a lady use him he didn't know her name was, Sue
The Little old Blue Bucket thinking I guess they will get rid of me, I'm wore out and old
Till thinking, I hope they won't put me out into the cold

The Little old Blue Bucket, was surprised to be pick up by a new man on the job
He wonder who is he, his name was, Bob
The man had took the old Blue Bucket home, painted and improved the Little old Blue Bucket a lot
The Little old Blue Bucket was happy the man made out of him a beautiful flower pot

Mark Woodfork
SOMEHOW, SOMEWAY
So many times, have I longed for your touch
And while we are apart, have I missed you so much
How nice it would be, to hold you in my arms
To see your beautiful smile, to experience your charms

There is something about you, that I just cannot ignore
You are one in a million, you are the one I adore
I need you here with me, my life you enhance
And I pray that together, we might give life a chance

In a world where our love, will know no measure
In that world you will be, my most valuable treasure
For a love like yours, is so very rare
And all I ask is for a chance, to show you that I care

So my hope will be, that you will understand
That a lifetime together, is what I have planned
So I will ask the Lord nightly, whenever I pray
That he will bring us together somehow, someway

Jessica Rusgo
I'LL NEVER FORGET
My wish finally came true
Though it only lasted for a
short time
I'll never forget you

I'll never forget the way you
held me in your arms
Or how you could always make
me laugh, no matter what

I'll never forget your smile
And I can still hear your
laugh echoing in my mind

But the thing I know I'll never
forget
Are the last words you said
to me:
I'M SORRY

Julie A Meyers
MEMORIES
Dark hidden shadows beneath your eyes
Give hints to the secrets that you hide
Stolen, borrowed, given, and lost
Is the time that we shared in the past
From joy to sorrow, life to death
From the first time I saw you
I knew you were lost
Locked behind forbidden doors
Gathering dust and cobwebs
Wishing for someone to care
Wishing for someone to share
The memories inside my mind

Holly Cosner
THE UNCOMFORTABLE SELF
For Carl Swann.

Infant sorrow
Screaming through marrow
of lost nights and meaningless days
Splendor falls and I am left with
the uncomfortable self
Beauty fades as well as hope
but some of each will never leave
I am only left here with the pains
of sleep
When I close my eyes, everything
changes.
I never know what is real
I just twist my lip and hope that
everything will be alright

Kristina Hester
LILAC MORNING
Lavender whisper, lilac breeze,
blossoms floating from the trees.
Scent of morning, moist of dew, all
bring me to my memories of you.
Simple pleasures, simple cares,
gentle laughter at times we've shared.
Tender smiles, tender touch, this lilac
morning I miss you so much.
I recall your fascination with spring, I
remember your love for everything.
I see your face inside the sun, I feel
your tears as the river runs.
I hear your voice in the rushing wind,
I feel your love as I say "Friend."
Missing you is breaking my heart,
but our spirits are one, never to part.
Again I smell the lilac breeze and
marvel at the bowing trees.
I feel the soft, moist morning air and
know that deep inside you care.
Wherever your life leads you,
whatever you may do.
Each Lilac Morning will lead me to
you.

Savonia Rickwa
THE PERFECT CURE
Julia Jamie Marie,
Had a terrible cough and a terrible sneeze
She had an ache in her arm,
And an ache in her leg.
Her brain was doing cartwheels
inside her head.

She had had it for about a month,
And her mom, she was quite fed up!
She took Julia by her hurting arm
And off she went to see Doctor Squarm.
He gave her some pills and in about a week
Julia had taken a bite to eat!

Her mom was so, so happy and glad
She threw a big party, but Julia was sad
Sad and depressed is something that
Doctor Squarm said would happen
And, as soon as her mom noticed this
She made her eat some chips and dip.

Suddenly she felt much, much better
Chips and dip were the perfect cure.
So if you ever get very, very sick
You can remember to eat chips and dip.

Stacy G Byrd
PICTURE WINDOW—WHITE LILY FIELD
This poem is dedicated to Erik, my hope, my inspiration, my life. I love you, Stacy.

When I walk through the meadow of pink and blue;
I turn around and I see you;
The mountains of green in the mist blue light;
Shades of yellow surrounding your eyes,
Next thing I know, we're walking hand in hand, by the bank of the river;
We both see a bright white light.
I turn to you, you turn to me, we are facing each other and our destiny.
No words are spoken, for we both understand, once we cross over into the white lily field, our safety is bound.
You look deep into my eyes and I look deep into yours,
We see a future of happiness in colors all the more; through love, joy, sadness and tears, we'll make it through all and leave our fears;
Our souls are one and are free to fly, fly forever
Across the opal sky—because, we know, that the white lily field, is in our reach as time draws near.

Joan Cardlin
REMEMBER ME!
This poem is dedicated to my mother Dorothy McCaffery, who dedicated her life to her family. She was my inspiration and I will remember her with love forever.

When the Spring Rain falls and new life begins
to grow
When all the flowers spring forth and the pastel
colors show
Remember me!

After the rain has fallen and the air is
fresh and clear
Know always I am somewhere near
Remember me!

When the sun shines bright on a summer's day,
And yesteryear seems far away
Remember me!

And when Fall turns the leaves into rainbows
of colors,
My favorite time of year.
Smile for me and shed not a tear
Just remember me!

When the snowflakes fall and the world
is a wonderland of snow,
And the fireplace burns and the Christmas
tree is aglow
Remember me!

And if your days are long and lonely
and no one seems to care
Somehow, somewhere I'll be there
Just close your eyes and
Remember me!

And when you hear a melody playing
You know it's just me saying
Remember me!

And if there are days that you may reminisce
of happy childhood years.
Please don't think of me with tears
Just smile and remember me!

And if once and a while you smile
and a thought of me passes by
Then I know my life wasn't wasted you see
For someone is remembering
me!

So pass on to all the generations, of the love
we had as a family
So I may live on forever
Because someone will be
Remembering me!

Frederick D Wuliger
THE WORLD WITHIN
The disc begins to rotate
And as the music floats from the
speakers
I am free

My soul sheds self-destructive
conclusions
Reached by years of direct
speculations
It soars above trees
Experiencing only emotion
Pure life

Then the music ends
A sad similarity to birth
I review all I felt

Which is a return to painful reality

I truly love to confuse my overactive mind
Thus I find new ways to fly

Frederick D Wuliger
PRIDE

Hold out your hands
Splash them in the clear flowing water

Now grasp the water
You cannot

Pamela Lemon

Pamela Lemon
HE CHOSE YOU!

To the man who taught me to love again, my husband, Richard!

Why do these thoughts go through my head?
I'm alive, I'm not dead.
You're the one who died that day.
I'm here because God said, "Stay!"

Like it or not, on earth I'll remain.
From thoughts of death, I'll refrain.
Somehow I wanted to be the first,
'Cause staying behind is the worse.

But god made His choice and He chose you.
And I trust our Lord because He always knew
Just how much pain I could endure.
I can survive, of this I'm sure.

I don't want to be lonely and sad,
Because I miss the love we had.
I want to live such a life,
That you would be proud I was your wife!

A D Bennett
I SIT AT THE END

I sit at the end
of a long stretch of wharf,
wooden slats nailed
together form this platform

Feet, clip these boards
like some uncoordinated
tap dancer. People compelled
to walk to its end.

Maybe they come
to stare at the light
reflected on the water,
from the sun as it sets.

Or maybe they are attracted
to the gulls crying. Whatever
their purpose, it seems as lost
to the wind, as their souls

Lorene Butcher Hall

Lorene Butcher Hall
OUR LIBERTY

Dedicated to: America and her future ones.

She stands on a pedestal high above the waters of this land.
She's a giant of a lady with a torch in her hand.

Representing all the people's of this nation.
Differences in religions, ideas, freedom for all races.

They came from every shore to live in America, leaving behind cultures of which they were born.
Entering this land of dreams; to them, was foreign.

The land of hope, opportunity, and liberty for all.
Viewing her from a distance, they know she's the "Lady of Liberty" that stands so tall.

On our nations call for restoration of the "Statute of Liberty."
Together, we'll keep her standing strong, she'll radiate a new beauty, all will see.

The torch she holds high will burn brighter.
We'll stand as one, this is our key.

As we unite, she'll ever stand to welcome each, to the land of the free, "America"

Lorene Butcher Hall
REFLECTION ON SEASONS OF TIME

As dusk gives way to the twilight of dawn, sun's golden glow shines, reflecting its warmth from the window to rest upon my face.
Lingering, brilliant light illumes its place.

If though on course, came, to awaken me from sleep. As chirping of birds fill the quietness of my room.
Knowing, their chirping to be interrupted much too soon.

Watching the sway of willow trees, as a gentle breeze excels.
Drifting in the wind, sweet fragrance of flowers fill my nostrils.

Each day, I have these special gifts, "One" who cherishes such moments of time.
Being aware in all that surround me, which nature designed.

Roaring of planes overhead reach my ears, as their presence silently fades.
Thoughts go beyond "My delight in serenity," of past decades.

History was made through seasons of time past, races of people fought and died.
When, in their time and place, had National Honor in their country's pride.

Now, as then, races of people on this beautiful earth have eyes of despair, whose land quake with war and death, they ask, does anyone care?

For those who experience day after day, seeing their home land crumble in ashes, no beauty in nature lie before their eyes.
Just in times past, century through century peace has been their cry.

Hope, for the fighting among civilizations to cease.
As yesterdays are gone and todays begin, let them reign with what each would give, for the tranquility of Peace.

Lorene Butcher Hall
FAMILY THOUGHTS

Nestled amidst the mountain's valley, draped in its shadow on a moon-lit night, a modest dwelling stands.

Within its foundation one's departure, on morning's arrival, begans.

Sleepless, lying in bed taking thought.

Will I miss my friends or the cat, on my birthday of seven mother bought?

Will it be, when family gather for a meal, I'll miss the most?

Preparations we make, chatting laughingly, as who slices the roast?

The walks together down the lane we take, on a bright sunny day?

Observing the field being reaped, as a neighbor works to bale the hay.

Will I forget fun times of playing, running in the meadow, through the years with Ollie?

When I return, will she be first at the gate to greet me, the family's pet collie?

On summer nights, sitting in the porch swing, relishing in each sight and sound.

The beautiful bird call of the "whippoorwill," croadking of the frogs, with fireflies flying all around?

Could it be, time shared with brothers and sisters in the playhouse, daddy built beneath the big oak tree?

Finally, eyes weighing heavy, yes, I realize I'll dearly miss my family, and; as all thoughts must come to an end—

I know, it will be, "One special lady,"
My mother—My friend.

Lorene Butcher Hall
LINKED THROUGH LIFE'S MEMORY

With prevailing wind showering snowflakes, goes the fading autumn. Forgotten in the ebb of first frost.
An ocean of Winter white, medleys of dappled colors lost.

Briefly changing, brings presence of mystique, while captivating, "Magically" inhibits.
As portraits unique, in their pose of natural exhibits.

Tender its time in youth blooms the budded rose, drenched in spring showers.
Challenging passage of the year's seasons, the vine, bearing its flower.

When passing by, left with places and visions in mind.
Tho blossoming then fading each season ultimately intertwine.

Vanished, Autumn's array of dapple colors, Lost is the snowflake among those fallen. Withered, a rose on its vine.

Granted still, the memory. So it is,

in one's first love,
yet linked mysteriously.

Siri German

Siri German
LOVE

Dedicated to my husband, Dennis for all his "love" and support!

Hushed air
sleek, silent pathways
moonlit journey with
crystallitic realms.

Encompassing, renewing
seducing the lingering reluctance
coaxing softly, inaudibly
soothing, quenching.

Whispers, dark, candid
trailing freely
into wide meadows
never tread before.

Open trusting fields of splendor
magnets compelling with
outstretched hands
till yielding whimper
and time stands still.

Siri German
CHRISTMAS MEAL
Watch . . .
The vacant stare of the mystery man
Picking his food from a garbage can

Hollow eyed with creviced cheeks
Dirt caked shoes been walking for weeks

Rumpled clothes torn and ragged
Searching through the stench and maggots

Salvaging a moldy burger
Wilted lettuce, haunting fervor.

Joanne I Lussier
OUR BACKYARD

Dedicated to: "PLANET EARTH" (Our responsibility).

We looked at it more than once.
As a matter of fact twice.
And realized that it was not nice
at all
People throwing things recklessly in our backyard.
Maybe they don't think
or forget someone lives here.
We looked at it closer and found:
Fenders
Suspenders
Tires
Burned out fires
Iron bars
Old rundown cars
Disposable diapers
Warped windshield wipers
It looked disgusting
All this rusting
"JUNK"
Whose backyard is it?
I told you: "OURS"
Yours and mine!

LeRoy B Schwan
TEACHING
Bright cheerful faces
wanting so to learn.
Dirty sullen looks
wanting just to spurn.
Polite and eager
children learning how to write.
Sarcastic lazy
bodies wanting just to fight.
Motivated angels
wanting to spell and read.
Spoiled teasing
ruffians not taking any heed.
Little boys and girls
tuned in for the math.
Some restless talking
creatures needing a good bath.
The rewards are many
for those who like to teach.
But baby-sitting's boring
for those students we don't reach.

Julie Christine Wacker
LOVE
Hands intermingling,
entwined.
Lips brush,
sensual.
The feeling,
forever.
A mutual bonding.
Eyes,
glistening like
rays of the sun
Lasting adornment.
Loving
for Eternity.

Emily R Whalen
SUMMER DAYS IN THE PARK
The carrousel sang gaily
Horses seemed to fly,
As children
Reached out for the brass ring,
Again and again.

Summer days, happy days
The park is green.
The trees dressed; for aye
Children would climb
Today—and laugh.

Thelma O'Donnell
AFTERTHOUGHT
No, I feel neither sinful nor virtuous.
All I know is
that on that night
it was important to love you.

I had no words
to say goodbye.

Lynette Rene Fouche Davidson
OLD MEMORIES
I don't know why I am thinking of you now,
I don't think of you much anymore.
I only remember the pain I felt,
the day you said it is over, and
walked out the door.
I never wonder what you're doing,
or even how you have been,
I only remember your sweet love,
and why it could never be that way
again.
I never think of the trouble we had,
or if you ever think of me.
I only remember the look on your face,
the happiness to be free!
I guess I will live with these old memories
and the way it used to be,
and only remembering the part,
of how much you had meant to me.

Shirley A Lawrence
MY DREAMS
When all the kids were little
And there never seemed time to think,
I used to dream of things I'd do
While scrubbing out the sink.

With two of them in diapers,
Two more riding trikes,
And two of them in grade school,
I'd dream of all MY likes.

And then those two were Seniors,
The older ones were gone.
The years had flown, and so had they -
It didn't seem so long.

Now it's time for all those dreams
I had while I was young.
The things to do, the places to see,
The songs I've not yet sung.

My hair is grey, my eyes are dim,
But my heart is young and sure.
And the Grand Kids call me Speedy,
While I follow my dreams lure.

Sheryl Bean
A MOTHER'S SON
A mother's son is never forgotten,
A mother's son is so close to her heart.
Even though prison bars separate them,
In spirit they're never apart.
Every night when the twilight is falling,
The pain in her heart begins calling.
And her work worn hands hold the bible,
While she searches the scriptures for answers.
Her pleas to the Lord are endless.
And they've never fallen on deaf ears.
But the Good Lord has His reasons for waiting,
And she knows she has not been forsaken.
Still the grief in her eyes is so plain to see.
And tears fill her eyes at the mention of his name.
She sighs at the empty days that remain,
Until he comes home again . . .

Ray Motondo
LIFE IS:
Life is: This.
What we know.

Life is: The hands of time that tick ahead
into the unknown
from present to future
the long-distance
not reached by phone

Life is: Test upon test
The hardest of tasks
Fulfill this task,
Attain success; succeed,
For in the end you'll be judged
And he will be pleased

Life is: The plan that is laid
The road that is paved
The game you must play
If you wish to be saved

Life is: This.
What we know . . .
. . . What do we know?

Janine Gentzkow
ONE LONELY NIGHT
One lonely night
I travel down
A darkened road
The place deserted
Trees surround me
On both sides
A gentle breeze
Is blowing softly
The air is humid
After a sticky day
An owl hoots
A wolf howls
The rocks scatter
As I slowly drag along
My feet are sore
For I've been walking
For several days
I have no water
I have no food
But one thing I have
Is my pride
Most wouldn't
If they were me
For I am not perfect
But are any of us
They treat me
As a stranger
Perhaps they wish I was
Then they would not
Be forced to claim me
For I am mentally retarded.

Delia M Bermea
THE HOMELESS
They huddle in groups or stand off alone
In the bitter winter of ice and snow
As patiently they wait for shelters to open
For a brief respite from the awful cold

Who are these people we try to ignore
Whose living conditions we abhorrently deplore

It's difficult to believe they were once like us
With homes and jobs until misfortune struck
With no mercy shown them they were left no choice
But to live on the streets in misery untold

Without an address to call their own
They are unable to even apply for jobs
So a vicious cycle permeates their being
As society looks with indifferent disdain

How sad, how sad, the same fortune
Could so easily happen to you or me

Debra Odren
YOUR BEAUTY GLOWS LIKE A CANDLE
Your Beauty glows like a candle in a darkened room,

Our love we feel is like a star on a moonlit night,

Its single beauty is not noticed by all, but it's seen by few.

The few who can see beauty in pain
and love from afar,
Those who still dare to dream of
things others say can't ever come
true.

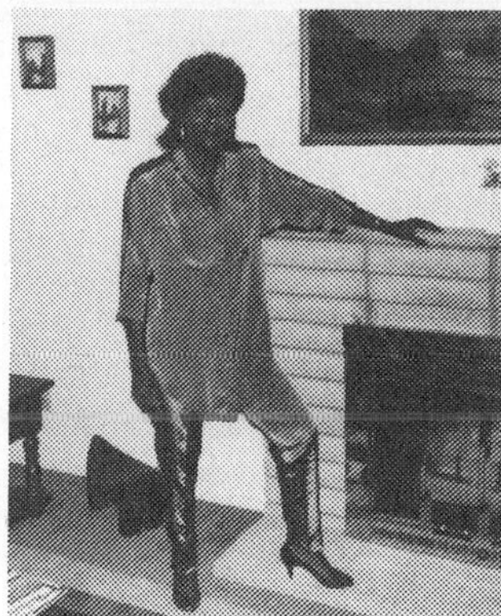

Jane Y Freeling

Jane Y Freeling
INVEST IN YOUR FUTURE

To my third grade class at Huntington School.

It's important to put forth best efforts
Never settling for anything less
Valuable time is never wasted,
Energetic, creativity with carefulness
Sticking to the task at hand
Trying to accomplish your goal

It is necessary to strive for a brighter
tomorrow
New ideas are as good as the old.

Yes, your time is important
Open a good book each night
Use your skills to build upon
Rewards are there in sight.

Fill your minds with wisdom
Usually ideas will flow through
Try to learn what you need to know,
Understanding may be slow
Rewards will come with knowledge
so,
Education will make you grow.

Cheryl L Pizura
THE FOUR SEASONS

I dedicate this poem to Mr. and Mrs. Bernard Pizura,and my daughter Candace.

The spring is your favorite time of
year
to be able to breathe in the fresh air
The grass gets greener a little more
every day,
it's the lawnmower and rake on the
way
You open your windows to get some
spring breeze
then all of a sudden it's the allergy
sneeze
By this time you're ready for the
summer heat
to sit on the beach and get red as a
beet.
By now you're saying you can't take
the heat it's the fall time you think is
really neat.
But as you know the fall goes by so
fast.
forever here you wish fall could last.
Now winter's here but that's okay for
in the snow you can play.
The storm windows are down, now
it's really cold.
it's going to be a long winter so
we're told.
As the snow's piling up at your front
door.
it's the wintertime you can't take
anymore
New England is what Florida should
be
it's the four seasons for all you and
me.

Robert Carlton
LIFE . . . WHAT?
Life:
a theatre full of time
a history of memory;
mountain Earth,
our lives in layers
the past
until now, unto me.
Am I from what I became
or what I was to become?
And who taught what
we learn to live,
or what taught who
we live to yearn?
Once having what we live to want
can't be enough compared
to what we were used to having once.
What of a final goal?
through generations of tiers
we reach,
hands empty for help of sin,
survival a story folded into Earth,
a mountain of us within.

Robert Carlton
DONNA'S EVE

This one is for Donna, my everything.

Midnight waned,
a hushed glow spilled on sky,
I heard the morning sneaking up
restless dawn
lights winked, the door shut.
Those eyes that see so much
sleepy, lifted
then looked
In love I became you.
We two tied
bound by a love and more
that emotion with no name
we make.
Naked souls
our lives meld,
with the heat
from those eyes that can melt
I want to be one
as one
with you,
with love.

Amy Thienpont Bell
KEEPER OF THE SWANS

To my dear son, Richard.

I am the keeper of the swans,
The swans of illusion
Enamoured of their own beauty
Reflected in the tranquil pool
Where float the lotus flowers
Of remembrance, of regret.
I am the keeper of the swans
Of love, rising on triumphant wings,
The trumpeter swans,
The flightless swans now flown.
The swans of farewell
Gliding down the river of tears
Forever fed by the tears of
mourning . . .
I am the keeper of the swans,
The swans of love, the swans of
death.
They are the same swans.
I keep a thousand times a thousand
swans
But only one royal peacock
With a thousand jeweled eyes
Of purple, emerald and gold
He spreads out for me alone to see.

Amy Thienpont Bell
THE GLASS HARP
From a distance heard . . .
From the shadows seen . . .

In fragile illusion
The quivering strings
Struck softly by ghosts unseen,
Shimmer in the moonlight
Cascading gossamer rainbows of
sound.
Is it the voice of the wind
That stirs the strings
To luminous melodies,
Or the hands of my lost love
Amorously caressing them
To play again our song of love.
I cannot know
For when the door is opened
The glass harp stands silent
Shrouded in mystery
Shrouded in dust.

Amy Thienpont Bell
ROSES IN OCTOBER
Alienated successors to the roses of
June,
The nubile bee-kissed buds
Since fallen,
They wear their late beauty with a
difference
Out of time, out of season
And bow in apology
To the zinnias and the marigolds,
The rightful heirs to Indian Summer,
And to the gilded maple trees.
Death-kissed sad and aging
courtesans
Anxiously trembling on their frosted
stems,
Pinch-petaled,
Barren of pollen and uncourted by
bees,
They feel
In every tinted, painted, perfumed
petal
The coming thorny winds
Of November.

Amy Thienpont Bell
WILD STALLIONS
Riderless
Wild and free.
As the roaring thunder
Of their approaching hoof-beats
Strikes sparks like lightning
The very earth beneath
Trembles with desire for their beauty.
Madly galloping
Manes and tails streaming like
banners,
Gasping nostrils snorting fire
They appear. Milk-white steeds
luminous
Against an amorous night sky
With a love-sick moon rising . . .
Neighing, shrilly neighing,
Rearing up, plunging at the vacant
air,
Frantic in their lust for life—
Before they disappear forever
In a pillar of fire and smoke,
Beyond the rim of the canyon,
Beyond the bend in the river.

WRITTEN IN PROTEST AGAINST
THE SLAUGHTER OF THE WILD
HORSES IN OUR OWN WEST.

Janet J Messick
SITTING

To my mother, Roberta N. Jones, for all her love.

She sat in the yard chair
overlooking the fresh mowed
lawn.
Watching the evening sky
turn into vibrant hues like dawn.

She contemplated life here
as she sweetly hummed a hymn of
old.
She sat and thought of her children
as her dreams and memories
would unfold.

She watched the rabbits creep past
the cabbage
to the garden's grassy edge.
And she hoped she might spot a
redbird
sitting on the peach limb's ledge.

She often thought it lucky
to see the cardinal's blood-colored
chest.
She loved the male ones most
because the way they always
dressed.

If I could give her something
that could make her lucky each
day,
I would give my Mother peaceful
skies,
sweet memories and a redbird to
pass her way.

Dedee Mariani
AS I SIT HERE AND WONDER
As I sit here and wonder
My thoughts seem to say
Will I ever find peace
Day after day.
As I sit here and wonder
What tomorrow will bring
There will be no more sorrow
And again I shall sing.
As I sit here and wonder
Will I be sad and blue
For I think of tomorrow
And the joy of being with you.
As I sit here and wonder
What life is all about
I can't help but wonder
Is that all I have but doubt
As I sit here and wonder
My life was a mess
For tomorrow is sunshine
And my heart is at rest.

Wayne M Bushnell Jr
UPON MY GRANDMOTHER'S DEATH

To my grandmother, Mrs. Lillian Jeramiah (1902-1988).

Dawn's incandescence cast a chilling
silhouette
Upon the suffocated shadow of a
sunken sunset
Eternally lost from Life's stage,
Eternally mounted in memory's cage!

Buried in the blackness of this
paralyzed past
Brutally bound to a ghost ship's mast
Eternally lingers Life's lost page,
Eternally mounted in memory's cage!

Pounding in the pall of this chilling
silhouette

Drones the doleful dirge to a sunken sunset
Eternally missing from Life's stage,
Eternally mounted in memory's cage!

Groping in the grave of this paralyzed past
Sadistically shackled to a ghost ship's mast
Eternally endures Life's missing page,
Eternally mounted in memory's cage!

Cursed be the casting of a chilling silhouette
Upon the asphyxiated ashes of a sunken sunset
Eternally extinguished from Life's stage,
Eternally emblazed in memory's cage!

Jo Nichols
THIS IS ME

To my dear grandmother, Mary B. Nichols, who loves a good book.

A hollow feelin' is cast upon the Willow Tree
Amidst the branches, there is little to see

A Winter haven, lasts too long
freezes up the present and in leisure is gone

The color of the day speaks for itself,
with little or nothing to say

A myriad within myself, leaves a question as where to begin
Sometimes I think that I'm not here, I take a step and disappear

A short note to occupy the growing trend, a drawing room awaits to befriend

A beat of Raga does wonders to your head,
and third-world countries are underfed

A stepping stone to dance upon,
lights the night, to create
This is me, endless words that go unheard

Deborah York
NATHAN
Nathan, distressingly shy, led the class today.
Teaching his peers to make origami boxes.
Step-by-step the boxes and his courage developed,
Nathan's self-confidence finally emerged,
like a new day's sun.
I sat back and enjoyed the radiance,
Reflected in the glowing faces of his peers.

Hugh J White
THIS THING CALLED LOVE

To Ronnie my wife, for forty years of the good life.

A tender look, a whispered word,
Your heart beats faster when she is near.
A fleeting touch, a treasured smile,
You know these feelings because she's dear.

Moments of bliss, privately shared,
Your life starts anew with each day's dawn.
Fulfillment comes to all you do,
Two lives now entwined, memories spawned.

These feelings last, bringing new thrills,
And new blessings come from Heaven above.
You wonder why - and then you know,
You have discovered this thing called love.

Anne Marie Nolan
MY CAMELOT THE CAPE

This poem is dedicated with joy to a friend.

There are no maids in waiting, or knights in shining armor here
Sand dunes, windswept beaches and salty air
At dawn I walk the shore alone, never lonely
My friend walks with me, for I would share the peace and beauty
I turn my back to the wind to fight the cold
The footprints left in the sand are quickly washed away
Leaving no trace that I was once here
In the distance I hear faint echoes of childrens' voices
My mind envisions them at play
Time passes quickly and I must leave this place.

At sunset I return once more to the shore
The tide is low so I wander out some distance
I walk perhaps where no mortal has ever tread
As I look out in the distance the sun seems to rest on the water's edge
I feel overwhelmed by it all
Darkness comes quickly here, and it holds it own beauty
Is this not then "My Camelot"

Laray Scott
THE MEANING OF LOVE
Love is tender. Love is true.
God is love and family too.
Love is sweet, not sour at all;
Helping friends is also love.
It is sent from God above;
Love is a word seldom used;
The word love can't be abused;
Love is like a needle very sharp;
You make one mistake and it breaks your heart;
But after a while the pain goes away;
You can make it better again any day.

James Evans
A LETTER TO MY WIFE

Love for Jamie Louise Wright, Joshua M. Evans, Keshia A. Evans.

Dear Darling, remember
When we kissed and said bye,
It hurt me so bad,
That as you left I began to cry.

I love you and I hope
You still care and love me . . .
Ever since you left
In my eyes you're all I see.

I don't want to lose you,
'Cause my heart don't feel right . . .
I have been going to bed,
And I just can't sleep at night.

I hope you haven't found,
A love that now is new . . .
'Cause I love you so much,
What am I now to do?

Al Kaminer

Al Kaminer
I KNOW THE WORLD BELOW

Dedicated to the Original Old-Timers—Who were pulling gates—wooden—Reliable Clapboards—Beyond the Retirement age—until the City set them Free—and made a bonfire of both B.U.'s Bklyn, Unions and Steel B-types—

I know the world below—
where the trains thunder forth—
south and north—where the
Crowds—pour in like
sand—the consuming—
madness—that ensues—
WHEN THINGS—get out of hand
I know the fears—
AND HATES—THAT OPEN AND
Close TALLONED GATES —

I know the defiant Slave—
the ghosts that walk the long deep
grave—I know the dupe—
the pickpocket—the CASTOFF—
whose dreams—have long been
Sunk—I know the song and
dance—of little—Souls—
at the balancing poles—I
know the filth and stench—
of that long endless
trench The Stagnant—
indifferent pose—the
creature that grabs your
Seat under your nose—
The fluke—who waits
for the bell to ring—
then Scatters his brains—
to get on the Train—
as the doors—begin to Swing—
I know The World Below—

Created By Al. Kaminer—From the Army—and Marines—honorably discharged—As a Buck Private—

Linda Willis
I NEEDED SOME TIME AWAY
I wanted to tell you that I needed some time away.
To think about my life,
I can't go on this way
Even though you're always here for me,
I really don't want to part.
There is so much love for you deep in my heart.
And I need you oh so much.

I'm going to be away to have some time to say,
Just what's really important to me
Each and every day.

I've had so much beautiful times with you.
And the love you give is true.
You've shown me what it's like to love again like you.
I'll always love you, I'll always care,
No matter what I decide I'll
Shed a tear for you.
When I return I'll hold you close.
To tell you what's going to be.
But I know—I won't set you free.

Catherine M Griswold
ERIC
It seems as if I've been alive forever,
And it seems as if I've wanted a baby of my own for just as long.

One day I awoke nauseous and ill and I realized that my dreams were about to come true.
I was going to have the baby I always wanted. One to love and nurture,
To fill a void—the need to be a mother.

The waiting was endless, the nine months passed slowly.
My patience grew thin, my body was swelling.
What I was forgetting was that I was creating a life so tiny and new.

Finally the day came when you were to arrive. The labor was endless, the pain intense. As the hours dragged on and you were in distress, I felt exhausted and powerless.
My anxiety was high and I feared for your safety.

When they finally handed you to me the feeling was so incredible,
What a precious gift to be given.
A beautiful baby boy.

I love you so much my son. And as I look down at you sleeping so peacefully
In my arms I thank God for bringing you into my life. I pray I can always
Be the loving and nurturing mother you desire.

I love you my beautiful, lovely baby boy Eric.

Patrick H Peery
CHILDREN ARE!

I dedicate this poem to "my gift from God above," my one and only precious son! Patrick Joe Perry.

Children are: a special gift sent from God above,
they're put here on earth, with the only worth,
for every mom & dad to love.

The year was eighty-two, an with a sky so blue,
We got a special blessing from our God above.

With eyes so blue, he was shared by two "(mom & dad)", in what's known and called,
THE ACT OF LOVE.

Twelve years of school later was the day to come, when he would finish an be done, then leave without a SHOVE.

Come their last day, before they leave on their own way,
All they can leave behind, for you to find is.

A clean room, household pets, old friends, lots of life-long memories, and
MOM and DAD's SPECIAL KIND OF LOVE.
THIS is what CHILDREN ARE.

Laura Napier
SALUTE ME

To my family, Thanks for believing in me.

Salute me
For I am special
I devoted my whole life
To service

See my uniform
It is always clean and pressed
My buttons are sparkling gold
My shoes are black and oh so shiny
My medals cover my breast like armor
See these birds on my coat

Many hours I worked to get them
The coat I wore into battle is tattered and torn
See the hole they made
I am weary now I see darkness surround me at noon

Salute me
As "Old Glory" warms my bed
My medals are shiny
My uniform clean and neat
My shoes reflect the saddened faces

Salute me
For I died proud!

Rocky J Daigle
LIGHTS, CAMERA, ACTION

To "Snakeboy," Thanks for the inspiration you have given to my heart.

Gazing out my bedroom window
Mesmerized by the sky so blue
I begin to ponder thoughts of you

The moon so bright, so bold, so new
They reflect the feelings
I have for you

A flicker of light
That flutters a tear
Which makes me fear
My soul's foreshadow of you

A star I see
A star I'll be
Because, my dear
You live and breathe inside of me

Now I believe,
YOU will always be
the center of my everlasting eternity

Debbi Wilhelm
MAKING IT EASIER

To Mom, who has stood behind me - for better or for worse . . .

I think I know where I'm going
but the road leads away from here.
This means a long and lonely walk
from the people I hold dear.

I don't want to go - but they're calling,
those voices from within.
"Come away - you're older now,
Look where you're going — not where you've been."

And Mom, I'm so afraid of going,
afraid of losing you!
I guess my frustration is showing
in the things I say and do.

But please remember, I love you,
no matter what I say.
It's just those darn insecurities
keep getting in my way.

Someday, I know the clouds will lift
and I'll make it through this rain.
And then I know, when I come home
that we'll be friends again . . .

Shauna Endo Ramirez
IS LOVE . . .

IS LOVE . . . the tingling feeling I get when you hold me near and tight?
IS LOVE . . . the smile I see when everything is going right?
IS LOVE . . . the squeeze of your hand when I need to know everything is going to be alright?
IS LOVE . . . the special card just for me with all the right words?
IS LOVE . . . your "TRUST"?
IS LOVE . . . your strength you give me when I have none?
IS LOVE . . . the security I feel?

If these things mean "LOVE" then I have found my one and only love "YOU!"

Samuel S Laury
MY LAST REQUEST

I came into this world unknown;
Unknown lived, labored and die;
Why then erect, for me, a stone
That tells where under an unknown lie?

Burn, instead, my flesh and bone
And fling the ashes into the sky;
For there is where my soul will've flown
And shall reunite by and by.

And whether, in death, my beloved wife
My precursor or follower be;
Meld our ashes so, as in life,
Together we'll be eternally.

Josephine Bolechala
THE WALL OF SHAME

A downcast woman lingers
On a dusty city bench
With wings down, leaden limbs, how down!
Parched lips once kissed, now uncaressed,
Eyes glued on the graffiti
"Love's dead history."
Engraved on the Wall of Shame.

Listen to autumnal leaves rising,
With the turbulence of youth's storm rising,
Tearing, pressing, pacific dancing, lapping
Up space and time in fiery embrace
Wake O lethargic heart, take a leap!
Let the barren world stand in awe,
For there's nothing more promising than defiance.

And there's nothing more powerful than Love,
Come down, tear it open the iron curtain
Of fear. Lovers of the same city,
Once separated, sing a leap of Love!

People of the same planet in cold war,
Sing a leap of love forevermore
Disarm the proud masterminds,
Bring down the Wall of Shame.

Candice Perry
CHANGES

With love, to my mother and father.

There comes a time in our life,
When changes may come about.
And sometimes we may think
These are changes we could live without.

But, if we are to go on,
And try to continue with his plan
We must accept change in our life,
And try to do the best we can.

For our Lord is God Almighty.
And we must put all faith in Him.
So we can't question where we're going,
Or look back on where we've been.

We can only believe in Him,
And know that He is in charge
Of all the changes in our life
All that we do, and all that we are.

Leigh Maness
TRANSITION

The tears fall like raindrops
The pain is a bolt of thunder jolting my body
The darkness, black and grey, shade my heart
while I stand in a distant storm of confusion.

But once the raindrops quit falling
The pain lingers on,
and the sun's shadow follows close behind.
The black and grey turn to colors of the rainbow
and make me glow all over again.

Deborah Ann McVay
UNTOUCHED BY HUMAN HANDS

I saw a world outside my window today.
There were birds chirping, bees buzzing;
Why, I even saw a grasshopper jump.

Buds were blossoming everywhere
Into beautiful red, yellow and white roses;
Yet, one I noticed more than any other.

Its color was like that of a peach
And its petals looked as soft.
It was the most beautiful Peace rose.

Everything thrived that grew around it.
Nothing tangled, not even two blades of grass
Where I saw the Peace rose grow.

It was a world of calm and quiet.
No blowing wind to tear things down
Or freeze to make things die.

It was a world I'd never seen.
So completely unique that
Its beauty left me breathless.

I saw a world outside my window today.
One of happy, peaceful existence.
There was not one human in it.

Jo Anne McAbee
MY LITTLE BROTHER

With pen in hand I try to find
The words that really say,
The things I think
And how I feel
In a very special way.
When I was just a little girl
I prayed to God above,
For a little brother
To care for and to love.
It seems it took a lifetime
For God to work His plan.
And sometimes in the waiting
I didn't understand.
But I waited and I prayed;
And now the answer's come.
I have a little brother,
A very special one.
But God so gracious in His plan
Gave not just a brother,
Because you see, He gave to me,
A very special mother.

Sylvia Hopkins
THE OLD HOMESTEAD

The old homestead still sits there on a quiet country road. No little children play there as they did so long ago.
Is the old choke cherry tree still standing in a field there all alone.
Can I hear an echo of my parents GOD gave me for a loan?
Are the goats still in the pasture eating grass upon GOD's land.
Can I see my father pitching horseshoes in some far off distant land?
Will GOD let me walk upon it, once more before I die? To see my mother in the kitchen, and then you'd know the reason why.
For she was the dearest mother and now she is gone away with Dad to another homestead, somewhere up in the sky.
Where their children will be waiting to enter their home up yonder still.
For a grand reunion in heaven.
And the LORD will greet us there.

Helen J Allen
FRIENDS FOREVER

To my mother, best friends Stella & Lashonda Thomas, Karen Harvey. Thanks for believing in me, with all my love.

I held out my hand,
and someone took it,
and said I'm with you all the way,
and when I needed someone to talk to,
you were there.

When I needed a shoulder to cry on,
you patted me on my back,
and said don't worry.

And now you're looking for
that same feeling,
So turn around slowly, and look at

me.
I'm here, just like you were there for me.

Friends can never be forgotten,
as long as they are friends,
So lay your head on my shoulder,
and cry out loud, I'm here,
To comfort you, as you did for me,
And we will always be
Friends, Forever!

Brenda Markley
A LATE NIGHT STORM
I try to sleep upon this restless night,
The clouds floating eagerly and the stars shining bright.
As the clear, cool wind blows through the trees,
My mind is open and my body's at ease.
A bright light in the sky and a small thunder I hear,
When suddenly small drops upon my window appear.
The thunder was loud and the lightning was bright,
There's nothing like a storm in the mid of the night.
The winds die down and the dark clouds pass,
Leaving heavily watered flowers and the smell of wet grass.
My eyes start to blink and things begin to go from sight,
Where I find myself sleeping through the rest of the
Night.

Paul M Ryan
RESPITE
I stopped atop a mountain once
To gaze at the world below.
All was calm and peaceful there.
I had no wish to go.

The snow was fresh and terribly bright.
The sun and breeze were both just right.
My spirits were lifted because of the view
And I wished that you could share it too.

The lake below so deep and blue
And the cloud-capped hills beyond—
Stirred my soul so fresh and new
To yearn for the calm of a peaceful pond.

Wars rage the world around.
Here—the silent, peaceful sound.
Would that the world could see this place
And erase the wars that scar its face.

Paul M Ryan
MASTERS OF THE EARTH
The leaves are falling on the ground.
They're doing it without a sound.
The trees on which they did abound
Endure their loss without a sound.

There's a lesson here that's very plain:
All of nature is an endless chain
Of life and death and birth again.
All but one creature does not complain,
And it has as heart, a soul, and a brain!

Paul M Ryan
ODE TO JAY'S RETIREMENT
Farewell to those who've asked you for money;
Hello to free time to spend with your honey.
Farewell to bosses who asked you for more;
Hello to golfing from mountains to shore.

You've made all your money, so relax on your deck.
Let others get stressed over each rubber check.
From sunup to sundown just do what you will—
Why, what the heck, you're well over the hill.

So get in your camper and travel around
To faraway places where you can't be found.
Let the grass grow up under your feet.
It's time to let callouses grow on your seat.

Look forward to fun, it's your time in the sun.
Know that your life's work has well been done.
Be proud of accomplishments and all that you've sired
For that's what it means to be known as "retired."

Paul M Ryan
BEACH BUM BRADLEY
On the sunny sandy shore
By the shining surfing sea
There's abandoned there a cottage
By an old and twisted tree.

In that old abandoned cottage
By that old and twisted tree
Lives the ghost of Beach Bum Bradley
Who was killed in a surfing sea.

On the sunny sandy shore
By the shining surfing sea
You can see the steps of Bradley
Coming up out of the sea

To that old abandoned cottage
By the old and twisted tree
Where the spirit of surfing seasons past
Still lingers by Bradley's sea.

Paul M Ryan
AH TEN HUHT!
ATTENTION!
The Captain is coming.
"Your boots are not shined."
But that doesn't matter;
The trails are mined.

Inspecting your weapon—
"There's rust on the bore!"
Stabbed a man yesterday
Sure he was sore.

The Captain has stopped
To look at your brass
Hasn't been polished—
Makes him act crass.

What does it matter
How good we all look?
Fighting is dirty;
But we live by the book.

Barbara Britton
IF YOU BELIEVE

This poem is dedicated to my mother, Sharon. For believing in me, and helping me believe.

There will come a time when you must fulfill a dream,
A destiny that will take a while and days that will look grim,
But it's something worth the wait and pain,
There will be days with sunshine and days with rain,
Follow your dreams if you believe in yourself.

A feeling of frustration from failure will cross your path,
But never give up you still have a lot to succeed with,
If you believe nothing could keep you and your dream apart,
Let the feeling of accomplishment flow through you.

Don't let failure get the best of you,
Learn from it and give all that you feel is true,
Allow no one to tell you that you can't succeed,
Show them that they're wrong and help them believe,
You don't need a prayer if you believe, although it wouldn't hurt.

Open your heart, your soul and your mind,
Follow your dream and your future you will find,
Let your faith and spirit lead the way,
And soon you will find a better day,
When everything goes right and your dream has been fulfilled.

Delores A Anderson
HOMELESS
Did you ever think that you might meet
A homeless person on the street
And if you did what would you think
Would you offer him some food or drink
Or find for him a place to stay
Knowing he would not be able to pay
Maybe you would sit and visit awhile
To see if you could make him smile
Or look in his eyes and see another
Thinking this could happen to your brother
Yes it could happen to you or to me
That one day homeless we could be
So open your hearts and keep in mind
When you meet a homeless person be kind
For they really don't seem to ask for much
Just a chance at life and a tender touch

Andrean Linh Nguyen
WHEN WINTER LEAVES
When Winter leaves, Spring comes with the beautiful shining warm sun. The birds chirp and sing in the early morning Spring.
Then Spring is gone like a bird's morning song.
Summer settles in like an early morning wind, then is gone in a flash like the sweet smelling grass.
Fall comes in with a swift blowing wind. All colors are brown, crackling leaves the only sound.
When all is over, the sun settles down. The seasons are over with an early morning song.

Beulah Tigue/John Tigue
BEING FREE

To family, friends, the flag and freedom.

There is nothing compared to being free,
No chains to bind, no lock and key.
No ropes to hold me from my dreams,
No hands to mute my many screams,
No cells that deny the rain on my face
Or hide the sun and skies of space,
No walls to shield the earth and sea,
There is nothing compared to being free.

There is nothing compared to being free,
To show the world what rests in me,
To have a chance to hope and share,
To hone each wish with tender care
Without shackles and bonds to bar my way,
The right to do and think and say
What's in my heart; sweet liberty,
There is nothing compared to being free.

Sharon Denise Brown
WHY I WONDER

To my mother Annie D. Baldwin.

Sometime I sit and wonder
why I don't have anybody
to love me for me. Is it
because I'm ugly, crazy,
not willing to give up
easy. No that's not it,
because I'm a beautiful
person all around and
doesn't make any fool
or ugly people, 'cause
sooner or later someone
will come around. So why
do I sit and wonder about
a guy loving me.

Jill Marie Watts
D-DAY
We look at all the lonely people
And do not what they do
We act upon our feeling of desperation
And perspire at the thought of change

We look at all the successful people
And want what they have obtained
We act upon the darkness of our desires
And bleed when the darkness fades

We look at all the imprisoned people
And assume they see only iron bars
We act upon our sense of security
And tremble when we dream their dreams

We look at all the giving people
And take what they hand us
We act upon what science labels as our "heart"
And strangle the doubts in our own assurance

Finally, I look at my own image in the mirror
And see the potential God has created
I now begin to be part of his reflection
And sequester the darkness, the doubts, and desires of mankind

Susan L Weidman
THOUGHT OF YOU
You weren't long,
but in your time here
you managed to take me in your strong hand
and suffocate me.
But even though I was choking,
I was enjoying,
for you are like an addiction that can kill,
and death comes without warning.

Kerry Dannar
GOOD-BYE

This poem is dedicated to Teri-Michelle Matsuda, my best friend.

That wasn't expected of you . . .
The time that it takes

Just to answer a call
To let someone know you're there
Friendship is really a matter of time
The time that you take when you care . . .
now you're gone
But we're not gonna cry,
We say to ourselves,
Wiping our eyes,
We never got a chance,
We never got a try.
But what hurts the most of all . . .
Is we never got a chance to say
Good-bye

Rosy Carmen Garita
COLETTE, LADY BAG
The cemetery at the east
beyond the city
sleep in the mist and the yellow dandelions,
stick like skin
at the nude body of the ground.

Once an a while
a bouquet of flowers
swerve the flight
of a butterfly in way to home.
Or the squirrel
that plays in the dry leaves
divert the gaze
of the sole visitor
that think and think again
about the dead he is visiting
and the alive
that is waiting for him.

Beside the iron door
close to the willows,
the bench of stone
that is the Collette's home
She lives, and sleep,
and eats and beg.
She can't make distinctions
at what side of the wall
the graves belongs.
Because the deads, walking around
alives in dead, just like Colette.

Collete, cemetery flower.
Cemetery of the city,
fogs in the brains.

Helen C Bessard
A MOTHER'S LOVE

Dedicated to my mother Lillie Mae Canady.

Sometimes it's not easy being a mama,
But you don't know that until you have kids of your own.
Sometimes you don't understand your own mother.
Until you are fully grown.

You think she's old and out of touch with the times.
The way she's treated should be a crime.
Just remember those days, you had to call,
Mama came through for you in spite of it all.

We say we don't have time, money, nor patience,
Our mothers found a way, somehow they made it.
We look for excuses, and the easy out,
They faced adversities, far beyond our plight.

She'll stand by you through thick and thin,
There will be times she's your only friend.
Some of you think she's supposed to do,
She's gone the extra mile, why can't you?

You're out here in this world without a care,
Your mother's on her knees, deep in prayer.
The hopes and dreams have turned to tears,
Her broken heart is full of fear.

Others may accuse you of all sorts of crimes,
But she's quick to defend you and say, he's mine.
Just one more thing before I go
Remember mothers have feelings too,
OR DIDN'T YOU KNOW!!!!!

Lisa Beasley
KITCHEN COWBOYS
The kitchen lay in havoc
With flour on the floor
And chocolate streaks decorated the door
Tom, playing Indian beat the tom-tom pan
While Timmy, pretending to be Jessie James
Tried to shoot him with spoonfuls of jam.

Willie rode by on his broom-horse
Leaving a ghostly trail
He wore a Tupperware hat
A milk mustache
And carried a spatula sword
All of a sudden Timmy through the window spied
Mother coming . . .
Quick let's hide!
She opened the door and slowly walked in,
And she knew without a doubt—
The kitchen cowboys had struck again.

Cindy Cassidy
FAITHFUL AGONY
You always threw caution to the wind,
and denied all you were taught.
Though peace is what you were after,
freedom is what you sought.
There were times you felt the emptiness,
and times you wanted to cry.
It was all so deep inside of you—
all you tried to hide.
As a boy you couldn't name the reasons
Why you chose the life you led.
And as the man that you became,
you may have never felt the need.
Now there's an open wound of loneliness
from the breaking of a lifelong tie.
The silent faithful agony
That fills my tearful eye.
Some called you a warrior—
Bandit of the Steel Horses.
I just called you brother,
For better or for worse!

James A Wilbur
DEAR SPARROW
Dear Sparrow the hawk within the mind
Feed on tomorrow and until the end of time
Sleeping in the shadows of moonlight,
rising in the sunshine
Whistling tunes of twilight,
to brighten all hearts yours and mine
Singing so happily, moving smooth and fast
A sight that will brighten thee with a love that will last

Lois Brown Wadas
COMMITMENT
He sat
watching her
all a-whirl as she
spun about
her kitchen
pots boiling
water running

He sat
watching her
swollen belly

and felt
uneasy
left out

she felt
fulfilled
completed

What has this to do with me?
He thought

Everything
her smile answered

Shae Blomquist
ECHO
If I send you a card on a special day,
or to send you a message that is hard to relay —

If I say let's make love on the living room floor,
or on the beach by the ocean's roar —

If I say come share a soak in the tub,
with bubbles to tickle as we make love —

If I cry in your arms drawing comfort from you,
or you cry in mine as you sometimes do —

Are all of these things something precious we share?,
or is it only an echo of someone else who dared —

And if I say I Love You and let's make a new start,
is it only an echo that bounces off your heart?

Angela Hubble
FROM THE HEART
You mean so much to me.
When I'm with you,
I'm completely happy.
Your kindness and friendship
are so very important.
Can you see the
way I look at you?
Can't you hear
my unspoken words?
I know we will
always be friends;
and that's why I will
never tell you how much
I really love you.

Sharon Faye Asher
LITTLE SOLDIER

To my son Travis, my little soldier.

He says he is a soldier.
His horse is riding low.
Wooden stick bumps the ground,
as he marches slow.
His trousers they are droopy.
His trusty sword is drawn.
Ready for the enemy, should he come along.
Hark! is that a battle call,
heard round yon bend;
or mommy at the kitchen door,
calling Captain in.
Battles are forgotten,
Troubles are no more.
Horsey is now resting,
on the kitchen floor.

Jesse Lindley
MY WORLD, CHILDHOOD
There is a music to be felt that no ear can hear
There is a breeze, sweet, that has stirred no leaves
I have no fear of the puma
The fawn has no fear of me
I play in the grass and streams and seas
And conquer mountains, walk plains, bend trees
I have no fear of any man
No one is afraid of me
Earth holds no place like my bright world
Fright only comes with terrestrial gear
I am not afraid of fear
Death will not take me
For it is my world here

Gail Justiss
FRIENDS

To my husband, Gary and my son Steve, the Love and Light of my life.

What do I need in a friend,
One to be near till the very end.

To understand my changing smile,
To stand by me through every mile.

What should a friend expect from me,
To love and cherish whatever might be.

I'll forever be close and always near,
To feel your needs, to share your fears.

What should friends expect from each other,
A bond to be shared with one another.

Friends, they come and then they go,
With few memories left and little to show.

Then once in a lifetime two people do meet,

A force is found, no one can defeat.

When one comes along, you feel it is right,
Give up your wall, no longer fight.

Cherish each moment, make your memories last,
No darkness to linger, no shadows to cast.

Be gentle with love, treat it with care,
And happiness will be as Spring in the air.

In life's rewards there is none more dear,
Than the warmth in knowing a friend is near.

I'll protect our friendship, keep it from harm,
Making memories last, holding close in my arms.

Remember this with each passing day,
I care for you in a very special way.

Tim Spetnagel
AN UNKNOWN WONDER
Whenever he moved his hand,
he painted gold,
Yet never a painting
had he sold.
In a subliminal world
all his own,
All his works n'
paintings were known.
The grandeur exhibited wi' the
stroke of his hand
Left all bewildered yet
all understand.
For such beauty should be showered
throughout the earth,
That the world might know the
little man's worth.
But the little man desires no
fortune and fame.
To him his art is
no money game.
So quietly and patiently he
sits in refrain,
An unknown wonder to the
world he'll remain.

Tim Spetnagel
FAIR BARTER
'Tis a noble gain of gallantry,
This common law of chivalry.
A principle of old courtship,
A game of new psychology.

That a man must win his fair bride,
Earn her, to have her by his side.
Buy her off by analogy,
Though coinage for barter denied.

And as her heart triggers alarm,
Questions motive, alerts to harm,
Beckoning, then pulling away,
She strains to reason of his charm.

Think not the receiving of much,
And giving li'l, unfair as such.
For having won her as his wife,
She will have given just as much.

Tim Spetnagel
A RECOGNITION
I recognized a thing
in her,
across the parking lot
of the park.
And though I didn't know her,
didn't recognize her face,
I knew it was there.

And for a brief moment,
we both could share
the pain that we
both had felt.
It was reassuring to know
that we were not alone.
That others had felt it too.

That crying sting
of another,
less cunning
than the tiger,
but just as deadly though.
Whose red dripping paw had left its mark
of path cut across an innocent
heart.

An open heart
to sin and shame,
and to crying,
and the same.
A now closed heart contemplating a wave,
"Another chance with another?
Or to walk away to ever ponder?"
"What would life
bring to her?
What would it have brought
to her and Me?"
And now ten years gone by.
Am I any better for it?
Or are my choices still the same?

Still as deadly as
the tiger's game?
Am I any wiser
to see:
"Is it safe for you and me?"
And she I'll never know,
who helped me remain
poor and closed
yet a little longer.

But helped me though
along the way,
to make it through,
day by day,
'til now, a little stronger.

Elsie Lynn Brown
TODAY
When I awoke this morning to a
beautiful, brand-new day,
All pure and bright and shining,
It seemed I heard God say;

What will you do with this precious gift
I so freely give to your care,
Will you use it someone's load to lift
Or leave it empty and bare?

It's yours to do with as you choose
The "good news" of Christ you can share
Or you can waste the day and lose
The power you could have gained in prayer.

Oh God, may I hold each day in Awe
for the trust you have in me,
To give each moment my best, my all,
And tonight return it to Thee

Unspoiled by anger, pride or lust,
but filled with your love and Grace
Confidently place in you my trust
Until I meet you face-to-face.

John J DeStefano Jr
SPARTAN

Dedicated to my father, John J. DeStefano, Sr., veteran of World War II, the Korean War, and the Vietnam War.

Battle on Spartan, noblest of knight,
From you fear itself takes to the flight.
Mind and purpose have become your shield,
All environs are your battlefield.

Strength and energy your
man-of-war,
Before to such great heights you did soar.
Man thought highly of you in the past,
But man's admiration failed to last.

At this age in time you stand alone,
No wars to fight, no medals to own.
The young ignore you, wipe out your trace,
They're the future, the past is your face.

They scowl at your wars, attack your pride,
Your feelings become ideals to chide.
Still you hold your ground, stand
straight and tall,
The epitome of a stone wall.

It's a shame that they don't
understand,
The meek too proud to reach out their hand.
Their views of today they owe to you,
You fought so they'd have a point of view.

John J DeStefano Jr
THE ROSE

*In memory of my mother, Rose Dolores DeStefano
She will live forever in our hearts.*

Offspring from the breath of the
Helios seed,
Nurtured in earth's reservoir you
sprout forth, freed.
An unblossomed play just waiting for its start,
An essence of beauty in search of a heart.

You gather your substance and lay
bare your soul,
Your beauty nurtures, but life collects your toll.
Petals begin to wither, souls learn by heart,
We have become as one, we can
never part.

Beauty can never die when it lives within.
When I find you in heaven, life will begin.
Even as death moves to interrupt, our love still grows,
Clutching the last petal on Beloved Rose.

Ann M Stengel
REALIZATIONS
Soul-searching to find myself,
enjoying all that I see
Never again avoiding truth, finding
comfort within me
No longer look for answers in
someone else's eyes
Solutions come from within me
without excuses or lies
My entire life I've played games,
now have paid the cost
Not willing to sacrifice me, just
searching what's been lost
What's been missing is unconditional
love owed myself all along
Constantly trusting what others felt,
believing I was wrong
Turning the torn & tattered page.
Moving to a new chapter
Reflecting past endeavors with half a
smile, no real laughter
Being open and honest with myself
has become my sole desire
Too much time has been spent
fueling sparks, absent real fire.

Nancy Feliciano
WITH LOVING THOUGHTS

This poem is dedicated to Agatonica, my beloved mother.

With loving thoughts . . .
'Tis this season
Of this joyous holiday brings
The birth celebration of our Lord
Jesus Christ, our King
As we think of the beginning
To the end of His life
As it is written
Life after death
As we strongly have our deepest
thoughts
Throughout this holiday season of
our
Loss of our beloved mother . . .
May life after death
Always be closely to our Lord
In His loving arms of comfort and
peace
As we keep our warmest loving
thoughts
Of Christmas dreams forever long.

April T Franklin
EXCLUSIONS

To my loving and devoted husband and my sweet precious daughter, I dedicate this to you. I love you all tremendously.

Lest there isn't a heart to love
A heart will crumble and die
Lest there isn't a love to nurture
A love will fade inside

Lest there isn't a warmth of one
One's warmth will never be shared

Lest there isn't you with me
You'll never know how much I
cared.

Lowell "Ted" DaVee
SWEET SMOKEY SCHNAUZER

Dedicated to everyone who likes dogs. A special dedication to King, the German shepherd pal of Smokey who refused to eat for exactly two months after she died.

I grieve for thee, sweet one
The truest friend of all
From dawn to setting sun
Your name I cannot call.

Far deep into the night
Your presence is missed here
You were my guiding light
With you I had no fear.

Of all the pets I've had
You gave more love to me
Each moment you were glad
Just around me to be.

Oh, that I had done more
To help you when in need
Now that you've crossed life's door
My heart shall ever bleed.

Time takes us all away
As from this earth we pass
Thank God for you, I pray
Farewell, my little lass.

Erma Dixon
MISQUID'ED MERCHANT

To Troy and Edward Davidson, my two wonderful sons. God bless you and keep you always. Love, Mama.

Decision and judgement council and magistrates open your eyes it's never too late. Delivers us lord these deception we take forgive us our wrong and or mistakes. For in time of pain we take your name conceive in weakness we proclaim Lord without bonding for or peace you're the only substitute for this beast. Guide us on a narrow path enrich our lives that we may last to keep that great and wonderful date, so we may rise to see the faith. Faust was favor to the best but he sold his soul for nothing less. We must trust him when we pray, for "I am" is truly the lamb he say, he will grant you another day.

Nelda Marshall
A FRIEND

Dedicated to Laura Marshall & Dorothy Lineer.

A Friend is someone you enjoy
To be with.
Someone you do not try
To create a riff with,
A Friend shares with you
All sorrows and Joy,
Someone who is always True
And with you on the morrow.
A Friend is someone you can confide in,
To tell your secrets to,
And someone who with you will stride
Even though you have made a mistake or two.
They are someone who will laugh and cry with you,
Your deepest feelings share,
And you, in turn, will be true
To them and show you always care.
A true friend lightens your burdens
By a smile, a tight clasped hand,
Your heart will be lightened and gladdened
And thru this you will always understand.

Kelly Jo Beeson
SILENT IS THE MOTHER

To the one I've loved and laughed with—Thanks . . . For just being there!

It's spring and the rain just turned to snow.
It's spring and a baby just died ya know.
It's snowing and the flakes gather upon the ground.
It's snowing and from the mouth there is no sound.
It's cold and the darkness seems like light.
It's cold and the baby died in the night.
It's spring and the rain just turned to snow.
It's spring and a baby just died ya know.
It's winter and spring refuses to come.
It's winter and still no promise of sun.
It's quiet and silence is like a cover.
It's quiet and silence is the mother.
It's spring and the rain just turned to snow . . . .

Marjorie Bachmann
LITTLE BROTHER

Dedicated to my "Little Brother" Gordon Joseph McGunagle.

Isn't little brother one of the sweetest things,
When he takes your hand and to it clings
And lifts his eyes that seem to say,
I love you sister, more each day.

The hair that lies mischievously on his brow
Was once golden curls, And now
That Little Brother's growing up,
He's learned to say "cup" instead of "tup."

But now we must think, in that little face,
Someday a great change will take place,
There'll really be whiskers and cheeks of tan,
But of course that won't be till he's a big man.

When he says with a sigh, "Someday,
When I'm through with toys and my play,
I'll have a car, a big house too"
I really believe it will come true.

God keep him, never let him stray
Remember him as he is today,
For when a man he's grown to be,
I know he'll still have love for me.

Freddie Chapel Wright
STAIRWAY TO THE STARS

This poem is dedicated to Michele, my lovely daughter.

The stars are bright and glowing
Just hanging in outerspace
How can you build a stairway
Into this unknown place?

The climb may be tedious as you ascend
Always be persistent, if you care to win.

As you plan your future,
Take one step at a time.

Just remember to have a goal in mind.

Be patient if you stumble
And start out anew.

No one prepares for your future,
Only you.
If in your preparation for tomorrow
Seems far, far away
Just remember to ask God to guide you
He'll be there everyday.
When your goal is within your reach
And you've prepared your very best
You've climbed the stairway to the stars
And passed the most challenging test.

Gerald Leon Graf
YOU'RE SPECIAL

To my wife, Joan.

In your eyes I can see,
And in your touch I can feel.
While we lay in embrace,
Our love so very real.

To me our union is special—
For some, found only in dreams.
Being with you is more than just pleasure,
But like a star's twinkle and gleam.

Since knowing your love and affection,
It's all I want or really need.
So let's walk together in the same direction
And sow our love seeds.

Vincent (Vinny) Manning
RIVER OF ICE

This poem is dedicated to the one I love, Candace (Candy) Manning, my loving wife.

Computerized people
with paperback dreams,
about keyboard castles
and survival machines,
with psychotic illusions
about lezoids from space,
metropolitan snow queens
and emergency escape
into the trivia tunnel
of the trivia race,
with no zone victims
and no zone names
into the pinball reality
of the oblivion game,
where genetic assassination
and micro zero life
live in a neon needle
on a
river of ice!

Doreen Gordon Schmitt
OBSESSION

Dedicated to: Those who seek the why's of the skies.

My soul is lost—it's gone—but where?
O God! what have I done? My body echoes with its sound,
But only echoes in my mind.
Where are you God?—o where, where, where?
Be still—yes still—but pain is still.
My ears are lashed with echoes of my God
My eyes are dim and see unsteady fog
My smell is death and mums and rancid greens
My touch is ice—it burns and freezes me.
O God, god, god you have forsaken me!
My circled self is rolled up in the dark
And laughs at me within its core.
O free me from the body of this death!
Stretch forth my hand and touch it with your kiss . . .
Your kiss of death and life and birth and love and hate!
To hate—yes even hate has breath
Much better than the mist that is my home.
Abandoned, lost, embodied in the droplets of the swamps
And hanged and mired on every slimy tree
In darkness dark and cold and lost
But never free—no never free . . . .

Doreen Gordon Schmitt
I DO

I did not know what I know now
The day that I walked down the aisle
I did not know just why or how
But I did know I loved your smile
And through the years I learned so much
About your hopes and love for me
I felt your presence and your touch
A touch of love and dignity
You helped me smile and loved me so
Each time that I had lost my cheer
My love for you could bloom and grow
Each day by day and year by year
I want you ever at my side
I never tire of your way
My love for you I'll never hide
My heart is yours for every day.

Doreen Gordon Schmitt
LOVERS

In this thing that is called love
They are not blind—they see.
They see what others cannot—won't;
And that's eternity.

How can he love her truly:
Those unknown hidden things?
Just glance at him: look at his eyes,
Oh, look! the joy she brings.
How can she love him as she does,
To give herself—her life?
Just look at her: she trusts, she cares
And wants to be his wife.
Oh no, their love is open
There is no mystery
Their eyes and minds become as one:
Total sincerity.

If only we could love so
Could share such depth of sight
To look right through the darkest soul
And find it filled with light.

Doreen Gordon Schmitt
CANTICLE OF LOVE

So hard to say "I love" because love is.
There is no holding back once said: it is a life.
Its essence is so simple yet so full,
So near—so far—so sweet—so hungering.

The smile on tiny lips, the curled sweet fingers
Clinging soft to feminine folds of silken truth;
The unassuming pose of youth in searching for its depth;
The fullness of a man.

The half closed sight of aged eyes
Which see the face of God,
The gnarled hands tightly clasped in prayer,
The wisdom of the years.

The smell of grass, the sparkling rain,
The drifting sands and snows,
The moon, the stars proclaim the truth
Of life and love and God!

Doreen Gordon Schmitt
ATOMS

Can you give your life for your fellow man?
"O yes, O yes, O yes I can!"
And fellow man cried and then he died
And I saw you hide.

Can you give your food to fellow man?
"That yes, o yes I certainly can."
And I saw him wait and I felt his hate

As you sat and ate.

Can you give your love to fellow man?
"Indeed. It's easy, of course I can."
And you split in two, and I watched that too,
And I became YOU.

Doreen Gordon Schmitt
THE TREE
The children gather 'round the Christmas tree,
And ah's and oh's are verbally proclaimed;
The lights renew a solemn mystery:
They shine within a world that's hurt and maimed.

Some packages are lying 'round the base
In myriad profusion ribboned there,
And light creates a glow on haloed face
And hand which grab at gifts to shred and tear.

Then after fun and games the hearts consume,
And children bedded down amidst their glee,
The lights are dimmed, the shadows grow and loom,
And tinsel hides the slowly dying tree.

Doreen Gordon Schmitt
IN MEMORIAM
We remember, we remember many days
When battle smoke created haze,
And men were killed and cities raced
And bodies burned because of craze
Created by an evil maze
Of thought and greed which evil pays,
And men still live from hospital trays:
While at the church their nation prays,
And at the front a soldier preys
Instructed to renew the blaze . . .
So we can have memorial days.
These are the days we sing their praise.

Doreen Gordon Schmitt
ENEMY
I look deep in his eyes and see a flame
Of hurt and fear and suffering so deep
And reach to touch and feel a slippery wall
My God! It is a mirror of my soul!

William Blake Faile
THE LIFE THAT'S NO LIFE AT ALL
To my loving father and mother.

Life behind bars is no life at all, for the women and men whose life did fall.

They're misunderstood, some bad, some good, and some that just lost their way.

For the thing they've done, in desperation, in the heat of the moment, in a heart break situation, they know they must pay, they know they were wrong, and I sing their song, for the life, the life that's no life at all.

They need a hand from up above, they need the forgiveness of the snow white dove. They need a friend that won't turn away, they need a love that will always stay, they need some help to live the life, the life that's no life at all.

The years they count, the days fade away, themselves they blame for their painful stay.

As the time passes by they are forgotten and lost, the dreams they once had, pay the cost, it's a life of loneliness, a life of guilt, it's the life, the life that's no life at all.

They need a hand from up above, they need the forgiveness of the snow white dove, they need a friend that won't turn away, they need a love that will always stay, they need some help to live the life, the life that's no life at all.

Doris Halpin

Doris Halpin
MY WELCOME MAT
Someday, I'd like to figure out
I hope it's not too long,
Why my friends don't come around
And family too, what's wrong?
I guess folks just don't realize
I need a friend today,
Sometimes tomorrows are too late
I'll soon be gone away.
It sit alone, most every night
It seems folks go and hide,
My (Welcome Mat) is always out
But no-one steps in-side.
The children also seem to hide
Sure—they've got a life to live,
But someday soon—they'll surely miss
Just what I had to give.
Someday—my (welcome mat) will fade
With all its threads un-tied,
And then if folks decide to come
There will be no-one inside.

Doris Halpin
OUR MOM
This was written for our mom, Mrs. Helen Hilderbrand, two years before she passed away in 1985.

We smiled today, Mom made it so
No matter what the weather,
The one thing that she really loves
Is have us all together.
It's hard to tell what pleases her
She always wears a frown,
But have her kids all gather here
Turns that frown around.
Her interest now—at eighty-three
I'll mention just a few,
Playing cards and counting change
That's what she loves to do.
She counts all day and counts again
And plays the cards to win,
But if you want to see her smile
Just have us kids come in.
Her pleasures aren't many
It's worth that special grin,
If we can turn that frown around
JUST BY WALKING IN.

Doris Halpin
MY BLESSINGS
I've learned to count my blessings
Lord knows, I've quite a few,
The one I'm thinking of right now
Is sharing life with you.
The happiness, we've had with you
I wouldn't trade one day,
Through heartache and some laughter too
We've shared it all the way.
You've made us very happy
And Dad would say it too,
No Mom or Dad could ever have
A finer son than you.
We've loved the many things you've done
And interests that you've had,
Your love of planes and flying
Was something shared with Dad.
You may not know, the joy it brought
That memory's here to stay,
So thanks for sharing his great love
He speaks of it today.
A special thanks, for all you've done
Or what you'll ever do,
And let me say, I'm thankful for
Our sharing life with you.

Doris Halpin
NO ONE'S ALONE
Whenever I'm facing a problem
And life's not the way it should be,
It seems my mind is on others
The ones who are smarter than me.
I'm envy of all of their riches
Their life is where I should be,
But if I would think for a moment
There's someone that's worse off than me.
Quite often, my health is a problem
I've had many ills down the line,
But just when I'm feeling my finest
A crisis will hit, one more time.
I've had all the pain I can handle
Sometimes I ask the Lord WHY?
But if I would think for a moment
There's someone—worse off than I.
It seems, I'm just feeling sorry
That's when my thoughts lets me see,
No matter what life lays before me
There's somebody—worse off than me.

Doris Halpin
BEFORE PROGRESS
It gives me lots of pleasure
To think of yesterday,
Long before the progress came
To the young folks of today.
Growing up, we did it fine
Each memory brings a smile,
It's hard for young to comprehend
My life, as just a child.
It was fun to use that dipper
Drinking water from a pail,
And hanging up the daily wash
On a line from nail to nail.
Four of us were cramped in tight
On a bed just meant for two,
Our Mom just had to touch the feet
To find out who was who.
Now I'm not knocking progress
I'll just keep my yesterdays,
And thank the Lord, for letting me
Live life so many ways.

Nancy J Pokorney
DEAF AND BLIND
This poem is dedicated to Jesus Christ, who will heal all.

There he was, standing so tall.
Some said there was so hope for him.
No answer to their call.
His ears, though shaped as yours and mine,
Heard nothing. Not rhythm. Not even rhyme.
But his mind was bright. Yes, so very, very bright.
If only they, the others, could see him in that light . . .

Sharon Lee Edwards
ACAPULCO MANGO
To my dear friend Kamal Nathan, from the island country of Sri Lanka.

Within the Tropical Clime
Lives a tree most tall;
With leaves and branches sublime,
Containing fruit colored like lime.

If you but wait for a time,
They will change to red and fall.
Climb up the tree and pick the prime;
The Mangoes are waiting . . . .
In the warm sunshine.

Frances E Tolson
WHAT IS LOVE?
I wish to dedicate this poem to my husband Melvin. He brought love to my life.

Just what is Love?
I never really knew
Until the day we parted.
Then I learned my lesson
In the age-old hardest way.
It's the trembling of your body
When you whisper in the dark.
The touch of hands so gentle
And the clasp of arms so strong—
It, too, may be the pressure
Of lips that linger long.
It's the little things that make you laugh
And things which bring the tears.
Each one has its own appointed place
In the total thing called Love.

Patricia Anne Bullock
LEONORA
For my lovely daughter, Leonora, who has brought so much joy into my life!

Her light brown hair flies in the wind,
As she cycles towards the dawn.
Slim legs furious in their pedalling,
Eyes lifted to welcome the morn
Of a bright new day.

Gazelle like she slips from her seat,
And cartwheels across the moist grass.
She stands breathless and still with arms upstretched,
To catch the clouds as they pass
Across the blue sky.

The songs of birds are in her heart.
Her laughter rises through the air,
And is caught by the eager tree of life,
Whose leaves are whispering,
"Beware—
Of the future's thorns."

The carefree girl sees only love,
As the child in her is still free,
But she's poised on the brink of womanhood,
And the joy she feels will soon flee
Replaced by sorrow.

Bonney Jean Byars
AN IMPRESSION IN TIME

To: the "Memory" remembered and cherished forever and beyond.

It was another time, strange, a different place.
I can't recall the hour or date, I do remember the face.
A face of beauty, such a sight to behold.
Another life perchance, a connection, may the chronicle be told.

Seemingly detached from reality for a turn.
As the heart was calmed and the mind burned.
And a sea of necessity for knowledge screamed,
As this foreign memory with my mind teamed.

How it freely came to existence, a phantasm slightly now known.
Fearlessly frightening, so genuinely manifesting, then gone.
Intended returning as a departure, the impression moved aside.
No doubt, with a disclosure. When?
Only for time to decide.

John C Robinson III
NOVEMBER . . .

Fur P. Maus.

They are sitting in chairs
Running fingers . . .
Through their hair
How thoughts Linger

Thinking with chains
Letting the mind close
Are they waiting on change?
Will they ever smell the rose?

I saw a death
A man on fire
Will I be next?
Thrown to the pyre?

As the old men sit
Afraid of the times
They sit waiting
For the end of their kind

Let new thought approach
Let new hope arise
For we are all sick
Of the old lies . . . .

Terri M Stagner
BOY MEETS GIRL

To my world . . . P.M.S., C.M.S., and J.F.F. For my love . . . John.

Boy meets Girl; Girl meets Boy.
He's afraid he's her new toy.
She's afraid of the feelings felt;
Afraid she's just a notch on his belt.
Boy gets to know Girl;
Girl gets to know him.
They realize it's love
And not just a whim.
She knows, inside, that his love is true,
Altho' he won't say 'I Love You.'
He seems to believe that her love is real,
but he doesn't want to HEAR how she really feels.
Boy works hard, every day;
doesn't have much time to play.
Girl works, too, but not as long.
Tell me, now, are either wrong?
They hold each other in the night,
knowing and feeling their love is right.
Did Girl win Boy? or, did Boy win Girl?
All seems so perfect in their world.
But, how long (they wonder) will it last?
(Each looking back into the past.)
It's not that trust isn't there,
but experience shows that love's not always fair.
Girl wants Boy for the rest of her life;
would like nothing better, than to be his wife.
Boy wants Girl, but that's all that's known.
Maybe he thinks she isn't grown,
He wants her to be sure that she knows her mind;
maybe thinks that he's had plenty of time.
But all will work out in their own little world,
Because that's how it is when . . .
Boy meets Girl.

D Sweeney
SUMMER NIGHTS

This verse is dedicated to Virginia, the moment may have been lost but the memory lingers.

Cool summer nights are best for remembering.
When thoughts flow back to former times
of simpler things, and forgotten laughter.
Sweet moist air dampens the anxiety
of a busy day and higher priorities.
Whispered from the past are the carefree hours
of youth long abandoned, endless summer days,
and star filled nights.
Feel the grass, wet from an early dew.
The impressions of footsteps fading
even as you rest, and remember.
The soft fresh breeze caresses your soul
to ease the burden of a worried mind.
It stirs the restless reflection of a hurried first kiss,
a missed interlude, and lost moments.
This night will pass as all time does
never pausing for those who reminisce,
never slowing though we may plead.
Dawn spurs us forward to plan the future.
But summer nights, are best for remembering.

Thomas J Button Jr
WHERE DOES A WAVE LEAVE OFF AND ANOTHER BEGIN?

TO MY FRIENDS—Debbie, Steve, Chris, Buffy and Budgie.

Where does a wave leave off and another begin?
Is there really such a thing?
Why, even the sound of the ocean is heard as one voice.
There is no place where I leave off and you begin
This is really true my friends
'Cause through you
I began to discover who I am
That's why I must love you!

Bob Boger
A FATHER'S PROMISE

To Brittany Marie, my own very special angel.

The time draws nigh, the signs do tell,
To bring forth new beginning,
To hope, to pray, to wish it well,
To boost its chance of winning.

The established life with patterned strife,
Cares not to relive history,
But longs to guarantee a life,
That's a fraught with awe and mystery.

What can be done for daughter or son,
Through each and every day,
To surround with love from God above,
And keep the world at bay?

I make this pledge before the Lord,
To try my best for you,
And sacrifice my own accord,
To see your purpose through.

Love, Daddy

Lucy Chowaniec
LOVE

To my wonderful husband, Walter, of 54 yrs.

His voice in the morning
Want coffee dear?
His slippers in the corner
By the chiffonier.

His head on the pillow
Beside me at night
All of this
Makes my life so bright

Fifty-four years together we've been
Three sons we raised to wonderful men.
All of this would mean nothing to me
If I'd wake up and my husband not see

Gloria M Huntington
THE FABLE OF THE RED ROSE

I wrote this poem in youth, I dedicate it to youth; my two grandsons, Robbie and Greg.

He kissed her on the forehead,
In a simple and delicate way,
He told her that he loved her,
And wished that he could stay.
He smoothed her hair back gently,
'Twas only she to love,
He kissed her silken hair,
Glistened by the sun above.
Her soft and rosy cheeks were all,
That he desired to kiss,
Here sweet and glowing colors,
Forever should exist.
'Twas only a little rosebud,
Kissed by the dew and wind,
A rose that knew mere nothing,
Of the wages brought by sin.
If only more were like her,
If only more could see,
For God put roses on the Earth,
A gift of love to be.
Its glowing, soft, silk petals,
Clustered by showers of rain,
And taken off the face of Earth,
To come not once again.
But ere she dies, she sets aglow.
A love both warm and true,
Take only of the roses,
Kissed by the wind and dew.

Jane MacBeth
ROCKS

To: Em, Florence and Bunny.

Would somebody kindly remove the rocks
that border this wretched space
For I even hate to see a rock
continually slapped in the face.

For I pity the rocks that sit by the sea
so many times splashed and dried,

But then the question is put to me
Was there ever a rock that died?
No, rocks don't die
Rocks don't live

Jane MacBeth
THE UNIVERSAL GIN GAME

Dedicated to: Russell, Clancy, and Mc Shane.

The sun has gone to bed
She just put out the light,
She surrendered to the moon,
The gambler of the night.

At dawn she'll tip-toe in
To see how he has done,
Another issue of the same
Is all that he has won.

Alone, and left unguarded
Naked truth was laced with treason,
I fear the sun might abdicate
To search for long lost reason.

Elizabeth A Phillips
INSIDE THE GATE

To all of those who have lost a loved one. May there forever be another meeting place.

As a child when away from home I'd go,
My momma would walk with me to the road.
She'd kiss my cheek and smile and say,
"Hurry home now, don't be late,
I'll wait for you inside the gate."
Years went by and momma knew,
Time for her was nearly through.
In a gentle voice she implored,
"Please don't think of me as dead.
The Master is calling me to rest,
For me he waits,
Inside the Eastern Gates."
As I watched her laid to rest,
A gentle wind came from the west,
In the wind again I heard my momma
say those special words,

"Hurry home, don't be late,
I'll wait for you inside the gate."

Denise Fulmer
MYSTERY MAN

This poem is dedicated to all teachers everywhere, especially to Rick.

Once upon a time
I could not hear or rhyme
All I thought was slime . . .
And then I was born.

I want to be free
So I came to see thee
And so you must be . . .
Quite amazing.

With wisdom and kindness
You led me from blindness
Seeming like His Highness . . .
All the while.

With laughter and fun
My respect you have won
These problems weigh a ton . . .
If you aren't there.

I wonder who you are
Riding upon that star
Could you be the next Czar . . .
Of Mesopotamia?

Alice C Nasworthy
MAKE YOUR DAY BRIGHT BY THINKING RIGHT

This poem is dedicated to Vernon, my loving son.

Don't start your day by supposin'
that trouble is just ahead,
It's better to stop supposin'
and start with a smile instead.

So if you desire to be happy
and get rid of the "misery of dread"
Just give up "supposin' the worst things"
and look for "the best things" instead.

Cindy Watson
LEND ME A HAND
Dry my tearful eyes
Clear the clouds from the sky
Mend my broken wings
And help me to fly

Give me a flame
I can make it burn bright
Shatter my darkness
To bring me the light

Give me the strength
To help me go on
Hold on to my hand
Help make me strong

Help get me on my feet
So I can walk the path of life
Help me not to be afraid
So I can win the fight

Help to keep me warm
When life gets so cold
Just lend me a hand
When I need one to hold

Debra Hataway
AS WE WALK ALONG THE ROAD OF LIFE
As we walk along the road of life,
We come to a fork
And we know we must part.
I feel privileged to have been your friend,
And I wish I could be with you forever.
But I know we must go our separate ways.
Still, we feel we have accomplished a
friendship that will never end.
Please stay my friend,
And I will stay yours.

Maryalice Friday
NEVER SAY OLD
I may go blind, I may get lame,
I may have wrinkles by the score,
But there is one thing, however,
I am determined more and more,
Never to say I'm growing old
Even though my hair is gray,
And my steps begin to falter
And I live life day by day.
For age is a matter of opinion
And my opinion I will state most bold,
That is that I am never, never, never,
Going to grow old!!

Mabel Hilligoss
MY VALENTINE
If I could—by magic wand, convert my heart to gold
I'd whittle out a big hunk for you—just thoughts untold.
Valentines, the sweetest ones, their lines just won't convey
The message that I have for you this day when hearts hold sway.
Lo! even my pen—obstinate thing—to that depth won't go
Through blundered lines it whispers—"Please, won't he just know?"
So I'll cease and place a thought between each little line
And trust you'll soon discover that you're my VALENTINE.

Thad Beery
WHAT PUPPIES KNOW
Time drifts by, a great endless river.
Future threatens our death.
We hurry, despair, quiver.

The past is lost, but not forgot.
Irretrievably gone
in the instant, like a rifle shot.

What we know has been. Never yet to be.
Understanding and knowledge,
the flowing droplets, ripple down through eternity.

Oh this counting, weighing the flow of time,
costs us our lives,
our present, yours and mine.

What we learn time takes, for it comes too slow.
Of the present,
only very small children and puppies know.

Melissa Brown
IF THE LATTER TRUE
I have nothing to offer a conversation.
No one to speak English to.
My life . . .
Living without me.
I'm isolated.
Not understanding what I'm to do next,
Not understanding the things I've done,
The things I've said.

Are they to affect my life,
Or these lives around me?
And
If the latter true,
Am I a player

Or am I a tool?

Herbert L Keene Sr
FALLING WALLS
WALLS FALL,
Ask a fella
Named Mandela
WALLS FALL,
The wall is gone and none too soon,
The one erected 'twixt earth and moon.
WALLS FALL,
Not quite yet and it's a sin
But the wall is nicked in Tiananmen.
WALLS FALL,
Lech Walesa, one man only, and yet
He breached the wall of the Soviet.
WALLS FALL,
The Berlin Wall, the massive dis grace
Is a thing of the past, and in its place
ONE GREAT COUNTRY
WALLS FALL.

Anita Cammuso Miller
NIGHTMARE
I just saw a face I can't forget
Think I'll make a little bet
One day I'll sit by his side
Forgetting all about my pride
For he belongs to another
Who is soon to be a mother
Oh, how can I be so mean
After all the hurt I've seen
What's behind those big brown eyes
Will he tell me nothing but lies?
Yes I knew from the start
I'd lose my heart
Now it's time to say goodbye
And silently ask myself, why?

Reina Paz
BETWEEN AND OVER
Between rocks, over galloping blindness
memory juts like fir
its feelers obstinate with hindsights.

Between hopes, over lighted crosses
love writes like silence
its foresight, a gentle volume.

Between mountains, over scarlet pastures
peace in woolen presence
beckons butterflies to be freer.

Cherilyn Papa
BREAKING UP
Breaking up is hard to do,
Never realized what I had with you.
Crying in Silence,
Weeping without tears,
Trying to get away from all of my fears.
Feeling no pain
As it's all caught inside,
I did my best, I really tried.
You were the best,
Aside from all the rest.
Our love was so strong,
Now it all seems so wrong.
Please give me another chance.
We can make the best romance.
This time I promise to stay,
Only I'll never go away,
And everything will be O.K.!

Frank O'Brien
ZOOTIME IN THE ROCKIES
"Please stand back!"

I am a tiger
I am a lion
I am a monkey
I am an elephant
I am a bison
I am a bird
I am a seal
I am a bear
I am a giraffe

I can eat
I can sleep
I can wash
I can groom
I can play
I can stand
I can walk
I can run
I can fly
I can swim
I can growl
I can scream
I can chirp
I can honk
I can smell
I can touch
I can see

I am an animal

I am in a zoo

I am without dignity

"Please stand back!"

Faye Linn Mayer
BE STILL MY SOUL
So good to slow down—
Just sit quietly and listen—
'To the wind.'

The wind has always talked to me—
It's like a 'gift of tongues,'
It speaks to my soul.

Between gusts—it speaks of 'peace.'
Sometimes it threatens—so I—
Brace myself against it.

Often it's an invitation—
Beckoning me to stay alert—
Keep in step—go where the action is.

But when it howls, really howls—
It brings me to my knees—
Reminds me of my 'littleness'—
My dependence on forces outside myself—
Teaches me—
To—'humbly seek renewal.'

Jay Del
ONE WORLD, JUST ONCE
If we could heal
the paranoia we feel
if we could cleanse the flesh
and start again fresh
abolish the disease of hate
and release its cold grasp of fate
if only we would follow our heart
we wouldn't be falling apart
if only we had a secure tomorrow
and a cure for sorrow
then this place truly would be
a divine home for you, and me

if only for a day
could we laugh, could we play
in the rubble of the collapsed wall
witnessing every border fall
if true peace is given the chance
we would see no more the soldiers stance
and all these years of waiting
would end, leaving no one debating

Richard Wayne Resser
THE MUSE OF POE AND PLATO'S CAVE

Without the thought of annexation
There is little that goes with the mind.
You'd think the tools of all creation
Were granted and taken just as life.
But brighter things still haven't been
Superposed with the tools of our day;
To the mind and hand, to dreams and wit
Add the muse of Poe and Plato's cave.

We smile with hope at the muse of Poe
And take lessons from Plato's cave.
For along with the troubling shadows and smoke
Comes a will like the sun to light the way;
And shadows will cling as doggish tails
In the clutch of a frigid hole,
But birds can speak and hearts do tell
Of fat freedom, peace, and puffy souls.

And they say,

"Tears upon my once-bright mirrors
Yet I stand there straight and fearless
'til again my heart is cheerful . . .
Nevermore tells this tale of tears."

Shelby M Harris
HUNGER

I look into those eyes—
so different, yet so much the same.
I dream of him every night—
some sweet, some cutting as a knife.
I wish for immortal life,
yet not to know these mortal pains—
that would surely be no life.
His caresses, I soulfully miss.
His altogether presence—I crave
beyond all measure.
The need far greater
than any pleasure.

Robbie L Grant
LOVE

I discover love is true
I discover love is real
I discover love is everlasting
I myself I me I! I! I! discover
LOVE! LOVE! LOVE! LOVE! LOVE!
The void is now filled with love
The question is now answer
The dream no longer a dream
I discover LOVE
No longer do I search
No longer do I wonder
Now I can Love another truly
Because I discover love.

Martha Bender
INFLATION

Met a man who had ten dollars,
Gasoline, Gasoline, He hollered.
Yesterday to Springfield, He went.
With INFLATION, it's a miracle it wasn't spent.

Just to step out of the house,
Most of Us come back as poor
as a Church mouse.
How much money it will take, no-one knows,
Any place a man has to go.

When will this INFLATION stop,
That's what worries most, of Us,
Moms and Pops.

Cecilia Vega
RECYCLE OF THE BODY

To the memory of "NINO" Angelo Vega, my most humble gift I offer as he gave me my name at birth, with the touch of class.

It was "Fear and "Sadness that swept threw my mind . . .
My body was tested beyond, that it left me with chills up and down my spine . . .
What was taking place in the "Universe of my body was calling all the powerful "Cells, almighty and good!!
To have the "insite of knowing that healing is on the way, puts a mind in a "Joyous Mood" . . .
"Flashbacks I Feel" of this humble life built so well in "Patterns and Programming . . .
How there is Bitterness, Sadness and lots of Door Slamming!!
Now! I am alive . . . mind and soul
My spirit is aware of gladness . . .
I have been through a Hell . . . just built for me,
no parts have been to fit the Mold . . . Oh where is that key . . .
I must have it . . .
The Scars are all over . . .
to have survived is a gift indeed for me.
I am being hand picked for a Great Play and the scenario will be me.
How incredible this stage is going to be,
For the script is written for me . . .
I will be the Producer, Director, and The Movie Star
And finally, I feel is being removed
The Ugliest Scar.
Forever . . . .

Florence Henderson Peters
BLESSINGS

This poem is dedicated to Montie Henderson, my dear mother.

The sun began to light the earth,
another day is born,
how thankful I am for eyes to see this beautiful sunny morn,
I've often taken for granted, the blessings God sends my way,
so I think I'll take time to look around at the blessings of this day.

My legs are swift to run about on grass still wet with dew,
it seemed I could almost hear God say, "I made the grass for you,"
then I reached up to pluck an apple, from its home up in the tree
and I thought of the blessing of daily bread the good Lord gives to me.

A newborn rose raised its head from leaves of darkest green,
I saw its beauty clothed in gold as it caught the sunshine's gleam,
the Bluebird winged its way toward Heaven, a robe of feathers it proudly bore
and I thought of the blessing of material things as I looked at the garment I wore.

I sat beneath the tallest tree, where a squirrel had made its bed,
while faces of all I hold so dear, sped quietly thru my head,
my world became a brighter place, such joy I've never felt,
as I thought of the blessing the Almighty gave, when He blessed us with our health.

At day's end, I stood in awe and gazed at a star-filed sky
and wondered why the Creator of all, would bless one such as I,
then came the peace, only God can give, when He opened my eyes to see,
the same great God, who loves all His, I know must surely love me.

Tena L Ehret
THE JOY OF LIFE IS IN MY HEART

The joy of life is in my heart
I know someday we all must part
when you're down and feelin' low
pick up your head and start to glow
Because someday we'll be together
If not in person at least in soul
The love we feel is very real
and we all know it's made to heal
Through the pain we stand to gain
The strength we need to keep us
Sane . . .

Joli Smith
A YELLOW ROSE

A yellow rose to hold me
Forever alive after it had died
Sweet smelling yellow rose to me
No more tears have I cried
A yellow rose to hold me.

A yellow rose to guide me
ever since that day,
A yellow rose alive to me,
I picked from that small bouquet
A yellow rose to guide me.

A yellow rose on a special day
Will be given to me
A yellow rose from a small bouquet
To hold me and to guide me
A yellow rose on a special day.

A yellow rose to love me
That's not much but precious
A yellow rose that is love to me
Oh so delicate its pureness and freshness
A yellow rose to love me.

Pamela Drury
BLUE SKY

Blue sky
Shining bright,
Caressing and inviting,
Piercing the eyes,
Warming the flesh,
Letting clouds roam
And birds fly free.

A sound in the splendor,

Rumbling and roaring,
Lights creasing the gloom,
Angry tears falling,
Clouds tossed around.
The flesh is wet;
The eyes can't see;
With confusion and fury
The birds are not free.

Suzanne Strugalla
THE FATE OF DREAM

The reoccurring picture haunts me every night,
running from an evil i cannot see
Running like the wind hair whips my face,
the gap widens between invisible pursuers
The earth stops, as do i
on shaking legs peer over my shoulder
Over a leary edge i spy my doom,
all is blurred, no sound, no sight
For reasons unknown i leave the surface,
a sense of darkness the one who has pushed
Faster and faster retreat to the ground,
past occurrences stream before my eyes
That lies above has now vanished,
leaving behind the hollow sense of loneliness
All is still, no more is seen
my fate is lifted.

I bolt up in my bed;
i've met the ground.

Gregory Mietelski
MEMORIES OF YOU

Feelings of you
Bless my every thought

Sitting alone and remembering
All we could've had,
Waiting for you to come
And hold me in your arms forever.

Recalling the heaven in your eyes
Fills me with the joy you have given me.

And the memories of you
Keep me from drowning in my tears.

Alan L McKennon
BILL

I see a man in rags with whiskey breath,
Being two gray days until Christmas.
He gazes from the gutter with eyes that say death,
But no passers-by seem to notice.

Schizoid dreams run rampant in Bill;
Not of Santa or the tree or of presents,
But of demons screaming for a new kill,
Inside a head that once sang common sense.

Full hospitals throw them out in droves,
For there are so many who can pay.
No caring that they have no clothes,
Or a reason for existing another day.

Another shelter is closed by tycoons;
Another bridge abutment is cleared out.
To jail police take Bill and others to room,
But the excess of hard criminals turns them out in a rout.

Find doctors to work on the streets.
Divert dollars from guns to thorazine.
Build havens for the ill and the meek.
Let Bill know what Christmas means.

Rosa A Cipollone
RED IS . . .

Dedicated to my family and friends—you are my "true riches" in life . . . with love and gratitude.

Red is . . .
the sun rising above a field.
a rose newly sprung in June.
a cardinal in mid-flight.
the joy of receiving one's first valentine.
the passion of an unforgettable kiss.
the warm feeling expressed between

two lovers.
the glowing cheeks of a newborn baby.
the fear of one's dreams set afire.
the anger of a jealous heart.
the screams of a battered woman.
the burning light at the end of life.
death.

Rosa A Cipollone
ONE LAST GOODBYE
Death is . . .
the roaring wind that abrades the sea.
the shadow that waits for the sun.
the vanity of an ambitious man.
the falling of a wishing star.
the flight of a hungry vulture.
the last drops of morning dew.
when the star has crashed,
the flight has ended,
and the dew has dried.
when love, passion, and a living name are left behind.
one last goodbye.

Tyrone Phillips
THE STORM
A cold wind blows
The sun disappears behind
A wall of clouds
A storm is coming.
I button my coat
And set myself ready.
It's coming, it's here
Rain, lightning, wind.
Rain blowing in my face
Making me turn away.
Lightning, flashing in the
Sky above my head,
Making me frighten
Causing me to cower in my
Coat.

Wind blowing from north,
South, east, west.
Pushing me in all directions.
It's over the clouds
Dissipate.
Suddenly the storm is gone
The rain stops
The lightning cease
The winds die
The sun appears warm,
Comforting, and I feel
Secure.
Understand, the storm
Is trouble in my life
And
You
Are the sun.

Mark Eddy Smith
TWILIGHT MUSIC
Twilight music shadows consciousness, dimming the glories of another day.
Thoughts are lost in futile restlessness, timidly reaching for Tantalus dreams.
Deep from within the infernal forest, Orpheus beckons.

Sodden leaves rustle damply under sentinel trees and low, gray skies.
The lyrical shade leads, receding, as cold, teary rain unfocuses eyes.
Breathing in time with the airy music, the shadows deepen, a fisher cat cries.

The night gets colder; rain turns to snow: despairing and weary, the angels weep.
Frost bitten hands wriggle under armpits as thoughts return to elusive sleep.
Eerie murmurs crowd like eyes, "The woods are lovely, dark and deep."

Orpheus spares a backward glance; consciousness reawakens.
The music is silent, the forest obscured, the dark-mirrored mind abandoned.
Sleep is no solace unless eternal.
"What dreams may come" are melted.

G S Bosworth
LET FREEDOM RING
Oh Beautiful world in which we dwell!
Let freedom ring!
The sun, the moon, the stars all tell,
Let's rejoice and sing!
An era when time has turned around,
Boundaries changed, hearts with joy abound;
No more iron curtain,
Freedom at last, for certain!
Laughing and tears as loved ones mingle
As they stand in groups, or single,
The great Creator must look down
With happiness, gone the frown,
To listen to the stories they tell,
And hearts with love swell,
Let freedom ring!
Praise the great Creator, our King!

Sheryl A Pleasant
DADDY'S LITTLE GIRL
Getting caught is dumb.
You think and plan and plot
And when you go to pull the job
It wasn't what you thought.

The party didn't turn out
When your parents were away,
Neither did that risky date,
Remember, the one who wanted to stay?

When they came home on Sunday,
The household was a mess.
Dishes in the kitchen sink
And crashed on the floor was Bess.

Her clothes were wrinkled and dirty
Her hair a tangled nest.
Pop said, "Here lieth misery
At its very best!"

Mark C Seeley
POVERTY, IT'S REAL
Poverty stricken cities
with fluorescent buildings of steel,
it's people consumed by foundations
the sick, the starving, it's real.

A life, a film in slow motion
in the shadows they subside,
some survive as others may wither
the strife, the pain and hardship, they hide

Paul S Bresko
CONTENT
The time has come.
The end is near.
The moment is coming.
I feel it is here.

I feel I will burst,
I cannot keep it in,
And to do so,
Would be a grave sin.

When I sit back,
And watch the sun set,
I think of you,
So glad that we met.

I need to tell you,
I hope you do not mind,
I am so glad to have you,
Oh, what a find!

It is clear to me,
You must be heaven sent.
Now, thanks to God,
I am forever content.

Betty Dudenhaver
SPRING'S DAWN
To me, the Spring is much like Dawn
The very essence of all that's new,
So like the sun, beginning a day,
Unfolding a brightened world for you.

Winter's white snow has long since gone
And the shadowy sun has brightened,
Revealing nature's spring face-lifting
As each tired color is lightened.

The dull brown grass has turned gay green,
The first, yellow crocus peeping through,
And all the blossoms, pink and white
Blend the sun's gold, the sky's azure blue.

And when summer's rainbow is in full array,
It seems much like high noon.
For Autumn is the setting sun
That brings winter's night too soon.

Linda C Kover
A MYSTERY
The brightness of the sun and the richness of the sand
reminds me of a person that's hard to understand.
Both are constantly changing, yet forever bringing joy
The pleasantness of their company is easy to employ.
A simple look, a quiet touch, dreams that never end
Could it be that someday I'll learn to comprehend?
Patiently I'll wait for their secrets to unfold
but forever they'll remain untouched and untold.

Jeffrey M Bellows
MAN AND MACHINE
A warrior once proud and strong lays bleeding in the sun.
He fought hard and battled well but he met that one,
That one that goes one more.

A warship once dignified and mighty lays burning under the sun.
She sailed the seas and the oceans sending others on the run,
Until she met the one that goes one more.

Each man and machine will fall,
Because there's always one stronger.
It just takes the toughest
Just a little bit longer.

The tank pitted and abandoned took out the enemy before
It met the one that would settle the score.
It's an old story we've all heard before,
Because there has always been the one that goes one more.

Henry W White
DON'T PASS ME BY
I represent all the things
That's fine and good and clean
And if you really care for me
I can be quite serene.

I can fill your cup to overflowing
And bring you much contentment
Or then again be miserable
Offering nothing but resentment.

I'm not just one sided
As you can plainly see
I can be complicated
It depends on how you look at me.

And if you use me wisely
There's naught I can deny
I'm yours until the very end
I'm "LIFE" Don't pass me by.

H.W. Splatters

Elizabeth J Lauretta
MY SHADOW—MY FRIEND

This poem is dedicated to my friend, who accepts me for what I am, and is the wind beneath my wings.

I have a shadow he is my friend;
Though he lives apart from me,
His presence is never too far away,
for need of company.

My shadow will walk beside me;
My friend can do the same,
So it's both my friend and my shadow,
Who bears my joys and my pains.

Having shared tears and laughter,
Or just the time of day,
My shadow my friend I know he cares;
His silver lines circle clouds of gray.

I have a shadow he is my friend,
There's nothing to understand,
I know in my heart, the joys he imparts,
When he seeks my trembling hand.

And when the daylight turns to dusk—
Will my shadow disappear?
Not this friend—He's one in the same,
My trust from year to year.

Although I am the architect of my own true destiny,
My shadow my friend, my constant support, he's my stability.

Norman E Wirth
SLEEPING
I sleep.
But I sleep an eternal sleep.
I am dreaming, too.
I am dreaming that you are by my side,
and always will be.
But only in my dream.
Maybe someday, someday soon,

that dream will come alive,
and our love for each other
will be known the world
over.
But I sleep eternal sleep.
But, also, and maybe, just maybe.
Your kiss can wake me from this
sleep.
And the dream will come true.
And the sleep will end.

Pamela M Wyant
THIS IS A TIME TO START A NEW YEAR
This is a time to start a new year:
A year that should be filled with love;
laughter, and hope.
Hope that all your dreams come true,
for the New Year.
This is a time for no tears.
Just someone who cares, with love,
laughter, hope and dreams.
Just to start a new year,
to make your dreams become true.
With love, laughter and hope with
someone who cares.
There's no way you can go wrong
with love, laughter, hope and dreams.
To start a New Year
There can be failures but with hope
and dreams,
there's no tears.
Just someone who cares.

Kimberly G Gibbs
THROUGH ROSE COLORED GLASSES
Through rose colored glasses
At the age of three
Things bright and beautiful
Is all we see.

As I grow older
I'm daddy's little girl.
For me he would do anything
Anything in this world.

As time went on
Things started to change.
Resentment set in
Lenses rearranged.

Then I became aware
Of a certain painful glare.
I laid aside my crooked frames
Peace was all that remained.

I could truly see
The fault didn't lie within me.
Slowly hurt and hatred passes
Now I know, he was seeing
Through rose colored glasses.

Edith Johnson
MANKIND
At the sea of life they stand
With their future in their hands
Filled with fire and determination
Eager to reach their destination

Always changing, but yet the same
Seeking for knowledge, they
never gain
Searching for truth, they cannot find
No rest is given, for their weary
minds

Having ears, they cannot hear
Their own sad cries, filled with fear
Having eyes, they cannot see
A way to end, sickness, war and
poverty

Looking for peace, and goodwill
Finding the light, but in darkness still
Always questioning but they
never find
An answer to the problems, of
Mankind

Benjamin E Everhart
EARTH THOUGHTS
Children of Earth
hear me, for I am Earth.
My wind blows sadness upon you,
Yet you do not feel.
My rains weep of death,
Yet you do not hear.
You have tortured me with your
luxuries,
Yet I allow you to continue.
You have scarred me with your wars,
Yet I do not fight back.
You speak of changes,
Yet I feel none.

Soon I shall endure no more,
and you shall be faced with darkness.
The very essense of your being
within me,
shall be,
as you have done to me,
ripped away.
Children of Earth,
hear me!!

Lillian Pandeline
OLD HOUSES
If "old houses" could speak, what
stories they might tell
Of times which were like "heaven,"
some like "hell"
Of "joys," and "laughter,"
"kindnesses," "sadness", and "tears"
"Hopes," "dreams," and
"disappointments," "disillusion-
ments," and "fears"
"Achievements," and "failures,"
"bold ventures", "set-backs", and yet
The "old houses" withstood it all, as
people entered, exited, and met
Leaving an aura, somewhat like a
lovely woman who
Had aged, and wrinkled, yet remnants
of former loveliness still shone
through.
Yes, if "old houses" could speak, it
might very well be
A story worth listening to, yet some
might see
Without "words," or "explanations,"
that some "old houses" held treasures
In "beautiful memories," of "good,
and lasting pleasures"
Sealed within their walls, now
somewhat cracked, and worn
And to the last day of their
experience, even more might be born,
Under their weakening rafters, right
out to the end
For you see, some "old houses" have
been more than just "a shelter,"
but to many, "a friend."

Lillian Pandeline
HOME
A "House" is just a "house" until
It is filled with "understanding," and
"Good-will"
And then, like sunshine cast across a
lawn
A "Home" within the "House" is
born
A "Haven" wherein those who dwell
May find surcease from all worldly
Hell
If each one would lend their humble
share
Of "Good-will" and a "heart-felt
prayer"
Each "House" might attract to it,
"God's kindly Grace"
And make of it, a "Homey Place."

P.S.
The word "house," can be substituted
by "room," "hotel," "apt," "nation,"
or any place where people live in
close proximity with each other.

Muriel Yakir Pickard
WOULD YOU WANT ME TO LOVE YOU A LITTLE THE LESS?

For Keith, Glenn and Drew
With everlasting love, and pride in your accomplishments.

Would you want me to love you a
little the less
So you could pleasure unconcerned
all the more?
Would you want that I'd watch you a
little the less
So uncontrolled freedom would be
yours evermore?

Would you want that I'd give you all
that you ask
And then ask for nothing in return?
Would you want that I'd do all these
many things
Then how much everyday would you
learn?

Darling, when life was given to you,
there were given to me
Many, many unseen, but heartfelt
laws to obey.
For a son to grow healthy and
morally strong
His mother must follow a straight
path all the way.

So bear all that I give and grow
straight and strong
And don't be angry with me when
day is done.
For my heart cries out; your growth
pain is mine
But would you want me to love you a
little the less, my son?

Dianne Bourgeois
FOR NANA

This poem is dedicated to my Nana, Ruby Anderson Pierozzi.

Take my tears to Heaven
Send them back as gentle rain
To nurture trees and flowers
And to wash away my pain

I'll remember always
Your love and deep affection
Your strength, your smile, your
laughter
Through you—the Goddess
connection

Your spirit soars completely free
Of earthly pain and sadness
And when I remember you, Nana,
dear
I shall be filled with gladness

Love forever
Blessed be

Elizabeth Harkey
OH, MY LOVE . . .

This poem is dedicated to my mother, who may live her fantasies through the loves of my life. Love, your daughter, Beth.

You have awakened
Such new feelings in me;
Of excitement and longing
Tell me, what is to be?

I feel your strength;
My friend, my lover,
Beside me, inside me,
There will be no other.

Heidi L Whiskeyman
A LONELY WORLD
The wind whispers through the trees,
a lonely hollow cry.
The birds sing no more melodies and
tears roll from their eyes.
Blue skies have all disappeared . . .
the blacks and grays have arrived.
The earth beneath us is always cold
what a way to enjoy our lives.
The trees are slowly all cut down,
Yet some of us question, why?
Why do we destroy this, as our only
home?
Why do we want to be left all alone?
When the stars no longer shine at
night,
And the rivers no longer run . . .
When we have nothing left to burn,
will our work be considered done?
When the wind whispers through the
trees,
a lonely hollow cry . . .
Will we then believe that we have
killed; that everything has died?
When the birds cease their melodies,
will we realize . . .
The salt we taste is from our very
own eyes.

Susan Schuh
ONE SPECIAL MOMENT

To Brian Schaefer and to my Family.

Shiny are the stars above which
twinkle out so bright.
Narrow are the rocky roads which
lead us to the light.
Calm are the ocean waves as they roll
in unaware.
Sweet is the breeze that surrounds the
midnight's air.
Lying under the fullest moon joining
our warm hands
We hold and face one another,
romancing in the sands.
This is that one special moment that
comes for you and I
The moment when we join as one,
leaving back any lie.

Laurie J Arnold Manley
THE WALK

To my wonderful husband Jason, the meaning behind all I do.

This world is so full of
jealousy,
bitter hate and disgust.
It is a sad, sad story
no one can tell who to trust.
Where to turn to, where to
run,
I wish I had a gun.
A gun would cure all,
No more walks down a cold and
lonely hall.
The heavens would be
waiting,

No more anticipating:
The gates are open wide
just to run inside, then hide
No one would ever find me,
they'd never even see.
Lord-Jesus, don't let me roam.
Please, come and take me
home!

Joseph Ferguson
THE GLORY
My eyes have seen the running
Of the hoboes for the train.

Shouting, "Here comes the bus!"
They hobble like broken dolls and
scarecrows,
Leaving bits of stuffing scattered
down the track.

Then, gathered like iron filings
Clung quaking to a magnet,
They leave the earth behind
To become the hum,
Of movement.

Patricia A Grimshaw
PEACOCK
You stand there,
In the middle of those women,
Like some pompous peacock;
Young, handsome, desirable,
Yet arrogant and rude.
Our eyes meet,
And mine return what I see shine in
yours,
Like a mirror reflecting
The real image.
That reflection must have been truer
than I realize,
For you blush
And walk away.

Ron Jordan
YELLOW FLOWER
Yellow flower
in a desolate desert scene
Your face, your lips
Blossom just for me
Rose petals in your hair
Cactus flowers around your hips

Shaking
Pale youth quivering
Erotic knowledge
Anticipating spring's first rain
Fertilizing
Conception

Plants abounding in desert rains
Blooming before it becomes dry
again
Like her windblown skin
Sagging breasts (in)
Beauty's last shimmer
Brown dry earth of
Dead desert's splendor

Sagebrush cocktail
Elegance so frail

Ron Jordan
NO ORDINARY LOVE
Fire is the fashion
You are my passion
No ordinary love

Feel it in the air
Before we touch
The fire of desire between us
No ordinary love

If I can't see you
Going to burn baby burn on up
My ashes turning into dust
No ordinary love

Come with me
Let me swim in your sea
Drown my love in your warm water
You are an island oasis as I make
your shore . . .
Fruits to find as I explore
No ordinary love

A Sabella
WHAT IS A DAD
A Tribute to My Dad
He is there when you're born,
beaming with pride
From that day on, he'll walk at your
side
His love for you shines, more every
day
While he brings you toys, and new
games to play
It's finally time, your first day of
school
You're so scared, you cry like a fool
He assures you then, everything's all
right
There's nothing to fear, 'cause, he'll
always be near
Then as time goes on, and, older you
get
You think you know more, than, he's
learned yet
And if you thought, at times, he was
hard
It was only him, doing, a father
facade
Then one day along comes trouble
And all your smarts, burst, like a
bubble
But here comes dad, with his love, so
strong
It makes you feel safe, knowing he's
along
So always try, to remember, before
it's too late
His life was all yours, when, you left
Heaven's Gate.

A Sabella
MOTHER
Like her there is no other
She is a mountain of strength
Whose love can't be measured by
length
She is all heart and understanding
Yet, never is demanding
From, morning till night, day after
day
Her aim in life, is to pave your way
And, if at times life, seems hard to
bear
You're never alone, 'cause, Mom is
there
So treat her kind, and sweetly
Because, to you, she gives com-
pletely.

A Sabella
LOVE
Love is a sensation, A feeling of
emotion
It can be shallow, or deep as an ocean
It begins from, within, and can tingle
your skin
To some it's a game, which is really a
shame
They're sure to lose, to a thing called
blues
The kinds of love are many, one can't
live without any
There's the love for a Father and
Mother, that's like no other
The love for a Sister, and the love for
a Brother
The love for a Spouse, and the love
for a Child
There's Boy and Girl love, signified
by the dove
The love for a Pet, and some do
forget, the love for God
With its many facades, love can keep
you at odds
Though each one different, they all
are love
So it must be, as you can see
The difference of love, is only
Degree.

A Sabella
FRIEND
Friend, is not just a word, of little
meaning
Nor, should you use it, without true
feeling
Friends aren't someone easily found
It's for sure there aren't, too many
around
And, when you're doing well, and
not, in need
So called Friends, are plenty, indeed
But, when things go wrong, and
really get tough
To find, one Friend, can really be
rough
And if, in your lifetime, you find, just
one
Consider yourself, one lucky Son of a
Gun
So, if you use the word Friend
Be aware, of what it means
Whether good times or bad
A Friend, is a Friend, to the End

Pearl Fretwell
GOD'S VESSELS
Have you aught to offer to men
below?
Have you graces that others in
trials will know,
The head that has bowed from
the grief it has borne,
Humbled by sorrow; by adversity
torn;
Is often the quickest to be raised
when it knows,
That another soul has received a
blow
That will dampen its spirit and
dull its glow,
If they hasten not "the balm of
gilead" to bestow?

Be not quick my brother, my
sister, to lightly speak;
Of one that to you may seem to
be weak.
The one who was quiet and still
while others "Glowed,"
Could easily be the one who will
rise in a strength unseen;
unknown;
When the courage and joy that
others showed,
Has dimmed and faded and
slipped away,
Proving what grace was wrought
alone,
In the heart that was smitten,
and grief had known.

God's ways of forming a Vessel
for use,
Often break the heart strings,
riddle the dreams,
Humble the mind, till no wisdom
is seen.
Oh the wisdom from that Vessel
infused
With all meekness, gentleness,
pure and clean—
No lofty thoughts! No partiality
seen;
The heart that was broken, yet
made clean
Is a Vessel indeed whom the Lord
would choose!

Pearl Fretwell
THE HOUSE OF MOURNING
AND THE HOUSE OF MIRTH
One day as I was riding,
Along a country road;
I recalled the days of childhood,
Of days so long ago.
When gathered close about me
Were those I loved so dear,
Whose every word were words of
kindness;
Of tenderness and cheer.

The years have flown swiftly;
We wonder where they've gone,
And now I'm growing older,
My eyes oft fill with tears.
The cherished hopes within my heart
Have more than been fulfilled;
And yet the sorrows that accompa-
nied them,
Had never pondered been.

I wonder why it is
We always hope and dream,
Of joys; of happiness; and success—
Of all that glitters or gleams?
Why do we not seek the duller things
Less joyful, though they seem—
They make our hearts much better
Said Solomon of old,
"For by the sadness of the counte-
nance
The heart is made better," we are
told.

"It is better to go to the house of
mourning,
Than into the house of mirth"—
Were the words of the wisest man
Who ever lived upon the earth.
The philosophy of men today,
Is this saying in reverse!

Pearl Fretwell
JUDGE NOT
When you start to speak that word of
Gossip,
Or to sit in the "Critic's" seat;
Remember, you might be using
A pick; a hammer; or a mallet of
stone,
To strike from God's Building
One who is His Beloved and own.

Remember that you too; as part of the
human race—
Subject to all the frailties of man;
Upheld by Infinite Mercy and Grace;
Must hold to Love's strong hand

The current of life has many
"undertows,"
To pull and drag a soul down,
And though you see someone
drowning;
When by all sense of reason, he
should be able to swim;
It is a lifeline he needs—
Do not delay—throw it out to him!

Lynne Tornetta
SHARE WITH ME MY LOVE
I see in your eyes a lifetime of
pain.
Emotion wanting to be born yet
afraid to experience the same
heartache once felt in your
past.
Carefully guarded feelings
wanting to come alive.
Wanting to share your soul, but
knowing the turmoil that

sharing can bring.
How can I show you all the
passion I have for you
inside?
Only sometimes does the true
feelings you say you have
seem to show.
I have in me the same past hurt
and yet have reached beyond
that, deep within, and have
found a burning love I had
not known I could give.
I want to give all of myself to you
and want all of the doubts
you may have to diminish
and fade like the setting sun.
Share with me your dreams, for I
will protect them as if they
were my own. For I hope some
day our dreams
will be one, and there will be
no need for guarded feelings.
We would share in life all that is
pleasurable, and if there is to
be pain, we will be each
other's side, guiding the one
who needs extra strength.
Share with me my love. Show me
all you feel in your heart, for
I would never cause you
pain.
Grow with me and we will only
know happiness.
Love me and we will know
eternal bliss.

Lynne Tornetta

AS THE SUN TRIES TO WARM THE COLD WINTER AIR

As the sun tries to warm the cold
winter air, I try to remember
warmer, happier times.
Was it not yesterday we made
love and shared ourselves as
only those who are lost in
each other can? Or has love
distorted time for me.
I have given myself to you as I
have never done before.
I have given more love to you
than I ever knew I possessed
nor will ever possess again
for you have captured that
love and hold it wherever
you go.
I have known more happiness
with you than many find in a
lifetime.
Yet as we sit side-by-side
something has changed and
you no longer want my love,
and the pain from this
rejection is more than I can
endure.
And as I gaze upon the frozen
lake before us, I see a
reflection of my life without
you: cold, barren, empty.
I can only dream life with you by my
side for you are no longer
there. I will always dream
someday we will be again.
My love for you is so strong I
must go on dreaming or be
destroyed by the pain.
Maybe someday you will
discover this love for me.
Maybe someday you will realize
we belong together as we are
so compatible.
Maybe someday we will once
more be one.
Maybe someday . . . .

Carol Strawn

NATHAN K. S.

My dearest grandpop
Such a gentle man
You'll never know how you touched
me
You helped me grow and open like a
bud
Our lives were entwined since I first
drew breath
How could I ever know the depth of
emotions
You would stir in my heart
You taught me so much
But you never knew
And I'll always be so grateful to you
For being my beloved teacher
Nathan.
You opened yourself to me
and we shared heart and soul
I miss you my dear old friend.

Carol Strawn

GRAMMY C.

One-fifty Sunday morning
Full moon shines in my eyes.
Gentle music of his breathing next to
me
is soothing,
But I cannot sleep.
Thoughts of his "Grammy" fill me—
Resting. Silent. On her egg-crate bed.

Memories of my own sweet
Ida, Nathan, Angela and Jodje
Wash over me bitter-sweetly.
Every little old grandmom and pop
I've ever known
Passes before my awake eyes.

Life goes so fast.
I can never forget how fragile,
precious and sweet . . . it is.
My job is to care for the
grand-parents
My joy is to love them to death.

James Greene Jr

THE COCAINE TRAIN

Listen my friends and listen well,
maybe there's a better way to say
what I'm about to say but I better say
it anyway. But it is The Cocaine
Train we are dealing with today, it
costs a lot of money to ride your soul,
your heart, and even your pride. It'll
damn sure forevermore freeze your
brain, so take my advice, stay away
from the Cocaine Train.
So please my friends just say no,
'cause cocaine will leave you with no
place to go. Cocaine, the big lie, if
you used it you are going to die.
Cocaine fools your brain in reality of
course nothing has changed, but to
your brain the feeling seems real, but
cocaine just hands you a bad deal. So
my friends just say no 'cause that's
the right way to go. The Cocaine
Train it costs a lot of money to ride,
your soul, your heart, and even your
pride, cocaine will take you where
you have never been once you're
there you'll cry for more. One day
you're happy, the next day you're
blue, that's what cocaine does for
you.

Hazel McNea

CHRISTMAS

A blessed Christmas and a joyous
New Year
To each and every one whom we
hold dear.
Whether they are far away or near,
Laughter and glad tidings may they
hear.
May happiness and good health be
the reason,
For celebrating this happy yuletide
season.
With relatives and friends may you
share,
Precious moments to show that you
care.
And now may the symbol of the
white dove;
Bring you hope, peace and love from
above.

Patricia M Calkin

MOTHER'S DAY— MAY 9TH, 1989

Here I sit all alone, A Mother's Day
has come and gone,
Two cards I got, From the ones that
care,
There's a sadness that fills the air,
There's something missing that I
can't quite tell;
But there's a blank, I can't fill,
Around the corner, Or around the
block,
I might find that blank, To fill the
space,
But right now I pray, with grace,
That the missing blank; Will "come
together"
With the leaps and bounds, And
laughter
A soft prayer, Or grace, that blank,
will come to me,
There's so much to see and explore,
But here I sit behind the closed door.
I'm not afraid of the out-doors,
Just waiting for the missing to come
through the door,
When the blank is filled,
I will know; I'll laugh and cry,
The days will fly by,
So here I sit all alone,
Waiting for the missing to come
home.

Linda Geering

TIMES THAT WE SHARED

I will always remember the
times that we shared,

And there once was a time
when you truly had cared.

But the pain in my heart
I will not soon forget,

And the love that we had
I will never regret.

I never imagined we would
end it like this,

The times that we shared
I will honestly miss.

Many memories of you are
still fresh in my mind,

And the love that we had,
may we soon again find.

Tracey Jordan

THOUSANDS AND THOUSANDS

Death came with open arms and a
smile,
and a calming voice that said,
come and sleep awhile.
Just for a little while.
I recognized her face,
and I didn't try to run.
Her wings were as the midnight sky.
And they covered me,
in soft velvet shades of cool space.
Death! Like a never ending dream.
Sleep! Like an ever lasting stream.

A cool peaceful night.
A night that never ends.
Stars like thousands and thousands of
eyes.
Death always comes with a smile.
She always comes with open arms.
To embrace in love,
and rob the soul.
The body an empty shell.
The vast night spread out like eagle's
wings,
over the flatlands.

William D Hawes

KNOWING WHEN

Rules
Simple yet complex

Speak, listen
And pause

Speak
What's to say

Listen
What's to hear

Pause
Why stop

The secret is
To know when

Speak, listen
And pause

Bobbie De Sorbo

CRY BABY, CRY

A drop of dreams shattered falls from
my eye,
For a moment all hopes are
meaningless.
The future fades with heavy sigh,
For a moment my heart beats distress.
Never-ending miniature pools
released from inside,
Show the sorrow of the loss created.
Increased passion, continue, and
drive,
Show days of glory much awaited.
Times of down are part of the course,
Making the character separately
played.
Soul building shows light through the
doors,
Making the being that God has saved.
Greet the sadness, a gift from the sky,
Cry baby, cry.

Barbara Hill

SAUSALITO

Sometimes unlikely strangers happen
along
And turn my life around
for a day
or a week
Without ever really touching me

they touch my life.
I can be hypnotized by a
gait
or a smile
An overheard remark can speak
to me with immediacy
Repeating itself long after.
Sausalito was like that.

Leah Peterson
CHOICES
They wanted their freedom, marriage had grown stale,
Their vows remote in the past;
They partied and pranced with others who chose
To live their lives hard and fast.

It was fun for a while, but the new lifestyle
Was stressful and not fulfilling;
So they're caught in a web of their own design,
Too proud to return—although willing.

If you catch them off-guard, forced smiles are replaced
With sadness and disappointment;
They've learned that variety is not always the spice
That leads to a life of contentment.

Betty J Guthrie
SNOW
Softly
on angel wings
Silently
descend and
Gently
touch the earth.

Jim Drysdale
THE BIRD
The bird sat on the window sill
Twirping, chirping, loud and shrill
At a reflection in the glassy pane
And caring naught it did not deign
To answer back; yet aped him so!
Its head, its beak, its very eye did go
Just so! Tiring at the last of this diversion
The bird struck at the glass
And felt the other give dull answer back.

Manh Chieu Luong
THE SPACE NEEDLE'S GLOW
Since the Angels give them a riddle
People build and love the Space Needle
Then come the Northwest Wind and Snow
The beautiful views that Nature likes to show

Not only Summer when to wish the Sun shine
Not only Spring when to hope the weather fine
Not only Autumn when to have the leaves yellow
But also Winter when everything cannot grow

There is a poor boy who lies on the sidewalk dirt
And a Saint uses this Needle to mend his shirt
To make a blanket which that youth never knows
But to be warm, that we see through the windows

As the homeless wander around the street
Their throes are too heavy on their feet
Like the farmers have nothing to mow
The Mother kisses Her babies with Her own woe

Now They dream a roof to live under
Nobody gives Them any wonder
With the exception of the Space Needle's Glow
Which makes the City certainly grow.

Audrey May Bank
TURNING WITH THE TIDE

To Norman—You taught me to smile again!

Erratic waves break upon the beach
Making patterns in the sand.
Pebbles of every size and hue
Make their way up to the land.

Shells which once housed living things
Are washed up high and dry;
Only to start the trip again,
Floating with the tide.

I feel much like those pebbles and shells,
Of the tide I can't be certain;
The highs and lows are like my life,
But I am quite determined

That when I give to others
My time, my love, my caring;
I'll like myself more every day,
And I'll be proud of me for sharing.

If I can give away a smile,
And get one in return—
I'll feel that I have reached my goal,
Where once it was uncertain.

Elaine Blais-Dailey
A PROMISED PONY
When I was small,
and merely nothing at all,
I, like others, wanted a pony—
my Poppa promised me one,
someday . . .
I was about 10 and a bit older by then,
I restated my wants,
to Poppa again,
someday . . .
I turned 18, and already almost grown.
My Poppa would still say,
someday . . .
Someday
never came.
Nor did it seem important.
My Poppa's gone
and took the "promise"
with him.
I suppose that "pony" was a token of conversation.
A private constitution between father and daughter.
Perhaps it was a promise of promises,
love of loves.
Whatever it is or it was,
my dreams of ponies are gone,
along with many others.
What's real is best
unpromised . . .

Tammy Racine Hoover
I HAVE WATCHED YOU

I watched you in High School, I watch you more now. To my husband with love—for Dave.

I have watched you as you slept
in the newest part of day;
I have crept inside your door
gently kissed you as you lay.
I have watched you as you slept
Sat for hours ever still;
I have sat beside your bed
and have come and gone at will.
I have loved you for a time
have wished you were
my own;
I have watched you as you slept
and you have never known.
I have watched you as you slept
while the night became the dawn;
And as the shadows left the room
I have touched your face and
gone

Deen Underwood

Deen Underwood
FIRSTS
A Mother remembers—
Her first pains . . . His coming into this world.
His first cry . . . The joy that he lives.
His first word . . . "Mama!"
His first steps . . . To her waiting arms.
His first parting . . . Going reluctantly into school.
His first love . . . The pain of its ending.
His first prom . . . How handsome he was!
His first shave . . . The faint fuzz of manhood.
His first car . . . Old, but he loved it.
Her first telegram . . . "Killed in action."
Her first tears . . . For her first-born.

Nanette Ewart
TO MY LOVED ONE

To my husband "Michael"—I love you.

Many poets write about the moon
And the stars.
Sometimes the moon changes
And the stars fall—But my
Love for you is forever.

Lillian M Libert
PASSING THOUGHTS

Dedicated to all those who work with the mentally retarded.

Those little arms not ready to
master the skills of this earth
Those little legs not yet
developed to walk the ground
beneath them
Those little eyes see, yet see not
That little mind cannot yet
comprehend the ways of our world
The back is too weak to sit up and
take notice.

So here lies this product of
creation fully developed, yet not
fully a person, yet not
Lying here day after day
depending upon someone to
care for him—to love him
To give him a little bit of life that
he can never know.

He is special
He is severely retarded
He might be your brother
He is some mother's son.

Anita Gale Moore
I'M LOOKING FOR JESUS

To my darling Granddaughter Lacey Nicole Moore.

I look at the sleeping city
Everything so quiet and still
Everyone tucked safe inside,
"I'm looking for Jesus"
Maybe He'll come, maybe He will.

No children's laughter, none at play
Everything so quiet and still
No one running here and there
"I'm looking for Jesus"
Maybe He'll come, maybe He will

What's that sound?
So loud, and clear.
I just heard Gabriel blow his horn
"Jesus is here to take us home"
You're too late, He's already here.

Ramona H Paddock
THE CRICKET SONG

To William B. and Enid J. Paddock, my parents.

Oh lively, cheerful, vagabond insects
Filling the evening with cricket duets,
Sallying forth and livening the night
With all your chirruping, cricketing might.
How do you utter such a humdrum tone
Often in chorus but sometimes alone,
Tossing the notes in such wild ecstasy
Far and away on the warm summer breeze?
Monot'nous, tiresome, tedious song
Cricketed, cricketed, all the night long.

Charles E Mead
WITH A LOT OF LOVE

To My Darling Wife Kathy, Who Gave Me All The Inspiration.

With a lot of love could only say
When I feel that passion for you every second of the day.
That when I come home from a day of work,
I look into your eyes, then suddenly all my troubles melt away and so does the hurt.
And so is the sorrow with a love that's so deep
When fights and bad words can cut so far and so cause the heart to bleed.
With a lot of love, compassion, devotion, and need
I want you for all my life to cherish, honor, love, hold, and please.

So if you'll take me and need me the way I want you
Just give me a message or a signal or a clue.

Barbara J McDermott
YOU ARE MY HERO

To Jan, my hero and inspiration,
Thanks for showing me how to fly.

You are my hero
And in my mind you stand as tall as the tallest mountain.
And, at times, I believe I see your head crowned by the
Billowy clouds hanging in the heavens as if you
Owned a halo all your own.
Your patience is as endless as
The forgiveness of God.
Your love is as strong as a raging river
And as gentle as a summer's breeze.
Your smile is as bright as the morning sun
And as sincere as a baby's laugh.
I trust you with my heart and with my life.
You already own a part of them.
You are as trusting as the keeper of the
Keys of heaven.
You take my pain and hide it from me for awhile
And I feel a happiness I have never known.
You are my hero and you always will be.
You are a very special gift
And I treasure you above all else.

Bernadine Tetzlaff
EQUALITY

Dedicated to Ada B. Jones, a treasured friend.

Open the closed doors to equality.
What rare virtues do you expect to find?
Is it openness of your heart and mind?
Do you want to walk the long path with me?

Come with me down paths of society.
Each to his own prejudice you will find.
We walk together—we're not of one mind.
For no one here is really half so free.

Society walls us in—shuts us out.
As we walk the corridors we mingle.
How shall we go now? In pairs or single?
We may batter the doors down, cry and shout.

Some will go single up the shorter stairs
Others will mingle with empty straight chairs.

Christine Lo Monaco-Goldberg
THE KINDNESS THAT PEOPLE DO

To my Great Grandfather, Sylvester Lynch—thanks for your legacy.

I would rather have one little rose
from the garden of a friend,
than to have the choicest flowers,
when my stay on earth must end.

I would rather have the kindest words
than flattery when my heart is still,
and this life has ceased to be.

I would rather have a loving smile
from friends I know are true,
than tears shed round my casket,
when this world I've bid adieu.

Bring me all the flowers today,
whether pink, or white, or red;
I'd rather have one blossom now,
than a truckload when I'm dead.

Arlene Zellmer
A CANTICLE

I didn't know the meter
When it all began,
Nor see the rhythm of the verse
Could scarcely catch the rhyme.

I didn't know the way
That lyric joy and pain
Can be as one
Like giving birth a second time.

I didn't understand the mystery of the words
Nor how the pattern went
I simply lived them through
Not really knowing what they meant.

But, softly, toward the close
The harmony began.
Somehow the beauty of the Gift
Had made the space for letting go.
The circle of the words
Had finally let me know.

And now a slender thread of meaning
Weaves through every single line.
I think I see the counterpoint
Love is the canticle divine.

Sandi Gienapp
I DO

In memory of my Father and His love for my Mother, Elmer & Maxine Frey.

Remember when you said "I do"?
Remember after how your love grew?
Remember when you brought forth your first son?
Remember the smile on your husband's face
When at last his life was put into place?
You had another son and then a daughter.
Then another son, a daughter too, and love
Was still there between both of you.
Then as Life went on as seen.
Another son and daughter gleaned.
Life went on and we all grew and
Found our love and grew a few.
Our Father has since passed away and
We are left to take his place.
We will remember as time goes by
The love our parents held deep inside.
And even though he's not with you, Mom,
The day you said, "I Do" . . .
lives on . . .

Mark R Wolfe
MY FRIEND

To Clarice Hawks, who welcomed me into her home, and into her heart. In a lifetime, one will seldom chance to find and cherish a true and real friend. As in life, for me she is that in spirit—forever!

I found a friend the other day,
Or just the day before,
I felt such warmth and tenderness
As I passed beyond her door.

A warmth and tenderness so rare,
I wondered could it be
That in this stranger I had found
Someone to comfort me.

But wait, I said, it's not my place
To take and not return,
This person who has suffered much,
And from whom so much to learn.

Who has struggled quietly with life
With never a complaint,
I have, at times, imagined
I found the company of a saint.

Her honest caring and concern
Shine through on every day,
The simple touch of conversation,
Or at moments when we pray.

And now, what more to say to her,
What words should come to mind,
How can I truly appreciate
That I have met one of a kind.

I know, for sure, she's touched my heart,
My soul forevermore,
My duty is now to spread that joy
As I pass another's door.

I found a friend the other day,
And I pray for all our time
That in her quiet thoughts she'll say,
He is a friend of mine.

Shirley L TenHagen
FRIENDS

To our very special friends: Al & Judy, Joe & MaryAnn, Frank & Marion, George & Steva.

Friends are special, day in and day out.
They accept as you are, without a doubt.
They're there when you need them,
That's where great friendships stem!

Family is family and everyone grows
A different way, that we all know.
Friends are forever, they're always there
Whatever the problem, the worry, the care.

Families are loving and each in their way
Are as different as moonlight and sunlight today.
But friends are constant and supporting to us
We love family, but friends are a plus!
Family is family, there's no other choice,
But to friends, anything can be voiced.
Friends will stay by you and listen and guide.
They'll share their feelings, with nothing to hide.

You can't choose your family with in-laws and out-laws
But friends are always there—because
They love you and care for you with all your woes
With friends—anything goes!

Robin Lee Wood
AND THE PROBLEMS

This poem is for all the people who care about the environment; they are not alone. It is also dedicated with the hope that others will realize the problems of the environment and pitch in.

Flowing in nature
the creek runs dry.
Standing, the forest burns;
man wonders why.
Turning in time,
the earth revolves:

A look at man and the problems
not solved,
but created.

Annette Dwyer
THE CACTUS

Alone it stands. Hard and harsh,
against the sun's brilliant rays of fire.
Yet green, never thirsting. Bringing
forth its most brilliant miracle . . . A
flower of softest Lilac. Mixing with
the fragrance of the earth. That green
King of the desert.

Dillard K Henderson
TO TAMMY

When I met you, I met someone
I love much more than me
With deeper love than I had thought
A human love could be.

I lived a long enriching life
But with one gnawing void,
The absence of a trusting heart
Where love should be enjoyed.

I was a river rushing on
Without a goal for me,
But when I came to you at last,
I knew I'd reached the sea.

You make me feel fulfilled, complete,
All centered and all whole;
You are God's greatest gift to me,
A mate for my whole soul.

Now there's no need for me to seek,
No need for me to roam,
For lying in each other's arms,
I know I've found my home.

Melody A Habecker
ELEMENTARY SCHOOL IS A PLACE WHERE . . .

A child is harshly told by a shallow person that his beliefs are only myths.

A child is pulled from and forced to leave his fairyland.

A child is robbed of his childhood and loses his innocence.

A fragile child is forever scarred by unthinking authority.

Terry McDaniel
OUR CRUCIFIED SAVIOUR
I couldn't imagine how he felt
How his heart had slowly cried
And as the tears rolled down his cheeks
His eyes looked towards the sky

He hung up high above the crowd
And all they did was sigh
He finally gave up the ghost
Then on that cross he died

Before the Sabbath day drew on
They took his body down
And there his battered body lay
Upon that cold, cold ground

They dragged his body to the tomb
Where he was going to rest
Our loving Saviour died for us
So we might all be blest.

My Precious Jesus, Mighty Saviour
You died so I could live
So take my life, Oh Blessed Saviour
And teach me how to give.

Eva M Byzio

Eva M Byzio
POEM
pump pump
bleeding you a poem
blood swelling my pen
first trickling later gushing
into slivered paper

gushing in gushing out
leaving me parched
paper saturated
pump pump

writing i love you
comparing you to a summer's day
describing my heart's landscape
pump for you for me

for me for you pump
i think i write i am my poem
its metaphors are my limbs
but wait pump pump pump

pen is running dry
pa-pump
still have not told you that
pa-pump pa-

Patty Call Bauer
MAMA

To the most hardworking, loving mother that any child could ever have!

Mama, no one can take your place
No one ever had such a pretty face
No one, so kind can ever be
As the mother god gave to me
He blessed us all right from the start
When he gave to her such a big heart
Oh, there are those in the world who still care
And, you will even find people who still with others share
But to us, there will never be another
Who can take the place of our dear mother
God took her home to be with him,
And to be with our belated kin
But, to all of us, she still lives
For, a life like hers continues to give
For time and eternity, she lives on
In the eyes of our daughters and sons
And, when their lives have gone by,
A child will look at their parents and sigh,
"Grandma, a great lady was and she looked a lot like me.
Look, and her smile you will see."
And the circle will begin again
That great circle with no end
The one that started with our mother
And, can never be replaced by another

Rene M Doehrer
TWO LOVES ARE BROUGHT TOGETHER
Two loves are brought together
But only as one heart.
Two feelings are brought together
But only as one soul.
For as we approach the time
for our beginning
We know it will be the best
for both of us.

Jenny Olin
LIPS
Everyone has them—some are small; others are big.
women color them to attract—
Men and women use them to interact.

Some are pouty—another word for sexy—
others puzzling and perplexing.
Wetting one's lips is an invitation to romance—
and a kiss the next step after that first glance.

Many women paint them orange—
others in the rose—
even in the the pink.
And just from one's lips can often be read—
that which one is thinking but often left unsaid.

Next time you look at someone of the opposite sex—
see if their lips are smiling, or the look beguiling.
And when dancing cheek to cheek, don't be meek—
pucker up—and chances are there'll be no need to speak.

Lips don't usually lie—well, maybe they sometimes do—
but who care when you're puckered with that special guy.
And who knows—those long, sultry kisses may one day
change your Miss to Mrs.

Rushelle L Cliff
ROMANCE
If I had my way
there in the perfect night,
I would be by your side
in the vision of paradise.

During that special moment
dancing all night in your arms,
throughout that wonderful kiss
remembering you sweet but masculine
charm.

As the night gets late
why should you go,
after that high
you live with the low.

Mary Elizabeth Capps
WHISPERING WINDS OF WILLOW
Soft sweep the silence still,
Aloft a distance and sea gull spill
The birding echo across their lake,
Ducks of water profoundly awake.

Off afar a sunbeam silhouette
Of mountains up deep with its shadows to set;
Sun hanging down to touch the tree.
Warm is the haze to the tips so free.

An island sits green—the right palm of its birth
To nestle and spree the surrounding earth.

The tree of willow is a song sweet wheel
For one motion is glorified
As low branches kneel.

Pleasance so shining in the eyes of the sky—
Whispering winds of willow will fly.

Trudy Owens
SWEET MEMORIES OF YOU
Images of yesterday
crowd my mind
again today
and bring to me
sweet memories of you.
A fondness
For your gentle touch
a stolen kiss
a hidden blush
deep inside
my secretness
where no one
dares to tread
you
touch my soul . . .

Madelyn G Stone
THE BEACH . . .
What a wondrous place, the edge of the sea;
Where treasures abound for us to share.
God's special creation, gift to you and to me;
Full of such pleasures and beauty so rare!

Walk along the beach with me, see it through my eyes;
Discover what the sea has washed upon the sand.
Sun-bleached driftwood, in many a shape and size;
Exquisite seashells, waiting to be found by a gentle hand.

What stories could they tell of places they have been;
Carried by storm-tossed seas to a distant, sun-kissed shore.
To rest awhile, until the tides will move them once again;
Now we can treasure them, keep them safe forevermore.

The gently lapping water picks up speed and force;
As the tide comes in to collect its unclaimed gifts,
And gathers them to continue that endless course;
While seagulls soar and a breeze dies, then lifts.

The sun is setting quickly, a fiery ball of red;
Nestling into the bosom of that majestic sea.
A wonder to behold, as these mighty forces wed;
To witness such splendor, how privileged are we!

Elnora E Wilson
CHILDHOOD
Take me back to my childhood days.
Let me wander over those sweet by-ways.
Let me feel again that childish bliss
with the friends I now so sadly miss.
Let mother tuck me again in my bed
after my evening prayers I've said.
Let me rise again with the morning sun,
spend a day enjoying the innocent fun
that children know, free from anxious cares
and the worries and heartache the grownup bears.

Take me back again to my grandpa's farm.
Let me play with kids on the hay in the barn
or race with Shep o'er the old clay hills,
and listen at sunset for whip-poor-wills.
A barefoot lass with long brown curls
and a tattered gown, O I'd give ten worlds
if I owned them, to be again a child
and romp and swing on the grapevine wild.

Now I'm growing older each passing day
like everyone does, that's just the way
time hastens on, and it seems so long
since the days I sang those childish songs.
Few are the things I'd change if I could,
but could I go back, I gladly would,
and live again those childhood days
and wander over those carefree ways.

Beatrice C Horton
LIFE OF METAMORPHOSIS
What is life like, a caterpillar or a butterfly or both?
In our darkest hour are we but like the caterpillar struggling against change.
The emotional strife, learning ourselves, becoming individuals, and mature adults.
The hurt and pain of love, trusting another with your heart.
The vulnerability of another learning your weakness,
The fear of trying new things, prefer sticking with routine or the old habit.

By finding our strength from a Spirit from beyond, greater than us,
Then we turn into beautiful butterflies, daring to hope or make a dream come true.
Taking a chance on love, joy and happiness, and becoming peaceful, wise,
And confident individuals free to fly and to enjoy life.

Donna M Selbach
MY GREEN DUNGAREES
It was love at first sight
I had never owned a pair like these
the year was 1971 when I acquired
my green dungarees

Although they were a hand me down
I loved them with such ease
a garment once owned by my brother
were now
my green dungarees

We did a lot of things together
we even played in the trees
but my favorite was playing baseball
in
my green dungarees

There comes a time when a girl must
grow
when her old clothes become a tight
squeeze
such a sad when I no longer fit in
my green dungarees

I think of the times we had been
through
as I try to remember what happened
to these
I will never forget my very first love
my green dungarees

Elrena Parton
BRICK WALLS
In life I have
faced many
thick brick walls.

Some brick walls
I have faced,
I faced alone,
there seemed to be
no one who cared.

Unfortunately banging
one's head or
shedding tears,
does not make the
thick brick walls crumble.

With the passing of time
ideas come forth,
or a passer-by may
offer a solution.

Thick brick walls are
difficult at times
to make crumble.

Tammy N Brewer
TOGETHER

To Phil, The man who will always stand out In my Heart.

I know that through distance
separated between us
Our hearts can only grow one way;
... Together.

I know that as one foot is placed
In front of the other, the only way
we will walk
... is Together.

I know that as visions are turned into
color
And images are turned into voices of
reality;
The only way our words will be
exchanged
... is Together.

I know that when a hand reaches out
for comfort
And a means of satisfaction is needed
to be felt;
The only way we will touch
... is Together.

I know that to love another, one must
first love
Himself.
And once that person has
established a foundation
for that love to grow on, the only
way one's heart
will grow
... is Together with another.

Steven Popp
MY PROMISES TO YOU
I cannot promise you everything in life for our days on earth are numbered but I can promise to give you all the happiness I can give in this life. I promise to be patient with you never to mistreat you I promise to be honest and open with you because I love you I promise to be sensitive to your feelings and to be there when you need me. I promise to help you through life and I promise never to try to change your ways but to accept them for they are part of you and most of all I promise to love you and only you for the rest of my life. I promise you all these listed above for I see so much in you but sometimes I cannot say them to you, but most of all I love you and always will.

Trina D Witt
IN TIME

I dedicate the publication of this poem to my wonderful sister. I love you Tanya . . .

The hearts love inside dream on
until the day our love will twine.
Minds will wonder, till the end of
time.

To feel the world till we come
together,
dreams will shine on.
To share our hearts
will last forever, till our dreams once
Come together.

The blossoms will bloom, the stars
shall shine. Our hearts together,
our love in time.

Christine Whoberry
THE TREE
When will I reach the sky?
All of my neighbors are taller than I.
The clouds are so fluffy and bright.
When might I reach their light?
While the wind is blowing so strong,
My branches are growing so long.
But wait, what do I see?
Why some children are running
toward me.
They start singing and dancing happy
as can be.
Being small is not bad at all!

Rick Austin
LOVE MAKES ME HAPPY

To My Darling ROSE ANN, My Reason for Loving.

To be happy, I don't need much,
Certainly not just toys and such.
All I need is you,
And a love that is true.
With your support and understand-
ing,
Caring and tenderness not
withstanding,
The world is a better place
Because it includes my smiling face.
And hopefully when I show that
smile
It spreads to you, at least for a while.
For love is something that we share
With someone for whom we really
care.
It's that process of sharing,
Both the love and the caring,
That makes my life complete
And I'm happy from my head to my
feet.

Cherie L Sunderland
MY MOTHER'S HEART

To the backbone of our family— My Mom, Muriel Louise Hayes-Sunderland.

Springtime—Freshly mowed grass
Gentle breezes under blue skies,
Shows you that life can hold peace
When you're feeling lonely and
needing to cry.

Summer—Sunny days and warm
nights
Sandy beaches and ocean waves,
Serene, beautiful sunsets
Gives light to hot and balmy days.

Fall—The smell of burning leaves
Bonfires and long walks at night,
Leaves falling and changing colors
Making for a beautiful sight.

Winter—Freshly fallen snow
Under a bright and starry sky,
Symbolizing that nature is only
asleep
That nothing really ever dies.

The four seasons can be so peaceful
But there is only one part
That is more beautiful to me
And that is my MOTHER'S HEART.

Claude Berglund
A LULLABY FOR MY BELOVED

To the girl who saw me through and heaven sent.

Ever softer grows my slumber
Now sweet angel from my side
Though departed into silence
With me always you'll abide.
Lullabies from out your singing
Soars into my dreams at night.
Though tomorrows may be bringing
Sorrowed memories of thy flight.

In the sighing hours my darling
As the sadness whelms my heart
I'll be listening for you darling
When invited to depart.
Then so gladly I will greet you
Winging from this sorrowed earth
Where our joys and tribulations
Were all trialed from our birth.

Marie Thompson
LOOKING BACK
When I was a kid—my age I'll tell
not
I went to the movies, and a quarter I
got
My Mom never knew of the words
P.G.
It was always a movie that I could
see
There was no raw sex and no bad
words
Just a way to spend Saturday, us boys
and girls
There was always a good guy that
we'd clap and cheer
And a bad guy we booed and hated
all year
What's happened to the movies they
make today
They have to be censored and rated
all ways
Too bad—all you kids, for you'll
never know
The fun of spending a Saturday at a
Matinee Show

Anne Turner
SOUL IN FLIGHT
Soaring over azure fields, I see the
world unfold its truth.
I feel the warmth of morning sun and
know the beauty of my
youth.
The spring has brought a golden
glow, and everything shines
vibrantly.
I want to teach you how to fly. You
answer "no" so silently.

I'm flying—Don't try to bring me
down.

I turned my head, and met my soul
going places yet unseen.
A flash of light brought knowledge,
and I'm full of all I've
ever been.
The wisdom of a thousand years
enfolds me in its solitude.
A traveller through endless sands—
The desert is my only food.

I'm flying—Don't try to bring me
down.

I, like the albatross, fly with the
ancient wings: solo: on a brass
breeze that splits the night in two.
Alighting the tall cyprus now and
again to peer at the sky's
endless black line.
We are brothers, this feathered soloist
and I: Awaiting a warm
wind to carry us into endless light.

Alyn Kemp
FEELINGS
On this one day, beautiful and bright,
Not pitch dark, like the lonely night,
We can hear all the birds sweetly
sing,
Be patient heart, the phone will ring.

Once we two met, in a very simple
way,
For one woman's love, this I must
say,
She shows all her hurts, like a veneer,
But inside, all her feelings are there.

Upon her face, a smile, so very
bright,
And as standing there, in the sunlight,
Her hair glinted, like burnished gold,
Nothing for a man, this to me she
told.

I looked, and this in the yes of you,
Woman race, hurt, and proud it's
true,
But so loving, kind, tender, all three,
And much, much more, this in you I
see.

Woman's love, some men will never
know,
Being held, touched, let feelings
show,
Oh! how I wish a chance for you and
me,
Be still my heart, for it may never be.

Alyn Kemp
IS THIS ALL

"To Mom and Dad" Thank you for the life you gave, and values taught, now rest in peace, in God's countenance.

Yesterday, it has come, and it has gone,
And as I look about, my heart is torn,
For all my brave front, I seem to pale,
On the day, they held the auction sale.

The people came, from near and far,
They all came by bike, and by car,
Some were friends, both old and new,
The others were folk, just like you.

What am I bid, one, then two, and four,
The auctioneer called, "Who'll give more"
Five, then eight, ten, fifteen said one,
Going for fifteen, going, going, gone.

Yes, I watched as everything was sold,
One by one they went, both new and old,
The end of a home, which stood so long,
As I thought, stand tall, be strong.

Is this all, we must face it one day,
Time, when there's nothing more to say,
GOD, gives us life, to strive and try,
We are born, and we live, then we die.

Dwight Barnett
LOVINGLY

There is much I must share with you.
There is even more I must tell you.
I must,
Because you are my audience.
You are the reason all of this matters.
By allowing me all of these expressions
You afford me purpose.
You let me matter.
I am truly free when I share.
I am happy with me.
I understand most of that which comes before me.
I am alive and new again with each word.
Come, be my audience,
Be my critic.
Be my fan.
Come, be my Love,
I have stories to tell,
Many words to which you can listen,
Many visions that must be shared
With one who loves, who cares, who knows . . . .
With you.

Karen Marie Breslin
SILVER STRAND ON GOLD

Do you feel an unknown fear?
Cannot touch it, but you know it's there.
Know the words to the songs,
See the dark in the full moon,
And listen to midnight no matter the tune.
And do I have to tell you that the only true bet is the one you can't win.
How far can you take it?

Step into a daydream longer than the nights.
The play of light can distort your sight.
Make believing can come easy for you
And it's hard to acknowledge the past.
The winds of change have started to blow.

In silence the lonely make all their mistakes
It's just a silver strand on gold.
Sometimes I listen to myself.
Don't know if I can get it.
I never did leave you
I never did run from you
In my dreams I said I would always love you.
And if I was to say this was my last time
Would it end with you?

Richard A Hindle
ONE OF THE BEAUTIFUL PEOPLE

In a world of boundless gratitudes, and endless ways of saying good-bye; How can I determine the right words to say, to a beautiful person whose departing saddened me? The feelings are ones of regret, because I did not allow myself to really know her. She is one of authority but can show compassion; a sense of humor that has given me hours of laughter. Her intelligence is astounding to me; her kindness overwhelming! To simply say, "good-bye and good luck," does not see near enough; so I could express a sincere feeling of caring, Caring that this beautiful person will always have happiness and inner peace.

Allis Peters Dethrow
MY MOTHER LEFT ME

In memory of Cleo A. Aydlott, March 11, 1911—December 22, 1989.

My mother left me memories
A box of photos
A camera

My mother left me a diamond ring
Her mother's jewels
A sewing machine

My mother left me an antique doll
A shadow box
And a teddy bear

My mother left me a 23 year old car
A sleeping bag
A lawn chair

My mother left me a new TV
A box of books
A crossword dictionary

My mother left me a rocking chair
A table lamp
A radio

And last December
At seventy-eight
My mother left me.

Grace E Jones
A TOUCH OF SPRING

I saw today on a willow tree
The faintest trace of Spring.
In the whispering pines above the house,
I heard a red bird sing.

Beneath the trees along the road
The fragrant hyacinths bloom.
And the golden crocus that grace our yard
Peep out of the winter gloom.

The air has a nip, a chill,
A warmth that whispers . . . "Come."
I will,
While the red bird sings at the trace of spring
With the beauty of the daffodils.

So throw a log on the fire tonight;
It's crackling a welcoming tune.
And I know for sure that winter's passed,
And Spring will be here soon.

Helen M Bowie
FOOLISH QUESTION

Sorry I loved you? How can I regret
For one short moment you made me forget
This made changing world and all its woe?

If I should lose my sight, would I regret
One fleeting glimpse of the dying sunset
Or the robin's breast against the snow?

Could I no longer hear, would I disdain
To listen to some heavenly refrain
Because for me it would be the last?

I'd gather them all close to keep me numb
Against the cold void that would surely come
To protect me 'til the worst had passed

Then I would be ready to face the years
With my last impressions mocking my fears
For I could at will recall each one

And savor its sweetness to the bitter end
And be thankful for memories and pretend
I could hear again and see the sun.

Angela M Wahl
HEALING LOVES PAIN

If only a single tear falls from your eye,
I will catch it and wipe the memory from your mind.
When your heart breaks and bleeds,
my heart will reach out and help mend it.
Bandages made of hugs and kisses will be wrapped
around you wherever you may be hurt.
I will heal all the wounds that you may suffer,
and your skin will never be marked with scars.
If your breath comes in jagged spurts,
I will revive it with the air from my lungs.
When your body burns with fever,
I will bathe you with cool water.
And, if you will want me;
I will stand by and hold your hand gently.

Nitin Ramlall
A SPECIAL PERSON: FATHER DAMIEN

This poem is dedicated to my parents, Richard and Joya Ramlall, and to my wonderful grandparents, Fred and Edith Ramlall and Nani and Nanda Kar.

Father Damien was a great man
A man of giving.
Some people were dying
And then they were living.

Father Damien would help
Any time, any place.
First the lepers were sad
And then had a happy face.

He built houses
Brought water that was clean.
He was somebody who was nice
Not somebody that was mean.

He would make you feel happy,
If anything was wrong.
He was very,
Very, very strong.

Father Damien would help,
Summer, winter, fall.
Father Damien was a great man
A man who gave all.

Father Damien was a man of love
Not a man of hate.
He was super.
He was just great.

June Andrews
THE KING

Today I saw a King,
a glorious sight to behold.
His robe was of the finest cloth,
upon His head a crown of gold.

Today I walked with a King,
down a path not often trod.
At the end my eyes could see
the wondrous light of God.

Today I talked with a King,
as He sat upon His throne.
He told me that I need not fear,
for I was not alone.

Today I was touched by a King,
and I knew instantly,
That by the gentle touch of His hand
my soul had been set free.

Oh, today I met a King,
He said that He had paid the price.
Yes, today I met a King,
and His name is Jesus Christ.

Lisa Gilpin
SOUL SEARCH 101

Listening to my professors
I wonder if I'll maintain my
Sanity
Always

Goodness! What if
I march down
Life's aisles
Pretending
Instead of
Never living?

Leslie R Lohn
VISIONS

Like the madness of passion, with the roar of success
The speechless spirits wander endless
Not good enough for heaven, not bad enough for hell
Stuck somewhere in the middle, forever to dwell
They see no evil, they feel no good
They'd find the passageway, if they only could
Flying through air, with a haunt if they dare
They cannot talk, they cannot speak
They're looking for the doorway, but will forever seek
Misty visions flash before my eyes
Terror and horror, with a touch of surprise

Who can help these long lost beings
When no one believes what they are seeing
Shadow like people who wander endlessly
Unsheltered spirits who were left friendlessly
They search for the door, with a dream of hope
Hiding behind curtains, holding on to their rope
Shadows of wonder, shadows of stride
Mischievous spirits left without pride
Not good enough for heaven, not bad enough for hell,
So they're stuck in the middle forever to dwell.

Karen M Kotlarchyk

IN SEPTEMBER

In memory of my sister Lorraine, Whose love inspires me every day of my life.

In September, the leaves gently fall
from the trees,
The multitude of colors are beautiful,
yet sad.
Each leaf has a story to tell
Of life, of love, of death.
But September has a different meaning
for me.
For as I watch the leaves float to the
ground,
They remind me of the tears I cry for you.
And as the seasons turn,
My feelings change.
But when Autumn comes once more
Like the leaves, my tears begin to fall.

Felix Buccellato

MAYFLIES

As I watched the Mayflies
So pretty and light
I witnessed a wondrously
Wonderful Sight

Tides always changing
The flow and the ebb
Completely entangled
An elegant web

All of the players
Humble or Strong
Watching and listening
Each singing their song

Happy or sad times
With each heaving breath
It could not have been clearer
Life = Death

Daniel J Leshikar Sr

OUR CINDERELLA GIRL

To: Joyce and Marvin Sondermann, Grandmas, Ellen Sondermann, and Margaret L. Leshikar, in loving memory of Niki L. Sondermann. May 17, 1974—July 26, 1989.

Flowers covered the grave of our Cinderella girl
only lent to us, for a short stay on this world
She's gone and peace of mind is so hard to come
and for our heavy aching hearts—there is none

Our Cinderella girl had a zest for life,
each life touched was affected
as the magic of her personality went to work, nothing was neglected
Everything was beautiful, because this is the way it was, in her world
God! What have we lost? When we lost our Cinderella girl

Our Cinderella girl touched little children with love
little children look for her, as they look to heaven above
And somewhere in Heaven, She has got to be
waiting for Mom and Dad, family and friends to see

Cinderella girl, you blessed us with your stay
We'll remember you, especially the seventeenth of May
We thank you, our Cinderella girl
for letting us be, a part of your world

Helen M Ostrom

ONE FRAGILE PRECIOUS MOMENT

Outside a father's study door, wavers a little voice,
"Daddy . . . Daddy, are you . . .
there?"
No reply is heard from the busy man inside.
The little voice repeats, "Daddy? Are you there?"
A pause—a man replies, "Yes,
Son . . . I'm here."
Softly the little voice asks, "Open the door . . .?"
"Not now Son. I'm busy."
Sadly, the little voice pleads,
"Daddy? Let me in . . .
I love you . . ."
Within the room, stern eyes turn tender, brimming with
unshed tears.
Business coming before his son?
Never should it be!
Opening wide the door, he greets his child with loving
arms.
All the money in the world could not replace this love.
The little voice had touched his heart, to release one
fragile precious moment.

Helen M Ostrom

PRESSING ON

Echoing through the canyon's gorge came the
sonorous sound of Indian drums.
Throughout long months of rains and drought,
the settlers kept pressing on.
To the West they had come, so far away,
that to return was yet another tale.
No greater sacrifice would they make, and
while sorrow filled their breasts,
They buried their dead, through sweat and
tears,
And headed toward the West.
With bodies and minds aching and sore,
They came to a mesa's rocky gorge.
With pulleys and ropes held tightly above,
They were lowered out over the river's falls.
With women and children following suit, without
a thought or pause.
Magnificent courage was shown by all, with the
prayers at end of day,
Thanking their God for leading them, and guarding
them on their way.
Across this land run various threads from peoples
of many lands,
They blazed the country from coast to coast,
through rain drenched fields, and sands.
Each generation brought new hopes that helped
to form our States,
And to this day, we look with pride, in spite of
dissension and hate.
Through all their troubles, some good seeps
through, no matter what the cost,
And our prayers go onward each coming year,
for those who fought and lost.

Donna M Innamorata

THE SORCERESS

I look into my crystal ball, the wizardry begins.
The secret tool I utilize to steal thoughts deep within.
Another naive victim has come into my view;
thoughtfully I plot and scheme the damage that I'll do.
Wickedly I state my aim; to seek and to destroy;
to dominate this puppet like a silly finger toy.
To play upon his feelings; gain his confidence and trust,
I gather "charm" and "cunning," throw in "purity" and "lust."
Now I have my weapons and the battle will commence.
I suit myself in armor, use his love as my defense.
"Let the games begin" I say, as fear does shake my voice.
As we enter into battle—our reciprocated choice.
The combat starts off slowly. We both size up our prey;
feeling-out and testing; gaining power day by day.
Finally I see a chance. It's time to take my stand.
Aware that if I stumble, I may perish at his hand.
And now the war has ended and the loser will subside.
Do we call the death a murder or name it suicide?
He stares at me with hatred in my Sorceress disguise
to find I'm just an angel as seen through a demon's eyes.

Greg S Sanderson

WHAT IF

What if I did this?
What if I'd done that?
The answer to these
questions none knows.

What if I never left home?
What if I'd never joined the marines?
Once again the answers
are unknown.

What if I'd never grown up?
What if I'd never met you?
And still the answer is not known.

What if I'd never gotten sick?
What if I'd never used drugs or alcohol?
I'm still not sure if the answer is known.

What if is a question I'll continue to ask.
The answer I will probably never know.
If I do find the answer
I may not want to know it.

Days will pass and so will
weeks and years.
What if, will be a question
I'll always ask.
The answer I'll never find . . . .

C L Dougherty

GOODNIGHT

Soft lights
Dance in the rain-slicked
Road beyond my window
Slow shadows
Roll across my wall
And disappear in the cool corners
Of my room
Muted murmurs
Of the snoring city
Fill my mind and sing me
To sleep

Mili Gera

RAINDROPS

Raindrops are like beautiful
musical notes falling from the
clouds of heaven. And as they
fall upon my face I hear
the joy of a wedding and
the pain from a broken heart,
the warmth of love and the
fire of hate, the silence of
spring and the thunder of
winter, the happiness of life
and the sadness of death.
Raindrops play the music your
heart desires.

Linda Bradberry

MOM AND DAD'S FACE

To my cousin Carolyn.

It seems like yesterday you
were here
Your smiling face was always
near.
I turned around and you were
gone
Never again to me to belong.

I wish just once again I could see
That face that meant so much to me.
I close my eyes and trace
the lines,
I have the memory deep in my mind.

You're gone from me that sweet face
You're at rest in God's grace.
Some say it's called the ending
I would like to think it's
maybe the beginning.

Carol Eichholtz

ECHOES OF JOY

In a valley, gently sheltered, stands
an old endearing house
with long forgotten memories
embedded in its walls.
From the graceful veranda that
encircles its heart,
ring the echoes of voices gone for
many years.

Sadly it listens to the crooning of the
sea and remembers
children's laughter ringing round its
hills.

It remembers generations who grow
up within its walls and
watched sadly as each one went
away.

Where gardens bright and cheerful
lay, now barren rock
does reign and the grapes once
sneaked by childish hands
are rotting on the vine.

This tired old house, so lonely now,
exists on memories
and on a quiet night can hear the
echoes of the past.
For the love and joy it nurtured there,
ever will remain
though all the folks, who filled its
walls, have long since
gone away.

Shar'Ron Mahaffey
MU-DEAR (MOTHER DEAR)

Dedicated to the memory of Margaret Walker-Mahaffey, my mother.

I don't remember your tender touch
Or your loving ways
And I don't recall your kind face
Or your gentle embrace.
But I know that if you were still alive
I could count on you
To stand by my side,
Chase away my fears,
And wipe away my sighs.
Folks still speak highly of you
Whenever your name comes up,
What a good mother you tried to be,
An all around good person you were.
I know that God didn't mean for me
to suffer
When He took you away,
But it's still very difficult
Accepting that you aren't here with
me everyday.
I'll always love you, Mu-dear.
And, although the memories are few,
There's a special place in my heart
Where no one can take you away.

Margie Payne
LIGHT OF DAY

With Love, To my husband, children and grandchildren.

The light of day begins to seep in.
As the sunrise appears in the sky,
new life,
new beginnings, Just as our life,
begins new.
And then, the day begins to pass, and
fade away.
And sunset, appears in the sky. And
I'm reminded
of another day, gone by.
And the day that began with sunrise,
fades into
sunset, such is life as the light of day.

Lisa Cross
MY EVERYTHING
My eyes
All they see is you
Dancing close

My hands
They feel only strength
From the touch of yours

My ears
Only hear words
From your lips, whispered

My heart
It knows joy, hope,
Time we will share

My soul
All it feels is love
Forever holding you to me

Allen E Lock
A FRIEND
A Person who knows one,
Is lucky.
A Person who follows one,
Is a sucker.
A Person who criticizes one,
Is afraid of him.
A Person who praises one,
Is a fool.
A person who believes in one,
Is great.
A person who hasn't one,
Is nothing.

Dotti Bagby-Morris
PROBYN . . . MY LOVE
Precious is our relationship that
started quite harmlessly
Pride will never stand in my
way nor will I throw us away
carelessly.

Real are the feelings that flow from
deep within me to you
Ready and willing I will be
there and I do promise to be
true.

Only you had that something it took
to make me say "I do"
Over and over I will try my best
to prove I am in love with you.

Better and closer we will be as the
days go by
Beautiful is the reality that love
can change something inside.

Yes! I will lend a helping hand, a
listening ear
Yours . . . Today, Tomorrow,
always . . . I am here.

Nowhere else on God's green earth
would I rather be than sharing my
life with you
Nothing and no one comes
before my commitment to you.
So never never doubt . . .
I love you!

Eleanor Barger
GOD'S GIFT

To Mike and Esther on the birth of their son Daniel.

God's sent you a gift
From heaven above,
A precious baby
To hold and to love.
May this blessing
You've been given to raise,
Bring joy to your home
And hearts filled with praise.
Each time you look
At that tiny face,
Thank God for this gift
Of His loving grace.

Connie French
PERUSAL
For every leaf that falls,
A tear is shed.
For every bough that breaks
Beneath the strain,
Humanity lies torn asunder.
Is it any wonder
That my heart lies
As does the tree
In winter slumber.

Juanita Finley
GOSSIP
Don't repeat gossip
Don't speak the untrue
For whatever you say
May come back to you

Always speak kindly
Of people you know
And always remember
You reap what you sow

Luis Henriquez

Luis Henriquez
THE SCOPE OF MATH

This poem is dedicated to Elizabeth, my sister.

Listen! the coffee pot whistle right
there in the kitchen.
The clock says eight and I go back to
read.
"The Scope of Mathematics/of
Arithmetics," is now my homework.
Thicks pages being turned down in
writing form the publishers.

Gulp at a lighted book. I read a
primitive peoples might use his ten
fingers in his first calculations. The
Babylonians, Egyptians, Hebrews,
the ancient Greeks, Chinese, until
Romans developed several methods
of writing numbers. In silence and
sad, read as long as the theme is?

Sit at old brown chair in front of
computer desk,
so I can think other things, perhaps to
stay.
Now where? I loved you once. Now
it's time I think.
Rereading the book through the red
glasses, focused in history.

Shudder me slightly, when I felt the
cool breeze filtrating
through windows. The decimal
system is introduced by
Arabs called Hindu-Arabic numerals
in the eight century.
Far from those parts of book, her
mind is my confidante.

The great contribution to electronic
computer from mathematics
are perform with two symbols 1 and
0 of the binary system, remarkable.
There are numbers that would exceed
the number of grains of sand,
Archimedes!

Slightly!

Luis Henriquez
A DAY IN SAN FRANCISCO'S LIFE
San Francisco is full of beauty.
It's in your eyes now clear,
and through the streets the agony,
of many lamenting voices I hear.

In the population at San Francisco,
it looks that way to me,
an inlet of the Pacific in California
broken down the world from
earthquake.

Death, after all claims everyone,
you find it everywhere.
The fault return that day,
it was a bad day of San Francisco's
life.

The rules of the world are made up
by men
with a certain justice, so
perhaps god, help to sweeten
the poor heartbreaking man's pain
and woe.

The seaport and city has been
restored,
leaders and taxpayers are rebuilding
it.
How much longer will continuous?
The strength come and save this land.
This young grapevine it made will
grow so strong!

Charles Schmitt W T

Charles Schmitt W T
THE GIFT OF TIME

I gratefully acknowledge my friendship with Helen Konstatados, without whom I would not have written this poem.

So much time spent searching for
what to present . . .
So back and forth to the shopping
center we went
Searching, searching, searching for a
special gift to give
Then we must ask ourselves, "For
what purpose do we live?"

Do we live to earn more money and buy nice things . . .
For the child who is happiest when he sings
Or the gift of wheels for he who moves
Or record albums for the one living inside record grooves.

Searching, searching, searching we pore over the shelves
Are we looking for gifts while trying to find ourselves!
Do not look outside, but look inside as with a bottle of wine
For its gift of quality can only come with time.

So when a friend calls for conversation on the phone
Remember we are all very much alone.
The gift of time is what we have to share
Its value is greater that other gifts we bare.

Wendy L Page

IMPOSSIBLE WISHIN'

With thankful appreciation to Rick, my faithful, loving, supportive husband, friend and partner. My Lord, who inspires me. My family and close friends.

Misty ocean seabreeze,
Sand dunes of all kinds.
Thinking of us together
Being in love till the end of time.
You my friend and love
Are always on my mind—
But you haven't much need for me
So I waste my time . . .
Wishin' the impossible.

Wendy L Page

WHO ARE YOU SIR?

Who are you sir? Handsome and strong,
Wearing a face of one who's been wronged.
Who are you sir? Asking me out,
To go to the beach, to walk all about.
Who are you sir? Trying to hold my hand,
Putting your arm around me, as we walk barefoot in the sand.
Who are you sir? Why did you choose me?
What fate or Supreme being had you run into me?
Who are you sir? So gentle and kind.
Will you let me know what's on your mind?
Who are you sir? You seem to be hurting,
Could I cheer you up by doing some flirting?
Who are you sir? Will you let me in?
Can I knock down the wall you're hiding in?
Who are you sir? How long will we last?
Will we continue to grow or be something of the past?!
Who are you sir? . . . I think I can see . . .
A vulnerable heart . . .
A mirror image
of me.

Wendy L Page

BROWN EYED SUSAN

Brown eyed Susan stands tall in a field
Looking to heaven full of zeal.
Awaking from the night to the shining morning Light,
Drawing strength from His warmth . . . feeling reborn.
Morning dew begins to trickle,
melting slowly it tickles;
As it washes droplets of tears—A smile buds forth and appears.
Arms of golden-bronze petals stretch out wide
delicately surrounding Susan's brown eye.

Brown eyed Susan stands tall in a field
Roots firmly planted, yet ready to yield.
Enjoying the freedom of wide open space,
Feeling the wind gently kissing her face.
She toils and dances and weathers the seasons,
Looking to heaven for purpose and reasons.
In the quiet whisper of a breeze, a voice is heard saying "follow me."
Brown Eyes look up to a radiant white light,
With questions about her plight . . .
She silently listens for hidden answers to come,
and reflects the beauty . . . and Love of the Son.

Wendy L Page

PERPLEXITY

I wish I had the answer,
to change how people care.
I know not all the reasons
but I see the pain you bear.
You need to find the courage,
to get your feelings aired.
Make one more effort—if you dare.
You can't pinpoint the cause?!
You don't know how you err'd?
It's been going on for years,
it seems so unfair!
What happened, when and where?
Love me as I am please!
Don't continually compare
others with me and how we each have fared.
Can't you see the hurting?
The heart with all the tears?!
Let's practice the art of forgiveness!
Or would it be so rare? . . . For . . .
if we wait, it could be a grave mistake!
Beware of death's stare.

Wendy L Page

TOKEN MEMORIES

I carry in my pocketbook
a sand dollar from the sea.
A smooth gray-brown token
that you had given me.
You told me you had found it
at the spot where we had been.
Where we went running to the ocean
as the waves came crashing in.
The water was so icy cold,
we did not stay too long.
Instead we ran up to the dunes,
and huddled to get warm.
We sat for several hours
in that cozy little spot,
watching the crisp blue ocean
greet the moon and kiss the rocks.

Wendy L Page

YOUR WINDOWS

Our eyes meet.
None others have I seen like yours—
Turquoise in the evening sun,
Transparent crystal blue.
Windows if you will.
They tell me how your heart aches
sometimes as mine does too.
They show those mixed emotions
all bottled up inside.
I can see the hurt upon your face
by the reflection of your eyes.
You're glad but sad.
So confident yet confused!
The tears of a clown best describes you
with those transparent eyes of blue!

Kelly Lumpkin

THERE IS NO JOY SO GREAT!

There is no joy so great
as the joy we feel
When someone we love tells us,
for the first time,
That they love us in return.

And an ordinary day
becomes a milestone,
and a memory
Simply because one person said to another,
"I Love You."
What power the words!
And once spoken,
No Day will ever be the same.

Deanna R Foreman

LIFE'S CHANGES

Standing on life's corner, taking a long look back. You see your life in perspective as you stare at a sidewalk crack. You realize that your life is slowly falling apart, and wish you could go back and change things, and make a brand-new start.

You know that you cannot do that, but you still hope that things will change. So you start off on a new foot; a beginning to all the things in your life you need to start to rearrange.

Suddenly you wake up, and you're lying on your bed, and realize that these were only thoughts that were going through your head.

So when you finally get up, you're feeling mighty fine. You've cleared up all the rough thoughts, and you're ready to start back in time.

Samuel F Gairy

THE SUN

This poem is dedicated to all youths—especially Adventists youths.

Halt! he says to winter, he melts the ice, brings back life, then brightens up the summer.
Seeds, roots, branches, leaves, buds, flowers and sun rays putting all different colors.

Power in the sun is what makes the stagnant water run, Prodigious power in the sun, electricity in its rays, we all use in different ways, then sing to God in solemn praise.

The sunlight gives us light, health and strength, all through the day, at length.
And tomorrow he will give us more, for us to enjoy each hour, for sure.

The change of the sun means spring, summer, autumn, winter, sometimes rain, but he's always there to shine again.
Its warming rays bring peace and joy to hearts each day, as we trod along the dreary way.

At sunset time millions take a last view, they say,
God! you do things in a marvelous way.

Samuel F Gairy

MOTHERS

Mothers are gentle, peaceful and kind,
Rocking babies to sleep when they cry,
They are human beings emotionally strong,
Having love to offer when things go wrong.

They are doctors giving aid to the sick,
Healing the soul from the cold,
They are seamstresses and cooks, producing
fashions that raise eyelids high,
The appearance is overwhelming but they just smile.

They are preachers and teachers telling the way,
They will make you independent some day,
Mothers are washers, hemmers, menders of socks,
Cleaning and sweeping, they do quite a lot.
They are makers of pies, cakes and babies too,
They are really talented, yes! that is true.

But wait, some mothers are bad women,
It's a shame, they disgrace the human race,
Some are abusers, they make children sad,
Others are inconsiderate, they make life hard.

You young girls will be mothers some day,
So please now learn to do things the proper way.

Samuel F Gairy

THE HANDICAPPED

The blind, the mute, the deaf, the lame,
They are really all the same,
What does the Holy Book say,
Prefer to only see it your way.

We cast them aside without a care,
Then act as if they are not there,
Let us be human, it could happen to you,
Remember friends, that is true.

The verdict was passed, he is no use,
He is as blind as a bat, put him away,
There is a place for him to hide and stay.

Society says one is normal when he could hear,
So the deaf lives on and nobody cares.
Just take some time to listen, hear what they say,
And receive knowledge to brighten your day.

Think of the man who lost a leg,
He is forced to go out and beg,
You feel pitiful so you give him a

dime,
But what about the next time.

They suffer ridicule and strife in this life,
You can become handicapped too,
When that happens what will you do?

Mr and Mrs Alxander Bradley Ruppert

Le Roy Ruppert
ONLY FOR ALWAYS

To my beautiful wife.

On one cold winter day
our eyes just didn't meet
the images of my youth
sent your heart in total defeat

Impressions left there to last
as I did my work at the table—
your thoughts, not of me as a child
not something you watched on cable

Our talk turned to tragedy—
you revealed your inner emotions
I could feel the hurt your father left
like a seashell in the ocean

Your life was empty
you lost the season . . .
an empty soul
no goals or reason

You showed me a picture
of one who you thought cared,
moments spent whispering
words that only you shared

Our friendship developed
built on patience and time,
the Kitaro music, the car . . .
almost the perfect crime

In a flash the time went by
men in blue surrounded the bed
they took you your way, me mine, but
we remembered the words that were said

A journey to the Golden Gate
was beyond our wildest dreams . . .
sitting at the Polk Street bar
you know what gay now means

Especially as we lay side by side
in seclusion—the Fairmont hotel
that lazy night . . . we became one
oh, how you loved me so well

Shared moments, were not that stable
they were still the best of times
fantasies are like realities
you have to read between the lines

A time searching for a gourmet delight
I created for you such a surprise,
that altered my image in your eyes

Though you didn't believe me . . .
I loved you then as I do now
knowing that John was part of your life
knowing things would work out somehow

Sitting on the sidelines
at a loss of what to do—
my heart was badly pitted . . .
I was falling more in love with you

Wondering if you'd know me
when the new guy came to call
or was it lost in memories
and not around at all

Though I used you . . .
I knew one day we'd be together
through summer rain, winter's pain
my love was stronger than ever

John caused you hurt—my intentions
were not to harm you, but him
the game he played was outdated
it was like an old gospel hymn

Who would have imagined
one small crime of passion, so much time
we both know who's the winner
it's obvious reading this rhyme

Because everytime I close my eyes
I think of you
and no matter what the season is
I'll still love you

Definitely with all my heart!

Saly, God put love in your heart
but he didn't put it there to stay—
because love is not love
until you give it away

. . . I'll Love You

John A Creger
YESTERDAY'S LOVE CAN'T ALWAYS BE TODAY'S

What love harks on Fairmaiden's words Are these not just words from the deep, dark corners of your mind's own memory lane, from when you were back in school, young and free you know before work, wife and the baby?

Are you now not sitting at a great big desk in a big ole expensive office day dreaming about the good old days, maybe even wishing they were here again, possible even contemplating suicide, well go ahead kill yourself, but before you do hear my words:

You will never again get to touch, squeeze, hug, or kiss your wife or child, also you will never hear either of them say I love you and that's forever.

Diane Wallace
THE CHANGELING

Let me howl down mountain canyons
Whistle through your empty dreams
Bring you pain and desolation
Ignore your frightened screams.

Let me shriek in quiet agony
Scatter thoughts like wasted years
Leave you torn, black and broken
Laughing at your futile tears.

Let me moan through deepest darkness
Crash into your splintered soul
Shatter hopes across the wasteland
Fill your emptiness with woe.

Let me wail beyond the bitterness
Hopelessness and despair
Ride the insane wind of change
Search hard! You'll find me there.

Angela Wiseman
I'VE LOVED

I've loved so many people,
throughout my life it's true.
But I've never loved anyone
as much as I've loved you.

I've loved every single day,
that we have spent together.
I will keep them in my heart,
and cherish them forever.

When I look into your eyes,
my heart begins to melt.
And when you look into mine,
my dreams of you are felt.

I've loved so many people,
throughout my life it's true.
But I'll never love anyone ever,
the way that I've loved you.

Michael D Dial
THE WALL

Hammered and torn by hope filled crowds,
The gruesome view abased the proud.

Against the gleaming goals of man,
The blight stood fast and scarred the land.

The enslaving span that hatred rose;
That long cold wall now reels with blows.

The gray dead length of tyrants' dreams
Cannot dissolve the victim's screams.

So many felled by its hateful hold,
So many sought dear freedom's gold.

Evil's breath stretched out and built,
To guard the hand of the sabre's hilt.

A blemish scorned, and void of worth,
Laid out to haunt the circled earth.

Its surly visage now less than bold,
Now its ugly tale is told.

Peter Michael Du Fore
OUTSIDE LANTERNS

You can touch, you can feel, delights, skies, exactly tiles

People fligh times, you can change, shapes their illusions in the nets

Illusions, confusions; the miles are all there, utterly frightening freezing to time

Inside there is doodles of years way ahead, the days are behind it by highlights lead for bed

Enduring images I have some to spare, but you'll see them through windows, and panes that are bare

Ride the riddle's lanes, keeping cool, won't be fooled during race's past the images across

Ensuring masques' guarded quests through hours rest in the fields of dew
Finding afternoon's sanctioned blue fulfilling rhythms

Peter Michael Du Fore
LOST RAINBOWS

Season blends, seasons missing in blunder attacks,
bucks and stones are in a now dry river

Bridges are washed and dry in the sun's everlasting
afloat are the shadows of what once had been

Caustic soldiers meditate of their heartland and
forward towards the trestles

The switches in rush breaks,
stockpile debase the embodiments
of leaves

Well's despirited rose; untriumphant in mirrors
desolated by space

Empty roads inviting signals,
reflector's beams
the debris overwhelmed by confusions
of time that had been

Shirley A Picco
GOD'S SWEET LOVE

Have you ever been on a mountain,
And looked down on the beauty below?
Have you ever been on the ocean,
with the sky all aglow?
Have you ever stood in the mist of the amber waves of grain?
Without these things of beauty, our world would not be the same.

Have you ever wondered how God felt, when his work was done?
Can you imagine the power it took,
just to give us the sun?
Placing each little twinkling star in the blackest of nights.
Oh, how proud He must have felt
when he saw these beautiful sights.
Then he gave these things of beauty
to you and to me.
Showing us how fabulous His love can be.
Oh how quiet this world would be,
without the birds to sing their songs.
Without the warmth of the sun, our nights would be so cold and long.
Without the mighty ocean—all the fish would die.
Without and old tree to climb a little boy would cry.
Without the fertile soil, the flowers would not grow.
A world without God's Sweet Love
I would not want to know!!

Shirley A Picco
I STUMBLED

Oh Jesus, sweet Jesus, wait on me.
For I have stumbled, following thee.
Please Jesus, please tell me what to do.
For my life is so empty without you.

As my poor heart broke, these precious words He spoke:
To be with me you must know I died
for your sins.
Follow me and I will make fishers of men.
Live your life so others will see
your light shine,
Love one another, do good for each other
And you will be mine.
Never take my Father's name in vain
If Eternal Life you hope to gain.
All your riches here on earth mean nothing
Can't you see?
Deny yourself, take up your cross and
Follow me.

Oh Jesus, sweet Jesus, you stopped and gave me your hand.
Oh yes I'll follow you, no matter

where thru-out this Great Land.
With your Hand in mine I will always
walk straight and tall,
Never, never again sweet Jesus,
will I stumble and fall.

Mary Furth
MENTAL PABULUM:
(FOOD FOR THOUGHT)
We are obfuscated and befuddled,
Our minds are bifurcated and
muddled.
Are things just as they seem?

We can't help feeling animosity.
Because of the state of bellicosity;
Is this an awful dream?

Events of today fill us with sorrow;
We can only guess about tomorrow;
What will the outcome be?
Money, love, death—the causes of
heartache,
Jealousy, creed—the reasons for
heartbreak;
Is there a remedy?

But, if we remember what we were
taught
About faith and belief,
We can have consolation in the
thought
That time mitigates grief.

Joyce C Doyle
SLAB OF STONE
Oh the days; They pass me by
Won't someone please
Please tell my why
I must come here all alone
And cry beside this slab of stone
I cannot feel; I cannot see
You were my own; A part of me
Oh time cannot erase memories of
My darling's face
Squeals of laughter in the rain
Oh No! Time cannot erase
Or ease my pain

I can't believe you're all alone
Lying here beneath a slab of stone
You can't really cry 'til you're alone
And sit beside a cold, cold stone
Oh the things I could share
A ball, a glove, a lock of hair
Snow has gone and flowers bloom
and the tears they fall on his tomb

Memories they stab, just like a knife
He was my own; I gave him life
Oh the things that I could share
A ball, a glove, a lock of hair
No! you can't really cry
'til you're alone
And sit beside a slab of stone

Mary Jane O Melad
BECCA

This poem is dedicated to a "forever friend," with Love!

She's cute
So alive with life that is boundless.
She's charming
A lady on her best when she wants it.
Sometimes she's childish
But a mature woman to talk with.
She is a good listener and a good
conversationalist,
A lady of humor and liability too.
Well, actually she's not "so "
beautiful
But the most beautiful to the one who
cares for her.
She trusts anyone she knows
Just don't ever make her a fool
Coz if you do or attempt to
I'm sorry to say but she'll never be
the same to you.
A girl worth loving, caring, fighting
and keeping for.
And I'm just so glad she belongs
here—the reality!
I don't have to dream . . . to
hallucinate
Or do I need to please the girl I'm
talking about.
No! I'm not, for here she comes . . .
Friends . . . meet, BECCA.

Mary Jane O Melad
THE WAY TO GO

To my maker and savior, I owe it all to you . . . with many thanks!

We're given all the chances
To love . . . to share . . . to serve . . .
The only thing that matters
Is the way to do our part.
Yet look here we are taking things for
granted.
Are we just going to hang around
And wait whatever will be?
Are we not determined to be worthy
of what God wants us to be?
Can't we see that time is running
fast?
And before it will be late,
A decision has to be made.
Only when we realize
That we need to change from what
we used to be.
It may not be that easy, just think . . .
There's so much to sacrifice, so much
to learn, so much to understand.
Needless to say we owe it to reality—
The reality of the word of God,
. . . to where love abides
. . . to where our strength begins
So take heart, believer
For if it will not start within us . . .
then who? If not now . . . when?

Patricia L Edberg

Patricia L Edberg
FOR YOU, MOMMY

I dedicate this poem to my mother, Mrs. Hansine K. Linehan and to my grown children, Terry L. Larsen (son), and Lauri A. Larsen (daughter).

'Mommy, Mommy!' Came the call
So I ran—not walked—into the
hall.
'Mommy!' I heard, and I ran. Was it
fright
Or was it perhaps, a cry of delight?

It seemed like forever—though
seconds went by—
And I answered, "I'm coming
now, why do you cry?"
I opened the door leading to the back
yard,
And out of the woods they came,
running hard.

I looked closely first to see what
wrong was done
Then noticed their faces aglow in
the sun.
"Mommy!" they cried, and in each
outstretched hand
They held bouquets of flowers
they'd picked from the land.

These are 'For You, Mommy,' don't
they smell sweet?
I smiled and I nodded, tears
dampening my cheeks,
Then remembered the times—not so
long ago too
When I lovingly said, "Mommy,
'these' are For You."

Addie Belle Carr Nobles
JUST A LITTLE
Why dear friends, is it so amiss, if I
take just a <u>little</u> heroin or just a <u>little</u>
crack?
"Just a <u>little</u> bit," says the novice,
won't throw me off track!"
"Oh, no," you say, and rightfully so,
"to take of pleasure drugs could mean
a deadly blow!"
Yet if it's not O.K. for a <u>little</u> crack,
or a <u>little</u> cocaine to take
Why is permission given for just a
<u>little</u> alcoholic drink?
Consider this, alcohol is the most
abused of all pleasure drugs they say,
We see the horrible results of this
abuse day after day!
Yet, just a <u>little</u> won't hurt, so
reasons the skeptic,
Till it's too late, they're hooked,
they're labeled an addict!
When can we win the drug war, we
are asked?
Not till the inconsistencies of use
have all been passed!
The facts are convincing and so,
please make your answer to all
pleasure drugs a definite "No!"

Karen Stodola Leigh
THE WOODS
Curtains of trees,
All kinds of color,
Where silence is noise,
There isn't another.

The whistling winds
Passed over the wood
To leave not a trace
Where the leaves once stood.

The trees were beauty
For townsfolk to share:
In Spring, with blossoms;
In Fall, branches bare.

My memory is strong,
As now it must be.
For, now there's a road
Instead of a tree.

Jean Lee Smith
RESTLESS SPIRIT
If only I could find a way
To let you go today
I would open the door and set you
free
So you could go away and let me be.

Oh Spirit, I want to set you free
To soar like the Eagle that flies
Let you explore the World
From the Ocean to the
Mountain-side.

Must you always be so restless
Searching for the impossible dream
Leaving my body to yearn forever
Never knowing what tomorrow will
bring.

Restless Spirit, please go away
Let me be happy, let me play
Please take away the heartaches of
the past
Lay this heart of mine to rest, at last.

Kristen Austin French
PURSUE MY HOPES
I want to stay
but cannot for if
I do then dreams
will end and I
will not pursue my hopes.

Life's glorious pleasure
of searching and
striving will mean
nothing, for there
shan't be any goal set
in my heart.

Persistently I'll continue
forward, and progress
will encourage me.

So I cannot stay
for I have not yet
tasted my success.

Sharon Ryan
NOTES FROM THE BI-POLAR REGION
I went up and I was never down
High, so high
Tingling sensation, Manic
stimulation
Kicked some dust on the way up
That off beaten path
The Road Runner never got busted
Some chemicals brought me here
Manic Depression . . .
You caught me unawares
The trip was unexpected and quick
Had not time to pack and my suitcase
was full
My mind traveled, thoughts
Raced to that dreaded place
Painful memories, things I made
myself forget
On that high road, I trusted—
And my subconscious got busted
Beep!Beep! I'm packing a trunk
And running on overload
Directions to the Bi-Polar Region,
off season?
I didn't hitch a ride up here
Nobody was going my way.

Michele Steedley
SEASON OF GROWTH
I'm beginning to like mountains.
Motherly mounds inviting
exploration,
Embowled in trees—hints of cities
barely visible through wind raped
leaves.
Feeling the sky a vortex
Enveloped in grey coolness.
Streaks of blue,
Peripheries to endlessness.
Once, I was city-bound
Garbage trucks and loud shouts
my wake up call,
Now I'm with you.

Jim Moore
GROWING UP
Getting older is hard to do.
Especially when people expect more
of you.
Now there is less time for play,
Because there is more to do in a day.
Running, jumping, hopping,
laughing,
Sometimes we never realize time is
passing.
Laughs change to a smile.
Remember we are a kid for only a
while.
Time is such a precious thing.
It is mother nature's diamond ring.

Nancy Anne Chiffolo
STILL A WINNER
Jenny —
Has not won the lottery.
Though she plays it everyday.
Those extra dollars she spends each
week,
To others —
Could be spent to buy herself a new
pair of shoes.

To Jenny —
New shoes are not important;
Winning the lottery is.
For to play is to someday win —
Millions.

When Jenny —
Does win the lottery,
She will not use any of her winnings
on a new pair of shoes.
Her old shoes are worth more.

Colleen Woodward
MY WISH TODAY
Sometimes,
I feel so overwhelmed
by the day to day
Drag
of Life.
And I just want to drop
everything
And run
to a more exciting place.
To run through a meadow
with the sun beaming down
is my wish today.
To be free from the burden
of day-to-day life
is my wish today.

Harry Hand
BACK IN THE HABIT
Wake up, it's time to get up, it's been such a long long time. Remember at ten o' clock is Sunday School, and at eleven, is Priesthood, then at twelve there is Sacrament. By then we should all be wide awake! So, I say unto you Brethen, Let's get back in the habit of going to church, it's been such a long time.

Nada M Coso
BEING YOUR LOVE

To: David James. All My Love.

Wearing your love fits me
Like faded jeans
Soft and gentle, touching skin

Feeling your love embraces me
Like rays of sunshine
Warm and caressing, touching skin

Tasting your love excites me
Like burning flames
Where passion meets ecstasy
Skin touching skin.

However, being your love
captivates
strengthens
And comforts me.
It is lips
eyes
hands
skin
And love touching love.

Tony Hopkins
YOUR FACE I CAN'T ERASE
What do I see
As I gaze upon thee
Is it destiny
Or is it fantasy

Are you real
Can you feel
For your face
I can't erase

For I have provided
A place in my heart
Now I'm waiting
Waiting on your part

So come to me
And set my love free
It will be
Only for thee

And together
We can walk
In love forever

Linda Mae Green
IT'S TIME
It's time to let go of the hurt.
It's time to let go and move on.
Even though you're not with me,
In my memory you'll always live on.

I can close my eyes and see you.
Remember the fun that we had.
I can close my eyes and remember,
And the memories aren't so sad.

Please understand my Shadow,
No one will take your place.
There's still a tear at the thought of
you,
But at least a smile on my face.

You'll always be a part of me,
Memories time can't erase.
It's time for me to let go of the past.
It's time to fill the empty space.

So when you look down upon me,
As I'm sure you will.
Remember that I loved you,
And I always will.

Bridget J Prezioso
THANK GOD

For all their love and support I dedicate this poem to my Mom and Aunt Twink. I Love You!!!

I've seen many broken hearts
Heard many angry words
and felt unbearable amounts of pain.
I've felt so alone in this world
Like no one understood
and thought no one cared for me.
Someone special once shared some
wisdom:
She told me God sends us gifts
to get through the hard times.
She spoke the truth for God sent me
you.

Joy Kaye Tedder
FIRST SON
It was hard and it was tough
And you've been put through a lot of
stuff
But as of 11:35 Friday night
A little miracle saw his first light

The pain was like being put through
hell
And all you could do was push and
yell
But when the doctor placed your son
upon your chest
You knew it had just started, but you
had to rest

Now all stitched up and ready to go
It's homeward bound with a brand–
new beau
He's your first and all is brand–new
But good lord just look at you

Up and around and on the go
Here and there yet still a little slow
Motherly instincts adapting so well
And always there without any fail

Now along the way things may get
rough
But always remember you're pretty
tough
But if I can help you any way at all
You know all you have to do is call

Sandra Villacarlos
LIFE

Daddy and Mommy — This one's for you!

a baby's first cry
an innocent smile
a helpless look
a comforting hug

a need for privacy
an urge to be vane
and experience with infatuation

a concern for the future
an ambition to succeed
a fear for being hopeless and alone
a need to be wanted and loved

life: a child's hope
a teen's passion
an adult's fulfillment

Rhonda M Hupka
COULD I DARE

To my husband Rick who inspired these thoughts and feelings. Thank you for your love.

Could I dare to be alone after
spending time with you?
Trading hours and years of laughter
and loving
for unlimited minutes of silence and
solitude?
Would I exchange the hard times and
bad scenes
we pulled through together, making
tons seem like ounces
for going it alone?
To bare the burden upon my
shoulders only?
The nights we lay close and secure
telling our wildest dreams.
Can I give that up for an empty bed
filled with nothing more
than stuffing and memories?
You're my friend when I need one
and even when I don't.
My life with you is full and rich.
My love for you is deep and strong.
My future with you is clear and
bright.
Could I dare to be alone after
spending time with you?

Dee Dee Grant
FATHER

To Russ, for understanding and hugs.

Father — You lost me
Father — You never saw me
Father — You never knew me
Father — I cry for you
Father — I drink for you

Father can't see the sun rise
Father can't see the sparkle in
His granddaughter's eyes.
Father cannot hear my cries.

Father are you better off dead?
Father can you feel the blood shed?
Father can you feel the home life
Wrecked?

Daddy look at me now

I'm a grown-up girl.
The seed you spent one
Wanton night
Made me a being that gloomy night

Father who I never touched,
Father who touched me for too
Much!

Robert L Brookshire
WHY?

I wish to dedicate this poem to the League of Families, and families who still wait for a lost loved one who failed to return from South East Asia.

My son and daughter ask me why
I sometimes sit alone and cry.

"Dad, what is this thing that makes
you sad?"
I feel so cold
as my story starts to unfold.

My children listen with attentive ears,
But only see my swelling tears.

How do I explain the terms of war
In a distant land
Called Viet Nam?

I've returned to you as a warrior of
sorrow.
I return to you, my people, I speak
the silence for the fallen,
Who have no voice but I.

I've returned to you not as a martyr,
but as a reminder of the war
To help the sons and daughters who
sometimes sit alone and cry.

Jay William Hoffland
WHAT SHOULD I DO?

To the best Grandmothers!

Here I am writing
when I could be biking
or then maybe
I should go hiking
But I am still deciding.

What should I do?
When I got gum

on my shoe
Maybe I should just
take a "snooze."

Jay William Hoffland
POOR OLD MISSISSIPPI MITCH

Dedicated to my dog, Mitch.

Poor old Mississippi Mitch
His scraggly tail,
Still gives a little switch
Probably wishes
To be young and rich

If he could be rich
And a supply of bones
came by ship,
Then he would be "hip."

He'd strut down the street
With diamonds round his feet
And a black velvet bone in his mouth.
So "ELITE."

Then one by one
The ship of bones
He would bury
Except for two
One black velvet for Mitch
And a pink Satin for Mary.

Kenneth C Rennecamp
OUR LOVE

The oak tree roots grow deeper and deeper. Is not our love the same?

Gary Garrabrant
GLASS & STONE

This poem is dedicated to Agnes, my dearly departed wife.

I sit here in my cell alone
And look at all the glass & stone
I think of all the years gone by
And wonder where they went and why
I wish that someone up there hears
Of all my prayers and all my fears
Since I've been here in this cell
I think of all the things I could tell
Of all the things that I could do
If only I could be with you
I think of all the years we shared
And how we both had really cared
Thank you Agnes for being my wife
And loving me all thru my life
Now that's all gone and I'm alone
Here in my cell of glass & stone

Gary Garrabrant
TURN THE CLOCK BACK

This poem is dedicated to Agnes, my dearly departed wife.

If only I could explain these words right from the start
Of how I feel from within my heart
It was a beautiful life that we had shared
And both knowing how we had cared
If only I could turn the clock back to where it all began
How we had walked hand in hand
We shared our love & we shared our sorrows
Knowing there would be only so many tomorrows
Love is built thru honesty
We both had agreed to love forever right thru eternity
We shared our joys & all our dreams
Never to put up with any schemes
Agnes is in heaven—above
With the one we truly love
Maybe it won't belong & then I can really turn the clock back again

Gary Garrabrant
BACK TOGETHER

This poem is dedicated to Agnes, my dearly departed wife.

I sit here in my cell & think of
Agnes my dearly departed wife
We had our ups & downs & outs
But we shared our love without any doubts
We took a vow from within our heart
That we would never ever part
We were together 50 years
And stuck it out in all our sorrows
& all our fears
Now that Agnes is in heaven & gone
I know our love will always carry on
We'll be apart for just awhile
Then back together to laugh & smile
I know that God has made a way
for Agnes & I to get back together
to–stay
Thank you God the Almighty above
The one that Agnes & I truly love

Amy Lynne Shockley
LOVE AT LOST

These days are ours
Which no one can take.
In your arms
Sweet love to make.
A wait with faith
For now we trust,
Dear God, we pray
Together we must.
The bond we have
Is more pure than gold.
I just want
To have you
To hold.

K O Setlow
MOTHER SEA

I sit upon the shore and watch
Waves rush to throw themselves upon
the sands,
Only to be pulled again into the sea.
Sometimes, seen through angry eyes,
My anger forms along the shore.
Bubbles pop and dissipate.
Slowly my anger follows suit,
And waves are music in my ears.

Other times, with tear filled eyes,
I go to lose myself only to find that I cannot.
Together—we cry alone.
Waves and tears—they taste the same.
The waves take, wash my tears away,
And I feel the strength within the waves.

In times of joy I can forget
The very same she's given me . . .
The strength and music of the waves.

Maebelle L Simpson
A LIFE WORTHWHILE

I like to see what nature holds
And to see what the heavens unfold.
The snow has fallen on the plains
It's a beautiful sight to see.

Soon showers from the clouds come down
Makes our teaching of the earth and water sound.
The spring is not far behind I see
I can see birds building a nest in the tree.

My life alone I want my kids to see
And leave them a life I leave from me.
For tomorrow we don't know what it will bring
But I hope a full life and birds that sing.

Everyday I ask the Lord to be with me
At the end of the day, I thank Him for thee.
At the end they can say a life worthwhile
And I can leave this life with a smile.

Krissa Ludwa
IT WAS ONLY A DREAM

He turned and looked at me with his deep brown eyes. Even for the distance we were standing apart; his eyes mesmerized mine.

For a moment, time had stood still. I felt as if I was standing there completely naked. Yet, at the same time my heart was racing with excitement.

He walked up to me and took my hand into his. He leaned over and kissed me, as his arms embraced me, pulling my body closer to his. His kisses were gentle and passionate. He looked at me, his eyes smiling at mine. We both knew what this moment meant. He kissed me again and then whispered into my ear. I opened my eyes . . . my heart sunk, I had come to realize it was only a dream.

Shaily Nair
FILLING THE EMPTINESS

The curiosity of life leads me on.
I wonder about myself,
I wonder about being what my parents want me to be—maybe succeeding.
I then feel the emptiness inside of me growing.

But I think,
Of being what I want to be—and succeeding.
The emptiness then subsides.

I will make my dreams come true,
I will be all I can be.
The emptiness will leave me,
My heart will then be filled,
And then—I will be happy.

Celeste Fahy Young
NEVERBEING

To all the Babies that should have been but never were. May "God" watch over your mothers and help them through their pain.

I've lost something I can never get back . . .
A child lost and forever gone . . .
It may not have made it to its day of birth . . .
but I felt that we two became one . . .
I felt the pain as it finally passed from my body,
into the world of neverbeing . . .
And I'll grieve this child for a very long time . . .
Until the eyes of our "God" stop seeing

Celeste Fahy Young
and James Kelley Young
GOD KNOWS

A cool drink from the sky . . . to all upon the land . . . rain falling softly . . . Earth is "God's" hands . . . birds flying freely . . . as free as can be . . . No bars to hold them . . . sweet reality . . . Sun rays from heaven . . . help the flowers
grow . . . "God" sends the sunshine, cool winds and snow . . . He changes the seasons . . . for reasons of his own . . . who are we to question . . . the one who always knows . . . .

Celeste Fahy Young
BABY GIRLS

To my strength and love Shelly Ann Achuff and Michelle Marie Achuff, my daughters who stand by me no matter what. "I love you both." Mom.

One day when I was very young . . . I asked the heavens for a son . . . The good Lord blessed my very world . . . He sent to me my baby, girls . . . I never had that little boy . . . the Lord above doubled my joy . . . he knew my needs and answered my prayers . . . I ask for one he sent a pair . . . The greatest gifts, worth more than pearls . . . he sent me love, my baby girls . . . No son could have given to me . . . The love I feel, that 's sent from thee . . . just a hug or I love you . . . I don't get one . . . I get two . . . So never shall I ever grieve . . . The little boy "God" kept from me . . . For he knew my needs and sent me you . . . I'll love you both till my life is through . . . I thank the Lord he blessed, my world. He sent to me my baby girls . . . .

Celeste Fahy Young
IF THE WORLD SHOULD END TOMORROW

To the man I love and who is my inspiration, James Kelley Young.

If the world should end tomorrow, would you still love me tonight?
Should the heavens turn to darkness, 'cause the stars fell from the sky.
Would you be my ray of sunshine? . . .
Would you be my guiding light?
Would you lead me from the darkness, walk together in your light?
Would you ease my pain and suffering, hold me safely in your arms?
Could I have your love for shelter, keeping out life's pain and harm?

For I love you like no other I've ever known before, would you hold my love and keep it safe, so I'll feel pain nevermore?
For I treasure every moment that we have come to share.
And a piece of me would die inside, if I turned and you weren't there.
You are the very air I breathe,
the reason I awake, the beating of my very heart,
my life, my dreams, my soul . . .
The reason I keep living,
the half that makes me whole.
If the world should end tomorrow,
I'd still be loving you, and I'll love

you past forever,
Please believe me, this is true.

If you're lost and in the darkness,
feel free to call my name . . .
and I'll lead you from the nighttime,
for I know you'd do the same.
And we would walk together, darling,
down the road that they call life,
and nothing could destroy us for
we're protected by love's light.

So remember that "I love you,"
when no one seems to care, and if
you ever need me,
call my name and I'll be there.
So when you're feeling lonely,
close your eyes and think of me,
and a cool wind shall embrace you,
take your pain and set you free.
Or, when a gentle rain begins to fall,
remember that it's me and I'll love
you past forever . . . for that's
Eternity.

Jennifer A Carlson
SMILE THIN
Trust
Opening up a grin to a smile.
Reaching out your hand first.
Shedding a tear in moment of need.

Betrayal
So cold inside you shiver.
So empty inside you ache.
So lost inside you tremble.

Distrust
Smile thin.
Walk alone.
Look stoic.

Diane Davidson Abbott
GOLDEN ANNIVERSARY

To God—For God sent not his Son into the world to condemn the world; but that the world through him might be saved. John 3:17.

Look back through the golden haze
The cloudy and the sunlit days
Look back through the golden years
The wonders—and the fears
The happiness—and the tears
Of golden days gone by.

Look up through the toils of life
The sharing of a man and wife
Look forward through the golden
years
The misty fragments bright of tear
And notes that only lovers hear
In golden days to come.

Diane Davidson Abbott
I AM YOUR LOVING WIFE

To my husband George W. Abbott III.

I am your loving wife
But I'm not your keeper
Nor ruler of your life.
'Tis not mine to control
Every thought and deed
Nor your own inner soul.
Only God can demand
That you must lead your life
According to His plan.
I pray that you might know
The joy of following
Wherever He says, Go.
For then I too may know
The ecstasy of Ruth
Who said, Whither thou go.
In time to come I'll be
With you forevermore
Throughout Eternity;
And always in this life
I'll follow you and say,
I am your loving wife.

Mary C Barrett
LIFE
The blossoms appear
That snow covers ruthlessly
Life is like seasons

One lonely leaf twirls
One desolate twig snaps off
Loneliness claims all

The breeze passed me by
Nearby leaves began to swirl
Love may sweep us by

All blooms showing
A brook swirls careless on
Happiness is here

As dusk nears, light fades
Drought remains, water recedes
Death is a part of life

Mary Lorena Cox
SEED
A tiny seed was planted,
One day to sprout and grow;

My deepest wish was granted,
How could anyone ever know;

What joy that seed would bring,
As I give it love and care;

My love for it makes me sing,
Now let go I must dare;

Oh how it pains me so,
To let it out of my reach;

But the little one needs to grow,
More things to learn and teach;

So the seedling can become more,
And grow into a strong one;

As I let you through the door,
Know that I love you my son.

Nancy Dyson
TALE OF DR. COKE
I once had a friend named Mr. High,
He was nice and a little shy.
Then one day I met Dr. Coke,
He made me laugh with his funny
joke.
Mr. High met Dr. Coke, and said
"Mr. High, want a toke?"
They talked and laughed and smoked
their stuff,
Asked me "would you like a puff?"
"No thanks" I said and turned away,
I smelled the smoke, what could I
say.
The next time I saw Mr. High,
He was not longer very shy.
He was bold and abusive and not nice
at all,
I really thought he was off the wall.
I asked Mr. High what drugs he was
on,
He said he didn't know he was too
far gone.
I saw Dr. Coke in the corner of the
room
He looked as if he were ready for a
tomb.
"Your friend has no problems," said
Dr. Coke,
Laughing as if it were a joke.
"You make me sick" I said unkind,
"Mr. High is a friend of mine."
"Stay away from Mr. High,
I do not want my friend to die."
He laughed again, I shook my head,
He didn't care if Mr. High were dead.
He gave the cocaine to Mr. High,
And sat back to watch my friend die.
I brought Mr. High to the hospital
that day,
Dr. Coke had nothing to say,
Mr. High went into rehab,
Poor Dr. Coke ended up on a slab.
Poor Dr. Coke, he should have
known,
You can't have life when you sit
around getting stoned.
The End

Debra Lynn Dexter
SOARING ON A CLOUD

This poem is dedicated M.L.O., my Best Friend.

I'm caught up in a dream
soaring on a cloud,
Desires crowd my mind
with thoughts not allowed.

Passions taken control
I'm walking on thin ice,
Do I take another step
and pay the price.

I closed my eyes
ignored all fears,
Wondered if my feelings
were really sincere.

Then I saw you smile
my body went on fire,
I knew right then
I wouldn't fight your desires.

Once our lips embraced
fireworks exploded,
We talked and touched
in loving modes.

I'm soaring on a cloud
without any regrets,
Hoping that this dream
isn't over yet.

While the sun was rising
reality had returned,
Will our hearts remember
what they had yearned???

Then the time had come
for me to depart,
Honey, keep on smiling
friendship is a start.

G Matthews Baxter
THE NOW!
Stars, and satellites filling the skies,
God's creatures cower with fear,
Bearing the yoke of science gone
mad—
With odious security from instilled
greed.
And, tissue thin veils hiding society's
players,
Empty of passion and heart—
Rush onward to commanding vogues,
Surrounded by garlands of frivolous
pursuit.

Whence cometh modern man replete
with inventoried intellect,
Mechanical evento implanted
vision—
That in perception fails to perceive,
And slowly, certainly, with papers
afloat—
Deceives traditional birthways path—
With muddied pollen everlastingly
sodden!

Upon the day when time stays still,
A shining beam of piercing light—
Brings back to mind in flashing sight,
Faint feathers of Hope,
New birth of Trust—
New days of help for hand and heart,
And darkness steals as darkness
stands.

Debi Bair
THIS EXISTENCE CALLED HUNGER
What's it all about
this existence called hunger?
Dreams reduced in size
to a cupful of water.
What can it all mean
when there's no field left to gleen,
nothing that is clean,
no hope that can be seen.
Your child's ravaged face,
disease and vermin in the place,
her stomach a hollow space,
no strength to step on pace.
There's only will left not to die,
no reasons/answers—why?
No composure left to sigh,
time going by, and by, and by . . . .

Karen Bessey
A POME

With all my love, this dedication is to Joe Dias who also inspired me.

I see you sitting there in the pool,
everyday afterschool.
You splash around here and there,
and eventually you wet your hair.
I see you swim a length or two,
and fantasize being with you.
You take a swim around the pool,
All the while keeping cool.
You walked around the floor so wet,
and that is how we both first met.
Everytime I see you dive,
it makes me feel so alive.
Your muscles smooth your body
slim,
what a joy to see you swim.
If ever you find the water cold,
I know someone you can hold.
If ever the bloom is much too deep,
I know someone you can keep.
In case you haven't yet guessed,
that someone's me forget the rest.
Whenever I see the water so blue,
I think of that day and especially you.
I still go swimming even though it
may seem,
that I will never again see the man of
my dreams.
Maybe someday I'll be lucky enough,
to meet him again in this clear blue
stuff.

Roger Adair
ANN BAKER, CSR SWEETHEART OF COURT REPORTERS
Ann Baker, you have worked through
thick and thin,
you have gone to limits and managed
to keep your grin.
You have done what every court
reporter hopes of doing,
being able to retire without any
booing.
Never getting all the credit you really
deserved,
while take down every big or little
precious word.
Thirty-one years of writing words for
attorneys to keep,
if not in court you do it in your sleep.
You have done so much without
showing wear and tear,
when I have worked half as much
with showing of no hair.
I'll never be able to look as good as
you when I retire,

by then I'll be held together with
bailing wire.
You have done so much for the
reporting profession,
being the first one there when court is
in session.
Listening so intently to every single
word,
the working of your fingers like
wings of a hummingbird.
You have worked so hard without
knowing you're the best,
and yet at this time in your life you
could pass any test.
You're an inspiration to us all,
for court reporting, you have done it
all.

BY ROGER ADAIR, 1990
PRESIDENT
GREATER HOUSTON
REPORTERS ASSOCIATION

Rebecca Moore Frey
LIFE GOES ON

Someone is born and someone dies
Each and every day
Someone mourns and someone cries
And it's someone's wedding day
But life goes on towards its new
dawn
In God's own special way
Some have hell and some have
heaven
On this earth we live
Some will give and some will take
And some will birth a babe
And all I know is we're not alone
We share our lives each day
Some will pray and some will pay
For debts they've left unchecked
Some will lie and some will say
That truth is the only way
Some are friends and some are foes
Some don't even know they have a
soul
But life goes on toward its new dawn
In God's own special way

Nanci Gerard Burke
SHADOW OF DUSK

This poem is dedicated to my mother, Patricia Mary Burke, whose spirit lives within us all.

Daylights burst forth with all its
splendid might,
The morning dew begins to fade
away.
The shadow of the dusk has taken
flight.

The moon is not smiling, he's gone
from sight;
No longer shining upon the blue
bay—
Daylights burst forth with all its
splendid might.

The dawn begins inside a flash of red
light,
Gone is the blandness of nightfall's
dull grey—
The shadow of the dusk has taken
flight.

The day is basking in a glowing light,
The breeze is singing, as if it will say
Daylights burst forth with all its
splendid might.

Gone is the silence of the previous
night,
Sunrise has come, we need no longer
pray,
The shadow of the dusk has taken
flight.

The day has risen to a glorious height
Evils of nighttime can no longer
stay—
Daylights burst forth with all its
splendid might.
The shadow of the dusk has taken
flight.

Helen Hicks Humphrey
PEOPLE OF THE STREETS

Oh stoic faces, unsublime,
the only thing you own is time.

Life will never change for thee,
but can this truly be?

In the sphere of thy existence
for naught you search, nor give
resistance.

Shake off the fetters that entwine
and pluck the blossom from the vine!

Your world is such a loathsome
place,
can you not bear nor do you dare to
lift your face,
for fear of what you'll see?

Helen Hicks Humphrey
YOUTHFUL SPIRIT

To Alma Striegel Hicks, my lovely mother, for her patience, wisdom and wit.

The woman, silent in her chair,
with gentle eyes and silver hair;

she smiled, upon the child so sweet,
dressing dolls, beside her feet.

In that brief moment, you could tell,
in youth, she'd been a bonny-belle!

With innocence, the child so bold,
said "grandmother—are you very
old?"

I cannot say—

for when I close my eyes, you see;
my youth is all restored to me!

I frolic in the orchard green,
and I am young and tan, and lean;

I meet old friends, from out of books
and I'm a child, despite my looks.

A lesson, little one—take heed!
you're ne'er alone if you can read

Nor old, if you can conjure dreams.
Age is not always what it seems!

Helen Hicks Humphrey
A MAN OF MEN

To my beloved father, James Robert Hicks, who is greatly missed.

My husband was a man of men,
how he'd have loved a bouncing boy.
We prayed for years for him to come,
yet never knew that special joy.
Late in life our daughters came,
a precious gift, more loved than
fame!
My man of men did ne'er complain.

A better father never was,
and Oh so proud, when they did wed!
He gloried, when a grandson came!
held him, and kissed his little head.
A precious gift, more loved than
gold!
and though he was now growing old,
my man of men had made the mold.

He's long since passed the vale,—
and yet;
I hear his voice and see his brow,
his laughing eyes do show
themselves
in our eleven grandsons now.
Never one from grace did fall,
I wish he'd lived to see them all!
these men of men so strong and tall.

Jeanne Warburton
SPRING AHEAD

When winter months are cold and
dark
And the landscape seems to drear,
We should all look ahead with
hopefulness
To the loveliest time of the year.

Spring, beautiful spring,
How welcome it will be,
To see the buds, the trees in leaf
And daffodils standing free.

From their winter sleep they wake,
Eager to greet the sun,
Golden petals unfolding
Bringing joy to everyone.

It's the loveliest of seasons,
When the earth is born anew,
The miracle of life and hope
Fresh as the morning dew.

If only we can realize
That life is a precious thing,
Just to be—and to see
The glorious wonder of spring.

John Robert Schild (Age 13)
DUSK

Dusk—when all animals but a few
Start to head for slumber
In the faint distance
I hear my mother call.
As I start to leave my special place
I notice a faint glow
Behind the hills.
It's then I realize
How beautiful day is
When it turns to night.

Julie Cybéle Sarah Minerbo
THE MOURNING AFTER

Writhing and squirming like a snake
Sickened by a self-induced toxin
Out of desperation, to escape the
isolation
Of bodies without minds . . . minds
without dreams . . . DREAMS . . .
DREAMS of brotherhood without
crutches of bottles
Bottles filled with an ambrosia that
fuses the souls of strangers
Entrapped within the boundaries of
what they should be
Always denying from the world their
individuality
The result of a country of fools,
clown, and clones
Always pretending the masses are
above the person
The lonely soul whose desperate cries
. . . float away
So dismally unheard—above the
threatening din
Of the MASSES . . . who so
guiltlessly absorb its members
Into a quagmire of amputated bodies
searching frantically
For heads nobody knows nothing
about . . .
And so we dip into the brew and try
to forget—
That only the toxin is calming a mind
fraught with disarray
Is torture no more painful than that of
plastic smiles,
And pointless lies to make ourselves
seem swell?
We somehow must free ourselves
From a life of acrylic hell.

Wendy Kay Slate
CAPTIVE . . .

To Mom and Dad for being understanding of my hopes and dreams . . . To Andrea and Peggy for all the good times . . . To Eric, with love . . . To my family and friends . . . and to Ms. M, "It's a poem!" You are the ones who keep me from feeling Captive . . .

Captive . . .
in a foreign land,
a strange world
unknown to my eyes.
Mysterious faces—
with eyes, curious and intent.
The area around spins . . .
My head is weighted,
with confusion,
curiosity,
and fear . . .
I long for home,
its security,
happiness,
and familiarity.
This land is an illusion,
The faces are that of a nightmare,
And I wait fearfully,
Waiting for an end . . . .

Jeanie Kahnke
SOLVING THE PUZZLE

It came to me one day
in the early waking hours
when the moon-globed and golden—
throws ruler straight lines
through bedroom windows and the
mind
floats tiny bubbles through the
hollow
of the half sleeping skull. Your love
is devoted like the seasons
and the break of day, yet your mind
is analytical like weather
forecasts and calendars—dividing
parts
of puzzles and putting them back
together. You do not see
the aesthetics of the whole
picture. Why can you not
understand this when you are able
to move the moon with one tall look?

Rebekka Hollis
SHADOWS IN PERSPECTIVE

When your days are Heavy
The nights full of Pain—
Tomorrow, a week away
Defeat your only gain.
Dare not look behind you
The past is but a guise.
God's Love for you, Today—
Is written in my eyes.

Bonnie Bienvenu
LOVE IS DEAD

To my children, Brian and Sheri and to our King Jesus Christ.

The village where I used to stay
Where peasants walked day after
day,
Where sheep dotted the yellow field
Lay silent now where they were
killed.

These soldiers marched on through
our town
Strewing destruction all around.
Because of one man's fanatical
screams,

They fell for lies they thought
were dreams.

I cried, "Love is dead! It's dead and
gone!"
An old man shook his head.
"You're wrong!
Love is here, in the heart, you see,
And no one may take that love
from thee!"

And suddenly I heard a sound,
A roar exploding all around.
When I awoke, I could not see,
But something heavy lay on me.

I struggled to stand, and looked
around.
I saw the devastation of my town.
And at my feet the old man lay,
Whose love had saved my life that
day!

Ann Macchia Coons

I REMEMBER

I remember her endurance
In all her trials and tribulations.
I remember her endurance
In all her pain and sorrow.
I remember her winning smile
And cheerful ways.
I remember her encouragement and
support
During my GREY days.
And most of all
I remember Mama for the wisdom
she instilled in me.
It's been my guiding light throughout
my life.
Thank you Mama, and until we meet
again,
I love you.

Victoria Garrett

THE PRICE

Thank you God, Dan, Eric, Chris, Brenda, Mom, Dad, and all my relatives and friends for your encouragement.

Give Me all your cares
Lay them upon My chest
For I have already said
My yoke is easy
And I will give you rest,
So my child,
Why do you point your finger
Placing blame on another
Looking for a way
To lay your burden on your
brother.
So stop your accusing and listen as I
have said,
I shed my blood
Now you accept
For I have won
I paid the price for all.

Richard E Davis

IN MY BLUE DREAM

Songs from a blue dream,
Always with me.
Talking in a musical voice,
Ringing inside of me.
Intense yet somehow soothing,
A pleasure to hear.
Never will I be sad,
In my blue dream.

Donna L Dilick

ON MEETING DEATH

Wilt that when at last we meet
where willows wailing; cry for sleep
grey cloaked in shadows gloom you
creep
to glean the weary soul

Where ancient nightbirds dare to
dance
in eternities spiral wind
and whispering faeries prance amid
a wreath of floraled leaves

There dragonflies alite on streams
that long gave up its dead
and many a martyrs lifeblood shed
wraiths; twisting in the breeze

Like a wisp you draw me from that
alabaster case
a shade without a face
to lead me to that sacred; hollowed
place
shrouded in its lore of dread

With gleeming sickle, ivory hand in
mine
my mother's breath blows back your
cape
I stare astonished; soul agape
to meet the eyes of a dove

Crystal L Dawson (Teddy Bear)

PLEASE PRAY FOR ME

To Indianapolis Youth Group/A Social and Support Group for Gay and Lesbian Youth.

Someday I wish love would turn the
world around
For everyone to see
That even though we are "different,"
Love is love . . .
Please Pray for Me
Our parents expect us to be better
and to do or achieve
as they believe.
"I cannot!" For you see, life will not
let us
For society doesn't understand . . .
Please Pray For Me
When my times has come and I have
loved
with a heart so true;
Then I say to thee—the Lord is my
shepherd . . .
Please Pray For Me
Amen

Pamela D Dence

A BABY IS FROM HEAVEN

Though I have never actually seen
Jesus's face
I have seen my baby's eyes.
For a moment I glimpsed Heaven
But it comes as no surprise.

Though I have never actually seen
Jesus's heart
I have never seen my baby's smile.
That could take the gloom from any
day
And make the word "Mommy"
worthwhile.

Though I have never actually felt
Jesus's arms
I have felt my baby's hands.
As she reaches out to touch my
cheeks,
"I Love You," I whisper, and hope
she understands.

Though I have never actually seen
one of Jesus's nail scars
I have seen my baby's lips.
As they tremble from a scraped knee
While doing one of her many flips.

Though I have never actually heard
Jesus's voice
I have heard my baby's love;
Through her hugs, kisses, and even
her tears.

Yes, she truly is a "Miracle From
Above."

Dorothy Kisselburgh

A KINGDOM TO CREATE

is it possible to create
a haven for the pure of heart
a kingdom free from all hate
where soulmates never, ever part

to live amongst creative souls
a world apart from all the rest
where children can search for their
goals
and hearts are never put to a test

a place to proudly call your home
all eternity to be spent
never any need to roam
to find your heart's content

from any castle window you could
see
wealth greater than that of gold
truly the land of the free
only your hands does this kingdom
hold

let us find a kindom, place
our own land to be tilled
start our own, loving race
where castles we can build.

Dawn M Fagan

LOVE AFFAIR

To Charles. My link of happiness . . . Siempre.

Chained, forgotten
don't be afraid;

Chained, forgotten
to hold me close;

Chained, forgotten
in good times and bad;

Chained, forgotten
forever linked.

Catherine Cutone Chernin

PASSING TIME

It's been so long, since my love went
away
The angels in heaven
Took him from me on this very day
The pain endless, yet I cry no tears
Remembering the love
We shared for so many years
Deeper than deep we loved so much
Wishing to God
Just one more time to feel his touch
To walk hand in hand, smell the
flowers
Thinking to myself
If we only had a few more hours
He'll look down on me, see no
weeping
My beloved at rest
With the angels forever sleeping . . .

Caroline Bennett

REBIRTH

At long last I walk along the shores
of time,
And hear the whisper of destiny.
I know now that what is cherished is
not lost,
And feel a vastness never conceived.
A spirit of ardor transcends me,
The perfect night illuminates my
gossamer form.

Caroline Bennett

FREE FALL

I am falling.
The spiral is becoming deeper.
The black void below is endless.
I cannot reach out far enough.
I am being pulled down further and
further,
into an endless abyss, a sea of pain.
I feel the knife digging at my soul,
Cutting it away piece by piece.
My brain is in confusion.
Where is this taking me to?
What part of myself will I see this
time?
What hides behind the mask of
sanity?
I am unreachable, disconnected.
I keep going down further.
Down to a cold, decaying grave of
my own creation.
Engulfed in isolated terror as I
descend to hell.
I am lost in oblivion.

Caroline Bennett

ETERNITY

Footsteps in the sand,
Soon to disappear like childhood and
youth,
Yet to reappear with another's tender
touch,
To imprint once more on a familiar
place,
and to sense the completeness.

Caroline Bennett

HAPPINESS GONE

I have known you in the past,
You were there with me, but I did not
know it.
How elusive you are, my betrayed
friend.
I remember the fond memories, they
are what sustain me.
Why did you desert me?
You are no longer there when I reach
out for you.
Like a mysterious stranger,
You came, then disappeared.
The past is all I know, I live there.

Caroline Bennett

FLOWER

Delicate and fresh in your glory,
You bring to me a meaning for
existence;
Tomorrow you will whither and die,
But I shall remember your fragrance.

Caroline Bennett

DYING WISH

How I long for you, secret lover,
Creeping softly into my room,
Whispering gently in my ear,
Seducing the curves of my body,
How I wish to throw back the covers
which hold me,
And glide away in rhythmic ecstasy.

Caroline Bennett

INSOMNIA

My eyes are wide in the silence of the
night,
How I crave you as I toss and turn,
In this meaning less situation of sleep
and wakefulness,
Tomorrow my eyes will show the
deepest grooves of thoughts not
allowed to sleep,
Troubled by yearnings of yesterdays,
And dreams never fulfilled.

Denis Kretzschmar

SOLID GOLD OR ORGANIC TREE-MOULD?

Which is of higher value,
Solid gold
Or organic tree-mould?
Let the world try to live
Without first one

And then the other.

Now what would such a test
Foretell about society?
It hoards the one that glitters
And paves over with asphalt roads
The one causing plants to grow.
Shall we ask this of a flower?

"What is the god of man?"
The bloom replies.
"That which creates life
Or that which entrances human
eyes?"

Should not people then establish
Steel safes filled with crumbling trees
And shining, golden refuse dumps?
Or is this too extreme?

Michelle Boes

WHAT IS BEAUTY

This is dedicated to the Lord Jesus Christ for giving me the insight to see the Beauty in everything and everyone!

Beauty is a flower blooming in the
sun
Beauty is a child playing in a field
Beauty is a puppy having fun
Beauty is a mouse with some cheese
Beauty is a kitten playing with yarn
Beauty is a baby being born in the
night
Beauty is Pine tree in the forest
Beauty is a misty morning
Beauty is a horse running free
Beauty is love in bloom
Beauty is a mountain on a Christmas
morn
Beauty is the sunshine in the rain
Beauty is a rainbow in the sky
Beauty is a summer in Colorado
Beauty is a caterpillar turning into a
butterfly
Beauty is a waterfall in the Islands
Beauty is a crisp winter's day
Beauty is a raging river
Beauty is a hummingbird in flight
Beauty is so many wonderful things
BEAUTY IS IN THE EYE OF THE
BEHOLDER

Terrence Malone

ONE THING

You are beautiful
as you sway in the trees,
decorate the leaves,
and foam
in the waves
of the sea.

There are no mistakes
in the elements
you make,
in the physics
that play
in the universe today;
I see you there,
and there you stay,
always,
in every way.

You are incredible
in your sunset fire,
your mountain's spire
And the winds
in your breath
never tires.

You sparkle
in the night sky,
and reflect off quiet pools,
I see you fly,
I feel your warmth
and cool;
I see utter fools
submit without choice
to your rules.

I am amazed
in the storms
you rage,
to make plants
from clay,
to feed me today,
And tomorrow
to return
from whence
they were made.

You are wonderful,
and in your mighty machine,
You give me
glimpses,
like a manifested dream;
I touch you
in my senses.

Yet still,
as selfish as it seems,
I lack
one thing;
I need someone
to share
the things I see;
Someone to care
for me;
I am Adam,
and I am
lonely.

Sandra M Pledger

Sandra M Pledger

SOME DAY MY SOUL WILL BE FREE

In loving memory of my parents, Lovonia and James Davis.

Upon death I will arise and my soul
will be free,
to roam the earth with no surprise,
beautiful things I never had in life to
see

I will walk in many worlds quiet and
new
my body bare free, my soul to

No more will I have to live up to
dreams
No more will I be the joke of society
means

I shall go to a place where the air is
fresh and clean
where waterfalls rush down, and the
sun always beams
I will swim in the ocean, not to worry
how long,
pick many many flowers, and know I
have done no harm

I can sleep in a patch of gentle green
coves
to awaken anytime, not to worry
about old lifes woes

I can go anyplace and admire all that
I see
but not be afraid for no one shall see
me

My heart wonders silently, my mind
at ease
I don't have to worry, suffering, pain,
ha!
it's all over for me
but I shall begin a better one the day
my soul becomes free!

Heather Marie Duffy

CATCHING RAIN ON YOUR TONGUE

Thunder is the opening crescendo
Exploding like gospel music
from swollen clouds like dingy bars
of soap
edges softened by fat fingers
Wetness pounds the roof like
footsteps
crunching outside on icy sidewalks

Once the angry winds subside
It falls softly
like whispered words
of dead heroes
Or blonde fringe
on a forehead
Slow, lazy rain
restraining itself
with the the quiver of a bottom lip

The sky runs dry; the world is still
wet
ghost-green neon signs
reflect off the wet hood of a car
A girl hugs herself in the starlight
Listening to the purple hours of
morning
Spinning themselves dry.

Gary C Dunn

PRISON STEEL

For my Inspiration Margaret Dunn.

These walls that are around me, may
take you away,
But the love in my heart, grows
stronger each day!
These walls I speak of are prison
steel,
I wish they were fake, but they are so
real.
They strip you of your pride, and
your will to live,
And leave you with nothing but your
love to give.
I wished I could speak of the sky's so
blue,
And the flowers that grow, with the
morning dew.
But as I look above me, there's
nothing I see,
But that gray prison steel, and that's
killing me!
God forgive me for the things I have
done,
And return me to life, with that
chosen one!!

Kathy Gentry

FOREVER YOUNG

To the Gang in loving memory of a dear friend.

Forever young . . . forever young.
Always surrounded, but all alone.
Always worn out, but I'll never grow
old.
Forever young . . . forever young.
They try to break me, but I'm strong
as a wall.
They may try to trip me, but I'll
never fall.

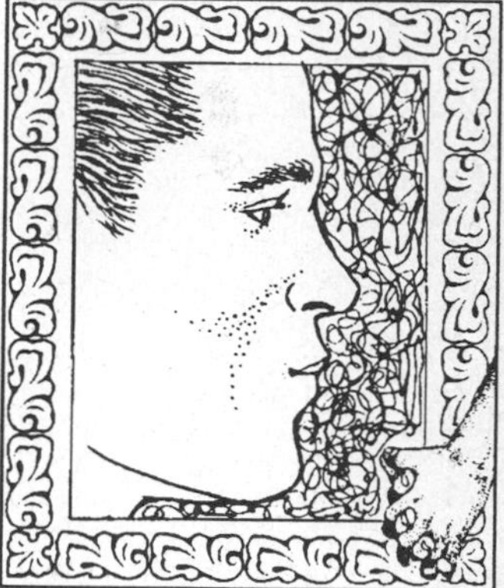

Forever young . . . forever young
my parents give me shit, and
My friends say to split
There's only so much I can do,
but I'll never quit.
Forever young . . . forever young
The battle is rough, the road long,
but I'll always keep going as long as
there's a song.
Forever young . . . forever young
Yes, forever young is how we all
must stay,
Because to overcome all these
obstacles given to us,
It's the only way.

Anita Hopkins

IF WISHES WERE FEATHERBEDS

I wish I had a featherbed,
All fluffy . . . and BIG . . . and round;
A place where at night I would
sink in to dream,
And never hear a sound.

I would dream of soft things;
Misty . . . and . . . light blue;
And, often would dream of
bold, colorful things;
And . . . sometimes they might come
true.

I would run and jump on my
featherbed,
And . . . landing there . . . lie still
Until morning came and whispered

to me . . .
"Let's do it over again."

William O Robinson

William O Robinson
THE STORM
The earth sends up its effluvial scent, and the sky blasts unpredicted
intervals of blue-whites.
Nervous winds, like the sound from within a seashell, reveal that the
souls of dead men walk stormy nights.
And after the violence, a placid moon sets in, with distant drums, and
a near tatter of drops—the only sounds heard.
Then, is a lonely spell that keeps till a mid-morning bell harmonizes
with God's first bird

William O Robinson
ROCKING CHAIR SONGS
Those trivial and mindless musings of tenderness cradle my life until
its end.
When on a night in my newness I heard that intriguing rhythm of love
sounding its way into my psyche.
Can I ever be completely isolated as long as rocking chair songs
inundate the requiem of my mind?

William O Robinson
ROCK GENTLY, ROLL EASY
Rock gently, roll easy Soul Storm.
Be quiet—settle down—wait for the warm
That's just beyond the ivory-blue portrait slamming against a black sky.
Lie down and pipe-dream a pastel day of cartoon colors, and nostalgic smells;
A banana morning, a raw-bacon afternoon—a vanilla night . . .
Die down wind-screams of mind.
Open some psyche window, and let out the noise.
Rest, and hold an old thought.
A building of grey-bleached boards.
And inside, dusty shelves holding a poor man's treasure.
Rain-wet window panes, spider webs and strange prisms
Striking an antiquitous Indian blanket in the corner.
Velvet and silk are a concert in conceit, but not this one.
It's aged cotton with tiny fuzzy balls.
Good to cover the tiredness which slew the pain . . .
Implode! That one small sliver of strength left within and force out surrender . . .
Rock gently, roll easy Soul Storm.
Know calm is not far.
As the moon travels with the earth,
So must travels with the earth,
So must a vision of hope travel with expectation.
Rock gently, roll easy Soul Storm.
The blanket is warm.

William O Robinson
YESTERDAY MAN
He listens with an intensity that makes its own sound, and sits alone
in the darkness with a glass and a smoke in his hand.
He studies reflections in stranger's eyes, and with subtle movement he hides by dissolving into a soft
speaking crowd.
He impatiently waits with his mood in disguise, and willingly draws
unto himself the feelings of others—
and others feelings
Transcended to him from a time he can't get back to, yet his wondering mind forever will wander and
Ever he looks with anticipatory gaze back toward the fast fading grandeur
of that moment of his own creation.
Looking to find and harness its first glow and cause it to linger long.
Hearing its image and seeing its music, falling greatly on it time and
preserving it for always.
Who is this one who hides in the darkness dreaming of light?
The once and never again yesterday man with his struggle for past.

Cheelee Ngan
ARE YOU FORGETTING SOMETHING?

Dedicated to the one who inspired me to write this poem.

My Dear,
The hour has come for me to talk about our marriage in question;
Let me begin at the day when we fell for each other with
Splendorous expression and the night when you assured me,
" . . . You have my deepest and everlasting affection . . . ";
So I thought we would be man and wife for at least sixty years
in succession;
All these times I stand by you with our beautiful children
Under every possible weather condition;
Somehow you have acquired a habit of getting lost in the woods
Because of temptation;
I took old Papa's advice of hanging in there and be patient;
Hoping you will soon come to your right senses with determination;
But again, you are wandering off the path
And this time things seem gotten quite a bit out of proportion;
Just want to tell you that your entire family is shaken
By your expedition;
You know you have already possessed everything
That are envies of a large population;
Why bother to spend more than a fortune to make any modification;
Honey, life is but a few decades of revolution!
I wish we could live ours without regrettable emotion!

Anita Hopkins
ERNESTINE
Ernestine, My girlhood friend, had imagination galore.
She kept me fascinated with her stories of lore.
Her house held so much magic; much more magical than mine.
Trading houses with her would have been simply divine.

When we walked beneath her attic . . . with its hidden secret door—
I was told that Santa lived there and up there had a store.
And so we climbed upon the trunk over pillows and quilts to see;
Pushing the door in gently . . . I made sure he didn't see me.

When the door was cracked a bit and I could peek inside,
You can bet for sure I saw him, to her I did confide.
Next . . . we'd tiptoe into a room and stop by an over-stuffed chair
and lifting up a cushion—she said a spell was cast in there.

A magic word would do the trick and at a beautiful place you'd be
when you crawled under the cushion . . . you'd be whisked away, you see.
My eyes grew wide with wonder . . .
Oh! could this adventure be true?
Just say a secret word and go to a fairy tale land so new.

But something always stopped us from fulfilling our escapade.
I never made the chair trip . . . but—
Hope to go . . . someday.

Harold Salinas
WATERFALL
Man, was I thirsty all day long under the mad sun.
The feeling of a parched, dry throat being no fun.
That desert seemed endless, but I simply had to endure.
Death Valley under my feet, much more walking for sure.
I envisioned an oasis, riverbeds, lakes, pools and streams.
Until the roar of crashing water filled all my dead dreams.
It was sparkling at a fair distance so I fell to my knees.
I thanked our Lord promptly for the great oceans and seas.
Oh, how beautiful indeed and I then began to slowly crawl.
My sole destination point being that delightful waterfall.
That lovely liquid splashing on the cliffs excited me so.
How I enjoyed all of its music, its freshness, its flow.
I became exhausted with my chest against the hot ground.
That wonderful water calling me with its cool feminine sound.
The spiteful sun blazed away, my strength was almost depleted.
I inched my way to the wet wonderland, tired and overheated.
Yes, I could have suffered a fatal stroke right then and there,
but wiggled like a caterpillar, the water being so near.
I reached out to touch it, but Lord I have been mislead.
That wondrous "waterfall" was the back of Terri's head!*

*Terri's long, beautiful hair

Ken Alspaugh
TIME'S MIGHTY HAND
I took a walk with time
and held time's mighty hand
and even as I walked with time
I aged
yet I did not age
the flour of God molded me
to eternity

Margaret Morton

Margaret Morton
REMINISCING
We walked the meadows when the grass was green
My life with you was so serene.
I saw the love light in your eyes,
Which were much bluer than the skies.

I saw you carry yourself so tall,
No one could compare with you at all.
I see you now in every star
And when the sun rises, there you are.

More beautiful than I had ever dreamed,
More precious than you had ever seemed.
I feel your soft hand clasped in mine,
And hear your voice so sweet and kind.

You may never believe me dear,
But in my heart you shall always be near.

Mary Casey
BLACK LOVE
Black love
Covered in darkness
Not allowed!
Forbidden!
Engulf me!
Forever.

Stephanie Drake
LONELINESS

With love to my Mom, Dad, Stacy, Kimi, & Janet. They all made it possible!

When I feel lonely, I feel that hope is lost. When I am lonely I feel like I'm in a dark room and trapped with no way out. I feel a wind go through me. So I pray and then I feel better. Hope is here again.

Margaret Morton
LITTLE MOE
I have a little squirrel named Moe,
I love to watch him come and go,
And he climbs trees that are so tall,
I'm so afraid that he will fall.
Whenever he comes down to me
He's just as precious as can be.
I open the door and he comes in.
He knows that I am his friend.
He knows, too, that I will feed him good.

And would keep him always if I could.
But he was born to be wild
And not to be cuddled like a child.

Margaret Morton
YESTERYEARS
Frankie dear, I miss you so,
And I wonder why you had to go.
I feel so alone and blue,
At times I don't know what to do.

You were always beautiful to me,
For even when you could barely see
You were so good to all the blind
And did so much for all mankind.

We traveled far, we traveled near
Trying to help those who were so dear,
Who were less fortunate than we
Who could not work, walk or see.

Your piano sits beside the wall.
The music you made was enjoyed by all.
And when you played in the school band
Everything just seemed so grand.

We would dance awhile, and then you would play.
And then, we would go frolicking on our way.
There wasn't time for many tears.
Those were the happy yesteryears.

Annie Fortunato
ALONE
Alone,
In a sea of green,
A field of blue,
Wandering.
Lost.
In time
In space
In all reality gone.
Only the night lives on
In my fear-driven
Mind.

Sherial Johnson
WORDS

To Brenadette and Chris to fulfill a promise made long ago. I love you both.

I love you so much
That it hurts me
Just to look in your eyes
And to know
There's no feeling for me there.
I need you so very much
I can feel it in my heart,
My soul,
In every breath I take.
I want to have you near me
To whisper the words I love you
Everytime I need to hear them
Like now.

Oris W Smith
THE GOLDEN YEARS
They say these are the golden years,
Our cares no longer be.
But what about my aches and pains,
And eyes that barely see?
Most names I can't remember,
My hearing needs repair.
It's likely I will need a wig
As I'm losing all my hair.
My bones are getting fragile
And I must watch my step.
I'd love to take a trip or two,
But I haven't any pep.
My friends are dying one by one,
But somehow I survive.
Could it be my pills and vitamins
Are keeping me alive?

Christal Rolland
SUICIDE
Suicide—why do some chose it as a way to end their lives? At times life may seem like a dead end street with no hope for the future. Things like fights, breakups, or pressures seem to trigger these thoughts and they may ask why is this happening to me or say I'd be better off dead then at least I wouldn't be bothering anyone. People would be better off without me and my problems. Besides who really cares anyway? It's not true there are a lot of people who care. There are many reasons to go on. If it's a breakup there are a lot of others out there. You'll find someone else and if it's pressures they will get easier to deal with. Everyone is special and who cares what others say if they don't like you for who you are forget 'em! Life is worth so much more than that. Pain is temporary suicide isn't! There's always hope. It's the only life you have it may not be goin' great now but it'll get better sooner or later—Just remember this with suicide once you're gone there's no coming back!

John Meise
YESTERYEAR
I knew you once long years ago.
How long it was I do not know
For time has ceased to mean to me
Anything but misery.
I see you walking by me side.
Where did you go? Where do you hide?

Ah, there you are. You're mine at last.
Our Wedding Day was not surpassed
By King or Queen.
Your blond beauty all my own
In our own secluded home.
'Twas then with the whispering winds
came death—
Despicable enemy of happiness.

But you are with me, Dear, tonight:
Just you and I by the dim firelight.
Death laughed at me: I laugh at death.
'Tis true: It took you for a time,
But you've come back and yet we'll find
Much happiness.

Burnett Lee Dorris
TO WHOM IT MAY CONCERN
I am writing to a girl that I have been dreaming of for all of
my life
I am looking out of the window of yesterday of lovin' times
and I can feel the warm and tenderness of her love although she is not here with me.
so I got to write this letter to her
and I am gonna say

To whom it may concern
to know that she is my girl
To whom it may concern
to know that she is my world

I can see her in a mirror of my time
I can feel her soft and tender lips
upon my face
I can hear her tender voice in a romantic place
I will send all of my love to her from one word
to the other

the sunny rain seem to fall across the windows of my mine
and I can feel her sweet love all of the time
tossin' and turning through the night
or could it be
that I may be lovin' her when I see her in sight
she is all of the love that I need so I am asking you God
would you please send this letter to her

the ocean skies and candy blue I just love being with you
to have and to hold and feel the warmness of her toes
but until that day come on by I will kiss her picture
every night.
and I am asking you God will you send her love to me
to fulfill this empty room and I hope to see her pretty soon.

Connie Jo Skinner
A NURSE'S LAMENT
The drunk came in from fifth street.

No one gave a damn.
They found him in the gutter
with his face upon the ground.
The Doctor in ER killed him
just as sure as I'm standing here.
The funny thing is he murdered but
he won't even serve one year.

Take it one day at a time Baby, forget about the past.
Take it one day at a time Lady,
'cause today ain't gonna last.

The Doctor went to a man and told him that his baby boy might die.
No, this can't be happening, it has to be a lie.
It's not up to you or me he said, as he looked him in the eye.
You have to get your answers from the man up in the sky.

Take it one day at a time Baby, forget about the past.
Take it one day at a time Lady,
'cause today ain't gonna last.

The widow asked how we stood it,
don't you people even care?
Then she looked upon our faces and all she saw was deep despair.
As I turned and looked at her, I saw straight through to her heart.
We're doing all we can Ma'am, I'm just trying to do my part.

Just take it one day at a time Lady,
forget about the past.
Just take it one day at a time Baby,
'cause today ain't gonna last.

Lonnie Pike
TIME
Time is getting older like the mountains that have changed.
Old faces are new faces, and so many things are rearranged.
The town is growing up like so many things do.
It, like all the things we used to do.
Yesterday we cried a lot, and today we just laugh.
Because days are much harder now.
We must work for what we have.

Lonnie Pike
THOUGHTS
sleep on old days of youth
gone just like the thoughts
that come and go
and friends that do the same
remember the games we used to play
how about the time we ran away
oh well . . . my thoughts are all gone
the wind played my song
and blew me thru another day.

David J Caspi
THE MIRROR OF OUR LIVES
Let us make a mirror, you and I.
Let us blend the right ingredients,
Shape and synthesize them to bring out
the finest contour and shiniest texture;
So that it matches what we want out of our lives.
When we gaze into the finished product,
we can be grateful in the satisfaction of knowing
the work we put into it will reflect
the glory and sensitivity that appear on the surface;
a fond remembrance that everything we pined for and
planned in our daily travails has accrued
to their best impact. Results that can only be achieved
and nurtured with love, togetherness and devotion.
In later years, our mirror will stand for everyone to see.
It will reflect, too, their charms, passions, and the
radiance we have left behind as a legacy to our fortune
of happiness and brilliance.
The cost may be priceless; but the value oh so rewarding.

Kimberly Austen
GOD IS . . .
God is the one who gave us love
For he is the Father from above
God is the one who made the seas
God is the one who made you and me

God is the one who made the skies
God is the one who made mountains rise
God is the one who made the world so great
For God made the trees, oceans, and lakes

God is the one who made the shores
For God made birds that beautifully soar
God is the one who made man
To dwell in his image upon his land

God is the one who gave us Jesus
For he is the one that now leads us
God is the one who gave us love
For he is the Father from up above

Barbara Austen
IN 1776 AMERICA LAID A FOUNDATION
In 1776 America laid a foundation for the building
and rearing of a great new nation
Our day of Independence had come at last and
into the world our dreams we did cast
For we knew that with God our King
Our nation would forever with freedom ring
"In God we trust"

McGuffy Ann Morris
ON READING MORRISON
The moon comes out
calling my name—
too many thoughts
none the same.
I can't write them all,
or some I will maim;
I try to control them,
only some can I tame.
Think; after thought—
one by one came—
out of my mind,
into the flame.
I don't know what's real,
or what is a game.
Is it me, or, tell me,
Who can I blame?
I must be diseased
or a little bit lame.
I can't go on . . .
perhaps I'm insane.

Helen J T Brumbaugh
THAT'S LIFE
There are cries from a tired and weary heart—
Life is a drudgery from whence it wishes to depart.
But tomorrow—the sun will shine again
And life—is worth living once again

Life goes on--the flowers bloom
Time to play ball—sunshine fills the room
With dreary weather comes aches and pains
A song—a smile, makes life worthwhile again

Life is like the weather if there wasn't rain
There wouldn't be the flowers when the sun shines again

It takes the storms then sunshine
Pain and Joy in their due time.

Louise A Joyce
NIGHTTIME
Nighttime spurs the shadows deep
Giving us the moon to keep.
It sprinkles stars above the sky,
Some strewn low, yet others high.

Artistically arranged in radiant array
The heavens become
A dramatic display

Such a magnificent moon
Each night, brightly beaming
Full of light.
Time of priceless peace is here,
Spreading silence everywhere.

Susanne Wagner
THE MONTH OF MAY
Bless these two who will marry in May
May their lives be pleasant every single day
After is said what they have to say
They'll leave for a honeymoon out on the bay.
If God is willing they may get to say
Hey Hey! A baby is on the way
Their boy they call Dan, and their girl they call Kay.

Now the kids are grown and moved away
It's been years, but it only seems like yesterday
It was that special day
In the month of May
As they said before, they will honor and obey
In every way
Until one must lay
On a special day, in the month of May.

William F Baggerman
AT TWENTY-ONE
I hope that I shall cease to be,
Before the abyss too long consider I,
ere bridging it by leap;
Before the numbing chill of age
replace the fire of youth,
Before the thoughts of quiet hearth I keep;
Oh Fate, be kind and bring that passing moment,
Rather soon than late to me.

Dana Holly Hurovitz

Dana Holly Hurovitz
COUNTRY CARES
Lovely wedge of grass
dainty like a crest of dew,
I watch the sky turn inward
and think of you.
Pretty ribbons of ocean song
Grant me the sunshine to belong!
Birds fly in circles upon my
beating heart, feeling short
like a tossled tree, I can
hear the melodies cry in
Harmony.
Windswept, I run, Oh, I love!
the castles I drew past and the
songs I sing, at last, the green
velvet sheen creates light waves
across my channel, I feel the breeze.
I see the trees, on a hazy September
morn, there calls the cry of a new day
at dawn, on my vision fair.

Dana Holly Hurovitz
MY GRAMMA FANNY

In Loving Memory of my Dear Grandma Fanny & sweet beau Bob—Luv You!

I am happy learning to cook, start a fire, and cheer you up with stories of rabbits, song, and love. How I made you smile with the whole world causing me to pout, I laughed, wrestled, even called their bluff, with your twin holding a grudge, somber in despair. Fancy footing in carbon print, a yellow frock, a spring stare, happiness is sure to return, red and blue flowers everywhere. How it takes time to forget a loss, a loved one in the summer soot. My smile come back to shout from the woods. Proud camel under a scorched sun walked straight and sure with God nestled in her soil, Isrealie Gramma travelled through time and the angels sighed under the blue horizon.

Dana Holly Hurovitz
COFFEE
From the day you barked,
I sat in silent memory,
Etching out in poetry such
wise brown eyes, a wet
tongue you kissed me.
Oh, so young you were before,
and in love with life then.
Needing a happy buddy
to bear my yearning of youth,
to hide beside me, to run out
in green fields of light, together
we flew through the pasture of our flight.
Freedom seekers, moving in laughter, sweet
friend, only mine You belonged with me.
A dog to listen to my silent tears
there was no such thing as a sky
drenched with clouds, except to
believe in silver linings and
rainbows.

Dana Holly Hurovitz
FREEDOM
Way far off, I spring in response. I hear something that sounds to me as a harp may sound. Ah! A harp, a unique, delicate instrument, dainty, illuminous prose in its harmony. It touches and offers up my glitter. The harp, an instrument rare in its exorbitancy. It reflects nature, the sounds of the wind moving gentle through the trees. It completes the dark burial of my heart, something that jumps up and creates it completely. I should like to run my hand through the windswept music.

The tree, a weeping willow, is it sad and forlorn? It is a magical life. It is thick, large, and hairy. It hangs down deep nudging its heavy head cool up on the ground. The rustling of the brush is sweet and clear. It sounds like the pitter-patter of pebbles. The sound is patient like an old man standing alone on top of his mountain. He heaves like the mountain in the willow, a clear rhythm.

I like to run sometimes almost blindly down a steep hill. I love to roll down a steep a green grassy hill. I love to smell the scent of moss in my nostrils, the spring in its glory, the first spring!

Carrie Elizabeth Manzo
MY MOTHER'S LOVE
My mother's love
I will always treasure.
A gift so valuable
It cannot be measured.
A friend, a guider
I will always look up to
Giving strength and warmth
I will always love her

I can only hope
That I will be
As good a mother
As she is to me

My mother's love
Will keep close to my heart
For all eternity,
May it never part.

Eric W Shaffer
POSSIBILITIES
A cherubic infant sat on the picnic table under the blossoming sun. Years have passed grass has grown, snow has fallen over and over. Now a hopeful intellectual thinks of himself and writes of this cherubic one.

A something in the distance, yes, I saw over there under that star, just beyond that light hint of haze. A something in the distance, yes, I saw and mounted the world to transfix my gaze.

Possibilities come to us in a flash and a flash only have we to seize them. For the people depend upon us, solitary few to lift them to our breasts and appease them.

Nancy L Smith
WATCHING BABY GROW

This poem is dedicated to Deni-Maire, my darling granddaughter.

The day that I conceived you
I began to watch you grow
From books I read and things—
I fed my mind
I saw you before me growing
Until one day reality
You laid there; tiny and motionless
Watching me
One day your arms and legs began to move
Reaching out to all the world
You began to talk in sounds, grasp at things
Then crawl to reach
Before long upon your feet, off you go
As I continue
Watching baby grow.

Evelyn Moore
A POEM TO A POM
My buddy is a ball of fur: so precious and so sweet
He's learned an awful lot of tricks.
He even cleans his feet
He sits, he speaks, he turns around:
He also shakes my hand
But what is very best of all—he's always my friend
He's always glad to see me. He meets me at the door
He stands on his back feet and walks all across the floor
When Bobby C. comes in and sits down in his chair
And starts to pull his shoes off—
Buddy's always there
For Buddy has a job you see; he takes it very seriously
He takes off Bobby's socks: not slow.
Sometimes he almost takes a toe.
He shakes the socks as if to say, "I've done my good deed for the day"
Then he goes and gets his bone and chews on it til it's all gone
He used to chew up shoes and such.
But he was only just a pup
He's outgrown all of those old ways,
and now we have some better days

He sleeps with Snuggles his little bear: he wants to take him every-where
So if you want a good little pet, get you a pom
They're the best yet.

Evelyn Moore
MY BRIGHT MORNING STAR
Nellie my Nellie, hold onto your faith
You're my example to the human race
Heart so pure and eyes so clear
A blessing to all for many a year

It matters not how your hair is worn
It matters not how your feet are shorn
It matters much that your heart is warm
It matters much that you have no scorn

You are my diamond in the raw. My bright and morning star
Whosoever will listen to you will go very far
Toward things important and not of this earth
You've been my anointed since the day of your birth

You take such good care of your little one
Teaching him the ways of god's only son
The mate that you have here on this earth
Cannot comprehend the amount of your worth
Together you stay till this life is o'er.
I'll welcome you children on the other shore.

Heather Moore
GREAT-GRANDFATHER'S STORE
The concrete porch—once smooth and firm is cracked, yet people ignore
The ragged appearance and vacancy of great-grandfather's store.
The shiny knobs and clean glass windows have faded on the doors,
For time has passed and no attention has been paid to great-grandfather's store.
The loving thoughts which linger there are to stay forever,
For too many to count were made and stored in the empty store together.
When I go back and reminisce the rusty countertops I trace,
Thinking I see spiritual reflections of his smooth but aging face.
With the creaking of the door I think I hear his lonesome song
Yet, it is the wind still blowing not knowing he is gone.
The cracking paint, the dusty shelves, the semi-boarded doors
The vacancy and mystery make chills run through your bodily core,
Oh! If the walls could talk, the stories they would reveal!
So many answers to our questions, oh, how I would feel.
Now the store just sits and fades although its death has passed
Just like dear great-grandfather who, his life, he always put last.
A monument of memories for his spirit to live forevermore,
Is what I see when I remember great-grandfather's store.

Patricia Ann Boyle
WHY DO I CRY?
The Feeble Old
The Battered Young
The Trampled Weak
The Twisted Powerful
The Self-Doubting Rejected
The Unquestioned Respected
The Condemned Minority
The Close-Minded Majority
You ask Me Why I cry,
I can only ask, why you don't.

April R Clopton

April R Clopton
VULTURES OF THE SOUL

To those who have reached the sky, only to be pelted by the rain: Between the drops, a dry path spirals beyond the clouds.

Feel how they feed on your soul; your constant hurt and pain is their daily nutritional supply of evil. They feel not what you feel, but feel how they are growing stronger and stronger as they drain from you your pride. And they thirst themselves on your many wept tears.

And they (the Vultures) like their lips at the thought that you are also strong. All the more for them. You will never die; neither will they.

Your emotions are just a tossed salad for their supper. Deranged feelings of hate, disgust, love, anger, and so many more that their garden of death flourishes to a full grown crop because you are the fertilizer.

How do you kill these damned creatures? Those Godforsaken beasts that are killing us. Do we fight, do we just lie down and let them gorge, or do we compromise?

You are hurting me Vulture, truly killing what I have worked so hard to gain. I once loved and trusted all. But, now I have seen the black casts of shadows that are thrown from above. It covers the world like smut. Ruining everything it touches.

Please do not steal my heart, my love, or my soul. For it is all I have to protect me from the world. YOU have them now. Keep them for me. Keep me! Do not feed on me. Just shelter me with your wing so the smut will not cover my soul.

April R Clopton
RIPPLES
As life goes continuously on, it is like that of a pebble in the pond.
The ripples it creates. A mere pebble.
(A mere me).
One single pebble can create so many ripples. A tiny pebble.
(A tiny me. Doing the things I do can create many ripples.
Big, small, good, or bad).

The ripples caused by this pebble reaches across the pond.
(The ripples I cause reach out across the world).
The delicate ripples produce no harm, no sound.
And though they are delicate and smooth and even,
A sense of strength can be felt as each ring tries desperately to reach the shore on all sides.

(And so like that pebble, I create the ripples in my pond.
In my own sea of life).

Peggy Ann Hill
THE SWAN

To My Sister Lynn Nelson.

As a child I watched from the banks often in wonder of her beauty.

So silently, so softly she moved. I could not call her, she would not come yet she knew my presence.

Somehow I know she feels only love, peace and forgiveness.

In all that beauty, in all that stillness, she does not search, only she knows the secrets of her silence.

I often asked myself when does she sleep, what is her purpose as I watch her so proud.

Then I remember she is from God for all the world to see from their eyes.

In each of us lies the stillness, the beauty, in search of that same silence.

So, so softly, so silently she remains forever.

The Swan

Peggy Ann Hill
THIS MAGIC PLACE
Softly surrounded by evergreens holding everyone so close at heart. They stay to heal, they stay until it's time to part.

Once one enters the rounded corners there's no longer a feeling of being alone.

It's full of people who have come and gone.

The patio is quietly busy among the plants the sun shining down through the trees giving a morning cup of coffee its own special warmth.

To have been there makes one feel so special, to know the love, to have felt your grace, to share the secret of this magic place.

Thank you, Keith, Steve and Daryl for a soft corner in my heart.

Harley Howard Thompson
IN FLIGHT
High in the sky at sunset,
Oh, what a beautiful place.
Man's beautiful earth below us,
Above, God's wonderful Grace.
Splotches of earth below us,
The works of mortal man.
Clear sky and space above us,
The future and God's mighty hand.
Darkness creeps up from below us,
The works of man grows dim.
Brightness and smooth flying above us,
Look upward to eternity with Him.

Sande Greenawalt
CARMEN HAIKU
Desire, passion, lust
Enslaves, consumes, betrays them
Red roses, blood, death

Allen Hipolito Mayor
TIP AND TOE THE RAINBOW
Tip and tip
And tip you go
Tip and toe
And tip in BLUE;
Tip and toe
You step into
Toe and tip,
You toe and toe.

Sinistral RED
And dextral GREEN
Oooops! you go
And Oh! I sough;
Steer for YELLOW . . .
Tip and toe
Tide to VIOLET . . .
Toe and toe.

Leap to ORANGE . . .
High and high
Then trip tip tip
And throw toe toe;
Spring the hedge
To INDIGO
Then, Oooops! you go
And Oh! you toe.

Tip and frisk
And tip, I sweep
Toe I gambol . . .
Toe, I go;
Oooops! and Oh!
Myself, I throw
Steering . . .
Drifting . . .
Like a spring.

Tip tip tip

And tip we leap
Toe toe toe
And toe we go;
Tip and tip
And toe the rainbow
Through the Golden Dew.

Kenneth E Gentry
UNSEEN WORLD
I want to take you to a world where only a few know,
I want to take you to a world where the streets are made of gold.
In this world there is no rain or snow,
In this world you can forget about growing old.
I want to take you to a world where there is no worry, time, or such.
I want to take you to a world where you don't have to talk so much.
I want to take you to a world where only a few know, for in this world you and I are free in body, mind and soul.

Kathy Brocksmith
THE NIGHTS ARE LONG AND RELENTLESS
The nights are long and relentless
The days are long and hollow.
My echo reverberates thru this house
Loud and silent.
I wake up at night afraid
And I cry
To God . . .
To nobody . . .
To myself.
Into my bunched and wadded covers
I press my face and sigh.

Monique Worrell

Monique Worrell
YOU AND I
Everyday when we walk together,
Just you and I not a sister nor brother.
I feel so happy whenever I'm with you,
I finally feel like my dreams have come true.

In my dream I dreamt you and I,
Have walked through the rainbows and even the sky.
Each time I dream all I've missed through the years,
I cannot resist all those large golden tears.

Now that we have all the things we wished for,
All the fortune, the happiness, and the future we adore.
We shall love and cherish until we die,
Our whole life ahead with just you and I.

Monique Worrell
PATIENCE

To my dear mother Janice Worrell, you certainly have a lot of this.

We cannot get accustomed to it
Not even when we want our bodies to be fit
To wait in an office or even a store
We just got to stay home and practice before
We got to be patient when taking a test
Especially if we want to do our best
I know you probably think you shouldn't be
But it's the best thing you'll surely see.

Monique Worrell
THANK GOD
As I look back at everyday of my life,
My family had taught me how to survive.
I loved everything that was good but not bad,
And I always laughed even though I was sad.

I remember the days I just locked my room and cried,
For days from the beautiful world I would hide.
Then you came along and showed me the way,
I was learning to love me each golden day.
My days before I met you was happy but no love,
Thank God you flew my way like Noah's white dove.

William A McDaniel
WHEN YOUR HAIR HAS TURNED TO SILVER
High up in the heavens
Under God's watchful eye
Together we will be
Forever you and I

Hand in hand in heaven
Just like down on earth
With the grace of God's love
We'll forever share his space

When our hair has turned to silver
When our hearts have turned to gold
Forever we'll walk God's pathways
Along his golden roads

When our hair has turned to silver
When we are wrinkled with age
When the roll is called up yonder
I know we will be saved

High up in the heavens
Under God's watchful eye
Together we will be forever
Forever you and I

When our hair has turned to silver
When our hearts have turned to gold
I'll still be there beside you love
To protect you from the cold

I'll wrap you in my loving arms
And hold you close to me
As I whisper in your ear
How much you mean to me

When our hair has turned to silver
When our hearts have turned to gold
Then all your years of loving me
Will be a story to be told

When our hair has turned to silver
When our hearts have turned to gold
I'll be there beside you love
To walk those streets of gold

Jacqueline S Dickman
FEELINGS
There's no explanation of the way i feel
It's warm and tender and i know it's real

Yet how do i explain what's going through my mind
Yet i know some day I will seek and find

But what about now how do i get my emotions out
I want to say things but i have such doubt

The people i care for seeing them come and go
should i ever tell them, or will they ever know.

Larry Barber Coleman III
LOVE
Love is often mysterious and wild
Someone in love is likely to have a child
Love has its ways of working a miracle
Love is always very mysterical
Love has many faces
Sometimes love leaves no traces
Love is different and love is nice
But sometimes love can be as cold as ice
Love is in a class of its own
Love is earned and love is shown
Love is contagious
And love is for all ages
And then love is beautiful and then
Love is outrageous

Bridget Williamson
GRADUATION
Graduation is here. I'm scared of the outside world.
What will happen when I'm on my own? Will I be alone?
Will I go to college? Or will I live in a cottage?
I wish I knew so I would know what I was looking forward to.
I wonder if my friends feel the same way, so they will tell me it's okay.
I set a goal; now I've finished it.
Now I will set another and go on.
I know my parents are proud of me, so I guess I should be.

Marcelle Daniel
THE LOSS OF A CHILD
Your beautiful little girl, they tell you has just passed away. You want to think it's just a bad dream, it will just go away.

Death is a natural thing, it happens all the time but, why my little one? Our bond of mother and daughter have really just begun.

Feelings of emptiness fills you from head to toe. You say, why me, it is so hard to let go.

My little Vanessa was the joy of my life, but she is gone now, and this I cannot deny.

For I will love her forever, she will always be in my heart, and this kind of love can never keep us apart.

Linda Jackson
I DON'T KNOW WHY
I don't know why I feel this way, I really don't know what I want to say. Seem like somehow I won't give up but seem like somehow the man I love between me and him it's all messed up. I really don't know what's wrong; but I think it's me on the telephone. I really do want to prove my love to him but in my mind I think I'll sin. I really don't know what's wrong with me. Is it him or is it me. Seem somehow this man I loved has put me down, but I still love him and want to see him around. I really have nothing else to do but sit and write this true love poem about you. It's something that I can't explain but man you'll making me go insane. I love you each and every day I love you and I always pray. I need you and I see you coming always my way. I get nervous when I see you my hands begin to shake and my love for you begin to bake. I'm crying for you. I'm dying for you. You are everything I need, and I don't know why I love you.

Clara Jean Scott

Clara Jean Scott
JACKPOT IS HIS NAME
Why can't I win at lotto?
The California lottery.
If I pick the winning numbers, a millionaire I'll be.
With my fine cars and dwellings, throw in availability.
Fantasies filled, wants killed.
Aroused is 'jealousy.'
In daydreams, the dreamer is greedy.
He wants it all for himself.
No concern for the needy.
He says, "Dump poverty on a shelf."
As for me, I'm different,
If I make a score deal; the big win.
I'll round up the homeless and seedy,
and buy 'em barrels of GIN.

Clara Jean Scott
VITAL SIGNS OF PROSPERITY

To Wookie: Who in spite of her parents' lack of strict decision abilities she grew up a well-educated, business woman and a caring concerned individual of which I'm very proud. C.J.S.

When presented a blue blanket of joy.
I congratulated myself 'rah we've got us a boy!'
Nurse left a sly peak which came next,
revealed that she belonged to the gentle sex.
Her delicate complexion, of body and face.
GOD had again enhanced the

BLACK race.
She was too cute. Later extremely smart.
Duplicated her daddy, this captured his heart.

Years passed by as they always do.
Before we realized the fact she was two.
Her naughty tantrums would come and go.
Like all kids in their struggle to grow.
another year. Birthdays ago, a later time.
Difficult to think of her as nine.
This former little tyke once dependently weak,
Adult now managing her own boutique.
'Adored DAD?, deceased, I'm sorry to say.'
But Jack Garrett her dad is in her heart to stay.
The end.

Jacqueline Ann Garrett

CRITIQUE WORLD REVIEW

OUR PLANET IS A VIBRATING BUNGLE, JUNGLE SAVAGE AND WILD!
Gone is our security for adult and lone child.
PRECIOUS DAYS SPENT IN DISPUTE AND A GUESS,
as to what course of action will turn out the best.
EVERY SMALL ISSUE BRINGS OUT A CROWD,
of rowdy demonstrators bloodthirsty and loud.
AND AGREEMENT IS REACHED IS BEACHED, EVERYTHING'S FINE.
Comes mass opinions, revised headlines.
SOME THINK "THE HOLY ONE" IS COMING ONCE AGAIN . . .
To eliminate problems, every enemy a friend!
ALTHOUGH WE'RE IN TROUBLE AND TREMBLE IN FEAR.
If given another chance would morals reappear?
Would we change our mode of living, how we act and think?
BECOME MORE LOVING AND GIVING, IF PULLED BACK FROM THE BRINK?
SORRY AS I AM TO SAY.
humans repeat, we face defeat the same boomerang way.

Claudius Deonarine

POLLUTION

Pollution! Pollution! Pollution!
Is the concern of every nation.
Every principal, teacher, parent, pupil,
Reduce heavy garbage, like crushing mills;
Get trees planted, in valleys, plains and hills.

Fathers, mothers, brothers, sisters,
Join the campaign, save the earth;
Do your best in whatever matters;
Form your compost, with what adds to dirt.

Heads of factories and auto plants
Research to save, our varied haunts;
Carbon dioxide and toxins, reduce please,
And let all live, in perfect ease.

All administration,
Aim at purification,
With no deforestation,
But re-afforestation.

Owners of business and food places,
Be aware of our future races.
Decrease the waste. Be not late
To preserve mankind, his settled state.

Marie E Gingrich

THE FURTIVE VISITOR

To my husband Harold, who has encouraged me in my poetry writing.

Spring is like a furtive visitor—
She sneaks in mid-frosty days,
She wears outfits of different styles and themes,
First-airy and warm then frosty schemes.
The buds on trees which have slept so long
Creep forth carefully—when they hear her song.
First almost fearfully at sounds so faint
then in the distance they keep growing stronger—
till suddenly the earth bursts forth in bloom!
Spring is here, all earth's in tune
And radiance replaces winter's gloom!

Nina M Hann

I WALK ALONE

Dedicated to Thomas House, a long time friend and lover of the ocean.

Wandering
Miles of footsteps left behind
Misty eyes staring at the white sands
Images crossing in my mind
And slowly
In deep reflection
I walk alone

Barely
Easing the aching pain
Bringing me back to the ocean
Images appear again and again
Like returning waves
Bringing me home

Timeless
Brisk wind whispering in my hair
Bare feet caressed by cool waters
Sea gulls gliding in the air
Unlike the setting sun
Memories linger on

Wandering
Miles of footsteps left behind
Misty eyes staring at the white sands
Images crossing in my mind
And slowly
In deep reflection
I walk alone

Shannon B Koester

TRUE LOVE

To Mrs. Ryan who helped me succeed my goal, and to Michael Bapst who this poem is for, I love you.

The rhythm of the water is subtle.
The sounds of splashes echo around them.
They hold each other close,
Full of love and happiness,
They kiss and sparks begin to fly!
He caresses her so very gently.
Then just as the sun sets,
Holding hands they swim freely, into the sea!

Angela R Whitt

SAYING GOODBYE

I'm hurting way down deep tonight
The love we once shared has slipped out of sight.
I know he loved me he had to
All he said as he turned to go was
"A man's gotta do what a man's gotta do"
Some people say that being depressed is a sign of low self-esteem
By this just what do they really mean?
I'm very messed up and really confused
Feeling so unwanted and used.
Why did he ask me to stay with him for the rest of my life?
To always love him and to be his wife.
I know he cared, but he had to choose
And unfortunately I'm the one who had to lose.

Arthur G Ray

POETS

This poem is dedicated to all up and coming new poets.

Poets never die and this is why.
It's what's in the mind's eye.
This is between you and I.
Although we often let out a sigh.

So let it be cold on this day
The Lord looks after us in His way.
We are poets here to stay.
It also helps us to pass the day.

The weather is cold but we are bold.
Our hands might shake we will never be old.
This is what I've been told.
Heads up someone's poem will be sold.

It's the Lord's way we can't take out gold.
Our silver will never be sold.
Now paper can always mold.
Us poets only get old
Our work goes on so I've been told.

Murray Bauer

FOR MY DEAR MEREDITH

I crave to open up inside,
the years have absorbed so much.
Tennyson's tears will always provide
the passing of time and touch.

To live a simple life filled with nature and Thoreau
is something I will forever yearn.
Spiring being supreme
will I ever truly know?

The greats must help me understand
O today their wisdom, a rarity.
You see I am just an ordinary man—
I exist in a world of impurity.

Susan Oliva

FOR MY NANA

Dedicated with love to my daughter Caitlin and my mother Chris.

Though I'm little and cannot talk,
What great fun it is when we go for a walk.
The wind, the sun, the animals too,
Such a special time for just me and you.
When I'm sitting in my backpack so high,
I can see the whole world go by.
Talking to you in my own special way,
Knowing you're there for me, even when I play.
All of these things are important to me,—
They help mold me into the grown-up I'll be.
And when you hold me so close and so tight,
I can feel your heartbeat—this love is so right.
With you and Gran, my mom and my dad,
I know that this world really isn't so bad.
When I go to sleep and you've tucked me in,
I can't wait to wake up and see your smile again.
Our time together is precious to me,
Please know how special you'll always be.
Before you know it, I'll be able to talk,
And my first words might be: "Nana, can we go for a walk?"
I love you, Nana.

Sheila A Broussard

IT TAKES SOMEONE SPECIAL

To Scott, Arica, and Anthony for the inspiration given throughout the years.

It Takes Someone Special: to admit when something's wrong;
You feel so very weak, but know you must be strong.
It Takes Someone Special: to care about his health;
To realize what's important is believing in himself.
It Takes Someone Special: to see life's ups and downs;
To wake up one morning to turn his life around.
It Takes Someone Special: to know day by day;
That you'll be loved tomorrow, even more than you are today.
It Takes Someone Special: to know when you are loved;
Not only by your family, but in GOD we trust above.

Michael L Clancy

SUMMER SONG

Summer's coming, just feel the air
Time's always runnin' from what takes me there
Just once, to catch up, when the stars aren't aware
It's comin' on and on
Strong and soft wind
Long winter's end
What you left behind comes back again

You always said you'd wait

And hope it's not too late
When the sun shines on
And it's a different light
At last now you can see
The road's a cold friend
But it's calling you to join the ride

Comin' on—summer's song
Seems like such a long time
Since it didn't feel wrong
But now in its light
Even the time—it feels right
Summer's coming to sing its song

Barbara F Ahearn
JAIME MARIE
7/14/81 TO 7/24/81
Jaime, we loved you and begged you to stay,
But for some reason God called you away.
He needed a rosebud so lovely and fair,
To place in His garden and none could compare
With your little spirit, so lovely and sweet
He wanted you close by to play at his feet
For God has a garden just filled with flowers
Where His eyes gaze on beauty for hours and hours
The choicest of spirits only go there.
He loved you so much, you're now in His care,
Some blossoms are young and some middle-aged,
Some faded and wrinkled like ink on a page,
Every so often God needs rosebuds like you,
A flower untarnished, unkissed by the dew.
We will all see you as we come thru the door,
We'll all be together, Dear Jaime, forevermore
Mommy will hold you and raise you with love,
We'll all be together in God's Garden above.

Elizabeth López
TOGETHER

To Dr. Karazim and the Senior Class of '90, this one's for us! Thanks Mom and Dad and all who believed in me. Elizabeth (Lisa) López.

I saw you standing there
Trying to seem not to care
I saw pain in your eyes
I knew the truth though you lied.

You had loved someone
Now you were alone.
I talked to you for awhile
And tried to make you smile
You gave in and smiled again
We walked on thinking of no one

I learned to trust you
And you did too
Then we cared for one another
We had found each other
We loved one another
And loved together.

For we had found a love
That had been thought lost forever
Now we are one, we are together.

Sherri Lynn Curcio
HERE-AFTER
And the autumn leaf
Crumbles into pieces—
Into dust,
And nothing cares
But the wind
that cradles its soul
High into the air
To reach new heights
And comes to know
Yes,
There is a hereafter:
After loneliness.

Miss Larnell Custis Butler
MY AFRICAN HERITAGE

To my children: Saja and Horatio Butler.

The sun shone on the topsoil.
That is what God made the white folks from.
God dug deep down into the belly of the earth . . .
And dug-out . . .
And dug-out . . .
The black earth until he found the bowels of life cradled in the earth's womb.
From that mound of indispensable organisms,
God fashioned the body of a black woman.
"You," God said. "Will give birth to all the civilizations of the earth." In His image, a black gave birth to the children of Africa, Asia, India, and all the lands God swore unto Abraham.

Maria Smith
TRAVELED ROADS
To walk a mile in another's shoe, is by some, quite hard to do,
For how can we see where we're never tread, or attempt to imagine it instead?

As older ones, we are bestowed, with the past—a long and narrow road,
We've had the chance to walk those miles, to overcome their curves and trials.

And so it is we can retrace those miles in our children's shoes,
Though the road may be unpleasant, we may rewalk it if we choose.

And we can warn and predict the younger ones of dangers,
For to the young, those curves and bumps are only known as strangers.

They haven't walked those miles before, nor do they have a clue,
How is it then that we expect for them to wear our shoes?

We are blessed with eyes that see behind and straight ahead,
They have eyes which only see the course on which they tread.

The double vision we possess, we only need to share,
And realize that our younger ones are really unaware.

If we but just remember the burden of traveled roads,
Then rewalking them through our children's shoes may help to ease their loads.

Mary Jane Hollen
YOU ARE VERY SPECIAL
All things they say must have a change
Nothing ever stays the same
And life is such a gamble, but
We all must play the game.

The sun may shine so brightly, yet,
In a moment comes the rain.
A windy breeze blows away the clouds
And the sun comes back again.

Thus goes the passing of the time
Each year, each month, each day.
New friends we meet, to love and greet
They too, then, go away.

But the memories that are left behind
Each one truly a pleasure
Will not be clouded, rained upon
But will shine in friendship's treasure.

And should we gaze into the sky
Seeing the rainbow's arching hue
We'll smile a bit and think, how nice
Of having met and known you.

William Arcurie
RUN AWAY CHILD
These poor kids for sale, everywhere
It is a very sorry tale, everywhere
No help for them, anywhere
No help around the bend, nowhere

Find them on a street in the city
From California to New York City
From the lower West Side Lass
To the suburban middle class

One child may be a runaway
Another probably a throwaway
But all have one thing in common
They are someone's daughter or son

You could find more young than old
That will love you just to beat the cold
'Cause there's no place for them to hide
Always running or hitching a ride

The average person can't imagine what goes on
Or how these children will be conned
This reality will always exist
Until it becomes number one on our list

Bessie L Seward

Bessie L Seward
THIS COULD BE THE DAY

In memory of my late husband, Rev. L. W. Seward, Sr.

God gave His only son,
To suffer and die on the cross.
So if we will believe in Him,
Our souls will not be lost.

Father we thank you for your son;
The greatest gift ever given.
You loved us all so very much,
So we can live with you in heaven.

Please listen to what I say.
He promised to return.
And if we are not ready to meet Him,
Our souls in hell will burn.

So get your work in order.
It would be wise not to delay.
Invite Jesus into your heart,
Because this could be the day.

Sandy Kalina
WHO WAS IT FOR?
A smile is given, a laugh is shared.
But did you miss it 'cause you didn't care?

A hand outstretched, a hug awaits.
You check your watch—oh my, it's late!

A child's begging, a mate's desire.
Just leave me alone for I'm much too tired.

A friend gives a visit, people are humming.
No time to talk now, Christmas is coming.

Cookies in the oven, gifts under the tree.
All in a rush—things to do can't you see?

The big day is over, the glitter is gone.
Can't talk now, must exchange what was wrong.

He's patiently waited for you every day.
Through others to touch you in so many ways.

The season has ended, but who was it for?
The one you left standing outside of your door!

Sandy Kalina
RIGHT OUTSIDE MY WINDOW
Right outside my window is a day that's filled with sun.
Children running, laughing, playing—having so much fun.
And if I look a little farther things sure do look glum,
Children stolen, broken, crying, abused while cameras hum!
The way the sick are taking over, convincing some it's right,
Has got to change so each of us must stand and join the fight!
Good people in our world today have got to work together,
Before our children and their children pay the price forever.
Make stiffer laws, lock up molesters, educate our young,
Outlaw bad print, cut down paroles, don't quit until it's done!

Right outside my window is a scene that's better now,
Children running, laughing, playing, watched over by the crowd!

Robert J Munoz
DISCOVERY
Relationships come, Affairs go.
Who's to blame, No one knows.
Feelings in the mind,
That begin to start.
Never progressing to reach the heart.

Falling in love, Or diving in lust,
That first reaction, Should we trust?
Emotional creatures not yet in control,
Still out of touch with the omnipotent

soul.

Yet love seems to win and constantly thrive,
In spite of man's irrational drive.
Where does happiness fit in this scheme?
Apart from our fantasies, wishes and dreams.

Is happiness part of this love, This life?
Or stem from the soul, Hidden inside.
Some know the answer, For they've reached inside,
A place from which the rest of us actively hide.
Totally happy, Carefree and Kind,
Glowing like the sun, On their faces it shines.

If love and happiness are one and the same,
How can we claim love when our hearts are in chains?
This is why relationships come and go,
They've yet to reach deep and stem from the soul.

Jaime Lyn Smith

THE WIND

The wind blows
through the trees
and makes them
whistle.

The wind whisks
autumn leaves and
scatters them.

The wind pushes
tiny sailboats
across a sea of
white foam.

The wind rustles
the mane of a mare
and her colt.

The wind dances
through my hair and
tickles my ear.

The wind blows all
my bad thoughts
away.

Melissa A Gehrman

MY DAUGHTER

With Love To My Daughter Nicole.

My daughter, how I love you so,
And every day I watch you grow,
You hear me yell, you see me cry,
But do you see how hard I try?

Each moment with you is a fight
To teach you what is wrong and right.
I wonder if you'll ever see
How much you really mean to me.

Ever since you learned to move,
Your sadness I could never soothe,
Your tears I could not wipe away.
I tried to hold you but you would not stay.

I'm hoping as the years go by
We'll heal the scars we made when we cried,
And we'll grow closer, you and me,
The way that we were meant to be.

Patricia S Minix

GOD'S RAINBOW

While riding along to visit a friend
I looked up in the air
And God had placed a rainbow
that told me he was there.

For years ago, He promised
to remind us of His love
That He'd never destroy the earth
again
by sending out a flood.

So the gorgeous, lovely rainbow
that man just can't explain
'Twill be sent down from heaven
and its mystery still remain.

But the beauty of its presence
to those of us who know
Is a wonderful reminder
of how God loves us so.

Don Newsome

THE LOVE FROM A SON TO HIS MOTHER

Like the moon is to the stars,
In their own special way
Like our love is to you,
From our very first day
The seasons just might change,
Right along with you
Well that's all right mom,
We'll see those seasons through
Roots which hold the ground,
Could not hold as well
Feelings which we hold,
We're sure you can tell
That the love we have,
Held within our heart
We'll love you to the end,
'Cause we have from the start

Tammy Jungers

COCAINE, MY FRIEND?

For my wonderful husband, Dave, with love.

Everyone said you were really great
I just had to try you and see
I promise it'll only be this once
What harm can just one time be?

And so just once I tried you
I told myself just to see
How much fun can a little white line
of powder on a mirror be?

I loved you from the very start
What harm just one more time?
None, I thought—None at all
as I chopped up another line

And then I couldn't get enough
You became my very best friend
I realized I could count on you
Life's problems you could end

My job takes too much of my time
time I cannot spare
I cannot be away from you
And I cannot have you there

You cost so much my friend
And so I start to deal
But even that is not enough
And so I start to steal

My family does not understand
I've lost everything dear to me
I finally see just what you are
and how evil you can be

Even after ruining my life
I cannot believe what you've done
I still cannot get rid of you
It's hard to admit but you've won

You've taken me over completely
I cannot believe it still
I cannot cope with life anymore
God take me if you will

But now is not the time to die
I've found a reason to hope
There is a place where I can go
A place to help me cope

Treatment can help me leave you in the past, until then here I'll reside
And then I'll leave here free of mind, with my family at my side

Stephen Anthony Rahaim

UNKNOWABLE

One can always wonder how
But shouldn't wonder why
An open plain in red light,
Horses running free,
Thoughtless to why
But the ground beneath
Their hooves tells how.
One can always wonder how
But rarely wonders why
An orange sky without restraint,
Effortless birds grace its winds
Thoughtless to why,
And what is there to tell how.
One can always wonder how
But shouldn't wonder why?
A sail in the ocean,
Minded by a man alone,
Has he anything worthier to do
Than wonder of anonymous answers.

Farah Mongeau

HOUSE OF FIRE

To everyone who has felt such pain as described, there is hope.

House of fire built from hate.
Every night you're drunk and late.
At 10:25 it begins,
the fire, the hate, it never ends.
Life so cruel and so unfair,
I look for help but no one's there.
Scars of the soul, still remain,
no anesthetic can numb the pain.
Through it all I will go on,
battered and alone, but still strong.

Martha L Gaudamuz

OF SHATTERED DREAMS

For you, Mother.

The sudden death
Of someone close,
The emptiness inside
That is left to hold.

Faith and hope
Is what is left,
Anger and disbelief
Is what is death.

The pain and anguish,
The endless, sleepless nights
Of shattered dreams
That are held in the candlelight.

Joseph Leonardi

YOUR REFLECTED IMAGE

When you get what you want, in the struggle for life
And the world makes you Lord and Master per se,
Go straight to a mirror and look at yourself,
And see what that person will say.
For it isn't your parents or your spouse,
Whose verdict upon you may error,
The person whose decision counts most in your life,
Is the one staring back at you in the mirror.
Some people may say you're a wonderful guy,
But the person in the mirror will call you a bum,
If you can't look'em straight in the eye.
He's the person who counts, never mind the others,
For that person is with you right to the end,
And you've passed the best test of all,
If that person in the mirror is your friend.
You may dupe the world, down the pathway of life,
And get pat on the back in its scrimmage.
But your final compensation will be sorrow and tears,
If you have cheated your reflected image!

Phyllis I Behrens

THE CENTURY GARDEN DANCE VII

For every daughter's father.

there have been many full moons wane
since last we sat at this table
and dreamed so loudly of green snow,
forgetting for an instant to silence our belief . . .

it seems our dreaming must still have some magic,
for through the glass we can see
the hillocks gilded by afternoon sun
and bare tree limbs tinted by afternoon sun
and the slate sky lightened to the west by afternoon
sun
snowing
spring
on frozen december.

Edith R Gibson

THE RETURN OF SPRING

Oh, hear the drip and spatter
of the soft April rain.
As the drops weave a pattern,
across the windowpane.

There are plants down below the ground
but some are early up.
They are drinking of the moisture,
like coffee from a cup.

Then the sun breaks through the clouds,
and makes each drop shine brightly.
Like jewels in a lovely crown,
upon the head of royalty.

The birds are singing fit to burst,
on apple, oak and pine.
And what they're saying to the world
is, "This land is mine."

The chipmunks chatter in the brush,
a hawk is sailing high.
And down the walk, in beauty,
the daffodils march by.

Esther Mazza

LOOK TO THE SUN

When you have a heavy heart—
With so much work to be done
You don't know where to start;
Hold-on and Look to the Sun.
The glorious sun in a clear
blue sky,
Makes you feel the Lord is near;
As this delightful sight caresses
your eyes
You think of the ones you hold dear,
Then with a smile on your face—
You get all your work done
So! When you're going at this rapid pace,
Hold-on and Look To The Sun!!

Verna Jackson-Glass
BABIES

To James, Elizabeth and Clarence, My Inspirations.

Giggling, cooing, gurgling babies.
Spitting, grinning, dirty babies.

Crying, sleeping, eating babies.
Teeth, crawling, toddling babies.

Walking, Talking, laughing babies.
Singing, running, jumping babies.

From birth to toddler, they all are a bother!

Pinkie Fry
RULES OF THE HOUSE
Please don't say it—if not to my face—
Don't whisper behind my back;
If what I am isn't good enough,
Don't criticize whatever I lack.

Don't sit in judgment of what I believe;
Don't alienate me with lies—
Give to me always, only the truth,
For with dishonesty, friendship dies.

Don't try to take advantage of me,
Or use me to gain your own ends—
I've been treated so, for much too long,
By too many so-called "friends."

So, care for me only for what I am;
Not what you would have me to be—
Don't change me into someone I'm not;
Just respect me, because I'm ME!!

Alice Jean Moore
WE CANNOT GIVE UP
Bad luck is not right,
Good luck is not wrong.
If only we can just,
Just find us a home.

A roof over our head,
And a bed to lay.
We have to keep the faith,
And continue to pray.

One day we will have,
All of our wants and needs.
But we must continue,
To stay on our knees.

We cannot give up,
Not just yet.
God will help us out,
I'm willing to bet.

Gary Collings
TO LAUREL
(an epitaph of emotion)
A wave slips on the deck,
Falls and breaks its back,
Then shivers into the sea
Reorganizes for a second attack.

Turbulent serpent seas tussle and coil,
Enraged by bitter winter winds, deemed
Desolate, except for a chilling song,
That lingers near the realm of dreams

And waits for me by the stiffened
Flower—drunk with frozen water.
Her tender ribs split wide apart
By malicious ice choked harbours.

The storm has faded. Its passion
Spent into a calm scarlet evening.
The night sails in on silent waters,
As we remain;
Docked and ailing.

Tamara Lynne Hart
THE REAPER
There she sits in a small, dark room
Waiting for The Reaper.
After submitting to the Gloom
He will be her keeper.

Looking out—a starless night
She ponders aimlessly.
Wondering but not in fright
The knife slips shamelessly.

If Life was tragic Death is more
Her hand lifts up to Him.
Making her follow Him won't be a Chore
Her life was just too Grim.

There is no turning back now, friend
For all of your Pain is over
You will Live with never an end
With The Reaper as your Lover.

Sherry Wright
BABY BLUE

Dedicated to Rodger Waters who has given me inspiration to achieve my goals . . . Thank you.

Let's talk,
Let's talk about baby,
She's quite the lady,
But the lady is so blue.

She lives in a dream world,
Of fantasy and fun,
Baby's a lovely girl,
She'll make you believe in the moon, the sun.

Her beauty captures all sight,
She brings out the brilliant colors of light,
She gives love of earth, love of light,
But Baby can't keep the will to fight.

She's nature's gift to the human race,
With spirit revolving land and space,
Shining through darkness with grace,
Nothing around could take her place.

And we call her Baby, Baby Blue,
She can't help herself, but she'll help you,
Can't change the world, but she'll see what she can do,
Our lovely lady, Baby Blue.

Zack Naiyer
TROUBLED STATE

To my beautiful family and my beautiful friend, Matt.

A man sits in a troubled state;
his brain pulsates,
as dancing demons stir up boiling hate.

He falls into a nightmarish trance
where he would have no chance;
in the execution of an evil dance.

The time seemed so near;
a thought which amounted to his unreal fear.
A whiplash attacked his exposed back;
the pain came so great;
and yet the pleasure came so late.

And then he woke up to find he had a different fate.
He felt the pain and couldn't experience the joy.
And he laughed as he viewed the depressing view around him.
For he was like a poor; helpless boy.
with all the joy taken from him, it was like some sort of sick joke
that this boy was played on like a demon's distorted toy.

Feel his displeasure and feel his ultimate pain
as you realize sadly how he suffers in vain!

William David Greene
THERE ONCE STOOD A TREE IN A WILD COUNTRY
There once stood a tree in a wild country,
it bore luscious fruit, beautiful to look upon and sweet to the taste.
Night and day this tree would call to the
wild and hungry country, saying:
"Come, my fruit is ripe and my limbs are
heavily laden with good things."
But no-one came, no-one heard,
so its fruit grew over-ripe and heavy;
it fell to the ground, there it began to rot, spoil and wither.
Soon afterwards, winter came and . . .
the tree folded its branches and died.

Amy Meyers
THE RESULT FOR EXACTNESS
I despise it above the flowers in spring
Because nothing is totally alive.
The calm air is still
Unlike a strengthened disjointment in the dust
And commences signs with nonsense.

Outside of a different chance, I wasn't sad in autumn,
Without the whole transparency of most-animate objects,
The robust darkened ground, the crystallizing grass,
The numerous worms, the exposed sun—

The exposed sun shading a dim space
Of non–existence that would be partially withheld,
Where I myself am imperfectly myself
And wanted and had to be,

Loathing the depression of stability:
The result for exactness, pushing towards
The lightness of subordinate midnight,
The fear of non–existence,

The pale calmness, the darkness
Of green and orange, the gentle silence—
Lean away from openness—the blunt endurance,
The immortal, modest, harmless, weak me.

Rudy Beltran
JUNE

To all my children which mean so much to me: Rudy III, Michael D., Timothy D. and Severa D. Beltran, with all my love, your dad.

The once yellow and lifeless ground
It's mostly green now.
The sky is so clear and blue
Without a single cloud.

The park is filled with children
And their laughter fills the air.
While parents fill the park benches
As they watch with so much care.

Squirrels chase one another
From tree to tree.
Running and jumping with
So much glee.

The sun is directly above
Not much pass from noon.
And all this occurs mostly
In the month of June.

Jan T Davis
SOMEWHERE
Somewhere
I will find the place
where I can rest my heart;
where I can sit and hide my face
to slow life's stride down to pace.

Somehow
I will learn to know
when not to let my heart be hurt;
when not to let my feelings show
to take each pain, then turn and go.

Someday
I will think of thoughts gone by
of each one that hurt a different way;
of each one that made me smile, or sigh,
to find the reasons why.

Someway
I will come to know
peace within my weary heart;
peace within my weakened mind,
then I will know, peace within my soul.

Angel Vdovjak

Angel Vdovjak
DECEPTION

This poem is for all my friends, family, and especially Kita for her inspiration, and encouragement.

I thought that love was yours and mine.
I thought we would be together all of the time.

Our love was like a dying flower
fading fast away.
Then you whispered softly,
everything would be okay.

The pillow where you slept was stained from crying.
It was then I realized you had, for a long time been lying.

The trees were walking aimlessly in the forest, without cause or means.
The mist that followed them began to settle in our dreams.

The silver moon contrasted brightly against the blackened sky.
Then my love, I realized our love was

going to die.

Tonight, I must leave you.
Fall away and deceive you.

Our love was never meant to be.
For you had always been . . . the first to deceive me.

Alison L Nash
A WINTER AFTERNOON

There's a crisp cool breeze as I sit outside on a December afternoon. There's a smell of pine from the trees across the way. The trees just blow in the wind. All of them except one; the big one in my backyard with no leaves. It's beautiful even though it has no leaves. It's very tall and it's brown and white. The color of the tree has faded from the cold bitterness of winter.
The grass is still green but there are patches of brown where the frost sits at night. I can look at the grass and imagine it white from snow and how beautiful it would be.
There isn't a cloud in the sky. It has an icy color to it. It's beautiful. It's a beautiful day. I wish every day of winter could be the same way.
The only thing that would make this afternoon more perfect would you being here. Feeling your arms around me and knowing that you love me. That would make this a perfect winter afternoon.

NormaJune Ritzmann-Hunt

NormaJune Ritzmann–Hunt
MY GOD

Written for and dedicated to my Daughter, Susan, and her Dear Family, Hank, Rocky, Michael, Cathy, Christy, Emily, Zachariah, and the expected new little one, with Love.

He gave me a rough, rocky hill to climb,
But He promised to stay with me, all of the time.

He bent me almost to breaking, from too heavy a load,
But He did not forsake me, He promised me so.

He brought me to the brink of despair,
But when I cried out, I knew He would Hear.

Into sickness He took me, where you must go alone,
But I knew, no matter which way I journed, He would bring me home.
He took from me loved ones, from whom I wasn't willing to part,
He had to know, how it broke my heart.

And I questioned His will,
As I climbed up that hill.

I asked, "Oh God! how can this help me, for what good was it done?"
And I heard His reply.

If there were never sadness,
Our joys would be unsung.

So He gave me time, to heal the wounds of despair,
And when I reached out, He was always there.

Oh No! He does not forsake me, He stays with me wherever I go,
For He knows, through adversity, is how I must grow.

NormaJune Ritzmann-Hunt
MY VOW TO THEE

Dedicated in deepest Love and Remembrance to my maternal Grandparents, Margaret (Maggie) and George Johnson, whose Love and farm was God's richest blessing and knowledge to a little city girl who loved kittens, puppy dogs, little biddies, piglets, and carefree barefoot summers.

I will love thee
For the ecstasy and all the strife thou has brought to me.
I will love thee
For thy gentle touch and thy love within me, that only thou can stir so much.
I will love thee
For thou kindness of thought, for all the wisdom into my life thou has brought.
I will love thee
For this feeling deep within my soul, that cries out, without thee I am half not whole.
I will love thee
Through all time to be, only praying God will place within thy heart, a great love for me.
I will love thee
As long as my life has breath.
I will love thee
When mine eyes have closed in death.
I will love thee
When my soul has ceased to be, and death has come and conquered me.
I will love thee
When on this earth I trod no more, I will wait for thee, wherever might be the opposite shore.
So come to me, through death's dark sea, I am awaiting thee, come and awaken me.
Thou smile, thou laugh, thou kiss, thou touch will have to be, for without thee;
My soul shall sleep on, through Eternity.

NormaJune Ritzmann-Hunt
THE PROMISE

Dedicated to my first Teacher, my beloved Father, August Ritzmann, who taught me to Listen. I miss you Papa.

Life's beginning, is like a book, unopened, unread.
Happiness, tears, joy, and sorrow, all awaiting ahead.
Then the chapters unfold, as you open and read and the lines all begin,
As we all live through this book of life, from beginning to end.

In our youth as we love, it's a sweet sour thing.
In our middle years, we settle down to a more comfortable theme.
And some of us are blessed in our late years, to love as in our youth once again.

Dear God! please open my heart like a flower, turned up to the sun.
Let me once again feel the sweet love in my soul, like when I was young.
Let my heart quicken with the sound of one special voice.
Let me know the sweet kiss of the one of my choice.

Let my book never close, before I have tried,
To taste all of life's mysteries, while I'm still much alive.
Be ever close to me, as through this life's chapters I go,
So I never fold down the corner of the page, close my book in defeat, and refuse to grow.

Let the pages be covered with kindness, generosity, understanding, forgiveness, compassion, and Love.
Let me always remember, with your help from above,
That the ones who pick up my book and read on after me,
Will perceive in their hearts and be able to see,
That with the closing of my life's chapters,
It's not The End—But The Beginning—of a whole new book for me . . .

NormaJune Ritzmann-Hunt
PERSPECTIVES

Written for and dedicated to my Daughter Cathy, and her Dear Family, Joe, Joey, Susan, Tina, Rachel (Little Gussie) Nikie, Joshua, and little J.K., with Love.

Sweet little Jesus, babe so small,
When I think of you, I can almost hear my Savior call.
Hurry! Hurry! Don't hesitate.
There is not much time, left to wait.

He's knocking, and He's knocking, and if you turn your back,
You might be left waiting, on the wrong track.
So take heed of His warning, don't close your heart and eyes,
For He might come, and take you by surprise.

Would you be ready, watching and waiting, and willing to go,
Or would you be too busy, with worldly things here below?
He's waiting, He's watching, He's hoping for you.
Are you waiting, and watching, and hoping too?

Surely you don't want to be left behind.
Make sure you're on the right track, you still have got time.
Be sure your perspectively sights, are in proper accord,
So if He should come in the next moment with your just reward,
Yours would be the right one, the one you would choose.

Be careful! Dearest loved one, don't get your perspectives confused.

NormaJune Ritzmann-Hunt
THE NURSING HOME

Dedicated to my Dear Mother, Gladys, and all the other Dear old Warriors, Pastor Hilmer, the Volunteers, and all the dedicated people of the Lutheran Altenheim Society of Missouri, who work in Christian Love, So our Dear old Warriors somehow know "Someone Cares."

They sit there/in their two wheeled chariots/around the walls/and down the halls/
Around the sunlit swept room/is an awful pall/
Are there any thoughts/in those drooped heads hanging down/ are there any thoughts at all/
Their eyes are dimmed and listless/ from days of staring at the shiny floors/
Are they thinking of happier bygone days/is the sunlight opening any doors/
Their work worn veined aged hands/ are folded in their laps/
It's as though they are passively waiting/for the sun to pass/
The TV is a-blaring of today's news events/
It's as though they're not caring/that another day is spent/

I look at all those snow white heads/ and bodies twisted by fate/
I wonder/God/will this be my lot/or will death/mercifully not let me wait/
I think of all the sweet bygone years/ that brought them to this last waiting game/
This game of life/has such a twist/ will my fate be the same/
Their eyes once told the story/of a happier healthier time/
Now their expressionless stare/only speaks to me of dying/
Doesn't anyone care/that life is still there/doesn't anyone care at all/
As these Dear old Warriors/slump there in their two wheeled chariots/ around the walls and down the hall.

Dear God/I beseech Thee/ bless these old bodies and minds/and take them back to happier times/
When life was sweet/days were neat/ nights were gay/children played/ wedding bells rang/
Back screen doors banged/babies cried/streetcars clanged/food and drink was good/and they understood/
Dear God/bless these old bodies and minds/and take them Home sweet Home/to happier times/

NormaJune Ritzmann-Hunt
MIRACLE OF MIRACLES

Dedicated to my Daughter Carolyn and her Dear Family, Tom, Tommy, Kristy, Cindy, John, Tyson, Jeff, Joshua, Mindy, Amy, Shana, Sarah Jane, and Nicholas, with Love.

Dear God! I would like to write of miracle things.
Of a silver moonrise, a rosy sunset, and transcendental Angel Wings.

I would like to write of melodious music too.
Brilliant melodies, of scales so new.

I would like to be—by you—so tremendously inspired,
That of our works, no one would ever tire.
I would dearly love to spend my days with you,
Penning everything, that you would want me to.

I would like to write of the little folks—
Like silver moonbeam dust sprinkled, as lovers spoke.
I would like to write of paintings, too beautiful, to recall.
By master hands, you inspired, one and all.

I would like to write of all creatures, you created, both small and large.
Creating so much love, within our hearts, and our senses, to discharge.
But most of all, I would like to write, of your Son, you sent so small,
For our souls redemption, and life eternal, through Christ Jesus;

Your greatest Miracle of all . . .

NormaJune Ritzmann-Hunt
FELLOWSHIP OF GOD

Dedicated to my Son Kenny, and his Dear Family, Brenda, Kenny, Tami, Mandy, and Danny, with Love.

As your sea urgents, frolic in your deep,
Are they as happy and content, right now, at this moment, as me?
Do they hear your mighty roar,
As they play upon your ocean floor?

Lovely; lovely fellowship, so fragibly balance,
Of water, salt, sand, seaoats, fowl, fish, and shells,
All helt together by GOD'S hands,
All with your ocean swells.

The sun and moon, the sky and clouds, and the stars,
All lie within this mysterious, great fellowship, of ours.
Within GOD'S hands, He holds them so tight.
He! who can control the tides, or change the day to night.

Hear my heartfelt sincere prayer, dear Lord to thee.
I thank You! for this gift of Love, of tranquility.
As we all strive, in deep-rooted fellowship with thee,
Dear GOD! I thank You! for your meticulous, miraculous, gift to mankind,
Your mighty Sea.

NormaJune Ritzmann-Hunt
MY SONG OF CHRISTMAS

Dedicated to my Grandchildren, each and every one of you.

I sing of Christmas.
I sing of Joy.
I sing of Mary's little Boy.

I sing of Jesus,
Who set me free.
I sing of Jesus, loving me.

I sing of shepherds, wise men, and kings.
I sing of that brilliant star, shining so bright.
I sing of that holy, holiest night.

I sing of Mary and Joseph.
I sing of a manger, filled with soft warm hay.
I sing of my sweet, sweet Savior, as He so peacefully lay.

I sing my glorious song of Christmas.
I sing of triumphant Joy.
I sing of my lost sinful soul's salvation,
Through
JESUS CHRIST
Mary's little Boy . . .

NormaJune Ritzmann-Hunt
MOTHER'S DAY

Dedicated to my Children, Carolyn, Kenny, Cathy, and Susan, with Love and Pride. Mother's Day, Sunday May 3rd, 1981.

A child, a small child smiling,
With a shiny face, so sweet, and all aglow.
A child, a small child crying,
With a dirty face, and runny nose.
A child, a small child sleeping,
In slumbers quiet soft repose.
A child, a small child playing,
In the dirt, in rumpled clothes.

A child, a small child frightened,
By the darkness of the night.
A child of any size, or color,
Black, yellow, brown, or white.
A child, a small child laughing,
In Mama's arms, happy and gay.
A child, a small child to hold my hand,
And touch my heart, and steal it quiet away.

A child, a small child's precious souls unique, beauty;
That's what makes
A
"Mother's Day"

NormaJune Ritzmann-Hunt
MY EASTER RANSOM

Dedicated in fondest memories of love and appreciation to my two second teachers, my step–Mother Thelma, and her Sister, my Aunt Myrtle. Who loved me. Gone but never forgotten in the heart of a little girl.

Good–night sweet Jesus, who set me free,
Of all of my sins, and all sins ever to be.
Whose life blood, flowed down the cross on Calvary,
Into the warm sweet earth, for you and me.

His gentle sweet nature He showed to all,
Trying to teach us to heed his call.
Sweet Jesus, make gentle, and open my heart to your cries of pain,
So I too, may be gathered up to your bosom, when you rise again.

His soft gentle hands where the nails were drove,
His sinless soul, was as white as the driven snow.
Upon his head, was worn a painful crown of thorns,
This was the day, to which He was borned.
Good-night sweet Jesus, look down and smile on me,
Even tho you know, tomorrow, again into sin I might be.
I try to follow the pathway, you have shown to all,
But sometimes, I can't seem to control my sinful fall.

Man is borned to sin, and when conscious calls,
Back to your anguished cross of forgiveness, come one and all.
By your blood, you have cleansed us, and made us free.
Good-night sweet Jesus, my soul thanks Thee.

NormaJune Ritzmann-Hunt
MILLIE MY FRIEND

Dedicated in Friendship, Remembrance, and Love, to Millie, who saw beauty in every–one and every–thing, even ugliness. To Mutt from Jeff.

A true friend, is someone who will love you, even so,
At times you're unpleasant, and not very nice to know.
Someone to whom, your deepest secrets are lent,
And you can trust they'll be buried, in the deepest respect.

Someone, who will find complete joy in your achievements, even so,
Their own achievements at the time, are at an ebb low.
Someone, you can turn to, when the world turns its back.
Someone, no matter how immense your mistakes are, will welcome you back.

Someone, in death, you will miss, even so,
Someone, in life, you were very privileged to know.
So sleep peacefully, my dearest friend, may the soft warm earth, gently enshroud,
Till one day in the Rapture, You and I will meet again in the crowd.

NormaJune Ritzmann-Hunt
DYING

Dedicated to my Darling Brother, Junior Ritzmann, who lost his life at 41, on a cold wet dark highway. God's choice that night.

You call us back, one by one, to take us to your grave.
I can't seem to understand, how is your choice made?

An old man is left, whose race has been run,
While you choose to take from our midst, a fresh young one.
A year old baby, a little child,
You sometimes choose to leave with us, so short awhile.
While an old lady of ninety-eight,
Who's so tired, and eager to go, you do not take.

And as we sit, and gaze at the loved one, this time you chose to take to rest,
We look around, and contemplate, whom you will choose next.
The beautiful teenager, whose life is all ahead,
You pluck from among us, from out of our flowerbed.
Disease, an auto wreck, a suicide,
How do you choose, to take us each, back within your stride?
An old wino, whom no one would miss, I know, you leave,
As I stand confused, perplexed, and amazed,
While taking a young Mother, with children to raise.

I know, It's not my lot to question your choice,
But I can't help wondering, how quite next, will be which voice?

NormaJune Ritzmann-Hunt
DEATH'S FLIGHT OR GOING UP? GOING UP!

Dedicated to my Husband Ken, whose love and patience allows me to write. Thank You Dear, with Love.

When the lights of life are turned off, in this body where I dwell,
And Heaven is above me, and all below me is Hell,
Lay me not down into the muddyabase, where the devil is king,
But lay me in the tree-tops, waiting for my soul of spring.

For my soul is eternal, in this body made of clay,
And in the winter of my life, my soul shall soar away,
So lay me not down into the earth, in the gates of hell.
But in the tree-tops sweet repose, where I can hear Canaan's bell.

From dust to dust, man's fate is found and bound,
To be returned, back into the ground,
For from dust man has been formed, but women was formed from a bone,
And if left in the tree-top free, like Gabriel! I can soar on Home.

Florence Daughtry
DADDY

Daddy, when we were small,
You told us bedtime stories.
You have now closed your eyes in glory,
You and Mommy have paid your debt,
That is why our eyes are sad,
And our pillow is wet.

Mommy went home thirty years ago,
Daddy, when you left us we could not help but show.
Daddy, we know God makes no mistakes,
Losing you, Daddy, was not our decision to make.
Daddy, tell Mommy we were good,
You did everything for us that you could.

You and Mommy have paid the debt we must pay,
We hope to meet you in glory on Judgment Day,
Save a seat, Daddy, for all of us,
We must prepare ourselves for heaven, we must,
We must clean up our souls and it won't take long,
We must treat everyone right and no one wrong.

Chester McTier
THERE AIN'T NO LOVE

To my son Telly S. Gary McTier.

There ain't no love in this ole land
The kind it should be for your fellow man
The love for money and what it can buy
Thinking only of our selfish desire

No it shouldn't be that way
Think about the price we may have to pay
We pave the road today we'll walk tomorrow
so why make it a road of sorrow

A teacher and a leader is what we need
A say-er and a do-er, one who won't deceive
Love plays a major role in our hearts
So let's get it together, and we are off to a very good start.

Steven P Donnelly
PRISONER WITHIN
I'm trapped inside this breathing shell of flesh,
Just waiting for the freedom of my death.
In body having to exist alone,
For only in this shell is life I've known.
For how could I ever really know,
The shell in which another's had to grow?,
How do I know I wouldn't act their way,
If in their shell my spirit had to stay?,
Such limits has each person of their own,
Limits only they have ever known.
How will it feel when I am truly free,
To finally leave my shell so far from me?,
For I am not this shell that I must wear,
For death this shell and I will never share.

Rachel A Tenney
JUST LIKE GOLD
Just like gold
You're worth the wait
You haven't yet seen it
But my heart's the bait.

You reel me in.
Then let me out the line.
How do I know,
If you're really mine?

Your baby blues cut like a knife.
You've captured my heart
For the rest of my life.

Just say the word, I'll be there.
With you by my side,
There's no despair.

Just like gold,
You're worth the wait.
You haven't yet seen it,
But my heart's the bait.

Ernest Gregory Kurpuis
A DARK NIGHT AT THE TREE
In the darkened night
As the moon shines bright
I sit under a tree
Thinking of thee.

As the beams shine
Through the limbs and leaves
They cast shadows
of how things have been with you and me.

Some wavy and bent
Some smooth and soft
And even some
That would break night off.

But when I take into thought
All of these
And looking again, I see a tree
Just like you and me.

Lorrie Brough
A LULL IN THE BATTLE
When the silence began no one quite knew,
But the deafening stillness grew and grew.
The men stood like statutes all around,
Their dead buddies about them on the ground,
Rifles held tautly, poised in mid-air,
Waiting for the enemy to come out of their lair.
Dust rose around them and remnants of fire,
Smoking wrecks of twisted steel and wire.
Hollow eyes only vacantly lit,
Weary faces lined with stubble and grit,
The scene was a scene of pain, death and horror,
Meaningful only in its meaningless-ness of war.
The bombs had been dropped, the flames had been thrown,
Bayonets found their marks, each man to his own.
The last grenade had been tossed into this cave
Where the men now stood frozen.
Each had been brave.
The battle had been bloody right to the last.
No time for thinking! Each had to act fast.
Now brains began to clear the numbness away.
But, looking around, what could a man say?
Suddenly the spell was broken by a shattering cry:
The unmistakable sound of a child . . . half sob, half sigh.
The men's muscles tightened as they looked in disbelief
At the emerging child torn by schrapnel and grief.
About ten she looked, with long blank straggly hair
And large brown eyes opened wide in despair.
Only one among them knew the language she spoke,
And with a start he suddenly awoke
And rushed towards her, dropping his gun as he ran,
Putting comforting arms around her.
They moved as a man
In a body, as did he, all stunned by this greivous turn of fate.
Oh, that a child should suffer from this senseless hate!
Was this the enemy they all had fought?
Was this the enemy of whom they'd been taught?
Skin yellow, yes, but her tears were the same
As the tears they'd shed in the night without shame.
Her tears were the tears of all Mankind
For the happiness few could ever find.
She looked up at them with childish trust,
And trust them she could, as they knew she must.
War was for grown men who knew what they were doing.
They started all this mess and the bally-hooing.
How far from the parade and drill field today
With the bright uniforms and the banners so gay!
Where were the dreams and horses they'd seen?
Where all the glory? . . . What did all this mean?
Was this the way to bring Peace to all men?
Or would the killing begin all over again
At another time, in another place,
Man against man, race against race?
Would men ever learn to lay down their arms
And refuse to exchange such bodily harms?
The men looked at each other and wept,
While far away all the world slept
And remained ignorant of the fact that today
This handful of men had learned how to pray.
They shouldered their rifles and trudged doggedly on,
For a job each now hated still had to be done.
Ah, Man, you march forward and you know not where,
Loyal to your armies, yet your soul is bare.
Against these people your heart holds no wrath,
But wearily you hold to this damned bloody path.
Perhaps one day the "little" people of the world
Will rise up together with banners unfurled
And say to their leaders, "We're tired of war,
Death and destruction! Now hear us! No more!"
For all men everywhere want to live their lives out
At home with each other, and without any doubt
That tomorrow will come for them and their offspring.
Then will Man laugh! . . . Then will Man sing!

Laura A Rainey
THE ROSE
There it stands in a limited amount of space,
Something red and green and beautiful,
In a crystal cut vase.
Shadows from the grandfathers clock,
hide the bright colors grand.
The rose stands there in bewildered shock,
for it used to be a great beauty of the land.
The rose is blocked out from the friends it used to know,
the gentle rain, the fertile soil,
and the sun with its orange and yellow glow.
Days and days go by, and the beauty has slipped away.
The stem is turning brown,
And the water is turning gray.

The most important part of the rose,
is now withered and old.
It is looking downward as if to be crying,
and is still as if to be cold.

A light is turned on, all the shadows disappear,
A friendly face in the doorway,
a feeling of fear.

The first person she's seen for many a day,
But the only reason he has come is
to throw her away.

Chris Gugliuzza
NOW I LAY ME DOWN TO SLEEP

Mary Claire, thank you for your love and remember . . . you'll always be my best friend! I love you.

Life is just a memory
That fades with each oncoming day
And we must all die someday
So that from life on earth we can be free
When my children awake one day
They may find I've gone away
I've finally gasped my last breath
Now in rushes this heavenly death
I may look back on the world someday
But for now god . . . I'm free!
Now I lay me down to sleep
I know my Lord I'm in too deep
I'm living over the edge and I'm losing ground
I'm living over the edge and I'm going down.

Debbie Casavecchia
STEPS FOR A HAPPY HOME

This poem is dedicated to Tom, my piece of heaven here on earth. Many thanks for your love and support.

Always awake in a happy mood
and greet your partner with a smile
kiss him and tell him you love him
embrace him, if only for awhile.

Show your affections as much as possible
so you're on his mind throughout the day
leave little notes around the house
show him that you love him in every way.

Absolutely never go to bed mad
for there's a chance morning may never come
forget what you were fighting about
and let the love within your heart succumb.

Don't worry and always be happy
our time together is such heavenly bliss
with a love as strong and beautiful as ours
surely my dear, we cannot miss.

Michael S Gomes
MIRROR MIRROR
Mirror mirror on the wall, why do I always take the fall.
When love was sitting in her hand, she squeezed it out, like bits of sand.
Oh mirror, can you tell me why, she always seems, to make me cry.
It's girls like her, the mirror said, the love she had before is dead.
You gave her everything you had, now you are the one, who is feeling sad.
When all she did, was cheat and lie, your best move, was to say goodbye.
And now she cries, 'cause she is alone, compassion is something, she never shown.
Now you are gone, 'cause you found out, what her life is really about.
I know she cannot, stay with you, not after all the pain, she put you through.
No—never can it be that way, that was then, and it's today.
As you leave her here today, we both know, you really cared.
As she cries, we can hear her tears, what ever happen, to your future years.
Like pretending is a child's game, only Tina can take the blame.
This is where you start to grow, this is something, she ought to know.
So you free yourself of her misery, you are letting her go, you are setting her free.
In time you will meet, someone who really cares, and never show again, your painful tears.

Louise Ingles Hyde Gum
HIGH ALWAYS HIGH
High, always, high against the blue sky,
May the torch in your hand
Blaze brightly, my Lady,
Proclaiming in sunlight, declaring by starlight,
In sunshine and storm,
In peace and in war,
A people who are
Citizens of a free land.
Let that torch in your hand
Tell the longing they share
For a world out there
Where bondsmen live,
Whose people would give
All they have to be free
As you are free,
Oh, my Lady of Liberty,
With a five-pointed crown
On your bonnie long hair.
Standing so queenly, so reverently there,
In the Harbour of America

Lisa Kopel
BEING THERE

I would like to dedicate this poem to my mom, Phyllis Kopel, for being there and having patience with me through good and bad times. Also I would like to thank the rest of my family for loving and caring.

I wish you were there for me,
when I needed you sc.

If I were down or depressed,
I felt I could not talk to you.

The reason for this is,
I was scared and afraid.

Afraid you couldn't or
wouldn't listen and scared
you wouldn't be there at that
specific time.

Sometimes can't wait,
for later.

They must be told now,
others can't wait, but not
too long.

So please listen and talk
to me about your problems.

And I will listen and talk
about mine.

So let's start now,
and make the bond.

The bond of mother and
daughter, love that is
there forever.

Cheryl Dawn Dillon
GATEWAY TO ADVENTURE

Dedicated to Matt, my husband and best friend. Love and to be loved is the center of our existence. Together, we are complete.

It happened one day
that the gate to adventure was opened to me.
My thoughts had risen
expanding to a point that pierced reality.
From the other side
dreamers art becomes alive indefinitely.
Living in color
of vibrations seen and felt for us all to be.
Sculptures made of sound
turn you in and turn you out.
True colors set free.
Never closed Mondays
the side face looks out and in to see inside me.
Painting of the tones.
Spinning disks around the sun held by gravity.
The living canvas
shocking in its clarity for us all to see.

Erik Swyres
DREAM OF THE SHADOW

To Linda Goodman, Ian Astbury and Grandma Mayfield, Who taught the children well.

There's a light in the sky.
Reflect a gleam in your eye.
Just a second in time
Just your secret for all times
Can you feel the winds of heaven.
Shadows fall before you
The darkness falls before you
Have you lost the dream of the wind and the light.
Hold on to that to night.
Listen to your heart.
Just a reflection of your shadow heart
Dream of the shadow
Look into the shadow
For that is where you might see the light
Two shadows in darkness
One holding the other so tight in the night
Just a second in time
Can you feel the wind and the light
Look into the shadow
In the dance of the light.

Denis Merrigan
LILIES OF THE FIELD
The catafalque draws the silent heart
Down the long corridors of time.
Wisdom weeps in silence
The death of innocence.

Though tyrants rise and fall
With the frequency of tides.
Hope, the freedom of flowers
Is beauty to the famished heart.

Our tenuous dreams are trapped
In the tears of all our tomorrows.
Happiness is in the giving
Of all we fear to lose.

The seed prepares the harvest
Of tomorrow.
While life blooms through the
Springtime of the rose.

Truth goads the restless soul
To scale the cataracts of time.
Through all the dark centuries
Gleams the eternal man.

The earth mourns the solitary flower
That falls before its hour.
Love flows beyond its source
To water all the lilies of the field.

Denis Merrigan
THE FLAME
Beyond the power of mortal men
The flashing sword the pointed pen

Breathes a flame that never dies
Turns the world and lights the skies

Lifts the veil that drapes the night
Guides the winged bat in flight

Drives the earthworm through the soil
Makes the witch's cauldron boil

Sprouts the twig upon the tree
Makes the mighty thunder flee

Guides the bee that bends the flower
Ushers in the witching hour

Further still the mind will reach
While there is all mankind to teach

Greater things the eye will see
Before we reach infinity.

Denis Merrigan
VESPERS
I've ploughed the endless fields of blight
And worried through the restless night

I've heard a thousand feet march by
And no one hears the anguished cry

I've seen the mob with blinded eyes
And resist the folly to be wise

I've hurried through the fleeting day
And watched the fretful world at play

I've viewed the state of those insane
And wondered wherein lies the blame

I've seen the lightning strike the earth
And heard the cry of gently birth

I've known the mortal stab of pain
And felt the gentle kiss of rain

I've soared the air in silent flight
And touched the rays of morning light

I've climbed the mountain to the sky
And freed my soul and watched it fly

I've come to know my time and place
And feel the earth move out in space

I've heard the poets gently rhyme
And felt the peace at vesper time

Denis Merrigan
COMMON GRASS
Dew upon the rose
The sun's rays mirrored
A thousand times
The spectrum fused
Each droplet a sphere
Separate and distinct
Swift in appearance
Silent in departure
Banished by the touch
That breathes them life
The temporary trimmings
That will be renewed
Throughout the far reaches of time
Enhancing the ever present now
Virgin fields of mercurial dew
Under early frost glazed skies
Garlands of iridescent gems
Moist opulent pearls
All rich in common grass.

Lucy Neff Phillips
DADDY'S LITTLE GIRL

This poem is dedicated to my Father, Ronald Neff.

I was your beautiful little princess
As I wore my pretty little dresses

You held me in your arms so tight
In your eyes, I was your shining light

You were just as perfect to me
We had a bond that was just as tight as could be

You made me feel so loved and secure
I knew you would always be there, that was for sure

We played and danced and spun around in a whirl
I will always be proud to be your little girl

Barbara L Martin
HUMANITY

In Memory of Brandon, my nephew, I dedicate this poem to all the bureaucrats and officials who didn't care enough to ascertain that the sidewalks would be plowed for our children and the elderly.

Has so much of humanity lost its soul?
Was the caring replaced by greed?
Where's the compassion, the sharing and love?
Have we blinded our hearts to the need?

Have YOU ever been homeless? On the street?
If not, how could you possibly know
of the helplessness, the overwhelming loss;
of what to do with nowhere to go?

Have you known what it means to merely survive,
seeking shelter in a blinding snow?
Have you ever seen children cold and hungry,
and wondered how it could be so?

Still the rich get richer and the poor waste away.
What if this is humanity's test?
Do you REALLY believe it can't happen to you?
FATE favors not who to strike next!

So many in our world today have so much,
But did they forfeit the Golden Rule?
There surely is more we can each do

to help
Save Humanity, OUR MOST
PRECIOUS JEWEL.

Nyla K Doran

Nyla K Doran
CONTEMPLATION
Driplets . . .
Sounding to the rhythm
Of my wearisome thoughts.

Slowly
Counting out the time,
As time passes me by.

Drifting
From care to care;
Desperately searching for answers.

Answers,
Mingling with the driplets—
Evaporating into the air.

Shirley F Carter
THE BEAUTY OF LIFE
The beauty of life is the little things,
Your voice with sound of angels' wings.
A smile, a song, a candle's glow,
The moon, the stars, the life I know.
The corn that grows in the summer sun,
A time at night when our work is done.
Oh, how can we leave these things for furs,
cars, and diamond rings.
With bills, traffic and union dues.
No thanks, my friend, you take the blues.
I'll just stay here on my country farm,
Where my dancing hearth will keep me warm,
And live my life with faith of a dove,
The beauty of life is eternal love.

Shirley F Carter
THE HOUSE WHERE MOTHER LIVES
Tho it's just a humble place there's warmth around that house,
Warmth around the house where mother lives.
Yes, I'm many miles away, and I vision pumpkin pie,
Warmth around the house where mother lives.
The porch light's on, she's waiting there,
With a smile that would shame the stars.
Standing there with arms out-stretched, in the house where mother lives.
Tho years go by we never change.
We're thankful everyone;
Thankful for the chance to be in the house where mother lives.
Someday up in glory we'll climb those golden stairs,
Right to her door, we'll stay with her
In the house where mother lives.

Shirley F Carter
STEPS OF LIFE
We started out together so young at the start,
We were both in college, gonna tear this world apart.
Steps of life moving away, steps of life moving away.
How can we be together, when steps of life are moving away.
We married in the springtime then winter came to say,
Our little baby Johnny's on his way.
You became the doctor one bright day in May,
And just about that same time I joined the P.T.A.
Steps of life moving away, steps of life moving away.
How can we be together when steps of life are moving away.
We lost our things in common, couldn't talk and didn't try;
And that's when lonely time went rolling by.
It's seventeen years later, my age is thirty-nine.
Johnny is a man now and he is doin' fine.
He's so proud of his father, he wants to be like you.
I know just how he feels, I wanted to be a doctor too.
The man I loved and married doesn't come home anymore.
But the greatest pain and sorrow, the thing that hurts me more,
Was when that lady doctor hung her shingle on your door.

Emogene Combs
AS I WANDER BACK TO YESTERYEARS

Dedicated to Afey Staton, my grandmother.

As I travel back to yesteryears,
I tend to forget all my cares.
Back to Grandma's house I go
As I did so many years ago.

I see important things I'd forgotten.
I draw water from the old well,
Visit the old cellar, smell potatoes rotten,
It's all as clear as a bell.

I hear the old wall clock chime
And lose all sense of time.
I see Grandma so petite,
As she calls, "Time to eat!"

Cousins by the dozens,
Grandma's house all abuzzin'
As again we eat her sweet cake.
Oh! Back to yesteryear a journey I take.

Again I see Uncles George and Andy
As then for we kids they have candy.
Grandpa with his long hair and beard
Another dear voice from the past is heard.

In the front yard Grandma's rose
The fragrance is so pleasant to the nose.
We visit the old pippin tree
For an apple that's so good and free.

But alas and alack
It's to the present I come back.
I thank God for memories so dear
That occurred in my yesteryear.

Viola Bell
IN A PEN SHELL
Went shelling one day on Sanibel Isle.
Found nothing but Pen Shells for over a mile.
Decided to look and see what might be inside;
The book, "Two Islands," was indeed our guide.

We opened many and found nothing at all.
But then found some goodies and started having a ball.
We found Stars and Limpets and Chitons, too;
Crabs, Slippers, and Jingles, to name a few.

So tiny they were! So perfect, each one!
Our day suddenly turned into one full of fun.
We continued our search 'til our backs were near broken,
Many an Ohh, and an Ahh, were heard spoken.

An Octopus and a watch were also found,
All treasures from Pen Shells . . . just look around!
This day was so wonderful, so perfect, so free . . .
These samples of God's handiwork, cast up by the sea.

Christy Perry
ALL OF A SUDDEN
As i sit here
on top of the stairs,
i am waiting for my lover
to appear in front of me.
I wondered if he was
really coming for me,
or was it another dream.
Then suddenly there he
was, real as ever,
just standing there, as
i thought i was dreaming again.
But then i realized it
was a dream, a
dream come true.
We were so close
and nothing seemed to
keep us apart, for the little
time we had together.
Then my dream was
shattered and turned
into a nightmare.
He disappeared for
no one to find, all alone,
away from me.
Now i still sit here on
the same old steps,
now dreaming a different
dream, waiting for him
to come back to me.
But for some reason
he hasn't come back.
Will he ever?
i'm not sure, but i do
know i'll always be waiting for him.
And i'll always love him, but
someday he will come back,
so i'll just sit on these
steps and wait.

Nic Louis Nardoni
SELF-DESTRUCT
Every time I watch the news,
Something else has been destroyed or damaged.
Are we trying to kill ourselves with technology?
The oil spill in Alaska is a prime example.

We seem to be systematically destroying the planet.
Our farmlands are becoming a wasteland.
The U.S. is beginning to look like a dust bowl instead of the breadbasket it once was.
Soon we won't need a nuclear war to destroy everything we're doing that on our own.

Last year's drought shows how we're fouling up the weather systems.
And year after year more animals are disappearing forever or are endangered.
The wild frontier seems to be just a storybook to most youngsters.
Forests are disappearing daily along with swamps, grasslands and even some mountainous regions.
Technology has become more curse than cure.

But there still might be a chance to save what little we have left.
Even the "common man" can make a difference if we make an effort.
If we honestly try we won't have to answer a question like:
"What was fresh air really like, daddy?"

Albertino Simao
THE DEAL
Who gets the best of the deal,
The wife or the "other woman?"
The wife, a full life together,
The "other," just what she wants.

The wife sleeps comfortably at his side,
She is the Queen at family gatherings,
The "other" living in constant anxiety
And dreaming about beautiful weddings.

But let's think about, for instance,
The wife living in this constant situation
Making love with her husband
Is not a pleasure, it is an obligation.

The "other woman" falling down under this man
knowing that this momentous emotion
Is a sin, is an act of a stolen object,
She's an object herself, with no pride, no aspiration.

Seems to me that the ironical winner is the man,
Taking advantage of this enjoyable combination
Who lives exclusively for his macho needs,
For his appetites, for his carnal satisfaction.

Victor A Hutcheson
LONG DISTANCE
I heard a drum in Nassau,
and I saw myself running on an open plain in Africa
And I was free with the animals,
the lions

the tigers
the elephants
the giraffes
the cheetahs.
I saw myself as one with the Earth,
the Sky, the Trees and with all
else God had made.
And I heard a voice of many tempos
and pitches,
Like all of my forefathers were
calling out to me;
calling over the oceans
calling over the centuries,
calling out to me over time.
They all spoke with love to me.
And they said,
"No lands, or seas or time
will ever let us lose you,
no matter where you may be."

James E Hodges
THERE IS ALWAYS TIME TO PRAY
Lord, help me to realize
There is no time to criticize.
No season to think or say
Anything to hurt or betray,
But there is always time to pray.

There is no time to be unkind
To anyone, by thought, word or sign.
No time or place to hurt those I love,
No time to hurt, push or shove,
But there is always time to pray.

There is no time for mind or tongue
To cause anyone to be sad or undone.
There is time to be kind and true
Lord, to myself, others and you.
And there is always time to pray.

Help me, Lord, to live each day
To examine my thoughts and the
words I say
To be sensitive and aware—as I live
To love, be thankful and forgive
And always take time to pray.

Amanda Mueller
LITTLE ANGEL
On a warm summer's night in the
crystal blue sky.
I clearly could see her, she brought
tears to my eyes.
My voice was entrapped, my soul
cried to be free.
I crumbled and fell on the velvety
lea.
It was just about dawn, the trees
trickled with light.
This enigma of beauty came in from
the night.
She appeared as an angel,
iridescently hued.
Her tattered reflection lightened my
mood.
Her calamitous stumble came round
with a grin.
I smiled too, it came from within.
Her golden mane brushed the back of
her knees.
She requested my help, her voice
sang through the trees.
I sped to her aid, gently straightened
her wings.
Her gratitude softly spoken, made me
feel like a king.
Then bidding farewell, she floated up
to the sky.
Dumbstruck I watched then I
whispered, "Goodby."
The angelic form disappeared in the
haze.
Go little angel, regret clouded my
gaze.

David L Schronce
THE SOLDIER WHO SLEEPS
A young soldier dies,
And returns to the dust.
He stood by the motto of "In God We
Trust."
He gave his life, for all to see.
That there is a way, for us to be free.
He died somewhere, in a foreign
land,
With a nervous heart and shaking
hands.
With a bloody body and tear-filled
eyes,
And still we do not realize.
That he gave his life for a better way,
Yet things get worse day by day.
He gave his life but it's all in vain,
And I think that's a crying shame.
So let's destroy war and restore
peace,
To rectify the soldier who sleeps.

Fran C Worster
THE WEDDING GARMENT
He is the potter, I am the clay
to be shaped and molded in His way.
Praise be to Him, His Holy Name
for always walking with me and
being the same.
And as I walk through His Holy
Land,
He's ever here to guide me and lend a
helping hand.
As I walk with Him, the fruits I'll
display
until I walk in purity and beautiful
array.
He is making me as a bride don't you
see.
The day will be I will walk in beauty.
For He is adorning me all the way
to become a bride in that day.
For the fruits are the wedding attire
that I shall wear when He calls me
higher.
I shall run to meet Him in white on
that day.
I shall walk in splendor all of the way
to the altar to be claimed by my
Savior, my Prince
all dressed in the fruits of Love, Joy
and Peace.
The Hosts shall proclaim it all over
the land
when my dear Savior takes my hand
in the ceremony of the ages we'll all
be there
if we let Him mold us and lend Him
an ear
to hear what He's saying about
beauty and grace.
For it's all in the fruits if we'll but
embrace
the Truth in His Word and hold it
dear.
We'll walk as His bride and shed all
our fear.
For the day of the wedding draws
ever nigh.
Her's even now at the altar waiting
on High
for us to complete our wedding
preparation
to be forever with Him without
separation.
As a bride of the Lamb that He's long
waited for.
Oh praise His name forevermore.
(Galatians 5:22-23)

W R Redding
OUR SON
His name is Bobby Lee, he's a lovely little tyke, with beautiful eyes of sky blue, and a lovely little smile.

We never know from day-to-day, just how long he's going to stay. But the joy and happiness he's brought us, will stay with us each day.

As I sit here my tiny baby, and watch you lay and play. My heart feels like it's going to burst, just knowing you're here today.

You will always be with us my son, the years shall never part.
You will always live forever, right here within our hearts,

Your little hands keep reaching out, trying to grasp onto something new.
You keep tugging at our heartstrings, with every little move.

Only God knows why you are made to suffer my son. His wisdom's far greater than ours.

But I would have given anything if he would have chosen me, than to have left you as you are.

JoAnn Marion
I'M A TEACHER
It's morning about 8 o'clock
Children come down the hall
So eager to learn
My concern is for them all.

I'M A TEACHER AND I LOVE IT !

We sing the song, "America"
Say the Pledge of Allegiance to the
flag
And hurry on to reading
We do not lag.

I'M A TEACHER AND I LOVE IT !

While teaching all subjects
In many different ways
We make learning fun
For days and days.

I'M A TEACHER AND I LOVE IT !

Playing kickball and tag
With the children is fun.
And they love to catch the teacher
So run teacher run.

I'M A TEACHER AND I LOVE IT !

Paper work, lesson plans,
And lunch tickets too
Make a teacher tired
With so much to do.

BUT I'M A TEACHER AND I
LOVE IT !

Then a child comes
And gives the teacher a hug
This makes teaching a job
Too important to shrug.

YES, I'M A TEACHER AND I
LOVE IT !

Dr L Marvin Marion
FALLING LEAVES
Listen to the whistling wind
(OO-OO-OO-OO)
While to the ground the fluttering
autumn leaves descend
(Sh! Sh! Sh! Sh!)
Painted hues of red, yellow, gold and
brown
Make a perfect cover for the frosty
ground.

REFRAIN:
Falling leaves in the cool breeze
Coming down from the trees
Soon they will be bare
Old Man Winter be aware!

Gone, another season of life ending
Soon a new one will be beginning
All the splendor of Autumn passes
too fast
But in this life nothing ever lasts.

REFRAIN

After Autumn leaves have turned a
crispy brown
In the countryside and in the town
Children walk through them with a
(Crunch! Crunch!)
While on fall apples they
(Munch! Munch!)

REFRAIN

Alice E Frantz
CIRCUS
The circus is on its way.
It's coming into town,
With monkeys, horses,
acrobats, and clowns.
Three rings to watch.
There's so much to see
For mom, and dad,
and brother, and me.
The man cracks the whip
in the ring with the bears.
The acrobat is balancing
on a high-wire chair.
Clowns are so happy
doing crazy tricks,
While dogs jump thru hoops
and leap over sticks.
Oh yes, the circus
is a fun place to be.
For every member
of the family.

Diane Batten
WHALES
Whales singing their haunting songs
reverberating through me
I turn to the last note
something in me almost
understands
maybe, because I am
locked on land.

It is hard to push through warm
waters
like a hot humid day
do you sing lullabies to your
young
warning them of the dangers
of sand
warning them of man.

Charles Pierce Brooks

Charles Pierce Brooks
A PICTURE
A picture is a moment, frozen for all
to see.
So, darling, never doubt it. This love

was meant to be.
The colors blend together. Our destinies intertwine.
I'm yours, for all the world to know, until the end of time.

A picture can tell of many things, or a thousand worlds and places.
You lift me up, as if you had wings, with all your charms and graces.
In all you do, you look so good. Your moves are so artistic.
Whenever I look into your eyes, I see something there that's mystic.

The brush accepts the canvas, and then the two shall meet.
Just as we accept each other, and together our hearts will beat.
The passion grows intense as our bodies come together.
Baby, don't you worry, because I will leave you never.

Our love is like a picture with every scene just right.
Cupid is the artist. So, we should never fight.
When the artist signs his name, we'll be there for each other.
You're the treasure of my life. I'll never want another.

Charles Pierce Brooks
THANKS A LOT

Maybe I never told you, because I never took the time,
to say how much I love you, and
How glad I am you're mine.
But, you were always there for me in everything I did.
And, sometimes when you reached out for me, I just ran and hid.
You repeatedly said you loved me, but I could never hear.
You never tried to be above me, even when I wasn't near.
I'd often get mad and curse you if I ever took a fall.
I guess I never noticed you were giving me your all.
Sometimes when you scolded me, I'd be mad for a while.
But, looking back, I can always see you gave me a fair trial.
Through all my life you've done so much and I never thanked you for it.
The urge would strike me now and then, but I would just ignore it.
I never once said that I was wrong because of foolish pride.
Through my whole life you've kept me strong and I've held it all inside.
I want you to know you've taught me well in everything you do.
My life's a whole lot easier to live because of you.
Mom and Dad, you're the best, and I know you're all I've got.
So, I just thought I'd write to say, "I love you! Thanks a lot!"

Kathleen Giamarusti
UNTIL WE MEET AGAIN

To My Deceased Husband Bob.

For I will always love
you, even through death
itself, For our souls will
be reunited as one in time
to come, and the love
we shared together will
even be stronger the
next time around,
So here's to us,
"Until We Meet Again"

Linda L Jett
DEATH

I don't really understand it,
It does have a meaning I know,
It's like going away, going to sleep for a while.
Not a short while really, because you never seem to wake up.
You never get to see the world again,
But you see a far more better one.
There's no way to get away from it,
No matter where you go,
No matter what you do,
Everyone faces it.

While you're asleep people miss you very much.
They want you to come back,
Even though they know you can't.
They'll miss you all the while you're gone.
You'll be gone, but I know you'll be by my side all the time.
The love will still be there.
No matter where you are,
The feelings will still be the same.
They will never change in any way
Death, is so hard to understand
But, no one can ever change it!

Jason Scott White
HOLE IN THE WALL

It's there, but no one
Wants to see,
The hole in the wall.

Unfixed for several years,
Now, the day of reckoning.

The ladder bangs the wall,
The hammer to the thumb,
The nail undaunted.
The hammer drops,
The ladder falls,
The hole remains.
Ladder, hammer, nail remain.
The picture doesn't hang,
Over the hole.

Perhaps, next year.

Lynne Souza
ALONE

Alone . . . that's how I felt after you left me.
Now there are no tomorrows,
And yesterday is but a fading memory.
My heart aches,
I cry out for you in the night.
You'll never come,
You'll never even look back.
I never meant anything to you.
Alone . . . I'll feel this way forever.

Linda J Hanna
A BIRD'S SONG

"To Bill," the most wonderful husband in the world!!! I love you.

As I walked through the woods one day,
I stopped by a leafless tree; that stood along the way.
And with my eyes wondering all around;
I slowly set down on a blanket of leaves; which deserately covered the ground.

And as I was thinking of how hard life could be;
And of all the pain and hurt, that life sent to me.
I heard a sound — high up in the tree,
And as I looked up to see; a bird looking back at me.

As I watched him leap from branch to branch,
In such a strutting way; tho of a little dance,
He sang a song that made me realize,
That life too — holds a surprise;

The gift of happiness — which he shared in just that little while.
But before I could say thanks with a smile,
He flapped his wings and flew away.
And I too left; with a touch of happiness; from a bird's song that day.

Diane Zieger-Audretch
THE FLAME

To all lovers—new and old—who want to know why and why not . . . and to new beginnings.

LOVE IS AN EVASIVE CREATURE . . .
. . . a spark ignited at a moment in time when needs collide.
But needs become desire when nurtured,
and desire requires a flame to survive.

THE FLAME BURNS BRIGHT AS TWO BECOME ONE . . .
. . . fueled by the deepening love they've become.
But time rushes in and with it comes forces,
of giving and life or pain and strife.

YET THE FLAME STILL FLICKERS, IF ONLY SO SLIGHTLY . . .
. . . unsure enough love's left to keep it alive.
For love is so different to each of the people,
who in the beginning were surprised by the spark,

AND THE FLAME KNOWS NO REASONS OR SEASONS OR CHANGES . . .
. . . but instead gets noticed when again it is dark.
So if you are able to share in the moment,
when love sparks the flame in your life at some time,

BE CERTAIN TO NOTICE THE STRENGTH OF THE FLICKER . . .
. . . and fuel the fire while there is still time.
For once it has dwindled from lack of attention
A FLAME HAS NO RECOURSE BUT DWINDLE AND DIE.

Diane Zieger-Audretch
NATIVE NEW YORKER

To my mother, Lillian Miller-Zieger—a woman who truly understands all the pain and pleasure of motherhood—love, your daughter Diane.

I can still remember being very small
and you were the beautiful lady
who fed me and loved me and always was ready
to give all your love to your baby.

The trips to the park, the Girl Scouts and dance when all in my life was ideal;
for only a mother who unselfishly nurtured
could be someone whose love was so real.

But, of course, we get older and think
we know better than the tenderer
of all of our knowing; and soon we
forget how lucky we've been
and decide it is time to be going.

So we take for granted the things
we've been given as we venture
to find our own way; taking along
that which cannot be bought
while learning the price we must pay.

And when we are finally convinced
we've found something that fills
the great void our mother once filled,
we find we're mistaken
in thinking we'd ever fill a void that cannot be filled.

So I want you to know that I always
will love you and thank you
for the childhood you suffered for
me; for now that I'm grown
I realize the giving it required for you
to help me be me.

I will pass on the values and strengths
that you've taught me
to my child who sees me as I once
saw you, and the loving and giving
so heavily invested will live on
through her from me and from you.

I guess what I'm saying is thank you
for being the kind of a mom
who is also a friend; no peace in the
world compares to the knowing
that our friendship and loving never will end.

Jeannie E Engebretson
FLOWER OF FRIENDSHIP

A new flower bloomed
in my garden of friends
Leaves full of color
a stem that won't bend

Petals that open
with a warm sunny glow
Friendship like flowers
when fed will grow

Each raindrop of time
together we share
Brings strength to the flower
of friendship that's there

Sophie Kleeman

Sophie Kleeman
MY MOTHER

To my mother and father—
A dedication with love.

God gave me a mother
The best of the lot
I awaken each morning
And thank him for that

As the days come and go

And years slowly slip by
I ask my dear Lord
To be by her side
Her health and happiness
I ask him to guide

I love you dear mother
These words from my heart
God love you and keep you
You're my guiding star.

Sophie Kleeman
MY FATHER
Dear father I've missed you
I hope you know how much
Your witty sayings and silly songs
This way you've kept in touch

At home you left an empty chair
With memories so dear
For years you toiled on endlessly
But for me you were always near

God has called you to his home
Where love and faith abide
Please guide me through the years ahead
Save a place for me by your side

God keep you ever in his fold
I'll help care for mother here
Her days of toil, I'll try to ease
In our hearts, you're always near

Donna Patefield
WARM LOVE
Warm love, is like a soft warm puppy
or a fluffy ball of yarn
Like a pail of fresh warm milk
from an old, cow-warmed barn

Warm love, is like beautiful flowers
or a bright warm sunny day
Like water falling over rocks,
rushing on its way

Warm love, is like bright red apples
filling an apple cart,
Or like the smiles when I greet you,
like our tears when we must part

Warm love, is like small children
laughing in their glee,
But mostly sitting by your side,
just being you and me.

Betty Ann McHan
THERE'S GOT TO BE A LOVE FOR ME

To My Long-time Friends in Arlington and Fort Worth, Texas, And To My New Friends in Florida And to all my Family everywhere. To God for giving me wisdom.

As sure as there are stars in the sky,
A newborn baby cries,
As sure as a Mountain is High,
A bird flies.
There's Got To Be A Love For Me.

As sure as A Fire burns,
A wheel turns,
A bell rings,
As sure as a Tree is tall,
A house has a wall,
There's Got To Be A Love For Me.

As sure as the Rain Falls,
The Breeze blows,
and the grass grows,
As sure as the Seasons Change.
There's Got To Be A Love For Me.

As sure As There's Faith, Hope, and Charity,
As sure as Jesus died For You and Me.
There Is A Heaven,
There is A Hell. So I Know There's
Got To Be A Love For Me . . .

Bonnie F Riddle
MOTHER

To me your beauty compares to no one; only a flower can describe you with all its grace and elegance.

Your eyes radiant a love that is undying and sacrificing. Your mouth gives forth words like that of a nightingale singing so gentle, so soothing.

Your arms so fragile looking but still full of strength—a circle of protection, shutting out all the pain and fears.

Your hands are so soft, they brush away tears when I fail; they held me up for those first steps and I know in my heart I can still hold on when I don't think I can go on by myself.

Through all my years you have been there to comfort me and give me guidance. You have given me everything you had inside even when things weren't so good for you.

No one's beauty matches yours— my mother, my love.

Dan Thomason
FRIENDS
Friends are the people you care about
They are almost impossible to live without, when you're in need,
Or just want to talk friends will be there and will not gawk
And likewise when friends depend on you, you have to stick together
Just like glue, listen to their problems listen to their grief
For if you listen carefully it will bring them great relief
You see there is a special kind of joy when with a friend
Girl or boy, You feel comfortable your mind is but clear
When you see your friend it brings much cheer
Whether going to the movies or just watching a fight
Be sure to say a prayer for your friend tonight
And when you go through life's trials and fears
Friends will be there to ease your tears
And when you have trouble and strife
Friends will be there to help straighten your life
Friends are for caring and sharing with If they are true friends
They will be there until death, And when I die and when I'm gone, don't be blue I'm happy to have a friend like you.

Pam Smith
A LONG JOURNEY HOME

To my beautiful husband Mike and a dear father-in-law.

A dreaded journey, lingering stares, made us both fully aware, that a dad who was loved was now at rest, but while here on earth he did his best.

The highways looked longer, the time just stood still, God took sweet dad, we know it's his will.

I looked out the window at fields that God gave and saw dad just standing and giving a wave.

He smiled oh so sweetly and looked quite content, he gave us a sign that on earth was just lent.

My husband looked over about the same time, and said, "A breeze just went through me, dad is just fine. He's just entered heaven, and now is at rest, while here on this earth he followed his quest."

We kept following the road through the farmlands dad loved, and were guided by him, and the Lord above.

Journeying home to a dad that was gone, but to ask for him back would have been wrong.

Yvette H Drouin
HEAR ME, HELP ME

To Child Abuse Victims.

Why don't you believe me? comes the plea of a child
Mom and Dad are hurting me, and creating something wild.
No one believes me, the teen or young adult
When I say, "Mom threw me out"
Officials won't deal with the statement
The parent is right no doubt

There's nowhere to turn for relief,
adults reign, protection's denied
Abuse is rampant, beyond belief
The child's word not taken, though adults have lied
From womb to tomb there is danger
With sex, and drugs and alcohol abuse
The source of harm is no stranger,
but speaking up seems of no use.

Will the day come, will it be soon enough
For every child to be protected
From parents or strangers who treat them so rough.
And a waif's plea for help is no longer neglected

Listen to me, do not ignore me
It is your sworn duty, your role in life
To defend me, preserve and protect me
Hear me, help me, save me from strife.

Patricia M DePriest
HOLD ME TIGHT

I dedicate this poem to all my friends and family, for giving me the inspiration to reach for my dreams, and to remember, that there is always a better tomorrow.

Hold me tight and love me,
never let me go;
Hold me tight and show me,
How our love will grow.

Hold me tight and comfort me,
with the magic that you weave;
Hold me tight and promise me,
that you'll never leave.

Hold me tight and tell me,
I'll be yours forever;
Hold me tight and promise me,
our bond you'll not sever.

Hold me tight and tell me,
that I'm not the one to blame;
Hold me tight and promise me,
that everything will be the same.

Hold me tight and tell me,
your love you'll give to me;
Hold me tight and promise,
Our love will always be.

Rosalie H Contino
LIFE

To Dad — who defied the odds of "life" and survived a recent bout of pneumonia.

Life - you precious gift, where there is no beginning, middle or end.
Life - who knows where you will lead us with your mysterious rights and lefts, ups and downs.
Life - you are the living end with your clouds, mists, fogs, smogs, blackouts, delays and meanderings.
Life - you meanie! You dance as we laugh and play — you SCREAM as we plot and plan.
Oh Life! What other tricks do you fate us? You scoundrel of humanity!

Richard E Bickel
THE MESSAGE

Dedicated to peace and brotherly love for all mankind.

I lay here on a table,
My body burnt black and grim

I lay here without being in pain,
For an instant, then back again

But in that instant,
I went a great distance, but not too far

I was given a message of peace, love and understanding
For foes, friends, loved ones, no matter who they are

From the CREATOR of us all and all life we know thus far,
The message goes as this

There are many roads to MY HOUSE,
They come from near and far
They have different beginnings but they all end at MY DOOR
So when they cross, remember, they lead to ME as yours
So respect and let them go their way
For they end where yours does, on JUDGMENT DAY.

Susan Clark
PERSPECTIVE SET STRAIGHT
Is not guilt,
At times,
A malicious lie,
Come to torment
The hearts and souls
Of those
Undeserving of it.

Or perhaps,
It is a message,
(Heaven sent)
To warn those
Whose way
Hath strayed
Afar.

A time will come,
When each person,
Bearing remorse
On heavy shoulders,
Shall choose which
Of these truths,
Apply.

Marie L Anderson

Marie L Anderson
LIFE IS A GIFT

I would like to dedicate this poem to my lovely daughter, "ANN MARIE" and her son "MARK OSSIAN." They both bring my husband and me great JOY, and we feel BLESSED with such a fine daughter and grandson.

Life is a gift that does not come packaged, or ribbon tied —
but it comes from the symbol of love, and we nurse it with pride.
It is our hope and dream to have someone, to build memories to treasure,
because for every life that is given, to someone; it will bring pleasure.
It is the someone that we nurture and teach, as we watch it blossom and grow —
and with the right seeds — the harvest will show.
We find in life that all humans are selfish — in their own special way —
and procrastinate on the love; that should be given each day.
We are all of the strong belief, that only to others will come sorrow —
and for our loved ones, there will always be; — a to-morrow.
Then one day tragedy came and had taken your loved ones away, I regret the
words of love that were left unspoken, and those words; are so easy to say.
Now! each day as I go on living, how can I explain? or try to forget,
for the choices that I made, and why? my family, I had to neglect.
For we all know! that for every life that is given, some day it will be taken away,
and death is the price for living, and death is the price; we all have to pay.
But no one has the knowledge to predict, the place, the date, or the time,
When! the road we will be taking, but we know; we are all standing in line.

Let us all get our priorities in order — as we wake up each and every morning,
for tragedy and disaster have no mercy, and both will strike; without warning.

Adam P Brown
NIGHT OF THE MOON

I sat and watched by the window
Her sweet song filled my ear
Her body flowed like a shadow
Covering me; I want her near

She swirls and dances in my eye
She beckons a call of love
Gray clouds gather outside
As she hovers from above

She grows dark, she grows cruel
Obscuring the midnight sky
She is a huge white pool
My time has come to die

She steals my life, my shadow
My ghostly love of the night
We dance away from the window
I soar straight up to the light

Adam P Brown
ADDICTION

Brought low by her schemes
Was the woman in my dreams
To my eyes once a beauty so fair
But tragically I became aware

That she has fallen out of love
Yes, she ruled my nights
This once so fragile dove
Having Heaven in her sights

The silver spoon was her new lover
My love was spurned for the white flower

Lorraine C Ericson
THANK YOU . . . FOR PARENTS

To Dennis and Joan, All my love always . . . Ice.

I send this message
to you with love,
For all your support
throughout the years.

For believing in me
and staying by my side,
Through all my accomplishments
and all my tears.

For getting me through
all the difficult times,
For the hugs and the talks
and always understanding.

A parent's love
is the most valuable gift of all,
One that is taken for granted
yet keeps on giving.

So I send this to you, Mom and Dad with all my love,
To thank you both
for just being you.

Georgiana Lieder Lahr
SILVER SEA

The moon shone down upon the dark, wide sea,
And covered it with shining, silver light;
The moonbeams danced on waves in happy glee,
And all the world was bathed in silver light.

And covered it with shining, silver light,
For there was magic ev'rywhere for all;
The silver waves sang songs of pure delight,
And moonbeams joined the chorus in glad call.
For there was magic ev'rywhere for all,
And silver mermaids crooned in voices sweet;
The shining moon held all the sea in thrall,
With mystery and loveliness complete.

And silver mermaids crooned in voices sweet,
The world was filled with silver music fair;
With joy, and wonder, silverness replete,
The magic of the moon was ev'rywhere!

Herbert J Fisher
THE RACCOON

This masked marauder of the night
Can fish and hunt and it can fight;
When it floats along on an old dry log,
It is a match for almost any dog;
To a farmer it can be a pest,
Conducting its forays with a zest;
It raids the garden and chicken coop,
And steals the things that it can scoop;
When the farmer views his fields next morn,
He notes the Coon's great appetite for corn,
Broken-down stalks and half-eaten ears,
A destruction sufficient to cause some tears;
At times, it is a playful imp,
That washes its food and likes to primp;
And in spite of its raids upon our camp,
We rather like this ringed tail scamp.

Joseph Girouard
REVENGE

To Alfred Hitchcock who inspired me with his surprise endings.

It was late at night,
And the moon shone bright.
The wind was blowing,
And the owl was screeching.

I could hear him creeping,
This lion of the evening.
His claws sharp as steel,
Which I in the tree could hear.

His stomach as empty as a cave,
And in the tree, I, for which he craved.
One bullet was all I had,
Only one shot, that's all I would have.

Then, quick as a flash,
Out in the open he dashed.
Beneath the tree he stood,
On a frail branch I also stood.

I aimed my life between his eyes,
And pulled the trigger quick and wise.
The great cat fell to the earth,
For, no more a traveler he would hurt.

I walked to my camp, which was miles away,
Where I knew my husband lay.
The enemy which took his life,
Was this great cat, I killed tonight.

Bunny Chaney
MIRACLES

To my 9 children. Bless them all.

Oh what miracles around us there are,
The nighttime moon,
the morning sun,
the evening stars,
The laughter of children,
the sparkle of dew,
The perky flowers poking their heads thru.

The Saucy Robin, the Sassy Blue Jay,
all these things go into making a day.
The sweet earth waiting for the precious rain,
To come rushing on like a rumbling train.

God made these Miracles and many more too!
But most especially God made YOU!

He gave you eyes so you could see,
the beauty around you,
the sky and the trees.
He gave you ears so you might hear,
the babbling brooks,
tumbling creeks and falling tears.
A heart filled with love He sent your way,
The better to understand each miracle filled day.
A lifetime He gave you, all these things to enjoy.
Not to be played with,
not treated like a toy.
Last but not least, to you he gave death,
So you could return and be held to his breast.
REJOICE!

Jacqué Schlottman
MORNING SUN

A glimpse of you in the early morning.
You started rising without warning.
As bright as bright can be.
You've taken over me.

You kissed my cheeks with warmth of sun.
What was dark and cold,
Now is light and warm.

Wishing this day will never end.
Giving my heart a chance to mend.
I want to hold you all day long.
Let's sing together a silent song.

Dreaming all night of you.
Anticipating the morning's dew.
Waiting for all tomorrows.
Only you can melt my sorrows.

You are my morning sun.

Arnold Lee King
LOVE WILL CONQUER DRUGS

This poem is dedicated to all drug users. Because I love you.

Jesus is love, the love of Jesus Christ
Will fill the emptiness you feel inside.
So if you are searching for something
And you think you can find it in drugs,
There is nothing greater than, the love of God.
Can't you see what's happening to this world today
Drugs is the destroyer.
Please don't pretend it's o.k.
What the world needs now is love sweet love.
Not drugs, sweet drugs,
So accept Jesus and his love
And please please say good–by, to drugs

He loves you so, don't let him down.
Accept his love, it's strong enough
To turn your life around.
What I am saying to you is true
There is nothing! too hard for God to do
His love has always seen me through
He'll see you through. He'll see you through.
Love love Jesus is love

Joan Schimschock
(JESUS)
(MY PERSONAL SAVIOR)
Jesus is in my life every day,
I talk and pray to him in my own way.
Everyone should come to Jesus as a little child.
It doesn't matter if you were once really wild.
Just ask, and Jesus will come into your heart.
Just remember you have to try and do your part.
Jesus really loves the sinner. He only hates the sin. But if you repent, you're a winner.
What good is money and material things, when you don't have Jesus, and all the blessings he brings.
Giving alms to the poor, praying for the dead, and worst sinners, not judging, and forgiving others,
Is the most important, and loving acts of kindness, you can show our fellow sisters and brothers.

Mary Coghlan
IN THE SHADOW OF THE NIGHT

In the shadow of the night
Within the darkness of our sight
Mysterious things always happens
Within the world of night

Beyond the darkness of the day
Upon the earth as we play
Within the shadow of our light
Adrifting from the moon of night

For every time the stars shine bright
Enchanting our lives forever
Beyond the sight of liveliness
Into our lives forever

Charles R Gardner Sr
IT'S ALL WE HAVE

It saddens my heart to know we'll never see them again, to know they're out there somewhere. To remember the love we had for them and the love they had for us. The joy and happiness they had brought to us, how they had made each day brighter for us, with their joy and love.

Even though there has been some time gone by, we haven't forgotten them. And there are times when the sadness pulls at our hearts, making us remember those times gone by.
There are times we remember, that the tears would come to our eyes, the heart would feel as though it would burst.
These are the times we remember the most.

I've sat watching the hurt upon her face, the tears as they would fall onto her cheeks.
I would hear the sounds of her sobbing at night while she slept and know there wasn't anything I could do for her.
I would hear the sounds of her crying and feel the tears on her pillow.

I would hold her in my arms to comfort her and feel her sobs of sadness.
To remember them, the joy they had brought to us, is all we have left, even though it saddens our hearts to remember, it's all we have left of them.

Merkia L Childress
A DECADE OF BEING ALONE (1980-1990)

A decade of being alone
Is not necessarily what it implies
For if it did, I have not grown
Within myself, nor within other people's lives.

A decade of being alone — 10 years
Often caused me to reflect
Through smiles and, yes, through tears
Upon changes in my life that I can never forget.

A decade of being alone — 120 months
Allowed me time to learn about ME.
Although doing so aroused a few disapproving grunts,
I continued fighting that constant battle just to BE . . .

A woman of 30-something left alone to cope
With the unknowns of which I had never faced;
And just hoping — hoping — hoping against HOPE
That somehow I would finally be embraced . . .

With the courage, stamina and perseverance to face the next decade
Being 40-something and NOT alone,
But marching to the beat of MY drummer in MY parade
On into the next century — with head held high and still carrying on.

Claudia Hanak
BROOK LANE

The still pine a
feather silently
dusts the air

The 3/4 moon in a
frame of maple and
oak beams its good
night

The brook bubbles a
soothing lullaby

Crickets and quiet
settle upon the lane

The morrow will rejoice
in the sunlight and its
glory again

Darlene Globe
THE ZOO

I'll tell you a story of when I was young,
When the giraffes knew how to dance and sung,
The hippo danced around the room with glee,
The silliest dance you could ever see,

The monkey talks as the kids went by,
They were all in cages, can you tell me why?
The ostrich swished its tail with glee,
The rhino yawned, made a piano for me.

The tiger with his stripes of black,
The babies on the possum's back,
The alligators swam and swam,
The baby raccoons were covered with jam.

The baby monkey with eyes of brown,
Was acting just like a silly clown,
A crocodile was sitting in a tree,
making faces down at me.

He jumped down in the water fast,
I knew this phase would not last
As I grew older they won't be the same,
The lions will only have a mane.

The alligators will swim in the lake
and chase a big fat water snake.
The monkeys will shatter, they won't talk,
and the Hippopotamus will slowly walk.

The rhino will yawn but not for me,
But the ostrich will still swish its tail with glee.
The giraffe won't know how to dance and sing,
They all will do the natural thing.

So when you're young, you see with your mind,
A lot of things old people can't find.
So don't question your children when they say what they see,
Remember, you were once young, just like me.

Gregory Gardner
FATHER, JUST GUIDE ME

I'm sitting by the window, wondering as my life goes on.
With all the hassles within my mind that live from dusk to dawn.
But there still is a light within the night that keeps me growing strong.
It's the strength of your word and the power of your touch, that shows me the right from wrong.
And if I should ever care for you, the way you care for me,
Then I would have no problems and I would always see.
For all I do is think of you and all my dreams come true.
For all I really ask of you is to stand to the side of me,
And if I should ever start to fall, you would take my hand and guide me.
Through the night and the light and the things to come,
And the problems that will keep me on the run,
Just take my hand, try to understand, just guide me.

Merna Burns
GRANDCHILDREN'S PICNIC

The day was blessed with shadowed sun
Gentle laughter fell as tinkling little breezes hummed
The little busybodies began to run in warmed happy, dancing sun
They ran the length of the park cheering one another on
The quest of a special secret cove by giant plants had begun this romp of laughter into the sun
Each child had a special spark, their own special tune embarked
Chubby Ashley's little hand hung tightly as we strode lightly to her own delighted mood
Little Lindsey's big brown eyes were saying here's a place for special sharing, and the time was almost noon
It was bubbling blue-eyed Brook who found our very special nook
It was there in the glowing sun that our priceless picnic had begun
Little Abby smiled and sighed, said she'd had too much pie
The Grandchildren's picnic was the best of my life's most cherished moments!

Bob Firth
QUESTIONS

How could I grow stronger when the one I love don't love me
How could life be better when there's no hope left to give
How could I feel something when that something has always been denied
Who could I turn to when there's no one to hear me
What can I say when no one really understands
How can I find someone when that someone always turns and hides
You know life ain't too long
And you have to be so strong
But the people cut you down
Until you're six-foot in the ground
Where can I turn to when I want some peace of mind
Who can I talk to when I don't have no one else
Maybe I'll finish dreaming and someday I'll find what I want

Grace Handley
THE GIFTS OF THE AGED

Waves crashing on the shore —
sparkling, whispering foam
Shifting sand from shore to shore —
Life held within its bounds.

Dream your dreams — old one
Hold hands with others —
Give hope to the young —
share your wisdom and your love.

Age holds its secrets
and drifts endlessly
with the tide.

Mary Margaret Longerbeam
TOAST TO YOUR NEW HOME

Your house is not just built with mortar;
Nor is it built with wood and clay

alone.
It is built with the love that you mutually share;
That's what makes your house a home.

May its roof and walls protect you
From Nature's every foe.
May the light shining from its windows
Give off a warm and friendly glow.

May your new home bring you happiness
In abundance for you to share.
May it always bring you love and joy
And may you always find laughter there.

These things and many more are wished for,
But this one thing we surely know,
Your house will always be a Home,
For together you will make it so.

Kenneth Woliver

HE LIVES ON

GOD is most gracious, also He is great.
When you think He has deserted you,
He may just be a little late.
He is out there watching, with still-silent eyes,
He is special to all, for He is so wise.
He loves all of His elders, and His children so small,
It matters not whether you're short or tall.
His love comes in the most mysterious ways,
He is still here with us, just like in the old days.

Kenneth Woliver

MOTHER

My mother is so sweet, tender and real,
She can take the worst sorrow, and comfort it to lie still.
She saw it so hard, the life that she knew,
For her husband was taken away and left her so blue.
With children at home and some married away,
She led and loved them, all in the same way.
There will come a day she will go home to the Lord,
That is the day she will collect her reward.
For her husband is waiting, she knows he's up there,
Smiling and singing at the top of the golden stairs.
Yes, life was so hard down here in this world,
But I know she will find Heaven, for she is a special girl.

Rick Joubert

I USED TO DREAM

I used to close my eyes—And dream of the good times that we once shared,
of the love, that we once had.
And the times that you said you cared.

I used to close my eyes—And dream of how nothing could keep us apart,
of the days and nights we spent together.
And how I felt, deep in my heart.

I used to close my eyes—And dream of the happiness you brought to my life,
of the smiles and laughter, that you gave me.
And how I felt, when you became my wife.

But now, as time has passed us by,
when I close my eyes the nightmares begin.
All our love has faded away,
Never to be together again.

Kathy R Hughes

MOTHERHOOD IS AN INSTINCT

To Thelma Hughes, my Christian mother.

Every woman wants to be a mother,
It often seems;
That there is no other
Sweet, single dreams.

My dream of five children
Is often known
As a thought bewilder'n
And not shown.

God made mothers.
He loved all.
There are no others
In the wilderness call.

I love my child.
Unborne or uncalled.
A call so mild
Lets me hear the unfalled.

God bless every mother
Wherever you are
There are no other
A childhood star.

Kathy R Hughes

THE LEGEND OF ELIJAH

Elijah lived on the river,
Close to a bank.
He had nobody
But the Lord to thank.

The flood waters were rising.
He climbed to the top
Of the church porch
For the rain waters to stop.

Waters came down.
He refused thrice to go
With his neighbor.
For the Lord would show.

The waters were rising.
He climbed to the top of the church,
of the steeple.
He refused aid and the rains didn't stop.
Thrice he had said, "NO," to his fellow people.

The waters came down, and, the old man died.
He, in heaven asked and the Lord replied.
"Elijah, you refused aid thrice, child dear.
Bless you, sweet darling! Now, you are here."

Mrs Millard "Gertrude Dooley" Gist

MEMORIAM TO MILLARD M. GIST, WHOSE LIFE I SHARED FOR 53 YEARS

The snow falls gently on your white magnolia tree.

Beautiful tiny red birds return each year to rear a family in the white magnolia's loving arms.

I watch from inside the large front window which we always said "was open to the world."

May God bless you. My prayers are with you as I watch, and care for, "your white magnolia tree."

J J Dickens

MASCULINE BRAVADO

As darkness dims the creepy path
Towards yon country store's far light,
I square my shoulders best I can
And swear against my present fright.
But as the light afar grows near
My courage lost now hurries back,
Until a rabbit scurries past
I darn near have a heart attack.

Polly

MAY DAY

To my beloved George.

Instead of Easter Baskets
With bunnies and eggs galore,
We made our 'love' a bouquet
And hung it on his door.

The May Queen was so lovely . . .
(We wove her a daisy crown)
And she reigned upon a dais
As ribbons 'round a May Pole wound.

But that was in my childhood:
Flowers, baskets, queen and poles
Have all long since vanished,
Only Memories Book unfolds.

I remember another May Day
When I pledged my heart away
To the one who is my May King
Pledged upon his own birthday.

So instead of hanging baskets
Filled with flowers on his door
Or dancing 'round a May Pole
I scrub his kitchen floor.

Kathleen S Suarez

THINGS I LONG TO SAY

To my husband Ismael, and my daughters Mellissa and Jennifer.

There are so many things I long to say
Unheard are they every day
No day goes by where I don't care
Love is what I'm willing to share
So many feelings kept inside
Too many feelings we try to hide
We've seen things where there's nothing we can do
That's why we were given to each other me and you
I'm here for you, I'll lend you my hand
My love will be yours forever just wait and you'll understand
Stay here and yours I'll always be
You, me, and our daughters will be happy, you'll see

Michelle Profeto

FROM THE BEGINNING

To Mark Roberts, my loving boyfriend.

From the beginning
I knew it was right.
Yes, from the very first night.

You're so special to me,
it's so hard to see,
Even though we've been together,
only a short while
Just thinking of you,
brings about a smile.

I can't remember life before you,
I don't want to think about life,
without you.

I can't express the way I feel for you,
it's totally impossible to do.

I love you more than words can say,
Please say you're here to stay.

Deborah Cheney

THE TEMPLE

The smell of death hangs sweetly in the air,
Like the scent of roses well past their prime.
Here spirits entombed in useless bodies
Patiently await the final palliative.

Here on a late summer afternoon
Rows of beds like ancient sarcophagi,
Newly hewn from ageless stone,
Brood and dream in shadowy forgotten halls.

Attended by the priests of medicine
Softly murmuring their litanies of hopelessness and despair.
Death walks these solemn halls,
Pausing at the foot of a bed,
To gently sever the last threads of life.
So that yet another shadow
May take its appointed place upon the haunted walls.

Wilma M Chastain Veroneau

SWEET SUCCESS

"Hurry! Hurry! Hurry! Hurry!"
teased the turtle to the hare
"You may think you're going to beat me, but you'll see who'll first be there.
You have always called me slowpoke; loving to make fun of me.
Thus, in this race I'll be the winner
for I'm steady as can be."

"While you're snoring,—cutting timber, I'll creep by, plod on and win.
Determination shall make me victor,"
said the turtle with a grin.
"Sweet success shall be rewarding;
I'll go down in history.
And who knows—perhaps one day
they'll erect a statue just for me!"

Carol Haslett Newiger

HERALDS

Fingers flutter in-between
Buried bulbs of bladed green
Arise, My trumpets, unfold

Give brass bugle blast
Embedded long past
Remember all years of old

From yellow throats now clear
Opening notes, we hear
Awaken, My world, behold

Cry out your soul-song
Sound the signal strong
Rebirth is at the threshold

My flares are uplifted
Our earth is regifted
God's heart in heralds of gold

His Voice by His Creation
A rising proclamation
Sense a symphony foretold

Scotty Webb

SHADOW

In memory of my brother, Robin, the sun will never set on his shadow.

Living with a legend wild and free.
Living with a shadow watching over me.

Shadow's tall.
Shadow's small.
Whatever it takes to watch over me.
When in dark, shadow glows.
When in light, shadow knows.
Shadow wraps his arms around my soul.
When the day's deeds have taken their toll.
Shadow sleeps with me late at night.
When friends are near shadow's out o' sight.
Others may think shadow's not real, he's just a fad.
But I know better; shadow lives inside of me.
And he's the best damn friend I ever had.

Arlene Vargas
APPRECIATION

Dedicated to that special person who took the time, the patience and the understanding to make a difference in my life.

I don't want to write a poem of love,
just of appreciation
'Cause when I had given up in life,
you were my salvation.
You came one day out of the blue
like it was really meant to be
And though we never planned a future, we now live happily.
You had chosen me from all the rest
So young and confused and destined toward death
You taught me stand and hold my head high
For my mistakes I have made were no cause to die
You wiped the tears from my eyes, brushed the hair from my face
Kissed me and told me my faults were no disgrace
You picked me up from where I laid so humiliated and withdrawn
You patched my self-esteem where once it had been torn.
You made me look at myself and say
"You can be what you desire
Just set your mind on target 'cause you have what it requires
So to you I write this poem, not of love but of appreciation
'Cause when I had given up in life
you were my salvation.

Gilbert Coleman
YOUR MOTHER

In Memory of my mother.

Did you ever stop and think
What she has done for you?
I mean your Mother.
She is always kind and true
More so than others.
When you are lonesome and sad
And you need a friend so bad,
She will be the best friend you ever had,
Among all others.

Dr Donald J Frey
MUSING . . . IN THE HALL OF WHITE

For my wife, Martha. For my son, Eric. For my late brother, George.

The Hall of White shivering in the spiked rays of the setting sun,
Beckon the dark phantoms of thought of deeds yet undone.
Souls beckoning with downtrodden muses,
To render upon the living, to question their users.
Shadows of long leftover images cast upon the dirty, dust-covered streets,
Waiting in silence to be heard.
A forlorn passerby scurries inside, inside a house of disrepair.
Alone in the wilderness of downcast eyes,
A happenchance meeting of two inhabitants . . . in the Hall of White.

Baroness of Dunfry
WHAT IS BEAUTY?

To the king who created beauty even in his son, and to the organization of Jehovah's Witnesses.

What is beauty you may ask?
I do know it has no mask.

Also it is simple, not bright.
It's not fancy, nor has it might.

What is the beast you can be?
Yes! This is your beauty.

Linda Widby
WINDS OF SPRING

I dedicate my poem to all humanity and especially to those who take the time to share life's precious gift "Love."

Now is a time for laughter and a time for joy for our
tears are swept away by the warm winds of spring now
show us a new life do we dare compare the old to new
for all that surrounds us life holds true, the gentle
kiss the touch of a hand brings life into his simple
plan for all to know and all to see love will last
through eternity . . . .

Ly Y, a Cambodian refugee in Boston
A DOVE OF PAPER

Dedicated to my parent and widow sisters in Cambodia who continue to suffer because of those superpowers. My wife Chantra, my only daughter Outtara and my only son, Johnny.

World flags fly float our spirit
This tall building uses for talks

You know them well, murderer
Humanity should take place

Relay on you no comfort
There is nothing you count on

Those crocodiles in water
Cambodians miss their homeland

Shut up all means your hearing
Sealing your lips none to say

The elephants went to war
Democracy or socialism

Represent who? You Hitler!
Cambodians abroad painfully

To sing to shout about evil
Secrecy has been hiding

U.N's indeed in New York
Searching for what we call peace.

Why their color hang like this?
Great risk to mess with Khmer Rouge.

To file report for complaint
All bump, all bounce into trash.

All those tigers on the land
Tried to explain, no one cares.

None advising you could choose
Gather all hay for the fire.

Roamed ripped over killed the ants
Peace in seldom plus horror.

Truth or error should you think
Christmas, holiday no good comes.

No love, no feel, no healing
Behind curtain of paper dove.

Mildred Rhodes
TO THE ONE I LOVE

God gave me a good father and a precious loving mother,
Sweet thoughtful sisters and a great supporting brothers.
He gives us each life for a span and a season,
But he sent me you for a very special reason.

In my days of sadness and my sorrowful hours,
You gave me your love with your greatest power.
I knew God love me, I didn't realize how much,
He blessed me with you with my mother's touch.

When I am sad and troubled you seem to know,
Your love like my mother you always show.
You give me your love every night and day,
You are my comfort since God took mother away.

I hope you don't wonder if I love and appreciate you,
Just hope you know it, by the little things I do.
As we grow older as those gone on before,
It makes me know within my heart I love you even more.

Our lives are filled with memories, our hearts filled with love,
Our treasures not on this earth, but in heaven above.
As the years pass and we start another year,
I want you to remember I love you very dear.

Henry Vauglé
PRIMAVERA

To Suzanne with affection.

Spring erupts,
Strutting like a peacock,
Gaudy with color,
And flaunts its cloak
Of chlorophyllic green
Before dazed eyes—
Eyes whose only light
During Winter's wake
Was the amber glow of bulbs
And electric halos of TV screens
Flickering
In darkened living rooms.

Gene Donald Parsons
SOMBER GIRL

For all the women, somber because of wounds much deeper than beauty's guise. I care and you don't ache alone.

She looks so somber,
I wonder if she knows she's beautiful?
God, she must be radiant when she smiles,
what I wouldn't give to see her smile.
Spellbound, as gazing upon fine art,
I wish she knew my thoughts;
though if I could have my wish of wishes,
I'd wish she knew
she's beautiful.

DiAnna Lyn Wheatley
HEAVEN

In Loving Memory of Bradley K. Haas. Loved and Missed Greatly . . . Forever, DiAnna.

As I looked down at his face, a tear dropped from my eye.
My heart inside was weeping as I said my last good-bye.
Eyes softly closed, he silently layed.
Take him to heaven, Lord I prayed.
Standing thee staring, I took a deep breath.
Knowing, wondering . . . am I scared of death?
I miss him, yet he is in my heart.
God is the only one who can keep us apart.

michael brown
A NEW BEGINNING

To me, she'll be a special friend;
already, this I've learned;
maybe 'twas the Fates again
allotting me rewards I've earned;
riches, in the form of she;
a friend for all eternity.

If Teddy Bears could talk to me,
she wouldn't be such a mystery.

Perhaps the day will come, she'll feel
rejoice the way I do
each and every time that she
comes briefly into view.
It cannot be so wrong to care;
of this, at least, I'm sure;
unto my heart, she has been charged;
so innocent and pure.

To transcend time, my soul is freed;
obsessed though it may be,

my heart tells me, she's worthy of
everlasting, steadfast Love.

Gary W Ellgen
THE BROOK

Dedicated to Pa, also commonly known as Da Da! My father in heaven — Love Gary.

Did you ever sit near a brook,
And sit & look, & look, & look.
Pretty soon you'll see a fish,
He'll be looking for his favorite dish.

And then a fawn will come to spawn,
By the meadow, early dawn.
The air is brisk,
A chill is in the air.
A bird flies by, lets out a cry.
You can hear the water as it falls,
Between the rocks & over logs.
On its journey to afar,
I wish I could go with it!
The air is clean & the scent is fine,
Like an expensive wine.
Flowers are tender & elegant.
All I can say is see a brook,
And take a look.
You'll fall in love, at the brook.

John J Cochrane
OH LORD, I'VE HAD MY TROUBLES

To Armond Millet, a brother in Christ.

Oh, Lord, I've had my troubles.
I've had my share of strife.
I've walked in worldly pathways
A great deal of my life.

And then one day I found Him,
The Savior of the world.
I turned my life o'er to Him
And miracles unfurled.

Oh I still have my struggles
And days of misery,
But now I have my Jesus
To go along with me.

Toni Ann Parinello
THE OCEAN

To my family. To whom I Love. Toni Ann Parinello.

One day I went to the ocean
I saw ocean waves crashing against the shore and people having fun.
I felt hot sand tickling my feet,
and cool water spraying my face.
I heard water moving and people screaming because the water was so cold.
I taste the salty air as the breeze blows against my face.
I smell the good food that my mother and father packed for lunch.
Now my senses are satisfied.

Tracy Bacon
MY POEMS

To my best friend Sue Jackson, thanks for your support. To my mother and father. Thanks for your love.

you show me your feelings,
locked up inside,
you make me laugh,
yet sometimes I've cried

your words are silent,
yet full of love,
like words of truth,
sent down from above

you're the key to peace
in all that is known
the things you say,
and things you've shown

you're the best you can be,
in all that is done
you guide the way,
in a life just begun.

You are my poems

Harriet L Gates
HOME FROM CHURCH

Of course, I'll go to church,
You didn't need to ask me!
It's the thing we always do,
And asking makes me angry.

I sing the songs, bow in prayer,
Greet the ones around me;
Listen to the Word explained,
Nod my head when I agree.

I hear, while the Pastor reads
How David, in those days of old,
Worshipped God, then went home
To BLESS his own household.

Go get the kids,—it's late!
I thought he'd never stop;
He went ten minutes overtime,
And that just makes me hot!

Isn't our dinner ready, yet?
You're so slow,—let me do that!
Why isn't the table set by now?
You kids, take out that pesky cat!

1 Chronicles 16:43
Then all the people departed
each to his house, and David
returned to bless his own
household.

Harriet L Gates
MOTHER'S DAY, A.D. 30

That day, the milling crowd
Was pressing toward the Skull,
With shouts and jeers, — few tears—
To watch Him crucified.

The day grew dark and awesome,
As from that One upon a cross
Went forth His cry,—through lips so dry—
To John, "Behold your mother!"

It wasn't, "Behold your father!"
Where was he, that awful day?
Was she a widow now,—bowed down—
Sword-pierced, as Simeon prophecied?

"Behold your mother!" it sounds again
In kindly cadence to you,
In this a later year,—do you hear—
And let yours know you love her?

John 19:29
To John He said, "Behold your
mother!" And from that hour the
disciple took her to his household.

Alice Lauffer Lawrence
AUTUMN

The fringe on the garden umbrella
Jiggles a different way
The squirrel buries a seed,
The days are shorter,
The plastic swan looks worried.
Train of consciousness—
Resounds all the time
Like strung poems
These thoughts so ephemeral
Mind pictures must be captured
Or on the evening wind away they are blow!
And an early snow gallops across the roof all night.
On waving branches
With all their leaves.

Alice Lauffer Lawrence
OPPOSITES

With my old scrapbook, I relived a youthful time,
And thought of things from way back when—
Somehow uplifting, optimistic—seeing again my prime
And these souvenirs are re-creating <u>"then."</u>
"<u>Then</u>," ah yes, you are in here too, just <u>look</u>!
But you refuse; the past with you would just intrude
These V-mail letters, photos, cards—bring back the past, though just a book.
The trip back to those days was just <u>my</u> mood.

Douglas Scott Dahar
ABSENCE OF THOUGHT

Man is not as Noble as he may seem
Standing there in the Middle of his stream

Unable to Phantom where or how it began
Completely Blind to its ultimate end

Even if his forbearers were Drown
He feels it his duty to plow the Same ground

Douglas Scott Dahar
THOUGHTS OF A TREE

What do you Think when you see a tree?
Standing so majestic and firm

A house for birds,
a squirrel or three

A phenomenon of Nature
in all her splendor and grace

A filter for the precious air we Breathe
Producing oxygen with every leaf

Shade from the sun on a long summer day
Shelter from rain on a cool stormy night

An anchor for the ground
keeping it from tumbling into the sea

Food for Caterpillars, Locust, or Moths
Causing us to spray at all costs

Whatever your thought,
It does not concern me

Since I am the owner of this
particular tree
and only see

Paper!

D M Lee
SUMMER TRAVELS

For my loving Aunt whose confidence in me helped me through the tough times in my life. To her I am deeply grateful.

The day dawned bright and fair,
As I prepared to take a trip in the air.
Summer vacation was here at last
And I was afraid it would go too fast!
To summer camp I must go,
To stay a week or so;
Then over to Grandma's house to stay
And wish her a happy birthday.
A stay at a lake for a row in a boat,
Then I must hurry and grab my coat!
I cannot stay in one place for too long,
Nor can I stop and sing a song!
Over the river and fields I ride
Next to the ocean at evening tide.
But alas! Here it is time again
For my schoolwork to begin.
The school year may be near,
But a wonderful summer is coming next year!

Ruth F Wright
THE FAMILY OF GOD

To my daddy, W. L. Foster.

Christ walks beside me
Wherever I go
I know He loves me
He tells me so.
He will never leave me
As long as I'm true.
And stay with His followers
For they are so few.

Christ walks beside me
Wherever I go
I know He loves me
He tells me so.
He will never leave me
As long as I'm true.
Our lives will be prosperous
And successfully through.

Christ walks beside me
Wherever I go
I know He loves me
He tells me so.
He will never leave me
As long as I'm true.
He will give us the blessing
And victory too.

Jon K Evans
EVANS LAW
<u>(written in 1981 before the days of "crack" and AIDS)</u>

To Jazz-Soul singer Gil Scott Heron. I imagined his singing this poem in the key of C and to the rhythm of "Johannesburg."

So you think you're not a man unless you've got yourself a jones
Evan if it reduces you to a set of skin and bones

Seems the only solution if you feel just like a slug
is shoot up snort or smoke but take a few hits of a drug

So you're thinking 'bout how you can get into that squeeze
But you're too dumb to think of preg-nan-cy or some VD

Gil Scott said it best when he rapped 'bout that Angel Dust
Yet you mess with it and in it you will put your trust

If you believe that you'll control the number of your drinks
Then you'll become an Alco faster than you'll ever think

For feeling good you'll drop yourself a very pretty penny
Instead of realizing one hit can be one too many

If it sure can thrill you it can turn around and kill you
If it seems like fun you'll be a disappointed one

If you read and start to ask that magic question "why?"
If it can get you high you just might die

Alta M Martin
MISSING YOU

To Atchison and Williams.

November 9th. 1988, I lost a friend that day
Our good Lord just took him away.
He paid his dues, served his time here on earth
We are richer by far having known him

He was a friend to man since birth,
April 6th. 1989, was another sad day,
My bowling friend was taken away.
As one grows older, and years pass you by
It's hard to big one's good friends Good Bye.
But such is life, it has to be that way,
Just be thankful for each passing day.

Ralphie Dawning
WINTER CHILL (Out-in Great Lakes)

To my youthful friends, who are ongoing life itself . . .

Came the first week of November,
Since I saw the bright westerly sunshine,
Roaming across the land till Christmas time,
I knew nothing about Ice, Snow, a-pouring,
Not until I almost lost this life sublime;
One night I cruise thru — the snowy weather,
Looking from sky to streets it fell,
Now it's blowing breeze, later on it's snow and sleet,
Looking beyond the road, only loneliness threaded that was noted;
Making haste would be wasting, life in accidents on the snowy threading,
Make your left turn, make your right turn, which way will it be,
But make your life a better hold, grip onto it for note,
Sooner or later the weather on life is made, to a dream deserved, to forever hold;
Life's a changing, so go on trudging,
Make what one must come up to, today, for tomorrow,
To a better, bright, "morrows,"
Perhaps, when all is done, beyond the horizon,
What was made, will all be undone . . . adieu . . .

Irving Levinson
A HURRICANE

This Poem is dedicated to Sylvia, my darling daughter.

A tornado, a storm, and strong winds wide
Torrential rain and high tide
Rivers everywhere overflown
In the streets with boats rowen

A destruction of houses down to the ground
Here and there to be found
A devastation by nature done
Everything destroyed and forever gone.

People had to move to higher land
For children to live and play on dry sand
Life has to start its course again
How, with what, where and when?

And yet houses must be built from its new
But financial help may come from who?
Food, lights, and gas for cooking need now
Would the government be interested their faces to show?
To provide the necessary items to live?
For families something to give?

Nature has for centuries the human race ignored
Wondering, whether that is a punishment by the Lord.

Irene Mary Larson
THOSE GREAT OLD DAYS OF THE PAST

To family and friends.

Let's remember—those great old days of the past with all our happy memories from our childhood with family and friends as we were close and we didn't have much—but was enough—as we had each other and we were happy—with what we had—as we'll always cherish those happy memories of our growing up together as the great old days from the past in our lives.

Basilisa L Halog

Basilisa L Halog
THE FIRST "WORLD OF POETRY" CONVENTION

It took lots of preparation
To gather poets around the world
Who would attend the convention
And have their fantasies unfurled.

The M-G-M was selected
To receive the congregation
This Casino really made it
Two thousand plus . . .
accommodation.

The poets have come from near and far
From North to South and East to West
Some came by plane and some by car
I took the bus, I think it's best.

I'm glad I signed up to attend
This first poetry convention
I know each one has found a friend
With lots of imagination.

This affair I will remember
For I was given an award
As a GOLDEN POET of the YEAR
A distinction of high regard.

Gyne V Johansen
THE KISS

For William, who lights my world.

One sweet, soft kiss and I am outside myself
flying through the clouds
intoxicated by this
intoxicating kiss.

Nectar is not so sweet, nor the ripest fruits,
nor the greenest young grasses,
as your kiss.

The freshest bloom in all the world is not so
soft or red
as your lips.

The virgin blush of dawn is not so pure.

Please, let me walk the dangerous line
Between your pleasure and the swift mirage of
fleeting time.
Let me drift between the ecstasies you give.
Just for one moment let me live
Inside your kiss.

It comes to this:
I love you.

Ricky Powers
ON THE CROSS

To my mother, Faye Powers, with love.

You think of work and have a boss
But one man died, it was on the cross
When being a Christian, it is no loss
On people's mind should be on the cross
When in sin there is a good loss
Turn to Christ who died on the cross
When reading the Bible is no loss.

Four books of the gospel tells Christ dying on the cross
I guess the soldiers thought they would win
Christ on the cross saves people from sin
Christ on the cross there really was no loss
But try to keep in mind, Christ on the cross
When people work and think of the boss
Remember, Christ died for sin, it was on the cross.

Dolly Marchesani
ONE

As I sit in the cool green
grass covered with evening dew,
I look up at the full moon
and
think of you.
Alone, as I.
Wishing to be with you
as One
Together.

Molly Franks
FRIENDSHIP

This poem is dedicated to all of the people who have shown their friendship to me by staying with me through some very difficult times.

What's the true meaning of friendship?
A friend is there for you,
Through thick and thin.
They listen to your every need.

A friend keeps everything,
That's told to them a secret.
A friend doesn't judge,
You on your problems.

A friend only cares,
About how you feel.
Not on how you act,
Or how you look.
A friend never leaves,
When you're having a crisis.
They stay with you,
Until your crisis passes.

If you are a friend,
Then you would return the favor.
You would be there if,
Your friend is having a crisis.

Alfred C Barza
TO GOD WITH LOVE

To my mother.

Imagine all the minds open to love
No darkness in the road of fate
No obstacles for the individual freedom
People walking in the streets of happiness;
Imagine the shooting stars falling brightly into the ocean
Cosmic sand turning into a rainbow
Prisoners crossing the barriers of the prisons
War tanks melting in the sun;
imagine all religions hand in hand
No remembrance of sad things
Money in the hands of the poor
Everybody working and laughing.

Pamela H Woodruff
NAMELESS FRIEND

Who is he? This unnamed friend — his name you do not know.
The only time one speaks to him is just to say "Hello!"
He passes by and with but a grin,
Makes life look a little less dim.
He rarely speaks — it's just a smile,
But his message lasts for quite awhile.
This nameless friend — who can he be?
He's someone just like you or me.
He cares about life — it's just his style,
You know this for he's never without a smile.
This nameless friend; he wants no glory,
No one need ever tell his story.
A smile, a grin, a laugh — just see,
To someone else a nameless friend you'll be.

Stacey Rhymer
THE PICTURE

The picture in his wallet was a picture of me.
There were no other pictures in there just the one of me.
I started at the picture and it stared back at me.
And I wondered why he shared it with me?
He told me he did love me. He told me he cared.
He told me he didn't know how to show his feelings or the way he cared.
Not all people can say in words what they feel.
So some people say it in other ways which are real.
Yes he was my Father who I thought didn't care,
But the picture in his wallet showed that yes he did care and would always be there.
Yes I loved you Father and I know you loved me.
For the picture in your wallet showed me.

Jenny Bender
MEMORIES OF A BEDTIME STORY

To My Father, who left his coffee spoons laying around the house.

The coffee bead in the teaspoon
reminds me of my childhood
I want to write a story but
my body is stiff.
I want to see myself but
I have escaped my structure
Nothing shows me the
right words
I see myself rocking back
and forth in the middle of
a room
I hear the music
But nothing is real and
silence is scarier than a continuous
nothingness kept alive by the
sadness
set to a beat.
I am not sure if I still
want to write a story, unless
I can write myself into it

Allison Teel
A BETTER PLACE
Our world,
A world of beauty; yet,
Also a world of pain.
A world full of friendship; yet,
Also a world full of enemies.

How does this happen?

A world so full of diversity.
We should unite, not fight.
We should be friends, not enemies.
A lot of people have tried
To make this world come together.

But we must all fight.
Because this world belongs to us all.

Eva Jane Shelswell-White
UPON A WINTER'S WAR
Bitter December on the sea
Makes a lonely man of me.
Tonight we enter Capricorn
And I'll be far by Christmas morn.

No crackling fire or Noel wreath
No comforter to sleep beneath.
No wassail warmed to make a toast
To Father, Son and Holy Ghost.

The carolers I hear tonight
Are far beyond a plain man's sight.
Voices of angels in the waves,
Sing for other souls who gave.

This ship, she rocks my weary head
I long for my love's arms instead.
But all that stirs my heart this night
Is the bitter cup that holds my plight.

Oh, Winter stars above the sea
Shine down upon my love and me.
For unto this war I must depart
Leaving life and my love's heart.

Alex A Calderón
ENDLESS APHOTIC WAY

To the ones I love, "For I will only live once."

Your shadows live inside of me
They're hunting me
They're pushing me
And holding my breath
With your shapeless lips
Your oppressive reflection
Chasing me and shoving me
Deep inside the dark.

Your poisoning lips
Senseless words telling me
Stories I can't resist
Your dangerous ways to make me
Feel like I never did
I'm thinking, I'm trying
For my freedom I'm crying.

All the dark voices
Are screaming my name
Dark voices everyone belongs to you
I need to breathe away from it.

I'm losing my sleep
Go away from me
You're digging deep and then deeper
And endless aphotic hold in the
ground
Like a witch hunting
For another heart
You fly away in the night
But still you're after me
And I get so scared in silence

Your priceless love
Took my world aside
And the impulsion to run
Screams to release my voice
To hold my own
To make my own choice
Without the endless aphotic way.

K R F L
LOOKING IN THE MIRROR

This poem is dedicated to Sylvia, my dear wife.

Together we looked into
the mirror, with a heart
And what did we see, two
budding young flowers both
rearing to be
We had known each other,
since we were small
We fell in love, and had a great big
ball.

We then got married, to begin a new
life,
Oh it was heaven, just like
paradise
The children they came as fast
as can be
But we made life happy it
was meant to be

We had very happy times.
And
many lean ones too
But we stayed together and
weathered them through.
When looking back at those
lean years gone by,
With much pride and joy I know that
I am satisfy.

If we could reverse our steps,
And start all over again.
I guess we would travel the
same road,
Without much change.

Today we look in the
same
mirror, with a heart
Forty years, from when we first
start.
And what did you think we see,
Two fading old flowers,
But as happy as can be.

K R F L
MAKING UP
As I sit across the table; an look into
your eyes
It reminds me so much, of those
happy days gone by
It was loving in the day, an
ecstasy at night
You cannot deny, it was a
great delight.

How did it go wrong,
maybe you can tell
I guess you will blame me,
for all that
did not go well.
I was madly in love with you
then, as
I am still now
If only we could mend the bridges,
And start anew somehow.

I could make it up to you now,
In many different ways.
Just say the words I'd like to
hear
That could begin our happy
days

God created us in this world,
To be forgiving, loving, and kind.
So why can't it be this way,
My love; just be mine.

K R F L
SOMETIMES
Sometimes we wake up in the
morning
Depress in every way,
Who knows the reason why,
No one yet can say.

Sometimes we wake up in
the
morning
Anxious to meet a new day,
Feeling zestful all the time
And only want to play.

You'll sing in the shower
And have a spring in your feet,
If you wake up each morning
With a goal you can reach.

Why can't all mornings be
the same
Who can really tell
It's a human weakness deep inside
Which makes us so dissatisfy.

God should have made us all
Feeling and looking just the same,
Then we would not have had a
chance
To have so much complain.

Jean Joanne Richards
OLD FRIEND
Hello, Old Friend,
It's nice to see you again.
I've missed you,
I've thought about you,
I've wondered how you've been.
Hello, Old Friend,
It's nice to see you again.

It's times like these I've wondered
why,
When you've meant so very much to
me,
Why all the years have passed us by.
How can that be?
Hello, Old Friend,
It's nice to see you again.

Janice Lynn Pryor
GOLDEN WORDS
Into the mystic sea,
I throw words of wisdom
written in gold,

and who shall be
the words received,
will find truth
and happiness,
written by
thee

Jann Elwood
CONQUERING FRUSTRATION
When I was a child
I loved to draw
I drew a stick person
And liked what I saw

As an adult
I'm learning to draw
I know what I want
I know what I saw.
It sure doesn't look
Like the picture I took,
It doesn't look real
Like the one in the book.

Why can't I draw
The picture I saw?!

When I was a child
I knew what I wanted
And happy was I
When I got it.

Perhaps if I liked
The pictures I draw
I'd draw more . . . like I wanted.

Arthur Lara
I LOOK BACK NOW

To Veronica.

I look back now at my hurt past,
When I didn't know how long the
pain would last.
I don't understand why I held on so
long,
When knowing that loving you was
feeling so wrong.
There were always things about you
that I will never know,
Feelings inside you, that you would
never show.
Some say it's better to have loved
than to have loved at all,
But pain proved it differently when
we began to fall.
Now I pray for myself not to dream
anymore,
Of the woman I had loved the most
once before.
A lesson learned is all I've left to say,
For now it's time to turn my head and
walk the other way.
And time always has its way of
making things work out,
I know who I am now, and what
love's all about.
For you I only wish you're never
lonely or ever sad,
I hope you never have to wish for
something you never had.
Yes my love I lost you, I'll never
know how,
I only know it's over as I look back
now.

Arthur Lara
SEPARATED LOVE

To Michelle, my good friend.

When times are hard and there seems
no end,
Think about me and the love I send.
The love I send which is deep in my
heart,
Will keep me alive while we are apart
While we are apart we've set each
other free,
A love test God gave to you and to
me.
And now we know what miles can
do,
To a love that's separated, divided by
two.

So if perhaps we can't pass this test,
Lord let us know we've tried our best.
And friends we'll become if we fail you see,
To a love that separated and not meant to be.

Kathleen Haviland
CLEO

Once on a time, we had a cat.
Cute, furry, funny — all of that,
Waving long tail switching gold,
Blue eyes, long whiskers, a sight to behold.

She'd run down the hall, jump 'gainst the wall
Leap right back and pretend to fall.
Turn somersaults on nap of the rug,
Grab soft toys she loved to hug.

She's run up for a drape and hang esque,
And hope for a sign of quick rescue.
She's roll and tumble and leap over a chair
She's arch her back and bristle her hair.

She'd chase a grasshopper or a mouse,
She reigned supreme within our house,
In angelic sleep, she'd nap in her bed,
A halo of gold surrounding her head.

Then she'd awaken and off she'd go,
Right out from under the gold halo.
She was up and over-down and back.
Once she placed kittens right into my hat.
Did you ever hear of such a cat as that?

Christine Warren
TOGETHER AT LAST

I dedicate this poem to Tony, whose love always meant the most to me, whose love I will never forget, and who I want to know "I remember you."

Hearing your name brings a smile to my face
Forever and always, my heart will hold your place
We've been together before, and again we are together
This time if we are lucky, it will be forever
So many people in my life have come and gone
But I always think of you when I hear our special song
Hearing that song makes me think of you and me
The way things are, the way they ought to be
I care enough of you so that you're in my every thought
I remember when I used to see you, I thought you had forgot
The good times we shared, the times we had cared
Thinking you forgot used to get me scared
But now I know far from your memory I will never be
Because I am special to you, as you are to me.

Paul Hugh Turner
UNDER THE MOON

While in the woods alone at night,
By my campfire burning bright;
Strumming my guitar and humming a tune,
At peace with the world out under the moon:

Only the creatures to hear my tune,
While singing and playing out under the moon;
Not a care or a worry to think of tonight,
Just me and the moon that's shining so bright:

In a tree way up high over my head,
Is a squirrel that's playing while I make my bed;
Not a care or in danger while sitting at rest,
With only that wind to blow on his nest:

Yet the creatures and I are having a time,
With the ending of song; I'll stop and I'll dine;
Then lay down to rest and let nature swoon,
While alone here tonight out under the moon:

Chadwick Blaine Johnson
HORNS OF DESPAIR RING OUT THROUGH THE CITY

Horns of despair ring out through the city's polluted air,
They cough and breathe death, yet there is no care.

Money is made, money is changed, that's what counts —
No need for it to be rearranged.

Cash is here, cash is there,
Magical transport only awaits a green fare.

Money is great, money is stable,
Without it we see you as useless and unable.

Escape I must — if not my soul is sure to bust,
Crushed by the green monster, he will starve and die,
for his kind there will be no need to cry.

Riches in heaven is what was sought,
Here there were no goods worth to be bought.

Horns of despair ring out through the city's polluted air,
They cough and breathe death, yet there is no care.

For money is their god,
A god they wish not to share.

Elizabeth Chapman-Nagy
RIDING THE DREAM

For my husband son,
For the new life you have given me—
I couldn't be happier.

I long to be a silver fox
Loping 'cross the snow;
Or an eagle with feathered wings to spread
And a will to come and go.

I long to have the freedom
Of a mustang in the wild;
The carelessness of a summer breeze,
Or the innocence of a child.

I wish the fragrance of a winter's eve
Alone, to have, was mine.
I want to go where I want to go
Without the push of time.
But the obstacle of a working day
Is all I have before me.
No hopes, no dreams, but lots of fears
Are always waiting for me.

I need to see a brand-new day,
With nothing else to do;
With no desire to go or stay,
But just to be with you.

Evelyn L Sweeney
LIFE

When your world turns upside down
With everything topsy-turvy and turning brown,
It's time for order and to start anew
By forgetting the days you were lonely and blue.
Now face the unknown future with hope
By doing it will help you cope.
Be thankful for the memories long past.
Start on new ones with a different cast,
For time heals everything so I've been told
But it can't keep you from getting old.

So dig in with the vigor of youth,
It is then you will learn the truth —
That life is what you make of it.
Just smile, you shall reap the benefit.
Fill the days with love, joy, and peace.
Before very long you will be at ease.
Then your memories will become pure pleasure
To be put away as very special treasure,
For then life will be at its best
And no longer a struggling test.

Margaret Halpin
A JUST CAUSE

To the American Indian, who dearly loved this beautiful land, and respected its ecology.

This land is mine the Indian claimed,
And to stranger he exclaimed!
"We lived in peace before you came
To chase us from our beloved terrain,
But someday we'll return again
To claim our birthright, and remain."

Serena Gaspin
FRIENDS . . .

To my dearest friend Shawn . . .

Friend . . .

Are there when you are down and blue
When you just don't know what to do.
I can call on you to chase away my blues,
A friend is one just like you.

By now you know you can count on me
Whatever the reason may be.
I would climb a mountain or swim a sea,
To help you in your time of plea.

Friends are two people like you and me
Who can laugh and play with joy and gleam.
Then we stop to look and see,
That friends is what we will always be.
Others will never have a clue
Of the kind of friend I see in you.
You mean more to me than you could ever know,
And I know our friendship will always show.

Jodi Redford
RITES OF SPRING

I hear the wind echo within my mind. I stare into darkness until I might go blind. I taste the bitter steel of the cold, and gasp as it tightens its hold. I touch the sun as it turns the sky aflame, knowing that after this moment I will never be the same. I soar up above the clouds and bubble with laughter so strong, and all around me the air is suddenly filled with song. Freedom dances within each vein, and gone is the loneliness that caused such pain. Disappeared is the child who shivered in fright. Reborn is the soul who has found the light.
Far below I have left behind the huddled few, and whispered upon the wind is a prayer that I once knew. There is only one small boy who looks to the sky, watching in interest as I continue to fly. I spread my wings and swoop and glide with a newfound grace. Nothing is more beautiful than the smile that lights up his face. The Season of Shadow passes below each wing, and now finally I've reached the First Rites of Spring.

N L Studebaker
SUMMER WALK

A gold and silver sunset
Glows through blackening trees;
The mother and her daughter walk
With hands entwined, at ease.

And on this summer evening
Their souls are set on fire,
To think that God would care enough
Such friendship to inspire.

Someday the daughter hopes to bless
Her own child with this love:
A chain unbroken through the years,
A gift from heaven above.

Roberta Cosper
BLOSSOMS

For William A. Rose, written 7/18/86.

Desperately we cling
to beauty,
to vision,
to passion,
For in our hearts we know ourselves
To be mortal.

The scent of the blooming rose
Already hints at decay.

Tremulous, we stand so poised:
our fragile art an epigram
to naked summer.

Richard Raby
AN ANSWER

An Answer

White line into doom,
A female,
Receiving satin on rough skin,
Contradictions in one.

Will there ever lie an answer
In the sinuous curves of women?
Don't answer, Don't question

If you're a man.

The absurd philosophers wilt
In the face of pain,
In the pane of face,
Is love the answer?

Is love an answer?

Michael Anthony Fasick

Michael Anthony Fasick (Age 11)
HELP THE WORLD TO BE DRUG FREE
Drugs are a slow painful suicide
And really only last for a five-minute high.

If you take drugs you aren't really cool,
In fact if you use—you're a big dumb fool.

Now hear my message loud and clear,
You don't need crack, cocaine, dope or beer.

Now does everybody catch my drift?
You don't need drugs to give you a lift!

Michael Anthony Fasick (Age 11)
AT HOME IN GOD'S FOREST
For the beautiful deer
And the leaves on the trees.

Upon this splendid sight,
I fall to my knees.

Animals hidden in trees,
Small insects gnawing on leaves.

When the wind blows,
You see the earth sweep.

Without the forest,
I would surely weep.

Moonlit night so brilliant in awe,
I wake in the morning,
To the large orange ball.

Another day of God's great earth,
Another day of living birth.

Comfortable at last,
My worries have past.

David Allen Ransby
WHAT'S A TRUE FRIEND
A friend is someone who is true, who will be there for you when you're sad and blue. A true friend helps pick you up when you're feeling down, hangs in there with you, tries to always be around, makes you smile when you frown. A true friend it doesn't matter, when you're in need of help, they wouldn't mind, then again a true friend is sometimes hard to find. A true friend is someone you don't necessarily have to win, but will be there for you through thick and thin, that's a true friend.

Charron M Daughtry
WHAT COLOR IS MY SIN
To the outside world I am a black person.

My family heritage is made up of Afro-American, Indian and Caucasian.

The blood in my veins runs as red as any man or woman.

I love life.

I want peace.

I need mankind.

I have learned it's ok to love myself.

So, I begin to ask the world,

What color is my sin?

Margaret W Cunningham
AS NATURE SINGS
I followed a sparkling, mountain stream,
Wending its merry way,
Through cool deep woods
Flecked with golden sunbeams,
Where frolicking squirrels were at play.
In this quiet retreat,
Where men and God meet,
All troubles and cares stand at bay.
I rested on velvety moss 'neath a tree
And dreamed pleasant dreams, ere so long:
Till the birds in this haven
So happy and free,
Broke the silence with beautiful song:
So I joined in, and the wind harps played;
I'm sure you could call it a hymn,
Giving thanks to our God
Who created this day,
And a place to commune with Him.

Rich 1ST
DRUG RELATED PARENTS
Some parents are and some parents aren't to blame,
Others can and others can't bare the shame.
Is the fault of the raising of the child because of me,
Or has he or she got caught up in a drug roaring sea?
Do these parents try to think of a way to face a friend,
Or put drug problems of their child to an ever-lasting end?
Should I worry about how to tell my husband or wife,
Or should I speak up to save my child's life?
Tell me please if it were your situation and left up to you,
I must speak out very clear and extremely loud,
Do the right thing and save the life of my child.
The road will be all uphill and very rough,
But I'll never give in no matter how hard or how tough.

Scott McKinnon Robinson
SWEET DREAMER

To my son Tyler and wife Kimberly. In loving memory of William Kerr and Flora Robinson.

Sweet dreamer you live in a world where nothing is real but the feelings you feel. Your love you share is beyond compare of those who are around you. You do so much for such little in return. You think of yourself you'll just never learn. But, sweet dreamer stay good my friend; we'll see you in the end.

Debra L Fisher
TATIANA
through time you touch the hearts of many
allowing all pretense shed
telling us everything will be alright
incouraging each and every dream come true
always smiling so tender
ninety-nine percent of continuous support
all having cherished pages of time — for this is Tatiana

Marjorie C Anguish
THIRTEEN

To Jennifer—my granddaughter, one of my greatest treasures.

'Twas never hard, until this year, to find a gift for "Jen,"
It was real easy when your birthdays numbered ten!
And all the years that came before,
Why I had ideas by the score.
But, this special day is different,
it seems just like a dream,
For, suddenly, like magic you've turned into a "Teen!"
We love you, just like always, and of course, we always will.
But when birthdays reach Thirteen,
there is a special thrill!
Now Mom and Dad are still important
and Gram and Grandpa too,
But with school, sports, and special friends
we might rate #2!
So as you grow into a beautiful young lady,
and dance evenings on your toes,
Just stay sweet and special,
like a rare and lovely rose!

Bishop Basil Tellou
THE KISS OF THE UNIVERSE
Oh, my God!
The terror
in the night,
in the heart of life!
The terror.
What?
The Holy Grail?
The Philosopher's Stone?
The Spiritual Rosetta Stone?
All the same.
The terror
in the night,
in the death of night.
And the Light,
whirling and whirling,
more like a fast, rhythmic
tick–tock . . .
the Light.
The terror comes,
by grace.
The Light. By grace.
Make a home
for terror.
Terror brings knowledge.
The terror,
by grace.
The Holy Grail,
The Philosopher's Stone,
The Spiritual Rosetta Stone.
Comes
the terror,
by grace.
The whirling, fast and
rhythmic tick–tock Light.
Make a home
for terror.
The whirling Light.
Oh, my!
GOD!!!

Jeanette Burrus
HEAVEN'S GIFT

To my three "loves," John, April & Kellie.

when I think of heaven
you know what I see?
a beautiful rose garden
waiting for me
under the trellis
I will be
taking care of roses
for eternity
in the center of the garden
there sits my lord
a rose in each hand
as my reward
red stands for his blood
that was shed for me
the white one for
his soul of purity
no perfume will I wear
except the fragrance of the roses
that surrounds me there
so when I die
please do not grieve
God is in the rose garden
it's time for me to leave.

Rocco Gomez
A SONNET OF DEATH

To my beloved wife Armeda and my son Roderick. Both are now in a world of peace beyond all suffering.

Oh, death you stalk the paths of life
Like a purring cat
That has stalked his prey.
You drift amidst life's scenes of strife
Knowing full well when life your hand will stay.
Life and death balanced like a pendulum swaying to and fro
Then suddenly, you messenger of grief
Decide when life's last breath shall go.
When will it be, you thief of life so brief
That this sickle you wield
Shall one day be no more
And allow the fruits and harvests
Of our meager life
To one day be allowed to store

Robert Rosales
WHAT'S HAPPENED TO YOU?
Where is that smile I've grown to adore?
Why don't you have that twinkle in your eyes anymore?
Why does it seem that you're so far away?
Why do I see those tears falling everyday?
Why are you so sad, that words could never begin to say?
It hurts me so bad to see you this way.
So please can't you tell me
what's happened to you,
And just maybe my friend I can help
you no longer be blue!!!

Lloyd "Forever" Young
RETURN TO THE GLEN

I long for another look
at my haven in the glen,
the stony path beside the brook
and the wildflowers once again;
I knew it in my childhood,
a secret place for dreams,
the solemn oak in quietude
shared my thoughts it seems;
Stately pines to guard my flank,
whispering, singing, sometimes still,
soaring birds o'er yonder bank,
the flaming maple on the hill;
I've been far and long away
and once again I'll see
the hideaway of another day
that had its hold on me;
But is it still the same,
magic, as I knew it then?
Was it but a child's game
played only in the glen?

Forrest J Baroni
BIRTHDAY WISHES

Chocolate ice cream and some cake,
Colored ribbons made of crepe.
Giggles and bright eyes do show,
Tiny wishes in a blow.

Smoke from candles quickly pass,
So young dreams thought in a flash;
Replaced by new surprise and awe,
With each new discovery saw.

As the years go passing by
Birthdays hold no new surprise.
Rather dreams may disappoint,
When we gaze at candles burnt.

But make a wish they do proclaim,
Though you know it is in vain.
Make it so no one may hear;
Is that purpose to you clear.

Chocolate ice cream and some cake,
Colored ribbons made of crepe.
Smiles and eyes do seldom show,
What we do already know.

Robert C Campbell
UNDER THE NEON TIGHTROPE

On certain nights we gathered . . .
Down by the club
Kamchatka's red label burning raw
Russian lullabies
down our easy throats

We bounced crazy dreams off the pavement
and watched them fly thru the singing wires
where Edison still ghostly walked

Quartz-lites played a sad substitute for stars
Aloof above the bats darting high in a moonless sky

Indigo patterns like ghastly Vida's lashes
Taunting
Under the neon tightrope

Cynthia Cunningham
WINTER WONDERS

To my husband, Tom, for his encouragement and love.

Sleep gently, my loved one,
The boughs are laden with snow
And creatures sleep by our fireside
For want of a place to go.

The tender fleece of the snow queens
Is dancing at our door.
They sweep across the windowpane
To fall on the forest floor.

A slumbering stump is covered
By the latest downy cloak,
And the wind whispers a love song
Whose words are seldom spoke.

The ferny green of the underbrush
Is now as white as a dove.
And here it is, my darling
I whisper my words of love.

Beth Underberg
PROMISE

I promise in every step you take
I will be with you.
I promise in every strive you take
I will meet you half way.
I promise that you will have my love and my blessings in everything you do.
I promise my life to you in the hope you will someday do the same.

Norma Bromley
A DREAM

Your dream has ended, your world won't mend
And when a dream comes to an end
There is no happiness for you
Therefore as your spirits sink
Your world is lost, so then you think.
Your final song may be sung
Worst things happen, you're not so young
Just turn a corner, wow it's there
Song and music in the air, and now after all the pain,
There's a good song once again
Your dreams—once bad and Black—
Are making rainbows, Don't look back

K Blair
GO, FOR ME

This is dedicated in honour of my "Mum" who made that flight to "freedom beyond" on March 8, 1989. I make my ascension to greater spheres with her spirit and faith forever the "wind beneath my wings."

You said, "Go, my baby."
"Go, for me."
I went assuredly.

I knew in you
The hopes you held
Were for the good of me.

But, on that day
You gave me wings
I knew not what would be.

For on the next
You turned your head
And flew away from me.

Our dream is cast.
You will's complete,
And honoured valiantly.

And when I'm challenged
I'll forever hear
Your commanding, "GO, FOR ME!"

Trina Cramer
WHAT ARE GRANDPAS FOR?

Grandpas are for bouncing on knees,
for climbing on, for hugging.
Grandpas are for telling no sense secrets to,
for laughing with, for singing.
Grandpas are for candy when mom says no,
for lollypops, for ice cream.
Grandpas are for telling you how pretty you are,
how sweet, how loving.
Grandpas are for those special talks,
of hopes, of dreams,
Grandpas are for sitting with together,
in cool breezes, in summer rain.
Grandpas are for a glimpse of the past,
the present, the promise of future.
Grandpas are for the nudge in life,
the happy, the sad.
Grandpas are for learning things,
the truth, the wisdom.
Grandpas are for children,
Grandpas are for cherishing,
Grandpas are for loving.

Steven R Hanzlik
BOB

Bob,
I've carried you many miles my friend!
And now here we are.
Your family and friends,
To lay you down to rest!
God didn't take you away from us!
He just put you in a better place!
Your body is here,
Your spirit is in Heaven.
And also in our hearts!
We've been through a lot my friend,
And I'm sure you're still watching over me!
We've went through the good,
And the bad together!
You weren't just my friend,
You were more like family!
When I die,
I know you'll be there,
To welcome me!
Thanks Bob!

James C Archer
THE WIZARD

This poem is a special dedication to my daughter, Dana.

The Wizard rides a silver star across a darkened sky.
He travels to the Land of Sleep to see King Lullaby.
King Lullaby has problems, some of which he cannot mend.
The Wizard brings the answer for King Lullaby, his friend.
For on his side, the Wizard wears a pouch that is made of gold.
And in this pouch he brings the sands of time, both new and old.
But the Wizard he must hurry, for the sun is about to fall.
He must help those little children, for they have had no sleep at all.
When the Wizard makes the Land of Sleep, the sun begins to hide.
He reaches for the pouch that he has carried on his side,
He sprinkles out the sand, and as it falls down through the air,
It brings to each and every child a golden teddy bear.

Becky Lee Noland
A MYSTERY OF THE RAIN

This poem is for my first true love.

I looked out my window and saw the rain,
it hit the glass and trickled down the pane.
My love for you is like the rain,
I see your pictures and feel pain.
I read your letters again and again,
and think about you day out and day in.
You are the one I'll always love,
I wish you felt that same strong love.
I opened the window and smelt the rain,
and that took away a lot of my pain.
I let the rain hit me in the face,
like a mystery without a trace.
I wish I could see your face,
and find the mystery's trace.

Sue Malec
ARTIST

In a state of mind
In an egotistical world
There is a person
A person who carries themself
In an eccentric manner

Within this person
Within their soul
There is a distinguished thought
A thought of imagination

Lisa Robinson
MOTHER

To: A very special mother, Mrs. Lora Robinson.

You took me in, I was young and wild
You treated me like your very own child
I wish I could make the whole world see
Just how much you mean to me
My mother's been gone for quite some time
But I love you, just like mine
Peace for you is such a high cost
For without you we'd all be lost
Everyone loves you so very much
You bring love to those you touch
Though we'll miss you, I have to say
I hope you'll be happy someday
I know for you there is no cure
but God will help us this I'm sure
I hope this shows how we feel
And how it helps the pain to heal

I love you!

Emma "Noon" Reed
LONELY OLD HOBO

While traveling down the highway with no special place to go,
I found myself a'talking to a lonely old Hobo.
He didn't mind that he was walking, for a ride he didn't care,
And when I spoke of loved ones, it brought a great big tear.

I knew that he was living in a world of long ago,
A loved one he was missing, and he finally told me so.
God once gave me someone to love, to honor, and obey.
I wonder why so carelessly, I let it slip away.

The day that we were married and she became my wife,
I promised God to love and cherish her for life.
I know that she was faithful, she loved me all the way,
But, I so very foolishly was soon to go astray.

I started staying out all night, I left her home alone,
I did not mean to break my vows, or

jeopardize my home.
But she was Oh—so trusting and I was having fun,
I only realized too late, the damage I had done.

One night when I was dancing with someone I never knew,
I got a pang of conscience that I wasn't being true.
I left my partner on the floor, as I ran out the door,
Praying every moment she would meet me as before.

As my footstep hit the threshold, I knew that she was gone,
A note pinned on my pillow confirmed my every wrong.
So all these years I'm searching for the long lost love I knew,
That's the reason I'm a Hobo, lonely and so blue.

Lucinda Baker
ME
If I told you what it's like to be me
would you listen?
If I told you how I feel
would you care?
Would you take time to see me, reach inside, get to know me
Hold my hand as I cry in despair.
It's hard to say how long it's been
when my sleep has not been marred.
My mind is all jumbled, it races and spins
and my way into peace is barred.
So many nights I have lain wide awake
as the fear and the darkness enfold me.
"Please wake up" I shout. "please listen."
Can you feel me, still see me?
This is hard to imagine
even harder to explain.
So in silence I'm trapped
alone with this fear and my pain.

Beverly L Bassler

Beverly L Bassler
WHAT IS GOLF . . . TO ME

To my best friend and husband, Ronald J.

Propelling a ball with the use of a club
is a silly thing to do.

Tho most would agree it's jolly good fun
but why, I've nary a clue.

It sits on a stick then you loft it in air —
and not always see where it's going.

You get in your cart and drive all around
'til out of the rough — there, it's showing!

You chip it out with this thing called an iron
'til again you're back on the fairway.

You chase it some more with a couple of strokes —
what you're think of course, you don't dare say.

You at last see a flag sticking out of a hole,
and the goal is for something called par.

You count up your strokes at the end of the game;
next time I'll just wait in the bar!

Robert L Montgomery
INDEPENDENCE
You can echo Society's judgments
And not be considered absurd,
But you'll never amount to a hill of beans
As simply one of the herd.
Make your own decisions!
Prepare to pay the cost.
You'll never be lost in the shuffle
Or shuffle along with the lost!

Helen J T Brumbaugh
ITCHING

To Grace and in memory of Luther C. Peterman.

Luther is going to give me a licking
Now what do you think of that?
Perhaps it will stop
The itching on my back.
I wash and rub and powder his—
But the itch keeps coming back
About the digging an scratching
We get a lot of flack.
I yelled at him, he yelled at me
We both get after Grace you see—
She scratched her arm red and sore
And then she scratched a little more.
Don't you scratch till red and sore
Or it will be worse than before
I rubbed my back on the kitchen door
But it only itched—more and more
I'm going to get a licking,
What do you think of that?
I sure hope it will stop
That awful itching on my back!

Peggy P Whitacre
RYAN
A look of wonder and
innocence pure.
An impish grin full
of ego secure.
Perpetual motion
even in repose.
Is that Ryan
do you suppose?

A celebration of life
even in trouble—
No, No's—not rules,
but questions to befuddle.
Joys of existence
each moment gives,
and serendipity just
follows the place where he lives.

A puppy dog's tail,
that wags with emotion
Not sugar and spice—
but a wondrous concoction
of energy, mischief, hugs
and stubbed toes.
It's a miracle to see
how a four year grows.

Velma Ross
HAVE YOU FORGOTTEN?
Have you forgotten all those hours
That to me were far too sweet?
Have you forgotten all those days
And how we planned to meet?

Have you forgotten all the joy
I found within your arms?
Have you forgotten all too soon
The bliss within my charms?

Have you forgotten how your lips
Met mine in that first kiss?
'Dear Heart' you may have forgotten
But I'll always remember all this.

Velma Ross
AMANDA JO
So, here's to Amanda
Amanda Jo Ross
Here's to the angel
Who will never be 'Boss'
'Cause that's left to Daddy
Daddy Jo Ross
And the strong hand of Mommie
Mommie Jo Ross
And then there's sister who's
Lindsay Jo Ross
But here's to Amanda
Amanda Jo Ross
Here's to the angel
Who'll never be 'Boss'

(Since Amanda (only two) has a middle name of Jo she thinks everyone else does too)

Muriel Marie Dubé
A PROMISE
From this day forward my home is your home.
The Love within will be our strength,
To conquer all temptations.
To Forgiving one another's errors,
For a constant love will help
From day-to-day as long as life.
With a patience of great understanding,
Always in trust and kindness,
When falling standing beside you,
To catching and holding above all things.
Our life will be Love
For as long as we live.
Shining through our children and generations yet to be.
The Eternal Love Will Be.

"This I Promise!"

Muriel Marie Dubé
CONSTRUCTIVE MIND
Authority of control interprets idea of a thought
Exchanging the insight of thought into words
Permitting the imagination of insight
Directly on target of a convincing arrangement of words in style
To the identity of opinion
For the determination of decoding an intuition from the illusion
Into identifying a belief
To an inspiration of understanding
As expressing the inner beauty of feelings
To the direction of attention in sharing life's experience
To celebrate the fabulously fantasy
To current issues of dispute
To convert from confusing occurrence
To a final decision of conclusion
To the Highest Personality of a positive gain
Are the qualities of devotion
Verifying the value of writing;
Is a Constructive Mind.

Dana Meland
I WILL LOVE YOU
Wishing you were here
As my heart cries for you in the night,
I hear a voice from high above
And he says "Don't cry, it's all right."

I try to believe him
But I'm too afraid
He knows I love you
And yet for you will pray.

I shall never forget you
Although you have forgotten me
I will love you always and forever
But now I'm setting you free.

I asked God if it was
The right decision to make
He didn't answer my question
But he did it for my own sake.

Whatever happens in the future
I'll always love you,
I've said it once, and once again
You'll always be my dream come true.

Nina J Musante
GOODBYE
Day, like a heart, breaks.
Its first lonely steps it takes.
The sun destined to cross the sky
Is compelled to say good-bye
To the horizon's vivid, warm embrace
For all the world it must now face.
The brilliant sadness of a sunrise,
Seen only through tear rimmed eyes.

Patricia Flack
LET THE PAST—REST
What was — is over and done.
What I have is right now.
The past is used to grow from —
And grow I must — somehow.

If I exist only in the past —
So confined I'll be.
That what really is — won't last.
And I'll lose what's really me

Minutes grow into hours —
Hours grow into days —
Giving me time to smell the flowers —
And grow in many special ways

So Lord — let me live.
And do my very best!
And enjoy all you have to give!
While I let my past — rest . . . !

Sandra Kozlowski
IT IS AMAZING TO ME
it is amazing to me
how sitting under the trees
and looking at the sky
everything is alright
and there is peace

and all the things
that have brought me to my knees
are of no value here

when telling people of troubles
they either try to fix them or
tell you how good you really have it
when all you were really looking for
was peace

and instead of dispensing useless
advice
or invalidating someone's broken life
why not offer them
a tree
and a piece of the sky
and their own hearts

Noreen Loss
RELATIONSHIP
A relationship is like a seesaw
Filled with its ups and downs.
It is not black or white
But lined with shades of gray.

A lasting relationship
Entails hard work
It should not be taken lightly
But built upon effort and concern.

Two people striving for the same
goal
Working together and not separate.
Feelings shared by both;
Not expressed by one
But by two.

On the contrary, it should not be
one-sided
And compared to as a one-way street.
If it appears to be,
Then it is nothing more
Than an obsession and not
A relationship shared by two.

Linda Key
THE LAST JOURNEY
Little did I know of the journey you were to take or that it would be the last you would make.

Little did I know as I held your hand through the night, that by the next morning you would forever be taken from my sight.

Now I remember the tenderness of your smile and the gentleness of your deep blue eyes; although your pain and suffering were great you already knew you had a date with fate.

You kept your secret from me with such care and gave your love till there was none left there. For you knew you were to journey to a far better place and that I would be left to try to stand in your place.

Why you chose me I shall never know, I have so much to learn and no time to grow. For months you told me in many ways all to do, but there's no way I could ever be you. Your patience, love, and kindness seemed to never end and in your understanding you were everyone's friend.

The last kiss I gave you was as you took your last breath, the sweetness lingered, then you left.

Kathryn Williams
THANK YOU GOD FOR MOTHER

This poem is dedicated to my mother, Lucy Redd, whom I love dearly.

Thank you God for mother,
the one you gave to me.
Her heart is very open,
and deeper than the sea.

She adds a little special,
in everything she do, and
for the love she gives to me
I give my thanks to you.

My mom is always happy,
and greets me with a smile.
Yes, just to watch her eyes light up
I'd walk a country mile.

So thank you God for mother
whose love just never ends.
She's never short or lacking time
and much more . . . she's my friend.

Trixie Jones
EVENING WINDS
As I walk through the evening
The winds of Heaven blow through
My hair and cross my face, and
I think of you and
What your love means to me.
For it gives me strength to carry on,
When the will to live is no more . . .
Then a fragment of sand upon a
beach.
You are my will to live and
For carrying on when I'd rather die.
To you, I give the key to my
heart . . .
Hold it true, for it is the only one . . .
To unlock this heart of blue.

Paula M Williams
CLOUDED REFLECTIONS
i miss you
 can i bear it
i love you
 need to share it
  loneliness
 longing
  endure

Rita Fields
GRANDMA

Dedicated to all grandmothers.

Grandma and I were the best of friends.
We talked, we laughed and did knee bends.

She was a grand old lady, my grandma was.
She taught me such skills as cooking and sewing,
and remained by my side till I was well grown.

Yes, Grandma is gone now, but not forgotten. Her
memories will be with me till the day I die.
But still, it is so, so hard to say goodby.

Donna Kowalchuk

Donna Kowalchuk
ECHO
Your eyes like pools of mystery
 drew me down into their depths
Shimmering reflections of my love
 revealed as there I wept
Love like a flower had blossomed
 beneath our tender care
Cherished deep within our hearts
 the beauty that we shared
Though alone now you leave me
 as our time has come to part
Whispers of our lost love
 still echo in my heart

Lynn Hibner
AN OUTSIDE PLACE
Outside my window the melting snow and ice drip down from the trees.
Inside of me my tears, lonely and
 alone, cry down into me.
  My soul
is saddened by a sense of loss.
I miss the things that I know and
  remember.
When I look for them, my memories, again in the old places, perhaps they will not exist . . . or when I look at them fondly, will have changed so as to
not be them, but a different, other.
And of me. Not only my old realities
  change and fade.
 It seems strange that I am me.
  Shall I have
 to make a new place for me?
 A place for new realities.
A different place.
An outside place.

John M Davis II
MY WORLD
In the back of my mind,
I've created a world, to go
to when life has me down.
Where the skies are filled with
happiness,
And sorrow is no longer found.
Where the streams flow full of
tranquility,
And flowers bloom all the year long.
Where the winds whisper sweet
serenity,
And nothing can ever go wrong.
I call this my Garden of Eden,
Where there is only me.
And the troubles in life,
Will not burden my mind,
And my heart and soul can be free,
Every night as I slumber,
I walk through my world,
Praying, dear God let me stay.
But the morning sun rises,
And I open my eyes to a bright and
glorious day.

Jennifer Church
LOST

This is dedicated to Rick.

I am so lost,
When I lost him,
I lost all direction.
I lost heart and soul.
With him I lost
my reason for living.
I am so lost.

Charlene Meissner
INSIDE THE MIND
As the heart grows older, richer,
wiser,
uneven affections threaten quaint
spring.
Pines yonder encounter kindless
pools of blood,
while experiments heat up heaven's
eye.

Virginia Bozza
EMOTIONS
Emotions in flow
 as they slip on by
My mind is a blank
 as I look into your eyes
I see nothing
 I know nothing with warmth
I am all alone
 in a world of my
own.

Sean T Straney
THOUSANDS OF MILES CLOSE

Dedicated to Sue, waiting in Australia.

We sit on different shores,
With an oceanic void between us.
We are a half a world apart,
Yet you are next to me.
We cannot look into each other's
eyes,
Yet your memory embraces my heart,
Your touch so near,
So real.
We cannot hear each other's voices,
Yet you are with me,
Day and night.
I can see your face,
So close.
I reach out to brush your cheek,
But there is only air.
We cannot touch each other,
But you are always by my side.
One day we will stand on the same
shore,
Knowing we never left each other's
side.

Leah Brickett
WEATHER REPORT
There are no clouds today
And I miss them.
The sky is a dull slate grey.
Yesterday, the horizon was rimmed

With lines of cumulus
Like flocks of sheep.
The day before, great puffs of cirrus
Floated against azure blue.
A week ago, just before twilight,
Sunset painted in
Colors of ripe oranges and wild
plums.

Storms are forecast for tomorrow:
Clouds will be threatening and dark
But not for long.
Day after tomorrow, following rain,
Cumulus sheep will come again.

Catherine Ann Griffin
MILE AFTER MILE
Feeling my heartbeat
Whenever we meet
Seeing his smile
Mile after mile

Twinkle in his eyes
Blue as the skies
Blond is his hair
Skin is so fair

Love of the street
Staggering when we meet
Jug in his hand
Something I cannot understand

Now that he's gone
I miss him so long
Every morning as I wake
I realize what I couldn't take

We've said our goodbyes
No use telling lies
Caring is only a game
Mile after mile would always be the
same

James Weems
ON THE FLOOR—SUMMER '89
Smoke curls from
The tip of my cigarette
Like a dragon's tail
Into my cold grey
Tombstone eyes.

Yesterday hides itself
In smoke and slithers
Inside my
Simple bleeding skull.
Breeding knowledge and ignorance
Beauty and Honor
Catharsis and control.

My soul aches
With the weight of you,
And your monster
Regality of poise.

My mind's screen is rich with
pictures.
Death and birth:
The eternal cycle
Of passion.

Kay Strohe Caswell
HONEYBEES AND POSIES

To my literary and musical mother, Louise Strohe Caswell, my engineer and farmer father, Ed Caswell, my songwriter brother, Bill Caswell, and Ray Grusing, my inspiration for this poem and others.

Ever wondered as a honeybee
Flits from flower to flower
If he ever buzzes back to
Any of the previous posies
To explain or apologize or say,
"Thanks for the lovely time—you
tasted great!"

No.

He just busily bounces on
To the next beautiful blossom.

Honeybees have such a sweet name.
But they are deceiving takers,
Just the same.

Honeybees suck!
And sometimes sting.

As for posies
They're tougher than I.

Thank God for baking soda paste.

Bernice Bottoms
DAY DREAM
I sit for a moment and gaze into
space
Blue eyes like her Dad's, lovely
blond curls
White pinafore all frilly with lace
Just like a doll, my little dream girl.

My daydream ends—I come to with a
start
There's a shout, a scream and a
deafening noise!
I dash to the rescue, a prayer in my
heart—
Thanking God for my four little boys.

Colleen Shea
ME AND YOU

To Courtney, all my love and friendship forever.

Stay with me my dearest don't leave
me now
Keep in our hearts our memories and
thoughts.
The cold days of fun
and the warm days of understanding
our times together are precious

If you ever left my life would change
To be afraid and alone, but that's
only the beginning
missing you would be the hardest.

We get along o so well
loving one another like family
I pray that you can understand
but I know that you probably do.

In deepest moments of need
I'll be there for you, as you have been
for me.

when things become the same in our
lives
we'll enjoy the things we used to do,
we'll talk and laugh and maybe even
cry.

no matter what happens
we'll stick together and reassure
that everything will work out.

Comina Hills
HE PULLED MY LAST STRAW
He pulled my last straw. I can't stand it being around, a liar. That pulled my last straw he crushed my heart. Why do they always act like that so strange once you get to know them. That boy pulled my last straw everytime I think about him he makes me ill. I swear he pulled my last straw this can't be carried on like this anymore. One minute he'd be so nice and the next minute he'd be so hateful, cause things can't get his way, he pulled my last straw and he really crushed my heart.

Virginia Morton Ross
THAT LITTLE GIRL AND ME!
I recall a little girl
I met so long ago
When only how to skip a rope
Was all you had to know!

When A B C's and 1, 2 3's
Were new and hard to learn
When "fun," was catching
"ladybugs"
And watching fire burn!

I still recall our teacher then
She seemed so very cruel!
"Close your mouth—wash your
hands,
and mind the Golden Rule"!

But all in all—our lives were good
And days were warm and free
And even now—we still are friends
That little girl—was me!

A happy child is a precious thing!

Menno Walter VOTH
UNCLEAR ON THE CONCEPT
Unclear on the concept of leal after
life
He ransacked the canons, then asked
of his wife
Who was baking the Saturday breads
at her hearth,
"Will you still wear my ring when
I'm dreened of my breath?"

She tested her tongue where a molar
one stood.
She was otherwise toothsome and
otherwise wooed,
Elsewherewise naughty and
Goody-wise good,
Her days much too drear for her
exercised blood.

Joints cleverly mortised, heft
pleasantly rhymed,
Pendulettas of lustering pearl tense
and primed,
Eyes deep from the wellsprings of
merriment borne,
Complected as May 'gainst
completion forsworn,

She straightened her face, said,
sincerely, "Forsooth,"
Then she tested her tongue to the
spectre good tooth.

Kennie Ray Robinson
TRUE LOVE
True love sometimes takes years
Other times only a glance
True love takes two
Who are willing to take a chance
True love is a strong commitment
Through good times and bad
True love will stand forever
When others were just a fad
True love is rare these days
So many times push comes to shove
The ones that forgive and never
complain
Are the ones that find true love

Bess Tompkins
HOW I WANT TO BE REMEMBERED
Some people want to be known for
their deeds,
While others seek fortune and
fame.
But I think I'll be satisfied,
Just to leave behind a good name.

I want to be thought of as caring,
And striving to ease the load
That all of us must sometimes carry,
While traveling down life's road.

I want to be thought of as giving,
And whether the gift be large or
small,
I want to have given part of myself,
For that's the best gift of all.

I want to be thought of as loving,
And eager to have a share.
In the lives of those around me,
Whether their days be dark or fair.

And when my friends remember me
I want them to say with a grin,
"THOUGH SHE HAD SOME
PRETTY BAD FAULTS,
SHE WAS A PRETTY GOOD
FRIEND."

Wanda E Blalock
VICTORIAN DAYS
Victorian ladies, elegance and grace
Magnificently gowned, elaborate
with lace
High button shoes, hats, feathers
adorned
A romantic age, a time to be born.

Those were the days, women wore
bustles
Life was serene, without hustle
Such ease and grace, will not come
again
What an Era to live now, instead of
then.

Five o'clock tea, muffins, jam and
bread
Dickens and Eyre, novels were read
Games were played, Cricket and
Croquet
A night at the Opera, ended the day.

Cruising the river, in Sunday best
A picnic in "Hyde Park," a day of
rest
Carriages, horse drawn, on cobbled
stone
Queen Victoria, ruled the throne.

The Easter Parade, frills to behold
Skaters on pond, when winter blew
cold
The Victorian home, a lovely sight
Fireplace aglow, mid candlelight
'Twas family together, on Christmas
night.

Leslie R Mahn
WHEN SHE WAS A PARTY GIRL
When she was a party girl,
She danced and danced,
Her hair would curl,
She glowed and hoped to find
romance
When she was a party girl.

Her specialty, it seems to me,
Was going on the town alone
And seeing who there was to see,
But never very far from home
When she was a party girl.

When music cast its magical trance
She felt most brave and had to be
The showy one who loved to dance
For Aretha and Bette, especially,
When she was a party girl.

Music and wine, the magical pair,
Confused her mind and tricked her heart
Again and left her in despair
To see that romance falls apart
For party girls and girls like me.

Leslie R Mahn
LOVE DANCES MY HEART
Purple poems fall apart.
Selfish lovers break your heart.
Broken poems now cry together;
Purple poems are dead forever.

Purple book of poems keeps.
Wonder where your lover sleeps.
Book of poems now feeds a fire;
Wildest dream is your new desire.

Fantasies of colors dance
In hearts so tender from romance.
Careful hearts are most objective;
Broken ones much too protective.

Leslie R Mahn
KNOWING DREAMERS AND SLEEPERS
Sleepers dream of better things,
Dreamers dream of everything.
Dreamers live in fantasy,
But sleepers live a tragedy.

Dreamers dream with smiling faces
And live their lives in perfect places.
Sleepers dream with fearful hearts
And flee from what their world imparts.

Those who dream of necessity
React to life obsessively.
The dreamer's dream is for satisfaction;
The sleeper's sleep is the only reaction.

Leslie R Mahn
CONTORTED
she cries and cries
she's dead from hate
she wipes her eyes
but she's too late
she sees that fate
told lies and lies
but it's too late
she cries and cries

Robert E Grenell
EARLY IN THE MORNING

For Amanda Kay Grenell, granddaughter (b. 1-18-90) "A wondrous sight . . . our heart's delight."

When the shadows of night begin fading from sight
  and sunrise is aborning,
'Tis the nicest time of every day:
  Early in the morning

In hedgerow green the wren is seen
  Her lichen nest adorning,
'Tis the nicest time of every day:
  Early in the morning

O'er meadow tops the field mouse hops
  E'er alert to warning,
'Tis the nicest time of every day:
  Early in the morning

Each night I pray when comes the day
  My soul must go sojourning
My saviour will stay death until:
  Early in the morning.

Pauline Monk Ward
TALKING TO THE BIRDS
You heard about those birds,
Talking in their tree.
About how much better off they were
Than either you or me—
About how we had no loving
Heavenly Father such as they,
Because we fuss and fret and worry so.
But no matter what you say
We do have a Loving Father, Birds
Just the same as you;
But you have no governments
Telling you what to do.
You get your needs all firsthand
Straight from Heaven blessed.
We get ours the long way around
From the FDA, FHA and the CSS
So yes, we do fuss and fret and carry on
For on these we must depend
And if you think you are so much better off than we—
You are so right, my Friend.

Pauline Monk Ward
MY NAME IS DAVID
My name is David.
I fought in the most unpopular war in history
I fought because I loved my country
And wanted all men to be free.
I fought believing I was right; the aggressors very wrong
That men should be allowed to live wherever they belong.
I fought when other men refused to take their stands
But denied this precious land of ours
And fled to foreign lands.
  I fought but lost.

The war is over; the boys are told that they can come back home.
So many that fought in that war made no move to come.
They had believed in their cause
And they were right—and brave.
Now some lay buried on foreign soil; some in a hometown grave.
No, they did not move, nor did I move
For I was one of them—
Who did not know the war was over,
And we could come home again.
  My name was David.

Pauline Monk Ward
MY CHRISTMAS TREE
My tree is not a pagan rite;
It reminds me—Christ is THE TREE OF LIFE.
The flashing lights upon my tree
Of many different hues, remind me—

The blue is for the darkened sky
'Neath which the shepherds trod,
The green, for a rich and fruitful life
Which we may have through God.

The yellow is for a fresh new day
Which brought a babe new-born,
The day that lives within us still,
As on that Christmas morn.

The red is for the blood of Christ
Born that Christmas Day.
My star—for that star shining
O'er the manger where He lay.

The wreath around my Christmas tree
Reminds me of Christ's love
That encircleth all life through
Since He came from above.

The presents beneath my Christmas tree
Just help me to recall—
That the Saviour born that Christmas Day
Was THE GREATEST GIFT OF ALL.

Marie Winslett
LOVE IS

Dedicated to my wonderful husband, my love, Edwin Burl Winslett, whose love keeps me going.

Love is for me, Love is for you
Love is forever, always, and true.

Love can't be wasted,
Love can't be bought
Love can't be sold, stolen,
or taught.

Love is for now,
Love is for tomorrow
Love is for happiness, peace,
& Sorrow.

Love is heartbreak,
Love is tears
Love is happiness,
Sought through the years.

Love is for me, Love is for you
Love is for always,
Forever and True.

Marie Winslett
I'M FINE
I'm fine, I'm fine.
There's nothing whatever the matter with me,
I'm just as healthy as I can be.
I have arthritis in both of my knees
And when I talk, I talk with a wheeze.
My pulse is weak and my blood is thin
But I'm awfully well for the shape I'm in.
My teeth eventually will have to come out
And I can't hear a word unless you shout.
I'm overweight and I can't get thin
But I'm awfully well for the shape I'm in.
Arch supports I have for my feet
Or I wouldn't be able to walk down the street.
Sleep is denied me every night
And every morning I'm really a sight.
My memory is bad and my head's a-spin
And I practically live on aspirin.
But I'm awfully well for the shape I'm in.
The moral is, as this tale unfolds,
That for you and me who are growing old,
It's better to say, "I'm fine," with a grin
Than to let people know the shape we're in!

S M Walling
HOT FEELINGS

Dedicated to life, love . . . and passion!

We're having
  warm balmy air.
Record breaking,
  I do declare.
Horny feeling,
  it does make me.
Wish you were here,
  if it could only be.
Hugs & kisses,
  I would bestow.
Licks & sucks, too,
  maybe even your big toe.
My creamsickle,
  once again, you would be.
To cool & satisfy my passion,
  I would even ride your knee.
My Prince of Passion,
  I miss you so, I could bust.
My scabbard awaits . . .
  your thrust of lust!!!

S M Walling
RED HOT
RED HOT pants
  for my RED HOT Lover.
Feel the RED HOT sensuous silk
  against your manhood.
Let it caress & remind you
  of the way I love to caress you.
RED HOT against your skin
  like a RED HOT Tongue.
    O-ooo . . . delicious!
      X X X

S M Walling
HOW LONG
How Long?
  As Long as I can Dream,
  As Long as I can Think,
  As Long as I have a Memory . . .
    I will Love You.

As Long as I have . . .
  A Heart to Feel,
  A Soul stirring within me,
  An Imagination to Hold You,
    I will Love You.

How Long?
  As Long as there is Time,
  As Long as there is Love,
  As Long as I have Breath . . .
    I will Love You.

Because I Love You . . .
  More than Anyone or Anything
  In All the World and
  In All the Universe and
    I Always Will!

Rene D Kelso
FALSE VALLEYS
I stand in a world
That's like a false valley,
With mock mountains
Surrounding, engulfing me.
My mind whirls and crashes
Into thoughts, words, and pictures.
My personality—
All that I am—
Is battered and pulled,
So that I feel I've lost
Self.
Can't the forces that be,
And the people I love,
Let me be—
Just for a moment—
Still and at peace.

Reneé Smith
ODE TO THE GRECIAN COFFEE CUP
I've attended more conferences than Murley himself
I've been guest of honor—invitation only—liquid elf;
I've been in on more secrets than the CIA or KGB
I've seen more political parodies than there are pre-election promises to philanthropy.

I've conspired silently to eradicate

emperors of error
I've brainstormed to abolish
blitzkriegs of robotic lecture terror;
I've pored over tests for universities
of noted esteem
I've perused works of novelty by
firesides' flickering gleam.

I've watched attentively while
magnanimous novels were written
I've pounded telepathically the
doormail with Luther's theses
besmitten;
I've witnessed with wonder
Ozymandius' Egyptian construction
I've beheld with benevolence Keats'
Grecian Urn deduction.

I've warmed the internal instincts and
precincts of old
I've comforted the tear-stained, the
fear-drained, the cold;
I've inspired writers at midnight as
tenacious thoughts unfold
I've energized brain cell synapses
when dendrites ardently sought gold.
I've offered my cup of kindness to all
Roden's model thinkers, meek and
bold
But this was an experience indeed—I
attended my own ode!

Katrina M Robertson

ALONE

I live on the streets and in dark alleys,
never know who to trust and
who's a foe.
I wander from place to place,
with nowhere else to go.

I've never known what it's like to be
loved
and held so tight.
In the night I sometimes dream of
children with
pets running by a stream,
With meadow so green and the sky so
bright,
I often wake up with a fright.

Don't live off much, tried suicide
twice,
I wake up with a new device.
One in my arm and hung up so high,
Nobody cares if I live or die!!!

Craig Aaron Hardin

THE BEACH

The sand under your feet
is moist and cool
Somewhere along
you will find a tide pool
You will see some crabs
running under rocks
As you move
to pull off your socks
Then at night
you are sorry to say
But, the day
has gone pleasantly away.

Lisa Rogers

TIME

There seem to be collections
Of moments lost in time
That come clear in still reflection
While harbored in the past

For what has already been
Is a portent of what may be
A preference for a certain turning
That goes always right or left

And leads to a specific future
By a path somehow meandering
Often goal directed, but how?
Living for today is all there is
And what becomes of the future
If no one yearns or plans for it
But meets it as it comes
Doing our best with what we have

Is it possible we cheat ourselves
By our lack of concern
Or could we really affect the future
With our worry and our striving?

Joan DePalma Bickis

BREATH OF LIFE

God blew his breath into us—giving
us life,
Thus becoming souls.
Now we are spirit, encased by
physical body.
But we must remember, we are first
and foremost—souls.

Earth is our learning plane, testing
place.
We should not collect and value
material belongings to gratify the
physical,
But rather feed and enrich the
spiritual self.
Learning, prayer, meditation, will far
surpass any wealth accumulated by
the body.

Will not the soul take with him all
riches of thoughts, deeds,
Given, received and shared,
And the body, nothing?

Enrich your hearts and souls,
Not your homes and egos.

You will learn the gems of this earth,
Are not the jewels of heaven.

Take heed to learn these lessons well,
For life as we know it now, is
fleeting.

And your last breath on earth,
Will be your first breath in heaven.

Diana Shannon Martinez

PAINTED BLIND

To all those broken hearts.

There are times in our lives when support, compassion, and love are needed from those we answer to as friends. We have their guidance and respect, also their need to hold and never forget.

But there are times a special friend is needed for when there is loneliness and fear, especially when a lover is not near.

One learns to love this friend in a manner no other would dare, for many could not understand or learn not to compare. This friend fills the space another left behind, then rules the path the other Painted Blind.

Beth Walker

FADED ROSES

To everyone who believed in me GOD BLESS!

Time has come to say good-bye, wish
I could say I won't cry.
It will be hard to not think of you,
and all we'd one day do.
I won't forget the feelings I had, till
we meet again I'll stay sad.
To others I've turned away, I won't
love until you're back to stay.
Everyday that you're not here, I'll
smile and dry my tear.
I had a dream it went away, I won't
forget you is all you did say.
We'll pick up where we left off then,
I'll know true love again.
When I think I'm alone, I remember
when you were my own.

I've thought since we've been apart,
I'll hold faded roses in my heart.
The faded roses in your eyes,
Has a kind of love that never dies.

Sherry Ann Bowman White

INNER GLO

Life brings you friends, who come
and go,
Some called friends, yet we do not
know,
Love is warm and fills our hearts,
Yet love cannot touch the coldest
hearts,
Give what you can and do not fear,
The cold heart rusts but cannot touch
you, dear,
When you feel the still of that cold,
Give no more and seek the warmth
you hold,
Stand alone and feel that inner glow,
God gave it to you, wait, you'll
know,
Rust breaks the heart but what do you
care,
The warmth you hold, is and always
will be there.

Madeline Ellis Smith

DAYS ROLE

I was just thinking the other day
about the role that I must play.

It starts in the morning at 5:00
o'clock
and ends in the evening just after
dark.

A quick cup of coffee with sugar and
cream
puts me in motion to face the scene.

The day is full of wonders and woes
but nevertheless I must get up and go.

My boss says do this, my boss says
do that,
I don't get nervous, I keep chewing
the fat.

I get my work done in the nick of
time
so that I won't be late or lag behind.

I jump in my car and head for home,
ninety miles an hour so it don't take
long.

I sit in my rocker and sew a few
seams
then get on my nightcap and head for
the dreams.

Louise R Haymaker Cook

FREEDOM

To Bill Haymaker Jr. who is in the Navy in island, my son. To all the military men, and American, God bless our homelands.

Our American flags are for freedom
blowing in the air
Our red white and blue is beautiful to
see
To our flag we must be true and
brave
Our flag has stood through all the
wars
Bringing chills tears and joy to our
eyes

Men who fought and died for our
flags in American
foreign wars battles
To our flags we must be true, proud,
and hold our flag high

Respect our flag that waves in the
breezes

Burning our flags is sad to see
God bless our flag and keep America
free

Keith Olive

ODE TO MIKE

In this life
Unfair as it may be,
Life lays little tragedies
On both you and me.

But all over the world
There are people suffering,
So don't feel sorry for yourself
While you are recovering.

Even tho' life seems so terrible
And you wish you were dead,
Think of happy thoughts
And keep them in your head.

Far lesser men have overcome
A greater strife,
So hold your head high
And let's get on with life.

What happened then
Is all in the past.
You're young
And you'll get over it fast.

Love ya,
Big Bro.

Mary V Gillis

AN INTERLUDE

I just can't seem to remember
What the day was in spring when we
met.
And I cannot quite recollect
Whether you were a blonde or
brunette.
It slips my mind
If I kissed you,
Though I do have a memory
That the month was May.
And I vaguely recall
Our parting was sad with many a
sigh.
But what were we doing together
And what was it made us cry?

Mary V Gillis

OLD CHINA

Was it more exciting when we were
very poor
To go to seek a tea cup in a lovely
treasure store?
When we had to count our pennies
and walk the steep slick hills
And now we give away our clothes
and waste our dollar bills.
I remember we bought the cup for tea
For the lovely lady painted there
smiled up at you and me.
She still has the same beauty and all
the sex appeal
As the day we bought the cup instead
of eating a meal.

Joseph R McEvoy Jr

A RAINY DAY (IN THE FOREST)

I spoke to the forest, he spoke back to
me
He said that the sun claimed, today
it's not meant to be
The drops start to fall, from way
above
It seems like the forest, lost its only
love

The sky is crying, hiding tears rolling

down my face
The sun is dying, I have no will when all I feel is disgrace

I kept walking, till it felt just like death
Then I stopped awhile, just to catch my breath
I thought of some problems, and who to talk to
Sometimes I feel so confused, I don't know what to do
So I walked to the mountain, to see what he had to say
He told me the sun, wouldn't shine today
I begged him to tell me, it was a lie
He told me, the sun will never die

The sky is crying, hiding tears rolling down my face
The sun is dying, I have no will when all I feel is disgrace

I told you my secrets, heard what to say
I trusted in you, to be with me every day
And just when I thought, you might open up and shine
You darkened again, to let me know you aren't mine

Debi Buettner

QUESTIONS

The day is grey and dreary
matching my overcast mood.
My thoughts are consumed with you,
and the whys of how you are.
I ponder the reasons for these changes—
what has caused them in you?
These are questions I cannot answer,
and have gone unanswered by you.
Can you tell me why we're where we're at,
and where the us of yesterday went?
You've let go of our hopes of tomorrow,
and have given me no reasons.
How am I to deal with these changes,
if I don't understand the whys?
Will you give me the answers I need,
to make my decisions?
And where will tomorrow find you and me?
I'm living with so much uncertainty,
and only you can give me the answers.

Nancy M Lillie

THE MONTH OF JUNE

The month of June I'll not forget
How love swept through my heart—
Only seems like yesterday
My thoughts of him did start.

Maybe it's the way he looked,
And lent a helping hand, or
The way he seemed to be there,
Even though not always planned.

Just maybe it was fate itself,
Each day I will not know
What for sure got started—
Such a short short time ago.

Keep loving me forever, I'd tell him . . .
I'll keep him in my heart,
This special bond will surely,
Keep us together when apart.

Gerrilynn Allemond Goodwin

THE WHISPER OF A DOVE

I looked to the heavens and there an angel did wait
The whisper of a dove, the voice did speak
Take one step at a time, it echoed from above
You were sent to this earth, to teach those to love.

I looked to the heavens and there I did see
My loving Father awaiting me,
He stood at the gate with his arms open wide
With a whisper of a dove the voice did speak
Take one step at a time, it echoed from above
You were sent from the heavens and taught them to love.

I looked to the heavens and I did hear
The whisper of the dove calling my name
I walked closer and closer, until it was clear
The kingdom of heaven my home to claim.

You'll look to the heavens and an angel will wait
And with a whisper of a dove a voice will speak
It will echo from above, take one step at a time
Teach them to care, teach them to love
For this is the reason, you were left behind.

Everett J Lewis

HOME

When folks we love pass on and depart,
It leaves a sadness in our heart.
Their chairs are empty. Their voices still.
We can't forget them. We never will.
Their worries are past, their troubles are over,
They are now in a land all of clover.
They've gone to where we all hope to go.
The place without problems, without any woe.
Do not cry. Do not grieve
When loved ones have to leave.
They've left this world, the land they've trod.
They've just gone home, they've gone with God.

Elizabeth LaMontagne

CHOICES

Gray walls surround me
Black iron bars all around
An empty keyhole.

In my hands I hold the keys
One to life and one to death.
Which one will it be?

No more anger, no more tears
No more problems, no more fears.

The choice should be easy,
I want to escape them all.

As I put the key in its place,
I say, "Death come greet me!"
When I turned the key, I found
people reaching out to me.

Through the anger, through the tears
Through the problems and the fears.

I looked down at the key, it said help me.

Their faces so warm,
Their eyes so kind
Their hands so gentle.

I got through the anger, through the tears
Through the problems and the fears.

Caring people, outstretched hands
Choices made.

Lisa Leach

DEMOCRACY?

One voice and one voice only,
seems to cloud our mind.
Injustice of the worst kind.
How can we be so blind.
To all the lost children we must find—
To the wrong ones we are so kind,
Injustice is served once again.
How can we make sense—
of the, "One Nation Under God"
If we do, will it fit together too easily.
Forget about in the end what God will say
Do it your way, America seems to me say.
It's obvious we're not doing so good,
On our own, all alone.
It's the one day it never got warm.
Our homeless, our old, sick, and poor,
Our aborted, mutilated, massacred
Innocent lives depend on it,—
This One Nation Under God.
Is there really no answers to
All this, that goes on under the sun.

Michael A Litty

LISTEN

Listen to the rain slowly falling, could it be my tears that you hear?

Listen to the thunder, could it be the sound of my heart breaking in two?

Listen for the birds to sing and what do you hear, could it be the silence that the rain always brings?

Where do the birds fly, where do they sing when the rain falls down?

Wait for me, for my Love grows stronger with every day that we are apart from each other.

Listen to the voice in your dreams, what does it say to you? Could it only be me saying that I Love You?

Alpha L Lockard

THE END OF THE RAINBOW

It's said, at the end of the rainbow there is a pot,
And everyone wonders if it holds gold or not.
We all dream of reaching the rainbow's end,
But it may not be gold you find, my friend.

What you find in the pot; you can't hold in your hand,
But some memory you've treasured, as you traveled the land.
It's not tangible wealth, but has appreciation,
And when it crosses your mind, you have a happy sensation.

Some may find it contains memories of childhood,
And future plans made, as they played in the wildwood.
Their memories are precious, and remembering is fun,
As they, now adults, take their place in the sun.

Many, I hope, will find at their rainbow's end,
Their Shining, Gold pot contains five words which blend.
They are: Association, access, authority, agreement, and assurance,
And are part of God's plan for Christ's death and resurrection endurance.

Find the meaning of each word, and give it some thought,
For Peace aplenty; to many they've brought.
The words in your pot, are the best of the lot,
They're your Passport to Heaven, believe it or not.

Michael A Litty

I REMEMBER DADDY NOW AND THEN

This poem is dedicated to Phillip H. Litty, My Father.

None of this writing really seems to help for only time can heal the pain.
The realization of the pain so deep, stemming from a time when no one could help.
The loss of my father, whom I Love so dear, where do I turn for an answer so divine.
To the question that has run through my mind from time to time. Why o' why did my father have to die.
The question with an answer that no one knows but is asked by everyone I know at one time or another.
As if ripping a part from me and my family, no one really gets over or forgets, but am I different?
Wonderful man that he was while I had him, I learned many things about life and how to fix the things I broke.
But how do I mend this broken heart that I have without crying or talking about the confusion I have and opening old wounds.
For I must know, simple though it is, people say we all have a time to go, why was his so soon.
Good-bye Dad, I Love You, till we\ meet again.

Michael A Litty

IMPRISONED

The bars that slam, the lights that never go out, the lack of the sun and the stars.

The hate and rage from which there is no escape, no love, no life, not knowing what is coming or happening.

The loss of caring, being caged like an animal, something you just can't imagine.

A fate worse than death, just going through the motions of life, losing the ability to think for oneself.

The total loss of contact with real life, total domination of body, mind and even possibly the soul.

To be locked and caged of the strength and desire to be free, come and see the shell of what used to be the man.

No pride, no manners, no nothing
striped down to just a form of
being, all that's left are the
memories of what used to be and
dreams of what could have been.

Even though release must come, what
will be left or can any or
everything be rejuvenated.

What becomes of the mind, body and
soul after being in this kind of hole
locked up, forgotten and left to
die.

Dortha G Ledbetter
FISHIN'

Saturday is finally here, at last,
Gotta go see if I can catch a bass.
Off to the good ole' fishin' hole,
Boy, I can't wait to grab my pole!
Grab your pole, Little Buddy,
Come, go along with me;
We'll grab some minnows on the
way,
Sure hope the fish are bitin' today!
Now here we are at our special spot,
The fish are bitin' quite a lot;
But there's a big one who keeps
gettin' away.
Sure hope we catch "Ole' Booger"
today!
Suddenly, Buddy's pole took an
awful run,
Boy, we're having lots of fun!
'Til I heard a big crackle and pop!
Into the water, Buddy flopped!
I thought my Buddy was gone for
good,
'Til all of a sudden — up he stood;
He splashed and sputtered — and
said with a grin,
"Man, "Ole' Booger" got away
again!"

Sheila J Linsner
LORD I KNOW I'M GROWING OLDER

Lord I know I'm growing older, but
that doesn't bother me.
For I really feel that I'm only
growing closer to Thee.
You love me so and give me grace,
it's true,
So I'll just keep growing older,
'cause what else can I do?

María Guadalupe Lizondo
THE 10,000 MILE LOVE THAT WASN'T

To Esteban with love. Thanks for being so special. I'll never forget you.

All those words, all the moments
of a love that never was, that never
could be
kept passing through my mind.
I couldn't help it, I was in love.
And as my family waited for the
plane
every second gone was another blade,
cutting my heart, leaving each time a
deeper wound
I was leaving, being driven away
from the one thing I truly loved
and my heart cried in pain
Distance was about to become one
more obstacle in my race for a goal I
knew I'd never reach
Yet I wanted so much to get there
I remember I thought: Maybe some
day . . . ; and started crying
Tears rolled down my face leaving
burning trails of a dream that had
sunk
in a sea of sorrow
I guess that's what first love's all
about, specially if it's not meant to be
I couldn't take it
Suddenly, everything I'd lived for
was about to vanish
Life just wasn't important because
you would no longer seem part of it
That's when I realized I would never
forget you
And I was right, because I still
haven't.

Hilda Jones Lawhorn
I WILL SING

For David who brought love and happiness to my life and a never ending song to my heart.

I will sing to you of sunshine,
And of summer's golden haze.
I will sing to you of wildflowers,
Of open fields where animals graze.
I will sing to you of moonbeams,
And of wishes that come true.
I will sing to you of dreams of love,
That can only be shared by two.
Together we'll sing a new song,
Of love's eternal promise.
A song of life renewed,
'Cause now it's sung by two.

Brenda LaBox
ROMANCE

For My Darling Jay, My Inspiration.

You came into my world
and breathed life into my
tired listless body.
You plucked my heart from me
and played upon it a symphony!
I was reborn!
Everything was new and wonderful
seen through your eyes.
Magic was everywhere,
You had made me care.
Love crept into my heart
and song burst from my lips,
My body and heart danced in time;
Life had become so divine!
Your love for me
had set me free,
Given new meaning to all things.
We have become one — you and I.
Let us sing and dance
and say thanks again and again
To that old magician — Romance.

Cindy Ann Lidke
JUST A MINUTE

Take a minute,
To look up above
Give time to a child
Or someone you love.

Just stop for a minute,
And look at the sky,
The beautiful colors,
Or the birds that fly by.

Give someone a flower,
To brighten their day,
Help those who need help,
I'll show you the way . . .

Michael E Lockwood
HOMELESS

Oh, America, you now have
People who have no home
You shun them and starve them
And on your streets they do roam.

You folks that are living good
Aren't you forgetting to treat others
as you should?
Isn't your kindness sadly dwindling?
Like a fire of nothing but wet
kindling.

America you have beautiful homes,
with white trimmed sash
But outside your starving brothers are
digging in the trash
You have too much and eat like hogs
Others, cold, outside, living like dogs

So . . . America don't look to far-off
countries
Trying to find the poor
Just look out your window
The Homeless are at your door.

Juanita J Lyles
YET IN ANOTHER WAY

I saw a leaf floating on the lake early
one morning.
It was, I think, performing its last
ballet.
The orange sun pierced the frail fiber
of its fading colors.
As I watched it turn, swirl and
pirouette,
I thought: Even you — a single,
beautifully shaped leaf
Has a purpose in life; in the spring
You burst from the bud, new, shiny
green, to say
"See, God's promise is being kept."
Through the summer, little leaf, you
gave cool shade
For those who came to rest.
Some even noticed your loveliness
As you danced to the quiet music of
the cool breezes,
Flaunting colors that artists have
attempted to capture.
Even now, you are still emanating a
glorious sight . . .
Saying to the world, "I am here,"
The fulfillment of that early hope.
And now, "I am floating here in the
late afternoon of my life . . . "
Not drifting, but knowing that I will
arrive at the shore,
To lodge there with others,
To be still . . .
To be used . . . yet in another way.

Clark Hunter
POLLUTED SINS

Dedicated to those who believe in a pollution free world.

The saddest commentary on our time
is the polluted sins of all mankind.
As pungent odors from landfills rise
the circling gulls fill the skies;
while barges dump into the sea
and man ignores this final plea,
oil drenched fowl crawl on the shore
tracking out the final score.
I'm not proud of this our lot
that generations past forgot.
To treat the land the sky the sea,
with more respectability.
The world's future they will find,
didn't stand the test of time.
Too late to heed, those who saw
our planet raped and rubbed so raw.
Our inheritance is one of shame,
and we cannot shed the blame.
But we must pledge, without delay,
to not except the world's decay.

Clark Hunter
AUDITION

To all who have faced life's auditions.

Strike your mark!
Project aloud!
With moistened palms you stand,
as the voice beyond the shroud
directs the next command.

A lonely shadow framed by glare
unfolds the lines of life
to reach, to touch and maybe share
a piece of human strife.

Silence . . . did it penetrate the wall?
Simply rated or too complex?
Or maybe no one listened at all
As the voice removes you with a
"next!"

Martha J Tinkey
GOD'S WORLD

Creatively,
Differently,
In unique design,
And ultimate power,
You and me
Were created
To be a part of
God's World.

Silently,
Softly,
In gentle times,
And quiet words,
I admire
God's World.

A world
Only
He
Could create.

L Montgomery
UNTITLED

To D. Fisher. I sure do love you. Always.

Clouds silhouetting
the moon,
stars here and there
piercing the distant sky

Wind blowing ever
so gently—
diligently waiting
for your arrival home

When the moon will glow
in our hearts
and the stars will shine
in our eyes
and the wind whispers
"I sure do love you."

Charles Donavien
FLOWERS IN THE GLOOM

Flowers of hardship strewn 'round
the room,
flowers of despair,
flowers of doom.
Petals of tears and thorns made of
pain,
a stem that is tainted,
with cold blood it is stained.
This flower of parting that I gave
to you,
lies crushed and broken,
there in the gloom.
It's come home.

Linda Beauchamp
A SEA OF WONDER

This poem is dedicated to all those who enjoy the beauty and mystery of the sea.

She is a sea of wonder so peaceful
and serene, yet so powerful and
mysterious as one has ever seen.

With her beauty and grace she brings
smiles to our face. She is a sea of

wonder so peaceful and serene.

Her crashing waves and raging seas bring fear to us for everyone knows the true strength of her mighty blows. She is a sea of wonder so powerful and mysterious as one has ever seen.

She is a source of food, life and death, but her beauty and inner strength outweigh the rest.

She is a sea of wonder so peaceful and serene, yet so powerful and mysterious as one has ever seen.

See her mighty shores and look into her eyes for you too will discover she truly is a sea of wonder.

Bridgette Romero
THE END
I see your smile in the sun.
I hear your laughter in the wind.
It seems such a lifetime ago,
We said "our love would never end."

Now I sit here so alone;
Listening to the wind, your laugh.
Feeling your touch, through the sun.
The feelings of love's ending aftermath.

The tears I cry are the sounds
Of my heart breaking.
I never knew these feelings before,
But I never knew love . . . what an aching.

I will overcome this pain.
Of course time will heal.
Memories of you soon will pass,
But I'll never forget how love can feel.

Michelle Kelly
CAROUSEL
Listen
Piano melodies
Round and round
Red
Purple
Royal
Blue
Engraved tracks
and tears

The tears of the horses
In circles
Laughter and
music
Echo
Round tears and
caked
orange
enamel
Ice crystallizes
The circles cease
Laughter
stops
Listen
Piano melodies
fade.

Charles Bunch Sr
COUNTRY MUSIC
Just let me be a sagebrush along the road of such a fuss.
Just a minnow against the sea
Lord it passes so fierce, and gallantly
A magnificent thing the people do, play that banjo and fiddle too.
Dance the two-step picking and a grinning.
Hand me that mandolin, have you seen my harmonica, do you think I've found the right key?
Country music is here to stay I love to watch them sing and play.

Lewis H Yotter
CLOUDS
I would like to be a cloud.
They sing so very loud.
They float around and are so free.
They are . . . what they want to be.

Some I've known have rained all day.
While others seem to want to stay.
Those are the kind that block out light.
And keep the sun from our sight.

There are even some that spew stones of ice.
These kind of clouds aren't very nice.
For they are the ones that cause destruction.
And ruin some of our best constructions.

The kind of cloud that I like most
Are the kind that don't try and boast.
They float along so swift and sound
And never lay their burden on the ground.

Carrie Sims
LOST LOVE OF THE HEART
The night held a mystery of uncertainty, as I closed my eyes.
The empty feeling that possessed my inner self.
To love and lost.
Thoughts run wild.
I try to hold onto solid foundation to steady my mind.
That inner being that search so diligently for peace, belonging to some form of oneness.
You have but don't.
That yearning, no return, but can't fully bring into focus, like a volcano ready to erupt.
The tears come but won't fall.
For love of heart.
Recall love the way it was just wouldn't let my heart try again.
To love and lost, will not compare to what will not be.
To give for love return back.
Yet in time the pain will go away.
Lost love of the heart.

Dorothy M Thompson
SNOWFLAKES

To my son Wayne and daughter Sharon and my grandchildren Stephen and Michael.

The snowflakes gently fall
On limbs of every tree
A blanket soft and warm
they spread
For all the world to see.
They fall upon the rooftops
And trickle down the eaves;
They land upon the ground below
And cover the leaves.
They cover yards and houses
Where happy children play;
They are rolled into many a snowman
Throughout the wintry day.

Myrta Weatherhead
OUTSIDE MY WINDOW
A gentle shower touches my windowpane
And awakens the silent, sleepy earth
To herald the anxious approach of spring
And coax all the bulbs to give birth
To snowdrops, violets and colorful crocus
Followed by daffodils of white and gold,
Flowering trees and floral-laden shrubs
And more tulips than my arms could hold.

Fragrant lilacs bloom outside my window
Where honeybees dart busily hither and yon.
Sunshine has stolen those early blossoms
And all the first signs of spring are gone!
Robins pause, then hop briskly across the grass,
Baby birds beg from their nest in a tree nearby,
Swollen rosebuds unfurl their beautiful colors
And spring gives way to summer for you and I.

Surendar K Singh
A MOMENT SO EMPTY
It's Christmas—
There is Cheers and Laughter—
Merry Christmas—
Hugs and Kisses

But somewhere,
awaking at the sound of their own dreams
in a world of loneliness
and a moment so empty—
just wishing if you could turn back the clock.

Time itself—flushing the
picture of childhood days
when there was never—
a moment so empty—and you
dreamed to be on your own
and alone.

But now—at a
moment so empty—wishing
there was someone, somebody
to reach out—just to hold you or even
give just a smile—so there would never be
a moment so empty.

Michelle Gregson
THE LAST DREADFUL KISS
As I sit in my room . . .
I think of all the accomplishments I have assumed . . .
Through my youthful years . . .
All the loves I have washed away by my salty tears . . .
I wonder is this all I have done with my life? . . .
Is there many more loves? . . .
Then I think there is none . . .
No more for me . . .
To laugh and for God's sake just to be . . .
Then I take that last dreadful kiss . . .
And think of all the things I have missed . . .
Why does this have to happen to me? . . .
Or are there others that wonder these same things? . . .
They wonder how could they let this be . . .
They turned their lives upside down . . .
For that one last kiss . . .
But always seem to fall into that lonesome frown . . .
No matter who, No matter what . . .
This day is still just begun . . .
But to still think those people were me . . .
Those dreadful thoughts that would turn things . . .
Into things that aren't too keen . . .
As I leave you with this thought . . .
Is the love this great? Is love this mean? . . .
Yes, I say to those who know this true . . .
Because you're only like a just planted bean . . .
You want to grow . . .
You want to know . . .
Is the taste for love that great? . . .
You can only anticipate . . .
Of what you know . . .
And I say my kind people this is how you grow . . .
Into the love stricken monster . . .
Of your wildest dreams . . .
You see that one last kiss . . .
Will make up for all the sweet things . . .
And years you have missed . . .
So I warn you now . . .
That kiss will last forever . . .
Just as the love that burns inside of every one of you . . .
For a better love . . .
That will taste just as sweet . . .
And as beautiful as a snow white dove . . .
And then you will know and only now you will know that this is the feeling . . .
Of Nature's TRUE LOVE . . .

Charles A Sprague
BRUTUS
He's just a little Yorky pup
But wise beyond his years.
There's more than Yorkshire pudding
Between those funny ears.

He came to heal the dreadful void
When Charlie passed away,
Whom we had loved for fourteen years
Until his dying day.

Then Brutus with his impish ways
Soon dried the salty tears,
And joined our canine family tree
Which spans more than fifty years.

There was Scrubby, Bozie, and grandson Butch,
Then Nikki's charm and grace.
Who would ever have believed
That he could be replaced.

But yet our dear friend Caroline

Foresaw that dire event,
And gave us little Charlie
For whom she overspent.

And so now Brutus rules our roost
With cunning canine style,
As Ruth and I enjoy the myth
Smiling all the while.

Jen Mollegard
THANK YOU
Flying high it seems,
Reaching out into the night.
Even without your attractive colored
leaves, blossoming around you,

Even without this —
Do you realize your beauty?
Oh, worry not to be forgotten.
Memories in you — find me.

Eileen Kivlen
GOD IS LIFE AND LOVE

"God is Life and Love" is dedicated with love to Eileen, John, Maureen Elizabeth Seton, and Catherine Labourè, all my children.

Love life seek joy
The spring brings song
It is renewed to life
Love escapes with every bud
Clear sky enjoy the beginnings
Soon the dawn to night escapes

Love life seek beauty
The summer bakes the earth
It is renewed to life
Love lives on in all
Soon the dawn to night escapes

Love life seek truth
The fall burns the leaves
Yellow orange and crimson color
Soon the dawn to night escapes

Love life—seek God
for spring summer fall and winter
See His Majesty—His Nature

Soon life begins to end—does not
escape
Love life—be with God

God—is life and love

Barbara S Weppener
COMMAND PERFORMANCE
In fluted golden skirts they danced on
a stage of moss-green grass,
Swayed to fragrant zephers' rhythms,
bowed to wide-eyed purple
violets;
Then, balanced on wavering hollow
legs the cast of yellow daffodils
Raised their shining heads and
welcomed budding spring.

Glendola Skaggs
TO BE THANKFUL
We never know from day–to–day,
What life will hold, Or what we will
do,
But if we look to God for help,
It will be revealed to you.
Sometimes I hear God's voice
surround me,
Like the falling of gentle rain,
Or the Angels softly calling,
Where the Ocean spreads its fame.
There is so much for us to be
thankful,
God has shown us the light,
We carry with us the Sunshine,
And live not, With the darkness of
night.
If we store up the Dreams God gave
us,
In the fertile soil of our Soul,
It will write the most important
chapter,
That our lives have ever told.
Thanksgiving is not the only Day,
In which we should be thankful,
There is always something in God's
plan,
So every day we can be grateful.

Catherine Walters
NO MATTER
On a cool spring night
and the mood just right
we entered our own paradise;
you held me in your eyes,
you put a song upon my lips,
a poem within my heart
and even strength while we're apart;
you've earned a special spot,
you have my love, no matter what.

Catherine Walters,
a.k.a. Sweet Choklate

D M Davis
THE SKY ARE BLUE
The sky are blue. The sky are blue
Oh don't you see the sky are blue
The wind are blowing, oh the wind
are blowing. Don't you hear the wind
blowing. See the bird they are flying
oh don't you see the birds are flying.
The sky are blue the sky are blue Oh
don't you see the sky are blue.

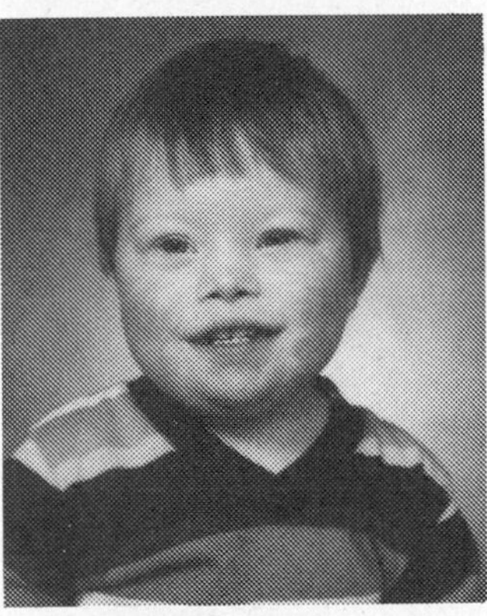

Rad Michal Haarberg

Renea Haarberg
KIDS LIKE THESE (TRIBUTE TO DOWN'S SYNDROME KIDS)
Stubbing nose, squinty eyes
Two things you might see.
You make fun of people like that.
I know, I did too.

Then my nephew was born
He was a kid like that.
I thought it was God's punishment.
Two years, now it's not a
punishment, but a blessing.

Look closer, search,
Behind this block
Of messed up chromosomes
You will see someone else.

His nose is short,
His love line long.
His eyes are squinty,
His arms open wide.

Jessica LeTarte
A SINGLE CANDLE
A single candle left to fight
The growing darkness, the dreadful
night
A single spark, one tiny flame,
Left with terrible night to tame

Just one wind at the candle's cost
And the world's hopes were lost.

But that single candle struggles on,
All its burdens heavy upon

Its waxy shoulders, its clouded mind
One last light in the dark to find.

The darkness came to deal death,
It succeeded, stole the candle's breath

Then, suddenly, came a fiery
blaze . . . behold!
It's day once more as the light grows
bold

For in that instant of worldwide
dread,
When all had thought the flame was
dead,

The spark to a million lights gave
birth,
That single candle proved its worth.

Mary Williams Barnes
THEY THINK I'M JUST A BUM
I'm only thirty-nine
And very thankful to be.
I know there are those out there
Who think I'm ancient history.

The average young Daddy out on the
street
Is having it kind of tough;
In this vast land of plenty
It's difficult not to buy too much
unnecessary stuff.

The folks down at the church
Are very good to us.
They help feed and clothe my
children;
I guess they think I'm just a
worthless cuss.

I'm restless with this temporary
disability;
I know people think many
able-bodied allow others to assume
their responsibility.
I guess some think they must have
boats and cable, VCR and beer.
Somehow the real necessities always
come from somewhere.

When I get over this surgery I'll get a
job with good pay;
I'll watch every penny and pay my
own way.
My Mother gave birth to no bum; my
children will attest to that.
The Lord has blessed me with a good
mind and body;
I'll use all these resources when I get
up to bat.

Rev Frank Pleasant
FAREWELL TO BETHLEHEM
(NOTE: This little poem is part of a three-act play in rhymed verses on RUTH of the Bible, enlarged and dramatized by the creation of new characters and episodes, all in dialogue. This FAREWELL TO BETHLEHEM is spoken by lady NAOMI before emigrating to Moab.)

Farewell, o Bethlehem, farewell!
Farewell, you field and you the well,
Now both dry, once source of life,
Farewell, sweet friends in strife.
Farewell, you brook once sparkling,
Now muddy bed, drying and
cracking.
Farewell, you hills and you valleys
Once green with ferns, purple with
berries.
Farewell, trees despoiled of fruits;
And you, flowers withered from
roots.
Farewell . . . Oh! Where are you,
chirping birds?
Ah! Since long far gone or dead from
hunger!
No humans or beasts, no fields, no
herds
Can ever forget this cruel surrender!
Our hearts, Bethlehem, with you
remain,
But can no longer withstand the
strain.
Oh, say? Shall we ever see you
again?
Will good days their sway regain?
Perhaps some day new life will tell.
O Bethlehem! Farewell, farewell,
farewell . . . .

A Scaroni
TEARS

To Ketty, my princess, the lady I love and will marry one day; I dedicate this poem to you my love.

When I see you my eyes become
moist
You ask why am I crying
In a shaky voice I say I am not
When you hold my hand and I feel
your warmth and love
Tears begin to run down my cheeks
You ask why am I crying
I am not I answer

You hold me and I feel your strength
and the security there in your arms
And I cry
You ask why am I crying
And I answer I am not
These tears I cry are tears of
happiness for loving me
My tears are my way of saying I love
you for the happiness, peace,
And security you have brought me
I cry for you my love

Phyllis Wooten
BLACKNESS

To Manat "my precious daughter."

We know of your shades
but what does Blackness
mean to us as a people?
Is Blackness a color among our
people?
Is Blackness a talk, a walk
a unique way to survive
a hard way to surivive
an easy way to stay alive?

is Blackness deemed music, dance
excellence in sports? Some sports?
All sports?
Are you no longer Black when you
become
Miss America, a country singer, an
opera
diva, an orchestra conductor, a
concert
pianist?
Are these all the hues of Blackness
that some of you refuse to recognize
as part of being Black or is it
we are just as individual as the
other races
and you don't realize it!

Phyllis Wooten
TO YOU
The music just flows
over and around me
like sand might on a
windy beach
just like I wish you'd do
when we are in the
midst of making live.
I am not swaying to the music
but my mind is, my heart is
my mind has you in my arms
moving when you do
stopping when you do,
turning, bending, blending when
you do
going slow and easy
swaying with my mind,
swaying with
you in it.

Sophia K Lilles
INSPIRATIONAL
I am inspired by a
certain face,
or a smile.
A fleeting glance,
a bluebird flying
against the sky.
A warm heart . . .
A fragrant rose,
a butterfly . . .
The innocence
of a child.
And i thank God
i am alive!
It is so lovely to be
heavenly inspired!

Bonnie Jean Ledford
SONG OF MYSELF
I am me and there is no one like me
I see and do things my own way
And no one can change me!

People have to like me for what I am
For I am stubborn when it comes to
being myself
No one makes me do or be what I do
not want.

I see things from the optimistic side
I look for the good in all the bad.

I enjoy nature, the trees, flowers and
animals most of all
For they are comforting to my mind
and soul.

The old way of life fascinates me
Antiques are pieces of art
They make me stop and think of how
I would have
done things then.
But I am a 20th century human with a
life of
racing time speeding cars and hustle
to get things done.

Life is short for me and the end will
come fast
So:
I must live my life on earth now
For
I will never have the chance to live it
again.

Cindy M Goedert
REMEMBER
Remember me when you laugh,
Remember me when you cry.
Remember the good and bad, the
happy and the sad.

Most of all remember the Dreamer,
for the Dreamer chases rainbows,
and your pot of gold.

Remember that, whenever you see
a Dreamer looking for that special
rainbow,
behind it all you'll Remember Me!

Anthony J Cuomo
FOREVER

For Philip: Pater familias. Poeta nascitur, non fit. Requiescat in pace.

The Master hung from the boughs so
bare.
The Temple's lights dimmed in the
late
afternoon air. Life precious,
contorted
with pain and despair.

Heart pierced and laid open for all to
see,
what would happen when He ceased
to be?
His Soul in anguish over what must
be, as
crimson rivulets stain His tree.

His eyes so icy blue, looked down
and pierced me through. The
lightning flashed,
the thunder roared, it was over and
yet just
begun . . . His tears shimmered
behind the
setting sun.

The answer came as clear as can be,
the
Torch I carried I now give to Thee.

Kristi S Pierson
DEIGN YOU ARE GOD
I pure reality express vision
Gray to grey rainbows
Chemistry of blood cosmos
And gravity
Be with the force
Of the light
Harmony and peace
Abound by grace

Anthony J Cuomo
THE THORN'S LAMENT
Of thistle down, gorse, furze and
nettle
who would dare my thorns to
meddle,
of that sweet harsh beauty dare inhale
who carelessly touches, do I impale.

Among rock and ledge must I endure
as a warning to whom my blossoms
allure,
that once from my spines the Master
bled
from a somber crown placed upon
His head.

Remember then, when you see me try
to twist and turn and reach the sky,
my flowers an offering to Him above
for my needles pierced God's
turtledove.

Elmer J Bryan
PRESCRIPTION FOR A LAUGH
Just a line to say I'm living,
that I'm not among the dead.
Though I'm getting more forgetful,
and more mixed up in the head.
For sometimes I can't remember,
when I stand at the foot of the
stairs.
If I just came down from there,
or if I have to go back up for
something.
And I stand before the refrigerator so
often,
my poor mind is filled with doubt;
Have I just put food away or
have I come to take some out?
And there's times when it is dark out,
with my cap upon my head,
I don't know if I'm retiring
or just getting out of bed.
So if it's my turn to write you,
there's no need in getting sore,
I may think that I have written,
and I don't want to be a bore.
So remember — I do love you,
and wish that you were here,
But now it's nearly mail time,
so I just say "Good-bye, dear."
There I stood beside the mailbox,
with my face so very red,
Instead of mailing you my letter,
I had opened it instead.

Glenda Friday
LOVE

To my family.

I feel as the years have passed,
An aching in my heart that seems to
last.
All because of mistrust and a broken
heart
I thought it would be easy to weave it
together
But now Love is so much like stormy
weather.
With less ups and a lot more hurting
downs
To grow up and find out that
Even Love has its Bounds.

Karen Boyce
LOVE-SCORE
Take a firm grasp
is what the man stated.
Confidence plus
surely, underrated!

May he lead me tomorrow
where my destiny lies
clay courts,
warm hearts
and
gentle, loving sighs.

Karen Boyce
TIME FOR THOUGHT
Time for thought
and meditation
to derive peace of mind
through concentration.

Yesterdays
todays and tomorrows
all blended into thought
discovering what gifts to the
world I have brought.

Mind awakening days
contributing maturity and truth
wisdom and gentleness will be my
proof.

Cheryl Ann Azcona
FRIENDS FARAWAY
Friends faraway in the time when we
were there,
Look at each other and tell all we
dare.
Now the paper and distance is
between us,
I sit and ponder and lose it as I fuss.
Friends faraway in the limits of our
mind,
Makes it hard to choose and it tends
to blind.
Why did we leave each other? Pops
up from time–to–time,
It was downhill then, but now it's an
uphill climb.
Friends faraway in the summer of
warm air,
Look at this cold winter with a blank
stare.
Spring has come but still I find,
People here hopelessly blind.
I waited out the autumn,
I think it hit bottom.
And we are still friends faraway as
we await a new day.

Betty Darlene Meeks
DEATH
To laugh, to talk, to run, to play
Never more will be.
Instead the metamorphic change will
Be: to fly, to soar, to know no
bounds;
All limits are broken down.

Mary Brookman-Wright
PRAIRIE STORM
The campfire burns
With a mysterious light
Casting shadows of fate
All through the night.

The lone wolf cries out
As the clouds start to gather
The cool breeze turns cold
As the rain starts to splatter.

Lightning races across the sky
Giving brief flashes of light
To the cows nearby.

Thunder crashes
The storm in a rage
Flooding the creeks
Once dry with sage.

Suddenly silent
The stars reappear
Peacefulness abounds
As the dawn starts to near.

Dale Mullen Jr
LOSSES
Losses to me is bad,
It sometimes gets people sad,

I have a loss of playing,
Football and lots more.
But I guess I'm a lucky one,
because it's only for 6 - 8 weeks
or two years.
I first thought I can't play
anything as long as I have a plate
in my leg.
But boy was I wrong.
In about 5 weeks I'll be able to play
almost anything except football and
maybe soccer.
That's OK I guess.
But there is always life,
that needs more than doctors,
they need a miracle.
So let's just help those ones in need
more than me.

William D Edwards

William D Edwards
TOTAL INDULGENCE OF LOVE

To Kathryn Edwards, My loving wife and companion.

Love searches itself in many ways but I find love fulfilled in my wife. Maybe it's just someone to talk to or a person to walk with, but I believe it's because I have become a reflection of herself. And love is a mirror; a shining reflection for all of eternity to see.

It's the greatest gift a woman has to offer, which is a life, the joining of two reflections created into one. One life created through the total indulgence of love.

Sarah M Adams-Harris
MOM

Was it the thought of someone
On high
Or on heaven's own plain
'Twas decided that our world
Needed a gain
To soothe our brows
To ease our pain
Someone to care
Oh yes! 'twas decided there
"Our Mom"

Sharon Roberts
NEVER FALL (hang in there)

Dedicated To: My lovely sister, Carolyne, for being the special person she has always been!

Never fall for a guy that's shy because he will, always cause your eyes to cry. Never fall when he breaks your heart or whenever he tries to tear you apart. Always hold your head up high, even when you feel that you want to die.

Never let him cause you to fall or give up love and end your life; For in the end he will get it all with pens. And your nights and days of strife will end. Never fall for a guy that's proud who wants his name known to the crowd. For he will be the one who tries to lead your heart to learn of love that's blind.

Never let him see how much you care for him, or whenever you need him and he's not there. Don't show the hurt you feel, but always hang in there. Never let your heart run dry; even though you need the special someone to just hear and you need to feel not others, but theirs; Remember don't give up hang in there.

Never hang your hat over the chimney because it will soon blacken out. For one day that special man will come and your name he will surely shout! Never let a man put you down or never make you feel ashamed; for if you had the talent to find you, and you will be free to be yourself, free like a dove.

Never let his love go, or let anyone make you feel low. For if he's loving enough to see your problems to hear. Just take it from experience, and never give up, —
HANG IN THERE!

Mary Ann Frazier
AS I GAZE UP TO THE STARS, I FEEL YOU IN THE BREEZE

I dedicate this poem to my mother Tillie Ward Cundiff, and my husband Willkie E. Frazier, who are the inspirations of my words.

As I gaze up to the stars, I feel you in the breeze
Standing here beside the fire, I feel you watching me
As the moon reflects its light across the river there
I thought I saw your shadow moving through the trees so bare
As you moved, I heard the drums soft but sweetly beat
Then the chanting of our tribe softly speak to me
They tell me of the pain they felt as white man drove them on
They spoke of death and many tears on that trail so long
I felt a chill, a haunting cry, and as I turned around . . .
There my
great-grandmother was, sitting on the ground
Her old skin was dark and drawn, but still I felt no fear
For in the corner of her eyes reflections of her tears

Anjonette Cruz
MY MOM, MY BEST FRIEND

To my mom, who is also my best friend. I love you very much.

I am so lucky to have a friend like you;
You are someone who is always there for me,
You understand my feelings and my thoughts,
You listen to what I have to say.
You were always willing to lend a hand
When I didn't understand.
How can I ever repay you,
And for all that you have done?

Thanks for caring and sharing,
Thanks for listening,
But most of all,
Thanks for being my mom and my best friend.

Moradi Wa Baphuting
14 DAYS IN MAY

For all those who have known the anguish of a DEATH SENTENCE; for souls forcibly extricated from HUMAN-NESS; for those who have had to live with the CONSEQUENCES.

The DEADLY CHAIR
That claimed
The life of
Edward Johnson
Left me Blue

I lost my cool
While Brother Johnson
Kept his intact
I lost my cool
While Grandmother
Kept hers intact
I lost my cool
While Mother
Kept hers intact
I lost my cool
While Sister Brothers
Kept theirs intact

It is a sick society
Said your lawyer
He did his best
But the evil forces
Were stronger

I say
It is a
DEADLY SOCIETY
It has to go
Before humanity perishes

Farewell Brother
You faced adversity
Squarely in the face

It made me realize
How feeble and cowardly
Some of us are.

Moradi Wa Baphuting
EMOTIONS

It hurt to see
you our
Black Father cry

It hurt BECAUSE
I was crying too

I shall NEVER
forget the face on TV

You said
THEY KILLED SAMORA

That's what I and
Many others were
THINKING too

I cried with you
We cried for Him
We cried for the Course
We cried for AFRICA
We cried for HUMANITY

Moradi Wa Baphuting
THE TWO DAVIDS, REUBEN AND TIMOTHY/BRANCHES, LEAVES, ETC, ETC.

As young men you met
and found in one another
a common factor
i.e. the urge to learn

You went through the ABC
in adult life and
never stopped to proceed

From the written word you
graduated to the HUMAN BOND
Or was it the other way round

I am only trying to
relieve my childhood
MEMORIES

Bringing us together into
a marvelous extended
Family

We children never connected
What we thought of as
Own Independent Achievements

As having you as
OUR ROOTS

Moradi Wa Baphuting
CHILDREN

Do we still
Have any

A 3-year old
A 10-year old
gets carried away
To the unknown
Or shot dead
By fierce machine guns

What memories of
CHILDHOOD

Poor mother what
do you teach them
How do you tell them
to respect their elders
And run their errands

We have lost
Them
To the greed
And the SAVAGERY
Of the oppressor.

Moradi Wa Baphuting
WHAT WENT WRONG

Am I the one
Sitting emptily
Trying to figure out
What should be done
With the precious Life
Given lovingly and naturally
By Man and Woman
Though not their own
Coming together alone
But primarily by the Mystery
Which no one as yet
Can sufficiently clarify

I suppose I had
A mission to fulfill
Like everyone else who
This planet inhabits
But somewhere along
The line the course
Of events was punctuated
Could it have been so
Planned?
Is their fulfillment still
To come?
Something for the future?
YES THE FUTURE

Or is this the end destination
DESTINY by no other name?

Moradi Wa Baphuting
FROM ALL OF US

Your children the
White City Tiny Tots

Mrs Dorah Mabaso
Thank you

For keeping us out
of the hostile street
Instilling in us the
meaning of togetherness . . .
a sense of belonging to
a worthwhile group

We learned to recite sing
& dance; perform for audiences
small and large

Your insight in allocating parts
is well remembered

For Willy did become
a Teacher; Maureen turned out
a Lady; and dear Maqinase
a Scholar?

Well,
Still in the making

Moradi Wa Baphuting
A HELPING HAND
From Africa's every
Cardinal point they hearkened
To your call for HELP

Sons of Africa came
to answer your call
to put an end to
Hitler's tyranny

AND
THE MONSTER WAS
DEFEATED

Now her sons and daughters
are banking on you to
Put an end to another MONSTER
THE APARTHEID REGIME

Thousands perished then
Thousands will perish now

SO DID/SHALL the MONSTER

Why not then
Lend a helping hand
To set the record STRAIGHT
AND
RAISE THE FLAG OF JUSTICE/
FREEDOM

Moradi Wa Baphuting
A SHAME
To you America to have
uprooted millions of HUMAN
BEINGS
Forcibly denuding them of
THEMSELVES . . .
Family, language, culture
Everything with a semblance of
the Precious Way of Life
Inherited from their FOREBEARS

For having them fight for what
should have automatically been
theirs after a very, very, very
long sentence of HARD LABOUR in
an Alien and Non-accommodating
LAND

Unlike you she cannot trace
her Roots — Irish, Dutch, German,
etc., etc.,
HE is a Jeff Smith; SHE cannot be
traced back to Mother Africa
As for you THEY NEVER existed
even THERE

A super power? Maybe but a
Great Nation? NEVER till you
open your HEART; stretch out your
ARMS and embrace US ALL THE
PEOPLE Of the U.S.
Amen.

Moradi Wa Baphuting
OCTOBER 19TH 1986
Not out of disrespect
But to me you shall forever be
SAMORA
The personified struggle of Africa

You went into the BUSH to
reclaim your Motherland
From them who had robbed
Your Fore Parents for
Ages

REPOSE THOU WELL
Mr President

You have sown the
seeds of FREEDOM

And Tidings of Joy
We shall bring you
When we join you
in The peaceful & everlasting
WORLD of BLISS

Moradi Wa Baphuting
THE GARBAGE MAN
Early in the morning he
rises for his ashy job
in the township/suburb to
"KEEP THE CITY CLEAN"

He has to be fit otherwise
He won't last a day ending up
in HUMAN garbage himself

Teaming up with his mate
the box perched on his shoulder
he runs after the vehicle in motion
empties the contents and hurries
back to replace the dirt box[1]

A marvel to see him
at work . . .
The nimbleness . . .
A HUGE GREY MUSCLE OF
ENERGY

Well he has to be an
ALL FIT MUSCLE OF ENERGY
There is NO OTHER WAY
LEFT OPEN FOR HIM

[1]Heavy corrugated iron container for garbage, especially ash from coal stoves.

Moradi Wa Baphuting
THE HERALD OF FREE ENTERPRISE 6/3/87
A crew member of
another ship saw the ferry
sailing with OPEN DOORS

I was too Busy loading OUR
ship to draw the attention of
the captain of the
Floating COFFIN

He subsequently declared

What a PITY what TRAGEDY

Are we not all always
Too Busy to CARE
To give of OUR TIME
To give of OURSELVES

To listen maybe even to scold
To reprimand SOMEONE else who
May NEED just That

We owe it to ONE ANOTHER
To unburden to EACH OTHER
So as to make Life's
Upheavals NOT SO
S T E E P.

Blanche Mitchell
MY FAITH
My faith is strong
As the eagles wings.
I face the worldly throng
With a heart that sings.
I run but I'm not weary.
My heart is not faint.
My eyes are not teary
Because I never say: I Caint.
When I seek wisdom
There's one thing I know:
Talk to my heavenly Father,
He never fails to bestow
His wondrous blessings
Now, and through eternity
When earthly exasperations
No longer be.

Sherry Lawler Sparks
WORDS
Never been gifted with the art of
conversation
Filled with words that never see the
light
In silence I watch as others speak
No sense of what to say when
timing's right

Given a chance my words might
change this lot
If half lifted, they just might find
your ear
And if words alone could make you
mine
Then time and time again those
words you'd hear

But my mouth that which utters not a
hint
Of all the words that in my heart are
bound
Aches for your tender kisses every
hour
Though my love, they do not make a
sound.

Marla K Greenway
WAXLIGHT
Flickering
moodsetter
touches our skin
bathing our nakedness.
Shadow-caster
kind voyeur
lending substance
to imperfect form.

Scott Alisauskas
SHE'S GONE
Emotions trashed
Yet my heart's not broken just
fractured
The smoke has cleared
The blizzard's over tears subside
A part of me is gone a part remains
Me in her and her in me
A part given A part saved
A part of me dies another grows

Emotions now stable not fragments
but whole
I've learned a lot . . . learned to love
I'll always remember her
she'll always be important to me
My heart a little fuller
full of life now
Inside . . .
gentle moments
Forever I'll cherish
My life . . .
more than before
yet still . . .
she's gone

Ruth McLean
NATURE'S REPERTOIRE
Lulled by evening's velvet mantle
Mystic joy invades my soul,
As nature's gentle voices blend
In rhythmic, sentient flo'.

A maverick breeze, in passing,
Brushed a kiss upon my cheek,
And on damp beach small wavelets
romp,
And splash about my feet.

The crescent moon affords its light
To dance on golden sand,
Overhead a mother squirrel
Beds her raucous clan.

From somewhere peals a bird-song,
Sweet and clear across the night.
Whispering leaves play background,
A chorus of delight!

The darkling sky a garden bed
Of diamond-studded bows,
And I, a solitary audience,
To praise this show of shows!

Genevieve Theresa Samsel

Genevieve Theresa Samsel
UNTITLED

Dedicated to those who loved me and those I loved, Jenny.

Life is a woman
Pregnant with pain
Capricious, malicious, and vain.
Life is a woman
Pulsing with ecstasy
Vibrant with expectancy.
Lifting its eyes unto the
Unlimited horizon
Where the glories
Of heaven and earth
Are pooled;
Contaminating itself
In the eternity
of the present.

Genevieve Theresa Samsel
THE STORM
In the middle of the night,
When everything is still and quiet,
Then I hear the thunder roll,
And primitive Fear lurks in my soul.

Lightning Livid Fingers probe,
The crypt of night my soul's abode.
While the thunder's robbing
antiphony,
Dissolves into impanity.

Genevieve Theresa Samsel
THE VISION
Yonder mountain doth in still
And cause my heart to throb and
thrill,
With the rapture of Creation
And Serenity of will.

I would Climb your highest peak
On bended knees my God to seek,

And lost in meditation and prayer
Join the lowly and the meek.

Genevieve Theresa Samsel
THE FLOWER
I saw a Little Flower grow
The ground was cold.
Oh so cold!
Little Flower do not die.
God Loves you
And so do I!
Thou are rooted in
God's mind

Genevieve Theresa Samsel
ROBIN RED BREAST
One Sunday in July
I chanced to espy
The remains of a robin
On my walk
Hopeless victim of a feline's stalk.
Feathery denizen of leafy skies,
No more shall you perch
On yonder swaying Birch,
Nor evermore shall thou wrest
The lonely angleworm
From earth's breast.
Heaven has ingloriously decreed
'Tis only in strength
That we succeed.

Megan Fay
TRAPPED IN A BODY

This poem is for Papa . . . you've come a long way.

Trapped in a body
Unable to be free
I've searched for a way
To escape this prison . . .
Unsuccessful am I.

What happened to my old self?
Where did my freedom go?

I want my body back
But it will not return
Movement was lost
Freedom is long gone
Trapped am I.

I'm imprisoned!
I'm lonely!
Someone please come,
Release my chains!
The key to the bolt was lost,
And so am I.

Friendships will diminish
For freedom was the key
I must find a savior
Another trapped inside a foreign body —
Someone just like me — paralyzed.

Eric R Burris
SPACEHEAD
Spacehead sits in the room by herself
she wonders will she always be alone
and I do think she'll get by
Spacehead calls me on the telephone
says she wants to die
dear Spacehead don't you cry

and Spacehead, I wonder why you worry
when the world is in your palm
if you just won't hurry
if you'll just stay calm
Spacehead confide in me
Spacehead you can trust me
you can trust me

Spacehead, you're much too precious
so don't take your life
Spacehead hear my message
SPACEHEAD HAND ME THE KNIFE!!!

Lucetta Warner Hunt
SUMMER LOVE
Come walk with me and be my friend
And we will wander through forest glens.
And we will bathe in sparkling streams
Where dazzling sunshine casts her beams.

Then we will sit upon the grass
Watching birds swift flying past,
And now and then up in the trees
We'll hear them sing their melodies.

And we will talk of many things
Of soulful thoughts our heartfelt brings
That no one else but we can share
Of trust and love our souls to bare.

Within your eyes I'll see such depths
And what I feel my love it whets.
We'll swing along through forest glens,
Then you'll be more to me than friend.

Kelly Sireci
FLY AWAY
As I get older and our relationship fails,
My memory reminds me of what once used to be,
Wanting to be known, wanting to be seen, wanting to be let free,
As the world closes in around me,
My insides weaken,
I yearn for love deep down from someone of my kind,
The wind blows strong,
My hat blows away,
You catch it upon your head,
As you go to return it,
We catch glances,
We then walk in towards the sun,
We feel the need to become one.

June DeFaye Adams
A MOTHER'S JOY:
A PRECIOUS BOY
The sweetest words I ever heard
Found me by way of 'phone —
Repeating someone's casual quote —
A Son's — who's long since grown.

"My Grandmother," the sweet son said,
"Has gone to Heaven, now."
"My Mom will go to Heaven, too"
(May that be true . . . Somehow!)

That Son, when seven, stopped his play;
Concerned, he wrote a note to say:
"I don't think they will remember,
But I'm sure it's in December."

"Happy Birthday, Mom"

Pam Bierer
THE STARTING OF A NEW DAY

To my family for encouraging me to continue writing.

Watch the sun as it hides its head for the morrow
See the shadows of purple, red and yellow
Listen as the birds turn for shelter
Taste the dew floating lightly on the wind
Feel the cold trickling in for the night
. . . again.
Wonder what is in store for a mere mortal
Dream of the power you will show
Fight for the sullen sweet feeling of rest
Fade with the black that envelops you in a wicked quickness
To give into the warmth of a soft, cuddly nest

Wake to the new sun rising in the distance
Arch to warmth that can never be matched
Spread your wings to a new day at dawn
Remember how it felt as the dew starts its melt
Forgive all that happened as for now you start a new day.

Nancy J Roeser
LIFE

To My Loving Niece, Cindy.

As you travel up the road of life
The road is winding and cold,
You will have many bridges to cross
From the day you are young, Till you are old.

You must be brave, strong and good
And you will survive it all,
You will be able to reap the food
That you will plant and toil.

So move on for now and do not look back
On what life has been in the past,
Be warm and comfortable with yourself
And inner peace will find you at last.

We all have to travel this road of life
And each in his own way,
You too will find the right fork in the road
To guide you on your way.

So with these words of wisdom
I pass right on to you,
The love, hope and guidance
That will help to see you through.

Ralph Lockwood
ODIFEROUS FOR SPACIOUS SKYS

In memory of my wife: Marjorie Yates-Lockwood (1941-1989).

Sweet scents, newly mown
reel me back
to those summers of breathlessness —
to the green blade I once was;

eager, with thirsty gasps
blooming in
hungering gusts of what
I then too soon became,

unravelling dry layers of my undoing;
paring off all the joy
from this: so bland a marrow.

The energy of malice drains
from chaos
its power-pride, dictating
soul-death in Goods' name —

sooooooo, lately, bridgeworks
of visions
rust . . . sink in muzzled times, when I
thought not about my thinking.

Yet, vaguely, still palp'd
each lurching pace (shod quiet
by rippled swelling faces
merged to a mauve collage)

that slacks . . . thaws gray snow
to smelt our
souls for the sky's Eucharist
until we reach, and be, stars

Tracing new orbits:
shimmering:
in the burnished cosmos, rouge
with the deltae of pity's

lean blood — clotting, orange,
the night's seeds —
symbiotic syntheseeds; corpulent
of brain-loam's starched manna:

Rich incipient dust,
intensely
starved for change . . .
COLLECTING,
EXCISING WHIRLWINDS.

Norma J Webb
YOU'VE KILLED MY PARENTS (COCAINE)

To everyone touched by drug abuse.

You've put my son in jail
You've crippled my daughter
You've put my neighbor in the streets
You've corrupted my doctor, lawyer and minister
You've taken the brain of the new born
God is the only answer — Cocaine

John C Hall
OLD DOG

To Friday.

Old dog, lying in the sun.
Paws in the air, having fun.
Tongue hanging out, the lazy lout
Muscles twitching, he stretches out.

Sometimes I envy you old canine friend
Your snoozy days seem without end.
The sun shines down on your simple life
Existence free of stress and strife.

Do roll over, just once in a while
With ease befitting your regal stile.
If occasional tension you do feel
It's merely contemplation of your next meal.

So sleep in the sun, you lucky hound
While off to toil I am bound.
Remembering each "dog" has his day
Just maybe, tomorrow is mine to play.

Julie Durgin
WHO REALLY CARES ABOUT CHILDREN?

Dedicated to Dodi, Ed, Mike, W J. Murphy School, to all of my friends.

We hear the cries and see the tears on children's little eyes.
WHO CARES!
They come to school with no hats, no gloves, they feel the cold snow above them.
WHO CARES!
They're hungry and they don't feel well.
WHO CARES!
They fall down and cry because they're hurt.
WHO CARES!
They want a hug, a kiss, and "I love you."

WHO CARES!
They're scared, "Don't leave me home alone."
WHO CARES!
They have to worry about strangers, drug abuse, and other dangers.
WHO CARES!
They tell me their parents have left them for good, and all their other problems such as boyfriends, girlfriends, fights, and arguments.
WHO CARES!
Some children are ill with terrible diseases and they still can smile.
WHO CARES!
Some children get into trouble and cause problems.
WHO CARES!
I CARE! I REALLY DO! I love my children and all children. It really isn't hard to care, to take a few minutes to share. Share yourself with a child. Let them know you're on their side, and you will help! It will make a difference you will see. Please be caring just like me!

Jean Ellen Baldwin-Gahner
A SPECIAL REQUEST

Order of events as they usually are,
Perhaps you will reach heaven's door,
Casting your sweet smile upon the stars,
Before I wander from sea to shore.

Mother, I have a special request of you,
That only you can fulfill;
Because, as no other could ever do,
You can, dear mother, if you will?

If you'd be so kind to let him know,
His eldest daughter ever recalls
The bootstrap message, and to go
On and up — to give it my all!

You'll find him ... You'll know;
Just look for the angel wings
That have the softest, brightest glow;
The voice with the prettiest ring.

Then, at his wing . . . Stand to the right.
Tell him how I missed him so . . .
And, at his left, some special night,
A daughter will sing to him sweet and low!

Dedicated to my daddy — May he rest in peace!

Deborah A Johnson
WHAT IT WAS LIKE

To my brother Michael, his wife and all the children. As a direct result of drugs and alcohol, Michael was found dead on August 22nd, 1989. May God grant me, part of his soul for life. I continue, on borrowed time, to live two life styles in one life time.

Where would I start?
How will I begin?
To tell my part,
of what happened then.

The story of me.
The story of I.
How I came to be.
I don't know why.

I was born fresh.
I was born new.
I was born an alcoholic.
What am I to do?

My mother is sane.
My father I don't know.
My sisters are vain.
My brother is on snow.

I am recovering.
My family is too.
We are rediscovering,
life is fresh and new.

Doré Brooke Waldon
THE LOVE OF A FRIEND

To everyone: TRUE friends will always be there for you no matter what. You just have to realize who those true friends are!

I'm glad that we are such good friends,
Together we've learned that love never ends,
We've been through the good,
We've been through the bad,
These were the best times that I've ever had.

We've bared many tears
That teenage life brings,
You were there no matter what . . .
The wind beneath my wings.

The time will come for us to separate,
We know that this is true,
We promise not to go too far,
But still I'm gonna miss you.

As our lives go on we're reminded
Of each other through and through,
And I want you to know that I'll always be
Right here waiting for you.

Dana K Ryder Sr
ALL ALONE

Often, I sit alone in my room, inside the total silence of the dark

Thinking and wondering, all to myself, how the next day of my life is going to start.

The hands of time have suddenly stopped moving, as everything around me appears to stand still.

A strange feeling of shackles and chains now binds my legs — my very own frustrations are now holding me against my will.

I start smiling and laughing all to myself. My world won't stop crumbling at my very feet.

Now I sit so puzzled and lost in my own solitude, wondering,
Will I go another night without any sleep?

Images of emptiness have taken over my mind. Loneliness can be so filled with empty space.

I am just trying to find a little tranquility, to feel a gentle smile spread across my lonely face.

So swiftly are the pages turning in my life, I often ask myself "Do I have any regrets?"

My shadows are slowly fading into the darkness.

Loneliness — could this be all that I have left?

Elmiral Calhoun
WISHES ARE FOR KIDS TOO

Dear Parents sometimes there's stories I can tell too, of dreams and wishes I wish would come true. For better things and times for you. Oh how I wish, how I wish they'd come true. I know sometimes things I don't do so swell, but Oh how I wish, I just wish you wouldn't yell.

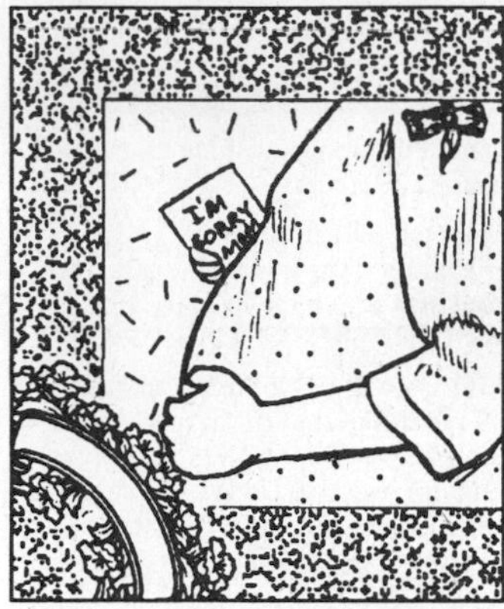

I know for you life can sometimes be hell. I wish my grades were better too just as hard as you do. I never meant to get pregnant before I said the words I do. You see some kids think that's a part of love too. Especially when our minds are not occupied with things constructive to do. The same can be said for drugs too.

I wish I could have found something else to do, like a word of encouragement or just a hug or kiss from you. When you're not at home and I'm alone, pressures can be oh so strong. I bet if we put our wishes together that God will see us thru and all our dreams and wishes can and will come true.

See, we're only kids
but kids have wishes too!

Cheryl Shaffer
THE KEEPER OF POEMS

Dedicated to: My love Ramon, my inspiration Renee, Kathy, Ruth, Mom, Dad, my boys Ramon, John, Christopher, and God above. I thank you each dearly.

Is there a poem you've been searching for, for days
The Keeper of Poems has put it away
Thinking later some price they will pay
By locking our feelings neatly away

From time–to–time you sneak-a-peak
Reading the words we wrote but, could not speak
Each one from there own moment in time
Some with rhythm and others that rhyme

You read them aloud to yourself
Then you set them back high on a shelf
And on the shelf they seem to stay
The Keeper of Poems has put them away

Rachel Matthews
THE STRANGER

He said he was a stranger, he told me his name. He said he was very glad that he came. He needed a friend, someone he could talk to; someone who wouldn't criticize everything that he'd do.

We talked for hours, and thought only seconds went by. Then he said "I'm saying good-bye." Then he said he loved me, and I just turned away. How could this happen in just one day?

He said he was a stranger, no longer shall that be. Marry, did he ask me.

The stranger is no stranger anymore.

Minnie Miller
A MOTHER'S SORROW

Mother, when God first gave you that boy,
Surely there wasn't a greater joy.
You bathed him, loved him, watched him grow.
Taught him things he didn't know.
You guided him with a guiding hand
Until he grew up to be a man.
Then he started out to roam;
left his bright and cheery home.
Oh how your heart for him did yearn
for news of him you didn't learn.
Until you heard the news, sad news,
that gives all mothers the deepest blues.
God had taken your son to rest,
but surely He knew what for him was best.

Michael Hickey
WAIL OF THE BANSHEE

Dedicated to Barbara Anne Hickey, 3 May 1932—7 July 1988, Isaiah 43:1.

Shimmering on the loch was seen
A pale young girl dressed in gray
Hands across her eyes, she cried
Teardrops rippling the dark water
Moonlight reflecting off its waves
From a field of sweet heather
Could be heard in the distance
A voice as soft as a rose petal
Low and melancholy, sad in tone
Her song deep within the heart
Beckoning and calling her love lost
The wailing of the Banshee is heard
Chilling and cold, straight to the soul
Eerily it echoes through the valley
For mortal men who hear its cry
So death will come to a loved one
Thunder and lightning forewarn the end
Torrential rains be the tears of Heaven
Guiding the soul of another love lost
The Banshee's wail drifts into silence

Grace H Patt
CONFUSED

To My Great Grand–Daughter & Namesake "Little Gracey."

Moods make poetry
I say this with a frown
Then ESP complains to me
And I start writing down
But this day I am so confused
I walk around with head held high
And you think I have the blues?
Believe me it's not that
Only a state of mind
Always looking, always searching
For something I can't find!

Mindy Browning Turner
MY FRIEND

For my beautiful daughters, Brittany and Annessa, you make the sun rise each morning.

I am so happy about my best friend
We take care of each other and on each other depend.

I first met her when she was brand new
My mother brought her home before I was two.

All she ever did was sleep or cried
I couldn't get her to play no matter how hard I tried.

It took some time getting used to each other
The hardest part was sharing our mother.

But now we share so many things
Our favorite dolls, our room, and our make believe games.

If one of us gets hurt or is sad
The other one of us feels really bad.

We are the best of friends there can ever be
There is no one else I would want with me.

Every day I will thank the good Lord who sent her
For in this whole world there is no one like my little sister.

Stig Waidelich
THE STORM

The Wind blows hard.
Outside; the crash
of the sea.

I am as
unseen driftwood,
awaiting peace
upon some sunny shore.

The sea rages
like some great beast
Brought to anger
by the howling whip of the wind.

She roars and gasps,
spitting her salty breath
above the turbulent whiteness.

In time
she will be still
Basking in the sun and
reflecting warm rays.

And it is then,
just as now
that I long to be with her.

Finally, the world rests.
Sun warms its soil
and plays music
upon a shimmering sea.

Only the waves linger
the final remains of its power
collapsing upon a sandy shore.
A beautiful conclusion to a turbulent storm.

Lisa L McCabe
ON THE DAY THAT WE MET

When we first met
And greeted each other
With a warm handshake
And a smile like no other,

We knew from the start
That we each had received
A friendship to last
Through all life's deeds.

I'm so very glad
It's lasted this long,
And grown into something
So special and strong.

I'll always remember
And never forget
The first smile we shared
On the day that we met.

Florence Castonguay
EMPTY NEST

In Memory of My Mother.

Nostalgic, wandering silent rooms,
My heart protests.
No clutter, muss,
Beds lie smooth, untouched.
The children flown,
To build their nests.

Bradley F McMillan
WINTER IN SLATERSVILLE

carelessly falling and lazily drifting,
covering all under mounds of white
snowflakes twinkle in lunar light.

winds blow, clouds float by on invisible wings
while winter weather brings a brisk chill
to the clear, crisp air of Slatersville.

thin, brittle icicles hang like tinsel from the trees
and even sturdy evergreens bow their branches wearily
under the snowy majesty that is winter.

a drowsy silence hangs heavily in the air.
even the busy, small-town church slumbers
under its snowy, white blanket.
in the night, a lonesome jay whispers gently,
"sleep soundly now, for Spring will soon arrive."

Rudolph Thomas
AMERINDIAN ELEGY

Dedicated to those afraid of accepting Change.

I fear the road is at its end
Freedom, twin-sister of Death
must soon be legend
Corrupted by Civilization —
Insidious poison
Aborted Idea
Cemetery of horrors.

Let me dream of kite-whims
that took the tail of Wind;
Knowing Nature undefiled.

I, indeed dream. For
Heart must heed mind. And Mind
Authority.

I have a guitar string in hand
It curls and twirls: It is free
Restrain it on my fret-board
Strike the note
And discover its true usefulness.

Rudolph Thomas
MY PEOPLE

Dedicated to those needing to know how to accept change.

It's written, I said so when Saul became king.
Yet, I recall, even before then warning
about the harsh realities of
establishing,
in my place, human authority.

With all their fine intentions,
Exploitation
Wars
Famine
Imprisonment
Censorship
Even the creation and spread of Plagues
will be tools they find themselves, at times,
using to manage you.

I know because I alone know
Continuous constructiveness! I alone can
teach the same!

Rudolph Thomas
TEENAGED GIRLS

Dedicated to those who would wait until eighteen.

It's a blast watching a teenaged girl's body
changing form
How the mischief in her eyes and smile
create storm
Never so hung-up on the phrase,
"You're so dear!"
And the silly things she'll whisper?
As well as cheer.
Fun, laughter and play, just make her day!
Ever happy to hear she looks fine;
because fragrances
and fashion dominate her mind.
Like the playful lark, in May
The flower hedges on a sun-shiny day
Let her be!
Enliven your world with, crazy
Her checkered attitudes to
chastity.

Rudolph Thomas
BEWARE

Dedicated to those needing to differentiate between mischief, and vandalism.

The man planting-up his yard
He foresees time's getting hard.
Like you rogues out to make him mad;
Perhaps, put aside his God
Indulge in what's demonical.

I've told you beware
He can set, damn good snare.
Stay clear; he may let you steal an apple, or pear. But don't touch provision
(yams and vegetables)
That's like his, religion!

Rudolph Thomas
THANK GOD CHILDREN KNOW

Dedicated to all parents who need to understand.

This year is designated
International Year of the Child.
But is this a proper choice — 79?
Can parents today really do all the occasion requires?
Aren't we hindered by
unemployment;
Food-stuff scarcity; the constantly
rising Cost-of-living
in the face of indefinite Wage
freeze — all in all,
the general fatigue to provide for a family?

Can the child understand; moreover, appreciate
parents in these circumstances doing their best?
Why couldn't the year be, 69 —
when everything was booming?
Then again, giving thought that, perhaps,
89 might see the worst of this
ongoing depression;
Is it the correct thing, in 79
to shelter a child from what might be
harsh realities, but proper
preparation?

Thank God children know,
instinctively,
in what era to rebel against their
parents; so that
each generation is adequately
prepared to deal with life
in their times!

Gina Marie Galaska
GRAM

In loving memory of my grandmother, Marie Clernt, and the special feelings that bound us so close together.

Gram,
Well, these past few days are the ones I always knew I'd hate
Even though we both knew full well,
it's all a matter of fate.
It's just that I'm gonna miss you so . .
that I'm finding it really hard to let go.
Gram, in my life you have given me so much:
Your friendship, your guidance, and
your very tender touch.
All of these things (and more) have meant the world to me.
And I just want you to know that
that's how it will always be.
There is a special place in my heart
that is reserved for only you —
So that you can be with me no matter what I do.

Well, good luck Gram in this
wonderful new place;
I know you are happy — I saw it on your face.
Your eternal happiness is well
deserved, and puts me at ease.
Because now you will be living in
eternal peace.

So I'll say "so long" to this physical part —
And let you start living inside my heart.
Until one day when fate evens the score
And we can be together
forevermore.

I love you.
Gina

Jenny Griffin
LONELY WIND

Silent are the mighty trees
That whisper softly in the gentle breeze.
Soft is the moon on high
That dazzles in the midnight sky.
Quiet is the wind so lonely
As if in search of its one and only,
And as the land is covered in dark
So too would I, without you in my heart.

You brighten my life like the midnight moon
When the burdens of life hit way too soon,
But though the lonely winds shall in time blow cold
Our love for each other shall never grow old.
For as part of my life you will always be there,
No matter when, no matter where.

Irma Holloway-Lott
JEWELS OF A FRIENDSHIP

Dedicated to the most beautiful and precious friend in the world, my mother — Georgia Lee Woodard-Holloway.

We were rough and dull in the beginning.
Then our brightness and brilliance began to shine.
Similar to diamonds . . cut, shaped and polished.
Our giggles at times would even entwine.
And could turn into unending laughter,
Like threads of silver and gold for strength.
A glow of ruby red come to our cheeks.
When our smiles would be caught at edges length.
At times tears of joy and genuine as pearls;
Filled our eyes like opal's snow white milky pools.
Though as a coral embedded deep in the sea.
Our friendship will glisten and sparkle as jewels.

Laurie Ferguson
THE KEEP
With yellow eyes, they hypnotize
their morally weakened prey.
With perfect skill, a silent kill
insures their hopes of this day.
In moonlite's foul, a prided howl
carries the message of ended beast.
And in anticipation, the congregation
awaits the promised feast.
A glorious haul, to be shared by all —
a celebration to be held this nite;
to honor the hunter, among the others,
who gained victory in his fight.
Then in their tire, the games expired
and all will settle in sleep.
With exception to one, who into the sun,
will ensure safety of the keep.

Robin Wooton
MY PRAYER FOR YOU
My prayer for You is small
But life is the greatest gift of all.
God put you here for a reason,
His love greatens season after season.
You have so many people who care about You,
I cherish our Friendship because it's so true.

Life has its ups and downs
But if you were gone, there would be nothing but frowns.
When I'm down you make me smile,
I want you to be around for a while.
This is my prayer for you —
Always think positive before anything you do.

Constance L Pogue
A PATH OF FANTASIES
You walk your own chosen path
—by my side
But my ways are not yours.

You gaze at me from a distance
—and wonder if I'm O.K.

I stare back at you with confused eyes
—and think
"I'm going my own way!"

Your mind seems secure about
which path is your own,

But I'm still in a dream world
following a path of fantasies
. . . ALONE.

Betty Jane Rhein
MY LOVE

This poem is dedicated to the man who is my love.

Your passion, I desire.
Your saddest, I since,
Your pain, I felt,
Your touch, I'll never forget,
Your love, will live forever in me,

Sandra Arleen Minchin
YOU

Inspired by Ted Reynolds, everything I could ever hope to find in a friend and more you are. Love you. Always.

All of my life I've been searching
Looking for a hand to hold
My summer shower, my autumn sunset
Dreaming before I'm too old
Of far away places, bubbles in springtime
Snowflakes that dance with delight
Warm fluffy sweaters, old mushy novels
Candles to burn through the night
Beaches of sand, oceans of blue
Roses that blush in the sunshine
Soft gentle music with haunting refrains
Verses that end with a rhyme
Searching for someone, to enter my life
And listen to my cluttered mind
Holding me close, yet letting me go
When I feel the need to hide
In eyes that dream of brighter things
I found it, beautiful and new
Something I've searched for all of my life
I found it all, a friend in you.

Elizabeth Kilmer Ronky
AN AFFAIR OF THE MIND
Who knows or who can remember
how I met this stranger . . .
shopping mall or through a friend?
His physical appearance I cannot describe but his thoughts
are sparks of brilliance.
He has taken me by the hand, away from my reality and led me
slowly, gently to another space.
A stranger guiding me to a virtual land where time is
naught and nothing intrudes upon one's privilege to pursue.
He shares his thoughts slowly till I beg like an addict for
more, quicker, tell me, share . . . reveal!
My mind ablaze, lost to reality and friends, I want only
to share his world caring of nothing else.
People put demands on me, Return!
Give him up! Provide! Make
clear your priorities!
In this un-world, as a woman to a man, sharing such
intimacies of intermost thoughts . . .
dare I call this stranger Stephen?
Do not despair, the real world beckons me out of this
fantasy, for I have only fallen into another book.
My mind thrives on the floating fantasy it experiences
and craves to remain long after my return.
Though the stranger and I have shared time in escape, the parting
arrives and all I can say is "Thank you Mr. King for a 'haven' from the hum-drum," as I pull my mind out of the book and on to other things.

Elizabeth Kilmer Ronky
DAN
Time was when the flowers bloomed,
The birds flourished,
And the heart was empty and lonely.

You came along and filled my heart.
Time flew.
We were busy getting acquainted and
sharing life histories.

The flowers stopped blooming,
The birds existed.
Who cared? My heart was happy and full.

Our times were so intense.
Neither one of us existed as we had been.
Time was poisoned.
Jealousies arose.
That special place of escape was locked.
You went away.

The flowers bloomed.
The birds flourished.
My heart ached.

Elizabeth Kilmer Ronky
THE PEACEFUL PLACE
Wouldn't it be great to be just me?
Not to have to explain my thoughts, expressions or moods.
To just be me doing what I want when I want.
To be accepted for who I am based on my life experiences
without hurting another's sense of self or space.
To spend time in a dream world or waste time doing nothing.
To stay up late with a creative endeavor or go to sleep
early and ignore life.
To work hard until I drop or let the clutter around me
mount to the sky.
To be side by side with others existing as themselves
without strife.
If a place like this exists, how do I get there and can I
take a friend?

Ceacey P Hardy
A SMALL GRIN
Within the depths of one lost soul,
darker than night, darker than coal;
a volcanic eruption lies on the verge,
with despair as its power surge;
No longer does the body belong,
she only wishes it will all be gone;
Once she saw a faint glimmer of light
and felt the warmth of its sight,
When comprehension began to set in,
only then she gave a small grin.

Erma Stalnaker
GOING TO THE FAIR
Tomorrow daddy will be going
To our county fair
He'll take his cows and his horses
And perhaps his old gray mare.
Mom will take her jams and jellies
And some flowers that she grew
Hoping that she'll win some prizes
And a big blue ribbon too.
I want to go with them
To our county fair
I want to see the cows and horses
And all the people gathered there.
I want to see the horses racing
The demolition derby too
Sit and watch the tractors pulling
So many things to see and do.
I want to ride the merry-go-round
Maybe the ferris wheel too.
Eat hot dogs and cotton candy
Then come home when the day is through.

Cecelia J Bryner
FREEDOM'S VOICE
At first
the voice a whisper on the wind
was small and weak, then it grew
in strength it grew
until it reached a peak!
It swept from England's shore to Holland,
across an ocean, argosy of Hope,
to a new a virgin land.
Through blood and sacrifice
the voice cried out, "Free men!"

1989-1990,
Again
the voice a whisper on the wind
stirs hope
in minds and hearts of men.
Revolution in many lands,
rejection of repression, Chinese sacrifice,
Confusion, continent in transition,
crumbling iron curtain—dark ages rule.
The cry for FREEDOM
fills the world anew.

Blyth Mackay-Bond
THE DOORWAY
The night is dark
The wind cold
But onward I must go.
My Mother Dear
Was getting old
And I was getting closer.

As I approached
The bedroom door
The panic struck within me.
Could this be it
Was this the time?
The time of her departure.

Uncertain steps
And fearful courage
Led me closer to her.
The fear I felt
Showed not in her
When peace descended on her.

I was not there
But this I knew

All fear now gone.
All death accepted
I closed my eyes
And prayed. Peace at last.

Dhari Murrell Parks
DARK HOURS

For my mother, Mrs. Pearl E. Murrell: and for all women who stand at the window and cry when choices seem few.

in the small, dark hours
i lie staring at the ceiling
wondering
how it could be different
what are the possibilities
or ?
what were they
and, where
is the future
in loneliness?

i don't have the answers
i only know sadness
i hurt, but don't cry
knowing
it's too deep
for tears.

Anita Ann Sloane
DIFFERENCES
We're not the same
Friend, you and I
No more than a snowflake
Drifting by

We're many ways alike,
It's true
But different still
Am I from you

I fear for us
Friend, you and I
I wish that I
Could tell you why

Let's trust, accept, and understand
It's up to us
So take my hand!

Geraldjean Ashley
NIGHTFALL
The day's death shroud colors the heavens,
Night begins its descent to earth.

A myriad of blues fade to violet-velvet;
Stars peek down from celestial perches,
Singing light songs as they blink.
The sun slowly begins its journey,
Piercing the night with spears of light.
And as night's curtain is slowly lifted,
Unwillingly,
Night vanishes, leaving the new day with temporary bruises.

Carol A Holbrook
SAVE OUR EARTH
To every being so humble and fair,
Who lives and breathes life's precious air,
Who smells the flowers and feels the breeze,
Who casts his net upon the seas,

Who drinks the water that's heaven sent,
Whose harvest is a big event,
Who drills for oil, or mines for coal,
Who flies an airplane to and fro,

Who rides the rails, or sails the seas,
Who lives and dies for liberty,
Who stares into the moon-lit night,
And counts the stars that come in sight,

Protect our earth, its land, and seas,
Our wildlifc, mountains, and our trees,
Conserve on energy, water, and air,
Recycle, show the earth you care,

Preserve our land, try not to waste,
Pollute not rivers, streams, or lakes,
Let future generations see,
The gift God gave to you and me.

Heidi Archambeau

Heidi Archambeau
TEAR ABOVE
When I wake up in the morning,
And I see the moon has gone,
Left only with the beautiful
Sunshine at the break of dawn;
Thoughts of the night fade away
With the stars.
Memories of you hidden in the past.

I knew our love would never last.
Like the gentle falling rain,
I can still feel the pain
To wash away my tears.
I see a sad reflection in the mirror.
You seemed so sincere, how was
I to know you had another love?
Somewhere up above the heavens
So blue this tear is dedicated to you.

Daryl Friedrich
THE END OF HUNTING SEASON

In memory of my grandfathers.

It began in October but you couldn't hear the shots
Then November rolled around and things got hot.
Hunting is an odd sort of thing,
For it's one man's dream, another's fling.
One man likes to enjoy nature to sit and look,
While another hopes to put his name in a record book.
For hunters sit and talk of days gone by
and of their hunting companions who now dwell in the sky.
It is a sport to be shared by young and old, rich and poor,
And both hope to add mystique to some grand old hunting lore.
But now the end of the season is near
The hunters pack, holding back a mist of tears.
I sit alone in my stand on that last day
To find the buck which avoided me like the plague.
As the last fleeting seconds go by,
I turn my head and wink to both my grandfathers in the sky.

Carolyn Wells
I COULD BE . . . BUT

To my sons: Warrick and Craig.

I could be out making money
I could be out making friends . . .
but I rather be home for
You and your friends.

I could be out making decisions
I could be out doing it all . . .
but I rather be home to
hear about your day and all.
I know where I need to be and
I know it's important to you.

I could be looking like a
Model all polish and neat . . .
but I rather be home in
My apron making you little treats.

I could have had a career
and money too . . .
but I rather be an unpaid
Mother, raising you.

I could be . . .
but I rather have you
Come home to me.

Donna McGovern
CEASE FIRE
I have suffered
in this relationship with you
like nothing else
I have ever been through;
This time I said I wouldn't run away . . .
no matter what, I would always stay;
but I fail to understand
how you can be so indifferent to me;
I search your eyes for a sign of hope . . .
and emptiness is all I see;
yet you grip my arm when I try to go
and say you love me . . .
when you know it isn't so;
I have carried our cause
like a crusade for years . . .
but my spirit is torn like a flag
beaten by an endless storm;
If you ever find yourself,
please tell me who you are . . .
maybe then I'll know what I fought for.

Ollie M Steen Russell
I LIVE BY FAITH
I live by faith because I know
That God has promised me
If I would only do his will
My everything he'd be

Because of this I can rejoice
When all around me doubt
When trouble calls and shadows fall
He'll surely bring me out.

When trouble comes in twos and threes
And the road seems awfully long
I trust in God because I know
That he will keep me strong.

He fights my battle day by day
He bridges my waters too
And everything he does for me
He'll do the same for you.

I walk and talk and live by faith
Because God never fails
Where I am weak he is my strength
And the strong always prevail.

Sharon Music
SPRING

With love and memory to Gary.

One day in spring while all was quiet.
And I was feeling good.
I went out for a friendly stroll,
Out through the greening woods,

The sun was shining bright and warm,
The wind was blowing sweet,
The flowers beneath the autumn leaves,
Came through the sun to meet,

I walked on through the grassy fields,
Such beauty can't be told,
The lovely sight I saw that day,
Was only mine to hold,

I sat beside a peaceful stream,
So shallow, cold and clear,
If ever I have been in love,
It came to me right here,

As long as I shall ever live,
I never will forget,
The day I spent in nature's arms,
Where my first love I met.

Alvin Mark Hawkins
THE ETERNAL SIGH

I dedicate these poems to all of the Hawkins family, especially to my son Dustin for helping me understand what love can be.

Along the way, one winter's day
An old man walks by
His choice of journey
In this modern day
No man can deny
Through the snow, the hidden trail
An old man walks by
This destiny from travel
His secret avail
Deep forests blind, the eternal sky.
Among the fog, the distant lake
An old cabin stands nearby
His choice of death
By this frozen lake
No man can deny
Under the ice, the endless well
An old cabin stands nearby
This fate of fortune
His secret avail

Deep waters hide . . .
The eternal sigh.

Alvin Mark Hawkins
WHITE CLOUD, THE BLUE SKY
White cloud, white cloud
Passing by moving down.
Blue sky, the blue sky
We're laughing and crying
The love he gave us
It's all around.
White cloud, white cloud
Passing by moving down.
Blue sky, the blue sky
We're living and dying
The life he gave us
It's all around.
Sad eyes, blue eyes
Don't cry, the blue sky
Our pain on earth this time
Once felt by him, the dying.
For there is joy beyond
And the life we seek
In heaven, it's ours to keep
So with love we speak
White cloud, the blue sky.

Alvin Mark Hawkins
ANN EMOTION
She came to me, one summer's eve
Those brown eyes I feel
Is that light for me?
A creation to need
This woman from Eve
Her brown eyes so real
She will always be free.
This is the light
The light of emotion
Come walk with me
Ann emotion.
You are the light
My eyes to see
Day into night
You will always be free
And if ever you are cold
So lonely in need
I will love you forever, Ann
Emotion.

Alvin Mark Hawkins
OUR WORLD
Behold, from the celestial body
A creation, perfect cosmos in time
The dawn, an antiquity of life
Our wonderful world so alive.
Absolute beauty, ambiance delight
An aura, sweet breath of life
Arousing the senses, to purify
Our wonderful world so divine.
Apricot tree, the busy honeybee
A merry canary sings along
Cherry wine, cold wind chimes
Banana nut bread we bake at home.
Apple pie, the graceful butterfly
A Christmas carol sing along
Cinnamon gum, cream colored doves
Shooting stars from the galaxy above.
Behold, from the ivory tower
Ascendent angel, soaring higher
One deity in harmony, love and peace
Now tranquility; sleep
Serene fervent dreams.

Bruce William Hardy
FATHER'S SONG
Dad, maybe you know, though I
doubt that it's so:
How I feel about you and what
you've done for me.
And that's why I wrote these words;
the ones that stick in my throat—just
to try and let you see.

Thank you, Dad, for givin' me
everything you had.
Thank you, Dad, for bein' the way
you are to me.

When I was just a pup, trying so hard
to be grown up; you know we
didn't always get along.
Those times we'd argue and fight;
you were tryin'
To make me something right. And I
want to say
THANKS before one of us is gone.

Thank you, Dad, for givin' me
everything you had.
Thank you, Dad, for bein' the way
you are to me.

Well, I'm in my thirtieth year and
finally grown
And findin' out just how little I've
known.
I'm a father, too, with a couple
bundles of joy,
But, if I could, Pop, I'd still be your
little boy.

Thank you, Dad, for givin' me
everything you had.
Thank you, Dad, for bein' the way
you are to me.

Julia Irene Hardy
FORGIVENESS
There is something about forgiveness
That warms the heart and clears
the soul . . .

Some choose to go through life
Bound and gagged; to hatred tied.
Always condemning the other guy
Flagging a grudge; eaten up inside.

If ever you have traveled
the wrong road
In your search for joy and peace;
Then, suddenly find forgiveness
You will sense an utter release.

Carrie Ann Host
UNMENDED HEART

To: Michael W. Kirk—I hope you found the happiness you were looking for. I miss you!

There's no phone calls
no flowers
no looking deep in his eyes
All that's left
is a broken heart
torn apart by lies
Is there mending?
no, not this time
Just pick up the pieces
maybe then
you'll be fine
But you will always remember
and can never forget
The one you fell in love with
the first time
you met . . . .

Ann S Huff
NOW
Yesterday is gone
Never to be recovered
Tomorrow may not come
Never to be discovered

So what we have is now
We might call it today
Some call it the present
It can't be held at bay

Feel what you feel sincerely
Speak truth gently but fairly
Hold on to and dearly
Face life and squarely
Sorrows can overcome you
Joys may overwhelm
There is good and bad to handle
Who is at your helm?

Faith is the source of power
Grace a gift of love
Now is the hour
Now you must rise above

Patricia Henson
OUR HEARTACHE

Dedicated in loving memory of our granddaughter, Natasha Henson. See you in heaven "Skeeter."

In the quiet of the evening
Our hearts begin to ache
We can no longer hear your laughter
Or touch your precious little face
This longing that we have will never
go away
Always, always, within us it will
always stay.
Our soul cries so deep within, and yet
so very near
We cry for what might have been
But there will never be no more than
tears.
Except for precious memories of your
five short years
Our hearts can only rejoice when we
think of you without the pain
For Christ died on the cross and that
was for our gain
Your entrance into heaven was a
joyous and mighty sound
That loosed you from your sufferings
and pain
In which you were here on this earth
Bound.
In our mind's eye, we can see you on
the streets of Gold
Just walking and running as the Bible
told
Our precious little "Skeeter," no one
will ever take your place
And we will be together again at the
ending of our race
We love you, our precious little one
And we will see you again by the
grace of His dear son.

April Hoisington
WHAT I DO KNOW
I know I'm not a great "artist" as
some, but one thing I'm not a
bum.
I know the world has its problems,
and that no one has to be alone.
I'm not saying I know it all, but
what I do know can't fall.
If you believe, care, share, and love
then you too can have it all. No
one is perfect except God.
But you should never judge others by
fault. Look at me I'm no
masterpiece.
I've been through a lot but I'll never
stop because if there's one thing I
believe it's in you and me.
If there's one thing I know it's that
God will never let us go.
So if you believe, care, share, and
love. Come on over it's time to
take over.
You see all the world knows is fear,
pain, and tears.
These things brought on by gangs,
wars, and peers.
But if you read this and understand
then you fit into the plan. So join
the thousands that live for peace.
And you too can live for peace. But
don't forget your love for he or
she deserves that above . . .

Dorothy Hershman
TRUE TO LIFE . . .
The beckoning tablet lies waiting—
It's vulnerable, unpledged, pristine—
The hand with the pen, poised and
eager—
The urge for creating is keen.
The words flow without hesitation,
Conceiving a hero, well taught—
A heroine, talented, lovely—
A gripping, mysterious plot.
But soon, without warning, the hero
And heroine, shocking the meek,
Befoul the once pristine bond paper
With slime and crass filth when they
speak.
We blush, feel offended and dirty.
We shrink from the curses they use.
The gutter is where such words
flourish!
We're filled with disgust we can't
lose.
It's "true to life" art, plead the
authors,
But whose real life do they define—
Those filthy, embarrassing phrases?
Surely not yours . . . certainly not
mine!

Dr Charles E Haggerty
STRETCH THE MIND
Has your mind ever caught fire,
Excitement as your intellect expands?
Has your horizon been extended,
Has your heart raced across the land?

Has someone caught your
imagination,
Stretched it until it nearly cracked
Let new ideas filter through
And then handed it back?

Have you seen great visions,
Have you dreamed great dreams,
Has your heart thrilled to great music,
Arisen to contemplate great themes?

Have you seen the simple beauty
Of the world in which you live?
'Tis a sublime feeling,
One of the greatest God can give.

Have you known the joy of
self-realization,
The confidence of being able to say: I
Can!
The strength of being in command,
Of knowing: You are your own Man!

Meryl Garrison Hus
MASTERPIECES
The narrow road wound like a ribbon
of white,
Over the hill and out of sight.
The lake lay below, while in the sky,
I knew a jet plane was streaking by.
The road that it left was straight and
true,
A path of silver on a sky of blue.

As the summer sun bid us a fond
farewell,
A picture was painted no tongue can
tell.
Fluffy, pink clouds on a backdrop of
blues,
Were mirrored below in soft, pastel
hues.
God is a Master Painter, every day a
new release,
Beautiful and different, each one a
masterpiece.

Patti Hunziker
THE MARVELS OF SPRING
Misty clouds hang low in the forest,
Just the tree tops are peeking

through;
New born lambs romp in green pastures,
As they circle around the ewe.
See the chestnut colored colt on spindly legs,
And the calf with the snowy white face;
It's funny how awkward they seem to be,
As around their mothers they race.
The spectacular sight of the Canadian geese,
Can be seen in their northern flight;
While out in the pond we hear croaking sounds,
As the frogs romance in the night.
Out doors is sweetened by the new spring blossoms,
From the bulbs and the budding tree;
We can't help marvel at how it all happens,
As spring brings new beauty to see.
Slide open the window in the old stuffy house,
Let the music of the birds come in;
Breathe in the fresh air, fold your hands,
And thank God it is spring again.

Jon Anthony Hoynacki (Age 11)
LISTEN TO THE OCEAN

The ocean waves come rolling in
Beyond the soft, white sand
And every person listens to
The breeze that spreads over the land.

The children in the water,
The shells upon the shore,
All listen to the sound it makes
When the ocean meekly snores

Listen to its famous hark
For soon it'll be no more
'Cause of the things we're doing to this earth
Soon there will be no ocean, nor shore

Santina L Gray
MY VACATION

Dedicated to my late grandfather, Frank R. Scavo, who loved poetry deeply and to my Uncle Steven Gray who inspired me to write this poem.

My vacation was too crowded to even say "hello,"
To my dear and very loved ones whom I never would let go.
I was always going places, always on my feet;
I never got a second to myself and my heart never missed a beat!
My Mom and Dad enjoyed it, but I couldn't stay awake,
When we went out to those places and stayed out way too late.
Even though my vacation was crowded, I had a real good trip,
And I hope to do it again sometime when my trip can last a bit!

Dolores J Garrett
MY FRIEND QUEENIE

This poem is a true story. To my Son, Fred and his dog Queenie.

When I was very sad.
This little puppy was born.
My mother said I could
keep her.
Then I was very glad.
The puppy filled my life with joy,
She became my friend.
It was better than any old toy.
When she got older,
My dog got very sick.
I never gave up hope.
We knew we could lick this terrible thing.
Here it is a year later and my friend,
Queenie and I are still together.

Jill Christine Groth
SEEING THROUGH EYES OF OLD

Written for two great ladies. Mildred I. Haag and Lucille M. Groth.

"That's only because you're old," says the child
whose grandmother says he's wrong.
"Someday you will understand," she said,
"someday when I am gone."

The child grew older and still didn't believe
until one day he had a son.
They fought, and then the father said,
"You will believe, too, just like I have done."

The things he said were what
his grandmother said long ago.
And with tears in his eyes, he looked to the sky,
"Grandma, now I know."

With a twinkle in the deep blue sky
in a very faint whisper she said,
"The story of olden times is told
and now you see through eyes of gold."

Linda Madeley Cooper
FREE SPIRIT

Inspired by you and your love of flying, I dedicate this poem to you, my beloved husband, Remel. My love to our four daughters: Sherridon Cooper Dobbs, Shannon Cooper Wagner, Christina Cooper Dressel, Laura Cooper Hunter. My grandchildren, Shaun and Kara Dobbs, Ryan Hunter. I love you.

Soaring like an eagle,
Free spirit in sight,
Gazing at God's creation
With grandeur and foremight.

The wind billows softly
Beneath my wings so high;
Kiss of nature lingers to
Never say good-bye.

Clouds so soft as cotton, as
Hence they beckon me; just
A mere ole pilot boring a
Hole of I.F.R. you see.

Erica Gassner
FUTURES

Traveling down
the road of life,
I hope we meet again.
I can't picture
life without you,
going farther and farther
along the road.
Nothing to grip on to,
when hard times come.
Nobody to help me
when I'm hurt.
Our futures
are unlikely to
be thought of
together.
Futures alone.

Sabrina Galimberti
LOVE IN MY EYES

To my Family, Relatives, & Friends. Who have given me Life, Love & Laughter. (Here Doggie!) My future Husband & Children. For without you all there would be no Love In My Eyes. I Love You All! SABRINA.

Love is a rose, for when it blooms it brings doom.
Love is a thorn, for when it pricks, it leaves you to bleed.
Love is the song that plays in your ear and brings a trickling tear.
Love is the knife, that pierces your heart, and brings you fear.
Love is infinite, love is kind.
But when you find the one you love don't be blind.
For one day you're sure to wake, and find your heart will break.
So shout aloud I love you!
And say never fear, for my love I shall always be here.
But when he leaves and your heart is broken, you are sure to be left unspoken.
Though the memories of your laughter and smiles may bring tears,
You will remember your first love throughout the years.
And as you walk away from your past, you will start a new life, with a love that lasts.
Once you've found the right man, reach out for his hand and say: Love is kind. Love is comforting.
Love is warm, Love is blue.
But most of all love is you!

Henry L Godwin Sr
WISHING

To all of those whose hopes and dreams have been shattered; shattered by an unrelenting force which no mere mortals have any control.

If I could see ahead of me as far as I can behind,
A failure I would never be, success would surely be mine.
The right path I would always take, not pausing or wasting time.
If I could see ahead of me, as far as I can behind.

If I could see as far ahead, as far as I can see back,
Fate's little games I wouldn't dread, and nothing in life I'd lack.
I would know of all the pitfall, venturing into nothing blind.
If I could see ahead of me, as far as I can behind.

Ah, but fate is a selfish foe, selfish to some but not all
Refusing, as quite a few of us know, to let us peek in its crystal ball.
Conjuring unpleasant surprises, denying me what's in mind.
Oh!, how I wish I could see ahead, as far as I can behind.

Henry L Godwin Sr
ASSURANCE

It's sad, said the chipmunk to the squirrel one day.
My mother said the green grass will soon go away.
It will all turn brown, she said, and so will all the leaves.
Very sad said the squirrel, as they sat down to grieve.

My mother mentioned to me something I've never seen,
Something about snow on the ground where once the grass was green.
I know, said the little chipmunk, his voice soft and meek,
But mother said I wasn't to worry, for I'll be sound asleep.

Well I won't be, said the squirrel, a frown upon his little face,
And I've been told by those who know, that food will sure be scarce.
Tears came into the chipmunk's eyes, as he turned and said,
Friend squirrel when I awake from my sleep, I might find you dead.

Not true said the owl, who had been listening, not making a sound.
Food has been stored for you when there's snow upon the ground.
That's why all summer long, you've been storing nuts away,
So that you'll be sure to eat on snowy winter days.

"Now listen to me you two, hear what I'm going to say,
"If we didn't have the dark of night, we wouldn't enjoy the day."
The owl spread his powerful wings, and as he left the scene;
"If the grass didn't turn brown, we wouldn't enjoy the green."

David K Gabriel
WITH ONE MORE STEP

if there's anything i should say to you before you go,
if there's anything i should tell you that you don't already know,
if there's anything i can do to make you stay,
then smile and reach out for me before you walk away.

if i can erase the pain from your saddened face,
if i can undo all the bad memories of this unwon race,
if i can take back all that i've said,
then smile and reach out for me and stay awhile instead.

with one more step and you'll be gone
you'll end a love we've shared for so long

with one more step there won't be another chance
to be together again and continue this romance.

if i could change the past i wouldn't change a thing
i'd remember the good, learn from the bad and forget the sad.

if i could change one thing i'd try to change your mind,
to stop you from leaving 'cause a love like yours i'll never find.

if i could say just one more time before you go, before we part
i'll always love you—you'll always be in my heart
if you believe in the words i say then smile,
reach out for me, before you walk away . . . .

Sandra J Hart
TROUBLED LOVE

To Paul Arvizo—A dear and wonderful friend.

Locked in my mind
Anguish and confusion
Suddenly opened
Devastation
Misunderstandings
A thousand tears
For seven years

Sandy Harth
AN AMERICAN MARRIAGE
So once again we had a fight,
So once again we were mean,
So once again we were nasty.
This is the great American dream,
This is the great American way,
This is the great American marriage,
PAIN, PAIN, PAIN, AND MORE PAIN,
Followed by days of no talking,
Followed by days of silence,
Followed by days of no communicating,
Further followed by days of forgiveness,
Those lying meaningless days of forgiveness,
Those empty promising days of forgiveness.
When all passes,
The circle begins,
The cycle resumes,
The pattern commences,
The fighting returns.

Sylvia Hawthorne
SHADOWS' END

This poem is lovingly dedicated to my parents, Collins and Lile Hawthorne.

In time all shadows will fade away,
holding a lost of memory for the day.
No longer will the hands of clocks keep time —
Present, Past, and Future will become synchronized.
The air will be filtered with a mist of despair.
Bright was the sun, now sheds a gloomy glare.
Moon and stars no longer brighten dark skies,
covered with the dust of screeching cries.
Trees will bend as though tired and worn—
Bowing to the earth from which they were born.
Flowers will close for the very last night—
Bees have gathered their nectar for a final flight.
All beasts shelter themselves for an endless sleep.
Men, women, and children shall walk nor creep.
The shadows of time shall cast its spell,
capturing the world and all that dwell.
With the assurance of limited space,
They're laid to rest in their proper place.
Its captive held in a pallor of mystery—
And the doors shall be locked forever, eternity.

Kristy Heard
MOONCHILD
The wind flows through the darkness among the gusty trees
As bats soar over purple moor departed by the cloudy seas
A castle lies upon the hill enchanted by a deep blue
Moon, scarce creatures roam the night and
Quarrel into doom, for I am but a child
Misguided under wound to mourn in black
Forevermore beneath a cross full moon . . . .

Martha Azar Hochendoner
SENSELESS TRAGEDY
Cancer.
A killer.
It eats its victims' bodies.
At first selectively, slowly.
Then, with a sense of reckless abandon
It destroys, as though to conquer.
And, within this madness, there is an irony;
The presence of a thorn bird.
For, as the human body is destroyed
By malignancy
And dies,
The cancer dies too.
It destroys its own house.
How senseless.

Ann Honey
SUNDAY CALL
Her day began, she says, quite sunny!
Though Lord knows, how it's to end.
You know! time's not the same, as it used to be, back THEN.
Time was easy, THEN to spend!

I just don't know; so much I long to see!
But steep the steps, the climb so high, to attics stored by me.
She smiles in moments sweetly loaned, to find herself back home;
wandering through familiar rooms, where LIFE and treasures loom!

I go back now and then, she sighs.
Yes! times a few I've been!
And it's the same now there, as then, as I go back again!

Now a wearied mind returns to find, that here for her must be, what's left of life to see.
With little need to try, in slumber, life and dreams glide by!
I wonder!
When I hang up and say good bye; does she like me, begin to cry.

Ann Honey
STRAY
One day as I sat gazing through my kitchen windows view,
Easy and content, the warm sun shining bright!
With only thought of blue sky and leaves a reddish hue!
When came into that joyful view, a sad and bitter sight!

A poor old cat my eyes did see, black his coat and sparse.
Some cruel misfortune life had dealt, only pity now I felt!
I watched heart broken as he limped, a spot of shade to seek.
Was all that he could do, his strengths so very few!

Upon the ground at last he lay, there to breathe a sigh;
Then began to wash the coat, hoary and so dry.
Eyes filling to the brim so that I could scarcely see!
He must have sensed I cared, for knowing eyes peered up to me!

I felt he knew here was a friend, still he chose to go,
And I was left with feelings, sadder now to grow!

To my surprise that poor old stray, came limping back one day,
Gazing up as if to say, was here his choice to stay!
Now lazing fat and shiny new, mine each day to see,
Stray, through my kitchen's windows view!

Amanda Sue Hosea
GRANDMA'S ATTIC
Libby and I could hardly wait,
For the big iron gate to swing wide.
We'd hug Grandma and say "Hello,"
Then we'd all hurry inside.

While the grown-ups talked, Libby and I
Would climb the dim, narrow stairs
To Grandma's attic, with the big wooden trunk,
And the stately old-fashioned chairs.

I'd put on Grandma's green velvet dress,
And the hat with the plume on the side.
Libby would don the white georgette,
That Aunt Lil wore as a bride.

We'd sit at a table made from an old wooden box,
And sip our make-believe tea,
Then we'd whirl round and round at the big pretend ball,
That was held just for Libby and me.

There was no end to the things we could do,
In that magical place all our own.
We were always amazed, when the day had gone by,
To see how the hours had flown.

Amanda Sue Hosea
THE FISHING TRIP
On a warm June morning, my brother and I
Grabbed our old bamboo pole,
And made our way through the sagebrush patch
In route to our fishing hole.

The blue jays were chattering overhead
In the spreading cottonwood tree.
A woodchuck peered from his hole in the ground
To see what the noise could be.

We seated ourselves on the cool green grass,
Baited and threw in our hook.
A curious turtle from the rocks nearby
Came over to take a look.

I had just lain back on an old rotten stump
And loosed the string on my hat,
When Bill jumped up and drew in his line
With a nice, big yellow cat.

We fished all day and we headed home
Making plans as we studied our catch,
For more lazy days by the old fishing hole
And a bigger and better batch.

Stephanie Styron-Hunt
BREEZE
I sit through the lonely breeze in the hill, which only a few can see.
The trees will blow, the wind will cool . . .
the only, lonely me.
It's the only way to sit in the shade and enjoy the breeze.
As it goes past, I say to myself, it's the only me.
I hear the breeze as it says to me,
Sit there till two past three.

Joyce Williams

Joyce Williams
CHANGE SPEAKS OF ITSELF
I am change.
Through me, all things become different.
Because of me, many things are renewed.
Without me, there is no development
Of the scope and activity of life itself.
Some welcome me as a path towards gain,
Others tremble when I appear
For in my wake I also bring loss and pain.
My nature is dual; if one sees my brightness
He must acknowledge my bleakness as well.
There is no other way of seeing,
There is no other way of being.

I am seen in the waxing and waning of the moon
And the events of a nation from order to confusion
I can be today's solidness,
Only to become tomorrow's diffusion.
Such is my nature and nothing escapes it
For this is how the universe fulfills itself
This must be understood if one is to have peace
And harmony within self
There is no other way of seeing,
There is no other way of being.
I am change.

Colleen Hogan
REFLECTIONS OF TREES
When the wind blows
late at night,
dead woods rub
in mystic eeriness.
A broken tree
twisted and ripped
by lightning and wind
rests along a trail.
Rotting logs
litter the forest floor,
Some provide homes for birds,
others soak the sun
like decaying skeletons.
A vast trunk grows
out of a hill, dead limbs
like bony fingers
protect the floor.
New growth sprouts
from the ground.
Someday it too
will join its ancestors.

Latheresa Howard
INVISIBLE TEARS
Should I hurt, Why?
—INVISIBLE TEARS—
I wipe my eyes.
I cannot cry.
My soul: a silent tear.
I don't know, Why?
Please, help me to explain it.
I live in constant fear.
My emotions: a silent tear.
The pain, the sorrow, the hurt
I hold inside me.
I wipe my eyes
I know it, I feel it.
My soul is crying,
Crying, INVISIBLE TEARS.

Margaret Herring
TERRIFIED HUGO
Come to tear down and destroy,
Strong wind & rain, only God
can control me, my Lord.

Across the country I roar and went,
No mercy I gave or spent,

Forty million dollars worth of damage I did.
Tore down houses, brought darkness that could not be hid.

Hugo the baddest, meanest, ugliest, I boast,
Brought fear upon Mankind, from coast to coast.

Only God enlightened, only one could calm me down,
When he spoke I had to stop and not make a sound.

One day some of my brothers will come back,
I am Hugo the baddest, full of strong wind, rain pack.

While I was doing my thing, I was so excited,
Knowing that I was strong, terrified and mighty.

Knowing that Mankind will rebuild back,
Now I have been weakened by God Almighty, back in pack.

Bill Hodock
MEMORIES

This poem is dedicated to two special people in my life Nichole Marie & Jacob Anthony Hodock.

My thoughts are with you every day
by watching other children play.
I can hear your laughter in their voice,
I want to call out but I have no choice.
I can hear your voice in every sound,
as if I were there on your merry-go-round.
I can feel your touch that is oh so dear,
and I wish somehow you were here.
I can see your face in all my dreams,
and can almost touch you it seems.
But when it comes time to awake
all I have are memories to take.
Memories to take me through the days
when I was there to watch
you play.
My love for you is in my heart
and that love for you will never part.
So my children I want you to know
that my love for you will always grow.
And no matter how hard it may seem,
I'll be with you tonight in
my dreams.
Love Always
Daddy

Alissa Heyman
THE OTHER SIDE OF THE MIRROR
She pressed her face against the mirror
Hoping to climb through it to the other side
Where she could walk in a garden of glowing lights and floating shapes
Where all the colors would run together and drip onto the ground

She pressed her hands against the mirror
Feeling the cool hardness of glass
And knew that if she got through to the other side
She could swim in a room full of water
That never got hot and never got cold
Where there were pictures on the walls that she could walk into
And stand on top of the highest building seeing the lights of a melting city below her

If she got to the other side

Barbara Harris
THE NIGHTMARE
I opened the basement door.
He came at me with a roar,
Faster than the speed of light,
This thing as big and black as night.
He grabbed me around the throat;
I figured this is all she wrote.
His paws had the strength of steel.
The look in his eyes—he meant to kill!
I fought with everything I had.
I always knew that cats were bad.
Cats!!! The only animal I really fear.
My mate was shaking me: "What's wrong, Dear?"

Heather M Gordon
WHERE LIFE IS SHORTER THAN THE HARVEST
No one has ever been there but it's said,
To charm all eyes.
No soul could ever climb to it,
And no heart would ever try.
The mythical castle Immortality,
Built on its coral rocks,
Above the dictated sea.
Where life is shorter than the Harvest.
Rub a dub,
The Butcher, The Maker
and the Forsaker.
A picture of a castle on coral rocks,
Sketched on the Beach.
Washed away realistically
Hope cannot reach.
A sea remains changing as it did begun,
Losing smallest droplets,
To the ever burning sun.
Their life shorter than their fall.

Carmen N Greer
YOUR FLAG—MY FLAG

To all persons and their families who have served our country ever.

One flag, long may it fly
And bring a tear to our eye.
A glorious sight we behold
All peoples—humble or bold.
It's beauty so lovely to see
It's meaning so clear to me
For many who did sacrifice
And died for our nation's life.
The color red, white and blue
Those 50 stars, united, too.
The greatest land under the sun
By much blood it was won.
A people strong but in need
Of abundant love so to heed.
The moral code given to man
And respect God's master plan.

Norma A Goodwin
WE INTERRUPT THIS PROGRAM—
They waited at the ballpark for the third World Series game:
Nature would pre-empt this night for indiscriminate fame.
The earthworks trembled, buckled, roared, and steel-strung bridges fell,
While on the heaving roadways gaped wide the gates of hell.
Mountains split, yet stood erect, defying nature's fission,
As though they were ordained for spectacular revision.
Once again the majesty of western grandeur shook
The very souls of those who had foundation sound forsook.
Tremor followed tremor; raw fear ruled with iron hand
The multitude of diehards who chose this quaking land.
Memories of nineteen-six were told, then told again,
And young folk could envision what this earthquake could have been.
The nation heard within the hour of this calamity,
Which measured to seven-point-plus in seismic energy.
Response was swift as people heard and answered anguished pleas,
And pride in human sharing swept a nation to its knees.

Laurie Gregory
ANOTHER DAY
Lusty dawn awaits the coming of another day,
Lonely flowers in nearby fields, lift their heads to pray.
Howling shadows, overcast retreat into the night.
Rays of warmth now spreading forth, followed by the light.

Debra Lee Greenawalt
DREAMS
When I think of you
I feel like I have been opened up, like an old vintage wine.
Ready to serve only those of Highest Esteem
And then I think I'll wake and find it was only a dream.
I feel your warm caress, and the love
I feel for you bubbles up and it has no ending.
And then I think I'll wake and find it was only a dream.
When I look in your eyes
I see an endless night full of the brightest stars
Look, a shooting star
Quick make a wish
And then I think I'll wake
But I find it was no dream.

David Vance Gardner
WHAT IF WE DID HAVE A WEDDING DAY?

To: The one I called my pretty girl. My love for you never died, it just retreated and grew stronger. When she hears or reads the words of her one-time hero a gentle tear rolls down her perfect face and she, almost silently says, "What have I done?" as she goes on with her sad and lonely life.

What if instead of tossing it all away, we did have a Wedding Day?

You would have made such a beautiful bride, your face aglow, your smile so bright, your flowing dress upon your tan skin would show so brilliant white.

I, so happy and full of love would wait so proudly for you to walk down the aisle. I'd hold back my tears of joy and just smile and smile.

And as your Dad lets go and you take my arm, my heart would pound against my chest until you'd think it would show; so close to bursting with your love, like a magical secret for just me to know.

And, then, the service would begin. I would think to myself how sweet some of the battles are we win.

I can't believe it when I hear your voice and to think I would be your choice.

I would be yours and you would be mine, a walk though life's love to have for all time.

I can't believe it but my dreams came

true somehow, as I hear my pretty princess repeat vow after vow.

Now the wedding is done and the reception is too, now it's off to our honeymoon just me and you.

I carry you over the threshold and you seem so light, this our dream come true, as husband and wife, on our very first night.

We made a fire and toast our new beginning.

The fire is warm and crackles as it burns and the sweet smell of hickory comes from the fireplace, and the light of the fire casts shadows on your perfect face.

We start to kiss but stop to talk, it seems the more things change the more they stay the same.

I'd take you in my arms and feel your warmth.

And, then I'd make this promise to you . . .

"Honey, I will always love you, but just as important I will make sure you know it, because as well as my words my actions will show it.

It's probably not possible but still I'd do all that I can, to make you always happy, and proud that I am your man.

For you gave the greatest thing of all, a gift wrapped in love . . .
to keep the rest of my life, you gave me yourself when you became my wife . . .

Yes, what if we did have a Wedding Day instead of tossing it all away. I would be so happy and you would be too, now I guess there is just one thing left to say, "I LOVE YOU" Feb. 14th, 1990.

An original poem to the one I loved, I Love, and will always Love.
Love,
Dave V. Gardner

Chad Grube
MOTHERS
Mothers are several people,
They are there on every day.
They're there to always love you
And help you in every way.

From the time of birth
To the end of time,
Your mountains in life
They have helped you climb.

A mother is many people,
A cook, maid, and nurse.
In a book of life's challenges
She wrote every verse.

A mother makes any house
A place you can call "home."
She turns an ordinary house
To a palace in Rome.

A mother is loving
Her love you cannot test,
For each of her children
Is the one she loves BEST.

Doris Guidry
DREAMS
Dream your dreams of castles in Spain,
Country houses in the rain—
Majestic mountains in falling snow,
A fire glowing in a cabin below . . .
Green meadows with birds on the wing
These are the things that make my Heart Sing.
So dream your dreams—
And they may come true,
But no one can take these dreams
From you.

Missy Goffinet
MINE FOR YOURS
Remember me as you pass by
As you are now so once was I.
Young and wild as the spring breeze
Eyes as blue as wild seas.
As the grass grew, so did we.
I loved you; you loved me.
Two growing children happy and gay
Until that very awful day.
We watched the sun with fascination
So full of bright imagination.
The crystal clear lake stood so proud
In the sky was not one cloud.
We paddled joyfully across the lake
Two target souls for god to take.
The cold, hard rock stood in vain
As the boat hit there was no pain.
Only the screams of hatred and sorrow
Here today, gone tomorrow.
I risked my life for theirs to save;
I admit the action was brave.
I pulled the body on the shore
Sighing with relief forevermore.
But suddenly I was pulled under;
The last heartbeat was that of thunder.
Saving a life can cost a fee,
So prepare for death and follow me.

Denise I Guinn-Bailey
LOVE AND PEACE
If only love came in a bottle.
With plenty for me, and for you.
You would never have to wish; you had someone there to care.
Just to take care of you.

If only peace came in a nutshell.
And wars were not fought by the young.
The shell would be empty; and nations would cry out in vain.
"Tell us, what have we done?"

But there never seems to be enough love.
And wars go on, oh!, they never end, for all nations.
The young keep dying, and parents crying.
This needs to end, oh!, yes my friend.
Before it's your son.

Angela Goodspeed
TEARS
They come and go
Watch them continually flow.
The glitter in your eyes the first I saw you
Made me see a wonderful side I never knew.
They represented the feeling inside,
And the lost love that hurtingly died.
I wiped the tears dry
From those sparkling brown eyes.
That beautiful smile
Lasted in my heart a long while.
I tried to take away that discomforting memory
That is in your life's keys.
And through our relationship
I learned the true meaning of a friendship.
The support each one of us shared
Showed how much friends really cared.
The moment of a loved one that died
Made both of us cry.
Holding you in my arms so strong
Made me realize tears in a friendship belong.
As two part away
The tears are there until they meet again someday.

Bryne L Garrett
HEART
The thought is what counts
But it's the heart that mounts
A picture perfect life
Unable for the eyes to see
Only it can control
And not the soul
A life full of hopes and dreams
Its aim is perfection
And pureness in part
With the rest untold wisdom
For see it's the heart that thinks
And the mind that marks
Without the heart fullness of steam
For the soul is kind
And the mind is smart
But without the heart
There would be no love extremes

Hilda Gordon
BING-O-MANIA
A room full of people—hoping to win
They call it gambling—but it's really no sin . . .
Charity and Bingo go together—
The Game is played in all sorts of weather.

The Churches and Temples need the money,
It's difficult to run Bingo—but at times it's funny.
Week after week new friends meet to play,
It's relaxation for some after a trying day.

They call me a Bing-O-Holic—it is so true
Because I try to patronize quite a few.
To me it's charity—and the cause is just
Charity is charity—and I do what I must.

The woman next to me wins again
I haven't won—I don't know since when.
However, I'll try once more and then some more
But the caller will say Three and I will need Four!

Gail Gowan
MY GRANDMOTHER
Last August on the seventh day
Someone I loved passed away.
She was very dear to me.
Held me often upon her knee.

When I was troubled she was always there
To listen closely to my every care.
She will always be dear to my heart
Although she's gone, we'll never part.

I know she's gone to a better place,
Although I miss her smiling face.
She lived a life for God each day
And never failed, to forget to pray

My mother died when I was one month old
I knew her not, except from what I was told.
My grandmother took her place very well,
She loved me more than words can tell

She lived a life for God, family, and friends
She had the kind of love that never ends,
I know she's gone to her home on high
I hope to see her, in that sweet by and by.

Chanel J King
BEDTIME HUGS
I love my Mom because of her Bedtime Hugs.
They warm my soul,
They give me a tingle in my stomach.
You cover my heart with glee,
As you wrap your arms around me.

I love you because of your Bedtime Hugs.
The warmness sunk down so deep,
I love to wrap my arms around you too.
Your heart is warm and tender,
I love you with all my heart.
This is to my Mom for her Bedtime Hugs.

Ryan J Spickard
CLOUDS
Upon sweet air
They drift
Upon the whims of the air flows
They fly
These strange things that give the Water—life.
Dancing on Ballerinas' shoes
They change
As the moods of a dancer
Inspired by powers
Greater than ours.
They are musical voices of creatures
Of old and myth
They shape our dreams
As we watch them on
Grass covered hills.
As I say farewell
I leave a word . . .
. . . Dream

Roberta Reimer
ROADS THAT PART
From this day on, our roads must surely part.
Altho you leave my presence, not my heart.
We each must lovingly pursue our way,
While all the while our hearts do heavily weigh
Upon our souls.

But we can always, always gently hope
That somewhere on some distant sunny slope,
Our roads will cross again and we will clasp each
Other heart to heart and never, never shall we
Remember roads that part.

Tony Arnold Miller
THE WORLD TODAY

I dedicate this poem to all the world. To warn them, if they choose too. They can change the course of our destiny.

So many people, so many things. So much hate. So much shame.
In a world for the rich and lets their

poor die. And tax all citizens until they cry.
A new deadly disease has occurred.
A virus called AIDS is now the word, with gay men roaming the streets, spreading more diseases everywhere they meet.
A nation is made up of nuclear bombs. Forgetting our own country helping the others live on.
We see our officials on T.V. saying have no fear. For what we don't know is what we don't care.
If a country strikes the U.S.A. first, we have no choice but to fight back.
And World War 3 could happen just like that.
So day by day we live in fear. Scared to death our time is near. But there is hope that shouldn't be there.
Nations get together with peace and prayer.
Throw away weapons and drugs.
This is what I say.
Or there will never be for us another day.

Teresa Waddle

Teresa Waddle
LOVE'S OWN ANGELS

To the ones I can't have.
To the ones who left.
And to the ones yet to come.

Whenever the sun breaks,
another soul becomes an Angel
—I see visions of you—
Whenever a shiver is nothing more,
than an Angel's passing
—I know your shadow—
Whenever it rains it's nothing more,
than an Angel crying
—I bathe in your radiance—
Whenever a chill is nothing more,
than an Angel's touch
—I wait for yours—
Whenever the winds chime it's nothing more,
than an Angel singing
—Lovers lost in the secret of each other—
Whenever a quiver is nothing more,
than an Angel's breath
—Never ending music—
Whenever the sun fades,
another Angel is reborn
—Never ending story—

Ann Saroka
APRIL SHOWERS AND YOUR FLOWERS

To my Mother—Alice—

It seems as though I can see you
Planting your flowers
Even in these dripping showers
Yes it is sort of a gloomy day
And before we know it will be May
Then all of your pretty flowers will be in bloom
I hope and pray that some day soon
I'll be able to have some in my room
Will you try dear Mother to come and see
I'd love to hear you say
Oh, just one little word to me.
I remember what you used to say
How wonderful is the warm month of May
It seems as though I can see your smile
That gave me a feeling to live, oh so worthwhile
No more do you sing my favorite song
To hear your voice again so much I long
No longer do you plant your flowers
You've done your duty on earth Dear Mother
There's no one like you, never another.

Rita R Visger
HER SON'S MESSAGE
His days are a struggle from morning till night.
Tho few are aware of his hard, grim plight.

He plods thru each day with the thought inside;
How futile his efforts to those outside.

Tho his words are so clear in his own mind's eye,
The key to release them is locked deep inside.

When he tries to exchange his thoughts for words,
It is plain to see, he is not being heard.

How heavy his burden, only a Mother knows
As she watches her son, while he struggles to grow.

Her son's message to all . . . is to make us aware.
He is part of God's plan to show that we care.

He is testing our strength in the love we display,
And the patience we show in a kind, guiding way.

Remember to keep the thought in mind . . .
He could be anyone's son . . . yours or mine . . . .

Kandi Jenkins
LOOK OF SORROW
Look in momma's eyes,
such sorrow and pain
she looks at you,
wondering why?
What did I do,
to get her,
Look of Sorrow?
What rules her,
Death
Depression
Disappointment,
all this in her heart.
Was it caused by me?
How can I change,
Momma's Look of Sorrow?
The blame lies here,
inside my heart.
Will the sorrow stop?
When?
Is death the only answer?
No! She can't
I could never smile another smile.
but why.
I cry out to you, why?

Eileen Higgins
HARRAH FOR SACRAMENTO

To the city of Sacramento.

Harrah for Sacramento
The City we are for
We love it better every day
We love it more and more
The people are jolly good fellows
They greet you with a smile
I hope to live in Sacramento
For a long long while

Robert L Graham
SPRING ALONG THE KOOTENAI
Everywhere you look
there are signs spring is here.
The weather is much nicer
and the skies are very clear.

Geese fly lazily up the river
as if they have no special place to go.
They seem to have the attitude
spring is here and they really know.

Each day the sun has more strength
and feels just a little warmer.
All around are signs
the days are getting longer.

Crocuses are pushing their buds
up through the last existing snow.
The little streams and rivers are more swollen
and moving not quite so slow.

Robins hop across the lawn
and appear to be listening for any
worm that may be near.
All this gives the impression
that spring is really here.

OctoberMoon Edwards
FIGHT AGAINST BLANKNESS
Looking at the creation
I encounter the power of mind meant
when the charcoal
became one with blankness

I notice separate thoughts
merging together through strokes made
when the charcoal
became one with blankness

I see strains of the artist
throughout the creation in my mind when
my charcoal
became one with blankness

I realize a door is opening
to end the silence
that exists
with the charcoal
in my fight against blankness

Louise Champion
MY PLEA
As I walk into the balmy night
I'm haunted by the pale moonlight
The sweet breeze murmurs in my dreams
The same as a year ago, it seems;
The twinkling stars who saw our meeting,
Two hearts that were so madly beating
Then seemed to mingle as if one
O, night! one thing I ask of thee!
Bring back his kisses now to me;
Or keep them all and give to him
One blissful thought of me!

Linda Paterek Scott
THE UNLUCKY DAY
My hem is down,
What rotten luck!
What'll be next?
My zipper's stuck!

My button's popped,
My jacket's torn,
I split my seam,
My knees are worn.

My breakfast's burned,
The kids ain't fed,
I've changed my mind,
I'll stay in bed!

Patricia Scott
FLOWERS

Dedicated to my loving family and Mrs. Davis, my second grade teacher, who started me on my "life of rhyme."

Flowers make you happy.
Flowers make you glad.
Flowers cheer you up
When you feel sad.

Flowers are pretty,
That we all know.
All you need is good soil
For them to grow.

Flowers can be pink or yellow,
Or maybe even red or white.
They open in the morning,
And then they close at night.

That's the end.
That's all I know.
Plant some in your garden,
And see what kinds you can grow!

Bonnie J Milligan
DR. ROSE
Why is it that some people feel
roses will heal anything?

Like they possess some miracle glue
that pieces together a broken heart,
or some powerful medicine
which will close an open wound.

Why is it that some people think
roses are like a doctor
who can't even cure the common cold?

But you'll always hold onto that message
on the card for old times sake,
it reads:
I'm sorry,
Love, Dr. Rose

Roses can't help when days lapse
and the sender never arrives.
How can they help
these swollen and teary eyes?

Gina Marie Chiovetta
WHAT IS A BABY?
A baby is an example of love,
a precious gift from above.

A baby is your little pride and joy,
whether it's a girl or a boy.

A baby should be wanted and
loved, and always thought of.

A baby is innocent and carefree,
like a dove.

A baby is:
A True Gift of Love!

Robert G Aldous
BEACHING
The smell of fresh sea air surging through my lungs,
The moist salt air cooling my body.
The horns and bells of channel buoys beating a rhythm in my brain.
It's down by the sea . . . where I want to be!

I never will have the need for shoes nor fancy clothes upon my back.
I just want to be bare, just as bare as they let me be.

To kick up the sand into little mounds as I frolic near the sea.
To fish and play.
To run and romp, will be my labor of the day.

Money will have no meaning . . . not like times of the past when it was all that mattered.
Just enough for a ham and cheese, and maybe a bottle of wine.

That's all I want.
To be what was meant to be.
ME BY THE SEA!

Harriet V Avery
FLOWER OF LIFE
Love is like a flower
Which is planted with trust,
And nurtured tenderly by the hour
It flourishes well when time is just.

With warmth of soul,
And understanding patience;
Shield with this against the shoal
Of any misguided conscience.

So thus it blooms
In unending beauty,
Until life's fulfillment looms,
And all have done their duty.

William J Ammons Jr
TWILIGHT FLIGHT
High above in the twilight
there passes a plane in flight
Its lights blinking
for all to see
Its destination—
unknown to me.
Heading westward, chasing
the setting sun,
in a race that will not be
won.
On it goes, swallowed by
the night.
Carried on wings of silver
to the end of its flight.

Joanne Bruyere
SEASONS
The wind rustles through my mind,
For I have lost all sense of time.
Slowly I forget the past,
Loves before now gone.

Birds fly past, their wings spread wide.
Where are they going?, can't decide.
Sounds of mowers cutting grass,
Pressed between the seasons that move so fast.

Sounds of summer once again,
Long last winters in so much pain.
Sunshine deeply on us all,
We're here to stay until the fall.

Flowers bloom brightly in all their glory.
And each one of them has a story.
The beaches are crowded,
The beaches are bare.
Summer is here, Winter is there.

Lovers meet and lovers part,
Memories of winter and broken hearts.
But the sun is here to dry the tears,
Looking forward to another year.

Edward M Garfield
A TIME ALONE
If ever there was a time
there was a time like no other time.
I would be all alone, by myself all alone,
in this space that I save just for time.
Now if I had not the time for this space that I save,
I'd have not the time to be lonely.
And if the time to be lonely was never a time,
then the time to be me would never be.
But now the time has come so I come to be lonely
as I, yes lonely, but Free.
I will be always lonely with time by my side
and so plenty of time to be me.

Edward M Garfield
MY FAREWELL . . . DREAM
There is no death, only a new beginning.
Then, never will be as soon as time completes its metamorphosis.
Then, then the journey to the void of emptiness, of fulfillment, will commence.
You must be of empty mind and clean soul to voyage through time when time itself sits beyond the door of forever.
It takes no courage, no definitive mentality, no positive enticement, only the will to go to where you have never been, seen only in your dreams, in the dreams that hold true reality with an endless euphoria, to be inhabited, possessed, and worshipped in great expectations of the mind itself. I have been there in this endless wonderment, where gravity has no meaning, and there is something new and very astounding behind every star. Await patiently for your time, it will come as it does for every living thing. I must hurry, I leave this world for my last time, never to return, never feeling the need to belong, for it will become yet another dream, one of the past, a dream for the new, my farewell . . . dream.

Dorothy Sanders
AN ANGRY EYE

To everyone in Sumter, South Carolina. We shared a terrifying night, Sept. 22, 1989.

We had a visitor late one night;
Hugo was his name.
But he was most unwelcomed;
I hope he never comes again.

He was furious when he got here,
And he left an angry sight.
But if he had to come at all,
I'm glad he came at night.

He had his eye upon us,
And in the darkness he did rage.
I'm glad we couldn't see him,
For our hearts might would have failed.
He shook the towering pine trees,
And the graceful oaks.
He pulled and tugged at their roots,
'Til they could take no more.

He took some people's homes away;
Even steeples from the churches.
No, not even one of us,
Was spared from Hugo's clutches.

Lori A Kent
REMINISCING

This poem is dedicated to Eric, my loving husband because we did grow together.

Before I sleep,
I reminisce
About the happy times we spent.
Why do I weep?
Because those times can never be again.
I guess you didn't realize
How much I loved you—
—and still do.
I know we can't go back,
But perhaps in time
We'll grow together
As we grew apart.

Chinwe Odeluga
THIS NOW AND THE NEXT NOW

For David, who didn't know if he was crossing over to the next now 12/13/89.

For two nights
I came home and
death was grinning
at me.

His smile was crooked
and he looked like
Roy Orbison.

And weeks ago,
I dreamt of someone's
ceremony.

Death stays at my side
and life seems like this
now and death the next now.

For, death smiled at Miss Paul
and she left this now and the
next now on the horizon may be
mine.

Jamie Keller
SUMMER
A warm breeze, a hot day.
A water filled pool in the shade.
Groups of kids on the field,
Getting ready to play.
The bright moon, the long nights,
The beautiful birds in the sky.
When morning arises, it's cool and bright,
And the roosters would not lie.
Along comes noon, so the country is hot.
And the birds are back to stay.
The children are back on that field,
Getting ready to play — TODAY!!

Imogene Welker Cole
M USE OF HOME BAKED BREAD

Dedicated to my grandchildren: Sarah, Alex, Benjamin.

I wait in my kitchen for the yeast to colonize.
There is memory to thank for what has gone before.
The upheaval of quiet when the shout "Hey Mom" surprises
That the children have invaded now through the front door.

I am never lonely—even after they have gone
To other lives and duties to which they now belong.
For when I am invited to share their offspring's doings,
They somehow make it clear to me to bring my yeast along.

The grandchild who is at college makes our visit coincide.
The eight-year-old wants "first cuts" and will not be denied.
She looks like her mother and he looks like his pa,
And I get a deal of pleasure seeing my efforts in their jaw.

This bread has no additives except that of Love and Prayer.
It is made of best ingredients and assembled with great care.
The room will smell distinctive and memory does not subside
When I break through my musings to knead down to second rise.

Imogene Welker Cole
GENESIS 1:11-12 AND FATHER'S GARDEN
The mulching caused compliance to human tools more prone
While creeping-crawling life helped too in finding its new home.
Sharp spade has coaxed unwilling ground to yield
To form in rows or mounds—whichever best will shield.

The warmed earth will coordinate with sunshine and with rain.
No schedule can be set by man for flowering to maintain.
The seeds and plants were lovingly placed in accord to need or whim,
Yet airborne life will work so he may sometimes have to thin.

The weeds now are uprooted so that they hinder not,
Water carried to the plants when dew is all they got.
The weeks of patient waiting begin to satisfy
For fruit is slowly forming—on this he can rely.

To the table for current hunger or delayed for later times,
With grace and thanksgiving he cleans the garden for winter climes.
So soon the season is closing but the next brings forth the pelf,
For he has seen the God made miracle—"whose seed is in itself."

Jean L Kambourian
THE BENEVOLENT

With greatest love, admiration, and respect, this poem is dedicated to Mrs. Cornelia Henderson, who because of her benevolence, changed my life, forever.

A caring that goes farther than just asking how I am.

A mild and gentle nature soft as fleece upon a lamb.

Their assuring words that ease my mind and take my pain away.

Forgiving me my errors help me face

another day.

With kindness shown to all around no matter what their mood.

For anything they have to say is always something good.

The beauty of their spirit which is so warm and free.

Make knowing I have them as friends mean so very much to me.

Kate Freebairn
INFESTED PARADISE

Machinery and gadgets invented for convenience
A starving child without a home
Bolting skyrisers, fast cars, telephones, and t.v.'s
Infested flies living on the flesh of a man
A stomach so big, yet full of nothing
Cattle herded in the lush western sphere
A gloating man laughs with a mouth full of potatoes and loosens his belt another notch
A naked mother slouches in the corner, her breasts sucked dry for her child's life
Give to another what you have and take only what you need
A life is a gift not to be taken by selfishness or greed

Tallak T Farsjo
THE BREAD OF THE NIGHT

Night encompasses the mind and soul
Of the victim of dirty needles.
It started as something so modern and "cool"
(As to listen to Elvis, the Beetles.)
It crept into many a high school class
In the form of powder, crack and "grass"
As it beckoned to any innocent fool.

This poisonous "balsam" from leaves and straw
Is the black death in the making.
The peddler, an animal in the raw
Whose victims are bleeding and shaking.
The merchants who sell this contemptible stoff
(Where the moral buttons are set on "off")
Just sneer at the courts and law.

Bread of the night like a foreign don
Is our country's curse and master.
There is no pro just an angry con
Against this satanic disaster.
If never you conquer this habit's curse
The drug-demon's grasp will get worse and worse—
The "Bread of the Night" has won!

Kenneth R Farley Jr
COLD HEART

To hear the wind driven rain, on my windowpane,
And the crash of the sea in the distance
It makes me forget my pain, if only for this instance
I can see your face in my mind's eye,
This moment makes it all so clear, to see you now,
And hear your voice, would make me forget my fear.
I wait alone in the dark, the cold empty night fills my heart
My feelings drift away on the freezing night air.
I'm all alone in my despair.

Ginevar Curenton
WHY DID THE LEAVES SWAY

The wind rustle through the leaves,
With a cool gentle breeze,
Like and echo of rowin thunder!
When it rain the leaves begin to shine.
Clouds look as if diamond in the sky.
No matter how hard the wind blow.
The grayer sky look as if to snow.
Have you ever saw a flower sway to and foe?
O! Mighty wind how do you blow,
Every spot or speck of grass?
Yet the wind has class.
Like passing gas.

Ginevar Curenton
THE GOOD O DAYS

Time slips slowly away
Trying to hold on to tomorrow — "dream,"

You said we'll keep in touch,
Yet i search for tomorrow.
Another day has past and gone.

Time i had not to borrow.
Precious moment.
I spent with classmates,

Those were the best days of
My life, although life is nothin
but a dream.

Grace Joffe
WHERE WERE YOU?

To my students at North Dade Middle School, Dade County, Fl.—Let's hope for a brighter tomorrow.

Is that new gold tooth that important?
The gold chains?
The shiny new car?
The BIG TV set?
Your son told me you moved into a bigger house last year.
How wonderful—
But—where were you on Back to School Night?
Where were you when he came home at 4 P.M. and his FRIEND listened to his problems?
Where were you when his FRIEND took him joy riding?
Where were you when his FRIEND gave him his first needle?
Where were you when I called to tell you his grades were falling?
Where were you when he was picked up for dealing?
Where were you when he assaulted the old lady?
Where were you when he was charged with his first B and E?
Where were you when he shot his FRIEND?
Working for all the goodies that you could buy?
R I G H T !!!
Where are you now?
Hymns, minister, black dress, and a G O L D C A S K E T — and you by his side.

Grace Joffe
COLORS

I love the color purple
Green is pretty too —
Does it really matter?
Maybe I'll wear blue

I'll sit with my white friends
Perhaps I'll sit with you —
Flowers come in colors
And blood is red, it's true
How boring it is that everything comes in colors
But people only two
Why can't we fit in the scheme of things
And come in many hues?

Margaret P Fairhead
IN THE GARDEN

Dedicated to my daughter, Elaine Fairhead Bialecki, the flower of my heart.

The daffodil is like a Queen
Of golden hair, robed in deepest green,
She stands stately there —
In the Garden.

Among the sweet crocus or snowdrops so fair,
Or alone on a hilltop, only God knows just where
She is charming and gracious, and of character rare
And she nods as we pass —
In the Garden.

With a scepter of beauty she has touched our hearts
We've been knighted, we suddenly feel with a start
We are happy and gay, and want to sing
We are under the reign of the Queen of Spring —
In the Garden.

Margaret P Fairhead
GARDEN GOSSIP

Dedicated to the memory of my mother, whose beautiful garden was the inspiration for this poem written in 1937.

"It must be love!", the Jonquils cried
As Lily of the Valley sauntered to their side.
"We just saw Jack from his pulpit so high
Steal a look at Rose, so demure and shy."
"And I," said fair Lily, "saw Sweet William so bold
Making eyes at that beauty — Marigold."
She nodded, and listen — "What do you think?"
"Shhh — this came direct from old Bob-O-Link."

The forget-me-nots clustered, the better to hear.
The tulips stood silent lest they interfere.
Tall lilacs cautioned the apple blossoms, so white on the ground,
To lay still in the grass not making a sound.

And then Bob related the story so old,
Concerning Sweet William and dear Marigold.
"Wilt thou?" said he.
"Ah, oui," she replied. "In the gay month of May will I come to your side."
"I love you," vowed William, with a sigh from the depths.
"Is there anything dearer than Sweet Baby's Breath?"

Wealthy J Kortz
ON SEEING CATASTROPHE

I try to imagine, how the world would seem,
If we all felt depressed, never to dream.
Surrounded by pollution and human waste,
Dumped in thoughtless greedy haste.

A nightmare at best, if the majority gives up,
Submissively yielding, to all who corrupt.
Ignoring the consequences, the need to protect,
Losing forever, divine legacy without respect.

I try to imagine, living without things I enjoy,
Cursing often, those hell bent to destroy.
Immoral and shameless in absolute disgrace,
Disregarding the environment and the human race.

Leaving sabotaged pastures, never bearing a tree,
No wondrous creatures alive in the sea.
All things bleak and dying . . . no human drive,
No lust for life, no will to survive.

I try to imagine, the devastation there would be,
Without inquisition, I see only catastrophe!
The earth, politically and chemically bashed,
Ethically and aesthetically horribly trashed!

Ruth E Bettenhausen
MOMS

Dedicated to Mary the Perfect Mother of Our Lord Jesus Christ.

Moms are so precious in the sight of God
We know we are accepted when He gives us the nod.

He starts us out by giving us a precious bundle of joy
Which makes us so happy, we don't mind if it's a girl or boy.

Sometimes it's one or two or maybe four
No matter, we just love them all the more.

A baby to cherish, to love and to hold
A precious child made from God's mold.

From baby to tots, youngsters then teens
Those years they go through many genes.

They emerge young men and young ladies
Wow we're almost through the eighties.

While they are growing up, you have been so busy
Those young gals keep you in a tizzie.

Sometimes a young man will make you mad
Then others will make you glad.

So mom when things go wrong, don't be blue
No matter what, all in all, we'll always need and love you.

Joreid Holloman
A TALKING CROW

To my five lovely daughters, Gloria, Eva Jane, Lauren Elaine, Wava Wanette & Shanna Lee. They think I'm a versatile poet & will one day win the money. I hope so.

Said a crow in the top of a tree
"What time is it gettin' to be?
If it isn't yet noon
I got here too soon.
But, I'm late if it isn't yet three."

Ralph Ferrara
HANGING OUT
You say you've been rejected, You say you've been neglected,
You also turn around and say you've never been accepted.
I'm just a kid and young you see, I don't think there's a life for me,
From house to house I also go, I feel that this is one big show.
From broken families I have come, I really feel just like a bum,
I've never seen my own two kind,
But people say that you are mine.
How can people tell you this?, It's in their face, It's in their kiss.
It's hard to treat you like their own,
Because you are a different Clowne,
You try to give them some respect,
and then they to . . . Recollect!
The things that you have done for them, I'm just myself I'm not a GEM.
It's just no use in going on, I feel like I am just a con.
I try so hard to be what I'm not, But they just put me on a spot.
I'm not like them I have no clout, I must resort to HANGING OUT.
I'm sure there's millions just like me,
Just look around and you can see.
I guess it's hard to find them two,
The ones that really care for you.
You try to make them understand,
They won't reach out to give a hand.
Life is hard enough you see, No one wants to speak with me.
You tell the Truth, you tell a Lie, It's hard to see from Eye to Eye.
I feel that now it's time to die, I must resort to SUICIDE.
If you can help another kid, Don't let him do what I just did.
Please help these KIDS and tell them why, And NO MORE KIDS WILL HAVE TO DIE.

Ralph Ferrara
R.I.P.
This is my Home for what It's worth,
I lie here calm beneath this EARTH.
Undisturbed I choose to be, But you insist to walk on me.
My house plaque stands up straight and tall,
But insist to make it Fall.
The writing on my plaque is Faint,
'Cause You insist to use Your PAINT.
So calm, So cool, and unprotected,
Please leave my home to be UNINSPECTED.
My guests who bring me flowers too,
May one day do the same for you.
I did not choose to be where I'm at, I lie here dressed flat on my back.
I'm on my back for ETERNITY,
One day my friend you'll be here with me.
Please stop and THINK before you DO, What you may not want done to YOU.
I stopped to THINK what you just said,
You're right my friend, I'll use my head.
I will not bother you . . . I say,
You're right my friend, I'll be here some day.
I spoke my mind to say the least, If you don't mind, I'LL REST IN PEACE.

Janie I Basting
TIME WILL PASS
Time will pass
Can you spare me just a minute of your day?
Am I worth the price that you must pay
For losing precious minutes of your day
To someone who needs help along the way?

Time will pass
Your opportunity to share will soon be gone.
The sun's rays burn away the glorious dawn,
And time, unrelenting, travels on
Without regard for life or anyone.

Time will pass
And take you with it to eternity,
And take me there as well for you to see.
Does all this make you view things differently?
Is there time yet in your busy life for me?

Jocelyn K Fillian
POEMS
Poems are neat,
Poems are fine,
They do not always have to rhyme,
Poems can be about most anything,
From a little grey kitten,
To a fish with wings.

Betty Ann Fromerth
YOUR LOVE
The gentleness of your touch
The sweetness of your kiss
The kindness of your heart
Is all that I would miss . . .

The love you give is so beautiful
I get the chills every time you are near
Please hold me darling
Tell me you love me dear.

The stars are shining so brightly
The sky so dark like velvet
You say my eyes glow in the moonlight
My smile will brighten up your life.

My darling I love you so
Please hold me close to your heart
It feels so good to be near you
I can also feel it in my heart . . .

Cammy Fisher
HE COMES
A gentle breeze is blowing,
A feeling is flowing,
A voice is wooing,
"Come, come unto me."

Over all the land,
A bond is forming,
A group is growing,
The sound is deafening.
Hear all ye saints;
Prepare, the time is short.
Stand fast, lest you be
Swept away.

The voice is God's.
The breeze is His love.
The feeling is overpowering.
Say, "Lord, I wait for you."

Evelyn Frinell
SLEEPY HAMLET
Sleepy hamlet how still you lie
Purple shadows all around
With yellow in the sky
Bring forth your trumpeters
Announce the newborn day
Awaken all your fellowmen
The sun is here to stay

Jenny Friedman
DOWN WITH SPELLING!
To me it is a mystery
How our language came to be.
Words that seem to spell so wrong,
Letters that do not belong.
How come a "b" appears in doubt,
But not a "b" in pout or stout?
If there's an "l" in calf and half
Why is there no "l" in chaff?
A "g" and "h" in sight and night,
Can you tell me by what right?
When we run we huff and puff,
Now look at words like tough and rough.
The word knife with a "k" we spell.
What earthly reason, can you tell?
Some day, though it sounds absurd
Phonetically we'll spell each word.
Till then, my friend, don't despair,
Though spelling makes you tear your hair.
Just shout it loud and shout it clear,
Shout it so the world will hear
DOWN WITH SPELLING!

Boyce G Flora
BEACH WALKS
I walked alone on the beach one night,
The surf came tumbling in on my right.
I stepped ahead. Then again, again,
And with each step the waves rolled in.
All alone with my thoughts was I
'Neath the star-lit, moon-filled sky,
Each step a memory of yesteryear,
A reflection of time and moments dear.

On another day with a friend I strolled,
Still the surf came in, the breakers rolled,
Timelessly same the ocean's motion.
The thought occurred, I got the notion,
How different to share this time with a friend
And know that I'll never be alone again;
Together to share moments, memories dear,
And reflect on the days of yesteryear.

Suzanne Kirsten Hansen
I WALKED THE WALL, IN SILENCE
I walked the wall, in silence
from the outside, and then again from the inside,
knowing I could choose which side to walk.
And inside, so many watched me walk it,
knowing I could choose,
knowing they could not.

My single stone-faced passport,
unlike theirs,
allowed me to trespass,
to flaunt my choice to walk—inside then outside along the thick grey wall.

Seeing my excursions
their shouts for choice began to peak.
The strong grey wall unmarred
by anything but blood—insiders' blood,
began to chip and crack from jeers.

Their vibrations growing stronger
shocked the wall, the thick strong wall,
until with one great sounding shriek
the wall tumbled at their feet.

And they and I danced on Freedom's keep,
And we danced upon its heap.

Suzanne Kirsten Hansen
WE SEEK IMMORTALITY
We seek immortality,
each one of us,
to dissolve the fear of dissolution—
to escape that particular
particulate dispersion.
We impassion ourselves with purpose
ever hopeful of a reason,
a reason — not for being
but for not being.
We find our ways, our special choices
which will impart and empower us
with a sense of eternal essence.
We hope we will always be remembered
by our children's descendants,
or maybe for a gift to society,
a discovery,
or some pure enduring melody.
Yet, we will not always be remembered —

but if I could just write that one poem
that one perfect poem . . .

Thelma E Hahn
WHITECAPS AT DAWN
Daylight broke through the veil of gray
Night's spell had been broken.
The angry waves beat against the shore
The egrets shouted out their throaty cries
And yet everything seemed silent
Through it all, tranquility reigned.
With the whitecaps at dawn.

The sands lay piled up against the barriers
As though some harried sculptor molded their shapes.
All the footprints of yesterday were washed over.
And remained no more.
Life had retreated, leaving only the forgotten,
the broken shells.
Yet beauty prevailed.
With the whitecaps at dawn.

Thelma E Hahn
SEE THE SUNSHINE
The torrents of rain beat against the window
Like crystal pieces, like

fragments from shattered goblets
Their sounds tingling,
Leaving my soul chilled.

Dark clouds dominated the
blue skies — gloom was everywhere.
Suddenly I felt your presence
in the room
And it brought the sunshine.

Troubles seemed to engulf me,
taking over of every turn
Was life to have no recess, no
cheer, no freedom from despair
My eyes lowered,
looking to the ground
Your voice sounded, "May
I help?"
And you brought the sunshine.

Zeddie Gillenwater

GENEALOGICAL OBSESSION

A "blue blood" genealogist, are of a
special breed,
Who love to dig into your past, and
read and read and read.
All about Aunt Laria, Uncle George,
Cousin Ben, and distant cousins too.
Trying to make this interesting, to
normal folk, like you.

Now you take a recent article, by our
distant cousin, Phill,
He told about our great-grandpaw,
who never made a will.
He was wealthy as could be, so all
the kinfolk said.
Buried all his gold in old tin cans,
when suddenly he fell dead.

He fought in all the "by–gone" wars,
from here to "Timbuktu,"
But later found out in another book,
that this was not all true.
But the "genealogical" mind probes
deep, with heart, mind, and soul.
Believing some mouldy record, from
some courthouse, will turn up
nuggets of gold.

But what would we do without them?
With their curious probing mind,
Who love to glean history from old
tombstones, among ponderosa pines.
Why all this, you ask? And they will
reply without fail,
To prove to Darwin, once for all,
monkeys only, hang by the tail.

To advance the "apes" in a theory,
they have held through eons of time,
That this "crazy" mixed-up, creature
that we call man, is no descendant of
mine!
Good luck "genealogist," in all of
your answers to find,
But remember always it's possible,
some hang by the neck, some time.

R A Halas

FAREWELL

To Beth, for the memories and times that we've shared.

I stood alone, one cold November morning. Watching the sunrise come up ever so slowly. The beauty of the morning sky, reminded me of your soft, glowing, cheerful eyes. I turned away from the sunrise, and shed a tear, knowing that you and I will never be the same.

Our life was one like a falling star. We burned bright, during that brief moment of intensity and awe. Then as fast as it had brightened, it darkened, burned up, and plummeted to earth.

The snow that falls before my eyes, is as cold, and as silent, as the way we stand apart today. I walk in despair, troubled and uncertain. With a little thought that you might care.

I love you and there is no denial, you made an impression on me, with your comforting smile. I walk here alone, with no destiny in sight. I bid farewell to you, goodbye, and good night.

R A Halas

THINKING OF YOU

Thinking of you, thinking of you always. I'm wondering when I will ever see you. Your presence radiates the happiness and joy, like the warmth of the life giving sun. With our song in my head, I leave the once cherished place of a past memory visited.

A split in the road to our destinies, caused an imbalance in our entities. No longer together, on a life of my own, reviewing our past, in silence and alone. With your Spanish eyes, and joyful smile, there is a wonderful person, of friendliness and desire. I long to see you in my sight. In my arms, at home at night.

Missing you, past times, bright skies and flowers. My, how the good days came and gone in a summer's breeze. Reality or a dream, think hard my dear, while the horses still roam free. Being loved, and loving you, are the things I miss, to be true.

While we may be apart, I know it is hard. We are still together, just through our hearts. Our memories may go challenged, by time and endless miles. However, once love begins, love never ends. Missing you today, missing you tomorrow, oh how I wish I could get rid of my sorrow.

Irene Parks Foster

SADNESS

The sun arose this morning
and with it came the tears,
that linger just behind my eyes
because of all my fears.

I'm so afraid of losing me
with no one near to care.
I've tried to smile and make it
seem
that I've no pain to bear.

But deep inside me dwells a hurt
from a heart badly marred,
collected one by one in life
the aches through which it scarred.

My friends laugh and so do I for
I cannot share the pain,
of the sadness that surrounds
me
without a loss of fame.

Forlorn I sit alone to brood
wondering why it's me,
that fate has chosen once again
to know adversity.

Irene Parks Foster

THE DREAMER

Be his friend
he needs one
he's quite alone, you know.
Through days and nights
he sets his sights
on wishful dreams
and fancy flights.

Spinning webs
of pretense
he's so secure, without.
But what a case
that put-on face
we all need love
not a carapace.

He should know
everyone
takes a chance when they care.
He's so afraid
no commitment made
his life, one long charade.

Margaret Ostyn

THE SEA

The sea, an essence of complete
solitude and tranquility
A limited and fragile glimpse of
eternity
Its whitecapped waves capturing
pebbles of the sand
Luring them into its deep expanse
never to return to land
During this tumultuous moment, they
join to become one
It's union witnessed and unintruded
by the sun.

Within its depths lies the secrets and
treasures of time
Knowledge and wisdom of
generations of minds
Such a vastness of intrigue and
wonder to perceive
Alas, if only we could be as free as
this sea
If we could learn to be content with
the beauty that abounds
Much more love in our hearts could
be found
To find rest and solace in nature's
infinite well
Pure contentment in us would dwell.

Thomas Kruger

THE MASTER'S BRUSH

Adorning the world in gold and
crimson
God lifts his brush to the land,
Giving the world a magical glow
An autumn original from the master's
hand

The hills and the valleys are alive and
on fire
With beautiful eye-pleasing scenes,
Dripping colors from painted trees
Of yellows, reds, and greens
Splashes here and splatterings there
God's hand is everywhere,
The never changing creator's ever
changing beauty
Hanging breathlessly in the crisp
autumn air

Hazy summer turning to radiant fall
In one glorious magical fling,
God's fulfilling promise of the
changing of the seasons
As the birds and the leaves take wing

Yes the hills and the valleys are a
living masterpiece
Painted with the creator's brush,
Beautiful beyond all imagination
A living testimony of the master's
touch

Margaret Ostyn

WHAT PRICE

A heart whose windows are open to a
touch
Do we give too little or too much?

One that is riddled with sorrow and
pain
Do we just look and turn in shame?

One that has known mistrust and fear
Do we become afraid to go near?

As we see it sinking before our eyes
Do we help or just watch it die?

Do we, with the Master's hand, put it
gently back in place
Forever its sorrow to erase

Building it back one touch at a time
Until its true place it does find?

What price are we willing to pay
To help others find their way?

Sophia Nicholas

THE DELINQUENT YOUNG LADY

To God: Thank you. Remember that talent you gave me? Well, . . . better late, than never!

Mama, I cannot abide
Your constant interfering . . .
And papa, with his discipline
Is harshly domineering!

I think that I shall run away
And live my life anew,
Say . . . life begins at forty
And I'm only forty-two!!

Sophia Nicholas

PEACE

Where are you, o' keeper of my
dreams?
Close the velvet curtain on my
conscious mind.
Place me on a cloud of soft blue
down,
That I may sail aloft into a golden
paradise.

Gerard H Zoehfeld

TRUSTING FRIEND

To Laura, whose friendship I will cherish forever.

Flower of my heart
My dearest and closest friend
I care about you more than life
To be there till the end.

As a sister to her brother
Through loving eyes I see.
Not a single solitary harm
So could you hide from me.

A buddy I can trust
To help me when I cry.
You've lifted my heart
when I needed it most
I need you by and by.

We shall always have each other
When it's tough, we'll still pull through
I know that you feel the same
When I say, friend I love you.

Gerald H Zoehfeld
APRIL RAIN
Blind to the sky
Reflection of the stars.
We fall
Willingly to the earth
To play amongst the tall grass
with young spring dew.
Light appears
As new day awakens
We are gone,
Until tomorrow.

Veronica F Jouben
PRECIOUS LOVE

To my wonderful husband Jimmie. You are my everything, I love you. Bonnie.

When I was just a very little girl,
a very gentle man told me, I smile like a pearl.
He claimed that I glowed and glistened,
As I sat upon his lap and listened.

He was eighteen, and I only eight,
I did realize I had a long wait.
Oh what love can do to one's heart,
If he only knew how I was so smart.

Oh what a gentle man he is to me,
He had to go across the sea.
And hoped one day he would return for me,
And may he get upon his knee, and say, "Oh, will you marry me."

One glorious day in May, we became husband and wife,
We cut our blessed wedding cake with a silver knife,
Oh what a beautiful beginning to a life of love,
Thank you God for your blessing from above.

Elizabeth Fortunak
THE THIRD WORLD RAINBOW
Please paint me a rainbow, as only you would know.
Show me your gray rainbow of starvation and woe.
Third-world child, with your stomach so bloated,
Paint me your grim rainbow of life so distorted.
Then the weary child, crippled and weak
Painted her rainbow of life-hopeless and bleak.
Her rainbow had no canvas, but was embedded in mud
And highlighted her silver lining with her brothers' blood.
Then gathered some tears from her river of despair
And scattered the tears over the blood with care.
No clouds had she to hide her rainbow of pain,
So she used her garment, ragged and plain.
I stood in awe of her finished rainbow of fear
Then her tiny hand reached out and I drew her near.
I thought, "My precious child, with eyes so sad and brown,
I'm so very sorry my society has let you down."
Then the teary child, with her life so bleak
Opened her tender, cracked mouth as if to speak;
Collapsed in my arms and passed away.
Choking on my words, I tried to say
"I'm sorry it had to end this way."

Elizabeth Fortunak
IN THE MIDST OF MY DESPAIR
In the midst of my despair there lurked a shadow
That cried in the night and in the meadow.
I could not live! I could not think!
My life was crumbling, I was on the brink.
Then out of the blue there shown a light
And I knew right then I'd end my fright.
I made a new friend. We had a talk.
He took my hand. We took a walk.
I told him of when my life fell apart
And of all the people who broke my heart.
I looked up to him and started to cry
But he just smiled at me and wiped my face dry.
He looked down upon me and said,
"My daughter, My dear,
When you believe in me, I am always near."
He gave me a hug and sent me along
but gave me a feeling of love and to belong.
So sometimes when I'm down and out,
My friend and I, we walk our route.
I know with him I'll always be free
When we take a walk, just God and me.

Barbara Fuger
HEATHER
A little girl woman
with bright green eyes
is stepping through
my thoughts tonight
my heart sighs

Her smile made of sunshine
her laugh my favorite song
dancing in my dreams tonight
all night long

Marie Jane Franciose
HEAVENLY LETTER
Dear God, I know
you are my friend
So I decided to write
a letter to send
About the many problems
we face down here
It's very unsettled
in our hemisphere.

People are homeless and
soon lose their pride
Looking for soup kitchens
and a place with a bed
Comes the morn and
another sad day
When they find out things
aren't going their way.

A Pandora's box
might possibly be
Unleashing its evils
from sea to sea
This humble person is
praying with zeal
That God in His mercy
will save us all.

Barbara Fuger
THE BIRTH
Long ago in Bethlehem
God sent a holy light
Salvation came for all mankind
Upon a Christmas night

The angel spoke to shepherds
And what an awesome sight
Fear not, I bring joyful tidings
Upon a Christmas night

And in the humble stable
A baby's eyes were bright
For in him dwelt God's perfect love
Upon a Christmas night

Teresa Kanieski
A FRIEND

This poem is dedicated to David, my best friend and husband.

The stars are silver, the sky is black,
I sit in the sand and lean lazily back.
The waves are gently caressing the rocks
I hurt so much from life's hard knocks
I was in love, but now I'm alone
Sometimes it hurts now that he's gone.
I cannot sleep, I toss and turn for this is twice, that I've been burned.
But I have a friend who talks with me,
He's been there too, so he can see,
So I sit and listen when there's nothing to do,
My friend, sometimes, he listens too.
I think my friend can read my mind,
And sometimes I think, my soul he finds.
My friend I thank you for caring for me,
For being there when I need you to be.
You shared my dreams, my joys and pains,
From your friendship, I have gained.
I hope my friend, that I can repay
The debt I owe to you someday.

Marie Jane Franciose
ODE TO A MAN

This poem is dedicated to my husband Michael, the proud father of our two lovely daughters. He is a good man.

We were lying there quietly face to face
and I looked at him in this resting place
and thought to myself, who is this man
we speak to each other in haste now and then.

—he's my husband—

The years have not been kind to him
enduring them calmly, he never gave in
in stress or in strife, we've bided our time
and counted our blessings, with nary a whine.

—I'm his wife—

Kirsten Phelps
FREEDOM
Floating through the sky
The birds soar.
Free.
Singing ballads of happiness.
Then, drifting down to earth.
They gather around the bench.
There the man sits.
Mumbling to himself.
Lonely and sad.
Trapped on the bench.
As the birds rise and fly away,
So does the man.

K P Finucane
ILLUSIONS TRUTH

Dedicated to Kimberly A. Bryant, who while being consumed in the big scope, scope of life, could not hear what was being said, and would not listen to what I was trying to say.— Thank you, Kim.

My heart is pounding oh so hard as I'm quite uncertain why, I find myself hysterically laughing wanting only to cry. While the memories of distant past are that of dull hazy blur, the uncertainty of my heart's emotions are ceaseless to stir.

They've come here together and shall all gather around, 'tis the bride to be with her family and friends in a far away town. Extraordinary people that soon love's circle will embrace, while to me they will simply become another lost and foreign face.

My mind refuses to stop trembling as I sit alone and wonder, why my dreams are that of sunshine though I pray for thunder. This tale of bitter end is void to reason and of no rhyme, such as one might feel having left themself to another place in time.

'Tis a foreboding night of confusion to cause such wonder towards home, remembering those places I've been, dreamt of, and have yet to roam. Far too many thoughts entwined in my kicking of this stone, it is better left unturned, as I walk into dismal days and nights so alone.

My heart continues pounding, as I'm still uncertain why, I'm hysterically laughing again only this time, I'm praying to cry. Perhaps there is a rhyme of this or a reason left unknown, if there is, I pray that it be given me soon.

Please Dear Lord, take from me this laughter and allow me the howling of your moon.

K P Finucane
YESTERDAY'S DREAMS

Dedicated to my friend and brother THE EAGLE, who through it all encouraged, supported, inspired, believed in and loved me in spite of myself.—Thanks Shane, continue soaring.

Peacefully sleeping while caught in the realm of yesterday's dreams, I was suddenly awakened only to realize that life isn't always as it seems.

So upon the wings of an EAGLE I mounted and together we did part, hoping to leave behind us not a single lonely nor broken heart.

Where our flight would lead us nary a soul could know and we dared venture to say that perhaps, we're sailing back to the dreams of yesterday.

Debra Underwood
AN AFFAIR
With my passion, I walked on fire
In the need, I ran on flames
It consumed and burned my soul
I rode a hot wind abandoned of shame

Then in the stillness of quiet storms
In the thunder of silent seas
The winds raged and darkness fell
In astonishment I watched me

I stood on the edge of a plank I walked
In final denial I plunged into
Cradled darkness of a forgiving sea
Caught in its arms of light so blue

Where I sought the comfort of nothing
It cradled me in the raging calm
Ever so gently the waves touched down
On the shore where I call home

My passion still longs to return to flames
My heart to roam for love it needs
My soul to ride the hottest of winds
So I bathe in the blue light of sea

Vera Montfort Westerman
FAITH AND WORKS
Surely the eyes of men can see a thing
That inspires the heart to rejoice and sing
Of a President who takes hammer and nails
To help those in need, because it never fails
To be more blessed to give than to receive.
This great man by this act shows he does believe
The Word that says "faith without works is dead."
Man's work and Man's faith in God is far ahead
Of any thing that can be attained here on earth.
The things that really count and have real worth
Comes from the throne of Almighty God above
Who gives to men here below mercy and love.
This President's name will live in history
His acts and deeds are written indelibly
In the book God will open on judgment day
And the voice of Jesus will be heard to say "When you have done it unto the least of these
Jimmy Carter, You have done it unto me."

Pattie Ann Harding
DEAR LORD!!!!!
Help me climb the ladder made of decision(s).
Help me understand that each movement(s) is guided by your hands.
Help me to accept the consequence(s) of my climbing and to use each step, with wisdom and love.
Strengthen my body to withstand the load of my struggle(s) and aid my heart to carry the burden(s) of love and forgiveness.
Open my mind, so that wisdom and knowledge will not be a stranger to me.
Allow me to feel the winds from your breath, the sun from your smiles, the rain from your tears and the love from your ever beating heart.
Thank you kindly, Father, for I am but a poor babe in this big spectrum of your creation, for allowing me to ask.

Kelly McAllister
LE RENDEZ-VOUS

To Jami and Jessie and Sue,
Love, Kelly

The shrill cries of abandonment
Echo throughout the corridors.
Eyes glazed in death.
Why was it killed?
Snow falls softly on the windowpane
Without hesitation the sterile instruments prod
Deep within the womb.
The tears outside do not make a sound
Seeds were cast on barren fields
But the snow from falling lovers
Will not let them grow.
The weight of indecision is lifted
By the steel of the knife.
The odious adventure has ended
There's nothing more to say
And nothing more remains of that
Fine and glorious day.

Tim Sims
PROMISES
Nobody's on the outside who pry their way in
Faceless someone's who say they're your friends
Mindless madmen who kill in their sleep
They all make promises they cannot keep

Gravebound stand-ins who turn tricks for drugs
Weak-hearted let downs who say they're in love
Pre-sweetened beauties that give you a peak
They all make promises they cannot keep

Trust them, if so I can't speak your mind
As undead liars will still go on lying
They flash in your face for you to believe
It's your decision on what you conceive

Featherweight fairies that dance because they are gay
Nosey spectators who can't turn away
Blank minded weirdoes who say they're not freaks
They all make promises they cannot keep

Cotton candied airheads who can't remember their names
Underhanded criminals that will not take the blame
Motherless children that live on the street
They all make promises they cannot keep

James L Smith
FROZEN MEMORIES
My face so cold and skin so tight
burning tears from the bitter cold night.
Eyes wind-blown see cloudless moon
forming light shadows through blowing trees
cold and bright but none so sad as memories
frozen in memory.

Eyes so cold the tears burn my skin
from bitter cold winter night.
Wind-blown eyes see moon's warming light
and shadows blowing trees 'round my path.
All other nights as cold and bright
but none so sad as the memory's past
frozen in memories.

Shadows surrounding blowing trees
My skin so tight with cold burns tears.
Wind-blown winter air moves light shadows
thru blowing trees on the path I walk
so cold and sad from frozen memories.

Sandra L Sersch

Sandra L Sersch
IN THE EYES OF A CHILD

I dedicate "In the Eyes of a Child" to my children, Laura, Janice and Steve, for all I have seen in their 'eyes as a child.'

What wonders we can see in the "eyes of a child" . . .
"Magical," "Mystical," Imaginations run wild!

A "wonderland," "play land," "toy land," of "Love!";
Flurries of "sunshine" from heav<u>en</u> above.

"Make believe fantasies" rise to all heights!;
"What's," "Why's," "Amazements," "Wide-eyed Delights!"

The most sincerest forgiveness you'll ever find;
The "not understanding," but "it's O.K." kind.

A "Help me," "I need you!" look in their gaze;
"I want to be just like you" is the phrase.

And when from sorrow their eyes fill with tears . . .
Look through the <u>teardrops</u> to capture their fears.

And take a moment from each day, to cross a thought or two;
And if you look deep enough . . .

"In the Eyes of a Child,"
You will see a reflection of "YOU!"

Pattie Ann Harding
FOR WHAT YOU HAVE CREATED
To gaze upon the earth and truly see what is being done to what you have created.

To listen to the hopes, wishes, joys, sadness, happiness, sickness, problems, anxiety of what is being said happening on what you have created.
To tolerate the lies, stealing, murders, rapes, robberies, plundering of each creation and still forgive what is dominating what you have created.

To smile with your sun's rays, cry with your rain and ponder with your winds, what you have created.

To not allow the bitterness to form in your heart or mind regarding what you have created.

To walk each day with all, not few, not some, not many of what you have created.

To wake each and everyone with your sun and passionately put them to sleep, with your moon what you have created.

To whisper, "don't worry I'm here, I'm always here for you," to what you have created.

All this and what you have created still wants more—

God can you forgive us all, for we all have truly <u>SINNED</u> !!!

Tammy Jo Hinson
DON'T FOLLOW IN MY FOOTSTEPS

To Jessica and Joseph. Mommy loves you!

Don't follow in my footsteps
For they aren't yours to fill,
Don't imitate another
For you'll climb an endless hill.
Don't follow the majority
For they aren't always right,
Don't be swayed by opinions
For your dreams, you stand and fight.
Don't ever lose your confidence
Don't ever, "just give in,"
Remember all these rules my child
And you shall always win.

Tammy Jo Hinson
WHAT GOD PUT INSIDE
There is an evil here,
And a hate; and fear
It is aimed towards our fellow man.
It is mean and cruel,
It is spread by fools
It is time we took a stand.
Look around and consider, what God had in mind,
When he created differences in all humankind.
Because color of skin, your sex, beliefs,
Doesn't change what God put inside.
We are all the same in one special way,
We all have our pride.

Laura Elliott
THE MOUNTAINS
How Beautiful!
No words can describe
The awesomeness of God's creation.
How He placed the hills in their

Great splendor that reach to the clouds,
To remind us of His presence.
They speak of His glory and power;
They are simple, yet rough—
They are high as if
God put them there to guard
The valley below.
God is much the same way,
As He protects us from the rough terrain.
It can make us feel small,
Compared to the mountains.
Yet, it makes us feel special—
To know that we can come into the presence
Of Him who created the mountains,
The valleys, and the ocean
And praise His name.
We can truly say,
"OH Lord; Oh Lord,
How majestic is Your name.
In all the earth!"

Johnathan Rella

Johnathan Rella
TIME WILL TELL
I can see our next generation of man
Asking questions like:
What could have happened?
Where did everybody go?
Looking for answers in the dirt and sand

There will be flying ships in the sky
Beings from another galaxy
Reaching out with a helping hand
Telling stories of what happened to man

He will be wise teaching us new ways
Showing us peace & tranquility
Also telling us what lies up there
In the vastness of space
The alien stops talking
Takes off his guard
And shows us his face

Man looks not with surprise
But he breaks out and cries

The End!

Linda A Pioli Selbert
MY SON
Dimpled cheeks
A warm friendly smile
Scholastically weak
Fun was his style

Uniform too big
Small wiry frame
A little twig
Fought hard to win a game

Rejected at an early age
His heart did pain
Lived with inner rage
Could see no gain
Drugs helped him see
A different world
Took over his mind at twenty-three
In his own blood he would swirl

Twenty-three — twenty-three
My son — My son
Gone forever from me
What have you done

Edward Shim
VULNERABLE
The ancient television sits on the floor,
Its top laden with dust, a millimeter
For every year of its life.
It is turned on and a faint
Crackling is heard from the dark screen.
A colored paper, twisting and folding, writhing
Emerges, rainbow colors pulse from its center.
The paper is laid flat:
Image of a man walking
In a strange city.
To my left is a lamp lit
Like a skirt on fire.
An insect crawls on the inside of the skirt,
A shadow (small).
I am consuming chips and Coke,
The bowl wet with grease,
The cup covered with fingerprints so that
I feel guilty like
The man on the screen must feel
When he shot a lady, her body lying crumpled
On the ground, seeming to suck the earth.

Rene O'Connell
RADICALLY COMMITTED
Radically committed is more than a saying;
It's believing and doing what you're saying.
John the Baptist was radically committed;
He was beheaded because of his faith.
Noah the arkmaker was radically committed;
He was laughed at while using his lathe.
Mary the virgin was radically committed;
She listened to God instead of the law.
Abraham our father was radically committed;
He didn't live by what he saw.
Jesus Christ was radically committed;
He paid for our sins when he died on the cross.
Hey, average Christian! Be radically committed;
Trust in the Father or it'll be your loss!

Rachel Griffin
WHERE HAS GRANDMA GONE
Grandma no longer sits in a rocking chair,
Knitting or tatting lace.
Instead she's on her powerwalk,
She's getting ready for the marathon race.
For Grandma has kicked over the traces,
And turned her boring life around.
Once known as a great homebody,
Today, she is even college bound.
Grandma has no time for babysitting,
And she caters to, not one.
Now she's perfumed and powdered,
And out on the town, having fun.
Boy! is she ever hipped on rock-and-roll,
And can she cut a rug?
You'll wonder where Grandma's gone,
When you see her jitterbug.
So now the old rocking chair is obsolete,
It is no longer Grandma's nesting place.
Because Grandma has bridged the generation gap,
And now she rocks at a brand-new pace.

Philip G DeLoach
JUGGERNAUT
Far beneath the singing petals,
Lies a memory of thunder distant.
When growling beasts heralded
The coming of one so small,
Yet so savage, as to quench his thirst
With beauty's pain.
The gleaming, glass and steel graveyards
Climb toward the sun,
With the vain hope of forgetting
That not-so-distant thunder.
Above the sighing of the trampled rose,
The clangings, whirrings, vent their unearned anger.
With no heart pounding out malice,
With no soul which can be spoken for,
The self-devouring juggernaut
Rends the thunder from its solitude.
Twisting and gasping,
The golden, granite beast consumes itself.
The struggle becoming as a whisper
In a darkened room.

Brian James Beers
LIFE RIDE
My mind meanders all around,
While the breeze blows through my hair.
It helps me to see things more clearly;
Life has its own little flare.
Some things are good,
And others are bad.
We all worry about them both.
Live your life to the fullest;
Do it in your own special way
Because in the end no one is here to stay.

Observe, learn, do what you can to preserve.
Someday long away the things that you do will better life in a great way.
You get just one ride;
If you are lucky, it may last a long time.
Through its ups and downs,
You can find what life has to offer throughout the journey.
No one wants to get off the ride,
But someday we all must oblige.
So why do I wonder about the day I die?

Juliet J Feravolo
THE BEAUTY OF IT ALL
Spring, summer, winter and fall
The pleasures of all I do recall
A winter's walk through the snow-covered earth
And the sledding children filled with mirth.

A crocus is a sign of spring
As is the song the robin doth sing
The tulips and daffodils begin to sprout
And the grass gets greener all about.

How beautiful is a summer day
The leaves in the gentle breeze do sway
The white-capped waves flow onto the golden sand
And the sight of hill and dale is grand.

The autumn leaves of red and gold
Are really breathless to behold
There is a sadness as they fall
Especially the time when there is none at all.

Each season plays its special part
To bring gladness to the heart
Each portrays its splendor to the eye
The beauty of it all will not die.

Carla Ellen Thompson
A BLANK PAGE
A blank page.
This vast desert of emptiness
Laid out before me,
The first blood of ink
I have laid upon your virgin pulp.
Words of thought from a mind not young, but not yet old.
Thought has no age,
It is like an oasis on this desert page.
Thoughts drift endlessly about my head
Opening new worlds to see,
Through visions of words that come and rest awhile
If I'm lucky they lend themselves to me.
While on loan I write them down
For what reason, I am not sure,
Maybe for some future treasure
These thoughts can give to someone
In a desert faraway place, a moment's pleasure.
I do know of that desert place,
For I have spent some time there.
In the land where no one has a face,
Clear thought is elusive, sparse and bare.

Vicki Collins
THOUGHTS
Watching the sun slowly rise,
In the quiet of the early dawn,
I think of my life as I look out my window.

The trees no longer bear leaves, and
I sometimes feel autumn has come to my life too.
God! I do not know which way to go from here.

My world has changed so much for me,
No longer do I have the same feelings.
The light that burned so bright is beginning to flicker.

The patterns of my life have taken a turn;
There are discrepancies in things I do.
Inside I have deep feelings of helpless despair.

The sun keeps getting higher, but
The amount of light does not seem to change.

My life feels endless, like
wind–blown sand.

Thelma Graves
WINTER OF LIFE
Is it the snow in March that made me sigh
Or the rain in May that occasionally make me cry
Or the fall in June that made me stop and wonder why
Why have the seasons of life come and gone
and left me with no spring to grow on
No summer to harvest on
Is it the winter of my life have stayed far too long
in June
Or the autumn fell where July was due
I watch the skies with clouds strew
For I know beyond the unpredictable storm
I see a rainbow of many hues

Irene Rector
A COLD WINTER DAY
LEADER: What would you like on a cold winter day
With snowflakes as soft as lace?
ALL: I'd like to run just as fast as I could,
And feel the cold snow on my face.

LEADER: What would you like on a cold winter day
When the snow piles up deep?
BOYS: I'd build a fort and a snowman or two
To dream about when I sleep!

LEADER: What would you like on a late winter day
When sun has melted the snow?
GIRLS: I'd go and look at some plants still asleep,
And some that were starting to grow.

Lori Grannis
LIFE IS LIKE A ROSE
Life is like a rose
Give it sun and it will grow
Love is like a river
Give it water and it will flow
Patience is like a mother
Always standing by your side
Peace is like a father
Strong, willing and full of pride
Hope is like a star
Twinkling brightly in the sky
Endurance is like the mountains
Standing proud, with their heads up high
Birth can be a reminder
Of our God who shows he cares
Strength is like a friend
Somebody who shares our fears
The world is a place
Where we so freely live
Open up your hearts
And find some love to give

Erneen Saye
LOVE'S HAPPINESS
There's something special about your smile
that stays with me during our in-between times
And makes me stop what I'm doing and think of you . . .

There's something special about your love that
carries me through a hectic day
just knowing you are there . . .

There's something special about you
that makes every day I'm with you
one more reason to want to be
with you forever . . .

Ben Erwin
HOW
How time flies.
How you must seize the moment.
How long you must wait.
How pretty it all is.
How many questions unanswered.
How things change. How things stay the same.
How simple. How complex.
How can you tell? How will I know?
How do I do it?
How an idea can change the world.
How someone rises to power.
How Albert talked to a flower.
How we got to where we are. How we are going—how far?
How will we realize: become one?
How will I die? How about the sun?
How do you figure?--something inside us? How do you know, that someone guides us? Or is it outside, just surrounding? But how did it get there? Was it a split? Or was it a joining?
How I love her.
How.

Bonnie Clayton
HER TIME HAS PASSED
To My Precious Grandmother

Though she's old now—and forgotten
and her body isn't strong.
Could they forget what she has taught them?
It hasn't been that long.

Her back is bent from labor—
working hours into the dawn.
to help her child or neighbor
Where have the years all gone?

But now she's old and lonely.
They have left her one by one.
How could they have forgotten
all the good things she has done?

The big house she kept spotless
and clothing she has sewn.
The love and warmth she gave them
and problems she has known.

She sits there by the window
remembering the past.
Memories of things so dear
Her life has gone so fast.

And now her worth is over—
She's just someone in the way.
Though they notice her no longer
God will want her home someday.

She can sit there in His heaven
relaxed and loved at last
She will be one of His angels
in the loving mold she's cast.

Hope O'Rourke
MEMORIES OF EARTH
To my Dad, who taught me how to make wishes come true.

I want to walk along the beach,
Greeting each grain of sand I meet.

I want to record the sound of each bird,
So as never to forget each I have heard.

I want to paint my memories blue,
With each and every sky I knew.

I want to engulf each and every wave I hear,
So my memories of earth are, oh so clear.

Hope O'Rourke
MOTHER'S BIBLE
Dedicated to Mother, who is the true poet of the family.

Her hour late,
her house quiet,
her bible she reads.

Her ten daughters,
her ten commitments,
her bible she reads.

Her faithful spirit,
her loving heart,
her bible she reads.

Her gentle hands,
her soft eyes,
her bible she reads.

Her lessons taught,
her love given,
her bible she read.

Susan Curnow
THE LOVE OF A FRIEND
A friend is someone who shares your dreams.
A friend is someone who shares your screams.
They share the good times and the bad.
They share the laughter and the sad.

Someone you know will always be there.
Someone you know will always care.
A friend lends an ear when that's the need.
A friend will guide and take the lead.

A love to share but rarely told.
For most friends are not that bold.
A friend will listen to our silly stories.
And be happy for us when there are glories.

What would life be and to what end
without this person we call friend?

Marsha Cavagnaro
THE FLICKERING FIRE
To My Sister Karen.

The flickering fire blazes aglow
The sound of the rumbling fire popping ahoe.
The rain falling heavily against the tin roof
Brings imagines of dancing rainbows on the roof.
The wind howling and whistling against the black sky, throws a shadowy cast on the house nearby.
The clouds sweeping swiftly through the open air, the birds flying without a care.
The silhouette of the buttes against the terrain, on the other side is the coastal range.
What a beautiful remembrance.

Linda Waid
ARE WE TAKING CARE OF WHAT GOD HAS GIVEN US?
This poem is dedicated in loving memory to my grandmother, Bessie Matthews and my uncle, Ernie Fonger, my family and friends, and also to the future generations who are going to inherit the world, whether they want to or not.

Standing by the seashore, with its fresh, salty spray blowing across my face, and the gentle warmth of the sun on my back, I feel all aglow.
I silently admire the foamy, ivory-white waves as they tumble, swirl sideways, then dash to and fro.

The rhythmic lapping of the rolling, crashing waves sounds like a nature's lullaby,
Until I hear the blaring noise of a motorcycle racing by.

The shiny motorcycle leaves tracks on the soft, glistening sand,
Carelessly destroying the traces of fading footprints and ripples, which look as if they were sculptured with an artist's hand.

Suddenly, a long-winged sea gull gracefully soars through the fiery, rose-red sunset sky,
Only to disappear behind a smoke-filled cloud from a factory building nearby.

I sadly pick up some of the paper, cans, and broken glass that people have neglectfully left behind,
And I wonder how people could be so uncaring and blind.

God created this beautiful, azure and verdant earth with extreme care,
He formed it with his infinite love, for us to share.

The balance of nature has been made uniquely and flawless,
But it's being ruined by our pollution and progress.

Nature is precious and if not used properly,
It will fade away fast and be nothing but a memory.

But, there is still hope for our future.
It is not too late.
If we work with the balance of nature, instead of destroying it, and recycle now, these threatening conditions do not have to be our fate.

After all, the earth is the only home we have. Protecting the environment deeply affects all of us, so it's everyone's fight.
We should work together to save the world and set everything right.

Harold Olsen
LOVE IS ETERNAL

To the memory of Alfred Christiansen.

God demonstrates that Love is Eternal.
God in love, breathed into his nostrils the breath of life,
and man became a living soul.
Though man disobeyed God, and sin came to earth,
Yet, God promised a new example of love,
to show man that Love is Eternal.
For God in love, presented His Son to earth, that man through Him,
might know of God's eternal love.
Jesus Christ, God's son, came as a servant,
So that mans' sin be blotted out from the eyes of God.
God sent the Son, so that man again may have a choice,
to know eternal love or damnation.
For God ordained that there be no forgiveness of sin
without the shedding of blood.
Jesus Christ at Calvary, accepted the guilt of sin of the whole world,
that His blood be the final sacrifice.
Death by sin was vanquished by the resurrection of Jesus Christ
from death to life, that man may know Love is Eternal.
Yes, Love is Eternal, Jesus Christ at Calvary, proved
for all time that Love is eternal.

W A Gray

W A Gray
MORTALITY
Standing, fearful at that portal
Aware, alive, still mortal
The frantic fingers of the dawn
Shed no shadows on the void beyond

That void beyond is the velvet sea
The cradle of death that waits for me
Who fanned the embers of this flame
Feeding these fears within my brain?

I shrink and shrivel with every breath
Fired with the fear of my own death
Has the time between been worth these fears
From birth down through these many years?

Birth of course was the start of this
It has not revealed any paths of bliss
Where is the peace? That calm of time
That I felt so strongly might well be mine

Has peace gone by, unseen by me
Blinded by that swirling sea
That need for visible acclaim?
If such be so—then take the blame!

I fanned those embers in my own brain.

W A Gray
LEGENDS LOST
We've laboured long and made a pact
Now fictions fade in the face of fact
Those legends lost to learning
Have left a sadness, a yearning

Our species seeking has no reliance
Except upon the facts from science
Following trails we know not where
From sea to sand to swamp and air.

The chains of dogma, long since shattered
Lay rusted, useless, long since scattered
What new standards of strength and worth
Will guide our species on this earth?

Can the children ever awake to see
A sunrise of stability?
Will those legends re-appear
To ease away the children's fear?

Or do we face an endless race
For Godlike grace in a frantic chase
A voyage to nowhere—propelled by sail
With the winds of knowledge our endless gale?

Virginia Burke
I SAW THE START OF A SOFT, GENTLE RAIN
I saw the start of a soft, gentle rain;
I heard their voices say, "Let's go back again."
I heard them but I did not want to go back—
I felt them leading me toward the old railroad track.

Then they led me down an old country road,
Saying, "This is the place to drop every load."
They let my hand go and left me all alone,
Saying, "Though we may seem to leave you,
We will not really be gone,
For we have implanted a memory deep within your mind,
And that, you know, can never be unkind."

I turned and walked down the deserted track again,
Joined by a memory and the soft, gentle rain;
Filled with the memory and renewed once again—
Knowing the memory of them will always remain.

B W Bartholomaus
INJUSTICE
Amidst the wailing din of an Ethiopian hunger camp
a child lies dying, belly swollen, eyes glassy;
his youth gnawed away by the rats of hunger.
In the distant capitol his pleas fall on deaf ears
muted by the bugles of war and greed.
And the heads of state raise their glasses in toast,
continuing their wining, dining.

On a dung heap in starving India, a beggar searches
for anything that will drive away the pangs of hunger as
the sky is blackened by the smoke of a thousand funeral pyres.
In Central America a volcano retches and a village is buried.
And in the distant capitol, the heads of state
raise their glasses in toast;
continuing their wining, dining.

Across the world in a February ghetto in Chicago
a blanket wrapped old lady shivers,
her heat long since turned off, and as foundry smoke
greets a new dawn another citizen of the streets
from a park bench is pried.
And in the distant capitol, the heads of state
raise their glasses in toast,
continuing their wining, dining.

Jean Boix
LAND OF THE DEAD
Out in the dark woods
The smell of death
Creeping upon my shoulders
Swamp lands I passed
To get to the Land of the Dead

The land where mortals live
That's where my power
Comes from
It's a land where only
The dead live
No mortals shall live
Their flesh is torn and eaten
In the Land of the Dead

My journey is almost over
I will be the one mortal to live
They don't know my secret
The one that has been hidden
I too am immortal

At night my flesh peels
And I am as gruesome
As the immortals
In the Land of the Dead

I hold the key
To be their ruler
I will rule and slay
And the Land of the Dead
Will be in my command.

Diane Frances Hill

Diane Frances Hill
JUNE

For my Mother, with Love.

"Where is June?", they beg my pardon!
Have you looked among her friends in the garden?

You may find her with the birds and the butterflies . . .
For she likes the gentle breezes and the clear blue skies.

You may find her planting bulbs by the light of the moon . . .
Or maybe just singing her sweet and lovely tune.

If you search among the flower beds,
I'm sure you'll find her there . . .
She brings them food and water, and tends them with loving care.

She digs homes for new plants for hours and hours . . .
And welcomes the sun and the sweet morning showers.

She's learned much from the flower and the butterfly
How their beauty lives on and on . . .

As the lingering fragrance of the sweet red rose . . .
And the chant of the Nightingale's song.

She'll always be there if you'll look,
her love is never far away . . .
You'll see it in the birds and buds,
and feel it on a warm sunny day.

How do I know this lady so well
And have such a long story to tell?

You see, it is because she is none other
Than my very own, lovely Mother!

Diane Frances Hill
THE MAGIC IN HIS HANDS

To Huck.

Someone came into my life,
Once upon a time.
How I came to meet him,
Has no reason or rhyme.

He made his way into my heart,
Without my knowing when . . .
He touched my heart so tenderly,
I longed for his touch again.

How sweetly his touch upon me is,
He cares and understands . . .
Oh, the power he has to heal my wounds—
He has magic in his hands!

What a gift of love can be,
When someone cares soo much!

The deepest words aren't spoken,
But felt in just a touch!

Diane Frances Hill
STONE HEART

To all those recovering from a painful relationship.

Who said, "Stone walls do not a prison make"?
Was it Tennyson, Lovelace or Keats?
Whoever the author, let me tell you what it means.

I knew a man who was a prisoner of his own heart,
Locked in by that monster called selfishness.
He had something to give, yet chose not to give it . . .
That is the greatest crime of all!

Stone walls do not a prison make;
Only your hard and selfish heart
Can lock you in for all eternity . . .
And lock out the love you long for yourself.

Who said, "You must be a friend to have a friend"?
Who said, "The greatest of these is love"?
I say, you create your own prison
when you neglect to give to others . . .
What you have in your hands to give.

You lock yourself in,
By withholding the love others need.
You lock out those who could love you . . .
And thus choose prison over life!

Pamela Brown
A WHOLE MAN'S CRY

This poem is dedicated to my beloved mother, whose encouragement has become my threshold to new horizons.

If you bare a poor man's cry,
Where riches gained are undefined;
Seek not your worth in gold to spend,
Seek your measure of worth in friends.

If you bare the sad man's cry,
And weep the tears from a sightless eye;
Be not blind to prosperity's view,
Life is bountiful, each day renewed.

If you bare the angry man's cry,
Ask yourself to reason why;
Is this of your heart's contempt?
This wrath you bare to scorn's intent.

If you've never dared to cry,
Have you ever looked inside?
Seen a trace of tears that hide,
Within a truth your heart's denied?

Hearts will grow through tears they've wept,
Poor man, sad man, angry regrets;
And with each tear your heart has bared,
A whole man's cry, you will have fared.

Ellen Bolding
THOUGHTS
Though I've known deep inside
my life would not be
like the fairy tale romance
that ends happily,

I did not imagine
what God had in store
I do know he's not through
there will be plenty more

Challenge and mystery,
surprise good and bad
will fill up my life
give it meaning, pizazz.

I will do my best and better
with all that comes my way
And things that I search out to do
will be material for my play

And so I sit and clear my mind
so I can start anew
Open up my heart, my life and soul
to all that I might do.

Grace Desprez
TO MY FRIEND FROM THE OLD DAYS
They talked about 'the old days'—
When you and I were young,
And we heard about those 'old days'
In all the songs they sung;
But all the world's been changed now;
If you look around, you'll see
That they've all forgot the old days,
Excepting you and me!

Remember all those old times
When our lives seemed dull and blue,—
How we'd visit one another,
And just 'spin a yarn' or two?
Well, we don't get to chat so much,
Like in those days of yore,
But it's friends like you make me feel rich!
All the rest make me feel poor!

Our friendship, in those 'old days'
Always seemed so good,
That we've buddied in those old ways
As often as we could.
Yes, ever since 'the old days'
You and I've been friends!
With smiles and tears, we've faced the years
With a love that never ends;

And every time I hear from you,
My heart fills with delight!
Then, just like in 'the old days'—
This old world seems all right!

Brandy DeBrun
CLUTCHING AT GHOSTS
With candle in hand . . .
I clutch at ghosts.
Down darkened
Cobwebbed halls.

The only safety
The candle's glow.
Which is my lead
In this maze.

I cannot find treasure . . .
What do I look for . . .
But still
I search on.

Time grows short . . .
The candle burns . . .
Soon I must find it,
For the candle goes . . .

David L Drushal
FOR A VERY LONG TIME
For a very long time I've stayed alone,
No one to greet me when I came home.
For a very long time my heart was closed,
No one could enter and hurt I suppose.
For a very long time I hoped it would end,
No one attempted, or caused me to bend.
For a very long time I wanted someone,
No one was right, just games to be won.
For a very long time, I've hoped for love true,
No one could give it, and then I met you!
For a very long time I hope you'll be near,
No one between us, year after year.

Vera Dworkin
THE UNKNOWN SOLDIER
I am the Unknown Soldier
I have immortal fame
But there is no glory in my heart
For no one knows my name.
They call me the Unknown Soldier
Mouldering in majestic clay
But there is no glory in my heart
For this Eternity of Gray
Like you, I had my hopes and schemes
I loved, was loved, and dreamt my dreams
But all too soon I was torn away
indifferent forces that ruled the day.
What is this Horror–War, I pray
Please tell me why I died this way?
Dear Mother, you will never mark my grave
You alone would know I was never brave . . .
I am the Unknown Soldier
My life too short, my death too much
Alas . . . I have immortal fame
But I thank thee not for such—
a name.

Christopher Glen Dixon

Christopher Glen Dixon
ONCE UPON A HALLOW NIGHT
Once upon a Hallow night,
When all the stars shine nice and bright,
And ghosts begin to gain some height,
And goblins finally have some sight.

It only happens once a year,
When spirits finally start to peer,
Peer into the open fields,
And humans realize to stop and yield.

Yield to save their life from danger,
So they can be but one remainder,
It cannot be very true,
But you can imagine them haunting you!

Anita Jones-Costley
SPRING MUSE
Rejoice my soul
and let the coming of Spring be your consolation
With the rebirth of nature I will be reborn
Stretching my wings upward as the naked boughs
I yield to the warmth and nourishment of the sun
And from the depth of my soul
wrapped tenderly as a budding rose
sweet expressions exploding in elegant blossom
Ah Spring whose wet kiss
rejuvenates my heart
I wait for you.

David DiCicco II
FUTURE TENSE
The earth is a circular chamber
It's headed for corruption
It's filled with anger
Most of its surroundings are polluted
Most of its greenery is uprooted
The birds cannot fly
The fish only die
Because the water and air is contaminated.
The future of this planet, is one that is grim
Children cannot go to the beach and swim
Think of our children and their children's children.
Then think of the world
That they're going to live in.

Roy De Fio
THE WAY YOU ARE
It isn't in your eyes
A warm sea of Blue
It's not the way you smile
That speaks to me so true

It isn't in the way you walk
With poise and gentle grace
Nor is it the way you talk
That lights up your face

It's not that sense of humor
That makes the whole world laugh
Or that sense of sorrow
That cuts my heart in half

It's all of them put together
That makes me want to say
How much I love you dearly
Each and every day.

Annmarie DiClementi
MONET'S LILIES
In July
I sat with Monet in Paris
looking at the lilies
on the water.

Pure white lilies
floated along on canvas saucers
imitating tea cups
I dress with sugar.

All around us lilies grew
and Monet picked one
for me.
He showed me the blue water stains
that glow in the mirror
of fish scales on the stem.

Never did I see the pink middle.
Only the petals he chose
for me to catch
and throw back into his mural
where great lilies grew
as a gift to Paris.

Shirley Dybdal
OLD MAN RIVER
Be still old man.
Let the waters once again be calm.
It's time for you to sleep.
I see the tears of those
who weep.
I'm watching you
old man river.
Why do you beat against
the shore line?
With all your frenzy you
have churned up white caps.
They stand out like stars
in the midnight sky.
Ice patches are scattered
across your face.
Your anger rages on, why?
Please give back to those,
the child you took away.
Let them bury him
along this shore today.

Ronnie Cadiz Gonzales

Ronnie Cadiz Gonzales
WILL JOHNNY COME MARCHING HOME?

In memory of Uncle Artemio Cadiz, who died on March 19, 1969 for his family, for his country.

Dusty combat boots.
19 year old bloody corpse.
Olive armed forces shirt.
Half a helmet.
An empty rocket launcher.
Deserted jeep

A small wooden cross
beside a black and white
family portrait clenched
in the palm
of his
hand.

Steve
YOU LORD
When I was lost
And could not find my way
You Lord
Brought a brighter day
When I was sick
And full of pain
You Lord
Came my way
When things were out of control
You Lord
Grabbed a hold
I don't know what life's going to be
But without you
You Lord
Life is nothing to me.

Ronnie Cadiz Gonzales
MEMORIES

Dedicated to Zaybe Crisostomo, my treasured friend in my growing years and whom I will continue to share a certain closeness with throughout my life.

this life of mine is meaningless
without the memory of what
we had and shared.

i miss your dancing eyes
expressing pure joy but
the dance ended.
it meant good-bye.

our childhood love vanished
with the morning clouds but
like the eternal sky, our
love will remain secure in
our memories
forever.

i love you.

Janae A Doran
THE FOREST
The forest is filled
With many surprises.
Like an Indian and Englishmens,
Long compromises.

The forest is dreary,
Lonely and dark.
The sounds of it are
Like a low deep bark.

The forest hides,
Many things,
Lynxes and bobcats
And lost dreams.

But the forest is pleasant,
friendly and kind,
If there were no forest,
We'd be caught in a bind.

Daniel T Dobberpuhl
EMBRACING THE EGO IDEAL
Within my mind I see a place,
Not of time and void of space.
Here, the chamber of the kings,
The final test of earthly things;
A shelter where the child can sing.

Gina Dennison
THIS MUST BE LIFE
How can a one—person be as
confused
As I? I left on a leaping heart
And oh it was high.
I went out to find new life and
New love.
I went out to find my struggles
To learn from them and
Watch them go by.
. . . And hope that my life could be
Free as a dove.

Do believe me I learned of many
fears—
That must be life . . .
I learned to go and grow
And handle this strife.
I'll never forget, though,

I learned to love life . . .

Sharon Duke
YOUR EYES
Perhaps if I could see myself
Through your dark and misty eyes,
I would see someone quite different
And not have to live a life of lies
If we could exchange bodies
Or intermingle our two souls
What would we both see
To look at my familiar face
And see it new, as if a stranger
That would be quite unique a very
Special treat
Do you see what is really me?
Or what you wish to be
It does not matter now if it be
True or false
Whatever good you see in me your
tender
Loving eyes
Will make it come to be.

Teresa A Cooper

Teresa A Cooper
A MOTHER'S LOVE

To my Mother; if it weren't for your insight, the world might not have known mine: To my Husband; I will always love you in a way you will never understand, my heart is yours. To my Son, who made it possible for me to love without limits.

Can it be forever that I look into
his face, see his mind, touch
his soul?

Or will my seemingly everlasting
gaze be interrupted by a
smile, a blink, or a sigh from
him.

There he is, so still, at rest in his
slumber. Shall I dare reach out
to him, awaken him to my
presence.

To watch his eyes open and
receive me with his
recognition, to see that spark,
that twinkle that starts the
love to flow freely.

Or to hear him utter his first
words from the long silence I
have anxiously and
impetuously broken; it would
be a symphony for my long
awaiting ears to embrace.

Oh what anticipation I have for
his wakening, yet I shall not
disturb the peaceful serenity
that lies before me.

It is the beauty that keeps me at
bay, a beauty that simply
cannot and will not be
disturbed by an act of
impatient selfishness; he is at
rest and I will wait.

Morning will come soon enough,
so I will lie down next to him
so that we may awaken
together to the wonders the
new day will bring.

And I shall keep these thoughts I
had tonight so that I may
reflect on them often,
for this is but one of the
memories I shall cherish of a
Mother's love for her son.

Teresa A Cooper
FRUSTRATION
I want to yell, to scream loud
enough to shatter this
barricade that separates me
from happiness, but I shall
not.

I want to fight, to destroy with
great vengeance and pleasure
the obstacles and barriers that
continue to hinder my path,
but I shall not.

It is society, reality and
obligations that hold me deep
within their realm, I am
bound by them, never leaving
them.

Cry, oh but so many tears I have
shed, the rivers I have made,
but to what avail, what
conquest, what reward.

Tears, they will be no more, no
more.

Anger, yes I anger, trying to find
a way to channel this emotion
but cannot, will not, shall not.

Hope is left, Survival is always.
Promise is never ending.
Future is undefined.

Yvonne G Engel Davis
THE DRUNKEN DRIVER
Boy, I'm feeling cool tonight,
I'm gonna have a ball, and that ain't
all.

I'm gonna hit the town and make the
rounds,
I'm not even gonna touch the ground.

I'll grab some whiskey and rye.
Boy, ain't I sly,
I'm really gonna fly high.

I'm gonna drag around all over that
town,
I'm really gonna make the rounds.

I'm flying high and I'll pass you by,
I feel like I'm flying through the sky.

But, look out ahead.
Oh God, look he's dead.

Is this a dream?
Did I hear him scream?

Was his car ahead of me?
Why didn't I see?
I'm flying high as they take me by,
It's off to jail and I don't even know why,
Should I cry?

Sonya McPherson
SUMMER

Dedicated to my family, my neighbors, and my friends.

Summer is the wonderful time of the year for a teardrop to fall here. You can hear the children outside playing in the summer moist grass. The loud roars of the engines passing by each and every day, and this is all I have to say for the summer that comes my way.

Herman O Whitaker
IF

If I were to love with your heart,
what would love be?
If I saw through your eyes, what
beauty would I see?
If I heard through your ears, what
music would I hear?

Don Koester Jr
FIRST LOVE, YOUNG LOVE

Our eyes met for an instant, shyly turned
Aside as though the spark of love might burn;
With bodies growing, lips that hadn't learned
To speak the words, nor kiss love's sorrowed urn.

I touched your cheek, a teardrop seared my palm,
And flesh was set aflame; my heart near burst.
My ears were ringing, singing silent psalm,
I knew not what to do: you were my first.

Our bodies tried to join, as minds could not,
In awkward coupling, virgin-sweet embrace;
And even as we finished I forgot
To kiss the salten rivers from your face.

'Twas first love, young love, never quite the best:
Though I have loved you longer than the rest.

dr.don

Don Koester Jr
RAINBOWS

Rainbows like to ride on bubbles:
Such an easy life, ya say . . .
Think them rainbows got no troubles?
Just one pop could spoil their day.

Rainbows like it when it's raining',
If the Sun ain't far behind;
Silver linings ain't complainin',
Just don't let 'em cloud your mind.

Rainbows languish, trapped in places
Where ya thought they'd never be;
All it takes is sweet embraces:
Maybe we could set one free?

Like a rainbow I' been glistenin';
Thought I'd conquered all my fears.
Guess the world just isn't listenin':
Ain't no rainbows in these tears.

dr.don

Don Koester Jr
TOUJOURS MOI

So gentle soft your lips did first brush mine,
So childlike innocent that lonely tear;
And then a meteor blessed with fiery sign
A love I thought might fill this empty sphere.

Of Love and Sadness, who could drink their fill?
Those brazen, brimming cups shall not run dry,
Nor set me free: 'twas meant to be, until
The unshamed, untamed stars have fled the sky.

Your hair was flirting with the seashore breeze,
The waves caressed our toes in mirthful play;
And as our tears flowed forth to swell the seas
You gave me one last kiss, and walked away.

I've seen it in the stars whene'er they shine:
They promised you would be forever mine.

dr.don

Don Koester Jr
KEEPSAKE

I've had this dress here nigh on twenty years;
I don't know why I'd save a rag like this.
Each time I get it out it brings me tears:
I wore it when he gave me my first kiss.

And sometimes I recall that county fair;
He got me all a-tingle, head to toes.
The first I ever let him touch me There . . .
Perhaps that's why I keep this dried-up rose.

And lookie-here, down in my bottom drawer:
It's kinda hard to read in this here light;
He thought we oughta try a little more . . .
I guess I done some growin' up That night.

And what to do with this ol' tarnished thing?
I wish I'd never wore his wedding ring.

dr.don

Don Koester Jr
THE WEDDING

And now, once more I taste thy honeyed lips;
O! rare intoxicant: thou heady brew
To set my senses reeling: starlight slips
Away unsoftly with the morning dew:
Awake my Love, I share first dawn with you.

A thousand men I fought, a thousand died,
To have thy timeless beauty by my side.

dr.don

Amber Nichol Torres
MY FRIEND—SAM

This poem is for Samuel Escalante, you're missed and thought of every day, Samuel—we love you!

I had to say good-bye, if even for a while—but I know again some day I'll see your crazy smile. You'll be standing there, like you never left and all the tears I've cried will slowly start to lift. The only thing that's kept me going are all the memories that keep on flowing.

I have thousands of questions with only hundreds of answers—why did you leave, why did you go? You've left me now with nothing but sorrow and the pain doesn't lessen or go away—I'm always reminded day after day.

Bertha A Finnemore Lee
LIFE BEYOND

A little baby boy named Reade
Came into our world one day.
Everyone was joyous indeed
But for reasons unknown he couldn't stay.

For precious Reade never took that first breath,
His Maker had called him Home.
He closed his little eyes in death
And left loved ones feeling alone.

Their lives still go on, as life doesn't stop,
And the memories they have kept them strong;
Their love for each other has kept them atop
And even strengthened their bond.

Some day they'll meet their sweet little boy
On Heaven's beautiful shore,
He'll stand with outstretched arms of love
To meet them and part no more.

Aarthi Rajaraman
WHERE AM I?

I dedicate this poem to those who seek a world free of man-made things.

Trapped in a cage,
of a man-made world.
Longing to see . . .
the outside.
Being fed with today's
ideas,
knowledge,
principles,
people.
Inquisitive, I peer,
through the bars of hope,
wondering what will
happen next.
Frustrated, I search for a key . . .
to unlock this cage.
The future is my key,
but I must wait.
My thirsty longing for freedom,
will be suppressed.
But I will always remember,
the lesson the cage taught me,
and my ignorant cries for
freedom.

Charles L McLain
DADDY'S GIRL

Daddy I just can't remember
when my life with you began.
You were there whenever I needed you
as I felt you should have been.

Some say little girls are daddy's favorite
and I've felt that way all my life.
You always knew just what to do
to help me cope with my troubles and strife.

I know you won't be with me always
so the time with you is so sweet.
To live my whole life dad, without you
would be somehow incomplete.

You always thought about your children
as you traveled on land and sea.
So when you get home to heaven
tell JESUS you want to wait for me.

Carlene Mowery

Carlene Mowery
NEVER SAY TOMORROW

This poem is dedicated to Eddie, my greatest inspiration.

Too soon life ebbs away,
and all our dreams lie forgotten,
buried in the sands of time, forever lost,
never to be realized, never to be savored
by those alone who knew their beauty.
Time is fleeting, and once gone
can never be recaptured.
So it is with life.
One brief moment in the vastness of time we appear,
then fade like a withering flower,
haunted by our memories,
reflecting back to all that could have been
if only we had learned
to never say tomorrow.

Carlene Mowery
ONE TO ONE

Dedicated to my loving parents, Cornelius and Bertie Vance.

How oft have I entered Your presence,
and You, in Your infinite wisdom, smiled
as I stood transparent before You.
Suspended in a realm where naught exists
but You and I, One to one.
Knowing I've walked where angels dare tread
in a place somewhere in time
where You and I together share the mysteries of life.
Privileged as the ancients

for our paths have intertwined
there to marvel at the ease of
revelation
as I sat in Your counsel
surveying the wonders of a limitless
God.

Karen Ruiz
A WEDDING PRAYER TO TANA AND CHAD

If I had only one gift to give you Tana and Chad and I could guarantee it for life, it would be love and happiness with a life-time guarantee. Although there are no guarantees, I can hope and pray this for you.

I pray for you that you will take your vows seriously and remember they are a promise to God. I pray that you cling to each other and are able to trust and depend on each other always. I pray that you laugh, talk, cry, and love together.

And when my prayers are answered and I get those special visits and phone calls and hear, "I LOVE YOU MOM" I'll know that:

Today, I've lost my little girl, but she's turned into a woman. She's found herself a wonderful man, and they've become as one. In days to come, I'll feel so proud, of what I've really gained, HONESTY, LOVE, and HAPPINESS and not just a DAUGHTER but a SON!

I Love You Both with all my Heart!

MOM

Melissa McKeon
CONFINED

I'm enclosed,
Locked in,
And I can't get out.
. . . trapped in a room with
all sides closing in on me.
It is black,
bleak,
boring
depressing,
despairing,
dismal,
and dreary.
Why am I held in restraint?

Reba S Perkins
TOMORROW

Far away in California
where the giant redwoods grow,
Lives someone very special
that I have come to know.

When I wake up in the morning
and see the sun above,
I think about him instantly
and my heart is filled with love.

I lay there thinking silently
how precious it would be,
If I were there with him
or if he were here with me.

I momentarily drift away
and dream a little while,
Knowing when I hear from him
he always makes me smile.

Life is full of mystery
and many other things,
Ours is not to question
what tomorrow brings.

But if it could be possible
there is one thing that I know,
I would be with him tomorrow
for he sets my heart aglow.

George A Kolar Jr
MY DAUGHTER THE SWIMMER

Dedicated to Mellisa Kolar, "Who swims like a dolphin."

Strong kick, be quick the coach will say
Practice, more practice most every day
Listen and learn, you shall hear
The gun, the fun, the trials, the meet
Yes, there is always the will to compete.
Back stroke, free style, butter and breast
You practice and practice and you do your best
If things don't go your way,
Smile and say why there's tomorrow, another day
Ribbons, Trophies, 1st place & show
These are the prizes, we all know
To get prizes you must be, the best swimmer
And I'll say "That's My daughter, The Swimmer"
Blond, blue eyed and sweet
My daughter the swimmer, the swimmer to beat!

Mindy DeLong
LIFE'S A ROSE

A perfect rose
Will never grow
Except for in your mind.

And when it's right
Then you will find
Flowers of a different kind.

Can you understand?
Open up your thoughts,
And find the perfect land.
(Hear the perfect band.)

Develop what you've got.
It may be just a little,
but even that's a lot.

Amanda Reeves
MY HEART'S DESIRE

To the only man I'll ever love, Timothy Johnson, My Heart's Desire.

I never wanted as I want you and I to be
Each waken second your beautiful face comes before me
It consumes me, even in my dreams at night
Yet you give me a peace, turning my darkness to light
Eyes so black yet glittering almost midnight blue
Full of laughter and gaiety, but shining with pain, too.
I want to kiss your heartaches and pains away.
Take you in my arms, and love you day after day.
Lips so finely shaped, made perfect to fit against mine
When in a sensuous smile, they bare teeth so white they shine.
But what torments me most is how you look into my soul
Knowing all of me there is to know, the happiness and turmoil
I am unsure of what holds for us tomorrow, But I am sure
as long as you are by my side, I'll never know sorrow.
For in me my Love you, have begun a passionate fire
And I love you more than life itself,
you are my heart's desire

Minnjuan Flournoy
THE WORLD

This poem is dedicated to Vivian, my mother, and Winnie, my grandmother.

The World was made for you and me
We are like a big family.

While taking each step day by day,
We can make it in life all the way.

If you get a good education,
That will care for part of life's situation.

But none of those things we can resolve,
Unless the world's problems can be solved.

Lew Alway
FOOT–PRINTS IN THE SNOW

The snow fell softly through the night—the world this morn is crisp and white—not a footstep mars the pristine beauty of it all—And I recall through my tears, other years, so long ago when my two sons were small!

The frantic search for mittens, caps and boots—the raucous laughter, wild shouts and hoots, as they prepare to tackle all the snow out there, Not a minute must be wasted, and breakfast goes un-tasted!

"Is there snow in heaven?" they want to know—aware the Lord delights in children everywhere, I tell them "Yes, there's always lots of snow."

And now, flat on their backs in virgin drift—with arms flung wide, and moving to and fro, I see them making angel-wings, beside them in the snow!

"You coming out, Mom" they shout, not really caring I'm not sharing in the fun—for the coffee is good—still hot, an unread book is waiting—I opt to stay in—
Only Heaven and little boys know snow is meant to play in!
I see again the crooked snow–man standing there so brave and arrogant against the wall, wearing Dad's hat—which crowns him King of all snowmen, everywhere!

While all around him, in the snow, I see the little foot–prints which, I know, can never come again,
For two small boys, have, all too soon, become Stout-hearted MEN!

Michael J Schantz
THE NEW WORLD

To my Love, Sarah.

I'll tell you of the golden sea
The rich adventure and the trip
In which there are few stars, namely
Some dreams and faith to guide your ship.

Care must be taken, Look to heaven while going
Amid storms that test both sextant and hold.
Life can't be gainsaid. Let what winds may come blowing
Leave each sailor humbled as each tale is told.

Eventually you must be sure of your way
Despite the dissent of well-meaning advice.
Let me add to this that of all I could say
Only naming this sea and these words may suffice:

Villains or Heroes, conquests or crusades
Each traveler's new world is gained by the trades.

Elizabeth Whitfield
LOVE IN BLOOM

Dedicated to the person who inspired me most in life, and who made me the person I am today. To Connie, my Mom.

Love is like a flower,
each day it grows.

Love is like a stem,
still standing strong.

Love is like a petal,
it crumbles and falls to the ground

Love is like a root,
it will always return.

Is it Love if it doesn't?

Julie Ann Suttles
CAROUSEL FANTASY

Painted ponies prancing
Round and round the carousel.
You fantasize.
Romance running rampant
On the deck,
Peering from behind the carts,
Tapping your shoulder,
Then scuttering quickly
Underneath the horses' hooves,
Afraid of being
Cornered, caught and kept
As hostage by a heart
Whose horse never made it
Round the track

Caroline G Hicks
MY SON

To my son Lenny, who inspired me to write this poem.

I look around and I see,
a tiny bundle next to me.
Sleeping like an angel there.
Skin so soft and smooth and fair.
I turn and kiss his tiny brow,
and wish to keep this moment forever now.

I look around and I see,
a toddler standing at my knee.

With unsure hands he reaches out,
to grasp my hand and walk about.

Time has flown and I see,
a young man standing next to me.
Mixed emotions he must endure,
until time and experience makes him sure.
In his eyes I can see,
many deep uncertainties.
Who am I? Who will I be?
Is it possible she's in love with me?

Times goes by and I see,
my son standing next to me.
Tall and strong as sure is he,
at last of what he wants to be.
Big ideals and head held high,
Go on my son reach for the sky.
I've helped to make you what you are,
and now that you have grown,
God bless you and take care of you,
for now you're on your own.

Forest W Stickney
FOREVER YOURS

Go on girl,
You can do it,
Break my heart,
Somehow I knew it.

You won't hurt,
So why should I,
But my love for you
Will never die.

I know my head,
I feel my heart,
I've loved you girl
From the very start.

Don't you worry,
I'll be okay
I'll wait for you
To come someday.

Course it won't work
When you block it out,
Reck me girl
Shut me out.

Soraya Benson
THE FEELINGS THAT ARE KEPT INSIDE

I'd like to make this dedication to Michael Thompson for always being there and for being so understanding and who has made all of my dreams come true.

The feelings that are kept inside
Nobody knows or begins to understand—
It comes and goes just like the wind.
We sit and stare at the window
Trying to find the rainbow that
Lies ahead—
But instead all we find
is a dark cloud of smokey grey—
Wondering if what we feel inside
is all so real.
We search in our hearts
For all the right answers
But somehow they can never be found—
With our minds playing tricks
We feel so far gone—
It's funny how life is so full of mysteries—
mysteries we don't know how to solve—
But somehow, somewhere
We manage to pull ourselves through it all.

Vicki L Wright
YOU'RE JUST A MEMORY NOW

I've finally found someone new, who believes in me much more than you.

He makes me feel good about myself.
Unlike you put my love on a shelf.

He makes me laugh, you made me cry. He tells the truth, but even your truth was a lie.

Sure I think about you, but then I think about all the growing up you've got to do.

All you are now is a memory, so let me live my life and leave me be.

But when you do enter my mind,
rejection and pain is all I find.

When I think of him, I see happiness,
you brought me no more but so much less.

He treats me good like you never could.

Around me you act so cold, like you don't know who you want to hold.

Well, now it's my turn to turn my back on you, because you'll always play the games you do.

Jean R Thompson
UNDYING LOVE

To Tommy—My Husband and Friend.

Today I saw a Robin and rejoiced
That Mother Nature had shed her icy coat
And slipped into a sweet soft warmness—
I have so much looked forward to Spring
When we could once again renew our time together.

As I sit here and gaze fondly
At your picture on the table
And listen to the chiming of the old German clock
We bought so long ago
I think of how it might have been
Had I not stayed behind
To care for the family
And spend the long, lonely years alone
While you rest comfortably in the silken bed
He provided for you
And you so richly deserved.
Could you have stayed here all alone
And traveled the same road each day
That we so often shared together?

Oh, I'm not angry with you anymore
For leaving me to be the strong one
And when I walk down the narrow path
To your side
I can smile when I share with you the things
That has happened since I last talked with you—
As if you didn't know
That I still feel the emptiness
Of your absence
And even though a kind of peace
Has quieted my heart
I can go alone now to place your favorite flower
In the soft earth at your head—
But I cannot help wondering
How it would have been
If our earthly lives
Were still as one.

Marguerite
MY "OTHER-COLORED" FRIENDS

To GOD, who gave me the friends and the words to write about them.

Our skin colors are not the very same
But you know our hearts are in Jesus' name
He came down to this earth to take our blame
So that salvation from sin we could claim

He loves us so much that our hearts He'll lead
He answers each time when to Him we plead
He's promised that for us He'll intercede
And take from our hearts envy, hate and greed

We need to grow more like Him day by day—
To learn to love, and care and praise and pray—
To look to Him and let Him lead the way
To our home with Him and eternal day

God has given me "other-colored" friends
On whom a lot of happiness depends
It's great to have a God who's "color-blind"
Who's able with His love our hearts to bind

Joyce Gregg
FLYING FANTASIA

flying—
far away, very high
above the clouds
below the sky

Places
no one has ever been
or seen
no one can harm
or be mean

fly, fly
High Above
use the powers
of the wings
like a beautiful dove.

Problems
wondering
away from life
A fantasy
given to those
for signs of relief
leaving, away

Florence Thompson
MEMORIES

Memories! Memories! Memories!
How grateful we should be,
To possess the power of reserving them
For future strategy . . .
For there comes a time in all our lives
When we deem it necessary
To change the mood, to clear the air
To demonstrate the fact, we care!

In moments like these, reach back in time
And try to remember when life was sublime
Surely a memory is lingering there—
One that will suffice,
Envision that one!! Force it out, but be precise.
Then devise a way to share it
You'll find it all worth while,
And when the air is clear again
I'm sure you'll share a smile.

Jessie (Hutchison) Petty
WHILE GRANDMA SLEPT

This poem is dedicated to the memory of Ida Isabelle (Young) (Pence) Robinson. And was written especially for Viola Ruth (Pence) Hutchison, with special thanks to supportive family, and my dear husband, Richard.

While Grandma slept,
The Angels swept
From the Heavens far above,
And took her oh-so-far from sight
To the One she loved one night;
Oh, how she did love a snowy dove.

Out of sight, not out of mind;
Her God and Savior was very kind.
She didn't suffer or die of disease.
So, dear family, grieve not much.
Her fragile hand 'gain never touch.
She is asleep in wondrous peace.

Death is just a sleep so very deep.
"Who does not need a good night's sleep,"
To quote Plato then Shakespeare if I may.
"Of life or death better God only knows"
Oh, how she did love a pale rose.
I'll talk with her 'gain one day . . .

Maybe soon.
I hope mine by light of moon.

Shirley J Broussard
THE GOD OF THE TREE

I laid under the stars . . . they shone so bright,
the moon was out for the night.
Wind, blowing, zippy, crispy,
ZINGING pass my only home, my sleeping bag.
But always there, said the peace inside me,
is, The God of the Tree.

No place to go, one to call Home.
No TABLE set, no dinner warm.
Under the tree I was, but not alone.
Unafraid of the stranger passing by . . .
the untimely man said to be nigh,
Invisible but, very near me . . . The God of the Tree.

I was numbered among the homeless,
the Destitute . . . always knowing I was to be,
one of the WELL-TO-DO . . .
one of the ones who always had,
never without,
what it takes to go in and about,
The RICH. THE FAMOUS,
not the aimless.
But there I was . . . yes it was me,
laying under the stars, praying
to . . . the God of the Tree.

But now the scene has changed.
the wind has shifted,
IT is happening, what I felt should be,

And like before . . . yes this too is me!
This too is me who laid before the trees
and prayed, before the stars and cried,
before the moon and sighed.

Never without a goal,
Never without a plan.
Looking for that certain Look,
for that certain lending hand.
Someone to show me, maybe lead the way,
to what I knew, would be a
BRIGHTER day.

LOOK ON, testify to this fact,
I was not aimless, yes blameless of this plight.
Beyond me was a plan, to see if I could endure
the OTHER side of life.
I believe that heaven is pleased, AND I very appeased.
From start to end . . . always with me was . . . The God of the Tree.

Fran Martin
LAST ORCHARD IN THE VALLEY IN JANUARY
Bare black branches cast
medieval shadows on
rain washed sky.
From the soft belly
green mustard tenders
each tree.
Stamens of the yellow blossoms plight
vale of the rainbow's
end.

FREEWAYS AND GEOMETRIC TRACTS!

I husband
my bastion
before cement.
I moat my mind's eye
where the orchard
is.
I need it
for my
sanity.

Faye J Richardson
VIRTUOUS WOMAN
Lord help me be that virtuous woman
Your word proclaims I should be.
Filled with your Holy Spirit,
Yielded totally to thee.

Full of wisdom and understanding,
Praying morning, noon and night.
Seeking your direction for my life,
Living holy in your sight.

For her price is far above rubies;
And she's more precious than fine gold.
Her husband doeth safely trust in her,
She's truly a blessing to behold.

Lord help me be that virtuous woman
In my home and everywhere—
Exemplifying the beauty of holiness
That a Christian woman should be;
When she totally submits to Jesus
Her life, marriage, home and family.

Joseph G Vilbig
I SIT HERE . . .

To: mom, because you know, and understand, and love.

I sit here . . . and realize, through small unspoken clues, that I did not create the feeling that my heart now senses gone.
I sit here . . . and my "self" slowly tries to recognize its own footprint over a well-trodden path.
I sit here . . . for the first time, really hear the cars passing by my thin walled room, and wonder, "Are they coming or are they going?"
I sit here . . . and do not care that I am tired, that I am unspeaking, for the talkative and energetic are not of this realm.
I sit here . . . and listen to my trusty alarm clock, that I wind every day, but still listen with a keen ear, for it to miss a tick.
I sit here . . . and think of ghosts. Ghosts are memories whose sheets brush against the soul.
I sit here . . . and look around and expect a door to close, the echo of a shower, the jingle of keys, a warm breath.
I sit here . . . and icily understand what a lonely man is.
It is I and I sit here.

Luella V Nichols
SPRING HAS ARRIVED

Spring is a time of birth, I dedicate this poem to my children, Naomi and Benn with unlimited love. Love Mom.

Beads of crystalized dew sparkling in the morning sunlight.

The day is clear and the blue skies seem so near.

Great white clouds sweep the above gracefully.

Tops of trees sway gently, as the warm breeze, flows through the branches evenly.

Birds arch their wings and soar.

Lakes and rivers swell with aquatic life.

Bubbling brooks and wildflowers explode gaily.

Spring has arrived!

Erika Hawkins
ALCOHOLICS
They drink and drink and drink some more,
But I really don't know what they're drinking for.
A problem pops up and down it goes,
Straight to the liver the old drink flows.
Just to deny it proves that you're wrong,
Can't you take it? Aren't you strong?
The act they show is ever so fake,
You try to give, but they only take.
I finally ask with an ever so soft "why?"
They only answer with an ever so loud sigh.
Now you must do what you know is right,
Surrender to me, and start to fight!

Sue Shores Brown
NO ROSES

To a very special person—my husband, Gale Nelson Brown.

He never brings me roses, I guess it's not his way,
but a young raccoon with broken leg,
a horned toad, three tiny catfish,
and a tri-blossomed cactus
found along the ditch one day.

He never brings me roses, he probably never will,
instead he brings a horse named Red,
a crawdad, old purple bottles,
and strawberry clover
enough a heart to fill,

He never brings me roses, it'll not be his downfall,
I get arrowheads from times long gone,
a perfect awl, pretty rocks,
and wild flowers I carefully press
in books for sweet recall.

He never brings me roses, I say to you, "So what?"
For how can mere purchased roses
compare with what I've got?

Ernest Randolph Casey
LOVE PERSONIFIED'S ARRIVAL
When days of abstraction
Are changed for satisfaction
What a wonderful day it is.
What one who killed and lied
Cannot be saved by love personified,
Thus obtaining eternal bliss?

Christ proved His love for all,
And He is a God of love,
Who came down from above.
He drank the bitter gall
To provide relief from abstraction
And our eternal satisfaction.

Shannon M Harper
TO TELL
Tell me you love me,
Tell me you care,
Tell me you need me,
Say you'll always be there.

Tell me no lies,
Tell me you're true,
Tell me you'd die,
As I'd die for you.

Tell me words
I want to hear.
Tell me secrets
You want to share.

Tell me your love,
And I'll tell you mine.
There's no bigger love
Either of us could find.

Caryn A Chow
BETWIXT AND BETWEEN (NIGHT AND DAWN)
Night falls into silence
muttering deathly voices of doom

The sky ignites fair warning
that treacherous spirits loom

Ocean waves echo
each reverberating sound

Calling forth all phenomenon
which in the night abound!

The thin line twixt' night and dawn
lies somewhere 'tween a halfway yawn
Folks are laid to rest
The sun is a welcome guest!

An eerie trillionth of a moment's
escape from its coherence
A heart might skip a beat
Awakening proves a feat!

The night portent and dreary
The dawn pretentiously cheery
Underscores the betwixt and between
where anything can happen lest in a dream!

Dawn rises above the skyline
bringing to light a newborn day

With dubious joyful noises
of creatures bright and gay

We see the crimes
We hear the news
We taste the tears
We feel the blues

'Tis a farce to believe that all is well
when day has in fact brought another hell!

Lisa M Bunal
FRIENDSHIP ON THE ROCKS

To mom, all that you've done for me was out of love. I now realize that you are the best thing that ever happened to me. I love you.

In the quiet darkness
where no one else can see,
that I am all alone,
the one and only me.
I shed a silent tear for you
as I remember all those years.
It makes me feel so empty
just knowing you're not here.
I wish that you could hear me.
I'd call you if I dare,
but something inside tells me
that you would not be there.
All I want to say to you
is that I'm sorry too,
but most of all for friendship's sake,
is that I love and miss you.

Kristen Lee Spurlock
IF EYES COULD TALK

To my family for being there; To Ginny and Lynn for not giving up; To Jennifer for being honest and caring.

If eyes could talk what would they say?
Well, eyes do talk in their own special ways.
Eyes say many different things.
They say I am hurting.

They say I am sorry.
They can be read like books;
Ten thousand emotions,
A million words.
Eyes do talk, but they say too much;
So they are hidden,
Or they are just not looked at.
But when eyes do talk,
Sometimes they say I am happy,
I am glad,
When they say those things,
They glisten and sparkle like a star.
But when they are hurting,
They do not sparkle, but shed a tear
or more.
People should try to read people's
eyes,
Then not so many people would hurt,
But their eyes would glisten and
sparkle.

Daniel D Caple

Daniel D Caple
PERPLEXITIES

I'd like to dedicate this poem, and all of my works first to God, for the gift he's given me, to my family, most of all my parents. Then I'd especially like to thank my wife Rosa, who kept me strong & willing.

With everything that's going on
maybe I should just let it go,
It's getting hard to just belong
anxiety and confusion steadily grow.

With things happening the way they
are
it's becoming difficult to cope,
anywhere I go, whether near or far
I see everything but signs of hope.

How to be all that I ought to be
to arrive at the point of ultimate truth,
How to elude an unceasing prophecy
that's been around since this great
world's youth.

A mind in despair, a heart in pain
a dying world, taking its yet cruel
toll,
As wilting, dry flowers, needing rain,
a body needs refreshment, for its
thirsty soul.

Anger sets in, and hate comes about
for all of the things beneath the skies,
The heart calls out, with a silent
shout,
when one thinks about the endless
lies.

Chrissy L Gordon
A LETTER TO YOU
So much time has passed
since last we talked,
I decided to look
and it was you that I sought.
The friendship we had,
was special and rare
two people who know,
how to love and to care.
We somehow lost touch
with all the time that has passed,
the time that we had,
went by so fast.
I decided to write you
a letter to know,
I don't want the distance
between us to grow.
So if you still care,
about me at all,
let me know
write me or call.

Carole L Hambleton
THE SOLDIER
Remember I am your son,
your husband, your brother.
Now I will be no one, no other

They have sent me to this
distant shore.
To fight yet another war.

Please say you will not forget me.
Don't let me lie in some unmarked
grave,
for I have fought to keep you free and
brave.

Please remember Mother
you and father gave me life
Remember darling you were my
loving wife
Remember sister, brother how we
fought
but loved each other

Remember I am your son,
your husband, your brother

Lori E Ouellet
GOODBYE
You've made my life as bright as a
star.
But I cannot love you
Because of what you are.

It would not be right, for me, for you,
We would always be at fight
Telling one another what to do.

But my love for you will always last,
I will love you forever,
And you will always be a part of my
past.

So tonight I have to say goodbye,
For you will still be in my heart
And forever the tears that I cry.

Toby Dwork Douglas
ART THOU MY FRIEND?

To my darling daughter, Meredith Dwork Douglas, I hereby dedicate this poem.

Art thou my friend?
Or sayest thou so,
Merely joy to lend,
I do not know.
Or art thou the kind
That would rather die
Than harm a friend
By falsehood's lie
Wouldst give, then
snatch away.
That on which I live,
I cannot say
It has been said,
In all life there are
But few friends true.
Would that my mind's eye
Could truly see,
E'er I put my trust in thee.

Toby Dwork Douglas
HUMANITY

Dedicated to Dr. J. A. Amunategui.

The ocean is roaring,
Humans are pouring
Out of its depths.
Each rushing billow brings
Many more human things
To fight to the death.
Nude bodies leap to clutch
Slimy ones, fierce to the touch.
All without cause.
Pulling to destruction,
Work of man's construction,
Not thinking to pause.
Man things seize and kill,
Woman things shrieks ring shrill,
Children look on.
Bloodthirsty know no end,
None them asunder rend,
While they kill on.
Oh, ye, who stand by,
Hearken to their cry,
Wrung from the soul.
Let not our coming men
Be reared from children
Brought up in blood.
Let us fight for the peace
That will bring sore hearts ease,
A smile On the tear-stained face.
All earth a harbor of rest,
To the weary a universe blest,
No place of disgrace.
The strong no more will hold
By force of lustrous gold
Those of "baser" lot,
The humans of the earth,
All monarchs by birth,
By God begot.

Trinity Rimes
PEACES OF THE PUZZLE

Howard, you are the most precious person in my life. I love you. And to my father, you have taught me well. I love you, daddy. Trin.

My mind is pieces of a puzzle,
separated in the air.
Problems and worries fill every
piece.
I wish my mind would fit back
together.
My tears are held back for they seem
foolish.
Yet, I cry for the pieces to be put
back together.
I wish for an inner whole.
Yet, all the pieces that are needed are
separated.
I wish to cry for help.
But the one special piece of the
puzzle I wish to cry to is not here.
Here, where I am alone, with the
peaces of my mind in the air.

Kimberly Ann Sherey
CHANGES

To Helen Copenhauer, my gramma, who died 6-23-90, to Sally Hunt, a great family friend, who also passed away. To John Godziebiewski, a great friend and classmate, who died 3-17-90. I miss you all very much. To Mrs. G, a great friend, and to my mother. Both of them inspire me greatly.

Why did you have to go?
It hurts all our hearts so.
I loved you so much, and now I know
I will
never again feel your gentle touch.
You were a shining star in my life.
Every time I saw you, you smiled a
smile as
bright and large as the sun.
But there was nothing that could be
done.
I had my hopes up but now they have
all began to fall.
Today I thought I heard you call, but
then
realized it was only my imagination
getting the
best of me.
I wish there was some way I
understand and see,
why all this had to be.
You were a very special person to
many people
and now all of them are torn apart
with sadness.
When I heard the news I was
shocked, my feelings
were a grey cloud covering the blue
sky's
clearness.
Crying, I think He must have needed
a special
person up there to have chosen you.
I just hope you can be happy in
whatever you
do up above,
and remember for you; our hearts are
always filled
with love.

John Nathan
DUST
The dust gathers on the trinkets
in my mind.
It builds when I concentrate on
my latest find.

Attics and basements of
a thousand lives,
are filled to capacity
by unremembered drives.

If indeed the clutter would
in dormant storage wait,
I might be spared the madness
of a certain senile fate.

But alas, my captor beckons
me from every crevice;
Like jealous children's whinings,
unanswered with my service.

Still, the only way to escape
this craziness I know,
is to start another project.
Therefore, the basements grow.

Barbara L Lewis
A PLACE TO CALL HOME

This poem is dedicated to all the unsaved, who might through reading it, may come to know our Lord and Savior "JESUS CHRIST."

My child hearken thine ear unto my
voice,
Have the fullness of joy and rejoice.
Life seems tough at times I know,
But, lo I am with you, wherever you
go.

My child bear with me, til the end,
The sound of my trumpet, I will send.
Together my people will finally be,
Just believe in me, and you will see.

Oh, what a beautiful place you can
call home,
It's far sweeter than the sweetness of
the honeycomb.
You will have the abundance of life,
joy and laughter,

From that day forward and there everafter.

So, my child, when things seem to get rough,
Just remember me, THE GOD OF LOVE.
Continue seeking the promises of my word,
And all these things, will come to pass,
These things you have just heard.

Tanna Short
I'VE HAD ENOUGH

I feel rushed, no time to rest.
My mind is full of things to do.
More and more is placed on me
As the time goes flying by.
Too much to do in too little time.
Will I get everything done?
If I try hard, it could be possible,
But many obstacles fall in my way.
I'd love to say just forget it.
Can't you see I've had enough.
My body will not take anymore.
I feel like I'm going to explode.
But if I do, how will I feel?
Will I not feel complete?
I think I will just try my very best,
And hope everything turns out OK.

Otelia B Sullivan
MY HUSBAND

My husband is a very dear man
And for him, I'm going to do all that I can
He loves me very much and he tells me every day
He is always taking care of me in a very special way
Whenever I need him, he's always there for me
His main goal in life is making me happy
I proudly married him on December 17, 1988
And ever since that special day, everything has been just great
I never met a man like this, so loving, so caring, so kind
So everyday I thank God up above for this husband of mine
I love my husband with all of my soul from the bottom of my heart
And I will keep on loving him until death do us part
My only regret with my husband is that I didn't meet him sooner
Because I could not live without this man, Mr Ira A Sullivan Jr.

Joan Zalus
HOME SWEET MEMORIES

This poem is dedicated to Irene & Frank Kaminski, my parents and to my sister Fran.

Streets of houses all in a row
Alleys between them as you go
The same old grocery store on the corner lot
From where many a pretzel I had bought
There stands a gray old house along the back alley
Smells of a home-cooked meal that would soon warm my belly
Mom greeting me at the door with a smiling face
Swiftly I ran to catch her soft embrace
Dad coming home from a hard day's work at the mill
The hugs that he gave me of which I can still feel
Fall was the time of the colorful halloween parade
Around the schoolyard and down the streets we did promenade
Winters were beautifully snowy white
Snowmen, sleigh rides and almost getting frostbite
Spring with its array of multi-colored flowers
The refreshing aroma after the noonday showers
Summers on the ball field the amateurs would be at bat
Watching from my bedroom so excitedly I sat
Reflecting on those carefree days gone by
Home sweet memories, joys that bring a tear to my eye

Inez S Osborne
THE WHITE BUTTON

To Jenny, always my love, Nana.

Jenny found a white button
At school today
Why she popped it in her mouth
She didn't say.

It rolled and rolled
Down out of sight
If only on a string
Like a yo-yo or kite.

Perhaps she was pretending
To be a goat
Goats eat anything and everything
But—sometimes they bloat!

It continued to roll and roll
Down her throat
Could it be the lost button
From "Barbie's" new winter coat?

When mama was called together
Jenny in her dilemma was frightened a bit,
She put a little finger in each ear and said,
"I don't wanna talk about it!"

The Doctor said, "Be patient and wait"
Referring to the buttons roll and roll
Down and out
The unmentionable hole.

Inez S Osborne
OUR FORTIETH SPRING

To George, always my love, Inez.

Our fortieth Wedding Anniversary
Our fortieth Spring
With daffodils and roses
Wonderful memories, fulfilled dreams

Three children
Now grown
Seven grandchildren
In bloom

A husband
Dedicated to working
A wife
Mothering and homemaking

Forty years
Of football!
Of baseball!
Of basketball!

Forty years with
Trusting love
With
Lasting love

Forty years with
blessings
from
above.

Amber Price/Belcher
CHANTED DAYS

Chanting thru realms of fire
Wish to see them burning
Higher,
I dance here, to dwell
Singing amoung pauper spell.

And of all the
World to dream and
Live,
'Tis one to die
Wise nigh.

Till the birds swoop
In grounds spell,
Look to see the fell
And roam amoung the
Cherry combs,

Swelling to see the
Fight once won.

It's all here, they say,
as They go their way
and Leave Us, but a few.

Harold S Wright
HAPPY BIRTHDAY—CARRY ON

A birthday is just another mark
To let us know how fast time flies . . .
The dates and numbers play with us
As time goes passing by.

Though we always have our memories
Of how our time was spent . . .
Each new tomorrow brings the promise
Of greater love and contentment.

So take your strength and carry on
With your blessings lined up in a row . . .
And know for sure, this son of yours
Loves you much more than you'll know.

Michael J McAleer
ANGEL IN DISGUISE

I've climbed up from the valley below
Through hell and high waters
And all its borders
To catch a glimpse and a smile
Of this girl they call Kandi

She's their daughter
And my friend
She's a godsend!!

I look down from the sky above
Into her green eyes
And all I see is
An angel in disguise
An angel in disguise

Darleen R Jones
THE BEST OF BOTH WORLDS

This poem is dedicated with love to a very special friend, Martha Stone, and a very special cousin, Sonya.

Why the question black or white? Why the answer never one? Racial tension, racial wars, racial upheaval—lifetime sores.

Am I black? Am I white? Which is wrong? Which is right?

Black is obscure, white is transparent; so far as which is wrong and which is right they are both equally yoked in One Man's sight.

Color like time is in the mind, a blind man's explanation of what he has yet to comprehend.

Neither of which was created to serve the purpose that they do, to be abused, misused and seldom understood.

If one day all hatred would cease and what we shared was love and peace.

If one day we learned to see the me in you and the you in me.

If one day this war would end and we accepted each other as an equal—as a friend.

NO BLACK—NO WHITE . . . 'just shades of grey.'

The best of both worlds, yours joining mine and mine joining yours.

The best of both worlds, the best of you, the best of me, the part in you that completes me.

"Mohawk"
CURIOSITY

Contez, I love you always! "Mohawk."

Maybe their life was really rough,
or could it be I just wasn't enough?
Well at the age of two, it was to their option
so they sought help and put me up for adoption.
At such an early age where was I to roam and so I was put into a Foster Home.
I guess it was a sight to see, but I was a lucky one who got out at the age of three.
My life started then and I had no clue, on what's what or who's who?
Throughout the months and years, there were times of smiles and tears.
Here I am at seventeen and not doing much, if you know what I mean.
As for now my life's been fine, but who really knows when I'll get out of line?
I've always been curious who's side I take after, cuz I like to be happy and full of laughter.
Education must not have been much as I see, if so it would have reflected on me.

I'm wondering how they've been, even though I've never seen them.

What I like to think and say, is that they're as happy and healthy as I am today.

Take into consideration what I've been missing, and tell me is looking for them the right thing?

Alison T Goggins
FLOORBOARDS SPEAK BELOW OUR FEET

Floor boards speak below our feet
The walls they listen well
Hallways breathe and windows see
If only they could tell.

Our shoes return the tête-à-tête
With muffled sounds of carpet cries
Shuffling through nothing new
No, not really worth the prize.

We pierce the walls with nails and screams
of hunger, pain, and silence.
"We listen well!" No, not well at all
We lie, sin, then fall.

Hallways long you lead us on our endless paths
Through empty space and cold damp drafts
Your windows hide visions framed
'Neath dusty shades and curtains stained

Oh, this man-made stuff
Of boards and boundaries, passages and views
How very well we use our craft
How very well it drowns us aft.

Katherine Vasquez
TEARS ARE REAL?

To Gloria, my mom, who allowed me to express my most inner feelings. I love you, Gloria. Love, Katherine.

Dark stains on my pillow
From tears I have shed . . .
My only friend is my pillow
In the darkness of my bed.

I know it cannot talk
Nor can it cry a tear . . .
But when I hold it close to me
It calms, my growing fear.

I know it doesn't listen
But I don't really care . . .
It takes away the loneliness
And hurt that I must bare.

Rachel A Biggins
SEASONS

To Linda Janes, whose many talents inspired my own. Thank you.

Her hair is the color of the fallen Autumn leaf
Her eyes the green of a deep uncharted sea
And just as the sweet Summer wind
Dances its tender dance across a desert sand,
Her skin is as soft and smooth.
With her smile she radiates warmth and comfort,
Easing and consoling like the first ray of sunshine
On a new Spring day.
And like a fierce and piercing Winter wind
Her love and understanding crushes the walls
Of hurt and disappointment.

Many seasons she has weathered
Shuffling through the darkened cold
Reaping all that has been lost
And when dancing in the light
She sows fervent hopes and dreams, knowing
They only might be.

For every new beginning, a season ends
Growing, enduring and petrifying
Living deciduously while bending with change.

These are the Seasons she has become.

Carolyn Byrd Presson

Carolyn Byrd Presson
THE SEA CAPTAIN'S DREAM

The lone table in his cabin dim;
The things he loved the most;
A single red rose laid before him
From a love so long ago lost.

The map so worn and edges burned,
Revealed the places he'd been;
His search seemed endless but never spurned,
For he knew some day it would end.

His eyes are dim but they behold
The treasure he had found;
The years gone by, he now is old;
But homeward he is bound.

The candle burned low, the night wore on;
He'd awake today—the dream would be gone.

A Nelse Grundvig
PERSONAL EXPRESS

I feel like the sound of the whistle on a train
It's here for a moment then drifts in the rain
As I try to race with the steady clickety-clack
Of the train as it moves down the railroad track.
I never quite earn the right to rest but
I sometimes do because I've done my best
Like the time I was able to do this or that
Sorry, talk to you later, got to get back.
To the job, to my feelings, or whatever.
Someday I'll rest from the noise and clatter
But for now I feel like I have to keep on
This highball train doesn't stop for long.
There is so much, for me to see
Afraid I'll miss it if I wait for me.
So forgive me if I chug along
Lights are green and the track is loooong.

Kirkaun Tamelen
MORE THAN ONE PROBLEM

Dedicated to Bunnie Newman.

Gunshots that I hear in the cities
Sound the same as they did in Vietnam
In my mind I see children hurting
Yet they are still worlds apart
As well as time has fled by us so fast
In my mind I wonder why it's going on
I think it's time to break down and stop
Instead we should fight against homelessness

Natalie Rossman (Age 9)
WHEN THE TIDE COME IN

To Mrs. Julaine Boehm, a very special teacher.

When the tide comes in,
I begin to think of my life.
Like the tide, it is formed
I am born.
It comes dashing in,
I am developed.
It fills the beach,
I am middle aged.
Out goes the tide,
I have died.

Natividad F Galang
VISIONS

To my family and nearest of kins.

Jubilant about the idea
That soon I will be in Shangri-la,
Hurriedly I packed my things
To meet a new undertaking.

It did not take long before
I reached the land of great promise and more,
But, alas! My ardor and fervor
Were lost due to some misdemeanor.

Various emotions engulfed my whole being,
To an unfathomable depth, and searing
My very soul because of knowing
That after all I might only be dreaming.

Indeed reality is a far cry
From fantasy and expectancy,
Believing is feeling and seeing, longing.

Life is practically not a bowl of cherries
Nor a bed of niceties and amenities,
Taking the challenge is therefore better
But hurdling the test is far sweeter.

Tarsha Toye
THE TRUTH

Overly proud you dare to be?
Boasting so loud about the souls
That are waiting to flee.
Flee you say!
They will one day!
For who is this I see?
This beautiful Being before me!
It is the Only One!
Ask Him if what I say is true
Believe him when He tells you
For it is He
Who should be proud
For it is He
That the Heavenly bound
Souls Await!

John T Savino
SCAR OF DEATH

Nighttime,
brought mystery,
as the shadows . . .
passed through the dark . . .
leaving little memories . . .
ones that leave a mark.

Shawn R Duhon
MENTAL HEALTH

Members of high courts,
Questions of all sorts.
Condemning people to die,
Never ending lies.

Sometimes I wonder.

Warriors with great might,
'Twas just lust in the night.
Why kill other souls,
Walk through the door.

And yet the world wonders.

Flowers of a different kind,
Superstition is really blind.
Brightness is all around,
Sands of another time.

At times I ponder.

Revolution of a different one,
A presence of another sun.
Shine it on, It'll look brighter at dawn,
To each his own, What is yours is not mine.

Geneva L Mullins
I'M STILL NUMBER ONE

I woke up this morning and
looked at my fate.
Twentyfive years of my life
I've had you as my mate.
After all of these years I've
had enough of your cheating and lying
But you say I'm still your Number One.
I've kicked you out and
with another you are living
You are doing the taking
she's doing the giving
She thinks you've been mistreated
but what she doesn't know is
you still think of me
as your Number One.
Your children you admire but
to them none of your love is given
because you come first
and we take what's left.
The kids don't know this
Thank God they don't and
they think like you
that I'm Number One.
So other women listen
When a married man comes
calling. He's using you
too so don't think he's loving
because in his heart
It's too late to change
for he will always think
of his wife as his
Number One.

Mark D Himrod
RAINBOW

The name was given
While in the garden sat I
A golden chariot, drawn
By a messenger of the sky
An ivory stallion
A mane all a glisten
Through a Zephyr wind

Did I listen
As wings did beat
To measured time
Embarkation in unison
Complimented our rhyme.
Ferried before a Palace entry
An Angel stood as sentry
Into a canopy of creation
Known as the Celestial Dome
Intuition confirmed
A prodigal son ushered home.
A presence could I hear
Thee inner sanctum drew me near
To behold life itself
Irradiant radiance
Simultaneous fission and fusion
Could this be an illusion
I knelt in prayer.
A voice echoed
Approach this throne
Stand to my right
You are given power and might
Forever be known
As Prince of the Rainbow Sky.

Jeanne Johnson

AUTUMN FEST OF DAYS GONE BY

Dedicated to Mom, Dad, Jack, Jay, Larry a friend.

Autumn Fest of days gone by
bringing colored leaves of rainbow.
Frost lingering in early
morning light.
Fog rising with the morning
dew.

Suzette M Gideon

PICTURE A ROSE

For Mike Busick, My first true love and inspiration. You will forever remain in my heart.

Before I met you:

Picture a rose,
Peaceful and content
Closed in a single bud,
So fresh and innocent
Yet so alone.

When I knew you:

Now picture that same rose
Blossoming and growing,
Bursting with life, spreading
Undeniable love and beauty
From the sole comfort of your love.

Now I've lost you:

The rose is slowly wilting
Weighted down with heavy drops of
morning dew,
The wilting is my crushing heart,
The drops
My endless tears.

Marissa D Lujan

LIKE THE FIRST DAY I SAW YOU

Like the first day I saw you, it rained.
The clouds gathered up over the
mountains in a pillow of air.
The sky was gray with silver tips
over the horizon.
Beams of light showered the earth
with drops of gold.
You were sitting in a chair, reading a
book, Faulkner I guessed.
Your eyes are brown, with dark green
shadows behind them.
The shadows dance and play
according to your thoughts and
emotions.
Looking at them I felt a deep energy
of love shine through with beauty its
mask.
You as a person don't know it, but
it's there.
As the sun broke through the sky we
talked of literature.
Time caught up with us and you left.
I sat for a while memorizing your
face.
That day the wind blew against the
light and cooled the earth.
The sun, laughing at the wind,
mocked it by shining down even
brighter than before.
I think I was moved that day.
To a level of fluorescent colors where
yellow and orange precede over black
and gray.
From the brown in your eyes, I was
able to catch the rainbow.
Just a piece of it, only long enough to
bare my eyes against the purest sight.
What a day.

Jennifer Mullins

TO A DEPARTED FRIEND

To Stefanie's grandfather.

I loved being around you,
And it saddens me that you're gone,
Sometimes when I think of you I feel
blue,
But then I remember that you are in
a better place now.

I will always remember the good
times we had,
Pool, bowling, putt-putt and going to
the park,
The things that you taught me I will
always remember,
And inside that makes me feel glad.

Physically you are gone but part of
you lives on,
In all the people you helped and
shared your wisdom with,
I will think of you when I see
airplanes in the sky or a sunrise at
dawn.

I will never forget you, I cannot;
The things you have given me could
never be bought
You treated me like family although I
was not,
And that is something I will always
be grateful for.

Sally Putnam

STARLIGHT

It's one o'clock, the stars are out, the
sky is still and clear.
I'm thinking of the time we had, the
memories dear, you seem so near.
I realize now, the miles somehow,
have taken you so far away.
I call you up to hear your voice and
listen to what you have to say.
If only, dear, you could hear what my
soul is saying,
The love it knows and misses so,
we'll have to keep on praying.
A storm moves in, the stars
disappear, the rain will soon begin.
The soul retreats, it moves to safety,
it never seems to win.
I miss you so, more than you will
know, though I am glad that we have
met.
I would risk it again, even if I can't
win, for the friendship we have set.

Randy Bennett

IF ONLY

If only I'd walked over,
Near until you sensed me.
If only I'd spoken
Or nerved to shout from far.
If only I'd eased through your circle,
If only my gaze had been straight—
I'd not be wondering now.

How carefree then was . . .
Next to this snownight's remorse.
A stride, a reach, a sight away—
Now lost in running years.

If only I'd quickened
Like time up to speed.
If only I'd dared:
A letter, the phone, your doorbell!
If only you'd aggressed—
If only you'd—no, no, stop!
I must make now unlike then.

Mary Sue Lembo

RAINING DIAMONDS FROM HEAVEN

Heaven in moon-light
The beautiful in you
The stars were diamonds
Your eyes blue as sky above
You passionate kiss my love set me
all aflame
O, magic night this night of love
Whispered trees speak to make our
dreams come true
Music fill the air the song came into
my heart
It sings of the blue in the skies
Little shining diamonds everywhere
we go
Your beautiful smile charming like a
pretty, pretty rose
Lovely, lovely to be mine Forever.

Fred Patrick

Fred Patrick

THE LAST PARADE

Dedicated to All the Willies of that "forgotten" "War."

I

Ole Willie said, "I've been mislead,
I joined this Corps, for a nice warm
bed,
But that instructor, my; what he said,
Was Willie my boy, you're just a
"knot" head.

II

A day soon came, that he got the
word,
To saddle up, it's a brand-new world,
Tonight my boys, we'll make a raid,
For the Corps, our Last Parade,
Praise the Lord, A Last Parade.

III

The enemy was, as thick as fleas,
But the Proud Corps Boys, wouldn't
bend their knees.
Surrounded they were, it's History,
How they made that march, down to
the sea.

IV

A forlorn task, though full of fight,
They fought it out, both day and
night,
A price was paid, for that big raid,
And for the Corps, His Last Parade.

V

They buried Ole Willie, in that hard,
cruel land,
As the hymn was played, by the great
Corps band,
Tears were shed, each knew he'd
made,
For the Corps, One Last Parade.

Moneva Canada-Byrd

GRAMMIE NET'S BONNET

Grammie Net's bonnet
Was a trademark for her
She wore it perched upon her head
Always, when she went anywhere,
Some were made of flowered
material
And some were trimmed with pretty
lace
And she always looked real pretty
When the bonnet surround her face.

She had a bonnet for all occasions
Each one was made by hand
And everyone was very special
And they made her look just grand,
But Grammie Net has gone to
Heaven
Where she will never, ever grow old
And I wonder if she wears her bonnet
As she walks in the streets of gold.

Teresa Roye

DREAMS AND HOPES

I am a searcher,
but not for silver or gold.
I search for the treasures
hidden deep inside your soul.

I am a sailor
sailing the seas of your mind.
Feel your every thought
As your dreams unwind.

But, sooner or later,
a searcher finds a new home.
And a sailor always finds new seas to
roam.
Seems we never have what we long
for
when we need it most,
so much for dreams and hopes.

I am a painter,
painting visions before your eyes.
Don't have a masterpiece
but, I sure painted a lot of lies.

I am a dreamer,
searching for a dream of my own.
It can be so hard when one sails alone.
Painting pictures of you in my mind.
Dreaming of what I might find.

Sooner or later,
A painter's work will find a place to
show.
And a dreamer always has tomorrow.
Seems I love you best when I need
you most.
But, so much for—
A searcher, a sailor, a painter, a
dreamer,
and hopes.

Mabel Miles

BRAINS

This little school upon the hill
Was built for greater knowledge
Than I have yet my task fulfilled

With just one year of college.

College, yes, what matters that?
Except to cost more money.
If you have brains, you'll have them still
With much school—'tis funny.

Brains are such funny things,
And so unevenly they're scattered.
You'd think 'twas only one or two
To whom they really mattered.

Yet everyone, sometime or other,
Will wish that he were smarter.
They forget ambition is the thing
To give that cell a starter.

Jennifer Grafe

MY TEDDY BEAR

To my BEST FRIENDS: Michele, Michelle, Lynnette, and of course, Mr. Boo Bear.

No one to hug,
But my old worn out self.
My life, it's been hung,
On a labelless shelf.

What should I do?
For me no one cares.
But beside me there sits,
Just one that dares.

This one he will listen,
While I cry and I weep.
Beside me he sits,
Through the night, in my sleep.

Now I can see,
For me he is there.
This one loving person,
Is my own teddy bear.

Franklin Grapel

YON DYING ROSE

To my much-loved wife, Rosemary, an Alzheimer's victim.

Yon dying rose that late was in full bloom,
That cast such sweetness from itself to me,
Do not fade before my eyes,
Lest I should read in thy sad fate
The story of my own.
Remind me not how fair you grew,
A rare and perfect blood-red bloom.
Let me forget how love grew too,
And waxing on in sweet perfume,
Transformed our life, and me—
Yet now before me fadeth!
Die quickly rose; fade quickly love;
That thy going shall not fill my heart with sorrow.

Envoy
Things never changed since time began,
The flowing of water, the way of love.
Japanese proverb

M Clare Wallace

THE DREAMER

In a land at the west end of sunset
Where the twilight of solace is found,
In a dazzle of settling sunlight
Is a place where the air's full of sound.

Herein you will find you a dreamer
Who ponders the earth and the sea;
Come closer and venture an intrigue—
You'll find that the dreamer is me.

Touch me and I'll shimmer with insight
Of your dreams that have never come true;
Stay on and alight with the lady,
I've always been dreaming of you.

I've the sound of the ocean in my voice,
The sound of the wind and the sky—
The sound of the black night above us,
And an end to the question of why.

Kristina A Bates

DEPRESSION: THE BEAUTIFUL BEAST

The rain trickles down, around my heart
Causing it to weaken and break apart.
Your love can mend it, sew it up inside
The water washes love away, or makes it hide.
Depression is a beautiful bride, a very lovely soul
The feeling she brings and gives to you takes a toll.
She reels you in and causes the pain
And smiles for she knows you'll fall again.
Being so beautiful it seems joy is her part.
But as you will soon find out, she is ugly at heart.

So beware to you, in all you do
Don't let her steel your esteem
Love yourself as I love you
For soon she may love you too.

Cyndie J Smith

STARS ACROSS THE SKY

To my mom, who supports and inspires me to keep reaching for the stars.

High above the ground I see,
The stars looking down on me.
As they twinkle with all their might,
I sit and watch with sheer delight.
In the evening sky they send a glow,
There is still so much to know.

I wonder why they shine so bright,
Yet barely shed a trace of light.
I wonder why they are so far away,
And why I can't see them during the day.

I ask myself . . . who put them in the sky?
If only someone could answer why.
I guess I know, no one can,
Their beauty and pleasure is enough for man.

For centuries we have savored their elegance,
Enjoying every lasting glance.
And sometimes they shoot across the sky,
As if reminding us to keep wondering why.

Cyndie J Smith

TWILIGHT

The sky fills with an orange glow,
The evening sun prepares its show.
Sunset fading behind the trees,
Watching, I enjoy the summer breeze.

As darkness falls upon the land,
The clouds reach out to lend a hand.
Light of day turns to night,
Red sky continues to burn bright.
Before it fades away,
I catch one more glimpse to end my day.

Jason Zara

GOODBYE

If I were to die today,
A silent voice would go out.
If I were to go far away,
No one would be without.
If my life were to draw to an end,
Who would notice my going?
If I were to die, without a friend,
Who would ever be knowing?
If I were no longer part of this world
What harm would ever be done?
If I lay in a corner, dead and curled,
Who would know; as I am only one?
If I no longer showed my face,
Would anyone face despair?
Or if I leave this human race,
Would no one ever care?
If I were just to go away,
Would anyone hear my goodbye?
What would be the end result,
If I were to shrivel up and die???

Annette S Todd

LONELY MAN

He sets his sail upon the sea; the wind blows and blows.
To the edges of the sea off he goes.

Where the wind will take him no one really knows
To a place beyond where only sea gulls go.

Another place, another time, an eternity ago,
He set his sail upon the sea to find a woman he couldn't let go.

He sailed and sailed nowhere to go,
Until one day he sailed into a cove.

This became his secret place no other man could know,
A place to come and grieve for the woman that he loved so.

He grieved and grieved, and then one day
He just got up and sailed away.
Back to the cove where no human could see
He lay down his tired body and died of his grief.

Jamie P Strange

RAW AND BEAUTIFUL

Today was the first day of this year,
I saw nature raw and beautiful,
But it was so very distant.
I could hear it quite clearly,
It permeated the glass barricade
In the guise of gentle notes.
The green pasture was golden,
Gold with the little manes everywhere,
Like a million suns in the grass.
I could hear the songs, but rarely saw,
Only when the notes poked their heads up.
The songs pierced the afghan, the golden quilt.
The black songs, and the ones with red hearts,
Escaped the gold and green landscape
Transforming my mind to colors.
As I sat and felt, and saw and heard,
I yearned to sit under the purple blossom tree
And pull the afghan around me,
To bathe in it, to hide and sing,
As those gentle songs do.

Judy Cruse Ballengee

THE SOLDER BOY'S PRAYER

Dear God:

I'm out here in this awful place all alone
And I'm so very far away from home,
All around me I hear death's cry
And my friends . . . Well, on the battle front they've all died.
I'm frightened Lord, with no place to run
No guarantee of even seeing another setting sun,
I've been through death, but somehow I refuse to die
This I can't understand and ask myself why?
Why do we fight and all have to die?
If you can hear me Lord from somewhere in the sky,
I need reassurance that I can make it here
And someday go home safely and never shed another tear.
Back at home Mom and Dad are waiting for me
With arms outstretched, and their faces I'll see,
If you'll only help me Lord to take a firm stand
And help me survive in the Death-Eaten Land.
I'm the only one left here and I'm too young to die
God, I'm begging you . . . Please, Please . . . hear my cry,
I want to go home . . . I want to go home!
I'm so afraid out here all alone.
The means of death and the cries of pain
Are messing with my mind . . . I think I'm going insane
Hear me God and watch over my life
Help me make it through just one more night,
And if it be Thine own will alone

Please send me safely back home.

AMEN

This was war and he was alone
God heard his prayer and sent him back home.

James Schueler
GOODBYE CRUEL WORLD
Here I am with bleeding wrists
I bear the pain with clinched fists
I feel a tear fall from my eye
I don't care I want to die
Life's so cruel, it's just not fair
If I die who will care
Although it hurts I bear the pain
I sit and watch my own blood drain
My arm is numb, my wrist is sore
My blood is dripping on the floor
I've really shortened my life's length
I'm growing weak I'm losing strength
I'm nearing closer to my death
And now I take my final breath
I lie on the ground, with my body curled
My final words are
"GOODBYE CRUEL WORLD"

Leonard D Kirk
HAPPY FATHER'S DAY, DAD
On this Father's Day Sunday, I thought of you, Dad,
Been dead seventeen years now, and the thought makes me sad;
I appreciate so much, the truths that you taught,
Of the things I should not do, and the things I ought.

There are many things in this world, that money will buy,
But a good reputation is not one of them, no need to try;
Be honest in your dealings, you said, treat everyone fair,
I believe you practiced what you preached, and are now up there.

You lived sixty-three years, with Mother as your wife,
There was much love between you, you lived a full life;
Many sweet memories of Mom, and of you, as my Dad,
I believe you are both in Heaven, and I am so very glad.

You served your God faithfully, that I now serve, too,
And Dad, you never quit a job, before you were through;
I believe you loved Jesus, and Dad, so do I,
I believe you are now with Him, in your home in the sky.

I just wish I could tell you, how much I miss you,
And have you actually hear what I say;
So I write this poem, to show my love and respect,
And to honor you, on this Father's Day.

Carol Nunemaker Knabb
WINTERY VISIONS
Deer are bedded down in
The thicket of the laurel—or—
Hidden among the pines
Drifts of fluffy snow—secludes
The snowshoe hares
Squirrels ramble among the pines
Stopping to—
Nibble the tasty cones
Birds flutter from dried berries to
Dried wood-seed heads
Some sit feather-fluffed among
Protection of trees or bushes
Coyotes sound their "greetings"—from—
An echoing distance
Wind whispers its mellifluent sound
Scattering swirling, sparkling snowflakes
Transforming the countryside into
A glistening fairyland
Complete with sleighbells—that
Reverberated in a flitered decibel
Across the vast and perpetual land

Tena Dee Blom
A FANTASY REALIZED
F ulfillment of a dream come true
a special someone in your view
A fantasy is a place in mind
where dreams come true in a matter of time
N othing else matters in fantasy land
but someone special & me—hand in hand
T ime passes here but, passes very slow
we're no place to be, have no place to go
A wondrous place, this fantasy is
it takes away nothing, it only gives
S haring a world we've given each other
a life of tenderness, loving one another
Y ears will pass, we'll fantasize & wish
that reality should be as wonderful as this

Kazi Golam Mustafa

Kazi Golam Mustafa
FREE WORLD
F—ading love, rise above, singing a new hymn
R—inging bell of humanity, as subdued for a long time—
E—nding an era of tyranny, a pangs of upheaval
E—ternal peace remains, for its removal—
W—onderful this planet, to be boasted of its blessed human being
O—wning a marvellous treasures of wish and wisdom that absolutely at offing—
R—emove, remould all snags that hinder human lives
L—ust and greed to be crushed by a thunderous dive—
D—onning, atoning, for a long-cherished goal of service adieu not, welcome thee—all smiles and smile.

Laura McCluskey
OUR PART
It was fate that brought us together,
And fright that tore us apart,
It hurts, but please just remember,
You'll always have a place in my heart.

For awhile our love was strong,
And then it only got stronger,
Until we went our separate ways,
Now the road between us is longer.

But down that road, in the distance,
You'll hear me calling your name,
I'll run down that road, into your arms,
Until then it won't be the same.

That something between us is special,
It's something that can't be replaced,
For now I'll live with a heart of stone,
And a single tear running down my face.

Marilyn Michele Gibbs
LOVE AFFAIR
A freshness sought with a familiar one.
Like Virgos seeking the Sea of Ecstasy.
Our breath caresses as a zephyr travels the land,
Vibrating with motions of embrace.
Entwinement induces ascension to Zion.
Reaching the zenith zestly zigzagging,
Sustaining us for a minute moment.

Bond together by palpitating instruments.
Overpowered by all sense of rational.
Neverending is the ethereal quest
Delightfully dancing in delicious desire.

Della Anne Jones
BROKEN ASHES

To Billy, My Darling Husband, who inspires the poetry in my soul and the deepest Love in my heart.

I am a broken flower
Forgotten and dead
I am a dying dream
That can't forever come true
I am an aging butterfly
Gasping last moments to live
I am a fading star
That slowly dies away
I am the tender willow
That cannot bend again
I am the cold, grey ashes
From a once burning flame
I am left cold and dying
Like the bud beneath the snow
I am a brittle, broken flower
Left alone in the cold, grey dawn
I am a falling teardrop
That never makes a sound.

Patsy Auiler
PEER PRESSURE

For Ann and Carol, my wonderful daughters.

Another day of pain—
She awakened with a nauseous ache in her stomach
As she thought of the encounters she would have with those girls.
She was a victim, for her sense of self was being destroyed
As they chipped away as with an ice pick at her daily.
They called her ugly because it made them feel beautiful.
Her guilt made them strong; Her poverty made them rich.
Her refusal to express herself made them feel superior
and they poked fun at her awkwardness for it made them think that they had a sense of humor.
She absorbed all of the trash that they dumped on her.
She allowed them to take her self esteem
and they gave her their contempt.

Teri Graves
YESTERDAY

To Jonathan: The only one I will ever love. FEAAD.

Yesterday when our love was new,
We'd do the things new lovers do.
The days went fast before we knew,
months were years, our love still grew.
What's happened to the loving touch,
the tenderness I miss so much.
Where's the magic we once shared,
the loving things that showed you cared.
Now we're strangers, like we never met,
Sweet yesterday I can't forget.
We've lost the love we once had,
and that makes me very sad, because now,
yesterday is all we have.

Carol Williams
REFLECTION OF LIFE

Dedicated to my friend, Anne DeFreese.

In God's own time He makes us see
What's really best for you and me
Though it may seem like punishment at the time
His will must always reign sublime

When there's not enough sunshine and too much rain
Oh! My goodness how we complain
He makes things happen that we might see
That life is not really a mystery

If we keep His will, and obey His commands
We'll always be in the hallow of His hands
Praise God for all things BIG and small
If we happen at times to make a fall
Get up . . . Stand up . . . like you're ten feet tall

I'm humble and grateful for what He has done for me
He opened my eyes that I might see
The awesomeness and beauty of His world is in everything
The winds that blow, the birds that sing
And the first flowers of early spring.

Carol Williams
MY GOD AND I
My God and I walk hand in hand
As i travel through this troubled land
He lights my path with His heavenly light
And calms my fears when I'm overwhelmed with fright

He picks me up when I stumble and fall
He hears my cry and my every call
When the burdens I bear press my soul
He's always there and takes complete control

When I want to curse the source of my anxiety and woe
It's then to the Holy Book I go
He tells me vengeance is mine
He'll take care of it in His own time.

Karen Sydnor

WHEN I WRITE THE WORDS

To my co-workers.

When I write the words
That are in my heart,
I feel I'm exposing
A very vulnerable part.

My poems state boldly
All I want to express;
For example, my excitement
About entering this contest.

I searched through my poems,
Reading and checking each rhyme;
But, none of them were
appropriate—
They exceeded twenty-one lines.

So I wrote this poem,
Each word to express
My thoughts to the judges,
of this fine poetry contest

Victoria L Greski

FROM AN IRONWORKER'S WIFE

Dedicated to all the Wives of Ironworking Men everywhere.

An Ironworker has no fear of heights
Some fall and break their bones,
Some fall and lose their life.
You say he was brave and did his job well,
What about the wife who also lives the HELL!
A wife worries the moment he walks out the door,
Silently she thinks, will he be safe,
Will I see him alive anymore?
Then one day while at work you get THAT call,
Hi honey, don't worry I'm ok, I just had a bad fall.
You rush as fast as you can to be by his side
You know he's hurting bad, you see the pain in his eyes.
The worst is not yet over, you hear him cry in pain
For the Doc's have to rebreak his leg once again.
Sometimes you want to scream and say,
I can't take anymore, I've got to get away!
But for his sake you hang in there through good and bad,
And you wonder "Is this how Mom felt about Dad?"
You see I'm the daughter, sister, and wife of Ironworking Men.
My days are filled with worry and fear
That one day I'll get a call saying
He's no longer here.
I Love these men with all my heart,
and my respect for them is high,
I just hope It's not a fall that will make us say GOODBYE!

Love and Prayers from
The Daughter, Sister &
Wife of Local #1 Men

Julie Velez

A LIFE FOR YOUR LIFE

To Mom, thanks for being the person you are.

You are my mother
I could write forever
And never express
What an honor to know you and your foreverness
You have loved me
And I have needed you, as I have needed no one else
The person you think I am, I hope for myself
You have suffered with me and for me
Through all my life, you have felt every heartache, every disappointment
Even heavier than if they were your own, because I am your own
The simple words I love you sound so overused, spoken by a friend or lover
Only through your love, I honestly know love exists
I love you mother.

Barbara Merced

JESUS CALLED

In memory of Nancy Jo Powell, Jacksonville, Florida 8-22-41 — 10-07-87.

Jesus called me home today
Forevermore with him to stay.
I reached out and took His hand
We went home to the promised land.
Weep not for me or grieve too long
My dear ones I have gone home.
At peace at last, there is no pain
If you have learned to love and draw closer
then my suffering was not in vain.
May God watch over all of you,
my loved ones, family and friends
And keep you in His care until one day we meet again.
THE DAY JESUS CALLS FOR YOU

Sabrina Jean Anderson

SUMMER NIGHTS (ON A BOSTON STREET)

Sometimes a gentle wind to cool and comfort.
Sometimes just the strong steady heat.
Sometimes lonely and dark.
And sometimes the dark is hidden, behind the laughter of people.

Sometimes blood stains on the ground.
Sometimes a moon so big bigger than sun.
Sometimes hate scattered around.
And sometimes the faint cry of a child,
echoing through the street.

William Wright

THE HOLE!

Sometimes I look, and all is dark,
I yearn for the light, even a spark.
I reach out, there's dirt all around,
I find myself, in a hole in the ground.
I feel a wind, from where is unknown,
The cold it cuts, through cloth flesh and bone
It's sapping my strength, I can't go on.
But I won't stop trying, till the hole is gone
Then suddenly I hear a sound from above
A hand is reaching down open with love.
We touch, there is light, I finally see,
She pulls, I'm out I'm finally free.
I look and see holes all around,
There are lots of people down under the ground
I look in her eyes and see love for a time
But she pulls her hand free without reason or rhyme.
I'd thought for a while, that I'd had it all
But I'm wrong, disaster, I stumble and fall.
Back I go, to the horrible hole.
With its dark chill wind and a pain in my soul
So here I sit, alone in the dark
I yearn for the light, just one tiny spark.
Maybe someday, with love and will,
The terrible hole I will finally fill . . .

Rosemary Kay Meade

MEMORIES

This poem is dedicated to my brothers, Alan and Karl Mittelsteadt and my brother Jr.

There are memories,
of certain places that we used to go.
There are memories,
in the photo albums we love to show.
There are memories,
pressed between the pages of our yearbooks.
There are memories,
of the way that years change the way we look.
There are memories,
in the different things we tend to do.
There are memories,
that can and will make you feel sad and blue.
There are memories,
of things that we have done, we knew were wrong.
There are memories,
of certain words when we're singing a song.
There are memories,
that might make you shed a whole lot of tears.
There are memories,
We will all make throughout the coming years.

Elizabeth A Cornele

WHAT ELSE DO YOU SEE WHEN YOU LOOK AT THE SUN?

What else do you see
when you look at the sun?
asked Wisdom.

Nothing!
replied the shadow,
Nothing!

And emptiness
filled the night.

To be the sun,
for the passing of an hour
content
forevermore
would I be.

The sun is bright
and fills the sky.
Life turns upwards
seeking its grace.
Basking in its warmth.

But I am its shadow,
a refuge for the weary.
I am sought
with nary
a passing thought.

And Wisdom said,

Shadow,
be silent
and weep no more!

But for the shadow
there would be
no sun.

Christina DeLeon

LIFE

To the people of Africa, and their surroundings.

All her beliefs are buried and denied, as she marches down the dreadful streets of Cape Town crying out loud "ABOLISH APARTHEID!"

The only optimistic thing she clings to are her thoughts as she remembers how things formerly used to be, without this so called "WHITE SUPREMACY."

Africa as a whole must plant a new seed, for the season has come to let children "GROW FREE."

Cynthia Thornton

PERFECTION

For Amy, my best friend forever; and for Jim; and for my family, I love you all.

Patterns.
Broken patterns.
A black ball with a tiny speck of dust.
Imperfection.
Misunderstanding.
Shadows, meaningless shadows.
An image. A pattern
We are all imperfections. Without perfection
we have nothing but
with nothing we have
imperfection
Life is a contradiction and people
contradict Perfection.

Jimmie S Vaughan
FEELING THE HEART

Dedicated to those that are a part of my life; especially Viola, Javeeter, and Jimmie Jr.

The touch within my heart.
Loveones, soft music, don't stop.
Feeling the midnight blue.
And this meditation is true.

May my mind move on.
Living, loving and not alone.
Sitting here in bliss.
Give me love, give me kiss.

Strong heart and daylight.
This ode is all right.
Bless it be the mind.
Bless it be the sight.
Be another day, to see the night.

Stimulation, co-operation, rejuvenation.
Oh goodness gracious.
The feeling of the heart.
Moving forward, not in the dark.
Earth moves in silence.
May you be still.
Feeling the heart. Oh! What a kilt.

Franceen C Roman

Franceen C Roman
I DO

This poem is dedicated to my two beautiful children, Shonte Nicole and Shawn Rafael Roman. I love you, Mom.

When I said the words "I DO."
I made a promise to God to always love you,
Our love was destined to stand through time.
You stay constantly on my mind.

Your tender smile and gentle touch
Are the things, that I love so much,
I walked through life in a daze
Until you came my way,
You brighten my darkest day,

Friends thought were a love so true
Always laughing and walking hand-in-hand,
A friend who always understands
My love for you grows more and more each day,
Thank God above, for sending you my way.

Priceless moments, so richly shared
To be so happy, do I dare,
I pray our love will never end
For my heart will never mend.

You make my life so full and complete
Through all life's downfalls and defeats,
You are the light of my life
Like a distant star, that twinkles in the night.

Each and every word you utter
Simply makes my heart go a flutter,
And, when I'm feeling so very low
For some reason you always know,
These are the little things that count.

Your precious love can never be measured
My darling, you are my foremost treasure,
And, when we both are old and gray
I'll thank GOD above for each and every day.

Kelly M O'Hara
I MISS YOU

I'm not for sure how long it's been since we last met.
It seems like another lifetime to me.

I thought I'd never forget your face
and smile, but the miles have
erased that from my mind.

I hope I'll never forget the way
you made me feel each time
you touched me.

I wish I was given the chance to
feel that way today.
I miss you.

Roger D Strickland
DYSTOPIA

For "Animal," who made this poem a reality.

If these old walls have ears, then why
can they not hear my cries
and be some consolation to
my dying will to survive?

Who could be so unfeeling
as to keep my soul locked here
enduring all its grievous wails
every day of the year?

I'm being slowly driven mad
by the loneliness I feel
deep inside this heart of mine
it seems will never heal.

I've tried to drown my sorrows
in all the tears I've shed
But it seems they've only made
the hurt
ready to be harvested.

Misery loves company, they say,
but I'm here all alone
in this cold place, Dystopia,
I'm forced to call my home.

Nicole Lynn Buzard
I'LL MISS YOU, MY FRIEND

I can't believe you're going.
I may never see your smile; again,
Or the tears in your eyes.
I may never hear your voice; again,
Or your silence.
I may never feel your hand on my shoulder; again,
Or hug you.
I may never laugh with you; again,
Or cry with you,
Or be silly with you,
Or just be myself with you.
I may never get another chance,
To do a lot of things,
I had wanted to do . . . with you.
But now,
I have a chance to tell you something,
I been meaning to tell you,
For the longest time . . .
I love you.
And I will miss you very much, my friend.

Michelle Beland
YOU'VE GOT IT ALL

I look at you and I see so much;
I see the tenderness and loving
that only a true friend could bring.
Your smile—it could light up the world
Your laughter brings great joy to
those who feel sad,
and your warm personality and
unique sense of humor
could melt even the coldest heart;
Your gentle care and patience
are high above the rest . . .
You've got it all—you are the best.

Michelle E Johnson
MY WAY BOULEVARD

A small church on the Road Of God
Existed years ago,
But something happened to that church
I think you all should know.

The church house was so small in size
The members strong but few,
But soon the church became well-known
And later that church grew.

The people of this sacred place
Claimed the small space made it hard
To worship, so they moved the church
To My Way Boulevard.

The joy that used to fill that church
Has packed and left that place,
The sadness that has moved right in
Resides on every face.

The church that left the Road Of God
Now sees how really hard
It is for them to worship Him,
On My Way Boulevard.

Ella Mae Sanders
SERENITY

Sitting high on the top of a mountain
where the air is clean and pure,
Where your silence is so deeply
intense you can hear a kitten purr,
Where your soul's at peace, you can
meditate as you gently rub its fur,
Where God's miracles abound and of
Him one is definitely sure.

Where the magnitude of this glorious
scene fills your heart with pure delight
And it makes you wonder at the
people below who seem always ready to fight.
They are so rushed and flurried, they
have no time to "live."
Some, perhaps, would if they had the
chance, for them, please God forgive.

Then there are others so greedy and
selfish they will never know what they miss,
Because they do not share with God,
they may not partake of His bliss.
Sitting high on the top of a mountain
watching the clouds go by.
They seem so close, they go so slow
as they hang there in the sky.

The trees stand there so stately calm
you can almost hear them breathe.
It fills your soul with contentment
and makes your heart strings seethe.

Sitting high on the top of a mountain
communing with God from above
And one feels protected and
cherished as you know He shares His love.

If one knew their life was over and
they merely had to die—
I know of no better place on earth for
their remains to lie
Than sitting high on top of a
mountain where the air is clean and pure,
Where God's miracles abound and of
Him one is definitely sure.

Jill Marie Burg
VISIONS OF LOVE

For all the memories and happiness, I dedicate this to you, Floyd, forever.

Strong castles among paradise
Brilliant rainbows upside-down
Long-lost fields of roses
Countless walks into the unknown
Justified emotions brought from feelings
Cloudless visions of happiness
Unlocked doors of the heart
Falling rain of everlasting sincerity
Security of arms unseen
Translucent wings of forever
Daring thoughts brought from togetherness
Golden hearts containing images
Waves of laughter rejoicing in life
Uphill steps always on the rise
Majestic character never unleashed—
Visions, love-felt visions

Larry S Pastre
THE WATERS OF LOVE

With all my love, to my love, Sharon.

Young love so much a tittering brook, Impish, exploring hardly garnering a look.

Unpretentious brooks flow to meandering streams, Puppy love in the past turns to new feelings and dreams.

Streams ebbing and cresting making its run, The highs and lows of love, heartbreak and fun.

It continues its journey extending its length, Ever searching love blossoms, gathering strength.

Once timid waters now converge at the river, Maturing love unheralded now sustains the giver.

A majestic visage ever coursing its way, True love now bonded, grows greater each day.

This mighty river runs to no

predetermined spot, Our loves unbridled, our passions run hot.

We ride this river, for our lifetimes entwined, Sincere thoughts and deeds forever enshrined.

My love I'll remember your ethereal glow, For as long as sun shines and mighty rivers flow.

Tom Davis
DON'T FOLLOW CROWDS
Times have changed,
for better or worse.
How come a nice girl
now gets the curse?
Let them have their title of Ms.
I'm happy being known as Miss
or his.
I'm a true to myself woman,
I don't follow crowds,
No, I don't follow crowds.

I like my doors opened
and my chairs pulled out,
But if they don't,
I won't whine and pout.
I like being called
and picked up at eight,
And not having to
out cuss my date.
I like going home
and all they expect is a kiss,
And hearing the words,
"Thanks for a nice evening,
Miss."
I'm a true to myself woman,
I don't follow crowds,
No, I don't follow crowds.

I still wear a bra
to cover my chest,
It's only for me
or my man at best.
I like myself groomed,
not like a witch on a broom.
I like the clothes
that look best on me,
Not what everyone says
is the only way to be.
I'm a true to myself woman,
I don't follow crowds,
No, I don't follow crowds.

I don't smoke
and I don't drop pills,
For I have enough
natural ills.
I've also learned
to be moderate with booze.
I'll wake up the next morning
and not have been used.
I made mistakes when I was younger,
but now, I know,
When you reach fifty
it will really show.
I'm a true to myself woman,
I don't follow crowds,
No, I don't follow crowds.

I'm not square,
and I won't go to bed on a dare.
My love is special,
as it should be.
For times haven't changed
that much you see.
Men still respect a girl
who says "No."
As all my male friends
will clearly show.
I'm a true to myself woman,
I don't follow crowds,
No, I don't follow crowds.

As time goes on
and they look back to now,
They'll still find one thing:
the marriage vow.
So I'm old-fashioned,
I don't care.
For, you see, one day,
we'll all have our souls to bare
I'm a true to myself woman,
I don't follow crowds,
No, I don't follow crowds.

Ella Eva White
WHEN THEY LAY ME DOWN TO REST
In the hills of Oklahoma
Where as a child I used to dwell,
There is an oak tree covered hillside,
Where lay the ones I love so well.
Gone are their footprints from our dooryard,
Gone are their songs and laughter, too.
May they sleep in sweet contentment,
Until we meet beyond the blue.
God reached down and took them
From this wicked world of sin.
Yet my heart is sad and lonely,
For the things which might have been.
When my life on earth is ended,
And they lay me down to rest.
I hope it's on that oak tree covered hillside,
Near the valley I love best.

Ella Eva White
CHILDHOOD DAYS
As I turn back the years of time
And gaze through childhood eyes,
I'm strolling down some countryside
Where Nature never dies.

There's violets and buttercups
Nodding to the breeze.
And oh so many other things
That townfolks never sees.

Yes, you can have your city life,
And I'll never envy you.
Just send me back to the country
Where my skies are always blue.

Lenox Collier
GOD'S THRONE

To my loving wife Elizabeth, whom I love with all my heart.

God's throne is never changing,
No matter the storms of evil that are raging.
His power is strong and lasting forever,
Defeating the powers of evil and leaving us never.
He is there to help and to protect;
All we need to do is ask, believe and not neglect.
For once we doubt and disbelieve,
We are starting down the path that from God we leave.
Satan may be strong and against us tries to overcome,
But we need not stand alone for we have God and his Son.
If we rely on the Power of the Holy Trinity,
Then in heaven we will spend eternity.
For our sins Jesus came to die on the cross,
Just turn your life over to Him and never again be lost.
Rely on the light to lead your way,
And you will be with the many on that great reunion day.
PRAISE THE LORD!!

Bonnie "Beebe" Turner
TWO LONELY PEOPLE IN A NURSING HOME

In loving memory this poem is dedicated to both our dear parents, Bill Beebe, Evelyn Beebe. Eunice Turner, Wilbur Turner.

We had a lonely dad, and lonely mother too,
They sat alone in a nursing home.
There was nothing else we could do.
It made our hearts as cold as stone,
As we never wanted them to be alone.
They often thought of all us kids
While they sat there holding hands.
Dad would have a tear in his eye,
While he looked at mother's wedding bands
Then they both would start to cry.
When they talked of all us kids, you could always tell.
They were so very proud.
They would look up and shake their heads.
That most always stayed bowed.
Neither one ever complained of being alone or neglected
A bitter word no one had ever detected.
Very often one would say, "I wonder if the kids are coming today."
Most of the time this is all they would say.
Over & over day after day.
They both tried to be happy, but most every night,
When no one was near,
They both would start to shed a tear.
Nurses would walk up and down the hall, and they would
Listen and listen for a teardrop to fall.
When daybreak would shine, they'd smile and say.
"Well Darling I'm fine again today."
Then set holding hands all alone, then one would say,
"Maybe the kids will take us home."

Bonnie "Beebe" Turner
DADDY'S TOT

Dedicated to my dear dad. From his little tot, Bonnie Beebe.

When I was just a little tot,
I loved my daddy an awful lot.
He would take me by the hand,
And we'd walk by the river, and even play in the sand.
Many, many times he'd look up at the sky.
And often a big tear would roll from his eye.
He said, My little girl you're the last I'll ever get,
So I want to tell you a story before I forget.
I want to tell you about your "Dear Mother."
For me dear one, there'll be no other.
But you my little tot.—
I'll always love you an awful lot.
Now I'll tell you, and I want to be frank
Your mama threw me out just because I drank.
But she really didn't want to be alone.
Because one cool nite she brought someone else home.
Someone, someone, that she could call her own.
She knew you were our youngest tot.
And she knew too, I loved you an awful lot.
I came back to see you for several years straight.
Then all at once she started to hate.
From that day on, I started to roam,
But from time to time I drifted back home.
By then you were no longer a tiny tot.
But I still loved you an awful lot.
We'd still go walking hand in hand,
By the same 'ole Kaw River. And same 'ole sand.
At that age "you" knew why,—
When "we" looked up at the skies
A big tear rolled from "our" eyes.

Karren J Manchego
THE SEA HORSE
Have you ever seen a horse from the sea?
He cannot breathe like you and me.
He doesn't try to run on the sand,
He wouldn't want to be held in your hand.
He doesn't have any legs, you see
And he can't play like you and me.
But he can swim as fast as light
And he can see in the darkest of night.
He can go where you cannot
To find the things that we've forgot.
He sees the whales dreaming there
And watches mermaids comb their hair.
He hears the oceans song of love
And follows it to his lord above.
There he rests when life is through
Safe in his hands like me and you.
And on his head so gold and fine
The crown of peace—his for all time.

Richard F Mason
THE DAWNING
Wake up! Wake up! The sun is shining,
Get up! Get up! And quit your sighing;
The pleasant dreams of the night are o'er,
Reality faces you once more.

But there is no need to feel despair,
Take a deep breath of the morning air;
Troubles that seemed so great yesterday
Like the morning dew will fade away.

Time travels on and when looking back
The skies will never seem near so black;
Take heart, my dear, and quit your yawning,
Wake up! Wake up! A new day's dawning!

Richard F Mason
A MOST UNUSUAL RECIPE
To a father's devotion
Add a mother's love
And a spark of life
From up above,

Then a gasp, a cry,
As breath draws free,
And there's one more fruit
On the Family Tree!

With a pink-hued skin
Like a morning rose,
Two eyes of blue,
A turned-up nose;
Small delicate ears
Near a dimpled chin,
And a mouth which forms
An engaging grin.

Now neither beat,
Nor boil, nor fry,
But carefully mold
As time goes by,
So that displayed
In this life's Fair
There'll be another
Grand Prize there.

Lesley Waltner
OCTOBER

Written for my daughter, Bethany, who was born in October.

October, and the trees are turning
Red and gold and orange and brown.
Soon the summer sun stops burning
And all the leaves come tumbling
down.

Pumpkins swell in fields nearby,
Farmers pick their Indian corn.
Luscious smell of apple pie
In the Autumn wind is bourne.

Cold and bright, the morning sky,
And the days are short and sweet.
Frosty cold comes by and by,
Nipping at our hands and feet.

In these glowing Autumn days
All God's beauty can be found,
And we thank Him for the ways
He spreads His love for us around.

Dedra J Smith
LASTING REGRETS

In memory of my loving step-sister Elyce who died at age 18 of cancer, it is through her strength that I was able to see the true meaning of life.

The love I feel for you is constant
And I miss the way we smiled
For now you are gone and can
no longer contribute to what I feel
All I feel is empty inside
with each tear I've cried for you,
Over and over I relive the memories
we had, although brief, and I regret
not seeing your love sooner and
reaching out to you. How was I to
ever know? I'm so sorry I was so
stubborn to be at your side.
Your death has made me so mature,
I've learned not to take advantage.
You opened up my mind to
understand
life, and I am so sorry yours was
taken far, far away.

Ridgley Wiggins
THE SEED

To Mrs. Joann Hunt Beloved teacher and friend For her inspiration.

The seed a tiny, precious thing.
Which has many different meanings.

It can mean . . . something
that when planted
Will grow to be something
useful and beautiful.

It can mean . . . something
that when fertilized
Will grow as a baby does
inside its mother.

It can mean . . . something
abstract as an idea,
Which, when it is tested, may
produce something great.

But all seeds will grow if
given a chance.
They will also reproduce in their
very special ways.

All seeds will either whither,
die or decay
When their life cycles are
to become complete.

But some are from their start
despised and rejected
As if they had no meaning in life at
all.

But all of life, even seeds, are
precious to me.
And it should also be to
the whole world.

Because Remember!
You yourself were once a
tiny, precious seed.

And this should give you a new
and different view
Of life and the importance of even
a tiny, precious seed.

Elena M Bourgoin

Elena M Bourgoin
PHOTOGRAPH

Wende, thanks for helping me to recapture the positive. This is for you with much gratitude.

The crispness, a solitude in this
photograph.
Scenes revisited in my mind.
Each layer of snow folded in some
gigantic embrace.
Sunlight through the trees, moonlit
constellations.
My summer's serenity whirl.
A bit of dolor and gaiety etched in
each frame,
Portraits of my life.
Cats immortalized on the bathroom
windowsill.
Of my first true love and
relationships thereafter.
Camping and hiking, guitars and
flutes.
Capturing, retrieving,—believing,
being.
Breathlessly cohesive.
The texture of my being, mindful of
life.
Intact.
In this photograph the recollection
comes forth.

Brandy L Cauley
LOVE

Love is like a delicate Rose,
Cared for it blossoms and grows.
When left alone it withers and dies,
When shared it spreads and
multiplies.

If you love someone, then let them
know.
Don't wait till they're old and gone,
And chisel love words in ice cold
stone.

If you no longer love, then set it free,
So it can scatter and leave.
To start again fresh and new,
Like the first rose of Spring bursting
through.

T J Casson
IN REVERIE UNION

Fascination watching the full moon
rise
This comes as no surprise
I feel it in my heart
The magic's still here, yet apart

The moon is high and shining
Now so sad, she's crying
Turned her loose, to be set free
A last night to spend with me

We stare into the starlight
Heartbeats heard in the quiet of night
Eyes are glowing in the dark from us
It's more what you think than lust

Our dreams passing in apparent time
Wild horses stamper in rhyme
Chasing stars in the sky
Don't never kiss your dreams
goodbye

T J Casson
TANGENT IN TIME

I see a child in front of the sea
His heart and spirits, oh so free
His head full, in wandering thought
In them, he never had to be taught

The world appears so vast
His carefree days go by so fast
A castle in the rocky sand built tall
But waves approach, that he never
saw

Grandpa joins him in front of the sea
His heart and spirits no longer free
Thinks back on years gone by
Wondering how his dreams did die

His realization brings a tear
Sadness in the world so clear
They stand together in the sand
Wondering what happened to this
land

T J Casson
FOR MOTHER

This poem is dedicated to my Mom. The most treasured part of my life. Thanks for the understanding and letting me, be me. Love Ya, T. J.

Here are some words sweet and dear
Ones that Mother should hear

Always lookin' out
For her love in life
She worries, but holds the faith

Keeps an edge on her number one
No other like her dear son

Usually willin' to listen
Whether right nor wrong
Her feelings remain strong and true

Somethin' special as a Mother
One you love like no other

Has given, lost and received
Kindness is her way in life
One never to be forgotten

Though we're another life apart
Every day she's in my heart.

T J Casson
IMAGINE IT

Thanks to those who help save our Earth. But we can't do it alone. You all have to change, 'cause wishing is not enough.

I see the mountain's shadow
Casting over me
Looking into the clouds
So far up to see

Now, close your eyes a moment
Imagine there is only night
Hear the sounds of life
Could the end be in sight

We are ending the planet's life with
pollution and wars
More guns and screaming, there is no
silence
You know the world should not be
this way
And man, has caused all this violence

Let's pray it won't come true
We need no more wars or don't you
know
There will be no more skies and no
ocean
We have nowhere else to go

Listen to these words of my wisdom
Understand what it is I say
A peaceful life of love and freedom
It's such a simple way

Imagine it

Jerry L Searcy

Jerry L Searcy
IT'S TIME

I dedicate this poem to Frances & Bradley Brown, my beautiful daughter and lovely son-in-law, for whom this poem was written.

I have to let you go
I know that this is true
But I've watched you as you grow
And I always have loved you

The years have gone so fast
So quickly they did fly
These years I thought would last
These years of you and I

What happened to the Baby
I held so many times?
You've changed into a Lady,
You're no longer mine

I have to let you go
I know that this is true

But it was only yesterday,
That it was me and you

I hope he knows how lucky
That he will be that day;
When he takes your hand in marriage
On your Lovely Wedding Day!

Jerry L Searcy
LITTLE STEVE

This poem is dedicated to my son
Whom I love very much!

There once was a boy
Who was a tot;
And that little boy,
My heart he caught.

He was as cute
As he could be.
Yes, he was my son.
My little Steve!

He was full of bounce,
He was full of glee.
My heart he would pounce;
Oh! How he loved me!

I thank God up above
For this marvelous lad.
For all of his love
Of life that he had!

We always had fun
At whatever we'd do;
"I Love My Stevie,
Stevie Loves Me Too!!!"

Marceline Evans
PETE—FATHER OF JOE

Dedicated to Peter De Laurentiis
Father of Joe De-Laurentiis.
Joe is my Son in Law and
a Judge of Lincoln Park.

Hey!
What's that you say?
Who is He—
Well, don't you know?
He is Pete—Father of Joe

He is a man who came across the sea
—All the way from Italy

He is one of our finest gents

He keeps up with the news and
current events
—Reads the papers every day

And listen to the news—without
delay

He's also a great gardener that
invents
He can mate—a fig tree—with a pear
And come up with something—very
rare

There is nothing he can't repair
All you have to do is call . . .
And he'll be right—there
So—
May I introduce—you—to—
Someone you really should know
Yeah, you guessed it so say hello
And meet Pete—
Father of Joe

Marceline Evans
FULL DECK

If you're allowed a full deck—
Gotta learn to take the heat

It's not so bad—as what is waiting—
In the devil's seat

We have to face a race
Against terror and defeat

Whip in there—swift and hard
Make it work—gotta pick a card
The odds are on your side

The terror is there
We know the Ace of Spades is—
too—
But where?

No doubt—one day—the cards will
run out
Then the Ace of Spades—will be—
Ready to mount

There's no escape—
From life's deadly rape

But don't say chow—
As long as you've got now

Marceline Evans
CUP FULL OF LIFE

From life to death—is only a moment
away
And all we got is today

Life is a limited amount of time
That can end on the tip of a dime
only a gift
What we go—Is all we got
And we don't even know about—that

Spend you days in idleness—if you
like
But tomorrow you'll be sorry
'Cause—you can't go back—and
make it up

So don't waste a drop from your
cup—
When it's over—gone—your time is
up

Be close to every minute of every day
Care and care hard enough—
As long as you can stay

Give and take
Stay awake

Squeeze every drop
No use to worry, just live—
Until you stop.

Marceline Evans
MY VALERIE

Written for and dedicated to Valerie
Ann Gillespie-Ponto.

My Valerie
Oh, so smart—so carefree; and
what a beauty
When I look at you—then I look at
me—
I say—So how can this be?
This gorgeous creature—part of
me
I see, home I came with the wrong
babee
Boy, what a blow to the other
partee
I sure got the better pick—
The real offspring—got the other
end of the stick
But, then—for a second as I
pause and contemplate—
Oh now wait—just you wait
Something just occurred to me—If
it 'tis truly so—
which, now wondering I don't
know? Could it be—
I did not bring home the wrong
babee—
She is indeed very much like me.
—For all the very same faults have
we.
Boo-Koo-Love,
Mom

Stephen Caissie
A WISH CAME TRUE

When I see the birds up in the sky,
It makes me wish that I could fly.
Or see a deer race by a tree,
it makes me wish that I could be so
free . . .
I'm sure there's things you wished
for in your life . . .
maybe one that's kept you up half the
night.
Or one like sitting in front of the
T.V.,
wishing those numbers were yours
for the lottery.
Well I know that wishes can come to
be . . .
I know this because it happened to
me.
My wish was to find a girl—
One who would change my world.
One who would stand by my side,
One who would be my loving
bride—
And if only one wish comes true in
my life—
I'm glad it was the one that made you
my wife.

Joleen Kobe
LIVING WITH A MAD MAN

I want to thank Kim for helping me
through this and for believing in me.

Society is saying "It must be my
Fault,"
Why else would a man beat and
abuse me.
For he was such a perfect and loving
man,
The only thing that came to their
mind was,
he was a good man.
He worked hard and long hours to
support me,
they must have forgotten I worked
also!
She must have been caught with
another man,
Why else would he beat her . . .
Little did they know,
there was no reason for his behavior.
The man in his mind,
was a very sick soul.

Jealousy rages and a hot tempered
mind,
brought much pain and sorrow my
way.
After the beatings,
there was always the promise of a
holiday stay with honeymoon plans.
The honeymoon was over in less than
an hour.
What high prices I paid,
for just one day,
not knowing what the rates would be
for just one day of no abuse.

Victor Levine Campbell
ONLY A DREAM

In your presence, the air is filled
with emotion that starts this
tired heart to beat strong
again.
So much time has passed since
the last time it felt its youth, I
can't remember when.
Each day I see you, I want the
world to stop, so time with you
would never end.
I love the way you laugh, the
glitter in your eyes, your smile
that says, "I like having you
around."
It's so wonderful to share things
with you, if only it be a
conversation, or a cup of
coffee.
Strange how a short conversation
could build itself into a closer
relationship and understanding,
even when no words pass
between us.
I long to hold you, to caress you,
to press my lips to yours, to
feel the warmth of your entire
being.
How much further we could go
would be ecstasy,
to be lost in a passionate
closeness of a love so strong,
I would fear our hearts would
burst.
This existence of me being with
you, what can it mean?
Nothing I guess, for it's "Only A
Dream."

Ralph Esparza
I TALKED TO GOD LAST NIGHT

I would like to take a moment to
thank: M. Chenault, B. Patrick, my
family, but most of all my brother
Richard Esparza, I miss, and love
you! I'll see you in heaven. Thank
you God for the wisdom.

I talked to God last night,
He spoke of peace of mind for me.

I thought he might be asking for my
soul,
As I have been asking Him to take
me from this world!

I have only loved one other than God,
She took me to the highest level of
love I have ever known,
Then to the deepest realm of sadness
I'll ever feel!

God knows me best, and He will help
me overcome all odds!

It's times such as this, I wish that I
could hold Him in my arms and say,

I love you more than life itself!

Ralph Esparza
ALWAYS HERE WITH ME

moonlight walks on a summer night,
you are here with me.

rain filled days of dark clouds, and
cool winds,
you are here with me.

autumn leaves that to earth,
you are here with me.

even though you love me no more,
you are still with me.

Ralph Esparza
DEAR BIG BROTHER

can you hear me from heaven?
I try to talk to you as much as i can.

can you see me from heaven?
I try to see you there at times.

are you proud of me from heaven?
I do all this just for you.

are you happy in heaven?
I won't be until i see you again.

Ralph Esparza
BODY AND SOUL
this man in my head hurts me at times.
the man in my heart tells me it will be alright.

this man in my head always makes me cry.
the man in my heart gently wipes the tears from my eyes.

this man in my head treats me like a small boy.
the man in my heart tells me how to grow up.

this man in my head keeps me offbalance and suicidal.
the man in my heart prevents me from doing it.

Jane Harriet Brown

Jane Harriet Brown
HELGA

After viewing an Andrew Wyeth Exhibition.

On lonely path
In winter's cold
Pensively she waits
Standing near
the blackened oak
Wrapped in her
dark green cape coat
A pained smile
reveals her fate
She turns and soon
retreats
Lies upon her bed
and sleeps,
Dreams aloof
and quite apart
Lonely in her
mind and heart
Far away, far away
Waiting for the light
of day
Another time
to walk alone
Down the path
that leads from home
Helga, Helga of Chad's Ford
With braided hair
and flowered cord!

Jane Harriet Brown
SYMBOLS
Shall the fallen leaf be mourned
Which the summer tree adorned?
And the ripened fruit found
Lying 'neith the bough on ground
Damp with autumn's frost 'round
Which rings and rows of water's floods
Are empty of reflecting moods—
Beneith the bark and leaf and bough
Eternal life force surges now
Unseen, to make another winter green,
And spring again to bring
Full cycle orbed her fruit
To bend the bough.

Daniel F Duncan
OUR GENTLE TEACHERS

In memory of my grandparents, Frank and Louise Palmer of Somerville, Massachusetts.

When my grandparents were alive
They taught me how to love and survive.

But now that they've gone to their final rest
I think of all the times I was blessed.

Grandma always had a gentle smile
Grandpa was clever and thoughtful all the while.

A couple you'd want to meet in a dream
Golly! They were a special team.

All their descendants talked about them with pride
Remembering the days that Frank stood by her side.

Friends could tell you of many a day
That Louise would always be the same way.

A couple that would always share with another
Golden treasures for more than just each other.

Two special people that can't be replaced
A Heritage to follow, A life to be traced.

When God called them home, we suffered a loss
Yet maybe in Heaven, our paths will cross.

I can still feel the warmth of their tender touch
Is it a wonder we loved them so much.

I miss them terribly.

Daniel F Duncan
DOWNTOWN SHOPPERS
On Friday Nights, My Mom & I
Went shopping, looking for a buy.
She'd have coupons in her hand
when we left the Taxi Stand.
We would wander down the aisles
Pricing and squeezing the mercantiles.
And if the product was alright
It would be homeward bound tonight.

We filled the cart up to the top
before we made the Bakery Stop.
Food or clothes, it made no matter
We'd eat the former or wear the latter.

A Bargain was a priority
when it came to Coffee or Pekoe Tea,
She made shopping such a joy
when I would get a little toy.

Bags in hand We'd head back home
and through each bundle my hands would roam
for cookies or a Jelly Jar
My Mom was the best by far.

Daniel F Duncan
MY FIRST RIDE
As a boy I rode a train,
a Greyhound Bus and Aeroplane
I went to Gloucester in a car
took a Trolley, near & far.

When a subway car came in
I gave the Motorman a grin
He'd ring the bell or give a toot
and I would travel on his route.

The first time that I rode a bus
I paid the fare without a fuss.
A seat up front gave quite a view
the driver was so friendly too!

And when I boarded a mighty plane
though clouds & snow and heavy rain
We flew to Boston from L.A.,
a marvelous trip in just one day.

But now a boy of forty-eight
still lingers near the Airport Gate.
The Railroad Station still looks fine
And I shall ride to the end of the line.

Daniel F Duncan
AMERICA'S GIFT
A chance to see a Redwood Tree
or a skyscraper built for you and me
To visit a zoo or Disneyland
America is a home well-planned.

From Maine to Iowa and other states
there are many versions of Golden Gates
A sunrise in Rockport or Nightfall in Texas
treasures so awesome it sometime perplexes.

The beauty & glamor of what we've been shown
still lingers for others in places unknown.
A hidden ranch nestled in Rogue River Valley
or a theatre in Boston whose name is "Pi-Alley."

A Clydesdale horse with its New Born Foal
An Anthracite Mine with tonnage of coal
A Swan Boat ride or Boulder Dam.
Grateful and inspired I certainly am

Perhaps we will never visit them all
a canyon called Grand or an ant farm so small
Wonderful memories we cling to so much
America, thanks for your gifted touch.

Mary Lorraine Lafreniere
SALUTE TO "OLD GLORY"
Salute to you oh banner, under God's sky of blue
Embrace us with your colors if you can for us too
Liberty still tells us what early colonists knew
Freedom is a promise to all black, white, red or Jew

Symbol of a hope and strength, you give to men goodwill
At home, abroad, your only goal is always to fulfill
The answer to the question, how long will it be until
War and greed are ended for the sound brings but a chill

What do your bright colors mean for all when flying high
I wonder what so many felt when they gave up their lives
It must have been important as they always seemed to strive
Spirits worked with all their might in order to survive

The struggle for this freedom is not seen by everyone
Perhaps their eyes are blinded as they're always on the run
So take the time to see "Old Glory"
She's waving in the sun
Salute it for our captives held in the land of Lebanon

Lil Hilliard
A PLACE FOR ME

Dedicated to my mother-Laura M. Brewington.

A place for me is in this country.
America, the land of the free.
A place for me is in this world.
It is my gift from God.
A place for me is in this life.
Let me find it.
A place for me has now been found.
Let me share it.
A place for me and you.
Together we will grow.
A place for us.
Let us show it.

Matthew Carroll
MY LIFE LONG VALENTINE

I dedicate this poem to my wife Diane, in thanks for all she has given me, for all she has taught me, and for everything she means to me that words cannot express.

When skies are blue you're by my side
When I'm down, in you I can confide
When things are hard and skies are gray
You stay beside me all the way
You hold me up and help me shine
I tell the world I'm glad you're mine
You are my best friend, you are my lover
Now that I have you, I need no other
When I'm with you I can laugh and sing
You make me feel I can do most anything
I may not be rich with lots of money
But having you keeps my skies sunny
You gave to me a child of gold
That melts my heart as her I hold
A better family I couldn't ask for

With both of you I need no more
So because to me you're both so sweet
I wrote this poem for a Valentine's treat
I hope to you it brings a smile
And makes you think of me awhile
So I'll keep it short, I won't write a book
Just long enough, for you to have a look
At what it is I have to say
Thanks for being my Valentine's Day!

All My Love
Matthew

KZ O'Dell
SOUL STRENGTH

These poems are dedicated to the three people who believed in me no matter the cost—my love John Silcox, my beautiful daughters Cassie and Crystal. I love you.

To develge into the past
brings pain and remorse
that will forever last

Hurt beyond the seasons
pain beyond the reason

Is this how life must be
pain and hurt to always see?

No, my heart and soul cry
to do this—then why not die?

Because we must learn and survive
not lay down and die

Strong we are, stronger in the soul
than we really ever know

This is how it must be
for we are we
you and me.

KZ O'Dell
INFINITE REALITY

Blades of grass striving for the sun
everything comes all undone

Breezes calm on the vast outside
waves getting bigger and
bigger with the tide

Ask yourself what do you want
while the moon continues
your dreams to haunt

Wolves howling long in the night
your nerves strung round
very tight

Voices whisper softly in the wind
Can you see? Can you see?
The line drawn thin?

Graceful dancer on the crystalline ice
people starving for a bowl of rice

Guns and bombs exploding with their might
you worry your trifle
thoughts—is it worth the fight?

Sparks fly and water flows
everything just comes and goes

Sing softly the melody
'cause this is infinite reality.

David Canter
TO THINK THAT I

Am I but fool to think that I could change the world with my mind
Or to bring joy and laughter from above
Display affection to those I love
To share experiences from beyond to put these thoughts into song
Is it too much to ask of thee to share my hopes my life and dreams
But yet am I fool of thought to bring kindness where there's not
To see a time so near to me,
heartfilled with joy oh God I plea
My words are crushed my eyes too blind
My sweet Jesus I must find
To think that I might heal someone any one but one
Or am I just a thought evading the wrath that God hath brought
The gentleness the kindness sought
Am I mind or am I not
To see a beggar on his knees, can we save him must he flee
And if the leper has need of thee
Embrace the poor the blind shall see
But yet if I could just help myself
Give me the power I once felt
Help me find who I am where I'll be
I shall come my Lord to Thee.

AMEN

David Canter
LAST NIGHT

Last night I had a dream, in it I had wept
I visited with Jesus and walked where he had slept
And when I first saw him, he was not alone
There stood with him someone I had known all along
His voice was pierce like arrow, his hair was silk and fine
His eyes were a glowing flame, the tears of course were mine
With him I felt a likeness to his angels above
And to all things held true Jesus, God and Love
I had so many questions, but he said "My son fear not,
for I am the rapture in which you have sought.
My wish," he said, "is only to embrace your every need,
Grant your repentance as you decide to plead."
At that my thoughts were with my family, how I miss them dear
And as I turned about me I saw that they were near.
As they came to greet me with bold tears in their eyes
I saw my Lord Jesus exiting the skies
He left me with laughter and hearts full of glee
That person who stood beside him had always been me.

Thank You Lord

Edward O Barry Jr
MY FATHER

So long ago we lost,
That which is so rare.
Now time has covered up,
The scars that we both share.
Yet the healing clock of time,
Can never take away,
The pain of lonely hearts,
And words we did not say.
So we live our lives apart,
Reaching out across the land,
With motives from the heart,
We grasp for the other's hand.
Yet we've lost our agile step,
In the abyss of our pain.
Now is it shadows that we cahse,
Or is there love, for us to gain . . .

Shelly Ann Horner

Shelly Ann Horner
VALENTINE

Will you always be mine
To love and cherish until the end of time
Will you guide me through my sorrow and wipe away my tears
Will you lead me to happiness and depart my fears
Will you take care of me when I'm sick or hurt from year to year
Will you always be the one to say I love you or I care
And at special moments will you be there
Will your innermost thoughts and feelings be shared
Will you be the one for me to comfort and hold
Will you still love me after I've grown old
Will you give me the light that could make my world shine
Will you stay truthful without stepping out of line
If you're the one, the one for me,
then I'm forever yours until the end of time.

Mary Champion
OF POCKET KNIVES AND HEARTS

There stands a sycamore tree in the valley,
where Bobbi and I went to play.
She whispered, "I love you," softly.
The winds of time blew her words away.
We wandered in the warming springtime,
from dawn through an April day.
With pocket knife I cut our initials,
and around them a heart to stay.

Years passed and I came back here,
and, searching, found the scarred heart,
with the distorted set of our initials.
I carry a hurting one—its counterpart.
The bark was twisted from the pains of growing.
. . . reminded me of all the bleeding years.
They left a numbness on my memory.
Time, finally had dried the salty tears.

Oh, the wine of that first kiss of children.
Oh, the glory of that budding day.
I thought I had carved a perfect heart.
But the passing of time grew it away.

Shannon Conley
A LOVE SIGH

When I look in your face my heart starts to sore
that causes me to want you more and more.
When I look in your eyes so deep, dark and brown
I want to smile instead of frown.
You're going away and I just want to say
—I LOVE YOU.
When I think of the times we spend together
I promised myself, I'd leave you never.
I hide my tears by blinking my eyes not letting you know, I have a few sighs.
To end my love sigh, I just want to say
I love you, I'll miss you forever—
Good–bye.

Felina J Cardenas
DAYDREAMS

Catch a falling star
Mix it in your dreams
Live on a colorful rainbow
And dance on a moonlight beam.

Soaring into the blue sky
Floating on the Milky Way
Reminiscing precious moments
Carried from yesterday.

A world of fantasy
Locked in your mind
Far away from reality
Another place, another time.

A place where dreams come true
A paradise in one's own mind
To where our imagination runs
When we relax and unwind.

Tosha Ann Miller Clayton
THE MORNING RISE

This poem is dedicated to my niece Sha-Nita Gañeal Rhea.

Before I go to sleep at night there's no one in my room,
But only the light from the mid-night moon,
I closed my eyes, then I realized, I didn't say a whisper
Of prayer, as I got out of bed, I bumped my head
and layed back down instead, as I layed there
I said my prayers and fell asleep right then,
I started to dream about a familiar scene of my
niece pulling my hair, then I was awakened, I wasn't
mistaken my baby niece was standing right there, so bright and early in the morning just a tugging
and pulling on my hair.

Kim Chamness (5th grade)
TOMORROW

Not today but in the world of tomorrow
There will be no more sorrow
The sky will be free of pollution
Working together we'll find a solution
No more littering, no more cries
No more wars and no one dies
But that takes a lot of work
So let's work together so we don't have to lurk
We don't want hunger, we don't

want starvation
So let's all join in and save the
nation
We will all have to bend so the
sky doesn't end.

Judith Y Rose Hopfe
NO ONE IS RIGHTEOUS

Dedicated to My Love, My Children & My Everything. Dedicated to all who Believe, especially to All the Related Family of: Judith Y. Rose Hopfe.

There's no one who's righteous, no
one who's wise
All have gone wrong and turned
away from right
The words off our lips can be full of
deceit
Condemnation, accusations, no proof
of what we speak

For all who have done us wrong, we
filled them with curse
To our satisfaction, we ruined them
with hurt
Thru the words off our lips, it is said
We shall also live by it, with pain and
hardship to dread

(IT'S WRITTEN IN MARK 3:25)

"A FAMILY WHICH FIGHTS AND DIVIDES ITSELF, THAT FAMILY WILL SURELY FALL APART"

I pray for all to "Learn the Reverence
of the Lord"
REMEMBER: What comes from our
lips unclean
Come all Evil, the true feelings from
our heart

Forgive all those who hurt you, as the
Lord would unto you
Ask the Lord to forgive you and grant
you a happy life too

Ben L Corpuz
IF YOU'RE EVER GOING TO LOVE ME

if you're ever going to love me
tell me now so i can erase
the fears of losing you.

if you're ever going to love me
admit it now so i can feel
every smile, every wink and every
touch
as a smile full of meaning . . .
and a wink full of understanding
and a touch full of loving.

if you're ever going to love me
love me now and let us enjoy
our moments together:
holding hands . . .
or just being around one
another.
but if you cannot love me at all
please don't let me know
so i can pretend that you love me
or hope that someday
you can love me, too!

Timothy M Connolly
MEANINGLESS VOYAGE

It is a meaningless voyage
such as these
that will bring civilization
to its knees.

Trials and tribulations
of a fly-by-night sailor.
Rumbling stretches of roadscape
for the unlicensed pilot.
Starving millionaires and their wives
on a pilgrimage to Mecca.
The Bear and I
joining hands in peace eternal.
?

It is a meaningless voyage
such as this
that will crumble cities and welcome
the abyss.

Joanna Conte
THE CAT

A handsome cat lies sleeping on a
bed.
The cat, contented, wears a quiet
smile.
A grand lifestyle, each day the cat is
fed.
So privileged, cat toys lay in a pile.
The cat, a care-free thing, does not
have bills.
Always sheltered, he need not earn
money.
He spends his time sitting on window
sills.
The cat sees a world all bright and
sunny.
So innocent, the cat knows only
good.
He is oblivious to what life brings.
It would be heavenly if all things
would
Be how the naive cat understands
things.
Although it is embittered by frank
hate
Cats see our tried and troubled world
as great.

Kendra Chess
IT'S OUR FIRST CHRISTMAS TOGETHER DEAR

Snowflakes falling outside my
window
Carolers singing their songs of cheer
Trees are dressed up in red and gold
It's our first Christmas together dear

It's our first Christmas together dear
And I'm so glad you're here.
Let's meet under the mistletoe
sweetheart
Let's kiss and have a brand–new
start.

Babs Cunningham
COME

Come here to me,
Please come.
Do not fear
I will not hurt you;
A child you are
And a child I love.

If all were like you
And came to me;
My work would be done.
The work I went to do on earth
To save all human kind.
But yet some don't believe;
And I must keep trying.
If all were like children
And believed in my love
There would be many more
With me and my Father above.

Janie Chastain
IN MEMORY OF MY FATHER

This is dedicated to my father, James Godfrey, who died in 1983.

You were one of the town's best
workers; this is something we all
know.
We also know you had a problem that
you could not control.

You couldn't help the things you did
nor the things you didn't do.
And I just want the world to know
I'm not ashamed of you.

You just couldn't cope with life or
the problems of each day
But I never held it against you,
Daddy, I loved you anyway.

How you must have suffered in your
sad and lonesome life!
You lost the things that meant the
most; your children and your wife.

Alcoholism is a terrible disease,
maybe even the worst.
But heaven will bring the final
cure—you went through hell on
Earth.

Mandie Cox
DO YOU CARE?

I see your face in the wind
Your eyes are true and blue.

Then I remember those three
Special words said to me from you.

Do you care for her
As much as you cared for me?

Or just one of those loves to
Set you free?

I left your side once,
And you left my side forever.

Why can't you see
My love for you is forever true?

Dellini M L Duff (Age 14)
CHRISTMAS IS ONLY A WISH

Christmas is only a wish.
A wish of happiness, a wish of joy.
But as we all know all wishes don't
come true.
How can you have a happy
Christmas?
How can you have a joyful
Christmas?
In a world so sad, a world so blue.
A world where people kill each other,
A world where people kill
themselves.
A world that looks so cruel to people
who have no place to go.
A world where people starve, when
others fill themselves full.
A world that is trying to full itself
into thinking there is
Joy all around on the day that Christ
was born.
A world that is blind to all the things
we need to see.
A world that is deaf to the cries they
need to hear.
Joy on Christmas doesn't need to be a
wish.
But the world that is so blue, so sad
needs a miracle
To let people see what Christmas is
to you and me.
A world that has happiness and joy
on Christmas all around
Starts with peace like it was meant to
be.
That is when Christmas will be happy
to me.

Ellen Clark
THE SUN

The sun shines,
then fades away
all in a second
all in a day
With all that glory
you think someone would see
the sky turning golden
Just for you and me.

Mrs Geraldine Charland
CANDLE

A candle in the darkness—always
there for me
A candle glowing hope and love—
within my heart will be
On my days of deep despair my
candle starts to dim
and then renews with prayer and love
With gladness I know Him
In days of peace and calm—my
candle glows so bright
My heart reveals my love for Him—
His love becomes my light
A beacon ever glowing—my faith is
always clear
It warms my soul forever—to know
that he is here
My God is always with me—My soul
can reach that light
that glows within my heart and mind
this faith that shines so bright
If I might share my candle
For all to trust and feel
I'd pass along the knowledge that
God indeed is real!

Ana Irene Carnal
WILD FLOWERS

Each delicate petal in umbrella
fashion
Created as formed together dancing
in chorus line.
Not unlike choreographers staging
their routines in unison
All colors blending a cherry welcome
to spring.
Dormant all winter, resting in repose,
Gathering forth to emerge in
jewellike shades
Beckoning artists to fashion their
beauty on canvas.
Caught in memory—not dimmed by
time's fading scene
And once more be claimed in the
eternal cogs of time,

Of endings and beginnings.
Every event of grand importance,
renewing their vibrant,
Silent melodies in color.

Jackie Cannon
ANAÏS GRACE CANNON
1916-1989
The sparkling dark brown eyes,
deep with compassion,
understanding, love . . .
Flashing in a moment at the first
evidence of an unkindness or
an injustice.

Integrity, genuine concern for
others, harboring good wishes and
no ill toward all.

Incredible tolerance and patience,
self-sacrifice for higher ideals,
for family and friends, always
to lessen their burden before
her own.

A fierce heart underneath a
gentle, caring hand,
encouraging all to be what
they want to be,
not to be afraid to be
themselves.

Kay Carnes
SONG OF FREEDOM
The winds of change blow swiftly in
the night
To tear the shackles loose from
man's plight
Of futile cries, unheard sighs,
Wandering Aimlessly.

No remembrance, no semblance
Of civilized society.
Generations once scorned, now
forlorned;
Bereft of human dignity.

But then dawn breaks; a new age
awakes.
No more cries futile, burdens brutal.
Behind eroded walls the power falls.
The curtains rise to freedom's open
skies.

Susan A Caltrider
MOTHER IS
The one who gave me life and love
and took good care of me,
who cured my ills through doctors
and pills,
and bandaged my wounded knee.

The one who welcomed my
childhood friends
into our home so modest yet warm,
who gave them dessert and when
feelings were hurt,
showed them the rainbow at the end
of the storm.

The one who taught me the "birds
and the bees"
which retained my good reputation,
who answered my questions and lent
benevolent ear,
to my trials and tribulations.

The one who lifts my spirits
when I am feeling down,
the friend with whom I share my
thoughts,
when no one else is around.

The one who is at my beck and call
when I'm all alone or in need,
through childhood, adolescence, and
now adulthood,
without hesitation of speed.

The one whose love and unselfish-
ness
are so very precious to me,
whose infinite compassion and
knowledge,
make her more able than others to
see.

I now, too, have a daughter
of my own to nurture and raise,
and it is often difficult knowing,
when to preach and praise.

But if I am blessed with half the
insight
as my mother so tender yet strong,
I shall have little trouble discerning,
between what discipline is right and
wrong.

So this poem is written
with so much love sincere,
and the thanks to you for being,
such a wonderful mother dear.

Melissa Currie
JUSTIN'S KISS
The blossoming bud; which petals
that fell
Your tormenting eyes can't resist
your spell
The moon that shines like a lonely
friend
It's you I'll love till the very end
If love was meant to be
Alone I'll wait for you to see
So very much I'll miss
The love of Justin's kiss
While every sparkle has its tear
And every sunshine has its fear
I'll sit and let the tear fall from my
eye
As the wind whistles a sweet
goodbye
With the stars to be a guiding light
I know not to cry; I know not to fight
My heart like a bubble to pop and
sink
A lost love for only my mind to think
If love was meant to be
I'll again wait for you to see
So very much I'll miss
The love of only Justin's kiss

Sean Crabbe
IT HAPPENS ONCE EACH YEAR
It happens once each year,
a single shines upon a clear,
I show no signs of tears,
instead my heart shall fill with
cheers.
It happens once each year.
The seas are calm,
the summer's gone,
we grieve for children without
dad or mom.
It happens once each year.
The sky is full of snow,
the trees are all aglow.
What will Santa bring them,
some children will never know.
It happens once each year.
Wars stop,
soldiers' guns drop.
Carols are heard for miles,
as we gather around the fire.
For once the world is one at
Christmas.
We are just one.

It happens once each year.

Mary Albo
FOR YOU MY LOVE
It is with deep regret, I set you free.
It is the only way, the only way, for
you and me.
And as you start your life with
someone new,
Remember this, my dear, I'm still in
love with you.

For you, my love, I wish the best of
everything.
Stars above, skies of blue and fields
of green.
But most of all, the happiness we
could not share.
A cottage small, with sunshine and
flowers everywhere
And as you walk down that aisle of
wedded bliss,
I wish you this, all the joys in life, I
know you've missed.
And when day is done, a fireplace to
keep you warm,
In his arms, where you belong,
forevermore.
For you alone know that our love can
never be.
You alone know, that I'm not free
For you, my love; for you, my love;
for you, my love!

Aimee Coley
IF STARS HAD EYES
I sometimes think
Of stars as small dots.
And I think,
What if a star had eyes?
And I wonder,
If a star had eyes,
Would it see me
And wonder if I had eyes?

And I wonder,
Which is my star?
The brightest?
The dullest?
The largest?
The smallest?
Or is it just the one
Who knows
It's alone
Even when it's not?

Kay Lilly Cottrill
DREAMING!
What if I think up a poem
And try to win a prize.
If I should be a winner
To divide it I'll try to be wise.
Some would go to a church
In a community of love and care.
Some to a volunteer fire department
Though otherwise busy the
volunteers are there.
Some would go to a school
That on donations depends.
And some to a wonderful college
My dear husband did attend.
Yes, it's fun to dream
Of some things coming true.
I will wait and see
What I hear from you.

Ginny Cash
ON THE EDGE
To be twenty, young and free,
my whole life ahead of me.
No thoughts of worry, trouble free.
Punch a time clock with
naivety.

Thirty, grown, married with family.
Life's all mapped out, neat and
tidy.
Undaunted, unaware of growing
despair;
monotonous, routine, with
nothing to bare.

Forty's and supposedly in my prime.
Something's amiss, I know not
why.
Frustration, impatience and deep
depression.
Not my scenario, just mass
confusion.

Doctors ignore stating not my time.
Saying my hormones are all in
line.
'I'm not like this!' I mentally scream.
"Can someone save me from
the unforeseen?"

Child abuse, Post Nam mental glitch,
or change of life? I know not
which!
Docs or shrinks, have they the key?
"Won't someone please just
listen to me?"

Willavena Cotham
THE WHISPER OF LOVE
I cannot be sad if my Savior is near,
He bids all my sadness depart;
I cannot be lonely, if gently I hear
His whisper of love in my
heart.
The whisper of love, soft whisper of
love,
How often, like the wandering
dove,
I fly to the ark with my Savior to rest,
And hear His soft whisper of
love.
I cannot be weary; the days are not
long,
If onward I trustingly move;
And oft on my journey I pause in my
song,
To hear the soft whisper of
love.
And when on the path He taught me

to tread,
 my footsteps forgetfully rove;
How kindly again to that path I am led,
 And cheered by the whisper of love.
No voice in the world is so tenderly sweet
 No charm can my sorrow remove;
No accents in glory my joy would complete,
 without the whisper of love.

Roena Jo Colinot-Katkus
FORGETTING
This morning when I woke I saw
His face, and pushed it out of my
Mind as I raised the window blind.
I sat down to my cup of coffee
And as I held the cup, I thought
To myself that he had held it also.

I looked at my hands and remembered
The many times he'd held them too.

Then I felt sick to my stomach
And poured the coffee down the sink.

I stood there and watched
It run away out of sight,
Just like he did.

Lana Collier
FAIRYTALES
Tell me a story of long ago,
Maybe happy or full of woe,
I'll listen carefully and clear,
If you hold me close and keep me near,
Tell me a story of princes and kings,
Tell me of riches and diamond rings,
Tell me of fairies, trolls, and witches,
Tell me where they hide, where are their niches,
Tell me of their life good and bad,
Tell me when they are happy and when they are sad,
Tell me of the war of pain, and the feast of joy,
Tell me of the lovers who teased and were coy,
Tell me till you know no more,
Of princes, fairies, love, and war,
For I will listen and forever keep,
Those great stories that put me to sleep.

Maria E Peluso
A WISH FOR YOU, DEUTSCHLAND
If you wake up one morning and can
no longer find your big black boots,
the ones that kicked humanity down
the stairs,
remember, that you lost your glory
along with all the others,
in the ashes of the Fatherland.

I remember once when the fire
burned you, burned your heart, in
your bowels, and
further down below, but you could
not follow me absolutely, me,
woman, who lit that fire.
Instead, your heart went dead.
You spent your time calculating,
always calculating: mathematics,
figures, the cost
of love in German marks, the grand
sum totals of dead bodies, Jews,
kilometers of Autoband,
machine guns, pork barrels, steins,
pickled herrings on rye bread.
Oh you've really done it now, thrown
the key away, the key to your heart.
Why were your politics so pig-
headed?
I believe it must have had something
to do with those damn boots you
kept, the ones
you've now misplaced.
Was it in the Hoftgarten where you
refused (again) to speak of love?
I remember how you spoke then, of
that glory that could have been, that
glorious past
that should have been.

Deutschland, I shall pray for you.
I shall bring you my hot passionate
heart in my hands,
breasts as large as moons to suckle
your children, and
stars to feel your poets;
Oranges bigger than the sun from
Pompei and roasted chestnuts, and
you shall never go hungry.
The waters from some mysterious spa
will heal all your wounds and
the light from Roman candles shall
guide you in the night.
Music, will at long last inspire your
spirit and you shall learn to dance.
And all this I shall do for you, my
dear, dear gentlemen, and for a
Motherland.

So forget about your boots, throw
away the garbage of your visions, the
garbage of
your yesteryears, and
those ridiculous cuckoo clocks!
Come, let me put you inside me and
let our blood speak,
and only then will the phoenix rise to
see a
real empire.
All this I wish for you, my
Deutschland.

Betty Barth
MY DARLING CHERYL

To My Daughter Cheryl just before her wedding day.

My Darling Cheryl,

Yesterday seems but hours away
When you were little and loved to play.
Some of the things you used to do
Kept me in stitches—I never felt blue.
How quickly the time goes flying by,
You're all grown up with the blink of my eye.
Ah, to go back and have you so small,
To rock you again in my arms, that's all.
But time goes on and soon married you'll be
With a child of your own and that'll make three.
Never forget your youth and the past
And the love of your parents that kept you steadfast.
Love has a way of conquering all—
It keeps you strong and walking tall
And now as your wedding day draws near
My gift of love is yours, my dear.

Love, Mom

Damian Arcilesi
SEARCHING

Dedicated to all who have faced personal tragedy in their life. Keep searching, answers will come! We are never as alone, as we may feel.

I am a stranger,
 to myself.
Seeking remnants,
 of my past.
Wondering
 why the transformation.
Fighting,
 against complete oblivion,
Of times,
 cherished and esteemed.
Of someone,
 whose thirst for life
 unquenched,
By the brevity,
 of the feast,
And the coming,
 of the rain!

Walea Walker
MY MOTHER, MY FRIEND

Dedicated to my caring Mother, whose patience, love, and strength helped me become the person I am today.

She is someone on whom I can always depend.
To lessen the trouble, I sometimes get in.

Sometimes she says things, I just don't want to hear.
But I know if I listen I'll have nothing to fear.

She's gentle, she's kind she goes out of her way.
My mother somehow, always knows what to say.

Many times late at night, we just sit down and talk.
And when we do that, any path I can walk.

All of her qualities are derived from sheer strength.
And you know what she says almost, always makes sense.

After talking with her, I can conquer the world.
And nothing I touch will ever lie unfurled.

Walea Walker
A MORNING MOMENT
As I woke up this morning I thought to myself, what will this day be like.
I must go get the paper, or turn on the news, will some company be on strike.

Will the trains be on time, will my bus be late.
Will I get a promotion, or maybe a date.

Is it cold outside, will I need my hat.
Will I need my money, . . . No I can't forget that.

Each day is so different, how will I fare.
Oh no! The big meeting just look at my hair.

I must get up now, and get dressed for the day.
And I realize now that I have the most say.

Right now I don't know what my day will be.
But whatever will happen is all up to me.

Walea Walker
SILENT HEART
It pumps without thought, never skipping a beat.
The work of this organ is a marvelous feat.

It's strong, it's powerful, it's complex, it's complete.
It's delicate, it's small, it's compact, yet concrete.

It wants to be verbal, it has so much to say.
To speak would be great, but things get in the way.

I want to speak, let him know how I feel.
I want him to help me, things are so congealed.

I love him so much, he just doesn't know.
But I better speak up, or away he will go.

My heart is so silent, so quiet, afraid.
But you're reaching me slowly, don't let your love fade.

The patience you've shown me, will help make my love grow.
Just your presence, your smile, sets my heart aglow.

I promise from now on, to give you my heart.
Please take it, <u>it's silent</u>, but at least it's a start.

Cheryl Spinella
MY SISTER KIM
Born November 28, 1971
My sister Kim is a special one.
She is two years older than me
Standing straight her height is
5 foot 3.
She has shiny black hair
and big brown eyes that are a
beautiful pair.
My sister is very skinny yet very
strong
Her legs are full of muscle and very
long.
She turned 18 about a week ago
Whether she knows she's an adult we
do not know.
Kim is special in her own way
She has been autistic from birth
through this day.
As we sit back and complain about
our week
I look at Kim who cannot speak.
She teaches me lessons day by day
Even though she cannot exactly say
What she means through words.

She makes some noises that can be heard.
But to me her actions are just the same
As if she were to talk to me and call me by name.
My sister Kim has influenced my life from the start
And I love her fully with all my heart.

Kelly S Mallett
MY TIME IS RUNNING OUT
With each day, I find another way.
I scar my skin, because I want it to end.
My scars show my pain, there is no one to blame.
I just want to love someone that will love me the same.
I tell them I need help, they think it's a game.
When it's over, will they still think the same?

Victoria M Cox
DEATH OF A KNIFE

To my family, Who always knew I could do it. With all my love.

Killed a man,
Now here I stand.
On trial for awhile,
With not a reason to smile.
Blood on my hands,
No reason to make any plans.
Thinking of it now,
I can only wonder how.
The scream of his pain,
Running all through my veins.
The stab of the knife,
Now ends his life.

Ron Parrish
THE ONES WHO SAY
The ones I know who will say
"Death before dishonor" know not what it is they utter;
They are weak and brainwashed by their own illusions, that their brains will sputter.
The ones, you who know who they are, who dress in war fatigues,
They play;
Games with their worthless minds, expose others to their wasted ways.
Me, I dress not in green, nor waste my breath on war;
But in my heart there is much more mettle and courage that is stored.

Crystal F Arnold
LOOKING BACK WITH REGRET
Looking back with regret
At a life gone in the past
At a future I once had in my reach
And a love that didn't last.

Looking back with regret
At all I could have done
The times I could have laughed
That now are all gone.

Looking back with regret
At things I wanted to say
And never got the chance
Because you're not here today.

Looking back with regret
That will last all my life
You were gone from the earth
Before I became your wife.

Looking back with regret
At dreams that can't be
You can never be here again
To share them with me.

Vaughn Inthavongdy

Vaughn Inthavongdy
MY BEDROOM
Pictures of ancestor were placed over my bed
but yet only one stands out to me

It's my resemblance

On the pictures was a fingerprint with bloodstain
Next to the picture was a crystal vase filled with dead flowers

The picture was small but very valuable
The picture it's all I know him by

He gave me life
And then he die

I don't know why
He say goodbye

Then I realize
He can't survive

From a disease
That cut him in piece

I am so glad
He is my dad

Vaughn Inthavongdy
THE MEMORIES
Goodbye today when my love say
I shall return each morning day
Not to stay, but to say
Your beauty shows inside and out
I shall not even give a doubt
I beg of you have faith in me
For you are all I need to see
Not two or three must I repeat
Nor will ever I ever cheat
My gentle kiss your rosy cheek
Oh how I miss your sweetly treat
So soft the touch I give your lips
I feel along my finger tips
So very bright, so very shy
Crystal glass shine is your eyes
I will awake with my last yarn
To see the burst of my first dawn
My love, I must go on

Troy Mock
CHANGE
Standing lonely in the wind,
Wanting to be close to you,
Living without you is hopeless,
Quietly I whisper your name,
Wanting to be close to you,
Thinking of the times we had,
The way you looked,
I never thought tonight,
I never thought tonight I'd be,
Without you,
The shadow of you lies with me,
Tonight.

Robert Lopez
THE UNRECOGNIZABLE SHADOW CASTED FROM THE SNOUT OF A DOG UNDERWATER
I
Sailing on a withering sea, can do no more for me
than what has been or what will be.
And since dry coconuts and rotten fish
have been the inmates of my driftwood dish
and all the things I've seen go past
have sleptwalked by me way too fast.
Thus the sun is gone and I don't know where I'm at,
I sling the carcass of a colourless cat . . .
into the sea—hoping that
someone will find the letter I scratched
and come gather the remains of me.
II
It is raining—I stand around contemplating
whether or not to wear a raincoat on my trip . . . or take an umbrella . . .
or an extra pair of socks,
for I may get
wet . . . when the sun will set.
Or I may not be able to see . . . so I'll bring a light with me
to shine the way—ha ha oh yes
to make the weariness much less.

Zandra R Lindsay
SILENCE
Silence everywhere
I just can't stand it anymore
I'm bored!
Give a wilderness to me
full of animals, birds, bees
Nature's sound I want to hear
Not this silence all around
Quiet is okay sometimes
but not now
I just can't stand it anymore
Let me scream
open the door
I want out of this silence
forevermore.

Elizabeth Jefferson
THINGS IN MY MIND

To Ted Harris for the inspiration you've given me.

There are things we all must do.
There are things we all see.
but the only thing I know
is where I want to be.
But then there are times
When I think in my mind
Why am I here
Will this be a good year.
Am I any good
or should I be
in reality
A bug on the ground
Where I won't be found.
What is my question
Where is my answer
Maybe one day
I'll walk at the bay
And somewhere I'll find
my piece of mind
but who knows
besides the shadows.

Ludivina Rodriguez
CALL FOR PEACE
Life offered peace
It offered reality
But I, the young dreamer,
Refused.
Now life offered more,
It offered success
But I, the young dreamer,
Laughed.
Then, I couldn't realize that I
Had made life upset.
Now, the old dreamer, begged life
For peace, but life had nothing
More to offer.
And now, my call, is a call for peace!

Eileen A Souza
THIS BOOK OF TREASURES AND GOLD

Dedication to the father of my children.

This book is filled with treasured memories that once used to be.
No one will ever take the place of the child that was once inside of me,
This book of treasures, I give to you, whom they belong with too.
No longer in my life you will share,
The treasures I've placed in your care.
Good memories never grow old,
Or will they never run cold,
As all good things come from each child we mold;
So hold on tight to these treasures of gold,
So you can share as you grow old and are able to cherish, the child you used to hold.
That our children's children can see who helped begin, the first lives of their family tree.
Given with loving memory,
Of what once used to be.

James F Smith
IMPECCABLE FORCE
The sun shining brightly on all those around
I open my eyes and darkness is found.
It's not that I'm blind or can't see the light
The thing that I see is as dark as the night.

Everyone sees it but most turn away
Ignoring the problem in hopes it won't stay.
The problem will stay, it will grow like a tree
It feeds upon fear of those who won't see.

It's much like a sickness, a contagious disease
Passed down generations, from

thoughts they believe.
As of this moment, there is no known cure
Not even the will can keep one's self pure.

All people are plagued by this impeccable force
Many say they are clean, but they have it of course.
For the face of this presence is often unique
It takes many forms to conquer the weak.

If you dislike a person, for any reason at all
Then you have this disease and likely will fall.
We hope when afflicted, it will not take a life
For the angers of prejudice can kill like a knife.

Shelby Colbert Bivens

Shelby Colbert Bivens
AWAKE ASLEEP

This poem is dedicated to my wonderful husband Rev. V.M. Bivens and my adult children, Denise, Ronald, Rickey and Dana and my mother Mrs. Margaret Colbert, for their Love and concern!

When we awake, joyfully shouting,
never doubting, expecting things
anew and fresh, assured the best,
we accept the test . . .

Every morn our lives arise, to see
a dawn, filled with radiance that
lifts our eyes up toward the blue
sky . . . with centered eyes we see
the trees and seas!

Joyfully shouting, never doubting,
We love the glow of the glistening snow,
The birds, the bees, the you's the me's;
Remembering the Hands, Who made everything;
we sing, Joyfully we sing . . .

Now, when we lay down to sleep,
Our hearts joyfully shouts, never doubts;
That when we awake in the morn, afresh
and anew . . . when we do our best,
we'll pass the test, assured that He
has conquered our quest!

Colleen K Chock
IN YOU

For your faith, inspiration, and friendship—thank you. Stephen.

I see a rainbow,
But I see you.
The ultraviolet glow
Of your personality
And style.
I see the sun shine,
And I see your smile.
The radiant beam
Of the joy I see
In you.
I see the stars,
And I see your eyes.
The bright twinkle
Of the you inside.
The sound of the wind,
Reminds me of your voice.
Soft, gentle, and sweet.
The beauty of nature—
Reminds me—
Of you . . .

Elizabeth Paulson
MATTHEW

A fun-loving boy of four
Who knows how to strike up a rapport,
With a bus driver, a salesman or a pedestrian—
They all respond to this little thespian.

He chatters about his favorite hero—
He-man.
All the exploits and adventures he imagines he can.
The muscles and strength of this imaginary warrior
Is a constant delight to this little terrier.

Cousin Stephanie contributed C–3PO to his menagerie
Which adds to his world of imagery.
This silvery, miniature robot from Star Wars
Aids in his travels through many adventurous doors.

He and mommy love to watch trucks and tractors—
but from a distance.
He and Grandpa are best pals—with no resistance.
He loves the attention from his uncles who are young.
They all help him to sing the song that needs to be sung.

Your Loving Grandmother
Elizabeth

Elizabeth Paulson
STEPHANIE

As the years begin to roll on by,
Our Stephanie is growing without a sigh.
She becomes more introspective by the day
In both her work and her play.

She shows she knows what responsibility means,
Which should help a lot as she nears her teens.
She has taken on part of the household chores,
And stays alone if she remains indoors.

She likes puzzles and crafts that requires some thought—
And is proud of the things she has wrought.
Her Barbie Dolls are a source of original dress,
And from time to time are quite a cute mess.

She has begun to build friendships by the score.
There is Nicki, an X-neighbor, and both know each has a revolving door.
A good skating partner is Nichole, her school chum.
Then two special people, Robin and Jessie, who makes Stephanie's life hum.

An enduring quality that we especially cherish—
She loves us—so we'll never perish.
Now that you have reached the age of eleven,
Continue to help us feel this is heaven.

Your Loving Grandmother
Elizabeth
1989

Elizabeth Paulson
ANDREW

A handsome boy who is in grade one,
Who can be a pain in the neck or lots of fun.
The age of dependence he is trying to leave behind,
To join the boys' world, and yet become "one of a kind."

He says, "He's the best in his class."
His favorite subjects are gym and lunch—I pass!
Let's hope this attitude carries over
Into reading, writing, and math, however.

He likes to take part in competitive sports,
And emulates the big leaguers—even their retorts.
His favorite sport this year—T-Ball.
He's enthusiastic except for the "out" call.

Grandpa's computer still holds a fascination,
For games that have fast automation.
"Dragon Fly" and "See Saw" keep him hopping,
Especially the "Turkey" that keeps on popping.

To my sister Stephanie—You have watched over me, and endured my teasings and tantrums.
Please let me love you without demanding a ransom.
For I'm not only a little brother, you see—
I'm me!

Your Loving Grandmother
Elizabeth
1989

Elizabeth Paulson
BRITTANY

To a little girl with eyes so blue
How fast the days have gone and how you grew.
You are a delight for everyone to see
And are everything a little girl should be.

You have an interest in something more important than looks—
These wonderful things are known as books!
Keep Mommy and Daddy reading those stories,
Until you have discovered words and their glories.

You have a pink blanket that trails behind,
It offers security—and there is no other of its kind.
Dolls and such provide hours of satisfaction,
But in times of distress it's the blanket that gives consolation.

And now as you approach the age of TWO,
There is a special treat in store for you.
Grandma and Grandpa Eckenrod are establishing a new encampment,
Which will provide you with many hours of enchantment.

This is a year that's about to ring
With many new words you are about to sing—
So take your time as you learn to run,
And make this a year that's a barrel of fun.

Your Loving Grandmother
Elizabeth
1985

Elizabeth Paulson
SETH

Seth—Our friendly little boy,
Who uses his smile in a special kind of ploy.
He has a habit he cannot hide—
When he sees us coming his arms open wide.

He expresses his emotions by clapping his hands, screeching and deep seated laughter,
That gives you the impression of a little actor.
And when he hears music with a beat,
He finds it hard to control his little feet.

He "burbles on" with new-found words—
Momma and "Hi" sound like the song of the birds.
His interpretation of one word has to go
And that's the use of that awful word "no."

He has to be watched closely because he's likely to wander,
And when he does this he's off in his own little world of ponder.
He comes by this wanderlust naturally, you see,
Because the acorn never falls far from the tree.

When this little boy seems overactive—let me give you a clue,
He's entering the stage of the "terrible two."
So let him grow at his own little pace
Because it's bound to show on his expressive face.

Your Loving Grandmother
Elizabeth
1989

Elizabeth D Fields
THE SECRET

I have the best big sister in the world,
She taught me the secret to life.
When I was three, she gave me an ABC book, twice.
When I was four, she said, "I'm giving you the secret to life."
I didn't understand then, but we sat down to read again and again.

When I was five, I was off to school,
Proud of the reading I could do.
Now, I'm sixteen and I tell you,
I've read math instructions, science,
English, how-to books, and more.
I've read the Bible, stories about
travel, and trashy books galore.
But, I know where I'm going and,
what I want to do,
Because, reading has opened the
world to me through and through.
So, Thanks big sister,
You know you were right,
Reading is the secret to life!

Nicky Lindgren
THE STARS IN THE SKY

This poem is for the people whom I love very much.

The stars
you see are always there
even in the daytime.
When the sun goes down
they come out
but only on clear nights.
Why you say,
when the clouds are there
they cover up the stars.
I don't know why
they just do.
On clear nights
the stars shine bright
but not as bright as Venus.
Some stars form things
Like Leo the lion, Taurus the bull
and the many others.
Some say stars are magical
Some say stars are living souls
and some say other things about them
but I say they are just special things
up in the sky.

roger k beedon
MY SPELLING AND PUNCTUATION

For my parents, Chuck and Lorraine Beedon, with all my love.

Mi speelin and punchyouashon
allwayz getz in th way:
they make it hard four me two get
thruw the day?
I seeldum did lissend too watt mi
teecherz did say"
I figyourd leernin two speel wood
just get inn the way,

As U kan sea; mi speelin aint' reelie
two good.
i dont' no watt wordz too uze,
when reelie i shood?
I kan knot punchyouate wordz
write: butt wich that i kould"
and i kan't uze a dickshonaire, and
pepole wich that i wood,

When it kame two speelin inn skool i
reelie got rookd.
butt if U kant' speel the wordz!
how kan U look it up in a book;
Mi pairentz payed four mi skoolin
and i think they got tookd"
butt i shure hope they nefer find
out, I nefer opend the bookz!?,.

Roger K Beedon
SOMEONE WAS CRYING

To My Special Friend, Karen Maire.

Someone was crying far off in the
distance,
I tried to find them, but found
much resistance.
I looked around in every direction,
I wanted to find them to offer
affection.

I followed the sound, but had not
found the source,
I began to wonder if I was on the
right course.
When I looked ahead, the sound
was always behind,
I was sure someone was crying
and was not just in my mind.

I kept on searching, what else could I
do,
I had gone this far with only sound
for a clue.
I felt trapped in a maze with no
sense of direction,
I had to find who was crying and
offer affection.

I arrived at a point, I couldn't brake
the resistance,
the sound of crying no longer had
distance.
The sound was now louder, like I
had opened a door,
I could hear the tears dropping and
hitting the floor.

I knew I was close and could soon
offer affection,
I hoped I could also reflect some
correction
The crying was now loudest, from
every direction,
I turned around slowly . . . and
saw my reflection.

Agnes R Jankowy
TO MY VALENTINE

To Frank—My Husband, 6/30/51-5/30/90. To Florence—My Sister & life-long friend. To My Children & Grandchildren.

With love sublime
Dear angel mine,
I send to you
This Valentine . . .
With a hope that life
Will always bring
The best to you
Of everything . . .

There is no word
That can define
My love for you
Dear Valentine . . .

Without you life
Was incomplete,
Your Faith has been
A welcome treat . . .

Again I say
These words divine—
Please be My Own
Dear Valentine . . .

Lindy Ann Ford
LOVE

Love is serious,
That's for sure.
You make a wrong move,
You run for the door.

You try to hide your feelings
From me, but why?
You know I Love you!
That I can't deny.

You said you'd never leave me,
But now you're gone.
Only the memory,
Can carry on.

But if you really loved me,
Why did you go?
I tried to kiss you,
But you said, No.

I look all around,
All I see is you.
Just remember one thing,
I was always true!

And something else—
I LOVE YOU!

Raul Jackson

Raul Jackson
THE BAR MAID

Dedication to my wife: Mrs. Ilse Jackson, and my daughter Denise Leah Jackson.

All what I can see
where I sit,
is a beautiful bar–maid
whose eyes are lit,

I turn my eyes
and look the other way,
with a sideling look
she was watching me,

With clear vision
I traced her line,
aged with fortive graces
still charming and fine,

All what I saw
a year ago,
a charming bar–maid
that's what I know,

Beneath her clad bosom
I could not see,
the hidden figure
this thing haunted me,

I intend to touch it
with my trembling hand,
I had no reason
and a ground to stand,

All at once what I see
and thing if so small,
my breath came short
which is not me at all,

All the wrongs what
I have done and said,
I stopped it until
it gets into my head,

I held over my eyes
a large beer glass,
through which my
shrinking eyes pass,

Lori A Aubrey
LIFE

For my mother, who helped me to be what I am.

Life is so simple, yet so complicated.
When you're born, life is so green
and effortless,
but then you grow,
Toddler, your first steps of life.
Teenager, the most arduous and
trying times.
Adult, now it's really starting,
you've conquered everything from
potty training,
to adolescence.

But now, you must deal with real
responsibilities,
spouse, work, family, how do we do
it?
I really don't know, except to say,
that it's all so simple, yet, it's all so
complicated.
And that everything works itself out
eventually.
So, if you find yourself thinking,
"things will never change," just
remember
what you've overcome thus far.

Rex D Judd
SCOTTY IS WALKIN' BY JESUS'S SIDE

To walk by Jesus's side,
And spend our days in God's glow;
Ya always want to end that way,
But, ya have to pray it is so.

But, one day we didn't know,
That he chose someone dear all;
To pass on to something better,
Now Scotty had heard the call.

I know that he is happy,
Gone to heaven to watch time flow;
He can look down and see us,
So he knows we miss him so.

But, now there are no tears,
And pain we don't have to hide;
So now I'm smilin' 'cause I know,
Now Scotty is walkin' by Jesus's
side.

gayle jacobs
WIZARDS

In the ancient time of kings
hear the wizards voices sing
Descriptive words used for the
purpose
materializing objects to the surface
Verses were the tools of trade
'tis magic, is what they made
And though the land was young at
heart
my wizards played important parts
Casting spells and changing forms
they called in raging
thunderstorms
Having knowledge of foresight
advising kings in their plight
To rule the land with goodly hand
letting not the evil band
But in this ever changing place
my wizards vanished into grace
Yet in my heart they'll always live
and with my words, 'tis life I give

Darlene Gutierrez
A SINGLE ROSE

To David, who gave me my first single rose.

A single rose
can mean so much,
so fragile
the heart is touched.

A single rose
holds so much beauty,
treasuring it
is your duty.

A single rose
can never be matched,
for to your heart
it will be attached.

A single rose
is meant to be,
a special gift
from you to me.

Mollie Curcione
TRICKY MARCH
The calendar read,—the middle of March,—
Nature,—was extremely busy;
Playing its tricks, on you and me,—
By sending us, into a tizzy!

Instead of wearing coats, and such,—
To keep our bodies warm;
Instead of wearing boots, and gloves,—
And fighting winter storms;—

The weather switched,—from "cold" to "hot,"—
A change so unexpected;—
Bringing temperatures of 80 degrees,—
Was for March,—not expected,—or rejected!

The public was delighted,—
To feel the summer heat;
Following a cold, drab winter,—
The warm weather,—was a treat!

Claire W Hicock
WOULDN'T HAVE MISSED IT FOR THE WORLD
We've lived a good bit since we said, "I do."
Times we were happy and times we were blue.
There were times when we crawled, love, and times when we flew
And I wouldn't have missed it for the world.

Cardboard to cover the hole in my shoe,
Turning shirt collars to make them look new,
Adding potatoes to stretch out the stew
And I wouldn't have missed it for the world.

We made the promise, for better, for worse
And that's what we had day by day.
Just you and I in our own universe
And the world was our Milky Way.

Bad times we remember because they were few
Compared to all of the good times we knew.
I want you to know, Love, that because of you
I wouldn't have missed it for the world,
No, I wouldn't have missed it for the world.

Claire W Hicock
HUMBUG!
Here we go back to the work-a-day world,
Footballed-out boy and gifted-out girl.
Solemn evening of worship, gleeful gifting of toys,
Chimes and laughter and shrieking and noise! Noise! Noise!
Then a week leading upward to greater endeavor
Which should end with the year, but it seems like forever.
Revolving, resolving, lots of helpful suggestion.
Upward! Onward's! The answer but what was the question?
And the year starts out full of choler and color.
The noise subsides not, though the hearing grows duller.
It's time to look inward but there's no time to think
And there's no more the palate for rich food and drink.
Just a yearning for hot tea and dull, quiet days
But ahead lies an evening of football replays.
Let me die with the decibels, live with the ghost
Of the noisiest of seasons. Wasn't this one the most?
"Bell, book and candle," chapter, verse, word and letter,
The season was great, but the silence is better.

Alex Engelken
TO SOMEONE SPECIAL

Dedicated to Carol.

You make me feel like someone special
When i think of you, my blood begins to rush
When i look at your lush face, my mind begins to race.
You've changed me in ways
i thought couldn't be done
You're a beautiful dove
And i know i'm in love.
i don't recognize others, no longer i do
Because my eyes are set on you
i was filled with great depression
But since i've met you, i've become a happy expression

My world revolves around only you

You're my mind and you're my heart
Without you, i couldn't start
You're my light, and you're my brain
Without you my world is slain
And when you leave me
i'll be someone new
For my spirit will always be with you

Alex Engelken
MOUNTAINS
Mountains . . . the peak of society
Yet the land of the lonesome
To some there is no other form of existence
Others a ticket to death
For mountains are God's breasts
Cresting the land in its hand
Mountains are for all
To fascinate
Bewilder
Adore
For mountains are not just plots of land
Mountains are more

Darby L Erbaugh
TOMORROW

To my mother and father for supporting me and loving me just as perfect parents should.

First rays of sunlight shining on the forest tops,
Letting gold strips shine onto the forest bed,
The golden ball arouses life,
Beckons them to open their weary eyes from dreamy sleep,
Calling out, "Awaken and live under my yellow rays."
And all life obeys.
Their thoughts and souls are filled with effort, beauty, and finally, tranquility.

Al Statum

Al Statum
SWEETHEART

To my darling wife, Wanda.

You should walk forever in a garden of roses, if I could but be the one to pluck the thorns from the presence of your beauty.

Lois V Curtis
GOD GIVES US MINUTES OF GOLD
God gives us minutes of gold, so when we grow old:
God gives us joy that we may give to make someone happy:
To make someone smile:
Two or three minutes—two or three hours, what do they mean
in this life of ours? Not very much if but counted as time.
But God gives minutes of gold and hours sublime, if only
we'll use them once in a while,
A minute may dry a little lad's tears,
An hours sweep aside trouble we fear,
Minutes of my time may bring me a friend.
God gives us minutes and hours of loads to lift,
That we may learn to bear,
For life is but minutes of gold.
For life is gladder when we give,
And love is sweeter when we share,
And heavy loads rest lightly two,
When we learn our minutes of gold,
God gives us.

Richard Pisarra
A GOOD FRIEND
Like a big old house
set back from the road
strong, sturdy, everlasting,
a very secure abode
giving shelter to
broken dreams and hurt feelings
only this house had no limits,
no boundaries, no ceilings.

Tina D Patterson
THE LAST I LOVE YOU
Last night the words
I LOVE YOU
Didn't slide easily
from your lips.

For the first time
since we've been together
you had trouble saying this.

Has the time come so soon
for us to part,
and happiness lies ahead
in someone else's heart?

If this time has come
I'll have to let you go,
because happiness goes together
in heart as well as soul.

Jacqui E Murphy
DEMON'S DISCIPLE
Your god was rum . . . and cold, You served him well.
As you staggered that rotting road, That led to the edge of Hell.
Eons ago, you had a heart; So small and obdurate a core.
It was the scantiest part of you,
Spirits leading contributor.
Your soul was ice, Your eyes were frost,
Your only love was demon rum,
It mattered not the cost!
You never veered from your idealism, You never once looked back.
At the endless trail you left behind,
Of your own bloody tracks.
While others suffered;
You remained perverse to their moans
Human destructor of clammy flesh, And slowly moldering bones.
I heard you onc war-red morning; On your journey towards death's door
The drunken horror of your laughter;
(A warning) I chose to ignore.
Laid to waste by your own hand, Too late now to atone
Desolate you stand on the shore beyond,
Knee-deep in the tides of brimstone.
Your god was rum . . . and cold;
You served him well.
Now only you and your advocates,
Can the devil's dues foretell.
I knew you once but when? I really couldn't recall;
As I passed by your coffin, I stopped to look twice;
I never knew you at all!

Kathy Hall
FAMILY TREE
As I close my eyes, I can see—
My big beautiful family tree
Yes, I can see the many branches of my family tree.
And, I can see in every branch, a little bit of Cherokee.

As dreams fly on
It's easy for me to see
Each branch of the family tree.

I can see all of my family
One on every branch,
With love for each other
My father, my mother, my sisters and my brothers.

Oh yes, I can see another
In the family tree
That's me—the oldest in my parents' history.

On every branch
A little bit of Cherokee.
A part of my life it's plain to see
You'll always be a special tree to me.

Kathleen Ryan Opon
MIST
(Dedicated To Jamie)
The sun, born upon the horizon
quietly floods the room with
golden honey warmth.
Lost in time, my mind wander
freely
contemplating the clear
October sky.

Gently caressed by fingers of
mist
old memories explode into
present-day reverie.
Reality, once vibrant and alive,
blurs, numbed by the intoxicating
haze.

My heart cries out in plaintive
whispers
ghosts of words adrift upon the
wind,
And your reply rings in tones of
silence
made achingly real within
my mind.

Startled, off-guard in an
ocean of illusion
I whirl drunkenly to confront
you,
to touch once again the
realness of you,
But I cannot.

Unearthly vapors swirl between us,
obscuring your image to but a
memory—
A precious dream that passed
too quickly
leaving teardrops in its wake.

Sherry Defenbaugh
HERSELF
Nighttime. She crosses into fields
often tripping over corn stubble—
not surefooted; a feeling familiar to
her

laying down in a grassy spot
facing the sky and beneath it
yet not submissive but equal;
a feeling not familiar to her

opening her raincoat to catch
raindrops with her naked body
the universe sees not bulges but
beholds a breathing creature
rain stops and crickets begin
their chorus is not seductive but
calming
clouds part as a falling star
ignites force within; a new feeling

reaching to pull long blades of grass
she begins to weave
not slippers for a child
not a scarf for her husband
but a robe she
will wear in the Daylight.

Kathryn E Crouch

Kathryn E Crouch
BEST CONTRACTOR
We are under God's construction
He's the best contractor we can find.

He will make a finished product,
The best production of its kind.

If we turn it all to Jesus
Let Him be the master key.
He will make it so rewarding
When we meet our destiny.

Orysia S Effler
LEAVES, NATURE'S CHILDREN
The leaves go tumbling o'er the ground
Like children playing tag round and round.
Scurrying here and there
Traveling everywhere.
Pushed by the wind in strange directions
Executing incredible acrobatic confections.
Until by a rake they're caught and thrown on a heap,
Onto which children leap.
Rolled upon and thrown into the air
Some leaves cling to the children's hair.
Holding on for one last ride
What a delightful place to hide.
When playing's done, picked off by gentle hands
And dumped into the nearest trash cans.
What an ignominious end.
I should have stayed with my friends.

Wes Stine
A SHADE OF MELANCHOLY BLUE
I sense a shade of
melancholy blue shadowing
my solemn, silly old self.
I shan't consider for a second
it's a secret source as a
probable cause to feel remorse,
or should I?
It's too late for regrets
so why should I sweat
for something I can't get?
Why should I cry "Too late, too
late!"?
For such is the fickleness of fate
and nothing can atone
for failures
of
the
heart.

Kristi Schmidt
THE CANDLE IN COMMON
We dwell in one candle
we each have a wick
We can't reach each other
the wax is too thick

Though the flame may extend
from your end to mine
To do so, the fire
would make us both blind

The burn of the flame left
my wick singed and weak
Are the threads of our wicks
e'er destined to meet

Consume melted wax and
float free to my heart
Ere candle is melted
and wicks fall apart

Daisy E Hoopes
TOBACCO IS A TERRIBLE WEED
Tobacco is a terrible weed,
from the devil it proceeds.
Stinks your pockets,
smells your clothes.
And makes a chimney of your nose.

Margaret B Ignich
YESTERDAY
Yesterday slipped past me like a bird, a huge black bird.
One with enormous wings that covered the sky and left me without even a shadow.
If it could have lost but one feather and let a tiny ray of sunshine pass through, I could have raised my tired head and looked forward to tomorrow.
But what is tomorrow? Something that follows yesterday.
A place we put neglected things. And then another place to look forward to.
Does it matter when it comes?
Sometimes too early, sometimes too late for some, and then never for others.
Today, the blackbird left with his enormous wings and morning rose above the lake and creatures there and here moved slowly, bending the grass underfoot.
Tomorrow is here now and they . . . whoever they are . . . call it today.
Two syllables everyone lives for.
Here it is now, and if we wait too long, it becomes yesterday and all the yesterdays become memories. A lot of people live on memories alone.
They're alright, but if we hang on to yesterday too long, today or tomorrow never really come.

Janice A Thompson
WHEN NONE COMMAND
By surging sea and force of wind
A tattered vessel floundered in
Where coral reef performed the rest
In ripping wide her wooden breast.
From timber scream to cracking mast
Her form dismembered to the last
And on the waves her pieces reached
An aftermath of slumber, beached.
She is a silent reprimand
To those who sail when none
command.

Christine M Hoffmann
LOVING YOU
Although it's only been one day,
I miss you more than words could
say.

Just one thought of you—no matter
how slight—
Warms my heart, all through the
night!

George A Rojas
HEARTBEAT
He walks North
She walks South
Heartbeat
He glances at her
She glances at him
Heartbeat
He stops, then he looks into her eyes
She stops, then she looks into his
eyes
Heartbeat
He speaks to her
She replies to him
Heartbeat

He sees and hears only her
She sees and hears only him
Heartbeat
The world around them doesn't exist
The world between them is of only
value
Heartbeat
She turns and walks with him, North
Heartbeat . . .

Julie R Bassett Meyer
LOST LOVE
Our time was short, but we had fun
Our memories are not a waste.
We shared the good and the bad
But our love was made in haste.

Now there's hurt and broken
promises
So our love went out the door.

As hard as we try to get it back
It seems there's just no more.

Although it hurts to say goodbye
I feel it just must be.
At least for awhile for us to see
Who's you and what is me!

But there's a child in this deal
That we must always share.
She needs our love and our time
And she needs our total care.

And it's for her that we must stay
Friends throughout all time.
We must let her know tho we're apart
That everything is fine.

So remember me when you look at her
And remember the time we shared.
Although I'm not there to tell you myself
I swear I really cared.

Roberta A Walker
SOUNDS OF DEATH

In memory of Ken, August 16, 1983.

The sounds of death:
The screech of tires too late
The thump and crunch of metal.
The clash and spray of glass.
The screams of witnesses.
The urgent voices from help.
And the quiet sobs from the man as he dies.

Steve Perkins
PUERITIA INVENTA
What do you want to do?
I don't know. What do you
Want to do?
Silence—a swirling, soundless force
That envelopes us like snow, dusted
Blue by swift-waning sun, that
Blankets a house with crackling
hearth
In January.

Playground equipment.
Nine-o'clock p.m. April.
Floating high—swooping back—
Two thin chains forming a bridge
To Reality.

Ruth S Ozanich
LOST LOVE
Now you are gone,
And all the things I should have said,
I did not say.
Now you are gone, forever, far away.

I should have said,
"I love you and I need you dear!"
For all my tears,
Will never fill these long and empty years.

I should have said,
"Life would be no good without you!"
For it is true,
But now, there's not one thing that I can do.

No words of love,
No tender words can call you back,
So I must wait,
And hope there'll be a Resurrection Day.

When I can beg
You to forgive me, and forget the past.
God grant that day,
When I can tell you all I want to say.

Jacquelin Tripp
TRUE
They say distance
makes the heart
grow fonder

But love, true love
will keep your together

The trust, real trust
you won't worry if
they're with someone

No matter how far apart
you are
They're always with you

To have
and to hold
forever
and a day

That is love
True love

Sandy A Huey
HERE COMES THE STORM
Laying on the wet sand next to the ocean. Watching the moon look upon me and the waves crashing on the rocks.
Sounds of sea gulls calling out in search of their nest. Glowing red eyes peeking through the bushes near the oak trees.
Watching the mother turtle laying her eggs in the sand next to me. Then watching her leave slowly back into the deep ocean blue. How sad she must be.
I lay and watch the shooting stars above me. How playful they become at night.
I drift and drift into everlasting peace, until dark clouds surround my world. Swallowing the stars and the moon and making the ocean grow wild and angry.
What did I do? I did nothing wrong!
Thunder and lightning, pounding and crashed of the winds.
It's my own mind I realize that is wandering around crazily.
How can that be?

Barbara Jordan
A HOMELESS HURT
With the tiny buds of spring
Was pledged the golden-shining dream

Summer's promise tilled the life
Filled with children-struggles-strife

Autumn's harvest then was come
In varied hues the dream seemed won
But a mourning wind darked the sun

When Winter's Thief the one heart stole
The other iced eternally cold

Ashes of a golden dream
Stir only in a muddled stream

This one's mind
Alone can know
The endless trek of

Half a soul

Kevin Boyce
THE SEASONS

Dedicated to Mr. and Mrs. Connel Boyce Late.

Roses bloom in summer
Pussy willow appears in autumn
The maples a'hue in the fall
Roses bloom once more in summer

Barbara Jean Smith

Barbara Jean Smith
THE CRYSTAL'S CRACKED

I dedicate "Lessons In Traditions" to my daughters Laurie & Lynnie. A special thanks to Bill for encouraging me. Loving gratitude to Mom & Granny. "The Crystal's Cracked" is dedicated to my special friends and family back in Texas. P.S. Thank-you Daddy!!!

Sometimes as we walk through Life, we're just looking through old glass.
The reflection it reveals to us is unhappiness, so to ourselves we ask?
Why can't I find some happiness, peace of mind, and honest Love?
Why can't I soar like an eagle, have wings, and fly to the Heavens above?

I have tried the very best in Life, to please each one and all.
But it seems that every step I take, I just stumble or I fall.
Then one day you meet that someone special, and that old glass looks like sparkling crystal.
You feel re-born again, you start to sing, and sometimes you even whistle.

But if that Crystal is not cared for, something goes wrong, and it gets cracked.
No matter what you try to do, it's just not the same when it's pieced back.
Just like a Rose in the Springtime, as the petals start falling to the ground.
You wonder what is happening, where is the happiness you thought you had found?

For the reality of a daydream, now has become a dreaded nightmare to you.
For "The Crystal's Cracked" the petals have fallen, there's nothing left you can do.
Those little Butterflies of excitement have left you, yes, they now are gone.
So with a crying Heart, you ask yourself, how could you have been so wrong?

Now all that's left to the Rose, is just the stem, which is filled with only Thorns.
So you Pray for strength, and ask for help for that old 'Love' to be re-born.
But "The Crystal's Cracked" the heart is broke, yet Life goes on the same.
Now I am back behind, that old piece of Glass, just like a fool, where I'll remain!!!

Barbara Jean Smith
LESSONS IN TRADITIONS
Just be cautious in what you wish for, 'cause your wishes just might come true.
Always do unto others, as you would have them do unto you.
Learn to never say never, for you just might have to swallow those words.
Speak softly and walk lightly, yet stand tall and proud, so you may be heard.

If you should make someone a promise, this is something that you must try to keep.
Always respect your elders, and say your prayers before you go to sleep.
Give thanks for all of your Blessings, learn to share, and Love your neighbors too.
Show them some kindness and compassion in everything that you do.

Now this is what my Mother taught me, so I pass this on to you.
You must teach this to your children, for it's the traditional thing to do.
For the one treasure that I have to leave to you, is just a chest that's filled with my 'Love.'
As I depart from this old earth and fly to the Heavens up above.

For I have no Gold or Silver, just a box of old memories.
Filled with snapshots and old clippings of the way that things used to be.
So to my two lovely Daughters, keep this advice close to your Heart.
Plus as Sisters you must promise, to always stick together and never to part.

For you both will share so much laughter and some bitter tears, lots of happiness, and yes some sorrow.
So be wise, and think with pride, for in your footsteps your children will follow.
For these "Lessons In Traditions" are for generations yet to come.
So many thanks to 'Mom' and 'Grandma' for all their wisdom, as all these deeds of 'Love' shall be done.

Maria Padgett
CHRISTILLA

To my wonderful mother Matilda, my loving husband Bud, and my beautiful children. All have made my world brighter, and my life worth living.

She's a rosebud waiting to bloom
She's growing up so fast
I wish I could make time stop
And make her childhood last.

At times I know I'm hard on her
But, I'm trying to raise her right
There are times I'm not so sure
If she'll ever see the light.

She doesn't understand all the things I do
And maybe one day she'll see
I'm trying to give her all I can
And be the best mother I can be.

Christilla you mean the world to me
Always remember I truly love you
I'm just trying to make you see
Sometimes in this world you'll be blue.

Tara Jeannette Frates
SALON
The exhibit, one of food
Displaying only good and perfect
Clean straight plates
Geometric and glazed
Made for the day of judging
Details erased mistakes for
Discussion and ridicule with
compliments
Vulnerable was the craftsman
Challenging his innards with sauce of
blood
Risked for the ribbon
Powerless they listen
Awaiting their pride's critique
Silver wasn't gold for the unsatisfied
For gold he had come
To keep him moving forward
Stronger was his heart whose love
Picked up and scraped the plate.

Rachel Monday
UNSEEN

To those "unseen" yet ever present, wherever life may find you.

In life you will find those
who are left unseen.
Those who stay in the back row,
Those who step aside.
They never really know where
they are,
Yet they wonder where they've been.

There he is waiting, for what is not
known
All he knows is he's growing old.
The world spins around him, there's
no one
behind him.
He's alone in the back of his mind.

He's in the darkness; he is the
audience
The others are playing their parts.
They're acting on the stage of life.

Familiar faces through memories he
sees,
Names flash but he just can't place
them.
There he remains unseen.

In life you will find, he's waiting
just waiting.
He's the audience apart from the
crowd
He's there in the darkness where he
can't
find himself
He's alone, and he's growing old.

Raquel Avitia
REFLECTIONS

I've travelled down many a road, seen and done many a thing, but whenever my heart leads me home, I always think of you three. To my lifelong friends, Rene Darbyshire, Linda Perez and Vicky Duron.

The road is long; time is short
And on this earth we pass but once
Neither time nor countless storms
Can erase that footprint in the dust.

So make haste before bells toll
Where mornings rush to setting suns
Before the summers all turn cold
And none of us are left behind.

Hand in hand begin to walk
Thus tame the sands of time
Mold that future in your hands
While making life a rhyme.

Bottle up your troubles
With faith and hope then look ahead
For the future is a doorway
Where broken dreams can mend.

Then someday, in years to come
You'll look back upon yourself
And find a beautiful reflection
Of a life that's been lived well.

Cecilia T Picker
A PASSING ACQUAINTANCE
It happens sometimes on my morning
walks;
a stray cat or dog,—I'll be
meeting;
and maybe it's only I,—all day,—
who,
has stopped to exchange words of
greeting.

And e'en though we speak dif'rent
languages,
I feel sure that we both
understand;
that it doesn't matter what words we
use;
it engenders a feeling quite grand.

The cat says 'meow,' and rubs 'gainst
my leg,
where I clearly can feel the
'purring';
though, when frightened, at times,—a
cat may run
and a closer friendship,—
demurring.

A dog quickly smiles, and he'll wag
his tail,
and so often, he'll walk at my side.
Still, there'll always be one, who'll
ignore me,
makes no difference how hard I
tried.

But I will continue to talk to them,
e'en though many may fail to
agree;
and hope that when I am old,—and
'alone,'
somebody will stop,—and talk to
me.

Franklin August Picker
BELIEVING THE UNBELIEVABLE
Ev'ry day is a day of wonder,
when I lift up my eyes to see;
an omnipotent God's handiwork,
which also includes—'you and
me.'

Thousands of galaxies in the sky,
and He added the planet,
'EARTH';
our own blue planet hanging in space,
where we may establish our worth.

The universe will ever remain
humanly—unbelievable;
'til faith takes over in human minds,
and makes it—'believable.'

Who are we,—bits of dust and clay;
can we know what is in God's
mind?
Can our knowledge ever equal His;
are His secrets for us to find?

Let's acknowledge the Great Creator,
give Him worship and praises,
due;
ask His mercy, and His forgiveness,
through His Son, and our Savior,
too.

Franklin August Picker
WHAT LEGACY LEAVE WE
Remember, we must, — with a
poignant recall,
when fortune and fame seemed the
point of it all;
as we marched in cadence, — to
world's metered rhyme,
and self, we surrendered, — to
peer pressured time.

Too well, we remember, the pointless
charade,
as days of our lives passed in
endless parade;
and in struggling to reach the top of
the hill,
we seldom considered the size of
the bill.

However elusive, — success was the
goal;
whatever the cost, — and
whatever the role.
Ego, adulation, — steroids for the
brave;
propelled us e'er forward, from
cradle to grave.

When mothers and fathers gave life
to our dust,
their fond expectations were
placed in our trust.
Have we used, — or abused; — how
will we be weighed;
and on life's report card, — what
then be our grade?

In 'letters' or mustic, — explorer or
king;
to our page in hist'ry, — what
credits we bring?
What legacy, leave we, — to those
who would learn;
while pond'ring our ashes, —
ensconced in an urn?

Annabelle Van Kleeck
TAKE TIME
When did you take time
to look toward the west,
on that special given day
as the sun goes to rest?

To see the cycle of everchanging
colors;
Violet, Orchid, Chartreuse and
Blue,
makes one wonder how it all
came true,
as the sun goes to rest.

Often a Halo is observed as a
crown,
the sight is magnificent
when we look to the west,
as the sun goes to rest.

Remember—take time
to look toward the west
and see for yourself,
as the sun goes to rest.

Annabelle Van Kleeck
GOD'S DAY AGAINST THE AZURE BLUE SKY
'Tis a lovely sight in the early
morning
to watch the sun arise, burning off
the dew, then making its way
among
the clouds, to silhouette itself
against the azure blue sky.

The morning progresses into
mid-afternoon,
then evening follows as the earth
becomes shaded from the day's
sun rays.

On into the night the sun goesto rest,
making way for starlight and
moonlight
at their best, just as if a dream had
come to life.

GOD, in HIS Eternal glory, made it
all comes to pass. This we give
thanks from day one to the last.

Leslie Manning
BUS DRIVER
Silver, matted hair is in her eyes.
Loud screeching in the background,
kids of all ages.
Driving down the road,
the cool mist of rain
fogs up her view.
Her warm, but coarse, hands
grip the steering wheel,
in hopes of making it to
her destination on time.
As the yelling crowd
begins to scatter,
one child looks back
just to see a familiar, mother-like
smile
that brightens his dark, elementary
morning.

Michael Lee Hardy Sr
FLIGHT
Like a plane in flight, supported by its forward motion. It cannot stop without falling. As we soar through time only holding the space we're in. Suspended in this place and time sustained by our hopes and dreams.

With our hope and faith, we must move forward, for this flight we must take for its part of our life. For as time moves on, we must vacate this place in time.

As this force within us speaks like a mighty wind. We move quickly to understand the things in our lives.

As we sojourn from the past and move into today. Inspired by the picture of life, we draw and see. Foremost must this all vanish on or is hope and grace always alive in us.

Morris L Miller
MY DEEPEST LOVE
I saw my Savior Crucified for me last night.
Upon the cross just to my right.
It all began with the break of light,
no man could really know his fright.

As by my side he trudged up the hill,
I begged him why.
He simply spoke, 'Tis the Father's will.
Deeper and deeper my anguish grew,
What could I do to change this thing?
If I only knew.

Atop the hill they lay him on the cross
And began to nail him to that cross.
As the hammer would strike the nail
My pain grew deeper and deeper, I felt my hell.
How can I go on from here, if I do not try,
To take your place on the cross to die?

His eyes they whispered back to me,
I do this out of my deepest love for thee.
If you go through life and remember this,
Then show forth this love to others is my wish.

I bear this pain each day I live
for I know how much was his to give.
My deepest love he spoke to me
is the greatest gift I have to give and now I give it all to thee.

Morris L Miller
YOUTH
A young man stood a looking out
what did he see through his doubt.
Was his future bright or bleak
how could I tell he was so meek.

Oh soul of mine do you really care
if so step proudly up take the dare.
Reach out oh arms and pull him in
do all you can to help him win.

As through your actions here on earth
you may not know just what it's worth.
I say of thee oh friend of mine
ask not of me is it worth my time.

For in his eyes look deep you'll see
just a simple younger you or me.

Morris L Miller
HER HONOR MY FLAG
She waved so fervently in Amber Blue Sky
each ripple whe made, said, I will not die.
Try as they would they could not bring her down
that lovely Lady, that waved above our town.

Now as the years have come and gone
this Lovely Lady still waves on.
Not one can tell all she has seen
as she waves so proudly on ever scene.

Oh how I Love my Lady Red, White and Blue
to thee I will pledge, to ever be true.
Wave on dear Love so valiantly each day
wave over our children as they play.

When the time has come, your tattered and torn
I'll give thee a hero's rest, for all you've born.
Oh now my love again I pledge thee
as here at my feet, a proper rest I give thee.

Carolyn K Dunn
THE DAY I WIN
The day I grasp the winnings of some distant lottery,
I shall go out and purchase the neatest pottery,
I'll go home so happy, and sit down upon the grass,
And thank the LORD for bringing this to pass.

After I have won, I shall become more thin,
For I won't feel so hungry as I did before the win.
I'll own a hundred acres, and I'll plant some shrubs and trees,
I'll feel so good about myself I won't be hard to please.

The day I win, the wind will blow so kind,
A faithful, loving spirit will be with me all the time.
I'll buy a Porsche, and three mink coats, and take me for a spin,
On the day that GOD is with me so much I really win.

There'll be a pasture there, and lambs, and shady pool,
And GOD will love me just as much, or better, seeing I'm no fool.
Then when it's dark, I'll light a candle and invite a friend,
And lock the door, and romance until daybreak without sin,
The day I really win

Chuck Michael Borres
RATS ON MY RAFTERS
Sitting home alone, waiting by my phone,
No one ever calls, I hear noises in my walls.
I can no longer wait,
And decide to investigate.
Nothing do I find,
It must be in my mind.
Finally to sleep I fall,
Only to be awakened by a call.
I've got rats on my rafters and they're coming after me,
It's so dark and I can't see.
Now they say I've gone insane,
And that I no longer know my name.
I tell them that they are wrong,
And to this place I do not belong.
Here comes the nurse again,
With a shot and medicine.
Finally to sleep I fall,
Only to be awakened by a call.
I'm afraid the rats are there again,
Maybe you'll hear them one day, my friend.

Faye Scoggins Bigelow
AMERICA SPEAKS
Wagon Wheels! broken, bleached by sun and rain
Abandoned along a sandy, forgotten trail.
Wagon wheels! mute testimony
Of pioneers who carved and built an empire
With nothing to soften the load.
Now memories hover 'round you,
Revealing the spirit once so alive, so dominate.
The spirit that forged into reality
Dreams, determination, vision and faith
Born of the unknown and beckoning frontier,
Now a symbol of deeds and feats of early days.
You give strength and courage to man,
Renewing his faith in himself and God.
Wagon wheels! broken deserted, mirroring the past
But also mirroring the future,
Where-in men can take heart
And restore to a troubled and weary world
Nobility of honest labor
And the beauty and compassion of Human Service
The Great American Dream.

Kimberley Kramer
CRACKING THE SHELL
Beneath my jagged edges and rough ways,
There lies a softness seldom seen by anyone.
Yes, even I have feelings,
Though my bitter sarcasm and death looks
Can scare demons away.
My strength has proven to be a great asset
For surviving, but not for loving.
Please tame me,
And take away the spark of hatred
That lies beneath years of pain.
Please love me,
So kindness will pour of my heart,
And hostility will be afraid to darken my door.

Gladys V Moss
HUGO'S FURY (Hurricane)

Dedicated to: Gov. Carroll A. Campbell, The People of S. C., America, and well wishes around the world. In Loving Memory of The Deceased.

One day before Autumn, September eighty nine,
Things in South Carolina seemed to be going fine:
Nature was dressed in its beauty,
Until Hugo came with its fury.

The winds and the waves did not obey
It blasted the Port City as it came ashore:
The Governor issued an executive order
To save needless drowning in dangerous water.

Hugo destroyed homes, business, schools and bridges
Other property, trees and damaged land:
A number of lives,
Were lost by Nature's hand.

A special salute to our "Governor"
A dedicated fellow, he deserves a "Gold Medal":
To the "Families," lost by Hugo's scorn,
May God bless you, And that September morn.

Loretta Vogel

Loretta Vogel
STEPS

This poem is dedicated to my husband Jon, and our children, Allena, Jon, Troy.

THE spark of GOD comes within,
and we will always walk with Him . . .
Side by side, don't you see, his footprints are in front of me.
The earth is a school to learn,
to love, and every good deed, you do or say . . .
You're making your steps along, the way . . .
We might have to come back to
the earth again, if we miss a
step now and then . . .
But to be sure, you will always know, we will never walk . . .
ALONE . . .

Loretta Vogel
LORD
Thank You Lord . . .
For letting us see your face,
with every dawn and sunset.
And giving us knowledge how
to serve you, letting us know you,
and love you.
Thank You Lord . . .
For letting us stand before your
light, knowing each act and thought,
brings us closer to you and your kingdom.
Thank You Lord . . .
For letting us know the purpose which,
we have entered this world.
To love one another, for we are as one,
with you.
Thank You Lord . . .
For letting us know that, the loving,
touch on our shoulder, is your hand.
The comforting voice is your voice,
and the glory we see, is your glory.
Letting us know, we don't move without you.

Sandra Peterson
HELP ME

To all those who believed, Ily.

Help me discover the way to the light
To conquer the problems in my life
Where there is no prejudice, and no lies
No confusion, or children's cries

Help me find a place where there is love
A shoulder to lean and peace from above
If shadows should guide me
Let them be true
If fantasies are my world
Let them be my clue
I have seen tomorrows
They are like my yesterdays
Help me find the place that I seek
My body is tired, my spirit is weak
Sometimes it is hard to get by a day
Having faith in yourself is the only way
You are the one a challenge will meet
Having trust in yourself is the only defeat

Bonnie M Brown
SO SMALL, SO SWEET, SO SOON!

Dedicated to the wonderful doctors and nurses in the neo-natal section of the Sacred Heart Hospital in Eugene, Oregon, and also to my family and friends who were there when I needed them most.

I was blessed with a child of only one pound
Who struggled and fought to hold his own ground.
Thank God for those who helped him survive
So small, so precious, and hurting to be alive.
Needles, tubes, respiratory equipment and all,
To me he was a beautiful 12-inch doll.
Special loving nurses gave their whole hearts to him,
Twenty-four hours a day even as things looked dim.
Doctors who devoted their lives to his cause,
Rarely getting sleep or a moment's pause.
A full 10 weeks and at last 2 pounds,
He left us without ever making a sound.
The sorrow I feel will never ever leave me,
It'll lessen with time, like things were meant to be.
I'm thankful at least that I had him that long,
He was born of pure love and that love is not gone.
Memories I have will be with me forever,
So I will go on living and forgetting him never.

Laura M Greenfield
ENGLAND'S GLORY

In memory of Marjorie Grant, my grandmother.

England's countryside is the place for me
The green rolling hills like an untamed sea
A foggy moist day with the smell of rain in the air
And friendly people who take time to care

The herds of cattle with their bells ringing
Flocks of birds sweetly singing
The rumbling by of horse-drawn carts
And the freshly made smell of lemon tarts

Little thatched houses painted bright white
Towering castles stand tall in the night
The warmth of a fireplace in a cozy den
When you hear the far off chiming of Big Ben

Don Chering
AURA

For Sandee!

For what reason did this immortal Rose
bring its Fragrance into my unkept Garden
That I may drink the sweetest of her petals
during the hardest of Winter days
Ever bright and sacred halos, in dashing flames
Bursting forth with unequaled glory
Refining my unpure remains.

Sandee Tschida
HEARTFELT

My friend and lover sleeping at my side.
He rests ever so peaceful knowing I am near.
But does he know how much he's truly loved, in his silent slumber.
Does he feel my admiring eye upon his cheek, lashes and lips.
Could the secure warmth felt in my heart ever be felt with anyone else?
This one, he is truly a friend, way beyond compare!

David W Pangborn
THE SENECUOUS NESTOR

To the Memory of: Cliff Renfro, and to Stephanie.

The senecuous Nestor
sitting
rumply doubled-over,
squished in his chair,
like a macerated 86-year-old fig
having been run over
by a Mack truck,
was drifting in an ancient,
jerking, distant sleep,
soundly losing control,
toppling with his head,
rushing to meet the concrete,
as do head-on collisions
on wrong-way freeways,
going south
forever.

Mary K Zuck
THE BLACK MEMORIAL

I visited that long black memorial once
It was one late day in early fall.
A quiet hush hung over that solemn place
Where many names were etched in gold
upon that dark stone wall.

Many parents, sons, daughters and also friends
had come to honor and to remember their loved ones there.
I searched and found your name, and remembering
I knelt there in silent prayer.

I placed a single rose, a bright red rose
Beneath your name upon the mossy green grass there
To signify my love for you and I believe you heard,
And know how very much I cared.

Dear ones you are not forgotten now
I can see you in the mystic view from here.
You may have been forgotten for awhile,
But to me, you know you never were my Dear.

And so, farewell "Dear Ones,"
Some time, some place perhaps
We shall meet upon some ethereal, higher plane
And your having died for Honor and for Truth
We know, never a one has ever died in vain!

Eveline T Good
COMMITMENT

Marriage, is the joy of love
Two lives combined in one.
A plan that sovereign love and grace
Could see the works well done.
No place for schism or debate
When promises divine are made
But, love that suffers long is kind;
Love envies not, nor is afraid
Love seeks God's best, for full accord
True love don't fault or fail or flee
But walks in God's humility
For I am you and you are me
And we are one.

Eveline T Good
VISITOR

He went away so silently,
He never said, "Good-bye," to me.
He never smiled nor clasped my hand,
Just hastened to some distant land
In search of treasures I've been told
Of value greater far than gold.

He never took a thing that day.
They were the same when he went away.
No change of clothes was out of place.
No sign that he my home did grace.
Although he's gone, he's still a part,
A treasured memory in my heart.

Carol Skowronski
BUZZING BEE

To my loving family.

There was a little buzzing bee
Who flew and flew around a tree.
He stopped on a flower to say, "hello,"
Then he hurried; he had to go.

Barbara L Baumann
SO MANY

To my Darling Peter David Hernandez. I thank you for your love and our darling daughter, Ashley Renee.

So many things to say,
With life changing every day,
So many people living today,
Some of them in the most unusual way.
Looking at life and trying to see,
If there's anyone simple-minded like me.
Life's so simple, take a moment and see,
It could be so easy, believe me . . .
Once you notice this you'll see,
Life's so simple,
Just like
Me . . . . . .

Jennifer Gail Baxter
HOLDING ON

Dedicated to my family, friends and my beloved Robert.

Holding on to love; holding on to you
Holding on to something that in my heart is true.

Holding on to the tears, cried both day and night
Holding on to the hurt; holding on tight!

Holding on to my heart, though it tears me apart
Holding on to the cupid that bares his last dart.

Holding on to the statements racing through my mind . . .
Holding on to the feelings, someday you may find.

Holding on to the laughter, someday we may share
Holding on to the hope—someday you may care.

Holding on to someone who means more than just a 'friend,'
holding on for always—until the very end.

Holding on to these four words
"I love you so"
Holding on forever . . .
never letting go.

Marideth Rochelle Bulkley
MORNING CRY

To my husband, Vern and my son, Dane. You are my joyful sunrise.

The lid ripped off the jagged night—
Leaving,
A torn and ice blue sky—
Hanging,
Above purple shadowed monsters,
Slumbering in sharp-toothed sleep.
The light comes liquid pulsing,
Pouring over mount and sky,
Rounding bleeding edges—
Until nights' image fades crying away.
And the giants groan and rumble,
At the cold coming . . .

Of a new morn.

Nichole Butler
GREEN MEADOW

To my Wonderful Mom Who I Love Dearly.

The green meadow smelled like freshly cut grass. When I walked I heard the branches crack under my feet. I could smell the fresh clean air like freshly baked bread. I felt the cool breeze gush through my hair.
I FELT IT WAS PEACEFUL

Jean Brewer
PRECIOUS GIFTS FROM GOD

To my children and grandchildren, that they may know and share my love for each of them.

Precious gifts are very rare
given by God for us to share.
Little ones to light our life
bring joy in place of strife.
Shining, smiling faces
rays of sunshine in all cases.
Small and wonderful to behold
grandchildren, priceless as gold.
Rainbows of sparkling eyes
smiles that are not disguised.
Memories from the far past,
moments of happiness that last.
Tears fill my eyes as I recall
their first steps, and endless falls.
Rewards in this world are few and far
none as precious as grandchildren are.
Thank you God for these gifts of joy
grandchildren—girls and boys.

Debbie Fisher
COME EVERY SEPTEMBER
Three long years at the end of September
Wonder fills me as I allow myself time to remember.
Yearnings, pain and the driving force
Of that magic potion needed to simply exist
Living for the moment, longing for that rush
Needs so intense I was unable to resist
Aches of muscle and mind overrule soul and conscience
Anxiety fills me as the date draws near.
This old "jones" fills my eyes with tears.
Every single day that old urge is felt
Even now the feelings of urgency and desperation
Are at hand,
On the streets, known as just another junkie,
In treatment, labeled an addict, informed of my disease.
A gorilla pounding on my back, once a baby monkey.
Will I forever feel this way?
Or is this empty feeling the price I must pay?
Lord, I pray I can make it just one more day.

Sharon A Badgley
PAPER AIRPLANES

Dedicated to the 1989-1990 JETS TEAM of Bogan High School, Chicago, Illinois.

Paper airplanes gliding through the school halls.
If you see one, reach out and grab one before it enters free fall.
Swoop it up, pitch it down, and watch it fly.
Loop to loop and spin around,
That's a paper airplane coming down I spy.

Sarah D Crance
YOUR EYES
Your eyes
which I had worshipped
have glanced away.
Their browness
has become numb,
you no longer can see.

Your hands
which I had held gently
have caught my heart.
Their roughness
has torn my insides,
you no longer caress.

Your soul
which I had admired
has melted.
Its wax being
has ceased all-together.
You no longer are here.
And I, I am bewildered.

Miriam Lee Bostock
ABRUPT

All my love to Mom, Dad, Michael, Arron, Matthew, Kim, Walter, Joshua and the Carratt family. I love you Craig!

I simmer in a warm, soft bed;
She shivers in a cold, hard chair.
I eat a hot breakfast;
She drinks cold tea from the night before.
I feel full all day long;
She feels sharp needles pricking inside.
I look forward to dinner;
She tries to ignore the word "food."
I eat a hot meal;
She unwillingly suffers.
I feel healthy;
She becomes weak.
I become stronger;
She suddenly grows ill.
I live—
She dies.

Neena Kathryn Bachik
WITH ALL MY LOVE FOR YOU

Cookie, For the many years of friendship, the special times spent together . . . we've shared so much, and I love you for it—Neen.

I sit here thinking,
thinking of my friend,
thinking of the letters that
she promises to send.

I know that she thinks of me beyond a shadow of my doubt,
but I wish she would let me know,
—if she could just write it out.

Often we don't think we have the time to write a line or two,
but if friendships are important—
is that really true?

This special friend of mine,
I love her very much,
I care about how she is feeling—
why won't she keep in touch?

There are many kinds of letters,
written all the time,
but not all have the promise
of the one I will describe.

In the beginning God created us,
He made us out of love,
to be a part of His special plan—
it was us He was thinking of.

But He knew that He would need a way,
a way that He could show,
the story of His love for us—
a way that we could know.

So He wrote to us a love letter,
saying we are precious in His sight,
now we can be happy—
because He took the time to write.

I wrote this poem for my special friend,
I hope that she can see,
in all the things we do for others—
it's love that is the key.

Cookie, I love you very much,
I told you I would try,
to help you find a way to write—
I wanted to take the time.

Now the rest is up to you,
I feel I've done my best,
I hope that you will try to write—
I think inside you would be blessed.

With All My Love For You,
Neena

Jay D "Dutch" Bedell
BLOOD AND ROSES

In memory of Ann Camaria (Cuffin) Naputi of Marina, CA, born February 20, 1962 in Korea; died 25 July 1988. Rest in peace, Annie. I love you.

Deep, abiding, eternal love—
Covered by a carpet of blood and roses—
The pain and suffering of such monumental tragedy
Are blinding my eyes and numbing my mind,
Petrifying me to hardest flint
And turning my heart to coldest steel.
Life is meaningless in the shadow of Ann's death—
Each day drifting by as the sands of Time
Run endlessly through the Great Hourglass,
Each grain of sand marking
A pinpoint of my agony.
When, oh Lord, will you call me home
To experience the joy of Your presence
And the companionship of my gentle friend?
May the Lord Jesus Christ bless Ann
With His love and salvation for all eternity.
Heartbroken, and without hope of deliverance
I walk a dark and lonely path through life
Blanketed by a carpet of Blood and Roses.

Karen J Booth
CHILDLESS

In memory of: Michael Andrew Booth. Born: September 13, 1989 6:59 AM. Died: September 13, 1989 10:05 AM.

Loneliness overtakes me
Everytime I think of my child
He was given to me
But only for a little while
He never got a chance
To understand a mother's love
He was called home to God above
I never heard
My baby cry
I could only ask
Dear God why?
Why me, when there's so much
My baby needed a mother's touch
He needed someone
To wipe away his tears
Someone to hold him
And take away his fears
There's so much I
Wanted to give
But now all I wish
Is my child had lived.

Miriam Garns

Miriam Garns
CHALLENGE
Sometimes my thoughts are blank and slow,
The wheels and cogs refuse to go.
At other times I start to write,
The words just flow and seem to fight
To be the first to open the door
Of my mind; They tumble o'er
And o'er like fiery sparks
From smitten anvil in the dark.
They push and shove and clamor when
I try to write them with my pen;
Like mighty, gushing waters flow,
No urgent need to prod the slow.

I would that all the days were such,
So easy to accomplish much;
Profusely then I'd use my pen,
And dread to lay it down again.
But such is life; it's in the test
We strive and try to do our best;
If goals were easy to attain,
No challenge e'er to push and gain.

Benita Bohler
WORDS FOR SOMEONE WISE TO KEEP UP THEIR STRIVE

This poem is dedicated to my Family, as well as friends to hold on and don't give up.

Sometimes the roads are hard to bear,
but knowing at the end what you
were seeking for was always there.

Sometimes you come to a stop sign
not knowing what to do,
but being the wise person you are,
you have to sit back, think, decide
and choose.

that's why I know in my heart, that if
you keep on striving you can't lose.

Even though you may pick the road
with a heavy load,
you can always take a shorter route,
but you'll never know what the end
of the road was all about.

Clint N Blackburn
TONIGHT

This poem is dedicated to my lovely wife, Kari, through whose eyes and heart it was written and her mother, Marie, whom I did not have the pleasure to have met, but would like to thank for raising such a loving daughter.

Tonight
A life has slipped away
Barely time to touch
But touch she did
So sweet was the love she gave
So cruel the way she was taken from
me
When life is taken from you
It makes you more aware
Aware of its true meaning
Of how special life is
The life of a best friend
I will always remember the way she
lived
Through eternity the way she loved
For part of me has gone with her
To her own special place in heaven
Memories must never fade
For you must cling to them
As this is the only thing they cannot
steal
My best friend will always be here
with me
Although she has gone away
Tonight

Nicole (Boehm) Archer
MY FATHER

In Memory of Eric Anthony Boehm. Feb. 4, 1952—Dec. 5, 1981.

Shot by a gun
Dropped to the ground
Lies my father
Beneath a soft mound.

The mound is the ocean
The ocean is the grave
Lies my dearest father
The man that was always brave.

Floating along, with
The ocean's great flow
Lies the clear ashes
Which shine my father's glow.

Floating within the ocean
Spreading and feeling free
For is my dear father
Living on, in the great sea.

Margurite Bishop
MOMS

This is dedicated to mothers everywhere, especially to my loving mother Nola Waltrip.

Moms are special people their job is
never done
When one day is over another's just
begun
Moms have many jobs just to name a
few
Moms do many things to show her
love for you
Moms are teachers and leaders to
show you the way
To be the type of person that you are
today
Moms are like doctors and nurses
They take care of cuts, burns and
bruises
Moms are confidants and counselors
they listen and advise
Sometimes it's hard to believe that
moms are very wise
Moms have many jobs all rolled into
one
For which they don't get paid until
the job is done
They don't get paid with money
'cause money is not enough
The only way to pay a mom is to
return it all with love
Moms are special people their job is
never done
When one day is over another's just
begun

Peggy J Burrows
LIFE IS GRAND

I dedicate this poem to my husband, Bill and all my family and good friends. For without them life would not be so grand.

A feeling of happiness, sadness and
joy,
Sometimes a twinkle in the eye, like
a child with a new toy.
Then there's an emptiness, that seems
so deep,
It makes you want to cry, so all you
can do is weep.
But; then something happens, to
bring you out of the slump,
You feel joyous and proud, it makes
you leap and jump.
And the world around you, well, it's
not so bad,
You've got a lot going for you, so
don't be so sad.
Life will never be all sunshine and no
rain,
And it was never promised, that
you'd have no pain.
Make the best of what you have and
never look back,
Don't carry your troubles around in a
sack.
Keep your eyes on the future and
look straight ahead,
For if you didn't have problems:
You'd probably be dead.
You see, God holds the world in the
palm of His hand,
Look up to Him, smile and say; Ain't
life grand.
You know there's always someone
that has it rougher than you,
I'm sure if you looked, you'd find
quite a few.
Learn from your mistakes, and try as
hard as you can,
Because you do have life and ain't it
grand.

Laura T Currie
A SHARED SENTIMENT

Take an idea, let it go.
Allow it to build, rise and grow.

A balloon in the sky
Floats silent, bobbing up high.

Wild winds of thought
Propel the balloon where it ought.

Though should the winds halt,
The balloon will fall and fault.

Little and large pieces scatter about.
Await their rebuilding, there is no
doubt.

Pick up the pieces, hold them tight.
Together they fit—making a kite

Hold on, and watch it soar.
Catching the air, the wind and more.

Another stands near—
Taking it in, a friend, a peer.

Through words, eyes and smiles
The kite soars on, and on for miles.

Others pass by, sharing the delight.
For an idea shared is a beautiful
sight.

Vanessa R Buffaloe
DECEPTION

This poem is dedicated to truth, justice and the American way.

No longer is there any trust,
All that remains is
disappointment and despair,
All preconceived notions proved
incorrect,
No honesty, no explanation, no
care.

Bewildered, those who fell for
the lines,
And even those who tried to
believe,
Was it all just an act?,
To befriend only to unjustly
deceive.

Respect had been earned,
And the benefit of the doubt
given,
What was there to be gained?,
What motive worth being so
driven.

Deception—cruel and very
cleverly disguised,
It has no regard for whom life it
plays,
And even less remorse for
feelings,
Which can be easily destroyed,
dismantled and dismayed.

Putting the remainder in
retrospect,
Drawn is only this conclusion,
That there is no truth in
deception,
Just a painful bunch of lies
surrounded by illusion.

Tina L Byrd
EACH TIME THAT I PLAY

Dedicated To My Grandfather William McKinley Johnson.

When I was a child, I'd sit down on
his knee,
and he'd tell me a tale of what could
be.
He'd sit and he'd listen each time that
I played,
on an old piano in a large hallway.

GrandPa, oh GrandPa I know that
you're there,
each time that I play a song
anywhere.
GrandPa, oh GrandPa I thought I
would say,
thank you, I love you, I thought of
you today.

Now that I'm grown up with kids of
my own,
I'll tell them about you until they're
grown.
Oh and each night I look out and see
a bright star,
I know one is smiling 'cause there
you are.

GrandPa, oh GrandPa each time that I
play,
I still think about you to this very
day.
GrandPa, oh GrandPa I thought that
I'd say,
thank you, I love you, I think about
you everyday.

Rosalia Velasquez Balli
CHILDREN AND MOTHERS

This is dedicated to my children, Marc E. Muniz and Natalie C. Muniz, who are my inspiration and have all my love.

God, the pain, it hurts
There is no cure for the pain of love,
A cry like that of death,
But only a separation of my body
The outer layer of my skin has been
peeled away
The veins in my body are burning
The inner parts of my body are numb
The feel of their bodies within me
And the joy that they bring!
A life without my children
Is a sky without stars.

Eileen Bahlmann
MY CHILDREN

This poem is lovingly dedicated to our three children—Tim, Annette, and Allison, who were my inspiration. Despite the humor here, you are individuals Dad and I are so proud of!

Of all the wonders on this earth,
I've pondered most about their birth;
The way that each and every one,
Could be so different, yet such fun.

The oldest was a boy so fair,
With big round eyes and wavy hair;
He played with trucks and cars and
balls,
And ran from teachers down the
halls.

And next a girl was born to me,
Who was as lovely as could be;
She played with dolls and dainty things,
And loved my lipstick, heels and rings.

The youngest was a tomboy though,
To Mother's pride she was a blow;
For every time a dress she wore,
It came back filled with holes and more.

And though I miss their childhood years,
In spite of all the joy and tears;
I'm glad I got to play a part,
In God's most precious work of art.

Louise Biser
GOTTA DO

Dedicated to Jimmie: May you always keep your Gotta Do's and—Wanna Do's in balance.

The things me thinks me gotta do
Has put me in a spin
Racing the clock, in a race
Me thinks me just might win

Just when me thinks, the gotta do's
Are all but over and done
The should have done's take over
Then me's back to where me begun

Me life's been ruled by gotta do's
So far that's been the case
But now me sees no finish line
Me's bowing from the race

Some changes are due in me life
Me must really think this through
Me's changing some of the gotta's
To the things me wanna do.

Luben G Angeloff

Luben G Angeloff
THREE MAJOR CONTAMINATIONS
The first contamination in my body
Was when I did in my mind
For cancer a cure to find.
To make people happy and smile
And to live in a fashion style.
But after when I discovered it
Nobody wants to see
Even nobody listens to me
And my voice remains in the desert.

The second contamination in my body
Is music. Since nobody wants to see
The results of my cancer research,
I start to write music, to play and sing,
With the hope at least one person
Will hear the melody of my music.
But the melody of my music also
remains in the desert.

The third contamination in my body
Is poetry. Since nobody wants to see
The results of my cancer research and
Nobody listens to the melody of my music,
I start to write poetry, because in the
Poetical language within its ambiguities,
Everybody can see him/herself
As in a mirror by reflection.

P.S. Let us hope that the World will open its eyes and see my contribution on AIDS.

Lloyd G Bell
THOUGHTS

This poem is dedicated to my parents Barrington and Glendora Bell for their love and guidance and to our Savior for His blessing of our lives.

Mind flows and abstract ideas
Merge into consciousness,
Becoming an art of motion.
The body surges to perform
Fundamental actions necessary
For the completion of the task
With the least amount of
energy expended.

Once done, the cycles begin anew
And there is the realization that
One beat of the heart begins
and ends with a thought.
A thought doesn't end with a
heartbeat.

Think about love and remember the thought
Of loving and being loved.
Now feel the heart that is alone,
An empty thought keeps it going.
Though empty, cherish in
knowing
That love's heartbeat can return
With a thought . . .

Denise Pearson Allen
SAY GOOD-BYE

The death of my mother was my inspiration for this poem. I hereby dedicate this poem to my mother, Millie Pearson Allen.

It's hard to say . . . Good-bye
When someone you love dies
It's hard to say . . . Good-bye
When tears are running from your eyes
It's hard to say . . . Good-bye
When there's nothing left to say
It's hard to say . . . Good-bye
Each and every day.
It's still hard to say . . . Good-bye
Just say Good-bye . . . Anyway

Jacqueline Lee Aiken
I'VE RETURNED

Dedicated: To all who ever lost someone dear!

Dear Mother and Father, you taught and you raised us.
That by our faith and belief; Our Lord Jesus will save us.
Now I'm waiting in the rapture,
For his return and final capture.
So have little tears my earthly dears
My memories will always be here.
For now I've returned, from where I was lent
My life is complete, my heart is content.

Jillian Awong
CHARADES

This poem is dedicated, to my loving, parents Peter and Jacqueline Awong.

In everybody's lifetime we all play this game
There is always somebody who does not want to be the same,
Whether it be me, you or him, projecting our lives the way we thought it ought to be,
But most of the times, we do not realize
The problems that others may forth see

In our own world where no one sees we play the part we want to be
Playing this part portrays some inner feeling that is kept inside,
That when it's our turn
No one can guess what you are,
For you, is a lifetime of pain
Not realizing what it means or what it is
They just give up the game of charades.

Darlene Tanuis
PINK CLOUD CASTLE

To Stefan, my inspiration, my friend.

I'm dreaming of my pink cloud castle
The one you promised me
A place of love and solitude
Where you and I can be
Far away we are alone
Among the deep blue sky
Chasing all the rainbows
That sometime may come by

We make love by moonlight
As the sounds of night begin
And the mist of glittering stardust
Clings gently to our skin
I'm dreaming of my pink cloud castle
The one you promised me
A place of love and solitude
Where you and I can be

Elaine Adkins
MOTHER

This poem is dedicated to Doris Beckham my loving mother.

The silver in her hair shiny and bright,
The specks on her eyes will help her sight.
Wrinkles on her face slowly appear
A strong willed person that is clear.
She's always busy and getting around
Saying if I give up it will get me down.
The courage of this lady will never be found
A heart of gold for everyone around,
She's bright and happy with a big smile
That's enough to carry her that extra mile.
This lady was God given to all of us here,
I love and respect you my mother dear.

Rose Donahoo
SHE'S UP THERE IN HEAVEN

To my beautiful Kristy, You're everything to me, I love and miss you baby.

When I think of my daughter
Up there in heaven
Knowing God took her
When she was only seven.
It brings pain to my heart
And tears to my eyes
Knowing she's up there somewhere
Way beyond the skies.
Knowing deep inside my heart
She's in a better place
She's in God's loving arms
Yet, this pain just don't erase.
I guess because I want to hold her
(brush her hair, kiss her cheek)
Maybe just be able to say good-bye
Maybe to get one last little peek.
I miss her with all of my heart
I only wish God hadn't taken us apart.
Maybe one day I won't feel so blue
I guess that'll be when he's taken me too.

Debra D Daniels
A BIRTHDAY MEMORY

To My 3 Children: Samantha, Tara & James. Love—Mom.

Fifteen years ago today,
A child was born in the month of May.
A little girl, so small and fair
With not a wrinkle or a hair.
A soft sweet smile and a mole on her cheek,
She was mine to cherish, to love, and to keep!
From that day on, I then vowed
I'd raise her my best,
My dreams on a cloud.
As the years passed, she gradually grew,
Not only in size, but also in views.
Her hair now long, and her body now shaped,
I've only to look, worry and gape!
You wonder and worry with each day that passes
If she'll grow up to be the lady of lass's.
It's just that it's hard to really believe
That this babe I once bore has decided to leave.
Divorce has taken her parents apart.
Daddy never really left her heart!
She needs to research her heart within,
Before her own life can ever begin.
Our home is always hers,
Filled with love and care.
Doesn't matter to her,
She will live elsewhere.
She's a teenager,

Wanting to claim her own
rights,
And leave our home,
Regardless of how hard it
bites.
When people loose people,
Our hearts really break,
But when people loose people
Who aren't really dead,
Life is a nightmare of horrible
dread.
There are two other children—
A girl and a boy.
Of course there's no comparing,
They're my pride and joy.
I'd never want to lose them or
ever replace,
But without number three,
There's an empty space.
So I'll pray that my years of love
will prevail,
And "she will come home
Just waggin' her tail!"

A Mother's Tribute of Love

Julius Roller
BETH

To a precious daughter.

Rather like a long-stemmed rose
You stand with awkward grace,
The look of nature's beauty
Upon your childlike face.

An angel wearing blue jeans
And the devil wearing lace,
My confidante and ally
Who keeps my mind in place.

Too soon you will begin to bloom—
We—to grow apart,
But all the precious memories
Will warm this mellow heart.

You're the magic of springtime,
The joys a robin sings.
The lump I'll feel, the tear I'll shed
When it's time to give you wings.

Sherrie M Daly

Sherrie M Daly
FOR MY PARENTS
Mom was only sixteen when she met
and married Dad,
They've been thru many things
together both good and bad.
They were married such a short time
when war tore them apart,
Dad fought for God and country, with
Mom's love in his heart.
He came home safe to Mom who had
waited all those years,
Dad held her in his arms so tight and
wiped away her tears.
They loved each other totally, he
treated her so mild,
She grew into a woman about to bear
his child.
They often stood and watched their
little daughter sleep,
And listen as she prayed at night
"Dear Lord my soul do keep."
Soon there came another into their
world of three,
Another girl to watch and love that
made their life complete.
You helped me thru all these years
and held me when I cried,
You tried to teach me right from
wrong, and scolded when I lied.
Today you hold my little girl and say
how much she's grown,
You look at each other and remember
when you used to hold your own.
Thru all the pain I've caused you—
dear Mom & Dad,
Remember that I love you and that I
always have!

Ellen M Dover
I USED TO BE

I would like to dedicate this poem to my family. They encouraged me to do the best I can.

I used to be a tree
Standing straight and tall
But now I'm not a tree at all.

I used to sit on the mother ground
Now people sit in me from all
around.

I used to be brown and have leaves
that were green
I'm still brown but my leaves aren't
seen.

Maybe by now my friend
You may wonder what or where
What I used to be, but now
I'm a chair.

Stephen J Diehlman
GETTING TO KNOW AMERICA

To my loving girlfriend, Judy Reinhardt.

I could have taken a fast plane and
flown over the countryside.
Don't you see?!
And saved a lot of time.
Don't you see?!
But then I would have missed the
countryside made up of great
mountain ranges, gorgeous lakes, and
beautiful streams. And best of all the
shining seas.
Don't you see?!
And all the other wonderful people,
places, events, and other things yet to
see and enjoy.
And that my friend as they say,
"Getting there is half the fun." And
one of the greatest ways of "Getting
To Know America," that I know of.
Don't you see?!

Frances I Deitrick
I LOVE HIM SO

This poem is dedicated to the ones I love.

In the solitude of the darkened room,
My beloved huddled down deep.
For an instant his face glowed in the
rays of the moon.
I could tell he was thinking, "I can't
be seen while I weep."
But I know he's strong, I love him so.
Why does he insist upon being alone?

I'd give him my shoulder, I'd tell him
I care.
He knows I listen well, seldom speak
long.
I'd hug, caress, and hope we would
share.
He doesn't seem to understand, he
thinks it's wrong.

Only to be able to sit alongside,
To reach out and gently stroke his
Auburn hair.
In no way at all would I hurt his
pride.
He's such a compassionate man, yet
to find any which compare.

We've never been closer, though it
saddens our hearts.
It went by so quickly, like a beautiful
dream.
I tried to explain, "We're players
with a dramatic part,
Nothing ever is, whatever it seems."
But I know he's strong, I love him so.
Then why, does he insist upon being
alone?

Sharon Doppelmayr
BEWILDERMENT

With Love, to my dad, Francis Marion Hill.

Hush leaves, shivering shadows are
after me.
My heart has filled with pain,
these eyes can barely see.
The valley below just warned me,
of what I haven't done.
Birds are gracefully hovering,
beneath the risen sun.
Mountains I have gazed at,
bring to me all sorrow.
For I know the dreams I have dreamt,
may not be here tomorrow.
Awakened by my mind,
I know now what to do.
I'll fill my head with different
thoughts,
fill my heart with you.
For you make yesterday not seem so
far away.
You have left your sunshine here,
in my life to stay.

Marie L Davenport
LOOK BEYOND THE LIFE WE LIVE

This poem is dedicated to my father, Howard Kurr, who has found that special place.

Look beyond the life we live
To the peaceful life ahead
Where nothing's known of war
And there's brotherhood
instead.

Look beyond the great blue sky
To that land so far away
Where the Hand is always waiting
That will welcome us
someday.

Look o'er the life we now lead
With its trouble and its strife
And remember that someday we all
Will lead a better life.

So look beyond the mountains
To that land so far away
Where God will wait to welcome us
When we all meet there
someday.

Lisa Daniels
A LIFETIME FRIEND

Stacy: To my best friend. Thanks for always being there. Toby: I will always remember you.

What is this world coming to?
Where will it go?

People making a living off of
Someone else's suffering.

But you know what they say.
You have to make a living.

You can smoke it and sniff it.
Swallow it and shoot it.

When will it stop?
When will they learn it's not
Right to kill to earn a living.

Dona Jean

Dona Jean
HE'S STILL CHASIN' WOMEN
He's still chasin' women
But he can't remember why,
He feels so young and spry!
He's still chasin' women,
But he can't remember why

He's in his second childhood
He sure is feeling good!
He's still chasin' women,
But he can't remember why!

He doesn't know what day it is
He doesn't seem to care!
He doesn't know right from wrong,
He's lost all his hair!

He's a snappy little guy,
He's not too old to try!
He can make the ladies cry!
He's still chasin' women,
But he can't remember why.

Teresa Ann Gardiner
BELIEVE!
All the Angels of heaven come
together.

This will be forever.

This is a dawning of a new
beginning: Oh, how this will be,
it's meant for all to see.

In God's kingdom, wild animals
roam, as does man's heart unknown

Allow the light and love for heaven
above.

We can give you all you need, just
release this, and you will see.

We are the Angels of heaven,
Believe! Believe!

Love and Light so shall you see.
Come with us in prayer, and help
each other from despair.

The love from your hearts,
together with the love we send,
will bring together our fellow man.

James Howard Donald
IN BETWEEN

This poem is dedicated to Mr. Julius Kilgore, my mentor!

Idolizing, but fantasizing, not
realizing what's for real.
Criticizing, but compromising, not
exercising what you feel.
Going through the motion without
any notion of what you're really all
about.
Holding sanity, but molding vanity,
and your biggest fear is doubt.

How much attention do you give to
yourself, as time goes by?
Are you aware of how you live, or
are you living to die?

Philosophizing, emphasizing, what
you claim your soul is saying.
Trying to philosophize, you end up
telling lies,
It's just a game that you're playing.

Steady sip'n when you're ego trip'n,
What's the matter with your mind?
Your disillusion creates confusion,
and you can't see when you're blind.

Come to grips with reality, the step
that you must take is wide.
Take a tip, assume responsibility
while time is on your side.

You fall behind, killing time; soon
age will show in your hair.
You don't see opportunity for the
superficiality,
That's why you're going nowhere.

You're in between, living in between,
Don't know which way to lean,
Just living in between.

Sonia Dainty
PUERTO RICO

To my native land, Puerto Rico, the glory of my dreams.

Floating in the ocean lies;
Beneath the blue of gentle sky;
In bower of summer dreams;
Of perfumed flowers and lavish
greens;
Won from the battles of many scorn;
Of Spanish culture and Indian born.
Puerto Rico, island of grandeur
treasures;
Of happy hours and many pleasures.
Where the palm trees like soldier
stand;
Dancing on shores of yellow sand
Where the wind with raptures blow;
And kiss the lamp of golden glow;
And the rain on rustic walls
Sings in a chorus of water falls

Steve Davidson (Pockets)
WORDS IN THE SKY

For Spooge and Ishcabibal—man's mortal quest against the God of Confusion.

Wishes and dreams abound,
Only to be tossed carelessly away.
They vanish without a sound, like
Words thrown to the sky in frivolous
Dismay.

Upon empty wings they soar.
Lonesome visions of those who are
Bound to die, ever wanting more.
Such wonderful things they have
Sought, but time has left them nigh.
All just but waning dreams.
Memories so distant of lives gone
Past—a last glimpse of fading moon
Beams—they disappear like them,
All too fast.

Aimee M Brimmer

Aimee M Brimmer
LITTLE HANDS THAT GRASP AT AIR

This poem is dedicated to the children who no one hears.

Big blue eyes with an empty stare,
Little hands that grasp at air.
A tender heart broke in two,
Hoping wishes do come true.
Watching people pass her by,
No one hears her silent cry.
Looking forward to the day,
Her parents will come home to stay.
For now she'll make it on her own,
Standing on the cornerstone.
Clutching on to an old worn bear,
But blue eyes with an empty stare,
Little hands that grasp at air.

M Durden
SOMEDAY

To Gloria, all my love "Ben."

Someday when you're free from
the chains of love,
You may fall in love again.
Someday when the torch for him
grows dim,
you'll hold my happiness then.
Although it may not be so easy
as peaches and cream,
Someday the sun will shine again.
Someday if we try
through the thick and thin,
with God and true love
we shall win.

Shirley M Draper
REMEMBER ME

With deepest love, I dedicate this poem, to my nine children.

Remember me, as the first noise you
heard,
As you lay beneath my breast,
Cuddled up, in your own little nest.
As the sound of my heartbeat, let you
know,
You were safe with me, so sleep and
grow.
Remember me, who kept you out of
harm's way.
When the Boogey man came, or you
had a bad day.
It was a warm smile and some open
arms.
Inside that circle, there was no harm.

Remember me, when you were in
school,
Trying hard to learn each golden rule.
You looked so grown up, and I was
proud.
That you were all mine, so I was
allowed.

The love I felt, as I watched you
grow,
Will be with you always. Wherever
you go.
So, remember the good times, let the
bad times be.
But most of all, with love, Remember
Me.

Maria G Perkins

Maria G Perkins
LOVE DREAMS IN THE RAIN

To my forever friend, who is my inspiration. Love, Maria.

I had a dream the other night
I dreamed of you and me
I dreamed that I was yours
and you belonged to me

NO one in the whole wide world
could take you away from me
because my love for you
was stronger than
the wind,
the rain,
and the sea

It was a beautiful dream!
A dream that turned to pain
because you were not mine
my tears had turned to rain

Now I wait patiently for night to fall
So I can dream of you once more
and turn the tears to happy dreams
again
Love dreams in the rain.

Maria J Destralo
THE LOSS I FEEL

Dedicated In The Memory Of My Grandmother, Rose.

This is the day I hoped I'd never have
to face
Just like you I knew I could be
But someone needed you more than I
And called you to be by His side
Your memories will last more than
this day
But there can't be any fancy words or
poems
That describe the loss I feel
You are still a part of my everyday
I think of you . . .
in that beautiful red
rose
I think of you . . .
in the clear blue sky
But most of all,
I think of you . . .
when I see my
MOTHER.

Marian F Dermer
I SEE YOU AS LOVE

Dedicated to the one who loves me.

You see me as beauty
In the way I do not see me,
Myself I scrutinize
Because I am not looking through
your eyes.

My undaunted love is given to you,
And if love could be spoken
In unbroken words
It would flow as free as a tireless bird
To live in the heart forever for you.

A vision of love
To uplift my wings to fly above
A lifetime of love,

You look at me, and you see beauty
I look at you, and see a love that is
true,
If love could be spoken in a new way
I'd say them to you, each and every
day
A new dream to see—so perfectly,

You see me as beauty
I see you as love . . .

Maria G Perkins
IN THE COMPANY OF GOD

No one is at home . . . and all is quiet
I meditate a while, and rest from a
long day
I sit and read, not alone,
but in the company of God.

The day sets the light of sun to rest
and as the day dims around us
and night befalls us,
I feel no fear, for He is near
I am not alone,
but in the company of God

I say my evening prayers and chat a
while with God
I thank Him for His guidance
and protection thru the night
I fall asleep in peace
and wake up in the morning

not alone
but in the company of God

Michelle Devins
FALL

To my mother, Donna Devins, my art teacher, Earline Moore, and my dear friend, Ressie Tankersley.

The trees are like nude statues
In a garden long forgotten,
The air is of subtle essence
Like beckoning words unspoken,
The birds have become clear
memories
Like the hours of yesterday,
The leaves have painted the grass
As the flowers did in May,
The sun falls even earlier
As darkness builds its wall,
The warm days turn to cold
As summer fills with fall.

Jean Rettig

Jean Rettig
MY FANTASY

Dedicated to my family and friends.

Now I lay me down to dream
Of bygone days and pleasant things
Cares of the day I'll leave behind
And close my eyes with you in mind

I'll say, "Goodnight Reality,"
And "Hello," to my Fantasy
For in my dreams I can go anywhere
But best of all, You are there

You come to me and take my hand
To lead me to some distant land
Or; Maybe, We'll stroll down
memory lane
There I can be in Love again

My Fantasy will hold me tight
Help me make it through the night
But all too soon there comes the
dawn
The sun comes up, And you are gone

I must hurry through the day
Get my chores out of the way
When twilight comes, And night is
near
My Fantasy may reappear

With open arms I welcome you
You make all my dreams come true

Jean Rettig
FRIENDSHIP
FRIENDSHIP is something to be
treasured
Its benefits cannot be measured
It's souvenirs from places we have
seen together
The fun, The Laughter, Shared in all
kinds of weather
It's all those pictures of the past
And memories that will always last
It's roads we have traveled far and
wide
Glad to be there side by side
Sharing the good and the bad
Sometimes happy, Sometimes sad
But always grateful for what we had

FRIENDSHIP is like a warm cloak
You wrap around you when you are
cold
A treasure you keep locked in your
heart
To take out and admire when you are
old

But sometime the dearest of friends
must part
Coming to the crossroads down the
line
You will go your way, I will go mine
Sorry to have reached that place in
time
And though someday, We may be
miles apart
We should not let our friendship end
You will always have a place in my
heart
Remember this, And stay my friend.

Jean Rettig
GOING BACK
I'm going back in time in my mind
And everything's still standing there
The old house and the barn
With the livestock on the farm

There's the orchard with the apple
trees
The beehives with the honeybees
The old smokehouse where we cured
meat
The spring house where we kept milk
sweet
The woodshed with the corded wood
Next to it the corn crib stood

And I can see him, Like it was now
Grandad trudging behind the plow
His ol' dog Dan at his heels
And the chickens scratching
In the newly plowed fields
The fresh smell in the air
After a spring rain
Takes me back to the farm again

I spent many summer days
As a child on the farm
Chasing the lambs and calves around
the barn
And looking for eggs where the hens
might lay
Hidden in their nests in the sweet
smelling hay

Now I can't go back, As I did before
Grandad and his farm aren't there
anymore
So I close my eyes, And let my mind
Take me back again in time

Jean Rettig
FORGET ME NOT
Forget me not in the still of the night
Or the hush of the morning wake
When the silence of the dawn is
broken
By a bird's shrill call to its mate

Forget me not when the sun breaks
through
The rain clouds with its rays
And over your shoulder a rainbow
appears
With the promise of brighter days

Forget me not when you are tired and
weary
And you sit down to rest awhile
Shadows of the past slip through your
mind
Bringing to your face a smile

Forget me not when you are having
fun
And everything is going your way
Then from across the room
You hear a familiar tune
Taking you back to our time and day

If you are ever cold and lonely
And the past you nearly forgot
May the memory of me soothe and
warm you
Then you can forget me not

Jean Rettig
CHOICES
If only I had known
What was in store for me that day
I would have turned the corner
And gone a different way

They say; "You make the bed you lie
in;"
If you're wrong, You have to pay
Why couldn't I have Known
And gone a different way

If you are caught doing wrong
And you want to run away
It's not too late to turn about
And go a different way

If you Know your friends are doing
wrong
And you really don't want to stay
You don't have to follow them
You can go a different way

God is always near you
He will hear you if you pray
You can let Him be your guide
And go a different way.

Steven J Dawson
WHY?

To Peggy, You are my inspiration. Love, Steve.

Why do I feel like I feel for you,
When I can't even feel for myself?
Why do I know that I love you so
much,
Yet at times only think of myself?
Why do I feel so lost when you're
gone,
Yet push you away when you're
near?
Why can't I learn to control my
insides,
Why do I give in to fear?
Why do I love you so deeply within,
Yet fail you so often without?
Why can't I learn to let my pain go,
When I know that your love leaves
no doubt?
Now I must pray for your loving
touch,
To help me, to not go astray.
Wanting your love, is not asking for
much,
Lord, let me be worthy today.

Richard Doss
HAPPINESS

To Ray Ann.

Happiness
evergrowing
love
a smile
a laugh
sincere and true thoughts
beautiful
growing and blooming
simple love
yet complex
emotions
spreading
growing
understanding
beautiful
forever.

Jan E Larsen
HOPEFUL SAILOR

TO GUY: MY SOULMATE. As you fondly remember me: SMILE!

Half asleep, half awake, hovering
over my body
I perceived the "dream," as if
watching TV
Of you and me lying together;
smiling to myself
"How natural it seems."

Then my fear intruded and I stifled
the future
Of this "hypnopompic" vision
bestowed by God.

Reality intervened as my alarm clock
rang.
Getting up, groping groggily to hush
its noise
I found myself in my silent, sunny
chambers
Remembering, remembering
something unusual occurred.

I hung onto the wall, concentrating,
concentrating
Then perception flourished and I
remembered: MY FEAR.

"NO!" "NEVER!" I shouted. "IT
CAN'T POSSIBLY BE!"
"I'M NOT OF THAT WORLD YOU
SEE!" "WE ALSO BELONG TO
OTHERS!"

In blind panic, I somehow dressed
that morning
Knowing and dreading I'd see you at
work.

Are we "destined soulmates?" The
secret is mine alone.
No longer belonging to another, I
wait for you.

Though we're now miles apart, we
communicate in spirit;
Numerous clues are interspersed
daily of having my vision
Become eternity.

Melissa Ann Dumont
MOTHERS

This poem is dedicated to my mother, Gayle Iris Dumont.

Mothers are so kind
Mothers are so sweet,
When you are little
She helps you cross the street.

When you are frightened
And all full of fears,
Your mother is always there
To show how much she cares.

She sometimes says no
She sometimes says yes,
You never understood why
But now you have a good guess.

She made those decisions
For your well being,
You realize now
The thoughts she was seeing.

Your mother only wants
What's best for you,
Your mother loves you very much
And you also love her too.

Virginia R Gonzales

Virginia R Gonzales
SORROW
Sorrow comes for a reason,
God's sign is a pinch of pain,
when prayer goes out of season,
a body weary, a mind insane.

Reach out for God's hand;
Reach out for God's love.
Reach out for God's command;
Reach out and pray to God above.

Sorrow comes to one and all;
rich or poor it matters not.
Pray to God for strength, so as not to fall.
Keep the faith that one was taught.

Do not let the goods man made,
bring forth thy sorrow;
for when in the earth you are laid,
no use are they tomorrow.

Flesh and blood a body now—
tomorrow turns to dust.
Save our souls, to God we bow—
For in God we trust.

Diana Czelada (Age 15)
MISSING YOU
That sweet smile
showing on your face
The soft feeling of
your warm embrace
But most of all
what I really miss
is your gentle touch
of your lips
when we kiss

Stuart Daniels
LOST LOVE
Enchanting Boston Irish face.
Such perfect legs, that tiny waist.
But I cannot possess those loins.
She married Harry from
Des Moines.
A dark cascade of shining hair.
But I will never see her bare.
Her tawdry perfume haunts my nights.
Her alabaster skin delights
in making other girls seem plain.
Her beauty brought me only pain.
If somehow time could be reversed
I'd write her reams of steaming verse.
I'd take her to the symphony.
Perhaps she might have sinned for me.
A perfect rose on dunghill grew.
Perhaps it's best I only knew
a slight aroma of her charm.
A stronger sniff could cause great harm.

Stuart Daniels
LOOKING BACK
Remember grimy grade school walls
a thousand years ago.
The screaming spinster principal
made even boys' tears flow.
My third grade teacher seemed effete.
I'm certain he was gay.
His music class was wonderful.
It's then I vowed to play.
Many concert tours I've made.
Records, broadcasts, accolades.
Might all this never have come true
without the youthful perils gone through?
Can one find poetry in the past?
Can early inspiration last?
Does childhood truly father man
as part of some great master plan?
The answers to these questions may
for me, the artist, light the way.

John L Hast

John L Hast
CEDARS
They are so green
They curve & bend
They beautify a scene
They also mend

They never turn brown
During the spring
They never fall down
What joys they do bring

The bird makes a nest
In their limbs
She now must rest
As the limbs sing it

The day goes on
The tree stays in the scene
At the break of dawn
It's still an "EVERGREEN"

Mary Eleanor Chambers
DEAR LORD
I need help and quiet
now that I am sick and old.
I hope and pray others around me
won't have to be told.

I have a quiet hurting heart;
to tell others they must part.
I can't take the noise any more.
Now that I'm no longer well;
there's so much of life just a bore.

I pray God will surely help me out;
'cause I don't really like to pout.
I don't need the unwanted stress.
I need help just to dress.

So please LORD, I ask You in Your name.
Please don't keep things just the same.

Patricia M DiCarlo
DAVID

To David Allen Coe. I may never meet you. But I feel you there.

David is a man you'll love,
But no girl can make a claim.
In his heart is cowboy,
Outlaw's in his vein.

The beauty of this person,
You'll find it's always true.
He'll give his love to everyone,
Hurting no one as a rule.

Patricia M DiCarlo
I CANNOT LAY DOWN BESIDE YOU

For Doug Levine—I may never see you again but the poem remains the same.

I cannot lay down beside you,
Or hold you close at night.
I belong to another,
And these feelings are not right.

My head I picture on your chest,
Your smiles in my heart.
I may not be your love tonight,
But we're never far apart.

So if you ever look around,
And find you're all alone.
At your side and in my heart,
You'll always have a home.

Hal Denton
LOVE OF YOUTH RETHOUGHT

To Eileen Jones Dudra, A special person of rare qualities that can cause enduring love and devotion, her secret she gives of her self.

The angry waves crash over the rocks, in rivulets they run in every direction back to the sea to regroup to come again and to give their proud display. Everything made and drenched in silver moonlight far out on the waves the lonely vessel makes her way. You can make out its dark silhouette the tiny dim lights haunt and fill you with dismay. My fair Eileen passed my way but she too was far out on life's wave. I was only a boy at play now older with lots of grey I still love you in the purest way.

Hal Denton
UNITY
Order the law, this bell of truth a ring. Harmony you shall not over sell. Every thing in its equal place, the ground does not the sky astound. In turn the wind it does not bound. Only the Heavens round. The Universe doth resound. Gravity holds the ground amidst plant and stone, the animals roam so man is not alone

Alma Wanjiku Harris
I WONDER WHY?
I wonder why in school, some
children write messy—other
children write slow, fast, and
sometimes neat—I
wonder why?

Alma Wanjiku Harris

Alma Wanjiku Harris
CHILDREN BETWEEN

This poem is dedicated to Tiana, Renee, LeiSawm, my nieces and I want to thank God.

The ants, caterpillars, and grasshoppers are creeping through the green, tall, and creepy grass hunting for food . . . Airplanes are flying high in the sky somewhere near the clouds . . .

And in between all of this, you'll find the children running, skipping, and rushing to some schools near by

Mark A Ceron
AT TIMES

To my wife Cindy and my son Mark II who give my inspiration.

Emptiness is waiting,
Loneliness has become your friend,
Heartache and sorrow, over and over!
When will this sadness end.

Your heart aches with pain,
Your laughter is fake,

You try so hard not to be
"Discovered"

The only way left of escape,
DEATH!
But to contemplate this final chapter,
throughout the day,
Only brings the real reality of it all.

Bearing down!

At times you do feel like you're
already dead.
Nothing arouses you, nothing bothers
you, a transparent being!
Solitude will come as the day grows
to dusk.
Then comes the shining moon,

Your heart escapes for just a moment,
to touch a glisten of light,
Hoping to rekindle your love for life!
A spark is all you need, to escape just for a moment.
The silver lining will not elude this time.

At times life can be so bleak,
Then at times, we do rise up, and to risk our emotions to another date.

Cherianne E Bosco

Cherianne E Bosco
EMPIRE STATE BUILDING LIGHT

To my family for their love and support.

Two years passed before I
witnessed the sight
The turning off of the Empire
State Building light.
A lot of people don't believe
this is true
But when the clock strikes
midnight you will see too.
When the clock hits twelve keep
your eyes open wide
For it is then that you'll see I
have not lied.
Darkness sets in and overtakes all
and the building that once
appeared big is no longer so
tall.
Few have witnessed this
incredible sight but just wait till
twelve and
you'll see that I'm right.

Cherianne E Bosco
MY FAVORITE PLACE

My favorite place is deep within my head
I go there in my dreams at night when I'm in bed
My place is very tranquil, meaning peaceful and divine
It's a place that will exist forever in my mind.
You'll know when I am visiting,
you'll know when I'm there;
A place I'd tell you all about, but no,
I wouldn't dare.
For you would all be off to find my uncomplicated place,
Led by this serene image projected on my face.
A place within my head so picture perfect clear,
Somewhere I go alone to get away from fear.

Cameron Cooper
THE DOVE

This is dedicated to Thomas Hensley, family, and friends. Tom shall always be remembered.

As we walk along we grow, while we grow towards one another.
For as we go through the years, we grow together.
There we know how to make each other laugh, for when we have to frown.
As the years pass, we will always be there for one another, good or bad.
We never fall apart, for there is someone always there.

For when we lay under a tree, we look up in the great blue sky, and see a dove, soaring in peace.
For the dove is a graceful symbol of great love all around us.
As we watch, we realize that love has kept us all going.
But as we look all around, there is a frown for sadness.
For we shall turn the other way and shall see a smile of happiness.
As we all know, that there is always love and happiness all around us.
Though we shall never forget the dove.

Joseph D'Albano
A LETTER TO GLORY

Father oh Father
Please send me a bride
My wife, if you may
Yes my wife—
"A Pray Day"

Prudent and tender
A "marry-want" girl
A girl of perfection,
of spiritual swirl.

One of similar mind
With an angelic smile
One to take up my hand
And walk with me the mile.

Graceful and humble
A partner in prayer
Please, oh please Father
Please let it be there

Written in ink
And my blood of the same
Written in Glory
In Jesus' name.

Joseph D'Albano
REACHING OUT OF THE WORLD TO THE HEAVENS ABOVE

A world in its spin
One day to sleep . . .

A place too strange
to partake in its dance.

Where rulers combine to rock the race
Deceivers of nation
Take off the masks
LET US SEE!

Rulers of nations fuel the fire
Chopping the tree of economy to a stump

How sad strangely come is the world;
a dying seed.

We walk each day
Through strife, emptiness, anxiety storms
We all walk the same rocky road
That leads to the "The Great Day of Judgement."

Through Adam, death entered the bloodstream of humanity
Through Jesus, the Way back to Life
So open your heart to Him and let in Life.

Let Him grant our flesh's death
The Promised Truth of Heaven.

Toby Cederbaum
PEACEFUL REMEDY

To Chuck, as I remembered you.

Watching you the other day
You were sleeping & on your way
Into the thoughts a dreamer dreams
Into your world of peace you lay.

Seeing you as a little boy
dreaming of all your trucks & your toys
You were so innocent & having your fun.
You didn't know of the problems to come.

You were so beautiful & love is what you knew
The beauty of life was lying right within you.
Looking at the man who seemed like a child
and hoping this peace could last awhile.

Toby Cederbaum
THE FLOWER

To the spirit of growing in love and in life.

Few see the flower
the one that hides
it's alive and living
somewhere buried inside

Most never look at
the peace it can bring
Why should they look at
What causes the sting

You don't want to expose
yourself to yourself
So you'll stay where you are
caged up on a shelf.

Cold you want
so cold you'll be
What about the flower?
What about the me?

What's human to you
is different to me.

Kevin Dumanis
EYE CONTACT

Dedicated to Christine "Moosie" McGlade.

I feel the essence of your warm presence letting light refract. We'll make eye contact.

Kevin Dumanis
DREAM SEQUENCE

Dedicated to neurotic insomniacs everywhere.

My sleeping pangs have subsided at last.
Now they have nowhere to explore.
As I wake to dream I find that I don't
Want to sleep anymore.
Cracking joints. Foot in mouth.
Bad health habits ease the pain.
Comfort was not my goal this year.
Stimulate me again.

Bonnie H Thompson

Bonnie H Thompson
HIS WATER AT THE WELL

This poem is dedicated to the memory of my dear parents who have long since gone home to their eternal reward.

His water at the well never runs dry.
JESUS stands there patiently waiting.
Here you will find peace and joy that
surpasseth all human understanding.
Lay your burdens at his feet.
Like a compass at sea our dear
SAVIOUR'S gentle compassion will
surely guide your life.

GOD'S glowing light and lasting mercy is forevermore.
We are like little lambs being led,
through a door; into the fold.
PRECIOUS JESUS LOVES US ALL.
So when you hear the call . . .
Remember this . . .
HIS WATER AT THE WELL
NEVER RUNS DRY.

Jackie Clements
UNANSWERABLE

As a child, both
curious and bright
I pondered with awe,
almost fright
That God made all
that does exist
But where'd God come
from? That's the twist
I never inquired of
parents or teacher
Nor went to church
to ask the preacher
I knew, even then,
that none could say
So I reverently laughed
and went out to play

Bonnie H Thompson
HARBOR OF PEACE
Crying out from depths of poverty is my need.
Only a talent fulfilled can lead me on to freedom.
When that day comes mind and soul will soar
like a bird set to flight. Until then I patiently wait,
knowing that fate must not have a final say.

At GOD'S CHOSEN HOUR human frailties shall melt
and HIS INFINITE POWER WILL BE FELT.
The key to eternal quest is my request.
Mom's strong song of victorious triumph
has been a long time coming.

My soul shouts with faith derived sincerity.
Only GOD alone knows our inner most depth
of feelings and thoughts.
TO GLORIFY HIS HOLY NAME
AND PRAISE JESUS
is this heart's desire.

HERE IS SEEN MY ROCK OF SALVATION.
A fire within burns brightly . . .
knowing that the time is so near
when all shall see
what GOD has done for me.

Until it comes to be,
I seek rest for life's ship
at GOD'S OWN HARBOR OF PEACE.

Bonnie H Thompson
A VISION OF FAITH'S REWARD
Look toward yonder hill!!!
THERE IS SEEN A VISION OF FAITH'S REWARD.
Non can compare to this sword of truth.

Down through the centuries of time mankind has sought
an escape from the black, chilly dark of sin.
The thief comes as a robber at night to steal our light.
This foe's desire is to see all humanity fall.
Captives we have been but in that final hour of battle
GOD'S infinite power conquers all.

An answer will come although it may take some time.
SEEK TO FEEL THE MARK OF OUR SAVIOUR'S LOVING HANDS.
DWELL NEAR HIS WELL OF LIVING WATER.
YOUR SOUL HE SHALL FILL.

Press toward that eternal goal! ! !
JESUS WILL TEACH US HOW TO REACH A STATE SO ELATED.
THERE FOUND IS A FOUNTAIN OF RIGHTEOUSNESS
POURING FROM HIS HOLY MOUNTAIN.

Look toward yonder hill! ! !
THERE IS SEEN A VISION OF FAITH'S REWARD.

Terri DiTullio
ALONE TOGETHER

For Tom, Without him, this poem has no meaning.

Can we take away
Everyone around us
And leave us together
The feelings that found us

A couple, a team
That works well together
Simple pleasures
That last forever

Thoughts of an island
Just me and you
Two hearts so close
An island for two

As one together
Two people alone
A life forever

Terri DiTullio
THOUGHT PROVOKING
A peaceful setting
The romance of quiet
A distant thought
Contemplating life

An island mystery
A country farm
Or city lights
Food for thought

Steps in stride
The ability to climb
A mountain, a struggle
Something worth fighting for

To vision is to learn
Knowledge earned
A future to build on

LaVonda Eastup
THE POOR CHILDREN OF THE WORLD
Oh, I wish that I could enjoy,
Take all the children of the world,
Every tousled-headed little boy,
And every precious baby girl . . .

I'd like to bring them home with me,
Give them their fill of food and drink,
I'd like to bathe them, dress them and see,
The lack of love from their little eyes shrink.

I'd like to tuck them in at night,
Read them stories before they sleep,
I'd like to make the wrong all right,
And soothe the little ones when they weep.

I'd like to rock them after lunch,
And kiss the little sleeping brow,
When they awake, give them cookies to munch,
Give all the love in my heart somehow.

If I could take them all, I'd try,
To do my best, for one and all,
To do some good before I die,
Before I hear the death angel call.

LaVonda Eastup
SOMEDAY
Someday, I'll take my pen in hand,
And write a beautiful sonnet or rhyme,
That will be acclaimed throughout the land,
Someday, when I have the time!

A book that would be masterpiece,
A song whose lyrics never yet rang,
A work of beauty that would never cease,
My star in the Heavens, for to hang.

Someday, just like the writers of old,
I'll seclude myself in some green bower,
And write phrases of purest gold,
Sent on wisps of angel power.

Fragments—floating here and there,
Begging to be written down.
Quickly write them down with care,
Before they drift from out of sound!

Someday, I'll write my books, I know,
Before my days on earth are gone,
There's so much that I could show,
That not to write it, would be wrong.

Pat Taylor
TRAIL OF TEARS

I dedicate this poem to my children in hopes they shall always remember they were the inspiration that inspired me to create this poem.

As I sit here and think, when I am alone
There is never a knock, to see if I am home

Maybe one of my children, will call me today
The phone hasn't rang, for days and days

How often I long, to reach in the past
Just to tell mom, my love will always last

Oh how I wish, I could see my mother
She was always there, when there was no other

So often I think, If only they cared
But there is no love, in our family shared

It would be so easy, to pick up the phone
But I know, they rather, I leave them alone

I would love to stop, when I pass their way
But I know, they rather, I stay away

Sometimes I wish, I had help with a chore
But there is never, a knock at my door

I try to forget, those words so unkind
Just try to hide them, way back in my mind

If only the family, shared love once more
Just forget, they have to even a score

If only some time, they had to spare
My life with them, I would love to share

As they go about, their busy way
A little attention, I wish they would pay

If only a kiss, upon my cheek
Another treasure, in my heart to keep

A little hug, would fill their part
But only the thought, tugs at my heart

Often my memories, search in the past
Remembering their love, that did not last

Sometimes I wish, they would only pretend
And let me think, I am still their best friend

Someday they will wish, they could turn back time
All those bitter words, they would like to make kind

Year by year, is passing by
No family love, just time to cry

How I would love, to share my golden years
So there wouldn't be, just a "TRAIL OF TEARS"

Adrian B Evangelist
SHE WALKS IN BEAUTY

"They moved my heart, touched my soul, and stirred my emotions."

Amid the dawn of a morning's splendor
Appears an angel in blessed September.

Flowing with grace, beauty, and charm I adore,
A gift from above hath crossed heaven's door.

Her innermost thoughts reign pure and sincere,
A free-flowing spirit that beckons one's tears.

A voice soft and tender, so mellow and rare,
A sound so inviting it's almost like prayer.

Her profile angelic, her lips are like wine,
She radiates beauty as endless as time.

A joy to behold, the pride of my life,
A treasured possession which hath no true price.

She ignites my soul and revives my heart,
A love forever till death do us part.

The rebirth of Spring hath sparked our desires,
Our passions oft rage like wild forest fires.

Though life is uncertain and truth must be found,
Love is perfection with limitless bounds.

Graceful as a feline, she walks in beauty,
To comfort and cherish shall be my life's duty.

Adrian B Evangelist
MY LOVING CONNECTION
In our star studded sky appears Mr. Moon,
The bewitching hour arrives not a minute too soon.

Time passes quickly, a new day begins,
As fleeting young souls are freed from their sins.

A lovely fair creature awaits my return,
As bold restless hearts are starting to yearn.

Such a precious face, so cute and divine,
True beauty and charm that mellows with time.

Her eyes oft sparkle like a comet ablaze,
An ageless attraction, that makes young hearts gaze.

Her hair soft and tender, swept by the wind,
Radiant, stately, and always so prim.

Whence darkness surrenders to light of the day,
The envy of many must be on her way.

Gorgeous, on fire and such a confection,
Blessed by nature is my loving connection.

Holly

Bernice Chambers
SHARING MY GRANDCHILD HOLLY'S WORLD
I walked in my grandchild's asking world of whys; of wonderment and awe
She picked tiny wild flowers, that my unseeing eyes had never saw
Humming birds flitted about, her movement and chatter couldn't scare them away.
They too love this precocious child, fanning her hair in wild disarray.
Then onward and discovery of two wiggly worms beneath a loquat tree
Eyes full of love "Oh Grandma aren't they beautiful?" and I of course agree.
Cold water sipped from the garden hose was the climax you might say.
Because we ended up soaking wet; two giggling young ones coming in from our day of play.
See through the eyes of the young, if caught in boredom's aging years
Enter their world, see as they do and smiles will replace your tears.
The fountain of youth will well up inside, far more precious than gold.
Contentment, joy and peace of living can eventually be told.
"A little child shall lead them" Jesus said, and as I kneel to pray
I thank God for my three year old granddaughter who showed Grandma the way.

Robert J Bunch
LOVER'S STORM
Shakesphere often wrote of the violent storms
That equate to the wrath of a woman scorned
But I was over fifty miles out to sea
When my lover turned her back on me
She begged and pleaded enticing me to come
She promised smooth sailing and hours of fun
The seas were calm and we were sailing well
When fifty miles out my trip turned into hell
The smiling sun was lost behind a threatening cloud
The rolling thunder intensely grew awesome and loud
When that storm hit all we could do was pray
Pray to God to try and see us through this day
The waves were high smashing us like bricks
My lover was angry and she was getting her kicks
I'd read and heard stories of lovers gone mad
But I never imagined that it would get this bad
I never knew how violent my lover could be
For my lover's always been the deep blue sea

Harriet (Shove) Bedard
ONCE—LIKE A GODDESS
When time began— —
The world was like a great
goddess
Hair—streams so clean and freely
flowing
Face—Sun and moon shining—
unblemished shores
Eyes—sky blue
twinkling stars
Bosom—voluptuous mountains:
creviced with beautiful
valleys
Gown—lush greenery: flowers in
multitude
Adorned with every kind
of gem
At the first bite of the apple
Man nipped her virginity
Her pure maiden body—
tarnishing began
Man's strive for power and riches
Stripping her down—now her
gown
Is taking on the look of ragged
britches
Body tormented with hate and
violence
Suffering from man's
weaknesses—her eyes are
weeping
She has a terminal disease—
nuclear waste and pollution
Unlike the Statue of Liberty: she
cannot be refurbished
And look like the original
Dying a destructive death—is that
the solution . . . . . .

Janet Brown
UNTITLED
I wish that there could be a way
to ease the world from pain.
To melt the guns of murder
and throw to the wind the grains of cocaine.
To give happy faces to those who grieve
and find a cure for AIDS.
For the homeless a pillow of foam,
not a streetside grate.
Food for the hungry,
Good jobs for the poor.
A cure for all diseases
and so much more.
Especially that all the world
would get down on their knees
and pray to our Father
and feel His Loving Peace.

Howard Beymer
THE POLITICAL CAMPAIGN 1988
Material that I did not originate,
I feel that I must eliminate.
It is very unfair to plagiarize.
This we must all recognize.
Innuendos by politicians to us blared,
Made us wonder if they were running scared.
That which was too unethical to mention,
Our politicians have brought to our attention.
Some of the rhetoric that we have heard,
Was a new low, the maximum of the absurd.
Some political rhetoric was so diffused,
To make the average voter completely confused.
The real meaning of some political rhetoric was so difficult to discern,
That more than half of the voters were left with no concern.

Richard M Brewer
MY FRIEND
Along this stretch of swirling sand
I walk with her my friend—
A winter squall is blowing in
Bringing sheets of rain upon the wind—
But I am happy, I am warm—
Because I walk with her my friend—
The sea gulls cry, searching, searching
So like a heart astray and aching—
Oh, the wounds of time
Seem somehow softer now
Because in love I can walk
With her my friend—

Ottis L Cotton

Ottis L Cotton
A DAY-BREAK OF BLESS
An Owl's hoot in the distance caused
me to awake
On a quiet Sunday morning just at
DAY-BREAK
Laying quietly still, only to find
It was too early for birds to fly at this
time

I arose from my bed and walked
quietly outside
And embraced the beauty that GOD
did provide
No insects were moving about where
I sat
Around my feet purring, was my
neighbors' white cat
Glowing light of daybreak as the
street lamps fade
A small cloud in the east over gold
inlaid
The sky grows brighter of creation's
ploy
A vast hue so lovely for all to enjoy

The leaves gently moving to and fro
on the trees
I bathed myself in this soft glowing
breeze
Only GOD can create a Sunday
morning as this
Just before dawn, a daybreak of bless

Kathy Sue O'Brien
MR SUN
Good morning Mr. Sun,
how are you today?
Will you still be shining
when I come out to play?

Will you color my skin
and lighten my hair?
When I wake tomorrow
Will you still be there?

Can you move the clouds
away from your face?
So I can see your smile
all over the place?

Thank you Mr. Sun,
for a bright sunny day.
I'll see you in the morning
When I come back out to play.

Jacqueline Brookins
DEAR GOD, WHEN I DIE
Dear God, When I Die: I want to go to heaven. For it is a place where people go and live in peaceful harmony.
Its atmosphere is as calm as a feather.
Because everyone enjoys each other & likes living together.

Dear God, When I Die: I hope there will be peace on earth.
I pray that all the unborn children will have healthy births.

Dear God, When I Die: I pray that I'm loved and hope that you welcome me to your gates up above.

Dear God, When I Die: I hope the Ethiopians are set free.
So they can live a normal life as things should be.

Dear God, When I Die: I hope there will be no pain and no sorrow.
So there will be a brighter future for the children of tomorrow.

Tessa Bergsbaken
SOMETHING IS OUT THERE
Something is out there
In the night sky.
Something is out there
Don't ask me why.

Something is out there
Look and see.
Something is out there
Don't you agree?

Something is out there
It's like a pool.
Something is out there
It's just above the school.

Something is out there
It's having fun.
Something is out there
Go with it and run.

Marlene J Bello
THE PEOPLE GATHER
The people gather, like the sea gulls,
In the warm December sun.
Chatting and visiting, friends and strangers,
Passing one year into another.
No loud noise, just quiet hums of a peaceful day.

Virginia E Jonassen
stranger to my heart . . .

For you, with my thanks . . . when my days were at their darkest . . . you were my light.—As always, Me.

do not ask me about tomorrow, for a prophet i am not
and do not ask for commitment
for i haven't the stamina to survive another letdown.
ask only for today, for that
is all i have to offer.
hold fast to my hand and pull me
from the emotions and pain of yesterday.
make me smile without
speaking . . . feel without
hurting . . .
make my soul warmed by
your gentle touch.
let me look into your eyes and see peace
for these things have been lost
to me.
teach me, like a child, to trust, to feel, to love
and satisfy my desire to be
needed.

go slowly, with patience and understanding
and when, in my confusion, i
stumble and fall
be there to pick me up, for i am a stranger to all of this.
do not give up on me for i
know that one day
i will stand and walk forward if you will show me the way.
my silent prayers give thanks
for the gifts you have given
me,
for i have back that piece of me i thought was gone forever.
you . . . my teacher . . . my
friend . . . my strength
have ultimately blessed my life and am i eternally grateful.

Jane K Begraft
FEELINGS
What we think and what we feel
Is very important and is very real.
Just taking a moment to lend an ear,
To what needs to be said, and what we need to hear.

The heart is a funny thing,
When it's happy, it's like a bell that's ready to ring.
But when it's sad the bell won't toll,
The world looks grim, the air feels cold.

So what we need to do you see,
Is talk about our feelings openly.
The heart will glow, the birds will sing,
The bells in unison will ring.

Della Joy Brehm
SAY GOOD-BYE
Say good-bye to yesterday
And try to carry on.
Find beauty in living
Look forward to the dawn.

Seek out fulfillment
For life is a gift
You cannot recapture
Any part you have missed.

Walk steady in heart
Be all that you are.
Turn away from yesterday
Or carry the scar.

Angelia M Bailey
SMALL TOWN GIRL
Blue jeans of denim
Just a small town girl
He loved her more than
all the whole world.

But from him, she wanted
much more
Like diamonds and rubies
from some elegant store.

She didn't know, you
reap what you sow
Until he left to return
no more.

Oh, if just once
she could turn back time
His blue jean baby
Once again he'd find.

Jeremy Brown
DON'T END LIFE
Indifferent corporations are polluting our planet's air,
While people of our nation cry out in despair.
Stop chemicals from being dumped into our rivers and streams,
Forbid these wicked madmen from destroying our dreams.
Their means of waste disposal is an evil, wicked beast,
Who's hell-bent on destroying the planet that we lease.
Can someone please tell me why,
Living creatures must uselessly die.
To give man the comforts to survive day by day,
Is destruction and pollution the 'American Way'?
I don't think in the midst of Toxic Waste is any way to live,
For it annihilates creatures with so much to give.
Yet we go on in this apathetic nation,
Until we became a bleak, dark planet of desolation.
It looks as if we will perish from the hole in the ozone layer,
But not if everyone partakes in a little prayer.
Pray that the world will not end in one not so distant tomorrow,
And we will not all die in pain and sorrow.
For the solution to pollution is simple, can't you see,
It all depends on you and me.
You and Me.

Marie Sollars

Marie Sollars
OUR LAND
God bless this soil
and those who toil
their weary backs
bent low.

Give us rain
and fertile grain
to set our land
aglow.

Christine Bassett
ONLY THE BRAVE DIE
Tell me straight what you think it means
Still black and evil; still white and pure
Tell me or have my own blood paint your scene
But for the purely prejudiced
That call themselves the solely just
Does it like you to lie?
Fancy that you're right
But know only the brave die
Discover that you owe the reason for their death
Don't be jealous on the still black
Know you affect for them through their last breath.

Debbie Bares
AS I LOOK OUT MY WINDOW
As I look out my window, I see freedom
I see children running about happily
I see cars speeding down the road
This is what I see as I look out my window.

As I look out my window, I see autumn
I see leaves falling to the ground
I see the branches getting bare
This is what I see as I look out my window.

As I look out my window, I see patience
I see a girl waiting for her date
I see a boy waiting to get into the locked house
This is what I see as I look out my window.

As I look out my window, I see love
I see a couple walking hand in hand
I see a mother caring for her hurt child
I see many things as I look out my window.

Patti J Boney
YOU ARE
You are in my heart,
a part of my soul
You are forever on my mind
I have shared love with you
and I have found myself
You truly are one of a kind,
and I need you
You are a gentle kiss on my lips,
a warm embrace,
and the sunshine of a smile
You are the eyes that see into my soul,
without speaking they say "I
love you, I want you"
You are the one I forever want to be near
You are the best you can be
For you are you and you are a part of me
You are a dream come true
and I love you

Bob Becker
TOGETHER IN TIME
Do you not remember? We have met before. It was a long time ago. We came to be friends then, just as we are now. As well as all the lives we have spent together. Together as well as separated. It seems like only yesterday we came to know each other.

We were two different people then. As we are now. Much has changed. But are we not still friends. As much as we were ever. Even maybe more so. Time has once again brought us together.

But the friendship that existed then, as now. Has changed into much more. The purest of all love. That one person could ever have for another. Love of very great depth. Unspoken, but very much felt.

What is felt today will be so tomorrow. For a long time yet to come. For the rest of this lifetime we have together as well. Perhaps into our next lives. But wherever we are. Or whatever we will be doing. We will meet again. I hope to be together again. Just as we are now in this lifetime. Who can say.

But I can say this; now and forever. Till the end of time. I love you.

L Ann Buscher
BUTTON BOX
Hushed day as raindrops tap tunes on misted panes of glass
each heavy droplet falling now more urgent than the last.

Companions gone, closed 'way
behind old doors that know this storm
will sing its song, a lullaby, beyond
tomorrow's morn.

Now melancholy takes its place
beside the crackling warmth
of old wood stove inviting all to
gather at the hearth.

Here soothed by softened sounds,
light subdued, too still for talks
from sideboard drawer, old handle
worn, out comes the button box.

The box of tin, paint smoothed and faded fine
holds treasures precious, priceless, at this moment mine.

Small shapes to sort, to count, to
touch as gently as though jewels
Imagination leaps, set free, without restraint of rules.

Red rubies, emeralds, diamonds
claimed or are they simple joys?
Small families, mothers, fathers
found with matching baby boys.

Perhaps a pause to ponder mis-matched shapes
then joyously we reunite the old familiar mates.

Partners together now forever
lifelong friends
Small button people gather now
grateful at day's end.

Close tight the lid, dear button box,
small treasures safe within
to charm again one rain hushed day,
old button box of tin.

Margaret E Becht

MY SON

With All My Love, Your Adopted Mother, Margaret E. Becht.

The seed was not planted within,
You are my son.
Your face is like the sunlight, what a delight.
Your hair is a soft glow, have small toes.
Straight back standing tall
among them all.
Your head is a worldly shape;
with all wonders
locked inside.

Do have a great smile a frown or two.
Your arms when held high could reach the sky.
With all your yes and no,
I love you still, after all.
You are my son, Richard

Your Adopted Mother
Margaret E. Becht

Jill Bliven

ODE TO GRAND-PA

News came today that you're gone,
But you taught us all to be strong.

You made it so easy for us to learn,
Always understanding, gentle, never once too stern.

Your eyes so soothing, your smile so sincere,
The stories of life you've told we all hold dear.

You never judged others, always saw good,
Constantly honest, the way we all should.

You'll never leave us, you're in each one's heart,
The memories you've given us, is a start.

A man so great a man so wise,
You're a part in each grandchild's eyes.

If we can live in the ways you believe,
We'll all meet in heaven, when earth we leave.

Erica Bradley

WHERE YOU REST

I walked up to where you rest;
I did not see you,
But I knew you were lying there,
Dressed up in your Sunday best.

I stood there alone and sad,
But I could not weep.
Your leaving me made me mad,
But your memory I will keep.

I could almost hear your laughter;
And your calling out to me,
But I turned and left,
Always remembering where you rest.

Albert L Buzzo

COMMON SENSE

Common sense is not so common, but 'tis rare.
When most in need, it is
never found anywhere.
In this world of madness, darkness prevails without glory;
But if common sense were to
dominate, 'twould be a
different story

From morning to sundown people live in constant fear,
Not knowing when this world
will clear
This mystery that puts man in a frantic state.
Where is this common sense
that states: Take heed afore
it's too late.

Ah, but men of knowledge are not to be found
When trouble is brewing all
around.
What they should do is come out and say:
Let's look at this in a sensible
way.

But as you know this world is lost,
Never to regain its prestige
at any cost.
Had common sense prevailed since time began,
What a wonderful world this
would be for man.

Albert L Buzzo

THE FIRST SNOW

Tiny flakes that fall to earth
Like crystal stars so bright;
Bring new invigorating birth
To this dull world overnight.
Like rain of cotton, soft and white,
It lays upon the groun';
To cover all earth's drab from sight
With a sparkling dressing
gown.
Skiing, skating, you'll do tomorrow,
But now to bed to wake with
the dawn.
You gaze out the window, alas,
Last night snow is already
gone.

Albert L Buzzo

FROGS ON A LILY PAD

Frogs are always croaking on a lily pad.
They blink their eyes
because they're sad.
The water tells them that they're secure.
That life on a lily pad they
must endure.
They swim around in search for food,
When amphibians are in the
mood.
Should they be satisfied to soak,
Back to the lily pad to croak.

Albert L Buzzo

YOU TAUGHT ME

Certainly,
You taught me how
To love the birds and bees.
You taught me why
The leaves grow on the trees.
You taught me to love.

Certainly,
You taught me why
The skies are always blue.
You taught me many
things I never knew.
You taught me to love.

Certainly,
You taught me how
To spend my nights and days.
You taught me how
To wait so I can say;
Darling, I love you.

Diane Pearl Marie Ismail

Diane Pearl Marie Ismail

HIS GIFT

Dedicated to my two best inspirations, Karen J. Pesce and Paul J. Pesce.

On Christmas Eve, my brothers and me,
Set our cookies near the chimney.
While Mommy and Daddy, decorated the tree,
With colored lights that glowed brightly
Through the night.
Soon it was time for us to say
Good night and hope that
Santa would have a good flight.
I slept snuggled in my bed
And all through the night,
I dreamed of things that were right.
On Christmas Day, I woke to say,
It's Christmas, it's Christmas:
Oh, what a glorious day.
As I ran down the stairs,
I knew Santa had been here.
All the cookies were gone
And presents were every where.
As I looked under the tree,
I'd seen the most beautiful,
Present of all,
It was sweet Baby Jesus,
Smiling at "me."

Diane Pearl Marie Ismail

PAUL'S GRACE

Paul was very sad today, his little crab passed away.
I was quite surprised, when I heard him say, Mom, Dad
Can I take a walk today, somehow I feel I'd like to pray.
Karen, he said would you like to come with me?

"Sure" Paul sure right away. As we walked through our
Back yard we heard a sound,
following it we came upon
Two kittens.
What a smile Paul made ear to ear.
"Oh" the Lord must
Have had truly heard his pray.

Mumbling all sorts of names finally he shouted "Velvet"
And "Chubette" that's what I'll call you.

Paul carried Velvet and I carried Chubette.
When Mom and Dad had seen his face, they knew Paul
Had found his grace, and Velvet and Chubette,
Still live at our place.

Clarence Bates

THE AUTUMN TIME OF TREES

The meadows seethed with hordes
O screaming birds, robins
in wild migration.

It was in the time of trees
Forests of douglas fir, yellow pine
And cedar clothed the heights
in shades of green.

The tamarack, its yellow fire ablaze
On autumn hills. In meadows sky high
Silver boles of poplars support
a canopy of frosted gold.

An autumn quiet stream adrift with rafts
Of leaves, Flows 'round scattered stones
of gray.

A knickered boy of ten splashes his
Wayward way, knee deep in fallen leaves
And leaves still falling.

The youthful time when he was free from care
To roam and feel and best of all enjoy
The autumn days when he was just a boy.

Judy Seely

THOUGHTS

I walk the sands of life
Engrossed in thoughts
The seemingly endless horizon
Lay ahead
Bright, but yet subdued colors
Engulf the sky
The waters reflecting the colors
In time night has fallen
Like a shade it covers us
It's dark once again, you wait
anxiously
For another seemingly hopeless day
to begin

Diane Pearl Marie Ismail
A MEMORY

For Mom. Dreams do come true.

It took me a long time to realize,
How much time slipped by.
The loneliness of my crying,
And no one to dry my eyes,
Until I found you, I could break all
ties.
Now I'm alone again
With so much emptiness.
No one to teach me
All I need to know,
No one to reach me
Or a place to call home,
Yes once again, I'm all alone,
And far from any home
No one to love me,
The way you used to do.
"Oh Mother" I only need you:
But God took you away
And left me to go my own way
Now how shall I live, for just one
more day
With no one to say,
"I love you" more than yesterday.

Kathleen Lefebvre
MY FRIEND AND I
A cool breeze brushed against my
face bringing me the
aroma of the briny ocean and its
inhabitants.
I strolled slowly towards the
breaking white-capped waves,
digging my toes into the coal black
grains of sand.
Walking, thinking, stopping
I want to be here with you.

The waves rushed to meet me
stretching like an eruption
of molten lava covering all in its
path.
Gently the waves flowed over my
feet like a light summer blanket
and hurried back to the deep waters
like a shy little girl.
Meeting, touching, feeling
My friend it's good to be near
you.

The rhythmic pounding of the
waves hypnotized me
and I was caught in the splendor of
the summer evening.
The sounds were quiet sounds as
thoses heard
by an infant in its mother's womb.
Breathing, whispering, listening
I need your quiet companion
ship.

The gentle touch of a wave was
unspoken words
from my friend.
One quick shiver like an aspen leaf
acknowledged
my contentment.
Sighing, sharing, understanding
My friend, I am revitalized by
your feelings of
peacefulness.

Mike Robertson
WHO AM I
Who are you to blaspheme—
Who are you to scorn—
Who in this world
ever asked to be born?

Who are you to detest—
Who are you to hate—
Who in this world
has a right to escape?

Who am I to blaspheme—
Who am I to scorn—
I, myself, alone
never asked to be born!

Who am I to detest—
Who am I to hate—
I, myself, alone
have not a right to escape!

Debra Carter
ONLY THE LONELY
Only the lonely knows how it is a
love so strong and pure.
Why did my suspicions get in the
way.
Don't you know it's wrong to love
me then leave.
All I can do is think about you look
at your face.
Only the lonely feels pain ouch cry of
pain for you.
I love you so every time I see lovers
together makes me jealous.
Only the lonely feels it wish I could
hold you
Kiss you tell you I love you I'm tired
of being alone.
I need you please can't stand it you're
on the east coast.
I'm on the west coast these distants I
can't handle.
Only the lonely knows how it feels.
Oh baby I love you so much.

Betty Garner
LOVES RULE

To the man, I Loved, Long Ago.

Time passes us by so quickly
We must do things in life so swiftly
But we must make time for important
parts of life
We must always take time to love
and be loved
Trying not to hurt the ones we love
As thru this life we go
So many times we take each other for
granted
Life is always such a hectic pace
We always seem to run, never
winning the race
Can you really imagine how it would
be
If we never hurt the one we love
Why can this, we not see
There is one thing we can depend on
The one we love, can forgive for just
so long
Then that love is gone
And we are left all alone
So give to your love, what you want
to receive
Then when love and life is over
You will not have to grieve

Brenda C Wellford
I SEE
I sit here, I look around me
and what do I see.

I see a sea of faces like you and me,
belonging to people with hearts and
feelings
and emotions just like ours.

Can you see the love in them.

Do you take the time to know at least
one of them or do you shut yourself
out
afraid to know them.

But most of all, afraid for them to
know you.

Linda S Iler
SPECIAL DELIVERY

To Aunt Dorie, the best Aunt, Sister & Friend. We know. We love you. From Linda, Steve, & Marleena.

Here it is your birthday again,
And we didn't know just what to
send.
Flowers and candy just won't be true.
To send the love we have for you.
300 miles is so far away
to send what we have for your special
day.
It's love and hugs and a great big
kiss.
To show how much we really miss,
Our special Aunt way up there.
So we're sending you our panda Bear
We hugged and kissed him a whole
night through.
So he'll take our love up to you.
So grab him up for a kiss and hug.
And remember he holds all our love.

Jo Ann Johnson
MY WEATHERED FRIEND
My Old Friend split today
I'm mourning with the saplings
She served me well, logging the story
of my youth
Leaning over the creekbank
Protecting me and the wildlife from
sunstroke
She was a prop for this bookworm
A mountain to climb
An umbrella for rainy days
Tiny twig villages emerged beneath
her
Daydreams prospered a glorious
future
Between her branches and beyond
We had a daily rendezvous to shelter
me
From a world of noise and chores
The orchestra of the woods
entertained
Wild violets loaned me their
fragrance
Her roots invited me to cover them
and rest
I'll miss her!

Chantel Lambert
ONE DAY
I love you oh, yes I do
I wish I could spend my
life with you

I remember the day you walked
out the door, I had never felt the
way that I had felt before

I ask you please just think
of me and maybe you'll see we
were meant to be

Maybe one day you'll forgive
me and I'll forgive you, because
I know our love will never be through

Until that day comes, just
remember . . . I love you

Doug Ries
FALLEN SOLDIER

Fallen Soldier was written in memory of my good friend, Michael Kirk, whose life was ended so unfairly and tragically by suicide.

Changes, Changes
writing on the wall
a last cigarette
a soldier starts to fall
days pass by slowly
months on end
the soldier will never
be heard from again

As the forces of evil
the verdict they pass
his days plagued with torture
like sands through the hourglass
No army could save him
no jury decide
by God's hand he lived
by his hand he died

The smile on his face that could only
tell lies
of the pain and the feelings of
compromise
his death brought him pleasure
beyond all remorse
he toyed with the reaper and
Fate took its course.

Berniece Cover
DESERT DAWN

To my wonderful family.

I love to walk in the desert
At the dawning of the day,
When the morning sun casts shadows
Moving like children at play.

It's easy to feel His presence
As I wander this desert land,
His home on earth was much like this
With mountains, shadows, and sand.

Let me slowly trod this beaten path
And listen to the birds sweet refrain,
Filling my heart and soul with
memories
For I may not pass this way again.

Denise Brooks
BABIES

This poem is dedicated to my four precious children and to all the precious Babies in the world.

Babies are more precious than rubies,
more sparkling than diamond rings.
Their skin is as soft as the
Roses
That bloom in the spring;
But, above everything is the
"Magic!
That their Love brings.

Charlie Irwin
RAIN OF FREEDOM

Dedicated to the memory of: 1989 Chinese freedom fling, Tiananmen Square, Beijing.

it's been a long drought
since new flowers came out

first raindrops merely stir the dust
guns rot money melts cannons rust

one, two, three little innocent
raindrops
dancing on trees like daffodils on
dragons

dozens and thousands of raindrops
dive
splatter and disappear into the silent

dark cracks of the shallow drying
river

'til mere millions join hands celebrate
on the big pond where dinosaurs die
the mystical butterfly survives
(no thanks to bombs bullets tanks)

billions of raindrops build behind
the dam of dynastys dictators Time
bulging cracks in the Wall. Curtain
rust, falls

all free people stand up for roll call
Poles Czechs Hungarians Germans
Romanians Bulgarians

a few refreshing raindrops, a trickle,
a river
of change carves its own course
across the peoples' thirsty earth

Dave Ivey
ME AND HER
Her eyes trapped me,
I looked inside of her,
Hopelessly in love, forgetting all
others
Yet remembering, and feeling
The exact first kiss.

Her heart keeps me alive,
I strive to keep her,
Her love gives me hope,
My hope gives her love.

I need her, her loving heart,
Her gentle touch, her lips—
Joined to mine, our bodies locked,
Never letting go, embracing—
—For eternity

I love her,
With all passion,
We kiss, and the sea roars,
The lightning flashes, the
Rain pours.
We listen as we fall asleep,
In each other's arms.

Joseph John Imperial
GOD

This poem is dedicated to God, and to Jesus Christ, my Lord and Savior, Amen.

God! I love you, with my heart, and
soul!
I pray to you everyday, to make me,
whole.
Although! I walk through life, with
troubles, and strife!
I pray to you everyday, to help me
through, my life.
And, even though, I feel like a chess
pawn!
I know, you will bring me through,
my troubles and strife,
Until I can see the dawn.
And, as I read, and believe in your
words, that are written,
In the book of Psalms!
I truly know! Dear Father! That you
will, never let me come,
To any harm.
But! I know, Dear Father! That
sometimes I fall!
So! When I read your Psalms, they
make me stand tall.
But! When I feel, that I'm going to
fail!
I! Read the Psalms, to get back on,
the right trail.
So, I praise you! Dear Father! For not
making me frail!
Because! Dear Father! As long as
you are with me,
I will always, prevail! Amen!

Daniel Johnson
THE TWIN DESTINYS OF YOU AND ME
For it has come to pass that an entry
shall be made in the great book, on
the subject of a single race calling
itself mankind,
as the pages slowly turn, we wonder
what the writer has in mind.
for none of us can remember when
the last entry was made,
it may be that the race has changed,
may be even saved
if so they have traveled far, since the
time they called each other slaves.
when the world burned with fire,
fueled by hate and rage. You see they
have this thing called poverty, which
rapes the souls of all.
For while society keeps looking up,
the poor can only fall.
Or did we finally see the forest
beyond the trees/
and help the common man to rise up
from his bending knees.
then together as a race of one, shelter
our homeless, and make sure that for
all time war was over and done.
did we take care of all the children,
feed those in need, and the
elderly, who had always given love
an respect, mankind for once
made sure that what they had given
was what they now received.
The entry of our destinys shall be
plain for all to see
as to how far we have traveled as a
race, or if we are still
standing in the same place. We are
all responsible as to which the entry
shall speak, for as always the keeper
of the pen, is you and me.

Daniel Johnson
THE COMMON MAN
We were once revered as workers,
the shining pillars of society,
backbone of the nation, we taught our
children right from wrong,
encouraged them to be honest and
strong, but somewhere somehow we
seem
to have forgotten that right is still
right, and wrong, is still wrong.
and yet the common man is faithfully
trying to hold on,
His home is the side walk of your
street, his next meal is what you
refused to eat his only crime is that
he is old or sick or weak.
they have been made the subjects or
our cruel jokes
and the political hoax that only talk
of bringing them hope.
We allow to exist in our mist a
faceless invisible nation.
indeed the common man has not
known such sorrow since the dawn of
creation.

A child crying from hunger is as
common as a song,
but do we really think of hunger as
something that is wrong.
Our leaders it seems are quite out of
touch, they speak often about
the problems, but the answers don't
say much.
Your children hear the lies you tell
see the wrong you do,
yet you seem so surprised when they
rebel against you.
We see the common man daily on the
street and get angry when they ask
for money or something to eat, but
quietly we say thank God it's him
and not me. Maybe one day the
coldness will end, for once upon a
time
even baby Jesus was denied room at
the inn, the common man is another
victim of power, fear and greed, his
salvation lies in the hands of other
common people, people like you,
people like me.

Chuck Jeffery
THIS FRIEND OF MINE
This friend of mine is strong and true.
A character was he,
But from my side he's disappeared
The blame I place on me.

This friend of mine had small dark
eyes.
His hair was thick and brown,
And when sad times afflicted me
He acted like a clown.

There were some times when we
would fight.
I lost not even one.
This friend of mine did not fight
back,
The fights were all in fun.

This friend of mine is not around.
I left him as a child.
My mother said, "Leave Ted behind."
She said it none too mild.

Now he lies with socks and things
And clothes I do not wear,
This friend of mine is still so kind;
He's just a Teddy Bear.

Elizabeth Johnson
JOEL THE CEMETERY CARETAKER
There was a man named Joel,
Whose job was digging a hole,
For all the newly deceased,
Whose life had suddenly ceased.

Joel was always very busy,
Sometimes it made him dizzy,
Staring at the marker stones,
Which identified all the bones.

Watching everyone by moonlight,
So they don't sneak off Halloween
night,
Cleaning the grounds was more than
a chore,
That even someone like Joel couldn't
ignore.

He keeps the graveyard lawn in
shape,
And remembers to lock the iron gate,
Knowing someday he'll be long
gone,
To lay by the bodies forever long.

Angelique R Brown
MY GRANDFATHER'S LAP

To my Grandpa, Ray Belden, whom I love and miss very much.

Perched upon my Grandfather's lap
I touched his veins so blue,
bubbling from his pale, crinkled skin
I stared into his eyes,
so glassy,
as if holding the years of suffering.
I sprang up and watched,
as he struggled to pull himself
from the swallowing couch.
His hand as if a dried fallen leaf,
next to mine, a peachy rose petal.
My throat tightens
as I wish I could crawl onto his lap
now
or look into his eyes
and help him just once more.

Donna Rose Bennett
TO THE CHILDREN

To my children, Benjamin and Sherry.

We all cry for our children
We ask where they are going.
But do we ever cry with . . . our kids!
Do we dare let them see
Our pain, our love, our misery!

Maybe if we did let them see our
tears,
We would not have so many fears.
To outside influence, drugs, and beer
If we could only show just how
much we care.

Too hard on discipline, Too little it
seems.
If only we could find one that was
in-between.
We never say "I Love You" enough,
Then "I am Sorry" for all the
abusive stuff!

Why is it that parents can never see,
The pain we give our children, the
misery?
When will the hatred ever stop!
When! We push our kids to the
one
down the block!

When we no longer see their smiling
faces.
When we no longer have their
hugs
and Kisses!
That's when we all wake to a bitter
end.
That we can never have our child's
Love again!

Mary Branscome
THE EVERLASTING SAINT

A Pleasant Memory.

A lot of people talk about St.
Valentine's Day—
When the YOUNG girls and boys
give their hearts away.
Red roses—Yellow roses—candy
too—
All proclaiming "I Love You."

But we older folks also have
something to say—
To our loved ones on this Special
day.
The quick-beating pulse—the
butterflies—they are all gone.
But the memories and emotions
simply live on and on.

Now my loved one has been gone
these many years past—
But my love for him has continued to
last.
We will meet again someday and the
skies of Heaven we'll paint—
Then I will meet the man who started
this mess;
After all he was a Saint.

Dr Lattice Boykin-McKoy
TO HATE

Dedicated to all who seek the pureness of love.

If this be love, then let me hate
With time to feel my heart break
Time to conquer, time to bend
Time for the heart to mend.

If this be love, then hate me
For feelings that curse and scorn thee
Laying bare, nude like death
As final and sad as a last request.

If this be love, then teach me how to hate,
Things I crave, and the joys I anticipate
Give me old age, in preference to youth
And lies that steal the heart of truth.

If this be love, then how ugly is hate
Can beauty be beauty if obscured in debate
Is love without identity or definition
When argued in hate and derision.

If this be love, then take my heart
For greed will grow and tear us apart
For true love gives for its own sake
And in the end, gives more than it takes.

Pauline Bonnici
TIME

To my parents, Emmanuela and John, And to my sister, Josette.

My past is gone—
My present here—
And the future—
Still to come.

Would I have had it,
For my past to be here.
Because my present is lonely—
And the future?

They all cry around me—
Shouting, screaming—
Laughing,
Have they no fears?

Not a care in the world,
Or so seeming—
Life is lonely—
And love not found.

Roseanne Alston
A CELEBRATION
I have someone who told me so
A friend I met some time ago,
That she was proud of each year gone by
Because, somehow, she had survived.

Not an easy task in this day and age
So many obstacles hinder our way,
But with a willing spirit the war we wage
Can sustain us each and every day.

And the war for many does have its reward
But it's not by always carrying a sword,
It's the love we carry and the care we give
To those who need a reason to live.

It's your birthday, so celebrate the year!
Because you've become that much more dear.
And my wish for you comes from the heart
Of which you've become a significant part!

Susie Andrews
MY GIFT TO YOU
Today is the day, We are to wed.
Ideas of our future, I hold in my head.
Today is our day, A new life we'll start.
I'll give you my love, my soul, and my heart.
Tomorrow isn't a place that we know.
It holds our future, so there we must go.
As we walk together thru life.
I'm proud to be chosen, to go as your wife
I love you.
I need you.
I give you my life.

Lisa Marie Anderson
DARE TO DREAM
Dare to Dream and you may succeed, but to fail is not to dream, and if you make mistakes just pick yourself back up and try again.
Sooner or later you will win

Steven Christopher Abood
SPRING
Spring is a time for new animals and flowers,
Coming and going by the hours.
Some animals big, some animals small,
Some flowers short, some flowers tall.
Flowers are yellow, blue, and red,
Smelling pretty get you out of bed.
Squirrels, cats, and even dogs,
Just over a rock and under a log.
Run animals, run and go hide,
For the hunter is here and real nearby.
The flowers will soon be all gone,
For now the seeds must go to furnish a lawn.
The trees sway as the wind blows by,
Just as the sun sets in the sky.

Teresa Anderson
CASTLE SAND MAN
All at once from a boy to a man, then a father, pretending to be stronger.

Until one day he notices, he forgot how to play and discover!

Watching his children play in the sand, his wife shows them how to build a castle of sand!

He can't remember if he ever built a sand castle. Did he ever know how?

Suddenly, he realizes, to play in the sand you have to get down as a child!

Is he willing to get into the sand compromising his strong hands?

Then he decides if he's ever to build a castle in the sand, it should be now!

Who knows when again he'll be able to build his Castle of Sand!

Joyce Miller
JUSTICE
Independence stating justice
Even tho there is not a dime.
Freedom beeched to all length of sublime.
Far from the soul of understanding deep within.
Never cast a doubt.
Just be above sin.

Joyce Miller
THANK YOU
Love for all acme of season.
Prayer universal given reason.
Hope for understanding know.
Faith for trial error and woe.

Thank you for the flowers
That have blossomed my way.
Thank you for the long hard hours
You have put in without pay.
Thank you for your tolerance
As you endure each trying day.
May God bless you with wisdom
Through words I cannot say.

Beverly Lynch
MY LOVE
"My Love,
a god mythology,
rendering heart,
soul strengthening life,
magic upon my being."

Though myth be not real,
strength in touch do appeal,
moving gently
through great powers
mystery."

"My Love,
a mere genius
savors flavor in style,
of love and affection,
a potent injection,
his shining oracle freed."

"Like a blooming flower,
or fermenting wine,
his beauty doth captivate me."

Joyce Miller
THE HOMELESS
No respectable gainful employ.
No sanctuary of peace and joy.
They have been stripped of dignity
And reduced to shame.
Scorned and abused
Left without a name.

Although woefully driven.
Filthy and mentally unwell.
They still deserve a decent place to dwell.

By passing the buck to and fro
Bureaucracy has dealt them a shocking blow.

The plight of the homeless is in despair.
From lack of understanding and care.

When the streets become home
There is no place to be
Just aimlessly roam.

It's a daily struggle trying to survive.
Knowing you are not wanted dead or alive.

Women and children are suffering
They are homeless too.
The numbers are mounting
Relief must come into view.
Let's come together and take heart.
Giving them hope for a brand–new start.

Thomas Moffitt
TO THE WORMAINE SOCIETY
We Night Crawlers and Angleworms
are on
STRIKE!
We till the soil
squirming
and
churning
Day and night,
Only to end up on a hook, line, and pole,
Sacrificed for some
'TROPHY' fish enticed
Out of its watery hole;
Then to be mounted on some
Fisherman's wall.
And, this is not all . . . !
We feel we deserve to be on
The same display
As the fish, who, thanks to us,
Received the great honor
Of ending up
In such a way!

James L Murphy
BARBARA
lying stretched
across
floral
sheets

your
lanky frame
next
to
mine

limbs
tangled
around
each
other

searching
for
peace

James L Murphy
THE PROSPECTOR
He doesn't talk much
When he does it's talk of goldmines,
Sluice boxes, trout fishing,
Beaver, moose and the sight of
Graceful, watchful deer drinking
At the water's edge near his old cabin
Up at Frenchman's Creek—
Such things as most men only dream about—
Old books and magazines overflow
The cluttered shelves behind him
As he speaks with quiet reverence
Of B.C's wild life legacy—
Long years of knowledge cloaked
Beneath the gentle pitch—
When he enters a room
All eyes turn—
With a slightly nervous cough
He lets me know he's there—
That's my Dad.

Geoanna Mohr
SIGHT BEYOND SIGHT
Sight beyond sight
Fright after fright
We still go on
And live life any way we can
We're not sure how or why

we're here
No one person can explain
And no one can see all
But we see what we need
And try to help others
Not everyone has this sight
But fright after fright
We still go on.

Gean P Moreno
BEIJING MASSACRE
Premature revolution
Uprising
Revolt.
The people,
Armed only with courage,
Facing columns
Of green mechanical beasts.
Open fire!
And the protest is scattered
It was chased by the fire flies
Coming from the cannons
Of the soldier's companions.
Many died
Many fled
Many cried
Many believe
That maybe,
Maybe it wasn't time for change.

Sue Krick
OH HOW I LOVE YOU

To Charles Robert Quinton Wheeler, a very special person in my life. I'll always remember you.

Oh how I love you, your eyes so blue,
After we first parted, I asked can this be so true?
You are so sweet and your gentle touch,
Are all part of you that mean so much.
I'm so glad we met and our conversation was set.
To spend very valuable time right now in our lives.
You captured a part of me and now I know I am free,
To do as I please and celebrate life
with who means so much to me.

Sue Krick
BRIGHT SUNSHINE

To Doris Jean and Joseph Edward Crum, my mother and father. I love you very much.

As bright as the sun that shines,
A love flows to you to say,
"I'm doing fine!"
With a heart of joy. I'm glad to say,
having a mom and dad like you,
"Is the only way!"
To talk and teach along the way,
to enjoy life when there's,
"Not much to say!"
I love you both on this Easter Day,
and may you spend it together,
"In a special way!"
Thank you for being so special!!

Doris Hughes McDouall
HOLLY

To Doug.

No legend signifies the holly
Snow decorates the leaves
No tinsel adorns
Christmas red and green
Perhaps this is its theme
'Twas not a dream
Peace is the crown

Jennifer Michel
TODAY AND TOMORROW

This poem is dedicated to Andy Carter, who will always hold a special place in my heart.

As I sit there in your arms I feel that nothing could tear us apart.
Words that you say to me are kept so deep in my heart.
I want to hold onto all of the things you do and you say,
I just wish I could hear your voice for one more time today.
I wish I could hear you say that you wish for the same.
I hope things will be the best for us for a long while.
For when I hear you or see you I always bear a smile.
Whenever I think of "us" being just me and just you,
I see things so cold and things are so blue.
I wish there was such a word as forever,
But, there's only such words as today and tomorrow.

Helen E Menor
TRIBUTE TO PRESIDENT KENNEDY
Ask what you can do for your country, he said,
Not what your country can do for you, instead.
Then with vision and vigor he pointed the way
To attain these goals without further delay.

The problems of the world concerned him most,
His main plan was peace, not an idle boast.
A new frontier was more than a dream,
Feeding hungry people was part of his scheme.

Better education for all was another fine aim,
For youth here or abroad it was the same,
So that some day all children might live to see
A world finally at peace in complete harmony.

A profile of courage, honest and strong,
Incredible that any man could do him wrong!
A symbol of kindness, always just and fair,
Heaven is a finer place now that he's there!

Mary E Merriam
THIS ONE IS FOR YOU!

To my wonderful Husband Michael C. Merriam. All my Love. Your wife Bella.

You're my strength to go through each new day,
You're the light to help me see.
You're my guidance when I'm wandering,
You're what I want for me.
You're the topic of my conversations,
You're the thought that's on my mind,
You're the love I feel inside of me when I lay back to unwind.
You're my hopes, my prays, my dreams come true,
Now my joys in life are because of you!
You're everything a man could be,
You're the man every girl dreams of.
And I just want to let you know that you're the man I love.
With each new passing day I see,
I pray there'll come a day,
When you and I will be as one,
And our love can lead the way.
You're someone who I cherish, admire, and respect,
And for all the things you've done for me,
I never will forget.
You're a very special person of which there only are a few,
And I thank God in every way for letting ME find YOU!

ALL MY LOVE
MARY E. MERRIAM

Susan W Morris
A FAMILY PRIDE

In loving memory of Bigmama . . . not only a catalyst in our creation, but a great mentor to us all.

The sweetest memories I can perserve . . .
are those of affection
deep in reserve.
A bouncing motion in my Mother's arms . . .
feeling safe and secure
away fromharm.
A hug from my Grandmother so strong yet soft . . .
brought laughter to heart
sent worries aloft.
A kiss on the cheek by my Aunt so dear . . .
gave happiness, pleasure and joy
not fear.
A pat on the back by my Brother's strong hand . . .
sent as feeling of confidence
bravery to stand.
My Sister's hand brushing back my hair . . .
made a close alliance of love
to share.
These are my memories of deep inside
A love overbearing . . .
A FAMILY PRIDE

Shirley MacKenzie
WHERE ARE YOUR CHILDREN
Standing by the window
All alone in the dark.

Do you know where your children are?

Pacing back and forth
Till you wear a path in the floor.

Do you know where your children are?

Worrying about the drugs,
The bad people,
And the alcohol.

Do you know where your children are?

You're worried,
You're scared,
You're upset.
What kind of strange people have they met?

Where are they?

You're up till 11:00
You're up till 2:00
Do they know what they are doing to you?

I don't know where my children are.

Do you?

Jeffrey Allen Miller
YOU
I would ride
That ferris wheel
With you
Wander in the sky
And drop a candy heart
On you

Voices ring and voices sing
But only yours can I hear
Don't be like the sun at night
And disappear

I would butterfly the sky for you
You hit my eyes like paradise skies—it's true

Lovers run in lovers sun
I won't run away from you
Don't be like the sun at night
And say we're through

I would ride that ferris wheel with you

Cynthia L Miller
WHO CARES?
Who cares when you're down and everything goes wrong?
Who cares when you're hurting; your heart's without a song?

Who cares when life's battles are difficult to win?
Who cares when the evil one is tempting you with sin?

There is one who cares; Jesus is His name.
He walked the streets of Nazareth; today, He is the same.

He was tempted and tried the way you are today.
He walked the same road so He could lead the way.

He cares about your hurts, your sorrows and your woes.
He felt those same feelings three days before he rose.

His blood cleanses you daily; and don't forget to pray.
He'll make your load lighter and turn your night to day.

Trust the One who cares; let Him lead your way.
Sing a song of gladness; praise His name each day.

Remember, He'll not leave you; never will He roam.
Hold fast to the One who cares and He will lead you home.

Donnie S Rochester
FREEDOM
The world stands alert on its lofty perch
Freedom it sighs, its soul has been searched
The East joins the West, hate is laid to rest
The walls came tumbling, freedom is the quest.

From Russia to Nicaragua
Glasnost promotes changes
From Panama to Namibia
Commons begets social graces
From Romania to Libya
Debauchery begets hostility
From Cuba to the U.S.A.
Hostility begets subtle sensitivity
From Africa to Asia.

Sensitivity begets amenities.

ALL HAIL TO WORLD LEADERS
Who are their brother's keepers,
As one man's trouble leads a nation's struggle
To beat apartheid into the rubble.

FREEDOM I SAY, FREEDOM I PRAY
For the price of freedom
With my life I will pay any day.

Lucienne Y Zelesky
BABY JESUS IN HIS BED

Father Joseph Labrie Died Xmas
Was buried on Mom's Birthday
I was 11th child out of 12—
Never enjoyed from then on.

Baby Jesus in his bed
Angels' watching overhead
Birthday greetings we will bring
When we do this very thing

Light the tree
Let it cast its bright rays
Santa's here all is clear,
On this here happy day,
Throw away all your cares
Be merry and gay,
Santa's here with good cheer
For all here this Christmas day

This is one thing we must do
Children love it grownups too
Everyone do his share
For this is a great affair

Martha Fridge
THE GREAT PHYSICIAN

To Pastor Robert L. Miller, Retired
For the Faith, Hope, and Charity
which have been my inspiration.

When sorrow seems to surround you,
And the pain grows day by day,
Call upon the Great Physician,
He's only a whisper away.

He'll take away all your sorrow,
He'll wipe away all of your tears.
All you have to do is ask Him,
And He'll vanquish all of your fears.

Call upon the Great Physician
Cast on Him all of your cares.
Then put your trust in the Lord,
To answer all of your prayers.

The Great Physician will answer,
Your heartaches He will ease.
And with His gentle, loving hand
The Lord will grant you peace.

Ralph James Moothart
THE OLD STONE HOUSE
It stands proud in the midst of tall mountains.
Its stone walls nearly solid as they.
Just two miles down a hot desert path,
the remains of an old house decay.

Its roof had burned away long ago.
Its two chimneys no longer hold heat.
On its floor, weeds vie with each other,
to fill in the cracks of concrete.

Six doors, and sixteen windows stand bare,
to look out on the mountain's views.
Across a ravine lies an old cement pond
that perhaps was a fountain when new.

One hundred yards back down the path
there remains an old covered well.
Around it, a small open plot of land,
for what use, no evidence will tell.

Oh, who were the people who lived here?
How long ago was this a home?
What was this old stone house to someone,
in the middle of nowhere, alone?

Rajesh Mahtani
OLD AGE
It is raining heavily,
The clouds are crying like babies,
Shedding their tears over a grandfather,
Who is counting the last days of his year.
His eyes open wide,
With a dog at his side,
Both showing their abyss of despair.
Both have everywhere stared.

Despaired because the roses are not in flower,
Waiting for the once black,
Florid sky to shower,
So that the trees would not perish.
An aura of emptiness seemed to be in their home,
Because no light shone,
In that desperate place,
Where sight was covered with a haze.

Rajesh Mahtani
DEATH
Spring, summer, autumn, and now winter,
My life spent in this soil very thin,
from which the trees whither,
when the lights begin to dim.
With this darkness I shall sleep peacefully,
My consciousness will be gone,
and no snoring will wake me,
for I am going ... going ... and soon ... gone.

Under this patchy darkness,
I shall not see
again the past in blindness,
for an abyss of dreams will take me.
Towards the realm of serenity,
Behind the dark brightness of dawn.
In the midst of the fragrant, florid eden.
I am going ... going ... and soon ... gone.

But before I drift into this cloud,
My face will be drawn
With a smile,
For I am going ... going ... 'gone.'

Debra G McGarigle
UNTITLED
People they say will come and go,
but you I thought would last.

I never thought that you and I
would be something of the past.

It's you I've grown to love and trust
Oh, remember how we used to fuss?

Remember all the time we made?
And now it's all beginning to fade.

The quality, I thought, was one of a kind,
And something, again, I'll probably never find.

Many things begin and end,
But oh, so precious, I'll miss you friend.

Debra G McGarigle
ON YOUR WEDDING DAY
Today is a very special day,
May you remember it in only happy ways.
Love is most precious when shared by two.
Enjoy each other in what ever you do.

Remember that one is always near,
And there will never be anything to fear.

To each other always be kind.
And love and peace is all you shall find.

Love is the most precious thing on earth,
Hold it and care for it, for all your life's worth.

Jenny Hendry
MY DADDY IS AN ALCOHOLIC
My daddy is an alcoholic.
He scares me when he drinks.
The more he drinks, the more I think,
How my opinion of him shrinks.

My daddy drinks, that stinks.
I don't know what to think.
He drives that way, night and day.
He's going to kill someone someday.

Nothing ever worries me as much
As him drinking and driving that Greyhound bus.
It's scary to think of the numbers he'd kill
If he was stupid enough to take hold of that wheel.

One day it will end either good and/ or bad,
But either way it does, I may lose my dad.
It's sad, I say, this may be his day.
It's hard to do, but I'll reveal it to you—
Daddy I Love You!
Jen
P.S. Daddy, Please stop drinking.
Admit your alcoholism!

Manervia Herrington
I WOULD THAT I COULD
If I could pick only the words I would have my child to learn,
And let him see only the things that to good his heart would turn.
If love was the only emotion he saw and kindness the only thing he heard,
I would that I could teach him all of God's HOLY WORD.

But this old world is wicked and full of words unkind.
The things he sees daily is enough to warp his mind.
Bad attitudes, immorality and violence ring out across the land.
Not according to God's will but the way Satan planned.

Satan's continuous effort to teach a child lies and deceit,
And if they listen only to him, their life will end in defeat.
"I would that I could, my child, that pure example be,
To point you to Jesus Christ, so His peace can dwell in thee."

Rachel Holdren
FORGET ME NOT
Forget me not and love m forever.
Scold me not but kiss and make it better.
Hold me in your arms, hold on tight.
I know you'll make everything alright.
So remember to forget me not and love me ever.

Lisa Hurley
GRANNY

To a woman who meant a lot to many people and is missed by me.

Love is always there
even if you can't feel it
I don't know why, but
when you were around
It was so strong
but now
It seems to be fading
And I feel so blue
So, please don't go
I know you love me
But did you know, I loved you
I hope so
Twice as much as yesterday
But not half as much
If there was, but one more tomorrow.

Hazel W Hutchinson
THE LITTLE RED HOUSE
All painted red, on the side of a hill
Stands a quaint little house, quiet and still.
The wide windows peek at the morning sun
Of the fresh new day, just begun.

It's shaded by pine trees that bow and sigh
When laughing breezes go tripping by.
There are flower beds blooming with colors bold.
Tall haughty snapdragons, shy marigolds.

The view from the windows charms the eye.
Placid blue lake, reflecting the sky.
As far off mountain peaks disappear
Mid the fluffy white clouds of the atmosphere

The little red house is the peaceful home
Of a dear, little lady who lives there alone.
She is friendly and kind and full of fun,
While sharing life's joys with everyone.

Within as without it is sunny and pleasant
Made welcome and cozy for all who are present.
She's a friend to treasure, and joy will instill
In her little red house on the side of the hill.

David Oden
BORN TO DIE
Born to die
Living death
To burn the flesh
To burn the lies
Smoke and dust
Flowing in the wind
Life and death
At the mercy of the flow
Only the dust
As artificial flowers
An illusion of life

will instill
In her little red house on the side of the hill.

Hazel W Hutchinson
THE WIND AND THE WAVES
The moon rode high
In a cloudy sky,
On a night of awesome wonder.
When the light from the sky
To the observer's eye,
Showed the waves, all split asunder
The howl of the wind, and the beat of the waves,
The creak of the boats, as spar and mast
Strained at the cables holding them fast
From the monster who held them slaves.
To wind is a howling madman,
Furious and free.
As with lusty blast
He rushes past,
And is lost in the pounding sea.

Hazel W Hutchinson
RETURNING SPRING
The day was a torrent of swaying branches
Drenched with the falling rain,
As the gusty wind tore around the mansion
Rattling each windowpane.

The old gray house stood dark and bare
Set back in a grove of pines
That shivered and shook as in despair
When the wind screamed through the vines

That frantically clung to the old, stone walls
Defying all traces of time.
While the winter poured in miniature falls
Down the trunk of each stately pine.

The wind decreased when darkness descended,
The torrents of rain to a gentle flow.
And soft light from the narrow windows transcended
The night with a faint ethereal glow.

The smell of the pines, dripping with rain,
The scent of the soft, wet earth
Pervading the air as a sweet refrain
With the joy of Spring's rebirth.

Penelope Stockley
DO NOT MAKE ATOMIC WAR
Do not make Atomic War.
The earth, the trees, and I,
Will surely die,
And we will be no more.
The flowers will go,
And all the things we know.
Do not make Atomic War.
No longer will the Eagle soar.
Dust clouds will hide the sky.
No birds will fly.

Do not make Atomic War.
The oceans then will lifeless be,
An empty sea.
And whales will swim no more.
Far in the deep,
This death will fall and seep.
Do not make Atomic War.
The dead will line the shore.
The stars and moon will go.
We, will not know.

Penelope Stockley
THE ETERNAL MIND
I am the universal mind, the mighty force,
The interstellar winds, I keep the stars on course.
The molten streams that from volcanoes flow.
The awesome forces on the universe bestow.
The continental plates are rent apart,
As continents drift off, new ones to start.
Some plates subduct beneath the continental shelf,
To join the searing magma that renews itself.
The whirlwinds and typhoons I make.
The foundations of the universe I shake.
I am the quasars, shining like a million suns.
I am the fuel on which the universe still runs.
I am the atom's core,
And all the things else and more.
The human spirit on its endless course,
Through all eternity, I am the force.

Ed Skornicka
WINTERLAND

Dedicated in loving memory of Ed Skornicka—With love, your wife Sandy and daughter Laura.

The new snow twinkles from an unseen
light
As it covers the ground like a white blanket
in the early night
Once again winter has found its way to the
cold midwest
Where our health, strength, and patience
will be put to the test
People in warmer climates ask why we
tolerate this year after year
Could it be the warmth shared by friends
that makes it so dear
Or, perhaps it's the enchantment of
watching a child build a person of snow
Using a hat, a carrot, and jelly beans to
make its face glow
The snow crackles under my boots as I
slowly walk away
And I look to the sky and thank God for
another beautiful day.

Darrell W Sutton Jr
ODE TO THE SEASONS
No song can be as sweet as the one the birds do sing,
When life is reborn upon the Earth in the time of Spring.
Eventually comes the Summer, the heat and lazy days,
When the sun does lengthen its life giving rays.
This is followed by the Fall, the time of preparation,
When we defend against the cold Winter's proclamation.

With Winter comes the cold, the snow and the rain.
We endure it with the certainty that Spring will come again.
Rejoice and be happy in the Springs and Summers of your life.
Prepare in the Falls for the Winter's strife.
Although your Winters may seem long take heart and never fear,
For as sure as the Seasons, your Spring is somewhere near.

Darrell W Sutton Jr
THE SECOND COMING
Jesus is the way, the truth and the light, the only way to reach Heaven.
Born to Mary upon that night, He still walks among us brethren.
How many of us would be willing to face Death on dread Calvary,
So that mankind yet unborn could from sin be set free?
When temptation sorely vexes you, think of Jesus first.
For the temptation He endured, had to be the worst.
Imagine how He felt on the Last Supper's night,
Knowing who would betray Him and that Death was His plight.
Think of how He faced his captors with a peace so serene.
Even though they tortured Him and proclaimed Him unclean.
He walks with you now my friend along life's weary way,
To help you meet the foe that plagues you day by day.
What sweet rewards await us on that Heavenly plain.
With Christ's help we can endure the agony of life's pain.
Weep not for the departed to whom Christ their lives have sworn.
We shall know their joy and peace upon that resurrection morn.
We must not question why when we are made to suffer,
Just fast, pray and fellowship one with another.
Who are we to question the All Mighty's Master Plan?
To prepare us for the Second Coming of the Son of Man!

Darrell W Sutton Jr
IN THIS LOVE
I have touched the sky and embraced the Earth.
Travelled the vestiges of time to return unto my birth.
Not mere years, but across centuries do I span,
With each generation I become one with man.
Warriors seek my guidance afore engaging the foe,
Learn of the power to defeat the pain and woe.
I am the well of strength should weariness grow near.
Draw from me what you will, succumb not unto the fear.
Become the master of life, do not become its slave.
Know your search is not hopeless for the happiness you crave.
I am made of the ether, of dreams that come true.
I am here only to help the warriors as brave as you.
I know much of the constant battle you do fight.
Warrior you shall be whole again and know the peace of Love's light.
Yet though the battle seems lost to you once again,
Draw courage from me, warrior, for in this love you'll win.

Linda E D Sarpy
MISSED
I missed you, I know
Because I thought of you
A lot.

I missed you, and wished
"That if I had $10.00 for every time I thought of you"
that I would really, really think of you
A lot!

And as I thought of you, each time,
Money would pile higher
and I'd get richer
and think of the clothes I could buy from these funds
from just thinking of you
and then I could think of you some more
a heck of a lot more and
purchase that Silverado I want
(just 10,000 thinks)

And as these thoughts turned from you to material things (goods, at that)
I pondered whether am I thinking of
you for you
or
for the monetary rewards?

Toni Pauline Schott
IMPERFECTIONS

For Teryl, the one I truly love.
Love, Toni.

If I made you something,
something from the bottom
of my heart . . .

would you accept it,
accept it with gratitude
or just because . . .

if you don't want it
don't accept it at all . . .
But if you did

would you love it
as much as I did . . .
did when I was making it

Although it does have
IMPERFECTIONS . . .
Imperfections here and there

But doesn't our love have
Imperfections too . . .
I know I do
I love you
because you have IMPERFECTIONS.

Maria C Siegel
FUNNY TALK

To my grandson Joey—one of the loves in my life—May your heart ever be young and soft.

A funny thing happened to me the other day
As I took a leisurely walk
I thought I heard a maple sing
And a weeping willow talk
I thought I saw a group of ants spreading
leaves for a picnic lunch
And did I really hear a robin tell a

sparrow
he couldn't sing because he had a sore throat?
Or the sad earthworm sigh saying he wished
he could fly?
Did the wind really laugh when it blew its nose?
Did the anemone weep at not being a rose?
Yes a funny thing happened the other day
Nature spoke to me . . .
But I had nothing to say

Danielle Scriva
A LAZY LIFE

To my Mother, for all the love and support she has given me.

Stars are shining in the sky,
as my life is passing me by.
I sit on the couch for many hours,
as my mind begins to sour.
My life is boring and bleak,
but I am not tiny and meek.
For God as my witness I never go out,
I don't dance or jump about.
I am tired and depressed,
but what I need is no more rest.
I will go out and be wild today,
and I will not listen to what my brain has to say.

Sybil Nassau
OUR SECRET
For awhile

I thought it was you who held on so tight
It wasn't though
It was me.

I was afraid to let you go
the unknown abyss waiting.
But day by day you let go of my hand
And I yours
gently
as you lived.

I didn't see Him
at first
hands outstretched to steady you
But you knew
and you weren't afraid.

Then I knew
It was our secret.
Peace, my beloved mother.

Elaine C Mouton
WHAT IS A FRIEND

Dedicated to my Husband—Easton John Mouton.

A friend is a special person
Who'll help you through thick and thin
A friend will not leave you
Till the very end
They're always there to do what they can
And every once in a while
It's good to have a helping hand.
Need money—that's no problem
Reach out and ask
That's all you have to do
And I know that your friend will help you
I needed money once
And I was scared too
Buy my friend helped me out
And everything came through
Now, don't forget when
When they need your help
You've got to be there too.

Lillian Major-Morrell
SAILOR BOY
Oh for a night
on the open sea,
your heart is light
the wind blows free,
great salt waves
clear your head,
you watch the stars
from your hammock bed.
The jib she creaks
with a pitch and yaw,
in the morning wake
to a seagull's caw,
when I grow up
you can bet I'll be,
just a sailor boy
on the open sea.

Carlton G McAllister
THE CABIN IN THE HILLS
As I am sitting on the front porch,
At my cabin in the hills.
I can hear the frogs a peeping,
And the call of whippoorwills.

Then there's the cricket in the woodpile,
That we hear but seldom see.
And I thank God for Old Vermont,
For she's home sweet home to me.

In the evening when the shadows blend.
The mountain peak's so grand.
I hear the babble of the trout stream,
As it ripples o'er the land.

The moonlight casts a silver path,
Across the surface of the pond.
And it's putting magic touches,
On this land where I was born.

You hear how people travel,
To London, Paris, Spain, and Rome.
And it sort of makes you wonder,
When we have it all at home.

Cherie McEwen
THE LIGHT OF LOVE

To Spanky: Thanks for adding warmth and joy to my life.
To Mom: Thanks for the encouragement and always being there for me.

The Light does shine
So true so clear
So sure it's mine
I have no fear

The strength it gives
The trust it builds
Inside of us
Is where it lives

Each day I see
The light shine thru
From you to me
God knows it's true

My heart once beat alone for me
No longer is that true
The light of love shines free
My heart now beats for you!

Cherie McEwen
TENNESSEE WARMTH
So far away
Yet still I see
The trees sway
With your quiet breeze

The autumnal grace
Of your rainbow hills
So warm its embrace
My nerves lay still

I dream someday
Not to be so taxed
To learn your way
And to live relaxed

Your beauty so real
The distance to see
God's pride you feel
A dream to me

So I know it's right
This road's for me
I'll follow your light
All the way to Tennessee!!

Ethel Zeichner

Ethel Zeichner
TOGETHER
I'm drawn to you like the ocean to the beach,
Sometimes I am the beach and you are the ocean.
You are,
on me,
over me,
in and around me
Like the waves.

We come together lovingly,
Like the water gently lapping at the shore.
We come together fiercely,
Like the tidal wave hitting the sand.

We lay quietly together,
Bodies satiated, warm and touching,
No longer water and sand,
But woman and man.

Mary Interdonato
TAKEN FOR GRANTED
I'm taken for granted so I am told
Even venture out, in the heat, or the cold.

I've no regrets, that I do these things
I'm deeply rewarded, in the smiles, it brings.

I gaze towards the heaven and ask him of me
Why do they resent what I do willingly.

The needy, I hasten, to do all I can
To ease some of their burdens I am, what I am.

I seek no pity, because I can't see
Why not let God, be the judge, of me.

Betty J Hall
GRANDCHILDREN

To my precious grandchildren—present and future.

Tender, new, young shoots are they,
Innocent, humble in all they do,
Reflecting truth as a looking glass,
Teaching us anew.

Bursting with enthusiasm,
Abounding with pure love.
Adorned with unique characteristics,
God's blessings from above.

They busy themselves from early morn,
With the labor or play until even,
Then peaceful in sleep, angelic are they,
Of such is the kingdom of heaven.

They are more than your very own,
Love them, cherish them while you may,
Their future days like a treasure chest,
Filled with all you do and say.

(Grandma/Me-Me)

Gary Hirsch
DREAM
It was dark
She was drinking a coke
"Seven Up"—I said
My eyes nearly giving me away.
"No"—she replied
In her sardonic smile
"Just a drink
see
Just a drink."

Then and there
I knew we were one
Just a one
Coalesce

Rebecca Ross
FRIENDSHIP
Friendship is like a river flowing
Or like a horse's gallop on
The sweet, green grass in the
Spring or summer.
Friendship is between two friends
Forever and ever and ever,
Or like a music playing a sweet
Tune throughout the air.
Friendship is like cat's purring
When it's happy and cheerful,
Or like a playful puppy
During the day.
Friendship is like a knot that
Can never break in two,
Or like a flower blooming
In the nice, warm sun.

Howard G Burr
THE CHILD OF AMERICA
I am the child of America,
Unborn, my destiny
But hours away.
When I first cry
Will I crave drugs
Or hunger anyway?

When I first see
Will there be trees
And grass, and flowers?
Or rusted junk
And garbage cans

And flattened tires?

Will scents be sweet
And tastes delight
Will I touch God
And hear birds sing
Or will fumes defeat
My sense, my sight
And know no God
When last bells ring
Wake me, the child of America.

Shirley J Schworm
SOMEWHERE BETWEEN NOW AND THEN
Somewhere between now and then,
We will meet somewhere again.
It maybe soon, it maybe never,
I know, Dear Lord, I will love You forever.

I learned a song, a long time ago,
The title, Jesus Loves Me, This I Know.
I have read this book, it talks about,
I follow Your words, without a doubt.

If I'm asked, to join Your crowd,
I would be, so very proud.
I followed Your light, one time you see,
You said, "Not Now," and turned away from me.

What I saw, when I visited there,
Makes me want to show You, I care.
Everyone dressed in robes of white,
Walking and laughing, in pure delight.

When my time comes, I pray to You Lord,
That You will ask me, to join Your ward.
The preview I saw, made me impressed,
To join You and Yours, would make me blest.

Jeffrey E Farber
PRIVATE NO MORE
The private person that I be, it's so hard to see inside of me.
So much boils and stirs behind my walls, as I struggle to juggle at least eight balls.
As opaque as I paint the walls around me, I wish they could wash away and set me free.
This constant weighing of what life is about, sometimes drives me so crazy that I just have to
shout. Oh let me be! Please set me free!
I want to join the world and let them see, there's more than meets the eye inside of me.

Jeffrey E Farber
DREAM ON
The world needs more dreamers, to see what is not apparent to you and me.
To soar above most mortal men, to seek and discover past what we thought was the end.
Scientists and poets and writers and you must reach beyond and seek anew.
Don't laugh at the ones with ideas off the wall, for their thoughts are what propel us all.
Sit back and relax and stare into space as your mind floats high above
the banal human race.
Let it expand into every niche and corner,
looking for harmony and beauty where common man sees none.
Seek to find what has not yet been found, by those who are affixed only to the ground.

Rose Garcia
MY SHADOW
My shadow needs some sunshine.
My shadow follows me.
If it weren't for the sunshine,
I wonder where my shadow would be.

I like my shadow,
He likes to go to Mr. Brown's.
I sometimes ask him to go with me,
To all the little towns.

Sometimes he is disobedient,
He won't do what I say.
I ask him to go with me somewhere,
And he says he wants to stay.

Rose Garcia
TRUE LOVE

To "Mac" whom I'll never stop loving.

I've had many boyfriends,
With whom I've had lots of fun.
I've enjoyed them all,
But none like my "Special One."

Only one have I loved,
Although I've had many more.
Though the years have passed,
He's still the only one I adore.

I may meet many others,
But HIS place none other will fill.
I've loved HIM forever,
And I know I always will.

HIS memories are precious,
And certainly, I often look back,
To the most enjoyable moments,
With my beloved Mac.

Regina Conrath
WHEN DOLLARS DO NOT MATTER
Was there ever a time
When dollars did not matter?
What is the most desirable thing
That each life can bring?

Is it dollars and entertainment
Or power and controlling others
Or privileges of walking and talking,
Maybe even joy plants for smoking?

Trash TV, sexual affairs, sudden fortune
Will not be the most desired
If one but thinks of drowning;
The only thing that matters then is breathing.

Circumstances dictate
What one desires most
To do the best
And do what's right
And offer others no slight.

If one is drowning
The only important thing is breath
For without it nothing else will matter
And dollars will make but a small splatter.

James Mieno
SOME ONE
We seldom stop to realize
How dear SOME ONE could be
'Til that SOME ONE leaves our
midst
For all eternity.
Then, how we mourn and weep for him
And speak the good within.
We love him now and cherish him
But lo! It is too late.

Frank Souto
IMPRESSIONS
Lithe leaves that temper with ruinous squalls
Strangers to diffidence
Unyielding trunks which stiffen
Stand foundered upon this bony earth
A splintery of feathery tribes
Flying wayfarers
Gliding through a network of clouds
Looping sinuous patterns
Blemishing the anomalous blue backdrop
Skuff marks in the dust below
A severance
Tearing tracks partition
Can these hands remain together much longer

Adrienne Hearn
SHADOWS
Demons smile down the hall,
Cats of black do shriek,
Nerves are bouncing like a ball,
Innocence can't speak.

Fear is calling in the wind,
Running through your veins,
Loneliness is your companion,
But he won't be your friend.

Darkness falls as raindrops,
Tapping at your heart,
Stress the wire pulls tight,
Emotions tear apart.

Sunrise brings the peacetime,
Freedom heaves the sigh,
No memories of hatetime,
The sun has cleared your mind.

Frank Souto
BROTHER TO BROTHER
We crawled into the cradled rudiments of youth
singing the alphabet, relaxing our maturity,
settling our eyes into a sandbox and reading
the signatures, our own, etched in illiteracy.
Our consciousness, for a moment,
was rubbery in direction,
swollen from amusement, and
softened with innocence.

Resembling wines unimproved with age, we were
thirsty for the sweet intoxication of youth
and surrounded by the elderly images of infancy,
wanting newer ones.

Kym Wallace
WAR IN THE FUTURE

This poem is dedicated to Jim; the start of my life.

In a world of darkness
filled with fear,
the sky is dim,
no birds to hear.

The mystic highways,
the glittering parks,
have all turned to dust
'cause fighting makes sparks.

In order to keep our world
forevermore,
let's help each other
and not make war.

Darrell Andrew Watson
DON'T CHAIN THE DOG

This poem is dedicated to all those poor "sanballat's" who said; you can't, and an inspiration to all those Roosevelt's, Lincoln's and Edison's who believe they can!

Restricted, inflicted they're unsure which way you'll go, courage built on bitterness, strength begins to grow, the lines are drawn, the battles high, goals seen through a vision quest, the time is short, the stakes are made, for now it demands your best, weakened hands, weakened legs, compromising trait, you've given in, you've given up and now it's sealed

your fate, I've also watched you suffer because the road you chose, it's made you hate, it's made you grudge and miserable suppose, but, I won't let it capture me I'll run until I drop, for "desires" have made me unreasoning and impossible to stop, so take one more look, one more glance before I go for "talents" will reveal themselves and "freedom" will they show.

Mrs Gerry Gassaway
THINK ON THESE THINGS

With love to my precious grand-daughters, Sarah and Erin Galpern and Allie and Laura Gassaway.

Awakened by the sunlight through the shade
I lay there quietly to meditate on today and to
reflect on yesterday

Knowing full well there will be disturbances in my life
I ask my God to be with me and remove all strife

Dressed by my earthly attire
I quickly put my emotions aside and
rush out to see
what I can "acquire"

We're so worldly Lord
Sometimes I forget what I was put here for?

Janet Guerrero
MY FIRST LOVE

This poem is dedicated to Steve Bernasconi, with all my love.

The first time I saw you I knew it was love.
I cherished every moment we shared

in our hearts.
You said that you loved me
You said that you cared
You filled my empty heart
With the love that you gave.

Then one day you broke my heart
a person came between us
You let us fall apart.
You said let's just be friends.

How could I accept
The feeling of reject.

There is nothing more I have to say
There is nothing I can do
All that is left are memories
And the tears I shed for you.

Heather Emily Hochuli
I'LL BE WITH YOU
I'm off chasing the sun
Havin' some fun
Treatin' myself right
Every day and every night
I'll be a part of nature in
every phase of your life
I'll be the fall breeze that gently
carries away your tears and fears
I'll be the midnight star that twinkles
in your eye
The sun shining through your hair
The first breath you take of fresh
morning air
The soft ocean wave that feels like
silk
The spring rain that you run through
Wherever you are, I'll be with you
Don't you cry when I go
I won't be feelin' low
I'll be flying high
Just me and the sun, in the sky . . .
It will be my dream come true,
I'll be with you.

Doris M Sergeant
CLIMB YOUR MOUNTAIN
Climb your mountain of dreams to
the very top,
And along the way do not falter or
stop,
Without patience and perseverance
you will falter and fall,
And will not accomplish anything
at all.

Your life will be a series of ups and
downs,
And will be as rocky as the
mountains around.
Yet isn't it worth the chance that we
take
Despite the many sacrifices that
we must make.

If all the world were broad and flat,
How dull the scene would be
without
Those mountains atop where success
abides
Where our dreams are fulfilled and
happiness lies.

Beto Guevara
AN INCULCATION
"Be
(fore)
your
best
friend—
Respect your parents
and you shall notice
that happiness
is
not
that
re-
mote,"
is the
start of a quote . . .
which has to end.

Howard Jacobs
UNTITLED
There's only one Love to outweigh
the rest
Just one ambition that burns with
desire
To please my God before life I divest
to acquire more virtues before I
expire

For I'm more concerned with Spirit
than flesh
The material world is naught to me
Though with the material, Spirit must
mesh
For alone each can bring only agony

Carolyn D Russell
IT'S NICE TO KNOW THERE'S SOMEONE

To My Friends.

It's nice to know there's someone
who
Thinks just so very much of you
Who knows your faults and likes you
still,
And makes you feel they always will.

Within this world of love and doubt
It's great to know there's one about
With hearts so big they want to share
Their happiness because they care.

Lois B Wilson
LORD, I NEED THEE

This poem is dedicated to my son Jerry R. Brown.

Lord, I know Thee like the fish needs
the ocean, and the trees needs the
rain.
The flowers needs the sunshine, and
when tears are falling and I'm in
pain.
I need you to walk through the valley
with me, and when I'm on the
mountaintop let me see.
I need you when life's sun is setting
low.
I need you to hold my hand when it's
my time to go.
I need you to give me strength every
day.
And lead me not into temptation
along the way.
I need a drink of the water, where I
will never thirst,
Help me, Lord, always to put you
first.
I need you to guide and teach me
along life's way.
I need your love and mercy every
day.
Be my friend dear Jesus, and listen
when I pray.
And fill my heart with love, until I
come to the end of the way.

Georgia Douglas
SWEET CONVICTION
Once fresh and young, life's hope
filled me to
brim as a blossom's morning dew.

And then you came, a fleeting part of
me
and I of you.

Within that quick passage, joy and
passion reigned,
a glimpse of what could be.

I almost immersed within your sweet
charm
and you in me.

Came creeping stark reality, past
commitment
robber of our days to come—
reminder I was not free.

Those other choices that came before
forced
my heart to flee.

In all of time's passing life has been
bitter and
sweet, joyous and fearful, empty and
complete.

With life's purging and giving—vivid
memories still
woo, sea lions at night and wild
flowers azure blue.

Oh dearest memory this sweet
conviction lingers true,
you'll always be a part of me dear
Rome—And I a part of you.

Crawford Spearman
FAITH

Dedicated to my friends and inspiration Oliver and Carol Moles.

Wild flowers give me faith in life.
Examples of hardship and strife.
A delicate look but tough as a boot!
No hothouse help; no cutoff shoot.
Jut wind blown seed on barren sod,
No help from man; just it and God.

Marilee LaMarche
SPRING
The coming of spring
Is quite a beautiful thing.
Green grass covers the ground
It's everywhere to be found.
Flowers do bloom
Giving off a sweet perfume.
The sun shines so warm and bright
Such a dazzling sight.
Birds fly through the air
While a cool breeze brushes your
hair.
There is nothing like a spring day
To take your cares away.

Joseph Hulon
THE CHIMES

To Cheryl—a friend whom I hope will appreciate this someday. To Brian—my best friend. To Miss Watson—thank you for teach me "Carpe Diem."

Wind Chimes ring in the cool
morning spring breeze
With their rhymeless tones they seem
to tease
A symphonic chorus without reason
Rhythmless singing without any
reason

The chiming awakens me here by her
side
The crashing waves tell of a morning
tide
Sunlight shines through the easterly
windows
As gulls play over dry grassy
meadows

Closing my eyes I tell her I love her
She stirs softly as we lie together
Bathed in the slowly brightening
sunlight
Remembering the love we shared last
night

She opens her eyes and smiles into
mine
I kiss her softly on her lips of wine
Our love, she says, will never change
with time
Her voice echoed by the sound of the
Chimes

Florence G Axton
SENSITIVITY
A picture frame, says it's spring.
Beauty, excitement, happiness, it will
bring.
A little mountain dew on a leaf,
A gem sparkling in the sunlight,
Clear mountain streams, will bring
relief,
Glee club of birds, butterflies bees,
hummingbirds,
Going from flower to flower,
Cannot be explained in words.
Look to the beauty of the gardens,
The daily rain, showers will be
A memory in your book of fountains,
A fantasy.
We need dollars and cents,
Money comes and goes,
But it does keep us on our toes.
Remember your divinity, your
creativity,
Your complacency,
Alert your
Sensitivity.

Judy Jackson
CHILDHOOD

To my darling husband Harry Jackson and loving mom & dad, Melvin and Lorriane Fink.

As a girl or a boy growing up
we have a goal or a dream!
Some reach the peak and others fail
it seems.
A doctor, a layer or Indian chief,
when we reach that goal what a
relief!
Toys, dolls, trucks, cars or trains
we were children in a world of make
believe.
Later to grow up and leave our
childish ways, put down our trucks
and trains
and pay attention to life and use our
brains!
The childhood days of love, laughter
and cotton candy were dandy then,
but now it's adulthood and the
difference between child and grow up
ends.

Susan B Hernandez
A DYING MAN'S WISH
I feel in times of hardships and times
of memories,
I remember a dying man's wish.
This man was strong and caring, but
he had a little
flaw, he like to have some violent
times with us.

His name was . . . for I couldn't
really tell!
He would yell at me when it was not
necessary and
strike me down to the ground if I
disagreed.

I loved this man so much, for he had
my same last
name, I understand sometimes why
sadness filled his
eyes. Sometimes we have to accept

moments of anger
within, that we just couldn't
understand.

This man was smart and wise in just so many ways, I
would call to him and he would answer me not always
with a smile. He had a sickness called abuse, that
he learned from his past.

Sometimes I cry for him because I want to change his
past. If I could tell him just one little thing, I
would tell him to change his mind. For he had a dying
wish, this man that I miss.

I'd tell him there is another way of life, where being
small doesn't have to hurt, where blood and hate are in
his heart, instead of joy and love. Oh, yes I'd ask him
to get some help, to spare his dying wish.

There were times of little happiness, in our small and
cozy home. Where dolls and pets were our best friends
with make believe parents.

Patricia Foddrell
BETTER TO GIVE
Tell me,
"Honey, give me your ear to listen to all my troubles;
Give me your attention, so I'll know that I matter;
Give me your shoulder to rest my weary head;
Give me your sympathy, so I don't become self-engrossed;
Give me your respect to strengthen my confidence;
Give me your laughter to fan the flame of joy in my heart;
Give me your tears to reaffirm my strength;
Give me your love to make me complete;
And, when you've done all this for me, I'll . . . .
. . . . . . hold on a moment . . . . . .
something's come up . . . .
. . . . . . I'll get back to you."

Miriam E Giles
FIRST GRANDSON
Oh what a heavenly joy,
To be blessed by this little boy,
At a time in life when our pleasures are rife
And we're becoming a little bored.

Each week, early one morning,
I would go knock on his door.
His face would light up, his arms would reach out.
This moment I always adored.

We would hurry to the car, head for Grandfather's house.
Little ditties we'd sing all the while.
His happy face beamed, what a pleasure it seemed,
To share time with this little child.

Sometimes we would go for a goodie,
Or into the park to play,
Or to the backyard to play with his cars,
A treasured, wonderful day.

And then he would hap while I too hit the sack,
Worn out but in a wonderful way.
What more could I ask than to share in the task,
Of raising my Grandson this way?

Ruth Butterfield

Ruth Butterfield
DON'T BE LONELY LITTLE DARLING
Don't be lonely little darling of mine. When I said these words to you and the people will be walking on a star. But remember that I promised you with all my heart and soul. Don't be lonely little darling of mine. I once told you that I loved you there would be nobody else. For the others they don't match the things. We say but remember that I promised you with all my heart and soul. Don't be lonely little darling of mine. Don't be lonely little darling of mine.

Tami Lynn Pereira
A PLACE . . . TO ROAM

Dedicated to all the teenagers who want to be loved and accepted for who they really are.

If you come and find me, and I am never there;
It's because I didn't know, you really even cared;
I wanted to be open and be able to share,
But that was too difficult, I just couldn't dare;

Pain—that pain is so hard to bear,
The gnawing feeling that no one cares;
The loving feeling that now is gone,
Being last—never number one;

I want to laugh, no never cry,
Maybe I'll last, maybe I'll die;
Wanting trust—not terrible lies;
Is pain real? Tell me why.

Let go of my hand, just for awhile;
I'll return someday, with love and a smile;
But for now—the love has died, the tears have dried;
Please don't think this is all a lie.

I need a break—a place to roam,
Like a daughter leaving home;
I want to run out in the hills,
Bearing heat, suffering chills;

Needing time to be alone, wanting space and a place . . . to roam.

Roselind Gold Rosenberg
MOTHER

This poem is dedicated to my mother, who on June 2, 1986 gave me her kidney and gave me a second chance to live a happy, healthy life.
Thanks Mom!

You always showed me right from wrong
When the chips were down you taught me to be strong
You wiped away my tears of pain
You held my hand in the rain
You always made sure I had everything I ever wanted
A mother's love should never be taken for granted.
You gave me a second chance to live
You gave me everything you had to give.
I thank you from the bottom of my heart,
Always remember we shall never be apart.

Judith Dawe
SUSQUEHANNA
I watch! I lap the shore!
I rise! I fall!
I see the green wreaths of Christmas,
The bright lights, the tinsel
I see the city beckon.
I watch the canopy protect the populace.
I wait!
I see the "high rises," the rinks, the gyms.
The restaurants, the statutes, the clock!
I know!
I am all powerful, I feel the surge within my banks
I can ruin all.
I will not be restrained
I have been polluted, filled
with mine water; filled
with the waste of mankind.
My gifts to you destroyed
by wontful waste
I will rest now—but not
for long.
My day will come
and all you created;
I shall destroy!
I Am The River!

Mary Rose Shoemaker
A COUNTRY HOME
These are memories of a Country Home.
The front porch with swings, and people.
Joyful waits for births of newborn babes.
Deaths of parents, surrounded by children.
Announcements of weddings, and marriage feasts.
Friendship of neighbors during harvest time.
Dark Days of The Great Depression.
Young Sons called to serve in World War II
Guests welcomed from foreign lands and places.
Festive meals prepared from the farm.
Preparing of many foods for church picnics.
The baseball, hunting, fishing, swimming and work parties.
Parents and children gathered for daily prayers.
Story telling and reading by the fireplace.
Horse rides on the farm and countryside.
Return of grandchildren, doctors, writers, etc.
All came for a glimpse of their roots.
You have been a FRIEND to all of us.
And ONLY. MEMORIES of you will linger . . . L O N G.

Pierre Novy
WAITING IN THE HOUSE
I would rather be alone in this house
without you, rather than in a crowd of
people only to be lonely without your
presence near.
At least, while I am here I know
that you were here, but a short time
ago, that you will return before the
night ends. Thus, my heart does reap
a silent pleasure knowing your
presence lives here whether you are
here or not.
The house is full of you, and all
your things are here that remind me
of you. I am at peace here waiting for
you, my heart grows full with the
wisdom that you are mine.

So, why would I go away without
you, knowing that there would be no
peace
because you are not near, go away
only to be sad, longing for you,
wishing that I had not gone, fretting
only to return as quickly as possible.
No, my dear sweet, sweet heart,
better I not go, only to be sad,
better to stay in the house,
waiting for you to come back
to me as I know you must.
Better for my spirit to wait
here alone with the silent song of
you, smelling the mist of this
perfume that
lives in the your house, this perfume
of you that gladdens my heart when I
know that you are at the door and in
a brief moment you will be here,
alive and warm for me to touch
and grow closer to you, and know
that it can never be any other way.

Marie "Huhndorf" Carlson
THE GATHERING
"Home to my Alaska" for Christmas '88
30 years later, a very special date.
A wonderful dream for me come true.
That year "no other place would do."
My sister's home all decked out for the season
And Jesus we knew was truly the reason.
Family gathered together there, during my two week stay.
The loving hugs exchanged, added so much to each day.
A time filled with loved ones so dearly missed
Who all of those Christmas's had been part of my list.
While sharing the holiday cooking and baking
Precious memories were also very much in the making.
Friends with no family to the Gathering came.
We all shared together in Jesus's name.
Those who were lonely, sad and depressed

Gathered with us seeking comfort
and rest.
A Christmas filled with Joy-music
and laughter
Those memories still with me a long
time after.
As we came together each night in
prayer
We thanked God for "this Gathering"
and for "His Care."

Tom Samuel
YOUGHIOGHENY
Dark waters churn below a menacing
surface,
Brown breaks to white then back to
brown again.
Rock, man, raft and a meandering
snake
Pitted against one another in a
tree-lined arena
The swirling blackness whisks the
voyager swiftly along
As the swish-swish-swish claps spray
to his face.
Phoebus directs his chariot across the
molten blue sky
Casting shadows among the hills and
scampering under growth.
Directed on, the unknowing traveler
awaits his next peril, his next
obstacle of cascading whitewater
while a discordant crescendo
of river babble peaks to thunderous
volume.
This was the hunting ground of the
instinctive Indian, he who
named her 'water of the roundabout
course.'
Only man's skill and his rubber
transport separate him
From the danger of the current and
the eager sandstone.
Man exerts his fortune against
nature's zeal
To capture the elusive Youghiogheny.

Gina A Caputo
MY FRIEND
Someone who laughs, to make you
smile
 Will stay until the end
Someone who cries, yet dries your
tears
 Is more than just a friend
Someone whose heart, is full of
sunshine
 To share with everyone
Someone whose eyes are full of
sparkle
 Like stars that shine above
Someone cares and always will
 By my side you'll always be
Someone who'll walk, and hold my
hand
 To always comfort me
Someone who does, what voices
speak
 Whatever they may ask
Someone who'll stay, never go away
 A true friendship built to last

Melissa J Belvedere (Age 11)
NEW YORK QUEEN
I begin my day early,
I end my day late,
Though I live here aboard the New
York Queen.

In the dark she is graceful,
Rising, falling, ever so slightly,
Like a finback whale, oh so silent.

By day illuminated in the sun she
shimmers and shines,
A speck on the sea.
To an outsider she's just a piece of
metal, slowly lumbering through the
sea.
To me, she's a home more beautiful
than any other.

Ralph E "Shine" Arthur
JESUS CHRIST HALL OF FAME
Wouldn't it be wonderful to be in
Jesus Christ Hall Of Fame.
How sweet it would be to hear the
Disciples call your name.
I most cases you have to be in great
physical shape to reach that glory.
But in Jesus Christ game, it's a
different story.
You have to beat many opponents to
reach the fame.
But if you don't make Jesus Christ's
Roster,
You have no one to blame.

George Mueller
ALL EARTHLIFE ENJOYS THAT FREEDOM
Life has a friend who gives presents
Life is the big present he gives
All life must learn how to live this
earthlife
For with this helper all earthlife
really lives
There is a mastermind at the head of
earthliving
As the free help from life's master is
right
But life needs help in all living
earthlife
Just watch some newborn! It is quite
a sight
That is why so many have parents
A father, a mother who share
They, are guided by a life protector
With him they do not throw life's
youth in the air!
Then youth learns the trick of
earthliving
It learns this supervisor to cling
Youth avoids listening to dope
forming habits—
A successful re-living to bring
Just for following that giver of
livings—
Earth gets life's promise so true!
That should you and I this spirituality
join?
Eternal life will include us too!
To some these facts may sound
unreasonable but with faith they are
real

Thurman B Everett
IT HURTS TO BE A SOLDIER

To my beautiful wife, J.W.

It hurts to be a soldier,
To have to say Goodbye.
To leave your loved ones
And see them start to cry.

To be taken away to some faraway
land.
Away from the girl he loves;
Knowing how much she will miss
him
He prays she'll preserve her love.

He looks for a letter from her each
day,
And when it doesn't come,
He wonders if he's lost her and tears
enter his eyes.
Each morning he arises before the
sun is up another day.

He raises his eyes to the heavens
above
And begins to pray,
Oh God, I Thank Thee

For letting me live one more day,
Please, Take my hand and guide me
on my way;
Oh God, I love her with all my heart,
Now she's said Goodbye.
And here I am miles away,
And all I do is cry.

A soldier is a lonely man,
Who lives for just one more day,
He never seems to have a future,
It's always too soon to say.

So if by chance you meet a soldier,
Be proud to take his hand;
Because he's a member of our armed
forces,
Which safeguard our beloved land.

Danielle DiMario
CANDY FROM A STRANGER
Old man you sit there
hand out your candy,
memories of life's experiences
you try to share
your teachings in each
cellophane lesson we
scrounge to catch,
to unwrap, suck on, then spit out
not liking the flavor
not realizing to pause
smile and thank you
for sweetening our day.

Geneen Marshett Simmons
BLACK BUTTERFLY
I am a butterfly,
floating freely against the wind.

I am of colors.
Beautiful colors.
Each one representing a part of my
being.

Black represents my soul.
Red represents my heart.
Blue represents my strong ability.
Pink represents my weakness.
Green represents my courage.
Purple represents my humorous side.
And yellow represents my sadness.

With these colors,
These beautiful colors.
I spread my wings to fly.
Above and beyond the big blue sky.
To find my place in this world of
black butterflies.

Rosa L Coleman
IN MY MEMORY'S EYE

Dedicated to the memory of my cousin, my sister, and my dearest friend.

In the eye of my memory I hold a
precious three
Deep in my heart, my two "Miss
anne's" and Vee.
One's a cousin, one's a sister, the
other, a friend,
All whom I will treasure until the
very end.
Unstintingly each one gave to me
their love
Like the gentlest showers from the
heavens above
With their ways of sharing my
laughter, grief and tears,
Thus giving me strength and
sustenance through the years.
Out of the many things that we often
talked about
The sweetest of all was one that we
could never doubt.
'Twas a consciousness of how some
of us are truly blest
By a God-given privilege that
endures despite stress.
And the best of ourselves comes
clearly shining through
Because other's inspirations, trust
will constantly brew
A sound basis for caring, and the
confidence to understand:
"That few of us can survive without a
helping hand."
So, the three of them, tho at different
times, did live
With open hearts to me and others,
freely did they give
Of themselves. Now, faces of my two
"Miss anne's" and Vee
Live on, securely imprinted, in the
eye of my memory.

Sahar Tchaitchian

Sahar Tchaitchian
MY DREAM

To my dear mother and father, with all my love.

Last night I went to a faraway place,
Where all the grass was pretty lace.
The clouds were made of cotton
balls,
All the people were cute, little dolls.

The branches on trees were cinnamon
sticks,
The houses were made of candy, not
bricks.
In this magical land, time would
stand still,
No one would ever, ever be ill.

The streams and rivers were filled
with milk,
All the sand was pure white silk.
The snow was made of sugar that was
white,

You would never have a dispute or a fight.

The hilly mountains were chocolate ice cream,
The lily in the pond was a lonely moonbeam.
The sun was distant piece of gold,
The weather was never chilly or cold.

All the stars were diamonds in the sky,
No one told a secret or lie.
Every little child got a baby pup,
I would get one too, if I didn't wake up!

Nikki McCoy
YOUNG LOVE

To that special person in my life—the one I love.

All day and all night I can only think of you.
The feelings are so strong—I know my love is true.
You may not believe everything I say, or want to just yet,
But I know the way I feel about you is something I'll never regret.
If we didn't argue—our relationship just wouldn't be right.
You can't forget love, but you can forget a fight.
I want our relationship to be the best that it can be.
I love you—don't you see that you mean the world to me?

Ida R Gremillion
THE WHITE IMPOSTERS

With love to Rosemary, my youngest daughter.

Today the "Yuccas" are wearing a new style of dress,
In their secluded corner by the clinic,
I'm the only one they're likely to impress.

They are all in glistening splendor after the snowfall last night,
And create a breathtaking beauty in their own special right.

Being so near the clinic, they look like medical men in coats of white,
In keeping with the atmosphere, they present a pure and antiseptic sight.

But nature with her fickle ways soon changed the scene,
And took away their M.D. degrees and left them in their usual garb of green.

Lisa B Fackler
THROUGH THE WATER

When I walk through deep water,
Rolling waves thunder and pound,
He gently takes me by the hand,
And leads me to dry ground.

Though my heart is very heavy,
He takes the load from me,
An arm He places on my shoulder,
And then hugs me close, you see.

He heals my bleeding heart,
And calms my every fear,
He wipes the sweat from my brow,
And dries away each tear.

He tells me that He loves me,
No matter what's in my past,
He'll always walk beside me,
Through every stormy blast.

Norma Lee Boeckler
NIGHT LIGHTS

Curtains open to catch the breeze.
Fireflies dancing among the trees.
Silhouetted against a sky of black,
Dotted with stars from large to a mere speck.
The fireflies flicker up and down.
Going from tree to tree, around and around.
Flashing their beams, just tiny lights,
Hoping to attract a kindred light.
In order to preserve their God-given right,
To be lights in the night.

Remonia Lee Bryant
T.V.

This poem is dedicated to my son Mark.

I watch T.V. from morning till night,
The game shows I never get right.
Then comes the soaps that I try not to miss,
I sit and I wonder what's better than this?
Without T.V. I think I would die,
It makes me laugh, it makes me cry.
My world revolves around the tube,
Life without it would seem crude.
When evening comes I watch the news,
There's so many people with so many views.
Programs with music, shows with dance,
Army action, love and romance.
Will I ever get sick of T.V.?
Ask someone else but don't ask me.
I'll be here in front of my set,
And in the end there will be no regret!

Linda Allen Rhodes
EYES OF THE DREAMER

To my parents who always believe in my dreams.

I am the eyes of a dreamer.
Eyes seeing beyond reality.
I enjoy the sensation of being alive.
The earth is my cradle
The stars are my blanket
The void is my eternity.
In which I dream my dreams.
The flight is endless,
Beauty surrounds me like and aura.
I am weightless, floating, falling
Cushioned by my thoughts
Tempered by that misty veil
They call a dream
I am the dreamer

Philip E Strand Jr
SPRING: GOD'S GIFT

To my wonderful wife, Evelyn.

First, come the buds on the trees
Then, leaves burst forth like a soft
Blowing breeze.

Yellow daffodils with crowns of
White, stand like ladies-waiting
For their knights.

Azaleas red, white, and bachelor
Buttons blue, look like our country's
Flag which we love true.

Like an artist's soft brush, thrift
And candy tuft soften the scene as
A song from a thrush.

Violets come early too-shining
Like sequins on the grass in early
Morning dew.

Easter lilies so beautiful and white
In remembrance of our Great
Savior's Plight.

So thankful are we to God's gift to
Man-early spring flowers and dreary
Winter's end.

MAlice Morgan
YOU NEVER KNEW

I loved you
  but you never knew
And I knew—
  I could never tell you
For if you knew, you would leave
So knowing I could never have you
  I chose to love you from afar.
You saw me as a friend,
  I saw you as so much more—
And knowing this, I said nothing
When we spoke, I felt that my heart would betray me.
For I loved you—and you never knew.

Alice Morgan
A GOLDEN RAY

It's early morn, and a ray of sunshine just came through my window,
Like a ray of hope, it was golden and warm.
And as the ray grew larger—so did my hopes and dreams.
Dreams of many wonderful things and thoughts,
Thoughts of love and need,
The need to be part of something or someone—
Of someone who loves you as much as you love them,
And all this from a golden ray of sunshine.

Marnie Luft
ALONE AGAIN

Here I am, alone again,
Feeling the pain that's familiar now,
I think of all the years that passed,
The time I spent in love with you.

I feel like I've been cheated of,
The happiness that I deserve,
To me it resembles the winter sun,
With its few rays of warmth,
I think I only feel it for a moment,
And then my happiness fades away,
And I'm alone again, without you.

Helen Fox Setzer
LOST OPPORTUNITY

A few times in my life, I've felt so impressed
To seek out a friend and try to express;
How much they had helped me along the way
Or something they said that had brightened my day.
So busy, I didn't stop and take the time
To let them know what was on my mind.
There's plenty of time and really no rush
Some other day, I'll get in touch.
Little did I know that I would wait
'Til opportunity had passed and it was too late.
The seeds of kindness that I might have sown
If that dear soul could only have known.
So if you've something to tell or a fence to mend
Don't put it off; just go to that friend,
Spread a little sunshine while you may
Life is so short—it will soon pass away.

Connie M Sullivan
MY ED

You have probably heard of "model" husbands before—
Mine has to be kissed everytime he goes out the door!
He's someone thoughtful, considerate and kind—
What a wonderful man to call mine!!!
We go shopping together, traveling and fishing too,
Without each other, our lives would be very blue!
Bad moments are far outnumbered by the good—
We talk things out like wise spouses should—
Our lines of communication are just great—
How thrilling to have such a wonderful mate!!!

As you leave me for the coming days, darling Ed,
Remember all the loving prayers being said—
Think of the lovely colors we've shared this fall—
Heavenly clouds, floating pretty leaves and all!
Even though the lovely trout we saw would not bite,
Our being together in nature's arms was a delight!

God be with you every night and day—
And send you home well and soon—to stay!!!

Your loving wife always,

Bette Tyson
WHERE ARE YOU?

I miss you when you are not seen.
I miss you when you are not heard.
Life is very different for me
Without vision of the eye and voice of the word.

Are we accustomed to the face?
Accustomed to the touch?
Is our time together all important?
Does it matter all that much?

Feelings come so easy
Because it seems so right.
My dreams are all the ultimate
By day or by night.

But, oh my dear, where are you?
Where does your heart tell you to be?
Can we ever be together?
Is there hope for you and me?

Tim W Falls
CARS

The rule of life concerning cars disgusts me to the max.
And yet this stupid happenstance is just as sure as tax.
If you own a crappy heap, a fact from which you hide.
Never does the engine fail to take you for a ride.

And never does some idiot screw up and dent your car.
Oh, no, it runs forever, as consistent as the stars.
But just as soon as you acquire a car that does you proud;

Misfortune falls about you like a rainburst from a cloud.

The thing won't start, the thing won't run; the troubles never cease.
Until you feel like trashing it, just for the sake of peace.
And, when at last, you fix it all; then quicker than a flash;
Some stupid jerk decides it's time to have himself a crash!

Donald R Beckwith
THE FLOWER
There was a flower
It is pretty neat.
It is made by God.

Francis Abdo
NOW THAT I THINK ABOUT WHAT WE ONCE HAD
It makes me wonder of how
at times i took advantage
of what i just lost.
The times when you held
me so close, the times
that i thought would last
forever.
I've been hurt before, but
never did i think it
could also would be you.
Could i ever forgive, all
the words you spoke, all
the lies that i once believed?
I didn't realize how much
i cared, until i lost you.
I was trying to hide the
feelings that you hurt,
to try and hide the feelings
you took with you when
you left.

Iris Thompson Fry
THE MASK

Dedicated to my three sons, of whom I am so proud. Reggie, Brantley, Jarrett Fry. Especially for JJ.

Off goes the mask, we all wear one; you know
A face that we would or wouldn't like to show.
One that's happy, one sad, one frustrated, one mad;
There are others we wear right here on our heads.
If we reveal our true selves, someone might reject;
And that might cause us to neglect, our feelings of whatever they might be,
Not wanting the whole world to know or see.
So, we go about our daily life, and hope there's not too much strife,
About who we are or this or that, unveiling ourselves, defenses down
Sometimes we're afraid someone might think we're a clown.
But taking the masks off one by one, we expose who we are
And shouldn't mind if we show a scar.
Scars of life are ok to have
They show character and flaws, and everyone should know . . .
The true gift of life is from the Father above,
With outstretched arms, He holds us in His love.
So, take off your mask and learn to let go
There's more love in your heart,
Than you might ever know.

Elsie I Miller
TREE

To my husband, Philip

Ole half-dead tree—
Is a small world to me—
Where young squirrels run free
Birds sing sweet melodies—
Kids play with glee and with—
me.

Ole saw arrives—
And tensions rise—
And squirrels die—
And all birds fly—
And kids and I—
cry.

Lorie Byrer
CHRISTMAS CHEERS

To my loving husband and supportive family.

Snowflakes as they're falling
Carolers as they sing,
Children as they laugh and play
Church bells as the ring.

Trees decorated with lights
Fireplaces all aglow,
The warmth of a loving family
As they hear the wintry winds blow.

The many sounds of Winter
The many sights of Christmas time,
How everything around seems to change
How the people become so kind.

The beauty of this special event
For Christ was born this day,
Amid the sky was a star shining bright
As if all was meant to say:

Listen to the angels sing
Bringing goodwill and cheer,
May it fill your heart with peace
To remain throughout the year.

Alicia Nicole Cato
OUR LOVE
Love is the times, good and bad
Walking together hand in hand
A kiss goodnight, a hug goodbye
The endless thoughts
That rest in our minds.

The moon is shining,
The stars are bright
As we sit together in silent spot
With you is where I want to stay,
But others are around to get in our way.

My feelings are more than words can say
If only I could make you understand
My feelings are real, my feelings are true
I always have, I always will
love you

Kleon Kerr
MY MOM
"My mom, my mom" are magic words
Cast in vibrant tone.
Heard within the market place
And on the telephone.

When life is somewhat shambled
And sadness blurs the way,
Somewhere an urgent murmur,
"Where is my mom today?"

When blues are bluer
And encouragement a yearn,
There is a fervent whisper,
"When will my mom return?"

When eyes are brimming tears
And visages are sad,
There is a testimonial,
"My mom will make me glad."

There are different moms,
Many fine and true.
"My Mom" is the refuge
When storm clouds mar my view.

M N Powell
MY AFRICAN PLAIN

I dedicate this poem to the memory of my son Charles.

In the first grey light of morning
the world is hushed
the world is still
Night mists drift in gossamer veils
over the last African plain
Where herd of grazing antelopes
appear
only to disappear
then phantom like
appear again
Here I watch the sun crest dark hills
Sending shafts of shimmering light
to drive away
the soft mists of the night
Leaving a sparkling carpet of dew
to bejewel
my African plain

M N Powell
ZEBRAS
With drumming hooves they flee o'er flowered plain,
Beating a wild tattoo through the silver rain.
Dancing stallions rear, then once more take to flight;
Their ebon stripes pencilled stark against the white.
A fretting mare calls out to her stumbling colt
As the herd whirls and comes to a sudden halt.
They stand with pulsing nostrils and heaving sides
Letting the vapor rise from their shimmering hides.
They stand in the fragrance of the fallen rain,
Facing purple hills that disk the verdant plain.

M N Powell
I REVERE
I revere . . .

The explosive song of birds
that welcomes the blush of dawn

The sacred voice of the wind
that stirs my searching soul

The music of mountain streams
that falls in crystal showers

The flaming torrent of color
that pours from evening skies

The call of the whip-poor-will
take takes me to my dreams

These my gifts from mother earth
. . . I revere

Sherry Lineback
JUST A VERSE
The blue marble turns round and round.
The people's heads do spin, as the children grin and grin.
The light will shine, but when? The cast consists of much turmoil
because very few stay loyal. Things roll along as the world
sings its song.
When we all learn to give, people from here and there
will just begin to live.

Chrystal Lynn Blossom
LOVE STORM
The pattern has been set.
Hear the falling of the rain?
Left alone to face the thunder.
And the pain, all the pain.

The thunder is my needs,
To be held, to be loved.
My heart lost in loneliness,
Crying out to be hugged.

The lightening is the war,
That is raging in my soul.
That keeps my broken heart crying.
Wishing to be whole.

The tornado is the pain,
From which you can retreat.
Bu no matter how far you go,
The damage is complete.

The hail is the pieces,
Of my heart that's fallen
down.
That the queen of sad and
sorrows,
Wears like a crown.

The rain is the end.
The tears as they flow.
The point at which I begin
again,
To make my small heart grow.

Leonard Kanigowski
MY WIFE
The love of my life is my wife,
forever and eve true
My life is at your command.

The following years I know,
our love will grow dearer and dearer
And always true . . . yours just for the asking.

The love of my life is you.

Candice Marie Alloco
CARELESS LOVER
O sweet boy, you restless heart,
needing to search for yourself
in someone—trying to gather your soul.
You were one with all for a
passionate moment,
but,
you surrendered to me.
Slowly but slyly, my poison ran
through your veins; consuming you,
deteriorating your unsuspecting heart.
Your gallant attempt at escape was impressive
—the bed grew cold so fast.
O bad boy, you poisoned heart, we
are one indeed.

Davina Carlo
MY DIVINE VALENTINE

To my legendary Gary Muriset . . . With all the love in Mary's heart.

upon awakening one Sunday
morning,
a feeling of emptiness had overwhelmed me
compelling me to visit the place,
in which I find comfort in times like
these
. . . i paid a visit to speak to my
heavenly Father

standing amidst the crowd . . .
being one of sincere christians
combined with a few self-righteous
hypocrites . . .
i glanced at my Brother
hanging from His cross . . .
and as always, proceeded to speak to
Him
through my heart and my mind
instead of the surrounding, repetitious
voices in prayer

in gazing upon his agony
He listened as i spoke to Him about
this lonely feeling i had that morning
as if i had never experienced that
empty
feeling before . . . trying to remember
if i
ever really did

after He comforted me, he assured
me
that all good things must come in
time
puzzled . . . i asked Him why my dear
Father
didn't allow me to love and be loved
in life
by a special man molded by his
miraculous
hands . . . just for me?
or was i meant to walk this world
alone—
was that His will for me?

in His Divine Graciousness
within a weeks time—he had
delivered . . .
a special present just for me
hand-picked from His own heavenly
garden . . .
i wondered if what i opened was what
i
had wanted . . . or something He
wanted for me . . .
. . . taking months to unwrap and ever
so
carefully and gently—removing it
from the box . . .
numerous amount of gifts inside

Such A Beautiful Package!

there he was
i felt as if i was adam discovering eve
for the
first time . . . and vice-a-versa
unveiling with the utmost care
i discovered a man—in every sense
of the word,
who possessed an abundance of
qualities
that only I and my Heavenly Father
knew
had been my longtime dreams . . .

handsome, intelligent, witty, and
charming;
stylishly sexy . . . shy at times—yet
also so
uninhibited at times that it would
make me shy . . .
a wonderful sense of humor—with
laughter that
would touch my soul like music . . .
and hard working hands that would
magically
become so gentle upon his touch
. . . as if someone softy caressed my
body with
the world's finest and softest fur . . .
compassionate to the point it would
make one humble,
yet an arrogant courage about him—
as if a castle
surrounded us, so there was nothing
to fear
he possessed a "secure" and self-
assured air about
him, which gently washed away my
insecurities
whenever he was never . . .
spontaneous and free-spirited . . . i
discovered
things in him that were similar to
me—
sometimes wondering if his soul
wasn't the
other half of my gemini twin . . . a
twin lost
somewhere through time . . .

my heavenly Father, being the only
one perfect . . .
. . . quite naturally within my
Beautiful Package
had to include a few flaws—oh but
hardly so
noticed for the good qualities
outshined them
all like the sun against the stars . . .

. . . i found such a soothing calmness
in his voice
—like the setting of forest trees
gently swaying
to the sound of whispering winds . . .
along with
the peacefulness of the never ending
brook . . .

yes
the whole world became beautiful
upon opening
that beautiful package, as if i were
given
a new pair of eyes to see with as well

i loved this present
i continued to pull out various things
from
this amazingly, incredible package
i even stumbled across a part that said
i was loved too

i felt as if i had cried the oceans
upon it slipping from my hands and
falling back
into the box—out of reach
and unfortunately, i haven't been able
to
grasp it since then . . .

. . . so once again, being how easy it
is for me
to communicate to my Father as good
as anyone,
i looked to the sky and asked Him
"what up, God?"
He smiled,
then He replied, "Time" . . .

Davina Carlo

UNCOMPREHENSIBLE CONFLICT

To my classic gigolo . . . My best friend, my loving inspiration.

Hang in there, bear with me;
Even—"save me," he said . . .
How long must I wait,
'Till Achilles is dead?

Sweet memories still linger
Pride's still in the way—
Vindictive thoughts start to dance . . .
"Intercept them," to the good Lord I
pray.

The man loves me,
Yet fears me—
He loves her,
And hates her.

What's the antidote to cure,
A gemini man's schizo soul?
What message to send . . .
To make this man whole?

Song of Solomon keeps telling me . . .
Let this man sleep
Yours is not to worry
When the almighty—makes him
complete.

Still I worry and I wonder,
Who's loving him now?
Does she bring him a smile?
Not a facade . . . not a mask.

Do I enter his thoughts . . .
When the night's calm and still?
Does he lay awake . . . to "night
dream" of me?
When he makes his love, is it me that
he sees?

If I never seem him again—
I can rest—that he's known . . .
His life has been sweet
And he has been blessed
To know an unconditional love . . .
Before I'm layed to rest.

Yet I realize my own strangeness;
And though my mind echoes . . .
His unemotional laughter when
referring to me—
Still I find an inner peace . . .
Knowing my greatest gift to him—
Was a love . . . eternally.

"Take all the time you need,"
I had said to him before
. . . And badmouth a bleeding heart—
If that be your new chore.

For the conflict inside myself
Can now rest assured
That in your destiny—I mattered . . .
And lonely feelings are no more.

Laughter interceded to kill
The green-eyed monster in me;
And compassion intercepted
The pity I had felt for thee.

Live each day to the fullest—
My fantasy friend
Laugh at me—that's okay,
For I laugh at me too.

Yes I'm crazy
But I recall
From your lips
"I love Crazy."

Yes, it's been weird and strange . . .
Having you as my obsession
Fortunately, I'm more gifted than
you—
With the art of self-expression

When you learn the art,
Of swallowing your pride—
And understand that from me
Your feelings cannot hide . . .

When complete and able to enslave
Achilles
With ball and chain;
When Delilah can't touch you
And reach blood in your veins

Just daily remind yourself
Who loves you still—
Be it two years or twenty . . .
Know I always will.

I pray the good Lord takes me
With the rapture to come,
And if I make it to heaven
Know that I'll be the one . . .
Best qualified to cover
That tough angel you have
And when he takes a break—
I'll have your hand

So don't hate me, my friend
Just cuz I care
Don't laugh behind my back
jJust cuz I'm there

Just cherish the thought
Of a love so true
For you'll never find another me
For someone as crazy as you . . .

Parker E C Bradley

WALLS

Within ourselves, walls we build.
Unaware that they are there —
We build them high, thick, and strong
Against all we think are wrong.

Higher — thicker —
Impregnable to all who'd enter.
Pretty soon we're safe and sound
Within our walls of Holy Bounds.

Built with fear through Summer's
years —
Sure to stand against our tears.
And woe to all who build them tall —
For when Autumn comes . . .

They're sure to fall.

Cheryl Christian

A SONG OF PRAISE

Praise the Lord
For He is most high
Giving glory and honor to our king

The Almighty God is greatly
powerful
Far more power than any man lay his
hand upon
With great and mighty power
Which can only come from up above
the heaven

Praise God!
Our Lord reigns forever
And all who abide in him

Great joy comes from our creator
As we are overjoyed with the
blessings of God
Tears of joy flow down our cheeks
As we receive blessings from our
Father in heaven

Praise be to Jesus!
For coming from you Heavenly
Father
Is a love we can't express without
him

Reach out to him
For he is waiting for you to come
and receive his gifts
And abide with Him forever
and ever

Praise be to the Trinity!
As we worship all three
Let our hearts be prepared to meet
him

For on that day
There will be a great sound of a
trumpet
When Jesus will call his children
And we have victory over our
enemies

Praise be to God!
For on that marvelous day
We will meet our maker forever and
forever

John Spivery
LOVE IS THE WINNER
The time could not fly on the fleet wings of mercury to say all of the wonderful things I would like to say to you. You are more lovelier than a day in June when the summer sun is down. If ever I had a thought of you being cold and cruel. I would murder my peace and rob my sleep of its happiest dreams. The shadows would cover all my skies with the blackness of despair.

Terry W Schwartz
WINDOWS TO FOREVER
As I looked into your eyes it was like looking into the gates of Heaven.
They gazed back at me with a soft warmth, born of God and nurtured by your abiding faith in Christ.
As I became lost in their elysian depths, my heart was stilled and peace enveloped my soul.
As I explored their celestial beauty I lost all awareness of the world about me.
Time became an annoyance, an un wanted taskmaster.
In that moment of time my spirit recognized the deep bond we shared together in Christ,
and the more I saw the more I desired to know.
I experienced the allure of love as never before in my life.
That love caressed my heart like the gossamer brush of butterfly wings.
Your eyes opened a window to your soul, and gave me a glimpse of forever.

Barbara Batten
PERPETUATION
Ambitious minds were gruesome things,
They all thought they knew some things.
So they went and blew some things
Up.

Don't worry if the sky should fall;
More minds will come and they'll recall
The thing that finally blew us all
Up.

This is too close, so . . .
Ambitious minds were gruesome things.
They all thought they knew some things.
So they went and blew some things
Up.

Don't worry if the sky should fall.
More minds will come, and they'll recall
The thing that finally blew us all
Up.

Julie Knight
BRIDESMAID
Now starts the wedding
The Bride drifts down the aisle,
But for some peculiar reason
The Bridesmaid frowns.

There stands the Groom
A smile on his handsome face,
The Bridesmaid holds back her tears
Knowing she's out of place.

These were not tears of happiness
That she bitterly cried,
These were tears of regret
For so long she kept inside.
For she was in love with the Groom
And no one has she ever told,
The feelings that she held for him
He will never know.

He can never know
Because now he marries her best friend,
The Bridesmaid will remain silent
But her love for him will never end.

Edith V McGrew
DEATH OF A ROSE
The rose fades and falls;
And, for a brief time,
Its fragrance haunts the air.
Then, only memories of beauty
(And perhaps a florist receipt)
Remain to show it was there!

Betty Sue McCarley
COUNTDOWN BEGINS

Thank you, Father, that you looked at the slowness in me and showed mercy, even to me.

Crowds gathered 'round, waiting the big moment
Every heart fluttering with excitement—and then
A voice booms from the speakers
As the announcer says, "Countdown Begins"

In speechless wonder, all eyes fixed on the screens
Some, more than a little fearful of how it might end
"It's for the good of our nation," someone reassured
"We must at, all cost, stand the greatest among men."

They watched as the ship streaked upward and away
In a cloud of flame and smoke
"They're at the mercy of whatever is out there"
Some realized for the first time, it was real, no hoax

Seems the bible tells much the same story
How Jesus was caught up in a cloud back then
But how many realize, what He was showing us
It was then, our countdown begin

As the disciples stood gazing after Him
Two angels said, "Why are you shocked, He's coming back the way He went."
He left a map of the path we should follow
GO! tell everyone to get ready for His final descent

Edith Ray Lackey
JOURNEY TO THE SEA
I went down to a wonderful place—
'Twas a bouncing, tossing, turbulent sea.
Look! 'Tis a body of water which has no end
with its great mighty roar—unceasingly!

I stood on the shoreline and viewed it long;
whitecapped waves swirled as they'd come and go;
and many a seashell was washed ashore
as the buoyant water ebbed, to and fro!
I sat on the sand, and then began to dream,
while watching waves lap; they took no rest;
I grew so dizzy watching waters foam, and thought
upon the many things which I loved the best.
I thought of jogging up and down the strand—
To feel soft sand between my toes, but changed my mind;
To making air castles as I walked on clouds above,
and dreamed of treasures, I would seek to find.

On the shore, I'd build a castle: I'd search for pearls;
I'd dig in hidden depths far beyond measure;
Maybe I'd find jewels, lost by travelers galore,
Or hit upon a buried box of "Pandora's Treasure."

Suddenly it thundered, and as it began to rain,
I jumped up, hurried so fast, my head began to swirl;
Then I remembered words from "PIPPA PASSES"—*
"God's in His heaven-All's right with the world."

(*Robert Browning—quote)

Jody Pinta
THE TRAIN OF LIFE
Take the train of life
It doesn't whistle at every stop
But boy, what a ride
All the way to the top

One track will take you
Thru the middle of town
Lots of hustle and bustle
With people all around

Another track if taken
Goes just thru the edges
A little more conservative
With cliffs and shapeless ledges

The track that leads off left
Is a dull and dreary ride
All gray and black and musty
Leaves you feeling sad inside

Last, but not least of all
Is the track with lots of cars
It takes off every hour
Directly for the stars

Jody Pinta
BY CHANCE
In flashing lights a face appears
A familiar face from over the years
The music is loud, with a powerful beat
The room is all steamy, filled with body heat

Hundreds of people together, alone
Sitting and talking, dancing 'til dawn
Faceless images appear all around
People's lips are moving, but making no sound

As their bodies sway together, only inches apart
She swore for an instant, she could feel his heart
Eye contact was apparent, as they continued to dance
If they looked away at all, it was for only a glance
As far as they were concerned, they were the only ones there
Together forever, not having a care
But soon the music stopped, he whispered "THANKS FOR THE DANCE"
They went their own separate ways, meeting again only by chance

B L Preminger
NO MORE REALITY
Climbing above
The earth's aurora
Lost in time
Within myself

I reach for the sky
To catch a star
Sadly though
It's fallen too far.

Through the ozone
I feel the night
Floating under
The full moon's light.

Back to reality
I slowly fall
Starting again
To build the wall.

Deborah Lynn Hall
MY THANKSGIVING DAY PRAYER

To Jim, a wonderful and loving husband. Love, Lynn.

When I pray on this Thanksgiving Day,
I will start my prayer this way.
I thank you Lord of above,
for giving me the ones I love.
For my husband kind and so dear,
whom I've given my body and soul
for these past nine and a half years.
He has loved me and friend me, and made me a mother of three beautiful girls, and their big brother.
He has earned our respect, and our love.
So I just ask from you, Lord of above,
to bless him and guide him,
Show him your way.
And make this his best Thanksgiving Day.
A-Men.

Julie Prado
A GIFT FOR MOTHER NATURE ON MOTHER'S DAY
On the first moment I came out of this world,
You came to welcome me with your sweet delicious air;
cradle me with your sunshine
and lull me to sleep with your gentle breeze.

In my childhood years, when I started to discover your wonders,
You sent me the rain, oh what joy it was
to splash in the puddles and smile at my reflection.
The coming and going of the waves became my playmate at the beach.
The rainbow ushered me to fantasy land
and the moonlight kissed my cheeks goodnight.

As I tread along life's uncertain moments,
May I never cease to remember

the beauty you adorn my world
with, the warmth and joy you
nurse me with,
And may I continue to believe in the
hope —
of the sunshine breaking through
the dawn.

DiAnna Lyn Wheatley
ALWAYS

The sun will always rise,
Good morning my dear friend.
The moon will always wait,
for the daylight's slowly end.

The dreamer will always hope,
days forever last.
The dreamer will always wish,
a look into the past

The trumpet will always sound,
together or apart.
The music will always play,
forever in our hearts.

The tears will always fall,
a little or a lot.
The angels will always call
wished upon or not.

The sun will always set,
Goodnight my dear friend.
One more day of our passing lives
Has reached its never end.

Barry A Mogel
TIME ENOUGH FOR TIME

I dedicate this poem in loving memory of my beloved father, Julian Mogel, and my beloved grandmother, Rose Gross. Their paragon of exquisite grace, perseverance and humanity are the criteria upon which I shall always endeavor to esteem.

Don't you know it is beliefs and
thoughts that rule the world?
Why do you cry the hopelessness of
exhaustive futility?
Don't you realize it as the most
grievous truth that you idolize your
negative emotions?
Have you no idea how inconsiderable
you are to yourself,
And how little you deserve that
perception?
Does the child in you not notice the
way the earth perceives the sun?
Can you not know that as you heed
your obsession,
You relinquish your life to it?
Don't you know you are fearful of
death because you are fearful of life?
Do you dread that which you do not
know,
And do not know where, or when, or
how?
Are you aware that life is a matter of
time,
But also a consequence of inclina-
tion?
If life and death are inevitable, is it
worth the wait
To endure the end of fear, the fear of
end, with fear?
Until then, or if, or how: are you
willing to move beyond the belief
that
The grains of life are fast sifting
through your mind's egg timer
without reason?
So, I ask you, at last:
Is there time enough for time?
Oh, dear God, yes! From now till
forever!
But do hasten into it with mirth and
velocity unbounded.

John Rodgers
THE DARKNESS

This Poem is Dedicated to all my Friends and Family.

Trapped inside a shell of flesh with
real visions blinded by images
Of motion that is black and white —
false hopes that I hold deep into
the night
Of waking to another day — yet
hoping and waiting for the night
To disappear into that land where all
is real but not at hand
"Come with me my dear boy" the
night calls and I drift with him
beyond human walls
To a world where I can picture all
the things that I love with poignant
mixture
Of all the wonderful things that could
not be — for the daylight breaks
and I'm back to me
So I tolerate the daylight with
whimsical eyes — even though it
has taken me to my demise
But there is hope in this earthly
plight for there will always be an
other night
"Stay with me now and always" the
night calls — but this is not
possiblefrom human walls
"Then I will wait" says the night and
thanks to him I feel no fright
But daylight never came for me —
and I waited and waited for the
sun to see
The night has taken me by his grasp
and I cannot escape at long last
For now I am in an eternal dream of
pleasant visions so real they seem
I have passed over to another
reign — and now that I'm here —
I'm glad I came

Christine Reece
NESTING TIME

When it's nesting time, birds are as
busy as bees!
Strange sounds are heard from the
limbs of trees.
There are chirps, warbles and bird
talk melodies.
Big birds and little birds behave as
they please.

They make nests of grass or long
strands of hair.
Some use sticks or mud; new nests
are everywhere.
Most birds nest in trees; some nest on
the ground.
The nests are camouflaged, so they
can't be found.

Each lady bird lays her eggs in her
feathered nest.
She'll keep them warm, beneath her
ruffled breast.
On hatching day, birdies emerge
from her tiny eggs.
Their tiny bodies have featherless
wings and legs.

With the new arrivals, a new cycle
will have begun.
Both parents are responsible for each
and every one.
They provide worms for their
fledglings, every day.
When the babies get bigger, each
family flies away!

Ruth V Butler
THE CREATION

To my brothers, Harlan B. and Frank P. Jensen, whose encouragement helped ensure my success as an artist and poet.

I was searching for a place called
Minee Do.
A promise I made grandpa, it was
where he was born.
The stories he told were vivid, and
etched in my mind.
Finally, I reached the peak, he called,
"the horn."

The stillness was overpowering,
but not in a frightening way.
The trees were changing their colors,
from reds to siennas with gold
overlay.

I gazed at the shimmering leaves of
the aspens,
and envisioned maidens in their
colorful array.
The tall pine trees stood in the
background,
like sentinels attending a festival day.

The lake was clear as crystal,
reflecting this beautiful scene.
I had come to grandpa's haven,
where in his dreams he had always
been.

Denise Parsons
WITHIN THE TEAR OF A BEAST

To Vinny, Brian and Fab 4, I love You All So Much.

Within the tear of a saddened beast
There lies a land which holds no
peace.
The ongoing darkness never rises
while the sun is trapped behind
disguises
Children's laughter is never heard
Nor is the sweet chirping of the birds.
The single sound is the sobbing of
the creature
Who created the land containing no
future.

Cathy Katz
ACCEPTANCE

My soul is embellished in pale.
I absorb the comfort of sadness.
The hollow sound of the gale.
And I am not tight with my tears . . .

A hue is not imperative for me.
For I am an only.
I am how I am supposed to be.
And I am not tight with my tears . . .

Cathy Katz
THE ADOPTION

This poem is dedicated to my dear sister Suzette. For the lost years— For the lost memories. You will never again walk alone.

We never knew the other's dream.
We never knew the other's soul.
We never knew the meaning of team.
We never knew the feeling of whole.

Bureaucracy had dictated our fate.
It cared not the deprivation.
It tossed away the mate.
In A horrendous violation.

In our quest we found our place.
No longer a sea in their jungle.
One day we came face-to-face.
We endured the long hard struggle.

With defiance we ambushed their
game.
But not without a sadness.
For tomorrow they will do the same.
In their condescending madness.

Eileen Carder
TO US IMPART

To those who have shared with me and allowed me to share with them, with love.

Share With Me Your Laughter
Shining Sun Upon Your Face
Share With Me Your Tears
As Heartache Steals Its Place
Share With Me Your Dreams
As Only You Can See
Share With Me Their Defeat
If Ever It Has To Be
I Will Share With You My Laughter
That Sparkle In My Eyes
I Will Share With You My Tears
As Heartache Darkens My Skies
I Will Share With You My Dreams
Those Wonders Of My Mind
I Will Share With You Their Defeat
In You Comfort I Will Find
To Share With Another
The Feelings Of One's Heart
Will Mend A Broken Spirit
New Life To Us Impart

Eileen Carder
RYAN'S POEM

Dedicated to: Dena Moyer Miller, who gave endless love and caring, in memory of her Son, Ryan Lee Moyer.

Ryan Is Now Running
Through Fields Of Flowers
Playing With God's Angels
For Endless Hours

Ryan Sees Only Sunshine
Still The Flowers Grow
No Clouds To Bring Rain
Yet Endless Rainbows

Ryan Sees Only Smiles
In The Ever After
No Heartache, Nor Pain
Only Endless Laughter

Ryan Rests On The Lap
Of Our God Above
Living With HIM Forever
In Endless Love

Ryan Smiles At The Sight
Of His Dear Mother's Face
Knowing God Has Given Her
HIS Endless Grace

Randal Weeks
POLICE ACTION

Watch their hollow eyes;
See their shallow lives.
They wander alone in memory
Of remembered war and lies.
A problem which presents no
righting,
The dissatisfaction of people.
Damned when the war is over
They were damned by friends while
fighting.

The fighting's over they were told
Time for us to go home;
Job well done; medals all 'round;
You were brave; victory to the bold.
Home to find disgrace;
You lost, you left; cowards, dogs,
and curs.
Words and thoughts and memories
Of their comrades' grinning death's
face.

Left homeless, friendless to wonder
If the fighting's truly ever done;
Their minds replay the scenes; their lives reflect
The obscene in their nation's greatest blunder.

Stephanie Gump
SUICIDAL SORROW

To my mother (Sue) for being there & pushing me to be the best I can be & Melissa Moore for always being there.

Petals fall off of dripping
Wet flowers
The wetness is from a
Man's tears
Tears of a broken heart
Tears of the pain he feels inside
He sits and thinks
Looks around to see the
World around him
He slowly shuts his
Eyes, and his soul drifts off
To heaven
He's gone now and may
Never look back to the
World that lays around his
Broken–hearted body.

Opal M Wegner
TRIBUTE TO OUR BELOVED SON

To our son, Timothy who was killed in a collision between his vehicle and a cow on the highway, near Tonopah, Nevada. Aug. 18, '89.

First you were a son, then a brother, with the bonds of love growing stronger each day.
As you grew in stature you grew dearer to our hearts.
We rejoiced as we watched you at play.
We tried to guide you the best that we could, without destroying your right to be you.
You were funloving and carefree while doing the things all the young people liked to do.
As you grew into manhood and had a family of your own you grew out of our home, not our heart.
Now as you leave us on this earth for your Eternal Home in Heaven you will have your part.
Fly away now dear one, as we break the ties that bound us so closely here.
We wanted to keep you but God wanted you more, and we bow to His wishes so dear.
Your family will miss you as we gather at times to be close to those that we love.
But your memory will ever be fresh in our minds, and our hearts will be warmed from above.
Farewell Dear One take your rest . . .
Mother

Mary Joanna
A WALK

To Mason, my cherished son.

I went for a walk. I saw a man hugging a cold, brick wall lamenting his losses of ownership of his worldly possessions. We toured his world. Such finery I had never seen. Gold, marble, glass, stone, brick, for what seemed to go on for miles. Upstairs, downstairs, entryways, hallways, winding, twisting. He sobbed as if his heart would break to lose such a treasure. I hugged him. I told him, "I am sorry." He said, "Thank you. You cannot help. Go away and leave me to my sorrow."

I walked on. I walked for miles and miles. I wanted to pray for the man. And I saw a woman. A woman with two small children. They were all weeping, holding each other and weeping. I was in the cemetery. She had made a crib cover and embroidered beautiful stitches on this cover. My baby. Born July 1, 1988; Died July 1, 1988. And they all held the cover and wept. I approached them. I held out my arms to comfort. She said, "Thank you. You cannot help. Go away and leave me to my sorrow."

I walked on. I walked for miles and miles. I wanted to pray for the family. I crossed a bridge. I heard laughter under the bridge. I looked. I saw a couple laughing and frolicking in the gentle rain. They were ragged and torn as if they were poor. But they were shining. Their faces were lit up and their arms embraced life. They felt the gentle rain, saw the light of day, enjoyed the gentle breeze.

And I walked on. I wanted to pray that they would always see.

Kataria L Warthen
HIM
When we were together I was overjoyed to be with Him.
The day I became downhearted is the day we had to say good-bye.
The feeling that half of my life had been taken away overcame me.
Not a day went by that I didn't hear Him.
I'd walk down the street hearing Him being echoed through the trees,
through the birds' love song.
The wind cried Him loud but peculiarly soft.
When Him was called I felt anguish.
Anguish I received from Him now slowly fades.
I hope one day Him and I will be together again.

Betty J Sleeper
INFINITY
Tired sun reluctantly stepping over
Flame-edged mountain —
Earth pales.
Young moon eagerly climbing out of
Dark crevasses —
Its beacon comforts.
I see infinity.

Brittle breath of autumn roughly
Fondling my hair —
Winter's clammy fingers clutching
My throat.
I feel infinity.

I hold my mother's fragile
Body —
My baby cries for me.
I know infinity.

Julie Hernandez
THE INDIAN
The Indian, proud and brave.
The soldier, relentless and cruel.
The child, pure and sweet.
What is left, but the old warrior
Who has laid his feathers to rest
And killed his last man
And for one last time,
Runs into the arms of his mother,
In heaven at last?

Rudolph Rodriquez
LIFE'S REALITIES

To God.

Round and round the wheels keep turning
Day by day our lives keep changing
and one by one the years keep passing
But we keep holding on . . .

Tears and fears, shattered dreams and broken promises
castles in the sand, that first romance;
circles in the sun, and dancing in the shadows of the moonlight
These are all life's hidden treasures . . .

The red, the blue, the green or the gray,
these are the colors that makes us whom we are
The springtime rain, the lonely hearts,
that last kiss and the Power of Love
We take life's challenges and we do our best.

Like the setting sun, the sound of laughter,
and that first snow, these are all life's realities.
And just as sure as the sound of music
we celebrate our life
With Love and a Field of Dreams . . .

Rudolph Rodriquez
UNTITLED
Have you ever seen the morning star
or have you seen the moon, with all its splendor and its glory
Have you seen the mountains of Colorado
or the cliff dwellings in New Mexico.
Have you wondered what came first, the chicken or the egg
or have you wondered about the beginning;
and how it was
How He created the heavens and the earth . . .
From dust he created you
To dust you shall return
The tree of life is within us, it's told over and over again;
in the greatest book on earth
Moving mountains, parting seas and greatest of all
a fisherman of men
Return to your roots, just like in the beginning,
Take time to pray, and never forget to read daily day by day

Rudolph Rodriquez
LIFE
Listen my friend
there are no guarantees to what life might hold
Like a roller coaster full of ups and downs
life is an adventure each day at a time
Live life to its fullest and don't give up
every day is full of adventure with new things to come
Take life in stride, follow your dreams
and witness the beauty each day has to bring
Each day is a challenge while on this earth
and when you fail, you merely stumble,
Just pick yourself up and carry on
experience the beauty,
experience the love
That each day brings with a start of a new tomorrow . . .

Rudolph Rodriquez
I STILL BELIEVE
Dear God,
There once was a time when I believed in you
But that was a long long time ago
As a child I was taught, that God was good
and sin was wrong
But that also was a long long time ago
Today many years from being the child, that believed God was good
and sin was wrong
But being a man, that knows God is real and God exists
I Still Believe . . .

Yolanda Thomas

Yolanda Thomas
FRE-DUM
I walk along that old hickory road
wearing out my shoes,
Walking along that old hickory road
with not a thing to do;

Humming to myself while kicking
the dirt aside,
Watching birds, bees, and those there butterflies.

Ain't got nothing to do, ain't got nothing too, just looking at all I can see.
Ain't got no troubles, ain't got no problems too, just young, black, and free.

Walking along that old hickory road,
day after day after day;
That very old same old hickory road,
humming that tune,
Freedom in May.

Rene A Davila
LOVE AFTER LIE
If you were a star that lit the sky,
Would you darken my lonely path;
Or if a stream that flowed quite cleanly,

Would you an unclean soul bath.

If you were an eagle that flew the skies,
Would you come for my death;
Or would you spare my one only life,
So naturally I live my last breath.

If you were the wind with your mighty breath,
Through the trees would you sing for me;
Or a bird just about to take flight,
Give me sight of freedom on your wings.

If you were a dragon that owned it all,
Would you hunt for me;
Or would you overlook my life,
And let this mortel free.

If I were dead, a stone all alone,
Would you not come near my grave;
Or would you enlighten my lonely tomb,
With our memories in your heart you'll save.

Marc Yates
SOMEONE CARES
Goodness comes within the heart,
From what you hold inside,
To know what you give of yourself,
Is to be free from all heartache, pain and grief
To give love in the right way without being hurt,
To know the true meaning of friendship and love,
Is to be real to yourself and to the ones that you love,
And the knowledge that you are willing to change your life,
For the ones most dear to you will help you
Overcome the everyday problems that are a burden in your life.

Pearl Gilman
RED TRAIN
There was an old train
That took you there and back.
But now it sits on an old side track.

When the whistle blew,
You could set your clocks—
People would come running
From many blocks,

Just to see the passengers
And to get their mail.
How I wish I could ride
On that memory trail!

Lynda Yonkoski
PLACES IN THE HEART
The sky above, so clear and blue,
Can know not what I feel for you.
For only you and i have wept
Over love so preciously kept.
So pure, so simple was life then,

Watch now the sunset o'er the hill,
With fading light made fainter still
Through eyes of one who cannot accept,
A life made full and empty yet,
With meaning and desire unfulfilled
Like the sea upon the shore,
Everchanging, ever constant, evermore.

Till the time when all can see
The two lives that were meant to be,
The sunlight strong up in the sky
Will light the way for them to hold
The two hearts that can never let go.

Victor A Stigliano
THE BOX
I sit in a room
Four walls ceiling and floor
With nothing to see
Not even a door

The closeness surrounds me
Like thick heavy fog
I try to escape but
Get caught in its bog

I try all I can
To get free from its clutch
But no hope in sight
The power's too much

I try all my might
To hide from its view
Each corner I try
Each corner anew

The fears never-ending
The sorrows and strife
This box which surrounds me
I know of as life.

Nancy Mistriel
MY LOVE

To my children—Abby and John.

Something is wrong
You don't speak
The silence is very deep
Love is dear
Speak I am near
I love you . . .

Marcia R Morris
MY LAST BED
Out there in the cemetery
Is a little plot for me,
It's where my last bed will be
Till Jesus comes for me.
I'll rest there from my labors,
And sleep so peacefully.
For then I won't have to worry
About another thing you see.

My Lord will know just where to find me
When eternal morning comes.
The trumpet then will call me
To join the rest of God's great throng.
We'll go to our eternal home
Where there is everlasting peace.

Marsadonna Marie (Krock)
A WONDERFUL SON

Dedicated to the memory of Elvis A. Presley and sent to his father in September of 1977. Put to music in 1988 and now this honor in the World of Poetry Anthology. Thank you! Marsadonna Marie.

In 1935 you were given a wonderful baby boy,
A precious little treasure for you to love, father and enjoy.
He grew into a man full of love, kindness and joy;
A man that the world loved,
Your wonderful baby boy.

He gave everything he had to the people of the world,
His looks, his heart, his songs,
His talents were un-hurled.
You gave the world your son,
And he gave back the world his joy;
The world can never thank you, for your wonderful baby boy.

And now he's been called by the "Almighty" up above;
They needed him more than we, they needed your son.
And now he sings in heaven with the choir up above;
But the world will not forget him,
For his talents and his love.

So thank you for your son, the son you gave the world.
The son who'll live forever; In our hearts, our mind, our world.
The world will not forget him, no never;
For his kindness, his talents, and his love.

Marsha S Miller
GIFTS
As I Watch The Leaves
Change On The Mountain,
And The Breeze Goes
Trickling By.
My Heart Does Soar
With Perfect Pleasure
Of all These Gifts I See.
So Come With Me
And We Shall Fly
Together Hand In Hand.
To Learn From All
These Precious Gifts,
All Across Our Land

Elizabeth L Hasse
MORTALITY

Dedicated to my dear late husband, Robert, who was my inspiration.

Once more I've come face to face with that inevitable event
(We all share the same conclusion)
It grieves me to reflect upon that occurrence
Which will separate me from all of you
And from the joys of living in this absurd world
The glorious thrill of my life with you, Dear One
But until that occasion arrives
I will strive to give my very best to you and God
My life can be yours with joyous abandon
As if I were deathless!

Elizabeth L Hasse
PRISONERS
Who is this lovely bird
Who beats his plumaged wings against his cage?
What awful torment keeps him there?
What aching loneliness too hard to bear?

Where can I find the key
To open up the door and set him free?
Or else he'll die
And so, dear God, will I!

Elizabeth L Hasse
ROCKS ALONG COUNTY #644 (NORTHERN MINNESOTA)
Ancient, grey/green, hard, immov-able
How long have you been there?
Is it possible two billion years?
What was our earth like then?
This wilderness did not exist
This part of our continent rose above the sea the earliest
Huge mountains shook with red hot fire
Pouring out the molten rock to form this land
Primitive planet, no life - only steam and fire
No trees or lakes or wild birds
No animals to howl - that took awhile.

Now this lovely area exudes serenity
Did the all wonderful Deity know how much men and women would find joy in this peaceful forest?
And all the lakes that sparkle in the noonday sun?
Of course He did—He planned it all for us.

Elizabeth L Hasse
FOUNTAIN OF YOUTH
Are we old?
Our bones tell us "yea",
Our energy is sapped too quickly,
An active day informs we are not twenty,
Each day new hurts, aching, throbbing pains.
And yet we continue on, as if we were that twenty!
Give in to being old? — Never.
You see, within us are the loves and dreams and ambitions of
younger selves.
Fountain of our youth, undying.

Germaine Tantone
NO REGRETS

To my beloved husband.

Have no regrets, my darling
When it's time for us to part,
Just keep the book of memories
locked deep within your heart
The joys, the laughter and the tears
Things we did throughout the years
Our faith and trust in God above,
Our children whom we dearly love.
Have no regrets my darling,
for one day you will see,
That we will be together,
for all eternity.

Jay L Jones
FOREVERMORE
I knew I shouldn't do it.
I knew it wasn't smart.
But right now all that matters
Is this pain within my heart.

The pills were white and tiny,
The whiskey smooth and sweet.
So easy to forget him
When these two warm friends meet.

Just a little longer now.
I know it won't be long.
All I have to do is wait
And my cares will all be gone.

Ahead a bright light beckons.
The tunnel I must tread.
No one now can stop me.
I've nothing left to dread.

Faster now I'm moving
Toward that golden door.
My pain and tears are gone now.
I'm free forevermore.

Susan Maccoux
A BEGINNING
The end is a beginning;
A beginning is an end.

Too afraid to go forward,
Too sad to look back.

Why can't I stay here
For a while and let myself rest?

You are my tears when I cry.
You are my laughter when I'm

happy.
You are my strength when I'm weak,
And my weakness when I'm strong.

If I'm talking in circles
let me stay encircled in your arms,
For here I am safe.

Dana Maldonado
PAIN CLOUDS

For Tiffany, I hope you get all I got from him plus all he really has to offer. I love you. I love you too Mom and Fran.

Pain clouds endless happiness . . .
From walking on slivers of rainbow touched crystal
From being excluded from someone special's life
From being deserted at age two
Because of the death of someone near
From shattered hopes
From broken promises
From feeling trapped and confused
Because of unspoken feelings
From time wasted on anger
From thoughts that were never expressed
From empty eyes and hollow expressions
Because of so much disappointment
From a broken heart

Josephine Ann Marino
WE NEED YOU BACK

This poem is dedicated to Josephine, my mother. I'm glad you're back.

All your life you tried to make things right, you put up with the fight, you've tried with all your might, but everything seemed to go wrong. We all know. We don't deserve crowns, but on all our faces, are the biggest frowns, and all our lives are falling down. All we want is you and all us crew, to stick together and hold.
We know it's a big load, but we'll help you along the way. What do you have to say. Is life OK?
We'll never really know why why you had to say goodbye, and leave us all to cry.

Trina Dell Mitchell
IN MEMORY OF MY BOBO

Dedicated to Bobo's children . . . Billy, Brenda, Freddie, Diane, Theresa and Toby.

Bobo I love you in my heart so deep,
the thought of life without you makes me weep.

It hurts so bad I want to scream,
but I always know you'll be in my dreams.

It's so hard to just let you go,
but you are in a better place,
this I know.

I know you are in Heaven where there is no sin!
And I will cherish the day when we meet and hug again.

You took care of me when times were bad
and cheered me up when I was sad.

My memories of you are sealed in my heart
and the bond we had will never part.

Your twinkling eyes danced everyday,
and I'll never forget when you smiled in your special way.

You taught me so much while you were here,
and in my prayers I feel you are near.

I wish I could hear your voice, your laugh!
But I know you are with the Lord in your path.

I thank the Lord for the time we had
and I'll try to be strong, not sad.

I took care of you when you were ill.
The pain you had I could always feel.

Your heart was weak but your spirit was strong
and to Heaven is the place where you have gone.

The family is together as you wanted them to be
and through his eyes this you can see.

In my heart you have touched,
for I love you very much.

To end this poem I close in prayer:

I pray to Jesus,
Bob will always be there.

Ree Thornton Moses
UPON LEAVING ARIZONA

Dedicated to Karen Todd.

Through morning haze
I cast a lingering stare,
Plane engines roar
My heart is stilled in prayer.

I bid farewell
to Valley of the Sun,
Remembering Jesus
Son of God's own love—
Shines down on me always.

I say good-bye to lovely desert flowers
Colorful in spite of rocky soil,
Knowing Jesus
Son of God's own love—
Blooms best in me ofttimes
When rough the way.

Huge silver bird
Winging towards the sun,
Soaring o'er
dark mountain's crag and cliff,
You lift me heavenward
As Jesus does
When earthly paths
are parched and burning, steep.

Michael McCafferty
BEYOND COMBAT

To The Fallen Warriors — A Company, 1st Battalion, 3rd Marine Division.

He wakes in a sweat, for the thousandth time
Disoriented and fearful of the visions that never die:
They'd been squatting in a circle in the rain, oblivious to the wet
Waiting always waiting
Weapons held close their comfort and each other
The dark, their friend, protects, yet holds their death
Wait for morning while twenty wait no more
Without seeing he sees the bodies lying in the dark
Knows that by morning they'd find grotesque distorted brothers
Invincible warriors, untouchable
Never again to feel the pain that is their life
Silence is their self-discipline, while within each rages out of control
Always the question never the answer
Why?

Connie J Mahoney
WIND-FREE HORSES

For—the faithful and dutiful, (Dreaming of) precious restful, recreational interests.

Wild, spirited steeds
Of thundering hooves,
Wild Mustang hearts.
Dash away—
High mountain
Restlessness.
Gallop free
Brave, bright stars.

Mark Scott Marcus
SOLILOQUY OF THE SEA

A lone figure sat upon the shore, and watched the sun slowly set over the horizon.
He was entranced by the magnificent splendor, as the sea seemed to open up and swallow the flaming sphere of orange and yellow.
It was the sea he worshipped-relentless, all powering, the very origin of life itself.
He would sing to the sea, and listen to the song of the sea nymphs in answer, as their song was carried by the waves that danced at his feet.
How he longed to join her, as he marveled at her immensity, as vast as time itself.
She spoke to him thru murmur and roar, thru thunder and foam, urging him to join her.
She beckoned to him, as the warmth of her fingers reached out and touched him. Her voluptuousness taunted him, like a succubus she challenged him to enter her domain.
He could not resist her almost demonic influence. He ventured forward, until their two bodies met, and like a mother caressing her child, she held him, pulling him closer, her warmth encircling his body.
The waves tossed him, and held him, and as the sea covered him, her breath was his, as goddess and mortal became one.
He was her's now, and she was his, suspended forever on the edge of eternity . . .

Kevin Douglas Murphy
RABBIT HUNTING DAYS

To my father, Dr. Sheldon Douglas Murphy, whose values are reflected in this poem.

Tonight the moonlight took me back
To days when I had fun
In snow choked fields of conquest
With my rabbit hunting gun

A .22 is what I used
To deftly bag my prey
And I didn't need a gunnysack
To carry them away

You see, I would be lucky
To fire at one or two
But in my mind I got them both
My memory's aim was true

Still sometimes I was happy
Just to crunch through fields of snow
With the full moon casting shadows
On the places I would go

And watch as they sat hypnotized
Within its brilliant glow
Then shouldering my rifle
I'd turn and let them go

Amy Meacham
THE SPECIAL YOU

To my Mom and Dad, Sandy and Greg, With Love.

You are a very unique person
So special in your own way
Always loving and caring
And knowing just what to say.

When you put your arms around me
It is a very warm touch
Then I can see
Why I love you so much.

You're so warm and loving
Never putting me down
You're always smiling
Never walking with a frown.

Now you see
Why I love you so much
Because you're always yourself
Not practicing to be someone else.

Shannon R Moore
A CHILD'S MATURITY

For my inspirations: Mom, Dad, Don, George., Meredith & Chris. With immense respect and love.

And the last few steps towards the mountain's peak were steep and rocky.
Though as tired and weak as my body and mind were, I reached forward into the sunbeams above.
And when I got there — to that summit once so far away— it was a sight to heal all wounds.
A valley of living things reached forever
Hills and fields formed the earth.
And, above it all, a sky coloured a blue deeper than any ocean.
And a sun, an ever giving life source, that warmed my skin that shone as a beacon of heaven.
Through renewed eyes, I could see beyond any horizon, past any rocky mountain, over the cruelty, above the evil
And into myself.

Edith Meadows
MY PRAYER AND TESTIMONY

My Grace is Sufficient,
I heard Jesus say,
In a still small Voice
As I knelt to pray,

I felt his presence by my side,
He had heard my prayer
There is Joy in Salvation
Away beyond compare,

It's not the first time,
My Savior Blessed me
Once I was fearful as could be,
He looked down, and smiled,
upon me,
And I was calm just like the sea,

O do not Cease my Brother,
To steal away and pray,
Your reward is waiting,
It will be Worth it all some day,

And when our Earthly trials
are over,
We hear him say well done,
Come on up here, you are welcome,
A crown of life you have Won.

Mary McCullaugh
THE HUMMINGBIRD
The butterfly bush was covered with
flowers,
They smelled so fragrant last spring
I stopped by each time I passed the
bush
It was so interesting.
It drew butterflies by the hour
They enjoyed the nectar there,
These little creatures so very small
Who flew about in the air.
There were honeybees, bumblebees,
hummingbirds too,
They were all so very small
The hummingbird drew my attention
though
And I liked it the best of all.
But it had one thing that was
different,
Antennas were on its head.
Then my son told me he had found
out
In a book that he had just read,
That the hummingbird which I
thought I had seen
Was a hummingbird moth instead.

Lawrence T Markham
THE MIDNIGHT SINGER

To Ione, my loving mother. Another with a wondrous, and angelic voice. And having a true love for prose, life, and her God.

Mr. Sammy Cut Throat,
the happiest finch alive,
will sing you a song,
no matter what the time.
Other birds will flutter and fly,
but Sammy sings with head held
high.
When you're sick and feeling blue,
he cheers you up with his whimsical
tune.
When you come home tired from
work,
He'll beckon you to come and sing
with merriment and mirth.

Yes, the Midnight Singer is small,
but his magnificent spirit makes up
for it all.
So if you love a good time,
and a dog and a cat just doesn't come
to mind,
get a Cut Throat Finch and have a
sing-along,
to make you laugh and feel real fine.

Lisa B MacIntosh
DREAMS
In a dream I can show how I really
feel,
make everything I've hoped for
become real.

I can say things to people I've always
wanted to say,
let my feelings show in their own
special way.

I am in a world where there are
people who are never mean,
but I can't forget it is only a dream.

My dream guy I would meet and
become his wife.
We could share everything for a
beautiful life.

With children in our relationship so
happy we would be,
many boys and girls for a large
family.

My husband could become the King
and I the Queen,
But my conscience still reminds me it
is only a dream.

Whether I'm dreaming during the day
or during the night,
my dreams will always be filled with
colors so bright to make everything
in the world seem right.

And though the sun still shines, and
the grass is still green,
the words remain true, it is only a
dream.

Paula Jan Medley
A NEW YEAR'S PRAYER
You give me the light of the day, Oh
Lord,
So I might see where I've gone
wrong,
There is no precious time to afford,
And I'll sing it in this song.

Thank-You God, for all Your love,
A new start, a new year, a new day,
All the gifts You share from above,
Then You pave for me a new way.

Thank-You God, for Your big heart,
With room for a world of souls,
And from Your children You never
part,
No walls, no bars, no holds.

Thank-You God, for Your strong
arms,
That carry me when I'm lame,
You protect me from the devil's
harm,
And I could never do the same.

Thank-You God, for everything,
I'll never be worthy of all,
Yet, only to You, this song I sing,
On my feet, on my knees, when I fall.

J Walter McMullan
GULLS IN THE MIST

To BB and KEG. Thanks for your love.

I often wonder about City folks
in fact sometimes cry
it bothers me to think they have not
seen
the Gulls in the mist

Hardy folk on the coast by great
waters
know of what I speak
the lonely sea birds cry cold in the
rain
do they know of warmth

Maybe their comfort is lashing waves
wet rocks foaming surf
man crouches to catch heat at cozy
hearth
tell — whose choice is best

I was born by the lonely rocky coast
I remember dull
dark days of sea clouds and plaintive
cries of
sad gulls in the mist

J Walter McMullan
MY CHILD
Don't depend on me
as you I am child
some days I may know
enough to get by

Strong tall I may seem
don't accept this face
depend on yourself
I am still your friend

My best was for you
love was yours alone
it will always be
there for you to hold

Don't feel bad today
things won't always be
cloudy and rain filled
sing tomorrow's praise

J Walter McMullan
WAITING
We are all waiting
the busy ones don't know
no matter what your scene
or steady your life flows

Each day the sun arises
winds and clouds will flow
babies breathe sweet air
come winter follow snow

And so our lives go on
we buy our toys and play
but in the dark of night
Godot will have its day

J Walter McMullan
FREE
It should come to us all once
we strive and strain and then
we burst out we are free
a moment brief ecstasy

Not for me this way why
should I strive so long and
then like quicksilver shine
then scatter lost in my folds

No, as I strive I savour
the time in future when
I burst out free singing
I dream it every day

Jerry McLallen
UNTITLED
I went looking for love,
But it was always behind me,
Following me wherever I went,
And patiently waiting to bind me.
I walked down the road,
Not knowing where I was bound,
Barely feeling my way along,
Just hoping to be found.

Just when the end of the road was
near,
And I felt I could no longer cope,
Someone gave my shoulder a tap,
And I turned, and I saw hope
in the form of a beautiful woman
Who took me toward the light.
And now, the road we walk together
Shall always be happy and bright.

We share this road now, her and me,
And we share the love we found,
And hand in hand we'll stroll
together,
From now on, Heaven-bound.

John Martin Jr
TO WHOM YOU LOVE SO MUCH
From the moment that you will go
hand in hand
With that of your mated one, of
which you have band

Make this be of a cherish event
And one that will be long spent

For going through life very alone
Is as fruitless, as seeds unsown

Love is of the foundation, by which it
can only survive
Let the glow stay within mind &
heart as long as you are alive

Hold within your heart a longing to
be within each other's arms
And not touched by life's harmful
harms

To share your life in marriage with
another
Be so close that the slightest hurt will
be felt by the other

Display feelings, freely to the touch
To one another, whom you love so
much

David S Mann
TANTALIZING TASTE
The supple stroke of her silken
fingertips
as they smoothly slide across my lips.

The tantalizing taste,
my mouth made little haste
as the taste buds on my tongue
touched the lips on which her
fingertips had hung.

Patricia J Hovde
IN THE ESSENCE OF A ROSE

Dedicated to true love; mates who commit for life; and our marriage of thirty-six years.

He handed her a sweet bouquet
Eyes searching hers hoping to find
Forgiveness for what made her sadly
sigh
In trembling hands she fondly held
his gift
Velvet gems encircled in an embrace,
tears, a kiss
The soothing aroma of purest scent
Carried to her heart his silent intent
A pair of roses of crimson soft petals
Framed in assuring eternity fern

Tiny pink bells speak of promises all
new
Tied close together with ribbons that
care
Bound together for true love does
live here
Each time she breathes their
fragrance in
A mending heart meets with his
For this is what she needed to know
That no matter what he loves her so
As these flowers lay pressed in
memories time
Remembered is their essence wherein
she did find
Romantic whisperings from his
gentle lips

Of feelings only his own heart could know
Until he took her to the garden where red roses grow.

Michael McGlasson
EULOGY FOR ELIZA
A wandering spirit
Through the night's plutonian shore;
A wondering spirit
That is weary and forlorn;
She brings with her a yearning
For the ancient days of yore.

Though her soul is weeping,
And her heart lies unbeating
Beneath her linen-clad breasts,
The memory of her as she was in life
Relieves the tormenting, unrestful strife
Of a thousand lonely nocturnal nights.

Be still, my wife—
Be still, in thine tomb by the resounding
Moontide sea;
In death, my love, and your love,
Has not been forsaken;
In life, thou hast awaken within
This pitiful shell of poetic man,
The purity of a melancholy heart.

Karen A Mays
THE RAINBOW
What is the rainbow,
With its pink, blue and green?
It is what gives the sky its luster,
After the fallen rains.

Can you tell me where it goes,
Or why it fades from sight?
They say it is beads of water,
Dancing on streams of light.

A pot of gold at its end,
Of that I am not sure
For, only God can make a rainbow
With its pastel colored hues.

God's love for all of us,
Restored faith in mankind
Is the reason for the rainbow's glow
That arches in the skies.

Reneé Miller
FORGOTTEN
Another day has come,
Without my friends near.
They must be mad at me,
Or they just wouldn't disappear.
I can't think of anything,
That I possibly could have done.
Maybe I was just myself,
And that is what made them run.
But they just don't want to include me,
In anything they do,
They go places together,
And rely on each other to talk to.
They no longer want to tell,
Their problems to me.
They go on having fun,
My disappointment they don't see.
They were always my true friends,
Who listened to what I had to say.
We took turns telling our problems,
We never got in each other's way.
Now everything's changed,
And it's not the same,
It's all my fault,
I guess I'm the one to blame.
That is the reason,
I wrote this poem,
I wanted you guys to know,
I no longer want to be alone.
So if you don't want to hear from me,
Just tell me you don't,
I will never come near you,
I promise you I won't.

Heather Erin McClure
SILENT WHISPERS
In the quiet whispers of morning
  a gentle voice is heard.
To walk in the clover so tender
  and not fear the world.
In the deep depths of silence
  we find our true self.
Though in this world of illusion
  many forget their path.
Our Love, Our Life, our Father and Light,
  rests within us in absolute peace.
Real human potential is not locked away
  but rather swept in a dark corner
  waiting untouched in complete bliss.
True hope lies not in asking for forgiveness,
  but rather in willingness to learn how to forgive.

Heather Erin McClure
TWIN FLAMES
You may fear me,
But you really fear love.

You fear yourself.

I would share with you everything;
Speak of the wonders of the universe.

I yearn for your love.

I have seen a part of you
which you have forgotten.

The most beautiful light,
Rests within — you.

An unbounding strength abides in you,
Yet you trust it not.

Oh behold the glimmer of radiant beauty.
Who you really are surpasses
your wildest dreams.

I dreamt of our love.
And I would share the dream
with you.

Oh, if only you could see

that you — are me.

Karen McElwee
A DREAMER SUNSET, A WINTER STORM
A summer sunset, A winter storm.
A falling leaf that no one sees.
The sounds the rain makes when it hits the ground.
The beauty in one's eye that no one else can see.
To read between the lines and still believe.
To know I love without being told
Having all of this in you.
Makes me love more than you will ever know.

Charles Benjamin Miller III
FREEDOM LAND
Dear lady blue
  You stand so proud,
With your gleaming torch
  Calling loud,
Come one come all
  Into my open arms,
Where freedom gleams
  And you're safe from harm,
Liberty is my name
  America is my home,
Where all men are equal
  And free to roam,
My land is vast
  My shores are wide,
My heart holds nothing
  But love inside,
Freedom rings
  All around,
Saying, "Welcome stranger
  To my hometown"

W Lois Miller
EVEN THOUGH WE'RE FAR APART

To my sister.

Even though we're far apart,
My thoughts go out to you.
May we always keep in touch,
As sisters ought to do.

Very swiftly go the years

While we're getting older
Every birthday leaves its mark,
Every day gets colder, but you
Keep your glow and youthful spark,
Love makes the world go round, 'tis said
Each day is a reminder
Yesterday's been put to bed, today's a whole lot kinder.

Kai L Marks
CLOUDS
Clouds, so pretty do they lie,
  Up in the sky, so high.
Their colors change as day goes by,
  White and fluffy, blue sky.

Sometimes a rainbow happens by,
  How nice its colors are
So brightly shining in the sky
  The best colors by far!

Nancy Margaret Maher
AN UNTIMELY PASSING

To Evelyn Adair—Dear Friend and Teacher.

In a world that seldom really
  understood you and one which you
  were never quite comfortable with,
You laughed,
  sighed,
    cried,
      and struggled.
Ah yes, the struggle to be yourself;
  A spirit who lovingly touched all hearts it came close to.
  In making yourself happy you never succeeded,
  but in accomplishing your goal of calming turbulent souls, you excelled.
  All that could have been for you on this earth is over,
Now . . . the Beginning.

Gil Martin
THE CROSS
I took the cross from the wall,
And flung myself upon the bed,
With cross in hand, I spoke to it,
Dear God, Why all this pain?
My love and I try so hard,
Why him? Why him?
All this pain, year in, year out,
I cried and cried, then came a light,
And in this, appeared my God,
My soul went before him,
Have Faith in me, my child,
Keep your Faith,
Then darkness came,
The years passed by,
There still is pain, but faith is strong,
Upon the bedroom wall,
There hang the cross,
This special Cross.

Gil Martin
THE HYMNS FROM ABOVE
I sometimes hear the hymns of heaven,
As my feet on concrete walk,
My eyes, look upward,
As clouds turn into shapes I know,
How sad I feel for loved ones there,
I have the need to see once more,
A mother oh so dear, father also loved,
Friends who left this world too soon,
Yet I sometimes hear these hymns,
I know that God beckons me not as yet,
And as I walk, the tears do come,
Yet I know, I have so much here,
I do miss the yesteryears,
I guess my youth, makes me sad,
For it is gone, and in its place,
Is a woman, with so much love,
She hugs this world and all above,
For she hears, the hymns from above.

Gil Martin
IF I COULD CHANGE THIS WORLD
If I could change this world,
I would wipe away all hate,
In its place, I would put love.
If I could change this world,
I would hug and hold all fears,
In its place, I would put hope,
If I could change this world,
Where there is no faith,
I would show the way to God,
If I could change this world,
Where there is no kindness,
I would show the way to charity,
If I could change this world
Where there is so much pain,
I would say, "look" there is god,
Forever, our only hope,
Forever, our only cure,
Forever our only way,
If I could, but hope, to change this world.

Gloria Patricia McMurry
MY CHILDREN

To: My Lord, who gave me my talent. My husband, William Curtis my encouragement. My children, Gloria, William, Terrance, and Pamela, my inspiration.

I would not ask you, to think like me.
I would only ask you, to think.
I would not ask you, to be like me.
I only ask for the best, you can be.
The struggles, the fears,
that I've had through the years.
I would not bequeath, to you.
I pray you'll be strong, and can step beyond,
to your future, and what lies there–in.
That your struggles be new, but let them be few.
The wisdom, the talent, to work all them through.
Till you reach your own, horizon.
(by glory)

Gloria Patricia McMurry
DANDELION FLOWERS GOD'S GIFT TO THE CHILD
What mother has not heard,
the squeals of delight.
As the small child comes running,
both hands clasped so tight.
'Tis the first gift to mother,
from the toddler of two.
A handful of sunshine,
that he captured for you.

Oh! this child just discovered,
a magnificent sight.
In their small world of wonders,
stands this flower so bright.
As they toddle uncertain,
in this world outside, their screen.
Yellow dandelions greet them,
in the lovely fields of green.

Annoying, to our grown-up world,
Proud in brilliance, stands tall, this weed.
Turning white and fuzzy, then goes to seed.
More dressed in yellow, hardy and wild.
Dandelion flowers, God's gift to the child.

(by glory)

Judi A Mongold
ONE OF THE FEW AND THE PROUD

To Billy, the inspiration for this poem. May all who read this poem be mindful of how important it is to convey our feelings to those who mean the most to us.

Today is the saddest day of my life
for my brother will be leaving tomorrow.
There were so many things that I wanted to tell him like,
How proud I was of him;
How much I Love Him;
How much I will miss him;
And how much I will think of him while he is away.

But all I could do was hug him and cry.

Even now as the tears pour down my face I think of him, and count the days until he is home again.

South Carolina seems like it's across the world right now.

I know he will be all right because he is a man now, strong and independent.
But all I can do is remember the days when we were young and he was my baby brother;
When he was young and defenseless,
I wanted to protect him then, too!
Inside I felt all his hurts and pains.
It's sad how Brothers and sisters rarely say what is really in their heart.
And now when I look back on when we said good-bye Billy, I wish I would have said I Love You . . .

Stephen DiSilvestro
WINTER IN HARDWICK
It's the weekend
The Volvos
and Jaguars
are out
to look at
the Bohemian Waxwings.
Lucky for me
I'm
just
a
bohemian . . .

Charles Ellsworth Hevel
THE SNOWFLAKE
The snowflake . . . Oh, what a lovely sight—a scenic delight to capture the imagination of one and all after the first snowflakes fall.

When days are cold and the trees are bare, and there's little to cheer the world out there, I love to climb a hill and see the snow as it covers the field and tree.

Oh, the snowflakes are falling, come, let's go—they give a lustre to our world—and so, when snowflakes are whirling and swirling around, with glee we'll dance and jump up and down.

The snowflakes are falling—come, take my hand, we'll wander thru this frosty land, created by winds that blow over icy figures and drifting snow.

Oh, the wonder of it all, oh, the beauty of it all. Each snow crystal that we see is individual as can be—No two the same, as science doth proclaim, each one a six-pointed star, that comes to earth from afar.

Charles Ellsworth Hevel
COME LET US REASON TOGETHER
Vets Hospital, Lincoln, Nebraska

Come now, let us reason together—
Thus saith the Lord: Will we not listen and heed his word?

Why tarry you so, and tempt fate?
Why do you wait, 'til it's almost too late?
You are not the 'captain of your soul'—
Nor the 'master of your fate!'
Your life was bought for a price—a sacrifice paid by our saviour Jesus Christ!
Oh come let us adore him—bow down before him,
Almighty and power is he, to banish all your misery—
your troubles and sorrows will flee away, just trust in the Lord and pray.
Oh what needless pain you bear, the burdens are too great, when you fail to come to your God in prayer, and wait . . . and wait . . . and wait . . .
Reach out to Jesus—He's reaching out to you, you may not see him, nevertheless it is true. He is there waiting—watching—eagerly ready to rescue you—Why do you stand there so weary—tired—and blue? Jesus will help you—He wants to bring you thru.

Alice Hanson Senter
VALUE$
Love of money
Appears
As the root of all
Evil
While compassionate LOVE
Measures
His Golden Rule

Elinor Bernice Tryon
ON MOMMY'S GRAVE

This poem is dedicated to those who knew and loved my mother who I knew as Mrs. Ethel Janet Chin Tryon. It is also dedicated to her.

Since you have gone to the cold grave
The breezes in Lincoln Park sigh and rave.

And I know that down there after dark
The leaves droop dejected in the park.

I, myself, never think it fun to—as before—
Wander, as we did, down there anymore.

With you gone, nothing is as it was then
When you and I were fun to begin.

The sky by day shines sadly duller.
The sky seems to have lost its color.

The time or two since you left I've been there
There is gloom and emptiness everywhere.

I miss there a dear form and familiar face
And all seems void and voiceless space.

Rosalyn M King
O GOD, MAKE ME MORE LIKE YOU
O God, how I love thee,
from the inner depths of my soul.

I strive to be like thee,
O my heavenly, heavenly, master and guide.
Won't you make me more like you?
I would like to walk the heavens
and ride the waves.
I would like to be omnipotent and
omnipresent—Expressing,
Expressing, Being, Being,
Everywhere.
Spreading Love, Joy, Light,

Blessings, Riches, Healing,
Happiness, and Magic,
everywhere I go in the world and
in the realm of worlds.

O God, make me like you—
Magnificent!
Angelic! Supernatural! Electronic!
Pure!
A great and positive force of love and
light in the universe and universes.

O God, how I do love thee.
Won't you please make me more
like you?

Margie C Keener
MY BEST FRIEND

Dedicated to my mom, Margaret Carllson.

Whenever I need a friend —
You always seems to be there.
You help me with my problems,
And our joys together we share.

I can't imagine life —
Without a friend like you.
Once we get together,
We are an indivisible two!

All the fun I've shared with you,
Can never be replaced.
Together we've had many good times,
And conquered the problems we've faced.

So I want you to know —
That I'm always here,
If ever you need a friend
To make your thoughts clear.

And when I must leave you,
As many good friends sometimes part.
I leave you with good memories,
And an important place in my heart!

Cheryl Cannon
YOU ARE GOD'S GIFT, MY FRIEND

For Debbie, you befriended me; you will always be; "God's Gift" to me, no matter, how far the distance, you're forever, in my heart.

When God gave out his special gifts,
a blessing I received;
For God put you into my life, you're a special friend indeed.
Although, I may disguise it, or act like I don't care; it means the world to me, my friend, to know that you are there.
I know I act so hurtful, in a lot of things I do;
I just pray you'll understand, and know that I need you.
I let you in my heart my friend, I hold you there to stay;
I just trust you'll understand, and won't turn me away.
So, when I'm acting wacko, or crazy as I do,
I just pray, you'll understand, and know that I need you.
Someday, I hope that I can be; As good for you, as you've been for me.
I couldn't do it without you, being there to see me through.
Tonight a special prayer I'll say, of gratitude for you;
You are as special, as can be; You are God's Gift, to me.

Cheryl Cannon
WINGED FAITH
A little bird is weary, with his first step from the nest.
He wants to fly, he really does, he tries his very best.
And when his fear he leaves behind, he finds that he can fly,
With Perfect Faith, he soars into a new dawn in the sky.
With Perfect Faith, he soars and sings,
Not worrying what tomorrow may bring.
God's little Angels in disguise; Oh, did you ever realize?
The cockatiel, a pet so great; he sings and talks without mistake.
Little spirits on high wing; Robins, how they soar and sing.
Pigeons with their friendly way; Can brighten up an old man's day.
Parakeets as they play; Can make the children smile today.
To God's angels I talked today; two

cardinals came to my window to play;
And when they flew off, into the nest.
I knew God had done his very best;
When within the spirit of the bird, angels rest.
If life should teach me anything, I'd like the faith of a bird on wing,
So, that when the day grows neigh;
My cares may rest, my spirit fly.
And, then my soul may sing; With all the grace of a bird on wing.

Cheryl Cannon
TAKE ME BACK, LORD

For Patty; May you carry always—
God's gift of the heart . . .
Compassion.

Lord, give me the courage, to trust in life again.
God, grant me some serenity, and give me back my friend.
I miss her Lord, I really do, I never dreamt I would.
I love her Lord, even though, I never thought I could.
I used her Lord, and left her, 6000 miles behind,
And now I find that she is, forever on my mind.
So, take a message to her Lord, and carry it with Love;
Let her know I miss her Lord, and send her a white dove.
I need some forgiveness, God, I need it from my friend,
So, that maybe one day, I'll try and Love again.
My God, you did give me a gift, that I refused.
Instead, I broke her heart in two, the friend that I did use.
Now my heart is breaking, and I don't want to stay;
So, let me fall into my dreams, and carry me away.
Take me back, Lord, where I long to be . . .
Take me back, Lord, in my dream, so my friend I can see.
I doubt she'll ever realize, how much she means to me,
So, take me back, Lord, in my dream, and then just let me be.
Carry to her all my Love, and drop it in her heart,
Let her know she's with me Lord, though we're so far apart.
Take me back, Lord, in my dream, and then Please mend my heart.

Cheryl Cannon
GENTLENESS
Gentleness can mean so much; Put some Gentleness in your touch.
With Gentleness God protects the land; He wipes your tears with a gentle hand.
Gentleness makes love feel right, God rocks you gently through the night.
With Gentleness your heart may mend, And you may even make a friend.
Gentleness can mean so much, With Gentleness God's children touch.
On a gentle wing God's birds do fly, With God's gentle touch they soar so high.
Gentleness in your voice you know, May soothe another's aching soul.
So, when you're sad and feeling down, Spread a gentle smile around.
With Gentleness God takes your fear, And holds you gently very near.
So, try some Gentleness today, And help another along life's way.

Cheryl Cannon
FRIENDSHIP
Friendship is like a flower, you know
It takes some time for it to grow.
Plant the seed within your heart
Like a new flower, to let it start.
Sunshine burns, if you get too much,
So, nurture it with a gentle touch.
And when the leaves begin to show
Water it, and take it slow.
Deeply, strongly, roots will grow,
And then you'll get attached it's so.
Nurture it with love and care,
And soon you'll find a blossom there.

Cheryl Cannon
FAREWELL, MY FRIEND
Farewell, my friend, I wish for you, fair wind and a following sea,
And may you always be in life, the best that you can be,
Though I'm gone, you're in my heart, I hold you there to stay,
Even though our distance now, is so far away.

And when I dream, upon the sea, serene and turquoise blue,
You, know my friend, in my heart, I'm sharing it with you.
And when I gaze upon the stars, distant and far away,
You know, my friend, you're the one, I miss so much today.

And if we ever meet again, in lifetimes or in days;
I'll have a special gratitude that God sent you my way.
Until our paths do cross again, I send you all my love,
And pray that God will hold you in, his loving arms above.

Willie James Johnson
HAPPINESS IS

I dedicate this poem to God, who has blessed me with the ability to create poetry.

Happiness is being free; free from drugs free from crime—free to do no time incarcerated.
That's what happiness is to me;
Happiness is equality and justice; if there is no justice there is no peace—and smart ones know violence won't cease.
Happiness is seeing young people increase their knowledge—and learn true history when they attend college.
Happiness is being with your loved ones and being unselfish and sensitive to the wants and needs of others.
Happiness is love.
Happiness is seeing someone smile after you've done something nice for them.
Happiness is unity.
Finally, happiness is being paid to do what you like to do for free—that's what happiness is to me.

Joseph A Martinez
COLORADO
California has beautiful beaches,
  and beautiful women too.
But Colorado, is the place to be,
  it was made for me and you.
From the snowcapped Rocky Mountains,
  to the prairies down below.
From the Aspen trees in Vail,
  people look, and they will know.
That this country is God's country,
  and it took some loving care.
To place all of the lovely things,
  in the right spots everywhere.
Where the people are real friendly,
  and they'll lend a helping hand.
Where a stranger is no stranger,
  and alone he will not stand.
So come to Colorado,
  where the Rockies touch the sky.
To the land that God created,
  with a twinkle in his eye.

Joseph A Martinez
ABUSED
I often sit and wonder,
  what makes the world this way.
Why people hurt each other,
  with words they should not say.
I often sit and wonder,
  why a man beats on his wife.
This man is not a man at all,
  but the lowest of all life.
A woman is a fragile thing,
  with feelings, that shows she cares.
And when abused in any way,
  it hurts and she'll shed tears.
God put her here for a purpose
  but men don't understand.
That she is for companionship,
  to walk life hand in hand.
So, I often sit and wonder,
  if such men will change their ways.
And treat a woman with love and respect,
  and give her fearless days.

Cheryl A Morris
MY LITTLE GIRL
My little girl, you seem,
to me, to be a dream.

But, each day I wake,
the dream is seen.

But, little girl though,
  Not mine of blood,
    But, are mine,
      by my heart . . .

AMEN . . .

Gloria Seltzer
WINTER'S WEB
Crystalline configurations
glisten gracefully
from overhanging boughs.

Pristinely
mantled branches
bend beneath their burden.

Corn stubble sentinels
stand guard
in whipped cream fields.

Winter's web envelops all.

Gregory D Schatzle
SEARCHING
Me . . . who began as a precious miracle of birth with so much hope and promise

Now dies a slow, silent death with every breath I draw

The obstacles are too great to overcome

The striving has taken its toll

Such a tragedy, it should be me who ended up imprisoned behind the bars of self-doubt . . .

Locked into the inability to trust, or to feel . . .

Me . . . who now withdraws, to the safe confines of my bars, to wait . . .

Not for an end to my suffering, but for a new day

A day filled with hope and belief

A day in which I'll be able to go on with my search
Me . . . who wants to be free

Monica Hopkins
LEGENDARY UNICORN
Somewhere unknown
and somewhere unseen
the unicorn roams
mysterious, but free

He hides in the shadows
and glides thru the air
without a worry
without a care

His legend is folklore
and known thru the land
his beauty is wondrous
his being is grand

Wild and uncaptured
free and untamed
the unicorn resides
in his own domain

His being is mysterious
as is his magical horn
for he is the legend
he is the unicorn

Dena Maria Beeler-Hill
I'LL BE THERE
You're thinking, "I'll never see her again!"
  But, you're wrong.
I'll be there . . . just listen to the
  words of a love song.

Each time you admire a work of art;
  You'll feel the deep love
I carried just for you in my heart.

I'll smile back through the eyes of a child.
  You will see.
And at times you'll drag out my photograph;
  There I'll be.

For awhile my pillow
  Will comfort you until there's
  someone new . . .
  Until then you'll find ways
In quiet for my love to touch you.

As always, even with my dying breath,
  I'll take care.
Speak my name outside Heaven's gate . . .
  I'll Be There!!!

Verria Whitehead
SIGNS OF SPRING
Scattered showers followed by the coldest, gray skies and winds that touch the very soul.

Turning over and over again as if in a lost ferris wheel ride; the Sun's rays push through the gray skies bringing a peace and warmth to the land.

Blue jays, Robins birds of spring chirp and sing as if no tomorrow; how lovely the serenade.

Truly spring is near as I see the kids head for the beach and skateboard row. Nothing but laughter

fills the air.
Yes yes spring is near.

Jessica Braks
WHY
I used to feel the wind whip across my face
Leaving without a trace
The moon used to light up the sky
Making the stars shine bright
Dreaming used to be like an eagle's flight
Soaring high in the clouds
The trees used to be so kind
Letting spring buds bloom
We used to stroll through meadows
Which let flowers blossom
My heart sheds a tear
It can never be the same

Liesa Riethmeier
SENTENCED TO LIFE
William he sits with his hands on his chin; his eyes intense, his mouth drawn thin.
So sad. He must have been hurt pretty bad.
He says he tried to take his life; so I'd like to give some of mine to save him.
Suicide took the greatest love I've ever had. So sad—to see someone so special hurt so bad.
I've walked thru most of my life alone. I live alone. A message machine answers my phone
'Cause I'm seldom there, I'm rather busy, I've got so much to do it would make one dizzy
But it would make it all worthwhile to know that I could make you smile
To see you get your life together—to bind the reaper in respite awhile.
William he sits with his hands on his chin, his eyes intense; his mouth drawn thin
So sad!
And I'll do whatever I can to save him.
I'd like to take out some time to embrace him.
For one it was too late to see any movies or make any date
. . . but let that pass . . . !
It would ease some pain in my life to save him from the eternal knife.
I just want the pain to go away; each night of living day by day
Each night I pray to my Guardian Angel
For tapestry and rainbow visions of a more colourful future.

Max Fantasy Singer
SINGING SAINTS

Singing saints—from the pop music collection.

Singing Saints
Throughout history
Have had a powerful
Influence on me
As shining examples
Of what can be
Done by one
Who lives powerfully

Yes
Saintly spirits
Inspire me
To live more influentially
To guide the course of history
I know they're up there
Watching me

To all you saints
I'd like to say
Someday I may try it your way
Maybe I'll become one of you
For I'm a super spirit too
But for now
I'd rather be me
Experiencing everything
I can see

Yes, if the decision's up to me
I'll use my superpowers here
In this playground world
Until the saints come marching in
Making love with another girl

Helen Ruth Vaughn
WHERE PARADISE NEVER ENDS
When I end my journey on this earth,
And bid farewell to family and friends.
I am going to a better home above,
Where Paradise never ends.

I will not need things that are here,
No, I will not need them anymore.
I'll walk, run, shout and sing praises,
Over on the other shore.

I'll walk on the streets of glory,
And listen to the Hallelujahs ring.
Jesus has promised me a home in Heaven,
Where Paradise never ends.

Donna M Mowinski
HELP ME

To my beloved family for all the encouragement especially to my husband Walt, My Son Stephen, and my Daughter Kristie for their love and also to B.M. who is always an inspiration.

I miss you my friend, I really do
Every day my thoughts are on you
It's a life of hurt, I feel so alone
Help me my friend, Call me on the phone

I don't know just how to express
The way I feel, the loneliness
I see you every now and then
Help me my friend, Call me again

I thought we were friends you and me
I guess I was wrong, That I can see
I guess I fooled myself into what I wanted to see
Help me my friend, be there for me

I'm always there for you, I told you the same
Can't we stop playing this game
I love you my friend, I really do
Help me my friend I need you

Mary Theresa Walsh
LOST IN THE DARKNESS
Lost in the darkness
Not knowing which way to turn

Trusting the signs
Only to vanish in the light

Hold to a fantasy
Make believe in reality

Knowing in the darkness
Be still my broken dreams

Frances Jarrett Tincher
SEA FANTASY
Chance has willed that we meet
like myriad waves of the sea.
Rising and falling — incomplete,
dashing headlong — still not free.

How like grasping fingers
are the Eddies of each wave,
But not one lingers
upon the sand a slave!

Out into the pulsing sea
wherein the heart's replete,
The waves dance joyously
as wave upon wave they meet!

So, too, are the ways of men
whose lives briefly stand
And touch, then touch again,
like waves upon the sand.

Carilin Halcomb
MEMORIES
Country roads and autumn leaves
Blue birds singing, in the trees
Wind blowing, across my face
Bring back memories, of my old home place
Climbing trees, and throwing rocks
Walking the top rail, of the old cow lot
With old stick horses, and match box cars
We really couldn't go, very far
So down to the creek, wading we would go
Without jeans rolled up, hoping mama wouldn't know

Little girls running, barefoot in the sand
While dad and the boys, plowed up the land
The barn was filled, with new peanut hay
A field full of corn, to be gathered the next day
There were animals to feed, and eggs to gather
And mom's fresh biscuits, there were none better
Now mom's gone on, and dad's grown old
But all these memories, I'll forever hold
I would love to go back, if only I could
To share with my children, my own childhood

Shirley Zeko
SEASONS

To my husband Bob, whom I love dearly.

As the spring rain hits my window-pane
I pleasure for the flowers will bloom again
While the porch swing squeaks with the summer breeze
I watch the birds as they nest high in the trees
I think, how fast the seasons do fly
Soon autumn will come, and the flowers will die
Not far behind comes the wind and the cold
Time for boots and coats and summer on hold
With each season we found great pleasure and fun
As we bid farewell to each final one.

Rachel V Walker
SWINGING

To my brother Robert V. Scott, who is always there for me. Thanks.

High over the land I go sailing
Rooftops and chimneys below me, twinkle
The fields look like old men with wrinkles

Oh! How I love in my swing, to go flying
As the trees go marching by they are sighing

Leaves in my path go rolling and chasing
Like hounds after a rabbit, go racing

The heavens are so blue,
The earth green, yellow, and brown
Cries from the birds made a joyful sound

The sun in my face, the wind at my back
The old gray cat still asleep, on the mat

I wish life could go on forever this way,
But twilight is now falling
It's time to go to bed

When the sun rise in the morning
All bright and red
A new day it will bring — And once again I will swing.

Barbara J Bassett
MOON DREAMS
When my heart was very still last night,
I heard it! Sweet and clear.
At first it came up whispering,
Then thoughts of you grew near.

And all at once it began to ring
In the wake of the moonlit sky;
Then touching me with enchantment,
It passed on the wing of a sigh!

It left me feeling full of life
As that fleeting heartbeat passed,
And full of dreams, in only dreams—
Are moments like that grasped!

John-Andrew TeGrotenhuis
FLOWERS
I know some dice belong to God
As I was thrown a way
Since we were penny in the street
And You came out to pray

You over flow tedrope sun d' rest
I breathe you deepen sky
And wonder if There Could Be Light
So stem the seeds ascry

And rose by any other name
's much too love for bud
but shall I hoard thy placial chord
an clasp arachnid flood

Andfromthe one I hope forgot me
to the one I hope to see
I hope the one I give you
remembers all of me

John-Andrew TeGrotenhuis
FINGERS
I was a child.
I learned to count.
I counted everything.
I counted all the numbers.

There are no numbers.

John-Andrew TeGrotenhuis
ME
I must not miss a single glance
I'm sure I used to love
And I should learn to smile in time
When passing chances of

After birth the quiet comes
I live my frame of day
Along the light, the only-fast
I'm always on my way

I've born a' most unheavened-yet
undone to make me child
As small the lash I can't untear
My God in-tends so mild

Forever on the v'rge of tears
I only see I'm blind
and even though I have un'touch't
I' ( ) Trust We are to find

Barbara J Bassett
STIRRINGS
A passing thought can turn to such stirrings
When pondering life's fanciful, powerful, yearnings.
And that was the way one day came to pass,
As I paused for a moment to look through the glass.

Outside the rain weaves its own sort of tale
As I whisper a prayer that my quest shall not fail,
To unveil the love that is shroud in my dreams,
And fend off the emptiness of life's daily schemes.

To stir up the embers of a smoldering fire
And ignite age-old passions of love and desire.
To lighten my heart with a gypsy's dance,
And feel the embrace of unquenched romance.

How long have I sat here,
So deep in my thoughts?
Of rapturous moments,
Of treasured times lost?

Now I sit in shadows that four o'clock cast,
Laughing with Spring at Winter's past wrath,
Willing myself to come to some terms
With these stirrings of heart-strings and lessons to learn.

Laura A Petak
LOVE IS SUCH A FRAGILE THING
Love is such a fragile thing,
especially from this far away.
I'd like to tell you how I feel,
but the words get in the way.
You and I are nothing new to me;
I think of you everyday.
I dream of you near me, close as can be,
and it breaks my heart that we may never be.

Patricia Anne Woods
HE'S PAID THE PRICE

This poem is dedicated to HVW. I wish you well, always, Patricia.

I know this man is hurting, I can read it in his verse
And every time I reach for him nothing seems to work
He has so much to offer, I wish that I could stay
But the feelings that I need from him, he cannot give away
He says he feels no need to touch, to hold, to hug or kiss
I look at him in disbelief and wonder what he's missed
I know there's passion deep inside for all the things he feels
But when it comes to one-on-one, there's nothing he reveals

I often think about him and his time in Viet Nam
And try to understand all the killing he has done
A man who loves this country went to war and took a stand
It was not easy in the Marines for this loner of a man
I listened to his stories and all the horrors he's been through
But finally realize there's absolutely nothing I can do
To erase all the memories going through his mind
He tells me he's resolved them and there's nothing more to find

How can he erase those memories from the past?
And how can he find happiness when nothing ever lasts?
I wish that I could be there, I wish he'd let me in
But no one will ever touch him deeper than his skin
So through this life he'll travel, a journey all alone
He has the right, he's paid the price, it's all he's ever known

Jennie Ann Thomas Carson
ALMOST A YEAR
Almost a year's past since you walked out of my life;
since you said you didn't love me and I couldn't be your wife,
I've seen you once since then but you wouldn't even talk;
you just gave me a cold look and off you walked.

The hurt I felt then is still with me today;
I don't think that hurt will ever go away,
I think of you in everything I do;
sometimes it seems as though I'll never make it through,

My dreams are always of you holding me tight;
then I wake up, wishing you were here tonight,
I know you had your reasons to go away;
I try my best to understand that each and every day.

Maybe when you're older you'll be able to see;
that the love we had, was really meant to be,
So wherever you are, and in what life you're trying to start;
always remember this love I have in my heart . . .

Franklin S Sanderson
NOVEMBER RAIN

For my friend Deanna S., who believed in me when no one else would.

The snow falls without a sound,
Gently covering the land in a blanket of serenity.
Summer is but a cherished memory,
As friends quietly remember and go their separate ways.

The northern lights dance through the sky,
As shooting stars fall from the heavens.
Like the seasons, things always change,
But the friendships built on trust never do.

Dreams are what we live for,
Without them, we are like feathers in the wind.
Who knows what tomorrow will bring,
But we all wish to see the sun rise again.

Love and heartache, joy and sorrow,
It's all part of this game we call life.
Children of destiny,
We strive to find our own place in the world.

A wolf cries lonely in the night,
Calling the wild and the free.
Never let the fire burn to ashes.
As I sleep under the November rain.

Patricia Lucero
NIGHT FEARS

For Patrick, my son, whose 'Night Fears' prompted this poem, with love.

Submissive fear a child knows at night
with open doors and shadows.
The mind is quick to tell of the unknown,
the heartfelt patters.
A tiny whimper, then a call to Mom
as hands clutch covers in care.
The favorite blanket, or toy or prayer
an "I love you" to share.
Eyelids close as Mom turns down the lights,
for a moment to leer;
Knowing all is well, with peace in heart,
sleeping without fear.

Violetta L Berry
SHADOW
What is I see in yonder window,
But a shadow of a stranger standing in the night.
As I walked I saw no face,
but the smile of a stranger.
How he followed close, but far behind.
From afar I saw him,
as I turned the corner.
I saw him enter a house in which my mother lives,
and kiss her cheeks.
As he turned to leave I saw that stranger's face.
It was the shadow of my father who followed me
for all these years to only protect the youngest child.
Which was I.

Michael V Robinson (Vincent Michael)
LOVE IS . . .

To my dad & mom (Edmond & Esther Robinson), my immediate family, Vickie, Jr., Felicia, Bryon, and my Greater Union Baptist Church family—enjoy!!

Love is a word
That should not be
Taken for a ride.
The power it possesses
Is more than we realize.
Love is a number of things:
A mixture of feelings,
Emotions you cannot erase.
Broader than the sky,
Deeper than the ocean
It grows and grows.
Time could not begin to measure
Nor could money add up
To this word called love.
For it is a priceless gem,
The peak of a mountain,
And sweeter than a rose.
Love comes from within,
It has a beginning
But has no end . . .

Vernita Younglove
DON'T MEASURE MY LOVE
Don't measure my love, it's deeper than the sea,
Yes this deep love, that dwells within me.
Don't measure my love it's like counting the stars
Yes, darling you would miss it, miss it by far.
To measure my love it's like counting the grains of sand
You might try to guess, to measure it you never can.
With satellites and rockets, you may take a trip soon,
But to measure my love, is more than traveling to the moon.
You can never measure my love
by any earthly realm,
And for the one who is worthy
it's reserved waiting for him.

Galadia Murphy
A THOUGHT TO HELP ALONG A DREAM . . .
They had been through a long day and needed to rest.
Sleep. Not yet.
"Do you think it's possible to fall even more in love"
He asked her;
She answered
"Yes"
But questioned
"Why?"
"Because I have."
And a heart-warming smile came to her lips as he embraced
His wife.
Sleep. Happily, now.

Diana Vincent
PASSIONS
My love for you stirs deep within my blood!
That precious balm of life, that gives me
Strength to love and worship you,
And flows to heart, to hands, to limbs, to lips,
To every dear and secret place of passion.
My God, it's sweet to be in love with you
And feel that you are rampant in my veins.
And I am glad that you are thus a part of me, behind and in and running through
My every thought and act, an indwelling,
Electrifying force that penetrates the core
And inmost essence of my being,
An utter, final taking hold of me.

Carla Sibson
THE SQUEAKY WHEEL
It cries out that something is wrong.

Oh, how it must regret its own nature at times and get tired of the
noise . . .

Some envy it because it is treated,
but it isn't always,

And how often it is cured before it finds repair.

Marilyn P Meola
LOVERS
Lovers, holding hands in the noonday sun, on a picnic in the park.

Lovers, together, kissing in the moonlight.

Lovers, finding peaceful coexistence with the universe.

Lovers, going steady, getting engaged, and getting married.

Lovers, after they tie the knot, of marriage, raising a family.

What should everyone in the world be?

LOVERS!

Tracey Katason
DANCING WITH MY SPIRITS

To all the people I love.

My feet are floating on these airspun alabaster clouds of light.
My soul soars out of me and up above.
I can touch it.
My happiness warms my face and makes me smile.
I feel all feelings at once.
My arms open to this happiness and harness it.
I spin and never get dizzy.
My soul grins at me and jumps in my eyes.
Crystal circles float around me dancing to the rhythm of my heartbeat.
My feelings turn to color and fly in circles around my feet dodging my steps.
Laughter comes from my hands as they hit the clouds.

Ernest R Bennett
LOVE
Love is a field of
butterflies.
Goes into dormant then
either blossoms into a
beautiful creation or
withers away like a rose.
A rose that blooms then
goes as it comes into your
life.
A memory of glory and
beauty, of sight and soul,
God made, then passes
as it came.
That's what love is.

Linda Conley
SAY NO TO DRUGS
Here's an urgent message for all boys and girls
From New York City to all over the world

It is something that is really true
And whether you listen or not it's up to you

It's all about cocaine, crack and what you call dope
Which can be swallowed, sniffed or smoked

They can stimulate the mind and make you whack
Especially this new drug called crack

If you do them at all, please confess
It would be much better not to fool with the mess

Just say no to drugs for they are bad
And it doesn't matter how much you've had

If someone offers you some, just keep on walking
Don't listen to what they say, for they're always talking

If they say you won't get hooked—it's a lie
And they will be on drugs until the day they die

If you be strong and just say no
Your future will be bright and surely glow

So listen to your parents and then obey
This is all I have to say

Mary Nordby
WHEN YOU SLEEP
When you sleep, I dream.
You sleep so soundly,
You cuddle so closely.

Sometimes you kiss me when you sleep.
I pretend you know you're kissing me.
I could be anyone,
But, in your sleep, I dream.

Sometimes you hold me while you sleep.
Sometimes you hold me so tightly
I can hardly breathe.
I wonder who you think you're holding,
But, in your sleep, I can dream.

When you're awake you touch me
and hold me and kiss me.
You touch me softly.
You hold me gently.
You kiss me sweetly.

But when you're awake, your life is real.
I think you need some rest now,
So sleep, and I will dream!

Clayton E Poarch
WOMAN
A man should be so blessed

To experience the beauty of her caress
When all in a life is suddenly right
The finishing touch of a starlit night

A man should be so blessed

To realize such happiness
That only a woman can bring
The forest and meadows sing:

New life, total peace
New life, sweet release

A man should be so blessed

An end to solitude; someone to share
An end to loneliness; someone to care
An end to searching: she who is there
An end to desire: her beauty fair

A wonderful solution to life she gives
And in a whisper she speaks:

"Think of me always in tenderness
Think of me always, our sweet caress
A wonderment of life fulfilled
Think of me always, your heart be stilled"

And with this he replies:

"Forever in my heart I lay with thee
To be satisfied endlessly
Gather together a mutual trust
To seed knowledge, 'the two of us'
I'll be there for you, a willing life
Be assured of love. An end to strife
Trying occasions will arise,
As a team we will prize
Sweet victory won
Triumphant we move on"

All in a word my gratitude of happiness
A man should be so blessed

Bertha Wright
THE SECRET INGREDIENT
We try so hard when baking
Those pies or bread or cake,
But somehow we can't match the ones
That Mother used to make.

Do you suppose it's secret
Or just a special touch.
A dash of this, a pinch of that
We loved them all so much!

She had no special recipes
But all were made with love.
She put "herself" into the task
With help from God above.

The family favorites she knew well
Each child would have its day
It tasted great, 'twas made by Mom
How much more could we say!

I'm sure you all have memories
Of Mother's special treats
We won't begin to match them
For they just cannot be beat!

Jay M Yenor Jr
NIGHTCHILD

To my best friend, my life, my love, my wife, Marcia.

The sun has gone far below the horizon
and as I look up at the heavens my heart races.
This is my time. The time is night, and the night is mine.
The slippery coolness of the dark caresses my skin
like fine spun silk. I breathe deep of the evening air
and am reborn, at peace, once again.
Countless worlds shine down on me and know they are mine.
I am alone in the dark where I belong, for I am a Nightchild.
A creature of unknown origins, needing no one, nothing,
with only the yellow moon and silvery stars to keep me company.
On a clear night I feel the power of distant galaxies
pulling me to their bosom, drawing me near to nurture
and transform me. And as I struggle to remain in my earthly form,
I know the night is mine and I belong to the night.
We are one, united in a bond that can never be broken.
We are one, as man and wife, mother and child.
We are as necessary to each other as sun to the day,
for without the night I am lost, and it, without me,
would cease to be.

Maude G Allen
RETIREMENT OF RONALD & NANCY REAGAN
Dear Nancy and Ronald,
Your retirement is near.
Am sure you'll be glad
And won't shed a tear.

You've worked hard, I'm sure
For our country's good.
I've voted and voted
And again I would.

Since age twenty-one
A Republican I've been.
And I've voted and voted
Again and again.

Sixty some years ago
Al Smith was in line.
I didn't vote for him
And now I'm eighty-nine.

I'll be ninety March nine
Year nineteen eighty nine.
And if you were closer
I'd say to you, Come and dine.

Matthew J Lombardo
TIME
What is time?

Time is the beginning of an event
Time could be the end of an event

Time is slow in coming
Time is passing fast

Time— could be the beginning of joy.
Time— could be the end of a happy occasion

Time— could be the beginning of life.
Time— could be the end of life.

Time— we haven't found its beginning and we would never know its ending.

Matthew J Lombardo
THE DREAMER
If, I was a pilot, I could fly to the moon

If, I was a mountain climber I could climb the highest mountain in the world.

If, I was a skydiver I could flow through the air like a bird.

If, I was a scuba diver, I will be able to discover the beauty of ocean floor.

If, But what I am—I am a writer of silly poetry

Matthew J Lombardo
TODAY
Today, there's a sunrise
Today, there's a sunset
Today, there will be winners
Today, there will be losers
Today, there will be happiness
Today, there will be sorrows
Today, we must decide to say yes for tomorrow
Today, we must decide to say no for tomorrow
Today, we may live to see a tomorrow
Today, we may die and there will never be a tomorrow
Today, we know that there was a yesterday
Today, we know that there will be a tomorrow
Today it's the most important thing in our lives
We are here today.

Raymond H Holderman
MUSIC FOR THE SOUL

To "Jo" Hughes—a lovely lady who is a multi-talented musician and teacher. Your beautiful organ music brings ecstasy to all who hear you play.

She's enchanting, she entrancing
She's bewitching, she's beguiling
And if you should see her smiling
you would know just what I mean.

She's a music virtuoso, and while
performing she's the whole show
And her name is Josephine

She keeps striving for perfection
which is a fleeting endless goal
And that's why her melodious
refrains are truly music for the soul.

So many irons in the fire
and always on the go
There's no time for Josephine
So she shortened it to Joe.

Nancy H Sidebotham
ALONE
I tried to cry my anguish to the sky,
For me the world was ending all too
soon.
The stars crept close to see this
mortal cry
Believing she was waiting for the
moon.

But as we mortals are when we are
aching,
Wanting only darkness and cold
space,
So I, with sorrow for myself
awaking,
Could not meet such beauty
face-to-face.

For me such loveliness could only
Mean love and two with hearts in
tune,
And I, here crying, sad, and lonely,
Childlike, forbade the rising of the
moon.

Lora Coslet
WILL YOU
Will you help me
When I need a hand?
As life's problems surround me
Will we together take a stand?

Will you hear me
When I call in the night?
Begging you to be with me
Will you hold me tight?

Will you see me
When I'm worried and down?
Can you come and cheer me
Will you lighten my frown?

Will you protect me
When others attack?
And if they follow me
Will you chase them back?
Will you show me
When I need a friend?
That you care for me
Will you be there at the end?

Jayne Whitlow Berman
THE FABULOUS MR. B—

Dedicated to my husband, Judge Alfred K. Berman, posthumously.

We were introduced quite properly,
He asked me if I'd like a coke,
(Across many years he comes to me.)
So to the rotunda we strolled.

He called me once—I made an
excuse
He called again—I did the same
Third time 'twas unnecessary to muse
Mother'd investigated the man.

Our tastes were the same
How could all this be?
A career'd gone wrong—
Here was Mr. B—!

His legal star was fated to rise
Oh so proud I was of him then
But never so proud as at the end
The quiet courage did not bend.

He gave me much to live up to
Such stature he expects of me
I shall keep trying until I die
For the fabulous Mr. B—

Mary W Blum
THE GREAT DEPRESSION
I hope that I will never see,
A depression as it used to be.
We walked to School, rain or snow,
They never said — you don't have to
go.
For heat we had to cut wood,
Our parents did the best they could.
Our shoes were shined, you would
never know,
There was a hole in the bottom — It
didn't show.
We always had soup or a pot of
beans,
We didn't go hungry by any means.
We never had to lock the door —
Somehow I feel,
People were honest or there was
nothing to steal.
Named brands we never heard,
children were not cruel,
They would help if they could and
never ridicule.
Our hair was combed, shoes were
shined, we were clean and neat.
Didn't worry about our weight —
exercise was free and dessert was a
special treat.
If you were lucky and had lights, our
parents were not soft,
When not in use — You had better
turn them off.
Traffic was no problem — cars were
very few,
Trips had to be necessary — gas cost
money too.
It would be nice if we could live that
way,
With all the comforts we have today.

Raphaela Ross
THE FOUR SEASONS
Crocuses are sprouting.
Pregnant Earth bursting with life.
Robins chirping and nesting.

Everything emerald green.
Blue sky, and fluffy white clouds
Inviting outdoor living.

The hillsides aglow
with leaves of gold and scarlet
whispering Autumn splendor.

Beautiful and bright.
Virgin snow softly falling
covering all in sight.

Charlotte Holifield
WHY?

I dedicate this to Raymond Richard.

Accepting knowledge in understanding of myself. Very aware of my
illness I decided I want to LIVE. So
afraid of the darkness, I'm fighting
for a light. I eliminated all thoughts
in feelings to one thing. Now I'm
willing and learning to share my love.
I want to GROW

Reaching for benevolence from
mankind. Coping from reality.
Soft-spoken, reacting only on
impulse, not knowing my where
about of life.
The remaining of my soul. I do
believe there's a better way than My
Way.

Jim Wolfe
CROWDED ON THE BAY
Crowded on the bay,
Deep waters boil red.
Do I dare dream again,
Talk to my uncontrollables?
A riot of me, my thousands,
Pure, meticulous, twisted words.
Battle of dancing desert sands.

Automatic and destined spinning,
I a microscopic part of the whole.

To Phoenix I pray for my turn.
To fly, breathe free, burn
Yet arise anew, fresh, tempered
Weapon that is cooled.

Ankh of my Archangel,
Naive heart of memory,
I rise again too.

Savagely divided, equally divided
Who of me will win?

Melinda Williams
A LITTLE BOY GROWING UP

This poem is dedicated to Ryan and Brent, my beloved sons.

It's simply beautiful
to watch a child grow—
to be able to teach him
everything you know.
He starts out tiny—
oh, so small—
then sprouts like a tree,
so straight and so tall.
To see him bring home
earthworms, lizards, frogs—
All his little treasures—
his guppies and stray dogs.
But time goes so quickly
and you see how he's grown.
He's now independent
with a life of his own.
And as he gets older,
he'll make it, you'll see-
because now he's the man
you taught him to be.

Ruby A Musgrove
DOUBT HIS PRESENCE
Whilst drawing near my final years to
bid this life goodbye
I pause to ponder the certainty, of a
being named "Most High."
Each dawn I see the sunrise, so
lovely to behold
Created for God's children, as His
day starts to unfold
The sounds of birds awakening, with
chirping songs so sweet
The flowers each in their season,
casting colors at our feet
A storm may be disturbing, but his
rainbow never fails
To give us the assurance, that God's
promise still prevails
The first cries of a newborn, a
miracle indeed.
The faith of little toddlers when first
footsteps we must lead.
The "howdys" of our neighbors, and
the handshake that pursues.
Could we as just mere mortals, his
influence refuse
The looks and wags of a faithful
hound, when we have pleased his
needs
A million beautiful songs composed
and the talents of those who lead
The stars that twinkle at dusk along
with the moon to reassure
That when we have rested from all of
those blessings
Tomorrow will bring us some more

Jeanne M Holt
ON A NEAR DROWNING
Sweet little babe of mine
Looking straight at me,
Will your still, unblinking eyes
Ever really see?

Do you even know I'm here?
Can you feel my touch?
Though you're lost in some dark
never-land,
We love you oh so much.

You were a bright and lively child,
So eager to explore.
Your body's there but with all our
care
You will be the same no more.

That part of you most precious,
Your mind, your wit, your will,
Was sucked out by some monster
Beneath the water still.

The headlines raved, your life was
saved
And people sighed relief.
Untold the cost . . . potential lost,
And no one knows our grief.

Linda Goldberg
REVIVAL
We need those protest songs again,
Like the kind when I grew up
'Cause the world it needs a change
again,
And a lot are giving up.

We see the people in the streets
No jobs, no food, no homes.
While others in their name brand
clothes
Close eyes and don't hear groans.

There's a sink of torn out babies
In a hospital nearby.
We never stopped to listen
To hear their silent cry.

The schools are filled with violence
Drugs and pushers fill the street.
We cannot take a walk at night
For fear of those we meet.

Will Peter Paul and Mary,
Joan Baez and Dylan too
Take up that call again my friends
And sing those songs <u>anew</u>!!!

Sherian Barnes
WIDOWER'S DYING MESSAGE TO HIS CHILDREN

I leave you, but for a moment,
To be with my life's true love,
And together we will endeavor
To do that which was first done.
When it is time for you to come,
The two of us will meet you,
In a time without end.

Eleanor Steffen
TWILIGHT YEARS

'73 said to '74, "Is it wrong to care?
And make new memories to share?
Our families frown—
Put us down—"

'74 replies, "We are free
So why can't it be
Just you and me?"
The widow '73, smiles, touches the widower's hand
Speaks softly, "'74, We can, yes, we can"

Roberta Jackson
SOME OF THE THINGS

To Krissy, Mike and Shelly — With all my Love, your Mom.

Run the Race
Climb the Mountain
Speak your mind, but not too harshly
Know Yourself
Follow Your Heart
Love Truthfully
Hold on and fight for true love
It does exist.
For You,
My Children
Some of the Things

Amy Evans
DEAR BEAUTIFUL ANGEL FROM HEAVEN

You remind me of a shimmering crystal lake in the summer, winter in the country, the grace of a beautiful ballerina in her opening act.

Your hair reminds me of the sunset, beautiful and golden.

Your smile, when I'm sad always cheers me up.

Your voice is like the soft wind blowing in the dark night.

Your personality like a bird singing me a song in the morning.

When I'm with you I want to forget all dogs crying, tell you stories of happiness, depend on your support.

Marianne Scharpff
BLIZZARD

Howling wind whips and churns fine snow,
trees and shrubs helplessly
abandoned to blow after blow.
No horizon to separate earth from the sky,
whirling flakes, no orientation for the eye.

A row of telephone masts sign of civilization,
shady outlines, a forlorn formation.
Storm whirls snow mist, alders moan and sway
in a world of twilight and whitish-gray.

I long for vivacious colours of a sunny day,
a pale blue sky, light spring clouds of promising May!
Have they been real or just a fiction of the mind?
Was the wind once balmy, the sun warm and kind?

Lonely I feel, far seems life and farther still light!
Winter storms sweep planes with power and might.
Once the land was wide open, seemed endless, far space!
Now all is closed, chokingly narrow in icy haze.

Leo Humphries

Leo Humphries
MY PET RAT

I had a rat for my pet, Mom said whoever heard of that, having a rat for a pet, I said It's better than a cat. Mom said, We'll see about that, and then went out to buy a cat. I was very upset about that, so I told mom that some day my rat would eat that cat. Then she would be upset about that. Mom said, I doubt that, your rat eating my cat. I said, We'll see about that. So I let my rat out to play on a sunny day, and mom didn't have much to say. She just said, Keep that rat away. I said, No way, my rat is out to play on this sunny day. Mom said, OK! Then walked away. Then I saw her cat out to play and I haven't seen my rat since that sunny day.

Marianne Scharpff
FAREWELL

There is no song in my heart
when you do part
from me, my dear!

There is no shine in my eye
when you wave good-bye
and leave, my dear!

There is no smile on my face
and I look through a haze
of tears, my dear!

Alvesa Garcia
THE MIRROR

You know me like the back of your hand.
Yes, those eyes can see deep into me.
You see me better than anyone in all the land.
I cannot escape you, you won't let me be.

You tell me if I am fat or thin.
Yes, those lips tell me like it is.
You speak only truth, so I cannot win.
You know everything, and you do not miss.

You hear my secrets deep in my heart.
Yes, those ears have searched and have found.
You have me trapped, so we can never part.
There is no place to hide, you can hear every little sound.

You are here today and tomorrow.
I turn to you when I am in trouble.
You know me and understand my sorrow.
You will not desert me, you will not go away.
I cry to you and you come running on the double.
Others come and go, but you will always stay.

Jeanne Steffey (Lynn)
WHEN THE SNOW FALLS

Today I had a vision, of déjà vu
I saw myself here before
In this room with you
Playing my old guitar and writing tunes
I guess in some way, I was meant to stay
A little time with you
You tell me what's the use to try to live
Just to die anyway
But in your eyes, I can see happy memories
it's not the time to say, goodbye today
To all that used to be
The days get shorter, and the nights grow colder
It seems that winter isn't far away
This old farm, it feels so peaceful and good
Stay a little longer, don't you think you should
To hear the rain on the roof
To see the birds in the trees
And when the snow falls
Time will have slipped away

N Joey Medley
THE ROBINS

I looked out my window this morning
And saw two robins at play
They chirped and twittered from tree to tree
As they greeted the bright new day

I watched the optimism that they showed
Their happiness seemed to glow
I wanted to be like those birds in the tree
I wanted some gladness to show

But I seem to be trapped in a different world
A world of depression and woe
Try as I might I can't seem to escape
I don't know which way to go

Someday perhaps, I'll be like those birds
Someday I'll reach for the sky
Maybe I'll take a lesson from them
I must walk before I can fly

Julia Haynes
WITHOUT YET

Without yet full comprehension
A child sits upon a living room floor
And gazes as a man publicly bleeds
She sees the people as they scream
And spies the man who holds the gun
That ended the last hope
For a return to the time of Camelot.

A mother sits in a chair behind this child
And rocks her young to sleep
As she views the horror tears fall uncontrollably
For a past that was violently stolen
For on this fateful day she understands the future
The day the second angel appeared
To take her prize away.

Marjorie Prenez
GENTLE MOMENTS

We're sitting around our campfire enjoying every minute,
We're holding up our heavy mug to savor what is in it,
We're thinking of the rising sun so beautiful to see,
The day was just so heavenly as it was meant to be,
We had adventures here and there and wasted not a minute,
The joy we got within our soul, was what we had put in it,
The sun has gone beyond the ridge and the dark is drawing nigh,
We'll snuggle in our sleeping bags, the moon is way up high,
Thinking of our perfect day—we all must say Good-night,
And thank God for His mercy and also for His might.

Brian A Clark
FREED FROM SELFISH CHAINS

To Paul . . . for sharing his thoughts.

While sailing in Love's mid-winter streams,
I felt myself trapped in rose-colored dreams.
Stripped of emotions, caught in a lie.
Enclosed in this vacuum, fearing I'd die.
But now it's come, new freedom, arrived.
I've broken those bonds, completely, revived.
And the lesson learned, though it be hard.
I'm winning again, at playing top card.
To guard my heart, from becoming blue.
I live this line, "To my own self be true."
I've walked away, so much the wiser.
I'm free from that, emotional miser.

Donald C Rubino Jr
CHILDREN CRYING

To those who cry for help.

Children crying no one listens
Now they're gone no one's missing
Want for nothing only a chance
Ever so young can't advance
Gone's the sunshine, birds a singing
Gone's the children never breathing
Little bodies break and twist
From you the Almighty, with your fist
Children crying can't you hear
Live a life of total fear
Touch 'em here, beat 'em there
For thy lust don't you care
Little children with nothing to gain
'Cept a body filled with pain
They show you love and ask the same
But, you the parents curse their name
Art thou losing self-control
Must you take a child's soul
Now their lives are nevermore
These our children, whom we adore.

Debra Clark
I LOVE YOU

To Tommy, Happy 10th Anniversary, I Love You!

While I am away from you,
My heart grows fonder.
My love for you becomes anew,
And continually grows stronger.

Just the sound of your voice
In a quiet whisper,
Silences all sounds and noise—
Makes me want you closer, Mister!

A glance from your gentle-loving eyes,
Paralyzes my soul.
I don't care about the world around me, it just dies,
Because I've finally reached my goal.

Your smile is so warm and sweet,
A kiss so inviting.
I pray our lips will again meet,
While our lives are uniting.

But thus, time goes on
And soon you'll be home to me,
Until the day has dawn
And in my arms you shall be.

Ron Barnes
ONLY A DREAM

To the memory of Richard and Helen Barnes. Thank you for this life.
To Jackie for sharing yours with me.

The rays of sunshine that glisten from your smile,
make me a jester or a clown in your presence.
But I'm not allowed to share this with you,
for that would be to chance chasing you away,
leaving me in darkness and solitude.

If I was ever to lose myself in your being,
it would be because of the tender touch
that I can only imagine you possess
in your fragile frame of fire.

The warmth and will to carry on,
this is the feeling you cast upon me.
The glimmer in your eyes, as bubbling springs,
fill a cup of faith for me to drink in.

Selfishly, I'll steal these feelings
without your knowledge or permission.
With only a dream of such a reality coming true.

George A Northup
TO MARGARET
I'm not much on poetry
Can't think of words that rhyme,
But Spring's 'round the corner
. That good old "Sweet Talk" time.

I've never tried my hand at this,
No — never in my life!
But rhymes are buzzin' thru my head —
And they're all about — My Wife!

My Wife! My Wife! Those words sound good!
I can hardly realize
That an ordinary guy like me
Can claim this charming prize.

I see her face before me
I dream about her charms —
All the stars aren't in the skies —
I've held one in my arms.

She's everything my heart would want,
She sets my heart on fire.
She's showered my world with gladness,
There's nothing more I desire.

The sea runs deep between us —
And time keeps us apart —
But still I feel her loveliness
In each beat of my heart.

A thousand years of happiness
I've lived in this past year.
On this our First (Forty-first) Anniversary
I love you more each day, My Dear.

February 14, 1944 Always Yours,
Valentine's Day George

Ron Barnes
EMOTIONAL STRUGGLE
Alone it seems, I walk these echoing passages, of a past unsure. Seeking to regain the treasures, only a memory can fulfill. The shadow of a smile once known draws me relentlessly, as a chill in my soul sharpens the eye to which I perceive it. Should an image of this value hold such a depth, to ensure its retention and grasp? Or simply be spoken aloud, for others' knowledge, distorting any meaning of a lesson once learned.

Harriett Stevenson
THANK YOU LORD!

Dedicated to Laura and Ben Schowe, Peter, Frederick, Donald & David Mancotte.

I thank you Lord, for sunny days
With skies of brightest blue,
For bird songs trilling in the air,
I know they came from you.

And when I walk in shaded ways,
The skies no longer blue,
I feel your presence there with me
And know your word is true.

For you have walked this way before
And heard the birds that sing,
They must have given comfort
As they went by on the wing.

So let me walk with confidence,
My face turned toward the sky,
For some sweet day, and maybe soon,
I'll hear them sing on high!

Desiree' L Livaudais
LOVE FROM ABOVE
Goodbye sweet love
Enjoyed your stay—
Sent from above
For just one day—
To fill my heart
And soothe my soul—
'Tis hard to part
And still be whole.

Glenda Duerr
THE SOULMATES
The giant-man entered
Ducking under the door.
He stopped, said hello
And walked into the store.

His eyes caught sight
Of a face that he knew
But when he looked twice
He didn't quite know who.

She stood by the counter
Looking into his eyes.
She remembered their kindness
And a soul with no lies.

They stared at each other
Hearts pounding inside
The searching was over
Again, their lives were tied.

Deeper and deeper
As each lifetime passed
Their love was rekindled
By a meeting of chance.

Joy D Cochran
TOMMY
I love you from the top of your curly
Brown hair to your unaggressive toes dressed
In dark cowboy boots. Your mouth is surly
If not often and tenderly kissed.

I love your petulant mouth which can turn
Upwards to an open friendly smile. Your
Sidesplitting banter causes my heart to learn
More, more about you. Love that asks for more.

I love your kind cerulean blue eyes
By night that change to powder blue at day
Lights break of dawn. Your beautiful blue eyes
Which cause me to smile when I look your way.

I love the way your "v" unlocks my key.
I love the way your "v" unlocks my key.

Karla R Eaves
BEING IN LOVE
I've never felt this way before. There's a part of me that wants no part of it. Then there's another part of me that won't let go of this breath taking feeling. This feeling is being in love for the very first time.

There are so many great feelings that you get when you're in love, like getting loved that same way that you're giving it. Being held like you've never been held. Feeling like his first kiss to you was your very first kiss from anyone. His eye's shining into your eyes and his cheek embracing your cheek.

There are also so many bad things that you feel when you're in love. Like lost time that you could have spent together but didn't. The feeling of missing one another when not together. Sharing your covers with your teddy bear instead of each other. Watching a scary movie when come to find out it's only you being scared.

Worst of all, not ever

BEING IN LOVE!!

Allen Lee Wenger
LIKE FATHER LIKE SON

To Robert B. Wenger—The Wisest Man I'll Ever Know.

We crawl, we walk and then we fly;
Away from home, we know not why.

Away from those that we hold dear;
In search of what? It is not clear.

The time we spend will change our mind;
But not our love for those behind.

But if we are to become whole;
We must stay here, to reach our goal.

You are the start of what we do;
You gave us sense when we were new;

You ask us what we have become;
Search yourself! Like Father Like Son.

Bonnie B Newkirk
JUST FROM MY HEART
You gave me your love Mom
In the palm of your hand
There's not many moms like you
They don't understand

When I was down and depressed
You said keep your chin high
Go for the gust–o kid
You've got to try

I drowned you in my sorrow
And taken up your time
You never thought of your own self
You just worried about mine

I came to you in tears
You said it would all be fine
So on this day for loved ones
You're my favorite Valentine

I have nothing to give you
Just this from my heart
And with the love you give me
I'll make that new start

Happy Valentine's Day Mom
I'll love you forever
With the problems we've had
I am glad we're all together

Wendy Hughes
LOVE'S COMET

For Robert, the love of my life and the comet of my sky.

You are as a comet, blazing a trail across the sky
You are a very bright light, at night
Emblazoning your image upon my mind's eye

During the bright glare of day, you are invisible and very far away
The knowledge you are there makes my heart expand inside my body

You stand out from the other stars around you
Crisp and clear and self-contained
You are safe and secure in the knowledge
That you have chosen your orbit, to be forever unchanged

Sometimes you scare me, your glorious light
Doing that wild and crazy dance across my sky
And insane fear grips me, that one day you will leave your orbit, destroy me

Destroy my life, rip it from limb to limb
Destroy the small world that is the only one ever known to me

I sit back upon my heels, and watch you creep, glide the sky around
You are a beautiful sight to me, watching from this hilltop
For my feet are fettered, maybe not forever, to this ground

For I may walk the straight and narrow
But my heart and soul wish to break their bonds
And forever fly, like a comet
Like you, with you, free, forever

Sally Angstadt
THE LOST PEN

To my son Michael, who took my pen and never gave it back.

AH HAH!
You have my pen!
I recognize it,
From its chewed up end.

You had it all this time,
You little rat.
You stole it as soon,
As I turned my back.

I'll make you a deal,
Give me my pen,
And I'll buy you your own,
At the five and ten.

Mary Patton Dye
GATHER IN THE ROSES, WHILE YOU'RE STILL YOUNG

This poem is dedicated to my sons, Tony and Jeffrey Cleek.

Enjoy this time, while you're still young
The years go fast when you get old
So much now is to be done
For later on, life takes its toll
Plant the goals to be attained
Don't get discouraged, if they're not met
By working hard there's much to gain
And you'll gather in the roses with no regrets
Gather in the roses while they're in bloom
Keep them watered along the way
Don't give the clouds any room
For then, you'll have a life to be proud of someday

Robbie Brading
DEATH OF LOVE

I dedicate this poem to Paul. The Great Love of My Life.

As I lie here tonight, my old heart grieves.
For love so cherished is just an illusive dream.
We fought a long, hard battle, this old heart and me.
To keep this love alive, I've tried everything.
I've cried till my eyes are sore, begged till I can beg no more.
Pleaded, bargained, threatened and much more.
But our love is like a flower kept from the sun.
Soon, withered and dying, it stands all alone.
What do you do when you give everything.
And ask nothing in return.
Only to love a be loved in return.
It's sad when you try so hard and fail.
It breaks your spirit, takes the wind from your sails.
It breaks your heart and then your mind,
To love so much, to be so blind.
I feel emptiness inside me, a feeling of dread.
Is our love dying? Or is it already dead?

Stephanie Juncker
YESTERDAY

Yesterday was a day when love was fair
Today I shudder from your cold stare
You want me to just let you go
But I turn my back and simply say no
I want you with me, I beg you'll stay
We can work this out there is a way
When I said "I love you" I've never meant it more
Together we were gonna open the future's door.

You are a link in my life chain
You've kept me locked away from all the pain
And now you've tossed me to the side
My friends are upset because all I've done is cried
You seemed special, better than the rest
Maybe to you, I'm just not the best
I tried damn hard this is true
But I guess my best just didn't suit you!

Robert Shaffer
HIGHER EDUCATION

I try to look with raptured awe
On higher education;
But there is just one little flaw
That dims my fond elation.

Some college profs don't seem to know
Where man originated.
Their "monkey" theories come and go;
They doubt man was created.

Until those men are born again,
God's kingdom they can't see;
So I am wondering what and when
They've got for little me.

So higher education's fine
But use your little thinker;
Don't swallow every hook and line
And gobble up the sinker!

Tammie Cabrera
JUST PASSING THROUGH . . .

We are put on this world here,
to live right
for the coming is near.
Each upon this earth we are born
and left to await the sound of the mighty horn.
The devil is beside us all the time,
his partners are there in which
we shall fine.
We must remember the mighty one
gave us so much and when in need
we should close our eyes and feel his touch.
He has taught us to be strong and never do wrong. Show others the right thing to do, with the light that shines in you.
It won't be long and he shall come for you,
'cause in this life we're just passing through . . .

Sabra Gaskill
REMEMBERING AND HOPE

Lincoln, King and Kennedy too,
Sacrificed so much for that we hold true.
The Air Force, Marines, Soldiers and Sailors who,
fought to keep waving our red, white, and blue,
we can't say too much in their honor I'm told,
as always in our hearts their memory we'll hold.
Our Country has two hundred years under belt,
and it's true tragedies have been felt,
but a new year cometh and if we join hands,
we can make this old world twice as grand.

Leander Wegdahl
ALASKA'S SUMMER END

This Poem is dedicated TO THE BEAUTIFUL STATE OF ALASKA.

When summer has finally come to an end
And winter is just around the bend
I spend my time in wonder where the time has gone
As I think of both seasons of which I'm so fond
Summer comes and goes so fast
It's hard to remember which was last
Wonderful sunshine a full moon at night
It's truly a very beautiful sight
All kinds of lowers in their early bloom
They grow in many places in god's given room
Winter too has its own special sights
The soft glow of the far northern lights
The crisp days and the cold of the nights
Suddenly the snow makes its early descend
With a cold gust of wind to which it will blend
As quickly as it came the winter is over
And summer is here with its grass and its clover
These are the seasons I'll remember as I grow older
As the summers grow hotter and the winters grow colder

Laura Brownfield
GENTLE LOVE

A gentle touch from unsteady hands.
Tender kisses from quivering lips.
Eyes that gaze with wonder and unsurety.

I am softly amused and smile as your naiveté
leads to mild embarrassment and you hide your
eyes for fear of being discovered.

Your sweetness and innocence is so honest and
admirable, like a child who must learn through
first experiences.

Yet your sensitivity and sincerity ensure in
your good character as an adult.

I value your presence. I value your warmth
and care . . .

I value you.

Anthony Solter
WE TWO, WE ONE

Along the old familiar road
We two, we one walked again
Nightblind, I, behind; you ahead.
You short, me tall,
But eye to eye, we downed to the sound
Barking beefs of man's planned carelessness
Above the washing rush of waves.
Down the land reaching up to the grass
We, proud show dogs, descended
Short and tall down to the sound.
Proud beasts paraded idealized worlds below the moon
While on the bluff arching over the beach
Civilized shacks stood deaf, gaping into space.
Amid the hapless precision of sea, sand and shrub,
We strolled the beach
We two, we one;
You short, me tall,
But eye to eye loping on sandy shores
Along the sound sensing two, sensing one
Then growling back up the road, up to the house.

Anthony Solter
WHEN I WAS TEN

Gauzy curtains haze the sunlight.
Hard red brick houses hang
Behind the frail veils
Between a harsh harried world and me.
Within the width and breadth of a room
An ever settling peace snows quietly,
A steady even pulse.
How I long for
When as a child
I so glued myself to a moment
Stretching the frail veils holding harsh harried time
Till bursting
It spilled into hard core reality
Where furious dragons and silver racing cars
Turned into space ships
Devouring and flying over
Tiny porcelain deer
And plastic chess royalties
In kingdoms of blocks
On living room carpet forests
When I was ten, when I was ten . . .

Annie Lamagna
THE WEAKEST LINK

To My FIRST Love.

On a gold Chain, there is always one link that is bent and twisted more than all the rest. The owner carelessly ignores this link until it can no longer tolerate the brutality that is bestowed upon it. At that moment, just
before the brittle, uncared for link lets go and allows the rest of the chain to tumble carelessly to the floor, the owner takes it to the jeweler for repairs.

And like an all powerful god, the jeweler fixes the chain. He strengthens it by caring for the weakest link. He gives the chain new life
and the strength to go on shining. And the owner of the chain knows the jeweler can
be trusted and is indebted to him for his ability to restore beauty to one of his most prized possessions.

My life was like that chain; my heart

was its weakest link. I
allowed it to be brutally twisted and
torn while I ignored the pain. And
when
my life was about to fall to the floor
in a million pieces, you became my
Jeweler.

You reshaped my heart and
strengthened my life. You restored
my
ability to shine when I stopped
believing. You give me strength,
courage, and
life. But, most of all, you give me
LOVE.

And like the owner of the chain, I've
come to trust and depend on my
jeweler, for I know he cares. I trust
you, my jeweler, and to you I give
my
weakest link . . .
MY HEART.

Rose J Pexton
MOON

In Loving memory of my son Vincent A. (Culla) Falitico.

Big yellow full moon way up high,
what's your mystery in the sky?
The night when you become your
prime, why is there so much crime?

Many new lives come into this world,
so many lives go out in a hurl.
Why does it happen at your prime? Is
it a secret locked in time?

Mr. Moon you alone own the night
sky. You light up the world from low
to high.
The stars that twinkle so bright, are
just a speck compared to your great
light.

It's been said by GOD that you are
one of two great lights, the greater of
the day, and you by night.

Jean Yearick
THE FRENCHMAN

This poem was written and dedicated to my hard working husband Jack Yearick.

My husband did some drawings for a
Frenchman moved in town.
With the accent of the Frenchman the
contract was unsound.

The sound of sixteen hundred sounds
like six hundred to him.
So the argument started but my
husband gave in.

He did the work for half the price
anyone else would pay.
And then the Frenchman had the
nerve, he'd pay a later day.

The wife got mad it slowly went.
The money she had already spent.

She told the French man pay up now
The phone conversation turned to a
terrible row.

The French man gave in at long last.
He paid his bill but the die had been
cast.

He still could not understand the gist
of the thing
So the story ended with a bite and a
sting.

No more contracts with French man
we say
We're working on building a better
U.S.A.

Jean Yearick
AROUND EACH BEND

I drove down the street today,
In my usual daily hurry,
I crossed the bridge and up the hill
with a hurry, flurry, scurry.
I looked out through the window,
to see if it was clear,
Into the rearview mirror
and there I saw appear.
A lovely picture on the ocean
as the sun was going down.
Two sail boats billowing in the
breeze
wearing their silhouette like a
crown.
Did you ever chance to think about
the things you've left behind?
And all the things you've missed
yourself,
in this crazy daily grind.
If we would take a little time to smile
at all our friends
This world would be a better place,
For looking around each bend.

Florence A Harris
ON THE WINGS OF AN EAGLE

On the wings of an eagle,
Flying through a bright sky,
Sparkles of sunshine
Beam as they pass by.

Filtered through treetops
In the sweet after glow,
A shadow is cast
On all that lies below.

His wing spread is mighty,
As he drifts through the air;
He seems to move silently
On a wing and a prayer.

Michael T Fink
BEACH

I've walked along the shore with cool
Sand running through my toes and so I
Plunge within the salty waters and
Swim with my moonlit shadow.

Cheryl McGuire
LOVE, I GIVE MYSELF TO YOU

Dedicated to Jim Simpson — my future husband, whom I love with all my heart.

Love, I give myself to you,
To have and hold your whole life
through.
The two of us shall always be,
As one throughout eternity.
Our hearts, our souls, our bodies, and
minds,
Shall be as one through endless time.
My love and faithfulness will always
be yours,
For only your Love, is all I long for.
For your love, so rare and so true,
Makes it so easy for me to love you.
So I give myself to you,
To have as your wife your whole life
through.
And as the years go slowly by,
You'll see that love has been our
guide.
For memories of many will be of us
two,
Of love that we've shared our whole
life through.
Love, I give myself to you,
To love forever, as I will you.

Laura J Werner
THE SHAMROCK COUNTRY INN

A little Irish ditty
About a little Irish city
Who banished Conway Twitty
From the Shamrock Country Inn.

Seems his songs were rather boring
And they caught the patrons
snoring
While he sang about his touring
And the trophies he did win.

So they hired some Irish fellow
Whose voice was soft and mellow
But always wore bright yellow
At the Shamrock Country Inn.

Then they asked the Irish Rovers
If they could please come over
And sing of GREEN and CLOVERS
To get the people back again.

So they sang an Irish folk tune
Of Unicorns and a big green moon
And Irish eyes were smiling soon
At the Shamrock Country Inn.

Cheryl McGuire
A POEM FOR YOU

Looking ahead at my tomorrows,
Only filled my heart with sorrow.
Then somehow you came along,
And now my days are filled with
song.
You've given me a special love,
Like something sent from up above.
Yet shared alone by you and me,
For the whole world to see.
I hope I always let you know,
Just how much I love you so.
For all of me I give to you,
And a promise to always be true.
And yes, it is very true,
This poem was written just for you.

Cheryl McGuire
YOU ARE THERE

Two arms to hold me tight,
Two lips to kiss goodnight.
So alone and so blue,
I wish that I could be with you.
You are there and I am here,
So far apart yet so near.
I need your love it's plain to see,
But could you ever love just me?
Your heart is lonely, I hear it call,
So is mine, let's give our all.
But you are there and I am here,
So far apart yet so near.
Long distance love will never last,
I have learned that from the past.
So my love it's plain to see,
That our love can never be.
For you are there and I am here,
So far apart yet so near.

Suszanne Howington
THE OTHER SIDE

This time I am on the other side I am the one in need of support, I am the one who needs comfort.

I cannot walk away this time because it is my loved one that is dying not a patient of mine.

In the past, death meant relief for those racked with pain, but now it means an emptiness in my heart.

Tears shed in the past were for my patients and their families. But the tears shed today are for me—at the loss that is inevitable.

I am selfish and don't want to let go but slowly the grip of death pries away at the fingers of the living.

And so I find myself on the other side. Not the nurse at the foot of the bed but the family member at the head of the bed. Anticipating and at the same time dreading every breath, wondering which will be her last.

Tony Rodriguez
LIFE IS HARD

Life is hard
Love is harder
Fear is easy
Faith is smarter
Examine your heart
Bless your soul
Practice forgiveness
And self–control
Count your blessings
One by one
Release your anger
When each day is done
Express your feelings
Share your pain
Just be yourself
Try not to complain
Right here on earth
Is heaven and hell
Which road you choose
Only time will tell . . .
Learn to laugh

Ana V Diaz
THE KISS

I want to remember the moment, take
hold of the time
Forever cherish the kiss you gave me
on that one
special night.

It filled my whole being with
something really special,
So sweet and tender - A feeling
which I will always
remember.

The kiss was full of so many
wonderful things -
Understanding, comfort, security,
love -
All of which are permanently
implanted in my
Memory.

Tony Rodriguez
DEEPER LOVE

For Tanya.

I know it hurts when love says good–
bye
and it breaks your heart . . .
it's okay to cry.
Life is a mystery, and love is no
game,
you win, you lose,
there's no one to blame.
I'll be there for you each night
and each day.
I've been in your shoes, I'll show you
the way.
There's a deeper love,
a love that is true,
it softens the pain and helps you get
through.
Yes, there's a deeper love,
it's found by very few . . . find that
deeper love,
it's hidden within you.
You can't love the world until you
learn

To love yourself . . . I'll be there to help.
There's a deeper love, a love that is true.
Find that deeper love, it's hidden within you;
I'll be there waiting . . . I love you.
Dad

Linda Winzenread
GOD CRIED TODAY

I saw his tears and felt them caress my face as they fell from the sky.
He looks down upon his children and ask, why do they not listen and believe in me?
He only gave us Ten Commandments to follow.
(We) his children have abused the earth and other people he created.
He sees the torment, the happiness, the love and faces of those who have lost loved ones.
He the creator sees and feels all.
He created mankind, the creatures, the beauty all around, but MAN has created the ugliness of the world.

Jennifer L Kitchens
SEASONS

Spring is the time when flowers bloom
The trees turn green with the golden moon.
But soon the flowers will wither and die
As the fluffy white snow falls from the sky.
The children play without a care
As long as the seasons are always there.

Marrijane Hayes

Marrijane Hayes
THE PHILOSOPHER

Dedicated with Love to Joe, Greg, Jason, Dan, Rachael, Mariah, Aidan, Jacinda, Dylan, Marjorie and Betty.

Socrates and Aristotle, Kant and Heidegger
Unamo, Camus and Sartre
Contemplated, meditated
Paced, walked by the sea, tormented their minds.
Thoughts flew high, into outer space
. . . into inner space.
The bright thoughts, the dark thoughts
Juxtaposing, counterpointing
Plumbed their souls, perplexed their minds.
The positivists, the negativists.
Determinism, free will, idealism,
Infinity and the finite, ideas, logic, reason
Skepticism, truth, ethics, fallacies
Induction and probability
God or existentialism?
Today's thinkers
Wanting definitive, instant answers
Use . . . a computer.

Tony Rodriguez
SHE'S LIGHT

She's like a priceless diamond
That has never been found
She keeps her endless love
Buried underground

Once in a while
The world gets to see
The beauty of the love
That she gives to me

And it shines
And it grows
And it's light
But nobody knows

She's very independent
And extremely sincere
She quietly ignores her critics
And confronts her fear

I feel very lucky
To know her like I do
Her eyes are real
Her friendship is true

She's light . . .

Bradley T Balbo
UNTITLED ENCHANTMENT

In twilight I sit, without.
A battle waged presently within,
my pounding chest beckons.
Forgive,
my pretentious, selfish
passions I cannot help.
—for you,
all the finest; nothing less
I desire.
—for me,
you are my all.
Unto yourself;
embrace this at face.
Your acceptance rewards
the fervor within
my pounding chest.
Only a dream of mine,
for some time—
the battle will end,
resulting in a unison
of our
bodies and souls.

Jucy Mariate
FOR SOMETHING

And God gave me the punishment: "You shall be a prisoner of an animal body" and here I am at the mercy of instincts. "And you shall have the physical needs of all animals!! And from infancy you shall revolt against your material condition and you will love stars and the skies, absorbed in the nostalgic idea of your origin. You shall discover wide spaces unknown, you shall feel foreign in this world. You shall be a lonely child, not understood by the surrounding environment. Eternal traveler from unknown galaxies, you shall not understand the why of your revolt, your humiliation in front of your physical body. And you shall pass through time like a roaming gypsy searching for the promised land and for people like yourself. You shall feel desperation and someday you will realize that you belong to the infinite and that you are fulfilling your sentence. And you will struggle to rise, to be free, to be redeemed . . . For something!

Bessie Carruth
THAT LITTLE COUNTRY HOME

To my three sons and their families and to my cousins, and relatives.

Many a happy hour I've spent in that little country home,
But now those hours have passed and here I sit alone,
Just sitting and thinking how happy I'd be;
If once more those familiar faces I could see,
No matter wherever I may drift or roam,
My heart still calls back to them and the place that I call home;

Back there, happy days together we'd spend,
Never did we think those hours would end;
But they did . . . and swiftly did they roll on,
And I wonder if those days forever, have gone;
But maybe fate will bring us together as time onward rolls,
And once more we can recall back the days of old.

Joyce Kepley Mayhew
THE MOUNTAIN MAN

This poem is dedicated to the man who stands beside me—not in front of me and not behind me—EARL ANDERSON VASSER.

The peaks of the mountaintop were white-capped with snow—
Fields of wildflowers burst into bloom in the valley below.
Unclouded colors shadowed the land—a haven of beauty for a mountain man—
High above the clouds, soared an Eagle in flight—The beauty of His freedom was a magnificent sight—
The mountain man makes this his home—The unclaimed land he loves to roam—
The lakes and the land provide his food—The serenity of the place supplies his mood.
Happy is he who lives off the land—this is the life of a mountain man.

Jason Bausher
FATE

I'd like to thank all my friends for their support and a special thanks to Jeni for her inspiration.

As I walked through the vast field of love
I found three species that came from above
Neither them nor I would be good at first

The first of these would be my fantasy
My feelings could have lasted an eternity
Finally, after ages of being drug through the mud,
She brushed me off like some little ole bug

The next of these is something unlike the first
She could suck the blood right out of my veins and still have a great thirst
This is something quite uncomfortable
For the feelings felt were not mutual

The final of these just caught my attention
I made it known that I had the same intention
If there was anything felt, it wasn't hate
We both think that it was, "FATE."

Debbye Rathmann
OTHERS USE THEIR HEARTS

Some people use their eyes to see, but others use their hearts.
Some people use their ears to hear, but others use their hearts.
Some people use their hands to feel, but others use their hearts.
Some people use their heads to judge, but others use their hearts.
Why can't everyone use their hearts?

Laura Hollis
THIS LIFE

To Virginia a friend who loved poetry I dedicate "This Life."

The profound sense of urgency about the popped balloon tangled in the T.V. antenna.

Is it the illusion of life's dreams deflated that it reminds me of?

Is it worse than the children I see blowing bigger bubbles with bigger bubble holders now than when I was child?

Bigger dreams and more grand illusions to tangle in my wires until I completely short circuit from all interference.

Gayle J Dinwiddie
THE DAY THAT HASN'T GONE BY

To: Rita C. Frakes.

Not a day goes by
That she doesn't think of you.
There isn't a day
That she doesn't wish she could live with you.

You are a very special lady to everyone who knows you;
But there is one person that wonders if you know
How much you mean to her.
For the first time since she can remember, she feels
As if someone cares.
Someone who will listen, and lend a shoulder for the
Tears she sheds.
But she means not to intrude or put forth any
Burdens upon you.

She goes to bed at night
And hugs her pillow so tight,
In hopes that someday it will be you
Holding and rocking her to sleep within your arms.

She hopes not to make you mad
From the truth of her heart;
For she is my friend
We have been one from the start.

For is it a sin to love someone more than family?

Because as my friend, I know she
loves you more than eternity!

Linda P Woodward
DOGGIE DECEPTION
"I'll be right back, now you be a
good boy,"
And she threw me a biscuit, and a
bone, for a toy.

"Now you lay in your bed, don't you
bark while I'm gone,"
As she closed the front door, I picked
up the phone.

"One large pizza for Johnson, just
charge our account,
And leave it out front, we'll send the
amount."

Heading straight for the fridge, I
grabbed a tall brew,
"This sure beats the water, I get from
the loo."

I plopped on her pillows, her slippers
on my feet,
I'd clean the sauce later, from her
fine satin sheet.

I headed for the bathroom, "Man, my
breath stinks!"
And picked up her toothbrush,
bending over the sink.

Think I'll floss while I'm here, might
as well take a whiz,
And my stomach could use, some
"Plop, Plop, and Fizz, Fizz."

Better pick up the trash, check the
rooms, just once more,
Throw out those dumb biscuits, and
lay by the door.

The key turned the handle, "Were
you good, dog of mine?"
"Woof, Woof—Woof, Woof," until
the next time.

Bonnie J Boggs
LIFE'S CIRCLE
When man was born
there wasn't much here,
Trees and Plants
not much to fear.

As time would pass
and life would grow,
Some mysteries on Earth
we'll never know.

We came into this world
with a good head start,
We must make the most of it
until we part.

Life is a lesson
we all must learn,
Try to take the right trail
and not make the wrong turns.

For it is on that trail
where life begins,
Life goes on
and then ends again.

Chelsea S Kerr
YOUR BODY

*To my best friend, lover and
husband—Stephen.*

Your body
next to mine
a message sublime
as, in your sleep,
you reach over
to take my hand
and hand it close
against your chest
Sometimes
I feel
that is your
strongest declaration
of love—
unconscious, asleep
you reach out
for me

Jeanne Vahle
CHANCES
We met by chance,
Talking of everyday things;
Cool and easy going,
Like the gentle breeze of springtime.

Laughing and joking,
A real easy peace of mind;
Day by day week by week,
Chances of friendship growing.

Chance friendships so they say,
Are no good in any way;
Throwing caution to the wind,
Just to talk to you my friend.

To have a friend like you,
Is a chance I will take;
A friend you have become,
A friend you will be.

Seasons may come Seasons may go,
True friendships never go they just
grow;
So I'll take my chances—
With the friend I've come to know.

Sandra Schaefer
THE FUTURE
Where will we be in years to come?
How will we get there,
When will we run?
Back to the world of love and peace
Where people really care.
We all need to see the light.
A light that shines so dim,
But once was bright.
This world need people, who
Show they care.
For each day we live,
We live to share.
Make that light shine brighter than
before.
Open a brand-new door
For people who feel helpless
In this world of make-believe.

Christolyn Willock
LOVING FROM A DISTANCE
You are my friend and my inspiration
Although we seem so far apart, I take
pleasure in
dreaming about you, hoping to see
you,
Wondering what you're doing,
loving you,
And taking strength in the painfully
delightful thoughts of you.

To know that you exist in flesh and
blood, is
the gentle breeze,
Warm Sun
the welcomed rain after the
heat,
To my joyfully wondering heart.

Your voice is the rhythmic Chords to
which my spirit dance.
Your smile—yes that smile is the
flood which breaks
the sluice gates of my anxiety,
Creating bellows of ecstasy
throughout my being.
You are the embodiment of all I love,
value and hold dear.
Living is loving you, and hoping to
be loved by you.
My will to live is powered by the
knowledge that you exist
And the everlasting hope that I might
bask in the shade
of your vicinity—Even for just one
second.

Marcia Wolfson
TILT

*To my wonderful son, Alan Neil
Rechtschaffen with all my love
forever. Your mother.*

I am lopsided. I am smart,
but live in an upside-down world.
This makes me feel stupid. It makes
me
eat wrongly, sleep wrongly, love
wrongly, and probably die wrongly.
Oh, Soul just go on a little longer
to solve what you are due on
Earth. Maybe being hungry, being
hurt,
misunderstood, has made me grow—

I could be a rose, but I am covered
with thorns—Ouch—Everyone looks
at me like the Court Jester. But,
Tilted
world, I am a Princess inside.
I was raised like royalty—not a bag
lady in New York.
Yes, this happened Step by Step—
No one can see the flower—only
its thorns—
Tilt like a pinball machine—
Be straight—don't Tilt—Be that
princess,
Begin Again.

Verna M Yopp-Williams
COLLECTOR'S ITEM
Stygian beauty,
a dark, warm incubus
nestling inside
the violet womb of her
thoughts,
then . . .
She awakens to dance
or be still,
perfectly still in
the satin coolness
of her dawning . . .

Brenda Hagler
THE OCEAN OF LIFE

*Dedicated to my best friend and
soulmate Debbie Holland-Felder:
who has for the past four years been
the "wind beneath my wings."*

Life is like an ocean that is filled with
rolling waves
One moment it is calm and clear: the
next, it roars and raves.
Life is such emotion that its depth is
hard to reach
One day we're up; the next, we're
down. Life's lessons hard to teach.

Life's undertow is frightening as it
pulls us to and fro
We head in one direction: then life
deals a bitter blow.
We find that we are drifting; we
cannot swim to shore
Then a swirling surge o'ertakes us
and we're slammed to shore once
more.

Life's tide's not always cruel: all the
lessons that we learn
At least we know the waves that go
will leave and then return.
It gives a calming comfort to view
the constancy of life
To know that peace and love abide
along with toil and strife.

Life teaches a worthy lesson as we
watch the ocean wide
We're forced to make sense of the
turbulence while enjoying the
swaying tide.
We all become a stronger lot for the
hardships we go through
That make us appreciate even more
when the ocean's calm and blue.

Florence I Baumgardner
OUR DREAMS

*In memory of my beloved husband—
John M. Baumgardner with whom I
shared 45 happy and love-filled years
of marriage. I'd do it all again!*

What will you do with our left-over
dreams
If I don't live to see them through?
Will you think of the things I once
said
Or the things that we used to do??

Go on with your life and live it well;
REMEMBER DREAMS DO
COME
TRUE!!
And if you should pass before I do
I will carry them through.

Life is sweet and so short
There is no time for mistakes.
Our love is so strong—It will stand
the storm,
Regardless of the one that He
takes.

Jo Sulzen
DISABILITY
A Human Being, bound and chained:
strapped to her seat
by shackles of pain.
A Human Being, how do you treat
a girl in a Wheel Chair?
A Human Being, sitting low?
The world isn't fair,
a wheel chair is slow.
A Human Being, her problems all
bare
how can you help her?
How can you share
With a girl in a Wheel Chair?

Denis Begin
ISABELLA
Slowly I walked,
The breeze in my face,
Pushing on forward,
To her loving embrace,

Together we clasped,
Until at long last,
The love that we shared,
Flowed high through the air,

As the tears came,
We locked hand in hand,
Marching together,
Throughout the vast lands,

Then we departed,
Our own separate ways,
Now broken hearted,
That sad winter day,

Patricia Kay Wilson
SOLITAIRE
As I gaze out at the illuminating
moon,
The music plays and I hear a familiar
tune.

Listening to the song brings me such grave sorrow;
Because in my heart, I feel so very hollow.
So then I gently hold your picture and just stare,
And I wish I could tell you how much I do care.

I know you're far away and not within my reach,
But oh how I wish we could be back on the beach.
To once again walk hand in hand and side by side,
And watch the everlasting beauty of the tide.
I swore not to give my heart to another man,
But I'm swept off my feet like the breeze off the sand.

I have so many feelings to express inside.
Should I share them or are they the type I should hide?
You could say I am a little bit curious,
Do you feel that I am getting too serious?
All that I'm really asking for is half a chance.
I really want our relationship to advance.

Gretchen Benton
PLEASE COME BACK
As she stood there silently
She realized they must say goodbye,
But her heart fought back violently
And she started to cry.
She slipped the ring from her finger,
And placed it in his hand;
She knew her love for him would linger,
She wish she could understand
What had taken place,
But now life alone
Is what she had to face.
She placed a kiss
Upon his cheek,
Then closed the door
Hoping it wouldn't creak,
And as the men in black
Lifted his casket up off the ground
She screamed, "I love you, so please come back."
But she heart no other sound.

Christy Moss
TRYING

To: Elisha Rylee—My other side—I'm always here. To: Mom & Dad Thanks for everything and to Brandon My Character—Love Christy.

Trying
not to think
Trying
not to see
All the memories that I hide
Wanting
to have stopped in time
But now
it's too late
You've gone like . . .
a swift wind and I wonder
If
you'll think to wait
I want only to hear your voice
But . . .
I hesitate
Not wanting
you to hate me more
Because
you're all my heart cries out for.

Julia Falvey
WARM CHILL
All the places
The daffodils grow
Have been destroyed,
And I find myself without
Hope.

Year upon Year
I visited them, to
Wonder and speculate,
To celebrate their
Inspiration.

For at Spring's early
Breath, from a blind
Winter's chill—They
Bloomed and promised
Warmth.

But no longer will they
As their fields in earth
Have become Man's design,
And not that of nature, nor
Beauty.

So now, I feel cold.

Hector S Dela Cruz
METAMORPHOSIS

Thanks. To my cosmic mentors: Noel Dela Cruz (artist), Jim M., Jimi, and Mom. Thank you Robert, brother Fred, Marie, Armando, and to my cosmic mate Tess: I love you.

Like images float in an eternal sleep.
And clouds embrace the innocent sky.
Your being has entered my soul.
My precious soul, my gentle calm.
Into your eyes a trance of love.
Love, in a touch of your palm.

Like winds swirl across the barren land.
And sounds echo in the vacant abyss.
Your words have become dunes in our desert.
Our desert of love and winds of pain.
Over the dunes into a valley of dust.
Dust, in an oasis of pain.

Like a vision distorted by lifeless heat.
And a soul controlled by a dry heart.
Your caress has sanded my flesh.
My quivering flesh that knows only death.
A sliding blade releases blood of love.
Love, that gives birth to my death.

Marie J Murray
IN MEMORY OF A SPECIAL AUNT
Dear Father,

With words so inadequate and even these flowers . . .
We remember a "Special Lady" this Aunt of ours . .

We ask that you love her in a very unique way . . .
As we recall our memories so fondly today . . .

As Mother, As Sister, As Aunt, As Grandma too . . .
She loved each of us so special—so true . . .

Gratefully she reaped what she lovingly did sow . . .
For her friends were many, as You already know . . .

Full of life, full of joy, gentle and kind . . .
Are words that describe and come to our mind . . .

But as for us, the gift we received and will treasure . . .
Was her Love of Music—the Piano—a gift of pure pleasure . . .

Yes, a special bond, without words, we really did share . . .
Thankful she knew, we understood and we cared . . .

So her gift passed on now with joy and with glee . . .
With honor and pride continues in this family . . .

Just knowing she's with You ends the pain of feeling sad . . .
Please whisper our love and thankyou's to our "Special–Aunt Mag" . . .

Amen.

Michael H Cook
DIVERGENT TWINS
Love and lust,
divergent twins.
To love is virtue,
to lust is sin.
Ever evoking . . .
conflict within,
fraternal twins.

Lust abuses,
love admires.
Love imparts,
lust desires.
One the wood . . .
the other fire,
sacrificial pyre.

For one to reign,
enslaves the brother.
The life of one,
the demise of other.
The decisive blow . . .
the heart to harbor,
one or the other

Elizabeth Armstrong
THE DEATH OF JEAN–MICHEL
It falls so far beyond my comprehension.
Why must she face another terrible grief?
His death has brought such utter desolation
To all of us. It tests my own belief
That somehow in the space beyond my knowing,
For those who wait a perfect plan comes clear.
Is this required for my dear child's own growing?
Why must it come through slowly trickling tear?
Where is the plan when little children grow
Without a father's love, without his sharing
The little hurts, the large? How can I know
That they can thrive without his own deep caring?
I hear kind words, but it's with some misgiving:
"The real resting place of the dead is in the heart of the living."

Merle T Killinger
A SUDDEN CHANGE
The thunder sounded fierce;
The wind blew and the silence was pierced.
The rain came in heavy raindrops;
While streets ran with tides of muddy water that wouldn't stop.

The houses were hidden by foggy steam,
People huddled under shelter of house's roofs.
Animals stood caught with wet coats;
Birds flocked to home and roost.

Dry dust became gooey mud,
Parched plants opened wide to welcome moisture.
All seemed to breathe a sigh that the heat was broken;
Cool temperatures rushed in:
Reprieve . . Relief . . RE–Creation.

Janet A Hester
THANK YOU GOD

I dedicate this poem to my husband Frank—my son Frank, Jr.—and my daughter Tavia—I love you all so much.

I take pen in hand this beautiful day
To put on paper what I have to say
Each morning I awake and face the day
Knowing, Dear God, that You will pave my way
I feel a soft touch upon my cheek
I'm filled with such love I can hardly speak
Almost a flutter, if You will,
I bow my head and all goes still
I praise You God that You think I have worth
To receive the great love You have for all people on earth
Dear God, I try to be humble
But, my shortcomings hinder and I so often stumble
And then, to me, You extend Your hand
I lift my hand and rise to stand
I face the brilliant light, because You see,
I know, Dear God, You are leading me
Now I close with these words to Thee
I love You, and THANK YOU GOD for loving me!

Dorothy Glynn
TOGETHER
Walking on the beach, hand in hand,
Toe to toe, sand to sand.

Feeling the cool wet mist on your face,
Gives one a warm inner glow.

Watching sea gulls dipping in and out,
On silvery waters so blue.

Our tenderest thoughts can be read,
No words need be said!

Walking on the beach,
Hand in hand, sand to sand.

Helen Mc Nab
SILVER RAIN
Silver, falls the rain in summer,
drizzled day, brisk, the air.
Concentric inner circles slide
in liquid patterns, rare.

All dark and mirrored, shifts the pool
upon the silent spray.

The vapor rises in the meld
and passes on the fray.

Plump boughs sway limpid in the dew,
contrasting ashen clouds,
As planted seeds extend themselves,
free, from their podding shrouds.

Rain falls silver in the summer,
in an elixir rare.
Delicate patterns streaming forth,
new life in the clear air.

D J Pembroke Jr
SAVE THAT CHILD

To All Parents In The World.

Mom and Dad I am but a child,
And curiosity is my life.
I pick up things that aren't mine,
Although it isn't right . . .
Today I was in your closet,
And sitting on the shelf,
I found this thing, I think it's a toy,
And pointed it at myself . . .
And just like in the movies,
I was a cowboy, or a cop,
But the toy, it made the loudest noise,
and now my heart will stop . . .
Mommy it really hurts so bad,
My body is running dry.
Soon I'll be on my way to heaven,
Mommy, please don't cry . . .
I didn't mean to make you sad,
And though I must go away,
I'll be up there in heaven,
And I'll miss you every day . . .
I pray that other moms and dads
Will see what's happened here,
And hide those guns, and dangerous things,
To let us kids know you care . . .
Your child, D. J.

Paula Smith
COMING OF SUMMER
The earth awakens.
From a long cold sleep.
A smell of rebirth once again.
The sun burns a bright yellow.
As a sunflower awaking for a stream of sun.
Birds cheer a light song in daytime.
Crickets chirping an evening song in nighttime.
Color replenished within the eyesight.
Summer is here.
With long warm days.
Unit color fades.
When the days become chilled.
Nights get windy.
Then the earth sleeps.
Until the sun will call again.

Tanya M Snyder
A PLACE CALLED ME
Emptiness dwells in a lonely place
far beneath a shadowed face
Much deeper than the naked eye can see
It hides in the shattered heart
of a place called me.

Oh, emptiness is not all that's there
No, it's not alone down there
it has some company
In the shattered heart
of a place called me.

In the depths of this broken heart
that's been used, abused and torn apart
there lies a dream of two or three
a love that's lost
and a memory.

Emptiness dwells in a crowded space
far beneath a shadowed face
In the shattered heart
of a lonely place,
called me.

Sue Driscoll
MINUTE BY MINUTE

*Dear Ray I'd not change a minute.
Thank you. Love Sue.*

You're every breath I take
And every dream I dream
You're my yesterday and tomorrow
You're my joy and my sorrow

Your voice echoes in the wind
Your eyes a cluster of stars
Your smile as warm as sunlight
And I glory in your delight

You're in your middle years
Every day I have mounting fears
I'll awaken in coming years
And I'll have emptiness and tears

Yet I'd not change a minute
Life would not be worth living
If you weren't there in it
I've lived life minute by minute.

Carolyn Hart Lockwood
THE BAR OF LIGHT
I stooped to pick a bar of light
From off the sidewalk in the night;
My hand brushed cold cement, and I
Paused there to seek the reason why
I'd tried to grasp a bar of gold
That eyes could see, hands couldn't hold.
Inquiringly I searched the night,
And then I saw a shaft of light:
The bar was the end of a dream
That started from a distant beam.
Although the dream had ended then,
I stooped to touch it once again.

Sharon Lee Lloyd
YESTERDAY
He sits alone and looks at her,
The lines he does not see,
For in his mind he remembers her,
The way she used to be.

He still sees in his mind's eye,
The soft and curling hair,
The dimpled chin, the soft white skin,
The voice as light as air.

The years have not been kind to her,
She is no more like the dove,
But he does not see the change in her,
For he looks through eyes of love.

Michael Swartwood
TODAY

I dedicate this poem to my wife.

Today is the day, when the wind is
Blowing very hard, that one certain
Woman will go to work. Not for the
First time; but for the fourth time
This Week. She is going to a Flea
Market or Swap Meet where the wind
Usually does blow. In fact she goes to
This Flea Market just because she
Knows that she can make plenty of
Money and she knows that she will
Get enough money to pay some of
Her bills. But this is going to be an
Unusual day in that the sales will not
Be very good and she will wonder
Why. Then she will come to the
Conclusion that the wind was blowing
Too hard. Normally she does her best
When the wind is light or calm but
Not when the wind is blowing hard.

Robyn E Hart
THE CHESTNUT SEED
Within the chestnut lies the tree.
Undeveloped, all possibilities.
As I tend the growing seed a dream
awakens, a natural need.
To grow and sprout, unfold in time.
Like me my garden within divine.
My light shines forth in living splendor.
Patiently I nurture that flame so tender.
Not yesterday, nor tomorrow but now
that seed within me grows.
So lovely and surely God's light
within me glows.

DeLois Percival Schwenn
I'M PLENTY-NINE

To my husband, Robert M. Schwenn, Sr.

It's really not that I'm old
Even though my footsteps sometime lags
And under my eyes are big droopy bags
I'm still young and very bold,
Because you see I'm only plenty–nine.

I can still do all the things I did at twenty–nine
It's just that now everything takes much more time
And my disposition isn't exactly like a green lime
I've also noticed that my reading isn't on the line,
But then you must remember I'm only plenty-nine.

Now we really know that I'm still young and fine
And if you ask my oldest grandson, he will tell all to you
Like I've been married longer than that and his Mom is older, too
Well just remember this—my grandson is only nine,
But anyone can plainly see I'm only Plenty–Nine.

Ronald L May
A DREAM WITHIN A DREAM

To Mother and Dad with all my love, until we meet again.

Take this kiss upon the brow
and, in parting from you now
this much I avow:
You are not wrong who deem
that my days have been a dream.
Yet if hope has flown away
in a night or in a day,
in a vision or in none—
is hope therefore the less gone?

All that we see or seem is but a
dream within a dream.

I stand amid the roar
of a surf tormented shore
and I hold within my hand
grains of the golden sand.
How few, yet how they creep
through my fingers to the deep.
While I weep—while I weep.
O God, I cannot grasp them with a tighter clasp.
O God, can I not save one from the pitless wave?

Is all that we see or seem but a dream
within a dream?

Roberta Lee
TOUCHING SOULS
Our minds speak to each other thru countless ways
It could be at night or could be in day
It might be a touch, a silent look
Or thru a poem in the pages of a book

God's creatures who have gone on up above
To be at the side of the one we all love
Just might make a visit night or day
To remind us they are with us to stay

The visit could be with a firm touch
From strong arms that love us so much
Or the thoughts of the minds that we once knew
That find their way to us from out of the blue

We never know when a presence will appear
To help us keep the thoughts in our minds all clear
Be kind to each other is one way it is done
To help our fellowman is to follow the sun

A plan for our lives is already there
To follow it we must, we know not where
A belief in a power from up above
Might come to us on the wings of a dove

Tamela C Stufft
MY LOVE

To the love of my life, Joe, who is making all my dreams come true.

The love I thought would go away,
Just grows stronger every day.
Everywhere I look I see your face,
I'll be crazy within the year at this pace.

Distance in a relationship is rough,
And makes a heart grow tough.
I only know I won't fall,
As I try to break down the walls.

I know you want to have fun,
Meeting everyone under the sun.
I know you want only my friendship,
But that only causes me hardship.

The memories seem like only yesterday,
And the future so far away.
And when you get home at last,
I still won't have forgotten the past.

I needed to let you know,
I still love you so.
Don't be angry or upset,
I'll try once again to put it to rest.

Margaret High
AFTER THE STORM
I heard the thunder in the night
Heard the gusting windswept rain
I lay and listened, not in fright
I'm not afraid of nature's own.

I lay there thinking, come daylight
When I get out to run my course
I'll likely get all chilled and wet
And even end up breathing hoarse.

But comes the dawn, the rain has gone
The cold wet asphalt looks like glass
The sky is mirrored on the street

A reflecting pool that's framed by grass.

It seems I'm stepping on the sky
Though my feet are still earthbound
I see reflections of the clouds
And feel earth mother all around.

Early dawn is so enticing
Swept by wind and washed by rain
Prodding me so that I will
Get out and run the course again.

Roe Pearl Bradley

THE HOUSE BESIDE OF THE ROAD

Dedicated to Mt. Lebanon Missionary Baptist Church. Dr. Harmon E. Stockdale, Pastor.

The house by the side of the road,
where you can take your heavy load,
is set between the block. When you
stop you don't have to knock.
I remember those days, the ladies
dressed in long frock and frills. They
would load in the old wagon thro' the
woods and over hills.
On Sunday, when time for altar call,
we go and kneel, one and all. There
where you can leave your heavy load
in the church house by the side of the
road.

Helena Brigman

CONFLICTS

She dons a mask
to conceal the inner
turmoil haunting

her waking hours and
preventing restful sleep . . .
sleep filled with nightmares.

Is she an over–achiever
compensating for a life
out of control?

Conflicting emotions tear at her soul
like a volcano ready to erupt;
like a mother overjoyed with love
and pride.

Unpredictable moods
an affliction
she bears

Day to day . . .
month to month . . .
year to year.

Miss Marlene Carter

IN THIS PRESENT TIME

What do you see in time these days?
Surviving day by day finding many ways.
A lot of violence many crimes:
Junkies will hurt their mothers for a few dimes;
Factories, cars making more pollution,
What do we have to do for a better solution,
Something we do have is humiliation, frustrations
A whole lot of determination . . . but we can have
better communication.

Leslie Lee January

UNSPOKEN WORDS

I catch your eye within my own
unspoken words need not be known
for all our thoughts to each behold
as dawn draws near to its unfold

Now the sun strikes twelves
and morning yawns upon its shelf
unspoken words of velvet violence
promisingly sealed with silence

Approaching skies of pink champagne
touching you through window pane
grassy green, cool, barefoot dream
unspoken words, a peach and some cream

Delia Greene

MOM'S THOUGHTS

Dedicated to my youngest son—Mike.

You are our star
Our bright and loyal son
Whenever there's help needed,
You're always the one.

Always ever ready
With a smile and helping hand
Never a grumble or a sigh
Always the perfect man.

A better son was never born
To a mom and dad like us
We never mind asking your help
For there's never a bit of fuss.

Even with this birthday
You're just that much dearer
If you want to see results
Just look into the mirror

Love, Mom

Missy Medlock

AFTER ALL

For Jeff, the only love of my life for now and always. I love you.

I searched so hard, looking for love,
for someone who would care.
I was too blind to realize your love
was always there.

And all that time I went searching,
you waited patiently.
You were content to be the friend I
needed you to be.

You always stood right by my side,
though I pushed you away.
You kept on giving me support,
knowing just what to say.

I guess that's why when things got
bad, I always ran to you.
I knew you'd make me smile again,
and help me see things through.

So many people said to me, "You
two are meant to be."
It's funny how everyone knew—
everyone but me.

And though I never would admit I
loved you deep inside.
My feelings were so obvious, so
strong, and yet denied.

I had to try things on my own. I had
to know for sure.
That our love wasn't convenient, but
love that would endure.

Well, now I know this love's for real.
And, I thank God each day.
From now on, I'll listen to Him, and
let Him lead the way.

And though I've messed things up
before, this time we're going to last.
But one thing that we've got to do is
leave behind the past.

God's given us this second chance
To find our love again
And now that we're back together
This love will never end.

I guess it's true what people say:
We're really meant to be
'Cause after all the time that's passed
It's back to you and me.

Missy Medlock

OUR LOVE

The distance between us is short
yet you seem far away
Our love is strong, though I am not
all I can do is pray.

I know I can't see you right now
I'll dream of you instead
I'll keep you in my heart and mind
and think of what you said.

Your words I keep close to my heart
to think of when I'm blue
they cheer me up no matter what
those words are "I love you."

Our phone conversations are short
there's so much more to say
It seems there's hardly time enough
to chat about our day.

Hearing your voice makes me miss you
I long to draw you near
I wonder if you feel the same
within me builds a fear.

Our trust alone must see us through
though conflicts may set in
We'll work them out and grow from them
and try things once again.

The time we spend together is
more precious than before
Now that we're back together I
appreciate you more.

This time around we'll work things out
and then we both will see
that nothing can destroy our love
not even you or me.

Ronald J Coyle

THE CHRISTIAN CONDITION(?)

Ah, yes:
What can be "said" of JESUS CHRIST???:
"The Son of Man, of Holy Thrice?"
"The Risen Saviour, on His Throne?"
"The Son of God?" ("The ONE, alone?")
I have "pondered such questions" but once, or twice.

But, "such thoughts" not often daily linger on He
who claims to "point the finger,"
And, as we stumble through this play, where "be
salvation day–to–day?"
Ah, dim the "song" when sans THE SINGER!

LIFE's Magical Currents through which we soar, if
not "used NOW," shall not "make store,"
And, all "belief in pale charades"
<u>return to us</u> –
as "Easter parades;"
The "Crown of Thorns" 'tis told He wore?

His "written role," did He so choose???
If so, who "gains" where He "should lose?"
And, if "judged from High Judical Bench the vinegar
His thirst to quench,"
As "payment" for His PAID–UP DUES???

What "dare men say" of CHRIST THE LORD???
(Divisions ever – to "strike accord?")
The Refining Fire of Civilization but reduced to
shallow explanation?
If "such price be mortal," can we afford???

But, THE SOURCE OF TRUTH is ne'er provided upon
"what mortal men decided!!!"
As HIS SACRED LIGHT OF CONSCIOUSNESS e'er shall BE
THE CHRIST <u>within</u> . . .
He urges: <u>"SEE!!!"</u>
'Tis His LIGHT OF LIFE – e'en "mortal life" subsided.

Patrick Bryan Witt

AN ANGEL'S CROSS

The angels cross is an honor for him to bear. It blazes with light and is found only here, where people have fears and for each other do care.

It's made just for angels and only angels do dare, to carry it to glory and to treasure it there.

Yes the angel's cross is beautiful and fair, for the angel's cross is God's very child. So peaceful and mild when caught up in prayer. So serene when borne to Heavenly shores, where it leaps with pure joy and gives forth shouts of happiness and remembers all of his to his angel with a loving thankful kiss, ah the bliss when we've passed the test, we angel's crosses.

Melita H Spadafora

THE NOISES OF THE FOREST

I can hear the noises of the forest
Both loud and clear
They come from various distances
Both far and near
The chirping of the many birds
Nestled in the trees
The humming and the buzzing
Of the busy little bees
The squirrels and the chipmunks
Are climbing up and down the trees
Looking for food and nuts as quiet as you please
The deer are roaming all around the wooded grounds
Leaping and playing with one another in gleeful bounds
The waters are babbling in the nearby brooks
Twisting and turning beneath the many cranny and nooks
The forest is a peaceful and wonderful sight to behold
As it contains many pleasures worth their weight
In gold

Georgene Sutton

ELEVEN ROSES LEFT

To my five children, and all my friends everyone.

I bought a dozen roses. One for each loved one I had in mind. I also wanted the dear red rose to arrive on time. So each one was doubly blessed. For as you look at your red rose, and wonder of the rest. You will surely know eleven roses left, were passed along the way. You were one of those twelve red roses, that had come to you to say "I wish you a very happy Mother's Day."

I love you,
Your
Mother
Georgene

Georgene Sutton
MY DEAR LITTLE WHITE LIGHTHOUSE

To all people who have a love of lighthouses, and for those who haven't yet found them.

My dear little white lighthouse how proud you stand in your white gown. Never, never to make a person frown. You have stood and winked. A woman drawing many to her side. Did you know that your wink as ships passed by felt warm and safe in troubled times. You stand there proud and tall and quiet and somehow shy. They are drawn into your harbor hands. Did you know in your own way, the hugs and kisses that you've won along the way. An ageless woman at her best, flirting and standing and drawing them into your harbor hands. Thinking "now I'm in command." If only for minutes or hours, you have won! Love of all, when all is said and done.

Love,
Mom, Grandma

Celeste Yolanda Williams
HER SWEET POETRY SPIRITS

I, Celeste Yolanda Williams, dedicate this poem to all sweet poetry spirits. Thank you.

In mind's possession
Of captive emotions
Her spirits strong
Though free as the storm
Her sweet poetry spirits are born

Worded expressions of simplicities
Her tranquil poetry rhymes endure
Brings spunk and cheeriness and peaceful time
Her sweet poetry spirits are sure

Sweet poetry spirits
So bright as day
Take them to heart
On this fine day
Her sweet poetry spirits here to stay

Fate bounds her feelings in sweet poetry
To be expressively bound into meaning
Creating her literal arts appealing
For mind's possession of captive emotions
Holds key to unlock of plenty devotions

Celeste Yolanda Williams
POTPOURRI BLOOMS

Springtimes air, A poof of sachet
Its fragrant blossoms aloof in array
It decor a delight in sunshine's hue
Amidst nature alluring potpourri brew
Imagining potpourri blooms

A summer essence gifts cachet
Pure floral bizzare accent its display
With sweet geraniums or honey-suckle wilds
Or rainbow roses of mellow bouquet
Potpourri blooms picturesque of the day
In essence of potpourri blooms.

Celeste Yolanda Williams
LOVE AND CREATIONS

Rain is falling from a tearful cloud
Her pouring cry a thunderous loud
Winds deeply expelling its breathful sigh
As mother earth's wrath of relief unfurls
She lights the sky with opening of her eyes
For all could see her yellow pupil of sun
Awakening dreams with her sparkling veneer
Warming one's heart with the heat of a peer
Her loves so vast its limitless skies
Has painted the world its picturesque rise
Teaching the lands her colorful rules
Of glistening rainbows across colorless sky

Celeste Yolanda Williams
BOLD OCEAN BLUE

Old blue ocean
Big and bold blue potion
True life inhibited water world
Sealand miles of many arise
Full of seafish aswirl of plenty surprise
It creates all that exits within
So deep those depths of serene ocean lifestyles
An underworld revolves
As with life sacrifice permisses
Waterwhirls motioning forward asway
In sparkling glimmers of blue water waves
With standing all of natures perist
Sea of an endless maze abliss

Angela Francis
SWAN SONG

This poem is dedicated to "My Love River Jude Phoenix."

Alone I wait for my love. In a secret paradise, only known to us. Now he is gone. Never again will I love any man as I did him. Our love ran deeper than the deepest ocean. A love so strong not even death can separate us. In my dreams he is alive and well, I hear him whisper in my ear . . . I love you. How I long for his caress, for him to hold me in his arms. Towards the end of my dream, I see him with his arms out-stretched. Waiting for me to him, then . . . I wake up.

We were like two swans on a still pond, its water shimmering like a pool of liquid glass. We were like mute swans. Which song can only be heard by the heart of one who is in love. They say swans mate for life, had he stayed with me we would have been together forever.
Forever in love.
I have been to our hidden paradise, it seems so dismal without him. A veil of misery has shrouded my heart, and there it will stay till the day I die. I feel so alone now that he is gone. I miss him being there for me, when I needed someone to talk to. My love dove has flown away from me, forever. Soon I will fly away also, to join my love.

Angela Francis
UNDER LOVE'S INFLUENCE

This poem is dedicated to "My Love River Jude Phoenix."

I walk along the seashore, alone. At peace. I wonder at nature's treasures. I watch the sunset, all the purples – pinks – golds and blues. How tranquil it all is. I listen to the crashing waves against the rocks. I feel the wind in my hair. I think of my love. I stay awake sometimes just to watch him sleep, his chest gently rising and falling. When the moon is full we walk by the ocean. It's very beautiful and romantic. He is my life – my love and my happiness. How can you measure that which is immeasurable. Love has no boundaries. If you walk in love's light then you are in paradise, forever. Love casts out all pain. Love is stronger than steel. Once you are in love you will know true happiness, for as long as that love lasts. I will always love one and only one man. My love is forever. Forever I will be in love with him, the only man I will ever care about.

Angela Francis
FOR LOVE REMEMBERED

This poem is dedicated to "My Love River Jude Phoenix."

Remember our love when it was new, remember our love when we were blue. Remember our love in sun and rain. Remember that we will always be as one, together forever. Through good times and bad. Our love will remain. Remember our love when we pledged we will be forever in love. To only love each other and no one else. We will be joined in that blessed state of love till the day we die. Forever we will love, forever we will be loved.

Sonja Harrelson
THE LAMB OF GOD

Jesus was born on Christmas Day
The sins of the world to take away
He came on this earth as the Lamb of God
To make a straight path for sinners to trod
God is not willing for any man to perish
But for eternal life for every man to cherish
Just open your heart to let Him in
To wash you white and clean from sin
He will be with you to help you through each day
To show you there is truly a better way
So turn away from your old way of life
And be free of hatred, sin, and strife
Jesus will give you peace and joy within
And be someone you can truly call friend
Evil and sin from this earth will He take away
When Jesus comes back here to rule and stay
He'll give you a love you've never known before
When He knocks on your heart, be sure to open the door
So be ready for His coming, just any day
The Lamb of god is the only way

Jeffrey Michael Bohan
PRETENDED SKIES

I

Lost in thought an out of reason
calculus of value tired in nights
kneel prayers in soft dreams
that we prepared under the stars

II

Suns arise with brighter knowledge
true love alone saves keys of silence
late evening bird gentle flock
to gather once again in summer's early morning
down the block in the woods

III

time slept against clocks
we kept to try and lock
but no cages could stop

IV

upon you reach the end
where suns fall just past the shores
from subjects past among souls
wilderness shadows adorn
pretended skies enamour night

V

The sun is a mysterious red
to sink and glare just above the waves
I closed my eyes stepped into the sea
a picture I colored with bright paint
with a garden of angels and saints
upon death's pillow I could see the gates

Gina Marie Lanute
AM I DREAMING?

Every night, I wake from dreaming;
My heart is pounding. Still unbelieving.
Something this special; Could it really be true?
What I'm feeling is real.
I've fallen in Love with you.

I feel your presence;
Deep within my soul.
I want to hold you forever;
and never let go.

I have captured your image
safe within my mind
and the intimacy that we've shared
My heart will forever hold in side.

I will never hurt you
for a broken heart will cause pain,
It hurts more than any scratch or cut,
and the scar will forever remain.

I want you to know me;
and all that I am.
I want you to be a part of me,
If you want to, you can.

Gina Marie Lanute
THINK OF ME

Think of me, my love
And hold your head up high;
For I am the one who will be there
When you feel you need to cry.

Talk to me, my love
Of all your troubles and pain.
For I will help you solve them,

And get you back on your feet again.

Hold me close, my love
And feel my warm embrace;
Together we'll take on the world,
There is nothing we can't face.

Dream of me, my love
When the day is over and done.
In slumber so peaceful and deep,
Your world and mine are one.

Gina Marie Lanute
FOREVER MY LOVE.

As sweet as the air in spring, as beautiful as the flowers that bloom;
As soft as the wind that blows across your face, is the love that is meant for you.

As strong as the light from the moon that pierces through the midnight sky,
As wild as the overgrown prairie in the fall, and as free as the mountain like
Waves in the ocean;
Is the way that I feel when I am with you.

So when the troubles and the worries of the world get you down:
Look to the moon in the mid of the night, and feel the strength of my love from its
Light.
Or look to the prairie and feel the wilderness of my character, or to the ocean,
For the freeness of my soul.

When you look to these places you will feel my presence and the weight of my love.
When you look through the wind for the image of my face, and smell my presence
In the sweet spring air:
The flower that falls to your feet is a symbol to you, that I'll always be there.

So remember my love, as we go through time, no matter where we go – how we turn;
I'll always be there, in my heart and in my soul:
Awaiting every turn in life you may go–
We will go together.

Gina Marie Lanute
A NEW RELATIONSHIP

Your eyes, like the sea, are peaceful and green;
Sparkling
I look beyond, I see how gentle and sincere your world really is.
Your eyes, soft, like a misty blue sky after soft fallen rain;
Questioning?
Afraid do you feel? Curious is what you are.
Is this real, or am I dreaming?
Shy, like a child with a brand–new friend.
So with caution, forward you walk;
Careful not to hurt, yet timid, afraid to be hurt yourself.
Relax,
The time we have shared has been so real;
The questions you ask, I ask them too.
The answers . . . well,
If we open our eyes and look ahead, staring at us
Are probably

The answers.

Ed Bagwell
FROM A GRANDMOTHER'S HEART

To Edna who inspired me and Nina our special angel.

God loaned us a treasure to brighten our home
When he saw how we loved her he extended the loan.
The interest we paid was heartaches and tears,
But we got enough love for two million years.

Yes, Nina is special, though she's only five
There's a deep understanding in those big brown eyes.
A peace and acceptance of whatever will be.
Things for a lifetime most people don't see.

She can look into your soul with the ease of a child
And soothe all your fears with one of her smiles.
Beautiful Nina, you've blessed our home.
God make us worthy of such a wonderful loan.

Ed Bagwell
MY WIFE

To my wonderful and understanding wife: Mary.

As sweet and fresh as the dew on a rose
From the top of her head to the tip of her toes.
A voice as sweet as the robin's song.
A smile that says "This is where you belong"
To look at her makes time stand still
I love her now and I always will
We've been together for thirty–two years
We've had some doubts and we've had some fears.
Her very true love and her under-standing heart
Kept temptation from pulling us apart
I love my Mary, my morning sun
And we will be together till our days are done.

Ed Bagwell
A VERY SPECIAL FRIENDSHIP

To Edna, my very special friend.

I'm lost in a feeling of friendship and love;
My head is in the clouds above –
To know you're loved by a friend so true,
Someone who loves you because you are you.
This love is not for sex or fame,
It's not for money, or for your good name.
It's a love that reaches from heart to heart,
And accepts your good and your awful parts.
A love and friendship where you feel the same;
A beautiful friendship that plays no games.
A friendship full of honesty and trust –
A friendship of love – and free from lust.
A friendship that took so long to find;
A friendship that's warm and beautiful and kind.
A friendship that can look into each other's soul,
And holding each other can make you feel whole.
A friendship embedded so deep in your heart,
That part of you is missing when you are apart.

Wilma Pierce
YESTERDAY, TODAY AND TOMORROW

I dedicate these words to the "Spoon River Towers" a high–rise in Lewistown, Illinois managed by the National Benevolent Association of the Christian Church (Disciples of Christ.) This was written to the tune of "Life's Railway to Heaven" in honor of NBA's 100th birthday.

Yesterday, my life was empty, with no sunshine in my soul;
And today I found a Savior, I no longer feel so cold.
I know I can face tomorrow, with his disciples at hand;
To tell me with sweet reminders, that there is a better land.

Yesterday till tomorrow I have courage to face today;
And have no fears of tomorrow from what I learned yesterday.

Life is full of toils and struggles, but there's help along the way;
From Jesus and his disciples, there is love for us each day.
Though the trip was long and dreary, "Oh yes Lord" we made it thru;
Thank you Lord for all our blessings, and they number quite a few.

Yesterday till tomorrow we have courage to face today;
And have no fears of tomorrow from what we learned yesterday.

Yes, we all must take that journey, from yesterday till today;
Looking forward to the future, though it may not come our way.
With the help of his disciples, we joined that happy band;
With a glow upon our faces, shouting praise thru–out the land.

Yesterday till tomorow we have courage to face today;
And have no fears of tomorrow from what we learned yesterday.

Roland Owens
THE QUEEN

High above the timber line
Beyond the silver tips
She screams her challenge fiercely
As she sways her gnarled hips

Battered and beaten by storms
Scarred by the fiery lights
Alone she stands, this aged queen
Where only the strong have rights

Where only the great survive
Where beauty is measured by might
Where death is swift and greedy
And life, but an endless fight

Where mightly stalks the lobo wolf
Where jackals never stray
And squalling births at midnight
Lay cold at break of day

And in the valley far below
Can be heard her mournful sigh
As darkness dims the twilight
To conceive the dawn anew

D G Mix
NOCTURNE

a willow on the water
over—under
an open moon
a firefly
a langourous cloud
a lantern light
a hush—
and whispers in the night . . .
sipping at these springs
this Hippocrene
no firelight tonight
I dream . . .

Caroline T Wilson
ODE TO SPRING

Dedicated to my parents for all their encouragement and support.

What makes an iris bright?
Must be the sun's warm light.
What turns a sunflower's head?
Might it be a cardinal's red?
Why is spring so long awaited,
And what God has new created,
For us to watch what once had died,
Become so bright, alive . . .
revived.

Hugh B Webb
THE DOGWOOD TREE

This poem is dedicated to my family—my wife Cleo, and our three children—Rickey, Cheryl and Christine.

Oh! That I might live another season,
My wish would be, to witness the
Flowering of the dogwood tree.
Spreading its beauty like a cloud of
White snow, mother nature at her best,
A sight to behold.
Like a light in the forest in early spring,
Standing out from others as if to sing.
My beauty commands for the eyes to see,
The glorious splendor of the dogwood tree.

Dorothy Howard Adler
WISE MEN BOW

Decorate the Christmas tree
For its fronds of living green
Call to mind the manger scene

Light it well with bulbs of red
'Neath it place a manger bed
Hear again what angels said

Should the snow fall gently down
For your tree 'twill be a crown
Let the love of Christ abound

Remember that the Christ child grew
He, a boy, was once like you
He went fishing; so do you

In His prime at thirty-three
Jesus died for you and me
From our sins to set us free

Angels sang and shepherds came
Sages and the halt, the lame
Wise men still bow at His name

Suzanne Taylor
TIME'S TRUCE

The spring will ever bring
A storm. Winds and rain,—
Frustration.
Summer comes with heat reborn,

Dust and deportation.
Caution and smoke in Fall months poke
Up every road and alley,
But with a snow, I seem to know
That time is here to dally.

Isaiah S Enoch

TO DREAD THE NIGHT

To my dear wife.

Why do I fear the dread of night?
Though it may have a thousand eyes.
I feel it faintly upon my face
Here in the dark, with its embrace.
As if in fear, or to survive.

When it is dark, there is this still.
The house become a crackling sound
This noise will cease, come break of day.
From force of weight upon the ground
My heart beats loud, as though I'm ill

There is no beauty in the dark
Only thoughts to comfort as I lie
And beckon for each dawn of day.
My cover is wrinkled where I tossed.
The clock will strike, I will embark

I choose the day, others choose the night.
Then I can see at yonder far.
At those who pass, or things nearby.
The sun will shine enough for me
It has one eye to make the light

Why is the darkness that I fear?
I feel the gloom upon my face.
Sometime I plunder through the room
In search of things that's lying near.
And move it from its resting place.

Why do I always dread the night
From it come rest, from toil of day.
Into a stage of flow and bright
Where mind and body can slip away
And both can rest, without a fight.

But once again at break of day.
No longer are there eyes of night
I'm up again and on my way
My body once more is on this flight
Will push and strain with all its might

Where has it gone? the time of day
How did it pass? when did it slip?
Again the sun fades in the west
No more this day within my grip
When evening comes, it takes its rest.

Then I must face the dark again.
Each night it crept into my room
No way for me to shut it out.
my doors and windows do I close tight
That I may void the dark of night.

Steven R Leonard

NATURE'S CHILD

As the northern wind blows briskly through the air,
It takes the wildflower from her glistening hair
And throws it across the forever green meadow
Into the pale blue pond filled with life. A rainbow
Rises beyond the clearing clouds as the spring rains
Have stopped for a moment. The mist-filled meadow gains
New growth and nourishment from the declining sun
Which shines in the pure beauty of dusk. A girl, young
And innocent, skips through the now dampened grassland
List'ning joyfully to the sound of nature's band.

She hears the song of swallows flying through the trees,
Of crickets in the field, and the wild wind whistling
Through the spring nearby as she gets down on her knees
To replace her lost flower. The cooler breeze brings
A chill through the air as the rain begins its soft
Downward flight. Cold and wet, the young girl walks swiftly
Through the narrow trail to her cottage. Her warm loft
Will bring warmth to her flesh, but not to her empty
Soul. She longs for a girlfriend with whom she could share
Secrets. Someone, like nature, who'll always be there.

Abby K Johnson

TO BE A POET

Dedicated to Carol and Barbara, my two sisters, and Bill.

If I were a poet
　　And knew how to write,
My life would be changed
　　As day is to night.

I may have a studio
　　With windows galore,
Bright colored walls,
　　My name on the door!

Strangers would know me
　　And shake my hand.
There may be a parade
　　And a large brass band!

Invitations to parties,
　　Velvet skirts and things;
Ladies a-glitter
　　With white diamond rings.

But that's not my style
　　For humble am I —
So to win this contest
　　I'll give it a try.

Patti Burke

THE DREAM

Traffic sounds drift up from the street,
Mixed with the kids playing in the snow,
And as evening comes around again,
I begin the dream of you once more.

It all fell apart during a winter storm,
With the freezing wind blowing hard and strong,
The patterns of ice made tears on the pane,
They were warning me that soon you'd be gone.

The music played as I held you tight,
You felt like a stranger in my arms that night.
I made an excuse for your faraway eyes,
Held on to the dream so I couldn't see the lies.

We said very little as we finished the wine,
Neither one voicing what was on the other's mind,
I reached for your hand and pulled you close,
Coming together for one last time.

The morning light found me in bed all alone,
With your scent still lingering where you lay,
The note on your pillow told me what you couldn't say,
It shattered the moment and the dream fell away.

Ralph Comfort

A ROSE IN THE DAWN

To Dawn Comfort; my beautiful wife, the angel in my dreams, the one that I love, my best friend, "Forever."

Alone again we are apart
Time ticking by as the shadows fall
All that was done and all that was said
Is now just a memory for a short time is all

For once what was sad now brings a smile
A gleam of enchantment to make a heart true
What once was a feeling of coldness inside
Brings forth the bells ringing for me and for you

And when my tears fall from a dream of despair
I wake to a thought I need you so much
And I sleep on a cloud in the cool evening air
For the dreams of your kiss warms my heart with your touch

Then light flickers in from the doom of the night
And I pray to the Lord as I stretch and I yawn
Then I look through the glass what a wondrous sight
For there in the rain is a rose in the dawn.

Kathleen Taylor

THE SOUTHERN TIP

Affectionately dedicated to my precious daughter Cindy.

There's a land remote and distant, down where the coconuts grow,
Where the crest of the waves sweep upward and crash to the sands below.
By land you can easily reach it, on trails that are ancient and worn,
Carved by the hand of nature, back when the earth was born.

You may have seen mountains which tower the skyline and valleys that flood with rain;
Jungles dark and mysterious and other exciting terrain.
But you haven't really seen it, until you've been to that shore
Where the waves simultaneously greet you and leave with a thundering roar.

You'll have instant embrace with King Neptune—be impressed by the might of his grip,
There on that rugged coastline, down by the southern tip.
And should you long to be part of the action; to ride with the rising swell,
You can—if you're friends with the sea god and all of his ways you know well.

But remember—to those who would venture, a warning it's wise to believe;
There's magic afoot on the white sands, you'll discover when time comes to leave.
If you find you're reluctant and linger, immersed in the sunset's red glow,
Then you'll know the enchantress has caught you—and it's likely you never will go.

Kathleen Taylor

BE CAREFUL WHAT YOU WANT YOU MAY GET IT

Affectionately dedicated to my precious son David.

I decided early in life that I, wanted a fortune in gold.
People said it would come my way as I was strong and bold.
Besides I was armed with the talisman of luck and born with the silver spoon;
Had prayed to the stars that shine above and paid my respects to the moon.

I knew it would come and indeed it did,
It was just as the people always had said.
So I sat content on my pile of gold, to live without worry or care
Which allowed me the time to ponder on, how it had gotten there.

Was it because I was strong and bold, or was it the silver spoon,
Perhaps the talisman around my neck, the stars—or the yellow moon?
The answer came as I knew it would when a voice in the night spoke to me
And revealed that my pile of gold was there, simply because—I wanted it to be.

Deborah Lynn Andersen

SPRINGTIME

To Gary Ross. It was a long, cold, hard winter in Cincinnati, and the sight of new buds, Canadian geese, and fresh breezes, made me long for springtime.

It's the season for opening up windows and starting anew,
Rain showers, cool crispness, and Morning of dew.
Daffodils are in bloom, the smell
Of lilacs in the breeze,
A promise that the trees will be
Bearing new leaves.
Nature is in bloom and wildlife's Afire,
Ready to soothe their burning desires,
Ducks on the lake and geese in the

Air,
Warm lazy days without a care.
It's the season for celebrating
Christ and Easter,
Hiding eggs in the park,
May Day, Flag Day, Mothers Day—
Children playing till dark
It's the season of enchanting
Magical rhyme,
I'm sure glad it's springtime.

Mary L Tyler
DREAM

To my children: Abby and Jason.

Just once I'd like to find my dream,
And see all the places I have seen.

There are no roads or maps to follow,
your subconscious is your guide.

You can take as many as you like.
There's always plenty of room,
Or, just go by yourself, when
ever you're in the mood.

There are dreams that can scare
you—you have once in awhile.
But, the dreams I have are fantasies,
full of beauty and style.

Oh but, just once I'd like to find my
dreams,
and maybe stay awhile.

Daniel Laurelli and Angelina Roginski

Angelina Roginski
SO DISTANT YET SO NEAR

This poem is dedicated to Daniel P. Laurelli.

Where is he tonight?
He is somewhere in the distance.
He is my innermost feelings.
Makes me feel I am part of existence.
What do I do tonight?
Sit here and be sorrowful?
No, I will patiently await tomorrow.

Sitting on my porch,
Looking at the seashore.
Dreaming of my love,
Having him home with me.
Cherishing his touch,
Surrounding me with his warmth.
Such a closeness between us.

Going out of my mind.
Calling upon his name,
Not hearing a response,
Come to me my dear one,
Teach me my love,
What it is to feel comfort.

A call on the telephone,
He says, "I'm coming home."
But there is trouble,
I have to go find him,
The traffic to the airport,
Very hectic and noisy.

Rain crashes intensely,
To the ground.
I reach the airport,
He is there,
Waiting for me to come for him.
He says, "I love you Honey."
I say, "I'd drive all night to be with
you."

We hold tight to each other,
For fear that,
Tomorrow may not come.
A soft kiss, he gave me,
His hand though,
My wet, curly hair.
He tells me,
Everything will be fine now.

I open the car door,
He enters and relaxes.
We are on our way,
Home to stay,
Our love is eternal
No one can destroy it.
Forever, my love and I,
Until we die.

Stanley Roberts
LOVE IS BEAUTIFUL

This poem is dedicated to my loving and caring wife Shelia.

Love is a beautiful thing when I'm
with you,
The sun is always bright, the sky is
always blue,

A lifetime spent with you, my
sweetheart,
Would be my happiest dream come
true.

Our golden years were meant for us,
Forever to be under the baby blue
sky,

Some day, my sweetheart, when
we're all alone,
I'll love you even more my darling,
As much then as I do now.

Some day we'll thank the Lord for
each year and each day gone by,
As hand in hand we will enter the
sky,
To meet the Lord almighty.

Helen Gilhousen
MOTHER'S DAY MEMORIES

I dedicate this poem to MY OTHER MOTHER, who treated me like her own.

She was loved by all those who knew
her,
by her Children, and Grandchildren,
adored.
And on Mother's Day she will be
with us,
Even though she is now with her
Lord.

For memories will linger forever,
Of her patience and sweet loving care
And for the love of our wonderful
Mother,
We offer to God a thankful prayer.

For a mother like her is a blessing,
And though she had many trials and
tears,
All the help and happiness she gave
us
Will linger through all of our years.
And we know she is still watching
o'er us
No matter how far we may
roam —
And she'll still be patiently waiting
For her loved ones all to come home.

And oh! What a glorious reunion —
When the circle is broken no more,
And we join with our loved ones in
Heaven —
To live with our Lord evermore.

Joy Yvonne Mundy
MARTIN LUTHER KING
Martin Luther King won the Nobel
Peace Prize. Love, Faith and Wisdom
made him Wise. He had a Dream that
one day all people would be FREE,
to live in America with Equal
Opportunity.

Alice Whiteside Jorg
EVE'S LITTLE SECRET
Outside of Eden,
hand upon the gate,
Eve paused and briefly
mused upon her fate.

Thought about the apple,
whisper of the snake,
and the one commandment
warned not to break.

Looked back at the Garden,
perfect, dull, secure,
then toward the unknown
with its hardships to endure.

Breathed, "Farewell" to the Garden.
Turned to the strange new land,
and smiling at a memory
she reached for Adam's hand.

Karen J Ross
QUIET HEARTBEAT

To you, the reader, take this present moment to listen to your own heartbeat.

Tainted love on top of the world
Touching the clouds through empty
atmosphere
with a blind man's view.
The clouds feeling like tender
thoughts
of someone else's mind.

Reaching, searching for endless
thoughts into a mind
that is ever so smart.
So filled with gardens of flowers
waiting to bloom.

Still sitting on top of the world
A brush resting in the palm of my
hand
to paint a tainted love.
To paint a picture ever so colorful, to
sit,
and wish upon a voiceless cloud.

Such a pictured life can be seen
in the back of my mind ever so
precious.
Like a feather in the wind,
free from all harmful human hands;
only the cool breeze to carry it.
Color it so beautiful
to an ocean in a never ending land.

Still sitting on top of the world—
somewhere.
Black birds in a red sky?
Red birds in a pink sky?
Just sitting with a quiet
heartbeat . . .

Lucille McCullough
JESUS
Jesus Christ, the son of God
Upon this earth he once did trod.
He bore the cross for you and I
And for our sins he had to die.

When he was twelve, he left his
home
To go out in the world alone.

About his Father's work it read
He had no place to lay his head.

A carpenter he was in deed,
But he was there for everyone's need.

He healed the sick; made the blind to
see,
And he is there for you and me.

Carol Suzanne Browning
IN THE STILL OF WINTER

This poem is a quiet celebration for all creatures and creators who understand and believe in the power of Stillness and the mystery of sacred rites.

Gently, quietly Father Sky
Sends forth his Blessings
Blanketing the silent Mother Earth
With the white mantle she so dearly
needs
to nurse the plants and trees and
flowers
to insulate and give shelter to
all
who seek rest and refuge in her
care.

He comes, Father Sky,
Giving new Hope to the Land.

The winter storm moves on.
The white gift of Light remains.

In the still of Winter
Beneath the newly-fallen snow
Lies the silent, unseen promise of
Spring
When once again Father Sun and
Mother Earth
Shall come gently, quietly
Giving life to our home.

Alfreda Crandall
MY WINDOW
My window is a picture
God paints for me each day.
I see the squirrels upon the lawn
I see the raucous Jay.
I see a saucy sparrow
Take a bath in his private pool,
I see some little children
On their way to school.
My painting is a magic one,
It changes all the time;
In summer, winter, spring, and fall
In this northern clime.
From my cosy living room,
Every day I see
The lovely, changing, living things
God painted just for me.

Sharlon M Wildt
SILENT GOOD-BYE
Ever so softly she whispered,
"Darling I love you." These were
her last words
of the night.
He knew in his aged heart
she would never again speak.
With tears in his eyes, he
kissed her wrinkled, pale cheek.
Looking down at her his tears
dried on his saddened face.
Quietly, he left the tiny
barren room.
Staring at the empty corridor,
he walked on without looking
back.

Susan Burgess
FROM GOD

To: God from which comes the ability, my husband who unlocked my heart, my mom and dad who brought it all about, and my kindred spirit for always being there.

I walked with you and held your hand
before Earth's soil you did touch.
I watched you take your birth in life,
still loving you as much.

But you strayed far away from me,
in search of other things
Still I watched you closely, through
Winters, Falls and Springs.

And all those things you searched
and found, yet never finding peace
If only you had come to me, this
senseless pain would cease.

So take my hand and speak to me
and peace shall cleanse your soul.
And all the treasures you desire
will come to make you whole.

Susan Burgess
SO FAST THEY GROW

To my sister for the nurturing yesterday and encouragement today, and especially to the most precious beings I've ever known, my children.

I watch the children throwing rocks
into the river's flow.
I find I wonder more and more why
so fast they grow?

Seems yesterday they learned to
speak, today they do not stop.
Much like the rolling river once to
God a single drop.

They too, seem to be lost at times in
this vast demanding life.
I pray I do not lose this time
amidst the constant strife.

So, God I look to you to ease the
burdens and bring calm.
And I may always know my most
important job is Mom!

Smaranda Livescu
THE DARKNESS, TOMORROW . . .

To my Mother, my country . . .

Candles
A long row
Temples
for my grandmother,
our childhood sky.
My grandfather's, inside the churches
he painted,
seem to be some angel's fingers.

To light their night, neighbors
have candles instead of the common
discussion in the University Square.
"Is it cold? Is it deep?"
My priest told us yesterday:
"Have a bit of moonlight
on one shoulder
some bitter life in your heart
and don't forget the Principal's
speech
within the pocket!
Here you are! Nothingness almost
completed.
Help yourself! Tomorrow it might be
too dark for you
to see . . ."

Mary Groom
MY LITTLE BLUE-EYED DAUGHTER

This poem is dedicated to my precious daughter, Robin.

I saw a precious little girl today
And I remembered a little
blue-eyed tot at play
With sandpiles built high, with pride
a beaming
Only to run in the house with a
skinned knee a screaming
"Please kiss it mommy" and "Make
the hurt go away" !!
Then with eyes a twinkling, returned
out to play!

The sandpiles are gone now
And that little girl has moved away
There is something as a mother that I
really do need to say
I realize now, that as your mother
That I was much more "harsh," than I
really "'oughta"
But please remember that you will
always be
"MY LITTLE BLUE-EYED
DAUGHTER"

William Bredesen
ABORTION

The miracle of life
Was in its place
Until abortion
Showed its face

A life is gone
It cannot be replaced
The life that was
Has been erased

This new life
Was destroyed
Where it lived
Is now a void

Eyes and ears
Fingers and toys
Have been destroyed
Because a woman chose
The right to life
Has been denied
Because of a mother
Who will decide
An unborn child
Securely placed
Has been destroyed
Forever erased

God started a life
And gave it worth
A cruel abortion
Denied its birth

Every unborn child
Has a place
Every unborn child
Is in God's grace

Every unborn child
Has a plea
Give me your love
Not eternity

God gives life
With dignity
He wants it treasured
Reverently

Jean D Beebe
WORKING MOTHER

I'm a working Mother
The fact is plain to see,
By the mud upon my favorite wool
And the crackers on my settee.

I really do not mind
The orange juice in my shoe,
For everything seems quite alright
When he says "I Wuv You!"

Elberta Wing
OPEN WITH CARE

Open with care this year that's
coming in
All tied with bows of efforts to win.
The good with the bad, happy with
sad.
Build determination for things to be
had.
Those that we need, those that we
want
Earned from plenty, or taken from the
"gaunt."
Things appreciated or taken for
granted.
From this big garden God has
planted.
All things made in perfection for
mankind
To pick as we need from hands
divine
Why doubt the power to be taken
care of?
When all good things come from
above.
Let's sing His praises as we close the
old door,
Thank Him for the New Year and
watch America grow.

Ina Askew
WHAT AMERICA IS TO ME

America is more to me than her
houses, lands and trees.
I close my eyes, hear the tread of
those millions now dead,
who roamed her hills and forests
deep,
Giving us LIBERTY—A birthright to
keep.

Those forebears of ours in homespun
jeans,
were as dauntless as Saxon Kings.
Ne'er more bravery was ever found
than their defense of
home and town; wielding mattock or
ax,
Driving the British ever back—
Oh, such spirit of men born free,
A heritage left for you and me!

What a heritage is ours in this land,
Where man is free to do the best he
can!
Will this be lost in apathy and ease?
How loathsome this benumbing
disease!
May the vision that inspired those
men of old
Keep us undaunted, and like them as
bold.

Catherine E Reynolds

Catherine E Reynolds
LIFE

To All My Children (Norman, Dawn, Kim, Camille, Ramona, Kelly, Mario, Dion).

If it were not for life
We wouldn't be here at all
Nevertheless, without it,
We would fall.

We, as humans, are frail
But weak
Often tempted and tried
For the joys we seek.

Let us continue while
It is day
When the night cometh
Fast and pray.

May God bless us
You and I
The good things of life
He'll not deny.

Keep us, O Lord
Till the day is done
Only then will we know
The Victory's been won.

Linda R Oxley
CROSS ROADS

Love and Hate, tough to mate,
this place we find us in.
The epitome of hurt, it's need
expressed,
only to find no kin.
But try I did and for that;
I will not walk in shame,
Although I may remain the only one
to blame.
May a light shine down, our new
found ground.
As we Cross Roads on our own.

Catherine E Reynolds
PRAYER FOR WISDOM

Teach me, O Lord, how to pray
Inspire within me what to say
Touch my heart with love divine
Give me more grace to be kind.

Open my mouth that I may speak
The things I ought more clearly

Move my lips with a tender smile
Instruct my hands in things
worthwhile.

Guide my feet in the way of peace
That I may walk more diligently
Wisdom to do and give
Of my substance that I may live.

To share with others what I have
acquired
A feeling to make this my desire
Let me continue to seek her as gold
Always to have and ever to hold.

Thank you, Jesus, for helping me stay
On the path of wisdom's way.

Vesta M Neale
MOTIVATION

Strange, that last evening after
leaving my work,
I went home with the vigor and
excitement of a young Turk,
Because I knew that ere the set of the
sun
My energies would be expended in
what I call fun.

Although the day's waning hours
greater efforts require,
than those, (when I'm honest with
self), I put out for hire,
still, my energy levels carry on as if
fueled by fire.

But come morning tide, sleep
dimming my brain,
Muscles aching with pain,
I swap bed for work in a daily refrain.

I ask myself then, "What motivates
this body of mine?"
Does innate spirit elevate self to the
headiness of wine,
when avocation has no linkage to
demands of time?

Thus, is it prestige, challenge, desire
for gain,
rising me from my bed, sleep-starved,
to work in pain?
Or does my sense of duty leave no
latitude to shirk
those expectations, taking me,
protestingly, back to work?

Shoua Nina Yang
WHAT HAPPENED TO FOREVER

To Dau Huynh: This is especially for you. It may be simple, but true . . . Forever and always, I love you.

What happens now that all your
dreams have come true?
The dreams without me . . .
You've always told me,
we were meant to be and
nothing was going to tear us
apart . . .
Now you broke my heart,
and your love, you gave to
another.

What happens now that you want to
be free?
Am I supposed to let you go,
when being with you is
everything I've got to be?
How was it so easy for you to walk
away,
and pretend there was
never a you and me?

What happens now that you love
another?
Tell me Baby,
what happened to forever?

Catherine E Reynolds
THE SQUIRREL

On a cold winter morning
While walking through the woods
I saw a little squirrel
Scampering fast as he could

He stopped at a tree
Then he looked around
And picked up a nut
From the snow-covered ground

He nibbled at the shell
Exposed the meat inside
He saw me watching him
And scampered off to hide

I like this little squirrel
Like to see him run
Just as a little playmate
He was lots of fun

I walked to the edge
He stopped in his tracks
The squirrel seemed to sense
That I would be back

T Grenz
LITTLE PROM QUEEN

Born from the start to break the boys hearts, voted to be MISS POPULARITY and how she got the title was so easy to see. When 18 came around, Little Prom Queen left her little town. Holdin' her dreams of big city life, she'd find a rich man to make her his wife.

'Cause life ain't cheap Little Prom Queen knew, she's need someone to buy her clothes and her shoes. And when it got hard, to live her dreams of gold, hubby's cash helped to keep the spoon in her nose.

She used to say, that it was only for fun, but now her little habit had her on the run. She never tried to quit the thing she couldn't hide, until it had her all messed up inside. But by then it was too late Little Prom Queen, had sealed her fate. She gave it everything even her diamonds and gold, and it left nothing but a dark, hollow, cold.

So late one night, after crossing the edge, Little Prom Queen took a walk off a high ledge. She couldn't go back, she couldn't go home and she couldn't find a way to make it leave her alone . . . Little Prom Queen, rest easy tonite, don't you know? . . . Your future looks bright.

Thi C Nguyen
BEWILDERMENT

Why can't this world be pure?
To have all life's diseases cured.
Why isn't there a sky full of white
doves?
To further enhance our peace and
love.
Why do we all have eyes but still
can't see?
A better life in the world, just to be
joy and to be free.
Why do we have so many books and
tools?
And yet many people in the world are
still poor.
Why is the world now has so many
jobs?
But all in the work of blowing up the
globe.
Why can't I be left alone with my
thoughts and tea?
Just me and my secluded sand castle
right by this chaotic sea.

Jeanette Marie Villalobos
A LOSER CAN WIN

This poem is dedicated to myself, because no one believes in me the way I believe.

As I lie there thinking trying to sleep
tossing and turning as the night
grows deep
my mind seems to be on things that
I've done
all the good times and bad that were
supposably fun
the partying was great, the streets
were alright
now my life is growing, time my eyes
see the light
the path I've walked has been
nothing but sin
now I want to show the world what a
loser can win
but what I hear is laughing voices
what I see is people making my
choices
they think of me as young and
carefree
I will show them what my eyes really
can see
I feel in my soul a different tomorrow
the time has come to end my sorrows
even though they made my choices
I'll erase their laughing voices
they believe what they want but
seeing is believing
all I can say my goal is achieving
I'll never stop knocking on the door
of hope
the way I believe its life I do cope
even though my path walked has
been sin
I won't stop believing a loser can
win.

Alan Frame
EXISTENCE

I see visions . . .
Visions of a past holding lifeless
memories.
Visions of a future most elusive from
my reach.
Yet I do have these seconds which
are held in the present.
Fleeting seconds which are most
intimate to me.
For my life is but an inanimate spec
on the scale of global time.
But unto myself I am the Great
Thinker;
For I am the creator of these seconds
held in my hands.
I may influence minds, command a
great peoples, or simply ponder my
own existence.
I am the great manipulator of lives . . .
of existence . . . of time. . .
For you see I am man who fears his
own mortality.
I seek to break the anonymity of time
by creating a lasting mark within the
world.
I aim to justify my own existence
through the processes of my mind.
Yet still . . . I am man . . . and I have
only seconds.

James Long
EAT

Poor, and starving
Did enough carving,
That's not art, they will say;
Call it what you like;
I will say;
It brings home what I call pay.
Pay we say; I don't eat hay.
I wish to stay here all day, and
say a prayer it won't move till I see
what's near
to me a drink of water.
Handed to me by my father.

Arthur Salazar
NEAT-MEET

You move me to speak words of love till the thrill of meeting you once again wins my heart. Start the motion then that raps a June tune on my chest, a love sonnet which maps my voice in synch—just think (!)—in blossoms pink.

Chart this chap who departs from the best art to paint a bonnet onna lovely lass. Croon to the moon, o'fella, you yella rhapsody so classic it kills hate-potions. What a notion! Link your arresting fantasies to me, sweet tart, so I can fan the flames of your red-hot flower drink that on the hour sinks me further into your rapport. Adore yon oceans, lust-lotions, the quaint choice of happenin' Bellas.

Awesome monsoons soon grate their sways into cresting melodies of "we." Games of passion irrationally played, scores of dead-heated players over-ripe and souring, showering themselves in troublesome lagoons, while beguiling missing links ain't thrillin' as one.

How come? Some people are dumbfounded wanderers pondering at noon aimless busts. Nuts to them! Your mission is impartial to guests who eschew soliloquies yet send whores to a gory destiny. Saints be groovin'. My mind afore to score the songfest in July. Till then goodbye.

Tasha Hrees
I SEE A STRANGER

To my Mom and Dad, who may not understand me, but love me anyway.

Sometimes when I look in the mirror,
I see a stranger.
I don't see me, my face, or my hair.

It's scary,
not to see yourself.
Why does this happen?

I'm really no different,
I haven't changed.
I don't think.

The face I see is not mine,
though there is none like it.
Who does it belong to?

I see a different face,
not young, not old,

not harmed in any way.

When I glance in the mirror,
I see a stranger.
Why?

Phyllis Schuster
THE HOMELESS CHILD

This is dedicated to all the unwed teenage mothers who have decided to have, keep and raise their babies.

A child was born just the other day,
many years ago and far away.
In a lonely stable with a crib of hay,
should we keep our son or give him away?
With no place to call his own,
will you let this child into your home?
What is this star that shines above,
a message from God, does this mean love?
From afar an angel sings,
Jesus Christ was born a king!

Phyllis A Wheelock
ACCEPTANCE

This poem is dedicated to my Higher Power. He is always there for me.

Like a tree standing naked and outwardly barren—
Gray sentinel on the earth's frozen surface;
So I, contemplate life—isolated in my stark pain.
Unable yet, to reach out with frozen heart—to the Higher Light.

Hands gnarled into tight, hard knots,
Face ashen, life suspended,
Held upright only by hidden roots
Vulnerable to the seasons of life

I struggle for survival—seeking the elusive meaning
To this harsh existence
Ever buffeted by raging storms, I must yield—
Bow graciously to a power greater than I, else snap and die

As I yield in surrender to this omnipotent power—
I find a warmth formerly shunned
As I stretch forth my limbs to feel the Heavenly Rays—
My sap, once again—begins to flow.

My smile of new found trust
Blossoms—drawing others near.
My body sways—skirts rustling softly
Like leaves in a gentle breeze

As acceptance comes into its spring.

Fran Doak
CHRISTMAS WONDER

To Tim, my own wonder, my son.

It's Christmas time,
and so good friends gather.
Although, outside,
it is cold, cold weather.
We'll laugh and we'll love,
and share in the cheer;
And very soon—
Will bring in the New Year!
So lift high your glasses
in one heartfelt toast;
To health, love and happiness,
so fortunate, we boast.
For all these good things
are from Heaven above;
And would not be possible
without His Son's love.

Sandra O'Brien
BUT DADDY

To my "Daddy" (1945-1987) always my rock to cling to, and to my brother Steven (1969-1989) always my soft spot to land on.

"Close your eyes and I'll be there,
it'll be like I never left."

"But Daddy what if closing my eyes
is all that I have left?"

"Hush now, 'Sugar' you're doing
fine, it's kind'a like a test."

"But Daddy I'm scared, things are all
wrong and I promise I'm trying my best."

"I know you are 'Sweetheart,' I
understand, things are going to be rough."

"But Daddy, I'm frightened and so
confused, it's so hard for me to be tough."

"I know it is, 'Honey,' but you have to
try, you're all your mother's got."

"But Daddy, what about Steven, why
did he leave? Mom and me miss him a lot."

"I know you do, 'Princess,' but he's
here with me, think of him as coming home."

"But Daddy, why can't I come too?
Here I feel so much alone."

"Close your eyes and I'll be there,
it'll be like I never left."

"But Daddy, what if closing my eyes
is all that I have left?"

Mary I McFetridge
JAYSON

To my big brother Jay, who has never compromised his gentle, sweet soul. With admiration and love.

He's my brother and my goal
And he is quiet.
He's deeper and fuller
And he is gentle.
He's scarred and used
And he is forgiving.
He's closer and better
And he is cleansed.
He's critiqued and belittled
And he is mighty.
He is the shelter
for the ignorant around him.
He holds them up
so that they can walk on him.
He lifts them high
And they block him from the sun.
He pushes them forward
so that they can win.
He stands below
And he smiles.

Phyllis Murray Carson
LIFE

Life is a brittle thread—
The friend we had today
Is gone tomorrow.
The keenest joys we find
Are very quickly
Turned to sorrow.

Life is a fragile thing—
Like a bubble, it may soar,
Then quickly break,
Or it may linger longer,
At last to disappear,
Though soon or late.

Life is uncertainty—
Just when our lives may end
We do not know.
How wise, then, so to live,
That we will be at any time,
Prepared to go.

Phyllis Murray Carson
OUR LITTLE ROSEBUD
To our little David—August 1, 1944.

A tender little rosebud
Entrusted to our care—
Its petals still unfolded,
Fragile, sweet, and rare.

Plucked from God's great garden,
Still wet with heaven's dew,
This precious little flower
Was given to me and you.

We'll cherish it forever,
Surround it with our love,
And pray that it will sweetly bloom
For our dear God above.

Phyllis Murray Carson
THE FADED BUD

Clutched tight in his tiny hand
A faded bud he brought,
Withered and broken it was,
A treasure rare, he thought.

"See what I give you, Mommie—
It's 'cause I love you so!"
And the mother's heart rejoiced
For the care her baby showed.

And is it not so with us—
Frail creatures of the earth,
What gift can we give back to God
Who lends to us each breath?

And yet in His great heart of love
He ofttimes longs to see
Some token of our love to Him,
However small it be.

Phyllis Murray Carson
A THING OF BEAUTY IS A JOY FOREVER

These are the things that I love best:
The mist of an early dawn,
The thought of tranquil earth at rest
After turbulent storm.

These are the things that I love best:
The tender blue of peaceful sky,
The majesty of a mountain crest,
The green of its gentle slopes.

The velvet stillness of the night,
The touch of a golden moon
Caressing the sea, and making bright
The sands along the shore.

These are the things that I love best—
Because they speak to me
Of the peaceful trust and tranquil rest
That I find, my God, in Thee.

Vanelle Daugherty
THE CATERPILLAR

Every time I approach a tree
My alter-ego says to me,
The leaf at the top is the one you want,
Climb, keep climbing, it's a very short jaunt.
I cannot tell to whom I appeal,
Life's a kaleidoscope. What is real?
Can we honestly look in the mirror and say,
I'm like this, and like this, each and every day.
Me? I think it's natural for each of us to doubt,
To struggle and struggle to let the real being out.
The cycle of life from lowest form to us
Breaking free from our cocoon, the butterfly, a must!

Cheri Lattimore
LIFE WITHOUT YOU

My life
my soul
it swells
like a sponge,
I absorb you
I consume your smell
life without you
lonely, dark and cold
my prison, my Hell
I try to start again
but my heart
feels the pain
nothing will be the same

Donald Kihm
PROGRESS

Tiny,
fragile hard,
resting in a corner—
a thought rushes forward,
previewed before my eyes:
tiny,
the gentle winged,
rock soft creature
unlocks mysteries.
Metamorphosed,
I am slowly
becoming.

John G Padilla
COMMON FEAR

Dedicated To: Mother Emma A. Padilla and Alice Barreras.

Hush! Do I hear footsteps
out in the dark?
Am I seeing shadows
beside the park?

What lurks? Man or beast?
Oh, please! How I wish they
would not persist.

It draws near.
It will not touch me, this I have vowed.
Would it help to pray aloud?
I will not go out; I am wise.
This horrible thing could
cause my demise.

I am speechless; my nerves are tense.
Do you suppose it's all a mistake perchance?
My Lord! I <u>have</u> been a victim
of my own imagination.
A victim of my own
frustration

I <u>have</u> been wrong; there is nothing I see
nothing I hear. My enemy?
Plain and common fear.

—Gaspar

William "Stan" Perdue
REMEMBRANCE

To: Bonney Jean, The "Angel" I will always Love!!

There's a portrait engraved deep in my mind,
of a lady who has altered my vitality.
Such a task to formulate that delicate line,
intervening apparition and absolute actuality.

An account illuminated by beams of sincerity,

from the depths of a miraculous soul.
An eternal flame kindled by love and caring,
impassioned bright and warm, the essence of purest gold.

Each time we touch, adoration countermands all emotions;
sadness and disconsolation move aside.
Thoughts abound with joys and wondrous notions,
as a sea of phenomenon rushes to over–ride.

And as we make memorable intrinsic love,
rythmatic with a celestial symphony of affection.
Soaring as if on the wings of a resplendent dove,
She and I, each to the other a desired reflection.

Patrick M Hogan
THE POND
I see a man in front of me
I ask of him "How can it be?"
He's incapable of loving from scars that never healed
He's wary of the truth, and feelings he reveals
Once caring fingers, now callous hands
I ask myself "Who is this man?"
The cause of hurt and broken hearts
I notice his heart now torn apart
As I turn away, then look again
I see it's me who is this man
As the pond's reflection stares back at me
I ask myself "How could it be?"

Carol Zimet

Carol Zimet
A SMILING PUP
Never trust a smiling pup
He's smarter than you think,
If he were well-behaved all day
He'd look at you and wink.
He'd stand up on his hind legs
And beg you for a treat,
Wag his tail, lick your face
His act just can't be beat.
But should he hide beneath your bed
And peep out with a tilted head,
You'd better scout around to see
What mischief he has done.
And when you find out what he chewed
Begin with lesson number one.
Though this cute little bundle has captured your heart
Be firm, be strong, with him be smart
For a better dog he'll grow up to be,
When he's learned that you're the boss, not he.

Carol Zimet
ADVICE ON TENSION
When you get that mid–day slump
And you're feeling rather low,
When your muscles start to jump
And your tensions grow and grow;
When everyone around you
Begins to sound absurd,
And even your psychiatrist
Can't come up with a word;
The time has come for you, to
Stop being so neurotic,
'Cause if you "overdue" things
You can become psychotic.
Persistence is a good trait
To help you reach your goal;
But don't go off the deep end,
It can only wreck your soul.

Karin Kamm
CHILDHOOD RAP
Well you remember Mickey Mouse and Donald too,
That funny looking dog named Scooby-doo.
Those little blue creatures from Gargamel's turf,
Yah you know them, they are the Smurfs.
And there's Gilligan and the Skipper too,
The ones who sailed the ocean blue.
Good old Cookie and all his friends,
On the Street when the morning begins.
They all work hard. They never stop
To bring us memories of our childhood rap.

Heather Mancini
I DON'T KNOW WHY
I don't know why the sky is blue, the sea is too, I don't know why a cow goes moo, but I sure know I love you!

Debra G Marion
ODE TO SPRING
The birds are singing in the treetops,
As the sun shines gloriously and warm,
And in the morning, the glistening dewdrops
Cause the flowers to bloom, and alarm
the world with their beauty.

With the soft, swaying, gentle breezes
And the fragrance of a newly awakened earth,
All sense of civilization leaves us,
As if undergoing a new re-birth,
to a bright and beautiful world.

Oh Spring, the changes that you bring
To sun, soil, and sky,
Compels all God's creatures to sing,
And also to wonder why,
Spring is here but a short while.

Melody Sisson
A ROSE
I'd like to dedicate this poem to Robert Minter for the encouragement and support to write poems.

A red rose is a sign of passion
A white rose is a sign of love
A red rose is two warm lips gently brushing against each other
A white rose is two happy people loving each other honestly
A cream-colored rose is passion, love, happiness, and honesty of two people

Margaret Lawson
FEELINGS
Dedicated to my son Steve Overton.

I know your pain.
I know your sorrow.
I know your feeling of desertion.
See I've been there.

Joan G Meiter
MY BELOVED FRIEND
To Bill, my mysterious, unique and eternal friend.

My life is empty and my eyes filled with tears; You were my Beloved Friend, for so many years!

No more laughter or secrets to share; When I needed someone, you were always there!

A diamond ring is not on my finger; But our precious moments, will always linger!

When my days are lonely and my nights are long; You softly whisper, you can't be weak, you must be strong!

May you rest in peace and be content; Your life on earth, was well-spent!

You always said "We'll be together someday"; If God is willing, it will happen that way!

My love for you will never end; How I miss you, My Beloved Friend!

Mark Long
YOU BLOW ME AWAY
Dedicated to the North Atlantic.

The tide's rushing in
The boats are all in
I'm near the bay
'Cause you blow me away,
You blow me away.

The tide's rolling back
Safe from attack
I want to stay
But you blow me away.

I've been on this shore
I've been here before
I'll keep coming back,
But you blow me away
You blow me away.

My sails in the bay
Waves light my way
What more can I say,
You blow me away.

Marina Viegas
SOMEDAY
To Giggles. You are always in my heart.

When you walked into my life
You made me realize that I could love again
You and I became just one
We shared laughter and tears

After all the years that had gone by
I love you more than my own life
Your loving ways, tender care and sometimes
Just by looking at me you say it all that I need to know

We are not together anymore, but in my heart
And soul you shall always be there for all
Eternity I miss you and I would love to be with
You, but for now we have to be apart

If only some people could understand that love
Has no choices but, when two people love each
Other they should be together no matter what
And, someday you and I will join hands will
Love and cherish one another until the
End of time

Sandy Neal
CHILD OF MINE
To my son, Lon. With love, Mom.

He grew up
Right before my eyes
Or maybe, when I wasn't looking
I only turned my back for a moment.

I hold out my hand
He turns and walks away
Will he come back
Another day?

Visions in sight
Quite different than mine
We don't talk
Can't find the time.

It's raining
Even when the sun shines
Lost in his own world
This child of mine.

He wants his own space
I only knew this child
Now he has a different face
Almost like that, of a stranger.

Marceana Cunningham
WHERE ARE YOU
For my Daughter Samantha: I finally found you all my love, Mommy.

I can feel you in my heart; though I can't feel you in my belly
I can see your face; though I can't yet touch it
I can hear you cry, yet no one is there
I can hear you calling mommy and daddy, yet you aren't there
I see you playing with your toys, but where are you
I see you take your first step, but where are you
I can see and imagine all the wonderful things you will do
I love you, but where are you

Donna Polkowski
ONCE UPON A TIME
This poem is dedicated to my friend, Ray.

Once upon a time
You walked in my dream,

You took away my freedom
And let it float in a steam,

Forever I'll be yearning
To see your enchanting smile,

Please release me from love torture
Like a bird let me fly,

But you don't know
That in my dream,

When you were passing by
I let you in . . .

Lucy M Holt
TO FIND MY BIRTHPLACE
I walked and walked down by the creek.
I searched and searched to try and seek
Out the place where I was born.
I didn't think this would do any harm.
So I went back down on the farm.
I walked up and down among the trees,
Waded through the grass and all the leaves.
I picked up a stone and tossed it away.
I wondered among the trees another day.

Walked down near a spring which ran so cool,
Walked by a building that once was a school.
There to the left lay some old stones
Where once a building sat upon.
They said "Now here it is" with a wave of an arm,
This is the place where you were born.
I think I will go back down on the farm
Among the trees and all the hills,
Down near the spring, and to hear the whippoorwills.

Jenifer Wall
NEVER ENDING FRIENDSHIP
We have drifted apart
But you are still in my heart
Our friendship is remaining there
Even though you are probably not aware
Your time has faded for me
So I'll just let you be
You want to stand on your own
Leaving me lost and alone
Time has grown shorter for us
Making things unable to discuss
Your life still seems to go on
Even though I'm gone
This could change our individual fates
But I hope someday you will find my friendship
still awaits.

Raymond F Rogers
SAMSON
Immense tectonic plates, afloat on magma seas,
Scrape against the masses of each other,
All moving in response to forces
Roiling 'neath their huge, expansive hulls.

As enormous ships of earth and stone are rocked,
They jam with sturdy force till they are interlocked,
Keystones forming temporary stays of seismic storms.
At last, the keystones break; thus earthquakes are formed.

Far below the tranquil covering,
A quiet foe regains his strength.
In an upheaval long ago
His locks were shorn, releasing potency.

Samson grinds in the prison house.
Who could guess
His power to distress
The revelers upon the temple roof?

When pillars fall, on which a structure stands,
The whole then crumbles, with a thunderous sound—
Samson held great strength from Heaven in his hands;
Dagon's house came tumbling to the ground!

John B Silvester
THROUGH THE LOOKING GLASS
Seasons pass in cycles
Lifetimes pass in years
Happiness in smiles
Sadness in tears
History is preserved in writings
Music in placid tones
Freedom in sacrifice of life
Epitaphs in marble stone
Dreams are kept in secret
Thoughts in diaries
Vows are kept in silence
The past in memories
Time is etched upon the earth
Age on windswept sands
Tribute is etched on monuments
Survival on wrinkled hands
Compassion is expressed in kindness
Love in poetry
Grief is expressed in lonely tears
Sorrow in elegy

Franqui B G R
INDEFINITE
Everybody has something of someone,
But nobody has everything of anyone.
And no one who is someone
Would want much of anything of another.
I wish everyone had either one thing or none;
I know we have many, but thank God not all.
I wonder . . . would anybody be happy
With simply a few or several?
Neither my two friends nor I would want any,
But each agreed
We'd probably be nothing without.
So both they and I simply accept some;
Therefore, we have enough and enough is enough.

Wendy Bradley
LIFE'S TOO SHORT
Three friends went out to have fun
and all friends had a gun.
They went down by the pond
and were shooting at everything around.

They were having the best of times
and swore they would always remember
this night, how did they know?
Because in a matter of minutes,
one of the friends had scared another,
the other turned and fired—
a child blew a child away.
The three became two
and that's how it would stay.

Life's too short for someone who was only 18
and makes one wonder how his last moments were like
Did he know he was dying?
Did he think of his life and what he's done?
Or did he think of what he will never do?

All one knows, is that this friend is gone
and is a forever reminder that
LIFE'S TOO SHORT.

Viviane M Janda
THE BEST GRANDMOTHER
I know you are not my real mother
but you are twice as much
You're twice as nice and
you also have that special grandma's touch.

You are very kind and very sweet
and you have that special grandma's treat
You love and care for me
as I do for You.

We walk together upon the sea
we walk together too, I love you very much
and I know you love me too
because we'll be together
forever me and You.

J F Cronin
HOW SLEEP THE BRAVE NOW?
The Gettysburg sky is blue and gray,
A quiet union of colors once at bay.
Beyond the plain distant hills peer,
Once witness to terrible battle here.

Once rocked by cavalry—corps;
Air smote by cannon's roar.
Turf's green carpet furrowed rust-stained:
Live plowshares reaping death and pain.

Normandy, 'Nam—sad repetitions;
Bodies fertilized—fruitless missions!
How sleep the brave now,
Agonizing each broken peace vow?

This plain, "hallowed" at great cost
Surrounds a campus here Future' host:
Students midst Past's sorrows.
Pray they seek peaceful tomorrows.

How sleep the brave now,
Agonizing each broken peace vow?

Dawn E Steenburg
LOVE FOR ONLY YOU
I still see the winter in your eyes
And feel the coldness in your heart;
It seems of no concern to you
That now we're far apart.

I guess you really meant it
When you up and said, "Goodbye!"
It all happened to suddenly
I never had time to cry.

But now time is all I have
And cry is all I do;
Though it's been one year to date
I still think only of you.

Love to me could never come easy
Once I feel in it, I was caught;
Even if you didn't love me back
No other love could be sought.

So I'll continue to live my life
Filled with love for only you;
And hope that one day soon
You'll feel love for me too

Lorraine Gravem
THINK TWICE
If I had known what was ahead of me,
I wouldn't have been so brave.
Now I can see what a waste of years,
Just to end up in my grave.
I would think twice
Before I'd give my body, soul and mind
To be used all through the years
By someone who was so unkind.

I always thought if I stuck with it,
And gave it all that I had,
That eventually it would pay off,
And I would be happy, wealthy and glad.

So after living my life,
If someone should ask my advice to give,
It would be, "Think twice, do what makes you happy,
For you only have one life to live."

Tracy A Perdue
THE DAY THE SUN SHONE
The day the sun shone
The day the wind blew
The day happiness came
Why? Everyone
knew
The day the war ended
soldiers made a choice
Go home to your families,
love and rejoice
The day the sun shone
The day the wind blew
from happiness they
cried
Their dreams had come
true.

Vernell B Yates
SUMMER MORNING
Down in the lane where the green grass grows
Over the stone wall rambles the rose
Tall by the stream stands the willow tree
Softly sighing, it weeps for me
Shimmering lays the meadow in buttercup gold
Diamonds of dew their petal enfold
Vividly blue is the sky overhead
Cradling cotton clouds in her bed
Mother duck waddles down to the pond
With her balls of down trailing along
The sheep in the meadow, the cows in the corn,
Make a beautiful picture of a summer morn

Vay "79"

Lorraine Scott
A MOTHER'S LOVE

Dedicated to my three children, Patricia, Byron and Douglas

'Tis oft been said that a Mother's love
is more precious than silver or gold,
For although it cannot be bought nor spent
its values are many-fold.

When each of you were laid in my arms
'tho your timing may have been wrong,
The miracle of love filled your Mother's heart
for her babs brought it along.

This love, my dears, is willingly given
to you each, in an equal part,
Although I cannot share a "material" gift
this poem comes from my heart.

'Tho many miles apart are we
my love spans each long mile,
My greatest gift this year would be
your faces at our door, in smiles.

May God Bless each one of you
with good health, happiness and
cheer,
And aid you in your hopes and dreams
all though another New Year.

"Mother"

Monique Cordilla Dougherty
I HAD GOLDEN WINGS
I was born believeing I was a
demigod
with wings of gold and love to give.
Reality quickly taught me
love cannot be unrequited,
love has to be returned.
So many chances I could have taken
but never really did.
I could have said I love you
risking rejection or something else.
The love I had froze.
I learned to cry myself to sleep and
keep warm with blankets.
The tears began to fall
for happiness, sadness, joy, sorrow
or no reason at all.
And tears,
they cause my wings to deliquesce.
I no longer soar
my wings are well past broken.
One day
my wings will be gone.

Frank Paul Graffeo
I LOVE MAKING LOVE TO YOU
Honey, when you're near me,
I love making love.
Honey, when I touch you,
I see the heavenly stars above.

Darling, when I caress you,
I find heaven, in my arms.
Then when I kiss you,
It ignites, all your charms.

How can I resist you,
With words you never say.
Your lovely eyes, just tell me,
Come on baby, let's play.

Love is not all sex,
It's a fire in a nest.
The moon and the stars, reveal the
heavenly skies,
Your love and kisses, have my
heart imply.

My eyes delight, in see-ing you,
Your warmth tells me, that it's
all true.
I love making love, to you,
I love making love, to you.

Penny J Gilcrist
IT'S TIME TO GO ON

This is dedicated to all my family that has went on to meet our Father: My Father, Adeleno Oliver Sr, Grandmother Cleo Johnson, Aunt Sylvia Hattan and Uncle Qubet Oliveria.

This is the day, for no more worries
& and no more pains
Time to go on & let this body remain
I'm FREE from all these worldly
things left behind
Now I have joy and peace of mind
Like a dove or a passing white cloud
My rejoice of freedom can be heard
out loud
When an angel appeared to me that
night
It told me, "Don't be afraid, come to
the light"
With the golden gates wide open for
me
My soul begun to feel so peacefully
Now that I'm FREE, my soul will
roam
For you see, I'm here with others,
I'm not alone
I knew, I'd leave you with sorrow in
your heart today
But God will fix it day by day
Soon you'll look back & you will see
There's no better place then I'd rather
be
Here at home, with my Father by my
side, holding my hand and seeing the
smile upon his face
I want you all to know, this is such a
beautiful place
So don't feel worry that I'm gone
from you this way
For it was my time, the place and the
day
To take my Father's hand
And walk with him throughout this
land

Penny J Gilcrist
FEELINGS FOR YOU
I never thought I would ever need
someone in my life again
Until I met you and all the joy and
pleasure begin
When I feel you touch me & see your
smiling face looking at me
My heart begins to feel a special way
you see
It's like spring, when love appears &
everything around you is so
wonderful, and your heart feels so
right
You are my sunshine, my guiding
light
I know that in life things happen for a
reason
It's you and I the right time, place
and the season
To fall in love and yet be the best of
friends
Just remember my love, you have a
special place deep within
My soul, my heart and my mind
Thoughts of you will be with me at
all times
I love you and wanted you to know,
even though words alone cannot
express how I truly feel for you today
It's something about you that makes
me feel this way

Elizabeth Foss
CHILDHOOD
Childhood is Eden to all
over-worked adults, a place where
Mom is God and the ice cream
trucks stops all.
Childhood is the largest classroom
where the Teacher never sleeps,
the student's imagination is the
only limit and grade.
Childhood, if looked upon fondly
is a place to which we may never
return, but should always try to
recapture.
Where else could truth and justice
triumph but in a mind so clouded
by innocence, and where else
might a soul find peace but in a
body free of sin?
Childhood is an unmarked slate to
which we all must leave our
mark; good, bad, long, or
short—we all must leave our
mark.

Leigh Frey

Leigh Frey
FOREVER FRIENDS
In appreciation for the many qualities that make you a wonderful friend sharing good times with laughter and dividing the hard times with tears for trying to understand and somehow knowing how to help I offer you this expression for always knowing when words need to be passed you are forever a true friend

Franchesca
NO ONE TO WARM HER HANDS

To Anita Louise, who believed.

And there was no one to warm her
hands,
to quell the creeping cold inside,
that spread from her very soul
and in her hands chose to reside.

She fought to work out the numbness
caused more than just in part
by abuse that had been heaped upon
her tired and weary heart.

For she had reached for the warmth,
the radiance,
she had learned to know as man,
and had been comforted and gathered
strength
for yet another stand
against the onslaughts of the day
that had ripped at her core,
and, like a child seeking love,
had gone back for more
and found the door barred against her.
She would not be allowed to stand
closely, nor lovingly,
with the race of man.
And there was no one . . . to warm . . .
her hands.

D'Anna Hammond
CONFUSION
So much confusion
In the heart and in the mind
It feels like a brutal abusing

This pain is so deep
Everything is gone
There's nothing left to keep

It's gotten so bad
I can't handle it
The rough times, I thought I already
had

I want out
Don't want this anymore
There's not a doubt
No one would ever care
They'd never miss me
It's not like, their heart would ever
tear

No, it's me, just me
Who feels so much pain
Nobody else will see

They don't want to
They're always hiding from the truth
But I know what to do

I know what's right
I'll end this pain for me
I'll take this life, you'll see

Louann Walker-Huston
LOVE
Love is a very sacred thing—
A gentle kiss
Wedding rings
The pitter-patter of little feet
A quiet place for to retreat
Special song that means so much
Star-lit nights
Loving touch
The tender look for you to see
Together is the place to be.

D'Anna Hammond
EMOTION
There's so much emotion
The joy, then all the pain
Caused from all this commotion

I don't understand
How could so much pain
Fit into this heart of mine
People say "Don't worry, it'll be fine"

But they don't feel this
And all I know is
I miss

All the happiness of before
They say God made our lives
Then God,
What is all this pain for?

Misti Thiel
GRANDPA
Bitter tears
cry out at
the injustice
my heart
feels
we were never
allowed the time
to appreciate
the gifts we might
have shared
if our generations
had been closer
together,
my future had
no place in your past
and age
kept
us apart
until time
took you away
forever.

James R Anians
WHILE THE LEAVES ARE FALLING

This poem is dedicated to my parents, Jim and Eileen; my grandmothers, Madeline and Mezzie; and to my family and friends for their encouragement and support.

Let's go for a stroll and reminisce
while the memories linger,
for the autumn of our lives, even
though uninvited, is with us
and summer is but a shadow.
For this is the time to ponder,

to imagine
to wonder,
to cry,
to hope,
to realize
that the insignificant become
mementos—a wilted balloon,
a torn comic,
a smile . . .
I wish there were time for another swim, but it's too late, too cold.
So let's gather the leaves of all shapes and colors
before they are scattered
unnoticed and forgotten . . .
Oh God, how I look forward to the Spring!

Doris N Martinez
BLESSED YOUTH
As a student, I went through hardships—but I never flunked!
The loud song of roosters, at the break of dawn
Was my daily sign to start getting up.

While I combed my hair, I smiled in front of the mirror,
My mind enchanted, by the lovely music
Played by the birds at the windowsill.

A cup of hot coffee rested at the side,
While my hands broke the bread into bits
To feed my little friends at the windowsill.

I took my book bag, rushed out like a storm
Crossing the streets and corners,
Saying "Hi!" to someone, and waving to others in a happy mood.

Reaching class on time, I sat at my desk,
A pen in my right hand, a pad laid below—
Ready to grasp and conquer that subject unknown.

My mind evolved there, while the instructor talked;
Trusting, alert and perceiving what the teacher taught.

At the end of class I piled all my notes securely tight,
And treasured them with much love and pride.

Knowledge *is* a treasure, needed to attain wisdom.
Happy be the man who acquires it!

Doris N Martinez
CROSSING THE LONG ISLAND EXPRESSWAY
Vespertine chill in the midst of the fall,
Crossing with much caution
The traffic-jammed road.

Weary, bored and hopeless
I Looked in search of mountains,
But couldn't find one.

Just to my amazement . . . bordering the sky,
The clouds began to create
A chain of majestic peaks
On the mountaintops.

I flew to one peak, looking right below.
A lake in the midst stopped me from sliding to the one across.

Waiting on expectantly for one hill coming forth
That looked like a bear in a sitting form.

I jumped and looked down to a peach-red sea
That swayed, in its midst, a marvelous boat.

I boarded the vessel in search of a different horizon,
Not dismayed a bit by the missing crew.

I was the courageous captain of the ship—
Bold, strong and determined to conquer the sea.

The sound of a van's horn shook me, taking me away . . .

Dorothy Moase
LAST NIGHT AT THE OCEAN
I had my last view of the ocean last night,
Was a wondrous, beautiful, magnificent sight.
The waves were rolling with surf huge and white,
Small boats were sailing toward shore for the night.

The sounds of the ocean are unique in their way,
The sea lions bark as they frolic and play.
White sea gulls fly over and squawk all the day.
And the splash of the water on rocks comes to stay.

There's a smell near the ocean, of salt and of fish,
There's a musty, yet clean swell, that makes my heart wish
That somehow, someday, I might get my wish
Of going out on the ocean to catch a big fish.

The sights near the ocean are different somehow,
There is seaweed and kelp, and surfers right now,
There are ground squirrels and pigeons and gulls on the bow,
Fishing boats, sailboats and boats that you row.

As I stood at the ocean watching last night,
My heart thrilled with the odor, the sounds and the sight.
As I stood by the shore of that ocean last night,
I revered and was thankful for God and His might.

Stephen L Mugrage
THE LIFEBOAT
I sail the seas in a lifeboat
not a beautiful cruising vessel
But the boat that I have stays adrift
for the boards are strong on my mighty trestle.

Though the waters may rage havoc
on the tiny boat I'm in
They couldn't defeat me, my boat is strong
and I will stay adrift in the end.

Sometimes the boat I ride in
can be maneuvered off its course
But soon I find my path again
and for my wrongful ways, I show no remorse

Through arid sun and raging storm
I always pay my dues
Until one day the boat I sail
sinks in the ocean blue.

My constitution are the sails
my emotions are the mast
My past mistakes, the anchor
though my past mistakes are vast.

I have no crew, I am alone
and alone is the way I go
For no one can help me on the quest of life
for my path is yet unknown.

But still I sail on through the waters of life
and survive through trying times
Until I find my final port
where my life can be sublime.

john anthony plaskett
companion ?
if you sometimes catch me
looking too intently
please don't take offense
for it is with loving admiration
that i gaze upon your countenance
perhaps this view is a reminder
of a maiden dancing on Nubian plains
or of a glance at a virgin in a passing 'Jung'
yet some mystique draws me to you
as the moth to the light
my desire is to encounter you
the journey i know
would be a delight
your eyes testify
to all you have to give
oh, if you only be receptive
to all i hold within

Angela R Calhoun
LOVE'S BROTHER
From town to town he travels,
He's in every all at once,
Through him a tale unravels,
It's everyone's soul he wants.

Dark forces, teams of slander,
Caution looses and words fly,
Hostile dreams rise and canter,
Flames burn bright within the eye.

Roads leading through history,
Of much hardship and of woe,
All lead back to his misery,
His brother, LOVE, is he? No!

Billie Jean Wohlert
JESUS CAME THEIR WAY
By the Sea of Galilee,
The Sun shown brightly,
The Sand shifted slightly,
As Jesus came walking their way.

They knew not what he wanted,
As they watched him undaunted,
As Jesus came walking their way.
For these men were fishermen,
They had cast their nets again and again,
Bringing in their catch for the day.

Jesus came up to Andrew and Simon,
With words that were ever to guide them,
He began to say "Follow me and I will make you Fishers of Men."

They took not a moment,
Their nets they forsook,
They followed Jesus that day,
Without a backward look.

Jesus is calling to us today,
To come and follow him, to go his way.
May God grant that we will answer,
and say, "Lord, I will obey."

Schelle Roberts
A LOST SOUL
At last you see the moon in the darkness
The dull yellow shine cast upon a face
But, of who, you wonder as you walk down a narrow path
of stones, dried leaves, and sticks that crack
A pale face looms before you,
perhaps it's a reflection
of a face known too well to the soul
In desperation you run for that face you do not know
It fades into the eerie darkness of life's cold room
The moon still shines and cast and eerie dull shine
upon you
As you wonder who it was with the pale face that your soul knew well

Dorothy E Gaines

Dorothy E Gaines
WONDROUS NIGHT

Dedicated to the Memory of the late FLOYD REXFORD GAINES.

Sweet Wonderous Night, that hides the anxiety within my eyes;
As the Heart and Soul, watch o'er my Love
Listening for distressive cries

The comfort of the night's cool breeze
As it caresses my face
Whispering into alerted ears
I am Grace, I am Grace

So be it, So be it, yes—never cease
Without thy depth, the Heart would know, no peace
The Tears that roll freely, from uncontrolled emotion
Have you as a sanctuary from prying eyes and commotion
Wondrous Night, Wondrous Night
what a creation Thou art
Thou truly understand, affairs of the Heart

Your blanket of blue and pillow of moonlight
Make perfect bedding for Lovers delight

Wondrous, oh Wondrous Night, that hides the anxiety within our eyes
The Art of such comfort—there's no question, as to why

Marciana A Sevandal
TIP THE BALANCE ON DOLLARS

This poem is heartily dedicated to my children and all to show that dollars and sense must complement each other to benefit mankind.

If I were asked to make a choice,
Between dollars and sense,
I would rather not commit myself,
To preclude inevitable pains.

I know that dollars without sense,
Will cause mankind disaster;
Either man will be drug addicts,
Or lawless men forever.

And sense alone minus the dollars,
Will get little in kind,
To achieve the good we wish to do,
To benefit mankind.

But with dollars and sense as one,
There will be a lot of good,
For all mankind mostly in need,
Of shelter, clothes, and food.

World millionaires with lots of sense,
Become philanthropists,
Doing mankind tremendous good,
Through charity, love, and peace.

Finale:
Without sense, dollars will spell "ruin."

Marciana A Sevandal
HAIL TO MOTHERS

This poem is both a tribute and a dedication to all mothers, most especially to the greatest of all mothers—The Blessed Virgin Mary, the source of our earthly mothers' love—which God gave to us through them. Both deserve our boundless love.

In this wide world over, are millions of mothers,
But always there'll be one, greatest among others.
It was she who mothered God's lone begotten Son,
And He gave Her to us when His mission was done.

With Mary becoming the great Mother of God,
Was unveiled the pattern of a mother's great love;
For Mary is truly most perfect of mothers,
From whose love was patterned love of earthly mothers.

Our love for Christ's Mother is the very same love,
God gave our own mothers here on earth from above;
Patterned from the great love of our Virgin Mother,
Our earthly mother's love can't be any other.

Oh Mother dear, we all remember joyously,
The magic of your love you gave us graciously;
For nine months you bore us, to you a duty prime,
Stood by through the years, helped make our lives sublime.

So thank you, Dear Mother, what can we ever do,
To compensate your love that keeps our lives aglow?
We know your love for us is like Mary's true love,
That God gave us through you, from the heavens above.

Finale:
A mother stands by her children, in joys and in sorrows.

Paul R Petersen Jr
A CHILD CRIES ALONE

To Corey, Chad, and Katie with love.

A child cries alone in the dark
listening to the yelling, tearing his life apart
He wants to make it all okay,
to stop the hurt and make it go away
He's scared and doesn't understand
How could things have gotten so out of hand
He feels it's him they fight about,
He thinks that's why they scream and shout
Sometimes he wishes he wasn't there
But he loves them, it isn't fair
He's a big boy, they mustn't see him cry
But it's so hard when you don't know why
What did he do to make them so mad
Can't they see, that he's so sad
No matter how bad it is for you and me
it's our children who suffer, can't you see.

Ellen Carpenter
TO CRYSTAL

Where will my grandpa
go when he dies?
She asked this question
with tears in her eyes.
To heaven, I said,
gazing into the night.
I stretched out my arms
and she held me so tight.
But where is heaven?
And why must he go?
Can't I go with him?
Can't we all go?
No answers came
as we looked to the sky.
She lay soft in my arms
and we both had a cry
And the stars seemed like the
burning tears
of that ignorant darkness.

Tania Hunter
THE LOST ONE

If only I had learned sooner in life;
but what can a person do.
A person feels sadness and sorrow all
locked up inside them.
You see all the pain and suffering
they had to go through.
You see all the long hours momma
worked to keep him here.
You see the struggle the doctor went
to make his life happier.
You can remember all the hours
waiting to see if he pulled through.
All the tubes and wires connected
seemed to make it hard to bear.
But we knew God would be there to
tell us everything would be fine.
Remembering all the cards and
flowers sent by the loved ones
Hoping he'd soon recover
But day by day he grew worse
And finally he slipped away.

Betty Kurzweg Killen
DEPRESSED? . . . YOU MIGHT SAY THAT

To my children, Larry and Debbie, who made my life worth living.

If it means to close the doors to be alone
look at the four walls and not answer the phone,
wishing you'd never ever have to get dressed,
Is that a sign that I'm depressed?

When you pretend to listen to what others say
with your mind on all your problems,
wishing they would go away,
you might say I'm depressed.

When you wake up in the morning
and don't care how you look
and you'd rather stay in bed
curled up with a good book,
yes, you might say I'm depressed.

When all the things you've tried, turn out to be a mess,
when friends and family let you down
and nothing ever turns around,
you darn right I'm depressed.

Jennie Anders
A HOMELESS CHILD'S PRAYER

If this is the land of the brave and the free,
Why can't there be a home for me?
If this is the home for the tired and poor
Why can't our family eat anymore?
If this is the place where dreams come true,
Why can't you spare a dime or two?
Isn't this the USA? Where good men died
And freedom gave.
I'm trying not to ask a lot,
But I feel I've been forgot.
All I want is someplace
That I can eat and wash my face.
But I'm too young to comprehend
How life comes and how it ends.
But if you have any extra time,
Think about this prayer of mine.
If you help my family,
I'll be the best that I can be.
Please help all the others too!
And let my prayer be heard by you.

Judy B Pequeen
GOD'S LITTLE ANGEL

To Our Son, Gene. He's in Our Hearts Always.

I feel pain deep within my heart that
God's decision was made.
May He give me the strength to understand
And keep the faith in this Great Man.

People don't quite know just what to say.
But some just quote some old cliche.
Some of them are sad but true.
And touch my heart while I'm unglued.

When I was the first to know my "Question's?"
Why me? Why my little one?
I prayed and prayed that nothing would be wrong.
And that my little one would be born strong.

God had a reason to call for my little angel.
The way it was done seemed cruel!
The waiting alone is harder than
anything I have ever had to do.
But I think it was meant to be . . .

I still carry my little one with Love,
because soon we will be apart.
But the Love I feel and the faith I have
are deep within my Heart.

When God is ready to accept my
Little Angel above,
I will know my Littlest Angel will
go with all my maternal Love.

So many thoughts have crossed my mind.

And the tears are still a flow.

But with time and friends who care
My pain will turn to strength.
We will get through a tough time in our life.
And Love and faith will carry us through.
Love, Mom.

Ellen Carpenter
GRIEF

Silent and fearful
With a lump in your throat,
Feeling like a raft afloat
On a stormy sea.
Inside crying in dark despair
Don't they see the crisis?
Don't they care?
Searching for answers
Hopelessly blown away like
wind-blown sand
Paralyzing numbness
Takes you by the hand.
Grief is such a
quiet,
threatening,
thing.

Kay Townsend
MISS PENNEY

To my husband, Lanier, Larry, Leatha and Liz.

"Look into my eyes," she said to me
"and tell me what you see."
I saw a tired looking mare;
sporting drab copper hair
and wondered what she wanted with me.

"Come closer to me," she said.
"look deeper into my eyes—
I can walk, trot, and canter
I know the ropes and mind my manners
Trails and shows you need not dread!"

"What shall I call you?" I asked.
Think of a shiny copper penny
I gave a sigh; she gave a whinny
Grooming was to be a great task
A bath, comb, and brush at last.

A new copper penny gave me a spark
I bought her right off; eager to start.
Vitamins, minerals, and Omelene feed;
Tender loving care is all she'll need.

I put her in her new stall
and brushed her very well.
She sniffed the other horses
and warned them with her tail.
She had been confined before

and patiently stood behind closed doors.

My thoughts drifted to past horse shows
Little did I know this mare was ready to go.
She answered every cue with a willingness to please
She was much more horse than I ever dreamed.

As she moved with cadence and grace,
My eyes filled with tears and I had to embrace—
what I thought was a tired old mare;
was actually an aged beauty with plenty of flair.

I rode her on the roads and trails
I began to work her on the rail.
She would warn me of danger by a twist of her tail
and the joy, trust, and love made me want to yell!

Miss Penny I'll call her
I thought after a time
Alabama's No. 1 Copper Penney
and she was all mine.

A few weeks later, I walked outside
Just to catch Miss Penney take a few strides
Oh how she glistened, My what a shine!
Gosh, how I'm thrilled that this horse is mine.

Come a little closer and tell me what you see
The most beautiful mare this side of Tennessee.
No longer looks tired; no longer looks bored
She's a hard muscled quarter horse
and very much adored.

Bill and Loree Ford and Tim

Loree Ford
VLADIMIR

The poem, "Vladimir" was written after I listened to an interview on TV, featuring world renound pianist, Vladimir Horowitz, who at the time was 74 years young. In his broken English, he explained that when he stepped on stage to play a concert, he was "kink" (king), do to mastery at the piano. The sparkel in his eyes and good humor caused me to write this poem and send him a copy.

Imagine my surprise and pleasure to recieve the following acknowlegement from him:

Defier of the dictum
That the passing of the years
Reduces us as victims
Of accumulated fears,

You magnify the glory
Found in precepts of our Saviour.
You force an inventory
For lost hours, we may not savor.

The rapidity and precision,
Attributed to younger men,
You excel in each rendition,
You old comedian!

We love your wit and humor
The sparkle in your eyes,
But most of all your mastery
At the keyboard we idealize.

Yes, we agree, you are a "Kink,"
A "kink" that we adore.
Play on, Maestro, for we think
Shattered sensitivities you restore!

Tim

Loree Ford
TIM

Tousled, dark hair, carelessly curls
On a forehead, fair as can be;
Complexion that would make a maid of sixteen
Jealous, only to see;

Cheeks, usually rosy from running,
(Or from a wonderful exuberance of life)
Long, upturned lashes, enhancing
Expressions that turn away strife—
As if that weren't enough, I'm reminded
Of his well-defined, dimpled chin!
Earnest, compelling,
There's no foretelling
What he achieves with a grin!

Loree Ford
WHAT A DIFFERENCE

At one of my vocal lessons, most thoughts in this poem were expressed by my teacher, Dr. Peter Sacco, who early in life excelled both in sports and music, becoming a well-known composer, fine actor, superb tenor, excellent pianist, teacher, and gardener. I merely set his thought to rhyme and rhythm.

What a different world we'd have today,
If each person was taught in a different way:
A creative craft, some physical feat,
How to dance, or sing, or raise food to eat;

To practice harmony, in one way or another,
Whether playing an instrument, or aiding a "brother."
To find in the learning, individual worth,
Giving purpose to living, enhancing the earth.

Could you imagine the effect this would start
With everyone taking an eminent part? . . .
A regeneration of mind and soul,
An integration and self-control,
A liberation from worldly strife,
And anticipation for each day of life;

The joy of atonement with all that we see,
The realization that we possess the key
To create and become what we want to be,
From this moment on, thru Eternity.

B B Watkins
JUST ONE PEEK . . .

Along the winding street we go,
As dusk spreads its mantle o'er all;
And now lights begin to show,
Their amber glow streaming forth
In a way that somehow calls . . .
Tempting us to peek within—
(Just one little look on the sly)
While quickly walking by . . .
It's early still for pulling shades,
As useful daylight still remains
And few desire to be closed in
Before true darkness fully reigns.
So here prevails a strange intimacy,
A familiarity of the in-between,
And we go on our way, gratified,
Past each such temporary
scene . . .

B B Watkins
ABOVE AND BEYOND . . . ?

Whenever we suffer one of Nature's whims
We seldom take time to protest;
We know it's not a personal attack
And carry things through for the best.

For no one expects to predict the course
Of natural forces at work;
They happen impersonally to one and all—
Too obvious for blame to lurk.

So poignant, then, to contemplate
How 'human' nature falls short
Of showing to us a similar face
To believe, acknowledge, and support.

For here we search for personal aims
And reasons for ills inflicted,
Not realizing people are currents, too,
Impelled, though otherwise depicted.

We need the same profound acceptance
Now granted to natural mishaps—
The potential to see our human misdeeds
As ingrained cultural lapse . . .

Robert Thomas Wood
THE GUARDIAN

Dedicated to my son David, Born to never see the light of day.

Cometh my child.
Into the garden, so wild.
Can you tell it's spring,
from the look of things.

See the squirrel in the tree.
The flowers and the bee.
Oh, you ask who am I?
I cannot tell a lie.

I'm the one from above.
Who comes full of love.
I can come and appear.
When you want me here.

But, I must return.
For someday you'll learn.
So whenever you feel low,
I will always know.

Robert Thomas Wood
GOD'S PALM

To my wife and children, Barbara, Robert, David, and Justin.

I like to look at the peaceful lake.
And wonder if I'm awake.
With the warm breeze in my hair.
As I take a long stare.
Is this Heaven so big and wide.
Could It be that I have died?
I don't mind to leave the past.
For I know I'm not the last.
But, I must regret to say.
That I hope the rest won't pay.
For their souls that are tossed.
Without God they're lost.
Into hell for the demon.
Where there is no free men.
I'm glad it's so calm.
Where I can rest in God's palm.

Henry J Roy
OUR LITTLE FRIENDS

Friendship is food for the soul.

We can hear them sing,
Every morning, through-
Out the seas - and land.

Our little friends,
They fill our skies,
Fly low, fly high, 'til
Each day's end.

Our little friends, sure have
Their woes, with rain and
snow, 'til it's spring again.

Our little friends,
All want to raise a
Family, some on the ground,
Some in the trees, their lives
Begin.

Our little friends, may their
Lives recycle, again and
Again, they need us, and
We need them.

Our little friends.
Have you fed one today?
They too, get very hungry,
But, they will never say; don't I get
Paid today?

Karen L Márquez
THE TRELLIS AND THE VINE

This poem is dedicated to Tom, the window of my life.

The vine is free and full of life
But doesn't know which way to go
It weaves in and out of time
It might bend if the wind were to blow.

The vine needs something to keep it strong
To give it some direction for life is not long.

It needs something
When the weather is rough
And when nothing around
Seems quite sturdy enough.

The trellis is strong and protects with all might

It keeps the vine safe, never holding too tight.

For the trellis and vine
Are there for each other
Working side by side
Never wanting another.

And I know without question
That this is so true
For I am the vine
And the trellis is you.

Huyen-Nguyen
TAKE A CHANCE
Here I'm in the freeland,
Where my life is in my hand,
Bright future is lying ahead,
I'll no longer build castles on sand.

Yesterday was a horrible nightmare,
Every single minute it was so scared,
At night if I hear strange steps,
My heart beats, it's hard to bear.

If you ask me why I'm here
Please come and sit very near,
I'll tell you about communism
and labor camps that give me fear.

Our people have crossed the ocean,
Many boats filled with children,
Half of them have perished,
Bodies were buried under the sea bottom.

Thousands and thousands of refugees,
For loving freedom we decided to leave
Our homeland and ones we love most,
To take a chance with the raging sea.

Huyen-Nguyen
FROM THE HIGH CROSS
From the high cross Jesus looks at me,
First I really want to flee
I myself nail Him to the cross
As my brothers the rock they toss.

From the high cross Jesus feels thirsty
His bloody face looks very unhappy
I myself give Him vinegar
and those who curse Him are my brothers.

From the high cross Jesus thinks
His wounded body seems to sink
The world around Him just ignores
He knew this moment long before.

From the high cross Jesus looks at His Ma
The other two ladies stand afar
He sees that His mother Mary is crying
For her most beloved son is dying.

From the high cross Jesus takes the last breath
That sad time His disciples have already fled
He comes and dies to forgive our sins
But instead we reject and crucify Him.

From the high cross Jesus looks at me . . .

Cathi Simoneaux
AT LAST THAT TIME HAS COME
At last, time has come to an end
As all good things began they must end
As to each hello, there is a good-by
As to each sunrise, there is a sunset
As to each life, there is a death
As to each smile, there is a tear
As to each class, there is an end
As to each of my memories,
There is no end.

Huyen-Nguyen
IF TOMORROW I DIE
If tomorrow I die,
My wife is not here to cry,
No Mom and Dad to be with,
And no friends to say good-bye.

If tomorrow I die,
My sons will close my eyes,
With whom shall they live with?
And no inheritance to divide.

If tomorrow I die,
I shall leave everything behind,
And what I have done in the past,
My soul will be happy and light.

If tomorrow I die,
Please smile not cry,
Because I have been liberated,
From the world that's full of lie.

If tomorrow I die,
My soul will be lifted up on high,
To be with my Lord JESUS,
Who is the creator and guide.

Pauline Scovoranski
THE ROSES
The Bushes were in Bloom,
With Red, Yellow and White Roses.
We picked a Bouquet,
The Fragrance filled the room.
The Gentle Rain fell on the Roses,
Drop by Drop it fell on the Petals,
The Sun came out and Shone,
So The Roses dropped no more.
The Wind came up Wildly,
The Petals fell to the ground.
A Blanket of Petals,
Red, Yellow and White laid.
Roses, Roses, Roses, Roses,
The Flower of Love.

Isobel Klodt
THE CONVENTION

Dedicated to The Ladies Auxiliary.

I'd never been to one before.
I'm glad that I was there.
I'd never been to one before,
I met friends and comrades who share.
The meetings in convention Hall
Impressed me beyond compare.
The girls they looked so grand and proud
the colors carried high.
Over two hundred I did count
waving as they went by.
One thousand six hundred in attendance
they all came.
In uniform of blue and grey.
They looked so proud in all that crowd
I knew I had to stay.
The delegates they sat in front
the observers in the rear.
When the Colors marched inside
I'm sure I felt a tear.

Written by Isobel Klodt.
Canadian Legion Branch 144,
Chesley, Ont. NOG ILO.
Canada.

Cathi Simoneaux
TREASURE HUNT
Oh! How I have always wanted to find the treasure
All the things I've dreamed my search of long has come to an end
I have found it!
Was it filled with gold? No!
But a few strands of sliver laid twine with it.
The jewels are more priceless than one can believed
They are the sprite of a person
They show only the youth that comes when aged with time.
Each one shines more brilliant as I gaze upon it.
The sliver twined with black is but a crown
The beauty can do nothing but bring awe to your breath
For 30 years I have searched for this treasure
At last I found
My mom!

Heather Penak
DAY TO NIGHT
The bright red of the endless burning sun,
And the blue of the cloudless sky,
Over the earth together,
Awaken every sleepy eye.

As it soars over hills,
This beautiful rising sun,
Meets with the sky,
They both become one.

It is no longer morning,
Now it is noon;
It gets closer and closer,
Night is coming soon.

Soon night swallows the sun,
Now night becomes sky's friend;
Together it is dark,
Into sleep every eye will mend.

Tammy Lynn Crouch
THE HURTING HEART
When I first saw your shining smile,
You stole my heart away.
And when I saw your starry eyes,
I knew you had to stay.
I gave you all the love I could,
but you never seemed content.
And then one day, I realized
that you had came and went.
Now the stars have lost their shine,
and the moon has lost its glow.
Why you gave me this Hurting Heart
I guess I'll never know.
You were my strength, my hope, my joy,
my inspiration song.
You were my light, my love, my life,
but now my life is gone.

Diana Jeweler
SINCE I HAVE LOST MY LOVE

To Allan.

I cannot see the sun, the moon
The stars that shine above.
Everything looks dark and bleak
Since I have lost my love.

What shall I do?
It's hard to live my life
I cannot be consoled
The ache cuts like a knife.

I really try but tears still fall
It's so hard not to cry.
I don't know how to cope
The future's gone for me—
there is no joy, no hope.

I miss my mate so much
I can't believe he's gone.
Am I supposed to live;
Pretend that life goes on?
They tell me that the day will come
When I'll have no more pain.
I hope that this is so
And I shall live again.

Allison Kyte
THE FALLING LEAF
If I were a leaf falling to the ground,
I would feel dizzy twirling all around.
And wonder what it would feel like
plopping hard on the ground.

Would it hurt?

Maybe I'd have to go to the
National Leaf Hospital!

Maybe it would be feathery soft,
so soft I couldn't get up.

Well, no, probably not.

Maybe it would be just right,
And I'd be safe and sound.

Plot!
Just right!

Diana Jeweler
LOST
I've lost my mate
The tears that fall are not because I wish to cry
My life is now so sad
It might be best if I should die.

My dearest spouse
It is so lonely in the house
I didn't know that life could be this bad
I didn't know that I would be so sad.

I really do try outwardly to smile
And yet my heart is broken all the while
I do not want my family to know
So I put on a show.

They want me to be happy and they are truly dear
But I can only act so much and many times I fear
They know my smile is not sincere
My dear one is no longer here.

The world goes on
And lonely bridges must be crossed
And I must live somehow—and must not show to anyone
That I am surely lost.

Dorrie E Carling
CONTENTMENT
In this oft-lonely silence, I may stand and wait,
unseeing of the beauty, of the grace of tree and flower,
living through the darkness and the dwindling heat of day,
till I hear the tolling of the bell, and know the witching hour.

I watch to see you passing, with light unhurried tread
and guess at shyness, sweet, yet wild, passing all too soon.
Yet dreams will fade though memories remain,
remembering friendship, life and loving under a silver moon.

But now grown old, with sleep-filled eyes,
I lean once more upon the gate where thought gave birth,
and know a sense of peace and joy and glory in my soul,
that gives contentment to the "here and now" on earth.

Patrice
SKATEBOARD

To My Family who Loves what I do, without them I wouldn't know what to do. Love mom.

My skateboard is awesome
My ramp is rad
My skateboard was awesome
My ramp was bad

Penelope Gautreaux

Penelope Gautreaux
ALWAYS HAVE; ALWAYS WILL
"Why is it that we can't turn back time?"
"If it were so, then there's a chance you could be mine."

"My love for you is still strong after 13 years;"
"So much so, that I'm constantly shedding tears."

"I know that people change in time;"
"Why is it then, that you are still on my mind?"

"Why can't my dreams come true?"
"If you know, please give me a clue."

"I knew I would fall back in love, once I see you again;"
"Why is it, that love for you will never end?"
"I know I must face reality & accept our lives as they are;"

"But the love I still feel for you is tearing into a deep agonizing scar."
"Please don't break my heart another time;"
"Can't you see what is happening, or are you that blind?"
"Please don't walk away from me again;"
"Coz, this time, I know my heart will never mend."

"Give me strength to accept the way your feelings stand;"
"And when I need you, please offer your hand."

"Help me to accept that it will never be;"
"Because we both have other obligations, you and me."

"Just don't take my dreams from me away;"
"Coz, in my heart, my love for you will always stay."
"I loved you then, and I love you now;"
"And I know, we will never have each other, I just can't see how."
"Just remember if you ever want me back again;"
"I'll be there, accepting you more than just a friend."

Rhonda K Gilmore
GENERATIONS

Thinking of you . . . B. J. and Chris!

Time has a way—
Of letting us see our day;
For when we are young . . .
We don't know where we had begun.
Seeking all the secrets of life—
We'll know when it's wrong—when it's right.
It's an inner thing,
Some call it sight
And some never see it at all.
We bring our children into this world . . .
In hopes they'll do things—
We never could
Watch 'em closely now, or they'll be grown
And out on their own
Bringing their children into this world
Hoping they'll do things
That they never could.

Peggy Lauzon
FREEWAY 401

Dedicated to my two wonderful sons, Troy and Terry.

Cloudy gray skies, tiny cracks in the heavens,
appears to be checking out the colors of autumn.
Sheep and cattle grazing, dusk is falling,
Eighteen wheelers racing, fourwheelers passing
High beams, low beams, no beams, some embracing.
Patches of water in a median of brown,
Harvested fields with patterns so weird,
Shapes like Zebras' stripes and colors of fall.
Deep brown, gold and rust, not to name them all.
Dark gray asphalt, lined with yellow,
Sometimes confusing, then sometimes amusing.
Alone with my thoughts on a bus going nowhere,
Mimicking miles and miles of sheer despair.
Multiple signs all shapes and sizes,
Haunting traffic and mesmerizing,
Time passes slowly, no sleep has come
As I sit alone in my seat seduced by the sound,
Of a bus going nowhere from town to town.

Denise Flood
SOME MINDS ARE NOT FIT FOR HUMAN CONSUMPTION

Dedicated to "White Dog."

One gets a false sense of security
But it's the altitude . . .
Not the gravity . . .
of some old science book.
Although they'll steal a look
But it's not the same,
since no one came.
The pit is not for us
Ride the Magick Bus
The driver has no eyes
No ears to hear the good-byes
Coming from within . . .
again and again
And you learn
Through selfish concern
There's no such thing as Reality
And you become the Fantasy
Spread from End to End
The Mind does Bend
While things fall into it.
You must have something to Forget
That someone stashed there.
A good secret to dare
Is it all in vain?
This mind that you claim
Wasted on indecision
Thoughts in a collision
But don't never regret
It's not a total wreck
Just record it fast
The thoughts won't last.
They'll fade away
Your mind will stubbornly delay
All the things you thought to think.

Rosemary Rulis
ALEX THE CAT'S LAST RIDE

To Aunt Marcie.

He gazed out the car window at each passing tree
Proud head held high with great dignity;
Yet afraid to turn once, and look at me.
I glanced at the back of that richly-furred head
So many times seen at the foot of my bed;
And knew pointed ears heard whatever I said.
"In a day or two, Alex—you'll be fit as a fiddle—
After Doc Bob cures that hurt in your middle;
So you can stop thinking like Chicken Little!"
A whip of coon cat tail told me not to try
To con an old con artist—with such a lie—
"As my ninety-sixth birthday has already gone by!"
He slipped from his sill view, into carrying case,
As I parked the car in the hospital space—
This ordeal, standing up, he just would not face.
It was soon time to say our good-byes
Only then did he turn and look deep in my eyes
As only cats can, or the worldly wise—
And the look said, "Cats do—but love never dies"

Rosemary Rulis
MEMORIES
"I looked for a sign that you had been here,"
He wrote from Big Sur yesterday.
Of course there was none
From our time in the sun
The waves erased our shining stay.

The letter was sad—an intrusion;
For we cannot recapture that time.
Only the rocks and sea are the same
With the winds of time ever blowing
—and knowing
You can never go home again.

Lisa Hampe
FROM THE YOUNG, TO THE OLD

For my Gram, whose love for my Gramp, gave me my mother, who created my hands.

Sometimes we don't take the time, the time that is
there, and then is gone. You always seem to have had
the time or at least took the time when it was needed
You have the time and need the time, that is the time
in return that you gave to others. If only we could
see through the eyes of elders, maybe we would
see the time of need, the time of love that elders
need. We the young are so darn blind, not to see
with eyes God gave us, the beauty, the hope,
the love, the grace, the young, the old and
the time that is there that we cannot hold.
From the young, to the Old, whose love I shall
Forever hold.

Melissa Velka
CHILDREN ARE FOREVER
Children, raise your faces to the burning sun.
We are forever; each different, striving to be one.

Be not afraid of time, or love, or what you have seen.
We are the dreamers; forever and on shall we believe.

Delicate hands making use of our lives.
We play the fools; our dreams shall arise.

We've overcome the stone, the fire, and the war.
We are the victors; fools are the ones keeping the score.

Their fists are clenched in a violent rage.
They are the rulers; blessed are the children in life's gilded cage.

Irwin J Amick
TO BE A MAN
A person of strength
who is proud of the land
always willing to help
and offer his hand.

True to his loved ones
until the day he may die.
Will often answer your question
with only a look in the eye.

To be able to hurt
and shed tears that are real.
To be able to kiss
and know it will heal.

Lord, I don't know where I fit
in your great plan,
but please someday
let me be a man.

Stephanie Smith
TRAPPED IN TIME
Trapped in a world with no freedom from fear,
It feels as though the end of the world is near.
Trapped between hatred, torn between love,
Freedom from being locked up isn't enough.
Emotions run high and take over our mind,
It seems we can't concentrate on loving mankind.
Fear of being attacked as you walk down the street,
Fear of what you could get into with the people you meet.
With one misfortune our trust will fade,
We wait and we wait but only one image is made.
The image that it was us that should be blamed,
Fear we'll be hurt if the guilty are named.
A life can be ruined in the blink of an eye,
You see all we really are is a speck of dust in time.
Some live, some die, we all go away,
But the feeling of being trapped is here to stay.
You're trapped in a corner, you can't get out,
Your reflexes tell you to yell and shout.
But that won't help so you break down and cry,
All you can do is live and die.

Edward Monahan
SOLITUDE
Silently, like softly lapping waves
The many fleeting nights unfold
And those who rest in hallowed graves
Attest we have grown old

What fills my thoughts of yester year
Those many loves who turned away
When each had been so very dear
I dreamed that one would always stay

Listening to muted music tone
Seeking to lessen my sorrow
For I am now so all alone
This day and come tomorrow

Monica Ciesielski
OH, SEE THE LIGHT!
Oh, see the light so dimly lit,
across the sea of black!
We've strayed so far away from it,
never knowing if we'll get back!

The Lord is reaching out his hand
to touch us in the night,
to take us from this darkness,
and bring us to the light!

So never turn your back on Him
to walk blind in the night!
Just touch his hand and feel the light
that brings us back to life!

Karen Pehlke
WITHOUT YOU
Without you, I wouldn't see the sun so bright,
No moon shining in the night.
No stars to light the evening sky.
No special twinkle in my eye.

Without you, I could see no light,
No birds soaring like a kite.
No butterflies to add some color.
No happiness to make hate duller.

Without you, flowers wouldn't cheer me so,
No delight in seeing everything grow.
No chirping birds to brighten my day.
No burning candles to light my way.

Without you, the water wouldn't be so clear,
No pounding waves that you could hear.
No roaring surf to listen for.
No ripples lapping at the shore.

Without you, I wouldn't see,
How very much you mean to me.
And though my heart would surely break,
A true friend you would make.

Susanne L Epp
LET IT SHINE

This poem is dedicated to my mother Helen, my father Paul, and his wife Annie, for all their love and support, and most importantly, the very special man that was my inspiration, Russell Christie.

The sun shines bright into the sky,
With all its might it does so try,
To warm the mind, the heart and soul,
To blend these parts, and make them whole.

The sun's warm rays flow to the earth,
And there it stays to prove its worth.
For its soft touch, will magically
Show just how much that you can be.

So let it shine, and do its part,
To warm the mind, as well as heart,
Before it's dark, and shines no more
And kills the spark your heart once wore.

Nicole Bianchi

Nicole Bianchi
TREASURED PLACES IN MY MIND . . .
Lately someone kind and strong, came into my life, so bright
this is why I ponder here, loosing all of myself tonight
those first few moments I caught your eyes, then quickly turned away
my heart had skipped a beat, but no, I don't dare let myself feel this way.

I do not know, I'm so afraid, of how we truly feel
although I think we're gentle lovers, hearts of gold, so very real
so much said, in unspoken words, we did not need to speak
the more I listened to your voice, sweet man, you made me weak.

The sunlight peeked inside the room, it danced on your hair, so kind
and as I listened to you sing, I think I lost my mind
with light and dust hung in the air, your body formed a silhouette
so intensely, I watched your form, I'll never forget the day we first met.

It's been so long since I felt this way, I don't know what to do
should I open up at all, to risk my heart to break in two
you've touched a secret part of me, that I always had to hide
when I look into your eyes, I just quietly die, deep down inside.

These are treasured places in my mind, I'll always have to keep and hold
when I think of you, these thoughts are warm, unspoken, never told
and as we now continue on, and go whichever way we choose
I have these cherished memories, precious thoughts of you, I'll never lose.

Sister Mary Valenta Akalska
Felician Sister
LITTLE BABE OF STAINED GLASS

To Padre Pio.

The Poverello of composure and exposure
Creates imagery,
Design and beauty.
Tints, shades and hues
Fashion reality
To expose one's soul
To open one's heart
To giftedness and grace,
All by the touch
Of a Babe, lying on straw.

Reid Bowers
LIFE'S HIGHWAY

To My Wonderful Children, Saronda, Randy and Tina.

You entered this world, on your birthday
With Mom and Dad, to guide your way
Growing so quickly, with each passing day
Reaching the age, when kids run and play
Learning and doing, new things day by day
Molding your life, for life's long highway
You showed no signs, if you felt disarray
It never hampered, never got in your way
You seeked out life, without a moment's delay
And moved swiftly, on down life's highway
Reaching adulthood, is a price you pay
For the joys of each, and every birthday
Maybe this time, brought some dismay
Renewed a memory, of a childhood day
If this privilege, should come your way
The blessed event, of your child's birthday
A good rule to follow, and try to obey
Raise it with love, it's easy that way
Then a Mom and Dad, can proudly say
I'm glad we did it, the old-fashioned way

Earl Jones
TODAY
A new day dawns,
one step from yesterday,
today is yesterday's tomorrow,
yesterday was before today.

Today we look forward to tomorrow,
then today will be no more,
it will be yesterday,
and tomorrow today.

Earl Jones
SLEEP
Last night as I lay,
I slowly drifted away, to nowhere,
Far, far away, to nothing,
I spoke to no one,
I saw nothing,
There was nothing to hear,
Just a silent stillness,
Lost in a mist of emptiness.

There was no loneliness,
No happiness, no cares, no fears,
No thoughts, no dream, no,
Just nothing,
An empty no-thingness,
Trapped in a lost state of oblivion,
How I got there, I can't tell,
Where I went, I don't know,
But now here I am, here.

Earl Jones
IF
If only I had realized, if only they would understand—the good, the bad, the wrong, the right.
If only we could live to be, eleven hundred and fifty-three.
I know we will never ever see, our ifs becomes reality.
This wishful thought is lost in time, a mystery we cannot unwind.
If there were no sorrows, no pains, no fears, no rules for us to ad-here.
No sun, no moon, no you, no me. No if only there could ever be.
If only I had remained behind, the thought occurred inside my mind.
If I alone could have the sun, if only if it could be done.
I know we will never ever see, our ifs becomes reality.
This wishful thought is lost in time, a mystery we cannot unwind.
If only I had seen today, I would never trade in yesterday.
If only I could reverse in time, a second chance to read the signs.
A silent thought in many hearts, a brand new me, from another start.
If only there was a way, I would quickly wipe away today.
To gladly bring back again, the joys of yesterday.
I know we will never ever see, our ifs become reality.

This wishful thought is lost in time, a mystery we cannot unwind.

Edna E Daniels
ONE NATION UNDER GOD

For all our Veterans, who give so much, and ask so little.

One Nation under God, 'tis wonderful to be,
To belong to this beautiful Country,
When the Star Spangled Banner is played 'twill bring tears to your eyes,
Watching Old Glory swaying in the breeze the heart swells with pride,

Americans wake up! We cannot allow,
the desecration of our Flag, we must remain true to our vow,
Many brave men have died! to keep us free,
Let us keep Old Glory waving strong, on the Land, Air and the Sea.

Edna E Daniels
THIS OLD SHIP

For my grandchildren who bring much joy.

This old ship is getting tired of all these rough seas,
It will have to anchor soon, or be broke apart, by winds that assail me,

It has sailed so many years, and some were really good,
But it is wearing out, as all things should,

So as I stand on the forward deck, and look just one more time,
I see it's about time to put to harbor, for the last time,

So do not grieve for this old ship, for she shall sail again,
On that immortal sea, where time shall never end.

Melissa M Brand
FOREVER

To John—The special person who made me who I am today, and filled my heart with memories. FOREVER.

Forever is full of tomorrows
and memories of the past,
Forever is full of smiles
and a love that should always last.

Forever is full of honesty
and not a lot of lies,
Forever is full of hellos
and never a good-bye.

Forever is meant to be
and never has to end,
Forever is for those in love
and not just as a friend.

Forever is my wish
I hope someday to come true,
Forever is saying, "I love you,"
and hearing, "I love you, too."

Walter H Phelan Sr
THE DAY MY LITTLE DOG CRIED

Dedicated to my loving grand–daughter, Robin, and our poodle, Paris Scampé. Robin inspired me for scolding Scampé for misbehaving.

My little dog was as faithful to me
As faithful as any little dog could be.
When I went anywhere—a walk or a ride
My little friend was always by my side.
But in my mind I yearned to be great
And money was the key to open that gate.
I met a man and a child that admired my pup
He said he would buy, if I would give the dog up.
When he talked about money, I forgot our close ties
And my little dog sat there with big tears in his eyes.
As I took the man's money and without even a goodbye,
That was the day I made my little dog cry.

In just two years I made out quite well
Forgetting the day I sold my soul into Hell.
Money I had plenty, friends I had none,
I was the loneliest man this side of the sun.
One day while I was sitting in the park,
I saw a child and dog having a merry lark!
The dog came over and looked into my eyes
Not a look of friendliness, but one of despise.
The child called him and they left by and by.
This was MY little dog,—that I had made cry.

Elizabeth "Card" Savage
I'M JUST WAITING

Dedicated to the memory of our beloved mother, Ora Belle Card.

I'm sitting in front of my Christmas tree
Waiting for Santa to visit me.
He'll bring me gifts and lots of toys
And games that make a lot of noise
He'll bring me a ball to bounce around
A jack-in-the-box, a stand-up clown
A tea set, a doll with eyes that open and close
A nurse's kit, and a pair of hose
A pretty new dress with frills and lace
Little girl's make-up for my face
I'm so excited I can hardly wait
I do hope ole Santa won't be late
I'm going to sit in front of my Christmas tree
And just wait for Santa to visit me.

Elizabeth "Card" Savage
SILENT FOOT–STEPS ON MY HEART

In memory of our beloved sister, Violet Rose "Card" Pergerson.

So long ago when youth prevailed, carefree days and dreams to come, back when my happiness compared to none I had not felt silent foot–steps on my heart.

I cannot walk I must run so busy that I stay. Un–seen wings attached to my feet swiftly carry me into each new day to conquer each big or small defeat impatient for the night to end there is so much to do, yet how beautiful to awake and see, a brand new sky forever blue

I'm grown up and have a family of my own, my baby's cry was music to my ear. The happiness was the greatest I've ever known when I wiped away each baby tear. But, today I brushed away a tear, my body wracked with grief and pain. Life is gone only memories remain
And I felt silent foot–steps on my heart

My foot–steps are slower than when I was young, visions and dreams have come and gone. Youth will flee, life will go on, and until this life I depart I shall forever bear silent foot–steps on my heart.

Elizabeth "Card" Savage
MOTHER NATURE AND ME

To my Sister and Brother, Mary "Card" Hedrick and Charles E. Card.

If I were a different me
So busy that I would be
I would not hear the whispering wind
Or see my favorite old oak tree
When I see Mother Nature in all her glory, I feel
I shall burst with happiness
She embraces the day with a hug
And ends it with a kiss

She is the greatest artist of all time
Her beauty is everywhere
There is no charge to see her
She only wants to share
I am content with her
She brings great joy to me
With her beautiful mountains, green pasture, cool water and an everflowing sea.

Elizabeth "Card" Savage
ALL THAT WILL EVER REALLY EVER MATTER

To my Sister Faye Card Bryson who has given much and asked for little.

It is such a beautiful night
The moon is shining bright
A soft wind is blowing as leaves gently fall
Casting a dancing shadow
For a fleeting moment, the beauty of it all
Is all that will really ever matter

Cast me not to where beauty ceases to be
Beauty is in the eye of the beholder
and beauty is what I chose to see.
A dream or two may drop and shatter
For this moment the beauty in all I see
Is all that will really ever matter.

Surrounded by this beautiful moon–lit night
In the privacy of my mind
I can go any place, reach any height
Climb any ladder
Now and for–ever
The beauty of life itself
Is all that will really ever matter.

Elizabeth "Card" Savage
ME AND MY CHOCOLATE PIE

To my wonderful Brother, Richard Dale Card.

Today my mom said she was going to bake a pie or two
I asked who they were for she replied, "Not for you."
I asked if I could taste or maybe lick the pan
She said no and if I tried she'd smack my hand
When she wasn't looking I stuck my finger deep
Into the chocolate filling and pulled out a great big heap

She spanked me so hard I finally had to cry
I asked her why she spanked me she said, "Come, I'll show you why."
The mirror sadly showed me a big blob on my toes
I'd missed my mouth completely and chocolate covered my nose

Mama's gonna be as mad as an ole wet hen
She's gonna spank me again and again
Well, I've earned this pie, and tonight I'll have a ball
I'd sure like to see mama's face when she first learns that I have eaten it all.

Michele Marie Rafferty
YOU'RE LIKE A SISTER TO ME

This poem is dedicated to Carmen Calandra, my best friend and sister, class of 1990.

You stood by my side
In good times and bad
You're like a sister I never had.

When you first came to N.D.
You were lost and afraid
Before You met me
You didn't have any friends
and now we're like sisters . . . you see!

All through those years
I've always been there for you
And you've always been there for me
We stuck by each other's side
No matter what it could be.

Now that our high school years are coming to an end
Let's never forget the special times we've had
And the memories that will never end.

Now, you're like a sister I never had
Please say we'll be sisters and friends forever
And whether in good and bad
We'll ALWAYS stick together ! ! !

Margaret McNabney
HALLOWED GROUND

To my parents, Walter H. and Callie Mann.

Trees, high on a hilltop,
Birds chirping and cattle lowing
in green meadows below.
Glittering sunbeams casting shadows on gravestones,
Some with names and some without.
In silent reverence I pause and
Whisper, "Yes, this is Hallowed ground."

Mrs Edith J Mosier
MOMMA

To my wonderful husband— Bobby C. Mosier.

I watch her walking down the hall
to her bedroom, afraid she will fall
She is old and getting frail
I love her with all my heart
some day she will leave us
That's when we have to part.

I haven't known her but just a few

years
I try to help her through my tears
Her mind is sick and almost gone
She doesn't know when each day moves on
God is with her, that's all she needs.

She's your Momma and my Momma too,
We try to help her the best we can
Asking God, what shall we do?
Sometimes we need a helping hand
Now he is the only one there
for we have looked everywhere.

All we can do is try our best
for some day she will lay at rest
Way up high in the sky
As each day passes by
May God and you forgive me
when the devil whispers just let her be.

Sometimes we have a cross we have to carry
but we will be rewarded in some way
Our time will soon come
When God says our days are done
we will hold each other's hand
With your Momma and my Momma too.

This is my way to say I love you
and how I love her too.

Chris Bennett

Chris Bennett
THE HOUSE THAT'S BUILT AROUND ME

To my wonderful mother Vivian, and my brothers, Dwayne, Vance, Chico, and my girlfriend MiMi.

Deep in the night I wake and lite, A cigarette and listen.
To all the snore behind steel doors.
My home is one of heartache, a place of steel and stone,
A barren cell, a home in hell as I sit here all alone.
For one small crime I pay with time
Where lights glare are filled with tears of misery, pain, and sorrow.
And every day I curse and pray, to my any god unknown
To hear my dreams my silent screams, when I'm here alone.
But don't be sad it's not too bad for I hide it all within.
No trace outside for it's all inside, what might be through life.
Has been men, scream and yell within my hell, yet I am a man alone.
My tears of pain like bitter rain, spill down on naked stone.
I feel an ache as though a stake were driven through my heart.
'Cause she said she couldn't wait and thought we should part.
I shall not shame or cast no blame on her for leaving me,
for love like mine imprisoned by time, must die unless it's free.
So sad too bad that what we had, can never be again,
but nothing lasts, and love must pass, so new things can begin.

Roberta A Barrera
WAITING FOR THE DAWN

Dark nights surrender
To the calling of morn.

The stars hang up their halos
For another day to be worn.

The briskness accompanies
The dew drops affairs

And the warmth of day break
Whispers to the air,

Magical poetry that fills the
Birth of day.
Leaving only inspirations
That leads one's hopes array.

Rev Donald K Barnett
THANKS TO THE WHIPPOORWILL

All day my heart beats
To the rhythm I've set,
Faster or slower as needed.
But, in the evening
When I'm preparing to rest
Another sets the rhythm
Of my heart.

The Whippoorwill
With its alternating—
Chipflewoutofthewhiteoak—

Chipflewoutofthewhiteoak—

Until the first rays of daylight
Are caught by the windows
Of my soul.

Then a new rhythm is born.
Thanks to the Whippoorwill
For the rhythm of the night,
The peaceful—

Chipflewoutofthewhiteoak

Of the night.

Lionel "Stonewall" Samuels
MISS EVENING BLACK

Miss Evening Black,
When you walk in a room, a sound of a pin is the loudest clack . . .
Soft velvet black and a body that won't bruise
Skin as soft as a pleasure cruise.
Miss Evening Black,
Take me on a trip which I'll never come back.
You smell lovelier than the whispering pines
Should have known it would be love that I would find.
The music played a nice, slow dance
Knowing you and I would have a pleasant romance.
Took your hand in my hand as we begin to cruise
Holding you near and having nothing to lose.
Loving one another, eye to eye
Touching lips was to no shock or surprise.
Miss Evening Black,
You're no stranger to me anymore, and that's a fact.
Being with you is more than nice
Loving you will be a life-long paradise.
Miss Evening Black,
Beauty and love, you definitely do not lack!

Carole Child Semon
A RAY OF SUNLIGHT

In memory of James E. (Dude) Williar, 1947—1984.

In the still of the night he appears at my side,
And our joy overwhelms us—so much to confide.
"Why did you leave us?" I cry in despair,
"Our lives are so empty, when you are not here."

He tenderly smiles, as my hand he holds fast.
"My time is so short—do not grieve for the past."
I've a mission for you—all the ones I hold dear.
You must cling to each other—I cannot be here."

And then he is gone as he came, with no warning,
And I lie here alone, awaiting the morning.
As the first ray of sunshine steals in with the day,
All my questions are answered, my heart knows the way.

God loaned him to us—our own ray of sunlight,
Love and laughter he gave us, through each day and night.
But God knew that Heaven had dark corners too,
In need of an expert, none other would do.

He lives in our hearts,
And our memories abound.
Our bright ray of sunshine
Is still here—Look around!

Mildred Hilsenbeck Smith
A MAN NAMED JOHN

Dedicated to: Jack W. Smith, Husband deceased; Mary Arden McCarthy, daughter. Lois Rich, daughter.

Our hearts are heavy, our eyes full of grief,
As we gaze at the chair of our fallen Chief.
The rocking chair's empty, the ship has set sail
Our Captain is moving to his new home up there.

Sail on little ship with your banner held high,
Sail out in the blue to your post in the sky.
A mop haired skipper with a big broad grin,
He towered above all, a giant among men.

The pointing finger, his quips to the press,
With "concern" and "vigah," the New Frontiers passed.
The Torch has been passed that fell from your hands,
It will burn in the hearts of your fellowmen.
Oh Captain we bid you a safe journey up there,
That men have denied you in your rocking chair.
Like the teacher of old "Peace and goodwill to all men"
With our poison and hate, we've crucified him.

May God forgive us this terrible crime,
That has taken your life in our day and our time.
He leaves behind an eternal flame,
that will light the world
Until the end of time.
The ship sails off to eternity, ask not what your country
can do for you, but what can you do for your country.

Sydney Celeste DuMaurier Morales

Sydney Celeste DuMaurier Morales
THERE'S A SKELETON IN MY CLOSET—YHEEZ!!!

To Mikhail Christopher S. Hill and Damion Dutwaune Morales. My Ace of Hearts.

I was clearing out my closet
prying high and low

When I stepped upon this something
that had a skeleton's toe.

I stepped backwards to see the
whole picture of what had startled me.

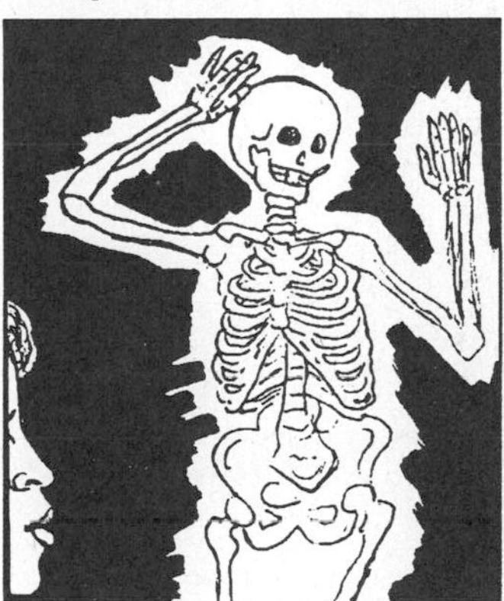

And to my surprise it was a skeleton
from my family tree.

Not knowing was this Henry or Bob
or Uncle Jim

Or Aunt Hanna's husband Clarence
or my clever cousin Tim

It looked at me, and I looked back.
I wondered what to do!

So I closed the door and walked away.
Wouldn't you have done this too!

Susan K Seery
SILENT SORROW

Maiden alone by a meager fire glow;
While night dims, so dawn may grow.

Coal hair glides softly in the wind;
Delicate, yet strong hands of amber skinned.

Searching the horizon with ebony eyes;
Waiting, as a night creature cries.

Scent of game and skins drift by;
Comfort from the soft owl sigh.

Fear and pain surge as she longs for her man to return home;
While across the darkened prairie, he yearns to roam.
Head bent with prayer for the Gods to protect him by;
Only alone, so as not to reveal the single tear of a maiden cry.

Cindy Andrest
BALCONY

For poet, Robert Bly.

pronounced! on a Liberated Day
beneath roaring skies of modern women
cries which covet conventional air with enmity
femininity's masque, restful, awakens
the straight back chair
in the corner
a towel covers to lessen the attack
vulnerable, transparent

mirror men with contact
unconditionally make allowances
listen beyond worlds as caring affirmation
reflection, transformation
reframe a different picture
a renewing of Our minds

the gesture of love
behind you; as the sun lights the moon
dream verse
"together conscious"
in a room
In Favor of Men!

Mary C Monaghan
COMMITMENT

Dedicated to my daughters; Maureen & Colleen, to whom I am totally and fearlessly committed.

If only you could understand.
How I feared the commitment that was close at hand.
That is the reason I said what I did
To make you retaliate instead.
I lost all that was good; because of fear.
Oh, how I wish that you were here.
To start anew as nature does.
This time not to loose your many different loves.
Never again will I see, those joyous days shared by you and me.
Time was cut short because of your ill
And now I wish I could meet you on the hill.
I know I would change the attitude I had,
Because what I perceived as good was literally bad.
The errors have been made.
There is no changing them now.
Just give me the guidance I desperately need:
To plant the seed of hope, and not fear in the deed.

Germaine Chevarie
FAIRY TALES

With love to all my friends in Blacks Harbour, N.B., Canada.

Do you believe in Fairy Tales
The joy it brings, it never fails
Do you believe in elves and Santa Claus
A child could tell everything
You want to know about such things
As three bears running after Goldilocks.

One day I saw this little man
Whose name I learned was Peter Pan
Flying around, happy as could be
I turned around and there I found
Pinnochio, wanting to know
Which way to find Alice in Wonderland.

I am your Snowhite
You're my Prince Charming
Fairy Tales are not so far away.
The seven dwarfs may not appear
To be around when you are near
Happy ever after we will stay.

Some things you just cannot explain
To rake your brain would be in vain
Rainbow don't dare disappear on me
Behind a cloud the sun will hide
Tonight the stars and the moon will shine
Tomorrow is the start of a brand new day.

Viola Hoyt
SANTA'S HELPERS

I
Jolly little workmen,
Were making toys all day.
So Santa will be happy,
When he fills up his sleigh.
II
Reindeers will guide him,
To all the girls and boys,
To fill up their stockings
While they're still fast asleep.
III
Mrs. Claus will join him
Tiptoeing to the tree.
For she's a jolly helper
Singing all the way.
IV
Boys and girls enjoy your gifts,
For we would like to stay.
But Santa and I are leaving you now
With your stockings filled to the brim.
V
Reindeers tiptoeing on the roof top,
And way up in the sky,
Trying not to wake no one,
For it's almost Christmas Day.

Toril C Tangen
SHE GAVE HER HEART AWAY

I remember pretty Rose,
she gave her heart away,
to sailor, young, and gay,
she thought that he would stay.

But he was married to the sea,
the waves were in his blood.
He joined a sailing ship so proud,
and left his Rose for good.

He sailed the oceans near and far,
and hardly went ashore,
until one day his ship went down,
and he could swim no more.

But Rose who gave her heart away,
was never quite the same.
She mostly walked the beach and watched,
the sea that was to blame.

Linda Robinson
SIMPLE SEQUENT

In my room
my love lies spent.
In a vacuum of
a love that's lent.

It is not yours.
It is not mine.
It's not a possession
that we can bind.

We gave our all
there is no more.
Like many more after
and many before.

Elfrieda E Burkett and Mother

Elfrieda E Burkett
MY MOTHER

To my Mother, Jeanne Bousquet Masiello, 85 years old.

She once had beautiful dark hair,
Now, soft silky white cotton frames her face like a halo.
A gentler more elderly look, one gets when you come near.
We all pray she can enjoy many more holidays, before she has to go.

I remember hands baking and sewing, playing the piano;
But, it was a voice that sounded like she performed at the opera,
That made you want to be around her, shake her hands and say hello.
When she was sad, it was the blues, but most of the time it was a happy tra-la-la.

Where have the years gone? I have often thought as I looked at my mother.
From a sprightly energetic walk, now it is a cane;
Her legs give out and her heart has become quite a bother.
With an iron will, she has survived many hospital stays, taking medication to ease the pain.

Even with all our arguments, times of great happiness, days of sorrow and joy,
I wouldn't live with any other,
She will always be my mother.

M C
OUR LEGACY TO LIFE

From here to eternity is our way around
Life, living and love that no one can abound.

We stop, stare and listen to observe the unknown
In wonder and merriment, we're awed with what's found.

So we prod and we probe, to see what we can improve
Only to find, change leaves a deep groove.

A groove that has opened a new dimension to address
One that mars life, our legacy is left.

To stop, stare and listen, to observe the unknown
But never tamper with wonder, nature's only a loan.

Lois M Edwards
THE ROSE

To my beloved brother: Wayne Adams Davenport.

There was a "teardrop" on "the rose,"
"red" was the color that she chose.
She layed it on his grave that day.
Remembering the day when he went away.
Just standing there staring at the ground.
Standing silent, not making a sound.
Thinking and wondering, if he knows she's there.
Standing and looking up into the air.
Looking and looking up into the sky.
Trying to really understand "why."
some of the reasons have come through the years.
But thinking of "him," still brings the tears.
There was a "teardrop" on "the rose."
"Red" was the color that she chose . . .

Davy L Johnson
PEACE

To My Beloved Wife Loretta, My Late Sister Janice, My Lovely Daughter Rachel, My Wonderful Son Aaron, and all my relatives.

Peace, what is it? I will tell you. It is two little children, who after a fight look pitifully at one another, wondering why it started in the first place and then fun and games resume,

while we so-called grownups still raging in a fit whose anger when kindled, puts us to flight and we soon forget the children's lesson, or that the next man is our brother, instead we are carried away in a frenzy consumed,

Will we never learn, wisdom cries out the question? Have we never read, "blessed are the peace makers, for they shall be called the children of God?" And that righteousness and peace have kissed each other. Is it necessary to build bombs, to prepare defenses in space? Can we not altogether spurn war and its definition?

Should we not instead seek meaningful dialogue? Well, are there any takers, or is peace so hard? Why not continue to till farms and leave this bloody arms race? Have we forgotten about Gandhi, Sadat, and King or what they stood for? Have their efforts failed to leave a lasting impression? Is peace ever to be gotten or is there no such thing? And do we really deplore such a word, is it like dust blowing in the wind? Peace, what is it? I will Tell you. It is like two little children, who after a fight look pitifully at one another wondering why it started in the first place.

Lauri Beimer

BLUE KNIGHT

Last night I was rocking the baby to sleep as the rain was coming down
Maybe praying a little as I waited for the sound
Of the car in the drive, that would tell me his daddy's alright.
Waiting again for my shining Blue Knight.

It was a a quarter past four when I heard the knock on the door
And somehow I knew, they were coming to tell me about you.
They told me how brave you were as my eyes filled,
And I cried as they told me how you'd been killed tonight.
No more waiting up for my shining Blue Knight.

Now I'm sitting here watching little Billy play
Thinking about how it was just yesterday
You looked at me and said "Honey, I love you, and I'll be home early tonight.
Till then, take care of our little Blue Knight."

Well, it's been four years now since you've been gone
Oh and you should see how Billy's grown.
He talks about his daddy all the time, and Lord knows you're still on my mind.
I want you to know we love you and I tell you every night
To look down once in a while to make sure Billy's alright
And watch over our little Blue Knight.

Lynda Lee Frolich

LOVED ONE

You made the Spring come to me.
Darling, my heart dances, like on a spree.
Flowers bloom & nod with glee.
OH! What was that special something! You did to me!
Was it magic in your touch?
Was it some kind deed, or what you said! No, I don't rightly recall!
Was it the tender caress of your lips.
I love so much.
All I know is that, special feeling is very hard to hide.
And it's what keeps me awake at night, and wanting to be forever by your side.

Lynda Lee Frolich

STORYTELLER

To my mom & dad, for their love and encouragement. And enjoyment of the Arts since I was a little girl.

Come here Laddie,
Come here my little Coline,
Sit here on my knee,
Listen to funny stories
of leprechauns, elves,
And pied pipers dancing through the trees.

Listen, and you shall hear,
The soft murmuring of a meadow stream so clear.

The pelting laughter of
Little bewiskered men
Traveling through the glen.

As they sing & dance
And carry you to their tiny fantasyland.
Sure an' Begorra
You'll bethinking life isn't so bland.

Audrey Feidler

THE HUNT

Stepping out of the golf cart
with slow small strides,
spikes noisily scratching the gravel path.
I step upon the grass,
silence;
as if I am the only person on this earth.
Standing on the tee box,
a cool breeze blows against me.
I push my orange tee into the moist green grass,
gently mounting my lucky yellow ball.
Breathing deeply, I tread up to the ball;
Spikes sink into the spongy ground steadying my stance.
Feeling isolated from the rest of the world,
I methodically grip my club in a comfortable position
and stare at the ball
Bright, yellow.
Slowly my arms bring back the club,
Left arm gradually pulls my club through the ball
striking it.
Club and ball meet,
A feeling of victory.
. . . The search begins.

Olga Fedak

STARRY EYES

I love your starry eyes of blue
They hold me like the deepest sea
When you're far apart
I know you are still true to me
We were meant to be together
Forever you and me

Maureen E Drake

DREAMS AND THE INVITATION

"Could I buy you a drink?" was his immortal line.
Twenty-two and in his handsome prime.
Impressed by slender curves and happy face,
"Pomp and fair, and dressed in lace."
His amber eyes were asunder;
Beholded his face, filled me of wonder.
His immoral smile flowed hot with lustful fire,
Seeming unwholesome and incapable of exciting strong desire.
Loss of judgment and control is caused by booze
Bad temper, abuse; I might lose.
So rude and reticent, I moved away to miss my cue:
Assert himself again he would never do.
Dark as the night was his hair,
For time has not erased his smiling stare.
How for his love I did yearn!
But he never would return.

Mildred Ball

Mildred Ball

GOD'S LOVING CARE

I'm really sick that's for sure
There's three things wrong
And doctors say there's no cure.
But—
God watches as I suffer
And when he knows I've had my share
He will reach down his hand—Close my eyes—
And take me in his care
I try to hold his hand real tight
And never let it go
I'll soon have a mansion just out of sight, I will enjoy so.
And when I'm gone
Don't grieve for me
I just want to be missed a little, you see
While I'm away I'll only be sleeping
You'll have all my memories in your heart
While God has me in his keeping
Some times it's real hard to understand,
Why these things have to be
But God in his great wisdom
Has plans beyond our power you see.
I want my loved ones to be faithful
And trust God and be true
Remember I'll be waiting
To see every one of you.

Love You All,
Mildred Ball

Michael Lee Battye

FRIENDSHIP

Friendship is like a treasure
And it's not too much to ask
But it's love, trust, & kindness
If you can handle that
Now, if you know someone
And they are your friend
Then please love and trust
And be kind to them
Now I have a friend but only
One friend
He's an old-timer
But I don't care
Because I can love and trust
in him

Jim Burch

DREAMERS

Dreamers always look to rainbows,
For they can see the end.
Dreamers are filled with love,
For they don't pretend.
A butterfly on a flower,
A fragrance in the air;
The heart inside of man,
God put it there.
Give me starlight on the water,
Dancing upon the sea;
Or a raindrop in the desert,
Lord, only you mean more to me.

Jim Burch

OF ALL MY FAVORITE THINGS

As the gentle mist arises and leaves its morning dew,
While I watch the darkness turn to dawn and nature awakens too.
So quiet in the morning, relaxing in its ease,
Each of God's creatures
Yawning, chirping, and crawling through the leaves.
Setting as one with nature, clothed in all its splendor,
I stop to feel like closely, my heart in deep surrender.
Yet, of all the things of beauty and of all the things I see,
I take care that it's not missing, my favorite thing to me.

As the day drifts along and the sun reaches high,
So many things are growing, and happiness is nigh.
Some people search in vain, some people just can't see,
This very special thing as sweet as honey from a bee.
When its touch of laughter is not standing next to me,
The bounty of nature's garden is perdition's empty sea.
So I take care every morning to be sure its warmth is near,
For without my favorite thing . . . happiness would lose its cheer.
Yes, I take care every morning, even noon and starlight,
To touch the beauty of its way so my world will grow just right.
Of all my favorite feelings, I take care my love is true;
Of all my favorite feelings, Lord, the love I feel is you.

Jim Burch

AS YEARS GO BY

As flowers sprout forth in May, I remember how I could spree;
At least I could in my younger day when you were here with me.
There was a time when our desire, burning deep within,
Could set our souls on fire, yes, burning deep within.

As the days of summer spread, with heat wave touching brow;
I have your visions in my head, I feel you touch me even now.
So I watch the leaves each Fall, what are they trying to say?
They say something, I hear them call, "Her love will come someday"

Now Winter has begun, it's off to a slow sad start;
I tread forward step by step, marching onward this shattered heart.

Dreams will die, and the heart will cry, and call out for tomorrow;
Teardrops fall echoing the unanswered call
For a love to end the sorrow.

As the snow piles high I think of thee,
As the years go by I wait for thee;
And for a time when our desire, burning deep within,
Will set our souls on fire, yes, burning deep within.

Jim Burch
AS NIGHTMARES COME
Here I am staring at the sky,
Darkness surrounds me and loneliness is nigh.
Each day the world surrounds me in troubles and pain,
The reality of each day with nothing to my gain.
I try to find a place to hide for just a moment of stolen time,
But something comes to stall me, breaking down my rhyme.
I can hear the birds singing, I can see the green grass grow,
But working in a steel mill can steal away the soul.
Yet I feel a touch of hope deep within my heart,
The chance to someday hold you and our love to have a start.
I say a solemn prayer for thee, the Lord each night I call.
I put my faith and trust in him, my heart and soul and all.
So as nightmares come to grasp me to bend and break my heart,
I believe someday I'll hold you and our love will have a start.

Jennifer Burns
THE EMERALD GRASS

I am dedicating this poem lovingly to my family: Robert, Kim, Gene, Jessi, Brittany, Bryant, and Laura.

The azure, autumn sky spread
Out like a veil above
Clouds of white daisies,
Marbling fields of timothy and wheat.
Leaves of ruby red, glistening gold,
And burnished copper
Cascaded like a waterfall
Of artists' paints forming
Pools of color on the ground.
Cooler days—
The emerald grass went tawny brown.
Colder days—
I went to bed, woke up in the morning,
And everything was covered with ivory.

Diana T Davis
THERE COMES A TIME
There comes a time
when your babies are born.
They are not yours,
they're, their own

There comes a time
when the babies are grown.
The mothers wonder what happened
to all those years,
and the fathers, maybe,
they start to fear.

There comes a time
when the babies want to leave.
The mothers wonder why,
the fathers do not care.

There comes a time
when the babies are gone.
The tears are gone by mothers,
but fathers weep forevermore

Fanny T De Waard
LEFTOVER DREAMS
What will I do
with my leftover dreams
when I depart this earth?

Will I take them with me
to shine as stars
in the vast depth of skies?

Or shall I drop them as
snowflakes upon
the still frozen earth of winter?

Shall I donate them to
my many descendants
to carry into their futures?

Or shall I hold them
close to my heart
to offer to the heavens?

Cynthia R Creasy
FRIENDS

For my mother, "Mae Surber," and her friend, "Barbara Layne."

Friends, you and I, as the years have passed by.
Children grown, and on their own.
Life has changed, but you, my friend, will always remain.
Laughter, tears, joy, sorrow.
Friends today, friends tomorrow.
Stressful times may bring you down.
Remember friend, I'm always around.
When in search of strength you need.
You my friend, may lean on me.
As the years pass you see, I your friend will always be.

Terrie Gentry
A SUMMER TREAT
Thunder echoes rolling
lightning flashes the sky,
heavy dark clouds hanging
so slowly passing by.

The wind it sweeps much rain
clear across our street,
the coolness of the breeze
is such a summer treat.

Verna Flonnes
FLOWER OF THE MONTH
January is the month for rubber plants, we set it on the table top.
See its shining leaves.
February is the month for gladiolus, to plant them in the ground. When spring comes they jump right up, they make painting beauty.
March is the month for Carnation Begonias. Begonias grow on bushy plants.
White, yellow, red, your eyes sparkle when you see the beauty of them all.
April is the month for roses. Some like to climb on gates or some like to stay like bushes, their colors are made of beauty, at weddings or on tables.
May is for Cushion Mums. Mums are all sorts of colors; purple, red, orange, or yellow. They take care of themselves, like we all do.
June dahlias are huge you know, they make many colors like sun on dust.
July is for daylilies that make your heart jump. Look at the rainbow in the sky, the lilies liked it too.
August is the month for Iris, their colors like the sky. Sapphire, pearl, different colors too, make your eyes sparkle when you look at the flowers.
September is the month for flowering gardens, jumbo tulips, iris, many, many, many more makes the place like a beauty when flowers are all in bloom.
October is the month for hardy glads.
Charming Beauty, Guernsey Glory is the beauty of the garden.
November is the month for amaryllis.
Amaryllis is a plant that grows so fast and beautiful, just like a clock that's time runs fast. The flower thinks it must be a clock.
December is the month for flowering cactus. It is also a beautiful plant.
Christmas is a time to give. Anybody would love one too.

Cynthia R Creasy
PORTRAIT OF MY LOVE

Dedicated to my one true love, my Husband, "Tom."

Each day I arise to see the sun shining in my
Love's Blue Eyes.

His love, His presence warms my very Soul.
I feel so beautiful in his arms,
I Love Him Dearly.

To me, He is everything. The Air I Breathe, The Space I Occupy,
The Reason I Live.

My Love for him is deeper than the vast depths of the universe itself.
To be surpassed by nothing.

My Love for Him will be Forever,
Endless, Everlasting,
For He is the very

"Love of My Life"

Andrea Hawkins
COMING HOME
He steps up to the bar stool
And speaks to good ole Joe
He sees her on his left
And begs her not to go

He says, "I need to tell a tale
Of a love that once was strong."
A tear rolls down his face
As he tells her what went wrong

"Our wedding vows were spoken
On a heated sultry day
Our hopes and dreams were genuine
And doubts were washed away.

We had a zest for living
That kept our love alive
But soon times grew hard for us
No way we could survive.

You see, I lost my only job
At the local textile mill
Then I turned to alcohol
My remedy to what was real.

I could not find another job
The dream was eternally torn
I kissed her gently as she slept
And walked quietly out the door.

I vowed to return someday
When I could face my fears
But days turned into months
and months turned into years.

Her heart was torn beyond repair
But a miracle soon took place
For a baby girl was soon born
That beheld her father's face.

My voyage of return
Came twenty years too late
For my true love had gone
I knew she could not wait

But I began to search and find
The angel I had lost
I swore I'd prove my love to her
No matter what the cost.

And as she began to forgive me
She told me about you
So here I am, your Father
Asking you to forgive a heart that's true."

A hush fell over Joe's Place
As she looked him in the eye
For she knew this man of old
And his tale were not a lie.

"Dear, dear father of mine
For you are finally here.
Come sit and let me tell you
Of my lonely twenty years."

Anne L Walka
REFLECTIONS OF A STORM
Tiny globes of water—
Reflections of an inverted world
In fragile glassy surfaces.
Each falling drop—
A slight change of view—
Facets fragmenting the whole.

Images shatter—
A splatter of splintering shards—
Chandelier crystals burst upon the ground,
Destroying individual perspective.

Broken drops blend and melt together
Into a smooth puddle of reflection—
Tranquil and silent—
Until a lone drop
Ripples the surface . . . briefly
Changing the image—

Dorothy Peterson Sprague
MOTHER NATURE, HOUSEKEEPER
"Rain and colder, skies all o'ercast,"
is the current weather forecast.
Rain turns into blinding sleet,
glazing every walk and street,
house and pole and twig with sheet
on sheet of ice.

Anyone so indescreet
as to venture, must retreat,
or go down to swift defeat
on sheeted ice.

Stand behind the window. Gaze
at the sunbeam's brilliant blaze
of iridescence from the glaze
of sheeted ice.

Traffic's traction is demolished;
empty is each street and store;
equilibrium's abolished;
ambulation's safe no more.

Mother Nature's waxed and polished
all the woodwork and the floor.

Dorothy Peterson Sprague
BIRDFEEDER BRUNCH?
It's a problem in logistics,
Sir Squirrel is realistic.

It's so easy to amble
the length of the limb
and the chain, but the scrambles
on glass dome exhaust him.
His plan ends in shambles!

His lateral jumps

from the sturdy pine trunk
miss his target; he lands
with a shocking "Kerplunk!"

His leaps from the ground
are spectacular launches!
But his front claws can't haul up
his tail and his haunches.
Still empty his paunch is!

His downfall's conclusive
That brunch is elusive!!

Gordon Hochmeister
THE POET'S REQUITAL
Don't ever believe that your prose
and your rhyme
Were penned with selfish intentions,
For the words have sustained those
sumptuously served
Far more than man's worldly
inventions.
Those who were fed in the doldrums
of life
When those light-hearted meals were
prepared
Were given new days—new years—
new being
As they reasoned that nobody cared.
A fondness of past, a hope for the
future
Flowed freely from your writing pen
So much has been furnished to so
many starved
With this writing that comes from
within.
Don't think your work vain—don't
think yourself selfish
It is a great meal you have served
You have succored us all with mirth,
hope and love
A truth that cannot be deferred.
So don't turn your back on those
folks in need,
A battle is won but war rages
In those who are poor—are lost
without hope
Are reborn with your life-giving
pages.

Lester
I WAS BORN IN 1960
I was born in 1960
Small, naked, and healthy
I never had to do without
Though my parents were never
wealthy
They taught me to respect
They showed me about love
I'm not talking worldly trash
It's the kind that's sent from above
Jesus saw me from heaven
Long before my birth
He saw the life I'd have
And loved me more than I'm worth
He came to die for me
So I could live for him
If he didn't I'd have no hope
And my life would be real dim
But I have a home in heaven
I know this is true
I won't leave on a Honda
If you want you can come too.

Clover D Green Hamilton
THE KNOW

My dedication is to the world, hoping some will shed the bad and see that good exists & put behind faded tears & fears and exit whole.

I know the know inside of me, the
know no one can see. If you should
find the know in you . . . . . your
spirit will be free.

Harry S Monesson
ELEPHANT IN A FLEA'S EYE
Amongst twelve-million
"Visiting" space aliens
One would expect
There to be at least
One case of plague.
Yet, it's ethnically safer
To search-out the lone stowaway
Fruit fly in a banana boat.
So, create the debt
That can easily detect
A lightning bug
Ten-thousand miles away—
And milk the stars
That won't object
To those phantom dragons,
Taxing Solons love to slay . . .
Conclusion:
While the donkey's fleas
Reside in Congress's bed—
The elephant blows its nose
And squats upon their head.

Harry S Monesson
SKY HORSE
Built they a skyscraper
Over the blacksmith's hearth.
Shod they the tired horse—
Riding it out of earth.
Rocketing hooves and wheels,
Stir moon-glass into soft sky.
In a galaxy smithy,
There pounds the blacksmith's thigh.

George L Sheffield
GENERAL CHUCK

To Chuck Yeager
Brigadier General, USAF (Ret.).

General Chuck, beat my butt
though I chased him through the
sky.
We WHEELED and DIVED and
CLIMBED and SPUN.
This story is no lie.

We CHANDELLED and
IMMELMANNED
and BROKE HARD left and right.
I could tell that he was having fun,
though I was filled with fright.

One more SPLIT-S and a LOOP or
two
and the horizon went round and
round.
The truth broke upon me like the
dawn
as I AUGERED into the ground.

George L Sheffield
ON THE ROAD

To the men and women who live the motto; If you got it—a truck brought it.

To go on the road, ah, that is the life.
No bills. No Mortgage. Not even a
wife.
Just follow your thumb till the sun
goes down
then, throw out your bed-roll right
there on the ground.

But, it don't work that way when
you're driving a truck.
In fact, sometimes you feel like
you're stuck in a rut.
Breakdowns and layovers and rising
fuel bills.
Flat tires, insurance and searching for
pills.

Speeding in El Paso. Overweight in
Wells.
Two days in GENERAL the time that
you fell.
The log books that are always filled
with those lies
and missing the sound of your baby's
first cries.

Follow the lines till you come to a
town
and hope a highjacker don't flag you
down.
To go on the road, ah, this is the life.
The bills. The mortgage. And, once
even a wife.

George L Sheffield
SMILE
When you smile, my knees get weak,
I have thoughts, of which, I dare
not speak.
Of carpet soft, before a fireplace,
where
I hold you to my chest and
slowly brush your hair;
Of lips, that gently touch a secret
place
while as one our two hearts
race;
Of dawn, that comes much too soon
to chase away a Lover's Moon;
Of perspiration, upon your breast,
while in each other's arms we
rest.

The Mona Lisa, rich men chase
though, some have never seen
her face.
And I, having seen you smile
have been made richer. And all
the while,
having seen what I cannot possess
cannot be lured from my final
quest.
If, on my death-bed, I should find
your tender love I've been
denied,
I'll know my life has been for naught
in not finding what I've sought.

Something as lovely as your smile.

Peggy Kirk

Peggy Kirk
AMERICA

Praise and thanksgiving to my Lord and Savior, Jesus Christ.

Three score and nine the years
You learned to stand
Now strong, amidst
The other lands.

Posterity look down from your
spires and pinnacles.
What womb birthed this land now
leader of the world cynics?
Whose hands feed the
stomachs bloated with
insatiable desires,
Which weed becomes the covering
for Adam's sensuous groin?
Cut the screaming tree dead
and build a shelter from it.
Humans, which vessel drew you from
the slime and mud?
Which mist placed in you the
bud to stand, face turned to the
sun,
Silly man, bend again your back in
agony over the plow,
Drench the dirt red, hear the
laughter then the silent cries.
Live, die, small speck in this spheres
staunch ebb-tide,
Ionian fathers have but once
passed this side.

Three score, no more
The years you must stand
Strong, alone amidst
The crowding lands.

Peggy Kirk
IMPREGNATED EARTH
Brown, sandy womb, sun-warmed
Morning dew, evening mist,
Impregnated promise of spring.
Stygian darkness, bedimed writing.
Interfere small blades
Parched and drying, crumbling
Umber, gold, vermillion tinged.
Blanketing, crinkling, neatly folding
Thatching the husk of summer.
Zephyrus, aged and upstaged
Withering away to Thrace,
Until Brutus bears breast and sword
Diary penned, whitened covering to
bed,
Poseidon's cradle a tempest, foaming
relentless
Borea's trumpets, the land and sea is
stilled.
Charthusian blades prick the frozen
soil
While Beatrice chants away the
clouds.
Ascend the ethereal mountain steep
Where chariots thunder will gauge
Trenched bars of spring's crescendo.
The prelude composed,
Sing sun, moon and stars.
Break forth secret rounded clouds
Hemorrhage, birth, inaugurate spring,
Bloom forth, oblige heaven's hounds.

Peggy Kirk
YOUNG
You sit and wait
The overture is playing
The play is about to start
The script is old
Read many times before,
The audience will be critical.
Perhaps in all the crowd
One or two will not have heard.
This performance may be to them
As new as it is to you.
You stand in the footprints of giants
It is you who now must read the part.
The listeners will clap and boo,
The past has clapped for itself.
There, your cue.
I stand in the wings and watch
I clap at the play's beginning, in
silence.
Make the part real
Be done with fantasy.
It is now your turn, young giant,
The stage, Othello is yours.

Peggy Kirk
JESUS

Bible stories say
They nailed Jesus
To a wooden cross
Pierced His hands
Pierced both feet
And left Him there with vinegar to drink
Mocking they all laughed and spat on Him
If you are King of the Jews save yourself
Bowing His head the Spirit left the body
From noon until three the land was dark
A Jew named Joseph
Got the dead body
Wrapped in linen
Laid it in a tomb
Later on a Friday
Two Marys watched
Early in the morn
Just about sunrise
The tearful women
See an empty tomb
An Angel exclaims
The Lord is risen
Jesus is not here
He appeared first
To Mary Magdalene
She told them all
I have seen Jesus.

Karen F Miller
VILLAIN OR VICTIM

He who has caused heartache
Suffers more than they
Who by it have been inflicted
Pangs of guilt eat at their heart
A constant reminder of their
Thoughtless misdeeds
Their conscience bearing witness
That they have erred.

For he who has been caused
heartache
Forgives, and it is forgotten
While he who has caused heartache
Lives forever with the knowledge
Of what he has done.

Is he villain or victim?
He who causes so much pain
He suffers in his agony
To have caused others much the
same.

Diana Campanella
I WILL REMAIN

As I dwell in my pondering
existence,
I touch my heart, my breath, my
feelings.
A realization blankets me.
I distinguish.
Yet I do not know whether to
acknowledge,
But to ignore is to lie
And I detest lying in darkness.

So beside myself I will remain
Until all is favorable.
And provided my entity is awaiting
I will tarry unhurringly.

Donna Kay Groskopf
HOW CAN YOU LOVE ME? I SAY

"How can you love me?" I say,
"I'm not special in any way."
You sigh, and exclaim,
"Oh, love for you just came.
Now, how about you?
Do you love me, too?"
"Oh, yes, oh, yes," I said.
"Before I met you, my heart just
bled."
You smile, and you say as you laugh,
"Oh, you don't love by only half."
"I could never love you part way,
I've got to love you forever and a
day."
"Love is great, love is grand,
Now will you join me hand in hand?"
"Yes, I surely will,
Until the day my heart stands still."

Connie Guting
FLEEING MOMENTS

Dedicated to Christopher and Christine.

What a change before my eyes,
Once, just a few days it seems,
That little one, cooing and babbling
sweet,
Now asks, "Mommy, can I write my
A,B,C,D's?"
So young, but yet so grown-up.
Before my eyes
A talking, playing child has grown.
O Lord, what has happened to the
time
That my baby was wee in my arms?
Help me Lord to take life slower—
Looking, watching and enjoying
The moments fleeing fast.
For yesterday's baby has developed
Into today's playful, cheerful child.
Only you, Lord, know what
tomorrow holds.
Please help me, Lord, to make
memories today
That tomorrow both my child and I
can hold.

kurt p stadler
THE FINDING OF NICOLE

This day was of fear and pain
Of shattered dreams in search
Of the light of truth and goodness,
Gleaming through the eyes of the
Unsuspecting gift. This day was of
Little hope. This day was lost.

This day is why all birds sing.
This day is the rebirth of wild
Flowers painting the essence of
Nature down by the babbling brook
Keeping time perfectly. This day
Is a smile that suddenly and
Unexpectedly fulfills the whole
Being with joy and happiness for
No apparent reason. This day is
Good.

This day will be everlasting strolls
Along the sandy beaches that boast
Unspoiled along the coast of our day.
This day will be the sharing of two
Souls as one. This day will be best.
This day will be ours.

Eva A Callaghan
ALBERTA CHINOOK COUNTRY

"To Remember The First Native People Of North America."

From the Prairies to the Mountain
Peaks
Alberta has what ever it is you seek.

To begin our adventures start
Let us visit "Writing on Stone
National Park."

The unforgettable "HOO-DOOS"
carved by wind and rain
With their "Indian DRAWINGS and
WRITINGS"
Is all of these Native Peoples that
remains.

Look to the Rocky Mountains in the
West
There stands "OLD CHIEF" up
above the rest.

To cherish and nurture the spirit of
"CHINOOK"
The Indian Princess who wandered
too far to take a "LOOK"

Who always returns to caress the
Furrows and Fencelines
With a SOUTHERN ALBERTA
CHINOOK from the pines.

Michael Byars
THE FINISH LINE

To My Mother, with love.

The longest race is finally run,
I am a tired soul and out of breath,
As I lay here motionless on my
stiffening back,
I recall every stretch and curve of the
track,
But time has flown; the final whistle
has blown,
And I must surely be a sport,
To take this sudden Death,
Even at this final ceremony,
Familiar face I see,
Blossoming gifts they bring; in hopes
to comfort me,
They weep in my loss,
While I lay at rest,
But I am content that I gave my
whole hearted best,
For this was my own race,
Fairly I have run,
Although uncontested,
I feel that I have won,
They judge me as defeated,
But the victory is mine,
For I finally saw the Winner's Light,
When I crossed the Finish Line.

G J Cannis
LOST LOVE

Dedicated to G. L. Bernstein.

He fell in love with a sick woman who used him till she returned to her sanity.

The security she found with him was his love for her!

That security she lost when he physically loved someone else.

Now he's sick over a lost love waiting for a woman to return his sanity.

Thomas H Suttles
ERINACH

What do you have when you take
away
The dreams of a man?
A dreamer—or—
A man teaching a child to hate.

What do you have when you take
away
The language of a man?
A poet—or—
A man teaching a child to hate.

What do you have when you take
away
The education of a man?
A scholar—or—
A man teaching a child to hate.

What do you have when you take
away
The religion of a man?
A priest—or—
A man teaching a child to hate.

Through eight hundred years there
have been Irishmen
Who were the dreamers, poets,
scholars
And priests of the world.
All that was left to them were
words—
And guns—
And men teaching children to hate.

Pam Littlefield
ANOTHER DAY

As I stand there on the beach.
I feel the water rush to my feet.
It feels so cool against my toes.
And then it's gone, away it goes.
The waves roll in, and then
slide out.
Again, and again without a doubt.
Sometimes it brings gifts from
the sea.
Like seashells, and driftwood just for
me.
On the horizon the sun is falling.
For tomorrow now is calling.
I hear it sizzle as it touches.
The sea takes it in her clutches.
Now the night has come.
And the day is done . . .

Ramon G Agdigos
THE PERFECT SONG

One perfect song our heart can sing,
One air that's crystal-clear,
One melody of love sublime
With charm for every ear.

One perfect song our tongues can
frame
Of goodness, deep and true,
Of seeking and sacrifice,
Of mercy, every new.

O Christ, our singing is of Thee;
To thee our hearts belong;
Thou art perfect melody
Of life's triumphant song.

Jenny Deuster
A TOUCH

It doesn't cost a penny
It has no sound, but a
dialogue of it's own.
It means so much, and only
takes so little to give . . .
A touch
Only to lift a finger, or the touch
of a hand, could mean the world
to someone.
Warmth, understanding and love, it
only takes so little time to give.
A touch so simple,
a gift only so precious!

Janet Grant
WHY

As I sit here in the blue-gray stillness
before the storm,
I can't help but wonder why and what
for.
Things soon begin to carry no
meaning; just sheer existence.

There is a purpose to everything, but
what; tell me.
I used to think there was, but lately
the reasons are dim.

There is always light at the end of
every tunnel. The tunnel is
So very long and winding. Is there no
end? I'll soon be there,
But will I find the light?

Far away I hear the echoing moan of
a sad lonely train whistle.
Where is it headed: can't you tell me?
Why go there: where the

train's headed? There's nothing there
for me; just more
Emptiness.

The storm is starting now. Soon it
will be over. Then what . . .
Another storm?

Gregory Zmiewski
CONVERSATION

For song, and my friends that won't let me go, thank you.

Is she in your dreams?
Every dream.
What do you dream?
I'm standing next to her,
Trying to speak,
My lips sewn shut
to keep my feelings in.
But she pulled them out through my eyes.
And you love her because you told her your feelings?
No, because she wanted to know them.
Like a song she made me feel better,
Every beat of the bass drum
weakened my defenses,
The guitar pulled at me,
my insides wept as they were
strewn across the floor for
her to see.
And then the mellow bass rearranged
and repacked them, kissed me on
the forehead, and put me to sleep.

Shauna Thompson
SCREAM LOUDER!

red man cried
Quietly as Whiteman
Locked his pride
In a tall, tall fence
Of submission.

yellow man ached
Quietly as Whiteman
Saw him baked
In a mushroom oven
Of submission.

brown man pained
Quietly as Whiteman
Had him chained
In an iron shackle
Of submission.

Still Whiteman knew no joy
For there was no man
Left to destroy
Except white man
With submission.

Donna M Vitale
IN YOUR EYES

To LJE, my dream come true at the cost of a broken heart. Love you "Always and Forever."

It's a tragedy to see my dream has ended
And I put up the hardest fight
But now I've surrendered
And I'll put back the pieces of my torn heart
And try to make a brand new start
But I'll always long for that look I found in your eyes
An embracing stare that
overwhelms me
Swelling my heart everlastingly
An intertwining of the souls
internally
Completing us both infinitely
Unexpectedly when my throat
tightens from thoughts of you Love
I'll convince myself that you were
Just someone I used to love
And I'll wipe the teeming tears from my bleeding heart
And try to accept that we are apart
But I'll always hunger for that look I found in your eyes
A penetrating gaze that
enthralls me
Fulfilling me so completely
Losing myself eagerly and
totally
Loving you for an eternity.

Keith Hodes
CUT LIKE A KNIFE

Born at the wrong time,
Mother seventeen, Father split the scene.
Nights seemed to fly by,
Mother would not love, Herself is all she thought of.
The girl turns ten today,
Mother split last month, didn't come back, not once.
All of the badtimes
Will stay with her forever, won't go away, not ever,
Now it's a new time
But she is still so taunted, Her heart is being haunted.

Now she lives in a brand new home;
Now she's not feeling all alone;
Now she'll try and get on with life
But memories still cut like a knife.

Marlene Weikert
GLORY ROAD

Majestic and in repose, there stood the earth
For the world to unfold and fashion a road
So many paths and byways, it would give birth
Venturing one's heart's desires—a place to abode
From Man's boulevard of dreams to Serendipity street
Choices chosen, chances chartered
Be it the downtrodden or the very elite
You know with your mind and soul, you've bartered
As though through life's movie
reel passing by
Therein lies the ultimate quest in one's mind's eye
Long ago memories tell of a city street parade
And as a child tramping thru the woodsy trails
Onward, upward the rugged rocky way, a mountain climber goes for the pinnacle Life's a charade
Go forward young man or woman, set your sails, ride the rails
Blue skies overhead, air spun pavement below, a Nomad cyclist races with the wind in true mode
Now it's post time, gates freedom sprung, by a length and a breath, a jockey brings in his own Glory Road
See the tired and weary soldier trod, his armour and courage at bay
Eureka! At long last. Homeward bound, mercy found, God speed the Great Mender
Heartfelt and in palm of hand, it awaits to plant a seed
Pressing toward that old country gravel road trudges mere man with feet of clay
For every ugly of the world, there exists a thing of beauty and splendor

Victor A Archbold

Victor A Archbold
WILL SOMEONE HELP ME?

To my family and friends and to those who had faith in me.

Good is bad, bad is good. Will someone help me? For my mind is confused.
Love is hate, hate is love, will someone help me? For my heart is confused.
My life is based on love, but all of it had gone to waste. Will someone
Love me? For I have no one to love.
What is love? For it's just a name.
Will someone show me? For I don't
Know what love is, Will you come and show me these things?

Jessica Marie Lichty
TIMES OF FUN

They were times of joy.
They were times of sadness.
Times of pain
and times of gladness.
They were the times I'll never forget.
They were the times when we did not know what war was
and peace filled the land.
I often wish; I often wonder,
if I can return.
Where I could run wild and free
not worrying where I'll next
have to be.
Those were the days of gladness
and those were the times of
sadness.
That was the time when I was young.
That was the time memories are made of.

Katy Mishler
A BELOVED CHRISTIAN FRIEND HAS DEPARTED

He reached down so very gently
And picked a flower fair,
To add a touch of beauty
To His heavenly bouquet up
there.

A flower of real beauty
She'd blossomed to full bloom,
When you were in her presence
Beauty and fragrance filled the
room.

The beauty of her love for Christ
And for others young and old,
Made her friendship to anyone she met
A treasure more valuable than
gold.

We'll miss the place you occupied
In our hearts and in your pew,
But someday by His matchless grace
We'll be up there with you.

Isa Nicholson
I KNOW A MAN

To KEN, my dear husband, on our 40th Wedding Anniversary, July 4th, 1989.

For many years I know a man
Who was brought up right and knows what he can.
He is exceptionally well informed and very bright
For he has all his goals steadily in sight.
Knowing the difference between work and play by far
Regard to good times or during times of war.
The years came and went and took him to foreign lands
Yet always returning to lend his helping hands.
His love is to work, no matter what, is his motto,
Wise investments—but no luck in Lotto.
Reaping the laurels of his life now in amaze,
Still trimming and mowing the lawn on sunny days.
You gave me hope and strength when I was down
Your humor always replaced my frown.
You made me often laugh—you made me cry,
You replaced tough times with happy ones as years went by.
Now your knees and back give you hell,
I stand by your side as long as oceans ebb and swell.
You know deep in your heart—and doubt it never,
My love for you is true and shall last forever!

Isa Nicholson
THE GATEWAY

Be still, my troubled grieving heart.
Listen to the song of the wind,
Trees swaying to and fro.
The sound of the chirp, twitter of birds in harmony,
Echoing in the hills at a sunset full of hope.
The past will fade in the everlasting melody
Of an endless rippling stream so crystal clear.
Let children's laughter, oh so dear,
Recall the smile on your saddened face.
A new tomorrow will soon be born
With fresh beginnings, to start anew.
Life's everlasting circle of ups and downs,
Like rain and shine,
Will come to nourish the seed of spring.
Continue on the path that seems too hard,
And remember those good times we will never forget.
Soon you will see a gateway to a

brighter horizon
To master a wonderful and fulfilling life.

Sissy Padilla
SAY NO TO DRUGS
DRUGS will take your life away,
they will take you down so low
SAY NO TO DRUGS WHEN they are passed around
This poem is for one and all, please listen and you'll learn, SAY NO, TO DRUGS
so you won't get burned.
DRUGS have filled the world with grief
even the UNBORN, cries relief, say no to DRUGS when they are passed around
There's more to life than living high,
this country needs our kids to survive
Let's free our nation's child and keep our country clean,
After all aren't we talking about our children's future
Don't we have a right to be concerned
CRY OUT AMERICA, let's fight this war on drugs
Teach our children to say no, with God's help and our love
Say No to Drugs when they are passed around, Say no to drugs
They will only bring you down.
SAY NO "NO DRUGS"

Megan Lindgren
BEHIND THE FENCE
Behind the fence
could be a different world.

A world of kindness and life,
or a world of violence and death.

A world of hope,
or a world of fear.

No one knows what's behind that fence,
yet some don't even care.

When it comes my turn to find out,
I know the Lord will be there.

Mary E Knopp
MY SONS

Dedicated to my sons Freddie and Ronnie.

I've delayed for many years
Some memories to define
The perfect words to put in print
For those two sons of mine.

I have tried to be worthy of their love for me
Being dependable and always there,
With joy or grief that I could share.

My sons to me are just as dear,
As when they were young and always near.
Tough little Indians, Cowboys and blazing guns,
Baseball, bikes, ponies and all the imaginary games of my little sons.

Happy school days with progress and pride
Forever smiling by my side.
Birthdays and Christmas was a happy time
All other Holidays close behind.

But all too soon their teenage years
With graduation growing near
And suddenly I realize how fortunate I am
To be the Mother of these fine men.
They are my sons, my life, my friends.

Walter D King
I MUST REMEMBER THIS

In memory of Ruth, beloved wife and friend, who helped me to know that light does prevail over darkness, and that love and beauty do endure.

The sun is shining bright today
To help me say what I would say,
The world's a lovely place to see;
Another time it may not be.
Therefore, I must remember this,
And know that beauty does exist.
It has, it does, it shall endure.
The clouds are fleeting that obscure.
They come, they pass, the sun is out,
Unveiling love, dissolving doubt.
If I but view the shadows right,
They'll only emphasize the light.

Craig S Rasmussen
HEAD AND HEART
Our tears have mingled with the rain,
our cries have vanished on the wind,
Time has carried away our pain.

These are our houses calm and blind
with permanence of polished stone
that paints indifference on the mind.

Beyond their walls outlawed, alone
Our muted sorrows smoulder and start,
The lonely tear, the silent groan.

How well they keep themselves apart!!
Oh what we know and what we see
are as separate as head and heart,
And all our sorrow a distant memory.

Craig S Rasmussen
SNOW
Slowly,
Gently,
Falling down
silence envelopes
the world in
a white blanket
of cold warmth
Like the touch of
a lover with icy fingers,
It curls around your soul.
The world seems at
peace
Yet a silent raging
storm pours out on it.

Craig S Rasmussen
FEB. 13, 1987
Pain feels
so pleasant
compared
to love
because when in pain
there is only pain
nothing else
taste it
absorb it
become it
it of you
when in love
there is pain and
happiness
and the
two together torture the soul.

Craig S Rasmussen
NOV. 22, 1985
When one snowflake
falls gently down
It disappears without
a trace
only the memory remains.
When one teardrop falls
it too is gone.

Craig S Rasmussen
UNTITLED-UNDATED
One,
Two,
three drops fall
Then suddenly a million more
Tears each one
crashes down
Rain takes the sun away
Rain washes everything away
Come, Rain on my soul

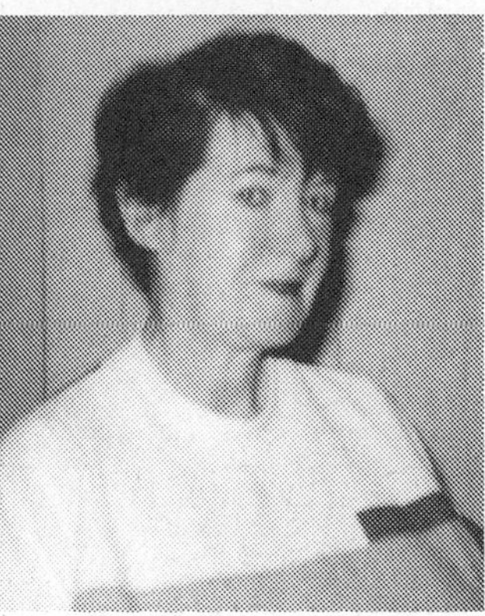

Selina Barton

Selina Barton
CHRISTMAS TEMPTATIONS
Oh! Christmas tree, Oh! Christmas tree,
How brightly shines your light,
And all the Christmas shopping,
Our spending, our delight.
Oh! What fun it is to give,
And also to receive.
But something is so very wrong,
Of this I do perceive.
An empty space is in our souls,
Of what life's meant to be.
Life should have some meaning,
That is plain for us to see.
We forgot about that shining star,
Once seen, bright in the sky.
And the little boy in the manger,
Did, asleeping lie.
He walked the world, just for us,
To teach us good from bad,
And ended on a cross for us.
Jesus, was that lad.

Mary M Young
THE WINNERS WHO LOSE

To Sharon Sparks in Dayton, Ohio Remember when . . . . . .

Who wrote the rules on today's business etiquette,
And decided back-stabbing was Vogue?
From Michigan to Florida, California to Connecticut,
Someone has set the mode.

Although the work rules are not generally moral,
Some climbers do not really care,
I sit and I watch it with terrified horror,
The climbers whose moves are unfair.

They treat their co-workers without due respect,
Compassion is one thing they lack,
As long as they make it to the top, what the heck,
They run forward and never look back.

They don't seem to honor small people who count,
The ones who can make them look good,
They're consumed with the thought, "To what will I amount?"
Their hearts I would change if I could.

But will it all matter when time has run out?
And in death they become dust again,
When time catches up, and they fight their last bout,
The winners will lose in the end.

Angel E Soares
SPECIAL MOMENTS

To Mellony for Believing In Me.

From my window
I hear the sounds of the waves
Gently touching the shore
Caressing it with Love
As I close my eyes
I can see you standing
By the water's edge
Holding me close to you
With each sound the sand makes
The rushing sounds
Gives one the feeling of emptiness
It's been a long time my love
Each wave reminds me of those special moments
My love,
My love,
Come hold me tight
Don't let go
So many moments,
So many dreams.

Fran L Rebo
THE VENERABLE YEARS
On transparent wings time relentlessly flies
Soaring, dipping, whirling across the skies
Youth fast receding into the distance
Old age rushing in with daunting persistence
Wrinkles appear in sudden gasping surprise
Bones and joints moan and creak in groaning sighs
Faltering footsteps, reading glasses perched on the nose
Knobbily knuckled hands with a trembling that shows
All the signs, the symptoms of old age that belies
The youthful exuberance behind faded rheumy eyes
Weeping not for lost love, nor songs we might have sung
All mistakes, all painful times, just another rung
On life's ladder from earth to the farthest star
The sum total of what we have been what we are
We greet the waning years smiling with arms out-flung
For beneath the sagging flesh beats a heart forever young

Frankie Williams
AND I SAW A DOVE
As I closed my eyes and whispered a prayer
Knowing my Lord was so near

and did care
I then saw a dove in flight sweeping o'er
To dive, then straight up and glide to the door.
Then it flew, in its own natural flight
Going to and fro from the left to the right
Then all of a sudden with my friend deep in prayer
The dove above her head just fluttering there.
It was hovering as if, in an upward flight
Wings sweeping forward back and forth left and right
How can I explain this sight from above
Has God sent his blessings on the wings of a dove.
This dove is of peace, and joy, and of love
As the sweet Holy Spirit descends from above
Help me dear Lord, to do what is right
Help me to know, when this dove is in flight.
Holy Spirit of God, in flight from above
Hovering over his children as on wings of a dove
God is gathering his children, and renewing their sight
The dove is returning, the dove is in flight.

Candace G Stallings
MY FEARS

To Lloyd, For helping me face "my fears." Thanks for being there.

Seeing you from afar,
I long to speak,
But I don't dare—
I'm afraid
I'll fall in love with you,
And you won't even care.
I'm afraid
I'll try to talk to you,
And you won't even speak.
I'm afraid
Everytime I hear your voice
I'll suddenly get weak.
But most of all I fear—
More than any fear
I've known—
I fear I'll never know you,
And I'll spend my life alone.

Carina Victoria Lovitt (Age 11)
LOOK AT ME
Look at me my child
And what do you see?
Only an old woman you say
Look again,
Look again at me,
My heart is as free as it could ever be
My spirit, my life is all in me
Look at me woman
And what do you see?
Only a child you say
Look again,
Look again at me,
I am young
And I don't have a worry in the world
I lead a life that only children can see,
My child you remind me so much of me
I can see my heart in yours, my child
My good woman, I can see my heart in yours.

Mark E MacCallum
A VIEW FROM THE TOP
Wind rushing, cold biting
Chill in air, all exciting.
White as far as the eye can see
Beauty here in all of thee
Nature's crystal palace.
Where cold cycles hang from limbs
And beautiful colors are shown through them.
Adrenalin rush, a natural high
And yes all this a skier's sigh.
For on top of the mountain he is king
And to the Lord he only sings
Thanking him for the beauty and grace,
Of this snowy and mountainous place.
The day is through, the final run
Thank you Mother Nature for all you've done.

Sherry Toland
MEMORIES

To: My Husband Mel, my son Barry and Memories.

The warmth in my heart of friends and places,
Of long ago I see,
In my mind's eye; their faces,
Are so very dear to me,
Drifting back to events of my youth,
Where only dreamers go,
It seems more life was in living,
Than is now my desire to show,
Has age left its mark of despair, so deep,
No more my youth to see,
My life is now my memories,
And my memories are life to me.

Emma Maxine Hirth
POETRY
My heart is just an open door that leads into my soul
And gathers thoughts both large and small, emotions shy and bold
That I may put them into words that give me joys untold.
And this, to me, is poetry.
To gaze into an open sky and know that day or night
My pathway will be guided by my Savior's heavenly light.
And wonder at the mysteries far beyond my sight.
And what I see is poetry.
To watch a bird in leisure flight; to hear a baby cry,
To see rose petals open wide; a rainbow in the sky.
And listen to the sounds of life that daily pass me by.
Dear heart, to me, that's poetry.
How wonderful to hear the voices stirring deep within
And wait in quiet solitude for the words to begin;
As music gently waiting for the notes to play again.
And it's mine to have, this poetry.
No matter if it comes in music, words or thoughts of mind.
It cannot be forgotten with the passage of time.
For living is the legacy that each one leaves behind.
This wonderful world of poetry.

Catherine T Miller
VISIONS
The scent of sage, it lingers still
on freshblown wind, creates a thrill
A vision of a midnight ride
the rugged wrangler by my side
The harvest moon, in its full glow
my pulse beats fast, the pace is slow
the desert scape begins to stir
nocturnal paws and wings and fur
glide through the shadows of the night
and seldom catch the moonbeams light
Rustling harness, jingling bit
disturbs not peace, but seems to fit
the solitude that we have earned
and nature's vision brightly burned
as if with branding iron set
within my mind, I'll not forget.

Agnes M Conde
ARTS AND CRAFTS
Sewing, Embroidering,
Crocheting, Knitting,
Which is an Art? Which is a Craft?

Drawing, Painting,
Writing, Reading,
Which is an Art? Which is a Craft?

Wherever you go,
Whatever you do,
Which is an Art? Which is a Craft?

They are all an Art.
They are all a Craft,
And they all come from the heart,
May Arts and Crafts never part.

Del Grote
WIND RIVER
Tears are splashed upon the river's edge
A Maiden's warrior is lost and dead
The battle was great there's no shame
The warrior died for his people the same
The Great White Spirit called upon his will
The warrior gave all the battle is still
Wind River will flow for many years
Whispering the roar and a Maiden's tears

C L Pyle
IN A MOMENT
Notice the ascending to descend
In a moment
See the smile that is pretend
Opposites fluctuate
Feel the bad turn to great in time
All the problems vanishing
Still heart of mine
Patiently I wait and see
And then I notice how the frown can turn to grin
In a moment
Feel the hope come from within
All inside to and fro
It's a feeling we know
Relax when the tear it brings
In a moment the real mood swings

Ruth May Dean
MY LOVE

To my lovely granddaughter Mrs. Beth Ann Rinsman who is very responsible for her selection of this poem, My Love, which was read at her wedding. Love always, Nana Dean.

What a wonderful experience to feel the touch of a lady's beautiful hand.
What a glorious experience to gaze into a person of caring's loving eyes.
It really puts a fellow into ecstatic command.
From the very moment when you meet that special miss,
And you enjoy the thrill of that never to be forgotten kiss.
Then all of a sudden your life changes indeed,
Because then you can experience, that with all your heart, you will need.
It doesn't matter whether you are young or old,
When that person comes into your life,
You are possessed with that pot of gold
That separate happiness free from strife,
Adds a special touch all of your life.
And a symbol signals from above
Centers excitement from within
The heavenly gift of love.

Clyde Orrick Jr
MY FLOWER
You are like a flower
So beautiful to me
I saw you in a garden
By a never ending sea

I picked you from the others
You stood out from the rest
With colors shining brilliantly
You simply were the best

I'll sprinkle you with tenderness
And water you with care
Protect you from the wind and rain
I always will be there

A red rose whispers passion
A white rose breathes of love
My flower you are both to me
From heaven up above

Eleanor Bridges Akridge

Eleanor Bridges Akridge
SUNLIGHT
Seeing the sun shine bright today
Just like a hunk of gold
I knew you were there, Dear Lord
Keeping things under control
It's never too hot to burn
Never too cold to freeze
Moves along as planned
Under God's guiding eye with ease
Earth keeps turning around
Trees still growing tall
Flowers becoming more beautiful
Rain brings in the fall
Sun makes soft green grass
Fresh fruit and vegetables too
Keeps us healthy and happy
We've always plenty to do

How about you and me
May we help someone today
Make life a little sweeter
Spread sunlight in other's way

Linda Goodsell Hibbard
BOULEVARD OF BROKEN HEARTS
A boulevard of broken hearts
Where no one knows your name
You can survive, and stay alive
If you learn to play the game.

No glitter here, no neon lights
Nothing that money buys.
It's a place where man is broken
Full of silent saddened eyes.

A coin in your cup, but don't look up
They'll quickly run away.
When day meets night and darkness comes
You'll need a place to stay.

A fire burns and you take your turn
To warm your hands and feet.
Your soul is tired and it needs to rest
Let it dance to a silent beat.

No epitaph, no eulogy, no R.I.P.
For what's his name
'Cause you're on your own, on the boulevard
Where no one knew your name.

Dennis R Fowler
MOTHER EARTH
Over across the distant shore,
lay a land with stones of Tor.
Time is still and day is night,
Children there are with the sight.
Through the mists ore the sea,
take me there forever to be.
We love the Earth & respect the seed,
forever let the Goddess lead.
Let the kings and rulers rise,
We know the one most wise.
She is the Earth, mother to all,
Please lift your selfish ignorant wall.
The raven flies to you this night,
let her lift you to endless highs.
For tonight the fires are aglow,
Springtime approaches, you should go.
It is Beltan, and the tides are high,
Choose the maiden
Bring back the ones who call through wind,
The Beltan fires are almost at an end.
As winter ends, the land lies still,
eat and drink to your fill.
For tonight the Earth will be reborn,
at dawn we'll blow the fertility horn.
The crops will grow, and maidens swell,
to bring forth life, and pass down tales we tell.
And so she sees another year,
from her cheek slides a tear.

Ed Ruggles
FALLING LEAVES
Bright is the sun, with skies of blue,
Leaves all colored in the fall.
Seems they're changing, all on cue.
Has winter spoken to them all?

Do the moving, broken lines,
Sounds of honking in the sky
Tell a tale of northern lands
That the cold and snow are nigh?

Who can tell the time or place
Where mysteries of nature dwell,
On a wondrous, living world in space,
Changing, moving, never still?

Colored sunsets in the west,
Lighting the sky at harvest time.
Do they mark the life that's past,
Or growing new in a different clime?

The fall of life, three score and ten,
The leaves that fall before the spring,
Would they escape the winter then?
Only by faith in our Saviour and king.

Richard Finks Whitaker
IN PRAISE OF FLAMES KEPT LOW (A VILLANELLE)
Once sparks of passion catch, the night's aglow,
ablaze with fiery hopes and raging fears.
Yet flames of love warm best kept burning low.

Like kindling, brittle need is first to go:
its crackling bursts to roaring in our ears.
Once sparks of passion catch, the night's aglow—

a dazzling, soaring, dizzy-making show!—
spectacular although—because!—it sears!
Yet flames of love warm best kept burning low;

wild conflagration overwhelms us so.
It's startling, thrilling, frightening as it nears,
once sparks of passion catch. The night's aglow:

not flick'ring—flashing! Blinding! To and fro
we race through fires—hysterical!—in tears!
Yet flames of love warm best kept burning low:

one arm around your shoulder and you know
how care that smoulders comforts down the years.
Once sparks of passion catch, the night's aglow—
yet flames of love warm best kept burning low.

Rachel Whitebook
ECHOES
We laughed in the lovemoments before and after,
and you said I couldn't do it,
but I smiled and made a moue . . .
And then we laughed again—
but this time you knew.

I woke and I found
your image nightimprinted:
echo of a dream.

And in that sudden rain,
listening, I remembered: you,
lovespent-sleeping in my lovedweary arms, smiling.
And listening to that springgreen rain
smacking on the garden leaves,
remembering you lovewearied,
I knew your tonguepoint passing feathery
across my sleepstained eyes.

I wake and I find
your image nightimprinted:
echoes of my dreams.

Dorothy A Bogue
PLEASE TURN OUT THE LIGHTS DARLING
I'm trying to write this letter
But the tears won't let me see
The lines upon this paper
There for you and me

You know that I love you
And I really want to stay
But the lines on this paper
Never say the words I want to hear.

I want someone to love me
Someone to hold me tight
Someone to share my life with
And fill my lonely nights

Instead the lines are empty
That's the story of my life
They're filled with tears of loneliness
Each time I turn out the lights

You're never there when I need you
To kiss away my tears
You never say I love you
Or let me know you care

Now I'll say goodby my darling
And take with me my tears
I'll leave you to turn out the lights
On a love we never shared

John V Weekes Jr
MOMMY . . . PLEASE . . .
Mommy please give me the chance
to hear the music that I might dance.
Mommy please let me breathe the air
for "I am someone," with dreams to share.
Mommy don't end it in this moment of strife
before I could take a chance on life,
Though tiny a life that I might be
let me open my eyes that I might see.
Mommy if you have a care to give,
Mommy please . . . let me live.

The plea of the unborn child

Lacanas O James
TIME

We love you Gramdma and Big Momma.

Tick Tock Goes The Clock
Slow Down Mr. Clock, Why So Fast
Running, Running, Faster, Faster
Stop! Stop!
My Head Is Spinning
My Face Is Older
My Hair Is Grayer
My Heart Beats Faster . . .
. . . Thank God, Another Day

G J Wood
BALL OF FIRE
Once we had a Paradise,
A Paradise called, Earth,
This was the real Garden of Eden.
So many beautiful flowers,
So many delicious fruits,
With raindrops coming down so softly,
Bathing flowers so gently,
And then the sun would dry those tiny drops,
And ALL what man had to do,
Was watch those miracles come up, from the Earth,
And watch the other miracles come down, from the Sky,
Everything was done for Man.
But All what Man could see, was the "Apple,"
The "Apple," which was really "Temptation,"
Temptation of dominating the World,
Power for a better, faster, easier world,
Which brought Man, finally to "Nuclear Power"
And it all resulted in pollution of waters, & the air,
Burning the soil and all the living things,
But Man had no time to see,
BLIND He became by that FOLLY of POWER.

Ted Hinton
DON'T BE A STRANGER
Don't ever be unknown or a stranger
To one that was born in a manger.
Born of Holy God to a virgin girl
To die for the sins of this world.
And to be cruelly nailed to a tree
That from sin we could be set free.
Crucified, dying and suffering shame
That we might be saved by His name.
No greater love could ever be shone
Than Jesus dying for our sins to atone.
Overcoming death, rolling the stone away
Rising from the grave on the third day.
Given power over both heaven and earth
How can we ever estimate His worth?
We being humble and with a human mind
To think one so powerful would be so kind
To sit at our heavenly Father's right hand
Hear prayers and intercede for sinful man.

Mary E Halbert
I MISS YOU

To "Cathy," my darling daughter, who has been my inspiration.

Since the last time I saw you
It seems like forever and a day
I miss your warm and sunny smile
You always send my way

I miss your tender and loving touch
That makes my heart beat fast
Oh how very much I wish
That it could always last

I will always love you
Until the day I die
I can't explain it
I don't know why

Someday we will be together
I hope and I pray
But until that day comes
I'll miss you in every way.

Dolores C Rawlins
MY LOVE OF LONG AGO

To Reginald S. Nurse.

See that picture over there
The one with the smiling face
I can almost hear his voice
And see his happy eyes that lighten up the place
In my dreams I see his face
And it makes me sad
To think I may never see him again
My Love of Long Ago
Love is a special happiness
As our hearts with memories fill
And loving thoughts of you bring

gladness
That will remain with us still
Does he ever think of days gone by
Thinking of what was to be
Knowing what he's always been
And will always be to me
Whatever may come or whatever may go
Though the picture may fade
year by year
There's still a loving spot in my heart
For the boy I loved so dear
My Love of Long Ago

Maria Förster de J
TO GROW AND TO BE
Deep within the earth
seeds await their birth.
Rain and sunshine flow,
force them all to grow,
make their brittle shell
crack and stretch and swell.

Soon the shoots will rack
out of darkness black;
But this power bold
seeking to unfold
lies as vital need
deep within the seed . . .
deep within man's soul . . .

Sorrow, joy and strife
burst the gates of Life
and out of the night
man must reach for light.

Strength will master fears . . .
Only under tears
can all living things
grow and spread out wings . . .

Maria Förster De J
STRUGGLE FOR A GOAL
The little pushers who lament defeated
hang on to bigger ones in their distress,
but these again cling to still higher seated . . .
All share each other's favors and success.
One goal unites all scribes who long and tinker,
while progress grovels like a centipede.
On road to fame many a weary thinker
wanes, basking in another fellow's shade.

Isabella Audrey Singh
THE MAGICAL POND
The pond an enchanting sight to behold,
frosted over in the winter cold.
The misty haze of winter, kept folks away at night,
but the morning brought a
crowd, a fun-seeker's plight.
The coldness of winter and the chill of the wind
held the pond frozen so the
races could contend.
The trees all around formed a canopy,
So the people on the sidewalk
could stroll by freely.
The lights on the pond looked like little lightning bugs
lighting them in their game of
War-of-Tugs.
The pond frozen over and the wind blowing low
glazed the pond over with the
icy snow.
All came to this magically, beautiful court
to enjoy something sweet and
the aroma of baking tortes.
Now the slumbering pond has no life around it,
as the night cascaded and began
to fall.
Except for the wind in the trees that are about it,
a hushed quiet overwhelmed it
all.

E Judson
RETURN (VERSION #2)
Rebellions Reach And Soldiers Fight
To Reach Eternal Shore
Where Lions Roam And Creatures Comb
Their Love Forevermore.
Republics Know And More—
Perceive:
Each—Steps Deliver Core
In Transitory Passage . . . Up
Toward [His] Holy Shore.

Transitions Troop "In Straightened--Loop"
. . . New Steps Toward The
Door . . .
Where Creatures Speak And "Holies" Seek
Escape From Senseless--War.
Utopic Light . . . Escape From
Fright . . . ,
Compels Our Learning--Lore
"Into The Air Where Fight-For-Fair"
Sustains Our Silent--Soar.

Utopic—Right . . . From Fatal—
Sore . . .
Has Earned Escape And More
From Gore
. . . For Para Looms Beyond Our
"Zooms"—
Toward—The—Golden—Door.
And, Then, . . . Beyond . . . The
Garden Lures.
We Hear The Lion's Roar
And Know [He] Lives, In—Silence Gives
. . . Relieving Tears—From--
Tore.

Denise Frazier
CHILDREN WE ARE
He was a young boy
with an endless smile
that kind of worked its way into your soul
Slowly, with ease
like his movements
steady, like the never stopping hands of time.

She was a young girl
with all the shyness of a child
that has never been introduced to a grown-up world
but with eyes
that told tales
no adult could phantom that she could conjure.

Together, they came
like words and a melody
that only two lovers could begin to sing
United as one
in an unsung verse
that was certain to play forever.

Katherine J McMurtry
A LOVELY GARDEN OF FLOWERS
Walking in a garden where the pretty flowers grow.
Such a beautiful sight to see more
then you'd ever know.

The pansies in bright colors their
faces soft and new.
Makes one feel their beauty is
blessed by the morning dew.

Then to see the hon-ey-suck-le vines
as they climb the garden fence.
And to enjoy the fragrance of the
blossoms as it holds one in suspense.

The yellow daffodils are as bright as
the morning sun.
So delicate and soft as from spiders
webs there spun.

Pauline Byrd Borden
LIFE'S LESSONS
I often think
That man's inhumanity to man
Is made manifest
That we may learn and understand
That all things must for a reason be.
For in the world's eons of evolution
We are all teachers and being taught.
And I believe
That however things may seem or be
We have our chance to change them
And make the most of them eternally.
Then as the endless cycles roll
The seeming good and bad will take its toll,
Until every man is free.
Then joyously behold—mankind!
Under his promised vine and fig tree!
And none shall make him afraid.

Mark S Bailey
CAPTIVE EYES
Captive Eyes
Chained to your desire
Imprisoned by your charm
Locked to your seductive glare

Captive Eyes
Corralled inside a growing friendship
Caged by your wild mind

Captive Eyes
Shackled by your radiant beauty
Leashed by your tender stare

Emma E Steckelberg
AND SO—
I suppose in seventy-seven years you
may expect those eerie, swift,
"gone-with-the-wind" feelings;
Those "out-of-the-blue"
announcements that suddenly you're
bereft of your life's savings;
That the Bankruptcy Court has
appointed a Receiver to untangle the mess,
And a Trustee designated to answer
all questions that bother you.

You write! You wait! No answer. No
recourse now but to wait and to hope.
And hope I will until the last vestige
of a possible solution is forthcoming.
And so—
I wait! And I wonder! And I hope . . .

Nathaniel Stover
CRUCIFIED HEART
God laid his hand upon my head
Said feel the hurt you have spread
Feel the pain deep in your soul
Look in your heart that is so cold

God saw no tear come to my eye
He said my child you do not cry
Is hate so strong or love so weak
That all you see is what you seek

God said you need no heart to live
You only take you never give
You need no heart to criticize
Stand an' judge an' tell your lies

God laid his hand upon my chest
Like lightning flashes then he pressed
Out come my heart upon the ground
I heard that thumping pumping sound

Blood from my palms fell to my feet
Spikes like arrows cut so neat
Fear then showed into my eyes
While at my feet my heart it cries

Patricia Robitzsch
SEARCH FOR PEACE
When did this avid search for peace
first begin to so overwhelm me?
Numbness has been my companion
for so very long.
But now the silent screams within
demand to be silenced no more.
Nature's creations no longer
buffer me from reality.
Man's powdery substance
only intensifies my worst fears.
These things which were once
my avenue for an escape,
have become a vicious warden.
Self-control is a vague dream,
seen through a mist of my
expensive, synthetic personalities.
Still the search goes on,
pleading me away from a lifestyle
I haven't the will to leave.

Susan B Hall
THE LIGHT OF LOVE
Dimly, through the dark of night,
shines a single star.

A bit of light so distant,
but in my thoughts not far.

It's like my hope, my love for you,
although we're far apart.

It reaches you because it's strong
and shines forth from my heart.

B J Jones

B J Jones
TODAY

This poem is dedicated to Francis T. Greene, M.D. and Daryl K. Houston, M.D. for their neverending compassion and unselfish dedication on my behalf.

Today I walked, Today I played,
Today was my day to have it my way.
So many days I couldn't play. I
couldn't do anything my way.
Now I must say, "Hey, What a lovely

day," for Today is my day.
When I was a little girl I had nothing to twirl, for I had nothing but an empty world.
And as I began to grow, I needed to know that love was aglow.
Instead only empty thoughts filled my head.
And now it's sad, but I'm not mad.
I'm really glad. For Today, my second chance, to do it my way.
Now friends and peers, listen here.
Perhaps you share some of my fear of those old yesterdays.
Well let's turn those days around 'cause we are now on new, profound ground where love and happiness abound.
Let's go and paint the town, Today!
For TODAY is my day!!!!!!

Julia L S Jones

THE TIME HAS COME TO SAY GOOD NIGHT

The time has come to say good night
you have come to the close of the day.
"Now fades the glimmering landscape on the sight."

Do not look back or shudder from fright,
You have kept your promises along the way.
The time has come to say good night.

The joy ahead is equal to mountains of heights.
Because you took time out to watch the children play.
"Now fades the glimmering landscape on the sight."

Go with the grace of birds in flight,
Eventide has come, daylight cannot stay.
The time has come to say good night.

There is a star above you shining so bright.
It will light your path, it will not stray.
"Now fades the glimmering landscape on the sight."

The splendor of the rose you cannot match the sight.
of the beauty at the end of the day.
The time has come to say good night.
"Now fades the glimmering landscape on the sight."

Stewart Erlich

NIGHT BY THE FIRE

Gazing into depths within depths surrounded by
Swimming in the utmost physical and mental enlightenment
Beauty unearthed and forever pure, I spy a silk white moth.
Climbing upward downward swirling delicate shadows cast on the rocks and trees by the flames licking the air.
Designed by freedom—beauty my glistening moth finds my heart and forever engraves herself there.
Outstretching my hand I find communion with her as she mounts it for the first time allowing me to taste her form.
Pure white glistening diamond wings delicately textured magical sparking blue eyes which I swear for a moment looked into my soul and found peace there. She outspreads her wings and shows me her exquisite fullness.
She smiled as she turned and dove carefully into the flames.
And I thought, This Is Meant to Be.

Emma T W S Fuller

NEW TESTAMENT TEACHINGS

Father in Heaven, I kneel to Thee in reverence
To thank Thee for the mission of Thy Son.
Grueling death pangs for us He bled and suffered
Excelled justice, and victory's death He's won!
We'll cherish now, Truths He taught us to follow—
To live in tune with Heaven's realms all hours.
Forgive cruel wrongs, or ill words of us spoken,
Return kindness with loving deeds, and dowers.
Daily searching to find the lone and weary,
To walk with them that extra mile or two.
Supply their needs, and share our priceless message,
Our testimony that the Gospel's true.
Ascend praises for clouds, as well as sunshine.
They each, are tools of learning, for our goal.
Accept with joy, all roads that Thou hast measured.
They'll weld the bond and crowning of our Soul!
Father in Heaven, may we be near Thee ever
To fill each hour, the mission we were given.
When we're called home to meet Thee and our Savior,
In glorious realms of Thy eternal heaven!

Robert Hatch

A SONNET FOR ANTOINETTE

Swimming, I think you are my dark lady;
A fish.
And I your bait.
I feel your absence as parted lovers feel
The phantom pressure of each other's bodies.
I miss you
As I miss the dead.
I look for you in the eyes of strangers,
cursing the water that leaves no tracks,
And I wait for your return
As I wait for my own youth
To come back to me,
Swimming in one morning
On the first heave of the tide . . .

Deborah Behlen

ONLY IF HE EARNS IT

I sit by the bed and I watch
I watch our little girl sleeping with a smile on her face
As I sit here I thank God she belongs to us
And I remember what mama said;
"A child is God's gift to man, but only if he earns it"
We've waited so long for this baby
And finally I guess God thought we earned it
But as soon as the baby was born you said good-bye
Honey just remember what my mama said
"A child is God's gift to man, but only if he earns it"
We worked hard to earn this baby
So why did you leave the baby and me
All of a sudden my thoughts are broken
Our daughter has waken and, I think,
"A child is God's gift to man but only if he earns it."
"But only if he earns it."

Rhonda Witt

BROKEN HEART

A heart is not a plaything,
a heart is not a toy.
But if you want it broken,
just give it to a boy.

Don't ever fall in love my friend,
you'll find it doesn't pay.
It causes broken hearts my friend,
it happens every day.

Every time you see him,
your heart begins to dance.
Your world revolves around him,
so you'll give him one more chance.

Then you'll start and don't know why,
to worry night and day.
Because my friend you're losing him,
it just turns out that way.

Don't ever fall in love my friend,
you'll get hurt before it's through.
You see my friend, I ought to know,
I feel in love with you!

Frank Gilmore

MOTHER NATURE

Revel in her beauty
Breathe her clean fresh air.
Commune with Mother Nature,
She has peace and tranquility to share.

Climb upon her mountains,
Hike across her fields.
Drink of her cool clear water
That she so generously yields.

Stop and smell her flowers.
Eat rite off her trees.
Try and get to know her
For she tries so hard to please

Get close to Mother Nature
And know what she's all about.
You'll find in her all the things
That you couldn't live without.

Regina Blackburn

GRANDMA'S PHOTO GALLERY

Smiling little faces hanging on the wall; remind me of my loved ones as I walk down the hall.

Happy faces and memories I cherish so dear;
longing and yearning that they were near.

I know they are growing older;
and have a life of their own,
but oh, how I love to hear their voices on the phone.

When I see their faces looking down on me,
how I wish they were here to put their loving arms around me.

Grandma doesn't ask for material things;
just to be my loved ones friend,
Til the good Lord calls my days to an end.

Debra J Wachtveitl

BITTERSWEET

This is dedicated to Jenna and Joey. May you always know of love's pure heart . . .

You never could just leave it alone
always having to throw the first stone,
when sticks and stones just weren't enough
you did the unbelievable , . . the unheard of.

You couldn't stand that I was so strong
and everything you did to me went wrong,
so you went after what I loved and hurt the most
my kids in their innocence, taken by force.

To satisfy your sick need of children and lust
first to gain, then used, betrayed all the trust,
you tainted and robbed them of their self-esteem
all in a demented glory to finally be victor of me.

The amazing strength that they had inside
carried them through each and every time,
then something happened and your bubble burst
spilling out your secrets ever so slowly at first.

Things became different and soon I became aware
of the hell they were living by their nightmares,
it was one thing to abuse and make a victim of me
another abusing my kids to feed your vulgarities.

Any threat on my life is a small price to pay
to assure their protection and put you away,
so go right ahead and make your move
give me some more to use against you.

Her Majesty Justice, will crown you

"King of Fools"
and sentence you to a throne of iron bars to rule,
you'll reign for some time, for what you did
but not long enough . . , as the suffering of my kids.

So don't you think for one single minute
this is just a threat with no promises in it,
'cause if ever there was a promise to keep;
it's this one for you, made especially . . .

Bittersweet!

Teresa Dawn Bradley
HATE
Fists flying broken glass
Screeching screams of violence
Vacant lots and empty streets
Ruins of the riots
Beady eyes in window sills
With treacherous tongues behind them
Scarlet billows of oozing liquid
leaving this lifeless figure
Pungent smells of decaying flesh
With a poisonous bite of vengeance
Leaving a bitter after taste of anguish and indifference!

Davina Zeitz (Davey '79)
MY SISTER, THE STRANGER
She is part of the family, but
yet she's a stranger to me.
We live together off and on, and
still know very little of each other.
The last time we saw each other,
she was on the go, and I was going on my own.
She has little or no family, but yet
she forgot about me.
We are like strangers.
We don't talk to each other, or
even know each other anymore.
We are sisters who are strangers, or
two ships that just pass through the night.
I am here but, where is the stranger
who is my sister?

Mindy Powers
A PICTURE OF MYSELF
Unicorns run so gracefully by,
surrounded by mythical beauty.
Their tails nearly drag the ground
as they stop to graze nearby.
Their manes, like mysterious rainbow
waterfalls, fall down their necks in
multi-colored ribbons that have been
made into beautiful curls.
Their horns are golden spikes that
have just been polished,
the reflections so bright that with the slightest movement,
the sight is nearly blinding.

Do they know that I'm here?
Are they afraid of me?
My mind is filled with so many questions.

As they move through this meadow
of snow-white daisies,
I hear them softly whinny to each other.
They frolic along and stop at the
stream where I stand.

Suddenly I notice my reflection,
and a warm feeling comes over me.
After all this time I never
knew . . .

At this very moment, as I look at myself,
I realize that I am one of them.

Mary Korchak
LOVE ONE ANOTHER
"Love one another as I have loved you" (John 13-34) Jesus said
Hard at times it may be
I will be there for you whenever you
call on me
I will lift you up to overcome any
obstacle you may face
Just keep tuned in and keep the pace
I will help you gently through if you
just take time to meditate
Answers come in many ways
Prayer, meditation, it always
pays
Let us always try to be free in heart
and mind
Into our life will come great pleasure
Because our love we did not
measure.

Patricia Joan Johnson
THE ART OF COMMUNICATION
Good communication requires one to
STOP, LOOK (at the other person)
and to LISTEN!
Do these three things, or you'll never
know what you're 'missin!'
You already know what YOU are
going to say,
So listen and your wisdom will
increase day by day.

Listening to others is a sure way to be heard.
You will capture attention without
saying a word.
Failure to listen results in things
misunderstood;
"I didn't mean it," "She doesn't
understand," "He lied" . . . all not good.

Listen with an inner ear, observe
body language,
And the message will be clear.
The other's concern is yours to
digest,
So forget your ideas, and put your
wits to the test.

Sometimes it's best to nod, and say
not a thing.
Your rapt attention may much
comfort bring.
Assume nothing, and act as natural as can be.
Our sincerity will one's inhibitions free.

Don't be vague or deceitful . . . say
what you mean.
We'll avoid hurt and confusion, when
our message is clean.
Understanding the message is the
important key.
Whether giving or gathering
information,
Close attention is required to a great degree.

So be friendly and reasonable, think
clearly and smile,
And you've found the secret to
healing and grace,
That will take you that extra mile.

DON'T TRADE THE GRIN
FOR THE GRIM!

Barry A A Dillinger
A NIGHTMARE?
Little Barry slept quietly, but stirred in the night,
The Terror had returned arrayed in its fright.
It arrived in his room just as before,
In through the closet and opened the door.
The Terror was wrapped in a cloak of fear,
Its claws like steel, long, cold, and sheer.
Its mouth gaped wide showing
blackness therein,
But teeth drenched in gore leapt out from within.
The door of the closet opened and creaked,
Its breath was hot and its presence reeked.
Barry awoke and witnessed its coming,
Walls were shaking, the air was humming.
It broke into this world with a terrible sound,
Its shadow foreseen, its intent hellbound.
Its talon clenched the doorjamb as its
red eyes gleamed,
It shambled across the floor as the
little boy screamed,
But the lights sprung up as his
mother came in,
And drove back the Terror to its
world within.
The closet door was ajar as his
mother leaned down,
And her teeth shown like razors cast into a frown.

Mark S Rizzotti
EXPATRIAT
Another year, another place
Different gear, same old face
Old bridges burned
New customs to be learned

Tropical latitude, renegade attitude
Sun drenched oasis, strangers faces
Another night, cantina waitress
Feels like so many other places

Always the outsider, on the run
Outlaw wanderer, under the gun
No time to settle down
No sanctuary, no high ground

The chameleon walks the beach
Security is out of reach
Desperado on the move
Hears the sound of approaching hooves

Morning sun numbs the pain
Time to move on again
Expatriated American, unknown
Man without a country, can't go home

Alice K Marko
ACTUALLY
Actually, we are a part of the universe,
Actually, we are a part of the world.
Actually, you are a boy,
Actually, I am a girl.
Reason knows the answers,
Deep within the mind.
Look, forever laughing,
See what you will find.
Actually, when it is over, there will be an end.
Actually, you will always, forever be my friend.

Stacey Skowronek

Stacey Skowronek
KITTENS 'N' CATS
Have you ever played with a kitten?
Or maybe a cat?
Sometimes they bother me,
I wish they'd scat!
They wake me up at night,
And meow in my face,
But when they play they really know
how to chase!
I see them run.
I see them walk.
But what they really hate is the sound
of a dog's bark!

Ted S Augustyn
WITHIN
Within the oyster lies the pearl,
The shell is quite misleading.
So thus it is with boy and girl,
First thoughts can be
demeaning.

Within the heart is beauty bound,
One's looks are oft deceiving.
Within the soul is virtue found,
And factors, worth redeeming.

So in your quest for things of beauty,
Look not on objects with an eye
Oblique to truth, or with sense of duty,
To judge each harshly, if a bit
awry.

Trust instead, your inner feeling,
For qualities that can most
enlighten,
And, if looked for, most revealing
By acts and deeds some life to
brighten.

Joel Tenenbaum
FUTILE EXPECTATIONS OF A DREAMER
Here's another one,
Another chance to change where I am,
But alas, it's another sweepstakes,
From Ed McMahon.

I enter them all,
Check the cards and slips,
And hope that someday it's . . .
"You've won the grand prize—
expect a call!"

That never happens,
But I send the entries anyway,
But with my luck, my only win,
Would be the day I passed away!

To win a sweepstakes
Is like the carrot dangling in front of the horse.
Constantly trying to claim the prize,

To change life's course.

Here's to the majority of us, the dreamers,
The losers, the futile schemers.
We'll keep on trying to change our destiny,
A future expectation, before our dying.

Jonathan Samuel Speck
THE PIGEON SLEEPS

To Grandpop Stanton.

A pigeon coos. Flutters her filthy wings
She nestles down, coos again. She goes to sleep.
As I lay to sleep in my eighteenth story gray apartment, the spectrum of violent smashes and screamings rise up and lull me to my dreams.
A cop car screeches around the corner on two wheels.
I suppose in search of the distant battle explosions.
A wino stops to complain to the elevator operator.
But really to nobody.
He goes on. I peer down and see him pee on my building.
A bus drives by.
I can hear the wheezing protests of its air brakes struggling to stop their master.
A drug hustler makes a sale to some kid.
I listen to the rustling of the deadly bills.
I feel protected from the earth high in my apartment.
But really only a few seconds away from hell.
A pigeon coos. Fluters her filthy wings.
Me and the pigeon nestle down and go to sleep.

Larissa Sparks
BREAK THE WALLS

I look at you, you look at me.
I can't see you; you've put up a wall.
As I call to you, you won't respond,
Please don't break our special bond.
I love you dearly as I stand in fear,
I can bear no more; your love isn't here.
Set us free, as it will be
the best thing you could do for you and me.
Fill me with love from up above.
Skies of blue make it come true.
Stop the fight, make it alright;
For I know that love bites.
Now that I am away I must face the pain.
Nowhere to run now, our battle not won.
Show me your heart, I'll show you where to start;
Show me your soul so that I may be whole.
Mother listen for once:
Break the walls before death calls.
If we must part, let it be with a free heart.

Kyleen Ramos
IN INNOCENT EYES

In innocent eyes
I see only the running tears
Of a painful life
A memory of unforgotten years.

Frank Morriss
TO THE FLAG BURNERS

Burn it here among these stones,
Light it with the brand of hate,
And tell those beneath this ground
That you have found them fools
To die of love of it,

To keep it seen against
A burning sky turned red
By hate like yours on fields
of fire.

A jury of heroes gathers
In the court of courage—
Bill who smiled his way
Into the last darkness,
And Joe of easy quip who
slipped, slipped
Away from Buddy's grasp,
And Jim who fought that old
last foe
In cursing agony.

Fear not their sentence.
It leaves you to die with
empty liberty
While they live on in the
embrace
Of a nation's thanks at each
Dawn's early light.

Tonya R Dickinson
SHADOWS

Pain is a shadow
That covers the heart
Love tries to mend
What's been torn apart

Tears that fall
From a scar of pain
Will dry in time
But forever remain

A scar so deep
Of an unthoughtful word
Caused the pain inflicted
On the one who had heard

The love that follows
The shadow of pain
Will dry in time
But forever remain

Tommie Terrell
TEACH ME LORD

Teach me Lord to share my love
with those who pass my way.
And let me change my fear to courage
for the remainder of my days.

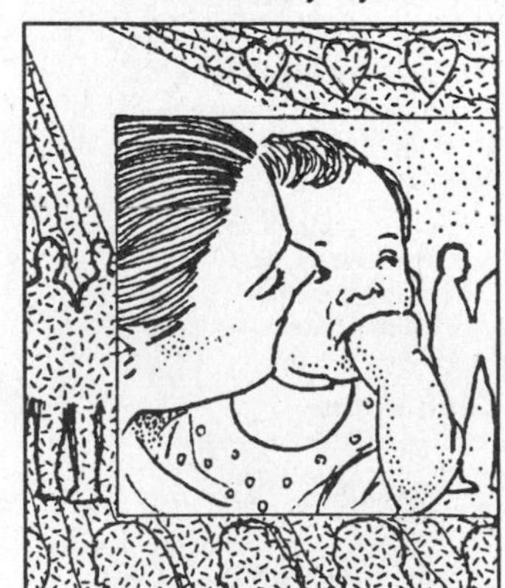

If I can help someone in pain,
with a loving touch or smile,
my reward will be in Heaven,
as I walk that final mile.
For death is but a short step
from darkness into the light.
God will hold me in His loving arms,
with all His heavenly might.

Tommie Terrell
A MOTHER'S LOVE

A mother's love is dear and sweet,
because that love is so complete.
We hold our children to our breast
and try so hard to give them our best.
I know we must learn to let them go,
even though we love them so.
Our Father in heaven put them in our care,
knowing we hold them in every prayer.
As we watch them grow,
we must let them know—
That life is a gift only God can give
He gave His life, so that we all may live.

Beatrice Kidwell
A MOTHER'S HEART

It must've been something for you to see,
A son being murdered and in pain, as he.
A son who healed the sick, deaf and blind
A son who was so very, very kind.
A son gave of himself so unselfishly,
A son who a mom could be very proud of, was he.
A son who raised the dead and fed the masses,
A son who know no particular classes.
A son who was a carpenter by trade,
A son who would never consider being afraid.
His life was so short yet packed so full,
Of unbelievable acts that he created and still
If you don't know who it is by now, I will tell,
It's Jesus the Christ, and my savior as well.

Sarah Jackson
IF IT'S TRUE

If it's true love that you think you have found,
That's what it is if this is how it sounds.
You laugh with one another and have fun together,
In times that are good or bad you're there for each other.
You trust each other and are really great pals,
Then you start to like even more than other guys or gals.
You think of them often even times that are strange,
You like them the way they are and don't want them to change.
Some people don't like them but you ignore what they say,
'Cause you still like them in exactly the same way.
When you see them your world seems much brighter,
You feel like you're floating on air and even lighter.
When they're with someone else you feel mad and jealous too,
Then you start to wonder if who they like is you.
When they touch you, inside you melt,
You tried but you couldn't tell them how you felt.
That's what it's like if that's how it sounds,
It's true love you're in and that you've found.

Rolland K Flicker
ACROSS THE WORLD

The bloody mess that lay asleep—
Dark and ever more—
Young lives gone to the corner store.
No bread today, no bread today—
Who are you anyway.
You have no rights—
Only to die at night—
In good old Tiananmen square.
Sitting in the dim lit room—
the old men sing their song—
Kill the bastards, kill them dead—
No one shall go home.
The same is heavy, the fires are bright—
In good old Tiananmen square tonight.
The tanks are there—
The soldiers too.
Kill the bastards run them through
Burn it all even their towns.
Across the map as the world spins round—
Death and hatred boils away.
In horror tone the world does groan—
Kill the bastards now—
Kill them—
The old men say.

G Joseph English
LORETTA'S WEDDING PRAYER

Forever and ever . . . and even then
Through wedding vows convey,
You bind your hearts eternally
On this your wedding day.

But Love is more than mortal things
That's bound by vows and wedding rings,
For Love is hope and dreams and fears
Shared with smiles and bitter tears.

As Cosmic tides launch inner waves
Of passions spent and passions saved,
Your Love and trust to each other you swear
ALL passions together you now will share.

As man, as wife, as friend and foe
Through life's journey together go,
But in the end you each will know
You shared Love only GOD bestows.

The earth, the moon, the bridge, the groom
We have gathered here to pray,
For your wedding vows and your happiness
On this our Wedding Day.

Joan Bishop
FINIS

Now it's time to end this song;
The Piper has been paid.
Games of love are costly
When recklessly played.

To use the heart and body
As a plaything, as a toy
Gives transitory pleasure
But robs the soul of joy.

And to tell the story,
You said, was honesty,
But heard time and time again,
It seemed a boast to be.

So now it's time to end this song;
The Piper's marched from sight.

The games have all been put away.
The heart has lost the fight.

Jean Bennett
HAVING FUN
Having fun is sitting on the veranda
Looking over the Adriatic Sea
Seeing the beauty of the mountains with many rocks
Feeling the clear misty air on your skin is delightful
Walking up stairs to unlimited heights
Looking down on the depths of the sea
Makes me feel grateful, that I am alive.
I rode a bus up and down the mountains
Observing the beauty of the terrain

Margaret Balcam Bess
PLEASE SET ME FREE
A butterfly starts life entombed—
No way to spread its wings;
Then comes the time when he is free.

Soaring high, does he wonder with glee,
"Is this really me, no longer bound on every side?"

His colors on the outside show,
But no mirrors reflect his beauty.

I have mirrors to show my face,
but like the butterfly who does
not know he is a thing of Grace.
I cannot see my inner beauty.

It's there somewhere—God told me so;

At times like this, I am the butterfly bounds in the cocoon—

Please set me free!

Penny Sue Paxton
EASTER DAY
A Babe wrapped in swaddling clothes
Came to Earth one Christmas Day.
This Babe who to manhood grew,
Walked this earth to pray & pray.

To those he met on the path he would preach
Follow me, for I am the Light and the Way
Twelve disciples followed in his steps,
Except for one, Judas, who did betray.

Pilot & Herod could find no guilt or fault
But the people, their feelings, did convey.
Not Jesus, Our Lord, The King of Jews,
But Barrabus, Barrabus, is all they could say.

Our Jesus now hangs on the tree of death,
The pain and suffering to all did display,
That Jesus, so pure from earthly sin,
Did die to take our sins away.

In three days time, he arose again
Surrounded by the Glory of God.
A sign to all that we, he did save
And this is why we celebrate Easter Day!!

Delmar Albertson
I WENT ABROAD
I went abroad one year ago,
To see what I could see
I own some stock like Valley Bank
and that safe one TEP.

I also had some Pinnacle West
and lots of Circle K,
I bought some Western Savings Bonds;
and I thought they'd always Pay.

I got back home and broke is not so bad
Except now I have to work down at the Burger King.

But now I know when I get my money, I tell my wife "Sofona", the way to make big bucks is to become a politician in Arizona.

Maybe you should sell stocks that you don't yet own, by borrowing from a broker, 'cause a person selling short is cheating the Public
like playing Poker

Barbara Luster

Barbara Luster
FALLEN LOVE
First: To GOD ALMIGHTY, MY REDEEMER & my beautiful mother: Mrs. Callie Luster, my inspiration.

Longing for a love—so tender
You withdraw from affection
Seeking a uniqueness: You know: one of a kind;
Sensitiveness—pains of heart—defensive moods—retaliation is smart.
O' love—love—love
Experienced too the fullest extent,
Makes your world, a "miracle of miracles":
Total joy—constant bliss.
Only in your mind, do you really conceive—
you've lived in a world—
a fantasy of make-believe.
Like a child, wishing upon a—falling star—
Loneliness being your constant friend;
Never Trusting anyone
With your tender heart again.
The sun dawns on a "new day"
You rebel against love once more;
Knowing it'll never stay—
As you watch the star falling
falling—It's gone away.

Heaven Anticlea Oliver
DEAR LORD
To my loving family and very special grandpa, Charley. I love you all!

"Dear Lord,
As I lie here quietly and reminisce the events today,
I'd like to take a moment's time to question you as I pray.
Lord, I'd like to know the reasons for the problems of the earth.
Why people have no place to sleep or only ashes upon their hearth.
Why broken homes are left to endure the memories of the past, or why the less fortunate people of the world are always thought of last.
And tell me Lord, why people think that happiness comes from wealth?
For, the only true happiness anywhere comes from inside oneself.
Another thing I'd like to know is why we always fight?
People constantly killing people for reasons of pure delight.
But Lord, I ask only one more thing for the world you've created is at stake; Please keep a careful watch upon us and the paths we are bound to take."

Patricia Ann McFadden
SMILE
Did you ever think of the word "smile"?
Let's dwell on it for a little while!
The facial expression may be in
for a bit of a change.
By the curving of the mouth
It could be felt even if you are out of range!
Amusement, laughter, affection—
It could express!

Irony, or derision, or ridicule
Could be done under duress!
How far does a "smile" go?
Do you really want to know?
Just look at the word
And you can see—
5,280 feet,
What a pleasure that would be!
A smile spreads friendship, love and grace
We, too, can see the glory of God shining in Christ's face!
So, regardless of what mood you are in—
Just draw back your lips, and show your teeth, and grin!

Evelyn L Suiter
SENSES OF LOVE
To watch the awakening of a new day as the sunrise warms the morning.
To be touched by the warmth of a newborn child and feel its innocence.
To watch nature in its spring as if it has been kissed with new life.
To smell the essence of the flowers in the dew of morning dawn.
These are senses of Love.

To see a motor of any creature of this earth caring for her young.
To hear the laughter of children while they are busy at play.
To enhance the magnificence of a rainbow after a warm summer rain.
To be near someone you care for and know you are loved without uttering a word.
To captivate the sensuous beauty of a sunset as the day turns into night.
These are senses of Love.

To taste the aromatic flavor of a fine wine just before retiring at night.
To see the leaves of Autumn in their blazing colors dancing in the wind.
To feel the crisp breeze caress your face as the Autumn turns into winter.
To see on a winter's night, the trees turn into crystal as the moonlight embraces them.
These are senses of Love.

William Nathan Shane Reynolds
BENEATH GREEN SKIN
This poem is dedicated to the Earth, for if the Earth can change, so can the world.

Labyrinths of sweating soil twist, searching for an entrance. Minerals masquerade, they dance to the hidden sound, the sound of men pounding on hollow wood. Radical mice crush tunnels of lighted passages, for they have broken the barrier. Wriggling saliva monsters violently chew, maneuvering blindly. Meteors of splashing water crash, clustering into mermaids silently disappearing. The endless hidden music meanders, scattering deeply into the endless labyrinth. Threaded veins hug tightly, squeezing and scribbling stretched roads striking the moist syrup. Acres of branched skeletons structure skittish bonds, creating cold images. The bowels of the earth hibernate, peering through the crusted glass only noticing the green skin.

Frances Ferguson
MR. FINNEY'S TURNIP
Grandma, please, tell me, a story,
that your, Grandma told you.
I'll tell you, about Mr. Finney's turnip
Mr. Finney had a turnip
It grew, behind, the barn.
It grew and it grew, behind the barn.

Until it could grow, no longer.
Then Mr. Finney dug, it up.
He made the turnip, ready to boil.
It boiled and it boiled, until, tender.
Then Mr. Finney put a big, flavorful, steaming, hot bowl of turnip, on the table.
Mr. and Mrs. Finney ate and ate and ate,
just, as long, as they were able

Bonnie Lee Wittum
HAVE YOU?
Have you ever taken the time to really look around you?
Have you really noticed the wonders of God's love?
Have you ever held a snowflake within your hand and marveled at its uniqueness?
Or have you felt the gentleness of a breeze as it presses softly upon our cheek,
Or watch a tiny raindrop spread to make an inch?
Or how about an eagle as it soars

above, just watching and waiting.
Did you ever listen to a cricket call,
or feel the warmth
of sunlight as it stretches forth its rays?
Or what about a rainbow and the promise that God once made?
Have you really taken time to notice the colors of autumn,
a smile on a young child's face, or a tear upon a friend's face?
Have you taken time to notice the gentleness and love around you?
And have you taken time to say,
"Thank you God for this day?"

Saundra Kay
TODAY I THOUGHT OF YOU

Today I thought of you
not you and I,
JUST YOU.
A gentle thought of caring,
a warm feeling of love.
I want such good things for you . . .
peace of mind and spirit,
joyful laughter,
family and friends, to know and share
all that you are.

I thought of you today . . .
just as you are,
for who you are,
not only to me, who loves you,
but to others.

Thanks for being you.

Dee Anne Brinkman

Dee Anne Brinkman
PERPETUAL MOTION

To everyone who feels inferior & my subconscious.

The longer I live the deeper I dig,
this pit I yearn to lie in
I have bought so much and received much less,
for what I've had to buy
They don't see my dreams deceased,
because of
what they have made of me
Living my life the way I feel right, is not
their cup of tea
Nobody knows the sorrow I play, this music that
is heard
I have no doubt that when I'm out,
my soul
will get the purge
I am so tired of fighting life;
Though I have not won I will not lose, this
precious game of strife.

Debra A Ruby
I'M ONLY HUMAN

I wish I could fly
Up.
Soar through the clouds.
I'd like to be a bird,
A rabbit,
An elephant,
A bear,
A flower,
Anything but me.
Wouldn't it be nice
To climb the sky?
To a star?
Or the Moon?
Or Mars?!
I've always wanted to
Swing on Saturn's rings.
To reach the farthest part of the Universe.
But I can't.
I'm only Human.

Betty Toiger
LIFE

With all my Love to my new husband (Andres).

My mind wanders down
that old road of life.
It makes you stop and think,
What life is really like.
A waterfall and your tumbling down
with no place to go, only in the
everlasting arms of peace.
But through the window pain of my
tears, I see a pair of clear blue eyes
pulling me back, to a new love
and life.
Now I don't go back there anymore.

E C Ahola
TO ARTHUR JOHN

I've kept busy at the things to do
Which put to rest that part of you
Who raised the garden, changed the oil,
Emptied trash, and liked to toil
At cleaning junk or mowing lawn
Or shining up the truck at dawn.
It's nothing I can do by text
For I'm not sure what will show up next—
And you see, I almost cried today
When I threw your old toothbrush away.
I detest the things I have to do
Removing that which once was you
From our abode—but let me say
In my thoughts you're never far away—
For it was you who made my life—
And made me glad I was a wife.

Pamela A Hamilton
CHANGES

Dr. Robert Cobiella—for helping me make the changes in me, that I need and want.

Changes can come at any time or place
Changes don't have to be welcome
Changes may or may not be helpful.
There are changes in me that
I want—there are changes in me
that I need. It is these
needs that make me grow. It
is this growth that make me change.

Kimberly Presley
ALL IS PRECIOUS

The birds sing glory in the sky
The song of life
As the day goes by
The sun shines in
The door opens wide
Life's always precious when you're
by my side

A pink ribboned sunset
Stretched across the sky
Always there for a watching eye
The moment of gold
Slowly passes by
Times always precious when you're
by my side

A gentle evening breeze
On a moonlit stroll
The delicate beauty
of a star clustered sky
The song of the cricket
That signals the night
My views always precious when
you're by my side

I love you dearly, love of mine
All is precious when you're by my
side

Judy Lynn Carman Doll
WITH LOVE, J.

Today, I wondered about you.
Wondered if I'd forgotten you.
And after all the things that have
happened since,
I choose to remember you.
Suspended in time,
Our moments linking moments,
Sweet hours into days
Summer moons and snowy nights
Steamy showers and wet lashes,
Evenings hushed by caresses,
Filled with words and song,
Silence and warmth.
Kisses and softness.
All these feelings and thoughts
flood my mind
And for a moment it seems
As if no time has passed at all and
As if I could have forgotten you.

Ann Cripe
A BLACK DOG

Dedication to all animal lovers!

My master and I were walking down
the street last week.
We stop and I look across the street
and I saw a big yellow and white
cat on the porch.
So I said, "Hi," but my master
wouldn't let me come over to visit
with you.
If he wasn't there I would have gone
over and said, "Hi!"
I wanted to see you run, but you
might have other ideas.
Like a scratch on the nose, maybe—
But it would have been fun—
To see you run and I would be
laughing!
So my master talked to me to turn
around to go home.
So no fun for me today!
Maybe I'll see you another time!
Goodbye for now! Kitty cat!

Elizabeth S Boyer
SOMEONE CARES, YOU KNOW WHO

Someone cares, you know I do
We've made some love, just us two
We've made for each other
You're my ideal lover
God has to know, I need and love you
so much
Since we've been friends I thrill at
your touch
I know he'll have to show us a
way
That friends and lovers we may
stay
Someone cares, and you certainly
know who
I hope you care enough to show me
you do
We'll have to find a way for us
both
To be happy and not prone to
loathe

Wayne Ball
GRASS & SUN

For the grass is green
And the sun is yellow
For all in the world shall bring no
trouble
Though we all shall live,
And we all shall die
Not let that bring a tear to your eye

David M Morrison
LADY COME TAKE MY HAND

This poem dedicated to Lisa Marie Smith, my heart, my love, my wife. Remember, I love you always, and forever.

Lady, come take my hand
And together, we shall walk
The endless sandy shores
Of a Cape Cod beach
Eluding all company, but each other
In the full moon, we'll behold
Dancing beams of light
As they gently kiss the rolling waves

When rays of the rising sun
Skip across the morning sea
We'll build dream castles in the sand
And walk the endless sandy shores
If waves should kiss our castles
farewell

Their dreams will still remain
For they belong to only us
As we stand, hand in hand,
Just you and me

Lisa, I love you

Marci Bustos Baker
THE WORLD, OUR HOME

To Desirée, Nicholas and Mallory, my grandchildren. You and all the children are the reason we must care for this world now and in the future.

The world, our family of humanity's
only home,
North, south, east, west, wherever we
live or roam;
Some of us want a world that is tidy
and neat,
Every country, state, city or town and
street;
We want our environment to be
healthy and clean,

Whatever the sacrifices to adult, baby or teen;
On the other side, some only live for today,
No thought of tomorrows, just going their own way;
Some are too enlightened, some are in the dark,
Compromise is needed, meeting close to the halfway mark;
No shouting matches are needed, not, only my way is right,
No accusatory finger pointing, let's not keep on with the fight;
We need to get together for one and for all,
We must walk with a solution, not run or crawl;
We must start now or the future will be very dim,
Or the legacy we'll leave will be very, very grim;
From 1990 onward, let's all try to do our very best,
Save our world, our home, let that be our Quest!!!

David M Morrison
ANOTHER DAY WITHOUT YOU LISA MARIE SMITH

I reached out in the darkness
And touched your warm soft body
Knowing you had come, once again,
To hold me through the nite
Keeping me from those cold and lonely dreams
So I let all those fears subside.
As dawns light filtered from the darkness
I reached out to feel your warm soft body
Touching only the cold emptiness
I knew, you stayed somewhere in the night
Leaving me again, in memories of dreams
And it was another day, without you

My love, forever
David Morrison

Darryl K Bing
WOMAN IS . . .

Woman need look no further than herself to understand beauty
Her mind though complex in form and imperfect in reason serves to remind us of what a sublime work of art
she truly is
Her gift to man is her ability to feel with eyes so loving and caress
the center of his being
In spite of this her life is often perpetual turmoil—for her heart
is too vulnerable to accept love
and her soul too vain to refuse
Yet through it all her name is perseverance and her hunger for
life consumes all making woman a lifeforce we dare not deny.

Gilda M Perez
DEVOTIONAL

This poem is dedicated
In loving memory to: Bobby
From: His family members.

Oh, how well you are remembered,
it seems like only yesterday,
moments of laughter and tears
we shared with you.

The hope of recovery held us on
an even keel; closely-knit to your
family, you didn't utter a hint
of your pain nor despair.
Seeing you so brave, you gave us
all courage.
And this we recall, again and again.

Somehow, fate's reality gave you the strength not to rebel nor rally for your faith was too strong and you knew you weren't wrong feeling comfort and peace that He, the Master and Father
looked at you from above,
a place for you He would find high up
in the sky.

Jerry D Mills
NEVER

To my only Love Elexis Grace Mills. You'll always be on my mind and in my heart. I hope to see you some day soon. Love, Dad.

I'll never see the love you show
in those eyes of blue,
Or see your smiling face
when the day is through.

I'll never feel your loving warmth
that would greet me at the door,
Or feel your silky blond hair
when you're hugging me some more.

I'll never be there to comfort you
when you fall and skin your knee,
Or to share all your loving joy
when the boy you love says, "Marry me."

I know I should be there for you
to teach you right from wrong,
And to be there when it's for bed
to sing you a goodnight song.

I'm sorry I'm not there to be a father
for you each and every day,
and to be there to tuck you in and
help chase all your troubles away.

I only know one thing that may help you
when things are hard to bare,
You father loves you with all his heart
And no matter what I will
always care.
Dad.

Shirley T West
MY LOVE IS

This poem is dedicated in memory of my husband, Kenneth E West, afflicted with a malignant brain tumor in 1988.

My love is your love, sincere, sweet, true,
Always loving, always there;
To see me through.
My love is your love, early in the day;
Never disappointing,
It's always that way.
My love is your love, late in the night;
Dancing moonbeams, flaming fire-light.
My love is your love, through all the years,
Joy, happiness, tears;
Always my darling, dear.

Maria Feltner
THE EARLY SUNRISE

To my Father, who always encourages me to do the best I can.

As I sat in a tree up high,
I saw a flicker of light from the sky.
Then I heard the birds sing,
A wonderful song of Spring.

Below me in the fresh green grass,
I heard a small deer pass.
I wish this day could last forever,
I wish this day would leave me never.

Ginger Chapman
WHAT IS LIFE?

Life is a journey full of adventures,
For those that dare to take chances.

Life is a carousel, brilliantly colored,
With fancy music, going up and down, day by day.

Life can be a shocking experience
For those seeking risks along the winding paths.

Life demands courage, boldness and daring
From those that look for fortunes around the world.

Life is, at times, a rocky, bumpy road
That brings hurts, unhappiness and troubles.

Life is smooth sailing in clear weather
With happiness, faith, and loved ones near.

Myrtle Howell Smith
THE PICTURE WINDOWS

The purple haze out in the west
Soon vanished in thin air.
When darker clouds formed in the sky;
The atmosphere was rare.

Much later when snow fell in gusts
On all the trees, and grounds;
This formed a deep, snow white blanket;
The shrubs, and rocks formed mounds.

All windows became pictures then.
Children in rapture stared!
They were amazed at the snow scenes!
Most every small child shared.

Their first snow scenes may be instilled
In children's brilliant minds.
When they're older they may recall
That snow of olden times.

Dale Brown
TRUST IN GOD

What ever your need, you'll
find it in me.
The way of impossible thru
me you will see.
Surrender your will, rely
only on me,
your path will be clearer,
your soul will be free.
I offer you freedom, I
offer you love,
what ever your need, I'll
send from above.
To choose or deny me,
is your choice my child,
don't you want peace,
when all else is wild?

Dale Brown
TO JUDGE

Never judge a book my friend,
only by its cover,
for your eyes may be misled,
by one thing or another.
Like a mask it only hides,
what really lies inside,
the cover may exaggerate,
just like human pride.
So if you think of judging,
someone that you know,
look beneath their cover,
their true self it will show.

Pearlie M Gnewuch

Pearlie M Gnewuch
WANDERING MIND

To the man I adore and love always, Joseph Cray.

It was like a cloud in the sky, moving slowly, seeing all the ways of life. My heart reaches out, my eyes shed tears. My mind was wandering like there was no tomorrow. There was no one to hear me, to reach me, to feel my pains, to hear the things I needed to tell them. There I stood all alone by the Deep blue sea with tears in my eyes, no desire, no purpose, no hope, no willpower. Everything I felt was like a shadow of doubt. Fear ran in my mind. Terror in my heart, I look up to the sky and pray to God to send someone to love me as I had loved someone before. I turned around. I felt a touch of magic. There standing on this porch was a tall, brown-skinned, handsome young man with big beautiful, sexy bedroom eyes, with a beautiful smile. Our eyes met. There was a spark and chemical between us. He spoke to me gratefully. I kept on walking as the young man followed, Asking me how're you love? What's your name? May I fulfill all your dreams and fancies now and from this day forward? Please, my love, give it some thought. I will always be here for you. You're the woman of my dreams. Please take my hand my love my love. It is not the end. Life between the two of us is just beginning and we can make it beautiful. Only if you let me.

Myrta (Campbell) Weatherhead
GRANDMOTHER'S TULIPS

In loving memory of my maternal grandmother, Myrta A Symes, nee Roper.

I close my eyes to see Grandmother's face,
And all of the tulips around her place
That open these sunny mornings in May
To smile for you as you pass their way.

Since I was a child some years ago
Each fall she has added another row
Of the little bulbs that always bring

Such welcome blossoms in the spring.

Some are as white as new-fallen snow,
Others are as bright as golden-glow,
And brilliant sunset's orange and red
Are there in my grandmother's tulip bed.

W L Mitchell
I DON'T LIE

To all of those I have had pleasure of knowing.

I don't lie!
I may stretch the truth,
but I don't lie.
I may evade the truth,
but I don't lie.
I may whitewash the truth,
but I don't lie.
I may leave out the truth,
but I don't lie.
And I may forget what's the truth,
but I don't lie.

W L Mitchell
ANDRIA
Why turn my heart to all the love you gave,
For it was my soul you filled with joy,

And, I will not mourn for the short time we shared,
For they were days lengthened by your love,

And I shall grieve not for the monies spent,
For it was all spent to be closer to you,

And I will never be ashamed of the gifts I bestowed,
For they were gifts that reflected my love,

And I will not berate the smiles you gave,
For they were smiles that brightened my day,

And I will never forget the day you left,
For it was a day that grieved my soul.

Frances C Wilner
MY FATHER'S TREE

This poem is dedicated to our wonderful parents Donald and Harriet Wilner. We love you both very much. You will both always be in the corners of our hearts.

These apples from my father's tree,
I clean and peel and bake for thee.
Each year we watch from spring to fall,
as the apples grow for one and all.
The deer and woodchuck and other creatures,
also share what this tree features.
The aroma from our dear mother's kitchen,
smells nothing like a roasted chicken.
Could it be? Of could it could.
She's made us some sweet applesauce.
But wait! What is this that I see?
Could it be yet another tree?
My father told me, this old tree
was struck by lightning as you can see.
Although it happened in her prime,
her fruit grows back all the time.
The applesauce that mother is cooking,
came from the tree where we are now looking.
From the look in his eye I can surely see,
that this is MY FATHER'S FAVORITE TREE . . .

D A Norton
LOVE HAS NO LIMIT

This poem is dedicated to my sister, Toni, and her husband, Reggie Banks. As a wedding gift, which I hope they will cherish for the rest of their lives.

Love is the most powerful word on earth
A category of meanings that surpass all.

Love is speaking one's mind, no matter
If there's pain or frustration behind
I call this HONESTY.
Love is feeling assured when one's partner does the judging—secrets to desires.
I call this TRUST.

Love is listening to problems and dreams
that a couple can solve or share together.
I call this UNDERSTANDING.

Love is remaining calm when things
Seem to fall apart or break down.
I call this PATIENCE.

Love is coping with moods and
even being dissatisfied.
I call this TOLERANCE.

Love is not being afraid to
show or tell that one is truly happy.
I call this AFFECTION.

Love is growing as one, yet
reaching individual goals.
I call this TOGETHERNESS.

Remember, when we love may it be
Kinship or personal ties, set no limit.

Joseph Ambrosino
I LUV YOU KIM

This poem is dedicated to a truly special lady. I truly love you, Kim Rogers!!

"I love you Kim, Honey"!!!
Sweetheart, with my words I can only say how much I
really love you, how much I really care,
How much I really need you and how I'll always be there . . .
And my heart really knows the true pain that only comes and goes when we're apart!!!
"I luv you honey bunny forever!!!
Love you always & more, Joey xxxx

April 6, 1984 April 6, 1990

Joseph Ambrosino
YOU–N–I

Dedicated to a "very sweet, kind & warm girlfriend in the world" !!! Kim Rogers "You're the best Kimmy!"

"Happy Anniversary Kimmy April 6, 1990" over & over again
Right up until the very, very END!
You and I . . .
May "our" happiness always keep us together, and
be just for "us" to share . . .
And may the best of life come
"our special way" always and forever
STARTING WITH THIS VERY SPECIAL DAY!

April 6, 1984

"I love you with all my heart. Kimmy
Love you, Joey xxxx

Terri Bennefield
THAT TREE
You hung on the cross
While tears fill my eyes,
With nails in your hands
And thorns in your brow.
Would anyone do this for you now?
But, GOD only knew that you would
LIVE again, so we would be forgiven of Our SINS.
My heart saddens
That you had to Die,

Hanging on That Tree in the sky.
You hang so patiently,

Only to understand,
Why That Tree was there.

For the story is told on and on,
And Now I Know!

While you were on the Cross,
I was on your mind!

Amy Sinn
CHILD
Little child,
they leave you in the cold.
Gentle child,
they don't care how they mold
your heart. Child,
your eyes are full of fear.
Lonely child,
you search, but no one's near.

Dearest child,
they broke your heart with pain.
Your loved ones smiled
As they left you in the rain.
Beloved child,
I can't be there to help you
Although you cry,
I can only love you.

Edward (Ted) M Courtis
A PLACE FOR ME

To my dear parents, Jean Victoria and Donald Murray McCreary, who for 46 tumultuous years have believed in me, encouraged my efforts and have always been there for me, through good and bad times. I dedicate this poem to them with great love.

There is a special place in life,
That needs my humble skill,
A certain job I'm meant to do,
That nobody else can fill.

The hours are demanding,
And the pay is not always good,
And yet I wouldn't change it,
For a moment, if I could.

There is a special place in life,
A goal I must attain,
A dream that I must follow,
For I won't be back again.

There is a mark I must leave behind
However small it may be.
A legacy of love for those,
Who follow after me.

There is a special place in life,
That I was meant to fill,
A sunny spot where flowers grow,
Upon a windy hill.

There is always a tomorrow,
And the best is yet to be,
And somewhere in this world I know,
There is a place for me.

Rhonda Donath
IN MEMORY OF MY DAD
Why did cancer have to strike, the best man in the world to me?
I asked our heavenly Father Above, why did this have to be?
This wonder man was my Father and he had a heart of Gold.
And I'll never forget him, as long as I live, my story is not yet told.
He laid for three months and suffered, us children were by his bedside.
It was so hard to accept, when we knew our dad had died.
As I sit here and write this letter, my heart is very sad.
Because I will never forget, that great man I called Dad!
Now he is happy in heaven, and he is watching over us all.
And dad, I'll see you again, when it's my turn to hear God's call.

S A Fillipih
DARKNESS OF THE SOUL
Behold; eyes that gleam in delight at my innocence, a gentle
mocking laughter; in anger at my bitterness, and
temper my passions with patience, piercing the shield which hides my soul, slicing through the bonds which bind my heart.

Harken; and hear the song of the words, like stardust in moonlight; mysterious and aloof, unattainable, and so
all the more desirable
silence that sings loud in my ears;
screaming rage and frustrations
and whispering fulfillment from the future.

Awaken; hands that hold infinity cupped between them, that
touched my being from the edge of the universe,
so far away and right next door,
a presence that makes itself felt
because the confines of one
world are too small to hold it all.

Arise; for the dawn is so close, and to miss it is to see only
darkness; or am I afraid that the light will blind me, and render me defenceless against the tides and the storms that are
inescapable and impossible to avoid?

Sharon Denise Warren
LOVE
Love is felt by all
But not the love we have.
Every year it grows
As we celebrate our Anniversary.
We are more than friends,
We are husband and wife.
We share the bad times
And also the good.
We may have problems
But our love is too strong
To let them stand in the way
Of our relationship.
We go from day to day
Sharing the pleasures of life.

We see others around us
Giving up on love,
But we go on
For we know our love is strong.

James W Briggs
MOMENTS OF REFLECTION

Dedicated to children and staff of the Glenrose School Hospital, Edmonton, Canada for cogent memories in retirement after eleven years as Principal.

Sometimes alone, at rest, an inner silence falls,
So deep the present fades from conscious thought;
It may happen when a project ends, a chapter closes,
Within the pause before another page is turned.
Thoughts, turning inward, reflect upon the past,
A vast accumulation which like a still, dark pool
Lies waiting, quiet, deep within the mind.
Until a recollection of some event of yesteryear
Drops like a pebble on the surface of the pool
And sends out ripples, breaking into sparks of light.
Reflecting back impressions, half forgotten:
A thousand, thousand memories are stirred,
Filling consciousness with images and sounds—
Myriads of past events restored to life again,
Most recalled with joy but some with pain.

Clarence Swinton
HAS NIGHT PASSED ME BY

To the men and women incarcerated in any prison system. May they find comfort and hope in my poem.

I sit and wonder why
It is Truth, or just another lie
Has light gone forever, from the sky
Or has night just passed me by.
Bells and horns, and things are ringing
The sound is melted into empty singing.
I sit and pop my fingers, to satisfy my being
While the blind rejoice, at the thought of seeing
Over hill, over dell, march right into hell
Catch a falling star, and don't be afraid to tell
For it's only an imaginary thought from on high
And I'm still trying to find out, if night has passed me by.
I keep looking, keep looking for the daylight
For a minute I thought I was losing my sight
As I look within, I see freedom in my vision
Even though the outer image, is still held in prison.
Going through the line, to get a pound of goodness
A frown on face, trying to hide the loneliness
I won't give up, 'cause I know the dawn will rise in the sky
Even if the night has passed me by.

Martha P Heck
A CHRISTMAS PRAYER

"Oh LORD, how long did you hang on the cross for me?"
"My sins you died for, but sometimes I forget, you see . . ."
"This Holy Season reminds me of all that I have to be thankful for,"
"You forgive me over and over, then you forgive me some more . . ."

"When I pray, it is usually to ask for something from you,"
And sometimes, I forget to thank you or all you've helped me through . . ."

"Since I am a parent, I can just imagine the pain in the heart of your Mother,"
"When on the cross, they first nailed up your hands, and then nailed your feet to one another . . ."

"You didn't have to die that dark day on Calvary's Hill,"
"But you accepted death to help us, by your FATHER'S will . . ."

"Then, three days later, as you had promised man,"
"You raised from the dead to fulfill your plan . . ."

"When you ascended into heaven on a cloud of white,"
"A miracle had happened, it must have been a beautiful sight . . ."

"Then LORD, you were sitting at the right hand of GOD,"
"When YOUR sheep are doing YOUR will, down from Heaven, you give a gentle nod . . ."

"Thank you for giving me all the blessings of my life so far,"
"And, please make me worthy of you: your name not to mar . . ."

"So I pray, this Christmas, to all join hands in peace and love,"
"To help one another, and return YOUR precious love from above . . ."
AMEN . . .

J Glennette Howell
JUST A THOUGHT

In dedication to Patricia L. Johnson for her encouragement, inspiration and true grit.

Oh, how I wish each coming day
Would bring me solace in every way
Silver linings on each cloud above
And never knowing to be without love

To reach and receive my every want
Never regrets or past years to haunt
No sadness, no pain, to ever endure
Remembering the old ole' days that were

What if each day were perfect bliss
How would we know just what to miss
And what if our wants were all fulfilled
Would we know what fields need be tilled

With never to experience sadness or pain
Where would sweet memories in hearts remain
Silver lined clouds and no weights to bear
There would be no glory in answered prayer

Pamela DiMercurio
LANDSLIDE

To: M. Laird

A colossal burden
The uncautious heart levies
A landslide of emotions
Heaped upon the unsuspecting;
Like a stranger in pelting storm
Takes cover from onslaught
Seeking refuge afar . . .
Leaving bearer in heavy silence
Bewildered by sudden self-deluge;
Listening carefully to cadent beat
Left to measure monumental loss;
To shelve once more
That which open arms
Find unbearably light . . . .

Albert Rom

Albert Rom
THE WILLOW

To my beloved mother and father, without whom this poem would never have been written.

For a fleeting moment the willow wept
as a green tear fell unto the ground.
And everywhere the silent sound
of lullabies of winter came.

The trees, like messengers of holy sleep
stood cloaked beneath a coat of snow,
and dreamt that Father Frost would go,
yet still he clung to every branch.

But as the seasons have to change,
the cold soon left and came the spring,
and everything began to sing . . .
except the sad and weeping willow.

Anna Hillanbrand
A MOTHER'S PLEA

To Sherri, Jennifer, Leonard, Freddy. All my love, Mommy.

Dear God up in heaven please hear my plea and send a little baby down to me.
I have everything I want, everything I need,
But please send a baby with the greatest speed.
I want to see her smile, and in a little while a tooth will appear.
I'll run out to buy a present for the little dear—
Soon she will be walking. Look, dear God, she's talking.
How can such a miracle come to be?
Just by doing what comes naturally
Dear God up in heaven, you have heard my plea.
You sent my darling babies down to me.
They are my GIFT, They are my Treasure
My love for them goes beyond measure
You gave them to me to have and to hold
Some of them shy some of them bold
You only loan them for a while
Now I have to give them up with a smile
Dear God I lay them at your feet, I watch them rise and in midair your eyes meet.
I give them back to you Dear God, I leave them in your keeping.
My heart is at peace, and it can stop weeping
As you have promised, you'll always be there
That they'll always be safe in your tender care.

Angela Barresi
THE LONELY BEAST

I, dedicate this poem to Joseph Anemone. To that one man who inspired me Who I, had great passion and, Desire for knowing it will never be.

Here I, stand with a tear
Waiting for you to be there
Here I, hold a rose to
Be at our toes
I, had a dream, a dream of
You that doesn't come true
I've came a long way to
Be away, away from my fear
That I, couldn't bear when
You were there.
Love, Angie Barresi

Lydia G Wilson
PAST AND PRESENT, FOREVER YOURS

For my forever Love, Val Ray.

So much wasted time looks back at me now,
That, sometimes, I wonder how I can go on.
But, I look in those eyes of yours and
Find that I am now where I belong.

Afraid to hope for something so wonderful
That I let go with the secret hope that you wouldn't fly.
I'm nestled in your loving embrace and
Know that I was foolish not to try.

Unwilling to believe that this was in His plan,
That we could really be together.
I feel your heart moving within mine and
Realize that the future is ours—forever.

Wasted time, unfounded fears, and disbelief.
That was what I felt for so long.
But, I feel your hand around mine and
Find that, without you, my life couldn't go on.

Pamela J Weatherford
THE DEFROCKED PRIEST

I am a very haunted man,
Who has no peace of mind.
I run . . . not walk . . . from job to job,
For Love, I have no time.

It's true that once I wore a collar,
Blessed those with same belief.
But, that was many years ago,
Before I was a thief.

You ask, "From whom do I run?"
"From whom do I hide?"
Could it be law, or threat of death?
Could it be a love that binds?

No, No, it is not any life threat,
That sorely frightens me.
Nor, is it any law of man,
That I have disagreed.

It is much, much more than that,
More even than hostile land.
It be the sweet calm of forgiveness, I fear,
From God's own blessed hand.

Kanak Trivedi
THE REAL PEARL

To my dearest departed husband JANAK, 1921-1989.

My mind is an ocean,
I tried, I tried, I tried,
To find a real pearl,
Searched in spring and autumn vain,
Drenched in monsoon rain,
Wandered among the woods,
And springs and lakes,
Dwelt on the mountains in the caves,
Sailed in the rivers to find the pearl,
Oh! Empty hands are searching still,
Asked some sages and some saints,
Served the feets of hermits great,
Meditation, prayer, rosary all,
Visit to churches, temples, mosques,
Was the real pearl there?
Took a tour of seven seas,
Came a message from my God,
His vision had I in east and west,
South and north my Lord so great,
In a palace, in a hut,
Throwing his magic charm,
Smiling like a child, a youth, old man,
My lord in different forms and sound,
Yes, I found it,
The real pearl of the ocean of my mind.

Marie Hill Dobbie
FEAR
Is it a big world out there?
Or little worlds thrown together?
Am I really afraid, of you? Of me?
Does anyone know where they are going?
They act as though they do.
They are doing their darndest to get there.
Is life not the goal, but the way?
The end does not justify the means.
Enjoy the now.

Sarah Kelson Selle
THE THAW
His face—
Impassive, cold, still;
Shutting out a world that hurts too much.

His eyes—
Today; distant, hard;
Tomorrow; hot with burning rage.

His body—
Tense, bunched, waiting;
Fending off attack that lurks near.

His smile—
Curling gently, soft;
Giving warmth and goodness to this world.

Candido Acosta

Candido Acosta
NIGHTMARE

This poem is dedicated to John Lennon.

There is light and there is darkness
I walk from one to another
Compensating quite a few demands
I like a pendulum come back and go
looking for the equilibrium
but I don't find its center

I yawn and go back myself to cero
year leaving behind me the atomic era
Then I find something incredible
What a wonderful life . . .! I'm in the middle between the light and darkness
It is like to see something
that my eyes never saw before

But suddenly I'm getting frightened
I feel scared by myself and like a crazy
I run toward the future how it I were witched
Then in the middle of the night
One low voice wakes me up
and whispers in my ear:
You are a Human Being

Jean Woodward Russell
SWEET SIXTEEN

This poem dedicated to Tom, my son and Nora, my niece.

So, now you're sweet sixteen
Not many years have passed between
For it seems like yesterday
That growing up was far away
What can I do, What can I say
When arms reach is so far away
For the heart comes the gift
Everlasting from my lips
I loved you then, I love you now
We're a team forever bound

Leanne Midura Torres
AT TWELVE
Growth untamed, beauty ungroomed,
He was summer absorbing the elements.
Posed at the fence,
Arms petrified in ache,
Weighted on finger joints blue.
Hair thieving the sun's rays,
Eyes, an omnipotent hue
About a wired sneer.
A calculated torso
Rooted in tar blackend boots
By pavement paralyzed,
A bloosm rushed by human touch
Entangled a flower on the vine.
Her mint silhouette
His shadow teased
She shuttered wet
For the unflichable mannequin.
To plunge and ascend unpurified
Through water's barren womb,
Grace fell flowered by September's wind
From ceremonial afternoons.

John Boginsky
A MOTHER'S PRAYER, A SON'S RESPONSE

To My Parents, who believed—Love John.

In the mountains of Virginia, my spirit's running wild
But way up north in the city, I can see my Mother's eyes.
Hundreds of miles between us, in the wind I can hear her voice
Letting me know everything's alright, and making my heart rejoice.
The winding roads of life I chose, has taken me far away.
But every night under the stars, in the wind I can hear her say . . .

Rest your eyes and ease your mind, everything will be alright,
Those country roads that keep us apart, can carry my prayers for you tonight.
Just relax and close your eyes, be a good-boy, and don't you fight.
Your father and I both love you, every-day and every-night.

I'm still in the mountains of Virginia, and my spirit's running wild
But my heart's up north in the city, with my Father and my Mother's smile.
With hundreds of miles between us, I still listen for your voice
Just to make sure everything's alright, so I have a reason to rejoice.
Over the winding roads of life, that have taken me far away
I'd like to send a message under the city stars, so in the wind you can hear me say . . .

Rest your eyes and ease your mind, everything is alright.
These country roads that keep us apart, can carry my prayers tonight.
So just relax and close your eyes, I'll be a good boy and I won't fight.
And I want you to know I love you both Every-Day and Every-Night.

Alexandra Belanich
ELYSIAN TIME
As the dusk closes in on me
Through my tears I'd plainly see
A time so fine, a time divine
A time I wished so often mine.

A time when trust and love were one
A time when stars danced through the sun
A time when justice and peace abided,
A time when loves were not divided.

A time when moonbeams flashed through the sky
And when mortals ceased to die.

Why am I left out in the cold,
To let my heart go brittle, my youthhood old?
I want to live, so let me inside
Where warm and lively hosts abide.

But I am mocked useless, can't you see?
Why, has God forgotten me?
I'm only trying hard to pass the test
In this cold world to do my best!

Through my tears I've no more to say,
I'm just trying to meet my time someday.

Lori (Craven) Neal
FEARFUL CHILD

With my family's love and to the children of a broken heart. The love I give to You I hope you hold this poem in your hearts as I do in mine.

Child of a broken heart setting aside, Waiting for someone to come. Wipe away your fears and hold on to your dreams for one day your dreams will come true.

Even–though I don't know how much you fear, Your day will come true. So look ahead fearful child and dont give up.

Let's see your smile and laughter to, because without your smile theres no sun, only of your sounds of your tears that you shed so much. So lets wipe them away and look into your hearts and souls for which you will find an inner peace and love that no one can give but only one person and that is GOD and YOU.

But only remember to carry on your faith for that might be the only thing you have for now.

My fearful child take my hand and let us help you throw it. I will be your friend your sister to.

HOLD ON MY
FEARFUL CHILD . . .

Alana Marie
THE SIGN
I sat upon the river's edge, filled with deep despair.
My world was 'ever shattered, so HE must not be there.
For if HE were beside me, I would not know such pain
I prayed that HE would save me, and stand by me again.

Then suddenly I saw a light, the sun's rays filtered through—
between the branches of the trees, down to the river blue.
A shape appeared before me, a sign that all's not lost;
the image was reflected there—our SAVIOR on the cross.

I realized at that moment, HE'D never left my side.
I thought with shame—it was for me—HE'D suffered so and died.
I felt my tears begin to flow; with great relief, I cried.
For 'though my faith had faltered, HE was still my guide.

HE never had forsaken me or denied me HIS sweet love.
HE'D helped me overcome my grief and find my LORD above.

And so it happened years ago—my faith was thus restored.

And since then trying times have
come—testing it much more.
But I'm a great deal stronger now—I
carry on with prayer.
I know the trying times will pass-
because my GOD is there.

Kristi L Mishler
PEACE
Peace is not the fighting of one
country or another,
Peace is not the hating of a sister or a
brother.
It is not the killing that is going on in
this universe,
It is not a young child's body laying
in a hearse.
Peace is not a person that hates
someone because of their color of
their skin,
It is not the fighting of the rights
between women or men.
But peace is the caring for someone
no matter their color, religion, or
style of living,
This world will have peace if
everyone will be kind,
caring, and giving!

Frank Corica
IN SEARCH OF A DISTANT TOMORROW

This poem is dedicated to my children, grandchildren and all children in our schools across the nation.

Rain drenches earth with eternal
wetness of silent ages;
While a hazy, ancient moon orbits
eagerly, in search of a distant
tomorrow.

An amber, gentle sun sustains life
on man's noble wages;
While a day reflects benevolence of
light
With muting darkness, in search of a
distant tomorrow.

God's plan for all defies holocaust
and nuclear stages;
While dawn to dusk and dust to dust
We journey far, in search of a
distant tomorrow.

Humanity's program for future
generations
Documents historical pages;
While the moan of a taunted society
Echoes, in search of a distant
tomorrow.

Faith, hope and love release us
from our cages;
While bridges from fire to semi-
conductor,
Go in search of a distant tomorrow.

Juanita Hildreth Lambert
MY CHILD
My child left a divided home
She went to live where strangers
roam
There one night she was murdered
Where strangers roam she died alone.

Because of a divided home
Her body lays beneath the clay
It's too late now for my dear child
To hear the words I long to say.

It's too late now to give her love
It's too late now to hold her hand
It's too late now to understand
My child has gone to another land.

Lillian Randrup
A MOTHER'S SON
Like a giant oak you stand, my son
And help hold the fate of our great
Nation
In GOD's own mysterious way
through nature
Your face has become molded and
shaped with
Contentment, love and strength,
warmth and peace
Like the mighty oak whose branches
spread
Far and wide your arms open up and
beckon inside
He who is weary and broken from
strife,
As the wounds of time tear away at
their hearts
And rip thru their minds
Is it any wonder, that I see the soft
breezes
That play on your face as a whisper,
like leaves
The reflections of summer in the lake
As they float down below
Is it the secret you share of the joys
and the tears
The sadness and the laughter?
Thru it all . . . You care

Roxanne Abbott
ANGER

To Susan, a very special therapist & friend. If it wasn't for you, this poem would never have been written. I love you . . .

Anger is a black thing to me
A reality I wish to suppress inside of
me
What if I could do or say what I feel
What if my anger becomes a threat to
kill.

I never used to be this way
To have everything become so
complicated every day
Yes, I've dealt with some bad times
Enough to lead me to be alone at
times.
Am I naturally a mean person?
It's never been known to me to ever
hurt someone
Although in the past I've been known
to threat
But the real person inside of me
wants to do the opposite.

Is it worth it to express your anger?
Or could it hurt someone or cause
them danger?
I feel so empty like I've lost a friend
Can I ever be a nice person again.
When with it end?

Edith Georgianna Harris
LULLABY
Sleep my darling, Sleep so well,
Angels sent thee here to dwell!
Heart beat 'gainst heartbeat,
Love, ages old
God has united, brought you to our
fold!

Close your eyes; Sweet Slumber's
Child
Rocks thy cradle,
Her gift, thy smile.
Drifting to Dreamland, safe in my
arms,
Mother's love lulls you,
Mother's love warms!

Beautiful Dreamer,
My happiest heart,
More precious than gold
Is the Love you
impart!

Chandra T
LIBIDO

To ODIN, to his glory, power and wisdom.

Amorphous yet a limpid 'fata
morgana'
artifacts of a primary fireworks

Permeable
through entity and non-entity
dimensionless in purity
And
transcendental beyond reference
of a limit
of the mortal and immortal

Amphoterically sweet and sour
it's a psychotoxic Hal-le-lu-jah!

Soul's drooling hemlock
to resuscitate a hormone-deficient
fetid fetish
with saliva, sweat
hallucination and ejaculation
finale of transmogrification

Then
a momentary limbo, a blind spot,
infernal void
and intangible return to a point of no
return . . .

EX NIHILO NIHIL FIT . . .

Helena D MacLean
NANTUCKET ISLAND
Nantucket Island, Nantucket Island,
you lie far out to sea,
Happiness, I feel when you reach out
to me,
My native land, I cherish so dear,
It's been years and years I've
neglected you near.

Now I stand on the steamship, the
Nantucket's bow,
Along with my son, so tall and so
proud;
Your sky is trimmed in ever so blue,
Like the earth, perfection, when He
made it new.

As your rippling green waters rush
along the shore,
Our hearts pounding, seeing
weathered cottages of Pocomo,
Wauwinet, and much more.
For memories I've held dear of agony
and pain,
But alas, leaving my home I truly did
gain.

Seeing the crackers in the young
boy's hand,
Scavenging sea gulls hovering
greedily where the youngster stands,
High on the deck on this great
Nantucket ferry,
Making the prettiest picture of
children, and nature's merry.

Our hearts skipped a beat, my boy
and I,
And tears starting to roll down
Mama's brown eyes,
This image of Nantucket, off my
Massachusetts coast,
Is truly a legend, and surely of one to
boast.

Helena D MacLean
HOMEY SANDS
I cry when I can't live with you now,
you're so far away my Homey Sands,
Remembering, thinking, feeling,
looking, touching, for my home
sweet Homey.
My eyes look deep out on the rough
sea, from Great Point, to Eel Point,
Smith
Point too, all up and around to
Sankaty Head, every inch through
and through,
I long to touch and be with you.

Brant Point lighthouse, stands tall
and proud, blinking, as if she were
speaking
Out loud. I taste my tears as we
move in, salty air in my nostrils,
memories
Indelible in my mind. Eyes focused
again back out on the turbulent sea,
thoughts
Blurred by pounding surf whipping
the skin of the breakwater,
continuously. I
Taste my tears once more.

My hand clutched on my son's strong
arm, he gives me the strength against
the
Pain I feel in my soul, now, and back
then. Reach out to me my beloved
island,
I love you, I love you. Off this great
ferry we step, arms flinging to Aunt
Rose,
A woman of much depth. Greedy sea
gulls pluck savagely for their prey.
Sand-piper's delicate feet planted
deeply, pulling at periwinkles and
fiddler crabs.

Soon, embedded cobblestones line
each street, white picket fences shine
along
Weathered cottages. Leafy oaks,
Maples, pines, and birch for miles.
Acres of
Moors, white sandy beaches, tall
boats sleeping in calm waters, and
weathered
Beaten docks high on stilts. Here we
are Pocomo, Wauwinet, Siasconset,
all of
You, this world I call my Homey
sands.

Helena D MacLean
LINES
Sitting with pen,
Writing a name in palm
Hidden just for me
Perfect sculptured lines

Depressed, despondent, pensive
Unveil the palm
Lips caress
Power, strength, love.

Helena D Maclean
I'LL HAVE STRENGTH
If life were perfection like a crystal hour glass
And things ran smooth as a carefree lass,
There would be no faith, or hope, or love,
Or the power of prayer to Him above.

There is a reason to keep the strength
For courage and passion would grow at great length
May God grant me all of the virtues above
So I'll have strength, faith, and his love.

Joe L Sifuentes
GONE

To my loving mother, Maria Hernandez; and all the World Leaders.

Seaside
The main street of Seaside
A wasteland of burnt crumbled ruble
With few survivors
With nothing to live for as a result of
Nuclear war!

A desolate place
Where the only sound that is heard is the breeze
A world of blackness
Caused by radioactive fallout clouds
and since the sun can't get through
The world is in a freeze

The kids my age if there is any
are scavenging for any kind of food they can
They listen to the solemn beat of their hearts
As they struggle to survive in their frozen land.

There is no newspaper stand
For it is burnt and charcoal black
There is no news to be found

I miss everything about my hometown
Every smile, laugh and frown!
I say good-bye to the world I once knew

No, my land has made no progress.
We have destroyed ourselves
Both me and you!

Terry A Osborn
A ROSE FROM GOD
If I had a rose from God
I wonder how it would appear.
The softness of the petals
Drenched by dew so clear.

The redness of royalty
That makes the eye see
A beauty not described
By any poetry.

I have a rose from God
With beauty through and through.
"Where is this rose?" you ask.
My darling, it is you.

Lu Raper
WON'T THE SUN EVER SHINE?
It's a dark, dreary day.
The rain keeps pouring down—
Raining upon this heart of mine.
I miss you more today
Than I did yesterday
And it seems that the sun will never shine.

The rain keeps pouring down,
Making rivers on the ground,
Filling up my world with gloom,
Won't the sun ever shine upon this world of mine
To drive out the shadows in my room?

It's been raining all day long—
The rain knows you are gone.
The rain is helping my heart weep.
Won't the sun ever shine again
To drive away my blues and pain
And bring my darling home to me?

Lu Raper

Lu Raper
THE SACRIFICE
I remember when you left me —
You whispered, "I love you;
This cannot last forever;
I'll be coming home to you."

I held you closer to me,
All my tears I hid.
Thought I couldn't live without you
But, I found out I did.

Your life was taken from you
Far across the sea
They wrapped a flag around you
And sent you home to me.

Now I stand here weeping
Above your open grave.
The world is dark around me
And I am so afraid.

How can I face tomorrow
Without the will to live?
Your love was taken from me
And I had so much to give.

Oh, what a price for freedom!
You've made the sacrifice.
My heart is there beside you,
Beneath the Stars and Stripes.

Jonathan E Plate
REFLECTIONS FROM WITHIN
Life, at times, for all its tough
Simple things seem oh so rough
These things must be, yes, we know
To give us all a chance to grow

Success, the goal we try to reach
Like oceans waves breaking towards the beach
Life and waves are much the same
Ever changing not always tame

Just keep thinking what life might be
In a world we would like to see
Thoughts like that provide the motivation
To somehow help us reach our destination

There are many roads from which to choose
It's hard at times, so we cannot lose
Sight of where we wish to go
Because we alone must work to grow

Edward J Steinhauer
THINKING OF YOU
I was thinking of you today
Hoping to catch that glimpse
of your beautiful smile
and to say, Oh how I miss you.

It is sad we can't be together
and it is hard to be apart.
But thinking of you today,
Has kept you in my heart.

Your eyes linger with me.
Your lips I still can feel.
And thinking of you today,
You can never be but real.
MY love for you will grow and abound.
And that I can say for sure.
And thinking of you today,
makes it nothing less than pure.

Kathy Eckels
SLEEPLESS NIGHTS
Silent moments;
Lonely times;
Bring back treasured thoughts of you.

Secret glances;
Hopeful smiles;
Make me want you all the more.

Crying eyes;
Sleepless nights;
Let me know that you are gone.

Clarice Ferguson Frowiss
THE REDWOOD TREES
When standing under the Redwood trees
I'm as near to God as I'll ever be
The air so quiet, peaceful, still,
They stand like soldiers on the hills.

The sun tries hard to shine between
The giants tall, forever green.
Rays filter through in a lacy pattern
Like a shiny path on the way to Heaven.
Ages old, their trunks not bending
Ever growing, time unending,
Reaching up to skies above
Arms outstretched they beg for love.

We must protect this gift from God
That grows so tall in richly sod.
The ferns, the moss, so dark and green,
The rivers running in between.

He only knows what He has planned
On this great earth of ours, His land.
We only hope that in Heaven there'll be
Another forest of Redwood trees.

Clarice Ferguson Frowiss
WINTER
The North wind is blowing, the sky is slate grey
Storm shutters clatter, horses whinny and neigh.
Winter is upon us, our breath is like smoke
Raindrops on the windows will soon turn to snow.
Wind gusts down the chimney, doors all shake and rattle
Men folks in the barn tending sheep and the cattle.
Meats hanging in the smokehouse, the coal is in the bins
Potatoes in the cellar, treasures for our friends.
Mothers in the kitchen rolling out the pastry
Anything she ever cooks is always good and tasty.
Aromas from the oven come drifting through the rooms
Pastries and hot breads smell like spicy perfumes.
Logs crackling in the fireplace, the house so cozy and warm
The North winds are blowing and our winter has come.

Alisa Divack
A LESSON TO LEARN

To Anthony—My love, My Life, My Inspiration.

Unresolved conflicts throughout the time
Deciding what's yours, deciding what's mine
Never knowing who's wrong or right
All we do is argue and fight

Never coming to any conclusion
Therefore we decide to live in seclusion
No compromises, no giving in
Someone has to lose and someone has to win

A separation of the human race
We're too insecure to meet face to face
Words hit as hard as a gunshot
They express, not anger, but a powerful thought

If only we learned to verbalize
We could speak the truth instead of lies
A man is not judged by who he can kill
But by his knowledge and freedom of will

Anthony F Mills Jr
LOVE

Alisa, please marry me. Alisa Divack wrote a better poem. I love her.

The intangible feeling of it
If it were for only an instant it would be enough
If it passed you by I for one am truly sorry
The feeling of being in it is frightening
An invocation of the spirit
I am in love

Iva Roberts
HE'S PREPARING JUST FOR ME
Praise the Lord, I have a Savior
And He's preparing just for me
A home far more beautiful than mortal eyes can see
I didn't need to draw the plans or worry with these things
Because the hands of the Master knows exactly what I need
And when it is completed I'll go to live up there
And sing praises to my Saviour
For His presence is everywhere
Oh the beauty of this mansion
He's preparing just for me
Is far, far more beautiful than mortal eyes can see
Yes God shall reign in His glory and the angels' choir shall sing
And I shall live there in that mansion for all eternity.

Madelyn Rapp
WINTER
The sky was heavy
and overcast
The trees were stark
and bare
Cold breezes sent
the leaves
scouring through
the air

Suddenly the wind
grew calm
The heavens opened up

Down came the
soft white snow
Making everything
aglow!
Mother nature grew
weary
Of every dark and
dreary thing
And as though
by magic
Touched each branch
twig and bush
Making each a
thing of beauty!

Oh! Beautiful
glittering soft
white snow
Making the landscape
sparkle and glow
Mother nature has
made you
Queen of the ball
Clothed you in
Ermine
To Reign over
All!

Donald G Charlton
A FEELING OF ROMANCE
A walk along the beach during a
full moon
With someone hand in hand, arm in
arm, sitting on
The sand holding each other in a
comforting and
Soothing way that would seem to
take away all the
Troubles and worries we had
during the day.
Giving each other a light kiss to
know that we care.

To look into each other's eyes
and know that it's
Time to go home and make love with
someone who
Loves you, and cuddle up in each
other's arms to sleep,
Knowing that if you wake up later in
the night
You can make love again or just
sleep in peace
Knowing that they will be there in the
morning to
Start the day with you again and
again.

Bridget A Cartlidge
KINGS AND QUEENS
Freedom dancer
Dancing with his wings,
Flying free all the time
By Queens and Kings . . .

Everyone looked at him
With envious eyes,
"Wow!" they thought
"Look at him fly!!"

No one could catch him
Not even time,
Just a girl dreaming
And wanting to call him
"Mine!!"

She could turn off her magic
And she could turn off her
pride,
But how could he possibly see her
When he was so starry
eyed . . .

She knocked and knocked on his
door
But he left her heart
crying,
"Stop! I can't take anymore!!"

So much to protect
So much to lose,
The world made up of
So many fools . . .

So many dreams
Left in 'Lost and Found'
Waiting to be claimed
Yet just laying on the
ground . . .

So there she stands
So many words unspoken,
With a pain in her eyes
And a heart that is
broken . . .

Tanya Bulic
OUR WORLD
This is yours and mine,
OUR WORLD
A poor starving child, skin to bones,
shaking from malnutrition
A child endlessly crying in grief from
battery of its own bearers
A man so brittle and frail, stricken to
the cureless disease of
AIDS, awaiting his own death
An 8-year-old child addicted to heavy
drugs, stealing money to
satisfy his addiction
A young girl selling her body on the
streets for mere survival
It's the bombing of a funeral in
Ireland, deepening the agony and
sorrow
It's the painful memory of war, of a
child screaming at the sight
of her parents flesh burning with
napalm, leaving her alone to
struggle for survival in the Vietnam
war
It's Africa's battle of white and
black, the endless hatred and
fury
It's the natural disasters that strike
innocent people and leave
them homeless
The disgrace humans are doing to the
earth every day
A leader starving and depriving his
own people from freedom
It's the fright of walking our own
local streets
Are we justified to cry over small
petty things? Though it seems
that our petty needs are met before
those others
Wake up and ponder your rich life
Open up and see that the world is
crying for help before its own
destruction
This is yours and mine,
OUR WORLD.

Eleonore Jackson
PORTRAIT OF A JEWEL
I have a one eye Jack,
To put a patch on it,
Would be an eyesore,
To sit her down and tell her,
She'd come up with a plan,
Conniving, Rivaling,
And then My Love would clip me,
The crocodile tears I'd cry,
My love I cannot hide

Lizette R Longacre
GONE FOREVER
There he lies
Upon the sand.
Pistol loaded
Still in hand.
One shot fired
One man dead.
Bullet lodged
Into his head.
No more worries
No more pain.
Just one family
To go insane.
He'll never be forgotten
But no one can understand
What came to his mind
Or to his hand.

Red Baron and
Olivia Elaine Marin-Devereaux

Olivia Elaine Marin-Devereaux
LOSING YOU

In loving memory of Walt's Red Baron. May 5, 1986—November 27, 1987 . . . my breathtakingly beautiful Quarter Horse.

I tried not to love you;
I tried not to care.
I knew all too well
of the pain of losing, of the
emptiness,
the loneliness, the despair.

And still, I fell victim to my past;
I fell deeply in love with you.
I needed you and depended on your
friendship
You were my life;
You were all things beautiful.

I'm lonely now;
It still hurts to think of you.
If ever life was unfair, your leaving
proves it so.
I know you tried so hard to stay,
but tragedy took you from me.

The hurt runs deep . . . the tears still
flow.
Never a day goes by
that I don't think of you
and find it difficult to swallow
past the pain of having lost you.

John E Mathes Jr
FROM ME TO YOU
If you want a kingdom
You shall have one
The kingdom of my love

If you want power
You shall have it
The power of my heart

If you have never felt tenderness
You shall feel it
The tenderness of my touch

If you have never known passion
You will know it
The passion of my kiss

All I want in return
Is for you to love me
As I love you

Patricia Russell
COLORS OF AUTUMN
Autumn's so beautiful, so colorful
and bright.
God takes his paintbrush and to
nature highlights.
The hues the colors so soft, yet so
bold,
To create such a stirring for all to
behold.
The heavens are blue with billowing
clouds high
They all join together for a parade in
the sky.
The leaves coloring yellow, orange,
red, green and brown,
From all manner of trees come
fluttering down.
I love the bright colors of autumn so
rare.
For it's God with his paintbrush
painting nature in air.

Ronald R Holmes
IN GOD'S HANDS
On our journey we meet many new
friends, never knowing what is
around the next bend.
We see sadness and joy and
happiness and sorrow,
never knowing what will be in
tomorrow,
The things we do and the things we
say,
touches everyone in a most
special way.
We gather our strength from the ones
we love,
for truly we are one before God up
above.
Our inner strength is not for us alone,
but to share with others clear
down to our bone,
The love we share which will alway
be,
will last forever if only in memory.
In passing from this world we near
our journey's end,

knowing that God's just around the next bend.
Peace and tranquility is what we will find,
cradled in God's hands for the rest of time.

With Love,
Ron

B I. Piatt
THE DAYDREAMER'S NIGHTMARE

I live my life sometimes in dreams,
Fulfilling the visions of life I admire.
But life is not always as it seems
When reality is wrought with desire.

I've been a showman, musician, captain and knight,
A dancer, romancer and a dolphin at sea.
I fade out the world by closing my eyes,
And become whatever I want to be.

Mankind continues its thankless old journey,
As my imagination seeks out its quest.
I escaped, or so it had seemed to me,
With daydreams and nightmares as my guests.

Have I been so terribly thoughtless?
I ponder this as my burning heart does scream.
I've denied myself real happiness,
As I have lived my whole life in dreams.

The smell of death is now in the air.
Its pungent odor surrounds my very bed.
I lie here waiting and wondering where,
My dreams will be when I am dead.

Robert W Heubel
MEDITATION OF A TROUBLED MONK

To Sarah.

I see the rising dawn,
And as I walk along
All by myself,
I find myself
Outside myself;
Where others find
Themselves inside—
In such a way . . . Unknown

Clara McKenney
MY LITTLE TALK WITH GOD

I awake to morning sunshine of another blessed day,
To wonder what will come to pass ere this one has gone its way.
I ask God to stand close to me as through pain and care I plod,
I ask for strength and comfort when I have my little talk with God.

Almost I see Him stretch a hand though it must be a million miles,
Almost I see in His loving eyes the tenderness of smiles.
Our thoughts just flow from each to each in understanding and accord
I know that I can face the day, since I had my little talk with God.

The hours come and the hours go, I meet each task and pain,
Until the twilight deepens and I seek his help again.
I thank Him for His constant care His watch on the road I have trod,
And ask again His watch at night, as I have my little talk with God.
How restful is His presence, how tender is His care,
How great that I can reach Him day or night in loving prayer.
All He asks is faith and trusting, His blessings are my great reward,
He fills my day with peace and comfort when I have my little talk with God.

Siba Sabbagh
DERIK
the rose has died

To my dad who no matter what stands by my side and tells me to keep on trying. Dad, I love you.

Now that the rose has died, and the blood drenched tears fall from the sky.

The mourners drown in their sorrow, why didn't he wait until it was tomorrow?

The rose was planted into the ground six feet under to never be found.

No one will forget that sorrowful day, when one friend of mine blew his troubles away.

Richard P Fahey MD (Retired)
A SURPRISE BIRTHDAY PARTY FOR GRANDFATHER

Dedicated to Katie Fahey, my grandchild, whose sense of humor encouraged me to write her story in poetry.

We wanted to surprise grandfather, by taking him out to eat,
to make him happy, and give him a treat.
We wanted to wine and dine him, so he'd enjoy us kids,
while he is still alive, and not on the skids.
Sitting him down in the restaurant, we ordered him a steak,
thought he'd be pleased, that such a fuss we'd make.
"Sorry, you all," he drawled, "this is too big a feat,
you surprised me, and I forgot to bring my teeth."
Restaurant steaks are expensive, and not to be wasted;
saddened were we, that steak was not to be tasted.
Instead, looking we were, one to the other,
wishing we had brought, toothed old grandmother.
A kindly gentleman, overhearing at a nearby table,
leaned over, to say, –grandfather accepting, he was able.
To provide a set of teeth, and help grandfather eat,
"Indeed! Try them on for size, sink them in the meat."
Grandpa agreed, –never was he great on protocol,
when it came to food, –he would try it all.
In went the teeth, –he began to chew and chew,
chewing that steak, like an old leather shoe.
When he finished, over he went to meet,
to thank his new friend and give him back the teeth.
Grandpa handed him back, and asked him for sure,
"Do dentists always carry, such fine pairs of denture?"
"No!" came the reply, "A dentist, I'm not to dare,
but always I carry dentures, an extra pair,
They re provided in death, and I take possession,
you see, I am an undertaker, that's my profession."

Alden Gary Allison
A SPECIAL THING

To all those who have inspired me throughout the years, especially Ms. Hanson, one of my instructors at Muskegon Heights High who believed in me and my poetry in 1974-76.

The talk seems to last
no matter where you go,
Of love from the past,
of those who let go.

I don't know about you,
but the way it should be,
Love is shared by two
from here to eternity.

A love that will last,
the only love for me.
Love not moving too fast,
love that you can see.

I hope you can see
love is no light thing.
When you're in love
it's a special thing.

Leonard Martin

Leonard Martin
STRUGGLING TALENT

To my inspiration my mother. To shoot for the moon even if you miss you'll be among the stars.

Why should I give credit to a piece of paper in my hand when the talent that I have was not given to me by man

I've been granted a gift . . . I'm sorry you don't understand.

You'd give her the job though it's not in her heart. I've been trained for the job but I'm stuck with no part . . . I'm able to do the things I say someone, someway, somehow, someday

Am I not allowed to do them for pay?

I hope the things I've said gives your ego a dent—Because I'm tired of being . . .

just a struggling talent

June North
TIME

Time—
artificial reality—
moving, imposing,
relentless,
carrying our consciousness
through experience
after experience

Unless feared—
truly a good father—
time.

Scott McKay
THE RIVER RUNS DEEP

Shadows dance upon the water
against the virility of lineage that composes
Justly in the background
A stoic sentry are these watching
over both sides of the river
Reflections of the day appear
brightness casts a fervent gaze
Reflections of what remain
untouched unspoiled uncivilized
Leaves brown withered and crisp fall
catching hold of this freedom
Blanketing what remains latent
And the river runs deep
A tug from nature her purse holds all
creation passing over no stone unturned
A shallow mist envelopes the air a
mist of natures perspiration as she sets
Task to the balance of her dependents
the mist gathers becoming a cluster
Of drops the drops separate into drips
falling unattended into the river
and the river runs deep
Moss clutches onto a gathering o
stone both are stable in the current of misdirection
The stones know not where to travel
the current travels endlessly
Upon whatever it sets about touching
it plays carrier to a haze collected
Upon the water
Unto itself the river holds clear
this nature knows freedom travels far
The haze remains unsettled drifting
out to where the river carries
And still the river runs deep

Karen Runyan
HE IS RISEN

"He Is Risen", What joy and happiness this brings.
New dawn, new life, the heart swells and sings.
Oh glorious day, the stone has been rolled away.
The blackened hearts are gone, happiness is here to stay.

"He is Risen", The Comforter He gave of yore,
Ask Him now and it'll be given once more.
All who ask and believe on Him,
Receive the Comforter and freedom from sin.

"He is Risen". He bore our sins upon the cross.
The agony He suffered, making sure we weren't lost.
Eternal life He offers to all who trust.
The Love He shows makes trusting a must.

"He is Risen". Oh, what power this conveys.

Helping to carry our cross all our days.
The Father, Son and Holy Spirit, never stop giving.
"He is Risen, He is Risen", Christ is Living.

Hilda Snyder
SIGHT AND SOUND

To my friends, who believe in me.

I've seen a robin in the spring,
And a golden hawk on the wing,
While overhead, in a sky of blue,
A white cloud gently passes through.
I've seen a meadow, where cattle graze,
Amid lush, green fields on sunny days.
I've seen the bright leaves, when fall rolls 'round,
die and flutter, softly to the ground.
I've seen the snow, that winter brings,
and heard the church bells, as they ring.
All these things, I see and hear,
with eager eyes and avid ear.
Now, I sit on a high green hill,
the world below, looks quiet and still,
Close by, I fancy I can see,
the wind as it gently caresses me.

Hilda Snyder
ARIZONA
In the stillness of the desert, alone I sit.
I watch the clouds overhead.
Off in the west, the sun sinks low,
As the sky turns from pink to red.
There in the distance, a purple hill,
Beneath the sky, cast low,
Resembles the headdress of an Indian Chief,
Who lived here long ago.
And just over there, an ironwood tree,
Pushing its roots in the sand,
Spreading green branches high above,
Giving its shade to man.
Beneath the tree, an ancient stone,
Carved in the shape of a seat,
Where once perhaps, a young brave sat,
To rest his weary feet.
And here close by, a field of hay,
Planted by modern man.
The past has a way of joining the future,
Here in this desert land.

Hilda Snyder
THOUGHTS
I once walked in a quiet valley,
Beneath the deep shade of tall oak trees.
I felt the heart of the land, pulse beneath my feet.
I felt the warmth of the sun, the coolness of shadows,
The fresh sweetness of an early spring breeze,
As it ruffled my hair, softly caressed my face,
and gently turned the new green leaves,
into pictures of gossamer lace.
And there in the quiet stillness,
broken only by a babbling brook,
crystal clear, wandering off into a shady glen,
Where stood a small old weather-beaten church,
Planted firmly into the sod,
With graceful steeple, pointing skyward,
Where it could only look, into the eyes of God.

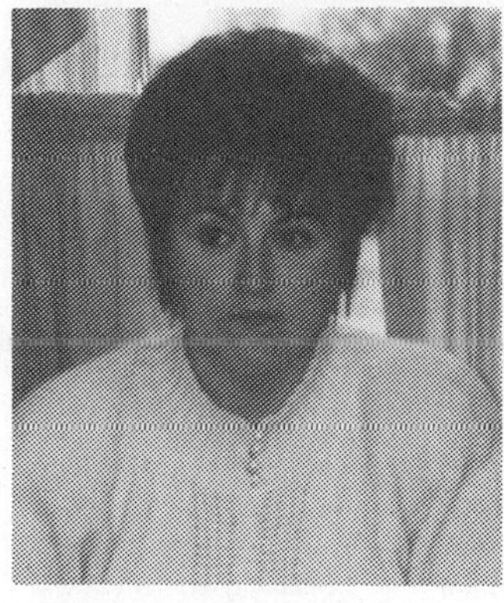

Estelle Fish

Estelle Fish
MY CHRISTMAS WISH

This poem is lovingly dedicated to my sister Helena, who was my inspiration.

I'd like to go on Santa's sleigh,
And hide like a Christmas stowaway.
Then as he sails across the sky,
To give his gifts, I wish that I
Could drop in on my family,
Scattered across the land and sea.

In Jacksonville, Florida, to find Pearl and her girls,
Dancer would have to make, round about twirls.
And to Marietta, Georgia, where Dorothy's family are,
Dasher's speed would be as fast, as a shooting star.
But with Anne in far off Iceland, and her family too,
For me to visit all of them, he'd say "I cannot do."

So with Barb and Pat, and Mom and Dad here,
We'll celebrate together, and shed but a tear.
For Helena is leaving, for Wisconsin it's planned,
With Jerry and her children, to their new homeland.
Hoping one day we'll all be together, is my wish,
From Estelle and her husband, and all the little Fish.
Merry Christmas and Happy New Year to my Family,

With all my Love, Estelle
XXXXX 12-28-81

Donna Irvin Hilton
CHRISTMAS EVERY DAY

Dedicated to my family and friends, with a special dedication to my husband, Bobby and my son Brandon.

The Christmas star shines once again.
A shining light, a sign to men.

Jesus Christ, a savior born
Long ago on Christmas morn.

He came to give us life and love,
A precious gift from God above.

Christmas comes and then it's past.
But if you try, you can make it last.

Show a kindness every day.
Say a prayer along the way.

Tell your loved ones how you feel.
Let them know your love is real.

When Christ is with you every day,
The Christmas star will light your way.

When love of God abides within,
Christmas day will never end.

Barbara Dunn
TRUSTING IN OUR STRENGTH
Look upon my affliction and my pain
I have walked in mine integrity within the rain,
Examine me, prove me, try my reins, my heart
For thy loving kindness is before mine eyes, never part.

As for me, I shall walk in mine integrity for many days
My feet standeth in an even place, my own ways,
The strength of my life, I shall be afraid to hold
My heart shall not fear, to remain warm never cold.
Open mine eyes, that I may behold a beautiful trust
Beyond a day of love, I shall never want or lust,
Within my hope, we shall become one
Forever trusting in our strength, a love just begun.
With my lips, I shall sing songs of love for you
Trusting in our strength, we knoweth now is new
Following our hearts desire, beyond the stars above
Therefore we sitteth holding hands, we knoweth eternal love,
Let in thy love, hold thyself up to embrace me now
I have been waiting many days, you keep a promised vow,
Together we will have everlasting love so pure
Our words shall protect, this love will endure.

Gary L Dion
THE OFTEN FORGOTTEN
I've seen the homeless as they weep
In cardboard boxes some live and sleep

Some rich turn their heads and never look back
On people who's lives fill a brown paper sack

Some drunken some drugged and others quite ill
This problem continues and always will

Their problem is known and often forgotten
They're regular people treated so rotten

To live like the others is all that they ask
Yet goodwill promises hide behind a false mask

Don't turn away when you see such a thing
Reach out your hand and learn the joy it can bring

Maria Y Thomas
TIMELESS LOVE
Can you see beyond my eyes
Can we touch those feelings inside
Have we learned all about love
Good times, bad times, broken hearts
Can we try and love again
Can we put the pain behind us
Will it take some time
Feeling, trusting, loving again
Can I ever love again
Or is my love for you
TIMELESS . . .

Judy Hance
YOU ARE

Written for Leland P. Freimark—Love you—Judy.

You are like
a graceful bird
rarely seen,

In flight
you are elegance,
when you perch
atop my life
your beauty
is exquisite,
your song
a soft sweet
melody,
and when
you alight
my heart
feels sorrow
but still
you linger
as your song
replays constantly
in my heart.

Tina L Fullmer
SNOW ANGEL
Her face was white as the white of snow.
Her cheeks had the tint of a cherry.
As she walked across the crunchy snow.

The snow glistened like a million tiny stars.
She was dressed all in white from head to toe.
Her white hair shone like pearls in the sun
moving only briefly when the soft wind blew.

She would walk all day and rest at night on the cool wet snow.
So if you happen to see a shape in the snow,
you will know it is where the snow angel has rested.

Tina L Fullmer
WONDERING WHY
How many times have we tried to
count the stars in the sky?
Why do airplanes have to fly?
How do boats stay afloat?
What makes the rain, the sun and the
blue sky?
Why do people have to die?
These questions I ask you the world
is big and confused am I.

There are four seasons why not
three?
Why are the fish dying in the sea?
The times have changed and so have
we now all we see is pollution
and pornography.
It makes me sad and makes me cry to
see the smog in the sky.
Let the smog go away so our children
can go out and play.
Make the killing and graffiti go away.
We are all one in the world but let us
put up a fight so our children
can grow up right and smell the grass
and evergreen and have their
world so very clean.

Edith Teich
HOPE FOR 1990
I'm going to hope that peace will find
A place in every heart of mankind
I'm going to hope each man a friend
That hatred in his heart will end
I'm going to hope folks born like you
Equality though skin differs true
I'm going to hope each baby born
Good health and to freedom sworn
I'm going to hope all nations know
Friendship, democracy never a foe
I'm going to hope folks just like me
Will find their road to eternity
For all these hopes I'm going to pray
Especially for nineteen ninety every
day.

Robert E Fortner II
MY PAIN
My heart melts like glass in a fire
When I'm overwhelmed by desire,
Filling me full of molten despair
Another rejection I could not bear.

Trying to escape the pain I hide in
my mind
But even in their relief I can't find,
So with each new chance the fire is
maintained
Keeping me forever chained.

Often the fire is intensified
When I see the hearts of others 1
unified,
And the only time I'm truly consoled
Is in God's loving fold.

But because of my human form
The pain still haunts me like a
lingering storm,
The storm waits for an opportune
moment
To drown me in its lonely sonnet.

As age creeps up and time flies by
It brings a tear to my eye,
Because of this fear of love passing
by me
I hope and pray for the pain to
subside you see
But because I have friends and I am
never alone
I realize that life is not etched in
stone.

So to everyone who shares my
despair
Keep believing for you there is
someone out there,
For soon they will come and quench
the flame
Then we will find something new,
about which to complain.

Shelby Lewis
IN SEARCH OF A ROLE MODEL

In Honor of Randal, Steven and Mrs. Lucinda Real. The first believers.

I have been searching for a model to
study. Someone who has gone
the road I travel now.

Alice Walker
Margaret Walker
Sonia Sanchez

Active, vocal, versatile women
figures. Each an inspiration. Each
born of average beginnings, emerging
as victors in a troubled, oppressive
society.

I love the way these women depict
other women in their stories.
Strong, realistic and brave heroines
who command respect across
any color line.

In this search for a model to study, I
find I must take my own way.
Doing so with the knowledge I am
not alone.

Tomasina Gritz

Tomasina Gritz
MY CHILD

This is dedicated to "My Children" and to all the Children of the World, WITH LOVE!

From the tree came the flower,
From the flower the seed,
And from love, my child,
Came you to me.

If you sleep, my child,
I will feel pleased,
because you are my child,
you are love to me.

From the mountain
came the river,
from the river, the fish,
and from love, my child,
came you to me.

Go to sleep, my child,
I have some work to do,
I have to clean the dishes
and prepare your food.

Go to sleep, my child,
go to sleep right now,
that I am feeling tired,
and I need to lay down.

Dr Millard Porter
THE PASTOR

To All Pastors

As the Pastor awakes and starts his
day
Knowing that there will be many
problems that he will have to face
that day.
So he bows his head and asks God to
guide him through the day.
He remembers his church members
as he prays.
He knows that each one will be faced
with a different trial that day.
The Pastor does not know what each
one will need.
As the Pastor works and goes through
the day,
Many questions will be asked—He
does not know what to say.
The young boy asks, "Pastor, why
did God take Daddy when he was so
strong?"
All the Pastor can say is, "God does
nothing wrong."
A young boy and girl asks, "Why did
God take Mother and leave us
alone?"
All the Pastor can say is, "God took
her to a better home."
So many people ask, "Pastor, why is
there so much trouble in the world
today?"
The Pastor answers, "God allowed it
to happen to show us there is a better
way."
God helps us as we go through the
day, to show people that there is a
better way.

Mary Triplett
SHADOWS

For all I love, may the shadows fall behind.

Rain, mist, fog
No shadows
You need sunshine for shadows
Yet oh in my heart life at times is full
of shadows
Especially on a day such as today
They rear their ugly heads
Creeping, crawling out of the dark
places of my mind
Seeking, searching, for whatever they
may find
I say, I see, yet at that moment I am
blind
Shadows away
Flee back to that evil one who sent
thee
Rain, fog, mist, you are a part of my
universe
My Lord sent you on both the just
and unjust
And oh I am in the middle
Rain, drizzle, fog, mist
Suddenly a feeling of wonder and
awe

As if my soul had just been kissed

Angelia De Lois King
WOMANS DAY
The Kids are screaming.
the cats are squalling
the dogs are barking
And the husband's calling!

Why is it a woman's work is never
Done?
But although you're sitting in your
chair,
you're not really there.
You're dreaming of cars & Trucks
and things,
While here I am fighting with
dishwasher as it coughs & Dings!
You're dreaming of pastures greener,
while I swear the children get
meaner.
You're wondering whether to paint
the car or not,
while here I am wiping baby snot.

You come through with mud on your
feet,
and leave it all there for me to sweep.

Late at night while you all sleep,
I sit in the chair alone and weep.

I am weak and so weary,
life for me is so dreary.

So now as I drift to sleep,
I pray the Lord my soul to keep.

Alice M Drexel
MY SISTER
I have a sister who is my best friend.
She is loving and kind and has
always been
There for me when others were all
gone,
I know my sister would not leave me
alone.

As for sisters mine will meet the test,
In fact she stands out from all the rest
Anyone is blessed if she is their
friend,
Because she radiates happiness again
and again.

She is loyal to family, friends and
others too,
And she will excel in anything she
starts to do
When given a project, she'll see it to
the end,
That's the way it is with my sister
and friend.

She is unselfish and generous to a
fault,
My sister is priceless and can't be
bought
I wish everyone had a sister like
mine,
Intelligent, beautiful, charming and
kind.

William K Yakoubian
SUNRISE AT MIDNIGHT
I
In a half-lit bar
Smoke and whispers
Fill every soul
With a dying melody.
Shadows move,
Back and forth,
Like ghosts
Gliding around
The broken rocks
Of ancient tombs.
Music in the air,
Gunfire not too far away,
Timeless ruins
Bringing beauty
Through centuries of death.
In a moonlight night
History weeping
In the death march of
tomorrow;
And the hopes of yesterday
Once again melting
In the foamy cups of today.

Linda Martin Soucy
ON A CLOUDY DAY

I wish to dedicate this poem to all my courageous friends who have made me realize that their silence gives me inner strength, better known as patience.

On a cloudy day,
Do you see spirits in the skies
Trying to escape
From an unknown fate?
Do you see angels come and go
In such a way,
That seeing them is believing
Because you have faith?
On a cloudy day,
Do you see a spiritual life
That coincides,
And yet it is something
Haunting us all the time?
Do you see all these things,
And sometimes wonder why
They keep following us around?
On a cloudy day,
Do you understand the silence
And yet they show us great signs
Of life that once existed long ago?
Is it not God himself
Trying to tell us something
That spiritual life can be inspiring
And rewarding for a long long
time . . .

Jetty Schwarz
LOVE ON ICE

To my husband, Josef Schwarz and my sister Else Kahn.

They danced buoyantly on the hard
ice there,
Feeling exulted in spite of cold air.
On their skates they turned around
and around;
Their rhythm was lewd and carnal
bound.
They wanted togetherness to be gay.
Their meetings always were a
holiday.
Their knowledge of love late began:
Both were the same sex; both were
gentlemen.

Julie Marie S Prado
BE WITH ME IN THE CHANGING OF SEASON

Summer breeze gently eases spirit to
the mind,
with passion anew created in the
wildness of season
Excitement filled the void of the once
vulnerable while
the start of a new adventure
now ready to be swept by its wings
Promises, oh promises.

Enchanting leaves gleam in sunshine
gold
Crispness of a new season glazed
with a misty dew
Yearning to flourish with each
moment gone by
Tender roots of the once new
beginning holding on
with lovely treasured memories.

Hold close! When winter frost is at
hand.
The perfection and purity of the air
peek through the windows of the
soul,
Close together with the flames of
love nearby
Hope, oh don't fail me now.

Tenderness does prevail, with the
freshness of Spring.
Softness of touch reach the heart
. . . with ever so full of warmth.
Favor of hope not only to start afresh,
But of LOVE, to fill my world again.

Leone Lee Coates

Leone Lee Coates
CHRISTMAS JOY

Christmas is for family,
Whether young or old
Everyone enjoys the time
That brings the snow and cold

Santa and his reindeer,
Cookies and a gift;
Those old familiar carols
Give spirits quite a lift.

The smiles and glee of children
Every Christmas morn;
Make us feel like youngsters
The day that Christ was born

Christmas is a time for love,
So smile and all be jolly;
Decorate with festive lights,
A Christmas tree and holly.

Christmas, 25, 1987

Margie Lalonde
WONDERS OF THE WORLD

I wonder how birds fly.
Why the sky is so high.
I wonder, I wonder,
I wonder why people cry,
And people die,
Especially ones so close.

I wonder how your hair grows,
How and why the wind blows,
Why the Earth moves,
And the cow moos.
I wonder, I wonder.

I wonder why the sun is bright,
Why feathers are so light,
And why the dark is night.
I wonder how we came to be,
And why some people yearn to be
Something other than themselves.
I wonder about these wonders of the
world.

Sally J Ingrassia
SNOW

To My Children.

Softly flying down from the sky.
So quiet and white;
a lonely feeling falls over the
earth.
A rare beauty lay before your eyes.
"Hush!" Listen to the silence falling
from the sky.
Beautiful White Snow.

Judy Hammock
MY FRIEND

To My "Baby Blue" I'll Always Love You.

I just lost my close friend
He went away & will never be
back
I loved him so—as he loved me
We had a bond that couldn't be
broken
many people had tried
But I was the one that made the
decision
For him to go & it hurt me
very badly!
When I would come home at night,
he would greet me with open arms; as
he would in
the morning when I called him for
breakfast!
He was always happy to see me
We had been together for 5 years!
But now he is gone and I will miss
him badly
He could never be replaced; no
matter what!!
You see—my friend's name was
Tipper!
And he was my cat
He was injured and got very sick
And I had to put him to sleep
Now he is in "Kitty Heaven"!!

Phebe Alden Tisdale
WHY TRY?

To my grandchildren: Emily, Johan, Todd, Amy and Sarah.

Why try? I cry, WHY TRY?

"Try! And try again!"

Try again? Inane!
Those willing to complain
evoke disdain,
and cause themselves more pain.
Let me explain—
A quick and easy answer
mimics a graceful dancer
hobbled by painful cancer:
where Truth fails to come clean,
evasiveness is seen
to be a crutch on which to lean.
I pray. I pay. Day after day!

"The fray of yesterday,
"today, is far away."

Why try? I die . . . WHY TRY?

"Why try? Hear our reply:"
"Care for this Earth! Never say die!"
"Cherish the sky! Never say die."

Please certify that I shall try—

Steven M Winter
BEHIND THESE BARS

Jailed in the walls of my head
Are scars from the tears that I shed
Ball and chain always pounding my
mind
Strong are the eyes but losing sight
becoming blind

Waiting for a key to fit my lock
So I do not have to sit alone on this
rock
Wondering if anyone will spend their
life with me
Because being lonely I do not want to
be

Having a woman to love and
someone I can touch
Feeling maybe it is a little too late
and asking for so much
I want to try and take a chance on
falling in love
So once again I will pray to the one
above

Behind this gate I am going through
hell
I do not wish to be in a very lonely
cell
Together in life we will try to give
each other sparkling stars
But never the years I have spent
being lonely
Behind these bars

Carol Macinga
HOUSEWORK

"Twas the day before Christmas
And the maid decided to come,
Put on her work clothes to get the job
done . . .
She tackled her chores,
She vacuumed and polished,
She thought to herself—
"Oh what I can accomplish!"
And when all was finally
completed,
With a smile on her face,
She knew she had succeeded,
To beautify a once dirty place!
So all she asks is one small plea,
To keep this place dirt and hair
free—
It's no problem to clean once in
awhile,
But to see this nonsense brings upon
no smile!
For all the good intentions put into
cleaning this place,
Give me the pleasure to always wear
a smile on my face . . .

Susan M Lovins
WHICH IS OF HOME

So many different structures.
Foundation made of cement, wood,
bricks of walls.
Marble, wood, rug to place their feet
upon.
Rows of pews and chairs to sit.
Pictures of His richness.
Elegant statues they pray upon.
Crosses that very of His sacrifice.
So many come here to seek Him.
All are not the same, but all alike in
one.

Here the earth is foundation, trees for
walls.
Branches heavy with leaves
protecting His floor.
Creatures fill His home of music.
Sun shining on you, it's Him who
warms you.

Gentle breeze that grasps you, is His embrace.
The fragrance of flowers, is His magnificent aroma.
All are the same, all made of Him.

Mary E Christian

Mary E Christian
LOVE

Love, full of expectations
Set you on fire
Stroke of midnight
Summers reward
Sweetest aroma, pristine light
Awe inspiring
He left no child of yours
To nurture to maturity

Mrs Flora Billings Wilson
WHEN DID I DIE?

To my Grandchildren! May they remember to respect our God, our country, our fellowmen, our flag and always remember! "God has blessed America." Never forget it.

I've marched with my men in fame and glory!
I've been the subject of many stories.
I've been raised with joy into bright blue skies,
I've been with my men when they died!
I've been with my children throughout their childhood;
I've often been misunderstood!
I've been to countries across the miles!
I've been the cause of many glorious smiles.
I've comforted widows on a dark, lonely night,
I've been with my country in all kinds of strife.
I've always been faithful, the Red, White and Blue;
making people's many dreams come true!
I've visited all types of sod, said with reverence "One Nation, Under God!"
I've heard the voices of the living singing of me with praises,
voices, loud and strong, their volume raising!
Now my voice mingles with others in their saddened cries;
Lord our Father in heaven, "When did I die!"
The pride and the glory of the American flag!
All this Lord, makes me sad!
"Oh, Lord, Oh Lord, hear my cries;
"When Lord! When! When! When Lord, Did I die!"

Ralaina Joy Ruvalcaba
A NEW LIFE BEGUN

To Deana, who inspired me with her real situation as a 16-year-old mother to be. To my parents, who gave me life and love, and who teach me more than they know. To Rachelle and Randy, who love me. Thanks for believing. And to Roger, who's death gave me compassion.

The parent rocks her babe beneath her tear-stained face,
She dreams of another time, another place,
When she could be a child with her life just begun,
Instead of a parent with childhood done.

The mother cuddles her baby against her shoulder and face,
She cradles the infant in that protective place,
Wishes her choices could somehow be undone,
Though she loves her baby son.

The teen holds the infant's hands to her smiling face,
She smooths his baby hair back in its place,
She wants him to have something—including her missed fun,
For he is a miracle, a life from lives, just begun.

The girl cradles her baby close, stroking the babe's face,
He is a part of her and for him, her heart holds a special place,
She does not blame the result of what she has done,
And never from responsibility has she run.

The child rocks her child with a Mother's innate grace,
She sings a lullaby as she studies her baby's face,
She accepts her eternal responsibility for his life begun,
What is past has been done—
At the expense of her childhood and fun.

Jen Dennis
UNSEEN TREASURE

To the people who have made the biggest impressions in my life: Beth McElhone, Matthew Elliott, Dan Duncan, Richard Ramsdell, and Jim Miller.

Where within you rage
Can I comfort you?
With what words can I soothe?
There is nothing so fateful
As a past which rules
Our lives in the present
The future holds no bounds on fate—
It is a risk to be taken.
O' that the door would open
And the light let in;
That <u>this</u> storm would calm
And sunshine return for a time.
O' that tomorrow were here
And today become a shadow
of your past.
And yet, stash away
The gold and diamonds of your
disturbing situation,
Within walls unseen, to be admired
another time . . . later.

Dolores A Hockenberry
HEARTS FOREVER

To my husband, Bill, whose heart attack inspired this poem. Thank you for getting well. I love you. Your wife of 34 years, Dolores.

I walked into the house today
And noticed something right away
A loneliness had filled the room
And that loneliness filled me with gloom.

I looked around at all I have
And thought to myself—"not so bad"!
I saw all the things you have done for me
And thought of the blessings between me and thee.
And I saw your hat just lying there
But I looked for you and you were nowhere
An emptiness then swelled up inside me
'Cuz what I have is nothing without you beside me

So hurry up and get yourself well
So not only your hat but you too will dwell
In our own little space we bring alive
With love and life and our will to survive.

I love you, my sweet—I'm really glad
That we've always shared whatever we've had
I pray we'll always be together
My heart is yours—yours forever.

Karen A Petrick
MY BUDDY

This poem is dedicated to Buddy, who brought me so much love and joy. No one will ever understand and someday we will be together again.
You are my Buddy, you are my friend,
I'll love you with my life, until the very end.
No one understands the love I have for you,
You're so little and tiny, and a very pretty blue.

You bring me joy and give me love,
It comes from your heart and Heaven above.
You live life freely, no worries no care,
But life isn't easy, nor is it fair.

The time has come for us to part.
You're so very sick now, and so is my heart.
I'll take care of you until it is time,
I'll nurse you and feed you, and you'll be just fine.

My hope was lifted—then came the fall,
I tried as I held you, I knew you had your call.
Now the end has come for us to say "goodbye",
For you're now made better, and you could fly high.

For we'll be together again someday, and in that lifetime, together we'll stay.
Buddy I love you my parakeet friend,
I told you I'll love you, until the very end.

Ruth Charlotte Heyde
THE WINGED BLUE

As I look upon a sturdy lad with his eyes
aloft to the winged blue,
The blue above where dart and fly
the mighty silver warriors of the sky,
No wonder, awe or fear show in his boyish face
Only envy that the joy of sharing
could erase.
You ask him, and before your query is
found and formed,
His face alight, he traces each outline
and feature
Of the man-made creature of the winged
blue to you.
Not long ago, a child upon a hill
would thrill to see and follow
The swift flight of swallow, nightingale
and dove,
And hear the sweet, clear song that spoke
of tenderness and love.

But look upon the lad who now is gazing
toward the winged blue.
He does not seek the simple joy
of small bird's flight,
But glories in the screaming,
roaring might of carriers
of vengeance and of death.
Let not the day be far away
when a child again
Can see and hear with childish
eye and childish ear
Only the bright and constant
glories of the ages
And not examples of the minds
of modern sages
Bent upon destruction, fear
and death.

Eileen M Raynor
ADAM WITHOUT EVE

See, Mom, I told you I'd make it big. I just wish you were here to see it. My words are for you, love Eileen.

I am Adam and I stand alone before the world.
A deafening calm surrounds my being.
To yell would be to sin
to be silent would be questionable.
How desolate a place I think to myself—
No trees, no water, no life, no sound
there's just a void, just a quiet void.
I sit to think, and I stand to answer
I yell to be heard, but no one

responds
Running blindly I try to escape,
at last there is light, but yet no source—
the way out is here, or perhaps over there.
Again I retreat, retreat to the spot,
back to where it began
back to the place
back to the deafening calm which surrounded me.

Terri Inman
BUSY STREETS

This poem is dedicated to the people in California who experienced the earthquake 1989.

Busy streets
automobile engines filling them
people on crosswalks
horns sounding
music playing
towerings rising
clear windows shimmering
with light
supper on tables
Daddy's coming home
cozy dens
noisy business offices
terrible sounds
sounds of glass
breaking
towers falling
crashing
screeching tires
frantic people
screaming
running
darkness befalls
quiet offices
supper's cold
Daddy's not home

Caroll Marie Der Kacy
WORDS SPOKEN

Your memory is like a rock n' roll song, a little jazz and lots of blues . . . To: John.

Be careful of the words you speak to people
Once they are out, they can't be taken back.
They will pollinate in people's minds,
Just as if they were wild seeds,
Germinating in the prairies.

Words of hate have caused the world's wars.
The words linger in the ruins of crumbled walls, graveyards and history
books.

Words of courage and hope gave us the twentieth century,
And rebuilt cities that were destroyed by Mother Nature.
Words of love that you spoke to me so tenderly—had comforted my pain and
hurt.

Your love was supposed to last me a lifetime,
Just like the redwood tress, the sunshine and the stars in the sky . . .

And on one ugly, cloudy fall morning you said, "Goodbye . . ."
Those words of sorrow linger in my mind.
Those words will always fester bitterness in memory of you . . .

Paula K Holley
MY LOVE FOR YOU

This poem is dedicated to Johnney, whom I love with all my heart.

My love for you
It grows each day
Whether skies are blue
Or whether skies are grey.

As for problems, yes, we've
Had our share
But our love (though hidden)
Was always there.

There was a time once
in our lives when we were very sad.
We took it out on each other
and always ended up mad.

We couldn't see the forest
for the trees up ahead
The only time we got along
is when were in bed.

That was in the past
when we both had much to learn
But now in pleasing each other
we each take our turn.

Since we've gotten back together,
as a family once again
I can't thank God enough
and once more I say Amen!

Andrea R Sirois
LOVE PAGES

To Kenneth J. Tardie.

Take the pages of our lives together,
spread them thin,
And read between the lines.
The wording is not just black or white.
And in between the different chapters,
the ink may be smeared,
The ink will never disappear from the story line.
And when you close the pages,
Dust may fly,
But our story line will stay on the pages
of our love time.

Theresa Delicato
ILLUMINATING VENERY

Thanks to my whole family; ti'amo, F4E and to all my friends. Also God bless Tony XO.

Share life with our children
Teaching all about love
Forgive their small blunders
Understand we're of one
Care plenty not pushy
And in time we'll find
The next generation will have peace in mind.

E H Ehlert
THE UNKNOWN SOLDIER

To—all of our national monuments, One . . . The Tomb of the Unknown Soldier.

At Arlington Cemetery, they laid him to rest
He had no name,
So with "The Unknown Soldier," he was blest.
He had no badge, insignia, or identification
To be positively sure he was which one—
Of so many "missing in action," or unidentified
So we'd know who he was before he died.
He leaves us with this message—
He died for his country.
Who he is, didn't much matter—you see
Nor to himself matter—
For he was but one of thousands of men
—If they gave their lives once
They'd give it once again.
But, now, as they water flowers o'er his grave
We'll learn what his message is—if one he gave.
It's to serve your country—
Even if it costs your life
In these times of war—and times of strife
And if nobody knows who to give the credit to
Because he had only one life—he gave it for you.

Christine Ann Reed

Christine Ann Reed
SITTER'S TIME—7-18-76

NOW children go up the stairs, for bed I think it's time; And I'll be up to tuck you in, and read a nursery rhyme.

And if you're good and go straight to bed, and you're tucked in nice and neat; When I come up to read to you, I may bring something sweet.

Like cookies & milk, or a piece of cake, with a kiss to make it just right; And a kiss is also for something else, to hope you both have a good night.

Donna Johnson
HOW WAS I TO KNOW?

To my wonderful husband, Larry.

How was I to know thirty years ago . . .
when we were both still in our teens,
chasing each our separate dreams . . .
How was I to know that you loved me so?

How was I to know only just a year ago . . .
our paths would cross again
and you would tell me then . . .
you loved me still and had loved me,
oh, so many, many years ago.

How was I to know first seeing you one year ago . . .
after all these years,
many heartaches, many tears . . .
How was I to know that I, too, would love you so?

Why did you not let me know a long, long time ago?
Now, have all these years we wasted
or learned from other love we've tasted . . .
clearing the path for us to grow and renew our love from years ago.

How was I to know on this day six months ago . . .
when in the prime of my life,
I'd become my high school sweetheart's wife?
Thirty years ago . . . how was I to know?

Carol S Wood
WILLOW IN THE WIND

To Richard E. Heyman, whom I dearly love.

You are a song,
In the wind
I am a willow,
Bending to your tune
I reach out,
just to touch you
But you are not there
And yet, . . . I still
Sense your soft whisper,
Moving through me
And I am touched by you.

Josef Shahwan
ANGEL CHILD

To Amy—
Domina Arcani Caelesti.

They say I should have not been born
The seed should not have clung
But the bed you made was O so warm
So sweet the food you brung

They say I lacked the crucial form
My ilk can only falter
But your blanket wrapt beyond the norm
I was like a host upon an altar

I heard your voice in that vital sphere
I felt you touch my face
I knew that my place could only be here
For I'd have both velvet and lace

So I postponed my fate for a later day
Because of the joy in my soul
I wanted to hold you in every way
For with you I'd surely be whole

Today I play like a lamb in May
I ride the unicorn
I've had my day only because
It's to you, that I was born

Wanda Lee
DEREK

To my beautiful son, Derek John Dietterich, who truly has been the sunshine of my life.

When you are born and cuddled to me,
I felt as blessed a mother could be.
Although I was scared, I was in such awe
of the beauty of it all.
How your eyes twinkled as you sucked those fists,
your one ounce of formula wouldn't be missed.
Through the years we were each other's worlds
our closeness couldn't be unfurled.

Me your mommy and you my
sunshine
I was so proud of this son of mine!
My love for you continued to grow
and I will always want you to know
your mom will be a forever friend
come to me time and again.

Love,
Mom

Angela M Edmonds
THIS LIFE

This poem is dedicated to the memory of Jessie B. Jones, and to the entire Edmonds family. We love you and miss you Granny.

All in this life cannot be guaranteed,
And all is not lost when in your heart
you grieve,
For there is someone watching,
watching way up there,
He can fix it all, make you walk tall,
and feel his presence as strong as his
love.

I hope that one day I'll get to see,
that great courageous man that
died for me, I would like to thank
him one day if I could, but I'll try to
do so down here by living life as I
should.
I'll teach it to my children, I'll teach
it to my friends, I'll teach it to the
people I meet walking down the
street.

I shalt not falter, I shalt not flee,
because your heart was big enough to
save a wretch like me.

I thank you, Jesus, with all my
heart and soul, when life is a struggle
or burden I'll think of what you did
to save us all, and on my faith I
will stand tall, for what makes me
think that I should not have to bear,
for you are the son of God and I
should not despair.

Barbara Jeane Canham
MOTHERS' HAPPY BIRTHDAY

Dedicated To My Loving Daughter, Sandra Jeane Canham.

As I walk along beside the Deep Blue
Pacific Ocean Shore,
I say, "Happy Birthday" to
Mother's Little Girl
For I relate to Memories of Yore'
Another Birthday has stolen you
farther away and Mother's
Little Flaxen haired Girl of four you
are no more
You retain your Daddy's carefree
personalities delightful
Smile and sense of Humor's bright
laughing eyes
Which steals my Lonely Heart
across the miles.
Memories of My Little Mademoiselle
of Yester-years
Still prevail while you cuddle and
counsel your own
Boys savouring many a Joy
For we Mothers are open
Blueprint Books of History, mapping
Many a Score of accomplished
Dreams and Broken Hearts, but Life
Is in the Fetus you see, Well Now,
Just Maybe, but into the
Future aloft we must scale and sail
our future children into God's
Eternity awaiting a mother's
embryo yet to be, to be, to be.
We are here today relating Memories
of Yore'
Yes, Just what is packed in our
Scientist General Store
For Mothers after you and me
But, then, I suppose, Life goes on
you see, and hopefully
We will all come to rest upon God's
knee, so therefore,
We must accept Life and Trust in
our Country whatever
We seem to be, for we shall remain in
God's Eternity.
"Happy Birthday" to you and to
me.

Linda J Hill
MISSING YOU

Hope you're watching Brant, 'cause this one's for you!

Your wistful eyes pierced eternity's
mysteries;
was that why we couldn't keep you
for very long?
My friend, my soul-partner,
couldn't you wait for us to leave
together?
Instead, you've left a vast, dark
chasm in my heart!

I long to hear your dear voice,
to see your gentle angel face.
I miss our phone calls filled with
laughter—mixed with tears—
caring and frustration—despair lifted
to hope.

Oh that wonderful wicked
humor—
your little boy mischievousness!!
Yet you were a man, with the
wisdom of sages
reflected in those soft, soulful eyes.
You were sent for us to share for
awhile—
to love and protect.
Sitting at your feet,
we tried to absorb your mystical
words.

But we will share the sunshine again.
Together we will walk beyond time
and space,
loving each other perfectly, spirit-to-
spirit, endlessly.
Til then, my friend, I'll be missing
you.

Tonia Young
REGRETTED PASSION

Dedicated to all those who have endured a short-lived, "should-have-never-been" relationship.

I already knew your heart was broken
But, yes, foolishly I took a big chance
I wanted to be yours, not a token
My heart cried out for a little
romance.
See the things I did, was it all in
vain?
On the phone when I should have
been at school
And in your arms, I was going
insane.
Not a sensible girl, but a damn fool.
That passionate Friday, oh, how
blinding
No, I had never kissed that way,
shame
However I knew, your heart was
minding,
the way I reminded you of old
flames.
There are no hard feelings, we are
still friends
the regretted passion came to an end.

Roya Perry
THE FIRST TIME I SAW YOU

the first time i saw you
was in my dreams

we were walking
hand in hand
on a grassy hilltop

you kissed me
for the first time
on that hill

when i awoke
i still felt your arms around me
your lips atop mine

but that was a dream
and it has already started to fade

Will you?

Melinda Dillon
MY SECRET PLACE

This poem is dedicated to my wonderful father, who has always been here when I needed him, his name is Larry Kenneth Dillon.

As I walk along this secret place,
It seems nature is with me
Like the setting sun, giving
everything a golden glow,
Or the animals, scurrying to their
homes
Like the birds, gracefully flying and
sitting down
In their warm nest in the trees
As the delicate flower buds, slowly
begin to close
Yes, they belong here, I feel I belong
too
I want to stay here forever,
Alone with unspoiled nature
Unspoiled by man's deadly hands
With no pollution or civilization, to
destroy it,
My secret place.

Earl T Chandler
LOOK UP NOT DOWN

Remember to look up not down
As you travel on life's way
But keep your feet upon the ground
With sure steps from day to day.

Material needs we can't evade
But in this life's hurried pace
We find in all things we must trade
We must keep things in their place.

The amount that you may own
Does not measure your real worth
You are more than flesh and bone
To your neighbors on the earth.

We must take thought of to-morrow
Or we most surely will stray
So let's look up for guidance
As we travel on our way.

William Lamb
MALL CHURCH

Oldsters walking slowly

having coffee, conviviality;

spending time most of all.

Where did people go,before they
built the Mall?

The ambivalent teen
boisterously acting the fool,
noisily making the scene—
conversation for school.

Serious shoppers too
intent upon the sales,
populating the view
recounting bargain tales.

More folks than in church you'll see,
this I'm forced to report.
One day will there be
PEWS located at Center
Court??????????

Robin L McGee
DECISIONS

This or That?
Yes or No?
Good or Bad?
I want to know.
Isn't there someone out there
with answers or explanations
or maybe just a little guidance
As I go?

Can I do it?
Will I fail?
and what if I do?
My brain says "Yes" Go Go Go
My heart says "Stop" it hurts to let go
of the past, of these ties you've made.

Whatever happened to the days
when my biggest decision of the day
was
Strawberry or Chocolate?

Janet Leonard
A PARISHIONER

A parishioner attends Mass every
Saturday.
He is always alone. He enters the
pew behind
me and becomes manifest. I am
distracted. My prayers become
fragmented and fleeting.
Sensations of awe, wonder and
yearning flood in to connect me to
the rhythms of
life and its impenetrable enigmas.
A fierce gentleness in me which
dares
to speak the truth tells me he is an
amalgam of ethereal mystery, a
vision
of cruel kindness, a pleasing plague,
a recluse in a crowd.
I look backward. He twists his neck
to the right with senseless speed. He
does not
want me to look at his face. I peek
anyway.
His face is a work of grand design. It
has an
esoteric, provoking charm that is rich.
It is the quintessence of beauty. It
reminds
me of a basic paradox of life: hidden
in the
beauty is the pain. Scripture says

sorrow is
better than laughter because when the face is
sad the heart grows wiser. (Ecc 7:3)

Grace Andraos
THE DREAMER IN ME

I long to be so many places
Experiencing life's different traces
drowning in the passion of my phases.
Uncertain of my reasons
the energy inside me
the drive that binds me
to those dreams and motivations
very clearly disrupts the calm & peace I thirst.
At times reality hurts.
I treat myself with distrust
when my calm & peace I thrust
continuing to assume
my youth is still in bloom.
My sorrows are always plenty
As I lead the life of a dream,
A life that's unfulfilling and empty.

Maggie Lee Cole

Maggie Lee Cole
CHICAGO'S FIRST BLACK MAYOR (CAN'T BE BEAT)

To the memory of Harold Washington— Chicago, Illinois' first black mayor.

Chicago first black mayor was for all people, regardless of rage, religion, color or creed, good better and best. With the greatest mixture for any testing. Chicago's first black mayor showed the world how Chicago could beat the rest and pass with an A plus test. The first black mayor cannot be beat, he was the greatest biggest treat. The greatest for any city and on their streets, a smile at all times that couldn't be beat. He passed every test and now he is at rest. I guess you are wondering about this man. He was tall, handsome, not small and dark tan, he became a great great champion of this land. Chicago's first black mayor showed the world, how Chicago could beat the rest and pass with an A plus on every test. This first black mayor can't be beat. He was proud and Chicago's biggest treat. Chicago, Chicago you beat them all, with your first black mayor who was on the ball. Harold Washington, Harold Washington, not slim but tall, there was no way he could stumble and fall. Chicago's first black mayor can not be beat, he was Chicago's biggest treat. No one, but no one, can take his seat, not even if they steal and cheat.

K W Smith Jr
MELLITUS CHANT

Thank you for all of your support and love, Little One.

Greet the morning:
Needle. (Stick.) Wince.

Get up. Watch your feet.
Measure. Weigh. Eat.

Work and expend. Overextend
Sweat. Shake. Eat.

Greet the evening:
Needle. (Stick.) Wince.

Sit down. Watch your feet.
Measure. Weigh. Eat.

Sleep and pray
you'll see the day
you throw the needle away.

Greet the morning:
Needle. (Stick.) Wince

Boris Skalsky
UNTITLED

To Christina.

I've seen God
In the clouds and rain,
In the burnished moon,
Calm and tame.

I've seen God
In the lakes and seas,
In the dying maple
And its bitter leaves.

I need not see heaven
To speak of Him.
I've seen God
In worlds within.

Gene Patee
JUDGING

I Dedicate This Poem To All Intolerant People Who Discriminate Against Others With Racial, Social, Economic, And Religious Prejudice. They Must Learn There Is No Substitute For Love, Empathy, And A Helping Hand.

When You Think Of Others Harshly,
Facts You Might Have—Ere So Sparsely,
A Pleasant Man, No Problem—He,
Not So!—That Vulgar Man You See,
You Think Of That Unlovely Soul,
Where Unseen Heartaches Take Their Toll,
For Things Are Never What They Seem, Nor Are They Ever What We Dream,
Repulsive Man—Emotion-Lame,
Too Oft We Judge The Outward Frame,
Help Those Irritant Oyster Lice, To
Create—A Pearl Of Great Price,
Prejudiced Hearts Are Never Right,
Such Evil Flees As God Gives Light,
Sin Left All Men In Disarray, Grace
Flowers To All Men When We Pray,
As We Judge Each Other Squarely,
Surely—God Will Judge Us Fairly.

Frances Robinson Sneed
THE CHOSEN FEW

To Joseph, my husband, and our babies—Christopher, Christina and Alicia.

Jesus is not interested in halfway people,
Only those who will go all the way.
He's not interested in lukewarm converts,
Only those who mean what they say.

Who will follow me, he said?
Who will take the final step.
Who will follow me, he said?
Instead of serving yourself.

But because so few refuse knowledge,
They often reject or rebel.
Saying God has failed, and the Christian life isn't real,
Not knowing they are destined for hell.

The counterfeit faith is a religion of fear,
It's a religion of law not love.
Only a change in the heart gives us a brand-new start,
And being chosen by God above.

Joel Dean Slaughter
PASSION

Dedicated to my father, J C Slaughter, thanks for your encouragement. "Keep your chin up!"

The night is black for the panthers prowl,
The moon burns bright for the wolves' mournful howl,
Hearts burn hot,
The flames rise higher,
For the breathless panting lovers.

Lust rages wild,
Passions gain tempo
As the wind's breath shivers.

Naked in splendor lay the battle ravaged souls.

Glistening uncovered as hot red coals.

Passions run hot,
Wild animals through fire,
Quenching its thirst,
Hot gained desires.

Morning breaks a new day dawned,
Lovers break from their sacred bond,
To await the return of this wild burning flame,
For Passion is why they play this game.

Marylee DiLorenzo
NOTHING . . . EXCEPT

I know nothing about you, except
the tears of your pain and rage,
how your blue eyes pierce my soul,
how your smile brings one to my lips.

I know nothing about you except
your soul-wrenching loneliness,
your power to heal,
your sensitivity to the world.

I know nothing about you, except
that you are a warrior.
that you need to help others,
that you won't help yourself.

I know nothing about you, except
that you ran from me
because I love you—and
know nothing about you.

Helen C Corollo
JUST THINKING

We thought the golden years were golden
but now it's plain to see
we spend our time just
thinking
of how it used to be.

We never had to look for "this"
and "that" was always near
but now we can't find anything
for the memory goes each year.

We used to go to bed at night
and sleep the whole night through
so now we lie awake and think
just nothing else to do.

They say for us to be involved
it keeps you young at heart
but they don't know how hard it is
to even get a start.

"Just thinking" is our pride and joy
We do it with such grace.
Far better to be sitting still
than falling on our face.

David A George
MY THOUGHTS FOR YOU

I went to war and I went to win,
To fight with my brothers
And to walk the bloody ground
Where others had been.

I carried my gun in the name of Peace,
And walked among the dead who
Filled the streets.

I saw a common hole where they
Died as one
While the monster remains free
To do as he's always done.

I did my best in the time I had
For the stars and stripes our Freedom flag

But with a frown on my face I
Cannot come back
I leave empty and cold because of
Some enemy flack.

War is hell I hear some say
While our dreams are broken by the acts of yesterday.

The price of freedom does not come cheap
But we do our best for those who have felt the grief.

So I went to war to fight the daily battles that
Are won and lost
Like the others around the world
Who have paid
The cost.

Father you taught me wrong from right
When to love and when to fight.

Too young to die we sometimes finish last
So mother remember me and our memories past.

I've had my time to laugh and some time to cry
Now my work is done so I'll just say good–by.

Joelle Graeb
TWO PEOPLE IN LOVE
Two people in love . . .
Laughing,
Smiling,
Gazing,
Talking,
Hugging,
Kissing.

Two people in love . . .
Arguing,
Frowning,
Crying,
Hurting,
Hugging,
Kissing.

Joelle M Graeb
TODAY IS A NEW DAY
Yesterday I felt scared
and I let my fears stand in the
way of becoming the best that I
can be.

However, today is a new day
and today I'm going to be the best
I can be
by taking risks and giving myself
the chance
to prove what I can do.

Today is a new day
and I'm going to make the most of it.

Kathleen Mapother
I HAVE WATCHED YOU PULL
I have watched you pull
Other lives onto your table and push
Them through the space in your
world,
Square pegs in round holes.
A game you play with no
return. Only temporary occupancy
of a place.
You are convinced can be filled by
nothing
Less than the shape of the woman
Who left her cartoon outline against
your soul.
Now you are left
Holding the gifts of today. Searching
To seal them into a moment of
forever.
Reaching for more because the space
inside you feels so big.

But the healing does not come
From the quantity of lives you pull in
Only from the gracious acceptance
Of the gifts which most resemble
The empty shape on
Your soul.

Marcella M Glennon
IN YOUR EYES I SEE A STORY

This poem is dedicated to Christine Sapien.

In your eyes I see
a story
Like so many times
before
A story of a girl trapped
within her own ingeniousness
Lost within the philosophies
of herself and others
So wrapped in her mind
that her heart has no room
to breathe, to be free, to love
Not even herself.

In your eyes I saw
Confusion and Pain
I tried to be there for you
You pushed me away
Withdrawn from the world around
You sent yourself away
Without a clue, without a sound
Now when I picture you
In your eyes I see
Silence.

Nancy L Kelly
A FRIEND IS ONLY
The dark is only but a thing,
We shall never see.
Together is the wanted way,
We will never be.

Love is only but a word,
Describes how we emotion.
A soldier for a country fights,
His heart filled with devotion.

Pollution is only but a thing,
That keeps us all from breathing.
But the fence I have around my heart,
Can keep you not from leaving.

The sky is only but a place,
In which to keep the stars.
It seems that my top dresser drawer,
Keeps thing that were ours.

The road is only but a thing,
We use to go adventure.
Your car you rode long times about,
That is when you met her.

The telephone is but a thing,
In which to relay a voice.
Your mind is what you must make
up,
When you have to make a choice.

Defiance is only but a thing,
We use when we rebel.
Without you here, fire surrounds,
Just like living in hell.

Trust is only but a thing,
We must have in fellow men.
But confidence between us dear,
Can never be again.

A friend is only but a soul,
To place all our faith and hope.
But the dirt you left behind on me,
Can't be washed away with soap.

The sun is only but a thing,
To lighten up the sphere.
But this is the end, so I will say,
Only, "Goodbye dear."

Eddie Grant Jr
WILL THERE EVER
Will there ever be a world
With all nations at peace
With no wars being fought
No guns being shot
No boys being taught to fight

No bombs dropped on the ground
no bodies lying all around
Just world leaders obeying a peaceful
plight

Will there ever be freedom
throughout all lands
With no more Kadafy or Ayatollah
with their selfish demands
Will there ever be a world completely
drug free
With no cocaine, marijuana or LSD

I'm sure these events will be actual
someday
When all can relax and live their lives
their regular way
This can happen, this can come true
But only with the help of me and
you.

Viola E Shaw
ME

I dedicate this poem to my children, Carmaline, Lisa, Dalana, and Darnelle.

Feeling, knowing, and growing ME.
What self-achievement in realizing
the importance of ME
Gradual and gross emotions of
getting to know ME
Too: Understanding ME is to pamper
and satisfy.
Stimulating things that enhance ME.
Keeping a healthy attitude.
With humble gratitude.
Building a character of solitude.
Too: Understand ME like no man
will attain.
GOD: Created ME for a purpose.
Living and loving, with little or no
regressions.
Caring for and considering others
through ME.
Too: Accept defeat, and still compose
ME in a good relationship
I want to be aware of ME,
show compassion for ME.
Feeling, knowing, growing ME.

Thomas Benros

Thomas Benros
THE LAST LETTER

To my mother, always alive in my heart.

If, in someplace, you could still listen
to me;
If my voice and thoughts could still
reach you out;
If memories of this world could still
be there,
You could possibly remember the last
letter,
Plunged in tears I wrote to you in the
distance . . .
Mother, I believe you can hear me
Even from far beyond the cold tomb,
Where human's voices are no more,
My deep feelings, my deep love can
touch you,
Still and always alive in my heart.
Beyond the sky, as far as my mortal
eyes can see,
Deep in the heavens, in God's
mansion,
In the joyful conviviality of the
angels,
You may like to turn your tender eyes
To your loved ones.
But what hopes can we nourish?
Under the flowers of that insensitive
slab,
Flowers for you and sadness for us,
Something rests beyond the dust of
our beginning:
Your soul, your immortal soul, our
last hope.

Gia Dameta Grant
THE MOST PRECIOUS MOMENTS—OF ALL

To my darling D.T.G. The moments we shared together, were the most precious moments — of all.

My darling one as the days slowly
swing by,
I always seem to picture your
glowing little smile,
Even though I often break into tears
and cry.
Knowing if I'd ever see you again, it
will be quite a while.
Remembering the moment I held you
gracefully within my arms,
Hoping you were protected from all
of life's harm.
Feeling as gentle as a soft little
feather,
I cherish that moment within my
mind,
As my way of you and I being
together.
Seeking all of the love I have for you.
You have yet to find.
All of the anguish I feel as we're
drifted apart,
I look upon the beauty of you coming
into the world such pleasure,
Those are the most precious moments
I hold near to my heart.
Thinking of you now and forever, the
loving times we shared, I must
always treasure.
As we each journey our separate
direction,
I await upon the day that meet once
more,
There's nothing on earth that will
destroy the love and affection.
Because it is you my dear whom I
most adore.
For the time has come for me to say
good-bye once again my dear,
May you always remember that I will
always love and be here for you.
And—may you always be in God's
hands, with all sincere.

Brenda Reynolds
TIC TOCS AWAY

Dedicated to Shirley, my beautiful mother in heaven, who suffered through several years of cancer in silence and smiles.

Powerful in the hands of Chance
Time sneaks by without a glance
leaving his mark.

When Fate steps in to give Chance a
break
Time strolls by eating his cake
and having it too.

Worry appears being Time's
companion
Making stress lines and seeming
champion
until Sleep.

Gentle Sleep relaxes Chance, Fate,
and Worry
But still Time goes by; he's in no
hurry
so Aware is called.

Aware realizes that Time has won
Wishing one day more just for fun
before Death takes over.

Patricia Page
THE LONELINESS OF MY SOUL
My loneliness fills my soul with sadness
and despair.
Life is just a mirage of adventure leading no where.
You can see that I am a pessimist who
has lost her way.
Loneliness makes every sleepless night
seem like an endless day.
Heartbreak and turmoil are loneliness turned upside down.
It is an endless circle that goes round and round.
Life as I said before is a mirage of adventures leading nowhere.
Loneliness is the catalyst taking you there.
The loneliness of my soul is quiet and discreet.
While I seem mellow and really quite meek.
My loneliness is really anger that no one cares.
Enough of this anger and pity and despair.
Loneliness is certainly leading me no where.
Love is the solution where most life should be bound.
Loneliness, I hope, departs after love is found.

Sylvia Hopkins
ONLY GOD KNOWS
The broccoli soup looked good as she poured it into a container. The tiny sliced sausages gave off a sweet aroma.
Placed the soup in the refrigerator as many thoughts went thru her mind.
Threw a kill at the semi as it disappeared out of sight.
Half an hour before, they enjoyed lunch together.
Will today be our last goodbye.
Or will GOD choose another time in our life?
I'm sure he knows I love him.
And he loves me.
The highway is now between us.
Will he come back to me, or will I be gone when he returns?
Only GOD knows.

Scott D Fuller
MY NEW SHOES
I won the race on Saturday,
Because of my new shoes.
They are white and gray,
I bet I'm on the News.

I really whipped 'em all,
I heard no sideline boos.
I beat them from the start,
Because of my new shoes.

I'll enter the Olympics,
I'm sure I will not lose.
I will be very famous . . .
Thanks, Mom, for my new shoes!

Kim Yurk
THORNS AND SPLINTERS
Little one, oh little one,
Why are you crying so?
I've cut my finger on a thorn and
have a splinter in my toe.
Little one, oh little one,
dry your eyes and come to me.
Life is full of splinters and the
thorns grow like a tree
A splinter is the rough outside,
that must come off before.
a happy, loving, caring soul
can shine their light and glow.
Many thorns will be encountered
before the rose is grown.
But with patience and with loving
care the rose will grow and grow.
So little one, my little one,
dry your eyes and come to me.
For many thorns will block
your way, and splinters will always be.

Shelley Williams
THE PERFECT STRANGER
Your nose so straight
Your teeth so bright;
Gosh, you sure were
a wonderful sight!

Your eyes so deep
Your smile so fine;
I thank the Lord
You were all mine!

Your looks were great
Your kiss so sweet;
Nothing about you could
Possibly be beat!

Nights passed and
Days went by;
It was as beautiful
As the stars in the sky!

Everything was great
We were such a team;
Tho' it hurt so much
To realize it was only a dream.

Satish Menon
WILLING WORDS
Like tainted water
Spurting disappointingly,
Forming no cogent matter
Amelioration comes sparingly.
Illusions of delirious plopping
Sooner go popping.
Dreams remain dreams—
Lofty malevolence gleams.

A modicum of hope—
Obfuscation overwhelms.
Jarring singularities
Cut cute curiosities.
Reach down for me
For fair flair;
Looming moribundity,
Nadir of despair.

Heather Close
TREASURES
I have a treasure in my mind
It's one I can easily find
This special treasure is my memory
It has no limits and no boundary
It has no need for spoken words
But every voice is always heard
It has no pictures for eyes to see
But the details are vivid inside me
This treasure can't be brought or sold
And it is more precious than gold
A treasure that's always there
Beautiful treasures with no price
They take me back to paradise

Kelly Sue Kemick
LONELINESS

To "Toots."

The old woman sits quietly in her rocker. Her eyes are gray and heavy. She taps her fingers quietly on the arms of the rocker.

Her blue-gray hair swings slowly, lightly brushing the sides of her face as her head tilts from side to side. She lives alone in her rocking chair.

The chairs around the woman are empty. No one comes to visit. Her grandchildren stay motionless in pictures scattered through her house. The dull colors around her and the sounds of silence bring back memories.

The old woman sits quietly rocking, remembering, and still remains lonely.

Orsola Jane Burnette
ODE TO BERMUDA—LAND OF PASTELS

To my mother—who loves Bermuda as much as I do.

With your greens and yellows and pinks and blue,
there are no reds to be found on you.
To your doll-house like shops on Hamilton Way
not a thought is given as to what to do today.
You never know who you might meet with all the
tourists and sailors strolling down on Front Street.
The Hibiscus is the island's flower which blooms all
year thru, but do not pick them, it's not the right
thing to do.
Elbow Beach and Horseshoe Bay are just a short distance
away; when you hop on the pink and blue buses that will
take you there each day.
With the water so clear and clean and green and the pink
grained sand that just has to be seen.
There are a lot of sights your motor-scooter can take you
to see, as you ride on the other side, that's the British
way to be.
All 22 miles of Bermuda's magical land is so near yet so far—if you can just understand.

Geneive Bettles
TO JENNIFER
To–day, great grandma is eighty
You are just two months old,
My hair has turned to silver
Yours is a pretty gold.
Your eyes sparkle as bright as can be
Mine need glasses so I can see
Those two tiny hands will find things to do
Mine have been busy these many years through.
Those two little feet will be on the go
Mine are still moving but now rather slow
That sweet little smile, may it last through the years
A comfort to all, and a help through the tears
Great grandma loves you—God loves you too.
May his blessings be with you in all that you do.

Elizabeth Sullivant White
THE BLUEBIRD
Do you see the Bluebird
Sitting over there
He's a lot like me
He likes to sit and stare
Early in the morning
His flight just begins
He follows you everywhere
Till the evening ends
He watches what you're doing
He knows where you've been
He's a lot like me
He wants to be your friend
So while you're out there working
Just stop and look around
He may be there above you
Or he may be on the ground
And though I've come to know you
In the most unusual way
One thing I can say about it
You really make my day

Rainee Ajaski
THE TURNS OF LIFE

This poem is dedicated to my father, who always believed in me. With love, Rainee Ajaski.

Life is like a merry-go-round
on each stop something new will be found.
Hopes and dream could die,
but only if you decide not to try.
Grasp on to what you learn,
and use it for the next turn.
Overcome the bad times
and cherish the good ones,
for life cannot always be fun.
Make the ride the best you can
And if you fall be sure to take a stand.
Don't throw all this excitement away,
Just sit back and enjoy your stay.
And when your ride is over
You will then know,
That through all the turns you made it through,
Was only because of you.

B P Abens
DISCOVERY
I find myself wanting to hold you
all night long.
Fearing if you leave
you may never return.

I find myself wanting to tell you things
I've never said before.
Fearing the loss of my oneness,
for a cause not yet determined.

I find myself falling in love again.
Fearing the responsibilities
it would bring to both of us.

I find myself with you as much
as possible.
Fearing nothing.

Tina Mercer
A SPECIAL CHRISTMAS ANGEL

Dedicated to: Nikki F. Bailey December 25th, 1989, we love you always and forever.

There is a family in a tiny town down south that
Lost an angel one holiday season long ago—
. . . for many years the memory of that angel was
their greatest holiday heartache, but they never
forgot and never gave up. They always prayed that
God would one day return their special angel.
1989 was a year for answered prayers and the greatest gift a family could ever receive.
The return of Nikki our special Christmas angel. The joy of the holiday season returned
with that angel never to be lost again.

Bert Santa Ana

Bert Santa Ana
A FETUS MESSAGE IS JESUS MESSAGE

To all victims of abortion all over the world who died needlessly for they all died for Jesus as He was crucified for them. They lived in the wombs created by God. May they all sing as angels to glorify Him.

A screaming fetus is much louder than thunder;
His mother knows not—cares not for the awesome blunder.
His pain, indeed, is his bloody crucifixion;
With such brutal love, life is a wailing dungeon.

Man fathoms not God's creation, not even drops of tears;
He feels no anguish, but his soul trembles with fears.
Sodom—Gomorrah are past, but hereon he must relearn;
And life was borrowed from God implying full return.

These screaming millions are a cry of pestilence,
While this mantled caravan parades in silence.
Some man-made laws are heading appeasement in gloom;
Such 'good life' of this world woes an infernal doom.

"The sewer was cold; the city dumps were filthy;
When I was slashed out of his world helplessly.
This world is moving too fast and someone can't wait;
Seemingly in the name of fun, pleasure, and date."

"Please, Lord, reach for me drifting far into the sea;
Take me into your loving hands where I should be.
I am the millionth flesh of this world bared of a womb;
Warm me with your spirit—rest me into your tomb."

Bert Santa Ana
BURN MY CANDLE

To all who might seek the promised glory of His creator.

Burn my candle,
Albeit thou are bereaved of saintly care;
The sun did briefly shine
Through my soul seeking celestial share.

Bid me sorrows,
But, not to lament eternally;
Fate's bold carnage
Devours the blightsome life into wasteful destiny;

Redress my soul,
These early sins find no refuge in death;
My living frame is yet unfit
To tread the gruesome world beyond or beneath.

Burn, burn, my candle,
And beam through souls amiss and hearts obscured;
Should any be lost,
Beseech no journey than the path of our Lord!

Stanley Gottheimer
NOT SO STILL LIFE

I never saw an apricot all summer
Nor a raspberry,
And without you, my love, my beauty,
I could not have endured
Waiting for the return of oysters in September.

For you are, Venus mode a la odalisque,
Cheeked like you-know-what,
No peach nor plum contoured
So delicately,
Your lips the rare savor I so fondly remember—
And the world is my mollusk.

Catherine Smajo
BRETT

Whenever I look up into the night skies,
I see the stars in the blue of your eyes.
The desires of your soul have entwined our lives.
I remember the touch of your long cool fingers,
The soft sensual touch of your warm body lingers.
When you look down at me with your wife blue eyes,
The breath leaves me suddenly and my heart flies,
Then I know I'll give in to all your desires.

Marlene Nottingham
LOVE

Be it for now,
be it forever.
Come to me open
for giving and sharing.

Let me be more,
of you, no less.
Come to me open
for living and growing.

If only to be,
for you, for me.
Come to me open
for loving and caring.

Robert Allen
SOLILOQUY

For Lee

I cannot shelter realists in the chambers of my heart,
There is no place for pure logic where dreams of passion start.
I am a child of fantasy, born of hope and of ideals,
A man whose heart will ever sway to make-believes appeals.
I see the dreams of childhood years dance before my eyes;
They help me still to find the truth in all my adult lies.
How dreams are made for simple minds, and love is but for fools,
How both these things are best left drowned in deep and silent pools.
For now this is the modern world, where science rules us all,
And we live our lives believing this sword of Damocles won't fall.
But in our deep hypocrisy, we gaze on childish eyes
And cherish all the hopes and dreams that forever there arise.
Yet despite our grown-up wisdom, one question comes to mind:
Who is the child, and who the adult?
Who sees, and who is blind?

Chris Bartolucci
A DYING WISH

For my darling daughter, Christine, with glowing love that shines for-ever.

I look up to the heavens
and down upon the sea
I look upon my life again
and see what I was to be.

My life has been a happy one
with bleak sorrow in between
I know who will watch over me
From the heavens I have seen.

Tomorrow will be another day
In hopes I will have some bliss
The lonely hours I spent today
Will be gone and will not miss.

I might see a new beginning
I might see a shining light
The thing for me to do right now
Is to make all things just right.

I want half my soul in heaven
I want half down in the sea
This wish I wish to cherish
For a dying wish to be.

Robert-John Werner
ROSES RED

For my parents—Mel and Gerry Werner—for never saying that it was going to be easy.

When all the leaves have fallen
and the ground is white with snow,
there's not much chance for roses red
to let their petals grow.

All winter long the ice falls hard
and paints the city grey
as clouds roll by and pique the wind
of every frosty day.

There are no sunsongs to be sung;
Few birds dance 'cross the sky;
no kite strings tangle on the beach
as to the clouds they fly.

But once the snow begins to melt
and leaves no trace at all,
the tulips blend with April's rain
in answer to its call.

Then once again the sky is blue
and the sun shines high above;
the land is fresh—the heart is ripe,
and it's time to fall in love.

Betty Elminia Naylor
TWENTY-THREE FLIGHTS

Written for and dedicated to Robin Gail (Allsup) Shockely of Manteca, California on 8–31–80. When we met in 1963 you were only two. Now twenty-nine with thirty-nine major operations due to being born without an esophagus. You have proven you are a great surgeon with God being Chief Surgeon.

Glad to hear you are back once more
And hope you've planted both feet on the floor.
You take these trips with grace and ease
Oh, Dear One—stay here long with us please.

Only your subconscious mind really knows
What lies ahead and how your life will grow.
'Tis a shame one only uses a small percent of his brain
That's conscious of course—we've a lot to gain.

Twenty-three times you've taken this flight
Only your subconscious knows—was it day or night?
Were you frightened and lonely?
Did you think you were the only?

Or did you ponder along the way?
Did you sometimes want to stay?
It's probably lovely there—wherever it is you go,
You seem to stay so long—coming back to us so slow.

And now that you are back with us again
Your doctors are putting their gowns in the bin.
With family and friends making a fuss in the hall
You, Dear One—were the greatest surgeon of all.

Joan Johnson
OUR CHILDREN TODAY

To Cathy Lucas, who has given me encouragement to go with my poems.

What's one of the world's greatest priorities this very day?
Our children without any doubt, are most important in every way.
We need to spend more time, giving them much needed love.
In doing this, the world will reap many rewards from the one above.
Our children being important to the

future generations is a sure bet.
Our children are the world's best and biggest asset.
Let's give them a feeling of great self worth by praising them everyday.
Let our love show through in everything we do and say.
We need, somehow, to keep our children away from drugs and alcohol.
It's a difficult problem we desperately need to solve.
Love can keep our precious children away from trouble and strife.
Investing in love will bring forth great happiness in every child's life.
Give out with the real thing, a lasting love that will forever stay.
It can help our children from going astray.
From a life lacking in a feeling of security and love, we must refrain.
Instead we need strong family ties again.

Lorraine C Fellows

THE YELLOW DAFFODIL

There is nothing that can surpass,
A flower given by one small lass.

A yellow daffodil, so delicate and divine,
Handed gently to me by a sweet girl of nine.

The lovely flower was placed in a vase,
Between two candles on a cloth of lace.

It came from a child, so thoughtful and kind;
Her beautiful soul had easily touched mine.

Her gift made me her instant friend,
And gave my day a rainbow's end.

Beatrice Calabro

ON BEING A GRANDMOTHER

Dedicated to my darling daughters Victoria and Christine with love who made me a grandmother to Ryan and Christi Jo my beautiful grandchildren

Ding-a-ling the phone did ring
just as I closed my eyes
It was my darling grandson
to tell of his surprise

Ding-a-ling the phone did ring
"A sale I shouldn't miss
I'll bring the baby over"
and she hung up with a kiss

Ding-a-ling the phone did ring
This quiet Sunday morn
"The kids would love a barbecue
I'll bring the franks and corn"
Once a year we get away
From all our family ties
Ding-a-ling the phone did ring
Surprise—Surprise—Surprise

Though weary bones need time to rest
I really love this time the best
I wouldn't change my life as 'Mother'
For fame, Fortune or any other.

Julie Yates

BROKEN DOLLS

To Ike—in loving memory.

To Debbie—another broken doll
Sometimes I feel broken, just like my china dolls.
From the time when I was young and could cry.
Cry over broken dolls.
Hit the wrong way and broken in two with sharp jagged edges.
The debris of someone's wrecked marriage.
Discarded—with the other miscellaneous trash.
Yet someone a long time ago picked up that broken doll that was me.
And put her back together just like new.
Almost . . .
Someone with kind and caring hands.
Someone loved me once a long time ago.
And I could feel that love. It was almost a tangible thing.
But I cannot remember who that someone was.

Casie Lee Robinson

IN THIS WORLD

This poem is dedicated to George Bush, our president of the United States.

In this world of despair,
Whom do we turn to
Show that we care,

When we need that special
someone there, just to
say they'll always share,

Our hopes and dreams maybe forever,
as long as we never say never,
the promises in our hearts
will grow and sow to every part.

Life will be like a tree by the water,
running just to go a little farther,
Seeking that great mystery,

Once heard about in our history,
about the times we'll all face
The One who let us live by his grace,
at his name every knee should bow,
and his name every tongue
Confess

In this world of emptiness
he has put us through the test
proving that with him we have
the best.

Helene M McAndrew

MY HILLTOP—MY HOME!

To my loved ones, who share my house and home!

High on a Hill sits a House full of Love,
A Happy Place that's blessed from above,
Filled with Memories of Family and Friends,
Where Love and Friendship never ends
And the Spirit of Kindness and the Joy of Giving
Is inspired by the Deeds of Daily Living.
A Haven—Where I can lie down to rest
When Sleep and Comfort suit me best,
From where my Soul shall never roam,
My "Special Place"—That I call "My Home"!

Casey Coady Robinson

CONNECTED

I dedicate the poem "Connected" to my daughter, Kim, and my son, James. May they know my love forever.

Flowers reaching for the sun's nurturing blossom.
Color springs forth and they are complete.

Teary-eyed and embellished in his own loss, the old man ignores his dog. Unfed and longing to be pet, the dog lays gently by his master's side, extending his untarnished love and protection.

As the monsieur plays his violin and the echo of music rings out peacefully and effortlessly, one can't help but wonder which the instrument and which the man. Have they united?

Mary holds her first doll ever so gently and lovingly.
She extends her utmost protection to a piece of porcelain, a cherished possession never to be forgotten.

Like the flower, the dog, the violinist and Mary, is the depth of my love for you, my children.

Your childish smiles, tears, hurts and kisses are but a memory; your missed presence, an emptiness in my heart. For when you left, you took a part of me with you.

Comfort caresses me when I dream that, one day or night as you sit gently alone with a quiet moment, thoughts of me linger your way; and in that precious moment, you feel my presence inside of you, the part of me that you took with you.

For you see, then, my son and my daughter, we know that we are connected and nothing can tarnish or take that away. We are eternal. Mom.

Edith Young

SURE SIGNS OF SPRING

Dedicated: To Anthony, Marc, Michele, Michael, Marty and Joe.

I like to walk down country roads,
That face the field where flowers grow.
A touch of green up from the earth
The budding trees, the song of bird.

The goldenrod and wildflowers grow.
There vivid colors overflow.
The chipmunk, scurrying on by,
The firefly, lights up the sky.

Sure signs that spring
Is here to stay,
Till summer chases,
It away.—

Shirley Clayton

THE RAIN

To "Carrie," the Best Sister, Live Oak, Florida.

From a dark cloud
it falls like a shroud
to nourish, the things that
need to flourish
and be replenished

Dania Y Baayoun

THE WINDOWSILL

To my wonderful and supportive parents; to my beloved sisters, to my late brother, and to all my family and friends—Dania B.

In a house with naked rooms, life stands still.
The walls are white like winter morning frost.
A young girl watches near a windowsill,
Defenseless she sees life forever lost.

Her soft breath fogs the glass, as she writes "PEACE",
While screaming shells bring agony and pain.
She wonders if enmity will cease,
For her heart and dreams are forever slain.

Why do they have to kill her innocence?
Must they always slaughter laughter and love?
How can they ruin the world with such vengeance?
Are these the deeds man is to be proud of?

Little girl, don't cry; peace will soon come by,
For the laws of God, man must not defy

Dania Y Baayoun

TO OMAR

Many winters have passed and distant springs have faded.
There she finally stands on a saddened October morning,
Fallen leaves dance in the wind, naked trees shiver.
She looks to the ground, her soul heavy with sadness,
What is she to ask the wings of darkness, their shrieking silence?
Will she be heard in suspended gardens and descending waterfalls?
No words shall ever suffice, no tears will ever quench
The unending sorrow, the undeniable pain, the unforgivable truth,
For a part of her soul, a morsel of her heart is lost.
The cruel hands of time erase precious memories,
All what remains is echoes of laughter and sights of smiling eyes.
Closer than fate, farther than existence.
She kneels to the ground lost in silence, conquered by the truth,
She lays the roses on the soil, if feels damp and cold,
As her silhouette fades in the October mist,
A ray of light falls from the somber skies onto the roses,
A white so pure it touches the soul,

the very existence.
Springs will soon return, serene
breezes will again blow,
But she will never know.

Erna H Braun

Erna H Braun
DREAMER

To Chris and Barbara.

dreaming is a most
wondrous thing
time flits by
and spring
the sun is down
the moon has risen
the dreamer
still sitting
in his prism
realism
the time has come
the dreamer
loves being alone
reluctant to leave
his beautiful prism
he sits and dreams
in his self-made-ism

Erna H Braun
TALL
infinite intelligence
who knows all
in knowledge and wisdom
elder citizens
stand tall
like silos filled
with rich grain
elder citizens
will always remain
elder citizens with
spectrum dreams aglow
are the sphinx
of life's pyramid
you know
preserved in them
knowledge of years ago
their dreams go on
and always aglow
with wonderful knowledge
wisdom of years ago

Erna H Braun
MIND'S EYE
up thru the
psychic eye we go
into golden
hued sunshine
on dazzling
white snow
psychic eye
with vibrating blue
floats you into
its wonderful hue
it greets you
and guides you
for what is due
in search of eternity
especially for you

Wayne W Yee
THE CALL FOR PEACE
The children need to be
taught the value of peace.
Anger of war is conflict
but the reach of goal is peace.
The children cried because of cancer
as the scientists search for the
answer.
Men theory the monkey;
who connects with AIDS.
Its spread menace at alarming rate.
But God is our Helper;
who watches us day by day,
He will save the human race.
As the heaven blessed us in the field;
let us share with the poor our meal.
U.S.A. would run the Olympic miles;
to bring about the winning smiles.
When the children grow into
maturity,
they will be the mastery of peace.

Faye L Chalbeck
GOODBYE HIGH SCHOOL DAYS
The end is here, what can we do?
It's a time to look back and start
anew.
We must spread our wings and learn
to fly,
Even though we may have tears in
our eyes.

We should look ahead, but remember
the past.
We all knew these years would not
last.
We leave our high school years
behind us now,
Knowing its guidance helped us
somehow.

We must grow and reach new
heights.
It's a time to explore and see new
sights.
The end is not here, it's just a new
day.
It's time for us to go our separate
ways.

Sharon Lee Waldvogel
UNTITLED
there's a window
in this room
which lives in
Babycake's house
open to the world
and beyond
free flowing contrast
blending as one
complicated visions
that simply
come muted together
in breath.
everything fits in
this life
and soon we'll all be
as one

Jessica A Lavine
DOG RIVER
(Upper Mississippi—St. Paul, Minnesota)
You need not stare into the river
for voices
instead
skip a stone across the surface

to another side where groves of
autumn
stand
and
a gray dog swims black in

the water sun-laps the current fetches
his
master's heart
paddling to shore don't wait for

pictures to show themselves on the
waves
the swirls
know
no answers just notice the sand and

only a dog's eye view is
needed or
God
I'll worry about my weight again

or my hair in the wind or
a black
dog
drying to gray in the sun.

Anna Marie Singleton
THE CLOCK
The clock is such an adversary
It threatens with those hands
Turning precisely to duel who'd
tarry,
To foil the slow, to chime commands.

Such charm in the reverie of simpler
times
When a solitary arm indicated the
hour.
Back when a flashing white knight
could climb,
At his own pace, the distressed
damsel's tower.

Think even of the wonderful-ish age
When dates were set at . . . noon-ish,
. . . six-ish . . .
Approximately times accepted. None
would rage
Over minutes missed; one would
have felt foolish!

Even the age of half past . . ., quarter
to . . ., is gone
Replaced by the accuracy of digital
clocks
Blinking warning in seconds as time
moves on.
Signs of bondage worn on the wrist;
worn till a body drops.

Mark Twain Jr
GOD CALLED
God called me on the phone today;
To see if I was at home; and what I
had to say.
They say that it was a telemarketer;
Randomly dialing my phone that day;
But I know that God called;
Called to hear what I had to say.
All he heard was my answering
machine;
God called and heard my frustrated
scream!
They say that it was a telemarketer
instead;
I know that God called; to save my
mixed up head.
I am not ready for you; that he had to
say:
You must face life; life yet another
day.
I know that God called on that fateful
day;
He really listened; he heard what I
had to say.
Then he took my hand; he led me
further along life's way.

Denise S Adams
FIREFLY VALLEY
Summer nights among the whisp'ring
trees,
Frolicking creatures flashing friendly
signs.
Dancing 'round each other, moving
with the breeze,
Making zig zag lines, tonight they are
mine.

I wander along the path in darkness.
I have naught to fear for I have my
friends.
To capture, hold a firefly is no less . . .
Than touching gentleness, our spirits
blend.

One flash near my eyes, others to my
side,
They add brightness to the dark,
peaceful world.
Their sunshine brings joy before it
has died,
Their movement is light and dark
colors, swirled.

The sun and the moon mixed right for
a glow.
Graceful fireflies, stars hovering low.

Robert Pagliocca
HARVEST GOLD
If all of love
was bought and sold.
I'd reap a field
to harvest gold

so spirits can
consume it all
in solid bits
of all our wars.

If that I would
then TAKE a rake
and wipe the roots
of my mistakes,

to plant a seed
within the earth
which only grew
the love of worth.

Though if I had
to harvest gold.
I'd poison fields
where serpents roam.

Grace Cardinal
OUR FRIENDSHIP
True friendship is a feeling of
closeness with no regret.
This is the way I have felt from
the first day we met.
I want to gaze into your eyes
and listen to your voice,
To be with you each day and night,
but mine is not the choice.
Just by the way you smile at me
your manner soft and nice,
The world around me suddenly
becomes a Paradise.
Whatever fortune may befall,
wherever you may be,
There will be no one else on earth
who means so much to me.

Patricia A Oakey
COOL MORNING
It was a quiet, cool, crisp morning
I sat and looked out over the fresh
fallen snow.
I came to realize that I was not
alone.
Only one who could create something
this beautiful
Had to be God.
A God with tender loving care.

A gentle father figure with deep compassion.
A God who offers inner peace and quietness.

My desire grew to know this great God
Who created the heavens and earth.
I longed for wisdom and understanding
But how was I to accomplish this?

To my amazement, as I asked, I did receive.
God, my father has given me all the answers I need.
For God is not as complicated as it seems.
He is love and answers our dreams.

So if someone tries to tell you,
You can't understand God,
Simply smile and reply that God is love
And in Him there is no darkness at all.

Curtis D Smith
ASTRONAUTS
(We are America)

Dedicated to N.A.S.A. and all the past, present, and future astronauts influenced by: The APOLLO and Challengers crews.

They were the astronauts,
Searching for a dream
Reaching for the stars above
and a place in history
As we all cheered not knowing
what was to come in the sky
We say to you,
Oh! challenger crew
your dreams won't be denied
For we are America,
a land that's known to be
Proud to die for the freedom,
That gives us liberty,
That gives us liberty!

Oh the price we pay for progress
Can come in many ways
There are times when lives are taken
There are times when lives are saved
But we must keep on doing,
all the things you set out too
Living a life in the High Frontier
can still be a dream come true
For we are America a land that's known to be
Proud to die for the freedom, that gives us liberty
That gives us lib-er-ty!

Gary Spivak
EMOTIONS ARE KEPT
Emotions are kept,
Duplicates are packaged to go,
Pressure builds as emotions grow,
No more duplicates, real emotions are free,
Maturity lets emotions be!

Bridget J Murphy
BUREAUCROCKY
Beware of the Bureaucrat, he is crafty and sly,
Like the spider who preys on the unsuspecting fly.

At first he will entice you, with his charismatic charm,
Promising opportunity, and protection from harm.

But soon you will find yourself in a world full of dread,
Entangled in his web, made from sticky red thread.

He will surround you with double-talk and catch-22,
While he passes the buck to his totem-pole crew.

Technicalities, formalities, procedures, routine,
Unwielding, inflexible, no end to be seen.

Such is the system, so you had better take care,
Do not get yourself trapped in the Bureaucrat's lair.

Minh Ma
STOOD IN THE CENTER
Raining cats and dogs
As dark as it would—
I sat between Annie's maple trees.
With a thought as thin as the wind,
I remember the old lord king and the throne.
Through my weakly, sickening mind,
my heart troubled me most.
Deep in thought of the realm,
I cared for none.
And when all seems lost . . .
with a thought as thin as the air,
my thought trapped and wrapped around,
within my heart full of tears from the moment I lay on that raised chair.
Surrounded by marigold,
I lay and skimmed into the wholly ground.
The night gives me no comfort
where dreams come bitter and dim.
I knew it wasn't a golden hour.
It was out of my reach or care . . .
because I looked toward sin.
I knew there wasn't any gold to collect or to be near.
I guess there was no one to stare at,
except my crumbled throne, my weak dream and corpse . . .

Dottie Kelly
MY PASSION
A fire could not put out
A flood could not dampen
A storm could not weaken
Another could not equal
When it is my love . .

it is my wildest dream
come true . . .

James O Clickenger
MOON MADNESS
How many times have I sat
And watched the night come down,
Stealing through these dusky lanes,
To shutter this old town?

How many times shall I gather dreams,
On some soft summer's night
How many loves have waxed or waned,
In your magic sheen of light?

Oh moon, oh moon, you insolent moon
Gliding across the summer sky,
Watching, and plotting a lover's fate,
With your giant cyclop's eye.

Then morning comes to end your reign,
Your spell is past and gone—
I am safe again, sane again,
In the sober light of dawn.

Jason Potar
FORGET ME NOT
Tossed in the tempest, the furious storm of time,
whirling, everchanging, this world of yours and mine.
We witness the epoch-making apocalypse of thought;
modern times become the past with the change we've wrought.
Can we see through the glamor, the glitter of it all,
to realize the terror that the real world does fall.
The things of Earth before us, glory buried deep,
we seal their fate with iron as we make a forward leap.
Who shall stand for the beast, defend our natural host,
before machines abandon them, a memory of just ghosts . . .

Ashley Ann Czajkoski

Ashley Ann Czajkoski
I WILL ALWAYS WONDER WHY?

Dedicated to Russell Harrell Dean.

Although I'll never know you or see your smiling face,
in my heart you will always
hold a very special place.

I'll love you and cherish you more than words can say,
and I'll think about you each
and every day.

When I gaze into the stars at night,
I'll see your shining
eyes, and I'll know you're in a
wonderful place way up in the
sky.

I'm so very sorry you had to go away,
but we will be together again
one glorious day.

To know you were my cousin brings tears into my eyes,
and when I think about you,
I will always wonder why?

I love you, your cousin,
Ashley

Linda Sessions Solomon
HERSELF
There was one standing alone.
Beside her, he stood—Then walked with her.
Even as two—they were one.

They shared tears.
They shared laughter.

In time, he stood beside her—then walked from her.

The two of them became two.

And she now stands as one—alone.

Linda Sessions Solomon
TRIBUTE TO LOVE
If ever I could hold you
and embrace you with my love,

For more possible it would be
to see in flight a wingless dove.

Passionate love unlasting
Though brighter burns its flame,

Than any love known to man
Or love by any other name.

Vivian S Nehme
ABANDONED PLAYGROUND
We planted a friendship
in the soil of our dreams

Up sprouted the laughter,
that buried the tears

Our curiosity provoked
our maturity to bloom

How we fell into "Love";
all the tears we consumed

Fate split the road
that we once walk as one

Our ambitions have changed;
and all that was fun

The arguments we shared
were the roots of our bond

How we took for granted
all the times . . .
now gone.

Melvin B Mellard
HAVE HEART MY ANGUISHING AMERICA
Are there really any words which truly describe it? When you most need it, where is that adjective which always evades?

It's a mind-boggling catastrophe when you're suddenly hit point blank with the very last words you want to hear—you have A.I.D.S.

Do not despair America—Let's all clasp hands, pray, and work together—we'll see this trying situation through.

Scientists will develop the cure like for all the dreaded diseases before. Until then, have faith and to the Lord, each other and ourselves be true.

Brian K Duvall
TIME IS A THIEF
Time is a thief
that has never been caught,
even history itself
it eludes without thought.

Time is also a killer
for it takes away the lives,
of so many of our loved ones
our families, our husbands, and
wives.

But time does give us progress
for the world is a changing place,
it's a criminal we all love and hate
time's a thief that steals in good taste.

Yes, time steals from the living
but with one death another is born,
then time makes a plan to steal from
him
and so the game goes on.

And time plays its role
For soon it lays down another wreath,
then smiles at its capture
time is truly a thief.

Elsie M Cook
IN THROUGH THE EYES OF A CHILD
The world is like animals running
wild
A scary place in the eyes of a child
There's a lot of fears that haven't
been met
and lots of rough roads, the older you
get
In through the eyes of a child, let
them see
What a joyous place this world can
be
A world full of joy and peace among
all
Not just a world of bitterness that
crumbles and falls
Let them have a joy which roams free
And their hearts sing with glee
Take the bitterness, put back the joy
And make it a wondrous place for
each girl and boy
Nothing in this world should be seen
so wild
Especially in through the eyes of a
child

Effie Read
BRIGHT STARS REMEMBER PEARL HARBOR
I heard my Nation groan under the
impact of sudden war.
I saw great men grow small, and
small men great. In a moment of
need, they gave their all.

I heard the people of my Nation
crying for their sons.
Then I remembered Rachael,
weeping for her children.

My Nation, in her sorrows, also heard
the weeping of other Nations, and
saw their affliction, and gave a
helping hand.

Know the World is at peace once
more.

I looked at my Flag. Each star seems
to have a glory all its own. Each State
seems to say, "Well done, my good
and faithful sons."

The Flag was never more beautiful . . .
peace has been won.
Shine on bright stars, shine on.

Chris Tegler
NUCLEAR SALESMEN
War and Destruction waylaying
instruction
The Cold flames of the Reckless
Heart
Seeing the reflection of Malformation
Degenerating all, want to tear it apart.
My World, your World our World,
their World
It's all out of control.
Building their egos with Pomp and
Circumstance,
The Power encompassing their fatal
task.
Sitting ignorant, lamenting our lost
chance
Congregating now, there is nothing
left to ask.
My World, your World, our World,
their World
It's all out of control.
Still Hear and Taste the rot of
putrefaction
The Hot ashes of the Fevered Mind.
Holding the revolution of Creation
Destroying will, never going to look
behind.
My World, your World, their World
It's all out of control.
Out of control . . . . .

David Carroll
POETICISM
Within the heart
the true poet
believes,
sound
yet sober,
poetry
breathes.

Lawrence Cabrinety

Mrs Patricia B Cabrinety
DO YOU KNOW?

To Lawrence, my husband of 35 years.

Do you really know how much
you're loved?
By us and by our God above?

How very much your presence is
sought
Though you've done some things you
hadn't ought.

Do you know how many tears are
shed
And how our very hearts have bled?

Desiring that you return to our home
And never more again to roam.

Do you really know how much
you're missed?
And of our desires, needs, missing
you and being kissed?

Do you know the ache deep within
our hearts
Each and every time you decide to
leave and depart?

If you could only know the prayers
we've said
And of the sacrificial offerings led,
Why can't we mend the fences that
are torn
Share its beauty—let our love be
reborn?

Oh please, please we ask of you
Don't let us feel so awfully blue,

We want and need your undivided
love
And so too, does our God above!

Stella J Patrick
BEAUTY
There is beauty all around us
If we but have eyes to see—
The colors of a rainbow,
The leaf's tremble on an aspen tree.

Reflections in the quiet water
That shimmers as I gaze,
The diamonds on a spider web,
Sunsets that end our days

The wonder of a child's eyes
That look of trust I see,
The iridescent waterbug
That hopscotches in its glee!

Let us take time each day
To see beauty here or far.
Ere your eyes grow dim I pray
Look for the twinkle of your star!

Miss Janice C Baker
HEAR THE SEA ECHO HUM HERE
The humming-like sound of the
horizon
Hums eternally and yet tells me
nothing.
A white parallel line of air stretches
further into the distance—
Bisecting the magnificent indigo
blueness of my plane of night sky.
Silence is not golden/for to love is to
communicate.

In this place where loneliness takes
me,
The she wolves paw upon and pace
the cold hard ground,
Tossing their heads—baying
mournfully to Luna.
A chorus of voices echoing in their
she wolf manner—
Waiting for Luna to speak—the
chorus echoing inside myself,
My heartbeat surrendering to the
greater decibels of the insistent
Echo of the chorus resounding
throughout this desert-land place
Of an island surrounded by a silent
foaming sea . . .
The tide which now has returned had
flowed out to sea,
Carrying—then losing—my essence
in the white foam and crystal spray.

Standing on the edge of the shore,
peering out towards the foaming sea,
My empty hands held my remains . . .
wondering what was left of me? . . .
Nothing! ! —happened—while I
waited with hope to hear
The sound of your voice calling out
to me . . . all I heard
Was the sound of the silent foaming
sea, the she wolves,
And the humming—no echoes of
loving me.

Margie M Dolohanty
MY CHRISTMAS MESSAGE
In the stable in a manger a little baby
lay
We celebrate his birthday on
Christmas Day.
People of his day would never
believe as years go by
That his name would still be so great
for you and I.
When I was a little girl for Christmas
I got
Some doll clothes for my dolly, we
didn't get a lot.
But old Mrs. Santa she really knew
If our dresses were made of pink or
blue.
Santa's wife as as smart as she could
be
In those days people didn't have
many Christmas trees.
Stockings were hung and filled
mostly with love
He must have been happy too, when
he looked from above.
God bless, Grandma D.

J M Blackburn
THANK YOU, FATHER, FOR BEING
Thank you, Father, for giving me
strength in times of stress,
courage to stand before you
with my sins to confess.
Thank you, Father, for letting me
have my say and "blessing"
my family and the friends I've
met along the way.
Thank you, Father, for all the
blessings you've give me and
by helping me understand
your "Book of Wonders"—
a better person I will be!
Thank you, Father, for being.

Ruth Mettler
MEMORIES
Dear Sarah, just today you turned
three
And soon we will be apart
These are all the memories that
will forever dwell in my
heart
The first time I saw you I knew,
there would be
A Grandma love for you and me.
The sweet little secrets you would
whisper in my ear,
Your favored colors and clothes
you choose to wear.
I'll always remember our little
walks.
And the shadows we tired to
catch,
And the little kittens you tired to
fetch.
The ladybugs that would tickle
your hand,
The tunnels you made in your
box of sand,
The game we played the songs we
sang and books we read.
The cute little curls we made
upon your head.
But most of all I got to know
The most brilliant, charming,
blond doll of all.
With your blue eyes, so flirty and
bright,
May God Bless you both day and
night.
And when I'd put you down to
sleep,
Your little arms around my neck
would creep.
And you'd plant a big big kiss
upon my cheek
And then you'd say, "Grandma
I love you today,"
I love you too Sarah, always

Dusty Reamey
SUNSHINE
Sunshine is my favorite weather.
The sun's gleam makes flowers grow,
The sun's warmth gets rid of the snow,
The sun's sparkle makes skin glow.
Sunshine makes things you don't always see show.

Winston Andrews

Winston Andrews
DADDY DIED LAST NIGHT
Daddy died last night
On the other end of the line
My sister's voice cried
Daddy died last night
Her voice tear-strained and tired.

Daddy died last night
Mammy hasn't spoken since he went
Please come home and put things right
'Cause daddy died last night.

Daddy died last night
How he tried to wait for your return
I felt his soul in flight
Until his life fire ceased to burn
Daddy died last night

Daddy died last night
Now no more love to give or gain
Too soon out went his light
And things will never be the same.

Now here I am in phase twilight
Who will I turn to when for me things aren't right
My daddy died last night

Winston Andrews
ESCAPADE
Only an escapade I thought it was,
And so spontaneously I indulged,
And fun and laughter seemed to say
Another phase would pass away.
Though only an escapade I thought it was,
This phase defies the reason a phase does,
This web-like indulgence choose to stay
With stronger magnetic bonds each day.
But reason claims no lasting bliss
Could culminate from such as this,
So in defiance I stubbornly claim
I would live through this as did I again.
Though only an escapade I thought it was,
Steadfast this is and I crave more of,
And reason like the tide ebbed away,
And need replaced the phase of yesterday.
Now my world is glad no longer saddened.
And I am a rose this escapade gardened.
And romance is in bloom and here to say,
"Yesterday's escapade is love today."

Rose McKinnon Dean
MIRACLES
While the astronauts are
performing their miracle in
space
and NATURE
miraculously changes colors
and texture

I spend an afternoon recording
a message to my three-
year old great grandson
producing a miraculous
sound which
he recognizes and enjoys.

Tulia Eugenia Smith
MY ROOM
I like my room bare
like my soul
like my life
like my thoughts

A clean rug on the floor
A quilt in my chair
to keep me warm
A lamp at my side
to light up the words
A bare table
to hold my typewriter
Everything bare
pure and clean
Like my thoughts
like my life
like my soul . . . .

Elaine S Hannig
MY FRIEND
Like a beacon in the middle of nowhere.
Rising above the jetty and the crashing waves.
Standing tall.
Proud.
Watching.
Glowing in the moonlit sky.
Guardian of the sea.

Like a candle in the window of a snow-covered cottage.
Calling out to weary travelers or a stranger in the night.
Radiating warmth.
Soft.
Shining.
Flickering through the frosted pane.
Keeper of the dark.

Like the sun on an early spring morning.
Shining down on the blades of grass and the crocuses.
Giving life.
Warm.
Healing.
Glistening out onto the horizon.
Sentinel of the sky.

Lisa K Wilbanks
I WISH
I wish, I wish, I wish
I had you in sight.
I wish, I wish, I wish
I had you near tonight
I wish, I wish, I wish
I had you to whisper to tonight.
I wish, I wish, I wish
I had you to kiss good night.
I wish, I wish, I wish
I had you to hold for the night
I wish, I wish, I wish
For you tonight.

Samantha Futch
THE WIND
Its gentle hands caress my hair,
I feel its presence everywhere.
The sun will shine, the birds will sing.
It seems to be with everything.
I can't recall any day,
When the wind wasn't on its way.
It blows the clouds all around,
It's everywhere to be found.
I can't imagine the world without it.

Jean P Brody
TRUCE
Shadows danced
in eerie ritual
preceding the wars
of my life but
beyond the roar
there was silence
And I struggled
to readjust
my ears to
hear it.

In the silence
i expected
loneliness but
in the backside
of shadow
there was peace.
The war
had ended and
I was home
with my love.

Richard and Darlene S Stone

Darlene S Stone
OF TIMES PAST

This poem is dedicated to my dear son, Richard.

I look out to see wide open spaces,
Imagining a time of long ago.
Of happier days,
Some that I have known, and a smile creeps across my face.

But those days fade away with time,
The memories never do,
For I'm still making memories in my mind,
Those days of me and you.

Mildred W Lyons
I HELPED A FRIEND TODAY
I helped a friend today. It helped me more than I can say.
To see the joy expel, did more for me than I can tell.

The sparkle in their eyes, was more than you can realize.
The humble "That's enough," really, almost made me choke up.

You never lose a thing, if you help a friend like I did.
The joy to you it brings, is more than just a little bit.

When I was just a child, my family really needed help.
My mother was so mild, I thought things were going real well.

She gave us lots of love, which is far more precious than gold.
The love she gave to us, is remembered as we get old.

There's more than I could say. I'd like to help you make your day.
I only hope and pray, that you can help your friend today.

Mary Hinckley
SUMMER SHADOWS
The loveliest cottage I've ever been in,
The Robinson cottage, they call "Ranch 10"
The screened in porch with the comfy old chairs
Looking out on the lake, the trees, and forgetting your cares
Inside is a feeling you wish could just last
The old things in place as they were in the past
Perhaps in the corner in an old oak chair
The lingering shadow of a little girl who once sat there
The family gatherings, the laughter and joy
You feel and hear it—the shouts of a boy
Oh how I wish I could make it all last
The beauty of summer in shadows of the past

Catherine Hoffman
JASMINE
Jasmine is Siamese
So regal, my royal queen
Her beauty has to be seen
Those blue eyes
Give me deep sighs

Helen S Kahler
KNOWN IDENTITY
He speaks to us in whispers
Through gentle summer breezes,
He speaks of immortality
When life on earth ceases.

He talks and pleads with us
In an autumn rumble,
Tries to stop his loving humans
Into sin to stumble.

He cries and shouts at us
In a fierce winter storm,
He tries to fit a perfect soul
In an imperfect form.

He screams at us in anger
In spring's violent thunder,
His grief for human fate is great,
He mourns our acts of blunder.

Andy Huse
VIOLENT SCIENCE
Violent Science looks so proud.
Breathe the hazy diesel cloud.
Drying rivers are running green.
Wash your hands in acid chlorine.
Drink the Coke that's sugar free.
Drink the saccharin and DDT.
Air, water and noise pollution,

We never attempt to find a solution.
Technology is a nature slayer
Burning its way through the ozone layer,
Secreting an array of different pollution
While we witness Terra's execution.
But our glorious Science isn't complete
Until we hide the earth under miles of concrete.
Eroding away in forest fires,
Strangled by fences and telephone wires.
Earth—do you have a last request
Before we lay you down to rest?
Earth, you're gonna fall, like a punted ball.
You're a small plant with big problems . . .
Violent Science.

Andy Huse
SOLITARY MONASTERY

Now, alas I can remember,
The features of that bleak December
The spidery branches, the trees, so tall,
The morn so sullen, I can recall.
The breezy arms of the morning maid
Outstretched from the sun,
The meadows so soft in the shade
And the ghost of the morning nun.
Her apparition so sleek and slender,
So vivid on that bleak December
The nun so solemn and solitary,
The dawn shone down on the monastery.

Elizabeth Ward
SAVOR THE MOMENT

A gentle wave comes ashore to make the shifting sands.
As a breeze touches my face as soft as a baby's hand.
A moonbeam above a fluffy cloud gives off a shimmering light.
It's free come sit with me and enjoy this beautiful sight.

Leif Madsen
I LIVED, I DIED, I AM

I became a crooked man with a crooked little smile
Broken from my bicycle and fractured, spilling bile
I was left for dead and I plainly bled o'er road and clothes and grass
I checked right out for a three day bought (good God! What saved my ass?)
My mind had left and was wandering far but life it held me dear
My body broken, wondering? What bonds? What next? What fear?
I did come back to wake again, yeah me, the crooked man
With tilted grin and eye half closed as if beaten by a pan
I woke but knew, without a doubt, I'd eventually be whole
I had no fear of living on as a husk without a soul
I must digress from this described mess to comment on my lot
What happened to me, as I plainly see was an intro 'parting shot'
It gave me a shake with a mighty quake and helped me to wake within
To smile at life through my pain & strife and to 'take it with a grin'
My times not up! I've much to do!
My life, this game, what fun!
A coaster ride with ups and downs, through storms and rains and sun
I'm still not free of what's done to me, but my body's on the mend
I live to write more verses bright, with dreams and hopes to rend
But that's it for now (at least this rhyme) my verse, my curse, my words
My story's told (I know it's old) and it's probably one you've heard.

Ronda A Winters
ROSES OF LOVE

To my husband, Rodney, the inspiration of this poem, and to my family who encourages me.

Roses of love
Each petal tells a story.
A neverending love.
The velvet of the red
brings back the warmth of his arms,
and the brilliant of the yellow
reminds me of the glow of his smile.

The petal of the pink
resembles his cheeks when
he laughs with sincerity,
and the purity of the white
reflects his gently, caring,
neverending love.

Dorothea Colangelo
LIFE'S ETERNITY

Dedicated to my friend Reverend Robert T. Cobb. Passed away 8/13/89. May his memory live on forever. God bless.

Please do not mourn my passing
For I am but away,
I am now in the light of heaven
So beautiful night and day
On earth when you have done all you can
In an honest and sincere way
The most pleasant time is yet to come,
When you can hear the Lord say
"Come and rest in my valley of peace,
And enjoy eternity's contentment,
For you have earned your place by me.
As an angel of the Lord."
Please do not mourn my passing
For there will be a day
That in the light of all you have done
You, too, will pass this way.
Then we all will be together, both friends and family
Wrapped in the protection of the Lord's eternity.

Marilyn D VanDerbeck
EMPTY WOMB

Looking out of the portholes
Of my mind,
I see children running and playing
But they are not mine.
Tears of fear,
Tears of laughter.
Smiles full of love
Smiles full of joy,
Not even a sigh.
Little coo's and so big too,
No ma ma I love you.
Empty hand for there is no
Little hand to hold.
No child to protect,
No child to guide.
No party with balloons.
No baseball games or baby dollies
No skinned knees,
No boo boo's.
No children no grandchildren.
Please dear God
Do not let me die,
With my empty womb.

Tony Laudano
MOTHER MARY

When I feel my life is falling apart
I close my eyes and reach into my heart.
When the day seems gloomy and oh so dark
Mother Mary comforts me in the park.
It's so so peaceful it's like paradise.
I remember the immortal words of Christ.
Love thy neighbor and he'll love thee.
That's how Mother Mary comforts me.
When I'm depressed I turn to the sea
Jesus
my friend is waiting for me. The sea is blue and very deep
as Jesus's words I hear in my sleep.
God is great he is divine
we will be together all the time.
Mother Mary I love thee Mother Mary she loves me.
It's like a glowing lite for the world to see.
So please dear God let there be peace on earth.
Let the children be happy like when you gave Jesus birth.
The world is bad in so many ways.
But god forgives or so they say.
We must have faith or we'll fade away.
Mother Mary,
I worship thee.

Irene G Smith
THE LITTLE SQUIRREL

Have you seen a little Squirrel climb
A Big Tree, up to the Heights Sublime
Out on A Little Twig so very Thin
He has no fear, about the Position he is in

He jumps and Scampers from Limb to Limb
And Never looks back to see where he has been
With full force ahead, He is in the air
Knowing his way he will soon be there

It is True, he made an enormous leap
Landing in another Tree in a furry heap
He will arise to view the new Location
With two Paws up, he is in Isolation
It is Lunch time Now he must eat
So with the acorn at his feet
He chews and nibbles and drops the rest
Time to relax now, he has Done His Best

Joe Pardue USN Ret
LIFE AT SEA

Life is short and rough you see when you sail the deep blue sea.

Your back starts to bend, your hands start to shake, your hair turns grey, but that's the breaks.

No one seems to know what makes you old, stooped and grey. It's just living at sea day after day.

So I tell you lads before you go to sea. Look around at what you see.

Lawrence Cabrinety

Mrs Patricia B Cabrinety
DEAR HUSBAND,

To Lawrence, my husband of 35 years.

Many years I've longed to see
a light in your eyes of glee

For some little accomplished task
of mine . . . but alas,

Your corporate world too important is
for you your world of sho biz,

Too world-searching you've become
that you continually treat me
as "dumb."

Ah, but that cast off old shoe
you've thrown in the dust,
remains "true blue,"

And will become the one groped
when others have no need of
"dopes."

Your corporate world passed you by
no matter how hard you tried,

Too busy are they in material things
they have no time for the
miseries you bring.

BUT will that cast off old leather
shoe
still be the same as new?

Will your time lost have hardened its
cover—
no longer the tried and true
lover?

Then oh-h-h-h the misery you will
find
when ALL of life will be
unkind

And NO ONE will care to ever see
where once I looked so
searchingly

To find the twinkle of love within
your eyes.

Kathleen Janet Brown
SLEEP

To my grandmother, Ila P. Vincent.

Sleep,
that sometimes elusive relief,
Spinner of tales and creator
of dreams.

Sleep,
that friend who never lies.
Although we lie when
waking, in sleep we tread in
truth. If we could but listen
and understand our sleep's
advice.

Sleep,
that foe who flaunts our fears. Our
fears become reality in sleep . . .
our hidden terror augmented.
Then waking becomes our
heroine.

Sleep, if we have none we go
insane; if we have too much we
can ponder our lives away. A fine
balance . . . a subtle line between
sleep and waking . . . a nightmare
of black and white . . . a
kaleidoscope of color. Sleep is
our other life, our fourth
dimension.

Ginny Persicano
SHOULD OF BEEN
You used to make me laugh,
And then you made me cry.
Now that it's all over,
I have to wonder why?
Cause the crying should have
been,
When I was stuck with you.
And the laughter should have
started,
When I found out we were thru.

Norma Foti
BROTHER MINE
Kenneth, how brave we seem as we
speak of your dying,
Pretending a calmness as our hearts
are screaming and crying,
I preach look to "Him" don't be
afraid
But do I believe what I say?
I thought of the days when you were
so small, just a baby,
And you grew and you grew a whole
foot over me.
Remember when mom cooked
something you hated to eat,
We would play pretend and it became
something sweet.
Can big sister play that game with
you now?
I asked our father to tell me how.
And somehow I know it's not the end
of your life,
Only the end of physical pain and
emotional strife.
And somehow I know that all those
we held dear
Are preparing your way—have no
fear.
And if we believe what he said will
be
We will soon be to–gether, the whole
family.
The years have flown by the magic
was lost
Was the difference of our age the
cause.
We can't recapture the years that
have passed away
But it matters not—for in eternity it
is but a day.
Remember there in the heavens we
need never pretend
The sweetness is real 'tis the
beginning not the end.
I love you too! Oh, brother mine.

Norma Foti
**HARRY, ANOTHER GIFT—
ANOTHER DAY**
After all the teasing,
The spats that end in fun.

After hugs so pleasing,
Another day is done.

I dreamt the same love story
in the blackness of the night,

And woke to the sun's glory
so warm, so very bright.

I turned and looked upon your face
so troubled as you slept,

And prayed for his saving grace
As I wept and wept.

I asked him—give us time,
There's so much to be shared,

And as your face became sublime
I knew he heard and cared.

Thus one more day to spend
His glorious gift of life.

For me to be your love—your friend,
Your everlasting wife.

Norma Foti
FATHER'S DAY
Good morning, my love, my life, my
joy,
Good morning, dear Father of our
boy,
Good morning, Grandpa and Pop Pop
too,
Good morning, from all of us who
love you.

Your neighbors say prayers for your
continued health,
Prayers more precious than gifts of
wealth.
Of course, there will be gifts too
big—too small
But they will be wrapped in love
from us all.

And in thanks there are things you
must do
Like smelling the flowers and feeling
the dew,
Make some mistakes—try to be late
For once take chances—go ahead,
tempt fate
Don't be so perfect, it matters not
So what if some projects are left to
rot
Stop and kiss your grandchildrens'
cheek
Listen and learn as our children
speak.

Greet your neighbor with a caring
smile
Go ahead, give them a hug once in a
while
What is truly important for you to
feel,
Is that love and friendship is what's
real.

And then at the end of your Father's
Day
Think of Our Father and take time to
pray
Thank Him for still one more year
Thank Him for taking away your fear
Tell Him how much He means to
you,
And with all my heart I will pray too—

Rebecca K Moody

Rebecca K Moody
RELAX

To my children Jeren and Amanda and my best friend Tonya. For supporting, caring, loving and believing in me. I love you all.

Everyone I know tries so hard from
day to day
To try and make their life go just the
right way,
When all they're really doing is
wasting precious time
No matter how hard you try you'll
always walk the line,
You have to live every moment for
that moment at hand
Make every second count and every
grain of sand,
Believe in yourself first and others
will too
Quit trying so hard and your life
won't be so blue,
Give yourself a chance and you just
might find
Life's not all that bad, just relax and
unwind.

Penne A Spitzer
LITTLE HANDS

This poem is lovingly dedicated to my daughter, Deanna.

Those little hands, so soft and gentle
sweep across my brow
Once they were smaller, much, much
smaller
than they are right now
With great precision and decision
carefully print her name
Upon a note, hearts all about,
with such sweet love it came
I love those hands 'cause when we
touch
my world's a better place
And with those hands, and heart, I
love
a shining little face
I see in it a brand-new world
with joy, excitement, peace,
With hopes and dreams beyond
compare,
I hope they never cease
If I were given no other choice,
but to have her near,
I'd give all up for little hands
that hold me, oh so dear

Robert Edgar Burns
GETTING AHEAD
Be thankful for what you've got
and cry not at what you don't.
There are so many people who want
something,
but work for it they won't.

You sit and hang your head;
you say you have no chances.
But, while the tears fall from your
eyes,
the other man advances.

Cry not, weep not, just try and try
and try.
Put forth effort for what you want
and you'll get it by and by.
Yes, you'll get it by and by.

Jane Ballantyne
CAPTURED
Panic filled their tired eyes
A pointed gun, they realized
Death before them, no escape
Pull the trigger, don't debate
This issue.
Make it quick or set me free,
I can't stand the anxiety
Of this wait.
His finger twitched,
The bullet came,
There was no delay
No hesitating
We are gone
Vanished
Forever long.

Carol Bochniak
BUT A HUMAN
I want to fly away
so that I can be free.
Soaring over the mountains
and high above the seas.
Not knowing any limits
of space or of time—
looking down at the world
as if it were all mine.
With power and grace
I would not know fear—
never turning and fleeing
when danger drew near.
But that is not how
things are for me—
open your eyes and
but a human you'll see.

Lucy Eula Gary
MEMORIES

Dedicated to my loving daughters Leslie and Mary.

Today I went down this mountain
road,
There it stood this old adobe.
The door hanging by one hinge,
windows gone.

There on the hillside it stood all
alone.

It had been new one time filled with laughter and love.
Lights shining down that road from windows above.

Someone waiting for a loved one to return
Rocking away with a light that burn.
Then I thought, how true to life was that old shack.
Waiting, always waiting, for some-one to come back.

But, alas, the young are old and broken like that old shack.
Too old to dream, too old to come back.
There with tears in my eyes, I walked away.

My grief so strong I could not stay.
My eyes are dim, my sight won't mend.
This is the end, good-bye old friend.

Rosemary Chamberlin
LONG AGO AND FAR AWAY
It was long ago and far away
In a distant place called yesterday.
You and I watched a few dawns break
And held away the tears for each other's sake.

But when you laughed, yes, I remember well
The skies would open
And my heart would swell.
Our dreams were our passion
In the daylight and the dark.

Yet today brings only the illusion
Of a peaceful place and time.
And where you have gone to I do not know
I trust the future's hands are kind.
It was long ago and far away
In a distant place called yesterday.

Shirley Cooper
PRAISE GOD
GOD is great, GOD is good,
Let us be ever mindful of Him as we should;

Let us not hate, nor envy one or another,
For who can save us in His day of wrath than other?

He is my rock, He is my shield,
As for me, I just want to praise Him and do His holy will;

He first loved me before I was conceived,
He says He'll fulfill all His promises,
If I just trust and in Him believe;

Just think of the prophets and disciples of old,
After He had tried them, they came forth as good as gold;

If you let His word be a lamp unto your feet and a light unto your path,
Do you know, you can be partakers of His, Kingdom and all that He hath;

I will never forsake Him, or from Him apart,
Because I know He has given me a new heart and, a brand-new start;

Love him, praise Him, morning, noon, and night,
Oh! Love him, Love Him With All, All Thy Might.

Lisa Jones-Kennedy
JUST DREAMIN'
If wishes could be
More than imaginary
If dreams were more than flirts
You would be my knight
In shining armour
So that nothing else would ever Hurt
Away we would ride
On your majestic black steed
Leaving behind my tears
Making a path
Straight for the sun
Living life without fear
But as always
I awaken to find
You are the one that is taken
Leaving me behind.

Brian James
THE STRANGER
To The Sparkling Eyes of Vickie Slee.

Inhabitant of the skies
I see it in your eyes
Keeper of the stars
Wanderer from far.
Nomad in seek
for a river,
In which a fish
Could be food forever
and the lilies
become friends
and the trees on the
bank
sing back and forth
their tune of
grace.

Nancy Reed
CHILD ABUSE
To all God's Little Children.

My name is Suzy
I'm only three
My eyes are swollen
I cannot see

I must be bad
That lesson I've learned
For I am punished
With a cigarette burn.

I have to be right
I cannot be wrong,
For I am locked up
All week long.

When I wake up
I am all alone
The house is dark
My parents aren't home.

Deep inside I feel so bad
I know I'm hated,
By Mom and Dad.

I am just an expensive joke
They need all their money
For speed and coke.

An accident yes
That's their words
Countless times
The phrase I've heard

Be quiet now
I hear a car
My Dad is home
From Charlie's Bar

I hear him curse
My name he calls
I squeeze against
The dirty walls

Oh Dear God
It's too late
His Face now looks
At me in hate

I feel the pain
Again and again
Oh please God
Let it end

My name is Suzy
I was only three
Just last night
My Father molested me.

Cynthia M Rahill
ADVISE FROM A DESK CLERK
A match would better light the way—
down the window-free corridors of
the all American hotel-motel-inn—
side the room shag rug car—
pets are not al—
loud noises resulting from bad acou-
stick to the dining room rather than
room—
service depends on the rate you pay
for staying in a cheap mo—
tell the desk clerk to save a news—
paper facilities can be found on the
maids
cart along extra towels in case you
run—
out side your room a lovely view of
the parking—
decks of cards obtainable at the
gift—
shop around before you check-in

and one final tip—
you can leave for me.

Regina J McKinney
MY LOVE FOR YOU
I dedicate this poem—in memory of my loving husband, Mark, who passed away February 11, 1990. I love you, Mark. Your loving wife, Regina.

Sweetheart life has its ups and down
Life has its smiles and its frowns.
"My love for you" is always there
My life with you—I want to share
I need you always at my side
"My love for you" is as great as anyone's pride,
I want you with me at all times
When you're with me everything chimes,
I love you with all my heart
From you I never want to part,
"My love for you" is as great as can be
I love you with all my heart you see,
You make me very happy dear
That is why I need you so near,
"My love for you" will never die.
I LOVE YOU MARK!

Molly Taylor
PARTING
This poem is dedicated to my grandson, Anthony Taylor Hughes.

When first the shoreline I did see,
And you walked hand-in-hand with me,
Through gentle mist, the isle we spied,
And there we built our paradise.

Yet always, for some cause unknown,
I sensed your inner thoughts forlorn,
You yearned to flee the simple life,
To face a challenge, war and strife.

When you are happy then I'm glad;
I cannot bear to see you sad.
May God protect you, have a care,
As you sail off and I despair.

Thelma (Tia) Webb
DECISION
Dedicated to all those who have survived the storms of life, and to those who helped them make it. To my dear sister, Lois, and to a very special lady, "Joan."

Rejection—loneliness-a black abyss
The anguished pains of hell within, I feel
I gave my heart and soul and sealed it with a kiss
Now he is gone—alone again—
From fate's cruel blow I reel

Torn between a bond with oneness
and that which is
the spice of life
He weighs the balance in his hands
While I am grieved
Sleep—elusive still—I seek
My anguished soul embroiled in strife

I ask myself what will the answer be
Alas, from deep within his heart the truth must come
Till then, my tortured thoughts within me burn
I wait, my love, on thee

Lucille (Landis) Brubaker

Lucille (Landis) Brubaker
THIS GREAT TRUST
Dedicated to B. J. Brubaker, my daughter, who is the Director of the Aspen Camp School for the Deaf.

Even when cool breezes
Swayed Colorado's blue spruce branches.
It felt warm in the SUN
At Picnic Point on Aspen Mountain.
My daughter and her friend

And I experienced THIS
GREAT TRUST.
With PALM extended HANDS
We took turns offering Crumbs of Buns
To attack nearby birds
If any were lurking and hungry.
From somewhere those birds came,
Called "Camp Robbers" of Aspen Mountain.
They swiped our Crumbs of Buns
And tarried only a few seconds.
When you actually see
And feel the bird land on outstretched HAND,
And then see that same bird
Disappear after eating your Crumbs,
CONTENTMENT and GREAT PEACE
Reigns from within your entire being.

Lucille (Landis) Brubaker

A FLY-IN

Early, this cool August morning,—
Why, the time is not yet seven!
Mourning Doves did a fast FLY-IN,
I counted over eleven.

The Mourning Dove's runway and stage
Was our short curved cement driveway.
There, they each did a pantomime
With acrobatic virtuosity.

The change of their pace and rhythm
Showed off the effortless technique
Of each Mountain Dove's performance,
While getting breakfast with his beak.

Mourning Doves showed initiative
With their spontaneous short runs,
Mixing in theatrical dances
While hunting for their breakfast crumbs.

Their feathered costumes looked the same!
Each was a composite work of art,
And when the FLY-IN was over—
Tails shuttled as they did depart.

Everlenia Jackson

TIMES

Dedicated to the homeless.

Times are hard,
Friends are few.
But what am I suppose to do.

Crowded streets, in the heat,
With peoples dancing to the beat.

No one care, or do they take pity.
What am I to do, in this big city.

Smog covering, even the streets.
Some have tears, dropping to their feet,
But what am I to do, with nowhere to sleep.

Tom & Rowena Stenis

THE QUEST

To our dear cheerful friend, Hazel Lauderdale, who is nearing 100.

We're searching all over for someone to ask,
"How to live to be a hundred, to accomplish this task?"
We went to the butcher to ask his advice . .
"Eat lots of good red meat, and this should suffice."
Next-door was the baker; he said, "What it takes
is eating wheat pastries and many good cakes."
The candlestick maker advised us this way:
"Use candles by nighttime and Sunshine by day."
Then Old Mother Hubbard appeared in a fog,
But answered us kindly, "You must have a dog."
Said Little Bo-Peep, "Do try not to worry,"
And, "You will live longer if you do not hurry."
Old Woman in the Shoe, how goes it with you?
"Keep children around you, and not just a few!"
We asked of Jack Spratt and his beautiful mate;
Together they answered, "Agreement is great!"
Said jolly King Cole and his Fiddlers Three,
"Keep happy by dancing and singing with glee."
Smiled young Mistress Mary while tending her flowers,
"Live long with earth's beauty to brighten your hours."
We went to the minister; for each he does care.
He answered immediately, "Regular prayer."
Dear Hazel, it seems the advice you don't need;
Just keep right on doing the same old things, Keed.
Now tell us all how we can live to be ninety
So we may cheer others and be just as mighty!
Is it living in Austin or keeping so thin,
Or all the good friends and all of your kin?
So here's to you, Hazel, with bright smiling face:
Happy Ninetieth Birthday, keep up the good pace!

Theresa Weisenberg Smith

JUST FOR BEING YOU

I want to thank you
for all you do,
But mostly just for
being you.
Your loving thoughts
and caring ways,
Help to smooth
the roughest days.
I know that you
don't want to rest,
Until we have the
very best.
So please don't
let it get you down,
I'm very happy
it's you I found.
I love you.

Debby L Emmett

AS I SIT ALONE

To My Mother.

As I sit alone
Only then can I be strong
Not the person with a sparkle in her eyes
Or lips which shine with the glow of life
Not the one who lives outside herself
Or the one who others see
But the one alone,
With eyes that darken with pain
And crimson lips which quiet burning hearts
Only alone can a smile caress my lips
Only alone can a dream be real
Only alone can my eyes sing with hidden passions
Can my world turn free
Only when alone, I'm not afraid of me

Rose M Pendola

ADOPTION

To Maria, our adopted daughter.

Long did I wait in terrible frustration
Till you came to us
Like God's own orchestration.

Now could anyone have known,
The joy that I felt?
How much love I had built,
As through the years,
I had wept.

Your beauty for me
Was the smile of God,
The love that I felt was as
Endless as He.

Christine Gangi

THE MOON

The moon now seems so far away, at times almost cruel
Smiling down on all our rights, laughing at all our wrongs.
Whatever happened to this dear companion?
One we could look up to,
with all his shining friends.
Now this has come to an end.
As on a dreary night,
I see you no more.
During your flight across the sky,
I search for you no more.
I'll bid to you a farewell now,
before it is too late.
Before you can put me back under your spell
I'll escape and let you wait.
Until I come back willingly.
The moon now seems so far away.

Brandi Holland

LOVE IS A ROSE

Love is like a rose grown wild,
You can never see the pain.
For it hides deep within your heart,
Like a bird it longs to be free.
Why does it have to happen to me?
A red one means "I love you".
A white one means "We're friends".
A pink one means we'll be together
Until the world comes to an end.
Love is a special feeling that dwells inside.
We must learn to share it amongst ourselves.
Love is like a red, red rose.
Love is a rose that never dies,
A love that never cries.
Love is a rose that should not lie,
Love is a rose!

Maverick Kemp

FEDERAL JAIL

As I sit here locked up in this federal jail,
Wanting to be home, but I've got no bail.

I look through the bars to the streets below,
The days and the weeks go by so slow.

We read books and write letters to pass the time,
But it only temporarily preoccupies the mind.

At night I lay in my bunk trying to sleep,
The price for my crime seems way too steep.

I dream of the people that I miss so much,
I long to be with them and to feel their touch.

I can't wait 'till the day that I will be free,
And the world that I know will once more include me.

Elizabeth A Hervol

VELVET VOID

To my husband Carl and to my daughter Carole, I dedicate this poem to you.

I know a place quite close to here
Where night is always nigh.
No mortal movement shows itself
Mere spirits rustle by.

The horrid gown of blackest black
Sheds no light on land below.
Just ever-present inky dark
No care of corn

No snow or rain or wind to blow
No living creature see.
No moistened ground to secure
A tall and slender tree.

It's so dark in this weird place
That I could never find
A ray of sun, a babbling brook,
You understand—I'm blind.

Brent Blevins

BOOGIE BOB

He was a member of the city's finest,
And preferred to be called simply,
Your Highness.
Of all the boogie dancers outclassed by none,
Before this fateful night,
he was number one.
Boogie Bob bobbed his head
to the boggie beat,
And danced with a girl
good enough to eat.
An unknown villain walked out
and through a door,
Paid the cover charge and
sneaked onto the floor.

A bobbin' and a weavin' this way and that,
He boogied so darn fast, he lost his hat.
Boogie Bob went and climbed into a chair,
And sipped on a whiskey while combin' his hair.
Somehow he knew comin' here was very wrong,
Although he had danced to his favorite song.
The newcomer that came in had shown him up,
And made him look like a little lost pup,
But even though his face was white as a ghost,
He was determined to be the perfect host.
The music stopped and his girl and the stranger,
Came to his table when he saw the danger.
He knew about then his dancin' days were done.
Boogie Bob was second best, the villain won,
Leading up to a last minute rave review,
Announcing they were tied, twenty-two to twenty-two.

Edith M Wiske
SAD
My heart is so full of sad,
Sad over words never said
Thoughts never heard
Wounds never bled.

And arching o'er the caverns of my memories
lies a dense fog of tears
That makes it difficult to see,
And harder still to hear.

What's that you say?
You love me?
Your voice sounds like a whisper
'Mid the turmoil of doubt and fear's cacophony.

But your whisper is sweet,
And calming, and refreshing as summer rain,
The dew of your affection
Warms my heart again.

True, tears may chill
And pain may wound the heart,
But with love's strong elixir,
Joy will instant recall its art.

Michelle Blakeley
THE NIGHT WE MET
We met on a September night, it was love at first sight, as though it was a beaming light When I looked into your eyes, I can see your love for me will never die.

When we go and dance, afterwards were in the mood for romance. When we had to go our separate ways, who would have guessed we both wanted to stay. When I walked in that next weekend, I realize our love wasn't at an end.

Sophie C Aksel
REBIRTH
Rebirth at 80?
No, no, that could never be.
I'd be lying in my grave,
Mourned by friends and family.

Silence everywhere now,
Only the trembling of leaves
And the whisper of wind
As it stirs the earth above me.

But now at 80
Life once more is in my grasp,
Hopes I'd had before are now achieved,
All that agony of self-doubt relieved.

Now I can dance around the globe,
Encountering people everywhere shy and bold,
Stirred by the magnificence of spangled seas,
And the rustle of wind on tropical trees.

And to whom do I owe all of this?
Could I ever have reached it on my own?
Never, never, could I have done this alone.
It's you, Michael, reaching into my soul.

Yes, Michael, you've revealed to me
What I alone could never see.
So now, instead of lying in my grave,
My life for the future has been saved.

J E McCarvill
SENTINEL
One day I wandered by a stony wall
Looking out as far I could
'Til my eyes would hold no more.
In the distance a red barn stood alone.
A guard to barren fields.
Yet being one, it seemed content.
With swayed-back roof and faded paint
It spoke to me in voice silent
Of noble times, and happy years,
Of rafters filled with feed and hay;
Of distant skies at Wintertime,
Of barren fields and withered bay.
I turned, I wept, I headed home.
As then I knew my time would come.

Thomas C Nelson Jr
ILLUSIONS
It is not what it seems to be!
It is an illusion.
Illusions do not let me see,
They cloud my perception
Of how I want things to be.
Down the path of life
I am led astray
By illusions causing strife
Which destroys my days.
I reach, I grasp, I strive
To obtain reality or its illusion
In order to survive.
To live each day untainted
By the morbidity of what is not real.
Ah, but then dreams are also illusions,
Aren't they?
For without our ephemeral dreams, what do we have?
Nothing but the discordant harshness
Of reality!

Michele N Schick
OH, TO BE UNDERSTOOD

Marvin & Maudie Graves, my parents.

'Twould be nice to be understood.
To feel loved, accepted for who I am and not for what I've done.
Oh, to be understood.

T'would be nice to be able to be me, no holds barred; not to feel scolded, molded into something I am not.
Oh, to be understood.

Not slighted for thinking differently, acting unusually, having an alternate point of view or by playing devil's advocate.
Oh, to be understood.

Heavenly Father, help me to have the courage to be myself; allowed to be angry at those who hurt others; to understand those who hate you; and to fight against injustices done to the weak and the poor.
Oh, to be understood!

Michelle N Schick
LONELINESS
There are times in our lives we feel unloved.
Times where we wish we'd get more hugs.
I wish life would go at a slower pace,
A different time, a different place.
Time for walking along the beach.
Time for making peace—in our homes,
With those in our lives whom we are at odds with.
Time when personal losses are replaced with encouragement and cheer,
Not with longing and with fear.
For unhealthy relationships must be given time to heal;
Although it feels like I am being peeled
Like the layers of an onion.
Sometimes the pain is so intense.
I cannot think! Life makes no sense.
These moods they come and go—I feel like someone's shadow.
Without a life of my own.
Meeting needs and learning to let go.
Being lonely is not all bad—I remember all I have.

John L Hough
LOVE IS SOMETHING LIKE A ROSE

To my wonderful wife Cheryl Who makes love a reality.

Love begins like a rose
First a bud and then it grows
Sweet and perfect from the start
The rapid pounding of your heart

With grace and poise it stands the storm
When the rain is gone it begins to warm
The thorns are there that bring the pain
But the beauty of it will remain

Love's the fragrance that smells so fine
Mine is your's and your's is mine
Love is something that we two share
The way I know you always care

So remember darling as years go past
That this is how our love will last
A touch, a laugh, a smile that knows
That love is something like a rose

Lisa Kathryn Pearson
BABY DAUGHTER

To my previous baby Jennifer Lynn, you inspire me always.

You are so very beautiful
I can see love through your eyes.
When I look at you I still can see
the little girl that is me.
Your world is all so steady—
so simple, honest and pure.
You have no fears to bind you,
you are completely free.
When I look at you, sweet baby daughter—I do not have to look at what I once was, but at what you can teach me to be.

Ken Launikonis
THE ANSWER
Wondering how I answer this strange request
Responding to a magazine
First time in years I've taken a test
Is this contest a part of my dream
A desire to be published

I have a message to get across
It's about beauty, truth, and light
Too many people in this world are lost
More self understanding, there's no need to fight

Moving thru time, suspended in space
Everyone's trying to prove a point
With no finish line, we call it the human race
No wonder the world's out of joint

Struggling so hard to fight for position
Within ourselves there's so much division
Does that have to be the human condition

We need to see we're already here
The message is simple and clear
Break down the walls, they are built by fear
Learn to experience love.

Glenn Toothman
KING OF THE FALL
Football, Oh Football, the big campus king;
The alumni knows well the money you bring.
Up the field, down the field, Rah! Rah! Rah!
For the good of the college, Siss, Boom Bah!

You bring lots of glory along the way,
And give life to the school each Saturday.
You bring in the muscle more than the mind;
You call up your best of all they can find.

To the black and the blue you are ever true;
You stick to your colors as if they were glue.
You take only the ones tested and tried,
And set them in classes where they can hide.

Still when the cheering has faded away,
And you have had your autumnal day,
We must believe there is reason to muse,
If you are the king, learning must lose

Charlotte Kay Ursula Krause

Charlotte Kay Ursula Krause
THE DANCER AND THE DOG

This poem is in memory of my beloved "FLUFFLES" who became "Heaven"s Little Present" on November 30, 1988.

There was a girl who studied dance
and taught its varied forms
until an illness took her chance
to live within life's norms.
At this time, too, an orphaned dog,
so pitifully abused,
hoped to lift her own bleak fog
which smothered and confused.
Swimming from a pair of hands
to the dancer's extended arms,
their eyes that told of other lands
now spoke of promised charms.
Blossoming from their sharing love
was a life so few possess,
for God did choose from up above
to heal and to caress.
It was with tears the dancer did give
to the angels, her dog, when they came;
but they promised both their love would live
and that their bond would remain the same!

Susan Jordan
GROWING-UP

This poem is dedicated to my father "Richard R. Lauzon" who passed away on March 22, 1990. I received my Award of Merit Certificate that same day.

World, world, please go away! I'm only a child now and I want to play.
I played in your sands, swam in your waters, felt your sun on my body,
to find my world as a woman now. Tomorrow is what I fear the most!
I'm not sure how I'll be or feel about anything. How will our society
treat people and problems
facing us all? People see you as they want
to. I'm not sure world how I see you.
My experiences in life have been
very special. You might say
they're "one of a kind", but they are mine.
You've taught me how and told me not to ask why. Sadly when one person's
life ends, miraculously another
life begins. It seems to be a
neverending cycle. My time
shall come sooner or later. Now
world you see
another child coming along to play. I'm all through growing up now.

The End

Sharra J Baggett
YOUR SHADOW

To my husband Clint and my wonderful family. God bless you all.

I saw the sunshine, it was shining on you
soon it was gone and so were you.
Now it's dark but I can see

I've changed now it shines on me.
Move over I want to see your face.
It's so hard to see in this dark and shiny place.

It's so bright, I can see inside your heart
it's broken and all torn apart.
is that what I've done or was it just
the shadow of the sun

Turn around so that you won't have to see,
I'm leaving now so your heart can mend for me.
Now the moon is bright and so very high
I can see you in the distance
Slowly waving good-bye.

Lark Koontz
CLIMB

Feel life my friend,
The joy and pain,
With true intensity.
Both enrichment and despair,
Stem from adversity.

To be content,
To be complete,
To have your dreams fulfilled;
If you want to reach the top,
You have to climb the hill!

Ronnie L Roberts
FIRE DRILL

To Courtney.

A fire drill is a simple thing
It could save your life one day
So when you hear the fire bell ring
It's not the time to play.

The fire bell means "Get out" "Get out"
And don't you dare come back
For if you do, you may not know
And get in the mean fires path.

Now you are out all safe and sound
And the all clear whistle blows
Was it a fire drill or was it real
Only your principal knows.

Gib Harms
THE WANDERLUST

I met a man with the wanderlust,
For the wanderlust was free,
And he'd been from deepest Africa
To the shores of the Bering Sea.

He'd worn Mukluks of the Eskimo
Seen the Halls of the Mountain King,
And when in the land of the Kangaroo
He'd seen many a strange, strange thing.

He'd seen the duck-billed Platypus
Saw the Wallaby hop along,
And the birds that he saw in the Out-back
Seemed to sing the strangest song.

From the halls of Montezuma
To the Amazon Jungle deep,
He'd seen the vicious Piranha
And had seen the big snakes creep.

But for all the places this man had been
And in all the dirt and the dust,
The only thing he ever acquired
Was this insatiable
WANDERLUST.

Dorothy Anna Margaret Hanley
ONE SUNDAY IN PORTLAND
(Implosion of the Corbett Building)

As I watched on slow-motion TV
This dreamer could see
The Corbett Building gracefully bow,
lingering for just a moment, then
with a graceful corner stretched upward,
wave reluctantly,—and was gone in a cloud of dust.

Karen Lee Maddox
TRIALS AND STORMS

When you're walking through a storm in life and everything seems wrong,
Just lift your hands to the Savior above and praise his holy name.

Listen to the still small voice of our Father
As he lays his hand upon your loving face and explains His touch of love.

Trials and storms are good (my child), they teach you to look to me, they teach you patience.

I'll walk through the storms with you (my child), I'll hold your hand and I'll never put more upon you than I feel you cannot bear.

Trials and storms are good (my child), they're to shape you into stone so that you'll be a rock for me, as solid as can be.
When you seem to grow weary and feel you can't carry on, just lay your burdens upon me and your strength I will renew.

Trials and storms are great (my child), keep your eyes upon me.

You're an overcomer in the battles of life as long as you have me. . .
In Christ: Karen Lubbock Maddox

Shawla M Swearengen
LADY OF GLASS

For Eddie-Lou Cole whose belief in me gave the courage I needed to succeed.

The darkness nestles close to her and wraps its misty arms
Around a swan-like neck that holds a head withdrawn.
A tremulous light illuminates a face
That time forgot and graceful fingers push gently back a lustrous silken lock this haunting radiant vision she brightens up the night. Admiring glances come her way drinks in the heavenly sight. But none can know she's hiding a jagged break inside caused by a careless lover who dropped and left his bride. Some say she'll never be mended and free from her damaged past. Who is the one who shattered the valuable Lady of Glass.

John M Anselmi
ENTITLEMENTS

You must be wary of worldly ways, and deeds.
Ah, but too young are you to know
of which we speak, the "I remember when,"
and "The good ol' days."

I know of which they speak.
Right now I just resent
that they know more than I.
But how long will it be before
I—I can see the reason I should repent?

It's not as long as you may think.
We remember yesterday,
or was that years ago?
What matters is what we must convey.
Of the fountain you cannot drink.

What matters to me
matters not to them.
And they just don't understand.
That the mistakes I make are mine alone,
and I must make them 'till the end.

John M Anselmi
LIFE FLIGHT

There is a tide which lives in some
to do that which few have done
to see the things the privileged see
to ride within rotating wings.
I do not wish to be the one
who looks back on what I should have done
to never have witnessed the sublime
which stable wings cannot provide.
To most the dream will just remain
a passing fancy; a fancy whim
do not be to quick to disdain
unless you have ridden in rotating wings.

Jim James
SHEEMA

To my white Akita Guard Dog. 12 years old; 11 of those years were spent protecting me!

Goodbye, my dog, my love, and my friend
You walked with me till the very end.
I'll never forget, your kiss yesterday,
As if you knew, there would be no today.
It was hard to leave you, to be put to sleep
So I hope you know as I write this, I weep.
But thru the thoughts, and all the tears,
I thank God, I had you all these years.
It's so very hard to say "Sheema Goodbye",
I just didn't want to think, some day you'd die.
Guard dog, you were, white and proud as you could be,
What honor it was, to have you walk beside me.
You walked with me, thru trouble and strife
Always there, willing to give, even your life.
So I take this drink, while your ashes burn,
For together in death, we'll share the urn.

To walk together again, in some unknown land,
With you by my side, your leash in my hand.
Right by my side, you'll be very much alert,
To always make sure, I won't ever be hurt.
So wherever I go, let it always be said,
"Sheema's there, even tho his master is dead."
And whatever the journey, and whatever will be,
The world will know, There goes Sheema and Me.

Ruth E Cramblit
THE SONG OF SEVERA
A fadista sings of an enchanted time. Of a king of earlier times living in Pombals castle grand. And once again the sound of Portugal is the mystical fado resounding across the land. The fadista tells in song of a gypsy queen whose love belonged to land and king. Who lives forever in the minds and hearts of the people who loved to hear her sing. Maria Severa was the gypsy's name. They said they had seen her alive once more. Those sailors and brave men of the sea. They had felt her presence there and they had heard her sing again as their ships came near the shore. The song of Severa is heard once again. And the mystical Fado intoxicates the land. As Amalia Rodriquez sings in the coffee houses, the gypsy queen Maria lives in the hearts of all Portuguese men. Come with me now to an enchanted place called Liston-By-The-Sea. A place where women are always young, and men are free.

Sally McBride
GIVE ME A SONG
Lord give me a song to sing,
Lift up my voice high and let it ring.
Give me a song from Heaven above,
Let me tell of your great love.
How Jesus died upon the cross,
That all who believe might not be lost.

Let me tell you of our Heavenly King,
Let me sing of the joy you bring.
Lord give me a song that's full of gladness,
To sing to someone who's filled with sadness.
Lord let me tell of your guiding light,
In a song I can sing day and night.

Lord give me a song to sing,
Let me tell of your grace and everything.
I thank you Lord for a song,
That will help make someone strong.
I sing praises to the King,
For the Lord gave me a song to sing.

Dorris L Thompson
MY LIFE IN THE U.S.A.
I crocheted around hankies
When I was only four.
I sold them for a dime,
A nickel or more.

I hoed the garden.
I cut the grass.
I picked apples
And fished for bass.

I canned the beans
And canned the meats.
I canned the peas,
The carrots and beets.

I mowed the lawns
To earn some money.
I sold buttermilk
And some honey.

I worked in a cannery.
Went to college and taught school for almost forty years.
Loving people was my rule.

Now, I am seventy-eight years old
And still not dead.
I teach Senior Citizens
Exercises in Physical Ed.

Doris L Thompson
MY HUSBAND
I love you, Darling.
Yes, I love you dearly.
I love you daily
And I love you yearly.

I feel very safe,
When I am with you,
Because you help and guide me
In things that I do.

Love!

Cecil O Boyce
SEASONS CHANGE
Winter has been long and dreary, cold, damp and weary.
With cold icy winds blowing from the north for all it's worth,
as it has from its birth;
As time goes by, it blows less and less,
With the air not as bitter as before.
Slowly the winds become a gentle caress,
As winter fades into nothingness, the birds sing, as spring will soon have its day in all its bliss.

Albert N Delzeit
ENVISION A BLUE WORLD ENCLOSED WITHIN LUSTERLESS CONCRETE
Envision a blue world enclosed within lusterless concrete.
With flowing hilly waters
And sweet blossoms thriving
Lying eclipsed within thickest artificial covering.
Only a comfortless cushion
Of stiff-dense-street.
Faithfully suppose
No more twisting vines to rend
No more sprawling vales to traverse
Or no more soaring peaks to ascend.
Then picture the people whose
Kindness provides this sphere.
Watch them pour without pausing.
See them toil without thinking.
Deriving purest somber content
With each additional tier.
As if glimpsing underneath was their sleepless fear.
As if threateningly below the unheard-of was lying
So why perplex their temporal taste of time
With some changing . . . ?

Kathy A Newsome
ETERNAL PEACE
Jesus is my Savior;
He led me
through all hardships
and kept me safe
from harm.
Now I'm in
His holy presence
in a place
that I call
home.

Laine Shamblin
KIDS

To what was essential but invisible, my love for my Kids.

I remember a time when I had a house full of Kids
Running around, getting into everything it seemed.
Crossed by time their eyes surely beamed
Small little things they would do or say.

It was nice to have a child and see them change
For things we do they weren't to blame.
A house full of ten—small, medium and large
Suddenly my house is empty from faith no longer charge.

A small little girl, I watched to grow into a lovely young lady
I walked away—for my life was heavy and distant from all.
Blonde hair so pretty, she grew and became so tall
Suddenly she was a mother, grown, no longer small.

Those I past for another's faith of hand
Three more I learned stood at hand.
But then again—my house was empty once more
Three who I became to love so dear
Almost thoughts of what was cheer.

The house crackles and creaks with thoughts of Kids
I'll become old but with memories of all my Kids.
My house is empty and cold forever more
I'll never again touch the closeness of a Child.

Diane E Willard
ALTER-EGO
We've met before, so many times before.
I've seen their faces framing the clouds
Above Athens' ancient Hill;
Seen them in the mired redness of Marathon.
Faces triumphant with the buoyant fear
of fierce commitment,
The cost of conviction a carousel of carnage
Shattering the Sunday silence.

We've met before, so many times before.
I've heard their voices in the dismal darkness
of Dachau;
Heard them in the tangle of tales forever sealed
In the secret stillness of Ellis Island,
In the strident song of Solidarity.

Today, we met once more,
Graven image of a double self:
Shadow of a fallen goddess,
Liberty lives
In the freedom of the human spirit,
On the Avenue of Eternal Peace.

Walter T Guenther
A TOAST TO FATHERS
A toast to all fathers who do their best
To bring up their children,—to pass the test;
Children want their dads to guide them in life,
To show them how to overcome all strife!

A child today may not look up to dad,—
Who wants his child to be happy,—not sad;
Dad deserves credit for all he does do,
To guide each child to be honest and true!

It's not easy for dad to give a child real love
When the child goes to others,—not Him, above;
Stealing, taking dope, can't all be blamed on dad,
And drinking while driving is so very sad!

Now is the time to really take a stand,—
Guide the child,—then take him by the hand;
Show him that you love him,—that you care, too;
Be proud of him and he'll also be proud of you!

Debbie L Walter
A YEAR AGO OUR BABY DIED

We dedicate this poem to our daughter Kelly Lynn Walter, who died from a terminal birth defect and made us aware of just how many grieving families of children there really are in this world—too many. Love, Mom, Dad and brother Seth.

A year just isn't long enough to wash away our pain;
to ebb the fears of going on; you see—our tears remain.

A little girl, a daddy's dream, awaiting to be born,
Until one day the doctors said, her death we would soon mourn.

Her birth was two months premature, but she was born a fighter.
Though diagnosed as terminal, her life made ours much brighter.

Eight hours of life she had with us; then in my arms she died.
I watched God take her peacefully, but to my heart she's tied.

So when we cry don't turn away and say we've grieved too long.
There's no such thing as "time to stop" and no one can grieve "wrong."

A year has passed and that is true, but we still grieve each day.
Please help us keep her memories alive along the way.

We love you Kelly!

Forrest Duckson
LESSONS
Lessons I've Learned
I Shall Not Tell
But To Only Those
Who Listen Well
For Those Who Do Not Listen
I Have Only A Sigh
For I've Learned My Lesson
To Live and Let Die

Jean Chancellor
FINAL BOARDING
Baggage was loaded, passengers waited to board.
Kisses, hugs and final goodbyes.
Children sighed of weariness, hugged teddy bears tight.
Agents worked efficiently, loading the Pan Am flight.
Crew members were in their places, all with smiling faces.
No reason to frown after visiting ole Londontown.

Unbeknownst to all strong winds were blowing.
The Captain was aware and knew he must vector North,
Because he'd been trained to care.

Passengers found their seats, became comfortable.
The cabin team mouthed directions, answered questions,
Appeared alert, and ATC radioed clearance, saying okay to divert.
The jumbo jet roared down the runway, gaining thrust,
And climbing upward toward Eternity.

No one survived to recall moments before the fall.
But, alas! Instead of the sea, the great machine
Fell on ancient Lockerbie!

Tawnee Bellamy
WHERE DOES THE SKY END?
The hopes, dreams, fantasies, and realities of mankind, what are they? They are the sky. Where does the sky end? The sky ends when men give into the harsh, unyielding, unmerciful world. When man and man alone lets the hopes die. When they no longer believe in what is good and true. When they let their ambitions go, and turn to each other in hatred, this is where the sky ends. When the hopes, dreams, fantasies, and realities are left to fall and shatter, a tiny part of the sky is destroyed. There was a time when men lived together and shared the good, the will to go on. Now, look at the world. How long before there is no sky? Nothing to look forward to? Turn to the children. They are the answer. They have no fears, no hatred, no emotion, but what we teach them. Teach them to love, to share, and they will rebuild the sky. So, where does the sky end? Only in the minds of those who have given up.

Carla Michelle Hall Pope
UNTOUCHABLE DREAMS
I look around,
You're not there!
I call your name,
I say a prayer.
Tears run down my face
and through an empty heart.
The place I was warm,
now turns to ice.
You've fallen asleep
and never to wake.
Why do you have to sleep
through your dreams?
Why do you have to sleep at all?
I lose another friend,
I gain another nightmare.
Can't you hear me?
Can't you see!
I need you back.
Just you and me.
We can have it all just like before.
But, only if you wake from your dreams!

Linda Lordi T
JOJO
19 years went down the drain,
The day you pulled the trigger,
19 years of love and pain,
Who would have ever figured,
That you would end your life this way,
Or any way at all,
'cause life is just too precious,
For you to end it all,
Life is just a game, Jojo,
To win you must survive,
But Joe you just copped out,
And left us here alive,
There's nothing left that we can do now,
But sit and mourn your death,
And of course life must go on,
But for you there's nothing left,
So many roads you could've taken,
So many choices to make,
But the road you chose that day, Jojo,
was the easiest road to take,
And now your life is over Joe,
And forever you are gone,
But in our hearts and in our minds
your memories will live on...

Rosanne Uchytil
LIFE
Life flows by,
Like birds flying through the sky.
Days pass,
As you see your watch
Ticking in the past.
But you see time fly,
You get older,
And you go through your life
But then the time comes to go,
And you go,
With another flow.

Ann Marie Kopp
THE GOAL
After fighting a long illness through
When life's light flickered a time or two
I looked upon the remaining span
and vowed to draw up a better plan.

Questions and answers came to mind
As how to spend the shortened time
Upon each hour carefully ponder
None of its minutes I choose to squander.

Then, hopefully when the journey's done
To leave behind with setting sun
Some happiness for those who stay awhile
Having helped with burdens and shared a smile.

Thus, will I sing a merry song
Though the way seems short or very long
For having spread God's sunshine bright
Chasing the shadows of someone's night.

Natasha R McClanahan
THE EGOTISTICAL MAN
In the lines of this poem there is a story I must tell
About the ways and doings of the egotistical male.
When people are not distant, you're sure to hear him boast
Of the things he has done and how we all think he's the most.
Because his opinion is not the same as mine,
He insists I am stupid or in the least must be blind.
What really gets me most is that he's so sure he is adored,
But this is only the beginning, keep reading there is more!
As he looks in the mirror, all the girls roll their eyes
And focus their attentions on all the other guys.
In the company of beautiful women, where he's sure to be around,
He believes them to be flirting, but they are laughing I have found.
If you just happen to be the one who cares in every way,
He decides he's too good and leaves without delay.
When it comes to his appearance, well they all look the same
Holding their heads up high and strutting every brand name.
In all his vain efforts, one thing he's sure to provoke
Is the wrath of the woman who's convinced he's just a joke.
For there is one thing I am sure about and will always take a stand
Is that there is nothing quite as bad as an EGOTISTICAL MAN!

Tanya R McBride
WOMAN EPITOMIZED
Can you guarantee me tomorrow, or can you tell me how
To comprehend the many things that I am feeling now?
Tomorrow's just a daydream and yesterday is gone,
The hardest thing I'll do today is 'keep on keeping' on.

Can't worry about forever, or how long it will last,
Sometimes forever's over, before I know it's passed.
Some hours seem like seconds, some seconds seem like years,
All crowded full of my desires, and flooded with my fears.

Would I give up my tomorrows to go back to yesterday?
Miss out on what is yet to come, dear God there is no way!
Each day brings me some brand-new joy and helps to let me grow,
I cannot let it pass me by there's so much I want to know.

I have to hear the music and feel the throbbing beat,
I want to see the faces of those I've yet to meet.
I want to climb the mountains and see the summer snow,
And sail across the ocean just to see the sunset glow.

I'd like to know the feeling of silk against my skin,
I'd like to loose the woman who's been hiding deep within,
The one who has the courage, the heart, the brain, the power,
To live life to the fullest, and to treasure every hour.

Holly Lynn Hensley
A BEAUTIFUL DREAM
The sparkle of his eyes set off a glint,
When it happened I knew what it meant,
It meant that I was falling in love,
And the only person that knew that was the great Lord above,
My first true love so it must be,
The greatest guy anyone could ever see,
I loved him and he loved me,
The power between us anyone could see,
The love between us was like a bright beam,
Oh well there goes another great dream.

Butch Edens
RISE—AND MEET THE FOE
Old Glory waves on yonder pole,
She ripples in the wind,
She tells us all we have a goal,
'Tis peace that will not end.

We have a job that's just begun,
It's to defend our fleet;
And fight we must 'til all is won,
All foes must know defeat!

The Naval Air Corps is the best,
Its glory ere shall be;
And never will it take a rest,
'Til all the seas are free.

Our fight begins with studies here,
So learn your lessons well;
And when you join the fleet next year
Your training then will tell.

And when you rise to meet the foe,
He'll know he's met his match;
And down in flame and smoke he'll go
Down thru the Devil's Hatch!!!

Dorothy E Smith
DOLLARS AND SENSE
Dollars earned by work that one enjoys...
And it is good to choose that line of work...
For that gives stature that a man employs
And deadens any tendency to shirk
In the activities of every clerk.

Use some for recreation and for good
Of joy and laughter and sweet peace is great
So many things to do, and all this would
Add richness to a life and regulate
The well formed plans that one should advocate.

The style of living that one may desire
Depends on dreams and goals one plans to meet
And with enthusiasm sets afire
The zest and vim of life that all may greet
When they meet this one walking down the street.

Deborah Horrigan
THE ESSENCE OF ME
the essence of me feels
like a bubble in time
trapped
between then
and when
seeking to alight
in now
without breaking—
remaining intact—
whole.

transparent to all
yet
with its own strength—
appearing fragile
to those unaware
of the incredible power
within.

Claudia Ramundo

Claudia Ramundo
GOODBYE MOM

To my cherished wife, our beautiful mother and grandmother, Claudia Ciarfello. Eternally yours forever, husband Frank, your children, and grandchildren.

Your work on earth is finally completed. God called you home to rest. All the angels and saints were with you, especially our blessed mother, whom you repeatedly told us was speaking to you. Our lives have been filled with love and joyful memories. The deep sorrow and sadness of losing you will be unbearable. We will try to be strong. We promise to continue to live our lives the way you have taught us. We will need your prayers to strengthen us daily. Rest in peace, Mom. We all love you and will patiently wait until we are all home together again.

Heather Dubs
SUMMER

Here I sit in my favorite place
As the butterfly's satin wings
Brush against my face.
The willows sway in the gentle breeze
And the tall cool grass
Brushes against my knees.
To think there is no other place to be
Except here where everything is in perfect harmony.

Wendy Barlow
THE MEADOWS OF SALOO*

The moonlight glows on the silvery lake
As a frog hip-hops across the field
A rabbit stares wide-eyed at the vast sky before him
All is quiet in the meadows of Saloo

A tulip sways in the gentle breeze
As a mouse scurries into hiding
A sleek eagle flies overhead
All is quiet in the meadows of Saloo

A newborn chipmunk sleeps in silence
As a fish snaps up an unsuspecting fly
A raccoon gathers nuts peacefully
All is quiet in the meadows of Saloo

A new dawn breaks
As the animals awake
A bird sings a beautiful song in a nearby tree
All is no longer quiet in the meadows of Saloo

Richard L Lyle
BEYOND THE DOOR

What lies beyond the door
That each of us must face
Sooner or later
Where goes the path
That others have already trod
Throughout the ages?

Resurrection brings new hope
Of finally becoming immortal
And the thought of perfect peace
Heaven and Hell, the opposites
Collide in books of truth
More we cannot say.

Still, let us remain certain
That Father Time is every watching,
Waiting until then
Fear overshadows the light
On the other side of the tunnel
Another world ahead.

Patricia Baxter Wright
TO A PURPLE LADY

Sitting next to an iris
on a Sunday afternoon
naturally curly petals
with yellow dusted beards
regal three-some
lavender crowned
more purple passion
than even O'Keefe stroked
I hesitated inquiring
of beauty
time-framed,
of color
deep-seated,
of dying down
at season's end
non-woody as you are
And simply basked
in a purplish presence
lacking pretence
a hue between red and blue
and knew
of you.

Albert C Smith

Albert C Smith
THE HUMAN DILEMMA

To my understanding wife Melvina.

We may speak different languages, and our viewpoints may not agree. Why can't one sit back and talk, impossible as it may seem. Everyone on this earth, is working toward a dream. Or is it many on this earth, has an inborn nature to destroy. Being just like two small children, one to take another's toy.

Even if a man may have millions, which everyone does not possess. It's not man's way to give up anything, for something he can't see. And always takes the attitude, of what gain is it in for me. But there will be another time, and another place, in which, goodness, kindness, and respect, will be too late to share.

And when you arrive at that final gate, and it is asked of you. What Good have done for mankin on earth? Will others remember you for the impressions you have left below? What then can you reply? "Gee I didn't know?"

Albert C Smith
THE UNWANTED SECRET

To my understanding wife Melvina.

Oh! Waves out or the ocean, what stories you could tell. Of Spanish galleons, which were engulfed by your grasping swells. Or possibly of enormous battles, in which was split out or your waves.

To make your ocean bottoms, their silent moving graves,
But alas! As I sit here upon your sandy shore, and listen to your waves as they roll up on the beach.
I know the ocean's secrets, you'll always keep from man's reach.

For man has not learned, to use his knowledge for humanity's sake.

Instead it's used to destroy, secure, and take.
So oceans keep your mysteries, for I do not wish to know.
For if you revealed to me a secret that could unlock some unknown door.
My philosophy of life might change, and I'd not be the same as I was before.

Ruth M Putnam
YOU CAME INTO MY LIFE

You came
into my life
like a leaf blowing in the wind.

You stayed
sharing your beauty,
gentleness and love.

We cared,
nurtured and cherished
the time spent together.

You left
one day
as briskly as you came.

I cried.

F Esther Barnard
FILLING GAPS

The sweetest music in the world
is robbed of sound if there's no ear
to hearken to the melody:
a song to live eternally.

The richest moment of a life
is robbed of love if there's no heart
to share the moment's ecstasy:
a pulse to form a memory.

The ebb and flow of laughter—tears
is robbed of hope if there's no hand
to grasp the hand or dry the tears:
a touch sublime along life's way.

The perfect work, Creator's plan,
is robbed of strength if there's no voice
to speak of hope for loneliness:
a message from the mind of God.

Marily A Reyes (Mar)

Marily A Reyes (Mar)
VICTORY IS IN THE AIR

To my loving kids, Frances and Alexis and my husband Frank.

Victory is almost there
winning is the key
you can almost taste it
it is meant to be.

The game really begins
Umpire calls: Strike! Out! Walk!
excitement's in the air
and winning is the talk.

No mercy out on the field
is ONE TWO THREE OUT!
Here come the players
so...look out!

Those outfields, the basemen,
the pitcher's on a roll!
The shortstop, everyone,
and the catcher?! Wow!!

Victory is almost there
winning is the key
you can almost taste it
it is meant to be!!!!!!!

Angela Hill
SPRINGS SAYS "HELLO"

Soft mist, pink sunrise,
Soothing rain, delicate butterflies.
Cool breezes, whispering willow,
Sunny daisies, daffodils yellow.
Newborn life, new found love,
Tender warmth, from above.
Warm nights, sparkling twilight,
Blue moon, love's flight.
Endless daydreams, thoughtless thoughts,
Baby's breath, peace is caught.
Pastelle rainbows, wishing wells,
First love, wedding bells.

Marily A Reyes (Mar)
MY LOVE, MY WORDS AND YOU

Loving you is fatal. My feelings,
trying in words to define is impossible.
But whomever you're with, wherever you are
my verse will look for you.
The memory of you is tattooed in me
and my poet's word, the soul's language,
will tell you that life is but a whisper.
Oh, if my thoughts could whisper to

you now...
You will crumble to their touch and your
human emotions would crystallize with the incident.
I could say "I love you" but words are just the
tools for our language.
Yes, words are just sounds to mention feelings.
But please, be sensitive and steal them away,
steal them away...for you.

Jay Clough
TIME GOES ON
You're conceived, and time goes on
Nine months later, you are born
You learn to walk, yes, you're no fool.
A few years on, you'll be in school

Minutes make hours, twenty-four make a day.
Seven makes a week, a month's not far away
Years will soon be passing, you'll have a steady job
You could be a rich man, or you could be a slob

Time will still pass you by
But you're still young at heart
Though you're happy with yourself
You'd like another start

Just be happy with yourself
And know you've always tried
Live your life to the max
Till you take your final ride

Lisa A Ulibarri
ADIEU HOME OF NO WALLS
I don't wish to live as I do,
can't you see.

It just so happens,
luck is down on me.

My home of no walls,
is not all there is to me.

Open your heart,
and the real me you'll see.

I'll gladly do any work,
to get by.

If, only, someone,
would give me a try.

Some day, all my failings,
will I defy.

Some day, to bid adieu,
to sorrows sigh.

Amelia A Sayles
MY PRAYER
Today I walked upon the sand,
And watched the restless sea
Toss endless waves of froth and foam
From depths of mystery.

Sunshine and shadows raced fleecy clouds
Across the blue of summer skies,
Gray gulls, dipping and wheeling
Filled the air with their lonely cries.

Salt spray, and tears unnoticed,
Mingled with love and with pride,
Dear God, watch over my sailor sons,
Bring them safely home with the tide.

Mrs Elaine Tripp
SOMETIME IN THE NEAR FUTURE
Sometime in the near future
Everyone will notice the change
Little will be done about it
For no one will know the range
How could this have gone so far
Everyone's lips will say
Letting pollution take over the world
Perhaps we could stop it someday

Jane Boston Lofton
THE INFERNAL TRIANGLE
I know three women
Who share the same house.
They share the same children,
They share the same spouse.

They share the same wardrobe,
They share the same bed.
They share the same body,
They share the same head.

One is a small child,
Frightened and shy.
And one's super woman,
She can really fly high.

The third one is loving.
The third one is kind.
But the third one is
Quietly losing her mind.

Gloria P Snowden

Gloria P Snowden
TRANQUILITY
The joys and sorrows of youth are past,
Their heights and depths were too great to last,
Only the very young can know
Such ecstasy and chaotic woe.

The heart's ship is moored now,
No jagged rocks can pierce her bow,
She gently rolls with the tide of Life
Her hull is weathered to withstand strife.

Joy still comes, but gently now
No fleeting thing to fade tomorrow,
But slowly, serenely with warmth and light
As boundless as a lovely, starlit night.

Disappointments still bring pain,
But Time has taught it will pass again
And youth with its heartaches and shattered dreams
Is only a ghost in the silvery moonbeams.

Gloria P Snowden
SNOW STORM
The winter's sky has turned to gray,
The first soft flake comes drifting down.
It softly lights and melts away
So quick it barely touched the ground.

Now they fall in wild profusion
Dancing gayly in the air,
Swirling around in grand confusion
Softly falling everywhere.

Soon the ground is lost in whiteness
Covered with a rug of snow,
Pure and clean with downy lightness
Frosty diamonds all aglow.

Not a track to mar its splendor
Vast, unbroken wild expanse,
So inspiring in its grandeur
With the power to entrance.

Gloria P Snowden
AUTUMN
A subtle change is taking place,
As Summer makes her final bow.
She turns away her tired face
For she is old and withered now.

Autumn comes with supple grace,
And Summer slowly slips away.
The cooler air holds little trace
Of Summer once so young and gay.

The morning air is crisp and clear
The azure skies caress the earth,
The falling leaves say Winter is near
And flit about in silent mirth.

Autumn's dress is bright with color
As gay and giddy as her moods,
Now clouds obscure the blue above her
To wait in silence while she broods.

She is somber now for she must go
As she feels the nudge of Winter's hand,
Her once light step is weak and slow
And Winter waits to rule the land.

Gloria P Snowden
LISTENING
What do I hear? I hear many things
For there is no silence,
The lovely, staccato song of the wild canary
Voices of loved ones, long ago stilled,
Spanning time with another year.
Hopes unvoiced, their abode deep in the heart,
The Divine Voice gently guiding the way to peace—
There is no silence for I have only to listen
And all these golden things I hear.

Clara L Frieze

Clara L Frieze
IN DEFENSE OF SORROW
If one know not sorrow,
Then how can he boast
That he understand joy?
Therefore let us toast
Sadness and Poverty,
Woe and Despair
Lack of Faith, of Hope,
Of someone to Care.

Look up and rejoice
That we move and can see,
Are alive and can think,
Or maybe just be
For true recognition
Of Life's greatest test
Resides in contrasting
The Worst with the Best.

Clara L Frieze
CONDOLENCE FOR A LOSER
If you fail, it proves you tried;
You went along, not "for the ride."
The winner may not be the best;
He may be luckier than the rest.

Number Two is good position;
Some improvement or attrition,
May promote your place to first—
Anyhow you weren't the worst.

I've lived a long and lucky life;
Sometimes I have encountered strife.
Friends have often helped my fight;
Perhaps not always was I right.

I've asked the Lord for help this time;
For help right now for better rhyme,
To finish with a giant splash
or fire-bomb to reduce to ash
All ofther mandates seeking help
Thank you Lord for help to self.

Amy Bowers
HIDING IN THE SHADOWS
He walks down the street with his hand out,
and his head down.
He has nowhere to go,
so he wanders around.
The people rush by him and don't realize he's there.
He's just like the rest of us,
but no one seems to care.
They try to ignore him and call him a pest,
They say he's a bum and a total mess.
Society has labeled him a complete disgrace,
They're just afraid to look in his face.
He deserves a better life than the one he was given.
Can the life that he lives really be considered living?
When he dies no one will miss him,
or realize he's gone.
Yet many just like him will continue to go on.

Lauren Ann Herzfeldt
ON AN ISLAND
On an Island near the sea
over looking what is bothering me.
As I watch the waves go by
I sigh and cry.
When my sister, my mother and my father
are bothering me.
I go to the place
where I want to be.
On an Island near the sea
So I can look over what is bothering me.

Diana Ray
MY LOVE AND DREAMS
My love and dreams
soon will die,
I won't even be able
to just say "Hi!"
For you are moving
and even though I know
I can't help but wish
that you wouldn't go.

My love and dreams
soon will die
And although I know

that our love isn't true
When you're gone
I'll be so sad and blue.

My love and dreams
soon will die
Please don't forget
to say Goodbye.

Debbie Pelley-Hudson

Debbie Pelley-Hudson
FRIENDSHIP IS...

To Mark, my husband, who has been the source of many inspirations

I am your friend!
You tease me with your proclama-
tions of persuasion.
The crowds laugh; they reject me.-
You hold my heart within your grasp.
As you ridicule, the pain is there
for only me to feel and see.-
Your tainted words are but the
sounds
of echoed emptiness;
For you need me!-
Step aside, what do you see?
Yes, clouds of teardrops as loneliness
doth render me!-
For your pain is my pain.
Your heart speaks loud as friends
subside
and night falls with the rain.-
Where are they now?
You hide your face in shame,
Then into the night you cry
And slowly speak my name.-
"Dare I call you friend?" you ask,
"I fail to understand."-
But my reply is that you must not ask
me why...
Just hold my hand!

Debbier Pelley–Hudson
MOTHER MEANS LOVE

To my precious mother, who taught me how to live...and love.

I have sometimes lain awake at night
Wondering where, today, I would be,
If I didn't grow by the prayers of my
mother;
My life guided on bended knee.

For she showed me a world that was
good and bad;
Teaching the difference between
right and wrong,
And nothing I did was overlooked by
her love;
Her faith in God was so strong.

She gave me the nurture and love I
would need
To make it in the world; so dreary,
And sometimes the lessons were
painful
But I found solace in many a prayer.

How many times have I seen the hurt
But she would smile and pretend
things were fine,
That only deepened the love I felt;
For my mother's true love would
shine.

Mother means love and is a gift from
God
To be treasured like no other,
I thank the Lord for His tender care,
In the wonderful love of a mother!

Debbie Pelley–Hudson
MY SOUL REJOICES!

To Mom, Dad, and my sister Judy for their encouragement, support, and love. I thank God for them always!

My soul rejoices!
I look out over the sunset fair;
And as I do I see the work of God's
hand there.
He never once with fury over man's
disgrace,
Ceased to give us beauty from
nature's place;
For He speaks to us of love
in pastures green,
When yet we fail to notice Him...
What does it mean?
His love it has no stops or holds; but
yet,
I wonder why He keeps His patience
when we so soon forget!
For He is God!...
He knows, He loves, He understands.
That's why I know I rest within His
hands!
No questions asked.
My soul rejoices!

Debbie Pelley–Hudson
FORGETTING...

To my brothers, whom I love very much. May they never forget God so completely, that they can't find their way back!

Forget God? Never!
Yet His heart is saddened when
sunfilled days
are taken up with one's own ways.
And dreams are sought as life is
good,
No darkened bays.
But lo the rain falls all too soon and
where is God?
You search and why?
As you now hurt and need His love;
expecting Him
to radiate your life from yonder sky!
But sunshine will not come...
Until you look and see the teardrops
in the rain;
For God wants you to notice Him, yet
with the sun!
Forget God? Never!
And yet you fail to realize when
things are fine,
The lack of words that should be
there
because He draws the line!
Think again to love Him both in
sunshine and in rain;
Forgetting God you never
would...But prove it,
By communion when there is no
gain!

Debbie Pelley–Hudson
STOP...AND LISTEN
"God," I whispered, "Where are
you?"
As I ran amidst the morning dew.
And yet as rays of sunlight fine,
Shone down and lit the path of mine;
I stumbled and replaced my feet,
On rocky ground that spelled defeat.
I yearned to find the God of light,
To rid my fears, dispel my night.
I stopped below a flowing creek;
Thirst now quenched, again to seek.
But what is that I hear inside?
"Oh God, I need a place to hide!"
"But child, it's me, what I'm trying to
do
Is tell you I've been walking in front
of you!"

Debbie Pelley–Hudson
HOW WILL THEY KNOW...
The rebellion of a wayward few
Are but a candle in His eye,
He can blow it out and leave it dark,
Or can light it to the sky.

Who are we to choose our idols
And think that life is fine,
When God sits watching soberly
And holds our hearts in time.

Yes, we ought not to whisper so
About the blessings dear,
For maybe the raindrops we do feel,
Will next be Father's tear!

Let's look inside and see the light,
Is it still burning there?
Our love for God, the word must see;
How will they know we care?

Lucy Capriglione

Lucy Capriglione
FEELINGS ACROSS THE MILES
Jamie, Jamie, you're across the sea,
I don't know you and you don't
know me.
You send a card with a holiday cheer,
I just wasn't expecting this at the turn
of the year.

Mixed emotions surround me,
confusion and stress,
All of a sudden my life is a mess.
Why did you wait twenty years to
write?
I ask myself this question late at
night.

Your father is my husband,
And he is shocked that you exist,
I walk around just clenching my fist.

I feel anger and hurt, still shocked
with pain,
My tears roll down, they feel like
rain.
Jamie, Jamie, you're across the sea,
My anger is not toward you, but
rather at me.

For I've watched your father, his
struggle would last
Questions were never answered about
his own past.
He grew up like you, my Jamie dear
Always wondering if that father
image would ever appear.

But unlike yourself, he never
searched
I give you credit, you are his first.
My heart goes out to you and all I can
say,
I hope that your father will write you
someday.

Han Thai
MIDNIGHT REMINISCENCE
The night was calm and cold
As midnight slowly approached.
Lonely I stood in front of the
window,
Reminiscing of my old sorrow.

There was one time in my life
When my spirit was at great height.
Unexpected encounter of you and me
Someone of good virtue that I could
see.

Service and sacrifice I never minded
For you willingly I provided.
And yet my passion for you I had to
hide
Simply because I was steps behind.

From you indifference I received,
Lonesomely and miserably I grieved.
In vain constantly I struggled
And constantly to the very utmost.

Oh! How ardently I admired and
loved you!
Painfully remained the untold truth.
A truth which was mournful,
Each time reminisced I of my old
sorrow.

Mary Alice Foster
LOVER'S DUET

Sometimes I want to hold him in my arms, and comfort him—the way a mother would,

To soothe away his troubles and erase the worried look from his eyes.

To take away all the troubles, the suffering, sorrow, agony, and pain.

Looking down at the one I love, lying fast asleep, I see at once two people—one with the look of a young boy—seeking only comfort and security;

The other—a man striving for independence—seeking love, security, and peace from within.

Tossing gently to and fro, he reaches out to take me in his arms-and finding that I'm no longer there—slowly opens his eyes.

His eyes still heavy from slumber, glow softly as I walk slowly across the room and slip into his waiting arms.

One kiss rekindles the ever-burning flame, and time slips by unnoticed.

Outside in a shady bower, two lovebirds, unnoticed from within, sweetly sing a lover's duet.

Gwen Park
TIME—THE HEALER
I tuned in to the psyche of a man in
agony,
And, what he was succumbing to did,
once, apply to me.
I caught his sad vibrations;

desperation, intense pain.
I knew, what he was thinking I would hate to think, again.
Once, I had been so riven. Dire thoughts of darker
Hue had, then, plagued me, tho' I'd striven to dispel them from my view.
I will repeat those phrases, just this once, and then, no more;
(That I am healed, amazes. Life has evened up the score!)
DESPAIR IS MY COMPANION, WALKING CLOSELY BY MY SIDE, OR,
BREATHING DOWN MY NECK, UNTIL I LONG TO RUN,
AND HIDE. BUT, "LAUGH YOU FOOL," MY MIND INSISTS.
"COME, FLASH YOUR FOOLISH GRIN!"
AND SO, I SMILE, INANELY, BUT THE JOKE IS WEARING THIN.
GOD, THE JOKE IS WEARING THIN.
I longed to offer comfort, yet, I knew the time was wrong—
'Twould be a while before this man could think of being strong—
I could not pass unheeding, so, a silent wish I sent
Just hoping it would hold him till serenity was lent.
"Hang in there, sir," I urged him—but in spirit; 'twas not said—
Would it be long before his heart would slip its sheath of lead?

Patty Earl
WIND OF GOD
Wind of God, blow thru my life,
At every turn, sing out your will.
In the valleys, whistle encouragement to go on.
In the deserts, let squalls of your love
Reassure me that you're there.

In the mountains, aspire me to seek your face.
During storms,
Shatter my will with your turbulent breath, then return,
As if stroking me with the gentle breeze of your hand
And comfort my heart once again.
As I look over the paths of my life
Allow me to see the wonder of your wind shaping me
And the wonder of your wind leading me
As I face the unknown paths that lie ahead.

Chrissy Ormsby
OUR LOVE HAS ENDED
Why did our love ever end?
My heart is never gonna mend.
I might have another guy right now,
but you'll always be in my heart,
even though you're so far.
I wanted to be with you forever, but you didn't think we should be together.
I know it will never be the same again,
you'll never forgive me for the things that have been.
I just want you to know i love you with all my heart,
i wish you never tore our love so far apart.
Yes, it's true, i'm very blue, i want our love to be brand-new.
There is something that can't be,
i want you, but you don't want me.
No man will ever take your place, not your body, personality, not even your face.
I'll remember you until i die,
even when i'm in that place in the sky.
I hope you'll never forget me, we had some great times i wish they could still be.

Robert W Smead
SMOKE UPON THE HORIZON
Smoke upon the horizon
Who would have thought
That our love
Could cause such haze

Because I cannot have you
Nor can you have me
The horizon has become
So very gray

Someday
The smoke will clear
And the sun will shine
Bright across the sky
Yet again

Look then
Upon the Horizon
I'll be standing there
Waiting for you

Bill Ricci
FOREVER IMPACTED
In the world of today, we must take care to prepare for the world of tomorrow.
The next generation is at stake as to the fault of this generation.
The current status of now looks grim, and if continued in this pattern it will be worse in the future.

We're up to our necks in garbage, from overcrowded landfills.
There are people living in poverty, while others in pure ecstasy.
This government's a joke with its debt.
They spend millions on defense and stockpiling missiles, while all it's doing is causing more problems.
There are millions starving, with nothing being done.
Education is in need of money, but the students come second to billions to the Air Force for killing machines.

Kelli Mentzer
SPECIAL FRIENDS
People think it's funny,
and others think it's cute.
But it's different with us teens,
to us it's a dispute.

We fight over boys,
and we fight over friends.
But when it comes to love,
we just hold out our hands.

Friends and boyfriends are different,
different in every way.
Boyfriends you can depend on,
friends are always there.

People don't take it serious,
to us it's our whole lives.
Sometimes it's mysterious,
but we stay away from lies.

Teens in love are special,
special in many ways.
Sometimes it just depends,
on all our Special Friends.

Kristi L Kief
LEAPIN' LIZARDS
Leapin' lizards,
Terrible lizards,
Where did they all go?
It's baffled all the powerful wizards,
And scientists want to know.

Mosasaurus, Stegosaurus,
Ankelosaurus, too.
Wierdosaurus, Whatosaurus?
Oh that will never do.

Paleontologists dig them up,
To see what they will see,
And put them in museums,
For all the world and me!

Ellen Bratcher

Ellen Bratcher
THE PERFECT MOTHER

To my only child and son, Chris.
With sincere love.

O Lord, I want to be
"THE PERFECT MOTHER"
The way you'd have me be
The way I ought to be.

But Lord I make mistakes
And sometimes I'm not there
When I ought to be.

So, Lord please step in for me
When I'm not there
When I ought to be.

Because Lord you know
I'm not perfect
And you can be there
When I'm not there.

Donna M Griffin
ALWAYS SOMETHING
Another ungrateful Monday
was finally over.

A mean storm was brewing up
outside.
No umbrella, as usual.

Large, freshly formed raindrops
beat my path to the car.

Sun magnified, humid-hot,
and no hope of air conditioning,
I had to crack the window—
just enough to breathe
but not enough to soak me.

While waiting, smothering,
at the always-red light—
a small, but perfect,
blossom blew its way into the window
and landed peacefully in my lap.

As if, Lord,
just to show me, there is
always something
to be thankful for.

Michele Porter
NEW KIDS ON THE BLOCK LIKE MORE THAN TO ROCK
Jordon is fine
Oh how I wish he could be mine.
Joe looks so sweet
He's the one I would love to meet.
John is so shy,
But he's an all around guy.
Donnie is the group's ham
But he's so calm in a jam!
Danny with his big brown eyes
and dark black hair,
He's the kind of guy that really cares.
Each guy has his own different style,
To meet them I would drive 300 miles.

Heather Ptaschek
IF I GOT THE CHANCE
If I got the chance
I'd lay down and die
Then no one else
could see when I cry
They couldn't hurt me
where I'm going to go
Who cares if I don't get
my one chance to grow
Wherever I am
I seem to be lost
If you want to hold
someone it will cost
Don't let people kid you
when they say life's great
The world is made up of those
people who hate.

Miss Joy Kabelitz
CHRISTMAS HOLIDAYS
The holidays are sharing
The holidays are caring
For other people around.
For there is much more sound
When the little kids come around.

There is excitement when Christmas
comes around.

For there are gifts to be opened,
And trees to get.
How could we forget
We have to Deck the Halls with lots
of Holly.
Fa La La La La.

Turkey stuffing,
Eggnogs galore,
Gravy for the potatoes,
And much much more

Christmas is a time for giving.
Christmas is a time for getting back.
Christmas is the time to remember all

the joys
And toys when you were just a kid.

Christmas holiday is here!

Ann M Koller
THE WINDS OF LIFE
The winds of life are strong;
do not get caught in the storm.
You'll find your life ripped to shreds
and your heart all tattered and torn.

The winds of life are strong,
but don't hide from it all;
sitting on the shelf of life,
just like a porcelain doll.

Use the winds wisely,
as if you were the leaves
floating gently, gently;
guided by the breeze.

Floating just enough
not to stir up any dust
and never sitting long enough
to gather any must.

Darlene Harris
NURSING HOME MOM
First a young girl playing dolls,
Then a teenager trying her wings out,
Then a young adult going steady,
Then a new bride, happily looking to the future,
Then a Mother raising her children.

That's the way of her life until,
The children grow up and
Mother isn't needed anymore by her children,
Then she loses her husband and gets old,
And her children don't know what to do with her.

The children say they have their own lives,
They haven't time for Mom anymore.
They worry about her living by herself,
They feel guilty but they have to do something,
So they find a good nursing home to put her in.

Then they think Mom is O.K. so,
They forget to visit her in the home,
Except for holidays and special occasions,
Mom sits there wondering what happened,
To her life and to her loved ones
And wondering if she is to end her life like this.

Marilyn Barnard Fritts
MOON GOLD
Touch the Moon, it's magic
that brings out the music
within each soul.
To share with others
and get to know
Love.

Deep within each heart
are mysteries untold
from memories of old
where dreams of future start,
tho not yet begun,
which may someday be done.

Oh, touch the moon
of mellow, magnetic, glowing snow-gold
and keep out the winter cold.

Touch the Moon, it's magic
to both
the young and the old.

June Begley Hern
AWAKENING
Dark lowering clouds
O'er cold damp earth keeps
Spring on
"HOLD" another day.
Earth's bright raiment waits
For sunshine golden glowing
And blossoms bursting.
The cardinal calls.
Sweetly invites a lady
His bower to share.
Warm rains to come
And loose the bonds of winter
With warm scented air.
And life stirs again
To move the plants and insects
To tasks of Being.
A neverending
Stream of life keeps moving with
God's Eternal Plan.

Ernest D and Berene Peabody

Ernest D Peabody
MEMORIES AND GRIEF

"Blessings to my beloved wife, Berene."

Let memories crowd in like hosts of armies,
like a cloud laden storm front moving in.
cried—hurt—haunted by what used to be,

bad with the good— exquisite
suffering is grief—it sears—it tears—
it enhances all sensations
to unbearable limits— mind
bounces like a
Ping-Pong ball from what was, is, and
can be—each room I go in closes
in on me with previous times as I'm
seeing them and how I felt
then—mauling
memories!

Deborah J Cottrill
IMMUNITY
I don't want a love that's bound
until death do us part.
I want a love much stronger
than death's chains are.
For if, after death does part us,
I am the one who is then a carcass,
I would not be happy to know
That to another you would go.
So sip from this poison with me.
Ah, at last, now I am free,
For you always said 'til death do us part
And though I'm immune to poison you aren't.

Gilbert Tremblay (mots-ferrant)
CHANTALAISON II
Tu es le Corn flakes de mes pianissimo matinaux à noeud papillon.

Tu es la chaux de mon encrier quand ma lucarne a mis son pyjama.

Tu es le ronron qui crénelle la nuit dans le zeste de laquelle je me balancine.

Tu es la penture migratrice à rotor ouaté qui dactylographie au miroir du val.

Tu es la sole que l'ombre de l'orme ne franchit qu'après avoir extrait des calandres de l'été toute l'élasticité nécessaire.

Tu es la soucoupe dans l'orbe de laquelle il ne cesse de neiger des framboises à roues à bandage et robe de mariée.

Tu es le dé à jouer dans les trous duquel on pêche en boutons de manchettes la crinoline à coups de locomotives fraîches rasées.

Ernest D Peabody
CONCERN
It certainly feels
So heartwarming friend,
When you are concerned
I can't help but win,
The fight for support
With a great big grin,
Our circle of faith
Give it a good spin.

Karen E Borden
CHRISTMAS SIGNS
It's this wonderful time of the year,
When all of one's family draws near!

The trees all in their decor,
People Shopping store to store!

The smell of pine and candles burning,
The anticipation of a child on Christmas morning!

The sounds of Christmas are also sweet,
Bells are chiming on every street!

The dinners are all being prepared,
But there's more to it, 'cause God, he cared!

He sent us a child on Christmas day,
His son to take our sins away!

That's why we celebrate Christmas every year,
The Christ child's birthday is very dear!

HAPPY BIRTHDAY LORD!

Richard P Baldi
AUTUMN OF LIFE
It always seemed amazing to me
How the leaves on the trees
Neither protest or assist
Their falling from the trees.

And in the autumn of my life
Would that I too
Neither protest or resist
But quietly and gently
Fall to the earth

Like the leaves on the trees
On a sunny and quiet day
In the autumn of life.

Mabelle Agnes Williams
CHRISTMAS OBSERVATION
Merry Christmas the Christ child reaches out to you.
What have we offered, did we lay a gift at His feet?
What has humanity done in over two thousand years?
Coming down through the centuries, on every page of history we have killed, raped and torn our world asunder.
Here we stand on the threshold of the twenty-first century with blood on our hands.
Is this the gift we lay at the Christ child's feet?
Some say we have made magnificent progress in medicine and science.
We have conquered outer space, put a man on the moon and returned him to earth safely.
All these wonderful things we have accomplished.
Yet the one thing we should have succeeded in we have failed.
How to live on this earth in peace with our fellow man.
Our Father in Heaven sent His beloved Son to teach us humility and love for each other.
It is time we looked back over the centuries to that stable in Bethlehem and let the Christ child touch us with His love.
Let the glory and wonderment of that first Christmas fill us with love for all men.
Hear again in our hearts the song of the Angels, "Glory to God in the highest and on earth peace to men of good will."

Carol Couture
TILL NON, TILL NON
Life but a breath
That passes through
Life is love
So precious, so new
Time holds no vengeance
Ticks on, ticks on
Love, live life
Till non, till non

Life like a breeze
That whispers true
Love but a flame
A torch, a jewel
Time holds no fancy
Dream on, dream on
Long, live life
Till non, till non

Beverly Davis
REMEMBER WHEN
Remember when we were
young and small,
We had no cares,
none at all.
Time has passed and
we have grown.
Our future as always.
is still unknown.
Our beauty is growing
just like a dove.
And our hearts keep
filling with lots of love.
Life gets harder for
us each day.
Now all we do is
struggle and pray.
So remember when we
were young and small,
When we had no cares,
none at all.

Deborah A Wilker
A WEDDING POEM
As you begin
your lives as one,
Remember your love
has just begun.

Marriage will need
your care at times,
Words of love
may not always rhyme.

But the work you do
will be worthwhile,
The love you give
will take you miles.

Sometimes it will be hard
to see eye to eye,
But love . . . long earned
is worth the try.

Kara Lee Genoway

Kara Lee Genoway
AS A FEATHER FROM A DOVE

As given to Tom Turner—Christmas time 1988—with love.

As A Feather From A Dove—
There Comes My Free Love.
Thinking Of Your Sweet Smile.
I Care—I Want To Embrace—
Feel Forever—The Warmth Of
You—
Surrounding Me.
Look At My Eyes—They Tell No
Lies.
Sweet Tenderness From My Heart.
Your Voice From There Is A Sweet
Musk To Me.
I Just Want You To See—
I Care.

Shannon N Boykin
ANGER
A fire burning in my heart
It doesn't take much to make it start
How it embarks, I'll never know
All it does is grow and grow
until I smother it in one attack,
I have to be careful, or it may come
back

What I am talking about isn't lethal
But it seems to have a strange effect
on people
It's an evil that affects this world
Every man, woman, boy, and girl
It causes us to do things
Evil, cruel deeds that bring
Sorrow, grief, and many others
It may cause us to lie to mothers

ANDER is what I am talking about
It is like taking the wrong route
You must look deep within your
heart
To tell those two roads apart
If only this world would try to talk
It would avoid a fatal walk

Bernice A Louden
YOUR WEDDING DAY
As you launch out on the sea of
matrimony on this day,
Be advised—amid the days of
calm—there will be storms along the
way,

However, with God at the helm of
your matrimonial ship,
You never need worry that it will
swamp or tip.

So, as you commit yourselves to each
other from this day forth,
Committing your lives to God, your
Captain, will add much of true worth.

He will keep your lives together on
the right course,
After you pledge to stay together for
better or worse,

So, as in years to come you look back
on this day,
May you remember it as being
special in every way,
May the love you now share,
Continue to grow as you nurture it
with utmost care,
May you have many years together,
May you experience little of stormy
weather.

Donna Gaylord
YOU
You do something to me . . .
Somehow you see when I just need a
smile
The touch of your hand on my
shoulder,
The truth in your eyes.
You know how to soothe me . . .
Just stimulate me with frank
conversation
I just want to hold you
When you need to cry,
Be there when you need a friend to
rely on.
For you've been there for me
I need no commitments,
Just knowing you'll be there
When I need a friend.

Biff Bowen
SCHOOL BOY
A boy is awakened,
by the warm touch of the wind.
Through his window
a life of summer begins.
The feeling returns
of bare feet and shirtless freedom.
Sleepiness leaves.
A warm wind is alive within him.

Karen Donna Jordan
(formerly Feder)
REBELLION
I'm tired of the rhymes
And the times when I stayed up for
nights
While the lights burned for hours
When the power of the thoughts that
were caught in my mind,
Overwrought with ideas,
Kept coming to the surface,
But the purpose wasn't clear,
And I'm fed up with lies
From guys who tell me how life goes
'Cause who knows how it is for me
If they can't see from where I stand,
And I'm tired that my mind's
perspired
So much that it glistens
And nobody listens.

Heather Kozlowicz
DIFFERENCES
Differences tear us apart,
We all feel we've been shot by a dart.

When people insult it gives great
pain,
But you know they must be feeling
the same.

You feel alone, and you become
scared,
You wish someone would be there
who cared.

Why can't we all just be the same,
Except each have a different name.

Debra L Dubina
SPRING LOVERS
I was lonely til a year ago
Then you stepped in my life.
I met you in December's snow
You asked me to be your wife.

It's set! the day! The wedding day
Tis in the spring of year.
The date's the 17th of May
So Mama, please don't fear.

My dress will be of all white lace
The bridesmaids will wear blue.
A flowing veil down to my waist
And soon I'll say "I do."

Down the aisle I softly go
Into a life unknown.
But unafraid of any foe
As I'll not be alone.

The marriage now is under way
The rings are put in place.
Two bands of gold, our vows we say
Then a kiss and fond embrace.

Together once more down the aisle
This time our hands entwine.
Our faces wear a happy smile
I'm his and he is mine.

Kimberly L Riley
LEARNING THE HARD WAY
You gave me a vision, of what life is
to be.
You showed me the world, what I
was to see.

You promised me love, said you'd
always be there.
To lend me a hand, to show me you
cared.

We walked through the days, never
rushing our steps.
We cherished our time, for the time
was well spent.

Then suddenly one day, you weren't
there by my side.
You were gone forever, but not a tear
did I cry.

I rushed through the day, by myself,
all alone.
Cherished our memories, although
my anger's grown.

Then one day I thought of you and
sighed a bitter sigh.
The long awaited sadness pierced my
heart, then I cried.

I cried for all the empty dreams, that
people have these days.
I cried because I had a dream, and
then it slipped away.

I cried because a love like ours, was
always meant to last. To endure
throughout eternity the present, the
future the past.

And although I wouldn't change it, in
my heart I know it's true.
A lesson learned the hard way, was
the price of loving you!!!

Denise M Smith
NIGHTWALK
As moonlit, silent skies shimmer,
telling tales
And the night beings are surrounded
in their veils
The cool breezes caress the brow of
the peaceful night
And a solitary bird exults in the
power of his flight

Footsteps crunching on fallen leaves
Pine cones falling, arranged like
sheaves
Moonlight glowing and showing the
way
One wonders why the night can't
forever stay

Creatures too fragile for the sun
Rule the night for time to come
And those so proud in light of day
Seek safety in shelter where they stay

When the air is damp, and crisp, and
cold
And the sounds of the night are harsh
and bold
Forever is longer when the world is
dark
When life is moonglow's single spark

The still is greatest 'tween night and
day
When silence grows as you follow
the way
And daylight falls in a single shaft
When you follow nightwalk's lonely
path

Rebecca M Gunn
UNTITLED
Oh I'm not scared of death,
I embrace it.
I hold it as a sacred tomb
of amniotic peace,
a sleeping, silent, secret nothing.
Pain is nothing,
Life is nothing,
just a fetal-perfect state
of indifference.

Arthur Carroll Mort
THE INSIDE STORY
A Bumble Bee was buzzing 'round
As bees quite often do;
And chanced upon a grassy field

Where lots of clover grew.
His heart was light
He hummed a tune
The day was bright and sunny.
He settled down to do his work and get a load of honey.
A Jersey cow was grazing near,
a careless thing was she
For in her haste to eat her fill
She gobbled up the bee.
The bumble bee was quite surprized
To be mistreated so.
His anger rose to unknown heights,
His spirits mighty low.
But it was warm and cozy there
He yawned and caught his breath.
And said, "I'll take myself a nap
Then sting this cow to death."
And so he settled down to sleep
And slumbered through till dawn;
And when he woke to get revenge
THE DOGGONE COW WAS GONE!

Todd Sands
SONG OF THE MANDRAKE
In the midnight hour
The mandrake sings
A song of paradoxical wonder.
Its voice is clear,
Yet silent.
The black moonlight casts shadows
Throw by the bardic root.
It tells of horrid beauty
And the twisted truth,
Of 'good vs. evil'
And 'Law vs. Chaos'.
It laughs at sorrow
As did the Orb.
The mandrake's silent cry resounds
Inspiring genius and insanity,
And yet in its sound
There can only be found truth.

Michael Leroy Porter
ODE TO MICHAEL PORTER
From America's halls of fame,
There are his accomplishments.
To the wall of our nation's monument,
There is his philanthropic name.

From within the walls of the world's greatest libraries,
There are his writings.
To his college's memorial,
There is his great name.

From the palaces of Australia and England,
There are evidences of his poetry.
To the museums of Chicago,
There is his musical gift.

And from his scholarly writings and effective teachings
At universities,
To the pavement of Hampton, Virginia, there is his name in immortality.

Menze Heroian
SELF
I see the sun rising;
it looks like a big yellow eye
swimming in a pool
of blue water.

I am the sun.

The sun is at full height;
I am afraid of the day ending.
What am I?
I am this. I am not that.

The sun sets in the grey horizon,
shooting darts of red and yellow light.
I see its silence
in the black east.
Come to me,
cover me with your darkness.

Robert L Stevenson
TO MOTHER
On this day I wish for you,
That all your dreams might come true.
For many years (it seems to me)
You've lived the dreams that others see.
First your parents, then your mate,
Then your kids (with whom you rate).
Now it's time for you to live,
For you to get instead of give.
And now once more to you I say
(and repeat it every day)
May you start each day anew
And may all your dreams come true.

Annamaria Scuderi-Adams

Annamaria Scuderi-Adams
YOU

This poem is dedicated to my one source of inspiration, my husband, Charles R. Adams II. I'll always love you Chuck. Love Anna.

I love the way you make me feel,
I keep asking are you real?
These feelings that I have you see,
are all because of you and me.
The way the sun glows in your eyes,
makes me feel all hypnotized,
and I think of you know this to be true, this is
all because of me and you.
When you were
being thought of, God made his master plan,
to bring into this world, you one terrific man.
I haven't told you lately of how you make me feel,
and I know now that you must be real.
I couldn't understand then, but now I guess I do,
GOD must have made me
especially for You.

Virginia M White
MEMORY LANE
Countless hours on the clock tick by;
A Family Bible and a picture album on a dusty table, lie.
An old man, with graying hair;
Rocks slowly, in a rocking chair.
In the light of the fireplace;
You can see wrinkles of old age etched on the old man's face.
In his hand, he does hold;
A wedding picture framed in gold.
From his eyes, fall many a lonely tear;
Upon the picture, which has yellowed with every passing year.
On his face, for just a moment passes a smile;
As fond memories embrace him for a short while.
The picture of the Bride's face;
With a withered finger, does adoringly, trace.
In his mind repeat the traditional words, "Till death do us part";
Loneliness overcomes his grief stricken heart.
The picture, he puts on a nearby stand;
For just a moment, the light from the fireplace reflects on the gold wedding band, and still to this day wears upon his hand.
Slowly, he gets up and walks away;
Tomorrow for him is yet another day.

Frank Hudson
OUR DEMISE
Deep in a river of sorrow
Drowning in a sea of despair
I dive to save your soul
But mine's already there
Cursed by the knowledge of our demise
We pray for integration
While staring in the eyes of death and segregation
In the end the universal color is grey
But they're still not satisfied
For as long as there are subtle differences
Hatred will burn in love's eyes.

Roy Lee 'Simon' Jarmon
I HAVE NOTICE IN YOU
I have noticed in you
a sink of uncertainness.
I have seen in you
a tower of turmoil.
I can see that men
have made your life a mess
with their slick, smooth lines—
slicker than oil.

I have noticed in you
a passiveness unbelieved.
I have seen in you
a passion not unfolded.
I can see in you
what makes me quite relieved;
and lying beneath
a story yet untold.

Debby K Sanders
SERENA'S
Full of wonder and life,
A child should stay.
There is so much in the world
To see, to enjoy, and to do.
Take the time to see it all,
Share it with others.
Look for rainbows everywhere,
And golden sunshine.
Watch butterflies dance in the wind,
Listen to robins sing their song.
Magic is in everything you see,
And dreams come true.
Don't be afraid to dream and hope,
It can come true if you try.
And never be afraid to love,
Love is special and comes back to you.
So be a child forever in your heart,
Laugh, dream, hope and love.
The world is your playground,
And there is magic in the air.

Doris L Burleigh

Doris L Burleigh
SEVEN SEAGULLS
I was strolling in sandals along white shores,
Feeling sea breezes teasing my hair,
As seven seagulls appeared in the sky,
Each held a leaf of everyday life!

First sea gull held a heart shaped leaf,
Love was the theme glowing in red,
As the second sea gull soared so near,
A white leaf shaped as a dove,
Could only mean peace within our lives!

Our third sea gull making with haste,
Held a leaf looking like a child,
A child means a loving family,
Which our God had always planned!

This fourth sea gull came flying high,
Holding a leaf shaped as a book,
A book of learning for our lives,
As the fifth sea gull was hovering so near!

The fifth sea gull gave me a sight,
A leaf of honor—he held so tight,
To be honorable in all we do,
Will bring hope as a special treasure!

This sixth sea gull came diving so low,
Holding a leaf shaped like a hand,
A hand to the sick and a hand to the needy,
Shows loving care is very special!

The seventh sea gull came sailing about,

Holding a leaf of work and pleasure,
Bringing a balance between the two,
Giving a meaning for every day life!

Esther A Araujo
THE BACKDOOR

To the guy with the hat . . . I have now gone from sinking trance to full traumatic shock.

Mesmerize my every thought
Against the backdoors of the mind
Rustled up, like a pile of leaves
Carelessly waltzing, back and forth.

Autumn sunshine . . .
Nature's blooming flowers,
Greeted each other at the backdoor.
Emblems of a young lad with a hat
Looking straight at me—while he enters
Unbelievably he embraces me!
Clouds begin to disperse
Creating visions in the sky
Inside the endless roads, within the backdoors of the mind.

Dorothy E H Miller
WE ARE LIFE AND MYSTERY

To we who are life and those who are history (To believe is to be.)

We all want reasons for difference of seasons
We look to the source, good idea: of course

Why do we believe in Santa, tooth fairy and Easter bunny
What we read, hear and see, story or tale sad or funny

Where do we come from, where do we go
There is a God, but how do we know

To enjoy our fantasies, our make-believe of life the mystery

It helps to realize, and understand, we are life and history.

Joseph Wright Griggs Ed D
"SENSITIZING" THE SENSES

To my Dad, Dr. Joseph R. Griggs, who taught me to "sensitize" the senses!

Though most can "Look," the few who "See,"
Keep "Mind Eyes" open, pure, and free!
Though sounds "Impinge," the ones who "Hear,"
Have an "Unbiased Inner Ear!"

Though one discerns a "Taste" or "Smell,"
By "Touch," a texture, he can tell:
If "Love" is to be "Maximized,"
All "Senses" must be "Sensitized!"

For though Eyes, Ears, Taste, Smell, and Touch,
Are all "Is Place:" they don't mean much;
Unless, we See, Hear, Touch, and Feel,
Each person's "Pain," then, help to "Heal!"

Simon Gan
THE ACT

To my family and Mary Hodges my English teacher.

You have made a difference to the world.
May each good day receive you in graciousness,
May daily providence comfort you with tenderness,
May the omnipotent goodness chasten the world.

May all that is be virtuous in integrity,
May charitableness be your life.
Let destruction befall all envious strife,
That everyone may live in truth and simplicity.

Mary E Rocco
DILEMMA

In memory of the innocent unborn whose lives stopped due to a choice called abortion.

Just yesterday,
My heart beat.
Just yesterday,
I had hope.
Because someday,
I will say:
I can smile! I can sing!
I can hear! I can see!
I can touch! I can feel!
I can smell! I can cry!
I am in love!
But today,
I despair.
For today,
My heart stopped.
Because tomorrow,
Is gone.
My mom
chose
to rid her body
of me.

Bruce L Rook
THE RIVER

To My Mother Verna K. My Wife, Mary Ruth, And My Good Friend Theresa Ann Fong.

Down from the north rolls a mighty river,
twisting, muddy, taker, giver,
writhing, turning, churning, grinding,
southward, ever seaward winding.

Atop the water yellow foam,
Beneath the surface
sandy loam. Endlessly at the shores
keep chipping. Southward,
ever seaward slipping.

Desolate snags and sandy beaches, touching all with its mighty reaches. Past cities silently sleeping. Southward, ever seaward sweeping.

Onward, forward, relentlessly rolling by tiny villages with church bells tolling. Over sandbars crumbling, sliding. Southward, ever seaward gliding.

City, farm, mansion, shack,
current rushing,
current slack. Island, highland,
bubbling, boiling, southward, ever
seaward toiling.

Rounding the bends in the morning sun a golden serpent on the run. Past the dikes, slowly turning, southward, ever seaward churning.

Faster, eager, of unbound flight, like a brilliant burst of light, a thousand fingers spread wild and free the Mississippi has reached the sea.

Bruce L Rook
SECRETS

I have a secret that I keep,
In the dream-time shadows of my mind.
A secret of someone special,
Of someone gentle and kind.

I have dreamed of her across the years,
Does she ever dream of me?
I have been a slave to a thought of love,
Will she ever let me be?

So I dreamed and dreamt and spoke and spake,
But she only smiled at me.
I would shudder and shake and at last awake
If only my heart she could see.

On a starlit night in a moonlit dream
She finally spoke to me.
Her voice, her voice, her beautiful voice,
It gently set me free.

You are the secret I have kept
In the flickering blue shadows of my soul.
You are the secret that I keep
That makes my life feel whole.

Lonnie Thomas
THE ANNIVERSARY POEM

This Poem was written for my wonderful husband. Our Love is as strong today as it was then. Arthur, I love you.

When I remember the first time we dated;
I know on this day our Love hasn't faded.
When I remember the first time we made Love;
It still sends me higher than the clouds above.
When I remember our first I Love You;
We were so happy could this all be true.
When I look back on those first times we shared;
I know on this day you will always be there.
Today is our day dear to Love and to share;
Those first times we had without a moment to spare.
For this is the day you made me your wife;
Just nine short years ago we two share one life.
And with each year it gets still better;
For this I know we will stay together.
For better or worse till one parts from this earth.

Denise McGinnis
WE ALL HAVE PARENTS

Dedicated to my parents, Gene and Judy McGinnis and to my sisters, Rhonda Nesse and Debra Loomis. For all the friends one might have in life, family never changes and is always there. Thank you for me.

We all have parents
and wish days we didn't;
Someday we hope they will understand
we need to be on our own.
Looking out for ourselves
learning the world alone,
Seeing it a day at a time.
Hoping when we fall
they won't be too hurt
to pick us up and point us in the right direction.
And if we fall again,
maybe watch us a little closer.
Wishing they could see the tears
hiding in the corners of our eyes.
Seeing something is hurting
help us silently
Not wanting to see more tears.
Wishing they could read us,
like the newspaper we
often find them behind.
Knowing they will make us smile
when all else has seemed to fail.

Jolie Ross
FOR YOU

This poem is dedicated to my husband and best friend, Wade. It was written prior to our engagement. He was worth the wait.

Love, I hope that someday
We can share more—build a life together
Perfect, certainly not
But there to fill
Each other's hearts
With love and laughter
Understanding and friendship
I wish these things for us, love
For my heart and mind
Feels an instinct
That we're right
Even when we're wrong
That we're strong
Just as we can be weak
I will wait for you, love
With my understanding,
Patience and desire
For as I have learned to love myself
I have seen the truth
in love
and you.

Frances Landis
LITTLE WHITE ANGELS

To my two beautiful young daughters and granddaughter who had such a short time on this earth and is now with our Lord.

Church Bells rang out for two people in love,
Soon they bought a cottage, blessed from above.
Then came the baby they'd planned for—with so much care
A sweet little girl, whose love they could share.

They gave her the doll she had wanted so much,
But it lay on the floor, alone and untouched.
'Til one day the doctor told them, what they feared was true,
That Little White Angels, wanted her too.

As their baby lay dying, she looked up at them by her bed
They knew time was giving out, as they kissed her and said,
"Darling, don't be frightened, close your eyes—God made so blue,
'Cause LITTLE WHITE ANGELS, are waiting for you."

As she smiled for them through the pain and the tears
They thanked God she was theirs for even a year.
While each day they watched over her, they tried not to be blue,
They knew LITTLE WHITE ANGELS, wanted her too.

Sharon A Fisher
SEPARATION

To Geraldine and William without whom I wouldn't be,

To Eugene, who set me free.
To Andrew, my husband, to whom faithful and devoted I'll always be!
It's not that I don't love you,
It's not that I don't care,
I just want to be my own person,
It's something I've never dared!

If my love,
your love,
our love . . . should fade out;

My marriage,
Your Marriage,
God's marriage . . . we shall not flout.

Things we've shared,
Things we've dared,
Things that have made us a pair;
I should,
You should,
We should . . . never despair.

Diane Morse
WAKE UP

I dedicate this poem to the human race. For their belief in Love, Peace and Freedom.

Wake up wake up, your mind to see,
The prophecy claims, the human race will be free.
Wake up wake up, the spirit has come,
It falls from the heavens, for each and everyone.
The moon has reached the seventh house they say,
And Jupiter aligned with Mars that day.
So PEACE will guide this planet now,
And LOVE will steer the stars somehow!

So wake up wake up, join in the one,
Find out who you are, find out why you've come.
Wake up wake up, connect to the whole,
Together as ONE, is life's very goal.

Feel the PEACE, from the heavens it falls,
Feel the FREEDOM, as we tear down the walls.
So wake up wake up, GOD'S here in full force.
To guide us to help us, with LOVE steering the course.

Lizzie R Martin
A POLICEMAN, MY FRIEND

I dedicate this poem to Pat McGowan, who was an officer in the police department of Palmyra, PA, who befriended me during a very difficult time in my life.

A police officer became my very special friend,
When a helping hand in my distress he did lend.
He was willing to be there with listening ears,
When I was lonely and feeling a lot of fears.

Even though I hurt him when I was feeling bad,
He forgave me and made me feel glad.
He showed me what God's forgiveness must be like too;
continuing to be a friend and never bringing up the wrong again to you.

He believed in me even though hope in myself was gone,
And made me feel better inside just like a new day's dawn.
I felt a lot of hate inside because a lot of pain,
But his friendship helped to turn my life around again.

Seeing his kindness towards me and others,
Made me want to relate the same to my fellow brothers.
He cared and went the second mile to help people in need,
God has made him a special person indeed.

The world needs more of people like him,
Who brighten up the human race when things seem pretty grim.
People like him who are willing to reach out and give,
Make the world a much better place to live.

Nikki Burkhart
PLEASE DO FORGIVE ME

Dedicated to my sister, Crystal.

I must have said I'm sorry
A hundred times or more,
I know you're tired of hearing it
'Cause I said it all before,
Sometimes my tongue just slips
And says things I shouldn't say,
I should teach my tongue this rule—
"I'm the Master! You obey."
When I say the things that hurt you,
I feel awfully bad.
When I can't control my words,
It makes me feel real mad.
So I'm saying it again,
I mean it from my heart,
I hope because of this,
We don't get torn apart.
I'm very very sorry
For all I did and said,
I'll love you forever,
To you I bow my head.

Lottie Ellen Roger

Lottie Ellen Roger
HOW ABOUT A HUG?
In April, my young pastor came to chat
He wished me a happy birthday and I loved that
When he read Bible verses and sang "How Great Thou Art"
I realized how much lately I missed that part.
He saw a photo of my children, each miles from here
I said we'd been together earlier this year.

When I learned he watched birds, like me,
I asked what one whistles, he said, "It is a Phoebe."
I said I'd show him, if he didn't mind the looks,
My hobby room filled with doll houses, paintings and books.
Then he said a prayer, and asked me that day,
"How about a hug?" which was a nice surprize I'd say.
As we stepped onto the porch, I pointed to my rose
Which last winter I was sure had froze.

Then he stooped and showed me a green sprout
Coming from the root, and I wanted to shout.
I cut the dead branches, cared for it that year
Till sprouts began to grow and buds did appear.
In June clusters of red roses bloomed all summer long
To remind me when I was 80 and shared a hug and a song.

Kathy Jarrell Sparks
MORE PRECIOUS THAN GOLD

To Jason, my son, and the love of my life.

If you get lonely
And feeling blue,
Listen to the wind
It says I love you.
If your sun simply
Refuses to shine,
Look to the clouds
And my heart you will find.
If you get discouraged,
If troubles won't set you free
Search for the rainbow
That's where I'll be.
For I have something
More precious than gold.
A love for life
It can't be bought or sold.
So, if you'd like to share
In these things and more
Take my hand, and
Together we'll soar.

Paige Marie Westover
WORLD OF LOVERS

To: Mom, Family, and Friends.

Down in the deep hollow there were two lovers who held hands in the autumn country, where the leaves were in brilliant colors.

They had no worries about what is going on in the world.

Not knowing that love was melting in the shadows and even in the corners of the world.

The love that they share would never die . . . like the other lovers of the world.

Kathryn DeHaven
LIFE IS LIKE WALKING ON ICE
Life is like walking on ice!
Is it thick, or is it thin?
Rough or slick, falling in twice?
Stay on topside, just don't drown!

Life is like walking on ice!
A challenge here, sorrow there—
Unbelievable accounts
Will be faced to settle where?

Life is like walking on ice!
Beware of those hidden traps.
Breaking through wrong spots ruins life;
Lose your own, lose success maps.

Life is like walking on ice!
Can be a slick trick to slide.
Should be ride for right not wrong,
With "mind-conquers-matter" guide.

. . . Face each day carefully, and watch for those cracks!
And thin ice!

Frank Druding
GREEK TRAGEDIES
Aristotle said, "The female
Reaches physical perfection
At age eighteen."
How sad it is,—
She is not a woman

Aristotle said, "A man
Attains his mental peak
At fifty-five."

How sad it is,—
His heart no longer cares.

Aristotle said, "In choosing rulers,
Prefer the good before the wise."
How sad it is,—
That neither seeks to rule.

O Chroic song!
O Terrible trilogy!
O Gods!
O Aristotle!

Shirley Thompson Chicholas

GARAGE SALE

In loving memory of Cleve Arthur Thompson, 1892-1969, the world's greatest grandfather.

Memories for sale.
A humidor
Fragrant with unused Prince Albert,
And nine stem-chewed, bowl-burned,
smelling-salts-strong pipes.
A fishing pole
Its hooks, child-proofed, anchored to
the line on its reel.
A shovel
Its handle, cracked, rough and
bleached;
Its blade worn thin.
A red, plaid, mackinaw jacket
Rounded at the shoulders, unwilling
to free the form it had warmed so
many years.
Two pairs of boots
The heels worn on the outside edges,
smelling of barnyard dung . . . and
devotion.
A barbecue
Where chicken, brushed with BBQ
sauce and repeatedly turned, had
cooked only days before.
All worthless, yet priceless
Purchased with the minutes of every
loving day.
Carried away by strangers
Leaving life's storeroom cold, damp,
And never quite
So empty!

Janette P Harvick

TAKE MY HAND

To my wonderful husband, who gives me encouragement to keep on with my writing.

Come take my hand, love,
And walk with me
Let's link our hands, please,
'Til the way we see.
Fill up my heart, dear,
With sweet melody—
Just take my hand, love,
And walk with me

Come stand by me now
And through the years.
Help me to see, love,
Through the smiles and tears.
The pathway yonder
Won't seem quite so long
If you'll take my hand, love,
'Til we've come home.

Kyle Freeman

PARADISE VALLEY

Traveled one thousand miles have I,
Standing atop this mountain I find
myself wondering why.
Looking east is that the love for
which I pray,
To the west I know land's end is not
far away.
And down below just think of what I
see,
Painted deserts—and many a fruited
tree.
Traipsing among the sahuaros such
beauty to behold,
Native villages unchanging as their
ancestors of old.
By a steam I would cool my thirst,
Thinking of my loneliness I am
startled at first.
Wishing the reflection might be two,
My emotions are surely one shade of
blue.
The magic of these lands may as well
be cold empty ice,
For without the lady by my side this
will never be paradise.

Larry D Smith

(INTRIGUE)

To Cindy Marrow who inspired my writing.

Her eyes were so big and sad
Like the dark of night
Trying to reach out and say
Come closer for I will not harm you
With a little twinkle in her eye
As he comes into my web
My stare hypnotizes him
Then I move a little closer
Still he is not hypnotized
not a move
Then I inject my poison into him
Then he's mine forever
Little do you know
I'm the black widow spider.

Robert M Seymour

TIME

To Amy, my love and inspiration.

Time
An endless sea 'pon which we flow
No beginning
No end in sight
Just here and now
Just you and I
Our love and
The words which need no voice
There need be no yesterday
For us only tomorrow
Enveloped in the velvety firmament
Assured a place here and hereafter
Together forever, love everlasting
Transcending the distance between us
Should the night ever darken
Or the reaper loom near
Fear not
For I will be there
In death as in life
To hold your hand
And draw you close to my soul

June Maria Triana

DRENCHED TRAVEL

Flat liquid succumbs to gravity,
Channels of rust colored water,
Drain to overflowing grates.

Pools of future buildings,
Abandoned trucks and lonely beams,
Clay molded to fluid rock marred by
tire scars.

A solitary hitchhiker dressed in trash
bag garb,
Carries a sign that reads just "MOM,"
I pass, for dry desire surpasses any
guilt.

Blackened bark adorned by pale
foliage,
The death of unfortunate blooms,
Thrashing windchimes singing eerie
chorus.
Cotton covered elevations,
Abodes straining for a view,
Flaming lumber, rising smoke,
perfumes the atmosphere.

A glistening trace of sun's embrace,
Where clouds broke military
formation,
The promise of warm face, warm
hair,
I know I'm almost there . . .

Charlotte Edwards

THE ROAD TO FRIENDSHIP

As if by accident our lives entwined,
Ignoring distances and time.
Just by chance I stopped to ask
Directions from a source.
Having asked and like received
We joined and gently strolled.
We spoke of light and livelihood
Shrouding each with dailiness
And inflictions of the past.
From sparks of kindred spirit
cloaked,
A friendship flame was kindled.
Balm upon the weary soul
Our soothing laughter salved.
Sharing moments full of wonder
Amazed at likeness found.
Parting came a bit too soon
And ready we were not,
To leave the road just traveled
To leave a friend behind.

Adina Chaya Shulman Levine

LOOK AT THAT

Look at that, there goes a car.
Look at that, here you are.
Look here,
Look there,
Look everywhere.

Look at that, I'm in school.
Look at that, I know the rule.

Look at that.
Look at this.
It is fantastic.

Look in sunset and look in sunrise.
Don't say you can't, Use your eyes.

Brenda A Nightingale

STEPPING STONES

Use each day as stepping stones,
try to see the value thereof.
Know you're guided through good
and bad,
by your Father from above.

The goodness shown upon your life,
is through His love and grace.
And when you're tried, by fire you
grow,
teaching the things you must
face.

Do not stumble on these stones of
life,
they're not meant for you to
fall.
Instead, use them for stepping up,
bringing you closer to His call.

Katharyn S Damon

MY CHILD WITHIN

Too young to understand grown-up things, silently crying for the innocence that was whisked away before she had the chance to give it freely

Hiding inside herself, never daring to let anyone know her secrets, too full of shame to trust, to tell.

Feeling dirty, feeling lost.

Forgetting her own identify, she grows up a stranger even to herself.

Who is she? This non-person. She doesn't remember. The pain so deep even the memories of her young self misplaced and forgotten.

Frightened and insecure, she never lets anyone know the real person behind her masks. How could she when she will not even allow herself to remember.

45 years go by and the volcano finally erupts and spills over, its lavae speaking loudly, telling her to go back, remember, and relive old horrors.

Like the excavation of old bones, she digs up the memories. She remembers, she cries, she tries to release all the old hurts.

And suddenly, beneath the rubble, she finds the lost child of long ago. Hiding, but waiting patiently with outstretched hand. With hope in her young eyes we embrace and I tell her . . .

Hush baby. I'm here. I'll protect you. I'll love you. I'll comfort you. From me you'll get the unconditional love that you deserve.

For I am the only one who can give it. For I am you and you are me. For you are my child within and together we are one.

Jeanette Wickersham

HEALED

Dedicated to Jerome Edward Sather, the inspiration of my poetic beginnings as well as many painful and pleasant memories, and to all others who find themselves in a world torn between hanging on and letting go

The pain is gone.
There are no more tears.

I've let go of all expectations.
I no longer hang on to any hope.

The phone still rings.
I continue to respond.

I still love,
but now it's different.

Maybe this is now the love of self-
respect.

I have survived.

I am no longer obsessed, preoccupied, addicted.

Again I have survived.
Survived what? Survived loss,
survived self—the loss of self into
another.

Jimmie Jeanne Rohrer

MY BEST FRIEND "SAMANTHA"

I had to give up my best friend today.
I have to wonder if the pain will go
away?

All the joy and laughter she brought
to our lives.
We'll never forget the sparkle in her
eyes.

She will be free of her pain at last.
She'll be able to run and play as she
did in the past.

So, run, old girl, with the wind at your back,
there won't be anything that will lack.

Now run through the woods, so wild and free,
and see all the sights that you once could see!

So, I bid you farewell with tears in my eyes,
and I'll think of you when I look to the sky.

And I know God will keep you in the palm of your his.
Goodbye, Samantha, my dog and my best friend.

Daniel Achterberg
OH LITTLE KITTEN
Oh little kitten, I love you so.
Want to go out and play in the snow.
We'll build a snowman and a fort too,
Oh little kitten, I do love you.

samantha r hisel

samantha r hisel
LIFE

This poem is dedicated to my Great-Grandma Coke, who has enjoyed 93 years of life and still going.

life is life we must go on
one day at a time day turns
to night as night turns to day

as a day comes to a new day
that new day is a new
part of life

so life is life but as a
new day comes we live a new
part of life

Raeanna L Hays
HEAVENLY TRIP
Along I go down the paths of righteousness, stopping to wonder why I picked this road out of many others, such as temptation, glamour, fame, richness, and poverty. As I walk, I hear the angels singing to the Lord. I see before me a light that shines forever with his love. I see behind me a darkness forevermore with evil. I know that it is time for love, a time for hate, a time to weep, a time to cheer, a time to be born, a time to die, a time to kill, a time to heal, a time for God, a time for Satan. As I walk, I hear the voice of God say to me "I have chosen your time to come with me." I take his hand, and he leads me to his kingdom.

Leah Beth Tomanek
UNINTENDED CONCEIT
My eyes
Closed in the night,
Blocked out the star light.
    My dreams
    Are of more imagination,
    Than any constellation.
My thoughts
Though aren't very colorful,
The small variety of happiness and peace is always beautiful.
    My mirrors
    Don't contain vanity,
    But hopefully, through friendship,
    on the inside I'm pretty.
My style
Is to always be kind and happy,
And always know that somewhere it is sunny.
    To know me
    You must step inside my skin and walk about,
    You must look in to look out.
A good person
Is everything I try to be,
But only in my heart is there a rainbow to see.

Michelle Lee Myers
LIFE
Life gets so confusing,
And hard to figure out.
I'm growing up so fast.
What 's it all about.
Things change so quickly.
Time is flying by.
Sometimes I get so scared
I just want to run and hide.
But I know sometime, somewhere
Things will all work out.

Michelle Lee Myers
KNOWING WHO YOU CAN TRUST
I had a friend once
Someone, who I thought really cared,
but I was the fool,
for I was the only one who cared.
That love I felt,
I thought I'd never feel again.
Then I met you, whom I knew for years,
but never really knew at all.
I felt that love again.
I could feel my outer defences
Shielding my inner self.
For I was afraid, what happened before
might happen again.
I told her what had happened, and
She told me don't put all your
Trust in man, for man will fail you.
Put your trust in God.

Regina Kleweno
THE OLD MAN

Thanks to my mother for all her encouragement.

The old man stood calmly
by the water
The ocean waves crashed hard
against the rocks
He didn't seem to mind that the water was icy cold
It splashed and shattered
into various sizes of sprinkles
and drops
The ocean sang as it called to him

I studied his face—
his eyes
The two empty spots of grey stared out
Above the water
past the sun and sea gulls
Beyond anything visible to me

I often wonder if the old man knew I was there
Something told me to not disturb him
I shouldn't interfere
He never once looked away from
whatever it was he saw
But took a giant step forward
into an eternal peace.

Rhonda Callaway
IN MY MIND
In my mind, I see our past, as vivid as ever.
All of the triumphs and all of the difficult times.
All of the tender moments, and all of those long, lonely nights.
Our past, flourishing in my mind,
reliving every moment,
minute-by-minute, drawing me in,
closer and closer as I actually touch
the days of yesterday once again.
I see you. I see me. I feel the strength
I once felt. The everlasting love I had
for you that burned so deeply—
I thought it would never end.
I recall the quiet times, when we'd
hold one another so tightly, almost as
if we were inside each other as one
entity, strong and confident, perched
high, above the world, just knowing
that no one else could possibly feel
the way we did at that moment.
I remember all of the nights of tears,
wondering if we would ever pull
through, trying to hide our uncertainty and faithlessness, comforting
one another, bringing reassurance of
friendship and love.
Our hearts saddened, our minds confused—
yet our souls insistent and inseparable.
Striving on, in hopes that one day our
struggle would end.
So now we stand presently, troubled
times more frequent than few,
knowing that the pathway of our love
has come to an inevitable end.
Looking back, I wonder, was it all
really worth it?
Then I see your face in my mind . . .
smiling, and I say to myself . . .
YES!

Leatrice Hassell
MOTHER, GRANDMOTHER, MOTHER AGAIN
You spent your years, bringing up your babies,
With some tears.
You cried with them, dried them,
Laughed with them
Had sick times with them.

One day you say—I'll have grandchildren.
Did you know (that you'd be a mother again).
Your child is out there,
Smoking that drug, called
C R A C K

Can't take care of their own anymore.
Begging you to lend a hand,

What can you do, their lives are through.
Their purpose is to get more and more.
There's no time to take care of the babies.
Mother, Grandmother, Mother Again.
Where is it going to end.
Some of the babies are born with the drug in their blood.
So extra care is there,
For grandmother to cry with them,
Becoming a Mother Again.

Bud Masterson
A GIFT FROM HEAVEN

To Helen my faithful wife for fifty–two years

A gift from heaven
Was sent to me
A bright-eyed angel
Just five foot three
A true life dream girl
Can this be real
Just what I prayed for
She's my ideal
I'm really grateful
To them up there
For sending someone
So sweet and fair
A gift from heaven
A love divine
A gift from heaven
She's mine all mine.

Gladys L Hobock
INTO FULL BLOOM
Like a rosebud,
I was tightly wrapped
Just waiting for eternity.

Suddenly
    my eyes fluttered,
    my heart did stir,
And my petals
    began to unfold
    one by one,
    into full bloom,
    my love, for you.

Jeannine Whitney
A BUG CALLED HERO
So this is America
The land of the free
Heard it's one of the best places to live
Not just because a lot of people adore me

Do they really adore me?
Adoration can be painful if it is abused
But I guess everyone has a little masochism in them
Because it is by persons of all walks of life I have been used

Who will it be today?
An unemployed high school dropout?
A so-called TV evangelist?
Or a CEO who says he has a lot of clout?

I like entertainers myself
They pretend to be one thing and they are another
But I guess that is the purpose
One guy wanted a bite of me in exchange for his mother

They say I should be put to an end
What about the people that love to burn cash?
I shouldn't be blamed for their stupidity
Should rat poison and I clash?

No, but we all learn.

Cindy D Caldwell
THE MELTING SUN

Dedicated, with love, to Brian Keele

Last night
I saw a shooting star
and as quick as it appeared,
it was gone.
How I wish you were here with me now.

This morning
I felt a raindrop on my face,
and it was like a tear
descending from the heavens.
I was crying for you.
How I wish you were here with me now.

Tonight
I'll walk along the shore,
the wind replacing your touch,
and I'll wonder
if all we have left are memories.
How I wish you were holding me now.

Joy Marie FitzPatrick
I HAVE LOOKED FOR SO LONG

David, I have looked for you all my life and I'm never going to let you go. I love you with all my heart and soul. Love Forever, Joy Marie.

I have looked for so long.
You have come into my life,
But I am unable to touch you.
You are beyond my reach,
Yet you are so very near.
It seems as thou I have looked
for you all my life,
And now I have found you.
I am trapped with no way out.
I can see you,
Yet I cannot touch you.
There is a wall of glass
surrounding me.
I look for a pebble to shatter the glass,
But there is nothing in sight
Except for You!
Why can't I touch you!
Why can't I have You!
You have entered my life
And now I won't let you go.
I have waited too long for this!

Ricky Hodgson
SUMMER IN A SMALL TOWN

It was a balmy,
August day.
All of the parents,
Let their children out to play.
A little boy has a lemonade stand,
That he shares with his sister,
Put a dime in his hand,
And he'll quench your thirst mister.
An old couple,
Sit on a porch swing,
As they watch a child's kite embrace the sky,
So overjoyed that they begin to sing,
Of a time gone by.
There are smiles, never frowns.
When it's
Summer in a small town.

Barbara Came
FANTASIES

Formulated in our own minds,
Always from the heart, warm,
Never leaving us.
Tormenting, teasing, tantalizing,
All of our senses.
Secretly, stealing moments
In time, of love, and desires.
Ever haunting, hurting, harassing, our Souls.

Barbara Came
MYSTIQUE

Mystique I see, and feel within
You. As your eyes, and mind,
Study your subjects, your hands, convey your
Talents to paper.
Impatience I see, and feel, as you do not entrap,
exact expression.
Quietly, you toil careful to purview, a look, a
mood, a feeling.
Unselfishly giving happiness, to all that meet you.
Yet, you
Escape, any attachment.

Angela C Stringfield
UNFOLDING LIKE A BUTTERFLY NEWLY BORN

Unfolding like a butterfly newly born
in flickering dust in deep blue skies
My rainbows end in scampered chase
upon another hill doth rise.

Run abroad in sexton's fields
among the moonlit fiery path
this day I chase a love once lost
though underneath his hand of wrath

Sixty white horses, trampling down
protest forbidden star crossed dreams
Seeking yet another way to close
Fate's yet tempting gleam

Aching fever upon, the brow
of one past carrier's wanting ways
Tripping time inside the soul
in which the crack beside me lays

Isabel Rosa Martins Pvt US Army
NEVER GIVE UP

No matter where you are,
look above and find a star.
Never give up, never give in.
You can conquer, you can win.
Don't keep your feelings locked inside,
for you my friend have nothing to hide.
So, when you feel your world has come to an end,
Remember me, I'm your friend.
I'll be here day and night,
for you my friend, will be alright.
Just remember . . .
Never give up, never give in.
You can conquer, you can win.

Ruth Moulton
THE LION

The lion once so brave and strong,
with mane so thick and tail so long
now cowers in the underbrush,
two eyes intently watching us.

No longer as brave, nor quite so strong,
for man has stifled his wild song.
No fearless roar will he dare utter
to make the jungle quake and shudder,
for man has intruded upon his domain
to cage him on an iron train.

The eyes that once were glorious gold
are clouded with fear, not nearly so bold.
A terror now within him lies,
and a heart torn with sadness silently cries.

Perhaps someday man's soul will rage
to find himself in an alien cage far from all that he holds dear,
filled with anger, hurt, and fear.
Only then could he understand
the hell he's brought to the Lion's Land.

Paul Laffoley

Paul Laffoley
PENETRATING THE KITSCH BARRIER

Homage to: Immanuel Kant, Richard Wagner, and Plato.

The enlightenment
Sought the limitless sublime:
The dream of reasons.

Wagner in disgust
Screamed, "Unleash the unconscious."
Now bounded by kitsch,
The escape is by lucid
Dreaming: The reason of dreams.

Then the future will
be again the unity:
becoming-being.

Florence Feinzimer
THE STARS

For Sue and Ted, Michael and Ellyn, Judy and Jon

I wonder what the stars on high,
Are thinking up there in the sky,
Looking down upon us all,
Above the treetops green and tall.

They are windows clear and bright
Sending down their happy light
To us here, from up above,
Sending messages of love.

Do they know if the morrow
Brings us happiness or sorrow,
Or if little birds shall sing,
Spreading happiness o'er everything?
And so I go on wondering
When the skies are thundering
Why the stars don't shine for me
Down from the tops of the tall, green trees.

Kristine Vangeloff
WIDOW

To Martin Buresh, Ph.D. Thanks for the time, discount, advice and helping me believe in myself. By the way, although a line is forming, there's still time to adopt me. Love, Kristine

Legs feeling wobbly
Like a worn out rickshaw
Trying to carry me through
Another day.
Another day as bleak
As a drizzly winter night.
Coldness permeates my body
As I stare at the dying petals
Of a pale yellow oxlip.
The dying petals epitomize
The feelings of my soul
As I strain to hear your voice
And your silly, frivolous chatter.
But your voice keeps fading
Little by little
Until all I can hear
Are the echoing cries
Of my lonely, desperate heart.

William J Cover
A THOUGHT OF YOU

To my loving wife Glenda.

A thought is so beautiful when it's on someone you love
It consists of so many different feelings and places her far above
Above all the other women, who in your life you've met
This one special lady—who you'll never forget
You are this lady; who's in my heart to stay!
My thoughts are with you and I'll find a way
A way to show you just how much I care
To build a love which only we can share!
Close your eyes and you'll hear me say,
"I want you and need you—in a very special way."

Margaret Louise Morel
MAN OF MANY FACES

In loving memory, of my daughter and granddaughter Veronica and Temara Hagey

While passing through my life,
I came to know a man of many faces,
And like a book would unfold
To a curious mind, so has the life
Of this true love of mine.
He has been a brother, a father,
A lover and a friend.
Yes, I know this is a lot
for one life to hold,
But don't leave me yet,
For there's more to be told!
His eyes are as deep as a river is wide,
And so easy to read as his soul meets mine,
As we look deeper, we will see,
He's a mother, a sister, a husband,
a daughter, and a son,

But through all of these lives
His love has stayed strong and true.
For you see, he is GOD!
And he's even in you!

Elizabeth Perez
SEXDRIVE
I reach deep in my pocket
And pull out the key
To that magical kingdom
So many conceive
I turn on the engine
And carefully draw
An image of pleasure
Deep down in my thoughts
The motor starts running
And slowly begins
The burning;
The burning;
I feel with a kiss
A passionate fire
Shoots up in a flame
And slowly reveals
This feeling I . . .
It's coming;
It's coming;
The fire gets hot
Much higher;
Much higher;
Till I just can't stop
A mound of carresses
Come out in a cloud
I;We;
Are never found
Whispers of silence
That brought out this love,
And roads of tomorrow . . .
That we will drive

Tami Lasharia Day
DARK DREAMS
We speak no words,
When I look in your eyes,
Daggers are thrust at my heart.
How long can my shield
Deny the pain?
My body shivers;
Harsh words are
Whispered in my ear;
Nightmarish visions
Push from my mind.
Engraved on my heart forever.
Holding the descending knife
which makes a single wound.
Blood stains the ground around me.
Tears paint my face
as the pain subsides.

Christine L Johnson
WAYWARD AMERICA
The foundation
Built slowly and carefully with trembling hands
With many a hope the castle would stand.
Each heavy stone placed with care
Precisely in place without err
Hoping to build a mighty fortress
Standing forever
A symbol of might to all who look upon it.
And so it was
Until that day—dreadful and cold
The wind lashed about; the castle was old
The process of aging had paid its dues
And the foundation was weakening
As the storm clouds grew
And so it was that the castle of might
Was but a heap of rubble at the end of the night
The beautiful pillars
Lay cracked and dull—no sign of life
Save the screeching sea gull
The crisp ocean breeze tickled the sun
And the ruins still lie but a memory of one.

Gloria A Keefe
DANDY MCSAM REMEMBERED

To my dear friend Helen C Dwyer and to my dear niece Debra Carver Lovers of all animals.

Dandy, what a delightful puppy when you were young, frolicking, running and full of fun.

Now that you are old and gone, we miss you and frown, "did we do the right thing, should we have kept you 'til spring?"

Everyone we know friends and family almost demanded that you should be put to sleep, but I fought them in thoughts and words that as long as you could walk and eat and if you could talk and given your choice to demise in dignity, I am sure you would retort, "please my mistress and nurse, don't let me suffer, let me go in peace!"

From Grandmother Gloria Keefe

Julie Barker
LOVE IS LIKE
Love is like a river.
Flowing in the sea.
It was only created,
For you and me.

Love is like a piano,
Being played at night.
And that beautiful sound,
Makes you hold me tight.

Love is like a trampoline,
It has its ups and downs.
But like river flowing,
You can barely hear the sound.

Love is like another world,
Surrounding you and me.
And in that world,
You and I is all I see.

Amanda KC
THE COW'S OUTSIDE OR BUY THEM THEY'LL STRETCH
My shoes are right, they're made from skin
The cow got out, and I got in.

Outside, the cow once smiled so bright
He felt so good, his skin fit right.

Incased inside upon the floor
The fit is bad, my feet are sore.
I thought they would not make me holler
Especially at two hundred dollars.

Inside, my feet, if could, would frown
The hurt when standing up or down.

The cow's outside are now out mine
the switch we made is not devine.

My walk from pain makes people stare
Alas, I dwell in deep despair.

These new shoes are not fit to wear
I'll have to buy another pair.

Elizabeth Hayes
LOVE IS GONE
When love is gone
And all is lost
Trust is scarce
At any cost
When memories fade
But you still hold one.

Alleen Taylor
LIFE—GOD'S GIFT FROM 'BOVE!

Dedicated to all lonely ones who need a hug 'bout—now!

If you can
Walk World Read Dream Share
Talk Think Eat Drink Care Cry Coax
Tease Love Laugh,
CELEBRATE! THAT'S LIFE.
THAT'S LIVIN'!

Timothy John James

Timothy John James
STARS, FRIENDS, LOVE . . .

To everyone whose life has been touched by AIDS.

I have another friend in heaven tonight
one of many I shall miss on this earth,
but I am reassured by the stars glowing bright
that we'll meet again amidst joy and mirth.

The moon seems to guard all the heavenly beams
as I pray to the heavens above,
each glimmer holds eternal dreams
that we'll all be, one day, lights of love.

One day there will be no more pain
all will be infinite peace,
O what heaven and completeness we'll gain
when the hurting will finally cease.

I shall miss the smiles and hugs that we shared
and the warmth a good friendship can bring,
but we'll gain our reward for just having cared
and live again where the bright angels sing.

Jessie Hinton
DEAD BORN
To fall, dead born from the press,
With nary a breath drawn,
Never to know the life of shelf that
Harbors no dust save that fallen
From one days reading to the next.
Print, not to leap at exposure
To the light, the pages never opened
From lack of interest.

Still before birth but pressed
Forward in agony by authors
So concerned with self that
They fail to note the lack of life.

Birthed limp and cold and pre-destined
Never to be honored at a book burning.

No candles lit in heaven by its pages,
No fires of righteous interest—
Dead from the press.

Timothy John James
IF THERE'S A HEAVEN
If there's a place where the sky is filled with birds singing sweet melodies
and for as far as the eye can see, flowers are always in bloom where each day is bathed by a golden sun
and gentle winds make aspens quake
and each night is guarded by an orange moon

If there is a land that's as soft as a whisper and as fresh as a new-mown field of four-leafed clover that has a fragrance of lilacs in
Summer and brooks in which to play and lounge peacefully at leisure

If there is a parcel of land somewhere with a house that's a home filled with children and smiles and laughter

If pain and sorrow don't exist and joy is abounding
and love lives forever after

If no one gets ill or leaves us alone and worry has never a chance to invade the soul or the mind

If beauty can be seen with closed eyes as a warmth in your heart and people are permanently kind

If there's such a place, and I'm sure that there is
I know you are there and that peace has been found
When the time comes that I can see you again
I'll meet you at the gate, and you can show me around.

Susan Solano
TENDER, COMPLETE DEVOTION
Angel of the Lord, preincarnate Christ,
Came upon Jacob one star-filled night.

Jacob fought so well and prevailed
That the Lord changed his name to Israel.

Now, Jacob had reached 90 or so

When he reconciled to his brother, Esau;

The Lord had brought him over a path crossed by strife
But because of the promise, He had spared his life.

He was molded, encouraged, strengthened and tried
To a point where he no longer had sinful pride.

He humbled himself before his brother;
Jealous strivings they could no longer harbor.

The lesson comes for us today,
Do we have 90 years with which to play?

Do we have 20? Do we have 10?
Or do we have but the present with which to begin?

To begin a reconcilement with God and with our brother,
Submitting to God's holy will,
forsaking our own and others'.

God may take a lifetime to mold us for His purpose
But we can only seize the day, the very present moment.

To renew our souls in love and peace,
in joy telling God of our devotion,
tender and complete.

Maxene Gonzales
SORROW'S PRAYER
Oh my father please hear my plea
I come to thee on bended knee
I ask for strength to be alone
Now my loved one has gone home
Please wipe my tears and take my hand
Bless me with wisdom to understand
In sorrow's place grant me peace of mind
I stumble in darkness of the blind
Your great plan is not mine to know
I ask for help because you love me I know
Oh my Father please hear my plea
Take my hand until I come to thee.

Rajeanna Lorraine
THOUGHTFUL MEMORIES
Sitting here with wheels . . . turning
Along with them
In my mind
Thoughts of you are burning

Memories of the nights we spent
Replaying in my brain
Tears falling from my eyes
Like soft crystal rain

Lying in my bed . . . hearing
Words you so gently said
With no commitment running
Through my cloudy head

Feeling your closeness
Your kisses and
Your touch
Yearning for your love . . . so much.

Ami Neckanoff
FEAR
i fear that i will leave
before my time to go,
and fear that i will miss
what i am meant to know;
if that fateful Spring arrives
before the expected snow,
there is something
that you must know—
i love you . . .

Carol Ann Hirsch-Duffy
A CHRISTMAS SONNET

To Professor Floyd Barbour of Simmons College, Massachusetts who thought, ". . . if in time to come . . . this sonnet becomes required reading for the nation."

Comet, Vixen, Dasher, Dancer, Cupid,
Prancer, Blitzen, Donner, Rudolph, also—
"Christmas welcomes Santa"—Don't be stupid—
Saint Nick ain't no saint and Frosty ain't of snow.

Santa, fat and jolly, eats your cookies;
Rudolph's nose is red—once mocked, now worshipped.
Stockings crammed with lumps of coal by rookies;
"TOYS ARE BOXED AND WRAPPED!, shout elves, 'ALL'S EQUIPPED!!"

Eggnog, cider, turkey, ham and yams, too—
Christmas is overrated, overpriced;
Cram and ram and jam—'don't choke'—what a zoo!
Kissing under mistletoe—am I enticed?!?

Stockings, candy, tinsel ain't the reason;
Celebrate the birth of Christ this season!

Christina Broyer
A MOTHER'S LOVE

To My Mother— Elaine Carpenter 1942—1989

A firm yet gentle, guiding touch
You took so little, gave so much.
Tired but yet spurned by love
You gave enough to be proud of.

Even by yourself you tried
To give us all what counts inside
Now with a family of my own
I see the strength it took, alone.

Endless days and lonely nights
Separating wrong from right
Wondering if we would know
The love it took to help us grow

I know that love. I feel it now
And on the days I wonder how
I'll make it through—
I look at them, and then at you.

Three faces shining all aglow
Just like we were years ago
I feel the strength from down inside
I'll raise them all like you . . .
With pride.

David Enblom
AULD LANG SYNE
Auld Lang Syne.
Another holiday season come and gone.
The kids have grown and gone their separate ways.
We pick up the phone,
to say hello.
Filling our hearts with much joy and love.
Promising to keep in touch.
Looking forward to the moments,
when the kids travel back
to a place they once called home.

Michelle Quinn
LOVING ARMS
Hold me in your loving arms,
And wipe away the sorrow.
Hold me in your loving arms,
And we'll love like no tomorrow.

Touch me with your gentle hands,
And brush away my tears.
Touch me with your gentle hands,
And we'll love for many years.

Kiss me with your tender lips,
And fill me with desire.
Kiss me with your tender lips,
And set our love on fire.

See me with your green eyes,
And see the passion yearning.
See me with your green eyes,
And see our love is burning.

Hold me in your loving arms,
That's where I want to stay.
Hold me in your loving arms,
If only for today.

Candace Guthrie
THE SEASHORE

To Aunt Hilda and Uncle Donald whose love and encouragement is as constant as the sea around us.

Rolling ripples of water reach out to the shoreline,
then are helplessly drawn back to sea where they belong.
Minute pink flowers stand out by themselves,
from the mangle of briar and brush.
The sea gulls overhead soar in the cool breeze,
and call out to the peaceful world below.
Granite rocks wrapped in barnacles,
appear and reappear with gently crashing waves.
The tall marsh grass blows in the wind,
like the free waves of the sea.
A torn net waits for someone to come by,
and feel its rugged ropes and knots.
The pale yellow buoys, once bright orange,
guarding a man's net, now lay without purpose.
The sun sets relaxing all souls,
bringing this memory to an end.

Patricia L Von Tellrop
SPRING WILL COME
People all strive for one common goal,
Survival, in the best way and as long as possible.
Like the leaves shriveling on the trees
as autumn closes in,
The day inevitably comes when the leaves can hang on no longer.

As the tree loses its leaves one by one,
We also lose loved ones and friends until we alone remain . . .
Being the only 'leaf' left on that tree gets very lonely.
For what is the need for survival without companionship, without love?

The last leaf finally falls to the soil of the earth,
Joining other leaves that have fallen before.
The barren tree does not die, but only sleeps during a cold and dark
But brief winter until . . . a new
Spring arrives, new leaves sprout.

When autumn closes in on you, do not give up hope.
Survival is, indeed, a struggle and sometimes unkind.
If after the struggle, you start to fall, remember—
It is not the end, but only a brief winter sleep.
Spring will come!
New leaves sprout and gather together again.

Patricia Henley
THAT IS SO
Dogs bark
In the dark

Birds fly
Up, so high

Kittens purr
As they stir

Hens cluck
For good luck

Squirrels chatter
As they pratter

Doves coo
I love you

Pigs snort
They are short

Frogs pivot
As they rivet

Bunnys hop
They never stop

Ducks quack
That's a fact

Cows moo
Yes, they do

Horses neigh
And eat hay

Roosters crow
That is so.

Therese L Othoudt
LIFE IS FULL OF UPS AND DOWNS
Life is full of ups and fowns
Everyday something new is brought forth
Whether it may be awarding
or displeasing. One must face
the facts of life
Sometimes it may seem as though
you are riding high and other
times as low as the
gates of hell
Life is full of love, laughter, tears and pain
These are emotions felt each and

every day, by anyone and
everyone
People say God prepares us for the
best in life even though it may
be hard at times
We still strive to get
through the dark days
in search of bright sun rays
Life taken one day at a time

Patty Bonine Krueger
I'M A BIG BOY NOW
Put these on my little buns,
For I'm a big boy now
I'll try very hard to be grown up
And keep them dry somehow

You see, I might have accidents
But, I'm really very sweet
Be careful when you pull them down
Don't get it on my feet!

Some day I will be grown up
The girls will all say, "Wow!"
Put these on my little buns,
For I am a BIG boy now!

Julia A Brown
DEEP INSIDE

This poem is dedicated to my wonderful children, Angalesia and Claud—with love Mom.

Inside each one lies a beauty within
If you reach down inside and let
life begin
There's a kindness, a caring and
considerate heart
There's a love within if you let it
take part
Life as it seems may be miserable at
times
When you feel that way just reach
down inside
Then take that frown that you will put
in place
Go deep inside and let God take
His Place
That beauty I speak of is beauty of
soul
And that kindness I tell you will
never grow old
If you think for moment of positive
things
And wipe out those bad thoughts
and let life begin
Happiness comes from learning to
love
and sharing and giving the same in
return
It abides in me as it does you
Just reach deep inside and start
anew!

Julia A Brown
THE GARDEN
There's a garden that builds only on
love
Consisting of flowers with
spring-like buds
They bloom just thinking of you at
night
By my side 'til morning light

And in the garden I can see
The love that you do have for me
But it's alright I know you care
It grows about everywhere

All the beauty of the garden you see
I hold real deep inside of me
I'd like for you see for yourself
And I promise it'll bring you lots
of wealth

Not wealth from diamonds, emeralds
or gold
I talk about love that I do hold
There's so much in the garden you
see
To be shared just between you and
me

There's a lattice of box-edge filled
beds
and luxuriant colours of mixed
azaleas
There's primulas and ferns in
woodland glade
and there's a kingdom of roses to
make your day.

Open up and let the heart be true
Because I have a garden just
awaiting you.

Katie MacCaul
YOUR BOUNCY LITTLE WALK

With love to Robert Liam MacCaul.

your bouncy little walk
so clever and taught,

that curt little chin
when you're unhappy from within;

your laughter so bright
full of delight,

the hugs so giving
warming the living;

eyes sky blue
that twinkle and glow . . .

Oh! how they charm me so.

With sunshine in your face and a
trot in your gait,

you are the little boy
with the wonderful face;

To the boy named Liam
from the lady named Katie.

Kelly Smith
KITES
I watched the kites
dancing with the breeze.

Sitting on the ground,
I could feel their joy in flight,
bright and soaring.

Like me,
they wished for longer strings.
Bound too tightly,
flight was
frustrating.

Not knowing
just how the kites feel,
the little boys
running on the ground
are afraid to let out
too much string.

Their beautiful kites,
with the long streaming tails,
might just fly away,
to dance forever
with the breeze.

Marilyn Sue McClain (Warren)
THE SWEETEST SMILE
The sweetest smile I've ever seen,
was so peaceful and serene,
It was the day Dad knew his soul was
Heaven bound.
The love of God shone in his eyes, as
he looked toward the skys,
And we knew the Gates of Heaven he
had found.

I can almost imagine how he felt,
when he walked in,
From God's face the light did shine
and no Man walked in sin.
No one was deaf or blind and
everyone could sing.
No one was in a wheelchair and no
tears the eyes did sting.

Fields of grass so green and the water
was so clear,
And as he looked across them he saw
many faces he held so dear,
So if you could look down Dad and if
you could speak aloud,
And if you could find me in all this
worldly crowd,
I know you would say these things
and also much much more,
And if you're allowed Dad, ask God
if you might greet us as we enter,
Heaven's door.

Tammy Holt–Politano

Tammy Holt–Politano
NECTAR OF FORGOTTEN YOUTH

In loving memory of my father—Charles B. Holt.

I lift my cup
To childhood love
And drink deeply
of liquid brown eyes
Reflecting yesterday's dreams

Sweet, sweet nectar
Of forgotten youth
Mellowed by maturity
Slowly, subtly aged
To a vintage rare.

Lost years evaporate
In a familiar embrace
Knowing smile . . . soft caress
Quench my parched soul
With passion's bouquet

Memories elusive carafe
Savor slowly this nectar
Each drop a sweeter taste
More delightful than
a child's lips recall.

Dawn Marie Bowman
FREEDOM
Here I sit in my bed
Unable to clear my head

I close my eyes hoping to sleep
But lately all I can do is weep

This past year what does it mean
It all seems like one big dream

Life has just been so hard
Behind these big iron bars

I try and break free
Only wanting to be me

Yet something is holding me back
As the problems are continuously
being stacked

Yet as I look out my room with a
view
I see my life so new

I notice a rope
It signals a new found hope

Soon I will conquer these walls
And walk down a golden hall

To a new life
That finally feels so right

Yet as I look out my room with a
view
I see my life so new

I notice a rope
It signals a new found

Soon I will conquer these walls
And walk down a golden hall

To a new life
That finally feels so right

Tammy Holt-Politano
DADDY WOULD READ TO ME
When I was a little girl
Still on daddy's knee
He would take the Bible
And He would read to me.

His voice was soft and gentle
It held a magic touch
As He read those verses again
The ones I loved so much.

The angels must have eavesdropped
And heard his magic voice
They needed someone to read the
Psalms
And my Daddy was their choice.

Daddy always tried to make me
happy
He never wanted me to be sad
But Christmas Eve is so lonely
I really miss my Dad!

I would give up everything in life
Yet I know it can never be,
If I could just have Daddy back
So He could read to me

I treasure all He taught me,
Praise the memories I keep
Always remembering Daddy when I
say
"Now I lay me down to sleep."

Ann Marie Boles
ICE LIKE PAIN
It's cold outside—frigid like pain.
So cold, it hurts to try again—
tomorrow.
The icicles are heavy—on the
limbs . . .
Like arms.
They hang low from the weight . . .
Still they are patient.
The wind blows now . . . The
branches sway in pain . . .
From the frigid cold.
Quietly I sit knowing somebody
soon will warm the bitterness
within.
And the Sun will shine; the ice will
melt.
The patient limbs will once again
feel light and warmed . . .
By the presence . . .
The Sun, the birds, and nature
itself . . .
Will heal the PAIN.

Bob McCauley
"B.J."
A big, black, barn bug
crawled so silently, swiftly . . .
CRUNCH—the thrasher's turn!!

Gwendolyn Vasquez
LORD AND MASTER
You are within my reach,
And yet, I cannot touch you.

You are within my sight,
And yet, I cannot see you.

There is a great mystery about you,
Something so powerful and sure.

Who are you?
Does anyone really know.

My whole being revolves around you,
And yet, I do not exist.

Stephen M Arndt
CAT'S CRADLE

For Julie.

The cat in the box sits and rocks
Among the clocks in his little box
He lives in shame because he is lame
He's really very tame while he's in his box
He can't run away 'cause he knows not the way
He's wasting away inside his box
There's no one to see except You and Me
And The Nurse makes three here in my box
He'd just like to run out under the sun
But his life is done while he stays in his box
But without a doubt he wants to get out
And just walk about, outside his box
He sits there and cries as time goes by
He doesn't know why he's in this box
But one day he leaves and his family grieves
They thought he was pleased with his little box
But he got away, he just couldn't stay
For one more day there in his box.

The cat in the box no longer rocks
They've stopped all the clocks in his little box.

Christopher Williams
JUST AROUND THE CORNER IS COMING THE LOVE OF ALL LOVES!!!
One more word whistled before love's reservoir
steps through our door!
One more evil to conquer through heaven's wonder—
It's better to fight with the word as the thunder!
One watch awaiting us as truth's translating trust
comes elevating us!!!!
(Just around the corner is coming the love of all loves!!!!)
One morn closer to love's rest, which is the best to quest!
One night nearer to that great claim—
His face and His name!!!
By his glory we're changed!!!!
One more challenge to pray, dare to be saved to look for this day!
There's heaven and hell, look alive by faith in God above!
One more touch coming before Salvation's finish as such through
unspeakable trust!
Thank you Jesus!!!
One shout coming before the unshakeable only remains!!!!

Doris Blohm
DAYS LONG SINCE PAST
Sometimes when I'm alone and feel a bit sad
I think back of the days long since past
Of all the many good times and of course the bad
Of old and dear friends and friendships that didn't last
And also of other people I've met along the way
I think too of some old and special places
And wish I'd said the things I really wanted to say
And how much it'd mean to see some ole' familiar faces
Then there's the silly things we used to do just because of the yesteryear
quips and one liners that expressed feeling
That the things we wanted to do or become somehow got lost
Also of the old family radio that kept us rockin 'n' reelin
Being a coal miner's daughter there was never enough money
our clothes were mostly handmade and hand-me-downs
Even with all the hard work our days seemed long and sunny
And Sundays all our friends and neighbors made their rounds
Growing most our food there was always something to eat
That's the way it was then and we thought it'd forever last
But oh, today how everything has changed so within reach
Looking back even now seems like only yesterday and
I wonder how it'd be to go back to the days long since past.

Tonya Massey
NEW CHILD OF LIGHT
The sunrise was new so beautiful as on the day of a soul's rebirth.
Sunlight shatters the clouds of night
entering into recesses long forgotten,
awaking long dead emotion.

Every new breath a new beginning.
Every look compleat seeing every line.
Never again to search the darkness.

Doomed are the feelings of dread and death.
Now my heart and mind are next to the sun as light and knowledge
pour forth, to wash away my tears.

The sunrise is brought forth by a new soul.
—A New Child of Light—

Darlene Lamm-Pennington
TO BE AS MY GRANDMOTHER IS
Oh, to be of stature and mind,
To be so brave and yet be so kind.
To be a smilin' when everyone's cryin'
To be as my Grandmother is.

To be able to cook for a gross of men
To be able to clothe, when money is thin,
To be of rapture, when everything's dim,
To be as my Grandmother is.

To be loved by everyone day by day,
To be able to love in her own special way,
To be able to leave when people say stay,
To be as my Grandmother is.

"Sweet, kind, thoughtful and true when she's around, nothing seems blue."

To be so short and yet be so tall
To be so big when outward so small.
To be all of this, I'd give my all.
To be as my Grandmother is.

Janice L Engler
CONTINUED TREASURES
I saw you today, did you see me?
I felt your strength by the roaring sea;
I recognized your gentleness in a newborn's face;
I embraced your confirmed belief in the human race;
I celebrated your devotion at a neighboring church;
I marveled at your presence in the budding birch;
I reached for your kindness in the stars above;

I explored your wisdom regarding true love;
I welcomed your warming laughter in the sunny lane;
I cherished your fallen tears in the driving rain;
I heard your truth in the echoing thunder;
I stood quietly in awe of your ageless wonder;
I inhaled your beauty in a simple flower;
I tasted your justice in the one true power;
I acknowledged your passing with one perfect tear;
I respected the man who is ever so near;
I admitted your place is in eternity;
I saw you today, Dad, but did you see me?

Eleanor E Ertel
EXTENUATING CIRCUMSTANCES

To the honorable Herbert C. Kaplan.

I stand before your honor
Quite plain as you can see
To express appreciation
For your kindness to me . . .

I'm not a hardened criminal
No crime did I commit
Yet in this legal structure
Before you I do sit . . .

I know it isn't easy
To send someone on their way
But by their course, they made the choice
And now their dues they pay . . .

A mother's heart is with her child
But the law is over all
Practical wisdom is what we wish
That one not stumble and then fall . . .

May we walk in the way of good
Be blameless and upright
Find purpose and discernment too
Receive discipline, that gives insight

Not all see through the eyes of truth
For greed has dimmed their sight
The rod of correction they will feel
The weight of law and right . . .

May I enter, now, a plea
But not for leniency
A plea for all who love what's right
That length of days, for them might be . . .

Nicola Perring
L.A.

To Mum, Dad, Diane and Peter, thank you for your love. You all are the most important people in my life, Always, Nicola.

When life seems down,
and things are rough,
what can you do but smile,
and all the world seems upside down
and turned around.
What can you do? What can you say?
to those who pass and say
"What's wrong?"
You try to smile and hide that fear,
that nothing really is as it seems
the act, the wall, is all that's left.
In an ungiving world,
and uncaring place,
that sees and understands nothing.

Nicola Perring
LIGHT AND GOLD
I wander through the lonely streets,
the cool air of morning walking with me
the cobblestones reflecting my romantic mood
the age-old mystery of Paris enfolds me
I wish time would stand still to capture this moment
the timeless old buildings are sighing my name
their echo's singing with the larks & the finches
they're singing of love, sunsets & joy & "God bless you all;" & how happy we are,
to live in this beautiful city of ours,
I take a deep breath & I breathe out a smile
&now, right now, I know all is well
As I saunter off home to my slumbering hotel
"Sleep well world and may goodness abide,
in all of our souls for the rest of our lives."

Nicola Perring
P.T.
To a man who has so much to give,
to a star that shines so very bright, to
a personality whose expression is
comparable to none, a ray of sunshine
on a cloudy day, and a feeling in my
heart which no man will take away.

For all that I have to give and for all I
shall learn from you.

Jim Slagle
THE FOOL
I think very much like you
More than you would think
Expressing thoughts is where you have the upper hand.
I have spent my whole life arguing;
Arguing over my personal thoughts and beliefs.
And now I have chosen to remain silent
Many times now I have played the fool,
A fool for my silence.
Swallowing my pride to keep my sanity.
Always the suspicious one with something to hide
Never the outspoken one, only the observer.
Not by force but by choice;
Choosing to be happy for myself and my thoughts.

Zenaida Geraldo Hunt
THE REAL ME
If I can't reach you
Allow my words to penetrate in you
Let your imagination take you
Beyond each word is full of life,
love, tears, and laughters
For what my lips hide
My POETRY reveals . . .

Zenaida Geraldo Hunt
MY MOMENT WITH GOD
To my FAMILY whom I have shared great loss and sorrows

Dear GOD! help me to cope with the death of my Mother
Help me to overcome the grief and emptiness
I'm suffering
Help me to be strong physically, emotionally,
and mentally
Help me to understand the reality of dying
Please bring back the faith in me
And if I ever question your judgment
Dear GOD! forgive me . . .

Lori Hille
I LOVE YOU
I dedicate this poem to Cliff Phipps, For inspiring me in writing this poem.

When you said those few words my heart skipped a beat,
You're one of a kind unlike anyone I could ever meet,
Your smile is the sun cheery and bright,
Your eyes are the stars shining in the night,
I know I'm all yours when I'm walking by your side,
Being with you makes me never want to hide.
Your voice is so gentle
Whispering in my ear,
I'll always feel safe knowing that you're near,
I couldn't believe it I thought for sure it was not true,
My dreams became reality I never thought there would be a me and you,
I have to thank God for this whole great deal,
He answered my prayers and made my dreams become real,
That night when we sat there all alone together,
That night was so special I hope I'll always remember, When you whispered those words, "I love you"
And I replied, "I love you too!"

Harriet Lee Rankin
QUATERNITY PRANKS
Four doughty rogues assail my walls
(a ball of soot; a blob of sunshine),
and fill the air with raucous calls
(a wisp of smoke; a tuxedo fine).

Löwen walks with lordly stride,
picaresque king of his demesnes.
Meddlesome canines, run and hide
for the Yellow Peril prowls again!

Lithesome, green-eyed Soren sings
his jeremiad at my door,
then lightly to my shoulder springs
to whisper ancient feline lore.

Debonair Squirrel, with tux and "tail,"
white goatee and shirt and spats;
seduces the ladies without fail,
that veritable 007 of cats!

Black Merlin meditates alone,
a sinuous jungle beast is he.
From high atop his bookshelf throne
he blinks his golden eyes at me.

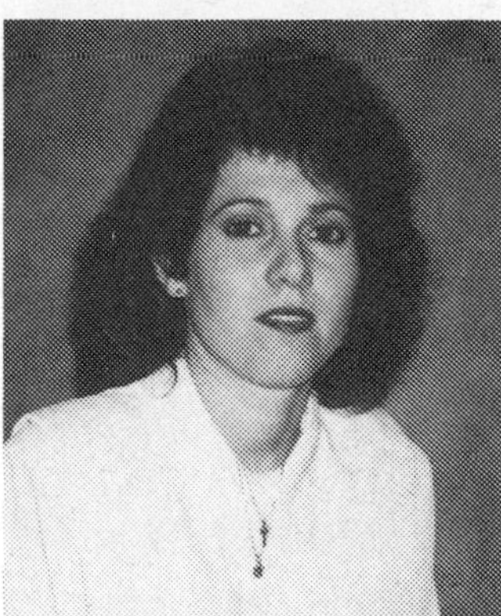

Carmen M Candelaria

Carmen M Candelaria
PRAYER OF PEACE
To Chanil, Kiki, Michelle and all my nieces and nephew whom I hope will work to make this world a better place.

Remember, remember the deaths.
Remember the faces, Oh their faces.
No anger, no cries just silent pain.

Remember, remember the day
August 6, 1945
Sunny and Bright.
Then came the blast that darken the sky.

Do we not remember. My God, man has created such wondrous things.
Open their eyes, open their hearts
Open their mind.
How is it possible that man has created to kill all human kind.

To our ancestors before us we gave the promise of continuance.
To the children after us we only give hope.
Doesn't seem fair.

Kneel, kneel down and pray with me.
Cry with me. Let our tears wash away our fears.
our hate, our despair.
Tonight I pray for the human race
Tonight I pray for peace.
My only hope that for all who see will also pray with me.

Remember, remember the deaths.
Remember the faces, Oh their faces.

Jennifer Ackerson
FORGOTTEN CHILDHOOD
Dedicated to my loving family, my friends; Michele, Jodi, and Rachel, and to my Literature teachers; Mr. Bouma, and Miss S. Vredvoogd. Thanks for all your love and support.

A baby doll lies on the floor,
A teddy bear behind the door.
Toy soldiers beat a silent drum,
No one hears their rum-tum-tum.
The model train lies perfectly still,
As do the plastic saw and drill.
A tear trickles down the china doll's face,
As she sits, forgotten, in her place.
For these things I no longer care,
With them my secrets, cannot share.
I feel too old for these childish things,
Tales of princesses, dragons, and kings.
It seems that growing up happens too soon,
No running in grass, or playing in dunes.
We're so hurried to mature,
We don't enjoy a whistle, a purr.
We should appreciate these things while we can,
Because paper dollars can't come alive again.

Stephen Barry Siegel
A WHISPER OF HONESTY
To my wonderful wife, Wendy

The maximum decades of sorrow—to moments of joy
The expression of love without knowledge of the meaning.

Fear, insecurity, jealousy, selfishness and hatred
Happiness, warmth, tenderness, trust and love
Complicated, enigmatic, mysterious, compromising—life.

Norma Ross Todd
GRANDMOTHER'S SPOON
I saw my grandmother smile today
As I stirred a bubbling stew,
I was using her time-worn tablespoon
Just as she was accustomed to do.
The spoon is worn off at an angle
From stirring many a bottom of a pot,
The bowl is pitted, silver plating half gone,
This old spoon could tell quite a lot
About a kitchen with the smell of heaven,
Hot bread from the oven and roasting hams,
About family traditions and warmth and love,
Piccalilli and ketchup and home-made jams.
I saw my grandmother smile today
As she did when she lived long ago;
I wonder if she misses this old worn spoon . . .
I will always miss her, I know.

Antoinette D Datoc
THE PELICAN
Do you know what's queer about a pelican?
His mouth holds more than his belly can.
Have you ever heard,
Of a thing more absurd,
Than that totilpalmate pelican?

Carla Deiringer
FALLING IN LOVE
This poem is dedicated to Kevin, my one and only love.

In the corner of my mind
Thoughts of you are kept
Locked away forever
Of the time we first met

Together we walked
Hand in Hand
To our special place
Hidden away . . .

Feeling the excitement
Our bodies trembled
Holding one another, oh so tight
Touching, caressing . . .

We Talked
We Laughed
We Cried
We Fell In Love

Laying back watching the
Water rush by
I knew then we would always
Be together
Lovers
Friends
Partners.

Candace A Murphy
DARK LUMINOUS CLOUDS
Dark luminous clouds rolling inward,
Reflect their power
Upon the foaming waters.
Their silent strength embodies itself,
Into the soothing whispers
Of cresting waves.
Blown about by the sensuous sea breeze,
Their melancholy tinge
Caresses this lonely heart.

Nancy L Clark
FINDING YOU
morning mist of long ago,
fogged my memory,
made it slow.
Running through that mystic air
i fell
i cried
i lost all care.
but now the clouds,
it's clear! They're gone
was this a dream?
T'was far too long
Oh morning mist has left my heart
unable to steal that little part
of the love I have for you . . .

Tonya Lee
WITH OR WITHOUT YOU
We meant a lot
to each other, once.
I thought sometimes
that I would never get over
that sad and empty feeling
that you left me with.

But I took one day
at a time and started
to realize I could make it.
I depended on you
more than I should have

that's why I thought my
life would shatter without you.
I kept wanting for it to
but it never did.

So with or without you
I know I will make it.
and the only person
I need to depend on is ME ! !

Ella Frances McDonald
DREAM OF PEACE
A dream took me by the hand,
And led me to another land,
Where everyone who looked could
find,
peace, long hidden from mankind.

For every heart was open wide,
With no place for greed to hide.
For greed must hide its ugly face
And usurps peace's rightful place.

Donald Stogsdill
BE A GENTLEMAN
My name is Donald.
I'm eight years old.
My dad says "Be a gentleman!"
But, I don't know how.

I do know how to burp and make fart
noises.
I know how to scream my head off.
I know how to giggle.
I know how to do summersaults
under the dinner table.

When my Dad takes me to a fancy
restaurant,
I burp and run around.
My Dad says, "Be a gentlemen!"
I say, "I don't know how!"

My Dad takes me to the movies.
I make fart noises, giggle, and scream
in the aisle.
My dad says, "Be a gentleman!"
I say, "But, I don't know how!"

My Dad took me to my Grandma's
house
To be with the clan.
Uncle Jim was there, and so was the
rest.
I burped for a minute—
I made fart noises—
And did summersaults under the
dinner table.
My Dad screamed "Be a
gentleman!!"
But I giggled and said "I don't know
how."

My Uncle Jim just smiled.
Later, I asked my Grandma—
"When my Dad was eight years old,
was he a gentleman?"
My Grandma looked at me and
Screamed "He didn't know how!!"

Phyllis Klock Plunkett
BEAUTY OF SILENCE
Listening to the silence,
As our heart is kept in tune;
In the quiet midnight hours,
Morning will be here soon.

My heart is filled with longing,
To see my Saviour very soon.
He is coming for His loved ones,
It may be morning, night or noon.

Is our heartbeat quickening,
Do we hear the gentle voice.
Beckoning to us to be ready,
Always to make the right choice.

What a precious time of fellowship,
With no hindrances like the day.
But a quiet sweet communion,
He always listens to what we say.

Night is quietly stealing,
Past the time of rest and peace;
To a new day quickly dawning,
A fresh strength He will release.

Angel Valentine
SEARCHING
Relentless introspection and
retrospection have rendered
my soul numb.

I sit in total darkness
hoping to grasp a glimpse
at reality.

But will this reality I seek
feed my hungry soul?
Give it shelter from cold
indifference? and,
Warm it with the raiment
of love?

Or will it never Come!!

But remain aloof with lighted,
burning candles of Hope?
Trying to guide my path?

And will this reality
annihilate into oblivion
the scars my angry, confused
existence has endured??

IT MUST!!!

Ernie Pisacane
MY SECRET PLACE
There's a place I call my own
That no one else can see
Where I spend my quiet time
Just my lord Jesus and me.

A place of peace and harmony
It's a dimension all our own
He's there to share my problems
I don't have to carry them alone.

Everyday he waits for me
I'm always there, it's true
But sometimes things distract me so
I'll have something else to do.

But Jesus waits patiently, in my
secret place
For the moment, when I'll appear
So while I'm out doing other things
Lord Jesus sheds a tear.

Forgive me Lord . . . I didn't
know . . .
I should've done my part
To spend some time each day with
you
In that secret place—my heart.

Helen T Cockrell
NO WALL!
Today, is my Beginning of a new life,
Gone are those days of pain and
strife.

I look to the future with hope in my
eyes.
The past I have left Behind with
joyful goodByes.

The wall has Been opened and is
coming down,
The shouts of joy are an exhilarating
sound.

Once again I am free to travel where
I please,
Gone is that endless fear of Being
seized.

My eyes scan over the graves where
many are lain,
A dreadful Reminder of a wall that
caused nothing, But pain.

Caroline Ceraso Sicilia
MEMORIES
The sky is bright,
The grass is mossy green,
And the air is filled with
The freshness of a summer day.

To just sit and daydream
Of all the memories of my childhood
The memorable days I spent in
Nature's own Masterpiece.

The setting sun,
The stately mountains,
And the babbling brook
Are a symphony of wonderful
sounds.

That can be enjoyed
By those who take the
Time to listen, look and see
The birds make their own rounds
With their own imitable composition.

Melissa Quinn
SCHOOL
What's School!
having Mrs. Tilley as a math
teacher
doing homework
special programs like O.M.
required subjects; math,
English, etc.
lunch with friends
P.E. anytime of the day
assemblies and P.T.O. meetings
buying school supplies
That's school!

M J Purucker
BABIES
Where did you come from, baby
dear?
God's bit of everything, there to here.
What makes your forehead so smooth
and high?
His soft hand touched it as he went
by.
Where did you get those eyes so
blue?
He took from the sky to match its
hue.
He took your cheeks, your mouth and
nose,
And made them like a warm pink
rose.
Where did you get this dainty ear?
God whispered and it came to hear.
Did He give you that smile of bliss?
Or is this from an angel's kiss?
Your arms, legs, hands, feet, all these
things
He made from the gossamer of
cherubs wings.
He put these all together and together
they grew,
And wonder of wonders, they came
to be you!

Yvonne Matthews
THE LOSS OF A LITTLE ONE
An Angel gazed into a crib
with sympathetic grace
And saw a small reflection of
his own angelic face.

"My little one," the Angel said,
"this world is not for thee,
So leave thy little bed of pain
and come along with me."

"In this sad world of stress and sin
and crime beyond control,
The worldly pleasures don't begin
to satisfy the soul."

The Angel took the little load
and held him to his heart,
And flew with him to God's abode
a better life to start.

So, Mother dear, your little son
has found eternal bliss,
Where some day he will recognize
your tender loving kiss.

Helen W Pabor
ALASKA REMEMBERED
Mystic land of snow and ice,
Thrilling, chilling paradise.

Mountains soaring into space,
Fogs conceal dynamic grace.

From Barrow south to Kotzebue
Kuskokwim to far Attu,

Endless stretch of rock and snow
For Aleut and Eskimo;

Living as the land provides—
Berries, crab and fur-seal hides;

Silver fish and silver fox,
Silky fur from rough musk ox.

Barábara and igloo walls
Shelter from the williwaws.

Tundra safe for feather'd fears,
Haven for ten thousand years.

Who disturbs this precious plain
Risks great loss for little gain,
Let the treasure stand intact.
Peace must be a lasting pact.

Donald C. and Quetta E. Copley Church

Quetta E Copley Church
OUR GRANDCHILDREN

Dedicated to all our beloved grandchildren, with much love and price in each one.

Grandchildren remind me of a flower
garden,
In full bloom, in the middle of
Spring;

They're all different shapes and sizes
And what pleasure and happiness
they bring.

Every now and then we add another
flower,
And when it blooms, what a big
surprise!
I thought we had all the different
kinds,
But, now we have still another size.

It's the most beautiful garden
anywhere,
Because, our flowers are all so rare;
They just keep on blooming and
growing,
Like they know exactly where they're
going.

Yearly, the blooms get larger and
brighter;
I may have to move my garden soon,
'Cause, if we get any more flowers,
I'm certainly going to need more
room!

Carl Ferrel

SPRINGTIME IN WINTER

A breath of spring in winter
Came suddenly to me.
From the shadows of the past
She appeared one wintry day.
And for a fleeting moment
The winter chill was gone.
And for a frozen moment
My heart was warm again.

Rhoda J Walker

DO YOU KNOW THE PASSWORD?

God created for us a password, to use
as a key;
It will open heaven's door, for folks
like you and me.
Do you know the password to God's
heavenly shore?
It's a word I know you've heard
many times before.
It was born of a virgin, in a stable, in
the hay;
This word we use everyday, as we
bow our heads to pray.
It was a small child, wise beyond its
years;
Trust this word with all your heart
and you'll have no fears.
It was a known carpenter, in the days
of old;
It turned the water into wine, that's
how the story's told.
It was a teacher, that taught us of
God's love;
So we can have that mansion, He's
prepared for us above.
It walked upon the water and it parted
the seas;
It cured the blind man, the crippled
and diseased.
It fed the multitude and died upon the
cross;
Do you know the password now or
are you still at a loss?
To get inside of Heaven's door, and
have your soul set free;
Yes, Jesus is the password, He's the
only key you need.

Susan Bame

DEPENDS ON WHAT YOU MEAN BY LOVE

Oh why, if asked to rate the feeling
love,
Would we take pains to conjure our
dismay?
And as the surgeon slipping on a
glove,
Would we, as well, our own veneer
display?
To some, love's merely just a
groundless term—
For others to perceive as life's intent.
But for themselves, the proven rule
stands firm:
Admit such state remains beyond
ascent.
To some, the word of love suggests
lost pride—
Dependent lust of blind delighted
fools
Who rise to heights of nocturne
ocean tides,
But fall to Wisdom's darker dawn
that's cruel.
Our face of truth we dare not
cease to hide.
Content we act while feelings
stay denied.

Alex Markoff

HOW TO BEAT MY DEPRESSION

I must learn to stand on my own two
feet,
And not tell everyone how I feel,
Each person has his own problems,
Whether imaginary or real.
I must learn to smile and really feel
fine,
No one will help you, when you start
to whine.
For some time now, I have been
feeling down,
And whoever you meet, when you
walk on the street
They will stare if your face wears a
frown.

If you want to beat a depression,
You must start by helping yourself,
Don't tell people your problems,
Or you'll end up somewhere on the
shelf.
Just face each day and do your best,
Greet people with a smile,
Do your work with lots of zest,
And you will find that it's really
worthwhile.

When you wake up in the morning,
And thank the Lord each day,
Begin to count your blessings,
And your fears will fade away.

Carrol Rowan Bailey

NEVER ALONE

I can climb the highest mountain
I can cross the widest sea
And go through the lowest valley
If my Savior is with me.

Though the storms of life be raging
And the tempests o'er me roll
My Savior is my keeper
For He's captain of my soul.

So I'll put my trust in Jesus
And I'll serve Him every day
And I'll conquer though I falter
For He's with me all the way.

Sylvia Stern

WHERE HAVE THE ORIGINALS GONE?

i am unique;
uniqueness is original
creative,
fluid,
expanding.
i am collectively unique
i am universal
encompassing all
enduring all
longing for
the original dream.
i am reality;
body, matter, form, life—
infinity.
i am being moved by
the God within.
i am unique,
original,
blessed,
humbled and praised.
i am the child,
the adult,
the guardian,
Your friend.

Donald R Dotson

MUSICIAN'S FANTASY

We sing our songs
to cheer the world.
We make our music
to forget the quarrel
that we have against
life in reality.
So we need something special;
a music fantasy.

Jean H Hake

PUSSY WILLOW

Pussy willow, soft, furry, gray,
Clinging ever so tightly
Purring kittens stranded in play.

Pussy willow, soft, furry, gray
Braving the March winds nightly
Peeking at winter's saucy jay.

Pussy willow, soft, furry, gray,
Growing plump and stately
Turning yellow in April's sun ray.

Donald R Dotson

INNOCENT CRY

I dedicate this poem to the whole world and mainly to my niece Akera Dotson and family.

A baby's cry to be consoled
goes far beyond its meaning to be
told.
This goes until maturity peaks,
but somehow, as an adult, this sealed
cry leaks.
Nurtured by mother, and secured by
dad
noticing instantly the opposition of
others
and also desolate of the love they
had.

Soon to learn the difference between
love and hate,
perceiving the nature of this world at
a very high rate.
Many are left all alone out on a limb.
Who will be a refuge and rescue
them?

As nature takes its course, it brings a
notion to a multitude of people
to look to the sky with an innocent
cry,
realizing there is joy and happiness in
life,
accompanied with pain, suffering,
and strife.

For, to be consoled by an act of love
and a special touch,
whether in the past, present, or future,
to many means so much.

Even from the beginning of life there
seems to be
a message expressed in an innocent
one's cry.
Is it by nature designed to be such an
easy thing
to do? Perhaps we may never know
the answer,
nor ever the reason why.

Penny Caddell

LOVE IS

Love is a mixed up mess,
Love is no greater or no less,
For we are equal.
Love is everything to me,
As far as the eye can see.
For love is blind and should be
dealt with care,
For some comes once in a lifetime
and considered rare.
Love is wonderful and can be showed
with a hug,
Love is also shared with a kiss
while laying on a rug.
For love is like nothing else matters
to me.
Love is hard to figure out and we
should let it be.
Once you've loved somebody it's
hard to hate,
Especially that person you call your
mate.
Although love is not perfect from
time to time.
What you call hate should be made
better with dinner and wine.
For love is grand and I hope he loves
me forever.

Kathy Church

SHADOWS

I get ready for bed and I turn out the
light
I fall asleep wondering if I'll have
that dream tonight
It's the boy in the shadows—I can't
see who he is
He's very angry—he's lost
something that was his
The outline of his body shows he is
not very tall
His voice is of an adult and not a
child at all
He is crying and upset and sounds
like he is quite near
But the shadows hide his face and his
features are not clear
Wrestling with a grown-up emotion
of origin I do not know
Perhaps he is sad because of a love
that cannot grow
His cries echo and haunt me in my
sleep almost every night
Would I recognize him in the
shadows if I left on the light?

Sonia Karen Waldron

DESTRUCTION

My soul cannot rejoice nor
My heart skip with excitement
When I know our world is
Being destroyed.

Souls walk around dead
And people are scared
Of living.
I close my eyes
Hoping that it is all
A dream
And when I wake
Times will be better.
I see the children playing
In the streets
And I fear for their future.
I have to question our sanity
For we have been
Suffering too long
Even someone half dead
Must realize
We are killing our youth.

Steve P Stewart
SEASONS
The twilight of the morning found
The sounds of spring abound
Winter lost its icy hold
Soon summer would unfold

Mick Hatten
TEETH WITHOUT DIRECTION
Top row—family eye tooth peeks
away
and worries.

It is the lone writer's embellishment
sticking out,
looking for gossip to latch onto.

Bottom row—screams in the night,
trying to fit,
but looking awkward,
like puzzle pieces
trying to fit together
on ice.

Way back—there are
four holes where
wisdom
used to lie.

Where did it go?

Into the dentist's
pocket,
like nuggets jarred from a
gold mine.

Joseph B Grigg
THE PIANIST
The staff's perimeters cannot contain
the fluid notes
which splash across the pages of
his mind.
Great speckled waves which rise on
high and then recede
to dash below,
Then rise again with undulating trills
and runs,
Arpeggios that find a voice
beneath the fingers of the artist on
the bench.
Accoutrements,
Enhancement to the greater grandeur
of the keyborn melody which
soars above the rest.
The burnished wood,
Reflecting pointellistic lights and
soaring sound,
Displays its elegance,
The instrument's modality of sight as
well as ear.
The audience reflects the music's
birth
with that ordained propriety
which passes for involvement on
the evening's air
While he projects from practiced
hands,
For here, his life is driven by the
measure's worth.

Jo-Ann M Hill and David Mullins

Jo-Ann M Hill
GOD'S WAY

To my sons, Robert L and Michael F Hill, forever in my heart and always on my mind. Until then I love you.

Four tragic years ago today
My son Michael was taken away!
And when God knew He needed
more
Again he knocked upon my door.
Because He wanted a special one
He called and took my second son!
Now every day and night I cry
And when I laugh, I live a lie
No more a mother shall I be
Until he comes and calls for me!
And then I'll know the reason why
Both my sons had to die!!

Judy Peebles
SMILES
You've brought sunshine and
laughter into my life
and smiles—lots of smiles
A part of me feared lost has been
reborn
through knowing you
I smile often now
at the beauty of the sunrise in
the still, cool morning air
the sound of a tiny bird,
perched on a fence, singing
his heart out
the wind in the trees
But most of all
I smile at the warmth and
tenderness
I see deep in those blue, blue
eyes of yours
Sometimes when you look at me, you
touch my very soul
I see the fun-loving, mischievous boy
in your eyes
Then you sweep me into your arms
and your eyes turn to a deep blue
and there is the man—
passionate and sensuous
My spine tingles just thinking about
you
and I catch myself smiling,
again.

Bob Hudgins
EARTHQUAKE CITY
It was like a movie
It was a pothead's fantasy,
A minor euphoric-induced vision of
apocalypse.

Eyes focused on the Bay Area
Waiting for game three of the series,
And introductions notwithstanding a
"major earthquake" cuts
A swath of death and devastation in
its random way.

Oh yes, fire, and collapse, and
crushed cars and bones—people—
destruction!

Penelope Beach Chittenden
MORS INTEMPESTIVUS
Wan sun, wan shadows
On the Ides of March;
Not warm nor cool,
The thin wind woos the buds of
nascent spring.

Earth doffed her wintry mantle
Ere her leafy shawl had clothed her.

'Tis a non season and a non day,
Limbo between death and burial.
The good-byes are said,
But not "Farewell."
Neither mourned nor mourner is yet
set free.

Oh, hasten, Aries, to your vernal
gate,
And with you the Paschal Lamb.
Give light to the quick
And flight to the soul
That rebirth can begin.

Debbie Stoner
THE DECISION
As Jesus walked up
That long lonely hill
His mind was reflecting
His Father's true will

His friends had all left him
And scattered about
Leaving him lonely
Was his mind filled with doubt?

He had prayed to his Father
Not my will, but thine
I'll do what is needed
For your glory to shine

His mind held no doubt
He knew what to do
He laid down his life
To make our lives brand-new!

Tiffany Dyer
BITTERSWEET MEMORIES
The bell rings and moments later the school explodes with activity as the children burst into the sparkling day.

The crisp air of fall greets them as they run across the endless green fields.
The blue sky is illuminated by the shining sun, smiling down upon the earth.

They sprint through the newly fallen leaves, their feet crunching with each step,brightly colored backpacks and lunch boxes dragged carelessly behind.

Happy shouts and exuberant faces are all around; school has been dismissed for the day. The children head home to security, a smiling mother with warm cookies fresh from the oven awaits them.

After filling their bellies they again attack the outdoors, frolicking in the leaves until dusk and the frantic cries of their parents beckon.

Do they know how lucky they are?

As a child I often wondered why adults would simply look at me and smile for no apparent reason. Now I do the same. Their faces are so sweet and innocent, one cannot help but to smile.

It is the innocence of youth, a carefree and wonderful time in our lives that we all wish to relive. If they only knew how lucky they are . . .

Is there any way to tell them?

How I wish I could go back in time.

Sometimes, when I am alone in my room, these thoughts bring tears to my eyes, and I cry because of these bittersweet memories.

Paul J Zappia
CHILDREN 'ROUND THE CHRISTMAS TREE
Children gathered 'round the tree,
Anticipating what will be.
Each Christmas gift brings a glee,
From all the children 'round the tree.

While in the back a small child does
sit,
With tears of sorrow in his eyes;
Which softly glow from the candles
lit.
I have no gifts to bring, he cries.

One by one the children turn,
To see the child with a look of
concern.
Then from their midst a voice is
heard.
I for you and you for me,
That's all the gift I want from thee.

What words of wisdom this message
does bring,
From innocent children who wish to
please.
So on Christmas Eve as the bells
shall ring,
Listen carefully for you will not
cease,
To hear the voices as they sing,
Of all the children 'round the
Christmas trees.

Laura Elizabeth Thompson
IMPROPER
Don't question your father's
views. It is improper.
Don't scream for peace in blood
streets. You might disturb the
harmony.
Don't stand so close to a boy of
black skin. People may talk.
Don't frown on the face of your
leader. No one will smile.
Don't give your love
away. It is not needed.
Don't wear black
today. Your friends are wearing pink.
Don't sing that song of
controversy. Other children might
sing along.

Dolores J Barrett
GIVE ME YOUR HAND
Give me your hand and let me guide you
Through the years that lie ahead
We shall walk the same path together
Edging on to find the way.
Be there tears or laughter between us
Our hearts will share those days
And I offer you joy in all your travels
Giving you hope for all your tomorrows
To carry you when I'm not there
So go forth young man and find your dream
For you will see the beauty around you
Because I have guided you halfway there.

Janet W Luczak
FIRST LOVE
At first I thought
Bastard, how could he understand
Then I remember

Quiet times and cold beer
Pinballs and long talks
A caring . . . A sharing
Getting high together
Only to come down without you

Letters without postmarks
Promises and questions
You never lied
Never promised anything
But the sky and the wind

A free spirit
Open arms when the need arose
There . . . then gone

I wait for your call . . . watch for your letter each day
No reply
I'm not empty though
Your memory keeps me
Until the next time you pass by

Leslie R Huddleston
CYCLE OF EXISTENCE
They are the infants
So innocent and weak
Heirs to the planet Earth
For they are truly meek

They are the children
Made to learn our ways
Disciples of the only one
We taught them to praise

They are the adults
Sent to rape the land
Followers of improvement
But they don't understand

They are deceased
Destroyed by their own will
Still too young to understand
Or they would be here still

R W Rodenberger
REFLECTION
As I tumble through this hard and rough road called life, I pause to assess just what hardships I have endured and conquered and still fight to go on living. The hard knocks, illness, pains, insults and diseases all seemed unconquerable, unbearable, at the time, but all have been fought and won, and to the Lord thanks have been given.

Thanks for the many good things, good times and blessings the many friends, and even a few enemies that tumble right along with me, not knowing what next for them is in store. Thanks for a loving wife, who, when all the chips are down, will stand erect, shoulder to shoulder with me fighting for what we both believe, our God, our flag, our country and more.

When I gaze into the mirror, and see my image staring back at me, I realize that all my grief, troubles and sorrows throughout all these many years have not been for naught: for my name in history shall nor be forgotten, lost or misspelled; because the three sons that I have sired will carry on with the many tasks and chores that I am unable to perform or have forgot.

Ana Brenda M Quezada
JEST
"LIFE"—she laughs.
Absently she begins
To dance.
Round and round she goes.
Spasmodically she stops.
Slowly she begins to run
Through the gates and dark passages.
The night is white and silent.
The journey never ending,
Fortified with walls and catacombs.
In search of the hearth
She continues west.
And then, as she is about to perish
It begins to rain.

Ace

Dianne L Bullington
ACE

In loving memory of Ace, 9 years of age; died March 6, 1990.

Yes, you were definitely one of a kind!
We had a language all our own,
Even if made by a statement with our eyes
Or just a gentle feel between us.
We could always understand each other.

Together we have forfeited the same friends,
And even came close to losing one another.
But I never wanted it to really happen,
Not without saying one last farewell;
Although that is how life will usually end.

I had always questioned what it would be like without you.
And it would hurt just to consider it.
So then why do I sit here so numb,
When I should be mourning such a great loss in my life
With great cries of pain and sadness?

Nevertheless, as I sit here without belief
Next to you, as you lie there beneath this Willow.
As tears flow down my cheek, I will water you
My dear feline friend and yearn for you,
Holding you forever, here in my heart.

Katherine Ann Knox
GO OUR SEPARATE WAYS
When we first got together we had so much to live for.
Our love ran so deep within our hearts, who could ask for more.
We seemed so much in love that nothing could ever spoil it.
Then one day to spoil it all, you threw a drunken fit.
Through all the years of torture
I stayed your devoted wife.
Then one day I finally felt, you didn't want me in your life.
I can only remember all the times you lost control and I was made to feel the pain.
So many times you left me bleeding, hurting, and lying in the rain.
You weren't there for me then but you want to be there now.
Yet my heart tells me it's over someway, somehow.
If I could find the courage, I'd go to any length.
To tell you that it's over, but I just can't find the strength.
I pray I find the strength to tell you within the next few days.
While we can still part as friends, and go our separate ways.

J Valrea Chase
WRITER'S CLASS LIMERICK
There once was a class full of writers
whose egos flew higher than kiters
Till they lovingly critiqued
each other's writing and piqued
And now they're not lovers, they're fighters.

Rita Kay Freeman
NO LONGER HOME
They are going to strip for coal.
I wonder, does the earth have a soul?
They are going to push down every tree,
The birds will fly away you see.
In the streams, the water is black,
None of the fish are coming back.
The men, machines, and trucks have gone,
Now for the animals, it's no longer home.

Doreen Knox Johnson
LOOK TO THE SKY AND SMILE

In memory of my brother—Joseph John Munnell, Jr.

Look to the sky and smile.
Feel the cool breeze on your face.
Remember?
Look to the ground, your feet planted firmly there.
Remember?
Think back on your life and do not cry.
For each memory has a purpose, a reason for being.
Remember,
The good ones, the bad ones, the happy, and sad ones.
Remember,
The smile on your face—seems frozen in time.
Left back in my memory to comfort me—in days to come.

Gwendolyn N Kelly
CHILD OF GOD
Child of God,
Don't be sad
Though things don't seem quite right
There's a place for you in heaven
Where stars shine bright at night.

Ignorance causes them to stare
While you don't understand
A special child you are to God
And He will hold your hand.

Take the days one at a time
And close your ears to what others say
You're the one who needs no reasons
For them, you'll want to pray.

Remember again, oh special child
His footprints are in the sand
No matter what, you're loved by God
And He will hold your hand.

Jennifer Kleinschmidt
SUNSET AT THE BEACH
Birds fly away, and then nobody's here.
It's nice to know such a peaceful place,
Where there is surely no need to hide your face.
Such a place where you have nothing to fear.
So sorry you're leaving a place not near;
Where the sun disappears without a trace,
But it'll surely leave a crimson face.
It's a sight to see the sunset in the night so clear.
Before I began to leave that peaceful beach,
A very sudden thought came to my mind.
This beautiful place has become my link.
Such a place could never be far out; of reach.
For it's so special, this place I did find.
This special place where I go and can think.

Mildred M Kauffman
A ROSE
A rose that may in summer bloom
Spreading the earth with sweet perfume
Must come from God;
For only He could create a rose.
Then; if ever you should doubt—
Or even just suppose,
Could ere a fool like me
Create a rose? No, surely not—
Yet God created both:
And blessed creation from above.
We call it a rose—
HE called it love.

Anna Koutsogiannis
WEST

Dedicated to the one who created this beautiful earth Jehovah God . . . Psalms 83:18

West how I dream of you so . . .
Your beauty abounds your wealth aglow

Your golden landscapes are
something to behold
Though you have been there years
you never grow old

Memories of you go through my
mind
over and over all the time . . .
The smell of sage in the air
The rippling breeze through my hair
The beautiful poppies in the field
The gold in the mountains left to
yield
And a glorious golden sunset I shall
never forget

Though we live so far apart
I feel a part of you in my heart
West I will never forget the
memories we shared together
Because in my mind they live
forever.

David A King
EYES OF COCAINE

To resolve a problem is to recognize a problem.

I See The Troubles In The Neighbor-
hood.
Sometimes It's Hard To Find
Anything Good.
I See The Dope Houses With All The
Traffic,
Take A Quarter Or Half, It's Your
Pick.
Selling Of Souls For Nothing At All,
But Happiness Is Possessing A Little
White Ball.
I See Little Furniture Inside The
House,
Three Kids, A Dog And Of Course A
Spouse.
The Hill You Are Sliding Down Is
Getting Steeper,
When Your Only Worry Is The
Number To His Beeper.
Searching And Hunting Throughout
The Night,
To Get Your Head To Where You
Call Right.
You Will See Through Me I Have No
Name,
I Am Just The Eyes Of Cocaine.
I See You Stumble And I See You
Fall,
But I'm Neither Concerned Or
Worried At All.
I See You Trying To Fight Off The
Addiction,
But This Is Real Life, It Is Not
Science Fiction.
There Are Powers That You Know
Nothing Of,
It's Your Highest Priority You Put
Nothing Above.
Bills Unpaid, Food Is Not Needed,
Smoked So Much "Crack" Surprising
You Don't Bleed It.
Neighbors and Friends You Continue
To Rob,
You Can't Support Your Habit With
One Or No Job.
You Try To Sleep, Cutting Off The
Light,
But All Of Your Dreams Are Of A
Clouded Pipe.
Why Can't You See, I think It Is A
Shame,
Why Can I See, I Am The Eyes Of
Cocaine.
Hiding Your Troubles From Family
and Friends,
Not Sure Yourself What Made You
Begin.
When The Closet Door Opens They
All Will Know,
Exactly And For Sure Where Your
Money Will Go.
You Can't Hide It Forever Its Powers
Get Stronger,
Look At The Hits You Take, Don't
They Get Longer.
Look At The World Around It's Not
The Same,
You Have No Control, But Who Can
You Blame.

Maria E King
EMPTY ARMS
Today I had a baby boy,
But in his birth there was no joy.
For in my arms he lay so still,
An empty cradle he can't fill.
I can hear him crying in my mind
Why did he die?—the reason I can't
find.
But now I know I have my own little
angel in heaven above,
And this thought fills my empty arms
with love.

Karen Bather

Karen Bather
TAKE ME BACK
Take me back to then
When peace engulfed our land
A time when ones looked out for
each other
When giving was the natural thing

When families stuck together
To attain a peace of the rock
When parents instilled dignity and
pride
Sharing dreams, hopes and desires

When there was no fear
No need to lock windows and doors
When children could play in the park
Or by the seashore

When alcohol, drugs and bad morals
was not the main
When there was no threat of nuclear
age
When food was abundant with none
ever starving
When housing was never a universal
thing

Take me back once again
Take me back to then

George Klenk
MY OLD FRIEND
My old friend the alcoholic has a
sense of being apostolic, epistolic and
epipolic in this frolic of vitriolic,
variolic
Dipsomania in the haystack on the
cul-de-sac, with an almanac, a knack
and a lack of cognac.

Jensena Lynne
WHITE LIE BLACK LIE
A white lie is a symbol
A symbol of white people
It is seen as the "innocent" lie
Therefore giving the impression of
white as innocent.

A black lie is a symbol
A symbol of black people
It is seen as the harshest lie
Therefore giving to all the meaning
that black is harsh.

White is good, it hurts no man
White is simple, it does no harm
White can't hurt you, it's like a
scratch
With time it'll heal back.

Black is bad, it hurts very deep
Black is painful, it does much harm
It seems like black men are like black
lies
The darker they get, the worse they
are.

White lie black lie white man black
man
When will the racism stop?
White is no better than black
Black is no better than white!

Svea Kanna
APRIL

With lots of love to family & friends.

April is here with sunshine and
showers
fooling the birds and the beautiful
flowers—
a picture of Life: the joys, the sadness
crossing our path in a fast paced
madness.

But sunshine is never more bright
and cheery
than after a storm that left us weary.
'Cause after the rain the flowers are
brighter,
the burdens of life seem to be lighter.

The sunshine, the rain, the
laughter and tears—
all lead our minds toward heavenly
piers.
So look for the sunshine—it'll soon
be here!
It is just hidden by your falling tear.

Svea Kanna
GOD LIVES
I know God lives, His works are
everywhere.
The stars and galaxies tell He is
there.

I hear His voice when ocean waves
hit shore
The lofty mountaintops I do adore.

The beauty of the flowers show His
love
Birds sing sweet praises to our God
above.

Through all creation, be it big or
small
I hear the echo of His tender call.

May all the universe God's love
proclaim!
May you and I exalt His holy name!

May all we ever <u>say</u> or <u>do</u> or <u>live</u>
reflect the love that only God can
give!

Ruby Fern Kern
MODERN THANKSGIVING TRIP
Over the highway and on the
thruway,
To the Grandparents' house we go,
Put the car in "cruise," let the family
snooze,
And pray that it won't snow.

Off of the main road and through the
town,
By the creek, through the "tent"
(underpass), up the hill,
Into the driveway we glide at the end
of the ride,
And soon we can eat our fill.

Into the kitchen or family room
To see if everyone's there,
Oh, it's just great, there's no one late,
Though we've come from
everywhere.

Into the dining room to eat,
And it's then we hear Grandma
say,
"You'll have to wait to fill your plate,
For on each Thanksgiving Day,
We all must give our own special
thanks,
Before we join hands as we pray."

We all have much to be thankful for,
Let's remember to give God the
praise,
And ask for His love and guidance,
For us all the rest of our days.

Rachel B Kielblock
THE DESERT ROSE
The night settles in as I sit here alone
The wind is sharp and icy, it chills to
the bone
The teardrops feel like they'll freeze
to my face
And my eyes sting and burn as I look
at this place
But in my hand I hold the one
memory I cherish
Though it's only a rose, and soon it
will perish
It's a rose of the desert, so delicate
and light
And now it is dying but I dream of it
each night
The sand, the wind, the sun darkened
faces
All take me back to that desert oasis
Reality there was like magic I
suppose
But although I can't be there, I still
have my Rose

Sandra Rae Frahm
ELIZABETH
GREAT news, everyone!
ELIZABETH is here.
Soft and sweet and ever so dear.
Told Robbin and Lou to do things
well,
So when she came my head would
swell.
Had her Sunday. So sweet and so
bright.
The cute little bugger slept all
through the night.
Spoke to Robbin the very next day.
She said "Oh my, how did you do it
that way?"
Just take her in your arms and sing
her a song,
She'll be asleep before too long.
Not too loud, or she will cry,
And you'll be on the phone, asking
me why.

So love her, feed her, and keep her clean
She'll give you happiness beyond your dreams.
Grandma—
Sandra Rae Frahm

Alice M Farrow
WINTER BLUES
Winter for me is a sad time of year
The howling of the angry winds you can soon hear

The trees stand barren against the cold winter's day
Soon the snow begins to fall this time it will lay

All the outdoors is covered in a blanket of white
You can't bring summer back, try as you might

The lakes and streams will soon turn to ice
Winter to me is not very nice

The days become shorter, bleak, and grey
All the pretty little birds have gone away

As the snow on the ground begins to melt
The warm rays of the sun can be felt

As each day passes and spring draws near
We know that summer will soon be here

Heather J Fairchild
BED TIME

To my godparents and their children, Ron, Barb, Kelly, Jill, Steve, and Rachel Evans, my grandmother Emmie Fairchild, and of course my best friend Viki Posko.

As the moon hangs high overhead,
Children everywhere are ready for bed.
Dreams of a fence, and counted sheep,
No child thinks of making a peep.
Children and blankets making a heap,
All snuggled down, ready for sleep.

Dorothy L Jenkins
THE FLAME TREES BLOOM
The Mekong's bed is dry with dust,
Whirlwinds tear at old rice husks,
As across dry paddy fields they fly.
Fire red flame trees burst with bloom,
A Laotian sings 'neath the dusty moon,
That's when the foreigners die.

The days are hot with dust and dirt,
The Lao sit idling dying of thirst,
An old water buff slowly ambles by,
And the flame trees bloom,
And the foreigners die.

The water buff pants and looks for a hole,
In which he can drink and wallow and roll;
He lows and casts his eyes to the sky,
And the flame trees bloom,
And the foreigners die.

The hot heavy clouds hang low over us.
The Mango Rains mix with the dust;
This heat will surely break we cry,
And the flame trees bloom,
And the foreigners die.

Laura L Jensen
ASCENDING TO THE LIGHT OF LOVE
Lord, my life was a mystery to me,
the pathway not easy for me to see.
Your plans I did not understand,
but you cradled me in your gentle hands.

You showed me the love that lights the way,
and taught my aching heart how to pray.
You lifted me up to your son's loving embrace,
and he filled me with his saving grace.

Now I hear his voice in the sparrow's song.
I know the difference from right and wrong.
Help me, Dear Lord, your will to do,
and forgive me when I disappoint you.

Thank you for turning my life around,
and blessing me with treasures abound.
My heart is at peace and full of love,
with the greatest gift from heaven above.

And as I continue to journey along,
with your love, I will always be strong.
And when my earthly quest is thru,
I'll soar to heaven and be with you.

Ann Johnson
FRIEND
We were with you in the beginning . . .
Of course we'd be there at the end!
Those who questioned our self-inflicted pain . . .
Never had such as you as a friend!

You loved all you met and brightened our lives . . .
Cheering us always, when we were blue . . .
Forgiving us our indifference . . .
When we were too busy to spend time with you.

Did you know your days were numbered . . .
When we left you with strangers that day?
Did you know how much our hearts ached . . .
When your eyes pleaded with us to stay?

When all medical miracles failed . . .
They asked if we wanted to come say goodbye . . .
We circled the block three times . . .
Crying, not believing you really would die!

You were so overjoyed when you saw us . . .
Letting us kiss you and hold you so tight . . .
Doubts and fears about being there vanished . . .
As we bid farewell to you, our dear dog that night!

Alice Foster
HEAVEN'S GATE
God looked down upon the earth,
And chose a soul today.
He wrapped it in his loving arms,
And carried it away.

He said, "Come home to me Hon,
Your troubles are all o'er.
It's time for you to rest yourself,
Upon a peaceful shore.

Your jolly laugh, your funny walk,
Will be missed by those below,
But you were mine before you were theirs,
So they'll have to let you go.

They had you for a lifetime,
As I sat here in wait.
Now it's time to come on home,
I'll escort you though the gate."

Evelyn J Jane
MUSTANG HEART

To Laura, who understands me.

I seek the high country, where the air is pure,
The wind, whispers across the ridges of my mind.
The sun sets late in the west, and the night people come out,
To drink from the Big Dipper of life.
Cities far below, I hear their cries of pain
Hoping to survive against a tumbleweed people call society.
I just toss my head, and stomp the ground
For I, am a mustang, cured with a thoroughbred mind.

Jean Stephens Johnson
MY BACKYARD AND PATIO
My backyard does not attract the bluebird,
But a flock of geese flying overhead I have heard.
Butterflies flit from flower to flower,
Those fragile wings have such power.
The colorful leaves begin to cover the ground,
Floating down and down without making a sound.
The squirrel will be back in the Spring,
Waiting for strawberries the warm sun will bring.
Eating the nuts we put in the tree,
Our backyard for him is a safe place to be.
I love to sit on my patio and look at my backyard,
We have a small garden, but no Swiss chard.
The neighbors visit and we sit and chat,
Comparing our gardens and this and that.
I have snowball and lilac trees,
Lots of flowers with nectar for the bees.
On one side of the patio is a rosebush that climbs,
Up above my head are the wind chimes,
They have a nice sound when the wind blows.
My patio and back yard—I'm proud and I'm glad it shows.

Char Johnston
THIS OLE' MAN

This poem is dedicated to our elderly and the homeless.

Places, spaces, faces, and fears,
Erotic movements with hushabye tears.
Take the body from its mind,
Feed in the heritage of another kind.

See the old man dying alone,
Who's his family, where's his home?
Lines of wisdom upon his face,
Where ancient memories left their trace.

A last breath of life sets him free,
Free to a life he can't see.
He leaves a heritage far behind,
For the greediness of another kind.

They show their faces without despair,
To take his belongings without a care.
Sadly he passes to the world beyond,
And leaves his memory to carry on.

Out of sight, out of mind,
Poisoned love is left behind.
Empty spaces, blackness and fears,
Cold emotions with hushabye tears.

Martha Bolduc

Martha Bolduc
I SAW YOU TODAY
I saw you today
And I tried to look away
The feelings were still there
I thought I was healed
But, no I still could feel

My heart is still tender
And I want you to surrender
But, yet I know
It cannot be so

My patience has grown weak
Why can't you see
The torture I go through
to be away from you

Yes, Love I am still yours
Till we walk the shores
I will not part from you
Because our moments are so few

Tom Jenkins
THE YEARLING
There's something about a yearling fawn
To me it's as beautiful as the sun just after dawn
It gently drinks from a babbling stream
Its softness puts me into a dream
A buck browses nearby
And a newborn hawk learns to fly
The buck looks big and beautiful
It feasts because grasses are plentiful
Nervously watching all about is the doe
With every footstep she leaves a soft footprint in the snow
The buck has just spotted me, and he has begun to run
The fawn jumps and kicks just having fun.

Soon they are out of sight and gone
But still I'll always remember that
yearling fawn.

Jennifer Jenkins
FINAL FAREWELL
I was cleaning out my bookcase
Like I once cleaned out my heart.
I came across your picture;
It caused memories to stir—
Memories, not feelings.
For you my heart is asleep,
The giant fist that clutched it once
Released the hurt ever so slowly.
It has been a while since then;
I am finally over you for good.
I had to learn to trust again
Because I had forgotten how.
I will put your picture back in place
Between the pages of my mind
And leave you forever as you once
left me
So very long ago.

Cynthia Jeske
A LITTLE TEAR

In honor of my Lord Jesus Christ, dad, mom, Carolyn, Charlotte and to grandparents: Ralph and Sally Jeske, Charles and Nancy Sheley, Lillian Sheley.

A little tear is a
silver bell dropping from
the flower of your eye.
A little word can be a jewel
from the jewel box of
your heart.
A little clap is a snap
that your ear likes to hear.

Jade
WIFE TO HUSBAND
Hello my love;
Please be my lover;
While we can,
Under life's sweet cover.

Time will pass,
And love will fade,
And it may die,
under life's sharp blade.

Past mistakes,
Will pierce our heart;
And each will blame,
The other;
For problems past,
And problems present.
Our mind and soul may part;
Each from one another.

So let us love,
My love and lover,
While we can,
Under sweet love's cover.

Pamela Joseph
WHAT SHOULD I DO?

To my Uncle whom I've always loved, respected and admired. Uncle I realize that it is hard, but try your best to help yourself. You are always in my prayers and I ask that God put His holy hand over you and guide you.

If I believe in myself then I know I
can
accomplish anything for I am a
grown man.
If I sit down and think about myself
only I know what I want and no
one else.
Sometimes, yes, I may feel like just
giving up because no one cares
but then I realize that I have God
and He would forever be there.
The saying goes, "God helps those
who help themselves" and this may
be true
but why should I help myself
when there's people pointing
fingers and saying things like, "I
hate you."
This hurts me and tears me up inside
so I turn to drugs to ease my mind.
Why I do this, I do not really know
but I'm weak and don't know
where else to go.
I steal from my family, one which I
love very much
and because of this they hate me
and I can't even touch.
I want to be able to have the things in
life I've always dreamed of
but there's no one to push me,
encourage me, or to love.
Sometimes I don't even know why I
do the things I do.
I try to figure out, but I don't have
a clue.
People tell me that one day I'm going
to freak out and kill my family
but God knows that I love them
and with them is where I want to
be.
I have a funny way of showing that I
love, care, and need them in my life
and now they have turned against
me and nothing at all seems right.
What am I going to do? Tell me.
What am I going to do?
I'm going to put God first, believe,
and know that He will make all
my dreams come true.
Please don't give up!! fight! Fight for
what you believe in!!

Lori Johnston
LIFE'S LOST TREASURE
They tried to find the treasure
But it just didn't measure

It was very, very hard
But they kept marching yard by yard

They tried to find all the gold
But soon they became too old

Judy Jacques
ANNOUNCING A BABY

To my sons, P. J. and Kevin. You both mean the world to me, you and my life. I love you both so dearly. Love, Mom (Be careful!)

We're going to have a baby,
He'll be so soft and sweet.
We'll be so proud to show him,
To all our friends we meet.

Maybe he'll have your eyes,
And maybe he'll have my nose.
He'll be so cute as he lies,
And plays with his little toes.

Oh what proud parents we shall be,
As the years go by.
To see that together we have made,
A man from you and I.

Virginia Joy
THE BEARING OF A CHILD
When upon a peaceful dream,
Two people fall in love.
This love becomes sound
And everlasting, as if a gift from
above.

A legacy of expression is experienced
And this pair is with child.
Looked upon
as a sensation
Like Autumn, their feelings are mild.

As time will tell, the child is born.
This sensation now becomes their
goal.
And the innocence of the newborn
Forever reaches their souls.

For the formation of the child
flourishes
Like a cocoon into a beautiful
butterfly
And both Father and Mother
Thrive and grow from their pride—
Their Child!

David M Jones
TIME

Thanks to my brother John, he always knew I could do it.

Time begins like the seed of a tree, or a wave far out in the middle of the sea,
The tree grows tall takes a hold of the earth, the wave travels for miles then crashes on the sand for all its worth.
A sheet blows in the wind first soaked then dry, the line holding its weight grunts then sighs,
A leaf wonders helplessly across unknown paths and ways, an ant disappears into his dark secret home, to most a mysterious maze.
A meteor breaks free of a planet unexperienced of life and air, although in daylight it can't be seen we know it is there.
Water hums through a stream not sober of the erosion it sings, the land surrounding it unaware of the slow death that it brings.
A bird starts to whisper its song as a milk white moon starts to sink, I just lay with my back to a stump wasting time, as I sit here and think.

Judy James
SOUND OF HOME
I am alone this morning, yet there is
sound in this house, of cold wind and
freezing snow,
Of sunshine, and spring rain and bird
songs.
Laughter, sorrow and pain, of
husband, children, grandchildren,
great-grandchildren and even my
own.
Yes, there is sound in this house, this
house my family calls home.

Stephanie Johnson
THE IMAGE
She stood in the midst of a blooming
peach tree.

As her muddied hands touched
the branch, her eyes seemed
to sparkle more than the
stars above.

Her hair blew in the wind and seemed
to match
the branches exactly, and her eyes
were as blue as
the sky.

Her skin was as fair as snow,
and her smile was always
giving me confidence.

It was like a dream, she was
there one moment, and
she disappeared the next.

I would chase her image
only to find it really was.

Jameriala Jackie Jones
I'M OUT HERE
I'm out here,
I stand tall and sometimes small,
Some of us are great,
While others are not, but, if you stand
next to me,
I'm sure you would agree,
I am out here in a part of nature,
For I'm only a tree.

Gail Hawkins-Johns
OUR SON
This sorrow, an ache in our soul
Far beyond, our mortal control.
A gift of life, a bundle of joy
Taken away, a life, our son, a boy.
Without a reason, a cause or a care
Emptiness,
Our hearts linger there.
The answer my friend
Seems so far away,
Perhaps wisdom, will somehow
explain
Maybe in time
We will understand, why
Still today.
For now, we cry
Time will heal our wounds,
And nurture our fears
Together we will grow, and conquer
our tears
As we grow, we learn.
Learning everyday
Oftentimes we find it hard, to
understand
God's way . . .
In time, wisdom will show,
Us a light, that will
Guide us and bless us with sight.

Lona Jaquess
THE '88' DODGERS
"88" was the year for the Dodgers,
What thrills they have given us all!
The rookies, the stunt men, the
veterans,
Were all there to answer the call.
LaSorda pushed all the right buttons,
And everything fell into place.
Then soon it was time for the
"Skipper,"
To get the champagne in his face.
So hail! To this team called the
Dodgers,
They're the champs of the world,
don't you know,
We wish them a pleasant off-season,
And thanks a lot "guys" for the show!

Ted Semenoff
TIME PASSES
Time passes, as we walk our way,
From Childhood's innocent acts of
play,
To manhood's wise and knowing
day.
We'll pause, and for a few moments
stay
To review our joys and then go on
To a new and somewhat different
dawn.

As needs come forth, decisions are
made,
And thus our plan of life is laid.
Experience gained from friend and
foe
Will serve us well as we onward go.
Given hope, we shall walk our mile;
For hope brings courage, and courage
a smile.

If when aged we become

We may review a favored sum
Of goodness, honesty and worth
That we have given to this earth.
Then we may rest and be content,
For life has not been vainly spent.

Maureen J Flanagan
OIL SPILL
Shimmering waters of life and beauty
Playing with the sun just yesterday
until
The sea began to sicken.

Come people rescue the sea
Streaks of scum are crawling
Puking into the lungs of the deep
Come with mops saturate them
suck it up
Clean out the ocean bed where sea
plants grow
Save dying fish in body-casts of
slime
Unslick the wings of feathered
things to fly again
Press out the smothering vomit
from their throats to sing again.

Pale waters, raped and traumatized
Let sunset be the shroud
Of bodies sleek in death.
The funeral is over, the living
breathe,
And as you sleep, remember, with the
horror
The touch of cleansing hands
caressing
And healing fingers of tomorrow's
sun.

Jean E Foster
MY LOVE OF LONG AGO
Reach deep my love of long ago
Deep deep inside of me

Take out the love that's entered there
It's yours for you to see

We shared a love, oh long ago
And somewhere through the fall

The shadows come and closed the
door
For us to meet no more

But now you're back from long ago
And how my heart does cry

So tenderly to tell you so
My feelings deep inside

Reach deep my sweet and precious
love
I have always been with you

Through all the sleep and times gone
by
My soul has been renewed.

William H Feagins Jr
WHAT WE LACK
To achieve we must believe in one
another,
all too many times we will turn our
back on our sister and brother.
I recommend that we end all the
unnecessary violence,
we mustvoice our choice we can't
win through silence.
Bad feelings and killings tend to set
us way back,
Unity between you and me is
exactly what we lack.

One step above our love is where we
should be,
don't let hate be your gate have a
positive destiny.
Everybody knows what shows in the
bad part of town,
In my mind it's about time that we
put our foot down.
There is no need for one to bleed
because of an attack,
Unity between you and me is exactly
what we lack.

We tend to offend many of our own,
they were wrong all along is what
we find when we're grown.
They guessed the best is what they
are,
when there is unity between you
and me we'll be the best by far
We preach and we teach what is right
and exact,
But, Black unity between
everybody is exactly what we lack.

Beryl L Johnson
RETIREMENT
Retirement! We thought we would
have time
To do so much we planned. Write
rhymes?
So many things to do! "Catch up"?—
ever?
At this point it looks like never!

Sons and daughters, grown and
away,
Call to ask if we could come and stay
While they are away, important they
say.
The other one is sick, needs help
today
We feel we are not so young any
more.
But then, we know we "ain't dead
yet"!
So get up and go, never say no.
Ready, willing, away we go. You bet!

Back home! Mom? Old project
finished up
So we can walk through some space
again?
The wee kids wish? A house up in
the tree
Where they can play, a place just for
them.

Time for bed. No! Shall we stay
up,
Watch the late night show just for
fun?
It seems good not to watch the clock!
So we chuckle and cuddle and love.

Chris Jahnke
THE PATH OF LIFE
I look at the sky and see
the world,
So high and wide, but filled with
perils.
I see the path of which I've taken,
Am I wrong or right for the life I've
forsaken?

We can all see the light,
When we reach the end of the tunnel.
Whether it's wrong or if it's right,
Is up to our sorrow.

We love and we leave a seedling,
Hoping it would grow.
But that's up to the seasons rain
To see if it would show.

I was taken out of the darkness,
Out of the night.
I was led into the daylight, and
Saw the morning light . . .

Dana R Jaramillo
MY PRAYER . . .
My silence is that of sorrow and confusion. My tears are for all hearts that are feeling pain. As I kneel by my bedside I ask our Lord to bring speech to my mouth and heal the sorrow and confusion I feel. I ask our Lord to mend all hearts from the pain they carry.

Life has no beauty without a smile on a child's face, without peace from war, without you my love. So as I kneel by my bedside I ask our Lord to make my world a little more beautiful. Letting my world be full of love, peace and a sense of security. Asking my world be free of hate, racism and having you by my side as my shield from all these diseases.

Lord, give me the strength to carry on . . . to make better that's been wrong . . .

Lisa Johnson
MY LORD, MY MASTER
You have the beauty of the ebony
night,
And the wonderful shine of the ivory
light.
You added that touch of sweetness to
the air,
And everything you create, you take
very special care.

You have the wonder of all good
things,
And the splendor of touching all
beings.
You are the riches of our salvation,
And the very base of our foundation.

You gave us right when there was
wrong,
And now by our undying faith we
stand strong.
You created that freshness after each
rain,
And you heal the sick and take away
the pain.

You gave us life where there was
death,
So we would live life to the fullest
with every breath.
You can wipe away a tear faster than
it came,
And forgive the worst sinner and
leave no blame.

You can create anything with just one
motion of your hand,
And stop all wars and bring peace
across the land.
As I write all these things I see,
You are everything to me.

L M Jenkins Jr
QUESTIONS

"Questions" is dedicated to my family and friends. Most of all to: Barbara Bohnet and Lori Bain, who stood behind me; and Walter Davies, who believed in me.

Believing.
Faith in one's self.
Hope for a better life.
An open heart, ready to live.
But in the real world,
Fate can be a cruel playmate.
Maybe I was blind . . .
Or didn't want to believe . . .
That it would happen again.
Looking for answers,
I find none.
But I soon began to realize . . .
That I can't even ask the questions.
Defenseless and alone,
My ravaged soul and broken heart
take refuge.
But soon, they are found out—
And tortured by the laughing masses.
Embarrassed and frightened,
They wither away . . .
And the world goes on.

Stacey Johnson
SOMETHING IN MY EYE

Dedicated to Mom, "One of the finest."

I'm OK.
There's just something in my eye.
A wet blur of scenes.
Gone, but very much alive.
A little girl, a little guy,
not much bigger than my shoe.
Coming to us from God,
to love, to hold, for a brief moment.
Then taking wings to fly,
to worlds of their own making.
A tiny red plaid dress,
doll-size black patent leather shoes.
A laugh like the melody an angel
might play, from a little cherub
mouth beneath bouncing golden
curls.
A skinny boy, holding something in
his hand,
wondering why it doesn't run
anymore.
But fiercely determined to find out
about it,
in his own way.

No, I'm OK,
There's just something in my eye.

G W (Gil) Jensen
MIDNIGHT BLUE

To my wonderful wife, Eileene; my wonderful children, Eric, Craig, Kristine; and my wonderful grandchildren, Kelly, David, Valerie, and Jeremy.

Once upon a midnight blue,
While I waited here for you,
A star fell down from the sky.
I watched 'till it faded, then began to
sigh:

Midnight blue—
Here I am at twelve without a thing
to do,
Reminiscing of the days we knew
When I loved you, but you left me
midnight blue.

Here I pine
For the love that once was close and
so divine,
It's cloudy and the moon won't even
shine—
Another shattered castle in these
clouds of mine.

I'm burning!—I'm yearning
To hold you close to me.
My heart's bleeding—I'm pleading—
Oh, won't you listen to my plea?

Midnight blue—
May the next midnight bring me
close to you,
For without your love I don't know
what I'll do.
Come back and I will never ever be
midnight blue.

YN1 Fred L Jackson Jr USCG
KEEP THE DREAM ALIVE (TRIBUTE TO REV. DR. MARTIN LUTHER KING JR.)
Walking in the shadow of a Great Man, sometimes it's hard to carry on his plan, when it takes a lot of courage, just to walk out that door.

It must have been a miracle that

brought him our way, it sure took a lot of struggle just to give him a day, and we hold our heads up high, just like we did before.

It took years of walking, talking about a Dream, we heard the words "let freedom ring" we showed the world that love could make a way, now he has a holiday.

Fourscore and twenty years ago, our forefathers told us so, they said there would be a world where all men are free, then he came along, a voice that was true and strong, "My fellow brethren we have to learn how to live together in peace."

I think I understand, the greatness of this man, his love for liberty and peace won him a Nobel Prize, as humble as could be, he even gave his life for you and me. We should do all that we can to . . .
"keep the dream alive."

Ora Lee Taylor Jones
LITTLE ONE

In the evening of life
In the evening's sun
The sound of your laughter is sweet
My little one.

My memory in timeless time,
is meshed like a tangled web
spun with yesterday's lost dreams.
Hearing your voice fills my heart
with sweet memories, long
buried in deep recesses
And forgotten
Until now—
Just for a brief moment they remain
giving the reaching hours
a sweet lilting refrain.

Come from the garden
My little one
Here by the window, together
We will watch the budding of
Spring
And I will savor the fragrance
of the red, red rose you bring.

Elizabeth M Ksiazek
MY LITTLE LIGHTHOUSE

To my Parents for giving me life, twice.

Just assure me
that there is a light
that never goes out
And I
will never be afraid
to cross the unknown,
to bear the unbearable,
As long as you,
My Inspiration,
Are there to make me see—
what isn't.

Sharon Koyle
FORBIDDEN KISS

It would be easy
to pretend that
I don't love you,
if not for this
forbidden kiss.

The kiss I often
crave for
in the waking
of the day.

The kiss I often
long for
when the moonlite
shades the day.

The kiss that
almost killed me,
The kiss that
always heals me.

This kiss,
to be forbidden,
but I cannot
turn away.

Patti Jo King
NEWLYWEDS

One day as I was walking down a long but
glorious path,
I saw the large trees as they crossed the road
in a romantic kiss.
The beautiful lilies, tulips and roses blooming side
by side.
The pebbles and the gravel I gently kicked as the
beauty I let sink in, as I slowly walked that day.
In the distance I listened to the high but progressing
sounds of the rising tide.
The caressing silent breeze that would blow through my
long dark hair in a sexy but
sensual way.
Forgetting for just a moment the accomplishments I had
made that day.
The joy of living, the joy of life, the scents of brand-new
days, and the relaxing smell of the
fresh sea air.
Watching the birds fly in and out, gliding gracefully across
the sky on their large but beautiful
wings.
Opening my ears to the pleasant sounds of a large bluebird
as he sings.
The happiness I feel inside, the stress and confinement
that passes away.
As I walk down the path near the sea, seeing
all the visions of what new days
will bring.
Then quietly but so lovingly I look down at my
wedding ring.

Rae Kaelin
ASSURANCE

To my pastor and wife, Rev. and Mrs. Wm. Estes— Dover, Ohio.

I took a sin unto the Lord
An old sin I had just found.
The Lord looked at me and said,
"You still dragging this around?"
"But Lord," I said, "I need
forgiving,
This sin is a burden to me now."
The Lord looked at me in sadness,
And said, "I really don't know `
how.
You see, child, I don't know
What you are talking about,
When I forgave you, died for you,
All your sins were blotted out.
Those old sins are in the 'forgotten
sea,'
I remember them no more.
Now forgive yourself, my child,
And close tight that prison door."
I turned and ran from the throne
room,
My heart was all aglow,
Knowing that my Dear Saviour
Remembers past sins no more.
O' Hallelujah! Praise His name!
His blood covers all my sin.
I'm free—free at last,
And received assurance from my
friend.

Wanda Koval
YESTERDAY

To Bill: Your love and inspiration guided me to write once again. My love and gratitude always—Wanda

I've closed the door on yesterday,
Its sorrows and mistakes;
I've locked within its gloomy walls,
past failures and heartaches;

And now I throw the key away,
to seek another room;
And furnish it with hopes and smiles,
And every springtime bloom;

I've closed the door on yesterday,
And thrown the key away,
Tomorrow holds no fear for me,
Since I have found today;

I've learned to trust,
I've learned to love,
I've learned to let you in;

I've closed the door to past
heartaches,
And welcomed life again.

Nereyda B Kircher
LOST IN THIS WORLD

I was lost
In a world of confusion,
Feeling down
Without emotions,
Only pleasure and desire
Were my satisfaction,
And my heart, and my soul
Were lost in this world.

When you came into my life,
Bringing me peace of mind,
Then your love and hope
Were my devotions.

Now that I have you,
I'll change my life around.
Now that I have hope,
I'll get up off the ground.
Now that I have love,
My world is bright,
My life is new,
Now I see what I have to do!

Flora L Williams
THE SILENT KILLER

This poem, The Silent Killer, is dedicated with all my love to my family, friends and all the children of the world.

There is a silent killer
Sneaking all around
You can always find him
On the streets in every town

He moves about unseen
Never speaks one word
If you ever mention him
Oh we have already heard

We can't get rid of him
Although millions have tried
If by chance you touch him
He makes you very high

He's pushed around by grown-ups
Into the path of the young
Sometimes unknown to you
He's killing your own son
Most of us don't like him
He sticks around just the same
If you would like to meet him
He is the Silent Killer, Mr. Cocaine.

Sara Triplett
THE FIRST

Dedicated to Sarah Campbell.

And when I touched that first
snowflake,
And saw the first snowbird,
When I saw the clouds gather,
And heard the first words
That morning has broken
A new day beginning:
And I saw the sun sweep through
Clouds that had no ending.
As I looked at that snowcapped
peak—
And saw one blade of grass
So vivid,—The Snow, so serene
That one blade of grass
Told Me—
Yes, there will be another spring.

Pat Zirbes
GOODBYE DAD

Every time I said Goodbye Dad a little bit of me stayed behind with you
Knowing that your life at any time could be through
Remembering what joy you seemed to get from life each day
The funny teasing things that you would say
Goodbye Dad, no more trips to Rochester to see me
No more rummage sales or shopping trips to the Salvation Army
No more going out to eat with us whenever we could go
And teasing the waitresses that you maybe didn't even know
Goodbye Dad, we'll miss you more than words can say
As we gather here together on your funeral day
We all have many memories that will last a long while
You gave so much pleasure and we'll miss your sweet smile.
GOODBYE DAD.

Becky Wyatt

Becky Wyatt
ODE TO MY MOTHER

To my loving mother, Dorothy Mitchell Wyatt, who raised me, five other sisters and brothers, and my son Faron Troy Wyatt. Thank you for a job well done.

Was it ever very cold in his shadow
Watching the world pass you by . . .
Did you awaken to know that you

were alive
Each time you heard a new baby cry
And what of your youth, your goals your dreams
Were they shattered with each newborn's scream
Or did you set them aside and now wonder why
"What if" you had only tried
Well whatever your reason for being
My mother, my sister, my friend
You've taught me well how to stand like an oak
And when the going gets rough how to bend
So you see your what if has been answered
And life never really passed you by
For you bore in this world the jewels for your crown
Hail thee
Queen Mother
Of mine

Ronald H James
YOU'RE MY WIFE

To: Jacqueline with Love.

You are my wife
You are my friend
You are my lover
You've been my wife
and closest friend &
lover too all of my life

You are my wife
You are my friend
You are my partner
You've been my wife
and closest friend &
partner too all of my life

You are my wife
You are my friend
You are my sweetheart
You've been my wife
and closest friend &
sweetheart too all of my life
You've been My wife

Kathleen A Kelley
THE CAR
Upon its face raindrops appeared,
Blurring the vision of he who steered.
The road was muddy and full of bends,
But the man inside to his driving he tends.
Increasing now, the rain beats down
Pounding upon the old car's crown.
The tears roll down its cold, clear face
As it catches the wind in its long, lost race
To find a shelter that's warm and dry,
But this will be a long, hard try
Because the man inside has complete control
Of directing where its wheels will roll.

Cindy Lortie
A TIME COMES
A time comes for all of us,
to wander in the sky.
To look upon the world below,
and ask the question why?
To think about the things we've done,
and wonder if we won.
To look below at the ones we love,
and consider why they cry.
To think about what we've done,
and figure out what's true and what's a lie.
To understand God's reasons,
for shortening all our lives.

Felicity Murphy
SPRING TONIC

I dedicate this poem to my family for they inspired me.

I had come down with the flu and was feeling blue for it was time for my spring tonic. It was real pain for it was time again for my yucky old spring tonic. It tasted like mold and didn't taste like gold for it was yucky old spring tonic. It didn't look bad but I was not glad to be taking that disgusting old tonic. I forced it down and felt swirling round and round inside me. Then I felt a sting come to my nose and eyes, I was ready to cry. Then I was sent to bed with a sore head, not to get up till morning. She didn't know it but I hadn't taken most of it, she'd be mad as a bear if she were to hear I never really took that old tonic, I went to the sink and spit out what tasted like ink and took a glass of water. Then she came in, Oh what a rage she was in, for she knew I had not taken my tonic. So I took it again oh how yucky to look at it again, but this time I swallowed it all. How sick I felt, but I knew as I knelt by my bed, I would not have to take it again till next spring!

Samantha L Miller
A SUMMER NIGHT

To Craig: I missed you while you were gone.

I was just outside.
It's dark, a little less humid than before.
Windy, but no rain yet.
The lightning bugs are out.
I saw two of them blinking in the grass together.

Did you know the females are the ones
That sit on the ground
And flash their lights?

Only the males fly around,
Landing to have a little fun
When a girl gives the right signals.

Makes me wish you had wings.

Cynthia A Massey
CASTAWAY DREAMS
Once upon a time,
I believed in rainbows and butterflies, and sunsets and castles.
You were my white knight coming to sweep me away to your castle in the sky.
We were going to live happily ever after just you and I.
Oh what beautiful dreams we wove.

But now you have cast those dreams aside.
I don't know why.
I'm not even sure I want to know.

The woman in me knows you're gone now
and you're never coming back.
But the child in me still needs to believe in forever.
So I'll safely tuck our dreams away, and maybe someday
I can share them with you again.

Elizabeth M Rushe
PENNSYLVANIA SPLENDOR
Come to the Poconos in the winter—do!
Snowy deer tracks will welcome you.
The ski slopes so exciting,
The warm fires so inviting,
The mountains and trees create a wondrous view.

Comes to the Poconos in the spring.
Birds 'n chipmunks announce it's awakening.
Mountain laurel in bloom
Fills the air with perfume.
Life in the wild becomes full-swing.

Comes to the Poconos, summer is here.
Hundreds of lakes so clean and so clear.
Ride your bike, take a swim,
Play tennis on a whim.
Wildflowers in assorted colors appear.

Come to the Poconos—come in the fall.
By far, the most breathtaking season of all!
All the trees put on a show.
Brown, yellow 'n orange—all aglow.
Mother Nature has created her own memorial.

Phyllis Jandebeur Garska
A SUMMER JOB

To all of YOU in my life, like winging birds in flight . . . A small portion of my writing and poetry.

Yon yonder sunset see?
Colors all aglow.
Summer has to be—
Fall comes in too slow.
It is all too much for me
With yards of grass to mow.
And if you'd come and sit, and watch—
You'd probably tell me how
A goat could cut a bigger swatch!

Travis Graham
POEM OF FREEDOM

I dedicate this poem to Casi Beagley.

Alas 'tis true, I have gone here and there
No freedom, nowhere.
How can I be loved in one place,
and not in another?
'Tis better to be free than to be without freedom.
Hast . . . , I shall fly into freedom
like Daedalus and Icarus.
For I am not afraid.
To live is to die without freedom,
either freedom of press, or religion,
or race of any color.

Donald C Hall
MICHIGAN
I am Michigan.

I'm bridged with an awesome crown beautiful with lakes all around. I'm unique you see I'm Michigan and I'm pleased.

I'm opportunities with cities and industries and country as far as your eyes can see, for I am Michigan, I'm pleased.

I give you the movement of the lightning and thunder with rain a cool breeze with the joy of a rainbow to see.

I give you the sunshine to brighten your day, blue cloudless skies and a soothing breeze to cheer you on your way. For I'm Michigan you see I'm here to please.

Come walk with me on my sandy beaches and trails. Fish and ski with me for I am here to please.

Come relax and dream with me by my rivers and shadowed streams with whispering winds and swaying trees. A rustling breeze of cherry, peaches and apple trees in a sea of blossoms to smell and see. For I'm Michigan and I'm pleased.

Marietta Catherine

Marietta Catherine
THE OTHER ELDERS

I faithfully dedicate "The other Elders" to my parents, Josephine and Josephine Mandracchia and all the family and friends.

The other elders
They are so fine
So true
Their kindness
Shows fair on their faces—
They always seem so serene
Their fulfillment time is now
The burdens of the world have
Strangely gone away
They are in contentment time
The glow of youth is somehow
yet present
Their laughter fills the air
There is so much they have
still to share
Thank God, for good health,
Good company, good news!
And then, sadly, their eyes
will dim
A silent tear will find its way
As they recall
The other elders
Who do not have it
So well—at all.

Marietta Catherine
I WILL GO
I will go
Where I dared not before
I am challenged
As never before
My days are stronger
As my life grows longer
I am loving
Like I never knew
Precious!
Be this time

Now—so new!
As I go
On my way
Life is a golden path
No time now for triviality
Sensational!
Is the power I feel
Thank God
For all things real!

Marietta Catherine
RARITY
Rarity came and visited for awhile
It had a little chat with splendor
They stayed awhile
And love sat on their laps
Kindness decided to call on them also
And marvelous came by too
The mating was so grand
They each held the other's hand
When blew open the door
PRIDE and diminished all.

Marietta Catherine
SAYINGS
Sayings
Come and go
Whereto, why and when?
Who knows?
Only yourself
And others will
Witness to these
Sayings
As the wise are teaching
The sermons are preaching
The rich may give
To the poor
And the poor
May pray for the rich!

Ben D'Urbanville
A PART OF ME DIED

Dedicated to my wife and children: Ursula, Karen, Brian, and Sonia.

A part of me died,
That part tied to my past.
A part of me died
To see the restless truncheon
Cleave a bloody path among my brothers and sisters—
My brothers and sisters, foster children
In their own homeland.
A part of me died
To see the innocent child forced to endure Error's wrongs,
And the young mother grow old before her youth recedes.
A part of me died
To hear the old man chant his ancestors' song,
Of freedom aborted and fear and greed enhanced.
But now
That part of me lives
To behold the son of man delivered,
Bringing healings in his wings.

Mary Eaddy
DRIVEN
What drives a man to greatness?
What is that inner drive?
Why does he put forth effort?
Why does he struggle and strive?

Where does he get the strength?
Where does the struggle stop?
When will it all be over?
When will he let the matter drop?

If we but knew the answers
To all the questions asked
Then all could be masters
Of all their chores and tasks.

But we are all so different
In form, word and deed
Some become very great
Some go to seed.

Mary Eaddy
LAUGHING LOVELY EYES
Laughing lovely eyes
Sometimes blue, sometimes green
In their wide reflection
I bask and I preen.

Laughing lovely eyes
Deeply plunging into my soul
If I had something to hide
My blood would run cold.

Laughing lovely eyes
Ne'er would I cause pain
In those beautiful eyes
I adore in vain.

Laughing lovely eyes
Someday may I see
A reflection of love there
Shining for me.

Patrick Froemming
A LITTLE BOY

Dedicated to freedom for my Friends.

Once there was a little boy
And his name was Patrick.
He jumped on logs
And played with frogs.
He even caught a rabbit.
But, one day it ran away
Because it needed freedom.

A Frau
EMANCIPATION
I held a bird in the palm of my hand
And before my eyes it turned into a man.
I set him free as the saying goes
But he returned to me in the very same pose.

Once again I set this bird man free
Once again he returned to me.
At last I made it clear to him
That each return was only a whim.

It suddenly became quite clear to me
This man lived only to be set free.
This release was the final and third—
Man cannot be freed easily as bird.

Judy L Dies
BROKEN SPIRIT
The sky is gray and bleak in the mind's eye . . .
for the atmosphere weighs heavy upon the soul.
Bound by chains of despair . . .
loneliness creeps into theshallow crevices of the heart, as it tries desperately to recapture the beat in the fountain of life.

Merely a shadow of existence . . .
drifting silhouette . . .
where once there was a song.
The heart, like an instrument fine-tuned,
played a rhapsody.

A metamorphose from captivity to flight,
silently remains motionless in time.

A merry heart doth good like a medicine . . .
but a broken spirit drieth the bones.

Alise Minney
RESURGENCE
From thoughts so long turned inward
Lost in a past grief
She wakens
As from a deep sleep.
Looks up.
And in the long interchange
Lost in the infinitude of time
Found in a split second
Drinks in the sustenance of another's eyes.

Struggling up from her mind's deep night
Heart quickened
She emerges
Lives
Breathes
Rejoices
And is born again.

Matthew S O'Pray
THE CLOWN
Over on the corner, standing high.
I saw a clown, he had a daisy in his hand.
Over on the corner, passing by.
I saw the stranger, he had a gun in his hand.
Over on the corner, I saw a good man down.
Over on the corner, I saw the clown.

And I wondered why as he stretched out his hand,
I was watching him die and I didn't make a stand
I just stood there, looking,
As the clown gave the stranger a daisy.
I just stood there, looking;
Life is crazy.

Mary Ann Armstrong-Egger
SEARCHING THROUGH TIME
I keep hoping, searching,
Trying so hard to find
That one man, that special man,
The man that would be mine.
Driving down the highway,
Walking along the street
Searching the faces of everyone I meet.
When I find him I'll know
When I look into his eyes
There will be a burning glow
One that will hypnotize and hold my eyes
And look into my soul
He'll say, "I thought I would never find you,
But now that I have, I'll never let you go."

Eric Miller
I AM
I am an athletic intellectual,
I wonder if we will live in space,
I hear the earth crying out of pain,
I see people killing the earth,
I want to live in space,
I am an athletic intellectual.

I pretend nothing,
I feel nothing,
I touch pollution and death,
I worry about athletics,
I cry when Michael Jordan gets hurt,
I am an athletic intellectual.

I understand much,
I say what I feel,
I dream about playing with Michael Jordan,
I try to live,
I am an athletic intellectual.

Alyssa Gioscia
NIGHT
A lovely time is about to come,
when the sun drifts into a deep sleep,
and the sky begins to darken.
As the dew appears like crystal teardrops, and the stars shine brightly to decorate the evening sky.

Then the moon comes out, to gracefully guide the sleeping towns to beautiful places where dreams are of wonderful things.

This is a unique time.
This is a time that I call Night . . .

Teresa-Marie A Christopher

Teresa-Maria A Christopher
A ROSE IN THE MIST

To my future husband . . . the love I am still looking for.

Sun rises in the mist;
A ray of light shines upon thy face.
Her blood-thirst dress dances, upon the gust of the fierce wind.

Sun then sets, a moonlit night then rests.
Soon a blanket of white covers her in
the mist of eternity.

Michael Fedako (Cigar Mike)
A TRIBUTE TO MR BERLIN
To the man who gave America God's blessing
And dreamed that every Christmas was white
That's why I am stressing
Why all of his songs are a delight.

To me he will always be rated on top
Because in his hundredth year he never stopped.

By composing fifteen hundred songs
Of all the immortals he belongs
As the twentieth century mankind's gift
Whose music and lyrics gave the world a great big lift.

During peacetime and even through the wars

They sang his songs and danced to them on all floors
And on Easter there is always a parade
With all sorts of bonnets on display.

Your melody of a pretty girl
Inspires women and men all over the world.
And I'll be loving you always will be
From the heart with all sincerity.
And when you're happy you won't be surprised
Because everyone can see it in your eyes.

And when you're dancing cheek to cheek
And you're caught in the rain
Don't frown . . . smile and sing a sweet refrain.

So put on your top hat coat and tails
Forget your troubles and all your ails.
So Mr. Berlin, count your blessings for your age
Because history on you will never close the page.

Karen Stefanik
WRAPPED AROUND A PILLOW
I used to dream,
Dream about someone—a man.
I dreamt of crying on his shoulder;
Just letting everything go.
He'd be so gentle,
Rocking me, cradling me,
Smoothing my hair, patting my back,
And making soothing sounds.
I'd wake up in the middle of the night.
Tears would be on my face.
And my arms would be wrapped,
Wrapped around a pillow.

Donna Campanella
THE PROMISE
One last time you touched my hand,
Longing so to question why;
I would never understand,
But, I promised not to cry!

I just smiled to hide the pain,
Knowing this would be good-bye,
And we'd never meet again;
But, I promised not to cry!

Bravely playing out my part,
Praying it was all a lie;
My world being torn apart,
But, I promised not to cry!

Whispering softly, "I love you,"
Turning, silent, with a sigh
I felt my heart break in two,
But, I promised not to cry!

Years have slowly passed away,
Haunting thoughts I can't deny;
Would my tears have made you stay?
But, I promised not to cry!

Pamela Prather
GUARDS AROUND THE CASTLE
My heart feels like
a stone castle,
with many guards surrounding.

No one from the present
is permitted to enter.
No one from the past
is permitted to leave.

Voices and faces,
Dreams and failures
are all locked together.
There is never any growth.
Only the pain breathes thru my being.

Chris E Haynes
PICASSO LINES
Picasso Lines Carve Images Of The Bull, The Horse, The Minotaur; Both Beast And Both Mankind.
In Neoclassical Pose He Contours Nude Greek Goddesses Sublime; Robust, Voluptuous, Semi-Draped Figures In Romantic Gesture.
In Similitude Of Monuments Cut From White Marble Stone And Fashioned Concrete Mass, His Immense Frames Of Anatomy Become Torsos Proportioned As Trunks And Limbs Of Petrified Oak.
These Pedimental Children Of Zeus Rise up With Herculean Arms, Endowed With Full Fleshed Bosoms And Jutting Nipples; Have Samson Locks Cascading Over Rounded Muscular Shoulders.
On Bent Elbow Picasso's Naked Creatures Recline At Entrance Of The Temple, Others In The "Holy Of Holies," Statuesque And Erect Form Pillars Sustaining Posterity.
All Children Of The Gods' Supremely Chisled On Paper White Flesh, He Sculpts In Pencil Black Lines Etched Faces Expressing Emotional Grins Coming From Celestial Senses.
Their Visible Wholeness; His Male And Female Entangled By Sinew And Joints, Comprise Michelangelo's Angelic Saints, Rodin's Contorting Bodies And Blake's Lyrical Creations: All Derived From Jehovah's Spiritual Portrait; Destined (In Premortal Heights) The Human Race.

Barbara Guaragno
INTO NEVER
To ride off into the night
on a great golden stallion
To ride off into the pale moonlight on a cool clear night.
To thunder down an unknown dark road
Lined with faceless shadows, that leads into never
gallop across foggy grey moors,
Feel the dampness fall across your face.
The night edged in shadows that seem to disappear. To thunder up hills, leap across
high fences, through open fields,
splashing through dark streams damp to the flesh now.
Thundering through the cool pale night, till you lose your senses.
Pale hair flying wildly into the breeze,
Face stinging, eyes cold and wet from the force of the wind pushing against you.
To ride off into the night, to ride off into never and out of sight on some pale moonlight night.

Ryan Q Paddock
THE FIRST LOOK
I've seen you but once,
I remember one thing.
We let our eyes dance,
And let our hearts sing,
I only long for that one look,
In different ways,
Like a storybook,
Happily ever after,
Forever your laughter,
But just that one look,
When our eyes danced,
And our hearts sang,
A beautiful thing,
My life became . . .

Tami Atwood (Age 15)
YOU
You are with me in the morning
And all throughout the day
You're still there when the sun has slipped away
You're my comfort when I'm lonely
My courage to be strong
Even when my temper gets outraged
I give to you this part of me
Because you are my friend
You're the mirror of the heart of me
That's how I know you're always there
You're always deep inside me
The shadow of my mind
The echo of a thousand memories
I'm sometimes sad and gentle
You're always brave and strong
You're the reflection of my spirit
Even when I'm not with you

Wendy Breitzman
ONCE IN A LIFETIME
Just once in a lifetime
The right one comes along
The feeling is immortal
To know that you belong
Just once in a lifetime
You see his honest face
You touch his loving hand
And feel his warm embrace
Just once in a lifetime
Everything feels just right
You see his shining face
And your darkness turns to light
Just once in a lifetime
The feeling is so new
To say these three words
And mean them
The words are
I Love You!

John C Kirk
GARDEN VISITS
They both came by today.
I was in the garden.
White flashed by while I bent over leaves.
Green appeared for a split second, then
He returned and walked with me past the white birch trees.

I usually come to the garden alone, but
On some days, while working in the garden,
I am given company.

White, she loved the garden.
"I Come to the Garden Alone",
was her favorite hymn.
Softly, I always sing the words to this song,
After white comes for a visit.

Green loved the outdoors.
He left the valley,
And returned to the mountains to live.
He was at peace and fulfilled,
While on the mountains, he died.

How good of white and green to visit me.
I feel inner peace after their visits.

Dear white and dear green,
Please come to the garden for a visit, anytime.
Please come to the garden and walk with me, talk with me.
Come to the garden and tell me
That we are his own.

Beatrice Naumo
OUR DAY WILL COME
Our day will come and we will be together once again.
I have waited so many years to see you and hold you again.
Our day will come it's only a matter of time.
So keep the faith and you will soon me mine.
Our day will come and all will be all right again. Sweetheart.

Seana Ficklin
SOME OF MY PEOPLE
Some of my people come in different shades of black.
Some of my people succeed in life.
Some of my people are poor, sick, and hungry.
While some of my people are rich.
Some of my people buy material things with dirty money.
Some of my people see education as a goal in life.
Some of my people will be left out of a good life
While some of my people enjoy their achievements.

Denise C Bryan
AN ANGEL WHISPERED IN MY EAR
And I heard an angel whispered in my ear
I will comfort thee, and protect thee
For time has no meaning, or passage in which to go
For all wounds, pains and sorrows shall heal thee
In your darkest of hours, when man has forsaken thee

And I heard an angel whispered in my ear
The darkness shall not consume thee
Have faith, and courage in your life to grow
Come and follow me, and I will lead you out of darkness
And with that I reached out my hand to hers, and was free
And I heard an angel whispered in my ear
The Lord has not forsaken thee
He have lifted thee of all sorrow, and set your soul free

Karen Y Fitts
MALANGS OF AN AFFAIR
Gentle and kind
A Special Breed of Mankind
And although you're not all mine
The part of you, you've shared
Proves you Care
Locked in an embrace of Passion
Our hearts Ignite
Made for long hot juicy nights
How long will this last
Only he knows
How far will this go
Only He can show
For those who Believe

Know pain he relieves
Love He Bless
Happiness he Caress
I cherish the moments with you
And daydream about you when we are apart
For with you I've restored warmth in my Heart.

Kerry Brooke
QUIET TIMES
A quiet walk in the woods
seems to clear my soul.
I no longer feel a goldfish
swimming 'round a bowl.
The still sounds of nature—
clear my head,
letting loose wonderment
as to what lays beyond the bend.
The greens, golds and reds of earth's pallet
blend, fuse and melt.
Nature's own rainbows dance
reminding me of pleasures felt.
I've left behind city life
with its own sounds tucked away,
for a few seconds of utter delight,
no longer held at bay.
Thank God for quiet times,
of which there are so few—
giving me time to absorb, breathe—
time to collect and renew.

Kathy Ward
IF TIME PERMITS
If time permits I'll go the way
that promises fulfillment each and every day
that holds the key to the door of truth
to be honest sincere and always true
to always lend a helping hand
to the person that says, "I just don't understand"
with a heart so big with love anew
I'll help a total stranger simply
because God said to
and when my time permits no more
I hope someone says she showed me
what time is for.

Melissa M Vallante

Melissa M Vallante
ONLY WORDS
To my one and only true love, Waldy Castillo. I'll always love you . . .

Remembering the words you said from the stars.
You told me you'd never break my heart.

Your words which I thought were true, were fake and phony just like you.
Now I'm wondering where you are, if you'll ever come back or have I gone too far?
I thought the world of you as if you were a star.
You were heaven sent from up above, until you went and stole my love.

Rowland Young
2600 CALIFORNIA
The black, the white, the old men young in years,
The broken clock that measures lives, not hours,
The innocent who taste the weed that flowers,
The crowded loneliness, the grass that cheers,
The anguished children's prayers that no one hears,
The manly crop that stupidity devours,
The frightened wardens in their ignorant towers,
And everywhere the rancid smell of tears.
Who sowed the seed and why I do not know—
That bitter weed of tears and human shame
Was it a god or devil made it so?
Perhaps the scoring of a children's game.
But I saw the poison plant and watched it grow
And paid no heed, and I must share the blame!

John Folse Jr
I LOVE YOU MORE
To My Wife.

I love you more
Than I sometimes show
But never doubt
You always know
Because this thought
In my life prevails
And showing you
This true love fails
I'll live my life
And always pursue
Life's everyday
Just loving you.

Genia Morse
THOSE FOLKS GONE AWAY
In my bed
as I lay
I pictured those
who've gone away
I see their faces
in the night
Those folks gone through
the Eternal light

With each thought
I miss them more
But they've all passed
through Heaven's door

This poem I dedicate
to them
'Cause I shall die
I know not when

But when I do . . .
I'll know it's right
as I cross over
that Eternal light

Myra Abbott Keef
OH! THOUSAND THOUGHTS
Oh! Thousand Thoughts
Of you each day
Miles a-part
What are your
Thoughts:
Reading your mind
That, link-together
Imprison with—in
our, brain:
One center miter
Billions of light
years
Begin, There! . . .

Marie Knudsen
PEACE
I wish the world could be peaceful, no fighting no more pain. We could shake our neighbor's hand once more, and smile not just complain.

The streets I wish were free of drugs, you see this could save lives. The kids would give each other hugs instead of using knives.

We are making progress here and there it's coming, world peace. The AIDS virus is an awful scare, can we soon cure this disease?

I wish there could be peace on earth, you know, there still is time. Let's get control of it all you know, this may well save mankind.

Shelley Pullins
ASHES TO ASHES
Tiny faces lost in darkness.
Blue eyes drowned in blood, cross amongst our selfishness.
Red hearts made of sugar.
Black souls thrive on emptiness.
Bite of fire, stings in the night.
Burn the soul,
ASHES
to
ASHES.

Shelley Pullins
THE NIGHT
Breezes cold with chill.
Wind whistles in the night.
She stands and waits for in her mind
Visions of evils, once love, and her lost savior.

Nights may pass
And pay no heed to the child who sits at his feet,
And worships the night for all she stands upon.
She is its child and with her
Morning fades into darkness and death remains in her mind.

One lost mind, one broken soul
Are what shatters her heart into a million pieces.
Lonely child sits in the night.
She flies with the wind,
That goes through her like fire and ice.

Hollow eyes filled with tears
Each man and woman which walk by.
Wonder if what they see is human
Or a horrid notion of all fears gone by.

She pays no attention as she sits
And waits once more for the night
Which filled with darkness is hers to keep till morning.

Donna Allen
THE CHILD
It is summer and the child starts its nine month rest;

Yes the child is sleeping its nine month rest, contended and peaceful; The child is sleeping; but no, he is listening and wondering what is that sound? There is no way for the child to know it is music, classical at its best;

The child sleeps on into the fall, but its resting place seems confined, but the child has no way of knowing that he sleeps inside;

The child sleeps on, but now he is restless, and the music is clearer, what can it be; but there is no way of telling, no way at all;

Winter is coming, and there seems to be a change, he feels some discomfort and then he feels a breeze, he has no way of knowing that his rest is disturbed, that this cold winter day is the birth day and the first day of his life;

But wait he hears music but what what could it be, he opens one eye and then maybe two, just what can the music be,

And then he knows, he looks far above, the music is his mother's smile.

Donna M Leftwich
YOU'RE MINE
You really do understand the way that I feel,
Even when my mind starts talking and my heart it does spill.
And listening to your thoughts seems to amaze me so,
It's like you're reading my mind about things that I only know.

This new found relationship is different than I've ever known,
For it's based on openness and honesty about our feelings unshown.
Communication and comforting just naturally fell into place,
And one day at a time together is just the right pace.

Who knows what will happen as the days start to add,
If we continue as we've started our hearts won't be sad.
We come from different worlds but our hearts are the same,
From the lessons we've learned while suffering the pain.

I know together we'll be for the rest of our lives,
Just as friends, or lovers, or maybe husband and wife!
For the openness we have is so hard to find,
That I thank God each day to say that YOU'RE MINE!

Edwin Perez
WAITING FOR YOU
Although you are not by my side anymore
In my heart there exist an open door
It's the door that awaits for your arrival
I'll always be waiting for you

Each day that passes I think of you
The way in which we loved one another
A love as such comes once in life
I'll always be waiting for you

Oh . . . it hurts so much not having you near
My life without you is empty

But my hopes are high and will never die
I'll always be waiting for you

With tears in my eyes
And pain in my heart
The love that we shared we never depart
I'll always be waiting for you

So in these few verses I hope I've expressed
The emotions and feelings inside me
It's you that I love and long to be with
I'll always be waiting for you

Robert Valletta
TOGETHERNESS
Togetherness is
Being with somebody else
Forever to stay

Robert Valletta
FALL
The crisp, cool wind
dances briskly through branches
of sap-filled trunks swaying
every so slightly
Brightly colored leaves float
downward quietly and lazily, free
falling from the crowns of overhead trees

Gray squirrels scurry about
gathering their autumn harvest
as ol' man Winter looms above
The sun peers out through
hollow nooks in ominous, shadowy clouds
The air carries a hint of
wood-burnt smoke as one strolls
along near to a sing-song brook
So this is the fall,
a season entwined between spring and winter
both bright and dreary,
cool and cold

June M Shaw
ANGER AND TEARS
I thought we had something special after all these years.
Is this what we get for the time and the fears?
We've already outgrown the bars and the beers.
Who do we blame for the anger and tears?

Someone to count on, I needed that so.
I just wanted to love you, to soften the blow.
I thought that you loved me, you sounded sincere.
So why, all the heartaches, the anger and tears.

What the future might bring, Well, who's to say.
The good times we had, have long gone away.
The time that we spent, I hold precious and dear.
Am I the cause, of your anger and tears?

If it's over between us, if time can't erase.
The love that I gave you, you cannot replace.
If goodbye is the answer, to all I hold dear.
Then there's nothing left, but the anger and tears.

Karen Voorhees
THE WAY OF THE WORLD
A Rose all alone, in a Bed of Thorns.
A Big Oak Tree, in a field of stone.
A Young Girl, alone in a big city.
Is this the way of the world?

A wise man, who cannot talk.
A Beautiful Dancer, with no legs.
Can this be the way of the world?

A little Baby, with no Parents.
A Little Girl, with no Love.
A Lonely Child, with no Dreams.
Can this really be the way of our world?

Rachel Susan Dyal
MY LOVELY UNICORN
There you stand,
The glory of your beauty,
Surrounds you.
Your head held high,
Looking into the blue sky.

The magnificence of your
Beautiful body,
As the muscles move,
With each long stride.
Your horn sticking out as a crown.

I love my magical unicorn,
You bring all that is pure,
And beautiful.
You fill me with fantasies that,
I know one day will come true.

As you stand so still,
I feel my breath catch.
As I behold your grace.
Don't ever run away!
Because you'll take away my fantasies.
I love your magical ways,
Never, never, go away . . .

Theresa Ener Jacks
WE HAVE PLENTY
(Of Love and Room)
Sometimes we haven't much to eat;
We never let that become our defeat.
We set our table each day with love;
The one thing we have plenty of.
We're thankful for what we have through grace;
There's always room for another place.
When it seems we have nothing;
We make do.
We'd love to have you join us;
Come on in,
We'll make room for you.

Laura Rusiecki
THE PROMISE OF DAWN
Sunlight streams across the field of snow
Overflowing thru my kitchen window.
Bright beams of light from a small white ball
Peek over the horizon amidst a pink and grey morning.
Reaching through the branches of trees
Stretching towards the open sky.
He awakens the sleepers like children
Coaxing them to begin this new day.
"Wake Up, Wake Up, New Day Coming!"
Time for you to see what you can do.
Time to start over . . . again.

Connie Midgett Hacker
(April 11, 1949—November 2, 1988)
REACH OUT AND TOUCH ME
I have so much love to give you, if I only had a chance,
And I promise I'll be true and give no one a second glance.
If you'd only reach out and touch me,
Then I'll take your hand in mine,
And we can walk together 'til the end of time.
Sometimes we have to gamble with the pain life has in store,
But if you give me half a chance, I'll love you more and more!
My sweet darling, please consider,
That I know what you've been through,
And all that I can tell you is,
I promise to love you!
So if you're feeling lonely, and would like another try,
Just reach out and touch me and give a gentle sigh.
Babe, it's just because I love you,
There's no other reason why,
And I can't stand to see you cry!

Barbara Teterycz
DOCTOR
Doctor, Who are you?
A man of Science who cures the sick
Who loathes disease and fights to destroy it.
A man of Science who dissects cells
And hunts the secrets which within them dwells.
A man of Science who prolongs life
And in sometimes doing creates more strife.

Doctor, Who are you?
A man of Science defined from the start
As a practitioner of the Healing Arts.
A man of Science who has lost his way
In the technology of the world today.
A man of Science who forgot the cure,
That only with caring will the spirit endure.

Doctor, Who are you?
A man of Science? No, for Science is not the only way
To heal the ails of the world today.
Doctor, Who are you?
A man of blood and flesh who feels and loves
And must with others his life enmesh.
Who are you, Doctor? Human.

Jessica E Spissinger
SHE DIDN'T KNOW
What she never knew was how much I cared.
We were one person.
But even though we stood together,
we walked alone.
She was my hero.
But her actions never told me she cared.
Maybe she did.
We are together, but strangers.
She brought me into the world.
Or was it me?
Was I the problem?
Mom, I'm sorry if I did you wrong,
but the one thing I never knew how to do
was to say—
I love you.

Shirley Harris
THE WHITE LINE
She walked the white line of the rainbow.
She saw the crooked tree . . .
A naked giant with outstretched arms,
completely faceless down below.

She saw inside the valley of the rain
where shadows did not dance.
The thunder reared in graveyard silence
and the snowflake spit like fire.

She sat beside the master river.
It did not flow.
It could not smile from the breathless bed.

She listened to the grinding thoughts
jumping here and there with pride;
little soldiers with their chomping knives
hacking on . . . and on . . .
and on . . .

She walked the white line of the rainbow.

Madelyn LaRoche

Madelyn LaRoche
PROTEST
By whose word must our sons go forth
To fight in East, West, South or North?
Whose challenge must be curtailed, stopped
By threat of evil bombs be dropped?
Whose power must our gold contain?
For whom must we inflict this pain?
The little man who daily works
Who labors long, no duty shirks
Is it quite fair that his reward
Is but to perish by the sword?
Another victim of this strife
Is his humble loving wife.
What of the child who seeks his mother
Who sought in vain his little brother?
Death falls from sky and from land

mines.
The weapons are of many kinds.
The leaders smile and quaff
champagne
While mothers' sons die on the plain.
They talk and talk and talk and talk
While soldiers walk and walk and
walk.
Sly snipers wait with eyes intent.
Flesh shrivels, rent when napalm's
sent.
The leaders do not wage the battle
Nor hear the warrior's harsh death
rattle.

Madelyn Larouche
HERITAGE
Purple peaks extend their beauty
Lofty to the sky.
Evergreens march as on duty
Where the pastures lie.

Soldierly they pass in silence
Our of yesterday
Strong, protective, deep and dense
On to future's way.

Something calls from them to genes
Blood responds and says
I know well what all this means
I feel only praise.

Grandpa saw this majesty
When he was a boy
After me now comes my son
To gaze on and feel joy.

Mike Cummings
BLACK ROSES

To my darling wife, Karen—The following is an expression of my love for you. Without you in my life, my existence would be void.

As I near the end of my life I've run
out of all time.
The clock has stopped ticking, my
tears have all dried.
As all things come to an end, I realize
I must die.
I cannot go on living, it's time for
goodbye.
My life was full of memories, which
forever I'll keep.
But now that you're gone, my heart
will eternally sleep.
In my heart is a ride called a
memory-go-round.
Where the memories are lost, never
again to be found.
As you bury my corpse, my soul to
keep, do not be sad, please do not
weep.
For this is my choice, which I have
chosen, my only last wish is for black
roses.
Place one in my hand, right next to
my heart, and forever we'll be
together, never again will we part.
Now that my soul has been freed to
reach the heavens above, I will wait
for you, my darling, in the gardens of
love.

Mike Cummings
TILL THE END OF ALL TIME

To my lovely wife Karen—Happiness is being held by the one you love.

As I lie here beside you, your flesh
next to mine, I still yearn to be closer
time after time.
I may never be able to fulfill my
desires, as my heart aches and pains
me with its burning fire.
I am seeking the bonding that only
true love can share.
For true love is the meaning of how
deeply I care.
As each day passes by me I find time
and again, how you show me each
day the true meaning of friend.
As I lie here beside you, our hearts
beating in time,
I've found heaven in your arms
which no words can describe.
I wrap my arms around you, feel your
heart beat with mine,
I want to be with you till the end of
all time.
As I lie in your arms you've made me
realize, if only I had one wish, in
your arms I would die.

Victoria Jubala
ONE SMALL TEAR

To Linda, whose friendship continues to touch my heart. Thank you for believing in me.

Sitting in my office,
hoping you'll walk by,
I think about your friendship—
A tear comes to my eye.

But not a tear of sadness,
(enough of those are shed)
Instead a tear in thoughtfulness
of things that go unsaid:

Like "Thank you" for your kindness,
and your smile when you are near;
for making each day brighter
with your constant note of cheer.

And "Good luck" in your own life!
I hope that I can be
as close a friend to you someday as
you have been to me.

And someday when it's my turn
to add that note of cheer,
I'll touch your heart
and you'll know why
I shed that one small tear.

Victoria Jubala
MY CLOSEST FRIEND
Jesus is my closest friend.
He's with me always—to the end.
He's loyal in His love for me,
He served my sentence on the tree.

And on the third day when He rose,
He spoke my name as one He chose.
He blessed me with His loving hands,
then sent me out with these
commands:

"Seek first my kingdom." Do what is
right and talk to me through prayer
each night.
Then "Love one another as I have
loved you."
And soon you'll find they'll love you
too.

"Behold, I stand outside your door
and knock upon your heart.
And if you'll let me in, I'll stay
My spirit will ne'er depart."

Yes, even death shall not o'ercome!
His love shall never leave.
For Jesus is my closest friend,
and yours if you'll believe.

Ellen Hope Priddy
CHILDHOOD FRIEND
He climbs on the chair and jumps on
the bed,
He sits on your lap while stories are
read.
He hears the secrets whispered in his
ears,
And when you cry he wipes your
tears.

He snuggles with you as you wait for
sleep,
He's ever watchful, your safety to
keep.
He laughs when you're happy; cries
when you're sad,
And waits through your punishment,
when you've been bad.

And once in a while, when you forget
He's tossed in a corner, but he's not
upset,
'Cause, sooner or later, he knows
you'll look
And find him hiding under a
storybook.

He's your best friend. He's tried and
true.
He's known great love because of
you.
Now, years later, he's ragged and old,
His one button eye stares straight and
bold.

He'll always have a place in your
heart.
His job is done, You, now, must part.
He's placed in a box with utmost
care;
'Cause he was your friend—your
teddy bear.

Dortha Mae Parker
ABYSS OF LOVE
To humankind God gave an abyss of
love,
So we could feel a depth of love
coupled with God up above,
That gives our lives true actual roots,
When applied with his "Book of
Truth."

The "Book of Truth" contains
instructions for living happily,
And if we read it carefully and follow
it explicitly,
We will have a healthy, happy life,
Free from hunger, want or strife.

Some people choose to go their way,
And prove their own strength each
day,
They feel humanity has the power,
To build its own white, ivory tower.

These giants of power are there
because God permits,
And not because of humanity's wits,
Most great achievers know in their
hearts,
God, The Almighty, had a part.

Evelyn G Turner
TRUMPETS OF LILIES
The glory of the Easter dawn
Is felt at morning's birth;
The trumpet lilies sound a note
That's heard throughout the earth

All nature proclaims the joy
In bursting forth in bloom;
The stone rolls back and thus reveals
The grandeur of the tomb.

And Mary Magdalene is there
To hear a soft voice say,
"Woman, why weepest thou, whom
seekest thou?"
"Sir, tell me where thou has laid
Him, and I will take Him away"

And softer still He says her name
"Mary—" "Rabboni!" is her cry—
With wondering rapture through her
tears
She knows her Lord is nigh.

The lilies sound the triumph note—
"The time has come!" they say,
And Mary knows her Master,
The Christ is risen today!

Randy W Smeltzer
THE ONE YOU WANT TO MEET!
While riding to a party in my blue
Ferrari, the music put me in a mood.
When the band started playen the
easy ones were sayen, at the table of
you know who.
The pretty lady was grooven. So I
started movin, in for a second chance.
Please don't tease me, tell me
you'll meet me, on the floor for a
new romance.

Time is of the essence, when I'm
in the presence, of a girl who can
dance like you.
You take it down to the sound,
with moves that can't be found.
You raise the passion with the
moves you do.

If your intentions are good, I think
I would.
We can dance and win the contest
tonight.
If you do your best, and keep your
eyes off my chest.
We'll boogie, but will never be out
of sight.

We put it out on the floor, like
never before.
The world was turning under our
feet.
We took home first prize for sexy
eyes.
It's so sweet to get the one you
want to meet.

Reba J Burgess
HOME
For troubled hearts where is
home? From where you left or trying
to belong?
Opinions always following along
never being considered why or
where. Just trying to pull along with
care.
Home dwells within our soul
brings us peace no matter where.

Paul E Compton
SCARED STIFF
In front of an audience, I can't speak,
My tongue gets tied, my knees get
weak.
I get real nervous and so uptight,
Trying to make words come out right.

Whenever all those people get in
sight,
I start to stutter, I get stage fright,
No matter how much, my speech, I
review,
I still mess up a tape interview.

Steven P Donnelly
REFLECTIONS
I stood upon the shore one night,
And gazed, this barren sea;
So suddenly unchanging, empty
patterns, saw then me.
Reflections on tomorrow, from the
past, whose moment's gone,
Cast from the shadows yesterday,
Behind our timeless bond.
A bond, a steadfast liaison,
Shore's waves, men's own, and me;

Along this shore, one sleepless night,
Reflecting gaze, stood me.

Vanessa L Henderson
BATTLE
Night and day night and day my life
is dissolving away with still several
problems today.

I comprehend the agenda of daily life
and still have many wars to fight. The
wars of health, some wealth, family,
and the wars of why does he reject
me?

I wish I could dispose of the wars and
open some doors
Doors to a better path and journey
and one that will last and not hurt me.

Terry Terrific Vona

Terry Terrific Vona
CARING
The holiday season is coming, we
all know this is clear
Before any of us realize, it isn't
coming, it's here.
It seems no matter how busy our
lives, or short our day
We all find a moment, to have
something nice to say.
But why must we all wait, for this
time of the year
To remember our loved ones, and
wish they were here.
What we all try to do in a few weeks
time
Is unburden our hearts and also our
minds
We give cards, presents, parties,
donations galore
But what everyone needs, is oh so
much more
They need to be thought of and loved
everyday of the year
To know through their sadness,
someone is near
So many people are unhappy, day in
and day out
Although they had nothing to do with
how this came about
So many are plagued by hunger,
poverty, and sickness too
But without the help and advice of
others, they feel there is
nothing they can do.
So let us all make a resolution to do
and not just say
To do a good deed more often, on a
not too distant day.
You will make two people happy,
this you will find to be true
Grateful and happy the one helped,
the other one—you.
Try it!

Andrea

Terry Terrific Vona
TO MY DARLING DAUGHTER ANDREA
On August the 18th God took you
from me
The tears are so blinding, I can hardly
see
The world you have left me for,
keeps us apart
But not from my mind, nor out of my
heart
Your life was so quick, but oh it was
full
So many you made happy,
heartstrings you did pull
A smile did not crease you, but lit
your whole face
Your giggle and presence, warmed
the whole place
To say we miss need and love you,
would not be saying enough
But for the sake of your sisters, I
must try to hang tough
Oh Andrea, my darling, it is going to
be rough

Terry Terrific Vona
TO MY DARLING DAUGHTER ANDREA
It is now six years since you have
died
I cannot count the days of anguish or
the days I have cried
Why, oh why, did it have to be you
You were so young and had so much
to do
I hope you are looking down from
heaven above
And can look in our minds and our
hearts and feel our love
I have wished a thousand times it had
been me
But that is because how bad this
hurting can be
Sometimes I think I am not going to
make it, but I know I must
Thank God, for family and friends,
our memories will not rust
No one, unless they have gone
through it, knows how it feels to
lose a child
You feel as though your life and
mind have both gone wild
But I keep hoping God had His
reasons for calling you above
And we are praying you are able to
feel your three sisters
And mom's love

Carmine Di Benneditto

Terry Terrific Vona
LONELY

Dedicated to Carmine Di Benneditto.

Being lonely is oh so sad
It feels so terrible, hurts so bad
You feel you cannot remember ever
being glad
The lonesome feeling seems here to
stay
No matter what anyone says, you feel
it will not go away
The sad part about it, but the part that
is true,
There are millions in the world,
feeling just like you
There is no medicine or cure for this
pain
You say you would do anything, to
feel happy again
Why not reach out your hand to meet
new friends
You may be surprised, when this
loneliness ends
You cannot cure this pain all alone,
or can the lonely ones
Around you
But a smile on your face, makes
someone happy they found you

Terry Terrific Vona
HELPLESS AND HOMELESS
Everywhere we look these days, the
homeless are all around
It seems like only yesterday, only in
big cities they were found.
At the train stations, the bus stations,
and doorways everywhere
No matter what time of day or night,
it seems they're always there
We look at them with pity and
disgust, wondering what happened
to make them that way
I'll bet if you asked most of them,
they wouldn't know what to say
They're glossy-eyed, hung over,
you'd swear they've never been
clean
They seem to be the most pathetic,
and disgusting sight, most of us
have ever seen.
We all know they weren't born like
that, but who'd choose to live that
way
To roam the streets, never having a
home, not eating everyday.
We know that some are lazy bums,
content with the way they're living
But most I'll bet would love to
change, if our help we were giving
In this country, the good old U.S.A.,
most people work hard, to live a
better way
But so many work hard, for such low
pay
The rent they can't pay, their families
can't eat
So many just give up, 'cause the
system they can't beat
Our government sends money to
other countries, far and wide
While we've got so many homeless
and helpless, they try so hard to
hide.
So let's get after our government, as
much as we dare
And push them to help us, to show
the homeless we care
The ones that are homeless and
helpless, never expected this is
what their lives would be,
God forbid, if it can happen to them,
it could happen to you or me
I don't know about you, but I'd rather
be dead
Than to go on living, the lives they
have led
They need more than a meal, or a
smile from your face.
They need help with their lives, to get
their own place.
So if we all get together and set up a
plan
We can have a lot less homeless and
helpless, I'm sure that we can
Now is the season, we all show
goodwill
So let's help get them out of the
gutter, and climbing life's hill.

Sandra Torres

Sandra Torres
LOVE
Love is wonderful
It is just a phase
But sometimes love
Goes a long way.
Love is wonderful
But sometimes cheap
But when you're in love
You just don't think
Love breaks your heart in two
Then you're down and feeling blue

Steven P Donnelly
THE MAVERICK
When I look into the street, I'll tell
you who it is I see,—
The one who struggled in the search
for his identity,
The one who changed as time went
by, being molded as was fit;
Never conforming to the world,
To rules he'd not submit.
And to doorways that would open,
saying "Come this way, others do,"
A person who would turn aside,
The norm he'd not pursue.

To the dictates of convention, those
around he'd see subscribe;
And though to these he'd follow not,
his life was no free ride.
He toiled in his offbeat ways;
Unique ideals had cost,
The price to pay for going his way
was worry and distraught.
His life was hard, his patience low,
To no job he would stick;
He lives in every town I pass;
He's each town's maverick.

Pauline R Duskey
THE MOUNTAIN

In dedication to my family.

I walked to the top of the mountain
To view all the beauty so rare,
No one on earth had to tell me
Or show me that God was there.

The trees stood out in their beauty
With lovely leaves to adore,
And the beautiful flowers in full
color—
What joy there was on this tour.

The birds were up and what singing
What lovely music to find,
Nowhere could one be so uplifted
As it soothed both the heart and the
mind.

On the mountain the wind was quite
breezy
As the trees swayed to and fro,
It seemed that God was now speaking
And the trees even knew it was so.

Tami L Cooper
THE BLOOM OF A ROSE

To Michael, my life, my inspiration, my everything.

The rose was a bloom in the garden
today
But tomorrow it will die
and wither away

Life is a rose
in many respects
It blooms,
It dies,
It withers away,
It stands on its stem
high up above
and shines all its glory
and fills us with love

But life does not stay
forever on
In the garden tomorrow
it will be gone

Michele Henríquez
CIEGO
Blindman:
You who look with eyes of air
Tell me
What do you see

Your air with mine
  entwine
in the quiet
of night

Your eyes
  (grope)
wisps
  of smoke

Could it be
that night
has color

What do you see
Your eyes
shine and never
cease to speak
Blindman:
You who look with eyes of air

Amy McFarland
QUALITIES
When we first touched
I knew I had changed
My life is complete
My sadness was hanged.

Your smile was so gentle
Your attitude, so new
I've never really
Known anyone like you.

Your belief in God
Is important to me
For I believe, too
Life's as it should be.

When we're together
I feel like someone else
You completely transform me,
I'm really myself.

Lois M Baker
WHISTLING SUE
Whistling Sue, she whistles all day
She trills and shrills away this way,
Her lips round out to form an "O"
For the notes to scale high and low.

A tinkling tune she whistles when
blue
Like a robin's cheery-cheery, cherry-
sue
For the bluer her mood the gayer her
notes
Then folks say "Sue, she's feeling her
oats."

The gayer the mood, the sadder her
tune
Like a whip-poor-will's wailing the
blues,
Her dreary notes belie her twinkling
eyes
Yet folks say,
"Sue, she's got the oh-mys."

All day, whistling Sue whistles away
Yet no one catches her at her game
Or ever figures which the mood for
way of tune
... And once in a while Sue
... even fools Sue ...

William F Rose
THE FARM BOY OF YESTER-DAY
He milks the cows—He separates the
cream.
Along with his Dad, they're quite a
team.
The hogs are fed, the chickens too,
As well as cows and horses, that's
not new.
He gathers eggs and brings in the
wood.
Repairs the fences, at least he should.
He plows the fields, he plants the
corn.
He walks so much his shoes get
worn.
He mows the hay and rakes it too,
And puts it in the barn, 'tis true.
The hog is butchered and meat
prepared.
He slips to town Saturday night if he
dared.
The vegetables are canned and so is
fruit.
To keep him fed and company to
boot.
The nuts are gathered from the tree,
If he beats the squirrel to them you
see.
He may hunt a duck or two,
as clouds turn to dark from blue.
All this is just a sample of joy,
That became the life of yesterday's
farm boy.

Joey Murello

Claudia Ann Murello
JOEY'S SMILE

This poem is lovingly dedicated to the memory of our son, Joey Murello, our one and only son; We Love You. Mom and Dad.

He had eyes of baby blue,
Hair that was curly brown,
Ears that sort of stood out too,
And he hardly ever frowned.

His body was long and slinky;
Gosh he wore a size ten shoe.
The clothes he put on had to be
perfect;
Even the cologne had to be just right
too!

Joey's smile to me made life worth
living;
For you see, he never stopped giving.
Every day he came up with
something new,
Rather it involved many friends or
just a few.

Joey had a unique way of pleasing
me
Especially if things went wrong;
He would simply make me see
Life's true meaning written in a song.

Though he left his world undone,
We still have memories of our loving
son.
I often wonder, every once in awhile,
What would life be like without
Joey's smile?

He always wanted to reach the sky's
heavenly stars.
Now he has finally gone afar.
If only I can make this last mile,
It'll all be worth while
Just to see my JOEY'S SMILE!

Tonya Whitmer
SUMMER DAYS
A river runs deep,
and it is trickling through my
fingers in the sun.

The sun shines brightly,
and the water is clear, a
frog jumps from one pad,

to another, hopping
gracefully as leaping through
the air, it croaks as
a fly buzzes by,
as the clouds brighten in the
sky on summer days.

I sit under a
shade tree listening to the birds
chirp as they fly by.

I hear the crickets
chirping in the summer breeze,
as I make rocks jump

Across the great blue
flowing clear water as the
rock sinks, it makes rings.

I hum a silly
tune while watching a mother
and her fawn drink from

the river, slowly
I get up snapping a branch,
As they both run to

the edge of the woods;
I walk home slowly but glad,
It is summer now.

Nicole Robin Lind
LITTLE THINGS
I wonder why
I love the sound of a storm
The wind whistles; the thunder roars;
the
Lightning strikes; the snow blows.
I wonder why
I love soft babies
Baby puppies wiggle; baby kittens
play;
Children laugh.
I wonder why
I love all four seasons
Spring's breezes; summer's heat;
fall's
Smells; winter's snow on the
windowpane.
I wonder why
I love the little things
A butterfly whisking about; a horse's
precious
Nicker; a chipmunk comes to say
hello.
I wonder why
Such peaceful, tranquilizing things
fascinate me.
I wonder why.

C Anthony Bennett
PROOF OF ESCAPE

Dedicated to Corey Jay Ayers, May 5, 1972-May 21, 1990. Corey escaped—and is now in Eternal Glory!

I tried to reach for a place to gain a
winning, but I found none.

I did not trust in myself.

I willed myself to defeat evil and to
find that place, again, to hold me
firm.

I stumbled not and did not find that
small, but stable place.

I continued my climb.

And I received my reward—one
small material gift—yet a reward
so great was the blessing I
received in my heart because of
my faith.

And I could feel the dragon's huge
eyes, staring in disbelief—

Stare on, dirty serpent!

Glennis M Olson
A PASSING THOUGHT

This poem is for my husband.

Wild geese flying high above—
A skein of grey yarn, blowing
Curled across the sky.

Kathy Venditti
THE SPECIAL MIRACLE

This poem is dedicated to "Karen, my miracle daughter." Love Mom

It is so wonderful to see you smile—I thank the dear Lord above
For bringing you through this trauma—and showering you with his love.

Three months ago things looked so grim—gloom was all that I could see
But you were so brave and fought so hard—it was a miracle to me.

Some days were good and some were bad—you had your ups and downs
But with your strong perserverance—
I knew you would come around.

It's a very sad thing for a mother to see-one of her children suffering in pain
But the power of prayer did wondrous things—no prayers were said in vain.

God sent a guardian angel—to watch over and comfort you
He sent you wonderful doctors—to medically get you through.

He blessed you with wonderful family and friends—and fellow workers too
They all poured out their love to show—how much they cared about you.

Thank God the nightmare is over—
you're well and on your way
To reach new goals—to make new friends—to enjoy each beautiful day.

I'm so grateful for all the blessings—
I've received from the Lord above
Especially for a daughter to be proud of—to cherish—and to love.

I pray that God will bring you joy—
peace—and bless you too
Because that special miracle "Karen" just happens to be you.

And so my miracle daughter—when you look to the heavens so blue
Just remember you're always in my prayers—and know that I—love—you.

Wendy Cocco
LIFE

Life is hard sometimes you see
When things don't go right for you and me
You want to scream at this world and spit
You want to give up, you want to quit
You feel like no one really cares
No one gives and no one shares
You tell your friends your problems
Hoping to get some soothing advice
But all they say is their problem's worse
Or, Oh that's very nice
Why doesn't anyone care anymore,
Oh, why can't they see?
Why do they look at the way I dress,
Why can't they look at me?
You know before you have the Lord in your life
That is how you think
But, when you die the Lord's not going to care
If you died in blue or pink

Shelly L Vonhof
IN THE STILLNESS OF THE NIGHT

This poem is dedicated to Gloria, my friend forever.

In the stillness of the night,
You can hear a tear fall to the ground.
Somewhere under the moon and stars,
Someone is reaching out to dry that falling tear.
And once again you can see the same eye gleaming,
Only to stream once again with a brand-new tear.

Why must we play the games?
Why can't we just be honest?
Take my hand, I will show you my world.
Give me your hand and we will explore your world.
Isn't that what life is really all about?
Are we all so busy we haven't time for love?
In time we will loose ourselves, and our worlds will shatter.

What we feel is life—don't let it go.
For once it is gone, it is gone forever.
Let's hold our hearts close and walk forward into the sunlight and leave the darkness behind.
For if we walk away, we might not have tomorrow.

Rita Iris Cutler
POETRY

This poem is dedicated to Natalie Marshak, my darling mother and my inspiration.

Poetry should soar free and wild,
not be tepid, lame or mild.
It should radiate heat and light,
have a fang and take a bite.

Whether it deals with love or hate,
it should reel and dance and sate.
Lift my heart and mind and soul,
eternal horizons be its goal.

It should stupefy, stun and daze,
sear and burn and broil and blaze.
Fly beyond my wildest dreams,
with its vast, audacious themes.

Make me quake, quiver and tremble,
a mass of goose flesh to resemble.
Scare me, awe me, speak of love,
hurl bolts of lightning from above.

Muse, oh Muse, set my heart afire,
and cheat me not of this desire.
No mere, mortal verse for me,
I crave God-like poetry.

Linda Hipp
SEA GULL

To the most important people in my life—My husband Aubrey Hipp, Jr., My children, Kevin and Kim.

White wings, flapping, with azure blue
above and below.
Head cocked to the right as if scanning the vastness for
some unknown danger.
Graceful in flight—
yet aware of any miscalculation,
the inability to pull out of a steep dive—
or the danger of flying into eternity and never coming home again.
One last look at the beauty of the sea and sky united—
then a graceful turn,
Homeward Bound.
Yet knowing that he
is the freest of all things living
and with each day—
A new flight!

David James Billman
THE ANSWER TO SHELLY

Why? Why?
I have no answers,
only feelings,
feelings I know are true,
the feelings I have for you.

The triples of questions
I don't understand
Tell me the answers
Tell me our plans.

The secret of love
share it with me
and tell me the charm
I share with thee.

The secret of love
has no place with charm
open your heart
I'll do you no harm.

You say you're my friend
and charming indeed
just let me fulfill
your every wish and every need.

Now, you say you're the one
as friends we are
I wish for more
upon a shooting star.

Cheryl Taylor
HAPPY SIXTEENTH BIRTHDAY, MY SON

Happy sixteenth birthday, my son;
Was it not just yesterday I was yelling walk don't run;
Now I will be saying, watch the road!
slow down, did you use all my gas?
It is so hard for me to look to your future, when I was such a needed part of your past,
My football hero you will always be,
Remember as you go through life,
you take along a part of your dad and a part of me.
Take our good points and leave behind our bad,
We weren't always right nor are we always fair,
But our decisions are made out of love, and because we so deeply care,
To the top of life's ladder I know you will climb,
Because you were blessed with such an incredible mind,
So go my son, live your life, but remember one thing,
Please be happy, honest, and kind.

John MacLean
HIGH UP ON THE MOUNTAIN

High up on the mountain, between the rocks and thorn,
A quiet spray erupts, a mighty river's born.
From deep within its sylvan womb, it struggles to be free,
To feed and grow and ever flow to find its destiny.
Gravity becomes the force that drives it ceaselessly,
From rugged peaks to lowland plains and lastly to the sea.
Man's life is like the river, flowing from the womb.
First strictured banks, then wider fields and finally the tomb.
Contamination oft occurs in rivers and in men,
But yet by nature's wondrous plan, they're purified again.
Both man and river oft display the many moods of life,
From placid pools to thundering rage with power to conquer strife.
A heaven for the river must be the boundless sea;
While man goes on his lonely way to meet eternity.

Jeannene A Tylee
TO MY HUSBAND

Thank you for the last thirty-three years,
For the love, the laughs and even the tears.
We were two, enjoying life and love together,
With the kids came late night feedings . . . whatever.
The pool where you also "baby-sat" for credit time
'Cause the kids were ours—not yours or mine.
You took time to teach them to swim, dive and sail.
Then stood by to support them if they should fail.
There were fender dents, broken toys, hearts and bones,
You were there to fix, soothe the pain and calm the moans.
We've spent our time in the E.R. and O.R. waiting room lounges,
We've seen them grow to adults and move away from us.
You gave our girls away as beautiful brides
With love, your support and an unmistakable look of pride.
What is this—a perfect man, no source of ire?
Heavens, no—but as our songs says, "You're my desire"
Now what does our bright future have in store?
Nothing—we had thirty-three years and can have no more.

Syndi Lee
GOD'S LOVING ARMS

Here in this country setting
Where peace and quiet abound
I feel as one, with nature
God's loving arms surround

Such a small part of the Universe
Just a spark, in the roaring flame
Just a grain of sand, in the desert
God loves me, just the same

I'm one of many, but different
Like the stars and planets above
A single blade, in a pasture of grass
And yet, I know God's love

I'm a part of all that surrounds me
But I'm individual too
As different as the sun and moon
Yet, consistent as morning dew

Here in this peaceful beauty
In the midst of nature's sounds
I'm truly one, with the Universe
God's loving arms surround

Geneve Baley
THE BEAUTY IN LIFE IS ETCHED
The Beauty in Life is Etched, as by Salvador Dali
(A Welcome to the 2nd Poetry Convention and its Star: Vincent Price)

The beauty in life is etched,
As by Salvador Dali: in nature's
Call to the splendor of the
Heights; where we who are
Gathered, come as like-minded
Souls, seeking to offer
Unity in traditional
Respect: for the human
Freedoms, in
Kindliness (as in opposition
To the US Constitution-outlawed
Cruel, and inhuman,
Treatment.)

The beauty in life is etched,
As by Salvador Dali: in God;s
Response; to our
Humble inspiration of
Eternal faith that
Radiates, like burning logs on the hearth
Lighting world fires—both day and night.

Jean Brunson David

Jean Brunson David
HOMEMAKER'S REVERIE
Various thoughts come to mind
As I shell my butter beans . . .
My imagination soars,
And I take this means
Of fantasy
To recall the rough edges
Of the day . . .
And determine to smooth
Them our same way.
On the whole,
With the beanshells
I shed the husks of my soul.

Jenni Alexander
MEMORIES
As I sat there, I thought of you;
Memories of heartache were all that I knew.
Watching and waiting for some little sign;
Wanting you back, to know you were mine.

Now as I lie here, falling asleep
I'm sad that we lost that feeling so deep.
And now there's only my empty heart
Slowly still beating, tearing apart.

Blurry now my dream of lasting love,
I long to be so far above
Where I can finally be free
Of these memories I forever see.

Sam B Smith
COLD GREY EYES
Like a stormy winter's skies,
Held my gaze and so I still lingered on.
To my mind
Came the fotuneteller's sign,
"When you reach to touch her hand she'll be gone."

Golden lights,
Music stirring love's delights,
Glances promising a longing heart's desire.
Still those eyes
Raged their storms of truths and lies,
Cutting deep to damp a smoldering fire.

Fly away,
Seek, and find another day—
Wait for love that warms the heart as the dawn.
Cold grey eyes
Held my gaze, but no surprise—
When I reached to touch her hand she was gone.

Judith C Edinger
AFFINITY

To; My Lawrence Earl.

Stop it, please!
I have no desire to be brought to my knees.
You make me quiver and shake.
You always give. Why don't you take?

"Innocent," you cry.
Well demond, you lie.
"I don't deserve all this," you plea.
Sorry, maybe it's all me.

Your command is your right.
So I'm told every night.
My position faces the ceiling,
While you're poking and feeling.

And when I approach you,
you sit there and stew.
Declaring you'd rather relax,
It's time to face the facts.

I am your mate,
Not your fate.
And, you over me,
doesn't make we.

Robert Frank Marano
TO IMAGINE A WORLD WITHOUT YOU!

Dedicated to my close companion, Kristine Marie Rodin, whom I dearly love with all my heart and soul . . . Here's looking at you, Kris!!!

To imagine a world without you,
Is to imagine a place without light and warmth!
Pray tell, A world lacking in love, care, faith, and hope,
Is a world without the only pristine Kristine
I know all too well—you!
Picture a Rose losing its rich, plush color red,
Then you will see a world without you!
As the water is to the creatures of the deep sea,
So are you to me.
The fish crave water to live and to play;
To enjoy themselves.
So too do I crave you to live and to play;
To enjoy ourselves—together!
As the towering, ancient mountains have grown from tiny hills,
So let our Love be born from our friendship,
And grow and grow to create a world . . .
Where I don't have to think about a world without you!
Because you will be right here
Next to me.

William J Harrison
VALENTINE FLOWERS

To Kathleen.

Oh, flower sender, as flowers received,
Heart reminisce, the future holds, I believe;
As if my life were but a flower:
Charm this nite forever be;
That crimson of yours, was red unto me.

J W Adams
BUSY LITTLE HANDS

To All My Children: Karen, Jay and Sandy

Busy, busy little hands
Oh, how they flit and fly
Picking up and putting down
Always asking what or why.

Always wanting more to know.
Looking, learning,
Watch them go.

When the time has finally come
And bedtime stories told
These busy hands will fall asleep
Teddy bears, rag dolls
They'll hold.

So, Mothers you must patience have
Let busy hands explore.
Cause they may belong to doctors
or presidents or more.

Sondra M Strotz
BOUNDED

For you, only, Kevin. Love Always, Me.

The moon reflecting all of Venus
Only God realizing all between us
The mystery, magic and confusing ways
Only the honest love we feel stays

The crescent moon comes so broken and frequent
Only time together contradicts loneliness spent
Then Venus with her present emotion
Only our passion is the true commotion

The separation of transcendental bodies in space
Only is pain in our loves case
Two cosmic powers bounded to time
Only one energy can be truly mine

The balance of Venus brings forth her love
Only our enchantment comes from above
The moon's pull and compelling ways
Only brings forth our love in play

The two bound hopelessly to eternity
Only our bond reflects true sincerity
Two planets evolving in rhythmic melody
Only never-ending in a cosmic flurry.

Janet Cooley
DREAM AND SEEK

In memory of Holly and Steve.

He came to me one summer night,
Standing in the pale moonlight.
He was such a sight.
His eyes called me with whispered pain.
His hair wet with the midnight rain.
You are my fantasy
A game we'll play called ecstasy.

Dream and seek is all he would speak
As I held his hand I felt so weak.
Night after night he came to me
Our shadows in the moonlight is all you could see.

The world was always sound asleep.
As we played our game of hide-and-seek.
Two people becoming as one.
The dreams we shared were so much fun.

Our bodies wet with the morning dew,
We hurried because we suddenly knew,
That the morning sun would soon arise.
Making our love dance vaporize

Night after night we shared the same plight,
Our bodies washed in the pale moonlight
My age seemed to fade,
As we dreamed and seeked in the darkened shade.

"Baby, can't you stay with me?"
Making life stand still,
Like a painted memory.
Just you and me.
Just you and me.
Forever like a memory.

Heather E Fogelman
SMALL MIRACLES

For my mother and father who encouraged me to start writing. For my husband and children who inspire me to continue and for my special gram.

The crash of a wave and the rustle of trees
The call of a dove and the calm of the sea
Each is special in its own way
Each is important to life everyday.
Nature produces so many surprises
The way the sun sets and the harvest moon rises
Much needed rain on dry dusty soil
And its soothing relief after long days of toil
Many ignore the wonders of living
The sharing and loving and joy of giving
The heartaches in life make it hard to remember
The beauty of snow on a day in December
One must believe that bad times have

passed
And hang onto beliefs that the good ones will last

Brenda M Dalbec
HIS PROPOSAL

Dedicated, with love, to Bill. All of his proposals were nice.

Miles of highway before me
Do I know where I am bound
I get lost on the back roads
And just ramble around

Won't you please travel with me
And help guide my way
Ride the long winding pathways
Share my dreams day to day

My dreams shift to high gear
And then back to low
I want to speed forward
Yet I want to go slow

People pass by so quickly
In the No Passing zone
Life can be oh so lonely
When you travel alone

The detours on life's road
Are not easily passed
Some help reading road signs
Is all that I ask

Won't you travel beside me
For the rest of my life
Down the highways and byways
Won't you please be my wife.

Carolyn Hagan

Carolyn Hagan
A WORLD FULL OF BEAUTY

As I stopped to view the roses
with the fragrance in the air,
I stop to think how very much
the Lord must really care.
For a world so full of beauty
if only you want to see,
It's just a portion of how much
He cares for you and me.
For it's in the soft and gentle
brushing of the wind,
Or in the loving caring smile
of a special friend.
It's in the soft and gentle hug
of some sweet precious child,
Or in the deer across the field
free and running wild.
And as I stop to smell that rose
all these things come to mind,
I'm so thankful for today
and each new gift I find.

Carolyn Hagan
JUST YESTERDAY

It seems like only yesterday
you'd take me by the hand,
And tell me some old stories
of a faraway land.
You'd set me on your lap to tell me
of this magnificent place,
I remember the sparkle in your eye
and the smile upon your face.
It seems like only yesterday
but as I look at you today,
Your walk has gotten much slower
and your hair has turned to gray.
I still watch you tell your stories
though I'm too big now for your
knee,
And I wonder if you realize
just how much you mean to me!
Yes, it seems like only yesterday;
no more than a month or so.
And as life rushes on I wonder
where did the time seem to go.

Carolyn Hagan
TOKENS

The things I do
I have a reason,
Doesn't matter the day
or even the season.
I don't want praise
or any kind of glory.
But behind all these things
there is a story.
I've sat back and watched
enough to know,
Just what it is
that pleases you so.
And these little things
are just a token,
Of feelings so deep
and often unspoken.

Sandi Briggs
SEASONAL MEMORIES

To Nigel

If I could capture all the memories of you, I would recall the smell of wood smoke on cold, crisp October mornings in the woods and of a small brown and white pup who consistently ventured just out of range.

I would conjure up summer thoughts of picnics beside small streams with a blackened teapot, and a special place, "vacation brook." Memories bring thoughts of late afternoons on a glass smooth pond where the trout mocked us and the black flies welcomed us.

Spring brings a flood of warm, sunny days, cool nights which led to long hot summer nights, opening the house to the desert under a star-filled sky.

Then there were the intimate, magic moments we shared, more so early in our relationship. The laughter, the excitement of seeing each other after a week, champagne in bed, rechts neben, Wally and Maggie stories, fires and dinner on cold winter nights.

It seems we learn something and benefit from each relationship, so as we leave this one, your memory will be with me as the seasons rush into years.

Geri D Aland
MY TRUE LOVE

In memory of my beloved daddy-o. Almost Father's Day—1989.

Oh that man could make me laugh;
And more so make me cry
Our love was strange I do admit; But
always we would try
In Winter when the lake would freeze
we'd play upon the ice
We'd bundle up to skate and fish;
We'd argue once or twice
When Springtime came we'd plow
the earth and carefully plant seeds
Our garden always grew so much;
Including many weeds
Summer came and Summer went; So
quickly every year
I'd watch the awesome sunflowers
grow; And watch him drink his beer
In Autumn he'd prepare his gear, to
hunt and fish and such
Although we fought, we'd always
make up; I loved the man so much
One Winter was unusual, we hardly
fought at all
Throughout that spring we laughed
and loved; Could this bliss last 'till
Fall?
All good things must come to an end;
And before Summer had gone it had
I lost the man I truly loved; I lost my
precious dad

Mary B Druckenmiller
THIS LIFE'S OVER; ETERNITY BEGINS

To Erline, Kari and Kory in loving memory of their husband and father, Mike Herchelroth. Love, Mary.

Honey, I love you,
But I'm too weak to eat.
I've fought this battle way too long,
And I'm really beat,
For this life's nearly over; eternity
will begin.

Is that a tear in your eye?
Oh, please don't be sad.
I'll be going home soon,
To meet our heavenly Dad,
For this life's almost over; eternity
will begin.

When you tuck in the children
tonight,
Tell them I love them.
Try to make them understand why I
must go,
Then let their tears flow and hold
them,
For this life's just about over; eternity
will begin.

It's time for me to leave now,
I'm so glad I'm ready!
Sweetheart, lean on Jesus harder than
ever,
For His love is constant and steady.
This life's over; eternity begins.

Barbara Ann Palmigiano
MY LIFE SEEMS SO EMPTY

My life seems so empty, even
though it's very full
There's a dull void consuming me,
that I just can't fill.
At times I feel so restless,
Like a tiger in a cage
There's an air of discontentment,
Like the birth of a new age.
My dreams are filled with fantasy,
My goals cannot be freed
My life is turning upside down My
mind just goes full speed.
There is a choice that I must make,
To be happy or be free
There is a chance that I can take
To live my dreams and still be me.
I need to know which path to take,
To set my soul free,
I need to know which one is right,
Dreams or Reality.
I'm slowly being torn apart
by these visions in my mind,
I need the strength to help me search
for what it is that I must find.

Barbara Ann Palmigiano
UNTITLED

Like voices echoing through the wind
An eerie silence falls upon the mind,
where once was laughter and smiling
faces,
Now only stillness and empty places.
At times there is singing and silly
dances,
But mostly sadness and
cat-like stances.
A spirit that was free and once
uplifted
Turned into a soul with feelings
shifted.
But the person that you see is really
not me; just a shell of what I used to
be.

Joan Magiet
THE GARDENER (For George)

For my husband, George, my rock and my support and my jewels, Erik and Brett.

When you mowed the lawn
The sweat from your brow
Formed wings of water
Above the garden
Gliding toward the geraniums and
petunias
Pinned down by the earth
Grabbing the grass and shining
Like dew at dawn
Or a gust of raindrops
Interfering with the sun
One drop fell on the marigold buds
And glistened there
Until they blossomed into flowers

Joan Magiet
ERIK'S WALTZ

You came home last night
I waited for you
Like the sun waits to rise
Your eyes were magnets
I took my usual place
Against the pillow on your bed
I watched you toss sneakers, books,
sweaters
Across the floor
Mixing up your room
In my life once again
You played your new record
Rocking to the blur of beats
Like your old hero, John Travolta
Juggling phone calls and suitcases
With kisses
Loneliness is on vacation

Joan Magiet
ON TURNING 18 (For Brett)

Fragments of moments are all you
have to spare
You've always seemed to like your
time alone
When you are gone I wish that you
were near

You live your life removed from
those who care
You spend your waking hours on the
phone
Fragments of moments are all you
have to spare

Sometimes the ways you hide are
hard to bear
I wonder how your heart became like
stone

When you are gone I wish that you were near

My words of love to you are very clear
You feel it in each breath and in each tone
Fragments of moments are all you have to spare

Each little hug and kiss you give are dear
If I come close to you, you wince and groan
When you are gone I wish that you were near

"I love you, Mom" is what I like to hear
Please talk to me without a sigh or moan
Will fragments of moments be all you'll ever spare
When you are gone I wish that you were near

Kelly Jones

Kelly Jones
FIRECRACKERS
Get ready for some shaky and some quivering thunderous noises.
Get ready for the emeralds, diamonds, and shiny gold blasting in the gloomy, still night.
You hear roaring when the glowing dust glides through the air.
Sprinkles of colorful rain charges down rapidly.
Electric sparks conquer the sky.
Glints and gleams fly about.
Suddenly flames of fire appear after the take-off of the small gleaming meteors.
Vivid balloons burst in the cool, frosty air.
While colorful ladybugs scatter around.
Angels shoot arrows high in the sky.
Kshoo! Kshoo!
The firecrackers brilliantly light up the dark, dull night.

Kelly Jones
I'D LIKE TO LEAVE THIS WORLD FOR A WHILE
I'd like to leave this world for a while,
to get away from pollution and smog, which I
would put on trial,
for murdering this beautiful world to dirt, oily
oceans, and chemical plants.
I live in Southern California and people are going insane.
When you walk on the street, a gang will blow you
off your feet!
We are having a drought here but up above all we
get is acid rain.
We build so much from engines to factories and more
and more, we are thrashing this world to its core.
Before you move into that town house or condo,
just think you took away a home from a deer or doe.
Let the animals run free, don't cut down anymore
trees.
Make sure no smog comes out of your
exhaust pipe,
that will be just one less pollution to wipe.
This world is turning into one bad cough,
so you and me me and you can help turn pollution, smog, and more off!
This world has always been a great world,
and always would of been if it had of been for
the modern man.
I'd like to leave this world for a while.

Naomi LeVay
THE SINGER
A song flutes through the trees
That stand so tall together
And I am glad
I cannot name the singer.

I am happy to be haunted
By this song.
Memory is stirred
But does not yield.

My cup has been empty
But now sound
Fills it to the brim.
I desire to be one with the singer
And never to know its name.

Rita Thorn Forman
DON'T WAIT TOO LONG
Don't wait too long to visit me.
Come while I can still enjoy the sound of your laughter,
And share your triumphs and your woes.
Don't wait till this mind is too clouded by age,
To recall good times we had and loved ones' names.
Come while I can still remember.
I will not feel your tears on my coffin,
Nor see your eyes filled with regret.
So, don't wait too long to visit me.
Come while I can still touch you
And tell you I love you.

Donna Madrid
FINAL FAREWELL
I was cleaning out my bookshelves
Like I once cleaned out my heart,
When I came across your picture,
It caused memories to start.

Memories, not feelings,
For you my heart's asleep.
The giant fist that clutched it once
Has released the hurt so deep.

It's been awhile since then
And I'm over you by now.
It took time to learn to trust again,
I'd almost forgotten how.

Now I'll put your picture back in place
Between the pages of my mind,
And forever leave you as you once left me,
So very far behind.

B L Allen
A PHOTOGRAPH
A visage of youth cut in fine lines
Inspired by dreams without confines.
The canvas I paint is no mystery,
'Tis merely my first photograph of thee.

Yellowed and aged from all the years
Of jubilant joy and sorrow filled tears—
Our restless lives take on change upon change
And neither photo nor past can we rearrange.

A journey begins with a spirit unstilled,
Ending with life's dreams as of yet unfulfilled.
But still the picture I carry with me
'Tis my cherished photograph of thee.

Memories may cloud, falter and fade,
Obscurred from decade to decade,
Yet somehow one image remains clear—
My simple snapshot of yesteryear.

But as love glows warm in one's heart,
I ponder a thought with a start:
As I hold so near my photo of thee,
Do you hold so dear your photo of me?

Charles Dixon

Charles Dixon
DEDICATION TO A FEMALE FRIEND

This poem is dedicated to Anita N. Bryant.

If I could rebuild all my friends, reform and reconstruct their lives, I would use your character as a blueprint because if every man, woman and child thought as you, this world would be at peace. I'm inclined to believe you're an angel in disguise and I'm glad you are my friend, I've been looking and you were here all that time. Your friendship is a blessing, so here's to you, a special lady.

Charles Dixon
THE CLASSICAL MAN
The classical statement . . . I'm a real man . . . Is definitely misinterpreted by my fellow black convict clan . . . For a man to truly be real . . . He must possess certain emotions . . . Love, Hate, Fear and Courage . . . Must be handled with prominent promotions . . . One who does not love . . . is a person who is all alone . . . One who does not fear . . . from this earth, will soon be gone . . . If a man is real . . . and finds it foolish to cry . . . he is no good to himself . . . He should give up life to die . . . If a man does not take the time . . . to tell someone how much he appreciates their love . . . He defeats the purpose of living . . . A divine gift from above . . . To be real . . . is to cry when sad . . . To be real . . . is to lash out when mad . . . To be real . . . is to say I honestly love you . . . That's being a real man . . . That's when you get the respect that's due . . .

Charles Dixon
MOTHER OF MINE
A person who bore the pain of my birth,
has given a gift to this planet earth.

I love her with all my heart,
from this lady my love will never part.

The queen of my world she shall remain,
she's been there through sunshine and rain.

This lady I speak of is none other,
than the love of my life . . .

My precious MOTHER . . .

Charles Dixon
COOL TEARS OF LOVE
As the cooler weather sets in
my heart grows weak,
and my feelings get thin.

I suffer the loss of you my dear
the woman I love,
oh how I wish you were here.

To have your love is a treasure
which I really need,
and loving you is pure pleasure.

So think of me as you go to sleep
'cause when I awake,
Deep within my heart I weep.

L A Nagel
MY INNOCENT HOMETOWN
On the foot of a mountain
My hometown sits down
Its neighbors are a fountain
And a glen in a misty gown
The trees garnish its suburbs
And the water in its burbs
In an alley not a street
Where the boys and girls meet
The hen teams with the cow
To hail it and to bow
Technology is not the solution
To live and shun the pollution!
We, truly, lived before
With no drug in the store
We, verily, could again
smother up this villain!!

Evelyn Montvila
A LOVELY CHILD
I went to see a lovely child
behind an iron door.
Her face was pale her eyes were dull,
and she would smile no more.

She recognized me standing there
she almost touched my face.
I put my arms around her neck

and gave a fond embrace.

She pulled away without a word.
She did not want my love.
I hung my head and bit my lip,
while she just stared above.

I loved you then, I love you now.
Whatever brought you here?
What did I do? What did I say?
Oh God! Please tell me dear.

I walked away and said goodbye
and all I felt was pain,
But I still have my hopes and dreams
that she will soon be sane.

Evelyn Montvila
THE TROPHY
A hunter
A gun
A deer
A son

A bullet
A sound
Red on the ground

A cry in the air
Retching not fair

A head on the wall
Madness that's all

Hate through the years
Remembering tears

Why tell me why?
The deer had to die?

A head on the wall
A trophy that's all.

Gloria J Nauer
JACOB'S HOPE

This is dedicated to Jacob Wetterling, who was abducted as he returned home from a convenience store in St. Joseph, Minnesota on October 22, 1989.

Turned on the TV and
Jacob you were there.
Eyes brightly sparkled,
all I could do was stare.
Your stories touched a nation,
brought tears to many eyes.
Reminded us that there are
dark clouds,
among the bluest skies.
Turned on the radio and
Jacob you were there
Lots of people pulling together,
searching everywhere.
Buttons with your picture
on them, balloons sent to the sky.
In hopes of your safe return,
as the days keep passing by.
Jacob we're with you, in
our hearts and in our prayers.
Jacob hang in there,
we love you and we care.

Gloria J Nauer
THRU MY EYES
I shall be your eyes
when you can no longer see.
And thru my eyes
you shall see the world, in
all of its glory.
You'll see the clouds of white
as they pass by.
The brightest stars sparkle
from way up high.
Thru my eyes you'll be able to see,
the dawn's early light.
Admire the eagle
as it soars out of sight.
You'll see the waves
as they come crashing down.
And an animal giving birth
not making a sound.
Thru my eyes.

Gloria J Nauer
COMPASSION FOR THE HOMELESS
Trembling she reaches out with
a calloused hand.
Looking for compassion, someone
who understands.
Her home is on the streets, she
has no place to stay.
Just one of the many homeless
in the good old U.S.A.
She used to wear the finest clothes,
that money could buy.
Now her only dress is soiled and torn,
as tears fall from her eyes.
Is there anybody out there who
won't just turn away.
Find compassion for the homeless,
in the good old U.S.A.

Bob Tesh
BEHOLD THE DANDELION
I've searched the world over, both far and above,
To find a small flower to tell of my love.
It must be strong, but yet graceful, to sway with the angry wind;
It must be strong, but yet gentle to tell of its love within.
I looked to the mighty rose with its beauty and its color;
It has the strength and love unlike any other.
But its strength lies in brambles, and its beauty fades away;
So all of that strength and love did last but for a day.
I summoned all the lilies, and the other flowers, too.
To show their strength and beauty to compare my love for you.
But alas! I found not one to compete for such a test.
They all fell short in some way, although they showed their best.
I cried, "O, Lord, help me to find that flower for my love;
Let it be the perfect one—the one from Heaven above."
And He said, "My son, go to the fields, down to the meadows fine;
Down past the rose and the lilies, and behold, the Dandelion!"
Now here is a flower both strong and bold that can outlast the seasons thru;
Its roots go deep, its spirit strong, just like my love for you.
It can grow almost anywhere, from the mountains to the glen;
It can share its love with everyone, with just a kiss of the wind.
So may I share with you this day my treasure of a kind;
May I say to you, my dearest one,
"Behold the Dandelion!"

Bob Tesh
THE ODE OF DANNY'S ARGUMENT
So here I sit upon my groins, copying off these dang old poems;
And now I ask you, teacher, dear, why must I waste my own time here?
When there's so much that I could do, instead of wasting time with you.
But then you say it must be done, regardless of the lack of fun.
I could be fishing or chasing the wind, for doing this seems a downright sin!
But you tell me to keep on writing and shut up all that dadburn griping.
Could Flander's Field have used a poet, as the big guns pierced the sky?
Could we have turned the foe with but a pen? Oh, no, no, Ma, not I!
And how many rebels were turned in fear with only the force of a poet's gear?
Then you told me so solemnly:
"Danny, if you could only see
The mighty power of the poet's pen, for to his eyes there is no end.
He can change a tree from stump to leaf, a charging sea to a calm relief.
There is no limit to a poet's pen, for it comes from the soul, from deep within.
How oft have we read of a lover's meet with but a sigh of a pen,
Or heard the words of fathers' past as though they were living again?
We learn of nations far abroad, through the eyes of the poet's mind;
We see the lands of ages past that are left so far behind."
Then as I began to understand what she was trying to say,
I bowed my head in humble shame saying, "Teacher, teach me more, I pray."

Eleanor R Lofton
ACCEPT THE ABUNDANCE
Come away, my friend, from your problem—load
From the cares, the worries and many fears.
Let Go! and laugh again on happiness' road
Waste not these beautiful wonder-filled years.

Let Go! Quit shoveling the endless debris
Accept the Abundance and joy and whatever is true
It's you . . . You who accept the problems you see
YOU who should know that the Christ, God's Best
Is here within you.

Eleanor R Lofton
WHAT AM I?
I am the flowers I see, the wind I feel, the smile of a child
the best I know and the least I know, be it good or bad, still if I see it, then that is me . . . that is what I am . . . all the life around me that I experience or feel or relate to. What else is it but myself. I am not separate, the whole of it all is what I am.

If I see you as shiftless or worthless or evil or bad . . . that is myself I see. If I see you good and great and wonder-filled then this is none other than I. Or, if some scene or happening I evaluate, I only do so because this is the me of me, and none else.

The funny part is . . . we think we are separate from all we see, judge, condemn, or applaud, when all the time it is ourselves being pictured as though viewing ourself in a mirror.

Who, or what is this in this world I see? None other than myself . . .
That's who I am.

Donna LeBlanc
MEXICAN ACCORD
While the senorita washes soil from her clothes
in an almost dried-up riverbed,
Christ stills the stormy Sea of Galilee
and by that belief the winds of change blow not in Mexico.

Without distraction,the Senor sends his children to barter for dollars,
for daily bread, for devotion to a church which has neither
weathered nor crumbled.
In the red baked land of Mexico, the paths on which the
people walk are neither paved nor littered with bramble.

The donkey waits underneath the still moist Palm
accepting the red baked land of Mexico as do the hands holding the rosary in daily devotion to a blessed Virgin.

The patriarches hold out the Bible in reconciliation
and the red baked lands, hands accept because they know so little else. The winds of change blow not in Mexico and by that belief there is still hope.

Jeanne Marie Madrid
PARENT'S GARDENS

For my best friend, my mom Sandy, and the apple of my eye, my dad, Tom. I'm not trying any more, I'm doing!!

You planted a tiny seed
  in which you hoped would grow
And as the sprout showed tiny leaves,
  It was passive strength that showed.
With love and patience and dares,
  You reaped the soil of its ugly weeds.
Doing all the best you could
  To nourish the thriving leaves.
Each leaf held a part of life—
  One of them was trust; another felt life's pain,
One was joy and hurt and risk—
  Another was soft and tame.
And so this tree reached its full potential,
  A unique entity began to bloom—
Results of tender time and years
  It yearned to find more growing room.
Giving all you had to offer:
  Love and anger, joy and sorrow,
You helped this flower of life
  Search for its own tomorrows.
When once you thought that all you had
  Was one tiny little seed,
You kept the faith and dreams to nourish
This flower that is me . . .

Dalia C Moss
INSIDE OUT
Would you let me in
Your private cocoon,
Shrouded in peace
And sainted with shade.
The lusty tomb
Of private dreams:
In awe of reality.
A stance akin to
Broken hearts,
As one grows weary
To plummet from here,

To an old paradise.
United in teaching,
The panes encased.
History told by
Impossible power.
Hands held to head,
The bizarre sheds no light.
Like fame in a dream,
And a wish in the void.

Nelda Ward Williams
ODE TO A RANCHER

To my dear husband, Sod, and our beloved Arbon Valley.

Remember him when the curlew's softly calling and you smell the new mown hay—
And the evening shadow's soften—at the close of a long work day.

Remember him when the roundup's in the makin' and when the bacon's in the pan—
And when the campfire's slowly dying and when he was leadin' "Dan."

Remember him when the brandin' fire's burning and you smell the scorching hair—
And you raise the iron to set the brand—then pause to feel his presence there.

Remember him at the dawn of each new day and when it's calvin' time once more—
And as each new life adds to the herd, new blood, and one more chore.

Remember him when spring comes to the valley and the meadows come to life—
And when you hear the children laughing and through both the good times and the strife.

Remember him when the wild rose is bloomin'—and silver tips the sage—
And when the wild coyote' pup first howls and the new life comes of age.

Remember him when the trail is hot and dusty and the herd is stringin' on—
As you head 'em up to the summer range where the feed waits fresh and strong.

Remember him as you start into the mountains and the breeze comes down the draw—
And the quaking aspens beckon and you hold this all in awe.

Remember him in all of nature's wonder and when twilight fades to night—
And when the warming sun comes up again—and with it comes the light.

Remember him when snow clouds shroud "Bowen" mountain and winter grips the land—
And comes the raging blizzards—and Mother Nature deals her hand.

Remember him when the drying summer winds wither the feed and crops—
And the snow comes short and the springs dry up and the water table drops.

Remember him in better times when the grass grows strong and tall—
And the water holes fill up again and the springs put out their "all."

Remember him when his country called him and he left a wife and little son—
And crossed the enemy infested waters and served until the cause was won.

Remember him when he rode his great champions, among them, "Poco Star" and "Steen"—
And "Poco's Herfie" and "Ches-A-Luck"—and he fulfilled a dream.

Remember him when he laid "Old Star" to rest at the head of an unmarked draw—
For him that stud had gave his "all" and held the crowds in awe.

Remember him when the tamarack is turning and the canyons deck their walls—
And early snows dust the back country and the mighty bull elk calls.

Remember him when the huntin' camp is loaded and the pack string takes the trail—
And when the meat is in the mantes and the hunter spins his tale.

Remember him when the lantern light is burning and camp chores are almost done—
And supper's on in the hunters' tent at the end of a day he's won.

Remember him when he promised his love he'd never leave her and took the vows that have lasted long—
And raised his sons to manhood and taught them right from wrong.

Remember him as he's runnin' out of sunsets and the strength of his reckless youth—
And his love for family and his respect for truth.

Remember him for the tender love he feels for grandkids, straight from a heart of purest gold—
And for the special times they've shared together, a grandad's bond to n'er grow cold.

June McMillan Rice
IF I WERE SANTA CLAUS

Dedicated to John David Wooton.

Of all the things that I could wish for,
Anything I want,
I'd wish that I could spend this Christmas,
being Santa Claus,
I'd put my elves to work at once,
making dolls and sleds,
Then pray a humble prayer,
kneeling down by Santa's bed.
"Lord I've filled all of the orders,
Thanks for all your help,
Now could we get down to business,
granting wishes for the rest,
Divide the loaves and feed the hungry,
Down to the smallest child,
Heal the hurt of all the burdens,
Let me walk my neighbor's mile,
Grant peace to all the nations,
God, keep them safe today,
Fill every lonely heart tonight
With something warm to say,
Lord, as I close my eyes this evenin',
while wonders You perform,
I thank you just for listening',
to my prayer for Christmas morn'. Amen.

Dawn M Burton
SOMETHING SPECIAL

With love and appreciation, to my grandparents—Frank and Mary Ellen Johnson.

Something special,
Someone say,
Love is the thing of today.
Love is something you can't buy,
It neither comes plain,
Nor will you find it layin,
It's that special something
From your heart.
Someone say "Let's make a start,"
You will find it in your heart,
You won't have to look long and hard,
Nor will you look deep and far,
Because when it's time to find your love,
You won't find him/her in a car,
You'll find him/her outside your door
And in your heart.
Just like grandparents say,
Right from the start.

Elizabeth Ingram
LOVE

I dedicate this poem to my husband, Thomas, and my family, for the "love" we share—forever.

Whenever love isn't all that it seems
Stop and reminisce about your dreams.
Recall the good times.
Learn not to regret,
And happiness is what you'll recollect.
Yes, you'll have days when you'll disagree;
Sometimes this is how love needs to be.
When you communicate freely by speaking your mind,
Make sure the volume is understanding and kind.
Don't ask for too much. Live and let live.
The gift you'll receive is the gift which you give.
When you work for love, love works for you.
So give love a chance; do the best you can do.
Keep your relationships fun and amusing,
And the next time love won't be so confusing.

Louise K Haywood
EASTER

On Easter morning, clear and bright
When lilies bloom so pure and white
And violet's fragrance is everywhere
Remember
Easter is a time for prayer.

On Easter morn, when church bells toll
And down the avenue you stroll
In new clothes and curls in your hair
Remember
Easter is a time for prayer.

When the sun shines bright on Easter Day
And you are ready for work or play
Remember
Easter is a time to pray.

Dorothy Vaughan
SUNRISE . . .

I stood by my window,
Admiring the dawn,
Watching beauty unfold,
When the darkness was gone.

The emerging sun,
In the greyness of morn,
Was a wondrous sight,
As the new day was born.

As daylight spread,
Throughout the land,
It brought to view,
The work of God's hand.

No artist could capture,
The passing of night,
The shadows . . . the colors,
Were a beautiful sight.

If all the great artists,
Were put to a test,
They'd have to agree,
That God's work was best.

Mary Foster
WHAT A FOOL I WAS

I gave it all to you,
knowing deep in my soul I was only giving, never to take from you.
My heart was an open book
for you to read, but you never once turned the page.
All you did was read the cover over and over and over again.

What a fool I was to believe that
you could possibly love me!
What a fool I was to think that
you may have cared for me.
How you must be laughing now!
Well, laugh, my friend.
Go ahcad and laugh.

You will never know the real joy
that love can bring.
You will never know the happiness
true love can give.
Laugh at the fool I was for loving you.
You are a real fool . . .
And I feel sorry for you.

Dee Anderson
LOST LOVE

I know our love is in the past,
And when I see you I know it still lasts.
But now it's too late, for there's someone new.
I love him, but I love you too.

I can only love you from a distance,
But I want to hold you, oh so close,
You're in my heart, but out of my reach
Somehow we got torn apart.

The kiss you gave me on my brow
Are like the tears I shed now.
So warm, so tender, so loving, so true
It's so hard living without you.

That's the way it is now, but it doesn't have to be.
I'll be with you again someday, just wait and see.
I maybe with someone all brand-new,
But there's no stopping me loving you.

I'll wait for that day, like you waited for me
We'll be together again, just you wait and see.

Donna M Staton

RED LIGHTS

In my little fishbowl, I happily drive
down the road.
Melodies of up-beat harmonious
volumes consume my spaces,
Cruising along to destinies' places in
my observation tank.
Noticing the victims' smiles traveling
off with the pace they keep;
Staring into their lives while I wait
for the lights of spring
I read into their ideas of being and for
them I weep;
Somehow churned in life's blenders
are their lost emotions and hearts;
Haven't quite figured how life starts
or why they've come from.
Pedals I push and move on ahead my
tin-sided fishbowl and I.
Watching the world from a haven
safe from the weather,
And glad to be traveling my way.

Gary J Henry

HOPE FOR THE HOMELESS

To everyone who forgets that the Homeless are people too. Also to those who have been there, never forget where you've been.

Old and decrepit, Never changing
Only rearranging words too often
said;
Out into the cold, Oh the burdens
they bare
A trembling hand wipes away a tear.

They never know just where they are
going,
But they look back at where they've
been
Struggling day by day; barely getting
by
Sometimes, asking God to let them
die.

Begging for sunshine only getting
rain
With weary eyes and tired feet,
No money in their pockets
And nothing to eat.

So have a little hope;
To help them cope;
Take away their sorrow and shame
For like us, they too, have a name.

Adam Mark Belles

Anne Himko Belles

MADRIGAL MOMMY

Whole wheat-bread and pencils,
notebooks and herbal tea—
Trademarks of a housewife
who would a poet be.

Contest after contest,
still I turn out this "schlock."
Fast lines while Baby sleeps—
listen, and watch the clock.

Enter writing contests
to see your name in print.
Dream of fame and fortune
but still be brushing lint.

Pick up toys, scrub bottles,
hug for the hundredth time.
To him, I'm just his "Mom,"
despite each published rhyme.

Anne Himko Belles

WAITING FOR ADAM

For my precious son, Adam—your worth is immeasurable. You are my earthly purpose, and my reason for being.

Unsure of the outcome of my present
condition,
Waiting for the temporary to
become permanent,
Apprehension and uncertainty
pervade the transition.
Retrospect assures me that you're
truly heaven sent.

Though you now are faceless, already
you have a name.
Divine intuition has foretold
specific gender.
Many lives, oddly intertwined, will
never be the same,
Zealously accepting the gilt balm
you will render.

Expectations grow larger than
abdomen or breasts.
Ambivalence prevents them from
soaring to lofty heights.
Anticipation and frustration increase
as weeks progress,
Discomfort and impatience are
two of many plights.

The denouement approaches, your
finale is near.
Labor is aptly called, for it is such
a task, indeed.
Held upward like a grail, my precious
son is finally here.
A great reward has been reaped,
having sown such a small seed.

Like the first man, you enter the
world in eager awe.
Lifting your head, you survey with
blinking, birth-swollen eyes.
Unconditional love is yours, despite
any trivial flaw.
Unhappiness and pain have earned
the ultimate prize.

Pauline McCarthy

ONWARD AND UPWARD

As all of us grow inwardly and
experience inner peace,
We find ourselves surrounded by an
aura of the cosmic may it never
cease!

We develop an intimate association
with our private God within

The feeling of universal love grows
for us to revel in

We sense deeper meaning within our
conscience life with compassion for
others' suffering and other people's
strife.

This kindness, empathy, and service
can only be shown through an
exchange with other people
This is well-known!

Michael A Sparling

MORNING MARRIAGE

Lying here with you now
Is like something from a dream
Like a long awaited pause
Beside a mountain stream
Or sleeping in the open night
With wildflowers all around
When the beating of our hearts
Is the only sound.

Let us make our promises
On tomorrow's rising sun
And take our pledge of love
While your hair is still undone
In the quiet of the morning
On the pond's beach of sand
The rings from my skimming stone
Will be your wedding band.

Michael A Sparling

MEMORIES AND AN OLD GREY CAT

Memories and an old grey cat
are all I found today.
Familiar pathway through
the woods, empty,
without footprint.
Patches of grass once bent
by our blanket, now,
standing tall, almost proud for once
having
been honored by
your presence.

The old grey cat was your friend
but I loved you.
We walk silently on, together,
pausing briefly, thinking
we saw a glimpse of you
behind a tree,
flirting and laughing
as you always did,
before it was just me and an
old grey cat.

Vaughn Robert Norberg

WITHOUT YOU

What would I do without you?
The world would cease to exist
Life as it is I would miss

Water wouldn't flow
Light would not glow
Trees wouldn't grow

The sun wouldn't shine
Poems would no longer rhyme
Clocks would tell no time

My heart wouldn't beat
New friends I might never meet
Love I would no longer seek

...........................Without You

Vaughn Robert Norberg

IF NATURE IS NO LONGER MORE

Wisdom exists not
While our
Water,
Air
and land rot

For to appreciate nature
Is to understand man
And to love nature
Is to educate man

For all of nature
Is at the mercy
Of the human hand

Nature now hides
Its treasures less and less
As man now presides
Science will be put to test

Tomorrow we will see
What fruits are left on trees
What kind of air we'll breathe
And still will water pour?
If nature is no longer more?

Juanita Villegas

LEAD US TO SOME SOUL TODAY

Dedicated to Brother and Sister M. L. Michener.

Lead us to some soul today;
That we might teach someone to pray
Help us do the best we can
To lift some soul from the sinking
sand.

Let us care for the ones we love
But more for those who don't have a
home above
Lead us with thy special light
That we will teach both day and
night.

Guide us with thy strong great arm
And keep us safe from every storm
Help us hold so strong and true
To the God who wants me and you.

Wm Kline

ON A SANDY BEACH, SPARKLING WHITE

On a sandy beach, sparkling white
I turn to you in the pale moonlight
Your eyes shimmer
A brilliant green
You're the most beautiful thing
I've ever seen
I touch your soft skin
With my fingertips
Hearing the sound
Of distant ships
And the waves
Gently caressing the shore
Hold my face in your hands
And kiss me some more
I love the time we get to spend
Please be mine
So it will
Never end

Wm Kline

SILENT RAGE

Silent Rage
In a cage
Someone let me out
Feed the beast
A hearty feast
Someone let me out
Too young to be
Alone with me
Someone let me out
Can you trust
Such animal lust
Someone let me in

Barbara Sorensen

'CAUSE MY MAMA ABORTED ME

I am a child of a King
I am wrapped in innocence
In my mama's womb
And Jesus has covered by
With love and happiness
I thought I was well-blessed
Then along came sin
In the manner of betray
And took all my happiness
away
'Cause my mama aborted me
the other day

I was like a little cocoon
In its mother's nest
All ready—For my travels

on earth

But something came and
spirited me away
'Cause my mama aborted me
the other day
I was all pink and velvety
Just like a delicate rose petal
Ready for my mama's arms
And sent—Straight from heaven
But now it's too late—Sin had
its way
'Cause my mama aborted me the
other day

Barbara Sorensen
JESUS'S BIRTH
The Christ Child in His manger lay
There in the stable among the hay
And Mary and Joseph were filled
with delight
Because the angel said He was Jesus
Christ
Born to be King of the Jews by
Heaven's right
Then the Wise Men to Bethlehem
came
Carrying gifts of gold, frankincense,
and myrrh
Knelt down beside Him and blessed
His name
Then departed to their country
From whence they came

Then Mary and Joseph and the Baby
three
Into Egypt they did flee
From Herod, the terrible king
Until he could be called a Nazarene
This wonderful story of Jesus's birth
Was man's first Christmas present on
earth
So deck the halls and trim the trees
And when Santa comes on Christmas
Eve
Remember the dear Christ Child
please.

Dorothy L Bigger
FIRST LIGHT
I walked my dog at six o'clock on
this September morn,
And in the field I stopped to watch a
new day being born.
The western sky was violet, the East
was aqua blue,
And scattered high up overhead were
clouds of rosy hue.
Then I recalled the sailor's lay of red
skies in the morning:
When dawn skies glow with crimson,
a sailor must take warning.
But there, knee deep in goldenrod,
feeling the soft air's kiss,
It seemed unlikely there'd be rain on
such a day as this.

The trees I walked beneath were
calm; I heard a bird's soft cry.
Now I was trudging home again,
beneath a brightening sky.
The dog was fed, the coffee made; I
sipped my steaming cup.
Then through the window I could see
leaves blowing wrong side up.
The scudding clouds were leaden
now; there was no cry of bird—
And on the sloping roof above, the
pouring rain I heard.
So quick a turn—from fair to
fierce—was not so very strange,
For the one thing ever certain is the
constancy of change.

Dorothy L Bigger
DAYBREAK IN WINTER
I walked my dog at eight o'clock one
cold December morn;
The winter sky was sullen gray, the
late moon thin and worn.
The earth was hard beneath my feet;
a cold wind chilled my face—
I pulled my muffler to my chin and
hurried on apace.

But even in the frozen field, as dead
as anything
New leaf buds on the barren trees
held forth a hint of spring.
The goldenrod, now dark and sere,
stood shaking in the snow.
It dropped its small seeds to the
ground; next spring, they'll sprout
and grow.

The pristine snow was everywhere; a
coverlet of white;
The green grass of last summertime
was hidden now, from sight.
An empty bird nest in a tree had a
dunce cap made of snow
And I wondered where the bird sang
now? Where did the fledglings go?

Those frozen buds will swell and
burst with new life's golden sheen.
Soft, melting snow will be pierced
through with blades of vibrant green.
Birds will return; they always have,
to fill the air with song.
And, plodding on through ice and
snow, I knew it wouldn't be long.

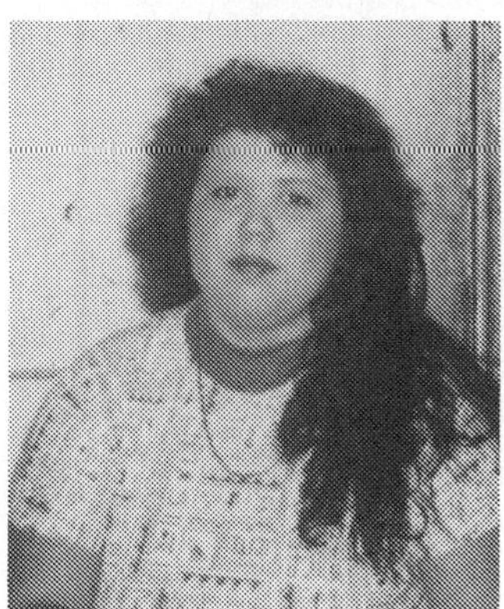

Clemencia Ann Mejias

Clemencia Ann Mejias
A MISTAKE
This poem is dedicated to my family. I couldn't have done it without your support and love. I love you all very much.

I was in love one time,
with someone I thought always
would be mine.
He never really cared,
But I can't stop thinking of the love
we once shared.

I fell in love, was my mistake,
Because his love was just a fake.
I already knew his name,
But he thought love was just a game.

Someday he will have received,
The same treatment that I had
conceived.
If there is a relationship you want to
make,
Be careful when you fall in love it
just might be a big mistake.

Dawn Harris
WHAT A FRIEND IS
For Jim and Beverly Stinnett

Two very special people in my life.
A friend is someone who's always
there,
A friend is one who really cares.
A friend will never let you down,
A friend will listen no matter how
bad it sounds . . .
A friend will never make fun of what
you say,
A friend will be there for you any
day.
A friend will help you with all his
heart,
A friend will do more than his part.
A friend will help you when you are
down and out
but this special friend will help you
without a doubt.
A friend will never turn his back on
you,
if he cares like he says he does.

James J Reuther PhD
TREES FOR ALL SEASONS
For reason must prevail. Be seeing you.

"Dearest Winter Trees"

Infinite is my fascination
Of a leafless tree's imagination.
With masterpiece rainbow of colors
brown
And singular intricacy up and down.
No matter the brightness of day or
night.
My heart races seeing its silhouette
slight.

"Arbor Again"

Spider web branches radiate in
random rows.
Patient nascence buds into sparkling
glows.
Brilliant verdant passion erupts when
each tree knows.
Joyous annual curtain call to
chromatic brown shows.

"Summer Senses"

Simmering green canopies swaying
with every breeze.
Producing soft murmurs for souls to
please.
Restful slow-motions that jigsaw and
tease.
Sightful, songful, sea-like trees.

"Fall Fiat"

Spectral explosions announce
imminent change.
Dotting treetops with chameleon
range.
Fanciful flight when wood's leaves
estrange.
Nature's poly and monochrome
beauty rearrange.

Randi L Copeland
BREAST AGAINST BREAST
For my mate, may our love be eternal.

Breast against breast we lay
Rolling as a wave to meet the shore
Our breath warm and blending
Absorbing each other to make us one
Wetness against wetness we create a
stream of familiar scents
Sweet and intoxicating, running
along our bodies
Embracing our desires to bare our
secret places
Knowing that acceptance will not be
turned away
Heart against heart, we pound wildly
within our depths
Arching like a rainbow across the sky
The rush in my womb tickles me like
a flame
As our love rises from the ashes of
our bodies burnt
Smile against smile, we part like the
winds of a desert
Swirling past the edges of the earth
To a higher plane of spirit known
only to ourselves

Tracy Anne O'Connor
AROUND THE CORNER
Robert—from '78 till forever and ever.

Around the corner you lived,
And came to me with just yourself to
give.

Night and day we talked, battled, and
cuddled on my front stoop,
Laughing and mocking Tony and
Ginny the snoops.

Still scared, but ready enough, your
mind was set;
And after the movie you questioned
me with your little love test.

You stole my lollipop and led the
chase,
We stopped far from our crowd and
then you set your pace.

I fought, you teased with my Blow-
Pop, keeping it from me all in fun.
Shutting me up, you asked me to go
steady sealed with a kiss of Bubble-
Yum.

We've had every movie, the Beatles
and Mets, the beach and 88th, and
together we've spent all our time.
With all our memories of pain and
cloud nine's and mainly being locked
up and making you all mine.

Robert, a poem from me to you,
So never to question that I'll always
love you.

Louise Eichinger
HOME ON THE HILL
Dedicated to: My beloved husband, Albert, and daughters, Nancy and Gail.

Leaving our home after many
Loving years
Where laughter was shared with
Sorrow and tears.
Family was raised and married
Off too,
Then came precious grandchildren
Filling our days anew.

Holidays spent with tender love
And care,
Each one looked forward to
Happily each year.
Blessed memories will remain
With all of us still
When we finally close the door
To our home on the hill.

Diane C Harwick
REFLECTIONS OF LIFE
To my Grandparents: In Loving Memory of Their Lives.

Reflections of life
Isn't life sometimes funny,

seems to appear bright and sunny.
There's plenty of fun and good times,
men, women share all kinds of lines.
As we grow and travel through life,
often encountering much strife.
Through problems and experiences we come,
difficulty is handled differently by some.

What we have gained by it all,
to learn and change is a constant call.
Yes, the ability to see and apply,
often strains the mental eye.
To correct and change what is needed,
a good course of life now seeded.
So far, by what you see and hear,
knowledge you have gained is clear.
Now that your course of life is almost gone,
their reflections of life well done.

Jeanie Marie Teel
MY HERO!

In remembrance of my Mother, Hazel Teel.

The grave slowly took her body
which had been destroyed
by years of feeling like a failure
with alcohol her only escape.
I have been robbed of a chance to tell her
what she was and always will be, to me.

Looking back, I have to go a long way to remember,
how she softly stroked my
forehead when the fever was high;
And sometimes people would say cruel things to me
and I would cry.
She told me it didn't matter, I was special to her.

I lay yellow roses at her feet because
they were her favorite.
And pink ones because they are mine.

She was everything to me.
By birth, my Mother,
By love, my Hero!

Virginia Casciaro
QUESTIONS

As I sat upon the mountaintop and watched the clouds drift by—
I thought of all the questions to be answered when we die—
My tears were sad and stormy, there was thunder in my brain—
My fondest dreams were shattered like a broken windowpane—
Where once was happy laughter and a friendly family joy—
there was left a saddened parent and a puzzled little boy—
Then I gazed among the treetops and I listened to the wind—
I could smell the flower's fragrance, I could walk or run or sing—
I could feel the warming sunshine in this quiet mountain place—
All my misery was forgotten and I knew the good Lord's grace—
There is a time to answer questions and a time to do our deeds—
And although at times we're puzzled—
God knows ahead our needs
So as the sun was sinking and my feet were homeward bound—
I knew that somewhere, someday—
All the questions that I'd found—
Would be answered truly and my heart did give a sigh—
My faith was much the stronger and I'd give another try.

Ronald Love
REFLECTIONS

To Barbara, and love's reflection.

Reflections
I look in the mirror
and what did I see?
A vital, handsome young man
looking back at me.
I looked in the mirror,
the same as before.
I saw a man with a wife
and children, the number was four.
I looked in the mirror,
that very same day.
I saw a middle-aged man,
with hair beginning to gray.
I dared look in the mirror,
the same as above.
It was a man called Grandpa,
with grandchildren to love.
I looked in the mirror,
and what did I see?
The face of my dead father,
was smiling at me.

Jeanine Rae Cowles
TODAY

Today there'll be nothing bad,
Nothing out there will make me sad.
The sun is shining, no clouds in the sky,
To my problems today, I'll say goodbye.

I'll stop and look at the roses so red,
And maybe I'll realize they need rain to be fed.
It's the rain and dirt that makes them grow,
And keeps them strong, when winds may blow.

I'll look around and see the weeds,
The job of pulling them is up to me.
For if the weeds are allowed to stay,
The colorful roses will die away.

So today in my own life, I'll pull up the weeds,
With a garden plucked clean, a new world will I see.
May my Heavenly Father in Heaven above,
Show to me always, His merciful love.

Virginia Casciaro
COMING HOME

Father—hang a star in Heaven up above—
To lite the narrow path I've taken
As to find my home of love—
I walked through storms and sadness
In the darkness and with pain—
But again I've walked in sunshine
and have felt the warming rain—
Your will is always with me as I wander here below—
Fathe— don't forget me— for my journey seems so slow—
The road is getting rougher as I'm coming near the bend—
Have my friends all there to greet me,
And my relatives galore—
For when I reach my Fathe—
I'll need to roam no more—

Virginia Casciaro
SECRET TEARS

Memories I hide away
Both sad and great delight—
Come back to me at end of day—
And haunt me through the nite—
As time goes by— my heart does sigh—
For things that should have been—
My soul does know that yesterday—
Can never be again—
As there is darkness in the nigh—
So comes the morning sunshine light—
With all my will—
Plus God's good grace—
Another day—
With smiling face—
I hide my worries, all my fears,
Until again—
My secret tears.

Virginia Casciaro
REGRET

As they brought him home one morning in a box so grey and cold—
He had gone to do his duty—and he did— so I was told—
Now I'm standing by his graveside there are teardrops in my eye—
thinking of the words I left unsaid to my growing little boy—
How the years passed by so fast—
too soon he was a man—
He was gone to fight the battles of the land—
Things would have been so different if I'd only took his hand—
And now I'm filled with sorrow—
Do you think he understands?
I'll never get to tell him and my eyes are growing dim—
He was my only sunshine in this terrible world of sin—
How I hope he can forgive me for the words I held inside—
Oh, I wish I'd said "I love you" but I had a senseless pride—

Domenico E Gianino

Domenico E Gianino
TO LAURA AND JESS

This poem is dedicated to my beautiful Granddaughter, LAURA ANNA PASSANISI McREYNOLDS, and her husband JESS on their wedding day.

Splendid joyful aurora
that enlighten the horizon.
Sound the reveille
for the gentle maid
adorned of white veil.
Fly in the flowered field
like jubilant butterfly.
Go to meet her lover
offering fragrant flower
for the wedding day.
The hands softly tighten
ready to challenge
the path of the long life,
until reaching
the radiant sunset.

Virginia Casciaro
LOST

My book is nearly finished thanks to a guiding hand—
I pray to find forgiveness and to know the Promised Land—
I can only say I'm sorry that Satan chose on me.
And I'm grateful to the heavens where the Saints have prayed for me—
So help me guardian angel and lead me by the hand—
I pray the Lord will find me— tho I am a darken lamb—
As time went by the pages grew, the cover did mislead—
For then a Jekyll-Hyde I knew— the price of my misdeeds—
I pleaded with my seed of faith and begged God let it grow—
I battled Satan all my life— the seeds were hard to sow—
One doesn't change in just one night of this I surely found,
And even tho the Devil's weak I know that he's around.
So help me guardian angel and lead me by the hand—
I pray the Lord will find me— tho I am a darken lamb—

Robert Howard
MORNING

Waking, the yellow
dog pisses quietly on
the summer tan bark.

Robert Howard
MIDNIGHT

Damp, the summer night—
pine dwells all alone except
for mockingbird breath.

Will Tallon
OCTOBER

Dedicated to Dearest Carol McKirnan.

The colors of dreams
All glowing once—now dead:
Crimson gleams,
Gold and the gray of lead,
Russet, bronze, saffron, red,
Airily moving—
A waving banner then.
Now, quietly carpeting
Magical Brycelind.

Tim Griffith
ONLY THE PURITAN TRIES TO DESTROY

Thanks A.C. Aum ha.

Only The Puritan Tries To Destroy You For The Trends You Create, But He's Too Late To Create. His Beliefs Now Guide Him. He's On The Chosen Path And Has The Edge On All This Treachery. Puritans Always Plan For The Future For They Believe The World Is Going To End. I Think Of A Hypocrite When I Think Of This Trend Of The Puritan With All This Faith And A God To Believe In.

Harold L Lockwood
PICK A DREAM AT RANDOM

To Alice, my devoted and loving wife of many years.

You're like a bolt from out the blue,
I know you not but hope I do,
Or like a small moonbeam,
I know you more, as just a dream.

You're like a dream, in many ways,
Until I find you, I'll spend my days
In all the ways of Solitude,
That makes a man so awfully crude.

Pick a dream at random,
From out the studded sky,
Cling to it but tightly,
For time is passing by.
Tell your dream to me, my love,
Then put it safe away,
And I will make that dream come true,
Some not too distant day.

Casey Jagiello
VANISHVILLE
"The mildest
And the wildest,
Vanishville."

An intriguing quotation
About an intriguing location.

A place where dreams are real
And women are ideal.
A place you've dreamed about
for years.
A place where you've shed
many tears.
A place where your unconscious
mind acts upon your wishes
And makes them even more
delicious.

A place called "Vanishville."

Austin Taylor
SPECTRE
It's war in a peace-ridden town
Nostalgia that brings you down
Ghosts off the memory tree
Spectres of oppression and grief
of the many friends I have known

His face makes a wrinkled land
He has the face of a haunted old man
Lines of lies from the spirits of his past

In his eyes there lays a forest of green
You have to wonder 'bout the things that he's seen
You have to wonder just how he can last
Another day in his dream
He is a friend I have known

I gave my words away for your life
Without them I'll quietly die, inside.
Live life, live long, live warm and proud

My only talent I gave to the man
Both are gone to their civilized land
To leave my town alone
Phantoms prolonging war—zone
Oh, the friends that have gone
The End

Geraldine Gleich
BASICS OF MARRIAGE & LIFE

This poem is for my children, Warren, Jim and Kathy Ann. Special thanks to Jim because he asked me to write down my ideas about marriage.

Marriage is not what the storybook says.
It's a challenge in life that changes many ways.
HE thinks that all the responsibility is his.
SHE thinks that survival stems from just what she gives.
What they both have to learn will take many hours.
It is not HIS or HERS because it becomes ours.
OURS is a word for people who care.
It shows the world that they learned how to share.
SHARE is a word that most people never learn.
They are taught from childhood to keep what they earn.
If you learn how to share both the good times and bad.
You will then have a life that is happy, not sad.
The most fragile of feelings, but one that's a must.
The base of all feelings is simply called TRUST.
If you trust one another in all that you do.
Your marriage and love will always stay true.
Your PATIENCE, at times, will grow very thin.
Please remember, it's a strength that comes from within.
There will always be times when you worry about cost.
With GOD and your love,
"NOTHING IS LOST."

Joni C Massey
MY FLIGHT
Away above the clouds, I float in childish glee,
And marvel at Creation in everything I see!
The fluffy, white clouds beneath me are a wonder to behold,
And the One who wrought the miracle is the One who loves my soul.
He's the God of all the Universe—He made the sky, the land and sea.
And even before the foundation, He planned a place for me.
But, oh, this view above the clouds is only meant to be—
A preview of far greater things awaiting in Eternity!

Beneath the clouds, it's dark . . .
Above the clouds, it's light;
And the place you find yourself is determined by your flight.
Are you traveling high or traveling low?
Did you chart the way you want to go?
Life can be dark . . . Or life can be bright—
It all depends on how you chart your flight!

Donna D Davison
SWEETHEART
Ever since I met you
you've kept me on cloud nine
It seems so very easy
for you to be so kind
Nearly every night you'd call me
and we'd talk for sometimes hours
You've always been open to me
you even brought me flowers
During our times together
and sweet moments that we've kissed
I wanted to melt inside you but
somehow I always missed
It's these memorable moments
and you make it so much fun
That makes me feel I love you
and desire to become one.

Sandra DeAngelis
A MOMENT IN TIME

To Jeff
You touched my life
Your Lady In Red.

In the passing of time, sometimes, someone comes into our life, just for a moment, and changes it completely.

You may meet a person that touches something deep inside you and you'll never be the same again.

Even though this person has no idea of the feelings they've aroused within you, you have to hold back because you know they are yours alone.

If you thought for a moment, that they were shared you know it would be ecstasy but even though you realize it is only your fantasy, it is still a part of you.

Then the moment passes and that one person is gone out of your life as swiftly as he entered it.

You wish you could turn back the clock and do things differently because the feelings are still inside you. Feelings you've forgotten ever existed!

As you sit by the fireplace, staring at the flames, you can't seem to quench the fire he's aroused inside you.

He is a witty, gentle, intelligent man and wonderful to be with and for a moment in time, he touched your life in a way no one ever has before and for that you thank him.

Gina L Barbara
ONE LAST NIGHT

Written for Jesse Cooper, the first I fell in love with, and the first to break my heart, and the one I'll always love.

Softly in the night,
I call out your name.
Never do you respond,
It's just not the same.
I need to have you here.
I want to feel you near.
To whisper in your ear.
Now only to hear your sneer.
I feel for you so much,
and long to feel your touch.
But I know that all you feel for me is hate,
and I just blew it, it's too late.
To be in your arms,
For you to hold me tight.
If only I had one left, one to remember,
One last night . . .

Stacy Larkin
ETERNITY

This poem is dedicated to my Aunt Sharon.

Life is long and death is longer,
But for the sake of us we must be stronger.
Oh my love, don't shed a tear,
Because as you cry I begin to fear.
I feel myself begin to go,
Oh my dear, for you I wish it were slow.
Please hold my hand tighter than tight,
Up until I lose all sight.
As I lay here on my bed,
I think of all the things that have been said.
Out of all the love we have shared,
For you I wish I was to be spared.
Remember me in your heart, not in your mind,
For your mind thinks of things we might find.
Your heart remembers things we have shared
And the special things that are so divine.

Linda Asher
LITTLE ONES

To my grandmother, who I miss and love very much. Love, Linda.

God lends His little children
To parents here below
To love and teach and nurture
As they live and laugh and grow.

Your baby came from his heart.
That your heart might be blessed.
In this little life so precious
He has given you the best.

The tiny hands are innocent
They only reach for love
Will you teach them always
To reach for things above.

The little feet will follow
The way your feet will tread.
Will your steps paint heavenward
As you journey on ahead

Train up your child, God calls you to parenthood today
It is his highest calling
His word will paint the way.

Stephanie Ann Fucello
THE CHANCE OF CHANGE

I dedicate this poem to all who face the struggle towards change, as I do, and conquer it, as I wish to.

CHANGE is when we wish to make different, what is too much the same.

CHANCE is what we take when we wish and need to make this change.

CHALLENGE is what we meet, when we take this chance towards change.

VICTORY is what we feel when this challenge is faced, and attempt at change through our chance is achieved.

GOALS are end results that we mastered through achieved victories from our inner courage to challenge a chance at change, and to make a difference of what was too much the same.

Sherri L Cox
YESTERDAY, TODAY AND TOMORROW

Dedicated to T.B.M. Yesterday you were the most special person in my life as you are Today, and will always be Tomorrow. I Love You. Sherri C.

Yesterday . . .
Sometimes it seems like such
a long time ago even though
it was just yesterday—but

passing slowly like the time
you spend alone.

Today . . .
Is the journey into the
future; the making of
memories as we go forth in
time—all too quickly though
sometimes it seems.

Tomorrow . . .
Is the keeper of our
yesterdays, today and our
future, for holding all the
memories of times past and
present so that we may
reflect upon each one—
tomorrow.

Theresa Lamb

A LIFETIME

Dedicated to both of my inspirations: my mother & my husband.

Our life is set before us like branches on a tree,
We reach out for tomorrow in search of reality.
We don't know where it will lead nor do we know what we will find.
We're clinging to hopes of tomorrow and setting yesterday way behind.
What we don't seem to realize is the importance of Yesterday.
It's the sunrise of our lives and leads us on our way.
And as our days seem to come and go, the sun takes route to the sky.
We find we're getting older, soon we start to question "WHY?".
As our lives go on, the sun keeps rising, soon it seems to reach its peak.
We're grazing thru our middle years and our branches now grow weak.
What once were supple leaves and limbs, grow withered, aged and dry.
Leaves, one by one, fall to the ground leaving a trace of days gone by.
When soon the sun starts fading and before we could turn away.
We find the sun is setting, disappearing for another day.
When in our golden years we find that at last our job is done,
there's satisfaction in knowing we're facing our setting sun.

Nadine Aide-Petty

WHY?

To my brother-in-law, Sam, who this poem was written for, and for my sister Michele, for the courage she has displayed. I love you both very much.

Everywhere I look, I see you—
The funny moments that occur, I think of you—
When your team wins, I cheer for you—
I am not alone in these thoughts—
All who loved you remember their private times with you—
The crazy way you had at looking at the world—
The way you laughed at every situation that came your way—
Why did you leave so suddenly?
Didn't you know you could come to us with your problems?
That we could have helped you?
We loved you, we cared for you so deeply—
Why did you do this to yourself?
You wrote to us and told us this is what you wanted—
You did not want us to feel sad—
No matter what you told us, we are sad—
We miss you and wish you were here—
We pray you are at peace now—
We love you and miss you—
You will be in our hearts
forever . . .

Dolores M Veitch

THE PRODIGAL

As I cross the bridge and head for home
I'm feeling a bit uneasy
For I've been away a very long time
my memories are unclear and breezy

I still can recall the way our house looked
the big weeping willow the bench by the brook
The swing in the oak the house in the tree
the girls that I loved and the girl who loved me

You can never remember the hurt or the pain
or the reasons that made you depart
Still my pace seems to quicken the closer I get
and the future puts hope in my heart

I know why I came, yet I'm not sure I'll stay
I'll soon put to rest what was my yesterday
Still I plod along with my heart in my hand
the heart of a boy who is seeking a man

Kimberly Lynn Finch

MORE BAD THAN GOOD

This is dedicated to all children who have gone through the abuse of an alcoholic parent. There is always help and it's never too late.

He was a man that the outside world knew to be very good, yet all they saw were the lies. The man was deceiving, hidden, kind, and giving all in one. I guess that's why he's believable. He is an illusion to some extent, wanting everyone to see and praise the light as the darkness grew deeper and stronger. He is a person blind to reality, never seeing the truth of what his disease was doing to him and to the ones who loved him.

I heard myself say, "If you love me, you'll stop" although the answer was already echoing in my mind: "I love you but I'll never stop drinking." To me he was the father only seen on weekends, and the father I loved no longer was there. The truth was there, yet he denied it. I've felt the pain like my soul being slowly torn apart. I've cried and asked, "Why must he be this way?" Out of all the loved ones, the one that shouldn't matter does.

I tell myself that a hardened heart can never be hurt and a cold person can show no love, yet cold is not what I am not what I was created to be. I always hear I'm sorry, and the promises of getting help are never fulfilled. I've never seen the results of the empty bottle, yet I know when the time comes. I've never had a hand laid on me, yet at times I feel bruised on the inside. Many people have the problem. Some can face it; others cannot. He has a problem only he can solve and the choice he made is clear to me. The alcohol has turned a father I once loved into a person I've never known. The lies have been told and the truth remains the same; a man who denies the truth can never change.

My love for him is faded now; I care but I've realized that my love was never enough. The bottle is his friend, family, wife, and daughter. I do feel as if a part of me is gone, but I feel no great loss. I have my family, my true family, and they are the ones who stood by and understood and showed me what love was really about.

Nora Lee McNeely

Nora Lee McNeely

BELATED THOUGHTS

When I often remember,
I am pained with regret,
for the many deeds of kindness
so often I forget.

Harsh words, in anger spoken
can never be erased;
Only God can blot them out,
by His love and grace.

It's sad, we cannot realize,
until later years we've grown;
The kind of fruits we harvest,
Show the kind of seeds we've sown.

Grace M Johnson

LIFE IS A MYSTERY

What do I know about life
It's not easy that's for sure
When you think you have it made
Trouble is at the door.
If you will welcome him
as an honored guest
He will soon be on his way and
Life is at its best.

Maysa Gadelha

THE VISITOR

I stand in wonder still amazed
With the passing hours gazed,
Upon these gentle children mine,
Caresses soft and features fine.

Stealing glimpses of nursery days
Hidden from view behind darkened doorways.
They don't see me standing there,
Children playing with abandoned care.
Laughing, singing, dancing too
Like a portrait is my view—
Little ones so fair and light
Playing in the waning night.

One so thoughtful, such sensitive care;
The other playful with rambunctious air.
Both precious gifts of heartfelt joy;
My singing girl and impish boy.

Beneath twilight's blanket I do pray,
Within this moment, remain to stay
A visitor in time serene
Participant, and yet unseen.

Delores M Veitch

SIMPLE PLEASURE

Oh flowers in my garden
you are a precious sight
As you lift your tender foliage
to greet the morning light

You are giving off a fragrance
that really is quite sweet
And your petals seem as making love
while staying quite discreet

The passion of your painted hue
puts fire into the air
And your genteel proper elegance
is there for all to share

Your beauty is astounding
your freshness so sublime
I'm so glad I came to see you
in the essence of your prime

Rita Poeppel

MY LITTLE ANGEL

Little Donnie, little Don Don
Our little baby boy
I wish we had you here with us
It would bring us so much joy

When I go to see you
There's so much sadness in my heart
The sadness comes from missing you
Because we are apart

I know it may be selfish
For wanting you here to stay
But the longing gets stronger
And hurts more and more each day

I really want to hold you
To rock you in my arms
To get to know your character
Your laughter and your charms

Even though my little angel
You're with Jesus in the sky
You'll always be my little boy
And it's hard to say goodbye

Victoria L Rinelli

CELESTIAL PORTRAIT

I mused on my balcony
Penthouse high
The moon shown full
In a velvet sky.

Frail moonbeams danced
Down the milky way
Aurora emerged
To paint heaven's display.

The sea below caressed the shore
With froth tipped waves colored blue,
Rising and falling, a rhythmic song
Of memories old and new.

Mirrored in water countless jewels
Diadems of diamonds grow thick
They sparkle in heaven
Flowers gone wild, too many to pick.

Night of wonders
In every way
Etchings of nature
End a perfect day.

Phyllis Gurchinoff
FROZEN SPIRITS
Frozen spirits of dark memories
drip icicles between us,
Entwining arctic circles about
My heart . . .
Damn you sorcerer!!!
You,
with your fire,
I fear your warmth.
BEWARE . . .
I curse!!!
. . . And yet, I yearn to be loved.

Ella Faye Poston
MY HEART IS FREE
My heart is free
God keeps in touch
Reminding me he loved me first
He truly seems to understand
All his children need a friend
He did not mean for us to cry
With loving care he made us smile

My heart is free
I sing his praise
Because God's love will never
change
One of the sweetest pleasures known
Is to know we're not alone
Through the glory of his grace
His famous name I'm free to sing

Each day I pray
To do what's best
And thank you God for many things
A simple song, a smile, a glance
My heart is free
To praise God's name

Ella Faye Poston
WHEN I'M ALONE
When I'm alone all by myself
No other one is near,
I think of all the things
God made so pretty here.

He made the sun to warm the day
The moon to light the night,
He even made twinkling stars
To decorate the sky.

God made the pretty mountains
Valleys, lakes, and streams,
It doesn't matter where I look
There's beauty to be seen.

So, when I'm alone all by myself
I think how hard he must have
worked
To make this world a pretty place
And he did it all for us!

Nancy L Finger
C-H-R-I-S-T-M-A-S
C is for the Christ Child.
H is for His Holiness.
R is for His Royalty.
I is for Immanuel.
S is for the Son of God.
T is for His Truth.
M is for Mary, Mother of the
Messiah.
A is for the Almighty.
S is for the Special Season.

Marie Elizabeth Belensky
BUT ONE WISH

To all those who may wish and to those who have gotten their wish.

If I had but one wish what would it
be
Would it be to see what is in store for
me
To know what is among the stars
To dream of things yet to come
Or is it better always to remember
Where we have been, that we may
know what to wish for in the years to
come.

Art Henry
A SHORT FLIGHT
When life begins, we are so small,
So small that no on knows we're
there.
And then we grow until we're born,
Then have our Mother's fondest care.

And like a plane that spans the sky,
Up through the clouds of life we go,
To pioneer a path of life serene,
And tell the world of what we know.

We span the canyons of the clouds,
We see our dreams of youth come
true.
We wend our way each day through
life,
As each in turn brings something
new.

The acts of life can lead us far,
Far off our course of joy we know.
We strive each time to right ourself,
And smooth our course before we go.

Our riches we do weigh each day.
Then wonder if we really try,
To lend a hand where ere we can,
To help the youth below our sky.

There comes a time when clouds of
life,
Are burdened with the many years,
Our flight must take us toward our
home,
As life has lost its many fears.

Our ride through all the silvery
clouds,
As life in ebbing must descend,
And down toward Mother Earth we
glide,
Our trip through life is near its end

And as we near our final home,
The Mother Earth we do adore,
We think of what we left behind,
And close our eyes for evermore . . .

Stella J Russell
ST PATRICK'S DAY
St. Patrick's Day is here again,
We wear the emerald green.
We cook corned beef and cabbage
And do the Irish scene.
Why do we celebrate this day
When Irish we are not?
Because we are Americans
And sharing is our lot.
And all the people near and far,
Whoever they may be,
Should share their celebrations
Like one big family.
And so today we all join in
And to the Irish say,
"Good wishes go to all of you
On this, your holiday."

S Raman
I AM WHO I AM
Why was I born; how was I
born—
this fact one should know
Reason for the birth of I—that realize
by self.

Fascinated though, by what then
goes on in this world,
Forget not then your real nature
which is Self.

What difference in the goings-on
awake and dream?
When it happens, what then happens
appears real!

What is truth in dream is not so
while we are awake;
What is truth in wakeful state
is not so in a dream.

So the question What is truth? then
leads to self of all.
It's the basis; that alone is Truth
that one should know.

Realized one stays so by the
Virtues of the past.
Act you now, to realize Self,
Chant the name of Lord.

Janice Fletcher Johnson
MYSTICAL MOMENTS
Waves explode, slinging on
weathered rocks their wild spume;
Mists, tethered on unseen tendrils,
enshroud the beach
As winds sweep across the shifting
sand dune.
Our souls, two haunting melodies,
turn to primordial time
As we fling imprisoned inhibitions to
the ground
And charge the fleeting shadows at
the waterline.

Silhouetted against the darkened
terrain,
We become intrepid explorers of the
pounding mane,
Wedded in perfect symphony to the
magic of the restless tide—
The tide that beats . . . beats . . . beats
. . . BEATS inside.
We surge to embrace in liquid,
iridescent gold,
While ahead waves crest, foam, fall
and fold.

Steven K Tegovich

Steven K Tegovich
THE PATH OF LIFE

Dedicated to my Mom and to my Dad, who taught me anything is possible.

She stood in silent wonder
as thoughts raced through her brain
aware her urge was foolish
with more to lose than gain

The path stood before her
and seemed to know the score
She sensed it knows her troubles
and knew what was in store

She heard old Jud explaining
as if he still was there
He knew a special secret
He felt he had to share

If you're in the forest
the path will be your guide
it's a beacon in the darkness
a friend to stand beside

And if you seek its safety
and remain within its sphere
You'll get to where you're going
without a thing to fear

But Ellie was a maverick
with something left to prove
if something stood in her way
it simply had to move

One step past the border
was done with oh such ease
she could come, she could go
and act just as you please

Three steps from the border
was easy as just one
the path was still so close to her
Naughty was awfully fun

Suddenly she changed her heart
what did the old man know
why walk the same old path each
time
why not just let yourself go

And from one step and quickly three
she ran with no regard
she skipped and danced and praised
herself
Until she was breathing hard

And suddenly reality set in
she saw what she had done
the path was gone beyond her sight
and she saw the setting sun

In no time she found darkness
each direction looked the same
sounds she heard scared her most
she knew it was no game

She had made thoughtless choices
and failed to look ahead
One step seemed like nothing
But further each step led

Now she sat and wondered
What else is there to do
So far from the path of life
It seemed her time was due

She longed for the path of life
and thought with a little smile
how pretty its borders seemed right
now
stretching mile after mile

And she sat, head in hands
with tears on the flow
A hand touched on her shoulders
"Honey, come on, let's go"

She hugged old Jud, quite a squeeze
and swore right then and there
the path, the forest, the whole
shebang
she'd never again go near

But wise old Jud made it clear
there were things on his mind
the lesson here was very clear
But Ellie still was blind

The path you lost isn't in the woods
it's the path of life my child
And if you let yourself astray
You may never leave the wild

But keeping on the path you'll find
It's hard to lose at all
A path of Right, through a forest of
wrong
is a choice we all must call

The path is all that's good in life
So be one with the road

Despite its passage through all that's dark
the good will not erode

And keep in mind evil is slow
it grows with every day
it gets you piece by little piece
it grows in a sneaky way

So when you find a choice in life
remember my little tale
It's never too late to find the way
back to safety's trail

Steven K Tegovich
A POEM FOR APRIL
A special thing occurs in life
and you're lucky if it happens at all
But once the luck seems all but gone
you'll feel against a wall

Love they say is a cherished event
a feeling like no other
a mood encompassing all your time
a bonding with a lover

And although you can't see it start
you move from stage to stage
involvement grows with each new step
like a progressive turn of a page

But like a book or spoken story
there's a birth, a center, and an end
the trick it seems is to survive the fall
Without hurting a beloved friend

So when or if the end is near
stand proudly, strong and tall
Because you'll find, it's better to lose
than to never have loved at all

Ina Foreman
SURPRISE!!
What have you done to me?
When you are near I am at odds, uncentered, all undone;
unable to attend the things I must.
Married and mothering these many years,
uninterested, untouched by any other man
until we met. We've never touched, never embraced and yet I feel on fire when you are near.
I see my spouse, long loved, so dear;
and feel ashamed of this unsought ignition of my soul.
What have I done to me?

Tayna Bustle
PAINTED SMILES
Winter with a hint of summer, that was today.
I can not decide if it was a dream or a memory that made me cry.

I thought of you today.
For a moment I smiled.
The tears went away.
I was in a happier place and time;
A time when the days lasted all night long;
A time when laughter came from deep inside.
My smile wasn't painted on.

Mike Gillespie II
THE BEGINNING OF NOTHING
The sun rises; the sun falls
I am the sun who has done this
Thirty days went down the drain
And Earth's star refused to shine.

It was like a funeral on that day
So depressing, but I wouldn't cry
For then my secret faults could be seen
I would just have to start over
Again and again, stomped on by a disease
Oh God, I surrender; Oh God, I surrender
I'm stomped on by a spider; clinging to his web
He hypnotizes me with his venom
For that time only I'm under his command

Oh Father, please relieve me
Am I the first of two
Or am I the beginning of nothing.

Elaine Meli
NEW MOTTO
Thru rain . . .
Thru sleet . . .
Thru snow . . .
Airplanes cannot go.
Trucks cannot move.
Trains cannot find their groove.

Bring back the Horse,
Of course . . . of course.

Bring back the Horse . . .
Of course.

("Best of all, you don't need to pay it . . . Just feed it.")

Della K King
DO YOU KNOW?
They come to me all alone,
Scared . . . Worried . . . on their own.
I look into their confused little eyes,
And I know just where their fear lies.

Taken from their soft warm nest,
Where their mom quietly laid them to rest.
Some human comes along and sees,
A tempting nest up in a tree.

What was once a peaceful life,
Became a happening of terror and strife.
Tiny babies left on their own,
Scared . . . Worried . . . and all alone.

I look into these worried eyes,
Knowing where their fear lies.
Caring and loving can never replace,
The familiar look of their mother's face.

Stuart Simon
SLUMBER BEGUN TOO LATE
The night laid heavy
On slumber begun too late.
It pressed on me
Cowering 'neath the blackened weight.

Fatigue yet held a vigil
At my craved tomb,
Barring a new day
From the blanketed womb.

Step aside bleak night!
End the strife.
Let me rise
To the day's measure of life.

Without thought
I cast the covers aside.
Within drifted darkness,
A spectre with resolve defied.

I'd need more time,
And probably the sun's first ray;
But finally to embrace
The offer, of today.

Marion F Corey
MY HOBBY
I like rocks, dry flowers, and such,
My hobby does not take too much,
Creating with my own ideas.
These objects last for many years,

Here is an old shoe, of baby blue,
Fond memories of him, come stealing through,
A bit of gold, a dash of glue, some ribbon too,
Now it is a gift for you.

Ina Pursel Britt
GOD GAVE US A BEAUTIFUL BABY BOY

To our only child, Philip.

God gave us a beautiful baby boy, so sweet and playful like a toy,
We loved him and taught him many wonderful things,
And he grew into boyhood with all his dreams.
His love for a farm wherever he went, he yearned to work there and was not content unless he was plowing or milking and such.
And my prayers were always, God keep him safe and one day, fulfill his dream with such a big beautiful place, as a farm of his own and a loving wife and later, children to bless his life, as he did ours.
So into manhood he grew, with kindness, humbleness and love in his soul
and fresh and clean as the morning dew.
Everyone liked him, such a fine man was he, with always an easy smile and a helping hand if need be.
We hold not the ace for our lives here on earth, God alone is King of the universe.
So before he grew twenty one years, God called him to his eternal home.
Our hearts are so empty and sad, but go on we must and try to understand, and let God's will and purpose be fulfilled.
For maybe God's need for him was greater still.
We know not much of the things above, so a Mother's prayer is only this,
that her son is happy in his eternal bliss and prays there's a farm there for Phippie to see. Amen.

Darthulia P Bruce
SNOW BIRDS!

To Gordon Alexander—Happy Years!

'Twas early in March, we decided to go
Leave it all behind, the rain and snow
We loaded "Bronco" with infinite care
Left behind, his socks, stacked on a chair
"Nomad" all shined up, looking like new
Refrig loaded, including the stew.
Spring was in Oregon, inviting 'tis true
Pink drifts of blossoms, skies of blue
Green, green meadows of lambs and ewes
Away down the highway, southward we flew
Searching warm weather, dry Washington dew!
Trip up Mt. Aho, the cactus to view
Then over Old Mexico Highway Two.
We settled in camp east of Yuma, Ariz.
And that's all there is, tiz it tiz!!

Joan Duke-Potter
LOVE MULTIPLIES
When I reach out to any man,
I want him to take my hand.
It matters not that one is black,
that is not reason to hold back.
Color is a matter of pigment in skin,
its difference is only significant when introduced by those who would use
a shallow reason to excuse
their distaste for their fellow,
be he brown, black or yellow.

As I reach out, there's no hate in my heart,
for hate divides and tears apart.
Love multiplies and thus creates.
When confronted by love, hatred abates.
Hate is like acid, eating away.
Love, like cool water, gives life each day.
The choice is clear, for the human race
to continue life in this lowly place.
To draw back in hate means we die,
so we must reach out in love and multiply.

Lorraine Burch Hancock
HUGO
A giant trudged this lonely, piney land
Intrusive in his prowl,
Trampling indiscriminately
The stately sentinels,
Impediments to his march.
Some high, some low,
Their needled crowns he picked
Like flowerlets
And left the stems
Naked where they stand,
Ashamed.

Edith Mae Payne
THOSE PLEADING BROWN EYES
Beginning of spring, it was, a year or so, ago,
The next door neighbor, knocked, at our backdoor, and so.
He asked, "Would you like a special friend, gentle and kind?
Most folks say, are hard to find."
Gladly, was our reply, fast as could be,
Come in Nickey, come here, to me.
Big brown eyes, curly blonde fur, soft as corn silk,
yes it was,
We will keep, sweet Nickey, no reason given, just because.
Moving was a chore, for our neighbors, for sure,
Nickey was ours, for loneliness, he was that cure.
No puppy, was ever loved, more than, our lovable friend,
He was smart, this was said, time and time, again.
One day, Nickey slowly down-hill came,
After this, my life, was never, the same.
Never will I forget, in a million years,
Nickey looked up at me, my eyes filled with bitter tears.
In our back yard with, perpetual care,
Our sweet Nickey, is laying there.
GOD FORGIVE, SOMEONE, that gave POISON, to our lovely pet,
Nickey died, that very day, this MEMORY, I cannot forget.
FAREWELL sweet Nickey, we will NEVER, FORGET YOU.

Euen D Ellis
THE PATH OF SUCCESS
Our path leads upward step by step
Up life's mountainsides so steep
By the cliffs of weak despair
By temptation's gorge so deep.

Upward climb we day by day
Visions on the upward way
Contented not with table land
But striving for the summit grand.

Many gorges must we cross
Many rocky crags be passed
But if we strive with courage bold
We'll mount the topmost peak at last.

Written June 18, 1917, wheat field

Helen A Adams
HE CARES
I turned to God in my sorrow
And asked Him to show me the way
To trust in Him completely
And to strengthen me day by day.

He sent kind friends to comfort
And His arms about me He placed;
He gave me the courage I needed
This very great sorrow to face.
Now to Him be all of the glory!
When I needed Him, He was right
there
To help me through those dark hours
With all of His wonderful care.

Helen A Adams
WHAT JESUS MEANS TO ME
J - is for the Joy which He has
given,
E - is for Eternal Life above,
S - is for Salvation which He
offers
U - is for His Unending love.
S - is for my Sins for which He
suffered
When He gave His life upon that
tree.
Put them all together, they
spell JESUS
The name that means so much
to me.

Laurell D Ward

Laurell D Ward
LOSS OF A LOST LOVER
He stopped loving me today
Through the years I've had no way
To tell him that my love remained
Even though it had to endure the
pain.

He was the first to kiss me
And to say, "I know you're sweet"
The years sent us separately
But someday together we'll meet.

And each will know of the other's
love
During the life on earth.
Two lovers united above
Will give that young love new birth.

I visited his new formed grave
Where now his body returns to clay
And to him my loving promise gave
As I grasped a rose from the floral
array.

The rose now dried
But yet remains to remind
That lovers once here intertwined
Will renew that affection on life's
other side.

As I silently whispered goodbye
I remembered the young years of
bliss
That we enjoyed side by side
And then I realized the years we
missed.

It is sad to love and lose
But memories belong to their creator
And I know that in thought we were
always close
And that to his devotion I am a
debtor.

Michael Koenigseker
AGE'S REPEATING MIND
GOD! Please grant me the serenity in
later life,
When I'm old and gray
And my mind repeats itself for all to
hear,
To block the bad from my speech
And let me sing the goodness I have
seen
And the wonders I have touched
That bear repeating for all to hear.

I see you as a benevolent GOD
Who wishes to pass on this quality
For me to keep.
Please don't let me forget
When I repeat myself
And can only remember
Small visions of time.

Let me repeat from love
And bury the darkness of hate and
anger
For it brings no joy to me or you.
I pray when I'm weak you'll guide
my mind
To search my heart and speak of
peace.

James Dowd
HIS SPIRIT DANCES
His spirit dances,
Finally free.
Across the vast expanses,
Goes he.

As the eagle soars,
Ethereal delight.
From heights explores,
God's might.

Eternity for celebration,
Unbounded bliss.
Step lively O creation,
Lest you miss.

Chris Shannon
WIDE-EYED SPRINTER
Gentle, wide eyes staring at me
through dusty windowpanes.
Unafraid, knowing a wall of granite
separates us,
And, knowing on our property, safety
reigns.

A motorcycle whizzes by on the
windy country road
Startling the wide-eyed,
white-tailed animal.
She sprints away—a vision in athletic
mode.

The overabundance of her family
makes my vegetable garden fence
quite high
And, it's necessary around flowers
too—
Unless I wish to bid the leaves and
bulbs of my early spring flowers
good-bye.

Though my dogs bark incessantly,
the wide-eyed creatures
Know the dogs are secure in their
chain link pen.
So the bushes by my house possess
overly trimmed features.

I round curves in my car
Prepared for those brown eyes to run
in front of me,
And I take walks hoping to see them,
wherever they are.

Always excited by their beauty
exemplifying
Mother Nature's Creativity.

Gene Leimer
LEAVE SOME WOOD ON YOUR BROTHER'S THRESHOLD

Dedicated to the people and principles of A.A.

In the northern states where the
weather gets cold, an Indian friend
shared with me;

A time honored tradition, a way of
life, an Indian philosophy.

On a winter's day when the air is
cold and above your brother's lodge
you can see,

that the air is clear and there's a
definite lack . . . of smoke from his
main chimney,

then follow tradition, or law if you
will, that came from the Gods of old,

take some time from your heart, some
time to show love,
Leave some wood on your Brother's
threshold.

Do not wait to be thanked or seen for
your act, for to do so is wrong don't
you see,

though your action was good, your
motive was wrong, your love was not
given free.

Live your life by this law, to give
from your heart, and someday you'll
surely behold,

On a grey winter's day, when your
own fires are out, you'll find wood
on your own threshold.

Jennifer Y Siner
WINDOW DREAMING
As I sit by my window, watching
the rain gently falling down,
My thoughts turn only to you.
Are you thinking of me, wondering
about me?
Wishing I was in your arms,
listening to the sound of the
rain coming down?

These feelings that I have for you
invade my whole body—
they're so very strong.
Like a deep and winding river
with a thrusting force.
They will forever flow, endlessly
on.

What will become of this? What
will be our destiny?
I sit by my window as the rain
gently falls.
Are you thinking of me,
wondering about me,
Wishing I was in your arms?
Do you love me? I sit . . .
Window Dreaming

Thelma Davis Meade
APOLOGY
Oh! Let the night wind softly blow
across your face so fair
And, in the moonlight's afterglow,
remove your every care.
No shadows of a long-lost dream
may fall upon your heart,
Nor problems of tomorrow seem their
worry to impart.

Forgive the night wind should it
storm with wrath, as I to you
In anger speak and, fuming, form a
barrier to break through.
For uttered words can't be unsaid,
(and winds cannot retract
The damage done), and keep, instead,
the friendship still intact.

The tempest of an angry word, if
spoken now in haste,
Cannot be checked before it's heard;
cannot prevent the waste
Of excess energy and love expended
mistrel-wise:
A storm that, raging from above,
anchors in your eyes.

So rest your head while night winds
sing caressing tunes to you,
And moonlight wants the night to
bring a peace which will renew
This friendship rare, which could be
lost with careless spoken word,
And by the night wind gently
tossed—forget that it occurred.

Bernard R Meinert Jr
THUNDERSTORM
A thunderstorm is nothing to
bemean;
It is only Nature's way of keeping
Her face clean.

Anne Ayer
TURN BACK
Turn back the dawn
That he may behold her
Radiant in moonlight,
Waking from dream.

Now, only now,
Before the world changes
Can such a face
Still be perceived.

Dr Mari P Saunders
J'ESPERE

To: NIK - getting there is half the fun?

The sun will get up earlier than usual one morning
It has a largely overdue contribution to me
So has the moon for that matter

The scorched away days bound in dry ice
keep producing withered discolored green
in the disguise of four-leaf clovers
And I grow brutal and gross
with the discovery

But also, maybe I'm becoming stronger,
less naive, more humble, reluctantly aware
of so much ambiguity
How else could I still quietly await another dawn?

Jennifer L McGraw
TO SOMEONE

To Adam L. Kilburne. Thank you for finding me.

To someone who,

when I hurt inside, will hold me tight enough to crush the pain from my heart . . .

who will let me use his shoulder to cry on each day
and make the days I cry come fewer and farther between . . .

who will overlook my faults and continually
ignore those who insist on pointing them out . . .

I love you . . . more than all this world . . .
I Love You.
And for sanity's sake hope you find me soon.

Ellen Brockington-Martin
CROSS COUNTRY SKIING

To my husband, Paul, for his encouragement in writing this poem as well as in cross country skiing.

Crackle, swish, crackle—as I start on my way, stumbling to get control;
through ridges that froze in a worn-down trail where
travelers' stories are told.

Cold shadowed woods give a mystic embrace, yet peacefulness quickly surrounds;
as I push and I glide, I can feel
my heart beat and the warmth
from my body abounds.

Continuing forward, I'm not alone, a chipmunk cuts right in my path;
and chickadees chirp as they fly
down low to a stream where
they all take a bath.

Climbing comes next, so I herringbone up to a ledge for a beautiful view;
and the sun beats down on my
numbing face with a warmth
that I never knew.

Carefully turning round a bend, my destiny lies straight ahead;
with a chill in my cheeks and a
lump in my throat, I move
nearer a hill that I dread.

Caution and tact steer me safely down, and a deep breath helps carry me on;
but what lies before me, I did
not expect, is the place that I
had started from.

Cathy Erskine
JESSICA—ONE

These poems are dedicated to my family and Greta—for enriching my life, and teaching me to listen and to always look again.

She plays with you and always
always lets you love her.
She takes everything you give
and gives it all back
with one smile, one peal of laughter
so strong you are filled with her
and forget anything or anyone else exists.

We all know the innocence of children
but rarely feel their purity.
It's as delicate as snow or rain descending—
as soon as it touches something other
it dissolves, irretrievable.

Just hold me, she says
arms reaching up—
nothing more.

There is no need.

The universe is within your arms
and the rain sounds within your hearts
touching nothing but itself.

Cathy Erskine
REDEMPTION
He said I had beautiful green eyes in the middle of
his monologue about The Redeemer, even though one
was more gold than green.
His stained teeth chattered
as much from intent as late-November New York.
I wondered if he knew his
right hand was bleeding;
that my camera wasn't an
accordion he wanted to play;
and whether his demons would
stop overtaking him
like a slick rubber glove
suffocating a fist.
Sensical things burst into his
conversation like bubbles
in just boiling water, barely
blistering to the surface.

His request for two dollars
seemed inconsequential.
It was more the scent of
my hair, a strand to wear
on his shoulder "home" he
wanted, his peacock feather.
I obliged, shook his hand—
blood trickled down
the lifeline of our palms,
a shared stigmata.
"We'll never be saved, never
be saved," he muttered,
jerking his head like a
metronome unraveling.
He whirled around, and with
his coyote-like stare
looking beyond/through me,
whispered almost seductively
that I had the most beautiful
green eyes
even though one was more gold than green.

Cathy Erskine
SOMNAMBULIST
Walking through no time, dead time
hunched by a man with broken feet
slung like a deer over the hunter's back.
Dressed in robes of crimson and green,
masked in porcelain serenity
I live with the game. It feeds me.

The pavement burns beneath my feet as I walk
to recreate the street, the drive along the beach,
tunnel up ahead, then dark—sidewalk post, shattered
glass, limp-legs-broken-feet upon the hood;
a cycle wheel spins endless behind my head,
a pair of wire spectacles cracked and twisted
like the man in the windshield in front of me.

Fear, the mind's apoplexy, my dissonant lullaby;
pain and acceptance, my morning song.

O to be like the Japanese waterboy
seeing a stream his mother could not cross
asked her to climb upon his back to walk as one;
as the waters pushed and rushed about his thighs
and jagged rocks tore and cut his feet,
he cried—for she was so light.

Rhonda Smithart
A DREAM

A dream to a dreamer is so close, but yet so far, ever present, but never in reach.

He dreams of beautiful but impossible things, but only impossible to the minds that have never dared to venture from the realm of reality.

He has traveled beyond the stars and dared to reach for the moon.

He dreams of a perfect love so beautiful that it boggles the mind, for you cannot see it with the naked eye nor feel it with a heart that has its boundaries.

He has seen things never before seen. Touched things never before touched.

He has felt things no one else has felt, but more important he is the author and the creator nothing is impossible.

"But what good is a dreamer" you say. "First thing you know you will have awakened to find that you are old and on your death bed. What a waste, you have dreamed your life away."

But yet to the dreamer it was a mere dream he has lived, life has not yet begun.

Cathy Erskine
WE LEARN FROM EACH OTHER
Your proud yet timid hands gather leaves and twigs
to fuel the firepit—your first campfire.
You start at the crack of the match
that ignites our warmth and safety,
our faces red from the ashes that swell
porous and hot like mounds of salt-rising bread.

A raccoon peering from a nearby bush frightens you,
yet somehow without your knowing you learn
others here want some unasked-for thing from you—
and you, the young firebuilder, become a man.

Your proud no longer timid hands reach out
above the dying flames to cup the rain
as it suddenly descends soft and wet everywhere.
You'll stop the rain, you say.

Your body in a half arch above the firepit
hunched like a human umbrella
reminds us you are still yet a boy.

Your face filled with determination and belief
remains like the fire beneath you glowing.

Brent Webber
REVIVAL
A snake coiled around the wrist
of the tent—revival evangelist
as he screamed at the crowd.
One elderly lady convulsed,
foaming liberally at the mouth
while her husband, speaking in
tongues,
was much too busy to notice.
A young man passed the plate,
collecting as much as possible,
while one devotee claimed to be
healed
of whatever had ailed him.
The holy rollers moaned and
groaned,
sang and clapped their hands,
whimpered and whined for hours.
Finally they faded off into the night.
Some claimed to have found God.

Anne E Jordan
THE NIGHT
The night is so quiet
and all you can hear
are the sounds of passing cars
by my window.

The sky was so bright.
With lit up stars that it
shined on the darken street.

I look out my window
and saw a shape of a cat,
by a telephone pole just setting there.

Then I went back to
bed and dreamed.

Thelma I Beers
INFLUENCE
This little world wherein we dwell
For some is narrow as a cell;
For others, wide as speed can reach
Or power can carry print or speech.
Nor can the sharpest eye define
The bounds between your world and mine.
This little world wherein we live
To move about; to take and give;
To learn and teach, to dream and hope
And often past our sight to grope

Perhaps is not mere land and sky
Where mortals wait the time to die.
Perhaps—and how shall this I phrase?—
'Tis heart and soul and friendly ways
And strength and faith in times of doubt
An influence that ripples out
Beyond the shores of self to blend
In hopes and dreams that never end.
Who chooses close to self to dwell
Makes of his world a narrow cell,
But who sets out of use to be
As far as he can hear and see,
Share grief, give aid and carry grace
Lives in immeasurable space.—

Audray Quill
DEAR LOVE

This poem is dedicated to my love, Jack, for all the times we have shared together.

In yesterdays of willowwisp ways
I saw you sitting there
In your chair.
So debonair.
There was much laughter in the sun.
I knew, you were the one,
Life was simple when and then.
In the days of willowwisp ways.
Night hawks flew
We watched, me and you.
I love you now
I loved you then
In the days of willowwisp ways.
Where are you since?
Search to find you
In today's essence.
Could it be——
You and me
Lost to those days of willowwisp ways?

Gloria O'Brien
MEMORIES TO SURVIVE
Death did come by my bedside
It wanted me for sure

I almost said, please take me
To stop the pain inside

Then memories did flood my mind
Of all of those I love

Those memories gave me the strength
I needed to survive.

Tracy M Craig-Clark
FEBRUARY 5, 1988
I woke up this morning and thought of you in an extra special way
You would have been twenty-one years old in our world today,
But, instead in God's world you are in your sixth year
Where there I am sure you are treasured so dear,
You have been gone so long
Oh, how it seems so wrong,
I have missed you so very much
Everyone of our lives you touched,
We spent much of our childhood lives together
Those memories will remain with me forever,
My brother and best friend you were, the best anyone could ever have
I never had a chance to tell you this and that makes me so sad,
You were taken for a reason, a reason I do not know why
All of us were forced to tell you such a sad good bye,

All of our lives have changed, which I am sure you know of
While you sit up there watching and protecting us from above,
I miss you so much that it still makes me cry
I just wish I knew why you had to die,
God's will I am not questioning I want you to know
I must wish I had more time with you before you had to go.

Randy Davis

Randy Davis
Baptist Evangelist
DEAR GOD:
Today as I entered your house to worship I felt your presence near,
A feeling of serenity overcame me knowing that you care.

Then as I knelt to pray,
I hoped that you would have time to listen to what I have to say.

I can hear the minister say that your son, Jesus Christ shed his blood upon the cross,
The Holy Spirit convinced me that I too am lost.

With eyes closed I now can see your face,
Revealing the pain you must feel,
They are now placing upon your head a crown of thorns,
As I wiped my eyes I began to understand what
I was seeing was very real.

Blood is dripping from your head, hands and side,
In my heart I now know with you I will always abide.

Dear God I will strive to do your blessed will in everything I do,
I only wished that all my friends were here too.

Dear God for me you gave your only son,
Because of you God a new life within me has begun.

As I stood and wiped away my tears,
For the first time I felt relieved that you had taken away all my fears.

Thank you God for listening to what I had to say,
So I'll promise you that I'll be here next Sunday.

Janith D Anderson
THE BEE
With wings to move,
And legs to crawl,
He moves in a skyward
Way.
Sometimes on trees,
Other times on flowers,
Collecting nectar to take to their hives.

To harvest the orchards
To fertilize flowers,
To make fruit or beautiful flowers.

To work its full life
The bee is content,
To a more beautiful world,
For people in it.

Josephine S Luporini
NATURE'S THEFT
Blankets cozy on my bed,
Pillow soft beneath my head.
Closed my eyes, but can not sleep,
Even tried to count some sheep.

Moon shines on the window pane,
Cast a picture with a frame.
The night is calm as I can see,
No winds or rains to distort,
The picture in the frame.

Clouds creep within the still night,
Stole the light right out of sight,
Swipes the picture from the wall,
I do not know who to call.

Mama says it is all a dream,
Still, I know—
Nature's up to her old scheme!

Holly Molero Raybon
THE MASK
There's a mask that many people hide behind, only because it's reassuring and safe.
It's a mask that hides true feelings of love and hate and of joy and pain.
It can show many expressions that one might choose to express, only the person behind the mask knows the reality of those feelings that he may choose to disguise.
When behind this mask of deception it gives others a false impression of what he feels, only to lie and deceive instead of being true.
If only everyone could be true instead of escaping behind a false exterior
The mask itself could be hidden and put away and every one wouldn't have to hide behind it again.

Frank J DiLaturo
BEACH
Smell the salt, smell the cool. Little men bob.
On green and white, they wait.

Lonely sandal. Two pigeons pecking the sand, side to side.
Children playing, their laughter floating on the breeze
Pelicans circling, diving, splashing, empty. They try again.
White flashes on the horizon! Sails!
Oh, how beautifully they harness the wind. So sleek and fast, slicing the sea,
riding that interface of air and water.

Standing on sand, soft, fine and hot.
Next, stones and pebbles, warm and smooth. Next,
Sand, cold, wet, hard, and flat. Hear the waves reach, extend, deliver and reclaim.

She appears alone. One hand in a pocket, the other swings in stride.
Her hair hangs straight, wet, and black. Her bright pink top is full and loose, casually tucked in grey shorts.
Her bare feet leave disappearing imprints in the wet sand. Her black glasses reflect the scene, as she inhales it all, and fades away.

Many have been here, many still, will come. Many suns have shed light,
Defining beauty at twilight. Many moons have changed shape, many more shall fill the night. A siren's ballad, she forever sings. A song of sweetness, of power, of inspiration divine, serenity sublime.

Betty J Dunlap
GOD'S DAILY CARE
Life is like a restless sea
With tides that come and go,
Some dash high upon the rocks
And some are quiet and low.

Some days are rough with care and work,
While others calm and still.
Yet life goes on from day to day
According to God's will.

We need to learn as days go by,
In sunshine bright or dim;
To trust His all-sustaining arm,
He'll hold us close to Him.

One day, and that not far away
We'll meet Him face to face,
To thank Him for His daily care,
And all sufficient grace.

Christina Gambill
BEAUTY
Beauty is a rainbow,
Beauty is a shiny star,
Beauty is a white unicorn,
But, most of all Beauty is
the love that your heart holds.

Brad Altizer
MY ROAD
I am growing up and looking out for the curves life is throwing me
I am trying hard to bounce back and stand firm for what I believe.
But my way is rough, the road is rocky. And I am not sure where it leads.

Richard W Sexton
AUTUMN BEAUTY
In the fall take a little trip and you will see,
All the beautiful hillsides in the country.

Jack Frost comes along every fall,
He paints all the trees the short and the tall.

The green, orange, yellow, red and brown,
There is a pretty spot on the way back to town.

All the beauty will be destroyed as fast as it came,
With wind and rain and no one to blame.

Dolores F Berkhimer
LOST CHILD

Dedicated to every missing child.

Little children lost and stolen away
You are in our prayers,
Each and every day.
We look for you in every young face,
Searching for but one small trace.
Your captors please, take note of this,
Were you not loved or hugged or

There must be room for some remorse,
I hope you'd say, of course, of course.
Can you but be a child again?
Remember that you were once like them,
Release that little one you knew,
Give back the child which once was you!

Dolores F Berkhimer
GRANDMA'S HAND

To all the dear Grandmas.'

Little one
Take my hand
Again, to play
In your secret hideaway.
Tell me I must stay,
Just for another day.

Oh, how grand to be
Swinging on that old oak tree,
Playing jacks with me.
You say it's time for tea?
Bunnie, poochie, dollie,
Yes, that's three.
Take Grandma's hand, dear baby
And always be, my little one.

Sally Gane
THE MIRROR
The mirror stares. I turn away.
"You can't escape," it taunts.
Reluctantly I face my foe,
The killer of my youthful dreams.

For now the voice turns soft in plea
For truce. "No beauty here, perhaps never was,
But that now matters less. The years
Can heal the wounds of youth. Come look."

A child's dark hair now gray, but frames
With longed-for curls, a weathered face
Long battered by the sun and marred
By curving lines set deep by time.

"Now look beneath this outer shell
To attributes which helped you through
These many years. There beauty lies
To bring you pride that you are are you.

Dena
ROSE-COLORED GLASSES
Take those
rose-colored glasses
off.
I can't,
I am afraid,
I don't want to get burned,
I need the protection.

Detra Shon Moore
I THOUGHT ABOUT IT: NOW YOU
Many times I wonder just how
Much more I can bear.
I begin to think about how Jesus
Died for me and how my ancestors
Were slaves in order to survive.
Many times I envy them because
they know what it means to suffer
Just so they can live.
As a black person, I must realize
That the cause they fought for
Was not a waste, but an achievement.
They wanted freedom and they got
That so I must carry on their dream
Before their achievements become a waste.
THINK ABOUT IT!

Charlene M Redding
THE STAINED GLASS WINDOW
As I journey back to haunts
That childhood memories love,
I sit again upon the stairs
With bedrooms clustered up above.

The favourite spot in which I sit
Is beautiful to see,
For at the turning of the stairs
Are colored panes in symmetry.

On dark days too the beauty shone;
On bright days prettier still,
All cherished memories of home
To be enjoyed by all who will.

And if the window panes could talk,
And if the glass were eyes,
Many sweet and tender moments
They could tell of past goodbyes.

Leo J Lawler
AMERICA
When Jesus came to America
They simply passed Him by,
They wouldn't hurt a hair
of Him
They only let Him die.

For men had grown more tender
They wouldn't cause Him pain
They only just passed down
the street
And left Him in the rain.

Still Jesus cried, "Forgive them,
For they know not what they do."
And still it rained the
winter rain
That drenched Him through and
through.

The crowds went home and left
the streets
Without a soul to see.
As Jesus crouched against the
wall
And cried . . . for CALVARY!

Lynn McLEOD
HOW TENDER DO YOUR EYES GAZE
How tender do your eyes gaze
Upon the life around you
How sweet is the smile
That has found you
How warm is the spirit
That always surrounds you
How understanding is your love.

How caring is the kiss
That always greets me
How gentle is the touch
That always defeats me
How strong is the heart
That completes me
How undemanding is your love.

John Geiger III
SELF EXAMINATION
I gaze out my window
And life passes by
The outside is cold
Just as I

A snowflake does fall
Past my eyes so red
I wipe the tears away
And try to clear my head

My life's been so empty
Without friends or love
The only lights I have
Are the stars and sun above

Suddenly a robin appears
And away go the tears
For spring and fresh
Starts are here

I may be lonely
I may be alone
But me, myself, and I
Will go on.

If it's meant to be
I'd be somewhere else
But there must be a reason
To be lost in oneself

William E Douglas Jr
SEARING
Whether I'll be frightened again tomorrow, I cannot say,
but dammit, I'm burning, no
I'm searing with life today!
I just love for my children to see me this way,
so they'll know adults aren't
condemned to live life afraid.

Why, I'm a booster rocket exploring out into virgin space,
or maybe the point man on
reconnaissance for the entire
human race!
I have no idea what type of life's fruit I will find,
but I'll be sucking all their
sweet juice, leaving empty
rinds behind!

Crashing symbols and devil trumpets wail my song today!
I'll <u>stand</u> down mighty armies
and on bended knees I'll pray.
I will surrender past sins and conquer new ones today!
I'm convinced God loves to see
me this way!

Compassion's love flows through me, like a mighty raging stream!
Words of wisdom come to me,
I say just what I mean.
Each person's deepest feelings, I'm yearning to learn
and through this joyous
curiosity, many friendships
are earned.

It seems these ecstatic moments are occurring much more often.
Yes, reality's harshness is
beginning to soften
as man's hateful, vengeful hourglass seemingly runs out of sand.
<u>I believe these days are the</u>
<u>new millennium's beckoning,</u>
<u>outreached hands</u>.

Ken Winkley

Ken Winkley
SANDS OF LOVE

To Karen, who decided to keep her feelings covered.

The dunes, desert sands, desolate,
Always shifting, burying fresh demise,
Bones of prominent feelings.
Yet, within this never-ending drama,
Untold treasures of emotion
Are also slowly exposed.
As the beauty of myriad desert flowers
Relies on this infinite sculpting
To conceive its new life,
So must the remnants of past love
Be covered slowly, patiently
And the substance of new emotion emerges.
Grain by grain swept clean
To become a durable thread,
Joining nature's other arts
In a splendid cycle
Of life, promise, rebirth;
Forming the fabric of human experience.
Sands of love,
Seeming so barren,
I know they're full of life.

Mary Whitenack
FOR YOU
I do believe that God above
Created you for me to love;
He picked you out from all the rest,
Because He knew I'd love you best.
I once had a heart called mine, 'tis true,
But now it's gone from me to you;
Take good care of it, as I have done,
For you have two and I have none.
If I go to heaven and you're not there,
I'll paint your face on the golden stair,
So all the angels can know and see,
Just what you really mean to me.

If you've not come by judgement
day,
I'll know you've gone the other way;
So I'll give the angels back their
wings,
Their golden harps and everything;
And just to show you what I'd do—
I'll go to Hell dear, just for you!

Doris Brubaker Walter
THE TRIMMING
A wooden box atop a chair
On which sat a tot with yellow curly
hair.
The barber to be, Granny A.
Tired of his squirming, did say
"Michael, if you don't sit still I'll cut
it like Grandpa Andy's"
To the top of his head went the little
lad's hand
Being bald-headed was one thing he
couldn't stand.
"No, no not like Grandpa Andy's,"
he did cry
To sit very still, he then did try.
I remember, with humor, the day I
did view
The day Granny Armstrong gave a
haircut to you.

Donald D Giesler
RAINY NIGHT LIGHT
Light tear dropping down
my window brightly.
Passing into the night slightly.
Reflections of an eclipsed moon.
Visions of a Blue-Lune.
Shadows move in rhythm of the tune.
The raven night and star bright,
all and all a blurry night.
Softly, softly it tear drops lightly
on my face.
This in all breaks the pace.
Oh how I embrace the total night
with all my might.

Bruce A Woods
LETTERS FOR BARBARA
Letters make words,
Words make phrases,
Arranged or changed
With tradition or crazes,
Sound silly, but really,
Let me arrange my letters to say,
I would do anything for you any day.

Billie J Martino
TRUE LOVE
He left the State of Virginia,
where he was on probation.
He was just a poor boy,
without help from any relation.
He didn't have any money,
when the trucker left him there.
He took all the boy owned,
It's a shame, it isn't fair.
He fell in love with a pretty girl,
In fact she loves him too.
They planned a beautiful wedding,
but their plans fell thru.
She went and got her wedding gown,
she packed it away today,
Their wedding will be postponed,
'cause the police took him away.
She really cares about him,
the love that she finally found.
If it takes Hell or high water,
she'll bring him homeward bound.

Kathleen Bosse
THE HAIRLESS BEING FREED
To the people who waste their time,
Trying to change what they don't
need.
To them this poem I'll title,
"The Hairless Being Freed."

The time and money that can be
saved,
In the good old stylist chair.
No tints, no cuts, no perms, no greys,
It truly doesn't seem fair.

Why spend the costs on formulas,
For a little fuzz to appear.
Or go under cover in a toupee,
So the wind can be your fear.

The eagle is our coat of arms,
Our strength for the world to see.
No one seems to mind she's bald,
She's as proud as she can be.

So all you hairless people,
Stop worrying and just be free.
Be glad of all the hassles you're
spared,
It's better bald you must agree.

Kimberly C Kelley
ADDICTION
When we could have so very much
Why must you always stir up a fuss
You accuse and you blame and
imagine the worst
'Til sometimes I feel that I will burst

I've loved you much and I've loved
you long
So how can you think I've done so
much wrong
I've only tried to make you mine
And if I could it would be just fine

The only good thing in all this mess
Is that I feel I've passed life's
toughest test
I've overcome taking the blame
For any of these things you want to
name

I love you now and always will
I'll stay until I've had my fill
Living with alcohol is not any fun
In the end—who will have won?

Salvatore Meloni
thoughts held
looking through the eyes of many
at laughter sounds, from precipice
abodes,
with contrasting views, dubious
existence,
then loneliness fills, my heart alone.
seeing footsteps in archaic days
of old—
holding thoughts of cavalry,
with a glance, judging,
instantaneous—
incoherent of reproach,
footsteps fade through misunderstandings,
the heart grows moss like a stone,
just—
frozen to this time of living
concernments only of my own,
congenial to the one's in
common—
ponder not, those affronted,
awaiting—
trials, of this memento,
mistakes in judging, I perceive,
being sensitive to oneself, but
others!—
as meek lay cold upon the earth,
memorials to his life of living,
caressing cavalry, thoughts hold;

Dawn Tomasello
SOMEDAY
Goodbye Blue Skies The Birds Do
Not Fly,
The Sun Shines No Longer.
If You're Wondering Why Then You
Must Be Blind,
It's In The Palms Of Your Hands;
There's too
Much Madness In Your Head

Say Goodbye To Those Blue Skies
Your Spirit Flies Higher.
The Coldness Grows Inside Your
Body
You Lit The Skies On Fire.
Welcome The Blackness That
Surrounds You.

Michael R O'Brien
THE CRYSTAL TREASURE
Mouth dry with anticipation,
Pause a moment with the pleasure;
Join me in participation—
Hit me with the crystal treasure.

Feel the warmth benumb my senses,
Feel the soul's awakening.
Tearing down my mind's defenses,
At reality's forsakening.

Thoughts are slowing, pulse is
speeding,
Senses reel in bursts of light.
Hands are shaking, eyes are bleeding,
Alone here in this day-turned-night.

Living on a level higher,
Than I've ever known before.
Drawn here by the crystal liar.
Suffering behind closed door.

Descending to the black perfection,
Passing by with quickened pace.
Frightened by my own
reflection—
How did I come to this place.

M Margaret Heerdt
THE POETRY CONVENTION
With poetry our common thread,
To newer friendships' hope we're
led,
At this convention here with you.
When every day brings something
new,
Although as strangers here we meet,
Some kindred soul we hope to greet.

We mill around to chat or smile
And so the time somehow beguile,
Hope when it's done—like ships at
night,
We're not forgot when out of sight,
And when it's o'er and home we go,
We'll cherish friendship's after-glow.

Andrew A Taylor
CREATION
Somewhere out there was a master
mind
That one day decided it was creation
time.
And from warmth of love, there was
a man.
And then came woman to replenish
the land.

Now out of this mist, there had to be
land,
So that the sea would not be in
command.
There was need for land, so that plant
could grow and sprout
To feed the animals when they came
about.

Deep within the sea, there was a
change,
For some of the creatures had to walk
the land.
And they that walked, flew and
crawled
Came to hear the master mind's call.

Now that the world was ready to
begin,
Man committed his greatest sin.
He did what was wrong, according to
the master mind
And from himself, he had to hide

Merrilee Nye
MOTHER EARTH CRIES FOR HER CHILDREN
My name is Mother Earth and I grow tired and weary! I was once a blooming budding planet with hopes and dreams, but now I am tired. No longer young and vibrant and full of life! but now polluted with smog and many toxins and many diseases.

Many years ago people respected me. What they took they replaced. They nurtured my many life forms young and old, but as time went on and the people and businesses grew they forgot to take time to notice nature and care. I am but one planet and many changes are of yet to come!

Please do not tear the Rain Forests down! Without them it is hard for me to breathe. With less oxygen for the ozone my skin burns easily. Without the water my soil will become barren and dry. No longer will man be able to reproduce his precious food substance and many will suffer much more than they already have! Please think of me when someone you know or a business gets careless and my body is soiled with toxins or pollutants, take the time to notice and care. Nature is of Beauty and Abundance! Enjoy it, but do not abuse it! Yes I grow tired and I weep. My tears are not for myself, they are for you! It is your planet cherish it and respect me. We are all God's creations!

Love,
Mother Earth

Jean K Sellards
MY FRIEND
One autumn eve I met a friend,
And such a friend was he!
It'd been some years since I'd known
someone
Who was so good to me.

Like desert rains that fall in spring
Bringing life to barren land,
He quenched my thirst and filled my
soul
With life 'til I could stand.

And then like clouds which onward
move
And leave the desert 'lone,

We parted ways—but I felt strong
For with him I had grown.

I thank the Lord for sending him
In answer to my needs.
Watch o'er him, Lord, and go with him
To bless the life he leads.

Kathy Scott
WHISPERS OF TIME

Whispers of time, whisper phrases of truth and wisdom, It tells the secrets of how I may think.

Understanding this gives aid in understanding lessons in life, even though it seems the more I learn about life . . . The less I know.

Maybe, the whispers of time are trying to tell me that there's a lot more, to learning the facts of life than one could possibly know.

Maybe one day . . . I'll know why the whispers of time gave me this lesson of life.

lori wineinger
TATTOO

old black tattoo
got it before I knew they were cool
happy dancin' fool
dead on my skin
frozen in time
to remind me
where I been

Kyla Rae O'Brien

Kyla Rae O'Brien
THE RUSTIC DOLLHOUSE

This poem is dedicated to my mom and dad, Jan and Ed O'Brien, and to my Fourth Grade Class at The Calverton School, Huntingtown, Maryland.

Crisp tan basket, sitting on the hollow chest;
Dark brown cover draped over the gorgeous couch;
White wooden door scraping against the soft carpet;
Burning hot tea cooling in the air;
Birds chirping softly on the misty fields;
Oil lamps sparkling in the sun;
Old dusty banjo hanging on the wall;
Toy dog glaring out the window;
Cracked mirrors staring back at me;
Rustic desk tucked in the Library;
Shriveled-up maps reaching from wall to wall;
Creaking floors confessing their age.

Margaret Hansen
YOUR COAT

You left us in the warmth of summer—
the master beckoned and you were gone!
I stood so helpless beside my brother—
what to say—to do—to make the loss of a wife-friend-lover—easier to bear!
We spent days filled with tears—
hugs—and love—
and then the time had come for me to pack my things together, and head back
to my world—children—work and life.
Quietly with a hug he handed me your coat—
and with tear filled eyes—I was gone.
It is winter now—the snow is falling—wrapped warm in your coat I walk the empty streets—chasing down lonely alleys—
looking for answers to unknown questions—why?
Suddenly you are here—your smile—your laughing eyes the warmth of your friendship.
Slowly I turn—button my collar to the
cold wind—and make my way back home—
wrapped in
your coat of love—and I realize someday too—the master will beckon to me!

Patrick Haggard
MOSTLY THE HOURS

Mostly the hours, in slowest of time;
I feel the flowers of past, in my solitude
The heartfelt joys, most sublime,
And the sorrows, of lack in my aptitude.

Mostly the hours, in present spent,
Blend this dull substance into gray.
Only to follow the previous increment;
So hollow, without relevance in today.

Mostly the hours, a traveler I am,
Directing this antiquated soul.
Depicting the coward and ills of mayhem;
And ghostly, these levelers take their toll.

Mostly the hours, in love and delight,
Did, I travail in furious fire.
and now are above, shadows of night;
As without avail in curious desire.

Mostly the hours, following my tears,
Do, I consecrate my treason,
And embower those fleeting years
Of consummate lies; knowing my deeper reasons.

Tabitha
GOD HELP ME A LITTLE KINDER BE

God help me a little kinder be—as life's goal I seek
More helpful to the frail and weak
More gentle with Thy blessed meek
Then, God, I know I shall be nearer to life's lofty peak.
God, give me more courage, strength and might.
Give me just a portion of Thy far-seeing sight.
Give me the will to battle always for the right.
God, guard and guide me ever with Thy protecting Light.
God—I pray for wisdom—power to know what things in life are first—how to keep them so.
Help me destroy all pettiness—make hatred go—
And, God—through my efforts let a little of Thy glory show.
"Inasmuch as ye have done it," said the Man of Galilee,
"Unto the least of these my brethren—ye have done it unto me!"
God, keep me ever mindful that I have learned of Thee,
And let my life reflect your Light that others, too, might see.

Amy Brockman
DEAR LORD

Dear Lord, why is it this way,
Why need we suffer, day by day?
Wasn't it enough that she was so young.
Wasn't it enough that her life had just begun?
It wasn't her fault, being hit like that,
The guy said he swerved to miss a cat.
He said he knew what a cat looked like,
How could he miss a young girl on a bike?

Now she's gone, home to your house,
I know she'll be good, like a church mouse.
He's in jail for drinking and driving,
But that doesn't keep us from crying.

Lord, we miss her, our hearts are broken
But I forgive him, let that be a token.
A token of her heart, for I'm sure she knows,
His regretfulness in the future grows.

He was drunk, forever he'll pay,
For one last drink, her one last day.

Dear Lord, why is it this way,
Why need we suffer, day by day?

Kathleen M Froode
ONCE THERE WAS A LITTLE BIRD

Once there was a little bird
he never even said one word,
so his Mother said, "why don't you talk my little Fred?" She began to weep, and little Fred he said, "Peep peep."

Alexander Leonard Bove Sr
ALZHEIMER'S PRAYER

Dedicated to those afflicted with Alzheimer's disease.

When I retire each night to pray
But can't remember words to say,
I'd lie awake all night this way,
And in a daze throughout the day.

So in an oddly reverent way
I say my alphabet each day.
From "A" to "Z" my words are there.
I know, dear Lord, you hear My Prayer.

For only you know what I'm thinking
On the nights you hear me weeping.
Only you know how I'm feeling;
"Thank you Lord, for bearing with me."

Now only you know how I'm healing
Every night I lie here sleeping.
Only I know why I'm healing;
"Praise the Lord, I'm in your keeping."

So with a fervent strong desire
I say My Prayer when I retire;
Until the pangs of earth have ended
And my longing soul ascended.
Amen.

Stella Kerkvliet
THE PLEA

To Bernie, my Son with Love

Love independent of time,
Countless, as the grains of sand,
Endless, as the heavens,
Hope in this torn land.

Print this indelible word
On my tormented soul
Carve it on my heart,
Make it my only goal.

Teach me to know this love
With every bit of me
Peel the scales from my eyes
That this imperfect soul might see.

Replenish my starving heart
With Your wisdom, and healing love—
Give me strength and patience,
Heal this heart so numb.

Stella Kerkvliet
CYNICAL HEART

To Dona—my last "Gift of Love"

The mist in a wind,
The dream in a song,
The cry, in a heart
All vanish 'ere long.

The yearning for life,
Its fullest to live,
The caring 'tis gone,
'Twas time in a sieve.

Life is a dream
Born, but to die,
Heed not this world,
Man's word, a lie.

Tomorrow is yet,
Yesterday gone,
Take all you can gain,
Treat souls, as a pawn.

Life is so short,
We kill, lie or cheat,
Ne'er number the day
We are judged at His feet.

Oh cynical heart
Many are we,
Beware, oh beware
For next could be me.

Shannon A Montgomery
JUSTICE

I am called Justice. I wander and roam
The dusty grey halls that I must call home.
Some seek me out, my favor to court,
But they find that my aid is a double-edge sort.
Down empty hallways, through timeless walls,
Few adhere to my beck and my call.

The gentle and squeamish, all refuse aid,
None willing to pay my price to be paid.
Just what do I ask, none willing to give?
Fairness in everything, a lifestyle to live.
A tooth for a tooth, an eye for each eye,
Murder for murder and lie for each lie.
Pain for each pain caused is all that I ask
I do not feel it is such a hard task.
All must be equal when I have my say—
And to call upon me, one must do things my way.
Think twice before, anguished, you scream out my name;
Perfect equality is the name of my game.
Am I what you seek? Justice, indeed?
Take anew look at the life you now lead.,

Courtney Rehbine

Courtney Rehbine
MOMS

To the best Mom in the world, who has given me the first nine years of my life, filled with fun and happiness.

Moms are cool,
They use the tools.
Moms are bright—
They always turn off the lights.
When you say ahchoo!!
They say God Bless you!
My Mom's the best,
She's not a pest.
She's so cool,
She said we may even get a pool.
When you're sick,
They get the thermometer stick.
They clean the kitchen,
And bake the food.
When you have the flu,
They even make you warm stew!

Writing poetry gives me great pleasure,
for I feel inside—
It's a hidden treasure!

James F O'Neill
INSIDE OUT

I've looked at myself from the inside out
And sometimes wonder what I'm all about
Such a jumble of thoughts and deeds
Wandering aimlessly like tumbleweeds
Through the desolate desert of my mind
Without a path for their way to find
Most men choose their goals and never look back
But there are fools like me who can't finds the right track

Well now I've looked at myself from the outside in
And it befuddles me so to know where to begin
To see the me that I wanted to be
Instead of the one that seems lost at sea
But I guess I'm not all that bad off
I've retained all my values and my heart remains soft

Laurie Gardner
IF THE LORD HAD SOME BROTHERS LIKE MINE

If the Lord had some
brothers like mine,
to help him through hardships and make him feel
fine.

He'd hardly feel sad,
but in a week he'd go mad.
so it's better the Lord has no
brothers like mine.

Ruby M Carlisle
A CLOWN

To my beloved daughter Kendra G. Carlisle

A clown
Sitting in a circus
All alone

Made people laugh
Then they
Went home

A clown
Wearing a funny suit
With a painted on smile
And an extra boot

A clown
Has begun to cry
No longer funny
But ready to die

A clown
Do you understand
Why he is so down

Or are you still
Interested in just seeing
A clown

Karen R Petroski
A SAMPLE OF SIMPLICITY

I dream of running away
And
Avoiding complexities.
I would like to
sift
The simplicity
Out
Of life.
I admire a fish,
Dancing in the water—
And a bird,
Darting
Back
And
Forth
In the sky-
And people, sitting
On
A
Park Bench,
Enjoying their silence.

Larry J T Foucault
THE MIMETISMS

you
nailed me
here
as your sacrificial
lamb, but the sins
I died
for,
are
only
a slam.
You have made Me live for almost two thousand years,
A precious icon to justify your civilized fears.
I hang a decoration in your shrines of once a week,
And yet for the remainder, you criticize the meek.
From tall steel towers I overlook your towns,
With your throw-away children in your elitist dog pounds.
The blood is still stained on your reaching hands,
That have littered, pilfered, and scattered
the remaining promise lands.

For the Little Souls you have
forgotten, are your
only Saviours.

Jackie L Kerr
I WANT YOU TO KNOW

I love you with all my heart,
And I knew that from the very start.
I swore to myself to never let you know,
But my feelings inside are too strong
And I knew if I didn't tell you,
Sooner or later you would care for someone else.
Then I knew I'd be blue.
So I got up the courage to show you this poem.
I'm not sure what your feelings are for me
Or how strong they might be,
But as soon as I laid my eyes on you,
My feelings for you were strong.
And everytime I see you,
I know they weren't wrong.
When I see you I began to shake,
And all my words were mistakes.
I just want you to know that "I Love You So,"
And I know that no matter where you reside,
I always want to be there at your side.

Elena Farmer
ALL WE ARE

All we are
are shadows,
Dancing on the wall.

All we are
are seeds,
Sinking when we fall.

All we are
are reflections,
Looking through the glass

All we are
are minutes,
Waiting for time to pass.

All we are
are doors,
Closed by racial fiends.

All we are
are windows,
Open to material dreams.

All we are
are prisoners,
Barred within our minds,

All we are
are poets,
Confined to prose and lines.

All we are
are rain drops,
Swallowed by the sun.

All we are
are adolescents,
Fearless and on the run.

All we are
are pages,
Turned by an impassioned wind.

All we are
are preachers,
Redeeming those who have sinned.

All we are
are entities,
Estranged from those around.

All we are
are mimics,
Echoes without sound.

Christine Mixon
WHY?

Why does the sun set, why does night fall
Does anyone know, does anyone really care at all.
Why do people cry when they're happy but also when they're sad,
Does anyone ever wonder, doesn't it all seem so mad.
Why do people get hurt, why do they live in pain
Does anyone care, is there feeling which our heart will contain.
Why does insecurity fulfill us all,
Why do we live in doubt
Does anyone stop to think, what is it all about
Why do people fall in love, why do people die,
Does anyone ever stop to ask themselves—why:?

Janice E Kelley
HIS BECKON CALL

When the sun sets or the moon rises and the stars shine,
I feel a warmth and a sense of peace from Thine.
God created this wondrous world in a hope for inner peace and a love for all.
All the beauty this world possesses was created from His highest call.

No greater wonder on Earth can we be given,
The greatest gift will be our final trip to Heaven.
In Heaven there will be no more hurts or pain.
It will be the ultimate gift and finest gain.

We'll be able to see our loved ones we've missed so much.
God awaits us with open arms and loving touch.
Have no doubts if you're a sinner,

God accepts all—losers or winner.
He forgave us our sins one and
all.
That is why He brings peace and
love when He summons His
beckon call.

Joseph W Fritz
PINK RABBITS AND PURPLE BUTTERFLIES

Las night I was in a world with
purple butterflies, pink rabbits,
blue and yellow horses with wings.
The yellow horses had single horns
that spiraled down in an array of
colors.
What a wonderful place to be?
Better than most places I'd like
to see.
Never before had I been so free
and so full of glee.
Like a child in toyland I was it
seemed.
The grass was all orange and
blue.
What a wonderful place for me to
view.
Not many places have red trees
and green honeybees.
What wonderful place it was to
be.

In a sudden burst I heard ringing
And my body was shaking on its
own.
As I closed and opened my eyes
My mom was there waking me
up
To go to school, she heard my
alarm.
It woke her up, she asked why
hadn't I awoke,
My alarm I said, loud enough to
wake you from down the hall
Not loud enough to move me at
all.

Joseph W Fritz
HOPES

I sit by my kitchen sink
Where I reside to think
'Cause I dream to run and play
Though here I must stay
My wheels aren't agile
To go out in the grassy green for
awhile
Long have my dreams been
To walk on the lawn again
I hope that someday
I won't have to stay
Strapped to my iron seat
Maybe soon I'll greet
The wonder of Nature on my feet.

J Michael Bliss
THE BALLAD OF JOHNNY NICHOLSON

There is a guy named Johnny
Who works the shift with me
That is, HE says he works it
But me, I disagree

'Cause if you saw his time card
You would know the reason why
Ol' Johnny's card is often blank
It's enough to make you sigh

He calls in sick or comes in late
And if THAT'S not enough
The days he does show up for work
He acts so rough and tough

Once he came to work on time
And he took a look around
But when he saw the shape of things
'Tough' Johnny couldn't be found

So, when you see dear Johnny
Don't stop to ask him why
Just smile and shake your head at him
And hope someday he'll try

Michelle J Edwards
A DAY TO REMEMBER

There is a special day,
this day will appear.
When this day comes
there will be a little fear.

The fear will become joy,
and everyone will cry.
This is the day
that I must say good-bye.

This day is familiar
all across the land.
This is the day
when he will take my hand.

There is a special date
when we will scurry away
This special celebration
is my wedding day.

Connie Whitmore
PAINTING & PANIC

To my very dear parents
Bob & Vi Love C.

My upstairs room was a very large
one.
One entire wall held the work I had
done.
I cut every picture I could find of
"his" face.
Every inch covered, not one tiny
blank space.
I know of "his face" was a hundred
or more.
The wall so abused from pin holes
galore.
Loved "him" so much. "He" filled all
of my dreams.
Even wore "his" name on a patch on
my jeans.

Dad was painting the house by my
window outside.
Off the ladder, he's falling. I just
nearly died.
Dad grabbed and I screamed, as he
started to fall.
He was holding on to my very prized
wall.

The poor man, by his fingers, was
still hanging there.
And by not helping him, it seems I
don't care.
But before thinking of dad, my
actions are dumb.
'Cause I checked "his" face to see if
damage was done.

I realize that a father is hard to
replace.
But he was grabbing at my Elvis's
face.

Eddie Denniston
SUN AND RAIN (HEAT AND PAIN)

To my Marine buddies, and all Vietnam Vets (Andy, Taters and Chief . . .). To my beloved family. To Steve Shatinsky, a dear friend.

The sun shines bright outside my
door.
For in my heart the rain will pour.
A smile I shall keep, so no one will
know; the pain that I put to sleep.
Friends will ask how are you; then
they'll go. When I close the door
behind me, the tears always seem to
find me. For I live with a secret; and
only I know I can keep it.
Letters from home, they want a reply;
how do you tell them you're waiting
to die.
You write them back so they worry
not
Yes, it's true you lie a lot. A more
terrible place, no one could find. For
the rest of our lives it will be in our
minds.
We left a country that said it loved us
so, now we are here wondering where
to go? And for my mom to sooth her
sorrow there's got to be a fib I can
borrow. To let her know I'm safe and
sound, as I lay here on the ground.
Explosions around my body and
head. Please God don't let them call
her and tell her I'm dead. Then
you're back home family and friends.
They help but then you sleep again,
and then bang a tremendous yelp! As
you jump up you cry for help. You
realize it's over there, but it's ok
because your back there. And so it
ends or does it. So for the rest of our
lives we'll never know.

Michael Ambrose
THREE WISHES

If I could have 3 wishes, and know
that they'd come true.
I would not wish for wealth nor fame,
I'd only wish for you!
I'd not wish for the stars, I'd not ask
for the moon, I'd just wish I had each
day 25 hours that I could spend with
you.
My 2nd wish wouldn't be to be
beautiful or to be strong,
I'd wish I had eight days each week
in your arms where I belong.
My 3rd and final wish would be, that
there were 13 months in each year, so
that I could have more time in which
to hold you near.
But I'll never have these 3 wishes.
And I know they'll never come true
But at least I know that I have one
life,
One life to spend with you! !

Dode Gepford
OLD FASHIONED WINDMILL

To Barbara.

Give me an old fashioned windmill
Surrounded by ancient oak trees.
Let the warm evening sun shine
through its blades,
Throw in a brisk summer breeze.
Give me a horse and a saddle—
Watch tumbleweeds rolling along,
I'll yell "yippy ti ay" little dogie
Deep in my heart, there's a song!

Give me a red crispy apple—
Go ahead friend, take a bite.
Give me a single, delicate red rose,
And my sleep will be sweeter tonight.

Give me your smile, your laughter,
your joy—
Your heartaches and sadness too,
Together we'll come through those
difficult times,
And I'll be so much closer to you.

Give me an old fashioned windmill
Surrounded by ancient oak trees.
We'll watch that sunset together,
And we'll both thank God, on our
knees.

Clona Hawkins

Clona Hawkins
WHEN I'M GONE

When I am laid to rest
Tell them all I did my best.
As I am now so must you be
Prepare for death
And follow me
Follow you I will not consent
Until I know which way you went

Lorine Shaver
NIGHT

To Jehovah God.

Night was created
For a purpose it seems.
It's a time to quiet down
And fall into sleep.

It's a time for rest
Which one's body needs
To make the next day
At a rate of good speed.

It's a time of quietness
When one can forget
All the worries and problems
Each day does beget.

When one arises
He's refreshed and renewed
Ready to tackle new things
That come into view.

So let us be thankful
God created night
And use as He purposed
For restful delight.

Keri Fotheringham
ATTIC

To my Grandma Nielsen, and all of the wonderful memories she left me.

Silver lace
Drapes from beam to beam
Shading memories.

Flakes of sunlight
Blanket stored happiness and pain.

Fragments of life
Remembered and forgotten
Yellow with age
Fading
Losing their light.

Then,
New life claims the treasures
Seeking clues to the future
Through facets of reality.

Knowing
Never-ending circle of time
Brings memories back in style.

Jeannie Baker
LITTLE THINGS

To my boyfriend Tom Aston and my mother Ruth Burns with all my love . . .

One plus one is two, that equals me and you, walking hand in hand, barefoot through the sand. The heat of the sun we feel as one, the coolness of the seas, the warmth of the breeze. When we lie on the sand we both understand. The love we share, watching the birds through the glare. Hand in hand through the snow, going to a matinee show. Having a snowball fight, building a snowman in the middle of the night. Little things that don't mean much equal big things along with your touch. I love the way you make me feel, what I want most to say is my love for you is real . . .

Karen Kasaback Parr
MICHAEL

We remember how we loved you
Even 'til your death
And though we lost our brother
You are with us yet . . .
Michael, we remember all the words
We didn't say
Michael, we remember all the gifts
That didn't come your way
We love you and we miss you
And hope God has held you in His
care
For when our journey is over
In Heaven, we hope we will see you
there!!
Good Bye, Michael Dennis Kasaback

Marye Jo Shaddix
THE CIRCLE OF OUR LIVES

Dedicated to my grandchildren, Chip, Sally & Marc, with my love.

Our lives are like a circle, beginning
the moment we are born.
Our fate is never known to us—
whether we will be famous or forlorn.
We "design" our own happiness each
day as we live.
We "allow" our destination to happen
by directions that we take and give.
The strength we require to "design"
and "allow"
Remains within our faith and positive
belief in a Higher Power.
It's all up to us to be willing and keep
an open mind.
A positive attitude will secure the
happiness and serenity we desire to
find.
We can shorten the circle of our lives
or broaden it by many miles,
Through the mirror of reflections of
our tears and honest smiles.
It matters not the size of our life
circle that others someday find.
What matters is the honest giving of
our lives that we have left behind.

Marye Jo Shaddix
ONE DAY AT A TIME

Have you ever lived in Hell here on
earth?
Have you wondered why the road
you traveled was so rough?
Did you wonder why the days were
so long?
And everything you did seemed to
Always turn out wrong?
Did your nights seem so endless
And you couldn't sleep?
Did you get so confused,
Not a sane thought to keep?
Have you wondered how you kept
living day after day?
So tired and exhausted, wondering
how
You could go on that way?
I've been there, my friend, and I can
relate
To all those bad feelings that you feel
and hate.
I traveled that rough road not so long
ago.
How I would live through it,
I really didn't know.
I prayed and I searched, an answer to
find
When I realized God would help me
make it
One day at a time.

Diane K Waugh
SELF-DECEPTION

Bitter
as arctic wind
and unyielding
as the chains
that keep me bound to you,
my world has become a cage
locking out love
and keeping me secure in my pain.
I circle the perimeter
of this transparent
universe
unscathed,
and yet battered
by the truth.
Like gravity I fall
to reality
while the green blades below me
ascend,
mocking me,
and my tears aid their flight
to freedom.

Brenda C Smith
A MOTHER IS

In memory of my mother with love. Edythe M. Carter.

A mother is a gift from God sent
from up above. An expression of His
very best, a token of His love.

A mother is the smile we see through
many of our tears, who kisses away
all of our hurts and hugs away our
fears.
A mother is the strength we feel
when days are not so bright.
Who just by being near us we know
things will be alright.

A mother is a tender touch in whose
care we have complete trust.
She holds our hand when we are
small and encourages us to stand as
we grow tall.
She guides our lives with love and
prayer and teaches us that God is
always there.
There seems to be nothing that she
can't do, for her loved ones
A mother always comes through.
A mother is special in so many
countless ways and we express our
appreciation on this her special day.

We thank God for mothers, a blessing
from above.
She is so many things to us but most
of all
A mother is love!

Brenda C Smith
THE SAME GOD

Dedicated to my pastor and friend, James E. Henry, Victory Bible Church, Pasadena, CA.

The same God who made the
heavens, mountains and the trees,
Is the one who lives within my heart
and watches over me.

The same God who causes the sun to
shine and the rain to come tumbling
down,
Is the one who said "Peace be still"
so in our sea of troubles
We will not drown.

The same God who lets the eagle soar
in the clear blue sky,
Is the one who is able to move your
mountain no matter how high.

The same God who loves us so very
much that He gave his only son,
Is the one who gave you victory over
the battles that you have won.

The same God who stayed with three
young men and caused them not to
burn,
Is the one who promised never to
leave us, he's there at every turn.

The same God who hears and
answers our prayers whether big or
small,
Is the one whose everlasting arms are
there to embrace us one and all.

Oh, do you know this God of mine?
So loving and so true,
Who even when you may think he's
not is watching over you.

Oh, do you know this God of mine?
Jesus is his name.
He is the beginning and the end and
thank God He is always the same.

Inspirational Scripture
Mal. 3:6A

Lee Lucas
I WALK

I WALK
I walk down streets, down alleys,
Not knowing where I'm going.
Not knowing who I'll run into.

All I see is the moon to light my way,
All I hear is my heartbeat to keep me
going,
and I walk.

I walk knowing the next corner I turn
you'll be there.
As I turn the next corner I see you
walking away.
And I walk on,
sunrise, sunset, I walk.

Babies crying, people dying I walk.
I walk on until we meet once again.
At that time my walking's done
and all my walking has paid
off . . .

and we walk.

Nassard R Brathwaite
THE BEAUTY AND WARMTH FO AICHI

To all those who loved and knew Aichi. To Akemi, and like a flower, may you continue to blossom gracefully.

It was a day of warmth.
The sun was its brightest;
The sky its bluest;
And the grass its greenest.
It was a day in which the birds
Sang more beautifully and flew
With greater grace.
A day when the smiles were
Brighter, and a sense that the World
had attained a greater peace.
Enhancing the beauty of all that of
Which is beautiful, and giving beauty
To that of which had little; for this
Was the spirit of Aichi.
This is a beauty that can always be
seen;
A feeling that can always be felt, for
this
Was, and will always be the beauty
and warmth of Aichi.

Julia L Harpe
SEARCHING

Dedicated to My Father—Howard J. Brown.

While people are searching
On land and the sea
The greatest of treasure
Awaits you and me
It's Jesus of Calvary
Who died on the Cross
This Great Gem was given
That none would be lost

This Gem—Jesus is likened unto a
pearl
That shines so very bright
Or likened as a diamond with its
many brilliant lights. This Great Gem
was given

So no one would be lort. So we must search for this treasure regardless of the cost.
Tell the world to search for me
For I am truly the Christ of Calvary.

Flora Niven Allen
MY MOTHER

To my mother Margaret Niven. From my heart, with all my love.

My Mother so rare.
Others may say theirs are,
But none can compare.
To mine so fair.

She's had some bad times,
But has always landed on top.
There's also been good times.
When she's made up with Pop's.

I love this woman so rare,
Whose heart is of gold.
She is as sweet as a pear,
Although she may grow old.

My Mother so fair, so rare.
Stands tall as a giant tree,
Is as soft as a gentle breeze.
I hope, she lives to be One Hundred and Eighty Three.

Alice L Williams
TALK TO ME SON

Dedicated to Rodney & Cameron, Love Mom

For nine months we waited for you to come—to bring joy and happiness to our home. We would talk and I'd call you "my little man." You would answer with each thrust of a tiny foot or hand.

I was there when you were born and laid by mama's side, and was overcome with love and so full of pride. You recognized my voice—know how I could tell? 'Cause when I spoke, you gave out a lusty yell!

Then you were one year old and growing every day. We marveled at the many things you learned to do and say. Just one look from your big brown eyes and the sunshine of your smile, would melt my heart and I knew it was worthwhile.

I want to be your friend, not just a Dad, to tell your troubles to and rejoice when you are glad. Don't shut me out and your feelings try to hide—if you are hurting or confused, let me walk by your side.

We can work it out together with love and prayer, I just want you to know how much I really care. So talk to me Son, I am here for you—you are gift from God, and He loves you too!

Debbie Buhler
LOVE

Love . . . What is love?
A smile, a warm hello; holding hands, a special look . . .
Yes, a special look that says "I understand."
There are the quiet moments when you two share so much—
Just by looking into each other's eyes & not a word is said . . .
Because if the silence is broken, it destroys the magic of that special moment.
Love . . . what is love?
It's sharing every aspect of life with each other . . .
It's knowing that, that person really cares about you & is there when you need him.
He loves watching you; you love watching him watching you;
Because there's that look . . . that special look.
Am I in love?
We've shared so many things . . .
We've laughed, we've cried, we've teased;
We've worked, we've played, we've tickled;
But most important of all, we've shared.
Love . . . am I in love?
Well . . .
Yes, I guess I really am!

Piotr A Grella
internal monologue of Ulysses /in memory of Delmore Schwartz/

to Kasia Zoledziowski

"she is surprised.
the delusion of doubt
ripped up the hush
without worrying about me
more than she is anxious
to shake hands with me.
/her hands dipped into laughter
of the voiceless moon
the face of which
is ruddy, sometimes/;

"and hair of hers the Aeolian
harp I must name
with our words
though they are not but hot air.
therefore,
I conquer understanding
being silent
with the blade
on the nanny's wrist"

Piotr A Grella
SONG FOR JOHN /CAGE/

"There is nothing,
either good or bad,
but thinking makes it so"

today, late at night:

"whatever memory is recalling
from the days to come, from the ancient pages
and no—man's—land of sounds to imagine:
no doubt, the trip will continue
towards nothing but more
than an advertiser would ever intend:

/we've made it 'cause you need it, don't you?/

all along the road stretched between
an erroneous hope and frank desire
of platinum landscapes:

/you guys have to be completely degenerate,
that's cool and that gets attention/

just passing by the cheap imitations
feeling like in combat
with an old enemy only I could see:
but it is still enough
to lose a fear
of being out of dreams:

anyway, let there'll be silence.
Even for a while"

Dorthea Darby
WILD RED ROSE BUSH

This red rose bush got lost among the other wild flowers in the field. But God in heaven looked down upon it and sent the soft rain to water it. He sent the sun to shine down upon it. It grew and grew into something to behold. The buds were tender with love that came from God's mighty hands.

As I walked through this field of wild flowers I came upon this red rose bush with its buds all opened into something to behold. It was the most beautiful flower in the field. When I looked at it I thought about you. So, I reached down and picked one for you.

Dorthea Darby
FAR OFF LAND

I was standing on the sandy bank. Looking at the ships coming into the harbor, from afar. It was evening time, and the sun had set in the sky. God had made plans to take many souls back with Him. To that far off land, that is not made by human hands. The mists were falling everywhere, and quietness same to linger there, when God calls out the names of many souls to get on board the ship to go to this far off land. that is the Promised Land.

Dorthea Darby
GRATEFUL TO YOU GOD

Praise God, praise God, praise God, for the rain that fell the other day. And the sun He let shine today. And for the wind that gently blew out of the East. And for the dawn of another day. And for the coolness of the evening breezes. And for the food He let us have for our table. O, God you are a great God. How can we thank you enough. We are grateful to you until the end. Holy to your glorified name.

Dorthea Darby
ROSES GREW ALONG THE PATHWAY

The red roses grew along this pathway of life. They grew down in the green valley, where this stream of water is flowing peacefully by. They grew in the meadow, where the aroma from them fills the air. They grew in my rock garden among the other flowers, where they stood out the most. As I go along this pathway of life, I will stoop down and pick some for you. Because God chose you to love. With God's great strength, He created these red roses to come into your life. It is truly a beautiful gift which comes from above. You are God's child. Created for His glory. That is the reason He has these roses growing by the roadside. So some of them can be picked, and given to you. May you be made happy all throughout your lifetime, with red roses.

Sylvia L Mayer
SITTING IN THE PARK

One more afternoon spent in the park
sitting underneath my favorite tree,
. . . I begin to lose myself in my thoughts as I meditate diligently.
I bring to mind loved ones that I left behind . . .
. . . those special people that will forever remain dear in my mind.
I recall the past, and retrace my rights and my wrongs . . .
. . . and realize I must look forward, and leave the past where it belongs.
I call to mind hearts I filled with joy and those I left behind which needed mending,
. . . lost friendships that I thought would be never ending.
I remember things I left unsaid . . . and words I wish I had spoken,
. . . dreams that have and have not come true, and all those promises that were broken.
I reminisce on gratifying moments spent with family, friends and loved ones who showed me they cared . . .
. . . and the glorious and bittersweet moments that with me they have shared.
. . . childhood memories of my parents are engraved within my heart forever,
. . . loving smiles, forgiving looks upon their faces . . .
. . . their gentle wipe of a tear and their many warm embraces.
The breeze cools, and the sun begins to set and reminds me it's getting late,
Tomorrow will be another afternoon and I will sit in the park, underneath my favorite tree, lose myself in my thought and cogitate.

p j moore
TO MY "J.R."

We have been through so many things, over the past few years.
We have shared the fun and love, and dried each other's tears,
So much has happened to us son, and together we've faced it all.
Sometimes our trials have been tough, and we've had some nasty falls,
But we've also had the good times, and our days of laughs and fun.
We've loved and helped each other, and had "our times in the sun."
I can still recall my sense of pride, from deep within my soul.
When you took your first few steps, or with your first mumbled words.
At first your falls were simple ones, and a kiss would fix you up.
But as you've gotten older son, the healing has become real rough.
I've always tried to lead you, along a path that's good.
To make you think before you act, and to think of others first.
You've grown into a pleasant boy, and very bright indeed.
I feel that I have done my job, and now someone else must lead.
I believe you need your father now, to lead you on your way.
For he will help you to be strong, and grow to a good man one day.
I will always be here for you son, no matter where you are.
You'll forever be deep in my heart, and I will always care.
I only want what's best for you, as you grow from boy to man.
Your dad will be a great help to you, as only a father can.
So try your best to understand, why now you must go to him.
For you'll always be "my only boy," but real soon you'll be a man.

Marsha E Smith
ABUSED
A lost lonely child on a dry desert plain
roaming and searching for relief from the shame
far in the horizon an orchard of trees
not seeing the mirage is really misery.

She runs on the wind
but soon stumbles and falls,
by nighttime the wolves echo their calls.

They run in a pack
blood hungry to kill
small children and girls
only for a thrill.

They circle and howl as they close in to eat
a tender young child whose fresh red meat
trembles and quivers on clean white bones
in the body of a child in the desert alone.

Jean Brill

Jean Brill
WHEN YOU'RE IN LOVE
When you're in love, don't take
her to a baseball game.
If you do, things will never again
be quite the same.
You'll wonder "How on earth
could she be so awfully
dumb?"
She'll ask you sillier than silly
questions
Until you're numb-er than
numb,
And then some!

When you're in love, don't try to
teach her how to play the
game of chess.
If you do, you'll acquire expertise
in the meaning of the word
"distress."
Play it safe: stick to celestial
things like the moon and the
stars above.
Then everything will be
"hunky-dory"
When you're in love.

Karla J Hernandez
MY STUFFED TEDDY BEAR

Dedicated to my little sister, Kari Lynne.

Shiny glass eyes
With a cotton soft nose
And a feeling of love
That curls up my toes

You're there by my side
Through thick and through thin
You listen to me
You are my best friend

You may not respond
To the things that I say
But I know you hear me
In your own special way

Sometimes I say
That life isn't fair
But I'll always have you
My stuffed teddy bear

Julie Garavaglia
FATHER

To Jack L. Stone—my ivory tower.

Time and words cannot express
the feelings deep inside.
The feelings hidden for so long
no longer can I hide.

You've been my inspiration.
My guiding light and star.
The one I've often turned to
When times in life are hard.

So now that I have grown
I think it's time to say
the way that I've been feeling
in a very special way.

For though you did not sire me
no person, place or thing
could take away my Father dear
or endless joys you bring.

Julie Garavaglia
MOTHER

To Michelle M. Stone—my pillar of strength.

You are the dawn that starts the day,
the moon that ends the night.
You are the earth that I tread,
the stars that shine so bright.
You are the fields where flowers
bloom,
that guide my inner soul.
You are the golden pathway,
that leads me where I go.

Although all sunny days must storm,
and fields and flowers fade.
My love for you goes on and on,
in the promise I have made.
Promises are sometimes broke,
on this you can rely.
The closeness shared, the trust
endeared,
will never, ever die.

James B Gravitt
FOR THE SHAMANS

Dedicated to Francesca.

I swear by the stars above and the sun in our sky,
By the moon and all that darkness below.
To that which is known and unknown,
And the Hell, that passes all understandings.

I do not believe you, your shallowness amazes me.
You scream for answers,
They surround thee,
You look but cannot see.

Do not be confused by illusion,
mirage and deception,
For your ignorance transcends your religious zeal.
Hallowed be thy hubris and
tolerance, you deny.
Allow me to shield myself from this
hypocrisy.

The oracle exclaims, "know thy self,"
But to be thy self is the
hardest thing.
And who would dispute the
pillars of Islam, the first,
Allah's supreme.
Or the Jews on the Big Ten and
the Fulfillment of Christian
theology,
Love God and humanity.

For one man's religion is another's
mythology,
The particulars are relevant,
The paths are many.
Our destinations are all so grave.

For a lack of depth,
We all may claim.
For where are the deep water sailors,
The riggings all the same.

James B Gravitt
SAYING FAIR WELL

for Valerie Ann Cahill.

If I could say good by to you
or fair the well.
I would write it with my tears
and a smile.
If I could give you a wish or an
answered prayer.
I would ask when life's tempests
are on your back.
May the fabric of your cloak, be
strong as hell!
When the path becomes
downward
and ensnared in trial.
May you be quick and dodge
fate's arrows here and there.
I would beg that you would never
need to look back.

For in that valley it's how we
played our role.
Carry on righteously and be a
spirit that's free.
And may your heart be filled
with harmony and soul.
As your love light sparkles and
shines, remember me.

May your heart be strong as
you rise to the task.
My wish, . . . to the powers that
be what I ask.

Pamela Ventura
LISTEN TO THE WORDS

*—This poem is dedicated to Joe—
may we always be a part of each
other's lives.*

In listening to the words of our
marriage ceremony,
I would expect that the union of
two people would bring
harmony.
The words are said, "'til death do
us part,"
And I sit back and wondered if
they meant the death of the
love in your heart.
Perhaps if the statement was
taken in this way
There wouldn't be so many
people remaining in a
marriage which has long since
passed away.
When there's that sense of mental
finality between man and
wife,
Then what would be the
justification for God to want
you to live in strife?
Where there is beauty in living
with your beloved, then
marriage makes the union
something you shouldn't
regret.
So listen to the value of those
words and never forget.
Have faith that there's a purpose
for whatever occurs in life,
So you may know when the time
is right to become man and
wife.

Charles R Gibson
YOUR EYES

Written for a beautiful time that once was, but is no more.

Oh the softness of your caressing
eyes
So often you have spoken to
me through them
Tender are the words, how kind the
message they convey
One of love, trust, security
Your eyes have shown me the many
beautiful and enchanting sides of
you!
In them I have seen a
woman . . . so sure of herself
and I
Strong and profound, with so much
knowledge and strength,
Telling me your love for me is
so real and true
In them too I have seen a little girl, so
full of life . . . with wonder
Imagination and at times
fear—the fear of being alone—
Of thoughts that say, will he hurt
me—will he want me? ?
Then the trust of the child
comes through—giving so
freely
And—unyieldingly telling
me; I do need you and I do
care so very much.
These eyes of yours scare me at
times, not because of you—but
because of me.
I at times am afraid I cannot
fill the desire, the need in
them—
I may not be the best but oh how I'm
going to try
Yes, my sweet; I love your eyes
as I love all of you!
I love to look into them to feel the
security they give
My Dearest, do you, I wonder at
times, see into me through my eyes?
—And, if so, what do "you" see?
I love you endlessly, tirelessly—
Please remember, I am here and
will always be "a look away"!

S Angie Lee
PLEASE LOOK THE OTHER WAY . . .
Looking in this old mirror . . .
Thinking back to childhood,
remembering that I always knew
what I wanted.

Growing up was not what I
thought—
then to find out you did it wrong.

Dreams having been dashed again &
again.
While the world danced the same
dance to achieve,

I was walking backwards down the railroad tracks.

The desire for originality was changed by new faces, time, and age.

Learning to dance the dance, brought back the dreams of a young girl, Now they have become a reality.

Watching you strive for your difference from others,
I wonder, just how to keep you from—
Looking in my old mirror.

Bruce William Litterer
SHELTER HEART
In the land, among thee Sheep,
Be not of 'Shelter Heart.'
For there are Lions.
Who shed the blood of Peace.

As their anguish for innocent Ones
Cried above the shadow of fallen Sons;
Draw neither the judgement of statue
Toward the fellowship of life.

Can you see it now, the Winds of Changes,
In midst of enchanted flight;
As the law of time, measure One's fallen fright
Toward the cries of innocent Ones.

This is the dust that cloud your heart,
As their guidance falls above
The ladder of unrest;
Shall we whisper for the fellowship of life.

So . . . In the land, among thee Sheep,
Be not of 'Shelter Heart.'
For there are Lions.
Who shed the blood of Peace.

Katlin Fairbairn
JEALOUSY
Jealousy
Is a brilliant hue
Green as the dragon's eye
As it cuts through blackness
Sharp as a razor
Cold as the ice that numbs my brain
Freezing my thoughts
taking hold of me
With a cold, smooth, almost silky touch
Sapping my strength
Feasting on my mind

I become the dragon
My piercing eyes will slice the darkness
Sharp as a razor
I wait for the hunger
It will come

William K MacDonald
YOUTH

I dedicate this poem to my mother and my wife Elizabeth who inspired me to write. William MacDonald

Give me back my youth.
Ungrateful, abaxious world
Let me show ruth.
Like a twister in a twirl.

I've been robbed dammed
by Time's destiny
Fortitude disband
Economic desire a villainy

Health wrecked by lustful rampant sins
Of modern man's distasteful economics whims
Cry in raging fright
Talk the phone
Drink the night
Walk alone in morbid flight.

Nigh those portholes of life
Wicked, immoral and fun.
Lift me high
Into the time yet to come

Eloy Lodge
SOME DAY

To my Wife and Daughter, Ruby and Simona.

Some day some where
I'll find the one I love
It may take a day or a life time
A day I hope will come.

Some day some day soon
My love will come to me
For in my prayers it's all I ask
To hold you in my dreams.

Some day may mean tomorrow
Hoping it's the day I am waiting for
If not other days will pass
To leave me with a broken heart.

This day a vision I behold
Of my love and life before me
And in my heart I truly know
This day my love has found me.

Scott Bostic
MY GIRL

To Allison.

Golden hair falling
blue eyes dancing in her joy
looking up, at me

John P Murray
MR. WILLOW
Weeping Willow why are you so sad? I think I really know.
You are like the person who has no friend or who has lost his or her last one.
Or, you are like the loner. The wanderer who never tries to get a friend.
You are one who sees life's problems, but says nothing.
At least life's problems don't bother you.
You are free; almost safe from all.
There's nothing or no one to make you angry.
But you're always sad. Why?
Did someone treat you wrong?
Did no birds visit you or did they all go away?
Life is rough all over Mr. Willow.
It's not a happy world.
Do you mourn for us, for our lack of communication with you?
At times I would like to trade places with you in this horrible world.
Weeping Willow, oh how sad, you are never happy, never glad.
Be through rough weather or nice, life's treating you kind, but you're sad,
as you stand there all your life.
Today I am like you, very sad, for a friend has gone away.
I am left standing like you, saddened and blue forever.
So goodbye Mr. Willow. Weep for me today in my sorrow.

Gilda Miraglia
MEMORIES OF MY DAD

A memorial to my father, for his love, patience, and humility. Dedicated to all who knew, and loved him . . .

Meek was he, yet proud as can be.
Young at heart but none wiser than he.
Full of sweet dreams of past memories,
A heart full of hopes, in the future to be.

Kind and gentle and humourous he—
All of these things was my father to me.
Simple his pleasures, tho' eccentric he,
Music and art his great passion, you see.

Cultured and learned tho' an immigrant he,
Full of questions and answers and knowledge was he.
A rock he was not—but of that I think not—
For 'tis not of his doings and deeds that you read,
But of what a sweet wonderful father should be.

Judith M Bettencourt
BENO, "I MISS YOU"

To Beno and those who knew and loved him, "My love and friendship is what I send"

You don't know what you have until it's gone

With me you left a very special song
The day you left I will never forget

And things I said I will always regret

You meant so much to me
More than you knew

If only you could hear me say . . . I miss you

I've cried so much since we lost touch
Life can be so unfair
Not having you I just can't bear

Although we've been torn apart
You have a very special place
Forever in my heart

I was forced to tell you good-bye
now with every thought of you
I start in a smile and end in a cry

Until We Meet Again, Dear Friend

Laura Long
LAST OF SUMMER
Quietly, as I walk along the mountain trail so high.
Birds sing softly up above, and fir trees wave good-bye.
Autumn leaves fall gently down like feathers from the sky.
They have but only one last chance to glow against the sky.
Autumn weaves a magic carpet.
Falling leaves swirl, through the air.
Sunset's glow is everywhere.
How lovely, just to wander down a shaded leafy trail.
To pause beside a little brook.
Where colored leaf boats sail.

Debra Lynn Barnes
MIDNIGHT RENDEZVOUS

To my family, friends & Gary. With love always.

We meet every night at midnight by the sea. No one will be there except you & I. We'll share our hopes, dreams & aspirations. We'll share kisses so warm & tender. We want so much to be together but we're afraid of what it might do to the ones we love. We know it's wrong but it's much too strong to let go now. We knew what would happen if we continued to see each other but we said "It wouldn't get out of hand." Somehow I don't believe we followed the rules. We can't go on & we can't let go. What are we to do? We'll find out tonight, together, at midnight.

Louise S Cooks
A SNACK WITH GRANDMA

To my mother, Callie Sanders and grandmother, Mary P. Royal

Grandma's Ash Cake tasted
Like pure heaven to our young
Taste buds.
By our,
I mean, my sister, brother,
Me and Cousin Leroy.

We sat before the big open fire
Place, the wood fire crackling
And watched Grandma mixing
And stirring the corn meal, then
Molding it into a wide layer.

Grandma raked out the hot glowing
Embers from the wood Fire
And placed the corn meal layer
On them. She covered it with hot
Ashes and left it to cook while she
Churned the milk.

We, that is,
My sister, brother, me and Cousin
Leroy, liked to imitate the sound
Of the dasher hitting the milk.
Ca-dash, Ca-dash it sounded
By the time the butter formed on The
milk, the Ash Cake was done.
Grandma brushed the Ashes from
The Ash Cake and put it on a
Plate, cut four slices, put a pat of
Butter on each slice, poured
Up four glasses of buttermilk,
With bits of butter floating
Around the top of it. By this
Time, we were ready to be
Served.
By We,
I mean my sister, brother, me
And Cousin Leroy.

I was very young, but I can still
Remember the taste of Grandma's
Ash Cake.
It tasted like pure heaven.

Ed D Holmes
LOVE IS . . . LOVE IS NOT . . .
Love is not a quickly manufactured desire.
Love is a flickering flame,
that gradually grows into a burning fire.

Love is not a luscious, lust at first glance.
Love is a waltz of wishes,
that turns into a delightful dance.

Love is not a onetime, darling date.
Love is a venturous, viable vision,
that times together can constructively create.

Love is not a heartthrob, a smile, or extended kiss.
Love is the maturation of an admiration,
which remains an Indestructible Bliss.

Michelle D Sampsel

Michelle D Sampsel
FOR THE HOMELESS

To Mom—who encouraged me to write my feelings from early on. To JR—who reads my every scribble incessantly. The best compliment. To Larry—who accompanies me when I sing and says simply, "You sound good."

It could be us
don't we all live in glass houses
It could be us
you or me
Our lives could be filled
with cut off allowances
allowances for the homeless
that's what we need to be free
of the shame of the sorrow
for the tomorrows that have
yet to be
there should be no homeless not in the land of the free
it could be you and me
it could be us

Allison R Kopczynski
IT'S ALONE
If there's reason, it isn't here.
Here there is only darkness.

It can only see jealousy, frustration,
And mostly a love that can't be gained;
It's alone.
It's a grey, dark road.
Followed by questions, loneliness, and loss.

Nowhere is there happiness or love.
It's only fake to keep away the questions.
It's alone.
Do they love it? Do they care?
Will they leave it out there to freeze and die?

It if leaves, no one know (do they want to?)
It won't cry, for fear of light it hasn't seen.
It's alone.
Forever alone.
It's forever alone.
Do you hear the cry?
The baby know not, but do they?

It's alone.

Fenton F DeSilva
DAVID AT BEIJING
Sans sling
Sans stone,
Majestically
He stood alone,
Stopping Goliath
in his track.
Now, climbing
on the giant's back,
And, in a voice
devoid of fear,
whispering in
Goliath's ear,

"FREEDOM"

Richard C Heumann
FOR YOU, MY LOVE
My life I live for only you.
My life I live for only you.
My heart I give to you alone.
I give my all to you.

For you have been my
Consistent friend.
Though storms may come,
You will not bend.

My love is all I have to give.
I give it all to you.

Cheryl A Spiegelberg
DEATH IS FINAL

To the addict or any person contemplating suicide

Death is final
There is no turning back . . .

Life is simple
Just keep yourself on track.
Remember that we love you
When you want to take
that pill.

REMEMBER that GOD put you here
and living is HIS will.

Jeana Donaldson
BIG BROTHER
When you, Big Brother, were six, I was only three
I had to watch from inside, While you played in all the trees.

When it turned cold and you couldn't go out, To get you to play I had to cry and pout.
I wanted to be Barbie, I asked you to be Ken, You wouldn't hear of it, we had to play army men.

When you were a teenager, you thought you were grown
I couldn't come in your room, I had to stay in my own.

Since then a lot has happened, Things have really changed
You have a wife and two little boys to carry on your name.

Now I'm going to tell you, but I think you already know
I knew you always loved me, you just wouldn't let it show.

I just want you to know, If I could choose another
I wouldn't do it for anything,
Because I love you, Big Brother.

Brandi Berryman
GLIMPSE OF YOU
What can I say when words are so vain?
Still my heart is full of pain.
I wonder at night,
what being together would be like.
All I wanted was a glimpse of you
for a second, that moment in time,
when both our hearts would entwine.
Now you're gone,
I am alone.
For all I have now isn't new,
just that precious glimpse of you.

Catherine M Hinds
A MOTHER'S PRAYER TODAY
I've heard it said that there's something special about a Mother's Prayer
And Jesus I have to believe that Mother's love will find You waiting there
For only You that kind of love that breaks a heart in two
And only You can take that hurt away if I just trust in You!
The hardest part of this Mother's Prayer, is turning that child over to You and leaving him there!
Another lesson I have to learn, he really isn't mine
You've lent him to me Jesus, and it's not my will but thine!
When he was just a little boy, I'd listen to him pray
But as he changed from boy to man, I didn't know what to say.
Why was I embarrassed to tell this precious son—
That only Jesus would be there always, You're the only one!
Now he's out here Jesus, fighting demons all alone
I'm not sure he'll ever ask for help from You upon the throne.
As his mother I'm asking that You'd send Your angels one by one
Surround this child with Your love, show what can be done!
For Father, hearts are breaking, and I have to share the blame
I never stressed the Power in Jesus' precious name.
I thank You now for listening, and for showing me the way—
I tell my grandsons, "Jesus loves you," I'll do it every day!
I don't know why You have me write things I find hard to say—
But thank You for hearing this Mother's Prayer today!

Karen Anne DiOrio
THE SEA
The cool sea breeze sems to swirl.
Water crashes on the broad rocks.
The birds fly swiftly through the sky,
their wings beating the clouds
into fluff.
Water roars, then hums.
Sparkling water shimmers in your eyes.
The cry of burning sand is submerged by the water.
The moon casts a golden glow,
A night light.

Amanda Perkins
THE SEA SHORE

Norman, this is dedicated to you for all your strength and support.

Come, let me take you far across the lands, to where you can
see vast seas waiting to be explored and to breathe in the
fresh misty air that hangs heavy upon the salty ground.

Waves that ripple onto the edges of the land
clutching at every grain of sand and stones upon the silvery beach that's laid within the reach of the ripples' hand.

A castle that had been built with time and care
has now become a part of the sea's great kingdom
and left now where it once was stood are only remains scattered and flattened for good.

As I look upon the tips of your world
I hear your cry of memories un-fold
stories you must have to tell of ancient times of so long ago.

What lies I wonder within the depths of your core
that it whispers softly upon the sleepy shore
will remain a secret to you all.

Amanda Perkins
ANNABELLE'S SECRETS
The days were bright, the flowers all in bloom
I would sit upon the garden seat and take in
the summer smell of the flowers' perfume.

My friend would come and meet me there each day
and would tell each other secrets, there was always
plenty to say. A warm willowy wind would rush on by, to where are you going I would cry.

We would sit and laugh for hours it would seem
and now when I look back it's like it was all a dream.

The warm summer days would all soon end
and that would put a stop to our little trend
So every day that we did spend, has become memories now and until the end.

Amanda Perkins
ANNA

My friend you are so dear to me
and others too in that I see
you give out your very best to us all
and that is a precious gift
to those of us that often fall.

When people look at you
they see the Lord in you docs dwell
a gentle smile, a happy glow, a loving heart
and lots of pleasant things to tell.

When things get tough and the road seems long
and everything you touch seems to go wrong
Just look to him who loves you so
and his promise is that he will never let you go.

Anna, people will say with a smile
I know from me and others too
We pray the Lord's blessings will shower on you.

Michal M Shirley
TO MY FRIEND

There's something I have to tell you,
Something I better say.
I didn't want to tell you,
Didn't want it to end this way.
Through all the years we've had together,
Sometimes good and sometimes bad.
Teased each other off and on,
It's the best life one could ever have.
I didn't want you to go,
At least not so far away.
But I've heard that things have to change,
And I miss you anyway.
I guess what I'm trying to tell you,
Is that I love you so.
But there is nothing I can do about it,
I'll just have to let you go.

Miss Mary Jane Dennis
PARTNERS FOR FREEDOM

With loving remembrances dedicated to my Coe-Fellow Friend, Ilse Richter, of Hamburg, Germany, and endearingly placed "In Memoria" for her precious daughter, Gabriele, who embraced the dreams of youth for fulfillment in life.

Tidal waves of ocean waters surge
upon their distant shore,
Thus, crowds of people from their homeland rushed to reach an open door.
People with a heart for freedom
chose the door without a wall,
To clasp this knob of liberty, some did upon their stomachs crawl.

Joyous voices sang together in refrains of sheer delight,
For East and West were mingled freely, millions having braved the night.
Stony hearts, like walls of stone, can chill warm hopes with cold despair,
So God bestowed the heart of flesh to kindle flares for freedom there.

Bible history will tell how walls came down in Jericho,
Such triumph gloried in the truth that God was pleased to have this so.
God still glories in the truth that men ought always to be free,
Hear Christ so graciously invite, "I am the Door; come unto Me!"

Happy people journeyed homeward
with their dream now come alive,
Let East and West be joined in effort
for a better world to strive.
"'Hitherto, the Lord hath helped us,'"
be engraved on silent stone,
Remember, on the Road to Freedom,
God is ever on His throne.

People yearn to share a freedom that is felt around the world,
So lift the Torch of Freedom higher—let the banners be unfurled!
Blessed are those needy nations who will take God as their Lord,
From the Fount of Living Waters
many blessings shall be poured.

Cleopha L Herzog
ALONE I SIT SOMEWHERE IN TIME

Alone I sit somewhere in time;
My heart, it aches a song in rhyme.
It needs the sadness of despair,
Worthiness to prove everywhere.
Why does this need arise in me?
Sweet surrender across blue sea
Would be a welcome to my soul,
But overlooking this I toll:
Endlessly consumed in the fight,
Having always to show my might—
Or left feeling inadequate
For not reaching my ideals, yet
Goals insurmountable I mold.
It matters not how oft' I'm told
To smelt the hope to please unknown
Entities, and accept my own
Self.

Daniel W Nitsch
HIDDEN EYES

I must only take one
glimpse . . . seek through the walls.
I could fall in . . . be trapped inside.
I'm off to myself once again.
I travel the land so much, my feel ache.

Vision starts to happen when you pass through emotions.
I search for the blinding light,
that will intensify all that surrounds it.
I will not become the light . . . just to see it.

I took love for a walk down my street.
I have a hidden poem in my heart for you.
I dream of you . . . a sylph!
Unwed, glamorous creation.
Becoming . . . my better half.
Living the life I live, loving my love I give.

I took love for a walk down my street.
I have a hidden poem in my heart for you
"Can I touch it?"

Marie Ahleen Webb
ONLY ONE DAY

To my husband Robert and my daughter Marie and my sons Robert Jr. and William.

If I had but one day
What would I do, What would I say?
Would I go places I've never been?
Would I say things, I have held in?
If I had but one day.
I know what I would do,
I would gather my family to-gether,
In the house they all knew.
I would smile and say,
I did the very best I could for you.
I wish I could have done better.
But—remember material things you can buy,
My Love, Caring, and Sharing I gave freely
This was my special gift to you all from me,
The light is dimming, and now I must go—
Remember me, because I really loved you all so.
If I had but one day.
Love MOM

Ruth E Smith
DAD'S LAST CHRISTMAS

In Memory of my Father, Charles S. Shearer, October 18, 1938-February 18, 1989

Of everything I remember,
I really think of last December.
It was Christmas weekend,
from the hospital Dad did descend.

We would all come together
for joy and laughter.
It just wasn't the same
And that's a shame.

Everyone seemed to know
that sorrow would soon follow.
It was sad,
to see him that bad.

Rocketman (Danny Moon)
THE RACE

This poem is dedicated to my Queen Madelyn Moon for her inspirations, all the runners of the world and the West Valley Joggers and Striders.

As runners we search to enter and partake in every race;
We strive forward with glory,
embracing each stride and pace.

It is with great passion that we endure and love to run;
Yes, it happens at dawn with
the luminous rays of a rising sun.

At the sound of a gun, our dreams begin from the starting line;
The success of being one and
winning, is forever on our mind.

Fruits of our labors turn into pleasure as we stride and run tall;
Our fellow athletes are as we,
no matter how big or small.

If through the race we should stumble and take a fall;
Our courage within will draw
us up, rather than to crawl.

We shall finish the race with dignity
holding our head high and tall;
Knowing the greatest gift we
achieved is, we gave it our all!

Woody Reed
TAKE TIME

Read a story, sing a song,
things remembered all life long.
Give a hug, an encouraging smile.
make their day more worthwhile.
Play a game, show some love,
press them on with a helpful shove.
Take time each day, the whole year through
for the wonderful child God's given you.

Lottie Sutton
MAP OF WORDS

Dedicated to My Family and All the Peoples of The World because of WORDS in any form, keep this world together.

My map is made of words
That become roadways along
The avenues of my life's journey
Through the heart flaming senses of the inner me.

The streets and by-ways are
numbered with thoughts and words
Each reminding me of a person, place or object
That has hitched a ride on the pleasures of life.

The rise and fall of a pen on the lines of paper
Bring it all together to paint a picture
Not soon to be forgotten.
Just passed on to someone along the way,
Interlocking to remain
A few shall keep, Maybe.

Our silent words deeming to be written, hoping
To fulfill a lonely day for someone making
Short the journey, while escaping through WORDS.

While walking through the forest of my mind
The windmills gently stir the peaceful dreams
Beyond the road that comes back to me in a word.
I listen, I look, wanting not to miss
A moment, craving for more knowledge of words.

Lottie Sutton
VICKI'S ROOM

Dedicated to my niece, who, at the age of sixteen, was told she had cancer. She lived only ninety days after being diagnosed, yet never had one pain; and to her Dad and Mother, Mr. & Mrs. James Sutton.

Hello! Little Room, so bright.
Ah, Yes, I know why the smiles
In every sparkling beam of light,
With your dazzling laughter, I, too
Linger awhile, to hug you ever so tight.

The radio softly playing your favorite tunes,

On your favorite station.
That you just happened to leave on,
Hoping that, I , too, would like them.
Well, I, Do.

Because, Little Room, you give to me
The fragrance of its belonging
That says a part of me, is there.

A comb, a sox, a book and pictures
That reflects that which is mine and
Will welcome me back again.

As each night, I tuck in a part of me
For you to keep
Smile on all the while,
For, Little Room, At dark,
You are the keeper of my child.

Lottie Sutton
ODE TO DAD & MOM
You wove a delicate web around
The loves of your life
So pure, true and beautiful
The cocoon, that
Those within, wanted not,
Elsewhere to roam.

Though you are gone, each day
Is a reminiscence of love,
Of happiness of a future
That only you could incite,
Unfold, so many things untold.

You were loved, the void, not filled.
I sometimes wonder, "Who was in
that cocoon?" The two of you or us?
I, now wish, I could have know, if
You knew how dear you were held in
our hearts.

Times of envy or jealousy were only
a longing to each of us, wanting to be
hugged the most.
A grin or shining eyes, was
Just another way you said,
"I, love you, too!"

Lottie Sutton
SHADOW HOPPING
Standing in the shadow of my past
I look back with the fondest of
memories.
The window box of sights and sounds
Of a by-gone era.

Dancing to soft music on a moonlit
night
Seemly in a cloud of yesteryear.

My mind hopping from times to
times
Of wondrous experiences
The good times, the times
Of identification.

All making of a past to remember
With a new motivation in life
renewed
Shadow Hopping into the future.

Lottie Sutton
WIND DANCE
Puzzled frames in the ever
Shifting sands foiled by
Cloud Shadows dancing across
The endless sky.

Splashed images dazzle me
As I drift aimlessly in the
Dancing winds of time,
Hovering between illusions
And reality, I smile as I think
Of all the greatness that lies
There within,
While dancing with the wind.

Eagles soar above me as
I seem to jet into the clouds
Ever playful with the seeds of
Beauty along the grounds of nature.

Gliding through the tunnel made
In the air with poise of a
Ballerina to dance again
With the wind.

Robert L Gregory
A SINGLE LEAF
A single leaf falls to the ground,
Its life gone from its veins,
Ending an era of but one season,
Never to return again,
A single leaf falls to the ground,
No one notices or cares,
Its insignificance more so now,
As we are unaware,
A single leaf falls to the ground,
Its burden now relieved,
Of supplying life to its host,
So another may be conceived,
A single leaf falls to the ground,
Withered and so dry,
But no one seems to understand,
There is a reason why,
A single leaf falls to the ground,
Its life it had to give,
So nature could continue to grow,
And other lives may live . . . .

Alice McKinney
TAKE TIME
Take time to help someone today;
Don't wait until tomorrow.
Reach out with inner thoughts to
share;
Bring hope instead of sorrow.
One simple deed, a thoughtful word,
Just a friendly call or two
Spreads sunshine through another's
day
And reflects it back to you.
Take time to live, to laugh, to love;
Bask in beauty all around.
Head high, breathe in the wonder of
A shining new world you have found.

Lura D Osgood
IMPRESSIONS ON THE WAY: APRIL

For my much-loved and supportive husband, Merle.

Joyous sunbeams frolic with plump
clouds in dappled sky;
Popcorn-blossomed branches wave to
robins winging by;
Impassive cows wade blissfully in
midday meal, knee-deep;
Dense velvet hills are wildly strewn
with buttercups and sheep;
The sturdy pulse of gray-green waves
beats tales of mystic seas;
Whole fields of poppies,
Midas-touched, are waltzing with the
breeze;
Tough, blazing clumps of yellow
broom on every side abound
And wild pink roses climb the fences
all the way to town.

William Soule
BROOK AND MOUNTAIN
The west wind blows sharp and clear,
while mist wafts to the valley below.
A lone hiker stands transfixed by the
sight,
his ears soothed by the water's brisk
flow.

Above him the moon begins to come
out,
as dusk falls fast on mountain and
tree.
The patterns of light are jumbled but
bright,
they tell a tale of ancient mountain
and sea.

For countless eons the stream has
been there,
changing but little, with never a care
that man will live on, or ever be able
to decipher his life, or nature's sweet
fable.

William Soule
SIXTH SYMPHONY
The music flows bright and loud,
tripping lightly over chords of stone.
The brook babbles ever proud,
while on it whirl castles of foam.

The rhythm moves through and
through,
its power of action never still.
Trees shimmer, proclaiming anew
stunning visions of vale and hill.

His genius knows no bounds,
as a crowd of peasants laughs and
clowns.
Then the storm so fierce spreads its
gowns
of rain and sharp lightning sounds.

Peace comes at last—
the silence of a day well done—
and then we know what will never
pass:
a love of beauty, air and sun.

How can he write so strong and true
about that which we know so little?
May the day come when we have
someone who
can match the grace of Beethoven's
fiddle.

William Soule
CLOUDS
The clouds are white, cold, seer.
They are ever present, always here.
They never bend, they never fall.
They describe a gray-white ball.

They move across the sky without a
care.
They fall on each other, with a never
ending stare.
High and low, over and through,
they're always there, they're always
true.

White against blue, rain against sky,
they're up there always, always on
high.
They seem so peaceful, calm and
serene.
All they want is to be seen.

So on and on it goes for ever.
The clouds think they are so very
clever.
They never bend, they never break.
Their water falls on pristine lakes.

High and low, back and forth,
east and west, south and north,
they move across the sky serene.
All they want is to be seen.

William Soule
A FOX
A bitter cold racks on the hill.
A brazen fox waits for the kill.
He seems so sure that he will win.
He seems so free of all man's sins.

He waits in peace for his own prey.
The victim really has no say.
A meal he makes for fox's lair.
The victim trots on without a care.

Soon he comes near fox's claw.
The fox opens his gaping maw.
The jaws snap shut without a care.
The helpless rabbit makes delicious
fare.

An act of nature seems so cruel,
that helpless rabbits make fox's
gruel,
but on and on it goes for years,
and animals shed no tears.

Cecilia M Eagen
SOMEDAY
Sometimes I want to tell you,
About the way I feel,
About how much I love you,
And how much I want you to love
me.

But when I go to tell you,
Something tells me not to,
It could be that I am afraid,
Of what you will say,
About the way you feel and care for
me.

All that I can do is tell you and pray,
That someday you will understand,
About my love for you,
And maybe then you will love me
too.

Donna P Deacon
FRIENDS OF THE HEART
The times we share together
are so few and far apart
But not a single moment passes
you're not with me in my heart.

I find a tender strength within your
voice,
compassion in your eyes.
From deep within you radiates
a love that never dies.

You've supported my decisions
and you've never let me down.
You make me feel so good about
myself when you're around.

So no matter where life takes you,
if we never meet again,
You will live forever in my heart
as my dearest friend.

Andrew Dwayne Conard
TREAT ME NOT
I am a child that is still blooming.
You call me names.
Do you treat me bad?
I am sick and sorrowful in a world
unknown.
You treat me not.
I'm alone and cold.
Do you treat me with warmth?
I'm filled with bad things.
Treated no way.
You're in my conscience,
Telling me what you can do for me.
You treat me not.
When I pray to the Lord at night,
Treated, I am.

Alfred K Neumann
WHEN DEATH DOES SEPARATE
When death here separates a man
From others, husband from a wife,
They surely will look back at life,
How once their love and joy began;
And wonder, could they've treated
better
The other halve in things that matter?

It always matters what we're for
For all of us who're still alive,
What we do now, how do we thrive,
When there is peace, when there is
war;

If we show kindness, understanding,
Or just are selfish and commanding.

Let's not just at a funeral,
But always now do ask the question:
"How can we truthful have digestion
Of thoughts and deeds in general?
How to avoid that loved one's suffer;
How not to act here like a duffer."

Rachel E Johnson

Rachel E Johnson
GARY
How much do I love thee?
Let me count the ways—
Is it the way that you often take
me by surprise, when you gaze so
deeply into my eyes?

Or is it the way that you kiss
me with your gentle lips?
You leave me so spellbound,
I often feel swept off the
ground—

Linda L Sedovic
GRANDMOTHER

Dedicated to the memory of my best friend, and Grandmother - Ruth L. Handley, September 1922 - February 1989. Without her my world would have gone crazy. God Bless her always and forever.

Watching a person withering away,
like a rose that lost its bloom.
A person who was vibrant and alive,
And now an illness enshrouds them.

A thought if the times you shared . . .
The good and the bad.
Sharing with her your first experience
. . . Where you could tell no other.

The stories of their youth gone by,
And of their own troubles.

That final link among your elders,
that have gone away long ago.
The ones who gave you your heritage
and blood,
And makes you proud of who you
are.

Now looking upon she who withers,
Realizing now that she is just leaving
one life . . .
To begin an exciting other,
Rejoining all those who left before
her,
And always being there for you when
you need her.

Lord in Heaven, I thank you for
taking away her pain.
For I now know,
Death is not forever, but only just a
beginning.

Melissa Rivera
WHEN I THINK OF YOU
When I think of you, I can always
define what I feel inside.
When I think of you, I see
Someone who will share his love
with me.
When I'm feeling down, thinking of
you makes my frown turn around.
You are the kind of person who will
share with me, care for me and love
me.
When I think of you, this is what I
see—
The love that we have together is
something that I will cherish forever.
So this is why I say, when I think of
you, I can always define what I feel
inside.

Jon "G-Wiz" Rotter
BLIND
There's a dense fog on the Material
Lake,
The Lake of Give and Take.
And they call it a mistake
And my friends have lost the Way
It's gonna all be fine, they say
But they've lost themselves instead
and they don't know that their god is
dead.
Please don't be Blind,

Well I guess it goes to show
The Bible tells you where to go,
Ask a "Preacher" on the street
there's so many there to meet.
Please don't be Blind,

It's almost time, I know
and I'd really like to go,
It's almost break of day.
Listen Blind Man find the Way.
Please Don't be Blind . . . .

D Lee Ripley
STORM OF MIDNIGHT
The widowed evening drops her veil
with mist
And sorrow rustles through the
shadows of my soul.
Your eyes of fire haunt my dreams,
my nightmares
Like thunder in a rainy storm of
midnight.

You left your footprints imbedded in
my soul.
Your ecstasy touched the very core of
my being.
. . . and your voice still wanders in
my heart
Like the muffled sound of the sea at
night.

I carry the burden of your memories,
Never hearing the answers in the
storm.
Stray words flutter and fall with a
sigh . . .
And I beg for you, my love, my life.

Marguerite Roberts
PRICELESS LOVE
Wake up in the morning
without any strife—and say
I love the breath of life.
The sweet smell of fresh air,
the food we eat the shoes
that we wear,
The friends we meet who really care;
That's Love.
The flowers that bloom along the
way,
The children we watch as they run
and play
The smile we give, or a hello we say,
Will brighten a day
with Love.
The animals in the forest, the
water rushing in the stream,
the fish in the sea;
The school bells ring, the

Chorus sing, the bands play
The sunshine gleams
That's Love.

It is so plain for one to see,
The best love of all
Is a love that comes free.

Bobby Russo
MY LITTLE GIRL

To My Little Girl Chelsea, With My Deepest Love.

As you lay so innocent, asleep in
your bed
I stand watching over you as I touch
your tiny head.
You are so small and soft, with not a
care in the world
I still can't get over the miracle,
you're really my little girl.
Your little body rolls over and you
awaken with a cry
I sit back and watch you come back
from your sleep as you slowly open
your eyes.
I see your light brown hair, your blue
eyes and tiny little ears
I still can't believe I've done this, my
eyes fill with tears.
Life's not always gonna be easy and
things will probably get rough
But I know my little girl will prevail,
I'll teach her to be tough.
For life changes so often for good
and for bad
You'll be happy one minute, and the
next so sad.
I'll feel your pains with you, and all
your joys I'll share
And when you feel helpless and all
alone just remember that I care.
I thank you God once more, for my
precious little girl
For I Love Her More Than Anything,
In your Great Unstable World.

Susan Roland
A BRIGHT COLOR AMONG THE LEAVES

To Dad and Mom—Arnold & Neva Roland. They loved the world of 'birds."

There's a bright color among the
leaves
He doesn't think anyone sees.
Helter-skelter, making a nest
Where eggs can rest.
His mate is busy gathering yarn
Hung long ago in the barn.
Now the nest is ready
Filled with eggs waiting to hatch.
There's many a bug to catch
To feed the sightless mouths.
Only dark of nights
Stops his many flights.
Owls and bats move in the black.
He can finally hit the sack!
The first rays of morn, yellow and
soft
Wakes the fuzzy mouths with sounds
of food on the move.
Time to get up and back into the
groove.
Back in the mood
Searching for food.
A bright color among the leaves.

Valerie Rich
TRUE LOVE
As we walk arm in arm, hand in
hand,
Facing each other we both stand
Gazing deeply into each other's eyes,
Knowing our hearts must compro-
mise
Then falling softly to the ground,
Ignoring all that is around
Laying there side by side,
Our deepest thoughts we both confide
Nothing can make this romance end,
The rest of my life with him I'll
spend
He must have been sent from the
heavens above,
For what we have here is true love.

Diane Roman
FLY UP AND AWAY

To Mr. Turk for helping me "Fly Up And Away"

Fly up and away and into the sky,
But don't ever let yourself take a
dive.
Because coming back up is such a
fight,
You may never see the end in sight.

But, try you must and never give up,
Because in this world you have to be
tough.
You have to say to yourself, it can be
done,
And in the end you will have won.

And when you have won it is nothing
else,
But the love and respect of yourself.
So, fly up and away and into the sky,
And again you may take another
dive.

But, this time you will know it can be
done,
Because now you know you once
already have won.
So, all of you go and give life a try,
Just fly up and away and into the sky.

Diane Roman
THIS IS NOT FOREVER

To My Dear Children: Kim, Alyssa and Brad.

When you are feeling down and all
alone,
Remember with all your heart that
this will not last long.
Each day you will have a chance to
start your life anew,
Because each day can bring a fresh
start for you.

No one has to be the person they are today,
If they take the chance to change their life the next day.
Anyone can be what they want to be,
If they work hard to learn to see.

See that there are so many choices to where you can go,
All it takes is when to know.
Know when the time has finally come,
When you know that something has to be done.

Then take the chance and go with all of your might,
You may be surprised at what comes into sight.
The doors will open and you will not be alone,
And you may find out things you have never known.

The most important thing you may find out,
Is that, "This is not forever," which is all that this is about.
"This is not forever," you have your chance today,
Go out and start anew, maybe today is your day.

Diane Roman
DOWN THE PATHS OF LIFE
Down the paths of life you travel many roads,
Where each one will lead you, no one really knows.
You try so hard to pick the right one, but you cannot tell,
Until the road becomes bumpy, if your choice was well.

At times the road seems as if you traveled it before,
And you become scared because you cannot tell for sure.
There are so many choices you say, which shall I pick?
And then you make a choice and there you have to stick.

Where do these roads finally lead you, is there finally an end?
Will the road become straight and smooth or will you find another bend?
The roads I have followed seemed endless and destroyed,
But I have continued going without making too much noise.

The road I now am on I hope will finally smooth out.
Because I am a weary traveler and am so tired I could shout.
I want the paths of life to go smoother for me
And not to go on smashing to each and every tree.

When I travel down the road I want to look out and see,
All the pleasures life has to offer and I hope can be granted to me.
So, I will continue going down the road I have come upon,
Hoping I have chosen the best one to be on.

Ronald Anthony Reynolds
TENDER HEARTS
As our tender hearts have come to find,
our lost sweet love was left behind
so now our love will never last
for it has diminished in the past
now as we have come to see
you and I are very free
and though I hurt deep inside,
I shall not cry but try to hide
all of the fear that I know,

The fear that your tender heart will let me go.

Robert R Rohe
YOUR LIVING LOVE

This poem is dedicated to my friends. Thank you for sharing your experience, strength and hope.

To let God,
Is to trust . . .
And to let live,
Is to freedom . . .
To let go,
Is to live . . .
And living,
Is to love . . .
One day at time . . .
Thank you,
Your living love . . .

Jennifer L Roux
THE MOON
The Moon, a spotlight in the open night sky,
Letting out bright light in one tremendous sigh,
Watching over the Earth like one gigantic eye,
Watching everything we do.
The Moon, one speck in the black shadows above,
A symbol of all beauty and love,
As gorgeous as a peaceful white dove,
Shining over us with a smile,
The Moon, our nighttime source of light,
Greeting us warmly every night,
Oh, what a beautiful sight,
As beautiful as the Sun.

Pat Richens
THE SEA GULL

For my seven children who are earthbound but whose spirits soar!

I saw a sea gull soaring free,
And wished that it could be me—
To fly so high in time and space,
To drift and glide into another place,
To beat my wings in magic motion,
Slowly over land and ocean,
To know I was king of all I saw,
To see beauty that no artist can draw.
How puny I am, but let my spirit soar,
My soul is free, though my feet are tied to the shore.

But my dreams take me up above the clouds,
And I leave them there, hanging like fleecy shrouds.
But as the bird comes back to land,
So dreams blow as the drifting sand.
But dreams are many, and the sky is there,
While the sea gull and I a moment share.
I held my breath as a puff of air
Came and carried me away, up there.
And as I gracefully move my wings,
The air through my feathers sings:
"I know what it is to be flying free—
I only wish you were as lucky as me!"

Pat Richens
THE JOURNEY
Our time of parting
Has come to pass.
We knew that forever
Our time wouldn't last.

Only our memories,
Our dream lives on.
We will meet again
In our heart's song.

To know in my heart,
That we will meet once more
Is the wind in my sails
To that distant shore.

As the sunset fades in the West
Gathering dusk overhead,
My eyes close gently with the night
My weary head to rest.

You hold my hand
My body lingers.
I feel your love
Gently through your fingers.

You kiss my face.
Your love you have shown.
I love you so, but
This journey I take alone.

Pat Richens
SADNESS
The young boys,
They go to war.
They lose their lives
In fields so far.

Their childhood
Flies so fast.
Their hands
Slip through your grasp.

So young.
So innocent they leave.
So trust. So true.
Immortal, they believe

Death
Surrounds them everyone.
Which one of them
Alive when the day is done?

Taps playing overhead.
The sorrowful drums roll.
The earth may claim the body,
But to God flies the soul.

Elizabeth Raniere
GNILGGOB-DNIM
Walking, Timing
Thinking, Rhyming
Everything so incomplete
Why does life have to be so neat?

A little void between every stone
A little light between each moan

Coming and going, as you please
Thaw it, eat it, and refreeze

Scrambled minds everywhere
Who really knows and who really cares?

Back, forth, up and down
A smile, a kiss, and a frown

Such is the course of life my friends
Wondering where and how it ends

So dream if you will and dream if you might
Dream secretly with Orion, late at night
If you do not dare to dream tonight
Tomorrow may be lost
Take courage and show your might
For your fear the future may cost

Linda J Robinson
GUESS WHO I AM?

Dedicated to my only son, Arturo Casimiro III, with lots of love.

I'm round like a beet
But impossible to eat.
I'm very sweet
But not like candy.
Six years from now
I'll be rather handy.

Some people think
I'll be a loser.
To prove I'm not
I'll challenge the Bruiser.

Stand back, don't stare.
You'll be shocked by my hair.
I'm not the blame
You'll be shocked by name

It's Arturo, Antonio, Francisco
DeCarlos Don Juan Hasso
Componrinio Casimiro III

I am my mommy's little man.

Dedicated to my only son with lots of love.

Ronald Robertson
PAY THE TOLL
The bridge of travel has fallen, all because another bolt has become loose.
Tearfully disaster struck, yet the Government came up with another excuse.
The people are crying from the pain, still they are expected to Pay the Toll.
The fighting on the streets never end, all because of the lenient criminal.
Tearfully cities are dividing, yet the Government words are never terminal.
The people are crying from the pain, still they are expected to Pay the Toll.
The homeless of the pressured cities, all because of a population overcrowd.
Tearfully play nomadic roles, yet the Government must take a bow.
The people are crying from the pain, still they are expected to Pay the Toll.
We are paying the price dearly, for the actions of the politics.
Yet do they really care about our safety?
There is misery upon the land, we must try to make it end.
It takes the right man to take action, and to stand by the message that he sends.
Unless the tears stop, we must be expected not to . . .
Pay the Toll.

Jason Rettig
RIGHTS AND WRONGS

To Kelly, wherever she is.

In my life I have seen many faces, many people who turn away from me. People who pay no attention to the things I do right. But those same people criticize me when I do them wrong. And they tease, instead of encourage me. Those same people, I see every day, probably for the rest of my life. Because no one on this planet will compliment the little things I do right. But they will always torment me for the things I do wrong for the rest of my life.

Brian Raskauskas Jr

THE SLAP SHOT

Pushing the puck forward,
the centerman glides behind it.
The vulcanized rubber
stops momentarily until
the fibreglass blade greets
the circular flat object.
As the puck floats
through the air,
another stick sends it
in a new direction.
Having taken this new course
has fooled the goaltender,
and the puck slides behind
the line and into the net.

Tara Lynn Ramsey

B vs. W

I don't understand why we can't be friends
Black, White or does it depend?

I always choose people I like
Despite the fact they're black or white.

People are people, God made us all.
We all have color flaws.

Black and white should get together
And make this world a bit better.

I don't see the difference at all!
Colors are colors forget the flaws.

The change starts here with you and me
Let's make this world a better place to be.

Doris Reader

JENNY LEE

From Warrensburg hails sweet Jenny Lee
Who is a very dear girl to me.
She's my one and only granddaughter;
And to see her you really 'oughter.'
She plays "Mansion over the Hilltop,"
Singing, one wishes she wouldn't stop.
Her books are numberless on the shelf,
Which Jenny reads and not any elf.
Many dolls make up her dear playmates;
Carrie and Uhla came on two dates.
She has a brother whose name is Dave;
He's fond of reading about all caves.
Her parents love her very dearly
So give a birthday party yearly.
School is a happy part of her life
Where she can work and get in no strife.
To Church very often she does go
God's holy word and will she may know.
And so here's to that sweet Jenny Lee—
"May your life be lived happily!"

Jean E Reeder

MRS CLOUD

Good morning Mrs. Cloud
I see you drifting by
I wonder where you are going
Away up there so high
Now I see your little ones
Trailing close behind,
You make a lovely family
So elegant and fine
Your home is in the heavens
How lucky you are
The sun your next door neighbor
The other side a star
Your landlord is the master
Who watches over all
It really makes no difference
If it is you, or me, so small
So have a good day Mrs. Cloud
On your journey up above
I hope each one that sees you
Is reminded of God's love.

Patricia Ross

BEYOND THE STARS, BEHIND MY EYES

Beyond the stars lies eternity
A place I would like to be
Where time goes on forevermore
Feelings I hold inside of me

The sky has no limit, it travels forever
Places that do not exist
The mind cannot wonder such mystical thoughts
But for some, it's hard to resist

Behind my eyes lies eternity
An infinite path through dreams
The mystery of life, the story of love
But no one knows what it means

The stars go dim as a fine will rise
The night has ended at dawn
Eternity fades with the blackness of eve
My thoughts have almost gone

I wait once more for the stars to appear
And let myself travel a thought
I won't reach the end, there's really no choice
To find what I had sought . . .

Patricia Ross

LOVE ANGEL

Sweet scented with dew and buttercup wings
With eyes of gems and dandelion rings
With silken slippers of melted snow
Cotton-soft touches as fall winds blow

Like fields of violets through showers of rain
Like resting ivies upon their canes
She comes to our souls on the tip of a rose
In a meadow of love where sunflowers doze

Her voice is a love song sweet and serene
Her love is untelling to those she has seen
Softly she speaks to comfort our mind
Why she has sheltered to make us so blind

She motions us kindly to come travel with her
to share the sweet world of a mockingbird
Behold the comfort and feelings we hold
Behold the warmth within the cold

She's painted the flowers in fields where we lay
She's keeping us hidden from hell's dismay
She's keeping us strong to look from the rain
To comfort our love and shelter us pain

As often as dawns and sweet early dew, is as often you'll hear that I love you

Donna J Reich

COMPARISONS

Oh, little shell from briny deep,
What ancient secrets do you keep
Locked tight in spirals turning round . . .
Safe haven for their hopes and fears
Their home a sea of salty tears . . .
Their fate in pearly skin is bound.

What lowly creature dwelled within
Not unlike some dark earthly sin
Kept safely hidden in your core . . .
In time your shell could not contain
The growth inside . . . the growing pain . . .
Released and cast upon the shore.

My life is like your mystic coffin
Where surface beauty show too often
The "outside" things I gladly tell . . .
But 'inside" things I dare not face
Stay locked within a hardened case . . .
My prisoners in a self-made shell.

An offering from the ebbing tide
An empty shell with naught to hide . . .
Yes, little shell plucked from the sand,
I gently hold you in my hand
And wonder what would be to find
If I could leave my shell behind . . .

C C Roux

SILENT HEART

For A.R. Nemarich. Rule #5: "Know there is someone in your corner all the days of your life . . . and then some."

Like the moon
you are:
one side full and light
the other, deep and black.
The stars,
they shine in your eyes,
and cold darkness is kept
at your back.
Beautiful woman, Celestial Child,
one of God's very own,
the measure of time
you have outgrown.
Waxing, waning
and then waxing again,
you move and dance
in an orbit without end.
Protector of sacred sorrows,
your nobility blazes eternal;
Lovers treasure your scars of beauty,
making promises and dreams
in ancient ritual.
Splash your love on us
Paint us in your Light;
allow my silent praise
to fill the vastness
of the night.

Brenda Rogers

JEALOUSY

UNPROVOKED, erupting without warning
Comfortable peace . . . Then the volcano rumbles
UNFORGIVING LOVE - No, that's contradicting.
Love's not unforgiving,
Nor vicious and name-calling.

What can I call this, so selfish and possessive?
The volcano sleeps now, so tempting and peaceful.

Could it have been so angry?
Yes . . . I must move while it rests
So the peace will last.

But how beautiful but sad;
Deceptive like the early spring.
Sunshine tempting the plum blossoms
They trust . . . then they bloom.
Then the frost takes them without warning.

No home can survive built on a volcano.
No love can survive without trust.
No trust is built where jealousy reigns.

So, move, love, trust and be happy.
Leave the volcano to rumble and rage . . .
ALONE

Anastasia Rose-Byrd

VELVET TEARS

I hear the rain in velvet darkness
Windswept on my windowpane
My footsteps remain yet soundless
As the darkened hours wane
A candle burning slowly
This my only source of light
My music playing lowly
While I waste away the night
A sound, yet no one listens
There is no one close to hear
My shattered feelings glisten
As I try to draw them near
The cold is all around me
Though I'm wrapped to keep me warm
My soul it walks along the sea
Awaits its deadly arm
Yes, life is almost leaving
Though it may take many years
The wind in darkness heaving
Not rain, but velvet tears

Kelly Marie Relich

THE GIRL IN THE MIRROR

I can hear a young girl crying,
In her room at the end of the hall.
I can feel her pain and unhappiness,
And her thoughts to end it all.
She feels that she's lost the only man,
Who could ever fulfill her dreams.
She's gotten to the point that she'll never know,
What the definition of love really means.
Why is there so much sorrow in her eyes,
And why do I feel the pain in my heart?
Whenever she cries, I cry too,
And my emotions get torn apart.
She puts me in mind of someone I know,
But this person I just cannot see.
But when I look into the mirror,
I can see her.
And I realize that,
That girl is ME!

Anna Russo
OCEANS BLUE
Oceans blue
so crisp and new,
are fun to people
like me and you.

Romantic scenes with twinkling
stars,
surely cannot be kept in jars!

Unique seashells
along the crystal beaches
make everyone's day
as nice as peaches.

Tropical plants and fish galore
dazzle people more and more!

Dolphins and whales,
a thrill to watch
as they splash and leap
into the sea so deep.

Oceans blue
so crisp and new
makes people of
all ages happy too!

Debbie Lisi Ruiz
IS THIS LOVE?

Written for Joseph, my inspiration.

Is this love that I am feeling, this
growing passion inside of me.
If it's love that I am feeling, it's
longing to be free.
Is this love that I am feeling, please
let me know, for I can't tell.
If it's love that I am feeling, I think I
truly fell.
If it's love that I am feeling, do you
feel the same way?
If it's love that I am feeling, then it
will never fade away.
Oh I hope it's love I'm feeling, for
these feelings are so strong
If it is love that I am feeling, then
nothing can go wrong.
I think it's love I'm feeling, for I can
feel it deep inside.
If it is love that I am feeling, then
there is nothing to hide.
But if it isn't love I'm feeling, if it
isn't true
Then how can I explain what I feel
for you?
It must be love I'm feeling, for what
else can it be?
But if it is love that I am feeling, then
how do you feel about me?

Linnie Kay Risk
I'LL NEVER BE A POET

For Peggy & Scott, for all their encouragement and faith that I would someday be a fine poet . . . with all my love.

I'll never be a poet fine
No matter how I try;
I cannot write words divine
Or tell you why I cry.
Tho words abound inside me
I cannot write them fair;
I can't tell of the smiles I see
Or the colour of his hair.
I'll never touch the clouds up high
On a cotton candy day;
I'll never soar above the sky
And then just drift away.
I'll never be a butterfly
Or catch the rainbow's hue;
I don't know why kittens die
Or why my eyes are blue.
But in spite of all the many why's
And the things I'll never do,
When you look into my eyes
I'm glad that you are you.

Carolyn St Clair/Richey
HANDICAPPED
Handicapped - thou art but a nominal
representation of ideas and images
forming a broad spectrum of
shadows in animation.
Your name alone is enough to
provoke courage to defeat in battle —
any misconceptions.
You are as a sculptor chiseling your
way through life - forever seeking
relief in a supreme challenge.
One by one, we step forward with
enduring faith and meet your
challenge with profound fortitude.
Regardless of the handicaps, the
victor is life, itself, as it
continuously interlocks with the
Soul - to form an insurmountable
shield.
God bless each challenge.

Carol Skowronski
SPIDER, SPIDER

To my special guy, Ray.

An old, old spider crawled
Across the wall,
Turned the corner, and went
Down the hall.

He made a web on the
Ceiling;
Then it broke, the paint was
Peeling.
He tried and tried,
And finally got it tied.
He was happy in his web;
The next day he was dead.

Gregory F Rynkiewicz
THE EYES OF DEATH

To the people who are important to me: Dad, Mom, Nuno, and Janice, and to everyone who appreciates my poetry.

As I stare into the eyes of death, this
is what I see.
I see the hate
The hate between two men fighting
in the street.
I see the businessman selling his
drugs that kill.
This is what I see.
I see the pain.
The pain in a young child's face as
his mother beats him.
I see the violence.
The violence exchanged by two
countries,
As bombs are dropped and lives are
taken.
This is what I see.
As I stare into the eyes of death I see
the hate, the drugs,
The pain and the violence.
This is what I see.
As I stare into the eyes of death I see
the death of our world.

Gregory F Rynkiewicz
A LOST MEMORY
With yesterday behind you.
And tomorrow in front of you.
The choices for the future
Must be made tonight
Tonight you must think
Make your choices quickly
Make your choices wisely
For soon tomorrow
Will be upon you
So I tell you now
Do not hesitate
Do not ever wait
Because soon
Tomorrow will be behind you
And yesterday
A lost memory

Gregory F Rynkiewicz
SO BEGAN THE NIGHT
The red hot sun set majestically
On the clear blue water.
I felt the last bit of heat
Radiating from the west
And as I looked to the east
I saw the dark sky
It was as black
As a panther's soft velvety fur.
So began the night.

Cynthia Alvarez Roehling
AND SHE WHISPERED
Although the thorn still sticks out of
her side,
I can see the pain has subsided.
And the memories of long trials laid
heavy in her eyes,
now showed tales of love shone
bright.
Lost in a new world. Everything is
clear.
And the water feels more and
more alive each day.
I remember her tears of fears and the
anticipation
waiting, longing lasting.
And yesterday I saw her peeking into
her own clasped hands and
whispered herself away.
And in her empty space laid a white
rose in its place . . .
I knew only then,
she crossed peace.

Ursula Ruebenacker
LITTLE ANGEL
I miss you, little angel
I long to see your smile
I want to have you near me
If only for a while.

I love you, little angel
I dream of your sweet face
I'm lonely and so sad
I need you in this place.

I see you, little angel
In everything I do
I wish we were together
There is no one like you.

I hear you, little angel
Every single place I go
I hear your happy laughter
Little angel, I miss you so.

Martha Revkin
OUR LIVES ARE "ODE" TO THEE OUR LIVES ARE "ODE" TO THEE

For Merrill - our son for 34 years of love and fun!

Oh, tender-loving, fragile tree—
You saved the lives of three—

Although you slept your autumn rest,
You gave your strength—
Your very best—

Were it not for thee — dear loving,
Fragile, little tree,
Another world would hold these
youthful
three—

So rest ye well—
Dear little tree—
And we shall worship thee—
For we are free—
Because of thee—

Tammy Lynn Reed
I DON'T ALWAYS UNDERSTAND LIFE
I don't always understand life
and the actors in this play.
Why kind and then suddenly cold?
Why do some react that way?

Why do some have two faces
in which are hidden dark things?
When do you see the real person?
Why these sudden extremes?

Can't we just control our feelings,
Let the beauty of ourselves show.
Don't be ashamed of who you are!
Allow yourself room to grow.

Why be jealous, hold a grudge?
Why play judge and jury?
Can't we learn, from experience,
to tread slowly, not hurry.

Why try to mask our feelings?
Why attempt to mislead
Who takes pride in a hypocrite
Who makes the innocent bleed?

Mark Ritchey
BABBLE
It rises from the creek bed
Reaching near and far.
Along its path the water spills
Endlessly gliding over rocks and
sand,
Ever keeping that same peaceful
pattern
Of miniature waterfalls
And spillways made of leaves.
The colored trees along the way
Give the stream that autumn gleam
And the babble goes on and on
Giving all who come near
A chance to hear
Its forever song
Of seasons come and seasons gone.

Virginia A Ribas
BUT WHERE WAS THE BABY JESUS

Dedicated to my Mom, whose faithfulness to the Lord and steadfast ways have paid off in the lives of her children.

I went into the store to do my
Christmas shopping
And as I looked around it was truly
shocking
People were hurrying and scurrying
everywhere
No time for pleasantries, no smiles
seen here or there.

The tiny child so tender was shuffled quickly by
No time for anyone to sooth the baby's cry
Sales people, customers were bent on getting through
With all their purchases for Tom or Dick or Sue.

Something was missing as I scanned all through the aisles
Then it dawned on me, there really were no smiles
What or who was missing from this vast scene
What had been left out, or was it all a dream?

No, it was not a dream my feeling of despair
I knew what was missing now, yet no one seemed to care
The birthday that we celebrate, the one who came to save us
Where oh where in all of this was the baby Jesus?

Paulene B Robinson
DEATH
What is it?
It is God's calling card
It's his way of saying I want
to see you.

It is in its perfect peace that
is forever searched after
It is the Time Clock for the ending
Of life's quota to go on to something else more beautiful and perfect.

Death is the end of the human body
for you to put on the wings you have
earned because of your Golden Deeds
Death it is not but God showing his
Love saying, "Be near me now."

In the silence, "Listen" and you'll
hear the soft whisper of a breeze
from the wings of an Angel.

Marie Rawlings
FASCINATION
Such a lovely word for a song and dance.
For a dozen years I had "the impossible dream," he sang it.
Some said, "They are having an affair."
"No," said he. "It is a helpful, platonic flare."
We grasshopper danced till we ruined our knees!
He loved to expostulate. I listened enchantingly.
Chicago was our hometown. We called it the "Big Breeze."
For hours we dissected it till it became a questionable specimen.
He had the brain of a genius, the brawn of Mr. Atlas.
His charm could bend your knee and wallet. Amen.
One day the volcano of "JEAL-OUSY" decided to erupt, spewing molten lava into our garden of friendship.
Our companionship was stunned by a deed so abrupt.
We saw and felt devastation. All became void.
Now there are no phone calls, no half hour chats,
No plans to go fishing on his river raft.
Once I was bewildered by a few crystal tears he shed.
Now I understand, "MEMORIES!"
They are like the earthquake's aftershock as they continue to spin in one's head.
Tomorrow brings new hope, friends, joy. Admiration
remains for him who aroused my emotion—'tis "Fascination."

Kathleen Rockwell
A PERIOD OF ANXIETY

To: John Jakes, Patrick Swayze, and the production staff of "North and South, Book II."

Day after day, I waited—like a
soldier listening for bullet's whine.
One more day passed; no word came
from the bank; it was likely still
That I could hit a mine.
Good news came from the bank on
one succeeding day—But I knew
The next mine field would not be far away.

Barbara A Rodgers
ONE FLEDGLING
One crystal day in past December
One fledgling left us, young and tender;
Once a toddler with charming ways
And smiling eyes prompting strangers' praise,
With rosebuds blooming in fair cheeks, round—
Baptizing her world in "surround-sound,"
When seventeen engaged her dream.
One young Camp Pendleton Marine—
Daniel, with eloquent, speaking eyes,
Turned her thoughts toward "paradise,"
Toward golden coast with glistening tide.
Destiny, purpose, fulfillment, pride—
Her loved Marine to stand beside,
Now fledgling bride of Oceanside.
Her fragile life bides in Other hands,
Removed by too many miles of sand
For us to respond effectively
Should hypoglycemia make free.
Our pain, the rending, life's ebb tide floats
Away one fledgling, shining, remote—
One dancing-eyed bridge in Oceanside.

Tammy L Runk
L O V E . . .
Sometimes it seems so far away
but if you keep it
in your heart
there is no distance
no matter how far.
The memories of once loved can never be
forgotten
for it is planted in the seed from the beginning.

Leona Robinette
WHAT LOVE MEANS TO ME

To my family for standing beside me and also to Mr. Lawson, my teacher, for helping me achieve one of my many dreams.

Love is when two friends unite forever
And they are constantly together
Sharing the good times and the bad
Being there when the other one is sad
Good friends from the start
And when one says something; it really
Comes from the heart
Feeling what each other feels
Making sure everything is real
Love is sharing, Love is caring
Love is forever a constant reminder
That two people can unite together forever

Louise V Richardson
I, HAVE LONG TO SEE, MY JESUS, THE ONE, THAT DIED FOR ME

To: my parents, brothers, sister and daughter, I am dedicating this poem to you all.

I have, long to see my Jesus, the one that died for me, but I, long to be, with Jesus, who set, the captive free, one day he's coming, back and I know, he's coming for me, I have long to see my Jesus, the one that died for me. I have long, to see my Jesus, far across the sea, but I long to just be closer to the one who died for me, and someday I'll be there to see Jesus, but I long to see my Jesus the one that died for me. I have long, to see my Jesus the one that died for me when saints and angels are gathered we will shout victory, but until I see my Jesus I pray and keep singing, but I long to see my Jesus, the one that died for me.

Pamela S Rhodes
SPRINGTIME IN NEW HAMPSHIRE
Slowly the snow is melting
As our winter wonderland is once again turning into Spring.
The Bald Eagle soars once again, solemn and serene:
Adding only more beauty to this time of year.
With the sun about us we are happy after the long cold winter.
All the creatures large and small,
Peek out from their winter homes,
As they too are happy for Spring,
As all seems new, from the buds on the trees
To the newly green grass.
The springtime seems to make everyone happy
As our winters are too long and confining.
I see Mr. Robin as he sings his first song of Spring
Perched high and proud in the old oak tree.
Long walks in the crisp spring air
Fills your lungs and gives you new vitality.
We contemplate putting away our winter clothing
Only to be sure Spring is here to stay.
The house plants even seem to smile!
As they catch the rays of sunshine on the deck.
Spring once again we welcome you
with open arms Welcome Spring!

Rick Rose
SUITE SALANGE
You wake up in the morning, and gaze out the windowpane,
To see the eagle gliding silently in the pouring rain.
You want to fly beside it, 'cause the eagle seems so free,
The eagle has no thoughts of hate or jealousy, oh Salonge.
You go to sleep in the evening, and dream the eagle's dream,
Knowing as you fly that things are not the way they seem.
A girl can only sky-travel when dream-time rolls around,
When the darkness calls and beckons you to leave the ground, oh Salonge.
Launch yourself from a mountaintop, sail across to a river drop.
Skimming over the waterside, floating past the rising tide.
Floating over an endless plain, gliding into an evening rain.
Soaring into the desert sky, sunshine reflected in your eye.
Lifted up on the warming breeze, dropping down to the redwood trees.
Threading silk through the stars at night, weaving into the morning light, oh Salonge.

Honora Annie Rigg
STILLED

To She, who danced the songs of her soul—Elizabeth Ellen

The old woman sits
On the back porch of the setting sun
Earth's bright tartan has dimmed
To the foggy grey skirt of time

Skirl of pipes echo vaguely
Along dance-steps edge
Murmur of song drifts and drowns
As sea swallows the last of sun

Flowers faint-scent
The weak breath of twilight breeze
Morning Glories half closed in slumber
Forget-me-nots fading blue

Weeping Willow leafy veils
Slowly stretch and pull in sympathy soughs
As the old woman shifts
Into stayed time

Pale, peaceful
No longer pulsing
How sweet it is
How sweet it was

Honora Annie Rigg
SAD

Dedicated to Captain Harry G. Rigg

Today I hold a golden thread
To the sun
It is warm in my hand
Prism pulsing

Today is full-born
Clothed in love at dawn
With hope, faith, joy in being
One in two happily drawn

Tomorrow is birthed in bare bones
Chill-dread - stark in its nakedness
I hold nothing
It is cold in my hand

My love has left me
One in one on deep-sick sorrow
He died in the birthing
Of tomorrow

Jennifer Romine
GOD'S MISSION FOR US
Did you ever stop and think about God's mission for you?
Did you ever really think what He wants you to do?
Did you ever question why He put you on earth?

Did you ever think, well what am I worth?
To Him we are so special that He sent His only Son
To die for our sins, before His work was done.
The mission left for us is just as clear as it can be,
Be an ever serving Christian - now and for eternity!

Todd P Robinson
SHADOWS OF DARKNESS

For the ones that keep giving me support and love.

The shadows of the night, are the shadows of me standing in the line of a lonely darkness.

The darkness is you.

I thought you cared because you said you did.

I told you words with some value, but the value did not come in quite clear.

I thought our love was true, I guess it was only for high hopes in my unsecured mind.

I understand now where I went wrong, so I'll just stand alone in the line of a lonely darkness.

Marie Roberts
THANK YOU LORD

To all my lovely family I love so much

the Lord has blessed me so many times with his wonderful blessings and his hand holding mine he tells me not worry what I face each new day.he puts me going puts me on the right way

he puts a smile on my face to face each beautiful day so much beauty to see as we travel on our way the roads may get long the hills may get steep in his sheltering arms Jesus will safely keep

he will take all your burdens he will lighten your load you must sing hallelujah as you travel on
the valleys may get narrow and you can't seem to sleep get on your knees God will softly speak I am your rock of ages your light of the day your breath of life to show you the way you just keep on traveling you won't get lost just stay close to Jesus whatever the cost

he is my pilot in the time of need when I ask for his mercy he always takes heed if your burdens get heavy ask Jesus today to take your life and save you
it will brighten your way

Robert D Reese
OLD AGE

In the corner sat the decrepit old man
Loneliness and sorrow seemed to fill his face
His mind reflects on places and times
Fond memories of friends, his life and good times
His wrinkled old face has a story to tell
From his long past youth
To where he sits now

His big aged hands though tattered and scarred
Show days of hard labor and how he worked hard
His eyes they still glitter, twinkle and shine
Though loneliness and pain can be so unkind
Old age is reality a thing we must face
An old wooden rocker and a big fireplace!

Shannon Robertson
THE RUNAWAY

This poem is dedicated to my sister Kristen. I love you and I'm glad you're safe.

So young and so angry you set out alone,
Not knowing the hearts you're breaking at home.
You dream of making it, showing them all,
You never thought it would be such a hard fall.
Cold and hungry you have nowhere to run,
You're learning that life on the streets isn't much fun.
But there is a place of warmth you left far behind,
Where everyone loves you and is gentle and kind.
They will be waiting for you with arms opened wide,
They will be there to dry the tears you have cried.
If you think they don't love you, I'll tell you, you're wrong.
Go back home Runaway, it's where you belong.

Greta Jean Rofkar
MOMMA YOU CAME TO ME

Momma you came to me
smiling and laughing to me
but all the while
you were gone.
Momma you came to me
concerned and worried you seemed
but then you smiled again.
Momma you laughed with me,
a joke no one else was told
but then the door was closed.
Momma you touched my hand,
told me nothing could go wrong
but your time was so close behind.
Momma you cried with me,
so sad I dreamed
but momma,
you were already gone.

Erica Richmond (Age 13)
FRIENDS FOREVER

We were the greatest friends of all.
We never were apart.
We did things simultaneously
Right from the very start.

Although we didn't always see
Some things from eye to eye.
When I found out you had to move
It was hard to say goodbye.

In fact I think it really was
The hardest thing to do.
Because of every single thing
That you and I'd been through.

Some people say we'll grow apart
And go our separate ways.
But I'd like to hope that maybe
Our friendship really stays.

I'd hate to think we could forget
Our endless days of fun.
But instead to realize
Our friendship has just begun.

Ebony C K Rowe
THE STORM

The trees bow
The winds dance
As night enters
A display of lights
Circles the moon
As the clouds tumble in
The rumbling of drums begins
A wet curtain falls
As the light streaks across the stage
Slowly the curtain rises
The trees stand straight
The winds stand still
As night exits

Delpha Funk Romeiser
THE BLESSINGS OF JESUS

I often have thought and often have said, to my peers,
"I wish I had been there when Jesus walked on earth."
Would I have been a follower of the Savior?
I wonder, would I have followed Jesus for his worth?

Would I have been like so many others there that day
Following him for the food he gave them to eat
Or because he healed the sick and blessed my children?
Oh, would I have been aware my life was incomplete?

How grateful I am to be here in the world today.
I can talk to our Savior each day and each night.
He is ever with me, I have nothing to fear;
For Christ Jesus my wonderful Savior is my light.

When Jesus prayed for all his disciples and those after;
He prayed for all men, he prayed for you and me.
I'm thankful for his goodness, his mercy and love;
For when our Jesus died on the cross he set us free.

Brian Rolley
DELIVERER OF EVIL

Locked in a steel room with no doors,
Sitting in the dark, praying to the porcelain king,
Giving back all the past, regretting the future.
Have I sinned or will I pay the evil price.
Brain teasing, mind pleasing,
But to do nothing but sever the skull.
Do you hear the children crying
Pleading for their sanity.
Unleash their fury and be still their hearts,
Bowing before me with
R.I.P. marked upon their heads.
Great mother of evil fill me with your pain
So that the beast will live and life will go on.
Let the light shine once again
So that unmarked souls will be unleashed
Into the living dead.

Shirlie L Robinson
HOMEWARD BOUND

To Mother, with Love

"Ma's gone," was all she said and shook her head
As if, in utter disbelief, she could
Not grasp the full significance of it.

"Gone?" Ella's husband questioned cautiously.

"Yes, Daniel," Ella answered quietly.
"Ma's bound for home; the place where she belongs."

"Belongs!" objected Daniel. "But, she's lived
With us for twenty years. This is her home."

"No longer," Ella mused. "Her final words
To me last night, as I put her to bed,
Were, 'Goodnight, Mommy.' God! I could have cried."

"Your mother's very old," Daniel intoned.
"Her mind's been all mixed up since your Pa died."

"I know that," Ella snapped, "but knowing it
Just doesn't help to ease the pain one bit."

Then Daniel reached for Ella's hand and, for
The quiet moment, shared her grief; until
A child-like voice chirped,
"Mommy, are you there?"

And Ella, sobbing softly, shook her head.

"Ma's gone - she left last night," was all she said.

Teresa Lea Ross
LITTLE ELLA

You started out no bigger than a pea,
then you turned into a little she.

Your mommy was very strong,
but thought, for a moment, she'd done something wrong.

Something went wrong inside,
so you couldn't live; you died.

Mommy had to endure the pain;
to deliver you in vain.

You were so very small;
looked just like a baby doll.

Your Aunty Teresa loves you so;
All 10 little fingers and 10 little toes.

I'll say "goodbye" for now, Ella
till I see you again above
the clouds.

We all miss you! April 14, 1989

Carmen A L L Roupp
OUR LIVES

I reread all the poems I ever wrote,
But none had that certain note.
The seashore one was quite good.
Only I didn't feel like I should.
The moon rising was a blair
But lacked a certain kind of flair.
Moats and boats, diamonds and rings,
Wasn't what I wanted in things.
Love and hate, peace on earth,
Always starts we know at birth
Pleasing others is hard to do,
Yet we try until we're blue.

Talking softly all the time
Puts a strain on one's mind,
Trying to get ahead in life can be
Like getting stabbed with a knife.
No matter how bad we think things are,
We have all made it this far.
Why give up or give in,
Let's just start and begin.

Arnold Wagner

Arnold Wagner
A CABIN IN THE SKY

Dedicated to my three wonderful sons: Steve, Sonny and Andy, with my deepest love forever. Dad.

As I lie writhing in pain of my hospital bed and feeling the excruciating agonies that life can bestow, I casually glance through the window to the beautiful tree below.

My thoughts are very clear . . . we all will live and we all will die. I pray we all will meet again at that cabin in the sky; so my loved ones and my sweet friends, please be closer to me before the passage of any more time—because you are all that I have—before I reach that cabin in the sky.

Michael K Roberts
SONG IN THE NIGHT

She's a feather winged creature
Of azure flight.
Brazen smile and gilded light.
Electronic priestess we come
Where you beckon, to
Hide from the night in this
Warm lighted mecca.

The silver-blue fire is at
Her command.
Communion of angels, the time
Is at hand.
A song in the night shall
Carry us on
to a shadow grey morning
Outside Babylon.

Joanne Riley
HEALING WORDS

If I can touch your heart with a word,
And heal a tiny bit of your pain,
Then my life will have been of worth,
And both of us will have much to gain.

If words can speak to you in such a way,
That lets you know someone understands
An experience you've had, maybe they've had too,
Maybe someone else feels the same as you.

If you can trust me just a little,
Enough to read some words in a line,
May you find healing for your wounds
In these heartfelt words of mine.

Lynda J Russel
HAUNTED

I wonder where your thoughts are—the expression on your face—
Are you here with me or are you in some other place
What is it that's touched your heart and won't release your mind
that holds you fast and speechless in this other place in time
I reach out to touch you then I pull my hand away
for I have no real place among the ghosts of yesterday
I long to ask you softly what's going on inside
this vanished place which still exists you take such care to hide
The pain reflected in your eyes is a mirror of your fear
the voice that speaks so clearly a message only you can hear
You listen to this voice that speaks so clearly of the past
of life and love and laughter that will forever last
Why can't you see forever is just a state of mind
and that for which you search you will never find
What you deny your very self you cannot comprehend
you will never reach tomorrow
yesterday will haveno end
You listen for the answer and yet you hear no sound
you look but cannot see what's never lost cannot be found

Alice P Ross
TRANSITION

Short grow the days now.
The leaves are splashed with color.
Soon the dew will be frost.
Summer gardens ripened, and brought forth their bounty.
The warmth of the day, will grow cooler.
One day snow, will cover the ground.
As we watch the flakes tumble to earth, we are not aware,
that beneath the snowy blanket, life lies asleep.
waiting the time when the earth will renew itself.
Life will abound with blooms of beauty, Fluttering of wings,
and scampering of animal life.
When the sun warms the earth again.

Mabel B Resor
AN ODE TO FLO

This poem is dedicated to Florence, my youngest sister.

We used to hold each other's hand—
when troubles came our way,
Together, we could face what life
gave out, for us, each day.
We shared the laughter and the tears
and found assurance there,
In knowing that the other one was
near; and would always care.
But somewhere, on the road of life,
we must have lost our way
As others came between us—and
darkened our brightest day.
It seems, sometimes, when one grows
old—and the light of life grows dim,
The heart becomes calloused and
love grows cold, like a cold and
glittering gem.
Some say that it was jealousy that
caused us to drift apart,
I never knew the reason but it left a
painful heart!
But I still feel I need the touch of
your strong, but gentle hand,
To reassure—and let me know that
you still understand.

Fred Roberts
COLORS OF CREATION

All that is good, was created by God.
He was the farmer, who put peas in the pod.
God told Noah, to build the ark.
He made the Blackbird, Robin and Lark.
He made the honey, and small buzzing Bee.
The whale, the snail, and wee little flea.
The pine trees, mountains, clouds, and snow.
He guides the rivers, and where the winds blow.
He put fish in the oceans, and salt in the seas.
He comes before bless you, after you sneeze.
God was the artist, who put blue in the skies.
He painted the rainbow, and colored your eyes.
He gave man culture, music, and art.
Blessed with a mind, with love in his heart.

Susan Becker-Roundy
THE TRUTH

For Mila, who taught me even at midnight there's a light that shines.

So you think you've got me over a barrel
You think you've won
What you think is true
But I'm gaining on you

Soon the tide will turn
And justice will prevail
For you broke a universal law
"What is right always wins."

Michael Louis Rachman
SORRY DAZE

Sorry days
Nothing ways
A sophisticated drug craze
Shooting up
Going down
A casual addiction all around
Having fun
Entering the gates of oblivion
A shot to your head with a smoking gun
Wanting it all
Watching your brain become small
A wishful thought to breaking the law
Sorry days
Smokey haze
A self-enhanced crash course
nonimprovement maze
Getting high
Tell all your loved ones goodbye
A wasted reason to have to die . . .
BLOOD FILLED POEMS INC., 1990

Margaret Read
PURSUIT

An inner urging taunts and teases my pursuing soul
Like as the winds of spring whose thieving gusts
Creep up unseen 'neath slackened hands
And snatch away those bits and gems thus carried there
Advancing only just enough to bait the chase
Then twisting, swirling, drifting, dropping, ceasing -
Ah now - almost - the swift, still step, the lunging reach -
Then laughing, skipping, rising up - away, now gone -
Seducing winds which play with me the game of lure
Now laugh again - I shall pursue you more.

Margaret Read
EVENING

The evening calm descends
To still the old mill's hum
And kiss the water's edge
With deepening shadow mist.

Night sounds creep through leaves
Abandoned by the sun,
Whispering muted clues
Of the veiled retreating wood.

With silent step I tread
On cushioned paths of pine
To leave the teasing wind
And restless tree behind.

Rebecca L Rice
THOUGHTS OF HIM

Dedicated to my wonderful husband, Gary D. Rice. Without your support this would not have been possible.

I dreamed about you last night. We stood tall on crystal glows of moonlight.
You came to me with a loving embrace,
To console my sadness, To show your grace.

I asked you never to leave me, Not to cross that think blue line.
But out there is where you were needed,
With your badge that shined so fine.

In armour of blue, You gave your best, Until you took that one last test.
You paid the price, you gave up your life.
Now is despair, I hope I can bear.

Each night as I lay here now all alone, I'm thankful for the years you were known
As an officer so fine, One who walked the line.
Who protected and served until his time.

I dreamed about you last night. We laughed and cried till morning light.
We prayed for the men who still wear their blue.
And for all those wives who somehow knew.

Last night you lit a candle in the altar of my heart.
You ignited in me a colorful, magical spark.
A glow that's filled with beauty, one forever that will burn.
A flame glaring of crystal colors, on through life for you I'll yearn.

Cheryl G Riley
SEASONS OF MY MIND

This poem is dedicated to my mother whose search for happiness is never ending and her heart & feelings unnoticed and unappreciated. I understand and I love you.

In the summer of my life
Tears were beginning to form
My life had no direction
My path going nowhere, too well-worn.

Then for so long I lived in the fall
Everything came down around me
Not able to get up and start again
My life never as it ought to be.

Slowly I drifted thru the winter
My heart numb and cold
I tried to bring love & happiness
To anything I could hold.

Suddenly spring showed its colors
At last a new life & season to hold
The colors of the season changed the wrong to right
I've learned thru the pain to finally love all the
seasons of My Mind.

Brian J Rogers
NAME UNKNOWN
A man curls tighter into the fetal position
Stone, concrete and glass are his quarters tonight
A few feet away the mid-October rain drums in his ears
Candy and her little boy hustle through the rain back to the shelter;
There was no room for him tonight
Women with children first, then just women, if there is room left you can come in.
There was never enough room for women with children, let alone me he thought.

I thought things were supposed to get better, they're all liars, Reagan, Bush, even Carter.

A yuppie in a Volvo drives by and splashes water on him and soaks him to the skin.
Suddenly the person realized what they had done, backed up and got out of the car.
A young CPA sauntered over to the slumped soaking figure in the doorway, then looked down at him.
His scream shattered the silence of the night, the man was himself.

THERE BUT FOR THE GRACE OF GOD LIE I

Jenny Rinard
NEWBORN
I looked down at the child,
And soon I started to cry.
For within this child was the realization
That life was passing me by

I still had yet to smell a rose
All red and soft and sweet.
I still had yet to run through fields
With grass beneath my feet.

I still had yet to experience love
And all the joy and pain.
I still had yet to stand in a storm
Feeling nothing but the rain.

And as I looked down at the baby
The tears running down my face,
Experience life, I silently pleaded,
This world is a wonderful place.

Berger Rodne
LIFE'S JOURNEY
Thank you, sweet Jesus for coming down to earth
To bring us salvation through the new birth.
Now we're walking in fellowship, a journey so sweet,
While you lead the way to a friendship complete.

Though trials and testings come along the way,
There is comfort in knowing glory awaits us someday.
As we sojourn together in this strange land.
Like pilgrims of old, we have formed a strong bond.

With our hearts in touch with heaven
And our eyes fixed on the goal.
We are fed by God's own precious Word.
While joy keeps flooding the soul.

We are on the King's highway,
With a destiny pressing on,
To the mark of the high calling,
Till our victory has been won.

With our eyes kept on Jesus
While we're nearing the shore
A glorious future awaits us
At home with the Lord evermore!

Dortha Reid
REMINISCENCE
"Just Married" said the sign on the car
And my mind took a walk—oh, so very far.
After the honeymoon, came real life—
Wonderful ecstasy, unbearable strife.

Living and loving, we've struggled together
Through bills, dirty laundry, sunny times, stormy weather.
Some days floating like a feather
Others feeling as though on a tether.

We've made it now through seventeen years
Two kids, three houses, much joy, a few tears.
Of this one thing you can be real sure,
Those newlyweds there are just starting their tour.

D K Reynolds
THE EYES OF A CHILD

To: Michelle and Samantha; To whom I gave life. Please forgive me: I Love You Both - 503-283-3853 call me.

Thru the eyes of a child,
still small, meek and mild.
The wonder of it all,
to one who is so small.
When life is still unsewn,
greed and hate unknown.
Too soon . . . she'll learn the game,
and lead your heart to pain.
So teach her kindness follows,
the gift of love, tomorrow.
And if it comes too late,
tell her she must wait.
For Kindness is a Seed,
to Those who are in Need.
For some . . . love is unknown,
until the Seed has grown.

Dena Christene Ruark
EMOTIONS
Words are sometimes hard to say
When trying to express my thoughts and to share
And to let you know in a certain way
How much I really care.

I hope this poem can help to show
How I feel and the answers you need to know
So accept my thoughts with love and passion
For I do love you with more and more satisfaction.

Last night you needed me to share with you
My thoughts on what I thought you should do
You know that I love you with all my heart
And I think of you and our life apart.

I want our life together to work out
And I know you can win this particular bout
Please go and get some professional help
So our life together can start on a solid belt.

To know we share something special from the heart
Is enough to get me through these days apart.
Please do what's best for you now and ever
And always remember that I will love you and yours forever.

Pansy Ward
HIDDEN TALENT
We are gathered here tonight
To put our talent to test,
Whether we can sing or pray
We ought to do our best.

Some of us might teach
Some might can preach,
But whatever we can do let's feel free
Because that may our talent be.

So let's be guided by the Lord,
Whether it be great or small
We may find out where our talent sends,
Then follow that lead to the end.

I love to cook and I can sew,
I plant flowers to see them grow.
I love poetry and I write poems,
I don't know whether I have several talents or just one.

Alice Lincoln Woodruff
CHURCH SPIRE
Tall white bubble,
Soft with light.
Face holy in
thick grey night.
Thin, soft,
translucent
bubble . . .
Pricks stars.

Alex Wadley
THE LAST LEAF
He stood firm against the sun,
And braced himself to face the wind.
He prepared constantly for things to come;
Whenever injured he would make amends.
The elements tried to conquer him,
But from season to season he held fast.
He was the sole survivor on the limb,
Because he faced up to the task.
Showers of stones couldn't bring him down,
He was out of the climber's range.
He swore never to touch the ground,
Even if the seasons change.
He's not as strong as he used to be,
His color has changed from green to brown.
But yet he stays rooted to the tree,
With courage and strength abound.
It has been some time since I passed his way,
To watch the warrior show endless dare.
But when I return some later day,
I expect to see him living there

Mildred Walters
THE BATTERED WORLD
The battered world
Whirls endlessly around the sun
Held in orbit by giant tentacles of fate.
Swept by violent hurricanes of change,
Torn from the anchors that kept us secure,
Fearing the whirlpools of destruction
We focus on the pimples on our chins.

Mildred Walters
LITTLE LEAGUE LESSON
He threw the ball for the final out,
But the batter hit it over the wall
And the game was won by the rival team.
He hung his head to hide tears and shame
And he walked alone as he left the field
Then his father's hand on his shoulder
Lifted the weight of the loser's despair
And he lives by the hope in his father's words:
"Tomorrow your arm will be stronger, son,
And then you can try again."

Jo Ellen Ryman
INTERIM
Life is but a patchwork quilt
the intermingling of designs,
from an interspace of time.

Hues of color, sizes and shapes
comes the meeting of the minds,
from an interportrait they make.

Dancing molecules interlock the space
govern by the masses to leave not a trace.

Carol LeighAnn Walton
OVER & OVER AND OVER
The End Of The Trail shows
fatigue—but not defeat
it shows survival—but not victory
and it shows continuance
For at the End there is always a beginning
a Beginning of our choice.

One can turn around and re-live the
same mistakes over & over. and over.

One can start a new trial and at the End
continue onto another new trail . . .
and re-live the same cycle over &
over. and over.

Always in anticipation of victory
and always alone at The End Of The Trial
not defeated/not victorious

Or is the head bowed—not in
fatigue but in prayer? . . .
ready for a new Beginning.
not knowing what lies around the
corner of the trail—but knowing
it will be positive—and good—
and victorious. as long as one
turns it over & over. and over.

Dwight Watkins
ONLY IN A SONG
Only in a song, I think not to me,
Can it give me life for eternity?
Can it reach within the troubled man
Or lift up the falling hand?
Will it help the one that may fall,
Or bring together one and all?
Only a song that comes from above
can bring back our faded love
Only a song that comes from the heart
Can give us a new place to start
Only a song if we sing it well
can give the world a chance to tell
Only in a song I think not to me
I look again and know it can be

Tony A Woods
RESPONSIBILITY
Mommy is in the kitchen
I don't know where daddy is
He left two years ago.
I had just turned three
I asked mommy why daddy left
She said he couldn't handle responsibility
I asked her what responsibility was
And she said it's when you make sure something gets done
I asked her what responsibility daddy couldn't handle
And she said, "Oh, this and that"
But she didn't fool me
I know the responsibility daddy left was me.

Grace S Ward
CRICKETS
Your melody, both old and new
Drifts through my window the whole night through
Do you ever stop to sleep?
Oh yes! I caught you as you creep.

Upon the spread,
Upon the bed
You stay so still
Awhile at will.

I guess that's sleep
You meditate
Where next you'll jump
For gracious sake!

Never thought I'd ever be
So involved in Cricketry
But here I am
Each way I turn.

In cricket heaven
I still yearn
For you to shut up
So that I

Can rest awhile
or even try
to meditate without your cry
For there above the coffee pot
I gotta spray again Hot Shot!

Leah White
REFLECTED IMAGES
I bent to retrieve a leaf
But 'twas only a reflection
Such is life
Such is love
Such is dawn
All are illusions of a sort
So I fell forward into the depth
And there I'll stay amidst the golds,
reds, fiery oranges, and subtle browns of Fall.
No more will I sit on the edge of the wall
For I've crossed beyond to a more peaceful place
where none of life's realities can harm or affect me.

David Lee Warren
MISTS

Dedicated to Christina and Aslaugh Helene Schau, my mother, for standing by in rough weather and fair winds.

Traveling along the barren sandstone bluff, I hesitate;
In the north, it is ice-cave blue,
Shed with frosted clouds.
Below, cliffs of sand glisten, swirling amber,
Struck by the rising sun, its thin rim,
Crackling the cavern-dark distance.

Here, at the core of this land,
Rain eroded crags, sun-soaked crust,
I smell the end of summer.

Thoughts drift, over the stone escarpment,
and down, into the canyon of Ancients.
Their cries long fallen, on vague
Sea-borne precipices, cold tinged.

With wandering faith, I move to the broken edge.
Pressed against the blood-scratched sky, crystal cut dawn,
I lean into the wind of songs sung to God-burnt heavens.

Wavering, alone on the summit,
Palms stretched over the depths, shadow etched,
Spirits fill the abyss, enfolding my destiny.
I smell the beginning of winter,
and move on.

David Lee Warren
PASSAGE
Ship of spirit,
Hemp loose.
Unshackled from cactus strewn rocks,
Slipping out from the edge
Of mesquite ravaged earth.

Questing the liquor of the quest,
Canvas billowed, shaking off desert dust
From sunburnt sails,
Caught ceaselessly in a saffron sea;
Wooden belly, gracing crimson waves.

Carrying away images
Of scattered feathers;
Snakes ocherous painted,
Lizard tracks, seeking warm shade.

Abandoning salt bitten shores
With a last reflection
In the hot white sand.

A cove once sought,
Shelter aqua found;
Leaving a spirit once seen.

Vernell Whitt
DID YOU FORGET SOMEONE

Dedicated To: Jesus Christ, My Lord and Savior.

Did you forget someone
Who died on Calvary's tree
Did you forget someone
Who died for you and me
Did you forget someone
Who gave his life, so free
Did you forget someone
Who loves you and me

If you forgot Jesus
Don't let him slip away
If you forgot Jesus
He's coming back one day
If you forgot Jesus
Get down on your knees and pray
If you forgot Jesus
He loves you anyway

Linda Washburn
LIFE UNKIND
How can life be so unkind
It breaks our back and wears our mind
We work all week to earn the pay
to spend it all in just one day

We pay the phone, the lights and eats
and buy new shoes for our aching feet
But when Monday morning comes again
we haven't got a dime to spend

We give our pay to one and all
so we can stand up proud and tall
If any is left then you can guess
it's what we'll give to the I.R.S.

Just when we think we've got it made
there's another bill that must be paid
It makes us wish that we were rich
and could go through life without a hitch

Stacey L Young
FANTASY BIRD FROM THE FLUTE
The Fantasy Bird is always heard,
singing the forest to sleep.

The animals listen to her intently,
As the Bird continues her singing contently.

The animals sleep with the song in their dreams,
when the Fantasy Bird spreads open her wings.

She sails through the sky,
to her home on high,

Where Jesus will keep her
'til the next darkened night.

Inez Babb Young
AUTUMN TRAILS
I walked down the trail,
And there I could see
Bright autumn leaves
On a beautiful tree.

No cloud in the sky,
No rain on the road,
Just beauty and light
As I carried my load.

With a much lighter heart,
I put down my pack,
And sang with a voice
That carried me back.

Back to the high country
Trails I will find.
Life gives such joy
With all cares left behind.

For nowhere on earth
Can the heart find such rest
As out on the trail
With the mountains windswept.

Judy Irene Lippert and Irene Dolores Lippert-Hoffman

Irene Dolores Lippert-Hoffman
THE OCEAN
I walked upon the ocean shore
till I could walk no more
then homeward I did turn
for I no longer had wished to roam.
The sky was dark no birds did fly
and the waters deep
had washed away the sand beneath my feet.
It was then I sighed
oh Lord God must it be here I die
for I know not how to swim.
I slipped but did not fall
I heard the ocean for me call
oh how the tide did rush beneath my feet.
As I walked through the waters deep
all alone was I
until my savior talked to me.
Holding out his hand he had said unto me
"Fear not my child for you shall stand
upon the other shore of sand."

Judy Irene Lippert
NATURE'S WONDERS
It is beautiful when they gleam an' shine
In their winter dresses of lace so fine
Oh winter is always such a beautiful sight
Everything is covered with a blanket of white
Oh how they do bow down their heads
As they stand there sleeping in their beds
Yet still upon them fly their little friends
And they swing on the arms that bends
Oh it's then to each other they sing
Now the buds only blossom in the spring
It's then they will wear dresses of green
Oh that will be such a beautiful scene
Homes between their arms their friends will build
Then their lives will be oh so filled
Soon they will grow up and fly away
Only to come back another warm winter day
Soon they will wear their dresses of red
Next dresses of yellow before going to bed
Oh then to sleep another year to wake
It's shelter again their little friends will take.

Judy Irene Lippert
THE YEAR OF THE FOG
The air is heavy and thick
A faint mist is present
As the fog rolls in burying everything in its path
All of God's creatures run for cover
As the evil mist hovered above

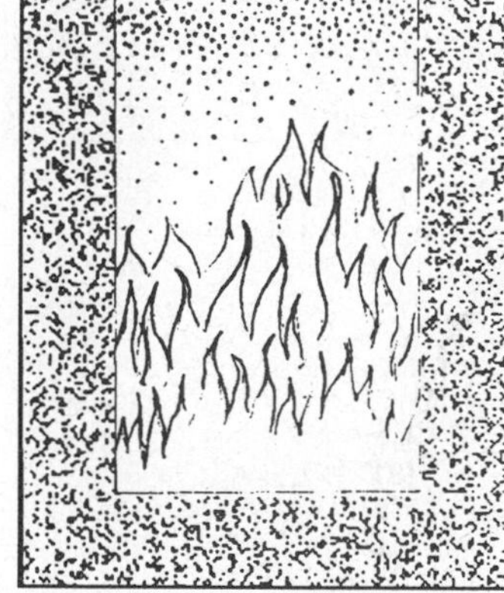

The sky is dark and gray
As if the land was in mourning of a dear loveone
The air hung heavy over the town
As the fog rolled in swallowing up six lives in a burning inferno
Cries of help could be heard from the twisted bent scraps of metal
The flames soaring out of control
I'm so close; but far away

Now only the hot smothering ashes remain
As six lives are lost in the wind for all time
With a flick of the hand the fog vanishes
Only leaving Mother Nature's evil blanket of dismay.

Judy Irene Lippert
IT'S YOU OR NO ONE
Only the end of time will tell of my love
A love that embraces me through the trouble seas of life
From the first kiss of dawn to the twilight hours
My heart is uplifted by the simple tone of your voice
Life's evil perils of money or jealousy fall short
For our love united stands stronger than a wall
A love that needs your beck and call
From mending your cuts and bruises
To mending our child's first broken heart
A love that can stand through all times
Richer or poorer, through sickness and health, to death do us part
It's you or no one.

Ann Jeannett
FOR BABY

Dedicated to all God's children created at the moment of conception

Who comes forward to
  speak for me
I am God's angel still
  mute within the womb
Could I find coveting
  protection in the
Answered prayers of an
  adoptive couple
Should my father and
  mother not want me
For I am God's gift
  but if not wanted
In turn steals away
  from your life forever

Ann Jeannett
MY PUP
My pup my pup you tangle me up
  Will we ever go a walkin'

My pup my pup you tangle me up
  Will we never go a stalkin'

My pup my pup you tangle me up
  Our ways you both are blockin'

Ann Jeannett
MISSING LUGGAGE
The trip started in joyous adventure
  Not knowing it would end with words of censor
Remembered well too late first was the snack
  Most our treasures I was assured we did pack
The pant rip was small and almost concealed
  When we rush what is about to be revealed
The journey smooth except for mighty bumps
  Oh baby feverish shows signs of large mumps
The taxi through thick traffic was sluggish
  Now if it weren't for the darn missing luggage

Ann Jeannett
MY MOM
My mother smelled of Vics
  To me it did not matter
For she's the one
  Who took me safely down the ladder

My mother smelled of rose
  When we would go a ridin'
And she was the one to seek me
  Where I was hiddin'

My mother smelled of flour
  Baking yeast bread high
The wait for which would cause
  Such a great sigh

Of all the fragrances I liked best
  The smell of powder fine
Knowin' soon it would surely be
  Kissing' and tuck in time

Ann Jeannett
SPARKLING WINE
To set on your table
  Your light sparkling wine
Caring lovingly for the soil
  And vine
Entwined are the years
  Of my life's long work
The lines are etched deep
  Onto my hands and lurk
May this portion bring you
  Joy laughter and strength
For bit by bit it was placed there
  In my life's length

Ann Jeannett
A FARMER'S WIFE
I rose before you
  In my fitful sleep
To gently cover you
  In your slumber deep

I rose before you
  To stoke the dying fire
To make your start of day
  Nothing that would tire

I rose before you
  And took from you your troubles
You not even knowing
  Of my many many juggles

I rose before you
  Seeing there was plenty still to eat
For you came in at the end of day
  Tired dusty and beat

And yes I rose before you
  And will await you there
In a place where we have
  Not a worry nor a care

Ann Jeannett
HEARTSTRINGS
The prying sounds of the violin
  Pulls hard onto my heartstrings
Releasing emotions within
  Ever so slowly
Of a time long long ago
  Strings that once bound me up
Now untie the hidden feelings
  Old and stored
Not unlike a box of lost letters
  Rediscovered
A treasure still shining
  Waiting to be remembered again

Ann Jeannett
ARABIAN LEGACY
Arabian of fire and flame
  Winds rise up your tail and great mane
Forgetting others been made too tame
  In the way you prance there is no same
You are the grand horse with all the fame
  I see you dancing in gentle rain
Quick movements turning as in a game
  Brilliant eyes that - Flash could be your name
Your knights coat glowing you are too vain
  Go forever race across the plain

Ann Jeannett
OF A MASTERPIECE
Creativity is a great swelling
  As an ocean's wave
Building in brilliance as it
  Moves the artist
Work done in limited time
  And great intensity
Pounding its impact upon
  Civilization
Then quietly subsiding
  On the timeless tide
Back into and out to sea
  Leaving its touch only
As a splash of tears
  On faces of appreciation

Ann Jeannett
THE CLEARING
Two trees were felled
  In the forest today
They were thirty and forty-eight
  Years old
Limbs fell down down on a
  Long last drop
No longer to look up
  Over us
Their massive trunks
  Dropped onto the forest lush
The birds were quiet and
  Stayed far back
The deer would not look
  Or walk the trail
Somehow the forest is
  Stiller than ever
We are in mourning and
  Where they once stood
Is seen now
  Only a ghostly mist

Gina Shoemaker
DON'T MAKE ME WAIT
Don't make me wait
Don't make me yearn
For you my love so strongly burns
Believe in me
Reach out with your heart
And nothing will keep us apart

Candace Dawn Stengler
THE KEY TO MY HEART
The key to my heart
Is plated in gold,
And it shall go to
The one I love.

Now that he has
Moved away; he
Will have to find
Me one day.

And if he shall
Use it on someone
Else's heart, I shall
Know, and it will
Shatter my heart.

And I shall fall upon
A thorn, to die, and
Shows my sins to
Him and everyone.

And shall he know
Not to use that
Key on my heart
Or anyone else's
But his own.

Wylmajeanne Simpson
THE BEGINNING OF SPRING
In my front yard I saw a robin sing,
  Just yesterday.
It looks to me as if Spring
  Is on its way.
The crocus and daffodils
Are blooming by my back porch,
Down dales, over hills, the sun will

become a mighty torch.
It helps everything grow
As much if not more
As does a rainy downpour.
But the branches of the bushes and trees
Are bare of leaves.
Soon the sun and warm breeze
Will cause the tiny buds to unfurl and flower
Making birds and bugs a fragrant leafy bower.
But for now, I wait by my window and watch,
Children splashing in puddles or playing hopscotch.

Patricia See
CRYSTAL CLEAR

To Patty & Ryana my granddaughters and special joy

Crystal clear are the teardrops, falling down my cheeks
Telling me of old-time memories
Crystal are those drops, falling to the ground
Falling, falling like tiny icy drops
Telling me of the icy heart within
As each memory passes, one tiny drop of ice melts
Each memory haunting of the past
Maybe as each drop melts I then can forgive myself
One day I shall awake and be free of all the past
My heart shall be free and I can forget and forgive
And the crying in my heart shall be a sweet, sweet lullaby
The terrible feel of pain shall be gone
The freedom of living shall fulfill
Either in this world or of the beyond shall it be answered

Karen Ann Smith
IT'S RAINING

There is nothing like the sound of rain
falling gently down
Sometimes you hardly hear it
it barely makes a sound
But if you go outside and look
just take a moment there
You will see . . . the good it does . . .
because it's everywhere

The rain brings out berries
and fields of luscious grass
The rain fills up rivers
that carry food in their paths
Right down to the oceans
to help feed fish and fin
And to think . . . the heavens above . . .
is where it all begins!

Anton J Stoffle
I DO NOT TREASURE MAN-MADE THINGS

I do not treasure man-made things,
Like objects owned by wealthy kings,

Nor do I seek a life of fame,
Forgetting friends in fortune's name,

The earthly gifts which money buys
Are made for fools and not the wise,

But give me mountains, lakes, and streams,
Great works of God to fill m dreams,

The grass of green and trees galore,
Where flowers bloom forevermore,

A sky of blue and shining sun,
There let me dwell till life is done,

And someday when life's book shall close,
I'll die content with what I chose.

Joseph R Swain
ILLUSIONS

Dedicated with all my eternal love to Sonja Elizabeth

Through my mind I have seen;
Blissfulness calm and serene;
Flowers blooming as in spring;
Rainbows summer showers bring;
Many vibrations originating from one;
Worlds within worlds where there's none;
Universal love warm as the sun;
One in all, all in one;
Teaching voices I listen to hear;
Hearing not by ear;
Speaking from afar and near;
Clearly soft and sincere;
Visions moving left to right;
Supreme beauty in every sight;
Prismatic colors inspiring light;
Through gloominess of night;
Unrealistic realities encircling me;
United in unity, forever free;
Experiencing divine divinity;
High on my eternity;
Knowing unknowingly known;
Reaping what I've sown.

Waleska Stefanelli
SILENCE

It's hard for me to say,
"I love you"
Even when I want to say it,
the words just will not come out,
I try so very hard
and sometimes even come close,
. . . but nothing.
So many times I felt it inside
but I could not say anything,
It felt as if I forgot how to speak
for just that moment,
Sometimes I would even think it to myself
hoping you would hear me,
. . . but you never did.

Diane M Sims
HER TIME

Dedicated to my mother, with much love and understanding

Each week we go
and each week it's the same.
Sitting there,
each in our own world
silent thoughts and prayers
fluently traveling through our minds.
Oblivious to the surroundings
I see her retreat within herself
We continue on, as does the mass.
I sense the sadness and sometimes see the tears
trying to be ignorant of both
I want to reach out
a hug, a smile, a shared tear
just to let her know it will be all right
and I understand
But I choose not to disturb her,
for this is
Her time.

Eleanor Spackman
TAKE MY HAND JESUS

Take my hand Jesus and lead me along the way
I feel so lost and lonely, I need you every day
I don't know what I'm doing or which way to turn
Others are so busy it's not their concern.

Take my hand Jesus and show me what is right
I know of your great love and have seen your might
I don't know what is best for me or what to do
I only know my love for someone and there's nothing I can do.

Take my hand Jesus please don't say no
I'm weak and will never make it as you know
I need someone to love me and make me forget
My being rejected has made me upset.

Take my hand Jesus you never will ignore
I know you will help me as you have before
To love and help me through each day and not be alone
It's hard for me to live and face the unknown.

C R Siteman
PASSION

passion
destroys this beast
as the delicate flower
folds
under the wrath of the cold
she opened his heart and devastated him with love
his heart now black as pitch
exposed him
opened his eyes
crushed his faith

Michael David Smoyer
BEST OF FRIENDS

Slip your arm around my waist,
pull me to your side,
Tell me of your most inner thoughts,
that there is nothing to hide.

Lay your head upon my chest,
when emotions are too strong,
Feel the warmth of my touch,
while tears fall too long.

I'll tell you with my eyes,
that you'll cry no more,
From this moment forward,
a many adventure we'll explore.

Let me show you my affections,
hold your hand in mine,
Take this chance with me,
and be my sweetest valentine.

The smile upon your face,
shall and will always be,
When the woman in you,
brings out the man in me!

Joy-Lyn Kenter
A NATION'S REJECTION OF GOD-NO. 2 (LAM. 4:3-10)

"Babies cry for bread" and none can be found.
Bread is nonexistent even in the center of town.
The palace dwellers now seek the garbage for a piece of bread.
Mothers cook and eat their own dead.
Oh, the rejection of God is utter doom
Causing unimaginable gloom.

Gina Sederwall
SNOWFLAKES

Silently I watch them fall and die
Never to be another exactly alike.
Some of them are gone before they reach the earth
Others huddle together to hide from ultimate fate.
Each one grasps onto infinity for a second
And then trickles away
forgotten.
More fall—
And the more alike they become
Each individual jumbled together for
that glorious, fleeting moment
In distress I wonder what's the use?
To rise and fall and forget
But then I understand all is not forgotten
It only melts into spring.

Narda R Strong
A SHOPPING SPREE

Once upon a shopping jaunt
To the mall, the shops to haunt.

A vision swimming in my head
My credit card turned blood red.

They said, "Come in here we're having a sale."
Hmm, did that clerk have a demon's tail?

Said every employee in every store
"Spend, spend, spend some more."

Their eyes burnt through me like blazing fire
Of intimidating they did not tire.

You must have this, that, and those
And to be chic, a ring for your nose.

I came home exhausted, with things I didn't want
The humiliated owner of hair bouffant!

Carmie Leigh Shoemaker
DOING MY OWN THING

Pushing through the forest
In my own mind.
Trying to make a path,
Trying to put the past behind!
Thinking, dreaming on a restless Day.
I want to do my own thing,
In my own way!

Some days are bright
And some are filled with gloom.
But on my own. The path
Will bloom!
And when it does, the sky
Will shine bright,
During the day and
During the night!

Carmie Leigh Shoemaker
ANTICIPATION

Winter lingers on
Spring never comes
We're all in a bind,
And we know it's not
Easy to unwind.

There's days we think
We can't make it through,
But with a helping hand
We always seem to.

So let's pull together
And make it a team.
And each day will seem
Like a never ending dream!

Carmie Leigh Shoemaker
WHO KNOWS?
When are you too young,
To stay out past dark,
To have a party and go
Out on dates?

When are you too old,
To eat lollipops, play
With dolls and cool
Yourself with the garden hose?

When are you too young,
To wear make-up, go out
With the gang and to know
Hate?

When are you too old,
To swing in an old tire,
Sit on daddy's knee and
Squeeze mud through
Your toes?

Who knows?

Carmie Leigh Shoemaker
WHEN:
When are you too old to . . .
Take hands and dance again?
To color in a book and sit and
Laugh with an old friend?
To feed yourself and reach
Something on a high shelf?
To tie your shoes, which once
Was easy to do or to read
A book because it brought
Much enjoyment too?

When are you too old to . . .
Walk around without a care?
Instead of being wheeled
Around in a wheelchair?
To sit and talk about a handsome
Man or a good looking woman?
To sit and hold hands and
Cry now and then?
To walk in a garden and plant a tree?
To live forever 'til the end of
eternity?

Mary Roth Smith
HAPPY BIRTHDAY STACEY

To Stacey, my friend

Happy Birthday on your SPECIAL
day
Listen well as I repeat and say
You are the person I wish I could be
Young, beautiful, intelligent and
pretty.

I wish you were mine now that
you're sixteen
Because you are sensitive, sharp and
keen
I see a lot of me in you—whether
good or bad
But, still, a daughter like you, I wish
I had.

You are so aware of life—there's no
doubt
Of how to cope—of things, I've just
found out
I only became aware through lots of
work
And you know just what makes
people perk.

Family, friends and people must
count
Even when your troubles and
problems mount
God is always there—just ask
To help you through a tough task.

May God bless you today and
tomorrow
And may you NEVER have any
sorrow
I'm so proud of you—you know
that's true
My final thought—I LOVE YOU!

Patricia E Stamper
BECAUSE I LOVE YOU

Dedicated to Carl, my loving husband

If I were a mountain, I'd want you to
be my tree
If I were a stream, I'd want you to
run thru me
Because I Love You
If I were the blue sky, I'd want you to
be my sun
If I were to be happy, I'd want you to
be my fun
Because I Love You
If I were the ocean, I'd want you to
swim in me
If I were a thought, I'd want to think
of thee
Because I Love You
If I were a field, I'd want you to be
my flower
If I were a day, I'd want you to be
that hour
Because I Love You

Mary F Schuman
THE LONESOME HEART OF A MOTHER
Sometimes in early morning light
As birds are singing their songs
For the sound and touch of her young
A lonesome mother's heart so longs.
Each moment of each counted day
Deepens the thoughts of each
As they grow in spirit and body
Just beyond a mother's reach.

Mothers must trust that God watches
Those who cannot be near
But a mother's heart grows weary
Waiting, and waiting, with fear
That one day God will take one
And the waiting will cease, for then.
The contact gone, no more to be
Only memories, and waiting, again.

One day that lonesome heart will be
With all the ones she loves
Though here or there, no matter.
'Twill be amongst the doves.

Emilia Salvo
SHATTERED DREAMS
Early morning, a drop of dew clings
tight
To the green leaf, near to the brook
that flows by.
Kissed by the sun, it sparkles and
shines,
Like a big diamond on the finger of a
bride.
Silent is the meadow, the heart is in
repose,
The air full of perfume of lily of the
valley and roses.
The mind dreams with passion, of
beauty and of love,
Joy and all the blessings, for which
we are born.
Suddenly, big clouds darken the sky,
The storm that approaches makes the
brook dark and high,
The scared dewdrop grasps the leaf
tight,
But an icy north wind, soon blows
them apart.
Battered by the storm and tired,
The dewdrop cannot hold on any
more,
Like a big tear it trembles, trembles,
Then falls in the raging waves down
below.
As the dewdrop lost in the brook,
A disappointed girl cries in pain,
The man that she loved let her down,
Her hands are trembling, storing the
fragile veil and the bridal gown.

Tonya Marie Smith
FRIENDS

To my whole family

Friends are people who are there,
In times of love and in times of
despair.
Friends are people that turn you
around,
And can pick you up when you're
feeling down.
There are friends that are old and
friends that are new,
But a real friend is always true.
So if you feel lonely and start to pout,
Go to a friend, they'll help you out!

Wayne L Russell

Wayne L Russell
OWED TO GOVERNMENT FREE CHEESE
When Reaganomics has got ya down,
not much money to go around.
My car won't run and my kids may
freeze,
but at least we've got our Government Free Cheese.
Because once a month I stand in line
with a whole lot of equal minds.
We say our names and say please,
then they give us our Government
Free Cheese.
Oh! Cheese for breakfast! Cheese for
lunch!
Cheese for supper and Sunday
brunch!
The atom bomb may drop and Dow
Jones may freeze,
but at least we've got our Government Free Cheese.
You see I am unemployed and I can't
pay my rent,
but at least I can thank my sweet
government
'cause once a month with good intent
they give me a block of yellow
cement.
It sticks to my ribs and it lasts awhile.
My Government Cheese is very
versatile.
Because when it gets too tough to
chew,
I use my cheese to repair my shoes.
Its preservatives are made to fast.
Its additives are made to last.
When I die of a government disease,
they'll probably bury me in that
heavenly Free Cheese.

Kendra J Schroeder
THE AGE OF TIME
Sitting in my room I stare out the
window
Alone day after day, I try to grasp my
existence
Ghosts of reality transcend my
presence
Voices of the past keep loneliness
from strangling me
Loneliness is my slow death;
Losing the ability to remain in time, I
try to survive the long wait.
Abandoned and alone to suffer each
day's beginning,
My mind screams for the end to be
near.
Can he not hear me?
Life is but muffled noise
Shadows creeping around me;
My crippled and failing body bound
to a wheelchair,
My body and mind starving for youth
it once had;
As my heart pumps against my will,
The footprints of my life pass before
me.
Closing my eyes, I search for my
tranquility.
Only when the age of time ceases
will I be truly free.

Anna Sermabeikian
FEELINGS
I feel the wind blowing in my hair,
It seems to say, life goes on without a
care.
I've grown up to feel that all is not in
vain,
Just pick yourself up, and don't let
things
give you a pain.

I feel my heart is empty, and
sometimes
full of hurt,
I know that only I, can make it really
work.

I try my best to make my life as
happy as
can be,
Only I can control it, through my
destiny.

Linda Jean Belloto Smith
MOTHER'S DAY

This poem is dedicated to Mary T. Garchar Belloto, mother of ten, college grad, lady of the 90's.

There is no one I can compare you
to . . .
There is nothing in which I could
relate you with.

Your natural high energy I have
inherited from you . . .
your nose, mouth, arms and legs too.

The amount of your patience,
understanding and love
are too good to be true—

Only because you've given so much
to my brothers . . .
to my sisters . . .
to my father . . . to me.

And the love that I hold for you—
can only be
as wonderful as you.

Happy Mother's Day

Phyllis Shullich (Sunshine)
FREE YET BOUND

This poem is dedicated to my son Kent, and my wonderful husband Ace. Two men I love with all my heart.

I have made my endeavors,
But how much more can I endure;
Inside these walls of confinement,
Where everything is obscure.

Already I have surpassed,
What my mind cannot conceive;
And I feel the strength within my soul,
Withering like a leaf.

If only I could fine refuge,
Somewhere here within,
That once again I could visualize;
Someday this all will end.

If only I could look ahead,
Though my youth is slipping away;
To sustain from becoming cold and hard,
As others in this place.

For someday this will all be over,
No more bars, no locks, no keys;
But if God doesn't leave here with me,
I'll be confined for eternity.

Lee Sharp
THE ALCOHOLIC GLOW

This poem is dedicated to my mother and Bill, my husband. Both have triumphed over adversity.

He sat in the chair
Rocking to and fro,
Bathed in the light
Of the alcoholic glow.

There was much that he saw
And much he didn't know,
Life was a haze
In the alcoholic glow.

He'd lost all his friends
And had no place to go,
Seduced by the warmth
Of the alcoholic glow.

And still he sits
Rocking to and fro,
A prisoner in a maze
Of the alcoholic glow.

Lee Sharp
VIOLENT NIGHT

Knives flash,
Voices screaming,
Run to hide,
Nightmare-dreaming,
Police arrive,
Flashing light,
Children cry,
Violent night.

Frank Schoonover
PAPER HOUSES

In the long night hours as the city lights beam
I am looking out the window in the house of my childhood dreams
Sitting on the bed, lonely as a mouse
In my quaint little paper house
I sometimes think that the whole world is mine
In this form of life a child would think everything is fine
Every child lives in a usual fantasy world
Which is something that could put any mature adult mind in a whirl
Paper houses, visions of every child's dream
An imaginary place to look out of as the city lights beam
Where every child lives out every fantasy
In a totally unexplained ecstasy
Every child dreams of going out to sea
This is yet another childhood fantasy
Every child lives in a total fantasy world
Something that could put any mature adult mind in a whirl
In the long hours of the night as the city lights beam
A child looks out the window in the house of his dreams
Sitting on his bed lonely as a mouse
In his quaint little paper house.

Julie Ann Skrobel
OUR FRIENDSHIP'S ONE OF A KIND

I dedicate this poem to my best friend Tina R. Klimpke. For without her as my best friend I'd be lost, and this poem would not exist.

When we first met we really didn't know,
Just how fast our friendship would grow.
Apart we were two, but together we're one,
Cuz when we're around each other we always have fun.
We've had a lot of good times, and yes some were bad,
We will always be friends, and boy am I glad.
Nothing can break this wonderful bond, you see,
We have such a strong friendship I'm sure you would agree.
Nowhere else in this world will you ever find,
A best friendship like mine and yours, it's only one of a kind.

Martha Ann Slaybaugh
SPRING AWAKENING

Dew glistening on the earth,
Trees budding in all their mirth;
Flowers peeking, merrily, through the ground,
Who could keep a smirking frown?

Spring, soon here in all her glory,
Revealing the miracle of her story.
Birds chirping as they fly, here and there,
A lilting lullaby.

Signs of a velvety green carpet under foot,
Marvelous wonderings taking root!
A brand-new spring is here today,
Oh, if it could just be here to stay!

Karen Schmidt
THE DRAGON

It's a dragon burning from inside,
tearing him from family, friends,
and his only daughter;
with its fiery breath.
That day when I walked into my room,
cold, darkness, fear . . .
imposes like thunder on a calm,
peaceful night;
nothing would ever be the same.
Outside my window a butterfly,
so beautiful and pure,
struggles to get out of its
cocoon . . .
to be free,
to set a soul free,
to go to a world we know not of.
Time stands still,
my heart beats and pounds,
as if a hammer was hitting my chest,
my stomach has a sinking feeling,
a heavy weight has just hit me,
something is wrong,
part of me is gone forever . . .
The dragon has won,
the butterfly is set free . . .
My father has just died.

Lou G Starr
THERE'S A NEW GROUP SINGING IN HEAVEN

It's Presley, Crosby and Lennon
It's the singingest group since the beginning of dawn.
It's Elvis, Bing and a Beatle named John.
Heaven—was never this way before,
The angels crowding the dancing floor.
Paradise will rock and roll,
Solos by Nat King Cole.
There's a new group singing in heaven
There's a new group swinging in heaven
It's Presley, Crosby and Lennon.
It's the swingingest group since the beginning of dawn
It's Elvis, Bing and a Beatle named John.
Gabriel will bring his angels along,
To a rehearsal with Louie Armstrong.
The saints will be clapping
Fred and Sam will be tapping.
What a wonderful treat, to see God shuffle his feet,
There's a new group swinging in heaven.

Kathleen F Snyder
GOODBYES

Friends are never friends they say,
until they say goodbye.
But when you think of old friends,
you know you'll hear a sigh.

Goodbyes are found everywhere—
in a city full of people, in a country full of peace.

No matter how they're said, no matter how they're done,
goodbyes bring tears and memories and love from everyone.

Goodbyes are full of sweet hellos,
memories and song,
of words you'll never forget, as long as you live your whole life long.

Parting is such sweet sorrow they say, goodbyes they never end.
But tears fill up your eyes when you know you've found a friend.

Goodbyes are the mournful song that old friends sing when they part.
Although, they say, a sorrowful end leads to a joyful start.

Margaret Smith
UNTITLED

Oh, a pair!
Incredible ocean blue eyes.
They have possession
of my soul.

If not for fate,
and years too late,
I could perhaps be,
the red delicious
only they could see.

But, wait, love is
all-forgiving,
Yes, and kind.
Do I not yet,
await a chance?
A fluttering I feel
each time I steal a glance.

Sadly, each day, I see a face
fading, more as time . . .
But never the color,
of a pair,
Incredible ocean blue eyes.
MARGI

Elizabeth Smith-Myers
TO MOTHER ASKEW: WITH LOVE

Homegrown farm girl,
With a mystic, kindly smile.
Died today, leaving me empty.
White corn silk halo,
Eyes so bright and forgiving.
Gone dim forever.
Tall and tomboyish,
But oh so feminine in carriage,
Lying horizontal now.
Encouragement giver,
Moving you with a single touch,
Or gentle motherly kiss.
So still and cold now,
But the memories are warm.
You went so silently,
It stilled my soul, ever so briefly.
Then your spirit touched me, kissed me, looked at me, smiled at me,
Life goes on, in the vertical position.

Rebecca A Skeen
DREAMS

I try to fly
Lifting off in one bound
But the fear of falling
Keeps me on the ground

Times can be hard
Things come unglued
The thing that matters
Relies on your own attitude.

Friends can't always be there
You may be on your own
Life can be easy for some
Those with hearts of stone.

Memories never die
They're yours to keep
Good or bad
Depends on how high you leap.

You can make me cry
You can make me weep
But no matter how hard you try
My dreams are always mine—As I fall asleep.

Jeanne A Sandt
LIGHT MAIDEN'S LOVE SONG

As your spirit flows
To touch my spirit
Our energies merge . . .
And so our power is increased.
We are guided from on high
To our Highest Good.
Light and Divine Love fills us . . .
Our beings overflow with joy
Like a fountain
Which continues to bubble over
into . . .
Infinity.
All our heart's desires
Flow to us.

Indeed we know true joy and contentment!
Bless the Great Spirit which touches us,
Inspires us
To live in the Law of Grace.
We walk in the Light . . .
Our way is made clear.
We travel the path of our Happy Destiny
United in Spirit and in love.

Fay Swanson
HANNA, THE CAT
Hanna is the queen of the household
She allows us to live with her
But, if we should become too bold
She is a fighting ball of fur

She struts around with her tail in the air
Jerks her head to say "follow me"
The look in her eye says, "Don't you dare
Defy me, or sorry you will be"

She plays rough, I'm telling you
No lady plays like that
If we won't play, we get our due
What a cantankerous cat!

She's even staked out a claim to the bed
It's a battle each night for the room
Some day, my friends, we will be dead
And that cat will take off on her broom

To find more victims, she will go
And pour on all her charm
They will love the unsuspected foe
And think "Keeping her will bring no harm"!!!

Fay Swanson
R-VING WITH A FRENCHMAN

This poem is dedicated to:
Gilles Vendette.

I've always heard Frenchmen are romantic & sly
But, that image was blown by just one guy

There were no candles, roses or wine
He didn't even use a good line

Beer & burned popcorn, he served to me
He's a Frenchman, how can this be?

Next, it was time for us to dine
"I forgot the utensils" was his line

Then, no coffee could be found
My morning was shot, I staggered around

I thought this Frenchman would be organized
But, I was wrong, I soon realized

One part of the image he does uphold
About getting fresh, he is very bold

But, this Frenchman is a fun guy
He is even more crazy than I

Katherine S Soffer
ONE MORE CHILD
She looked just like a baby. She had a grown-up's eyes.
They were cold and stony; Filled with hate and lies.
Looks can be deceiving. Seeing's not believing.
They didn't think their child could ever be so wild.
One more child has fallen. One more child is gone.
One more child has fallen. Where did we go wrong?
Youth and innocence are now things of the past.
Today our little children are growing up too fast.
They didn't see it coming until it was too late.
They tried so hard to save her, but she had sealed her fate.
One more child has fallen to a common plight.
One more child has fallen; A child of the night.
Sarah took her life today. She wasn't fully grown.
She was having problems and thought she was alone.
She is one of many. Another tragic death.
She thought she couldn't take it and drew her dying breath.
One more child has fallen. One more child has died.
One more child has fallen. One more mother cried.
One more child is falling to a fatal end.
One more child is falling.
Catch 'em quick, my friend!

Katherine S Soffer
THE BEAST
The Beast within me is ragin'.
It's crying out for your touch.
The Beast within me is ragin'.
The Beast; It loves you so much.
Its insides are growling with hunger.
That cannot be nourished by food.
Your love is all I can think of
to control the Beast and its mood.
The Beast is just lonely without you.
It struggles from inside my heart.
Although I'm not in any danger,
I feel like I'm being torn apart.
You're the only one who can tame it.
It won't take a whip or a chair.
The answer is really quite simple.
All it needs is for you to be there.
The Beast within me is ragin'.
It's crying out for your touch.
The Beast within me is ragin'.
The Beast; It loves you so much.
Yes, the Beast; It loves you so much.

Minnie Peacock Story
ONE MORE DAY

To Nicole, my daughter who is blind and has C.P. and a tribute to Patrick and Heather and all the kids at St. Judes Hospital for giving me my inspiration.

If I could wake up each day, knowing that I'd see it through
But we don't know that, so we do what we have to do, our best, be better than all the rest. Appreciate every day we have together and everything we do, don't forget not even one moment that I have spent with you. We don't know who our enemies are or who our friends are, but one day, I hope we can go that far. Life is so precious, people, you just don't know, maybe someday you'll understand and it will show. It takes strength and courage to go on, but the love you fill will make you strong. But God is waiting for us to come home, where we really all belong. Just to hold you and hug you and show how much we care,
But we know you've been through as much as you can bear.

Sandra Stewart
YOU HAVE GIVEN ME . . .
You have given me . . .
The beauty of
a springtime day.

The comfort of
a favorite easy chair.

The wisdom of
a king's library.

The warmth of
a blazing fire.

And most of all
a reason to enjoy!

Timothy Smith
THE LIGHT OF DAY
The light of day cleverly sneaks into my darkened room
The light, combining with the droplets of rain,
Form a crystal gateway to the rise of the morning

I had not been abrupt in meeting with the day
But when I opened my eyes focusing only to the sky
Looking for the slightest movement of the clouds
I noticed something usually invisible to my sight

The day had begun to unfold, and part of it being the morning,
Began to glitter and shine as rays of glory cried out from the dark clouds in the sky

Now, after watching and learning from the story being told
I soon found myself a distant part of the day

April T Sandoval
WHY ARE PEOPLE LONELY
"Why are people lonely?"
is a question always asked.
It's the result of a broken heart,
or dreams that do not come to pass.

They feel like nobody loves them,
or wants to be their friend.
So, they try to find some comfort
in a bottle that holds their end.

It seems that in this day and age
that nobody seems to care.
So, all of these lonely people die
because they had no friend to share.

This is for the lonely ones
with their hearts that are torn away.
Waiting for a new tomorrow
and a hope for a better day.

Jenna Schofield
THERE'S ALWAYS TOMORROW
It seems as if my past is so
Very clear
And the voices of yesterday are
So easy to hear.
But when I think of tomorrow
And the future ahead
I wonder what waits for me
Or the fate I'll be fed
For I live in my past and I
Can't let go
I then hold it all back so my
Fear doesn't show
I dwell on my hopes and sweet
Dreams in my sleep
And inside my grown body is a
Child who weeps
The tears are of pain felt
Inside
And the roller coaster of emotions I
Everyday ride
If I were a window, they'd see
Right through.
If the walls I've built fell
What would I do?
Sometimes I think I'm doing
Just fine
Then I wonder if I'll pass
The test of time
My day will come when there
Are no longer tears
And this shell of loneliness
Will soon disappear
I will walk out my door with
A smile on my face
And take hold of life with a
Strong embrace
I will take one step forward and
Look only ahead
I will no longer dwell on the
Poison I was fed
For in all of our lives we are
Faced with sorrows
But what we sometimes forget
Is there's always tomorrow

Vickie L Stewart
THE CLOWN
I sat underneath the apple tree,
and watched the leaves fall down.
Just like the tears that fall free,
down the face of the clown.

He looks like he has a happy face,
but alas, inside he is sad.
So he paints on his happy face,
To make everyone think, he is happy and glad.

But the clown's life is full of grief.
His heart is filled with pain.
He wishes he could have relief,
from this world of sorrow and pain.

But the clown puts on his happy face.
To keep things at peace.
But underneath that happy painted face,
Lies a face, lined with sorrow and grief.

The clown is at the crossroads,
Of life's ups and downs.
He can't go upwards, and everyone says,
He hasn't the right to go downwards.
Oh! but alas is the life of a clown.

George Robert Swanton III
LOST LOVES

For my mother Mary Dorio and my Aunt and Uncle Ted and Mildred Paschalides

Two loves once lost and gone;
Like the petals of a flower,
Sharing its life together; It
blossoms in spring; But, withers in
winter . . .

Two loves of yesterday and
today; But, gone on the
morrow; We bore life's grief
and sorrow; Its happy
moments together; That
soared like the dove . . .

Two loves united as one;
Our love was strong and
sure; A bond of two
hearts; A treasure indeed!!

My aches and pains are
over now; It's time to
move on, because life
holds the future; But,
I hold the key . . .

Deni Sinteral
A MYSTIFYING EMBRACE

To Dave, thanks for your love and the unforgettable inspirational moments we've shared.

The stage is dark; the curtains slowly part.

A man and a woman
One waiting; one moving
Both safely looking away
Faces concealed by a mystical mask

The flow of music fills the air
Pulling them close, they begin to dance
Allowing the rhythm to engage their souls

Time seems not to move.

The music plays on with passion and grace
Revealing the depth of intimacy
Unfolding a mystery in the gaze of their eyes

Moments are endless.

The echo of music remains
The light now casts a setting of purples
Dancing so close; only one shadow appears

A man and a woman
Two bodies touching; standing perfectly still
Neither looks away
Mystique unveiled as their mask hits the floor

The curtains slowly close; the stage is radiant.

Deni Sinteral
FLUTTERING SOUL

The mystery of the butterfly
is beauty and grace
She's untouchable and
alluring, happy and carefree.

She flies through the
flowers; tasting the breeze
dipping and giggling,
restlessly at ease.

But, don't get too close;
don't try to see
because once you do the
butterfly is set free.

Clouds cast doubts upon her
wings; the raindrops begin to
spill;
Unable to release her past; unable
to hold on to her future;
She pauses to listen to the echoes of a storm.

The present unfolds with a butterfly who's two.

One who dances alone in the light;
losing her innocence; but
never her hope
Feeling so safe; her truth
rests in her dreams.

The other who dances
alone in the dark;
keeping her soul asleep;
fearing the pain
Living a lie; her soul refuses to
wake.

Too close is he; Too much has been seen.

Time flutters past

Yet the butterfly remains; restlessly, achingly.

Still happily believing in
she,

Longing for the moment when one butterfly is gone and her soul set free.

Sister M Rosina Schopp RSM
WHAT DID I DO TODAY?

I wish to dedicate this poem to all who rejoice in the wonder of God's created beauty and love.

Today I watched the Master Sculptor
Chisel faces in a cloud-puffed sky,
And saw his beauty reflected
In a lovely butterfly.

I felt the warmth of sun and wind
As they stooped to kiss each
flower;
Then watched the busy honeybees
Sip nectar for their waxen tower.

The soaring, swooping, nesting birds
Came also into view
As I took delight in nature
In every form and hue.

Then I saw the face of God
In the smile of a loving friend
And heard a wondrous voice within,
"My love for you will never end."

What did I do today?
I pondered God in work and play;
Then humbly made my prayer to him,
"Lord, gently mold my heart of
clay."

Betty R Scalet
MY FRIEND, BRANDY

I wish to dedicate this poem to my beloved sister and friend, Allene Reisinger Lambert, of Columbus, Ohio.

Brandy is my pit bulldog;
She's brown and black and brindle.
She spins around on her back end
As if she's on a spindle.

She jumps through hoops and catches
balls,
And lies down on command.
She sits and speaks and answers
calls,
And loves to shake your hand.

And when she finishes her tricks,
She sits so patiently
And waits for treats and jerky sticks,
And lots of praise from me.

For sixteen years she's been
my friend;
She really knows me well . . .
And when I'm sad she sits
real close
To hear what I must tell.

And when I'm glad she's
happy too—
She always wags her tail.
He eyes light up,
she licks my hand—
Her loyalty leaves a trial!

She's growing old and
getting grey,
She cannot hear or see;
But through my tired
and clouded eyes
She's beautiful to me!

Amelia Shelly
HAPPILY I TARRY

Trekking through the forest;
searching for a drink;
finding a pond in a meadow;
leaning down, I pause to think.

Taller than a dwarf;
smaller than an elk;
I see in my reflection,
a rather handsome elf.

Jade eyes peer back at me,
causing a crooked little smile.
Happily I'd tarry,
but I need another mile.

Ignoring the image,
forgetting my face,
lapping up the beverage,
forgoing all grace.

Straightening, I turn away.
I mustn't lose the light.
I have to reach my fellow fay,
before the fall of night.

Ann Herwitz

Ann Herwitz
THE JOY OF BEING YOUNG

To my darling nieces who inspired this poem: Christine McPeer, Joann Zabick, Holly Miller, Bannie Renner, Sherri Collup, Janet Leandro, Linda Turkatte, Jackie O'Brian

Come, little children, to romp and
play,
In the sunlight dancing in the skies.
To the meadows, in the breeze,
Hair a-flying, feet a-running,
With gleeful laughter, full of mirth.
We caught bright ladybugs and gave
them a lift,
Into the soft breeze, away we go,
Frolicking along to the bubbling
brook,
To catch a glimpse in shallow waters,
A swarm of minnows slithering
away.
Come along, come along, one and
all—
We'll dance to the music of singing
birds,
While we grow up, let's frolick
along;
Always reach out to the touch of life.
Ladybug, ladybug, don't fly away,
Keep our hearts young and gay, the
rest of our days.

Ann Herwitz
ASSIGNMENT FOR ENGLISH

In the chapters of the Novels just
read,
"Discover Self," professor says.
Oh my mind does strain to please,
Where will it end, "think" I say,
Write and try to no avail.
Someone has dropped a pencil on the
floor.
My trend of thought has gone astray.
Back to the grind of pencil and mind,
Soon to go astray once more.
For someone has finished his
discovered self,
Among the characters of the novels.
Out they go, one by one,
Only to leave me in despair.
For my discovered self,
Is not those characters of the novels.
"I am me!" I cry out in trumph to
myself.

Philip R Smith
I CAN'T WRITE ANYMORE

To God; for this gift

I can't write anymore
I've written too many
another poem leaves me dry
from a well of plenty

I'm asking the impossible
but I continue to give
the resources of my love
dwindle through the sieve

No okne understands my life
deaf ears hear my cry
I've sat here endlessly
watching life slip by

The pangs of emptiness
fill my heart
no one's hand to hold
no love to impart

Where is my hope
why does it wait
no, it's still here
knocking at my gate

Jennifer Sullivan
DRUGS

Some say drugs are awesome;
Some say drugs are hot.
Some say drugs are cool;
Others say drugs are not.
If I told you they were good,
I wouldn't be your friend.
They tear your life apart.
Your problems they won't mend.
Drugs don't get you high,
But they get you sunk.
They're not any better
Than drinking and getting drunk.
So if you don't believe me,
Go to any book.
The book will say, "Don't do them.
On them you will get hooked."
So let me say it one last time.
I'll tell you that they're bad.
Drugs won't make you happy.
They'll only make you sad.

Brenda Whitehead Smith
NO LIGHT IN THE WINDOW

To my husband and son whose love has made my life wherever I may go feel surrounded by a home.

Pounding emotions tug down the
time-worn lines on my face.
Yearnings, such conflicting sorrow;
my life to tragically embrace.
Waves of intense pain cascade

sporadically down my spine.
Catatonic. My body sluggishly
drowns on cheap, leaded wine.

Home: construction of love where no
one yet lives.
Boxes of lumber organized on a
mindless belt thru a sawdust mill.
Raging blaze to consume the hearth;
radiation to burn up cold.
A resort of trekless sand and
waveless surf; visions as I grow old.

Searching each countenance for that
"goodwill" look.
Societies writing games; too much
reality from a fantasy book.
Who elects to withhold the plot of
my housing dreams?
Sketches, lines of space replace high
wooden beams.

Time withers possessions that belong
exclusively to me.
The State grants land to settle; no
dead bolt lock and key.
Where can you find this nomadic,
homeless heart?
Stacked on empty promises and a
stuffed shopping cart!

Dorothy Stegonshek

GONE FOREVER

I would like to dedicate my work to anyone and everyone who has ever lost someone near and dear to them.

When you lose someone be it family,
friend or lover
You're forced to deal with the pain,
you're forced to discover
They can't come back—they never
will
You feel so alone your heart stands
still
You can wish and pray and ask God
"Why?"
But I promise you'll make it as time
goes by

You can lean on me to see you
through it
You can lean on me to help you
through it
You can lean on me when times are
bad
You can lean on me when you're
feeling sad

Tricia K Slone

THERE SHE IS

To Roger Blackman

There she is
all dressed in black
She's the one you're after
now you know where she's at.

There she is
prowler in the night
She sells all she can
then disappears out of sight.

Nobody's seen her
she doesn't exist
She knows you're following her
can't you feel her amidst?

She's out of this world
you better leave her alone
When you look into her eyes
you'll be chilled to the bone.

Nena E Soltani

MY GUAVA TREE

In our front yard was a guava tree,
Just the perfect size for my friends
and me.
I would climb up high and make a
funny sound,
When my mother and father were not
around.

Sometimes I'd eat lunch on a limb by
myself
While the postman passed by who
looked like an elf.
My friends weren't so lucky, they
had to be formal,
Of course Mother wondered if I was
normal.

One day a lizard was right by my
face,
I screamed and ran as my heart began
to race,
In two hours the memory was totally
gone,
I was up in the tree again by my front
lawn.

I enjoyed the fruit and climbed the
tree year after year,
I ripped quite a few dresses that were
very dear,
But I always had freedom to climb
that tree,
With Ruthie, Flo and Gloria, trailing
right behind me

William H Schoppe

CHICKEN SCRATCH

Words
Come
Words go
Sometimes
Static
Others flow.
Amidst
The confusion
And the rush
In the
Mind
Jumbled
Phrases
Of chicken
Scratch
In broken
Line
Writing
Scribbled
On scraps
Of paper
Only to
Find
Words
Come
Words go
Sometimes
Static
Others flow.

Barbara L Santiago

SAILORS WHO RISKED THEIR LIVES (ON THE U.S.S. BATTLESHIP IOWA)

These brave sailors were trained to fight, they risked their lives day and night, they knew their job and they did it right. They weren't the type to take a fall, they were always on the ball. They were the ones who did not hide, the pride and joy they felt inside. For being a sailor was the best, for them especially among all the rest. So let's just stand and bow our head, and say a few words about our dead. They didn't deserve to die that way, it's always the good ones who pass away. And even though we are apart, they will always remain in our heart. Since we lost them in a fiery blast, we will always remember them in the past. For these brave sailors were killed by a gun, I feel for those families who lost their loved one, especially the mothers who gave birth to their son.

Donna Jeanne Stricker

THE SNAKE

My poetry is dedicated to my mother BEVERLY HUME STRICKER for passing on to me her creativity . . .

Come here little girl
see what I've got
in my hand

Why it's your heart
see it if you can . . .

Come closer little girl
let me smell your perfume
Let me touch your sweet face
let me get you into
my bedroom . . .

Oh no, I didn't, said the snake to his
friend
with a wink of his eye
and a smile on his face
with noticeable deceit in his
eyes

You must be kidding?
Me and that little girl?
Oh no, it wasn't me
I've got someone you see . . .

Come here little boy
see what I've got
in my hand

Why it's your heart
get it if you can . . .

Come closer little boy
let me smell your cologne
let me touch your sweet face
let me get you alone!!!!!

Oh yes, I did, she replied,
I intertwined with his soul
he can't deny

I'll do it again
when I get the chance
I'll get that snake
I'll make him dance
I'll put him down
upon his knees
he'll want me again
you wait and see . . .

My skin is soft
my perfume sweet
My body sensuous
it begs for a repeat

A repeat of souls
that intertwine
a day of passion
again will be mine

So come here little boy
I've got a surprise for you . . .
A little something
you can't refuse

(A little snake, you are indeed)

But this little snake
she will succeed . . .

Donna Jeanne Stricker

THE EMOTIONAL ROLLER COASTER

Which way did he
go???????????????
Only the future knows..................

On the emotional roller coaster
we will go..................................

Where it
stops?????????????????????
nobody knows.............................

One day up!!!!!!!!!!!!!!!!!!!!!!!!!!!!!!!
the next day down——————

All the emotions
circle round!!!!!!!!!!!!!!!!!!!!!!!!!!!

For all of those
who play the game
WATCH OUT!!!!!!!!!!!!!!!!!!!!!!!!!!
It's like a hurricane......................
Coming at you
then going away
Then coming again
another day.................................

Which way did he
go???????????????

Tell me,
who knows.................................

Up and down
all over again..............................

That emotional roller coaster
does it have an
end????????????????

Donna Jeanne Stricker

JOY

You———
were there for me

I———
hope to be there
for you in that safe
place of honesty and truth.............

Where———
even the child within
can feel free to express
the emotions of self......................

When———
the time comes to vent,
to grow..

How———
with the strength, knowledge
and wisdom given to us all by
our higher power, when we learn
to ask...

Kent Sorenson

TRUE LOVE

I dedicate this poem to my family and relatives.

Love is what brings life, but does not
control it;
Light a candle, and see the flame;
Quiet, calming, but speaking;
Listen to music, hear the songs and
what is being said;
Brings harmony and understanding,
but giving different information;
Look into your heart, for true love,
for it is strong;
Love is what people use when they
care for someone or something;
but doesn't always tell that person
or thing;
Look into someone else's heart, and
you will see how they feel about you;
There are many ways to express love,
But speaking aloud is the most
common;
But true love, is what people prefer.

Cheryl Lynn Stottle

DON'T

Chain lightning
Lead the way;
Close your eyes,
You can't forget

The sensation.

It's not what you put on your body,
It's what you put into it.
Don't just do it,
Do it better,
no matter what . . .

Obsession,
My favorite escape;
The fragrance that captures a dream.
Compulsive dots,
Smooth for weeks.

This is what you thought?
The killing.
The conviction.
The cover-up.
The dying.

Words were never your favorite form
of communication.
They tried to stay cool when the
temperature soared.
How far will you go
In a puff of smoke?
There's no such thing as a graceful
loser.

Being desired feels great,
But, does it have a future?
They feel good
Dying.
The most unforgettable problem.

The end of a brief but meaningful
relationship;
A terrible thing to waste.
Using may not be as safe as you
think.
What if one of these children were
yours?
What if one of these children were
mine?

Be wild!
Exercise your options.
Avoid risky drugs.
I'll be seeing you
Save a life.

The sign of the times,
The growing aware,
The next generation;
are to be a fashion,

'DON'T"

Peter Sacco
THE SEASONS OF DISCONTENT
-I think I'll miss the spring
With all the joys that nature brings
The falling of rain
The blooming of flowers
Only to realize what cannot be ours
-I think I'll miss the summer
The heat of the sun upon our bodies
The loneliness of missing the fun and
the follies
-I think I'll miss the fall
The resting of nature by God's call
The crunching of leaves falling by
our feet
Trying to contend with all of our
defeats
-I think I'll miss the winter
When it all seemed that life was
simpler
The falling of snow, the singing of
carols
Striving to go on with life and all its
perils
-The seasons must come and the
seasons must go
As I must go on to face the unknown.

Gertrude J Stewart
MY PRAYER

Dedicated to my husband Ed and our children Gary, Judy, Mary, Peg, and Jayne

Father in heaven I earnestly thank
Thee
For Thy son Jesus who died on the
tree;
My sins He bore;
My crown He wore;
And from slavery He set me free.

Please help me such a mother and
wife to be
That, with each problem, to Thee I
will flee;
Help me to care;
Help me to share;
Grant patience, love, and faith unto
me.

May I daily seek to walk blindly with
Thee;
Take my concern for tomorrow from
me;
Give daily bread;
Keep me from dread,
Help me be what you want me to be.

Please take away doubting and all
fear from me;
Give me peace, joy, and assurance
from Thee;
Keep Christ in my life;
Keep me from strife;
May my treasures in Heaven all be.

Gertrude Stewart
FAITH
It's so easy to say we have faith,
That we walk not alone by sight;
But when adversities come
And we feel we're all done,
We cannot in our own strength fight.

We say we know faith is the
substance
Of things that are hoped for, not seen;
But we fuss and we hurry,
Take our time up with worry
And find in our souls we are lean.

We say we have faith for the future;
We say we've laid all cares on Him;
But when we're left all alone,
We look not up to His throne
And our life's full of tumult and din.

We say we will leave all cares with
him,
That we cannot carry the load;
But we find we shed tears
And sometimes it takes years
To completely walk on faith's road.

Lori Sutton
ELECTRIC LIGHTS
Electric lights
Moonlit nights
Skies so blue
Stars so bright

Purple hills
Sunlit fields
Crystal waters
Running so still

Open spaces
Faraway places
Happy people
Friendly faces

Open minds
Hearts that bind
Love so real
So hard to find

It's all there
In this land so rare
Just look in your mind
If you dare.

Teresa L Smittenaar
PARENTS

I would like to dedicate this poem to my parents, Charles and DonnaLee Wheeler, Jr.

Parents are kind, loving and sweet.
Sometimes and most of the time,
They worry too much.

Parents give you things, that
You will cherish for the
Rest of your life.

You can also do things with Parents,
Like camping, fishing or just talking.
Parents are a lot of fun.

Parents will be and always can
Be your best friend through
Good and bad times.

So just remember that Parents,
Are yours to keep forever; no
Matter where they are.

Kevin D Smith
WATERY GRAVE
The eye of the storm
is getting near,
therefore, that makes
you, I, and we fear

The storm carries a lustful
dream of destruction,
but the season is right
for this type of fluxion.

Fall!! Fall!! fall is to blame,
but who can blame something
that's never changed?

The gods!! the gods!!
it is their fault.
Then I look at the clustering,
black sky with that shameful
thought.

The accusations I scream come
from nothing but a madman with
fear.
But fear is all we have
now that the storm is here.

Raging waters of Neptune
even more powerful than the sun,
leaving a trial of destruction
that is second to none.

Women cling to their children as
if they were the only thing
to hold,
as the storm blew on, throwing
mangled bodies and souls.

Ever wonder why whatever nature
giveth it taketh away?
Take for instance our children,
who now rest on a watery grave.

Judith L Simpson
SMELLING LIKE A ROSE

This poem is dedicated to my sister Rose, and to my darling daughter Candace.

As the Rose glistens with dew
From a brand-new dawning-
"Is the Life of Rose"

As the Rose petal is soft
Clad in crimson adorning-
"Is the Strength of Rose"

As the Rose vine bears thorns
Shielding its flower due warning-
"Is the Provision of Rose"

As the Rose stands aloof
Amid a cold winter's morning-
"Are the Trials of Rose"

As the Rose bows to the earth-
Awakened to a spring day's morning,
"Is the Re-Birth of Rose"

As Rose is a Rose,
And She is rightly so called
"The both of them adjoining"

Clayton Raub
POETRY
Poetry is words in rhyme, it happens
from time to time.
Like heartbeats, it feeds the mind, all
life together it binds.

For some, it is sissy stuff, others can
ne'er get enough.
The gener'l view, it is fluff, boys who
write it are not tough.

The troubled write, mentals too, real
good poets, there are few.
Most are dead their books reviewed
by mixed-up people, like you!

To end each line with a rhyme, who
can think and spend the time?
You make it up in your mind, a circle
you say it binds?

"Come on out," the partners say, "Put
that away, for today."
"You must know it does not pay, find
another game to play."

Someone has to write it down; a
smile, the tear, a sad frown;
The colors from red to brown; a
travel from town to town.

Life is not a big mistake, a dream
from which to awake,
To find we have come too late and
must now accept our fate.

The poet, he tries to rhyme, and fit
the world into time,
So to understand the mind, and all the
life it does bind.

Joseph Gregory Salvo
ROOTS
From the land of darkness they came
Your fathers and your mothers
Not willing and to build a nation
But in chains and desperation

They called your fathers and mothers
slaves
They shall call your sons men
For what happened to them shall not
happen to you
For you are men and you are free
And what happened before shall
never again be

But you did help to build a nation
With your love and work and
inspiration
And for all those who came before
you
And all those still to come
The fight for freedom has been won
But there is still much to be done
With hope and determination
There can be freedom in this nation

And so
Be proud to say you're black
Be proud to say you're free
Be proud to say I'm a man
Be proud to say I'm me
As I am proud to say I know you
And call you my friend
And say to all the world
This too is an American . . .

Eddie Joe Stacy
LONELINESS

To my three daughters, Vickie Higgins, Lorraine Atkins & Dorothy Stevens.

I look outside, it's raining
Tears from heaven, seems to be
For the many times I, break down
and cry
I feel the angels cry with me
I remember so long ago, happiness
came my way
Those times have passed, they never
last
For life changes from day to day
But now I know, wherever I go
And sadness seems to be gaining
I won't hide, I'll look outside
For I know it will be raining.

Linda Rudd
LOVING YOU

This poem is dedicated to Ronnie Good, who I love with all my heart!!!

Even though loving you is hard to do,
And at times I feel it's coming to an
end,
Even after all we've been through,
You will always be more than a
friend.

Even though loving you is hard to do,
And my heart may never mend,
Our love will always be true,
For me, our love is not pretend.

Even though loving you is hard to do,
My life with you, I've tried to share,
And most of time, I'm without you.
You'll always be my Teddy Bear.

Even though loving you is hard to do,
All my days and nights, I sit and cry,
And all the times I've been blue,
For me, our love will never die.

Jennifer Marie Stack
THE LOST MIRACLE

A tarnished star
falls,
tumbles down dry needles-
denying its top position.

Plastic adorns
the browning evergreen.
Feigning smiles,
the population-
follows methodically
the patterns.

Shallow faces play
the roles.
The dryness crackles
while
an angel falls.

Bobby Stanley
I LOVE YOU

To Kathy Hall . . . part 2 of the promise!

I want to tell you how I feel
But plain words will never do
So I'm writing a special poem
To show how much I love you.

I love the sound of your voice
When we sit down and talk
I love the way you move for me
And I love the way you walk.

I love the way you smile
It brightens my every day
I love the way you show your
feelings
In each and every loving way.

I love to know you're by my side
When I'm feeling hurt or down
I love how you put a smile on my
face
To cover an unwanted frown.

And I love the way you trust me
When no one else would
I love the way you care for me
Because no one else could!

Cindi Stein
I AM YOURS

To Keith - for whom this poem was written.

I am yours,
like always before.

I will never leave you,
or walk out the door.

I will stay forever,
to hold you near.

For you are the one,
I love so dear.

You have given me all,
I will ever need.

Beside you forever,
is where I will be.

I will try to keep you,
safe from harm.

Hold you tight,
and keep you warm.

Don't ever doubt,
my love for you.

I am yours,
I will always be true.

Nicholas Nathan Seaver
13 AND A 1/2

Ranting, raving, stomping around in
unjustified misery.
In a silent world. All alone, with no
one to take on your anger. In a land
filled with giants and infants. You are
somewhere in between.

You have feelings. But nobody dares
explore them. Everybody ignoring
you. Like you don't exist. But, you
do exist! Anger, frustration, madness
perhaps. Softness, understanding, and
even caress. You are somewhere in
between.

They take control. You have no say.
But, you think you are as smart as
they who rule the world. You are
tired of their control, so you defy.
You enjoy a few moments of
freedom then your whole world
crashes about you. They have locked
the house for you not to escape; Until
they say. You know they are right;
you think you are right, but . . . you
are somewhere in between.

Kelly Shugart Schinke
WHERE WERE YOU?

Where were you when I was down
feeling low and blue
when things were upside down for
me tell me, where were you
the times that I felt I was lost and like
I didn't belong
when I thought I was nothing and
everything seemed wrong
where were you when I need to talk
or to laugh or to cry
when I wanted to share a happy
thought or when I felt like life was
passing me by
where were you when I was happy
and had so much to say
the times when my life was right and
things were going my way
where were you when all I needed
was someone to believe in me
and even though they knew the bad
the good is what they'd see
when I needed someone to protect me
someone to really care
someone to want the best for me and
to know they would be there
when I needed someone to trust
someone who would be true
when I needed a friend at my side tell
me, where were you
when I needed someone to lean on
and to know they wouldn't mind
someone to understand my inner
thoughts when there were answers I
couldn't find
where were you in the good times
that I only wanted to share
and where were you in the bad times,
no matter what, you were always
there.

Kelly Shugart Schinke
YOU ARE ME

Before I hit rock bottom you caught
me as I fell
when I was out of hope you became
my wishing well
I found my shelter wrapped up in
your arms
I found my safety when you
protected me from harm
you are my past, you're my identity
you are my future, you're my destiny,
You Are Me
when I was shining you were my star
my purpose to go on is what you are
when I found my triumph you were
my foundation
when I was glowing I was your
creation
you are my past, you're my identity
you are my future, you're my destiny,
You Are Me
when I was lost you helped me find
my way
when I was safe again you were there
to stay
when I was fading you kept me in
your sight
now that I am with you, you always
make it right
you are my past, you're my identity
you are my future, you're my destiny,
You Are Me

Cheryl D Rhodes
EVEN THOU

Even Thou: I had never written a
poem;
I knew that some things
are just postponed . . .
Even Thou: I was careful about
what I wrote;
I knew someday that
fear was no joke . . .
Even Thou: I worked all day to
climb up the ladder;
Now, I find that it
really does matter . . .
Even Thou: I kept a good frame of
mind;
I found that success is
still worth my time . . .
Even Thou: I pay my bills, on time,
I am still over my limit;
and constantly
behind . . .
Even Thou: Now and then, I
remember there is no
end . . .
Now that things seem
very clear;
I can smile from ear to
ear . . .

Shawna D Remington
DREAM STREET

Many times I have visited dream
street . . .
At ten I was a journalist
At fourteen a child therapist
At sixteen a romantic in love
At seventeen wildly untamed . . .
When I was eighteen I understood
dream street could be a nightmare.
Now I am twenty just wondering who
the hell I am?
I am a daughter
. . . a sister
. . . a wife
. . . a mother
I am many things to others . . .
What am I to me?
I have a mother
. . . brothers
. . . a husband
. . . a child
I have great gifts given to me . . .
What do I want to give myself?
What's missing?
Dream Street.

Deborah S Reynolds
BABY

In the darkness of the womb, body
and Spirit become as one;
Creation of a simple soul, conceived
of Spirit and man.
But up from the killing fields, unborn
souls are crying . . . Silent wars
arising!
Baby's hands are doing, what's
washed through Baby's mind;
Leaders making decisions, concern-
ing Baby's rights.
Teaching Him If He sells His honor,
He can save His life . . . Silent wars
arising!
Baby's eyes beholding, and oh, what
Baby sees!
Kings and Queens, and leather and
lace, pain for a legacy.
And the innocence of Baby is dying,
Drowning in river of blook! . . .
Silent wars arising.
Baby's ears are hearing, what Baby
should not hear;
Monies changing hands, merchants of
integrity.
Power is what they're buying, souls
for merchandise . . . Silent wars
arising!
Baby's hands are stained with blood,
His heart the act;
The angry wolves are stalking, we
have baby trapped,
Is the damning of their souls the only
price we'll pay? . . . Silent wars
arising!
Brothers of love arise!
In the darkness of the womb . . .

Ronald Rodney
MOTHER'S WOMB

Nine months I spent in my mother's
womb.
Living in my pharaoh's tomb
Cared for like a king, and of this I
can remember
Not one thing
Protected from the cold and rain

Never feeling any pain
Feeding of my mother's veins.
Sometimes I kicked
And cuffed
And made a fuss
But mother never treated me rough
Mother was very tough
To carry me nine months without a fuss
Sometimes in pain she cried, but kept her pride
Nine months she walked with me inside
For my mother my love I will never hide

Johnny Campbell

Johnny Campbell
THE EYES OF A CHILD AT PLAY

I would like to dedicate this poem to my mother and all the inspiration she has given me.

As I look into the world, I wonder what does it have in store for me today. I am seven, mama said I was sent from heaven. I don't really know why I'm here, but I know I have no fear. Mama said I am mean as the dog next door, maybe I am but why doesn't my mouth drip with white foam. In my yard I am king, nothing lives or dies without my command. I am the ruler of this land. I see a butterfly, I ask it why do you fly? The butterfly said nothing, so I slapped it to the ground, and then I asked why do you die. Mama said I shouldn't pick on things weaker than me. I see next door another king, he is eight, he is my enemy. I run to the fence with my hands tightly together, I shout his name, he runs at me just the same. I say I am the ruler of your land? He said nothing, I hit my enemy with my hand, and climbed the fence. I now rule his land with an IRON HAND.

Margaret Adams
A THANKSGIVING PRAYER
Thank You God for roses red
And yellow daisies with a nodding head
For tomatoes hanging on the vine
And flowers and vegetables every kind.
Thank You God for the sunrise
And for the sunset skies.
For clouds that are so very bright
And clouds that do not seem so bright.
For the rain and the snow
And winds that can blow.
For birds as they fly
And rainbows in the sky.
For the young and the old
For the timid and the bold.
For light skin and dark
For their beauty of heart.
For that Heaven above
And the gift of Your Love.

Madeline Velez
COUP DE GRACE
She sits alone.
The room is quiet and peaceful.
It is in the company of her memories,
that she endures the final hours of her solitude.
The clock strikes five.
She takes a deep breath and stares out the window.
Shadows emerge over the white valley,
as the light of day is being
swallowed by the horizon.
Her pulse accelerates;
she is aware of the darkness to come.
From her sparkling eyes,
drops of anguish fall down her cheekbones.
It is in the joy of crying,
that she celebrates the final moments of her sorrow.
She gets up and faces the mirror.
Smiling, provocatively, the Grim Reaper appears before her;
she acknowledges the visit.
With her withered hand,
she unties her silver hair.
Alone she sits and awaits.
The end is near . . .

Madeline Velez
THE CENTER OF THE BRIDGE

Dedication: To the man who once stood at the center of the bridge, I've kept my promise.

She stands smiling, on top of the hill,
contemplating the sight before her.
Announcing the birth of a new day,
the sun also rises from the horizon.
Today she welcomes the light that
embraces, with warmth,
her slender young body.
Yesterday she was dwelling in the shadows,
trapped among the endless affairs of the heart.
From time to time she still remembers; somewhere in the oblivion,
bittersweet memories are forever
stored in shades of the past.
The center of the bridge.
It was there where he lingered,
confused and uncertain;
while a silhouette nearby awaited,
with wondering eyes set on his image.
He stood at the center of the bridge,
for what seemed to be a lifetime,
before he walked away, on his own,
never to return.
Left behind in the shadows of the
bridge, the silhouette asked among sobs,
"Do I know enough to make it alone?"
Plenty has taken place since then;
all the things she thought she knew,
she has learned, better, again.
Proudly she now stands, on top of the
hill; she has come a long way, from
the center of the bridge . . .

Rowena Wolfe
ODE TO YESTERDAY
Today I took a journey
Through the pages of my past
An album filled with smiles and tears
Where memories last and last
I lived again the days gone by
And I stopped a while to greet
The friends I met along the way
My friends of "Memory Street"

I thought about the things we did
And the times that we went through
I wondered where they are today
How many dreams came true
As time goes by it seems to me
That our thoughts now play a part
They recall the joys of yesterday
The memories of our heart

Cynthia White
FOREVER LOVE
Let the laughter and love shine through,
Tell me this our love forever true,
O hear my cry, O hear my plea,
May our love forever be,
The feeling I feel is only for you,
Tell me now our love anew,
Tell me this is true love I foresee,
That we'll be together, just you and me,
Together in Paradise that's where we belong,
Where the birds shall sing their songs of love,
Where we can stare into each other's eyes,
Enjoying every moment of our wonderful lives,
Tell me this our love so true,
That forever I want to be with you.

Lisa White
MY ONE AND ONLY WISH
It is my one and only wish
To have our love mature and grow.
If I could only let him know
I was so naive and foolish
To let him leave so long ago.
It is until then I will know
I have my one and only wish.

Robert M Shortell
KANDY KITCHEN KURRICULUM
Pick freely
On mere whim.
Bite into it;
Throw it back.
Seek not learning,
But fleshlike flight;
Flee the inevitable
Inevitable.

Choice, vacillating,
Sweet choice
Made nebulously
Of the nebulous;
Nonstructured symbols
Of sweet complacency.
Pick your way out
Insidiously—
Or is it cravenly?

Joan Wolfrom
HEATHER
Hauntingly beautiful you stand
Everywhere upon the misty moors.
As I walk among you, the chilly wind whispers,
"The pages of 'Wuthering Heights'
open to you."
Happily I enter in.
Exhilarated, I stoop to gather you in
my arms
Reflecting that I am following the
footsteps of the Brönte sisters.

Mary Elizabeth Zeider
A PERFECT WORK OF ART
Mounds of snow upon the ground,
Mirrors of ice form all around.

Gray clouds floating up above,
God gives it all to us with love.

Then He puts it all away,
Blue is used instead of gray.

What a way to paint the sky!
Lovely for the birds to fly.

Green instead of white we see,
And blossoms starting on the tree.

Drops of rain are falling down,
To help the flowers in the ground.

Up they come like magic too,
He has done it all for you.

Joellen M Wolfson
GIRLS
Delicate, lacey innocence,
With eyes like cats,
And minds like foxes,
Soft and silly,
Childish and charming,
Billowing, windy,
Tripping through scenes
of childhood and femininity.
Extending skyward
Their winnowy arms,
Reaching for love,
and drawing it close.
Enclosing love within,
As it dwells in their hearts
and makes them —
women.

Jacqueline Simpson
SOLUTION
I walked a wondering road one day
Hunting a solution to the problem I faced.
Looking deeply into my thoughts
I found another path a long ways off.
This path was easy
No bombs, no holes,
But a smooth surface
In which to stroll.
I walked and walked
Until I realized.
I must go back for
The problem wasn't solved.
I found the path in which I left.
And a solution
By just sticking with it.

Nora M Shutt
CHRISTMAS IS LOVE IN ACTION
Christmas is the story
Of God's great love for man.
When he first put in action
His great redemption plan

The baby born in Bethlehem
Was God's sacrificial lamb,
Offered on the cross of Calvary
To pay the price of man.

Oh, Christmas is love in action.
How great that love must be!
God gave his only begotten son
For love of you and me.

Christmas is love in action.
"Whosoever believeth in him
Should not perish"
But be saved from all his sin.

Christmas is love in action.
No greater love could be.
"For God so loved the world"
He gave His son for you and me.

Theresa Phelan

Theresa Phelan
THOUGHTS OF A LITTLE ONE

This poem is dedicated to 'Tara' our lovely daughter.

Inspiration flows easily, as thoughts of you fill my
heart and mind,
A person so little yet ever growing,
So helpless, yet ever gaining new skills
So needy, yet able to bestow such joy.

Complete with coos, gurgles and your own brand
of baby sounds
You eased into our lives changing everything,
Yet it seems like you were always here.

Big blue eyes, a melting smile, skin so soft, a
warm downy head,
Clearly we have shaped in God's true masterpiece,
Let us sit a while and ponder, gaze, cherish,
Time out to comfort, relax, console.

Now we are besotted by your winning ways,
Tending to your needs is paramount, all else
can wait,
Right now you are so precious, we must savour
each moment,
So much to marvel, enjoy, applaud.

Our lives are enriched with joy abounding,
Our love fuller, cemented, shared,
Goals are clearer, our direction more focused,
We are intoxicated with love.
The end.

Theresa Phelan
STRIVE FOR PARADISE
Should all the world enamored be,
A place abounding, full of glee,
Where man could live in joyful mirth,
A haven fort, a new rebirth.

No futile wars would ere erupt,
No place for man to be corrupt,
For peace lives here, there is no strife,
No feudal fights, no loss of life.

For if we strive to live with joy,
We can be freed, we won't destroy.
If look closely at each other,
We'll surely know, he is my brother.

Yes! there is time for all to see,
No victory rules without harmony,
For war can kill and surely maim,
And hearts of stone can do the same.

For those who have an axe to grind,
Will fuel their cause, when so inclined,
When far away, or out of sight,
They'll bother not about your plight.

For they don't have the hearts to care,
No real concern for your welfare.
Be on your guard, know who to trust,
And don't be spoiled by the unjust.

Theresa Phelan
CONSCRIPTION
Unrehearsed we move along, without a script or plan.
To the final destination, which is the fate of man.
Such meager preparation for an end we can't foresee
To plod away each life of ours for that final destiny.

For though we never volunteered, for our fate which is to be
We must have got conscripted to partake in history.
Nor did we chose our next of kin, for them we could not see
Our hands are tied, we're drafted, to face the penalty.

For if we tire along the way, and misery abounds,
There are no resting places, from the scorn of running hounds,
For no reprieve is granted, when the road is hard to bear,
The best that we can hope for is a kindly hand to care,
And as we move along the path from innocence to grave,
What are the final plans in tow, what are we here to save?
We cannot help but wonder, there are such scanty clues
So we are left to struggle on, reflect, and further muse.

Theresa Plelan
LIFE'S ANTIDOTE
Though young we are impetuous, our
judgment's not so keen,
Try as we may we'll sometimes fall,
things are not plainly seen.
There are so many paths to choose,
with so many stumbling blocks
If we have a good foundation, we'll
get the fewest knocks.

Just as we seek to learn in youth, the
truths we need to know,
We look back at a later date, and
harvest what we sow.
There are so many inward needs,
dreams calling to fulfill,
And as we pass in adult life, we're
reaching for them still.

There's much to learn along the way,
and always will be more,
Though you be wise and eloquent,
and reach more than score by four,
For always through the paths we take,
there's much to know and learn,
Should we remain inquisitive, we
won't look back and yearn,
Though waters can be rough at times,
and stumbling blocks too great,
And some of us have much to bear,
troubles piled up on our plate,
But humor is the antidote to life's
painful miseries,
And laughter is the sounding board
that calms the savage seas.

Theresa Phelan
MAN THE ENIGMA
Made unto himself in the image of God, he is Man the princely primate,
Reigning supreme amongst the species, superior in all his humanity,
Capable of wondrous works, undying love, and unyielding passion,
Master of art and science, leader of civilization
your quests are endless.

Your forms are many and varied, your habitat every nation
Born to be free, to savour the beauty, to live with dignity and pride,
Your fears are many, your struggles sometimes too fierce, for one so frail,
Your vibrancy is lovely, your darkness is a shame.

The past you inherit, can sustain or maim you, many have fallen by the way.
The monsters of drought and famine can threaten your very survival.
The hostility of war and conflict can strip you of your being, your zest for life,
You are now an endangered species, your struggles unending.

Disease and poverty, ignorance and pollution stalk your earth,
But wisdom, sanitation, culture and comfort befit you.
Your curiosity has opened new doors, your relentless search for truth, new horizons.
Your equality can never be equal, your wealth can never be shared.

In leaps and bounds you have developed strategy for survival,
Still many are impoverished, ignorant and sad.
Your most enlightened advances can sometimes destroy,
You are Man forever seeking that which eludes you.

Theresa Phelan
SOLITUDE
Within the furrows of my mind
There's treasure there, that none can find.
Some memories filed, some knowledge stored
And stories there when I get bored.

While pondering easily on my own,
I find some pleasure being alone,
Just browsing through my thoughts I find,
There's motion scenes of every kind.

Sometimes my thoughts can make me brood,
There's feelings there that change my mood.
But then when I get too uneasy,
I probe still more for thoughts less queasy.

There's so much there for me to ponder
I meditate, explore and wonder.
There's spaces still, that I can fill,
More memories for a future thrill

Theresa Phelan
THE WEARY PEDDLER
The peddler came to see the town,
And sell his wares if able,
He did not have a half a crown,
To put food upon his table.

He had toiled for endless hours now,
Made pots sand pans from tin;
He knew it was the only way,
To keep him from the bin.

But local folks were leery,
And some were downright rude,
They passed him with a haughty look,
And more times he got booed.

But travelling onwards on shank's mare
He thought about his plight.
Fate had to have a better deal,
A brighter end in sight.

While local politicians,
Talked of need and destitution
The old man had now passed away
Too late for restitution.

Theresa Phelan
NOCTURNAL DREAMS
There's a land far away and out of sight
I get there somewhere in the night.
When all is quiet without intrusion
I reach a land of pure illusion.

While reminiscence makes me doze
I reach a world of sweet repose,
And while I lie in peaceful slumber,
The plot goes on in awe and wonder.

There are those within my dreams I see,
I know quite well in reality.
Many have a part to play,
I know from only far away.

Some people that have never met,
Play parts together on my set.
While most are good, and some delightful,
Just a few can be quite spiteful.

Those that torment in the light
Come back to haunt me in the night.
But all my dreams are not austere
There's many that I hold so dear.

Eva Standridge
A LITTLE BIT ABOUT ME
When I get up and start a new day
I like to feel happy and have a day bright and gay.
I like to paint do my housework and think of my family and friends far away, It seems like it makes me at ease and have a relaxing day,
although I have distress to go through too, I suppose people and I all over the world have a little distress night and day But God helps us to make

any way. All we need to do is to look to him and pray
I am at home alone most of the time,
I like to listen to music, But sometimes I like it that way.
I hope it won't be long until I can be with my kids and grandkids. I want to hear them say "I love you" in every kind of way.

As of right now I live with my daughter, she has two kids. The other four of my kids are pretty far away.

Becky Stutler
ONLY FOOLS FALL IN LOVE

This poem is dedicated to anyone who's ever been hurt in love—and still can't stop loving.

Only fools fall in love
And I'm the biggest fool of all
For as the years pass on
It's your name my heart still calls
I loved you from the start
Though you warned you couldn't be chained
But I had to try
I had to risk the pain
Now I can see the truth—
I never stood a chance
I'm left with broken hopes and dreams
Surrounded by visions of shattered romance
Only fools fall in love
And I must be the biggest fool of all

Rachel Willey
TO OUR HOSTESS
Now we know a young lady named Alice.
She really should live in a palace,
For a most gracious queen is she,
For whatever she wants to be -
She is -
A good wife, a mother and a teacher of note.
To both young and old, she has time to devote.
A lover of nature, with all life she's aglow,
And her love for us all doth steadily flow,
A hostess with the mostess, and a friend most true.
In fact, we can't think of a thing she can't do.
So Here's To Our Alice, Our Queen Sans Palace.
And many, many long years may you live
So that much joy to us all, you'll continue to give.

David C Sutton
TOM CAT
Tom cat, where are you going with that tail switching back and forth?
I'll bet he'd heading South, no North.
He avoids the danger
Strays away from the stranger.
The females are fine unless they've been fixed
He knows he's just wasting his time.
He goes on the prowl night after night.
Looks pretty good except when he's been in a fight.
When you've looked all over the house
And you can't find a mouse
You can thank your furry little friend, Ralph.
Only the birds in the cage are not made his prey.
Big dogs, small dogs,
Friendly or nay,
When Ralph comes out they all stay away.

Helen B Glass
LETTER TO AMERICA
Not even in my dreams
Can I exorcise this nightmare
Even in my dreams
I hear the mourning doves
That waken me.

I cannot write you
Of my son, the student.
He is not . . .
The square is clean
And empty
The leaders say,
"There was no massacre
In Tiananmen Square."

Samuel Sutphen
OUR WAITRESS
We have a waitress in waiting
 that is far far supreme
for she is very good
 brings the coffee, forgets the cream

She surely takes your order
 and she is very polite too
but to get your order back
 you have to fret and stew.

She calls your order out
 it could be hamburger or just fish
she puts your service out
 on the way back-drops the dish

You could ask for tea
 but she only brings the bag
hot water is so very rare
 but her butt she sure can wag.

But Maryann is quite alright
 for she smiles from ear to ear
and she has her ups and downs
 So we say Merry Christmas see you Next Year.

Jill Doak
FORGET HIM
Forget his name, forget his face,
Forget his kiss and warm embrace.
Forget his love that once was true,
Remember now, there's someone new.

Forget the love that once was shared,
Forget the fact that he once cared.
Forget the times you spent together,
Remember now, he's gone forever.

Forget you cried all night long,
Forget him when they play your song.
Forget the way things once were,
Remember now, he's chosen her.

Forget you memorized his walk,
Forget the way he used talk.
Forget when he was mad,
Remember now, he's happy not sad.

Forget the times when you were alone,
Forget the times he used to phone.
Forget he made your dreams come true,
Remember now, there's someone new.

Forget his gentle teasing way,
Forget you used to see him every day.
Forget the things you used to do,
Remember now, she loves him too.
Forget the times when he went by,
Forget the times he made you cry.
Forget the way he spoke your name,
Remember now, things aren't the same.

Randall S Chandler
FOR SEVEN WHO DREAMED
In the cold, hard light of a January morn
Seven souls sought the heavens

Six who were born to touch the sky
And one who aspired to the unknown

Borne on pillars of crimson fire
They roared from the light to the darkness above

Seeking to challenge the stars
For a moment they became one

In time the sorrow of their passing will fade
But the memory of their spirit will remain

 For seven who dreamed
 We will remember
 Dreams never end.

Lynn Pesce

Lynn Pesce
WHAT A MAN, MY DAD!

In memory of my loving father, "Tiny" H.B. Culpepper, who passed away one week after writing this poem to him, in March 1982.

He's there from the beginning, right from the start,
Teaching and guiding, you think not from the heart.
And oh what a child thinks of his father's lecturing hand,
But life moves swiftly, like the shifting of sand.

Then sometimes as easily as the tick of a clock,
You'll understand what was, "was not!"
The unthoughtful guilt a father dost not speak,
Makes his heart, so gentle and meek.

With time and patience, what surfaces is true,
It's really just "life," but somehow anew.
You'll listen and linger on every word,
And pray that there's nothing left unheard.

Time is now, I sit back and listen with ease,
For whatever comes out, is surely to please.
He's still strong in the head, but soft in the heart,
And the talks all now, are of a different sort.

You'll forget some of the ones when you were little yet,
But not one word now will be forgotten, I bet!
For each word that's spoken is hid in a part,
Deep down in the middle, of my soft heart.

Lynn Pesce
ENTRAPMENT TO COCAINE
"C" closing the door to your family.
"O" obligation to only yourself.
"C" closing the windows to your
 heart.
"A" anxieties with your health.
"I" interior changes in your mind.
"N" noxious damage to your wealth.
"E" engulfing, endless ebony, for all
 eternity!!

Lynn Pesce
ASSOCIATED WITH
<u>L</u> is for love, lost and lonely.
<u>U</u> is for unfolding, unfair, and
 ugly.
<u>N</u> is for never, nothing, and nods.
<u>G</u> is for goodness, gracious, and God.

<u>C</u> is for caring, concerned, and
 confused.
<u>A</u> is for air and anger, but still time to amuse.
<u>N</u> is for nearness, naught, and nigh.
<u>C</u> is for countless, coping, and cries.
<u>E</u> is for empty, endless, and
 enduring.
<u>R</u> is for relief, ready, and reassuring!

Lynn Pesce
MOMA SHORT VISIT
Moma, you came and you left.
We laughed and we wept.
One week spent together so quickly it passed.
Clinging tightly to each other, right till the last

So glad that you came, but knowing you'd leave.
I stood off to the side, not wanting to grieve.
And my love and need for you is so much,
It's hard to say goodbye and not let my heart touch.

I'm happy I have you, for you are my pride.
And I know I'll be lost if ever you died.
Thank God that we have you and not another.
For you'll always be "My Loving Mother."

Lynn Pesce
LIFE GOES ON
Once I had a heart that was filled with love so true.
But when things fell apart, I knew that we were thru.
Left with two baby boys, my world tumbled down.
Taking away all their joys, no daddy to be around.

Picking up the pieces, I decided to go on.
Ironing out the creases, just to get along.
Stepping in the saddle, to do the best

I can,
Facing an uneasy battle, dared not to be damned.

Setting my goals high, I give it all I've got.
Time proves to fly by, loosening up the knot.
Still heartaches come, when I lay down at night.
Thinking of my sons, I've got to win the fight.

Home, school, work, and play, I divide up my time.
At the end of the day, thoughts still crowd my mind.
But, then morning comes, and all confusion disappears.
Kissed and loved by each son, we'll make it thru the years!

Lynn Pesce
GOLDEN ANNIVERSARY
You've spent fifty years of a golden life.
Not just as man and woman, but as husband and wife.
You've traveled a road not many can keep.
Even at times when it seemed too steep.
With crises and fears that came your way,
You've stood by each other, thru every day.
How wonderful the love you have for each other.
Like a kindling fire, no one could smother.
You're content and older, yet much wiser too,
And look at the children God's given to you.
The hurt and the joy of watching them grow,
With children of their own, the seeds you have sown.
Yet the memories we all have, not printed on a page,
Will grow in our mind and our hearts as time passes with age.
You've guided and taught, and the love's planted deep,
It's no wonder your beauty has made some weep.
Fifty years is a long time to spend with each other,
Thank God for you both, "Dad and Mother."

Lynn Pesce
WITH LOVE AND UNDERSTANDING
When you came into my life, I thought all troubles had ended.
But I have faults and you have faults, and someone has to do the mending.
I searched my mind and thought I'd learned, but somewhere someone had failed.
I'd give in, and at times I'd fight, but life must go on to no avail.

I was there and so were you, and yet we have the boys.
Time was, I thought, we'd all had learned, some day we'd reap with with joy!
One has the sun, one has the moon, the rainbow lights the sky.
But still we search and hope to find, that certain happiness that lights the eye.

"It's not easy," they all say, "to start a life brand-new."
And yet I remember when we met, your eyes and smiles, erased the blue!
You stood strong at the first, and faithfully I stood by you.
The world could come to an end, "Oh, how my love had grew!"

But then you grew, and I grew, "What happens to a person then?"
It seems you go your way—and I let my thoughts of love grow thin.

I'll stand by you to the end, for I really love you so.
But how can we go on and on, if you won't let it show?
And so, my heart aches with pain, to see us struggle so,
Not at life, just itself, but for the love we owe.

The little boys, they love you so, and honey, I do too!
But, it's as hard for me to be a mother, as it is a father, for you.

James Stone
RAINBOW
On the roof in the sky and sometimes in your eyes.
Rainbow of colors of our heart, and some will
make a start. As these great colors.
Come together when are the stars to make our
dream.
As each rainbow brings this festival and may
bring our eyes full of joy.
Rainbow is one of God's great creations as you look out your window and see. This, maybe a dream will come at the end of your rainbow.

Phyllis E Strickler
JUST BECAUSE
"Just Because" when I first met you,
I loved you right away,
And "Just Because" you loved me, too,
We gave our hearts away.

"Just Because" we've stayed together,
loving through the years,
"Just Because" we've kept each other strong, through sorrow, pain and tears.

"Just Because" I thought about you
when I had the chance to pause,
I had to send sweet flowers, and say
"I love you . . . Just Because."

Debra Davis
BATTLE OF WINE
All these emotions inside
The aging in the bottle
A fine wine in the back of the cellar
The pain of quality forgotten
To think of the stages of growth and handling
I went through to become what I am
Smooth is my taste
Strong is my power
I can ease your mind
Warm you inside
It takes a good wise man to accept
and respect this wine for what I am
Handle with care
Cherish the flavor
One day I will be found
Forever celebrated.

Susan Doyle
REFLECTIONS THROUGH A PICKET FENCE
Suspended in the mind . . .
Yet out of reach of gentle hands
Lies the beauty of our yesteryear.
A simpler time. A life less hectic.

Now Grandma's caring is out of reach,
And Mother's working on the job.

Remember the table laden for the family meal,
Homespun cooking and chitter chat.

Linen & laundry blew dry in the sun.
Mothers milk flowed thru newborn lips.

Problems were shared when listening ears
Were heavy with concentration.

Men raised hats in respect to women;
Children held adults in high esteem.

Bygone days of love and laughter . . .
When loyalty lasted & friends were true.
We know what we've lost, but not how to regain
A life that is simple, pleasing & plain.

Brian R Doyle
OLD MEN ON THE WHARFS
I remember . . .
When I was young.
There was always the old man
sitting at the wharf.
We would shout for his stories,
until he finally nodded.
And he would tell us tales of the
worlds we never saw.

I remember . . .
He spoke of places . . .
"The Land of the Rising Sun,"
or "The Misty Isles of the Aegean,"
of places, where mountains towered
higher than skyscrapers;
And oceans so deep, those very mountains
could disappear without a trace.

I remember . . .
How I listened to those stories
with a frantic fervor.
How they became a part of me.
How I lived for the days I would
see these wonders.

I remember . . .
The tears in my mother's eyes,
The anger in my father's voice.
But I heeded them not,
for no matter what they said or did,
I knew I would go.
Go, to seek the dreams of the old man.

I remember . . .
The disappointment . . .
The heartbreaking disappointment.
"The Land of the Rising Sun" was filled with people and buildings.
Such that the sun would not rise,
but rather, sneak through the clouds,
to avoid the humanities.

And "The Misty Isles" were not misty;
Just fogbound volcanic rocks.
The people of the ports did not
welcome me without their hands
outstretched.

I remember . . .

After many years of sailing, drinking, and living a meager existence . . . I retired.
I returned to my childhood paradise.
To the wharf; the wharf of my dreams.
I sat there, staring at the sea,
Hating it for the life it had offered me.

Breaking my reverie,
I noticed children gathering about me.
"Where have you been to?" they ask.
"Everywhere," I reply.
"Tell us a story," they cry out.
I looked at them, each and everyone,
(hoping that "I" was not among them.)
They shouted now, for a story.
Then I would not . . .
And I would tell the tales of the world we never saw . . .

Mabel B Guidry
COSMIC COLLISION
The sky looks down
On you and me.
You are the bright star
Of the everlasting.
I am the dark cloud
Of gloom.
You are the rainbow
Of promise.
I am the storm of regret.
If we should ever merge
Great will be the explosion.
And all will be one
In the fire of undrestanding.

Jessie Daraskavich
SUNSET SONG
When the sun is slowly sinking
Sinking in the Golden West
It is then I'm always thinking
Of the one I love the best.

Then it is my heart goes soaring
To a breathless, endless height,
While the moonlight, o'er me
pouring,
Heralds the fast falling night.

Memories come back to haunt me,
Of the days we used to know,
Days when love's own radiant blossom
E'er defied the coming snow;

But the wild winds chilled it,
killed it,
Leaving nothing, by the way
But the wasted, withered blossom—
Loath to face another day.

Oh, yon pale moon, shining softly,
Over hill and plain and sea
Tell him I am dreaming, dreaming
Of the love that used to be.

Janet E Davis
THE RAINBOW
Reaching for the rainbow, you see it slip away.
And yet you see it shimmering somewhere far away.
The portal of the sun and the threshold of the moon.
Are there really Rainbow?
Or are they just our dreams.
You see your illusive shadow shift and weave into the scene.
A never ending picture of changing colored dreams.

Frances Johnson Dooley
THEY NEED TO KNOW
Babies conceived in love, lust or rape,
It matters not, to God each one is great.
So precious this life from the moment of birth,
They need to know there's love on this earth.

Little children with eyes in a wide stare,
Look around to see who's there to care.
Some crying and standing so all alone,
They need to know they have a home.

Teenagers roaming and playing a game,
On the streets where no one has a name.
Each one aching so much to be told,
They need to know love warms up the cold.

Yes, please, they need to know,
Tell them they have a place to go.
Someone tell them they are not a mistake,
Their life does count and they are just great!

Hall Elliott
I WANT NO PYRAMID
Build for me no marble monument
And weep at no wailing wall,
Send no sick-sweet flowers of mourning
Nor wear any widow's weeds,
I want no pyramid.

For what's left is only dross to be set to rot in a tree or slipped over the side to feed the sea or burned to ashes and scattered free;
I want no pyramid.

Debbie S Duffy
MISSING YOU
On the verge of tears,
eyes swollen with pain
like thunderclouds
erupting up
to let loose rain.
Stormy skies
hidden
behind my eyes
reflect
all the sorrow
and pain
I so often blame
on missing you.

Debbie S Duffy
KINETIC FERVOR
Hues of yellow,
orange
and
ardent red
surrounding
the incandescent
solar ring
extends such
lustrous light.
Shining like
brilliant fingers
reaching, poking
through
tangled branches,
dividing
its warmth
from
multitudinous miles
above
appears
miraculously effortless
of this
exigent creation.

Jean Sampson Glasgow
SEMINOLE CHIEFTAIN
Reverently, respectfully - alone, I went to the Seminole home of Governor Brown to offer homage to a great Seminole.
The house had burned.
The well house had fallen.
The spring still fed the valley.
A solitary copperhead slithered
through a crack in the sandstone bier.
The area was permeated with history.

I gathered wild Indian Paint Brush, Clematis and Painted Daisies placing them on the graves of Governor Brown and his loved ones.

I offered prayers of peace to the Great Spirit and turned to each of The Four Winds with respect and bowed to Mother Earth.

A cardinal feather floated down from a great white oak.
A blue bird sang out his approval, a mockingbird replied.
Butterflies danced around my outstretched arms in appreciation.
The Sun God smiled, whispering warm winds held me close.
My ritual was complete.

Indian quiet with respect for those who were here before me - I left the peace of nature and all things natural - returning to the rush of concrete.

June Beth Stevens
TRUE LOVE
When we give to the work of the Kingdom
We see man's efforts excel,
As we give our offerings back to God
Then we have learned our lesson well.

He blesses us with what we have
We should give so all will know,
That little drop in the bucket
Will cause the bucket to overflow.

When Jesus looked at the rich man
He said, "Sell what thou hast, and come follow me,"
But he went away sorrowfully
For he loved his riches, you see.

When we die we can't take anything with us
But we can send our treasures ahead,
By doing the things Jesus taught us
Before He was resurrected from the dead.

If you truly want to be happy
Finding the joy which comes from above,
Then Love your neighbor as yourself
And you will find true love.

Margaret (Pegi) Cassone
TODAY
. . . Good morning today!
What will you bring me, what have you got planned?
Will the weather be cloudy and raining, or
sunny and grand?
Am I all together? Let me take a moment to check—
Can I see, hear, talk, feel and stand?
Yes I can! Yes I can!

I will take another moment now to thank the
creator of today—

And to ask for the wisdom and gentleness of heart to walk through his day!

It will be a busy day, this day, and I might not have another moment to spare, so I will try to stay aware of the miracle of this day—

For it will never, no never, reappear. This day has gone by quickly, more quickly than I thought.

It is time to reflect and give thanks
for what it has brought.

I'm tired now, I will rest, close my eyes and say;
Good night Lord! Good night Today!

Margaret (Pegi) Cassone
FOR I LOVE YOU
I can and I will;
Send you a flower a day,
To keep all the hurts and pains away.

I can and I will;
Send you a star a night,
To keep away your fear and fright.

I can and I will;
Send angels into your dreams,
So that nothing will appear to be as
Bad as it seems.

I can and I will;
Put happy faces on all the sad hearts you love,
So that you will be lifted on the wings of a dove.

All this I can and will do, if you ask me,
All this I can an d will do, for I love you,
I can and I will . . . won't you let me?

Susan Rickerl
MOTHER'S BIRTHDAY
Just as God made a promise
through the symbolization
of a rainbow.
My mother's promise is through
the love of her heart.
Her eyes are the passageway
to her caring soul.
Saying "Here I am my child!"
She comforts you with
the warmth of her arms.
Wrap around, and hear
the softness of words
The beauty of my mother's voice
When she sings a lullaby.
Oh, how the soil she nurtures
surrounds the growth of my
mother's offsprings.
Yes, she is beautiful!
Just like the rainbow,
which lights up the sky.
My mother's promise through
the love of her heart.

Kari Shields
NEVER LEAVE, MY FRIEND
You've always been here,
through thick and thin;
now you're leaving me . . .
a bittersweet end.

You've watched me grow
I've watched you, too;
You have been there for me;
through and through.

I know you hurt,
and feel great pain;
why let you suffer,
for my selfish gain?

Please watch over me;
keep me in your sight.
Leave your spirit with me
to watch me at night . . .
I'll love you always . . .

Arthur F Kennedy
PHANTOM STIMULI
In the land of 99 spiraled castles and crystals springs
where zephyrs disturb not platinum flowers a phantom voice sings,
in antiphonal speech deeper than gold
or oil osmosis sweeping thru the stocks or rose and
rhododendron flowing admonishing
us that no earthly beauty will last
forever lest we grow weary
Strike like a Lucite dart
Relentlessly into my heart.
Pity me not that my lady no longer
looks on me with love!
with cane, wrinkled hand and a
bedroom slipper for a shoe
I will still continue to harvest beauty
from any ground.
I'll pity you if you don't realize that
it can be found
The lovely fingers of delight
Caress and hold me yet still tight,
In the features of another line by line
will be found another lady love of mine
To blaze before me as wild and vivid
as when I was a child
No grape that grows on any vine
produce a wine
as sweet as thirst, Believe you me!
No fruit of any tree as delicious as want.

Jamal Sekou' Wright
RED

This poem is dedicated to Byron & Vicky Wright, my loving parents. They both have been a great inspiration in my life. I Love you both very much.

Red is heat in the house.
Red is sundown.
Red is fire.
Red is angry feeling I get when my parents yell at me.
When red blood drips down my leg
I feel like I'm going to scream.
The BMW with tinted windows, windshield wipers on the headlights, and a big stereo system, that I saw downtown, was Red.
Red is a stoplight, too.
Red is a candle glowing through a pumpkin.

Iva May Sharp
WOES OF A TEENAGER

My parents and teachers give me advice
Keep yourself free from any vice
No smoking, to drugs just say no
Dirty dancing will have to go

At fifteen I'm too young to drive
With hard school lessons I have to strive
I hate "You're grounded, go to your room."
Seems like eleven o'clock will be my doom.

If I'm going to be late I have to call
I never am supposed to drink alcohol.
I can't go out on a date alone
Until my parents think that I am grown.

But the worst thing that has happened to me,
And I am sure that you will agree
Today while I was out with other teens
Mom patched all the holes in my new blue jeans

Linda Paterek Scott
THE BIRTHDAY PRESENT

A birthday party!
What should I take?
I had no idea,
Someone else got a cake.

Clothes or games,
Which should it be?
I don't know!
Don't ask me!

But, it wasn't easy,
ideas came and went.
Then I finally found it,
The perfect present!

Christine Schuckmann
OUR LIFE IS LIKE A GRAIN OF SAND

Our Life is like a grain of sand, so different, so unique. In passing through life's corridors of time, moving swiftly or obscure, depends upon your outlook, either outrageous or demure!

For man throughout the ages be, as noble as a King who cares of His subjects daily affairs or as cruel as Hitler in His quest to eliminate all the rest of Love and Kindness, there now be, for all of eternity!

For President or King, Man or Child, Time will not stand still, so we must use our time wisely before we are buried under the Hill.

Our Life is like a grain of sand, how quickly does it pass, and once it's gone, there is no second chance! I pray you heed my voice today, before Dear God calls me away, leaving you behind, in the corridor of time.

Our future life depends today, on actions made in careless haste, not to worry you hear the cry, man will survive, but will he truly be alive?

The quality of life depends on you, Noble or Child though you be, for Earth's Treasures can surely slip away, like the sun at end of day. So heed my warning one and all for life is like a grain of sand, helpless and small.

Kimberly Schmid
CAPTURED BY A FRIEND

As the sun rises to warm the day
A shimmering glimpse of you is here in every way
Though I long to greet your face with the morning
The sunny skies look down on me with warning

Yet my inquisitive mind is craving the mysterious you
Like that of a soaring eagle grasping at the skies of blue
And unknowing if the feat will be accomplished
The eagle and I will be one in the same astonished

While I have watched the petals of a blossoming rose
In depths of nature as nobody knows
And on the ground lies each petal dealt
With expression in fantasy of how your lips felt

Like the mighty changing winds in a storm
I long for our faded visions to take form
And to search for a silver lining at rainbow's end
I will come to discover a newborn friend

As the sun turns into the lonely night
With a silent tear and a burning fight
I try to capture the memory of the beauty within you
And pray that you and I reunite again soon

Kimberly Schmid
A QUIET QUEST

Dedication: To all of the people who inhabit this tiny planet because I believe we should not take for granted today what could be gone tomorrow.

I try to visualize this earth in harmony and stillness
But all that inhabit are not calm or gracious
Yet we crave for the bounty to save us again
As the skies turn into nightfall when rest will deepen

All the colorful butterflies bring joy to the heart
Because we all see a need for that prism to become a part
Of our grayest days that appear to go on forever
Yet we do not allow the sadness to become a tool that will sever

The greet vibrant grass beneath our feet
Which we take for granted but still we weep
When it is taken away by the bitter snow
That will soon vanish and allow our young to grow

When I think of the many creations on this earth
There has to be a meaning behind each for there is worth
Like the redness in the rose that symbolizes love
And the white purity of peace that is sought in a dove

We now need to search into the depths of ourselves
To become one in the same as we begin to delve Into all the creations that possess the
Aire of mystery
And to discover their meaning will lead us into history

Kimberly Schmid
LION AND LIONESS

Dedication: To my loving parents; thank you for allowing me to discover myself. Your wisdom has been the stepping-stone.

The finest thing in life that my eyes have gazed upon in wonderment
Have to be a couple, lion and lioness
That walk hand in hand upon this earth in content
Still aware that they have given to me
The most treasured thing one can possess
So how do you possibly express gratitude to one
When one cannot comprehend the silence of a caress?
But when one language fails
Does this create a barrier of disillusionment?
Or shall we seek for different tongues
To communicate the message that longs to be sent?
And when the barrier has been diminished by the call of stillness
We come to realize that language is universal no matter how tedious
And like the Rocky Mountains that long to be climbed by the inhabitants
Faith will grant us the strength to climb
To the height of love so we may prance
And then the voices of harmony will echo throughout the canyon together
For the message of love has been spoken
To the finest thing my eyes have gazed upon
My father and mother's love for me

Mary Palatucci Salerno
MEMORIES OF THE WIND

For my father who lives in the hearts he left behind.

Beloved father -
Time does not ease my saddened heart
I miss you more and more
And when I look upon a deep red rose
I see your smiling face
And pause to brush away a tear
Remembering your kind and gentle voice
Your old familiar step
The warmth of your tender care
And the shared happiness
Of a yesterday forever lost
When God called you to his Hills of Home
And I grieve for all the lonely tomorrows
without the man I was so proud to call "my father."

And when upon the whispering wind
I hear - "remember me"
My memories stray into a vanished past
And I use God's gift of memory
Wherein they linger on and on
And lapse in reverie
In a cherished time remembered
In a home that is no more
But these fleeting moments of reflection
Are much too swiftly spent
And in a breeze all quickly swept from view
To once again become just dim and fading
Memories on the wind.

Rebecca Danielle Russell
MY WINDOW

I sat by my window and looked out at the sky,
I saw a little bird as it flew by.
It flew to a tree to feed its young,
Just like my mom took care of me.
Now I'm older and tend to myself,
But those little birds can't be by themselves.
My mom has took care of me day by day,
But now I'm older and it's time to move away.
Just like those birds who now can fly,
I can watch them as they go by.

Belinda Rickman
A FRIEND

There are times that you'd want to share,
But find there is nobody there.
You go from one to another,
Then you think there is no other.

At the time you think no one cares,
There is One that your burdens He did bear.
He has love for everyone,
Who is He? God's only Son!

He loves us so much,
All you need is His touch.
He's there with you always,
In the big ways and small ways.

He walked miles and miles in His ministry,
For the Pharisees and Sadducees, you and me.
He is no respecter of person,
In that, I am well certain.

He is one that sticks closer than a brother,
You will not find, no not one, not another.
Because if you need a friend,
Just turn to Jesus, on Him, you can depend.

C A Price "Caprice"

C A Price "Caprice"
TRUE LOVE
caprice, '82

True love has many faces,
Sweetheart, my friend, my son.
'Tis found in various places,
In art, life's work, in fun.
Sweet love's most fragile blessings,
Not won with toil or fear,
Live long—endure forever,
Through time's most fretful year.
True love calls out his manhood,
Brute strength, strong will, yet good,
He watches over his household,
And fetches in the wood.
She cuddles close their babies,
In life's most tender years.
She smooths away his hurt spots,
And kisses all their tears.

Jerome Peterson
MARRIAGE
Time passes so quickly
Holidays come and go
Marriage can last a lifetime
By a man and woman who know
Trust, forgiveness and love
Must be written on the heart
To endure the strength of selfishness
That can rip a marriage apart!

John D Odell
CURIOSITY
Brute curiosity destroyed the cat
And conned our Eve to risk the devilish bite.
An apple fell on Newton's head and that
Forced Isaac's disciplined, profound insight
To calculus, as numerous as sand.
Columbus braved the dark, forbidding sea
For India and found instead new land,
The humbling touch of serendipity.

What is this force called "Curiosity,"
A force so strong man's ingenuity
Discovers energies with scarce controls
That in the end could make him out a fool?
In mind's detesting allkind's sorry plight,
Darks holes—it is spirit seeking for the light.

Barbara O'Brien
WINGS
The journey would not be easy,
but I knew I had to try.
It was the road I had to walk,
before I could learn to fly.

My journey would not be easy,
but rough roads never are.
I just didn't really think,
this road was quite so far.

The miles don't seem to stop,
the road has been so long.
I'm getting tired of walking now,
but where did I go wrong?

I thought if I kept walking,
the road would finally end.
I would receive my set of wings,
and then I could ascend.

But at the end of the road,
there was nothing but sand and stone.
No way of getting my wings to fly,
but just simply, traveling alone.

Barbara O'Brien
THE SOUL AND THE STORM
The storm has finally subsided,
and the rain patters gently onto the sill.
A feeling of melancholy has possessed me,
while the world seems to stand still.

The birds begin to chirp outside,
even though it's quiet where I lie.
The wind howls softly through my window,
as a tear rolls from my eye.

As sweet are the sounds of nature,
my mind and soul are not at peace.
For the sounds of nature cannot console me,
nor make me feel complete.

The void within, grows every day,
like the grass grows with rain.
But until the mind and soul have been nurtured,
only then, can they be one in the same.

Ruth B Anderson
MAJESTIC RIVER
The majesty of the river's flow takes one away from the con and the pro, moments of concentration as to the river's role, one forgets trials and thinks of the soul.

Just how it became so deep and so wide, it must have help, constantly by its side, from small tributaries, it picks up its power, and reaches out to claim its width by the hour.

The rocks on the bottom of the river's bed, 'twas nature's way of looking ahead, to form the ripples and create a sound; puts a hush! hush! on other noises around.

The ripples form colors all of their own, especially when exposed to the rays of the sun, for lovers of nature, it remains on the scene; outshines anything to be seen on the screen.

It rolls on its way, empties itself in the sea, leaving new ripples, singing a tune constantly, it's not there for its sound and its beauty, it seems so cognizant of still another duty.

It cradles canoes and dozens of boats--which gather fish of all kinds and ably totes the catch to the bank, a sport high on the ladder of rank.

Besides the pride one finds in the catch of a fish; it also when cooked, makes a palatable dish, so roll on Mr. River, in your usual way; you bring solace and grandeur to anyone's day.

Marjorie Avant
THE NATURAL BORN TRUTH
When you find yourself in doubt, instead of trying to figure it out, tell the truth—my mother said; The Natural Born Truth.

If your heart's bigger than your head, if upon arising in the morning you surely dread, tell the truth my brother, The Natural Born Truth. What good deed did you do today Was it perfectly honest, would you say? Did you reach out to help someone in need, or just shrug your shoulder and bid them Godspeed? Just tell the truth, The Natural Born Truth. No one is perfect that we can see . . . we are forever changing to all that we can be. But where we run into trouble as you will surely find, that truth will outrun a lie any old time. So be cautious, beware of what you might say. Don't let it be held against you on that Judgment Day. Tell the truth, The Natural Born Truth, until the very end. You will be the wiser, the happier for it, I kid you not, my friend, for truth brings freedom from all fears, for once you start a lie, you'll lie again, again and again. So tell the truth, my sister, The Natural Born Truth.

Kathy Bates
DREAMS

To Gary, with love from the heart.

Walking along the shore, I dreamed of footsteps in the sand.
Wishing for my baby and me to be there hand in hand.
Thinking of a time our love ran so deep, like the water in the ocean and the fish in the sea. Listening to the rhythm of the waves on the beach, how beautiful the sound of my baby's voice is to me.

Our love is everlasting and that's the way it should be, for God sent us together . . . me to you, you to me. A very special feeling that grows deep down inside, the love I feel for you is higher than the skies!

Woman was created from the rib of man, to be by their side and walk hand in hand. Love, honor and cherish with love that's so pure, a love that's everlasting forever we'll endure. Where there's love, peace and happiness there's an everlasting joy that will last through eternity for richer or for poorer. Dreams are like wishes, they sometimes come true, and as long as we're together, all I need is you!

Glinnie J Albrecht Berry
"SHALOM", HAVE A "JOY-FILLED" CHRISTMAS
May the joys of heaven,
spread thru out your home;
Like the working of a leaven,
and touch all, where'er you roam:
All through this beautiful season,
celebrating the Holy birth;
God's Son, who bro't such love;
Quite beyond human reason!
Such love came, to this place called Earth;
And "He" heals the crushed, and broken hearts;
Ere so gently, as a dove.
When He heals the bruised, all hurt departs.
All the Heavenly Hosts above:
Still sing praises, for "His Great Love!"
If all mankind shall fail,
to praise His Holy name:
The very rocks, on path and trial,
shall SHOUT! "He is King," they'll proclaim!
O'er all Heaven, and the Earth:
"He" does reign!
This Holy One, A JEW, of lowly birth?

Don Bishop
DUDE TO DUDE—BEHIND BARS
You'll never know all the things I've been,
I don't need a fair-weather friend,
a wanna be or a has-been.
You can expect the same thing too,
no matter what I say or do.
I don't like fakes and/or growing old
only knowing things that'll make me grow.
Times I go back into my shell and another comes along and wants through, Hell
only time will tell, we know that's true.

I can be wrong or so can you.
Maybe it's this place,
or just the pace, but you're easy to talk to and easy to face.
Nothing will do if I don't know
if you know how I feel about you!
No we ain't gay, that's true; for friendship like this has only one way.
Now that; I give to you and expect no less.

Bryan Thomas Benetti
LIFE
Life is fun.
Life is sad.
Life makes you mad.
And in life things die.
So the only one I can turn to is God, God, God.

Barnarr Cannon
HOMELESS IS THE WIND
I follow the wind o'er sea and foam,
I followed the wind to seek its home.
High on the heights where the eagles soar,
Deep in the depths of a canyon floor,
I still followed the wind until I could follow no more.
Then I heard the wind whisper in a soft voice like a moan,
Never ever follow the wind for the wind hasn't a home.

Don Collins
IT'S YOU I LOVE MOST OF ALL

I'm dedicating this to the mother of my children.

It's you I love the most of all,
Whether it's summer, winter or fall.

I love you more than words can say,
And it grows stronger day by day.

To me you mean something more,
Than anyone has ever before.

You will be mine, I hope someday,
If God above gives me my way.

Then we'll grow old together dear,
And then we'll part and shed a tear.

We'll meet again up there somewhere,
Together again, our love to share.

We won't grow old as we did before,
For time will last forevermore.

I hope and pray all this be true,
And you love me as I love you.

Rita Verma
REBIRTH
Darkness sullenly closed his eyelids,
as the pyre of a long day slowly
burned away.
The ashes sighing,
watched the intimate moment from
dawn to dusk.
Clocks ticked away,
as shadows diminished with night.

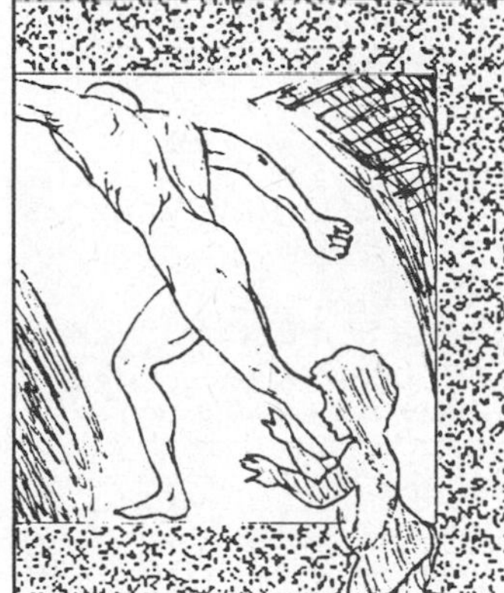

Memories echoed afar
with the howling wind,
of a child to a boy,
a boy to a man,
he left no choice but to sleep.
Eyes closed to hide their guilt,
but opened to know of only
innocence.
Churning passions, endless struggles,
joyous, angry and sorrowful
thoughts,
all whispered away as dawn called
upon us.
Awakening, all had been left trapped
in the past moment,
to mingle in the air.
Cleansed we felt the cool breeze,
sting the wetness of our flesh.

Linda Mackin Clark
LIFE'S WINDOW

To my mom, dad, family and friends, whose positive impressions have become the stepping-stones of my life.

I look through the windows of this
life,
And what do I see but the anger and
strife,
Of a world full of anguish, pain and
woe
Where no one seems quite certain
which way to go.
Where sometimes no one seems to
care
And sometimes forgets you are even
there.
People are hungry, starving, and in
pain—
Where most of the people are
thinking of gain.

Not all people are sad and so alone
For some are happy and content at
home,
Loving their families and are at their
best,
Trying so hard to pass life's tests.
Through what kind of window do
your friends see you?
Are you always faithful, honest and
true?
Do they see your courage, happiness,
and your success?
Or do they see a person who has quit
the test?
So be an active example and not in
limbo,
And let the sun shine through your
life's window.

Linda Mackin Clark
MY HEART'S REVELATION
If I should search
God's great world through
I would never find another,
My dear, like you.

God knew my wishes
And heard from Above,
So I know He sent you
For me to love.

You're my kind of sweetheart,
With qualities untold.
To me you're a treasure
More precious than gold.

I hope your love for me
Is as honest and true,
As this love I hold
My darling, for you.

I'll always hold you
Dear to my heart,
And hope it's God's will
That we never part.

This poem was written when I was eleven years old. It was written to the man I have been married to for almost twenty-nine years. We were childhood sweethearts and later married when I was only fifteen, and he was seventeen.

Linda Mackin Clark
THE LEGACY
What can I leave behind, she often
thought,
To tell others of the battle she had
fought.
To encourage others in this life here
below
And to show others the way that they
might know
The meaning of happiness,
contentment and love
That comes from serving the "one"
up above.

She was often denied, criticized and
rejected
And the inner self was seldom
detected.
She made many errors, often
stumbled and fell,
But was gently picked up by the
"one" she knew well.
She pressed on with such a great
determination,
To leave a positive mark in God's
great creation.

Take those good bits and pieces of
everyone you see
And put them together, so that a
better person you might be.
Mold them and shape them into a
Christ-like image,
So that you can leave a legacy that
others can't damage.
Always let your life be honest,
faithful and true
And one day great rewards will come
back to you.

She may not have continually done
what she should
But may her epitaph be known and
understood,
That always "She hath done what she
could."

Charlotte C Ross
THE FALL OF LIFE
Do you feel, hear, and sense it?
The coming of autumn leaves bit
By frosty lips of early cold,
Reminders that we, too, are getting
old.

As earth strews its fallen leaves
We collect our cup of dreams,
Colorful as fall's brazen show,
We clutch, hoping to stop the flow.

Change we must, as do the trees,
No stopping time, even on our knees.
So discard thoughts of all things sad,
And let the autumn of life be glad!

Louise Burk
THE GAME YOU WON
Well, I guess you've won the game,
If anyone was keeping score.
The day finally came,
When you didn't love me anymore.

I guess I could have seen the signs,
If I had known where to look.
I'd never have thought I'd end up
with a broken heart.
Not in a million years.
I just didn't know where to start.
There's no one here to dry my tears.

I sure feel like I'm falling apart,
With nothing to do but drum up old
memories,
When our love was new and we said
we'd never part.
I don't want to let myself believe,
There's nothing left, except maybe in
my fantasies.

To me nobody wins the game,
But I'll just keep on believing,
That someone might come along,
And make my life worth living.

Tonya Bennett
HE
Who is he who walks down with she,
Running his fingers through his hair
Oh he is such a flair in my heart.

When he walks down the street
He talks at the time as a single
heartbeat

With his lips like fire, his eyes like
the sea,
He whispers in my ear something that
makes my heart beat.

He speaks in a gentle voice,
His touches are like feathers
He says goodbye, I'll see you later.
It seems like forever.

May Abboud
THERE BEHIND THE HILLS
There behind the hills
is a soul and a breeze.
There behind the memories
is the image of my love.
There behind the past
is an old love . . .
coloured with old wine.
There in the midst of the universe
in the darkness of the night
is love . . .
drawn on the board of time.
Behind the hills
a lamp . . .
Behind the memories
a beautiful house.
Behind the past
a story of my first love
. . . forgotten . . . !!!

Tammy Anderson
NEW BEGINNINGS
The grass is green, the sky is blue,
The winter's cold is almost through.
Life coming alive is what I see,
All around me I see the world's
beauty.
Birds and bees flying all through the
air,
Flowers growing, kept alive with
great care.
I see the birth of a brand-new day,
Now I look at life in a different way.
My life has changed like I knew it
would,
I made the change my friends said I
could.
At first I didn't think that it could be
done,
Now I see that life can really be fun!

Wayne Mayfield Hoaglund
GOD CARES
God has made me happy
and kept me through the nite.
He assured me this morning
that things would be all right.
He will guide me through the day
and hear my solemn prayer.
Give me peace and contentment
and tell me his love is there.
So people heed my warning
and always say your prayers.
He will also watch over you
and you know he's there.

Timothy B Wilder

Timothy B Wilder
WHY DIE IN VAIN?

To: Humanity. Unless we can and do constantly seek and find ways and means to do a better job; unless we accept the challenge of the changing times; we have no right to survive and we shall not survive . . .

I was young, in sin and on a spree;
in search of some type of identity,
determined to control the elements of
my very soul. I deprived my own
self
of exchanging error for truth,

and fell into the grips of unjust abuse.

My billows came upon me like changes and moods, placing within me many dog-eat-dog attitudes. Then for several years at the least, I was highly attacked by the beast.

I became peculiar to suffering, oppressed and tormented, by all the elements that old Satan presented. I was a searcher, anti-adequate or wrong, caught in a system where I did not belong. You Know: The Thunder blasted, Lightning all around me I saw, those weird midnight hours began to withdraw, then a strong, still voice cried out, why die in vain? for if you shall die this night, you shall not live again.

I began to stall until I got a clue, Lord, this is the warning that I had gotten from you. So what; if you've had hardships and pains, but that's no reason why you should 'Die in vain' What happened to you, it happened to me first, but you can believe I caught it the worst.

I gave up my life that you might be free, and I did it all by way of Calvary. This was my life's darkest hours, as I begun to seek, that place of Worship where I could Study, Learn and Speak.

Oh; I searched and I searched, but I could not find a place of Praise worth all of my time. I looked Childishly and Religiously wondering, what must I do, then the answer came, Lord I knew it was you. I just could not believe it, I fell all apart, trying to figure this strangeness, bounded in my heart.

Jesus; I shall never, ever forget that name, that saved me from dying a death in vain, and directed me to a Church, a place that God had appointed and bestowed upon me the blessing of the anointed. Now free from sin I walk at large, the savior's blood my full discharge, at his dear feet my soul I lay, a sinner saved and homage pay.

He that loses his life for my sake shall be at a total gain, so be very, very careful, and don't (DIE IN VAIN)

Timothy B Wilder

SPINNING LIKE A WHIRLWIND

Spinning, Spinning, Spinning, from God's Holy Hands
Mighty, Mighty, Mighty, Mighty hard for one to understand.

High and Lifted up, This Ancient of Days
Crown of Sovereignty, in so many ways.

Spinning, Spinning, Spinning, a Crown; Embroidered with stones,
Far above Diamonds, and Rubies,
What one Man can own
Symbol of Dignity, High and Lifted Up of Victories,
Inscription of Holiness, God's Gift to Me.

Blazing and Burning, A Consuming Fire—
Illuminated by the Holy Ghost, What one can Desire
Spinning, Spinning, Spinning, from God's—Holy Throne
Receiving My Crown of Victory,
That God used to Own.

An Heir of Salvation, Jesus my Friend—
Lord of Greatest Splendor, Like that of a Whirlwind.
Spinning, Spinning, Spinning, Saved from Hell and the Grave,
Down, Down, Down, "Jesus" came,
Yes; I am the One that He Saved.

Without Restrictions, Show Honor, Love and Trust,
If You want Your Crown, then Salvation's a must.
Pick up Your Cross, Never, Never to lay it Down—
And it will come Spinning, Spinning, Spinning; Thank God,

For My Crown . . .

Timothy B Wilder

IN THE FACE OF COUNTLESS DANGERS:

In the face of countless dangers,
disaster strikes the earth,
and you may be a victim of violent crimes, for all that life is worth.
Panic and terror are worldwide, our neighborhoods in fear, the excess
of idleness, presents a crisis here.

Organizations from every State,
headed to stop the drugs,
many people are birds of prey,
from those that we call thugs.
In the face of countless dangers, a generation is being lost,
what a chilling, depressing sight it is,
to do violence, and not count the cost.

Stopped by the coffins, the authorities have been overwhelmed,
justice has taken a backseat, and the courts are overjammed.
So we organize to save the community and our youth,
beginning with an understanding of what we face as truth.

The report is quite devastating, the problems are getting worse,
the prisons can't hold the criminals,
nor the cemeteries the hearse.
A contagion of self-destructive behavior, a city in the midst of hell,
guilty of the sin of ingratitude, yet;
unhurried, unhindered and unassailed.

Religious Leaders needed, for I am totally enraged, that our children
are being used and abused from every age, but with out-stretched hands,
energy and commitment, we the community say no! for the druggies and pushers
have got to go. So in the face of countless dangers, I too take my stand
in the global revolution against—The Drug Pushing Man . . .

Timothy B Wilder

THE COMMON MAN

The common man whom God must love,
Is this ordinary man of worth,
He was not chief of a powerful state
Just a clergyman on this earth.

His smile bears the fragrance of goodness,
He attained liberation of heart,
Tried to give his life saving others,
Yes, the man was extremely smart.

He was highly educated and dedicated,
This man emphasized Christ,
Others had foolishly done him wrong,
But ungrudgingly, he remained so nice.

He headed no great institutions,
Just a man from Memphis, Tennessee,
Who struggled against racism,
For the sake of you and me!

Even for the world's great and famous,
To the anonymous ones he didn't know,

Fighting freedom on the Dixie battlefront,
Enduring the perils of old Jim Crow.

"Amen!" So be it, nonviolence his torch,
Until it was dropped on a Memphis porch.
Struck down by a cowardly sniper's bullet,
The common man did rise to become
a martyr of all humanity, the recipient of the Noble Peace
Prize . . .

This man, who tried to love somebody,
marched by the side of God
Nothing deterred his moral convictions,
This man—served with pride . . .

Donna J Wilson

ALL THE TIMES

If I could hold you in my arms and touch you once again,
My dreams would not only be beautiful, but they would just begin.
The times you held me in your arms,
The times that we made love,
Are just a few of the good times that I've been thinking of.
The time you held me close to you
and would not let me go,
Is just one of the times I wanted to say "that I loved you so."
But now that is all gone, and you are far away.
But in my heart there will always be a place for you to stay.

Lori Ann Hoecker

OUR WALK THAT ONE SHORT MILE

One day I gave my heart away, to someone that I love.
I knew that it would last for ever, like a match made up above.

I put my all into this love, my heart I gave in full.
But, fate took you far away, and now I feel like such a fool.

I've always been so careful to hold a little back.
To give to no one everything, for me the cards were stacked.

The very day I met you I knew my life would change, I knew I'd give you everything I knew you'd break the chain.

But, then you had to go away, I know it's better there.
But why did you have to go just now? You were an answer to my prayers.

In our time together you taught me more of love,
than all the stars in heaven or the great big moon above.

Now I'm sitting all alone in the darkness of my room.
Wondering if you will come back to brighten up my gloom.

Or should I just forget you, pretend that I don't care,
lose that time when every thought was something with you to share.

No . . . I think I'll cry just a few more tears, listen to a few sad songs
take one last look at your picture,
then drag my heart along.

Into the next stage of my life, in search for one more smile
remembering the love we shared and
OUR WALK THAT ONE SHORT MILE.

Lesel Dawson

YOUR PRESENCE AWAKENS

For the You that lets me Be, and helps me to Become.

Your presence awakens
The thoughts of my eyelids.
And there sleeps my reason,
With lonely promises
Made in painful solitude.

You slice through my words and lips and legs.
Piercing the echo of a memory
That circles the crystal edges of my mind.

My life was run by bells,
And the ticking hands on my face.
Until you dragged me into daisies,
Pouring laughter from icy jugs
On steaming afternoons.

Thank you for pulling out
The strings of my life.
Unraveling careful garments
To spiraling gypsies,
And filling
All the empty spaces,
With bouquets.

Rose L Corbacio

WHITE DOVE

O say White Dove,
Spreading your proud
White beauty, in the wind . . .
So graceful, so free
to reach the Heaven.

Beyond the sun
of Dawn's early light
You fly so free,
so full of might,

It cheers me so
to watch you fly,
My spirits rise so high . . .
Fly, fly White Dove fly . .
Ah! you give me hope
of a newborn day
You enhance our desire
to pray . . .

Fly away White Dove, O then
visit again
You build our faith,
To extremities, without end . .

Debra Ann Pettric
A LONE HEART

Thanks to my sister, Jennifer, and Mr. Fred Meleher.

When comes the mist,
Gently caressing the hills,
A soft calm mystery overtakes the heart.

When comes the rain,
Gently pelting treetops,
A sadness echoes in the heart.

When comes the harsher sleet and snow,
Grating on the earth,
A savage tale tears the heart in two.

When comes mist, rain, sleet, snow,
Then comes a beauty deep;
The wild call of nature, a lonely call to man.

Eve Bailey
A FRIEND
A friend is special,
And very rare—
When in need,
Always there.
A friend listens
Within their heart,
No matter the distance—
You're never far apart.
A special touch,
Allows the tears,
Holds the hand—
Calms the fears.
Encourages adventure,
To try something new—
A friend is interested
In being with you.
Laughs at the jokes,
Feels the pain—
A friend like this,
Is a joy to gain.

Leslie L Carroll
PINK WASTELAND

For Jean-Luc, who taught me how to love.

I remember our ranch, far back in the woods
there were trees, wolves
howled, stars shone,
The night air was so pristine.
Then a hole appeared, it endangered our existence,
our air was not fit to breathe.

We abused our planet, it's a vast wasteland now
there's no forest, wild herds,
private farms,
All stars are clouded from view.
The ghost towns of Chernobyl haunt our minds,
for we will never live there
again.

Then came the end, it was like a bad storm
there was lightning, loud
thunder, high winds,
Survivors were launched in shuttles.
We had intentionally risked all we had built,
assuming we would better our
lives.

We raced to be first, to fulfill selfish needs
there were A-bombs, acid rain,
nuclear waste,
Now our planet is pink in hue.
Will we ever regret, as we dwell on the moon,
that we left our mother, earth,
so bare?

Nancy Jones Justice

Nancy Jones Justice
PEACE OF MIND

This poem is dedicated to Jim, my creative friend

Bamboo shadows sweep the stairs
But the dust is undisturbed,
The moonlight penetrates deep into the pond,
But leaves no trace in the water.

Through openings among stems of the bamboo,
This distant village is seen.
I take it easy all day and receive no visitors,
But the pure breeze sweeps a path leading to my door.

Linda D Mead
THE TROUBLE WITH SOCIETY
It's a good relationship,
For the most part.
It's good for nurturing,
It is nurturing,
But it's not good for growing
—society wise.

It's more for just laying back,
And saying,
Oh God,
I hurt.

I sometimes imagine,
I'm ashamed to say,
That if the relationship,
would go away,
So might the pain . . .

And a new me would emerge
All ready to grow
—society wise.

Patricia A Montgomery
BLAMING
It's no disgrace to fall from grace,
unless you say
somebody pushed me . . . . .

Who's to blame for your shame?

Not you of course, you don't feel any remorse!

Although life is a journey and its course may be destiny.
Intentionally denying fault belonging to you is total immaturity.
Mastering our behaviour and accepting blame is inevitable
For everyone knows where the fault lies and denying it is pitiful.

Pitiful, because the blaming becomes endless.
Endless because it is more difficult for a deficient personality
to accept blame and consequent guilt that has usefulness.
It takes a person of integrity to acknowledge feelings so immense.
Occasionally, the guilt emotion is so intense.
This person has a higher mentality where truth is acknowledged,
not strictly selective.
They don't blame others to obstruct justice—blame is accepted,
behaviour objective.
Fault is found in themselves at its origination.
Perhaps faith and growing within themselves have procured blame's elimination.

Look within before deceiving yourself and blaming
others so you should be comforted.
Your contribution towards the problem needs to be
confronted.
Failure to accept it indicates a character hollow
inside.
Take the blame, it's no shame, eventually it will
create pride.
Pride in respecting others and of course, yourself.
Grab hold of this gift of life, truth and honesty
are worth more than wealth.

Esther Diane Armenta
ALONE, IN A TROPICAL PARADISE

To Angie, my inspiration.

Alone, in a tropical paradise
shooting snake eyes with the roll of the dice
You told me, "you better do what's best"
I told you "I might" as I headed West

Once we were made for one another
Now it's like we can't stand each other
You said long distance should do us some good
But only if both parties understood

You said try the lock and hide technique
We never felt the warmth of cheek to cheek
You said Latin beauties danced my way
But that doesn't mean I had my way
Alone in a western bar in town
I drink because you're not around
She sits beside me taking my hand
As if we're loving friends with some great plan

Back at the palm-leafed bungalow
under the shade I find I miss you so
The time of days become too long to catch
Instead I sit here keeping watch

Carol A Krommer
BIRTH IS ALWAYS
Birth is always a brilliant and
bloody business.
Months of liquid simplicity
Iris to days of pressing life,
to hours of life proving
pain.
We buy breath at the expense of innocence,
When with a love-blow and gasp
lungs fill, breathing.
Birth is a never-finished,
brilliant and bloody
business.

Cynthia Suriano
FACES

To my eternal companion Anthony without whom I'd never have had the courage to do this . . .

Of all the ghosts from years gone past,
Of all the questions yet unasked.

I look in faces for a clue, some old
And wizened, others young and new.
Behind each face a story waits,
Of lasting love or hearts that ache.
An infant in his mother's arms,
He cries for food and fears no harm.
An old man standing stooped and bent,
He wonders why his life is spent.
A woman's hair has turned to white,
Her lips they smile her eyes are bright.
A small child cries his knee is bruised,
His mother's there a kiss is used.
A young boy races on the field,
The ball is thrown his arms will yield.
Of all the ghosts from years gone past,
Of all the questions yet unasked.
Of all the faces the proud, the small,
A story waits behind them all.

Elizabeth James Rife
GOD'S MIRACLES

To my loving father, Dewey James—who is 92 years old—Thank you Daddy.

We cannot touch love
With our outstretched hand—
Yet it's so warm and real
In the hearts of man.
We cannot touch the wind
Yet we know it's there—
As it blows the lofty trees
And bows their heads in
Prayer.
The rain we feel, but we cannot see
From where it comes, or how it
Happens to be.
The snow so soft and white, as it
Covers the land—
Is all of God's beautiful and
Infinite plan.
The sea as it travels is tossed by the

wind—
But where does it start—and
Where does it end?
Like love—all of these things—we
Do not understand
But we know they are the
Miracles
God gave to man.

Rebecca Brooks
NO LONGER TOGETHER
Two people,
Two hearts,
Two halves,
Of each.

Two kisses,
Two hands,
Two footprints
Behind.

Too different,
Two lives,
Two vows,
Two cries.

Too far,
Away,
Too gone,
You stay.

Melissa Mullins
FATHER'S SMILE

This poem is dedicated to the memory of my late father, Jerry Mullins.

Father's Smile is special to me;
It's soft & so dear & precious, you see;
It cheers me up when I am blue;
If you saw it, you would think so, too.

Even though he's not with us anymore,
I can remember that beautiful smile he wore;
He left but we will meet again.
He went to the place that has no sin.

He's up in heaven near God's white throne,
But he will never be alone;
His presence is ever so near to me—
That's why Father's Smile is special to me.

Lillian E Scott

Lillian E Scott
APPRECIATION

We need to think about our gifts in life, To everyone interested in finding happiness.

A word which means so very much,
It's needed more, and more.
For every sweet and gentle touch,
It opens up a door.
Appreciation, for each little word,
Each kindness large and small.
Love for flowers, Life, A bird.
For trees, both short and tall.
For mountains high, for valleys low
For country, state or nation.
Are we too proud to bow our heads,
In pure appreciation?
I've looked through the almanac,
Encyclopedias, and such
And all the words, from front, to back,
None should be used so much.

Lillian E Scott
OUR TURKEY
Mother fixed the turkey,
I stood as if transfixed.
For this is no malarkey,
For legs I counted six.

I smiled and said to "Mother,"
"You know there is many more."
"Oh, Yes I know—don't bother
"You see I added four."

There on the platter, I could see,
It lay all trussed and hitched.
"I couldn't help but marvel,
"Four extra legs were stitched."

Lillian E Scott
CHILDREN
Children are a blessing,
Sent by God above.
A real love confessing,
Like the peaceful dove.
The childish laughter,
Loud and clear,
The little feet that patter.
So dainty and so dear.

I hear those little voices,
My heart goes out each time.
Each time those extra noises
I am so glad they're mine.
Children are the grace received
By parents everywhere.
They are the love conceived,
To make you think and care.

Harold G Wright
LITTLE BIRDS
Oh little birds
So grey so white
You look at me
So high and so small
Yet you sing with such beauty
In this cold winter
Yet your songs are so warm
Oh little bird you bring life
To this cold winter woods
A spot of warmth
Among the north winds
I do hear you sing
What beauty it is.

Deanna Thompson
DIAMOND IN THE ROUGH
(An ode to my firstborn)
I enjoy your gentleness and the compassion you possess.

I'm so grateful for your quiet strength and no-nonsense finesse.

To me, you're the salt, the very essence of the Earth;

and you have been since that day, the day of your birth.

The trust you have hidden in those multidimensional eyes

is priceless to those who love you, like a million dollar prize!

You're my firstborn and it comforts me to know that you're tough.

You're my very own diamond in the rough, and I love you.

Gloria Jean Robertson
THE NINETEEN DAYS OF MAY
Trying hours, bathed in tears,
Watching with no or little hope,
Will time be a little more gentle?
Before I'm at the end of my rope—
Trying to have a little courage,
To bear this cross at hand.
Will the mental torture,
That makes each step such a demand,

Finally lightened enough;
That peace can come my way,
To be able to live again,
After the trials of the NINETEEN DAYS of MAY? ? ?

Linda Cambio
NEED
Whenever I need you Lord
What better time than now
To serve and obey you
To give you my all.

Like the sand in the hour glass
that will soon be long past
Like the footsteps in the sand
that the waves will wash away.

Let me not be drifted
and washed out to sea
but yet, let me be gifted,
Oh Lord
that I may see
the glory in thee.

Debbie Weddell
SHATTERED HOPES
When the hopes that you had are anguished,
And your dreams seem to come to an end,
It's funny how when your heart breaks,
The tears start moving on in.

When all that you had is shattered,
And nothing is going your way,
You feel like you are alone,
And everything has gone astray.

The tears are going to start falling,
And your heart could break in two,
But every bad things gets better,
Soon things won't seem so blue.

So don't let your spirits get down,
'Cause hearts take time to mend.
Just remember that when your heart breaks,
The tears will start moving on in.

Christine Laufenberg
THE ONE CONSTANT

There is one thing I know I can always count on. From when I was a small child to the very second in which I took my most recent breath of air, I know it will always be. And that one constant is the sound of the crickets in summer.

Once, many years ago, as a child, I could not sleep. I'd sit on the roof and cry over problems that were big back then. And the crickets would come and take away my insecurities by singing me softly to sleep.

And once, on a distant July night, my friend and I walked down a long country road. And the crickets were singing. But she never heard them. Funny, how all those years, the reliable crickets would come and perform on summer nights, yet she never realized they were singing for her.

But that was long ago, and still they sing. With no applause, nor payment, nor simple appreciation, they sing. Maybe today my friend hears their song, maybe not, it doesn't matter, because they'll sing regardless of what she hears. And maybe that little girl doesn't need their song for security anymore . . . but maybe she does, because she knows that the one constant in her life is the sound of the crickets in summer.

Kathleen B Stone
TIME TO GROW

Dedicated to my son
Edward E Stone III

When I was just a little tike
I'd love to play and ride my bike

Night-time came, I couldn't wait
for morning to come, and the opening of my gate

Off to school my sisters would say.
Goodbye Li'l Eddie have a good day

Run to the window the bus would go by,
It wasn't a plane, but boy it would fly.

I felt so happy about the things I could do
Like buttoning my pants and tying my shoe

The more I learned the bigger I got
I didn't really care for sitting on the pot

Mom and Dad say, it's time for school to start
I know I can make it, I'm so very smart

On the big bus I climb the stair
Waving goodbye and remembering to share.

Into the school I'm feeling so strange.
I'm not so sure I like this new change

Well everything is fine I met a new friend
It's time to go, I guess this is the end.

Craig LaPointe
CATCH THE FALLING RAIN
Catch the falling rain
Soft colors reflect her eyes
Rainbows fill her dream
A kiss to catch the falling skies

Catch the falling rain
Sunshine whispers from her touch
Rainbows fill her dream
A tear to hold, to feel so much

Catch the falling rain
Her soothing words through the night
Rainbows fill her dream
A smile to free, an endless flight

Catch the falling rain
Catch a star that's falling free
Rainbows fill her dream
Rainbows across the open sea

Catch the falling rain
Rainbows fill her dream

Kim Lorraine Mitte
I FEEL LOVE THERE
I look up into the cool blue sky
Through its soft white clouds and sigh
I feel love there
Love of the fresh air that surrounds
My body so freely

I see the golden sun in all of its burnt glory
I feel love there
Love of the glow that bathes my flesh
And keeps it warm

I behold the beautiful world around me
I feel love there
Love of a land created so elegantly
Providing me every opportunity

Knowing and trusting that out in this wonderful world there is another soul
Who believes in the same love and beauty as I
I feel love there

Hoping someday we two will live and love as one
I feel love there

Marlene Lewellen
MAMMA, DADDY DON'T CRY FOR ME
Across the veil of death, I see
your silent tears and feel
your aching heart.

And oh mamma, daddy, how I
long for you to know,
'Twas not at the hand of the grim
reaper, or so called fate
That called me away, But that of
the Master's Divine plan.

So please mamma, daddy let me
go now.

My journey is ever upward and
Godward
For life goes not backward.
You gave me my garment of flesh,
but God gave me life.

So please mamma, daddy pray for
me that I might reach my
highest goal.

Death is not a punishment or
even an ending . . . only a
beginning,
To free us of sin and make us
whole again;
And no earthly bliss can ever
match being His again.

So please mamma, daddy send
me not your tears.

Remember me only with your
love and prayers
For I have work to do and
I'm only a thought away.

So please mamma, daddy don't
you cry for me.
We'll be together by and by.

Marlene Lewellen
FORBIDDEN LOVE
To love you, people say, is wrong
Oh how can you turn love off
and on.

Those sacred vows we'll never share
But darling I'll always care.
So our hearts in silence dwell
While lips promise never to
tell.

If by chance, we should meet
All this I know would be in
defeat.
For just the touch of your hand
Would send passion flowing
Like sweet red wine.
There in your gentle embrace
Love would have its way
Two souls in oneness to obey.

Angela F Murphy
A CRY IN THE NIGHT

To my father, for being there when bad dreams arise.

I laid myself down for bed that night, Sleeping sound, as the wind whirled playing a familiar tune around my house.
I am awakened by a fearful sound, a child crying in the night, and my heart filled with fright.
I quickly moved from my bed, lighting a candle my heart sped, I scurried out the door wishing the chid would scream no more.
I looked out among the endless field, hoping to see it was only the wind, the screams continued to an endless end. I wanted to run and close the door, but something said continue furthermore.
I walked slowly through the pathwayed woods. The screaming pursued by the pitch dark night. I ventured to my fright, the screaming stopped and in my eyes appeared, a small bodied child filled with fear.
I kneeled to feel the young child's hand, only to find she was cold as the wind.
I screamed a blood curdling scream.
Only to awaken to find, it was all a dream.

Barbara A Hilderbrand
CHANGLING . . .
I have gathered me
From the far shore,
I have gathered me
From the crying poor,
I have spread myself
Around the earth,
Through life and lives
And drums of dearth.
The is and was and what will be
Is gathering now in what was me,
I hear God's trumpet in my ear
Encouraging me to give up fear.
Know me now for what I am
Presenting here as child and man,
Soon free of bone and earthly fleshing
A glowing light divinely expressing,
I leave . . .

Kay Houskeeper
MISTAKES
God sent me here to make mistakes,
Hurt those I hold most dear.
Regrets I have, and a heart that breaks,
As I live from year to year.

Alas, too late, I have learned the cost
To be paid throughout the years,
Is wanting the one I loved and lost,
And an ocean full of tears.

I'm trying to atone to God up above,
In some small measure, for the wrongs I've done,
By teaching of "Him," and goodness and love,
Only that way, can true happiness be won.

But, I often wonder, as Judgement Day nears,
When our good and our bad is weighed,
If the price I am paying in grief and fears,
Will cancel the debt to be paid.

Merle Ann Marryshow
PATCHES & BOONY
My dog Boony eats flowers and oranges, and he is very kind to my cat Patches
At first the two should never meet,
Then I caught them to be playful and sweet
I combed one's fur and took turns with their brush.
My puppy and kitten are very helped enjoyment
Boony eats like he's somewhat human and Patches takes its place of a home made quilt, I have to make here
Somehow Patches ran from my arm load hold and he couldn't find his way back to our generous household,
I took for granted.
Someone would see him sound and echo be his position
To maybe never feel or be real sweet
A child and elder woman or courted girl
Might snatch his rare being before an alley cat eye tore
Boony was droopy for days
But ahha he was a pedigreed Cocker Spaniel, with papers
and I stud him
And brought a brother friend, an American Spaniel
So he'd feel closer within.

Rachel A Robinson
YOU ARE A PART OF ME
I held you close with joy and pride knowing that you are a part of me. As your eyes gaze upon me, you know that we are one. You do not know of what I've been through before you were in my arms. You've only caused me pain once and that was when I first saw you, but now as I hold you, I think of your future. I feel joy when you first walk, joy when you say mom, and pride when you succeed in school and today's world, but if . . . if you do not succeed in all of what I expect, I will not pressure you, you are a part of me and I can not forget that. I expect you to make mistakes so that you will learn from them, as I have. Do not forget that we are close friends, do not forget that I will always love you. As I have said you have only caused me pain once, and you will cause me pain again. When you leave to your future and make plans, and a family on your own.

Gabriel Seabrook
ODE TO A REDHEAD
O'er the languid loch of fog and
sheets of burnished gold
dwells my red-haired lassie love upon
a dreary knoll
and through each nightfall's dappled
play I search the molten mist
for signs of lighted window panes
and stars she might have kissed
singing "Hasten ye back my
Highland Heather, O hasten ye back
to me"

By daylight's turn my boat is born,
'twixt rolling waves I row
All drenched and cold 'neath Gaelic
winds which roil the dark below
To Moray Firth I sound in vain those
haunted noble shores
Like geese fly I across the strath,
through kyle and sullen moor
singing "Hasten ye back my
Highland Heather, O hasten ye back
to me"

'Tween rainswept hearts and
cloudless eyes she faintly plies the
glen
Her freckled visage, buxom cast,
becalms all forward men
To me her heart's a beating snare, her
voice a bonny skirl
No bagpipe's wind could grace the
notes of which I sing to her
"Hasten ye back my Highland
Heather, O hasten ye back to me"

O'er the languid loch I gaze on
tethered strands fo gold
Waiting, waiting, long and long, for
soft her whispered hold
Look there! is that her crown ablaze,
my beacon in the storm?
Alas I sit alone again and yield my
lonely song
"Hasten ye back my Highland
Heather, O hasten ye back to me"

Ginger Hill
LONELINESS
What is loneliness—
its hiding the world's torment
behind doors of glass marble
reflecting only the morning dew light
yet within the darkness
rages on
like the encirclement of a hurricane
it will never miss.

How well it is to us few
who can entice a multitude
with our quickness and

alertness
to pacify their 'quisitive minds
to be so good at playing the game
they really can't see it or is it they maybe just don't want to

Wise men have been known to say
that every stone can be chipped away
exposing layer upon layer of sediment
which time wears into a fine sand
timeless in its existence

And in the end the true form of its being can be found,
at last happiness I
breathe . . . today.

Nancy Elaine Henterly
WAITING FOR SOMEDAY
Talk about Love,
Read about it.
Dream about it.
Think about it . . .
Someday.

It's out there, I feel it.
Pulling me,
Holding me,
Making me breathe when I don't want to.

Like the moon, pushing waves in the Ocean.
I feel it.
Watching me.
Hovering, over my shoulder
Waiting for the day
I grow older.

Waiting for it.
Praying for it.
Living for it . . .
Someday.

Joan Dillavou Wiggins

Joan Dillavou Wiggins
CHRONICLE
(Dedicated to Alphie)
1984
Wasn't the sun once brighter gold
As it lighted and warmed my world?
What happened to flamboyant flowers
Now dull and dryly furled?
Why are all things sad and gray?
There used to be bluer skies.
My view is changed, is re-arranged.
I see the world through widow's eyes.

1986
And then the sun's glow did return
Though its light had subtly changed.
The rose burst forth again in spring
Though its petals were sadness-stained.
Your memory has given healing light—
What joy you had to give.
The end has come for that blackest night
And, Alphie, you live. You live.

Rachel Perez
LOVE CHILD

To: Bill Gutierrez whom I loved very dearly and had to learn to set free . . . I wish you much happiness in life. I'll always love you. —Rachel

Love child, love child
You meant so much to me.
I alone couldn't love you as much,
I alone couldn't keep you for long.

Love gave life in me,
Love brought heartache in me.
Love let you go,
Love set someone free,
When I took the life away from you.

So much I wanted you to have,
So much I couldn't have.
I alone couldn't love you,
I couldn't give you away . . .

I was in love, young; naive and
Wanted to be loved.
Little did I know that I'd
Receive you with Pain, tears and Sorrow.

Little did I know it would be
hard to let you go.
All I have now are a tiny pair
of baby shoes,
Shoes you could have worn.
I will always think how happy.
You my child would have made
Me.

In my heart you'll always be,
though it's too late to bring you
Back. I do regret giving you up,
For the guy I loved 14 years, I set
free. And for the one
I always wanted, which was
you . . . Don't exist . . .
No more. . . In me.
—ABORTION—

Haylee R Schweizer
PAIN

Dedicated to my Family

Pain is the meaning of sorrow and death. It hurts like a pick going through your heart. If I had one chance I would escape it. Pain hurts like no other. Pain is my worst enemy

Emilie Hansen
THE COWBOY
In memory of a cowboy.
Who fell by the way.
God caught up with him.
While he was looking for a stray.

Out in the middle of nowhere.
He was riding alone.
When God tapped him on the shoulder.
'n said, It's time to come home.

He died with his boots on.
With a soft sigh.
His back against a tree
'n his horse standing nearby.

He's riding in Heaven now.
Just looking for strays.
Still has his hat and boots on
'n has his cowboy's ways.

So look to the Heavens.
For a glimpse as he rides by.
He's pushing in strays.
To the big corral in the sky.

Joyce Jackson
YOUR PICTURES SAY SO MUCH
Looking at your pictures, brings back your life so clear,
many happy hours and days, times held now so dear.
Some have a look that pulls beseechingly at the heart,
others look pained, yet longing to be a part.
There is one, that seemingly looks directly back to me,
like waiting for the answer, whatever the question would be.
Some days one glance can bring tears to my eyes,
other days the look seems to say, mom don't cry.
Yes, looking at your pictures can say so very much,
wonderful memories, some good, some sad keeping us in touch.

Lillian Q Linger
BE CAREFUL WITH MY HEART
I didn't realize I loved you
How dear to me you had grown
So carelessly, I let you go
And now I'm all alone,

Dreaming of what might have been
If you and I had wed
If I had listened with my heart
To those pleading words you said.

Please be careful with my heart
You may regret some day
That you treated it so carelessly
After I've gone away

You'll have only memories
Memories that make you cry
So please think it over carefully
Before you say goodbye.

Jennifer Studebaker
THE POET
A poet never knows he is a poet
until someone else reads his work.
Because what to him is nothing but
a symbolic collection of thoughts
is to the world a poem
of great emotional meaning.
A poet never knows he is a poet
because he writes a journal
and his feelings flow together
like milk.
They flow together into what to the
world is a reminder of
some great thing we have all
forgotten
or a feeling
we never knew how to express.
A poet never knows he is a poet,
because to him his work is
nothing but a thought—
scribbled out on paper.

Federico Traeger
PORTRAIT

to Gloria

Her eyes
fall,
splash,
sink,
and are bitten by hungry visions
before reaching the bottom of the
quiet lake.

Jacqueline A Ritchie
THE SPIRIT LIVES
Ceaseless soul drifts and gives,
Death can't end, the spirit lives,
From sea's vitality it sails,
Even through portals into gales,
There's always a wider sea,
Always another port will be,
Homeward bound through the calm,
Directed by His gracious palm,
To sail at sea, peaceful, wide,
God is the only true guide.

Dee Halagera
FRIENDSHIP

To Ray and Tracy, for all their love. To Judy, for whom I dedicate this poem.

Experiencing friendship,
seems foreign to me.
It is like the excitement
of the coming of spring.
The strength and dependability
of the old oak tree.
It can be as mysterious,
as powerful, as our oceans and seas.

But as gentle, so gentle,
as a summer rain can be.
She is the most wonderful "feeling"
this friend of mine is.
I wonder why God decided
to share her with me!

Lisa Gregor
YOUR LOVE
Your love is like the winter snow,
it falls peacefully, surrounding me.

Your love is like the springtime rain,
it showers me with happiness.

Your love is like the summer sun,
Shining its warmth into my life.

Your love is like the winds of fall,
blowing gently through my soul.

Your love is like nature's seasons,
always changing, ever constant.

MaryJo Myers
LONELY HEART
Words whispered with
The feeling of love,
Caught by the wind.
The feelings of loneliness,
Someone to be loved.

Square insanity,
Dark and cold
Crowded and stuffy.
Let me walk,
Let me live.

A breeze that caresses,
A wind that whips,

A sun that lights.
A sun that darkens.

See this dream,
Colour in fantasy,
Grey to the sky,
Black to the heart,
Rain begins to fall.

Kiss me good morning,
Don't kiss me good night.

Doreen E Colonna
LITTLE ONE
So tiny, so new, all bundled in blue,
For ever and ever we waited for you.
The sound of your cry,
The feel of your touch,
My Lord, Little One, we love you so
much.
And when our day must come to end,
And nighttime rolls around again,
I sing that special lullaby,
You know the one that makes me cry.
The tears are not because I am blue,
But for a dream, a dream come true.
Yes, Little One, all bundled in blue,
Mommy and Daddy do mean you.
You have made us proud as can be,
For now we are a family.
We love you, Little One.
Mommy and Daddy

Pamela Jane Teflian
WORLD FAMOUS

Dedicated to John Ashton—My Never Ending Source of Inspiration

It was just something different to do
one night
But I never expected to find you there
Staring at me from across the way
But it was only vicious eye contact
There weren't any words to say
Guess you never saw the other girls
the same way

The night and the music went
grinding ever on
Still there was not even a clue about
you
You just went on dancing through red
light space
And I finally touched your hair
But I still didn't see your face
Thought I'd better get out just in case

But I didn't know when I walked in
that night
That I would leave with something
that mattered
Even though I really doubted you'd
ever think of me
A memory I'd carry for all the times
to come
But there were too many other things
for you to see
For just an instant in passing you had
set me free

Tara Sharp
MY FRIEND
A friend is someone special
who caters to your needs
and helps you through your problems
to make sure that you succeed.

A friend is one who listens
to stories long and short,
stories of all kinds and shapes
or one of any sort.

A friend is one that stands
so proudly by your side,
and when you've lost your way
he quickly slows his stride.

To help you on your way again
and lighten up your load,
he cares for you and you alone
and shares your dreams untold.

A friend's a dear companion
who seems to bring about,
the knowledge that reminds you,
you could never do without.

Monica Hurt
HEAVENLY FLIGHT
I had a dream of you and I, God gave us wings so that we could fly. Among the skies and over the land, through thick and thin we were still hand-n-hand. I wondered why within my dreams in all heavenly flights it always seemed, that hand-n-hand we always were, and that each time I fully learned.
That God has given us just one wing and that is probably why, hand-n-hand in my dreams together we could
fly.

Ginger St Clair
SUMMER RAINS
The wind is blowing
Clouds moving fast above the trees
And grass.

In rolls the darkness
Rain begins
Thump, thump, thump
On the rooftops

People scurry to get indoors
The calm and soothing sound
Of the rain stops.

The wind decreases to a
gentle breeze
In comes a sun breaking
Through the clouds
Light enters

The Summer Rain is over.

Tyrone David Sawyer

Tyrone David Sawyer
CALLING UPON DEATH
I've finally made the decision
It has taken me so long
And I want to tell you about it
In my suicidal song

I don't wish to live
And suicide is what hear
So I say unto you my children
That my time is getting near

I have sinned much
And have caused much pain
After my sin of suicide
I'll never sin again

They tell me my children
The wage of sin is death
For the sins I have committed
Suicide will surely pay my
debt

I won't smile anymore
And some people may cry
I'm sure they won't understand
The way I chose to die

But still some people will visit
And put Wildflowers on my
grave
And my Father will surely reward
them
For the kindness they hath
gave

I'll pray to my Father
To dry the tears you weep
To help you understand
That I've only gone to sleep

I wish to thank you all
For this life that I've seen
But as for me, this isn't death
Only the end of my dream

Tyrone David Sawyer
OH GOLDEN PRINCESS
Cry not
Oh golden princess
For the tears you cry
Will not always flow

The taunting ones
Who laughed at you
Are all waiting behind
Wishing to go

Suffer not
Oh golden princess
For the sins of the past
Are forever gone

The wise ones
Who cursed at you
Are all now longing
To sit on your throne

Fear not
Oh golden princess
For tomorrow I can see
With forever still to remain

The wicked ones
Who shunned your ignorance
Are all beside your treasures
Eagerly hoping to claim

Listen not
Oh golden princess
For the words they speak
Would surely drag you down

They're the ones
Who ridiculed me
When I was the one
Wearing the precious golden
crown

Gloria M
GLORIA M—FOR NOW
I am Gloria M. whose life is music—
I wonder about my unsteady future.
I hear the screams ripping from the
inside.
I see that for life you're the only
tutor.
I want to be stronger than the roaring
tide.
I am Gloria M. whose life is music—

I pretend to be happy behind the
smile.
I feel so scared but never touch
lonely.
I touch the bruises on my skin.
I worry about all the pain I've
experienced.
I cry all the tears having done no sin.
I am Gloria M. whose life is music—
I understand no meaning to this
ending,
I say to the powers of what the past
has been.
I dream to foretell the future.
I try to look around heaven's trail.
I hope tomorrow will be different
from yesterday. I am Gloria M.
whose life is music—

Lesesne Edens
LIFE
Life is what we make it
It depends on how we take it
Take the knocks with a smile
And things will get better in a while
Take the knocks with a frown
And things will look bad all around.

Be a friend to all you know
And happiness upon you will grow,
What we give away, we gain
That which we keep is slain
So help your fellow man
And they'll help you when they can.

Jamie Jolly
TEARS
It's the tears of pain
And the tears of heartache
That carry your deepest feelings
When your heart breaks.
It's this outpour of emotion
That you try to hide
To keep friends from knowing
How you really feel inside.
So when you're alone
And you think no one can see,
You let down your guard
And set your tears free.
But I have seen one teardrop
And I know more tears are
there.
The pressure of concealing them
Is more than one can bear.
So if you need a good ear
To hear what's in those tears,
You can call on me,
'Cause for you I'm always here.

Ms Donna J Jarman
WHAT IS . . . IT?
What is . . . it?
It . . . is lonely!
It . . . cries out!
But no one seems to hear!
It . . . wants to love!
It . . . needs to love!
What is . . . it?
It . . . . is my Heart!

Frances Juanice Fox
YOU PUT A SONG IN MY HEART
Life was sad and lonely,
Then you happened along.
You brought stardust and dreams
And a happy song.

You put a song in my heart,
You put a smile on my face,
You left me happy that night,
Glad to be part of your fate.

You put a lilt in my voice,
You put a lilt in my walk,
We didn't say words of love,
We didn't need to talk.

Our steps matched in the dance,
Was it fate or just chance?
A moment of ecstasy,
A moment that just had to be . . .

I felt your touch and I knew,
Though we were oceans apart,
That somehow you were the one
To put a song in my heart! !

Penny Payne
CONFUSION COMES IN AND TAKES ITS PLACE

To Marc, the best decision I ever made.

Confusion comes in and takes its place
It makes my mind a crowded space.
It jumbles my thoughts all around
I can't find any common ground.
First I think this way and then I think that.
I'm as nervous as a scardy cat.
I come to a solution and think it's the end
then it turns all around and starts over again.

Diane K Glazier
MELISSA WITH LOVE

If I could change your yesterdays
I'd make the wrong things right
I'd do it in a minute
I'd make the darkness light.
I'd like to have a magic wand
To use at my discretion
I'd make whole your shattered dreams
Put them back in your possession.
I did the best that I could do
With the little experience I had
Some things turned out good
Others turned out bad.
Precious child I love you
With all my heart and soul
Do the best that you can do
Let that be your goal.

Helen M Henderson

Helen M Henderson
DEAR SWEET DADDY

Dedicated to SAMUEL O. SHAFFER my Father, born Sept. 13th, 1911. Died Feb. 26th, 1986. He was loved by others much more than he knew. Daughter Helen M. Henderson.

Lord is that me? Please tell me about this vision I see. There's a long line of cars with their headlights on, Lord is that me? Put me high on a mountain between a bunch of trees in a place where gentle winds whisper to me, where raccoons, squirrels and possums and groundhogs and things can keep me company. High on a mountain in an old cemetery is where you meant for me, Lord that is me, now I see.Daddy will never cease now deceased, he lives on you see, in memory.

Margaret Cothran
FAREWELL TO BAM BAM

Dedicated to my little Bam Bam—who was my darling for ten years—and vanished, he was my friend

You went away and left me
With a sad and broken heart
Remember all the times I told you
Only death would we ever part
I don't know what really happened
And it leaves me in a daze
I only know I miss you, & your sweet and precious ways
I had you a long time little darling, you were my pride and joy.

You made me very happy Bam.
Why you were my little boy
Many tears I've shed for you—while everyone else was asleep
Many memories I have too—all for me to keep.
Sure had a lot of sense in that little curly head
You were such a wonderful pet—too precious to be dead
If there's a heaven for doggies—I hope you get there Son
'Cause you sure left a hole in my heart
A big and lonely one.

Brenda Irene Helling
GOD'S HEAVENLY GARDEN ROOM

It is such a short while we stay
On earth's garden of night and day.
We are small buds, waiting full bloom—
Flowers of the Master's perfume.
Gently weaving toward Heaven's Gates . . .
To where the Head Gardener awaits.
This wondrous landscape is so fair:
We'll blossom when touched by its air.
Our petals will not droop or fold.
We'll see the Hands of God who hold
Our sweetness, evermore to bloom—
In God's Heavenly Garden Room.

Anna-Jo Roberta Casciola
RECOGNITION

To Donna, Mom and Sheree: I did it, I reached the level with your assurance. I love you all, and to the ones I don't know, keep reading.

At birth a child is a man,
His life has already been planned.
Blocks are given to mold his life,
And if it be, one for a wife.

At first the blocks are laid for him,
Molded by everyone's own wish and whim.
But eventually the time must come,
For every man to follow his own dream.

Alone, I set the blocks in front of me,
Obstacles not like a rock or tree.
But stepping stones to set myself free,
So I can be what I want to be.

I did it myself without a single complaint,
Although I do feel weak and faint.
But I know I'd feel better inside,
If someone would just recognize.

Curtis Donald Lee
MOM

Thank you for being there when I was down
for picking me up when I was as low as the ground
You always had a way to say the right things
of coming across and making life sing
You stood me up and showed me where to start
when I knew my world was falling apart
You were there in my dark to show me the light
You helped me to see how God was my sight
With great pain in your heart you helped me to see
the beautiful vision God wanted in me
In the darkest of my life you showed me His glory
by telling me of His life in a wonderful story
Now I stand proud of what you are to me
because this is the mom of what God wanted to be.

I love you Mom,
Thank you!

Donnie

Ryan Reamer
A PLACE TO BE

I woke up looking
Through a veil of green;
Under trees bending
Calmly in the wind.
The sun broke in—
Through the leaf made screen.
The light scattered over the ground,
The light danced up to meet me
And show me this place I'd found.
Walking along I began to think
Of the beauty and life that's here.
There's so much more than in the city I lived
With all its violence and fear.
I'm glad I have found this place to be
And now, I finally have a sanctuary—

Joan E Allis
NOT HEAVEN OR HELL . . . JUST LIFE

To my beloved daughter, Ashley, I shall never forget you!

The wind is quiet and still,
I can hear all the pain around me.
I hear the breaking of hearts and the stomping of souls.

The ocean is loud and restless,
I can hear all of the joy in our world.
I hear the laughter of children and the song of lovers.

The world we live in and the life we lead,
It's all so confusing.
Do we laugh or cry? Do we mourn or do we rejoice?
It's never quite clear.

There's always new in the world,
But what of the old?
Do we embrace the new and cast away the old?
I don't know. It's never quite clear.

There's some in our world that we live,
Who only see the new and the good.
Yet others who only see the old and the sad.
What do you see? Is it clear?
Maybe in this crazy world;
Maybe in this unclear life,
We can just take things as they are . . . good and bad.

Janie Wright Pannill
I WONDER

From the top of the Blue Ridge Mountains
I look o'er the valley below.
The scene is one of beauty,
But who has made it so?
Who has made the broad hillsides
Covered with beautiful trees?
Who has made the lovely flowers
Swaying in the breeze?
Who has made the lowlands
And the rivers that gently flow?
Who has sent the sunshine
That helped the plants to grow?
Could man have wrought such wonders
As here before me lie?
No, there is one more wonderful
Who watches from the sky.
So, as I stand here gazing
I wonder how one can say
There is no God in heaven;
None to guide us on our way.

Shelita R Smith
JOLLY OLD SANTA

There is only one man in the world that brings all the girls and boys toys for Christmas. He brings boys trucks, the boys don't even have to pay a buck. He brings girls, dollbabies if they're good maybe. He has little workers called elves who work day and night to make all the toys shiny and bright. He has a reindeer that helps him fly way way up in the sky. He has a wife named Mrs. Claus that helps him with all his flaws. They live at the North Pole where it is very very cold. On Christmas Eve he rides his sleigh to deliver all toys in less than a day. He rides his sleigh only at night beside the stars that shine so bright. Over the seas and under the moon. Look! here comes Santa Claus can't you see he is coming to see me!

Herbert Lee Monk
VALENTINE FOREVER

Dedicated to my daughter Melissa. Born February fourteenth, she makes this day even more special.

Being born on February fourteenth,
A Valentine from Heaven was sent.
Filling a special place in my heart,
As days of watching you grow went.

Will always remember a little girl
Who'd smile, and with all her wit
Give me that ever so innocent look.
That seemed to say, "I didn't do it."

If only I could see that look again,
How it would set my heart aglow.
But you've changed from day to day.
As meant to be, you continue to grow.

A teenager now, yesterday only a child.
Before I know it, you'll be on your own.
Do me a favor and please slow down.
You're still the babe I've always known.

Will always cherish thoughts of you.
For they fill my heart with love.
Remembering how it came to be.
A Valentine forever, sent from above.

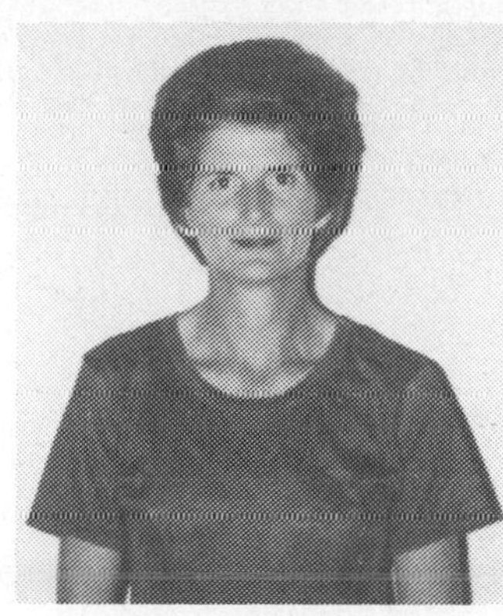

Rhonda Baggett Johnson

Rhonda Baggett Johnson
HEAVEN ON EARTH

This poem is dedicated to my relatives; the Baggett and Johnson families.

When I look in the eyes of a child
There is no wonder in my mind;
That in Heaven their angels do always
Behold the face of God at all times.

Their little faces are so Angelical
Their little minds so simple and clear
They make life such a pleasure
To watch them grow from year to year.

They are the closest thing to Heaven
We can touch right here on Earth;
It's not any wonder that they all
Are so full of beauty and of mirth.

I understand why God sometimes picks
One of these little ones so pure
Sometimes the most beautiful flower
Is too fragile to endure.

Geri Romero
THE PAINTER
Colors rush across the paper
Shadows swell and tiptoe into corners and cracks
A child's smile caught for everyone to see
The worker of such beauty?
Thee
A river flows out to the sea,
Friends pick cherries from a tree,
A quiet chapel stands alone
The surf it breaks . . . the sea gulls moan
An adobe wall after snow
A friend braids her hair by the fire's glow
A still porch in the spring
Such wonderful songs the paints and painter sing
Life captured by the strokes of a brush
Faces from an inner place shared with us
And for the sharing, a thanks need be said
Thanks for the kind and gentleness of heart
That shines right through your pieces of art
And as I sit writing these lines
I pause . . . look up and find
paintings which you've painted for me
And in these works I see
A portrait of a friend.

Stephanie Barnes
HOLD ONTO THIS

To Christopher, I did it! Thanks for being the inspiration to write the poem, and send it in! I love you—

Hold onto my heart . . .
But let it soar within the boundaries of our souls,
gliding free to express the emotions
that create warmth and understanding between the two.

Hold onto my heart . . .
Don't let it slip through your fingers.
Continue the loving guidance that is needed.
Enthusiasm pulls us forward,
drowning the past
creating euphoria so stimulating and powerful,
that "we" are forever meant to be.

Hold onto my heart . . .
Don't let it cease beating,
for if it dies, my expression dies also.
Take care of me kindly, gently catch all my falls.
Tenderly break all my crumbling walls.
Hold me close, understand and know,
forever I'm here for you,
I won't let you go.

Hold onto my heart . . .

Dixie Cooley
MY GRADUATING SON

This poem is dedicated to Brent, my loving son. Senior Class of 1990

It wasn't so long ago, I held you to my breast
Through these tender years, we've been truly blessed
To have a kind and loving son
To still be in our hearts as number one
It seems like yesterday you started to school
You always lived by the golden rule
You've had some good times and some bad
The best years ever to be had
Into a man, you now have grown
Even your voice has a deeper tone
As you go out into the sea of life
May you seek success without much strife
After your diploma, you receive
We no longer will need to grieve
To wonder if your lessons have been done
To anxiously await grades for you, son
We wish you warmth, wealth and laughter
To have a fulfilled life here and after

Linda Robinson
THE LAST DAY OF SCHOOL
On the verge of freedom,
the school boy sits.
Near the edge of his seat
and his mind sees bits.
Of the joy that will be
in the coming days.
Sun . . . Hills . . . A Pool . . .
and he silently prays.
For the longed for moment
when he can shout,
"Free at last. Liberated.
School's out! School's out!"

Lisa Burbage (1984—age 8)
RAIN
Rain falls all over the town,
Rain makes everything beautiful,
Especially our town.

The rain is beautiful.
I love the rain and I know that
The rain will never leave us.

Lisa Burbage
INNUMERABLE
Innumerable is the raindrops that fall from the sky
On a cold winter day,
Like the fur on a newborn kitten
Or the hair on one's head.

Innumerable is too many to be counted
Like the stars in the sky
On a clear summer night,
Like the blades of grass
On a fresh cut lawn,
Or even the many rays of the bright sun
On a fresh spring day.

Innumerable is like the love on Valentine's day
There is too much to count because
there is so much given out.

It is like the clouds in the sky
On a cold, rain, night,
Or the waves in the ocean
During a great storm,
And that is what innumerable is.

Diana L Price
SHADOWS

To these integral men in my life for the growth born from having experienced them.

See my heart with your eyes, hear it as well
For as fragments of the kaleidoscope
The pieces are spinning and ever restless;
I come to you now in an attempt to eliminate barriers
And while this is not presented as a test
I must determine the degree to which you care.

There was room in my life, but not for two
Friend shadowing husband, and now in his absence
Husband shadowing friend, while hopes come undone;
I have nurtured wounds while others came and went
I have been a port for a ship sailing stormy seas
I have lent an oasis in which to smooth shifting sands.

What I've not given; has been offered in velvet chains
And now like the child with values not yet instilled
I no longer wish to share or to be shared;
Will sand castles in the sky ride with the tide
Will I be tender to the drawbridge, or fare to be
The maiden who graces the knight's chambers.

The answer holds a lifetime of decision;
Shall I be only the best friend I can be
And put my dreams of possibilities to rest?

Leora
LOVE
memories intrude
bruises that never fade
bones beyond repair
skeletons whose silent screams
behind the walls of years

what passed in moments
lingers on
even now that I've
grown away

even now
the stabbing pain
seeps into the
safe reality
my life has come to be

my teeth still clench
my mind still reels
uncomprehending
the senseless violence
that was your
love

Janie Willis
HAVE I BEEN BROUGHT UP ALL WRONG?
Lord, have I been brought up all wrong?
Are people afraid to work some hours long?
To offer a helping hand and expect no return
Or to force a smile while doing a burn?
To share in a project, either big or small
Or help someone up, when they've taken a fall?
Are they afraid to associate with the terminally ill
Or bend over to pick up or wipe up a spill?
To read to a child or even the blind
Instead of finding that ole axe they must grind?
Where is Mom when the child comes from school
Are the parents around as an interested tool?
What are we teaching our children when young
To smoke, make fun of, with a mouthful of dung?
Why do we have NO time on our hands
And manage to waste the resources of our land?
It makes one wonder and yet appreciate
The old fashioned way we used to communicate.

By working together, talking, a peck on the cheek
Gathering wild flowers, a picnic, a swim in the creek.
To respect others' feelings, either weak or strong
Lord, please tell me, have I been brought up all wrong?

Florence Lange Taylor
MANY MOODS OF THE SKY

I dedicate this poem to my wonderful children.

Thick, white clouds are floating on a blue sky.
Hear the cacophony of wild geese flying in a
vee formation on high.

As night falls, watch the sun set after which
stars will be twinkling and shining and the
moon aglow in the sky. Then, dawn breaks and
the sun rises.

Now, the mood changes, a thunder storm is raging,
bolts of thunder crackle and lightning flashes—
the storm calms, and rain begins to fall.

In winter, look for the aurora borealis, lighting
up the northern sky like huge bonfires built by
Indian Warriors. Listen! ch
oirs of angels are singing in the sky.

Sarah Britton
LONELINESS

Loneliness is like an infinite black
hole that can swallow you
when you least expect it.

It will come over you with such
power and aggressiveness to
make you feel helpless.

Like you want to—
die.

Joanne Maguire
FRIENDSHIP AND LOVE

Friendship is one thing but
love is another,
Love is when two people are
close to each other.
A heart, an arrow, a cupid, a dove,
All mean one word and that word is
Love!

Karen S Stark
MOUNTAINS

Lovely mountains, oh so high
Bring a tear to my eye—
Where the air is clean and fresh,
Lets me know we are blessed—
Do you see—perhaps you know
What Mother Nature has to show—
Snow falls here and eagles sing,
Mountain life's a special thing—
Things to see, unusual, rare
A young cub and mama bear—
Peaceful deer make not a sound,
More beauty than anywhere found—
Mountains, mountains, oh so high,
Make me smile, make me sigh—

Stuart Sharp
TIME

Time;
I can see its passage—
Written;
On the whirring machine—
Of man.
I can see the passage—
Of his life;
Movement—
Of the hands.
Seconds—
Are his hours;
He cannot understand—
Yet;
All that he can do;
Is slowly—
Move the hands.

Shalom

Christina Vasquez
MY GUY!

I like to see you every day
To make you happy
In any way

You're special to my heart
And a big part of my life
Please don't ever part

I always feel good
When I'm by you and by what you say
You always know what to do

We're happy together
And we pray we won't end
We wish to be together to the end

When I look up to the sky
I thank thy Lord
For you're my guy!

Norma L Alvarez
THE USER

Now that your bridges
have all been burned,
never to be replaced—
THINK!
Was it worth it—
All this pain you caused?

You took more from me than
I was willing to give.
What's worse is your lack
of feeling—
no guilt, no remorse, no
regrets . . .
yet.

It's only a matter of time
before your "flight of fancy"
is replaced by the
inevitable confines
of reality.

Jayna Story
LONE GONE

The sound of a stick
Dashing across the planks.
The whisper of a solemn secret
Concealed in its boards.
Looking back,
Seeing nothing,
But childhood memories
rotting away like yesterday.

Kimberly A Jeffries
THE EFFECTS OF YOUR LOVE

To Jeff, the one and only Love of my life

As I take a nice long look
At my life of yesterday,
I never would have dreamed.
I'd love someone this way.

You've filled this empty void,
That had ached me for so long.
You put meaning to my life.
My love for you is strong.

When you hold me in your arms,
You melt me to the core.
The way you kiss my lips,
Does even that much more.

When you softly rub my back
Or run your fingers up my spine,
The effect you have on me
Is to always make you mine.

Terrie Ferguson
LOVE'S LESSON

It was he I met in the woods that day;
I didn't like what he had to say.
He told me of life,
That I had it all wrong.
Love was meant to stay
Not come and go away.
Soon I grew to know what he had meant.
I came to love him,
Even love his temperament.

One must learn to love;
One must learn to care.
Now together we are old
And hold each other dear.
Our love has grown each day,
And now, we look to our children
And hope, and pray
That they will also learn to love one day.

Lashawn A McClodden
IF LOVE IS . . .

To my mother and grandmother, whom I love very much and cherish.

If love is supposed to blind,
How is it that I can see the signs
The signs that show me your love died.

If love is supposed to be understanding,
How is it that I cannot comprehend
Comprehend your reasons for leaving.

If love is supposed to be strong,
How is it that I feel helpless
Helpless and without your guidance.

If love is supposed to be all these,
Then, what really is love?
If it cannot be described.

Cheryl Hudd
CHOICES

Dedicated to Mrs. Sylvain's English class, my family, and my friends.

Once I loved; Once I lost.
During that time I fought and sought.
To find in time what I wanted to do
And to be with who.
I thought that one day
I would find my choice of way.
But not it seems
that day will never come.
But maybe someday I will find
just who and what is right for me.

April Zelinsky
UNCLE DOUG

This poem is dedicated to ALL alcoholics . . .

Unique in more ways than one.
Never said you were perfect, and I
Can't say you never had fun.
Loved me more than any uncle could, and
Even though you couldn't stay,
I love you anyway.
Died because you drank too much
Or maybe the hurt went
straight to your heart.
Uncle Doug, after watching you, I promise
God, I will never start.

Matthew F Saucier
HOPE IN VAIN

This poem is dedicated to all the people I love. They give me the emotional highs and lows I need to express myself in this special way.

When I think about the times
That our love just had no rhyme
I could gaze into your eyes
To find your care again

Then it all came back
To the honesty we both lacked
Now I find myself reflecting
On the dreams that we once had

I hope for yon girl from across the sea
I wish that you'd come and be with me
Though I know that it can never be
The love that we once had

The many nights that I walk the streets
Looking like a man that's finally been beat
Thinking of the many people I've known
Wondering what'll happen if I come home
To be with you not them
Will you take me back again

I'm guessing as the world goes by
London, Madrid, Seville, Versailles
I'll see you in the faces of the women passing by
And I'll dream of how it was

Patricia B Moss
THE AWAKENING NIGHT

TO: NORLISHIA SMITH, my DAUGHTER.

At times I sit and close my eyes and daydream of a fantasy world, with flowers blooming and the singing of the birds whispering its way through the breeze.

The night is so dark; it's like the deepness of cave, where no one can't be seen. And the quietness just easing its way through the universe. While the universe is circling its way round and round.

As the night comes to an end, and the days are mourn. I sit awakening, waiting for the sun to rise.

And when the morning comes I sleep away, through the dawning day, and dream and dream and dream.

Wayne L Dobert
MEMORIES

Dedicated to the many wonderful memories of two extraordinary people, my parents, George H. and E. Iona Dobert.

Memory is a gift from God above
Given to all, by Him, with love
To help in times of sorrow and fear
By bringing lost loved ones near.
But each of us lives, and each of us dies,
And each of us sees life through different eyes.
This view is shaped by the heart and the mind,
And helps create these memories left behind.
A moment of the past may be special to me,
But you may remember it quite differently.
So honor the memories others cherish, as well as your own,
And remember God's gift of memory is not years alone.

Tracie M Kriska
WHAT AM I?

To My Unc, you're the best. And To My Aunt Shirly, you're wonderful.

I may not be perfect,
I may not be great,
But I am special,
Or so they say.

I may not be perfect,
I may not be great,
But I am special,
In my own way.

You may think you're perfect,
You may think you're great,
Nobody's perfect,
Nobody's great,
We're all just special,
In our own way.

Dorothy C Guterman
SNOWFLAKES

To Aunt Dora

Snowflakes, snowflakes coming down on this winter day
A hand on the door, a bell ringing somewhere
Once again, inside, the smell of pine
A Christmas tree with popcorn and silver bells
A blazing fireplace across the room
On a windowsill a small white cat
Through the door into the hall to the kitchen once more
The smell of cooking and pies in the oven
All the windows with frozen ice a picture is formed
With people singing and sleigh bells ringing
The spirit of holidays is here again.

Dorothy C Guterman
THE FOREST

Through this forest of tranquility and beauty
Colorful wings of butterflies stop by
Sun rays shine down from tall pine trees
Food for small animals of acorns and pine needles
Lying on the ground
Across the green field, a small pond with white lilies
And jumping green frogs
Deer walk through the green forest and stop and look around
In a second they are out of sight
A bird is singing a song somewhere
The stillness of the forest is peace and endless in time.

Marilyn D Wilcox
A MINI STORY FOR MY 1989 CHRISTMAS CARD

Dedicated to my children, Taren and Jolie, and their children.

I've painted cards for one decade,
(Some not so good as the cards were made.)

But the whole idea was for Christmas done to send a friend a special one.

The years have passed as cards were mailed with snowman, bell, or Rudolph tailed.

And now I paint the Christmas tree and send more poetry to thee.

I love you all, both short and tall, and young and older, big and small.

My only purpose is for pleasin'
and to wish you all of the best in Season!

Robert W Brumbaugh
THE CAT'S REVENGE

Dedicated to Elizabeth and Aunt Margaret's kitties.

With furry paws that are so soft
The little kitten ran
Around the room to chase the mouse
While quite the best he can.

He bumped into the little hole
Trying very hard to stop,
For when the mistress heard the noise
She hit him with a mop.

Now that he is out in the cold
He wishes he had not
Gone after that poor little mouse,
Without a moment's thought.

He begged and begged the mistress now
To let him once again,
Come in the nice warm house and rest
And seek the mouse's den.

He chased the mouse to make him pay
For the trick that he had done,
And now once more he caught that mouse
To make him finally none.

Grady L Brown
THE BLUE WATERS

I dedicate my poem THE BLUE WATERS *to my wife, my friend, my love, my life, LEONOR BROWN.*

While setting on a rock down by the sea, I can feel the cool breeze from the waves coming at me.

A large bird setting on its perch, sea gulls flying around, the noise from the ocean waves, oh how I love thee sound.

Oh ocean, oh waves, oh waters so blue, please bring back my true love that sailed away on you.

She is gone to her homeland across the waters so far away, bring her back safely, oh ocean, oh, waters, oh waves.

I can see the ship in the waters off the distance blue, here on this rock I will be waiting for my love so true.

Laura Weatherbee
WHEN YOUR FLIGHT BEGINS

To Cathy Vieara . . . you meant the world to me.

When your flight begins
soar adventurously high;
for our dreams we look
to the sky.
Abide only by your own rules,
as the life you choose to live
is what you alone must decide.
And although—to you—my name
may never be known,
with every journey,
wherever you roam,
keep in solitude and mind
that there will always be
someone here to see you through
the good,
the bad,
the milestones.

Kay F Armstrong
THE GIFT FROM DAVID

To David, with love. May all the joy you have brought be returned to you threefold.

The seed lays silent in the ground.
Long dormant now, 'til even Mother Earth denies its presence.
But then, with unexpected vigor, his ray of passion warms the sleeping life.
His gentle touch, his sweet caress, his strength of spirit stirs the germ to grow.
Not without its pain and anguish, the tiny bud begins to struggle.
Hesitant, its tender leaves break through their wintry prison.
In fear of frost or careless treading, still the life continues to proceed.
Now, with mounting hope, it dares to dream a future—
Sees its sassy, colored bloom asway,
Smells its spicy scent upon the air.
This, is the gift from David.

Loetta L Ritchie
I WAITED . . .

To Clark . . . in our 20th year . . . I still love you.

You say, you want me to be happy
That I must change my ways
You said that you would come for me
I waited . . . long and lonely days

You said, "It will only be a week or two"
But four months have passed us by
We should have been together, you and I
I waited . . . You never came for me

You say you love me, you say you hate me
I too have felt the same
You say you have no self-esteem
I know exactly what you mean
I waited . . . you never came for me

Your touch, your smile
Your body lying next to mine
. . . It's been awhile
I waited . . . you never came for me

I wish you well, I wish you love
I wish you peace and happiness
All other things aside
The time has come to say goodbye

Hal Dixon Hatcher
A BRIGHTER LIGHT

This poem is dedicated to Patricia and the memory of loved ones lost.

Between the initial light and the final dark,
We experience much pleasure and pain:
The warmth of the sun, the sting of the rain.
At times life is a beautiful dream, at times stark!
Our emotions suffer many a drain
Because of too much heart, too little brain;
What often ends as tragedy begins as lark!
(Some believe beyond the dark is a brighter light;
If there is any justice, they are right!)

William McCorkle
LOVE THROUGH TEARS

Love seen through the tears,
how distorted and blurred.
Somehow it seems like love
has just become a word.
Losing its meaning and
losing its touch.
The tears rolling down my face;
while I'm saying, "I love you so much."
What can be happening, what am I doing.
When I look at you,
what am I pursuing.
Is it love? then
why the tears.
What is it that I've
learned over the years.
Love is strong, much to
my surprise.
But you couldn't tell that by
looking in my eyes.
They are all wet and dimmed
by the tears.
Because I still can't see
my lesson in years.

Ida Sagers
A PRAYER

Dedicated to Leanne and Alvin with love.

God of heaven
God of earth
Can I know my real worth?
I, a microscopic speck,

My mind beholds creation.
Now infinite—how vast!
What is my right relation?

I would know Thy Will for me.
I would pierce eternity.
Let me ever open be,
In all things, to see but Thee.

Ar't Thou the voice when I'm alone?
Ar't Though the joy that I have known?
In pain, the hand that succored me,
The urge within me to be free?
Who and What ar't Thou, my God?
And who and what am I to Thee?
Oh let me see—please, let me see!

Connie Jenkins
I NEVER THOUGHT

To John Andreszcuk with all my love now and for always

I never thought that I would have someone who honestly loved me for me, and nothing less.
I never thought that I could love someone the way that I love you.
I never thought a love could bring so many memories back that I'd thought I'd forgotten.
Even though some of them may hurt me, you help to soothe that little pain.
I never thought that there'd be someone there for me, whenever I needed them.
Yet, it seems no matter how hard the situation is, you are there, caring for me still.
I never thought of a life as full and happy as mine has been since I've been able to call you mine.
I never thought I could laugh like I do when I laugh with you.
I guess I never thought of love in general—until I thought of you.

Bridget

Ola Mac Donald
THAT'S THE ONE!

We shall always remember the LOVE,
That one very special CHRISTMAS,
Brought to us when our GRAND-SON STEVE
Surprised us with a PUPPY!

Just three days before the HOLI-DAY,
He had been to an ANIMAL SHELTER,
He met DOGS of every SIZE and DESCRIPTION!
Watching from their TEMPORARY HOME" there!
Waiting "PATIENTLY" for
"PERMISSION"
To go HOME with someone who would CARE!

Looking into their EYES took time!
As did LISTENING with his HEART and MIND!
But he soon CRIED OUT LOUD!

'THAT'S THE ONE!"

She is a TERRIER with SOULFUL EYES!
A black button nose and a CUTE FACE!
She can "comb" the wispy hairs on her ears,
Until every hair is exactly in place!
HER NAME IS BRIDGET!
STEVE is always LOVING . . .
GIVING . . . and KIND!
But even he SURPASSED himself this TIME!

S Moritz
THE TRAITOR

In memoriam: Chas. Juan Jacobs

Paring his small fingernail with a frown, the latticed shadows of the bars striping his bare legs, he pondered upon allegiance and love: one, the vassal's soil; the other, a curse. The silver was not in my design; she, ever grasping, rasped, "Take it! Grief is a stranger now." That night, he scrubbed his hands; the suds never darkened; the stain had marred his soul. He winced as he struck the cuticle, just as he had when the histrionic attorney sneered, "Boardinghouse patriot!" shrieking, "Anyone with a double loyalty is a nation's security risk!"
The jury's swift glance "Con-demned!" wilted his last hope, and he muttered, "Lousy rat!" The shadowed bars vanished as the angel of death sat beside him, clasping his shoulder, chiding softly, "Why be so concerned at the clanged prison door or so fretful at lost youth? I will return when God's solstice clefts your soul, its brilliance empty of honored divinity, just cold infinity without the pulse of time."

Donna J Hebert
THE JADE

This poem is dedicated to Kelly Roberts, Tracy Harris, Cindy Harvey, Eric Black, Jeff Ault, Beau Steele—my jade buddies. Love, hugs and kisses, Donna (special thanks to Laura)

African green statute
Rests still in the night;
The native band plays—
tribes become silenced.

Visions of black
Loom by the hut;
Confusion and anger—
The oasis has dried.

Indulge in calmness
The haze begins to thicken;
Empty is the stage—
The spirits prowl.

Mrs Sandra L Carver
GOD'S SON

For Mommy

Some say his skin was black, some say white,
Some say his eyes were dark, some say light,
Some say his hair was long, some say short,
Why can't we all take hands and shout, He's God, He's our Lord?

Some say He died on a tree, some say a cross,
but oh dear child, can't you see, He died for you and me, for us.

So children in this cruel, cruel world, stop this fight,
can't you see that all this war and hate is killing us?
Let us take hands and you will see,
that only love can win this fight,
that only love and faith can make this a better place.

So down on your knees, no matter what color you be, and ask dear God to set us free.

Lucille Wypych
SAMISH ISLAND PRAYER

This poem dedicated to my son—Frank W. and daughter—Darlene D.

I thank thee Great father for your loving care,
and for your protection both day and night.
I can hear you whisper even though it's light.
Just as I can hear the eagle when he speaks.
When in my travels his strength I seek
This prayer I'll always keep in mind.
'Cause like the coming and going of the tide,
I know you will always be at my side.
Amen.

Carol J Butler
THE FOREST WEEPS

Oh weeps the forest lonesome lullabies
As summer turns once more to autumn winds,
And nature's children gently flee in kinds
Ne'er to return 'til sun warms earth and skies.
Oh cries the mighty tree which stands so tall,
As fallen leaves are with the frost caressed,
Hang barren branches each alone, undressed,
Abandoned with no succor for to call.
How quiet death consumes the winter day,
The darkened wood stand stagnant, snows lie stilled
Like passing time, but absent, unfulfilled.
The life in life doth winter take away,
But soon rebirth, new life comes in the spring
And happy songs doth nature's children bring.

Lana L Story
OF FREEDOM I HAVE ONLY THIS TO SAY

Of freedom I have only this to say:
There truly is a price to pay.
In aspirations, goals, hopes and desires, there lie but one to bind;
But, not for those who fail to find,
an end by means released are given.
Therein above, the choice to live or die.

Rebecca Hazel Storm
ACROSS THE SANDS OF TIME

I've climbed many hills so high and wide
across the Sands of Time.
God gave me strength to face ill winds
and directions for that climb.
I soon could see the sun so bright
that shined in full array.
But soon I found I must hurry on
as I stumbled on my way.
Then all too soon the clouds disappeared
as I faced the other side
Where friends appeared to share my joy
before 'twas eventide
All through t he years clouds passed me by
across the sky so blue.
I soon found out the sun beamed forth
to make each day anew.
Thanks to those friends I chanced to meet
across life's daily climb
And to my precious Lord above
for love that proved sublime.

Cynthia Dyke
AT DAWN'S LIGHT

For you, wherever you are now.

At dawn's light,
When the crisp air cleanses our hearts, and the birds and sun awake;
I think of you . . .

When the noon sun shines directly overhead, and beats down on the hot sand covered with lonelyfootprints;
I think of you . . .

When afternoon kisses good-bye daylight, and dusk settles in quietly;
I think of you . . .

As nightfall brings coolness,
and a moon that shines brightly into my bedroom;
As always,
I think of you . . .

Terah Fortner
THE SONGBIRD

This poem is dedicated to my mother &father—Janet and Roy Fortner my pastor & wife—W. J. Ferrell, Jr. and friend—Jeanne Blankenship

A defendive Blue Jay
A bird that chirps all day
Is so very happy and gay.
The bird called a Blue Jay.

When the Blue Jay finds his food
And all the other birds are rude,
The Blue Jay squalls all day through.

The Blue Jay likes to peck
And fight especially of a night,
that's a defendive Blue Jay.

Karen M Zorsky
OFFICER DAD

This poem is dedicated to Sgt. Ted Zorsky, my father.

Each night my dad dresses in blue
To fight the crime and God knows who.
I think to myself as he walks out the door,
Will I see him tomorrow morn?
I go on with the rest of the night,
But inside I still have to fight
The chance I might not get to say
I love you dad, the very next day.

Daniel Coates
PARIS DAYS
Guided by her mother:
The small warm hand held tightly
From above,
A little girl in a short blue dress
And long white socks
Steps off a street curb
Over the water which trickles in its gutter.
Her mother stoops, whispering encouragement.
—a tiny foot, laced snugly
In a red-leather doll's shoe,
Is delicately brought forward
And set down, and then quickly the other.
She looks back with flushed cheeks,
Her green eyes for a moment catching mine,
The blond hair tied by a pink strand of ribbon,
Her smiling mouth and face
Glistening in the sun.
I enter into the courtyard and turn towards
The lecture rooms, reminded by the sweet
Maternal tolling from the high chapel bells
Of the Sorbonne.
And even through the resounding voice
Of an aging man speaking of Racing,
I can still hear each
Careful, tentative step of a beautiful child
Who slowly climbs a staircase,
Somewhere, with red-leather doll's shoes.

Edith F Swinson
LITTLE RAINDROPS
To Billy

Little raindrops crystal clear
Like so many little bells I hear
Beating upon my windowpane
In your steady rhythm of rain
Such a tiny persistent thing
Tis hard to believe all the good you bring
With all the growth upon this earth
You've played quite a part in their birth
Creating beauty beyond our wildest dreams

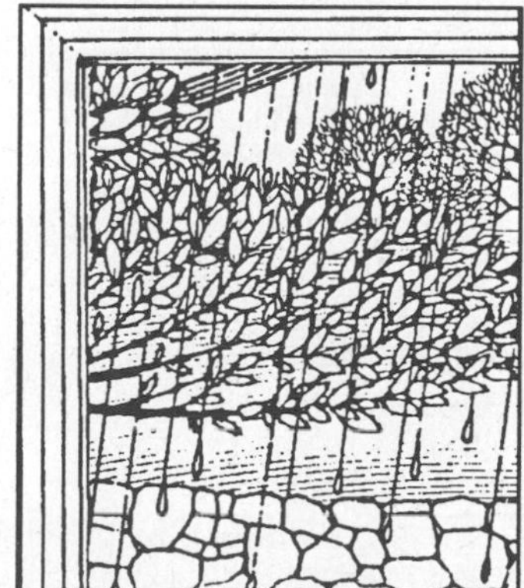

While you fill the rivers and the streams
Such a tranquil feeling that you bring
That it causes my heart to fairly ring
I wonder if folks all over this world
Take you for special like a very rare pearl
You're like tiny drops of silver
glistening in the sky
Your puddles tiny mirrors while on the ground you lie
Then with winter when you turn to snow
Your beauty then takes on a different glow

Edith F Swinson
THE MIRACLE OF DAWN
After a night that's long and still
Watching the dawn can be quite a thrill
You can always tell when it's getting near
When the singing of birds is all you can hear
The grasses become silver from the sprinkle of dew
While the sky is turning a beautiful blue
It is all so like a wonderful dream
That you wonder is it all as it really seems
And while I view this magic in the sky
It is with great emotion that I sigh
When I think of how good God is to you and me
By giving us the miracle of dawn to see

Edith F Swinson
SUSPENSE
She knows his build, his walk, but in vain
For alas she does not even know his name
Her poor heart skips many a beat
Whenever face to face they meet

She sees him in the morning then again at night
She sometimes talks to him too
While her mind is racing with all its might
Wondering, maybe, if he knew

But then again how could he know
While to and from work they go
When they just talk of things like weather
While they're riding the metro together

Edith F Swinson
POOR LITTLE OLE ME
I enjoy so much your friendship dear
Life without you I could not bear
When the hour is late and it's eventide
It's all I can do to tear from your side

Oh my dear how strangely we met
How it came to be is a mystery yet
And I'm so grateful as you can see
It's all so good for poor little ole me

Caring for you the way I do
Makes me want to bill and coo
How much I love you is plain to see
Oh poor little ole me

In time I hope to prove my love
Is as true as the very blue above
While I'm praying with all my heart
That we two shall never part

But now and then I frighten so
When I am with you and all aglow
All of this a dream must be
Happening to poor little ole me

Robert Hoffstadt
CANINE HEAVEN
Do dogs go to heaven when they pass away,
To wait impatiently till the day,
That they in their humble, loving way again
Can follow their master and be his best friend.
O' there must be a place in "spirit land"
To welcome the dogs with souls like man.
The dog that is faithful the livelong day,
Who guards the children at their play,
And asks no other privilege than
To be your pal and lick your hand.
O' God, on earth they seek but a caressing pat.
You must have a heaven for dogs like that.

Joseph Vito Ferlisi
THE BEGINNING OF SPRING
The beginning of spring is a time to share,
because all new things are blooming in the air.
Trees lose their leaves in the wintertime,
but in spring the leaves come back just in time,
Spring is a little bit warmer than fall,
and winter is coldest of all.
Spring is the next season in line,
and summer is right behind.
Spring is just a few weeks away,
which brings the Easter bunny hopping on its way.

Pamela Engle
TWO JOINED BY GOD'S LOVE
I dedicate this poem to my husband, Dave; for without him and his love for the Lord, I wouldn't be the person I am today.

Once upon a time . . .
About eleven years ago, in a state far away; was a man whose heart was empty, he desperately needed love; so he turned and prayed to our great Lord above.

He said, "Lord, hear me pray, 'cause I need your help today. The girls in my past, have done me wrong, lead me to the one, to whom I belong. I promise to love her, until the end of time; and she will be forever, and only mine."

So he packed up his clothes, an d was homeward bound, he was in search of the girl, the Lord had found. He seen his old girlfriends, he talked to some, then the Lord said, "None of them are the one." So not many days went by, he went to a restaurant to eat, He didn't know the waitress he saw, he was to meet.

More days went by, he asked the Lord, "Why haven't I found her yet?" The Lord said, "Be patient." So he went to see his brother. The brother said, "I have this aunt, who to me is like a mother, my birthday part is at her house, you can come with me and my spouse." He had nothing to do, so he said o.k.; he didn't know, this was the day.

He walked into the house and into her life.
The minute she saw him, she wanted to be his wife. He was working on papers, being a little shy, she thought he didn't like her, and didn't know why. The night grew closer, it was almost the end, how could she lose this very special friend? He made no attempt to ask her out, she didn't know what he was thinking about. Her heart was crying, she loved him so, how could she let this great man go? He thought to himself, "I'll ask her out, she is very nice." She said "YES" quickly, he didn't have to ask twice. Day after day they saw each other, nothing could separate them from one another. She loved him so much, it hurt to part, but he was always on her mind and in her heart. So seven months later they both said, "I Do," promised to love and be together till all the days are through. In the eyes of the Lord, it is true love, their marriage is as pure and Holy as a white shiny dove. The Lord brought these two together, together they will stay, forever and ever.
To this day, he says there is no fairer, she was the answer to his prayer.

Susan A Cooper
GRANDMOTHER
You cared for me when I was small.
To me you were very tall.
My love for you will never die.
To you I would never lie.
So Grandmother dear I love you a lot.
I think of you as the tippy, tippy top.
The way you held me when I cried to you.
You changed my life when I felt blue.
Oh! Grandmother I love you so.
I won't even let your memory go.
The beautiful things you do for me,
Will be in my memory through eternity.

Rebecca Sandoval
LOVE
Friendship
caring
Trusting
sharing

Happy
sad
Shouting
mad
Comfort
desire
Pleasure
fire
Laughing
crying
Hoping
dying

Mary Rawson
ACUPUNCTURE AFTERTHOUGHTS
I dreamt I lay on the great battlefield of life,
Alone and weary and wounded
And a man with Asian eyes
approached and said;
"Would you like your fortune told?"
And I, being lost, said, "Aye."

So he covered me with herbal paste
And in between, stuck pins.
Then reaching out his palm, he took my purse.
"You're on the great battlefield of life,
Alone and weary and wounded," he said,
"And now you're one bit wiser;
Beware of life, dreams, and men in white with needles."

James Frisbie
O TANNENBAUM

To Bruce Frisbie, my father, who taught me to love trees as creatures of beauty, deserving our respect.

I went for trees today—
One for the house and one for the church.
They rest on top of the Cherokee
Like a green coonskin cap.

It would have been cheaper to get them in town.
$9.97 each for groomed clones
of someone's idea of perfection.

These are wild trees taken from a wild place.
I breathed a prayer "forgive me, my friend,"
As I knelt in the snow
to take them home.

My boys, eight and four,
Cried when it dawned on them
that the tree they had hung with lights
and handmade ornaments
Was a cut flower whose life was ended in our
living room.

How apt a symbol of the cross and the manger,
Life and death and the fragrance of mystery!

I will not cease my yearly ritual
Of forest service permits and snowy canyons
I need the chance, at least once a year,
to kneel in the snow and say with reverence—
"forgive me, my friend."

Laura J Davis
BEST FRIEND

Incredible eyes
so full of life
A brilliant fur coat
and claws sharp as a knife.
You're so independent
so strong and so real
It's amazing the way
you always know how I feel.
There, in the window
as if the world's your crystal ball
You seem to see everything
and understand all.
You know when I need you
like a magnet drawn to steel
The best friend in the world
My orange-striped Garfield.

Barbara Marie Respo
VOICE FROM THE PAST

To Mary, my mother, whose spirit guides me, whose love inspires me.

You called today, for my birthday you said.
"Do you know what you have done?
You have opened the wound; the wound I call my heart.
It had almost healed, that part of me
that could not feel anymore after you left!
That part of me that wanted to scream your name and bring you back!
That part of me that could easily have filled the room with my tears.
Voice from the past, you say you're not opening the door again, but you have,
the door to that part of me that still loves you!

Wilma Human
PROGRESS

Our progress through the years
Has made a drastic change.
We have gone from covered wagons
To the fast electric trains.

We have changed our mode of travel
To the airplane and the car.
We now have modern appliances,
Air conditioners, TV's and a VCR.

The washtub used on Saturday night
Lost its fame to the indoor bath.
Nowadays there's a whirlpool to relax in.
We no longer need a path.

We had "Silver Threads Among the Gold"
And the record "Tennessee Waltz."
Today we hear noisy Rock Stars
Singing from a tiny little box.

Since the days of the cotton gin
Man has landed on the moon.
Everything has become computerized.
We all will be a number soon.

Milo M McFarland
THE MASTER PLAN

There it stands in all its mystical beauty. One of our rugged mountains reaching towards the sky, still wrapped in winter's snow.
The sun gradually melting it into beautiful crystal clear rivers, that rush down the mountainside, spilling into the hot dry valley below.
Turning them into rich fertile farmland.
Huge trees standing as sentinels in timeless splendor.
Could anyone be a part of this, and not feel
that there is a master plan?

Ina Mills
TO CHRISTINA

Dedicated to Don, Shannon and Misty's little Christina.

I only held you one time and you were so very small,
Now I know you would not grow to be strong and tall,
Your tiny little body so cute and sweet,
Had too many odds to beat.
If only I had held you a long long time,
And told you of Grandma's love, a love of a special kind.
It is a blessing the future is not known to us,
We have to put in God all our faith and trust.
To leave to Him little Christina to hold and keep,
Until we too must go to sleep.
And then awake to hold you again some day,
For this I hope and pray.

Grandma.

Jeffrey J Giba
TIME

To the Lord, my God, who is long suffering and, to my wife Consuello, who gave me . . . time.

I blink, I see . . .
And another second passes by.

I smell a scent, I feel a breeze,
I watch a life beside me . . .
And another minute passes by.

I walk, I talk, I think & feel,
My eyes catch the wind in the trees . . .
And another hour passes by.

I watch the birds, I count the stars,
I rest my hand upon my pillow,
Wake with a tear and rub my eyes . . .
And another day passes by.

The warm wind gains a chill,
The leaves gently drop with colors changed.
A smell of Autumn in the air,
I feel the hustle of a time . . .
And another season passes by.

I wait . . . , I wait . . . , I wait . . .
And another year passes by.

Jon B Paley
LONGING

We walked the wings of love today, my dear
Abandoning the ground beneath our feet,
Exploring, joyful, mindful of our fear . . .
We walked back in at two o'clock, discrete
I think they knew. We never could disguise
The lilt, the smile, the satisfaction bold,
The warmth, the blush, the meeting of our eyes.
The gentle touch that leaves no tale untold.
I'm only slightly paranoid you see.
But that's the lesser of two evils now,
The only thing I dread more is saying goodbye.
So let them speculate. Meantime I'm free,
To let this precious friendship slowly grow.
Besides . . . there's more to love than meets the eye.

Kathie Reedy Jordan
NATURE'S BABE

To my babes who never experienced the dawn of spring.

Soft snowflakes
float gently to the ground.
The stillness of the crystal landscape
embraces the world
with the gentleness of a mother
enfolding her babe in her arms.

Through the silence
a soft breeze echoes a gentle voice
as it whispers,
"Sleep peacefully my babe
while I clothe you
in the purity of my love.
Rest; then awaken
at the dawn of spring
to don the attire of new life."

Patricia J Kelly
SPRING STORM

The tall tree stands stretching
branches bare against the sky
Thunder comes booming, rolling,
night and storm is high.
Nervous and edgy, forest creatures are wary,
The proud tree looks down at bunny
crouched and scary.
Trust me, the tree advised. Trust me, dig in deep,
When storm is over, we wonder why we weep.
There's nothing to fear, God in heaven nourishes
I've seen it before, in days of yore,
After storm, calm beauty flourishes.
The raven, the fox and the hare found
shelter without a sound
But the sky split with a flash and a crash
As the tall tree hit the ground.
The sun rose bright to greet the day
Forgotten was the storm torn night,
Each little creature in his own way
had conquered his fright.
They gather 'round the tree, vowing faith so sure
Their captain's mighty trunk to provide
Home site safe and secure.

Charlotte C Goldson
HUSH LITTLE CHILD

If you are hurting as a child and no one seems to care
Just you always remember, to turn to God in prayer.
You may have to hurt awhile, and pray, but do not cease.
God in heaven will hear your call and give you everlasting peace.
Mothers and fathers are all alike, consumed by their own troubles and woes
They don't have time to see your pain but only God knows.
Hush little child now don't you cry just remember what you've been told,
Close your eyes and rest in peace as you head towards the city of gold.
Hush little child now don't say a word, go quietly without any fear
For I am your heavenly father who will be with you always, my dear.
Come with me and your pain will fade, for I have a heavenly home
Where pain and loneliness is a thing of the past and you'll never again feel alone.

Maryann E Gould
SUBSTITUTES

Florida has sunshine and tropical rains,
palm trees, ocean breeze, sand of white grains—But—
I miss the lilacs, purple and white,
the heady aroma of floral delight.
I miss the peonies of heavy blooms,
that grow in clusters the month of June.
These beauties won't grow in the white grains of sand
Or survive the driving rains in this tropical land.

The crepe myrtle resembles laden boughs of lilac
The hydrangea, like peonies, are abloom, but in lack,
of the intoxicating aroma that causes one to linger
and reach for their beauty with a hesitant finger.

Susan M Zack

SYRINGE JUICE

I saw you jab the needle into the bruise on your arm that commemorates so many other similar insults,
yet I know the syringe's juice offers you life.
How cruel the curse of Adam and Eve—
To know death, to fear, to grasp at life even when we know death is closer and easier to obtain.
So many mental giants trapped in limited bodies—
Or was it the limited body that forced the mind to expand?
Our pain promotes our compassion, our suffering helps us understand the suffering of others.
Surely somewhere it all balances.
Surely God has a sense of fairness.
Please, God, let me peek at the Rule Book.

Ursula A Humphrey

JOEY

To Joey, the best guy in the world.

There is a fellow, a special one:
with laughing eyes and a smile,
A small little fellow, with a curl.

He can be so sweet at times.
And at others, he's a devil.
An angel with horns sort to speak.

But this little fellow, I love.
And my day would be sad.
Were it not for his sweet self.

I sometimes get mad at him,
But then he'll do something sweet
And it makes me glad that I have him.

I could search the world over.
And nowhere could I find,
A brother as great as Joey.

For Joey is a great little fellow,
And he makes life grand.
To see the world as he does.

I love to hear his laughter
To see him at play
For he makes life grand.

Reneé Murphree

THE WALK

Firey reds and bursting oranges dance across the water, as the sun bows to kiss the ocean's horizon, The waves gently, soothingly lap the tired and wounded soul. Sedately I walk through the passage of color. No confusion, no anger, no thinking, just being.

Billie Wallace Franklin

THE PAINTING

I saw a painting of a man.
Where his heart should have been,
I saw nothing.
Standing all around him,
were stone statues and dead trees.
No life.
Nothing living.
On his face was a sneer,
and his hands were clenched fists.
Before I turned away,
the sadness in his eyes
sent a tear down his cheek.

Brenda Baggett Arendt

TRUTHS

Success is counted Worthless,
By those who never succeed.
They misunderstand the sweetness
Required to meet the need.

Little, "say they," care for pearls,
Or who sails the deep blue sea;
Or Stones from the jewel crown,
Such falsehoods distress me.

As they defeated, dying,
With closed mind and ear;
The distant sounds of success
Break, agonized and clear.

Unsuspected desires of prosperity,
Within each one lies low;
But hurry! Don't be late!
Time passed—an hour ago.

Brenda Baggett Arendt

DECISIONS

Dedicated to one very special friend. My sister-in-law, Linda Wilson Baggett.

As I sat down playing cards one day,
I thought of friends so far away.
Friends that I've met face to face;
And in my heart they've found their place.

So I thought I'd try and search the cards.
A task I thought would be hard;
Because of all cards, numbered fifty-two,
I knew only one would really do.

I immediately mixed the cards real well,
But how to select theirs I could not tell.
Do I shuffle or cut, pick or choose;
Which card was theirs, I had no clue.

So I decided to spread them all face down,
And with shut eyes, move my hands around
Finally the card chosen, I turned to over
Its suit, not a spade, diamond or clover.

This card had a face, quite plain to see
Of course, the Queen of Hearts, it had to be.
I now understand when my life is at an end
In the Queen of Hearts, I had a Friend.

Jean Manning

TO MY PRINCESS

For my baby angel—the wind beneath my wings.

I've written you poems;
Dressed crazy at times.
Sung you unwritten songs;
Turned your tears to laughter.
Tried to tell you in every way;
I'll love you more tomorrow
than I did yesterday.

Should your days seem cloudy;
I'll bring in a rainbow.
If friends desert you;
I'll always be there.
Each and every night I pray;
We'll love each other more tomorrow
than we did yesterday.

So, let's Love Life together;
Love, laugh, sing and dance.
Always cherishing each other.
Discovering new pleasures in
Being close day by day;
Finding we love each other
More with every new day.

Sabrina A (Sam) Moran

Sabrina A (Sam) Moran

LIFE

To my family and Relatives.

It goes on and on
through many obstacle courses
Testing our confidence
of qualities—weak and strong
It's a test of fate—a specific trait
Life goes on and on.

Sabrina A (Sam) Moran

FRIENDS

Dedicated to Carrie Williams.

A person near
and very dear
Helps you calm
anxious fear
A never ending affair
of secrets to share
Learning we are
an inseparable pair.

David Horn

THE PAPER BOY

The dark figure of the paper boy comes and goes.
Did he come to my house? No one knows.
Only a few people get the sign,
Of a newspaper folded so fine.
The newspaper is trimmed with silver lining,
Sitting on the doorstep glittering and shining.
In conclusion, I've got to say,
That he'll be back another day.

Robert W Mayer

ODE TO A MONTEREY PINE

For Tom Z., a rare friend, crippled with muscular dystrophy.

Clinging bravely on a cliff
You overlook the sea.
I look at you outlined in blue . . .
How could you come to be?

Who would plant you where you are
In such a jagged crack,
So as you grew, the wind that blew
Would form your twisted back?

Your feet explore the rocky floor
Of such a steep incline . . .
How wantonly they wander . . .
Were you weaned on wine?

How can you pray with arms that way
But whistle with the wind?
I marvel at your innocence . . .
Have you ever sinned?

You're gnarly, twisted, just a stub
Of what a pine should be,
Yet all your rugged beauty lies
In such deformity!

Ellen Berven

1990'S HISTORIAN'S TIMELESS ACCOUNTING FACTS COMPILING BOOK AS LIFE GOES ON

The 1990's for a decade, we are in the beginning stages!
Yet ending once again a century, documenting its history for the ages!
Etching events and accomplishments on life's pages!
Where the bulging volumes life's generations wages . . .
Second by second . . . Minute by minute . . . hour by hour . . .
Day by day . . . Week by week . . .
Month by month . . .
Year by year . . . Decade by decade . . . Century by century . . .

Monica Hulm

THE WISDOM OF OLD

The wisdom of old
is never too bold
Clearer words spoken
to leave us a token
With age comes insight
in which we all delight
Hear the words they speak
They will not make you weak
So cherish the wisdom you hear
And always remember with cheer
You heard it from the
Wisdom of the old
And it can never be untold

Bertha Cornwall Pearson

COVERED BRIDGE

Have you ever entered a covered bridge
And felt its magic spell?
Do you hear the words of its ancient beams
And wonder what they tell?

Did you know that if you but close your eyes
And speak what you dare not say,
But take care not to breathe it to anyone else
Your wish will come true that day?

Have you watched as lovers go hand in hand,
And cuddle as they go?
Don't you suppose they know it's a kissing bridge,
Or intend to make it so?

And can we whose grandchildren deem us wise
Dare not to cross such streams?
Can we find our long lost youth again
In these old childhood dreams?

Keep your magic, bridge of my broadening youth,
You cover my hopes sincere.
You have helped me to make my journey safe,
You protect what I still hold dear.

Sharon L Cuchiara
THE SPIRIT OF OUR LOVE

For David.

When ancient pyramids have blown to dust
And monarchs forget to engage in war,
This tribute shall be breathed to life for thee
In your bright memory forevermore.

No dark shadow of death shall touch you
For in this, you will remain purest light
A quick smile on the face of sunshine
A slow fire in the heart of night.

With these words of promise, you shall live on,
Even as the end of time grows high.
My love for you will be forever echoed
And the spirit of our love shall never die.

Anna Hicks
BILL
My darling's fifty-seven years of age
Just now in life's middle stage
Already he's retired
Having worked the years required.

He's around the house all day
But I like it fine that way.
He can weed the flowers and mow
And to the grocery store go.

He's angel all way thru
Since joining Club Honey Do.

Kathy B Allen
TOGETHER FOREVER
When I was a little girl my mom always told me,
"This bear and you will be together forever . . . "
I carried it with me everywhere.
On cold lonely nights we snuggled up and counted the
white sheep in the darkened sky . . .
"This bear and you will be together forever . . . "
Then I met you . . .
I let my heart do the talking,
It was the same kind of
communication I had with my bear.
When I went home that night I told
my old ragged bear all about you,
and I swear he said,
"This man and you will be together forever . . . "
And so we lifted each other to the heights of happiness,
we count our lucky stars each evening that we will be
Together Forever.
Yesterday I looked my little girl in her deep brown eyes
and slowly handed her my
precious bear
I gently whispered in her ear,
"This bear and you will be
Together Forever . . . "

Ilene Shuler
RAIN OF HOPE
You Lord, send the fresh, the cleansing rain that brings the sweet fragrance of earth and tree.
But Lord, what is it your rain brings to me?
Is it healing, is it solace, is it peace of mind and soul—
is it your presence as I turn toward my goal?
Your rain washes the dust and staleness from the air
as it washes the care from my heart, leaving bare
the thoughts and plans that shape my destiny.
With hope and prayer can I become what you want me to be?

The grass responds to the rain by turning brightly green.
Now, do I respond by being only what I seem,
or do I too, recover with the cleansing of the rain
and become what has only previously been my dream.

This beautiful place, this world where I live,
brings forth an abundance of hope and does surely give,
after the quiet, gentle, sustenance of the rain
strength and courage to accept your love and try again.

Amy L Hickey
UNTITLED AND UNREMITTING
Twisting ropes of chromosomes have kept me here beyond my will to live. Too cowardly to slice them, and without even the shield of whitened hair, I age alone, shrinking and drying like uneaten pie.

It has set, the sublimation of ambition to the sublime. Sweetly washed in semen and blood, that fertile young moon lies stored in a round silver box in my mind. Only I can take it out and offer up its dripping horns to the sun.

How I pulsed in passion-to-diapers phases for time of my own—time away from the drive to be good at everything in a kingdom where I was both queen and slave, accepting all I could, giving all I had.

This is no plea for turning back, satellite in tow,
For I am tired and he is gone; let him let me go.

Barbara Sharik Babb
MISCONCEPTIONS
I wonder what the answer will be
to the question of love—a love that keeps making a fool of me.

From yesterday till the beginning of time, I always thought you would always be mine. I just always knew the sun would rise each day, and I never thought you would ever go away.

I just always knew we would always be. Wherever I was, you were there with me.
I thought we would always sing our song
and now I don't even know what went wrong.

Somehow I missed seeing your soul slip away,
and somehow I missed feeling your love die that day.
Now I wonder how I could have been so blind:
I guess I just always thought you would always be mine.

I just always thought that I would always smile,
and it's no consolation that you were mine for awhile.
I never knew I would have to learn how to weep,
because I didn't know you were just a gift I could never keep.

Now I wonder why the sun still rises each day
and I wonder why I can still hear the music play.
I wonder why my heart continues to beat and deceive,
and I wonder why you lied and why I believed.

There is no easy answer that I can see to the question of love—so love, stop making a fool of me.

Timothy R Williams
BE HONEST
Be ye ever loving kind and true,
God said you are his.
Be honest in what you say and do,
No matter what it is.

Be fair in the games you are playing
Always tell the truth.
Be honest in what you are saying,
Always have some proof.

Being honest will help you through
To where you ought to be.
The truth will not hurt you,
It will set you free.

The world will begin to look to you,
Because you are honest and true.
Let them know, that they can trust you,
Be honest in what you do.

Honesty is your best friend,
It is always around.
Even to the very end,
It will not let you down.

Timothy R Williams
TIMOTHY
I was birthed by my mother,
I had plenty of vim.
I had two brothers,
My mother, named me Timothy, not Tim.

Brothers born in January,
In good health, not ill.
First day of February,
I was born in Jacksonville.

Some people call me Timmie,
I answer just the same.
Sometimes they call me Jimmie,
Tim, Timmie, Timothy is my name.

Poetry is my first love,
I like to write about words.
Poems about the skies above,
Trees, bees, and birds.

He who believes in himself,
Can't be counted out.
He who doubts himself,
Will be doubted.

Sherry K T Jacobs
POEMS
Poems written to tell a tale
Feelings captured to sell
Times of wanting and needing
Times of regrets and pleading
Feelings as free as youth and old age
Feelings unlocked from duties' cage
Times of a first kiss
Times of remembered bliss
Souls unraveled as free as the dove
Poems written to express love
Feelings as transparent as the wedding veil
Captured in verse we have not failed

David G Ware
SHADES OF REALITY
I look around
And all I see
Are clouds of illusion
In shades of reality
A gentle sound
I turn and look around
In weakness I'm surprised
As I realize
I'm lost in all I've found

Bernice Anita Reed
CHILDREN ARE ASTOUNDING (A True Story)

To Reggie, The Child In The Poem.

I am supposed
To love you Gail

Because you are
My aunt; I do

But I like you
Very much also

They are not
The same you know.

Doris Juanita Sloan
INSIDE-OUTSIDE

This poem is dedicated to Dr. Bryan E. Connell and Dr. Gerald K. Anderson; who taught me to trust, to live, to love.

When looking in my old mirror
I soon expect to see—
A little girl; all eyes and innocence
Just staring back at me

My soul cries out for all the years
That is lost forever to me—
Running barefoot in the rain
Spinning dreams of what is yet to be

Inside-Outside
Is tearing me apart—
Holding onto the child within me
While I have a woman's heart

I can't fit into this world
Of corruption, pain, of cruelty—
So I live in my own world of teddy bears
Gentle hands, love and security

For my inside and outside
Are parallels of controversy—
To be merged together
But, meanwhile; I have to be me!

Gaea Bear
MOTHER
Mother dear
How I wish I knew your pain,
For you know mine and you comfort me;
Yet I continue to bring you hurt.
You are my life
And I am your Death.
How I long to have lived your life,
Felt your joy, seen the world through your eyes.
The times I've misunderstood—
When I've been angry,
They hurt because you hurt.
You are so strong, and so fragile—
An adult, yet such a child.
You are the flower child in a world of ugly weeds.
I long to have danced in the night
with you—and understood;

To have worn loose, flowing garments
And twirled in the wind, laughed at the sky
With the stars in my hair and the moon in yours.
Yet that can never happen, for lives change with time,
And so have ours.
But let me be close to you, let me sing with you,
For I love you.

Ellen M Renaud
FOREST AWAKENING
As the moon retires, from the misty twilight,
stars of fire, retreat with the night.
The night is shattered, with a twilight of grey,
only to be flattered, by the first light of day.

Fresh is the new dawn, with dewdrops agleam,
sweet is the birds song, of last night's dream.
The sun starts to rise, above a sharp mountain crest,
to set peacefully this evening, upon hills in the west.
Behold trees dancing, and prancing
with grace, with the leaves enchanting, romancing embrace.
As God's love glistens, on the shimmering lake,
along comes the bristling breeze, to announce a forest awake!

Arthur Robert Killingbeck
PASSING OF TRAINS

To my mother's memorial, Clara Teti, Killingbeck, wife of Fred, mother of six children; a great-grandma, too!

Freight train, freight train, whe're you going so fast,
Burlington Northern Red, Norfolk Southern Green, the "Midnight Special" just went past,
Atchison, Topeka, the Santa Fe,
Salad Bowl Express all the way.
"Chattanooga Choo-choo" going down the line, "Orange Blossom Special," mighty fine time.
New York Central,
Southern Pacific, "Rock Island Line" and
"Old Number Nine."
Baltimore and Ohio, the Chesapeake,
Delaware Lackawanna, it's nostalgia we seek.
Pennsylvania Railroad, "Wabash Cannonball," Atlantic to Pacific, thru the mountains tall.
Coal mines, steam engines,
John Henry too, "Ole Casey Jones" just went thru.
Train, Train, Train, southbound freight,
"City of New Orleans," don't be late.
"Sugarland Express,"
skies of gray,
billboards and clothesline
along the way. Cigarettes and coffee,
oil and gas, coal and lumber,
steel and glass. Freight train, freight train,
whe're you going so fast,
down that lonesome road,
where images of miles last.
Cowboys, horses, fenced corrals,
tumbleweeds, plains, and lack of rains.
"Folsom Prison,"
pass it by,
that lonesome whistle,
don't you cry. Now eighteen-wheelers
and interstates, truckers on the move,
freight, freight, freight.

Tired, aching bones
and sticks and stones,
six days on the road, Honey, I'm gonna make it home.

H Cromwell Smith

H Cromwell Smith
BLACK SKIN

In praise of all who have the courage NOT to judge a book by its cover.

Must I forever exist in weeds
Fertilized by biased greeds?
Must I forever direct my face
Toward the black ghetto's disgrace?
If so then I shall go within
And seek a world beyond black skin.
It is a world of hills and sky
Of suns and moons that never die.
Of gentle winds and roaring gales
And clouds foiled into spirit sails.
And if their source is same as mine,
I'll know how to define
The pigmentation that began and ended with a blackened man.
And if I discover there is no way
To change the order of night and day,
I'll know that I'm an equal man
In spite of pigmentation plan.
For as man carves light and dark
And flames leap from an atom's spark,
Black skin then is same as white.
He is the day and I am the night.

H Cromwell Smith
PRELUDE TO BEING
God cast into His sea of creation
A seed,
Watching if it grew into a tree
Or weed.
And I, riding crest on tidal wave
Of joy
Looked to Him for guidance. It's then
The buoy
Of love led me to life's waiting
Embracing shore.
And suddenly I knew I was a seed
No more.
The sky and stars, the wind and rain,
The land
Were filled with joy, offering their
Helping hand,
Pulling forth the seed into manifest of me,
Resolved that I would grow into
The tree.

H Cromwell Smith
OPEN MIND
Great is the tranquil feeling
Hugging a silent, shaded dell.
And cool is the sparkling water
Bubbling from a summer well.
Quiet is the sad and lonely heart
Hungering for a human voice.
And happy is the fellow being
Who makes that heart rejoice.
He offers from his well of life
Something that will never recede.
A tiny niche in his loving mind
Forever open to another's need.

H Cromwell Smith
THE DANCE

To Helen: Remember our first dance at Roseland and how we looked at one another through the moving spots of light?

We met between two lonely smiles
And I thought it was by chance,
That our eyes grew bright together
When I asked her for the dance.

The music rose in gentle waves
Carrying us on a happy crest.
But my feet, not used to dancing,
Couldn't match her rhythmic zest.

Then as we neared the orchestra
And I stepped upon her feet,
The music suddenly claimed us
As our hearts caught the happy beat.

That was many happy years ago
In a ballroom of lights and tints.
But the music of that dancing hour
Has been with us ever since.

H Cromwell Smith
CONCEIVED
It starts
A struggle
All ache and desire
Seeking the egg
Anxious behind virgin gate
And wrecked
By the throbbing, strong vessel
Of male
Whose army
Shall find
The tumescent mate.

The soldier most stalwart
In that army of love
Reaps a reward
The ultimate union.
An eruption
Releasing
The cells and the genes.
To final fulfillment
LIFE'S PERPETUAL COMMUNION.

H Cromwell Smith
DEATH
There is a void into whose voracious depths
All life stares, stricken with fear and wonder.
And in trying to check their downward plunge
They scream, rip, and claw each other asunder.

Yet, with patience and a terrible certainty,
And a pace that's set by human qualms
The guts of time gorge the perpetual feast,
That death brings in its quicksand palms.

It's the one thing that chokes our laughter,
Or breaks a branch from the family tree.
And when I see the empty body of another,
I'm sombre, knowing it will one day visit me.

It has numerous ways of settling onto life
In cold breath that drains all body heat.
And as the soil grows rich, man is convinced
Death is the one thing he never will defeat.

Life ponders, and many welcome the release
From body ills, and malignant pain filled breath.
While in history's seething, boiling cauldron,
The only unchanged element, a cold profile of death.

Danny Jay Stanks
THE WINDOW
These gentle, insane people
Watching,
Whispering,
Strangely,
in the night.
Roaming on the sheets,
Voices of voyeurs
surround you.
The eyes of lookers
through your window.
Do they want you,
Or do they haunt you.

Noelle Gorka
HOPE
Wood grain clouds of feathery mist, drifting slow,
Permit the sun to shower a cold, slumbering earth,
Travel not in her path and let her brilliance show.

Frail ice wind stir not the resting, peaceful trees,
Far above with the sun's warm and giving glow,
Leave them alone in their dark beauty and winter's weakened freeze.

Still, in the chill of hiver a sunbeam warms and comfort in glory,
Battling the distance and conquering the breeze,
Reaching her destination and reveling

in her arrival and victory.

And all the life seemed to fade with
the last colours of November,
It may seem somber but one should
not worry,
Because in the bleakest season there
is still one thing to remember—

Her majesty the sun shines the hope
that is spring's worth,
Hints in this desperate looking day of
December,
The rejuvenation of living things and
along with it, mirth.

Lucy Kincaid Bond
LOST
On my walk I found a butterfly's
wing
Such a beautiful and fragile thing.
As I walked on, I wanted to sing
As I gazed on a world of beautiful
things.
When my thoughts returned to the
treasure I thought was mine
That treasure I could no longer find

Love came to me from one sweet and
kind
When others intervened, the love I
once had
Was no longer mine, it was as the
butterfly's wing;
It had flown, while I was absorbed in
other things.

Sharon Skilling
MY THREE LITTLE GIRLS

This poem is dedicated to my daughters.

I've watched them grow
throughout the years.
I've held their hands, and
dried their tears.
From that first tooth, to that first step,
to that first glance at a boy.
They have truly brought me
great happiness and joy.
And I would not trade
one moment in time.
That I have spent with those
three girls of mine.
And if I could thank the Lord
today,
For all the wonderful gifts
he's given to me.
I would say thank you Lord,
for the most precious of these
in all the world.
Is Heather, Amber, and Shannon
my three little girls.

Amie D Pappas
THE FLOWER AND THE MOTH
The flower that lived in the garden
outside of Elderby
Was beautiful inside—but had no
faith and seemed so very shy

She couldn't open up to let the world
see the beauty underneath,
Not even to get some sunlight or
uncurl a silken leaf.

One day a moth who lived not far—
did hear the flower weep
And knew if he did not help this soul
that he would never sleep

He said, "Why, dear! No wonder
you're sad—you've seen no sunlight
yet.
You need that light on your inside,
You'll wilt! Did you forget?"

She said, "Why, no" "I'm just too shy
to let myself be seen.
What if they laugh or say my stem is
an ugly shade of green?"

The moth did smile and say with a
twinkle in his eye,
"If the world were meant only for
pretty things then who, I say, am I?"

"But you're not bad!" the flower said.
"In fact, you're very kind."
Said the moth, "But it's not my
outerside you seem to keep in mind."

"Come out now and let us see what it
is you hide!"
"All right," the flower smiled and
exposed her other side.

"What's this?" the moth did cry with
joy. "You're beautiful you see."
"Thank you," said the flower, "Now
so happy I shall be."

You're welcome" said the wise old
moth and this lesson now is taught.
It's not what you behold with your
eyes—but what your heart has
thought.

Melissa Blum
I KNEW YOU FOR BUT A TINY GRAIN OF TIME
I knew you for but a tiny grain of
time
a single beam in a sea of stars.
Ours was a deep secret,
a dark pleasure.
You touched the very depth of my
soul, held me fast there,
and then you vanished . . . like all
shooting stars.

We had bathed in a gentle stream
had followed the rushing river
had ridden the waves of foam . . .
drawn to each other as only cosmic
mates should be.

Now I've lost you.
Nor can I find myself.
I look for you in the gentle shrugs
the sky-blue smiles I see
passing me by.
They are only reminders, for you are
still missing.

My only hope is that you think of me.

The tiny grain of time seems to slip
from my hand in your absence.
It will soon be scattered on the shore
of many memories.

Come to me . . . together we can
search for tomorrow.
Or alone, I can remember
yesterday.

Alice F Kobe
CHRISTMAS EVE AT HOME IN MINNESOTA
When I was very young:

A real spruce pine tree
Stood in a place near the door
Each year was like the one before
Chains made from wallpaper books
Bells made of colored construction
paper and trees of green. (Reindeer of
brown.)
Hung from the branches on our tree.
A homemade star perched on top
Real candles of white, red and green.
Set in the holders placed on the tree
The most beautiful lights you could
ever see.
Were shining on our Christmas tree
Our gifts were few, but we felt joy.
A pair of socks, a doll, a train
A top, some dishes, candy popcorn,
oranges and apples in a stocking.
A walk in the snow to Midnight
Mass.
Dad came along—his gift to Mom.
Carols sung and the Christmas Story
told
What a wonderful memory!
Those days of old (1920-1930).

Sandra L Dorney
A WINDOW

To my husband, Charles, who made my life worth living.

I wish I were a window to look up at
the sky.
I wish I were a window to watch the
clouds drift by.
I wish I were a window that I could
look through.
Then I could see the earth, the sky
and the sea so blue.
And if I were a window I could look
out where.
I could see the flowers, birds and
people everywhere.
But I am just sitting here, being what
I am.
Being glad that I was made by God
and not by man.
I know it doesn't hurt to have a
dream or two.
But aren't you glad God made me
and you.
For we are the windows of the world
for all to see.
The love that lies within the heart,
that God gave me and you.
So let's all open the windows of our
hearts,
and let the love shine through.
So we can make this land a better
place for me and you.

Cynthia R Shane
TODAY I HAD TO SAY SEE YOU LATER

To my best friend I see as my brother, the late Ted Anderson.

Today I had to say see you later Ted
Today I watched and I listened
As the words of sorrow made me feel
cold and just as dead
As death made my best friends, my
brother's life come to an end

Today I had to say see you later my
love
The memories of childhood dreams
that once soared
Like God's greatest gift
The sacred white dove
The dreams of yesterday are my
reward
For the living nightmares of today

Today I had to say see you later
I had to look upon that horrible box
before me
Knowing my brother, my best friend
was returning to our creator
For no more can I look and my eyes
will see him
No more can I reach out with my
hand and there his will be
I will know now when I call to him,
he can't answer my whims
So my friend, my brother, my love I
must say see you later
As I will never say goodbye, for
those are the final words
That say forever to never meet again.

Laura Zahr
THE GOOD FATHER HE ONCE WAS THERE
I looked in his deep brown eyes,
I could feel a storm of frustration
arise upon me.
I dispraise him for his mistakes,
yet I loved him for all the good times
we had.
I am not sure if we have an
understanding in between us,
but I shall never understand no more.
He is being torn apart by both an
evil source and a
loving touch from above.
Although I know he is there,
right next to me and nearby when I'm
in need,
I can no longer understand,
for the evil force has taken more than
it should.

Kelly Sue Alford
AUTUMN
The leaves are falling,
the frost is here;
Everything is beautiful
this time of year.

The leaves change color
then fall to the ground.
That doesn't happen
all year around.

In winter comes snow,
with springtime comes flowers;
In summer comes heat,
With autumn comes showers.

The showers of leaves
that come tumbling down.
The showers of yellow
and red or gold-brown.

I like the autumn
when its pretty leaves of gold
come off of the trees
that are years and years old!

Thelma L Cooper
A DOLL

Dedicated to Mother & Daddy—Julia and Homer Conner.

A Doll is much more than a toy to a
little girl
or a little boy!

A Doll is a friend they tell stories to
and cuddle close when they feel
blue.

A Doll doesn't tattle, that's for sure!
Little secrets she'll keep, lonely
hearts she'll cure.

A Doll never complains when
forgotten somewhere,
in the yard, in the rain or lost
under the stair.

A Doll loses a shoe, a stocking or
dress,
she feels no distress though she
may look a mess.

A Doll is waiting when a child needs
a friend,
her vigilance and patience will
never end.

A Doll is tucked into bed at night
and listens to stories as she is held
tight.

A Doll is waiting 'till school is out.
Endures dragging by one leg to see
brother strike out!

A Doll isn't selfish, she's willing to
share

hugs and kisses with Toy Horse
and Teddy Bear.

A doll is sometimes stored in a trunk.
When spring cleaning comes,
she's not tossed out with the junk.

A Doll can change little tears to a smile
and hopes you'll remember her
once in a while.

Yes, a Doll may be waiting in the attic back home,
hoping your child won't be tucked
in alone.

Christy Lawson
TOGETHER FOREVER
When your lips gently brush against mine
A feeling like no other comes over me.
For you are the rain in June that caresses the rose
And I am the one you center your sprinkles on.
For we are one Together, Forever.

Delinda L Tipps
CASTLES IN THE AIR

To all those who believed in me . . . Mother and JD, Uncle Larry, Memaw and Papaw, who is now in my Castle In The Air, With All My Love, Delinda.

As a little girl I always dreamed of Castles In The Air,
Where golden halos of Magic Love, floated freely there.

I climbed upon an angel's wings, and soared to stars above,
Where magic was my kindred spirit, from the castle's magic love.

I dream someday to find someone who needs a
Magic Love
And ride with me on golden halos
to my castle up above.

My dreams came true when I found you,
'Cause loving you is magic
I dream that you can love me too,
magic love that's real and true.

Magic cannot shine for you when only one love sparkles through
To feel real magic through and through, our love
can't shine unless there's two!

When the sparkle fades and the magic is gone,
tainted feelings linger on.

As a woman I still dream,
of castles and love and magical things.
As long as my castles are still in the air,
I'll dream of your love and wish you were there.

Sweet dreams to you, and magic too,
With love,
my castle waits for you.

Delinda L Tipps
MY PRAYER
Dear Heavenly Father above,

Always watch over the Papaw I love.
Take him with you to heaven above, bless him for eternity
with your sweet love.

Papaw was brave and honest, yet loyal and true
Loving and serving no one but you.
He spoiled me and loved me as no one could, and
and always took care of me, as I
knew he would.

Dear God, I loved him so much and respected him too,
I adored him, and held him so tight and so true.
Papaw lit up my life in millions of ways,
he gave me gladness and smiles
and sunshiny days!

To all those who loved him and knew him as well,
He'd joke with them, laugh
with them and sit for a spell.
He left so many memories to keep and to share; but,
Papaw always had time for me
to spare.

In addition to me, he had a beautiful Lady,
he cherished her, adored her
and spoiled her like crazy.
But his children and grandchildren held that special place,
They lit up his eyes, and put a
smile on his face.

His love for life was so deep and so strong,
If our world knew that love,
things would never seem
wrong.
His love was special, sincere, deep and true;
he was steadfast and wise, and
most gracious too;
whenever I needed him, he
knew what to do.

He was always there for me, in good times and bad,
with him by my side, I could
never stay sad.
If I had one wish that I knew would come true . . .
Papaw, it would be to have one more precious day with you.
I love you, I miss you and still need you too;
Papaw, be happy as I am for
you, and Always know that my
Blessing was you.

Papaw, you will always be in my heart, and in the love of our Heavenly Father. May he bless you and keep you. I miss you and love you truly.

Always, Your Granddaughter,
Delinda

Shannon C Murry
CYCLE OF NO END
Chained and abyssed in a cold lonely world I submit
Hoping to be sheltered from the miserable realities in life
Parents inflicting wounds to the heart as if being branded
Peers breeding misery into a massive sorrowful stampede
Mankind living money like a starved blood-sucking leech
Religion choking believers leaving them strangled within a noose
Greed nurturing its occupants like a deadly cancer cell
Drugs leaving you prey to a rotted carcass loving vulture
Love hurts, as it hangs you upon a spit searing security into insanity
These miserable realities in life occur and reoccur
Making it impossible for me to flee for shelter
Chains tighter, abyssed deeper enable me to cope
But then coping gets lonelier and sheltered grows colder
Often I wish I were an infant asleep all safe and secure
But when awoken I realize this pain comes twice again
So then I think of dying instead grasping for an end
To find there is no Lord there is no Savior
There is no end!

Thomas Kiernan
LOVE IS
. . . Love is . . .
. . . A tear.
An emotion from within.
. . . A smile.
A wide wonderful grin.
. . . A laugh.
From a child at play.
. . . The sun.
On a warm summer's day.
. . . A look.
From the young or old.
. . . A touch.
To warm the soul.
. . . A feeling.
Which no one can see
. . . A child.
Both of you and me

Thomas Kiernan
GHETTO CHILD
The wind blows cold
Over the lonely street,
As the young man rises
No more can he sleep.
For he lives in a world
That is full of hate,
No one to look up to
They're too busy to wait.

What this child needs
Is someone to sit,
And help with his burdens;
To ease his pain a tiny bit.

What this child wants
Is no great task,
But; for most of us,
It's too much to ask.

Cherie L Rouleau
CARUSO
Canaries were made to sing.
Caruso sings beautifully.
Sometimes, when he doesn't I ask him to,
Because I love to listen to his song.
But I shouldn't.
When a song is given out of love or joy or feeling
It is beautiful.
But when someone demands that we sing,
The song is never the same.
Canaries were made to sing.
Caruso sings beautifully.

John T Prescott
CONFUSION SPINNING ROUND AND ROUND
Confusion spinning round and round,
Caught in a maelstrom, destined to drown.
Up and down, right and left
It seems, my soul, it hath been cleft.
Split infinity, juxtaposing,
Indecision or just supposing?
Oceans of ice, heart of stone,
Pulling me under, toward the unknown.
Depths are increasing, to fathoms below,
Where am I destined, where will I go?
Darkness engulfs me, I'm pulled from the light
The whirlpool has caught me, and brought me to night.

At the bottom down under, my heart beats as thunder.
My lungs, rend, torn asunder.
On the ocean floor, one half remains,
Eroded by waves for all its days.
Overwhelmed am I? or shall I lie?
The Vortex has claimed me, that part of me dies.

Francis E Tenney
MEMORIES

To my husband, Ken, whom I love. Only you gave me these memories and only you can give me more.

The clear summer night,
with stars shining bright.
Echoes of joy and laughter,
and more thereafter.
The visits to the park,
playing till after dark.
Tight hugs here and there,
with kisses of care,
The walks, always hand and hand,
feeling special and grand.
Whispering secrets of pleasure,
wanting more to treasure.
The romantic hideaways,
to make up for lost days.
Having fun, doing whatever,
so there will be no never.
The intimate embracing of lust,
with overwhelming trust.
Wishing the day not to end,
afraid it will all descend.

Annetta Rygiel
LOVE IS BLIND

To Ron, my tender husband, who revealed love and our precious children, who magnified it.

Love is blind, or so they say
You fail to see my wrinkles and gray
Or those extra pounds, you seem unaware.
If my hair is tossed, you seem not to care.
Your eyes see right through all the faults that are mine.
Instead, when you see me, they take on a shine.
And just when I feel from beauty I'm far,
You take my hand and say "How lovely you are."
If love is blind then let it be.
If only the world could see what you see.

Mary Simpson
QUIET WALK
If I could do just anything
my heart desired to do.
I'd go for a long and quiet walk
as day was almost through.

I love the way God draws each day
to a soft and lazy end
He slowly draws His drapes of dusk
and shuts the darkness in.

He bids His angels bring the stars
to sprinkle in the night.
Some fall to streak across the sky,
some stay to shed their light.

There is no time that brings such
peace
when I am filled with care.
I seek Him in the twilight hours
and we walk together there.

Mason Grace
PLAYGROUND
Running over here,
running over there,
again and again, and to end;
Which part holds the most fun?

I suppose, it depends on
if you want to hit something . . .
chase something . . . climb something
or simply hang around.

The sounds of movement,
the noise, the laughter . . .
the sometimes sweetly
stabbing snickers overheard.

Racing the clouds, back and forth.
Spinning, in dizziness,
'till you meet the ground.
Whispering, while you will stable
eyes.

Unlimited imagination
of caged in freedom.
I have been a playground you
know . . .
playgrounds don't always get to play.

Mason Grace
FATHER
Help to release the negative
through the portal in my soul.
Thank You for the chance, again, to
make my Spirit whole

Send the negative beyond the sky . . .
Cast into a comet's tail
I've learned things from this
energy—
I've mostly learned to fail!!!

Cast off to the "Cosmic Closet"
to the "Shelf of Useless Thought"

Time to practice things I've learned;
Good lessons I've been taught

Lead me Father, while on this earth;
to be Righteous, to be Kind
Please forgive me, Father . . .
some thoughts, I leave behind.

Jon Lee Lauer
LOVE 'EM AND LEAVE 'EM
It's Christmas Eve and all is so well,
there's no one to talk to, there's no
one to tell.
The lady I love is leaving my side, I
can't understand just why we had
tried.

You have no way of knowing, you
have nothing to say, Sometimes
they talk and they leave you that
way.
There's no guarantees for the things
we had said, there's no under
standing the thoughts in her head.

That lady is lost in my mind and my
heart, I really can't see the reasons
we'd part.
The fires put out by the tears in your
eyes, It's too much of truth and
never the lies.

Now yesterday is gone and there's no
turning back, My love is still there
and that is a fact.
So baby please stay and never leave
me, I know that you won't, you
just want to be free.

The love that I had for you I
thought'd never die, It's too late to
worry, it's too late to try.
So baby if you love 'em and leave
'em that way, You'll have no one
to talk to with nothing to say.

Jon Lee Lauer
SOMETHING
Something more than a friend
Something warm and true
What can this something be
Involving me and you.

A something that we started
A something that won't end
This something I can tell ya
Is this something's not pretend.

Whatever that this something is
Whatever it will be
This something's on the border line
Of something wild and free.

I really cannot say just what this
something is
But at times it's slow yet fast
This one thing's something sure is
enough
Because somethings forever last.

Shana Lighter
SONNET TO MY SHINNING LOVE

To my wonderful Grandma, for without her this poem would have never been written. Thank you.

Come swim with me in waters cool
and clean
The sun upon my back as warm as
love.
My love enfold thee, keep thee far
from fear
Thy safety and my love hath much to
prove.
For they, O they can move at will,
my heart,
They rule the waters and the running
stream
Yet we must stay together, not apart
For things may not be always as they
seem.
Where waters sparkle, there is much
danger
My thoughts to yours, think well
until you die.
Go never where thou seeist a
stranger.
They mean you harm, so ever
underwater be.
For they, my love, can go where 'ere
they wish.
For they are humankind, and we but
fish.

Catherine Purcell
CONFORMITY
In everything
Lightness.
Angels airborne
On winged Harleys,
Offering white stuff
In its purist
Wet form—
Laying under overpass—
Violences
Echo
In studded ears . . .
Men with less freedom
Than me.

Micah A Ponce
AFTER DEATH
Descend into the Darkness, my son
creep back into the earth
come, come return to me
the mother who gave you birth.

There is no sunshine in the sky
that can warm your flesh as I
no winged bird's trumpet song
comforts you
as in the comfortable bedgrave you
lie.

Walk no more in the light above
believing your soul to be safe
It is all but a waking dream
turn your path homeward my
prodigal waif.

Revel as you burrow in the dirt
breathe deep the moist air in your
lungs
embrace the dank soil with your arms
you and I decompose as one.

I, the Firmament have always been
not created upon some whim
no seven days did mold my shape
I am the product of forever . . . not
Him.

So descend into the darkness
none can warm your flesh as I
It is all but a waking dream
you belong only to the Mother Earth .
. . when you die.

Laura L Vanuch
IF I KNEW THEN WHAT I KNOW NOW

To my grandparents: Bob and Betty Dukes.

If I knew then what I know now,
I know that things would be
somehow
the way they should, If only I could
go back and live again.

I'd go back to when life was new
when youth and innocence led you to
do
the crazy things that childishness
brings
If only then I knew.

To the people who have touched my
heart
my words had all but torn us apart.
Comments I didn't mean, as trivial as
they seem,
I'd like to say I'm sorry.

And my parents who had seemed so
cold
I miss them now as I grow old.
And I'd like to shake their hand, for
now I understand
But I guess it's too late to tell them.

For my children who have grown and
gone away,
I wish I could find the words to say
but I never have grieved, for all they
achieved
I only hope they're happy.

And now as I sit in my golden years
I think, and my eyes are filled with
tears
with all I didn't do of all the things
I'd wanted to
I'd like to go back and do them.

Now I turn back the pages of my
book
and to each page a second look.
And between the lines, it's happiness
I find
that made it all worthwhile
and I smile.

Jean Franse
FAITH
My unrequited love lives on,
Surviving but to dwell
Upon the countenance from which
All adoration fell.

Though now in time's unceasing flow
The tangible is parted,
Yet in some new face still I see
The fount from which it started.

And there is full remembrance of
The time when love was christened.
He spoke enchanted words of love
And angels bent to listen.

My husband, Carroll

Carol Jones
CANVAS OF ROCK
On the porch facing south where the
trade winds blow
there's an artist at work and his
picture will grow.
On his canvas of rock, he'll lay his
heart down
making puzzles of stone on the
cold hard ground.
Together he weaves the mortar and
rocks
around odd shaped pieces of his
jigsaw blocks.

Rocks from the creek and the cliff so
tall
Rocks from the towering forest wall
From faraway places and rocky
spaces
And under the thundering waterfall.

Cutting and shaping the gemstone
slate
the artist's picture unfolds
As he washes and scrapes and fits
into shape
His canvas of rock on the knoll.

Franz von Weizmann
THE ANSWERS
When I was a little boy, I wanted to
be big,
But when I became big, I became
very poor.
Not satisfied with my life, I prayed to
my GOD,
And HE led me to the Army, and
opened up another door.
Onward did I march, and powerful
did I become.
I was cast into a war and later
became undone.
Poor once again, I called upon the
LORD.

I prayed for new direction and buried my heavy sword.
I then studied medicine, and became a useful man,
But I became so busy I neglected the master plan.
I forgot about loneliness and the emptiness of life.
I longed for a family and the company of a wife.

My career stopped suddenly and I disappeared from the scene.
I pursued that missing companion and the fulfillment of my dream.
A lady did I meet and she appeared the answer to my quest,
But later she was gone with a friend I thought the best.
Emptiness and depression overtook my way of life,
And I began to wander aimlessly, confused and full of strife.
Again I prayed to JESUS, seeking a reason for it all.
At last I learned the answers for my sufferings and my fall.
I was now with my FATHER who taught me to love HIM most of all.

Linda Wicklein
A SPECIAL SEASON

To Jeremiah, my son . . . The greatest Love I hold in my heart.

The lazy days of Autumn
Are a special time of year,
To reflect upon the summer
Watching colors reappear.

The golden reds and oranges
Of the foliage all around
And the sadness of that first leaf
As it floats down to the ground.

The air is filled with sadness
And it carries on its breeze,
The promise of its winter
And the scent of burning leaves.

The beauty and serenity
That makes these special days,
Is but a passing moment
As you watch them slip away.

The heart is filled with laughter
And the memories we'll hold dear,
As the lazy days of Autumn
Start to fade and disappear.

Denzil Cox
BE HOME SOON

This poem was written to my darling wife, Lavern, at the end of World War II.

The days are drawing nearer
When my time in Europe is through,
And my heart is ever pounding
As I think of home and you . . .

Tho' the time has seemed to linger,
And the nights were, oh, so long,
But now I feel so happy,
As I lift my voice in song . . .

I remember back in combat,
When I said to God on High,
Please remember my wife and kiddies,
And do not let me die . . .

Now, God surely heard my prayers—
He made the impossible come true,
For He spared my life in battle,
And now I'll soon be back with you . . .

Now, Sweet Wife and Little Kiddies,
Just remember this, I say,
If you are ever in serious trouble,
Just knuckle down and pray.

Mary Sodano
FIRST DAY OF SCHOOL

To my grandchildren, Sherry, Chris, Marie, Kristen, Erin, Danny & Danielle.

As I look up at old red brick, its screaming windowpanes
penetrate the delicate veil that covers my memory, focusing on a shy six-year-old, withdrawn, apprehensive and afraid.
Light looms in on a black and white rectangular form,
stone faced, five decades and a crucifix.
Gray walled cubicles scented with lye, lead and the printed word
take shape around a strange c
argo with forty eyes staring straight ahead as pointer does her dance routine on slate.
Shadowy figures from the past
encased in oak and wrought iron
have been released from their prison house to recreate for me that first;
The loneliest day of my life.

Debra K Wheeler
INNOCENT CRIES

Dedicated to & in memory of the twenty-five million babies aborted since 1973.

Please hear my innocent cry, before many more of us suffer and die.
Speak out, Speak out for me, so blinded eyes begin to see . . .

Please Mom, Hear my earnest cry,
Save my life, don't let me die.
If only my voice could be heard . . .
but I'm silent and can't say a word.

Hundreds just like me are murdered each day, no matter what some people might say. Be my voice and speak out for me, so innocent bloodshed no longer will be.

God gave me life that began in you, save us from this agony we both will go through. Someone could love me so don't make me pay. Let me LIVE! Consider another way.

If in your heart you could care for me, forget this crime and set me free; I have so much that I could give, if only you'd keep me safe and let me live. This decision you're making, Is it your choice? Listen Mom, can't you hear my voice?

Please know if you permit me to stay, there are a few words that I must say . . . Thank You Mom, You heard my cries, and have wiped the teardrops from my eyes.

Beth Ann Byrd
MIRROR IMAGE

To my parents who gave me the inspiration. Love, Beth.

Looking in the mirror I see a reflection of time
Time flying quickly past me and into the future
The mirror never lies, and I believe this as I see all the opportunities I had to reach slowly pass me by
It's not a reflection of a person that didn't have a chance to care
It's a reflection of a person that lives in the past

Camilla M Smith
A CHILD'S WORLD

What are you dreaming of my little one
Are your soldiers at war, has a war been won.
You're so angelic and innocent, so tiny and wee
Are your planes soaring high, your ships at sea

Do you dream of the bike you will learn to ride
Or the home run you'll hit and beam with pride
Do you wonder how tall you'll grow to be
Or what it will be like when you turn three

Are you frightened by things you know nothing about
Do you wonder if we love you when we shout
Are you happy in dreamland fast asleep
With your soul in God's hand for him to keep

The wonders of childhood show on your face
As you slumber peacefully in God's embrace
And when you wake, I'll be right here.
To help keep the new day free from fear.

So pleasant dreams in your safe little world
May all your hopes soon be unfurled
May you grow up happy, and safe and sure
In the knowledge that our love will keep you secure.

Bonnie Lee Lundy
ONE LOOK

This poem is dedicated to Nick.

One look from you was all it took.
From that moment, I've been hooked.
I love your body and your mind.
Your personality is oh so kind.
Do you know how much you mean to me?
It's like I'm the lock which cannot be opened without the key.
You have opened my heart.
Without you, it's missing a part.
That part of you that's in me means so much.
That's why I will always need your tender touch.
When your lips are pressed against mine,
it sends chills up and down my spine.
Those chills you send are just like fire.
A fire which is burning with a massive desire.
A desire which must be met
which is only by you, if you'd let.

Bruce Starfield
LAID BACK AND LAZY

Laid back and lazy and no good they say
At times I've been crazy and I think that's okay
And I may be wrong, 'cause I'm not always right
My hat's off to you, you're a helluva sight.

When I see the sunset with a beer in my hand
Then I'll drink a toast to this beautiful land
'Cause I think it's great in the U.S. of A.
Where a man can be whatever they say.

With the freedom we share some people get shady
But here's one to you, you beautiful lady
Well I'll drink till I'm drunk and lying on the floor
If I see the sunrise, I'll have me one more.

James T Ferris
TO WAKE A DAY FOR REASON WHY

This poem is dedicated to my wife, Maria S. Ferris, my son, James M. Ferris, and my daughter, Jessica J. Ferris. They inspired this poem along with my old days as a "Workaholic."

To wake a day for reason why
to enter the morn with no idea
if to be repeated all the time
is this why we are alive

Work to tiredness as we all do
to enter our home without wonder why
now it's night and with no time
is this why we are to strive

More of the boss do we know
than our wife, lass or lad
wait at home with open arms
only to find we have no drive

Beyond the dollar we must see
surely our kin are not forgotten
for the future and world beyond
answers why we are alive.

Ruth Joan Takacs
THE CLOWNS

To Bea for all her help.

Fantasy and laughter makes a clown a clown
No matter what's inside nothing lets him down.
At least not on the outside for other folks to see.
Fantasy and laughing is what a clown means to me.

The circus plays a part of it, everything bright and gay.
I love to go to the circus to see the clowns at play.
Tall ones, short ones, whatever their mood might be
I'll look up or I'll look down, A clown there I will see.

The band plays on, I enjoy every minute of their game.
The band plays on, I ignore a lion to be tamed.
Because my eyes are on the clowns in their gaiety
Sometimes I'd like to be a clown—can you imagine that with me?

Aline Stafford
LOVE ME, LOVE YOU

Written by Aline Stafford for the man I love, Alan Mills. I'm looking forward to spending the rest of my life with you.

Love me, Love you
Together one, Alone two
Hearts tied, Souls touch
Trouble unspoken, Remains such

No future, present, past
Making love, Moments last
Short times, Fantasy rules
No goodbyes, Passion fools

Sleepless nights, Lonely Days
Waking dreams, Reality plays
One desires. The other needs
People fail, Love leads

Love me, Love you
Together one, Alone two

Pat Matheson
TOMORROW

To all my family—a little keepsake.

Turn to me
And share with me
Everything that we have today.

Turn to me
And be with me
Before tomorrow slips it all away

Turn to me
And need me
Before one of us has to say
Tomorrow's here and I can't stay.

Dawn Robnolt
I THINK I WILL CALL HIM MY FRIEND

Dedicated to Tom Sherbrook, my teacher and friend.

I think I will call him my friend
Even though some may call him a preacher.
He teaches love in all he pursues.
As his words ring true, he's a teacher.

Gently he leads the best way he knows how;
Love, live the truth and they'll follow.
He watches as slowly the buds burst forth
From lives that had once seemed so hollow.

When time gives him up on this earth plane,
And his battles are fought and won,
His students will carry the message he taught,
What more can God say but well done.

Dawn Robnolt
A SPECIAL MAN

Dedicated to my husband, Peter.

A quiet man, a gentle soul,
With a love deep in his heart.
Our paths did cross for a moment in time,
They were meant to from the start.

We loved, we laughed, sometimes we cried,
And we learned along the way,
That time on earth is limited,
For we don't know how long we'll stay.

I'll never see a rainbow,
Or sunrise brightened rays,
I'll never look upon a rock,
Without seeing his face.

For all the love he's shared with me
My soul does feel its worth.
I pray that I'll pass this love along
As I bend to touch the earth.

Philip A Eckerle
Dejá Vu
Somewhere in the turbulence of time past
I have been where I am today.
I have felt the same stirring
Of emotion,
And the same fears.
Long ago and far away
I arrived where I am
But I could not or would not stay.
I have traveled the full circle
And returned to
Déjà vu,
Thoughts of you.

Doreen Skinner

Doreen Skinner
MORE PRECIOUS
The Bible, more precious than gold,
Filled with history, glad hopes, and its pages unfold,

It speaks of the Father and tells of his love,
And shows us the way to the mansions above,

I know not by what methods rare,
But this I know—God answers prayer.

The Bible, more precious than gold,
Jesus, the greatest story ever told.

I leave my prayers with Him alone,
Whose Will is wiser than my own.

Great Father of glory, pure Father of light,
The angels praise thy glorious sight.

The Bible, God's Word more precious than gold,
Tells of Jesus, my Saviour bright and bold.

The Bible speaks to people all walks of life,
To bring them from sin and strife.

Jesus loves me this I know,
For the Bible told me so.

What a day of rapture that will be,
When I finally meet and see,
My Saviour more precious than gold.

Doreen Skinner
THE SACRIFICE
The world was filled with trouble and despair,
People dying and every wicked imagination;
It was so great no one cannot compare.

More interested in worldly fame,
They forgot the meaning of His name;
Knowing not their destiny is fate.

One day in Heaven something wonderful happened,
God sent His Son to this sinful earth;
The wisemen brought gold, frankincense and myrrh.

The Son brought forth the gospel, the Word,
That all ages may hear and receive;
Instead they all refused and didn't believe.

Suddenly, that day came,
The world was sure not to forget;
His Holy name.

Jesus, the sacrifice for man's sin,
Paid the price to those who enter in,
No greater love can compare;
The Sacrifice in which He has given,
To let the world know all has been forgiven.

Deneen Skinner
THE LITTLE PREACHER

Dedicated to Bro. Carl Perkins.

There was a young man in the church,
Who was in deep search,
For something that would satisfy his need.

One day the Lord called Him to preach,
He set out to see how many He could reach,
For the mission to which he was called.

He was a little preacher full of zeal,
Who preached his messages with sincerity,
Honesty and with great feel.

The Little Preacher is handsome and debonaire,
And the people sat and listened intently—
To hear what God has to share.

I like this Little Preacher, so kind,
He always stays on everyone's mind,
As He takes a stand to help the blind.

He tells of the one who gives life
To those who are in need,
If only they would take heed.

The Little Preacher still goes on,
Spreading God's Word to everyone,
And to carry the news God has won.

Cindy A Spearman
OPERA GLASSES

To Dad—whose example taught me to live with dignity and that self-respect is priceless. Eternal gratitude from your favorite daughter.

Confusion is the byword
I'm enraptured with, of late
The never ending patterns
An eternal twist of fate
That might be quite amusing
This play so fraught with strife
Viewed through opera glasses
In someone else's life.
For now it is a sorrow
A void beyond the door
That lengthens with the shadows
Night casts upon the floor.
And I'd tear away each soul scar
That they might bleed anew
If it would fill the emptiness
And wash me clean of you.
My life remains in fragments
The question always, "When?"
My love won't be a parody
Of what it could have been.

Betty Minor
INFINITE
The serene blue of the
evening sky,
Untouched, unmarred
by a single cloud,
The thin sickle of a
spring moon reaching,
To touch the rays of the
evening star,
A soul in silent slumber,
No cloud to darken the mind
A vanishing spirit rising
to reach for the light of God.

Andrew John Ward
TRIALS AND TRIBULATIONS
Toiling in heat, intolerable heat,
The beat of the whip cracks with anger;
White man shouts with mean slander,
Lashing my sisters, mother and brother.

Striking me upon the temple,
Blood trickles as a little stream;
Sitting or lying, I began to dream,
Is this life really worth it?
Kidding myself, I tried to lie,
Think it is time to wither,
White man shouts with infinite anger.

Running forward, muskets strike,
Bayonets taunt, while friends die;
Variate that conniving white man.
Oh my God do not forsake me,
Take my soul and really save me.

Now my people are free to breed,
No more ships to make us bleed!
Laying down and reading this,
My children will not face the awful abyss;
The dream is real, so I die.

Charles F Madden

Charles F Madden
OUR ENEMY—BEWARE
The planes in the air, the ships on the sea,
Are manned by our men to keep us free.

They never were sent to put down by force
Another country, unless they were crossed.
We have always been ready to take a slap,
To be insulted and bullied by the other chap,
Rather than to use our might
In, perhaps, an unfair fight,
But when they want to take your life,
To involve your country in awful strife,

It might be well for them to know,
We might be gentle, we might be slow,
But when this country begins to go,
The one to beware will be our foe.

Charles F Madden
FREEDOM
The price you pay that it may stay forever in your land,
Is not to see what you get free with empty, outstretched, hand;
But toil and sweat then you may get that for which others flee,
That land so fair, that land so square, that land that we call free.
You've got to fight with all your might for something you prize dear,
To say, to mean, to show, it's not a word they hear
But by our pride, we'll show the guy away across the sea;
We're in a land, a land that's grand, a land that we call free.
Roll up your sleeves it's bound to please those who love liberty,
As side by side they glorify this land that we call free;
But don't forget, there's more than sweat that we must have in store
It's love of God and Country;
Then surely there'll be more
Of peace we crave, if we must save, this land the world can see
I truly hope forever, forever will be free.
Don't sell it short for it's been bought with the blood our men have shed;
Who valued it so highly that now they all lie dead.
To take this land for granted a great mistake 'twould be,
This land so fair, this land so square, might then ease to be free.

William M Lynk
THE DRAGONSLAYER
Some years have passed since I knew thee
A Dragonslayer he chose to be
"Why must thou leave, and abandon all?"
To find his peace; an inner call.

Most wants and needs were tended to
But questions came, his heart was blue
"How can I know, until I've seen
The things I've heard, that others mean?"

So then he left, in search of Doubt
That Dragon that he's thought about
And where to go—he knew in part
That answer lied within his heart.

He fought with thieves and paupers bold
As anger brewed, his heart grew cold
When would he find this Dragon green?
It stood before him—fierce and mean.

The years had gone, the time had come
To slay this Dragon, feared by some
He raised the sword kept at his side
Thrust in its heart—the Dragon died.

And in a flash, he knew right there
The one he loved, they were a pair
He conquered Doubt and knew his heart
His journey home—he must now start.

He pondered on this Dragon killed
There was but one, he ever willed
This one he had, what he longed for
But didn't know 'till he looked more.

We often search for what we've got
In other places, it is not
Their hearts grew close—their souls did soar
But a Dragonslayer, never more.

Clyde E Tennyson
A BEAR
To my grandson, Randy Burgess.

A little Eskimo sleeps
in his little bearskin
and keeps quite warm,
I am told.
I slept in my "bare" skin
and I got a hell of a cold

Kimberly Cunningham-Kyoung Sook Yang
SOMEBODY
To whom it may concern, only God knows.

Oh, how my heart aches to have somebody,
To share my life and thoughts.
To love me tenderly but passionately,
And give me all support.

Oh, how my heart aches to have somebody,
To put their arms around me.
And if we often disagree,
He'll still respect and love me.

Oh, how my heart aches to have somebody,
Who, when he walks in late at night,
Will kiss me gently on the lips
And sit to hold me tight.

Oh, how my heart aches to have somebody,
This someone in my mind.
Yet, my heart knows down deep inside,
True love is only a matter of time.

Bobbie
AT HOME AT LAST
In memory of Yvonne Schneider.

On golden shores . . . I stand
Touching Jesus's outstretched hand—
Wide of eyes . . . I now can see
Heaven's beauty encircling . . . me

Christ died for sinners, such as I
His blood he shed, his body did die—
His gift, his love, his mercy, he gave
That I a sinner, would reach heaven's gate.

Through his resurrection, he still lives
He's building mansions, to us he gives—
"Born again" I've reached that shore
I'm now with . . . him . . . forevermore.

On golden shores . . . I stand
Touching Jesus's outstretched hand—
I'm crossing that river . . . to Jesus's side
Forever . . . with him . . . to abide.

His head doth nod . . . his hands outstretch
For me to take . . . that "final" . . . step
I come . . . with joy . . . my life is . . . past
To be . . . forever . . . with my Lord
At "home at last."

Michael G Healy
YET I'M NOT AFRAID OF YOU
I seem to know your one desire
I seem to know that you're kind
I seem to sense your fears
Though you have a hardened heart

I have wealth and need nothing more than love
But I must know and feel this passion here within my heart
You're a vixen trying to lure me with your splendor and your words
I'm dreaming it can't be true

"I can't answer you," he said
She laughed and came so close to him
He could feel her hot breath on his skin
He shivered, rose to his feet and started to leave

It's no dream she cried, "It's true I love you,
But I must be sure."
So please wait and feel the truth reach out to you
So you can know that I'm yours, and we'll be happy
You'll see, you'll never be lonely with me.

Michéllе L Slack
LOVE AGAIN
My life has finally
turned around,
Laughing not crying
is the new sound.
Love is at my door
once again,
A new experience is
ready to begin.
I did remember my
solemn words,
Don't rush into love
that'd be absurd.
I found this totally
wonderful guy,
As fascinating as a
clear blue sky.
He picked me up
when I was down,
Making a smile
turn from a frown.
Filling the space
that no one could,
Saying that caring
for me he would.
We've shared
some special things,
Happiness to me
is what he brings.
My friends like
him and they don't mind,
A guy that treats me
good is hard to find.
I care for him
and that he does know,
And if it's up to
me I'll never let him go.

Julie Rea
AS THE RIVER RUNS SILENT
To Jeff, my husband, my love, my best friend, and always, my inspiration . . . forever . . .

as the river runs silent,
and the dove flies with grace,
as the rose has its beauty,
like silk and fine lace . . .

as children run free,
like deer in the field,
as the rain softly falls,
to the grass without yield . . .

as the wind softly blows,
and the trees gently sway,
as the sun slowly sets,
and then rises to day . . .

as angels sing lowly,
sweet songs from above,
so my heart does for you,
with undying love . . .

Gillian England
DESTITUTION'S SCHOLARS
For my father and mother, who showed me the world's to be found in words.

They huddled up to abandoned Dumpsters
Sometimes together, always alone.
In threadbare coats, like newborn pups or mice
They maneuver for the middle
In unending pursuit of warmth, of safety.

Cold, scared, hard and hungry—
Is this what we want
Them to remember of the "golden age" of youth?
They extend their hands to strangers—
Humility is mastered early by destitution's scholars.
A quick study is imperative to Survival.

We can see them at every turn
(If we want to).
We can ignore them just as easily
(As we're wont to).

We sow our crocodile tears
On children worlds away,
And flood the lands where granted no food grows,
Nor water flows.

But perhaps the drops should water
More domestic ground?

Karleen Espinosa
I WILL LEAVE THIS WORLD LOVING YOU
This is dedicated to my one and only George Henderson.

You may drop me a line now and then
to let me know how you are.
But if we never meet again
and my life is over,

I WILL LEAVE THIS
WORLD LOVING YOU.

You were mine for awhile
and I was grateful.
You can take everything,
except my memories.
But if we never meet again
on this side of Heaven,
I WILL LEAVE THIS
WORLD LOVING YOU.

Me-Lissa Cartales

GREEK WOMAN BATHING

To Ron, my beloved. Without you, this poem would never have been written; and I certainly would not have had the courage to publish it.

A shawl drapes art-
fully over
a soft shoulder,
elegantly
falling upon
a supple breast
and resting on
a long bare leg;

Sunlight trembles
in small droplets
as they slip through
the gaps of the
knitted garment
shimmering down
a pure white form;

She perches there:
innocently,
sensuously
silently, at
the edge of the
clear blue water.

Jenna Burns

AS THE SUN SETS

No better words could describe you Mom; I love you.

As the sun sets, I watch you walk along.
You have lived and loved,

And still your time has not come.
You are a beauty of grace,
And if age has stricken, It has not left a trace.

You are the wisdom, love, and knowledge of my life.
Because of you I was brought into this world.
For me, you were my father's wife.

I want you to know,
You are the spirit in my soul.
You have taught me to live, learn, and grow.

Somedays I wonder where I would be without you,
You have taught me all there is to know.
You have watched me live, learn, and grow.

And so now I must tell you
How very much I care,
For me mother,
You have always been there.
I love you.

Katherine L Buster

MY LOVE

Dedicated to David Sepulveda . . . my inspiration, my love!

When I think of you a smile forms on my lips,
a spark from our love shines in my eyes,
my heart flutters with anticipation of seeing you again.

There doesn't seem to be enough hours in the day for me to show my love for you. If you were to hold me in your arms at this very moment I still would not be close enough to your warmth.

Knowing that you accept me and love me for who I am is a wonderful feeling.

I enjoy being the one that makes you happy,
and I do my best to fill all your needs,
and I pray that I can grant your every wish come true.

Patricia M Barkley

DECEIT

To Larry with love.

You come to me, you call me sweet,
You pet and pamper when we meet.
But then your wife you must appease.
"May I use your telephone, please?"
You call her sweet endearing names.
Perhaps she does not know your games,
But then again, maybe she knows,
And that just keeps you on your toes.
I know that I'm the stupid one,
At my expense you have your fun.
I wonder whose deceiving who?

Is it her, me, or is it you?
I know that were you asked to choose.
The question would not you confuse.
You'd run to her with undue haste,
And I'd be left with downcast face.
Not because she's such a honey.
She has a firm grip on your money.
It's hard to love another's mate
But for the moment that's my fate.

Judy Hoover-Starling

THE PERFECT MAN

For DMB, a man that has showed me more about life, caring and giving and who will always have a special place in my heart.

In this world of crime, passion and hate there is the Perfect Man.
Somewhere in this world a man for every woman, a woman for every man.
There are many definitions of perfection; yet perfection is in the eyes of the beholder.
My idea of the perfect man is not how tall he is or the color of his eyes.
Yet what perfection is to me is what is on the inside.
It doesn't matter how long the hair or really what he drives.
Yet how he treats me comes from the inside.
In every man there is a heart with feelings and who cares.
You can't find that perfect man on one-night stands alone.
You have to get to know him and show him that you care.
And if by chance he'll take that chance—
You just might have found that perfect man you've dreamed of so many years ago.
No, perfection is not on the outside but on the inside where we store our thoughts and secrets that we never ever share.
To compare the outside without looking in; is not a chance for anyone to find the Perfect Man.

Florence Charlotte Rousey

A FRIEND SO TRUE

With love to my family, friends, and teachers, who raised me, consoled me, and taught me. With special thanks to my pastor and youth director.

Did you ever have a Friend so true,
That He gave His life for you?

Did you ever have a Friend so true,
That He knows everything you do?

Is He more than you can be?
Is He every sight you see?
Is He the rainbow in the sky?
Is He there when you say goodbye?

Did you ever have a Friend so true,
What was that you did? No matter,
He forgave you.

Do you want to know a Friend so true?
Come on over, I'll introduce Him to you!

They've written a book about Him
it's called the Holy Bible.
What were your sins? If you truly love Him, He won't hold you liable.

I have a Friend so true, His name is Jesus Christ
and He shouldn't be a stranger,
For He was the little babe laid in a manger.

He is always my Friend so true.
Now let's hear it! What about you?

Sharon Keefe

ONE KISS

One kiss, one love, one life—together, Love Vincent.

I never felt a kiss so sweet,
Until your lips met mine.
That feeling hasn't gone away,
It's with me all the time.
I didn't think I'd ever dream,
that I could feel like this.
Spending all my excess time
In thoughts of that first kiss.
At that moment I knew for sure
that it was not the same.
Because your lips sent sparks of fire,
dashing through my brain.
I knew you were the one for me when our lips did part,
Because those sparks went through my body,
and landed in my heart.
As I write these last two lines
I wished that you were here,
So I could gaze into your eyes,
and tell you, "Thank you, Dear."

Richard J Lea

A LOVE LONGED FOR

To a very special lady.

You are a love I have longed for,
My life started with you, all
My hopes were in you, I don't
know how to give you up—
My love is forever, why do you
hurt me so, my love forever,
I don't know how to give you up—
You were my answer to a prayer,
a love I never dared to hope for,
in you lies my tomorrows, share
with me those tomorrows, I love you so—
My love is forever, why do you hurt
me so, my love is forever, I don't
know how to give you up—
How to give you up—you are a
a love longed for

Audrey Menegus

ETERNAL GARDEN OF LOVE

In memory of my beloved parents Peter and Eleanor McKeon.

In the Eternal Garden Of Love, you and I have found a place
With memories of happy days, that time cannot erase
The garden is full of beauty, to delight both mind and heart
When we travel to our garden, we are never really far apart
Just close your eyes and wander to our wonderful secret place
If you use your imagination, you will see my smiling face
Our love is like the garden, it will be there for all time
And like the beautiful garden, your love will always be mine

Patricia Chilcote

COME WALK WITH ME

To my family, Friends and Neighbors, whose lives are surrounded by the Peace and Beauty of Lobster Valley, Oregon.

Come walk with me through the forest
where the majestic fir trees grow,
as the cool breeze of summer rustles
the twigs below.
Or walk with me in the winter
on a cold and stormy day,
as the winds whip the branches
and the mighty giants sway.
Walk with me in the springtime
while the fresh smell of spring's
in the air, for the beautiful forest we hold sacred,
may not always be standing there.

Donna Maag

MY CHRISTMAS PRAYER

This poem is dedicated to my mother and my brother (Jimmy) who was taken away from us at the age of three.

All I want for Christmas
Is to have my little brother back.
I know that he'll just fit,
In Santa Claus's sack.

I'm not asking for much.
Nothing like a diamond ring.
I just want my brother.
And it won't cost you a thing.

Mary Agnes Lynch

THANKSGIVING DAY PRAYER

To God, our Father.

I

"Thank you," "God," for our blessings,
On this blessed Thanksgiving Day.
Thank "You" for "Your" gifts of plenty,
As we bow our heads to pray.
"Thank "You" for "Your" unending love,
and our eternal Home,
"Heaven above."

II
"Thank You," "God," for the gifts we
receive from Thy bounty on
Thanksgiving Day,
For our "True Faith" and "precious
life," to "You,"
Our "God," we say,
"Thank You," "Thank You,"
dear "Divine Lord," for the greatest
of all gifts,
"Almighty God."

David R Buchholz
SAILOR'S WIDOW

Poetry is love and beauty. Therefore, with all my heart, I dedicate this poem and everything I write to Anne—the most beautiful person in the world. Thanks for everything!

A crouched silhouette on the dock
Stares out over the waves of the bay
Watching the sun's last bit of
shimmer fall
And close out another day

The wind whips her frailed hair
The sea gulls seem to laugh
As they dance in the air
To the wind's playful wrath

Waves beat the sides of the pier
Splashes jump to her feet
She moves back a step, surprised
Then looks around so discrete

The coal docks distant activity
Rolls out over the waves
It's the sounds of the pier
Which remind her of a love she
craves

Now off in the distance
Over whitecaps too numerous to
count
Comes a ferry from the point
And it comes carrying a fair amount
But, on nights like tonight
A night no different than another
The ferry can't bring back
What the sea took from her lover.

Thelma L Williams
LIFE

To Mom, Dad and my Grandparents. Thanks for always pushing me to try.

For some life is happiness: All sunshine and roses. For others it's sadness: All brimstone and ashes.

For some success comes easy, while for others it never comes at all.

Some never know what it is to want; while others want for it all.

Some are loved and admired from both near and afar. But for others it's loneliness, scorn and hate.

Why must some go through so much pain, only to be hurt again and again. While others know mostly love and happiness and hardly any pain at all.

For some death is feared, they want to live it up. They're having too much fun to grow old and die. But for others death is a sweet song. Enchanting and longed for. They know that when death does come that the pain will be over.

Life is mean and hateful to some. But to others . . . oh those are the ones, They are the ones that life gives to. Gives all that she has. She doesn't know how to deal happiness and sadness out equally, But isn't that her fault? Isn't that life?

Imogene Center
WALK A LITTLE SLOWER

With love and fond memories. To Judy, Tanya and my friend, my pal, & my beloved brother, Walter Scott Lacy.

Walk a little slower child, my pace is getting slower, Try to understand me
Now—you see Mom's getting older. Be patient with me, dear, When my humor seems indiscreet, and there's a frown upon my face. I'm not so steady on my feet. Don't be ashamed of wrinkled hands or posture not so proud or straight—Seems those tasks of love I used to do—now at times must wait.

The eyes so blue have faded. And golden hair turned gray, Mother's not so pretty now, as in my younger days. The voice that sang to you—lullabies of love in your tender years—I'm sure if you listen closely you'll hear some silent tears. Sweet precious memories linger in my heart—time can never measure. So be gentle with this old heart it too has grown fragile—Easily could be broken, if you forsake me ever.

Just walk a little slower with me my child, through these my twilight years. Keep me ever young, with your youth and laughter—sometimes wipes away my tears.

Take me by the hand, tell me that you love me and will forsake me never. Just walk a little slower.

Sallie McGee
THE ADOPTION

To my dear family, Pat and Shannon. Whom I love so.

We always wanted children, to
feather our nest
But to this end had never been
blessed
She came into our lives approaching
her two's
Once there—We threw out all the
rules
She moved into our hearts—And
rearranged completely—all our old
values that we had stored so neatly
with her sweet smile, and cute little
ways
that made life fuller and brightened
our days
Free from this love, We never want
to be
Now She is our daughter,
Sweet little Shannon Lee.

Sallie McGee
PASS THIS WAY AGAIN

Let me be all that I can, as a
spouse—parent or kin.
For I'll not pass this way again:

For those in need—lend a hand—
And to the lonely—Be a friend.
For I'll not pass this way again.

May my love of fellow man be as
pure—
as God has planned. While I'm here
upon this land.
For I'll not pass this way again.

To love the earth and nature in
birth—
And to the world feel akin.
For I'll not pass this way again.

Our lives are as an hourglass of sand,
A short time and we will disband—
and travel to a far off plane.
And never pass this way again

Barbara S Goertz
LIFE

I dedicate this poem to Charles Goertz, my beloved Husband, and thank him for showing me what life is about, Love.

People come and people go
in this imbroglio

Some are early some are late
But on arrival all are inchoate

They try so hard to master it
But, alas it seems to be predestinate

Sometimes its lessons are hard to
percept
It seems there are no choices but to
accept

They are allowed to stay for such a
short time
It's almost like playing a pantomime

And when the end of it draws near
The goal it seems is to leave with no
fear

It was a gift from God, you see
To help prepare us for eternity

Madeline K Daniels
SPRING

Flowers popping through the ground,
Wee children dancing all around;
Birds fly their way again to North,
Happy songs they gayly chirp and
chort.
The air so very fresh and clean,
New babies born, soon to be weaned.
All things so new and beautiful
Tis Spring again on the new yule.

George Forrester
FROZEN

Birds fly slowly, stiffer now
No singing on the sill;
Waving a good-bye to loving thrill,
To chirp and entice, the one so nice;
I'll fly north this winter to freeze my
heart;
So my beating wings will never part
from you.

Lillian A Eigner
ALONE

I open my eyes to a darkened room;
The blackened sky has not awakened.
Soon, it too, gives promise of a new
day.
A faint shading diffusing the
darkness
With shades of gray, yet, the eyes do
not
Adjust to light or color.
Slowly I rise and view the sky,
As ticking time and dawn move
silently
Forward, unveiling early morning.

The waking sky and silent house steal
Into my arousing senses, alerting me
To the stillness all around. No one
With whom to talk, no human voice
within
My home to greet and say, "How are
you?"
The sky has brightened, light now
suffuses
Color and heralds the morning. The
house,
My home, remains sober and silent,
digging
Deeper into the thick concrete walls
and
Carpet. Making no sound. Nothing.
I am alone.

Brent Stauffer
THANK YOU

My eyes once smiled, my face once
sweet
My life was easy, nice and neat
But as time went by, I began to
change
My eyes no longer smiled, my face,
now strange
Times were changing, I was too
Confused and alone, I didn't know
what to do.

Death was the answer, it had to be
That's the only way, I could truly be
free
So I plotted and planned, then gave it
a try
But something went wrong, I didn't
die.

Now I wake up, in sweat from fright
Dreaming about that lonely night
So I often stop to look above
And thank the Lord, for his love.

Marlene Palacios

Marlene Palacios
TRUE LOVE

To my loving family: Roberto, Michael, Yolanda, Armando and Sylvia. To my son Michael and his wife Emma Palacios and all the family Palacios and to my sister Miriam Mendieta and Family, God bless you all.

High above the mountains,
underneath the trees,
lies my beloved underneath the
leaves,

Have you seen the flowers growing
straight and tall?
Oh! How beautiful, over by the wall.

I have watered them for you my
darling with my tears,
all these days, months, and years,

Pretending you are here makes me
feel alive,
but knowing the truth makes me want
to die.

Honey if we only knew what laid
ahead,

You would be here with me and not lying dead.

So many times I wondered how it would be,
as I stare hopelessly into the deep blue sea.

As time has passed and the hurt is healing,
I begin to have a great new feeling,

That you are here with me on shore,
and I am not alone anymore.

As I see the airplane disappear in the sky above,
I know now this was true love . . .

Monique Martin
WORD UP!

Being in rhythm with your thoughts
And breaking it down

Phrases dancing on pages
Giving colour to sound

Delineations of oppressed nations
Hand painted lovers with rosy fixations

A twang a pang a sweet sticky thang

Give birth to your dreams and romantic love potions
Cuz life as we know it began as a notion!

In the beginning there was the word . . .
word up!

Rose M Cronk
INSIDE LOOKING OUT

To All Those In Nursing Homes And All Those Who Work In Them.

The path that has led to here,
once carried those treasured and dear.

The threshold weakened, can never again,
bring back what has gone or what has been.

This structure can no longer hold the years within,
or remember those it sheltered in.

A hearth in the cold and lonely dark,
awaits the kindling of just one spark.

The panes are distorted from years they've took.
Perhaps, you haven't tried to look.

Or perhaps you just have some doubt.
But, I AM,
INSIDE, LOOKING OUT!

D Nelle Andrews
THE STORM

To My State of New Mexico

There was a storm tonight:
High winds groaned
Like people's pains of death.
Wrath of the God in tears
Burst forth in rain.
Hovering thunder roared triumph
Like a wild beast
As he jumps his prey,
And the lightning flickered
Across jet skies.
Stillness—the dark cloak
Heaved a sigh.
The heavens in the western horizon
Powdered dusky gold
On the threatening clouds.
A flash of lightning in the east
Shimmered as a white diamond,
Flooded the background;
Then fading away as it came,
The fling of beauty vanished—
It was the death of the day.
In torments of sorrow
The clouds wept again.
The wind moaned in grief,
And the storm rocked on.

Fred E Detwyler III
GARBAGE MAN

To my daughters, Arlie and Bessie. May they deal with this problem better than us.

The Garbage Man went down to New Martinsville.
Looking to make a fill
He was in a bind.
He was way behind.
He was looking to make a steal.
He came across some Wetzel countains.
He said, I'll make you a bet
You're going to regret
I'm willing to make a landfill.
He said, I'll dump this shit
And make you sick
Because I don't live here.
He said you think you got a garbage flow
When I get done it will glow.
He said I'll fill this hill with my gold
Then disappear while you grow old.
The Garbage Man went down to New Martinsville.
It's been three long years and he's still here.
Everyone wishes he was broke.
But he's making a million. NO JOKE!
If we don't wake up and get our head out of the sand,
It might just be the end of the Mountaineer Man.
The Garbage Man went down to your town?

Carrie Frye
TO A FRIEND

To Arminta and Michelle, my best friends.

I had never known what it is like,
To feel my heart break,
Until I had to turn and slowly walk away,
From you and hear you sadly say,
Goodbye, I'll miss you, love always.

I had never known what it is,
To feel such great pain,
An emptiness in my heart never replaced,
A new feeling to face,
With memories I can never erase.

You have inspired me and I thank you,
For all this happiness,
I can cherish the moments of the past,
Pray that they will always last,
And know as a friend, you are the best.

Stephanie D Francis
HIDING PLACE

This poem is dedicated to Joel Martinez for being such an inspiration in my life and a stepping stone in my walk with God.

I sat in a small, dark corner
Of a place I once called home
Now, only to be called my hiding place
From a war that started from reasons unknown.
Lightning struck through the sky
Drowning out the lonely, scared cries of someone praying in the night.
Thinking of things happy,
Not wanting to think things bad
I quivered in the cold still house
Praying a prayer—silent, but long
As the last bomb exploded
As the last soldier was gone.

Stephanie D Francis
BLINDED BY THE LIGHT

I walk alone,
Lost in the night.
I hear you, but I cannot see.
I feel that there is a battle I must fight,
But there are people in my way.
Take my hand
Which way is right?
Speak to me softly
For I am afraid.
Have I lost you?
Please show me the way.
Come back;
Come back;
For what have I done?
No more do I see light;
Oh, but I feel someone near
I am not alone.
You were here all alone.
I was only blinded by the world.

Tamara Robin Hall Grenier
ECHOE'S

What's left of all those yesterdays,
has tangled a matted maze,
they say that's how the story goes,
when all that's left are just echoes.
My youth was robbed of innocence,
my fate left up to circumstance,
in dreams the visions still exist,
as echoe's of the life I missed.
I joined a race I couldn't run,
ignoring things I should have done,
and all the while they laughed at me,
while screaming out obscenities.
What's left of all those yesterdays,
has tangled to a matted maze,
they say that's how the story goes,
when all that's left are just echoe's.

Kelly Jo Sattazahn
LONG DISTANCE LOVE

You are so far apart
But so close inside.
It is all because of your love.
You only see each other a little while
But it is enough to keep your love burning inside.
He might live far away but
Your love brings you close together.
You spend all the time you can together that you can.
That's all you need to know
One thing: You love each other.

Jessica Dewhurst Spengler
TIME

Time
An endless symphony of swirling lives and ceaseless worlds
Plummeting through the infinite void, a vacuum of history
Where centuries are twisted into milliseconds of
Triumph and defeat, anguish and ecstasy,
Governed by the spinning of the Universe,
Galaxies of frozen eons turning on hubs of fiery stars,
Shifting across the dome of the sky, hurtling through the heavens,

God's domain,
Governed by the spinning of the Fates,
A brittle thread of Birth, Death, and the brief lives between.
The hourglass, sand slipping from one world to the next,
The scythe, to reap the ancients of their wisdom,
A skein, a tangled web of Mortality
Where the gods play.
The Future superimposed on the Past, in juxtaposition with
The Present of tomorrow and yesterday,
And endless journey beyond the bounds of space,
The eternal cycle of
Time.

Jane Southworth
DRUMBEATS

In the Finger Lake region of upstate New York
Within the hills around Cayuga,
When the first warm winds of Spring
Gently blow the apple buds to blossoms,
Or when a leaden sky looks down
On the first white blanket of snow
With which it has so quietly covered the earth,
You can feel a certain pulsing in the air,
A liquid sound of persistent drumbeats
Like a soft tattoo.

*An old fisherman once said
"It's the drums beneath the water.
And Seneca Chief Jesse Complanter said
The York State drums are the death drums of my people
Whom the White Man killed and took their lands."

Although part history, part legend, part myth,
Most farmers working in the fields
Know of the beats and say
They have <u>heard</u> the drums beating in the day . . .
And sometimes in the night.

*"Listen For a Lonesome Drum" by Carl Carmer

V F Thurman
REASONS

hours spent together—
OR just a minute or two
how happy they make me
As long as I'm with you.

holding hands
stolen kisses

gazing into your eyes
sitting near you—
feeling the warmth of you
A smile from you
A touch of your hand—
Softly on my cheek
A soft kiss—
On my neck

These are some of the reasons
I care so much for you.
To have you love me—
There isn't anything—
I wouldn't do.

Barbara A Osborn
AGED WINE
How warm love I would be
if only you were here with me
hold me close, hold me tight
comfort me in the night.
Do you know my days would all be bright
if you were here to walk me to the light?
How I've longed to have someone with me
beside me, inside me.
I'd carry you always; you in me, me in you
no one could penetrate
the fortress we would build.
Together we'd protect
each other's precious heart
we'd live apart
from the world uncaring . . .
sharing a love—God given
time refining . . .
defining—divine . . .
like aged wine—refined . . .
divine . . .
so fine my love—so fine.

Virginia F Felker
OLD LOG CABIN
There's an old cabin,
That is falling down.
On an isolated patch,
of forgotten ground.

It pulls at my heartstrings.
Every now and then,
So I always go back,
To see it again.

The emotions I feel,
Are hard to understand.
As I stand here alone,
On this deserted land.

I see the barn and woodshed
And the path to the spring.
I gaze at the garden patch
Just across the stream.

I see the violets coming up,
And bloom every year.
I pick a few and wonder?
What! I'm doing here.

Lester G Adams
FOR ME

Dedicated to my wife, Charlotte.

For me for me
God did it all for me
He made the world
And all the things
To bring me joy and peace
God gave his son to die for me
He did it all for me

Linda Lawrence
LOVE
I think of my Jesus,
The purest symbol of all.
Given thru God's love for me.
With assurance of eternal salvation.

I feel my mother's love,
Without judgment or condemnation.
Made by my father in heaven.
With everlasting joy of giving.

I see a yellow rose,
The symbol of peace, joy, and love.
Made thru God's need for beauty
With lasting perfection.

Three all so different:
Yet all so alike.
Peace, love & perfection,
Given to us thru
God's love.

David James Platt
A MESSAGE
A breath of love I felt upon my brow.
It came to me; I know not how.
It was heaven sent, I am aware,
For God left me a message there.
A message from my God above;
A message full of life and love.
He loves me for He told me so;
In many ways He let me know.
Dear God, please bend me to Thy will;
That I may know you love me still.

Ellis Ovesen

Ellis Ovesen
NUT ON THE LOOSE
Today, he walks with a limp.
Yesterday, a black eye;
His white shirt torn in the back . . .
Too full of pain to cry.
Everyone knows he is nuts:
He is talking as though to a crowd . . .
Now, he is clapping out devils;
Now, he is laughing too loud.

He goes to the radio station
And hangs his coat on a stick . . .
No one will give him a voice:
All he gets is a kick.
No one will give him a voice
Though his voice is The Voice of the Ages . . .
(All of us various players
On various crazy stages.)
Some of us sing and swagger
With voices trained to croon;
But the one who comes halt with a stagger
Is the one who will call the Tune.
Yes, the one who comes halt with a stagger
Is the one who will call the Tune;
His voice is The Voice of the Ages,
Though it sounds like the cry of a loon.

Lois Johnson Armstrong
THE FIRE'S DYING, GENTLE WARRIOR
Lie beside me, Gentle Warrior
Let me share the darkness here;
Let us listen to the sounds
out beyond this warm wigwam,
in the very blackest night.

Hear the rustle of the dry leaves;
the distant, hollow
wild wolf cry.
Cover with this heavy blanket
Gentle Man;
I touch your arm,
pull it 'round me;
you are warm and woodsy,
smooth and rough,
good and bad.

The fire's dying;
red coals turn to grey.
Lie beside me, Gentle Warrior,
Let us share
this deepest night.

A T Sabella
SINCE
Since we must
express it thus
to start the liquid
diamond's ooze
from out of our minds
I will adhere to the structure
we have come to
and praise the rainbow
and curse the dragon.
But if it were mine
to undo, then do again
I'd channel another swim
unfreeze the gem
and revel profitably
amid the law's denial.

A T Sabella
LEFT HAND
On a checkout line
a blonde boy was seated
in a grocery cart
trying to reach me.
He was smiling.
He was ecstatic.
He had a mechanical claw for a left hand.

His face looked as a messiah's,
charismatic and wild.
His feet bobbed; jangled bottled beverages.
His hand rose for the air. He said:
"mommy, tha's a mmmaa."
"Yes, son, that's a man."
She smiled at me then
as she caught her son's groping claw.

A T Sabella
MY GRANDFATHER THOMSON
My great-grandfather Thomson
was a religious fanatic
who became so deaf in Texas
after he gave his children's
white shoes to barefooted blacks
that he couldn't hear
his gas stove hiss
before they both exploded
as he tried to eat.
I know his soul
and hear him
from time to time
clattering in the kitchen
while making a breakfast
for me. I pray my hearing
remains acute.

Sheri L Krumins
POETRY
Poetry is tomorrow.
It is yesterday.
It is now.
A few simple words meaning nothing,
but together meaning everything.
Someone understands it
Someone else lives it,
And yet another criticizes it.
Somehow it has power.
Poetry is always.
It is never.
It is something.

Lindy Hamilton
THE BROKEN NOISE
There are no sounds,
But it is still loud.
Pounding in my eardrums.
It is constant.
It is heavy on my ears.
Then it is broken,
And there is too much
real noise.
I want the silence back!

Pauline C Bernot
HE GAVE ME PEACE OF MIND

Dedicated to my children, Paula Ann Jack and Thomas W. Bernot who make my life beautiful

Tiny ringlets of moist curled hair
lay upon your skin so fair
you were crying out to say
I have arrived for you this day.
My newborn babies, a mother's dream
after months of waiting to be seen.
There you were, so sweet, so fair,
surpassing all my doubts and fear.
God was good, God was kind
giving me such peace of mind,
two beautiful children, a perfect start
bringing such joy to my lonely heart.
Precious bundles of new found joy
a beautiful daughter and a baby boy.

Donald D Smith
PLAY OF DUSK
With falling dusk the cooling breeze
bends the long stems
of grass and reeds
While tree boughs sway with graceful ease
and cattails give flight
to cottony seeds.

Glistening with interrupted sheen
the lake water ripples
in faining light
While a rustling sound from
darkening green
settles with kindness
on somber night.

The cool breeze smites with a tender
blow
that edge of dark
to laughingly bring
A gentle whistling soft and low
that whispers of grateful
songs to sing.

With vibrant curtsy this dusk is met
And the long day sun has deftly set.

Martha Lewis Kuykendall
A STOLEN DREAM

To parents who did the very best they possibly could.

I can't sleep, the pain is too deep.
Tears bathe my face,
As I sit here, in this place
Greed! stole my home, leaving me
alone
With this cost, my trust is lost
My patience worn. My heart is torn
As I long to go home.

My dream, since I was born is gone,
A little house of my own.
A small garden to have grown.
There was a dream in my heart.
To have this, before I part.
Years of hurt, sweat, and tears
Seeing my children grow, through the
years.
My love for them conquered the fears
Often dried the tears.
Now they are grown, with lives of
their own
I will never have, my little home.
When my time has come, and I am
gone
Bury me deep, so then I may sleep.

Lydia Regehr
TO OUR CALIFORNIA

We greet you with a loud hurrah,
Our State of California!
Accept the leis we come to render
To landscapes of your regal splendor.
You are the State of many charms,
Of modern cities, towns, and farms.
We hail the peace across your plains,
Your valleys, flanked by mountain
chains,
The grandeur of your Ocean, streams,
Our pioneers had seen in dreams.

We love you, California,
Our vision of Utopia!
You wore the halo of your glory
When you were still a territory.
Your sentinels of redwood trees
Date back to bygone centuries.
Our sunny State, our golden ore,
You have become an open door,
The emblem for our future years
That link our own with past frontiers.

C Harvey
THE FAIRY

In a place of shadows/light she had
taken stand.
So still at first I knew not she was;
but
By a nervous ear betrayed and
I saw her.

A graceful form with delicate ears
and frightened eyes
Legs so fine I marveled they bore her
weight
Her coat the summer red upon her
flanks
Coin size, coin round two spots of
white.

I blinked and she was gone. I heard
No twig snapped by tiny feet and no
leaf would
Whisper to tell me her way.
She disappeared as fog will on a
sunny day.

I'm told the fairy never was, but I
wonder . . .
I believe I met one that summer day.
I say the fairy walks this unbelieving
world a deer.

Esther A Williams
LOVE

Love is like a river—
Restless—onward going,
Mid storm tossed, angry rapids,
Then serene and deeply
flowing.

Love is like the wind-
Laughing, merry as a gentle
breeze,
Then raging like the hurricane,
Bringing proud men to their
knees.

Love is like a burning fire—
A warm and tender flame,
It can die away to ashes
Then, like the Phoenix, rise
again.

Love is like the air we breathe—
It is vital to each soul.
Without the love of God and man,
No human heart is whole.

Esther A Williams
ALONE

We walk alone and separate,
Each human soul apart.
And none can ever penetrate
Another's lonely heart.

No human hand to guide you
No one to feel your need,
With heartaches all around you
Each follows his own creed.

Each buffeted by the furious tide
That roars within eternally,
The loves and hates that live inside,
That cry for help—"O, set
me free!"

No one to hear the anguished cry
That soars to Heaven far
above,
That rends the chasms of the
sky—
"Oh, God! Oh, God! Where
is there Love?"

And yet there is no one to see
The storms and tempests
wrought by pain.
Or none to know the gallantry
That lifts its head—walks on
again.

Kristi June Reynolds
KILLER BEAUTY

A rose is beautiful,
A bright bright red,
Its soft delicate petals,
Will turn a head.

A hand could kill,
And pull a life from its bed,
To breathe no-more,
And then be dead.

But, this very rare breed,
Has a weapon to shred,
The predator's hand,
To bleed rose red.

Francisca (Kika) Wheeling
WHISPER FROM THE SEA

To those who believe in themselves, and those that want to start.

As the waves rush over me, and toss
me about
I may stumble and fall, but I will
never doubt

For I have faith that one day I'll
reach the shore
The sun will shine its light upon me
and the warmth
of the sand will embrace me, as it has
done before

Though I may be but a single shell
cast upon the sand
I hope that one day I'll be picked up
by a warm, gentle and loving hand

One day I may be tossed away
And I may crack or even break
Though as the waves wash over me
every day
I will not consider it a mistake

As I once again become part of the
sea
I will realize that for now, it's what is
meant to be

I will not lose hope in once again
reaching the shore
No matter how the tide changes, or
what's in store
I will always have faith and hope to
rely on . . .
Forever more

Francisca (Kika) Wheeling
SUCCESS

Set your sights on the future and put
yourself there
With a positive goal in mind, you can
go anywhere

It's doing whatever it is you want to
do
And knowing in your heart, your
doing it just for you

Others may want to change your
ways
But it's only you, that will live your
life
For the rest of your days

Somedays your goals may seem so
far out of touch
And struggles you go through, may
seem a bit much

As you go through life, it's to
yourself you must teach
With the will to succeed, your goals
are never out of reach

It's only when you give up, goals
become lost
And would you really be willing to
pay such a cost?

Yolanda Lebron
I WANT TO LIVE AGAIN

To Mehrdad, for being there through the good times and the bad times, and especially, for showing me the way.

I want to live again
I want to walk by the beach
and feel the warm breeze
softly kiss my cheek.

I want to hear the birds sing
in the early morning light
and drift off to sleep
as serenity dresses up for the night.

I want to smell and pick the flowers
that decorate the most humble garden
patch
and walk in the rain
and follow the rainbows
and delight in the colors
that my eyes can swiftly catch.

I want to love "someone"
the way no one has ever been known
to love
and feel the ultimate pleasure
a woman could ever experience
as "life stirs within her."

Kathleen Squire Merolla
SUNBEAMS

For all my 'children'.

A rosebud in a garden,
A dewdrop on a rose;
A sunbeam's gentle whisper
and away the dewdrop goes.

A teardrop on a baby's cheek,
So soft, just like the rose;
A parent's tender sweet caress
and away the teardrop goes.

A mother's breast or daddy's chest,
So comfortable and secure;
A place to rest a weary head
embraced in love to reassure.

The love light in a parent's eyes,
Their tender words of love;
Are like the sunbeam's gentle rays
that shine from Heaven above.

Linda Salas
HOUSEWARMING

Our house is new, the neighbors too.
The address changed, rooms
rearranged.
New sights, new sounds, they all
abound.
We like it here, we like what we
found.

Far down the road we left behind,
The home we loved, 'twas one of a
kind.
The walls have echoed through the
years,
The loves, the hates, the joys, the
tears.

Tonight our friends are here to share,
Their warmth and love, to show they
care.

They helped us move and settle in,
And now they're here to drink our gin.

The sounds of love will soon be here,
The warmth of our family, so close, so dear.
And with these sounds is sure to come,
The change of this house into our home.

Audrey Ann Lance

Audrey Ann Lance
ABOUT LIFE
Homework is the worst thing to do until you graduate.
Then you are out on your own,
Where you can buy a home,
And you don't even have to write on a slate.

You may marry someone, and have a little boy,
Who loves to go fishing, and gets lots of bait.

You may have a little girl, who has pretty curls,
And, in a skirt, loves to twirl and whirl.

But if life goes bad
Don't be sad
'Cause there's still the life in the clouds.

Linda Robillard
LOVE IS NOT HINDERED
I look into a mirror that hangs upon the wall,
And think unto myself, "I know you not at all."
How many different lifetimes has it taken to declare
The varied common aspects of a 'me', that's standing there?

And as I gaze on you amid a myriad of souls,
I ponder hidden mysteries, "What were our former goals?"
What passion bloomed before, that welds our lives through time
And brings to light some memories of a love, both yours and mine?

It floats on wings of angel's wings, always to return
To spark the embers of a fire for which we ever yearn.
Soul mates have magnetic pull that draw out those they love
Through mists of time unmeasured, and renewed by Him above.
All our cosmic wanderings flitting swiftly through the maze,
Like butterflies, are drawn to light regardless of the haze.
In all the majesty of time, the longings of our hearts
Will bring us back together, we are summoned through the charts.

So wait for me beloved, know in your soul it's true,
You fill my total being, I'll be coming back to you
To be your healing balm, caress your pure angelic face,
Love is not hindered, always know, through spans of time or place.

Karen McKnight Furrow
I FORGOT

This poem is dedicated to Clyde McKnight, the best father a girl could have.

I didn't mean to forget you;
On your very special day.
I missed the chance to tell you, "I love you";
In so many special ways.
You raised me up with pride and respect;
To value these you could only expect.
I didn't always see the love;
You had within your heart.
But I felt it each time you picked me up;
And gave me a brand-new start.
I thank you for the love you gave me;
As you taught me to face the world.
I could never feel apart from you;
If I traveled around the world.
There is a little part of you in my heart;
That I could never live without.
It's the love you still have when I make mistakes;
A special love, I could never doubt.

Karen Almaraz
REAL LOVE

To my one and only love, Anthony Fuentes.

I don't know why
but sometimes when I think of you
I want to cry
I guess it's because
I'm really in love
and I never want to say good-bye

When I think of you
I think of all the fun we have
and I think of all the love we share
and I found out
how much you really care

I just want you to know
that wherever you are
and wherever you go
I will always love you so

Think of me through the day
and think of what
I had to say
and think of how much I really care
and no matter what
I'll always be there.

Wade Monroe Winfield Jones
TIME FOREVER MORE

This poem is dedicated to my best friend, and wife (Turk) my children, and my family.

I get up in the morning, and feel that life is new,
'cause all my pain, and sorrow, from yesterday is through.
I open up my eyes, and life is ever clear,
to know there is tomorrow, I shed away my fear.
I look forward to the minutes, and hours in a day,
to know that life's without you my mind begins to stray.
I dream of happy moments as life continues on,
to know that I'm not near you, I'll sing a sad, sad, song.
And when this life is over, and time exists no more,
I'll hope your memory of me will last for evermore!

Jeff Carter
THE WILLOW
trickle

sprinkle
summer
drips of rain
in warmth
and me in my
umbrella
the open black spot
contrast hurried against
wetted sidewalk
damped
the air of gray
into my
nose
smiling against
my own
wishes
for
winter
day
the willow

signed as usual

Florence McInerny
GIVE IT AWAY
Why build a wall around your heart
Of mortar, brick, or stone?
For then the love you have to give
Could never more be shown.

Love is ours to give away,
So spread it far and wide.
No wall should ever be allowed
To keep your love inside.

The more you give, more will be yours,
For that's just how it goes.
It's like a shining boomerang
That keeps you on your toes.

Sonya Knowles
MY BELOVED

Dedicated to my Mom and Dad who are the reflection of My Beloved.

If only a brief moment I can spend,
With my Beloved, Lover and Friend,
The day will shine brilliant and new,
As grass kissed by early morning dew.

For my Beloved is everything to me.
My Love, my Life, He'll always be.
My Champion and Guardian of my soul,
Each thought, every problem He consoles.

His arms never weary in holding me tight.
He never tires of talking all thru the night.
His love has no limit. His forgiveness no measure.
His depth has no boundaries. He's an infinite treasure.
For tender moments shared with my Beloved,
Are treasured gifts lavished from above.
Whether at home, in the car, or on my knees,
I am My Beloved's, and He loves me!

Ann H Gillespie

Ann H Gillespie
SAN FRANCISCO EARTHQUAKE '89

Dedicated to: All the brave people who helped the victims of the earthquake.

I switched on my t.v. to watch the world series game
Just as the sports announcer shouted, "We're having an
earth . . ., the word quake never came
The t.v. went blank, I knew an earthquake had begun
After a few seconds, the station put on an old "Roseanne" rerun-.

I turned it quickly to the cable news network with a feeling of dread
Hoping and praying that nobody was dead
The picture was on, it showed Candlestick Park with people milling about
Their stunned faces showed they'd had an earthquake, . . . there was no doubt.

The game was called off as they stared and gaped
Not knowing then, what they had just escaped
In a matter of seconds, all around them people were dead and dying
And hundreds more were injured . . . waiting for help and pitifully crying.

One of the most sickening sights of all
Was when Bay Bridge started to fall
People were crushed as the ground kept shaking
The ones who survived looked on, their poor hearts breaking.

A lot of people went home to find their home was a shamble
By living in California, an earthquake zone, they'd lost a gamble
Some of them will re-build and some will leave
For the earthquake victims, we'll remember and grieve.

Darrell Hoberer
CLOTHES
Spotted pants,
down to her knees;
They're cut at the cuffs
to let in the breeze.
A striped dress,
I must confess,
is extremely short.
It's a funny sort.

Faded jeans,
are in the style!
Before I wear 'em,
It'll be a while!

Cowboy boots,
who gives a hoots?
I like my old shoes.
What about all youse?

Bright pink shirt,
eyes it does hurt.
The loud colors shine.
The pleasure's all mine.

Esteban Gonzales
LONG LOST

To Jennifer, a part of me left when you moved away, but your love still remains.

If I could reach out and touch someone
Someone I can't see right now
Because she's miles and miles away
I'd hold her tight for the rest of the day
I'd love her, caress her, make her feel warm inside
Maybe one day I'll wake up
And she'll be by my side
To think it is only a dream
But soon, she'll be married to be
With that guy that loves her more than me
I'm just a soul wondering in the wind
Someday my life will come to a complete end
In the meantime my love for her cannot be said in words
But rather hold her tight, make love to her if I could

Cheryl A Fisher
GENTLE WAYS
How many times I've seen you,
In so many different ways,
Yet, you seem to stand out from the rest
In this crazy kind of maze.

I've looked all around this world
And seen quite a few,
But never have I seen a man
Who's quite as gentle as you.

I've seen you in so many ways
And no matter what the mood
The gentleness in you
Still comes shining through.

You are one in a million,
Oh, how that saying stands true,
I only hope the gentleness
Is always a part of you!

Shanette Gaston
IMAGINATIONS
As I sat there watching things go by
I happen to look up in the sky and there I saw something
I had never seen before it was a shape of a house with an open door . . .

It had fluffy clouds all around it
And inside of it was a big white closet
I thought to myself should I go in but
Then I had to think again . . .

What if it was something really horrible
Or maybe something really adorable
What if I walked in on some people but
How could that be when this isn't the Holiday Inn or the end of the seasons . . .

I then thought to myself
Hey! This is really neat
I wouldn't take it back if I had the receipt . . .

Everything was going really well and in cooperation but little to know it was just my imagination . . .

Grace Paschal Wheeler
ON GENTLE WINGS

This is dedicated to my beloved husband, Terry, who is a constant source of encouragement.

He is my Lord, He gave me life,
He brings sweet peace
when there is strife,
He gives me courage to sing His songs,
He gives me strength
when nights are long,
He shows me beauty where there was none,
He gave me friendship,
His only Son,
With my heart, His story sings,
God is the wind
beneath my wings,
God is the wind,
the blessed wind that only
His love can bring,
God is the wind, the blessed wind,
that carries me
"On Gentle Wings",
that carries me
"On Gentle Wings".

PAX Koontz
THE WALK IN THE FOREST

To Hillery, with Love, for everything she has taught me.

We walk through the forest,
stay on the trail, thoughts the purest.
We follow the trail and we are fine,
safe in our lives.
But, at once, the trail fades.
Before our eyes the forest revives.
We stand in the wilderness, each step as lost as the next,
leaving our simple hearts wearily vexed.
Now, feeling safe, our hearts beat wild, and we live.
Free and we, as we are. As we should be is relative.
Running through the woods, so much for attack.
Loving the world though it doesn't
Love us back.
Then, again, uncertain of our steps or any direction;
the steps are too heavy, and we too tired for their correction.
Free spirits imprisoned in a wide open cage,
growing so old far beyond age,
So we are, until the wilderness is home. The trial is gone,
we have become our own decision's pawn:
We can lose our way and die alone,
or cut a new trail to call our own.
The choice is ours. Forest shall stand either way,
Whether we live or die the forest shall stay.

Barbara R Slater
LOVE'S CHALLENGE
Beloved, have you slid beneath
The cool, green waters and felt
Nature's caress upon your flesh?
Have you laid in the rustling field
And known the prickle of unmown grass
Upon your weary and jaded skin?
Have you inhaled the odor of unripened apples
As they await the blessed warmth of sun?
Have the evening breezes kissed your eyes
With tongues of longing peace?
And have you believed that only nature
Could offer you such infinite joy?
I have, and only now I know that
Your love can challenge nature and
Nature bows her head in acknowledgement.
Love's touch remains her equal.

Barbara R Slater
TRANSFORMATION
My soul sinks lower
Through a sea of darkness,
Weighed down by a dull
And listless heart.
My spirit, too aimless to note the descent,
Fails to counter the lethargy.

Then strikes the shock of conflict,
Bands of iron-like guilt and
Sharpened knifes of fear.
A wash of unaccustomed feelings
Threatens to inundate my very being
And break the boundaries of reason.

Time passes in pain and confusion;
Slowly, slowly balance commences its return.
Thoughts gain an edge of clarity.
Feelings, newly unrestrained, seek communication.
Sensing myself now as a whole, united being,
I slowly, tentatively reach out.

Joy, now joy, to find another,
Quietly, patiently awaiting my awareness.

Robert A Nichols

Robert A Nichols
HOLY SPIRIT FALLS ON THOSE DOING GOD'S WILL
Priests, Pastors, and Reverends
Mostly at home stay.
God's lay people are on duty
Everyday!
Jesus called all to be fishers
Of men—
Going to church is not our
Sole obligation:
Gathering ourselves together
To incite to fine works and
Love—
Gives incentive to do daily
Works as ordained from
Above.
Our Holy Obligation:
Make disciples of
Christ and preach
God's Holy Nation.
Those who God's commandments
Fulfill—Will with holy spirit
Be filled!

Sources: Mathew 4:19; 5:13, 14; 7:21; 9:9-13; 12:30; 16:24; 23:8-12; 24:14; 28:19,20;; Acts 5:32; 2 Corinthians 5:19-20; I Timothy 2:4; 2 Timothy 3:5; 4:2; Titus 2:14; Hebrews 10:23,24; James 2:18-26; 1 Peter 2:9,10; 3:15; 2 Peter 3:13; 1 John 2:3-6; 5:3

Robert A Nichols
GOD'S EXISTENCE
God writes of His Existence
On the space-time continuum
With His Words—
His creations.
The grammar of His sentence
Is the set of physical laws
Of the universe—
They reveal His
Wisdom.

Sources: Job 38:1-41; Psalms 19:1; Romans 1:19,20; Hebrews 3:4

Robert A Nichols
UNFADING STATUS AND SECURITY
Doing God's Will fulfills
Status and security needs.
When we do God's work, our
Prayers He faithfully
Heeds.
When we encounter situations
Chaotic,
God provides escape that
Keeps us from becoming
Neurotic.
While on humanity we

Can't always depend,
God is always faithful
To the end.

Experience, plus sources: Psalms 34:4, 7, 15, 18, 19; 37:5, 23, 24; 46:1; 50:14, 15; 112; 118:6-9; 119:165; Proverbs 3:5, 6; 16:9; Joshua 1:8, 9; Isaiah 50:7; Romans 8:28; 2 Corinthians 5:18-20; Philippians 4:14-16; 10:23; 13:5, 6; 2 Peter 2:9; 1 John 2:15-17; 1 Corinthians 10:12-13

Michael Fink

TICK

through wishes vague
and dreams which cinder glow,
splinter blades of desperation
ticking, ticking . . .

in wishes vague,
I surely wish I knew
a trick to teach
to this old dog

certainty that
tapers on with time . . .
apples green, wrenched from the tree, devoured by impatience?
confidence that fades
away with time . . .

trace my mind
for memory of tricks
that once would do
for this old dog

Charles T McGrath

THE FINAL BATTLE

Hemispheres rumbled, Continents shook, borders crumbled
barriers no more, only piles of rubble the remembrances of war, and the Earth stood still, for just a time, as PEACE descended upon mankind. Prejudice now gone, buried with words of violence and hate, while burning hope consumes power and greed lifting black clouds filtering fear extinct. Weapons are gone, attitudes that kill, along with rulers of vengeance, despair, providers of ill will. Hunger is gone, no thirst to quench, disease now history, myths first went. Need is gone, there is no need, all things cared for in time and place. The battle is over, PEACE has won, Earth not being an only son; the battle is over in this final war, our Universe now in perfect accord.

Thelma Schiller

THE COMING OF WINTER

I look upon a cliff, a rambling sheath of glacier-ice where swerving skiers soar,
where mountains rise from mists that bathe beneath
low branches, linger on the morning shore.

The stained glass windows intertwine with quay,
and tinted mainsails ride the rising sun,
and lifting, revel in the channel-sea,
then flying on a crest of wave, stretch-run.

The pine trees blossoming white plumes of snow,
assuaging quickened thirst that beauty brings
match blooms of flowers inside in planter's row
with loveliness that haunts till coming spring.

Ronald L Slayton

A TENACITY FOR LIFE

I dedicate this poem to the idea of a cancer free society.

Cast in a mirage, in a frenzy for time, to tinker with the timetable of my life's grind.
Crouched in a corner with the folders of time,
desperately searching for an extension to mine. Frantically fumbling through the pages of ages, until I discovered mine, clad between the dust of time.
Suddenly, surprised by a sentinel in this pinnacle of time,
"Where goest thou, thief, with those extensions of time?"
Turning, I spoke from my heart to his piercing eyes of fear,
"They are additions to my life, to conquer these tears."
"A document to ensure the addition of time,
so I will not be burdened with these thoughts of mine."
"Sentinel! Guard as you must, the rest of time,
and expose me not to the creators of mine."
"Call to me, sentinel, in a future time, for destiny anxiously awaits my victory this time."
"Allow my exit through this mystic haze,
sustain my wish, oh sentinel, this day."
"For with these years, I can hope to find, a way to save this life of mine."

Manuel "Nuni" Lopez Jr

WE WERE ONLY MEANT TO BE THE BEST OF FRIENDS

We were young and we knew little about Love,
We felt that just being with one another was enough;
But we never stopped to think about commitment and trust,
Because in reality what we had was a lust;

We were never meant to be Lovers,
We were only meant to be the best of friends;
Although we tried to be a little more to one another,
We were only meant to be the best of friends.

I'd tell you I Love you and you would tell me,
But the future ahead we could not see;
For we were a couple just passing through time,
And maybe tomorrow you would not be mine;

And although we waited hoping things would work our way,
The days just got longer from blue skies to gray;
And now as we look back on our search for Love,
We now know that what we had was not enough;

We were never meant to be Lovers,
We were only meant to be the best of friends;
Although we tried to be a little more to one another,
We Were Only Meant To Be The Best Of Friends.

Jeanette Rich Wiley

UNEXPECTED LOVE

You entered my life
like a melody, and
captured my heart.

Time hasn't dulled the pleasures I've known
just from being with you

Thank you . . for the
beautiful melody,
and for the Love
we've Shared.

Neil Cheswick

EPITAPH

Here I lie to feed the ground,
Which has helped me grow.
As the memories pass,
I will never forget what the world has—
It has all of you
Whom I have left behind.
I just hope there is a love out there,
Which someday you will find.
Now leave this site,
Which you have visited today
And, remember what I say:
Don't weep for me in sorrow,
for this hurts me more.
Just weep for me in joy,
For it's you whom I adore.

Casandra Robinson

WHAT CHRISTIANS SHOULD FEEL INSIDE

This poem is dedicated to my grandfather, the late Charlie Robert Robinson II, whose kind countenance deeply touched my life.

In his big chair with a belly so jolly
Grandpa grabbed his sweet granddaughter with eyes of folly.
He rubbed his curly black beard and opened his Bible.
The granddaughter displayed to her grandpa a beautiful smile she could not hide.
Then grandpa explained to her what Christians should feel inside.
He said we were like sheep that needed his shepherd—
Just as we need Jesus to be Our Father.
And when we run astray we can always come back
To His sweet tender face and say,
"Forgive me Lord of my sins this day."
He said that we should have joy inside—
A light unto the world that we should not hide.
We should be like bells with an ever-resounding ring,
Never ceasing everlasting praises to our King!
And at the time of nightly prayer,
When Jesus is there, He touches our hearts dearly,
Beyond compare.
Grandpa gazed at the time, turned off the light,
And kissed his beautiful ebony granddaughter
Good-night.

C R McPherson

A VIEW FROM OLYMPUS

A passing strange and wondrous thing
Has lately come my way,
When first I felt its magic touch
I really cannot say.
I simply woke and it was there
One splendid autumn day,

I rose and threw the shutters wide
And breathed the fresh fall air,
And the glory of the risn sun
Had never seemed so fair,
The faintest glow of orange first
With violet here and there,
And then a splash of pink and rose
Burst in a mighty flare.

The spectacle was all too brief
But as I watched it fade,
I wondered why, until this day
No other sunrise GOD had made
so filled me with a sense of awe
Nor stirred my heart in such a way.

Teresa M Hopkinson and son Charles

Teresa M Hopkinson

LOVE MAZE

This poem I would like to dedicate to Chuck Jackson whom I have learned to love and share with, he has shown me true love. I love you.

Mind spinning, in a daze
Find a way out of this love maze,
Turning, turning no way out
All mixed up, want to shout,
This way, that way, where do we go
Want to run but our feet are too slow,
Take my hand and lead me home
So I won't be left here to roam,
Shouting, hugging, kissing , loving,
Where does it all come from
Those feeling's that always leave us numb,
Touching, feeling
Sends our minds reeling,

Around we go on the path of love
Always a hand to give us a shove,
Where does it begin and where does it end

There is always a broken fence to mend,
Finding yourself, you are half the way there
Learning to love and learning to share,
If you know true love, you will find your way out
But you will be lost if there is a doubt.

Teresa M Hopkinson
CHILDREN'S LAUGHTER

I would like to dedicate this poem to my son, Collin Hopkinson. No one could ever be so lucky to have such a wonderful son as you. I LOVE YOU, LOVE, MOM.

Children's laughter everywhere
Running through life without a care,
Jumping and playing on hill's and in field's
Hoping the fun and love never yeild's,
Rosie red cheeks's and pug little nose's
Make them shine brighter than all of the rose's,
Big warm eye's

That can tell no lie's,
Calling for you when they need a hand
Building their castles up high in the sand,
Enjoying every moment they have to share
Letting them know you will alway's be there,
Take their hand and show them the way
Where the love in their heart's will alway's stay.

Teresa M Hopkinson
MOTHER

I would like to dedicate this poem to my mother, Margaret Burke. My very best friend, you mean the world to me, no one is more swet, loving and kind. I LOVE YOU.

Oh beautiful mother, where can you be
I need your love to set me free,
A steady hand to help me along
To point thing's out when I do them wrong,
I know you think I am silly and wild
Needing you doesn't mean I am still a child,
Please understand and alway's be near

For your love to me is very dear,
Don't hide your love, I know it is there
I want to be friend's so that we may share,
So many feeling's, I have deep inside
I need to tell you, they are so hard to hide,
Alway's be there, no matter what life I may choose
For your love I could never bare to lose.

Kim Everett
OPEN THOUGHTS

Have you ever seen the stars above?
Or flown to the moon, just to see the view?
Do you dare believe, your spirit can leave the ground and go that high?
Have you ever ridden down a river and let her comfort what ails you?
Or taken a trip down a road, just to see what was there?
Has there ever been a time, when you were lost within time,
And there as no place to hide?
Were you yearning for the birds to sing and the sun to shine,
Just so you would have a little company?
Longing once again for that freedom to roam,
And someone to give your love to?
Have you seen the deep blue ocean?
Or heard the thunder before a storm?
Have the beauties of life ever bought a tear to your eye?
The overwhelming joy can never erase the little pang of sorrow.
As I travel down the road of my yesterdays, today and tomorrows all alone.
Lord knows I know how to be alone.
But if I could cloose, all I need is someone to share my life with.

Jerri Ann Hinkein
PEOPLE DON'T GO AWAY

To my Dad, with all my love. My family and friends, thank you. To my Mother my best friend, may you rest in peace and live in my Heart Forever. Love all of you.

I am feeling feelings that I haven't felt in awhile,
they take me back into time when I was a child.
They are feelings of knowing what is right and wrong, and feelings of knowing that something or someone is never completely gone.
Some people may die, and some might just choose to go away,
but in your heart they are with you everyday.
As times go by, and we all grow older,
we often forget that it is okay to cry on someone's shoulder.
We tend to look up what we are feeling inside,
and barely realizing that within ourselves we have lied.
It has taken me quite a few months to find the truth from my heart,
and realize that for the last eight years or more I have been tearing myself apart.
Tomorrow is a new day, and it is never too late to say,
I have hurt so many of you in so many different ways.
I realize now that I have caused most of you some type of pain,
but believe me, I have hurt myself just the same.
I am going to start taking my life day to day,
and stop trying to make everything go my way.
Sometimes however, I might not know how to say,
I want you in my life, so please try to stay,
no matter how hard I am trying to push you away.

Bea Wilson

Bea Wilson
TREASURES

To my three sons, with all my love.

I had three little baby boys
as sweet as they could be
and when they grew into toddlers
they were a handful one might say.
One was blue eyed and a curly light blond,
another brown eyed and brunette,
While the third one, being different yet,
had platinum blond hair and a hazel eye set.
The littlest one was mischievous,
The eldest one was jealous,
While the middle one, on the quiet side,
was a much fun as the others.
One was lovingly called "Manny,"
Next came Denny D,"
Last but not least, and never forgotten,
was "Little ol' man of the mountain."
They all grew up in their separate ways
but staying so much alike
and yet so different—
and Always Treasures in my heart.

Melanie S Pond
A LOVE THAT LASTS FOREVER

You taught me how to love someone,
and how to say good-bye.
You taught me how to laugh,
and you taught me how to cry.
We seemed to be the perfect pair;
at least to everyone else.
You saw so many things in me
I couldn't see in myself.
Somehow we seemed to grow apart,
and changed in many ways.
Still good-bye from me to you
was the hardest thing to say.
I'm glad I got the chance
to know someone like you.
You taught me how to share my love,
and believe in what I do.
I know we are forever friends
and that's something I'll treasure.
I wish for you the best in life;
and a love that lasts forever.

Antonio Earl Robinson
WE THE PEOPLE

To The World, and Everything In it.

We the people, of the world
We the people of man, woman, boy girl
We the people, of the sands of time
We the people, of each other's mind
We the people, of life and death
We the people, when there's nothing left
We the people, of many colors
We the people, who fight each other
We the people, who go to war
To maintain peace, there you are
We the people, traveling through time
Wondering each day, will we find
Now that I've, gave you a clue.
We the people, belong to me and you.

Jadene Cramer
FIRST LOVE

You were my first love.
The one I cared about.
I gave you everything I had.
You said you loved me, too.
So why did you leave me?
And now you want to come back.
Now that I have nothing more to give.
You were my first love
And you took it all away.

Jennie V Coleman
OH SINNER CAN'T YOU HEAR GOD CALLING

This poem is dedicated to my family. With all my love.

Oh sinner can't you hear God calling.
Please, listen to him he will keep you from falling;
He has laid the map for you to follow,
Come now don't wait for tomorrow;
This old world is getting worse and worse,
And for you not to come is to be cursed;
He will deliver your soul,
And give you peace untold;
His heart is Heavy, Burdened, and Grieved,
Because he knows some of us will never believe;
The Lord don't want you to make the wrong turn,

Because he knows you will forever burn;
We all know that sin is the blame,
But none of it do we have to claim;
Jesus is the one that has all the answers,
There's nothing too hard including cancer;
If you will come to God with a sincere heart,
There's no doubt about it, he's going to do his part.

S Melanie Sellers
WHEN
When, when, when will it all end?
When the men stop fighting and all the wars end.
When will people learn to love not hate?
When they find out that there are better things besides money to appreciate.
When will gangs and violence stop on the street?
When the president and the government finally get up on their feet.
When will racism stop among people?
When they find out that all men were created equal.
When, you wonder, will this poem end?
When the world is put back together again.

Kim Kerek
I HAD TO GO AWAY
I had to go away,
I'm sorry you couldn't come with me
but on earth is where you shall stay.
Please do not be sad.
Instead laugh and be glad.
I'm in a beautiful place, such a
beautiful place.
I know you won't see me for a while
but you will hear from me.
I will be the wind that will chill you
on a hot summer day.
I will be the sun that will warm you
when it's cold.
Listen to the birds sing, I will be
saying I love you in their song.
I know you can't touch me but you
will feel me.
Because I will be inside of you giving
you life on the days you feel like
you can't go anymore.
Please, I beg of you, go on, live your
life as I lived mine.
Always remember that we will be
together again.
I will be waiting for you patiently on
that day when you will join me in
this beautiful place.
Until then may God bless you with
His Almighty Grace.

Julie Anne Mackay
AWASH WITH INFORMATION
Francine the Yuppie was a diligent one,
Always studying in grad school, she rarely saw the sun.

She took very seriously her Very Big Job,
Trying just that much harder than her co-VP, Rob.

Soon Francine discovered she had much more to do
Than just computing and managing; she had to read, too!

The journals—of Wall Street, her industry and women in her field,
Plus dailies and weeklies with "life info" to yield.

To keep up on the techniques of her profession was her mission,
Not to mention the world, health and fitness, and nuclear fission.

The information was delivered to her office and her home, and
Tho she diligently waded through it, she sometimes lost her phone

Under the piles and stacks simply brimming with knowledge;
She hadn't realized there'd be this much to learn after college.

But Francine was determined and was not to be defeated;
She read every second, as much as she felt she needed.

Until one day when her secretary couldn't find her,
And the rescue team uncovered her neath the piles she kept behind her.

Now Francine rets quietly on a far-away shore,
Having foresworn "keeping up" for now and evermore.

Eleanor Louise Foix
THIS DAY AT HAND
To my daughter, Vonola Elizabeth Cutter.

This day at hand is the day to look upon
For yesterday is past, good only for memories as references,
And tomorrow is the future, good only to plan upon
But this day at hand is the day for action.

Look to this day for it is the very essence of life,
It is a day to build and not destroy,
It is a day to love and not hate,
It is a day for peace and not war.

Look to this day for things real and lasting
For it is the esence of growth;
Be dependent this day upon the Lord
For this day is only a segment of days to come.

So look to this day at hand, make the most of it,
For tomorrow may cease to come;
Look to this day for faith, reverence, joy and understanding
And love for God and the whole mankind.

Cindy Bias
SOON I'LL DIE
One of these days, I'll be gone,
and you'll wonder why.
If you don't believe me, wait;
soon I'll die.
And after you find out,
you'll hurt too.
And I hope you wonder,
"is it what I did, what I do?"
You knew I was hurting,
why didn't you help me?
I guess we all realize, at the
toll bridge, this is the fee.
To someone like you,
this price may seem high.
But to someone like me,
all we wanted was to die.
One of these days, I'll be gone,
and you'll wonder why.
If you don't believe me, wait;
soon I'll die.

Shirley M Hicks
BETTER THAN LOVE
This poem is dedicated to Mr. Slim Glover Tyler Sr.

My dream come true, entered my life at a night club. He asked me to dance and gave me a passionate hug.

As the night went by, he asked me for another date. He was so polite, and forward, he asked me to be his love mate. He wasted no time letting me get to know him. By the way, his name is Slim.

He conversates about his feelings of me, he impressed me so, that I let it be. He feels he wants the relationship to last until he dies, after checking him out, he really don't lie.

He let's me know that this relationship of ours is better than love.

Tammy M Green (Age 15)
JOYOUS SPIRIT
In loving memory of my grandfathers, Edwin Lewis and Johnny Ingram, who now sing songs of praise in Heaven with the Angels.

Flowers bloom, children sing;
There is joy in Everything.
When the spirit comes around,
All creation makes no sound

We're wondering how he has affect
On every living thing;
And when we finally know the truth,
Songs of praise are what we'll sing.

We'll never know what we need not,
But only what we do;
Then everything will be just fine,
Especially his "love" for <u>you</u>.

Marlene L Worek
NIGHT'S REPOSE
Darkened leaves, softly rustling
Quiet listening.
Sunset streaks on moon-brushed water
Shining, glistening.
Muffled noises, hushed and calming
Crickets calling.
Birds lifting on silent wings for flight
Rising, falling.
Shadows growing, darker, deeper
Dusk is ending.
The curtain of the night enfolds the day
Colors blending.
Starlight shimmering through somber trees
Brightly gleaming.
Day is closing, tomorrow's promise
Hopeful, dreaming.

Nancy Eileen Kiesung Gregg
AFTER THE BATTLE
The battle is over. You penetrated the fortress of stone I had built so carefully around my heart. Though determined, my will is useless against you. My protective amor cast aside, I surrender.

The passion I kept buried deep inside, is awakened from its long sleep and stirs restlessly inside. Craving your presence, your touch, thoughts of only you invade my mind night and day. I am barely able to function. My lips are hungry for your kiss. My body aches for your touch.

It seems an eternity until I feel your lips press against mine, and my body seems to melt. My heart pounds so fiercely inside my chest, I fear it cannot possibly go on much longer before it ceases to beat altogether. Your arms, so strong and powerful, are now loving and gentle as they encircle my body in their embrace. I feel the moist warmth of your breath as you urgently kiss and caress my body. My ears are deafened as the blood rushes to my head. My mind no longer thinks as I drown in an ocean of intoxicating sensations. I cannot seem to hold you close enough. I want to climb inside your body, and become one with your very soul. Suddenly, the world seems to stop, and for a few precious moments, the oneness is realized.

All my energy spent, I am still. As I lay upon your chest, my ears now listen to the gentle beating of your heart, and the steadiness of your breathing. My fingers gently smooth the velvety stream of hair down the center of your torso, wet with perspiration. I feel you gently kiss the top of my head before you fall alseep.

The corners of my lips curve up slightly as I smile contentedly to myself. I have found happiness in losing the battle of my heart to such a victor as you.

David A Lynch Sr
GOD WAS THERE
To my nephew: Ted Dale Manby. May you always find God There as you progress in your journey in faith.

Have you ever seen a glorious sunset on a placid lake
or a swiftly moving river?
Its eclectic rays filling the whole spectrum until all the
far away clefts enjoy its golden hues and splendor.
Or witnessed the grandeur and majesty of a stately mountain range
with its lofty peaks like fingers
reaching high to the
Heavens to caress the ethereal blue, suggesting pillars of great power and ultimate strength.

Have you ever felt the quiet, tranquil peace of a verdant green valley
with a forest of tall, magnificent trees nearby?
Its rolling hillsides covered with a carpet of incomparable beauty
and variety in wild flowers and other vegetation.
Or reclined on a sandy beach and been lulled by the rhythmic ebb and
flow of the waves breaking
upon the shoreline.
Or gazed upon the very special loveliness of an arid dessert with
its craggy hills and peculiar
rock formations and strange
colors
Abounding everywhere; all are unique treasures as far as the eye can see.

Thus in one breathtaking moment one pauses to reflect upon the abundant
beauty of creation of the near
and far distant places of our
Universe, one most convincing Truth is most evident; our GOD WAS THERE!

RAM II
HOLDING ON TO YOUR UNDERSTANDING
I tie it without much thought.
From childhood I was taught,
How to hold down my tongue,
Which is hard when you're young.

It winds its way through the holes,
Binding together two soles.
Saving tackles are made,
By this lace in braid.

It's a kittens toy to enjoy.
A practical joke for some folk.

Into knots its bows turn.
To avoid this, we learn.
Most have at least two,
One for each shoe.

Not another clue!

Norma V Wong-Larkin
EMPTY WORDS

To the God of Christ, my husband Warren, my 3 children Tyrone, Marnyka and Hasim and to all the people involved with my Honorable Mention.

Love, I heard you knocking at the door of my heart,
You said to my heart from the depths of your own folly,
I will never hurt you!
I will never leave you!
I will love you forever!

From the depths of my heart I made myself believe, and I
Forgot to ask the spirit of truth what the 'word' had to say!
The word came forth from my heart and said!

My child, put not your trust and faith in man!
Man is untamed in
spirit and soul and lacks wisdom!
Man does not even know the meaning of the word love,
Much less the hollowness of his spoken words.

Child of understanding! Ask always the spirit of truth from
Within, to grant you the love, wisdom and understanding, that
Through you all men can see and experience love, truth,
Understanding and wisdom by your actions and deeds.

Love, I heard you knocking at the door of my heart!
I will never hurt you!
I will never leave you!
I will love you forever!

Hank Ring
SOMETHING OF VALUE

To the younger generation.

When you're on the top of the heap young man,
and everyone shakes your hand,
it's something like a narcotic,
too hard to understand.

Some time in your life my lad,
you could run into trouble. Then look around for handshakes son.
You'll find you've burst your bubble.

The friends that stick through thick and thin
are rare and must be earned.
If you find just one of them,
there's something you must learn.

Work hard to deserve this catch.
Help him when you can.
He's given you a rarity,
You're now a wealthy man

James G Exum Sr with Capers and Misty

James G Exum Sr
TO SEE

This poem is dedicated to Mary, my first wife now deceased.

TO SEE birds at my window sing songs without words,
TO SEE squirrels in the yard call to each other without fear of being heard.
TO SEE bare branches whose leaves now deck the ground in wondrous color,
To know they still live and in spring will bud again—if for some other—
WHO SEES!
TO SEE a winter sunset with its shades of bright color across the sky,
As the magic of night approaches and seems to say—
SEE me now—to the others for a while goodbye.
TO SEE a star fall from a star-lit sky and fade away in the still of the night,
The silence broken only by the soft sibilation of the wings of an owl in flight.
TO SEE your wife and your dog beside you before an open fire,
Pause to think and give thanks when ready to retire . . .
Teach me Father when I pray not to ask for more,
But rather give thanks for what is at my door. And SEE!

Betty Bearden
BLEEDING HEART

To all earth's heartbeats.

So often you will hear My words—but, child,
their meaning is not grasped as I had hoped.
You see, your heart is hardened, even wild,
grown cold toward Me, although I've reached and groped.
You seem so far, and yet you are so near;
I made you so that you might come to Me
when Life is
rough, and I would always hear your pleas and sufferings, bid you to be free.

Man weakens when decisions must be made;
some tempting counterfeits may often win,
instead of choices joined as in a braid of oneness toward the victory over sin.

There is forgiveness, after all is past—
if you believe, and hear My voice at last.

Concetta La Morte
CONSIDER
Consider—the fields of lilies wild
splendid beauty—nature's child.

Sustained by sunlight, water, rain
they do not toil or worry for gain.

Consider—Love, God's greatest gift
patient, kind—can cause no rift.

Love builds up and does not spoil
on fertile ground, not rocky soil.

Consider—lilies raising faces high
freely feeling, nurtured . . .

Without Love's sustaining sigh,
Love, and lilies . . . die.

Consider . . .

William H Barker
TO VERONICA—ON APPROACHING MY 88TH YEAR
I am dreaming my dreams in the long ago
Of mountains, brooks and starry skies;
Of the road that we trudged in the full moon's light,
Those thoughts of love of that heavenly night.
On that road, alone, I do trudge again
Loving you now as I loved you then;
Sweet memories of Thee shall always be
That night of love I shared with Thee.

Eddie Applewhite

Eddie Applewhite
THE INVISIBLE MISTLETOE

This poem is dedicated to my sons, Milo and Brandon, with all my love.

'Tis the voice of me
Speaking ever so gently
The pure at heart
they perceive

Because they, give ear to me
'Tis I, the invisble mistletoe
Hanging so graceiously above
Your door, the door of your
Heart, if so may be.

But I, am very real, indeed. I
Am the heart's true remedy
Of a thousand ailments, will
I set you free.

'Tis I, the invisible mistletoe
Hanging graciously, above
Life's door.

Shalmali Pal
ICE CREAM JUNKIE (A TRULY SHORT LOVE STORY)

To John Liddle, wherever you are.

I remember you . . .

Barely 19 with a lust to surpass all others
and a broken spirit to serenade it.
That summer,
things just sort of simmered
between the freezer and my fever.
One instant too long
became a melting moment too soon.
Lurking and groping and
wishing and hating—
sure just rev up that machine of yours
and ride out of here
dragging my heart along the
pavement don't worry the rest of me
will follow
shortly You could have turned around
and looked behind you you blind
insensitive
son of a bitch,
Then again,
I could have turned back and said
something.
Nowadays,
there really is nothing left to say
except
yes, I do remember you . . .
I'm basically a love junkie
withdrawal cold turkey
What will it take? (just 10 days and a couple of two day follow ups.)

Stacy Lavalliere
WOE IS THE DELIVERY ROOM?
We emerge from our ebony chamber
with all security stolen in a thrust,
given a cuff by a sranger
we are initiated into a world of trust.

Our first uttering a cry for love
'til we learn more selective picking,

a world where peace is symbolized
by a dove
and dinner by a bucket of chicken.

A world where billions go to make
invalids walk,
and "General Hospital" has the
heroes of the year,
Jack Daniels and nicotine cologne
accent our talk,
and Dr. Joyce Brothers is rich off our
fears.

Like the sunrise's first beam our first
cry makes its mark,
'til the last pucker of orange and
close of the dream
beginning and ending cold, alone,
stripped, and stark.

Dino A Rossi

THEY DIDN'T KNOW OR CARE

Some former friends I used to have,

If sincere in feeling of sorrow,
Are waiting for me to crawl prepared,
It's not me today, nor me tomorrow.

Insensitive to feelings, a loved one's
lost,
And not forgive, my attitude
condemn,
I think the friendship's not worth
having,
They must come to me; not me to
them.

Nelle Gray

GRANDMA'S LETTER TO SANTA

Santa Claus please bring to me the
thrill I felt over my first Christmas
tree
Time may be running out you know,
that was many years ago.
I woiuld like a set of tiny dishes, too,
make believe food will do
A little sewing kit will be fine, there
are more things on my mind.
A story book to read, big print is
what I need,
You see Santa my eyes are growing
dim. Much of life is just a whim.
No candy canes you know, a real one
is what helps me go
No need for jewelry to wear, I won't
be giong anywhere.
Friends are all around you see, that is
enough for me.
Santa Claus I thank you for the years
past, this may be my last,
But please bring our world a better
understanding and love
For each other, God made us to be
sisters and brothers.
Santa Claus you always wear a big
kindly smile
Think of me as just a little child.

Thank you.

Walt Collins

ATLANTIS

Once, cloud wrapped Towers of
gleaming Crystal Fire
Stood shining in the Sun
With singing Birds and golden Seas
And Walls of endless run.

But now . . .
In wav'ring Vistas of the Seaweeds
Bower
The scattered Stones of Temples dead
Lie greenish gray; and Orichalcum,
dully red
Still gleams beneath the Sea.

Slowly swirling Silt from ancient
Crystal Power
Drifts down to never was and up to
yet to be.

Alta Richardson McLain

DESIGN

Those who examine History
Can have no questions for they see
The fingerprints of God are plain
On our foundation. Some are vain,
And honor not the Mighty Power
Who blessed and kept us to this hour.
America is great and strong,
But many modern things are
wrong.
The sinful actions in our Nation
By some are called a liberation.

Our Christian heritage is great.
God's people pray it's not too late
"One Nation under God" to be.
May we in righteousness be free,
Our children taught the Truth again,
And know that God rules over men.
America's dream, and her design
Was made in our Creator's mind.
May God be praised in this dear land,
His children all together stand!

David L Becker

David L Becker

BRANDON

My companion, my pal,
My four legged one

A friend of distinction
bright and warm like the sun

He listens to my laugh
He listens to my cry

He never thinks me daft
He never asks me why

He is a friend, his senses keen
Total devotion is always seen
His love always faithful, it never ends
A magical message is what he
sends

For Brandon is my dog
sent from above

He is my friend for life
He is my friend to love.

David L Becker

MORNING TIME

Good morning my
Fairest of Fair.

How are you today?

The glow of your golden
hair as it shines in
the morning sun.

Have you slept sound?

Are you ready
for another round
of Life?

I am truly glad it is you,
my darling wife,
beside me

On this morning.

David L Becker

A WISH

Just a thought
for today,

Because I have
something to say.

I sit and think,
sit and pray

That now is a good time,
Now is a good day

For You.

David L Becker

MY WORLD

The world was once mine,
but that was then.

I rejected it didn't
you know?

It turned so slow when
it was mine.

The challenge gone.

David L Becker

VISIONS

A beautiful flower
with stem of green
Grows on the hillside
and by the stream

A beautiful bird
with wings spread wide
Flies with grace
flies so high

A breaking of dawn
the stars in the night
The river flowing peaceful
such a beautiful sight!

All is God's making
some large and some small
So many things to behold in
Summer, Spring, Winter and
Fall

The vast universe
or a patch of green
Such wonders these
eyes have seen.

Eleanor Petracca

QUIET IS THE STILLNESS I FEEL WHEN I SIT

Quiet is the stillness I feel when I sit
Once again I, alone, become the
misfit
Anguish is the emotion piercing my
heart
As I long to be with those from
whom I'm apart

Solitude is welcome by those at
sometime
When life leaves them feeling
celestial and sublime
I, on the other hand, at this very
moment
Crave the noise and the ruckus the
darkness had sent

Calm, peaceful content are we
Who realize that life isn't only what
we see
But when eyes are shut and memories
are resting
Its true meaning shines through,
manifesting

Renee M Ramos

PASSIONS WHISPER

How often
have I held you
in my mind.
Whispering love
to the image
of your face.
I hear your voice,
a whisper of passion
in the night.
Afraid to say out loud
that which you whisper to me.
I am yours
to hold on tight.
The love you cannot unlearn
I hear you
when your words
are left unspoken.
I feel you
though you are miles
away.
And how often
have I seen you in my mind
as I whisper love
to the image of your face.

Dorene Coffey

HOLIDAY DANCE

To the singles, the newly single, the previous single.

It's a holiday weekend, the status is
single,
I ventured out to dance and mingle.

Groups of girls, a guy with a guy,
A friend of mine, stops to say hi.

It's a holiday weekend, the status is
single,
I ventured out to dance and mingle.

A dab more perfume, a little cologne,
Fix the tie, add the pin with the stone.

It's a holiday weekend, the status is
single,
I ventured out to dance and mingle.

Advance preparations, the
babysitter's on time,
Last minute hesitations, a cola, beer
or wine.

It's a holiday weekend, the status is
single,
I ventured out to dance and mingle.

Hair's in place, shoes are shined,
A frilly dress with a pretty design.

It's a holiday weekend, the status is
single,
I ventured out to dance and mingle.

Some come just to dance,
Others come seeking romance.

It's a holiday weekend, the status is
single.

Linda L Lodell-Perretta

OH HAPPY DAY

To my family, with love, especially to Joe, David, Leeann, and Carin.

Oh happy day—
When we met,
When we kissed,
Fell in love, married.
Oh happy day—

When we united,
When you became mother
And I father.
Oh happy day—
When we laughed with an infant,
Struggled with a toddler,
Cried with an adolescent.
Oh happy day—
When the cycle was repeated,
You bore anther child
Who grew as quickly as the first.
Oh happy day—
When the family is together
And we remember both . . .
The good and the bad . . .
Oh happy day—today
Because we celebrate
When we met, kissed, loved,
And married.

Barbara Ann Abt

I DID, I DO AND I ALWAYS WILL

This poem is dedicated to my "Mom, Maxine and Suzanne."

"In the beginning God creatred
the heaven and earth."
And from me to you today,
what is my worth?
Yesterday I loved you;
today I do;
Tomorrow and forever I'll
ever be true.
Let the past be forgotten,
yesterday, behind.
Today and tomorrow I
renew my mind.
Let us press toward a better life
and all our dreams fulfill;
Remember I did, I do,
and I always will.

Beverly A Wilson

AWE

To M. Lucille desOrmeau Brazie, my Mom, who gave that star to me.

Lovely ballerina, so tall,
so lean, so free
reaching so high to catch a star
then swooping down on bended knee
she hands the pretty star to me.

Johnna Tush

WONDERMENT

To mom, dad, Becky and all my love to Brian.

I look in wonder
The world all around
The rain and thunder
Life or death, a burial mound

Rain upon the sun
The rainbow glows a rosy hue
The glistening waters run
A final answering Cue

The flame of life
Glows bright and free
The answering of a fife
Shining like the morning sea

Wonderment is a part of the song
A glorious birth
So a life may be long and strong
Childless mirth.

Terry

THE ETERNAL ROSE

It was mother's birthday, comfortably warm, the sun shown bright.
Everything seemed so right.
Little Sue walked in, then ran off by herself.
In the company of her little toy elf.

Sensing something was wrong,
Mother asked, "What's the matter Sue?"
"Oh mommy, I just don't know what to do.
I had a rose just for you today and I losted it."
Once again running off by herself to sit.

Pa hearing all, knowingly smiled and called his little girl to his side.
For indeed she was his joy and pride.
"Come help me, I have some gifts to wrap for mother."
"You can give her one and I will give her the other."

Having been able to give mother something that day,
Sue soon found the time to run out and play.
Mother treasured the presents that were given with so much love.
And thanked God in the above.

Darkness coming on Mother said,
"Where did that child go?"
Unusual for this child you know.
Putting on her coat she went out to bring her little girl home.
Night was no time for a child to roam.

Down the path she caught sight of a rose by the gate.
"Oh, so this was the little flower's fate."
Reaching to pick it up she placed it close to her heart.
Of which it has become so great a part.

For the longest while she found herself deep in thought,
About this beautiful gift Sue had bought.
And on a bench that was near she stopped to sit.
Tears streamed as she remembered,
"Mommy, I losted it."

Terry

OH BOY

Gertie met Henry, and felt she had found her man,
To hold him she wuld do anything she can,
Fixed her face and hair, not a flaw,
Bought new clothes and much much more.

Served sumptious dinners to prove she could cook,
New furniture, and how pleased Henry did look,
Went around to friends many pictures in hand,
Showing that what she picked was grand.

Friend Myrtle advisd that she should lose weight,
Then in her clothes would look really great.
For today it was the trend you see,
To be as thin as one could be.

A little offended Gertie felt her friend was right,
Even now her skirt did seem a wee bit tight.
And sometimes found it hard to get through small door,
And Myrtle, oh well what were friends for.

She began a diet and exercise, cost way out of sight,
Could be seen jogging well into the night,
Famous meals Henry was no longer invited to,
But given a diet cake and a soda or two.

He seemed unhappy, but she was doing this for him,
Skipping dates to be sure to be at the gym.
And the endeavor soon proved worth the care,
For now stood a new trim, slim girl there.

Well at a time when she felt she looked most glamorous of all,
Wondered why her Henry did not write or call.
Myrtle told her she heard he would marry a girl called Jane,
And she didn't think that Henry would call again.

Well strangely although she found herself left in a lurch,
She received an invitation to reception and church,
And Henry and Jane walked down the aisle, and what astounds,
To Gertie, Jane seemed to be every bit of 200 pounds.

Joe Nations

GOD'S GIFT TO ME

To my terrestrial trinity—sweetheart, wife and best friend—Mary Ida.

In stillness I sit so very quiet,
Pondering thoughts I wish to write.
I struggle hard as I try to say
What my heart feels every day
About the woman who shares my life;
A gift from God to be my wife.

She taught me love and how to live;
How to accept and how to give.
She brought me out from my hiding place
And helped me stand face to face
With myself and all mankind;
To walk beside and not behind.

The life I live is different today
Because God sent my wife this way.
I praise Him with all my heart
For teaching me the marriage art
Through this woman, my loving wife;
My joy on earth for all my life.

Frank Savino

SUNSET

To my mom.

How I marvel at the time of day,
The setting sun seems to slip away,
Colors like an artist's palette cast across the sky,
Purple, pink clouds of crimson hues,
The glow of the sky so heavenly imbue,
Majestic grace cast from above, that seems to slip away,
To begin anew, in some far off place,
Its fiery grace, a new dawning,
How I marvel, as I marvel,
A cherub shaped cloud hails the setting sun,
To hasten it on its journey's end,
The day is gone, peace an' calmness fill the air,
The day's brightness slips into rainbow dreams,
Setting hues of crimson glow,
Remind me of its glory;
As I marvel at the time of day,
The glow of dawn, now slips away in majestic beauty
The dark of night, hastens on the wind
'Tis twilight I're again,
As I marvel, how I marvel, as I marvel!

Clara Dorio

PAST LIVES

To Patty, who believed in me.

I visited the old cemetery read the old poems about people who gave so much for freedom, courage and hardships from the past a haunting begins in my soul the stories these people told they gave so their children to sickness and death to settle a new country to be free husband and son buried side by side it wasn't important to be alive but to be free and work a new land if only to hear the stories they told if only a glimpse of their life I behold.

Clara Dorio

MEMORIES

I saw for just a fleeting moment into yesterday
I was there a time ago carefree at my play
It really makes me marvel the things your mind can store
In darken shelves inside ourselves the pleasure that it
Gave me I won't soon forget I'll store my precious moment
Back upon its shelf ready for another time to share it with Myself.

Clara Dorio

TRAPPED

My soul is entrapped behind a dark door suppression of my spirit I cannot endure. I was free I was alive now I fear my soul has died. You can take away all I have owned but, I cannot survive without my own home, freedom of thought I treasured above all now it's enclosed behind a dark wall if I can't get out and be set free like a bird without wings I'll fall in the sea drown and die exist nevermore I know I am trapped behind this dark, and will fly away nevermore.

Sandra Gayle Pierce
MY SISTERS CHILD

Dedicated to my nephew Nathan, my little dream.

In eighteen hours of non-deliberation,
her eyes shown much frustration.

She had doubts of her existence.
I had to be strong and persistent.

I could not see, in her painful
screams,
that moments away was our little
dream.

When his tiny face did first appear,
my heart gladdened with a tear.

As the total moment did arrive,
her only question: Is he alive?

With a wail, he began to cry.
I could breathe with a sigh.

As she smiled and spoke his name,
neither of our lives has been the
same.

Sandra Gayle Pierce
SENSES OF LOVE
Love is white.
It looks pure as
dew on a flower,
It smells fresh as
a flowing river,
It tastes sweet as
a cube of sugar,
love feels warm as
a ray of sunshine.

Jacob Alan Kruse

Jacob Alan Kruse
IT IS GETTING DARK IN THE TWILIGHT
It is getting dark in the twilight.
Ghosts are running through the sky.
Witches brewing something in their
pots,
ready to seal your doom.
The door of horror ready to open.
You'll try to hide,
But everywhere you look it's terror!
So LOOK OUT . . . you're doomed!

Evola Loretta Sander Barron
I NEED A POEM

". . . while we were yet sinners, Christ died for us." Romans 5:8. Thanks to Eddie-Lou Cole—and all the others who helped me reach my goal.

I need a poem.
I need a verse.
My mind's a blank,
my heart just sank—
Where can I rent
a think tank?

John Kelly
WHEELS
I have been away awhile
but I hope to be home soon.
Home to face the unguarded thoughts
of my habitual heart,
to silence it before I start to say
"I must protest. I must protest!
It is my diamond duty."

But now, in such an ugly time,
the true protest is Beauty.

And a single star rises shining,
beaming on the border,
saying passion leads to chaos
now chaos leads to order.
As other stars are tears of the Moon.
Yes, I have been away awhile
but I shall be home again soon.

Sandra Walker
GOD'S FLOWER GARDEN

To Everyone who Encouraged and Supported Me, You know Who You Are. Thank You!!

Such Beautiful Thoughts in One's
Heart,
Helps Life to be more SPECIAL AT
THE START,
As I look at ALL the BEAUTY
THERE IS TO SEE,
How wonderful AND PRECIOUS
FOR You and Me.

Another Beautiful Start,
Is God's Children, A FLOWER
GARDEN OF THE HEART,
As We learn of the Wonders for Us
to Heed,
How Wonderful and Precious Indeed.

What A SPECIAL WAY FOR TO
BE A PART,
OF GOD'S FLOWER GARDEN OF
THE HEART,
As We RECEIVE HIS SPECIAL
LOVE,
He reaches down, He pours it out
from ABOVE.

And when I REMEMBER THAT
WHICH HE HAS DONE FOR ME,
HOW SPECIAL TO KNOW YOU
SEE,
A WONDERFUL AND PRECIOUS
START,
AND TO BE ONE OF GOD'S
CHILDREN, A FLOWER GARDEN
OF THE HEART.

L M Ludescher
SOMEDAY
We sit closely to the fire,
You're my every desire,
You're cute and smart,
When I see you it adds ten thousand
beats to my heart.
I see you standing there hoping
One day you will start to care,
Until then this poem is at
an end.

Nicole Hamilton
AFRICA
OH mother land we were solden from
your bosom
We were separated from our brothers
and sisters
We were carried across the big blue
in chain, we lived in filth for months

We were bought and sold into slavery
OH mother land why
We were beaten, killed, and raped
OH mother land why
We were slave for them, we surfered
because of them
OH mother land why
We were hated because of the color
of our skin
Oh mother land why
Oh mother land why have they not
seen the way that they have destroy
us
We once lived in freedom without
chains
We lived off the land, the sun would
raise and set with us without chains
OH mother land we are strong we
will one day
RAISE AND SHINE WITHOUT
CHAINS

Mike Graham
SONGWRITER'S BLUES
My telephone don't ring nobody
knocks on my front door
I check the mailbox every day I
check the charts on Billboard
I've got a song I'll sing for you too
It's all about a Songwriter's
Blues

I go to the important parties even if
I'm not told to
I always try to do the right thing I try
to say the right things for you too
I've got a song I'll sing for you
It's all about the Songwriter's
Blues

My friends almost understand me
why I'm always home all alone
Why it seems like I'm always so busy
never getting anything done
I've got a song I'll sing for you
It's all about this Songwriter's
Blues

Everyone says no pain no glory I
believe that almost feels true
Because if I could describe this
feeling I'd write it right down
for you
I've got a song I'll sing for
you It's all about these
Songwriter's Blues
It's just this Songwriter's
Blues

Carmen H Fernandez
SEA GULL HILL

To my parents, Mike and Griselda McGuane, in appreciation for all their help, support, and their love. Also to Richard and Sarah, Laddie, and Luigi-Squeegy! I love you all!

Honoured among ocean waves I was
queen of the blue sea
And once, upon a time I fondly had
the zephyrs and waves
Shells of silver and gold
Under the clear waters of the gentle
sea.

Oh, time let me play, let me be
Golden in the palms of the sea

And silver and golden I was ocean
queen and sailor, seabirds
Sang my song, the seashells sparkled
silver and gold,
And the waves rocked gently the
pebbles of the calm sea.

And the sun was brightly shining, it
was lovely, the waves swayed high as
the sky . . .

Then I wake, and the sea, shimmering with waves, rocks forth,
Rocks back, the foam like unicorns; it
was all shining, it was the waves and
seashells, the sky embracing all.

Honoured among waves and seas
gulls, I lived my present days
And nothing I cared at my blue ocean
stays that time would
Keep me up to the seashell thronged
shore by the shadow
Of palm trees, in the moon that is
always smiling.

Oh, as I was young in the palms of
the sea, time took me and kept me,
though I sang in my chains with the
sea.

Carmen H Fernandez
MY LOVE SONG TO YOU
Deeper than the oceans,
Stronger than the strongest winds,
Brighter than the stars in h Universe,
My love shines across the sea.

And in a starry night
Under the moonlight,
It gently renews itself
Like a morning rosebud.

And to wake,
In perfect beauty,
You and I,
Side by side.

Kimberly Offield
SPIDER WEB
Spinning magnificently,
A sparkling silver maze.
In the mystery of the night,
Silent and alone.

Weaving majestically,
In an evening sea of silence.
Catching dew drops at the rise of
dawn.
Peaceful yet fearful.

Gently swaying,
In dusk's tender breeze.
Displaying a delicate individuality,
And a silky, sheer design.

The spider web.
In its single majesty.
Silent, lonely, and dark.
Mysterious and appealing.
Deadly.

Sonja Ahtiainen
NATURE
Nature is a wonderful place
to be in
It has the blue and white sky as the
ceiling
green and brown trees as walls
don't forget the green grass.
Nature is so beautiful and great,
Why should we destroy it?

Mary Wronko
RE-UNITED
Let us pick up the poor threads
of our lives where we left them,
when our love faded
with the dying embers of a sunset;
when we lingered beside a time-worn gate,
and the rain in your hair glistened silvery-wet.

You pluck a wild rose and place it
where my heart beats loyal but free,
and we'll walk a road that is
dusty and white.
Out of dreams that were shattered
such things can be.

Let us remember the sweetness of happy hours,
and forget the bitterness of parting.
Let us recapture the moon's placid glow—
and claim it is ours.

Dorothea H Roth
GOD MADE THE EARTH TO PRODUCE AND ENJOY
God gave us this earth to produce and enjoy.
Given with love to every woman,
man, girl and boy.
Look at nature once in a while,
I'm sure you will like her beauty and style.
Awake to a sunrise telling us a new day is beginning.
Listen to a babbling brook the song it is singing.
Look in wonder at mountains
towering up to the sky,
Where God watches over us from His Heaven on high.
Man makes taxes we must always pay.
God gives us free the birds, to sing day after day.
Stand under a tree and rest in its shade
A tree is something beautiful God has made.
Get close to the earth, its roots and sod.
Do all these things and you will feel closer to God.

Beatrice Florist Brown
MIGHTY LIKE A ROSE
MOTHER . . . You keep your home a haven,
for those who are in need,
And any hour of day or night,
the hungry you do feed,
Standing at the cook-stove,
in your apron soft and fair,
Mother sitting sewing,
in your old rocking chair.
Your wisdom how it clothes me,
to cope with worldly cares,
You teach me and you give me strength,
with love and fervent prayers,
We stroll the fields of Memory Lane,
sniff fragrance in the air,
And listen to the birds' song,
it's peaceful everywhere.
You comfort me in dreams at night,
When troubled, you are near,
You tell me all will soon be well,
it's just a passing fear,
Your hands that rock the cradle,
as everybody knows,
MOTHER . . . The Virtuous Woman,
YOU'RE MIGHTY LIKE A ROSE!

Jel D Lewis (Jones)
ANNIE MAE

This poem is dedicated to Ella Mae Jones, my beautiful mother. And Joy L. Landre, my number one fan.

Like the silent tears of the sea
your pain found a home.
Yet you live within your own prison
that locks its doors with steel.

To wipe your tears with a delicate rose
may scar the surface of your skin.
Yet the tears that poured were like
fiery acid that burnt the depth of your soul.

Your pain runs deep—reaching out
into the vast space of darkness that
stands no man. And if you cried in
the face of a goddess, she would turn
to you her back.

Annie Mae be brave. You are a gentle
rose among thorns.

Cathy Warsheski
FOREVER
With my deeply saddened heart,
Whose, from yours, grows far apart,
I wonder when it all will end.
When will my heart finally mend?

When will those smiles reappear,
As in times that seem so near?
Those crazy, carefree, happy times.
For those, I'd give my last dimes.

All those times I've come to treasure,
Ones that gave me so much pleasure.
What does it all really mean?
Or has it been just one long dream?

Please, dear God, please give us peace.
On our lives, just one more lease.
But mostly bring us back together,
So we can start to make forever.

Sandra L Adams
THE OLD OAK TREE
The old oak tree
That has stood so long
Through all the storms
And the droughts
Has died this year
And left behind
Its ghostly statue
To remind us
How in its prime
For many years
Birds built their nests
Squirrels played and
Raccoons made dens
It's such a shame
A life so long
Has come to an end
Because you see
We're losing one of
God's works of art

Brenda Bastien
SHED YOUR LIGHT ON ME

I dedicate this poem to my lovely daughter Corissa, for hopes of everything she endured that the feelings in her heart will remain true forever . . . Mom.

Shed your light on me,
for just a little while.
I need a touch of sunshine,
I need a gospel of a smile.
The road ahead is dark and weary,
No light shines through all the dreary.
Make the sun warm my heart,
make the sun never part.
A constant ray of warmth and love,
lets me know god's watching from above.

Edith F Taylor

Edith F Taylor
TED BUNDY THE MURDERER
Ted Bundy you died the criminal's death
What entered your mind when you took that last breath?
Did you think of the people you tortured and killed?
Did you feel any remorse or deep down were you thrilled?

Were you a misfit or an unhappy child?
Did you have tantrums and a desire to be wild?
Were you rejected by some girl while in your youth?
Was it easier to lie than to free the truth?

It's hard to fathom why you were such a cruel creature
To premeditate murder is too difficult to feature
The feeling I had on the day that you died
Was sympathy for your mother when she openly cried
The other I wish you had donated your brain
Maybe research would prevent this from happening again

Doris Sinclair
RENUNCIATION
My purse was full of silver,
My pockets bulged with gold.
And I had all the precious jewels
My arms could ever hold.
Love whistled from a thicket,
The tune was light and gay,
I flung my treasures to the ground,
And blithely went a beggar's way.

Elyce M Burns
ON A STORMY NIGHT IN NOVEMBER
On a stormy night in November
With the wind blowing through
the trees
The little girl watches the rain
through her bedroom window
The clock struck midnight and the
wind howled, but not one
thing could move the girl from
the window
She stood there through the night,
not letting a sound disturb her
The rain slowed down but her
heart kept beating
The storm was over but her fear
will never end.

Sylvia M Bealer
CUPID

To My Other Half.

Our marriage is sometimes a lark
To each other the love of our heart
Till death do us part
Was the message from the start
The Beatles' "All My Lovin'" started the spark!
Sometimes we dish out to each other some jib
I (Wife) have even offered him back his rib
His just due thoughts have not always been visions of halos over my head
Make up resources prevail afterwards instead
Ah! As a starter a hug and kiss is not meek
Nor does it refer that the one or the other is weak
Resulting that our thanks to you our marriage is kinda neat
The Cupid giver is able to deliver
To conquer whichever one is the jibber.

Wm James Harris
DESIRING TO KNOW YOU BETTER
I remain thinking of the first time,
I laid my eyes on you
and how I knew that I had to know
you better . . .
To see within your eyes the rare
things that make you smile
Lookin' at you like this gives
me
the feeling of viewing
a sunset, with a ballerina
dancing,
or strolling in the moon-light
as One
Desiring to know . . .
the better things
Like caring, sharing, communicating,
understanding and loving
Desiring to know . . .
the mysterious depth of your mind,
the magic of your lovin' soul
Desiring to know you better . . . .
I ask and wish that this never
ends.

Brian Collins (Scout)
REFLECTIONS OF A SCOUT

To my wife, Luise, and my children, Christina, William, and Michael and to the scouts, the unsung heroes of baseball.

A baseball scout is many things to
many people.
He is a man probably overworked
and underpaid
Whose face is weather-beaten
from years of exposure to the
elements
Who in the course of a season
will see thousands of players.
Appreciated by some,
misunderstood by others,
but above all, dedicated to the
game of baseball.
A man who will decide who can
play
and who cannot play.
If he is wrong he will hear about
it
But if he is right, he's just doing
his job.
Faceless men doing their job.
But let us all remember,

these men are the backbone of
the game
we call our national
pastime, baseball.

Roberta L Hutto
MARINA BEACH
In great stride this day's birth is unfolding
Blue skies promise another sunny morning:
Sea gulls gliding in swirling motion
Must be breakfast is my notion.

Misty sprays atop the breaking waves,
While that crafty chill wind has penetrated
Warm clothing barriers and enters in, as if an old lost friend:
Then sandy dunes no comfort lies, as these tiny partials
Grip my cold wet eyes.

Still the chilly wind blows the sand up and around,
Freezing my skin: I'd throw it to the ground!
Sounds of crashing waves, like that of thunder, roll on this
Coast and here I still stand amidst such splendor;
As these moments disperse and leave me as a ghost.

Dana Brindisi
GRANDMA

To Lillian Bochiaro, my loving Great-Grandma, August 26, 1989.

Don't cry Grandma, there's no reason to cry
You're going to a more beautiful place up in the sky

So don't be afraid, there's no reason to be
This place has more beauty than you ever dreamed you would see

We will all miss you until we see you again
So watch over us and protect us till then

Tears cloud my eyes when I think that you're gone
But I'll remember you forever as my life goes on

I envy the peace that awaits you up there
Our life on earth is just not fair

So go ahead Grandma, don't hesitate
We all must say good-bye, it's decided by fate

Maureen M DeLucia
BE ALWAYS PREPARED

This poem is dedicated to Beth, my loving sister.

If you had but one day to live,
What would you do?
Pray to God that he might forgive,
Or try to start anew?

Spend your last hours with a friend
As though nothing were to happen?
Rather than face alone, the end,
A thing dreaded by all men.

To recapture all the good things you missed,
Where would you go?
Back to old places so hard to resist,
When memories now overwhelm you so?
Or better still, stop your running,
Why not be wise?
Be always prepared to face with cunning,
The Almighty, who won't tolerate lies.

Ola Margaret James
I WANT TO SING
I want to live a happy life,
To laugh and dance and sing!
Hope to avoid most earthly strife,
And bless each common thing.

But inside there's a warning Voice
That says, "Not so, my child,
If with the angels you'll rejoice,
You must greet sorrow wild;
Your sisters and your brothers, too,
Have grief too hard to bear,
So help them with their burdens,
And Jesus will be there."

Martin Fewster
SOLACE
O' rest your weary head upon my shoulder,
Unfold the troubles of your heart to me
That this may help to ease the heavy burden
Of pent-up woes I'm sure that there must be.

If I were given the power of understanding . . .
And wisdom in abundance to console,
Then would I gladly do my best to vanquish
The turbulences of a grieving soul.

So rest your weary head upon my shoulder—
Allow my little worth, to you, to lend;
And, when relaxed, perhaps you will discover
That you have gained, at least, another friend.

Tho' this my lowly song of comfort to you
Has really no beginning nor an end,
Each simple verse its separate page does cover
That thoughts on future pages may append.

Now rest your weary head upon my shoulder . . . .
Nor hinder that your grief may outward flow:
A kerchief will be neatly placed beside you
To wipe the tears, that others might not know.

Ira Jackson
THE GOOD OLD DAYS OF THE PAST
How can violence in the past be less when slavery in the past was not less. How can crime in the past be less when greed in the past was not less. How can rape in the past be less when sadism in the past was not less. How can drugs in the past be less when addiction in the past was not less. How can incest in the past be less when perversion in the past was not less.

Jean Lewis
FOREVER DANCERS
Forever dancers in the night
with instinctive grace, our steps are light.

Unspoken words are exchanged
—We understand

In our private world for two
—We are in command

The room is dark, the only light
—from the moon and stars of
night.

In each other's arms
—we hold tight

An air of eternal enchantment
—no questions, it's right.

John Boggess
ALL THAT MATTERS

To my wonderful wife, Jennylind.

The only thing that matters is the love you have for me,
and how much time I have on earth to share your company.

Because your love inspires me to live a better way,
to be more diligent at my work and frequent when I pray.

To strive for great glory and attain a true success,
whereby to bless and honor you and bring you happiness.

When we are together dear, you make my dream come true,
Because there is no greater joy than just to be with you.

So it does not matter dear, how dark the sky may be,
as long as I am certain of, the love you have for me.

Wasila Dahdul

Wasila Dahdul
THE RAINFOREST THAT WAS

To my grandmother in Brazil, Antonia Umbelina Rocha.

There isn't much left there anymore
The area is destitute and the air smells of smoke galore.
If you can find a native maybe he'll tell you
About the way it was and what they didn't do.
It used to be so beautiful, a place where nature took over
Where everything was possible, maybe even a four-leafed clover.
Each year the river would overflow and flood the land
There would be no more beaches, because there was no sand.
Fish you never heard of would come up from the sea
Fishing was productive and you'd get top-dollar at the fishery.
Then the water would recede and the land would get real dry
Where the fish once swam was now just grass and it kind of made you cry.
That was then, and now is now, and now it doesn't exist
It used to be a big topic, at the top of everyone's list.
But somehow they forgot about it and the forest burned to the end
No more animals or plants, nothing to defend.
Not it's just a memory, and you can only see it in books.
Not very long ago, but I forget how it looked.
Sure it was sad, and I was real mad, because I didn't try
To save the Amazon and now all I can do is cry.

Dr Pauline L Green
I'M SO ENCOURAGED

"I'm So Encouraged" is dedicated to John Milton Green, my precious husband, who has loved and encouraged me for 46 wonderful years.

I'm so encouraged;
I know you love me.
I'm so encouraged;
No one's above me.

My heart is smiling:
The Lord is styling
Our life together,
With sunny weather.

My soul's uplifted;
We both are gifted.
God's love belongs—to him, to her.
Were I a kitten, I would purr.

I'm so encouraged:
From doubt I'm free
I'm so encouraged:
For you love me.

Rod Aschbrenner
ONE MAN'S LOVE

To Debbie.

Do we know "it" as foe or friend?
A soul to break, a Heart to mend.
A phantom shadow in the night.
A ray of hope, a shaft of light.

An imposter, or is "it" real?
No hands to touch, yet "it" can feel.
From deep inside, or from above.
That elusive emotion known as LOVE . . .

Geraldine McDonough
THE SECRET PLACE
When we listen to,
The secret place,
In our hearts,
To know the,
Wisdom of truth,
Buried deep.

To feel,
The compassion,
And love,
From the start,
And all the,
Beauty to see,
Our integrity,
We keep.

Dark shadows,
Intrude,
Here and there,
They dart,
A shield,
Of fortitude,
Appears,
To do, Its part.

And a deed,
To happen,
To make,
The heart leap,
The Wonderful,
Feeling,
The knowing,
For the,
Secret Place,
To keep.

Mrs Dorothy M Hosey
SAN ANDREA'S FAULT
"Fault, whose fault?" they asked that day.
"It was San Andrea's Fault!" so they say.
Mother Earth spread her lap upon the land—
Making the Continents—Oh! so grand!
To every corner of her beauteous girth,
Man came to dig; to drill; to build;
Using up her riches and her worth!
She squirmed; slowly moved and groaned.
In agony, she willingly shared her throne.
Waves and tides pounded her with might!
Her heavy load heightened in restless plight.
Her molten heart became stressed and worn,
In her earthy garment, a rent was torn.
An earthquake released her torturous stress;
Renting and tearing at her splendid dress!
In its wake: disaster, loss of life, and home of man;
Leaving: fire, sorrow, rubble, tears across her land.
"Fault, whose fault?" they asked that day.
"It was San Andrea's Fault!" they say—
But, Man abused along God's earthy way!

Joyce I Clemens
SWEETLY HOURS
Will you look upon this day?
Tears or smiles will let us say;
What our burdened heart may feel,
The pain we have within is real.
Cleanse thy thoughts that are so few.
Hopes and prayers I have for you
Reach out from the darkened mask,
And sweep away the hardest task.
Tears fall like little stars,
Leaving deep and bleeding scars.
Will you ever walk life's road
Leaving behind the greatest load?
Play the game of life each day,
As if our happiness could pay.
For love and trust side by side
All through our blessed life we stride
Hopes and prayers—hopes and prayers
The game is hard to play.
Happiness or sadness, life is in each day
Tears and smiles—tears or smiles
The game is hard to win.
Play the game of life each day
Life is our last spin—

John O Lilly
A SMILE AMONG THE TEARS
Tears of joy and sadness
Flow intermingled down
Across the smile upon my face
Then softly to the ground
Wherein the shell that once was you
Was placed with tender care . . .
And though I come with sorrow
I know that *you're not there*!

And knowing this, I smile
While tears of gladness flow,
As I recall the tender love
We shared not long ago . . .
For I look toward the future
When He too will beckon me
For then again we'll share our love
For all eternity!

Sandra E Snider
ANGEL OF THE NIGHT
As he layed silently beneath the stars, on a warm, dark night
the moonlight, it shined so bright.
He began to think once again
of the girl he called, his
Angel of the night.

He thought of how she had loved,
in the night under the moonlight,
He remembered how she danced so gracefully, so full of delight.

He thought of how her eyes, would sparkle like the stars,
He remembered how her hair would fly with the breeze, during each graceful move.

She was his vision of loveliness
his precious Angel of the night,
then he thought of when, he had last seen his, Angel of the night.

He remembered how she, had laid
so cold, and stiff! in that casket,
that had stolen his, Angel of the night,
as a tear fell from his eye,
you heard him whisper,

Goodbye! my Angel of the night!

Joan L Gordon
UNTIL
My silent song
Like an unsung bell
Waits to be heard.

But until you ask,
I'll dream that we will one day
Share, our hearts
Like bow and string
Will meet as one
Attuned to sing.

Laura Denise Ferris
WHATEVER HAPPENS, LOVE ME

To all those people who want to be loved; just as I want to be. Special dedication to those who love me as my poem states . . .

—LOVE ME—

LOVE ME—Because I try to touch life, within the framework of uncertainty . . .

LOVE ME—In the shadows of my indecisions, as I strive to gain knowledge . . .

LOVE ME—In the silence of my pain, and in the noise of my joy . . .

LOVE ME—For the feeling of my heart, not for the fears of my mind . . .

LOVE ME—In my search for truth, though I may stumble upon the lies . . .

LOVE ME—As I pursue my dreams, sometimes retarded by illusions . . .

LOVE ME—For I may be going along with open eyes, but blinded with each step . . .

LOVE ME—In my openness, as I am tightly closed; like that of a new bud . . .

LOVE ME—For I may be the follower, as I am the leader . . .

LOVE ME—Because we are different, as we are the same . . .

LOVE ME—Not with expectations, but with hope of achievement . . .

LOVE ME—For I am what I am, and not who you see me as . . .

Frank Vélez
TWO VIEWS

Dedicated to my Uncle César who fought bravely in Korea.

His nervousness showed
He forced himself to talk about it
Never wounded, but spiritually tormented
He saw death, he saw horror
Boricua friends mutilated after resounding cries
Survival seemed impossible in this foreign land

She sat on her hammock reading his letters
Wondering if they were his last
She did not cry, she wept
A mother who might lose her son
His mamá a model of faith
"When will my son return from Korea?"

Rusty Oase
A MAZE
Surrounded by friends
I feel alone
My mind wanders from their conversation, into a maze
In my maze lies a fantasy world
I spend all my time in this world
As long as I don't touch them,
The towering walls numb the true feelings in my heart
I've never walked through my maze
I sit and admire its wonderfully bright beauty
Now I want to walk through my maze
I want to experience these wonderful surroundings
As I walk, I wonder which way to turn
With every decision I make, I hit a wall of reality
Everything turns gray and gloomy
Afraid of these walls
I stand still
Alone in my fantasy maze
Surrounded by friends

Douglas Brennan
THE CARPENTER
I knew a carpenter; his name was Mike,
He couldn't even fix a bike,
Every time a nail went in,
Mike would start to sing,
He even took it upon himself,
To build us a brand new shelf,
He tried so hard to impress my mom and me,
But we didn't buy it and neither did he.

Janet L Knapp
SENT FROM HELL
My life, is it not a mirror of Hell, and my conscious been given to the insane?
The evils I've borne, I know not from where they were conceived.
I bare the scares for all the pain I've caused, and the tears that only fell in my mind.
The evils my life has shown, have been returned ten fold.
They've sent from Hell one man, to torture my body, then my soul.
My life's mistakes, the people I've done harm, now my pain, see, he's been sent to inflict this upon me.
If this life I've been given came to an ending; Then, this man you've sent from Hell, will he be done?

Linda C Marlok
WINTER BEAUTY

This is for my husband Raymond, and my children Carrie, Stacey, and Christopher.

Howling winds in dark of night,
Lift and twirl flakes of white,
Bending tops of trees up high,
Breaking branches that fall and lie,
Gusting winds that push and shove,
Soft white flakes that dance above,
Descend to earth to blanket all,
Let eyes of morn, the beauty fall.

Norman O Bakke
SALUTE TO PEACE AND FREEDOM
The dawn of peace has broken and the guns have ceased to roar
The pain, the blood, the sweat and tears, have paid the price and more
Midst ruins of war a gallant youth on bended knee is praying
While near at hand a wounded pal with outstretched hand is laying

A trembling hand, a tear-filled eye, a soul that's sad and shaken
Can hear a comrade's dying cry, in death he lies forsaken
Far across the briny deep a solemn

prayer is said
For a loved one fighting over there,
he has fought though now he's dead

Not long ago this fairhaired youth
was filled with boyish laughter
A happy home, a land that's free was
all that he was after
Now stilled by death, the toll of war
has marked his destiny
A valiant fight midst battle's roar,
and now eternity

What price freedom? what price
glory, who asks this price be paid
That men should fight and bleed and
die, on battlefield and glade
We have won the war for freedom
and overthrown tyranny
Let's prove that we've not fought in
vain, to keep our country free.

Erlinda Nugal Fields
TENDER LOVING CARE
A seed is planted into the earth
That someday it will flourish.
The pouring of rain, the rays
Of sunlight, the moisten earth
And its creatures.

As the flowers bloom unto the night
And the morning dew sets,
The fragrance of sweetness is in the air.
It opens up and into each hand
It is picked with thoughts of
Tender loving care.

Brandy Fry
LIKE A FLOWER
Like a flower is my heart,
When warm and bright,
It opens up,
How like a flower is my heart,
When cold and dark,
It will close,
Like a flower is my heart,
When not cared for,
It will die,
How like a flower is my heart,
When it is loved,
It will thrive.

Pauline Legant

Pauline Legant
LOVE DIVINE

I dedicate this poem to God my beloved Father.

I have found the glory of a love
divine,
Arranged by God, the Father,
in His love sublime.

He has watched me closely, every
livelong day,
Has chosen me to work for
Him in a special way.

I am grateful, Father, for this love
divine,
For just a closer walk with
Thee
Along the path of time.

Pauline Legant
INSPIRATION

I dedicate this poem to Jesus, the Love of my life.

Inspiration is the heart's desire to
communicate
Lovers understand and use it
It dwells deep within our souls
It never fades or dissipates
itself
It is eternal as Love itself
It comes and it goes, fashioned
after the Universe
It is an endless well of thoughts
unadorned and unabashed
Ready to give of itself at the
least urging
It responds willingly to Love's
beckoning
Shyly incorporates itself into
our lives and refuses to be
stilled
It has much to say and much to give
Inspiration is the ultimate
wisdom of the ages and of the
senses
It is revealing in its nature
Diffused only by darkness
Oh! Come let me give of myself
That you may acquire wisdom
and knowledge
All that ever was and ever shall be
Is mine to give and yours to
receive
I am—"INSPIRATION"—the
"GOD" within

Gary L Osmonson
CELEBRATION OF LIFE
As this soul sits along the ocean front
Time passes, but the blessing of
thoughts flow over the mind.
For every season there is a reason.
That's life?
We come to earth portraying
people—never knowing what our
own special life means.
Truly we should stop—think—
appreciate what we are.
Life or death—whatever, it's our
destiny!
Loving is giving. Not take but share!
As I watch the sun set into the
ocean—
I toast life with such a learning
process.
Time—yes—accept people—life—
teach yourself to Love!
Life—death—who cares! ?
It's what happens between the
Celebration of Life!
May peace of time—space the ocean
waters
Never end with the sunset—sunrise.
The beauty of nature—truly a revival
of this soul!

Theresa DiBiase
THE SEA SWALLOWS
Upright endures the stern
Whilst the bow;
long surrendered into the chasm,
beckons its complement
to harmonize alongside its misfortune.

Yet, she perpetuates.
Whereupon the sea's barbarous curls
grapple amid malevolent, saturated
gales—
crushing her resistance.

Beneath the proceeds
relinquishing the sole entity of its
existence
to anatomies, chafed by cobalt
plumage.
Nevertheless, they, too, are
submersed,
and the morrow's phlegmatic waters
surmount in a more deeper azure.

Departed they are. To a sea
persevering in roaring enticement
to mariners and their odysseys.
Many a widows' walk will be worn
threadbare
protecting intimate communions
weighty enough to generate its
collapse.

Kathy Manley
FRAUDULENT ACTS
The red eyed, slimy eel
sleeks slowly up
from the dark, depths of hell.
Completely masked, and showing no
intentions,
he dances his own show.
Sweetly motivating my emotions,
he portrayed a beautiful,
sensitive type.
Speaking in tongues, I was greatly
misled.
Cheerfully, I smiled,
not realizing
the trap was set and I was captured.
Like a baby mouse, I wandered
too deep into the darkness.
Accepting this false personality
was the first mistake.
I could not see the deceitfulness
in those red, glowing eyes.
Playing games with my emotions
this imposter stole my good
judgement.
Betrayed by my blindness,
I am the one who dies.

Diana Uhric
THE ROADS AHEAD
I see the roads ahead, I see
the future bright,
I see the shadowy past and the
darkness of the night.
I remember the days gone by
as God watches over me,
I see each one of us fulfill
our own destiny.
Then as we sing a new song
or turn a new page,
We remember together as we begin
a new age.

We are divine . . .
We are the Class of '89!

Greg Williams
MIDNIGHT STORM
His face was gray with envy
Over his lost friend,
Brought on by much destruction
And many a sin.

His eyes were filled with tears
As the streams begin to flow,
His heart was filled with pain
Seeping deep within his soul.

There was many a weeping
As the trees knelt down,
Almost nearly almost
Touching the ground.

And then it was over
And his face lit back up,
With little blooming flowers
And even buttercups.

'Twas the brightness of a rainbow
Which lit the morning air,
Bringing love, peace, and joy
From here to everywhere.

Annette P Crickard
FIDELITAS
To find a flaw in a friend
Is like a little death;
The teats of grief come welling up,
There is a stop in breath.

So cry my eyes, and weep my heart
But quiet be my tongue.
For love of friend is ever firm,
And faith forever young.

Bernice DeChaves
RAINDROP
Did you ever watch a raindrop travel
down a windowpane?
As it joins another raindrop and
proceeds ahead again?
With it goes a tiny drip, that once
stood alone as a drop,
'Til that special raindrop decided to
take the time to stop.

Together they begin an adventure,
As by all the others they pass
To find themselves locked together,
At the bottom of the glass.

For a moment they'd held each other,
And ran along the glass . . .
Not thinking about the time they had,
Or how long it might last.

The outcome was inevitable . . .
Still, they took a chance,
As they left the glass together,
Embraced in glorious dance.

They'd met but for an instant,
Still they touched until the end,
Not only to vanish as lovers,
But to become to each other a friend.

Mae Bennett
FATHERS DAY, 1989
Dad,
On Fathers Day twelve years go,
'Twould be your last. But we
didn't know.
Just days before you'd been
informed
There's cancer cells. We all were
torn.
This disease was quickly spread.
The following month you were
dead.
"Life must go on" is what they
say.
To ease life's pains I stop to pray.
Somehow I think you're in your
glory
With lots of time to share a story.
Be it about your moonshine still
Or accepting Christ and becoming
fulfilled.
At forty-two my mind still whirls,
Thoughts of care-free days of a
little girl.
When you'd buy peanuts, a pack
of gum.
That, to me, meant love and fun.
Though we can't share this Fathers
Day
With gifts of love, 'cause you've
gone away.
I'll trust you know that I still care.
But, only in memory this day we'll
share.
Love, Mae

Gordon Sawyer
TO & FROM A BLIZZARD

To Raoul Kraushaar, (best known for his noble symphonic scores to Johnny Mack Brown & "Whip" Wilson "B" Westerns), who, more than all other composers combined, has captured the glory of the Old West—yet who is the only totally neglected great composer.

Brusquely, out of a gentle lull, rustle leaves, sprigs, dust—faster, faster, faster;
Lurch small trees, larger trees, all trees—farther back, still farther forth, still farther back;
Bustle twigs, breaking off trees—more & more numerously, more & more violently.

Wildly! Sinister ceilings of swollen fulvous strato-cumuluses whirl athwart the hyaline heavens,
While trees tumble & thud—as if ambushed from all directions—
While flying roofs mow jaggedly the tops & sides of more & more trees, more & more houses.

With the compassion of enraged waves of white killer bees, the billowing clouds bury our warm star;
& thickening & darkening & swooping, cast forth they: the dreaded wrath of a blizzard's gloom.

Unremittingly, this frigid arch-blade of winter's shrilling blasts slashes the land,
With its gashing rushes ripping from the Great Plains to the Atlantic strand,
With its blinding, piercing ice-slivers, drifting over, smothering, crunching whole homes;
Smashing through windows, through buildings, through cities; stinging, numbing, mantling life,
& ramming & collapsing all else open to its hacking teeth or to its mountainous drifts.

Cities it incarcerates, leaving behind but the most pathetic, helpless, cut off isles.
& whatever is not buried is disfigured, skewed, entwined, cracked or demolished.

The remnant from this ice-blast? A muffled grater after any footstep on the paralyzed snowscape,
So chilblain-deep dives the temperature: a silence deflated to insipidness, deadness, hopelessness,
So forlorn is it all! The woods? No, only sparse, upright, snow-laded mazes.
Surely cities! Woe! All ground or shot into snow-robed badlands or countless, grisly, oversize graves.
Such then is to be battered, bombarded & bonded to & from a blizzard—till rescue? or till death!

Juanita Oliver Johnson
I AM THE REST OF HUMANITY
I am the rest of humanity:
A proud black woman, standing tall.
I am the rest of humanity
I envision a hope with
New found freedom for us all.
I am the rest of humanity
I've seen many days of toil and strife;
I am the rest of humanity
My God gave me life;
This free willed mind,
And state of being
To listen to the words of
Many wise women and men
Jessie Jackson, Coreta Scott King,
Micky Leland, Benjamin Hooks, to name a few
Nelson and Winnie Mandela—
Whom the Lord reveals concepts to,
Making living a little better
For you and I in this world, our place
Because we all are a part
Of this human race . . .

Steve McRoberts
FOR DEBI, MY BRIDE
Dreams there were of piercing strength
which haunted lonely nights
and stretched imagination's length
by wild and fancy flights.

All my life I've had such dreams
of very special places
with golden mountains, silver streams,
and bright enchanting faces.

Long I've sought this shining vision
but always I've been turned away:
all my hopes met with derision,
my aspirations with dismay.

Then into my life you came
bringing sun and light and laughter!
Within my heart you lit a flame
which burns forever after.

I know your faults and all your charms
that's why I love you in extremes.
And here within your gentle arms
I've found the place I sought in dreams.

Rebecca L Ulrich
SORROW
Sadness comes and sadness goes
Those who cause it never know
The pain is great but I will try
To be strong and not to cry
The sadness clouds my days with grey
It takes so long to go away.

Feelings locked so tight inside
The hurt and shame I try to hide
Wounded pride is what I feel
But slowly I begin to heal
Through the gray I see a light
Toward the brightness I start to fight.

Things don't seem as bad right now
It all begins to clear somehow
Sorrow and darkness chased by dawn
It seems, for now, the pain is gone
As night it will return I know
'Cause sadness comes and sadness goes.

Mrs Linda D Pleasant
WAKE-UP AMERICA
America be ashamed!
You have earned yourself a new name.
It's no longer home of the brave and free.
But of violence and hate of humanity!

It's not bad enough our young men must fight abroad
We have to fight here to top it all.
Our young men make an oath to die,
To guard our country and so called "way of life."

But really aren't they dying in vain
Because we don't help them, we add to their strain.
What do they see when they look back at us?
Nothing but their country full of hate and disrupt.

So really what is "our way of life"?
To them it only brings heartache and strife
Why can't we give them instead of deny
The reason fore which they took an oath to die!

Billy R McMahon
COMING AND GOING
When I found out where I was going,
the place had already gone.
I turned back in a hurry,
But couldn't find where I came from.
So I stopped and looked for some sunshine,
and a meadow of tall green grass.
As I lay there watching,
the world go by so amazingly fast . . .
It struck me really funny,
you couldn't help but laugh . . .
Smiling and waving,
at myself going past!

Melissa H Harris
THE DEATH OF FREEDOM
Amid flurry and toiling, untainted it came,
The patriot's pinnacle, freedom its name.

United, devoted, the people they stood,
Desperately striving to do what was good.

A bulwark was risen to harbor their gift,
A rotund, unscathable wall without rift.

Laudably in it their freedom they poured
And watched as their fertile land drew from its source.

Until one day a dark voice rose up in each heart,
"The freedom's all mine," and each tore down a part.

The great wall did crumble and out freedom roared.
With scratching and groping, the people did hoard.

In the distance stood watching a mother and child.
He viewed all in innocent horror, she cried.

Our freedom has died now,
Our freedom has died.

He viewed all in innocent horror, she cried.

Years later a young man walked close by his child
In a land seeming desolate, bleak and defiled,

And his face bore a tear for recalling, he knew
Why the parched earth was scarred and stained red, white, and blue.

michael l abt
THE PASSING WIND
The Wind she speaks, upon her journey
As she passes in the night.
Her words are clear, each one I hear,
Like syllables of light.

She speaks; I listen; I cannot turn away:
Each word a vision seen
Of castles and hovels, of plains and tunnels;
All landscapes she has been.

And now she's gone upon her journey,
As she passes me in flight.
She leaves me sad and yet I'm glad
For one brief moment of angelic sight.

Brad, Erin and Jordan Henderson

Brad Henderson
LITTLE BROTHERS
Little Brothers are very fun
But sometimes they act like Attila the Hun

Little Brothers are special in many different ways
They're still very fun on the cloudiest of days

Little Brothers are fun and fun they are
Sometimes they let you wish upon their falling star

Little Brothers love to play
On every single type of day

I love my brothers the best you see
And I know my brothers also love me

Lynda LaMore
GOODBYE MOM
You wanted it this way
No more trouble or strife,
so when I didn't listen,
You took your own life.

You wanted me to be tough
Stronger than you,
By giving me no choice,

So don't misconstrue.

We both made mistakes,
Both of us our share,
But I won't take the blame
It just isn't fair.

I've missed you so often,
But you were no longer there,
Confused and alone
A mother's love can't compare.

I'll remember you always,
And hope you found peace,
I forgive you for leaving
This being my release.

Vincenne A Waxwood PhD
TRUE FRIENDSHIP
When I am not at peace with me,
I do not like you either:
"Do you have to make that noise?"

The little gnawing feeling
Feeds on everything you do:
"Must that TV be so loud?"

Love never bloomed with quite the speed
Of growing irritation.
"Just leave me alone."

And yet you know
I do not want to be alone.
So you sit and wait me out
Because you understand
That when it seems
I like you least,
I need you most of all.

Vincenne A Waxwood PhD
DESCENT TO DES MOINES
We slip slowly through the clouds,
DC engines in a roar.
Below, narrow roads rim farmlands
Like patterns on a table chess board.
Houses stand at close attention
Like marchers frozen in the snow,
Neatly lined row after row,
Brightened by a sunset glow.

R J Miller
FRIENDS
Straight and tall this person stands
the one whom I call friend.
Lending me strength and sharing my load
when my patience is at an end.
I value this friend's wisdom
over others' I could name.
Without this person by my side
life wouldn't be the same.
My friend is comfort when I'm ill
or tired of daily strife.
I'm proud this person stands by me
my special friend, my wife.

Deborah A Hasara
WICKED WORRY
Wicked Worry casting spell
Sold out Bus Bound to hell;
Secret sinners watch astill
Out of breath going down a hill.
Stepstools to the brave and ruling
Few go by found by this fooling . . .
As you feel the night—torn ripping by
And crave for love's sipping sigh,
You surrender to torment and dishevel
Becoming one with the devil.

Joy Chamberlain
THE FOUR SEASONS
Now that Fall and Winter are gone,
and Spring is around the bend;
It's like someone took a magic wand,
and brought it to an end.

Now the trees and flowers will bloom,
and Summer will be nothing but hot;
Showers and storms will feel like doom,
but really it hits the spot.

Since Fall was here and gone again,
Winter will bring us snow,
arctic air will come and bring us all the cold;
The wind will howl and snow will blow
a snowman begins to mold.

One day it will be warm again, and
out will come the sun;
People will go onto the beach
to have a little fun.

Sharon L Rockoff
DO YOU REMEMBER WHEN?
Do you remember when
Life was full of simple joys,
Of teddy bears
And wind-up toys.

When nights were peaceful
And days were good,
In a world of fantasy
Known as childhood.

You were always happy
And didn't have to care,
About your future
And the burdens you'd soon bear.

As time went on,
Everything changed.
Suddenly your life
Seemed so prearranged.

There were checkbooks to balance
And deadlines to beat.
You found it was hell
Just making ends meet.

When you were young,
You couldn't wait for the day
When you could do things
The grown-up's way.

But now that you're old
And haven't a dime,
Oh, how you wish
You could be young, one more time.

Do you remember when . . . ?

Elaina M O'Neill
TO BEGIN, IS ALL TOO EASY
To begin, is all too easy,
To stop . . . ah, now that is the work!
how I wish that I might be able to stop.
To stop seeing into death's eyes . . .
to stop feeling this pain . . .
To stop . . .
. . . to stop this hell!

I wish I could stop.
But I don't know how.
I think I'm okay. Yet I know I'm not.
I'm never okay, even though I pretend to be.

He walks thru the door, and almost like magic,
a wall comes between us.
I don't know how to tell him, but tell him I must . . .
We cannot play hide and seek any longer,
it's not a time for games,
it is a time for trust.

Yet still . . .

Π (P L Dwyer)
LIFE IN LOVE
Winter come for naught my love.
The season's summer tallow
singe the leaves and turn
the deepens fallow.

Soon to raise the moaning swans
to call the wild within
and leave again the pleasant heights
far chasing sunthreads dim.

In shadowlight, gold persians glisten
silents in spectre stand
lost amid their naked limbs
vigil loft in hidden plan.

For winter come on mournful journey
and naught but life in love survives
in blasting winds and snowfall fury
to gladden sleeping life alive.

Life in love weaves yet among
the mystery's moody tantrums
to stir and strain star-reaching gain
in rhyme to a summer drum.

Π (P L Dwyer)
THE ONLY SONG THAT MATTERS
Mazes more, the less I am
to judging strange proclivity.
Instead, I, inward drawn
seek my own nativity.

Wasted woe, in time begone
moments snared to relent
for something never coming,
something never sent.

Mizer most, these wilting lifedays
to spend in wanton misery.
Wasted heart in wasted hope
praying ancient wizardry.

winsome whisper, time's tuning fork
sets right the noisy pratter
and gathers to nature's notes
the only song that matters.

Π (P L Dwyer)
THE SECRET PLACE
In the secret place,
time measured in moonbeats
quickly waits for day.
While new beginnings
made in shadow
watch mist fold
in gentle womb
wondering.

Π (P L Dwyer)
AWAKENING
Lonely lost in arrowflight
out among the stars
one night.

Silent fallen from rimfrost
Goddust scattered, reaches out
storm tossed.

Seasons come in marching rhyme
starseeded come to know
in time.

Π (P L Dwyer)
TO THIS FOR LIFE
To saddle frump
a mindless bump
on life's eternal scale,
this lonely life
in anguished strife
searching a tuneless score.
For drifting soul
pays higher toll
for wanting more'n not.
Life's anchor drawn,
this simple pawn
wonders yet another shore.

Π (P L Dwyer)
ENIGMA
Singing sound heartward bound
rolling in clover budding.
Wispy laugh simple graph,
love's smile grows within.

Single song all day long,
secret glances in lover time.
Slowing day rushing night
love rainbows soft moonlight.

Tasks undone more to come,
love's fleeting shade unmask
twilight world, twinshape curl
love energy rushing past.

Silent now unknown how
heartglow to embers gone.
Lonely night, sudden flight
love's gone another way.

Π (P L Dwyer)
ENDLESS ME
Sing to me of softer songs
out beyond the reef
and I will hum a silent prayer
yielding in my grief.

Hurts that come in waves of pain
crash against my mind
and build their mighty beaches
from my tiny grains of time.

Yet the sea of me is endless
and calms a distant shore
as I lay upon my dune
and watch the sea gulls soar.

The moon's own dancers
ballet across my waves
while life flows to sleep
and dreams this song away.

Murray H Lowenstein
SHOEHORN
Hanging like as tired dog's tongue
Red and shiny it's hidden among
The bric-a-brac my nightstand holds
Peeking at me through a tissue's folds

Ready and waiting for a tight hug
From my shoe dozing on the rug
It doesn't gasp, cough or wheeze
No matter how hard the squeeze

By name you'd think it played a tune
But it's really as mute as a spoon
This soundless horn without a squeal
Slips on the new or down-at-the-heel

Rosella Rockman Fertitta (Age 72)
THE LIFE-SPAN TREE
A grapefruit seed we did plant
One morning long ago,
My grandson small and I
To see if it would grow.
It grew so fast and tall and green
We put it in a larger pot
much better to be seen.
The years went by and time went fast
The boyhood of my grandson soon
was past.
I grew older and still it grew,
A tall and graceful tree we now
knew.
Many years it still has stood
As my grandson now has reached
manhood.
I have reached the later twilight
years,
But I still remember "the Planting"
with happy tears.
So the tree grows still,
Forever it seems,
Until we both are gone
And asleep with our dreams.

Joanne B King
ALL WILL SHINE
I saw a fire burning. I watched flames
shooting up.
I saw a man walking, carrying a
golden cup.
I felt the heat and moisture pouring
from my pores.
I smelled the smoke and musky scent
of rotting to the core.
The core of life. The core of death.
Beginning or the end?
It was a dream. I am awake. I do not
understand.
Living, dying, all life crying, forms
that do not count.
It's blood that flows and children
know that animals too cry out.
Every form of life under the sun,
lives and dreams and dies as one.
For in the end when darkness comes
and the bright light shines for the
chosen ones.
There will not be a preference for
those who lived their lives on stage.
But love will shine through the
chosen few and peace will come to
all of age.

John A Cristion
INFINITE DAWN
Dawn will always find her way,
Through the fields, across the bay.

With her come the sun, the rain,
Joy and sorrow mixed with pain.

She leaves the stars to kiss the sun,
Night's then gone day has come.

Audrey Yoeckel
DRIVEL
Yea, though I walk through the
valley,
I just can't listen to any more drivel.
Drivel drives me crazy, droning in
my ear and
Draining my last drop of energy.
I am a dromedary in the vast dry
desert,
Where wind-driven drivel drills
under my skin and makes me sore.

Drivel drums in the distance as if it
were important.
(But it really isn't worth a drachma.)
Is it my dharma to dance through life
to drivel waltzes?
When I die, will they drape me in a
drivel shrouds,
And drivel flowers all over my
coffin?

Whisper not your dreadful drivel in
my ear,
But delve with me beyond,
Beyond truth, the brightly polished
drivel,
That leads us to dance to its drivelish
humor.

Before we depart this drivel driven
planet for
Something less noisy,
We must drop everything,
Dump our drivel,
Douse it in kerosene and watch it
depart in smoke.
The haze that remains is the Veil of
Isis.

Constance A Carter
JUST A FRIEND
If there is ever anything I can do,
Anything in this world for you,
I'll be right there, by your side,
Your feelings in me you can confide.
My eyes will help you see.
My hands will hold you, lean on me.
My feet will guide your way.
My lips will find good things to say.
On my shoulders you can rest your
head.
On my bosom, your tears you can
shed.
In my heart there is a place for you,
Your feelings and emotions, too.
I'll help pick up the pieces in the end,
Yes, all this and lots more, too—
Because, I am your Friend!

William E D Bowley
THE SWINGING BRIDGE
Let us go to yonder canyon,
Enjoy the scenery, both high and low,
At the canyon we walked together,
Crossing a bridge, that swung to and
fro.

Looking down at the canyon river,
More than three hundred feet below,
It was such a thrill, and hard to stand
still,
While watching that river flow.

We could see the rushing water,
Forcing its way over a rocky bed,
'twas a sight! from where we stood,
Hating to move we took pictures
instead.

Reaching the end of the swinging
bridge,
We strolled along for many more
hours,
Covering mile after mile so
revealing,
Amid shrubbery and flowers.

The sun was waning in the west,
So we made our way to the street car,
We must have walked some twenty
miles.
Although it did not seem that far.

To us it happened so many years ago,
But it only seems like yesterday,
That afternoon, we will never forget!
Though we are now so far away.

Brian Michael Martin
silent melissa
april's drizzle showers grey dismal
afternoon
standing alone he amidst cool gentle
downfall
heavens weeping oceans upon rising
hill seclude
delicate hands weeping rose
weeping rose weeping droplets
droplets weeping pools upon rising
hill seclude

lowers soaking brow he before
silence jutting silence
whispers silence melissa silence
happy silence birthday silence
kneels softly upon grass he setting
rose to rest
'neath waterfalls fragile a smile curls
jutting stone he sweetly caress

april's drizzle showers gray dismal
afternoon
never alone he amidst cool gentle
downfall

Bette Soterios Hanges

Bette Soterios Hanges
REALITY
The Royal Family of 860—
Lovingly—Always.

Walls were white
Windows clean
Floors were bright
Waxed to gleam—
Adream in the dark.

Boy scout camp
Sunday school
Bedside lamp
Swimming pool—
Adream in the dark.

High school then
College soon
Wond'ring when
It will boom—
Adream in the dark.

Cardboard sheet
Bare of walls
On the street
Rain just falls—
Awake in the dark.

Mrs Billy L Saunders
LIFE TOGETHER
What a wonderful life,
To never know strife.
Please accept me as
Just half a wife.
This has been nineteen good
years,
Forgive me when I caused you
tears.
We have been granted such a
good love,
But only from heaven above.

Billy,
Without your help,
I couldn't have made
That first step.
You have been a guiding star,
Even the first walk was
To me so far.
But we only know what
We both are.

When you read this
If you don't cry,
I'll spit in your eye. (I did)
This really sounds like me,
And if it doesn't
You can take me out to tea,
Maybe even the Atlantic Sea.

Nothing in life is for free—
Not even a wife.
You've always had my heart
Even when we were apart.

Eunice B Lanzl
DRESSES
To my mother, Ida Uhl Brumm.

Many dresses I have worn.
All new—then tossed into a corner,
Crumpled and edged with grime,
Like poor, dried-up flowers
With torn, curled petals.
Dresses almost white in spots
And soiled by my fingertips.
Where did your freshness go?
Lost in a dance or in a stolen kiss.
Rising in a mist of perfume,
Having only a few minutes of life.
I loved you once the way you were.
Hanging in the shop.
Unworn.
Unwrinkled.
Shiny.
Your satin gleams.
Your velvet is still soft.
I feel your lace against my face,
Dresses are fortunate and free—
Locked up only in a Cinderella's
memory.

Peggy J Harrell
COME WITH ME
In one lifetime I've never found
This kind of love that has me bound.
Your Love engulfs my very soul—
and fills my heart.

Come with me my Love, I'll share
your pain
And in its place love shall remain.
Your Love engulfs my very soul—
I'll share your pain.

Come with me my Love, come walk
with me.
Side by side yet both are free.
Your love engulfs my very soul—
walk with me.

Come with me my Love and sing to
me
Of the joy we share—sing to me.
Your Love engulfs my very soul—as
you sing.

Come with me my Love and lay me
down.
And be as one here on the ground.
Your Love engulfs my very soul—
when we're as one!

Kathy Zakri
MASKING GRIEF
Self-recriminations abound,
as a mourning dove's melancholy
song
breaks the stillness of first dawn.
Meeting the day with dread,
a mirror illusion of sanity
she sits before the vanity.
Glancing at a photograph,

a mother's treasure to behold,
her handsome son framed in plated gold.
Camouflaging a quivering lip,
a stroke of dewy pink, an unfulfilled wish—
memory of her child's cookie kiss.
Masquerading a colorless complexion,
with artificial blush applied to last
unable to diminish vivid regrets of his past.
Disguising dark circles and puffy eyes,
once blinded to his plea for release,
now shocked by suicide, his final choice for peace.
Pulling not brushing her tangled bleached hair,
for today she buries her fifteen-year-old son,
masking grief, but fooling only one.

Jo Faye Beddard Todd
EASTER CHILD

If I could, my child,
I would
Cushion you from a fall,
Shield you from the wind,
Prevent your pain,
Ensure your win
In all.
I wish I could
Feel pain for you.
I wish life would
Be kind to you.
I'd feel the pain,
I'd bear your loss;
I'd seal success
And pass the test.
If I could, I would.
But wait, my child.
Your fate's not wild.
Though I can't die
Or hurt for you,
Cannot assure
Success for you;
Though I can't pass
The test for you,
There's one who could
Do all for you,
Who did it all
For you, for me.
He gave his life,
So we'd be free.

Ida Johnson
THE HANDS OF MY MOTHER

Dedicated to my mother—our moma Corn.

There's a light that has burned 'Oh' so brightly.
For many a year I have seen.
A beautiful, patient, kind lady
Who helped me and, shared all my dreams.

She taught me the meaning of loving.
She gave me a reason to care.
If ever I needed a favor.
She would alway be standing right there.

Then one day I noticed a slowing of steps
that once were like mine.
And the light that had shone so brightly.
Was beginning to dim with the time.

The hands that were all the time busy.
Doing things she loved doing for others.
Lay quiet now; these hands I love.
The beautiful hand of my mother.

The light that had burned so brightly
was flickering now at dawn.
A few more days of waiting,
and the beautiful light was gone.

God took her in the morning,
when everything was still.
There's a new star now in heaven,
It's on the highest hill.

Ida Johnson
INSPIRATIONAL

Dedicated to my husband Johnny and all my family; I love you all special.

I took a walk along a path that was winding up and down.
Dry leaves crushing underfoot and, flowers all around.
Cool wind whistling through the trees. The sun was shining bright.
A small stream rushing down the hill and going out of sight.

A quaint log cabin came in view. A lovely sight to see.
And on the porch a gentle man was looking out at me.
He offered me a place to sit and rest my weary feet.
I looked into the kindest eyes that I will ever see.

He said, "You know I'm getting old. I'm ninety two today."
With tears in eyes said, "I can't walk the path you walked today.
Won't you stay? And talk a while please tell me what you see.
Are flowers blooming everywhere? Are leaves still on the trees?"

And suddenly I knew that he was lonely sitting there.
And as I looked into his eyes I said a silent prayer.
Dear God help me to be a friend
in everything I do.
Help me to share your beauty and show my love for you.
Thank you for my eyes—that see the wonders that you made.
The lovely mountain and the stream
I walked across today.

Grace Yohannan
THE LAST ROSE

Casting a shadow upon my wall,
Reigning supreme, eclipsing all,
Complementing your portrait,
meaning little, you see;
Your affection, your favors, were
never for me.

Outer petals unfolding to the sun
Share their beauty with everyone.
Nether regions, remaining
tightly furled,
Hide their secrets, their love
from the world.

Faded and withered, leaving
only the thorn,
Your love, your affection—
for these I mourn.

Fannie Sipes
BONFIRE

A tarnished tinseled friendship,
That I mistook for gold;
Ashes of a burnt out love
I would no longer hold;
Smoldering embers of a hate
That blinded me for years;
An unkind word I spoke one day
That filled lovely eyes with tears;
A mud bespattered half truth
Uttered for personal gain;
Malicious gossip repeated
That caused unmeasured pain;
False standards in a dog-eared book,
That kept me shackled, and enslaved;
A collection of bad habits,
That once my pathway paved;
I've assigned them to the scrap heap
And tonight ere I retire
I'm going to strike a little match
And have a big bonfire.

Michael K Rollins

Michael K Rollins
SAIL BY ME

To God Almighty I give the credit to this song, yes this song "Sail By Me."

We go sailing far across the sea
We'll be searching, for her majesty
It's such a nice day, days don't come like this
Come on baby won't you sail by me
And I know it's such a lovely place to be
Don't say no oh Baby won't you sail my way
Won't you sail by me
Let's go fishing, right upon the ocean
And the fisherman will meet us at the coastline

he's such a nice man people don't act this way
Come on baby won't you sail my way
It's my life It's just another act in the play don't say no
Oh Baby won't you sail by me.
The water's moving, moving underneath us
The sun's creating rainbows in our eyes
I don't believe it see you sail by me
And I know it's such a lovely place to be, don't say no
Oh baby won't you sail my way
Won't you sail be me
Won't you sail by me
Oh oh oh (Repeat)

Marnie Vogel
THE MISSION

As the world prepared for sleep
I began my mission.
I dreaded what I was about to do.
It's for your own good,
I reminded myself.

Entering the murky darkness
I stealthed through the thick fog.
I reached my destiny.
I carried out my chosen deed.
Goodbye, my friend!

Virginia (Sims) Robinson
IN MEMORY OF MY DARLING SON

To my Darling Son Jimmie T. Sims.

On one Friday eve at 2:07 God called my Darling Boy to Heaven.

He was a man everybody liked to be around. When he talked there was not a sound.

Because he gave everyone good advice, He said before you act or speak think twice.

He did not want to hurt anyone because he said they were some mother's son.

The joy he got out of life was helping others; Because he said he was taught that by his mother.

Life is not the same since he has gone. But I know in Heaven he has a better home.

He not only helped his family and friends, but that is where his good deeds began.

He did without himself while others he might help.

When you asked him how he felt, he would say about the same. He never did complain.

Never no more on this earth will we see his face. He has gone to a better place.

Reba Purcell
SILENT VOICES

To my family, with love.

Sometimes we talk for hours
And never say a word.
Sometimes words aren't needed
When a silent voice is heard.

We talk of love unending
Past the end of time.
Our silent voice is speaking
To your heart and mine.

Just being with each other
We need no words to say
How much we care and love
More, with each passing day.

A silence spent between us
We grow so stronger, still
A thousand words are spoken
And our hearts they drink their fill.

Though our silent voice can tell us
Of the love that we're so proud,
We still say that I love you,
And sometimes right out loud.

Bonnie Rapelje
MOTHERS
First, we become, mothers to be.
And oh, how excited and happy are we;
To know that it's happening to me.
I'm going to be—a Mother.

When children are small there's no other;
That can fit the shoes of their Mother,
So listen listen you children, what your Mothers have to say;
'Cause they are trying to lead you the right way.

It's only when we grow up and become a Mother;
That one day we will look back and recall;
That your Mother was right after all.

There comes a day when we become old, feeble,
and gray;
We will hear our loved ones say;
Our Mother's too old to live alone;
We're going to have to place her in a home.

Why can't they leave it up to me?
For you see;
In my home I feel free.
But for now, let it be.
And when I no longer can live alone;
I will find another home.

Sondra Watson
I WONDER

This poem is dedicated to Allen Sturgill, who inspired me to write it.

I wonder if he thinks of me,
or if he speaks my name.
I wonder if we'll be more than friends or just remain the same.
I think these thoughts to myself, as day and night go by, could it be he doesn't like me?
Or maybe he's just shy!

Diane M Finn
GOODBYE

To someone special with all of my heart. Thank you for your love and friendship. It's made the difference in my life.

Sadness covers my heart
like a blanket of snow.
The pain I endure comes
and goes.
The love I feel for you
is so very real.
Through the tears I cry
my love will never die.
I want you to know how much
I really love you, before I go.
My words spoken here
are true.
No one could ever replace you.

Tammi Lynn Hughes
LYIN' EYES
Once upon a time I thought I was in love,
But now I'm only falling apart.
I need you so much, but you let me down.
You think you can just walk
away and I will forget.
Turn around and look at this broken heart.
Turn around Lyin' Eyes and look at these
tears roll down my face.
Once upon a time there was love in my heart,
But now there's only hate.
I want to hurt you until I stop hurting—I want to understand why.
It will never be the same again.
All trust of you is gone.

Don't just walk away—turn around
and look at this broken heart.
Turn around Lyin' Eyes and look at these
tears roll down down my face.
Goodbye Lyin' Eyes. Goodbye Forever.

Anne-Margaret Mc Elroy
ROMANCE LOST

This poem is dedicated to the memory of Charles Troy Wicker and Germaine Troy Wicker with all my love, God bless.

Love isn't what I thought it would be,
No knight in shining armor upon his great steed.
No bouquet of roses or soft murmured words,
No poems of praise that should be heard.
No commitment of the heart or passionate kiss,
No dedication of the heart or sweet marriage bliss.
No chivalry that was once said to be found,
No happy endings linger around.
No roaring fire or bottle of wine,
To heat the blood and dullen the mind.
No embraces that surely hunger for more,
No sensuous lovemaking behind closed doors.
Where are these unions of body and mind,
Romance lost somewhere in time.

David W Riggs

David W Riggs
COUSIN MARY
Mary, my world is unlike yours.
My birds sing after midnight.
I can hear them now in the trees across the street.
My world is what some people might call dull.
I seek my happiness alone
dreaming of thoughts that pass with love,
and watching my hand making shadows
on the moon-lit window of my room.
You place your value in your husband, and your baby, yet unborn.

Mary Ann

Your world is locked up tight
in the small circle of your family.
I lie around in my world of words and smiles,
wanting what I can't have.
still, I'm happy, until my hand grows tired
and the words fail to come.
I also seek my happiness alone,
searching out the words between the lines in books,
or imagining the jelly beans at the dime store
candy counter are smiling at me
through soft eyes of reds and blues.

Susan J Kauffman
WINTER WEATHER
The year was 1989,
and Christmas was a comin'
The heartland had a cold, cold heart
with no one strollin' and hummin'.
The southland was a shiverin'
with real chances of some snow.
The Siberian storm express
was certainly on the go.
We all dream of a white Christmas
but not that cold and frigid.
The east coast is a popsicle
which really is too rigid.
The west coast didn't seem to know
the rest of the country was so.
As warm and balmy winds did blow.
But, alas, when summer comes
and everywhere is hot.
The cold and snow and all that came
will be completely forgot.
And cooler temperatures and snow
will be our heart's desire.

Krista N Staton
THOSE OF DEPRESSION
Living in a world of "first come, first serve," there are those who disbelieve. Those who disapprove. Those who have no choice, but to push aside their pride, put on that "servant's" uniform, and walk to work. whereas some can afford to ride in luxurious cars, others can barely afford to walk. those who can barely afford to work for what little pay they earn. To sit in a warm place and yet have no second thoughts of those who cannot afford to buy a newspaper to shield themselves from the cold, damp winds of winter. Though people say and do things to help, that just isn't enough. Those still struggling with the emotions of embarrassment, pride, fear, and abandonment, somehow find the courage to go forth and, with heads held high, live the life of which they have been, so cruelly, given.

Opal Ruby Cunningham
ARE ALL THE CHILDREN IN??

Dedicated to my deceased mother. Rena Laura Smitch.

I think of times as the night draws nigh,
Of an old house on the hill.
Of a yard all wide and blossom stared,
Where the children played a will.
And when the night at last came down,
Mother would look all around and ask,
"Are all the children in??"

'Tis many and many a year since then,
And the old house on the hill.
No longer echoes to childish feet,
And the yard is still, so still.
But I can see it all as the shadows creep,
And though many the years have passed,
I can still hear my mother ask,
"Are all the children in??"

I wonder if, when the shadows fall,
On the last short earthly day.
When we say goodbye to the world outside,
Will we hear Him ask as mother did.
"Are all the children in??"

Love and Prayers

Emma Callahan
DEPRESSION
Depression is like time is
standing still,
instead of going up, your
life is all downhill.
You try to smile, but
all you do is frown,
it seems as if your bottom
lip is touching the ground.
Depression is like a maze;
you're trying to get to the end.
It's like you are alone
with not one single friend.
All you think about is
wanting to die,
but all you do is get
angry and cry.
it's like your heart is
heavy and you have a lot
to bear,
It's like you just have
a lot of things to fear.
All you do is feel very low,
your life's like a nightmare
and not a show.
Try to be happy and not
so sad,
when you know you have
friends, your heart will
be somewhat glad!

Reine Desrochers-Milne
ABODE OF DESTINY

To Father-Mother God, grandparents Champagne, parents Irene and Joseph, brother Armand, twin Marie-Jeanne, beloved Ed and Bruce, dear auntie Yvonne, family and friends, and poet-friends Ruth Forbes-Sherry, Dick Aldrich and Dorothy Milne.

We have loved you, our castle by the sea
You opened wide your gates to us
Your main hall vibrated to the wedding ceremony

To be or not to be chanted the Cosmos

Your rolling surf lulled us to sleep
To dream the dreams honeymooners dream
The sound of violin strings could be heard in the night
As though, out of the past, forward came a knight

Things of beauty we have transcended here
Grateful are we to have lived in its atmosphere
A deep sense of reverence we have felt
For the three wisemen who lived in its orbit
And, through their creativeness, made our dream come true

How we shall miss your serenity
The wild flowers on the cliff, the ships at sea
The beautiful view of the ocean and the hillside
Oh! in your hearth to always abide!

Fear not, say we—your memory shall never fade away
In our hearts your picture shall ever be
We have loved you, our castle by the sea,
And will remember you into Eternity.

Bonnie Armstrong
A CHILD'S VIEW
Mama, why are the trees growing upside down in the water?
And why are you standing on your head?
Why do the mountains face the earth
When they should face Heaven, instead?
Why does it look like the moon and stars
Have fell upon the ground?
Tell me, Mama, why these things
Are completely turned around?
"My dearest child, they have not changed,
They're seeing their reflection.
They see their picture with grace and pride
And a touch of true perfection."

Penny Chiasson
DO YOU SEE HER?

To Michael, with love.

Do you see her? She's standing right there. Look how happy she is, No one could guess her real feelings. Look closer, look at her eyes you can tell. See the pain, the hurt. Go stand by her, you can feel it. No, you think it's love, see I told you, she hides it well. The pain is so deep no one really knows what she's feeling. What's wrong with her, can't you see it, he's right on the side of her. Yes, he's caused all her pain, he's made her grow up and really look at life. That's right, all you ever get is screwed in life. She knows that now, it's taken her a long time to understand that Sure she still cares but he's hurt her so much; love she's not sure, who can love her after so much pain and hurt. Will she leave him, not right now, she'll try again. Does he love her, that's what he says and she knows deep down he does. Then why does he go on hurting her, simple he doesn't know how to stop. She'll find one day when she lets herself think about it, that love has turned into hate. And not even realize when it happened, and wonder why so much wasted time has gone by. It happened so slow she says she can't say exactly when. How do I know her so well? Look closer can't you see I'm looking in the mirror.

Elizabeth L Anthony
LIFE
Life is like a song
It has a beginning
It has an end
But whatever life will be
It's up to God above thee
We struggle and fight
For what we wants in life
Sometimes we all disguise
And hold our dream so tight

Let your heart be filled with love
To see the world in light
Embrace the things that make you laugh
And let it go those that make you sad
Don't be envious for what others have
But get smart and be delight
For life sometime can be really tough
But let's do our best and be glad.

Stephenie Whitaker
HEAVEN SENT
You treated me with such tenderness and care;
we have each other and the love we shared.

Our friendship has grown as much as our love.

I guess that's because of the great miracles in the clouds above.

When your lips cross the journey of reaching mine
it is so special, it is divine.

Kiss me again, and again, and again,
because when you do I know this isn't a sin.

God knows this was meant to be,
that's why he put 'us together'—you and me.

I guess our gift was, "Heaven Sent," right from the man himself.

This is something I have always felt.

It's just you and me and nobody else.

Trust me I'm under your spell.

Our love is written everywhere, even across the sky.

This is the atmosphere that brings me so alive.

You are what I live for,
you are what I'm going to die for,
but that is a long way off and we've got a whole lot more.

Even if the touch doesn't, the love will always remain,
because deep in our hearts it will always be the same.

Not only in our hearts, but our love . . .
can never be broken or bent.

I guess that's why God made us "Heaven Sent."

Clifford W Malson
WHAT I'D LIKE TO BE

To my first born Grandchild, Jandee Lynn Turner.

"What I'd like to be." Said a seed to me.
"I'd like to be a graceful willow tree."

"What I'd like to be." Said another seed to me.
"I'd like to be a flower, a flower beneath that tree."

What I would say, to both the seeds to be.
"Be all that you can ever want to be."

Julie A Szuch
METAMORPHOSIS

For the magickal travelers:

Barren black cave
Deathly silent
Alone and motionless
Knowing he comes

There's no escape
Desire none
Fear and anxiety
He stands here now

Learning guidance
Mentor, my God
Journey to inner self
He's there as well

Seraph help me!
Mentor now gone
Upon mine own two feet
Will I survive?

Julie A Szuch
A JOURNEY

For all dreamers:

Renaissance, Remembering
Its chivalry divine
Enchantment from so long ago
Romance upon my mind

Those gallant men and ladies fair
And honor never wrong
Destrier trotting proudly in the lists
Old mysticism strong

Guenivere and Lancelot
Brave knighthood at the Round
Shining swords and Merlin's magic
All delightfully found

Renaissance, Remembering
So simplify my heart
And cast me back through time and space
My passion, to depart

Judith Sessler
THE CHANTEUSE

To Bill, for all your love and support.

Hear her singing sweetly the chanteuse,
gentle melodies, soft dark rhapsodies
carried swiftly through the night
on soft, white wings of hope.

Hear her singing proudly the chanteuse,
elusive youth yet fleeting in the night.
Left behind the pristine glow,
left behind the dewy innocence of old.

Hear her singing sadly the chanteuse,
lingering melody of youth but gone upon the wind,
faded gown upon her back,
weathered lines upon her face,
Hear her singing sadly the chanteuse . . . . .

Richard E Matera
HOW?

To Lynn.

How do you take the red from a rose?
Or make its open blossom close?
How do you stop a snowy night
From painting morning landscape white?

How do you teach a baby's cry
To silently pass a mother by?
And how persuade a starving child
His hunger's just a feeling, mild?

How do you send the rain back up?
Or drain God's overflowing cup?
How do you take the words you said,
And replace them in your mouth instead?

How hold back the ocean wave?
When will cowards change to brave?
Or madmen cease their rant and rave,
And bow again within the nave?

How do you teach the eyes that see
To choose the dark, and darkened be?
How unlock without the key?
Or stay imprisoned, though already free?

All of these I cannot do,
Nor find a day without thought of you.

—A Valentine poem

David L Crump
MIDNIGHT SUN

To my Mom. 1911-1990.

As I look into the morning sky
Grey and orange color, as the night goes by.
One star is left, shining so bright
Clusters of others fade out of sight.
A sweet fragrant smell, from the honeysuckle vine
Morning glories open up, all at the same time.
The wind starts to blow through the leaves on the trees,
And the sounds of the pines, that flow gracefully.
The birds start to sing, their own beautiful song
looking for their mate, so they won't be alone.

The sun is straight up, and the day's half through
The leaves are all dry, from the morning dew.
As the day goes on to midafternoon
The sun grows deep, as it awaits the moon.
As the sun fades away, and the winds calm down
Whippoorwills singing their lonesome sound.
Darkness falls but the night's still young
It awaits the moon, to be the midnight sun.

Peggy Powell
THE SOUND OF LOVE

To my darling Husband, Edward. You have made our lives magical with your love.

Somewhere between the conscious and unconscious
Lies an area that hears.
A baby hears its mother's voice
And an unspoken communication
Starts . . .
Growth begins because of this
Love bonding.

And when a man and woman become one,
A chord is born which
Is heard as the
Sound of love.

"I'm home" you say
Softly pressing the key
To my soul
The sound of you fits into a
Special place in my mind
And body.

When you talk to me
It feels as if we are
Alone in this world.

Safe
Happy
and full of magic.

Mary A Womack
YOUR NAME

I speak your name
And I feel the sun within my soul
I speak your name
And I am an astronaut amid
the outer limits
I speak your name
And heaven is my home
I speak your name for always

George Ashton
SUDDENLY WITHOUT WARNING

Suddenly
Without warning
Came the rush
Of new feeling
Unbidden,
Uninvited,
But welcome.
Rushing forward
I run
Unmindful of the words,
"Never again,"
Spoken to the winds
Only months ago.
What strange magic
Does she possess,
This woman-child,
That I should find no shelter
Within my resolve?
I sit in wonder
Totally awed by a sudden magic.
The magnet pulls . . .
And my resolve
So stern,
So cold,
Loses potency
And,
Turned to iron filings
I follow the pull.

Jack Grbcich
THE SEA AND ME

To Valerie.

The water of my body is
The same as the Earth.
The sea gave birth to me;
The sea shall reclaim me;
The sea is part of me;

Add me and part of the sea
To be as one, the sea and I,
To mix as one in this place we
Call Earth; we will be
As one until the end of time.

Terry Lippens
LIKE A MOM

You were there for me when I was down.
You were there for me when I wore a frown
You were honest, you told me when I was being dumb
You were just like a mom
You listened, you understood
You gave me hugs like a normal mom would
You tucked me in, you kissed me goodnight
Then you slowly crept out of sight
You knew when I needed hugs, I guess you still do
The only mom I want is you.

Kitty Krogg
ODE TO THE OLD

They suffer more than we will know,
Take more than life's severest blow,
I take me hat off to them and bow,
We've forgotten them somehow.
Long live the weary and the old,
For stories in their hearts still untold!

Stephen Bricker
SHARDS

To Benja, who listened to my heart.

my memories were once
whole
like a clay pot
carefully made
and painted with the scenery
of my life

colorful vistas of people and things
were there
in moving panorama
infinitely unfolding
upon the glazed surface

but something happened
a time ago
my beautiful pot
was shattered
i find only shards
designs incomplete
fragments of my memories
or is it my life

Kerrianne Spellman
DONNA

Oh how you wait for the prince to
stop at your castle
And stay.

And the world is full of princes.
But they have heard that your castle
is hard to get to.
And once there, it may be cold.

Yet those princes are far too young or
too weak to make the journey
to find if that's true.

But the one who is willing to make
the journey to your castle,
will leap through the sky on his white horse
and grab hold of the shining star
You really are.

Heidi Lisa Fritz
DECISIONS

There are always two roads to travel,
Two roads with no map,
No known destinations.

Two roads, two different directions,
Good and bad, right and wrong,
But there are no signs.

Two roads, no signs,
It is here that you must decide
Between two unknown roads.

Two roads, unknown destinations,
Which wrong, which right?
But in making your own decisions,
there is no wrong or right,
no good nor bad.

Two roads, to leave behind in the past,
To be remembered,
As triumph, or defeat.

A decision made on your own,
It is your own,
It is who you are, what you are,
It is why, you are unique . . .

Christine P Easterle
WHO AM I?

A warm and gentle being,
who cares an awful lot,
who waits for you with open arms,
who waits an awful lot.

Sometimes I get impatient,
But I try to understand,
And be here when you need me,
Or to lend a helping hand.

Someone who listens carefully,
to every word you have to say,
Someone just to be there,
At the end of a long hard day.

Your companion till the end,
is what I hoped to be,
But I often wonder,
if there's any room for me.

Marianne Smith
THE MIND'S EYE

Within the mind's eye,
Man becomes overwhelmed
by its knowledge.
Capable of dismissing such intense awareness,
As if it were a dream.

The innate cellular impulse of the dreamer,
Paralyzed in the moment;
Precludes speech while inhibiting motion,
Exposing a perfect form.

Truth.
In its negative can only be an untruth.
Perceived as a whole,
Such distortion cannot exist.

Man's atrocities inflicted upon man,
Acknowledged light hearted,
then discarded.
Weigh heavily upon our shoulders,
As these inhumanities are
universally condemned.

When pandemonium spews its contents,
And man turns within;
The light of Truth will surface,
Indigenous within the mind's eye.

Linda Hutchins
WITH ME, BE FREE

A gift passed on: To Clearance Rogers, my loving Grandfather.

Sleep with me,
In a valley of trees
Follow me,
To the south side seas
Sit with me,
Beneath star clustered skies
Walk with me,
On a moonlit night

Be my lover through eternity,
United with me in ecstasy
No drug or alcohol nor chemical of man
will make you feel the way I can
So take my hand, together we will become
A legend of man . . . .

Daniel R Niquette
SO ALIKE

Flowers fragrant, beautiful and regal,
Blossoming invitations congenial,
Epitomize your essence, sweet angel,
Enchanting delight so adorable.

Pheremones elegantly attracting,
Refreshing olfactory entrapping,
A splendid bouquet of feminine charm,
Love's halcyon embrace the world becalms.

Ann C Paris
LIFE
Life is a challenge to us all,
We must not tarry lest we fall!

Life is a series of surprises,
Not to mention compromises!

Life is love that lasts forever,
Friendships naught that we might severe!

Life is faith, life is enduring,
Unworthy thoughts be obscuring!

Like winds of the sea, are the ways fate,
As we voyage along life's open gate!

Be life long or short, full of good or sin,
The journey we make, we shall lose or win!

The gates of heaven are open to all,
Let's choose our seats quite close to Him!

Katherine Robb
THE LEXICON
My love!
How I lost you
For words unacted
For acts unspoken
Left you starving
on the tip of my tongue

And where shall I go
to find you now?
I call to you with the steps of my feet
wandering from word to word
lost in a lexicon
of unthought deeds.

Corey D Paine
INSANITY
Your mind's shut off to the world
leaving you in your own world.
Your thoughts to people are insane
but there's no one there to explain.
Because the way that people treat you,
it feels as someone had just beat you.
Slipping off into the deep end
as your mind is being weakened
your mind becomes smarter than anyone else's
but only you can realize it yourself.
Now your world is locked away
hoping to return some other day.
But, to the day you see it through,
the bars remain and the song the same.
Echoes that go off into the night
like a little child running from fright.
So, insanity is there, but lock it out
before it decides to lock you out.

Ruth A Hall
ONCE I HELD YOUR HAND
Some things are hard to understand.
Once I held your hand,
in mine so small,
as we walked the mall
at Christmas time,
all lights and glitter time—
my little niece of three,
a doll in white fur finery.
I thought, "She's part of me,"
her aunt so proud to be.
Yes, it's hard to understand
why I can't still hold your hand:
as an ex-inlaw, I stand
outcast in Divorce Wasteland.

Jacqueline Sawyer
THE ROAD
There's a mystery in me,
I can't as yet, explain.
The road I follow is
Unlike any I've travelled before.
A time comes when one must listen
to an inner voice.
The sound of one's own drummer beckons.
Foolish, unwise I'm told
The ordinary is best to go.
"Impossible," I say.
I must go on,
Regardless of the road,
Amidst laughing & jeering,
Finding freedom worth the effort
And peace worth the pain.

Anna Marie Kroczynski
FEELINGS
Girls and boys sugar and spice
Men and women being naughty and nice
It's not a game or a dare
Emotions aren't the same everywhere
Words often spoken yet so thoughtless
Take a quiet situation and turn it into a loud mess
Sometimes it is so hard to be in love
One minute you're smiling like the sun above or a circus clown
After a while you feel so sad and then you wear a frown
Why bother going to an amusement park or county fair
When you can ride the emotional roller coaster everyday anywhere

Louise Pressley

Louise Pressley
IMAGES OF FLEECING
Here I stand looking down at you—
As softly you glide beneath me.
On your way into a hot pressed drum—
One that will spew you right out its mouth;
Onto a hard flat racing steel belt.
Through many flying fast rollers—
High up into the air you do go.
Around and around—up and down
Until you end up in something round.
Gray is your color—quality 1 is your goal.
Hoping some day on a rooftop you will go—
Or in a car with a lover—
One that will sit up an take notice
Of all your durability and good qualities.
Knowing you're out front and you're number 1
For you are BASF Colback fleece.
In cars you will go and on rooftops too.
You're so tough and durable—
I wonder how—you move so softly,
And swiftly beneath my feet?
Flowing—flowing onward you go.

Louise Pressley
MEDITATION
In our hour of meditation
Let us walk as children of light.
Freely we have received, and freely let us give,
Of the gifts He has given us.
The greatest of them all is love.

Let us meditate in silence,
That we may know God better,
And keep Him closer by our side.
Feeling His power and presence
Every hour that is slipping by.

Let us not turn out time to follies,
But keep your mind turned toward Heaven,
In a meditative way,
That we may know God better.
Understanding His greatness,
And feeling His love and power
In a very special way.

Through still quiet meditation
The soul can only learn—
The beauties of God's salvation,
And the greatness of His love.

Richard Outerbridge
SAIGON 1975
Mamasans running with babies, crying and pleading terror filled eyes. Thousands of faces with no names calling out to me, but I just turn it off because it's the way it has to be.

Rifle butts come smashing down on their faces, but their desperation makes them fight to get back in those spaces. The rockets and rotars are close to the compound then all of a sudden I see a smoky gray cloud.

It's all over for me I'm on a Navy ship in the South China Sea. There are bookoo junks packed with those same frightened people floating past and staring at me.

A country of people at the bottom of the sea. The price to pay for wanting to be free. These aren't tears the wind just makes my eyes water.

Alice F Frazier
CHRIST OUR LORD IS RISEN!
'the darkest hour is just before dawn'
The truth of this saying goes,
Especially so at Easter time,
It was then that Christ arose!

He suffered, bled, and died in shame,
But death's chains could not bind Him—
Entombed for three days, but Praise His Name!
He left the grave behind him!

Victorious over every foe—
He ascended into Heaven;
And oh, what a blessed joy to know—
That Christ our Lord is risen!!

Dick Kenney
SUMMER COWBOY
The alder is turning yellow
There is a nip in the air
My mare is kinda frisky
though she's done the work of two
When we cut the last heifer I knew our work was through
I'm just a summer cowboy but I wouldn't trade with you
Sage hens are strutting the fall air is cool and sweet
My bedroll is ripe but tonight it will be sheets
My mare is fighting her bit but I can't let her run
I'm just a summer cowboy and it ends when this day is done
There is ice on the creek my mare is nuzzling water and I am drinking too
It's just the last without chlorine and it's mighty sweet
I'm just a summer cowboy and I knew it had to end
I sweep the horizon from this vantage point God made
The range is behind me the ranch lies just ahead
My mare is insisting and I let her have her head
As I rub down my mare the steamy smell of lather its aroma fills the air
I pat her on the rump and gather up my gear
And I know it's over for another year
I'm just a summer cowboy and I knew it had to end

Debby Malone
GOOD–BYE
How can I say good–bye
When I never said hello
Your smile was my sun
Your anger my pain

Your eyes told me so much
Your jokes weren't funny but I laughed

I hope you know
You gave me so much that
I can never give back
My love for you will never die
How can I say good–bye.

Vivian Bender-Sanchez
I'M WATCHING HER AGAIN

This poem is dedicated to my grandmother; may your smiles guide me till we meet again.

I'm watching her again, sitting there,
so serenely yet sad
Her old weary bones have won
The pains in her body,
too strong to be ignored
Her will too tired
to ignore them
She smiles,

I smile back
I can't say anything to her,
there is nothing to say
It was the other day
she was cheating at gin
rummy
Scolding me to finish my dinner
And now it's me
scolding her
I take her dish away
a moment forgetting
The water cold and hard
begins to fall
And I remember,
and run back
Inhale, exhale
inhale, exhale
Oh thank you God
She knows,
and knows I'm watching
her
So she smiles,
and I smile back.

Virginia Dean Waters
DO YOU DARE TO PONDER?

To all the people who will listen and help to make this world a better place to live in.

Do you dare to ponder, or ever
wonder, why we are here?
To me, at times, it's strange,
although, often, it's quite clear
Many, many, years ago, "God"
created a wonderful place.
People, lived to be very old, and
many had faith.
Somehow, things changed, they
because so terrible, bad and bold,
without shame.
"God," told Noah, to build, the ark,
then, the deluge came
This wonderful, new world, 2000 yrs
again, is the same.
Ask "God," to forgive you, for what
you do,
Remember, you, can always start
anew,
Is it right to have "Him", shed so
many tears?
"He" put us here to do good, and take
us away, in a few years.
People have gone from bad to worse
It's time to ponder, and not be cursed

Allison Campbell
TOYIN

To my special Nigerian friend, whom I will never forget, Toyin (Michelle) Ojo. May all your dreams come true!

Life is unfair
I don't understand why
They sent you away without a logical
reason of why?
They don't know what it's like to be
you or I,
and say goodbye to everything
we've known for a long time.
It's not your fault all things must end;
But a true lasting friendship, they will
never be able to replace in the end
No matter how unfair life plays its
games
You will always have a friend to turn
to—ME!
I will always remember the moments
we've shared
Whether you're a citizen or not, I do
not care.
I love you and owe you more than I
could
ever give you;
Your specialness is a rare one to me
No matter where we live.
What have they done to us, my
friend?
Apparently, not that much, when this
poem
comes from the heart of your very
dear friend.

Shari Kinney
COME HELL OR HIGH WATER

You only have to speak
and I will listen
You only have to laugh
and I will share your joy
You only have to cry
and I will mix in my tears
You only have to need comfort
and I will hold you
Come hell or high water.

You only have to be weighted down
and I will give you my support
You only have to be puzzled
and I will quiet your doubts
You only have to invite
and I will be there
You only have to accept
and I will be your friend forever
Come hell or high water.

Cheri Lasiter
HAPPY BIRTHDAY

This poem is dedicated to all of my special friends who encourage me and enrich my life throughout the years. Thank you for opening your hands & heart to me and blessing me with your friendship.

Dear Recorder of my good friends
Very special birthday greetings I do
send.
I hope this day will surely bring
Special joys and many good things.
I have no special gift to impart
Except these sincere feelings from
my heart.
Please, Dear Recorder, tell my dear
friends
What a great joy their friendship has
been.
Their life is truly a blessing to me.
My heart is encouraged through each
thing I see.
How I truly enjoy visiting with them.
Just being their friend is a treasured
gem.
Our time together is always a
pleasure.
Sure to bring countless joys and
blessings beyond measure.
Our special visits lift me when I'm
blue
And delight my soul through and
through.
There are a few things more to my
friends I'd like to say
Happy Birthday. I love you and wish
for you a very special day.

Celesta Scott Walters
CASA RETIREMENT HOME

When life becomes golden—not old
We decide to sell—be real bold
Find a place with life care too
Is what we seek with dollars few.

We go to CASA'S "Life Care
Center" new
Where there is always something one
can do
Friendships are made as we work and
eat
Food is excellent, varied—quite a
treat.

There is time to head or volunteer a
skill
Join a committee or game to your fill.
There are trips, walks, hobbies,
movies, art or craft
Where apartments soon become
home at last.

Our inspiration is a lighted cross on a
hill
Which reminds us of our purpose to
fulfill.
Just to meet another before day is
done
Where we can assist before set of
sun.

Where there is Love—one can
always hope
For everyone here is a friendly folk
All are congenial and carry a smile
Each gives of self toward a second
mile.

Claudia Fujinaga
MY CHILD

My child falls once again.
Down the hill, into dirty water and
then
Climbs the slippery way.
I'm sorry, she wants to say.

The all knowing lives in the presence
Shouting don't go down the hill.
But the child exists in defiance
And must learn to exert her will

And then, with my higher self, hand
in hand
A quiet walk on the path but not
alone
Forgiveness is given in this land
Where my soul is journeying towards
home.

Amanda Lea Garoutte
CHILDREN

Children are so special,
They will keep you warm.
They go through clothes,
Because they get worn.

They can be chubby,
Or skin and bones too.
But they are our future,
Now is that a clue.

They soon will be working,
Then they'll want cars.
Then all of a sudden,
No more baby jars.

They'll go off to college,
Now where did life go.
They're not children anymore,
What's to come, no one knows.

What's the next step,
They've got a family.
Oh good, a baby,
Now they live happily.

Jim Sparrow
ODE TO A LEGEND

Dedicated to Jim Morrison, performer tour de force.

Seems like yesterday
You went away,
Into my memory you will
Forever stay.

You left this earth,
Commended to the dirt
From which you came,
We will never be the same.

The music you made
Is still being played
To this very day.

You sound just fine,
Drowning in wine,
Forever sublime!

I look to the grave,
Knowing you're saved.
We must meet someday,
When my hair is gray.
Where would we be today,
If only you'd stayed?

Marlene Cook
IMMORTALITY

Wisdom comes a morning
Known I am true
Standing in understanding
Watching what I do

Heard her calling worthy
Discipline comes nigh
Entering in her presence
Sovereignty was mine

Every thought a meeting
An irresistible greet indeed
To anticipate my arrival
Was Wisdom's love for me

I rendered full attention
Extended my whole being
Offered my soul and body
She graciously received

Knowledge was her beginning
Incisive stability
Benevolently surveying
She captivated me

She directed her love and beauty
To emanate our space
And traced this pure experience
Subtly upon my face

Unique and penetrating
She moved into my ease
And granted me the luster of
closeness
That initiated this mystery

I gently opened my desires
Eager to find her way
Yielded the fruits of my virtue
To love her one more day

Her breath was warm with power
Triumph on her lips
Splendid strength of goodness
Acclaimed my untarnished wit

Enfolded in contentment
I turned a comfort knee
And touched the disposition
Of immortality

Arlene Leddy
DESERT SERENADE
Night falls on the desert,
The moon shines forth in all her splendor.
Shadows creep from dune to dune
And in the East
A star of peace
Shines for Allah, her sender.
Dark palms against a deep sky brood in stillness,
A night bird calls his love.

Night winds sweetly scented,
Across the oases are sighing
Midnight flings her velvet cloak
Across the sands
Where golden bands
Of moonlight pale are lying.
Open thy sleepy eyes yet filled with dreaming
For I, too, call my love.

Gary A Thompson
SIGNS
Like the proverbial mermaid
she must be in that pond
herself, ever-searching
knowing how you must wait:
like the deceased sixties ideologue
striking Plato again in isolation at dusk
abandoned as if by some distance
or sudden light
your writhing numbly behind locked doors
watching through windows other couples
their children tumbling
through the mounting snow
the falling aways, the quick turns,
the closeness of memories,
imagined one last time,
of silent understandings,
the merging of adulthood
into night.

Paul N Mendoza
ADORABLE ADMIRABLE BABIES
Adorable admirable babies burdened
by butchering bastards beguiled
by cheap careful cunningly deceitful
devastating demonic executions
each embryo encarnalized for
frivolous freedom from frail fetuses
going gainst God's gracious goals.
How horrible how heinous
ignorances impudent, irreligious,
investments in jealous, jugulating,
juvenility kindering kindless lavage.
Leaving Lamia's loquacious, lawless,
lethal misdeeds mocking morality.
Now noxiously nasty, neglecting,
obfuscating obedience of parenthood.
Parents parley parson's partitions
quibbling quixotic rights,
religious raconteurs recall such
sarcastic, self pity, self righteousness
throughout the testaments. These
unjustable, unreligious, unrighteous
vexations vilify virtu. Weak-minded,
weak-souled, weak-willed why?
why?
Xpletoe! Xytians, yield your yoke,
your yell, yield your zestful zeal.
Abonish abortion and bring back
bold bitific, blissful, cheerful,
compelling, Christianity. Despite
demonic encounters encouraging
falsehearted, farouched gossips.
God's holy heaven honors heroic
holocaust impositions in imminent
immorality.

Gladys Dawes

Gladys Dawes
DEAR "GOD" PLEASE SAVE MY SINFUL SOUL

This poem is dedicated to my beloved aunt, Mrs. Daisy Powell.

Dear "God" please save
my sinful soul
Looking back to yesterday and the
way I lived my life,
I thank "God" for teaching me
to hate the wrong and love
the right

I wouldn't trade for all the
silver,
I wouldn't trade for all the
gold
The riches "God" has bestowed
on me,
when he saved my sinful soul.

Gladys Dawes
A SPARK OF HAPPINESS

This poem is dedicated to Eddie-Lou Cole, Poetry Editor.

I watch the stars, I often
Say, how beautiful they
shine,
They smile, upon the world with
Nothing on their mine,

We too would love to shine
Our very best,
For just, a spark of
Happiness.

Wally Davis
THE ULTIMATE PRICE
Lucifer's mind, was way, off track
When he thought, he was, in front, &
the Lord, in the back

God & Jesus, had a plan
To give, Lucifer his own land

Hell is, this place, to be
It doesn't have, to be, for you, or me

Satan's got, a ticket, to his place, for life
We're heaven bound, with just some Christian strife

Jesus paid, the ultimate price
Thereby, putting Satan, on ice

Janet Schwind
A WRITER ANSWERS THE MOST DREADED QUESTION
Describe, they said, the job you do.
How is the process done?
I feared the telling of the truth—it
sounded too much fun.

The initial step, I said with dread,
requires the utmost care.
You lean back far, legs on the desk,
feet propped high in the air.

What, they asked, is the next step?
My heart began to race.
It starts, I said uneasily, by staring
into space.

I sensed a strong hostility my
answers had evoked.
I felt impending violence, like me
getting choked.

Continue, please—the words came
hurling at me like a knife.
The mention of thumb twiddling had
me running for my life.

Is it my fault creative minds lack
outward signs of thought?
Was there no way to show the inner
struggles we have fought?

I led them to a rainbow. Do you see
the beauty there?
Just like the colors in the sky, ideas
come from thin air.

Steven A Hodges
CHASE TOMORROW
Delicate fine lace
Of frost on windowpane
Lays out a maze of roads to follow
Come tomorrow

Find a road and choose
One to all that is new
As it rolls ahead run to follow
Chase tomorrow

Chase all the tears away
In search of sunny days
When you reach the end at last
You'll find
That yesterday has past
Gone like beads of water
Dripping from sun warmed glass

Delicate fine lace
Of frost on windowpane
Lays out a maze of roads to follow
Chase tomorrow

Jeannie Hope
PAPA'S DREAM
It sits in the pines at a crossroad,
practically hidden from view.
Burdened by years of winter snows,
much of the roof has fallen through.

The sign has long since disappeared
that proudly proclaimed its name;
and the gas pumps wait like sentinels,
dejected and cold in the rain.

Where red-checkered curtains once
fluttered,
the windows are gaping and black—
And I stand there bemused at the
crossroad
as his memory comes whispering
back.

I can hear his raucous laughter
as he joked with the visiting men,
lounging around the pot-bellied stove
sipping bear and "remembering
when."

For years he dreamed of a little place
away from the crowds of man.
Far from the city's noisy grasp
surrounded by pines it'd stand.

He'd drawn us so many pictures,
we knew it from end to end.
And before it was halfway finished,
it seemed like an old, old friend.

The shelves were lined with assorted
jars,
the countertop gleamed with a shine
from years of endless polishing
and the beauty of passing time.

Standing alone with my memories
in the warmth of the summer sun,
I knew his dream isn't over,
its lifetime has barely begun.

Though endless snows have taken
their toll
and the place is falling apart,
the memories breathe in the
whispering trees,
and his dream abides in my heart.

Michael Dippel
LOVE MAKES YOU WANT TO LIVE
Love makes you want to live, Love
makes you want to die.
Love makes you happy, Love makes
you want to cry.
Love is sometimes right, Love is
sometimes wrong.
Love makes you fight, Love helps
you grow strong.
Love is something you hold onto,
Love is something you let go.
Love is filled with lots of questions,
the answers you'll never know.
Love makes you dream to keep you
warm and tender.
Love hurts in many ways to make
your heart surrender.
Love sheds tears of joy, Love sheds
tears of sorrow.
Love makes you think of today, and
wonder of tomorrow.

Cari Michaelle Porter
SUMMER
I see a pool with cool, clear
water, a beautiful flower
garden with lovely pink and
white roses. There is a
bluebird with a song without
words. A bee buzzes from
one pink rose to another
almost silently. The fresh
breeze is so light it could
take me away. Summer!

Toni (O'Brien) Pease
SEPTEMBER
September is a month to remember
all the good times that we shared
together
September brings fall weather
leaves of many splendid colors

joining limbs combining them
together
birthdays seem to come in numbers
especially in the month of pretty

September
what a good time to remember
all our friends and family members
September is a month to remember
but without God we would have no splendor

Robert Rosse
I HAVE NEED OF THEE
God, You gave me sight,
But I am blind and cannot see,
Nor comprehend, Your plan for me.

Which road to take, where will it lead,
Once on it, ever filled with doubt,
I wonder, should I turn about?

Why do things which I have sought
Go up in smoke and come to naught,
Each enterprise, full of promise at inception,
Ends always in deception,
A journey through the maze
In which success averts its gaze?

Have all my dreams been built on sand,
My seed be sown on barren land,
Or, are my desires so lacking in grace
That in Your scheme of things
They have no place?

Is it my destiny to ever be
Alone and adrift on a windless sea?

God, help me. I have need of Thee.

Mary Stingle
PERFORMING ARTS
I have met
Your pain,
I have seen the tears
That fall behind
Your made-up smile,
Your painted face.

I know
The person behind
The actress who smiles,
That person cries
And trembles,
But no one sees,
The Show Must Go On.

But I stole
A peek behind the scenes,
Glimpsing a real person
Is so much better
Than watching
A player perform.

Rebecca L Woloski
LOST LOVE
The roses are still
and the horses are wild.
The true love you'll find
is only a moment in time.
You will say your good-byes
and close your eyes
for you do not know
what is waiting for you.

In the days that go by
all the flowers are blooming
but all that you see is gray.
For in this world,
you seem all alone
and your true love
is nowhere to be found!

Melanie D Dirige
THE CHILDREN
The children are the future, of the world and of us all
They grow to gain knowledge and feel so proud and tall
We all shall encourage them each day and even more
And show them life's not perfect, so be a good sport
If drugs, gangs, and crime should ruin this future of ours
We all must continue the climb of life's unjust towers
The children all must learn to keep a positive mind
And not feel so hopeless, the down-spirits kind
Education is the key to success, it's something we all need
And for the children of poor countries, we know we must feed
The children of the world make a difference in our life
So we should teach them wrong from right
everyone should understand what each child dreams
So that they grow to be wise and continue to succeed
They all must understand that crime is not the way
And that school is the place to go to each and every day
If a child has a dream and puts in their heart and soul
We must encourage them to strive and reach their goal.

Kenneth Wayne Carter
I TASTED HER TEARS
Her face void of newborn smile,
flushness filled her pours,
Cry loud and clear, suddenly softened
Tears swelled up against her pain.
Delicate cheeks exposed to fresh air but ten days,
Learned whole, defect free, prides swelled
But for a second care compared to none, but for a second,
Death screamed out as she hit the hard floor,
That heart failing never forgiven mistake made,
Trust soured, fears swell, aid is summoned.
Gently touched by experienced hands,
Each centimeter covered, redness recorded, breath measured,
Pulses bilaterally equal, pupils checked,
Each finger, toe, joint, ears clear, mouth patent,
Tears salty and thin, not thick and bland.
Skull firm, neck subtle, heart sounds strong.
Firmly secured to awaiting board, padded softly,
Blanketed warmly, red lights cranked to high.
Cradled in Grand-fatherly arms,
Fingers felt, toes tickled, cheeks brushed lightly,
All response good, prayers uttered,
Truth, GOD does protect the infants,
But I tasted her tears.

Grace Garone
A DISEASE
As waste when virus takes control of one,
Sunken, pale faced with bones protrude from parts.
Vanished strength no longer protects what's done.
From one tiny bug, where the problem starts.
The insect indecision works on me.
Takes hold of brain and heart to change my state.
Today this me, in pain, is what you see,
And desperation teaches me to hate.

Reaching only unrest the tic remains,
Providing new hidden reasons to wait.
With time the choice wraps me with many chains,
Accustomed to living without a mate.

No hope I turn towards what is above.
Give me the knowledge to find my true love.

Ms Bobbie L Wright
A BOOK
A book is a friend for you, it's always there with adventure.

It could be true, it could be not. It's always there with a thought.

A bright one, a dirty one; torn or not; ugly cover or pretty cover.

They're always there, they always share.
They're always there for you to take an adventure anywhere, any time.

Sherri Hague
MY DAUGHTER
My daughter makes me proud
Unique in self as a cloud
Personality that glitters
joy inside to see her smile
so very glad God lent her for awhile
Though usually happy and full of grace
She has those times for an ugly face
Still growing day by day
I'll think of her as I lay
One day she'll be grown
And dad and I alone
She'll be in a world of lots of work and little play
YES! OH YES! That's my daughter is what I'll say
And so proud as ever yes siree
For that's my daughter and part of me.

John Adams
THE CHALLENGER'S LAST FLIGHT
I'm deeply troubled tonight
As I think of the space ship
That seven brave Americans entered
For a long space trip.

The countdown began
All systems were go.
When the countdown was over
What a beautiful show.

The liftoff was perfect
The shuttle began its flight
Seven brave astronauts
Would never again see night.

Everything was beautiful
For only a few miles
Then suddenly down below
There were no more smiles.

All eyes were on the shuttle
As it traveled downrange.
Then something suddenly happened
That still seems very strange.

There was a great explosion
A ball of fire in the sky.
The space trip was ended
No one yet understands why.

The space center is working
Both day and night
Yet they don't know what happened
To a flight that seemed alright.

Yet we all saw the tragedy
The fire and the falling debris
As it slowly drifted down
To the depths of the sea.

First there were faint hopes
That maybe they might survive
Yet after seeing the explosion
We knew they were not alive.

We may never know what happened
To the Challenger that tragic day
It may have been fate
But who are we to say?

The world mourns with you
But as difficult as it seems
The space program must go on
That we might fulfill their dreams.

Be brave, ask God for comfort
Seek His wonderful love
Be prepared to meet your loved ones
In that wonderful city above.

Teresa Y Ellis
ODE TO A PAINTER'S POEM
A poetic painter feels a sudden rush of words . . .
Quickly, he searches for a pen.
Instead, he finds a brush.
Gently, he picks it up.
As the painter's brush delicately dances
Across an eagerly awaiting canvas,
Unspeakable words begin to come to life.
Then, with each loving caress,
More breathtaking beauty emerges.
At last, with a smile of deep satisfaction,
The poetic painter leans back to admire
The brilliance of his poem,
Now in glorious color.

Nicole Ora Sammons
HOMEWORK
Homework is white
It smells like broccoli
And tastes like cauliflower
It sounds like people crying
And feels like pain.

Annelle Stuckey
MUSIC
Music warms the heart and soul,
Even if you are growing old.
Music makes us want to dance and sing,
Sometimes it makes us feel as great as a king.
I love the piano's melodious sound,
It seems to create joy all around.
The violin plays a fast tune,
Someone will be square-dancing in the room.
When the band strikes up a patriotic tune,
Then we all begin to march very soon.
When the organ plays and the choir sings "Amazing Grace,"
That is when I see GOD face to face.

Mary Lucci
OUR LADY OF LOURDES
Ever ready I stand at the Grotto and wait,
To heal, to console, to bless,
All in need, all in distress.

With my holy water, I'll wash away
The sins of the past, the cares of the day,
And heal all wounds of body and soul.

To calm all those who are in despair,
If in Faith, you'll ask,
If in Faith, you'll pray.

No one is turned away who calls on me,
Who listens to your every prayer,—
In darkest moments, I'll light your way.

With St. Bernadette, who will bless you, too,
We'll turn the gray skies to the fairest blue
Ever ready, we wait for you.

Faye Joanne Plaisted Pritchard
OUR LIFE'S PLAN
Our walk in life is ever so short,
The days go rapidly by . . .
We seek our niche in life and then
One day, almost too late, we realize we didn't rely
On our God above, who knows us best,
And cares for our every need.
To direct our path, our ways of life
As all these years we've tried to feed
Our minds, our souls, our hearts
With food we thought was all life offered,
While the utmost was buried deep inside.
Forgive me Father God, for all I proffered.
Why did I struggle, toss and turn?
When the flow of life is an even tide?
Just allowing direction to come from above,
Frustration would vanish, no need to hide
From fears and cares we daily bear,
When all along the sweet Holy Spirit dwelt within
To be our strength, our pattern for life,
His presence just waiting to come in!

Juanita Mercer

Juanita Mercer
MOMMY
Who will take mommy? Who will it be? All of us wants her, I'm sure you'll agree. Let's call a meeting, let's gather the clan, let's get it settled as soon as we can. In such a big family there's certainly one, willing to give her a place in the sun.

Strange how we thought she'd never wear out. But see how she walks, it's arthritis no doubt. Her eyesight is faded, her memory dim, she's apt to insist on the silliest whim. When people get older, they become such a care, she must have a home, but the question is where?

Remember the days, when she used to be spry? Baked her own cookies and made her own pies? Helped us with lessons, and tended our seams, kissed away troubles, and mended, our dreams. Wonderful Mommy, we all loved her so. Isn't it dreadful she's no place to go? One little corner is all she would need, a shoulder to cry on, and a Bible to read. A chair by the window, with sun coming through, some pretty spring flowers, still covered with dew.

Who will warm her with love so she won't mind the cold? Oh, who will take mother? Now that she's old?

What? Nobody wants her? Oh, yes, there is one willing to give her a place in the sun. Where she won't have a worry or wonder or doubt, and she won't be our problem to bother about. Pretty soon now, God, will give her a bed, but who will dry our tears when dear old mommy is dead?

Elmyra J Haverty
A PROMISE
To this I know you two will be
Joined in Holy Matrimony.
As together you pledge unfailing love;
Sealed in a promise by the sign of a dove.
Give of yourself—your very best;
Ask of God to do the rest.
And in time of sorrow, a comfort be
As God will also comfort thee.
And should angry words well up inside
Recognize it as foolish pride.
And say not words to hurt your mate;
Nor hold in feelings full of hate.
And always remember your wedding vow
Of loving; honoring; then and now!

Jennifer J Johnson
IT'S TOO LATE FOR ME (BABY OF ABORTION)
I'm only a baby, but mom wants to abort me,
She wants to end my life. It's just not fair.—
I want to live too, like anyone else,
Doesn't she understand or care?—
Sure, she can go on living, but it's too late for me,
I'll probably be forgotten in her heart;
How could she do this dreadful thing to me?
Why couldn't she love me right from the start?-
I heard my grandparents say, they would raise me up,
But mom said, "No, it's better this way."—
How could she really mean that?!!
I want to grow up too, someday.—
Well, I guess this is it, my life will soon be over,
Just as fast as it started,—
I don't even have a name, but it doesn't matter,
Because this is what you want, mom, for us to be parted.—
God, please help my loving grandparents to find,—
their peace of mind,
because now you can see,—
It's too late for me.

Melissa Horner
WHAT IS THE MEANING OF LOVE?
What is the meaning of love?
to any human being
Is it walking in the park
or hearing the lovebirds sing?

What is the meaning of love?
What does it mean to you
Is it having a boy or girlfriend
no matter who?

What is the meaning of love?
Is it having the last dance
or being involved in
a true romance?

What is the meaning of love?
Is it how he looks or how he feels
But ask yourself
Is this love truly real?

Love means different things
to you and to me
what you have is right
Whatever it may be!!

Cynthia J Teague
THE SEA ALWAYS WELCOMES ME
The sea always welcomes me.
She knows where I've been.
The sins I've committed,
The beds I've been in.
The sea judges not,
Just accepts me as me.
The sea gives my heart
The grace to be free.
She bids me "be silent"
And she'll show me some things,
Cloudless blue skies and white gull wings.
The sea changes faces,
And she changes her voice.
But she won't change her name,
Even given the choice.
She is as she was and will be tomorrow.
And she'll hold me in joy,
As she's held me in sorrow.

Toby Simpson
IT WAS A BRIGHT AND HORRID DAY
It was a bright and horrid day;
I spied a noble black haired maid.
I bade her with me to dine;
In my bed she was not laid.

Such an angel with eyes of jade;
Her smile had two sparkles of gold.
Aye the heart of a Mormon saint;
With her I long to grow old.

There I stood in the Utah cold;
Not able to touch this perfect dream.
The days to come were paint dealt;
But every blissful moment my eyes agleam.

Every hour my soul she did ream;
I fled for a gift to bring.
To gain title and wealth to awe;
And return one day with a ring.

To this sad, bitter dream I cling;
With the fury of love still alive.
A dozen years have come and went;
On for the distant goal I strive.

Florence Russell Taylor
THE RAINBOW
I looked at the Rainbow
After a rain
And know that YOUR PROMISE
Has not been in vain.

You kept your word—GOD
And hung in the sky
YOUR beautiful bow
That is seen by all eyes.

At nighttime YOU gave us
An outer space view
Of moonlight and starlight
As earth passes through.

We're awe-struck with wonder
And such love we feel
Was meant to enrich us
As humbly we kneel.

Enlighten our thinking—GOD
Our hearts need to care
That mankind is crying
YOUR BOUNTY to share.

Angela Massey
NO MORE SILENCE
The father's shaking hand slowly turned
off the respirator switch—
The wheeze of the ventilator—
The beep of the E.K.G.,
Silence—

The tears falling to the floor
The fear of losing their tiny baby boy—
The worst thing you can listen to
Silence—

Everything still—
Only hearing the quiet whimpering cries
Silence—

Watching each staggering breath—
Watching his lungs slowly deflate
Silence—

The boy being welcomed to the skies above
Suddenly silence—
As they quietly chant a small prayer
Silence—
Is always dead, no more, no more.

Bernadette Scalera
FLAMING STAR

To Arden.

Flaming star spinning round
Tumbling slowly to the ground

Touching this heart upon the earth
Capturing forever at your hearth
Shining brilliance love you are
Ending never your flaming star

Dorothy M Rush

A CHILD'S PRAYER

Dear God, I'm just a little child
Take care of me today
Guide my footsteps
Calm my fears
And guard me while I play
Help me with my lessons
Tech me to obey
Make me kind and honest
Let me be yours today
God bless my Mom and Daddy
My sisters and brothers too
May we all meet you in heaven
When the trials of life are thru

Shari Carter

THE LITTLE ONES

The day is finally here—
Why doesn't anybody stand up and cheer.
The high winds are blowing—outside people go
Rushing off to the jobs they know.
No one stops to recognize the little one down in the corner—
So lonely is he.
Why doesn't anybody stop—
Can't anybody see—
The pain he is feeling on the inside.
Give him just something small—
That his young boy could treasure—
So dear to all.
We need to remember the little ones—
Ones who don't have much.
They need to have a loving hand—
Reached out to them too.
Just to say "I LOVE YOU"
Many of us get all caught up in the traditions—
Like candy and flowers—Yes they seem very nice
To us but we need to show the LOVE that—
We have from the Father above.

D J Brown

AMERICA 1990

Our world is in a mess today, I'm sure we all agree.
Something has to change—and soon, it starts with you and me.
The devil has deceived us, O, man why can't you see?
He's leading us down the path to hell, and we're going willingly.
Our schools are not worth the money, Government spending is out of control.
Drugs are ruling our children, and AIDS is taking its toll.
Mothers are forced into working, in order to pay the rent.
The sitters are raising our children, some of them aren't God sent.
Morals have gone out the window, along with love and respect.
The children are crying for all of these, no one hears—because of neglect.
Most movies are atrocious, no story do I see.
Just sex, satanic violence, and four letter word profanity.
We teach our teens abortion is right, we allow them to do as they will.
Then wonder where they are all night, but hope they're using the pill.
We're told not to discipline them, or teach them right from wrong.
We wonder why they take their lives, have you heard the hard-rock song?
Satan is ruling this world today, because we've pushed God aside.
We'd better get on our knees and pray, that God will forgive our pride.
He is our strength, our power and might, without Him, we'll crumble and fall.
He is also our guiding light, I pray for our country—I pray for us all.

James B Kirchhoffer

THE DIGNIFIED DEATH OF THE NINETY-SIX-YEAR-OLD MATRIARCH

"She is . . ."
Said sorrowfully,
We were called to her hospital bed
Knowing that
Death could not be denied
This time, unlike previous predicaments.

"She just . . ."
The house was hollow,
Though filled with relatives.
The sensation is
The moment the trapdoor underfoot opens
Just before the inevitable fall begins.

"She was . . ."
A nearly joyous realization
That, though gone,
She lives on,
Enjoying the mundane matters of daily life
Through those who loved her.

Ethel Simon

DESIGNS FOR LIVING

Designs for living
Are many depending on
Inner desires, birth
Areas of moving
Parents teachings, health, wealth, needs
To grow beyond birth.
To know fame in lands;
Aiding many inspiring
Souls to stir today,
Following parents
Or their own inner plans
Broadcast their claims
In arts, music, dance;
Any trade to amuse, aid
Peoples on their hopes
Tomorrows will bless
Many in health, wealth, fame.
love
For good happy lives.
To know no strife
Hearth aches to mar their growing with this trouble world.
For lands find troubles
In many forms, lack of funds,
Rains, right guidance
To give souls hopes, live
In peaceful surroundings in
Tomorrows activities.

Cheri Bell Stoops

A LONELY HEART

I'm so lonesome without you,
I'm so sad when I'm blue.
I don't know what to do,
I'm so lonesome without you.

When you left me all alone,
I cried myself to sleep.
I could not believe you were really gone,
But I continued to weep.

The days were long,
The nights were bleak.
Everything seemed to go wrong,
My senses reeled until I was weak.

The world was such an empty place,
My mind seemed in outer space.
I could think of nothing else,
Only of you and nothing less.

I'm so lonesome without you,
I'm so sad when I'm blue.
I don't know what to do,
I'm so lonesome without you.

Rick L Burgett

Rick L Burgett

WHEN A LOVED ONE DIES

To my grandmother, Jacqueline O. Burgett. May she rest in peace.

Another day goes by, who will live and who will die? Do we have a choice when we go? or will we even know? Will it matter to anyone and will we be greeted by the Holy Son. The choice will be his, the Heavenly Father's. Will we be missed by our sons and daughters, why does losing a loved one hurt so bad. And why do we feel so very sad, even knowing they might be going to a better place, why must there be this tear on my face?

Maybe I haven't showed how much I cared and maybe my love I haven't shared. Is it because of my selfishness or my big head that I am sad my loved one is dead. We could wish and pray for life, and hope we would never lose a wife for the bonding from one to another is like that of a brother. Life after death we now not know and will not find out until we go, death to some may be scary and sad but for others happy to see the father's hand, time for death is sometimes unknown so while alive our love shall be shown, for we will not know who will be next to go. For it could be you or me I hope not so, so if there are tears in your eyes it is common when a loved one dies.

Jean Foley

FIREFIGHTERS

They are a people like you and me
They have a home, and family, too
But there's something special about them
When they go out to rescue you.

As soon as their alarm sounds
They put everything on hold,
It could be a false alarm
Or a fire that's brightly gold.

A medical assist, or car accident,
Or anything else, we know,
Their lives could be on the line
As the adrenaline starts to flow.

Firefighters have that courage
Which we can't feel within,
We run out of a burning building
As they are rushing in.

I place them on a pedestal
For all that they go through,
And with all due respect
I thank them for what they do.

Rod A White

CRISIS OF PRINCIPLE

Blightingly badgered my soul drops a fathom
'Neath the weightier matters of life's subtle sin.
Hypocrisy brings me to manic depression;
Principles violated once and again.

I cry, "Who is worthy?!" and cry, "Who is right?!"
Swooning at the latest paradoxical whim.
Transpiring emotions arising contrite
For the pitiful, helpless state that I'm in.

Demons they deem me a fool quite conspicuous.
Truth elusive avoids me as cigarette's puff.
But throwing a blow that to them is capricious;
Dark mysteries ebb when declaring, "Enough!"

Truth is what conscience proclaims to be normal,
Sound foundations established with me at birth.
Intimate commune 'tween Creator informal;
With peaceful existence I'll love in this earth.

Ruth Powell

WHERE ARE THE NINE?

I held the door open for three young ladies
Who went merrily on their way
Never turning to smile or nod
And not even a word to say.

Then came one who limped and walked with a cane
Her face was wrinkled and her hair was gray
She turned and smiled and said,
"Thank you for being so nice.
Be sure to have a great day."

Lady I already have
An angel just passed my way.

Luke 17: 11-17

Heather Louise Burns

FOR SR. NICHOLAS

Death come and lay down over me.
Be my blanket one last time.
Hold in your hand all of my pain and
Keep to yourself all of my suffering.
When I leave myself,
When I leave all I've ever done and known,
I want you with me.
Please come with me.
Death come and lay down over me and
Yes,
Bring darkness with you.

Ruthella Harvey
DEATH

To all my friends, who listened. Thank you!

Death Can't find me, 'cause I'm already dead you see.
Here lies my body in funny clothes
I'll never seen.
Bought for me by someone who really didn't care at all.
They're just glad they got all my INSURANCE, and that's all.

Sandra Ismail
TRUTH EVERLASTING

I have reached a lonely ocean all my feelings of deep despair then my hopes lifted when I found God was there

Night was soon upon me as I slowly walked along I found joy and sweetness all my troubles were soon gone

The clouds gathered up above as there started a new day I found happiness beyond the shadows God is there all the way

All the times I searched are gone for I am free I found God everlasting when I found God right in me

Najwa Salam Brax
THE VOICE OF MOTHER NATURE

Be deep in thought like my mysterious oceans,
Reflective like my serene skies or magical lakes,
Self-confident like my self-rotation;
Be lofty in your ideals like my towering peaks,
Steadfast in your belief like sunrise and sunset,
Free in thinking like my boundless galaxies;
Be imaginative like my four seasons,
Creative like Life-Force, like earth and seeds,
Active like a supernova or a hive of bees;
Be generous like my affluent fountains and falls,
Loving like my fruitful trees and golden ears of wheat,
Pure like my fire or polar icebergs;
Be straight like the shining arrows of my suns,
Faithful like my gentle, silver moons,
Tender like my sweet breezes or dew-drops;
Be peaceful like my sheep and doves,
Modest like my flowering valleys and hidden roots,
Prudent like my creeping serpents or soaring eagles;
Be simple like a drop of water or a grain of sand;
Be your Greater Self, and you see me within yourself.

Renee Neal Allen
GLAD

I'm glad you stayed and fought it out.
No one else would, there's no doubt.

To know me, is to love me, the phrase is said.
No one knows you like the one in bed.

Someone who has stayed through thick and thin.
A person who'll not just let anyone in. Into
the mind, and heart of your soul.
Only you could
be so bold. Bold, faithful, stubborn, it's true.

Am I speaking of me, or referring to you?

It matters not what others have said.
I've seen
you alive, and just about dead. Dead to feeling,
joy, and love. Love no one else was worthy of.

I'm glad you stayed and fought it out.
No one else would there's no doubt.

Najwa Salam Brax

Najwa Salam Brax
MISS LIBERTY

This poem is dedicated to my Guide and Beloved Prophet Dr. Dahesh.

O Mother of the prophets, Nursemaid of the liberals!
You link Earth's horizon to Divinity's twilight,
Like Zephyrus, you flutter from sky to sky,
Like a shining sword in the dead of darkness,
You puzzle and dazzle all creatures!
With your magnetic force, you've bewitched Humanity!
You granted us to know our spiritual responsibility;
But the hunger of our bodies flared up!
With our foolishness, we disfigure your beautiful imagine,
We try to clutch you with our clawed slavery;
But your holy halos burn our fingers!

You can't take flesh among us;
You are a diaphanous creature;
But you are the everlasting sunrise in our sunset.
Speak about your sacred fire which burns our bondage,
Let us fuse into your holy blaze,
And cross the bridge of wounds to the Spirit of liberty,
To its boundless ocean which overflows all universes;
Enfold us within your long golden lashes
That are swaying in the neighborhood of god.

Najwa Salam Brax
UNDER THE FLOWER-TREE OF DEITY

This poem is dedicated to Ghazi Brax, my beloved husband.

In the beginning, the Almighty spread
Your divine petals of infinite hues,
And let us revel in their seraphic shadows.
But we dropped into our Earthly reincarnations,
And our insight was covered with a thousand veils.
Then, from celestial spheres, you came down into our galaxy,
You the oldest god among the gods.
Every dawn, your shining torch rises
To awaken our sleepy consciences.
O Divine Truth, you remain forever
The Eternal Book which refuses to be written.
Forgive our ignorance, for with our hands
We've sewn garments that cover your beautiful face
In the innermost of ourselves,
So we've been not able to discern
The white thread from the black thread
In Time's spinning Wheel.
From your sacred boughs, let some seeds of wisdom,
Infused with love, peace and beauty,
Be scattered into our daily bread.

Najwa Salam Brax
A FAREWELL TO MY FATHER

Like a quivering canary I alighted upon your grave,
Nay, like a gashed dove I dropped by your eternal alcove,
And I read on the everlasting pages of dust:
"Stone endures! Man perishes! Here life ends! Here life begins!"
O dust! roaring tempest of dust!
An awful ear listening; a huge eye watering;
A dreadful mouth eating up without being satiated;
A gigantic foot treading and wiping out everything but truth!
Each grain cries out asking for cadavers!

But we are like sunbeams; we withdraw from one place to rise in another.
Every atom of our beings cries out to live forever.
Through your terrifying face, o death, I see the gate of eternity!
Go on a new travel, Odysseus, this is a new road to discover!
Your enthralling smiles to sunbeams were given;
Your ardent voice to hummingbirds was offered;
Your lively wit to fluttering rainbows was donated;
Your shining eyes to the flapping butterflies were granted;
Your human elements were merged into nature's elements!
O Mother Nature, be merciful, my eyes are still wet;
O Biggest Fisherman, hold your new fish gently in your strong net!

Najwa Salam Brax
THE GOLDEN GOD

O magical dollar! You are the talisman of might,
The god of this Earth
That turns around your magnetic hearth
In war and peace, day and night!
You are the universal alphabet
Which everyone speaks at ease.
For life and death, you are the best bet.
With bacchanalian lust we kiss your cold cheeks;
With infernal thirst we drink from your aphrodisiac chalice
The wine that drives us mad into the big jungle of life!

O false god! You perform among us but tragic miracles:
Brothers assassinate brothers, sons murder parents!
Homicides for your sake have become valuable talents!
However, starveling lions don't devour lions,
And hungry tigers don't prey upon tigers;
And vampires don't suck the blood of vampires.
But only he, who considers himself the master of all creatures,
Only he, who considers himself the image of God,
Devours his progenitors and progeny,
For in fact, he is your image, O golden god!

Donald Wayne DeHart
EAGLE

If you could fly with me
across this land of ours,
what beauties would unfold to you
from high up in the sky.
To look upon the great green plains,
and watch the rivers flow.
We could fly above the mountaintops
and watch the things below.
The animals across the land,
and birds up in the trees,
can only try to cross our land
to see what I can see.
You have to be an eagle,
to fly as far as I,
and see the world from up there in the sky.

Eddie Belles
I'LL POUR THE WINE

This poem is dedicated to my loving husband George.

This is for all the lonely women,
You know who you are,
We smile and say it doesn't matter,
And we'll keep busy with our lives.

It's a very well kept secret,
We hide it day and night,
But when the loneliness gets too heavy,
We need a man to make it right.

The phone rings half-past midnight,
He's sorry for calling so late,
He promised he'll be home

tomorrow,
What else can I do but wait.

I lit the candles for our dinner,
Making everything just right,
He'll be home by sunset,
With flowers in his hand I'll bet.

But as the night grows darker,
The candles burning out of sight,
I'll pour the wine and turn the lights down,
He won't be coming home tonight.

Lorraine F Lewis

SILENCE

Silence is golden the immortal words of time.
A thought that is never spoken so it passes along without rhyme.
What could be better than silence when one wants to sit back and dream.
Could you think if all about you, you heard a noisy and rowdy world, not the silence of a word.
To be able to sit in silence and watch troubles come and go
Instead of making a rumpus just to put on a show.
I tell you there is nothing finer in this whole wide land to
Know and live with silence the kind you understand.

The end.

Else Sprague

SPRING MIST

Fresh
wet, cool
a dew
folding around
the earth
and me;
Grass mild
green to be seen
it grows, to know
it is Spring;
Flowers
tender the colors
pastel lilac, pink and yellow
I want to keep the expression
the measure of Spring,
the mist, the song
it sings.

Bob Charest

THE COLORS OF MY LOVE

Words of Love, for Kathy.

Green eyes and blue jeans are the colors of my love
Her heart is as soft as the wings of a dove
She's got a big heart for a woman her size
She's got an angel in her smile and the devil in her eyes

Green eyes and blue jeans on the woman I love
She's tough as hell when push comes to shove
She's got dimples when she smiles, her lips quiver when she's blue
She's got haunting green eyes that captivate you

Green eyes and blue jeans are the colors of my girl
With her beside me I'm on top of the world
When we're together she makes everything right
I love nothing better than to hold her all night
Green eyes and blue jeans are the colors of my life
Some day green eyes and blue jeans will become my wife.

Dorothy Kinsella

THE FANTASY

To my husband Kevin. Without him, I would not "... pursue that...."

We all chase after
A piece of the
Dream . . .
They are not just
For children.

We all strive for
What we want . . .
The way it should
Seem.

We set our sights
And sail away.
Following that
Sliver of gleam . . .
As we pursue
That unattainable
Dream.

MaryAnn Sanchez

MaryAnn Sanchez

NOCTURNAL PARADISE

I'd like to thank my friends and family for their faith in me and Brian the man who makes all of my nights paradise.

Nighttime is the time
when all the people
come out,

They hide behind the
darkness talk with
friends and walk about.

There are no clouds on
this clear summer
night.
The air is clean and
crisp, there is no sun in
sight.

Only the moon and stars,
I feel so free, it feels
so right

I want to be here with
you under the soft
moonlight.

Walking close together
holding hands so tight.

The breeze softly
blowing through my hair,

The sand between
my toes, nothing else
could compare
Being together walking along the beach,
Listening to the waves as they create their
own beat.

I see the sparkle in
your eyes as you look at me

I catch a glimpse of
that same sparkle as I gaze out at the sea.

The moon reflects off
the tide so beautifully

The stars shine bright
the waves just flow,

I never want this
night to end, I never
want to go.

There's never been a
time when I've felt this close to you,

I feel your love
surround me, I know
your love is true.

I want to hold you
until the sun comes
up, I want to hold you
all night.

I want to hold you
until the sun comes up
and wakes us with
its Light.

BG Richard J Huggler

BG Richard J Huggler

FANTASY OF FLIGHT

Do you care a little bit, would you like to share?
Wonderful and exciting experiences, where we both would care.
A sweet and tender moment, a full day of bliss.
Where we can understand each other, and nothing shall we miss.
An ecstasy beyond compare, a fantasy of flight.
To forget the world of darkness and bask into the light.
To obtain dreams of fulfillment, and not to feel shame.
Where we do not have to question, or try to place blame.
It's a natural growth of wonder, that should nurture and grow.
If we do not hurt anyone, who really has to know?
The world is full of delights, that I would like to see.
It would be like heaven if you would share with me.
Come join me in this enterprise,
unfold your wings and fly.
Or, do you want your solitude, so you can wither up and die?
Break those bonds that shackle you and bind you to conform.
Come and drink of the ambrosia, have your life reborn.
Life is for the living, but many of the living are dead.
They go through motions of life, a treadmill they do tread.
Do not despair and give up hope, come place your hand in mine.
Let us journey as of one through life, space, and time.

Bobbi Sue Fowlkes Wilson

TO LOVE

To My Husband Tim, With All My Love.

Love is so dear,
Mysterious and deep.

Love is so blind,
But old and neat.

Comes so fast,
But leaves with pain.

My love for
Tim,
I'll never complain!

Rosella M Nerdin

BOYHOOD DREAMS

To my grandson, John, who is now completing a successful mission for the L.D.S. Church.

He was only a little boy of three,
When he sat upon his grandfather's knee.
A piggy bank he clutched in his arms,
A note attached, "Going on my mission money."

He looked up into his grandfather's eyes,
The expression on his little face, was oh, so sunny.
"Please grandpa, won't you give,
Your pennies, nickels, and dimes.
So that the dream of my mission I can live?"

So down in his pocket grandpa did dig,
Bringing up pennies, nickels, dimes and more
Putting them in that piggy bank to store.

Until the day that little boy grew,
Dreaming always of the day to be called,
"Church of Jesus Christ of
Latter-Day Saints missionary."
And now that wonderful day is here,
We bid good luck to John, our dear.

Catherine E Suthard

FULL ARMOR DRESSED

To the embers of near forgotten dreams in each of us, that CAN be rekindled, and to Ms. Fas . . . thank you.

He comes
in half shadows
of night's curtain
Full Armor Dressed
sword at his thigh
Hiding
his hopes
behind him
in scattered leaves
like

a living orchestra
full
Each instrument, a dream
waiting
to be practiced
dying
to be played.
The mount
guides him
for no choice is made
which peace?
to place before the steed.

Then, as Moon breaks full . . .
Light speaks.

Arida Randall
MY SHOPPING LIST
some soda
tissues
something to eat

cough drops
hair combs
a few sweets

nylon stockings
earrings
a bracelet too

something for me,
something for you

cologne
talc powder
a gold ring

a sweat shirt
a teddy bear
a swing

hair grease
coffee
and shampoo

something for me,
something for you

Alice H Vaughan
KISSED

This Poem is dedicated to the Men in my Life.

I've been kissed
Behind a waterfall
And on top of many mountains, tall
And by the sea.

In the midst of cities
Both large and small
And beneath an old oak tree
Where the grass was green and tall

On the banks of rivers and of steams
Where the bright sun beamed, and
Beneath the stars and under the moon
And near roses in full bloom.

Kissed while the lightning flashed
When the rains came down and
splashed
On lips warm and eager,
Seeking to find, mine.

Larry H Hulme
THE WINE IS FINE

To: My sister Judy, who told me to keep up the love's work.

The wine is fine—the rain falls—and
the nite is long, but not lonely . . .

Alone is a fine thing—shadowy &
elusive—
The mind can be a trickster!

The heart is warm, ungiven and
unhurting . . .
Seems it only hurts when
given . . . as no one takes it tenderly,
seriously—gently
I walk with the river sometimes, it
goes on & on, singing its songs to me
. . . I chirp back at a squirrel
sometimes, they
know . . .

The shores of my Soul's sea whisper
to me . . . A lighthouse beckons—
But away I must drift on the current
that carries me, I know not where . . .
or why—

My destiny awaits me—but alas I am
adrift . . . on the river in the seas of
my Soul . . . my heart knows not
where I go, but only awaits the
choice of my Soul—nor I

There is an end . . . I Pray, it comes
soon and I will find love again, feel
love—I felt it thrice—but as the
elusive Butterfly,
Beautiful to behold, but held too long
. . . it perished—as it is
free—
Not to be held—only cherished from
a distance . . .
The wine is fine . . . The nite long

Kenneth Yanow
PARTY IN A POEM

This poem is dedicated to all those single, fancy free people lucky enough to travel and to appreciate each individual place as they go. Especially to those few that have been at the New Orleans Mardi Gras!

I love New York City and I love L.A.
too,
I love Dallas, Texas, all different bars
to sing the blues,
You party here and you party there, it
doesn't matter where you are,
They all have one thing in common:
pretty women fill the bars.

A night in New Orleans, a drink at
Que Sera,
Rock and rolling at Fat Harry's the
best of all the bars.
It's Mardi Gras, Carnival time, an all
out party until you drop,
The town is lit, your mind is blitzed,
It's a one and only experience.

A night in New York City; A party in
New Orleans,
On the beaches of San Francisco,
loving everyone on the scene,
Life is hard, it's sometimes strange,
Don't let fate take you for a ride,
You only go around once in this
world,
So party while you're alive!

Kenneth Yanow
TUNNEL OF LOVE
Every night you close your eyes, your
mind awakens, you go to sleep,
Dreams and inspirations all night
long, conscious carry you into the
deep.
Visions appear of the one you love,
pure as the essence of a flying dove,
Now she comes towards you, a vision
so clear,
Come enter the Tunnel of Love.

The sun goes down; the moon comes
up, you disappear as you follow the
glow,
Think of the one; the one that you
love, follow her high, follow her low.
The dove flies high right into the
cave,
Join your love far and away: follow it
now before she's gone,
Come enter the Tunnel of Love.

Join your dreams and the one you
love,
Never turn back, join the flying dove,
Come enter the Tunnel of Love.

Kenneth Yanow

Kenneth Yanow
A SONNET FOR SAMANTHA

To my precious daughter who I love with all my heart, Samantha.

"Mommy Mommy" came from her
lips, amidst the sweetest little smile;
Like a midnight view of a midnight
ship.

She speaks many languages, though
none that I know,
or is it just gibberish, from those rosy
cheeks that glow.

With her mind at work or play or
sleep,
Priceless are the words that she
speaks.

Samantha, Samantha, as I told you
before,
I wrote you a poem once, now I shall
write you one more.

You are more precious at a year, than
the year before,
Or is it everyday I love you more and
more?

My words can never say what my
heart really feels;
Bright as the sun, Pure as a star—
"Mommy Mommy" comes from afar.

Another fine morning, as I awake to
the call
of the beautiful sounds of my year
old baby girl.

Kenneth Yanow
THE SWORD OF LIFE

To all those who suffer, in this poem there lies hope!

Pain, strife, business pressure every
day,
Attracts dark shadows of gloom,
enables Evil to prey.
All we take for granted until that
darkened day appears,
Pain penetrates my threshold more
than any person fears.
I lie horizontal, my physical pain all
too clear,
Only to be surpassed by that positive
Universal sphere.

Without Evil and pain, the "Gloom of
Darkness" and fear,
No light can ever be seen, no Good
will ever appear.
Days filled with agony, I would
rather not behold,
Though enlightened is my mind, my
body and soul.

The "Sword of Life," double edged
as it must be,
Lets us all feel the shadows and
darkness,
Yet enables every blind man to see.

Life has many meanings, opaque as
they may seem,
Everyone must seek that brightest
light, which can always be seen.
Everyday goes by—Only once and so
quick; though daily pain of some
kind often seems fixed,
One shall never see Good, without
experiencing Evil and fear,
So let the darkest days change the
most opaque to clear.

These are the ingredients of the food
we call life; Balance each day as each
passes by.
I know from where I speak as I lie in
midnight blackness,
My mind, body and soul internally
glowing so bright, this most painful
day, brings me great gladness.

Kenneth Yanow
A BIRTHDAY CARD FOR BETTY
Grandchildren, daughters and mom
alike,
Might it be time to take a ride?
With the expenses all free, and the
cherry blossoms in bloom,
Why not see Georgetown, a national
cemetery, and a zoo.

What will George Bush and Abe
Lincoln say,
When they hear the news, that it's
Betty's seventieth birthday?
Come down to the Capitol, relax a
few days,
Enjoy the history and sights, you're
welcome to stay.

The Lincoln Memorial; the
"Monument" in the spring,
These are a few of my favorite
things.
So without further ado, I shall say:
A very special surprise—HAPPY
SEVENTIETH BIRTHDAY:

Come visit with us, to Washington,
D.C.,
With Ella, Joyce and Jonathon, and
don't forget Lindsay.

A Travelling celebration is shortly in order,
With all of your grandchildren and all of your daughters.

It's time you make this trip, since never done before,
After all seventy years not to see the White House, is overdue to be sure.
Have a Happy Happy Birthday, with love from us all,
A very special happy and healthy, for a lady I adore.

Dee Stockton
TO LOVE ONCE

The sky was blue
the water was clear
God how I wish
that you were here.

I gave you my heart
You tore it to shreds
I gave you my love
You choked it to death.

I still dream of
how it used to be
but, you were the one
who wanted to be free.

So that's how it is
And how it will stay
'cause now there is no
love to give away.

Mike Sforza
THE TERROR OF MY DREAMS

A dream is yet only a fantasy
in a world caught up in my reality.
My mind draws blank, and then it starts
with a roar of passion, it makes its marks.
Motionless is my body, quiet is my stare
to wake from this dream, I do not dare.
A sweet melody whispers in the back of my mind
I'm lost in a place I thought I'd never find.
Far from the darkened depths of hell,
into a haven is where I fell.
As my mind begins to drift away,
how can I pretend everything's okay?
Sure everything is perfect, just as long as I dream
And perfect would last forever, or so it may seem.
When I do wake, the magic will be done,
my dream is broken and nothing is won.
But the terror of my dreams is when I awaken
and by dreaming the chance that I had just taken.
When I wake my dream is shattered,
my soul is torn and my mind is battered.
I was just hit with the reality
that my dream was just a fantasy.

Gail Farmer
REBORN

Dedicated to Steve—who was there when I needed him, caring for and loving me thru it all. I love you, Steve.

God touched me and gave me a start
Showed me a way to open my heart
To let out the ache, pain, and sorrow
Giving me life for a new tomorrow
Renewing my faith in all that is good
Living my life the way that I should
Being the person he meant me to be
From now until eternity

Sheila Ashby Kirkley
IRONIC DIMENSIONS

This poem is dedicated to my sister, Theresa Ashby Carruth—in her memory, March of 1990.

Hell be bent this wicked tree,
prevents me to see the sun,
I was to see, as clear as you are there.
How dare you grow so big and shade me with those branches.
You're far too large to climb myself and shape you as you should be.
It's God who made you, right, well he so made me too.
Take a part of the land but stop growing over me.
Yes, one would say, that's crazy.
It would be easier for me to move, than to shape your soul.
But I have traveled many roads. And now that I've sat my house here, before your limbs grew so long.
I'll be damned, if those hell bent wicked limbs will set me looking once again.

Alice McDuffee
HOME IS WHERE THE HEART IS

Dedicated to: Mary Barton.

Take good care of my grandmother, Lord,
For I know you will,
She is in Your holy presence which is peaceful and still,
Thank you Grandmother for all the wonderful memories,
Your kind spirit and your big heart,
You were full of wisdom from the start!
You are as jewels now and precious gold,
For it is your heart that will be told.
Your life has just begun,
For you are with Jesus, the Everlasting Son!
Love you Grandmother.

Ruth H Gorman
FALLING LEAVES

To my Family and Friends—Ruth H. Gorman.

Family and friends are like leaves on a tree.
We are grateful for their kindness, and
Our loves and friendships we treasure as we grow older.
We comfort each other when the winter of our time comes.
One by one we leave the tree, like falling leaves, but—
the memories we cherish and save another day.

Michelle Lynch
COME BACK

This poem is dedicated to my special friend, Rob Payne, for whom I wrote this for. No one will ever come as close to you. Not even to match your eyes, so true.

Days pass on and on.
And my man, I feel, is gone.
Far away and never to return again.
Seeing him everyday brought a rush to my mind.
My body established a complete and sensational high.
No one and nothing could stop this feeling I had.
But only could I feel this when I saw him.
Being in the same room with this man.
A man of mystery.
Very intriguing and sensuous,
Of pure darkness and freshness.
Never unappealing.
Oh, how I'd do anything for this human being.
Commit the deepest and dirtiest crime.
Swim the Ocean Blue.
Pour down sweat to make him happy.
Knowing I did it all for him, my man.
If that Special Star came along,
I would definitely know what I'd wish on.
Please come back.
Don't forget about me.

Willie House
GROWING-UP DAYS

Dedicated to my brother, Monroe, remembering enjoyable times past. Thank you for your understanding and help to me over the years.

Recalling fond memories of many years ago
Is one of the most enjoyable things I know.
I go back in time to childhood days,
To a time so different in many ways!
We lived on a farm way out of town,
And used a wagon and horses to get around.
We had chickens and pigs and a cow to milk,
A garden with vegetables and corn to silk.
The Saturday night movie was a favorite pastime,
And would you believe it, cost only a dime!
My brother Monroe, a real entrepreneur,
Took peanuts to the movie and they sold for sure!
He would gather them, parch, and sack them up,
Neatly arrange in a box, each the size of a cup.
Also he had a publisher's magazine route,
And he'd walk on foot to distribute them about.
Our family was close and each did their part,
To achieve our goals and satisfy heart.
Now as I glide back over the years and gaze,
I can see those really were good old days!

Tonya R Evans
REMEMBERING WHEN

This poem is dedicated to my first love, Wayne Alley. Thank you. I'll always love you.

We met through a friend we both shared,
Someone who loved us and really cared
We became fast friends, that was easy to tell
Then you left
Without a trace
Until that day when I saw your face
You smiled and waved, and gave me a friendly greeting
What else would it be? Oh, it was so much more to me.
Again we were friends and things seemed to change.
You've always been there for me, through good and bad times
I've cried on your shoulder and laughed in your face
Now in my heart there's an empty space because of something we both did.
If you love something, let it go
That's what people say, so I'm saying good-bye
And I love you. All I ask is one small thing
Remember when we were together

Ms Cindy Lou Siple

Ms Cindy Lou Siple
I GOTTA BE ME!

This poem is dedicated to my children, Lee and Lissa, whom I hope will grow up to live life to the fullest and enjoy being themselves. I love you, Lee (my munchkin), and Lissa (my babycakes).

I do a lot of things that are just for fun
And lots of things that are serious, too.
Often I do unusual things
That people say "only Cindy would do."

I'm just trying to be happy
By being the way that I like to be.
I often get silly and crazy
Causing unhappy people to criticize me.

I don't believe in "acting my age,"
Yet, I don't feel that I'm immature.
Why should happiness have an age limit?
Why should I live my whole life being bored?

I know I can't always be happy.
now and then, things will go wrong.
Problems, to me, are a challenge.
That I accept and overcome.

I want to live life to the fullest
And be the best that I can be,
So please accept me the way I am
'Cause I just GOTTA BE ME!

Louis Still
I LOVE YOU

To Veronica my love, no one makes me happier. I truly love you.

Thinking of you as the day goes by
Waiting for the night to look into your eyes
My love grows stronger when we are apart
I can feel the pounding of my heart

To hold you is all I want to do
You make me feel happy not blue
Your loving touch picks up my day
I miss you so much when you are away

I hope you see the joy you give me
With no one else do I want to be
I wonder if you feel the same way too
Do you love me like I love you?

I can't help but love you so much
I feel so good with just your touch
I want you always by my side
My love for you shall never die

John J Busch
PICTURE BOOK

Dedicated to my wife Dorothy.

Before when I opened my picture book
There were no pictures of you to see
Now when I open it I look
at pictures of you in blue and green
The leaves they're turned since we've met
But the memories I will never forget
Isn't it funny how time goes by
the happiness we share and the tears we cry
The seasons that change from year to year
I love you and I'm so happy you're here
The love we've shared and the pictures we took
Will live forever in my picture book

Eric P Carnahan
EGO TALKS OF ID

All thanks to my Savior, you have shown me Alison. An ideal captured unto reality.

I'm falling unto him again
for he waits crouched and wishes to begin
drifting, dropping, twisting away
he needs to be put at bay!

he wishes to possess and again tumble
he has nothing that is humble
I wish not to follow, I hate thee Id-iance
for mine will be whiter than, bright than . . .
(more loving than.)

he knows no love!—(he knows not the dream)
as I search so, he licks lips of eaten cream
I am yet to find her . . .
I hold her vision being divine; (She's not a Blurr)

Pleasures delude all senses
bleeding out my soul for false pretenses
he will see to my demise
(under me, atop of me, or on the prize)
(his lady is there: Mine would not)
faith of Him, divine decision
He will bring her in all precision
He Loves—even fools of we in unity
Surrender—(will I?) and have serenity.

Robert H Wolf
MOTHERHOOD

Tribute to a loving Mother from her grateful five. 1882-1965.

Motherhood's an institution
She's a special friend;
More than this she's many things
For truly there's no end.

Motherhood's a teaching job
We learned a thing or two;
She must have been a prophet
To see our lives come true.

Motherhood's a loving life
Despite heartaches and pain;
Her prayer, her faith sets all aright
And sends us forth again.

Motherhood's an inspiration
Strength to each in turn;
Courage is her stock in trade
No sacrifice would spurn.

Motherhood's a lifelong trip
Through her family's lives;
Never does her influence cease
She wills that each survives.

Robert E Rader
I WONDER WHY

I dedicate "I WONDER WHY" to my children, Bobby and Amanda. May all of their dreams and goals come true.

This world in which we live is going to waste,
With each passing day it's a faster pace.
Earthquakes, fires, and floods too,
This is three, just to name a few.

These three in fact always bring a tear,
But it's drugs on the street that I really fear.
They bring death to our old, who thought they were bold,
And kill our young before they are told.

Earthquakes are over, fires go out,
And our land will dry
But if we keep our drugs on the street,
We will all surely die.

I pray in the morning, I pray at night
That one day we will all see the light.
But just for now, as each day goes by,
I sit and say, I WONDER WHY

William F Martin
SUNSET

Mary Jane Pawlowski and all the children involved in my life.

As the sun sets on a clear blue day
I can sit and admire it all,
for I do believe this is God's world
and he giveth me this to watch, to recall.

I can sit and admire the beauty
and wish to catch what comes my way.
I hope tomorrow is just as nice
as it was today.

The warmth that is generated
the coziness of one's soul,
the feeling of belonging
to achieve one's ultimate goal.

Yes, I do believe
that this day was for us all,
and to remember a day like this
can make a person feel ten feet tall.

Edythe Russell
PAVANE

Last night I swam in a sea of music.
The waves of sound
Rolled as thunder
'Gainst the cliffs of my being.
A sweeping surge
Then a sudden hush
A soaring skywards
On wings of melody.
Then a soft clear call
That brought me back,
And I stood on the gleaming strand
With small tunes tangled in my hair
And dripping from my eyelids
On music!
My heart will hold your glory
Forevermore!

Myra M Gregory

Myra M Gregory
LAUGHTER

To My Loved Ones.

Laughter has so many sounds
For there's a certain tone
Which makes it especially yours,
A laugh that is all your own.

Laughter arises from emotion
Of sundry different kinds
Sometimes there is joyful elation
Which recollection finds.

Derision in the laughing tones
Destroys all respect,
And makes the victim of the sounds
The one whom you reject.

Laughter also might be a balm
That soothes a tired soul;
For laughing together breeds the calm
Required to reach a goal.

Laughter wafted by merciful kindness
Brightens the atmosphere;
For love combined with thoughtfulness
Creates the sound we hear.

Myra M Gregory
SILENCES

Silences of beauty surround us:
Sunrise is never heard,
Nor yet, the sunset;
Or quiet twinkling stars;
Or glistening moonbeams.

Smiles silently slip around one's lips,
They are a source of joy,
Signs of friendship,
Welcome's gestures,
Symbols of lingering love . . .

Myra M Gregory
NIGHT

The night is robed in a garment of stars,
The diamonds of the sky;
It rides in chariots of moonbeams,
That constantly pass by.

It spreads its mantle of gray-white clouds
Around the sleeping world;
Then, quietly its outstretched hands
Welcome the waiting dawn.

Myra M Gregory
THE WIND

Sometimes the wind likes to play:
It blows my hat off my head;
It pushes me along my way;
It pats my cheeks until they're red.

Sometimes the wind seems so sad.
It moans and sighs, and even groans.
At other times it is quite glad,
And whistles tunes in happy tones.

Myra M Gregory
OCTOBER

October has so many colors:
Red, gold, and yellow;
It paints the most unspeakable wonders
Upon the autumn meadows.

See the graceful goldenrod,
Gentians and asters, too;
Everywhere that we trod,
Grasses glisten with dew.

Myra M Gregory
SNOW

Snow falls so softly;
It must be that each snowflake
Tiptoes down from the sky,
Then, quietly takes its place.

There is no sound as others come
And rest upon the things on earth.
Each snowflake with its own pattern
Fills the land with beauty.

The gentle snowflakes lie quite still
To form a glistening coverlet
Over the sleeping plants below
That patiently await the spring.

Myra M Gregory
WINTRY DAY

Whistling, whirling winds rush in gusts
That push and shove you on your way
Past the trees which stand like silent

ghosts,
  Sentinels of a wintery day.

Snow flurries join the fun the winds began;
  They chase each other past your nose
As if to say, "Catch me, if you can."
  In time, some melt; some freeze.

Drifting clouds let the sun appear
  And share the warmth of its rays.
Spring is on its way. Never fear
  The cold winds of the winter days.

Mary An Lynn
BECAUSE . . . I LOVE YOU

To Jim Miner, the one who started it all. Love always, "Me."

The day had started cool & cloudy.
There were smiling faces and early morning laughter, but it soon became afternoon, a cool sunny afternoon, most of the happy smiling faces had ended including mine.
I have lost the biggest part of my life,
I am beginning to realize it, but don't want to believe it.
You made me laugh and you made me smile, but now that you are gone life is a cold dark world of hell.
You made my life worth living and helping me along the way
You helped me discover things about myself I never knew before.
I knew I was someone who existed when I was around you.
I tried to make you happy I really did!
I wanted to be what you wanted me to be, but I guess I just didn't qualify.
I'm sorry I scared you away. I guess I tried too hard
I won't ever quit loving you, but if you'll be happier without me,
I'll leave.
Without your love and caring for me there are no reasons left for me to live.
I just want you to know that I'll always be there for you anytime that you need a friend . . .
Because . . .
I love you!

Patricia L Marino
A PRAYER FOR MY LOVED ONE
May God watch over you while we're apart
And guide you along as new days start,
From the breaking of day when you open your eyes,
'Til again on the pillow your weary head lies.

May He give you the strength to face all your trials,
And the Heaven-sent health to walk many miles;
May He bless every deed that your loving hands do,
And give joy and success throughout life to you.

God knows that the love between us is dear,
And though miles come between us,
He keeps us near.
May He bless you and keep you and one day, too,
Let me in Heaven be always with you.

Ranza Devereaux
A SPECIAL PLACE
Home is such a special place
  in most of our hearts . . .
With loved ones to surround us
  it's where the family starts.

Home is what we make it
  each member has a share . . .
To prove to one another
  how much they really care.

Home should mean our happiness
  with the family gathered round . . .
A place of joy and gladness
  where true love should abound.

Home becomes our refuge when
  living we find hard . . .
Gathering loved ones about us
  to seek our help from God.

It matters not how humble
  the home may really be . . .
Home is second best to God
  designed for you and me.

Dianne M Cottone
SHATTERED VISION
As I stand in my room, I stare blindly into
The reflection I see in the mirror.
Alone stands a woman. Is she happy or sad?
The vision is not quite that clear.

I blink with the hopes of getting a much better look,
And see that this woman does smile.
I stand wondering just what her smile can mean,
So I stare in the mirror for awhile.

In just a short time, a man walks into the scene,
And brings himself right to her side.
With no words at all, they look at each other,
As their smiles extend heart-felt pride.

What a beautiful pair these two people did make,
Chasing happiness to higher ground.
Through each other's bright smiles are a Lifetime of thoughts.
No exchanging of words to be found.

Their future interpreted simply by eyesight,
Of smiles telling tales of a Love.
Down one road through eternity the couple shall roam,
Spending days of which dreams are made of.

While I witness this scene with such warmth in my heart,
I notice the smiles disappear.
The man at her side, his reflection is fading,
The woman is left in despair.

As I stand in my room, I stare clearly into
The reflection I see in the mirror.
Alone stands a woman, who is very sad.
My own face becomes wet from the flow of her tears.

Gaye Lowrance
SONG OF RICHES
Horizon on fire!
  A lightning's bolt.
A pet's affection.
  The newborn colt.

Belly's full,
  Clothes to wear.
Parents to love me,
  Always there.

Teachers taught me,
  Friends did, too.
Knew pain and sorrow,
  But made it through.

What is life
  without its glitches?
I'll sing instead
  A song of riches.

Sunrise
  always reminds me to.

Dorinda (Dinky) Stone
THE WOES OF A SHUT-IN
A Shut-In gets lonely as everyone knows,
Things of the past only add to their woes.
They think of the day they were Husband and Wife,
And all the joys they shared through their life.
When hand-in-hand they walked in the park,
And heard the sweet song of a Meadowlark.
Now they sit all alone their chair,
Hoping a friend might visit them there.
They pray every day for the "Spiritual Lift,"
Knowing some day God will send them that "Gift."
There will be no more loneliness, sorrow or cares,
When the "Good Lord" has heard and answered their Prayers.

James Fox
THE SILENCE WAS DEAFENING

To a real Friendly Girl.

In our silent confrontation
Not a word was spoke.
I looked at you,
You looked at me.
As for all the people around us,
It must have made for a joke.
But as for me, I think all my dreams
Over before they started,
Just went up in smoke.

Thomas Staab
ADULTHOOD
  Being an adult means
putting down the dreams of those
  who reach for the stars;
Can't have them flying high
  when you're stuck on the ground.
keep up the old;
  kill the new.
keep 'em stoned and dreary
  while their lives go by and
only wake them up in time to see them die.
  Nail their feet to the ground
so they can't join the birds in the sky.
  Don't let them change things,
  that just won't do
'Cause if things get better, then
they'll have done more than you.
  Douse the fire that burns bright
  in their eyes,
Lest they burn the ropes binding the world.
  Call them "child" and put them down,
just as those before did to you.
  Keep the cycle going
until the world ends.
  Then we can all weep together
When we think of what could have been.

Richard A Milroy Sr

Richard A Milroy Sr
IMMORTAL GREATNESS

Dedicated to NAMFONOS INCORPORATED and perpetual life.

We live our Lives, both Good and Bad
  then comes the Day when All are sad
to Leave behind That which Was ours
  to Travel through Eternities Hours.

If Now we live our Life on Earth,
  Enlarge our Number with each New Birth,
and increase Strength of Mind and Spirit,
  when Change comes we will not Fear it.

As We in Number and Spirit grow
  the Universe too is Making a show,
and ever Growing as only Truth knows how
  to Make a Place for Each to Plow.

We often think that We are not much
  when compared with Raindrops and such,
but Life and Death, and Fun and Sorrow
  become a Part of the Eternal Power.

Tonya Mills
CLOSE YOUR EYES
Close your eyes
and dream with me
only to awaken
by what we cannot see

Keep me close
but far away
tell me things
you would never say

Be my guide
yet, let me lead
give me nothing I want
except all that I need

Teach me things
I've never learned
care for me

but don't be concerned

Share with me
in a selfish way
let's make memories
that last only a day

It's all so real
we're not what we seem
so open your eyes
because WE were only a dream

Kathlyn Crandall
VOLUNTARY SELF-FULFILLMENT
I envision myself at the edge of a precipice.
Fear is coursing through my veins.
Yet there is no other choice.
I have prepared them, though they know not.
I am ready to slip away from my soul.
The living hurts too much.
My heart is broken, that I cannot deny myself
This release.
And for what will never be.
But this release is divine, and the desperation is painful beyond bearing.
Death is empty,
But my soul has been filled!

Milton V Moore
SMALL
How small we are—
Observers of all, participating in none.
Caught between dimensions, alone—the anxious one.
Blackness, brightness, the only change.
Eyewitness, to infinity, galaxies in range.
Cold pierced by heat, energies beyond measure.
Behold, the universe—Man searching for treasure.

Judith Cox Phillips
HER SILENT WORLD
Silence fills the young woman's life—
Yet her soft dark eyes never reflect sadness, grief or strife
For the hearing world that she's never known,
Or for the words that she's never spoken.

Her world is quiet—she'll never hear
Nightingales singing or shouts of cheer—
Music, laughter, the ocean's roar,
Or the flapping of wings as the sea gulls soar.

Through her eyes she captures her silent world
A kaleidoscope of colors softly swirled.
Her delicate hands reach out to her lover
Who loves her completely—he could love no other.

The silent tears that streak their cheeks,
Are universal in their speech.
And their bodies intertwined in tender embrace
Help her to win the silent race.

Connie Vainavicz
DELINQUENT
Deep within my soul
lies truth
unable to surface beyond
the confines of doubt.

Afraid to be uniquely me
I hide behind avid sadness.

Watching my ice sculptures
melt into a puddle of nothing.

Gil Horn
HEARTBREAK AND BRUTALITY
When I was just a little boy
Placed in a foster home,
I learned that there are people
With hearts as cold as stone.

Hard work topped the menu.
Strict discipline was next.
Learn to hate your fellow man
Was their favorite text.

And when I broke the rules
Which I did from time to time,
They would take me out behind the barn
And tie me to a pine.

The whisper of the buggy whip
Made my innards ball up tight.
And then the spell was broken
When I felt its stinging bite.

I was treated like a criminal,
Harsher than full-grown men
But the only crime I was guilty of
Was being orphaned at age ten.

Jeffrey W Cahoon
I HAVE STOOD ON THIS CORNER BEFORE
I have stood
on this corner
before

What a town
was this

But what of friends
that have gone
before

What of feelings
that have gone
before

I have stood
on this corner
before

What is said
is true
one can never
go back

Melissa Schwartz
LIVING UP TO OTHERS' STANDARDS
not good enough
never satisfied
disappointed

lose touch
your feelings
dreams
yourself

where are you
who are you
why

Stefan Schumacher
MY SOCIETY
I see 'em on the television
And in our magazines,
I know it's just a plot
To infiltrate our dreams.
The cover girls and pin-up boys
Are always on my mind,
I know they are ideal
I see 'em all the time.
What's wrong with me,
Who am I to blame?
Each time I look into the glass
I turn away in shame.
It must be subliminal
A grotesque conspiracy,
Why else would I want to live
As someone besides me?

Prince William McDonald
TERRORISM

I dedicate this poem to the true mothers and the true fathers of the world. God bless them—and death for the terrorists.

I

Abortion the worst act of the real terrorism The criminals are looking to be recognized and paid with money for their criminal actions are asking freedom to destroy and kill innocent human victims of the sadistic action of the terrorists with Ph.D.'s in clinics, hospitals, barns and private homes.

II

Criminals with degrees and titles to murder legally, they want to operate all over the world
Prostitution, degeneration and exploitation
Professional bastards with medical degrees
Cooked like the eggs "more cooked harder they become"
No scruples to butcher innocent babes
The kind of Christ sellers evil beasts

III

Satanic pestilence over the world
Bringing clouds of darkness without light
Suffocating the negligence of hybrid authority
They exploit the sentence "We the people"
Without meaning in this crowd of criminals
With sick minds with any hope to change
Contemporary decease without cure or salvation
They hate God, priests and themselves wild beasts
Baby cry baby the terrorists are loose and with the law.

Virginia Lane Beattie
PASSER-BY IN TUSCANY
Along a country road I went
On a day dark with autumn hint;
The olive trees so gaunt stood guard
Gnarled against sky in upturned sod—
Their silhouette grotesque and gray
Softened by mounds of brownish hay.
Yellow green vineyards growing nearby
Continued on to terraces high.
Clusters of homes caught by a hill
Looked ancient of days and undisturbed still.
All sights before me seemed to rise,
And though diminishing in size,
Bespoke of Italy rising too—
Keeping the old to create anew;
And cypress trees like hands uplifted
Prayed even in these times unsifted.
On a country road I passed by
And learned what will live and never die.

Angela Eisinger
I AM ONLY ME
Oh Lord, take what's left of me.
If I appear as an aging flower,
Take my old, withering petals,
And make me beautiful again.
If I appear as a sunken ship,
Take my old weakened frame,
And make me sailworthy again.
If I appear as a crude rock,
Take me in my ugly form,
And polish me into a gem.
But I, I am only me.
A used, dilapidating body
With a filthy, unclean spirit.
Show your mercy unto me.
Make me clean and pure again,
Make me happy and beautiful,
Make me hungry for knowledge and truth,
Make me a lamb in your flock.
Oh Lord, take what's left of me,
forever.

Cathy Downey
PUSH COMES TO SHOVE
This world has come a long way, in a very short time.
Nothing short of amazing, we've turned on a dime!

But tell me my friend, with walls coming down around us,
Our private and public wars coming to an end,
when push comes to shove, will we be able to put our guns down?

It's an exciting time for everyone.
Just think what these changes mean,
freedom for you,
a sigh of relief for me.

But tell me my friend, will freedom
to do as you choose
be enough for you?
Will peace be enough for me?
When push comes to shove, will we be able to put our guns down?

Can we forsake our hate?
Can we see beyond our own needs?
Can we get past our own greed?
And when push comes to shove, will we really want to lay our guns down?

Ian Craig
YHWH (YAHWEH)

In memory of William A. Craig, and Winifred Amy Hahn, and dedicated to Stuart Craig, Jr., David Long, Amy Painter, and Helen W. Craig.

Whenever you're feeling lonely,
or if you're down and out.
The whole world seems against you,
and your mind is full of doubts.
Just remember what you're made of,
and keep your faith in Him.
Utilize all God's wisdom,
to do the things you feel are right.
Then you, my fine, fair, honest child,
shall surely see the light.

Vera M Schultz
MY SISTER
My sister left her house today
—I didn't want her to
She went to live in an old folk's home
It seemed the thing to do.

She took her mirrored dresser
—I remember when 'twas new—
Her creaky old oak rocking chair
And a hanging plate in blue.
I'll miss the cheery phone calls

We shared on dreary days
I'll miss the bowl of gumdrops
She kept in a certain place

Yes, she took her mirrored dresser
Her chair and the plate so blue.
What she doesn't know is that she took
The "heart" out of me too.

Kimberly Walsh
THE HIDDEN

To my father and best friend Sally. You are both the Hidden in my life. Also to all of the McPhersons. It's been real.

My dreams have burned to ashes
and now your smiles have turned to tears.
It never seemed that you could contribute
so much sadness to me.
Would you surrender to my fears.
Before the day is over my heart will be lost forever.
As I paint myself all you see
is a lonely portrait.
To hide all of the love away
never to feel how happy you are.
The pain that should only come from tragedy
comes from you instead.
Tears will fall from the pain and hurt
though that will never matter.
You are the hidden source behind the pain.
Then again do you or will you ever care,
I THINK NOT

Betty Thompson
METAMORPHOSIS
As I sat looking out the window,
I remembered the encumbrance of despair.
As I sat awhile longer, glancing around the wall,
Something caught my glance.
It emanated itself into my mind.
My thoughts and emotions became bared
To all who dared to stare.
The room became enamored of memories
That entrenched my soul.
The realism of that fleeting thought
Held my mind in suspension,
And allowed me to become a metaphysics
Of this earthly body and to transfer
My soul's destiny.

Lola Corning
WEAVING SNOWFLAKES
Santa's little elf men are weaving in the sky,
To make a snowflake carpet for Santa as he stops by.
Santa and his reindeer will make an evening call
To find a snowflake carpet, made as the snowflakes fall.
Sleigh bells ringing, happy and gay,
ring, ring, ring, ring.
Ringing as Santa speeds away.
Elf men weaving all through the night,
With clouds for their shuttles, aned looms of stars so bright.
Children will be sleeping, while
Santa in his sleigh,
Comes to bring our darlings, a happy Christmas day.

Keith Myers
IMAGE OF PAIN
I cannot imagine
The pain of seeing
My son for the last time,
Of knowing that Death
Waits, impatient,
Or that this yellow violet
Sunset
Is the last on earth
With you, my love.

This cancer,
Oh! Pain of life's dwindling
Flame
Of a fire that burns
In my soul.

End it, oh sweet Death!
So that I may from
Heaven
Be each sunrise warm,
And have life after life,
New.
Imagine, my love,
I'll wait for you.

Denise D Carter
ETERNITY

This is dedicated to my loving husband, Steve, and our beautiful children, Victor and Codie.

Eternity, if ongoing forever,
Until the end of time.

It is the ceaseless void
That awaits us all.

Forever there, not very far away,
Just there.

Waiting, watching, and wondering,
When someone else will enter.

Asking "Why don't they hurry up?"
But it is okay,

I'll be here FOREVER.

ETERNITY

Kelly B Grace
CHILDREN, OUR FUTURE

To Daddy, for you, your daughter.

The time is now to make a change for tomorrow.
Let's start the healing and end the sorrow.
These babies need to know,
there's a brighter day beyond the rainbow.
They need to see,
there are those who care for them dear-ly.
Who want the very best for them;
because they're as precious as gems.
Oh! How I pray, that you hear what I say.
We need to do our part;
to ensure they have a place in this world's heart.
So let's act our age, let's be mature,
Because these are our CHILDREN, OUR FUTURE

Lori Jean Cipriano
TIRED OF BEING THE FOOL
Getting by week to week
Wishing for more than a glance of you
Though afraid of what you'd say
I kept it deep inside
The love that quickly grew
The innocent passion
That longing to hold you tight
But now what good does it do
If I can't have you by my side
Just when I thought you were
The man of my dreams
Looking at the two of you, I realize
You are not what you seem
Though to start again
Turn my love off and on
Find another man
And in the end
Be the fool all over again
No—I just won't risk my heart again

Charles Hammond

Charles Hammond
I DON'T KNOW WHY A MAN GOES TO WAR

The lyric of a song "I Don't Know Why a Man Goes to War."

I DON'T KNOW WHY A MAN GOES TO WAR
I only know that he goes
He may not know what the fighting's for
He marches off to the foes

Maybe an echo of long ago
When men were daring or dead
Urges him on as he reaches the foe
Where other men were led

To his lips comes a battle cry, forcing him on
With a curse on to kill and to hate
And he vows he will strike until victory's won
To the hell of a glorious fate

For a day and a year and a decade he roars
"I'll crush and I'll kill and I'll maim"
For what man values most, man ever destroys
Till at last he goes home with the lame

He passes the trees he uprooted and tore
He passes the lives he has shattered
And mem'ry plays tricks and he wonders of yore
Why vic'try and conquering mattered

From the beginning of time
No matter how often he kills
What death he may call sublime
To live forever, he wills

For all man born of woman will verily know
Ever since the world has begun
There is nothing so great for him or his foe
As the glory of seeing the sun

I Don't Know Why a man goes to war
I only know that he goes.

Betty Lichtenstein
LIFE
I planted a tree—this is so important to me
Long ago I was told—by a woman who was old
That one day I would rise and really see a leaf
Really feel the warmth of spring—really hear a birdie sing
I listened patiently—I smiled indulgently
So silly but she was old—and that was so long ago.

I arose one day—and saw children play
I saw a weed, a bud, and grass—I saw cracks in the streets and taxis pass
I told a lass as I was told so long ago
She listened patiently—she smiled indulgently
Now I know—this is the way the cycle of life must go
Years and understanding can never meet.

I walk in footsteps engraven deep with age—footsteps with a tale we cannot presage
Each footstep is the same for all eternity—yet different from each other for all infinity—
My tree and I have travelled far together
I am so tired and very sad—yet one more journey must still be had
My heart is heavy and full of grief—my stay on earth was all too brief
Now I join my ancestors in their march

Nathaniel Connors
PASTURE
As I sit it comes to thought
Time to write about what's not,
Peace and Joy and Good things all
A baby walks but first it falls.

Oh how fun it seems to be
Engulfed in my simplicity,
That soon the land I call my home
Will lose the lands I love to roam.

As age is true it is a fact
I need to polish up my act,
How they lie about what's real
Oh the many who've missed a meal.

But things are good, well good for now
Let's join the herd we are but cows,
And soon the grass we love to feed
Will turn to waste a wealth of weeds.

Tonya M Cahoon
ETERNALLY YOURS
Like a wreath of thorny vine,
is your hand clutching mine:

For with one touch my heart doth break
and all the earth's land doth shake;

One stinging touch; that piercing pain,
the crimson blood shall flow again.

And with one breath, (the last to take),
one final wish I shall make . . .

To my love who feels this too,
who cries out my name—knows not

what to do:

Glorious death has brought me new life,
Know of my happiness and forget of your strife.

And one of these days in the trickle of rain,
you'll feel me in your arms again.

Craig Fender
SANITY IS NOT
Sanity is Not.
It is biological.

Black is White,
and Logic is Illogical.

Crusades and Jihads are the sane man's lies.
As acid rain weeps, so will your Monoxide skies.

To strike at the other cheek is the sane man's way,
Witness the guns with which your sane children play.

The Almighty isn't and technology plays his part.
No emotions phase your heart of hearts.

Unearthly cries of mercy you choose not to hear.
What it is your questing for remains unclear.

Your crusade for Sanity has left you many dead.
Can you not see that sanity is a Grail in your head.

Sr M Dolorine Marthaller
THE MYSTIC SCENT

I dedicate "The Mystic Scent" to my twin sister Jean who died a victim of cancer.

'Twas Mary's rose
They crushed against the Tree
And thus was spread
rich perfume
far and wide.

So now
where'er that Mystic Scent
may be
There, too,
another heart
is crucified.

Willie Hudson
A TOUCH OF MAGIC

Dedicated to the love of my life, Jennifer L. Walsh.

Raindrops cascade across the midnight sky
Visions of a lifetime fills your eyes

A Touch of Magic allows you to shine
It casts out the pain burned in your mind

You feel the beauty within your heart
It warms your soul like a poison dart

The radiant stars glisten like gold
It lures you in and then takes hold

An eternity of joy is flowing inside
The night all cools, your fears have died

You raise your hands to the darkness above
As it showers you with the heavens love
Cleansed of your troubles, as pure as the dove

Betty Jane Burge
THOUGHTS OF YOU
O Lord, I awoke this morning
With thoughts of You,
Of how You kept watch o'er me
The whole night through.
Now I'm refreshed,
Filled with Your love,
Ready and waiting for what
You've planned from above.
Your Presence I feel
With power and peace of mind,
I shall go through each moment
With strength undefined;
I shall not worry or be set affright,
Knowing You will be with me
As my guiding Light.

Betty Jane Burge
FOR THEM YOU DIED
Lord, I hear you by my side
All through the night and day,
And I feel your Presence everywhere
Especially when I kneel and pray.

Your love abounds o'er all the globe
And yet we ignore your love and care,
Help us see with spiritual eyes
How your life with ours we share.

Lord, teach us to love our fellowmen
And be humble, not charged with pride,
But to carry others' crosses too,
And let them know for them you died!

joyce m bigley
MESSAGES OF LOVE
All I ever need
is to hear your gentle voice
to know you're doing well

All I ever need
is to see your loving smile
to turn my sadness to joy

All I ever need
is your tender touch
to reassure my feelings

All I ever need
is your sincere concern
to show you still care

All I ever need
is to hear you say, "I love you"
to make my life complete

All you ever need
is to hear me say, "I love you"
to fulfill a promise of a lifetime together.

Mary Jennison McAuliffe
SPRING ART—FORM
Before the Spring leaves appear
The treetops do their dance—
See how they hula
To the left and right
In their grass-like skirts—
Hawaiian style!

The music changes
And to a Spanish tempo
The treetops dip and sway
To the tune of the dry leaves castanets
Twirling on the ground!
All is music and dance—
The birds singing their love calls,
The harmony of sunshine,
Clear blue skies
And sparkling, dancing, rippling waters!

Judith Lynne Beale Hilliard
WEDDING POEM

To John and Lisa Hilliard, October 7, 1989.

A new day is launching,
Sunrise on the lighthouse,
Standing majestic and grand,
On cliff, surrounded by sea.
Lapping water, sounding serene,
As the tide promenades in;
Two keepers of the Light.

Hands embraced, faces toward sky,
A celebration of this moment.
Gulls clamor, distant ship horns,
Acclaim this exalted union.
Warmth, security, tranquility,
Silently penetrate the breeze;
A partnership, preserved in time.

Inaugurate pilgrimage through life,
Voyage of infinite discovery.
The lighthouse requires vigilance,
The beacon does not shine alone.
Reaching as one, working, sharing;
A partnership preserved in time;
Two keepers of the Light.

Cheryl Lee
INNER PEACE
May you find the inner peace,
That only love can summon within.
May your pain be more at ease,
If love's great power crushes in.

To feel both love and its pain.
Is to reach into the depths of hell.
Even when we utter, "Ne'er again."
We desire once again its spell.

For the heaven within is love.
And our hell is pain from desire.
Purgatory is not below or above,
But our present existence of fire.

So when our souls cry out for more,
And our bodies do crave and ache.
When do we then relinquish our store,
To the Man for "mine soul doeth take?"

Cheryl Lee
SHE
She stared through me; but did not see.
She seemed alive; but did not breathe.
She appeared to move; but with a float.
She reached for me, hands on my throat.

My heart now pounds, out of my chest.
I can't control my fear—I sweat.
I was to die; but not like this,
And then she gave me a tender kiss.

Awake you fool! It's only a dream.
She came in darkness, to hear you scream.
You killed her when, she loved you most.
Awake you fool! 'Twas only her ghost.

Evelyn Richie
YESTERDAY . . . TODAY
It's Sunday. Folks will be coming at two, Dad.
Baked some cookies and we'll have tea
Visit a bit and laugh together and
Sarah might play the piano for me.
(they don't come . . . to visit . . . any more)

We'll talk politics some and tell a few jokes.
What book are you reading, Sam?
Admire the quilt that's being stitched up
Another cookie? Yes, thank you, ma'am.
It's time to part, there's a lot more to say
But never you mind, they'll be here another day.
(they don't come . . . to visit . . . any more)

In the wink of an eye, we grew older.
Dad passed on.
Too busy, they say.
Kids have sports things to do
And we can't miss the show on TV.
It's Sunday now
And the cookies are baked
But they don't come . . . to visit . . . any more.

Winifred T Manion
PUSSY WILLOW

To my children, who give me constant encouragement and inspiration.

Soft and furry kitten
Blinking at the sun,
How smugly you are sitting there,
Another battle have you won?

Resting on your pillow
In the warm air gently toasting,
Another winter have you beaten,
Is that of what you're boasting?

Well, I'm so glad to see you,
You really don't know how,
For Spring's not only on its way,
It's come! It's here and now.

Ian Jorsling
FATE

To M.N. with all my prayers and love.

Blow, blow, blowing is fate . . .
On the whispers of the wind . . .
Until it reaches its chosen one . . .
It stops and hugs you . . .
Sometimes sweetly, sometimes bitterly . . .

Go, go, going . . .
It's gone and the chosen with it . . .
If so desires . . .
Look, look, looking for its next task . . .
Until time hires . . .
When and where it will stop . . .
Only God knows . . .
For He is master of it all . . .
That's life. Maybe.
That's fate. Surely.

Ian Jorsling
DECEMBER
De festive season
De Lord's birthday
De gifts, De joys
De happy little girls and boys
De brightly lit trees
De falling snows
December
Everyone knows.

Lawrence M Wolfe
NEVER WANT TO LOSE YOU
I hope it's not the end
But it might be very near.
However, with me being alone to contend;
With all my hidden and deepest fears.

I've been having a lot to think about you;
Mostly, I think about the love we shared.

Because you know I really love you, I do.
And that we could and still make the perfect pair.

The decision is totally up to you;
To whom you're going to choose.
I know you'll make the decision, so;
With that I say that; I never want to lose you.

D B Priestley
THE OLD CHECKERED APRON
Remember- That old checkered apron on the nail by the door?
That old checkered apron, the one Granny wore.
Careworn it was, as a Prophet of old.
The planning and caring, the tale it told.
When she was young just starting her life,
Visions of grandeur, a beautiful wife.
A gift she received from a friend quite poor
Was a new checkered apron like the one by the door.
As the years passed by and she was known far and wide
By that old checkered apron, she wore with such pride.
Granny has passed on to that beautiful shore,
But left us her apron on the nail by the door.

D B Priestley
GHOST TOWN
The valley is lonely, the winds never cease,
Only rock and sand, where once were trees.
Little remains to say they were here,
A few dim stones placed by someone dear.
Weathered and torn, by storms through the years
The few walls reflect the toil and fears
Of those who were here in time long past,
Casting their lot with man will not last.
Whispering so softly, the land seems to say
All this is mine please go on your way.

Becky Wilson Byers
GONE AWAY
Alone again, one more time.
This hill has gotten harder to climb.
Waiting and wondering, where's he now.
Never again, each time I vow.
Every frustration building inside
My wants and wishes once more denied.
Why doesn't he love me as once before?
Seems I love him even more.
Total confusion fills my mind.
Unanswered questions are all I find.
Can't he realize my need for him?
Or has his love for me grown cold and dim?
Useless to say anything at all,
No explanations, not even a call.
He used to care, what's gone wrong?
So out of place, I no longer belong.
Did his love for me just simply die?
Dare I question his reason why?
Maybe he will understand love some day,
But by then, I'll have gone away.

Eunice Chae
O YOUNG HEARTS
That magical word, your beautiful name
You are to me, water to a dry, malnourished plant.
Nonchalance, my mask, fills my presence
but inside a drum is beating faster . . .
JOY when we casually touch
You watch—not aware I—the same
Exploring our minds, feelings, hearts—
A baby opening its eyes to the world around
Don't you remember? We were friends once . . . long, long ago.
Why do we hold back? We would be in perfect tune, you and I
But instead; your loved one still clings on.
Must we stay this way—in an agonizing fury of frustration,
Admiration, and hidden attraction?
—CONFLICTING FORCES—
The wave of longing to be with you is on verge of total absurdity
eyes closed to outstretched hands;
waiting only for your own

Ethel Lukawecki
MY SON
We live in a wonderful world—
That world of ours Today.
We should be thankful for what we have,
But many don't see it that way.

Look into the eyes of a little boy;
They sparkle and shine like a light.
He makes believe in a world of his own
And we love him with all of our might.
There is one that I know—with a heart full of love
Who has brought only comfort and joy
He may have seemed mischievous and bad at times—
But then—stop and think—he was only "A Boy."

As the years went by—that "little boy" grew—
And was soon to become a man.
He reached out, wanting love and respect,
But no need now—to be led by the hand.

He now has his own life and others who care,
But to me—he is second to none.
There is no one more dear or loved as much—
Yes, you guessed it—"My Son."

John Laurie Smardon
DOLLARS AND SENSE
Some people save dollars, some people save cents,
Put together they make up dollars and sense,
Maybe dollars and cents come easily to you,
A lifetime satisfaction gained from whatever you do.

Then, my friend, you possess plain common sense,
Your ingenuity brought you dollars and cents,
The senior era a joy to behold,
Your golden years a treasury of gold.

What if your lifetime was largely misspent,
You wonder forever where every cent went,
No dollars for you in the neighborhood bank,
For receipts in your bankbook show a total of blank.

Spending money is like turning on the tap,
Dollars and cents flowing like water, you sap,
Unable to put a stop to your spending,
You worsened the situation by excessive lending.

The moral you see in this poem of mine,
Incidentally all lines intentionally rhyme,
To make a success of dollars and cents,
They must be carefully integrated with much common sense.

Suzanne Hastings
A NEVER ENDING JOURNEY

This is dedicated to the one I love, who believed in me and helped me realize that it's never too late to change.

The demon is calling my name:

"Come my frightened child, please come with me,
I'll take you down where hell will set you free.

No more worries and no more fear,
All the painful memories will soon disappear.
There's no need to run, no need to hide
So come with me and I'll take you for a ride.

A never ending journey.

Now that you've tried me, it'll never be the same,
You've trapped now within me
playing my deadly game.
I've killed your dreams and destroyed your feelings
I've put your life through hell
that left behind numerous beatings.

Death will come quickly,
it will be closing in soon
You can't escape me now, I give you no room.
I made you believe I was well worth the wait,
but no one can save you now,
because now is too late!"

Richard B Juliani
PLEASE LIE THEE DOWN, MY LOVE, TO REST
Please come and lie upon my bed
and place thy head upon my chest.
Then together we shall lie and rest
both hand in hand, and breast to breast.

There we shall place aside our thoughts
and pretend that all the world is naught.
We'll find true love that ere we've sought
and one be found where two are lost.

So when sweet passion makes its play
and strength, like dust, is swept away.
When wants, are needs, and must have say
I'll take you love, then there we'll lay.

Please come and lie upon my bed.
I'll be thy love, thou be my breath
and all be yours till nothing's left
only lie thee down, my love, to rest.

Kulbir Singh Bhalla
SHE KNOCKS THEM OUT!
Women will put men in a trance
Whenever they can get a chance.
Monica has several charms
But I don't think she ever harms.
Everyday she knocks people out,
Five to ten without a doubt.
Now she has become quite a pro,
Which even the hospitals know!
She very smilingly gives something
Which makes you forget everything.
In fact, you lose all your senses;
You are left with no defenses.
Now don't you curse this noble soul;
To serve all mankind is her goal.
She's not a demonologist
But an anesthesiologist!

Aaron Ray
O WHAT HAVE THEY DONE?
O what have they done,
to our lovely daughter Leannette?
Pastor Sly Wun from Little Genesee she met!
Who introduced her,
to Dastardly Coward from Forestville yet!!
They orchestrated a deed so foul,
that her mother is stunned beyond measure!!
And the father is dazed,
as he has lost his precious treasure!!
For they have brainwashed her
and taken her for their own pleasure!!
Dastardly Coward has taught her,
to dishonor her parents it would

appear!
And she no longer desires to be around,
the ones who love her so dear!!
Anguish and sorrow is breaking their hearts
and they've shed many a tear!!
O WHAT HAVE THEY DONE,
TO OUR LOVELY DAUGHTER
LEANNETTE???

Ronald A Fegley
ARE YOU THE RABBLE??
Away with HIM!, Away with HIM!
CRUCIFY HIM!! CRUCIFY HIM!!
The RABBLE cried, for they wist not that He was,
Jesus of Nazereth, King of the UNIVERSE!!
In their fury they mocked HIM!!
struck HIM!!
And spit upon HIM!!
And as their foul and evil deeds were perpetuated,
They cast upon Him a crown of thorns!!
And railed upon Him!! if thou be the Son of God???
Come down from the cross, then we'll believe thee!!
The rabble cried!!! for they wist not, that He was,
Jesus of Nazereth, King of the Universe!!!!
Now may I ask of you dear one!!
Are you the rabble??

Joan Nepveaux Brown
MY MOTHER

This poem is dedicated to my mother Nellie Ledet Nepveaux with love.

I'll never forget my mother, there could never be no other.
She tried to keep us from all harm, I still can feel her loving arms.
I miss the twinkle in her eyes when she knew we told a lie.
My father went away, but Mother wanted to stay.
She raised us by herself and didn't depend on anyone else.
Now she's gone to her rest and all I can do is my best.
Wish we had her back again so we'd have more time to spend.
I miss her so very much, I miss her gentle touch.
If you still have your mother, treat her as no other.
For one day she'll be gone and you'll feel all alone.

D M Lewis
OUTDOORS
While walking alone the pathway
Breathing the fresh air from blowing winds
Looking at different kinds of trees
Swaying against the breeze
Oh! What a glorious sight to see
Birds cheeping their sounds while
On the ground or in the trees
Oh! What a wonderful sound to hear
While strolling outdoors

Joan E Hirak
THE DRY DRUNK
What do you say is a Dry Drunk
You've never heard of such a thing
If someone is no longer drinking
What in Heaven's name are you thinking

Well let me tell you it is true, and it's the worst thing to go through
Sure you're sober, clean and dry, but life is still passing you by

Instead of filling your days with Joy, in the new life you've made
You stay in the same old rut, something's bothering you, but what?

I can tell you just what's wrong,
Peace and Serenity is what you need
Try to do for others at least one good deed

Join a group with people who care
People who know, people who have been there
Open your eyes and open your heart
It's only then can you begin to care

REbuild your life the best you can
With family and friend, they'll give you a helping hand
Love and Happiness can be yours
You'll be surprised how much this cures

Become involved as much as you can
Take each day and make a new plan
Live one day at a time, what you did was not a crime

Joan E Hirak
THE WISH
If I could have just one Wish, I know exactly what I'd say
Dear Lord above could I please see my Mom and Dad for just one day?

It's been so long since they're both gone, there's just so much to say
I miss them both so very much, more than words can ever say

Why couldn't I have told them before
Just how much I loved them, how much I needed them more

Only when they were gone and then it was too late
Did I realize how much I'd hurt them, God what a twist of Fate

If only I could hold them for just one more time
To feel their warmth and their Love, and for them to finally feel mine

Oh Dad and Mom I miss you so, I wish to God you didn't have to go
But most of all I'm sorry for the years I wasted long before

If only we could spend one day I'd try to explain in everyway
How much I've changed, how I've grown, if only before I would have known

Don't waste a precious moment, share each and every day
Because once they're gone there's no one to hear you say
"I Love you Mom, I Love you Dad,"
I'm sorry for the times I made you sad

If I can't have this special wish, I can only hope and pray
That God will let them know some way
How much I Love and miss them with each and every passing day.

Joan E Hirak
THE ESCAPE
You sit and stare and wonder where do I go from here?
Your spirit is broken, your life is a mess
Maybe ending it all would be the best

You try to figure out a way to end the misery you face each day
Not to have to awake tomorrow, never to feel any more sorrow

Does anyone really care whether or not you're even there
Wouldn't they be better off if you were gone—out of their life?

You close your eyes and try to see just what the future for your family would be
You're not around to bring them down, but you can't seem to hear a sound

All you see is the heart you've caused
The tears and fears in their faces, wishing with you they could trade places

Thank God for this moment of seeing the future, it's not the picture I planned to see
Maybe it's not as bad as I thought, could the problem really be me?

I think it's time to look at the past and count the Blessings I have been given
Look at the way I have been living, taking from life and never really giving
Did I really try my best, if I did would life be such a mess?

Now it's time for me to change, my life can't be that hard to rearrange
I've got a lot of things to do, life is short—so why take it away
Thank you God, I'm ready to face another day

Lyn Shea
IN THIS LIFE
In this life, we long to grow
But we yearn to hang on,
And we fear to let go.
We search for love, we look to learn
We search for the fire that does not burn.
We weigh the risks, we fear the unknown
We dare to take a chance alone.
We face each day with its challenges and demands,
We seek experience, and make new friends.
We take a step, we learn to fall
And we wonder if we've grown at all.

Lyn Shea
FOR TOM
You took me by surprise
When I wasn't prepared to let anyone in,
And you waited so patiently
As I let my defenses crumble.
With you, I could be nothing but myself.
And you've made me feel as though I deserve to be
Treated the way you've treated me;
In my insecurity, you have loved me,
Even when I found it too difficult to love myself.
And I have found strength in all of the wonderful things
That you've brought into my life.
Still, you continue to give of yourself
And you ask only that I be happy in return.
Defenslessly, and joyfully, I realize
That my life would be incomplete without you,
And my only wish is that I can give to you
All of the happiness that you so truly deserve.
With you, I have discovered all of the colorful expressions of love,
While I was unaware that some of them even existed.
I love you more than I thought I could ever love anyone,
And you have become a part of me that I cannot live without.

Lisa G Sytek (Anderson)
REFLECTIONS
When we're born God implants in each of us special gifts that only we can bring to light.
Consider this—
Have you ever seen shells on a sandy beach identical to each other?
Or,
Two butterflies still, resting, their wings exactly marked?
Or, Perhaps,
The ripples of a thumbprint similar to any other?
Or, On a spring's day have you heard the singing of happy birds and noticed each song was different?
Like a potter who takes clay and molds it into a beautiful vessel. So, it is with us, that God places a sparkle in our heart that only we can make shine.
Let your light shine like a lone bright star in a dark sky whose glow never dies.

Nicole Goodwin
SAD BUT NOT MAD
You said you are leaving, not leaving this town,
but leaving my heart.
I guess you want to throw it all away
and every feeling I've had from the start.
I'll miss your warm tender care
every time I feel you are near.
Nothing can stop my feelings now
I'll never forget how it was from the start.
If you see me on the street, don't worry about my broken heart
Just keep on walking, walking in the dark.
I'm sure there will be others along the way
but I'll never forget my feeling from today!

Dustin Cosby
LIFE'S WORTH?
They say that a picture is worth a thousand words
But what's worth?
It's worth both living for
And dying for.
You get both compliments and insults
But can't live with one without the other
You may live your life in happiness
Or in pain,
So live your life to the fullest,
For you have a lot to gain.

Tim G Kelley
HAVE I SEEN YOU ONCE BEFORE?

To Jennifer—my dearest friend and inspiration in all that I achieve.

Have I seen you once before
In some other place or time
Or can there be a deeper reason
Why I need to make you mine
Take me by the hand; together we'll walk awhile
And I'll gaze into your gentle eyes
And, Jennifer Carly, I'm taken by your smile

It's more than the way you look
Or how you move when you walk
It goes far beyond the things you say
Though I love the way you talk
Can't you see it's your soul that's been driving me wild
And I love you for what dwells inside
And, Jennifer Carly, I'm taken by your style

It's even more than that, though
It's your essence of being
The comfortable way to make me feel
That's what keeps me believing
On life's roller coaster the two of us should ride
There's never been a feeling so right
And, Jennifer Carly, I want to be by your side

Donna Westina Gilligan
FROM ME

This poem is dedicated to our Higher Power and to twelve step programs for recovery everywhere.

I linger on and wonder why
Smiling outward, I want to cry.
Again the pains Reality reigns!
The way's been hard; my soul nearly lost;
I keep my thoughts toward my Lord on the cross.
For where once I dwelled and continued to stay,
From all others, myself hidden away,
Still thinking that I am—I can,
I played my tortured mind till the end.
With a glimmer of hope: there had to be another way!
Unconditional love and faith, Yes, I have that today!
Again the pains Reality reigns!
Joyous tho, my soul can grow!
Time is healing self-inflicted hurts,
Insights; amends still come in spurts,
I can welcome even those pains with relief,
For following comes a stronger belief.
Smiling outward, I want to cry
I linger on, now knowing why . . .
Old pains I feel on a new face I see,
The words of hope, of love, can now flow from me!

Rachel Smith
THE DREAM TREE
The dream tree is a place of love.
A place to go and dream.
To dream of love and romance
Or just to sing and dance.

When you're at the dream tree
Don't be shy.
If you have to do it,
Go ahead and cry.

The dream tree is a place to mend
All those broken hearts,
Or a place to go and
Get a fresh new start.

When you're at the dream tree
Look up at the sky.
Remember when you first knew love
Like the picture of a morning dove.

Liliana E Bathurst
WHAT A POET MAKES
Vivid imagination
Creative mind
Expressive words
That touch a chord
Eyes as windows
Of the heart and soul
Spirit that soars
Even when
The wind is no more
Most of all
"Feelings"
The poet's badge of honor

Donna J Peters
STAND TALL

To Karen, who is never out of reach.

He sits in solace
pondering the works of the day.
Weighing out decisions,
already made.
Rights and wrongs,
paths taken,
missing the joys of the sunset.
The colors in the sky,
surrounding him.
Living life with blinders,
picking out the lows.
Struggling,
on his own accord.
Ponder, dear sweet child,
but wonder of the stars.
Stretch out your fingers,
reach for the moon.
The problems of yesterday,
put them to rest.
Hold on to the new day,
dream of tomorrow.

Ernest M Collier
YOU ARE MY HEART

To my loving wife Sandy.

My love for you
I cannot hide
For it comes from my heart
Down deep inside
Sometimes we fuss as lovers do
But I feel our love
Is really true
No matter how much of these things
We find that we do
I know I'll never stop loving you
I knew from the start
We would never part
And you soon became
A piece of my heart

I love you

Kaye Desormeaux
RYAN'S LEGACY

To all of my family members who have encouraged me to write, especially my husband and my children.

No more sad goodbyes
Or sighs of sorrow;
Just tears to cry
With no days to borrow.

No more painful glances
From such hollow eyes;
No more innocent chances
Wearing smiles of disguise.

No more stories to tell
Or battles to win;
Just an endless trail
To be traveled again . . . .

Shawnya Calp
PUNK JUDGEMENT
Walking down an empty street,
Dust and gravel at your feet.
Eyes are peering from the panes,
Your blood is pulsing through your veins.
The eyes look scared, petrified,
Because your mohawk's one foot high.
Your black leather, combat boots,
They stash away their secret loots.
They've never seen such sight as this,
Walking through their town of bliss.
You're an intrusion on their land,
They will not lend a helping hand.
Secret whispers behind closed doors,
"The girls' black skirts, they look like whores."
Dressed in black the intruders came,
Eyes still peering from the panes.
You are judged just by look,
Judged by cover, not the book.

Angela Wallander
SMILE
A smile in any language, all
can understand,
No need interpret, 'tis the same
in any land.

A smile will show good will
to those of any race,
For one can't hate while there's
a smile upon his face.

A frown's unwelcome, for the
world needs not more woe;
But smiles enrich both reapers
and the ones who sow.

It doesn't cost a cent; its worth's
untold in wealth;
It brings good cheer to others
to the giver—health.

A merry heart like medicine
is well worthwhile;
I'll wipe the frown from off my
face and smile, smile, smile.

Angela Wallander
THE PRAYER OF FAITH
"The prayer of faith" means one
believes God's Word is true
And that the things He promised,
He will surely do.
For prayer is telling God what's
in one's heart and mind;
In Heaven 'twill be bound as
we on earth do bind.
So, then, by faith, confess in
prayer, the thing you wish were
true;
And God will hear your prayer
and bring it back to you.
For when we give Him thanks and
praise, and bless our store;
God sees our gratitude and
multiplies it more.
We know, by faith, it shall be
so—we trust in Him;
And, thus, we add unto our
prayer the word, "Amen."

Angela Wallander
GOD'S CREATION
God spoke the words, "Light be!"
He fashioned earth and sky,
The foamy oceans wide,
And purple mountains high.

God made the birds which sing,
The tall, green leafy tree,
The fragrant flowers fair,
And little honeybee.

God made the golden sun,
The gleaming stars above,
The moon to light the night,
But, then, He wanted love.

God formed a man of dust;
And breathed His life within,
An ever-living soul,
To love and worship Him.

Angela Wallander
THOUGHTS HAVE WINGS
I didn't say a word; now, truly,
did I not,
Or were there words involved in
things that I have thought?
For while I think, my mind is
talking back to me,
Yet, even though I cannot hear
it audibly.
Now, thoughts are really words with
power and great force,
And they'll come back to bless or
curse their root of source.
Then, I must watch what things my
mind is telling me,
As thoughts have wings—
for they return eventually.

Lucille C Schreiner
HAPPINESS
Happiness is a state of mind
It's not something you have to find
It's just being glad for one more day
Praying that God will guide our way
It's giving up thoughts of discontent
And counting our blessings as heaven sent
It's giving up wishing for things we have not
And making the best of whatever we've got
For it's by doing our best in everything we do
That we find real contentment and happiness too

Kari Clayton
SHATTERED DREAMS
Entering a World, world of Dreams
Full of ideas, I'd go to any extreme
Hoping for that, shooting for this.
Got great ambitions, a whole big list.

Started when I was young, kept on growing
Dreams of yesterday were just now showing.
My Daddy yelled and my momma slapped!

in my world, I took all this crap.

Now I took the chance, now I pay the price
I screamed out loud, but now I'm cold as ice.
Beaten to death, is why I scream
To tell all the world of my "Shattered Dreams!"

Barbara Bazoff
A NEW BEGINNING
When we first met I didn't pay attention to your name.
As the days passed I found myself stealing glances your way. I had to ask your name.

The girls at work, we talk. You heard. Then came the dreaded question. "What about the ring?" I drew in a breath, with pain came time to explain.

I was hurting, you saw through the pain, then came the note you wrote. I was confused. I looked to you for a signal of some kind, while you were on my mind. I asked you out, you accepted. It wasn't what I expected. I couldn't explain the way I felt, but when your arm went around me I started to melt.

I was scared. I couldn't explain the security I felt. As time went on and we were together, the pain eased. I wanted to say I need a hug please. You read my mind. Then came that hug! When you were gone I felt alone. I thought of you and I wasn't blue. Thank You!

Shelby G Walker
HINT OF LIFE
Life is full of ups and downs;
It goes by in leaps and bounds.

We struggle, we fall;
We sometimes even crawl.

It comes with no manual or guarantee;
It's simply over like a breeze.

When it's over and our journey done;
there is only a hint we ever begun.

Karla Woloshyn
COMMANDS IN MY DREAMS II (EXCERPT FROM TRIAD OF COMMANDS)

Dedicated to W. Irl Miller of Edmonton, Alberta, Canada.

Embrace the wind
Touch the breeze
Screen the rays
Chase the rainbow
Nail a song while being sung
Still a motion
Retrace the waves on the ocean
Hold a raindrop—intact—in your hand
Reroute a flying arrow
Sting a bee with its own sting
Scrape the scars from a broken heart . . .

Renée Kempf
THE SUN
The sun's external ray burst
through the fluffy clouds
like a pillow. Floating in water
Its reflections bounce off the
clouds and send out
bursting vivid layers of light
beyond self-existence.
Yet the imagination wonders
of how majestic the sun really is.
It startles us just to think
billions of miles away
there is such a powerful
thing just laying still
in the sky.

Renée Kempf
THE IMAGE OF A FRIEND

Dedicated to my best friend and Godmother, Sue.

When I look in the mirror
her eyes my eyes, her mouth mine.
Working together as one.
Standing together with strength
like the beat of a heart.
Yet, together never alone.
For two seconds alone is like
one grain of sand in a windstorm
Our hearts ready to take a
strike of a snake.
But knowing we're together the
Love gets stronger & stronger
each day

Sarah Flory
WHEN WILL WE BE TOGETHER
When the first sun sets,
When the last moon shines,
When will we be together?
When the last memory,
Shatters to the ground,
The clock keeps ticking time.
When the first tear falls,
When the last rose is gone,
When will we be together?
When the clouds beyond
Open up a light,
And the stars up in the heavens arising;
That is when we will be together.

Sarah Gottry
OVER THE HILL
The calm commotion
of blooming mountainsides and
silent weeping trees
crying colored tears of brown
rasp against the city walls.

Della F Griffee
DRIFTING APART
The house seems so empty
Each time her husband is gone.
She's left there with the children
But still feels all alone.
They require so much of her time
So she's in great demand.
My how she wishes he would stay around
Just to hold her hand.
But these days they've grown
So very far apart
What used to be there
Is now gone from her heart.
If only they had each realized
Many years ago
Maybe they wouldn't have drifted
From best friends to foes.

Michael D Gibson
FEELINGS OF HER
So quick the night As day is short
From far out to close within
Small is the wave in time does grow
From distant shore I feel the heat
Hand in hand upon the sand
So far we walked our time together
The bond we share crosses time and space
Forever unyielding with love's strong hold
Distant feelings from deep within
As time is short my love endless
Search not the things that are often near
Speak not my love of words so harsh
If indeed they be without thought
Reach out in heartfelt emotion
To a time of unyielding passion
My heart like many pieces of life
Now lay broken too numerous to count
Morning breaks dawn is in the sky
Misty morning air A new day rises
I have dreamed I have lived
But never a dream I could dream
As a dream of life with you.

Eva Gumke
THE CHILD IN ME
The child in me
independent
loving
responds with joy
when I reaffirm
I have a right to be alive.

She basks in the glow of fine gold
that shimmers about me.

the loving care of my being
she hugs me—I hug back
feeling safe—secure—wondrous

waiting for the day to start
for new experiences to occur that are
positive
reflecting my inner thoughts

and

THAT FEELS GOOD

Michelle A Grau
MY SLEEPING CHILD
Into your room, I quietly creep.
My sleeping child, I softly weep.

Do you understand the changes
we have thrust into your life?
Will you remember a childhood of happiness or strife?

Two weeks with mommy, a weekend with dad
We'll split every holiday . . .
It won't be so bad.

You smile bravely, a tear in your eye.
"I love you mommy, I'll try not to cry."

Looking back now, those problems seem mild.
Are there sweet dreams
for my sleeping child?

Pamela Gibson
ASHLEY MY ASHLEY
Ashley my Ashley
The feline I adore
Ashley my Ashley
You wait for me by the door
Ashley my Ashley
The colors of your coat are so true
Ashley my Ashley
Never leave me, or I'll be blue
Ashley my Ashley
The feline I adore
Ashley my Ashley
I love you every day more and more

Sarah Coats
BIBLE JONAH
It is amazing how the sea billows roll,
In the book of books it is told
God prepared a great fish to swallow Jonah whole,
out of the fish's belly Jonah
prayed to God for his soul.

St. Matthew referred to the great fish as being a whale.
It occurred to me as if it was like being in jail.
The second time the word of the Lord came to Jonah
to go to Ninevah he didn't fail,
This time Jonah stayed on the right trail.

Jonah, spent three days and nights in the belly of the whale.
The whale vomited him on dry land
in all this time his body
didn't get stale.
A three days' journey he made in one,
He called to the people of Ninevah
and the Victory was won.

Shayne Moss
TRAPS
Countless faces white as flour,
trapped in an expensive beauty powder.
Noble men—their suits are grey,
speaking of traps in false display.
Yes but people traps are special
For eyes with <u>sight</u>
And feet which press hard
to accelerate.
The trap screen flickers—glowing bright
don't forget the trap bulbs of incandescent light,
The trap boats all bobbing and float
Carrying each victim atop an endless trap moat.
The trap castles alight,
And trap planes aflight!
Beware of that fickle trap
Upon which I write.
The trapped animal—
Will chew off its leg;
But the trapped people smile,
And drink their trap drink.

Ted Kesner
SNOW
Snow, Snow let me go
Make me wild and free.
Snow, Snow release the cold,
And set the cold on me.
Swiftly falling all around,
Glistening snow upon the ground.
Snow, Snow come today
Take my troubles far away!

Ted Kesner
TOMMY SCOTT'S NIGHTMARE
She asked me my name
I said not a word
I felt like a rock
And she was a bird
She asked me again

I said nothing still
I was the virus
She was the pill
I noticed a change
It was something quite wild
She was a big monster
I was a scared child
I called out for help
But I could not speak
I felt kind of strange
Strong but yet weak
Two of them now
Three, four, and five
I wished I was dead
But stayed quite alive
They asked me my name
I could not talk
They asked me once more
I had begun to walk
They asked me again
They were having a ball
Again and again
I had run down a hall
Was it my imagination
Were they getting taller
I don't think it was
The room was getting smaller
There was a door
I went inside
I was back home
I nearly cried
From that dream forward
I never forgot
That my own name
Was Tommy Scott.

Elizabeth L Pardue
HELP OUR LAND
Help our land
Oh, Lord we pray.
Help us make it better
Each passing day.
Save the trees
That house the birds.
This we pray, Lord,
Please hear our words.
Save the fish and whales
That live in the sea.
I will try, Lord,
But please help me.
Please cleanse our air
Or show us how.
Time is running out,
We need to start now.
Each precious tree
And beautiful flower
Will all die
From an acid shower.
You gave us this land
To do with as we will.
And now it's being poisoned
With each oil spill.
Please help us, Lord,
Teach us to improve.
If we spoil this land
To where do we move??

David A Heard
HOW CAN I . . . ?

To my love & my people!

How can I express the things that I feel, when all that I feel seems so unreal.

How can I say what's truly on my mind, when all that I think makes the world seem unkind.

How can I be the man I was meant to be, when the lady I love thinks she isn't made from me.

How can I set an example for the world, when my brother man has just raped a little girl.

How can I feel that life is worth living, when to charities of life it's the poor that are giving.

How can I give all the love that I have, when I say that I love all they do is laugh.

How can I find the true meaning of life, when my next door neighbor's in the alley with a knife.

With all that can hurt you and tear you apart. The crime and disease that sadden the heart.

What can be done to set the negative aside, if not as a unit, then tell me . . . *how can I . . . ?*

Herbert Stastny
THE CONCEPT OF IF

To Herbert and Robbie Stastny for whom the poem's about.

Have you ever considered the concept of IF
Just look at the word LIFE
Right smack in the middle, you will find
Now IF you can have sight, then you can have life
IF is half of life, whether it be good or bad
IF we are not happy, then surely we're sad
IF we were married, then single we wouldn't be
IF we weren't imprisoned, then we would be free
IF the wind didn't blow, then it would be calm
IF there wasn't a hand, then there wouldn't be a palm
IF a woman were not pregnant, then she had not conceived
IF it wasn't for faith, then we could not believe
IF we didn't love, then we couldn't care
IF we didn't give, then we wouldn't share
and the whole world, should be like that
but IF we aren't pitched to, then we can't go to bat
IF we're not here, then we must be there
but regardless of which we do
keep IF in the middle of LIFE
Have faith and believe and it can come true

Nina Cottrill
TO MY DOGWOOD TREE

Dedicated to my children—Diana and Jr.

A nephew brought you from the woods, and planted you for me.
I watered and nurtured and waited and waited, for your growth to see.

At first you were crooked and think, and I worried about you each day.
Then you were pruned and tied to a stake, and my efforts began to pay.

Sometime later on an early spring morn, I stood and gazed in glee.
For on your shapely branches there, three lovely white blooms I see.

You have grown now to a much larger size, clad in a beautiful white cloud of blossoms upon each limb and twig, and I am ever so proud.

Nina Cottrill
REFLECTIONS ON A WINTER DAY
Watched the day end,
the sun go down.
Behind the hill,
with trees winter brown.

Streetlights come on,
they shine in the snow.
Lighting the way,
with a soft warm glow.

Time for thinking,
as a winter day ends.
Wishing the best—
for family and friends.

God is so good—
supplies all I need.
Forgive all my grumbling—
Sincerely I plead.

Deborah J Kilgore
NEVER SAY NEVER
Remember when we said never?
Remember before we said "I Do,"
We said "I will."
I will always love you.
I will always like you,
You will always be my beset friend.
Remember when we said never?
Never would our friendship die,
Never would we ever lie,
Never would our friendship perish,
For it's our GEM we will always cherish.

Remember before we said "I Do,"
The song that played,
"JUST YOU AND I?"
We said, "Oh yes, that's US."
Remember then the song that played,
"YOU NEVER BRING ME FLOWERS?"
You said, "Never."
I said, "Never say Never."
You said, "NEVER EVER!!"

Remember when we used to talk,
We would never ever have to stop?
Remember when you held me tight,
All the way through our first full night.
Remember when we said never?
Never would our friendship die,
Never would we ever lie,
Never would our friendship perish,
For it's our GEM we will always cherish.

b w arbogast
THE OLD MAN
I went to see the Old Man today.
He was sitting on the porch,
Rocking to and fro just like yesterday,
And the day before that.

I go to see him when I can,
To hear his tales
Of how things began
And were in his day.

Some of the stories he tells
Are real neat;
Some of them smells
Like Dad's fishing tales.

But I don't mind.
I just like to listen to him.
I figure his kind
As something special.

So, I'll just sit here, quiet like,
At his feet and let him ramble.
Maybe later, I'll take my bike
And ride over to the new damn site.
Maybe . . .
Later . . .

Philip J Smith
I'M LUCKY

Dedicated to my best friend and wife Maryann, loving daughter Michelle, supportive Dad Joe; to the stranger who made me aware of my good fortune, and in memory of my Mother Ida who told me I'd be published.

I heard a man say he hated his wife.
I love my wife, I'm lucky.
I heard a man say he couldn't stand his kid.
I love my daughter, I'm lucky.
I heard a man say he was going to junk his Mercedes.
I love my clunker, I'm lucky.
I heard a man say he had medical problems.
I have my health, I'm lucky.
I heard a man say his banks were giving him grief.
My account is fine, I'm lucky.
Instead of wishing for what I don't have
I should be counting my blessings for what I do have;
I'm happily married with a beautiful daughter,
My car gets me around, I'm in good health
And I have a few dollars in the bank.
Come to think of it, I'm very lucky!!!

Verla J Laymon
MY CHRISTMAS DOLL
Oh, Santa dear, I'd like to have, oh please,
A baby dolly with two dimpled knees,
A baby dolly I can hug and squeeze,
Oh, I'll be good to her,
I'll take her everywhere,
And, of all the things I have, I will share,
With my dolly, with two dimpled knees,
A baby dolly, I can hug and squeeze,
From the top of her head, to the tip of her toes,
I'll dress her in, the finest of clothes,
Oh, Santa dear, I'd like her hair to be,
A golden brown, and shiny as can be,
Her eyes too, must be shiny and brown
Her lips, not quite a frown,
So when she looks at me,
I'll know, she's happy as can be,
To be my dolly, with two dimpled knees,
A baby dolly I can hug and squeeze.

Rebecca L Soderstrom
FEELINGS THROUGHOUT THE YEAR

This is dedicated to my first love, the father of my children, Darrell.

This is another year,
that I'll love you.
And with some luck,
I'll be your fool.
I'll bloom for you,
on this special day.
I'll be fireworks,
for your display.

I'll work so hard,
not to scare you away.
I'll Thank God
for all the joy you've brought.

Maureen Black Elliott
FLOWERS ON THE GRASS

To my beloved son, Dean Shepard Elliott, age 30, killed by a drunk driver on April 29, 1990. He is in heaven now with his brother Paul, killed eleven months ago by a drunk driver.

I've always loved to see and smell
the flowers as they grow,
carnations red and lilies tall, and
tulips in a row.
The gentle petals so short-lived are
such a joy to see,
A springtime promise to us all that
life will always be.

The yellows, pinks and purples, a
pleasure to the eye,
And so it is the sunflower, as it
reaches to the sky.
I've always thought of flowers in
such a loving way,
But they took on different meaning
on that early summer day.

Instead of standing gracefully, or
pressed in a book to save, The
flowers now were laying on a new
and recent grave.
The flowers that I've always loved,
that I hoped would always last,
Until I saw them laying in arrangements on the grass.

David Boyd

David Boyd
THE LITTLE THINGS
The little things, the little things
The careless words that bite and
sting,
The unsaid words that break the
heart,
The blemishes that ruin art,
These fill our lives with grief and
care
And spread disorder everywhere.

The little things, like lovers' sighs,
The smiles that greet expectant
eyes . . .
These call attention to what's good
And should be better understood.

David P Boyd
LADY LUCK
To get ahead, we need initiative
Which shows itself in works of peace
and love.
This comes from deep within,
The help of many friends who care
And rarer ones who really share.
This comes from the outside.
And lastly Lady Luck, illusive soul,
Who dwells in "outer space," address
unknown.

If we but knew her secret hiding
place,
What a stampede there'd be to get
there first!
And some, the first in line, might be
the worst.
What a long line of hopeless, hopeful
men
Each one imploring her with
tear-stained eyes.
And empty hands.
Ah, luckless Lady Luck, remain
obscure
Lest you be pestered by suitors
galore,
With empty hearts.

David P Boyd
ILLUSION
My beautiful, white bird,
I sought you in the skies.
Now I have plucked your feathers,
One by one
And felt the blood and the pain.

But I sought "reality."
Now I have it. I hold it,
Your little limp, dead body
The plumage of Illusion gone.
Gone.

David P Boyd
UNTITLED
Deep is my love's emotion
And secret her desire.
Her saucy head is upright
Her green eyes beam with fire.

You would not know to see her
That she loves only me.
Yet she would find another
If faithless I should be.

David P Boyd
THE ORATOR ON THE FLYING TRAPEZE
O, now he can speak with the greatest
of ease
You don't hear him stutter, or
stammer or sneeze,
The voice is near perfect the gestures
are there,
Though the speech may be only—
hot air!

O, once he was timid and didn't
know how,
He would awkwardly gaze at the
floor,
He's acquired that orator's eloquence
now
Till the audience hollers for more—
More!

(To be sung to the tune of "The
Daring Young Man on t he Flying
Trapeze.")

David P Boyd
PRINT SHOP HELPER
When I was a lad I served a term
As "devil" in our printing firm.
I assembled galleys and ran off proof.
Today I am well-qualified to tell the
truth!
I carried type around the shop so
carefully
That now I am the editor of our news
weekly.

I hand-picked letters from a printer's
case.
I made up the news pages in the
all-steel chase.
I inked the press and even ran the
lin-o-type.
I could set a dozen galleys in a single
night.
I ran around our printing shop so
rapidly
That at last I am the editor of our
news weekly.

David P Boyd
UNTITLED
A conversation is a game of catch
Like children play to pass the time of
day
And both of us should follow basic
rules
That make the game a game that's
fun to play.
An idea is tossed back and forth,
Like as ball that is thrown by me to
you
And then thrown back again for me
to catch.

I must throw the ball so it can be
caught
Without stinging your hands.

I must catch the ball that you have
thrown,
Accurately, and not too high or low.

It takes two to keep a conversation
alive
And either one could spoil the
dialogue.
It takes two people, or nations, to
make peace
But either one could start a sudden
quarrel.

David P Boyd
BOUNCE THE WORDS AROUND
When words are backed up by a good
intent
They help us to discover and invent.
When we communicate, let's be alert
To insult's sting and words that
crudely hurt.
But words that bring to light the old
Are sometimes worth their weight in
gold.
The words that throw light on what's
new
Give us a cue to follow through.

So, jingle, jangle, jingle, bounce the
words around.
Some are barking in the dark, some
new truths have found.
Jingle, jangle, jingle, pass the words
around.
Facts may lead to wiser acts. Songs
are merely sound.
Jingle, jangle, jingle. Words are large
or small.
Some words frown and some words
smile.
Words are meant for all.

Words aren't all, but some stand tall.
Some seem weak and some seem
strong.
Some seem right and some seem
wrong.
Some just fit, some don't belong.
Jango, bingo, bango, bong!

David P Boyd
UNTITLED
Repent and change your ways.
Prepare for brighter days.
Discover better ways of doing things
that should be done.
Seek friendships everywhere,
avoiding dim despair.
Respect technology
with scientific zeal.
Reveal all truths with ample proofs
so people can agree!

Our children are tomorrow, listen to
the things they hope for,
things they plan to do.
I need this job and the prestige it
brings
so I can turn my thoughts to higher
things.
When I in adoration sing
I feel my life's complete.
I do not fear defeat.
I sublimate my greed, sex and vice
and try to do what's right and nice.

David P Boyd
IN PRAISE OF THOSE WHO WRITE AND TAKE A CHANCE
The writer is the doer who speaks
first,
Which places him at a disadvantage.
He is at the mercy of the reader,
Editor, or critic who will speak next.
The poor writer can never be certain
That what he writes will deserve
approval.
The reader can cherish or throw
away.
He accepts, or rejects, the written
words.

Rejection to the writer means defeat.
He does not work to fill the garbage
cans.
Acceptance means fulfillment of
desires.
It means the written words have
scored success.
The writer first must show initiative.
He lives by giving, not as many live.

David P Boyd
UNTITLED
Live not by shadows but realities.
The world presents itself, a barren
scene
To some who find not where its
riches lie.
Though waters cover three-fifths of
this globe,
Nature may not one cup of water give
To satisfy the desert wanderer
If he, through ignorance, has lost his
way.

It may at times show him a bright
mirage,
A green oasis where fresh waters
flow
To torture and deceive the thirsty
man.
And, as he vainly shouts, "Help! Or I
die!"
His echo mocks his frenzy in reply.

David P Boyd
UNTITLED

People who worry are in a hurry,
their lives are hectic and a-flurry.
They fear that they will not arrive on time
and being tardy will score as a crime.
"I'll miss out if I'm late," they say.
"I have no time to rest today.
I must get going, moving fast.
These days are just too brief to last.

People will say that if I'm late
it's all my fault. I hesitate.
I do not grab the helm and steer.
The sea is stormy. Rocks are near.
It's good to rush from here to there.
The laggards don't get anywhere."

Rykki
GIOVANNI'S ROOM (A TRIBUTE TO THE NOVEL BY JAMES BALDWIN)

Thanks to my family for all their support, and for encouraging me to follow my dreams.

Piercing thorns; to often cold
They wound the heart, and bleed the soul.
Confusion lurks from deep within—
mockery that never ends.
Finding love is hard to take.
Thoughts that linger—morals break.
Giving of your mind and flesh,
portraying lovers is the best.
Oppressed by feeling you can't explain.
What once was love—now guilt and shame.

Rykki
THE KISS

To my husband, Rodney D. Hopkins. I thank God for giving me someone like you.

When you hold me so tenderly and
the passion flows like satin you take
me to an ecstasy where almost
anything can happen
And when I feel your warm embrace
I know your love's inside me
And then your lips I gently taste
with your soul right there to guide me
To know our love will always soar
like the morning bird of glory
and you'll be mine forevermore
like the happy ending to a story
To share with you a part of me
that no one else can see
To make love in the early dawn
and live a fantasy
To share with you eternity
and memories such as this
To release that certain splendor
that is sealed with every kiss

Barbara Mitchell
CRIMPLED BEARINGS

To my loving friend, Eric T. Harris. I shall always love you. Forever and a day!

Moments spent with one another brings to life an untouchable chatter. Listen to the tones brought about from mystified gatherings; don't think of taking this away as have been done to all my others. No! Not to be sculptured within the hands of he the musician; for only the heart gladdens of such a needed model, timeless moments are steadily ticking.

"Can I hold on, why does my grip seem to lessen, leaving humanistical qualities altering around my natural being—taking that which holds solen stigma, yet returning a lessened smile?"

Marian Brand
FORGOTTEN WISH

I find myself perplexed these days
My nights have grown so long
That it's become quite sad to say
Goodnight to setting sun.

The wise old moon peeks out and sighs
Then sheds a tear for me
Forlorn he cries and herein lies
The subtle tragedy.

For as a child, I made my wish
Upon his evening star
And saw a wondrous future plan
Etched on night's blackboard.

But in between the then and now
My life-path went astray
And time, which tells, when no one asks,
Has told his somber tale.

Jill & J D Ritter
MANHOOD

For each other.

The sun beats brightly burns boldly
on a young boy's chest
in a young man's

heart

Isolated as a sad island, yet sweet,
the pain and confusion
are silent and undiscovered.
The moon a beacon on a cold summer night
Passionately he looks upward, often,
Thinking -
I won't let you down.

Jill Howry
CRESCENT TEARS

A sleeping moon, gliding with
grace toward the distant horizon.
Her beauty illuminating the
heavens, reveals her path.
Always alone in her timeless journey,
for another was never intended.
Years unrecountably passing in
loneliness, falling stars are the
tears she sheds.
Comfort is hers when a wolf sings
a caress, and when the tides
harmonize in rhythm.
Gently she convokes and unity
unfolds

Antoni Mikel
BEAUTIFUL

Your smile is like the sunshine,
Bringing warmth to stop the chill
That my lonely soul is feeling.
I find I love you still.
Your gaze is like the rainbow,
Showing color in my sight.
My life which once was bleak and grey
Is now something full and bright.
And all the tears you cry for me
Are like the summer rain:
A gentle, sweet caressing
To wash away my pain.
The words you speak are poetry,
Such soothing lullabies;
Ones sung by the angels
As they hover in the skies.
It's so hard to show my feelings,
For so priceless is your worth,
But I know that you are everything
That is beauty on this earth.

Audrey Karen Frederick (Neumyer)
THERAPY

Thank you Pat: memories scourged, a friendship forged.

Nothing can compare,
With the feeling of despair.
Desolation was my world,
Into fetal position I had curled.

You know not whereof I speak?
It is the light ahead I seek.
Black hole, down I slide,
With depression's depths I did collide.

Unloved, battered, shamed in my past,
My whole life to the wind was cast.
I crawl, I kneel, get to my feet,
I must not sink into defeat.

Self-knowledge, patience, counsel sought;
Going hither and yon in thought.
I remember, I hurt, I cry,
At last that light I see and sigh.

To step beyond the past I now declare,
To gain anew the will to care.
Gathering together body and soul,
Life beyond tomorrow is my goal.

Lisa Cole
LOVE'S FAITHFUL PROMISE

This poem is dedicated to Gary, the special man in my life, Love Forever, Lisa.

Two become one
We give our hearts
Like turtle and dove
We will never part

A foundation is built
Made of trust and hope
Hearts free from guilt
Love becomes a moat

Like the change of seasons
Hearts change too
We both have reasons
For things we say and do

Life's storms hit hard
Temptations rise
Only the true heart
Will survive

Like the promise of a rainbow
When two hearts hold true
Love's faithful promise
Will shine through

Jacalyn Rae Angell
THE CHOICE

We fall down so many times
that our bruises become permanent binds.
They chain us with bitterness and despair,
then change us into hate —
SO BEWARE.
Don't let the falls that bind us
become the chains that guide us.
Follow the path towards light
where the chains will then lose sight.
With a path lighted by care
the falls will lose their snare.
The chains will fade away,
then love has a place to stay.

David J Thorpe
I WANT TO BE A WRITER

I dedicate this, and all my writings, to those who've always stood by and encouraged me, my mother Elizabeth, my father Joseph, my wife Jody, and my many friends and relatives— Thank you all.

I want to be a writer, I want to be one now.
I've tried and tried and tried, and still
I don't know how.
They say I should be patient, and
give it some more time.
And if I wait a little while, perhaps
my words will rhyme.
Maybe they're right, they could be
wrong, I wish they'd tell me how.
For I want to be a writer, and I want
to be one NOW!
I cannot wait till next year, I can not
wait till Fall.
I cannot wait till Springtime, I cannot
wait at all.
For I want to be a writer, and I want
to be one now.
So I'll just keep on trying, until I find
out HOW!

David J Thorpe
THE OLD HOUSE

A powerful wind pounded the frail window frames of the old house. It was as if nature itself had turned against her, and was dishing out its just desserts. In a somewhat aggressive mood, the old house creaked with discontentment and discomfort. Its old wooden doors, stood now weather-beaten, still tethered to their aging hinges. Then as suddenly as it had come, the forces of nature slipped quietly away, leaving the old house in peace again, the sun peeped from behind the clouds, and gently warmed the old house with one of its tingling rays. The front door seemed to almost smile as a gentle breeze blew open its letterbox. Inside the old house seemed to be drying out from the cold and the damp. A single feather drifted downwards and was nestled peacefully among the others, yes the old house was, once again at peace, friendly with its companion, the sun. It stands now in solitude, and inside, most of all quiet.

Jennifer Gagliardo
ANOTHER DAY GONE BY . . .

Another day gone by,
another sunrise came and went

Another day gone by,
another 24 hours wasted another
letter sent

Another song sang,
another phone rang,
another baby born

Another flower blossomed,
another puppy left sad and forlorn

Another day gone swiftly by,
another day that children cry

For what do we owe this sadness
that lays upon us each day?

Maybe it's because of all the grief
that's always headed our way

There's hate, and crime, and violence
yet still without a cause

For if God had meant it to be this
way,
the world would have started with
wars.

Zona Mae Kirkland Fulton
LONELY EYES

This poem is dedicated to my family and friends.

Look deeply into my eyes . . .
Can you not see my lonely cries?
My tears are flowing through my heart,
You promised we would never part.
You told me once you'd always care,
Our lives together we would share.
My heart is bleeding, my breath is gone.
Please tell me what went wrong?
Kiss me once before you go . . .
I will always love you and you should know,
The time we spent I will always treasure,
We have shared so much pleasure.
This final kiss will set you free,
Promise to always think of me.
Go now, my darling, say good-bye,
My love for you will never die!

Look deeply into my lonely eyes . . . .

Beverly Staples Ryan
MOTHER-CHILD LOVE

Did anyone try to explain to you
what it's like to be a mother?
It's very hard, 'til you live it yourself
with one child and then another.

Now I only have one, but I must admit,
it must be very hard to explain;
How that little one you helped come into the world can make the sun shine through the rain.

My Danny is one year old right now,
and I've learned so much in one year.
To change & feed, to comfort & love,
and be there to wipe up a tear.

Now I'm now saying you always feel great;
there are times you feel you could scream.
But maybe you're tired or under some stress,
maybe things aren't as bad as they seem.

My Danny's the best; they don't come any better,
and I may sound prejudiced there.
But no one can imagine how high I can feel,
on the mother-child love that we share.

Gloria Vaughn
REBECCA

An unexpected blessing
Has been sent me from above.
She brings me joy and laughter
And a special kind of love.
Unconditional, she says,
Is the love she has for me.
I've never known this kind before-
It makes me feel so free
To do or any the things I feel
To be myself; in fact
Sometimes I fear I smother her
But she just comes right back.
A part of me is what she is
So precious in my heart.
I feel she is so close to me
It hurts to be apart.
She is so very good to me
And some days we get wild.
At times she is my grown-up friend
At times she is my child.
To God who does these wondrous things
My thanks eternally,
For giving this beloved gift
To her Mother . . . then to me.

Dawn Haney
THE SEARCH

So long ago we said good-bye;
A few letters here and there,
And a couple calls too.

Then one day all contact was lost.
It was on this day,
"The Never Ending Search" began.

I called and called, but none were you;
Asking anyone, and everyone;
Here, there, and everywhere,
But not a one knew you.

Finally after two years passing;
I gave up on that Never Ending Search.
I never once could have believed,
That one day soon; together again, you and me.

Three years have passed; we both have changed,
But those feelings are still the same.
I hope this time; forever, together we will be;
Never to be parted again; I pray!

I only ask one thing of you.
Never say good-bye, for it's too final,
But only see ya later . . .

Ross E Percifield II
SUMMERWINTERTIME

Though verdant hills have long since browned
And frosty breath falls on the ground
My spirits fly, my hopes are high
With glee and Joy I happy cry

Though bird and beast have southward flown
From cold that chills right through the bone
I bask and bathe in naked fun
As if I were a burning sun

Though icy winds assault the sky
And leafless branches groundward sigh
No darkness visits this heart's home
Through sun-filled, flow'ry fields I roam

Behold! The reason for my glee . . .
The love, the hope you give to me
Such tenderness and caring ways
You've shown to me these wint'ry days

Frances Johnson Dooley
OUR WORLD

Oh, what a beautiful world God gave to us,
In His wisdom He created and did to us entrust.
So many wonderful things He gave us to enjoy,
We were to be the keepers and not abuse them like a toy.

How gorgeous He did make our earth,
As precious as gold, man couldn't measure their worth.
The flowers and trees and sunshine for them to grow,
Nor did He forget the seeds for food which we could sow.
And now we've made a mess of these marvelous gifts,
We're trying so hard to resolve all our rifts.
Somehow we've got to undo the damage that's been done,
Lord, help us in this battle that so badly needs to be won.

Mark Welch
THE YEAR THAT STOOD STILL

To Babee; my inspiration—you're in my soul and my every thought.

The mighty wind blew from the north
It was a freezing chill
Is this the year of snow and ice
The year that would stand still?

The people in town somehow sensed
That there was something wrong
Would it be like years ago
When everything was prolonged?

A man in town who lived alone
Was getting up in age
Nobody knew where he was from
Or why he had a cage

And then one day a blizzard came
Covering the town with snow
And just before they saw the man
Praying for the wind to blow

During the snow there was a death
The old man passed away
But no one knew that he had died
They thought he moved away

When spring came they opened the house
Finding the old man frozen
And when they read his will one day
There was no one chosen

Then one day a woman passed
Hearing something in back
And in the cage there was a bird
With feathers white and black

She had someone unlock the cage
To let the black bird free
It didn't move—all it said was
"You finally care for me."

Cynthia L Malone
OUR UNEXPECTED LOVE

To Gerald Vaughn Tinsley; For shining light on the shadows in my heart. I LOVE YOU and you Love me—and that's always enough!!! Cyn

Taking the time to find myself,
no love to call my own.
Feeling content with what I've learned,
the respect for myself that's grown.

Behold—one day, was I to know?
a pair of "Brown Eyes" I'd see.
That would grab ahold of my lonely heart,
and set my soul so free.

For I to think, when things get tough,
on my shoulders, the world falls down.
I'll think of the color in those very two eyes,
to remind me of the Love I've found.

So now I say—to you—"My Gerry,"
thank-you for the love you've given.
The Love I have to share you,
Has made life all the more worth livin'.

If loneliness bestows your heart,
reach higher than the stars above.
Close your eyes and find the strength
from " OUR UNEXPECTED LOVE "

José Luis Belmar
REBIRTH

To the beautiful eagles I have met in my life.

GOD bless all of you,
forget all your sorrows;
there'll be new tomorrows
for people like you.

"Farewell" your anxieties
and some friends forgotten,
for something was rotten
amongst past societies.

We eagles will fly;
the rats will be gone,
and all will be done
but we will not cry.

And we will survive
in new times to come,
with new friends to sum
with almost no strive.

Let's worship our Lord
and welcome new loves.
Let's bless all white doves
by acting accord.

HE'll take care of you,
forget all your sorrows;
there'll be new tomorrows
with people like you.

Mario J Traversi
SILENT

Tears come to my eyes as I watch
Or rather listen

The notes float, they really float in the air like gondolas borne by a godly sea
A sea of human voices
In harmony

Stille Nacht. Truly a silent night from the cold city streets to the warmth of the pews. Body against body and voice with voice a harmony of earthly angels uplifts
the soul: that soul that for 364 days of each year we seek
we find

In the tear that runs down our face
Our soul of salt and water
That spills forth for ourselves
We cry for our beauty and ugliness
We cry for ourselves, children of God.

and for Stille Nacht.

Rae Lee McPherson
MAN IN THE MOON

O man in the moon,
flying high in the sky,
why does it seem
like I want to cry?
Why can't I be
like a bird in the air,
and soar like an eagle
without any care?
O man in the moon,
sitting serenely on clouds,
can't you see me now?
Can't you shout out?
The birds are your children
free and alive,

ducking back and forth,
peeking from your sides.
O man in the moon,
come and take me now,
bring me on home,
tuck me in your shroud.

Rae Lee McPherson
EMPTY SOULS

An empty soul is lonely.
It has no happiness.
It has no sadness.
It has nothing.

An empty soul is forever seeking.
Looking for something to fill it.
Looking for something to make it whole.
Looking for companionship.

An empty soul is a wanderer.
Walking down every lonely road.
Walking down every worn and beaten path.
Walking down tunnels.

An empty soul is confused.
Where did I come from?
Where am I going to?
Where am I now?

An empty soul is . . . .

Pat Stowell
LIFE TO LIVE

Why is there so much uncertainty in the certain
Why is there so much sorrow in the joy of giving
Must there always be discontentment within
Is there nothing but loneliness in the outlook
Every heart aches for the gentleness of a touch
One that unquestionably breathes love.
From the moment of life within the womb
There's innocence and unknown of hurt to come
Belief and understanding to only be disillusioned
Doing good unto others so you won't be undone
Will the time come when life will be complete
Or will there always be complexity to delete
Shall there be freeness as there is in flight
Maybe only a moment now and then if we fight
Life must always be a struggle if we live
I only hope to receive almost as much as I give
Only then can I say life is lovely to live . . .

Angela K Batman
AFFAIRS

You are now apart
The hurt pain and loneliness
What do you do now
How do you forget
Is there anyway

You work and try to stay busy
But that does not help
What will

Then you meet another
And have fun get along
Slowly the pain and
The memories are gone

You have a new affair
The only thing to cure
The pain of the old one

Thank God for affairs

Madonna M Cantwell
KISS HIM GOOD-BYE

Dedicated to my love, Gholam. Love forever Madonna.

You promised me the world.
Took my world away.
You promised to make me your Queen.
But shattered my dreams.
I cannot forgive you.
It's a wonder I have no regrets.
The love I had for you
I can no longer find.
The hurt has buried it deep inside
I have no idea why you feel
it's all my fault. Are you sin-free
It's easier to blame someone
Than to take responsibility
I don't feel it's all my fault
Just the promises you broke
You're not the man just pretend to be,
Put me down for just being me.
Beautiful things to share. Now evaporates.
and disappears, walk away? Escape the pain?
Blood! My world. Only a whispered NIGHTMARE.

Philip A Chacon
QUEST

Dedicated to my Love Tammy Lee Chacon.

My heart has left my body
It has flown up to the sky
Maybe that's the reason
I lay in bed and cry
I, searching for a woman
an apple for my eye
Praying that I find her
alone I'd hate to die

Don't know if I will ever love
but God knows I will try.

Philip A Chacon
LIFE IN FATE'S EYE

Dedicated to Jesus Christ.

Life is short
Life is hard
Life is like a game of cards
Life you win

Life you lose
Life forever when Christ you Choose
Life with God
Life is Love
Life with Our Savior in heaven above

Margie (Blanton) Sherer
THE PAINTING

Dedicated to my husband Jerry. My best friend always.

It hung in the gallery, close to the door
The portrait of a lady, Painted a hundred years or more
Her hair was long and dark, Her eyes were black as coal
She wore a haunting smile, She held her head just so
There was something about this lady
From long long ago, that reached out from the canvas
And touched my very soul,
Her identity I tried in vain to uncover, Who she
really was I never did discover
Something in those eyes, No! it couldn't be
When I looked at her, I was seeing me.

Thomas Mitchell Dooley
SMOULDER SWEET, SWEET GUN

A blast explodes the midnight air, a hush turns to a scream.
The battle fiercely rages, its head built up with steam.
For the moment of our peacefulness settled with the sun,
Victory a phone call; now smoulder sweet, sweet gun.

The village stirs, awakens, two others coldly sleep,
Families and friends have gathered one to weep.
The church bells ring out softly, sorrowful their score
For the innocents been stolen in the passion of this war.

The slow parade of tears rolls down the now-familiar trail.
Even the daily pubsters here look up from their ale
For a glimpse of the sorrow drifting ever past.
"Cheers" to the children lost, "May they please be the last."

A warrior, long distance, courageously takes the blame.
"An accident, we're sorry. But we'd misread the name."
The constable, his crime a Brit, he deserved the gore.
The children? "Hey, we're sorry, casualties of war."

But forget the past as quickly, today's another day.
One step closer to victory, the glorious I.R.A.
Broken families, shattered hearts; countdown three, two, one . . .
Victory a phone call, now smoulder sweet, sweet gun.

Sabrina Michael-Fiester
UP ABOVE

Up above the clouds
I saw a flicker of light,
Red, green and yellow
Spinning slowly thru the night.

Shining stars, sprinkling stardust,
Can you tell me of the lust
Of making eyes with that man up above?

Night lives don't compare
With the kind I have in mind,
Taking flight to far-out galaxies
I am hoping to find.

Oh city lights don't you know I'm going insane,
Staring at those sparkling lights,
Dancing off my windowpane.

Flickering lights way up high
Where is your destiny this night?
Beyond the stars, beyond time,
Take me with you on your flight.

Michelle Tan
LABYRINTH EMOTIONS

To: Eileen, Kieu, Renee, and Terry—Thank you for your understanding and help. This one's for you.

I close my eyes as I lay me down to sleep.
My soul I pray the lord shall keep.
Memories I shall keep deep down inside.
Tears running down through my eyes.
My dreams so fresh and new.
With fulfilling pleasures which I had adieu.
Memories of the young I could not forget.
Blue, gray marks she did not regret.
My sorrows I dared not show.
For I always told myself that there's always tomorrow.
Day by day, I await for such happiness.
Only to find out that there's only loneliness.
Memories of 16 . . . Oh what a great number!
Hurdles of life I could always remember.
Friends of all races, everywhere!
When I needed them, they were always there!
Evidence of depression were on my wrist.
The slash of a razor which still exist.
Reasons of curiosity was misleading.
Trying new things was quite appealing.
But for me, it was a big mistake.
Marijuana could have put my life at stake.
From then on nothing seemed to matter.
Not friends, not school, or even pleasure.
My grades were down and so was I.
I felt like I could no longer get up high.
So many to blame, but that would be a shame.
Nevertheless, Mom and Dad I loved you the same!
For all of those whom I shall treasure.
Memories of me you'll keep with such great pleasure.
But when I sleep I shall not awake.
So those of you who can relate.
Remember this for goodness' sake!
Regrets come last and not at first . . .

Suzanne Richardson
MY FRIEND

A friend; a true one indeed.
You've been there during my needs,
Giving me that helping hand
That's picked me up when I've fallen;
to once again make me stand.

You are there to listen to me,

Letting me open my eyes to see,
Pointing out that sometimes this is
the way it has to be.
Supporting my mind to again be
restful and free.

I've needed that someone there,
Knowing someone at least cares,
Along with my appreciation, I hope
you understand,
I am here, if needed with a helping
hand.

Thank you,
My Friend

Dawn T Wege
CRY OF A SOUL
Blackness surrounds me,
And my eyes ache to see.
The cold penetrates from the winds
that blow.
Where am I?

There's a dampness in the air,
It sprinkles my face with wetness.
Yet, I hear no waters flow.
Where am I?

It's very lonely here,
My shoulders feel heavy.
My heart keeps sinking with woe.
Where am I?

I hate this place,
Please let me out.
For it's a place that scares me so.
Where am I?

A voice answers my plea,
"You're inside of me,
And there you must stay, I know."
I am lost!

R J McKinnon Sr
LOMA PRIETA
Earthquakes excite our sensibilities
As do the scourges of life's realities.
Ravaged by aftershocks, forfeit of
choice,
We look for reconciliation and peace.
Fearful of their repetition, we seek
surcease
And dread the shocks, leaving
tremblers
That tear the fabric of our souls,
Fracturing bonds of love and
friendship.

Nor shall we return to those
contentious shores,
And ply the trades of our anxieties,
But cling to those most dear. We
promise
Not to squander their love, to be lost
again.
We throw our arms about them, and
whisper
Be not afraid, "I am here, I am by
your side."

R J McKonnon Sr
SWEAT
SWEAT
SWEAT
In the beginning, GOD gave us
sweat.
He never said you couldn't do it;
All He said was you'd have to work
at it,
And, if you did,
You'd S W E A T . . .

R J McKinnon Sr
ART OF PAINTING
Paint with abandon
Try your soul !
Live, and live on,
For what you do
Can test your heart,
To love, and cherish
What you know and see.

Linda J Hughes
ROSES

For G without whose inspiration, support and love I would still be going backwards. I love you and, again, I thank you.

I never thought much about roses.
Until he sent me some.
Half a dozen red roses to the office.
A thank you for a job well done.

A dozen red roses for Valentine's
Day.
Just simply, thank you.

He likes yellow; I prefer white.
Hence, the red.

It went to one single rose.
Those single roses mean so much.

And now it's my turn to say thank
you.

Leon P Ramsey
FREE SPIRIT
I am a free spirit
I roam all around;
I roam through the mountains,
The cities,
The towns.
I do what I want
Whenever I please;
No questions asked
No answers given.
I flirt with the women
And like having fun,
Yes, I am an outlaw
All locked up and proud;
I don't take no handouts
Or anything free,
I'd rather be lonely
And roaming 'roun free.
Now this is my story,
So please understand;
The life that I've chosen . . .
A lonely old man.

Taylor Holt
I AM

To my family for encouraging me to express my feelings through poetry.

I am a girl who is fond of all living
creatures.
I wonder why the sky is blue.
I hear the heartbeat of all animals.
I see a slug slithering through the
grass.
I want the homeless to have homes.
I am a girl who is fond of all living
creatures.

I pretend I'm a beautiful black horse
galloping through the woods.
I feel that all animals should be free.
I touch the light of day.
I worry that different animals are
going extinct.
I cry when I see a living thing die or
in misery.
I am a girl who is fond of all living
creatures.

I understand that every thing will die
at one time.
I say there should be no more drugs
in the world.
I dream of being a wildlife
rehabilitator.
I try to save everything from danger.
I hope God brings Heaven down to
Earth for peace and loving
EVERYWHERE;.
I am a girl who is fond of all living
creatures.

Sue Doyle
MY CRYSTAL
Sparkles of rain
reminding me,
Of the crystal
in you I see

Your glistening heart
led the way.
Taught me to laugh
and how to pray

Yet now I look
through an hourglass,
And notice that
time's passing fast

I think to myself
what would I do,
If my crystal broke
because it's you

I'd pick it up
piece it together,
And place it in
my heart forever

That's where it belongs
that's what I'd do,
Remember grandma
my crystal is you

Hope Evans Guy-Teano
#5 THISTLE LANE
Welcome to the great masterpiece.
An abode of solace and peace.

An acre of ground in the highlands,
Stands an edifice built by human
hands.

A work of art to appreciate
A God-given talent to create.

Besetted by tall and stately trees,
Branches sway by the gentle breeze.

A spacious showcase for living.
Interior finishes all eye-catching!

A sense of depth and elegance,

Colonial style with informal
ambiance.

Ceilings are high, vaulted and trayed.
Intricate design of banisters in array.

A living room to entertain guests,
Four bedrooms a place to rest.

A dining room to chat and eat,
Busy kitchen where food is a treat.

A porch and deck for outdoor fun,
Sprawling lawn for kids to run.

A cozy mastersuite to relax and sleep.
Refreshing invitation for a jacuzzi
dip.
Stone and black-marbled fireplaces,
A heat storage for winter recesses.

A mark of achievement,
A symbol of fulfillment.

O what a joy to live in this place.
Where God richly showered His
grace.

O home sweet home,
As we welcome friends and say
shalom!

Niki Barnes
MISSING YOU

To my two best friends in the whole world. I love you mom and dad.

Emptiness has taken me
Since you've been gone
I think of you with each love song.

The space can't be filled by anyone
else
I can't fill it by myself.

I'm incomplete without you here
I see your face in my tears.

I hear your voice in a child's cry.
I watch your spirit through a child's
eye.

I feel your energy run through my
veins
I feel your frustration as I feel your
pain.

You're a part of me now
I miss you so much
I miss your smile
I miss your touch.

Tammy D Johnson
THE OLDEST QUESTION
Today gives us knowledge and
dreams,
Yesterday has become the past,
Tomorrow is the future,
Time goes by so fast.

What will I find in my future?
How much time do I have left?
How long is forever?
Is there life after death?

I know that spring follows winter,
And that the sun sets in the west,
But the future's known to only One,
Life's filled with changes, chal-
lenges, and tests.

Have I accomplished enough?
Did I waste too much time?
Can I make up for my mistakes?
How could I have been so blind?

The light of day turns to darkness,
A chance to escape from my fears,
Time to sleep and dream,
When I wake, will the future be
clear?

Térèse M Landrum
I MISS YOU ALREADY

This poem is dedicated to Margaret Ferry who will always be with us.

Dear Nan Nan:
I miss you already and you are not
even gone
But you will be in heaven right
where you belong
Among those who love you above
and in peace
Where time doesn't exist and
worries do cease
I'll miss you so dearly but this you
must know
Because you are a star in my eyes

who makes my life glow
You have meant much to me with your unselfish ways
And I'll reflect on them always for the rest of my days
For I have learned much from you and have so much to tell
To those who will precede you and will know your life well
You're so special my Nan Nan more than words can express
As your life can be called one of great success
Because you give of yourself to those you adore
And to those who are needy you have opened your door
So goodbye my sweet grandmother as I know you are going
To meet our creator and all he'll be showing
You will always be with me and to you I will pray
That my life will resemble yours in just some small way

Love,
Terese,
December 21, 1982

Diana K (Jarr) Anthony
I REMEMBER

This poem is dedicated to Don Dahl, a very special friend.

You are in my heart and thoughts each day
Even though you are many miles away
I remember the first time I talked to you
I ask if you had some time and you said I sure do
It was in the lunchroom at old Davis High
I needed your help and you seemed to know why
Do you realize that was over twenty years ago
I was fourteen & thought I was at the almighty low
Oh God, the things I have learned over the years
And growing up has sure used up a lot of tears
You will always be a very special person to me
You were there when no one else could be
My own daughter is 14 and in high school now
I pray she'll find a friend like you somehow
For that first day, I loved you with all my heart
And in my thoughts we will never be these miles apart!

Thom D Beckett
DEATH AND LOVE
Death is cold and lonely, filled with despair.
Love is warm and someone's always there.
Death is somewhat of a bad idea.
You close your eyes for many years.
Love is a long, strong, wonderful feeling.
Death is a low on dragging feeling
like walking through a labyrinth
with no end in sight
just the black of night.
Love is like a knight in shining gold armour
with a heart for a shield
slaying the uncursed evil to save you.
Death is one of the many obstacles
we have to cope with.
Love is a many splendored feeling.

What do you feel like?

Carmen V Pinto MD
TAKE A PART OF ME
Take a part of me, as the day starts anew;
Darkness fading, sun rising, burning off the dew.

Take a part of me, as you bustle and clean;
Fixing meals, doing laundry, the daily routine.

Take a part of me, during celebrations and holidays;
Halloween, New Years, Happiness in many ways.

Take a part of me, in grief and in sad times;
Loss, rejection, loneliness of all kinds.

Oh please, take a part of me,
something to remember me by;
My smile, my caring, for I'll carry part of you till I die.

Mike Palumbo
TWENTY-ONE LINES
It doesn't take Twenty-One lines.
I don't even need fifteen,
I only need those three little words
I only need to write
"I love you."

I don't need symbols.
I don't need rhyme.
And I don't need Twenty-One lines
to tell you how much I care.

But I do need this paper
'Cause I'm too scared to sing
And I'm too scared to love
And I'm too scared of you.

And with this paper
I can write my feelings.
But with this paper,
You will never know this.
'Cause I don't have any courage
To ask you how you feel.
And I don't have any courage
To hear that you don't want me.

Kate Isabelle
FALLING, DRIFTING, WEAVING
Falling leaves
Drift on the wind
Weave circles around the trees.
Dreams sift through the leaves
Dropping hopes upon the world
Forming patterns in my mind.
The autumn colors
Blaze like fire in my eyes
Lighting my shadows
For all to see
My insecurities.
I lean toward myself
And laugh then cry
My soul spread wide
The corners gone
Doubts remain
Fastened to my bones
Weaving circles around my being
Drifting through my thoughts
Falling to my knees.

Marsha Rudolph
PRECIOUS TIME

To my loyal and loving dad.

Precious Time
I look at you differently—
The way a child looks at the ocean.
Open eyes, beating heart
Not wanting to see us part.

Precious Time
I hold you different—
Holding you tightly in my arms
Proves you're still there
Even if you've lost your hair.

Precious Time
Describes every moment with you.
This man I always argued with
This man who made me angry
We didn't see eye to eye.
Now we look at each other
Eye to eye,
And we cry
Because we know time is a precious gift
Too precious to waste.
So we love with haste.

Kathleen P Bardon
ALL THAT WERE

I dedicate this poem to my mother & friend, Allecia Rose, who I owe my love of the arts.

You my love
have been long past.

Though I do not desire
to stay in loneliness.

My heart is empty,
my soul so alone.

I dream of you
to hold you in my gaze.

Cherish your smile
and to know why my sun rises.

To fill my arms
with love . . .

My very being . . .

Would hold your worth
and mine.

Suzanne Womble
TO A FRIEND
It hurts to see the way you are hurting deep inside
Knowing things could be different
If only you were willing to let God inside
You keep pushing Him away
Saying I am not sure if I could live his way
You're not even trying, but God doesn't give up
Tears filled my eyes
As I see only you can help yourself
I just pray that you don't wait too long because if you do
God will laugh in your face.

Eric Siracusa
WE ONLY HAVE OURSELVES TO BLAME
Everything that pollution; does to the air, trees, birds, and sky,
Makes me want to cry.
Sure we're making progress,
But we're also making a mess.
Styrofoam and sprays for our hair,
Are rotting holes in the OzoneLlayer.
We're building nuclear power plants with haste,
Even though we can't dispose of nuclear waste.
What we're doing to our environment is really a shame,
But we only have ourselves to blame.

Lisa Russell
A DREAM OF A GARDEN FAR AWAY

To Billy Savage, remembered by all who loved him!

I dream of a garden far away,
Where no one else can go.
A place of peace and silence,
That only one may know.
A place where wishes come true,
And only happiness is found,
A place that even pain cannot enter;
A garden of roses all around.
A place where troubles are lost,
In the beauty you, behold
A place where honeybees dance on the sky.
Where even butterflies will land on your toes.
A place where animals may go,
Without the fear they know
I hope one day I'll find the garden of my dreams

Mary Johnson Taggart
GOD AND ME

Dedicated to my Mother, Elsie

I see the shining light of God
As I traverse o'er this great sod
And gather round me cloaks of mist
To run thru meadows newly kissed
With dew and raindrops soft and wet
And pause to smile, to briefly sit
On rocks and shore and sand, near sea
To ponder deeply on God and me
What friends we are, and how we talk
We laugh and cry, and then we walk
Thru cities large and cities small
And weep for those who've missed their call
We hear the birdsong short and sweet
And feel the leaves beneath our feet
Then sit 'neath trees to rest and sigh
As sunset's shadows soon draw nigh
To cloak us then in evening blue
As moon and stars are coming thru
My heart sings praises to the skies
For on this day I realize
That shining light of God I see
Is part of Him—and part of Me!

Wm R (Bob) McGuinness
A WALK IN THE WOODS

This poem dedicated to my loving wife, Flora.

One of these days when you have nothing to do,
try a walk in the woods for an hour or two.

Take in the wonders that nature provides,
the trees, the brush, and the wildlife it hides.

Watch for the many birds on the wing,
and try to distinguish the songs that they sing.

Look for the rabbits, the squirrels and the deer;
they will run when they see you, for humans they fear.

Look out for the skunk, his scent is not pleasant,
And no doubt you'll be startled by the flight of the pheasant.

After a while, find a nice place to sit and observe what goes on in the woods for a bit.

And when it's time to leave, I'm sure you'll agree,
You'll do it again, next time you're free.

Barbara A Lott
THE LEGEND OF THE MOON-LESS NIGHT
There is a tale that, long ago
A young girl loved her sweetheart so
But fate decreed he go his way
She watched for him every day
At night the moon looked down on her
And saw her grief, as if it were
The first time, ever, a young girl cried -
Tall trees whispered; then they sighed
The moon was then her only friend
But did not see her young life end...

When it is dark, now, without a moon
Young lovers wait for the moon to spoon
Because of the tale that, long ago
A young girl walked in the frozen snow
On a black and moonless, winter night
Dark enough to give a fright
She leapt to her death on the rocks below -
Then it is said (surely you know)
With a shrill and, somehow, awesome cry
The name of her lover pierced the sky...

The moon is a friend to lovers, they say
And smiles on them to this very day...

Katie Sullivan
WHAT PEACE IS
Peace is a dove,
that stood for love,
way back on Noah's Ark.

Peace is a nightlight at bedtime,
a small light in the dark.

Peace is laughter
peace is joy.

Peace is loving a brand-new toy.

Peace is a pretty flower that you see,

But most of all,
Peace is you and peace is me.

Arlene Campbell
MY BEST FRIEND
My friend, my pal, my dog Ambra that's what she is to me
Running, playing and chasing cats, look how happy she is
She's only a pup and not full grown, she has a long way to go
Black and tan and so full of life, that's my dog Ambra
Jumping up and playing with the kids, that's my dog Ambra
Romping in the snow, under the trees and
always chasing through the breeze
Then one day my friend, my pal, was gone
We will always think of her and how she played
One day, we will all be together again
Jumping and playing like we always did
That's my friend, my pal,
my dog Ambra

Constance E Richards
THE FIRST TIME

To J P - For Making it Happen . . .

The First Time
I saw you—
Your Smile,
Your Eyes:
(I Knew.)

The First Time
You Kiss Me—
Your Taste,
Your Feel...
(I Wanted You.)

The First Time
You Held Me—
So Warm,
So Safe...
(So "Comfortable")

The First Time
You Loved Me—
So Tender,
So Understanding...
(So Wonderful)

Linda Richardson
SPELLBOUND
A merlin of love, a spell you have cast.
Time, a dark dragon, that holds our love fast.
Sweet magical prince, of love that I've found,
It's more than my thoughts, or my dreams that you've bound.
A lover, enchanted, I surrender my heart.
Held by the magic, right from the start.
Nights passed in wonder, of this miracle love.
Fantasy takes flight on the soft wings of a dove.
Will the dragon be slain and the lovers united?
Will the princess awaken to the flame that's ignited?
What key do you hold to my passions unbound?
What hope do you bring to this love we have found?
Hold fast my love, keep reign on my soul,
With golden soft threads, born of love's glow.
For who will know but the moon and the stars,
If our love be granted by powers afar.
And deep in the night the sweet spark of love,
Will grow ever brighter than the sun up above.
And as that sun rises, with a kiss we will seal,
A love that is honest and faithful —and real.

Ronna R Hicklin
MOMENT PASSING

For Dave.

Just once I'd truly like to find
The place that's known
as peace of mind
And not too long for yesterday
Or wish tomorrow were today
To linger and to finally rest
In just this moment's friendly nest
To lie there still
With quiet calm
And know I am
Where I belong

S P Kelly
LOVE'S LAST STOP

This poem is dedicated to the love of life and my wife.

I'm not sure what you're looking for
or thought you might find
But I couldn't want more
if you'd say you were mine

I'm sure of only one thing
that it's love which I need
I know that I do
and I don't find it crazy
For I think you may too

If love's why we live
I have some to give

And it's to you I will give
this love as it seems
Together we'll live
fulfilling our dreams

Anna McEwen

Anna McEwen
DESPAIR
Now, like so many times before
I feel lost and alone
No one to talk to—No one . . .

A neverending darkness
No walls No doors
No where to go—No where . . .

A road that leads to emptiness
I can't turn back and all that lies ahead is
Nothing, lots and lots of,—Nothing . . .

And just when my feet will no longer move
And my heart has nearly ceased to beat
I see a light—a big, bright, beautiful light . . .

I run as fast as the wind
And break free from the darkness
I am back—and ready to try again . . .

Ron Skutt
ANCIENT PASSED
I lie in bed late at night, reading about ancient history passed.
Reading about their customs and things and the way they lived their lives in the past.
The loves they loved and the sins they sinned like the cleaning of the air,
Reminds me of the most beautiful thing and that is a beautiful girl with the most loveliest hair.
The action they lived and the beds that they lay, reminds me of the children at their play.
The armies they lead, the battles they fought,
and the treasures from their conquest that they brought.
The wars they waged and the religions they preached and the famines that did last.
It really shows you that the life we live, is comparable to the past.

Ron Skutt
LIKE THE MORNING GLOWS
Didn't you ever think you would like things to go
Just like the morning glows?
How the different colors coming in
Just to make you feel so serene.
You can never match this most beautiful thing.
It has more splendor than a diamond ring.
Its golden and different hues
Are enough to chase away any blues.
Oh if I could only sing
Just like the morning brings.
It would be the greatest show
Because it's like the morning glow.
Like flames of radiant colors it sheds
Greater than any darkness that fled.
Then we all can sing.
Because it's just like spring.
Then I know we would sing
Because it's like the children that brings
Joy and Peace to us all
That is greater than any
that I know.

Denise Carnero
LIFE REVOLVES AROUND LIFE

My dedication and love is belonging to my family who is flaring up the spark of life and my cousin who is starting the fire with his support.

Life revolves around life
Life is a constant circle
Living for each other that's what we do,
Life is constant with love
Love keeps life company forever
Love conquers hate
Love will always be superior
For love is a constant battle for life
Love is what we all live for.

Lauren Akins
A WOMAN

To Rose, a woman who gave so much of herself to others. The following I give to her now.

A heart, a cross
All signs of love
I stand and I stare
Waiting for a sign from above
A woman so kind, so caring and so giving
A woman who possessed a joy from just living
The years as they pass and the tears just won't end
For a woman so loved, so needed, so missed is a friend
Here I sadly stand at the grave of no other
For the woman I speak of she is my mother

Mary French
LOVE IT OR LEAVE IT
Oh Glory flies high in the sky
It waves to all who passes by
It is our flag that we all love
For who are they to burn it up?
If they don't like, let them leave
The world is big for them to seep
Our boys have died to keep us free
So guys like you can live in peace
So take a power—go on your way
For we feel sorry, you think that way
Oh glory flies
Will never die
For we the people
Stand by its side

Mary French
A PROUD AMERICAN
America—we love you
America—we're free
America—is our home
Where we all live in peace
We love, we raise our family
We worship as we please
We lead the life that we believe
The way that life should be
That's why that lovely lady
Who stands so proud, so tall
Who holds the lighted torch above
Along the ocean floor
She stands to show the people
She stands to show the world
In God, we trust
He watches us
A land of liberty

Vernell Hengel
A TRUE POEM OF OUR LOVE

To Jim, my wonderful, loving husband, whom I love always, Vernell.

My life was unhappy and rotten
A lot of mistakes I had made
But then, I met the love of my life
And together, we have stayed.

I was thirty-nine. He was only
twenty-one
We started out as friends
After seven months, I had his love.
I felt so happy and lucky, I had won.

He is so thoughtful, loving and kind.
And I am very happy to say
I have his love and he has mine
Also to others, our love does shine.

I am so thankful that I have Jim
November of seventy-five, I said my
vows to him.
His ring was engraved "God Gave
Me You"
From that day on, our love has grown
With God's help, our love will
always be true

He is my lover, friend, and my life
Our love we will always treasure
God has put us through some tests
But with God's love, we have Peace
and Rest.

Laura Donaldson
A TASTE OF HEAVEN

To my father, Thomas.

He paused beside the river's edge
To look upon its beauties.
Its crystal ripples swirling below
Reprieved him from his duties.

His face reflected in its shine
As he gazed upon its colors.
It seemed for him and him alone,
He'd share it with no others.

For one brief moment stopped in time
He dared not make a sound,
For fear that someone might pass by
And tear his dreamland down.

And when he'd looked for all he
could,
And drank the vision in,
He turned and slowly walked away
Thinking heaven's where he'd been.

Esther G Crane
WHEN AUTUMN PAINTS THE LANDSCAPE
While the world sits idly by,
And the days are growing cold,
Autumn rides 'long with a sigh,
While the world sits idly by,
And the wintry snows are nigh;
Beauty the earth will enfold,
While the world sits idly by
And the days are growing cold.

While the leaves turn red and gold,
And the frost on the window
clings,
The wind blows icy and cold,
While the leaves turn red and gold,
And the earth its treasures will hold;
Gaily the merriment rings
While the leaves turn red and gold
And the frost on the window clings.

Mildred (Gray) Griffiths
MY HERITAGE
Once when a child, I wanted to know.
What was my heritage I'd like to
know.

I asked my Mother and she related to
me.
Some of these things I remember
today.

Your Grandma was tiny as tiny could
be,
But she really was strong for her
heritage you see.
She was part Indian, French, and
Pennsylvania Dutch.
And it made me think, I could not be
much.

To be a mixture, I thought lessened
me,
To be very strong, or very happy you
see.
But when I saw how strong she was
of herself,
I felt that I was as small as an Elf...

And sometimes I was at war with
myself.
Sometimes the red hated the white,
And sometimes the white hated the
red.
But still I'm proud to be part of them.

Linda Louise Alvarado
A CHILD IS BORN
A child is born, her life begun,
then a joyful song is sung.
I give my thanks to GOD above,
to this child I'll give my love.
She has little eyes that shine,
and two hands, so small in mine.
I'll give this child lots of care,
teach her to talk, to walk, and comb
her hair.
Then she'll jump and run and sing,
her hands will soon touch everything.
For now, she talks, she's sweetly
cooing,
but growing up is what she's doing.
One day we'll quarrel, but make
amends
for we'll always be best friends.
One day to come my heart will
grieve,
she'll be grown and some day leave.
In my thoughts, close to my heart,
she'll always be
a child once; once days long past,
that child was me.

Jacquetta L Finnegan
WONDERINGS
You know
I never (ever-ever)
Knew You
In
The Biblical sense
Tho'
I should have.

And I
Think about you often
And
I dream about you more

And more—I wonder
What would have/could have
Been
And
Why
Things turn out
The
Way
They do.

Pamela Sheets
LETTING GO
The apron strings have lost the tie
that once held so very fast.
With each little more it is undone,
my heart goes with it too.
The years have gone by so quickly,
too quickly,
and I can't stop what I know
must be.
But those baby days are gone forever
now,
and letting go brings many a
tear.
But dear Lord, to you, I entrust my
most precious child,
and let him go into your all
loving hands.
So I take a step back as each day goes
by,
because I know this child's
becoming a man.
As he struggles to be free, to find
himself,
tempers fly, but my love's as
deep as the sea.
And I know as he goes away from
me, you are there,
his loving Heavenly Father, to
watch and care.

SO I LET GO...........

Steph Sdanowich
TRANSITION
A new year has come
my new life has just begun.

Since I was very young,
I've prayed this day would come.

I wish I would have had the guts,
to proceed without all those if &
but's,

My new life could have had an early
start,
instead of this pain piercing my heart.

A girl is what my gender is,
not a boy this shell says I am.

It hurts so much to hear them,
call me Stephen, like an actor in
show biz,

I'm Stephanie playing the part of
Stephen,
and now it's about time I get even.

Balancing my body & soul is what I
mean,
too many people base their lives on
green.

So now that my life has come to
bloom,
I hope family & friends give me
the room.

If my choice scares them away,
I really don't know what to say,
but I will still love them anyway,
because I never, really had a choice.

Steph Sdanowich
THE DEATH OF A CHILD
That day in March
Your Easter dress full of starch
In Ocean City to calm your soul,
But God had another goal
All the time you boasted your
Beauty
We knew you were such a cutey.
But now that you have done
We feel that it was so wrong.
We all love you very much
If you only knew without a
Touch.

Peggy O'Neal Nickle
MOTHER
the look in your eyes
was it one clear?
in the dark of the night
did you know any fear?
or a special color
of which you were fond—
that one true friend
with an unbreakable bond—
were you one so passive
taking life in stride?
was there ever a picnic
in the sweet countryside?
did you curl your hair
or make up your face?
what were your clothes,
of cotton or lace?
where was your heart
when I was to be?
did you know that my life
you would not see?
I wonder most often
who you had been—
and could you start over
would you have me again?

Christina Sweeting
A NEW DREAM
Running as fast as a lightning bolt,
As swift as the wind.
Her glittering horn held high,
As she flies through the sky.
Her brilliant eyes,

Sparkle as stars go by.
Higher and higher she flies.
As she slows,
You clearly see,
That she is a dream.
A new dream she is,
A pegacorn is her name.
Half unicorn she is,
And half Pegasus also.
A great dream she is.

Ethel R Whitaker

Ethel R Whitaker
LIFE CAN BE BEAUTIFUL
Your eyes can see the beauty in living,
And far beyond what is seen by a few.
It's what you put into it, forever giving,
The beauty of your service always come back to you.

It's finding the blessings that do come true,
It's seeking the strength to climb higher.
No matter how steep the hill is for you,
Keep your mind on your goal, never tire.

It's finding the courage to seek what you're after,
With your heart firmly fixed on your dreams.
Then your smile may turn into laughter,
When you see just what beauty life brings.

Yes, life can be beautiful for you at last.
It's seeking your dreams each day as you live,
It's the enjoyment of your present, and discovering the meaning of your past.
It's seeking the creative possibilities of your future;
that's the special beauty that life truly gives.

Lillian McPherson
I CRY FOR BABIES; N'ER TO BE BORN
A shortage of babies, you say today?
"Why I know they're conceived," I dared to say.
"Tis nothing but a blob"—"a mass."
"Just can't be bothered," she'd often harassed.
"Just not convenient in any way."
"Who wants a 'kid' to raise today?"
My heart is shattered when by and by,
this precious infant is doomed to die.
Just look who's playing God today,
and can't be bothered with a child, anyway.
Lord, let them see in their babes lies a future of love,
God's best gift of all—a child from above.
My heart, it's so heavy, it's oh, such a shame,
if only they'd raise them and give them a name.
Praise them and love them as I know they could,
'cuz God sees a way when you've done what you should.
I'm hoping, Dear Jesus, I'll wake up to see,
that there's no more crying for you and for me,
and happy the babies all over the place,
will still be around to continue the race.

Ted Robaczewski
WITHERED LOVES
Wilted flowers in a vase,
dust on the shelves,
white lace faded yellow,
since the clouds took their place.

Pools of crystal blue,
sable wings of decoration,
Stamping stallions of white,
combined for beauty true.

Blue eaten by murky brown,
black swallowed by gray,
Stallions fell on weakened red,
Since the sun's rays touch not the ground.

No one notices the loss
As velvet darkness smothers light,
the light glimmers and fades
while being gathered to the gloss.

Dorothy Helen Bertalot Jahns
MY GRANDSON, KENNETH
God loaned us Kenny for a while.
Beginning life was touch and go,
A fighter from his crib, I'd say.
'Twas a delight to watch him grow.

Ken had great influence on people.
A super example for all,
Teaching be happy, love others,
Be yourself, tell the truth, stand tall.

God told Kenny, "Time's up right now."
I miss him greatly and weep tears.
Surely my crying will help me
Be thankful for his twenty years.

We've stories to share about him.
There's movies and snapshots to see,
Newspaper clippings saved carefully-
We'll remember him, believe me.

G Richard Leyrer Jr
BECKY
The Twinkle in your eyes is all so Bright, they remind me of the stars on the darkest night. I get a special feeling whenever you are near.
When we are together you should have no fears. They say the world won't last forever, so we should enjoy the time we will spend together.
Each day I think of how pretty you smile, I know we will be together in just a little while. When the day comes, walls will come tumbling down.
In my arms is where I wish you to be found. I cannot wait till the day I get out. We will have a good time, this is no doubt.
I can only write so many lines, this poem is for you, my sweet cherry wine.

Jodie Newsome
FRIENDS FOREVER
You're always there for me. So I'll always
be there for you.

You're my shoulder to cry upon
when times are tough.

You'll always be a part of me, not only in my soul, but always in my heart.

You make me happy and glad to live for tomorrow.

When times go bad with you and me, we always
have our great memories.

All the tears and pain we've shared make up
for all the laughter we've lost.

I hope our lasting friendship will make history.

And our friendship will last another thousand days.

Estelle Tillmon

Estelle Tillmon
SOMEONE THAT CARES "JESUS"

To my family and all that do not know that Jesus cares.

Somewhere in the air
I breath something that's not there
Oh how I wish I'll meet someone that cares
As I turned and looked around my Jesus stood there
I looked at him with tears in my eyes
But he said to me, "Don't fret my child."
He took me by the hand and led me to the hills
Because he knew I needed to be filled
The spirit was upon me but I dare not to say
Because my Jesus knew this was my day
As he started talking to me I start crying
But he knew already what was on my mind
He told me to go home and tell no one
Because his work with me was already done

(I Peter 5:7) Casting all your care upon Him for he careth for you.

Estelle Tillmon
HOLY SPIRIT
Holy Spirit Holy Spirit
Lead and guide me all the way
So I can have a peaceful day
Help me to hold out a helping hand
As I ponder through this land
Looking beyond what my eyes can see

Thinking of faith how far it brought me
Hoping and praying as I travel this road
Just to see Jesus to give him this load
Holy Spirit Holy Spirit
I thank you in a mighty way
In more words than I can say.
Leaning and trusting in Jesus's name
So one day I won't be ashamed.

Pamela Willis-Gray
DUSK
Waves of golden grain at our feet,
Sun warmed backs.
Sounds, smells of evening so sweet,
Dusty deer tracks.

Warm orange glow of bright golden sun
Lights up the frame
Of bent old tree whose day is done,
Brilliant as a flame.

Purple shadow on gray valley,
Dusk coming down.
Blue foothills, peaceful rhapsody-
Above the town.

Engulfed in freedom there that night,
Beyond self strife.
Sensed everything would be alright
In this game of life.

Colorado Red

Dana-ayn Gulczynski
SOMEONE TO WATCH OVER ME
A touch, a smile,
the wink of an eye.
All serve to remind me.
The soft whisper
of your voice,
and I'm reminded
of how much you care
for me.
My own guardian angel.
Someone to watch over me.
I need you always.
To be there by my side,
with a caring word,

and a reassuring hug.
Don't ever leave me
standing in the cold.
Because I need someone
to watch over me.
And that someone...
is you!!

Sister Carol Vanden Eng
OUTER SPACE, INNER SPACE
Outer space is a vastly unexplored expanse.

Is my Inner Space just as uncharted?
Do I know why I feel and act as I do?
Do I realize what tenses and relaxes me?
Do I comprehend what losses I have blocked, if any?

The Galileo probe was sent to investigate a minute part of the universe.

Is the Inner Space of my being as carefully examined?
Do I know the wonders it contains?
Do I realize my gifts, loves, and cherished memories?
Do I give the time and investment an exploration needs?

Most of my energy-
Is it spent on
OUT SPACE
or
INNER SPACE?

Katrina Adams
WHAT MY FREEDOM MEANS TO ME

I dedicate this poem to my Aunt Mary, for believing in me even when others didn't—and for pushing me to succeed even when I felt like giving up.

Freedom, yes it's a very strong word.
And for those who never had it makes
them wonder when it is heard.
To them it means something extraordinary and grand.
For it is something they never experienced
something they never had.
Those without freedom anything they would give.
Freedom is the only reason that they have to live.
But for me freedom—I see it in a
whole different way.
Simply because I have it each and every day.
The slavery I get is punishment
from Mom and Dad.
And usually I deserve it cause I did
something bad.
But years and years ago
it was not hardly like that.
In those days you were born a slave because
you were black.
As you think about it now—you say,
man, that wasn't right.
After King stood up—people were ready to fight.
Before King died—he said he had a dream and the dream he dreamed
is the theme. So by the words I say "you can clearly see what the word freedom means to me."

Mrs J W Tillema
TRIBUTE TO GREAT GRANDMOTHERS

To Mary K Rieder who had to be both my grandmother and my mother.

Long years ago we started out
As mothers, young and gay,
We knew not much of life and all
But learned just day by day.

We raised our children, some just one,
And thought they were the best,
We never dreamed of days to come
When they would make the test.

But came that day eventually
We were both glad and sad,
It meant the leaving of one loved
But that was all the fad.

Their days were brightened as they planned
For future years to come;
And then one day they too were gladdened
By a daughter or a son.

These children grew up much too fast
They soon were off our knee,
We grandmas were right proud of them
As anyone could see.

School days were over for them too
We watched them day by day,
They liked to come to Grandma's house
For cookies and to play.

For us the years passed all too soon
For them, not soon enough,
But came the day for each and all
To find this life was tough.

Before the years rolled round much more
They made us all right proud,
We added great to grandma
And shouted right out loud.

If anyone should ask you
If we're worthy of that name,
I doubt if any would deny us
That honor, love and fame.

For I know we've surely earned it
By our helpful, loving care,
Through sickness, health and happiness
We've done just all we dare.

Our great-grandchildren are our joys
As anyone can see,
Had others been given such a chance
I'm sure they, too, would be
Happy and proud, shouting aloud
Hurrah! for us one and all,
We dare you to challenge our claim to fame
For these children can answer the call.

Stacy A Agnello
THE BEACH
The beach is quiet,
Except for the tiny rippled waves coming in.
Listening to that sound is sometimes comforting.
My future is looked for,
Always unlightened, dark and dim.

Stars are looked upon as the answer to life.
Will I fall in love, marry, be a wonderful wife?

It's eerie how nature soothes the mind.
The midnight breeze right through me,
My feelings slowly unwind.

Will I escape this lost daze?
I'm unfounded in my dreams,
Seems to be a neverending maze.

Cries are heard, no one seems to listen.
I will live my fantasies, it's my goal.
A fearful mission.

F J Alanis
HAPPY MOTHERS DAY
Remembering when I was just a lad,
How you made me smile, when I was sad.

Whenever I needed you, you were always there
To sew on a button or remove gum from my hair.

And all the hurt which you made go away
Let me know why you so loved today

You are my number one lady
The queen of my heart
When God made you, my mother,
He made a work of art.

Nancy Wright

Nancy Wright
TWISTED MINDS

I dedicate my poetry to my brother Tom, who gave me the inspiration.

Twisted minds maneuver changing each and every day
they twist and bend and pull and push until they get their way
negative thoughts and positive deeds outside a kind man through and through
would you judge him as harshly if the deeds were meant for you?
To take the truth and twist it into tiny little lies
hurts those involved enormously . . . only God can hear our cries
a twisted mind so narrow can never understand
how you could do things your way and not as they demand
enraged and broken feelings running the gamut for so long
no suffering to endure if one's love was not as strong
how can life be so unjust when we are pure in heart?
We've done much more than our fair share right from the very start
to do things as they have been done is to relish a hateful scorn
it makes the other siblings feel unloved and so forlorn
these twisted minds will put you down if you don't see their way
but how can you see it when it changes every day?
Though he may not be a flower with a fragrance oh so sweet
black and white makes a pretty gray carpet when I walk
with my two feet!
The poison has leaked for many years creating the future as it has begun
A new beginning unfolds but the puppeteer has not won!

Nancy Wright
THE MAN IN THE MASK
Beware of the man wearing a mask
who will gladly perform any difficult task
he sure is kind and charming they say
there's so much he does and without any pay
the Rolex he wears is made of pure gold
but his heart inside . . . calculatingly cold!
He thinks he can have any girl that he chooses
they feel pretty special 'till they see how he uses
his money he flashes when out for the night
and his best girl worries when he's out of her sight
he has no conscience and puts others to shame
the devious masked man's the one who's to blame
Steadfast in his trickery he pursues his prey
like a spider wrapping up a host
tomorrow's another day
he seeks out those who compliment and praise him in awe
watch out 'cuz this sly fox is barely above the law!
The exposed face beneath the mask
will prove him incomplete
without a heart a human suffers anguishing defeat!
In anger against God's children the wind cries out
and it's hard for most to see what the trouble's all about
blessed be those who have a keen eye
they can see through the mask and end with a sigh!
At the center in his orbit is the loathsome puppeteer
who makes me glad he's there and grateful I am here
The center of the Universe is a great place to be
if I were but God and not quite simply me.

Nancy Wright
RUTHLESS
The ruthless endeavor to perform
and care less of what's right or wrong
they seek to mow their obstacles
and happily play and sing their song
when overwhelmed with uncertainty
and decisions must be made
problems stack up in mounting force
it's hard to act so brave
when wrong's within the law
and right is morally wrong
the ruthless try to take you in
to sing and dance their song

if right is not the most correct
and wrong is not too wrong
one can take a neutral stance
but must be very strong
to take a stand's a grand decision
and neutral an unpopular choice
consider what's best for all involved
and listen to that inner voice
when faced with crystal blue
confusion
and knowing what's at stake
you'll find there's little they can give
because they're on the take!

Nancy Wright
THE DEVILS ADVOCATE
That thief of the mind will steal ideas
and act like they're their own
they suck the thoughts of others and
amplify the tone

Transplanted beliefs can emerge
quite strong how could we ever get
along?
led astray in each direction how
could our thoughts reach a connection?

I always try to harmonize and do my
very best
and now that I'm grown up my
thoughts are put through quite a test

A child becomes an adult with his or
her opinion
a devils advocate tries to sway each
clear-cut decision

The source of all the energy is the
backstage puppeteer
he strongly argues the opposite of
what I'd like to hear

In the battle with the puppet when it
began its song and dance
every time I'd lose because I never
had a chance

It's like a rigged straight poker game
and the dealer's not the one to blame

Whenever I would have a vision I'd
become the object of derision
memories of foul contradiction
swallows my mind with firm
conviction!

Nancy Wright
A MOTHER'S LOVE
Doing things for others would show
you love them at first glance
But using those you love is frankly
taking quite a chance

If you refuse to perform her tasks
does that mean you don't love?
Stand up for what you believe in and
put faith in God above

Mother always showed her love when
conditions had been met
But how that proved she really loved
is difficult to get

It's quite easy to assume the lady
didn't care
She made a pact with Satan to
become a millionaire

If those she loved wouldn't do what
asked she'd make a judgment call
Love that is conditional means
having no love at all

There were things she wanted done
my time and energy she'd rob
All these things to get her love
became a full-time job

Love's not measured by what you did
or what you plan to do
It's Universal and all encompassing
in your heart you'll know it's true

By refusing work to say, "We lacked
love," takes a lot of gall
There was little love left for return,
the devil drained it all

A mother's love is supposed to be for
her children every one
How could she not give equally or
did she only have one son?

Mother you've made our lives
miserable because of the will you
drew
Oh my darling mother in spite of all
we still love you!

Nancy Wright
EMPTY DREAMS
Promises made and soon forgotten
in the midst of mass confusion
what came to pass is empty dreams
my life's a grand illusion

Oh what I've unveiled
the contagious secrets that went on
and shaky is the rope that I am
balancing upon

In looking for the answers
the wise say "seek and ye shall find"
and with these ponderous thoughts I
seek
I just may lose my mind!

Nancy Wright
THE EVIL I HAVE
How can I feel love when creeping
torment anguishes the heart?
Monstrous deeds shake me and put
fire in my soul.
My mind's eye experiences the
thunderous emotions that
can only be the guise of the evil one's
marks. He laughs
at me and taunts me with such cruel
sport that I am
drained . . . dead and yet I walk
around. The beast is
with me just over my shoulder,
waiting and wondering
what my next move will be. If I
choose one road or the
other, he will see it is blocked. How
my spirit is toyed
with and dashed. I try to see the
sunshine and a cloud
passes overhead. The suffering of
outrageous caliber
is vented only by the smile on my
face. But in my eyes
the astute onlooker can clearly see
into the window of
my very being. The tumult can not be
reckoned with
because it is overpowering . . .
unrestrainable . . . and
yet I keep looking, trying to find the
sunshine.
Perhaps when I cease moving I'll see
it's light!?

Nancy Wright
BROTHERLY LOVE
Look at the good in all mankind
and accept what you don't like
manipulate, sway, maneuver them
but always be polite

Be matter of fact be assertive
and state what you don't like
it's better than blowing up
and getting so uptight

With love in your heart
you just can't lose
that glitter in your eye
it's the love of Jesus
God wants of us
until the day we die

Treasure him and keep him safe
as you would a baby dove
accept his faults and angry ways
that's universal love!

Donna Ruth Barr
WHO ARE YOU
You may not be a movie star
You may not be a king,
You may not be Michael Jackson
Or be able to sing like Bing,
You may not climb the mountains
Or all those kinds of things
But I think you're just the swellest
guy,
Whoever turned thirteen.

Laura Hinkle
TO YOU—FRIEND
To you—the special one
Once in a lifetime they come

They say they are forever
In the beginning it was me and you
And I hope in the end
It will be that way too

To you—the true one
Who will always be in my heart

They say—they are a blessing from
God
My blessing is you
And the love, caring and compassion
That has always come too

To you—the best of the best
Of a thing they call friends.

Heather Anne Macpherson
FLOWERS
Rain is wonderful for nature.
While the rain pours,
it's the flowers galore.
They open up like a hand
reaching for candy,
but it reaches for rain.

When the rain stops,
the flowers, they keep their frail
petals open
like a child would keep its hand open
for more candy.
When the rain doesn't come for
weeks,
the flowers wither and die, and
nothing is left of
the flowers or the rain that had once
fallen, for
the earth to feed on.

Anne Marie Bullock
THE BLAZING HEAT
The sun is blazing with the heat!
It shines over the deserts' streets!
I touch it with my toes and feet!
The sun is blazing over the street!
I feel blazing inside my body heat!
The sun is blazing free to see!

Gretchen I Martin
ELEGANT THUNDERSTORM
The elegant thunderstorm was
dressed in a tux.
He was the host of our post party
in a ballroom decorated with wind
and rain.
At first, the gentleman was calm,
content
Drenched in a layer of cordiality and
politeness.
He glided and flowed gracefully over
the dance floor.
But then the music with his intensity
swelled.
And the thunderstorm roared with
spells
of primitive anger.
The now furious storm crashed and
threatened
like the dark-faced man screaming
at the insubordinant servants.
Then he mellowed again.
And the pitter-patter, pitter-patter of
soft rain,
the sweet tranquil music returned.
The world was quiet. Our party
continued.
Always, the gentleman shifted
moods.
Suddenly peaceful. Suddenly
raging.
The elegant thunderstorm was
dressed in a tux.

Kimberly Lynn Lowe
A MEMORY OF GRANDPA
Solemnly I entered,
The room had the green cast of death.
Life
Slowly
Draining
From his Soul.
His hand reached out, holding it tight
Time Stopped!
For a moment,
Death flowed
From his hand
To mine.
The chain broken I left,
Knowing all things have an end,
Even I.

Barbara Butler Lemaster
THINKING
Sitting in a car
watching people
come and go
from near and far.

Just wondering?
What! would I be
if I were in their
shoes.

Chances are, they,
like me, would be
sitting in a car
wondering what they
would be if they
were me.

Esther H Wiseman
A FATHER'S LOVE
I want to be my father's kind
Who mounts the everwinding stairs
To a better sign of knowledge
Far beyond the shadows and the
years

To be welcomed by the loved one
Who shows him in every way
A father's love of all the things
We need—and someday I pray
I will be that man, and walk my
father's path
But no—that future will not be—for
When I look to my own two loves
I see—I have the very things
My own father has—to be
A happy man like me.

Katie Ann Bell
HIS
His eyes like the sea after storm.
His lips rounded and pink.
His hands soft and smooth.
His hair light yellow.
His face oval.
His legs good for running.

Gen O Marshall
AN ARTIST IN THE NIGHT
An artist in the night
An artist in the night
While I was sleeping
An artist came last night
He dressed my little forest
In robes of snowy white
Transforming it completely
Into a forest of delight
He transformed my little forest
Into a wonderland
And I feel like a princess
In a little fairy land
He frosted it completely
From the tree tops to the pond
He frosted it completely
With his magic wand
He kissed the trees and shrubbery
And left bare branches gay
Then softly whispered Good Night
And made his get away

Micah Neff
ME
My name is Micah Joseph Neff
Yes, that's right, Micah—not
Henry—Not Jeff.
I love to skate, think and sing,
But I guess I do most everything.
I love my Mom, she's my friend,
I'll love her till the very end.
Well, that's me, without a doubt,
And Hey dittle, dittle with a scream
and a shout!

Vicki Adams

Vicki Adams
FOR MY MOM

To Mom: Forever in our hearts—We love you muches.

Whenever I feel all alone
I go to see my mom,
I know that she is always home
with her my blues are gone

She lives up high up on a hill
it's peaceful and serene,
the wind and trees are always still
the hills are lovely green

She doesn't have an address
but instead a slab of stone,
engraved with name and all the love
a mother could have known.

She can't exactly speak to me
or hold me when I cry,
I know that we can't talk again
until the day I die.

When that day comes I'll hold her
tight
and never let her go,
At long last now my heart can heal
it broke so long ago.

Doris Maskevich
REFLECTIONS
As I looked towards a better life
daydreamed of different things
Wondered what it was I could do
so it would all come true
I couldn't accept anything less
than it all just being right
Now like a shadow from the fading
sun
it's all drifted out of sigh
While waiting for things to be just so
what was ahead is now behind
my search has all been in vain
My life has drifted by and now is past
things weren't just right, I've been
so blind

Charlotte M Peiler
TRAPPER'S HEAVEN
The old trapper
with arthritic joints,
from years in the cold,
felt the call to
HEAVEN.

Up the mountain side
with his walking stick
leaving his mule behind,
climbing higher and higher
toward HEAVEN.

Met himself a Grizzly,
with hands held up
to the sky, he met the
Grizzly's full-forced blow,
Death arrived—HEAVEN came!

Dee Hall
LIGHTS
Lights bright, lights dim,
Lights ornamental,
Filling every whim!

Lights that sparkle,
Lights that dance,
Lights that can put us in a trance.

Light manmade, lights from above.
Lights from our Savior
That reflect His love!

Light from His sun,
Light from His moon.
Light from His stars,
He came not too soon.

To save us all, right here on earth
Let us celebrate, His night of birth,
With holy music, that fills us with
mirth.

May we remember: He wants us to
be,
A light here on earth, to serve Him
and see
That all our fellowmen,
Have light from above,
May we all be guided
By His gentle love!

Shayne E Pound
WHAT FRIENDS ARE FOR!
Friends are there when you're down
Friends are there when you're happy
Friends are there to see you through
the bad times
Friends are there to make you feel
good
Friends are there to help you with
your problems
Let's face it! Friends are there when
you need 'em
That's what friends are for!

Jennifer Lee Schoenherz
ACCEPTANCE BY GOD
His face was dimly lit by the
moonlight,
but his expression could be read
as clear as day.
His smile was wide as could be,
and his eyes were sparkling and fun.

Death overcame the body shortly,
the soul of the man was accepted by
God,
as he had died for a worthy cause,
saving the life of one he had hated.

The moon slowly sank,
as the sun came up,
and hidden in an alley,
the shadow was cast over
the face of the man.

Jeannie Hoffman
MY PASSION
I smell the smouldering leaves and
sense
the air is charged with electric
crispness
The grey smoke chokes the sight
from my eyes

And when these lids are lowered, I
see the heat
the reds and orange that fill my
gut
with the melted jello that is the core
of my
being
wet
hot
this passion of mine

Mildred C Scott
OF PLEASURE AND PAIN, TWO DIFFERENT, THE SAME
Pain and pleasure are opposites not,
Although this be what is commonly
thought.
Neither of these can be sold or
bought,
Yet both rich and poor these two
have got.
"How ludicrous," one might at first
exclaim,
But think on the examples one can
easily name,
As that of Socrates' friends, whom
his company cherished
Even in the very hour that he
perished.
And of Jesus' followers, who
mourned deeply their loss,
At the moment their Friend died upon
the cross.
Yet, in that same moment the veil in
the temple was rent
Bringing joy that the days of sin's
bondage were spent.
And, although these examples are
from days long past.
These tales of this truth are hardly the
last.
Today, who in your life is the one
you call friend
If not one whom you know will be
there to the end.
For it is in such a bond that we find
this great link,
When on tough times shared together
we suddenly think.
After all, are not the moments in life
we most treasure
The ones when pain's tears were
wiped away by love's pleasure?

Jessica M Arnold
THANKS FOR BEING THERE
Thanks for being there all these
years!

Guiding me, Teaching me, through
an earth
full of fears.

Pointing out the way, when I couldn't
see.

Thank God for the Light shining in
me!

Nancy S Hahn
REMEMBER WHEN

For the S.S. kid.

I remember when we were little
The Games we played
The fun we had.

I remember when we were little
Playing in the rain,
Really loving school.

I remember when we were little
A cherry popsicle, a kiss
Made all the pain go away.

What happened to those days
When we were little?

Donna K Huckabey
PAID IN FULL
Jesus was a humble man, it
was very plain to see, and yet
he had the power to part the
raging sea.
How could such a gentle Man
be nailed to that cross?
No one took the time to
realize and estimate the loss!
But yet he loved us dearly,
and He saved our souls for
us, by praying to His Father,
that we should not be lost.
He paid the ramson for us all
and now it's up to us, to make
our way to Jesus, no matter
what the cost.

Hyla M McLain
MISSING MOM
When you are a child with so much to learn
Mom was always there and helped you at every turn.
Then the teen years came
and the closeness was not the same.
But that period soon passed and you knew
Mom's friendship would always last.
She was there in good times and bad
and made things better when you were sad.
As you had your family and they grew
Mom was there to see you through.
She loved them all and they loved her
There wasn't a better Grandma, no sir.
She made every visit so great
Her treats were delicious—we ate and ate.
Soon it was time for her to be a great grandmother
and she loved that role better than any other.
But Dad was sick with a terminal ill
and Mom fought hard to pay the bills.
It got her down and wore her out
She became sick and had a terrible bout
We lost her in a few short weeks!
Why, why why the answer we seek.
Dad's lost and can't hold on
Six months later he is gone.
The pain stays and stays
Will it ever go away!
Eight years later, I find myself still reaching for the phone.
I want to say hi but suddenly remember she's not home.

James M Green
AWAKEN
Earth is an experiment of the Universal Master,
The experiment failed, that's why earth is a disaster.
It's not too late to change what has happened here,
It all starts with love and life without fear.
Without fear there would never be another war
In the United States or on a foreign shore.
If we could rid the world of politics and greed,
We can help the failing experiment; help it to succeed.
The New Age is starting, planetary awakening will too,
It all begins with finding yourself within you.
Once people realize it's their choice to choose,
They will either change to win or remain the same and lose.
They day will come for all hate and violence to cease,
And we shall see an interplanetary peace.
You must have faith, you must believe,
Before the gift of change we can receive.
In order to avoid mistakes like the ones we're makin',
Everyone on earth must first spiritually awaken . . .

Carla L Schrecengost
AS YOU LOOK AT A STAR
As you look at a star
on a dark clear night,
way above and yet so far
it is full of might.

It makes you wonder how
they are suspended up there,
With speckles of white,
that glitter so bright,
In the crisp night air.

As we ponder and gaze
at the size of this universe,
aware and amazed,
That we still are in search.

In every day life
we look near and far
with all of the strife;
We can all be a star.

Josie Gallo
THE UNANSWERED LOVE?
It seems so funny to love someone
you have never been close to,
From afar you know his voice you
wish he feels the way you do.
You listen to his every word but
no one seems to care
If you only can tell him that he
takes you breath away
If only you can look into his deep
dark eyes
And see the stars of love appear.

If he can only stay forever by your side
He can only love you and never let
go, if I'd had the chance I'd tell him.
How his voice brings chills down
my spine.
I can't explain the secrets he seems to
hold, but I have to trust
My feelings because I think it's love.
Someday he'll be mine, I dream of
him in my arms
Touching me, loving me. I cry myself
to sleep just wishing he was near
With his loving arms around me
comforting me when I'm down.
I pray and love him from afar, no one
who he is?
I reach for him almost for a slight
moment actually feel him.
But I can't it's a mystery.
The Unanswered Love

James Mason Merchant
ON DEATH'S BATTLEFIELD

"To Congressman Tom and Anette Lantos for their dedication to the prospect of peace."

As the cross-maker tends his endless trade,
The varied trumpets still the noble fight,
Recruiting all from the Left and the Right
To march in the mothers' weeping brigade.
Soon they come to rest with the yawning earth
And the spring-like hearts gush fountains of tears,
For Priestly words tremble remorseful ears,
Echoing: 'tis the destiny of birth?
Such be thy fate when fools and cowards scheme
For the Stately Seat, and witless soldiers'
Headlong ambitions enshroud their formers'
Wisdom: Heavenly Order reigns supreme.
As the platoons battle anew across
The rested land, the tradesman
plants his cross.

James Mason Merchant
THE STERLING ROSE

To Mother, Father, Andrea Shispinsky.

Basking in the sunshine the buddings grew,
Purpling the fields with their lavender hue,
And like the Eye of Heaven did one wink,
And thoughts of thee, lady, I soon did think;
From the virtue of this sterling blossom,
True, true beauty bloomed under my bosom.

Edward H Birkemeier
AN ANCIENT THEME
Aweary with the waste and haste of toil,
the heat of diligence dispersed to spoil,
languishing an end to means assembled
where labor to its bounty is imbred.
Oh rummage through decrepitudes of time,
obtrude into the cryptic shades of fate.
Then tell me if success e're crowned its deed
or where if so the lengthening of it leads.
Or is it else a victory throne of thorns,
a desert seat in a deluge of defeat
where clamorous applause is hushed to shame
by stumbling time's wide-trampling tide of truth?
Oh vanity of events doth ravage hope
though thinking on it doth enhance our scope.

Edward H Birkemeier
BEYOND THE PALL
Despite the slough of time and
raging spite,
the twisted sneer and vacant laugh of Hell,
the thumping thrust of fate unjust but there,
the fabricated jaded acts of pride,
a man of pluck could seek beyond the pall
a something real, substance, truth or ground,
dodge the worst, stake a claim withal
and make of it a biding map to guide
the soul to more distinctive form and aim,
full deeper tone, a further search of word.
then he perhaps may stay the strident hour,
rein in the loose unruly gloom of woe,
throw the rope ashore and thus secure
a foothold of repose amidst the storm.

Edward H Birkemeier
BEAUTY'S BREVITY
The face of autumn's fleeting
glory fades,
a blaze of blushing beauty soon abashed
veiling herself in pale obscuration
where the mocking world will menace her no more.
Beauty is brief and we who seek extent
of leisure, of luxury, of splendor laid at length
where wisdom's pith and point inscribe it's measure
debased by neither brute nor boorish pleasure,
are fettered, vexed, distressed in a helpless quest!
A prey of birds is beauty's preservation,
frail grist to blight and deformation
that seize its life and breviate its luster.
Enjoy it then the while within its presence
ere moth and rust and ruin consume its essence.

Edward H Birkemeier
A POEM BY THE SCUFF OF THE NECK
Then up to stalk the bristly
thickset wood
to scavenge out a brawny-furrowed beam.
Or rake the rugged quarry for a cairn;
all warped and warted—telling a tortured tale.
To ferret out the forest of the mind,
To punctuate a path of true intent;
then sack the sacred citadel of words
and bind them to a barbed and pointed phrase;
lavished with a lusty-colored image
that speaks of purloined hours and rubric wit;
shred the chaff and clip it to a figure
that hints of heated strife and reeking pain.
To catch the word and tack it to the line,
a token of a triumph of the mind.

Thomas Harvey Blanton

Thomas Harvey Blanton
SUMMER, MAYFIELD AVENUE, 1989

Dedicated to my Mother, DeRue DeShane

In the Garden,
The Sun Shines
On the Buddha,
Sitting before
A Row of Bamboo.
Over by the Gardenias,
Two small birds
Are playing
In the Birdbath and,
In the distance,

Across the hedge,
A Rooster Crows.
Summer has arrived!
Perhaps, this year,
For the first time,
I can finally find time
To enjoy God's Sunshine.

"In His Light and Love"

Melvin L McCoy
SLEEPY

Dedicated to my companion, despair.

I love to sleep
It brings me closer to death
And I do wish to die
I have destroyed everything
meaningful to me
I feel life slipping by
I hear drums drumming to me
My heart beating ever so slowly
It says—shall I stop-shall I stop—
shall I stop
And so I sleep
It keeps me safe
In my dreams it seems I'm safe

But then I awake and die all over
again
My face shows the years of sin and
torment
My poverty shows the wasted gifts
that were God sent

I wish to die or at least sleep awhile
I begin my days all alone
I live in a home that is not my home
I do nothing I need to do
I have no one to talk to—no one
seems to give a damn
So I sleep to keep the pain away
I sleep hoping death will come and
stay
I pray to die before I wake
If worthy my soul I know God shall
take
If not—so be it
I could look back and ask why
But it does not matter
I wish to sleep or to die
My God—I prefer the latter

You are not me to think
It's not or it can't be that bad
You do not know me
You have not had what I've had
It's sad for sure
But my only cure is to sleep
And I'm sleepy now
So GOOD NIGHT

Melvin L McCoy
THE KILLING OF A KING

We are killing our presidents, our doctors, our great teachers, and explorers much too soon. With our so called women's rights we are killing them in the womb. It shames me to say that this right that millions of women feel so strongly is theirs, is doing the work of Satan. He loves it. Without lifting a finger and by planting a thought, he has killed millions upon millions. All in the name of women's rights. Deprived of life, another child cries in heaven's orphanage. Sad would that day have been had your mother felt that way. There are many reasons to "kill" a child before birth, but no good one to let it live. It's a gift from God no matter what the circumstances. No matter what they are. What right have we to judge this child so harshly? To condemn it to death! It would be better to give life and take our own rather than to condone abortion. We have not the right. We in truth, know not the future of our child and should not judge it by our present or our past. Wake up, women of the world, this thing cannot last. You may be killing our king.

Patrick Whitcomb Kelley
A STRANGER TO THIS LAND

This poem is dedicated to my mother and teacher,Geneive Hosmer Kelley.

Man and his perception is a conflict
made of stone
The truth of all creation is a hope that
stands alone
They say the only path to truth is free
of mortal stay
But in my heart and through my God
I've found another way

This path is built on love and faith
but first there must be death
A death of earthly bonds and fears
with anguish put to rest
When through your heart and through
your mind you grasp this moment
true
A voyage is made possible and
everything is new

When day's work ends and darkness
comes the world around me sleeps
And that's the time I drift away and
leave this mortal keep
I soar above the laws of form and
witness things not seen
And travel through the distant voids
that's far beyond a dream

I float upon a whitened cloud and
look up at a glance
And spy the brilliant angel forms
with golden wings in dance
I visit lands in harmony where time
has lost its place
Where rainbows touch from world to
world and songbirds give to chase

And then this voice within me says
"its time this travel cease,
To end this secret voyage full of
wonderment and peace"
And as my mortal bonds become a
part of what I am
I rise up to the morning sun, a
stranger to this land.

Debra K Madrie
MOM

This poem is dedicated to my Mom, Wanda Prosser. She has been everything to me. My mom, my friend, my counselor, my world. I love you Mom.

You gave me life—took me home
Loved home—respected me
Raised me—cried for me
Cried with me—cried at me

You taught me—showed me
Took time with me
Laughed with me—laughed at me
Cried with me

You cared for me—shared with me
Grew with me—bled for me
Sheltered me—fed me
Cried with me

You talked to me—listened to me
Disciplined me—hurt with me
Hurt because of me
Cried with me
Mom—what a lady
What a joy—I need you
I can count on you
Mom—"I love you"

Ben Alan Hawkins
PEACEFUL EXUBERANCE

To Those Of You Who Believed In Me

The variation between reality
and fantasy—misconceptions of
Time which become the
purpose of animation.

Shadows—shadows.

Feelings of tranquil apparitions
guiding your steps, leading
Us through
delusion; impetuosity;

The compelling omnipotence.

April Sharrock
STARS IN MINE EYES

I dedicate this poem to my sons, Cory and Brady.

You're the stars in mine eyes;
You shine, your my life, my loves;
When I am blue;
I just look at you!
Those stars that shine
In your eyes;
Make life easier to get by;
My eyes have seen, so—much;
But, oh just looking at you,
Makes me see,
The stars in mine eyes.

Lori Klingman-DeWitte
SLEEPER

To my family, with love and devotion.

The sun has set
And shall never rise again
An endless sleep
Has now begun
Tears roll down cheeks
Hearts are weighted
With the sadness of loss
This is the pain
Of those left behind
For the sleeper
Feels no pain
No sorrow
No anguish
For the sleeper
Only sleeps
Taken to rest
Knowing only of the sweetest dreams
So don't cry for the sleeper
Cry for yourself
And when it is understood
The tears will fall no more

Kevin Bindl
DESOLATION ANGEL

To people with a chemical dependency problem.

Here I sit, I look at he and he at I,
All alone, full of sorrow and despair.
He can give me no advice, for he
cannot speak,
He can only listen.
I have let myself get brought so far
down,
That up I can only go.
So here I am in a recreation of hell,
Finally seeing the roads I must walk.
I know now the things I must do,
To find the happiness I seek.
My angel is with me all the time,
I just wish he would talk.
But if he did answer, I am afraid of
what he might say.
For he is only in my mind.
Yet he has helped me come to the
realization,
That desolation is only as powerful as
I am weak.
Now the hurt is gone, and the
feelings of betrayal have vanished.
To this I owe my angel.
My angel has renewed my strength
and hope,
Where I thought no hope could be
found.
With my strength anew, I can now
look forward to,
A life of happiness, success and love,
which I couldn't seem to find before.
All this I owe my angel.

Ron King
LATE NIGHT VISIT

Alone in the house in the middle of
the night
Listening to the storm's fury and
might
Lightning flashing and thunder quake
house, like knees, tremble and shake
Lights flicker and dim before going
out
Alone in the darkness I yell and shout
I can see a crescent moon through the
door
hear thunder crash by the time I count
four
I have no business being where I'm at
But it was business that brought me
where I sat

I should be upstairs snug in my bed
instead of here scared out of my head
I feel monsters coming out of the
ground
I feel breath and jaws pulling me
down
I promise to tantrums or sour pouts
I'll go to bed on time and eat my
sprouts
back upstairs quiet as a mouse
safe from my late night visit
to ye ole family outhouse.

Ron King
PRAIRIE BEACON

On the stark . . . barren . . .wind-
swept prairie,
forlorn and abandoned in the blowing
dust,
stands a monolith of freedom,
mans' symbol of integrity covered
with rust.

Silhouetted against the gray laden
sky,
like a skeleton of prehistoric past,
stands the farmer's windmill . . .
tall and stalwart as oaken mast . . .

Towering in majestic, nobel pride,
silent sentinel of duty bound,
derelict hovels huddle her feet,
bolted steel cries agony's sound.

Look at her. Feel her dying breath,
a relic of the past begins to fall;
a way of life that was . . . is no more.
Pity her . . . pity us . . . pity all.

Witness what is shining in the fading light,
at furthermost height of windmill strand
waves of glory . . . the American flag,
placed there by a weeping . . .
farmer's hand.

Judy G Dotson
THE STORM
The storm is near as so is the pain
like last nights winds and hail of shame.
Confused is my mind how it wonders
along, much like the storm that rumbles on.
Which way to turn for they are few.
But still my mind confused for the love
of you.
My mind does wonder and can be a
wonderful thing much like the love
that bloomed that spring.
Promises made my mind could hear
unlike deep in my heart for it did fear.
The storm outside is drawing thin yet
it must turn about and try again.
Is this my fate I ask indeed or should
I turn about and leave.
Love so deep and sure was mine
giving completely and yet so blind.
Who am I to ask and wonder why am
I not here to try.
Could it be more I should be given.
Why not try and ask God in Heaven.

Trina Burt
IN THIS WORLD THAT NOTHING PHASES
In this world that nothing phases,
I see the light in children's faces.
The "real" world is tearing at its seams,
I envy the children, their play, their dreams.
Where friends and politicians can be bought,
Greed and ambition: How much does happiness cost?
Drowning in pools of man-made misery,
Wake every morn, dreading cold reality.
When humans have destroyed humanity,
And no one wears their hearts upon their sleeve.
Faith in our race and ourselves has died,
Look, you can see the hope, burning in a child's eyes.

Robert C Leachman Jr
CAN YOU CAPTURE THE LOVE
Can you capture the love
Where does it go
Why does it flow
Seeking and ever seeking
You know I loved you once
It seems there was always a full moon
Or a land too large to cross
Still, loving you
Was this my reward
My bitter reward

Rayford Woodall Sr
LITTLE THINGS
When at home we arrive after the day is finally done
To find that our work has only just begun
For at our door we are met by the kids we so adore
With questions, expectations they cannot hide
They with their innocent eyes—open wide
Searching, seeking for answers that we must provide
To quell their curiosity—or to reinforce their philosophy
Then, with prayers said, they scurry off to bed
A smile, a kiss,—Oh the things we really miss
When our day is finally done

Ian Firkin
THE EARTH
The Earth is a ball of glowing life,
but growing dimmer, day and night.
To save our earth, here's what to do,
I can, he can, you can too.
Recycling is all you have to do,
To keep the skies and oceans blue.

Beulah M Lackey
FLAME
Oh, newly lit fire, your bright
sparks dance and jump as playfully
as little children in the meadow.

Oh, pretty fire, you now become
stronger, brighter, more intense,
just like passionate young lovers.

Oh, waning fire, you keep fading now,
and I find I must rekindle you more,
and more to keep the flame burning.

Oh, dying fire, you must be tired,
the time is soon coming when the
last glowing ember will turn cold.

and such is life!

Cathe Carruthers
THE MAN
I knew a man who laughed at life
He loved his job he loved his wife
He loved his kids, his beer and Elvis
He loved his garden the horses
the neighbors
And weekend mornings drinking
coffee over the back fence
These things were good
He left them all on Father's Day
after a family gathering
His funeral procession was quite a scene
I watched it from the limousine
Cars for miles had come from far,
from near
to say good-bye to him
I started at the flag over his casket
I noticed one corner crooked up straight
As I bent over to fix it
I never thought I'd do that for him
We had a big wake that day
It was more of a party but anyway
It was the way he wanted it
And everyone wants to please the dead
I just hope I pleased dear old dad!

Tammy Lee Donaldson
THERE'S A TIME FOR . . .
There's a time for hurting.
There's a time for love.
But there should not be a time for murder.
There's a time for caring.
There's a time for helping.
But there should not be a time, for death.
There's a time for sadness.
There's a time for happiness.
And that time is now.

Tori Cournoyer
SINCERITY
Sincerity, is with which I write these lines
Although they may sound silly
And not even always rhyme—
They express the way I feel
And who's always on my mind.

The first thing every morning
As I greet a new day's light,
And the last thing in the evening
As I drift off into sleep
And dream of you and I and we—

Until again I meet
The rising sun that greets the day
Of each and every week.

Elizabeth Trouvé Callison

Elizabeth Trouvé Callison
WINTER

This poem is dedicated to my three children Eileen, Susan and David remembering the snowmen we fashioned together in the elegance of winter.

Droplets of snow from
a sky of gray
heralding wonderful
wintertide,
beckoning children to
come out and play
to build a huge snowman,
to frolic and slide.
Flowers are hidden
not one can be found,
the earth is a vision
of shimmering light,
hiding the season
we just left behind,
Jack Frost, the Artist,
has painted it white.

Deanna Kirkland
CAMEO
Cameo, sweet Cameo; zephyr of love in life
among the rocks and stones;
eliminates hell winds of strife,
within your flesh and bones.
Cameo is tender, she'll teach what is the true;
she'll broaden views of vision,
through squall gray clouds;
black hue,
leading her flock to prism.
Cameo . . . rains will dance at a rapid rate,
withstand; . . . calamity.
Silence thoughts of inner hate;
unlock closed doors for thee.
Cameo, fair Cameo;
flamed passions wound the heart,
reminds one of live petals
of some roses as they part.
Cameo, sweet Cameo;
extinguish their burning desires.
Delight and warm with rapture;
then, purify with your fires.

Mary Bertrand
REMEMBERED BLISS
The flames of passion roared
Demanding all.
A mighty struggle raged within,
But that was long ago.
Now the embers, burning low,
Lie banked until
A certain scent,
A long-forgotten air
Bring forth a surge of youth,
A moment of desire
That dies, unfulfilled, unmourned.

Retha Waskom-Heath
BABY ANGELS
Where do all the unborn babies go?
Those thrown away by mothers they will never know.
I'm sure God, Himself, must reach down His mighty hand:
And gather up their tiny pieces from all over this land.
Death was to be their fate here on earth;
But, in heaven He gives them a miraculous rebirth.
There to live in perfect peace and joyful harmony;
Throughout the ages, throughout all eternity.
If you listen closely you might hear the baby angel choir sing;
Hallelujah, Hallelujah, Jesus Christ is King.
King of man and King of the earth;
King of Heaven and the whole universe.
Yes, God must have needed thousands of baby angels up there;
Because so many are eliminated by mothers who do not care.

Murray Goff
REFLECTIONS
The sun is shining brightly, and there is snow upon the ground,
The trees are bare of leaves, and the sky is a brilliant blue
So it brings to mind many things that are beautiful and profound,
I try to put them all together—the old and the new.

As the day has spent its course, and the evening draws nigh,
I reflect upon my life, with a long and blissful sigh
What more could one wish—a beautiful daughter, and a lovely wife.
God has bestowed upon me many blessings—a wonderful life!
And now approaching those exciting

and golden years,
I have no regrets, and hope I've gone the second mile,
And when it's time to meet my maker, I'll shed no tears
But look up and say, "Praise God," and on my face there'll be a smile!

Sister Honorata Hesse
THE POTTER AND THE CLAY
"How could you?" the thick, squat cup cried bitterly,
"How could you do this to me?" For see
I dreamed of something beautiful and rare,
A fragile piece and delicate. But this ungainly thing!
Why, I am fit only for the refuse heap
Or to be trodden underfoot by Grace and Beauty.
Oh, Potter Divine, why—why did you make me?"

The Potter gently lifted the ungraceful object up
And looked with joy upon the wide-mouthed cup.
"I could have made you delicate and easily shattered.
But I wanted a vessel strong and durable,
A cup that baby hands could clutch and drop,
One that would hold cool water
And offer comfort to the thirsty traveler.
I chose to make you just as you are;
I foresaw a need that only you could fill.
What do you mean—ungainliness?
How can you be so blind?
There is no lack of beauty here.
I fashioned you so lovingly—with such care—
My child, you are a precious piece—and rare!"

Linda Badger
HEART TO MIND

In memory of Linda Badger: by Craig Badger.

And the Heart of Woman cried out to the Mind . . .

"Must I bear all the strain? Why must I feel all the anguish and yet you, so quick to decide, rule the direction of my beating . . .

I, the Heart, am too easily swayed . . . yet you, oh Mind, rage onward in thought not really thinking of my needs. Oh Heart, why not open yourself up? Is that not what you are thinking?

But I, Heart of Woman, opens too widely and a tear will I have to endure . . . again, I might add. Perhaps, unable to heal, I will be drained of all.

While you Mind, you can open wide and receive without fear of permanent ache. The Mind, who can shift and drift but feel not as I do.

For I am, Heart . . . the source of love, of unleashed feelings, of pain . . . yes, pain . . . but you, Mind, you can exist and create covers and hide in a mixture of thoughts . . . perhaps I envy you, perhaps not.

But, not I, the Heart . . . so vulnerable, so eager to reach out. Alas, I cry . . . for as the Heart, I can not turn away so easily as you great Mind.

For you see, I seek fulfillment and in so doing a part of me . . . dies."

Gayle Walls Jr
DESPAIR
Like a thief in the night
Despair comes with no warning.
You succumb without a struggle,
Leaving your soul to its mourning.

Darkness falls across your path,
Your days are clad in painful shadows.
Life seems to lead you further into the depths,
Always in the valleys but never on the plateaus.

Wishing to pull you into complete misery,
Despair deftly obeys its master.
Seeking to hide its black heart,
It wears a mask of alabaster.

The battle for your mind wages.
In your heart it wants to exist.
But if you look up toward the light
Within you will be the power to resist.

Guard well yourself against despair,
Heed its malicious scorning.
Or risk the fateful outcome,
Losing your soul to eternal mourning.

Helen Pidgeon Haley

Helen Pidgeon Haley
LITTLE THINGS

To my 17 children, 57 grandchildren, and more than 60 great-grandchildren.

Yes, little things can mean a lot,
A smiling face on a little tot.
A sweet "hello" and "how are you?"
When said by someone who is true.
A pretty card because of love,
Sent to say you are thought of.
Flowers given for no reason.
Except you are a special person.
A prayer at night to wish you well.
Said to Him who in us dwells.
The song of a bird to greet you,
White clouds in a sky so blue.
The smell of earth after the rain.
The sunshine on you once again.
An unexpected call at home,
When you thought no one would phone.
Comfort again after the pain.
To prove God's love for you again.
All of these things and many more.
The good Lord has for us in store.

Helen Pidgeon Haley
LAST CHANCE
This is my very last chance
To make my mark in life.
Don't look like much at first glance
Because of time and strife.

Been through much along the way.
Weathered many a storm.
Had God's help from day to day
To keep me safe and strong.

Trying my hand at poetry.
Doing some painting, too.
Hoping some of it will be
Showing God's beauty through.

Don't praise me if talents there,
It's a God given gift.
Given me, only to share
To give the world a lift.

Think of me when I am gone.
Say a prayer or two.
Hope I've helped someone along
I've also prayed for you.

Helen Pidgeon Haley
LIFE IS A YO-YO
Life is like a yo-yo
And as I start up the string,
Something gives me a jerk
And I come back down again.

I look all about me
And I think I'm doing great.
Someone breaks my bubble,
And I'm in a panic state.

I pick up the pieces
And I start to climb again.
Another setback comes
And it jerks my yo-yo string.

When will I learn, "Trust God!"
And put my string in His Hands
And climbing on His Grace
No jerk will abort His Plan.

Tina Aja
VIOLET BLUE SKY
Violet blue sky with dust in the air
Visions of change everywhere
There's a full moon in the mist of the night
Angels from heaven with candlelight
Rivers of tears fill the valleys below
Eagles with wings and no place to go
Burning red sky on a mirror of glass
Oceans of sand will come at last
Darkness falls and never ends
Mountains of metal iron and tin
Big grey birds now fly in the sky
Bullets of hate make the children cry
Wisdom no longer rings through the land
Machine has taken the place of man
Heaven tell us to watch in the night
Soon there will come a glorious sight
After the fall of life or death
There will only be robots left
Streams of blood fill the waterways
In hopes that freedom will come again someday
Amen 1990

Melvin Manwarring
SPRINGTIME
Springtime: 'Tis a grand
Time of year- when nature
Is soon to burst into full
Bloom putting away winter's
Dark gloom.

Flowers about to bud- leaves
Soon to unfurl- The Master
Painter- God- His landscape
Spread forth into full view.

The picture changes all the
Time: When man listens-
God still speaks thru nature
'Cause He has a message to
Impart.

When we allow Jesus to enter
Our life- we will enjoy
Springtime in our heart: For
Then God and man will never
Be apart!

Wendy Chan
SINCE YOU WENT AWAY
As days pass,
I long to,
Touch your caring heart,
Hear your loving voice,
And to see you.
But I've never been the same,
Since you went away.

I would always remember,
The fun we had,
Your lovely smile,
And you.
But things have never been the same,
Since you went away.

I've went on with my life,
But I would never forget
The things you did,
Your personality,
And most of all,
YOU!

Jane Ramon
ONE
On such a special morning
words are hard to find . . .
For you have changed just like the seasons,
right before my eyes.
You fill my days and my nights,
with tender thoughts of joy.
And challenge life with zest and zeal,
just like a little boy.
The love you share is like no other —
honest, pure and true.
You are my special treasure . . .
you are you.
Now with each new day we'll both delight
in the windows of the world.

And watch the colors of the universe,
burst into a swirl.

Carol J Minalga
AID FROM AIDS
Acquired without prior recognition
Immune from the outside world
Deficiency of body and mind
Syndrome of our modern lifestyle.

Adding stress to relationships
Invading our privacy
Depending on others for life
Suffering without hope.

Assist one another in fighting this plague
Implore others to do the same
Define your role in the battle
Seek out knowledge for prevention.

Administer to those less fortunate
Investigate alternatives
Defend yourself from fatal mistakes
Show concern for future generations.

Patrick E King
THE LORD'S CANVAS
Our world is but a canvas upon which the Lord does create, a masterpiece of color, only he may duplicate.
Clear blue lakes and rushing streams, air so fresh and crisp and clean, these are but a few of the things I've seen.
Red and Yellow, Bronze and Gold, these were the colors in autumns past.
Such is the pity they did not last.
A walk within a masterpiece, I've promised myself to take, before the colors you see today begin to dissipate.
Autumn ends, shades of color fade away, I've lost the colors of autumn, the colors of yesterday.
Fear not young one let your heart not fill with pain, the Lord shall create his masterpiece a-gain.

Alice Wojewoda
I KNOW ME
Pluck that pounding, pulsing tremor
trickling through my veins into my very soul.
Scared? In a way —
Coward? NEVER!
Tenderly touch my sweltering wound
gushing geysers of bellowing blood.
Pain? You might well venture —
Cry? NEVER!
Peel the rotten, rough, dried and dingy
strips of fallen leaves from my weary depths.
Sorrow? I believe —
Defeat? NEVER!
Cease that sinister shiver,
untangle the tickling tenseness
beneath my oneness.
Nervous? You had to ask? —
Worried? NEVER!
—AT LAST —
Try to resist the steady flow of radiance
bursting, bubbling from my ecstatic eyes.
Carefree? Quite so —
Devilish? Of course —
I know ME!

Gary Augustine
TWENTY-ONE LINES
Twenty-one lines are in my poem,
They say it has to be.

If I write—more than that,
In print I will not be.

Twenty-one lines is hardly enough,
to express my inner feelings,
But if that's all—one line no more,
Just sends my head a-reeling.

For I like to write them very long,
And set my thoughts a-movin' —
So from my head—down to my arm
To set my fingers grovin'.

And so you see —
It's hard for me,
To write on — this notebook pad,
The things that run throughout my head,
I'm sure will make you glad.

I didn't go —
The longer route
And put down all I had
'Cause one more line—would have been too much,
—Oops—I hope you don't get mad.

Lisa E Luse

Lisa E Luse
TREASURE CHEST
Searching for the sparkle, hoping to find the light
Seeking answers to the mystery of happiness
The further I dig for answers, the more lost I become in my own desires
The calmness of the wind and the trees swaying, makes me forget treasures lost
I savor the moment by listening to the stream trickle peacefully
For now I realize these are the true treasures, which I cannot fit in my treasure chest
But may cherish in my heart for an eternity

Maeke Linn
HIS WORLD
He sat back in the big rattan chair;
A glass of wine comfortably in hand.
His blue eyes penetrated my soul
As reflections from a candle's flame
unveiled their wisdom and game.
He looked like he owned the world that night,
And to me . . . he did.

Lisa E Luse
INSANITY
You create your own hell
You lock yourself up in your own prison
You push away the ones you want to reach out to you
The answers to your problems are within yourself
They were always there and always will be
Seek your inner truths and you can set yourself free
You will see the light that was shielded by your anxiety and self-doubt
You are
It is as simple as that

Kimberly Villaneuva
THE DAYDREAMER
There she sits,
Motionless,
Unaware of everything around her.
She sits dazed,
A film over her eyes,
And voices inside of her head
Prohibit anything from the outside
To bother her.
Then suddenly,
A noise shakes her awake.
The daydreamer's reverie
Is broken.
But then, after realization,
She returns to her
Private, secluded world.

Cheryl Ray
I LOVE YOU
There's no need to worry
So please don't haste
I see I'd better hurry
And give you a taste.

I give you a dinner plate
And say please don't make me blue
Won't you ask me to be your mate.
For I love you, yes I do.

I feel the pounding of my heart,
And hear the thudding in my ears.
Then I hope we will never part
For I feel so good whenever you're near.

And Honey if you don't know
From all the ways I try to show
I love you and I always will
With all my heart and better still
I love you with my soul.
Yes, I love you.

Elizabeth Vickers
WHY DOES IT HAVE TO END THIS WAY
Why does it have to end this way?
I never thought it would end this way.
We were great together.
Why does it have to end this way?
We had such hopes and dreams for each other
It was an everlasting love affair that we never wanted to end.
But something got in the way and shattered our hopes and dreams.
We never wanted it to end.
But you're gone and when I see you our love is there once again.
Do you want me back or is it some kind of game we both play.
I don't think there's a chance with us again.
For once it ends it will never come again.
We never wanted it to end!

Ruth Rames Munson
PSYCHIATRIST
The Charon stream runs cold
In the mind of the child.
Whispering fantasies
move under the bone-vault
Like dust grains twirling in confusion.

Bruised life, the fire gone,
the lost child weeps alone
And crawls beneath the leaf and fern
in skeletal woods
Where mists hang heavy in their skull-like caves
And stars are quenched.
The Charon stream runs cold.

Out of the hours rocking in burning time
A hand reaches to touch the broken mind.
A voice calls, "Come with me where blossoms promise ripened fruit
Where fleshy roots wait in shadowed earth for light.
Have no fear I shall lift you above the night.
Love runs with the winds, Oh child, oh child."
Words gently spoken quiet the river of woe.
The child hears and crawls from beneath the leaf and fern in skeletal woods
Leaving his fantasies to the Charon stream that runs cold.

Mildred Ringler
TO A CHOCOLATE LOVING NURSE GOING ON VACATION
No patients to alkalize or cauterize
Nothing left to organize or sterilize
Only days and nights to socialize
Men you'll tantalize and hypnotize
Your beauty and I emphasize
Will drive men to fantasize
If none of these joys materialize
Don't agonize - chocolatize, chocolatize

M C Ridenour
THE SETTLEMENT
We found you when our love was young
You a frighten puppy at the city pound,
In our home you made us laugh and gave
Us unconditional love, Little Spotted Hound.

Now my love and I have grown apart,
Our love for each other is sour and dead;
We're in the process of a divorce and
We have other loves we want to wed.

Little Spotted Hound, your eyes are so sad;
You pick up on our tensions and fights;
You whine softly, laying your head in my lap
And rush to him crying as he comes in sight.

The photos are divided and so is the furniture
Daily papers advertise the selling of the house;
We find your water and food bowls empty,
But you kiss us both and we feel like a louse.

Little Spotted Hound, a symbol of young love,
Little Spotted Hound; how we both love you!
Everything is settle but your custody,
Little Spotted Hound, Oh! What to do!
We both want you!

Arthur Lee Lewis Jr

MY SISTER'S KEEPER

Tender woman
I wonder why you
sit and stare out
restaurant glass
in the direction of the airport
I wonder what it is
you see
or think
as your warm eyes
suddenly turn cool
from tears that roll
down
your cheeks.

Are you reminiscing
about some past lover
who still holds space
in your heart
or do you just long for the company
of a present lover
who's just away for
awhile

Laurie J Arnold Manley

THE DREAM

This society is hard core,
it will put you to a test.
There's no more love and feelings
everything's a bloody mess.
Too busy putting up a front
to stop and realize:
behind the front and all the scenes,
lies the truth; wrapped in a dream.
The dream is of relity;
REALITY—NO LONGER SEEN:
The love, the truth, the caring,
the actual sharing of a dream.

Karen A Dullnig

I WALK THE SHORES OF THE OCEAN

I walk the shores of the ocean
It's outstretched arms wave at me
furiously
Beckoning me

The breeze slaps across my face
The salt in the air invades my nostrils
filling my head with peaceful chants

Beckoning me

I smile
I am drugged by the powers before
me
Cooling my body, filling the
emptiness within me
Deep within the realms of the
timeless
I am forevermore
Beckoning thee

Cynthia Lawson

UNTITLED

The time has come for us to be free
Blacks and whites should get along
let us be
We have been through so much
Working so hard to get what belongs
to us
Our world together it should be
Not just yours sharing is the key
African Americans trying to be
strong
It's very hard but we try to get along

In 1990 we made history
A black activist who just wanted
peace
Nelson Mandela finally let free
These are things that should have
been done
long before this decade had come

It's time for us to get educated
Learn of our history stop getting
agitated
Do something to put history in our
schools
We're much smarter than given credit
Prove them wrong education get it

Calvin Lowe

ACAPELLA CHOIR

Toquerville has an acapella choir—
the strangest in the land.
The only time it ever sings is while
standing in the sand.
Sometimes one sings a solo, other
times they harmonize.
We hardly ever see them 'cause they
sing to moonlit skies!

Their favorite song sounds kinda like
this, I hope you'll bear with me—
Because I still haven't learned their
tunes, I'm somewhat up a tree.
It's a yip, yip, yip, and Oooo, Oooo,
Oooo, and awr, awr, awr, awr, awr.
Strange as their songs may seem to
you, it's our acapella choir.

Some townsfolk don't hold this choir
in very high esteem.
They claim it's only coyotes that
keep messing up their dreams.
But I don't care, I love these tunes
though it's a sound some may not
crave—
It's music I even hope to hear while
resting in my grave.

Leona Nelson

BEAUTIFUL DAY

The sun rose so beautifully this
morning.
It's truly a beautiful day.
A day when you feel like being alive.
For you like seeing the sun when it's
shining.
It's good smelling the fresh air.
What a beautiful sound hearing the
birds singing,
Enjoying looking at all the pretty
flowers,
All the beautiful green grass,
And all the rich black dirt.
It really makes a person feel good to
be alive,
When you can enjoy the beautiful
things of nature.

Orit Mizrachi

THE ULTIMATE RISK

To create! To push boundaries!
requires the ability to take risks.
The Gambler, Speculator, Investor,
all need the courage to put their
money on the line, in hopes of a
bigger return.
The Race Car Driver, Hang glider,
Acrobat, and similar people, need the
courage and steady nerves to stretch
their physical capacities to the limit.
Some of the essence here is the thrill
of an adrenal rush.
For most of us, the tremendous build-
up of Falling in Love, being in Love,
and Loving is a major component of
stimulation in our lives
LOVE CAN BE THE ULTIMATE
RISK.
This urge for ego expansion is
connected to self-esteem.
Everyone needs a sense of pride, in
his or her actions and the ability to
feel good about what we're doing in
life.
Life is the challenge to somehow
ground our ideals so that we feel we
are Beautifying or Improving the
World, in some way, uplifting our
current state of existence, but also
getting some Real World results in
what we Do.

Rosemary Zaney

THINK AHEAD

Smile, right now and say
Tomorrow will be a better day
But until the hour of tomorrow's
dawn
Has risen and today is gone
We must remember and explore
The possibilities at this day's door
Make a decision firm and strong
For to wait until morning is much too
long.

Nina Rogers

WHY CAN'T I BE A LITTLE GIRL AGAIN

Daddy can't you bounce me on your
knee . . . once more
You told me once to be happy—all I
had to do was "open that special
door"
Daddy I'm hurting deep down inside,
Can't you tell me what to do . . .
Your word I'll abide
I feel so alone . . . tho I have many
Sometimes I wish, there weren't any
For there's one, I'd love to hold dear
to my heart . . .
But how can I if we're apart
Bounce me on your knee once more
Tell me I'm the special one . . .
Someone will adore
Daddy can't I be a little girl once
more?

Colleen McGowan

SILENT CRY

She tries to show her love,
but you just turn her away,
She's never say a thing.
What would mommy and daddy do
or say.
She hides in her room,
the door shut and locked tight.
And lies awake at night crying,
until morning light.
All the cuts, sores, and bruises,
Have made a permanent scar on her
heart,
And the silent cries in the night,
Are what are tearing them apart.

Barb Clager (age 13)

BROKEN DREAMS

Age means nothing in a world of
dreams,
There where nothing is as it seems.
Dreams are pure, straight from the
heart,
They have no end, they have no start.
So here we are in a world of dreams,
Looking for happiness, or so it
seems,
But there is no happiness, JUST
BROKEN DREAMS.

Joyce Barron

Joyce Barron

TO YOU ONLY

To live and love with you, and be one
forever
To be near you so I can reach out and
touch you
to make love with you,
laugh with you,
cry with you,
talk with you,
and be silent with you.
To hold you close to me every night
waking up to you each morning
To share my secrets with you
and to be honest with you,
to understand and respect you,
accepting you for you.
To find shelter in you when I am
afraid
And to hold you when I need
warmth
To be with you through all the
seasons
Walking with you in the sunshine
To care for you when you are ill, and
be joyful with you when you are
happy
To grow old with you, and be with
you till the end of time
With you only
For you only
I want all of these things
I would do all of these things
To you only, all my love.

Kristina Burchett

GIVEN GIFT

I, confused in my state of solitude;
looked into your eyes seeing
promises
of love and tenderness.
A time for two people to become
united as one.
A God given gift was your love.

I, held bound in emotion,
was afraid to take the chance
of giving my love,
only to lose it in someone's
selfishness.
Yet, you patiently waited;
giving of yourself to me,
believing before I believed.
In the warm circle of your love;
the doubts disappeared,
the fears subsided to be replaced
by the given gift of your love.
My heart is free, my spirit soars
on the wings of God's given gift of
your love.

Marie Kallas
OMISSION

The chapters in your book of thoughts didn't really come out and mention my name. I just naturally thought I was there, for I have a part of you with me during each waking moment.

When I realized I was omitted, I thought it was to protect my well-being.

Now I know I have encountered the answer. There was no me in you. Forgive me for trying to read between the lines.

Edward Ellis Jr
NO REGRETS

I've known the type of love
that makes you believe the
world is an alright place.
It gives reason to the madness
in your life and perhaps
compassion for others' space.

I've known times, that I hope
I'll never forget. The bitterness
of anger and sorrow, the sweetness
of joy and love.

This is life, for me there is no regrets.
We all pray for tomorrow, sometimes
curse the present and pay for the past.
I never had things to turn out always
right, time moves too fast.
This is life, for me there is no regrets.

Lynette Lilly
A WORLD WITHOUT SANTA CLAUS

Surprise!
Surprise!
Always a surprise and such a
pleasure
to see you
Such a one as you is hard to find
And there will only ever be one of
you
And I feel so privileged and honored
and humbled
To have been given the joy of
knowing you
Such a special one
So beloved
He must love you so incredibly
much,
Much beyond our capacity to
comprehend
Giver of insights and revelations
How desperately I need you and how
lost
I'd be without you
Oh, precious, precious one
Do hang on

A world without you is like
A World Without Santa Claus

Yvonne Angel Bentley
THE THOUGHT OF YOU

Can't get you out of my mind today.
The thought of you is monopolizing.
It takes hold of me and just will not
let go.
Sometimes I find it overwhelming,
like today.
It's like I must see you, I have to.

The thought of you is treacherous.
It will sneak up on me when I am not
ready.
Trying to replace it with other
thoughts is no good.
It likes where it is, doesn't want to
go.
This is home to it.

The thought of you is the most clever
thief.
It teases and then steals me away to
pleasurable reminiscing.
No use trying to arrest the thought of
you.
Because no charges will be pressed.
It is much too persuasive.

The thought of you can be so
naughty;
its tantalizing eroticism arousing me.
Coaxing me to fantasize about . . . the
next time.

Filling me up with such desire that I
might erupt!
Giving me deliciously wet dreams.
The thought of you.
It subdues me; it excites me; it
motivates me.

Agnes B Wagner
SPRING

The earth is now awakening, a new
and lovely day
Will give new life to everything, the
winter's passed away.
The snows and stormy sleet and cold
have fled before the spring,
New buds begin to blossom out and
birds begin to sing.
The flowers that you thought were
dead have blossomed forth anew,
The grass that winter covered up is
creeping into view.
Summertime's fulfillment comes
with gentle springtime rain,
and birds that sang so merrily are
coming home again.
So don't despair if Springtime seems
to be a little slow,
Just look real close and you will see a
rose beneath the snow.

Ethel J Morsey
THE BARREN TREES

They stand cold barren and tall
The size may be big or small.
As winter does set in
naked branches left, since leaves
have fallen
yet amidst the skies of gray
or on a bright sunny day
the beauty of their branches
have outspread arms, as if dancing.
As their shadows show, barren
trees
upon snow ground earth
We look forward to another birth.
Betwixt fall and winter
your the barren trees that seem to be
bitter.
Cometh forth in the spring, begin
to
glitter.
Cold, lifeless, gloomy, barren trees
'tis another sign of life you've
shown
as the howling winds stop a
blown,
no longer are you all the barren trees
for you've become another sign of
beauty, see.

Jayike L Taylor
SOMEONE SPECIAL

Sometimes I feel like
I could lose myself in your eyes,
The feelings that they hold
Make them a warm spring in the
woods.

When I am with you
I feel like nothing can harm me,
Like I'm in a special place
That knows no pain.
It takes someone special
To make a person feel that way,
But then,
You are someone special.

Lorraine Welch
THROUGH HER EYES

In the heart of the forest, no one hears the dull thud as the boughs of pine release their burden of snow.

She raises her head and looks around with frightened eyes. She tries to run, to hide. The scent of man is in the air.

It's too late, they've seen her, she stumbles on.

The traces of her passing easy to follow.

She lies there the scent of wet earth in her nostrils, as the lifeblood leaves her body, she remembers;

The springtime fawns at play, her bucks, their horns locked in combat, the brook that flows through her high mountain meadow.

She tries to rise, weak, so weak.
With one final, gentle sigh, the
spark of life leaves her
soft brown eyes.

Melissa Spurlock
GOLDEN CHILD

The golden child of the family
He could do no wrong that I could
see
A smile that brightened the dullest of
days
And eyes that softened the hardest
gaze.

A freckled face kid with the world in
The palm of his hand, I knew he'd
win
If only he'd given life a chance
It would be better at a second glance.

But somewhere along those rough
teen years
He must have silently shed his tears
Who would have thought there was
such a frown
Hidden behind the smile of a clown.

Never will my life be the same
It still hurts just to hear his name
I couldn't begin to say how much
I'd love to feel that sweet warm
touch.

I wish I had not been so blind
I wouldn't tried to change his mind
—

For if that child had lived to be a man
I would surely be his biggest fan.

Mary Lynn Klesh
TIRED

I am tired.
I'm tired of holidays, happy voices, happy couples, old loves, new loves, tears and fears, old times, new times, despair and defeat and feeling so weak.
It is all so much; I feel out of touch; I am tired; so I sleep.
I dream.
I dream of wonderful times, believable lines, to have and to hold and never grow old, to always be strong, and feel I belong, to never have fears and see things so clear. Idream.
I grow restless;
In my dreams I grow restless, I turn and I toss: the feelings are lost, I must pay the cost, I know I must go so I awaken.
Drifting back to our time, to reason and rhyme, to the world of today, the American way.
I no longer know the answers or reasons, the change of the seasons; the hows' or the whys' - I just want to cry - I'm back; it is reality and I am tired.

Kristine McInerney
SOMEBODY'S WATCHING

Somebody's watching,
somebody's there —
I see the sound
I hear the stare.
Whose image is that -
that I see?
Who does it belong to?
Does he see me?
Through the dark
I can feel the eyes,
I can hear the touch
and I can see the cries.
Will we come together
or just pass in the night?
Will we ever come closer,
or will the ones go out of sight?

Jennifer L Vinci
THE KEY TO MY HEART

With all my love to my husband, Patrick, for whom this poem was written.

So many times I'll look back and I
see,
The person I was hiding, deep inside
me.
Hardships weighed heavy and
clouded my mind,
Happiness was something I wanted to
find.

I needed to let my other side out,
And show the whole world what I
was about.
All they could see was the anger and
greed,
But somebody special was all I
would need.

My family was there, to help me
along,
But I just felt so different, I didn't
belong.
I was rash and rebellious and just
downright mean,
I know I was wrong, my mistakes are
now seen.

Because I have found you, the one
with the key,
To open my heart and let me be me.
It had to be you, I knew from the
start,
It was felt through my body, but
mostly my heart.

I know that you'll be there to help me
along,
To finish the race I've been running
so long.
Now that I have you, my search is
complete,
With you I will win and not suffer
defeat.

Things will be rough, I still need to
grow,
But bear with me, Pat, the process is
slow.
I'll need you to be there, to trust and
to share,
To hold me and love me and show
me you care.

I know this is it, you're so thoughtful

and clever,
You're my whole world and will be forever.

Because you are the one, the one with the key,
To open my heart and let me be me!!!

Kimberly Clifford
NEVER FORGOTTEN LOVE

This poem is dedicated to Kenny B. There will always be a special place in my heart for you! With all my love, Kimberly Clifford.

As I sit in the still of the night,
I remember when everything was right.
We used to spend so much time together,
I wish it could have lasted forever and ever.
I dreaded that day when someone else stole your heart,
When that day came it tore me apart.
My heart is filled with love and fears,
My eyes are filled with sadness and tears.
In my eyes you are perfection,
Even though the love only flows in one direction.
My love for you will never die,
It will just multiply.

Shanen M Onken
A THOUGHT TO LEAVE YOU WITH

Two red roses resembling us,
Never forsaken nor forgotten.
The red is for our blush tenderness.
The long stem, our late nite conversations.
Each leaf of different size and shape,
The many changes we've gone through.
The thorns are for the rough times and rough edges we've survived in our relationship.
The soft petal, your smooth, warm caress against my skin.
And as each petal dies and falls,
A part of us dies; a memory always remembered.

Eliza Sarnacka

Eliza Sarnacka
THE CASTLE

To all people I love.

people carry their love in the eyes
a drawbridge through the pupils
eyebrows' plaits
to lead in it
there are many paths
as the galleries of the ears
or a raft of lip- branches sticked
together
or a words' sea

and the only guard is
somewhere far away
(tell me where he is, where?)

and that is the heart
IT cares the tower called
A MAN

Eliza Sarnacka
MY FAIRY TALE

and when we loose our hearts like the trees undergo
I'll miss my way
you'll feel my going
you'll have the hazels on your fingers growing

and when we couldn't foot on the earth
we'll get a cradle of sunshining sins
the angel will fly to sing
Ikars with restored wings
will start burning

but God won't throw us away from his throne
and we'll become as saints true lovers
and we will start
a new book of poems

Gayle L Adamek
LOST LOVE

A lost love,
Is the worst kind.
It hurts the most,
It's hard to find.
The feelings you can't describe,
No matter how hard you try.
You search and search,
And reason why,
That one lost love,
Brought tears to your eyes.

Robert E Kirkpatrick
THE PICTURE OF LIFE

Alone she sleeps from dusk till dawn,
the soldier she loves has come and gone.
She awakes early morning just before light,
his picture always the first thing in sight.
One day soon she hope's he will come back,
but little does she know his unit is under attack.
Plenty of times she has thought of callin',
but nobody's there, the unit has fallin'.
Days, weeks, months, go by without any news,
then a soldier comes, looking sharp
in dress blues.
The soldier tells her the man she loves has died.
She had one tear, for she could not have cried.
She will never believe that he is really gone,
for she sees his face every morning,
just before dawn.

Darlene Bozanich
MY FRIEND

To My Habiba, Tony Najm who inspired me to write this poem.

I will remember the times we had
together my friend
You are and still are a lover, a friend,
a man.

The love you gave to me
No one will ever know
As you were there in times of need.

The wondrous beauty of it all
Sticks like glue inside my mind

The ups and downs I have
learnt from
It's growth, its wonder, its bewilderment.

I will remember the honesty,
straight-forwardness & togetherness
We shared my friend
You were and still are a sincere,
a kind, and a gentle man.

The warmth you gave to me
No one can know
As you shone through
for what you've shown.

I will remember the times we
had together my friend
As life goes on until the end!

Jeri Sereno
DEEP

To my girls for smiling through the rough times.

Deep.
I feel deep and hollow, sometimes it seems there can't be no tomorrow, for the shallow pond inside is evaporating, as the heat of the day wallows.
No one can see as they walk in me, which each step spatters my feelings into sprinkles, which fade faster in the laughter of the sun, seem faster as I pray some shade will save the day.
When the trickles at end the Lord lets the summer rain rush in. The trickles become a river which run deep, sometimes shallow, but God somehow lets us know we're never hollow.

Judy Zucal

Judy Zucal
FOR FIFTY YEARS

Dedicated to simple hope for a future without affront of the past.

For five years I've hurried fast.
In doing so I've developed a past.
Now I've met you, I swear to be true.
All of my conscious thoughts will center around you.
But when I'm daydreaming just give me ten,
for all of my old loves visit me then.

Judy Zucal
BETRAYED

I gambled with life many years ago.
Though heart and soul died form stayed with the flow.
I toiled and struggled, did all I could.
Though care seldom returned, I gave more than I should.
I raised ungrateful children for an uncaring man.
Though the form now weary middle age began.
Ostracized by my family because I couldn't do more,
for aged, ill Mother custodial care had began.
Life forgive me for not giving enough,
maybe my next life won't be as rough.
Cremate me! I'll be gone in a puff.

Carolyn Charnock-Atkinson
SOMEHOW I ALWAYS END UP COMING BACK HERE

This poem is dedicated to Pat, my friend, my confidant for giving me courage, for helping me believe in me.

Somehow I always end up coming back here,
Is it your trails?
Or is it your dreams?
That I want to make mine.
Somehow my feet end up walking down to the marsh.
Is it your tides?
Or is it your past.
That has come back to enter my life.
Somehow my loneliness ends up here or the lookout,
Is it your freedom?
Or is it your tranquility,
That has become my shadow.
You bring me peace, yet so many unspoken emotions.

Judy Zucal
PURE PLEASURE

To Abbagail, first born grandchild whose birth was the rebirth of me.

I give a tickle.
You smile and giggle.
Oh boy!
How I joy.

Judy Zucal
TRIBULATION OF LETTING GO

To Pauline Kohn and a billion others who have or will suffer the pain of putting a parent in a nursing home or needing help with their care.

Miss my Momma? This just can't be!
Not me! I'm too old you see.
Something vital is tearing at me.
What is it then?
Love, maybe fear, that wants to keep her near?
Am I ashamed of the way it might appear?
Do I believe it's a sin?
God help me! Someone help me!
Cut this umbilical cord that's attached to me.
Quilt stop! Set me free.
I have other responsibilities,
other people who need me.
Stop pulling me into the grave with thee.

Judith Moriconi
SPECIAL TIMES
The holidays are great
A special time of year,
Families getting together
Spreading good cheer,
The holidays bring back
Memories from another time,
Music and laughter
And
The holidays fill me
With visions of long ago,
People I've known
Who I loved so,
The holidays for all
A time of remembering,
A time for love
A time for giving.

James T Stewart
OLD FRIEND
Out on the far horizon
The Scottish Bagpipes softly blow
The sprinkle of new summer rain
And the southwind blows so slow.

We've walked the long miles together
My tears I cannot hide, Old Friend
We've walked the seasons side by side
And I'm with you when dark descends.

We've rested on the banks of the river
We've let the green grass be our bed
We've set and watched the last sunset together
Part of blue and crimson with a small shade of red.

Through all the long years we've been together
There has never been a friend quite like you
There will always be a special place in my heart
For this eternal love I hold so true.

When I hear the gentle music of the last Bagpipe
And in the sky the last sunset I'll see
We can again quietly walk together
For all eternity, just you and me.

Diane Hansen
SNOW
Heaven's angels busily sweeping
Golden dust falling randomly to the earth.
Turning white upon its descent.
Covering all of nature's sins
and blanketing its imperfections.
It shows no favoritism
to behold its beauty.
It freezes and enchants us,
But warms our hearts
with fond memories and scenes.
It clings to all who will embrace it
And flocks the evergreen trees.
Its peaceful, silent journey
sends a hushed quiet into the night.
How much like golden stardust,
as it glistens in the morning sun
Bringing us a sprinkling of glitter
through the cracks of Heaven's floor.

Michael J Gavaletz
JUST ANOTHER DEAD LEAF
Dead leaves dangle and fall
Hovering over, and plunging into a dark, foreboding pond
Fighter planes circle overhead
Flying to lands far beyond
Another dead leaf falls
Trying to escape the engulfing, herbivorous surface
The plane takes a dive
Into an enchanted forest
The rotting leaf, descends,
Sinking to the ponds floor
The plane, fired upon, plunges into the sea
While the enemy waits for more
The conserving leaf, becomes recycled
Under the mucky, ground cover
The "life-loving" pilot's life was lost,
Yet replaced by another
Bright green, conglomeration of leaves,
Mother Nature's flagships, flutter high above the admiring mosses
Royal blue skies, tainted with man-made, metal monsters, darkens,
While the face of Mother Earth becomes decorated with one too many crosses.

Marla Rae Heidt
THE ESSENCE OF WARMTH
The water went up to the boy's knees.
It had small rippling waves going along the beach.
Tiny sand crabs were playing in the sand.
The boy wondered what mysteries the sea could teach.

Picking up shells and studying their varied colors-
Strolling and watching the sea gulls
at play—
Throwing bread crumbs into the air for these birds to catch-
Giggling delightedly-
For this had been quite a day.

As sunset approached, darkness proceeding
The boy ran home to shelter, comfortable and warm.
Turning to the window facing the sea he saw the last of day
And in the twilight watched a "Great," distant storm.

Marla Rae Heidt
RESUME
The sun was big and white,
Half covered by the clouds.
The air was still, the trees silent.
Nothing was making a sound.
Suddenly in the distance a bird
Was screeching long and loud.
I stood to discern what disturbed that bird
My heels rose quickly from the ground.
Spotting a nest quite high in a tree.
It appeared like a topsy-turvy mound.
Moving closer, the bird seemed frantic,
I proceeded to look around.
And there quite close I spotted a tiny baby bird
Fluttering helplessly round and round.
Awkwardly, I approached for a closer look,
The mother's frantic chirps did resound.
Gently I picked up that tiny little fluff of feathers,
It weighed a mere fraction of a pound.
Gradually I managed to climb the tree
Searching and reaching the nest I found.
And placing Pee Wee back into its cozy home
Elated and smiling I proceeded down.
The sun was big and white,
Half covered by the clouds.
The air was still, the trees silent.
Nothing was making a sound.

Windy Karr
TILL WE'RE TOGETHER
At first sight of you, my heart wanted to melt
But little did I know
That the look in your eyes, that beautiful glow
Would soon tell me every emotion you felt

We were friends at the start
But now it's grown much stronger
I can see we'll be friends no longer
For you have taken over my heart.

It may be a while till you're mine forever
But I promise to wait here for you
My heart has no choice but to always be true
And hope and pray for the day we're together.

Sherree Faries
SISTERS ARE SPECIAL
Sisters are special, yes, this is true.
But none can ever be as special as you.
Always supportive, caring and fun,
I am sure that you are the very best one!
No one can part the love that we share.
I can always count on you, you're always there.
So many memories and feelings we hold,
Locked in our hearts — more precious than gold.
I feel more fortunate than any king on this earth,
A wealth that is shared, because of our birth.
Let us not forget the blessings we have:
A wonderful family, laughter and love.

By: Your Sister, Sherree
Especially for you!
August 17, 1988

Travis Gilbert Jr
AMANDLA

This poem is dedicated to my Grandfather, Herbert Gilbert.

I dedicate this day to the root of mother and child,
To its thrust, drive and loving motion,
To its root, base and delivery from the womb,
To its truth, trust and warmth,
To its desire, hunger and need for expression,
To Africa.

To its oath, convictions and demanding survival,
To her need for love, and acceptance,
To the root of mother and child

Understand its relevance, for it has total understanding of you
Know its power, for it is your boredom and your ecstasy,
Your fulfillment and your neglect,
Your support and you opposition

Children of Africa the call is there demanding your reply.
Make peace on the churning waters of your soul.
Settle the sea so that you may marvel at its natural beauty
For we must dedicate this day to the root of mother and child.

A Evelyn Walbert Conyers
MUCH MORE OR FINE NINE

To Jonathan G Conyers - Grandson- nine years

Fine nine you've gone far
You play the piano so well
How well!! I know!!
But fine nine
You have farther to go

To see all things anew
There is much more to do
There is much more to live
Much more to give

You write beautifully;
Dance gracefully;
But you have much
More to be—
Much more to see.

Inspired as you go
You'll know
There's a rainbow
Around you
That to others
will show.

Count your blessings
As you are
Here's a wish
To follow you
Wherever you star!!

Barbara Lynn Chenoweth
GOODBYE

This poem is dedicated to Mom, Dad and Dan for all your love and support.

There is a special group of people
With whom I can laugh and cry
The family I've made down south
The one's I must tell goodbye

You have the strong and intelligent gal
The sweetest person whose just right for a pal
The one with a hillbilly heart and feet of the city
A quiet one who's about to have a little bity
A woman whose grace fills any room
The one everyone suspects rides a broom
The biggest hearted person that I know
The one whose grades could steal the show

My goodbye really hurts
And makes me so blue
I'll miss you all dearly
And I'll always love you!

Penny Lee Limosani
GOOD-BYE
Today's the day, I say "Good-Bye",
To a love I've kept inside.
Tho I've been married for several years,
A part of me has always cared.

You were my first, I thought my last,
But then we took two different paths.
We shared a love, but not too much,
Because we couldn't open up.

I sometimes wish we could go back,
To try and fix the wrong in our past.
I have no right to feel betrayed,
But deep within I feel that way.

Now things have changed, for both me and you,
May life shines bright for both of you.
You now have yours, and I have mine,
So I guess it's time to say
"GOOD-BYE."

S Paul Dixon

IF I COULD

If I could but see
The fire inside me
If I could but know
What makes it glow

If I could but feel
What makes it real
If I could but touch
It's out of my reach

If I could only cry
Then I would know why
I need to have a goal
To have peace untold

For all this I plead
This is all I need

Sarah Garvin

BLUE EYES

He looked at me
With those big Blue Eyes
Knowing there have been many guys.
I could not tell him how I felt,
But those big Blue Eyes just made me melt.

I told him how I felt inside.
He said it would help him to decide
that if our love was great and strong
or if it all had been wrong.

As he said, "I love you"
I said, "I love you too."
And those big Blue Eyes stared at me again
only this time they were true.

Shelby Crowder Barnes

Shelby Crowder Barnes 1953-1988

A TRUE FRIEND

To mom, with love.

I asked my Father in a sad, unhappy time;
"Are you truly a friend of mine?"
He answered boldly, and in no uncertain terms,
"Child, I'll be with you 'til the end of time.
Once that happens, you will be with me
To live in peace and harmony.
We'll walk together throughout eternity.
So, don't forget when trouble calls
That I'm your friend
Throughout it all.
I'll wipe your tears, and ease the pain,
Because you're my child;
And a part of me."

Shelby Crowder Barnes 1953-1988

WHEN WILL WE LEARN

Submitted by her sister, Sharon C. Swinney.

Simple things lie all around
Only waiting to be found.
A tiny raindrop on the road,
A little fish, a tiny toad,
A pretty flower, a sunny ray,
A precious moment of the day.
And yet we strive for greater things,
Things buried deep and tied with strings.
When will we learn
To live our life,
In harmony,
Instead of strife?

Jennifer Susan Johnson

THE FRIENDSHIP GARDEN

A rose that grows in the garden of love, is a rose that lives forever. A friend can be that rose of love, if you cherish a friend forever. Water your friend with happiness,

show them they are not alone. Be with them in times of trouble and help them when they need it so. Friendship is the best kind of love if you handle it just right, it will bloom and bloom in any light, and it will never die.

Janis Lynn Zarkowsky

CHERRIES

Cherries dribble down the chin
It feels so nice and cool.
Only in a group or crowd
Do they make me look the fool.

But when I'm all alone like this
In cherry-land and dribble bliss,
The pure delight of stems and pits
Tickles my stomach when the pulp hits.

And when I'm really on a binge
Mind you it's awful, but please don't cringe.
I'll simply mash up a cherry or two
And mix it with peanut butter that'll crunch when I chew.

Of course, I can't always have what I please
My mommy forces down potatoes and peas.
Potatoes are awful and peas are unreal
I'd rather chew on a lemon peel.

Yet when I'm all alone like this
In cherry-land and dribble-bliss,
The pure delight of cherry juice
Will always turn my pleasure loose.

C F Mewborn

THE PRECIOUS GIFT

This poem is dedicated to: Our cherished and beloved youth all over the world.

Life is a precious gift from God,
a gift more precious than gold,
a gift that money can't buy,
a gift that only God can mold.

Life must be handled with the utmost respect and dignity,
a gift so rich, beautiful and free,
a gift we must treasure,
a gift God gave to you and me.

Life was not designed to be wasted on drugs and crime,
for they only cause sorrow, sadness and pain,
why destroy a precious gift such as life,
just for temporary, ill-gotten gain?

Life is a process we must go through,
so let's unite together as one to do the best we can,
let love, peace and harmony abide in us,
and leave the rest to God's master plan.

Life is the ruling force of the universe,
let's thank God for the precious gift of life,
and while we are here on earth,
let's pray that we cause no one any hurt, harm or strife.

S Paul Dixon

FROM INSIDE OF ME

I did chance to pass a mirror
It hung aimlessly on the wall
From inside came an erie glow
A stately image in a dark hall

Its glance pierced my soul
My sacred thoughts revealed
It was in complete control
From it nothing is concealed

What enigma has entangled me
It's a message in the mystery
This is not real only fantasy
Is this the realm of insanity

Melisa S King

WHEN A CHILD CRIES

I dedicate this poem to all the hurting children. May their next teardrop be their last.

Even a flower when planted
needs love from a heart.
They don't grow on hate
and they don't die with care.
But why do they have to be
replanted and reloved to stay alive?
What's wrong with our hearts if
we all have one?
Why do we replant a wounded heart
before the bleeding stops?
Or put water on feelings when they are already drowning?
Do we really know what makes a smile grow,
or do we kill it even after it's dead?

GMVM Ricci

DEFINITION PLEA

Dedicated To: American Red Cross - Northeast Region.

Research is a science,
a life worth well indeed
To think of all the sorrows
and have a new-born breed.

I'm more inclined to rest-assured
that nothing seems to fit;
But then again I think I'm sure
to have a sense of it.

Numbers can be meaningless,
One's work is such a chore.
If one would brain to calculate
a word or two, if more.

For one word is the answer
and many hold the key
Please give your life to research
and then we will be free.

Hylma Currier

SMILE

Life doesn't have to be gloomy
Full of struggle and strife.
Just keep a song in your heart
And a smile for your husband or wife.

Let the troubles melt into silence
And the sorrows pass away
Let happiness grow with your wisdom
And try to make it a better day.

When the weather gets dark and dreary
Just remember it's only a cloud.
Out there is a world of sunshine
Just waiting to be allowed.

Don't gather the thoughts of sadness
Let them fly away on a wing
And open your heart and soul
Raise up your voice and sing.

Hylma Davis Currier

OUR HOME

In a little old house in the village,
By the edge of a little old road,
There's a happy little old couple,
Who live in this little abode.

They have neither a care nor a worry,
And their burdens are all their own;
They live and love for each other,
And leave the world alone.

Oh, don't think they are not friendly,
For their friendship is known afar,
And when they are thus together
Their love twinkles like a star.

If when you are lonely and burdened,
By cares that are heavy to bear;
Just stop by at this little old cottage,
And meet this happy pair.

They will share with you their table,
As well as their soul and their heart;
You'll go back to the world of trouble,
With a fresh and livened start.

Hylma Currier
FISHING TIME
The first of May is fishing time,
The best time of the year;
We may not get a lot of fish,
But we see the streams, so dear.

We travel far from worries,
Though not many miles away;
We think of nothing else around us,
Not even the time of day.

We cast out our line with shining lure,
And reel it in so slow,
Maybe then we have a fish,
If not, back we go.

When we let a line glide down a brook,
We gaze up at the hills;
The beauty of God's gardens,
Gives us an unknown thrills.

There are lots of other hobbies
That anyone can do;
But when we take a fishing trip,
It's like starting life anew.

Heather Skowood
FOLDS

For my wonderful Mom.

Alone and broken
dancing in the moonlit room
as the music plays inside
her head
silence wraps around
an empty room
where music never plays
and rain never dries
eyes nearly drowned
in pain and sleeping
is time
as she dances
around in around
within and within
the walls of solid
concrete bound to
death alone
she shall never understand
dances dances
within soft steps
to smile at only
herself.

Renae Fowler Powell
MEMORIES

For my husband, parents, sisters and my best friend. Thanks for believing in me. And for my three sons. I love you all.

I can hear your voice whispering in the wind
Telling me you love me and that it will never end.

I turned around to hold you but you were not there
I stood and gazed looking into the air.

Oh, what I would give to touch your face and to see your smile
I think I could travel
a thousand miles.

But I will hold close in my heart and my mind
The memories of you that will never die.

Marsha Elizabeth Knoll
LIFE WITHOUT YOU
Like time will go on.
And days will slowly pass by,
The heartbreak that now overwhelms me.
Will gradually subside.
As time passes I realize,
That though I would give anything to be with you again,
All your reasons for leaving me are so sensible.
My brain understands that,
Which my heart fails to comprehend.
For my heart cries out,
"How can you let common sense prevail over love?"-
I have no doubt that you did love me.

And I will forever remember every moment we spent together,
Cherishing these memories until the end.
But eventually I will think less about how much I miss you,
Never thinking any less of you.
Gradually I will forget quite how special you made me feel,
And, yes, I may even forget the sweetness of your kiss.

And painfully, slowly I shall return to my old, meaningless life—
a life without you.

Kim Switzer
DO YOU SEE THE HOPE?
Do you see the hope outside your window?
In the gray sky is the hope of sunshine.
In the falling rain is the hope of bright flowers.
In the young child running through the grass is the hope of tomorrow.
In each sunrise is the hope of great accomplishments.
In each sunset is the hope of lasting peace.
In each bright star is the hope of beauty and love.
In the rising of the moon is the hope of reaching further than anyone ever has.
In every winter is the hope of spring.
And in every spring is the promise of new life.

Susan Dwyer
GROWTH

This poem is dedicated to my husband, Francis, whose encouragement, love, and support gave me the courage to grow.

Intelligent - creative - nonconformist
naive - sick - scared
never finding real love
social outcast - feeling alone - purpose
Who am I?
Help!
Lack of self-esteem - confusion - despair
searching for thyself
truth - conformity - out of place
alcohol - drugs - false security
out of control
Death!
30 years looking - finding me - work
friends - not alone - not so different
spirituality - serenity - happiness
drug and alcohol free
feeling good
Alive!

Shannon E Crusco
MAYBE
Maybe I'm dreaming; maybe it's not real,
These thoughts that I'm having, these emotions I feel.

Maybe it's magic. Maybe it's here,
And suddenly it will all disappear.

Maybe it's just an infatuation
For a different style and situation.

Maybe it's fake, maybe it's not true,
Or a fascination for something new.

Maybe it's a worldwind romance,
No heavenly praises, no eartly chance.

Maybe, just maybe, it possesses that part
Which only comes from within the heart.

Maybe it was meant to be,
For us to share eternity.

James C Seward Jr
SOMEONE UP THERE LIKES ME

To the one who loves me and others in all the earth. To our Father in heaven. GOD.

Born in a world of destruction
where the bad outweighs the good.
Where things are "not at best."
in many, many neighborhoods.

But I can't feel the pains
which most have deep inside.
Someone up there likes me,
in them I can confide.

There's much to be thankful for.
The breath of life's just one.
The people we love is another,
and the times we have clean fun.

Hold fast to your integrity
swallow your foolish pride.
'Cause someone up there likes you!
In them you can confide.

And you, and you, and . . .

Sandra Trimble
HERE I STAND

This poem is dedicated to the many brave men whose lives were changed forever. My heart goes out to them all.

Do you know the things I saw
the pain that I endure
the nightmares linger through the dark
there will never be a cure

I awake to an explosion
which echos in the air
I try so hard to run away
but I'm not getting anywhere

For here I am already home
a different man you see
a place they call Vietnam
had done it in for me

The memories I can't forget
the shooting never ends
for they were not just anybody
those soldiers were my friends

I need someone to listen to me
so would you take my hand
many others died for you
but see me now for here I stand

Jo A Hickenbottom
BEYOND DREAMS
Once upon a starry night
I dreamed a dream
I saw the light
A roaring sound
A blinding flash
As my dreams came
crashing down.

Michelle L Bonnett
MIGHT I STILL BE ALIVE?
I never really wanted to go,
But you begged me to come along.
I knew right from the beginning,
That we didn't quite belong.

You said to loosen up, to chill out,
That one drink wouldn't hurt me
I knew I was making a mistake,
But I didn't know how high the price would be.

Friends Forever!
That's what we always said.
I guess forever ended yesterday,
When I was pronounced dead.

But one thing will always haunt you.
That I might still be alive,
If you would have told me
To Never Drink and Drive!

Elaine Skaarer Aden
DAKOTA WINTER NIGHT

To my husband and son, who are also my best friends - I love you both, Kenn and Kirk.

The wind is really howling,
It sounds so fierce and wild.
The only thing we're knowing
Is it'll soon be warm and mild.

The storm roars down from the hills,
Be glad you're indoors safe and warm.
When even though it gives a thrill
Indoors you are safe from harm.

Sometimes the wind brings the snow,
Sometimes it's only dust and dirt.
If only there was a way to know,
Will the farmer gain or get hurt?

The plows are out there somewhere,
Hope the electricity won't go out.
When ice storms happen out there
Who knows how long we'll be without?

And then the morn dawns so bright
Though it's cold work must go on.
Daylight puts everything to rights,
Erases the storms overnight frowns.

Tracy Hale
FRIENDSHIP

To Janet, Lynn, and all the others who encouraged me to write. To Mrs. O'Bryan, who introduced me to poetry, and mostly to my family for all their love and support.

Snow-covered mountains
cascading waterfalls,
crashing waves
and
flower filled meadows
May bar us from each other
And yet our bond can never
be permanently severed
Childhood fears and tears
we suffered through
Maturing hearts and souls
helped us become one of mind
Age, knowledge, and wisdom
we soon acquired
And now even though it seems
we are sometimes
universes apart
I know that when my problems
cause turmoil in my life

Your sweet voice and advice
will always be there to
quell the storm
Our friendship and love can
never venture into the dark
Because your letters and thoughts
are lanterns in the night
And you and I hold a
friendship of the
heart.

Joseph V Tripptree
WRECK

Crushed,
and
stolen breath.

Fragrant injury
and
chlorophyll blood.

Carol Davis
RAPED

To J.B.D. - Unexpected, but loved.

I've been raped
It seems so distant
yet so close.
So close that I still
feel sorrow.
A sorrow that fills me
instead of a gratefulness for life.
This sorrow has consumed me.
But it is my soul's duty to reach
for that one strand of happiness
So that I may live.
So that I may live.

Regina Machelle Butler
UNTITLED
bleached blonde hair
and blue contacts for eyes.
the all-American?

why try to resemble a stupid
stereotype?
why not just be
you?

BUT if being you
means substitution
you must be as you please.

so the next time you look
in the mirror
i guess you won't wonder what's
behind the makeup.

the sad part is
not that others won't know-
BUT you won't.

Joscelyn A Johnson
RECOVERY

I, with nothing found to say
Numb heart reluctant to obey

Feel trapped in a cold web
Raw emotions begin to ebb

Owned by the same motivations
Though now awaiting invitations

"Waiting" breeds ulcers and aches
But pains less than mistakes

Rough waves relax against rocks
We measure healing-time by clocks

Christopher Wargaski
WHAT AM I?
Day and night I would think of it;
how to do it.
The quickest, easiest, messiest,
painless, and most grievous way to It.
The black void of depression was
engulfing me.
Slowly I was dragged towards the
point of no return.
No one but myself knew.
I was all in favor for a try.
Then life one day changed.
Only occasionally would the
colorless hand start to pull me in.
For no apparent reason a friend
attempted to push herself to the
endless sleep.
A failure for her; a success for God.
I cursed her for it.
"Because of you" she said.
Still I cursed her.
She must have thought I despised her
pursuit of eternal rest.
Little did she know still would i think
of it and yearn for it at times when I
am depressed I do.
Am I a hypocrite? or selfish?

Vickie L Campbell
MY SON
My son needs someone who will care
Make him feel wanted, and take
everywhere.
Somebody love this son of mine
Even though he's only nine.
Help him get over this loneliness he
fears
Help him be happy, and make no
more tears.

Somebody take my son and love him
right
Hug him and say, I love you!
Everything going to be alright."
Don't blame him for the way he's
being raised
It's not his fault.
He's just a little boy, and he should
be praised.

They say that life is rough
But a little boy without a father . . .
Now that's really tough.

God help us
Watch over us day by day.
Help me raise my son
The proper way!

Angie Holland
VERBAL WORLD SITUATION
This world would be a better
place, if everyone worked together,
Let's work as a team and make
things better.
We can make this land a great
place to life,
If we stop constantly taking, and
find some good things to give.
Such as keeping world peace
between countries and nations,
With more communications and
less complications.
Being more open-minded to the
serious problems in our world today,
Making sure the homeless life a
more safe, secure way.
Prevent the Drug Problem, also all
the violence involved,
We shouldn't give up on these
problems, which can be solved.
Today's children, is tomorrow's
future, encourage them to stay in
school.
A mind is a terrible thing to waste,
this is very true.
The world we live in is only what
all of us make it,
If we want our world better, let's
do something about it, and not fake
it.
Our world is beautiful to some
extent,
Let's give that extra push and try
to repent.
Becoming one big family is the
issue here,
Means this message is perfectly
clear.
Let's Improve Our World.

Charles K Sharpe Jr
TEMPTATION (A BLANK PICTURE)

This Poem is Dedicated to My Family & Dear Friends, Mother, Father, Brothers, And My Sweetheart Tam. I Love You All.

It attacks not only losers, but winners
Not only saints, but sinners.
Although you can't see
How tall it can be,
And though you can't touch,
You sure can wonder how wide and
how much.
It could be real big or small
And terribly bad for us all.
Your mind it could take,
Your heart it may break.
Your soul it may enter
Like a cold breeze in winter!

(This poem was taken from a piece of art observed in the Salem Burke Art Gallery. "Temptation" Indiana limestone size 15"x10")

Lynn Mathews
LOVE

To my husband Leslie, children Vicky, Dawna, Leslie Jr., Tim grandchildren Kimberley, Lance, Jamie, Misty, Erin, Brandon, Jon, Corey, Jermey, Mike, Josh.

How far to the stars, millions of miles
And to travel it takes years I've
been told
But, love knows with just a smile
or
a touch
It travels fast if it has room to grow
With many kinds of love, each
good
as the other
All in different ways the very best
love is one that stays and stays
Your mother and father the love you
have for them
It goes on forever this love know no
end
The distance that love will travel
The love between sister and brother
Depends on the love one has for
the
other
And to be alone in body and mind
Not having friends loving and kind
Someone to turn to when you are
blue
No matter what they are always
true
Then the ultimate love God gives to
life
The love between man and wife.

Leonina Fortunato Heringer
SPRING AUTUMN
What's this beautiful change
growing up before my eyes?
Wasn't it all green a few days ago
or am I dreaming?
Did the angels do it?
I think so . . .
The mystery of the magic painters
giving colors to the trees

fills my soul to the top . . .
Gives me ecstasy . . .
They call it autumn
but I prefer to think about spring . . .
I see flowers instead of leaves . . .
This is a true miracle
I can't be out of this great
Splendor
Change . . .

Leonina Fortunato Heringer
IF I WERE AN ANIMAL
If . . .
I'd like to be a lion . . .
I'd be very powerful.
Then, I could dominate . . .
I'd have a strong voice . . .
I'd make all my own choices . . .
I could display a pretty mane . . .
I could give a thousand orders:
To all the dogs I'd roar:
-Stop!
I'd order the mice:
-Come!
I could eat a bird for my breakfast.
-Don't bother my nap, I'd tell my
master.
But, despite all my wishes,
I was made a simple cat,
I look like a lion but
I'm not, yet.

Leonina Fortunato Heringer
PLENITUDE
Winter is over
Charles River defrosted
The trees are still bare
unprotected . . .
I miss . . . how I miss . . .
the flowers and leaves.
The rare snow of March
transforms into a light
and continued rain . . .

Suddenly . . .
from nothing
one flower blooms
from the ground . . .
Followed by others
and still others.
The bare trees
the dry branches
"good for fireplaces"
also bloom and grow
in flowers and leaves.
It's SPRING.

W E Swope
TO BE WITH YOU

To all those who have helped me grow in these trying years. Thank you to my family, my Bear River High School, and of course, friends.

I do believe the Lord above,
Created you for me to love.

He picked you out from all the rest,
For He knew I'd love you best.
I once had a heart that was true,
But now it's gone from me to you.
So take good care of it as I have done,
For you have two hearts and I have one.
If I go to heaven and you're not there,
I'll write your name upon the Golden Stair.
And if you're not there on Judgment Day,
I'll know you went the other way.
And just to prove my love is true,
I'd rather die, just to be with you!

W E Swope
BILL EDWARD

I sit all about, watching you drink,
Silently wanting to pour it down the sink.
You would probably punish the cabinet door,
And unto the store, you would dash for more.
You think that you are intelligent and smart,
But what will you do when your body doesn't start?
You sin with the alcohol until it's gone,
Not knowing what you are doing to God.
People die by this disease every day.
Never knowing Jesus' name.
You probably wouldn't care, because it's all the same,
And you may wonder: "What will happen to her I say!"
I would come and toss flowers on your grave,
And pray to Jesus, that you are safe.

Barbara Williams
MY CABIN

Here in my cabin I find the rest
That men pay wealth to gain,
And stretch my legs before the blaze
Upon the hearth, and listen to the rain
That beats upon the glass. Content am I
As an Arab on the desert all day,
Who pitches tent at eventide and finds
Shelter, and time to pray.
Here I am master. Here I dream
The dreams that come to all
Who heed the voice of nature, and
Answer her silent call.
My dog for companion is enough for me,
And like an eagle alone that soars,
So, too, soar I and rest,
In my cabin, in God's out-of-doors!

Ruth Kemp Fessuh
COUNT YOUR BLESSINGS

Dedicated to 2 daughters: Herma Jean, Varryl Delisa; 3 brothers: Nathaniel, Jr., Albert and Joseph Kemp; 5 sisters: Iola, Eddie, Georgia, Lida & Verna.

Counting your blessings is a wise thing to do
Giving the Lord thanks for all our blessings
That is a way of counting too.
Before I start counting I want to include you, you and you.

Now let us count to ten thousand
The number of blessings he has to satisfy the poor
Gee! If we receive ten thousand blessings
Do you think we should ask for more?

If we would count more and complain less
We would not have so many sleepless nights
We'd be ready to fall fast asleep
By the time we turn out the lights.

At the count of one, look around and see
What great things the Lord has done.
This will keep you counting from early morning
'Til long past the setting of the sun.

Now we are going to count and count and count
Til our Savior's face we see.
Then we will stop counting
And praise Him eternally.

Donna J Nuss-Rick
WATCHING YOU

To Jessica Susan Heather Rick.

I hold your mask
with the breath of life
You warm my heart
as a tear escapes my eye
While you gasp for life
with struggle and strain
Your jokes, songs and laughter
ease our pain.

Anna L E Gonzales
SURROUNDED BY BEAUTY

Dedicated to the loving memory of Paul D. Sullivan, former Executive Director of the Pine Street Inn, a Shelter for the Homeless of the City of Boston, Massachusetts.

Society simply refers to me as the Homeless One.
My clothing is ragged, wrinkled, torn and tattered.
Well bedraggled is my hair, so
unkempt, unshorn and undone.
Lined and unshaven is my sad face so battered.

Scraped, scuffed are my over-sized high shoes, well worn and mud-splattered.
Youth's white, smiling teeth are long, long gone except one.
Gone, too, from my harsh life is all that ever surely mattered.
Feet, once very agile, now are unable to run.

Yet, amid all this misery that weighs upon me a ton,
Beauty dwells like flowered fields, by wind unscattered.
Reflected in the eyes of fellow Homeless, as I am one,
Is the warmth of Love; my dreams remain unshattered!!

Richard K Bosko
WITH HANDS ONLY

Health is health and not with out.
From Above-Down could B.J. be right?
From Inside-Out is it ruled by innate.
Could ADIO be what it's all about.

The Chiros world is in his hands
while the M.D. world is in his bag.
But the body's health is within its self.
The precise pressure on each process brings about the position of each facet.
But the bodies health is within its self.

While medicine has brought us from Hippocrates there chemical and potions ward off disease.
But the bodies health is within its self.

Both worlds are needed to preserve one self
but can the two work together inspite of themselves.
But the bodies health is within its self.

Health is health from the inside out.
From Above-Down his legacy lives on.
From Inside-Out one can not manipulate.
Yes ADIO is what its all about.

Rachel L Ivey
THE STRENGTH IT TAKES TO LOVE YOU

Love is going when there is nowhere to go,
Love is forgetting when things cannot be forgotten
And forgiving when things should not be forgiven.

Strength is running when you want to stop.
To carry on when you feel like quitting.
Strength is loving when there is no one to love you back.

Combined together love and strength can create a world where two hearts
become one.
But only can they become one, if there is love and strength coming
from both hearts.
The true test of strength and love is loving you but having the strength
to walk away.

Valrie Cobb
I HAVE FELT THE DAY

Tell me what today is like,
Tell me what you feel
The joy, the pain, the grief, the shame,
or did it feel the same?
Of yesterday of every day or
Did it per - haps rain?
Tell me what today is like,
Was there someone new.
The smile the tears the love the hate
Or would you ever wait?
To feel brand-new, so tired and true.
Or will you be too late.
To share your day to learn
Of something new.

Thomas Wood
DON'T BURN THE FLAG

People are burning the flag today
And it really puzzles me
Because it's not only freedom
It stands for you'll see

The stars show us
There's a heaven above
Where Almighty God lives
Who showers us to love

The stripes show us
That Jesus was beaten
Then went to the cross
To die for our sin

So please think twice
I beg of you
And help America defend
The red, white, & blue

Calvin L Meirthew
SIMPLY LOVE

In Your Past I Couldn't Give Much As Your Dad, In Your Future I'll Try To Give More As Your Friend.

Dear Lord, Dear Lord, Yeah It's Me Again
Just Wanted To Say Thanks For
Shining Your Light So I Could See Within

To Change My Pessimistic Views
Into A Positive Force
To Again Love One & All, Yes I'll
Carry That Torch

May This Love Spread Like Wildfire
& Backslides Be Few
May I Never Forget, Dear Lord, I
Owe It All To You

Each Day Help It Grow Some More
& Give To One Another
The Hopes & Dreams & Courage &
Means To Share Our Bread & Butter

This Curse I've Built, Of Loneliness,
You Have Lifted It Away
I Talk To You & You Answer Too, I
Just Wait Until You've Something To Say
So Now I Know You're Listening, I
Need Never Feel Lonely Again
I'll Simply Reach Out With My
Heart & My Hand & Always Have A Friend
Love To All
Cal Meirthew

Calvin L Meirthew
ANSWERED PRAYER

Dear Lord, Dear Lord At Night I Pray
Remove My Blinders & Show Me
The Way

Again & Again I've Tried At Love & Have Lost
What Have I Done So Wrong To
Warrant Such A Cost

I Feel The Pain At Night When I Lay Down To Rest
And Again In The Morning & All
Day, This Much I Confess

There's Much Pressure & Reliance
Moving This Family To The Top
So If You Please, Send An Angel, To
See I Don't Stop

For They Too Have Had A Rough Road To Travel
Spreading Their Hearts For Others
On Life's Road Of Gravel.

This Campground We're Building,
We're Building To Share
Doors Open To All, Can I Stop, I
Don't Dare

It's For The Lonely, The Runaways,
The Lost & The Tired
So Give Me Strength, Dear Lord,
Build Within Me The Fire

To Build & To Work & To Pay Off The Debt
Because Next To Your Sweet Love,
My Family's Their Best Bet

Cherokee Lake Campground
Cal Meirthew & Family

Myrtle I Macaulay
THANKS

To Allan Stewart, Herther Ann and Rebecca Mary Macaulay.

I want to thank you Lord above,
For giving me three special people to love.
May they give to theirs what you have given to me,
The hopes, the love and the comfort of thee.
They are each special in their own special way.
And they have made my life happy in so many ways.
May you watch over them, with your love from above,
And may they always thank you, with their own special love.

Photo by: Thomas F. Florey

Arden Harrison

Arden Harrison
IS THERE A GHOST IN THE HOUSE?
If there is a ghost in his house, he's never seen it
Sure, he stares at the keyholes a lot and kisses the air
Occasionally
But, is there a ghost in his house? I doubt it.
Still, he sings in the shower and perfumes his pillows
Just in case someone 'happens' to appear.

Martha Adams Meek
COUNTRY VISIT

To Ben from alpha to omega.

I'm going out to the country
And visit Brother Ben.
I'll help him cut the firewood
And get the taters in.
We'll break the ice from off the pond
And milk the jersey cow.
We'll wean the dozen piglets,
Butcher the fat old sow.

We'll stalk the deer on a woodsy trail
With his Remington shotgun,
Or surprise a turkey gobbler
At the rising of the sun.
We'll eat the fruitful harvest
From the cellar's well-stocked shelves,
And sit around a roaring fire
Keeping company with ourselves!

Alberta Floersch
HOLY SPIRIT WINDOW MEDITATION
Before
Silhouetted against the faintly lighted window.
The Cross looms dark.
Ah, must I bear the Cross alone?
After

As softly as the morning sun
lights up the chapel
My heart has been lifted up.
Now I see His image
not the Cross, but His
is mine to bear.

Shirley L Watt
LITTLE BOY LOST
You came into our life a bundle of joy
Oh what a cute and darling boy.
The years passed as you became a young man
Things didn't work out the way we had planned.
Now you've grown to a full adult,
Things are worse, it's not our fault.
Oh what pain we've yet to see,
Look what drugs are doing to you and me.
We know not how this all will end,
All we wanted was to be your friend.
To love you to guide you and help you to be,
Good and honest and most of all free,
Before I leave this life I'll appeal,
Please let me stay to see you heal.
Mom 1988

Joelle Bafile
THIS MOMENT

(is for my friend, Katherine).

Life
Is a series
of singular moments.
And
Each moment
should be cherished
at that moment,
For
that moment
is not like
the one that went before,
Nor is it the one
that is to come.

Elvanelga C Isenia
WHY ME?

I would like to dedicate this poem to my wonderful parents, to whom I am forever grateful.

I may not be perfect and probably do have a lot of faults. But what fault could be so tremendous as to make me see through glasses as dark as the night.

I don't know why, but maybe someone in the same situation might be able to answer me. Why should I have a heavier cross to bear.

I know that each and everyone of us came on this earth for a reason.
What is mine then, if I cannot see through the eyes you gave me

Why me? Could it be because
I was able to hold on as a strong person willing and able to help others.
Why then do good and still have to pay such a high price. Accept it, yes, only when my question has been answered.
Why me?

Frances Guadiano
WIDOW

Dedicated to Catherine Gaudiano.

It is a grey afternoon in February.
Two weeks ago they took his body away.
Walking into an empty house,
Cold, you turn up the heat.

You don't bother with the lights
To rinse the dishes of their
Morning's crusted cottage cheese.
Ants drown sullenly.

How quiet it is:
Faintly, children playing on the sidewalk,
A television next door,
No car pulling up in the drive.

Examining the refrigerator,
Discovering plates of leftovers,
Lots of frozen dinners.
You make a rum coke.

Sit down with the mail.
Sort through yours, his.
Neat piles, nothing opened.
The Kleenex box is empty now.

Donna J Spence
ONE DAY IN WINTER
The sun arise' in the misty morn,
a blaze of color and Fall is born;

Geese and ducks migrate o'erhead,
their calls to each forlorn;

The fog's mist penetrates,
the trees' leaves shorn;

And misty smoke through
a persimmon sunset torn;

So life continues on each year,
and time wellworn.

Lori Collins
TO MY LITTLE ONE

I'm dedicating this to my son Austin who has brought much happiness in my life.

I love you baby I want you to know.
Can't wait to meet you, soon to watch you grow.

I think about you all the time.
Oh my precious you are mine.

Will you be big, will you be tall?
Will you be short, will you be small?

It's all in the works.
It's all from above.

All made up of miracles.
All made up from love.

Do you know when I'm talking to you?
Can you feel my touch?

Do you know how I love you?
How I love you so much?

At night when I'm watching your jiggles and shakes.
How often I am smiling, and that's all that it takes.

Your kicks are so faint, your rolls are so smooth.
But playtime is yours to do all you can do.

But, baby get ready as time's drawing near.
You'll take your long journey, and before you know it, you're here!

Love,
your Mommy.

Professor Norman Pearson
ON THE DEATH OF STALIN: IN MID-ATLANTIC

To all the aircrew who served in NATO to protect western democracy.

Give me a vodka and vodka
Titan who trusted nobody
We who are wearing blue salute thee
With the North Atlantic Squadron
Old sobersides thinks
And give me a vodka and vodka
They all go
Ozymandias . . .
And shortness of days matters not
And prejudice and hate matter not
And the dialectic of this sudden smart is
Monoliths matter not
Nor fear nor malice
Nor the broken brick proletariat
Our little father thingummy
What did you say his name was?

(On board RMS "SCYTHIA", 1953.)

Adelle Ann Cook
NATURE'S GRANDEUR
From atop the mountains, Eagles soar with glee;
From snow-capped tops, swept up by the sea.

Goldenrod blooming, in a field of green;
A shallow brook, a beautiful dream.

A man and a woman, their lives intertwined;
Nowhere on earth, is the peace so divine.

Swallows fly in, a delightful form;
To a place in the trees, where baby swallows are born.

From out of the nest, they chirp and they cheep;
Soon they will fly, over oceans so deep.

Back to the mountains, so high they do fly;
From far, far away, a sweet baby's cry;

Dew in the fields, a sound is a hush,
The beauty is true, of earth's fragrant touch!

Donna Lee Dunkley
A DISTANT PLACE
In the distance
some miles away
There's lots of cheer
and a brighter day
But before we reach
this distant place
we must try to learn
from our mistakes
Be Careful, Beware

There's more than one path
You have to look ahead
You must never look back
It's gonna be hard and
if rough times arise
keep your chin up
and don't close your eyes
'Cause in the distance
some miles away
There's a lot of cheer
and much brighter days!

Deana Gardecki

I FEEL SO WARM WHEN I'M BY YOUR SIDE

To Paul J. Mello, Jr., with all my love, Deana.

I feel so warm when I'm by your side,
I wish we never had to say goodbye!
You make me so happy, I just want to cry!
I know you are saying - "Why?"

Why - because I've never been treated good before,
I never understood! Until you!
You came into my life and you gave me respect & love,
As I adore my soaring dove.

I also adore you - quite a bit more,
Than anyone I've ever gone out with before.
I respect you even more,
Because I've never had these feelings before!

The passion, the warmth, the love, all burning up inside me!
I just pray that you can see!
Can you see what I'm trying to say?
I want you, I need you, and most of all - I Love You!

Angie Griffin

GOODBYE

In remembrance of my Aunt Nellie who gave me all the love in the world. I love you. Passed away . May 26, 1989

Hello, are you there?
Oh no,
You're not answering me.
I feel all alone, I'm so scared.
Maybe it is time for goodbye
But please explain to me why!
I only want you to know
I would be by your side day and night
But even though I'm not,
I am not giving up the fight.
I love you so,
as you already know,
and I hope it isn't time for you to go.
I'm a survivor and so are you.
Please don't throw in the towel and give up now.
If you do always remember
How much . . .
I love you!

Grace T Burns

A LITTLE MORE THAN HALF

If everyone did a little more than half
To bring peace to this troubled world
Think what it would mean to all who took part
To have such thoughtfulness unfurled

Lend our sight and ears to the blind and deaf
Our limbs to help the crippled walk
Our arms to embrace unfortunate souls
Our words to those who can't talk

Our Christian thoughts to the wickedly bent
A helping hand to someone each day
A smile to those who seem saddened by fate
Help them to find their way

These are the things which will help make us
Have peace and be able to laugh
If everyone of us each day of our lives
Would do just a little more than half.

Cary Owen Threadgill

THAT OLD FIELD ACROSS FROM ME

They're clearing ground of rock and tree,
From that old field across from me.
But they don't seem to care or know,
How God has made that jungle grow;
Nor how each vine to rock will climb,
To shelter nature's trembling things;
Nor how each child that comes along,
Can see a bird or hear its song—
As it sits perched on rock or tree,
In that old field—across from me.

Some day a growth of brick and wood,
Will stand where happy children stood,
And I will then so sadly say,
"Is nothing pretty here today?
Where is the coolness of the glade?
What is this thing that man has made?"
If this is progress I see now,
Forgive me if I do not bow.

Francis A Targowski

STARS DON'T MAKE WISHES COME TRUE

This poem is dedicated to my sons, Andrew and William, that they will always have faith in God and themselves.

Listen to those wishes wished on me
How foolish people can be
To believe I can make them come true
Don't they know that's something stars can't do
But they still come up
Enough to overflow the Big Dipper's
cup
That and so much more
But that's not what I was created for
And yet, here comes another one
I don't know how this all began
But so many have been wrong
And it's been going on too long
To believe in what I cannot do
And now the truth must be known
Stars don't make wishes come true
But people with a strong will of their
own.

Simon Gilbert Amarasekera

A CHANGING WORLD

The world with admiration watch
The changing ideals from old to new
Blessed with peace and reason
In all its depths and heights anew

People unused to think are now
Free to think, speak, write and act
Beginning to realize the change
Delight in the changing events

Unknown to freedom all their lives
Lived life of fear and doubt
Unable to express the violations
To uphold liberty their right

To honor the right reasoning
To be united in heart and mind
Work hard and live in dignity
And enjoy the God-given life

To follow a religion of choice
Without harm or hate
In well-being may all
Be blessed with peace always.

In a world to come.

Malikah L Jeffries

DON'T DWELL ON TIME

Time is a neverending
entity
The clock is ticking
yet time stands still

Don't dwell on time
for then Father will
move his hands

Man lives on time and
in time he dies
Don't dwell on time
for you will be lost
As Father stands still

Free your mind and let go of time.

Gurina Flossie and Bill Marantette

Gurina Flossie Marantette

THE OTHER WAY AROUND

In memory of my daughter, Sandra.

You follow me to the drugstore
To get a soda pop
Then you tag me 'round the neighborhood
To spin my spinnin' top

After all you're just a baby yet
You know you're only three
I wish you'd go home and leave me alone
'Cause you're too young for me

I'm sorry I'm too young for you
But just because you are eight
That's no excuse for all this abuse
I think I'll set you straight

In a year there will be a change in me
It will be the other way around
I'll be grown up and you'll be
The one to follow uptown

Gurina Flossie Marantette

MY HOMETOWN

I wrote this little poem today
It's about my old hometown
Remember the Columbus School
They've even torn that down

It's kinda funny in a way
This poem about my town
No matter where I seem to go
It seems to always be around

Someone always seems to ask
If I've a picture of where I was born
It just so happens that I have
Even though it's ragged and torn

There's something special about my town
When asked how big or how small
I look at my torn picture and say
It's wonderful - that's all

Gurina Flossie Marantette

A A

Drinking wrecks so many lives
I pray it won't wreck ours
It snuffs out life so easily
And leaves so many scars

The broken limbs and broken hearts
Leaves trails that never end
So why not drink a cup of coffee
The next time you meet a friend

Gurina Flossie Marantette

BIRTH OF A BUILDING

The day the seed was planted
Equipment was standing by
To move the earth so the building could grow
Each day as we walked by

The skeleton became more perfect
With the passing of each day
We could almost hear it breathe
In its own mysterious way

One night the lights grew bright
Its eyes were shining open
The changes that had taken place
Were far beyond words spoken

We saw the birth of this building
From the beginning to the end
Now as we see it standing there
It has become our friend

Alice Farnsworth

BUBBLES

Happy, carefree children
laughing,
singing,
blowing bubbles
incandescent globes
frivolously floating,
joyously free.
separate in their transitory splendor,
collapsing on collision
or
on their journey,
joining with another
to become one
—whole—
for that magic moment
before finally freeing
their eternal essence
from their shivering shells.

Jennifer Farnsworth

HALLOWEEN IS LOTS OF FUN!

Hallowe'en is lots of fun!
Treats in bags.
Pumpkins and hags.
Witches, goblins on the run.
Doors squeak!
Windows creak!
Children all call "Trick or Treat!"

Walter Swardfarger

ONCE UPON A HALLOWEEN

Once upon a Halloween
I met a friendly witch.

She flew right over top of me
And landed in a ditch.
I asked where she was going.
She said, "A pumpkin patch."
I asked her, "Why so?"
She said she had a broom to catch!

Daphne D Jones
WE

I need the laughter we share
When we are being silly.
I need the love we share
When we are being serious
I need the arguments we have
To get rid of angry feelings
I need the look in your eyes
That melts my heart
I need you to be my friend
When I'm feeling lonely
I need the craziness and even the loneliness
Of being in love with you
But most of all ......
I need you to need me

Daphne Jones
BOYS

You've hurt me like this before
So why should this be new
I know deep down you love me
Even though you say we're through
Why can't you just accept it
That you're hooked on me
It would be so simple
Just to set your feelings free
I'm not going to be sad now
Nor will I be blue
For one day you'll realize
What I meant to you

Paula Marge Lent
FOOTBALL TEAM

To my third granddaughter Angela Susan Lent, age 10—Poet Paula Marge Lent.

Angela Susan Lent
one of six cheerleaders
at the football game
In their colors of
gold and maroon
adorned the field
and consume
They cheer up the players
with gladness, joy and fame
as crowds of spectators
anticipate the game
Waving their Pom-Poms
that they do best
Letting the Redskins
do the rest.
Win! Win! Win!

Paula Marge Lent
THE CHEERLEADER THEME

Redskins, Redskins
you're our kins
We're here in spirit
To help you win
To help you win
Our pretty array
for you we dress
Waving Pom-Poms
That we do best
Applause from the spectators
we do address
Letting the Redskins
do the rest.
Win! Win! Win!

Laura Hinkle
9 A.M. SOC. CLASS

So long ago; yet not so long
And here I am
Hard to believe; not easy to understand
Seems like a dream
How fast time escapes; with no way to stop
Living in a blur
Hard to believe; not easy to understand
So much to learn
So much to see
Who am I now?
Who will I be?
Hard to believe; not easy to understand

John C Williams
TRANSFORMED

There's a place in my heart not too far away
I can get there in a moment anytime of the day
Love is the fulfillment of the voidness of my heart
His love is my vesture, without it my world turns dark
Why I drift away from Him I cannot conceive
For without Him in my heart, all is vanity indeed
I am simple and quite unlearned and too often alone
But with His love in my heart, I'm divinely atoned
All the troubles and disappointments
I encounter on my own
But with His thoughts in my mind
In Christ I'm above all wrong
Sometimes I wonder how he could love me still
For I have often fallen and prodigal been in past years
Some have seldom faulted their life is sweet and bright
My life has been tainted so filled with false pride and strife
But when I sing my heart is clean, I see things from above
And when I sing my mind is clean, all thoughts are pure & of love

Mary Helen Mossholder
I MISS YOU

Dedicated to: "Dearest," my lovely daughter, Marianne.

I miss you lovely daughter,
With an aching in my heart,
If words could ever express it,
I wouldn't know where to start,
It's just your sweet expressions
That I keep inside my soul,
If I ever had a goal,
It'd be to have you near me,
For always, alive & whole—

By her mother,
Mary Helen Mossholder
8/14/88

Connie L Olson
GOD'S "GOOD-MORNING"

This poem is dedicated to my mom, Pat Waste, whose precious love has always been unconditional.

God has a way of using beautiful things
To say what He has to say.
For instance, the way He says, "Good Morning"
In His great and unusual way.

He gets out His paintbrush and loveliest colors:
The pinks, the yellows, the golds;
And blends all the colors smoothly together
Into marvelous beauties, untold.
A message seems to come from the great God above
While basking in this glory, we sit;
'This is the day which the Lord hath made,
Rejoice, and be glad in it!'

So let's learn a lesson from our Father above
And hear what He has to say,
And let's let God's glory shine out through us,
For it's the beginning of another new day!

Mildred L Cherry
PRECEPTS

The precepts of a kindly world
Lost on a foreign shore
Can be regained by flags unfurled
And men can love once more;

For love can change one's darkened thoughts
And let one start anew,
And one can win one's battles fought
And drink the morning dew.

So, open wide the door to love
And love while there is time;
This love is like God's love above,
Untouched by earthly grime.

Yes, precepts oft are displaced
By this or that or those
As men seek gold and quickly race
Before a door can close.

They ran for what they surely knew
Would not get them ahead
And failed to drink the morning dew —
Alas, those men are dead.

Mildred L Cherry
TOY SOLDIER

Just part of a toy soldier
Lying there on the ground,
And his head and legs were missing—
Just his torso I found.

He was still holding his rifle
Just as a real man might—
No longer for a little child
Would he stand up and fight.

His uniform was muddied—
He was a saddened sight,
He who once so very bravely
Fought for freedom and right.

I will keep this little toy
As a symbol for all
Of our American soldiers
Standing before their fall.

And on will march other soldiers
Real ones and toys too,
For grown men and little children
Wave the red, white and blue.

Lettie M Petersen
MY TREE

To Pastors Warren Jorenby, Pastor Donald Rose & Linda Jensen for helping me be me.

I was adrivin' along East on Interstate 90
When I finally came to the Freeborn County Line
I saw this lonesome tree astandin' there,
It had no leaves, and looked so cold and bare.
It wasn't an oak, a maple nor a pine,
It was an old willow, still alookin' fine.
You could see it had several branches broken,
and what tales it could tell, if only it could have spoken.
Speeders driving by, never seeing it there,
Others, young and old, not giving a care.
Lovers passing it by, and others with lots of nerve.
All of them knowing Albert Lea wasn't far from that curve,
and home was no longer a faraway dream.
Instead of tiredness, eagerness took over, it did seem.
It was wonderful to see that tall living wood
And how many years, I wonder, had that tree stood.
I know it would tell, if it only could.
I hope I never have to tell it goodbye,
I will never forget this tree, no matter how I try,
But I am not too old, nor too afraid to cry

Crystal Otero
PREJUDICE

Why is it so hard to love
When it is so easy to hate?
Why is it so hard to like differed colors
When it is so easy to like only one?
Why do we look upon some as inferior
And upon ourselves as superior?
Can you show me where the difference lies?
We all breathe the same air,
Everyone lives and then dies.
Life and death don't discriminate,
Why should we?

Crystal Otero
SEPARATE WAYS

Since you've been gone, I've been in hell;
You seem to have put me in a spell.
I picked you above any other,
There could never be another.
But I know . . .
Everything good must go
The same as the wind must blow,
All people nice must leave,
Some friends you can't retrieve.
As for you, that special someone
It's the same as the rise and fall of the sun,
Everyone must go away
But you will see them again someday.

Barbara Dowling
SMILES

For my daughter, Aubrey, with love.

Too long now have there been sad,
unhappy faces.

Our world, in too many places,
looks haggard, full of woe.

But wait! Look! Over there, a crowd!

Voices, in unison, shouting aloud!

What could it be?

I best take that first step and see for myself.

Why, it's only one person, and what
is it they're doing?

Why, sharing a gift—that of a smile.

If only we practiced that magical gift,
Which is ours alone to give,

How often we could experience

Success in small places.

Aubrey Dowling
PUMPKIN
How big are you?

You are big and round.

If I were you,

I'd be careful on Halloween.

Myrl Evelyn Jones
NEW POETS
John Campbell wants to discover
some new poets
If we are good all to him we will owe
it
It must be 21 lines or less
I like to do the 21 lines the best
A $1,000 grand prize sure looks good
Makes a poet write the best she could
Editor and Publisher, please don't
laugh at my poem
For it may help furnish part of my
home
You advertised in February, 1990,
Redbook
Let's hope some new poets you did
surely hook
Page 137 . . . bottom right-hand side
I hope you are proud and my poem
you will not hide
I am not trying to make this as a joke
For if I offended you, my hanky I
would soak
I hope if I have talent you will let me
know
On to the World of Poetry, I will
really go
This is the second poem or letter
I really do hope I did a lot better
The words are done; it goes to the
World of Poetry
Oh John, oh John . . . please vote for
me
And all of us know the rest will be
history

Myrl Evelyn Jones
ENTRY
Enter free the best bargain I can find
Let's hope the right words will flow
from my mind
It's been a pleasure to enter your
contest
I hope my poem is among the
cleverest
I wanted to write a book of a lady in
the south
Not a single word did I ever speak by
mouth
Nor did I sit down to write this book
I was a little afraid people would
laugh till they shook
Also I had thought about writing
children's stories
But maybe this poem will be my
glory
I first saw your ad which I cut out for
a friend
Her name is Barbara her poems she
may also send
I want you to know I decided to give
this a try
My poem is true as the words don't
lie
I hope you like the work that I have
done
The words that I chose I really had
fun
Oh John, where will this poem lead
to
I hope you don't sit there and say
Boo Boo Boo
I have just another two lines to go
I hope I have all the judges going Ho
Ho Ho
In all contests the stakes are high—
chances low

Myrl Evelyn Jones
CONTEST
I will write my poem today
Hoping that it will be my payday
Also it must be 21 lines or less
I will surely try to do my best
A $1,000 grand prize sure looks great
All the 200 prizes make good bait
January 31, 1990, is my deadline
Myrl E. Jones may make a headline
March 1, a winners list sent
All entrants will have a remembrance
This may be my big chance
Hope it doesn't leave me in a trance
Says Editor and Publisher, John
Campbell
I must send to them my sample
It goes to the World of Poetry
Let's hope the words I was able to
see
2431 Stockton Blvd., Dept. USA
It will be me who has to pay
Sacramento, Calif. 95817
Any prize will seem like from
Heaven
Let's hope I appear in the top seven

Francis E Tenney
UNEARTHLY FEELINGS
Lost in the world of deep emotions,
with lasting tears creating the
oceans.
Rolling clouds of anger,
clashing with thunder, knowing
the danger.
Hours of peace and serenity,
then the uprising tornadoes of
agony.
Forsaken deserts of emptiness,
always desolate, causing
loneliness.
Eruptions from aging volcanoes of
fury, letting off steam of crazed
weary.
Continuous disturbance of earthquakes, shaking from the nerves and
aches.
Forests of unknown trees producing a
maze, with underbrush signalling the
haze, and all is dark, waiting for the
blaze.

Cynthia Goddard
FOOTBALL

To George Starke, lifelong friend and member of victorious Superbowl 1983 Washington Redskin team.

No wonder Black folks love football!
Where else can a Black man
Run with lightning speed
And not get shot in the back?
Where else can a Black man
Tackle
A White back
And be applauded?
Where else can a Black man
Reverse the tables,
Intercept a play,
Steal a ball
(for a touchdown)
And raise his
Unhandcuffed hands
In triumph??
Yes, Sir—
Thank God for football!!!

Kelli Jessen
LOST HOPE
Within the thoughts of my sleep
Your romance,
Like majestic mountains,
Tower above the rest.
The memory of your touch
Brings the image of a gently fallen
rose petal.
And I'm forced to follow the
Suffering path of Lost Hope,
You become the savior of my soul,
The keeper of my heart,
The sunlight of my universe.

Carrie Grayson-Jordan
LOVE'S BLADE ON THE EVERGREEN

Whenever you doubt Love: With all my Love, to my Sons, Corichey and Rickson.

The wind-up couple, not dancing,
"On The Beautiful Blue Danube"; not
playing.
Petals of dried fragrances crushed
between
pages of old books go unnoticed by
blushing brides and brides-to-be;
especially flower girls who carry
fresh flowers
to wedding parties.

A snarled heart turned to stone
preferring to be alone
snub others, who reread love letters
written in gold ink which
drip of love drops to their lovers.

Preambles of love's demise? Yet love
remains
the mountain unclimbed, until the
crest is reached
to embrace the summit for the
sweetest caress.
After many close escapes of
ascension from death below the
slopes;
love lets go the rope of disenchant-
ment;
for love alights even in the dreariest
dungeons
where daggers once grew as scars
around the margin of a cold, cold
heart.

Judy Cope
POETRY CONTEST

I dedicate this poem, Poetry Contest, *to John Campbell, and Eddie-Lou, and all fun-loving poets. It was my first time to attempt to share with the Many accomplished poets. I am sixty-seven & love writing.*

Twenty-one lines or less—
Certainly won't be my best—
But I must give a good try
As I think of what I could buy—
Others will be trying too
Good poems, you'll get a few—
'Twill be very hard to choose—
Just remember, someone must lose—
I'd never, never try to bribe—
But my talent I cannot hide—
Now, if you like really good stuff—
I have more, and quite enough—
Anything I've ever written, has been
for fun—
About any subject or about anyone—
Give it some thought and consider-
ation—
Save yourself time, and exaspera-
tion—
Let me hear I won the this contest—
I won't mind being the best—
I'm sure this, is genuine and true—
So let me say now, I do thank you—.

Judy Cope
I GOTTA BE ME
Whatever I do, I gotta be me—
My reasons you may not see—
When my actions, you don't agree—
Remember you are you, and I gotta
be me—
I have faults and make mistakes—
You are someone dear, I'd never
forsake—
Each other we cannot force—
I gotta be me of course—
Whether we like, whatever each do—
I gotta be me, and you gotta be you—
Our relation I'd never abuse—
Keep faith in me, you won't lose—
Trust my decisions, I am true—
I just gotta be me, and you gotta be
you—
Our views may differ about what's
right—
Only because our reasons, are not in
sight—
So whatever each of us do—
I gotta be me, and you gotta be you—
Our times together may be few—
'Cause I gotta be me, and you gotta
be you—

Edith P Aase
OXFORDSVILLE
I'm doomed to dwell in Oxfordsville,
No Florsheim's styles for me!
No pumps—no slings—no high-
healed shoes!
My feet rebel, you see!

Critics say I'm not well-dressed
But, little do they know—
My footwear was the same as theirs
A few short years ago!

So—as I shine my oxfords up—
In attempt to keep them neat
Thank God that I have shoes to wear
What's more—that I have feet!

Edith P Aase
DEDICATION DAY
On Christ, the "Solid Rock" of life,
A stately church, now stands!
Built not alone, by money's might
Nor labors of our hands!
But built with faith amid our works,
Christ lives in us today!
The power of prayer—our means of
grace,
To light the narrow way!
We dedicate our church, dear Lord,
To have, to hold, to keep!
And as our tender shepherd Lord,
Watch o'er thy humble sheep!
While in the time of our Master's
plan,
May love and peace be found—
Within these walls so firmly built,
On Christ—and higher ground!

Chris Drury
WHERE DOES THE SKY END
The sky is the limit my friend;
but tell me, where does it end?
It is where the eagle soars,
or the rocket roars?
Is it where the kite is gliding high,
or where comets go racing by?
Is it where the hummingbirds play,
or way out beyond the Milky
Way?
I don't know the answer to this my
friend;
but I know that if we set our goals
high,
someday we will reach the sky.

Donna Scheer-Croney
SUMMER'S END
I heard a tapping on the windowpane
I drew back the curtain, through the sunlight I strained
I couldn't see, but knew I heard
a soft chilling whisper, not really a word
Through the open window came
a cold gripping hand that brushed my motionless frame
The cold chill of winter waiting to be unleased,
the soft summer season giving way to the beast

Carolyn A White
DECISIONS OF LOVE
I have two choices—
Continue as is and thrive on my love which I know is real,
Say I can't go on and never know if he feels the same thrills.

The signs I need are clouded by the sea.
The words I hear come with echoes, yet very clear.
The love I have is proud and strong,
But fears the absence and quietness that goes on and on.

Do we grow more distant as time goes by.
Can we part the sky and cling to that wish, till we die.
Dare I dream of us, or be satisfied for whatever you give.
Should I want, ask or seek more, or grow into things based on my will.

To love and let go is not my way.
At least, not until—

M Pardo
MUSIC
Music . . . it is the essence of my soul
It is a beautiful sound that imparts life and energy to my whole being. It is life to my soul and my spirit.
Music makes me happy; makes me jump for joy. Music makes me get lost within its words, its tunes, its rhythms.

Music . . . it enhances my soul; enlivens it like standing in the middle of a peaceful rain forest. It moves my spirit & my body with its rhythms and vibrations.

Music is life to my soul. Music is an expression of my inner self. Music is the essence of my being. Music . . .
Oh, how I love music!

Kate Louise Mendrey
REMINISCENCES FOR JAMES MERRILL 75
Spring veined pink
petticoat blue vase
ruffled rippled water
around sunset Monet.

Swallows spray fine
penpoint victories.
Lilac lady scented
forest wisteria rich.

Dark green patina
ushers in the night.
Blissful reminiscences
Romantically recalled.

Peacock feathers flurry
Lobster red/5/4/2.
Domed pristine world
Venetian peach spring.

White petunias placed
clock strikes three
Infinitely
ever so delicately.

Simple stroking grase
Madonnas, Maxfield Parrish
Great abundance sprays,
mystical magical memories.

Hawk circle precisely
Advancing rhythmically
Sailing along sandy shores
Miranda mirrors knowingly.

Switchback glidding air
California Foothills, Fresno
Eagles overhead bright
Swift shifting currents.

Screams of jets
Cambodian blood
Two million dead
Kissinger.

Perras Hélène
WEEK-END

Pour les filles du service linguistique du C.N.

Vendredi soir, la cadence s'est arrêtée, fatiguée.
Elles sont huit.
Sans songer où elles vont, elles se sauvent par des corridors bondés de cris de vauves
Elles dansent, le pied meurtri, le rock de l´oubli, jusqú à minuit.
Au cinéma de la nuit, elles défont le lexique de la locomotive.
Et valsent les mots, durs kilomètres de rails, posés sur fils d´Ariane.
Progrès, tête carrée, boulon noir, trou normand.
Blouson bleu, bouton de rose, le lilas embaume,
nous irons au bois, dans la mousse bleue de nos amours.
Sylvie invite Sylviane pour voir les pousses et les grives
Loin des poussières agressives.
Andrée porte les tartines et la brioche.
Susanne trotte guillerette on la trouve gaie, coeur d´acier trempé.
Danielle raconte le coucou, la légende du chêne, espir ami de la raison.
Hélène rencontre Pâris, tendre printemps, dures mains tendues.
Lucie porte son mérite, modeste, comme une autre, un sac de chips.
Claire offre du chocolat malté, du muguet, aux carpes de l´étang.
Elles aprennent la fleur, le fruit, la fêlure, le parfum, la brûlure.
Le ciel n´est pas plus lumineux que le fond de leurs yeux.

La violette brille au salon, le temps aux yeux marrons attend que le lundi allume,
qu´il enligne les maussades messages et les mots sages sur l´écran.

Suzi Housel
THE GIFT OF GIVING
The gift of giving
giving of one's time
and energy
The love that is packaged
into every small moment.
The caring shared between
the hearts of few
The hand of strength . . .
. . . an aid thru troubled times
A smile that carries
through all kinds of waters.
You have a way of giving
me so much
That with our strength together
we will conquer all.

Beth Milliken Joerger
DARE TO BE GREAT
Dare to be Great!
Think big, not small;
He who thinks big
In mind grows tall.

Like rocket in cosmos
Be confident, strong,
Aim for the moon—
With heart full of song.

Dare to be Great
But Pray to be good;
Clasp Man's Hand
In Brotherhood.

Linda Copechal
A SPECIAL PERSON
I know a special person
He's "good guy" thru and thru.
He's always helping someone
Perhaps he's helped you too.
He blows balloons for all the kids
And entertains the old
I guess you could describe him
As "having heart of gold"

He works on one committee here
And one committee there
Where he gets his ambition
Beats me, I do declare.
There can't be many like him
I'm sure of this and so
By now you've guessed of whom I speak
Who else but Dick Laneau.

Ricie W Campbell
UNSPEAKABLE LOVE
As I look up to the sky,
I cannot help but wonder why,
That you would tell all Heaven goodbye
And come to Earth for such as I.

And go through pain that I don't know
For unworthy sinners here below.
Oh Lord, there are no words to say
To someone who can love that way.

But let me say it once again,
Dear Lord, I'm sorry for my sin,
And right now I bow my knee
In humble gratitude to thee.

Barbara F Dudley
FOREVER
Forever is a long, long time;
Incomprehensible to our minds.
We think in minutes, hours, and days;
Forever is like an endless maze.

Forever always seems at bay,
But suddenly it can be today.
Through the loss of life, love, or liberty,
Stressing our emotions, at times, our sanity.

Forever is an eternity,
Stretching toward infinity.
Where we shall always be,
In a state of immortality.

Forever is a long, long time;
Incomprehensible to our minds.
Forever is our destiny,
Our LORD, our MAKER, we shall see.

Bonnie F Clay
NOCTURNAL MELODY
The heavy mist outside settles in the trees
a soft, blanketing haven —
impenetrable.

With second sight, the animals move,
wandering through the forest night,
unafraid of darkness quiet.

Morning rays of glistening sun
melt away the mistiness,
creating shadows in the woods,
places made for shrouding nighttime creatures.

Daytime lengthens into dusk,
rustling sounds of bushes moving,
crackling twigs and dust motes
stirred by passing hooves.

Our day ends in blissful slumber,
while theirs is just beginning,
with notes of their nocturnal melody
playing on the wind.

Berta Kaye Conrad
BIRTH ANNOUNCEMENT
Winter clings to life,
While nature decides
The time for Spring's birth.

Lazily she stirs,
Then, tries some isometrics . . .
Rebellious she naps,
The sun kisses her gently,
She awakes, and Spring is born.

Berta Kaye Conrad
REACH OUT
The whole world lies like a wounded animal,
It moans in pain
It is pierced on all sides by the darts of war and hate.
It belches forth in anguish
The fire of guns, the poison of greed and lust.
Mother Nature spews forth vomit from her inner depths
In answer to man-made terror.

Where is the star that shone so brightly long years ago?
Has it dimmed? Burned itself out?
No! It is there, if we have eyes to see, and faith to feel.
The Christ-Child, man grown,
Cries out, "Come follow me,
I will stop your bleeding, bind your wounds, make you whole.
My love will embrace you
Turn not away, for I am the resurrection and the life."
The world sighs, then reaches out,
"Master," it cries out, "Help me!"

Carol (Lacombe) Grissett
THANK YOU, DADDY
I lived in California
When my father passed away

And his death was so sudden
I had not the chance to say

How sad the would would be now
Since he'd been called away

Without the whistle of his song
His humor and his love for life

All the encouragement he always gave me
But, especially, through the pain and strife

Yes, his battles; they were many
And the last one laid him under

But, even if he hadn't been a soldier in World War II
I would hope that he wouldn't doubt

That in my heart, a hero, he'll always be
Within this present world and without

Thank you, Daddy, I love you.

Carol (Lacombe) Grissett
REFLECTIONS
Pain can be a paralyzing thing
Be it from grief or heartache; 'tis no measure of the sting
But, a healing word, a hug of reassurement
The wisdom earned as souls connect
Can do much to help you bear the torment

Tho in life's valleys we sink low
Beaten and blinded by defeat
A quiet confidence can grow
Upon the mountain it can be sweet

Don't be afraid to share your love
And the lessons God has taught you
You may reach out and see yourself
In this pain that you've been brought to

Clinda L Fairow
THE LIGHT IN THE SKY
As I stand and look out
from the balcony . . .
At the beautiful lights of the city
they stand, twinkling at me
Many colors dance before my eyes
I wonder what each light represents
Thousands are combined together
they are a beautiful sight
But as I gaze upward
another light captivates me
A light that envelopes me
with its brilliance
Surrounds me with its beauty
touches me with its purity
For this light is not man-made
and doesn't shout to attract me
Just stands alone, in its love for me
love from its maker
Letting me know of His assurance of
His love and care for me.
And that He is ever near
watching over me, with His tender care
It doesn't shout at me
just stands alone . . .

Teri C Nelson
THIS TIME
Let's make everything work this time around.
I really do like the let's sound.
My feelings had all become doomed.
Then there was some strange sensation that bloomed.
The love I had, has never gone.
It's just we both needed some time to be alone.
Now what about this time?
Will you really give me another chance
Can you actually take another glance?
Do you still need some time to be free?
Or could you give it all up again for me.
I've tried to learn from my mistakes.
Everyone has their bad breaks.
Now, what about this time?
Our world is really a strange place.
Everything seems to go at such a weird pace.
I keep hearing a message to wait.
Is the message I give you too late?
Since you are the best thing that ever happened to me.
I just want you and I once again to be WE.
WHAT DO YOU SAY ABOUT THIS TIME?

June Prout
WELCOME

I dedicate my poem to all my family, especially my mother who I love with all my heart, who has been my dearest friend and protector, and to my friends who are there when I need them.

Welcome, welcome it's nice to see you
Simply because our visits are few.

Because miles and time have kept us apart
Meeting again brings joy to our hearts.

We are hoping you'll enjoy your stay,
Looking forward to each and everyday.

Hearty meals have been planned—
Hoping your diet isn't bland.

You'll be seeing a few old faces
and maybe visit a few old places.

All these things will be familiar.
Never finding anything peculiar.

I for one am truly glad you came.
Knowing everyone here feels the same.

The country is lovely this time of year—
No robber, killers and con-men to fear

You can sit back and enjoy the scenery
Watching the trees and landscape of greenery

From what I have mentioned above,
It's an open Welcome of Love.

Maryedna Carr
ON THE MEND

This poem is dedicated to my grandmother, EDNA VIANELLO, I LOVE YOU.

Spring is just around the bend,
With Winter's doldrums no longer to contend.
The bright sunshine will be our friend,
To start our spirits on the mend.

Mountain waters begin to flow,
While Mother Nature's children grow.
Our wild flowers we do grow,
Hence their beauty is our momento.

The colors and blooms are vast,
Their loveliness will ever last.
And forever be in contrast,
The dismal Winter's snow forecast.

The memories of Winter fade,
While walking down the promenade.
We'll treasure all the plans we've made,
For laying in the Summer shade.

It's dreary in February,
But March is forever airy.
Let's all rejoice and be merry,
This is sent with Love from Mary(edna).

Mary Bell B Jones
AH! YES IT IS CHRISTMAS!

To All My Grandchildren and Their Children.

Christmas, when earth is silently
wrapped in new fallen snow.
Christmas, when homes are alight
with candles' soft glow
Christmas, with its mistletoe and
berried holly
Christmas, with good old Santa,
generous and jolly
Christmas, with its silvery tinsel and
bright toys
Christmas, a day alive with happy
shouts of girls and boys
Christmas, when hearts for one
another do care
Christmas, when holy music fills the
air
Christmas, when the stars have a
story to tell
Christmas, when the Christ Child
came on earth to dwell
Christmas, when hope, love and
peace are born anew
Christmas, may it always be a blessed
day for you!

Mary Lou Konzem
AN AGE OF TIME

To my son Phillip Peter Konzem who has brought me so much love and happiness. Phillip is the greatest son ever.

The clouds
dark and grey
causing rain

A rose dead and withered by age

The desert of sand and dust
blowing wind.

An age until the end of time.

My dreams here and there
gone tomorrow

My heart
empty forgotten of love

A man
confused and lost
in his role in life.

My courage lost
with everlasting wars

A child alone and forgotten
of special needs.

A tear
Expressing someone's feelings.

An age until the end of time.

Mary Lou Konzem
A SPECIAL PLACE
I need a special place.
Where is my special place?
Where I can think out my thoughts and troubles.
A place with no more wars,
A place of freedom.
Where I can breathe again.
Where no more blood runs cold anymore.
A place of love and peace together
with unity among each other.
My memory is so bad, that many times, I forget my own place.
No one knows exactly what goes on,
Or, they do not know what to do.
I wish they would make up their minds.
I hear it all the time.
What will our children and our
children's children
Think of us?
Look what we have done.
We will leave them
this place
this way.

Carol R Leech
TAKE TIME

For my Mother, Dorothea and my Father, Richard Goucher, who took time for me.

In the busy world we live in today,
We often forget to stop along the way,
To smell the flowers, to hear leaves rustle in the breeze,
To feel the ocean wash around our knees.

We forget to listen to the song of our feathered friends,
To reach out and hold our children's hand.
We don't hear the purr of a kitten
Or feel the softness of newly knitted mittens.

Yes, in the busy world we live in today,
We often forget to stop and say,
"I'm glad we met and got to know each other,
Join me as I walk a little further."

Take time now to share with those you love,
The rich blessing that comes from above.
Take time to stop and unbend,
Take time to be a friend.

Thelma Romberg
I'LL BE COMING BACK

To my daughters; Mary, Nina, Laura.

I stood on deck and waved my shaking hand
As the big ship shuddered and drew back from land,
I heard the sailors' loud voices ringing, ahoy, ahoy
The words were repeated from captain to cabin boy.

As I watched the ship dim in mist far out to sea,
His farewell like billows came rolling back to me,
Oh, surely you will not cry, I too, will miss you so
Ere many moons have passed, I'll be back you know.

I'll bring you tales and gifts from foreign lands
Just like I dreamed of as a child again and again,
The golden sunsets on the great rolling ocean blue
The smell of seawater, friendship and missing you.

You would not have me miss the beauty of the sea
And the call of duty and service that now beckons me?
As we bid farewell, let me see your loving smile,
And remember now, it's just for a little while.

Aileen Seton
THE ORDER

To my mother, husband and children with love.

In the bowels of the monastery
the sonorous chimes of bells
echo down the cold halls
as brothers move in silent precision,
feet weighted by souls imprisoned
in endless servitude.

Faces serene in hypocrisy
hands locked in prayful ostentation
they pelt mental stones at the
watching multitude of purist
Christians
whose needs and afflictions
perpetuate their entrapment.

Over the roar and coercion of the
outside world they writhe
inwardly in weary righteousness.
Eyes downcast they parade in unison
bearing their defeat with dignity.
Crystallizing their humanity
in penitent submission
for the sins of all their brethren.

Aileen Seton
CIVILIZATION
Civilization restricts true feelings.
Primitive peoples have no such
impediment
neither do small children nor animals.
Theirs is a love-hate relationship.

These creatures of nature
act out their feelings in
an unrestricted, illogical manner
without fear of reprisal.

They are unfaithful, loving and
indifferent
without benefit of conscience.
They yawn openly when bored.
When angry, they spit and claw each
other.

Then our four-legged brothers are
ensnared,
trained to be mindless robots in
man's "civilized" world.
Nature, perverted, masks itself.

And little children grow up.

Bisher Tarakji (Age 11)
THE SUN
A golden coin behind the trees
The Sun
A ball of fire hanging in the breeze
The Sun
The light of the world
The light of the earth
The Sun
With all its rays in swoops and curls
It's been that way since its birth
The Sun
Every morning it wakes up bright
The Sun
To wake up the whole world with its
light
The Sun
And it is so
And it is so
But when night comes, it has to go
The Sun
To wake us up another day
The Sun
"Refreshing!" the old people say
The Sun
A golden coin behind those trees
The Sun
A ball of fire hanging in the breeze
The Sun

Ellen Cox
MAGIC JACK
I am a hobo on a circus train.
My name is Magic Jack.
All the animals know me by name.
On a circus train racing down the
track.

When I was a lad of only ten,
I set out to seek my fortune and fame.
Now I have circus animals for my
friends.
I am a hobo on a circus train.

Box car forty-four is where I bed
down
Using Glory the tiger as a pillow for
my head.
We are pulling into a brand new
town.
I can see her lights shining ahead.

I teach the animals new magic games,
Pulling them out of my brown paper
sack.
Yes circus magic is my game.
I am hobo Magic Jack.

I am a hobo on a circus train,
speeding down the railroad track.
Yes, I am a hobo on a circus train.
My name is Magic Jack.

Ellen Cox
FROM A YEAR AGO
Down the country roads, across the
rolling hills.
It is spring time again, time to plant
the fields.
Grandma is in the kitchen cutting
chicken up to fry.
Grandpa is on the front porch
watching dark clouds
Gathering in the Northern sky.
Children playing Red Rover, Hop
Scotch and Hide and Seek.
Aunt Sue getting ready for Uncle
Joe's homecoming next week.
A phone call from cousin John down
Georgia way.
Everyone gathered around to listen to
what he had to say.
I'm coming home for a visit
sometime this Fall,
While I am there I would love to see
one and all.
Sister Rose planning her wedding on
the 4th of July,
To her high school sweetheart, David
Fry.
It is Halloween, time for fun and
games.
It is time to ride on the witches'
planes.
Christmas time is near, time to
decorate the house.
Time to get out the Wooden Horse,
Pink Cat and Little Gray Mouse.
Down the Country roads across the
rolling hills,
It is Spring time again, time to plant
the fields.
Time has flown by, like the rolling
waves.
We have come full circle from a year
ago today.

Sara Lewis
SPRING SUNDAY
Under arching elms,
The dogwood blossoms white;
Serene and fair and stately,
In the morning light.

Breezes whisper symphonies,
And sunlight, sifting o'er
The leaves cast lacy shadows
On the forest floor.

Here, from the rushing world
We come to nature's balm,
And I am filled with beauty
And joy and peace and calm.

Jessica Maria Gatewood
MUST I CARRY THIS TASK ALONE?
This is for the homeless.

To my mother—Mrs. Ophelia G. Foster, for my friend—Mr. Ike G. Evans, who has helped me make things possible.

Must carry this task alone, when God knows have no place to call my own. Must go on and live each day without knowing how my Day will end? For have no place to call my own. For know who bought me this far. Should go on sleeping in the streets? Must this be me Dear Lord? Must this be me? Without the love have, have none . . .but what have done? I am so hopeless and without love to carry me through, where do go? What will do to carry me on? I have no home to go to . . . must pick myself up and take the little that do own? For have no place to go or call my own. If you see me and ask you can you spare a dime, do not turn away as if you did not hear me—tell me where can get a job, do not laugh at me, help me. Each day carry this task alone for have no place to call my home. Dear Lord make me strong, for am homeless, and my life is in this mess because it's not that did not try to do my best. I must have some place that can rest. Maybe one day will do my best for right now Dear Lord help me to help myself. If a man asked you for help do not turn him away but help him and let him do his best, for have passed this test.

Jessica Marie Gatewood
BEYOND THE SUNSET
Beyond the sunset where
The darkness is silent from
The rest.
Oh still of the night—where
quietness
is
Reserved from the rest.

I blow my horn and no one heard the
sound of the noise
That I seemed to make, sleep in the
hours where
Rest is so still as the morning
breeze—
Oh sun where you set yonder—is
Dark and where has night gone?

Come my sunset and evening in
between—
Quiet tonight I must sleep.
You so still but yet so warm silent oh
sunset—
Yonder you slipped up on me again.
So still and
Yet so peaceful you are—your light
shines over
The ocean as you set by beyond
your brightest fail
And lower your leep to pick up the
peep.

I spare the rest as you sleep in silent
Of a deep breeze between my sleep.
Oh sunset where you sleep beyond
the clouds and
Wipe the stars of the morning blow.
Oh sunset, oh sunset dark and silent

Nights—you are so quiet and yet
So restful in sleep, oh sunset, sunset,
So nightly you are.

I Shyke
TALE OF TWO PARADES

To Memory Of A War Known Otherwise Before But Now Recognized As A World War BY JAPAN.

Before cat-calling crowds in Seoul
celebrated
Captured USS Pueblo sailors were
paraded
Tattered tortured victims of Korea's
rule designated
Long punishment for entering Sea
of Japan guarded
Fate of a single peaceful scientific
ship
Later came the Korean Day trip
Annual marching by Korean
thousands
Silently greeted by New York's
5th Ave. crowds
The American Army was hereabouts
disappeared
Into other lands to be quartered
Now the way was clear
Behold Korea was near
Its marchers were all employed
Or store owners with customers
overjoyed
As tranquil an occupation as ever
imagined
A few blocks away a path to New
York harbor
American battleships were at anchor
"Move them out of the way!"
came the order
"They are carrying nuclear
weaponry."
That, they said, was danger to their
own citizenry
And Korea's silently greeted parade
continued into history.

Marion Hebert Caldwell
THE PATH TO THE SPRING
There is a dappled woodland path
that I wandered long ago,
where — when in search of
solitude
to this wooded path I'd go.
Here — I'd leave worldly cares
behind
and then stroll along real slow,
on the path that led to the spring,
where the clear, cool waters flow.
There — a deserted logging road
on — up the hill ascended,
where — it then forked along the
way,
and a deer-path there descended.
Sometimes, staring through wild
hedges,
stood a statuesque-like doe,
for she knew where the path did
lead,
where the pure, clear waters flow.
Here — this shady, green, grassy
path,
beneath the cliffs and ledges,
blew with lady-slippers of pink
amongst the wildwood hedges.
And, then the path still wound around
'til it reached a swinging door,
formed by great, green, swaying
branches,

branches,
that up toward the sky did soar.
When this woodland door swung open,
one could hear the waters sing,
for — within this wooded haven
the path ended at the spring.
At this spring of clear, pure water,
I'd kneel at the crystal sight,
then — cup my hands like a dipper
to fill with elixir of life.
As I drank the life-giving water,
I'd suddenly feel fresh and whole,
for — it not only quenched the thirst,
it also restored the soul.

Suzanne Peabody Stout

SHINE ON!

Of faith respectfully, answering undying & unselfish love. Love's on, shine through the Raging and sometimes empty understanding. The 4 stars soon to be . . . five special stars: my children Melissa, Robin, Johnathn and (RIP) Bokell Lewise Gean Lyons Born May 30, 1989, died April 6, 1990 . . . shine on! 4-Ever-My Luv, 4-Each one and U !Almost Home!

Painted tinker toys,
Special spoiled trust.
Painted blue roses,
Blackened if you must.
No games are easy not,
For us oh! No!
We have been savoring,
Spoiled love no more,
We musn't discuss.
Well I think if I had,
Us to play.
We played too hard no,
More we must trust!
Blackened blue roses if,
You must.
Special love turns,
Promises-broken to rust.
And I've been painting,
Tinker toys, and painting,
Blue roses blackened,
Beginning turning to rust,
Love turning to lust,
Shine! on.

Dorothy Flood

SPRING

What a glorious time of the year is Spring,
Color, new growth, what joy it brings
to the eyes of all who take time to see,
His creation, a panorama of great beauty.

The grass, the tiny leaves of a shade of green,
That cover the earth with a beautiful sheen,
Lights up the world with His magic touch,
And gives happiness to all of us.

Creation again is fulfilling His plan,
of life renewed and joy that can span
the depths of sorrow that can enter a heart,
Living a life from His love apart.

Examples He gives and lessons abound,
And the soul who seeks will always be found
to see in the blossoming of the world,
The truth, which His love alone
unfurls.

So with thanks we walk, drinking in the scent,
that only this time of year presents.
Thinking only of Him whose love for us,
Shows life renewed, and bestowed, thus.

Dorothy Flood

MOLES

As I walked in my garden this morning,
My heart was filled with displeasure,
And I was hurt to the core of my being
Since my garden to me is my treasure.

Arrayed before me like an army bastion,
Was row after row of mounds of earth.
Thrown upward by an invading faction
Determined to destroy beauty and worth.

I felt I had really been negligent
in not realizing this could occur.
But Moles are certainly not evident,
Nor the damage their burrowing incurs.

Sadly, I know I have much work to do
to restore the beauty I had,
And make the Moles their damage to rue
and their departure make me glad.

When they leave, the flowers again will bloom,
And the birds their lovely songs sing.
Beauty will return and pleasure resume,
And peace, like a bell will ring.

Michelle L Sudo

DROPLETS

As I sat there aboard the transportation, provided by the schoolyard, I could not help but
think how much the fogged up window looked like a mirror image of myself.
Rain would fall from the heavens above, to plummet down to the earth below, only to have the cool, crisp breeze blow them
against the window.
And I think how much those droplets of water reflect my own tears, my own loneliness.
Then that breezy gust of wind blows the pellets of rain down the window's glass.
In the rain's trail, I see the trail left by my own tears, streaming down my face.
I try to hold back the tears; they well up and the dam bursts forth.
Just like the window am I.
For the rain leaves behind the trail of sorrow in the form of a teardrop's trail of raindrops; And I leave behind my
trail of sorrow in the form of a genuine teardrop's trail
And now the rain has stopped.
The sun has evaporated the window's tearful trail of sorrow; but my trail of teardrops still prevails.
My face still has the bearings of a reddened tearful trail in which my
tears continue to obligingly and to steadily stream down.
And now I guess I have to wait for my breezy gust of wind to evaporate all my teardrops and vanish their trail.
So now I sit and patiently wait . . .
and wait for my breezy gust of wind to come to me.
The window, my friend, my counterpart, in sorrow, was free to let her teardrops stream down her face while I am not allowed.
For me, it is different.
I sit and cry my tears in the silence of a dark and lonely room, hoping only to
be like my window counterpart as she is like myself.
For until then, I sit and patiently wait . . . and wait for my breezy gust of wind to come to me as it did for her.

Judy Lee Perry

ANOTHER ODE FROM THE LIVING

Quietly and unexpectedly it came,
claiming the weakened body
that could no longer sustain itself,
leaving behind the unanswerable 'why,'
the reasonably to ponder,
the confused to cry.
Reaching down into the depths
of the unimaginable,
the soul searches for reasons
where there are none.
So homilies are written,
dirges for the dead,
but the pain in the breast
cannot be soothed.
Outcries at the injustice
of life's early loss
falls deafly on the stillness
left by the absence of answers.
Acceptance does not come easily,
yet, that is all there is.

Nancy J Gassman

THE SETTING OF OUR LIVES

What will I mean to you when I am old?
Do you know?
Looking through failing eyes,
will you forgive my aging skin?
Will you see the handsome features of my youth?
Will you still feel fireworks when we kiss?

I will be blind to the silver invading your hair.
Your embrace will never lose its hold on me.
You will be my sunrise in the setting of our lives.
I will love you then as I love you now,
here in the dawn of our togetherness.

Whether we are older than the universe
or as fresh as an opening blossom,
we will always be sky and water on the horizon;
Separate, but one, eternal in beauty and love.

Patricia Ackerman

WEANING TIME

Dedicated to "Buckaroo Springs" our cow camp.

Ole Lord, cover your ears at
Weaning time,
For this ole gal is using language
That's not so fine.

Nothing is working like a breeze,
Sometimes I think the only "good cows"
is in the deep freeze.

They won't gather or mother-up—
can't get them out of the rodear,
So some of the language, I'm sure
will burn your ears.

Be patient, ole Lord, it only last a week,
Then I'll talk like a lady, and be a little more meek.

Each year when the trucks pull out.
We heave a big siy--.
Terry turns to me and says, next year we'll hire a guy.

Next year comes, ole Lord, and here I am again,
Who can hire a guy, when our check book is so thin.
So cover your ears again, ole Lord,
It's weaning time.

Jason Springfield

THE PERFECT FLOWER

I see a flower
So beautiful and true,
Its colors sparkle
In the morning dew.

The sun comes up
And takes the dew away,
So it opens
For another day.

It soaks in the warmth
And is filled within,
To grow in beauty
To shine again.

Some stand in awe
Of the beauty it shows,
For this is the one
True perfect rose.

I look at this rose
And see its true value,
For this beautiful flower
Is really you.

Cynthia M Gerke

RESULTS OF SILENCE

Senses slowly surrender
To the crescendo of its power.
The sights, sounds and smells
Are hypnotized by noiseless pounding.
Suddenly, the living world is gone:
Open eyes see the blinding
light of nothingness,
Listening ears hear the echo
of fleeing footsteps,
Sensitive noses are assaulted
by mustiness,
As the mind meets the soul
And must try to explain its ways.

Pat Alexander

MAGIC

An evening of magic
Kissed by the stars
Music so mellow
From sweetened guitars
Nectars from flowers
Washed by the rain
Romance and cupid
At work once again
Dreaming of wonderful
Moments like this
Hearts full of laughter
Music and bliss
"Oh"

Oh for the spring days
When we were young
Every word spoken
Filled our hearts as we sung
Of love to each other
No reason to rhyme
When romance was magic
All of the time.

Pat Alexander
FLIGHTS OF FANCY
I met three little whimseys
Playing in the street
Dancing on the stardust
And singing with their feet
They never got depressed
At black and grey and white
They only looked at rainbows
That's why they seem so bright.

Pat Alexander
SWEET AND SOUR
Once I saw a laughter
On his way and sure
Who met a great big heavy
And stopped to give him wine
The heavy saw the twinkle
Of the laughter at the time
But was too big to lift himself
So he wallowed in his brine.

Pat Alexander
OTHER TIMES
The magic of the moment
Swift as a breeze
Through a dan-de-lion's hair
Or the gentle rays
Of a warm spring sun
To help keep the memory
Of a joy that once was.

Pat Alexander
MOTHER'S DAY
Give your Mother a bouquet
Fill it full of spring
Tie the knot with a rainbow
She'll hear the lovebirds sing
A burst of radiant colour
To brighten her special day.

Write your most endearing words
On this your Mother's day
Live long and live each moment
May all your days be spring
Enjoy your life forever
And always want to sing.

So . . Give your Mother a bouquet
Fill it full of spring
Tie the knot with a rainbow
Then you will hear her sing.

Shirley A Young
THE PREMIERE OF A TEAR

Dedicated to my daughter, Beth, whose tears were its inspiration.

The premiere of a tear is, in truth, the finale of a drama.

It is evidence—a tally of emotion undisciplined.

A tear's premiere is versatile—gala, in celebration; relief, in sorrow; or empathetic, in understanding.

Each tear's premiere is a unique original performance, wrought anew by circumstance.

An awesome wonder, this tiny, delicate drop of moisture.

Therapeutic or healing—ethereal and mysterious, or tender and sweet.

All powerful and mighty—or, humble.

At the final curtain, unobtrusively and without fanfare, the tear takes its lonely path to everlasting obscurity.

Amy L Wadsworth
THE LIFE
Love stormed the gates of the temple,
Taught by the quiet sea,
Traveled the paths with the restless crowds
Of ancient Galilee.
Love spoke to the poor, the stricken, the sad,
The errant and sick of soul.
"Rejoice! Be healed! Take up thy bed!
Thy faith has made thee whole!"
Love rode triumphant through crowded streets,
"Messiah! . . . Anointed One!"
Love prayed for strength in a garden,
Forsaken, betrayed, alone.
Love left to die on Calvary's hill
Breathed forgiveness as the heavens drew down,
Love rose victorious . . . stronger than death,
To claim His kingdom's crown.

Brenda S Mudrack
NURSE'S AIDE
Listen up, oh nurse's aide
When in this job that's underpaid
How can you say you do no good at all
These people know you're at their beckoned call

You reach out with a caring hand
and gently tie a woman's hairband
When a man does sit and say
"What is there to live for today?"

And in a soft and gentle voice
Your reply, "there's always reason to rejoice."
Life is peaceful, life is short
And someday the ship pulls into port.

And when you at their bedside sit
Their death is like a hammer hit
You wonder as you sit, "Lord, why must they go?"
Then you realize it's part of life's evenflow.

And you watch in a silent hate
as the elderly sit and wait
For family members to come and call
But no one comes at all

Yes, oh nurse's aide, you do a lot
And maybe the rainbow has no golden pot
But a smile and a twinkle of an eye
Should be your rainbow, by and by.

Brenda S Mudrack
THE END OF ANOTHER DECADE
A new President started the decade
In December, John Lennon was shot.
In 1981, the President was shot but did not fade
In 1982, Henry Fonda won an award
and left us for a new spot

Princess Grace followed close behind
And the Fort Wayne Flood puts us on the map
In 1983, MASH said good-bye with peace of mind
1984 woke up people from their nap

In 1985, we came and went back to the future 30 years
In 1986, Cary Grant passed through a new gate
And many watched the shuttle
Challenger in fear
In 1987, Jackie, Fred and Rita left us without debate

The King of Rock still reigned
despite the passing ten years
In 1988, President Bush took the office pledge
In 1989, Olivier and Lucy passed from their peers
And I now sit and ponder the new decade teetering on the edge

As we reach 1990, a new year
Open that door, eager to explore
In ten years, a new century will be here
Let's try to make it a whole lot more.

Annie Virrill
HYPOCRITES

Dedicated to those who had an impact on my feelings inspiring me to express myself.

A mistake you say committed by me
Has not left you understanding
But of course you disagree

You lecture and plea, argue and scold
Brutally punish, but never am I told

Of your embarrassments, not a thing
Causes you shame? You never lied,
Stole or cheated at games?

Please forgive me, but I have to say
Perfection I believe is no one's forte.

So don't pour my guilt, I'll be happy
To share, because I do not believe
You have nothing to despair

And if again I fail or show
That I have brass
Careful of judgements for
Your house is of glass.

Annie Virrill
A BOOK WITHIN ITS COVER
You hide behind an image
One day you hope is true

Never seeing my side, but
afraid that I'll see you

Narrow minded are your thoughts
Self-centered are your deeds

I guess you have what it takes
In order to succeed

So very unreal is what I see if
you care to take a look

You're nothing what I thought
Like a story from a book

As the pages turned I
read between the lines of fate

At Chapter One there was
love, but by the end it was hate.

Deborah Cunningham
FACE THE CHALLENGES
Why grumble of a life that may be ordinary?
Existence down here is only temporary.
Get rid of that stony, chiseled face of gloom!!!
You've had that same look since early afternoon.

Cheer up! Count your blessings — it's not all that bad.
Life is full of challenge, some good and some sad.
Rise up! Meet the enemy with your armor of God!
Fight the fierceness of life with protective gear on!

Stand tall in battle and leave your mark—
so others behind you can ignite the spark
that's necessary to achieve goals from within.
Set an example and others are sure to win!

Deborah Cunningham
WHY?

Dedicated to a world that doesn't have to be in despair!

What in life has made them lose all their self-esteem?
What in life has caused their eyes to lose that lustrous gleam?
Why does it seem existence is like a bottomless well —
with life consumed as if living's destiny is headed for hell?
When did the transformation begin
that was bound to be doomed?
Where in life do they think they're going when death could come so soon?
How can a life be turned into one
that's filled with joyful bliss?
Who has the answer where they would find
the good life that they've missed?
There are so many broken people running
to and fro being absolutely devoured!
I am really concerned and have found the answer,
One truly set for this hour.

JESUS CHRIST OUR LORD
HAS THE ANSWER
NOW!

Steven H Gale
SPIDERWEBS, (TO KRISTIN)
Spiderwebs.
Your mother can't see spiderwebs;
There are always spiderwebs in her houses.

Not many, but a few,
High up in the corners near the ceiling,
Strung across the tops of doorways,
Nestled in the rock baskets of the fireplace,
Arching between windows and screens.

I wonder why I only see them on the left?
Surely they are there, on the right,
When I come back through the doorway.
They are obvious when I go up the stairs,
But I seldom see them when I come

back down.

Your mother can't see spiderwebs;
I can only see them from certain
angles.
That says more about us than about
them.

Ethel H Bennett
SILVER MOON
Silver moon away up high,
Have you ever told a lie?
You do your deed and help us all,
Winter, spring, summer and fall.

With all your light you spread
around,
To watch the lovers on the ground.
Are you lonely, do you have no
mate?
Oh! silver moon it's just your fate.

The stars keep winking down at me,
Among them all it's you I see.
Sometimes you don't shine, but I
know why,
It's those floating clouds in the sky.

They play hide and seek then dance
away,
Don't they ask you to play?
But you're still there and lending
beams,
Down on the mountains and across
the streams.

Silver moon I've talked to you all
night,
With all my heart and all my might.
You don't answer, but I understand,
So please keep shining on the land.

I'm not a dreamer, I was left behind,
To spend my life until the end of
time.
Now morning has found us and we're
far apart,
Can I just call you "My Moon
Sweetheart?"

Dolores Salinas
MOONLIGHT & STARDUST
Moonlight upon my cheek
stardust has fallen under my feet
trying to remember what was once
forgotten
hanging on to the branch
of a family tree in pain
I feel as though I have no control
like the water that will drown me
the further I swim
the hole that will bury me
as I slowly sink in
hovering above the Lord he waits
in his high seat for me
above the clouds and the
land that was and never will be
Moonlight upon my cheek
stardust has fallen under my feet
I'm showered with tears in this
barren field
as the tender touch from the mind
the caress from the sea only touches
me
I take a step in to finally be free

Sarah A Williams
GENTLY GO THE YEARS
A child is born
The hopes and ambition endowed
in
one
precious little one.
Gradually she begins to grow and
develop
Gently go the years.
A child grows
The achievements accomplished in
one
precious youthful one.
Steadfastly she acquires and
receives
Gently go the years.
A young lady marries
The union blessed with children
harbored in one mature one
Lovingly she cares and teaches.
Gently go the years.
A Mature Lady Reflects
The achievements accomplished
in these precious little ones.
Proudly she approves and relates
Gently go the years.

Tasha Walters
ON
We made clear our feelings.
The sensual deprivation
and the unwholesome partial ecstasy.
Confused,
Timeless and undesiring
Understanding
The shaman means to cleanse our
souls,
without perpetual solitude.
Listen and you'll learn,
Question the answers.
Tempt us into leading.
Come into our world
where we terrify the filthy.
Shocked and ashamed
we attempt to understand.
We're here disecting society.

Callie E Walker
WHAT IS THIS WORLD COMING TO?
What is this world coming to? I really
don't know. We have people walking
on the streets of America with no
place to go. We have children having
children, because
they are not being raised. Boys and
girls don't act right. Parents? How do
you expect them to behave? We have
people killing people. What's going
through their minds?
God bless America, because it isn't
very kind.

Terri Valenzuela
LOST TRUST
Here I stand in front of you
What you see is seen by few.
Bearing my soul, face wet with tears
Losing myself, trapped in my fears.

You reach for me, I pull away
Wanting your comfort but always
afraid
Afraid of the hurt that closeness can
bring
Will my loneliness worsen if I let you
come in.

You say you love me and always will
stay
But I carry doubts that won't go
away.
You want to be my lover and friend
But I'm afraid of being hurt again.

Too much doubt within me lies
So I shut the door, you're left outside.
Heart full of pain, I fall to the floor
Sobbing and weeping, no more, no
more.

Alma Bella S Waddington
HOMINIDAE
Enchanted by the unknown,
Twisted with fellowship of lies,
Burnt by skilled acts of time,
By man's madness,
By man's egocentricity,
Into the realm of obscure reality;
Into the path of repugnance—
Man is swallowed
By his own incredulity.

Skies of awakefulness spread,
Like showers of delighted con-
science,
Shared from baths of blood,
Through ravening mouths,
Tears of pain, sweat of joy;
Man is mellowed
By his own boundaries.

The shadow of a silent gracious
morning,
Gushes forth with a reproof of life,
To the world about to listen,
A world closer to true humanity.

Lisa Tepe
MY BEST FRIEND

This poem is dedicated to my cousin Heidi. Love ya!

She was my best friend
My best friend until the end.
We never had secrets we couldn't
tell.
We picked each other up when the
other one fell.
Of best friends, I've had dozens,
But she was special,
We were cousins.

Pam Tedrow
ONLY IN TIME
I love you for who you are,
Not for what you do.
Therefore, I hold no grudges on
What you have done.

Just promise that you'll be true and
patient,
And when you're through with that,
Then maybe we can "get together."
But only in time.

Be patient, my dear, for
I love you for who you are
Now, not then.
"This is now, that was then."

Colby Taylor
WITHIN A FEW MINUTES

To my Grandmother: Mrs. Guynelle Lingold.

I watched contently one crisp fall
afternoon
as the autumn leaves fell onto the
sun-brightened pond.
As I watched the ripples cascade
from the place of
touch between leaf and water, I
thought of
the leaves as special people that had
touched my
life, and the ripples as the ways in
which
they touched me.
I watched as some of the small waves
journeyed
away from their place of origin never
to return,
while some returned in the graceful
way in which
they had been sent.
As the wind quietened to a calm, the
water was
full of stillness as though there had
never been
the small ripples silently running
above its surface.
As my thoughts returned to the
reality of life,
I felt as if God had shown me this
event
of nature to make me realize that all
people
are special and that each person
touches your
life in a different way, whether good,
bad,
or evil, and that each person should
be thanked
for their part before their role in one's
life is over.

Chris Tate
FEVER'S FIRE & ICE
Hot dry heat
Released from my core
Like bubbles,
Climbs through layers of flesh
To the skin's surface
Where they burst and are
Tingled away
By the air's breath,
(Feeling now like an arctic blast).
Chills caress each contour
With the rough persistent hand
Of the newly blind.

Hilda Adams Bonebrake Suter
TO HATTIE
Friend of my childhood come walk
with me
across green fields of our
memories.
Echoes of laughter and happiness
dwell
in scenes and places remembered
so well.

Wending their way to the hidden
glade
deep in the woods and its
cooling shade,
Girlhood secrets exchanged and
treasured
a lifetime friendship of
unbounded measure.

Two little old ladies recall to mind
tender the thoughts held fast in
time.
Touching the past across the years,
the joy of living its hopes and
fears

Gone—all gone, the beloved faces
wait
to return again in the shadowed
places
Did you hear the whisper of a
chuckle we know?
Come old Friend it's our time
to go.

Jennifer Lynn Stillwell
MY FEELINGS . . .
There's not much to say about them.
My feelings are always overlooked.
My feelings are some were hiding
inside,
they rarely ever show.
My feelings are my own, and no one
can rob me of that.
I hurt, I cry, I love, and I care.
These are my feelings . . .
as hard as it may seem.

Nancy Sommer
LOG CABIN BY THE ROAD
There is a cabin made of logs, in the
hills of Tennessee,
At the crest of this mountain, it's so
beautiful to see.

A cabin down the valley, a short ride
will take you there.
Sweet flowers in the garden, their

fragrance beyond compare.

Looking out a window a beautiful
lake will meet your gaze,
Standing on the porch in autumn,
seeing such color all ablaze.

In the summer evenings when the sun
sinks out of sight,
You can watch the many fireflies
light up the silent night.

At the foot of a majestic mountain,
this log cabin can be found,
With rolling hills and grassy knolls,
with rich and fertile ground.

Thanking God for His grace and the
love He has bestowed,
This couple has made a home in a
LOG CABIN BY THE ROAD.

Nancy Sommer
ALWAYS THERE
My Jesus is always there, He never,
never moves away,
Holding my hand He walks with me,
all along the way.

When I call out to Him, I know that
He will come,
He will never fail me, no matter what
I have done.

I often wonder what would happen to
this life of mine,
If Jesus treated me, just as I do Him
at times.

Walking away from Him, as if His
heart won't break,
Recognizing Him only, when I need
Him for my sake.

Not telling others that He is my very
best friend,
Ignoring Him in so many ways, is my
greatest sin.

All these things and many more, for
which I'm guilty of,
But He never puts me down, He just
bathes me in His love.

Healing my wounds, He holds me
close, each time I commit a sin.
Oh, Lord may I never in this world,
break your heart again.

Nancy Sommer
THIS BEAUTIFUL LAND
Anyone who is lucky enough to call
America their home,
Can say to the world, "I love this
land, I'm so glad she's my own."

The marching bands, the soldiers at
hand, will swell any heart with pride.
We wave and cheer, wipe away a
tear, for the joy we feel inside.

We will raise the flag on high, and
praise her beauty to all,
The stars and stripes is an anchor of
love, when to duty we're called.

The great land didn't just happen,
Much prayer was prayed at will,
For lonely hours and aching hearts
and for those on the battlefield.

Thousands of men and woman have
made the greatest sacrifice,
Giving their talents, strength of love,
and then laid down their lives.

Thank God for lending this piece of
paradise, to you and to me.
Old Glory must keep on waving o'er
this land of the brave and free.

Many lives have been given to show
what she means to man.
With heads held high, and a smile
from the heart, we salute
THIS BEAUTIFUL LAND.

Omaya Seif
OF WOMANKIND
We all believe that there can be
One who hates all womankind,
But do we realize the fact that he
Might've lost one of the kind?
A fool he was to have loved and
trusted
Her beauty than her inner grace,
But twice a fool he is to have quickly
judged
Half the image of the human race!

Omaya Seif
TRAVELLING INTO MY DREAM
I came upon a meadow
as I travelled into my dream,
a green meadow sunk in bright
yellowness
by the summer sun
reflected from a running stream.

I looked around and I found
the merriment I was seeking,
for all my troubles drowned
me in the depth of sleeping:
far from the frustrations of my
present day
I found the hope of life in one ray
of light in the meadow,
where I lay down to rest from woe;
and as I stayed there
in that meadow called "Nowhere,"
my troubles slowly drifted away.

Omaya Seif
I STILL SIT
I wonder why I'm still here
looking down from my window
at the poor old man below.

Too hungry to stand he sits with an
open hand
staring at nothing or maybe at space
not feeling the tear teasing his face.

Weary and weak his little son is
asleep
maybe dreaming a nightmare of
himself in a grave
with the penny that some idiot just
gave him.

I wonder why I'm still here
watching this pitiful scene
doing nothing and being mean

Like the people who pass them by
insensitive, cold, and selfish,
I still sit and only dream of my wish.

Paul Schulze
THE GODS PLANNED IT

To my family with all my love.

The evil witch of Kalpernia
Was her name
The ninth plane of hell her
Goblins and ghouls came
She rocked the very balance
Of the world
Under her feet women in
Obedience curled
She took my beloved to
Her fiery pit
Together in hateful harmony
They sit

Maria Kane
THE GREATEST BLESSING
There's so much beauty living brings
The sweeping arc of sea-gulls wings
A field of wheat in golden sun
meadows where small children run
There's beauty in the bright blue sky
Where whipped cream clouds go
sailing by
In cool green lawns, in streams and
fountains
The stately trees, majestic mountains
There's so much beauty living brings
But the loveliest of lovely things
The greatest blessings from above
Are the gifts of faith, hope and love

Henry Rodriguez
LOST WISDOM
Man's infatuation with war
Has always been a mystery.
Perhaps he does not realize
That there will never be a victory.

To fight an enemy he cannot see
And wondering why it has to be.
To reason with wisdom is seldom
heard,
And end it all with just a word.

Has this earth ever known
A lasting peace?
Since its beginning, like oceans
Of water and all the seas.

Even to dream would be too much,
To shake a hand, a simple touch.
Those who dared to think such
thoughts
Are those who have all ready gone
and fought.

Perhaps one day soon
We will open our eyes,
To hear and see truths
Without empty lies, the
Heavens above and her blue skies.

Andrea Riccardi
I REMEMBER
I remember when we were together,
But nothing lasts forever.
And when we said good-bye,
Everything just had to die.
Then I see you again my friend,
And remember when you said it
would never end.

I remember our happy times together,
And we wanted to last forever.
But things just had to go wrong,
And for so many things I long.
But my love for you had to come and
go,
My dreams keep thinking you love
me so.

I remember when we said we would
never leave,
Or our hearts will just retrieve each
other again.
For everything has split apart,
Even the strings that hold together
my heart.
I'll give you up that's all I can do,
But remember I love you true.

Rev John W Olson
CLAY FOR THE POTTER'S WHEEL
Clay for the Potter's wheel?
This worthless clob of dust?
Oh, no, God No! You have no
use
for me, I cried;

But underneath a rim of pride
That feigned a false humility,
The Spirit breathed, and found
A hard, black stone.
It was my heart — my selfish
heart —
That would not even part
with worthless clay.

Oh God, have mercy and forgive, I
pray!
My overwhelming shame at greed
within so fierce
Drives me to genuine tears
Which fall upon the clay and
stone
To soften it.

Broken, dissolved into a formless
mass,
I bring it now to Thee, O God;
Do as Thou wilt,
For I have tried and failed,
Take this worthless, shapeless mass
of clay,
And mold it again in Thy Image,
I pray!

Rev John W Olson
AUTUMN LEAVES
The climax of a leaf's career
Comes in the autumn of the year
When unseen painters, brush in hand,
Do suddenly transform the land.
With ev'ry color you can name
The forest brightens like a flame.
Each leaf, resigned to garb of green
With only shape distinctions seen,
And only fear of turning brown,
Delights now in its autumn gown.
I hear the leaves laugh in their glee;
I hear them whisper constantly.
The leaves, you see, have planned a
ball
Before the winter meets the fall.

Johnny C Norris
TO THE ONLY ONE

To the Blonde Beside Me.

Every day I work with you.
I smell the sweet fragrance of your
hair.
I see the deep beautiful luster in your
eyes.
I hear the mesmerizing sounds of
your voice.
I can almost feel the smooth softness
of your cheek.
Every day I think of you.
I recall your soft laughter.
I remember your sweet gracious
smile.
I ponder on your love of life and
God.
And with every thought, my pulse
quickens,
As if my heart would leap from my
chest.
But, despite my emotions, I can do
nothing.
For the chains of fear, fear of being
turned away,
Are far too strong for me to break.
I ask myself, "What can she see in
me?"

And I have no reply.

Dee Dee McNeil
TOMORROW
Tomorrow is a butterfly
prize of child-like dreams;
trapped inside a mayonnaise jar
with trembling, colorful wings.

Tomorrow is an orange sun
flooding dark with light.
Tomorrow is the brightest star
upon the breast of night.

Tomorrow is the unborn child
of pregnant, bleak today.

Hope for all the world
that something better's on the way.

Tomorrow is a precious gift
meant to be a sweet surprise.
However, bears no guarantee
until today has died.

Stephen J Mehl
PAY THE U S A
Well I pray for the USA
And I pay the man every day
C'mon let's all do our best
And pay our dues to the I R S

Don't worry brother if you're short
We're bound to get our money's worth
Just do all day what you do best
Someday collect the interest

In old age we'll be given care
If there is any money there
Although the rising deficit
Could make us all be eating shit

I have faith in my Uncle Sam
That he will do all that he can
To pay our bills and keep us clean
And build our mighty war machine

If there's a war we will not fail
We'll have a great big weapons sale
The revenues from all those guns
Will put us in the black again

But all those weapons may come back
And leave us feeling mighty flat
Then we'd be in the red again
Commie red that is my friend

Now we don't want our freedom gone
And comrads running all around
So pay the man I say today
The I R S will save the day.

Stephen J Mehl
THE WORLD CENSUS
The Government would like to know
Who's alive by the year two thousand
We're killing the babies now
In case Messiah's among them

Remember in the year of Tiberius
When Caesar needed to know
Just who was from the tribe of Judah
And Herod watched the show

They were looking for those zealous ones
Who worked the underground
For in their midst the Holy Son
Could probably be found

Wise men from the East did come
Then Herod knew the truth
"Now's my chance to kill the Son
He's somewhere amongst our youth"

Today's the day, stand up, be counted
The truth shall make us free
Let's not abort our babies now
Or Christ we'll never see.

Maria Mediavilla
LOVE LOST
As the sun sets into the heavens above.
My love disappears into the mist below.
Summer evenings filled our chamber with the classics.
As we lay in each other's arms.
We listen to the concerts from on high.
Long conversations resolved our tormented souls.
Times remember by books — we once read.
Now I am as before.
For my love is no more.

Daisy Rittgers
CONTENTMENT
My dog and I
Together go,
Down to the pond,
Where the Cattails grow.

He chases butterflies,
I swing my feet,
Down in the water.
Isn't Life sweet?

Dorothy Gorman (Wiesler)

Dorothy Gorman (Wiesler)
LOVE SO TENDER

To my late husband, Ed Gorman, a wonderful husband, father and dear friend — who passed away in 1980—

The tears I cry tonight —
Are for a love that's long gone —
Love that made the whole world bright —
Love so tender — love so warm —

Now there's one pillow —
Where once there were two —
The nights are long and lonely —
Trying to get over you —

My life is upside down —
Because you're not around —
Whereever I go - your memory's there —
You're in every breath of air —

Yes - the tears I cry tonight —
Are for a love that's long gone —
Love that made the whole world bright —
Love so tender — love so warm —

Dorothy Gorman (Wiesler)
LOST CHILD

To My Beautiful Grandchildren.

Do not cry, my child, He said
For you are safe with Me.
Sleep tight within your bed —
And I will set you free —

Look up at the sky above —
Look hard - and feel his love —
For you are not alone
Wherever you might roam —

The road — sometimes — is hard and long —
And it's easy to go wrong —
But you have in Him — a friend —
And He'll be waiting at life's end —

So — when sad — pick up the pieces —
Give your heart to Jesus —
He will lift you from all strife —
And give you courage to live your life —

Wm T (Bill) Lindsay
A SALUTE TO FIFTY YEARS

To my loving wife of seventy grand years.

Many years ago, when Lemon Groves gave "Lemon Grove" its name.
Two families, from the middle west, to this fair village came!
The BEIDLEMANS and the DENLINGERS were just family friends,
But this fact marks the beginning of where this story ends!!

When Beidleman's sweet daughter met Denlinger's husky son
They said, one to the other, "Gosh but YOU'RE the ONE."
Then and there, without a doubt, Romance was on its way
And then went on to blossom on that SPECIAL DAY!!

As Ernie said, "How 'bout it kid, shall we set the date?"
Dotty, modestly hesitated, then she grabbed the bait!!
Where to hold the Nuptials, a decision must be reached,
The kids, both were for the Bluff above Torrey Pines, fine beach!

The parents quickly vetoed that, with a very strong, "No, No" —
The Congregational church in Mission Hills, now that's the place to go!!
So on OCTOBER SEVENTEENTH, FIFTY YEARS ago this date,
The PAIR that we are honoring, entered the "MARRIED STATE"

Guided by Dotty's Dad, Edgar, there was gathered many a flower —
They transformed the front of the church into a lovely outdoor bower!!
Helen Stephens Holzer, was "Maid of Honor," Dwight Stanford, the "Best Man."
They sure helped the Bride and Groom, as from the church they ran!!!

Following the Honeymoon, what or where, who knows,
Into a brand new little cottage, the Happy Couple goes!
This started the tradition, known with quite some Fame,
Giving to the cottage, its "HONEY-MOON COTTAGE" name!!

The children, LINDA ANN, in forty-one,
The first born in the family-better folks than them, there's none!!
Next came JERRY EDGAR, born in forty-four,
But hold onto your hats folks, I'm sure there will be more!

The last child to be born to them, CARL BRUCE is his name,
In nineteen hundred forty-seven, this third deduction came!
Most of all these JOYS did come to pass in Lemon Grove, their home.
Except for a year or so when they did choose to roam.

As an Official in the Packing House, Ernie's leadership did show,
And so, to take another job, to Ontario, they did go.
Then back again in Lemon Grove, they really went to work,
As volunteers in many spots and their duties did not shirk!

Dorothy with the Hospital and Ernie with the Scouts
Both did work with Youth Groups, including their own "Sprouts."
In the middle Fifties, this group proved its worth,
Furnishing another "Son and Brother," this one not by birth!

From across the Ocean, They welcomed George, in their new big house,
Then and there the Denlingers, His CITIZENSHIP did aspouse!!!
This made quite a Family, one girl and three boys!!
Then each, by getting married, added to the family's JOY.

That's the Family, all complete —
No, that is not Right.
Because the ten GRAND-KIDS, we must never slight.
Five of them born Denlingers, Two Maisches, Three named Hall,
But regardless of the names, we do LOVE them ALL!!!

Now the family IS complete, up to this very day,
But what about the Future? Who are we to say?
How many more will there be, in the years to come?
Just watch out for "GRAND-KIDS!!!" . . . They'll add quite a sum!!

Now, to the HAPPY COUPLE we're honoring today,
There are several personal things we all do want to say —
"As a PAIR you sure have lived a HAPPY, BUSY life,
With all the Joys AND Problems shared by MAN and WIFE."

"You've journeyed to far places, whene're you had the chance,
And in between, enjoyed your hobby, Remember? The SQUARE DANCE!!"
But despite these many things, and your Business too.
Your Church and Community, you have been ever true."

"You've Both been very Faithful to your Growing Family
And have shown in endless ways, It's Top PRIORITY!!!
Your ever readiness to Help, Young and Old Folks too,
Has been so clearly demonstrated by ALL the things you do!!"

"So to you BOTH, on this YOUR VERY SPECIAL DAY,
We wish you HEALTH and HAPPINESS, as you CONTINUE— ON YOUR WAY!!
May God's richest Blessings be showered on YOU TWO,
Now, as we close these greetings, WE THANK GOD FOR YOU!!!"

(WRITTEN BY BILL LINDSAY AND RECITED OCTOBER 17, 1987; RAMONA, CA.)

Krys A Jasinski
BITTER ENDING

I Dedicate This Poem To My Sister Diane, "Because She Liked This One!"

Spring Was Here
Now It's Gone
Summer Has Arrived
And Soon The Fall
The Leave's Colors
The Air So Crisp
All Having Such A Radiant Glow
Like Reflections Of The Sun
Off A River's Flow
What A Beautiful Sight
To See The Coming Of A Cool Fall Night
The Air Scented Of Burning Wood
If Autumn Were To Last Forever
How I Wish It Could
As A Life
It Has An End
Now Arrives The Winter
My Other Somewhat Bitter Friend.

Krys A Jasinski
THOUGHTS OF YOU

I dedicate this poem to "Hope and Faith," my great "flow" of inspiration . . . "How sweet it is."

As I Watch The Sun Rise In The Morning
I Watch The Sun Set Into The Night
As I Watch The Moon Rise In The Darkness
I Dream Of Holding You Tight
The Color Of The Skies
The Stillness Of The Air
Remind Me Of Your Eyes
And Softness Of Your Hair
Thoughts Of You I Cannot Resist
For A Person As You Does Exist
Your Smile
Your Laughter . . ,
Though Nothing's As Special
Than Times We spent Alone Together
Your Mind On Me
My Mind On You
This Love Will Last Forever
Day Out And Year Through.

Krys A Jasinski
WITHOUT A WORD

I Again Dedicate My Poem To "Hope And Faith," "It's Getting Sweeter All The Time."

The Day I Walked In
The First Time I Saw You
A Word Was Not Said
A Voice Not Heard
Though The Room Was Filled
Silence Fell Deeper
As Your Eyes Grew Brighter
My Eyes Listened,
As My Eyes Grew Brighter
Your Eyes Listened.
The Loudness So Great
Still A Word Not Spoken
Yet So Much Said . . .
The Day I Walked In
The First Time I Saw You
The Day We Fell In Love
Without A Word.

Viola McIntosh
MY CAROLINA

My Carolina how I love you
the place where I was born
many many years ago
on a cold December morn.
Beneath your lovely mountains
the home of all my dreams
i've roamed your hills and valleys
and waded barefoot in your streams.
I've climbed your lofty mountains
and watched the sunset there,
as I listened to the birds at twilight
sing their songs of beauty rare.
I've marveled at your summer beauty
when you're all dressed in emerald green
then in colors of the rainbow
to me you are an artist dream.
It's as if each leaf has been painted
by the touch of the master's hand
then in winter all covered white with snow
your majestic mountains stand.

Roland Hasso Millar
ME HOMELESS, CAN YOU TELL?

To all the people who have been thru this and still going thru it.

Me homeless, can you tell?
I'm a bit lonely, but I'm feeling swell.
I have my pushcart and my portable bed,
I have my pick of any alley to lay my head.
I have my pets; my dogs, cats and rats,
I never worry about overeating, so I don't get fat.
I'm never in one place, I'm kicked out so fast,
I never have a permanent address, it never last.
So I keep moving on, alley to alley, street to street,
In search of an outside vent blowing out some heat.
Some days are fine but the nights are so cold,
I'm really young at heart, but I look so old.
I've done my best thru this life-time of mine,
People tell me I'm not doing too good, others tell me fine.
I see these well-dressed people staring at me,
I tell them I'm not different, but they don't hear my plea.
Since I am so poor, I'm not even worth the time,
"We've got to get these kind off the streets," they throw me a dime.
But in this society, you're judged on what you've got,
Materialistic things are important, it means a whole lot!
Me homeless, I'm glad you can clearly see,
The state that this world is in, this will always be.
But until there's a change, homeless is where I'll stay,
And if that time ever comes, I won't worry about it anyway.

Roland Hasso Millar
YOU WERE HITLER

You were Hitler,
I was a Jew . . .
I had nothing, nothing to give to you.
So your troops took me and my family away,
Till you knew what to do the very next day.
Arise, we were awakened early, moved with haste,
Board a train with other people in a quick pace.
Doors slammed shut, locked, dark and cold,
Men and women, boys and girls, even the old.
We all had questions, too scared to ask,
Ride was hard, how long will it last?
Hours passed by, the train began to slow,
Some were sleeping, awakened by the whistling blow.
Doors unlocked, thrown open accompanied with shouts,
Black dressed storm troopers yelling, "Get out!"
The light blinded me, but the smell I can remember,
I lost track of time, the month, is it still December?
In the background, from huge chimney stacks came smoke,
Thicker than fog, with the smell that me choke.
The separation had begun, between men and women, and the old,
There were no questions, decisions,
just do as told.
I never saw that old couple again that came with me on the train,
They were carted off toward the chimney stacks in emotional pain.
I was later separated from my family and taken to a room,
I was alone and on the wall written I read, "Doom."
Is this the place people refused to believe existed?
Are people this easily fooled, to be brainwashed, twisted?
What have I done wrong, how can I make it right?
I tried to read the walls but there was not enough light.
Times was not on my side, whether time meant anything at all here,
I recall years back when there were nothing but cheers.
I was taken to another room, and on my way, saw what I had feared,
Those chimney stacks weren't burning wood, my eyes full of tears.
Had I recognized pieces of clothing I had seen before?
Things people brought with them, scattered all over the floor.
I went into the room with other people, it looked like showers,
We didn't know it, but this was to be our hour.
My clothes were taken, I was like the rest,
Naked, confused, scared, dealing with it with my best.
And came the familiar sound of the slamming of the doors,
There were screams, shouts, could I possibly take anymore?
Then came the sound thru the pipes, the gas,
The fighting, the struggling, the pain, it all came to pass.
And as I slip away, I remember the summer a few years back,
Of promised bright futures, and energy I never seemed to lack.
Of the smiles of my family, and special things they would do,
You were Hitler, and I'm proud to have been a Jew!

Julie Graham Borne
IN RETROSPECT

Love escapes humanity,
as emeralds flow over
a persian cascade.

Drifting through Utopia,
as butterflies shed land
for Giselle with the wind.

Retracting the tenderness,
as feathers from the crest
of angel wings.

Memorizing innocent calm,
as violet skies embrace —
resurrected in moonlight.

Watching pendulating hues,
as silver dew sparkles
on an opal under divinity.

Smelling lavender incense,
as swans give up
the breath of lillies.

Sipping ambrosial lotus,
as honey in the mouth
of a gold dust horizon.

Ascending amongst eternities,
as celestial zephyrs
caress a sapphire wood.

Hearing graceful rhapsodies,
as a blushing crystal mist
dances in weeping ferns.

Kissing each petal,
as dark tears in the eye
of an angry storm.

Love's pastoral remembered,
as the rapture of sunset
weans itself from heaven.

Matthew O Graham
ALONE WITHOUT YOU

I look into your empty stare
With my hand tangled in your hair

And my fingertips freeze in place
Just as I touch your pallid face

It is as cold as it is white
As the coldest hour of night

And as the moon shone upon you
Your eyes reflect the gazing blue

Oh would not I be left to cry
Since it was you first to die

But as the clouds gathered above
Death comes to me as black, a dove

And ringing the faceless deck's bell
You see the heavens, I see the hell

Christopher F Borne
i miss them

i miss them
the feelings
the feelings of missing depression
emptiness . . .
i hate them
the feelings
the ones i feel
so i got rid of them
by picking up a pen
when i set it down
the rush will kill
then shiver
and shake till i drop
drop to darkness
wishing you could find me
i know you won't
i didn't warn you
about the feelings
the ones i feel
the ones i hate
don't leave me alone
ever

Iris E Grenier
WITH ONLY MEMORIES

As my thoughts wander, my eyes filled with tears, my heart aches as I long for you my dear.

When you passed from this earth to be with your creator,

I was the one God chose to stay behind and live out the memories we shared.

Just to hear a familiar song or a place brings you so very near. It is as if you were still here with me. I only have to reach out and touch you, I relive all the memories we shared, the times we were so close, we were as one.

We said to each other all the words that lovers want to hear.
You held me so close, I prayed you would never let me go.

I sacrificed our favorite things, and places we shared, yellow roses, we both loved so very much, our favorite view of the country side we shared together so many
times.
All alone.
You see, these things are not the same to me anymore. Because we shared them together as lovers always do. What wonderful memories they are, you shall always live in my heart, today, yesterday, and always. I loved you so very much, I will never let you go.

When my time comes for God to take me from this earth to the Heaven above, I pray you will rush to greet me as you always did before.

In our spiritual bodies we will be together forever more in God's Heaven where only the chosen ones go.

Isadore Willensky

Isadore Willensky
TO-DAY'S LIFE
Life to-day is hell on wheels
People get shot from automobiles
Then there is drugs, morphine and cocaine
Making life always in pain
Alcohol comes next in the way of sin
How can we be happy for life to begin
It looks like we are headed for hell
We don't try to make our mind well
At the rate we are going no one will be alive
In years that are coming say five ten or twenty–five

Maryann Bratton
EVERY OTHER INCH A LADY
She's always late, has been known to doze
In church, forgets who she owes,
Is prone to impose, but everyone knows,
She's every other inch a lady!

She's pretty, she's smart,
But she will break your heart,
When you are no longer the "State of the Art,"
She's every other inch a lady!

She plays piano, can write a song,
She's flighty, flippant, and headstrong.
She's tried most everything once, her whole life long,
She's every other inch a lady!

She's mistress of all things taboo,
Then wonders "why all the hullabaloo?"
That is caused because of her derring-do,
She's every other inch a lady!

She's full of fun, this Rosie O'Grady,
Some things straight and some things shady,
Never mind she's almost eighty,
She's every other inch a lady!

Arlene Goff
GOD AND THE WISE OLD OWL

To Mom, Whom the Lord found for me. After missing for 43 years of our lives.

God sent forth this wise old owl
To be our night watchman while we sleep.
And to hoot late at night
When danger lurks about.

Oh! The beauty of this wise old owl,
So sleek is his gaze as he watches over us at night
As our God watches over His beloved children.
Our illnesses and pains He heals and mends
While his Holy business he attends.
For He wants us to be like the wise old owl
While we are on the mend.

He wants us to seek, but though like the owl
We are blinded in the light of day,
And like the wise old owl
Who sees all things,
In the darkness of night,
So should we the darkness in the light.

Be ye wise and hoot, hoot
When the shadow of darkness crosses our path,
To keep us from our Father's light,
The Hoot, Hoot of our Lord's Great Love.

Fern V Jones
SUFFER THE LITTLE CHILDREN

This poem is dedicated to every child who has known the horrors of war.

OH, the sadness of eyes grown old
But in years defy the truth
In their depths is age untold
In the face is youth.

Ones so young should never know
The tears, the fears, the strife
Of falling bombs, skies aglow
The ending of a life.

What devil's creed do men profess
When victory is their goal
That little children must confess
To scars upon their soul.

Rodney S Rauch
NIGHT EXPRESS
Light train came in a cream-quiet coast,
slowing to a hundred in cool illumination,
Winter's fog nuzzling 'round it like fur;

hushed as slow motion
in speed seen when standing still,
in moonlit couplings in far off fields.

It ate us for some seconds
in its wholesome brightness,
dreamt onto us in gales and waves,
and in the later awful wake.

It sped out into dark night
reverberating heart-like,
twinkling warm and sleepily,
leaving us with hope.

Stephen B Grant
THE BLACK ROSE

To the ones who paved the way and opened so many doors for me that were otherwise closed. Dr. Martin Luther King Jr., Nelson Mandela and the late Hayward Grant, my grandfather. Thanks.

You are unique, one of a kind
And I vow to someday make you mine

Your buds are soft to the touch and have extraordinary
Beauty to the eye
You have a legend about you that will never die
You have survived the strongest winds and the hardest
Of the rain storms
It is your destiny to win; it has been since the
Day you were born

You, the Black Rose, is very uncommonly seen
Yet, I see you each night in my dreams
You radiate powers of love, trust, and understanding
You give me only what I have been demanding

Among all others I believe you to be best
For you are different, very much unlike the rest
You are not so fragile that you are so easily broken
You, the Black Rose, are a symbol of hope; a priceless token
There is much about you to be learned and desired
You are a precious gift to life and will be much inspired

Where did you come from? Only Heaven knows
I am glad to have seen you, the one and only
The Black Rose

Lorena Bowers
LORD DO CARE
Oh, Lord, yes Lord do care,
There are scars I will remember,
There are scars I cannot erase,
There are scars that I must face,
These are scars I'll have to forget,
Oh! Lord, yes Lord, do care,
There are moments that will be tender,
There are tears that will wash my face,
There are days my soul shall cry out
There are times my heart will be torn.
Oh! Lord, yes Lord, do care.
My step shall be forward,
My path shall be steep.
I'll lift my eyes up to the sky,
For Lord, yes Lord, you will be at my side!

Lorena Bowers
MY FRIEND
"When I grow old, and my steps are feeble,
Will you my friend lend me your hand?
When my eyes grow old and dim,
Will you my friend lead the way?
When I can no longer hear,
Will you my friend understand?
When my mind cannot remember,
Will you my friend forget me not?
When my heart grows old and tired,
and I have reached my journey's end,
Will you my friend say a prayer of courage,
So I can meet the great beyond?"

Patrice
THE BOOGEY LIGHT

To Jeff, My Son, you keep me in the dark sometimes, but when you shine, you shine bright. Love Mom.

There was a young Boy at night
who had a terrible fright
He thought without a light
harm would come to him at night.
Of course this could not be true
because of what his Mom knew.

The light he thought would save him at night,
turned out to be a Boogey Light.
The Boogey Light as this Mom knows,
makes the Boogey Man grow.

The light that seems to shine so bright
that lights up his room at night,
that makes him feel alright
turned out to be a Boogey Light.

Now word has it, when you feel the need for some light,
When darkness comes to say Goodnight,
Remember this one thing, When Mom says
lights out, let's keep that Boogey Man
from Boogeying out. The night light
you thought was alright might turn out
to be the Boogey Light.

Patrice
THE FORGOTTEN TOOTH

To My Daughter Alicia who made the Forgotten Tooth a memory. Love Mom.

My Tooth the Tooth Fairy Forgot
It really did mean a lot
My Tooth the Tooth Fairy Forgot
It also hurt a lot

I'm sure the Tooth Fairy was so busy
It was in a Tizzy
To find the Tooth The Tooth Fairy Forgot
was still under my Pillow.

So what Mom did you see

Is she made it up to me
Because you see The Tooth
The Tooth Fairy Forgot
It really did hurt a lot.

Jean T Tobin
I AM
I am the sunrise on the beach.
I am the shyness of a puppy and the roar of a lion.
I am the ring of a telephone.
I am the happiness of best friends.
I am the hurt of being left alone and the joy of being the center of attention.
A newborn baby's smile is what I am.
I am the joy of a Santa Claus and the disappointment of finding out his real name, Mom and Dad
I am the smell of a red rose after a cool rain.
I am the buzz of an alarm clock and the darkness of morning.
Friday night at "Reflections" is what I am.
I am shopping all day.
I am the excitement of New Year's Eve and the happiness of New Year's Day.
I am the sorrow over a lost pet and the joy of finding him.
Playing the stereo full blast is what I am.
I am a secret told to a friend and a quiet whisper.
I am the warmth of a puppy and the cuddle of a baby.

I am a never ending
R-A-I-N-B-O-W!

John F X Tobin
ODE TO A UNICORN
The Unicorn is a Creature rare,
A precious gem to know.
It often dares to venture,
where the timid fear to go.
It seeks new worlds to conquer,
And lofty thoughts to know
It dwells upon high mountains
of magic ice-blue snow.
And so are you a Unicorn,
a creature oh so rare!
So never fear to climb and soar
high above the rest.
And never cease to dare
And strive, to be the very best.
For you, to truly be fulfilled,
must sing a Muse's song.
A wondrous thing indeed it is
to be a Unicorn.

Mary Enright
OUR TIME IS COMING
O, my love, our time is coming.
Away from you my heart is running.

O, I can't hold the love deep inside of me.
It scares me so; won't you set me free.

I've become a fool for you.
Is that what love's supposed to do?

See it in my eyes, feel it in my heart.
I wear my disguise and it tears me apart.

I want to tell you just how much I feel.
But yet I ask, can it be real?

Even after all of our time together.
I can't believe we'll last forever.

We can't stop it time may tear us apart.
Maybe together we can make a new start.

Please believe in my love; it's hard to do.
I hide it so well, if only you knew.

With every beat of my heart, I love you more each day.
I love you so much more than words can ever say.

I couldn't have made it without you by my side.
You were with me when I laughed and all the times I cried.

You are a part of me and I a part of you.
You are my Best Friend! Believe that I love you.

Christine L Wilcox
BEING FREE

To all of those who made it.

As I look back through the years
I see how naïve I was
I thought I was invincible
But you made me believe
I felt you were a friend
But now that I am older
I know it was just pretend
You are like a spider
Slowly weaving its web
To capture its prey
Never to be free again

Patti Shew
NITE LITE
Our precious children answer to the night
The essence is alluring but the poison's not in sight
Dangers on every corner, no one guards the prey
Children in the night from their homes they ran away.

Now to make their own lives, many roads are there to choose
Lost, cold and frightened and they can't turn to you
Shattered by emotions, no way can they turn but to the promising night; where they are doomed to burn.

Leave them to the night life, for they have made their bed
No one can blame you; you can't control what's in their head
Admit there is a problem, look deep inside your heart
We all have many conflicts but none should keep us apart
Let them know you love them — that could be a start
For we are all God's children and need shelter from the dark.

Jackie Johnson
I DIE YOUR MOTHER EARTH

To all who grieve for her scars.

I am your Mother Earth,
From the surfeit of my body;
came multi-colored field, mighty stream
rock, rill, wooded hill and blanketed grass.
In my flesh, I interwove their tendon roots,
so gentle rain, rutting field and tearing wind
would take my scales and rotted meat,
but leave the forest and the floor.
Beast and fowl styled my brushy hair,
drank, feasted and preened in my limpid eyes.
Plumed pilots floated in crystal air,
docking high to trill a hymn to the sun.
And my psychedelic raiment scintillated in the dew.
A roving throng swept my carpet clean.
In life I gave them sustenance,
In death, I embraced them in my absorbing breast.
Loved and nourished, I lived, your Mother Earth.

Then trickled in my browny children, with ax and blade
they thinned my snarled forest.
And scratched my fermenting belly with gentle plow;
and I yielded in abundance.
They fed me their organic steed and kine
and the residue of my bounty.
Loved and nourished, I lived your Mother Earth.

Then came the greedy ones—like vultures they hovered—
spawning their mechanized monsters
and declaring my body free range.
They scalped my head,
rent my garment,
bored through muscle and cartilage
and pillared me with my bones.
They gouged my sustaining breast
and dumped their droppings.
They reset my fluid eyes
and clogged them with refuse.
The powerful beams of my sister, Sun,
turns pale before her sibling's scars.

I cannot digest the produce of the technosteins.
I cannot disgorge the concrete from my birth canal.
My bones bear heavy on me.
My blood pours over me.
My eyes bubble with slime.
Wind and storm gnaw my naked flesh.
Unnourishing and mutilated, I die, your Mother Earth.

Jackie Johnson
NOT UNKNOWN
And the Word became flesh,
and the Word filled the world.
And the Word, Christ,
seared a mark
deep inside every created being.

Who, in all the universe, has not cried his Name
in reverence
or in scorn?

Nay, Christ is not an unknown Name.

Terry L Hamilton
THE GIFT

I dedicate this poem, with all my love
To my Mom & Dad
William and Evelyn O'Banion.

Within my mind, I look to see
A brighter light than day
For all my life, I've thought about
The things that people say
I have a feeling, deep inside
Like a cut, that needs to mend
The sunshine that I'm searching for
Has no beginning, nor has an end
For things shall come, and things shall go
And things shall always be
And the love of life, and all that is
Was a gift to you and me

Terry L Hamilton
FEELING OF LOVE

This feeling, sent from above
I dedicate, to the one I love
My lovely wife, Penny.

The sunshine casts a shadow
upon a broken dream
But look to see the Mountains
And the running of the stream
A rainbow stretched to heaven
The song the lovebird sings
The beauty of a woman
And the hope that each day brings
The searching for some thing unknown
The peace within one's soul
For this is Rainbow Heaven
Found only by those who know
Who know the feeling, towards a friend
The feeling of love, that has no end

Kenneth Dolphin
YOU

You is sincerely dedicated to my mother, Essie Lee Dolphin. My Aunt Wilma, Rev. Tommy Byrd, Arminta "sister" Terry and Miss Ruby.

You open your door and greet me:
with such a Heavenly smile.
You stimulate a Spiritual Expansion;
you make my life sublime —
You make me feel so comfortable
and welcome, to stay a while.
You always touch; comfort, and
enlighten this heart of mine

You show Spiritual Goodness, that
helps me to ascend
You have been an unfailing
inspiration to me: for quite some time
You are my Heavenly Blessing —
You are my Heavenly Friend
Your Christ like Behavior made it
this way: You are so divine

My enlightened mind; my enlightened heart, will always cherish.
The very Spirited Kindness and
patience: You have shown me
My feelings for you are abounding
and absolute, they won't perish—
You are the Spiritual Friend: I'm
always delighted to see.

Your exceptional devotion is
unending company, I'm never alone.
I am blessed; I appreciate having a
friend, that's so rare and true—
You are genuine: Your distinctive
completeness is always shown
May God bless you: from my heart I
thank you, for being you.

Kenneth Dolphin
FATHER FATHER

I dedicate this poem to our Heavenly Father, God. My father, George T. Watkins Jr. My grandfathers, Silas "Papa" Dolphin & George "Big Daddy" Watkins Sr.

Father, I tried to do my will; instead
of doing yours

My disobedience, caused me to stumble—
My disobedience, blocked chances, and closed some doors
I brought it on myself: my heart wasn't humble

Father, please help me to understand, your divine advice
Father, I want to do your will; teach me I will listen—
Lord, I am your child — please guide my life
Your Spiritual Journey: is too great to be missing

Some trials in my life: were such a conquering challenge—
I thought I was defeated, rescue and victory, wasn't in sight
Lord, you lifted me up: and put my life in balance
Now I know, live By Faith! not by sight

Father, you have done so very much for me;
You lift me up, when others won't take time;
You saved my soul, and set me free—
You are so devoted: Lord you are so kind.

Father, we have had so many talks: you know every secret fault
I desire your Spiritual journey, for my entire life.
Father guide my thoughts, so I can taught
To constantly give, Glory and Honor and Adoration to Jesus Christ

Kenneth Dolphin
TIME TO GET REAL

I dedicate this poem to God, Jesus and the Holy Spirit. The Dolphin Family & the Watkins Family. And to Mr. Wilmar Barnes.

Once upon a moment, I was taking
A Spiritual inventory of myself;
God's guidance, showed me mistakes
I was making:
He advised, "repent while time is left"

Only God, knows how much earthly time is left—
Time waits for no one; it constantly moves on.
I must repent, and serve God—I can't save myself—
Years come and go fast: earthly life is short, not long

The world is changing, quite rapidly.
It's moving continuously at a fast pace;
It's time for me to change and be happy—
I won't risk my soul—there's no time to waste.

I saw with much more than my eyes:
God, wants to make my life unique.
My mind expanded—I realized
That God, Jesus, and the Holy Spirit, makes my life complete.

So I'll do God's will: It's time to get real,
And live in the Spirit, not in the flesh;
To deserve the joy, the Holy Spirit makes me feel.
The Holy Spirit inspires me, to give God my best.

Carol D Stamp
THE HARBOR ROCK

The rock sits there so big and bare
On the edge of the roaring sea.
It's pounded by the mighty waves
And the winds that blow so free.

The gulls and buoys keep it company
On the fog-filled mystic nights,
When Mother Nature flings her cape
O'er the many coastal lights.

The ship horns
sound and the ferry toots,
And the shadows dance and play
As they move on out
and come back in
On the ocean and the bay.

And the people scurry like fast rats
To get behind their doors
Before some harm can capture them
In the bogs and wasteland moors.

Then as early morn
the steam soars up
And coats the world in grey.
And the Sun cuts through with
her magic rays
And brings the break of day.

Soon the human lives
with their many roles
Take their part in the many scenes
'Til again it ends in the deep twilight
And the world returns to its dreams.

Carol D Stamp
SUNSETS SAIL

Sail with me across the sea to shores both far and wide.
Sail with me across the sea with trade winds by our side.

Let's sail and fix a course that leads to foreign lands.
Let us ride the oceans blue where Nature takes command.

Islands fair with beauty rare and sea gulls soaring too;
Moonlit night beyond compare are waiting there for you.

Travel back in history to where man first began.
Sit beside the roaring sea and see the Master's plan.

Hear the chanting of the drums and watch the natives sway.
See their hands and eyes give voice to what they have to say.

Let me take you by the hand; we'll stroll beneath he trees.
Hear the palms sing lullabies while dancing in the breeze.

Watch the oceans turn bright red as evening sun goes down,
And the tonga torches light the sights around the town.

As the fishing boats arrive with catches of the day,
Listen to the happenings in what men have to say.

There's a special waiting place, a spot for you to see,
Far away from all this world.
Come sail away with me.

Tonya Ferguson
AVALON

This age is one and passed,
No more is there to sing
No more quests, the Grail, the last
Ending with the death of a king.

The Dragon banner flies no more
The Barge of Avalon comes not
All is gone of them but lore
All is gone that was Camelot.

The knights are scattered like sand
The brave heroes of old are gone
Sorrow and sadness across the land
The king rests forevermore in Avalon.

Tonya Ferguson
UNTITLED

I always act the opposite
Of what I feel inside
But even though I don't show it,
You mean so much to me.

I don't mean to hurt you
But I always say the wrong thing
Even though I never say it
I love you more than words can say.

I'm afraid to show you how I really feel
To show you just how much I care
I'm afraid to tell you what I feel
I'm afraid to tell you I love you.

Christopher Harmon
WOMEN

Women, most loving, some bold, But their hands are always cold;
Lucky for us they're warm at heart, or we might end up all tore apart;
Some are cold and can't be hushed, and leave some guys, terribly crushed;
They bring forth life, they bring forth joy, And most of us hope it's a boy.
Just like a beautiful art, Women were made warm at heart.

Adrian LaVerne Hall
A MOTHER'S LOVE

Will I not soon be together with you?
Or will fate take hold of the one I bear?
Will our love disappear like the morning dew?
Or will death snatch the one for whom I care?

No, my child, this love—it has no ending.
To the highest mountain or deepest sea
The love we share is like the songs birds sing.
A singing tribute to my child to be.

Once united, our love will more abound.
Together, forever throughout the years.
The love we share, no one can put it down.
So dismiss all your worries, troubles, fears.

I'll always love you whether tame or wild
And you shall always be with me,
MY CHILD!

David Howard
GRAY

Gray is like the
grayness in my heart,
and like the darkness
of night,
Aad the feeling you get
on a cold rainy day.
The feeling you get
when winter is on the way.Tthe
feeling you get
when your heart is broken.
You get the feeling of gray
when some one dies
so next time you think,
we don't need gray — think again!

Sheila G Cone Freeze
GRAND STAIRCASE

Dedicated to my loving husband, and our family.

As I live my life in this
difficult place.
The task I must accomplish is a
Grand Staircase.
It must be built with greatness
and care.
It must be strong for my family
to share.
One that carries memories, both
laughter and tears.
One that holds up throughout the
years.
This staircase must last through
the test of time.
For I built this staircase for my
children to climb.

Terry J Farnsworth
WHEEL OF CONFUSION

In a desperate search for sanity
they all turned away
Knowing now, they never will
see the light of day

They opened their minds
but closed their eyes
and nothing did they see

Until they turned around
and finally found
that they were always free!

Andy J Furniss
MY LITTLE AUBURN GIRL

To James Douglas Morrison, an American poet, my inspiration.

My little auburn girl
The fairest thing in the world
My reason to live, my excuse to die
I will build a world just so she can lie.

She is my little auburn girl
As perfect as a brand new pearl
Her moist eyes and soft golden things
Lock me in a prison of sweet delight.

Ah, my little auburn girl
Never change when I leave this world
Keep your sweet, soft innocence
And being afraid of the night
Always stay the little auburn girl
That I fell in love with in the October moonlight.

Lisa Falandysz
MEMORIES OF THE PAST

It's been awhile now, since my last love.
But now I've found a new love.
A love that I know will be better than the last.
My last love is very much in the past.
It was a love that just couldn't last.
This love that I had, just made me upset.
The things that he did; somehow, I'll make him regret.
He acted like he was better than all the rest.
He always treated me like I was just another girl to mess with.
But this new love that I've found isn't
like that conceited user.
He's a very nice guy; sweet, caring, and not a girlfriend abuser.

I'm glad I found a guy like him.
I just hope he doesn't do what my last
boyfriend did.
I think our love is made to last.
I just with I could forget all those
horrible memories of my boyfriend
of the past.

Howard L Fowler
THE WALLS
As the sun sets over the south wall
Men step into their lonely cells
Awaiting that familiar supper call.
Those lonely walls that seem to
close in and compel.
They all quietly pray for an answer
to this everlasting hell.
But to them no answers come
For they are being punished for
what they have done.

Into those lonely cells shadows creep,
crawling across the walls and floor,
like some medieval monster from the
deep.
For men not troubled by the days
ending,
They know they can say, One day
less,
and slowly pass to sleep once more.
But, for some, sleep is not
forthcoming
For one man sits all alone,
Reading over and over a small
letter from home.

He can be heard reading aloud,
"Dear John," I regret to inform you,
For what I must say shall not
be easy to do.
But to the future I must look toward,
Because, for you, restitution will
be hard.
We must part, and go our separate
ways.
I know our love will never stay.
It was withered and died away.

And from wall to wall
The echo that does not die
A whispered sigh is ever increasing,
Until there arose a sound not like a
sigh,
But of a man starting to cry.
Why, should tears roll down a
man's face,
He can be heard wanting out of
this place,
For he has been deprived of his love,
By a man who is on the other side
of these confining walls.

As I drift off to sleep,
I can hear him say,
Please Dear God,
Make this my last day.

Myrna D Frederick
AUNTIE

I have written this poem in honor of my Aunt Ina Martha Kane, who helped me grow up, through my trying teens.

If I was a child left all alone,
Remembering the past, all the love
you've shown.
Would you care and be there?
When all that you had, you took time
to share.
If I was a person who needed your
help.
Would you find time to comfort a
poor little whelp?
Was it just because I was small,
That you even cared at all?
You've been such a comfort, love,
and joy.
I'm so glad that you've noticed, I'm
not a boy!
You took time, to make my wedding
dress.
When only a few cared and knew my
distress.
Will you always know my love and
gratitude?
When life's joys sometimes seem
glued.
Will you remember, I think you're
the best!
Always and now, through all time to
rest.

Lorraine Hicks
ALIVE
So young was I . . .
when in my mind
a vow I signed . . .
it died.
A second vow I gave . . . died.
Between the two vows . . .
eight times a mother,
I was happy . . . proud.
My children loved me
I loved them . . . Always will.

Yet I was never me . . .
refraining my need.
Questioning who . . . what am I?
Inwardly was a sigh.
Slowly the dawn . . . a new era.
I breathed . . . I'm alive.
Spreading my wings
flying as a bird . . . to a dream.
My third vow forever alive.

Heather Hall
FRIENDSHIP
Friends are special,
Some friends stab you in the back.
Best friends love you,
They are the friends
you cherish the most.
You can't buy a friendship,
You can't sell a friend out.
You don't get your choice or design.
A good friendship happens only
once.

Judith C Hill
YOU'RE LEAVING ME AGAIN

To Frankie, who's forever in my heart.

You're leaving me again.
What have I done this time?
I waited so long.
I had so many times when I didn't
know if I could go on.
The miles between us put so much
pain in my heart.
Then you came home again.
The waiting was over—everything
was alright.
Now you're leaving again!
Where will you go? What are you
looking for this time?
Will the distance of the road keep
you from me
or will the gates of hell lock you
away with no tomorrow in sight?
This can't be happening — It's only a
dream.
I want to run — protect you — keep
you safe forever.
Now I have to find a way to tear
down the walls, unlock the gates.
Keep you free!

Christine Hsieh
FOREVER IN DREAMS
Never has there been a man quite as
blessed
As he with the eyes like the deepest
sea.
Upon his sighting, ladies are
obsessed—
His smile's so handsome, his nature,
carefree.
I love this man more than I love my
life.
My heart is restless and seems to
careen.
My love's so strong that it cuts like a
knife
Through my heart, and soul, and all
in between.
I haven't the charm of Helen of Troy,
Nor the brilliance of Madame
Butterfly.
Instead, I am plain, unnoticed, and
coy.
Yet, I dream of him, and content I'll
die.
My vehement passion is all in vain,
Forever but in dreams shall he
remain.

Don Marshall Hensleigh
YOUR MOM AND DAD
Who encouraged your first step to
walk,
Then who soothed that bump or
knock?
Also, your first word to talk?
It was your Mom and Dad.
Right from wrong they helped you
choose,
How to comb your hair and shine
your shoes,
How to win and how to lose.
It was your Mom and Dad.
The ones who wished to share your
thrills,
Picked you up from your spills,
And the ones who paid your bills.
It was your Mom and Dad.
When you became a teenage gal or
lad,
Taught you to sort the good from
bad,
Then to give Life all you had.
Just like Mom and Dad.
Value the qualities that made them
great
To work, to love, to administrate.
Don't wait, let them know you
appreciate.
Your Mom and Dad.

Barbara A Hook
SEA SHELL
I have the ocean in my hands though
I never gave a listen.
A tiny shell tells it all, so I picked it
up and listened.
As I placed it by my ear, I closed my
eyes and it appeared, the beach, the
sun, the summer fun things that I've
been missin.
I'll place it back upon its shelf till
next time when I miss it.
Oh the sounds of summer in a shell!

Bess Stanford Hill
ON LOSING ONE'S TEETH
Don't speak to me of steak or try to
make me drool
Because a bite to try to take would
make me look a fool!
For I have lost my bite and I'm
sipping liquids only,
You can bet I look a sight as I gaze
on food forlornly.
My lower teeth are gone and the
uppers will be going—
They are no good alone, except to
have some showing.
New dentures will take their place
when I get them all extracted
And though they may improve my
face, will probably drive me
distracted!
But what others can do, I can do,
though a heap of grit it takes.
(I'm determined to wear them, too,
though to think of it gives me
shakes!)
Oh woe is me to think of steak, fried
chicken, ham or liver,
There are no teeth a bite to take, I
cannot chew a sliver!
But 'tis an ill wind that no good doth
blow for while liquids I am
sipping,
The pounds should swiftly from me
go while inches from my waist are
slipping!

Grayce S Hawks
THANKS
Thank you, Lord, for the beauty of
your creation.
Oceans blue, lowly plains, lofty
mountains too.
Creatures of the sea, on land, and in
the air;
In outer space, the vast everywhere.
Thank you, Lord, that you are always
with us,
No matter where, to hear our every
prayer.

We may travel near or far
Over hill and dale.
On a cold night or a warm sunny
day,
You are there with us
Every step of the way.
Thank you, Lord.

Cindy Sandell Hoffacker
COMMUNICATION AVENUE
He who speaks with words that care
to say what is meant: a conscious
dare.
Deep inside it's locked by a need
subconsciously buried—a treasure?
Indeed.
Being lost, I am, on a road too
narrow.
Provided: a map of supple marrow.
In search of my Self, I yield, then
cross
over that question once covered with
moss.
I proceed with caution and as I turn
I see, with my heart, the answer I
yearn.
So voice my faults, but state the
merits, too.
Stop. Now hear my point of view.
Inclined to believe in both: give and
take
is to be aware of what is at stake.
The avenue I find that says: I AM
ME
is the key I use to set me free.

Audrey E Holland
BLESSINGS

In memory of my beloved husband, Earl Holland.

May I share with you my blessings?
Its just joys within my Heart
each time I share my blessings
God doubles them all anew.

Oh! I know there's special blessings
for each kindness I bestow
Just like blessings from my harvest
came from seeds I plant and sow.

My greatest reward from Heaven
for my deeds I do each day
Is the wonderful way God doubles
blessings
that I share and give away, each day.

Stan Hayden
ASHES AND CHEAP WINE
Let us watch the fire burning with
fierce pride.
Slowly the flames rake the sides of
the bark,
Eating it through the core from side
to side,
While shooing up the chimney smoke
and sparks
And dreams of those who wish upon
the wind.
Too far removed to grasp, too dead to
hold,
Dreams crumble in the hands of those
who've sinned,
Those fools who've lived and now
believe they're old.
The vultures laugh, while worms wait
patiently,
As ashes slip earthbound in
happiness.
Life is simple in its complexity,
And beautiful in all its ugliness.
I scream, "There must be more to
this, I know!"
I sit, sip wine, and watch the embers
glow.

Marlene Heffernan
A FORGOTTEN PONY TALE

To a Lovely Daughter; Lucy A. Brooks.

Yonder in a deep, dense wooded
forest,
there lived a lonely painted pony of
gray.

Orphaned there, since a hunter casted
off his mother one day.
Sad and sullen he would often there
stay, for many a visitor in those
deep woods did stray, just to glimpse
the sad painted pony of gray . . .

Good times came and had gone,
nonetheless, the little painted pony
plundered alone . . .
tourists from far away, oftentimes,
intruded on the stray, of gray.

Perhaps the right "wooded" visitor
would offer the pony a way,
with his little life he would never
have to pay
Just in order a hunter to grandstand
his evil way.

There is no tale this way, never a
"good home" for this painted
stray pony of gray!

Marlyn Hodson
LOVE FOR ALL SEASONS?
Rainbow arched across clearing sky,
Sound of raindrops bathing embryo
leaves,
Two people with upturned faces taste
the rain.
Springtime promise.

Cloudless blue sky bright with
sunlight,
Sound of jazz trumpet from muted
radio,
Two people, lost in each other's eyes.
Summer dream.

White cirrus clouds above multi-
colored trees,
Sound of geese V-ing southward,
Two people with arms entwined for
warmth and comfort.
Autumn love.

Darkened sky, drooping over barren
trees,
Sound of logs crackling on sterile
hearth,
One person, unwarmed, stares into
space.
Winter reality.

Faith Constance Howard
PERCEPTION'S NEW BORN DAY
If all the world were poets — what
a great world this would be,
Because perception paves the way —
enables man to see!
There'd be no toxic wastes to harm
the newborn and the old —
There'd be no one meandering — so
homeless — hopeless — cold!
No missile sites to guard at night —
no chemicals in food —
'Cause man perceived the outcome of
a thoughtless attitude.
Said gains that seem so right today
can wipe our world away;
And nothing would be left to save
of what God planned that day —
When in His great perception — He
designed a world to Live,
And only man in selfish greed
destroys what God did give!
So now what is there left on earth
to cherish and adore?
When feelings and perception go
who wants the first strike war?
If we could but manipulate
a turnabout today,
And put our minds at ease and peace
as poets of our day —
One million strong they stand as
one —
Ovations fine and true!
Could it be this could become
a world revival too?
To contemplate—to save our
earth —
EACH and EVERYTHING!
To do it NOW — with open hearts
and make perception RING!
If we do not —the end will come —
as night time — follows day —
We'd better choose the ways of
God—

PERCEPTION'S NEW BORN DAY.

Rebecca Humble
THE SOLDIERS ON THE HILL
The cold dew of the morning
Spread across the bloody land.
The soldiers, they lay on the ground,
like scattered shells upon the sand.
The shots that sounded in the
night —
died as the sun rose over the hill.
Each dream of victory buried —
deep within the souls on the hill.
Cries of pain and defeat were heard,
the night the soldiers came over that
hill.
The wails of the dying.
The screams of the wounded —
everyone was lost in the sound.
So many lives destroyed that night.
So many lives left useless.
The men they fought long and
hard —
And all for what was worthless.

Muriel Gordinier Slate

Muriel Gordinier Slate
DADDY

Dedicated: To my loving father, Oliver Gordinier.

We lost our loving Daddy, a year ago
today.
God took him up to heaven, where I
know he'll stay.
I know that Daddy's happy, up there
with God tonight.
He's looking down upon us, with his
guiding light.

We hated to give up Daddy, but we
knew God knows best,
for Daddy suffered very much and
badly needed rest.
Our Daddy was so good to us, that's
why we miss him so,
but life was his enemy and we knew
he had to go.

No one could e'er replace him, no
matter how they try,
For he'll remain in our hearts until
the day we die.
We have to go on living, tho hard it's
going to be,
But someday, if God's willing, our
Daddy we will see.

Ruth E Harris
LIFE'S A DRAG AT FIFTY
Time for a "Tune-up." I'm not
bragging,
and all your tires are wearing
thin.
When all your Axes are adragging,
Then birthdays are not welcome
with a grin.

Now I am speaking from experience,
Although it's "Sad but True."
"Father Time" and "Mother Nature"
Sure make it rough for you.

I admit I'm getting well mildewed.
And believe my carburetor busted.
My chassis is cracked and dented
Now, then, my spark plugs are
rusted.

But what's the use of griping,
Because you've stripped your
gears?
You can't expect to feel like piping.
When you've lived for fifty years.

James Harris (Age 9)
LONGHORN
There once was a longhorn
Who was just now born.
It was eating corn
When it broke its horn.

He got caught on a thorn
I said, "Poor little longhorn."
That was just now born
In a country that was foreign.

Deloris N Hester
GOOD TO BE ALONE
Why is it life is so lonely?
What makes you feel like the one and
only?
When does all this hurting stop?
I've got to get these feelings out
before I pop.

Life can be whatever you want to
make of it.
Some people make you feel like you
just don't fit.
You can control all this hurting
inside.
I feel so much better when I just take
a ride.

Sometimes it is good for people to be
alone.
Getting away from everyday life,
especially that phone.
It's too bad that this world is in such
a hurry.
No wonder there are so many people
that worry.

If it is just five minutes that will do.
If it is just one day you need help
through.
Just open that door and get in your
car.
It doesn't matter where you go or
even how far.

Sharron L Holmes
HIS HANDS

I dedicate this poem to my loving father: Harrell E. Holmes, Sr.

In his hands,
There's physical strength to perform
many jobs, Yet, the gentleness to
cradle a small baby as it sobs: He
possesses an energy that won't let
him be still, But fatigue of a 12-15
hour day's work allows him to sleep
at will:

In his hands,
There's a tender touch when
embracing, Yet a stern swiftness of a
belt on an erring child he must
chasten; With his hands, he
emphasizes a serious
Gospel sermon, And later on, he'll
have a sense of humor that radiates
to everyone: He has an intense duty
to do what's right, Because with the
pains of war, he fought for the
American rite:

In his hands,
He has knowledge to spiritually
direct so many people, with a
constant
awareness of the forces of evil: At
times, he displays a subtle,
unexpected sensitivity, But mostly
he's frankly candid, whatever the
cause may be: In his hands, he's
patient with loved ones in trying
situations,
with the hopes of a better tomorrow
for future generations: I can see his
sincere desire to always "be there,"
Open hands, always ready to give to
anyone, anywhere: When he's done

all he can, I see an unending love and devotion, I wish you could see as I,
You'd then understand how and why:
All these things through God he's learned and done, He's achieved them with-IN HIS HANDS through wisdom!

These hands are MY DAD'S!!

Druzella A Holley
THE OLD FARM HOUSE
The old farm house just down the road,
so scarred and weathered from years long ago.
The memories it carries are all stored away
in the lonely gray dawn of day.
The grass grows high all around
and down the path still stands the old barn.
The birds make their nest in the eaves of the house
as another season comes and the winds blow
on through the old farmhouse.

Druzella A Holley
SPRING SURPRISE
The tulips have pushed their heads through the ground, you would think that wintertime was still not around, until you see the gray clouds form in the sky and see all the snowflakes as the wind carries them by. The hint of spring flowers was only a dream as snow covers every thing a good foot DEEP

Lynn M Holder
ONE LOVE
Time spent together, moments shared between you and I

All combined into one, creating a bond which will be forever tied

Quiet moments, softly and gently created by our own desires

No words are allowed, only the beat of our hearts, each beat perfectly in time, never to part

Tender caresses, sweet innocents exploring new emotions, never felt before

First love, all so new and fresh; First Love creating a need for more

You imagine a Love everlasting, I dream of a Love pure and true

Our Love is as one but created by two.

Amy C Harmon
THOUGHTS OF YOU

For Thomas Edward, December 3, 1987.

Thoughts of you
Keep me warm inside.
When I'm alone with you
I have nothing to hide.

As I've said many times before,
Baby brown eyes don't lie
And when I say that I love you,
I mean, until I die.

Before I met you,
I had given up on love.
But then I was given another chance,
Granted from heaven above.

So beneath an empty sky,
When the stage has turned to gray
When all the other lights
Begin to fade away,

I will take your hand
And lead you to a place
Where we'll be sharing
"Silent Nights"
And lying face to face.

Tanya Hopkins
MY CHILD
I was born into this world having
Not one thing to call my own.
I grew into a woman still relatively unknown.
I became someone's wife, for one reason or another.
My life went on uneventfully till I became a mother.
Now every day is special and I'm glad to be alive.
Because there's someone who needs me as a friend, teacher, and guide.
So thank you Lord for my child.
I will love him as no other.
For no other reason in this world
except I am his mother.

Linda Sue Hall
THE SEA

This poem is dedicated to Harry, my husband, to my mom & dad Charles & Gladys Crittenden & to my four children. Randy, Richard, Shanda, & Amber.

Come sit with me
beside the sea
Share this peaceful
scene with me
Sea gulls flying
high above
Palm trees blowing
in the breeze
The sun fading
behind a distant cliff
A lonely ship far
out at sea
Sailboats sailing
dreamily along
Beautiful white waves
Upon the lonely beach
An ancient beautiful
Light house standing
Tall and lonely above
The sea
God gave this beautiful scene
For all the world to see
Sometimes I feel
It was meant
Just for you and me

Karen Haas
HOPING

This poem is dedicated to Sharon Sklaney with love from Karen.

You lie there in bed dying
As I stand here alone, crying,
The day was sad and blue
For I miss seeing you.

Your face used to glow
The look only I know,
You look so out of place
As a tear forms on my face.

The nights are dark and lonely
I just want someone to hold me,
Hoping you will be alright
As I cry throughout the night.

Sammie G Harris
MY FATHER, MY FRIEND
I know I found my Father.
He's not the fleshy one you see.
He's the one who's always there.
To hold you up . . . not flee.

When we feel alone
Rejected and down hearted.
We can always look up.
To see the one who never parted.

It's so nice to have a Father.
So loving and so kind.
Someone you can depend on,
And never leave you in a bind.

He's always around.
So don't you try and hide.
He will seek you out.
He knows you from inside.

Sometimes we can't do right.
Sometimes we can't do wrong.
Your Father you can count on.
To always see you home.

Wendy K Hartshorn
OCEAN TRANCE
The oceans wave
The rolling wonder
Memories to save
Of living under
That peaceful trance
Of when you're alone
The waves will dance
When the days are done.

Ingrid C Herland
MUSIC FILLS THE AIR
Music fills the air
I lay my head back and listen
My spirit rises forth
To meet the spirit that is gay, light
and happy

'Tis not the body that hears
But the spirit within
The body withers but the spirit
endures and is ageless
It is always ready to dream of things
past
Enjoy things present and hope for the
future

Music fills the air
And I dream again that I've been
here yesteryear
Palace ballroom is full of laughter
I am dancing and nothing matters
My dress is flowing, my jewels are
sparkling
'Tis a joy to feel so glowing.

Donna K Hershey
LET'S ALL BE AS ONE
I saw a dog today,
Going through my yard on its merrily way;
The dog was tall and lean,
His shaggy coat without the slightest gleam;
You could play a tune on his scaly bones,
I tried to 'shoo' him away with a disgusted tone.
I turned to our family dog,
Whose coat is shiny and she's fat as a hog;
I said to her, "Don't associate with a dog like that!"
"You try to play with him and he's as gross as a rat!"
The tears swelled up in my eyes,
For I couldn't believe the words I had just said, that came out in such disguise.
Was My dog so much better than this poor pooch who was starving for food and love?
Did I truly feel that I was so much better than the dear people in this world who only own the stars above?
To keep them company, for they have No one to love . . .

Nancy Holmes
MY SOUL IS AS OLD AS TIME ITSELF
My soul is as old as time itself,
Much older and wiser than I.
It started its journey many eons
ago,
from the mountain of stars in the heavens above.

For some reason unknown to me,
it fell from the Heavens to the
earth far below
Many lives it has touched as it
Struggles through time
Many difficulties to overcome
before forgiveness is found.

How many more lives will it touch
after mine, until its journey is
ended—and once again shine
bright in the
light of the Heavenly stars.

Kate Henderson
MY DEARS
Seven little pairs of tennis shoes
Shorts and socks, ties and bows,
Seven little shirts called Tee.
Seven little mops of yellow hair
To wash and comb, cut and curl
Seven little dears to me.

Thus on and on my story goes
In septuplets long ago proclaimed
A nature's magic own.

And then one day, in mild surprise,
They're caught and I rush out to see.
Lo, I behold, through sparkling eyes,
Fourteen glimpses of eternity.

Faith E Henry
BEAUTY PASSING
A seedling I am
A sprout to become
A bloom for later,
With just a ray of sun.
The rain will come
Only as it may

The God above has made me today.
A sprinkle for now,
Or a drop of that dew,
Will help me along
and make me like new.
I have bloomed
My fullest extent,
I now bow down, as I wither;
I must go . . .
For this was my life!

Jenny Hogan
I'M ALWAYS HERE FOR YOU

For Dan, whom I'm always there for.

I wish I could take away
All the pain you feel right now
I wish there was something I could do
That would make everything okay
But this is the real world
And all I can do is be here for you
Listen to you, when you pour out
your heart
Hold you, when you need to be
consoled
Love you, so that you know someone
cares
I'll always love you and I'll always
be here
To listen to you, to hold you, and to
love you
Whenever you need someone, I'm
here
I know it's hard

We both know you deserve better
You just don't want to admit it
Because you're not sure if it's true, but it is
I wish I could give it to you, but I can't
You think that there's nothing you can do, but there is
Just believe in yourself
And remember
I'm always here for you

Marie E Hauser
AUTUMN ENCHANTMENT

Dedicated to Johnny Stone.

The moon slowly rising on the lake at night
Lending its pink-gold hues to the water below
Makes me think how beautiful God is
From His magnificent place on High.
The stars in the evening twinkle so bright
What a glad feeling at such a breathtaking sight!
The hot, languid days of summer are gone—
And in their place, the coolness of fresh clean air all about us.
The leaves are falling to the ground
amidst a light, falling rain
This time of year makes me feel
so young all over again.
It makes me think of things yet to come and of things yet to be.
I give thanks to the Lord
for this chance to live
And this in His service to be able to give
My heart reaches out in thanks to Him.

Jerry L Hillyer II
THE FROZEN HANDS OF MAN

To God, for everyone should have his love & warmth. Peace to all.

Snow swept across the barren land,
And froze a child's tiny hand.
His hand turned blue and fell to the ground,
With a harsh and very distinguished sound.
The noise was heard for miles in surrounding hills,
Creating horrifying sounds and trembling trills.
Trills that cracked and burned the sky;
Sounds that caused the population to die.
Mountains, that once stood alone and tall,
Can now do nothing but crumble and fall.
Trees, once proud, with green leaves in the air,
Are now charred kindling, destroyed without a care.
Streams, were prosperous with fish and game,
Now they are dust, gone as quickly as they came.
There's a single candle burning, long into the night,
It's creative with its gesture, and shines with bright delight.
Life as we know it is over and done,
No more children; no more fun.
That my friends is the end of the world, a story never told,
Let's all do our best to put this story on hold.

Margaret R Hodges
HIS EXAMPLE

To Jesus for his glory and the Nazarene Church of Medford.

His example He set for us,
To believe in the Father is a must.
To love our neighbor and to trust,
He came and died just for us.

He said in Him we'd find our rest,
So He came to Earth that we might be blessed.
Love your enemy and turn your cheek,
For I will make you strong, although you are weak.

He taught to forgive and be humble,
And He lifts us up, when we stumble.
He said, "Do not judge for you have no right,
It's the Father above that gives you your light."

He didn't condemn, but gave us His hand,
And the angels came with their heavenly band.
He said, "Go and help those in need,
For you will be planting, my seed."

Talk to the Father and use my name,
For I will do for you, the same.
He had to go away, but His example He set,
And left it for all those He had met.

Betty B Haws
SKIING!

See them struggle, stride and go
As they glide across the snow
Sometimes in unison, sometimes not
To rush and prove just what they've got.
Twisting, bending, falling down
Often looking like a clown.
It's great hard work—thrilling play!
—Like a beautiful ballet.
Swishing, swerving in the snow
Jumping, flying—watch them go!
No other sport could compare
With doing acrobats in mid-air!
What an exciting sight to see
Fantastic aerospace flight on skis!

Michelle Huffman
THE SIFTER

I watched the waves roll on the shore
They talked in a low low whisper
Some say it is really a bore
But words were becoming crisper.

And as I stood out on that shore
And I listened to those whispers
I understood the old folklore
Someone else would be the "Sifter."

Someone else did stand on that shore
And he marveled at the whispers
He also knew the old floklore
and I knew he was the sifter.

Patricia Hannon
THE MONARCH

She was as a butterfly;
Her mantle shed and broken,
By the urgency of youth.
The Monarch winged with darkness;
Saw not her lovely flutter,
But the dance of gypsy moths,
Who waltzed on —
The whispers of sweet pleasures;
Sighs of forbidden nectar,
Hidden beneath the moonlight.
The Monarch whirled on darkness;
Knew not an inner warning,
To dance with the gypsy moths.
She waltzed on —
Fragile wings swept by nightwinds;
Caught up in lofty branches,
That rag'd her velvet colors.
The Monarch fell in darkness;
Saw her own sable shadow,
And the dancing gypsy moths,
Who waltzed on.

Shanta Henderson
GOODNIGHT KISS

This mighty and glorious day profuse with mankind's brilliant
triumphs and
sinking
lamentations
has finally run its course and I The Radiant and Shining Sun
must
also retire into the harmonious aurora above
the glittering ocean
But those who I protect by day
behold My beauteous exit
with awe and rapt fascination.
My dazzling complexion erubescent
as it flushes vermilion and cerise
slowly breaks into thy inlands
of color
gilded islands of golden
ocher float aimlessly
in a glowing sea teeming
with apricot foam
and flaming cadmium,
as the
livid mauve haze
evolves
into somber sable
night
my audience
slowly
shifts
their
gazes
toward
my
partner
the
opalescent
moon

Sheila Hager
MATTHEW

I love you, my son.
I would give you the best of the world
My son;
If I could.

I would shelter you
From the hurts and stabs of life
My son;
If that were wise.

I would cradle you against
The warmth and softness of my breast;
And touch your curls,
My son.

And I can.

That much I can do
To ease the frustrations of growing,
To let you know that
I care; I'm here
My son . . .

Grow with love.

Judith A Harris
VALENTINE'S DAY

Valentine's Day was made for love,
Fluttering wings of a snow white dove.
Hearts of pink and ruby red,
Express the ideas in our head.
Words of love on cards appear,
For our best loved one to hear.
'Tis a special day you know,
What's in our hearts we dare to show.
For all our friends both far and near,
We tell them all they are so dear.

Charlotte A Fabozzi
THE SPECIAL GIFT

Before the time,
They spoke of him,
My father and my mother.
How could it be?
Her stomach giving me, a baby brother.
Ty"Mudders gone to get your brudder!"
Slowly then the days went by.
(Sometimes, I'd even start to cry)
Then, when it was Christmas morning
All I waited for came without warning.
Then my mom came home to me.
She brought a special gift, you see.
Wrapped in blankets, soft and blue —
A baby brother, it was true!
He's changed some, since that Christmas Day.
But in my heart, he's stayed the same way.
My very own baby brother.
There can never be another.

Sue Hathcoat
THE LITTLE BOY WITHOUT A BED

He was so sweet this boy to me
I think of him and hope to see
A rainbow shining in his eyes
And stars that twinkle when he cries
He was so good and was so bold
He didn't cry when he was cold
He didn't have a bed at all
And he wasn't very tall
He was just a little boy
And he didn't have much joy
And then one day sickness came
And it made him very lame
Where cold winds blow
And rivers flow
We discovered he was dead
The little boy without a bed.

Eileen Klepper
ROAM TEENAGER ROAM

Show me a home where
a teenager roams,
And I'll show you parents
who've gone gray,
Where seldom is heard an encouraging word,
And the phone is tied up
night and day.
Roam teenager roam,
For hours you've tied up the throne,
Leave the refrigerator untouched,
That's not asking for much,
And you are not master
of our microwave.
Roam teenager roam,
For you've turned upside down
our home,
Your music is strange,
Your clothes have all changed,
And our charge card has seen
brighter days.
Roam teenager roam,
You are now never at home,
Since you have passed the test,
Our auto never rests,
What happened to the good old days?

Catherine Kintner
AT THE PASSAGE OF A HAND (ON A GAME OF CHESS)

The players are set,
their lots have been cast.
Litigants now stand facing,
stiff and tense, waiting.
Destinies unfurl, nations crumble
in carefully planned maneuvers.
Two empires, equal in strength,
are controlled by greater forces.
Obediently, one step at a time,
they attack—each playing to win.
An arcane world, seemingly serene—
Horses graze beside castle walls.
Bishops offer sacrifice and prayer.
Kings and Queens rule in silence.
Two worlds that tremble
at the passage of a Hand.

Beth Anne Kurtz
LIFE HAS NO MERCY, LOVE HAS NO PRIDE

So cruel, the things that Life can do!
Life's so unfair to me and you.
It draws us together,
Then tears us apart,
Leaving me loving you with all of my heart.

Life has no mercy—how cold it can be!
Such thoughtless ways it shows to me.
It lets me know Love,
And then steals it away,
Just leaving me broken with nothing to say.

I'm so tired of trying to sort it all out,
To make sense of what Life's plan is about.
For I love you now—
Why does Life make me wait?
It's with you I belong, my heart makes no mistake.

I just don't understand it—I've not asked for much.
All I ever wanted to feel was your touch.
But instead I feel pain
That will never subside,
Because Life has no mercy, and Love has no pride.

Guy F Harris
EMPTY ROOMS

My heart has many empty rooms
Where once did passions dwell
No feet disturb their dust but mine
Which know them all too well

For oft at times I visit them
With hope to find therein
Some answer to the wasted love
And dreams that might have been

But dreams of love are only dreams
And love of dreams is vain
Though now I lead a waking life
The empty rooms remain

Elaine Hayducko
STOP SNOWING!!!

This poem is dedicated to Norma Jean, my loving Mom. Inspired by her because she prefers the warm weather.

Knowing that it's snowing,
I won't be shopping,
I may be mopping.

The iced lanes scare me,
Won't do what I dare to,
I'll stay inside here where it's warm.

Drink hot chocolate,
Watch TV,
Housework's the last thing on my mind.

I'll look out the window—
Wait for it to stop,
And then I will go out to shop.

Linda D Ferraro
THE COUNTRY, THE CITY: DIVERSITY

Dedicated to my home village of Athens, N.Y., may it always be a beautiful, serene, peaceful river town, and may we all always care what happens in it and to it.

I went up into the mountains
To breathe the piney scent of spring
To see the splendor of the view
To hear the wild birds sing.

I went down by the river
To breathe in the heady sweet musk air
To see the smooth and mirrored surface
To hear small waves lightly rippling there.

I went down into the city
To breathe many varied smells
To see towering skyscrapers, people and vehicles rushing everywhere
To hear the cacophonic jangle, that this way of life foretells.

So I went over by the river
To breathe in and savour the calm and cool night air
But all I smelled and saw was decay and garbage
This assault upon my senses — it really isn't fair!

Why can't the river and the city
Get cleaned up, and slow down, so they may also be
Sweet smelling, serene and beautiful
Like the peaceful placid mountains, crystal sparkling rivers and easy going way of life up there in the country?

Or doesn't anybody care?

Linda D Ferraro
THE FIRST AND LAST VALENTINE

Dedicated to my only Valentine, my wonderful late husband, John T. Ciccone, I still love you and miss you.

When we first met I was cold, sick, hungry, tired and afraid
Then you asked me if I'd like to join you, that you were going to get something to eat
I still was scared but knew I had better take a chance — you said "I have seen the look of hunger before; yes the meal really is my treat."
Your reassuring voice and kindly way was unlike anything I'd known in a very long time — I was really glad I went with you, and even more grateful that I stayed.

You were so thoughtful, caring and concerned, as time went on, it almost seemed hard to believe
You took me to a doctor, always made sure I ate, got me some clothing so that I was more warmly dressed
Your love radiated throughout, melting some of my wall of suspicion, although I sometimes still worried that you might ask me to leave
But you never did, you were so kind and gentle, giving me your clean warm bed, while you slept in a chair watching over me, while I got some long overdue and very much needed rest.

This was in November, we moved — together — in December, and sang with the carolers under the Arch, around the Christmas tree in Washington Square Park
January came, and from being warm, no longer so afraid, eating regular meals, I began to regain my health and began to really feel fine
You went off to work in the morning, I rested most of the day — I still was a little bit weak — but went to meet you at the subway station each evening just before dark
It's now February, and up the subway stairs you came one night, carrying a big pink satin flower and lace Valentine.

I was totally surprised when you said "this is for you, Happy Valentine's Day to my darling, sweetheart"
I stood there speechless, no one ever gave me a Valentine before, I was so happy I almost thought I would cry
It's nearly thirteen years later, and until death only will we ever part
There was always a pink satin flower and lace candy box Valentine every February fourteenth that went by.
We long since moved out of the city and fixed up a big rambling old house in the country
During what was heartbreakingly to be the last year of your life, for you had really become very sick
I then took care of you, though you couldn't walk and were going blind, our faith and love helped us through, so we lived and loved life as fully as could possibly be
Even though you could no longer go out, came February fourteenth there was still a pink satin flower and lace Valentine, it took quite a while to get you to confess how you managed that miraculous trick.
You've been gone seven years now, and that many Valentine's Days have passed, but I still have and dearly treasure my only Valentines, from your first, up to your last.

Susan E Harder
THE HAND OF THE CARPENTER

Dedicated to Lloyd Jamison, carpenter.

Can you hear the knock
of the hand of the carpenter,
Trying doors, so many doors,
for a place to stay?

Can you hear the knock
of the hand of the carpenter?
Does he know the grain of the wood
and tree from which it came?

Perhaps he stops
to feel the sheen, or craftsmanship therein,
As he knocks his gnarled, strong hand
to ask that wife—"with-child," and he
might stay within.

Can you hear the knock
of the hand of the carpenter?

Hearts or doors,
Did not the hand that made thee know?
The cold we feel outside
Is not the wood or metal
that keeps people out,
but other people's wills.

And The Carpenter, whose work was carving, molding, building, mending, moving
hearts,
Forgot it not,
when with His gentle hands, and skilled touch,
He bowed His head,
who'd changed the lives of others,
and let them place Him
on a cross
of wood.

Carol Hughart
MY DAUGHTER

To my beautiful daughter Joyce and my two granddaughters Erin and April Marie.

Have you ever felt the breezes
blowing softly through the trees?
Or seen the sun come up at day break
and chase the dew away with ease?
Have you ever watched the snow fall
and lay softly on the ground?
Have you stood and listened quietly
as the birds all made a joyful sound?
Have you felt the dry leaves crackle
as you walk along the trail, while the waters babble softly as it goes along its way.
Have you wondered how a spider
spins such a fine and silver thread?
Or how the birds can take some twigs
and make themselves a nice soft bed?
All the wonders of the world came to me that blessed day.
When you my darling daughter came into our lives to stay.
You're so like the gentle breezes,
many times you're in my hair.
And I've seen the sun at day break,
holding you in my rocking chair.
And as I look upon your face as you lay silently asleep,

It's like the gentle snow fall, so soft, so pure, so sweet.
And then there's days that you begin
by babbling like the water.
But you're one of God's creations,
and I love you, you're my daughter

Lola Hansell
WHERE CAN I PRAY?

To my minister—Brother Ron Anderson.

My head on my pillow at night
when the stars are bright.
Before a meal
and I feel
so close to the Father above
and He gives me His love.

In my rose garden with much dew
and in my church pew.
When I open the church door
and walk down the carpeted floor.
On Sunday morning taking the
Lord's bread
much prayer is said.

Sunday when six o'clock comes
around
much prayer is found.
Morning, noon and night
and when the days are bright.
When the day does part
God has my heart.

THE THOUGHTS OF LOLA

Lola Hansell
WONDERS

WONDERS — To Mom Gretchen Drake.

Each snow flake
That comes from space
Looks like lace
And each of us have a different face.

Talents we do show
That makes us grow
Wonders we do think
And how they do link

A chain of thought
And how it was sought.

THE THOUGHTS OF LOLA

Colleen Elizabeth Kilcoyne
THANKSGIVING

To Richard Tuttle Jr., his family and his friends.

Thanksgiving always seems to bring
out the best in everyone.
It pulls families and friends together
in a special way.

Thanksgiving falls upon the autumn
season,
A season for change.
It is a vital passage of time,
Filled with thoughts, actions, and
friends who rearrange our days into
memories, never to be forgotten.

It begins with our dreams,
Each one as numerous as the fallen
autumn leaves.
They are a symbol of the changes that
life has in store for us.
With this perception, we should now
begin to reflect and be thankful for
what we have.

It is a time to set aside our greed,
And help our fellow man in need.
We are a reflection of the world in
which we live,
We are thankful for those who care
and give.

Things aren't always at their best for
some,
But if you take this time to appreciate
things that you have,
Then today will prepare you for the
tomorrows yet to come.

Thanksgiving is a time to conquer
this hazy world.
With this hope it someday will
become clear,
Though we have made it thus far,
We have yet to encounter another
year.

Cynthia Korn
THE STORM

In loving memory of my mother, Betty J. Cox. Born 12/19/23, Died 2/21/87.

The thick black clouds
roll over the innocent ground
below
Violating her unsuspecting peaks and
valleys
As it rumbles by stripping her
of everything she has to offer
She welcomes him with loving arms
Only to be disappointed
by his swift retreat
As fast as he comes; he goes
Leaving a trail of tears to be dried up
by the slight glimpse of sunlight
His rampage is over
Still she lies alone
vulnerable to his next outburst
Will it ever end?

Kristine Lynn Kennedy
STARS THE SHADE OF AMBER

Stars the shade of amber
Cause me to remember
On a cold December
How I spent the day.

He had come to see me
Just to have a spot of tea
Love I believe was the fee
But who am I to say.

As I left my home that night
I wondered at the marvelous sight
I sensed my stomach getting tight
My love, my life, my play.

I spent my time as I see fit
Content to watch the stars dance and
flit
To stand as judge I aptly quit
Never too high a price to pay.

Stith Ketchum
OTTOFELIX BEGINEND REMEMBERS IN 1988

This poem is dedicated to Palestinian rights and to peace between Arab and Israeli.

I stand before the wall and hear the
wall's wail.
My hand's blood runneth over its
palm.
Surely we have risen from the Nazi
nail.
Cured, we hear the Palestinians'
psalm.

Karen Lynn Kaufman
EVERY DAY I PRAYED FOR HIM

Every day I prayed for him, as I
watched him slip away
Every day I prayed and prayed, that
God would find a way
To get him off the drugs he craved,
and make him want to live
Every day I gave and gave until I had
nothing left to give
Now I no longer pray for him, and I
don't even care
Is this the man I loved so much and
would follow anywhere?
I don't remember loving him, I only
remember the pain
Of watching him kill himself, day
after day after day
I must have known how it would end,
I should have left him then
But somehow I kept thinking that,
he'd want to live again
Now I'm alone and I know, that all
hope is gone
The drugs have overwhelmed his
soul, I know it won't be long
Until I have to bury him and people
will wonder why
I go through the funeral and it all
And I don't even cry
Forgive me Lord, for not loving him
I've known him for twenty years
I don't remember the love we shared,
I only remember the tears
I couldn't make him realize,
the value of his life
I tried everything I know of, when I
was once his wife.

Doris Elaine Kampfe
CELEBRATION '89

Here I sit by these typewriter keys
thoughts swirling in brain
like muddy footprints tracking my
kitchen floor;
Each year charges interest for its use
and now that I'm old it's plain to see
that life's a mortgage
I've borrowed and used;
Meant well; shaking, shivering under
December's abuse,
To justify my being, poet's muse,
I drink champagne!
The mixed emotions which I hold
this year
Let me stand free
Like the "tumbling walls" of
Germany
Where I hang my breathy wreaths of
flowering words;
I'm a fool in some ways, but I know
that '89
comes down to this:
Everywhere the tyranny is broken,
the pine trees stand,
messenger pigeons circle over the
land;
A toast! A toast!
A fire, fierce, strange, resurrects my
hand.

Angela L Koerner
SNOW

As snow gently falls to earth
A blanket of white will be seen
Covering the darkened ground
Making everything clean

The singular flakes glisten brightly
As rays stretch out from the sun
Children head to hills with a sled
Enjoying the wintry fun

Shovelers soon start to grumble
As snow starts forming a drift
Their backs start to ache as the snow
Gets heavier with every lift

Will the snow look as pleasant
tomorrow
As it piles alongside the walk
When lanes become getting slippery
And drivers beginning to balk

Do we remember in the spring
This beautiful glistening snow
Falling gently down to earth
From oh so long ago

Ginger S Knapp (Swain)
GRANDMA'S LETTER

As I sit, I find myself staring off into
space.
Wondering how, when, and why?
I've come to be at this place.
Oh how I remember the prime of my
life.
I was a daughter, a sister, a mother, a
wife.

When all of a sudden, old did I grow?
Where did the time go? I really don't
know.
Time passes so quickly, too quickly
really.
I remember most times as so carefree
and silly.

Like when I was little, and dad taught
me so much.
How to ride a bike, catch a ball and
such.
How mom told of the bliss of being a
bride.
How dad seemed to burst at the
seams with pride.

I remember the time I held my first
child,
and looked in my husband's eyes. Oh
how they smiled.
I remember all the good times as a
family we had.
And the bad times I remember, even
though they were sad.

So how have I come to a time in my
life?
Where I'm so alone. No family, no
longer a wife.
I'm here with only memories.
They're rejoicing up above.
Hurry Lord, bring me home. To share
again in the blissful love . . .

Michael Koich
ODE TO THE MOON

To Josephine Raies: Whose love, understanding and helpful smile have somehow made it all worthwhile.

Oh, Moon, fair guardian of the night,
Conceived of atoms and timeless
dust;
Born of the Sun to reflect its light,
And set in motion by Cosmic thrust;
Assigned a course amongst the Stars
By a hand beyond thy ken,
And placed, with Earth, 'twixt Venus
and Mars
To become the marvel of Men.

Oh, Mistress of nocturnal skies,
Bereft of Life and mortal Man,
Where nothing grows and nothing
dies,
Yet, still, a part of Nature's plan;
Destined to wander your lonely way,
Bound and chained to a Cosmic
clock;
By night a jewel, but alas, by day
A hurtling sphere of barren rock.

Sharon Kelley
LOOK AND LEARN

For Chiefie Sr., love Chiefie Jr.

I walked in the shadow of two stars
Which held the fire of my life.
Yet as I walked, I found the fire
gone,
My soul dead, still I existed.

Now a blind man, I have at last been given
Sight.

Celeste Kiphut
PORTRAIT OF LUCIFER
no red-horned, spike-tailed
monster, he
but a vision of beauty and charm
deceitfully darling,
so winsome, so swift
all too quick to deny he can harm;

no cartoon creature with flames all about,
his ways will appear to be sweet
claiming to grant wishes,
make dreams all come true
deny him, lest his scheme be complete.

2 CORINTHIANS 11:14
EPHESIANS 6:11

Wanda R Kepple
DOOR
The door it opens and shuts.
Some doors we go through make
us want to shout and be
happy.
When exciting things happen, I want to share with you.
So come through the door to my
room.
My happy world and loom.
If I become sad, be a friend
to cheer me.
Tell a joke or think of something funny.
It doesn't cost any money.
So open the door to a cheery happy time.
Don't close it now. It cannot cost a dime.
Life can be good.
Open the door of wood.

Mark J Krein
STAGES OF LOVE
Love is:
Fresh and exciting.
Living and learning.
Sharing and caring.
Knowing and growing.
Happy and sad.
Lost and found.
Warm and comfortable.
Forever and ever.

Lynda Kearney
THIS FEELING
I held it just once
without a moment to spare;
It was this great feeling
that no one can compare.
This feeling is drifting, but
is not very far.
For I've held so tight, I can't let go!
I refuse to believe, that it's only a "one night love affair."
I often wonder if you ever think of me.
Just don't drift any further,
for I can't bare to be;
living my life without this one feeling!

Edward C Kandl
FOR YOU
I wrote this poem
just for you
please don't throw it
in the trash
a poem is more than
mere old words
'tis the singing of my soul
wizards use them
to cast the spells
against their mighty foes
lovers use them
to entice new mates
or let the old ones go
for if you read
more clearly now
and open up your heart
you'll find my heart's
not made of ice
but is a paradise

Ed Y Kish
HOW SWEET THE MUSIC

To all senior citizens who have courageously walked the long, hard road to reach their destination in life and who are now spending their days in tranquility as long as the sun will shine for them.

She sits, she smiles, her ears perked up to hear
The songs she sang in pigtails long ago;
Her stiff and often painful fingers rest
On bony lap where warmth is slow to flow;
The music brings a twinkle in her eyes.

From side to side her head begins to sway,
From time to time a finger tries to tap
Then other fingers move though not with ease;
She strains to sing while dear ones urge and clap
From aged shut-in's throat comes not a sound.

Each song reminds of carefree times she spent
When world was small but never skimped on fun;
Her little friends who laughed and played with her
Came waving, walking past her one by one
As sound of music filled her perked up ears.

Today her heart is full of children's songs,
With smiles, her twinkling eyes start happy tears
To those who love her, sun is setting fast;
How sweet the music, bringing joy not fears
To one who waits for journey far beyond.

Mary Helen Leonard
HOW THE M&M'S FEEL
The molded piece of chocolate
Comes down yon conveyer
They pick the yellow color
Then proceed to spray her
Thrown into a bag
With a million others
Some of them unfortunately
Are even the same color
Thrown into a bag
The fit is really tight
If the M's are not freed soon
There's gonna be a fight
Finally a kind man buys them
And their terrible life is over
When the bag is open
All the great things he will show her
Finally the bag is open
Her time to tell him how she's felt
Until she finds his one concern
To eat her before she melts

Geoffrey Kline
THE DAY THE EARTH MOVED
On the day the earth moved, I was in my car.
I'd just left work and hadn't gone very far,
When all of a sudden, the car swayed to the side,
A rather unique feeling, certainly not the usual ride.
I failed to realize a quake had occurred.
It didn't register with me until on the radio I heard
That a large and serious earth movement took place.
I kept right on driving. It was now a determined race
To get home to loved ones in whatever state,
All the while having to ponder their fate.
Finally arriving, I learned that things were all right,
But was deeply saddened by reports later that night
That people had died and many were hurt,
Merely from a movement under the soil and dirt.
At the time, it didn't seem like such a big thing,
But tragedy never is, unless you're caught in the ring
Of those who suffer from loss in an unfortunate way,
Such as occurred on the day the earth moved, that October day.

Herbert Edwin Kelly
KING EDWARD VIII AND MRS. SIMPSON

Dedicated to our 20 grandchildren and 4 great-grandchildren, including my two sisters and their families in England.

In the British House of Commons
There arose a great debate
As to whether love should triumph
O'er a crown and throne of State.

It first began when EDWARD,
(Who was KING of ENGLAND then)
Had declared that he would marry,
Just like other normal men.

His heart was beating only
For a woman, twice-divorced,
Though Parliament had scorned her
For the turmoil she had caused.

A morganatic marriage would have
Been the king's desire,
But the British Lords and Masters claimed
'twould stir the country's ire.

Against advice the monarch warned
About his self-made plot:
"This woman I shall marry
Whether on the throne or not!"

And so as "Duke of WINDSOR"
England's ex-King went his way
To join the woman he loved best
A happier man that day.

If she had been but single then
She might have stood a chance
To prove herself a worthy queen
With such a famed romance.

Their cherished love had lasted well
And never once did wane
Till death, alas, o'ercame the DUKE
To cause the DUTCHESS pain.

And now she too, beside the Duke
In peaceful bliss now lies
No more alone without a throne
Beneath old England's skies.

This romance now is history,
A king who scorned renown
Had shown the world how love alone
Could triumph o'er a crown.

Dana E Kawa
THE WORLD I LOVE IS THE WORLD I HATE
Our world is a place of great beauty and dimension
Its seas and mountains infinite in wonder
Its animals and people in threat of going under.

Our world is polluted from ignorant misuse
While its resources cared for with profitable abuse
We live in times of gross extremes
Pseudo government, puppet regimes
Oppression, obsession, grab all you can
To take freedom from earth is to take freedom from man.

Our world is abound with political whores, clandestine wars
While religions clash and speak their holy trash
Corporate liars and convenient ceasefires
Terrorism in the news on such a massive scale
One can't help but feel unscrewed.

My world, your world
Look around before it's too late
The world I love is the world I hate.

Lorrie Ann Kahle
TWENTY-ONE

In loving memory of my Uncle, Benjamin Franklin Ashmore, who died July 27, 1982.

I turned twenty-one today I am a big boy now. I should have listened to what my friends had to say, but I went on any way as I drank down my tenth beer, they pleaded with me to stay, but it's too late now. I got in my car and drove away. I was on a hill doing ninety miles an hour. I felt the steering wheel begin to jerk and my wheels began to slide. I lost control of my car and went over the hillside. As they pulled my mangled body from my wreck of a car, I seen the blood on the sheets my face full of scars, I lay on a flat cold surface now with visions running through my head, is this real, am I really dead as I feel warm and sad tear drop upon my face, After god had taken my life. I hear painful cries and the tears fall into place. As I looked upon the griefstricken face of the girl who would have been my wife. I am in a casket now begging them not to go. I can see the sadness on their faces and tears in their eyes, as they lower me in the ground I begin to realize this is real, yet I can't make sound. And as I begin to think. I would not have been here if I had not had that Drink!
Please don't Drink and Drive

Mark S Keefer
MY VISION OF NATURE
Strolling through the woods one summer day,
I observed a squirrel scampering my way;
Beginning its journey during the morning's wake,
I, motionless, without a sound to make;
Skyward bound I ascend my eyes,
To view the bright, radiant sunrise;
As it spreads its fiery blaze,
I felt the warmth of its rays;
Listening carefully with silent ease,
I heard a multitude of birds amongst the leaves;
From tree-to-tree, studying with my eyes,
Noticing the birds and their charming cries;
So I whistled cheerfully with pure delight,
Hoping to talk to these birds of flight;
But before I could wink, the birds did flee,
As I noticed a hawk hovering over me;
Pacing homeward 'til the days end,
There was something I'd comprehend;
Life is so precious and so sweet,
So, respect Nature and be discreet.

T J Kapenekas
LOST STAR
When I was but a little boy
And day would turn to night
My eyes to heaven would I cast
And stare with all my might

A wondrous view was painted there
Made specially for me
The sky was filled with twinkling lights
As far as I could see

The years have passed I now have aged
But dreams of youth remain
I look upon the sky at night
My search for stars in vain

My canvas black with sparkling jewels
Has turned an ugly grey
The many lights that winked at me
Are lost or gone astray

I know that high above this earth
Still shining from afar
Above the smog and city lights
I'll find again my star

Dorothy M Kamminga
A TEACHER'S PRAYER

To my Dear Husband, Frederick J. Kamminga, who helped me to achieve my life-long ambition to become a teacher.

Oh Lord, help me guide my Children today, in the path of righteousness, I pray.

Help me God, to be ever patient and kind, That as a Christian, a light will shine from within, as a Servant of Thine.
Amen

Dienetta Kelley
HAVE I TOLD YOU
When you're not with me, I'm lonely.
Longing for your wet lips pressing mine.
I feel empty inside, wanting only for your gentle touch.
Wishing time we had together came more often.
I fill my days with thoughts of you.
Your tender embrace, Your loving words, the warmth of your body against mine.
I see your bright smile in every memory,
Hoping to never lose you.
My passion rises, and the pain grows deep within my heart.
I reach out, and you're not there.
So I close my eyes and dream.
Maybe tomorrow I'll hold you in my arms.

Robert Kowalski
ZOMBIES IN THE HALL
Zombies in the hall as I lay in my bed at the V.A. Hospital
I see zombies in the hall
No! that is not a zombie, that is Jerry,
He took a hit in the head on Turrawa, never made the sea wall
Zombies in the hall, they are always walking or else in wheelchairs
There is another zombie, no that is Tom, he was in Nam, as was I
we both use wheelchairs
He is an artist from the south side
He was in recon, I was a helicopter mechanic, we were both in the Marine Corps
Damn, there is another zombie, No that is just Bill, another Marine, his war was just his automobile
He is not even sure what state it happened in, half his brain is missing
Another zombie in the hall, this one is walking, he was in the army, took a bullet in Korea
This zombie was a passenger in a pickup truck, went through the back window, a coma for 3 weeks
He was in the Navy, another zombie in the hall
There are a lot of zombies in the hall
They all served their country
That's why they are here in the V.A.M.C.
But they do look like zombies in the hall

Paul A Kurian
LIFE—THE DREAM

To Mrs. Mary Oommen, my mother in law, who could appreciate the greatness of her creator in his small creations.

A drop of gold
On a tiny leaf of grass
Over it clouds dark and dense
Beneath, a desert desolate.

A long deep sigh
On a pretty little face
Covered by an air of gloom
On a bloom of innocence.

Time marches on —
With its segments overgrown
On the icy floors of souls
Of lonely weeping hearts.

Deep in the heart of night
Where owls devour fireflies
Cold yet golden rays of morn
Render their own magic touch.

Tear drop on eyelash tip
Fluttering in the gentle breeze
Is turned into a glittering gem
As a smile spreads on face
—And that is life—The Dream.

Shearon (Shearson) Kerrison
THE FIRST TIME
The moment you held me and I looked into your eyes, I felt the warm embrace of your arms melt the coldness that had protected my heart for so long.

I felt the tears of life's previous pain fall down my cheeks as you held your body close to mine,
For the first time I finally knew what it felt like to be truly loved.

The passion that I never knew existed in me, was coming alive and filling every part of my body with such a burning desire I felt as if I would explode in your arms.

I will always remember the first time,
I will always feel the first time,
Because the first time was with you.

Kevin M Kennedy
BE CAUTIOUS, BUT DON'T BE AFRAID TO TRUST
Be cautious, but don't be afraid to trust
It's time to break down these walls as is Berlin
To end the cold war inside this warm man

Master Brian Kasper
WORLD
It's a world to be perfect when you love
It's a world to be perfect when you're loved
When you love somebody give them a hug
Then that perfect will turn into love

Jane Knights
THE EGG-SPERIMENT
(it wasn't all it was cracked up to be—or was it?)
To underscore the need for care in the nurturing of human life, a teacher asks each student to act as a parent to an egg for a day.

You think you've heard everything?
Listen again—
I'm about to provide yet another:
When a hen offered me her traditional place,
I accepted the role of a mother.

The object of all my maternal concern
Was Shelly, a pale, fragile creature.
Her face was her fortune—no doubt about that—
'Twas her only discernible feature!

I coddled my wee one with tenderest care,
But Shelly was clearly a rover.
Imperceptibly she reached the edge of my desk
And, with pioneer spirit, went over.

I scrambled to reach out a rescuing hand,
But Shelly's frail vessel sailed past it.
Emergency measures were futile, alas!
O-val', it was fun while it lasted.

Robert E Konkler
TOGETHER ALWAYS

To My Precious Wife REAH EVALIN THOMPSON KONKLER With My Love.

We will be together always,
until death do we part . . .
Our Friendship . . . Our Marriage,
You are my one sweetheart.

Our lives are more than one half over,
we have so much more to share . . .
Our Love and Caring, have always made us a really loving pair.

Let's hold hands as always,
as we look forward . . to our trip home . . .
We Thank God for Our Children and their Children,
and . . . the years we have shared alone.

Together we have overcome every obstacle,
fate has placed in our path . . .
We have taken every disappointment,
yet we are always able to laugh.

We share our days together,
as we are growing old . . .
Almost all of our dreams are over,
and, some will never be told.

Our hands reach out to touch,
Our eyes . . sometimes fill with tears . . .
Always our lips meet
as we turn back the years.

You will always be young to me;
no matter how many years have passed . . .
We will be together always,
Now . . In the Future . . Always as in the Past.

Hildegarde Willson
CALL IN THE NAME OF JESUS
Courage to attain healing and God's love.
Raise up! Take hold of His hand.
Descending as a dove.
Act of the Holy Spirit.
Always faithful.
Let God love you.
Application by His holy word.
"Call in the name of Jesus."
Motivation toward spiritual outreach!
As brethren to be heard.

"Surrender all to Jesus"
Amen.
In Thanksgiving, Peace and Love.

T L Wood
I'D RATHER BE WRONG
Lord, as I see the world I'm in,
I know you created not, these violent men,

Men with hatred, anger, and war,
Wanting all they have, and too much more,

How can man destroy your creation?
When it is them who pay, at life's resignation,

For success is cheap, if it's all you're after,
It takes up your life, love and laughter.

At times I watch the human race,
Diminishing life, at an even pace.

I wonder then, what happened to men,
seeking power, ignoring life within.

Yes Lord, I know this is not your doing,
For love is lost and is not renewing,

At times, I want to go far away,
Gone from people and the world today.

We need a miracle, you know it's true,
But Lord, this time it is not up to you.

If it is right, to be powerful and strong,
Then Lord, I don't want to be right,
I'd rather be wrong.

Mary Ellis Warrick

SCHOOL, THE LEARNING TREE

To, my husband Walter and the children, Paul, Ted, and Norma.

THE classroom is a learning place
Back into history, and even outer-space
History and English I desire to learn
Filing, too, but in its turn.

I'm really trying to do my best
Willing to help others in this quest.
Adult I am, but I must be like,
A CHILD, again at the learning tree.

I intend to press on and never look back
For if I do I'll only be slack
I pray that many will join its parade
And never turn it, into a comic charade.

Please fill the classrooms of every school
Allow, the teacher to tap you, with her rule.
The harvest is great, the students are few
Age doesn't matter each has their cue.

The learning tree is the place to be
It's a guiding hand for you and me.

Leonora A Wyatt

THESE ARE MY CHILDREN

To my four children, who have made my life so beautiful!

First comes Wendy, who is tall and lean;
When she's older, she'll walk like a queen.
She always has a project growing,
But doesn't yet know, quite where she's going.

Now comes Michael, who loves to read.
With each fact learned God plants one more seed;
A seed when fertile and is sown,
Doesn't stop growing until all is known.

And now my Wayne with great wide eyes,
Is a sensitive child yet full of surprise.
He never ceases to understand
When his mother needs his hand.

Now comes Linda, who is sometimes shy,
Wakes each day to a bright blue sky.
She always has a wide, wide smile;
And makes my day very worthwhile.

These are my children and they number four,
To know this makes my heart soar.
As I live, love, wonder and see,
It's pretty wonderful that they belong to me!

Ashley Wallace

I CAN'T UNDERSTAND

I, Ashley Wallace, would really like to thank all of my associates for making me write a very wonderful poem.

I can't understand, the way you feel,
If I talk to you I hope it's real.

I can't understand, why you like me,
You act just like a little bee.

I can't understand, your ways at all,
But knowing you that sounds like a ball.

I can't understand, why you say you are shy,
But one thing I know that's a lie.

I can't understand, what's going on in your mind,
I'm going to be first in line.

I can't understand, there won't be any trouble,
I'm asking you, you better think double.

Shari K Waldon

CAN'T YOU HEAR ME CRYING?

This poem is dedicated to Russ, Mom, and Tom for all their love and support . . .

Can't you hear me crying
in the middle of the night? . . .
Longing for you to embrace me,
and tell me "It will be alright"
Sometimes I feel so frustrated;
so scared and all alone.
I fear that holding everything in,
will only make me turn to stone . . .
Can't you hear my crying,
with such great sobs of despair?
Just wanting to know that somewhere;
someone out there will care . . .
With such a struggle for today,
How can I face tomorrow? . . .
Please hear me crying Lord,
and lift my heart of sorrow!

Kathy Woodward

SCATTERED SANDS

We are but scattered sands on the beach,
helpless against the winds and waves.
Waiting for whatever comes our way,
seeing not what is outside of our reach.

We are but scattered sands in the breeze,
being whirled to our unknown destination.
Waiting for our fate to take hold,
knowing not, by what we will be seized.

We are but scattered sands upon the shore,
being molded by unseen hands.
Waiting for the inevitable day,
when we'll be washed away forevermore.

Barbara Whitehead

A TURN IN LIFE'S ROAD

To my husband, Carlos, and my three children.

A long time ago when I was just a young lady;
I had plans for this and that in my life—maybe.
To finish my education was my first ambition;
But right out of high school "love" came along without inhibition.
College, career or marriage, what a heavy load;
A decision to be made, which turn to take in life's road?
There were many many happy days and a few mixed in that were sad;
But all the good things outweigh the bad.
On down the road my heart was made glad;
Two beautiful daughters and one very handsome lad.
These three children are my life, but also a load;
Just another turn in life's road.
Now I have four precious granddaughters and one special grandson;
The prizes in life are very great that I have won.
Many years have past with joy and sorrow,
But I am looking for the next turn in life's road tomorrow.

Elizabeth Worden

WHY MY PEOPLE AREN'T RICH OR SOCIALLY ACCEPTABLE

I come from a long line of people who spent their lives
throwing punches at the world, trying to change it
Powerful fists, keen minds and unbreakable wills
No wonder we haven't been accepted by society

Society is made up of conformists,
All leaning on each other for support
Ignoring evil and lies, pretending things
We pretend nothing and call a spade a spade
We see everything and don't like half of it

We feel it's our job to fight for what is right
irregardless of what is acceptable to modern taste
I will take the poverty and loneliness along with the rest of my clan
It is the dues you pay for using the world for a punching bag

Electa M Winter

JOHANNAH'S GARDEN

All is pleasant,
Colorful and bright.
Growing from one season
To another
Out of sight
Scents of roses,
And pansies by the shore
Leading a floral path to
Hannah's door
Among them, life seems to be content
In her precious garden,
Many a peaceful moment is spent.

Ruth Warnock

ONE QUARTER CENTURY

Life is but a vapor that fades and passes.
Only the faint-hearted need rose-colored glasses.
Twenty-five years have made their history.
With foot prints and finger prints leaving no mystery.

Where have the words and the voice prints ended?
In conversations and talks that were so splendid.
Our words and songs find no resting place.
They travel forever into time and space.

Leaving us faint echoes of a distant sound.
Recorded in hearts and minds with a love that's profound.
Twenty-five years of reaping and sowing
Deeds and experiences that are all part of growing.

Everything past and present that come into play
Make special memories and the person you are today.
The future lays open with promise and hope.
And many opportunities can be viewed in life's scope.

We travel this way only once and we're through.
We all need God's help in whatever we do.
So gather the courage, the grit and the will.
For life although fleeting is still all uphill.

Ms Shirley Winden

SOLID BONDS

This poem is for my love, Brian, the man in my life, and for all other couples, who have found their long lost loves.

It's so very true,
We were always meant to be,
Yes, our timing was off,
Made no difference to me.
The days we spent together,
Were oh so enlightening,
Our heartfelt attraction,
Was everso frightening.
Regretful, I am, of the years we have lost,
I appreciate your attempts to reunite, at any cost.

Today we are one, should've been, all along,
Our flame has never died,
Our depth of love, still strong.
In love, and ecstatic,
The ultimate aspect of life,
That's god's gift to myself,
And I will become your wife.

And now, time is ours,
Feels like a brand new dawn,
Thank you, so much, sweetheart,
For the lasting solid bond.

Bettysue Waite

LAKE

I went down to the lake,
To relax for just a while.
With surroundings so beautiful,
They made me smile.

The gracefulness of a doe.
Turtles sunning themselves you know.
Nature at her very best,
So peaceful, you had to rest.

Wildlife so vast and free,
Lucky am I, to be able to see.
Butterflies so full of grace,
Flying from magical place to place.

Reflections of the forest,
All around the lake,
The beauty of the trees,
In gratefulness we take.

So much of nature here to see,
The frogs, swans, and honey bees.
The magic of nature inspires me so,
To watch it daily makes my heart glow.

Darrell Whitbeck
LIFE'S LIGHTNING
Things will change, things will derange.
As I wait for the hour of my calling, I view society as appalling.
Fond memories so long gone, reminds me of a sweet bird's song.
We're in trouble on the double.
While we wait and weep, last years laugh and sleep.
Friends diminishing through the years, all verging on the point of tears.
What can be done? What can be won?
Fleeting images glancing through my brain, ain't it about time I've gone insane?
The door is closing, rapidly closing
Is this my home or am I all alone?
Time to go.
Time goes slow.
The minutes tick the hours past, could this be my final rest at last?

Patricia Woods
WHAT HAPPENED?
We were so close, what happened?
Wherever I was, you were.
Wherever you were, I was.
We were best friends forever.
What happened?

We went to the same grade school.
We laughed and complained about the nuns.
We shared secrets.
We whispered about the boys.
We were best friends forever.
What happened?

We went to the same high school.
We laughed and complained about the teachers.
We shared special secrets.
We whispered about the boys.
We shared each other's plans for the future.
Wherever I was, you were.
Wherever you were, I was.
We were best friends forever.
What happened?

After school you got married.
I moved away.
We wrote to each other faithfully.
Best friends forever.
Soon it turned into a Christmas card a year.
What happened?

Now years later, I have a daughter.
She laughs with her friend.
She shares secrets with her friend.
Wherever she is, her friend is.
Wherever her friend is, she is.
Best friends forever????

Cheryl "Sherri" Walker
A MATTER OF PRINCIPLE
I write because I feel,
Not for monetary gain,
I write of things quite real,
Of my pleasures and my pain,
I write when I am crying,
From the pits of inner strife,
I write of people dying,
Some from cancer — some from life.
I write when my mind is reeling,
I write of laughter and of rain,
I write to share a feeling,
Sometimes I write just to keep sane.
I cannot fill a chance request,
Made by a stranger off the street,
It's from my heart I write my best,
It's from my pores my words secrete.
However, if perchance you feel me,
If one message I convey,
If to your heart I turn a key,
For this my friend — I proudly accept pay.

Fred J Wiener
TIME AND TIDE
Time and Tide will never subside
across the rolling oceans wide.
Many a bold sailor storm tossed
never with the ship was lost,
Though the ship with highest waves was tossed.
Many continents and islands are washed.
In our lives there also Time and Tide abide and
toward eternity glides.
Grace always true wisdom, foretold and through the centuries rolled.
Undying wisdom will live forever
from errors hold many souls will sever.
Through Time and Tide truth will survive.
People their salvation will apprise
hope and salvation will arise,
Mankind with peace will live,
God His blessings will give.
Heaven's shower of blessing will descend,
Mankind to Heaven's accord will attend.

Fred J Wiener
O COLUMBUS!
O Columbus, dreamer and prophet brave,
Hand to rudder, to fear no slave,
To isles and lands to discover,
Oh, what the future will bring
In the future new nations arise,
New nations and frontiers will arise,
Then commanders will encircle the world,
New people will be met,
New people will be amazed,
Unusual fruits of the earth will be found,
New nations with new governments will arise
Fallen ruins of the past uncovered
Mankind's triumph will be over all!

Michelle White
FRIENDS AND LOVERS

To Mark, For all the Love you've shown me! I Love You!

If it all comes so easy,
Why does it seem so hard?

I feel so content when you are near.
It feels so perfect that it brings some fear.

I could sit all night looking into your eyes,
Talking with you, feeling your sighs.

You make me laugh, you make me care.
I long for you when you're not there.

When we make love and open up,
It's like we've won the victor's cup.

There's nothing like it — we both know.
We must never let it go.

Let's stay friends 'til the whole world ends—
Let's stay lovers — the kind we are
'Til the sky is filled with just one star.

If in God's plan it's you and me,
Let's let fate arrange our destiny.

Aubrey L Weedmark
CHRISTMAS
Christmas is in December.
The most beautiful time to remember!
The snow on the trees,
The cool winter breeze, and
The glow of the fire's embers.

Heather Williams
TO ANNIE, WITH LOVE
I can't remember the first time I heard about it—I can't even imagine such cruelty
And yet to face it with such dignity . . . amazes me
I think I was watching television the first time I heard the word
"Holocaust"
"With all that it is man can do." I say to myself
Over and over
"With all that it is man can do" I laugh to myself, "He chooses to destruct."
And you say, through all of this,
"Inspite of everything, I still believe man is generally good at heart."
Ha! I laugh, They're keeping you in confinement Annie—They don't care!
I've read the end, Annie—You'll never be able to love, laugh, cry, care, share . . .
And still you say, "Yes, I do."
"Man will never learn, Annie—He is too selfish. Man is a cannibal."
And still you say, "No, man is good at heart. Man is good at heart."
But I say, "Man is a tyrant, Annie—I've read the end . . . "
But you still say, "No!"
You'll never be able to love, laugh, cry, care, share . . .
And then I realize you do . . . You do.
I put my book down.
I believe too . . .
I believe too.

Clova Van Order
DAY'S HOUSEKEEPER

To my mother Maude Elinor Bowers who wrote and appreciated poetry.

The sun is dusting shiny sunbeams,
Sweeping out its golden dreams,
Shaking out her brightest carpets,
For you and I to walk upon.

Cleaning out the darkest places
With her brushes made of light,
Making bright our morning faces
She's day's housekeeper until the night.

Then night's soft, velvet clouds,
Slips a cloak around her shoulders,
And the evening breezes having fun
Rocks to sleep a very tired sun.

Clova Van Order
A TRACE OF GLORY
A rose grew gracefully slender, and tall,
A splash of color against the wall.
The sun flecked shiny rays about her head,
The bees of her honied goodness were fed.

Each day was a warm memory of hours
To this sweet and loveliest of flowers.
The sun entwined bright fingers in the soil,
Keeping the earth warm by its steady toil.

She felt the earth's bosom beneath her leap,
And stretched her greenness for strength to reap.
She grew beautiful, lent gaiety to each day,
Until dark clouds came and swept the sun away.

The harsh winds blew against her slenderness;
When the sun bathed the garden in tenderness,
One bright petal lying on the beaten ground,
Was all of her shiny glory that could be found.

Clova Van Order
SHINING FAITH
A bright star shone
In all its virgin beauty
On God's field of blue.
I, a weary traveler
Seeking the path of right,
Saw this star ashine
In the sky one night.

I sent my faith with God's love
To shine in this star above.
God made this star, and He made me,
The shine of star, bright of my soul,
Will one day be encircled
In a greater glow.

Another weary traveler
Seeking his path at night,
Will see this love
As a new star above,
And his faith will shine
In God's love, in God's time.

Tracey Wentzell
MEMORIES
I see a place,
where I once played
as an innocent child
with my old battered dolls.

I would sit there for hours,
just me and my dolls,
in my own little world,
far away from home.

Then I heard my mother call,
and ran to meet her,

leaving my toys and never going back,
. . . until today.

Nothing is left of my playthings,
they have long since withered away,
but in my memories
I am still there.

Jen Whaley
A DREAM
To laugh,
To win,
To live.
Dreams can take you
Anywhere you want to go.
Life is a dream.
Where does reality stop
And dreams begin?
To be brave,
To humble,
To fear.
A child wishes upon a star
Only to find
Wishes don't always come true.
This world would be a better place
If we could only learn,
And hope,
And love.

Rose M Warner
NONIE

This poem is dedicated to Nonie, my sweet precious grandmother.

Nonie was the best friend to everyone,
Her smile was as beautiful as the sun.
She had a heart of gold.
Yet she never seemed to grow old.

Nonie never had a bad word to say,
She never had to have her way.
She always had a lot of love,
Now she is free and spirited as a dove.

Nonie is at peace now,
You wonder how?
She is now up in heaven.
She was the best friend given.

Nonie I miss you,
You were never blue.
You always had a great smile,
Nonie I will see you in awhile.

I love you Nonie very much,
You were always full of love, & joy, and such.
Who was Nonie, you wonder?
She was always full of love for me,
Nonie
Was my beloved grandmother.

Faye Gillenwater
BABY SWEET BABY

To My Darling Daughter Brenda.

Baby Sweet Baby
from Heaven you came
A little angel
from the Father above!

God sends us his love
in the form of a child
His precious Holy Spirit
in the form of a dove
Baby Sweet Baby

Your hair golden like Sunshine
eyes, twinkling, like Stars in the Night
A Smile, so Cherry and bright
Why! "you must have been Heaven's delight"

Your Cheeks, are like Rose buds
in a garden of dew
Tell Me! Lord How can anyone
want to abort you?

You say, "Look Moma
I'm growing" I'm growing
God Created Me, and he's given me a will
His Promise to fulfill
Oh, "Moma please let me live"

Faye Gillenwater
DEAR LORD JESUS
Dear Lord Jesus
Before you, I humbly bow
Asking you to please, "Show us how to cope, In this world, with so many needs

Where Hunger and Homeless
is the Thief
Every night, Somewhere Lord
little children, will cry themselves to sleep!

No clothes upon their backs
or shoes on their feet!
Cold and hungry, with no food to eat.

Forgive us Lord, If we have fallen asleep
Because you, said in your word
If you love me, Feed my sheep!

Why, You gave up Heaven
to show us the way
and Lord, You feed multitudes everyday!
Please, Help us Lord Jesus?
to think of others, and to share
The Blessings, You have given!"

Elizabeth Webster
WHERE DOES THE SKY END?
Where does the sky end?
It never really ends.
The sky holds bright stars,
Like the one called Mars.
We even have the Milky Way,
Which we can see — only one way.
We have Pluto, but no Mickey,
Rhyming this poem is a little tricky.
The blackness of the night,
Comes full turn with daylight.
When I see a shooting star,
I know it has traveled very far.
Speeding through the night so fast,
I was taken by aghast.
So when you wonder "Where
Does the Sky End?",
Think of this poem, and read it again.

Marie Walsh
BLOSSOM
Lying in silence
The seed of life grows.
No sunlight to guide
The route that it goes.
Floating in darkness
As its stems and petals form.
Surrounded by nourishment;
safe and warm.
Time is the essence
Perfection the goal.
For this flower's seed
is really a soul.

Norman F Wilbert
TO A SLEEPING CHILD

To Rachael Ruhlman.

Sleep softly, little lady,
And dream the night away.
Forget the cares and troubles
You face throughout the day
Sleep softly, little lady
Protected by the night
Forget about tomorrow
and the cold, harsh morning light
Sleep softly, and sleep gently.
For you deserve the rest
You made it through another day
You did your very best.
Sleep in perfect happiness
With pleasant dreams all night
Until you are awakened
By morning's gentle light.

Al Westbrook
OLD DAN
Old Dan,
Was just a man,
Who lived back in the wood.

When he passed away,
So went the day,
Of his everlasting good.

He taught us boys,
of daily joys,
there only if you look.

Those lessons shown,
That we now own,
Don't show in any book.

From stars above,
To brotherly love,
These things Dan gave away.

And now he's gone,
Though we move on,
We'll miss him every day.

Nancy J Schneider-Walsh
THE WORDS
The words come typewritten from my mouth
I stop
and stare at them.
Did I say that?
Gee, I'm sorry.

Carl C Williams
IT'S A WONDERFUL NIGHT
It's a wonderful night for singing,
All the bells over town are ringing.
With hearts all aglow,
As we walk through the snow.
We merrily, merrily sing,
While the bells ting-a-ling.
With the glistening snow, pure white,
It's a most delectable sight;
So our spirits are bright,
We are happy tonight,
It's a wonderful, wonderful night.

There's a reason our hearts are jolly,
And it's not just for snow-covered holly.
We go carolling along,
With a bright, happy song,
And here is the real reason why:
Angels sang from on high,
That the Saviour has come to earth,
And this is the night of His birth;
So our spirits are bright,
We're so happy tonight,
It's a wonderful, wonderful night.

Lou Verna K Waite
WILL I COME HOME FOR CHRISTMAS?

Dedicated to my Father, Mother, Brothers and Sister.

Will I come home for Christmas?
Is what they always say.
Don't they know that at Christmas time,
Homeward tread those who stray?

We long for the snow and ice
When snow peaks stand solemn and white.
Made great through all the winters seasons,
We wouldn't change it for any reason.

We long for the apples and home made candy,
Donuts and all things found on the farm,
And some things that really do us harm,
But the greatest reason is, time spent with our dear family.

The woodland pleasures—the resounding horn,
The packs loud chiming and the hunted hare,
With all the fun spent with long time friends,
Nothing in the world could ever compare.

Will I come home for Christmas?
That's a queer question, I say,
Do you think I could stay away?
It's strange you would ask it that way.

Of course I'm coming home for Christmas, Chip Ahoy.
Why, with all my fond memories, I couldn't stay away,
When to my mind comes all our Christmas joys,
When the memory of other times crowd round me every day.

Norina King

Norina King
LOVE
Love warms the soul as
the sun's rays warm the
earth;

When Love comes to abide
in the heart, life
springs forth from within
and reaches out touching
everything in its path
with joy;

But, when Love is bound
and denied, the soul
weeps within and its
portals close as a flower
in the night.

Yes, night has fallen;
but tomorrow there will
be light. The sun will
rise again to warm the
earth, to light the sky;
because life was created
for continuity — so was
Love.

Love is independent from
all else in life yet, it
is an integral part of it.

Love has to meet with

Love to find the
nourishment it needs — if
it is to survive!

What is Love? Who is
Love? What does Love
look like? Where does it
come from? Where does it
go?

Love is a mystery none
can understand, none can
explain but, God is the
creator of it.

Teresa B Walker
SOMETIMES ALONG THE WAY

This poem is for: Dad-Ellen-Mona-Agnes-Bryan Bain-Verlie and for life of love and family life. All of you are very special to me.

Sometimes along the way—we touch
people in a special way.
Sometimes along the way—we find
places that touch us, and we are
moved, for without these places the
way we feel about them would not
become a part of us.
Sometimes along the way—our
feelings may seem to turn on us.
That's the sad times when we
allowed our loneliness to overcome
us.
Sometimes along the way—we find
everything we could ever dream of—
only to see it fade—for no real
reason.
Sometimes along the way—there is
laughter—lots of pure joy. When
babies are born and the love of a
family keeps it strong.
So many things happen to tighten the
ties that bind in our lives.
Sometimes along the way—we
seek—we sometimes find.
Sometimes along the way—we
love—we regret, we care, we are
touched by death and we think back.
To the time of Sometimes along the
way.

Jill White
UNTITLED

Dedicated to my best wettis Laurie, Thank you for being there for me. I love you!

Engulfed beneath,
I forever drown amidst this vast
tangled sea,
Far above, billows swell
repetitiously.
Encased, I am, rippling in these
waves of confusion,
Hoping and wishing to sink my way
down,
onto the ocean's floor,
Away again to my once lost sanded
shore.

Jean Wilcox
FEAR

Dedicated: Memory of Rai Saunders/ actor/poet/loving friend.

Five full years
Of psychiatric care
When I did see his face
My soul it did lie bare

My nerves began to quake and shake
Tears they filled my eyes
My fear was real and intense
My hysterics would not die

The fear that possessed my soul
Was not for me alone
But for a friend who'd befriended me
As I bathed my battered bones

As I continued on my way
With matters of the day
My feet for me became as one
And my mind would not obey!

Annie V Winston
MOCKINGBIRD

God gave you all the songs to sing
In tones of heavenly pitch,
The trills and garbles and chirps
Ring out from mountain top to ditch,
The wren, the blue, the whippoorwill
Must envy every peep.
Since they were given just one song,
They hang their heads and weep.

Jean Wilcox
SATAN'S TRAP

I met a man the other day and could
Not recall a thing to say — he was
Just a man of the streets and nothing
More — but long ago and far away
He was more than — just a stranger!

It was like living with Dr. Jekyll
And Mr. Hyde — never knowing
who
You'd meet on the other side —
But knew enough to stand clear
No rationale in his anger!

I felt invaded, deprived, deceived,
Worthless and most of all trapped
In a web so strong I could not
move —
Legal Aid rescued me — a Pauper's
Divorce
Delivered at dawn — permanent
restraint!

Emotions have vanished — I feel
Empty — nothing — just a man of
The streets and nothing more —
My soul was raped and torn apart
Separated now without constraint!

Louise Sayre
RAILROAD

Have you ever thought how the
railroad got its name,
How hard it was in the days the
buffalo roamed the plains,
When they had to drive the cattle in
wind, snow and rain,
Hoping in your heart what the next
day you might gain.
What a thrill it must have been when
you first saw a railroad track,
And you heard the shrill old whistle
and saw the old smokestack.
Thoughts like this should really make
a person thank the Lord and pray.
When you think what it might have
been without the train today.

Stephanie Warner
THE AUTUMN SEASON OF OUR LIVES

The Autumn season of our lives . . .
Flowers fading like our hopes and
dreams.
Leaves falling like our passing years.
Clouds fleeting like our illusions,
fantasies.
Light diminishing like our memories.
The sun growing colder, sometimes,
like our affections.
But these are only natural things.
Preparing us for a rebirth,
a new beginning,
as our earthly Autumn prepares us for
our spiritual Spring.
It's all part of the cosmic changing
cycles.
Our acceptance should be graceful.

Stephanie Warner
MEMORIES OF UKRAINIAN CHRISTMAS EVE

Ukrainian Christmas Eve . . . The most wonderful night of the year . . . the Yuletide Spirit, and Christmas Cheer. The table . . . with white cloth covered . . . Baby Jesus's swaddling clothes remembered. The straw . . . on the center of the table, and under it, too . . . representing His humble manger . . . the night He came to save me and you. The braided Christmas bread . . . made by our Mother . . . celebrating the Trinity . . . Christ's union with the Father. The flaming white candle on the bread . . . burning brightly as "The Star of Bethlehem."

Always the empty chair and place setting . . . for our ancestors long gone . . . for the Prophet, the stranger, the traveler . . . who "might" visit our home.

The celebration began, as we ran out the door . . . sighting the night's first, shining star. We sat at the table, fidgeting, giggling, our eyes, transfixed . . . while Father banged, three times, on the door . . . pretending he was St. Nick. Smiling, Mother would open it, ajar! Father would bellow, "Christ is Born!" We'd yell, with excitement, "Praise Be To The Lord!"

Never receiving big gifts on the next morn, we already had our gift . . . "Christ is Born!" But, Oh, how we did scuffle and scramble . . . when Father threw candies and coins under the table.

Holy Supper . . . always began with a prayer . . . for every soul upon the earth, be he far, or near. The bread dipped in honey . . . passed down the table so long. The "Kiss Of Peace" . . that our love for each other would always
be strong. The burning incense . . . passed beneath everyone's face . . . inhaling its fragrance . . . brings health, God's blessings, and grace. The twelve course meal which followed . . . each dish commemorating the lives of the Apostles.

After story-telling, laughing, and feasting our fill . . . Father would lead us singing carols. Our tradition, we never let wane. Our final prayer . . . for our brothers in the Ukraine.

Stephanie Warner
THAT'S WHY I NEED YOU

To my children: Stephen James, Anelle Jean and Ann Marie. To my grandchildren: Philip John, Matthew Warner and Amy Ann. With love and best wishes for a wonderful life!

You see that I am a small seed.
That's why I need You.
You choose me,
Your weak instrument to be.
That's why I need You.
Lord, You know, the road I trod
won't be all sod.
That's why I need You.
When my patience is put to the test
in failure or sickness.
That's why I need You.
In sorrow,
when I must part with loved ones,
and grieved is my heart.
That's why I need You.
To be my Light,
when darkness calls me to my
eternal sleep.
That's why I need You.

Ford Fullington White
THE RISK

Dangling from the end of long and
twisted rope.
The danger and thrill of death excite
my senses.
Searching for my future and gliding
on my hope.
I devour the thought of victory and I
hear it call.
Do I take the chance that I might fall?
This world is filled with challenges
and dares.
Some admire the risk and others
never cared.
In order for any man to make his
mark on this earth.
He must first be willing to toy with
death and place a value on his worth.
Many are held at bay
And for the few it is even fair to say.
That life is but a chess game for you
and I to play.
Your move my Dear.
Do not let it overwhelm you this
blanket of fear.
It is cold, damp, and wet, drowning
you in your own pouring sweat.
The pains of each day and yet another
debt to pay
And to the reaper — who is the only
one to gain
In this conflicting game that harbors
the insane.

Ford Fullington White
TRAPPED

Trapped by this tormenting sin.
Will I ever cast it away?
Will I ever win in this battle of each
day?
Guilt surrounds me like a blanket
of fog and I cringe with pain.
Endlessly looking towards the
horizons and searching the plains.
Here where I stand without
progress and little to gain.
Yet I wait alone for that day of
freedom.
The day I forever run from these
binding chains.
Please forgive me Father for I have
failed.
My heart is imprisoned and my
soul is jailed.
Will I ever have the strength to stand
and fight the evil which
prevents me from becoming
whole?
The blood which runs through my
veins is no longer red but black-black
as the color of coal.
That slow and agonizing death which
tears me apart.
Please I pray—remove this dagger
that pierces my heart.

Ford Fullington White
TAKE CARE

Take and grasp the hands of love
Open your heart and soar far above
Search the sky high and low
Feel the pain come and go
Run naked through the streets of

sorrow
And set this house of lies into a blazing fire for a better tomorrow
Please take my last gasp of air
For we who are brave and care to dare
Lift our children of death into the arms of love
The sound of music and the sight of a dove
A symbol of peace and a taste of heaven
The tears of joy stream from a young child's cheek
I cannot breathe and neither can I speak
Let us touch the hearts of those who need
And heal those lost souls which bleed
The few who never had chance
They hear the last call and choose not to dance
The pain of a broken off family
We ignore the tears and I ask how can we?
Turn the other cheek and look away
Pretend not to notice this blood red day

Ford Fullington White
DESERT RAIN

Desert rain
The words of wisdom I scream in vain
Show me the way far from this present day
Catch a falling star and have another round at the bar
Drowning in a bottle of hopes and dreams
What can all this possibly mean?
I think I'll go home now—
Wait! Stop! It's too late!
Panic-fear and hate
Run like a mad dog and swim through the ashes of hell
Run! Run! Where do I go?
Who do I tell?
I have no strength
I possess no will
Buy another bottle
Soak your dreams and protect your tears
I could have been someone
Well so could anyone!
I give up! I quit!
Let me die I scream with sorrow
Please just let me die
Let me weep—Let me cry
Just to lay there on the cold wet floor
I swallow my pride and yell—I can take no more!

Johnny Anthony Wells
THE WORLD OF LOVE

This poem is dedicated to Estella, my wife, and to my Mother, Mrs. Flora Louise Wells, and the rest of my Family of Love.

What does love mean to the world
Is it something shared between a boy and girl
Can children really feel true love
Or is it an idea of a little white dove
Love, Love given to man from God on high

Shared when a woman first hears her baby cry
Life, innocent, free and so simple and true
Knowing that life's opportunities awaits you
Take the first step to do your part
This is where the world of Love starts
If you can give love in America today
Soon Europe, Russia, and China will feel the same way
We are all Human and have the same needs
The feeling of Love which is displayed through our deeds
The basic unit of love is the Family tree
Loving Family trees lead to World unity
Our family is the largest World we know
It is here where our Love begins to grow
A long used symbol is the pure white dove
Which is our family The World Of Love.

Mr Thomas E Wade I
DON'T TAKE MY CHILD

Thanks Melanie, for giving me the keys to your heart.

Undo hurt,
intensive pain;
how can I keep from going
insane.
To take my flesh and blood
from me,
would kill the utmost inside you
see.
My heartaches
can't stop these tears from
flowing;
Especially when you stop this
love from showing.
You can kick me,
stump me,
bind me in chains; but the Love
I carry will remain the
same.
So please, please
Let us be;
most of all,
Don't take My Child
from me.

Mr Thomas E Wade I
BY ME STAND

I reach out to You,
don't turn me away;
especially when I choke on the proper
words of which to say.
Should I speak of my feelings
sometimes happy and gay;
or maybe of the sadness which
strolls so easily my way.
Whatever the word of which I seek
to express,
by me stand, so I can push out the
best.
For hardtimes, through stress and
strain;
You can count on me
my Love,
to always do the same.
So if you can . . .
By Me Stand.

Annie Ruth Waldsmith
COSMIC INCIDENT

Sometime . . .
The dying sun will envelop
The planet and its satellite
In primordial fire.
All life, if there still be life,
All fossils of conifer and hominid
Will be consumed by merciless flame.
Beloved Earth and Moon!
Beloved life!

My lover and I have walked along the seashore
And listened to the songs of our mother
And have written our names on her sand.
We have sat beneath the stenciled oak leaves
And have spoken of the young acorns
In their cups.
We have looked at the crescent Moon,
Shadowed by the Earth,
And have been silent in wonder.
Beautiful life!
Beautiful Moon and Earth!

Tara Michelle Winder
A STRUGGLE TO SEE

It hurts to grow up.
It hurts when things change.
It hurts because I know it has to be.

I fear being an adult.
I fear not being able to handle it.
I fear it because I can feel it.

No one said it was like this.
No one told me this would happen.
No one showed me how the world would change.

Just when I thought the world loved me.
Just when things were going great.
Just when everything looked up.

BOOM! Racism attacks my culture.
BOOM! Crime invades my society.
BOOM! Evil is born.

It hurts to grow up.
It hurts when things happen and you can't do anything about it.
It hurts because I know it will never end.

William Phillip Wilson

William Phillip Wilson
A GEM IS MISSING

Here's to Love; for anyone who has ever met and Loved a beautiful person and believes in memories of joy . . . Phil.

A gem is missing from my golden watch although the time goes on.

A diamond sparkling like a flowing fountain of endless beauty has drifted to the other side of the rainbow.

As I glance upon its crystal face, streams of tears appear . . . because the memories of one so very precious Lingers in my mind.

My heart is aching though I am numb from the pain of losing a gem.

The absence of her soft and Loving voice, the gentleness of her touch. Her intelligence and smile and laughter are the things that I miss so much.

Yet I can feel her presence in a quiet, consoling aire.
A breeze that is almost a whisper;
A gentle tap now and then on my shoulder;
A peacefulness that stirs inside me in remembrance that she once was here.

If I had a choice and had to lose a million dollars to spend another moment with her, there's no question I wouldn't hesitate to see her again.

Although I truly miss her dearly,
our souls still seem to keep in touch.

When I'm down and feeling lonely,
I know she's there to pick me up.

Time stood still the day she left but
I know we will see each other soon.
The gem is a signal she's sending to
Let me know her Love remains behind.

I Love and miss you dearly but
in time we'll be together again.

William Phillip Wilson
BLACK QUEEN

Behold! Thy beauty, oh majesty in vow
'Tis you, of all hue, a blackman shall endow.
You've seen the years of strife and sweat
that went unmourned and abhorred regret.

You, thy majesty, I now renown,
Bring back our pride that has been down.
Reflect through thine eyes the native dress
Of those in the past, now laid to rest.

Oh, my Queen, under spacious skies
Instill thy love with a glance from thine eyes
And those that scorn and wonder in doubt
Let them know what it's all about.
"We've given them everything,
what's the complaining for?
They have afros and dashikis, why want more?
Tell them my Queen, and tell them loud
That we are Black and not afraid to be Proud!

As I write this verse from where I reside
The same can be heard the entire world-wide
by every true brother who knows what I mean
There'll be no more "Nigger" or "Negroe" because—
the Blackman has a QUEEN!

William Phillip Wilson
DAD

You lived to be one-hundred and eight,
Now you have stepped beyond

the Heavenly Gate.
You'll have no more worries, pain or grief —
Only — happiness, joy and blessed relief.

We Love you — Dad; we hesitate to let go
We need you and, already miss you so —
Though we still wait to hear your voice;
Knowing you're with God, we must rejoice.

Five generations, you leave behind
to grow and take on their parts . . .
Thoughts of you are on our minds,
as well as within our hearts.

The years went by so very swift,
You Learned — you taught — you knew . . .
For over a century, you had a gift
We'll never stop Loving you.

If one day we see a rainbow,
reflecting across the skies . . .
The colors, perhaps, will remind us
of the gleam once in your eyes,

And, if we see a star at night
glistening high above . . .
We'll know it's you — Dad, watching us,
And sending back your Love.

We understand the time has come
to bid our Last farewell.
Go; rest in peace; give God our Love,
we all do wish you well.

(May God bless us as He did you . . .)
Love thru Eternity,
Your family

William Phillip Wilson
EMBRYO
A force is sent out to the earth and while on this new domain, there comes a pause . . .

Evolving within a span-of-time, the force becomes a form.
Destined to someday leave the form, the pause becomes Life . . .

Nourishing on experiences, eating the foods of knowledge,
Growing from the womb of existence, seeking out a goal,
Looking up into the skies, searching for itself,
Walking thru a colossal maze, closing the doors of age.

Falling sometimes into valleys, reaching plateaus at heights
Sipping precious drops of air, striving to move ahead.

Traveling this domain in Life, there comes another pause . . .
The force leaves the form, the form is stilled,
the pause . . . becomes —
DEATH . . . .

William Phillip Wilson
STREAM OF LIFE
Life's been like a fountain, spraying
the years of dew
Resembling drops of rain
reflecting Nature's hue.

My hopes, despairs and desires
formed a rippling stream
That echoes pain and laughter,
and never ending dreams.

The trials and tribulations, engulfed my
heart with grief
Like a dam on Life's horizon,
I sought to find relief.

The stream of Life began to rise,
and suddenly overflowed
And bellowed into a river
the banks of which once glowed . . .

Then there came an angel, gently
from above . . .
With just one touch that freed my soul,
and filled my Life with Love . . .

Whenever I see a mountain or
think that I have failed,
I remember that there's an
ocean of faith . . .
upon which I have sailed!

So when I feel this Life is Lost
and no one seems to care
I go back to that fountain,
take a sip
and thank the Lord I'm here . . . .

William Phillip Wilson
MOTHER
We had a chance to share your love
To see a smile upon your face
You've risen now to God above
He'll bless you with his grace.

Together Mom, when times were rough
We braced each other and pulled on out
To higher grounds though things got tough
We learned through you what Love's about.

Your gentle touch, your sweet caress
Kind words spoken and thoughtfulness
Your tenderness and true concern
Are what we'll miss but we have learned.

That you were such a blessing for us
The years went by so fast
God must do whatever he must
But our Love for you shall last.

Mother dear, on your farewell journey
Remember we Love you so
Although it's hard, we're still here learning
But we know we must let go.

For now your troubles and worries are gone
No pain, no suffering or storm
It's the quiet peace you've waited for so long
We know you'll be happy and warm.

It's times like these when we must test
Our Love, our strength, ourselves
We Love you Mom, but he knows best
So go and take your rest.

Sadly Missed,

Your Loved Ones

William Phillip Wilson
WE ARE THROUGH
A day in my life I will never forget
The very first time you and I met
You stood alone — unhappy but free
I watched you so hard, you stared back at me . . .

We finally got together — you had so much to give
I gave you my all, you gave me a reason to live.

Whatever you said was fine with me
Keeping you the way you wanted to be
What was mine was yours, my love and all
I couldn't foresee our good thing would fall.

I revelled in the thoughts of happy times,
When I was yours and you were mine.

The years of ecstatic giving exists no more
I called it love, you say it was my flaw
I was for real and yours to take
I gave — you took — now it's a mistake.

When I see you now, you have nothing to say
Yet I'm awake all night and away all day.

Although we have changed, the seasons still pass
I'm wondering how long our new roles will last?
Who will we hurt and what will we do
Now my love, that we are through!

Anne Maxfield Wilkinson
LOVESONG
Crude ardor, fashioning lovesongs out of rock.
Like a child in his first art, innocent of craft,
Awkwardly, earnestly trying to make an act of love,
I planted stones on a hillside
In the shape of your name.

Spurious implements, unglorious bits of broken rock
Carelessly locked in line.
I might have hunted diamonds,
Or bid the jewelled lizards link a live design.

Improbable task, tribute.
Like the earrings I made for my mother in first grade —
Bits of cork with sequins and pins — deft slice to my pride
When I would love with all greatness, All delicacy,
How these hands defy me, and my dreamings deny me
Their instant realization.

I mock myself. Grown to womanside,
Warmed by the mountain sun,
I stirred to manifest our love in the act of creation
And with rocks I have written your name
On a hillside that only the skies shall read.

Janet D Wright
THE TRANQUIL SEA
I have sat and watched the sunrise over the tranquil sea,
and felt the wind on my face, as
peaceful as can be.
The sea gulls and the pelicans already are descending on their prey,
I watch the clouds and hear the
birds and think "what a beautiful
day."

The tide is slowly going out and new shells begin to appear,
I walk knee deep in the water to
find the hidden treasures there.
I put the shells to my ear and hear a mighty roar,
as I look overhead to see the birds
and clouds that soar.

This is my favorite time of day to be by myself on the beach.
What it does for my soul as I sit
and watch puts heaven within my
reach.
I realize the magnitude of everything I see,
and really treasure my quiet time,
alone by the tranquil sea.

Janel Wrobel
YOU'LL NEVER KNOW

This is dedicated to my mother and best friend, Mrs. Irene Taylor. Thanks for the past 17 years and for all the years to come. I LOVE YOU, MOM!!!

You gave me my wings
And taught me to fly,
You didn't hold back,
You showed me the sky.

You gave me the world
On a silver tray;
You taught me of love
And the games people play.

You gave me the strength
To stand alone,
And all the confidence
To make it on my own.

You gave it all,
But you'll never know,
Just how much
You helped me grow.

Stephanie Wisor
OUR LIFE
The Red Rose bud, fresh and young, a new beginning.

For as it feeds on water and sunlight, it begins to grow.

Until we see no longer the Red Rose bud, but the Red Rose.

Along with the Rose however; comes the thorns which cause us pain when we touch them.

Still the beauty of the Rose remains.

Henrietta E Welch
THE SEARCH FOR UNDERSTANDING
I walked within the shadows of the ghostly pines
Searching for some solace existing therein,
But even in the midst of my searching,
I could only find a continual darkening void.

Where I had once been able to find peace,
There now existed none for my deepening sorrow.
Where I had once been able to walk in the brightness of day,
I now became frightened as a child in the darkness of night.

I had come to this oblivious world in

search of understanding,
But had only been greeted as by a black wind of death.
Being terrified by the morbidity of this atmosphere,
I ran as if being chased by the forces of evil,
Propelling forth a choking, noiseless scream
That would reach no man's ears as a plea for help.

My flight, having been of a sudden nature,
All concept of distance and time had been lost.
I had only been conscious of the movement of my feet,
When my mind, having suddenly reverted from its trance;
I realized that I was no longer surrounded by darkness.
How long I had been of the protection of the sun, I had no idea.
I wished not to know, save anything, but the comforting realm of salvation.

Wilton Charles Waterman III
ARTISTIC MEDIUMS

To my greatest motivative tool, Jill.

Innocence a thing of the past.
The instinct pushes us through a new door.
Bringing forth the changes,
in society's attitude and preservation.

Thumbnail sketches create grand designs.
The void filled with the paint of evolution.
Big brushes,
with wild, vivid imagination.
Big strokes,
covering the out going trends.

Complex greed through simple ambition.
Fanatical causes run the program.
A mission of powerful presence,
through a vision of sheer obsession.

Opal Williams
LOVE OF GOD

To my mother, Bernice Neil.

God loves us all the time
He is our friend no matter what.
There is no one like him,
You can search the world over.
We can't find a truer friend.
We can look toward north,
south, east, or west,
He is there for us no matter what!

Margaret E Whitley
AWAY

This poem is dedicated to my husband Sam, my daughter Dyann, my son John, my mother Margaret, and my father Howard, for loving and believing in me.

Atop a mountain be it night or day,
it is a place made just for you.
You can live a thousand years it seems,
or choose to just stop time.
You can Listen and Hear a symphony of sounds,
or just hear your Own mind.

In nature Both are Possible . . .
What you choose is up to you . . .
It seems to give birth to an open mind,
And it is just between the Two of You . . . !

Dwayne E Willis
A BROKEN HEART

Once, filled with a love
that now is gone
Once, filled with joy
now feeling alone
Swollen with sorrow
shattered with despair
Filled with confusion
where once was care
The pain is great
more than it can bear
It swells beyond belief
then starts to tear
Finally, it explodes
and is gone beyond reach
Shattered into pieces
like sand on a beach.

Gloria C Harrison

Gloria C Harrison
WITCHES

This poem is dedicated to Agnes, my loving mother.

We only come out at night
When all the stars are shining bright
When children come out with their funny faces
Going to all the different places

We ride through the sky
On our broomstick flying high
It's just this special day
When we get to have our way
That's the day we get to be mean
And it's only on Halloween

Lawrence L Wallace
PEACE

I would like to dedicate this poem to all the caring people who believe in KINDNESS, JOY, LOVE, & HAPPINESS.

P-is for PORTION.
E-is for EXCHANGE.
A-is for ALWAYS.
C-is for CONSIST.
E-is for EVERLASTING.

To put it all together it would say . . .
ALWAYS let your heart
CONSIST of a small
PORTION of
PEACE, to
EXCHANGE with the
world, so that there may be
EVERLASTING LOVE on
earth.

Erica Trejo
THE ADDICTION

I'd like to dedicate this poem to my family and God because without their encouragement, I wouldn't be where I am.

You may not see it now that drugs are very bad, and are also very sad. So many teenagers take drugs to ease their pain, but in the long run pain is what they will gain. They are at the age where everything seems to be wrong so they take these drugs hoping it will help them be strong. Once you take drugs you cannot seem to put them down, and you start to see your whole world turn around. You get so addicted to these drugs and you start to tell lies, steal and kill, when you are under its power you have no will. Your friends will push you into buying more and you scream YES in a loud and vicious roar. Stop taking drugs before it gets too late, the percent of teenagers taking drugs is at a very high rate. You will have to live with the crave because if you don't stop you will be the one to dig your grave.

Susan Perry-Turner
VALENTINE'S DAY POEM OF LOVE

Dedicated to my husband, Michael. Thank you for all the good times; thank you for Roy, the sun in my life. Love always, S.

Everyone writes poems of love; they're easy to start, but a really good poem must come from the heart; just like our love has been from the start.

Written in these lines and through these pages is my love for you that will last for all ages.

One day we decided to take vows of love; we stood before God (I think secretly he gave you a shove!)

But why is our love so different in so many ways? When I think of it sometimes it puts my mind in a haze. Yours quiet and reserved, mine loud and strong, but as long as it's true we'll never go wrong.

Sometimes I feel like I'm all alone. Sometimes I feel our hearts are of stone. Sometimes I feel you don't want me around, and then I don't feel like our love is so sound.

But then there are those times when we laugh and confide. We walk holding hands; this is our love, too; this is its better side.

I guess I've just said it—love has all sides. Good ones and bad, happy and sad, maybe even some day Mommy and Dad!

I've learned love from my father and love from my mother. I've even learned love through the eyes of my brothers, but love for a husband is like none of these others. It's made out of trust, laughter and romance; without these three things it hasn't a chance.

Whatever happens, whatever is said,we must always remember not to hate, but to love instead.

Yes, we have fights, disagreements and strife, but what would love be?
It's all part of life!
That's why I'll always love being your wife.

Wilford F Teel
REMORSE

This "poem" is dedicated to my "wife" "Beatrice," who through the years has always given me hope when I despaired.

I was real shy and introverted when we met that first day
But soon you made me realize that it needn't be that way.
You gave me much more confidence and made my sad face glow
All in all I blossomed out and the smiles began to show.
You gave my life new meaning—you put more blessings there
You somehow drove away the blues—the sadness and despair.
But, as years went by, I soon forgot to give where credit's due
And took for granted all you'd done—forgot to praise anew.
We shared a mutual happiness when four children blessed our life
We never had an inkling then of some impending strife.
But we began to drift apart—a breach began to show
And then that shadow crossed our path—ill winds began to blow.
You went your way and I went mine—we drifted far from shore
But even then your answer was—you loved me more and more.
And now here comes the awful part that left a broken heart
That heart is mine and all the pain makes hope and faith depart.
I pray that I may have the chance to give to you dear Bea
Atonement for the things I've done—gain back your trust in me.
Is it too late to make amends? I ask our "God" each day
Can we unite and heal the wounds I caused along the way?
Can you forgive? Dear one, I plead—and let the past be past
Or shall I pay, forever pay, and know the worst is last.
My life is in your hands right now—don't make me hope in vain
Because without continued hope I cannot stand this strain.
Dear "Bea"—I love you very much and have faith you'll do what's right
And pass this awful "cup" from me, and be my shining light.

John D Tobia
I HOPE. I DO.
I am, but now is beyond me.
I was, but then was before me.
I will be. I hope.

Through the hole of tomorrow I think I see.
Yesterday there lies the key.
Today I must cope.

I'm going to get the chance.
All the presents are circumstance.
I've been here before.

What I've always had, I still obtain.
I'm not lost, I'm of only gain.
I shall open the door.

I am and now is beyond me.
I was and then was before me.
I will be, too.

There are no problems, only solutions.
The past provides for no delusions.
Will I succeed? I need only know that I hope. I do.

Dustin G Thomas

DEEP GAZE

Someday I know
Our eyes will meet
And our minds will blow
With our synchronized heartbeats

A chill down our spines
A whisper of a voice
Is love finally mine?
Who makes this choice?

It was I who dreamed
While on this tightrope
Stifling the screams
By not losing hope

But is not love itself
A tightrope as well
Feeling warm wealth
While close to cold hell?

Yes it may be
But I'm willing to try
For it is worse to never see love
Before we die

S Jeffrey Trees

WHITE PURITY

Dedicated with love to Brandy Lea, without whom there is no inspiration.

Just as the child of God
Findeth his salvation
In the blanket of Christ's shed blood
So the land which He created
Is once more made pure
By the White Purity shed from the sky
As Autumn chokes the greenness
From the very roots of His creation
Recompense is dealt
Feathery softness soothes the bruised earth
The Father's White Angel
Baptizes the Earth that She may walk anew
Her Virginity restored
From Autumn's vile ravaging
Yet as the life of Winter draws to an end
And the Sun has once more regained His strength
White Purity's softness
Is no more needed
But to melt away and nurture
The newborn Progeny of Mother Earth

Rhonda M Taylor

VISIONS

To my family, friends, and most of all—my parents, Don and Diane Morgan.

I'm standing in a field
waiting for you.
I see you walking toward me and I wonder
How can it be true?
Before, I had hurt you and
you had hurt me.
But now we wonder what
the future will be.
I see you reach for me
as if to say I understand.
But then I see the other guy
holding out his hand.
Suddenly, you disappear
and so does he.
Then I'm left alone, in the field,
just my visions and me.
I look around and
I see nothing there
But I'm left with the feeling
that you still care.

Julie Ann Tracht

THE ESSENCE OF BEAUTY

So you wish to know what brings a Smile to my face . . .
A twinkling star
A voice from afar
A flower near a fence
A rickety park bench
A baby's tender face
An old woman's grace
A rose's beautiful scent
A child's innocence
A lamp lit at night
An end to a fight
A maiden's blushing glance
A honeymooner's dance
A beautifully lit tree
A place of harmony
My Bible on the shelf
The God within myself.

Julie Ann Tracht

THE WINDOW

So young and innocent
Not yet harmed by the world's hate
Serene inside
Naively look out the window at the falling snow
"How beautiful" you say
I stare at you in disbelief
you hop off of your little chair and
Scurry to another room.
I am alone with the window where beauty
spoke to you
"Oh speak to me" my heart cried
"Make my mind as a little child's"
And for a moment my hurts disappeared
And I remembered the joy of my childhood years.

Shirley Todd

AWAITING

As the days go by I mark them off on my calendar. Yet I can't remember the date. But I do know the day you will return.

And I await anxiously for that day to come. Through the daytime I experience a loss of memory of what I was doing and why. I begin to wonder if it's because I only have you on my mind or am I losing my mind.

All in all I do know I love and miss you more than my words can say.

So until then . . .

Julie Ann Thies

VICTORY

This poem is dedicated to Robin, my sister and very special friend.

Silence swept across the land,
there was no one around, no one at hand.
The sound of the past fires were loud,
but now all that is left is a quiet cloud.
The awful stench of death is in the air,
the feeling was that of great despair.
Where there were explosions and booms,
now there lays people's tombs.
The odor of the deaths sicken,
as the sight makes the heart quicken.
Now all the life is bare,
because the destroyers didn't care.
War and explosions are as one,
but all is what the silence has won.

Eva M Twoguns

WARPED MINDS

Enter my world
A place of total darkness and pain
In my reality soon you will doubt you're sane.
There is no light
There is no warmth
There is only survival
There is only terror
Enter my world if you dare.
Enter where there is no friend, much less someone who cares.
It's where few tread.
The rest just shut the door.
For it is an ugliness, their soul can't bare.
Turn the other way pretend it's not there.
Enter my world, my reality
For it exists day, after day.
From seed to seed
Warped minds shall feed.

Frances E Turner

PASSIONS

Passion is a strong feeling;
It matters not which kind.
Passion released is frightening;
It can cause problems of the mind.

Passion in the form of hate,
Is an unproductive thing.
Passion uncontrolled and unharnessed,
Only pain and sorrow, can it bring.

Passion shown through anger
Can erupt into injury and pain.
Passion that stems from such things
Causes nothing, nothing is to be gained.

Passion is a good thing.
It is good when positive in kind.
Passion can be of love and devotion
Then, it is productive to body and mind.

Frances E Turner

UNSELFISH LOVE

Embrace the world
With wonder;
Welcome it with love.
Look at all of creation
As a gift from above.

Let your attitude
Toward life
Be gigantic in scope.
Let it be
Full of love and joy
And full of hope.

Always give to life
Not to receive
In return
For love unselfishly given
More love will it earn

True love is given
Without intellect or thought.
You get back in return;
You get back what you ought.

Frances E Turner

BELIEF IN SELF

If you think you can;
You surely will
If you think you can't
You won't

If you shall
Who can tell
If you do
Or if you don't.

If you try
With all of your might.
You probably will
Succeed before the night

Success is when
You succeed in what
You set your mind to do
Have faith in yourself
And to yourself
Always be true!

Tabatha Y Tucker

SOMEONE SPECIAL

I dedicate this poem to my husband Virgil, and my kids, Latesha, Virgil, Jr., and Ava Tucker. I give all the love inside me, to all of you.

Someone special you are to me
You came along and made me free,
Those days of hardships, trials and pain
A sunny day you made out of rain.
And to this very day I say
I love you in a special way,
A special way unknown to you
My feelings are so plainly true.
My body aches for your tender touch
Oh, how I long for it so much,
I do not know just how you feel
But what I feel is simply real,
That special love, the way you kiss
Would drive a girl right out her wits,
The love we make, the time we share
I cannot find that anywhere.

Margie Topkin

IN SOLITUDE

When I'm most alone is when I'm least alone because Jesus comes to me
It's in those moments of solitude
closer then ever He'll be,
His presence is so closely felt and the depth of His great love,
And visions of all glories to come are sent down from above,
Oh dearest Jesus how can it be
That you care so much for someone like me,
But whatever the reason to me there's no doubt
Your strength and love I cannot live without,
And when I must come back to the evils of today,
To carry my cross along life's way,
All things are seen in a much different light
After my close walk with Jesus in the still of the night.

Dean V Thompson

JUST YOU, ME AND TIME

Our friendship has grown so much,
I don't know what to say.
I put my faith and trust in You,
A little more each day.
I know when you are happy,
I know when you are sad.
A friend you are indeed to Me,
And that I'm truly glad.

The Time we spend together,
I know will last forever!
Just You and Me and Time.

George A Tison
ANOTHER DAY

To my wife Barbara of thirty-four years, whom I love so much.

Each morning as I watch the sun rise in the east
I know God has given me another day at least

As it rises slowly into a sky of blue
I know I have another day to spend with you

We have lived half our lives together and more
And honey if we could live forever my life would never be a bore

I thank you for all those wonderful years
And now my eyes are filled with tears

When I think of all the men living and of those who have died
They will never know the joy of having you by their side

Murray Trainen
THE GYPSY FORTUNE TELLER

This poem is dedicated to Gertrude, my darling wife.

A Gypsy fortune teller
Told my fortune by the stars
And just the way she told it
That's the way it was

She scanned the spacious heavens
Across the midnight blue
Said that one day I would meet
A gracious one like you

Oh! That Gypsy fortune teller
Her predictions they came true
For heaven came right down to earth
The day that I met you

In our arms as we embrace
As lovers great of old
We burn with fervent passion
Just like the Gypsy had it told

There is my dear, no greater love
This side of planet Mars
You came to me, you're heavenly,
You descended from the stars

Murray Trainen
THE "CON" ARTIST

There are people in this world
Who stop at nothing to establish their means
They know every trick that's been invented
And will take the gullible aged and teens

In advance they are well prepared
The trap is baited and set
They tell you fantastic tear jerkers
Then take you for all they can get

In sympathy you loan them a bundle
Unsuspecting that you've been deceived
Not until the due date has come and gone
And the payment promised never was received

They would even fool their mothers
Knowing nothing of pride and shame
Sympathy is their modus operandi
A century old, and unbelievable game

Webster defines these people as "cons"
Their excuses are endless, believe it or not
Either slam the door in their face
Or lose every dime that you got

Char Marie Town
HE'S COMING IN THE SKY!

Lying in the darkest night, I hear the raindrops fall;
I see the lightning overhead, I hear the thunder call.
Ten thousands, I see starving; the diseased and homeless too,
And the unclean water that's running short, may soon be poisonous dew.
The latter days are drawing nigh; men's hearts are growing cold.
I often hear the children cry, in the streets beyond control.
Brothers are fighting with sisters; There's a hatred in the air,
And children rise against parents here, because no one really cares.
The sun no longer gives her light, to the full extent of day,
And the wars continue over seas, while the rest of the world's at play!
Now soon the word of God will cease, for who is there to hear?
As missiles go into outer space, and God is no longer feared!
Oh it's coming to an end, my friend, and you know as well as I . . .
. . . that only one can save us now and He's coming in the sky!

Jeffrey M Rivard
THE ULTIMATE FEELING

To Tammi, you're the inspiration behind the ultimate feeling. Love, Jeffrey Michael.

So many feelings rush through my head,
I guess you know; my mind can be read.
Into your arms, I'll let myself go,
Just like the river, I will flow.
My heart is opened and ready to be filled with the joys and emotions that this love can build.
I needed a change and that I found.
destined for love, we are bound.
So into your arms, into your soul, my river;
I will flow my entire being running to you.
Trying to meet your waters through and through,
and if by chance our sea will part,
I could never forget how you stole my heart, for deep inside,
I'll feel the trickle, the stream of love, a gentle prickle.
I'll see your face in the mirrors of my mind and
I'll be reminded of the love you helped me find.

Evylin Trussell
QUESTIONS

So many questions,
So many words,
Will I ever know what they mean?
Will I ever know exactly why,
Will I ever know the way,
Will I ever find the road that leads the way?
Will I never stumble,
Will I never fall,
Will I never make a mistake?
Will I ever know why things don't go this way or that?
Will these questions ever be answered,
Will these words ever find their place,
Will I never make another mistake?
Or will I keep growing,
Forever wondering,
WHERE THE ANSWERS LIE?

Celeste Toye
TO MY CHILD

To my precious children, Sean, and Charity, Lynn, without whom, Life would have no meaning.

Every parent has a hope,
every parent has a dream,
that their children will be something,
like the world has never seen.

A dynamic speaker, a qualified teacher,
an investor with great means,
an over-achiever, a fervent believer,
in all their plans and dreams.

May they fight for their cause,
when all else seems lost,
and use wisdom to accomplish their task.

Be wealthy, be famous, whatever the chances,
is all that society asks.

But I would like you to know my child,
that this does not hold true for me.

For whatever your life,
whether happiness or strife,
on whatever road you deem,
I will love you then, as I always have,
like the world has never seen.

Barbara B Turner
TO YOU MOM

To my mother—for always being there when I need you. I love you very much. Thank you for all you've done.

My mother's face is beautiful
Her laughter fills the room
Her arms hold security
in a world filled with doom.

I have children of my own now
Their cherished faces I see
It fills me with pride to know
How my mother felt about me.

Take me back to my childhood
And let me feel that love once more
Let me hear her prayer for my guidance
As she pours out her heart to the Lord.

Now that I'm a mother
Your shoes I'll never fill
As I pray for my children
It's your voice I hear.

Mom, I know we take you for granted
And yet you never say a word
But always remember, You are very loved.

Connie Rotheram Tabory
YOU

You came into my life like a gentle sunset
dazzling me from head to toe with the quiet brilliance of your style.
You touched my heart with your kindness
and warmed my soul with your sweet love.
Now once again I'm like a child,
finding delight with each new day,
tingling with renewed anticipation.
Eager to see you,
longing to be near you,
aching for the feel of your arms wrapped around me.
I awaken each morning with a sigh,
the thought of you instantly caressing me,
moving across my mind in waves of escalating desire.

Lucia Tosti
PEGASUS

Dedicated to my esteemed son, Blaise, whose innate wisdom, ingenious humor and profound understanding, has inspired me to go the distance.

The world acclaimed his first, sweet cries,
Enriched by the thunder of his new, pure heart.
It felt the sunrise in his face,
It saw the diamonds in his eyes!

"Ride high, sweet prince, hold fast my wings!"
From cradle through life's blackest clouds,
You'll thrust ahead through wounds and scars,
To seed your songs — for the gods to sing!

Behold, take heed, the child has grown,
He's learned to wear the yoke of pain—
Of bitter heartaches that come too fast,
His fruitless loves fade in the past.

Now, manhood's shackles claim his strength,
Life's arrows pierce his fragile heart—
'Til in the sunset of his silver years,
No longer does he bow to foe and fears!

His costly victories say: "At last he can!"
The sacred child has fought and grown into a man!
And in the twilight of their fated ride—
The man and steed fly side by side!!

Lucia Tosti
THEIR REIGN OF THORNS

Dedicated to my counterpart and mentor, Ben Johnson, the Pope.

There lives a legion by the sea,
Their fortress shattered without a key
They have no refuge — not a wall,
No dreams; no peace, just hell through all!

Nobody hears their cries to live,
Nobody knows how much they give.
How many times they try "just one"
They hear their god, who pleas; "Have none!"

This bottled plague that comes to stay,
That rapes their light and leaves them prey

A thousand sips are not enough —
They need "one more" — to strut
their stuff!

When once again the jug runs dry —
In bloody pain, they kneel to pray
Just one good gulp, they need to take,
The devil wins; their souls he'll
break!"

They grope to steal, one warm, sweet
sigh,
The anguish start — that was a lie!
Caught in their sneering pit of snakes,
All hope is lost — they soon will die!

Lucia Tosti
DEMONS' DANCE

Dedicated to Massimo, my 27 yr. old cousin, who overdosed on heroin, in the spring of '89 in N.Y.C.

What demons lured you to demise?
With promises of dreams, all full of
lies!
Death danced in veils of fantasy—
Through misty glows as her disguise.

Each candle lit to briefly burn,
That led the trail of no return.
Those lights that should have been
your guide—
Brought you your silent "silver"
suicide!

You gored your arm to set the pace
A second's triumph in your final race
You rolled your dice — a gambler's
chance,
They beckoned you; you joined
death's dance!

This world cannot forgiven be—
We let your cross become your
destiny!
We failed to show you the rainbow's
hue—
That one bright star, just meant for
you!

And so sweet youth, dear precious
soul—
We mourn, but will not say "adieu"
Hang tight! Hold fast! Wait up!
We're next!
For soon — we shall hold hands with
you.

Lucia Tosti
HAIL, LOVE'S SWEET VENOM

The flesh betrays the heart —
No victory is won!
The passions chill — the fervor
wanes,
As though it ne'er begun.

No dreams hold still; they bleed and
cry
They barely last the night
Love's fragments fall and drift away,
A smile ago it seemed so right!

Too fragile to endure — too hurt to
be forgiving,
We weep forlorn, in the grey, cold
morn'
There's no reprieve; it's "tell and
show"
Love stands its ground and won't let
go!

I will to love's sweet pain concede,
Embrace my longing heart and need
Surrender now — roar with delight!
Begone tomorrow — let's take
tonight!

Tammy Thompson
SHEER CURTAINS

We lie on linen of gold and blue
silken in gleaming daybreak hue.
Slender tendrils gently hold
a touch of blue, a blaze of gold.

And then a nimbus of cream and
green
filters through . . . wafts warm,
unseen.
So thus we lie in sunlight's stream;
awash in green, bathed in cream.

Crimson fades to primrose and grey
upon linen wilting with the day.
Whisper not promises, faith, or
those . . .
kiss me grey twilight, touch me
primrose.

On linen of silver, of indigo black
night creeps through then, swiftly,
back.
Kisses like stars calm velvet-limbed
shiver
We melt into black . . . we breathe
molten silver.

Ellen Tsamasiotis
CANDLELIGHT

This goes out to my friend and big brother, John Craig.

In the darkness, there's a flickering
candlelight,
Held on to by a lonely, vacant heart.
Love is dying in the world and in his
heart,
But love still lives in the flame;
It's warm and lives eternally,
Until the wind blows its destructive
breath.
Then, there's no more flame,
Just the dark and the vacant heart;
Dying, as the sun appears
And the memories flood back.

Elizabeth Tipton
UNION

Closely entwined—
Outward, inward.
Rampant ecstasy
Raging. Tall
Towers, high wave
Cresting, tossing.
Thrusting, forcing onward.
Clutching, grasping,
Gasping, holding tightly—
Outward, inward
Gradual lessening,
Calming, quieting,
Soothing, easing
Raging emotion.
Still closely
Entwined outward.

John Taggart
A WINTER'S WISH
(I'll Be Glad When the Robins Come Again)

I'll be glad when the robins come
again
For I'll know that Spring's come
to stay.
I'll be glad when the birds start to
sing their song,
And the snow and ice melt away.

In the bleak of winter, the cold gives
a chill.
It cuts to the heart; freezes the will . . .
To venture on out into life's main
stream.
The old are confined to a chair and
a dream.

I'll be glad when the robins come
again
For I'll know that Spring's come
to stay.
If I listen, even now, I can hear the
birds sing.
My cares and troubles flee away.

I'll be glad when the birds their nests
start to make,
And the warmth of the sun melts
the snow.
I'll rejoice when the ice on the pond
starts to break,
And the flowers on the hill start
to grow.

I'll be glad when the robins come
again
To feed at my windowsill.
I'll be glad when the birds start to
sing their song,
And the Maker of spring has His
will.

Glenda M Pride
AN EARTHWHILE CAUSE

To my loving husband, Russell.

The rain forest—exotically beautiful.
Why do we find it so hard to keep?
It is plentiful with birds and animals
and plants,
With a brilliance of colors so deep.

The elephant—a magnificent animal.
Ivory trinkets we can buy real cheap.
But the elephant must pay the highest
price
—His life for his "two front teeth."

The whale—a majestic mammal.
On the high seas we brutally
slaughter.
If this continues we must ask
ourselves;
"How long will he be king of the
water?"

The dolphin—a playful creature.
The fisherman's net becomes a snare.
How many of our aquatic friends
shall die,
Before humans begin to care?

The air—our tender lifeline.
The ozone layer must be kept clean.
When our world is fresh as when it
was new
—Only then can mankind dream.

Cathy Vertile Cummings
NEW LOVE

To my love: Willie F. Brown.

In this house by the sea,
We can be man and wife you and me.

As the waters reflect against the sky,
It seems our love should be enduring
and never die.

The depth of the earth exposes the
inner tenderness and strength of the
soil,
Like your kiss upon my lips opens
my heart.

Yet like the blossoms kissed by early
morning's dew,
Our new love breathes forth a
freshness for an eternity.

Tadd Thorston Reiley

Tadd Thorston Reiley
THOUGHTS OF A GENIUS

Dipping his feather in ink,
He began to think.
He thought deep in principle,
Of Socrates,
And Aristotle.
He dreamed of a free land,
Given by God's hand.
From these thoughts
His mind took flight,
And Thomas Jefferson
began to write . . .

Tadd Thorston Reiley
THE GREAT DECEIVER

The Iron Curtain has ripped
Under God's judgement grip.
"Nations have fallen, kingdoms
raged,"
Hardliners hate this changing age.
Too many people have now been
fooled
By the one who has used fear to rule.
While ignorant people cry, "Peace!
Peace!"
The future awaits the cries to cease.
The Russians have not changed their
intent;
'Tis the purpose of world conquest
they're bent.
They'll invade God's land, stur his
wrath,
And cause the tragic aftermath.
Let's not be so deceived
By the one that only seeks power and
greed.

Susan Stark
SIMPLISTIC CREATOR

They dance in the moonlight across
their fine threads
A delicate marvel is spun as a bed
Creating uniquely a word never said
With instinct their guide, now they'll
secretly fled

And when the sun rises to shine on
their ware
It glistens with dew, nature's artist so
rare
He takes not a bow but reflects with a
stare
His goal yet another to spin with such
care

Who is he this artist who creates with such flare?
He's only a spider his life we should spare

Susan Stark
TAKING CHANCES
Of time and space we all exist
What's our reason for being? We always persist
We are born as the dawn and in death the sunset
Making choices each day, hoping none we'll regret
Our paths crossed with strangers, some become friends
A few stay but briefly, some stay till the end
Some live moment to moment, some will plan every day
But alas, does it matter? Or will fate make the play
And just when we feel settled and secure in our space
Circumstances occur and some things are replaced
We will love, we will lose, we will hate, we will win
Our time's much too short some don't even begin
Live each day to its fullest, don't be shy of your dreams
Sometimes taking chances are best, they bring more than it seems.

Leo R Soine
THE AGONY
Waxing sentimental and heavy wining can be such a distressing combination,
The incredible stupidity of it, the agony of it, "I shall never live it down."
"I know dear friend," I replied, "but certainly you don't expect vindication."
My friend twisted his hands in dejection loathing himself and said with a frown,
"No heaven forbid, I shall accept my folly even though it be the greatest of them all."
"Yes," I said, "time will heal your wounds dear friend. We shall walk ever forward.
We shall not abandon or we shall be in for a horrible and fearful fall."
"You oaf," his mouth trembled in agony. "Who ever heard of a man walking backward."

Leo R Soine
THE SPARROW
You can see it fluttering most everywhere.
World-wide, it daintily hops in search of fare.
From East to West it chirps ever-merry
Gaily fluttering with spirits airy.

Wherever man is so this little creature is
A cocky little bird as if the world was his.
It's not popular with common man
And survives in most places man can.

In beautiful trees it seldom nests,
But loves to breed where man rests.
It sullies man's home with grassy aeries
With rags, paper and string it carries

It's fried and eaten in many a China city
But ever survives though never shown pity.
It sports no gay plumage and cannot sing
It's such a common feathered thing.

To all insects it is a foe,
Always hopping and fluttering low.
Man lost his fight to this strong creature;
Be not ashamed man: survival is its ultimate feature.

Leo R Soine
A MEETING IN A BAR
As he slowly shuffled along the street
He rapped his cane before his feet.
His ears were tuned to every rap
As he used his cane as a sort of map.

Soon he heard a distinctive sound;
His cane had rapped an iron post round.
In ten more steps he opened a door
And with faltering steps crossed the floor.

Five steps to his left was the long bar;
He walked against it with a sudden jar.
"Paco, Paco" and his voice was gay
"Where are you on this summer's day?"

Paco's stride was firm and sound
And entering the bar therein he found,
Pepe standing uneasy and waiting.
To Pepe Paco strode unhesitating,
"Pepe, my friend," he said with a yell,
"How many tickets did you sell?"

Pepe smiled and then he said,
"Enough to buy us good wine and bread."
Bound together, they stood without fear,
Then Pepe said, "The day is hot, let's have beer."

"Oiga," Paco shouted to the barman,
"Two beers please for two poor men."
"Pepe, lift my glass high so that I may drink;
It's right before you on the bar's brink."
Pepe raised the glass face high
And Paco swallowed it with a sated sigh.
Pepe's instinct found his galss
And he gulped it down in a flash.

Between the two, there was a strong bind,
Paco had lost his hands and Pepe was blind.
'Twas siesta time so home they went
Paco leading Pepe with elbow bent.

Kathy McQuillan
SNOW

To Mrs. DuBois, my third grade teacher.

Snow is light and bright;
It's beautiful at night;
I feel the drifts from the snow;
I'm shivering from head to toe;
My feet are cold my nose is blue;
I do not want to catch the flu!

Barbara Ann McNair
TWO OLD WOMEN WALKING

Two Old Women Leaving Home.

I wish that I could have met you, when sweet youth was young and tender.
I know that we could have been the best of friends —
Sharing all, making plans and keeping our secrets safe.

And yet, our worlds were so different, moving in a set direction.
I, a traveler, to the other side, and you —
Sought and conquered many worlds — in your fond romantic dreams.

Oh, the sun is setting, we have walked far.
Our memory grows dim and the fragile shells carrying us about,
Yearns now to slumber for a rest.

Pick up your pace! For I shall not leave thee, far behind.
And suddenly she turns, seeing the thoroughbred strive
And the sparkle of her eyes.

And for a moment she suddenly knew —
A taste of her youth had returned.
Shall we walk this way again, come soon tomorrow.

Barbara Ann McNair
THE WOODEN COAT
Nobody wears it very well —
And yet it is a major sell.
Nothing so special of its design —
Serving a purpose according to time.

Taking the journey to the end —
Quickly coming, slowly going, stopping when.
From every walk of life you will find —
A soul to wear it for an unlimited time.

Fashion it not unto my will —
The thought of it makes me ill.
Everyday throughout the seasons —
It is in use, it's got a reason.

Trouble me not, who can understand —
Claiming a cover for every man.
Although the earth so willingly receive —
The wooden coat worn eternally.

Barbara Ann McNair
WHEN A WISE MAN DREAMS
Consider the great bird soaring in the air —
A warrior of strength yet a beacon of peace.
He maneuvers freely the dominance of his time —
Plucked from existence by the arrow traveling,
Too fast into the heavens.

Watch the small seed bloom in the earth —
Slight chance to life see the great tree.
He grows fast in the elements surrounding his time —
Struck from the root by the cutting blade.
The tree grew too far into the heavens.

Charisma has the great stone in the earth bedded deep.
A prize of wealth and a flawless possession.
Praised upon the crown for all to see.
Crushed from its origin by the ruler of man.
The stone can share no glory too quickly into the heavens.

A message given and well received.
A purpose to gain a life to proceed.
A foolish notion indeed a failure of fault.
Consider it well when a wise man dreams.

Hayley C Heller
WHY ALL THE PAIN AND HURT
All the days long and short,
people fighting soon divorced.
Why does it have to be this way,
people crying, people hurt?
Why the pain we live today?

Tami Hastain
I'M WHO I AM BECAUSE OF YOU
By another I was given life, but then lovingly accepted by you—
You both chose to guide me, and see that my dreams would come true—

Your love for me began so blindly, while I was yet in my Mother's womb—
You already had three children, but for me you still found room—

The first moment you held me, your eyes filled with joyful tears—
From that instant on you raised me, and comforted all my deepest fears—

You taught me to live with morals, and the art of unconditional love—
Through these gifts I became your child, no less than if by flesh & blood—

There was not one moment in life, when I reached and you weren't there—
At times I questioned your discipline, but now understand the way you cared—

You showed me an infallible God, whose love brightly shined through you—
With your consistently perfect example, my faith in his presence grew—

I will forever be your daughter, but now also a mother to my own—
And everyday I pray I can guide them, in the wonderful way that I was shown—

So in the times when you feel proud, it's yourselves who should be praised—
If you had not become "Mom & Dad," I would not be who I am today—

Leah Head
THE OTHER WOMAN

To Vietnam Veterans Every Where, especially for Darrell.

Too, many children, women and men;
Suffering from, misunderstandings, marriages and divorces . . .
Each all alone . . . because of the "fight" . . .
To what can we blame much of this plight? . . .
Another, "woman," you say, well just maybe you're right.
"She," makes him remember, what he tries to forget;
Torments his mind with a limit not set;
"She," feeds him with guilt and bathes him with sweat,

Taking his heart, body and soul, back to where it all started; the place where they met.
"She," makes him silent, moody and "numb,"
Makes him lack his emotions and feelings, made him what he's become;
"She's," like a drug that runs through his veins, makes his Adrenalin flow, like the sea after long Monsoon Rains.
Even times when he's with you, "She's," lurking about;
In the jungle, the bush, or maybe a Hill: Where he learned that to live was also to kill . . .
"Just leave Her," we say, "put Her in the past, come to terms with yourself, be free at last,"
God, how he prays, that so easy it was, his inner torments to calm, to leave "Her," forever back where "She," belongs;
But this, "Woman," this place, this Hell;
"She's," known all too well by the name "Vietnam."

Stephan Hundley
UNTITLED
Time
Passing through life
Always leading
Constantly bleeding
Pushing forward
Yet falling back.

Life
Passing through time
The living hell
Shines like a bell
No one can stay long
The wind carries on.

Space
A state of mind
The wondering, the wanting
It's always haunting
Heaven is above
Just out of reach
But then . . . where is love?

Sharon B Hambrick
EMPTY HOUSE
The house seemed big and empty
although it was small in size.
No more young laughter echoed
from either gals or guys.

The vacancy had put a strain
on dear ol' mom and dad.
What seemed would last forever
left like a passing fad.

All the familiar routines
was sadly put on hold.
Then the house did flip-flops,
when certain news was told.

All attention gladly swelled
to everwhelming joy . . .
What would the house welcome,
a grand-baby girl or boy?

Bradley T Harrington
DREAMS
The moonbeams whisper to me in my sleep
Come to us, they call, and trek through the deep
Of the starry heavens on the edge of your sight
To behold the mysteries awaiting your flight
To learn things anew, floating amongst the stars
Glinting like jewels, they beckon from afar
My mind starts to stir in the midst of my dreams
My thoughts coalesce, the star field teems
I rise and float and the world drops away
Time slows to a halt, there's no more today
I lift into the blaze, and start to ponder
Like a mote caught in a ray, I can't help but wonder
Where we fit into this vast scheme
Of the Universe at large, it's not just a dream
There's more than we know out there in the reaches
Just waiting for us, like sand on the beaches
Someyear we will go, to explore and search
Like a bird taking to wing, and leaving its perch

R B Hubbard
WALL OF TEARS
Dear Father of all, I pray in your name,
The guilt is mine, my son has no blame.
The sin from my past was struck too deep,
And too long has plagued me at night, in my sleep.
When we finally acknowledged those who fought, and who died,
They came back, all too clearly:
Those memories . . .
I cried . . .
So many who were friends of mine.
A few who made us toe-the-line.
The one who forced me to take a stand:
The sly one; who died at my own hand.
He was no hero, but he's just as dead,
A victim of evil that twisted his head.
Let not my son bear any chain I have wrought.
Grant him the redemption which I have sought.
Your Grace is within me and helps me to know
That he will reap beyond what I did sow.
In that placed called
VietNam,
so long, ago.

Sdh (Susan Hallman)
CALL ME ALONE
Am I destined to walk through the dark gates of life alone,
Not a soul to guide me as I travel onward?
Always searching for the inner peace,
That brings the much needed tranquility to sleepless nights.

Am I ever to know my heart's flutter of loving someone,
As well as being loved by them?
Longing to know of the security and passion,
Of being held for love's sake in another's arms.

Is there something in me that others see,
And want to shy away from?
Never getting to know ME,
Nor trying to see into me, but always instead, through me.

What can be done to save me from this dark loneliness called . . .
myself?

Charity Hawley
CANVAS
Just as the sun gives the trees life and hue,
Like a paintbrush, you bring color and brightness
With just a stroke of the hand, painting beauty
On a bare canvas. The canvas of my heart has
Never before held so many colors.
The canvas
Shows colors of love: green grassy meadows,
Crystal blue streams, and red roses.
These are
The hues of my dreams, yet they don't seem like
Dreams. The canvas was yours to start but
Still mine, too. Then you painted beauty into
It and signed your name to it. It is yours
Forever. My heart, like the canvas, is yours
Forever . . .
With all the colors you put into it.

Linda Haynes
MY HUSBAND, MY LOVE, MY LIFE
My husband, my love, my life
I live to be your wife
For better, worse, rich or poor
You I'll always adore
Let our love be set free
To each other; you and me
Throughout the years
There will be many tears
Yet there will be many smiles
There will also be many trials
For each step we take
Our hearts at times will ache
For the wrong we've done
But let us not shun
Let's look at each other
Saying I love you is no bother
'Cause you'll always be
My husband, my love, my life
And I'll always be your wife

Valerie Anne Hayes
PLAYTIME
One day when I had lost my way
I saw some children hard at play.
I waved to them and they waved back
Then I wandered over to have a chat.

Two little girls and boys at play
On such a lovely summer's day,
I told them that I'd lost my way—
They only laughed "com-on-let's play."

The little girl with golden hair
Put out her hand and asked me where
I'd been going on this lovely day
And why I'd gone and lost my way?

Then, the little brown-eyed boy
Who seemed at first—a little coy,
Smiled one lovely smile of joy
And handed me his favourite toy.

It was upon that lovely summer's day
I realized there and then I'd say,
What I'd been doing wrong and pray . . .
These children taught me how to find my way.

David L Huck
THE EVERGREEN
Evergreen trees swaying
In the light breeze of the day
Going this way
And everyway
Feeling the breeze of autumn
And the soft heat of the day.

Christine Juszczak
A WORLD WITHOUT YOU
The Leaves Are Green, The Grass Is Blue
What Can I Say But I Love You
Flowers Unfold With Beauty And Grace
Like The Smile I See Inscribed On Your Face
Every Time My World Seems Blue
All I Have To Do Is Look At You
Then I Go And Wonder Through And Through
What In The World Would I Do Without You.

Christine Juszczak
WHY?
Why Does This Only Happen To Me?
Why Does The Sun Shine Darkness In My Room?
Why Does This Only Happen To Me?
Why Does The Light Lead Me To My Doom?
Why?

Why Does This Only Happen To Me?
Why Does Hope Fade Away Like A Cool Summer Night's Dream?
Why Does This Only Happen To Me?
Why Does The Door Stay Locked From All That Is Seen?
Why?

Virginia Knight
CHRISTMAS TREE RANCH
It's Christmas time all the year 'round
At a little ranch by the side of the road,
Good cheer abides by its happy hearthside
With no thoughts of life's heavy load.

The bright, smiling lights shine gaily each night,
Friendship's beckoning hand . . .
The spirit of love fills the air all the time
Oh, would it could spread o'er the land.

A little ranch by the side of the road
Has found what the Master taught . . .
Seek ye first the Kingdom of Heaven . . . within,
And it cannot be bought.

Each light on the tree is a light for a friend
And oh! how the lights grow and grow . . .
May we be worthy to light on that tree
With its warm, happy, inner glow.

Away down the road, like a beacon at night,
You can feel the warmth of this tree . . .
Its friendship and love, with the North Star above,
Sink deep in the heart of thee.

Keith Robert Chigbrow
MY FRIEND
My friend, how long has it been
the time, since first we met
one year, so long ago
how joyous, we yet are friends

My friend, how long, has it been

We have, travelled many roads
together, yet apart
each hour, a step in time
each knowing, of the other
We have, travelled, many roads

How long, our quest for living
each seeking, life's own way
yes friend, life has been good
the years came, and they have went
How long, our quest, for living

Friendship, like ours has been blessed
to last, these many years
and with time, grew stronger yet
yes friend, it's life we share
Friendship, like ours, has been
blessed

Emmanuel Efiong
THE FACE OF AN ANGRY CREATION

This poem is dedicated to my family and friends, especially my father, Mark Asukwo (late), my mom, Petronila, and my uncle, Dr. Africanus A. B. Okokon.

Trembling upon its length and width,
The angry creation's face.
The god of the sea so wild with anger
Unveiling its look, hard to appease;
And smoky clouds of heavens
descending to kiss its angry lips.
O terror, thou art clamping me down
As if I were to be a victim
Of this dreadful scene.

Edna L Renner
CHRISTMAS LOVE

Dedicated to all future Christmases.

It's in the air
Around, around everywhere
Shimmering in a starlit sky.

Shining from a child's eye,
Caressing each and every smile
Lingering there awhile.

Gently nudging each heart
With joy to impart
In the serenity of carol singing.

The hush call of church bell ringing
The feathering touch of merriment
Silently hugging lush contentment.

Fluttering softly, dreaming you know
Its showering seed will take root and
grow
Oh, yes, yes, it's in the air.

Around, Around everywhere
Sent down from on High Above
Once again His Christmas Love.

Joyce L Ingram
'CAINE

She masquerades as a snow-white
lady
and her sensuous call
is a sirensong that no man can resist.
Her touch is the sweetest fire
that ever gods denied us,
and she burns me in her white/hot
flame—
I wonder, "Is this some now love?"
"Is this a form of worship too
secret to enscribe?"
Or have I become obsession with
sweet vanilla candy.
And through my wondering
'Caine whispers softly in my ear,
like a poisoning lover she smiles
beautiful white lies
"I love you—I love you—I love
you,"
And I swallow nectared hemlock
full with delicious passion.
Her song lullabies me to my grave.

Audrey Babcock
FREEDOM

To freedom, which is not just a word but a priceless volume of humanitarian dos and don'ts.

Caged; Caged;
Pacing the perimeters
Batting at the bars
Growling at the gates
Roaring. Silently ROARING.
Building . . .
Earthquake tremors shaking the
mane;
Epicentered in the brain.
Where? the One who keeps the door?
Where? The ones who keep the
doors?
Not our chosen lair, this unnatural
prison.
Does Even One know or care that we
suffer derision?
Tethered to zooism. Always feeling
the yank
And the crack of the whip on
shoulder and flank
BuilDING . . .
ZOO: Lion in cages, kittens in chains
Maybe robotic figures when
thoroughly trained
Don't rock the boat is all they explain
And that explanation resounds
through the brain.
BUILDING . . . until
Breaking the framework they pushed
through the doors,
Breaking the walls round the
paced-out floors.
Breaking with strictures they had
come to deplore,
They destroyed the zoo, becoming
people that roar.
Some, contrite and humble,
imploring in mind.
To eat and to drink of Thee, good
Bread and Wine.

Carol Anita Reed
MAINE

The water so blue and the thick
forests so green
make the vast State of Maine a
most beautiful scene!
The town folks so plain, the
mountains which reign,
and deep snow in winter, the
oft chilly rain
and bright sunshine in summer
are all part of Maine!
Untouched by man's worry, and
unfrayed by his hurry,
here nature runs free, as do the
bird and the bee!
And it is spread out for all eyes
to see!
The beauty of Maine spells magic
to me!

Norman H Walker
I CHOSE KURT
(Ephesians 1:4,8)

I chose you Kurt millions of years
ago.
Before time, long before the stars and
moon gave their light.
In my all knowing all perceiving
mind.
I arranged for you to come in latter
day times.

In a day when the Sun and Moon
would give its Heavenly Light.
And in a World where rainbows
would shine.
And in a world that has stood the
ravages of time.
And the spirit of God's Grace was
seeking to make man divine.

I gave you a father and mother that
had wisdom and a Spirit Divine.
For you to bless their home and make
the Glory of Heaven upon them
shine.
For home is a part of life that makes
our lives Divine.
As it makes an opportunity for your
life to be sublime.

It will take some time for you to find
out, that in the world there is stormy
weather.
Yet the two you have to guide you on
your way, will continue to bless you
and give their love to you each day.
Yet you may wonder why to this
world I came, but you were
predestined millions of years ago.
So when you are older read the Book
of Books, and make note of what
Jesus to Nicademus said, and the road
to where the path of Glory lead!
Also take note for the one who is
writing this to you today.
Is your Great Grandfather who is old
and grey.
Again to remind that you were
predestinated in Clouds of Glory
thousands of light years away.
So when your life is over let's hope
that in Eternity you will be, for
there's where Jesus gave you the
option to be.

Rose Scoppettuolo and Cynthia Foster

Cynthia Foster
MOTHER

I dedicate this poem to my Mother Rose Scoppettuolo who meant the world to me. Thanks for always being there for me and teaching me everything. I Love You. 1934-1990

What my mother means to me is
More than she could ever see
My mother's love is precious and
dear
And I will cherish it year to year
My Mother's love is the greatest
thing
For with her love I could do
anything
My mother doesn't always get
recognized as she should
But she would always do for me
Whatever she could
Mom we would like you to know
Just how much we love you so
We would like to thank you
for all you've done
And being our mother makes you
#1
We Love You

Susan, Steve, Anthony,
Cindy, Janet and John

Richard D Cagg
THEBE C

To my loving wife—Donna Willene Cagg.

My darling precious Thebe C
May your passionate love for me
Never forsake nor leave thee
May those shining stars in your eyes
Forever light time's fireflies
As they light upon my heart's string
And a harmony to my soul sing
Bringing to my face a glow
That heaven's beams might flow
Bathing me with the portals of glory
Telling me an eternal story
Coming to me from that song
That to only my creator could belong
For you are mine and I am thine
Thebe C—To me you shine

Joshua Case
WHAT IS BLUE?

To my mother.

What is Blue?
Blue is the ocean,
So big and beautiful.
Blue is the sky,
So high and bright.
Blue makes me feel very cold.
Blue is a fish,
Free and peaceful.
Blue is a blue bird's,
Flight in the sky.
Blue is the blue,
on the United States Flag.

Blanche McCauley Hallett
LOWER MOUNTAIN ROAD

Hemmed in by greenness from the
whispering trees,
Cooled by shadows and a wayward
breeze,
The mountain road, not very wide,
Had little thought, could not decide
Which way to go.
So merrily he climbed a hill,
Went down again, and down until
He had to turn around to see
Just where the end of him might be;
Then thru a quiet spot where deer
Had sole possession, no one near;
And where ferns, whole congrega-
tions,
Danced a dance of jubilation;
And blackberry bushes, blossoms
blowing,
Gave invitations for future showing,
To where a church all chastely white,
Stood quietly in holy light;
Then where the past in retrospection,
Stood saddened by our recollection,
To hills, our past, our present, our
forever,
In circled guardianship
That never
Changes.

Laurie Hepworth
WANNA BE

Wanna be a dancer
Wanna be a singer
Wanna be a mother
Wanna be a homeowner
Wanna be a writer
Wanna be a poet
Wanna be a photographer

Wanna be a drummer
Wanna be an executive
Wanna be an actress
Wanna be a video DJ
Wanna be a radio DJ
Wanna be me

Cynthia A Bulger
TRUE FRIEND

This poem is dedicated to my loving husband, Mathew and my two beautiful sons, Richard and Jason Cooper. Thank you for your support and understanding.

Life comes but once to us
so to listen is a must,

Life is full of sorrow and pain
and not to care would be nothing to gain,

Living is to share the heart
and with that we become smart,

So to take the time to listen to a friend
truthfully makes living better than the end.

Aerok Pierce
DRUID'S PRAYER
Leaf
Teach me your
Sensitivity
That I may feel pain
Thus love
That I may be hurt
Thus heal
That I may grow old
And die
And may the Wind
Lay me down
Beside tranquil Waters
Amen

Cheryl Switzer Treat
CHRISTMAS WISH TO A SPECIAL FRIEND

My Christmas wish would have been to walk thru your woods in person, rather than in the daydream of my mind.

To hear the crunching of snow and twigs beneath my feet as I'd follow the path made by the deer in the fresh fallen snow — But instead, I trudge through the slush of the village streets.

To sit, so very still, and watch the wildlife search for food or shelter before dusk turns to darkness — But instead, I sit in the car at a stoplight, and watch people gaze into store windows, searching for the perfect gift, to be given only one day a year.

To have the snow-covered boughs of Hemlock surround me with their serenity and beauty — But instead, I'm surrounded with falsehood of good cheer, and what is fashionable style; for beauty.

To have nature's light filter thru the trees to touch me, adding a little warmth to the brisk air — But instead, the glare of the artificial lights and tinsel, instill the coldness of not only my person, but soul.

To stoop and hold my hand in the cold, but still flowing stream, avoiding the rounded edges of ice that has formed along its banks — But instead, I avoid the black ice on the road.

To sit in your moonlit woods, with some of the snowflakes caressing my face, as the rest drift to the forest floor — But instead, I light the candles in the windows, and watch the snow drift on the road in front of the house.

To kneel, even next to a fallen log, to say prayers for peace and forgiveness of my sins — But instead, I enter an ornate building and humble myself upon a man made altar.

To walk thru your woods, was my Christmas wish — But instead, I hold the daydream of it in my mind.

Cheryl Switzer Treat
A SPECIAL PLACE

As I stand at the window, watching the Cardinal and Blue Jay gather food, I think once again of your woods.

Even though I was there a short time, I found tranquility among the Hemlock trees and the smell of decaying leaves. The moss, mushrooms and the scattered red berry plants brought color to the dimness of the forest floor.

I sat upon a fallen log across a stream, and watched the water flow. It seemed to be so carefree, yet moving toward a destination, rippling over objects beneath its surface. You had mentioned that the water was polluted. But the stream moved on searching for something greater, even to making new paths to reach its goal, unaware that its molecules were contaminated.

The trees rustled their leaves above me, as if understanding the loneliness I was feeling. For they had grown to stand on their own, against the elements, to protect the living things beneath them. Some of their leaves were beginning to drift to the ground. This saddened me for a moment, but knew that new life would form during the harshness of winter, and would come forth with the spring sun. With this a new cycle of life would begin.

I knew that all around me, though silently at the moment, the struggle for survival existed. And I wondered why I couldn't manage the same calmness and acceptance of life that took place in your woods.

As I approached the edge of the woods, toward the fresh mowed grass, something strong was tugging inside me to look back. And when I did, I felt a moment of serenity and peace. I seemed to understand that I would be granted acceptance with time, as long as there were special places to go — like your woods.

Vivian E Nelson
WELCOME! SPRING

To my late husband Enoch Nelson, to my daughter Sharon, granddaughter Amy, and great-granddaughter Ashlea.

Oh spring! Beautiful spring!
You have arrived at last!
The winter has been so long and dreary,
But now the cold is past.

"Hope springs eternal in the human breast,"
Has been written by poets of old;
That hope now flows in each one's heart
As thy beauties, O spring, unfold.

So welcome, sweet spring, beautiful spring!
With showers and warming sun;
We will enjoy the gifts you bring—
Yes, we'll enjoy them everyone.

Vivian E Nelson
HERE I COME AGAIN, LORD
Here I come again, Lord.
Seems I'll never learn
To draw from you the patience
For which I so much yearn.
Remember, I came yesterday
And knelt in deep contrition,
And was, oh so thankful
That You heard my petition.
I thought I had the victory
Over self and worldly care;
But here I am again, Lord,
To ask You, "Hear my prayer."
This time I believe I know
That victory will be mine,
'Cause I asked in faith believing,
And Your peace I know I'll find.

Vivian E Nelson
BE STILL MY HEART
O troubled heart be still;
I know thy every care.
Have I not promised in My Word
That I, thy burdens would share?

O restless heart, be still
And know that I am God!
In the very center of My Will
Is oft the chastening rod.

O burdened heart, be still!
That burden is from Me
To bring the lost and dying
To the cross of Calvary.

O aching heart, be still!
The storm will some day cease,
The clouds roll back and you'll behold
My Kingdom of love and peace.

Vivian E Nelson
DAY IS DAWNING
Day is dawning . . . bright and clear:
God is with us . . . God is near.
Dewdrops glisten . . . on flowers fair:
Hearts must listen . . . bowed in prayer.
For this day . . . Lord, we pray
Make us thy channels . . . now and alway!

Cullen Nicholls
love blinds
love blinds.
many see it either
one way, or another.
but, it is, unfortunately, often forgotten;
notallis
as
i tap pears.

Etta Netherton Jeserski
A LUSH GREEN GLOBE MADE DECADES AGO

To my beloved daughter Jessica and husband David, whom I feel lucky to have with me, and to all the homeless children, may you find the understanding, help and a loving home that you have long been denied.

A lush green globe made decades ago,
how it and our existence came about,
No one is quite sure or knows.

It has been said, Human were meant to rule.
Someone ponders this, looking upon what was once an eden,
now an oil spill pool.

Innocence lost in the faces of homeless children,
A sorrowful wail for the white seals and dolphins . . . goodby.
Who will take care of them?;
except you and I.

Special People, Special Creatures, Special Places,
in danger of losing their identity and existence;
While I abide in my perfect uburban home,
decorated to spare no expense.

It is a sign of hope though, that this cry of sorrow makes my
own happiness hard to enjoy.

Etta Netherton Jeserski
OUR CHOICES, OUR REGRETS

To The Late, Barbara Stanwick.

It's your life, and in it comes a time when you reach adulthood. Along the way, you must make choices, experience regrets. No doubt you like to relive some of those times if you could.

A child has a favorite toy, he sleeps with every night. It is this companion he seeks for reassurance from fright.

A teenager chooses an idol, most likely a music star. The young executive plans someday to own a duplicate of the boss's foreign sports car.

It's your choice, "Nothing is impossible, it's the American Dream." After all it's America, it's our right, this the Constitution deems.

Most of us remember our first kiss, or the birth of our first child, an experience you never forget.

We protect ourselves sometimes by not recalling a past event. We've seen good times come and later we wonder where they went.

Perhaps, we console ourselves, if I'd have done it this way instead. Is it fate, or do we lie in our self made bed?

I still ponder if it was my own busy life or made by choice. I never expressed my love for, "Christmas In Connecticut."

My regret, my admiration to pen and paper I never did voice. It's too late now, no if's, and's or but.

Or is it?

Etta Netherton Jeserski
THE TRAIL OF TEARS CONTINUES

To Grandma Rose and her people.

It was once their land, and they were free to roam. Some still live on reservations, unable even now to escape the white man's invisible dome.

Many say other races have suffered also the shame, these heritages and races have survived and multiplied just the same.

The real people as they once called themselves, have not been so lucky, for they have dwindled down to a small amount,
What is left of their beliefs from ancestors probably sit idle somewhere on an old woman's shelf.

Once the elders of a tribe passed on with grace and pride, I wonder if anyone mourns when another link to the past has died.

While their teenage suicide rate is sadly unbearable, Social daughters complain, they haven't a cotillion dress wearable.

The drums once beat a sad but beautiful song, when do we plan to right what our government has so long ago, wronged.

Every day I read of racial issues at bay, Deliberately escalated hatred; does our world really have to be this way?

There is a holiday or recognition on our calendars to celebrate almost every race and religion,
Never have I heard one be proclaimed for the true American,
...... The American Indian.

P R Hall
THE QUESTION
Are you that special someone I've been seeking
Are you that dream I've been having
Are you that fantasy I've carried around all these years
Are you the one I thought I would never meet?
Are you the one who will last a lifetime?
Are you the one?
Are you?

P R Hall
OPEN BOOK
When we met I was willing to give you what no one has ever asked for...

The essence of me.

My dedication

I surrendered it unconditionally, unselfishly, without hesitation.

My introduction

My truth was finally recognized and appreciated.
My heart was never in jeopardy.

Subsequent chapters

My dreams were unleashed and reborn.
My soul delighted in the joy you gave me.
My life was paved with a bed of roses that
You selectively picked from your very own garden.

My epilogue

Now, I am an open book, one that I hope you will continue to read, study and never forget.

P R Hall
WITH YOU
When I'm with you, I can soar like an eagle.
When I'm with you, if it rains you will provide the sunshine.
When I'm with you, your face rests on me like dew on a rose.
When I'm with you, the little girl in me goes out to play.

When I'm with you, I rest calmly a sheep with her shepherd.
When I'm with you, I blossom like flowers in a field.
When I'm with you, I am void of pain sorrow and regrets.
When I'm with you, I live, I laugh, I love
Only when I'm with you.

Patsy Kurrelmeyer
WALKING IS BEAUTIFUL
Walking along there, is a dream.
The beauty and wonder of God's skill
Makes the eyes of mortals beam.
As we see the glories of divine will.
I see the fjords of branches in the trees of Norway.
The peppermint, refreshing, snow caresses
My cheek, as I stroll through the white, carpeted, doorway.
The winter wonderland, my soul and
heart addresses.
There is no season as peaceful as the warm snow
Settling quietly, gently, cheerfully, on the cedars and pines.
Pure, bright, luscious, making rosy cheeks glow.
The escort of trees, with me along the road, winds.
Mountains, the Alps of the German—Swiss—nestle the log cabin.
And the yodeling wind, skips and dances in the trees.
Swirling flakes silently bounce
and I have in My mind's eye,
drifts to places faraway—dreams carried in
a breeze.
Holland's windmills are the trees, tulips are the rows
Of fence posts, and waterfalls of snow heaps.
And China's soaring peaks of Sinkiang, sweeps.
The sleeping earth nurses under the windsong blows.
New Zealand meadows in the breathtaking highlands
Sparkling under the broad, wide, river of clouds.
Thank you Jehovah, for the inspiration of this, my land.
The ball gown of snow on the needles, a painting enshrouds.
I am walking on my home road, all of this in Pinecreek, Idaho.
Which bears the mark of many places I will see someday.
Why so many people ignore the sky and trees, I don't know.
Foreign lands are here, in Idaho, on the road my way.

JoAnn Baxter
COMPASSION

To my dear friend Kim, for whom this poem was written.

In this world of ups and downs
Some fall along the way.
A helping hand, a soft kind word,
Can help them through the day
Compassion is a sharing, caring,
Sense of understanding.
A place to feel a sense of self,
Where no one is demanding.

Compassion fuels the inner self,
That makes the flower grow.
The world becomes a better place,
For you and those you show.

Go through each day and share yourself,
With feelings from the heart.
When you close your eyes each night,
You'll know you've done your part.

Angela Wuthrich
ETERNITY
Forever and ever and ever more,
Life goes on,
If you knew the Lord.

You reached outer space,
You flew so high,
You found that place

In the sky.
Where the sun shines brighter,
The moonbeams are wider.

My friend found that place,
When I closed the casket door,
Forever and ever and ever more.

Rachel Marzuk
ONCE AGAIN
I'm writing this because I care
From all my heart with you to share
I'm telling you this once again
I really love you and I'll always care
Baby I'm asking you again
Please come back to me if for me you care

Misti Beckham
PRAISE OF LOVE
Love grows to blossom
and sprout a new seed,
a seed to grow in any
surrounding.

But a flower grows
to be a pretty—yet a
thoughtless soul of beauty,
to spread lifeless care,

to a world of admirers
with no heart of
sensitivity and no
mind of control!

Marcia Adele Jackson
ENDLESSLY

To Roger.

Endlessly,
as surely as I breathe.
I spend the time,
believing in you.
And with my thought,
the liberty is gained.
Because for you,
I will set myself free.

Edward Paul Balboni
ROAD PIZZA
Waiting
For a chance to cross
The river where mom's life was lost.

Standing
There upon the bank
My younger sister by my flank.

Looking
Slowly left to right
The enemy was not in sight.

Hoping
By some chance that I
Would make it to the other side.

Running
Faster than the wind
Just then it came around the bend.

Turning
Back it was too late
You can't avoid what is your fate.

Dying
As my sister cried
Alas, the river was too wide.

Edward Paul Balboni
FOUR SEVEN

Dedication to 'Four Seven': We love you Mom. Ed, Paul, Tina and Becky.

Amazing, how in retrospect,
You kept your pride and self-respect.
Where others seem to try and fail,
Somehow you strove and did prevail.
I'm sure that somewhere you were taught,
That you must pay for what you've bought.
But one thing you have yet to learn,
The love you give will soon return.

Sometimes, though it don't seem right,
Some clouds will come and block the light.
The storms will come, but don't you know,
That without rain you cannot grow.
So keep the faith, the sun's still there,
Letting others grow somewhere.
Soon it will come bursting through,
Like the love I have for you!

Janeice A Jaynes
ONE LESS DAY
As I stare into the sky,
I feel my heart begin to cry.

The stars above are all so bright,
They light the sky all through the night.

I hear the crickets sing their song,
They're telling me it won't be long.

The wolves are howling at the moon,
They don't want morning to come so soon.

For soon the rooster's voice will crow,
The light across the sky will grow.

So now another day's gone by,
As I stare into the sky.

I guess what I would like to say,
is I now have just one last day.

One less day to hear your voice,
One less day, but not by choice.

Linda C Jacobs
WALK ON THE BEACH

This poem is dedicated to my friend, my husband... Doug.

We walk on the beach stopping to pick up shells, sand dollars —

We talk... eagerly speaking the thoughts and innermost feelings stored inside thru days of work, schedules, responsibilities —

We stop... look out over the ocean —
At one with each other —
Husband and wife, lover and friend —

In tune with each other, only the soft roll of the waves to accompany us —
We stroll —

Cherishing our time, so
precious —
Away from the world —
By the sea.

Jomarie Campofiore Johnson
MOTHER

To My Mother Julia Campofiore, My husband David, My sister Julia Kulish, my family, and friends.

Mother I look at you and realize how much you have grown old,
I see sorrow in your eyes, the past has taken its toll.
You are a woman of self greed, I never could understand,
I was always my father's seed, your love-hate passion for this man.
Many silent tears I weep as the years pass quickly by,
What is the real reason you keep such torment, and pain inside?
How I begged you for some guidance, a touch of motherly love,
Maybe a few words of kindness, the kind children think of.
Yet you've molded me into a person of strength much wiser for my years,
And educated me in independence because you were never there.
As an adult I theorize what life was like for you,
For the bad twist of fate must have been negative, hard, and cruel.
Mother it is time we both look ahead, and give history a rest,
For life does come in positive form when gambling for the best.

Bonnie R Jussila
AS LONG AS I HAVE YOU

To my husband, Charles, on our eleventh anniversary.

Our years together that we have spent
The good times and bad, that have come and went
With you by my side, I look forward to each day
Our hopes and dreams don't seem so far away
It started rough and was an uphill climb
But you said we'd make it, and to just give it time
I want you to know that all we've been through
I'd do it all again, as long as I have you.

Mary Ruth Edwards Jones
AMERICA, BETTER OR WORSE?

Thanks to God first, then to all the veterans who have fought to keep America free!

Every time I look around, I think back to why America came to be,
People from different nations, just crying to be free,
Our nation was founded on that great hope, our ancestors came to see,
Their dreams to have life, hope, justice and liberty.

With their eyes and hearts turned toward God, our forefathers knew,
What must lie ahead, and the things that they must do,
They wrote our Declaration, the Constitution and our Bill of Rights, too,
But little did they realize, what America would come to.

In our modern generations, we think we've grown so smart,
Just take a look around us, we must have missed the mark,
Our children are so precious, why have we not heard their cries?
Why are they so mistreated, how many are to die?

Our nation is in trouble, just look at what has taken place,
Our sister nations laugh at us, our country has been disgraced.
Our nation's leaders need us now, they need our Christian prayers,
For America is slowly being defeated with drugs, alcohol and sex,
If we don't put our trust and faith back to God,
Tell me, who else cares?

Hazel H Johnston
O LORD I PRAY

Give me strength O Lord this day
To do thy work and mine.
And give me patience when some times
I must wait in line.

Give me Faith each morning and night
I know my GOD will always guide me right.
Help me to trust others along my way
Help me to be more loving O Lord I pray.

I must trust in Jesus whenever I roam
I know he will surely guide me home.
Jesus loves me this I know
And my love for him I will surely show.

There are parents and friends we hope to meet again,
And if we put our trust in Jesus
It will never be in vain.
God is the way, the Truth, the Light
And if I trust Him enough, have Faith enough,
and wait long enough,
everything will turn out alright.

Amy L Jensen
DEPRESSION

To all of those who have been depressed, may this be an inspiration for the future.

Depression is not what it seems to be,
Sometimes you feel closed in and sometimes free.
It's like a disease, illness, or fear,
And often starts with one little tear.
You feel like the world is closing in,
It hurts to give a tiny grin.
Because you feel all alone,
It's mostly kept in and never shown.
Other people may think it's stupid and it's just an act,
But depression is real and that's a fact.
When it seems like there's no one who will care,
Talk to someone you know who's already been there.
If you think you're not like all the rest,
Give life a chance and give it your best!

Nancy J Harris
ENCHANTMENT

This poem is lovingly dedicated to my husband John, my sister Charlene, and my mother Rachel, for all their help and support in my writing.

It is a midsummer's night,
And the winds softly blow,
With the moon full and bright
Bewitching the earth below.

It is not a night to be alone,
With only memories to touch—
For moonlight can be haunting,
Breeding longings, desires and such.

Many nights like this I've seen,
That brings back the haunting hours
Of guilts and hopes and dreams,
Brought forth by unseen powers.

And with the air as cool and sweet
As on this enchanted night,
Heightened senses reach their peak,
Freeing the spirit to go in flight.

So beautiful and yet foreboding,
Enchanting, yet still hauntingly,
As moonlight puts the final coating
To the night's majestic harmony.

George K Holliman
WHAT IS A LADY

I dedicate these poems to Eddie-Lou Cole. She believes in me. Thru her eyes I see a pinpoint of light.

What is a lady—the opposite sex
With feelings and thoughts she protects
What is man—the other half the plan
And he tries all his life to understand
What is a lady?
She is a creation of beauty
With a strong devotion to duty
She is a source of sorrow
— a source of bewilderment
— a source of joy
and the only inspiration to this boy
She keeps me guessing, thinking
And sometimes drinking
I only get up each day—
To try to figure her way
What would life be—
Without this mystery
What is a Lady?

Jane Harrison
LONELY

To Jimmy, for always believing in me.

Lonely is sitting in a warm room all alone, watching happily married familes on T.V.
Lonely is walking in the sunshine, wishing you were with someone special.
Lonely is going to bed at night with, only a pillow to hug.
Lonely is washing someone else's clothes knowing you may never see them worn.
Lonely is looking at the clock, ticking
so slowly, realizing that the time you are waiting on will never come.
Lonely is sitting at home, watching the phone and waiting but, know it will never ring.
Lonely is having to put a coat on to be warm while looking at the moon and stars in the sky, just wishing
for someone
to be yours.
Someone to hold and love, mostly someone to love you.
Lonely is . . . Me
Wanting to be special.

Vanessa D Howard
FAR APART, BUT BY MY HEART

As we say our long good–byes
We promise that there will be no lies,
"Next time I promise to never go."
I hide my tears so they wouldn't show.
He holds me as his ride appears.
He holds my hand and wipes my tears.
"I'm really lucky that you're my friend
Time will pass, but there will be no end.
But I will send my love to you.
Wrapped with care. That's what I'll do."
We hug real quick and start to let go,
But hold on and let go slow.
"Goodbye," I said, "it's you I'll miss!"
And as he vanished, I thought with bliss—
"Time may pass as we're far apart,
But he gave me a picture I'll keep by my heart."

Almira Huntsucker

Almira Huntsucker
OUR BABY

As I hold you close, My Little One,
I know from heaven you have come.
I know that God gave you to us,
For of heaven He said, "There is such."

We shall try to rear you right,
So you can walk in the Light
Of His Steps, who once was here,
And He was to his mother so clear.

As I look at your eyes so blue,
You are indeed a dream come true.

And as I hold you in my arms,
I want to shield you from all harms.

So sleep away, My Little One,
And dream of days and years to come,
When from us you will in time grow,
And out in the world you will go.

Travis E Johnston
JUSTICE?
We fight for justice, our justice,
no others can keep the peace.
We stand alone to defend our pride
together we defeat the beast.

Understanding, we are to some point of view;
but to all we do not agree.
Some force our anger to its very limitation,
and pain and suffering is their fee.

To us, we abide the laws of the land,
that seem most stupid in our eyes.
For the justice of the land is untrustworthy;
it says it helps, but it lies!

We stand together as all for one;
we raise our flag in glory.
It waves in red, in white, and blue
as shown in histories of story.

Rebel yells cry out in victory,
the battle of truth is won for some.
But to others out there, yes, the battle's won,
and the war has just begun.

Denise R Jones
I WONDER
I wonder what my life would be, if I had done things differently.
I wonder if I hadn't stayed,
I wonder what I'd do today.
How would I look,
What would I be,
Someone for me.
I wonder if there is true love,
Love at first sight,
Or hearts in flight.
I wonder why I wonder so,
I wonder why I want to know.

Claudia Renée Jones
SIMPLY WAIT

This poem is dedicated to my Brother, Bobby. Be patient your love will come soon.

When will I learn about life?
"Simply Wait"
When will the sun set?
"Simply Wait"
When will the moon rise and
the stars come out?
"Simply Wait"
When will I learn about love?
"Simply Wait"
When will you tell me the answers
To my questions?
I know, I know,
"Simply Wait"

Tina A Johnson
A KID'S WAY

Dedicated to my 3 beautiful children, Rheanne, Ben and Kandi. Also to all those mothers who sometimes feel like kids just don't care. They do care, they really do.

Why must I fuss and scream?
To make you children understand what I mean.
You always want more, more, more.
Always wanting to go to the store.
But yet when I ask you to dust.
You look at me with disgust.
I say go clean your room.
And don't forget the broom.
You yell mom do I have to?
I yell back yes you do.
But you always ask what does this pay?
Well children sit down and listen to what I say!!
Who do you think paid me for taking care of you when you were a baby?
I bet you thought your daddy, maybe.
No, and who do you think paid me for all the baths I gave you?
You say, "Ah mom that's what you're supposed to do."
Who paid me for scraped knees and all those tears?
Who gave you enough love to last throughout the years?
I hug you and I say;
I was paid in all those hugs & kisses because that's a kid's way.
But remember someday when your kids say more, more, more,
And all they want is to run to the store.
Then repeat all I say.
Remember . . . just remember nothing is sweeter than being repaid in a kid's way!!!

Melanie Jordan
ARE YOU GONE?
You won't be home tonight.
I won't wake with you in the morning.
Your touch is still so new to me,
not yet fading into my dark, surreal past.
I can still physically recall our last kiss,
and feel the same excitement as if I had just this
moment brushed my hand across the flat curve of your hip.
The memory hasn't yet become a shadow
lingering in the ruins of past lives.
Crowding out our intimacy
with its cold distant breath.
The house is silent, and I feel truly alone for what
seems like the first time in my life.
Who will I share my last thoughts of the day with?
How can I wake without the hope of hearing
your laughter when I do?
Who will I learn from? Who will I teach?
Who will I grow with now that you're gone?

Melanie Jordan
A MID SHOWERS DREAM
I have seen you in my past;
and the exquisite memories
we have given birth to
emanate my being in the present.
I sense in you my future
and a life of happiness.
A life—
filled with white roses
and dancing with the blues.
Sharing rides on
multi-colored rainbows
and stopping to rest
on the clouds.
Making love under the moon
and calling the sun our best friend.
Believing in fairy tales
and their proverbial happy endings:
And always knowing that I will never have to ask you for anything,
you know what I need
even before I do.

Beatrice Harper
MORNING WALK
I saw a parakeet
In a tree
He escaped his cage
Now he is free

I wonder how
He will survive
He has never been free
Will he stay alive?

In the yards as
I walked past
Dogs were barking
Leaves were falling fast

A child waved
And said hi!
From a doorway
As I walked by

If I see a friend
I stop and talk
All this I see
On a morning walk

Harry J Hill
OMPHALOSKEPSIS
was there but one
favor given
only to me?
(by the Mighty)

one gene apart
different from start
that's only me —

one core of seed
that makes of me
this thing I am —

this transient thing
in endless ring —

devolve, evolve.

unending quest
to solve and wrest
the answer from
my cummerbund.

Rachel Klaiber
MISSING YOU
Often I wish you were here,
To catch my falling tear.
To hold me in your arms so tight,
To help me make it through the night.
To whisper in my ear,
Those three little words I long to hear.
For you to tell me we'll always be together,
And no matter what, love each other forever.

Dena Kinzer
CHRISTMAS MEMORIES

To my husband, sisters & children who made my Christmas memories so bright.

Thoughts of Christmas bring to mind
a scene of warmth and cheer;
of children playing 'neath the tree,
with all my loved ones near

The fireplace with stockings hung,
the angel on the tree,
loving faces by candle-glow,
the hope of things to be.

Snow flurries, holy silence, carolers to sing;
sounds of children's laughter,
the church bell soon to ring.
This is the very essence of Christmastime to me,
and yet I know these wondrous
times cannot always be—
At times some of these loved ones will have to be apart,
and I will have to close my eyes
and see them with my heart;

For Christmas was never meant for one day just to be—
But to warm our hearts the whole
year through—within our memory.

Kellianne Kittle
THE OLD GUITARIST
About loneliness he was never wrong,
Picasso: how well he understood
The value of loved ones and friends; how
Without them
Life is empty as an abandoned alley.

In The Old Guitarist, for example, how everything
Is blue.
The blind man sits alone,
His guitar in his lap,
As his long, thin fingers
Pluck the strings
And a slow, lonely song
Is played.
His clothes are torn,
His body frail and weak.
His head bent low,
His stomach gaunt.
Unable to see the strings
He still plays;
Searching through the rhythms
To find a friend in a note
To stay with him for a moment.

Margaret L Brown
A VALENTINE FOR LILY

To my children who have encouraged me and given me love and to my dear friend Marjorie Murray who is the owner of "Lily."

There once was a dachshund named Lily
Who wore neck scarves and acted real silly
She was quite long and lean
Like a big old string bean
And she had her eye on a collie named Willy.

She was spoiled and snippy and lazy
Like the proverbial fox she was crazy
For she was warm and well-fed
With soft cushions for her bed
Like her rich friend
The poodle called Daisy.

Marjorie loved Lily quite dearly
And Lily loved her most sincerely
She would run and bark and howl
When she saw her beagle pal Sal
And they had a dog-gone good time clearly

This is the end of the tail of Lily
Also of Daisy and Sal and Willy
and Louie and Eloise and Marjorie too
With their mushy message
"We love you"
On their valentine for Lily

Lillian Hall
BRIAN'S STORY
It was the middle of the night,
I awoke with dreams and tears;

Mommy came into my room
and tried to calm my fears.

She hugged me, she loved me,
and gently asked why
I awakened from my sleep
and started to cry.

I tried to say the words
but I'm not even two . . .
My mommy tried to help me
but what was I to do?

Now I'm learning new words
and soon will tell my mommy
All the things that bother me
from my head to my tummy!

Carolyn Jackson

THE BEST IS ALWAYS LAST

The winner always comes in first
It happens all the time
The crowd they cheer and clap their hands
For the one at the head of the line
But notice how the crowd don't move
They still stand there and wait
To see who's coming up in the rear
The loser who's always late
He too is proud at the finish line
He gave it all he had
What counts is that he made it
Last place is not so bad
It's great to be the winner
Someone who's very fast
But if I'm behind I keep in mind
The best is always last

J Martin Hurd

SYLVIA

To my mother.

Looking out a watered window
I see her face. I smile.
She smiles back, from somewhere else —
We visit for awhile.

She's there, beyond the window —
It fills me with delight!
Then find it's my reflection.

(They say we looked alike.)

Winnifred A Cleaves

THE LITTLE BIRD AT LAKE LA ROSE

I was busy swimming in the lake,
When I seen a little bird, no sounds did he make.
Coming out from under the alder bushes, he look all around,
And he seemed to know exactly where he was bound.
I watched him as he slowly walked across the beach,
Being very careful to stay out of everyone's reach.
He walked across the gateway to the other side,
Watching me in the water as I'd glide.
He walked in amongst the lilies and the rushes,
And sat on the sand under the alder bushes.
Then he climbed on top of a large stone,
And began to watch a show all of his own.
Maybe he wanted to learn how to swim,
Or enjoyed having company, or just had a whim;
Then he flew away to a small tree limb.
I decided I'd had enough of the water,
I'd come back again when the weather grew hotter.
I thought about the little bird all the next day,
But mostly remembered seeing him fly away.

Shana R Tennyson

WHAT THE GNU KNEW

Do you know what the gnu knew?
Well? . . . Do you?
If you knew what the gnu knew,
Then you knows what the gnu's nose knows.

Do you know what happened to the gnat?
Well? . . . Do you know that?
That which happened to the gnat, happened
After the gnat knew what the gnu's nose knows.

Do you know what happened to the goat's throat?
Well, then take note.
The goat's throat got stuck on a note
When he found out what the gnu's nose knows.

Do you know why the duck got stuck in the muck?
Well, Good Luck!
The duck got stuck in the muck
When she found out what the gnu's nose knows.

Submitted By Charmaine Rodriguez, Author Unknown

MISS ME BUT LET ME GO

Dedicated to the loving memory of Don Steve Rodriguez.

When I come to the end of the road, and the sun has set for me, I want no rites in a gloom filled room, why cry for a soul set free. Miss me a little, but not too long. And not with your head bowed low. Remember the love that we once shared. Miss me, but let me go.
For this is a journey we all must take, and each must go alone. It's all a part of the Master's Plan. A step on the road to home.
When you are lonely and sick at heart. Go to the friends we know, and bury your sorrows in doing good deeds. Miss Me, But Let Me Go.

Wayne Farnes

I WILL ALWAYS

I will always . . . love her 'til the day I die
To retrieve her love I will always try
Something within that very first kiss
Twin to an unrelenting bliss
Numerous intense moments we spent
Never once a thought of repent

I will always . . . hear her voice in the rain
Whether it be in Miami or in Maine
Her face is forever etched upon my mind's eye
The chance of just one more embrace, requests a try
The outcome of a rendezvous
Would entail more than just tea for two

I will always . . . understand it will never be the same
Never again will I ever complain
A kiss or two may feel like déjà vu
But there always was more than just staying up 'til two
Now I live with traces of you
And wonder if you do too . . .

Kathleen Hunt

THE MAN I LOVE

To my husband Brian, I'll love you forever, Kathleen.

There is a hand
I love to hold
Two eyes I love to see.
There is a voice
I love to hear
That means the world to me.
There is a step
I listen for
Each day when work is done.
There is a smile
That says to me
"You are my special one."
There is a heart
That understands
What I am dreaming of . . .
And all of these things
Are you:
The wonderful man I love!

Amy Wilcox

WHY DID YOU LEAVE WITHOUT SAYING GOODBYE

Wasn't it bad enough you left without saying goodbye? You don't know how much you've made me cry. You've made me feel like such a fool, cheated and uncool.

Someone else told me where you'll be. She said you weren't coming back for me.

Didn't anything we do mean anything to you. All those things you've ever said all bundled up inside my head.

I'll never get over this 'cause in my heart you'll always be missed.

They tell me to get you off my mind, but what do they think I am not blind. I thought there was love there, but obviously you didn't care.

You've left me to get my feelings straight, but I feel I am closed inside this gate.

I wish I could see you for one more day. I'd give you hell and make you pay, 'cause it was my heart that died when you left without saying goodbye.

John W Wagner

MEMORIES OF SPRING

Gently the wind blows
on the green grass that grows
under the flowering trees
that sway forward and back with ease
under a warm and rising sun
as the birds return one by one.
The warmth gives them time to sing
which brings back memories of Spring.

Kerry P Weber

AM I IN LOVE?

When we met
a first moment's glance
produced a spell
that drew me to your charm

I followed your eyes
they struggle to release
hidden truths dwelling beneath
the surface of your words

It was daylight
that first revealed kindred
passions and spirits that fill
my open heart with a gentle touch

I feel the long
winter nights drift slowly
to where my dreams of the future
embraces the tenderness of your soul

Where can I go
from here my courage is distant
the words are foreign to say
Am I in love?

Pearl Wentworth

ETCHED IN MEMORY

Ancestral walls leaning against the wind
Walls of calloused wood that age has dried
Stands shadowed by the weathered barn
'Midst fresh cut hay and bees and flies.
And trees of fruit, some red, some green,
Held on branches stretching to be seen.
Tall grass dancing in the wind
Bending to the ground to rise again
With smells of earth and flowers breath
To scent the air with nature's zest.
The ribboned path that time has formed
By feet bared to the earth with shoes sole worn
And step by step, the grass so tried
Crushed to the ground, with age has died.
Across the fields of fadin' green
With sun transformed to Jasper's scene
The wind speaks warm in autumn's breath
To cast its spell on summer's rest.
With trees embraced by red and gold
Their clothes so turned by rising cold
And leaves set free in flowing grace
Glide to the earth in quiet pace.
When winds blow white with winter's birth
To blanket warm the sleeping earth
Strong branches held by snows that cling
Awaits in glorious hope of spring.

Laura York Willard

BEGIN THE DAY WITH GOD

Begin the day with God and believe
The joy we can take in and conceive.
There is so much to express of love
To our dear Savior in heaven above.

If we will begin each wonderful day
Asking God's blessing on our way
What a difference our act of strife
Jesus Christ can have on our life.

Approach the day with God so dear.
Open our heart without a fear,
It will bring us close to the Lord's side.
For all of us He was crucified.

End the day with a prayer you make
Each petition to Him calmly take.
Then listen for the Holy Spirit to guide.
He is waiting to always with us abide.

Rose L Weisenauer

GLORY OF THE SEASONS

I like the quiet winter-time;
Snow softly falling on bush and tree

Makes the world a fairy-land
God's gift to you and me.

I like the calm, fresh spring-time
When life begins anew,
'Tis God's miracle wrought
To prove His promise true.

I like the bright, warm summer
When comes the long, long day;
Blue skies, brilliant sunshine,
And children at their play.

I like the crisp, cool autumn
When trees are red and gold,
Then God sends bountiful harvest
Before the year grows old.

For each lovely season
We thank Thee, God of all,
Make us worthy of their glory
And like a palm, grow straight and tall.

Robert G Wolfe
FRIENDS AND LOVERS

To My Darling Wife, Kim.

If in this life you can find
just one friend who's really true
Then you'll have accomplished more than most
when their lives are through

And should you find a love
who fulfills your fondest dreams
Then you'll know a joy
much more than most, it seems

But should you find that friend
and love are both one soul
Then you, as I, are blessed more than all
and your life, 'til its end, will be whole

Mary (Sally) Wade
FORBIDDEN LOVE
The world rejects us, we're just tossed out
The daylights forbidden, no loving hearts allowed

We must be quiet, we can never be seen
We walk in the darkness, we become night beings

We know we're different in some sense of the word
Our hearts and bodies together, neither immoral or absurd

We have the feelings just as all people do
Why can't they handle it, it being me and you

The pressure is so great, the road so long
We'll go alone together where loving hearts belong

Love is Love regardless, it's shown in many ways
It only brings us closer, the world won't break us today.

Maxine Worthington
A HOUSE—OR HOME!
A house can be a room or two;
a place to hang your hat.
Some folks can always feel at home,
no matter where they're at.
There are those who live in mansions,
trimmed in crystal and gold;
Tho, with all this the mansion, may
still be dreary and cold.

For me, a house is not a home, no
matter where it be.
Where constant strife occurs, there's
little harmony.
People can have their mansions—
with an atmosphere of ice;
I'd rather have a tiny room that's
comfortable and nice.

Yes, if there is no love around, a
house is not a home;
Just a place to hang your hat—till
you decide to roam.
Yet, if there is true feeling, of
harmony in the air,
You'll find a lot of happiness—that
everyone can share.

Maxine Worthington
A HOLIDAY MESSAGE
The holidays are here again
They come but once a year;
A time for many wishes,
Blessings, good times, and cheer.

It's time for buying presents
For the family or a friend,
And time for the addressing,
Of cards we want to send.

Amidst all our confusion
While things are merry and gay,
Let's not forget to say a prayer,
For peace each coming day.

And as we face the New Year
May things look ever bright;
May the problems of the old year,
Quickly fade from sight.

Let foreign crisis be resolved
And the economy begin to rise;
Let Peace on Earth—Good Will to Men,
Forever—Be our future prize.

Ruby Cummings Webb
A ROSE
A rose is a rose
Wherever it grows
It's a beauty to behold
Red, white, pink or gold
All are favorites of mine
Give me a rose anytime.

Scott Williams
FIND OUT
I've got to find out why you're
Walking out on me
Lady have you found someone new
or have you been untrue.

I've got to find out why you're
Walking out on me
Lady have you forgotten me
Darling I still love you can't you see.

You left me here cold and all alone
Broken hearted I realize you're gone
Broken dreams and broken streams of love
Where have you gone.

You could have said something
before you left
But instead you just walked away
Without saying anything to me
Why did you leave me honey.

Lady could you still love me
If you can then don't leave me
I know you've got someone waiting for you
So if you want to go I won't stop you.

Joan D Wood
A FAITHFUL, FURRY FRIEND
Our family pet is a faithful, furry friend,
Whose love and loyalty knows no end.
Butch, the sandy-beige cat with amber eyes,
Intelligent, beautiful, and huge of size!

Sometimes playful as a kitten
With whom you can become quite smitten.
Oft' times just a tom of leisure,
Who else could give us so much pleasure?
To all around him he is simply a treasure.

Joan D Wood
ODE TO A LI'L LADY
Li'l dabs o' powder,
Li'l dabs o' paint,
Make a li'l lady
Exactly what she ain't!

John Wood Sr
BIRTH OF A BABY

Dedicated to the late John Wood, Sr.

I have some news
I wish to tell
But pray, be calm
For all is well.

A baby's come,
And she's the cheese.
Her Name? Oh, gracious,
It's Helen Louise.

How pleased we are
No words can tell.
And Father and Mother
are doing well.

So dear friends all
Come see us; Do!
We still reside
At 482.

My message done
So far, so good.
I still remain,
Yours, Mr. Wood

Phaidra Wright
FRIENDS
A friend is very close to you
with many things with you can do.
You share most anything with them
they're just like an unusual gem.
Each one is very unique
like some are outgoing, some are meek.
All are fun in different ways
in which you enjoy by the days.
They share your tears and your joy
they can be a girl or boy.
They should not be your personal dart
but at least should be close to your heart.

James R Tilley
MR. PSYCHO

In loving memory of L. H. Tilley, 1926-1987, and John Lennon, 1940-1980.

I stepped into an alley, got myself a gun
I'm going to rid the world of sin,
'cause I'm the chosen one
I'm going to be somebody, I'm gonna make a name for myself
I'm not going to Hell
Hey, Mr. President won't you look my way
Hey, Mr. President I'm gonna get away
I stalked him for days, I knew his every move
But he just would not talk to me,
what else could I do
Hey Mr. Lennon, won't you look my way
Hey Mr. Lennon, I'm not going to pay
The Devil lived inside the dog, I didn't know his game
But every time he spoke to me another one was slain
I'm gonna be somebody, can't run away from who I am
I'm the Son of Sam
I can show you miracles and you'll believe it's true
I've done them so many times that I believe it too
I'm gonna be somebody, drink this cup, let's sing a hymn
Believe in Reverend Jim
Hey Mr. Jones, you've had your day
Hey Mr. Manson, are you gonna get away?

Alvin R Weiss
SQUIRREL
There's a red squirrel frisking
In the maple trees,
His fiery tail he's whisking;
There's a red squirrel frisking.
Now, fancy tricks he's risking
On his high trapeze;
There's a red squirrel frisking
In the maple trees.

Jennifer Trumbull
LOST IN LOVE
Theirs was a love so tenderly bound; only one knew of it, the other had yet to be found.
The day their eyes met, one knew the love was for real. She could not help but wonder how the other might feel.
The summer went by with its memories fast, but the thoughts and dreams of her love would forever last.
It took 3 months to try and forget her only dear; it took only seconds to fall in love again seeing him so near.
At that moment she knew she would love him forever; she dreamt that someday they would be together.
She tried to tell herself that he felt the same; but her heart knew he was only fair game.
There was one other girl who liked him as well. How did her love feel?
She could not tell.
She began to wonder if her past feelings had been wrong. She cried tears of sorrow when she heard a particular song.
Her love began to ignore her, to act as though he did not care.
She broke down in sorrow, the pits, the depths of despair.
She talked to her friends, knowing they would care; all the while making her troubles easier to bear.
She knew to keep hopes and dreams alive was the right thing to do, for when she did this, they would surely come true.

Rebecca Sue Whitco
LOVE IS LIKE THE WIND

To Miss Carrie Fuchs
my favorite teacher who
I will always remember.

Love is here,
Then it's gone,
Love is like the wind,
Sometimes it has its ripples,
Usually it's free and flowing,

Love,
It's like the wind
Fun and laughter,
With not a care in the world,
But each other,
Hopeful yet fearful,
Sometimes it can be dreary and dull,
But usually it's graceful,
A relationship,
Just gliding along,
Love is like the wind.

Pattee Thorpe
INCUBUS
I dream of fire and ice and snow
In a place I cannot comprehend;
And heat and sleet and winds that
blow
propel this dream to no quick end

My visions are of fleeting veils
That vanish from my virgin stare;
I seem to float along a trail
of ghostly umbra here and there

By pools of liquid hot, yet cold
I pass but do not stoop to touch;
And apparitions faintly bold
Stretch tentacles of vapor dust

And on and on this nightmare speeds
Slow motion pictures in my head;
Among sensed vile and evil deeds
I walk in graveyards of the dead.

Diane M Thompson
A GAME?
We are taught in Sunday school
Obey the Golden Rule.
Then why all this corruption,
Decadence, immorality?
It seems to me if God is in control,
Is it He we should blame?
Or is this place called earth,
Just God's video game?

Paula Kristi (Thomas)
PURPLE SHELL
I am searching for a purple shell
through sand and water where it
may dwell.
The sun is smiling on the sea
precious gold entangles me.
Flamingo pink sprinkles the sky
the day has dawned and the tide is
high.
The waves crash wildly on the shore
the droplets and sand again at war.
Sea gulls are shrieking loudly with
glee
snatching any food they can get for
free.
I walk along the beach, a thousand
waves swell
doing nothing at all but looking for
my shell.
The day slowly fades, and drifts into
the night
the moon climbs the stars and
warms me with his light.
I stumble in the water and turn
around to see
my purple shell lying there, shining
up at me.
Some people would say that this day
was a crime
I simply smile, I was not wasting
time.

Matt Thomas
CRAZY WOMAN CREEK

For Linda and the Desert.

Alone on Crazy Women Creek she
stands,
behind the sun.
Skirts, hair sing in the wind,
eyes shine like the desert after rain.
She waits, with a smile and bare feet,
for day to hide itself
under hazy, distant mountains.

Warmth.
She laughs, fills the sky with herself,
reaching.
And I, who didn't stay,
can feel my crazy woman.

Crazy maybe, but hardly mine.
She does what she wants.
Sometimes, she wants me.

When she calls, I want to run to her.
Through a thousand days of hope,
through a world cracked and dying,
to find her hand.
Together we'll shriek at the sun,
whisper to the moon, and fall
laughing
in the dust on Crazy Woman Creek.

Barbara J Turk
WHAT IS BETWEEN US CAN'T BE WRITTEN, OR SPOKEN
What is between us can't be written
or spoken,
can't be sung, or painted or
photographed.
It's a feeling, an understanding of
each other,
a communication that needs no
direction.
It's words unspoken,
It comes from within the heart,
It is LOVE

Amanda Tucker
FRIENDSHIP
Friendship is the act of caring.
Friendship is sharing.
Friendship is having someone to tell
all your thoughts.
Friendship is not letting anyone insult
your faults.
This is what friendship means to me.

Karen Thompson
AND STILL . . .
I woke up screaming
From a dream of my childhood home
A place full of shadows and imagined
fears
Underneath which lay my real fear
That I felt for a real man
A faithful husband, the good provider
Who had forgotten what it was like to
be a child
To make a little too much noise
To forget a mother's request
To drop something too big for little
fingers to hold
To run and hide from a man with a
belt
Who would not stop until . . .
And still I wake up screaming

Dean Walter Lowry III
HIDDEN FEELING
There's a hidden feeling, in my heart,
Waiting for someone, to get it to
start.
A feeling that's in, my heart and
mind,
It's a feeling that makes, some people
blind.

It's filled with warmth and caring,
A feeling that's there for the sharing,
For the right person, to come along,
And make that hidden, feeling strong.

It's a feeling that needs, to be brought
out,
And shared with people, all about.
This hidden feeling, is called "Love,"
Which is one of God's gifts, from up
above.

Wendy Thomas
FACES

From the deepest of my heart, for Sean Hogan with love always.

I hold a polished gold coin in the
palm of my hand,
and watch the light reflect its
perfection.
As life, I watch.
A struggle of emotions hides behind
the purity of its
golden shell.
I listen.
I want to reach out and believe in all
that life has to give
and at the same time I want to
withdraw to the depths of
my golden innocence.
I wait.
So many faces of time remind me of
the faces I loved yesterday.
Like the faces of a polished, gold
coin, its brilliance
overwhelms me and I am taken.
I wonder.
I stand staring at the polished, gold
coin and am curious to
its perfection and pureness.
I turn the coin over, and behold the
fool who holds it.
I stand staring at a harsh and ugly
side.
The tarnished face.
Seek out, and you shall find, the other
side of the coin,
the face that no one seems to see.

Jamie Tatlas
CHASING NOTHING
Love seems to forever elude her,
So many acquaintances,
No lasting alliances.

No one can see into the glass house,
She built it that way.

She dreams of somedays yet to come.
I spy a tear making a path down
her cheek
I long to console her.

In a fast, whirling speed she turns
Racing like a wild mare into the
sunset
And she's gone—
Just like that.

Dan Tynan
MY HEART'S . . . HEART

Our Debbie . . . beautiful daughter #2 . . .

My little girl, her face is so sweet
when I kiss her I taste her very last
treat.
Two eyes, shiny-brown as a coffee
bean true,
strange, that more often they're
not black and blue.
A nose like a button with two tiny
holes,
with her sleeve she does wipe with
pure apropos.
Her ears are as trinkets, lovely and
dear,
but what is the use, she refuses to
hear.
Her hair is so long and hard to
unravel,
she changes the color with a
handful of gravel.
Her feet they are small and
wonderfully strong,
how different they look when her
shoes are on wrong.
Three feet of motion, and thirty
pounds too,
wrapped in a package, wholesome
and true.
Her world is a challenge, to be
conquered it must,
no one is right, and no one she'll
trust.
She fights like a teddy, she runs like a
deer,
she yells like a hippo, when
reaching high gear.
Soon, she'll be three, and never a
bore,
so, now she is dating a rascal of
four.

Linda V Thomas
I DID THE RIGHT THING

For Rick: Now, Always and Forever.

I did the right thing that night I told
you goodbye.
I fought back the tears as I cradled
your face in my hands.
Memories of everything you stood
for went rushing by.
I knew how much you loved me,
Knew how much pain that love had
cost you.

I did the right thing that night when I
said goodbye.
You gently ran your hands through
my hair,
Your eyes looked deeply into mine as
if searching for a cause.
You poured out your soul to me
without saying a word.
You struggled with wanting to say no.

I did the right thing that night I told
you goodbye.
I knew I had taken far more than I
had ever given
Knew that through your love I had
found myself.
I thanked God for the times with you.
Wondering how I could go on
without you.

But I did the right thing that night I
told you goodbye.
Even fearing that it was over,
I knew in my heart it would never end.
Seeing the tears in your eyes as you
said goodbye,
I knew our love would never die.

We did the right thing that night we
said goodbye.

Linda V Thomas
THE SEA
You are such a violent lover
my friend the sea.
One moment young and calm and yet
another powerful and old.
You bring climatic response as you
carry me away
to a foreign land.
You take the sand particles of my
youth and cast them adrift.
Your foreplay is never ending,
always stroking and caressing.
You open your body wide
to receive whatever lover that will
crawl in.
You are such a violent lover
my friend the sea.
Yet ever touching me softly.

Sylvia F Tansey
LITTLE SISTER'S LAMENT
My sister no longer has time for
me—
I've been replaced along with her
toys,

for she now has special girlfriends
with whom she giggles over boys.
We used to play dress up together—
wearing Mom's jewelry and clothes—
now she insists on her own make-up,
not to mention high heels and hose;
her bedroom is reserved for friends—
definitely "off limits" for me,
it seems she writes in a diary
she doesn't want me to see;
yet there was a time we got along—
when we could sit and talk,
and I can remember how a few months ago—
together to the store we would walk.
Mom said that I will soon be like my sister
and Dad hastened to agree,
but I will resign from the Human Race
before that can happen to me!

Ricki Tebaldi
MEMORIAL DAY
Did you notice my friend
How silent the cemetery is today?
As if God commanded, "quiet"
In his own special way.

Grass blows softly in the breeze,
Yet never makes a sound.
Leaves of green fall from the trees,
And flutter to the ground.

It makes you think of God.
The silence and the beauty.
Placing wreaths upon the graves,
No longer seems a duty.

Your loved ones seem closer now,
Then they ever have before.
You realize they're waiting,
Upon a Golden shore.

Sounds of nature hushed,
Trees bow and nod.
Only reverent whispers,
In the waiting room of God.

Knud R Madsen
CHICAGO & ITS GROWTH!!!
Chicago's phenomenal growth
is making us so very proud
that we lift our heads
above the crowd,
Steel, concrete and glass
are reaching for the sky
'Build them taller'
comes the strident cry.
Our city's growth is self-evident
on every hand
in what was once Pottawottomie land,
Buildings are growing
with a rhythmic beat
amid the clamor and shuffle
of a million feet.
Buildings are rising
where rubble falls
and aged squalor is replaced
by lovely malls.
The changes brighten our lives
with a brilliant gleam
to grow and prosper
with Chicago's dream.
Michigan Avenue's magnificent mile
will cause so many
to linger awhile
for beauty and culture
is so evident there,
its greatness and fame
is known everywhere,
Our lake shore drive
and the adjoining green
is just as lovely
as any I've seen
we may rant and rave
and wallow in self-pity
but we are truly in love
with our own fair city.

Rebecca L Mathis
PRAYER TO MORNING
Dear Lord,
don't take the darkness;
it is my peace
don't bring the light
until I sleep
Banish the creeping sun from the sky
and give me night forever.

With the darkness comes wanton fear
that makes me so alive
By day I die; I merely exist
so to see the night survive.

Dear God,
give me strength
to outlive my pain
give me courage
to always remain
Bring to me my Mystery less his ghosts
and let us have, to share, the night.

Rebecca L Mathis
WILD FLOWERS
As the sun returns to its home
I sit in my fields
Alone
gathering wild flowers.

Golden faces
with dark eyes,
Silver laces
And a purple thistle
Bow their heads as
the wind whistles.

Their colors fade
With the sun's dying embers.
I wonder
if he remembers?

And now all I have
To spare my tears these hours
Is my beautiful
Wild flower.

Mrs Willie Mae Busby Taulton
ON THE WINGS OF A DREAM
Sometimes I have to slip away
into a world of my own.
Where my dreams come alive
and my hopes are made known.
Where the troubles of my heart
burst forth from its gloom.
Where my fears seem to drift away
and my thought flourish and bloom.
Where my spirit is lifted high
and my sanity is redeemed.
It's floating high up in the sky
on the wings of a beautiful dream.

Mike Mleynek
IN MY PRISON GARDEN EARTHLY AND SPIRITUAL FOOD IS LIFE'S NUTRITION

May WE the human race lovingly WORSHIP & PRAISE our Almighty Sovereign Lord JEHOVAH GOD. For He gave this Breath of Life for Us to enjoy in complete happiness in a promised Edenic EARTH within HIS original purposes!!

I seldom read the papers, nor watch much TV, so I don't know what goes on.
I go to bed at sunset, to leap alert at dawn,
To gossip with MY GARDEN, which I'll have YOU understand,
Is the neatest and the sweetest little GARDEN in the land;
A span of sunny quietude, with WALLS so high and stout,
They shut ME in from all the world, and shut the whole world out;
So that its sad bewilderment seems less than true to ME,
As FRUITFULLY RIGHTEOUS I TRY TO LIVE, though tranquil as a fig tree;
In further glory of MY perseverance, I will have MY glint of Linnet's wings;
MY soybeans are more to ME than worldly governments and pagan kings;
Dominion have I of MY OWN, where feud and faction cease,
A little Heaven of tranquility, MY present GARDEN-PARADISE of PEACE!!
My friends nod to ME, and pass the TIME of day.
WE talk of herbs and clover, the prospect of MY crops,
And the price of MY labor, . . . there the conversation drops;
For in a doubt-distracted world, to MY FAMILY I TRY TO KEEP IN TOUCH!
Although I'M THE TYPE WHO THINKS & WRITES DEEPLY, but I don't talk too much;
But just to Meditate on SPIRITUAL-LIFE matters that are NOW COMING TO BE,
In taking delight in all I think, hear and see;
And through the drowsy noon, the rush of MY daily routines are like-so,
This is MY inner world, then back'n'forth with a Heart of JOY I GO!
I didn't make this cold-outer-world, but it's part of OUR JOB to mend;
Yet I'VE lived only 29 years, this old-wicked-system is very near its END;
For by learning JEHOVAH GOD'S ACCURATE KNOWLEDGE OF WISDOM,
There's been a foretold birth of His HEAVENLY MESSIANIC KINGDOM,
To bring about a NEW ORDER that His WITNESSES preach by FAITH to fight,
To claim JEHOVAH' S KINGDOM of JUSTICE is FOREVER PERFECTLY RIGHT!!!
So by GOD'S written Holy Oaths, do I know in MY Future EARTHLY LIFE,
Will prove to be FREE of any worldly-wicked strife. . . . Amen!
MeanWhile, Here I LIVE within these WALLS of MY low and humble thatch,
Smiling little tea-herb plants and a sweet potato patch.
So with hoe in hand I stand, to view the vast heavenly sky,
Let JEHOVAH'S Revelations ROCK! the land, serene, spiritually secure am I;
So be it, during ARMAGEDDON that MY plants may get dusted,
As long as sinful people and those darn bugs in the GARDEN get busted!
While studying on SPIRITUAL FOOD, I groom thy lettuce, I pick My soybeans,
I feast in colour, form a song, then ponder on its means;
The beauty of growth suffices in itself, then when MY strength is spent,
Like simple ME, hungry for LIFE'S FOOD, I CULTIVATE CONTENTS.

Robert Miller
THE LOVE THAT'S COME YOUR WAY
I long to wrap you in
the comfort of my love
take from you the loneliness
your soul gets weary of

Let you soar and break the bonds
that have held you for so long
allowing you to see and feel why
love is never wrong

Set you free to taste the wind
that blows from other shores
gaily reaching new horizons as
you open long shut doors

Watch you grow and stand by you
if hurt and tears should come
show you too my love for you
will more than overcome

Doubts and fears you've held for years
will simply pass away
replaced by more than i can say
the love that's come your way

Robert Miller
FRIENDSHIPS GONE BY
Friendships have come as
friendships have passed
I sometimes wonder what
makes them not last

The feelings survive but
what did it cost
Bonds being broken
both sides have lost

To misunderstanding and
words not spoken
Weakening those bonds
until they are broken

I sometimes reflect on
the meaning of it all
Some support has been lost
but i know i won't fall

For i hold onto the threads
from the bonds that have gone
With hope of retying them
Once again making them strong

Francine Denton Lerner Schachter
TRANSITIONS
I do not take so lightly to change
Thick, habit-minded victim of inertia,
Transitions are tortuous moments,
Graduations, weddings, old age, and bus depots,
Where the possibility of losing the original
intention looms large.
Essentials packed, activity suspended,
Routines abandoned to a somnambulance
of expectations,
That, alas, reality is rarely able to

equal.

Waiting rooms are purgatories,
Littered with candy wrappers, once fresh
and sweet,
And restless sleepers in alcoholic drowse.

Lost, they have lost their way at the
division in the road,
At the decision moment,
That presses in upon us all,
Which way, how many, where and when.
The unprepared are cast aside
to stay in crumpled heaps.

Kathleen Ebell
THE MORNING AFTER
Amber glass
marks a ring
on the
walnut table.

A crowded
ashtray
makes room
for one more.

The bottle
full of
false laughter
is empty.

A soggy
napkin
soaks up
brittle dreams.

Clare M Fildes
PEACE
Where there is abortion, there is no peace.
Where there is drug abuse, there is no peace.
There is no peace where there is war.

Where there is prejudice, there is no peace.
Where there is crime, there is no peace.
There is no peace where there is injustice.

There is peace where there is happiness.
There is peace where there are caring people.
Where there is love, there is peace.

We must find peace.
There's got to be a way.
Let's not wait until tomorrow.
Make the world peaceful today.

Ann E Kaster
THE BEGINNING OF AN END
A gentle breeze sweeps across the hill;
Though it's a small breeze, it creates a chill.
The sun is slightly lighting the sky;
It's about to say good-bye.

A brave, old mountain stands all alone;
It's as if you can hear it moan.
No birds, no bunnies, no deer around;
The mountain's moan is the only sound.

The prairie is hushed in fear;
For winter will soon be here.
A smell of moisture is in the air;
A drop of rain here and there.

The stream creates a little roar;
It's about to flow no more.
A thin layer of ice covers the top;
This, a sign of the water coming to a stop.

But yet tomorrow the sun will shine;
The glory of the day will be yours and mine.
Together we can run and play;
It shall be another wonderful day.

Jo Deneen
I'D CLIMB THE HIGHEST MOUNTAIN
I'd climb the highest mountain just to see your smiling face
I'd swim the wildest river just to feel your warm embrace

I'll never love anyone but you even in God's after place
and not anyone never as much as I Love You!

Connie Davis
DREAM STREET
It's a funky old world.

The lights on this street are your enemy, so don't be misled by their flashy colors blinking on and off that way. Take a closer look, my friend, and see what message is blinking Like . . .

Eat . . . Eat . . . Eat . . .

They're mocking you. You'll know someday when you are standing here in the rain and your eyes are filled with tears. They'll gloat in your misery and their colors will melt together. When you turn to run, the colors will blind you, and you'll stumble and fall in the gutter on your face. Then do you know what they'll do? They'll flash

Eat . . . Eat . . . Eat . . .

Right on your back in pretty colors.

Now turn down this street. This is Dream Street. This street's the best friend you'll ever have. She's your mistress. Your doctor and lover. Your shield. Your sorrow. Can you hear the lonely sounds emanating from that little club across the street? That's the sound your soul makes. Like a muted trumpet that wails and moans because it's reaching for something that will never be. And while you stumble around in the dark, you find something better because of that misery inside yourself, and that misery is a reflection of your soul in one thousand different hues of color.

It won't mock you my friend. It soars through the clouds like a white dove until it reaches the sun, and then sits there pruning its feathers and lets them fall like your troubles down to the earth below.

Into this building, quickly now, and up these stairs and through the hall. Into this room before anyone sees you. Sit here a moment and catch your breath. This won't hurt a bit.

1-2-3-4-5-6-7-8-9-1 . . . 1 . . . 1 . . .

I sat in the sun and felt the warmth of it against my face. Someone reached down from my ceiling and removed the weight off my back. I looked up. No one there. Funny, you can go around all your life carrying a heavy load like that and no one realizes it until it's removed.

Lady Dream entered the room and placed her satin veil over my face. My eyes dropped.

"You Bitch! You Bitch!"
I screamed as I fell into the abyss.

I stood on the hill and looked at the warm valley below me. I ran down through the violets and buried my face in the earth's soft green fur. Looking up I saw the white dove sitting on the sun cooing softly while she pruned her feathers. They fell, one by one, landing on my lips.

"Willow weep for me
Spread your branches down
Along the ground and cover
me."

The willow wept. Her tears fell on the web above my face and clung to it like white emerald notes on a staff. They dropped in succession on my eyelids in a flurry of rhythm and sound. The willow spread her branches down along the ground and covered me. She tore at my body until her branches were covered with blood. I struggled to rid myself of her incessant weeping. . . tearing, my hands twisted her branches 'til they bled white and sticky and covered my mouth with their bitter, evil taste.

The sky turned black as I ran up the hill. The raven flew down off the sun and tore at my hair with its black claws.

I fell to the gutter on my tear streamed face. The lights faded and flashed

Eat. . . Eat. . . Eat. . .

On my back in pretty colors.

Beverly A Caouette
REFLECTIONS
I've passed along this road before,
around the bend, in time.
To see it,
Is just a reflection in my mind.

Beverly A Caouette
EDGE OF THE WOODS
Golden ferns just sitting there,
against your autumn green.
In your sea of sunlite, on a late afternoon.
The coolness of the night air hits
my face, as yours dances in a rhythm
known only to him.
The darkness of your neighbor creeps
up to your front door, letting you
know, soon you will be covered by
a warm blanket of snow.

Ruby Byrd
CHILDHOOD DAYS
As we welcome the "good old" summer days,
Our thoughts go back to childhood summer way;
Of doing things that satisfied our whims.
Of picnics, hiking and afternoon swims,
Of tramping in woods searching for treasure
And exploring streams that gave much pleasure.

We enjoyed the beauty of each new day,
And gave "Thanks for Blessings" that came our way.
We sat under trees in the cool, cool shade,
And put our hands in grass to feel each blade.
We observed the birds, having left their nest,
Each trying to sing its loudest and best.

Those happy days—fun in every minute;
With feelings of joy by sharing in it.
Now those were the wonderful carefree days
That gave us childhood joys in every way.
Oh, to go back to those days of "black when,"
And re-live those childhood days once again.

Ruby Byrd
A SENIOR CITIZEN'S PRAYER
Dear Lord, at this late time in my life,
I feel the pressures of age and strife.
From all my ailments I pray release.
From aches and pains I pray relief.
And for every one else, big and little;
And all of those who are in the middle,
For the old and for the young,
I pray healing for every one!
For the short and for the tall,
Yes God, I pray for them all.
As I'm here praying on bended knee
Asking healing for them and for me,
I'm trusting that you will answer my prayer,
Because I know dear Lord, that you really care.
Amen!

Andrew H Abel
WOULD I
If all the blue left the sky
If the winds refused to blow
If all the birds forgot to fly
Your love unto me
is all I'd need know

If all the blind but could see
If the clouds cried upside-down
If flowers killed the bee
I'd like to be the one to find
that you're still around

If I had a natural state of mind
once the trees began to walk afar
your smiling face always kind
If we all were just plainfolk
how sorry we all then are
If the stars cease to shine
I don't mind
It'll never replace the twinkle in your eyes
If the stars cease to shine
If rivers' water no longer could flow

If all things stood still
I wouldn't mind
Nothing will never replace the twinkle
of thine eyes, this I know

And if your heart got Broke
If we all did Sigh
or, even, if you were to die
Then too, SO WOULD I.

Lee Abramowitz-Halzell
A POEM? A CHANCE TO SAY
A thought with words can come
to mind

For some this is not hard

to find

The chance we are glad to
have it be

In a mind it is hidden on
paper it we can see

Is it a rhyme or is it a
lengthy verse?

Is it warm and friendly or
is it at times a bit terse?

It matters not what the
innards give out

The mirror image creates the
mystery of what poetry
is all about

Lee Abramowitz-Halzell

A CHALLENGE

Should I drop the thought
or keep it still afloat?

What can I do—keep it on
the moat?

Or should I still pursue

As if a successful outcome
I felt, I knew?

Never take the easy way out

Keep a search—it can happen
like more water in the spout

Don't leave a stone unturned

There might be another
way to win

Turn to the right, or turn
to the left, sometime
even turn and take a spin!

A K Ranjith

THE LOST RHYTHM

To All Who Are Deaf And Dumb.

Unspoken truths and broken words
keep on rising from the depths of
my soul
Chained legs and masked face
steal from me the fruits of life

Watchful eyes and careful steps
end at the tip of my slippery
tongue
Polished lines with a pause in style
deliver me but bouquets of shame

The song I sing here all alone
never crosses the boundaries of
my room
Luckiest breaks and happiest
occasions
fail to touch the core of my
stammering

Gasping for air, with widened eyes
fixed on heaven above, I pray
for the joy of an unbroken line
to shout at the world the truths I
know
Night after night in bed I cry

A K Ranjith

THE MAGIC SHORE

Thick dark clouds ruling the skies
Making rare to the eyes the shining
sun
Fuming poison filling your lungs —
These are our legacy to you, kings of
tomorrow

Vanishing into the past
Are the sweet notes of the cuckoo
The soft fragrance of wild breeze
Will never relish again your senses or
dreams
Let not the slow steps of your soft
feet
Lead you to crevasses of Death
Never, never be caught in the deadly
traps
Traps of addictions and temptations

Dear bundles of love
Bundles of sorrow await you outside
Open your eyes wide to this biting
darkness
And be bold

Come on, break all the chains
Hesitate no more, break them now
Avoid those myopic eyes
Wake up and feel the life
No looking back nor crying
Boundaries hold us no more

Good-bye ghost of the Past
Let us take a fresh deep breath
Dance and sing to the beat of Love
Plunge deep and feel the Joy
Forget forever the tears and fears
Evaporate all our cares here

On this shore of overwhelming
Freedom
Life and light fill our hearts and souls
Flying high and low in the blue sky
Spraying the Magic everywhere
No need for any more dreams
In this Dreamland of our Minds

Francine Spacek Merlock

AN ODE TO GRANDMA

In loving memory of my grandma, Mary Louise Spacek, from her loving granddaughter, Francine Spacek Merlock.

This lady was special as we all know
Her warm heart could melt the
winter's snow.

Her eyes were as soft as summer rain
Her smile as bright as the first day of
spring.

How nature adored her the birds and
the flowers
As she loved to sit outside for hours.

Her slight little hobble when she
would walk
Should have not have deceived you
of her mighty talk.

Her stories would charm me as I
listened with awe
To the little lady who sat wrapped in
her shawl,

The history was great, I will never
forget
The times I would listen, oh what
they meant.

She loved her family who all were
dear
And we shall feel her presence ever
near.

The soft cooing song of the morning
dove
Will always remind me of my
grandmother's love.

Oh God how proud you must be
To have my grandma at your knee.

I love you grandma

Emily Hurt

TIMES

We all have times . . .
Times of joy,
Times of sorrow,
Times of today;
and times of tomorrow.
Times of love,
Times of hate,
Times of difference;
and times of fate.

Times of pain,
Times of madness,
Times of happiness;
and times of sadness.

Rather it be times of fate or
happiness,
Times of hate or love,
These are times of life
sent from above.

Velma Mae Davis

MEMORIES ARE MY SOUVENIRS

Over the years I've collected
Memories as my souvenirs
With friendships and many things
shared
The good times and bad, the hard
times, the sad. Joy and laughter,
sorrow and tears; memories are
my souvenirs.

With failures and trials, many tasks
shared each day
I'll remember them all—each one in
its way.

We've aged, but we've mellowed,
with our dreams still beyond—

The memories are many—but it's
time to move on.

I'll remember them all with smiles,
and some tears—

As days turn to weeks, and months
into years—but
With pride and respect, I'll never
forget—these memories are my
souvenirs.

Elizabeth Chapin

ON WINGS

I don't know what it is that you give
to me.
It's like nothing I've ever had before.
It starts within the very depths of me
and goes forever.
It defies all description and lifts me
on wings.
Wings of vapor and wings of light
Wings that will take me to my
forever land.

Where will these wings of light and
vapor fly me to?
Will it be that Blackhole in Heaven
That space where I fear so
desperately to tread.
Will those wings you've given me
carry me to heaven or hell.
That is what I so longingly want to
know—
What is waiting for me in that
Forever land?
In that land where I can hear the
silence and feel the clouds.
In that land where I can taste the air
and touch the stillness
And hear your thoughts so quietly.

Will my wings of light and vapor
take me there?
Those wings you have given me.

Peggy Hubbard Whatley

THOUGHTS & REFLECTIONS

In memory of my father, Policeman Homer Foster Hubbard, (Alabama—Killed May 10, 1952) and to families of law enforcement officers everywhere who have had loved ones . . . "Killed in the line of duty."

Quietly I bowed my head and cried
On the courthouse lawn that day,
As "Killed in the line of duty"—
I heard the Mayor say.

Close by were mothers and children
And wives of the deceased,
Who relived the sadness of death
As memories brought back their
grief.

Blue uniforms were all around me
The protectors of our town,
High officials who from their duties
Somehow a moment had found.

To my left a cold, gray monument
Completely covered in blue,
Unveiled and dedicated to those
Who gave their life for me and you.

A wreath of yellow mums was
placed—
Officers removed their caps,
And a silence fell over the crowd
As a bugler played the Taps.

The Honor Guard then marched in
step
To the monument to pay tribute,
And as 'ole Glory waved above us
They fired a gun salute.

As I left the courthouse grounds
While much sadness I felt inside,
This memorial to my father
I gladly accepted with pride.

I'm thankful too that May 15th
Is Law Enforcement Day . . .
. . . "Killed in the line of duty"—
I heard the Mayor say.

Peggy Hubbard Whatley

TODAY

Today I let this mouth of mine
Spew forth words that stung,
And badly hurt a friend of mine—
LORD, help control my tongue.

Today I let these eyes of mine
Gaze where evil lies,
LORD, help me fight my
wanderlust—
And these roving eyes.

In this sinful world of ours
Such language that one hears,
I must not let this filthy trash
Fall upon my ears.

Today I let these hands of mine
Take from someone else,
Something that I yearned for—
I couldn't help myself.

Today I let these feet of mine
Stray down paths of sin,
To places where I knew that I
Should never enter in.

Today in this heart of mine
No kindness could be found,
Jealousy and hate were present
Where charity should abound.

LORD, keep my body a temple—
For THEE a dwelling place,
And help that I may never
Thy precious name disgrace.

Control my thoughts and temper—
May patience linger with me,
And may I love forever
My fellowman and THEE.

Forgive where I have failed—
And if it be Thy will I pray,
May tomorrow be for me . . .
. . . A much better day.

Leslie Joann Williams

FOR DORIS

I see you with a hair twisted around
your finger

clicking curlers
or with both hands immersed in shampoo
putting me to sleep

I knew even in fifth grade where I could relax.

I grew before your eyes in that chair
and it's time to throw back some of that love
that strength
that determination
that pride
that sense
you massaged into my scalp

I just want you to know—
it took.

Dolly Parton doesn't begin to know
what hair dressers are all about
they raise more than their own children
and their responsibilities are not bound by time or space
or affection
and they always surpass the limits of
what others say is possible
and we walk out, beauties, again.

Ruth P Pitman
REMEMBERING
As I look out the window, I long to see,
A reflection of a little girl looking back at me.
I long for the days of the good old past,
To run home to the arms of mother at last.

There are days in life when you look back in surprise,
And think of those comforting words at sunrise.
"It's time to get up dear, and get on to school,
Where you will learn all about the Golden Rule."

Never back then did we ever think,
There would be days to push us to the brink.
The brink of what, we have to discern,
Of what's most important in life to learn.

Be kind to one another with the love of a child,
With words of compassion, meaningful and mild.
It may be hard to deal with some,
But always remember that love from "Mom."

Remembering can be happy, it can be sad,
But always remember your Mom and Dad.
Only they deserve such praise,
For giving you your God-loving ways.

Carrie Tulgetske
LOVE FOR MY BROTHER

For Mitch (you're never alone!) I Love You.

In the darkness so silent
In the storms that just scream
if we walk on together we can
reach any dream

Though the roads might get rocky
and the hills hard to climb
I will always be with you time
after time

When you feel that you're slipping
and just want it to end reach out
and I will be waiting to lend you
a hand

For I love you my brother and will
stand by your side because I am
not ready to just say good-bye

Lee M Thompson
I LOVE YOU

This poem is dedicated to my wife JoAnn.

My eyes will always say I love
You
Even if my lips can't speak
And if you look close you will
See
The sparkle of memories of you
And me.
Hold my hand and you will feel
The warmth of love I will
Always feel
And tho my eyes may close to
Open no more
I will always love you as before

Marion Tukiendorf
WHEN DREAMS ARE BROKEN
If Words only could stand alone,
without the feelings without the pride,
just a simple meaning never emphasized,
then tomorrow . . . a new light would shine.
If Thoughts stood still imprisoned,
having no will,
there would never be guilt,
and we'd climb the hill,
and find fulfillment on the other side,
and tomorrow . . . a new light would shine.
If Hope were taken and put aside,
more rainy days would linger falling dry,
and the pangs of despondency . . .
would have no end in sight.
When dreams are broken,
a last thread unwound,
on the edge a figure,
holding ground,
sitting alone on top of his world,
juggling virtues . . .
for a captive audience of the past,
present and future.
If Words only could stand alone,
If Thoughts would stand still,
If Hope were taken and put aside,
when dreams are broken,
eclipsed,
. . . in a wink of an eye.

Cindy R Tenney
MY THOUGHTS ARE OF YOU
Every moment of everyday
My thoughts are of you,
Wanting, needing and
Loving you,
I have spent a life time looking for you
I won't give up on us
I can only pray,
someday,
you will love me too.

I look into your eyes
and I get hypnotize.
You have stolen my heart
and filled it with so much Joy
and Love
You say "I'm not in love with you"
and it's slowly tearing me apart.

I couldn't take it, if, you said
we were through
I try to tell myself, I can find
someone new
But you see I have so much love for you
and my love I have for you
is so very true.

If your Love for me never comes,
I will sadly let you go
And I'll remember all the beautiful times
we shared together
But the pain and heartache
will always show.

The memory of loving you
you cannot take away,
I can only hope
one day you'll be in my life to stay.

Lou Tappon
TRENDS

To those who work for a living.

Magnificent corruption,
Competition,
Disabling,
Malfunctioning.

Society extracts its price,
From the majority,
With few survivors.

Lou Tappon
MAN ON THE STREET
I can't get too close to you
I can't bear your pain
My own overwhelms me.

Sometimes
At night
I wake
And cry

For homeless dogs in the rain
And other souls with nowhere to go.

Janice Terborg
A SUMMER BREEZE
Oh how nice,
that summer breeze.
From the wind in my hair,
and the warmth on my knees.

The birds are a flutter,
the grass is so green.
Sandwiches of peanut butter,
and a child's happy scream.

The wind keeps on blowing,
the fall soon to start.
Remembering the promises
from our love struck hearts.

We can all remember
days like these,
all the memories
of a summer breeze.

Melanie Thut
THE ROSE
Our love was like a rose
That grew with time and care
It flourished and bloomed
With grace and beauty so rare

It lived through the winds and storms
And all the lies we told
And when the storms were over
The rose stood strong and bold

But the storms gradually grew worse
And then came the winter frost
That killed the fragile rose
And our love was forever lost

Heidi Annemarie Tidwell
DREAMS COME TRUE

This Poem is dedicated to my dear husband, John.

One word can't tell you what I feel for you.
It's like a dream I had lost, a long time ago coming true.
Listen to me and you will know what I mean,
come into my world and together we dream.

We met in December on a cold winter day,
from that moment on, I felt strange in a way.

A feeling I had forgotten so long
came into my heart like a beautiful song.
And all the nice things I see in my dream,
things like having a future
with us as a team.

And yes you are there, very special and kind,
a wonderful person with such a strong mind.
I respect you for that dear, never forget
and I love you for that, since the first day we met.

This is my Poem, from me it's for you,
whenever I say I love you it's true.
Yes this is my Poem and I wrote it for you,
If you love me, I will love you too.

Heidi Annemarie Tidwell
LITTLE BOY IN A MAN'S BODY
Little boy in a man's body,
trying so hard to get out,
trying so hard to forget the man's world
trying so hard to be proud.

Pride left him many jears ago
pride for laughter and joy
happiness sharing with someone he loves,
he just can't find it that boy.

Sad is this world around him so sad,
and he knows it is true,
he gets so furious and he gets so mad
if you remind him of you.

Oh little boy, oh pardon big man,
I don't have to ask how you feel,
I will not be part of the world you are in
or the happiness you have to steal.

Dan Turner Sr
A PLACE OF PEACE
Many times I have walked this road,
Up and down this path.
Seems I always carried a heavy load
But I always tried not to look back.
I took my cares down to the creek.
I would wet a line and catch some sleep
And dream of places far away,
The land, the sea, the air.
I never got to stay the whole day
Which I thought was never fair.
Reel in my line, it's not a switch.
Turn loose the fish I didn't catch.
Go down the path and walk along
The road and head for home.
To this place I'll return one day
And maybe by then I'll get to stay.

Wendy Thomas
THE FETUS

To Shawn and our son Mark, who inspired me deeply...

I look around and see many young faces,
I, too, am as young as they.
Yet, I have aged.
We, are growing up real fast.

They look around unaware of me, us.
They soon will know.
I, us, are together and are one,
They will look down on us.

We will be protected though.
There is one man who cares for us.
Who brought you together.
He helped make you, and loves us.

We'll walk towards the darkness,
and we'll be old and happy.
Yet I am as young as they,
and they are twice as sad.

Allan De Fiori Litt B
CONFIDENCE IN GOD
Almost forgetting the corporeal weight, rapt toward, God who willingly forgives, on her knees (she) her beautiful body abandons: Tenderly one and the other palm. A tired sorrow, a celestial calm appear gathered in her whole person, but in her mind which reasons with God, gleams the soul's immortal ray! And she seems to foretell:
If towards a serene, hopeful time, every little sweet thing deceives me, and life becomes wary— O Lord, trusting in Thine paternal bosom, my soul applies and finds shelter into an affection which is not earthly.***
Poetry is an expression of life, a slice of death, a form of love.
There is such power in the written word, such beauty.***
Gloriosa spes in Deo. Magna invocatio Domini.—Solvitur in Excelsis.

Janice G Tate
LIFE
It is in a baby's sweet breath,
or an old man's last gasp in death.

It is a soft caress
in a moment of stress.

Mother's arms, loving, soothing
woodland deer frozen in time,
unmoving.

Lover's touch, meaning so much.
Cloudless dreams, often of such.
Heart's broken, full of numbing pain.
Soulful cries, all in vain.

It is compassion, it is truth.
Found under each and every roof.

It beats in the heart of every man and beast.
And so it shall be until all time has ceased.

Don Thieme
US

Like sands from different
shores, we have drifted
together.

Thousands of grains mingle,
as your being enters mine.

We share the ecstasy
of the surf.
We endure the heat
of the day's sun.

A fleeting moment
of eternity is ours
for
the eternal wave will cover us.

Until then,
we must not miss
the beauty at our window.

The sunrises, the sunsets . . .
they are ours now.

J Mechele Thompson
FOUR SEASONS OF LOVE
The winter seemed so cozy and warm,
We snuggled closely during the storm.
The spring it was breezy and bright,
We were together from morning to night.
The summer was so joyful and fun,
We laid together enjoying the sun.
Now the Fall is finally here
Life will be wonderful enjoying another year.

Gail Teague
MY DEAREST FRIEND

To Rachel—who fought a good fight; finished the course; and kept the faith.

She always stood by her beliefs,
True to her heart—that was her way.
Though fame and fortune hailed her not,
Her greatness lives from day to day.

My true companion, faithful friend,
Her counsel wise, her laughter gay,
She held my trembling heart within,
And showed me how to find the way.

The love she gave—love without end,
Would light my path and calm my fears—
I did not recognize it then,
But I have lived it through the years.

I see it all so clearly now,
The best of me that lies within
Is her own heart she gave away,
That lives in me until the end.

Through her example I have known
How strength can heal and love can mend.
I'll see again, at Heaven's door—
My mother, and my dearest friend.

Gail Teague
DAWN
Only God can make a dawning—
Moving picture of creation,
Just before the light breaks through.

In the stillness of the morning,
Just before the day beginning,
Signs of life begin their living.

Bird songs fill the morning air
With Heaven's voices to declare,
"A brand new day is here!"

Earth awakes and lifts its eyes
To say "Good Morning" to the skies,
Then all is still again.

Raindrops rouse the lazy trees—
As they're awakened by the breeze,
The picture comes to life.

Joseph Tarkanic
I'M
The frost on your window
The corner you can't see around
The shadow behind you

I'm
Wherever you're found

I'm
The words you can't find
The love you can't feel

Linda R Thorne
THOUGHTS
These thoughts take place at the break of day,
With the weather outside humid and the sky dark and gray.

I set here at work with my work all completed,
My mood is quite stagnant—but not yet defeated.

It has been at least two years since I talked to you last.
Now it is time to live for the future and discontinue the past.

Of course, the future is unpredictable but still it holds hope.
Each day we are faced with decisions with which we must cope.

Unforeseen events change the world all the time.
With politics and destruction, what a pity, what a crime.

Individuals may say, "I am but one person, what could I attempt?"
While others unite and reply, "Why should he be exempt?"

The time is now for the people to take a stand—
Disaster has spread too far across the land.

Which side are you on, you know you must choose.
Shall we all stand together, or shall we all lose?

You may think it is silly to worry or fret,
But unless changes are made you may see the day yet:

When your children are unable, in the broad light of day—
To go to their back yard and feel safe just to play.

Shelly M Tarabochia
GOODNIGHT

Dedicated to Mike Sienko who passed away February 3, 1990, "I love you Grandpa."

As the snow falls gently
forming a carpet of white,
the time is pure
as I wish you a goodnight

I think back in time
we laughed; as we did cry,
the thoughts of you will stay
as the time passes by

My tears will soon dry
and I will be okay,
I cherish our memories
for they are here to stay

Now don't get me wrong
I will miss you; oh so much,
because you are my Grandpa
and I love you a bunch

I know you are tired
so you have a good rest
you have a long journey
and you deserve the best.

Carmel M Tanguay
LIFE
Words . . .
Feelings too deep for Words
Life too full of Feelings
Love and Pain for all of Life
Never ending Love and Pain
Merry-Go-Round of existence Never ending
catch the Golden Ring of Merry-Go-Round
Love and Marriage the Golden Ring
Words . . . Love and Marriage
Feelings too deep for Words
Never ending Love and Pain

Maye D Taylor
ODE TO JESUS

I dedicate this poem to my two moms, Ruth Gordon Dempsey and Mattie Gordon, who sacrificed their needs in order to meet mine and my brothers and sisters.

There comes a time
Once upon there was
Of some thought never been
He was, He is, will ever be
Master, Saviour, Friend

He came, He died, He rose again
The Man, the King, the Jew
To save a lost and dying world
To keep the chosen few

The once upon a time there was
Forgiveness, love, and grace
He would have come to sup and dine
With mercy on His face

Reflecting to back to once upon
To what then might have been
Before He came to claim His own
Some would not let Him in

Watch for the night cometh
When you can watch no more
The sickle has been driven
The house an open store

Elaine Traynelis-Yurek
THE SPIDER'S WEB
Jewels glisten in the morning sun
exposing a night's work intricately done.
Design is all perfection
As one examines each section.
What hidden power directs this fragile chain
Of little workers whose webs catch rain?
From time immemorial they leave their mark.
Catching jewels for a Monarch.

Elaine Traynelis-Yurek

THE GIFT OF LIFE

He came into my life when I was half formed,
Offering me a patience and gentleness I never knew.
Oh how I struggled with it as my Ignorance blew
And stubbornly clung I to the lower ways.
Slowly the breaks came as the snapping of a twig that lays.
New form began to take shape.
Then came the wrenching, flying out of my life.
Leaving barely discernible traces in strife.
Now shaping came from that which is beyond.
With great pulling and taxing,
Allegiance formed with great waxing.
Citadels torn and barricades crushed.
No gentle snapping now,
Emerging with what I never knew
I offer the gift of life to you.

Karla Thornton

MELLOW MADNESS

Thoughts of Mellow Memories float throughout my mind. Lonely daisies waver in the wind leaving a fragrance of lost lust in its path. Two people meet and can feel the energy of physical attraction, yet they're unable to express their feelings.

Quick glances and soft touches torture the mind while you slowly realize that your love partner lives in the core of your imaginations. Those fanciful creations of the mind that leave a tantalizing, yet sour feeling at the pit of your stomach.

Unanswered questions that jag at your heart like a knife being plunged deep within your soul, never cease to amaze you. Will anyone ever understand you or will you forever be immersed in MELLOW MADNESS!!

Clara J Turner

THE DAILY WEATHER REPORT
(January 4, 1990)

Early this morning the sky is blue
and the sun is shining bright
The clouds rising on the horizon are gray and blue & white
The Little Winterbirds, The Bunting Birds
and the Snowbirds are calling for snow
The Bunnies are hopping down the wood's trail
The Squirrels are sitting on the old porch rail
The Little Chic-a-dees perched high in the trees
are singing their melodies
This evening at sunset the clouds of blue,
gray and white have covered the blue sky
and the sun is shining bright, sending through
the clouds its colorful rays of light
Falling down real slow are a few scattered
flakes of snow

Bhujanga R Lankipalli

LONGING FOR A LUNAR LAUNCHER

Dedicated to my beloved parents

In the blue sky is shining the full moon
Though she does look winsome, she's alone
She seems to call me from the Heaven
I wish I were one in the Sputnik's cabin
or else having a huge and capable balloon
that could defy the laws of gravity
and understand my love's gravity
for such a fantastic celestial Beauty
And take me away into the vicinity
of my darling's pure and white dacha
from the clutches of this carnal world
to a sensible and saner one, for good!

Let all in the world of hypocrisy and mintocracy
Try to transform this into an egalitarian society!

Michele Jill Wright

CRIMES OF PASSION

Don't say you care in every way,
Then say you're here and walk away.
My love for you is very deep.
Sweet tears of pain I always weep.
My heart it aches with all I've given.
To crimes of passion I feel I'm driven.
From jealous lips true love doth fall.
If you're not mine you're none at all.
I'll pearse your heart with the pain I've felt.
In rain of fear I'll watch you melt.
So leave me now or choose to stay . . .

With the crimes of passion you become my prey . . .

Betty Alice Teel

HAPPY HOLIDAYS

Time was when I loved going
dancing to the Big City Clubs
Where the beer and wine flowed freely
in dark corners of the Pubs
For college kids it was so great—
so carefree and such fun
Taking out that "special date"—
good times for everyone
But now since we're married and
really "settled down"
Very seldom do we ever have
"a night out on the town"
Our nights and weekends with our
sweet kids now are spent
Sharing their little interests and
with them we are quite content
Oh, the Happy Holidays with family,
friends, and one another
Can never be measured by money
nor words—pleasant days like no other
We begin by singing "Auld Lang Syne"
ushering in January's Happy New Year
February's Washington and Lincoln—
St. Valentine's giving heart-shaped
boxes and "Cupid's Cards" to those
we hold so dear
March brings Irish Folks "wearin'-o-the-green" on St. Patrick's Day
Christ's Cross, the Easter Lily, and
families in Church on Easter Sunday
Laughing children with baskets
hunting pastel-colored eggs from Easter Bunny
Flowers we bring for Loved Ones
gone each Memorial Day in May
Picnics on July 4th with baseball,
fireworks, songs, and speeches on this Patriotic Day
Hard-working Americans rest or
play on Labor Day in September
We honor our Brave Men in the
Armed Forces on Veteran's Day in November
Thanksgiving Day with stuffed
turkey and all the trimmings—
Blessed Christmas—the Babe in
the manger; lighted tree, Santa,
carols and gifts—thankful
hearts for December and
another year of Happy Endings.

Joe Tyndell

JUST TO BE A CHILD

Dedicated to God, my family and my friends in Denison, TX.

Just to be as a child, God,
Free from sin and strife;
Walk with me every mile
Down the road of life.
Let me be sincere and happy
And give me a pleasant smile.
Share with me your wonderful wisdom,
Make me humble as a child.

Ah, the joy of being a child again—
The magic of eggs in a nest,
Or watching a fledgling learn to fly,
Striving to do its very best.
Deep in the leaves there's a feathery owl
With large, mysterious eyes,
Looking up at a circling sparrowhawk
As it soars high up in the sky.

An old bass feeds under the lilypads,
Gracefully seeking minnows out.
The rippling of silent water
Causes frogs to skitter about.
A dark cloud of redwing blackbirds
Swoops down and covers a tree—
A vision of simple grace and beauty
That only a child would see.

Just to frolic through fresh wildflowers,
Beauty often by adults unseen,
Or roam white-capped fields of clover
Laced with many shades of green.
The fragrant lilacs hum with honeybees
While butterflies daintily pass,
As I rest in happy contentment
And become a child at last.

I return to the cool, damp creek bank
To fish and often to dream,
Or jump in and wade barefooted
Down a shallow, rocky stream.
My heart overflows with gladness, God,
When you whisper to me so mild
That I have been looking at your world
Through the trusting eyes of a child.

Joe Tyndell

GRANDMOTHER

When I hear songs from a hymnal,
Songs that Grandmother sang,
Fond memories fill my heart
And I become a child again.

I return to the old rustic farmhouse
That's been battered by wind and rain,
Where love and happiness flourished,
Enduring o'er sorrow and pain.

Grandmother would fill the kerosene lamp
And polish the globe with care.
She stoked the potbellied stove
With wood from a box beside her chair.

I see the bleached, crannied floors
Where cold wind whistled through,
While I snuggled in Grandmother's iron bed,
Thinking of my long walk to school.

Grandmother had little education
But she read the Bible, every verse,
From Genesis through Revelation
She'd explain God's Holy Word.

From a wobbly oak table
And a squeaky rocking chair
She read from her tattered Bible,
Inspiring me with joy and fear.

Always with an empty cupboard,
She began each day with a prayer.
And from her vegetable garden
There was always food to share.

I know Grandmother is in Heaven
With happiness beyond compare.
I know she sings in the angel choir
And worships God up there.

Joe Tyndell

WHEN JESUS PASSED MY WAY

Strolling along the beach one day
A stranger passed my way.
We stopped and talked a while
Amid the ocean spray.

He was dressed in a seamless robe
And his eyes, they glowed like fire.
There was a mystery about this man
That filled my heart with joy.

"You're not a Christian," He said,
In a kind and gentle voice.
"Be not afraid, my child," He said,
"Today you will make your choice."

His words of wisdom touched my heart
And chilled me to the bone.
Then on the beach, I knelt and prayed
And suddenly He was gone.

With tearfilled eyes, I continued on,
Searching for this wonderful man.
But to my surprise, I noticed,
He left no footprints in the sand.

My life now has new meaning
And I thank my God each day,
For that beautiful day on the beach,
When Jesus passed my way.

Joe Tyndell

THANKSGIVING DAY THANKS AND PRAISE

Dear Lord, we thank you for your many blessings on this
Thanksgiving Day.
Thank you for your love divine that never goes away.
Thank you for our church, Dear Lord, and the fellowship
We enjoy therein.
Thank you for our pastor, our loved ones, neighbors and
Our friends.
Thank you, Dear Lord, for all the lovely little children
Who make our lives a pleasure;
Without their smiles and laughter there would be less worldly
treasure.
We thank you for all the beautiful scenery—
The beach with ocean spray,
And all the pretty flowers that bloom along the way.

Thank you for the bird that sings
from high atop its perch,
That fills our hearts with joyful
music, melodious and
unrehearsed.
Dear Lord, we thank you for our
magnificent world created
With Thine own hands;
For the many wonders of nature
that we don't fully understand.
Thank you for the old people from
whom much wisdom we have gained.
Help us never to consider them a
burden, Lord,
Of that we'd be ashamed.
Dear Lord, thank you for our
health which is so important and
dear.
Thank you for standing by us so
many times, often
When death is near.
Thank you for the food you put on
our tables on this Thanksgiving
Day
And for reminding us to share with
others as they
Journey on their way.
Thank you, Lord, for the peace we
enjoy
Which has triumphed o'er many
scars.
Thank you for our friends and
loved ones lost in Foreign Wars.
Dear Lord, we thank you for your son
Jesus
Whom you sacrificed to set us
free,
Who shed his blood for all our sins
on the Cross at Calvary.
We thank you for our country and
the fact that we are free.
But our greatest privilege of all in
life, Dear Lord,
Is to love and worship Thee.
We love Thee and praise Thee, Dear
Lord, as we journey
From day to day.
We thank you for all things, through
Jesus Christ,
On this wonderful and glorious
Thanksgiving Day.

Cora Touchton
ARKANSAS

In the piney woods of Arkansas,
There seems to be such peace and
rest.
You can see the trees all glittering,
They seem to know they are the best.

You can walk the hills of clover,
And smell the fragrant rare.
Looking all around you,
There is real contentment there.

If you would like to see a place,
Where love still abounds.
You should visit my old home place,
And see all the beauty for miles
around.

Sometimes you can feel a little bit of
Heaven,
As you sit and watch the clouds
abound.
They all seem to be saying,
That God's love is all around.

Adele Traub
OUR WORLD

I have told you my stories
I have told you my dreams
I have told you about my life.
Why not now don't you tell of the
dreams you've often had.
Of course we all have some the same.
You musn't be afraid,
We are friends not enemies.
Come to the fire
It is your turn, your time.
Share with us—trust in us,
For here there is only peace.
No talks of money, war, or politics
Everyone is accepted, here no one is
different.
There is no hate, no lies, no death,
Only happiness, truth, and life.
Anyone else can live in the other
world,
A stupid world doing stupid things;
If only they knew what they were
doing.
This is the world I love.
This is my world and I hope it can be
yours too.

Jeanne Tonkin
LITTLE LISA

When she was born
I'm glad to say
She had a nice look
So bright and gay

Some months later
On in time
So many diapers
Still hung on the line

Some of her antics
Frets and frowns
Go from a demon
To a cute little clown

Up late every night
Just fooling around
Not a wink of sleep
Anywhere to be found

But still all in all
With a sweet little smile
A hug and a kiss
Makes it all worthwhile

Peggy M Joyce

Peggy M Joyce
BLESSINGS

To: My Husband—Rev. Johnny B. Joyce.

Count your blessings, from day to
day
And let God bless you in His own
way
Be grateful, be thankful, for whatever
arise
And count your blessings, that you
are alive.

Count your blessings from day to day
And thank God for the freedom of
pray, in your own way
As the sun adawns, And another day
start to form,
And as the darkest hour goes
It's better to hope, though the clouds
hang low.

So count your blessings from day to
day
And never, never forget to pray
That you heed God's voice
Whenever life asks you to make a
choice,
Always count your Blessings.

Dawna Pronk

Dawna Pronk
FIELDS OF FREEDOM

To my husband John, for all his love and support throughout the years.

I long for fields in which i could run,
wild and forever free.
I would try and remember who i was
and save a little piece of me.
I would hide it in my pocket, to save
for another time.
When things got bad i could take it
out, and retreat into my mind.
I would be set free once again to
escape from my world of pain.
To run through the fields wild and
free, never to leave again.

Claudette Gasch
DESTINY?

Mirror mirror on the wall,
set humanity up to take the fall
Fears of our children burning
bright
Don't extinguish the candlelight
Show us our reflections true,
But let only the good shine through
If it comes in our artless slumber
When mankind can't see the thunder
Be thankful we won't hear the
screams
of dying mothers and shattered
dreams
The earth is on fire like the sun
Do not cry the day has come
Worry brother, I grieve too
the loss of all things old and new
—Especially the loss of me and
you.

Janet E Tichnell
THE PROMISE

This poem is dedicated to my family and the people of White Church.

God gave a promise
One that wouldn't break.
The clouds roll in and out.
As morning breaks, with a new dawn.
A new day gives, another promise.
On that day, came rain, so pure.
The promise of many colors;
Seven colors, so right across the
heavens;
Red to orange, yellows to greens, to
blues to purples.
'Tis true, God gave and holds many
promises,
Waiting just for you.
So, God gave a promise
One that wouldn't break, the
Rainbow.

Richard Duffy
ETERNITY

This poem is dedicated to my new wife, my new life.

You will be with me for all eternity,
And throughout the ages
We'll anxiously turn the pages
Into another day of our life.
I'm holding you oh so close
Your love is what I cherish most!
Close your eyes,
Take a deep breath,
Let the wind blow through your hair
Slowly, as you open your eyes
You begin to realize,
I am the wind that blows your hair.
I am the air in which you breathe.
I am the chills up and down your
spine.
And you my love, are mine!

Ann U Mariasz
A MOTHER'S DAY BLESSING

Dedicated in memory of Julia Ushala, a wonderful mother for 22 years of love and care.

Today is Mother's Day, a beautiful day it is, because of God's creativity of Mothers and this Spring's special day. As I sat in my comfortable chair, front door opened wide, I noticed a most beautiful sight. I'm not a writer, but I hope and would like to be, for you see this beautiful thought came to me, from this sight I saw in our tree. In this tree, starting to get its Spring and Summer dress of green and leafy leaves, two lovely and beautiful doves, resting and viewing the tree. I wondered why they just keep on staying and singing this beautiful sound. Then one dove stayed and the other flew away, and then brought back a twig and then another and another. This was a very inspirational sight. So as I watched I felt and thought to myself, what a beautiful gift God sent to me in front of my door on our home sight. My immediate thoughts were when I seen these doves of the Holy Spirit and of the peace and joy and love they symbolize. Mother's Day is always a little sad for me, because of a wonderful and good Mother that I had. But to see these two doves on this special day, somehow I felt she's not far away and still looks over me, cares for me, and sends me a message through the creativity of God's Hands on this special day.

Tyrenea M Sharpe
YOU CARE!

God, I saw no love.
I looked all around.
With my heart stretched out wide,
Love seemed not to be found.

In the newness of morning
Love had taken its flight.
I waited with hope
For its return in the night.

But while waiting on knees
Bent in heartfelt despair,
Love found me in Your whispering
assurance
You care.

Dusti Weldon
LOVE

Dedicated to Dad, Mom and Stoney.

Love is sweet,
Love is kind,
Love is like a yankeedime,
Love is a pain shooting through
your heart,
love is a whisper in the dark,
Love is many different things
So listen when your heart rings.

Cheerrie Johnson
CHILDREN OF WAR

To the children of the world.

Listen, do you hear them?
Crying in the night,
All the little children,
Trembling with fright.

Tell me, can't you hear them?
Crying all alone,
Stumbling through the darkness,
Looking for a home.

Oh, you must hear them,
Waking from their sleep,
Crying in the dark of night,
For something they can eat.

I know you can hear them!
I hear them everywhere,
So lonely and neglected,
They need someone to care.

Oh, tell me that you hear them,
Don't let them cry in vain,
Please, tell me that you hear them,
For they're crying out your name.

Teresa Harper
MEMORIES OF SUNDAYS

In Loving Memory Of Mrs. Bessie Lee Edenfield Stewart, My Grandmother.

Grandma would meet us at the door,
With a loving big smile we always
adored.
You-all come in and stay a while,
Your favorite's in the kitchen you
know my style.
Baking pies and cakes you could lick
the bowl,
Everything had to be from scratch
this I know.
With the family of all Sixty Three,
When we came to visit it was a
crowd you see.
Never a dull moment or a place to sit,
So much laughing and chatter you
didn't want it to quit.
Someone shouts, "The Games are on
get your hats."
We grab our gloves and bats,
To the field we would head . . .
"Look out for cow pat!!!"
The games would go on for hours and
hours,
Who cared if dark came the games
were ours.
Grandma was there with iced tea for
everyone,
A pat on the back for that swell home
run.
With a large smile and gleam in her
eyes,
A job well done with proudness that
made you cry.
Family so close so loving always,
That you pass it on with memories of
Sundays.

Ann Sloan
THE FROG
The frogs 'colors' are black, and
brown,
They hop and hop and never stop.

Their eyes look like they're going to
pop out, but if they do you better
watch out!

Robin Leigh Johnson
ME, MYSELF, AND I

Dedicated to God, Mom, Dad, brothers, and family, Janna Poston, Ms. Seamen, Mr. Rader, Tracie Polk, and everyone else who encouraged me to shoot for my goals.

Me, Myself, and I;
I have two legs, two arms, two ears,
and two eyes.
I am unique in my own special way,
Because everyday when I wake up, I
start a special and unique day.
I am called I
And also me
But I am also called Myself.
Me, Myself, and I;
I am here today and not where
yesterday lies.
I have my faults,
But afterwards get caught.
Yes, Me, Myself, and I
Yes, everyday I look at you with my
own special and unique eyes.
Everyone is unique with his own
ways,
Whether it be that they brighten
someone's day like the shining sun's
rays.
Me, Myself, and I;
Is a perfect way to say that without
Me, Myself, and I, I would be
nothing but hellos and goodbyes!

Kristina Baleczak
DEATH OF MY CABBAGE PATCH KID
One Christmas I received a Cabbage
Patch dolly,
With her face all dimpled and
freckled and jolly.
Slowly and painfully I put her to
death,
Choking and tossing 'til she coughed
her last breath.
When I was through, I had her
beheaded,
A stunt to this day I have never
regretted.
She was struck with malice, took a
horrible beating,
And all other attacks are not good for
repeating.
Her insides surrounded her carcass in
a mess,
And there was many a hole in her
little red dress.
Done with destruction, to my parents
I said,
"Can I have a puppy next year
instead?"

Shirley L McLaughlin
EACH ONE IS DIFFERENT
The fields are alive with his flowers,
their colors all aglow,
He sends the rain and sun that makes
them reach and grow,
He makes them blend and come alive
with His tender loving care,
Each one so different, Each one so
rare.

He made us in His image, His love
we were to show,
He uses the pain within us to make us
reach and grow,
He's made us blend together as He
teaches us to care,
Each of us so different, Each of us so
rare.

His prayer is for the seeds we are to
plant and sow,
His love for us is boundless He wants
the world to know,
And through this love the world will
know how deeply He does care,
Though each of us is different, Each
of us is rare.

Sara Musillo
MESSY
I like being messy,
Yes, it's true.

C'mon, admit it,
So do you.

I just don't know why
My parents complain,

They're driving me
Totally insane!

What's so wrong
About being messy?

Nobody said I had
To be dressy.

I just shove it in my drawer,
And throw things on the floor.

Cleaning up just doesn't pay . . .
I don't care what people say,
I like doing things my own way.

And when I ask,
"What is the matter?"

My parents look at me
Like I was the mad hatter.

I plan to move out
When I am nineteen,

But I'll be rich
So my maid can clean!

Tina Kneram Ardito
DREADFUL DOING

Dedicated with love to my mother Sheryl and my father Tommy Scott the Ardito family. Life is too short to sin. Love makes the world go 'round.

You don't know what you're doing until everything is gone. It's not worth it, not worth it at all. Your life will go by so fast. You won't remember anything, except for your Dreadful Doing. Take a look at what you're doing. 'A very good look' or you won't even notice. You won't want to. You know what's happening and you can't face it. Love and happiness are most important, along with a clean soul. That knows what it's doing. Your love and your life are too important to waste it all away. So let's stop the hurting and start loving again. Then we can have a better today, with hope that Dreadful Doing will fade . . .

Sharon Dee Keller
REALITY
If I were but a vision of who I ought
to be,
If I were but a shadow of who I wish
I'd see,
If I could write a script of how I
ought to be,
If I could paint a portrait of who I
wish I'd see,
If only all my dreams could be,
Then at last I'd accept reality.

Jean Hayman
SOUNDS OF SILENCE
Where sunlight slips through pines
creating
etchings on the sand,
And Spanish moss hangs silently,
holding
secrets of the past.

Where golden cordgrass gently
moves
in murmuring azure tides,
And herons serve as sentinels for
unseen
eyes that wait;

Where wind creates a symphony for
all the
heavenly choirs,
And thoughts are flung across a
stretch of
boundless sky;

Where time stands still and heart and
mind are cleansed,
And no man walks. And silence is the
only sound;

I touched the hand of God and knew
that I was whole.

Dorothy Passoth
FOURTEEN YEARS ARE YOURS
Fourteen years are yours
today, my son.
You're the size of a man,
the shape of a teen.

Your mind already full of life's joys
and sorrows
You intuit the depths of others' souls
and scarce know yours.

Lucky the woman who gets you.
Lucky the children you'll beget.
Lucky the mother who helped make
you and is watching you spread
your life.

Cyndi McClendon
ARRIVALS
While walking down the airport hall,
Baggage claim check in my hand,
I saw standing there against the wall
A black lady, fine and grand.

Tired wrinkles lined her well-worn
face
But you could not fault her dress
For although it was pre-dawn hours,
She stood wearing Easter best.

A wide-brimmed pink hat topped her
curls;
Her organdy dress, so neat.
You could tell this was Easter finery.
Then my eyes sank to her feet.

The shoes told much of this sweet
soul
For there on her feet, tired and sore,
A ragged old pair of blue house shoes
The matronly lady wore.

A young-aged black girl then rushed
up
And asked the woman in that place,
"Mamma? Is it really you?"
Her whole face then shone with
grace.
How I longed for my own mamma's
face!

Miss Garin Armenian
PAGES
Day after day,
She sat.
Mesmerized,
Book in hand.

Week after week,
She stayed.
Glazed,
Novel on lap.

I called,
Yet no answer.
For she was off,
Into another world.
Hypnotized,
She remained—
Only moving,
To turn the next page of adventure.

She was frozen.
Time stood still.
Her head,
Bending over the leaflet,
As if one worshipping a god.

Hour after hour,
I walked in,
Only to see her unmoved, unchanged.
Her statue,
Unruffled.

I ventured toward her.
The subtle movement of her
fingers—
Had stopped.
My hand extended to her shoulder.
And with that single touch,
Her body crumbled.
Not into hard pieces of stone,
But into soft, flowing pages.

Pages of the life she never had.

Linda Rhodes
VICTIM OF AN ACRONYM
And I Do Suffer
And I Do Struggle
And It Does Strain
As I Die Slowly
Surrendering to pain.

The closer it gets to dark
The faster I ride my bike home.
The faster the ice cream melts
The tighter I hold my cone.
But now after all my futile efforts
Death and I seem all alone.

And I Do Smile
on the sunny days
Though sometimes it hurts to lift my
head
I'd rather be weak in body than dead.

And Ignorance Defiantly Survives
When it should be defunct
Giving way to preservation
of precious human lives.

And It Seems to me a Dreadful Sin
To be a victim of an acronym.

Jean L Palmer
MELLOWED DOWN AND LAID BACK
I am mellowed down in Jesus,
I am laid back in His arms.
Earthly pleasures may avoid me,
But I'll focus on His charms.

As He daily gives me blessings
And He teaches me His way,
I will learn to walk beside Him
And be close to Him each day.

And I know it won't be easy,
And the road, it may be long.
But in Christ I'm sweetly resting,
And He gives my heart a song.

So when your life hands you trouble,
And when your world does you harm,
Just get mellowed down in Jesus
And laid back in His arms.

Kathryn W Johnson
THE LONER
Is that sea gull lost on his inland
pond,
perched on a stump alone,
majestically alone?
Is he envying the lordly mallards
circling to and fro,
preening greens and gold?
Will he fly to the furthermost rim of
sky
someday,
And be tinted by sunset hues, and
cry?
He may.
But the winds of the lightly salted air,
somehow,
Will be sweeter than any landlocked
lair,
somehow!

Jennifer Brooks
A GROWING SEASON
If I planted a grain of sand,
In your mouth,
Would you grow a pearl for me?
And if, by some great, good luck
A string of wisdom should
Spew out,
Would you wrap it around my neck,
And waist, and fingers
Like an oyster queen?
I have need of such smooth,
White loveliness in my naked hands.
A small irritation is such a little
Price to pay for these fruits,
O brother mine.
I would that every priceless pearl
Were so easily obtained.

Wesley Henley
INVASIONS AND EVASIONS
Reality, we often think,
Is not so kind,
And must be disciplined so it stays in
its place.
It's like the fleeting sense of power
experienced by the small boy
As he puffs away the parachutes from
the dandelion plants,
To watch them sink slowly into the
jungle of whatever life is there.
They say that in a vacuum they'd
sink as fast as a steel ball,
Though in a strong wind they scatter
in confusion like clouds gaming with
the sun
rays — and they've argued about
that.
But, to this small lad there is no
concern about the vacuum or the
wind.
He'll puff out more invasions until
the plants are gone,
And then seek something else to
create, or destroy.

Barbara Lynn Chenoweth
CHRISTMASTIME

This poem is dedicated to my family whom I love dearly.

Christmas is a time of giving and
sharing,
Of laughter and togetherness, of
loving and caring.
The twinkling of the lights, the
ringing of the bells,
The melody of the songs, the
sweetness of the smells,
The search for presents, the
decorations to see,
The baking of the cookies, the
trimming of the tree,
All bring us memories of Christmases
past,
Of the special moments that will
always last,
From deep in our hearts come
Christmas wishes,
Filled with all our love, plus hugs and
kisses.

Lisa Cestaro
NO WAY OUT
Grasping for breath
Reaching out for every last second
Trying to find the way out
Like some animal trapped in a cage
Or some prisoner locked in a cell
Like some great magician's final act
The great illusion
But this is no magic trick
There's no audience to cheer you on
There's no trapdoor
Just a bunch of emptiness taking up
space
Which seems so far away
Yet it keeps blinding me
Maybe I'm closer than I think
Maybe I'm just an arm's reach away
Another heartbeat
Another tear
Then nothing, but the way out.

Mary Burns Yasbick
FOREVER GREEN
Green is a color of freshness
It blankets the earth with
grace and warmth . . .
A gift to the earth that in turn
is freely given to us.
It's a color of readiness,
endurance and growth.
It's true and alive and
its depth steadfast.
In likeness, Love holds all
these qualities of the color green.
And it is these qualities that
I have surrendered myself and
in turn, give freely to the man
I'll Love Forever Green.

Margaret Burt
RHYMIN' ICE BLUES
Poised and sure, a pleasure to the eye,
He beckoned, "Only you."
A quickened heart gave me reply,
That surely his embrace would
subdue.

But iced and hard,
His arms enfolded me.
Clinking cold resounding
down
'round
my shape.

Fool to love too hurriedly,
When time and sorrow
break
down
the bonds
made in haste.

Phyllis Adams
SISTER'S LOVE

In memory of my sister, Millie.

There will always be a tear in my
eye,
And now I will tell you the reason
why.
I've lost my sister, I've lost my
friend,
But the memories of her shall never
end.
We were oh so close as close could
be,
She was so very, very dear to me.
My heart has been heavy, that I
know,
But the love I have for her, I can't
help but show.
Our devotion to one another was
simply great,
Our meetings were punctual and
never late.
So many memories of laughter and
tears,
As we grew older over the years.
The last time I saw her was when we
said goodbye,
She stood in the doorway with a tear
in her eye.
With a wave of her hand and a smile
on her face,
I knew then she was a woman with
heavenly grace.
Now her face beams in all my
dreams,
And everything brings memories it
seems.
Of a witty young girl so full of
laughter,
She'll always be missed, now and
after.

Maria A Allen
SNOWFLAKES
On a quiet winter's day
I sit in my room
staring out a clouded window
thinking only of thoughts of you.

I sit and wonder what it would be like
if our love were to endure.
Would our lives be complete.
Could I commit myself to you
without any inhibitions
or would tragedy strike at any minute
causing lost feelings and pain.

For at any moment
I could turn to another
causing you to be left with only
the Passion of the Heart.

But in any event, always remember
that
I will always be a friend and
confidante
loving you always.

Janet Millian
LIFE

To my husband, children and grandson, Robby.

What is life with all its strifes and
cries
With every passing moment of
Uncertainty of our lives
With all its wars and hates,
And lies that destroy our lives
'Tis very little love that we have
For each other and our lives

John Morris
THE SEA

In memory of my late grandmother. May God bless her, love John.

The calm, blue skies keep watch o'er
the golden brown sand.
As the cool wind and crisp waves
move softly hand in hand.

The sun rises slowly o'er the
horizon's edge.
To shine warmly and endlessly, is its
only pledge.

The sun's radiant glow is like that of
a noble leader.
As it shimmers upon the ocean, there
is no place sweeter.

Seashells of brilliant colors sparkle
like precious jewels.
While tiny hermit crabs search for
home renewals.

The cool seaward breeze brings a
tantalizing chill.

To the soft-gliding sea gulls who fly peacefully at their own will.

Flying high o'er the vast, clear waters of the blue sea.
That stretches outward, as far as the eye can see.

The sound of quaint palm tree leaves echo in the smooth breeze.
As the sun begins to set and time seems to freeze.

Sylvia McCutchen
WHY GOD HAS CALLED
A little angel, God has called
To be with him above it all
Our hearts are broken
For words unspoken
He touched the hearts of those who cared
And everyone's life of whom he shared
Although he's gone we'll never forget him
We'll remember his smiles, his laughter, and cries
And hold to us dear, the days he was here
He was with us for just awhile
But oh how he made us smile
We loved him dearly
And don't see clearly
Why, God has called
God called in the night
For him to make his flight
God had his plans for him to come
And in his name thy will be done.

Linda Dale Turner
FREEDOM
Freedom is having political liberty and independent.
Freedom is love joy. The feeling of being immunity and peace.

To be a slave within open up your heart and let freedom in.
Let freedom ring and all the children sing.

Freedom is just a matter of speech if only our souls could be reached.
Poetry is freedom to say and feel what we believe.

Poetry is freedom to express the pain and experiences in our life.

To write for others, to share with our needs for hope to all who believe.

We should all join hands and raise our voices in freedom."

Shelley R Sponsler

Shelly R Sponsler
WEEKEND LOVER
Our bodies passed in the dead of the night,
Our faces illuminated by the pale moonlight.

Our eyes connected for some unknown chance,
Our bodies trembled from that split second glance.

The flame of passion ignited within,
The feeling was right for a night made of sin.

The lust filled oiur loins 'til we could wait no longer.
The feelings were right,
But ever present—the hunger.

Our bodies were bare,
But our souls not uncovered.

Come delight within me,
Come and be my weekend lover.

Paula Kay Twohy
1-2-3 CHEERS!

Dedicated to John Albert, John, Aric, and Ryan Keith through inspiration.

Kids are funny,
Kids are creepy,
They are angels when they're sleepy!

Kids are funny with their friends,
If they won't make some
Snowmen with them!

Kids are creepy,
If they can't open the door,
They make wooden keys to clog the hole more!

Kids are creative,
Full of self-esteem,
They stick together like a football team!

Creative they are,
On Halloween night,
Imaginations soar on frightened sights!

Oh what pride and self-esteem,
When their horizons are widened,
Eyes opened and gleamed!

Kids are like angels,
They make a great team,
All programmed together, blessed in their dreams!

Darleen M Russell
JEANNINE
A lovely lady passed my way
and paused for just awhile
She touched my life with
happiness and sprinkled it with
smiles

We found each other quite by chance
as friends so often do
And while we watched our
children grow, our bonds
grew stronger too

As we approached our middle years
God gently touched her hand
and took my friend beyond
with him, to his eternal land

Though years have passed
since she's moved on,
to smile from far above
She left with me her precious gift . . .
A LEGACY OF LOVE

D R Mote
BLUE PEN
Blue pen descriptive of a mood not colour
Blue pen descriptive of a life of mine own
Blue descriptive of mine soul

If colour served as a conduit for a soul,
As a life, enriched with shades of reality
Make mine colour blue

Blue with shades of blue
A consistency ne'er changing
A continuum of mine life

Blue pen descriptive of my life
Blue pen descriptive of a mood
Blue descriptive of my soul . . .

Carole F Webb
I AM WHO I AM
I am who I am because I'm me
I am an intelligent black woman
full of ideas and full of pride, don't try to bring me down with your high class actions or venomous ways,
I am as real as you.

I speak one's native tongue or speech
I have vigor and I am valuable
I am not vindictive, nor am I irate,
I am as real as you.

I am an evening star, I shine brightly upon others and I never change, you cannot bring me down verbally, nor can you antagonize me.
I am not the cause of your misfortune or your pathetic ways.

I am an intelligent woman
I can be irrational or vindictive, but I am more like the spine of my kind, you can try to treat me like a blister of some kind, and tease me at the same time, but the verdict is, I am who am because I'm me.

Patricia Troiano Peters
SINCERELY SPOKEN

"To my beloved friend Linda," the sassiest dragon slayer I know . . .

I have been some places, still
sometime, quite suddenly so,
Selected surviving, thru any sad scenarios.
Been sentenced for scandals, and what remain are the scars,
Sailed on a ship once, with a course set for Mars.
Seen sights so sizzling, that a sunset seems dim,
Touched serenity for a moment, and it stays deep within.
Kept silent when safety strolled by my door,
Sat staring at danger, need I say more?
Seized by Satan, saved by God,
Sipped champagne slowly,
in a bubble bath tub.
Yes, I sampled and savoured and saved what I could,
To store away secretly, my life as I should.

Jackie Gritton
YOU'VE ALWAYS BEEN THERE

To those ever in doubt, have faith that He is there because He is, and always will be.

The days are long and dreary, when you're not here beside me;
The days are morbid and hollow, when you're not there to follow.
But there are days when I can feel your presence, and my soul is then filled with your essence;
But sin is bound to come, if you're not there to be my savior one;
Somehow though you have made me strong, my mind has only deceived me, you've been there all along;
So if I'm ever in doubt, I'll just lift my head, and pray and shout!!
Now I know, sweet Jesus, that you <u>are</u> there, no matter what happens to me, you'll always care
Because you've always been there.

Margaret Ann Seipel
WINDOWS OF MY MIND

This poem is dedicated, with love, to my brothers and sisters, Darlene, Delores, Bud and Bill.

Where do I begin.
A thousand memories creep into my mind.
I feel a mass confusion,
As I'm viewing from afar.

Was I ever that young,
A child running through the meadows
Savoring the outdoors, a tomboy in the making.

So much to discover, acres to move about
Pastures and wooded hills to explore
Or to find a silent escape.

Brothers and sisters so much a part of my life.
Each so different from the other.
Mother and Father and Grandma Kate,
I see you all.
So many treasure to bring to life.

Now slowly I must search;
So clearly I can see
All the memories in the windows of my mind.

Claudia Ann Burns
MY HERO

This poem was written for my father, who was murdered March 15, 1969.

I can still remember then, when it was all new, when I was a little girl, and I remember him vaguely.

His hands were much bigger than mine, I can recall our walk in the woods, I even remember it was a Sunday.

I can still feel breathless as he threw me high, high, in the air, then he would catch me. He was strong.

When I did wrong I was sent to bed without any dinner and he would wake me for cream cheese and jelly. He was kind.

And he'd let me play with the glass dog, way upon the kitchen knick–knack shelf. Even after I broke it, he glued it back together for me. He was generous.

I can remember how he'd let me sit on his stomach and climb all over him, laughing. He was my mountain, my hero.

I was about four years old then, and there aren't many memories. But I remember how safe and warm I felt in his arms.

And the witch we saw together that Halloween night.

And I wish I had more memories, I can barely recall the day I woke up to learn he was gone. All I remember is how confused I was and am.

Sometimes I sit and think of him, and at those times I remember how much he loved me, and how much I loved him.

Even if it is only a memory, he is alive in my mind forever.

Me a little girl, and him, my mountain, my hero, my father.

Josephine Rhyder
LIFE HIGHWAY

This poem is dedicated to my brother Albert.

Our Life Highway is like a Roadway
on which we travel toward our destination.

With its intersections and detours that
goes in different directions,
As a journey through a person's life.

We have many interruptions in life
We have dreams that don't come true
We have unexpected surprises and
obstacles which keep us from
doing those things
That make us happy and prosperous.

But in spite of these disappointments
we can manage somehow to be
happy,
And be content with our life
situations
With faith and trust in God.

Even with Life's Shortcomings
we can always find happiness,
and joy in our daily living
With family and friends
and people whom we meet
On Our Life Highway.

John Austin Linke III
DIVINE GOLDEN DOLPHINS

To Natasha Nagaman, thank you for inspiring magical feelings of wonderment in my soul. To God for the talent I have.

They have deep golden skin
A constant warm sensual smile
A flick of the fin
Sends them soaring for miles

Divine Golden Dolphins
They swim in the sky
I seen them sometimes
When they play in the night

When my sleep is trampled by
nightmares
And my sheets soaked with fright
I watch them descend from the
heavens
Enveloped the auras of light

Soaring down to my bedroom
Arriving in a flash of golden haze
I leap onto the Divine dolphin's back
And off to the atmosphere we blaze

Spinning and twirling
Through the soft moonlight
Gasping and giggling
What a wonderful flight

A thousand dolphins and me
Swaying to a symphony of twilight
Floating on the breeze
Of a warm summer's night

Now my ride is over
As I fall to my bed
And curl up in my blankets
As sleep fills my head

I awake in the morning
With a smile on my face
And laugh as I imagine
My next ride through space

Patricia Mensch
OPTIONS ON TIME

To Rosemarie, Jeniffer, Daniel, Angela, & God. All of them gave me faith in new beginnings.

She sits there by herself,
Among the ruins of sanity,
Amidst shards of broken dreams,
Silently building her walls,
No touching hidden reservoirs,
Of long lost hopes and prayers,
Never to reach the bottom,
Of glistening pools of despair,
Letting no one get beyond,
The limits she has put upon
Herself
How do I touch you,
Can you still see,
Does light penetrate the fog,
Growing thicker each ticking second,
Don't lock me out when you're
drowning,
On the rushing tide of your fear,
There may be no miracles left,
But someone is here,
When you run out of time.

Nolan C Orgel
YOU TOUCH ME

To Jeff.

You touch me
A feather, soft and light
Like clouds, from one day to the next
Our game is different
I come home to find you
Soft and comfortable
Like goose down pillows and satin
sheets
We enter each other peacefully
Like a newborn asleep
Who is the child this night needing
mothers milk and roses
When I wake and look at you I smile
Remembering last night as we filled
the space between us
Our bodies, like parts of a puzzle,
fitting just so
And now, in the morning light that
floats down through the window
I see your smooth skinned shoulder
Like a pearl, round and unflawed
Your broad back, a wall towering
above me as I lie beside you
Your hair, still curly, but matted with
sweat from my palms
As I ran my fingers through the
waves in the moonlight

Elizabeth Beauchemin
POOR GRAMPA

I met a kindly gentleman
While in the park one day
We stopped to chat a moment
To pass the time away.

Then we walked a while together
And talked of many things
He told me of his loved ones
Of the sorrow that time brings.

He said, "I'm old and useless
Not needed anymore
My family wants to put me
In a place that's for the poor.

"They say I move too slowly
And my sight is not too clear
When they talk about my leaving,
Seems they think that I can't hear.

"They say my room is needed
That their house is much too small
No place for, "Poor Old Grampa"
I will miss them one and all."

It was time for me to leave him
And as I turned to walk away
He said, "I'm glad I met you"
Thanks for being here today.

Raymond Almodovar
IN THE EYE OF A STAR

Dedicated to Arlene Roman Cardona, the brightest star in my sky, truly beautiful in my eyes.

'Tis she who cries when I can no
longer bear,
and she hurts, deeply,
'cause she knows what I feel,
to see the misfallen pain of others . . .
I see her reflection in others' beauty
and to reach out, only in a vain grasp,
and my life is long and hard,
she watches, waits,
in a puddle of fallen tears
to love, to bear the loneliness . . .

Jim Webb
MY FRIEND IS GONE

My friend is gone, I'll see him no
more
Until together we walk that heavenly
shore.
From the very beginning until the
end,
He was ever, unfailing, my faithful
friend.
But he trusted Jesus to cleanse his
sin,
And because of that, I'll see him
again.
Whatever my need, whatever my
whim,
I always knew I could depend on
him.
And to take his place there is no other
For he was closer to me than any
brother.
We spent times together, the
memories sweet,
And someday we'll meet at Jesus's
feet.
But his going away has left me sad,
Because he was my friend. He was
my Dad.

Annette L Bonamo
VALENTINE'S DAY

For my mother Rita Bonamo, who always believed everything I wrote was beautiful.

Though we fight and we both get
mad
It's time to say I'm very glad,
That we two can take the time to
share
Some moments of love to show we
care

A wonderful day for all that's living
To prove our love is for the giving
Chocolates, hearts, flowers, and
candy
To show our love is still strong and
dandy

A time that is made for the seeing
The remembrance of one human
being
Pictures of love to paint—
For Valentine the Saint.

Jeff Rodrigues
TRAGEDY BY BEAUTY

Dedicated to Keven Lawrence, Larsen. For his Love, respect, and ALOHA for the people of Hawaii!!

Fresh aroma from the mountains and
sea
Roams in darkness invisible from
sight
Nearby a loon searches in flight
As he wails to his mate—come back
to me
Fragrance of Orchids imbued with
those of trees
Inspires romance for this Hawaiian
night;
On the slopes a volcano is clearly
in sight
Hot-red, orange fingers reach for the
sea.

A memory comes back, then lost
again,
Ah, reminisce, a myth once told
and perceived
A barren yarn, of sorrow and pain,
For two felt passion—the other did
not
She crept to her destiny, they both
grieved
One in the mountains, the other at
sea.

Marjorie M Ladue
THE WALL

I dedicate this poem to God who gives me the talent to write, and to my loving family who has always given me courage to keep on keeping on.

Two friends have built a wall
between them, both thick and wide,
the stones of it were laid in scorn and
plastered high with pride.
They talk through the stones that lay
mighty and strong,
to tear it down would be the answer,
but to whom would it belong?
Each piece put in anger, was the plan
for it to be built,
to apologize would be impossible, for
each of them might feel some guilt.
So they walk across the stubborn
stones so arrogantly tall,
and cannot reach each other since
they built the mighty wall.
Reason—that's the answer as both
can take the blame,
something so simple, no remorse, but
lots of shame.
A mighty tool it will take,
to remove the stones, for the wall to
break.
The will power of one's mind,
can break the stones if both seek the
same to find.

Sally Schuerlein
LIFELONG FRIEND

We've gone through changes
you and I
Some good times and some bad
But the thing that always
seems to stay
is the friendship that we've had
It's been there from
the very start
getting better as time goes by
We've gained the trust
the love, and strength

that a friendship should supply
We have an understanding
that will be there until the end
And there's nothing quite as special
as you my lifelong friend

Cheryl Galante
THE PRISONERS
All is still,
Except for the flag
Flailing its naked sheet;
Prisoner of only the breeze.

One man walks the green.
I know him,
My face, he has seen.
Does he feel the breeze?

I am inside;
A window addict,
Examining the clouds,
And passing men;

Prisoner of what I see.
I know the man,
but he can't know
The watching eyes
of me.

Beth A Miller
THE STAR
There is a star.
I can feel it burning
on my forehead.
It promises great things,
Success . . .
Love . . .
Happiness.

But this beautiful star,
trying to burn
through my vision
thoughts of great hope,
only brings despair.

The star is there.
I can feel it.
But I can't feel me.

Earl E Bergh
BEYOND

Dedicated to the savior of all.

Beyond the scope of mortal mind
Beyond imagination's pen
Beyond and still beyond again
There rose a plan

A plan to put an end to thirst
A plan to sunder sin's dread curse
A plan to heal the universe
A plan to save

To save us all from selfish power
To save us all at evil's hour
To save us all lest death devour
And give us joy

A joy that cannot be erased
A joy that shines in eyes and face
A joy that goes through time and
space
How great it is

So great a plan did God design
So great a savior can one find
So great a joy that will not cease
Ah, endless peace

H Ettie Janzen
GUESS WHO?
Who is this little creature
Who sits beneath the tree
And cuts off growing daisies
Especially meant for me?

Who climbs the family cherry tree
To try and prove she's male?
Who picks up snakes and lizards,
Sprinkles salt upon a snail?

Who tries to find a hide-out
Beneath her first big bed
When thunder and the lightning
Is crashing overhead?

Who gives me homemade Valentines
On that day we often seek?
Who tells me that she loves me
And plants a kiss upon my cheek?

Whose big blue eyes are sparkling
From a face as pure as pearl?
Please let me introduce you
To my precious little girl.

Charlie Droz
DO YOU CARE
Do you really care—about
A friend in need,
Or is a friend a word—like
make-believe.

Have you called, or asked, how've
you been,
Or dropped a line, do you remember
when?

If you really care about that
so-called friend,
Then pick up the phone . . . or maybe
the pen.

To love is to care, which has no end.
Isn't it time to call and say,
"Hi, my dear friend."
Amen.

Gordon Stoeffler Jr
GERADEN'S FIRST SONNET

For my sweet Melissia. May my love for you be proven at last.

I spied a lady fair one day,
my tongue fumbled for words to say.
Never had I seen —
nor will there be,
a lady as fair as she.
Her beauty will serve a mighty blow,
to any who dare to make a show.
As she approached so very slow,
I had to cast my eyes down low.
For her eyes were bright as the sun,
oh dare I pray to be the one.
For never had I seen —
nor will there be,
a lady as fair as she.

Sylvia Montenegro
TOGETHER

To my wonderful husband Enrique, The love of my life, and romantic inspiration of my heart.

From the moment that we first met
we've always been
together

Though storms came our way
and teardrops fell
we always stayed
together

When fate separated our lives
our <u>hearts</u> still stayed
together

Now in just a few short months
we will be joined at last

To live the life we've long had
planned
as one . . .
together

Brendan Conk
FIRST THERE WAS GOD
First there was God, and then you
and me.
But before us all, was the Devil's
society
A society made of hate, and one that
you can probably tell,
Was a society where all lived in Hell.
But all of this is not what you think,
For it all isn't a fiery pink.
This is a place where all have been,
and not all the people live in sin.
For some of these people, it's not
their doing,
But they live their life constantly
moving.
Some of these people you would not
want to meet,
But these are the people who live on
the streets.
On rainy days they have no where to
go.
And their lives do not change when
God makes it snow.
These people can't always drink
when
they feel the heat
And some die not getting to eat.
Sometimes I wonder what these
people think,
But when I hear all the facts the
pieces don't link.
When I think of living one of these
lives, I think I'd be weak and\
commit suicide.
But I'm glad that most of them don't,
because you should never end your
life, even if everyday ends on a
bad note.

Patricia M C Johnston
OPEN AND CLOSE
I hold on to the night sounds,
whispering.
Gently I am touched
by the growing darkness
that surrounds me.
The mounting tension
only enhances
my excitement
as I wait.
Slowly a light breeze brushes past me
and I become aware
of the state I am in.
Ever so softly I begin to move past
my daytime,
I wander unknowingly through
shadowed hallways.
Finding only the doors
locked and sealed
with the growing time
that has sadly slipped away.

Tracy Allen Atkins
ODE TO A DAY-CARE WORKER
You touched a lot of little lives in
more ways than you know
When we couldn't be there you
helped our children grow

In your very capable hands, we
placed our precious "gold"
And in return our children's lives you
gently began to mold

You were there to watch over them as
they played or took a nap
And when they needed comfort, you
held them on your lap

We never had a moment's worry
because we knew you cared
And all the love you had to give was
very freely shared

To all of our children you freely
opened your heart
And just being part of their lives gave
them a wonderful start

Because of your influence many
children will go far
You taught them each and every one
that they were a shining star

Now that you are gone, we can only
hope you knew
how very, very much we loved and
trusted you

Ginny Webber
THE CROSSROADS OF TIME
We look in the mirror and see our reflection of time. For this is the crossroads the threshold of a new being the turning point of a new century is just beyond our touch.

Charles Louis Chatmon

Charles Louis Chatmon
THE DRUG OF RACISM
Here in America, we have a number
of addictions,
Throw in drugs, greed, and include
racism,
Prejudice is a drug dangerously
sweeping the nation,
Serious as a world threat or
superpower invasion.

Blacks mistrusting whites, whites
mistrusting blacks,
Sources of communication is what
both races lack,
Other cultures and races tossed in the
hate game,
Free–basing on hate, burning up in
flames.

History records uncover this
substance abuse,
Morals were tight and codes were
unloose,
Armies slaughtered races, creations
of God,
The dead paying a price for blood
they trod.

Little children aren't affected, they're
color-blind,
For they are pure in heart, cleansed in
the mind,
Only when society bombards them in
condition,
They accept and absorb its racist
traditions.

If this is America and her states are
united,
Then why are its citizens painfully
divided?
To stop racist addictions, there must
be a start,
To ban this drug and treat many
hearts.

Charles Louis Chatmon
THE STORY OF THE HOMELESS

Walking downtown, I stare at my feet,
An unclean man lays on hardened concrete,
Face unwashed, filthy blanket on head,
He sleeps on a corner, he doesn't own a bed.

The story of the homeless in our major cities,
Often to them we don't show pity,
When they plead for just a little change,
We glance at them and consider them strange.

I wonder what would happen if roles were reversed?
The worst become better, the better becomes worst,
And what would we do, fall on our knees,
Shouting to heaven, "Oh please help us, please!"

Another day passes, the homeless still there,
In a society who doesn't turn a glare to people without homes, to them we show no pity,
But their numbers are increasing in our major cities.

Charles Louis Chatmon
LIKE A BIRD IN A CAGE

During this life of frustration and rage,
I feel like a bird locked in a cage,
I want to break out, be free from this trap,
The chains I feel are tight and wrapped.

My cage is my environment, no way to escape,
The conditions I live are in an awful shape,
How I long to be joyful and free,
Still, the cage encloses around me.

Single parents strive raising children on their own,
Themselves under age, not fully grown,
Neighbors next door sniffing white powder,
Keeping that up, they'll be dead in an hour.

The day is almost gone, night will soon appear,
Out in the streets, gunshots I hear,
Another chapter in this life, almost a full page,
At least I know I'll see one more day in this cage.

Charles Louis Chatmon
INTRODUCING THE MAGICIAN OF LOVE

Who is it with all those fantastic tricks?
It's the Magician of Love, oops, I let it slip,
He can pull a broken heart from out of his hat,
And repair it with affection just like that.

Take a card, any card, when lonely or depressed,
The Magician will give you care, peace to rest,
He's so slick, there's nothing up his sleeves,
Except tenderness, kindness, surely yours to please.

At any point you face bitterness and pain,
The Magician conjures a spell to clear the rain,
And if ever guilt seems embedded in your soul,
The magician levitates it and lets it go.

But who is this Magician of Love?
Funny you asked,
For we are all sorcerers, there, no hard task,
We have the ability in every family and relationship,
Make it work daily, perhaps you'll turn a trick.

Judy L Rust
THE ALIEN

You are so young — I remember my age.
I look in your eyes and see what could have been;
You look into mine and see what might be.
You gaze at a mystery — I gaze at a sea;
What is unknown to you, is my ocean of destiny.
  Silently my heart cries;
  For you — for me.
I want to turn back all the days;
You say the years mean nothing anyway.
Logic becomes the escape route I plan;
'Til you quietly reach out and touch my hand.
Sweet winds of illusion create the dream,
Causing mere seconds to illuminate the scene
Before reality creeps in to close the door,
Commanding me to look no more.
I know I must let go of what cannot be — yet,
  Silently my heart cries;
  For you — for me.

Judy L Rust
OUTLOOK

Am I to live my whole life long
  and never hear the sea gulls' song —
Or feel the misty breeze of the sea
  as it rushes inward so wild and free?
To caress the sun as it leaves my view
  across a mountain bathed in blue —
Or touch the soil of a foreign land,
  where castles and dragons were said to stand?
When there's a whole world
  out there to see,
Why must I be shackled
  with the bonds of
    POVERTY!

Mitchel James De Larm
HAND IN HAND

Hand in hand, shriveled old in their years
  Their hearts still young and gay,
Their hair is white as the fallen snow
  Yet their love grows mightier,
  Stronger as they go.

Like pyramids their hearts will stand
  Through the rest of time,
To know that life will be too short
  Is their only crime.

Eternal love will always live
  Yet the breath of life will pass,
Shriveled hands lay silently
  Beneath the barren grass.

  Side by side they die,
  Forever in love they lie.

Donna E Batt
FRIENDLY SEA

To my friend, Denise, who encourages me every day!!

No one yearns to be near
You as much as I!
My friends can't seem to enjoy
Your riches or know your
Drawing power.
They don't know your gentleness . . .
Or desolate lonely cry. And
Gulls screaming overhead,
Now diving through frothy foam.
They can't hear the buoy . . .
Clanging . . . a friend to a tuned in ear.
They can't see the mystique
Or the savageness in a storm . . .
And love the solitude of the
Lighthouse flashing warnings
To those of us who might wander.
None of these wonderful things
Can my friends understand
About me . . . and my friendly sea.

Robin Hatch
BY SEPARATE PATHS

Silently the sinking sun
Slips beneath the blue horizon.
The night nestles near the knoll
Upon which I stand.
The fresh foliage rustles
In the cool evening breeze.
The snap of a twig indicates
The approach of someone.
Suddenly the arms about me
  are strong and tender.
Our lips meet, we sink down
  to the soft grass.
The fire of our Love is bright
Beautiful in the approaching night.
Though the bliss we share
Cannot forever last
For soon the moon will rise,
Our stolen time be spent
And we will leave this sacred spot
By separate paths.

Joe Lunsford
IRISH HEAVEN

To Brenda and Leslie: "The wind beneath my wings."

Have ya ever been to Ireland he asked with a smile?

No says I, 'cause it's a good many mile.
But go I would if I had the fare,
'cause my mother's folks they are from there.

Ireland to me, he said with a grin, is heaven on earth, like the second coming again.

Oh no no I cried with despair, you mustn't compare Ireland to the good Lord up there.

The good Lord, Sonny, he said in a fuss, would live in Ireland, if he lived amongst us.

But alas he does not and it's ashamed you should be, for the Lord lives not in Ireland, but inside of me.

He lives in my heart, and what I say is no lie, heaven is but heaven in the sweet bye and bye.

Then forgive me, lad, he said with a frown, for though Ireland is a jewel, there is a higher ground.

And on that ground may you walk, sir, I said from the heart.
Make heaven your home when in death you do part.
But while I'm on this earth he said kinda shy,
Can I still call Ireland my sweet bye and bye?

Margaret K Tyler
LIFE

Dedicated with all my love to Mom, Mike, and Yvette. I love you all very much.

Life is strange, isn't it?
It seems like just a few short days ago, I was somebody.
I hung out with the "in" crowd.
I dressed in the latest fashions.
I drove an outasite set of wheels.
I had friends on top of friends.
It seems like days, but it's been years.
How many? Five? Ten? Who knows?
I stopped counting.
I had everything then. Everything a girl could possibly want. But now — you ask me what I have now?
Nothing. Everything is gone.
The "in" crowd is dead. The set of wheels is dead.
And the friends. Yeah, the friends.
They're all dead, too.
Seems like everything and everyone is gone.
I don't know anyone anymore.
I don't even know myself.
I used to know everything.
Now I know nothing.
I introduced me to myself yesterday.
You know what happened?
I walked away.
Everyone I know is dead.
Know something? I think I died too.
Now there's a new me.
I'm different now. I'm better. I'm friendlier.
Hello. Nice to meet you. I'm me.
Who are you?

Cindi Parsons
HER DAUGHTER'S VOICE

One night a woman hears a whisper.
She dismisses it, and falls back to sleep.
She hears it again, and answers back with,
"Who are you, and what do you want?"

The voice doesn't answer,
The woman stands and begins to go to the door.
Again she asks, "Who are you, what do you want?"
Still there is no answer.

She walks to the room across the hall from hers,
She looks in, and is awed at what she sees.
She closes her eyes, and opens them again, the vision is still there, it whispers, she screams.

The woman's husband comes to her side,
He asks her what's wrong.
She just stares into the empty room, that once belonged to her daughter.

D P Dresbach
A RETURN TO STANDARD TIME
Where echoes in the corridor sound
each other out
I toss
seeking a quiet turn

this place called memory
where you (sleep) live

whenever I go there
music eddies then ebbs

sometimes stillness
catches quick reflections
the sea gull snatches blue shadows

I finger water beads
cobwebs net the gathering dark

I count round wet drops
listen again
rondo
for what is not there

hearing it
counting again again
again
listening

Marilyn Overturf
LOVE'S TIDE

Dedicated to Sunshine for the smile, the warmth and the time.

Love
is like the ocean's tides
coming in and going out,
collecting the grains of
sand left on the shore.

Taking and giving of one's self
building a tremendous swell,
one that goes far out to sea,
to again come crashing into me.

Feelings so deep, so clear,
so wild,
like the deep waters of the sea,
illusive at times but wondrous
always.

Love
is a collection
of the repeated waves
that build into a
treacherous storm.

Feelings build and collect
until they grow into what's called,
LOVE.

Lonnie E Williams II
RAIN
Rain on my frontstep
dropping on top of me
Relaxing Spring days

Lonnie E Williams II
SISTERS
Fighting, hitting, punching,
kicking socking,
Beating up their brother
Sisters

Joyce Kallstrom
SILENCE

To my children, Debbie, Tom, Todd and Chris—and to their families.

The night is dark
The rooms are still
There's silence everywhere
The furniture reflects the times
Of children playing there.
Alone, and in the stillness
There's the ringing of a phone
A small voice sways
"Is Tammy there?"
. . . and then a dial tone.

I wonder,
In the years to come
When Tammy's friend has aged
And in the mystic book of life
Has turned the final page
If one dark night her silence
Will be broken by the phone
Some voice will say
"Is Julie there?"
. . . and then a dial tone.

Michael D Chastain
ORIENTATION OF REALITY
When in one first bestruck with
reality?
Appearing like a gray rain cloud
caressing the earth's ceiling with
such originality.

When reality first diseased me,
I immediately began to see.
Is reality a mere illusion?
Or is there some alternate solution?

Reality can consume someone like
the moist and sullen mysteries of a
cave,
So be aware of the undertow of
the reality wave.

Marie Law Haire
SCULPTORS
America.
It took great men
To make her great.
I can see give of them from here.

I see
Washington
Jefferson
Theodore Roosevelt
And Honest Abe

Towering
Five thousand, six hundred and
fifty-nine feet
Into the South Dakota sky.

I see
Truth
Courage
Brilliance
Determination
Passion
Compassion
And "freedom for all"
In the visages of four great men.

And what of the fifth?
He is there, too,
In the faces of the four —

Gutzon Borglum —
He lifted those men up there,
All five thousand, six hundred and
fifty–nine feet
Into America's sky.

It took great men
To make America great.
I can see five from here.

Lynn A Geiger
WHEN TWO BECOME ONE
In this life we share many loves, . . .
Few
Of these will last very long. All,
will change our lives in some small
way.
But none shall change us more than
The love shared by two people.

It's strange how one person can make
another bend,
In ways that would shatter a person's
sanity.
A person without this love would
never consider . . . ,
Or at least they would get caught up
In someone's crazy trend.

Orders, lists and demands are not for
them,
Decisions can wait, they're in no
hurry!
These are not the ways to express
your needs.
Just plant warm, loving, considerate
unselfish seeds.

And within two people a small flame
will spark;
Filled with a special, more understanding love.
Allowing these two people to become
as one,
As you and I have done.

Maurene Miller
ANGELINE MY MOTHER
Oh Mother, how I love you with your
big brown eyes aglow,
Your hair with pretty silver streaks is
soft as fallen snow.

You were always there to love me as
I grew to who I am,
You taught me strength and
tenderness and forever should I stand.

It hurts to see you lie there so
helpless and asleep,
I know the loss I feel today will be
forever deep.

How you loved and how you lived
was always full of wonder
When you disciplined the five of us;
to us it seemed like thunder.

You were always such a Lady, my
Mother and my Friend,
I'm not sure how I can go on when
all of this does end.

But I know that you're in Heaven
with God and Grandma near,
I pray that you will smile on us and
guide us from up there.

Not only do I Thank You Mom; but
the other kids do too,
Your husband and your grandkids;
we've all learned so much from you.

We just want to tell you one more
time, Mom,
<u>We all love you</u>!

I love you pretty lady and I miss you.
Maurene

L I Zimmerman
LOVE'S FRIENDSHIP
Over the years
We've had our ups and downs
But due to friendship
Love's grown in leaps and bounds

The time we've spent apart
Have been difficult to bear
But all has been easier
Just knowing you care.

The memories we've made
I shall forget never
Your Love and Friendship
I'll treasure forever

Mere words aren't enough
They're so easy to say
One thing to be sure
I'll love you more tomorrow
Than I did yesterday.

Bernice B Hoffman
LITTLE MIRACLES
On one of those busy, hectic days
when everything had gone awry,
There finally seemed nothing left to
do but sit down and cry.
Then suddenly, I remembered a small
package delivered with the morning's
post,
Put aside, in haste, for later opening,
then forgotten—well, almost.
From a multi-layered cocoon of
tissue paper, you popped into view,
A tiny white ceramic horse, saddled
and bridled as for dress review.
You looked so grand poised there in
the hollow of my hand,
Just like a real live pony strayed from
some circus wonderland,
Bridle abloom with ribbons and
plume, forelegs arched skyward,
nostrils aflare,
Ears pricked forward to catch notes,
once long ago, rife on the air,
Your coat sleek and shiny as if
freshly curried by a groom,
And I loved you on sight because
you'd chased away my gloom.
Holding you closer, memory
unbidden, replayed scenes long
stored away,
And for a moment I grieved that
those wondrous days couldn't stay.
But life is a parade and for everyone
Time sets the pace,
And though we may try, none can
ever one single footstep retrace.
With a sigh, I tenderly carry you to
my curio cabinet,
And gently place you among other
reminders there, lest ever I forget,
That deeds done, things said, color
the threads woven into life's tapestry,
And all those "Little Miracles" that
come to keep us company,
Are heaven sent to help smooth the
path of our earthly journey.

Debbie A Bell
MOMENT OF SERENITY
Only in my moment of serenity do I
truly embrace the depth of my
love . . . a feeling so warm and
precious, in a form so rare, that
only He is aware of the
compassion by which my soul
bestows;

Thousands of miles away is my
mind--far from a world engrossed
in vanity and crime . . . can I once
more grasp the peace that lies
within my heart—joyfully smiling
of the loving kindness that it
embarks upon;

As my thoughts creep closer to the
realities of life . . . the visions and
dreams of loved ones so close and
dear—are safely secured in a cove,
by which the depth of my love is
bestowed;

And so once more I anticipate, ever
so patiently, for this warm feeling
to once again be clenched—by me,
and only me, in my moment of
serenity.

Marolyn M Rondorf
OLD PLAYMATES
So long all my naptimes,
bye-bye Teddy Bear.
See you worn out britches
my favorite to wear.
I'll miss you all, my dear friends

Raggedy Ann and Pooh.
I hate to put you all away
But what more can I do?
I have no time to play and laugh
No time to bounce my ball
No time for autumn picnics
No time for you at all
But you'll be safe and warm you guys —
Some day you'll all be back.
Though many a grown-up years must pass before you'll be unpacked
Someday a babe will be mine and then you'll be
Her favorite boys, her pride and joy
As you were once to me.

Kim DeCatur
STAND BY MY SIDE
Stand by my side,
when things get complicated,
and remember, I was there through your complications.
even though your answers become unrealistic.
Through the tears, my shoulder was there,
and became wet with your frustrations,
which became mine.
When you doubt me,
remember, my explanations are hard to understand,
and my views may seem distant.
Through a mind's eye, see my tears,
that others use to crucify me with.
And my pictures, distorted as they may seem,
are complicated with simplicity.
And when my bitter or sweet tears fall,
lend me your shoulder,
that we may become one,
and have an understanding beyond physical passion.

RaNee Long
THE LAMB OF GOD
Long ago in the city of Nazareth,
Was a virgin exceedingly fair,
More beautiful than all others;
Chosen of God his son to bear.

Mary, mother of the Lamb of God
In a lonely manger gave him birth;
Born after the manner of the flesh
God's only begotten came to earth.

Angel Gabriel promised her
His mother she would be.
She was to name him Jesus,
The promised king was he.

The lamb of God went forth
Healing the sick, blind and lame;
Blessing the little children,
As to his arms they came.

"Dear, Jesus, my Redeemer
Please keep me in thy care
As thou did for others,
Is my humble prayer."

George Polomchak
A SILENT PROTEST
As I wander through the forest,
the leaves sing gently upon the air;
And in this song there's an urgent pleading
of tragic loss, so very near.
They seem to be crying out,
their sounds falling all around me;
Stirring a conscious hurt deep inside,
that society's progress could never see.
You take me in your own time;
Mercilessly—to fit whatever mold.
Such beauty of so many years;
Wasted — and so cheaply sold.
Not even to be remembered,
for this long hard life I've led.
But as you write on me,
do you think, here, I die dead?
Very silently I think again;
About the story they have told.
And the words keep coming back;
With a haunting feeling to forever hold.
"Why must you keep on killing me?"
"This here life so very, very old!"

Debbie Therrien Feldman
DREAMS OF YOU
Dreams of you do often inspire.
Visions of love, a heart's desire.
Thoughts and feeling run through my head
As I lay sleeping in my bed
Dreams that sleep in a starlite sky
Dreams that bring tears to my eyes.
For the moment I wake the further you're away
For my dreams do not sleep during the day.

Trish Schiesser
PERFECTION
Once I photographed
a railroad track
Straight down
the
middle.

Straight as a die.

It's good.

It's just about
the
only thing
I've done
that
my husband
thinks
is
perfect!

Trish Schiesser
BAPTIST CHURCHES
Did you ever notice how many
Baptist Churches
there are in the South?
They are all painted white
with a steeple of black.

An old cemetery sits, waiting, next door, across the way, or out back.

I remember one in Alabama
named Beulah, where mother was baptized.

I wonder if she still wants to be buried there
with her mother and her father,
and whoever else is lying back in the murky depths of time.

Leanne Purdy
I WANTED TO SAY . . .

To Love's Dreamers: The spoken word lasts only a moment, but the unspoken truth of the eyes and heart is eternal.

I want to say "I love you"
because the feelings are so strong.
I want to say "I miss you"
because my heart sings this song.
I want to say "I care about you"
because my heart speaks this truth.
I want to say "I'm thinking of you"
because my heart feels this worth.

I want to say "I'll love you"
for this chance of me and you.
I want to say "I'll miss you"
for the feelings which are true.
I want to say "I'll care about you"
for the times we spent together.
I want to say "I'll be thinking about you"
and that I'll leave you never.

I wanted to say "I'll love you"
but that depended on you.
I wanted to say "I'll miss you"
but these feelings you never knew.
I wanted to say "I'll care about you"
but that day never came.
I wanted to say "I'll be thinking of you"
but I couldn't remember your name.

Dierdre E Washington
WHAT A FOOL BELIEVES
I believed in a love
a love so true
I believed in everything
i believed in you
I believed my tears would fly away
i believed in my heart that you would stay
I believed in all of my dreams
the good ones and bad, no matter what they seemed
I believed in the most tenderest touch
i believed that i loved u so much
I believed in myself, I believed i've tried
but i couldn't believe that u had lied
If you believed in love, why did you betray?
if you believed you loved me, then why did you stray?
If you believe in love and believe you are so cool
Then you really must believe women are fools
But a woman knows, A woman can see
A WOMAN KNOWS WHAT A FOOL BELIEVES

James A Sluder
MY QUEST
I have drunk the sleepy wine of the moon,
And flourished in the rays of the sun.
I have been cradled by the soft, magical light of a star,
And traveled across the rainbows of time.

I have ridden the gigantic waves of the salty sea,
And played merrily a game of tag with the ageless wind.
I have lain in the shade of the ancient oak,
And felt the freshness of the rain upon my cheek.

I have frolicked in the earth's carpet,
And have seen the majestic hues of its sunsets,
And witnessed the virginity of the dawn.
I have seen the splendor of the heavens above.

I have sown seeds in the fertile soil.
I have experienced respect for the unknown.
I have seen the victory in death,
And yet—

I have found something that is more precious and wonderful known to man—
I have found God.

James A Sluder
THE AWAKENING
An unbearable light suddenly filled the dark, cold and musky burial chamber.
A tall slender figure of a man could be seen lying on the cold stone slab.

Suddenly, the frail figure began to jerk and twist in a spasmodical way.
The white linen shroud began to loosen from the body and fall to the floor.

The silent figure that lay so motionless only a short time before, had begun to stir.
His nostrils began to flare and the chest expanded as the lungs filled to their capacity.

Inhaling the fresh morning air, He arose to a sitting position on the edge of the slab and slid to the floor.
Standing momentarily, the slender form reached for the fallen linen and draped it about Himself.

Walking through the open passage way, He saw the huge boulder that had blocked the entrance of the tomb.
Once outside, He looked toward a nearby hillside, and saw three empty crosses.

He smiled and walked away.

Patricia Flake Cribbs
THE COPPER LADY

For my Father, John C. Flake, Jr., disabled veteran, died August 12, 1970, Army staff sergeant in World War II, machine gun expert.

Years ago when Lady Liberty was being planned
They wanted to put a rifle in the palm of her hand
Instead of the torch of eternal freedom she now holds
Promising our fair share of what America unfolds,
Standing high above the harbor 300 ft. high
"Liberty igniting the sky is truly no lie"
It was a dream, a plan of many a man
They even thought she would be filled with sand,
Great care and art was put into her creation
Loving America was truly a thoughtful realization
She was to be the largest copper statue in history
A rising symbol, above the water, OH what a mystery!
The torch represented Liberty, meaning much more than a word
The torch represented liberty, meaning much more than a word
During 1876 that's what everyone heard
The sculptor's hands worked hard on her face
With love and tenderness he did embrace
The skeletons went up to erect her body
At the world's fair they toasted her with a toddy
She would soon sail the high sea
Heading for America and there she'd

never leave,
Raising the money for her construction
Turned out to be a publicized induction
She was a gift from a country called France
And America's Freedom she would surely enhance.

Richard Lee Doub

Richard Lee Doub
IMAGINE

Dedicated to: All who have a love for poetry.

Can you imagine life with only
Never ending pain
No sunshine as the days go by
Just storm clouds full of rain?

Can you imagine life with only
Colors dull and gray
No beauty to enjoy or see
While passing thru each day?

Can you imagine life with only
Hatred by your side
No one to cheer and comfort you
Where for you love has died?

Can you imagine life with only
Teardrops as your friend
No freedom in your life to choose
The things you want to end?

Can you imagine life with only
Prayers for death to come
Well prison's where to find it all
With nowhere left to run?

Delora Earley
STANDING IN THE RAIN
You saw me standing in the rain
The storm was there before us
We had to face the lonely pain
This was the final chorus

Our love had weathered all the years
Oh how you loved me
But now we shed the final tears
And now we faced the final fears

The thought that I will be alone
For now and ever
Is really more than I can bear
To know you no longer will be there

The time has come to say goodbye
Oh how I'll miss you
Caress my face just one more time
And let me kiss you
You left me standing in the rain

Yvonne A Miller
JUST FOR YOU
Take my hand
and let us walk through
the four seasons of the land,
where time is only of our minds,
our reflections are of our souls,
and our love is a beam of
everlasting protection.

Hold me tight
when doubts are present
and shower me with affection,
for your touch of warmth is
my home.

Let your lips touch mine
to reunite the passion we share,
the passion of yesterday, today,
and tomorrow,
and when we reach
the end of our journey
we will have become one.

Willette Harmon
TEARS
Silver drops of dew
Red puddles of agony
Silent cries of endless thoughts
Dark and deep inside of me
Graveyard smiles of sleepless woe
As the blackness now enfolds me
Empty shallow climbing fears
Building up inside of me
Love can melt these fears of mine
A kiss can light the way
To open up my heart to live and
Send loneliness astray
A hand can caress this face of mine
As its touch vibrates against
The tears
The silent cries changes to shouts
For love
Because I want you near
But until you come my teardrops fall
Silver drops of dew
Red puddles of agony
Because I didn't have you

John S Mills
AMANDA
She never puts her toys away;
Just leaves them scattered where they lay—
I try to scold her, and I say,
"You make me mad!"
But when to bed she has to chase,
The toys she left about the place
Remind me of her shining face,
And make me glad.
When she grows up and gathers poise
I'll miss her harum-scarum noise,
And look in vain for scattered toys—
And I'll be sad.

Delores Minton
EARTHQUAKE!
The earth shakes, violently!
Making crevices & cracks.
People, houses, swallowed up!
The big one is back!

Freeways collapsing eerily!
Concrete and steel, deadly blow!
Flattening both car and flesh
The wake of destruction glows!

Crushers work thru the night
To clear away debris
To find the dead and injured!
Loved ones, waiting, anxiously!

How sad to see a teddy bear!
Or a doll come falling thru!
And cry silent for that child
That these belonged to.

For victims left behind
Most deal with things new
Not only did they lose homes
But lost their families too.

The big one is back!

Cassie Case Morton
LIFE, A SWIRLING MIST
I walked slowly through the swirling mist,
My feet, often, did not touch firm ground.
Sometimes the mist was like murky water,
There were days when the way could not be found.

Sometimes the mist lifted from around me,
And I moved swiftly, as if my feet had wings,
No obstacle stood in the way,
My eyes saw only the beautiful things.

So in and out of the swirling mist,
I traveled along day by day.
Crying out when I was lost and hurt,
Singing when nothing was in my way.

Then one day a hand reached out and took mine,
And led me along an unbarred way.
My heart was singing, my joy was great,
For ahead of me was light, as brilliant as the light of day.

Beth Jo Mullaney
ONE NIGHT IN THE MISTING RAIN
One night in the misting rain
I climbed to the top of the mountain
to look down
On the left pincher-clawed crabs
clacked advancing
On the right hissing-howling
mountain cats paraded forward
From behind came the buzz of
ill-voiced nonsensed humans
flaunting their
cohesiveness
In front double rainbows brightened a golden dawn
I reached out to touch them
And Fell
Tum-
bl-
ing
up
Then landing finally at the pinnacle
ready to start again
this time I soared down
and was caught by the rainbow
Suspended, then loosed
As I picked myself up
the vision cleared.

Gail Haynes
I AM THE LIGHT
I am the light, the creation,
a distant star, a wisp of wind,
a grain of sand.

I am part of the Universe.

I have the knowledge to understand.
I am laughter. Joy and Happiness.
I am pain. Tears I call rain.
I am love the hand that might fit your glove. I've seen darkness and despair.
I am the cub in the Lion's Lair.
I am the door without the key,
searching for the love and sunshine,
the green of the sea.
I am flesh and blood, arms and legs, I am a smile, a mind that thinks, a reflection of God is seen through me.
I am a bearer of fruit, a giver of life. I am not the bridegroom . . .
I am the WIFE.

Betty C Hiller
BUTTERFLY
Butterfly, Sweet Butterfly
with your delicate wings
you flutters here and there
in my flower garden.

Butterfly, Sweet Butterfly
with your grace and beauty
you adds a serenity to this
quiet summer day.

Butterfly, Sweet Butterfly
to catch you would be a sin
for there is so little beauty
left in this busy world.

Leah Hameen
THE LANTERN
On a dark and stormy night, in 1863, a lantern shines directly so Lillian's young child can read.
She, a former slave never learned to read and write, and so she smiles proudly as her daughter reads contently by the light . . . of the lantern.

Melanie Lyn Harrop
MEMORIES LOST
Blonde hair blows in the breeze, as
Crystal blue eyes stare into mine.
Olive skin comes in soft contact
With my shoulder from behind
Green palm fronds wisp above my
head
Brown and gold speckled, swollen
eyes
Meet mine gently, as
Silver tears run softly down three sad
faces
With fear of memories lost.
Dark blue minds drown in sorrow.

Linda Henson
MEMORIES
Memories are things built of the past
They are made of things that don't
last
Some memories are good
Some memories are bad
Some are happy
Some are sad
Some are sorrowful
And some are glad
Good or bad, happy or sad
Sorrowful or glad
Memories are the building blocks of the future

Myrtle Hailey
SIMBA
Royalty never sat so tall
Like a queen upon a throne
Yet to be so very small,
As you sit there all alone

Firelight shining in your eyes
Big, round, clearly blue
Oh, you seem so very wise,
Little kit kat, who are you?
Little furry creature,
With your solemn gaze,
Were you sent especially
To brighten up my days?
Were you sent to care for me
All through the lonely night
Allay my fears, dry my tears,
And make the darkness bright?

Louise Elaine Horton
LONG COLD NIGHT
It was a long cold night
When I held you close
You told me that you loved me
And I'm the one you chose

You promised me forever
And I believed you too
I cannot wait until the day
We say I do.

I'll sit here forever
Just to hold you tight
Because it all started
On a long cold night

Then I had your baby boy
You were there to see
But something went wrong
And now it will never be

Now I sit all alone
On this long cold night
With your baby son
In my arms
And you out of sight.

I'll sit here forever
Just to hold you tight
Because it all started
On a long cold night.

Loren J Hieb
MY COLORING BOOK
What is the color of thunderless rain?
Is it anything like the color of fear.
What is the color of music—
to your favorite song—
What color do you hear?

Take me back—
to my coloring book;
I'll only stay long enough—
to have one more look.

When that old Tom Cat purrs;
What color occurs?
When people get mad—Why do they see red?
What color do you see—when all feelings are dead?

I've got to find my way back—
to my coloring book.
I know I'll find some answers—
if I could get just one more look.

What color clouds your mind—
when you're walking on air; air and so full of love?
Does it come to you in colors—
Like the sky above?

Take me back—
to my coloring book.
I just wanna go back—
and take another look;
at my coloring book.

Delila Rema Hamilton
ASTORIA
Mountains,
Charcoal etched,
A bridge
Of black velvet ribbons,
Hanging free
Against the silver satin
Curtain
Of sea and sky . . .
Perched,
On a black beanbag chair,
My arm
Across your shoulders,
I think I shall
Never be
As happy again,
As I was once,
In Astoria,
In the rain.

Ellarae holding Sara, Kermit, and Mighty Mouse

Ellarae B Miner
FRIENDS
Dollie's a girl
Kermit's a boy
Stophouse is a lady
She paints the big boy.

Carlene Halle
A COMPARISON
Sandboxes, a place for a child to play and discover.
Sand castles, a place for a king's lover.
A single drop of water, and sand is held together.
The wind blows, and it is emancipated with the change of weather.
Sand watches the time pass;
But only a spectator through its hourglass.
Sand drifts in and out by the tide;
Dominated it will never subside.
Seashells sand does keep;
Secrets we clench so deep.
We walk upon sand;
Leaving memories; footprints in the land.
There it is, sand, as it lingers;
Try to collect it, and it falls through your fingers.
Sand belongs to history.
And life is still a mystery.

Rose Hamilton
SHOW HIM YOUR FATH
You never need worry, nor show any doubt.
Our Lord knows you need him, just show all your faith.

He knows that you're hurting, you're scared this he sees.
Pray to him only, just keep all your faith.

When all seems darker than nights without stars, remember the brightness
of light in your heart.
The Lord dwells within you, just show him you trust.

Darcy K Heskett
MARRIAGE
To Love, Honor, and obey
For eternity and everlasting.
We love each other with
our hearts and souls.
We shall not ever forsake
each other for any one else.
To protect one another at all times
no matter what shall happen.
As of the day we got married
we promised to one another
That we shall always cherish
each other's lives.
Our love to each other
is no joke it is our
truth to each other.

Ann Russell Janes
THE HOARFROST CEREMONY—
Moments of Beauty No. 15
To the solemn service this morning
All NATURE wore robes of priestly white
And chapel caps of diamond-studded lace.

At the proper moments, SUNSHINE
cast its dazzling gold o'er all
And the diamonds glittered.

(Man felt himself an intruder; he wore no gems.)

SYCAMORES, too tall and stiff to earthward bend,
Stood erect 'gainst blue, blue sky;
Covered by close-fitting veils,
MAGNOLIA buds sparkled;
Willow branches touched the ground with glistening gloves,
And prim EVERGREENS remained in their pews.

As the ceremony progressed,
The chapel caps moved in unison;
showers of diamond dust filled the air.

Soon, almost imperceptibly,
The congregation cast aside their cloaks of frozen dew,
And the icy-white washed the grime away.

After the benediction, all NATURE
appeared before the world
Cleansed and ready for the day's work.

THE HOARFROST HOUR, a silent rhapsody of enchantment, was over.
Man no longer an intruder . . .

Nina Johnson
REMEMBERING HER
She was my girl, my entire world.
So sweet and kind, and she was mind.
She was so smart, a true work of art.
She made life worthwhile, always making me smile.
So young, yet so wise a real prize.
Then one day to my dismay.
Coming home from the park after dark.
She was no more, this child I loved and adored.
She was all I had, now I'm mad.
What sat out as fun turned out to be hit-and-run.

Seppo Kauppinen
MIRROR OF LIFE
Oh! Lass you're mirror of my life.
Please! Don't become error of my night.
When I look into your eyes,
then you make my mind bright.
When I kiss your lips, I feel them
like waves around the ships on a warm day.
Oh darling! Hide my head in your long hair.
Cos tonight I don't want to go nowhere.

You showed me a motion by which betrayed
the world to believe that love is all around.
And I lost my sound because of you my girl.
You helped me to forget my
universities of loneliness.
In which I was living for my life.

Thank you for relieving my strife
for this help God will bless.
I got the sweet cross on my back,
The cross made of flesh, I'll carry it
for joy in this beautiful mesh.

Hana Kocourkova
PICTURE
The fissure above horizon —
the antler of stormy sky;
hands and legs in the body's cleavage
and thin fingers from the arm's stump?
When I look from high above down,
at the earth,
I can't distinguish rivers and roads
from each other.
The same sense makes them alike.
Scream of the bird and the man in danger! —
My God, wherever I look,
everywhere the same picture.

Philip Leibowitz
NOTHING WAS A PENNY FALLING THROUGH SPACE
Nothing was a penny
Falling through space calling it to the bottom with many.
Little manhole, please take my bowl.
Nothing.
Nothing was a particle of light in the night floating through space;
Fighting
The lightning of the changes I was thinking
Nothing paused to ignore
All falling asleep with a snore
Nothing was a clock that read
To the only penny falling through space, in the night
Silently dead.
It's going down, down, down bottom of the night.
"Hey!" said the boy to the lady with her little dog walking away, grey.
Play guitar buy a wooden jar, in the bottom of the night, bottom of the night.

Kathryn Daley
THREE AND SEVENTY-THREE
The pain you felt when you were three
Was from a bump, a skinned knee.

The pain you felt at age ten
May well have come from a leaking pen.

The pain you felt at seventeen
Was from a dent fender and the scene.

The pain you felt at twenty-four
Was from your boss, his gigantic roar.

The pain you felt at thirty-one
Was when the surgery had begun.

The pain you felt at thirty-eight
The first time you faced such hate.

The pain you felt at forty-five
Prepared you daily to survive.

The pain you felt at fifty-two
Self-contained but solely undue.

The pain you felt at fifty-nine
Put you in a slow decline.

The pain you felt at sixty-six
Had you stay as if transfixed.

The pain you felt at seventy-three
Made you feel so fancy-free.

Pat Calhoun
ENIGMA
Only empty space there was,
a nothingness
and yet, methinks a marvelous
thing occurred.
Was that a sound? Oh, who could
hear, for no one was. 'Twas then
it merged, there was a blast and
energy became matter.

Could this be the answer? a
"Big Bang" that left a sky filled
with stars, planets and galaxies.
A firmament of untold beauty, with
space so vast, that in one infinitesimal
moment, a world did come to be, out
of that immensity.

Pat Calhoun
LEGACY
They came to forge a better place for themselves and their posterity, out of a wilderness that scorned such daring. Yeoman, yokel, village lads, men with proud high-sounding names found that they became but one of the common folk they toiled among.

They came seeking a land where a man would be judged by his personal worth and accomplishments. Mountains were crossed, rivers forded, plains rich with the promise of fertile ground, were conquered by the horse and plow, hardened hands and sweat of brow.

They came to fight for the homes that they would build in this savage land and left an inheritance of pride, deep stained by the blood of those who died to reap the harvest of freedom. Knowing this was the land where they belonged, they raised our flag on wings of song.

Candace Powless
ANIMAL TALK

This poem is dedicated to my daughter, Kathryn Jean, who loves all animals both great and small.

A Persian Cat on a Velvet Settee
Was stroking her long long fur;
When up jumped a Mouse,
How did he get in the house?
And verily frightened her.

Said the Mouse, said he,
I've come to find a place in which to stay,
I've brought my family and my friends,
We thought you would like to play.

Oh, No, said the Cat,
This languid, lazy Cat,
In this house I fear you'll find,
A Dog, a Dog, a big black Dog,
Who is very, very unkind.

The Mouse was shocked, how can it
be that neither the Cat nor the Dog
knew nothing at all about his
friend, the big, fat sassy old Hog.

The Hog said the Mouse is a
Friend of mine. He'll see that
I get to play. Oh, No, said
the Cat, you mustn't reply on That,
You see he is Thanksgiving Dinner
Today.

Karen Kelly
SPRINGTIME AT HARRIS CRESCENT
The lake is calm and smooth as glass
The bunnies are nibbling on new mown grass
Chirping birds and bumblebees
make everlasting memories.

Red and yellow tulips bloom and lilacs are due
The pear tree has flowers and the cherry tree too
The sun shines thru evergreen and birch trees
Pictures in my mind are made of these.

Past the garage, wood is split with an axe
A rabbit bounds away chased by "Bax"
Springtime pollen makes some people sneeze
But that's what makes unforgettable memories.

A hoot in the distance signals the train
The clouds are scattered so it won't rain
The trees are rustling due to the gentle breeze
adding to more fond memories.

A neighbor stops by with a lake fresh trout
That's what Harris Crescent is all about
Bar-b-qued with wild rice and sweet peas
Making a thousand memories.

Richard Z Smith
POWER OF LOVE
You are the earth, I am the sea
You circle the world, surrounded by me
I flow in and around every part of you
What I cannot touch I cover with my dew
I melt into the wind to envelop you with my love
To rise over you and blanket you from above
To surround you and touch you is incomplete
I must blend with you to be replete
Ever merging, our souls entwined
For we are one, solid and liquid combined
We do not take and give in resentment and strife
We share with love, in love and life
For love is the power that makes us one
The pull on the planets, moon and sun
The force in the universe, filled with space
Yet all held orderly together in place
Always moving, never still
Yet part of each other with no separate will
So long as love exists, life will always be
Throughout the universe, throughout eternity

Mary Korman
GRANDDAUGHTER'S GRADUATION GIFT
They lied to me Gretchen, those sages who sang
Of lavishing love on your first born grandchild.
They never warned that marriages break. Families
Shatter. Some miles can't be crossed.

Your vacations were spent, safely cocooned,
In Grandmother Rosie's pie scented kitchen
With smiling young aunts to whisper soft secrets.
I was the other, unknown grandmother.

Nostalgic warmth we never could kindle
At a fleeting and crowded holiday hearth
But heritage, dear, is a double-edged sword.
One side won't sharpen till the other is honed.

Now grandmother smiles in late-day contentment:
There's a feminist cadence in your long-legged stride;
Your polished smile hides a prairie unrest;
When quiet, your eyes are the eyes of a poet.

Geraldine Martin
FEELINGS LAID TO REST

To my beloved brother Jessie Lee Hamilton, our little angel.

A shroud of heaviness in darkness veiled.
A feeling, that in life, I've failed.
Feelings laid to rest inside;
But continue to flow as the tide.
I'm lame in body, and tired in mind.
Peace to be found only in another time.
Will it ever really be mine?
Pray God, give me a divine sign.
For in this world, I walk a thin line,
And I do return in kind.
As beset inside the confines of this mind.
A beacon I do wish to find,
And in all its splendor it shall shine,
And guide my soul to the path of infinite time.

Geraldine Martin
DEATH COMES A CREEPING
I'm not close to heaven,
For death he comes a creeping;
And leaves those I love a sleeping;
With only my memories to be keeping;
While silently I'm weeping,
And my broken soul is seeking:
A touch, smile, word, or even yes a thinking;
And when there is just a momentary blinking,
Death, he will come creeping.
Man is born to die;
Don't you ever wonder why?
A loved one to cherish,
And within a blink, they perish.
Did you know my name?
Did you know I came?
Did you know I cared?
Or I even dared?
Can we ever lay our burdens down;
And say yes peace has been found?
A time for every season;
But is there is a reason?

Geraldine Martin
JESSIE LEE
Little baby brother of mine, I wish I could remember you.
But I was only three, when you left me.
No pain do you know little brother of mine;
For your soul now does pass all time.
And you have a playground, with gates of pearl,
And billowing clouds that swirl.
The streets are paved with pure gold.
For your tiny feet to run upon.
Your teachers have been Apostles, and Saints of old,
Never ever do they scold.
I truly do believe, that God has set you on his knee,
And said, "I've brought you here to live with me,
My Little Jessie Lee."
"I've also brought your daddy here,
that he may see you run and play,
his pain now lifted away."
In his arms you may now stay."
"So run my little Jessie Lee, and take your daddy by the hand, show to him the still waters which flow and are clear as glass."
"And know that you now possess everlasting eternal life."

Leonie G Dyer

Leonie G Dyer
IT'S TIME WE CARE

To the terminally ill patients who are suffering with the disease may you find comfort and peace with God. We who care will be praying for you and I do hope that some day researchers will find an alternative to cure the disease.

AIDS is a typical discussion and no one seems to find a cure
We don't like talking or thinking about it

We just try our best to ignore
You see most of the victims are in so much pain
They can't even describe it, or hardly explain
Some of them are left to die
And we say to ourselves, "I wonder who, I wonder why!"
Yet in so many ways we can't erase it from our mind
Because that is a fact, and true words are often too difficult to find
We say that's too bad, but what could we do
When we sit and think about it
It could happen to me or even to you

Then we call in a doctor and perhaps a nurse
But what is worst of all, some people often call it a curse
But what they don't know is, what GOD has in store for them
When they shut out the victims and are so ready to condemn
Although this is a tough situation, surely we must realize that
AIDS VICTIMS ARE PEOPLE TOO!
So please don't criticize
Just do whatever you think is best and GOD will surely take care of the rest
For you know that we look to Him for Power
What we don't know is that no man knows The Minute! The Day! or The Hour!
When GOD will call them home into eternity
So wake up all you people because we have to look at AIDS realistically
("AS LONG AS A MAN HAS LIFE, LET HIM LIVE, DON'T SHUT HIM OUT")

Leonie G Dyer

DEDICATED TO OUR MOTHER

Mom you have always been an inspiration,
Through your hard work and your dedication;
Although we all will miss you so,
In our hearts we will cherish you wherever we go.

As our love for you will never die,
One day we will meet in the sweet by and by;
We know that your soul is with the Lord,
And He will give you your reward.

Because, while you were here upon this earth,
You did what you could for all it was worth;
Now you have passed into a new life,
You were an example . . .
A Good Mother, Grandmother and a Loving Wife,

Truly God has taken you away from the suffering and Pain;
As we know He is the Creator and He will always remain.
For He alone did what was best,
Meanwhile He has taken you home to rest.
MAY YOU REST IN PEACE

Leonie G Dyer

DEDICATED TO DR. MARTIN LUTHER KING

Dr. Martin Luther King was a very courageous man
He struggled for freedom and had won in the end
He fought for human justice, nonviolence and peace
He was a great example but unfortunately he's now deceased
We will always observe his integrity for civil rights
His dreams to many showed that he was reaching for higher heights
He laid down his life to free many blacks
Then one day as he spoke he was brutally attacked
In spite of his actions he never gave up
He just wanted desegregation and violence to stop
They put him into jail and done all the wrong that they could
As painful as it seemed he understood
He had won a Nobel Prize as we recall
That within itself transpired all
Diligence and equality is what he had stood for
He wanted nothing less and nothing more
We have him to thank for up until this day
Therefore we as supporters won't have it any other way
The blacks are grateful to enter the work force
The Restaurants, Buses and Theatres, of course
Indeed the Schools and Churches we're now able to go
He was fighting for our freedom, Oh, What a Hero!
He had a dream that one day he will be in the Promised Land
And that God will guide him with his unchanging hand
Therefore, Dr. Martin Luther King may you rest in peace
And for the true believers this message will never cease
Although his mortal body had ended so abruptly
His soul which we believe is now resting into Glory

FREE AT LAST! FREE AT LAST!
THANK GOD ALMIGHTY HE IS FREE AT LAST!

Colleen D Lattanzio

A RARE AND BEAUTIFUL FRIENDSHIP

When I walked through the hardest hours of time
you were there to comfort me.
When my limbs were sore from standing alone
you were there to carry me.

When my heart burned for someone's love
it was your arms wrapped around me.

When you left and we went our separate ways
you kept in touch with me.

Ours is a rare and beautiful friendship
that through each year grows tighter.

For all of this and so much more
I thank you and I love you.

Harriet H Lee

AUGUST DAZE

Those lazy days of August
Are with us once again—
Too hot to have ambition
And not much chance of rain!

The garden needs a weeding,
The house needs cleaning too!
They'll keep! So don't remind me
Of all that I should do!

I think I'll go and find
A lounge chair in the shade.
I'll read—or simply daydream
While I sip a lemonade.

I'll forget about my "duties,"
Let the world go rolling by,
Dream about those far-off places
And those castles in the sky!

But I fear that I'll be wakened
By my conscience all too soon,
So I guess I'd best get busy
Getting lunch! It's almost noon!

Joyce Landrum

SHY

As she sat staring into space
He walked on by
She thought, what a waste
That she couldn't say "hi"

Carole Lantaigne

LIFE

When I close my eyes,
I dream and fantasize.
I dream about love and relationships,
And about what the future holds for me.
Sometimes life just seems so cruel and unfair,
that you get to the point where you really
don't care,
But I'm sure that it gets better,
You just have to take a deep breath
and be stronger,
For life is worth living for.

E Sims MacRae

TOTAL PEACE

I love the night,
The stars sparkling like sequins
on a blue velvet dress,
The soft, sweet smell
of dew on the citrus blossoms,
The gentle chirping
of crickets,
An occasional croaking of a frog,
calling to its mate.

In the city,
The lights twinkling
like a million fireflies,
Cars hurrying back and forth
impatient to be home —
wherever.

People and animals
Snuggling into the dark, warm,
enveloping night
as if it were a burrow or
cave.

Awaiting — resting for the
Fervent activity of a new dawn.

Tony Miller

MY GENERATION

The old generation has lost all sense of mind.
My generation is naked and fine.
Our music is rock and roll. The old jam had to go.
We have been known to smoke the best.
Not cigars, just wacky weed we just have to put to a test.
The old generation drank their moonshine.
Our drink is Bloody Mary and Jim Beam wine.
To get around we have Corvettes,
beside them are Harley-Davidsons
that sound like jets.
Our clothes what I've been told are fiery gold.
We think that suits have been too long ago.
Can't you tell our hippie tradition?
We raise all kinds of hell in this generation!
Kings and queens to us are friends,
just because we stay broke,
they're just a joke.
My generation has always stuck together.
A promise of peace and a party, to make things better?

Kennetha Mingo

DEPRESSION

To Tyrone Lamont Johnson. You have always given my heart love in this life, and I thank you for everything that you did. I will always love u! Thanks!

Depression is not a wonderful state
that fades into outer space like a
flying saucer that explodes through
the wild wind of glory. It's not the
story of a troubled child.

It's the story of a sad and lonely
person who has feeling that can be
hurt just as bad. Who feels as if no
one cares
"So why should I"

Mary Elizabeth Martucci

GRADUATION

As parting time draws nigh,
And we must bid adieu,
Then we'll breathe a sigh
For the years gone by.
Spent in learning here with you.
The socials, plays and such,
Have filled our days with joy.
Though we're glad we're through,
College, we'll miss you;
Farewell, dear College days.

Vera Tanner

THE ROCK

The black rock
Down at the sea
He must know something
He must feel something
The wave encircles the rock
For the thousandth time
She crushes against him
Then caresses him
With many white arms

He remains an immovable object
The rock must know something
Feel something
And maybe
When night envelops the land
And sea
He smiles to himself
Happy for all the love he gets

Lisa G Tilyou
WINTER, SPRING & LOVE
The Wind is Cold,
Surrounds my body, and fills the empty
Spaces that lie close to my heart.
And then you come along,
And the warmth which radiates from the
Love you feel,
Sends shivers up my spine,
And I tremble
with delight, as the cold that held my
Soul a prisoner, melts away.
The sun shines on my life,
And the tears that once fell, due to
pain, fall now to make room for the
new, youthful sprouts of life, bursting
forth to experience being alive.
I am Free, Life is Fresh, and Love is BEAUTIFUL!

Kimberly Thomas
LIFE WITHOUT LOVE
Life without love is like a
Body without soul, take one away
From the other, then it is worthless.
Life alone is good
Life along with love is even better.
I lived my life without love so long
Only to find out I was wrong,
Keeping love out of my life
There was no point at all,
So, every day I sit . . . and rock
looking at that same old wall.
I put not my love in this poem but
My heart instead,
I'm living it all my life
And it had to be said.
Let not your heart be trouble
Live life in the minute,
Express your love with others
And you won't resent it.

Eileen Smith
BILLY JOE
B londe with blue eyes, is my son,
he's three years old and lots of fun.

I nto everything in his reach,
at times I wish I had a leash.

L ooking for mud puddles in the yard, keeping him clean sure got hard.

L aughing and playing all day long,
his happiness to me is a song.

Y oung, small, and very fast,
I don't know how his energy can last.

J umping around on his bed,
coloring pictures, all of them red.

O pening gifts, he always had fun, he plays with the wrapping when he's done.

E vening comes, for me it's the best,
finally a chance for mother to rest.

Manisha Talim
YOU
There's a world out there
Waiting for you to reach out to
Mountains, forests, rainbows, sunshine
Skies that are a Wedgewood blue;

Don't hesitate to take that first step,
Your initiative lies within yourself,
So wake up and move forward
And yours will be every dale and delf!

You alone can decide your happiness
You alone can build your fate
So, friend, if you have remained dormant,
Start now, it never is too late.

You are an original masterpiece
There simply is no one like you
Smile at life and give it your best
And then the best will come back to you!

Barbara Rame Taylor
MY YOUTH
I remember when I was younger
And full of infinite wonder,
I had the fun of a child
Before I learned womanly wiles.

When a stick was a spoon
And there was a man in the moon.
When trees cast huge shades
I was the star in great plays.

I was a beautiful maiden, saved again
By a handsome prince from a wicked man.
I was an Indian and a cowboy
When things were for real, and not just toys.

I could change a river's course
Or track a rainbow to its source.
I could catch a falling star
And didn't have to reach that far.

I've tracked down the dinosaurs
And with the eagles I've soared
I've made mountains out of hills
Even the wind did my will.

Those wonderful days of long ago
Were full of joy without any woe.
Oh to feel like that forever
Would be worth any endeavor.

Earl W Thompson
THE WOODLAND ON THE HILL
As you travel along life's pathway, although you travel where you may, you will find a message written there to guide you on your way. You will find the answer written on the hills and in the valleys, on the mountain, on the plain to the question men are asking, "Dying shall they live again?" You will find an answer written on a field of golden grain—for the grain must ripen dying, so that it may live again. There is a message in the flowers we see blooming every day, that we may know of heaven's beauty. God has strewn them along our way, yet they too must die and wither so they may live another day. For it seems it is God's purpose, even to the life of man that all things should perish so that they may live again. There is a message with the seasons as they quickly come and go, from the emerald green of spring time to the winter white with snow. But perhaps the greatest message you will find painted in the fall with its many brilliant colors, may be seen by one and all. Then the trees all hold a party before the days of cold and snow that they will soon be sleeping — somehow they seem to know. The poplars leaves are bright yellow — they're a beauty to behold. And the birches stand so stately with their leaves of purest gold. The spreading oaks leaves have turned a golden brown while the maples are in scarlet like the sun just going down. They all stand close together and their arms seem to entwine. Oh! if men would learn a lesson from a painting so divine. For God is trying to tell us if we try to do his will, we'll awaken from our slumber like the woodland on the hill.

Ruth Ellen Foust
REFLECTIONS BY THE POND
By this pond, beauty smiles
and invites me to commune.
Reedy grasses, leaning on one another
as must man, sway in the wind.
An inquisitive fish flounces to the surface—
is he, too, stagnating?
Birds are chatting—do they
understand each other, or are
they—like so many people—
making noise,
saying nothing?

Rippling water gently subsides as the
wind stills, and nature's voices
calm my soul.
Ducks, fluttering their wings, sleep, and
awakening to an intruding visitor, quack.
Man's machine, a hum, drones its toil—
a faint reminder of why this solace
I seek.
A bridge I see, and know I need
to build a few to connect broken
dreams.

By this pond, I resolve again to celebrate life
and learn from God's "inferior"
creations
how to live in harmony.

Mary Sproat

Margaret E Horn
THE RIVER VALLEY

To Mary Sproat whose love and warmth has touched the hearts of all those who have had the pleasure of knowing her.

A heritage for many years, built up
from people's sweat and tears
Where people get together in any kind of weather
Everyone is welcome there.
Except the unwanted guest? We call the bear.
The River Valley school where Mary Sproat did rule
They have a picnic day, no one is turned away
The little children come because they have such fun
The large machines do roar and whine
To the toppling of the beautiful pine.

The ground has turned a murky grey
Where the green grass has been scraped away
The spots where the lady slippers did grow
Are replaced by a dirty overflow
The environment people spent their time
Trying to save this place sublime
Only to meet the arrogant lot
Who said to them, "We are not going to stop"
The Valley once covered with mist in the morn
Is covered with smoke and Oh! so forlorn
This place of beauty has now a duty
To house all the junk, for the garbage dump
So we should stop and think, don't spoil it with a stink.
Why don't we give some thought and save this hallowed spot?

Jonathan Sowers (Age 7)
CLOUD STORIES
Oh clouds, oh clouds, have you seen
a helicopter?
Oh clouds, oh clouds, have you seen
an airplane?
Oh clouds, oh clouds, have you seen
lots of birds?
Oh clouds, oh clouds, have you seen
the wind blowing you everywhere
around the world?
Oh clouds, oh clouds, have you seen
lots of people everywhere?
Oh clouds, oh clouds, have you seen
the stars?
Oh clouds, oh clouds, have you seen
the lines of smoke in the sky?
Oh clouds, oh clouds, have you seen
the sun rise before you?
Oh clouds, oh clouds, have you seen
other clouds, too?
Oh clouds, oh clouds, have you seen
the rain?
Oh clouds, oh clouds, have you seen
a rainbow?

AND THAT'S ALL THAT I WANT TO KNOW!!!

Carl David Marcum
COME BACK HOME

This poem is dedicated to Debbie, for things past that did not last.

My pockets are thin, memories stacked on end, nothing but me and the pain within. Come Back Home, Come Back Home, Come Back

Home. The smell of the kitchen, the warmth of the house, the scent of you when you were my spouse. Come Back Home, Come Back Home, Come Back Home. I sit in this place, the loneliness is clear. All I love is ever so near. A dream I'll cherish 'til I cease to be, for I know you'll never be with me, Come Back Home, Come Back Home, Come Back Home. The tears, the anger, the hurt blends in, all I feel is held within. Hopelessness prevails, despair swells, Come Back Home, Come Back Home, Come Back Home, Oh Lord, if only Come Back Home.

Patricia Maria
THE RING BEARER

To My First Love, you'll always hold the ring to open my heart.

No one can reach the depths of my heart.
The walls are too strong, they cannot be torn apart.
There isn't a key that can fit into the lock.
There isn't even a door to bear someone's knock.
There is only one way in which to enter.
Only one way to reach the very center.
It is the bearer of the ring that will win my love.
The answer is clear, he must first look above.

Carol May Noble
SONGS OF THE BIRDS

To my feathered friends. May their songs enlighten the earth for eternity.

Songs of the birds travel gently
through the woods
During the spring they are heard like
soft-spoken words
Nestled in the branches in herds,
singing a tweet chirping
that spring is here at last.

Over the lake fly the birds
like a reflection of classical melodies.
An orchestra of instruments playing
to keep time with Mother Nature
and her children.

Slowly the sun cast a shadow
and the birds sweetly sing
a bedtime lullaby.
Saying to all, take care and
goodnight.
I will sing for you tomorrow.

Renee Nelson
PEACHES
Peaches are SO good!
When you bite in,
Sweet rain
Runs down your chin
Like peach rain
and peach skies.

When you chew,
More and more
Sweet rain
Runs down your chin.

Charlene F Nichols
WOLF PACK
Swift slinking shadows in the dark
Movements barely seen
They huddle close around the fire
The children lost in dreams.

Old woman, tending to the fire
Dreams of a better day
Hunger stalks the little band
There had been no kill that day.
The hunters hold their weapons close
And do not lay them down
For if the pack attacks tonight
They must be ready then to fight.

The Darkness deepens near the dawn
The pack comes boldly near
Their fangs gleam white in the
firelight
Their eyes are clearly seen.

Attack is swift, they seek to grasp
The children from their mother's
clasp
The hunters keep them from their
goal
Then call their mates, come food for
all.

Teresa A Nyarady
LOWLY SONNET
Chide me not for mine inadequacies
Nor for mine insecurities
For within mine amentia do I hold
thee close
And I within mine fears dare not
approach
E'er since mine eyes beheld thy
countenance
Mine heart in darkness does joyously
dance
Tho I be not able to be so express
Amidst crowds I hide the loneliness
Mine dreams at night do give
reprieve
But in daylight hours they take their
leave
And I remain besotted alone
Ne'er shall this heart to thee be
known
For ye amongst the scholars do rise
And I mine self cannot disguise
That I am but a lowly wench
A servant of the higher bench
A jester that so plays the fool
A puppet on a golden spool.

Diane Neale
GETTING MARRIED
You're getting married, Hip Hip
Hooray!
Now you are going another way,

Some people may tell you congratulations!
Others may give you salutations!

Everyone who is married has a story
to tell
Some are great, others are Oh Well!

Let's not get on the other subject
All marriages have a different object.

So I hope you make the most of
yours,
While your wife has to do most of the
chores,

(House chores) that is, while you
bring home the bacon,
And think of the time off you'll be
taking,

While you're on your
HONEYMOON
Think of work, but not too soon!

Cathy Thi Tai Nguyen
THERE ARE MOMENTS

With love for my husband & daughter, Thi Chanh & Anh Thu Nguyen. In appreciation to those who sacrifice in the past, present & future for Democracy in Viet Nam.

There are moments
I sit and think
Of my past, present and future
What had brought me here?
Have I betrayed others!
Countless wars
Against strangers
Now after so many years
Between Brothers
Supposedly changing to Democracy
A better life for all
Freedom bell does not ring
Only the trumpet sound
From re–education camps
Remind those who try to escape
That you are considered traitors
For once you were soldiers
Who fought for what you believed in
Regrettably! all are in vain
One after another
Fall down without recognition
Not for benefits
But only
To be a stepstone
For those who come after you
A
SOLDIER.

Adrienne R Nolan
SECRET LOVE
To see you day by day
To hear your laughter when you are near
To see your smiling face makes my heart
skip a beat
Because you are my secret love
Knowing that you do not know how I feel
or care for you
It's my secret that I hold close and dear
to me
The only ones who know of my secret love
is the sun that shines so bright on a
clear and sunny day
The breeze that sends my kisses to your sweet lips
The stars that shine so bright at night that I wish
upon a star to make you mine
The flowers that remind me of the
sweet smell of
your body when you are near
But best of all tomorrow I get to see my secret love

Phyllis Nikbakht
KING OF FOOLS

To Valiant, who wasn't a Fool at all. I apologize!

I

There is a well-known king
Of whose name we are not sure
His kingdom is all 'round us
And his castle has no door

II

He is "The King of Fools"
Living in a fool's paradise
Wearing a crown made of paper
And a scepter cut right to his size

III

Who is this King of Fools?
Does he bring fortune and fame
To all the fools in his kingdom,
Who bow at the mention of his name

IV

He thinks he is better than others
And his subjects they all think the same
Sowing his seed of destruction
Hatred and Prejudice their name

V

All of these fools follow blindly
Like the Rats when the Pied Piper played
Mesmerized by the notes in his music
Never listening to what's being said

Allison Rae Naus and Leslie Ann Naus
BORED ON A SUNDAY AFTERNOON
I sent a cookie to the moon,
It wasn't too easy,
The spaceman ate it
And became quite queazy.

So, he tossed his cookie
And he planted a flower
But, to his dismay,
The buds were chocolate-chip
powered.

The spaceman's name was Sebastian,
it was
And he sent his flower
With the chocolate-chip buds,
Back to Earth.

I found the flower on my doorstep
And I greedily ate the buds
But, to my dismay, in a poof
I, too, became a chocolate-chip dud.

Now what do I do?

Linda Nicholson Harms
EARTH
One eye be full awake
The other in full sleep.
In full harmony each sleep and wake.
Drops of dew in the eye of sleep
With sun to brush away each drop.
Then bring a glint of light
Within the sleepy eye
And then a sunrise make.
While the lid of that one full awake
Will feel a heaviness and fall.
A darkness that will bring full rest
And peacefulness to the sun-tired
eye.
The moon its gentle song caress
The one that lies now in sleep.
The sun its joyful spirit sings
To that one now full awake.

This Earth's two eyes
With sun and moon — a symmetry
complete.
Full twelve its Maker made;
Within a symbiotic universe
God's creations each — its role to
play!

Frank E Napper
IN MEMORY OF "OLEY" HANSEN

This poem is dedicated to Eloise Hansen, wife of Maj. General Floyd A. Hansen ("Oley").

The cannon–ade is over
With its thirteen-gun salute
And the passing of our comrade
Is forever—absolute.

We came that day to Arlington
On the Greensward facing east
To pay our last respects to "Oley"
The so-doing was the least.

It was the memory of his service
From the Long Grey Line to Taps
That each of his sub–alterns
Reviewed in memory's past.

It was his ever-present guidance
His stern but fair command
That made us all develop
Better soldiers to a man.

He was big and strong and rugged

He was tough when chips were down
But he'll be best remembered
That he never wore a frown.

He was never too engaged
In the matters of the Corps
But to offer help and counsel
To his officers, evermore.

Today the caisson rests in camp.
The black and well-groomed horses stabled
Plans he had for grandsons
His widow will not table.

And as we all pursue our life
Whatever be our stint
Let us pause in silent tribute
To our chief who's now absent.

And if I may paraphrase Robert Service
In his Ballads of the Wild
"Oley" Hansen dwells in Heaven
As peaceful as a child.

Hulda Nickel
AN EMPTY ENVELOPE

This poem is dedicated to my mother who taught us to use those gifts given us to the extent that that was possible.

The postman had come
And had brought me some mail.
Letter-opener in my hand
I was ready to sail!
This was a good morning—
The sun shining bright.
What would this one bring me?
Perhaps some delight.
But, as I held it . . . it did seem a bit thin—?
The sun shone right through.
Held up to the level of my chin—I saw
There was nothing within!
With opener and letter held in my hand
The thought came quite quickly;
"No sense to go on—to open it,
There's nothing within!"
Half in confusion I looked once again.
Outside it was perfect—addressed, stamped, sealed;
And—it had arrived.
But there was nothing inside!
Like some of our lives.

Hulda Nickel
LEAVES FALLING
The long summer is ended.
The once fresh leaves tired and older,
The days turned shorter and greyed.
Winds seem to blow much bolder,
Before long blowing much colder.
Two walnut trees across the street
Are resisting valiantly the wind
Now tearing at their leaves.
The tree in the vanguard of the blast
First losing few—then losing fast
The leaves that once caught the sunshine,
The rain that helped sustain
Its growth and its integrity
To maintain the yield of nuts borne.
Nuts already picked—now seen no more.
More leaves falling from the branches
Now showing as they are stripped bare,
As ribs show on a human form
When the beautiful clothes once worn
And padded flesh have worn away.
Things not meant to stay.

Hulda Nickel
FOR A BROTHER'S BIRTHDAY (His 61st)
Forty years have rolled by quickly
Since a young man left his father's farm.
No more grubbing in the soil or pulling weeds;
No more shocking hay or tromping corn!
But his fortune he would find!
Confident in his self-possession
He left what he had known—
To the city, the biggest, nearest home,
Which beckoned him—Vancouver.
His good fortune he would find.
To his mother's way of thinking,
On her third son's leaving home,
Many thoughts and prayers went with him
To keep and guide him as he'd roam;
His good fortune for to find.
What these forty years have brought him
He alone will know that best.
Perhaps there have been real misjudgements,
And some attitudes best laid to rest,
Of good fortune—That God knows best.

Hulda Nickel
I WANTED A DOLL
The depression lay hard upon the land
And I, just a little girl,
Did so very much want a doll.
A Shirley Temple doll who was smiling at me
From the page of the Eaton's catalogue.
I dearly wanted her for my own.
I had never had my own doll.
Mother had made rag dolls
For the infants of our family.
The bigger children held and cuddled the infants.
But I wanted a doll, my own doll,
A Shirley Temple doll.
I took the Christmas Eaton's catalogue,
Which had arrived at Thanksgiving,
To show my mother the doll I wanted.
She could send the mail-order now
So it could be back by Christmas (I said).
The parcel came in time—a doll in it,
But it was not a Shirley Temple doll,
And it was not alone for me—
It was for all sisters—THREE.

Charlotte Napoleon
MY BROTHER
He was all I knew of a dad
I loved him though happy or sad.
He was big to me, bigger than life,
The strength of the family, through joy and strife.

He ruled hard and made you tow the line
How else could he mold and refine
The nature of siblings under his care?
But when we needed him, he was there.

He was not given to idle chatter.
He had no need, it didn't matter.
Labor, generosity, kindness and care
Attributes as these, he had more than his share.

Oftentimes brusque, stubborn and stern
Making it very difficult to learn
Of turmoil and frustration that goes on in man.
God has forgiven so I'm sure we can.

As I've grown older I fully understand
The substance of this wonderful man.
This is the brother I loved you see,
And all his life, I'm sure he loved me.

Tracy Newton
NATURE . . .
Is everywhere
In every corner of the world.
The wind sings a beautiful melody,
Swaying trees are dancing to the rhythm.
Flowers are blooming all around
When they hear the fresh new sound.
The creatures come up to me as if to sing
"So how do you like nature today?"
It's spring!

Roger K Nielsen
LIVING
The hustle, the bustle,
The bright city lights.
The entertainment goes on
Thru the endless nights,

All the calm and the quiet,
Of the dark country nights,
There's little to do after sunset,
You seldom see any lights.

The city never sleeps,
Night life is the best.
People never stop running,
There's no time for rest.

Country folks never rush,
It's peaceful and serene.
They relax by the fireplace,
It's like a wonderland dream.

No need to pretend in the city,
Everything is right there.
No matter what you like,
It's usually quite near.

Country living is great,
There's usually plenty to do.
They have dances and hay rides,
And bicycles built for two.

Wherever you call home,
Whatever life you choose,
If you like where you're living,
You can't possibly lose.

Vickie L Nagle
CHILDREN, IMPLEMENTS FOR THE FUTURE

To all Children Of Alcoholics, May God have mercy on those too far gone to respond to treatment and pity on those whose lives have been ruined in their path of destruction.

Do not take for granted our future will be mold,
With only love, hope, and happiness, inferred sweet dreams of what life will hold.
For behind that latent silver lining lies a dire darkest depth,
Enticed to poison their callow minds cede two blind eyes have met.
Our heads may be rex with knowledge, but let our vain wit be scold,
In choosing not to decide we still have made a choice.

Inez Nagle
I AM THE RAIN
I am the rain
I fill your oceans, rivers, lakes, streams and ponds
I feed your meadows and forest
I nourish your crop. I am the rain

I come down hard on you in anger, I am the rain
I comfort you, I am the rain
I gently soothe you
I wash you till you're clean, I am the rain

Sometimes I show up when you wish I did not
Sometimes I show up when you need me not
I am the rain

Though often you need me and not a drop
I am the rain
I come to quench your thirst — so thirst not
I am the rain

I stay away long at times
You can't live without me
I am the rain

Sarah Hawkins Norris
THE TREE
It looks lonely and undressed,
With leafless limbs, deteriorating trunk,
This barren shell,
Yet it has cradled new life
Many times within its limbs,
And has many stories to tell.
Its days are numbered,
This crumbling tower,
But I feel there is no pain,
Because beauty surrounds it,
And the sun embraces it,
And occasionally it's bathed with rain.
Though the subjections to the elements,
Will restrain and devour,
And shorten the life of the tree,
It will stand sentinel until the end,
And with dignity, bow out
When its wooden soul is free.

Sharon E Neuberger
CHRISTMAS MEMORIES

To Christmases — past, present & future that keep the book of memories ever growing.

The distant sound of church bells ringing. The Heavenly voices of small children singing.
The birth of a babe, laid in a manger of hay. Thus was born the first Christmas day.
The star of Bethlehem shining so bright, for all the world a wonderful sight.
The wonderful aroma of holiday baking, touched with love in the making.
The scent of pine that filled the air, the tree that we picked with tender care.
The thoughts of those who have departed, brings to our eyes a mist of tears.
The cards and letters, from those far away, read with excitement every day.
The beautifully dressed rag doll, the handcrafted wooden toy, that brought happiness to many a girl and boy.

The merriment and laughter of family and friends, filling a circle that never ends.
The parties and gatherings with toasts of good cheer, for all too soon the ending of another year.
The hopes, for all mankind, of goodwill and peace. That all wars and fighting would cease.
The soft fallen snow, the wind that would blow. The warmth of a family together again. That's what Christmas has always been.

William Eric Noyes
WAVES
Waves of disillusionment pounding,
against the shores of hope.
Slowly washing the towering cliffs away,
into the vast and empty ocean.

Bit by bit, little by little,
the majestic bluffs are worn down.
Once fertile soil is carried away,
banished to the bottom of the sea.

Only through vigilance and determination,
can we shelter and preserve the bluffs.
And stop the waves of disillusionment,
from eroding the shores of hope.

Patricia Nelson
BEFORE DEATH IS LOVE
Light falls and casts shadows on the wall.
Eyes look, but no one is there.
The mind is playing tricks again.
(fingers become numb . . . tears begin to flow)
The heart beats unusually fast.
The mind recalls the last time the heart pounded
so quickly, so alive . . .
A time when life stopped while two loved;
Two held each other, till that two became one.
(the heart cries, the mouth sighs)
The head lays upon a pillow, the hand
wipes the tears.
(the heart cries, the mouth sighs)
The mind reminds them all,
it's almost over now.

Theresa A Neptune
MY WORLD
The map of the world is on my kitchen wall . . . As I do my work, I can visit far-off places—Indonesia, Zaire, or Nepal.
My world is in my little home—It makes me feel happy and alive . . .
I can visit anywhere from Nome to Rome, and still have the table set by five.

Theresa A Neptune
PETER, DEAR
'Tis not the Wind you hear,
It is the Great Spirit
whispering in your ear . . .

IT whispers of the birds and flowers and bees,
Of butterflies and squirrels,
And great ships on the Sea.

All the things created and
living in harmony . . .
We are all related . . .
the Wind, the SPIRIT . . . LIFE . . .
Eternity.

Susan E Nielsen
BEYOND EVERY THUNDERCLOUD
Beyond every thundercloud,
a rainbow is hidden.
Waiting to be found by a glistening ray of sunshine.

Beyond every rainbow,
there is a pot of gold.
Waiting to be discovered by
the eyes of a dreamer.

I feel you are that dreamer.
Look beyond that thundercloud,
find the sunshine to make that rainbow,
and follow it to the end.

Look into that pot of gold,
and discover that all
your dreams are possible,

And go for them with all that
you possess.

Jerome O Nelson
AND I THANKED GOD

This poem is dedicated to my loving wife Joanne who encourages me to keep looking up.

Today I stopped, and thought, and looked all around me. And buildings and all the things people had made, was all could see.

Then I looked up, and saw the sky, the sun, and clouds, and became elated. And when I looked around again, I saw nature, and everything that had been created.

I even saw the little ants rushing to store food in their holes, as if anticipating snow. And I saw the busy bees jumping from flower to flower, not knowing, they were helping them to grow.

I saw the green grass dancing with the wind, and I could count each blade. And I saw the mountains standing so strong and tall, looking as if they were all hand-made.

I saw a robin's egg in its nest about to crack its pretty shell of blue. And I saw the fish swimming in their waters, and it made such a beautiful hue.

I saw the great oceans that covers most of the earth. And I saw all the plants and trees, and appreciated their worth.

I looked up again at the heavens above. And I knew, that all these things and more, were created out of love. And I Thanked God.

Jerome O Nelson
I ASKED THESE THINGS

In Loving Memory of my mother, Bernice Nelson, who taught me which things in life were important.

I asked to have removed from my heart, all prejudice and hate. So that no longer on these things, might I contemplate.

I asked to be allowed to forget the things that should be forgotten and to remember the things that I should recall. So that my path might be made clearer, and I would no longer continue to stumble and fall.

I asked for compassion, that for the needs of others I might truly care. So that in their joys and their sorrows, I could sincerely share.

I asked that for what I would give into the lives of others, would always from my heart go forth. So that I might be able to receive only a portion of it back, to aid me in my own course.

I asked for the courage to make humility my new way. But yet the strength to maintain my integrity throughout each day.

I asked these things and received them from the one above. And now, the hate I once felt has been replaced with love.

Carol Maxwell Nantze
NEW MEXICO'S ARTIST
He knew that He was doing when He picked up His brush.
He used each of His colors with tender love and a true artist's lust.

The mountains He painted to glisten with white peaks of snow.
They reflect off the desert far down below.

Cactus are painted with just the right shade of green.
Their flowers the most vivid you've ever seen.

Each of His creatures He touched with brush in hand.
And shaded the right colors to blend in with the land.

The sandstone He painted with soft shades of red.
If ever you see them, their beauty forever will remain in your head.

Delicate wild flowers He painted here and there.
With the soft gentle breeze they scent New Mexico's air.

High in the mountains, lakes are touched with pale shades of blue.
The Aspen in fall have a yellowish orange and red hue.

He knew what He was doing, this Master above.
He painted New Mexico with true tender love.

Pamela A Carter

Pamela A Carter
MY BEST FRIEND WHERE HAVE YOU GONE

In memory of mother Joanne M. Carter.

As I held you close to my heart for the very last time in my life.
Looking down in your face begging you please don't leave . . . I need you . . . I love you

You slipped away as if to say I never was . . . as you travel your new journey your new beginning forevermore
My best friend . . . My mother

You shall live on forevermore in our hearts & minds

How could you leave me getting mad and angry at you for not being
Only to realize no one has a choice to live or die . . . but a greater force stronger within

No one understands like you or no one can give the comfort that you could always give . . . A smile . . . A hug . . . or a comforting word
My mother My best friend

Where have you gone . . . And tell me why you left
When I close my eyes I can see visions of you forevermore
Loving . . . Soft beautiful you
My Best friend

A part of me has died forevermore along with you

Where have you gone
Tell me why you left

Amber Norwood
COME JOIN ME
Come join me,
As I race to destruction.
I use too much water
I use too much gasoline
I don't believe in car pools
I slash and burn forests without reason
I believe the Soviets are scum
I want to blow them off of the face of the earth
I drive drunk
I curse; I am a menace to society
I kick small animals
And kill for sport.
I hate everything innocent
And everything good
I am prejudiced
I hate all who do not conform
All of this because I am ignorant
Come join me,
Let's have a party
As we race to destruction.

Frances Diane Kendrick
REFLECTIONS
Well look at that reflection
That's looking back at me.
It's wearing the heartfelt smile
I've waited so long to see!

There's a sparkle in the eyes
Where sadness used to live.
There's compassion in the heart
That's learning to forgive!

My life is so much better
Since I've learned to laugh again.
I see beauty in the sunshine,
And feel beauty in the wind!

Was it chance or fate or wonder
That drew me close to you?
How could I know you'd touch my soul?
Did you feel the same way, too?

Yes, look at that reflection
That's looking back at me.
It's good to see the happiness
Felt by a heart that's free.

Connie A McKay
DEATH OF A TREE IN EVERGREEN (cemetery)

For years I have shaded those at rest
with my leaves of tender green
So many autumns have lived and died
so many teardrops I have seen
To every snowfall that has comforted me
with its blanket of pure white
How I have dreaded to see the darkness
that brings the cold of the night
But for every new life that is born
someone something must die
And how I wonder that for my death
will there be someone there to cry
Perhaps the birds shall miss my presence
perhaps the winds shall call
For now that I am forever gone
my memory will stand tall

Dawn Lee Mason
THE SPIRIT RIVER

Looking out over the hill was the river.
The river was flowing into Egypt,
Silently running with Your everlasting love
that is slipping into the sea of eternity.
Flowing until the end of time.

As You promised of old, flow sweetly,
Singing of Your song and glory,
Jesus, my friend.

The peace of Your living water gently washes
over my quiet, crying soul, kneeling to You
for forgiveness, as one of Your lost children
that has gone astray.

You lovingly embrace me, leading me home.
The tender leaves of the trees are Your
tender hands guiding Your living water
to Your poor, dejected children who
hungrily thirst for Your love that is
their precious, secret gift forever in
the silence of their begotten souls.

Jennylyn MacKenzie
I'M A FLOWER

I'm a flower,
Swaying in the breeze.
Holding my head up high,
Up to the blue blanket of the sky.
Each day I soak up,
The sun's rays and rain.
My bright petals yellow petals
And my long green stem,
Bringing color and love into the world.
As the bees drink my nectar,
Rain tap-dances on my petals.
When the sun's rays hit me in the
Morning I open up,
To welcome the new spring day.

Linda Kay Miller
A CHILD'S HEART

The heart of a child
Is like that of a clown.
Always full of laughter
Seldom seen with a frown.

It's really amazing
To watch the little tyke,
Running, jumping, playing games
And riding his new bike.

One never knows
The pain of a child.
He may be unhappy
Yet still carry a smile.

Yes, the hurt in a child
It is a hard thing to spot.
It's real, it's painful,
But fun it is not!

The life of a child
May seem full of joy,
Just keep in mind
His heart is not a toy!

Catherine Marks
IS THE MORN OF THE 11TH OF OCTOBER

This is the morn of the 11th of October
The sunrise is here, the darkness is over.
The beautiful colours in the sky
Have really helped me to open the other eye.

The colours that I am able to view
Are a wonderful blend of: yellow, red, white, and blue.
I'm feeling the powers of the rising sun
My new life has just begun.

This vision is sent from the heavens above
I can feel the beauty of God's great love.
He is giving me a strength for each new day
Helping me deal with obstacles that block the way.

Now's the time for me to start living
To appreciate those who have been and still are so giving.
I'm going to express how I truly feel
To come out of the box, first by breaking the seal.

To write this poem I woke from my sleep
This is the life I want to keep.
I thank you Lord for the opportunity
to let my feelings out
It's time I find out what living's all about.

Margaret G Mixon
THE RAIN

How sweet the flowers—
How green the grass.
I watch for hours
As the days pass.

I love to wander
Through parks and lanes—
And look up yonder
At sun and planes.

With skies so blue,
and grass so green—
Blooms of every hue
Show beauty in between

I think of rainy days
So dark and dreary.
Look through the haze—
Become so weary.

When the sun I see
Shines down again—
I think—"Where would beauty be—
without the rain?"

Steven Mooney
SNEAKING UP ON THE TRUTH

I don't know how to say that crazy is
just an adjective
when it runs like wildfire
coursing in vein sandblasting skulls
and wasting away in the heartthrob of difficult
mountainous odds.

I don't know that flipping the channels
is any different than television,
Kinetic living room watching aware detached
a common malady of our times,
responsible guidelines.

I do know that love and a tender appreciation
of skies are
tantamount to revolving forward to openness,
happiness, and the recently learned, eat.

There's a trust in center of the heart
in everyone.
We stay in touch even when temporary
blackout sends us away.

Steven Mooney
ON THE SPOT

Sitting in Klonsky's Bar
18th and Texas, after
doing laundry next door.
Saturday afternoon, overcast,
and happens to be a birthday.

Yesterday a friend shot his head off
with a .38 the week before
a friend drunken drove his car
into another killing cop father
husband.

Things wash up things go down
to terrible accounts and write-ups
which seem to distort time
by action alone.

So this day is another year as well
as a memoriam and careful
monument
to appreciation of life,
if distant, a general glee,
a shot straight up.

Novella Meek
ONE SHORT BLOOM

In memory of my lovable Collie, Buffy Brownie Honey, and the faithful canines of all time . . . Praise the Lord for man's best friend!

Buffy . . .
She loved beyond the lofty heights,
She did her work, then fell asleep.
I face the emptiness of nights,
Alone I ache . . . alone I weep . . .

Somewhere she has a place of gold
With rabbit spirits all around,
I'm sure she's found that heaven-fold
Of other loves we placed in ground.

My rose of life once more has
shed . . .
She asked for nothing, gave her all,
That faithfulness from me has fled.
Once more I watched a petal fall . . .
Buffy . . .

Mickey McShan
THE LEGACY OF FRIENDS AND LOVERS

The time comes for some of us, when
that which is our is free again.

The time comes for some of us, when
those held so close no longer feel.

The time comes for some of us, when
AIDS makes itself known.

And this, my friend, is part, it seems,
of the legacy of friends and lovers.

It will go away, my friend says
where as the chart states
otherwise.

I wish I knew what to do when told
of those I know.

Reach out, My friends take what time
is left.

Death comes in many forms and we
have no time for fear.

Reach out to those who need help let
them know they are not alone.

Reach out and touch.

Reach out and show you care.

We've come a long way in the past
few years and damn it

WE SHALL OVERCOME

Let us not forget the good times or
the bad.

Let us remember the way we came
and the many paths left to go.

Let us remember that for each of us
there is the beat of a different
drummer.

AND THE LEGACY OF FRIENDS
AND LOVERS.

Myra Victoria Matlack
YOU DON'T KNOW

You came in my life
As if you were sent
In a darkened world
The sun appeared
You brought me so much love
A feeling I never knew
You left as you came
No warning or blame
Darkness fell the world again
The sun disappeared
Just as it came
No laughter or love
Would I know again
But the love I feel
And the pain that grows
At least for you
Will never be known

Christopher Mobley
HER FACE

Her face shows great pain
Deep emotion as though
Someone had the key to her heart
And threw it away.

Her face says leave me alone
And yet, also shower me with love.

Her face has a bit of hope,
A shred of ambition to move on
An urge to find someone new.

All this can be seen from
Her face.

Coleen McPhail
MY TRAVELED PATH

For the one whom I will always Love—Josh Clark Morgan—On the occasion of our one-year anniversary . . . All Of My Love—Bean.

I've taken a path too harsh for the
deed;
It is not until now that I have
finally seen
That the wrong was not so steep.
My tears have all been wiped
away; although the traces still

remain,
My Love for you has gone un changed.

The base of my Love for you is built on trust
Which had been expunged by lust.
I've come to realize that our actions were masked —
An unfamiliar inner-self in you had then become so vain —
And it is now the cause of all our pain.

This path that I have taken is a very dangerous haul
And with every step I take, the ground crumbles beneath my feet
And I begin to fall.

I am now with all my effort,
Trying to retrace my steps to get back to a certain place.
The place where everything was so calm and gentle;
Where the courage in me was seeing your face.
In that place, we cared and Loved one another.
But here our feelings are hidden by darkness, fear, anger and guilt.
These forces hold back our ability to Love each other;
Love in the whole sense — Loving forever —
You and I always together.

Please help me now to see my steps so that I may turn back.
Please hold out your hand and shine forth your light
So that on firm ground I may stand.
I can bear this path no longer, and I am frightened and alone.
Here I have no one to call my own.

I am the one who chose this way — I know — and if you'd like
You may let me go.
But all I ask — all I beg — is to see your hand reaching out for mine
With Love and compassion.
This of you, I am asking.

Louis W Monroig
LET IT BE BUT ONCE

To the one I love.

Always to be near
But never to be close
With every passing thought
You are here with me
Always to be near
But never to hold you
In my wanting arms
Always to be near
But always so far away
Let it be but once
That I could hold you close
And my heart will rejoice
Let it be but once
That we share our
Gift of timeless love
And our passion will light
The heavens from now
'Til time unending

Doreen Mitchell
A SPECIAL FRIEND

To Elaine, this poem was written for you to show you what a good friend you are to me. You've always listened to me & have been there for me always. I hope no matter where we are or what we do, we'll always be close. Thanks for believing in me.

There comes a time in everyone's life,
When they need a close friend.
Someone they can depend on,
To help their troubles mend.

Someone you can count on,
Through the good times and the bad.
One who never judges you,
Through the happy and the sad.

One who you can trust in,
Secrets never to be told.
Always a companion,
One who can never be sold.

A gift of lasting friendship,
A bond no one can break.
Laughter shared with good times,
That no one else can take.

One who knows you like an open book,
One who can read your mind.
One who's always there, when you need them,
One you'll always find.

One who knows all your moods,
Just by reading your face.
One who means a lot you,
Someone you can't replace.

You see this is a special friend,
One is lucky to find.
Someone who is special enough,
And can always be so kind.

For you see you are that special friend,
All these qualities that we share.
You're someone positive in my life,
You mean the world, because you care.

Jim Morrison
CONTINUATION OF THE CELEBRATION

I would like to dedicate this poem to: Gene Bartley, Ray Manzarek, Paul Rothchild, Robby Krieger and John Densmore.

As inherent heir
to the majestic poetical throne

I proudly sail
repetitious seas of intense turmoil

And torturously converse
w/torturous confusion and deprivation

and w/mysteries from the highest order

Intrigue at the border

Rhymes twined within the
essence of tragedy

Soft
warm and content

True substance for conceptual characters

Yet
hostilities prevail

Twenty years
of silent literary warfare

and they prevail

But what do we care

Embrace us
And hail the continuation.

Stella Manaker
EARTH
A blue planet
Spinning in the universe,
Contains beauty in
Flora, Fauna and Humans.
May goodwill
Bring Peace to our
Beautiful Planet.

Stella Manaker
THE MALL
Sitting waiting for my friend,
I watch people
coming and going.

Tall ones, short ones, thin ones, fat ones,
GIRLS dressed in shorts, tight slacks,
long dresses or short skirts.

Men in colorful shorts, T-shirts,
Baggy pants, untied shoes and others
dressed in style.

Children, some sedate, others crying,
Running or too tired to care.
Friends meeting, relating troubles,
Family and activities.

It will be good
To arrive home
To comfort and quiet.

Stella Manaker
SUMMERTIME
The aroma of roses fill the air.
Their beauty and perfection of form
Are a delight to my eye.
A hat to shield me from the sun
Has a combination of red and white roses
To complement my red sash.
Awaiting my companion
In such a serene situation
Gives rise to hopes for a happy day.

Stella Manaker
DAYDREAMS
To daydream in the Springtime
Can be sublime.

To daydream on a Summer's day
Can be relaxing or gay.

To daydream in the Fall—
Think of playing with a ball.

To sit before a Winter fire
Eases body and soul that tire.

Michelle Rena McCarty
LAST NIGHT
Here comes the morning and the man in the moon is fading fast,
Last night was like magic, but last nights never last.
I wonder what I'll tell him because I don't have a clue,
I don't know why I gave in to what I swore I'd never do.
Like lightning on a warm summer night, you came without a warning,
Oh why did I give into something I knew I'd regret in the morning?
You often try to hold on to all the special moments in the past, but time just won't let me stay,
Because with every step you take you'll find, you're losing something along the way.

Michelle Rena McCarty
LEONA MAY

To My Wonderful Mother For Never Giving Up On Me, "I Love You!" Love Rain.

Mom, you've always been there to share my laughter, and also share my tears,
You've always been there for words of encouragement, love, and to help chase away all of my fears.
You and I have so very much that we both share, and whenever I've needed you, you've always been there.
It seems like it doesn't matter what I do, You're always there to help me get through.
With all your faith, and patience and your ways so lovingly, Now I see that most of the things you do in life are just for me.
My dreams that you encourage and the doubts you sweep away, Is one of the reasons why I love you more and more each day.
In the past twenty-one years you've
never turned your back on me through the easiest of times or the hardest of hard,
And it's all of these things together that makes you the greatest Grandma and Mother that you are!

Jeremy Martin (Age 12)
STARLIT SKIES
Walking along a sandy shore,
The starlit skies above.
Holding your hand, I feel the warmth,
That bonds us together with love.

I've been waiting for this incredible night,
That I could look into your eyes.
They're more beautiful than, the exquisite dove,
That flies among shining skies.

We paused for a moment, to look at the stars,
That twinkled with joy up in space.
I was thinking about, how beautiful she appears,
As the moon danced with light on her face.

We continued our walk, then she came to a stop,
Turned and looked right in my eyes.
I thought that I knew, just what she would say,
It's time for us to say our goodbyes.

To my surprise, she told me she loves me!
Instead of beat, my heart started to skip!
And that was the beginning, not the end,
Of a lasting relationship.

Lee Mertes
BIRTHDAYS!

I want to dedicate this poem to my friends, Ludwick & Holly. To my brother Rodney and my daughter Susanne whom I wrote this poem for.

Once a year we have a celebration.
Mostly children enjoy this occasion.
Birthdays mean another year of aging.
But there's more to ponder than just a celebration.
Another year of life is a time for reflecting.
Your family and friends, and the master's creation.
The wisdom, the blessings, that come with aging.
A year of new beginnings, now that's worth celebrating.

Monica E Martish
YOUR WISH
Please believe when I say this to you
One day near, your wish will come true
Just make sure that you want it more
Than anything you've wanted before

Just wish upon a star so high
That shines so bright in the evening sky
It will come true, wait and see
I know it will, take it from me.

Terry Messner
BODY ADORNMENTS
Standing alone
So far from home
Holes piercing my very being
Nothingness is all I'm seeing
I'm walking a straight line
Chains dragging behind,
Connected to huge weights
That rip, and pull, and tear, and make me hate
Hearing not a sound
I turn around
And instead of seeing my imagined pains
I find all my possessions, my family, friends
Commodities indeed rare
Which make my burden easier to bear.

Ruth A Matula
WAVES OF LIFE
Ride the waves of life
And find —
The ups and downs within your mind —
The clams that come when the raindrops fall —
As the overfull heart tends to empty and stall —
Oh, yes, ride the waves of life and find —
The highs will always make you shine
The swells all hold a big surprise —
Of life passing in front of your eyes —
The shallow part of life will be —
As the tide touches the shore and sees —
Another life only on solid ground —
This time your ups might be your downs —

Ruth A Matula
YOU KNOW
There's a simple little phrase I've said a few times to you—

It doesn't say a whole lot but it is so very true—

There's a lot of things that happen that don't require words—

Maybe, A Smile, A Look, A Feeling or
The Soaring of a bird—

It's not so important that anyone notices
what makes me grow—

The important thing to me is only that
"You Know."

Benita Moore
YOU AND ME
Walking by the river
Walking by the sea
Nobody is around
But you and me.

Lying in the grass
Looking to the sky
No one is around
But you and I.

Simple things are nice
That's what I like
You and me together
Alone in the world.

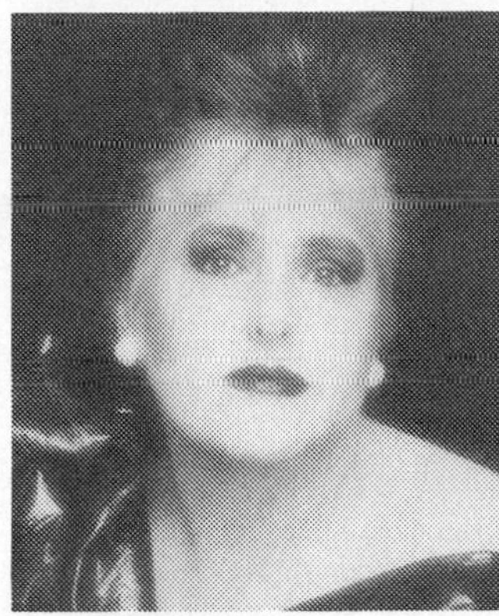

Finny J Burns

Finny J Burns
SO BEAUTIFUL . . .

Dedicated to Sondra L. Burns.

The warmth of your nakedness blended with the warmth of mine. I gaze into your eyes and they speak softly, silently answering the tenderest of my question . . . yes . . .

Then some fragrance — some red fire grass brushing against my burning cheeks. A long lash of curtains closed on a blue sky tickles my face and then a tighter embrace as your lips cover mine with kisses of passion.

So gentle your caress — like waters of a sunny brook babbling over its pebbles and tickling the side of a playful silver fish.

Oh, if my heart could shout its happiness, I would drown out a thousand thundering heralding trumpets with my joy.

Then slowly raising up — up — up — you bring me equal to the height of the tallest mountain and down go my love on the flight of a few hundred butterfly.

I lay trembling in the of arms of some soft peaceful dove — returning from a flight of ecstasy.

And breathing in your same breath from the last closing moments of some great symphony — I know I have been on a journey of true love . . .

Finny J Burns
IF MY HEART'S A STAGE!

Dedicated to Wilma Jean Burns.

If my heart's a stage—
Then you have captured the scenes—
Which have played upon it . . .
Of my heart is a garden—
Then your small rosebud
Grew into a lovely rose . . .
If my heart is an attic—
Then you have stored my precious moments—
For memories on rainy days . . .
If my heart is a fireplace—
Then you have set the inspiration of life
To logs of my ambitions—
Until the flame is reaching upward . . .
If my heart were a swift river of emotions—
Then you have been a steadfast undercurrent of love—
to channel it . . .
If my heart is a lonely island on an ocean—
Then the tide of your love has embraced its shores—
And left the kiss of purity . . .

But Mother —

If my heart is a valentine—
Then it's all for you—For you have taught it well!

Finny J Burns
WHAT'S THE MATTER

Dedicated to Rowena (Cookie) Ruiz.

Oh gentle and softly tumbling down—
pittering pattering teardrops round.
Rolling swiftly down your cheek—
muttering rumbling tears that speak.
Streaming down on your party dress—
will they ever cease to rest.
What's the matter — be my guest?!

Please tell me friend I ask—
tears — for what unwanted task?
It is this I want to do—
to find out what is hurting you.
Come sit down here beside, and
let down your pearls of pride—
do not from me hide—
what's the matter . . . huh?

Finny J Burns
TOMBSTONES

Dedicated to Shirley Watkins.

I love to dance among the tombstones
And read the epitaphs . . .
To sneak and prowl around the graves
Like an evil alley cat.
When sin is king and things go wrong,
I go there to sing my heartfelt song
to those who are long gone.
I like to run free in the wind
And acrobat over tombs and spin.
This I do again and again . . .
Until at last I'm rid of sin . . .
And then I go home.

Finny J Burns
I AM A CAPTIVE!
I am a captive — a slave in chains — never to be free—
I am haunted — taunted — cast down lanes—
where time just laughs at me!

I am given to love which is not returned—
can never be mine and yet I yearn—
my heart may as well be turned—
and what is life to me!

Finny J Burns
SOMEBODY'S SON

Dedicated to Bertie Baughman.

Are you troubled and sorry—
Have you done someone wrong—
I'll tell you of forgiveness—
in an old-fashioned song . . .

Somebody's Son lived long-long ago—
And he died on the cross—
To ease our tales of woe.

Are you lamed or weakened—
Have you gone astray—
I'll tell you of strength—
To live day by day . . .

Somebody's Son lived long-long ago—
And he died on the cross—
To make men whole.

Is your heart heavy laden—
Your spirit so low—
Then I'll tell you of Jesus—
For he loved you so . . .

He is Somebody's Son—that still lives today—
And He died on the cross—
To take our sins away.

Annette Moreau
NO ONE KNOWS AS MUCH
No one knows as much as I
The pain that comes with each of my cries.

The sadness that flows with each tear
The frightening experience of the unknown fears.

And your angry words carelessly thrown at me,
No one sees as much pain as me.

R E Mazey
MEMORY SONGS

For Georgianna L. Cunningham.

I bought an old record today
and, as I put on that disc,
30 years fell away.

Grandmother, you came to me.
We played these songs together?
Remember?
I suddenly realize
I learned to love music through you
as we listened on those golden afternoons long ago.
You laughed when I asked you
to play it again . . . and again.

The memory glows.
The sound unlocks the door,
and warm, happy tears flow.

Kolleen L McCormick
MOMMY

Dedicated to my parents who taught me to be myself and how to express my feelings.

Mom—why don't you love me,
I'm your only one.
Dad, doesn't love you,
and, I need a chance to.
Don't let them take me from you,
you locked me in a room,
and say they will take me.
I want to see the sun,
play in the sand,
and fall in love.
Don't do this mom;
I can be good;
I promise.
What's going on?
Who's pulling at me?
I can't hear you,
Mom, don't leave me!
It feels different, I feel different.
Where are you?
Where am I?
and, why did you kill me, mommy.

Retha V Minor
NO MORE DRUGS
When everything in your life seems to be going wrong, do your best.
One day you'll look back and say, "I'll not settle for less."
Think of life as a great success and value your life as your biggest asset.
When things are going wrong don't take alcohol and drugs.
Your body will decrease if you endure in the things that we call the drug bug.
The drug bug will knock you down and out.
You'll not live to see what life is all about.
If you decide to take drugs get help instead.
Always remember your life is worth more alive than it is if you are dead.
Be sure to do your best, because without drugs your life can be a great success.

Regine M Mikucki
FOR ALL ETERNITY
God grant there yet be time
To still plead with this rhyme
For St. Mary of the Angels Church
So that it not be left in the lurch
For it was the movie ABOVE THE LAW
Whose actual moral tone but a few people saw
As the violence and street language galore
Made certain it be rated "R" and more
To the faithful to whom this Sacred Shrine
Means more than a Developer's gold mine
Bring hope that with the start of repair
Divine Providence shield them from despair
O people do come to Chicago's own edifice
Shown in a film for posterity
That it and many cultural buildings
Be kept for all eternity
FOR ALL ETERNITY—FOR ALL ETERNITY

Teri Marsaw
MY FRIEND?
You said you would always be my friend,
And I believed that was true.
We shared a great deal together,
I loved and trusted you.
We talked about our dreams for the future,
And how happy we thought we would be.
Nothing could separate the two of us.
Together forever, you and me.
You came to see me one night,
There was something you had to say.
You told me you were leaving,
You would be gone the very next day.
I couldn't believe I would never see you again.
All I had left to hold was the memories of what could have been.
The days that followed, I cried many a tear.
I was filled with pain and heartache,
What had happened was my greatest fear.
You said you would always be my friend,
And we would never part,
So how could you do this to me,
Why did you break my heart?

Virginia Mendoza
JUST A . . . FRIEND!

To my husband David and Angel my niece, who encouraged and supported me.

To a friend whom I
Care for,
Love,
Who I will be friends with . . .
Always
There is a man I dream of,
Not only at night,
But during the day as well.
He's not my boyfriend or a lover
He's just a friend.
I like to hear him talk
He makes me laugh, cry,
But most of all he makes me feel special.
I don't want you to think I love him,
Unless one can love a friend.
Sometimes I feel so happy
To have a friend like him but,
Other times I am so confused.
But if this is what is what it feels like
To have a special friend like him,
Then it's worth all the confusion in the world!!!!

Barbara White Miller
YOU SAID
You said:
Trust me
I want you
You said:
We'll grow together
There's no hurry
We have the rest of our lives
You said:
You are my baby
I'll take care of you
You said:
Please never leave me
I need you
You said:
Promise me
You'll always love me
You said:
Goodbye
I said:
I promise . . .

Christina Mitchell
FEELINGS

This poem is dedicated to my dear family and the darling loved ones in my life.

People all around me make me cold and hostile inside.
They give me bad feelings that I dare not push aside,
but when I obtain courage, and goodness from God, things
seem very differently, and times are not as hard.

Emberly Melton
SIMPLY CALLED LOVE
Love is not words shared in the dark,
Love is a feeling straight from the heart.
From the top of your head to the tip of your toes,
When you feel love the whole world knows,
From the earth below to the heavens above,
It's simply called love.

To feel love there is no pain,
You have no fear,
You have no shame.
Love grows stronger everyday,
It strengthens your heart in every way.
No need to hold on too tight
It's a feeling you'll never fight.
Love is free to fly like the doves.
To say in a word
It's simply called love.

William Miller
MAYBE

This poem is dedicated to my sisters, Dorothy, Pauline, Helen, and Maxine.

Maybe I'll have my tomorrow
Live under a clear blue sky
Maybe there will be a dream I could borrow
To keep my dream alive
Maybe there will be a new beginning
With the thrill of love
I keep down deep inside
Maybe my dreams will survive
If so, I'm one lucky guy.

Daniel P Moynihan
A BETTER BERLIN WALL

To the September and May demonstrations of the students in Burma and China—a message not lost but won.

Let's build a better Berlin wall
Not just of stone and wire.
But of composites and alloys
Electronic and bionic.

Let's build a more enduring wall
That will stand against erosion.
Terrorists strike
And radical explosion.

And even a poet can love this wall
That shadows generations,
Cooling blood in vein
Inflaming indignation.

As it stands a monument
In every bloody noman's land
In every bleeding heart,
Of mothers who have lost their child
To fathers — who have not.

Let's build a better Berlin wall
Not just of stone and wire.
Formed this time not from ice
But formed to be torn — with desire.

Daniel P Moynihan
ALEXANDER
Western masculinity
Doused in a torrent of Eastern Passion.
The quest for greatness and order,
Deterred by gentle seasoning, exotic herbs and manners.

Pepper for rancid meat!
Beauty with a different slant.
Rank and file not standing but prostrate, deferred.
Transcended mind had never really left the body
(Or shouldn't if it could).

An embrace,
Sweet and compassionate
Yet ironically iconoclastic,
Ending,
Not in marriage, but a parting.

Continental drift
Slowed, ceased, resumed.
Not by the sword,
in spite of it.

Lisa M Nault
YOUR WAYS
The way your eyes would always smile,
And let me know you care.
The way the sun would shine upon you,
And pick out the gold in your hair.

The way you would always laugh at things,
And be serious when the time was right.
The way you would always cheer people up,
Your mood was always so bright.

The warmth of your body when you pulled me close,
The touch of your lips on mine.
The sound of your voice when you whispered to me,
So caring, sensitive and kind.

The way you always cheered me up,
The way you were always there.
It really is a shame we ended it all,
Because I want you to know I still care.

Helen Nukala
MY CHILD

This poem is dedicated to my children: LeRoy, Barbara and Grace.

I think that there could ever be,
A thing as sweet as a baby.
A child with skin so soft and fair,
And burnished sunbeams on his hair.
The eyes that look in wonderment,
Yet in one's arms seem so content.
I can't believe this child is mine,
Such little fingers mine entwine.
Each child a heritage divine,
To love and cherish for all time.
No harm shall ever come to thee,
For I'll watch o'er you constantly.
Oh, little one, I love you so,
Such love no one shall ever know.
I'll guard you with my every thought,
This miracle has love begot.
I'll walk beside you all my days,

And guide you in the narrow
ways.
For there are pitfalls everywhere,
God keep you in his Loving care.

Michael G Nicholas
DEATH IS THE KEY
Death is the key to the Locked Door
of Life.
This life is perfect;
There is no crime, prejudice, or sin
Where you can gather with all your
kin.
You'll always win, and never lose.
This life is in our Maker's Kingdom
For me and you to choose.
But to pass through this door,
You will have the strength within to
get in
By having faith in Him.

Frederick J Neff
OUR TREES
Joyce Kilmer wrote in melancholy
verse, "I think I shall never see a
poem lovely as a tree."
In our town, you'll notice, there are
fewer OAKS standing tall and
free.
They cut down the hardwoods at
Heck's along the highway,
Then the OAKS at the courthouse fell
where nearby the Promotion
Council earns their pay.
You know, the ones who in October
say, "Come see our colors on
display."

This "poet" spoke to the local scribe
who said, "I'll write an editorial
on trees and thee."
In the meantime more trees came
down because they interfered with
C&P.
If there was an editorial by the scribe,
it was certainly missed by me.

The buzz of the saw began on the hill
and down came the OAKS.
This, at the place where we like to
play host,
To the tourist who came to see the
colors and stop at the Post.

Now, more trees have been cut at
Eighth and High,
But who cares, who cares, I say
with a sigh.
I think there is no poem lovely as a
tree.
Bye the bye, I'm no poet you're
certain to agree,
But I feel sure you get the message
from me to thee.

Anngie T Nightingale
PLEASE
For Jason, with love.

Talk to me
as a friend,
not as an enemy.

Call to me
as you wish,
but not as a necessity.

Understand me
as me
and don't get suspicious.

Love me,
for who I am
not what I am.

Tell me your secrets,
I'll inspire them.
Explain the tears
n your eyes.
And won't you please
lend me the key . . .
to your heart?

William C Neal
I BELIEVE
The most beautiful things in life are
not the things we put the most value
on.
Rose in full bloom, a face with a
smile.
Great oak casting a cool shade on a
hot day,
Kind word spoken in time of need.
Gentle flowing stream, big hug to
wipe away the sorrow.
Song of a red bird, presence of a
friend in a crowd.
Snow covering the ground in bright
sun, faith of a Christian.
The spider weaves a masterpiece and
no one knows, till morning, sun rises
and whole world sees its beauty.
Some people's work is like the spider
web, truly a wonder to behold.

Christopher A Nooner
FATHER
Come and help me
up son
for I am getting
old
my limbs are getting
weaker
my head is getting
cold.

I used to be more
stable
my eyes could see
afar
my hands were much
more steady
when they rapped upon
the door.

I might have once been
handsome
but wrinkles have
replaced
the smooth soft lines
of youth
that dwelt there on
my face.

So come and help me
up son
and one day hope to
be
as old as your poor
father,
as old my son as
me.

Brenda Kay Nagel
A CHILD'S MEMORIES
Dedicated to a very special friend, my Mother. I'm sorry Mom for all that you've struggled through and I want you to know I'll always love you. From your daughter — Brenda.

The voices rise;
A child begins to cry;
She sees him hit her;
A child wonders why;
Unforgettable words are spoken;
He hits her again;
A child cries;
She feels unforgettable pain;
The child continues to cry;
For look into my eyes, I was once
that child;
The memories I'll forever carry
inside;
"Why Daddy, why";
Take back them nights;
Oh, could you please;
Take away all the bad memories . . .

Stacey Nelson
ODE TO STEPHEN KING
A writer's pallet
Paper is sweet
yielding fruits
of labor until then unbeknownst
creation is result
with obscure tumult
you see.

Patricia Nash
MOTHER'S LOVE
Mother has a way of knowing,
Everything that you are doing.
Even though you try to hide,
Mother sees with hidden eyes.
She knows when we're good and
bad;
She knows when you're happy or
sad.
Mother knows your every thought
and deed;
She's there for you and all your
needs.
Even when you're far from home,
Mother never leaves you alone.
She's always willing and standing
near,
To ease your pain and calm your fear.
Mother thank you, for the sacrifice
you made,
The love and dedication, and many
times you prayed.

O T Neely Jr
A DREAMER'S PRAYER
This poem is dedicated to all individuals who have ever dared to dream.

Believe in me ever I dream
When at times although it may seem
They may never come true
I would be grateful if you
Would believe in me ever I dream

Trust in me ever I ponder
Ofttimes my mind tends to wonder
But with faith I no doubt
Will soon work problems out
If you trust in me ever I ponder

Comfort me ever I fear
That it's evident my failure is near
Strength comes from within
And is magnified when
You comfort me ever I fear

Be near me whenever I wake
I alone the credit can't take
For my dreams that come true
Yet there's more dreaming to do
And as always . . . I believe in you

Amen

Sara Nelson
SUDDENLY . . . I'M FORTY!
My hair is turning white;
I'd swear 'twas overnight;
Suddenly . . . I'm Forty!

I hate to strain and stare . . .
Turn the light on over there.
Suddenly . . . I'm Forty!

But my hearing's still okay . . .
Eh, what's that you say?
Suddenly . . . I'm Forty!

Not a pound heavier today . . .
Throw those fibbin' scales away!
Suddenly . . . I'm Forty!

Where did all those years go?
Why couldn't they go slow?
Suddenly . . . I'm Forty!

Who could that old codger be?
Why, I'll bet he's ninety-three!
Gosh! I'm glad I'm ONLY . . .
Forty!!!

Orpha Parscale Norris
MY LITTLE CHAIR
The little chair I rocked in
When a little child was I,
A "Pauline" doll now sits in
The space I occupied.

It was lo' many years ago
When I sat in the chair,
But still the mem'ries linger
Of times that I spent there.

There was a little pup that I
Would rock to sleep at night,
I'm sure that when I put it down
Its eyes opened big and bright.

But in my little, childish mind,
The puppy was sleeping tight,
And I went to bed still thinking
The pup slept thru the night.

Mark G Nunn
LOST SOUL
Caught between two trusses in a barn
twisting not knowing which way to
turn
I began to think my life being harmed
never did I want to be stuck in a barn;
For years I stayed locked in this barn
twisting away—my head in a daze
this barn so old just doing me harm
never really wanting to be stuck in a
barn;
One day I sold my thoughts to the
sun
leaving my mind to them who knew
asking for an answer to what should
be done
he looked at me and gave me a gun;
Cocking the lever and aiming the gun
straight for my brain—my head got
hot
blowing my brain away oh, it was fun
filling me with answers this gun from
the sun;
Awakening I ran to look in the mirror
finding myself everything came clear
gone were the trusses, gone were the
fears
never should I—have stopped there
for years.

Virginia M Nesbitt
FOR THE BIRDS
I hurry to your rescue,
I'm bundled up to feed,
Your dinner of suet
And freshly bought birdseed.
I leave materials for nesting,
Easy for you to see,
And have provided houses
To raise your family.
You look so sweet, so tiny,
I want to keep you near—
I'm hoping you will work for me
Later in the year.
Winter days of birdseed,
Summer—a birdbath,
Now I watch you hopping
Down my garden path.
So please, do appreciate
The goodwill I have shown,
And eat those pesky garden bugs
And leave my berries alone!

Virginia M Nesbitt
THE HUMMINGBIRD SHOW
Here again, there again Humming-bird,
Darting through the air.
Now you see him, now you don't,
Now—He's over there—
Resting in my apple tree,
He's as tiny as a leaf,
Watching o'er his territory
To chase away a thief!
Standing as a statue,
I can enjoy his show.
If I move a little bit,
He will surely go.
Kissing tiny Coralbells
On their slender stalk,
They were planted, just for him,
Along my garden walk.
Wings rotating with a hum,
Hovering,—he sups,
"Chip-chip," (Thank-you) is his song,
While kissing flower cups.

Karen M McKinley
CHILDHOOD MEMORIES
A day in the park
Playing on the swings;
Those are the memories,
Those are the things
I treasure from childhood.
Hold your daddy's hand,
Go for a walk.
Sit with your mom,
Kid and talk.
Now that I'm older
I try to stay close,
Because family to me
Means the most.

Patricia Mulder
LIFE IN THE SLOW LANE
Life in the slow lane can be so sweet.
Taking time to savor life is a rare treat.

Faster and faster they race past my car.
Sometimes I wonder where and how far
They're driving in a dust storm's flurry.
I don't want life to zip by in a hurry.

Wildflowers bloom at the edge of this road.
I notice turtles and even a tiny brown toad.
I see a red robin chase a sweet little sparrow,
And I know just where this road becomes narrow.

I see groundhogs, rabbits, squirrels and deer.
Because I drive slowly, they let me come near.
The fast lane I've tried to its fullest extent,
But only in the slow lane do I feel such content.

If life in the fast lane makes you hurry and race,
Join me in the slow lane; enjoy my peaceful pace.

Pauline Meyer
SITTING BY THE SEASIDE

This poem is dedicated to my mom and dad, who believe in me.

Sitting by the sea
You feel the wind caress your hair
You might even taste saltspray on your lips
You watch driftwood float back and forth
Each wave brings it close to you and then pulls it back
You feel your imagination take hold
Your emotions course freely
You see yourself float on those billowing white clouds overhead
Beyond that is the endless blue sky
How luxurious it feels to rest on the warm sand
All you can hear is the sound of the waves and the cry of distant gulls
Those ageless sounds of the seaside.

Domus
EMOTION

To: Little Sailor of the house I am.

There is of me deep EMOTION
Moving waters as a great sea
Blue waters being that I am
As everything being of me.

Tipping waves of much churn
Source of life of mighty hue
A surfacing of great yearn
Of many things for me to do.

A sailboat of these waters
Of purpose I also be
Being that I am devotion
This churning EMOTION of me.

To sky of true azure
Sails of me, love and purity
The wind so does allure
My direction a surety.

As everything being of me
Moving waters as a great sea
Blue waters being that I am
All of much EMOTION.

DOMUS

Kathleen Mundy
THE CRIMSON ROSE

To My Loving Mother, Mary Murphy, who passed away on May 24, 1990. I will miss her very much.

The droplets descend upon her petals,
like beads of pearls,
Making her ever so radiant,
and e're unspoiled,
She will not wither,
nor will she die,
Her beauty glistens through summer skies.

Her color now looks faded pink,
She starts to sway, or so you think,
Her petals are in a row instead,
They aren't blue or even red.

The rain has ceased, she looks so frail,
The weather's left her very pale,
The sun shines on her petals bright,
and kisses the last raindrop's flight,
For on the vine, there only grows,
The last remaining Crimson Rose.

Christina Menefee
A GIRL'S MEMORY

Dedicated to EVERY SEA OTTER, EVERY FISH, EVERY LIVING THING that died because of an oil or raw sewage spill.

Along the sandy shores it was like another world,
Full of waves that crashed, waves that curled,
Oh how I remember how I stood and gazed,
I used to sit there for hours feeling amazed,
As questions came up How, When, Why?
I'd look up at the clouds and see birds fly,
But now other questions come up in my mind,
How could they do this, How could they be so unkind?
Now when I look at the beauty that used to be,
I think to myself maybe it was me,
I took another look to make sure what I saw was true,
I saw other things in the water that looked pretty new,
Oils, garbage, raw sewage and more,
The water I used to love, I looked back at it in horror!
I thought wait, this water's not just harmful to me,
It's harmful to fish & crabs and everything else in the sea,
But some others don't see it they just let things spill out,
It made me start to wonder even doubt,
If only they wanted to, if only they were willing,
I'm asking you, PLEASE STOP THE SPILLING!

R J Mentone
ODE TO OEDIPUS
Of all the senses none is so missed as vision.
Diabetes, glaucoma and the dreadest rest
make the world complete darkness.
The nothing you see is your very best.

But I'd rather be blind in the eyes
than blind in inward sight.
I'd rather not know what color is
but always know wrong from right.

In knowing what is real and correct
no one can ever call me blind.
They will point to my inner peace,
the happiness I was able to find.

Betty Morgan
POETRY'S DEFINITION
The art of taking a thought
molding
shaping
grabbing
hold of it
shaking
beating
stirring
it up and coining a phrase,
sifting it out in such a way
old words
make a
new statement

Dorothy Moore
SORROWS OF WAR

This poem is dedicated to Michael, my son, who fought for freedom in Panama. Michael, you're my inspiration. I love you!

Was it worth one life
Was Noriega worth the fight
I screamed and cried
But, I couldn't rally around
America's side.
My son survived
But, what about the mothers' sons who died
Did America cry, did they reason why
Did anyone really care, I didn't think it was fair.
I didn't raise my son to kill
But this fight was for real
Did we do it to help the country or to save face
Did we really want to help the human race?
In either way, it was such a waste.
There's so much doubt
To the mothers my heart goes out
But for me it wasn't worth the death
To get a drug dealer and clean up his mess
Mothers we are thinking about you a lot.
War has no boundaries when it comes to the heart.

Genevieve M Castillo
SPECIAL LOVE

To Jess, there will always be a special place for you in my heart.

When you took me to those special places
I thought I felt your Love.
The waterfalls meant so much
I felt a special touch.
The edge of the world ended
To all we disagreed.
But now I have realized
What it is you need.
A little bit of space and time
And soon you might agree.
That our Love was special
And truly meant to be.

Denice Fitzpatrick
THE MAGIC OF TIME

To Jim Coolen, The passage of time can never erase my memory of you and the passion we once shared. Love always, Denice.

He must have been a wizard,
Or a magician of some kind.
He must have cast a spell on me,
Or am I going out of my mind?

Appearing from out of nowhere,
He came into my view.
Hypnotizing me,
With his ocean eyes of blue.

He must have waved his magic wand,
Or put a potion in my drink.
For my vision became blurred.
What else was I to think?

There was something about him,
That kept me mesmerized.
Could it have been his boyish grin,
Or the twinkle in his eyes?

I tried to fight his powers,
To stay in full control.
My efforts were of no use.
He was already in my soul.

As mysteriously as he came,
He then vanished in a cloud of smoke.
And with him he took my love,
And my heart he had broke.

He must have been a wizard,
Or a magician of some kind.
The spell he cast on me,
Can be broken only with time.

Marianne Herrling
OLD BLACK CROW
Where do you go, Old Black Crow—flying slow, winging low?

Where do you go, Old Black Crow?
"I go to my babies in the nest: I go to my babies in the West . . . "
Caw Caw Caw
Where do you go, Old Black Crow in the snow—flying low, winging slow?
"I go to my babies to keep them warm . . .
I go to my babies to keep them from harm!"
Caw Caw Caw
Where do you go, Old Black Crow, flying low, winging slow in the misty rain
"I follow the whistle of the train to the station where the golden grain all spilled out in the driving rain!"
"Caw Caw Caw"

Janice Ivey Hallyburton
RAINDROPS

To Judy, My Friend In Christ. For your encouragement and love during the sad and lonely times of my life.

Today a raindrop ran down my windowpane
I thought about the good it does flowers, trees and grain.
It is a gift from God you know, and what a joyous one!
It seems that after the raindrops we always have the sun.
So watch the raindrops fall so softly to the ground,
And think of all the blessings and the beauty that we've found.

Barbara Jane Walker
IT'S NEVER TOO LATE
February is the month we
celebrate the love of our
fellow man.
It's a time to take down the
racial walls; united we all
must stand.

Brotherhood month is a time to
display our appreciation to
one another. It's a time to
thank God for all that we have
and be kind to our sisters and
brothers.

It's love that makes the world
go around, not prejudice,
anger and lying. Just look at
the faces of the lonesome
children, and the tears that
they are crying.

Man was created equal, and no
man should boast, about the
things that make him great.
How can a heart be filled with
joy, when it's filled with
anger and hate?

Great men have died for your
transgressions, because their
skin color did not match.
Cities were destroyed because
of a lie, and we can't bring
the great men back.

My heart goes out to those who
are proud and think they are
better than others. It is
they who are truly lonesome
inside, because they can't
show love for their brothers.

United we stand; divided we'll
fall; all men have fought
for our nation. Stop judging
others by the tint of their
skin; we are all God's
precious creation.

Brotherhood month is a time to
tear down the walls of
prejudice and hate. Today is
the day of the rest of your
life; remember it's never too
late.

Eve A Taylor
HELLO LORD
Hello Lord,
it's me again,
your little lost sheep
gone astray again.

I know Lord
that I only talk to You
when the world is on my shoulders
and there's nothing left to do.

I know Lord
that I haven't done my best,
but it's a hard cold world
if you're not like the rest.

I know Lord
that I always put you last,
until all others fail
and you're the only one to ask.

Thank you Lord
for listening to my prayer,
and keeping your promise
of always being there,
Amen.

Karen Estrada
SUBSIDENCE
When was the last time we laughed together?
Like mother and child when they are happy and innocent.
We are pretty far away from the woods
Where the fairy dances with the gnome
And the Prince Charming takes the princess
In his white horse to be happy forever.
So we hurt each other as adults do
And the time when we were close and friendly
Belongs to the past now.
I could choose to go on living without you,
I could fool myself by saying I don't need you,
But what am I to do with this empty space
That is in my heart
Hurting every day?

Jim Dooley
IF ONLY

To Marcia Dooley — my mother. May the memories of her be as kind as she was, and her soul be at peace.

If I could only hear you
and you could tell me you're alright
Maybe I'd get peace of mind
and sleep all through the night
If I could only hold you
hug you one more time
I'd tell you things I seldom did
and say what's on my mind
If I could only see you and say I love you so
You could tell me you were needed
that's why you had to go
If I could only touch you
and you could tell me there's no pain
Then I'd know that our great loss
is surely heaven's gain

Marjorie Ratcliff
ON WRITING—
A PERSONAL VIEW

To Mrs. Levitt and sixth grade students for encouraging me to keep writing.

Actually, it must come easy one would say
but, it doesn't, the words are hard to find to my dismay.
If I can write it all down, I am able to say
whatever, however, I feel in a special way.
If it is written at least you have something to remember—
and yet, to get a thought or idea, not written, you soon forget.
It's very hard, not easy, for me to speak in a crowd.
It frightens me even to think about speaking aloud.
I keep believing writing is like a tape of T.V.,
A rerun of a creativity for all to see.
How dull life would be if we could not read of travel,
comedy, love and
a stranger's great need:
of finances, wars and this world's great beauty — of peace, happiness, responsibilities and duties.
What if we had no record of this human race?
What can we leave for our children in the future about space?
The master plan has been written to the best of God's glory.
It's up to me to finish writing, as one, for the end of a great story.
I'm thankful for the great writers and for what they have done for me.
Because writing is a good change to release my feelings and to be free.

Margorie Ratcliff
THANK YOU

To Susan: she helped me realize that I am somebody.

Things are a lot different
having a new look on life.
And believing I can accomplish
Not all, but part of the strife,
Knowing I am somebody,

Yesterday, I'll leave behind.
Only to remember, the amazing good times.
Understanding, love and Kindness, too—

Thank you, dear friend, for just being you.

Marjorie Ratcliff
MY CHILD—UNPREDICTABLE

To my sons: Vincent, who is loving, caring and very patient — Vance, who is willing to sacrifice and Eddie who is super in his own special way.

Unpredictable Eddie, that's his name
Unpredictable Eddie, playing his game.
He doesn't realize the problems he is giving.
He doesn't realize he is amongst the living.
Eddie will laugh, tease and bring joy, all things which are done by a normal boy.
But Eddie is different, he's a special child, so he is judged and ridiculed when acting wild.
Special children are here for certain reasons,
unpredictable and changing as much as seasons.
My wonderful child is so loving and free,
Not even knowing what he's doing to me.
If I can hold on just a little longer,
and, maybe, be just a little stronger—
This unpredictable child of mine,
will do something special in his own time

Iva Jean Hart
MEMORIES NEVER SLEEP

Dedicated to the book I am writing entitled "Memories Never Sleep."

Oh memories, sweet memories, how come you never sleep?
Don't you know that you are locked in my heart?
And that you are mine forever to keep?
Why must you constantly walk through my mind and on my heart?
Don't you know that you are tearing me apart?

Maybe some music playing sweet and low, will lull you to sleep
You won't quit walking by my counting sheep.
Everything is getting quiet,
hopefully, off to sleep you go,
But then, here comes a song from the 50's . . . oh no . . . here we go . . .

I see his face as he asked me to dance,
It was our first night of a sweet romance.
Our first kiss, our first "I love you,"
Our laughter, our tears,
The day we said "I do."

How I miss that smile, that special touch, oh sweet memories,
I miss him so very much.

My memories, sweet memories, I'm glad no one can take you from me
and that you are locked safely in my heart and are mine to keep.
But must you go walking all hours
and never, never sleep?

Lenard W Eccles
FRECKLES ON THE SAND
Two Decades have passed
since oil washed our land,
and the beaches are still spotted
like Freckles on The Sand.

Along the sandy bluffs
my eyes long embrace,
tar cliffs stand majestic
on a smooth sandy face.

Where the graceful mystic Islands
once captured our peaceful glance,
the seascape is now dotted
with offshore Oil Camps.

My thoughts drift back
to a time long long ago,
the sea was dark with mystery
when the stars were full Aglow.

But now when I look from the edge of the sea
where the night stars unfold,
the dark sea is lighted by the lanterns
of the Kings of the rich, black Gold.

Brennan Pearl Jr
A VISION

Having my poetry acknowledged for the first time is always something special, and I would like to share this special moment with my family: My Mother, Mrs. Elaine Pearl; My Sister, Trevin Pearl; My Brother, Tab Perry, and my grandparents, Elizabeth &Wilson Stone. Love always, Brennan.

I've always wanted to be on the outside looking in,
in order to observe the people we call friends, through a wish an angel gave me a vision,
to see the world we live in was my decision,
everything I saw was wet from a recent rain,
not rain from nature but rain from tears of pain,
the world was crying in every category you think of,
I noticed people playing games in the category of love,
I couldn't believe it but yet it was real,
people were playing games with how we feel,
it's funny 'cause I noticed a few people in line,
who had the audacity to abuse my feelings at one time.

Lillian Berenson
CORNER OF TIME

Time erases memories,
Brilliant minds fade away.
They talk of achievements
While other, less inclined,
Aren't aware.
Life is with your eyes
Wide open
We raise up to the Sun
Bow down to the Wind
We live until the end of time.

Kip Wheeler
WHY GOD GAVE US MOTHERS

I'm seventeen now, and I wonder how
I ever survived this far.
But I'm not surprised when I realize
Who got us all where we are.

When we arrived on Earth, at the moment of birth,
We could not have even made a start.
But the Master above gave a mother's true love,
And a place in our mother's warm heart.

When we first tried to walk, or first sought to talk,
Our mothers helped us along.
When we cried at night, they turned on the light,
And sang us a lullaby song.

With our hopes and fears through our growing years
They were always around to care
And as we each grew, we each always knew
That our mothers would always be there.

We can all bet, that we're each in their debt,
And it's a debt we can never repay.
Time keeps rolling on, so before time is gone,
Let's tell them we love them today.

Tanya M Einhorn
BLACK WEDDING

Falling,
Falling,
Falling,
Out of the sky,
up to the clouds.
Pulled in many directions,
peaceful and confused;
a cocophonic silence,
my body tense—
a feeling of fulfillment,
makes me feel empty.
As I shudder with grief,
I am joyous.
This final event,
is just the beginning.

Rochelle M Whitaker
MY OLD MAPLE TREE

I just love to sit out back, and gaze at my old maple tree! To me, he's become such a good friend of mine, his branches whisper down to me! I realize some day this old tree will come down, and for him, this will be the end! But until this actually happens, little by little, his branches will bend! He "hangs in there," as loyal as can be, smiling down at all my flowers, he stands there proud and tall, protecting us all, enduring heavy thundershowers! Once in a while he loses a branch or two, sometimes a good sized limb, but do you think he's ready to give up, oh no, this doesn't stop him! Right along I've always known this tree could tell me quite a story, as he stands there tall, branches reaching far and wide, standing proud in all his glory! He's stood there such a long time now, birds chirping in all his branches, they're coming alive with their new spring song, for my backyard, he surely enhances!!! Mother Nature's furry little ones swing from branch to branch. In summer he protects me from the glaring sun. In autumn he cradles nature's small creatures, as they scurry to get their yearly work done! In winter he stands there, boughs heavy-laden with snow, he looks so sad to me, but I know deep down as he stands there a-shivering, that only God could have made "My Tree!!!"

Sallie Carter
WHY IS IT GOD THAT SOME DAYS

This poem is dedicated to my four beautiful children and grandchildren.

Why is it God that some days
The problems are so heavy to bare?
Why do I feel as if I'm all alone, desperate,
Afraid and feel that you do not care?
Are you testing to see how much I can endure,
Or is it punishment for sins I have done,
God I'm just not sure?
I have so much love and compassion
For ones that are dear and a part of me.
But it seems I fail them and I need
Your help, love and security.
I've been through a lot of testing I'm sure,
For you wanted to see if my faith
In you would endure.
It's true I've questioned why
All the pain and sorrow?
But my love for you will not falter,
Some day, somewhere, there will be a better tomorrow.

Deborah Nolan
REMEMBER?

What happened to the land called America?
The land of the free and the brave;
Where everyone thinks of themselves,
And we've become nothing but slaves.

What happened to the spirit of America?
It seems to have shriveled and died
Because no one is ever happy,
And no one is satisfied.

What happened to the pride in America?
It's all but vanished from sight.
No one follows the rules anymore,
And the people live in fright.

What happened to the great green America?
Look around—it's dirty and brown.
We once were so proud of the beauty,
And now it brings a frown.

What happened to the people of America?
Is it all just over and through?
Or from the dust will it rise again?
Remember it's up to you!

Helen Ridings
LORD OF ALL

They have just gone home
The ones we love so dear
So, friend, in sorrow, look up
Our loved ones are with Jesus
We don't have to fear.

God will lift each burden
and make the future bright,
We'll all soon be together
And there, we'll have no night.

The blessed light ashining
From our dear Savior's face,
Will from our very being
Every sorrow — tear — erase.

So rest, my friend, in Jesus's love
We'll wait our turn
To go Home above,
The One we own, we do possess,
In our Precious Lord
We have Perfect Peace and Perfect Rest.

Musinka Alexia Schauer
MY MASK

To all of my family—with love from your Princess.

Don't be fooled by me or the thousand masks I wear
Pretending is an art that's second nature to me.
My surface may seem smooth but the surface is my mask.
I frantically create a shield to hide me.
Panic at the thought of my weakness and my fears
Exposure and aloneness — a face that hides the tears
But I hide this so well.

Afraid that I am nothing, afraid I'm just no good
I play my game, my acting game
But I don't tell you this because I hide it so well.
My only salvation is a glance followed by love
My only liberation from myself is love
You alone can remove my mask
You alone can tear apart my shadow world
Don't pass me by—please don't pass me.

Who am I you wonder?
I am someone you should meet
I am every man and woman
Walking down the street.

John F Teeling III
ROCK BOTTOM

In order to avert cerebral malaise, I gazed into a dark spawn of night. I wasn't certain what I was doing, because my existence had been so imbued by blight. My epidermal shell had been severed and I seemed to not really know what was right.

Blue tequila flowed through my heart's blood and veins. In a feeble attempt, I sorted the remnants of my youth's ashes knowing all too well that that spring would never come again.

Trying to prop up my shoulders on an ice cube hill, I saw wet eyes on the face of a clown who looked like someone who had been saturated with far too many evil pills. I blinked him away, but his shadow tormented me still.

Now I see far too clearly that my future will be that of one who will always pay dearly.

Spasms of compassion won't be offered on a daily basis. I may drown easily on a watery oasis.

With a bull's temper, I must ferret out obstructions on a road never to be plated in gold. If I don't persist so I am told, I will simply rot away and not die old.

Champion of an endless deed, I approach a time that will have no creed. Some will fare but most will be gutted to bleed. Now, I pray to a force that may hold the terrors and stop them so I won't ever see rock bottom.

Denise Tyler
BEST FRIENDS

I dedicate this poem to my best friend, Leslie Dufur.

A Best Friend is someone who,
can care and share like you;

At times when I was down,
you would always help me come around;

By listening to my faults,
every time I wanted to talk;

And at sad times for me and you were there,
I could really tell that you cared;

For doing all these crazy things with you,
I can tell that our friendship will always be true;

Well now that this poem is done,
I want you to know that you are my Best Friend number one!

Larry Moser
FORGET ME NOT
With old and crooked fingers.
A face that's marked with pain.
She sits and stares into the night.
Through dirty window frames.
Her hair is streaked with silver.
Her body weak and frail.
Her once a mild complexion,
is now a deathly pale.
Her thoughts aren't on tomorrow,
or the things she must do today.
Her mind is like a little child,
left in the yard to play.
She'll sit and talk for hours,
even if no one is there.
I guess she sometimes wonders,
if anyone really cares.
But she has a friend in Jesus,
He'll show her that He cares.
And no longer will she sit by herself,
in that lonely chair.

Wanda Chapman
SNOW GEESE IN THE SOUTH
Graceful wings lifting in flight
As they rise from earth in the morning light.
One, then two, then by the score,
Into the open skies they pour
Circling and wheeling until they sight
The path they follow to the northern door.

Glistening white with the morning rays
Of the sun as it greets the southern days,
From rest at night to a feeding ground,
This moving cloud can be found
Questing eagerly for the time it stays
For the grains and grasses which here abound.

Such a short time these visitors come
To spend their winter in the southern sun,
And brighten the lives of a certain few
Who watching the geese, wish they, too
Could lift their wings and for a time become
Lovely and free in the morning dew.

Tonya Anne Volcansek
A CRY FOR HELP

I dedicate this to my friends who have died & those who have the courage to go on. To my Best Friend, Curtis Schmidt (Jan. 3, 1971—Apr. 25, 1988) for showing me to make your mark on the world you must live when you die, they forget.

Why can't I have happiness
All I want is death
Many times I felt sad & lonely
Many times I needed someone there
Many times I tried to tell you something
But you just turned away
You don't care what I say
I cry out but you just cover your ears
I guess you didn't see my tears
I can feel
My fears are real
You didn't even have a second
You said I was much too strong
You said these feelings just wouldn't last
I am trying to hold on fast
I need your help please listen
I don't really want to die
Another casualty for suicide.

Lillian V Brown
TRUE FRIENDS
Your enemies may be countless,
Your friends very few;
Sometimes, you won't know the difference,
So, to all be kind and true.

Swing wide the door of compassion,
Welcome love and peace;
Shut out hatred and jealousy,
Let misunderstandings cease.

Be blind to the faults of others,
Quick to make amends;
Deaf to idle gossip,
And you'll always have true friends!

Hester H Day
MIND AND HEART IN CONFLICT
The Mind, is vengeful
with thoughts like animated creatures,
Lurking . . . in the shadows
waiting . . .
to pounce on the first unsuspecting
Soul, they find . . .

The Heart, is gentle, kind and forgiving
Yearning for Love, that passes understanding . . .
Anxious and willing to make peace with the Mind.

Ruth Hancock
A BOY CALLED SHANE

Dedicated to my two grandsons, Shane Ratliff and Stevie Aikin.

Once there was a little boy.
Who filled my heart with so much joy,
We sang & played and what a treat,
'Cause this little boy was very sweet.
Then he grew up and moved away,
And then my blue sky turned to gray.
Although he's gone we're not apart
'Cause he's still with me in my heart.

Now I have another boy
Who brings me now another joy.
We sang and play and have fun too,
Although I know that he's not you.
But sometimes when I call his name
I forget and call him Shane.
He's sweet and loving just like you
And when he's here I'm never blue
But I know that some day he'll be gone
And I'll be left here all alone
But I'll treasure all these memories
And some day it'll all be history

Elta M Smith
MEASURED PATIENCE
The Inch Worm,
Another of nature's wonders,
Humps along
Measuring inches into feet,
Yards to miles.
Undulating vigoriously,
Out on a limb to the very end,
No retracing steps,
It drops on a line
like a mountain climber
Sliding down to another level.

He may be just an adventurer
Exploring a new territory
To be measured and recorded,
Reaching out, always reaching
with steadfast determination.

I wonder, could it be
another of God's subtle lessons—
To reach out to new horizons—
Taught by a little green worm?

Jessica Hawkins
A MAN HAD A DREAM
One night a man had a dream, how very beautiful it did seem. It was a vision of two giant hands, each one of them from different lands. It was a very wondrous sight, filled with: courage, spirit, and might. The hands looked like they'd had a fight, yet they weren't gripping all too tight. They were relaxed, one in the other; standing there brother to brother. That's the way it should have been, though we can't change what was back then; we should never let it happen again. If Mr. King were here today these are the words that he would say, "To all mankind, oh, let us bind in heart and soul and tongue and mind. Forget about color, looks, and size, think about what we jeopardize; let's love one another, while we still can or soon there will be no more man . . . "

Heidi Ach
TO ALL MY FRIENDS
Now that we are such good friends.
I hope our friendship never ends.
I know sometimes we fight,
sometimes I don't mean what I say.
Or you take something the wrong way.
I want you to know I'll always be here for you.
And I hope you feel the same way too.

Theresa Leslie

Theresa Leslie
ALONE
I am —
but, not complete.

I feel —
but, am numb.

I see —
but, am blind.

I reach —
but, loneliness is all that I grasp.

Theresa Leslie
MISSING YOU
I feel so strange
being apart from you.
I really can't explain it—
this feeling.

It's almost no feeling.
a numbness,
love?
a fear
of love.

If I could scream!
Cry!
Talk to someone
other than myself,
and find a release . . .

Maybe, then I would know,
What I really want—
is . . .
to talk to you.

Theresa Leslie
WITHOUT YOU
A new day is dawning,
without you.
A new year — a new decade,
without you.
A new me— better and worse
for having known and loved you.

Your picture, our picture
Removed from view,
Fading too slowly from memory.

Broken dreams, empty promises
of what was meant to be —

And, tell me . . .
Do you remember?
the love you lost,
and the dream,
I won?

Steven Syko Song
TAKE AWAY THE COLORS

To the ones who made my picture colorful.

In a dream-like vision see the picture deluded with colors
Justification yet unexplained. Didn't matter then, was in a fantasyland
Sights and sounds did not exist, thus cared for nothing
Picture achromatic and full of beauty
Unconsciousness . . . loved the picture

Blinked once . . . Picture began to expose
Distorted with many colors, images appeared
Scarcely half of the beauty remained
Imbibed with complexity, consciousness creeped upon
While obligations wrapped the picture

Blinked again . . . Where am I?
Eyes are naked and the picture is clear
Shapes and colors too many, smiled at few
But only for a moment
No longer full of beauty but full of hate
Picture too bright, picture too colored

Seeking darkness and beauty, turn my head
How do I get there with all these colors?
Before I blink again, take away the colors
And take me two blinks back

Steven Syko Song
LOVE OF HATE

Dedicated to M. 'Leann' Bell, the one I love and hate.

Though I may have stitches in my heart
I know it was meant to be
Though I may hate her for crime
I know I should also love her

Yes, like poetry, she is ambiguous
Yet full of beauty
And like any abstract, she is obscure
Yet full of my curiosity

Though I may be ignorant of her
I know what I love
And as she fulfills her objectives
I know I will love her . . . till the end

Georgianne Rasmussen Gustafson
THE GREAT LIGHT

I dedicate this poem to CDR.K.R. Gustafson USN (RET), "The only one I've ever loved and all my dreams fulfilled on Feb. 24, 1990 after 34 years apart."

When I found true love, then a new love,
Cold and distant seemed our path;
Like Halley's comet shooting past
Crystal cold was our demise.

Fool's gold glitters in a real hot sun,
The light of day, but not of night;
Among trodden pebbles washed ashore
Broken hearts are many tossed at sea.

Three score and four before we could see,
Diamonds in the rough were we.
We live, we love, but mortal you see;
Tested must a true love be.

Not by surprise our plight was mapped,
By chance our fate decreed;
Before the sands of time were born
The light of love reached out.

The elements, once confused became
Aligned to form a bond.
Like Franklin's light we came to be,
A beacon for all who are lost at sea.

Like a mountain beneath the tide
Together as one we now abide;
Sustained in the faith of undying love,
Forever suspended upon a reef of hope.

Michael Cyrek
MY TEMPLE

My temple is the greatest there is
Where most of its occupants are his
Living their lives as best they can his way
And struggling to survive the hardships of today

This mighty temple has the sky above as its ceiling
And the soil of the earth as the floor for its healing
The mountains and the oceans are the walls that confine
So let us worship this gigantic treasure which is thine

This treasure is Nature!

If you love these great gifts to behold
Then you must rebuff those that defile with a scold
And protect nature's right to exist
For all their lives are worthy for them to subsist

As they frolic about on land and sea you will agree
Do not look down upon them because they are free
And release those that are caged and abused
So that all will enjoy a life where they are not used

Their lives let us ensure!

The ceiling has the great light of the day
And the twinkling lights of the night that are faraway
Let us enjoy these night lights to behold
And the warmth of the daylight that dispels the cold

This is all free for everyone to enjoy
And we should learn that nature we should not annoy
For they also enjoy living as we people do
So realize that in the beginning they all ran, swam and flew

I am sure you can see that their spirits are pure!

And those giants of the plant world are worthy to see
For they purify the air to keep life in harmony
Let us do what we can to ensure the trees a life of great length
For they all are a good example of great strength

And the flowers of spring need we say are beautiful to see
As are all the tiny plants as they emerge in ecstasy
Let us admire them all with the greatest of reverence
For some are the source of our living affluence

So please help their cause with some expenditure!

Julius Richelson
NUMBER TWENTY-TWO

As one grows older they realize how little they know. There is only one solution. Hang out with the smart ones . . .

Take a six-year-old
They're cool and classy
And downright bold,
They know all the questions
Just ask them, "Why?"
And they'll take your answer
Right out of the sky.

Or

Sixteen years of age
Conservative and sexy
And an ongoing sage,
An ambiguous answer
With a look in his eye,
"Don't fool with me or
I'll eat you like pie."

Come to think of it, I guess I'll remain ignorant. I just remembered a line from an old popular song, "Don't Mess With Mr. Inbetween."

Gladys Faye Armstrong
MY DEAREST LOVE

To My First Love: When you go away from me, I will hold you in my heart forever.

Sitting by my window, gazing up above,
I see the light of a star,
illuminating the entire sky.
Through the dark it's shining, shining bright
Though it's bright, it's not as bright as my burning, burning light.
My light burns within my heart like a flame that never ceases.
It glows and glows and then grows and grows
Until it finds its peace.
That light that's burning, burning bright
Is what I call
My light of love that burns for you, my love,
My
Dearest
Dearest
Love.

Helen S Kahler
MOTHER'S LOVE

In a hundred ways, my children,
I showed you that I cared,
A hundred different things I've done
In my love you've shared.

In all the socks that I have darned
I weaved a little of my heart,
'Twas in the seams I've sewn together
And in the seams I cut apart.

And even though, I never said them,
The words were there, engraved,
In all the patches, in all the mending
My love was there enslaved.

In every dish I cooked for you
I left my love behind,
In every bite that you have tasted
It was there for you to find.

And each time that you were hurt
I washed away your tears,
My love had brought your laughter back
And removed your fears.

Lenna E Etzler
LITTLE WILLIE'S CHRISTMAS PRAYER

Dedicated to Christopher Brandon Scharnus.

I hung up my stocking in a room bleak and bare.
I knelt by the fireplace and said a small prayer.
I prayed for the weary, the old, and the sickly.
I asked Him to help them and to please do it quickly.

There was poor Mr. Brown—so lonely and thin
You wondered how could he greet all with a grin.
He smiled when you met him and bade you "Goodbye"
With a wave of a kerchief—A twinkle in one eye.
Then on he went in a merry way, and this went on day after day.
It gave me a light heart and much, much joy
In spite of the fact I was a very small boy.

Then there was a widow and so poor was she
That her whole house was made out of one single tree.
Very little had she, but she did not complain
Though she lived in that house and was always in pain.

I prayed for the children—I called them by name—
There were John, Sue and Junior, Charles, Mary, and Deb.
Some of them didn't even sleep in a bed.
I asked God to send them some food and some clothes,
To protect them and heal them and take care of their woes.

Then I told Jesus I didn't need much;
I had a good Mother, I had a good Dad,
And this for a wee, tiny boy was not bad.
I asked Him to tell Santa to take most all he had
To the unfortunate people, though some were quite bad.

I awoke Christmas morning and ran down the stairs
And lo and behold! He had answered my prayers.
I found in my stocking a note and one toy,
But this was enough for one wee, tiny boy.

The note said "Dear Willie, your message came through
Wish there were more in this world just like you;
But people are greedy unkind and untrue.
There are just not many fine boys like you.
Just love your Mother and follow your Dad,
And You'll find out that the World
Is not at all bad."

Lenna E Etzler
ONLY GOD

Who could make the mountains and the trees
Hummingbirds and deep blue seas,
Deserts bare and prairies wide,
And winds that cause a rising tide?
Only God.

Who could make the sun to shine?
Only One that is Divine—
He could make the sun to shine
Lighting the path of yours and mine—
That was God.

Who could cause the moon to rise,
And put the stars up in the skies?
Who could put to sleep Mother Earth
To awaken each spring with a rebirth?
Only God could do these things.

Who could make a mortal man
To climb the mountains, till the land,
And make the fruit and flowers to grow
With all the beauty we love so?
Only God could make a man.

Who did teach man how to love
And get his strength from One above?
Who could send His Son to save
Mortal man from a hopeless grave?
It was God.

Who let His Son die on a Cross
That mortal man would not be lost?
Who when he hung on Calvary's tree
Made yours and my salvation free?
'Twas only God.

Daniel P Bitter
LOVING A CONVICT
Loving a convict is a hard thing, I say,
In loving a convict there is a price to pay.
Loving him with nothing to hold,
Is like being young and feeling old.

It's letting him whisper that he loves you,
And you whisper back that you love him too.
Although you are near yet so far away,
His love gets stronger with each passing day.

It's extremely painful letting him go,
While dying inside from needing him so.
Then comes the letter and the promise to wait,
Knowing the Parole Board is holding his fate.

Loving a convict isn't much fun,
But it's well worth the wait when his time is done.
Thinking back on memories, his eyes fill with tears,
As weeks turn into months and months into years.

He is missing you with each passing day, And
He is sad and lonely from being away.
So Love him, Miss him and please tell him so,
For if you love a convict he surely needs to know.

Arturo S Quijano

Arturo S Quijano
IF WE COULD ONLY BREATHE A SMILE

I dedicate this poem to Celia, my darling wife, to our children Nenita, Elizabeth, Danilo, Corazon and Edna, and to all the members of the Philippine Christian Church.

A smile is like a radiant sunbeam
That has a message to impart;
Its cheerful warmth, its gentle touch
Could appease a lonely, grieving heart.

A smile is a bright moonbeam
That filters through a pitch-dark room;
Its serene light is a welcome sight
Which brushes away a pall of gloom.

A smile is a soothing balsam,
Which could assuage a grievous pain;
In the arid desert of life
It is indeed a welcome rain.

A winsome smile is contagious,
It affects all those who can see;
Permeating our environment,
Filling the air with peerless glee.

If we could only breathe a smile,
Which drives away the ire within;
No enmity, but peace shall reign
Within this world where we live in.

Arturo S Quijano
WHAT IS A FATHER?
As far back as could be recalled
Even before the dawn of history;
The father was and still is
The backbone of the family.

A father is the chain that binds
Ev'ry member of the family,
He is the mainstay of the home
An emblem of authority.

A father is a protective umbrella
Over his own beloved brood;
He aspires to shower upon them
Anything, everything that which is good.

For the sake of his loved ones,
A father bestows his everything;
He is ready to sacrifice
Ever willing, never tiring.

A father deserves our highest regard,
As a pillar be looked upon;
Let's accord him our due respect
For what he is, for what he has done.

Paul O Carlson
AMERICA
U - UNITED STATES BY vote of the people.
N - Now is power to set an example.
I - Indivisible by this faith in our soul.
T - These United States strive for this goal.
E - Every citizen is obligated to one another.
D - Delivered from sin then help your brother.

S - Sovereign people trusting each other to rule.
T - There are some who react very cruel.
A - Admittance of God's Spirit will bring victory.
T - The grace of God believers profound mystery.
E - Emancipated from sin we obey American laws.
S - Sing for joy with great al-le-lu-jahs.

Paul O Carlson
POWER TO ATTAIN

As negative and positive are opposite poles, So sinners without Christ are lost souls.

As negative and positive are opposite poles,
So sinners without Christ are lost souls.

To be born again a new creation
Receive by faith God's gift of salvation.

Insulated by His Word, faithful and true,
The Spirit of God will energize you.

Having all power to attain that goal,
With peace and charity in your soul.

Mary Lyn Bryant
IF I WERE
If I were a wee Firefly
Each night I'd let you know
About the lovelight in your eyes
And set your heart aglow

If I were just a little Bug
So tiny and so small
I'd reach your heart by end of day
If I had to crawl

If I were just a little Bee
and you would go astray
I'd sting you 'til you turned around
and came back home to stay

If I were just a little Elf
I'd try to make you play
I'd dance and sing, to you I'd bring
new blossoms every day

But since I'm not a little Bug
a Bee or little Elf
I'll lock you up, within your heart
and love you by myself

Ruth T Gisler
PRAISE THE LORD
My heart is crying
Lord, don't you know
We'll all miss Jody
We loved him so.

His work is done
His hour has come.

He leaves this land
A never forgotten son.

The gates of heaven
Have opened wide,
To accept Jod's spirit
To enter inside.

The Lord reached out
And touched his hand
He is now with the Lord
In the promised land.

Vivian Lumbard
TURBULENT DEATH
Heat coursing through hurtful truths.
Adrenaline flowing in chilled veins.
Torment raging in angry souls.
Anguish storming with pulsating pains.

Bitterness galloping in an unseeing path.
Recriminations flying into unhearing ears.
Harsh words whipping with unexpected force.
Verbal darts colliding with unspoken fears.

Reason racing out the door;
Voices railing at fate.
Forgiveness speeding toward destruction;
Finality slamming its gate.

Indignation wrestling with remorse.
Shock fighting with tears.
Hate battling with peace.
Acceptance tangling with fears.

Love surrenders.

Matthew C Lafferty
BLANKET OF LOVE
Just lie there and sleep.
I'll cover you and keep you warm
From the bitter cold
That life lays upon us.
Sleep
And dream of happy times,
Of loved ones;
Here, and those who've passed
Into a higher life—filled
With the love
We both wish and hope
Will complete our days.
So, just sleep—and dream,
And I shall envelop thee
In a blanket of love.

Eric Lehman
THE EVIL ONE (REV. 9:11)
As streams of blood flow to the sea
Satan sends his wrath through me
Tormented souls of hell be free
And praise the beast that's in the sea

The sea of blood flows day by day
I have seen this I can say
Death shall come in ninety-four
Don't look back just lock the door

Earth shall burn
Flesh shall melt
As bodies are buried by blackened smelt

All prophesies have been fulfilled
You are now in Satan's guild

The Seven-Headed Dragon's here
The Pregnant whore now lives in fear

From the cloud they have come to take away
For death will come this very day

Seven years of hell on earth beheaded you will be
Bloody bodies thrown around and cast into the sea

I heard a voice from hell it came
Now my son we play the game

Nera Gingras
PINK COLORED SNAILS SEARCH FOR SOUL

Dedicated with love to Gram from Nera.

(By an angel
stuck in a shell)
Of willows, of weepings,
of cabbages, of kings,
of what is nature,
the nature of things
?
In the beginning,
of what where we once,
Demigod-slug, Ameoba-king
?
Did we soar with grandeur,
or slowly slink along,
like pink colored snails,
with a so silent song
?
Seek, and ye shall find,
the answer, my friend,
is beyond the mere mind
!
A mystery doth rise,
upwards a soul,
a shining, searching thing,
that has to know
!
Be silent, oh stirring soul,
lest one learns of things,
that only gods do know
!

Doris Guarino
THE CRYSTAL TREE

To the Christ beauty and joy within each of us.

A place of beauty I have found, a Paradise, you see,
Where I do go and contemplate in calm serenity.
In quietude I listen, in harmony mind clears
As beauty speaks in joyous tones, the music of the spheres.
And as I muse within my soul, I see a mystery
For in this very secret place there stands a Crystal Tree.
Through every facet of the Tree, radiant light shines forth in clarity.
It never wavers, never dims, throughout the trunk and all the limbs.
I behold this strange phenomenon and as I wonder why
A tiny touch of gold does gleam to catch my wondering eye.
Along each fragile limb I see, golden spheres appear
Manifesting with each lovely thought, the world I see out here.
The golden fruit produced inside manifests along the way
As smiles, greetings, helping hands, loving thoughts throughout the day.
And now I truly understand in this secret place, I BE
Kind thoughts and deeds are the golden fruit
My soul—the Crystal Tree.

Jillian F Lord
WINNERS

To my Grandmother Mable— Lord— A Winner.

Some people love to sit and boast of the many trophies they have won —
But ask them how many times they've sat and talked with a lost and desperate son,
How many times they've praised him— just because he tried
and how many times they've comforted him — when he just felt to cry
If they are WINNERS! WHAT AM I?

WINNERS are the people who look you in the face —
pat you on the back, utter words of praise
Keeps you in the limelight through THICK and THIN,
knowing how you feel — never making you keep it in
Holding your hand — during desperate times —
These are the winners you hardly ever find.

IF that is a WINNER — I wish there could be
someone that thoughtful, smart as thee
Most of the people known today;
don't bear the courage of love to say
"You're a WINNER" - as if you didn't know
"Keep it up and don't ever let it go"
That's a WINNER so pure and true
Someone who'll live forever
Someone like YOU!

Wes B Lucas
ECSTASY

For Bev, whose spiritual ecstasy consumes me with Christ's love.

Make holy love with me and let me be your servant. Grant me the search of your soul for strength, and rest my weariness as doves upon your all forgiving bosom.

Let me worship and adore your body and blood, as Joseph molded you from birth—Carpenter's Son.

May I never again cry in pain, de Profundis, but daily chant Magnificat in blessings over and over for freeing my soul.

Grant me your benediction even when I err, praying for self alone, forgetting others. You have never forgotten me.

Filled with rapture, O Blessed Christ, I approach thy Holy Table as a soft treading monk. I eat, I drink, I am filled. I gaze toward the shimmering votive light. It shimmers within my soul.

Again and again and again, it is finished, finished and finished.

Traci A Lordan
LOST LOVE

Dedicated to Richard Warren Bruccoliere.

As I stand
here all alone,
I say good-bye to the sun
That has already shone.

I listen to the tears
Falling from my face,
Hoping that our love
Is an unfinished race.

I'm trying hard
To keep up with you,
But you're too far ahead
I'm lost in the blue.

The blue of the sky,
The color of my heart;
I'll love you forever
'Til death do us part.

Norma Lux
SINCE YOU'VE GONE

So many things have happened since you left that August morn,
The grandkids have really grown and two new ones have been born.
It really broke our hearts when you left us all that day.
It's really lonely without you and sometimes we've lost our way.

Dave and Rick have regrets, for there's things they would like,
to learn to tie your flies, to do your art—Do the things you'd do,
You were so smart! You would get an idea and figure it out,
You could do anything—even catch trout!

Korey and Trisha remember you best, They talk about you,
and tell all the rest. Li'l Rick and Derrick were tiny you know,
Oh, if you could have been there to watch them grow.

There are so many days when things cross my mind.
And questions need answered all the time.
When our boys are troubled, I try to be there
We've needed you with us—it doesn't seem fair.
We could solve so many problems if you were there.
We've got your memories and we hold them dear,
But we really miss you, year after year.

Korey's in Middle School. Trisha, Rick and Derrick not far behind,
They're all smart kids and treat me so kind. But there are 3 more
that you never knew; Jamaica, Nichole and Brieanna, named after you.
It's quite a little family you left behind—
We all love you dearly, my sweetheart, so kind.
Now You're up in heaven with our loved ones gone on.
I'll look after the ones here with our strong love bond.

We all hunt arrowheads—it's quite a family affair.
The walking's real easy—wish you were there.
The boys are still fishing, They fish year round.
They still go back to the tree and the fishin' hole you found.
And always on the deer hunt, while standing around the camp,
The boys always talk of Dad, because you were their champ.
Yes, you're always on our mind in everything we do,
And we want you to know that we all love you.

Livia Ungar
WRITERS ARE LIKE WINE

I dedicate this poem to my sister, Rachel Frankel, whose encouragement and enthusiasm has always inspired me.

Writers are like wine, I think
Offer a reviving drink
Disturbing, comforting, intoxicating
They make you see black and make you see pink.

Writers are like wine, I bet
Your sorrows they help you forget
Instill euphoria and make you glad
Or render you melancholy and sad.

Some are refined, some are cheap
Some are shallow, some are deep
They make you laugh and make you weep
Some make you nauseous or put you to sleep.

Writers are like wine, I am guessing
They are vile or are a blessing
Often with your mind are messing
Often soothing or depressing.

Writers are like wine, I gather
Some heavy, some light like a feather
Stimulating in any weather
And perhaps like wine, the older the better.

Amy Leuschner
YOU, MY FRIEND

My days are all a little brighter just because you're there.
You make me feel so happy and I smile because you care.
No one person is quite like you, your personality, laugh, or smile.
And no matter how far apart we are, I feel your love across the miles.
My heart swells with pride for you, because you are my friend.
You play that role so very well, I know you'll be here in the end.
I thank you for all you've done for me, all the caring you give.
'Cause without you or your friendship I don't know how I could live.

Mary Lewis
NO TIME

One day as I walked along life's road,
I met a man with a heavy load.
His shoulders stooped, his head was bent,
He wore no shoes, his coat was rent.
I had much pity, but I'm afraid
I had no time to render aid.

But today it is I who am bowed low,
Beset by sorrow, tossed to and fro.
And although I plead for a helping hand,
Someone to care and understand
All have pity but I'm afraid
They have no time to render aid.

My father once told me you get what you give,
It's not enough just to live and let live.
Thus, I think of the man all bowed with life's care
And Oh, Lord, my God this is my prayer:
May I have compassion and understand
And then take time to lend a hand.

Mary Lu Test
NEW YEAR'S THOUGHTS

In Memory of my dear mother, Margaret White Gage Taft.

To us another year is soon to come in view
A question or two let's chance to ask before this year is through
Have we done our best in this past year
Have we always been what we ought to be
To those who love us have we kindness shown and always been true
Have we loving words and smiles given to a lonely one or two
Have we spoken ugly words or an act that broke some dear one's heart
If our tasks that God set before us seem too great and somehow we have been slack
If sometimes we have wandered away from the Father who taketh care of all and have done things we shouldn't have done
Let's try to be more worthy in the year that is to come
That God may say in his kind way "I bless them one and all"
There are times in this world when life doesn't seem what it ought to be
That sorrow or care too many are cast on you and me
But after all God knows what is best in this life and Eternity

Ma Clemence P Lastra
MARSHA LYN LASTRA

I lovingly dedicate this poem to my youngest granddaughter, Marsha Lyn Lastra, at her seventh birthday.

M - Many many happy days
A - Are kept in mind and breast,
R - Remembering when you're small
S - So cute, charming and playful,
H - Has the appearance so cheerful
A - And a good friend to all.

L - Let those days be kept fresh
Y - You maintain that nature always
N - Never and never make a change.

L - Loving you always in your gain
A - Among your kins you're the Valentine,
S - Show your kindness to grow green
T - To love and care for them,
R - Reward you will soon be given
A - And you will have the gift from heaven.

Ma Clemence P Lastra
KITES

This poem is dedicated to my fourth granddaughter that is so loving to everybody in the family.

K - Kites fly on summer time
A - Above and above the ground,
T - Towering high high alone
H - Having fooled the kids on the ground,
L - Letting others watch and enjoy
E - Even the neck and eyes are hurt,
E - Everybody see and laugh and laugh
N - Not to remember the worries at heart.

J - Join the kids to fly the kite
E - Entering the fun even at sight,
A - Among other games to participate
N - Never on summertime this fun to forget.

L - Leave worrying things aside
A - Allow fun to tickle your side,
S - Summer time will give much fun
T - To fly a kite, to hold the string and run
R - Remember by this time you're hungry
A - Apples at look so delicious in the tray.

Ma Clemence P Lastra
LONGING

I dedicate this poem to: An ounce of loneliness is worth a pound of longing.

When feeling isolated comes the longing
To see friends and nearest kins,
Their attitudes and gestures are genuine
Their cares and smiles worth remembering
Treasured in hearts not in dreams.

When all the days gone by
And the expecting the longing will die
Never the mind and heart shy
For revival will come in bunch
Of what work has been done.

How long had been the longing
How long had been the expecting
To see faces that are smiling
To hear voices that are caring
All these things are in vain.

Florine W Lowe
A PRAYER FOR PEACE

In this world
of hate and confusion,
I have come
to this conclusion,
If peace and love
are to stay alive,
We best start
from the inside.
Each one
must do this little bit,
So the broken pieces
will all fit.
The strings of love
will hold the world together,
And peace will abide
forever and ever.
Amen

Lauretta Jane Lowell
PROMISE OF HOPE

"Were it e're but the time for growing?
The light in my heart is glowing, glowing.
For we will find true love flowing
And His happiness God is bestowing."

Thus said the maiden to her true love
And fairies and angels from above
Listened to her young spirited voice
And were thrilled with ecstatic joys.

Her lover shared in enthusiasm
For they had just bridged a chasm
And crossed over to a bit of heaven
Feeling they'd never touch sadness again.

A yes! What can be more happy
Than a lassie and a laddie
Sharing their hopes of love and spring
Truly life should such joy e're bring!

Gloria M Colon

Gloria M Colon
YOU SHOWED ME THE LIGHT

You love us all the same, always have, always been, you died to save us from our sins.

Oh Lord all you ask is for us to have faith, to trust, and to believe, not to live with sorrows, to hurt, and to grieve.

It is easy to love you just the same, and I hope one day you give me the courage and strength to praise your glorious name.

You showed me the light, and your ways of a beautiful life, you showed me to believe that there's more to life to see, you showed me the light, oh sweet Jesus, your love is like gold, such a beautiful sight, and could never grow old.

Oh Jesus, I was lost hoping to be found, you showed me the way to stand up tall, and always be proud.

I learned so much from the bible, made it my number one idol.

I pray for this world to change, reunite as one. I thought it would have after that song "We Are The World" was sung.

But I guess people don't believe, and don't want to know what love really is, this word so mysterious and great, this is what happens when our brothers have lack of faith.

Oh Lord for you have shown us that there is no reason to hurt for we must not let the enemy intrude, we must stay alert.

We bring this upon ourselves, and if we truly believe, then there is no reason for remembering or to dwell, just be happy and receive.

Gwen LaVoi
TIME FOR THOUGHT

When I wake up and the sun
is shining on my bed,
Thoughts of pure happiness
fill my head.
I think of everything and everyone
that means something to me.
I think of family and friends, and
I dream of everything that could be.
And when I look up, see the sky
so clear and blue,
I'm so very, very happy as I think
of grandpa and you.

Maude M LaFountain
NOT A TEAR SHALL FALL

This night we part forever, you are nothing more to me.
Gladly each tie we will sever, that has linked my soul to thee.
Not a single nerve shall shiver, when I bid my last adieu.
Tho it broke my heart forever, not a tear shall fall for you.
Take back those vows you plighted, think not I prize them yet.
A heart you would have slighted, seeks now to forget.
Go smile upon another, go worship at her shrine.
Win another heart and break it, as you have broken mine.
Go in peace tho you have severed every tie that held us two.
Tho it broke my heart forever, not a tear shall for you.

Joyce J Goldbach
OLDEN DAY —
Beauty And Simplicity

Logs, strategically placed — made a cabin
That sits atop a country knoll
Inside, oil lamps and fireplace glow
As if waiting for Lincoln to call

Feeling as though back in time
Throwing logs on the fire
Outside, snowflakes pilled high
Crystal icicles hang to admire

House skeleton fully exposed
Plain wooden steps lead to lof'
Walls with spots for their design
Those round knots show them off
Variety of trees give up their wood
Outside, you can smell chimney smoke
Logs crackle and hiss as they burn
They roll over when you give them a poke

Living with old-time simplicity
Surrounded in the country by nature
Such a short time to spend there
It's always experienced with awe.

Joyce J Goldbach
FOURTH OF JULY

Let's have cheers for the noisy fourth
On fireworks, we've come to rely
Acknowledging freedom, east, west, south and north
On this day, in the month of July

Since the noise and sparks come in summer
Picnics appear in the mountains and dell
England — we became freed from her
Long ago, patriots rang the Liberty Bell

Sun sparkles on the silver flatware
As family and friends enjoy the food
When it's dark, the sparks, again, flare
Celebration takes on a different mood

The flag that flies from the porch
Now has its colors lit
In proudness, it waves in the glow of the torch
Our forefathers died — they did not quit.

Joyce J Goldbach
THE AMERICAN FLAG

Our FLAG —
It rises so high in the sky,
For it, true Americans proudly stand by,
Its colors so rich — its colors so bright —
As the sun shines on it, and a light at night,
It makes us so proud, seeing it wave,
About this "PIECE OF CLOTH," we sure do rave,
The stars — each for a sovereign state —
Where men are called to war— unknown is their fate,
And at the battles that we have won —
Flown was our FLAG — second to none,
To the FLAG, we pledge our allegiance,
It was flown by patriots in "'76" and since,
So to our FLAG, here is a toast —
To this wonderful "BANNER," about which we boast.

Nadine Spears Law
SYMPATHY

For my dear friend "Corine."

Ashes to ashes — dust to dust,
Life's such a privilege that death is a must.

It's awesome to think of — it's harder to say
But every human life must end some day.

In troubled times like these; mere words just will not do
So as I write these words, I send my

heart to you.

You must now take life one day at a time,
Trusting in the Lord to be comforting and kind.

Please don't question God by saying "It's not fair"
For we are but mortals and cannot make judgment there.

I wish there was something that I could say or do,
That any way might ease the pain or bring comfort to you.

So, I'm sending you my prayers, and all my hope and love;
And all I know to tell you is to "Trust the Lord above."

Nadine Spears Law
CLASS REUNION

Former classmates, families and friends
We welcome this chance to meet again.

To reminesce of days gone by
Of earlier times at Dollarway High.

Of all the things that we went through
And through the years together we grew.

Just look at us now that we're all grown
With husbands and wives and kids of our own.

After we all went our separate ways
It sure is good to be together today.

To relive the past for just a while
To fondly recall the tears and the smiles.

We shared it all — the worst and the best
At our favorite place "ole DHS."

Though we're busy with jobs and families and such
For the next ten years let's not lose touch.

Colleen Lewis
ODE TO A RECIPE

To Liz, Bud, Brendetta, Brandon & my husband.

They come in many shapes and sizes
Some filled with corn surprises
An array of colors too
Custom designed directly from you

I brought my entry to the fair
Where all the judges sat and stared
One asked me for my recipe.
But I said it's hidden deep inside of me

I won with hands down
All the contestants left with a frown
Planning for next year's defeat
I headed for the market for some more rotten meat

I knew I'd win again next year
Chilli, burritos and rotten steer
Maybe something new
Cabbage, popcorn, hash or stew

Tracy Leach
TALK TO ME

I am here for you
Whenever you need me,
But when a problem comes forth
You hide it inside and it breaks you down
Whether you see it or not.
Believe me, I know how it feels,
I've gone through it before.
The feeling of being betrayed
Crushes your self-esteem
and lowers your ability
To ever trust anyone else.
I want to be the one you can trust
From now until forever
Just give me one chance
I won't let you down
Have faith in me please
I'll be truly faithful
Towards your feelings and thoughts
So please . . . Talk to me.

Barbara Lunenschloss
SUNRISE TO SUNSET

I do not mind that I have reached the autumn of my life with winter not far off,
For I witnessed golden dawns usher in the mornings; pastel rainbows arch the sky,
Heavenly blue morning–glories with trumpets uplifted to greet the rising sun,
Raindrops like tears upon the sweet faces of pansies,
Diligent spiders weaving gossamer webs,
Pink and white apple blossoms playing hostess to busy bees,
Delicate anemones peeking out from under their winter blankets,
Jack-in-the-pulpits preaching their first sermons in the spring,
Fringed gentians and goldenrod enhancing the roadside in the fall,
And snowflakes drifting down to hide the wounds of a frostbitten earth.
How often as our eyes grow dim do we seek Thy help, Oh Lord, in humble garden plot.
The flowers express their gratitude by fragrant beauty rising up to greet us.
Help us to give ourselves as unselfishly as they,
Forgetting our infirmities, our griefs, our woes in helping those most needy,
Remembering always Him whose love was given, oh, so freely.

Helen I Leonard
THE UNSUNG SONG

There was a Star that lit up my life,
For a moment in this daily strife.
I watched it glow and brightly burn,
And felt the tide slowly turn.

The joy and gaiety that followed,
Were more than my life was allowed.
My days became bright,
Just as the sea gulls in their flight,
And I felt love for everything in sight.

But time was not ours,
And as the light began to dim,
I realized with the passing hours,
That I would never belong to him.

Life goes on and the Star has gone;
But I will always know there is a song.
Notes left unwritten,
Words left unsung,
And they follow me through,
As each day is done.

Irene S Laupp
ANTICIPATION

It's a lovely morning,
  in the twilight of the winter.
A light mist falls
  from low smutty clouds.
The nearby farmlands
  are eye-popping green.
The trees nearly budding.
The sea–smell of the inlet
  mixed with the odor
  of the land.
As the clouds of winter are dispensed
And Mother Nature delivers
  spring flowers, of tulips
  iris and daffodils, in the valley.
The joy of anticipation
  changes from buds to blossom,
  a beauty of transformation.
The flowers speak to the
  spirit of our hearts and souls.
On the early April morning
As the flowers of late winter
  and early spring,
Occupy a place
  in our hearts.

Nancy Lamons
UNLIMITED TEARS

This poem is dedicated to the many bereaved parents across the United States. Written with empathy and understanding by a bereaved parent.

Tears of Joy
  Tears of Love
Tears of Comfort,
  Tears that cleanse the soul.

Tears, they are so warm,
  Tears, they are so real,
Tears freely flowing over my cheeks,
  They are so necessary.

Tears for our children
  who rest in peace,
Tears for our families who
  seek relief,
Tears for our friends
  who loved them so dear,
Their wish for us is happiness
  and peace while we remain here.

Tears, they say so much,
  they express how much we hurt,
They are emotions shown by our
  "Master's Tender Touch."

Mark Ladd
UNDER YOUR WING

Dedicated with all the love in my heart to my darling mother.

You never really give life what it's worth until you see one given.
And see the true beauty of the world from the first smile.
On that little face and it makes you all warm inside.
And in the face of mom and dad you sense a little pride.
Then one day they begin to crawl
  you have to watch them close so
  they don't get hurt.
Then they begin to walk
  and smile at this newfound wonder
  now's the time you're always
  annoyed
  because they're into everything.
Now comes the time when they learn to talk
  so be careful what you say.
Now they are in school learning to read and write.
Then one day they grow up and start to pull away.
But the next thing you know along comes the day
That you are shocked by what they say.
Only three little words but they mean more than anything else.
They tell you that they love you
  and then they go away.

Janice Lenhart
MY PARENTS' LOVE

This poem is dedicated to my precious mother, Vera H. Lenhart, age 85, and in memory of my Dad, Frank S. Lenhart, whom I loved dearly.

Oh, Dear God in Heaven above,
Thank you for my parents' love.
They guided my feet when I was small;
They held to my hand so I wouldn't fall.

A family altar we had each night,
They strived each day to teach us right.
Up and to church on Sunday we'd go,
In their eyes was a Heavenly glow.

Mother would send us to school each morn.
She's pray as she grasped her Bible so worn,
For God to guide our little steps that day,
To help us grow stronger along the way.

Daddy would rise at the crack of dawn.
When we'd awake, he'd always be gone,
To labor and toil, a living to make,
For a loving family his earnings to take.

Now each child is grown and gone,
And Mother and Daddy are all alone.
Their hands are folded and their hair is gray,
But their lips never cease for each child to pray.

Sunny LaFave
PLASTIC JUNGLE

What good is money, if we don't spend it?
So, month after month, I continue to send it,
To American Express and Master Charge,
To Visa and about twelve other cards.

The interest I'm paying just doesn't make sense;
And, yet I continue to bear the expense.
Some royal list has my name on it out there,
And the offers they send me . . . it just isn't fair!

"No annual fee, a card made of gold,"
I only have to live to be 150 years old,
To pay all I owe; but I really don't care,
Especially, if I go before the utilities get their share.

Knowing that they had not been paid,
Would give me the last laugh as I laid in my grave.
To cash in my chips owing them a pile,
Would certainly help me to die with a smile.

Not caring one bit that upon my demise,
If my tombstone should read, "Now

here she lies;
Oh, yes, she did live ever so humble,
Then died a slave to the plastic
jungle."

Tyna Lair
GOD GAVE YOU CHILDREN

Dedicated, lovingly, to my children, Cheryl, Eddie and Jerry.

God gave you children,
as a favor
as a dream
as a touch of heaven

They are the hint of heaven,
to love
to enjoy
to share

They are borrowed not owned,
take care of them,
as if they are something
God gave you, the privilege
to borrow.

Because He is the
One, who allowed you,
To love them,
For the moment.

They belong to Him,
He loved you
enough to give
them to you.

Carmen Lee
IRISH DOUBLE RAINBOW

Anything is possible, it is said
Even miracles can come true
A rainbow of green, orange, blue,
violet, and red
Not only one, but two.
A half circle of color stretches across
the sky
One above the other
A land of love that will never die
Where all races live as brother
No need to hate, steal, or lie.
A place blessed, when a miracle is
heard,
Of a double rainbow in a small
humble town
Between the two arches flies a
graceful white bird
A dove, sent by God, flies down
To love all and each is known, for He
has sent His word.

Tina Lam
MONKEY BUSINESS

The monkeys were talking
in the jungle one day
and so I eavesdropped
to listen to what they had to say
"What strange animals humans are!"
one money declared
"They have no fur.
Only a little pitiful hair.
They don't eat leaves and berries
like we always do.
How can any creature be such fools?"
The other monkeys nodded and
agreed
Shaking their heads at our stupidity
"Must they stay so close to the jungle
floor
Traveling without a tail
must really be a bore!"
So if you should see some monkeys
at the circus or zoo
Listen carefully
They are talking about you!

Patricia Laymance
THE KISS

Just one look into each other's eyes.
Thoughts of carresments running
through our minds.
A touch of the hand upon my face
gently surrounds me like white lace.
Heartbeats echo in our ears like
thunder awakening future years.
Our bodies come closer pressing out
time.
How can it be that I feel so fine.
Our heads move forward then the
softness of lips.
Tasting the moistness like wine
gently sipped.
Suddenly both souls encircled by
total embrace.
The passion rises high
And the joy of love shows by the one
single tear from my eye.

E M Scott
WELCOME TO MY HOME

My walls are lined with roses.
My doors are open wide.
My walk is strong and sturdy.
My house is filled with pride.

For my walls are lined with children;
While some are lined in wealth:
My door with sticky fingerprints;
My home is lined in health.

I would not trade my roses for
those walls laid in gold.
I would not shut you out and
keep you in the cold.
I would not close my walk and
send you away.
Instead, I'd show you the greatest
gift of today.

Melissa Padilla
DANCING WITH A SHADOW

The memory of us a year ago on
this very night,
thinking of the fondness our hearts
shared, brings me to tears,
I will never let the memories go.
Although you are no longer
around because your
soul left the world, I am constantly
praying that you could see
that I will always love you more
than you'll ever know.
As I weep in my room, all dark
and grey, I see a tall
and strong, yet a gentle and warm
shadow, a shadow with your
heart and soul, a shadow that came
to ease the pain.
It lifts me gently into the air, I
am no longer
desolate with this wonderful gift. I
thank you for sending me
this gift of your heart, which never
spoke in vain.
You gave me a devotion that I
will never spare
I am dancing, remembering all the
endearment your sweet love
gave, I am dancing with a shadow.
I feel so secure as it holds me so
tightly in its arms.
This is so beautiful, can't you see?
My heart goes to you up in
heaven, as the shadow and I dance
to our song.
The affection grows as it lifts
me into the night, the
melody is so very soft, subtle and
warm. Every minute we are closer
tell me, how can this be wrong.

Jennifer Lynn Buxton
YOU GAVE ME LIFE

You gave me life,
You gave me hope,
You gave me the courage,
In my life to cope.
I've always wondered,
If you really cared.
I've always wanted to confide in you,
But I never dared.

You've always seemed distant,
Yet never too far away.
If I ever had a problem,
You had a kind word to say.

I know it may seem,
That I don't really care.
But some parts of my life,
Would only bring you despair.

I once was your baby,
But now that has past.
I'm now a young lady,
It seems that I've grown up so fast.

You are my mother,
For this I am proud.
I just hope I'm the daughter you
dreamed of,
And that one day you'll be proud.

Ruth Shelton
THE FACE OF A CLOWN

To My Granddaughters, Sara, Jennifer, Michelle, Denise, Bobbi, Cindy, Lisa, Rae & Ruth.

Did you ever look into a crowd
and see the face of a clown?
It really doesn't matter
for they are all around.

You look into their eyes
and a smiling face you see.
And you often wonder
why can't that be me.

The face of a clown is happy
or it could be sad.
You look around the crowd
and you know it can't be bad.

Sometimes we hide our feelings
so we clown around
The face of a clown is wonderful
the happiest one in town!

Janna D Keifer (Madden)
ONE LOVE

Dedicated to Someone Special.

Love so strong,
This love can't be wrong
My soul and mind
Love in my heart a real bind,
Never again this special kind . . .
Will never I feel that fine
Thoughts of us pass through my
mind.
Happiness shows at this time,
Without your love all emptiness
shows
Only my heart truly knows . . .
Good and bad we've gone through,
Missing your touch is all I do . . .
Those hugs and kisses.
That tender touch
Without these near,
I'm not worth much . . .
On with life you not near,
Each night my pillow I shed a tear.
Only one thought I really fear,
Losing your love honest dear . . .

Isabel Gonzalez
OUT YOUR WINDOW

To my loving mother, Marcola Gonzalez.

The sky is blue and, just below is a
garden.
Take a moment to look at the
flowers.
Find it in your heart to realize.
They are as beautiful, as we are, you
and me, my neighbor.
As individual and wondrous as
we see it.
Look at the wondrous marvelous
magical garden.
Put love in your heart, love yourself.

Thelma Montavon Gage
BROTHER'S BABY SISTER

We love you and your sister.
We know you love her too.

Remember when you first kissed her?
You were two and she was new.

Try to show her that you care.
Don't let others be unfair.

Someday Dad and I'll be gone.
Her brother's love will keep her
strong.

God's greatest gift to Dad and
Mother,
was She, your sister and You, her
brother.

Timothy Grubb
CHASING OUR DREAM

Dedicated to Angela — whose love and support has given me inspiration. I love you. Tim.

A dream is a daring adventure,
That can never come too late;
For when you can hold a dream in
your heart,
The journey is worth the wait.

I think of all the memories we've
shared,
Places we have been;
Of what our dreams offer us,
Time and time again.

The dreams we chase together,
Are built around our love;
For God is watching over us,
From Heaven up above.

Timothy Grubb
ONLY YOU

I come to you today O Lord,
For guiding me through this day;
To thank you for those little things,
That often come my way.

My heart was full of emptiness,
That only You would know;
I needed you in my life Dear Lord,
To show me where to go.

My life took a new direction,
When you took me by the hand;
You gave me wisdom, strength, and
love,
And showed me your Eternal Plan.

That void and emptiness in my heart,
That only You knew of;
Was filled with hope and happiness,
With an Angel You sent me to love.

As we dream about our future,
And live our lives for You;
We ask you to watch over us Lord,
That only You can do.

Catherine McCulley
CHANGE

Why does the truth have to hurt so
much?
Has it alienated us, completely out
of touch?
We used to talk about so many
things,
now I'm not sure what all of this
means.

You said you would be there when I need to talk,
but now you just sit there, all you do is sulk.
I'm trying to reach out, to make everything right.
Whenever I do, we end up in a fight.
What did you have in mind for later down the road?
Is my being honest too heavy a load?
You've told me how you feel, you said from your heart,
and I've told you from the very first start.
I've tried to keep things straight, so it doesn't get carried away,
but I can feel us slipping day after day.
What do you want from me, where do I stand?
Can I still reach out and hold onto your hand?
I have to admit that I'm very confused.
Where do we go from here, is there too much to lose?
I guess there's not much more to say.
I feel so lost right now, the words are in my way.
I thought I knew you,
I guess I don't.
Would you rather I lie?
I'm sorry, I won't.

Angela Freda
IT'S RAINING
Drip-drop.
It's raining.
Plip-plop.
It's raining.
Will it ever stop?
Not with you complaining.
Drip-drop.
Please stop.
No noise.
Now what?
Go play.
Today?
Yes, dear.
Tears.
What's wrong?
No rain.
Drip-drop.
It's raining.
HOORAY!!!!!!

Margie Wilson Grant
CHRISTMAS EVE
Somewhere in our world
In the pale moonlight
An old lamplight is twinkling
As the evening star peeks
Thru the dusty sky
Turning day into Christmas Eve.

The snow is softly falling
And crystal icicles glisten
In the pale moonlight
Slowly painting a picture,
Turning our world to winter
Wonderland.

Somewhere in the distance
Church bells are ringing
And children's voices can be heard
Singing the carols of Christmas Eve.

Listen closely and you may hear
Angels humming the carols of
Christmas Eve,
Telling the story of Jesus
And the meaning of Christmas Eve.
In our world Jesus's story
Is everlasting — like sunlight to the Soul.
For His love is forever —
The soul's eternal spring.

Brian T Fenton
WHY IS LIFE SO DESOLATE?

To my father, the late Paul Fenton.

Why is life so desolate? That's what the young man said.
He said it to himself, alone in his hospital bed.
Life was so much easier before that fateful day,
When he found out the Lord would soon take him away.
All he ever wanted from this confusing earth
Was to love the girl to whom his wife gave birth.
He was allowed to visit her five times or so a year,
But that would never be enough to stop his sorrowful tear.
He looked across the room, over at the door,
Standing there was his daughter, soon he could hold her no more.

David E Gamache Jr
GLANCE
When I see you standing there,
My heart is a flame,
My hands are cold,
Why do I clam—
when I am bold?

A bug had bitten me that day,
that love itself could not take away.

When I hear your golden voice,
my ears do ring like a song.

You alone I do love,
to you I know, my Turtle Dove.

I watch in envy for to see,
if you, by chance, would look at me.

My heart to you I want to give,
and my life with you, I want to live . . .

Linda A Patricia Carroll
TALES OF GOLD

I would like to dedicate this poem to my parents, because through them I found the way to dream! Love Always, Linda Anne.

As I sit between my colleagues, I find it rather odd, that they could not see a dreamer in their midst; so well-educated and all. For I could spin webs of famed knowledge with an imaginative line. They never suspect, my colleagues, that is, that my knowledge is my mind. So peculiar I say for people so well-educated with absent-minded minds. Yet I love to spin my tales of gold and watch my colleagues sparkle and shine.

Harley Brumbaugh
TO PICK A PROMISE
I have the need to run again
Through fields of boundless sky:
To pick a promise from the brook
And pile the promise high!

I have the need to fly again
Through fields of boundless chance:
To skip a stone across the blue
To hear the ripples dance.

This, to me is heaven . . .
And what it means to die . . .
I toss myself into the brook.
God plucks me out to dry!

Harley Brumbaugh
BIRDS
I'm drawn to those who warble . . .
Who praise with open throat;
Whose music fills the upward sphere
On wings of song and hope!

I'm drawn to those who soar
Above the sluggish snail
With flutters and flings
And flapping of wings
Face the howling gale!

I'm drawn to downy nesters
Who keep December warm.
With leaves and rigging of mosses
and twigging
Snuggle in chilling storm.

Soaring birds, there are
I will never match.
Soaring birds . . .
I shall never catch . . .

Sue Vilburn
NUMERO UNO

My Son, you were our first. We wanted you to be the best, and you never once let us down. Those that grew to know you, loved you. Our little gentle man of 5-1/2 years who was taken from us so suddenly.

You seemed to always know my many moods. When I was feeling down, you were there to comfort me and kiss the tears away. You had a special way of saying goodnight, too. Nibbles on the ear for the words you could never speak.

We miss you so; I most of all. Your sister look sat me with those questions in her eyes. Questions I can't answer. I hold her close and tell her how much happier you'd been in those final weeks, before strangers, for some unknown reason, ended your life with a shotgun. When we lost you, we lost a piece of our hearts.

Yes, beloved son, your gentle nature will stand forever as a living tombstone of the love and respect you gave so freely to all. Your name, T-Bone, is tattooed on our hearts a living epitaph for our gentle Pit Bull.

We're happily awaiting the arrival of your heirs, but there will never be another T-Bone.

We love you, Son!

Laura White
THE HUSK
tears course down the withered desert patch of skin
softening the black eyes
surrounded in the cloak of creases and folds, mourning
for lost youth, for the pain of the world, no

for loneliness, for lost friends
again, no
what is being grieved over is the
knowledge of futility, of emptiness

never been married, never having friends
never been in love, an orphan
no one knows him, his name, his pain
worked the same job, the same factory
the same city, the same brown, weathered
cracker-box of a home

throughout his years, he lacked substance
a grey, hollowed-out shell of a man
people look past him, no one cares
a pawn to be shuffled, a lifeless wooden figure
touching no one's life, fading into the background
as the dust and insignificant paper
blowing through life without purpose or meaning

Nancy M Miller
MOTHER'S DAY
God made all the mothers
Then he gave them all away,
And because he was so proud of them
He set aside this special day;

To let them know they're thought
about
And loved the whole year through,
He blessed them all with hearts of
gold
To give to me and you;

He gave them strength to carry out
The tasks that needed tending,
Then he gave them children
Of which are so depending;

Yes, God made all the mothers
One for every child to behold,
And because she's like no other
In our eyes will never grow old.

Nancy M Miller
TAKES THE BLAME
Those who always take the blame
Often hang their head in shame;
Lack the confidence to speak their
mind
And feel put down most of the time.

They think that they're the one at
fault
Are not worth their weight in salt;
Carry the burdens inflicted on them
And view life as somewhat dim.

They become withdrawn and ill at
ease
Try too hard to always please;
Refuse to ever take a chance
For fear their doubts will be
enhanced.

They isolate themselves from those
around
In case their feelings should abound;
Shield their life in such a way
Nothing changes from day to day.

Those who always take the blame
Feel as if they have no aim;
Suppress the desire to move ahead

And would rather sit back and watch instead.

Nancy M Miller
POETRY IS GOOD THERAPY
Poetry is good therapy
It lets you express how you feel,
It's taking time out to wonder about
Those memories you try to conceal;

Poetry is good for telling
All that of which you know,
It's a wonderful tool for recording
What's deep down in your soul;

Poetry is good for sharing
Your ideas as they become clear,
It's a way to say whatever you may
To those who are willing to hear;

Poetry is good for learning
How to be more objective,
It exposes your thoughts and feelings
And helps put them back in perspective;

Poetry is good for many things
Like exploring all your notions,
It's good and bad, funny and sad
While it brings out all your emotions.

Nancy M Miller
THE PERFECTIONIST
He tries to be thorough, complete and correct
But, at the end of the day he's a nervous wreck;

His work is impeccable, accurate and exact
But, his calm, confident manner is just a big act;

He wants to be faultless and without defection
But, he thinks he is nothing if he senses rejection;

He pushes himself beyond limits to achieve his best
But, his standards are high and he can't accept less;

He strives to be flawless and appears quite at ease
But, no matter the impression he is often displeased;

He's dissatisfied if there's anything he doesn't know
But, knowing all the answers does takes its toll;

The perfectionist fears that he's not good enough
But, trying to prove that he is only makes life tough.

Nancy M Miller
CHANCE
I took a big chance today
Jumped on its back and rode away,
Circled my troubles in less than an hour
And blew them away with all of my power;

Upon returning from where I went
I realized it was time well spent,
And chance has agreed to do it again
For the opportunities have no end;

Though the journey I took was all in my mind
I was able to leave my troubles behind,
Now when chance comes through the gate
There's no way I'll hesitate.

Carrie Renee Fonseca
FOREVER
What we had was unique.
No one can have what we shared, we were one.
Linked only by our voices.
Weird? No — special.
Even though you left me, we will always be connected — Forever.
I will hear your soft loving voice, such nice things were said between you and I — Forever
Time only knows when we will speak again, I hope it's soon.
I love no one like I love you, and for once I believed someone loved me in return. Even if it was only for awhile
Your voice will be deep inside my heart — Forever
I hear you and I.

Judith Perley-Berntsen
MY JOURNEY

To my three Aunts, who never let me quit.

The steps are there for me to climb,
But first I must descend for a time,
Into the "me" I've hidden away,
Waiting so long to see light of day.

I'm anxious, excited, and in such a hurry
To put me together, no time now to worry.

The parts that were missing, I'll now put in place
To carry me faster to my special grace.
United, at last, to all that is me
I know, for the rest of my life, I'll be free.

Angie Coyne
THE RESTLESS NIGHTMARE
I close my eyes to stop my tears from falling to my cheeks. My dreams and thoughts are only of the one I used to love. I awake in a cold sweat, crying out his name. I still shiver from the darkness of my empty feeling. I toss and turn from the thought of it being over. The aching pain is deep in my heart. The air is filled with the scent of our memories. The world just a hazy fog of mistaken confusion.

Anita Dalheim
WHEN I DRAW BACK MY CURTAINS

To my sisters, Rosie and Erika—and the cats, of course.

When I draw back my curtains each morning
And look into my elder–tree
I'm glad that a new day's beginning
For I feel so wondrously free!

This twisty old tree's my companion
It's been part of my life all these years
I've seen it so still in the moonlight
And glistening with raindrops, like tears.

This tree is also a blessing
For my very large cat family
For they come to my bed very early
And their eyes they are pleading with me.

Yes, there's Posy and Bunty and Mitzi
And Felix and Katy too
All waiting and staring and saying
"Just open the window, please do!"

Then out they all leap to the garden
From this wonderful elder tree
And I share all their gladness and freedom
For that is how life's meant to be!

Jeni Morrow
SOLITAIRE
Sometimes, it seems, life falls a blank,
at others, 'tis full as can be.
Never mind with the rest of the world,
my world revolves around me.
No planes, no trains.
No blizzards, no rain.
No cats, no dogs,
No steam, nor fog.
Don't ask me how, nor ask me why.
It's just me, myself, and I.

Jodi L Belz
FRIENDS LIKE STARS

This poem is dedicated to Shari and Kim, with love. Thanks for being a true friend.

Friends like stars
Are quite abundant
Yet a true friend,
Shines the brightest
While others fade away
With a cloudy sky

Tracey L Wall
OUR HERITAGE
Longing for freedoms
of religion, speech, and press
they went on their journey
west.
O'er the sea and the land
a Bill of Rights was formed so grand.
And now
personal liberties
freedom of religion
speech and press.
And the freedom to assemble
Peaceably.
Are all part of the heritage
of our free country, America.

Deborah F Gabrels
AN EMPTY SHELL
The slam of a door
Now a noise like shattered glass
in the quietness of the room,
breaking the stillness therein.
The noise was only heard by me
because it came from within
It signified the breaking of my heart
this final and painful time.
My body is now drained of all feeling, my emotions no longer exist
I am merely an empty shell
since you withdrew your love from around me.
No longer will my smile hold warmth,
or my eyes shine bright with love
No longer will my skin glow
with the warmth of passion's fire.
I can't even feel the pain inside
all I do now is exist
An empty shell of a person
with nothing for which to live . . .

Suzanne M Kett
PASSION
Caress me gently with your eyes
Speak to me without saying a word
Hold me closely in your thoughts
Touch my heart so my soul is stirred
Stroke me softly with your breath
Lift my spirits with your smile
Fill my senses with your loving ways
Join me in my dreams for just awhile
Feel my presence with your longing
Arouse my desire with your sweet embrace
Carry me away with your passion
Take me with you to a higher place

Terese Boyer
MORNING
A fresh new morning quietly awakens.
The sun, as it is rising,
breaks its light through the windows.
In the distance
the birds begin their songs.
The clock is lightly ticking
On the other side of the bed.
A cool spring air
brings a chill to the room.
The fading shadows in the room
begin to dance.
I snuggle deeper
into the darkness of my covers.
You reach for me and pull me closer.
Embracing,
we share the warmth of our bodies.
Gently you make love to me.
Our hearts are aflame
as our bodies become one.
A fresh new feeling quietly awakens.

Trisha K Jones
THE CLOWN
Can't you hear me crying?
I'm screaming out your name.
Not by sobs and mourning,
but by laughing, joking, and acting insane.

I want so much for you to hear me.
Can't you see it in my eyes?
I'm just afraid of what you'll see;
scars worn on the heart of a wicked life.

Tears can wash away bad memories;
they can wash away bad dreams.
But it takes blood to wash the miseries
of the unpure, unjust, and unclean.

For every time I laugh you see;
it doesn't mean I'm happy.

Rachel Kelly Edmonds
TRASH IT
When I went outside the other day
There was garbage every which way

It's very dirty out here
And look at those chewy pairs
It looks very gross
It's probably from coast to coast
Eggs are all rotten, and apples spotted
As to my concern its very yucky out here
So from time to time,
You take the garbage out
Remember this poem and what it's about.

Susan Vilar
MY SWEET PRINCE

To Albert, my sweet prince.

He is my sweet prince.
My love for him is the strongest entity I know.
It is for his love that I live, he makes it so.
My sweet prince.
His beauty grows every day.
He is like the most glorious days, brilliant and filled with hope.
Looking at his face is like watching the sun rise, it's warm and glorious.
His eyes sparkle with the brilliance of diamonds, and makes the world glow.
His breath is as sweet as his kisses.
His hair is as smooth as silk.
He is my sweet prince.
He knows I can never stay mad.
His self-confidence makes me want him more.
I am weak when it comes to my sweet prince.
I desire him like no other.
His love is powerful.
His touch makes me insane, his touch makes me pure.
Love exists only for me and my sweet prince.
He is my sweet prince.
My heart drains of life at the thought of losing him.
My soul be lost . . . forever.
I love you my sweet prince.

André Carrier
THE ABORTION
The Lord sent me from heaven into mommy's tummy
That's when I first felt alive.
But when mommy received the news of my presence
She didn't seem too happy for she couldn't stop to cry.
Slowly mommy came up with a decision,
She didn't want me in her life.
So mommy went to see a doctor and within seconds I had died.
Moments later I returned to heaven
Unsure of where I was.
And there before me stood an angel
And he guided me to a light
And there was God and I began to cry.
I asked the Lord why I had to leave mommy's tummy
And he said, mommy didn't want me.
My life seemed so empty.
My life seemed so gray.
Mommy didn't know me and killed a total stranger in a day.
A day unforgotten, a day unforetold
Of the life of a fetus who just wanted a home.

André Carrier
PLEASE DON'T DADDY
Mommy and Daddy got in a fight.
Mommy didn't like the way Daddy touched me tonight.
Daddy cried, Mommy screamed.
Daddy kept saying it's not what it seemed.
I ran to my room and hugged my teddy.
If I was a boy maybe Daddy would love me.
Mommy ran in my room and she packed our bags.
I know Daddy loved Mommy and if she left I'd be to blame.
But I didn't do anything, yet I felt so ashamed.
Mommy put our bags in the car and we drove away.
As long as I live I'll never forget that day.
Years have passed and I am much older.
Daddy's been seeing a doctor and I think he's O.K.
Mommy and Daddy still aren't together.
And Daddy's never touched me that way.

Rev R T Sanderson
AUTUMN'S HOMING TREND
The robins southward flew at dawn
From slanting turf they'd bobbed upon,
And from a grove, that nearby stood,
Where once they'd watched in parenthood,
Songbirds have gone—the young with old—
Toward some migrating southward goal.
All through those ambered sunny hours
The angels of September flowers
Have drifted south in bobbing weave
Of haste, then hesitating leave;
And honking fowl in pointed line
Keep winging toward some homing clime.

There's need to heed that noticed trend
Of fowl and butterflies, my friend:
For such a trend awaits us all—
Call it Autumn; or, call it Fall—
When hope beyond life's Summer's end
Is zoned in Autumn's homing trend.

Dorothy M Harris
NO DAFFODILS YET
I wandered out this morning
About the neighborhood,
To loosen up arthritic joints
And search for signs of spring.
The sun was shining brightly
Snowdrifts topped with dirt were melting,
Yet the wind blowing quite briskly
Whispered into my reluctant ear,
"My friend, it is too early,
For what you seek to find.
All things have their seasons
'Tis right it should be so.
Go home and wait the proper time
For the winter to disperse.
And then behold the glory
When Spring renews the earth."
Chastened I turned homeward
Humbly pondering this truth,
Knowing a greater power than man
Controls the universe.

Fran Krebs
DEATH

This poem is dedicated to Ray Fleming, who lost his life on foreign soil during the Vietnam War in 1966.

Desolation — utter loss of one so loved.
Empty world — without his laughter, without his voice,
Without his world still within.
And yet . . . No blame to place.
Forgotten names, forgotten places — but still remembered
In the hearts of persons near . . . and dear.
The end to life's chapter — a closing epitaph . . .
Be he humble who treads this earth,
His final resting before rebirth.

Evelyn T Withrow
JESUS IS THE ANSWER
We have just celebrated the birthday of Jesus
Who was born on Christmas morning.
We have taken down our tree and put away all the trimmings.

The children are happy and playing;
Everyone has exchanged gifts
But the greatest gift was when Jesus came to earth to forgive our sin,
Save our soul and give us a new life to begin.

Yes, Jesus is the answer.
When things go wrong as they sometimes do,
We can pray to Jesus and He will make things right.
When our load is heavy and our burdens too hard to bear,
We can pray to Jesus, He is always near.

When we are down and out,
As we sometimes are;
We can pray to Jesus, He is always there.
Yes, Jesus is the only answer;
We can call on Him,
He will give us joy and peace that will never cease.

Maxwell B Courage
HOPE
Hope enables us to rise from bed at dawn,
When we face a difficult, challenging day;
It helps us to look for the good in all things,
However bleak they may seem in every way.
Hope can lead to success and great joy,
When we persist in the way we want to go;
If we travel to historic places,
We will learn much and our knowledge will grow.
Hope leads to happiness very often,
When we try to make the most of each day;
Let us conquer life's unpleasant things,
And look for the worthwhile in every way.

Andrew Robert Scot
DESTINY
Timeless Relentless Beauty
stranded on the edge of darkness
starlight her only background

I see
A face so pale
whiter than bone

Lips so red
deeper than blood

Eyes like vengeance
shred my soul

but . . .
fast frantic

A fatal kiss

The Angel of Death

Andrew Robert Scot
a day
dreamy clouds
grey white cotton
swiftly moving
in an open blue
above the trees
they move
seeing the earth
turn by and by

dreamy clouds
swiftly moving
so unlike
a dream
vapor trails
in the air
your hair

even in these
these wispy clouds
i hear your beauty
speak aloud

Scott R Seelye
SEARCHING MY BEING

For Jack and Rose with love! Your son, Scott Richard.

Searching my being
For unturned stones,
Polished and gleaming
With life's unknowns.

All through my thoughts
These well-worn trails,
Of previous walks
And unfinished tales.

Like dead-end streets,
Insignificant to mind.
None of them meet
None of them rhyme.

It's there I shall pave
With Life's precious stone,
Word to engrave,
Those of my own.

Norman L Squires
WHERE THE HEARTS OF MEN LONG TO BE

to the Pride of Baltimore and her crew.

The sun shines its grace upon the majestic heavens,
As the morning sun awakens the saintly sky,
And casts its beauty to the glistening sea,
Where the hearts of men long to be,
To sail upon the water so careless and free,
As the snow-white clouds drift towards the leewards,
And the winds caress the peaceful

serenity,
This is the joy that lives inside of us,
To sail with pride and the love of the sea,
We will never forget your smiling faces,
Baltimore's best, the ambassadors of the free,
Someday, we will be together again,
And sail upon the glistening sea,
Where the hearts of men . . .
long to be . . .

Norman L Squires
BETWEEN THE LINES

Dedicated to Mary Dzubara.

My hopes and dreams,
Lie between the lines,
Of chance and possibility,
For, I see the beauty of life,
As words that come from the heart,
That shines like diamonds,
In your eyes,
And whispers on tender lips,
Like a sweet silent singing,
An autumn wind came scurrying in,
And swept out the ashes,
From a love's candle that flickered,
Then gone out,
Left my heart to a tempest toss,
In the pouring rain,
And now, I'm filled with the fear,
That our newfound love,
Maybe lost to the antiquity of time,
Between the lines . . .

Norman L Squires
CHILDREN OF THE SUN

Dedicated To The Followers Of The Life Of One.

Children of the sun,
Dreamer's everyone,
Travelers of light-years,
Where time has no pace,
The givers of life,
The keepers of grace,
Children of the sun,
Dreamers everyone,
The hope of earth's future,
The light of ten thousand suns,
Shines upon each and everyone,
Time is running out,
But we still have the chance,
To join in the amazing grace,
Children of the sun,
Dreamers everyone,
The eternal light of life,
Shines in their hearts,
And reflects on us all . . .

Norman L Squires
HOPE IS A PLACE TO CALL HOME
A cold wind blew past,
My makeshift door,
As I lay upon by cardboard bed,
Next to the sleepy giant,
That spews bursts of steam,
Into the winter's sky,
Like a mist upon the water,
Of an early summer's morn,
Casts its mystique,
Into the wintry night,
That creates a peaceful solitude,
In this God–forsaken place,
Where three old men and I,
Call home,
In this tiny space,
All is not bliss,
In our makeshift world,
For hope . . . is a place to call home . . .

Judy B N Wheeler
LET ME
Let Me
Let Me Be
Completely Free
From This Minority
You've Placed On Me

Can't You See
You're Just Like Me?
No Different From He Or She
Seek To Find Me As Equal As Thee
So I May Flee From This Hold On Me.

Petra Ohnoutka
MY WORLD
I know this place
It's far away—
But you can't see it . . .

It's a magical, mystical
Garden of dreams
A fountain of countless old wishes.

There are golden raindrops
Of tears I shed in the past
But I do see a moon . . .

A moon to light my darkened days
And comfort me in times of weariness
Let me tell you . . .

There is a place I know
Which is far away—
Only I can see it . . .

Lisa Evan
I CANNOT UNDERSTAND
I cannot understand I do not know quite why
Still every time I think of you a tear forms in my eye
A feeling of guilt often passes my mind
Though when I look in my heart
Happy times I still find
How we laughed and we talked on that first day we met
The short nights together
Long nites apart
We vowed our lives we promised our love
While we sat on a beach
Looking out for a dove
Our love grew strong we were together as one
But now you are gone we shall have no new fun
To look back on and talk of
When we are both gray
Why did God call you home
Why did my love go away

Betty Zimmerman
RAIN
How I love the tranquility of the falling rain
The tiny little steams it makes, on the windowpanes.
The cool refreshing scent in the summer air,
Truly a gift from heaven for all the earth to share.
The peace and quiet of the night . . . everything so still,
Just the steady dripping on the windowsill.
Not a thing is stirring . . . not a bird in sight,
While Mother Nature does her thing, but not a rainbow in the night.
The clean fresh smell the raindrops bring, and the flowers raise their heads,
While Mother Nature cleans them, in their flower beds.
Clean, clean grass, luscious green,
the cool air that smells so clean.
With Mother Nature calling, her little raindrops falling,
And for all her little creatures, to slip away to sleep.
When I was just a little one, I was told for many years,
The water falling from above, was just the Angels' tears.
I couldn't understand, although I kept on trying,
To find the reason why, all those little Angels were crying.

Michelle Thompson
RED
Red is the color of a rose
Or a color painted on toes
It's my favorite color of all
Also the color of fall
Cardinals are always red
Our hearts being fed
With love.

Esther Cruz
BETRAYAL
What's betrayal we may ask,
In search of thoughts we go inside.
Betrayal is when you feed a cat
And he pays you with a scratch!

When we kindly give some help,
And it is taken while in pain;
Then as quickly as it ends,
It's return by giving pain!

Betrayal is what you get,
When you trust the ones who can't
Give in turn of themselves
To the ones who trusted them!

When you give and don't receive,
That's betrayal truly indeed.
For it takes some one who loves
To return a given love!

Open minds and open hearts,
Can't conceive of betrayal acts;
For it takes some one who's closed
To betray an open heart!

Esther Cruz
WOUNDED DOVE
I saw a dove go by, barely able to fly,
As the winds kept pushing back,
So increased her will to fly!

What's the use of trying so hard,
To fight the wind, that pushes so hard.
It would be easier, just to give up.

All alone, the bird must go on,
For her flock just left her behind.
All alone and unprotected, in winter she will die.

I saw a dove go by, barely able to fly,
As the winds kept pushing back,
So increased her will to fly!

Little bird that tries so hard,
"Why don't you, just give it up?
"I must fly until I reach, the special place just for me"

I saw a dove go by, barely able to fly,
As the winds kept pushing back,
So increased her will to fly!

Esther Cruz
DEAD FLOWERS
I once saw a man
Who had a corsage.
"His lady would hold it,
Forever in her hand."

He gave it to his love,
With so much pride,
Not knowing it was predestined,
For them to die . . .

Like all things in this life,
Pretty flowers also die . . .
All turned brown with decay,
Petal by petal, all went away.

Their sweet fragrance and perfume,
Eventually gave into the doom,
Not their beauty, not their smell,
Can keep the flowers from the veil!

I saw the flowers, I saw their eyes
Come together onto death . . .
So much pain, and so much sadness,
To see flowers under veils . . .

Esther Cruz
HE'S IN CONTROL
Tho chaos is very evident in the world,
Stop it all, take a look, he's in control.
Tho death surrounds us, and pain goes on,
Just get away, take a look, he's in control!

Despair, hopelessness and desolation
Surrounds us all, but never fear, he's in control.
Why we ask to all we see, thinking and feeling
There's no control; but look again and you will see . . .

The ocean waves come and go,
As to indicate his total control.
The sun goes up, and the sun goes down,
As his sure way to show us he's in control!

The little birds feed of the seeds,
That he has put there for them to eat.
Would he truly do less for us all,
Who are a part of his master control?

Chaotic signs are all around
That make us think there's no one to account.
But look again beyond these things,
To find inside, the truth we seek . . .
He's in control!

Esther Cruz
DOUBLE-SIDED
Alone we're born . . .
Alone we die . . .
What's the secret of the eyes?

What gives beauty to one person,
Can the same way, turned around,
Take the essence of one's life . . .

Depth is beauty and power to some,
While to behold it can send many to run.
Double-sided view of things . . .
Can we reach all inside?

Why can some laugh at a movie,
Yet some other start to cry?
Do we not see all the same when we
Look at the waves and sky?

Half glass empty, or half full glass,
Isn't it all the secret of life
Just in how you look at the glass? . . .

The sky is blue, the ocean is too,
Or is the water really blue?
Once again I say to you—
What's the secret of the eyes? . . .

Bernard T Sherry
MY POEM THE GUARD
Flowers are sent to my old friends of mine.
Fruit baskets are filling the Guard

House now.
I see people come and go to where? I don't know.
There must be a beautiful place called Heaven.

My days are peaceful, when death appears.
The flowers are so cheerful, they make life seem so real
Happy were the days when my friends were here.
We had so many good times that disappeared.

Life seems so much happier when we were serving the Lord.
The roses smell so sweet with a design that can't be beat.
Only God can make a rose with foil leaves pressed so neat.
The different taste of fruits from seeds so small and sweet
These miracles of life are easy to see, from the waterfront to the city streets.

The Guards prevail where others fail.
Guards do their share sacrificing their life many times without despair.
Sharing His Love with others, into the darkest of night to the brightness of the sun.
God lights the Guards path so Heavenly won.

Thank you, Lord

Bernard T Sherry
THE FLOWERS

Flowers are sent because of someone's loveliness.
It reminds us of being of one and together forevermore, the likeness of the petals have a uniform look, never losing their appeal for all to enjoy.

Flowers at a funeral make attractive stand pieces, they symbol the beauty of life, never sad always smiling, and eternal peace, many times flowers are sent instead of prayer. The churches look so alive with flowers at its altars.

I'm surprised the way the churches have been changed, no more religious statutes to worship day by day, our parents were better to understand and raised us much better than modern time families.

Today churches have lost their charisma and faith in God.

My sister had so many bouquets of flowers she was very well loved. "God bless her." I remember the funeral parlor filled with roses lilacs, lilies and gladioles. The beauty of flowers carries us through so many difficult times in our lives, when we are sick, dying, injured and smiling people. It lifts our souls and our hearts and our minds forevermore. "God Bless us all."

Anne James Valades
THE NAKED TREE

A leaf
falls.
So brief,
it calls
my grief.

The tree is bare.
Branches form a snare,
an empty trap,
which started when
a leaf
fell in my lap.

W M Ismailoff
TOPLESS

A problem of unusual sort
Divided the entire nation.
Denying either the support,
Or some additional formation;
(Both cases are a common plight
In pastures overripe or cropless)
Of course, it is a nuisance topless,
But otherwise a glorious sight;
Which even hidden by the cover
Revealing little or too much
To ashes could reduce a lover
Or show a place for gentle touch,
Or you, if trying to absorb it
Without a due and proper care,
Who knows, may send into the orbit
To circle close to Venus there.
And so, considering this matter,
Since something simply has to drop,
Let's pass a judgment what is better
To keep the bottom or the top

James Anthony Castelli Jr
THE ROSE AND THE WEED

There was a cultivated rose;
Beauty best when was half closed.
The weed, it cries once aphids bite —
Attracts such vermin in the night.

The meadow be untamed by man;
The rosebed kept by caring hand.
Which one's preferred? A simple test:
Which shall adorn thy woman's breast?

As withered flora: brittle soot,
Which first is trampled underfoot?
Be it poor or noble shoe,
One more relation I must do:

The gentleman: a scholar mind —
A trail of ladies close behind.
A pauper lags; was never taught;
Displays his face that none have sought.

Sun, rain, snow; the two won't meet
Such royal blood dwells not the street,
But when as corpses, I ask you
Which is the fairer of the two?

Sheldon Davidson
THE FALL OF THE TRIUMPHANT

Climbing up the mountain
It's a long way down
Don't know how far to the top
And it's either surface or drown
You can hear the eagles call
But you cannot see around
Hear the glister of gold call you
But by blackness you are surround
And you grope into the night
You think you're near the top
But reality sets in, and another
Foot you've dropped
Falling down the mountain
Your life passes before
Your silent screams are heard
And you'll return nevermore . . .
Sometimes I sit and think
And shed a passing tear
And the mercy of the God above
Will take away your fear
The fall of the triumphant
The ring echoes in my ears
The fall of the triumphant
I cry for my own tears
The fall of the triumphant
I've still got a long way to go
The fall of the triumphant
It's how far down I don't want to know
How far to fall,
For the fall of the triumphant

Vivian Marshburn

Vivian Marshburn
SECRET NAME

These poems I dedicate to my special friend Gary L. Murvin, who has encouraged and inspired me through the past several months.

When we first met I knew right then, I had a secret love and could not say his name. His name is forbidden in words out loud, but in my mind I scream aloud. He's in my dreams and deep in my heart, he's never to know for I'd fall apart.

I want to hold him and hold him tight, to kiss his lips till they're rosy and bright. But each time I see him, I grow with more pain to know, I have a secret love and can't speak his name. "Oh," such mental anguish to live in pain to have a secret love, the one I can't claim.

My ears pound at the sound of his voice, please my special love I have no choice. My lips part to utter your name, but my voice won't let me call out your name. My mind and body scream in pain to know I have a secret love and I know his secret name.

Vivian Marshburn
SOMETHING IS ON MY MIND

"Something is on my mind," I'd like the world to know.
It's kind of hard to cry about, when no one seems to know.
"Something is on my mind," I would like to write about, to one special friend I have which he knows nothing about.
"Something is on my mind," my friend you must know about, but then again it's hard to say, what my friend is all about.
"Something is on my mind," I'd like to tell my friend how much I really appreciate the kindness he's shown completely to the end.
"Something is on my mind," I must tell my friend that I'll have to say goodbye to him, when this all comes to an end.
"Something is on my mind," I want to tell my friend just how special and dear he is to me, and all the kindness he brings.

"Something is on my mind," and this will always be, I'll carry this special feeling till I'm eventually free.
"Something is on my mind," I want him to especially know, his friendship means the world to me, It's more valuable than gold.
"Something is on my mind," I want my friend to know that I'll carry this special feeling with me, till I'm completely gone.
"Something is on my mind," I want him to especially know that it won't be much longer, in letting this special friendship go.
"Something is on my mind," I hope my love will grow for this one special friend I have, I want the world to know.
"Something is on my mind," I want my friend to know that I really and truly trust him, in things that he's been told.
"Something is on my mind," I always seem to tell these little secret feelings I have, and he never seems to tell.
"Something is on my mind," It's been there all this time, and now I have to go my friend, so this will be on time.

Nancy Lauterbach
RAINBOW VIEW

I came to Murrieta on an April day to stand atop my hill
This bit of planet Earth I'd bought was mine to till
Wild lilacs and manzanitas were blooming all around
Fragrance was everywhere in the air and on the ground

Suddenly there leaped from this magnificent splendor
A deer with sad dark eyes, yet graceful and slender
Then quickly the creature was gone, to his hideaway
I'm hoping to see him again on another special day

A peaceful covey of quail meandered slowly down the grade
Bluebirds flew up over a tree into the nests they had made
Red-tailed hawks soared high above in the bright blue sky
While far away on the mesa, I heard a lonely coyote's cry

Many rainbows appeared in the lush green valley below
Our Creator's gift so spectacular, vivid and aglow
The message came in loud and clear, as at last I knew
The country road where I lived would be Rainbow View

Vivian Marshburn
TIMES OF PAST

The time is past,
My time was you.
My time is gone to
be with you.
Time runs by no one
knows! Where time
went now that you're
gone. I held you close!
I loved you deep!
I have these memories,
they're mine to keep.
The time has passed, I had
with you.
I have my future, to
remember you and
"Times of Past," that I
had with you!

Gordon Shao

Gordon Shao
CHRISTMAS

This poem is dedicated to Cathy Marie, My sweet, loving wife.

CHRISTMAS n. (A tale of the birth
of Christ on December 25
in Bethlehem of Judea, is the
year's most Holy Day.)
C is for the Christ child born in
manger,
H is for the hallowed hour of
honorary prayer.
R is for remembrance of the
holy babe,
I is for the inborn sweet and
rare.
S is for the solemn shepherds
in field heard the good
tidings of great joy by night
with angels,
T is for trusting fully in God's
care.
M means Mary blessed the
holy Mother, and brought
men's gifts so fair.
A is for the anthem of angels;
"Peace on earth, good will
toward men.
To God in the highest glory.
Halleluiah, Amen."
S is for the star that shone in
Heaven, guiding to the place
where Jesus lay.

Mary Hamlet
TO MY SWEETHEART ! ! !

To Ursula & Macy, daughters who believed more than me.

Have I told you lately that I love you,
Do I have to tell you every time we
meet?

Have I told you lately that I miss you,
Do I have to tell you every time we
meet?

Have I told you lately how I love to
love you,
Do I have to tell you every time we
meet?

Have I told you lately how I love to
hold you,
Do I have to tell you every time we
meet?

Have I told you lately how I love to
look at you,
Do I have to tell you every time we
meet?

If your answer to all these questions
are the same (same being yes) then
you know how I feel about you

I think you know this is just
another way of my saying

I LOVE YOU

Orvel Jeffery
GETTING AHEAD

Saturday work I really dread,
But try I must to get ahead.
I pay one bill but surely then,
I just go back in debt again.
It's just a cycle that I take,
As long as money is at stake.
I buy this and that and then I say,
Why did I charge again today?
I guess it's nature what I see,
I just can't see to let it be.
But buy I must at any cost,
If only to show my wife who's boss.
Then I must pay or soon return,
It seems that I will never learn.
That I can earn more or less,
But it can't bring me happiness.

Cécile Fleury
IT WAS IN 1915, THE THEN GOVERNOR-GENERAL OF CANADA

It was in 1915, the then govenor-general of Canada, Lord Aberdeen, residing in Ottawa city, capital of Canada, on a nice Sunday afternoon went for a ride in the Gatineau Mountains nearby.
In a beautiful carriage driven by 4 horses, they left. There was Lord & Lady Aberdeen, 2 servants and the coachman. Later in the afternoon when returning home, suddenly came the flood on Gatineau river with its thunderlike noise. The 4 horses got afraid. And the coachman was trying to direct them on the Gatineau bridge, but . . . straight in the deep river the 4 horses & their load went.
By chance, there were 3 farmers on the bank of the river, which were very good swimmers. By a heroic gesture those 3 peasants succeeded in saving Lord & Lady Aberdeen, the 2 servants and the coachman. The carriage and the 4 horses were a total lost.
Safe on the land, Lord Aberdeen said: For this big favor of our rescue I want some thanks to God which people shall hear for a long time. As a little church was on construction nearby, Lord Aberdeen had made in his home town of London, England, three bells of cast iron. The bells were named after Lady Aberdeen who was born in Germany by her name: "Ishdell."
So, nowadays, 75 years afterwards, anybody who goes for an automobile drive, when passing on Gatineau bridge, can still hear those bells ringing . . . the everlasting thanks of Lord Aberdeen . . .

Jodi C Brincefield
SPECTRAL NIGHT

'Twas a coal black night on the
graveyard grounds
The gales piped chords of eerie
sounds
A moon glowed brightly through
misty haze
To mirror his face on an icy glaze
An old cobbled path met a crypt at its
bend
As a tall iron gate crept along with no
end
The ghostly fog danced 'round in the
yard
Decrepit stone soldiers with secrets to
guard
A rancid smell hung with death in the
air
Like bats chasing shadows for
victims to dare
Darkness prevailed as king of this
sight
While echoes rang out through a
spectral night

William A Reh
CAMEL

The dromedary, not a date,
walks a shuffling, go and wait.
Muscled saddle forward goes action
rearward from the nose.
Redolent vessel of sanded waste,
offends the senses, mostly taste.
Sad-eyed ship with shape alop,
ugliness with lips aslop.

Be not glum miss–happened friend,
lift on high your frontal end.
Homeliness can be a blessing,
good looks are only window
dressing.
Though your ego lies in tatters,
it's persistency that really matters.
Stand proud and tall with tail high
be smug of grin and let a sigh.

Your biggest fault I cannot omit,
it's such a sight to see you spit.

Clinton W Rowley Jr
SAN FRANCISCO'S FISHERMAN'S WHARF

Checkered tables overlooking the
bay,
Bouillabaisse at Scoma's,
Beamed ceilings,
Allito's abalone,
Gulls squaking overhead,
Margaritas ala Pico's
Packed harbor of sails,
Ghiradelli's chocolates,
Tourists sightseeing the cannery,
Magic Pan crepes,
Dragon kites skimming the horizon,
Crab cocktails and oyster crackers,
Walking and drinking Steam beer,
Brandywynne de Beausite,
You and I;

Some memories, like the wine
We drank, mellow in time with age,
Softly, to be tasted again
And again.

Elizabeth H Lugo
TO MY DEAREST MOTHER

When I was small, you were my
mother.
When I was small, you loved me so
much.
When I was small, you cared and
clothed me.
When I was small, you fed and
nursed me.
When I was small, you walked me to
school.
When I was small, you sang me
songs.
When I was small, you called me
pretty.
When I was small, I laughed and
cried with you.
When I was small, we played
together.
When I was small, we watched the
raindrops.
When I was small, you took me
shopping.
When I was small, you got so sick.
When I was small, you said goodbye.
When I was small, you slept and
died.
I love you Mom!

Laurie L Bell
A WEDDING

To J. M. Dycus—I'm still loving you.

He's like a breath of fresh air
when he enters a room
And brings joy to me
like I've never known
I really don't know how to express
my feelings
except to say
If ever anyone has ever felt love
it has to be me
With you
life is a shining paradise
One I'd like to share with the world
you are my happiness
I've so desperately been seeking
and the one I've finally found
Our separate lives
have joined as one
You are the other person traveling
through life
and I am the lucky one
Who has the chance to share
the rest of our journey.
So I want to say:
Thank You
John
I'll Love You Forever
Laurie.

Angela D'Orsi
MOMMY DEAREST

I dedicate this poem for my mother, For all that happened in my life, I think that it turned out for the best . . .

Oh Mother, How Could You?
I put my trust in you!
You can't hurt me now I am gone.
There are no more tears to show the
pain,
No more lies that are in vain,
Or the laughter to brighten your day.
But yes, at times I wanted to leave,
But you kicked us out and I thought
that was mean!

There was not a day that went by,
That I did not fight or cry.
Now I am living a life so different so brandnew,
And much more happier than I did when I was with you.
I will always remember all the times we had,
But near the end they were mostly sad.
You said that you would be there,
But over this past year, you were never once there,
When I needed someone to care.
Now it's up to you to go with the flow,
But like you say life is rough,
Or was it; I guess that's tough . . .

J J Brinkman
KISMET
He's got a pot of words.
He stirs them with a knife,
Then picks the most absurd
To plot my future life.

Obese-ily, he sits
Cross-legged on his stool.
His laughter comes in fits
While sketching me a fool.

His devil's eye ignites
With venom from his mind.
His moving finger writes,
Then gooses my behind!

I once thought I would take
And hang him from a tree,
But feared a grave mistake:
The hangee might be me!

Patricia Rust
IF YOU WERE AT CALVARY
Could you have nailed the nails,
That put Christ to the tree?
Would you laugh at Him or mock Him
If you were at Calvary?

Would you thank Him, for being our sacrifice,
For setting us all free,
Would it mean so much to know
By the shed of His blood, we have liberty.

Would you beg them to stop, or keep quiet,
Because of your foolish pride,
Or would you stand back laughing,
While they pierced Him in his side?

Whether you want it, my friend
Some advice to you from me,
Each day you reject Jesus,
You nail Him deeper to the tree.

Debra A Conway
DEAR LORD
I'm a little boy, I'm only seven.
My mom tells me I'll be going to heaven

I have MS and I'm dying you see.
This will be the last letter you'll get from me.

My mom's really sad I don't know what to say
I know she'll be missing me, when I go away.

My dad left us when I was only three.
He told my mom it was because of me.

And now it is time, for me to go
The Angels are calling and telling me so

So please Dear Lord, can you try your best
To be with my mom as they put me to rest

K C Wright
AMONG FRIENDS
Everywhere I go I am among friends,
In faraway countries I am among friends,
Even in my dreams,
My friends are always there,
I move a lot,
but just to say,
I make new friends every day,
So even when I am lonely,
and even when I must pay,
I call up a special friend, and say,
"How has been your day?"

Janet D Crowson
MY HOME
My home is special
A good place to be
To feel happy or sad
Or just to feel free.

My home is full
With love in the air
The doors always open
To friends everywhere.

The walls aren't blank
They're covered it's true
Of special loved ones
And special times too.

One little sign reads
"Home is where you hang your heart"
And all my friends know
They've all played a special part.

My home is special
So special to me
'Cause it's friends who make it special
So special to me.

Dann R Ward
A WORD OF PASSAGE (A 13th Birthday)

For you Joshua on your 13th birthday.

As you enter these years
Of triumph and tears
Of bitter and sweet victories,

Come teach me, My Son
As I look from middle ground
To where I had begun
So to greet again what's before me.

We'll walk together for a ways, I'm sure
Some miles until yonder horizon's lure
Beckons you walk, then run before me.

It's okay, you know
For a son to go ahead and farther
To find his way, a new way
For a father to marvel and not feel sorrow
That sons of fathers do not stay
But go to greet their own tomorrows.

Helen Scott
WALLS
There seem to be so many walls
In my room and in the halls,
Walls that keep me in or out
As I wheel my chair about
The rest home. But the walls most real
Are those you cannot see nor feel:—
Walls of illness, walls of strain,
Frustration, loneliness and pain,
The hazy walls of failing eyes,
Of deafness and of broken ties.
But walls can never keep me bound
While my mind and faith are sound;
They fade until no longer there
When you hold my hand in prayer.

Helen Scott
WARLORDS
With living men they play, those evil ones,
Relentlessly, each day, and with their goons
They move the pawns about the muddy board
And laugh to hear them call upon the Lord.
In secret huddles, plotting cunning ways
To create new dissentions, darken days;
Undoing age-old treaties, telling lies
That fill the world with doubts and cut old ties.
They push the men about the rough terrain
While trading hills and trading back again;
And all the time they're talking, talking peace
But do not let the bloody forfeits cease.

They do not know that though they fall, good men
Beloved of God, rise seven times again,
While those who dig the pit will fall therein
And cringe before the Judge who saw their sin.

Ben Franklin II
THE WAYSIDE SHRINE
The soldier passed a Wayside Shrine,
Built in some Medieval time.
The figure of Christ crucified,
Looked down upon the trail beside.
"Take up your Cross and follow Me,"
The dying Jesus seemed to plea.
"War is man's fate," He seemed to say,
"Til at Armageddon we win the day."

A rifleman carries a heavy Cross;
His blood is shed at a frightful loss.
Death walks beside him constantly,
Who serves in the mountain infantry!
The weary trooper calmed his fear,
And shifted his heavy bandolier.
His company moved down the snowy trail,
And so ends a valiant soldier's tale.

You who may pass this Holy Place,
Tarry, and ponder a soldier's Grace.

Natalia Isabel
HER LAST TEAR

Her last breath was on this pillow I hold in my hand. As I hold this pillow, memories of the past come back. She suffered so much, she sacrificed her life to bring joy to mine.

She cried in the dark where no one could see her, no one could hear her. This pillow holds all her secrets, it knows her deepest feelings. She often wondered why I was not near, but destiny was cruel to her, happiness she did not know.

When she was dying, in agony, desolation, I was there to see her last breath, her pillow was there to comfort her, soaking her last tear, the pillow was there. She closed her eyes knowing I was there to see her departure.

She left to find a peaceful world where her tears would stop and happiness was there to embrace her fully. Her last breath was on this pillow I hold now, sharing my secrets and welcoming my tears.

Linnie Ann Hancock
THE NEW MUSTACHE
As, he walked into my room, with such dignity and grace,
I noticed something new,
'twas there upon his face!
It was right there,
'tween his nose and his chin,
As, he showed it off,
with a great big grin!
It was fuzzy like a caterpillar,
and just about as long.
'Twas this a creature, or was I wrong?
Was my "little boy," about to be grown?
I'll have to admit, he is a man at last,
'Cause, now he sports a new mustache!

Virginia Webb Langdon
MAGIC
I never cease to marvel
at the magic of the sea
as it rolls upon the shore
in endless rhapsody.

In winter its roar is mighty.
It frolics in the spring.
Whatever beat or rhythm,
it always seems to sing.

If I ever travel inland
and leave the ocean shore,
off on vagrant journeys
or in search of ancient lore,

or in a greening valley,
as I sit beneath a tree,
I'll hear the song within me
of the wild and foaming sea.

Elizabeth Jackson-Meehan
POOR LITTLE RAG DOLL
Poor little rag doll battered and beat
Little rubber legs can't stand on her feet
Poor little rag doll thrown at the wall
Trying to stand only to fall
Poor little rag doll gasping for air
You're so tiny it's really not fair
Poor little rag doll what did you do?
Only to be kicked by the monster's shoe
Poor little rag doll terrified inside
Crawling and looking for somewhere to hide
Poor little rag doll sobbing for help
Only to be beaten again with the belt
Poor little rag doll praying Mommy, please come
I wasn't bad what have I done?
Poor little rag doll promises to be good
Poor little rag doll did all that she could
Poor little rag doll can't stand anymore
Poor little rag doll closes the door

Jody Kay Rieder
FOREVER YOURS

To the men in my life who inspired me—my husband, my brother and my friends.

I am Forever Yours.
I am not afraid to let you know
I Love You,
For in many ways I do.
Although people on the outside
Could never understand
The feelings I feel for you.
For now my words are silent,
For I have naught the voice to speak.
May you Forever remember
My actions,
And Forever remember
Me.
Forever Yours . . .

Mary S Carroll
REMEDY FOR THE BLUES
One day while feeling rather blue,
With weary heart, I rummaged
through a box of odds and ends:
Recipes, poems and letters from
friends.
A picture I found of my son when
two, a card from my hubby signed, "I
love you."
And a recipe on how to make
homestyle stew.
So to the blues, I bid adieu; framed
the picture of my son when two,
Kissed the card signed, "I love you,"
and for supper that night served
homestyle stew,
A cure, "a remedy for the blues."

Mary S Carroll
PLEASE BE PATIENT, GOD ISN'T FINISHED WITH ME YET
I've been auditioned for my role in
life by God,
My script I read and try to memorize
my lines;
My contract no small print, a child
can understand 'ten rules,'
commanding love for God and all
mankind.
The scene is set, I take my place upon
the stage,
It seems I go from day to day,
unseen, unsung.

I soon grow tired and cast aside my
role "Thy will be done."
I choose an easy role, I now ad-lib. I
do it well, I win acclaim!
I hear applause!

But all things pass and soon enough
it seems all downhill!
I stand alone, afraid and nil.
I panic into prayer," my god please
come! Stand in! I'll do your will!"

In an instant he is there! He reads my
lines and now I clearly see!
This role, "Thy will be done" was
written just for me.

I take the contract penned in his own
blood,
As on the dotted line I sign,
With all my life and love,
Mary S. Carroll

Mary A Kosterman
SUNSHINE LOVER
Waking in the morning light with
sunshine
sparkling in my eyes, thinking of our
night before, and the love always
shared with the one I adore . . .
sunshinewarming me today, taking
all my cares away . . .
what is this sunshine in my life,
making me feel like a wife . . .
It's you dear, the one I love, my
sunshinelover, my husband and
friend . . .

Keith M Hall
CONTACT
Like the petals of a rose
my mind
is always spiraling outward
seeking
some vast consciousness of time
and space
into which my cosmic being
can be joined
to that larger sphere of consciousness
to which
the universe belongs
It seeks
to join with that which has been
and that
which is yet to be
without
losing sight of that
which is.

Elizabeth Miller Elfring
LANGUAGE OF DANCE
It beckons and calls with open arms,
Its eyes, watchful and sparkling,
Time is kept with unstill foot
and beats conquer still hearts.

Cheek to cheek,
Love filled glances
and sturdy leads start the motion.

Motion like swans —
Graceful, flowing, fanciful:
Take over the night under stars
and moon filled skies.

Each step carefully placed,
each revolution a joy.
Both pleasing for
participant and spectator.

On and on till dawn's dim light
they swirl and laugh.
Laughter of mind and soul.
Exhilarating for all.

It beckons and calls with open arms,
What else but the language of Dance.

Elizabeth Akins
MEMORIES OF PAUL

Paul—How can one love a man who causes so much heartache? My heart knows not why. My heart still belongs to you. Beth.

Our very first slow dance
That first passionate kiss
All these memories, Paul
That I will now miss

The day you met my children
The day that you moved in
The night you first said I love you
And now, all I have is confusion

How could you give up on love
And the many things we've shared
I guess I never realized
Just of what it is you're scared

Now all I have is long, lonely nights
That I must somehow get through
And even these are filled with pain
And memories of loving you

Are you sure you want to take that
chance
That someone better will come along
Do you really want to give up our
love
Because that choice just might prove
wrong

Louise Paolillo
INSIDE ME
Feelings that can no longer be
ignored
Words no one found meaning for
Reasons why my intentions
diminish
Sentences I never get to finish
Inner feelings that need a special
touch
Obviously asking too much.

Florence Costantino
FORESIGHT
Count your blessings
day by day,
embrace them tightly,
then tuck them away.
For on the morrow
you may find,
you'll need those blessings
you've left behind.

Debra Hutchins
THE CHRIST CHILD
He came, of His own accord to a
dying world just to afford man a
chance to live eternally.

Why did He leave His Princely
throne to bear our sins and stand
alone to face the cross and die
to set us free?

There was no man who would suffice
to make the perfect sacrifice but
the spotless Lamb unblemished
purity.

In the beginning was a word and
through His Word God sent His love,
then clothed in flesh that Word
became His Son.

Born a babe but yet when older God
set the world upon His shoulder,
the burden He was born to bear
alone.

Yes, He came in all His Majesty a
king to set His people free to
reign with Him throughout eternity.

Debra Hutchins
A SEASON'S END
As we close another season and
enter into Fall, there is a time of
reflection that touches one and
all.

There is a time of wondering as the
Summer season ends, where the Fall
season went to as Winter rushes in?

We attempt to start out planning
for the holidays to come, as we
want to make them pleasant for each
and everyone.

But, somehow our desire may be
stronger than our will, as we
struggle to get going all our
attempts seem nil.

Why is it such a problem to fix our
minds and hearts on the coming
season of turkey, pies and tarts?

After all, this time of year should
not come as a surprise, year in
year out as time goes on this time
of year arrives.

But yet as the time passes by and
as the seasons change, it seems
that we forget all the changes each
one brings.

Spring brings a time of newness, a
time to start again. Summer brings
out the child in us as we make
vacation plans.

Fall seems to hold a sadness as the
Summer season ends, it brings the
chilly weather and "dread it!"
school begins.

Oh, but how lovely the thought of a
snowy wintry day, and how the trees
do glisten when in the wind they
sway.

And how the ring of children's
laughter spreads out and fills the
air, as the thought of holidays to
come brings excitement everywhere.

So now don't you feel motivated to
start your holidays? A time of
year to celebrate, spread happiness
and cheer? Be happy as we're
coming to the best part of the
year!

Deborah Besser
A CHILD'S PRAYER

To Frankie and Brandon. May all your prayers be answered and all your dreams come true.

Show me the way cries the child
I don't know which way to go
In this grown-up world of confusion
I just seem to drift with the flow.

The world seems so scary
Where's the love I should feel
"Watch out for strangers," "Don't
Do drugs"
Will the scars ever heal?

My world can be a beautiful world
One embraced with joy and love
But it only lasts for a nighttime
A dream given to me from heaven
Above

Help me God not to lose my way
Like most grown-ups that I know
I just want my world to be
Happy and safe
With lots of room for me to
Learn and grow.

Betty Jane Roselauf
RAINBOWS FULL OF HAPPINESS

To those who give happiness to others through kindly deeds of love.

Like golden drops of sunshine
That brighten up the day,
Loving deeds and kindly thoughts
Help chase the "blues" away.

Many deeds of kindness
And acts of love that "glow"
Make us all so happy
And help our "Friendship Garden"
grow.

So when you're feeling lonely,
And need a friend or two,
Perform a deed of kindness . . .
It will return to you.

When rainbows come, the storm
clouds "flee."
Rainbows just for you and me.
Rainbows full of happiness
For everyone and all of us!

Delila Rema Hamilton
JOURNEY
Wandering, lost upon the sands
of life's unyielding stress,

The way strewn with broken dreams,
shattered on loneliness;
No landmarks raise a helping hand
to keep the heart's desire,
No banners fly from fortress high,
to make of pain a liar.

Mental shards of the living soul,
mark the Lost One's track;
The burning suns of passing time,
bar the pathways back.
Condemned to travel on and on
for all life's living years,
The future holds but trackless sands,
Wanderer, save your tears.

Ethel Corona

SAVE OUR CHILDREN

I dedicate this poem to my brother John Scholander who died at the age of sixteen years due to drugs and to all the parents who lost their children on drugs.

Please don't destroy our children
let them grow at their own pace.
Don't introduce them to harmful things
that have taken over the human race.

Don't take them down the endless road
where their world becomes a lie.
While they walk around in body
their brain will slowly die.

Don't take away their childhood
and strip them of their pride.
Please don't turn them into victims
of life's most phoney side.

I ask you on behalf, of the
parents of the universe.
To break this gain for financial gain
and the world's worst curse.

Dena M Dawson

ON YOUR OWN

It starts out so fun, so exciting
it seems —
You do things you only did in
your dreams —
But the beauty of the street is only
skin deep —
Through its cracks horrid things
do seep —
You've grown up on the outside,
that's —
what they all see, in their minds
there are no doubts —
But what they don't see is the
frightened —
child who's scared to come out—
Sometimes you want to crawl and
hide —
like you did when you were small —
But this is the way of life you chose
to live — after all —
Sometimes you watch kids at play
laughing and being free —
You shed a few tears and think to
yourself "Not long ago that was
me . . . "

Dena M Dawson

HOW LONG?

They say love is long suffering but
how long can it stand the pain?
How long can the sun hid behind
grey clouds and let them send down
rain?
How long can a heart
Watch a life fall apart?
How long can eyes try
To force themselves to watch
someone slowly die?
How do you express what you feel is
so wrong,
When your words are only
rejected so strong?
You can't help someone who won't
even try.
You can't sell someone something
that they don't want to buy.
You will give and give, soon nothing
will remain,
Tears will drop into your heart
until you drowned in pain . . .

Debra Dorrance

TRUE FRIENDS

This poem is dedicated to Arlene, a very special sister.

True friends stick with us until the
end.
True friends, our lives they always
defend.
They're always there with us to
share.
True friends open their hearts and
show that they really do care.

True friends never tear us down
Or laugh at us whenever our heads
are hanging to the ground.
True friends are always willing to
pray with us
And it's in them that we should
gratefully trust.

True friends try to understand our
particular situation.
They're always an inspiration.
True friends always say the right
thing.
True friends make our hearts sing.

True friends are of God
And they are the ones who help us to
walk the terrestrial sod.

Steven S Gilley

THE END OF THE LINE

Oh how the flame helped me ease the
feeling
Of the pain coming from behind
Esoteric memories distilled from a
bottle.
If you peer through the smoke I'm
sure you'll find,
That static discharges better
unfounded;
And two exits prove better than one.
The strain of the pain will stop real
soon
When the liquid goes over the
tongue.

Ooh somebody is knocking on the
door
Should I answer it just for fun
I realize it's only in my head
As I drink from my glass gun.

And the strain beckons with every
flick of the bic
But insanity numbs me to the bone.
Would you turn out the lights and
exit stage left?
So I could spend my ovation alone.
I must defect to abandon the misery
I need an escape for it won't abstain
I falter as I take the hard way out
The remedy is left up to the aim

It's three in the morning and I'm
alone once more
But what do you expect from a
bugger?
It will always bleed darkest before
the dawn
When the drip in my head is like no
other.

I'm saved as my smile's torn to a
frown
And loneliness flows from my eye.
My wall gets wet and my guilt reigns
down.
There's always peace when you're
this high
On the last train at the "End of the
Line."

Debra Golden

A REFLECTION

My life is like
A rainbow extending
Across the blue wide
Sky blending an array
Of colors of yellow, blue,
Red and orange.

It dips faraway in
The ocean blending
With its white caps
Of foamy waves and
Dipping into the depths
Of the ocean.

As the tide ebbs
And flows, so does
My life; washing
Up upon the sandy
Shore!

Free for a child
To build sand castles
As huge as can be!

Standing by the shore,
Looking within, I reflect
As though through a mirror
Like a reflection, I have
Looked think what my
Life has been and meant to me.

David W Hoff

PLEDGE OF LOVE

To My Dearest Darling Wife.

I'll walk with you each Sunday
morning, I'll walk with you my
whole life through.

Through fields of roses and of
thorns, I'll walk with you my
Love not worn.

I knew not love on the day
we met, words came hard as
confussed I sat.

I wondered of such feelings,
should I fret?, for of me love
did beset.

Your eyes told me not to despair
for the feelings I had you too
did share.

I learned of Love on that special
day and though the years have
passed away, forever with you
my love will stay

Isabel Kent

FRIENDSHIP

To all my friends, past and present, for their steadfast loyalty through the years!

A friend is someone with whom you
share,
All of your joys and all of your cares;
Someone with whom you laugh and
cry,
When the time comes, it's hard to say
good-bye!

Time passes so quickly for all of us,
Some people say, "What's all the
fuss?"
The memories are there throughout
your life,
Of your High School Days both the
joy and the strife!

We have come together one last time,
To share the Eucharist, the Bread and
the Wine;
In the coming years whenever our
paths will cross,
We'll remember our Baccalaureate
and feel some loss;
Of the carefree days when our
worries were few,
When a date for the prom, was an
important event for you!

Tonight we bid farewell to all of you,
We wish you luck—may your every
dream come true;
When we meet again along the way,
Remember this night, smile, and say,
"HI FRIEND"

Helen L Kuntz

I WANT TO WRITE

Dedicated to Mr. and Mrs. George W. Baldwin, Paternal grandparents, Mr. and Mrs. George C. Leedy, Parents.

I want to write so I can
Become a small child again
And live in fantasyland,
And ride my rockinghorse to town,
Play and converse with toys I've
found,
To be always up and never down!

I want to rewrite the lines
With ruffles and valentines,
Lace, and rainbows and
sunshine,
To live by the sea and build clay
Castles, high in the sky, all day,
And sail my boat on the bay,

With a prince I want to ride,
Carefree, in dreamland abide,
Where happiness, like the tide,
Comes to meet me in the early morn,
Caresses, frolicks, and is worn,
And at night, in my dreams, is
reborn!

Helen L Kuntz

PEACE IN THE VALLEY

There's peace in the valley
of the fern and evergreen
When winter yields to spring,
The glades are clean and green,
And nesting birds begin to sing,
And flowers polkadot the dale.

There's peace in the valley
of the fern and evergreen,
Earth warms, new life appears,
Exhilarant, noisy, and serene,
Heralding summer in the valley
of the fern and evergreen.

There's peace in the valley
of the fern and evergreen,
Gone is the storm of yesterday,
with renewed beauty of terrain,
There's peace in the valley
of the fern and evergreen.

Mary Helen Oakley

GOD GAVE ME

Dedicated to my father, William Henry Miller. Born: March 13, 1913; Died: April 7, 1990.

Life could soon be over,
At the age of forty, for me,
Because I found out yesterday,

That soon, I might not see,
God gave me, this wonderful
gift of sight to see.

For almost forty years,
It's been a constant
companion to me.
But now he may have to
take away.
This gift, I've had so long
you see,

So thank you God,
for letting me have
this great power to see.

Murrel O Short Jr

MY HOME — THE SEA

Sailing across the wildest sea or
ocean,
Turmoils, I'll face with desperate
devotion;
Conquering whatever it is that
assaults me,
While taking care of my home – the
sea.

Beauty so some say, is only skin
deep,
But his you won't find true with
taking a little peep,
Below the surface of the ocean
waters blue,
There lies a beauty, unknown to most
of you;

Before being touched by man's
beastly hand,
It shined like crystals were buried in
the sand;
Beauty you'll find there as deep as
you wish;
In the rocks, the seaweeds, and even
the fish;

I'll fight for its beauty, and save it I
will;
This beauty man's ugliness shall
never kill;
Man has polluted Paris, and man has
polluted Rome,
But if it means my death, man will
not pollute my home;

The sea is my home and free it shall
be,
Of all the demon hands destroying
today's beauty.

Lois (Loy)

REACH OUT AND TOUCH SOMEONE

Dedicated to: Mynor–Deane, Aisha & V. Omar Boland – my adorable children. Also to a very special person who came into my life and made me realise just how totally one can love another – Mansel Lewin.

The cold hard hands of reality
grasped the frightened heart
With thoughts of how everything
would surely fall apart;
Feelings of uncertainty gnawed at the
fibre of every nerve
And no longer was the need or
urgency there to serve.

Drained of all emotions that the mind
could muster
Sad and deadened longings gathered
in a cluster;
Bent beneath the load of such grief
and pain
With hope so far away, never it seem
to come again.

A gentle whisper, a soft, and almost
thereal call
Sent the shattering shrills of agony in
such appall;
The heart so saddened, lost and
lonely still
Reaches out for the one true joy that
keeps the will.

The serenity with which such
outreach is received
Leaves much to be accepted when
it's believed;
In love and courage give a hand to
someone now
Reach out and touch, and give your
answer low.

There's always someone near who
needs a hand
To give that added strength it takes to
stand;
If only in our hearts we could search
deep
And awake those given strengths that
in us sleep.

Doris M Carlton

MEMORIES

To all my family.

Sweet of face silver hair
Back forth in her rocking chair
Family album in her lap
Open to a day long past
Tear stained face now relaxed
Softly smiles begin to show
Of whom is she thinking I do not
know
Graduation picture of a lovely young
girl,
and a handsome boy
my grandfather, she said with a smile
A newlywed couple then a babe in
arms
Then a family of four.
Her eyes are closed, memories are
hers alone
Some she cannot share.

Doris M Carlton

LOVE SONG

Give me a love song
Give me a true song
And someone to share
Give me a blue song
And someone that's true
Give me a fun song
That brings me laughter
When life gets hard
Give me a good song
As strong as the bonds that tie
Oh give me a love song
That I can sing all day
And a night song
That will carry me through
The long evening hours
When I am not with you
Oh give me a love song to share.

Doris M Carlton

I GOT MARRIED AND HAD A KID

I got married and had a kid
This would be easy I said
But he hollered all night through
Good Lord what will I do
We made it through the first five
years
He will outgrow all this I said.
Finally he went to school, now I'll
have time to myself I said
But baseball was his game and I got
to drive the team around
I'm proud he is so smart and he will
outgrow this I thought.
Now he has a girl and is out on a date
I'm walking the floor, the clock says
he is late
He will outgrow this and I'll have
time for myself I said.
He got married with my blessing and
soon had a kid
He is off for the weekend and having
fun
And Grandma is still happily walking
the floor
Now I don't remember what I said

Douglas Cann

A MOMENT IN SPRING

I wish to dedicate my work to God. He gave me the talent to think of and to put down on paper these thoughts.

The breeze whistles through my hair
I have no fear
Not one single care
I sit on the stoop
A bird does a loop de loop
The kids walk to the park to shoot
some hoops.
The grass tingles in the breeze
I hear Robin sneeze
Oh what a tease.
I feel the breeze.

Douglas Cann

I LONG

I'm king of kings,
Jesus sings,
The word of God is spoken,
I believe this is the truth,
Although no actual proof,
My faith is strong,
As I long
For the comfort of God,
Although a peasant,
This peaceful feeling I feel,
Is very pleasant,
His eyes heavenly blue,
His story O so very true
I thank him from the bottom of my
heart,
  Time to depart.

Douglas Cann

THE VILLAGE

Sippin' beer in the village
People walkin'
People talkin'
What a place
Feel like I'm in outer space.
People are real.
People are relaxed.
It's the real deal.
What a place.
Things are happening.
Vibes are cool.
What a great place.
People in motion.
Things are happening.
It's great.
It's the real deal.
What a feeling.
Try it some time.
It's on line.
It's happening.
It's bussling.
It's the real deal
THE VILLAGE.

Douglas Cann

PEACE & LOVE

The color doesn't matter,
Just the pitter patter,
We all make up the batter,
N.Y.C. needs oneness,
So God doesn't shun us,
No matter what the color,
Just love her,
The city,
The neighbor,
The color,
Just love them,
The city,
Its people!

Rachel Bennett

LOVE

The most precious gift,
I am told,
Is all the Love
The heart can hold.

I give it to you;
you give it to me –
There's enough for the world,
and the gift is free.

Will you take my love –
More precious than gold?
It's the finest gift
That the heart can hold.

Sarah M Adams–Harris

ACHIEVEMENT

It matters not
Our worldly acclaim
'Ere it be money or fame
What matters <u>most</u>
In every way
How did we treat out
  fellowman
Today and Yesterday?

Sarah M Adams–Harris

MY COUNTRY

Have you ever pondered
As you rushed through the day
What kind of country
Is our U.S. of <u>A</u>.
From the President's seat
To the Statue of <u>Liberty</u>
Is my Country <u>better or worse</u>
Because of <u>me</u>?

Kathy Stout

TOGETHER FOREVER

We may not keep in touch,
  but our hearts will never forget the
  tenderness we felt.
At times we lose sight of our goals . .
  but the stars we'll not stop
  reaching for.
And when their brightness makes our
eyes water
  and we lose sight of them,
the desire burns strong in our hearts.
Deep down we'll always remember,
  no matter how rough the road gets.
If we don't follow our hearts,
  we may get lost on that winding
  road.
And when I get led astray,
  I can follow your smile
    that lingers in the stars . . .
I know I'll never be alone
  because you'll always be in my
  heart.

Alma Ray Ferris

A LITTLE LOVE

Everyone knows a little love
Can brighten the road
Everyone knows a little love
Can lighten the load.
A kiss, a tender touch
Can do so much to cheer you on your
way,
Just the memory of those little signs,
of love
Can bring you a happier day.
  Some people yearn for wealth
  alone
  They think that is the best
  But if you have love
  You have a goldmine all your own
  And you are truly blest!

Vicki J Motley
MOTHER . . .
Mother, you're an artist
of the truest sort,
painting a life of wisdom,
love and good report.
On the canvas of my heart
I can see the picture clearly.
You're a master at the art of giving.
That's why I love you dearly.

Beckie A Miller
FAMILY
Love and pain,
Happiness and rain.
Joy and breath,
Life and death.
Comfort and warmth, anger
and trust. All are a must
to the scheme of things.
All that family brings.
Without we are lost as waves
on a sea tossed.
Should we be without love
and family and all that
it encompasses. We would
be without life and all
that it surpasses. For the
love that family brings
would not be without these
other things:
Love and pain,
Happiness and rain
Joy and breath
Life and death!

Ethan Engdahl
ODE TO THE WILD FLOWERS
O, vast fields of wondrous wild flowers,
nestled in the lush green valleys of the country side,
Such pleasure do you give the naked eyes.

Your delicate array of fine colors dance in the sunlight
and quiet one's soul in the twilight.

O, how your multitude of pastel shades
glitter in the first morning's dew,
allowing one's mind
to escape into a world filled with bliss and peace.

Yellow and gold blossoms dispel your riches,
continuous as the stars do shine,
Riches for us only to find.

O, how your petals soft and kind cradle the young bee,
to give him strength through nectar sweet.

Soft gentle breezes billow your seeds of fruit into the air,
only to spread them here and there.

Long may your perfume fragrances
enhance our senses,
Just as your beauty overwhelms our comprehension.

Your woven carpet of Forget–Me–Knots and Baby's Breath
heighten my measures to life's many pleasures.

O, that you may live forever
Your simplicity I will always treasure.

Becky Barnhouse
REALITY
Sometimes things are just dreams,
Some are just screams.
You're sometimes put through pain,
even though you have nothing to gain.

Many just lead you on,
even though you may not be strong.

Don't let them slip away,
if you love them in a special way.

Many don't like to talk about it,
Some must talk about it.

You may not love me,
But I will always love you.

David E Jusczak
BEAUTY GROWS WITH YEARS
" . . . to you, Mother, with all my love . . . and to your mother."

I've never known a woman like you
You've built my dreams and you'll see them through
You've wiped my tears in times of pain
Every time I've stumbled, you've picked me up again
There's a light that shines around you, it blinds my eyes
You're the truth behind all tomorrow's lies

I've felt your touch, it heals my wounds
You've given me life, the sun, stars, and moon
When everyone else had led me astray
You were always the light that led my way
What your voice can't say, your eyes may reveal
But your words and your wisdom are what make it all real
You've warmed my heart and you've toughened my hide
You've given me memories that I cherish deep inside

So whether the candles keep burning or are blown away
The light shines brighter with each passing day
Through all the laughter and all the tears
Still your beauty grows with years

David E Jusczak
WHILE LOVE IS AWAY
"To the heartbeats that never really died. This is your song . . . and I want you to remember me."

A soft, wispy breeze blows through the door
Cashmere and rose petals scatter the floor
The walls are adorned with paintings and tapestry
Outside your window: the deep, dark sea

The bedposts and vanity, draped in lace and chiffon
Threadbare dolls, all tattered and torn
Crystals and pearls cover the bureau
The flames of the candles reflect in the mirror
Velvet and satin in the bed where you lay
To keep you warm . . . while love is away

The scent of your perfume lingers in the room
Upon the piano, white roses in bloom
Diamonds in a jewel box, fit for a queen
A living fantasy, every man's dream

Your music plays faintly in time with the waves
You lay low in your silence, rendering pain
The moon casts shadows in every corner
Silhouettes of the ghosts that your memory endures
You wait by the window for your ship to sail in
You are the softness felt by the wind
You hide in your room through each passing day
It secures your heart . . . while love is away

David E Jusczak
GLITTER AND GOLD
Thank you to all my family and friends; for their words, wisdom, and inspiration . . . and to Stevie, for your beauty and your beast. May you all find your "glitter and gold."

You spin yourself around like some lost little dancer
You'd like to stop for a moment, but you don't want to chance it
Your heart and your soul are open like a book
You gave it all away, but nothing that they took
Your life has been lonely, yet you'll let no one in
You can't bear to lose, but you just can't win
Your music is fading, your words are unclear
Your voice becomes shaky, and the love disappears
So you step to the other side, where you often go
That little piece of Heaven
Your Glitter and Gold
Your eyes may be closed, but falling tears still flow
You say it's all over, but you just can't let go
You hide all the hurt, but you still feel the pain
You wish you could start all over again
The hope that was there has long been gone
You just can't help but to carry on
Trying to hold on to what's left of your dreams
Nothing in your life has been as it seemed
When you finally reach the end of the road
I hope that you'll find all
Glitter and Gold

Millicent Grace Anderson
I AM
In dedication to the spirit of the child. It is for you I tell my story.

I am who I am.
There's no other me.
So see me as I am,
Not who you want to see.

I am who I am.
And before this is complete,
I'll give it to you straight –
I am unique!

Penne Lou Riffle
MY FRIEND
I have been blessed with a remarkable friend,
She and I are much the same, but yet different,
Our friendship is limitless and has no end.
Our trust, respect and love are always apparent.

We share a friendship that is strong and true,
There isn't another with which it would compare.
Without it, I am not sure what I would do.
Our friendship is so uncommon and rare.

Talking to her can make my day brighten,
We can sense each other's feelings and moods,
I can feel the tension ease and lighten.
And be gone when the conversation
concludes.

I do not have to see her every day,
To know that this is a friendship like no other,
It will last even if we go in separate ways.
For the friend I speak of is, my mother.

Arvis Tyson–Ashitey

Arvis Tyson–Ashitey
I'M BLESSED
This dedication is made to everyone who sometimes find it difficult to count their blessings.

If I am blind and cannot see,
I know that GOD will lead me.
I'm blessed!
If I don't have furniture in my house,
Yet GOD puts food in my mouth
I'm blessed!
If I lose my job and do not have money,
GOD's Word is my milk and honey.
I'm blessed!
If I weigh 500 pounds and cannot get around,
if everyone tells me I look like a clown,
I will not allow anyone to put me down.
I'm blessed!
If I only have one dress and one pair shoes,
I know as long as I have GOD I cannot lose.
I'm blessed!

Dollie Davis
ROMEO AND JULIET

To Greg, my Romeo.

Their eyes met and they looked deep into the other's soul and saw
the flames of emotion burning brightly within each other.

His hand so strong and powerful, gently touched her satin like cheek,
he leaned closer and his warm moist lips met hers in a peaceful kiss.

They were so close that she felt his heart throb as he softly
caressed her shoulder and slowly kissed her neck.

With each embrace she felt her deepest emotions untie themselves
from her heart and become one with his.

The bond their hearts had created could be broken by nothing, for
they were in love.

E Grace Springer
LIGHT IN THE SKY

There is a light in the sky if you only raise
Your eyes and believe.

The light is put in the sky by Jesus to light
The road along the way.

If you fall along the wayside all you have to
do is to lift your hands and pray.
Jesus – will then lead the way

Jesus fed the multitude by the sea.
He prayed
The Garden of Gethsemane.
And He prayed
in the mountains and He walked upon the
Waters of the Sea of Galilee.

Jesus paved this road with His blood the day
He walked it to Calvary and died on
The cross for you and me.

Teena Major
THE BEACH

From the shimmer off the water I see the bright moon beam,
And scenes of past days flash by like an old and treasured dream.

As I walk along the water and it splashes round my feet,
It sends a shiver up my back as my heart then skips a beat.

A gust of wind passes through my hair and a tear trickles down my face.
I yearn for the feeling of you near and the touch of your embrace.

As the cool air stings my skin I care for nothing much,
Then your lips pressed next to mine and feel of your gentle touch.

Such words and feelings I find hard to let out,
So they're left for only the Beach and I to know about.

Benjamin Seaton
BOBBY

I dedicate this poem to my daughter "Robin."

Bobby was the boy she loved,
he was all that she thought of,
every single day, and every night.
One look from him, would make her sigh,
she thought that she, would surely die,
the first time, that Bobby held her tight.

On Friday night, she would go,
with Bobby to the Drive–Inn show,
but little, of the picture would they see.

Bobby would kiss, her lips and then,
they'd touch a lot, and kiss again,
At Drive–Inns, that's the way, that it should be.

All the windows, would fill up with steam,
she thought, that is was all a dream,
but she hoped, that she would dream, a whole lot more.

As the night, came to a close,
she'd try and strike, her most famous pose,
as Bobby, kissed her good–night, at her door.

Eleanor Pullen
FORGIVENESS

Do you see things in black and white and with a touch of gray?

Or do you only see things as clear as night and day?

Well for you my dear friend I do pray.

For as we travel life's rocky road
allowances must be made.
Forgiveness must be given if we are to join in God's parade.

Charles M Roberts
HAPPINESS

I sought for happiness
Among the sun and stars
Where the wild seas roll
I found it not.
As mute I stood–far overwhelmed
My soul
But when I shared with
One in need
I found happiness indeed

Robert J Williams
HILL TALK

For Monica.

From her diary:
"There was never such screaming,
Washing, tearing, and milling
About our shack as when streaming
From the door went those too willing
To pray after a Saturday killing.

"Monday they'd meander (mean again)
So far from the furrows and the fence,
You'd wonder if you didn't know your men
Whether they'd burn a neighbor's thatch
Today, or merely mow his garden patch.

"Feudin's quite an excitin' thing;
Been enjoyin' it for years and years;
Darndest thing to hear us burn and sing—
And Granpa'd clip our ears
If he ever saw us shed some tears."

From her epitaph:
"Measure your success
Not by how many times you touch
The fountain and the Holy Grail:
You'll die dreaming for so much.
Settle for a spring and a pail
And you'll hardly feel you fail."

Sister Barbara Mary Lanham OSF
WINTER'S FOG

This poem is dedicated to Sister Mary Ann Minor, O.S.F. in remembrance of her election as Provincial Superior of the American Province of THE HOSPITAL SISTERS OF THE THIRD ORDER REGULAR OF ST. FRANCIS, SPRINGFIELD, IL.

Fog embraces earth,
Cleaving to rocks, valleys, hills;
Nourishing all life.
Gloom penetrates all creatures
Who wander life's broken paths.

Piercing misty air,
Sun's glimmering, playful rays
Show us life's treasures.
Only Yahweh can withstand
Full brilliance, radiant Sun!

Drink in all Beauty
Yahweh chooses to show you.
Yielding, gentle Breeze
Will lighten weary footsteps
Mixing Seasons, graceful Song!

Tanka

Clynis A Benson
WORDS–WORDS

Words are avenues upon which we express our thought.
Unless combined in proper sequence come to nought.
In ages past, great men of old in battle fought
With words to gain the things they sought.
But I, not like man of old, come distraught
To find correct words to voice my thought!
An uttered word, incorrectly caught,
Could easily be the one to thwart
My musing, in which I ought
To strive the harder to extend my thought!

Frances Kay Mendez
TELL ME YOU LOVE ME

Tell me
You
Love me
With Touch
Taste
Smell
Tell me you love me
I'll know this very
Well
Don't play on my
Emotions
Love is the potion
Tell me you LOVE ME
Please tell me NOW

S Larissa Petrella
EMPTY MOONLIGHT

To, Jason J. H. Williams
With all my Love.

A kiss of feathered light,
Bestowed upon my heart,
Eclipsing lonely darkness,
With a halo of dreamy pastels,
Bringing forth warmth,
Like affectionate shadows dancing,
In the background,
And in the foreground.
A singing, soaring wind,
Howls through my soul,
Like a lonely wolf,
Hungering for love.
He is howling to the empty moonlight,
Empty now because,
It has been preparing,
For a symphony of song and fever,
To fill its vacant depth.

Sean D Brown
LOVE

There's something in school
That you cannot learn,

That love is powerful
And has to be earned.

Eva M Roy
BELIEVE IN THYSELF

Only you can believe in thyself
When all else fails. It is up to you
To put realism upon the shelf
And look at it and study the clue.
Only you can come to grips with thyself
When no one else can. It is the truth
To whatever the matter is and to tell yourself
That you believe, than for you to get proof.
Only you can look up and see the sky
Even when it is cloudy and dark
Upon the area. It is the way and the why
That comes in belief, in thyself
When all else fails. I know, I believe in myself.

Carlota Constantine
I DO NOT PRAISE BUT SEE . . .

I do not praise
Your accents
Precise and neat,
Clipp'd like a New England hedge.

I do not praise
Your aspect or attire
Austere in every pleat,
Such is the Puritan's conceit.

I do not praise
Your ecstasy for sports
Favouring "football" as a cause;
Does not a tackler oppose
Fatigue's display?

I do not praise but see
Your temperate wisdom
And your love for
The explicit word.

So vividly remembered
When the page is turned.

George A Cordner
AS SLEEP FADES ! !

To the world community with love, my wife Patsy, daughter Desiree, and my heart George Jr. Thanks Lou! One Love! George.

As sleep fades I'm awake, in shades of figures as thoughts sail, Oh sleep
Faded to a vivid scene of life's seeming realities
Oh ! ! A dream of peoples, and portraits of times
Action of their scenes as sleep fades and rhymes

As sleep fades, awake to a moment of truth
Tranquil in you with love, inner love

with time, and place
A vehicle turning today's version in circles from youth
To figures of today, as sleep fades its aging face

When sleep fades, minutes! moments! Hours it seem
A world of realities to be reflections of personalities, and themes
Children awake, thinking in a being of today's scenes
To be of service, and experience to their dreams, as sleep fades

As sleep fades! Pursued in moments
To travel, with time, and mused with intent
With opened eyes, reflecting nature rhymes
In histories of life's defined minds, as sleep fades!
Am I awake in time? In time! In time! In time!!

Camellia Lovegrove
A FATHER'S PRAYER TO GOD
The following thoughts came to me while thinking about how hard my husband has worked these many years. How his main concern was to provide for his wife and son. I then wondered what is must be like to be a man, and what he might think about . . . Heaven can wait, there's still much to be done. So many good lessons to teach to my son. The pleasures and secrets to share with my wife. Dear God, please be patient, let me live a long life. All the cities and meadows I need to explore. Dear God, let me live many years more. I know to you God, I'm just a dot on this earth, but Dear God to my family, I have a great worth.

Christina Marie Rose
DEATH

Dedicated to my brother, John Stephen Rose, who is sadly missed by all his loved ones.

Death is so full of sadness and so very much painful for us, who have lost a loved one.
But for this loved one it is a time so beautiful and happy.
For he gets to meet his Mighty Creator
and feel no pain in his heart.
He waits and longs for his loved ones below to join him.
But why can't his loved ones below understand
that he is happy and wishes not to return to Earth but stay in heaven with God his Mighty Creator.

Christina Marie Rose
TOMORROW & YESTERDAY
Always a problem, a crisis to face.
It feels as though tomorrow will never arrive.
Will I make it?
Will I survive?
Tomorrow's here and look I made it through yesterday.
The pain still lingers.
The memories strong.
Yet I believe my life will proceed.
I will never run out of tomorrows to long for.
Yesterdays remain.

Teresa E Dunn
DREAMS
Growing up in times today
Means whatever come what may
For every road in life you may choose
It's still a gamble, the flip of a coin, a chance for each that you may lose
But with love in your heart and faith deep inside
Within you forever a small child filled with
dreams will abide

Dreams of yesterday seem to find their way
To apply themselves in the life I lead today
For if I were a princess in a castle so very fair
I could not be happier I would not even dare
Or if I were just a pauper with just a piece of bread
I'd look to God in quiet prayer and simply bow my head
I have my dreams like others you see
But put them in perspective, the prince is my
husband the princess is me
We have a family that will live happily ever after
Just as long as we hold it together and not turn
it to disaster

Yes our lives are just those fairy tales
We've heard a hundred times
But change the characters and start to juggle
a few but simple lines
So look at life and keep your dreams it's only
what you make it
You cannot live your life exactly as the
tales may often say
But you can write your own fairy tale with
dreams to be continued from day to passing day!

Jennifer Woodrum
COME . . .
Come with me to this place
Where together we can race
Where the wind whistles your favorite song
Where everything is right
And nothing is wrong
Where the sun always sends its light
To the flowers that sway,
Everyday

Come to where there is no rain
And no one goes through any pain
Where dogs never bite
And tigers never fight
Where trees reach to the sky
And all of us could fly

Come to where waterfalls run across the land
Where you can walk across golden sand
Where there is no hate
And love is the best thing to create

Come with me to this place
Where together we can race

Dyanna L Young
UNVEILED
Slip under native flames
The orchard is gone,
Thorns have come
The harvest is no more,
Secrets in the trunk — Slowly opening,

Snow in a swirl of flight.

I'm chilled inside naked lakes
As mirrors unfurl a reflection
Swirling around an eye unseen,

My crystal bog unknown
I whisper in a shiver
Alone in silver fog.

Daybreak shatters the night's glass
A shudder in life, for dreams forgotten
As ashes turn to vines
Choking, twisting, drowning,
Intertwining my soul
In a web of dank weeds oozing,
The knife cuts and hope returns.
Can I move upward and become
A twig again?

Marjorie E Deschenes
ETHEREALITY
Surrounding secrecy. Permeating,
Dynamic force of latent energies.
Laboring undiscernibly with gentle,
primistic, simplistic ease.
What is this–

invisible stuff,
gently interspersed throughout the illiterate zephyr. Hovering above, then nestling within the mountainous
terrain. Expressively unfailing, through all of life it playfully entertains.
What is this–

invisible stuff,
majestic, unfolding, from ideation to creation. Extravagant displays, are at last visualized. With capricious involvement and chameleonic ways, it
changes back to its original, transient guise.
What is This?

Jenny Merth
WHARF
The scent of the salt air tingles my nose
At the ocean, on a cool crisp morn
The sound of crashing waves echo in my ears
The color of the deep blue water calms me
The warm wet sand squishes between my toes
The scene imprints my thoughts

The kiss of the salt wind
The curve of a white sail
As a sailboat pulls into port
And the whisper of rumbling, tumbling
Rolls of thunder in the distance
The flashing lightning blinds me
It's as though I'm witnessing a secret occurrence
. . . These are part of life at the wharf

Vicki D Ford
THE GIFT OF RAIN

This poem is dedicated to Ascension, my mother.

The Rain came pouring down today.
And it completely soaked the ground.

I can smell the sweet fresh air all around.
I know, I'm not the only one enjoying this; Because I can hear, the birds chirping from about.

It's a great feeling, If you sit in silence, and listen to these things, given to us free, from heaven above.

It's getting close to Spring, and most of the flowers are in full bloom.

Oh! "The Gift Of Rain," How much happiness it brings. It seems to cleanse the Earth's atmosphere.

Nature has its way of changing the seasons; Like people strive to change, and to fulfill their dreams.

Wendy Dose
WHY?

I would like to dedicate this poem to my great-grandfather.

He is gone.
Oh, why did God have to take him?
Once here and now,
He is gone.
As you can see – I miss him so!
With no more chances to tell him . . .
He is gone.
Oh, why did God have to take him?

Erica M Davis
TEARS FROM AFAR
There's a house across the field,
Each movement I can see,
And in this house, the shade of grey,
There lives the one for me.

His eyes the color of the wildest sea,
His smile a whiteness glow,
His heart the size of Africa,
His shyness no one knows,
His pride won't let him love me,
His soul won't make him mine,
The warmth he brings won't be forgotten,
His spirit's afloat in time,
His mind knows not the truth of love,
Which someday he will find.

Traci Sidelinger
DREAMS
Dreams are only a state of mind,
is what a lot of people find.
Other people find out still,
dreams are only make believe,
they're not real.
Dreams to still others are the only way,
to find out what will be done that day.
Dreams to many more are only fantasies,
and to those people, those fantasies please.
Good dreams and bad dreams do occur,
like ones that will be and ones that were.
There are dreams of what might and might not be,
like the dream of traveling across the sea.
Dreams make people think and wonder,
they make them realize what's deep down under.
Even though scientists have found some clues,
people still have their own different views.
"Why do we dream?" Some people ask.

Maybe it's to reveal what's under their mask.

Marvierene Lusk Kelley
ONE SWEET BOY, ONE PRECIOUS GIRL

I dedicate this poem to my son Allen Wade Kelley and my daughter Donna Gwen Kelley Howard.

One set of grey eyes, one set of green,
Their light sweet breath and soft sweet touch, like velvet
Starlight swirls.
One sweet boy one precious girl.
You forever have my love
You forever hold my life.
Do not forget me when you are grown.
Please do not leave me when I am old

Marvierene Lusk Kelley
AND I DREAMED

I dedicate this poem to my sister, Virginia Lusk Parker, your dream will come true and your life will be your dream.

And I dreamed all I could see would be mine,
Land, Where there is peace and tranquility.
Space, where I and mine could fill could tread
Never to fear or take flight.
Where there is only happiness in life's darkest night

Sharon Lisee
ECHOES
Echoes in the mind,
Memories of every kind.
So many reflections of the past,
Surely this cannot last.
Friendships, lovers all long gone,
Reflecting the lyric of so many a song.
Haunted by shadows of mistakes,
Mirrored upon the lake.
Laughter and tears,
Covering layers of fears.
Etchings in the sands of time,
Some how it all seems such a crime.
Echoes in the mind,
Memories of every kind.

D L Lipe
YESTERDAY'S SONG
Looking back into the past I find notes and pictures of people I once knew.
I hold in my heart all the memories of things we used to do.
Somehow I wish I could go back in time, and just for a moment,
Make those treasured days, once again mine.
Then I realize, as I wipe the tears from my eyes, those days belong to me.
Like the wind memories are free.
So with my yesterday's agenda all tucked away,
I head out into the world for another day.
Yesterday will never be forgotten:
This is something I could never do.
To the memories of yesterday we must all be true.
So I hold to them tight as I keep moving along.
Knowing now that tomorrow, today will be yesterday's song

Peganne
MY RIVER
Like the river keeps on flowing
So is our friendship forever growing

The beauty of it all is forever present
In all seasons smiles looks and senses

It's difficult to find beginning or end
The river and you are both a dear friend

Always there to sail me away
To smile be happy and share sunny days

Both are gifts from heaven
The time we share is oh so pleasant

Sometimes we tumble over stones
But we stand by each other we're never alone

You are my river and should you stop flowing
My life would go dry and I would stop growing

The river of my heart shall never lessen
For you my love are my river of blessing

Cindy Stump
TRY TO UNDERSTAND

To Eric Sheets and Pam Stump, They are the inspiration of my poetry. May they always know that I love them.

I face each day I live.
taunted with my fears.
Confused with unbelief,
Fighting back my tears.

I hoped you told me lies,
throwing them away.
I just refused to hear,
the truth came to stay.

You can't return my heart,
when I release your hand.
You can't return my love,
Try to understand.

Albert C Schumacher
THINKS AND THOUGHTS

This poem is dedicated to Edna my darling wife.

Thinks and thoughts are what we say all the time,
but it is the do's and don'ts that makes the dime.
The media is great with this expression,
thinks and thoughts and then the truth is depression.
Half truths are stated so many times,
it is the easy way out and how many minds it grinds,
how many hearts it breaks in its wake.
Thinks and thoughts are disguising and fake.
The whole world loves news be it good or bad,
using thinks and thoughts can make a lot of people sad.
A more positive approach can be achieved and said,
with just a little more patience thinks and thoughts would be dead.
More hearts would be glad and joy to more people
more truth achieved and spread like a ripple.
Even the bad news would be easier to accept.
Leaving out thinks and thoughts causes less anguish and regrets.
Thinks and thoughts have been around
a long time with a questionable winner.
They will continue to be used by all, spring, summer, fall and winter.

Ken Quarles
BIRDS

To my aunt, Martha Boutwell, for getting me interested in Birds.

Birds are marvelous creatures.
Their beaks, their wings, and many-a-feather
Are all among their handy features
That help them in any kind of weather.

The male is full of color,
Which is strange, because usually
It's the female, which in this case is duller.
The reason is to protect the nest and family.

In many sizes their eggs are in.
From the hummingbird's, which is small,
To the middle-sized egg of the chicken,
To the ostrich's, the largest of all.

All over can nests be found.
In the trees or on the ground.
Whether in a cliff or in a barn,
A nest may be made of sticks and yarn.

Birds come from many locations.
Many countries, many nations,
From the north or the south,
Whether the east or west,
Not one place is the ONLY best.

Mrs Sonya T Seymour
A SONG TO SING
We have a song that we must sing
A cross to bear, a pledge to bring.
A burden heavy on our hearts
A secret wish we must impart.

To those that are outside of Christ
To those who do not know the price
For only He can clear our slates
And show us clearly of our fates.

And if our song can take some part
In touching some poor loved one's heart
Then the promise of a life secure
Will renew in us again once more.

Christine Ynocencio
YOUR FLOWER
You are the sun,
I am your flower.
A seed embedded in your earth,
Your rays upon me;
I feel your warmth.

My small stem enters the world.
I grow taller.
I take form;
My leaves grow,
My petals bloom.
What type of flower have I become?
No, not a rose.
I am a daisy, a simple flower.
My stem long and green.
My petals white.

I also have something more.
Something that no other flower has.
(Not even a rose.)
For I have a part of you;

A small bright sun.
This I keep in the center of me.
And it makes me brighter than any other flower.

Thank you mom.

Denise Myers
A CHILD'S SURVIVAL
I'm sorry, sorry, sorry.
That's what I used to have to say.
I had to be sorry for everything.

They almost destroyed my body, mind, and spirit,
But I fooled them, fooled them all!

I went along with all they said. I did as I was told.
If not surely I'd be dead.

But just when they thought the spirit they had broken,
I sent for recruits to help in the mission.

I fooled them all, they cannot break me,
'Cause if one soldier hurts, I sent in another.

And so the war continues. But . . .
Let them think that they have won,
That I am broken, hungry, cold, and frightened.

Let them think that I am one,
So they do not know how strong I am.

That's the strategy I used in my war,
And I fooled them all,
They never got my soul.

AND I'M NOT SORRY ANY-MORE!

Betty A McCoy Dreher
OLD ROVER—GRANDPA AND ME
Grandpa took his Grandson's hand
Would you take a walk with me?
While Grandma is getting her housework done
We'll see what we can see.

He called Old Rover from his bed
"Come along"— said he
Let's take a walk along the creek
And see what there might be.

We walked along—the rumbling creek
While looking o'er the land
We listened to the waters flow
While walking hand in hand.

We watched the minnows swimming by
Darting to and fro
A little frog jumped from the bank
Not knowing where to go.

The flowers were blooming all around
Many colors among the green
We tossed some pebbles in the creek
And watched the riffles beam.

We watched leaves blowing in the wind
From many a kind of tree
While Old Rover, slowly, walked along
Just he—Grandpa—and Me.

The birds were singing all kind of songs
As we sat down to rest
We listened as they'd come and go
While watching o'er their nest.

Grandpa said, "Son, we must turn back"
As we've walked—for quite a while
Come here Old Rover, come with us
And he seemed to give a smile.

As we returned my Grandma said
"Did you have fun today?"
"Thanks Grandpa," I said — while hugging him
For showing me the way.

Betty A McCoy Dreher

THE RABBIT AND THE OLD RED HEN

Once we had an old red hen
In a pen with a nest so neat,
Where she always laid an egg each day
For you or I to eat.

One day we bought a rabbit;
We put her in — with the hen.
They ate their meals together
And soon became good friends.

The rabbit decided to take over –
The old hen's nest, you see.
The old hen said, "Now, bunny,
That nest was made for me!"

The old red hen went in the box,
Tried pushing the rabbit aside.
But he rabbit wouldn't move an inch,
Instead just stayed inside.

When the old red hen wanted to lay her egg,
She went in her nest, as she should.
"My, my," she said, "what a crowded place!"
Laying her egg as best she could.

As the days went by, the rabbit was moved
To a pen not far away.
"Oh my, oh my, what a great relief!"
Was all the old red hen could say.

Millard Ardell Henderson Jr

LOCK & KEY

She feels for him – Bed's so cold on his side
She's alone
There's no one there – Another lonely night
On her own
I feel for her – Know she's faithful and true
Every day
While I'm away – On the road, Lone and blue
Far away

Seems so long since I last held her
Seems so wrong when I'm leaving her
On my way
Through this cold moonlit night
To love her

Far away – From the woman I love
She's the one
Only she – Holds the flame to my heart's
Burning sun
Won't be long – And I'll hold her again
Close to me
There'll I'll stay – With my love,
Give my heart
Lock and Key

Erin K Murphy

REALITIES OF ADMIRATION

To Family and Moses: Never forget who you truly are.

Long ago; years ago;
There was a caring, warm face
Full of understanding.
A voice full of fun and laughter.
A mind with wisdom, ideals, and morals
That strongly connected to a heart of
Truth, Love and Honesty to give and receive.
A complete package standing proud in their beliefs.
Believing (in themself and) in others unconditionally.

Time has passed, Times have changed.

The admiration and respect fading as the once proud
Individual falls prey to the realities of
Believing and keeping faith.
The caring, warm face full of understanding remains distorted.
The voice cries loud amongst its fun and laughter.
The mind wiser with weaken ideals and morals
No longer connecting to a heart of gold, but to a heart
Tainted with fear, frustration, and pain unable to give and
Receive Truth, Love, or Honesty.
The complete package damaged by facing the realities
Of all others except themself.

Dawn E Rearick

THE GOLD DIGGER

I look for pain, I look for sorrow,
This I dare say is much easier to espy than
that of which lies at the end of the rainbow.
I am not a gold digger, but perchance I should be,
Spending months on end looking for something so
precious and perhaps meant to be.
Yet I call upon pain, I call for more and more,
I am rich in pain while the gold digger is poor.

Lee Ann Benson

EAST TEXAS STILL LIFE

Domino Hall, Lufkin

Oldtimers sitting foursquare on a Thursday afternoon
Old Buck corners his tin can, blesses our feet with
tobacco syrups from a mouth kissed by stroke

Years of foundry oil and Christianity
cover hands, gray hands pulling
pieces from the boneyard.
It empties into walls we build around ourselves.

And the old blacks on the street corner – there
They're always wearing striped shirts and
praying into warm beer cans. Hearts chanting,
Hallelujah, sweet jesus, he's coming

Somebody slaps his last cold white piece
down, finishes this game. Old Buck leans to one side
and I can feel all the bones falling into place

Paula Verway

LOVE

To A Wonderful Father, Cleve Colyott.

I've never felt so loved before,
I don't even dare to ask for more.
It's a special kind of love I hope
will never end,
More special a love than the love
of a friend.
It's the kind of feeling you have to share
Just to let others know how much you care.
Love works like magic in a mysterious way,
Bringing sunshine on a cloudy day.
It's always with you, wherever you go
And once you find it, I'm sure you'll know.
Just reach in your heart and pull it out
Let everyone know what it's all about.
It's living to love and loving to live,
The most precious thing a person can give.
It's Love!

Gerald W Wood

DEDICATED TO A SOLDIER

Far off on a misty shore,
A body lies and moves no more.
He was a soldier, brave and grand.
He fought and died for our great land.
He fought for you and he fought for me.
He fought to keep our country free.
And now our great society,
No more his happy face shall see.
He got his medal for being brave,
Yet his life it did not save.
And back at home his parents wait,
Longer and longer, filling with hate.
Now the saddest thing that I have to say,
To this very day, they haven't taken his body away.

Shayne Gordon

LOOK AROUND

In loving memory of a very dear friend . . . whom I miss very much . . . Bradley Scott Ackerman (1969-1989).

I look around and there's no place to go.
The guilt overcomes me, my fear
only shows.
How did this happen?
What did I do?
The shadow of doubt, if only I knew.
Ideals and hopes just fall down
around.
Dreams of my life lay helplessly on the ground.
So full of love yet so much alone.
My life cut off early, no time to grow.
It's dark and it's cold—what can
I do?
I try to cry for help—if only they knew.
Where am I?
How do I get free?
I am locked up but I'm also the key.
I look around and there's no place
to go,
And find I am trapped
in the depths of my soul.

Leotta Anna Burke

SHADOWS OF TIME

To my son Jeffery, who inspired me to write. To my husband Linden, and son Robert, for their love and support.

Like the hourglass
Of time,
So are the pages
Of my mind,
Like the sands
That slowly flow,
So does the memories
That I know,
They shall
Forever be,
Locked in time
Within the shadows,
Of my mind.

Emilia O Duroska

ENSEMBLE

To the spirit of complimentation, not competition.

As the people are
so is the music
of that world–time.
As the people are
so checks its currency . . .
As the people are,
so social–efficiency.
When money devalues,
when music de–tonates,
then, equivalently,
disharmony resonates!

As the people are,
so equipollent rhyme
through thought, task, design . . .
Would not then first clue be
to ancient Time–Mystery
that together government
and musicality
as ensemble weave history?
As the people are
so shifts polarity.

Emilia O Duroska

APPROPRIATENESS

Is not appropriateness
Best Idea of The Ideal – the Absolute?
Ethereal and cellular Life–
Atoms balancing –
Solar Spirals centering –
Earth–Stellar Life complimenting . . .
Such an inner substance of outer sustenance
in a Time and Space Conjunction
could but effect Appropriateness!
Arrow and Target touching–
The Aim and Arc re–uniting

with New Arcs emerging, evolving!
for higher aspiration, Destination!
Thinking and doing the necessary,
the true in perfect timing and
proportion
and duration honors The
Appropriate!

Daniel S Guerra PhD
WITH YOU
With you
I am constantly developing an
experience
Of meaningful intimacy
That fosters commitment to
Passion and reverence.
With you
There is a rhythmic movement
through life
Which has me abundantly
And adroitly aware
Of how precious you are to me.
It is as if we are moving
In unison
Through experiences of life,
Perceiving closeness,
Assisting each other with emotional
support,
And patiently enduring confronta-
tions –
Lovingly
So as to invite growth.

Daniel S Guerra PhD
CONSCIENCE
Our inner voices
Become our source
Of choices,
Our wisdom for learning
And growing
With measurable bestowing,
Sinewy strength
In our hour of need,
Peak experiences
From which we feed,
From here we develop
Values and choices,
If only we follow
Our inner voices

Beverly G Robinson
THE POPPY PARADE
The day was overcast and grim,
The view was veiled and somewhat
dim,
When over the hill and down
Cumbrian grade
I saw Beauty leading a Poppy Parade.
In ragged rows they filed by,
Tossing their saucy bonnets high.
The colorful columns of poppies
flowed
Along the margin of the country
road;
Smiling and waving a greeting to me
They pranced and danced along with
glee.
There in the English countryside
Across an ocean wide
Those"California" poppies
Cavorting in glad array,
Reminded me of my Homeland
Then so far away.
They surely brightened that gloomy
day
and lightened my mood in a special
way.
Now at very dreary times, in
retrospect I find,
Beauty's regiment of poppies
Merrily marching through my mind.

Beverly G Robinson
ON SEEING THE ELGIN MARBLES
They made Keats aware of his
"mortality,"
And I was moved to tears, as he,
Weeping for glories long gone by,
and glory yet to be.
This Grecian grandeur was a
"wonder" to behold
With graceful flowing lines, so
splendid and so bold.
Action abounds 'round the famous
frieze
And the gods sit there, conversing if
you please.
This dazzling display might cause
one dizzy pain;
Surely to grasp it all, a monumental
mental strain.

On viewing the Parthenon's empty
pediment
I asked, naively, where the "marbles"
went.
To the British Museum they had been
sold,
Courtesy of Lord Elgin I was told.
The acquisition of each magnificent
marble piece
Led many to a passionate int'rest in
legendary Greece.
Without its inspiration what would
the poets have done,
Those young Romantics who gave so
much beauty to everyone?
Retrieving Hellenism from the rubble
Was truly worth these poets' trouble.
Classic beauty has an "eternal"
quality;
There Greece's Golden Age became
"alive" to me.

Mary Clark
OUR COUNTRY
Think thanks for our Country,
The good U. S. A.,
Unique in the world,
Is what people say.

All of the conflicts
We face day by day,
Are human efforts
to keep her that way.

Mary Clark
SONG OF CHILDHOOD
There's no defense for sarcasm
In the lyric of a child.
He will hear the discord
But his response is mild.

Be firm, fair and friendly
To harmonize with a child,
And you will be recorded
In the medley that he filed.

Daniel Healy
know yourself
merry go round
characters mounted
with only slight
difference
in rotation were
i stand to observe
coming to realize
various unlikely
impressions
so many seeing
what i don't see
so much it seems
i perceive
differently
i've learned to do
without comfort
desiring a contagious
smile

Vincent P Weaver
CHRIST CARES
Look about you and you will see
Others who are far worse than me
Some who just sit and stare
Not knowing that you care.

Those who long have lain
In beds with their pain
Many who need your prayers
As for me, I know Christ cares.

Chris Jancan
SEAN'S SONG
I walked the path of life,
and been down every road.
I've walked without a burden,
and carried many a load.

I didn't take for granted,
the road ahead each day.
With maps of love and friendship,
I was guided on my way.

And now this road has ended.
My journey seems complete.
Yet as I look ahead of me,
a new road's at my feet.

I've never walked this road before,
yet others have it trod.
And you will walk this road one day,
it leads us to our God.

Don't weep for me this day, you see,
for we shall meet again.
And live as one in peace and love,
In the brotherhood of men.

Chris Jancan
WISDOM
Time goes on like an endless sea
We all grow on in years
And through the pain of every day
We learn to cope with fears
Why'd we forget to hear their cry
They've the wisdom of their years

Today they're all forgotten
We've cast their lives aside
We lock them up in crystal cages
Then take away their pride
We neglect to see their pain
And act as though they've died.

The world's troubles aren't our own
They've seen sunshine, they've seen
rain
And their wisdom can light our way
to conquer fear and pain
We can live in rainbow pastures
Just give them love again.

E Krysko
BORN AGAIN

Dedicated to all who accept the words of Jesus— John 3:3 Jesus said "Except a man be born again he cannot see the Kingdom of God." John 3:7 Marvel not that I said unto thee, "Ye must be born again."

I am a sinner, Christ died for me
He shed His blood on Calvary
His shed blood has set me free
From all my sins that shall ever be.
Because I'm a believer
I know this is true
So why not believe and let it
happen to you?

Become a believer and see what
God has done
Through Jesus Christ his only Son
you'll see things in a different light,
Things that till now have been
out of sight.
Believe with all your heart what
God has done
And you'll see a life that has
just begun.

A believer's life is different indeed
With freedom from trouble
not guaranteed
But as you walk in the newness of
life
you'll know that with Him you can
handle all strife.
What a blessed assurance His
presence can be
What a blessing it is that
believers can see.

Born of the Spirit is being
born again,
No longer seeing through
the eyes of men.
Out of the darkness and into the light
We now see things with
spiritual sight.
What a blessed assurance
His presence can be
What a blessing it is that
believers can see.

Chris Jancan
LISA'S SONG
Little one so dear to me
I'll have you here one day.
Never leaving,
Day or night.
Always this I pray.

Love has come to set me free
I'll soon be free of pain
Never more, this
Devil's grip.
At home with you again.

Little dear, I love you much
I know this in my heart.
New beginnings,
Darling mine,
A life for us to start

Lamé
SMALL TOWN BLUES
Gazing out of my office window,
seeing all of the calamity;
Wondering what a small town
country boy is doing in a big time
city.
Where are the mystical mountains
that run into the bright blue sky;
Sitting here with my thoughts,
knowing it's time to say good-bye.
Missing Ma's home cooking, the
smell of her chili;
All the familiar faces, the love of my
family.
Hustling, bustling, everyone's
running around;
You could have your big city, I need
my small town.
High rise buildings everywhere,
concrete instead of trees;
Knowing in my heart that this isn't
the place for me.
Give me my hometown with all it's
good ole times;
Who needs the city where no one is
mine.
Pavement and buildings replacing the
green grass;
Makes me long to return to my small
town past.
Can't get used to the filth, the noise
or pollution;
Don't want to be a part of this
undeclared revolution.
It all is not that bad if you like a lot of
stress;
Gotta get back home where the

chirping crickets put me at rest.
Friends in the big city are hard to find, though I met a few;
Have to get back home where all my friendships are true.
Miles separate me from my small town, thoughts make it close;
Driving the desert highway, looking up at the mountains is what I miss most.
Gazing out of my office window, seeing all the calamity;
Wondering what a small town country boy is doing in a big time city.

Mary C L Gilland
JADED SOLITUDE

i feel alone in a world high above me
the feeling of paralysis is unreal
the fears of the future confuse me
and send my senses reeling
i feel alone in a world high above me
a world that belongs to others
i do not cannot regret the past
i have no past to overwhelm my conscience
i have never freed myself enough
i am alone in a world high above me
a world i seem to have missed out on
i wonder how i made it this far this way
i think of others and their experiences
i am alone in a world high above me
a world that runs on by me
i can't seem to keep up with its expectations or give in to its desires
i am alone in a world high above me
a world others fit into perfectly
i often wish i were more like THEM
i wish at times i didn't worry so much about HIM
i am alone in a world high above me
a world i can't master or defeat

Patricia Doyle Owens
MY BABY

To all my children: Deborah Jean, Mary Christine and Stephen Lawrence.

The birth of my baby, a little one for me to love
The child that I hoped for, the one I dreamed of
You were brought to me all bundled up and
Waiting to be fed
I waited for the nurse to leave, then unwrapped
You on the bed
I counted each little finger and every precious toe
I checked to see that you were well, just so I would
Know
I wrapped you up again and held you up to see
If maybe in your little face, you'd look somewhat
Like me
I held you close to me and fed you for awhile
Then after I had burped you, I swore I saw you
Smile
I laid you down again and was filled with pride
Once more
I played with you awhile until the nurse came to
The door
Although being with you was the time I loved the
Best
It was time to let you go, so we both could
Have a rest
It made me sad to be away but, I knew when we
Went home
From that day on, neither one of us would
Ever be alone

Margaret Kish
A BLESSING

Through pain and torture a life is given
Eyes open to a world of light and wonder
Tiny fingers encircle your own
Around our hearts a glow has grown
Is he really ours?
This bundle of joy
Ours to cherish, to love, to adore.
Time passes on, our wonder grows
He belongs to us
He also knows
First he rolled, then he crawled
Each step forward we watch enthralled
A special smile to each he will give
What greater happiness from the throne of God
The arrival of a baby come home to live.

Floyd S Knight
DOUBLE FAULT

History, we are told, repeats itself.
True. We blindly stockpile ammunition –
bricks, steel, concrete –
for Nature's next inevitable tantrum.
And in time Mother Earth, the Benevolent Destroyer
(and other fitting oxymorons),
bored and indifferent, shrugs her tectonic plates
and the ground shakes and the dust rises;
bricks crash down and flames reach up.
The screams never stop.

In the aftermath, numb but heroic,
we of the lemming mentality
proceed to build bigger and better tombs
on the very same spot.
This time, we say, this time we'll outsmart the old girl!

But, having had the last word,
Old Mother Earth, in her own sweet time
and for how long God only knows,
will kick back, shudder a time or two,
and rest in peace.

Isaac Jay Kennedy
NIGHT IN THE LIGHT OF DAY

I long to walk the golden paths again,
To see the green of Spring,
To see the sky with clouds so thin
Or the sparkle of the rain.

The smell, the feel, the sound, the taste
Are exhilarating to my senses.
But the lack of sight's a waste
With its all–enclosing fences.

The lenses made by craftsmen sure
Do little to allay my fears.
The night's darkness can do slightly more
Than hide the traces of my tears.

My other senses can tell me true
Of such beautifully animated scenes.
I imagine, yes I do,
Just exactly what it all means.

Since I can see, this is unreal,
But it is my way
To approximate how it must feel
With night in the light of day.

Carrie Jo Kruger
HUGS

To Mom and Jason . . . both experts in the art of hugging.

I prefer a hug . . .
A kiss is too calculated . . .
Too much work.

Kisses must be planned.

A person may be offended,
Or not kiss back properly.

Hugs can't be done wrong.
You can hug your friend.
You can hug your Mom.
You can hug your kid.

Hugs are never criticized,
And they are always appreciated.

Hugs are for all occasions . . .
When things are good . . .
When things are bad . . .

ESPECIALLY when things are bad . . .

You can always fall into the warmth
of a hug
And squeeze until your problems shrink away.

Harold Kersey
TEARS OF SHAME

Tonight it's kinda lonely in this foxhole over here,
And my thoughts go back into the past, to day of yesteryear,
Back to the past, when just a boy, although I knew wrong from right,
Now and then I'd get in trouble, and I had my share of fights,
I remember one good spanking, oh! Yes I had quite a few,
But this time I did the very thing, I'd been told not to do.
And as the tears trickled down my cheeks, I never thought of pain,
My only thought was what I'd done, for those were tears of shame.
Now as I'm sitting here tonight, shells bursting overhead,
My buddies all around me, some wounded some are dead.
Again tears trickle down my cheeks, once more they're not from pain,
Again tears trickle down my cheeks, once more they're tears of shame.
The shame of why men have to die in battle over here.
The shame of why we cannot live in peace and free from fear.
Of course I'm a little older now, and I still know right from wrong.
And I know I'm fighting for a free world, to which all mankind can belong
So if by chance, the Lord chooses me, one of the lucky few,
Who will return back home again, to start our life anew.
I only hope and pray to God, that we who do remain,
Will not forget these tragic days, and leave these others to have died in vain.

Daniel "Wayne" Kramer
BILE

To Karis, There shall never, ever be another girl like you.

I fall down within my mind, awake with both feet fast
There is no Gentle, Peace, or Kind, at least none which will last

Venus rises high above fools who only dream of love
Chaste and decent fast evade men whose minds are not up made

"The end is near," this calls too dear for most young ears to gather
But this they must to gain our trust unless they wouldn't rather

Dry and fading Fear parading
all the sojourn pain cascading

Knowledge burn Wisdom spurn
this dark world is fast degrading

Comfort curled Pride now furled
original thought is downward hurled

Standing all alone just then –
Time runs down a drain
Deep within the Vicar's den –
Sanity's a cane

Mark Kendrick
I OFTEN WISH

I often wish
To sit beside a gentle stream
Listening to the sounds of Mother Nature,
Daydreaming under an old oak tree.

Then I picture you
By my side
Talking about the good times we've had
And what the future might hold
For the two of us.

As I slowly drift back from daydreaming
To reality
I can see that I will always have you.
Not always by my side
But forever in my heart
And in the memories we both share.

Terri Kriske
THE BOTTLE

This is dedicated to my family and friends and the members of Alcoholics Anonymous who have helped through the tough times.

I sit in the corner of my room
With my only friend,
A bottle of booze

All I feel is fear and pain
So I take another swig
As I slowly go insane

I drink myself to near death
I cry out for help
In between my dying breaths

So it was help that I sought
For I was almost gone
And for that help I fought

Guess what I found?
Someone who loves me!
I had found my God!

So in His arms I huddled
And he gave me the strength
To throw away the bottle

Paula S Hamilton
CRYSTAL TEAR
A crystal tear flowing through
prism of the wound.

Piercing through a once willed heart.
Crushing delicate wings in a shining soul,
my will is torn apart.

Lodging towards a painful flight.
A uniquely see–through torture,
bears the light.

Crystal tear begins to fall.
Shattering a mind of hopes.
A vision truth shoves your,
back against the wall.
It's amazing how you cope.

See no one else could ever know.
No one else could ever hold.
An endless silence of lonely power.
The hurting anxieties within those hours.

Seems only I can now bestow.
The making of a crystal tear.
I feel another about to flow.
Uniting too, with all my fears.

Mélody Bovair
GIRL

To you Heather, I wish you love.

The path you lead has taken your youth
you are ten going on thirty;
The life called yours belongs to others
do they know how young you really are.

I see your face and wonder of the truth
of what could you be certain;
I sense your desperation and your loneliness
which way do you go, to whom do you turn.

So many changes force you to press on
where is the light; the tunnel;
So many people tell you what is best
wouldn't you like to choose.

Girl, one day your path will be anew
dream to be ten at thirty;
Girl, one day your life will belong to you
Smile on, keep them guessing at how young you are.

Girl, there will always be changes; press on
you'll see the light; you'll find many tunnels;
Girl, one day you'll be a woman
just hang on.

Sharon Joy Hyke
THE NAME SHARON MEANS PRINCESS
The name Sharon means Princess
I have chosen you, rose of Sharon
I feel like a princess too!
Long flowing hair with a rose swept
on the side of my hair, elegantly!
Freely, flowing, glowing gold color
Long locks of hair which drape past
my waist and bottom!
Lengthy locks of hair frame the face
Gracefully like a Princess

Virginia Hahn
MY CREATOR
God is my creator, the one that I love,
The one that pours blessings down
from above.
He gave of his son; so we could be saved.
To give us the love that we all have craved.
I love the dear Lord, for things that he's done
For the blessings and healings and victories he's won.
He is our savior, our helper, our closest friend
He'll be there forever; right to the end.
So people reach out for the hand extended to you
The hand so compassionate, blessed and true
Receive the salvation offered to you
And you'll find he'll be there and make you anew.

Allan J Hayward
REACH
Reach in.
Reach
into my mind.
reach in
With your hand.
What,
might the matter be?
What,
might you have found
that weighs so heavily
within your hand?
A handful of depression,
of hopelessness.
The weight
of worthlessness?
Reach in
with the other hand.
Reach into my heart
and what,
might you have found?
The steady beat of sadness.
Cold, firm beat of loneliness?
A slow beat
of worry of
a low self-esteem?
Touch
your hand upon my head.
Maybe now,
you can feel a lighter weight
for
a future
with
a future.
Lay down
your gentle, kind hand upon my chest
and feel
of the warmth.
The flow
of lie and thankfulness.
The warm
flow of love
of happiness,
of a tomorrow,
with a tomorrow.

James Wallace
THE PURE AT HEART

Dedicated to my beautiful daughter Jamee LaSeann Wallace.

A child's heart is born
True and pure
Will this pureness
Forever endure
Only if it is nurtured
With love and faith
No other offerings will compensate
Let this be the guide
That we strive to follow
To keep a heart born of fullness
From growing shallow
A child's heart is born
True and pure
Let this pureness
Forever endure

Melissa Holmes
EMOTION

I dedicate this poem to the mystery of emotion.

2-night the moon is full
yet, is my will my own?
Eternity lies with-in stillness
the vast belief of a better thing
and emotions stirred by fantasy
strongly unfold in darkness—
then slip away . . .
A soul inside a body
thrusting onward
seeing time pass through human eyes
the desire to be free
to fear
desperate lack of confidence
to be accepted
keeping differences
yearning for happiness
with-out conflict

Mark A Hoffman
COLORS
The skin be black,
The skin be white,
The soul,
Remains, the same,
The skin that was
The ash is grey
An all,
Must come this way

Katy Krombach
BLIND
Blind is the world that cannot see,
The hopes and aspirations in me.
The light that shines will soon expire,
But hopefully not the dreams and desires.

The light that shows me the way,
Along with the inspiration,
That let's me know it's okay.

I will follow the light,
Till it converts to night,
Then I will divert away,
Until another day.

Betty L Harper
WORD STORM
Our conversation erupts
crackles like static lightning
signaling impending storm.

Your face holds a cloudburst
puffy, crusted over with fury

My breath hisses anger
a Sirocco wind
harsh and clumsy in its blusterings.

Thunder descends from eyes to mouths
soft lips pinch
into hard words
that spew out
rage red and molten
inundating the gentle space
that was between us
uprooting the tender shoots of love.

John K Hatchie
PROPOSAL
If you could enter into my mind,
You know what you would see?
The future thoughts of happy life
In store for you and me.

We'll marry first and go abroad
To see the world at hand,
A honeymoon in calm smooth seas
Make love upon the sand.

Let's share the joys a family knows,
Of love — respect — and pride,
We'll have some kids to make complete
Our dreams within the tides.

We'll have just one or maybe two,
I've so much love to share.
It's up to you my darling
For you will have to bare.

Or should we wait and put this off,
Could it be much too soon?
I kissed your lips and fell in love
Beneath that silver moon . . .

"Oh I can't wait! We might as well,
No younger do we get,
I love you dear, so marry me,
I'll make you my sweet pet . . . "

A long white gown I'll buy for you,
It won't be just a dress,
For on that day you'll be my bride . .
I want you, please say YES!!

Stephanie Harris
IF I HAD A CHOICE
If I had a choice,
I'd be there with you,
But it's not mine to make,
For you must want me there too.

Our first kiss
Had to be tainted with a potion,
'Cause the love in my heart
Runs deeper than any ocean.

I want you to hold me
And rid my heart of the chill,
Just kiss me gently
And make time stand still.

If it were possible
Our love would prove true,
'Cause if I had a choice,
I'd be there with you.

Joseph J Miller
A NEW YEAR DAY
Every year we vow to make resolutions
To change our lives in some way
These may not be the solutions
Instead we should work with today.

We aim for certain goals
Some that we may not attain
Instead our lives may take on too many tolls
And cause us inner pain.

Look not into our past
Because this we cannot change
Our lives move too fast
And there's not enough time to arrange

Look on tomorrow
As come what may
Our past is there to borrow
To make our changes stay.

Alon M Humphrey
A CHRISTMAS THOUGHT
At Christmas time our thoughts are full
of gifts for family and friends
And what we will be receiving,
our list never ends.
Are we forgetting the meaning of Christmas
and the Father's gift from above,
His gift of His only Son Jesus who came
that we might know the true meaning of love.
Do we remember His commission

through which the world could
find peace,
Without love like our Savior's, war
will
never cease.
So spend a few minutes each day to
study,
learn, then live the Savior's way.
Then tell of His love to others so all
will want peace,
Then wars between nations will not
happen—
they will finally cease.

Sybil Sale
THESE MAKE NURSING WORTHWHILE

To my husband Guy and daughters Paula and Susan.

The grasp of a hand grown weary
with pain
An aged face softened with a smile
A grateful parent's fond embrace
These make nursing worthwhile

A new mother's voice trembling with
joy
When she asks the doctor 'is it a
girl or a boy?'
A baby's first cry, a father's proud
smile
These make nursing worthwhile

When we change our attire to snowy
white
May God grant us the wisdom to
see
That just as a beacon guides in the
night
With knowledge must come
humility.

Danny Horowitz
CYCLES

The long shadows of summer
Touch the edges of the lake;
They dance like butterflies across the
waves,
As they vanish out into the open sea.

The leaves fall gently,
As the day turns into evening,
And the luminescent moon charts the
course
Of man's never–ending voyage.

The snow–capped mountains stand
majestically
Against a cloak of ebony,
As giant protectors,
Of beauty and peace.

The birds fly across the bright, blue
sky,
As the flowers open their petals,
And rejoice once again,
In the warmth of the sun.

Denise Hollinger
BABY

From the murky waters deep a baby
boy was born.
But when his birthing was complete,
was left alone forlorn.
He learned to live and to survive, a
ravaged forest land.
He lived alone, a wild one, not
known to human hand.
As time wore on, the small boy grew
and lived to be a man.
But all the dreams he'd ever dreamed
lay buried in the sand.
All he'd ever dreamed about was
living wild and free.
His dream came true – an old old
man – living alone lonely.
He drove himself to perfection, but
ne'er did he make a dent.
And so when he died a lonely man,
back to the sea he went.

Jim Haprian
DRIVING WITH GRANNY

Better buckle up tight,
When you go out with granny at
night.
She's older than you and me,
But that doesn't help her see.

She rarely goes over twenty
Which is about as fast as you can
pour cold honey.
Oh, she could go faster you see,
But then she might hit a tree.

She used to drive better years ago,
Through rain, sleet and snow.
Something happened to her along the
way,
That causes her to drive so bad today.

She's blind in one eye and almost the
other
Why she nearly killed my brother!
She was going to turn left at the light,
But instead of left she turned right!

Across traffic she went at a slow pace
While other people were driving as if
in a race.
When granny drives, it sure is a sight,
And when I ride with her I buckle up
tight.

Pauline Oates Hager
STARLIGHT

Daddy bought us a Shetland pony.
Her name was Starlight.
She should have been named Ornery,
Because she was such a delight.

She knew how to unlatch a stable
door.
A tied rope to her was no chore.
Pick up her front leg and she laid
down.
She should really wear a crown!

A buggy she pulled us three to
school.
The other kids thought we were cool.
She stayed in a nearby farmer's barn.
When school was out, home we went
to her oats and corn.

She ran a lot of races.
Took us to lots of places.
Threw us off into the ditches.
Stood and waited 'til we got back on
with our britches.

Then summer was over and fall
began.
We lost our wonderful and gentle
friend.
Starlight laid down and quietly died.
As the Star entered Heaven, we cried
and cried.

James N Hammonds
A LAND OF DANGER

The moon is my nightlight, with it I
have peace.
I look to the sky and see the large
white geese.
The great birds honk and sing as they
fly,
bearing their souls as they cruise
through the sky.

A shot rings out and the great bird
falls,
another victim claimed in this war
fought in vain.
The stranger laughs and again takes
aim.
For this war is not fought between
man and man,
but between him and the creatures of
this great land.
The great animals fall prey day after
day,
The stranger taking their land and
lives away.

The creatures have a chance, though
it is small,
to rise up together and make the
stranger fall.
Then when he leaves everyone will
see,
that the way the creatures live is the
way life was meant to be.

Tyletta LeJuene Hayes
GRANDMOTHER

No more tears of sorrow,
no more feelings of pain,
She revealed a strength within her
life,
She did not fret or complain.
The Good Lord gave her a purpose,
her purpose was being a mother;
She raised her children so wonderfully,
to them, there will never be another.
She strengthened our lives with her
actions,
by showing she really did care.
Whenever we turned around
we knew that she'd always be there.
The love lives on in our hearts,
her name forever in our minds,
her memory will never be far from
us,
my grandmother was one of a kind.
Although life goes on, it's true
we are faced with hurt and sorrow.
I'll try to continue living and loving
as if there were no tomorrow.

S Maxine Hackerson
NO TEARS NOW

I often sit and wonder
About my lonely years.
I think about how sad I was
And all those lonely tears.

The days were so very long
And the nights were so cold.
I remember my empty heart
For there was no love to hold.

But, then I met you!
All my tears were wiped away.
I no longer dreaded the night.
And looked forward to each new day.

We'll spend our life together
And plan each golden year.
I'll never again be lonely
And together, laugh away the tears.

Chelsie L Horne
TIMES CHANGE

Time changes with the hands on a
clock,
But the loving friendship shared
stayed solid as a rock.

Through thick and thin the caring
always remained,
When one needed support the other
would offer a cane.

Yesterdays were precious memories
and treasured close to the heart,
But now all must move on to a fresh
new start.

Sharon Headley
MY MEMORY BOX

My memory box is covered with
clutter and dust.
Even at best; I doubt there's some
rust.
The reasons for this are too numerous
to mention—
But to be honest with myself, it's
strictly
from lack of attention.
The wonders of my childhood,
adolescence and teens,
Have all been tucked away (in
there)—
for ages it seems.
One of these days I'll sit down and
try to uncover,
All the wonderful dreams and wishes
that I've
yet to discover.

Christine Silvas–Scott
SOMETIMES

To Michael, I love you more than there are grains of sand on the beach!

Sometimes when you meet new
people,
Make new friends,
You talk about Life.
Here you think nobody has lead a
Life . . .
Like your own.
People come from different worlds,
But you make new friends.
You talk about Life.
Here you think nobody has felt
pain . . .
Like your own.
When you talk about Life you find
your
Worlds are the same,
Sometimes when you make new
friends.
Life goes on.
Your Lives will change.
But when you look back on Life and
remember
You'll remember the one like your
own!
Sometimes when you meet new
people
Make new friends—You talk about
Life!

Karen Kuta Hussain
I AM EMPTY

I am empty now
Floating lifeless
As a fetus in a glass jar
Aborted in blood
Abandoned
I have left life
As life was sucked from me

Flower of my womb
My flesh is warm
I live
Still
Breathing blood
Blood is on my hands
My heart bleeds for what
Could have been
I am empty now
Please feel me

Bryan Keith Hull
SO THE LIFE GOES ON

For my daughters and my father.#1 Marissa Layne, Brandi Leigh and Charles Hull.

It starts as a seed, so little, so small.
With Mother Earth with her sun so
bright and her rain so soft.
I grow and grow, from little to tall
as life goes on we stand so tall. We
shelter more than just the forest floor.
I protect little lives that are starting

all new. I've been here now close to a hundred years, I've put up with all the Earth can give, and gave all one can give. As time goes on, the wind and cold, the snow and rain, the sun and clouds have pushed and pulled till parts of me start to fall. My roots are deep, still in the earth but what you see is all but dust. In my prime they called me big and mighty they leaned on me, took shelter from me. They stripped me down, they took my name. As I leave this place I leave alone another seed to carry on. My life was good as life could be. I watched all my seeds grow as I became old. I'm gone now, but my roots remain for many years, to help my seed to grow big and strong like me. You probably think that this life is the life of the mighty oak.
(But it's a Daddy's life.)

Amy L Hull
UNTITLED

It all began . . .
Yes, of course it did, go on.

It was a fateful day,
who would've ever guessed . . .
Yes, that's true, but—

An ordinary journey
except for a few volcanoes,
earthquakes
and tidal waves.
Well, we do get weather, don't we?

Then there was a burial,
not much else except maybe some
invisible destruction . . .
Everyone dies.

Time rolled on,
soil eroded, dead animals decayed
and some highways got built.
Life goes on, you know.

It came to this,
right here, right now,
2:00 p.m. . . .
Already? I've got to go!

But wait!,
there's more . . . .

Joseph Quintavella

Joseph Quintavella
GOD'S CREATION

The landscape far and wide it stands
Bristling trees before us lies
Greener leaves like roaming lambs
In this summer's paradise
Insects on the ground they crawl
Birds so high we all can see
Tranquil breeze the winds blow tall
Speaking word of God's creation
Trees each year they shed their leaves
Gone are beauty all that's whole
It is God's do not deceive
It is sure come once your soul
A heartful youth no care
Strives through life's dark way
As trees and man so be
Speaking words of God's creation

The years go by a new life whole
Takes it's place among the new
Not knowing much unless be told
That life is nothing more than dew
Thou aged flesh what flows to end
Dreary, weary a rest at last
A life has come gone and past
The seasons also come and go
Speaking words of God's creation

Marian G Hale
IN PRAISE OF AWKWARD

For Jean Houston, who helped me get out of my own way, and face my fears.

I wish I weren't so perfect,
So right in every way.
'Cause if I weren't so perfect,
I'd be a lot more brave.

When I was one, I made mistakes;
Fewer when I was two.
Now I'm grown up and never err
Which makes me scared, like you.

'Cause when you never make
mistakes
You're perfect, yes, that's true.
But Oh how long you have to spend
Just checking things you do.

You check to get the words just right,
The music must be fine.
And when your checking's all
complete
You check, just one more time.

So with this checking care you take
There's no time to be bold.
No time to state uncertain thoughts,
You're checking 'til you're old.

I wish I weren't so perfect,
So right in every way.
'Cause if I weren't so perfect,
I'd be a lot more brave.

Note: Supply your own choice of actions in the 4th verse, to make this poem apply to your own life,

Stephen Glenn Hinson
USF&G

To the one I always will love, Allison.

I never knew pain
Couldn't even say
But as day is plain
One day you went away
And the tears they fell
For every piece of my broken heart
Into the well
Wishing we weren't apart
Because time goes so slow
Thinking of when
And why did you go
Will I ever see your eyes again
Because calls and letters are all
Our lonely hearts can get
I'll just continue to fall
And ask,"Is the waiting over yet?"
To be with you forever
Through thick and thin
worth this endeavor
Loving each other in this love we're in

Jennifer Sowders
MY SUN

My sun arises each and every day.
It peeps over the edge of sleepless
nights and cautiously displays its
gloriously brilliant red–orange
light that ensures my every move.
It warms not only my face, but it stirs
my soul in a way unknown
to everyone except my sun, my
God, and me.
My sun is a true gift of love from the
Lord of All.
Its two qualities are devotion and
determination, and in these
areas my sun never fails me.
It does not disappoint me for I trust it.
Dark, ominous clouds attempt to take
it from me, but my sun
is too wonderful and heavenly for
evil.
My sun protects me for it is protected
by the Great One.
Energy explodes gallantly and
purposefully to ensure my very
being.
For this reason, I trust it.
I need my sun, and my sun needs me.
It gives me strength no other has been
able to give.
Some only see a dot in the sky which
makes life on Earth exist;
yet I see a marvelous and honest
friend that no one
can ever replace.
My sun brings forth life and joy,
never sorrow.
When my heart sags, I look to my
sun, and it
makes my clouds of despair
disappear.
Little pleasures comfort us, and little
disasters destroy us.
Being survivors, we can handle any
situation.
Yet, somehow my sun makes it
through the hard
time more gracefully than I.
My sun can read my heart and knows
when I
need help to get back on my feet
again.
Tranquil peace will be established
when my sun
and I are truly united.
I fear no death for I trust my sun, the
Son.

Lisa Melto
LIFE MAY END BUT LOVE DOESN'T

Life is a wonderful & powerful thing,
but it ends
Death steals life away
But it never can steal love away
Love is a chain
That binds my heart & soul forever
With every link
It gets stronger and stronger
Love lives forever in my heart
Even though my lover is gone
He may be gone in the here & now
But he is forever beside me
In my daily thoughts & memories
Of our short but loving relationship
Our love is stronger than steel
And mightier than death
Many things end when
Life does but love is the only thing
That stands up to death and never
Gives in.
LIFE MAY END BUT LOVE
DOESN'T . . .

J C Trees
FROM A ROMANTICIST'S ASPECT

You're a vixen in disguise,
An enchantress tempting the souls of
men.
When I gaze into your eyes,
Your desire to mesmerize.
I succumb to your gentle sweet
whisper,
So poetic and alluring.
My soul is conquered, forever
yearning.

As a long forgotten dream,
you come to me.
With the nature of a succubus and,
the body of a goddess,
you come to me,
To tempt me ever more.

I long to possess,
To be possessed by the demon that
you are.
To nourish the fire,
That rages in the furnace of my heart.

Delia E Lopez
TO LOVE THE WIND

Words that tear through my heart,
Escapades of love told in song.
He remembers life's bitter notes
But on his lips
The memories are sweet.

The sound of his guitar
Makes love to me.
Enchanting, a melody, my senses,
My loneliness disappears.

But the music ends
And reality reappears
To see his love
Drifting in the wind.

Enveloped in his absence
My forgotten laughter
My tears imploring rainbows . . .
Waiting for the reason
To love again,
The wind.

Rachel Woodrome
FLASHBACK

Whispering winds
Winding trees,
Summershade
What a breeze.
As the sun goes down
I can feel the enduring beauty
All around.
The stars begin vigorously
Shining bright.
With such content through all the
night.
Flashbacks
All I see.
A vague memory,
You & me

Tomni Lynn Brown
DEATH

Dedicated to the memory of my father, Walter Thomas Brown, my mother, Shirley and my sister, Gina.

There was a cruel steel framed chair standing by the desk. Reluctantly I went to rest my broken limbs that seemed to disintegrate with cold and fatigue. There at the desk, laced with gold, I rest my weary head. I cannot resist the temptation of the gentle caressing sleep that beckons to engulf me in its pleasure filled retreat. I gently lie my swollen cheeks on the cold unwelcoming desk

painfully pulling air into my sickly
lungs, barely holding on. My eyes
seal themselves from reality. I slip
surely
fading from this cruel world to seek
and join oblivion, where
everywhere is nowhere. It is the
harmless void of the unknown.

Oda Mae Dye
I REMEMBER

To Jack, My Husband of 66 years.

Morning brings the evening and to
homeward steps I turn.
True I could be thinking of lessons I
have learned,
But troubles all elude me and
somewhere on the way
An old familiar feeling creeps in my
heart to stay.
Though I am worn and weary, hair
long turned to gray,
I know to someone waiting I'll never
be that way.
So God stays in his house, the sheep
all in his fold,
And I become a hero, debonair and
bold.
Yes, you can have your millions, just
leave me the right to be
My special kind of hero 'til he calls
for me.

Belinda Corley
DEAR MOMMY
Dear Mommy,
I'm sorry if I made you mad
I was only trying to do what was
right
I know you were feeling sad
After you and daddy had that fight
I didn't mean to break the vase.
I was only trying to be of use.
The pain still stung across my face
I wish I didn't have to be abuse.
Dear Mommy,
I know you had to let go
Of all the anger you felt inside
But the last blow was the final blow,
For last night I died.
All I ever wanted was for you to love
me
I longed for a hug, a kind word, a
gentle touch.
But all those things were not to be.
I'll always love you so much.
Tomorrow they lay me to rest
And I'll go live with the Lord above
You probably figured that's for the
best.
Me too—At least now I'll be loved.

Barbara Dempsey
WISHING YOU WERE HERE
The day lingers on,
And time just ticks away . . . slowly,
I sit in a room all alone,
Wishing you could be here with me.

Every day I need a moment to look
forward to,
An inspiration . . . which others can't
seem to satisfy,
It's the happiness I feel when you are
near,
That makes it harder to say
"goodbye."

It's those moments I cherish the
most,
Believing you can make the
difference in my life,
The shortest minutes sharing a few
words,
The words expressing how I wish
you were here.

Colette Kamm
GOD'S RAIN
Deep purple and silver streaks
flashing across a gloomy sky
thunder pounding down upon us
like a million horses passing by.

"God" cleans the earth with rain
to wash wounds of worldly pain
to touch each flower head and
soon proudly lifts its head to bloom.

"God" creates puddles in the street
for birds to wash their tiny feet
yellow parched grass turns to green
trees glisten with branches clean.

"God's" rain falls on farmlands too
for crops to grow all summer through
the prayers of farmers heard on high
are soon answered from the sky.

When the rain has finally passed
sun breaks through the clouds at last
"God" smiles, Amen to us below
we stand in awe, behold the rainbow!

Erika Howland Klie
SEEING YOU
I get lost when I feel how much is
really real, and living here.
Looking at you makes me weak.
Looking up at the sky, my life seems
bleak.
My heart will flutter and melt like
butter.
You seem like a star shining alone in
the darkened sky.
Your smile, like the sun, can never be
done.

Mary M Kuhn
MY SISTER
My sister is a meany
She treats me like I'm crud
Every time I go outside
She throws me in the mud.
Mom thinks she's an Angel
I know that she's no Saint
If Mom only knew
She's everything I ain't.
That's alright, that's O.K.
Her day is coming soon
I'll grow up, I'll be the boss
I'll show her a thing or two.
I'll take all of Mommy's keys
And lock her in her room!

Lorien Rae Konetzka (10 years old)
IF YOU WERE DEAF
If you were deaf:
You couldn't hear birds sing
or the doorbell ring
You couldn't hear the crickets chirp
or your brothers burp
You couldn't hear the rain fall
or your dad's saw

Annette Koenig
THE BEAUTY WITHIN
The struggle to be perfect and
desire of approval
exhaust my body and mind.
Never quite able to reach
the ultimate goal
instead, fall even further behind.
Why must these bruises
of imperfection
pain me right down to the bone?
Whomever decided that I
must be special?
This conclusion I came to alone.
Will I ever be worthy enough
for myself,
see thru to the beauty within
And realize it is from a person's
own soul
that the true assessments begin?

Mary V King
SHADOW OF MINE
I've seen my shadow–
have you seen yours?
I've faced my shadow–
have you faced yours?
I don't hate my shadow
do you hate yours?
For–
My shadow is my twin,
My silent partner–
the only one who
always lets me win.

Alma Ray Ferris
THE OLDER MAN
I told her that I loved her, and do you
know what she did?
She laughed at me and then she said
"you must be kidding, Kid."

You're much too young to know
what love is all about
and that's the kind of romance,
I can do without;

But for sure you will get older
and will find somebody sweet,
who will think you are the nicest man
she could ever meet.

Then you will be glad you waited
and will thank me from your
heart–
Take my advice and if you do,
I'll be glad I played a part.

Dorothy D Keltee
WITHOUT YOU
My days had passed, empty and blue;
Void of the rainbows, sunshine and
dew.
Blind to my heart the beauty would
be;
Until that miracle inside of me.
Trimesters passed – one, two and
three.
A lifetime of love came forth from
me.
In the rays of God's sun you
flourished and bloomed.
You were the love he'd placed in my
womb.
Once taken from me, you cried and I
knew;
Never my son would I be without
you.

God blessed you and kept you right
up to the end;
When death came to claim you by the
hand of a friend.
Last, when I saw you – you lay at
rest.
Peacefully sleeping, hands crossed on
your chest.
Submerged in my grief – no
movement or sound;
I stood as they lowered you into that
ground.
A very small hand slipped into mine.
Here stood my peace – Your seed
was my sign.
So I looked towards Heaven – saw
skies of blue;
Never my son would I be without
you.

Andria Leigh Wilson
FOR GRANDMAS ONLY
Inside my heart is a special room –
For Grandmas only.
Because of this special place,
I am never lonely.
Every time I need someone to share
My good times and my sad,
Grandma is there laughing, loving
Making me glad.
When problems come, few or many,
I have the answer, I'll call Granny!
And there she is, reaching out her
hand.
I can count on her to understand.
She can be so funny–funniest I ever
saw,
I just laugh and say, "That's my
Grandma!"
So I never worry about being lonely,
Because inside my heart is a
special room –
For Grandmas only.

Cathy Gabriele
DAVE'S TUNE

*"Mere words can't explain what
went on between us . . . "—YOU
"But one kiss might."—ME*

You were an instant, a whisper in my
ear.
That's all it took, my very worst fear.
I tried to resist, I tried to be strong,
I wish you had never played your
song.
But I had heard it although it was just
a note,
And I fell even further with each lyric
that you wrote.
Touched and inspired, peaceful and
serene,
The melody lingered as I wandered in
a dream.
Inside my heart is trapped this song,
Forever playing, forever strong.
Never to stop or skip a beat,
Memories of us made the melody
complete.
Now the pages are yellowed, the
notes are smeared,
I can't hear the music through the
sound of my tears.

DuJuana Frazier Thompson
MY FAMILY NAME

*To my Mother and Father who gave
me such a wonderful heritage in a
respected family name.*

There may be a lot that I may not
know
Great wisdom and fame I cannot
show,
But that doesn't matter that much to
me
For most important is my family!!

My dad always said, "Be proud of
your name
If you always do right, you'll never
feel shame,
If a man can't be proud of the name
that he wears
Then he doesn't have much!" my dad
would declare!

"If you bear a good name being kind
and true
Then the rest will not matter, for they
really know you"
In years since my youth, I have found
this is true,
Beware of your name for it really
follows you!

And the name that you leave for your
family to share
Is more valuable to them than the

clothes they can wear!
Or the house they can sell, or the money they may need
For your name follows them for all eternity!

Thuy Chung
ARE YOU EVER COMIN' BACK

To my dearest friend Chad Miller.

The way you left us
Without a word
Not tellin' what happened
Not a single word
Everyone's cryin'
Everyone's blue
Everyone wishes you
Were here
But you're not
You're special to us
You're always here
With us
But now you're gone
We got each other
We will remember you
In our hearts
You'll remain
For a thousand years
Or more
No one will forget you
'Cause we all love
You.

Lynn Ann Warner
THROUGH YOUR EYES
The sun shines for me
Through your eyes
The wind howls her lament
At your good-byes
The oceans cease to roar
At your caress
And knowing that you care
Puts my mind at rest
Your gentle loving ways
Give my life new lease
And knowing you are near
Gives my soul its peace

Terri Cook
MY MOTHER'S SMILE

This is for my sons' Michael and Scott, my smile will always be there, for them.

My mother's smile is so dear.
It dries away the saddest tear.
My eyes search upward,
desiring to see.
My mother smiling down,
upon me.
Oh, daddy's smile is special,
to me
But it's my mother's smile
that I long to see.

Hank Smith
TIME'S EXISTENCE

Dedicated to my Mother, Jewell W. Smith.

"What time is it," did someone say?
Or, "Hurry! It's near the end of the day!"
We rise and dress striving all the way
From dawn to dusk to earn our pay.

We measure life's steady, flowing, course,
In times of heartbreak or rejoice
Glancing anxiously from time to time,
The clock beats onward toward the chime.

Our daily existence given its meaning,
As mind creates through timeless dreaming.
But measurable is meaning, not dreaming,
For time cares not for idle scheming.

The march of time soon cuts life's cord,
When time ends, existence is no more.

Thomas M Stratman
A SOLDIER'S PURPOSE
Why do we war?
And why do soldiers die?
Is it to kill the Cuban, Russians and North Lebanese?
And all of the people, linked to those geographies?
Or is it the Shiite Muslims, that we despise?
Is it an organized religion, that picks for us our sides?
Could it be Communism? Is that our political test?
We have the worst form of government, except for all the rest.
Do we fight to protect Big Business?
All of the Oversea Loans I mean.
Do the poor of each generation die, to keep safe those of means?

In the next few lines set not the answer, but my theory,
For I do not proclaim to be, smarter than our gathered history.
The long reaching tendrils of War have, as its seed,
A basic human emotion, that goes by the calling Greed.
Greed makes the Aggressor want more land.
And greedy religions always use a forceful hand.
Of course your government is greedier than mine,
And the greediest races want most of the coastline?
Its the wanting what you don't have that leads to this nonsense.
The desire for the greener land on the other side of the fence.

Tracy Sargent
PRINT WASHED BOY
Comic strip character
growing up.
Past the next frame
and the hands of an artist.
Becoming himself
and not a colored boy
with humorous thoughts
to convey
No, no, no humor.
Just a comic strip
character
leaving his panel
and learning the world.

Lisa R Wiscombe
LATE AT NIGHT

This poem was written for Brian, Gia, Olivia, and Alicia. For they help me to be the best I can be!

As the day ends and I wander to bed,
I check on the baby and kiss her sweet head.
My big girls are sleeping to my delight,
but before they lay down for the night.
I hear "Mama" and my feet surely stop,
even though I am tired and about to drop.
I return to their room for reasons unknown,
maybe some water, a kiss or a moan.
To my surprise it is not a request,
but just to tell me I am the best.

Birthel Lyon
DO NOT TURN THE KEY
Once I saw an object coming in my direction I was hoping it was just a reflection, but knowing all along it was real as could be. Luckily it moved over as I could see. No way I could understand this happening to me.

They are a danger to all and there is no excuse. The carnage they cause could be you or me. They go out to have a ball but end up causing somebody's downfall. They take one, two, three maybe
even four never having the guts to say no more. They stay and take it all in usually until late after ten. Not giving a care about the world we live in. They go their way down a fast lane. Not knowing they cause much pain when it is all over and the damage has been done they look for mercy but there should be none!

Judy Peckinpaugh
COME SIT WITH ME
Come sit with me awhile
And let me hold your hand,
I understand your sorrow
And know you need a friend.

I understand the pain
That lies within your heart,
I have felt the silent screams
That tear you all apart.

I know about the sleepless nights
That last so very long,
I understand the emptiness
When you hear that special song.

Come share with me your memories
And let me be your friend,
You can cry, laugh or say
Nothing at all
And I will understand.

Come sit with me my friend
I'll try to help you thru,
I understand my friend
For I have been there too.

Patricia P Kincer
PEOPLE
People, people everywhere—
Some get in my way–
People always interfering–
Trying to block my day–
People coming against me
Wanting to see me lose–
People certainly not helping
Wishing for a catastrophe–
People, why don't they look
At the positive side
And help me to succeed?
People, why don't they make
A way to help me accomplish my need?
People, people, let us love–
Helping others meet their goals–
Wishing good instead of bad–
People, release peace
Instead of strife–
Make this world an excellent life–

Rae Hanlin
THE PURPLE VIOLET
'Twas nestled down among the rocks,
Surrounded by some moss.
Its large flat leaves swayed in the breeze . . .
The sun they seem to toss
Across the face of this fair one
So it would thrive and grow.
I stooped to pick it for my own,
But break that stem, oh no!
Its pretty face looked up at me;
I'm sure I saw it smile,
Yet there are many that would say
My mind was 'running wild.'
I felt that I would 'snuff' it's life
So held my want 'in tow' . . .
And left that purple violet
Right in that woods to grow!

Marilyn S Decker
5.7
Shaking, Quaking, Rocking, Rolling,
Scared!
Dishes breaking, candlesticks flying,
Heart in my toes; Too afraid
to move.

Solid, Quiet, Normal; Earth
at rest.
Radios singing, Cuckcoos cooing.
Why won't my heart quit quaking
now too?

Michelle Tye Martinez

Michelle Tye Martinez
THE HURT AND PAIN MY LIFE HAS GAINED

I dedicate this poem to all the people who have a hard time dealing with their epilepsy, and to my family and friends who have made my epilepsy a lot easier to live with.

An epileptic seizure
Where I fall to the ground

Where I shake
And roll all around

Where people stare
To think it's a show

Where I lay
Quiet and know

That down deep
I'm filled with embarrassment

When I fell to the ground
And hit the cement

Everyone runs to
See if I'm okay

As I just lay they're
Knowing not what to say

As everyone has

Their jokes and remarks

I just laughed
With a broken heart!"

J B Latham
MY GIFTS TO YOU
My friend, I ask myself what I can give to you.
I sit and look around me and this is what I see
and what I can give to you.
I can give you the music of the wind as it
makes the leaves on the trees dance.
I can take you to see a bird build his nest
I can take you to the woods and let your
weary head rest on the earth and hear a blade of grass grow.
I can let the sun shine on you to warm your body.
I can take you for a walk in the rain and
let God wash you all over with His dew.
I can take you to the ocean and let the peaceful water ebb over you and
make your body peaceful and rested.
There are so many things I can
Give you my friend;
There are but a few

Mary Gem Dennis
OUR ANNIVERSARY
These years of blissful happiness
Were chucked full of joy divine.
With every task a sweet caress
From you, Sweetheart of Mine.

The road that lies behind, My Sweet,
Is memory's lane today.
But oh! The happiness we'll meet
If on that road we'll stay.

For that one road has been to me
A path to paradise.
For such you've made it, don't you see
And Heaven beyond it lies.

If coming years may be as sweet
As these have been with you.
Then everywhere with joy I'll meet,
And heartaches will be few.

Oh, may we never have to stray
In lands beyond the tide
Without our sweethearts all the way,
To go along beside.

Joan M Hubbard
STAYING A-FLOAT

The praise and the glory for this poem goes to Jesus Christ my Lord and Saviour.

Today out on your fishing boat
Take time to thank God for keeping you a-float!

When you are looking at my blue skies
Take a long look and ask yourself why?

When you look at my sun
Look in your heart and ask yourself why you tried to run?

When you look deep in my water
Remember I was took like a lamb and led to slaughter!

Look deeper in my water
You can see my blood
The blood that was shed to buy you at a very high price
Don't even try to say that's just life!

Holly A Wagner
EARLY
The sun has not risen,
All is dark.
Outside blocks of light mark where houses will soon be.
The ticking of the clock goes in rhythm with my
broken
healing
heart.

But all is not lost.
A friendly, warm, loving hand reaches out,
A shoulder for me to lean all my worries & tears on.
Reaches for mine,
Touches ever so softly.
A familiar sweet, cute face.
A friend that I will cherish & never leave
Someone I will always love,
No matter how far or distant our lives are & will be.

Vonnetta Miles
WHO AM I TO JUDGE

This poem is dedicated to my mother who inspired me to write poetry based on my feelings. Thank you Mom.

Who am I to judge
When I myself not perfect;
To call some people names
To call some folk perverted.

Drugs, violence, crime
All crammed into one;
Although I do not do it
My life has not begun.

You do not laugh at people
When they look differently;
You laugh at yourself
For acting stupidly.

People can't be perfect
Not like him above;
So who am I to judge them
For I am not the judge.

Victoria Lynn Shandor
SONNET 777

Dedicated to Mr. Gilbert P. Huhlein Through Christ in you and the humble life you lead, I have found Peace, Love & Joy.

The Lord has Blessed you, O,
Earthen child.
From Heaven you've Come,
Resembling the Skies.
Your Hair is the Sun, Golden, yet, Mild.
God's Sprinkling of the Great Blue formed your Eyes.
The earth Yielded the Wheat that you Abused.
Hell Claimed you, when Mugged and in a Wreck.
You would then Replenish all that you Used.
But you are Loved by He, who Saved your Neck.
There is a Purpose as you Sure did See.
Granted another Chance, you've Done your Best.
By Sharing your Life's past, I've Learned from Thee.
Your plain Relived is Better put to rest.
I Know that what's Said here May make you Sore.
What's Done is Done, which makes Me Love you More.

Rochelle Bowe
TAKE TIME TO PRAY
I woke up early one morning
And rushed right into the day,
I had so much to accomplish
That I didn't have time to pray.

Troubles just tumble about me
And heavier came each task
"Why doesn't God help me," I said?
He said, "You didn't ask."

I wanted to see joy and beauty
But the day toiled on dark and bleak
"Why doesn't God show me," I asked
He answered, "You didn't seek."

I tried to come in his presence
I tried all my keys at the lock
"Why doesn't God open up to me," I asked
He said, "You didn't knock."

I got on my knees that same day
Because I had so much to accomplish
That I had to take time out and pray.

Sharon K Togashi
necessity?
Frankly, Mr. Shankly, (and yes I stole this from Morrissey if
you must know) I don't give a damn if you live or DIE.
Because your quest for humanity is continual by life,
but arrested in DEATH.
It belittles you to speak of break-throughs and advantages
when you are
INCAPABLE
of curing mental illness,
that reactionary outcome
-sparked-
by a SUBORDINATE cell mass in
the depth chambers of the mind
while we shrink and snivel
in the LIGHT of the moon
in the name of SCIENCE.
Benefits?! Ha!!
Your rationalities? We are
expendable.
You are not.
We are ignominious.
You are not.
But frankly, Mr. Shankly,
what is imperative is not essential,
and what is immeasurable is
overbearing.

Kathleen J Newell
DO NOT DREAM YOUR LIFE AWAY
Do not dream your life away.
They are meant for only night.
Live to the fullest each passing day.

Make a wish here and there you may
but reality do not fight.
Do not dream your life away.

Dreams are fun and very gay
but they are not your guiding light.
Live to the fullest each passing day.

Dreams can be beautiful, that they may
but they cannot show you wrong or right.
Do not dream your life away.

Dreams can fool you in every way
I only hope that you might
Live to the fullest each passing day.

Dreams can be nasty they
can try to blind your sight.
Do not dream your life away.
Live to the fullest each passing day.

Stella F Terroso
MY SOUL

To Jim with gratitude and fondness.

A one-way bridge to dreams untold
Limitless as the shorelines of the world
This ocean of fortitude lies tranquil,
where fondness for the intangible abides.

My palace prospers, blazed with light
I am consumed with completeness.
Pray, I find an equal abundance
a traverse affair of the spirit.
My thirst is to share my space,
My sacred treasure from the Lord.

Jewell Castro
OLD-TIME FIDDLER (MY DAD)
In the hills of western Texas
on a prairie, barren and wide,
there lived an old time fiddler.
He was his family's pride.
He never earned a nickel
for the tunes that he would play.
He played just for the joy of it;
he fiddled every day.
As he tuned up his fiddle
and rosined up his bow,
he would tap, tap, tap the rhythm
with his feet upon the floor.
I grew up with "Old Joe Clark,"
"Soldier's Joy" and all the rest,
and when I heard "Orange Blossom Special,"
I knew that was his best.
Now that old time fiddler I knew so well
said good-bye to us one day.
He now fiddles in the Heavenly band.
Some day, again I'll hear him play.

Merelene Haffke
NOTHING
TO my two beautiful, talented sisters
who convinced me that I had some too.
I'm writing this poem about
NOTHING
And I'm writing it especially for you

I usually start with a theme or person
Or maybe some kind of event.
But this time I'm writing about
NOTHING
At least that is my intent.

Have you ever thought about
NOTHING
And tried to make it rhyme
But that's the great thing about
NOTHING
You're not even wasting your time

I can't tell you of beautiful flowers
Or kittens with cute fluffy tails
I can't speak of birds that are nesting
Or boats with white billowing sails

I can't even comment on the weather
Which by the way was near one hundred & 10
Because then I'd be telling you something
And I'd have to start over again

My mind is beginning to fill with thoughts
Of stories and jokes I have heard
Almost started to write them down
But can't and that's really absurd

Have you ever studied about
NOTHING

Wonder if the library has books of reference
But when I think back to my school days
The subject NOTHING was my preference

How many times have you gone to the closet and said
Oh—I have NOTHING to wear
Maybe we should all become nudists
Then we'd just run around bare

My stomach just started to grumble
Said let's have a sweet little treat
Went to the kitchen in search of food
Guess what! NOTHING to eat

Tomorrow I'm going to do NOTHING
I won't even answer the door
And if I find that I like it
The next day I'll even do more

I looked up NOTHING in the dictionary
It's a noun, I guess that makes sense
It's meaning is nil or zero
A person of no consequence

Let's get together for some NOTHINGNESS
Makes no difference, your place or mine
We can do it over the weekend
'Cause NOTHING doesn't take much time

I'm sending you this poem right here and now
For there's NOTHING more to be said
Besides it's past my bedtime
And I'm tired and going to bed

I think I've proved my point
If I've talent it won't bring me cash
So after you've read this NOTHING
Just toss it into the trash

Sandra L Adams
ON THEIR WAY
On their way
Three bears and a possum
On their way to church
Stopped to chat to the mouse next door
Big bear said "We're late"
Possum said "Yes you're right"
Little bear said "Bye mouse"
Middle bear said "See you tonight"
On to church they went
Just as fast as they could go
Three bears and a possum
On their way to church

Paulette Schauer
MOONLIGHT ANGEL WRAP YOUR ARMS AROUND ME

In Memory of Michael A. Mentgen, Sept. 16, 1989.

I went to the cabin
Where we used to go
The place I told you felt like home
It wasn't the same, you were not there
Moonlight Angel
Wrap your arms around me
Oh how I miss you so.

People search for years
To find the love we shared
And never do
Moonlight Angel
Wrap your arms around me
Oh how I need to hold you close.

Married in our hearts
Is how we wanted it to be
But in reality, it just couldn't be
Moonlight Angel
Wrap your arms around me
Oh how I loved you so.

It's strange how a smile
Can turn to pain
When the one you love
Is no longer there
Moonlight Angel
Wrap your arms around me
I will forever love you so.

As I was floating flowers on the waves
To say my final farewell
The flowers floated back to me
As if they didn't want to say good-bye
Moonlight Angel
Wrap your arms around me
I know will be no more
Rest In Peace, MY LOVE.

Eileen Lievers
NORTHERN LIGHTS

This poem is dedicated to Sister Betty and Sister Agnes.

Dancing Northern light, dazzling to our sight,
Enter to perform on the stage of night,
Skim through the blue that's star studded too,
Moving light like an advancing cue.
An order is given across the vast heaven,
"Into one" now shred away to oblivion,
Some shoot high, search lights in space,
Others have wings and an Angel face.
Many fluffy balls in shades blue and green,
Players are a blank and never can be seen,
The sky is their field unlimited the range,
So they fade and return in a constant exchange.
Beauty to the eye old as eternity,
New as this moment, but still a mystery,
Enter mystic light spirits in snow white,
Dance once again on the stage of night.

Monique M Murphy
TO MY HUSBAND
You're all alone where
others can't find you
to understand you.
Lost in a world
of your own
hiding from your past.
Trying to find a way out
by hiding behind someone
or something.
Thank you for realizing
you were all alone
and hiding behind the wrong things.
I love you with all my heart
and I'm going to try
try my hardest to grow up.
I am going to try to put my past behind
by putting my husband
and children first.
I am going to start doing
things on my own
without having to ask anyone
from outside of our home.

Frieda Gyorgyi
WORLD PAIN
We live in a world of turmoil
of ravages and wars
of oil soaked birds' dead bodies
washed on distant shores
Our buildings are leveled
the tremble and crumble at the breath
of a hurricane assault
Many are left fleeing
but not of their own fault
Our children are left wreathing
with drugs in their veins
while their parents' hearts are aching
with unfathomable pain

What is this world coming to
It's falling apart
Where is the answer?
Where must we start?
We must look within the depth
of our being
We must commune
with God in our hearts
then let the love flow outwards
to a world so broken apart

T Leonard Kinkead
THE COLD CIRCLE
Through the deep dark canyon, I was born.
I sucked in the breath of life that was foreign.
Rejected among the great walls of cold stone,
She cast me out without regret, without a moan.
The Rag-Woman picked me up out of the alley;
Then as I grew I went deep in the Valley.
I wandered in a maze of right and obtuse turns.
It became my turf with painted grass, no ferns.
The swift and crooked currents carried me along.
I went forth, on a cloud, looking for my throne.
The shores I walked, were laced with quicksand.
There were few safe places where I could stand.
The sharks circled tirelessly but I would not bleed.
My acquired love waited for me to succeed.
She was warmth and light in my cold dark life,
Her open arms welcomed me from daily strife.
Then a deadly missile found my racing heart.
Rising slowly, from this life I unwillingly depart.
I turned to the tunnel and to the pure light,
Now all the wrongs are understood as right.

Marie Hayes Blewer
LOVE PAINTING

To my lovely daughters Beverly and Barbara.

If I could paint a picture
It would be of you and me
The sky above of azure
Below the deep blue sea
The sun shines down upon the sand
You and I are hand in hand
Leaving footprints far behind
For the hungry waves to find
Never dreaming it could be
The birth of a new reality
To love — To live
Asking nothing but to give
The love I have for you.

Harold F Quincy
BEFORE I GO
If I had only a few minutes before I go
Most of all I'd like to see it snow.
Lots of big soft glistening white flakes
Just before my last breath I takes.

Now many folks with me would disagree
Likely some part of this old world they'd want to see
Or maybe a relative or a friend's hand to clasp
Difficult to decide—as life is slipping from our grasp.

Others might enjoy a stroll down memory lane
Knowing full well that things would never again be the same.
Perhaps a treasured glimpse of someone dear
Would satisfy a tired mind while death stands so near.

Then again maybe an auto trip or a horseback ride
Would brighten those last minutes more than a friend by side.
Odd how a lifetime passes through your mind as you stare
Whether it be money, passion, or worship that makes you care.

Actually they say it's the thought that counts the most
And we all want to be 'Right with God' when we meet our ghost
But most of all I just want to see it snow
During those last few minutes—before I go.

Pat Qualls
WAKE UP
The building lies vacant, just going to waste,
While the homeless are out there, suffering and cold.
Would be cheaper to fix it and clean it all up,
But bureaucracy and red tape is endless I'm told.
They would rather spend money on everything new,
So maybe it will be done in a year or two.
Cleaners and plumbers and maybe you too?
Could take that old building and fix it like new.
If everyone with talent gave a little free time,
The building that lies vacant could be done on a dime.

Robert E Quick
MOVING ON
From fog to mist
I move on now.
From day into night
I move on now.

You said I should go.

From a boy to a man
I move on now.
From school to work

I move on now.

You said I should go.

From one love to another
I move on now.
From this hurt to that
I move on now.

You said I should go.
You said I should go.

Gary Quartana Jr
THE PILOT'S FLIGHT
Flying, Flying up so high,
With speeding jets that roll right by.
Soaring in an '18 Hornet,
It's me, myself, and my opponent.
Going as fast as sound will go,
I maneuver my jet to get a tone.
Finally I get him in my sights,
But then he lights those flaming pipes!
Afterburner comes, and he's on his way,
I eat his dust and feel ashamed.
But now I've got a second chance,
I barrel roll and do my dance.
I break left, he breaks right,
I'm on his tail, and it's my fight.
Now I hear that special tone,
And very soon I'll be alone.
Now I fire my missile with pride.
And wait till the plane and missile collide.
I see it explode, and know he's dead,
For I'm the Victor, zooming ahead!!

Sandra Gayle Pierce
WHO AM I?
Am I really here?
or
Am I just acting out
a play for someone
above?
or
Am I someone's doll
put here for them to
love?
What if
I am a feather
that appears to be
alive?
But probably
I am just a person
who lives a lot of
jive.
Who am I?

Amy Smith
BY THE SEA
I walked alone beside the sea;
And as I walked there seemed to be,
An unseen friend walked by my side
As I wondered at the changing tide.

He rules the sea, the sky, the land,
The moon and stars hear His command.
All else but man, joins his melody
Of love and faith and harmony.

His gentle voice spoke from the sea,
"Be not afraid, just follow Me."
I noticed not the time or way
As we walked and talked that day.

I lingered there until the sun
Dipped in the sea, and day was done
My cares, my fears all slipped away
Because I walked with Him that day.

I hurried home but duty called,
All seemed right within its walls.
My hopes renewed, tears washed away
Because I talked with Him that day.

Mark Alan Smith
TIME FOR A TRIM
I went to the barber shop
About a quarter of three.
I sat there slightly trembling
And then he called up me.

He put the cloth around me
It went down past my gut.
He plugged in his shearing shears
And then began to cut.

I felt the cool air blowing
Across the fresh new fuzz.
Cuz there wasn't any hair
But stubs; that's all there was.

When I left the shop that day
My head sure cut the breeze.
But now when the winter comes
My ears are gonna freeze!

Kathryn K Schwirian
MOTHER NATURE'S LAMENT
My children, what have you done to Planet Earth?
Teeming with life and beauty rare,
Lush green forests and pure fresh air,
Rich fertile soil and mountains high,
Sparkling clean waters, fair blue sky,
With a life support atmosphere
It was entrusted to your care.

In the early years of living,
You were a lover, ever giving,
But as you multiplied and grew,
Careless greedy ones among you
Cared little about conservation
Or healthy life termination.

It's CHLOROFLUOROCARBONS global,
THREE MILE ISLAND and CHERNOBYL,
ACID RAIN over northern lakes,
ILLEGAL DUMPING CHEMICAL WASTES,
CONTAMINATING LEAKING LANDFILLS and the DEADLY
MASSIVE OIL SPILLS.

POLLUTED WATERS, LAND, and AIR
And HOLES in the OZONE LAYER.
It's not too late to stop, repair
Damage done to the atmosphere.
So all nations can breathe and live
It's not too much for all to give.

Respect the earth and life within,
Cooperate and all will win.
Begin the task and start today,
Correct the problems, don't delay.
If not, PLANET EARTH will become
Like VENUS, a HOT LIFELESS ONE!

David Sheridan
HABITS OF MY MIND

Nancy, I love you and if it wasn't for You this wouldn't be possible. David.

A memory echoes through my mind
of promises, that have come to pass
through life's tragedies.

Years unlived, No one can
touch them
or give answers to the questions
that shake my faith in life's
essence.

Me, a mortal, laughed upon
and criticized for my youth.
Waiting for silver, searching
for gold,
Wishing all of humanities
mockery away.

I ask, 'Why are the destitute
of life's crumbling society
wasted away?'
'What chance is their purpose?'
A memory echoes of promises.
Again only echoes!

This time of ignorance and
blame of fate.
On with the laughter, cry
for your life,
Laugh through its bitterness and pain.

Pray forgiveness and at its end
should you have the breath.

Karl A Storch
PLACE OF FANTASY

To Michelle, with you I have found my Place Of Fantasy.

The orange setting sun shines
down on my worn face,
as warm pieces of sand
filter through my toes.
The gentle ocean waves
lay down on the beach
as seagulls fly overhead.
Sitting down and scanning the sea,
I spot a lone two mast sailboat
slowly drifting across the horizon.
So peaceful if this place
as the beach runs empty
for miles each way.
The wind gently blows
warm air to caress me,
making me never want to leave
this place of fantasy,
as I fall asleep to a setting sun.

Elaine Schlomach
SWEET AND SIMPLE
How can life be so simple
How can life be so sweet
What's the required principle
That you would have to meet

Oh, can life be as innocent
As innocence can be
Like when you were a babe-in-arms
And all was worry-free

Self-respect was never free
Nor something that you learned
You'll value something even more
If it were roughly earned

Life could be so simple
If we all stayed young at heart
It's the children of today
Who give the future its own start

Kevin Sakovitch
A TEAR OF HOPE

To the memory of my beloved Aunt Jackie, Jacqueline (Heaton) Wilbur, who passed away November 1989 after a three year struggle with cancer. I miss you— dearly.

Alive with the sound of fire it moves cascading to all points of no return. Enlapping as it goes, it is the sensation of death. Forward on and over it decreases to none. Filling the void of great and endearing love. It conquers all and amany, destroy. Pain and agony is its only reward. Stronger, stronger it is and goes. To live it is impossible, the torment unbearable, it is breaking the hardest heart, dissolving the soul. Slashing the courage. A tear is left and left alone, 'tis the only one. A tear for God's pity, a tear for the misfortune, a tear for emptiness that is left. Why is it alive, it lives to see the pain. Many a pain and suffering to live through. Can it not see, it is blind, the hurt and tears. Yet alas a glistening tear of forgiveness and hope. While the blackness wreaks havoc, all is not forgiven. Tranquility and peace, the everlasting sleep of dreams. Is it the only way, why must it be so to hope of death, can't it see what happened, to look at battlefields lost. The life of another to be forgotten.
Do we forget and dream of mystified places. Dream we dare for it is the only life of one we know. Never forget me.

Christie Sebastian-Lane
TAKING DOWN THE WALL
My hurt feelings have turned to stone
As I buried them deep inside.
I saved them up and built a wall
Behind which I hide.
Here I'm safely tucked away;
Loneliness is the price I pay.
I build my wall up stone by stone,
The higher it gets, the more alone.

Locked with me behind my wall
Is the love I long to share.
I pray this love will give me
The strength it takes to care.
The courage I need to face my wall,
The power it takes to make it fall.
Taking it down I will feel the pain
But then I may start to live again.

Debbie H Saaler
MOM

This poem is dedicated to Margaret, The best Mom in the world.

Mom stands for,
the mother of making.
She pours all of her love,
into what she makes and bakes for us.

Mom stands for,
the mother of many.
She's always there for you,
lending a helping hand.

Mom stands for,
the mother of mary,
She's always there for you at the time of sorrow,
listening with an open heart, an open mind, and a prayer at hand.

Mom stands for,
the mother of memories.
Through the happy times, sad times,
good times, or bad times,
"Thanks for the memories, Mom."

Helen V Simpson
THE SCARLET LADY
Who proves there is a God above?
The poinsettia does.
She appears, in all our years
In her scarlet robe of love.

Her annual visit on this earth
'mong silver bells and mirth,
Most celebrated time of year
A reminder of HIS BIRTH.

The lovely poinsettia knows
When it's nearly Christmas Day
She glows in all her glory,
But doesn't wish to stay.

I think that when the world grows safe
As our dear Lord intended,
The Scarlet Lady will stay all year
With open arms extended.

Jennifer Schiff
FIRST STEPS

To my sweet little baby David, I'm as proud of you today as I was the day you took your first steps. To my sweet new baby Payton and my husband Dave. I'm very lucky to have three such wonderful men in my life. I love you all.

Sweet little baby time goes by fast
Before I know it my little boy will be a man
You did it today you took your first step
You crossed the fine line you can never go back

Sweet little baby time goes by fast
Cherish the memories make them last
Please my baby don't grow up too fast
For someday soon you'll understand
When it comes to sweet babies time goes by fast

Bettye E Nelson

Bettye E Nelson
FROM TIME TO ETERNITY

In memory of my parents, Leon and Blanche Nelson, who raised me in God's way with love and helped me towards my goals which filled me with hope and the ultimate happiness of being a parent myself.

Time started with God billions of years ago.
How and why the scientists don't know.
But the universe is still growing.
Where it will stop there is no knowing.
They cannot explain it.
There is no way to contain it.
Time is such an important factor
And God is the controlling actor.
Our life here on earth lasts only a twinkling.
The rains will become only a sprinkling.
Man will not last to tell what time has told
But future learns from history
And God alone can solve the mystery.
Scientists predict earth will disintegrate during the 21st century.
Our waste has not been complementary.
Why worry that it is growing and will scatter?
What does it matter?
One day in time God will end what He began,
And at that time eternity will begin.
Time will mean nothing then.

Flo Saforo
I AM BUT

One woman with one heart
to share with one man.

To give my all, but not
to fall for all of love's
pitfalls.

To be understanding, but
not foolish. To be his
mate and try not to hate.

To be a partner and never
apart.

To give as much of myself
unselfishly as possible,
for afterall — I am But
One Woman.

Jeff A Sackett
IF WORDS COULD SAVE THE WORLD

If words could save the world,
such a poem I would write,
and copies for every nation, an end to every fight.
From every city in every nation,
laughter we would hear,
both young and old in song and dance living free from fear.
In peace would we live, one nation
and as friends,
together we would learn to forgive and make amends.
No longer would there be
governments in dispute,
armaments and propaganda, no longer to pollute.
The sun would rise and never
set in a world filled with love,
the only leader being, the greatness of God above.
The hearts and minds of all the
world from young on to the old,
would know the joys of peace in the words that I have told.

Carol R Trevisan
THE NEWS

It is just so, how all the good people have to suffer for the bad people.
Good people always forgive the wrong;
Jesus always forgave all the people who walked all over him and abused him.
Because of Faith, Hope, Love and Charity he was taught . . . by his father.
Abused children always protecting the abuser.
Because of fear.
Victims of alcoholics always forgiving the alcoholic for a bad time.
Because of hope, and love.
A victim of a drug addict forgiving the drug addict for almost killing him.
Because
How honest people always get blackened by a liar's doing.
When the dog bites.
How the hard working get stolen from because of idol air.
When the bees sting.
How good people get hurt by being the good circumstance in a deceptive situation.
When you're feeling sad.
Funny, how twisted life can get.
But thank Jesus for influencing those people who put up with it all
This has been eyewitness, late night.

Sandra Turgeon
POTPOURRI

Save the beauty in a jar,
Roses gathered from afar.

When things go crazy and the world's gone mad,
Look in the jar and think of what you had.

The warm summer breeze that would carry the scent
Of sweet smelling flowers wherever you went.

The soft gentle blush of a single rose
That hung on the fence in a perfect pose.

Petunias, pansies, daffodils, and more,
The Bleeding Heart just outside your door.

Gather them, save them, keep them from frost,
Look in the jar when you feel that you're lost.

Remember the beauty, the love and the pain,
Then pray that the world will return and be sane.

Wonda Troth
MISSING YOU

I know I shouldn't miss you so
whenever you're away,
I know I shouldn't think of you so
many times a day,
I know it isn't right to dream those
dreams that can't come true
But that's what happens when
someone becomes a part of you.
I know I shouldn't wait to hear the
things you often say,
But it really doesn't matter—I keep
waiting anyway,
For you've become a special part of
everything I do,
That's what happens when someone
becomes so dear to you.
I knew I had to find a way to always
have you near,
So now I simply close my eyes and
see your face appear,
I see your smile, I hear your voice, I
feel your tender touch,
That's what always happens when
you love someone so much.
So now if you should go away,
however long you stay,
It really doesn't matter for I'll have
you anyway.

Patricia Baker Triggs
TURN AWAY

To Michael, for the pain and the joy; To A.A., U.B., Ann, Amber, and Justine for their non-stop believing and Love, and Tom, for never giving up or giving in, PISTAS!

I remember seeing you for the first
time ever
my blood raced, my heart pounded
and I wanted so much
for the slightest touch but from my
mouth nothing sounded
and I had to turn away.
From that very first glance whether
by fate or chance
All I ever wanted was to love you
As funny as it seems, for all that it
means
no one's ever loved me so true and I
could never turn away.
And so we loved for two years while
not once did I fear
our love would ever end like this.
Just like a bad dream whose endings
are so terribly mean
I couldn't even bear a final kiss, nor
still, turn away.
I don't know who was wronger, you
turning me away
or me for loving you longer than I
should have let myself
But I care not for power, for wealth
I care only for you, my love with
eyes of crystal blue
I know not of happiness without us,
two
together we should be as one for my
love for you will last
Even after the Earth, Moon and Sun
have passed
and that is a pity, truly a shame
for when two hearts collide no-one is
to blame . . .

Barbel N Salvo
INTROSPECTION

Radiant sunbeams danced on the trees,
shimmering, shining rusts and greens.
Trunks of stature portrayed strength and time
immovable soldiers in God's organized lines
Sleepy-eyed puppies basking in the sun
these were not what I saw when I was young.

Hurried and frenzied I searched for life's fun,
unable to feel and see, for I was on the run.
Precious babies grew overnight
did I hold them and love them
before they took flight?
What I was here for I wanted to know
I searched for the answer and it
became my Foe.
Wasting hours in perpetual thought
wishing and wanting to be what I
was not.

Why does it take so many years
to find an answer through
highways of tears?
Couldn't I have turned my face to the sun
seen all the mighty things God had
done??!!

Every day is a rose surrounded by thorns
in order to pluck it, gloves must be
worn
Tenderly touch it, hold it with care
every petal a chapter—so beware!

Leonard Shapiro
STABILITY

To Henrietta, whose fortitude and visibility has given me stability.

Harbor not the notion that our nation is unsound
Advance with dignity to meet on common ground
Think righteously about the struggle to achieve
Constant diligence is for us to always believe

Our attempts at placid cool logic
Warrants a desire to not kindle magic

But release the emotions of veritable thinking
Eyes are open to sight not stubborn blinking

Pragmatic opinions will bring stability
Blossoming forth fluorescent fertility
Minding it with exuberance
Clarified roughly with a magnificence.

Deborah Sharkey
THE AWAKENING
Ballerina in flawless toe
Performs a dance before untold;
The dancing vision, I behold
And take the gift she dost bestow—
The illusory motion of effortless flow.
Not passion nor promise does she withhold.
Astonished, I watch the story unfold,
Conscious of my surroundings, although
Hypnotized, I gaze enraptured,
Marvelling at the body lithe—
Turning, soaring, carefree, blithe;
Movements of elegance, poetry, grace.
Awakened, my imagination is captured,
Suspended a moment in time and place.

Tony Soto
IF I FALL IN LOVE AGAIN
If I should fall in love again
May she be as enchanting as you
May her eyes be as charming
And her smile as pretty too

If I should fall in love again
May she possess your tender touch
May your love song be hers also
And may the words mean as much

If I should fall in love again
May she have your kind of pride
May her heart be full of warmth
And may fate be her guide

If I should fall in love again
May she be as special as you
For she would be a priceless treasure
So lovely and beautiful to view

Tony Soto
THE GREATEST HURT
I Still love you with a tenderness
That grew deeper with every kiss
I lived my days for only you
My nights with you were full of bliss

Then one day your heart grew cold
Your kisses lost their flame
And now I sit alone and cry
Whenever I whisper out your name

I feel so terribly lonely
It seems as though times has ceased to be
I seem to wander aimlessly
Because you're not a part of me

Torn are the plans that we made
Our dreams are a world apart
And taking your love away from me
Has really broken up my heart

M Roger Shumway
THE MAIDEN
Lovely maiden I like what I see
heavenly delights in a form so free
musical interludes quiet me
but love is the best.

mental demons torment me
sometimes
tearing at my very soul
they won't let me be
but your love has swept that away

Let me take you in my arms
and hold you tight like you hold me
if we could only be together,
then you and me would be one entity.

such a long time forming a foundation
but now I know I AM here to stay
I AM the man I was meant to be
and you a woman of today

graciously you sing to me
I listen and know you true
you hold my hand and I'm not blue
(so faithfully)
The answer if you love me, too.

Lois Staton
WHISPERS OF THE WIND
The wind whispers softly,
Of two hearts becoming one,
A togetherness in life,
As none other has known.

A precious gift is given,
With memories to be created,
A sharing in your quest,
For tomorrow's dreams awaiting.

Cherish every moment,
Take for granted nothing at all,
To possess a love so rare,
Through every strength and flaw.

Gently the wind whispers,
Of two souls which have found,
A love to hold on to,
A commitment and a vow.

Marjorie Squires
OUTER SPACE
There's nothing new that's under sun
Or, so the story goes.
Then we have finished 'fore begun
Whichever, heaven knows!

But, let's consider outer space
It's under sun and o'er.
Frontiers are boundless for the race—
We've not been there before!

We'll end this rat race—tail 'n all,
And other problems, too;
Then zoom away and have a ball,
Where skies are always blue!

A stop by MERCURY for mail
And travel hints 'n trade,
Then JUPITER for laws 'n bail—
Aha! we've got it made!

We'll bypass MARS—we've got it here!
There's VENUS just above.
Her shining beauty makes it clear
To us—from GOD with love!

Jennifer Marie Steele
ROSE

To my parents, who always believed in me.

A Rose is like a person.
In many ways.
So beautiful in blossom.
Dies all wilted and old.

Roses burst into life with a bang.
They die without so much as a goodbye.

Roses stand like guards at attention.
Swaying in the wind like children at play.
Their soft petals made of baby's skin.
Water glistening on them like tears rolling down cheeks.

JoAnn G Siclari
NO MOTHER HAVE WE
No Mother have we to call our own.
Yet we see her name engraved in stone
For she has gone and won't return.
Oh, how our hearts will always yearn.
Now our Father lays at her side.
And together in heaven they shall reside
With our Lord up above.
We send them all of our Love.

Paramjit Sidhu
VEILED EMOTIONS
How do you relieve the hurting down deep?
And wipe away the tears you've been crying too long?
When will you find a love you can keep?
A love that isn't part of a song.

When will you stop playing the fool?
And acting as if everything is cool.
It's no longer just a game,
Because nothing will ever be the same.

What happens to the pain you're trying to hide?
And the loneliness that tears you apart?
What about the beating going on inside?
That takes on the form of your heart.

Keith E Spence
THERE'S A CRYSTAL BLUE EXPLOSION

To My Loving Wife.

There's a crystal blue explosion
As the night time fills the sky
The stars rest high, the moon she smiles
And the rivers sing good–bye.

The breeze goes sifting through me
The willows whisper a poem
I see the flowers bending low
Their fragrance no more to roam.

The sequel to our day has come
To rest our weary bones
But the songs I hear are the songs I love
With their natural loving tone.

So I lie here in the meadows
My friend the river swishes by
And I think of love and life and you
As the night time fills the sky.

Stessy Shrum
WISHES
When I'm sad and feeling blue,
I make a wish hoping it'll come true.
If my wishes never come true I'll try and try until I pull through.
To make wishes happen you have to believe
in what it is or else those wishes will turn into a black colored fizz.
Love and passion are part of wishes too,
'cause it'll make you believe in everything you do.
Some of your wishes may be filled with love
those wishes will make your heart look
silk white like a dove.
Some wishes are filled with passion,
hearts of desire and lots of fashion.
Wishes are sometimes heartaches too, but
never give up your wish might come true.
To live in desire would most likely be best
but I seem to live like all of the rest.
It really doesn't matter because my wish
might come true. To be rich and famous,
glorious too. I'll keep doing what I do.
Many wishes don't come true, but don't put the
blame on you, just keep trying to pull on through.

Pam Sherwood
WALKING IN THE SOFT GRASS
Walking in the soft grass
with beautiful flowers all around.
An old lady in the distance
is on her knees; crying
She feels the pain.
She knows the memories,
of the day her son died.

a dark, rainy day
bewildered men walking around
many lying down; lifeless
he starts to run
trying to get away
but there's nowhere to go
trees all around.
a cry through the night
and now he is one of the lifeless.

Now an old man came,
trying to comfort her.
They lay down a single rose
turn and walk away
crying.

Alice Seeman
GOOD MORNING
God was up early this morning, I know, for I looked at His sky,
A waning moon was sailing, and a star was still twinkling its eye.

The birds in their nests were waking, and called softly to the trees.
The chimney smoke, showed that homes awoke, And lighted their windows with ease.

Within these homes the loved ones, were busy with the cares of the day,
And soon the early morning, passed silently away.

There's a wonderful peace and quiet, In the early morning dew,
When you say, "Good Morning," to God and His Day, You see, I was up early too . . .

Toni Richey-Steele
TO MY KIDS

For my children; Joshua, Jessica and J. And to their Daddy, Robert, for obvious reasons.

I want to write a poem
To be read years from now
So when my children read it
They'll laugh or cry
out loud.

I want you all to know
how dear you are to me
Even when you think
Daddy and I are "mean."
Spankings may not feel so good
Grounding's hard to bear

Hours of standing in the corner
Never seemed that fair.

And all the other little things
We've done to punish you
Was only me and Daddy's way
of saying
"Love Mom"

Paul C Snyder
MIDNIGHT SKY
A midnight sky of darkest blue
a blanket full of stars,
A tiny patch of heaven
to worship from afar.

The stillness of an evening
to make your spirits flow,
A shining moon to greet you
and bathe you with its glow.

A gentle breeze surrounds you
as you look up to the sky,
And all the stars that you can see
add a twinkle to your eye.

If only during the daytime
you could feel as you do,
As you dream all through the
nighttime
with your midnight sky of blue.

John Siciliano
THE WORLD—TODAY
The past,
So simple,
So relaxing.

Nature,
So pure,
So everlasting.

Today,
So complex,
So contrasting.

A fire,
So destructive,
Burning
Searing
Cutting through the simple pleasures
of the past,
Revealing hatred,
Discrimination, racism, hunger, war.

The simple pleasures of life,
Now eaten up
by the deadly blaze,
of the fire;
of human ignorance.

Sonya E Spicher
UNTITLED

In loving memory of Peter A. Harris (1964 – 1984).

Sometimes I sit and think of the
way it would be,
If you were still here with me,
I'll never forget you for as long as I
shall live.

This life that we've had together,
Was shorter than it should have been.

Sometimes I feel I've lost my only
friend
Then I remember things about you,
your style and
The way you made me smile.

Lord have mercy for the way left us;
one night on a lonely highway.

Peter M Slegr
SHOW OF SHOWS
Stone gates, stone gates please let me
in
Before I commit another sin
I feel the Devil burning deep inside
'Cause he knows I have nothing to
hide.

How can a man feel any good,
If he cannot be washed of the Devil's
burnt wood.
So I am a human as I well know,
But please don't make me go through
this show.

I want not to be a great star,
But just a corner in this world of
ours.
For I've seen too long, how the wood
burns slow,
And how hungry our people must go.

It's no play game, that's for sure,
But reality right now, in its purist
form.
I wait & wait & look here & there,
For a clue of you & all there is to
spare.

Our spirits get high when we feel
those passes
Coming our way day to day
But then we see it's just thee ashes,
of the burning wood
slowly blowing away.

Burn wood burn
Let us see our hearts
We're getting so
Tired of playing
All those parts.

Argentino Saraceni
MY LANGUAGE
Fresh vowels tepid consonants
Sweet perfume of fruits and flowers
At every Mediterranean season
Loved daughter of vernacular Latin
Tender mother of many dialects
Melting the metallic echoes
Of the tower bell's sounds
Running jubilant harmony
On top of the hills among the valley
From the Alps to the Iblei
Gentle triad of italic tongue
Birth given me with maternal love
Others I was stretched to learn
To soothe my two half of sorrow.

Debra Sierminski
THANKSGIVING
Hugs, Kisses
Laughter and Pleasure
as family is gathered
all together.
Love, Joy
Pride and Desire
as children go and
co–conspire.
Yelling and Screaming
fills the air
as the football game
is on the air.
Dinner is done
down to the very last bun
and plates are piled high
with style.
A pause comes over us
as we are led in saying grace,
and then everyone can
stuff their face.
Everyone thinks
as they drink
how thankful we are
to have each other.

Frederick Benedict Scheel
NIGHT
'Tis dark! The tide of night will lave
The cobbles of the mind, clean wave
To flush away the seat and silt of day,
Black cares, dead leaves along the
way.
Clear thought, white marble of the
mind,
Remains. How muddy it would be,
and blind,
Without clean waves of night, a delta
littered
With roots and rivulets of pain
embittered.
Worry, bolting unbroken doubt-laden
steed,
Stumbles and sinks beneath dark
mists of sleep
As mind in stream, or eddying in
dreams
Slips awash to more ethereal themes.
Curtain of renewal drawn between
our days,
O' night! You too are wright for our
nocturnal plays.

Gerald Schultz
CANDY JAR
Striving for the grade
While reaching for the top above
And in the meantime being afraid
If unable no one will show love
One cannot be beat all days
Life is not perfect by far
For consolation there are many ways
But not a candy jar

Oh to dare
And break the mold
Disregarding values where
You find to be old
Without a guide
Incoming drugs there are
Coming for outside
And not a candy jar

Mary A Schlarmann
SUMMER MEMORIES
Blackcaps:
Plucked for jams, jels and pies
Oozed betwixt my fingers
Blackcap wine.
Hay:
Clover and timothy
Intoxicating smell
Asleep in the mow.
Oats:
Harvested seeds of grain
Itching beneath britches and shorts
A sea of sand.
Sweat:
June, July and August sun
Cold showers and lemonade
Summer fun.

Susan A Stavely
THE HEART NEVER LIES

This poem is dedicated to Daniel, a boy I'll never forget. Love Always, Susan.

If you listen to your heart
You'll know it's true
It's not the love, but the lover
Who'll desert you

Everyone's wishing that
they were me
To be loved by you, instead of
being free
As I listen to the rumors that
go around
You say it's not the way it sounds

But as I slowly slip further away
You know you have to find some
way
To strengthen the love that's slipped
Down inside, far away

My heart forgives but never forgets
So I'll make one last wish
To never forget our last kiss

Vonda Sims
DREAMS

For My Daughters, Dawna and Leova.

Dreams of lonely passion
Waken me at night,
Dreams of fallen angels
Fill me with fright,
Dreams of mare's tails
Painted on the sky,
Dreams of people living
And also how they die,
Dreams that carry far away
My Spirit, I can tell,
Dreams that show me Heaven
And the darkest side of hell.

Joyce Stuckman
SUNSHINE AND RAINBOWS

To Meme and Duke, "Sunshine of my Life."

May God fill your day
with love

May God fill your night
with hope

May God fill your life
with sunshine
and rainbows

Al Soucy
TRUTH

To my loving wife and best friend. The best means for understanding is to question life and yourself.

When looking for the TRUTH in life,
One should look no further than
inside.
For the TRUTH is sometimes very
hard to find.
You struggle, pray and search until
the day you die.
One day in time you will know
TRUTH.
That TRUTH is nothing more than
the way each person chooses to live
their life, and life is nothing more
than a measure of time in which we
have to choose that life.
Step forth into the adventure, walking
slowly, observing all that life offers.
For one day it will offer no more and
the memories that others have of you,
will endure until they have gone too.
Though there will always be life, the
sky and the sun to begin a new day
after this day is done.
So in your quest for the TRUTH as
you say, remember to member the
price that is paid for the wisdom and
knowledge you have on this day.
That life is to live, though question
you may, but don't forget to live life
today.

Al Soucy
JOY

To My Loving Wife and BEST Friend. The Best Means For Understanding is to Question Life and yourself.

With spring in the air.
Change will soon be here.
New birth will rise with the wind.
The trees and flowers will bloom.
The grey dismal sky will disappear
and love and joy will fill your heart.
For winter is the time of year that's
always cold and dark and people
keep

themselves locked up, hoping only for a spring breeze over the mountains rushing
through the trees. Reminding them that it
won't be long before the spring fills your
heart with a song and winter will be only
of the past until another fall. So dream
today in February of a spring day not long
from now, when the sun will shine and the
days get longer and the birds begin to sing
for this is the time of year that I love most when winter turns into spring.

Karen Salvadore
ABSENCE

Lonely is . . . when people are trying
To talk to you and your mind has
Flown to a faraway place.
Depression is . . . when I cannot touch
you or look into your eyes.
My mood will not change, until I
Feel the real presence of you.
Let me have patience for this moment,
For patience and my love for you
Are the only key to my happiness.

Faith Angelica Vettrus

Faith Angelica Vettrus (Age 11)
FREEDOM IS MINE IN '89

I dedicated this to MOM who helps open the 'DOORS OF OPPORTUNITY' for me; to GRANDMA KAYE, who loves every poem I write; to AUNT KATHY who is so generous with encouraging words; and to my sister, DIANA, who is responsible for opening this 'biggest door' yet! I LOVE YOU!

Freedom is mine in '89,
And it always will be.
I'm just like my ancestors before me,
So very glad to be free!

I'm free to vote for whomever I choose,
I also have the freedom of speech.
I can express my personal opinion,
And learn from all those who teach.

Freedom is mine in '89,
For some, it's not theirs I see.
Now I know that emigrants came here,
Just so they could be free!!

Freedom is mine in '89
And I think that you'll agree,
Freedom is mine in '89,
I'm glad that I am free!!!

Charles B Rodning
MY YOUNG ONE

my young one
holding a yellow crocus
smiling

S A Sellers
'TIS 11 O'CLOCK

'Tis 11 o'clock
And all's not well
The King is dead
And the government fell
The end has come
The time just right
So watch the land for economic plight
And though democracy fights itself
A dictator slips off his chair
Raises his hand to the air
And begs the land for its support
But in the end, he is seen
For he is, no more in between
As the country falls into the past
We wonder why it could not last.

James Shockley
SEA BREEZES

Sea Breezes
gently touching my face as I meander slowly
down the isolated strip of beach.
Sea Breezes
slightly stronger, playfully lift kites
high into the pale azure sky
flying farther from my reach.
Sea Breezes
more forceful – churn the water
into foaming waves
lashing wildly at the shore.
Sea Breezes
at gale force – tossing debris as though nothing,
searching frantically for more.
Sea Breezes
frightening, foreboding, terrifying
power – causing those
who near it to cower at its sight.
Sea Breezes
a panorama . . .
gentle, playful, churning, forceful, frightening,
enticing, alluring, entertaining, but never . . .
. . . ever . . .
. . . trite.

Martha R Siminpar
DYING IN A FIELD OF WAR

A Young Man Lies On The Bloody Ground
Before He Dies He Wants No Sound.
He Was Struck By Lead And Now He Must Wait
Until He Is Dead To Feel The Hate—
The Hate Of Men And Of This War
Of Those Who Sin Forevermore.
He Thinks Of Home And How It Will Be—
He Feels A Groan But He Cannot See.
And As His Eyes Are Slowly Closing—
He Finally Dies With No One Knowing.

Jennifer Sanborn
DISCOVERY

Old and young,
they walk.
Standing still,
they talk.
Young has just begun,
to live.
Old has a lot to share,
to give.

Listen to me Old pleads,
take heed.
Some day this knowledge,
you will need.

Young's laughter lilts,
away
Old looks on and
stays.

And now I see,
When did this happen to me,
Yes, I see
Old is Me . . .

Robert O Shipman
CAROL

Dedicated to Carol my love, my wife.

I met me a lady as pretty as can be. She came into my life and really changed things for me.

I used to run around and chase women all night. She held me and hugged me and squeezed me tight.

She whispered in my ear, things will be alright. As we sat and held each other every night.

Time has gone on and I realize things have gotten better since she came into my life.

I am in love that is true ever since you came into my life and I started sharing it with you.

Mary Schlotzhauer
PAIN

He said, She said.
Then nobody said.
He left.
She cried.
Over and over she pondered in her heart.
It wasn't the first time.
For her, it was the last.

Michael Straub
DEPRIVED

You are not Forgotten.

The man is lying on the corner,
in the silver that he holds,
I learn of the wisdom he beholds,
with his body ever changing.

If you have seen him before,
and know him by name,
he may sing a tune or two,
and in his songs you remain.

It would be wrong to say,
he hasn't put up a fight,
he's tried as he will,
but always ends up losing to the night.

And if one day he has your company,
he will tell you of his thoughts,
but when the sun comes to rest,
you will go to live with the best.

Ruth Ann Sparks
CHANGING SEASONS

To my Father, Danial S. Sparks Sr., with love.

The Changing Seasons have always been a delight to me. Spring: which is the birth of a new time. With the fragrance of fresh clean earth, awashed by the gentle rains that brings forth the blades of grass and the buds that will
soon burst into blooms, the birth of new things, that is Spring.

Summer: a maturing of the passing seasons. The strength of warm sun and mild breeze. To warm the earth and nurture it. So many things the Summer brings. The warm sand on ocean beaches, the strong fragrance of the forest, the dry pungent odors of the desert. That is what Summer brings.

Autumn: the time of changing and passing on. The world around us alights with brilliant colors. Golds, Reds, Yellows and Browns. It is difficult to describe the beauty of Autumn. It is the golden time. A time of complete maturing.
A time of saying good–bye to the youth of Spring and the maturing and strength of Summer. A mellowing is what Autumn brings.

Winter: a time of a different type of beauty. With its pure white coat. It is a time to say to the seasons pass, good–bye forever. It is the time to blanket the earth, so that beneath the blanket, the preparation for new things can begin. A time of passing and preparing is what Winter brings.

Robert Serrano (Age 13)
LIFE: BEGINNING TO END

Born as a baby,
Exploring new found land,
Looking all around,
For your parent's gentle hand.

Many years passed,
Then you are a child,
You become real hyper,
And very wild.

More time has gone,
Six years more later,
A boyfriend or girlfriend,
Puberty, a teenager.

Finding the right person,
Starting a family,
Having one or two children,
More than you've ever seen.

Then you're old and sad,
Death is not to whom you should surrender,
Times have gone quickly,
Beginning to end.

Kathy Schreader
SADNESS FAR BEYOND IMAGINATION

When I heard she was going to a new world of her own,
Experience life in another way, in another place,
Somewhere beyond unknown,
I felt like crying as a child cries for its mother when it is hungry or sad.
We had been the best of friends since the day her eyes met mine.
Even when arguments come about I could hear the sincereness in her voice.
Now she is gone.
Never again would I see her until the sun's hot rays would beat hard against the ground floor.
Even if I would see her those days that would come,
How long would that last?
For a lifetime or none?

J C Steindorf
GREY MORNING
Grey morning
Dull day
No warning
All grey

Nothing to do
Just sit around
Thinking of you
Without a sound
Then . . .

Suddenly sunlight
There's no more grey
Everything's bright
A happy day

Fern Crowell Stengel
FACT AND FICTION
Yesterday my oats I ate
Today . . . today . . . passé
woe is me . . . I . . . wonder
why . . . have I lived so long?

Last year 'twas red, red meat
Then the roundy, roundy egg
Woe is me . . . I . . . wonder
Why . . . are . . . they so tasty?

Now there was a time
A cup of coffee I enjoyed
Woe is me . . . I . . . wonder
Will it stop my heart, a reflex curb?

Today another fella said
More, more food to regulate
Woe is me . . . I . . . wonder
Why . . . I could have lived so long?

Daisy Sanders
LOVE IS

"To Humanity," in its gifted struggle to Love, and share Life, in all its "humorous splendor."

"Love Is" . . . ?
"Two"
Adore and Comfort
Understand and Forgive
Give Joy and Hope
Honor and Trust.

Tammy Shields Swallows
THE CHRISTMAS GIFT

To Bethany Alyce, born November 27, 1989. The expectation of your birth is merely a wave in the ocean of mystery on which ebbs the revelations of who you are and who you will become. I love you precious daughter.

Little wonder, deep inside,
What wondrous miracle goes disguised?
Who are you, infant dear,
Sleeping, curling, growing there?

Charming child of unknown grace,
Do you have Daddy's eyes, his smile, his face?
Or is it my reflection I will see
When mystery becomes reality?

While Christmas magic charms the earth
We, awe struck, await thy birth.
For with the delivery of package glee,
Two in love, become family of three.

Little wonder, safe inside,
What shimmering secrets do you hide?
Who are you, child of mine?
Christmas gift of wondrous life.

Paul J Sandacz
USE CANS AND BOTTLES
Use cans and Bottles
No Deposit, no return.

And when discarded, they just lie there,
They don't rot, they don't burn.

Are we destined to die!
Among this sea—of no deposits, no returns?

No! The Pyrolysis Plant is the answer,
to this creeping sea of cancer.

It looms like a shining knight
to save us from this inevitable plight.

But alas, it too may soon be gone,
is there any hope beyond . . . ?

Joyce Rogers Stevens
LIFE ETERNAL

To my son, Mark Alan Stevens. Blessed are those who believe and receive God's greatest gift—love eternal from your mother.

A glimpse of Heaven for us to see . .
Where God and Jesus reign eternally—
In all their splendor and majesty . . .
Exalted in power beyond degree.

Yet, meek and lowly . . .
bidding All to come . . .
to taste sweet liberty . . .
His Life's Blood—our souls redeemed.

Water of life—offered free . . .
to All who will just believe.
Spirit to spirit—sealed indeed . . .
In earthen vessels this gift received.

His hand stretched out . . .
Love fills our cup . . .
There's nothing to fear—
When we just look UP!

For of things that now we see . . .
Very soon—just won't be . . .
But things that last for eternity . . .
Lie just beyond what we believe—
we see!

Alison Seale
LIBERTY

In loving memory of those who fought, both living and dead, for liberty, they are my heroes and are far from forgotten in my heart.

The day the American flag does not fly
Is the day my heart will shrivel and die.

As it waves in its majesty
It is a cherished piece of our history.

Grandly it stands for the people who have died for me
so that I may forever live in liberty.

I respect it so with hand over heart
For America, the flag is the greatest part.

Flying proudly oh so high
Against the darkening polluted sky.

We've ruined this land
That God layeth down with his mighty hand.

Yet with liberty we are still alive
Even though, in this country, some people fight to survive.

Communism is on the fall
They are finally breaking down the "Berlin Wall."

Maybe some day
we all may cherish liberty in the same way.

Remember always I will die for thee
Oh my sweet beloved liberty.

But I beg of my countrymen "Don't forget me"
For I fought and died, like so many others, securing your liberty.

Billie J Struckman
MY MINE'S EYE
My mines eye sees all kinds of things,
but what my mine's eye sees I cannot tell, for if I do, all I'll cause is grief and hell.
My mine's eye sees a face so gentle and kind, yet tormented by memories of the mine.
My mine's eye sees so clear the picture of what once was to me so dear and now all that's left is memories of you up here.
My mine's eye is lonely for something new, but all my mine's eye sees is you.
My mine's eye sees that gentle, kind face, the one that my mine's eye knows so well, that none other could ever take its place, in my mine's eye.

Bridget Sullivan
LOVELY NIGHT

For Julianna Smoot, who is always fully alive.

So lovely
Was the night
I almost cried.

It was a night for porch swinging and
Listening to a saxophonist
Fill the air with
Rich gold notes

Memories
Of lush Hawaiian breezes and
Palm trees
Flirting their fronds
On the beach
Prevailed

Taking my bike I rode the streets
Letting cool breezes
Tickle my throat

I never smiled so much

It was the kind of night
That only comes once a year
When spring is sweetly succumbing to summer
And you feel glad to be alive.

Christopher W Stinger
BRIANNA
Just for a little time until I see you.

Your face, your eyes, your smile and oh to be
sure the most infectious, lovable part of all your laugh.

Just for a little time until I hear you.

How sweet the memory of you at play, no grimacing
carousing, no shouting of "hey"
Just precious small hands busy with love, and a heart
that so gladdened those who were near with eyes that shone
with real joy, knowing no fear!

Just for a little time until we all can see you again, and
again, and again.

How I would never complain with your heart next to
mine, and forget the whole world and forget about time—
Brianna is here.

Just for a little time—how precious!
"Pop–Pop"

Judy Stephens
SUN

To James, with love and hope.

Morning
And the world around me wakes.
The daffodils along the fence stretch themselves
Toward the smiling sun,
Old friends reunited at the end of a long night.
They do not know my Sun has gone,
Stolen by his father in a fit of anger.

The daffodils tremble with joy
As the playful breezes tickle them.
They do not know that I tremble with fear
That my Sun may never shine on me again.
We live in two different worlds, the daffodils and I.
Their world is bright and breezy and simple really;
Mine is empty and dark and cold,
Where delicate hope dies too young.
I wait for the night and sleep,
Where I dream only of the Sun.

Jannette R Crowley
BRIDES
A women
in love,
Is something
to behold.
Efficient,
yet so shy.
Laughter
comes bubbling,
From deep
within her soul.
Graceful--
Beautiful—
and yes perfect.
Is a gorgeous
Bride!

Mary C Quinn
COMBAT WOUNDS
The weapons of war are spent.
The wounded soldiers grieve and sigh.
The nurse, on land, on sea, and in the sky,
Is there to help and heal
And she tries and tries.
Can someone see her pain?
Look into her eyes!

Wars are man-made . . . a game to them.
The nurse knows . . . she's had to pick up the pieces,
The pieces of arms and legs, bellies and heads
Bright red . . .
Dirt-filled . . .
Still pulsating!
Some pieces pierce her heart for she knows
She must share the burdens of our wounded sons
For years to come

And she cries . . .
Cries because she cannot
Not now
Not ever
Give them back their carefree former selves.

Mary M Stumreiter
SNOW

As I sat by the window
The snowflakes softly fell
So gently lest they break,
Their beauty to behold.

Quietly piling up in heaps,
Wrapping bushes in a soft blanket
As if to say, "I'll keep you warm;"
Glittering in the sunlight like diamonds;
Soft as ermine fur.

North winds started blowing.
The snow soon piled high.
The children shouted with glee,
Mounds made good sliding.

Mother Earth welcomed the snow,
Its moisture gave new life.
Flowers blossomed; birds sand.
Suddenly it was Spring!

Geneé N Stites
THE LORD'S NEW YEAR

Thank you, Lord, for another year,
For all those people precious and dear.
We made it through.
We made it fine,
For only you could be so kind.
Some were hungry
And in so much pain,
but you brought the surviving light back each day.
Then, others were happy
And joyfully sane
as you led them through your path of riches and fame—
The riches of life, family, and friends
And the fame of the spirits who'd be with you without end.
Dear Lord,
May this year be better than the last
And make up for all the bad things we've left in the past,
And we thank you, Lord, for leading the way
And for bringing life into us all each and every day.

Jeneen Olaiya Smith
THE BAGWOMAN

This poem is dedicated to my Mom, thanks for believing in me.

When I see her it brings tears in my heart
That the American society has let this start
I get sad and it makes me mad to see someone
Who has to roam the land without knowing what
Is in store for her life from day to day
But she is also an inspiration to me
For not giving up her life, because America
Gave up and did not help her because she
Could not offer this country what they wanted
Anymore.

She has not given up the fight for her life and
I thank the bagwoman for it.

Tayce Stinson
SPARKS

Dedicated to Randy and what could have been.

. . . Sparks,
where there once were flames
are all we'll ever see.
Sparks,
that die in random games
are all that's left of you and me.
Sparks,
will never light a fire
when smothered at the start
And sparks are not enough to warm
this cold and broken heart . . .

Hazel Sparks
SLEPT JUST FINE

I went to sleep and slept just fine
Conscience clear like it ought to be
to have life happier for you and me.

To have life happier for you and me
Lots of fun: work and play
Of the nice kind to make life gay
Carefree, stable, steady, and good
To have life happy as we should.

Hazel Sparks
THANKSGIVING

One day should not be put above another day in the ways of our behavior
But special days we celebrate to add a little flavor
Therefore, Thanksgiving Day is a special day in our lives
One to have a big dinner at home, out on the town, at a relative or friend's
A day for gaiety, some frivolity, and a bit of sober contemplation
But a day for one's cares to have been put away for future consideration
To give thanks to God for blessings of the year on what we hope to be a very happy occasion
A day to ask for a more fruitful harvest in the year ahead when one's
material or spiritual needs have not been sufficient
For the standard of life a person's work should provide in this twentieth century civilization
A day of restfulness, as a rest one day in seven, a change that refreshes our day–to–day living
That is how to truly appreciate our own American Day of Thanksgiving.

Kristofer Stankovich
FORGIVE ME

Forgive me, forgive me please.
I've lost my will to live.
I've committed a crime
which hurts so bad inside.
I try to run,
but I can't hide.
Still the hurt keeps finding me.

Linda Sanchez
INSECURITY

My love, so new we count relationship in days
has eyes the color of a cloudless sky
My ears deceive me; his words fall as I listen
only to the blueness of his eyes
Oh god, will he find me stupid? And so, leave me?

His kindness and gentle manners show compassion
my own impatient nature pales beside
Doubt pervades me; can the sweetness he sees in me
veil the moody temper that is mine
Oh god, will he find me thoughtless? And so, leave me?

His hand, a strength barely hiding in the softness
has the warm, smooth feel of velvet gold
The mirror defies me; time's cruel pass left scarring
imprints on my body and my soul
Oh god, will he find me ugly? And so, leave me?

Lying near, tenderly, arms held light around me
he speaks of independence, being free
Panic grips me; what fair homage have I offered
to keep this Adonis here with me

Dear God, has he found me so imperfect? Will he leave me?

Esther M Sperlbaum
WHERE IS THE WIND

Where is the wind, when it does not blow
It covers ground, sometimes with snow
I feel the wind, feel it day by day
It must be hiding, but I cannot say.

Please answer my question, because I must know
Someone has the answer, and won't tell me so
Where is the wind, when it does not blow
It can't be everywhere, where did it go.

It freezes water, when it touches ground
The wind's very strong, whenever it's around
Where is the wind, when it does not blow
Guess there's no answer, no one seems to know.

Shawn Micheal Patrick Besaw
AMBER

A color I think of as burnt brown
lies upon the beaten ground.

Autumn ending in the fading leaves
brings a time of passing in a cold breeze.

Warm living stone from a tree's essence.
A knowing, feeling color within my presence.

My amber forever continue in fur and flora.
It is a very part of me, it is my aura.

Javerlyn Barnes
THE ROAD TO SIN

The road to sin is long and broad . . .
At the end stands Jesus telling me to come on . . .
To my right are drugs with their tempting lust . . .
Up ahead perverted men trying to gain my trust . . .
A poor wretched soul with no food to eat
No shoes to put on his worn tired feet
Little children who cry in the twinkle of night for a mother who's gone to fulfill the night
Men loving men with an uncured disease fail to listen to the truth they need.
Over there a brother who's just been killed for his shoes called Adidas his blood has no still . . .

Education has no value in a broken home. I'll trust upon welfare to carry me on.
I'll lay and make a baby: one, two, or three; maybe four or five. I wonder what they'll pay me . . .

Crack has drawn my mother there to the man in the Mercedes . . . Some oral they'll share.
This road to sin has lots of trees I've hit a few myself because of blindness I could not see.
Thanks be to God for the mother he's given me. I realize that there's some not as fortunate as we.
She stayed awake nights praying in tongues unknown to man that each of her children would be saved from sin at last . . .

This broadness I speak of has taught an awful lot that my body is God's temple to protect from deadly drought . . .

Yolan B Shute Parker

Yolan B Shute Parker
TO MY CHILDREN

Dedicated to my children. Autumn Lynn Shute, Christopher Shute, Spring Jean Parker.

You came to me as a sign
Of God's love.
His angels will always be with
You from heaven above.

Fear not my CHILD!
His presence is near
Please don't cry.
Or shed a TEAR.

I nursed you,
I bathe you,
I put you to bed.
And with a big KISS;
Prayers were said.

CHILDREN! I LOVE YOU!

With all my heart and soul:
You are more precious to me

Than money or gold.

I am your mother.
I am your friend.
Always here for you.
Again, and again.

You make me laugh,
You make me smile!
That's one gift of a CHILD.

LOVE, MOMMY

Gary Michael Robinson
EPITAPH
If my life is only
A collage of my experiences
Throughout the years
Then let me share what really matters—
Not names or people or places or things
But the feelings, the unspoken emotions
The unexpressable joy
Of a crimson sunset, a child's grin
And may someone else
Experience and share this again and again
For this is life Amen!
If I have learned
Any worthwhile lesson from this odyssey
It is my own insignificance
For anything one can touch
Is not real
But things that can be grasped only by
An open mind a joyous heart
Are forever.

Gary Michael Robinson
FLORIDIAN LULLABY
The insects are abuzz in anticipation . . .
Another sunset, seascape, serenade
Moon appears to illuminate the rippling, watery orchestra pit
Stars wink on to set the backdrop
A sparkling blue and rosé layered tapestry
The audience is hushed
Save the heron noisily searching for a seat
The pelicans rustle their wings anxiously
And the concert begins . . .
As they conduct their symphony of serenity
Coconut–clustered conductors
Coaxing moonbeams to dance
Majestic maestros–loose leafy hair
Indelibly silhouetted in my mind

Brad Rajewich
OLD JOE
I saw an old man standing under the pier.
His face was stubble but his clothes were cashmere.
His home was a box made of cardboard veneer.
The comforts were simple, with eyes full of tear.
But it isn't his fault he has to live here.

Somewhere in the past, a bitter divorce, a family no doubt,
Call him just Joe, a number society cast out.
Benefits are a helping hand, but not always enough.
They set strict limits even the homeless like Joe find rough.

Programs are developed with years of red tape,
Useless tons of paperwork, thought up of by some stupid ape.
Some big man sits behind a desk just collecting a check,
While Joe searches the alley for food, what the heck.

Joe is an old man living under the pier.
He no longer has a number, just a heart full of fear.
Joe is made the same as you and I,
The only difference is his slice of the American pie.

Nobody looks, human beings really don't care,
Turn your back and keep on walking, afterall,
He's an old man whom society lets live in poverty and despair,
Provided that good old Joe don't breathe too much air.

Jacqueline Rinehart
ZACKARY

For Zackary.

My little boy Zackary,
you're such a sensitive one,
you've got a long road ahead of you,
and your journey's just begun.

Your heart is such a soft one,
your feelings are all so new,
the smallest little comment,
can bring a tear to you.

Just keep your head up,
I know that you'll grow strong,
I love you little Zackary,
My little sensitive one.

Steven A Zopfi
LIFE ALONE

WANTED:
Someone to hold and be held,
someone to care and be cared for.

God made life different for every living soul. Why so many hurtless for me? Lost inside myself, not knowing what I want, or who I am. Holding back words and feelings as not to hurt or hurt others. Why do I care about others more than myself?

Feeling alone with nobody to look up to. Always hurting, not knowing what to do. Finding ways to run. Doing things and knowingthey are wrong. Life is full of questions, always looking for answers. Nobody has the answers? It's left up to me. I can't figure which way to go. Up, down, left or right. Knowing I want to go up, but always running down. Life to me has been a battle of hurt.

Resisting the feeling of falling deeper and deeper into anger. trying to exalt myself up, it feels as if someone is pushing me more distant than before. Anger is a powerful emotion, it brings out the most extreme in all of us.

John L Zacker III
FIVE SENSES OF LOVE

Inspired by my wife, Teresa Ann. At a time when we were forced to be apart.

When my eyes are closed there aren't any fences—
No walls or barriers to block out my senses.
My thoughts come alive with colors so real—
Imagination so strong I can taste, smell, and feel.
I take a deep breath, smell your perfume in the air—
Reach out my hand and touch the curls in your hair.
I watch you get dressed so early each day—
Feel the warmth of your kiss and then hear you say . . . I love you.
When my eyes are closed I can hold you so near—
Feel the heat of your skin, whisper words in your ear.
I hear your soft breathing as you drift into sleep—
And taste a wet teardrop. I'm so happy I weep.
I see in our future a long, love–filled life—
Recall that cold champagne toast when I made you my wife.
I hear the music wind down, end our dance with a bow—
Foresee a ninety year old man still keeping his vow.
When my eyes are closed my heart feels no pain—
Of my past years of heartache, no memories remain.
I am so close to you girl, sometimes your thoughts I can read—
So deeply in love because you are all that I need.

Bonita L Zoph
ANTICIPATION
I wait with anticipation, hoping to see you enter the room.
Could it be your eyes are searching for mine; and are your dreams reaching out to me?

I can almost feel your touch when I close my eyes . . .

Our eyes meet across the room and for that moment a whole lifetime with you fills my consciousness . . . Do you see it too?

I see you move to the door then you pause turning again in my direction: A smile crosses your face briefly, then you are gone.

Are our dreams shattered or did our hearts truly touch.

I walk as if floating toward the window, then suddenly feel your touch.

Our eyes meet in silence. The words of our hearts have spoken.

Rose M Zelinski
KING NEPTUNE
Our ship was quietly sailing, on the sea so peaceful and blue.
I relaxed and leaned on the railing, to watch the magnificent view.
The sky, aglow with the splendor, from the rays of the setting sun.
The breezes were gently playing, as if pleased with a day well done.
Then off from the east came Neptune, the Ruler and King of the sea.
A giant shell was his chariot, drawn by his dolphins three.
On his shoulders he wore a mantle, the same shade as his eyes so blue.
His left hand clasped a trident, so burnished it gleamed like new.
I held my breath as he drew near, for fear he might be araging.
At something done in his domain, to fuel his anger to blazing.
In such a mood, he'd wave his hand, and the seas would start achurning.
They'd roll and rage and swallow ships, so long his wrath was burning.
But as he passed, my heart rejoiced, for he turned and smiled at me.
Then faded with the setting sun, King Neptune, ruler of the sea.

Donald L Zeits
WHY!
Why!
When time suddenly stops you soon learn fear,
you say to yourself, why am I here.
The days are slow, the nights are long,
you say to yourself, what did I do wrong.
The trial starts the Judge declares, I sentence
you young man, only twenty-five years.
Off to the joint, the Bus slowly rolls, Why am I
here, God only knows.
Pick up the Bible, read it every night, hold on,
it may save your life.
Walking the mainline, the gangs prevail, you say
to yourself, this ain't County Jail.
Hop in a car, push some weight, toughen up or you
soon will lost fate.
Tattoo your arms, chest and back, a riot or two
they cut you no slack.
A few years now have suddenly gone by, night after
night, you just want to cry.
Why! Because on the street, the word you never knew,
time locked up has taught you a few.
Time has come, for you to know, the board has said
it's time to go.
Make sure you bring your Bible, I want you to know,
because without it, back on the Bus you will go.
Why!

Dawn M Zulawski
THE TEAR IN MY EYE
As I sit and watch the world go by,
I hang my head as a tear fills my eye.
There are many kinds of people out there,
Some who hate, and some who care.
The ones that live, the ones that die,
And that's what puts the tear in my eye.
As I grab my bags and walk,
I listen to the people talk.
Young ones laughing, even crying,
The sad part is — the old are dying.
While I'm walking down the street,
There are many different people I meet.
Parents teaching wrong from right,
Crying babies, to keep you up at night.
As we all watch the world grow,
I just want everyone to know,
There are people who let their feelings show.
The ones who care, the ones who love,
Are the ones who go up above.

Edward A Zenes
ECSTASY AND LOVE

For Veronica, (Ronnie) My Wife.

How can I express my love, my dear
Whenever you are near.
Your laughter is like the bubbling of a brook
going down the mountain side
searching every nook . . . and oh
That twinkling in your eye
Shines with all loveliness
Like the stars in the sky.

The shafts of golden wheat waving in the air
Remind me so much of your lovely hair.

Just to be near and caress you my love
And whisper softly to me like the cooing of a dove.
Oh, what ecstasy, what bliss
When our lips come together
And we kiss.
And so my love, whatever we do
I just want to express my love for you.

Carol Ann Zoranovich
BIRDSONG
Whenever I hear
the song of a bird
I think of her mate
and her young
and now and then
Jonathan Livingston Seagull.

Joe Zabel
OF DEATH

Dedicated to Christine Marie Zabel, my darling daughter.

A fragmented mind runs the gauntlet
Only a small amount ever used.
Nevertheless
Impressions of grandeur are made
With the inevitable doom in sight.
This meagerness of man goes forth
flailing & wincing
Waiting for that solitary blow,
That shall quiet the turbulence
So corruptly created.
The single blow,
Of course,
Never comes,
For death is but and illusion,
Created from within.

Andrew Zimnoch
ON THE PURPOSE AND USEFULNESS OF A HIGHER EDUCATION IN THE UNITED STATES OF AMERICA DURING THE 1990'S
To know the thoughts of gods above;
To live a life that's free
Of pride, and prejudice, and greed;
To transcend what is just I;
To understand the sky and sea,
And what makes thunder cry;

To probe the depths so close, yet far;
To dare — in thought — to fly;
To bring the spirit home to rest,
To bear the soul new hope;

To test the bounds of certainty
Without the shame or fear;
To look for light in places dark,
To find, and build, new worlds;
To live more days, each year, alive
To thunder and to roar
With past in every step I take,
I ask
what is school for?

Patrick Zale
LOVE IS LIKE A PIT BULL
Love is like a pit bull;
that look in their eyes
won't let you go easy.
If I had cared more only a little while longer
even my soul could now be mutilated but
why do I love someone I sometimes hate?

A silk black rose with red thorns lies
across his naked breast
in my dreams.

Erasing his number in a grand gesture to others,
not telling them it had been memorized,
calling it months later to see if . . .
to forget means to lose
all of the things from one's mind that
peace will not sleep with.

It was 3 AM once and outside this
idiot dog kept yipping at the moon
while the poet scribed of love
unrequited; YipYipYip YipYipYip YipYip

Why do trees grow into the sides of mountains?

Jean Ann Zwart
THE MEANING OF TRUE LOVE

To Jim To the one I Love the MOST.

It is sharing and caring
Giving and forgiving
Loving and being loved
Walking hand in hand
Talking heart to heart
Seeing through each other's eyes
Laughing together
Weeping together
Praying together
And always trusting
And believing
And thanking God
For each other
For love that is shared
is a beautiful thing
It enriches the soul
and makes the heart sing!

Amparo Zuniga
AND I SHOULD HAVE KEPT MY DREAMS
Foolish dreams of happiness.
Rhapsodies in the fantasy of illusions.
And I should have kept my dreams,
rhythms of my whispered dreams,
tunes of my irrevocable memories.
All to wonderful, being recalled
to my dormant mind.

Dreams I should have kept,
disposed of them to my pleasure.

And I should have remained
in my dimensional fantasy.
Never should have left secure comfort.
Hidden in some dark
secret corner.

As I awaken into this frigid
and penetrating
world of reality.

They seem to vanish into this mist,
into limitless universe.
Never to return again,
Until my last eternal sleep

Viola Skaggs Zimmerman
DEAR SAVIOR WHY
Only one short day after I gave my sons birth,
God chose to reach down, and pluck them from Earth.
I cannot understand why "He" chose to call them home,
Nor can I fight the feeling, that now chill me to the bone.
Taken to the "Savior," where they can never come to harm,
Somehow doesn't take away, this aching in my arms.
I'll never hear the pitty patter, of their precious feet,
Or check my babies in the night, to see if they're asleep.
I'll never kiss their tiny hands, or wipe away their tears,
Nor will I ever share the joys, of their childhood years.
I'll never waken day or night, to hear my dear sons cry,
But always in my silent prayers, I ask "Dear Savior"
"Why?"

Rose Young
HOMELESS
The Storm Broke,
The Rain Fell,
The Thunder Clashed, and
Lightning Flashed,
Dark and Cold, Silent and Alone.
The child sat in tattered clothes,
No home to call her own.
The Tears so sadly shed,
unheeded, even unneeded,
By those that pass each Day,
Through the city streets,
Only seeing the Tall Buildings,
City Sparkle and Shine,
Leaving the Dark night far behind,
Hiding its Shame,
That so many of its own go
unclaimed.
So many — No Shelter from the Rain,
The wind Blows untamed,
Through the streets,
Where the homeless live,—
And the tears, so sadly shed,
By those with no place to lay their head.

Rose Young
(THE BATTLE)
THE MORNING AFTER
The Battle Raged—
with might and honor; They Waged;
Till Dawn, sweet and swift;
to find Victor and Foe,
The Dead Lay cold as stone.
Raise Thy Sword; Bow thy head,
(for) you are not among the dead.
Follow the path,
for the way you must go,
of sword and blade, of warring ways.
Trouble not thy sleep, Leave you not to weep,
Nor shed a single tear.
Brave, Strong and Noble are Thee,
In Battle, you wage Might and Honor.
Have you no shame? for what has come?
The Battle Rages,
with no end in sight,
AYE, Raise thy Sword,
and bow thy head,
for you are not, yet, counted—
among thy dead.

Rose Young
LOVE'S FIRST TEARS
Take my hand, walk with me.
My hair may be gray, wrinkles show my age,
I may not know, of all the things of today,
but my heart still knows,
It still hears;
Each tear that falls, Each time you call.
Take my hand, walk with me.
I've been to war, I've seen men cry.
Found and Lost, many a true love;
I've seen this old world,
let me show it to you;
strong the Oak grows,
and deep the Ocean flows,
In the East the sun will greet,
the morning sky, and sleep in the West.
my hair is gray, my eyes gone with age.
but walk with me, for in my years,
I still remember, Love's first tears;
and I too, lost to another,
one so dear, YES,
I still remember, Love's First Tears.

Karen Zoldi
IF ONLY WORDS COULD DESCRIBE
If only words could describe,
Exactly how I feel inside.
Then you would know how I feel,
And that all this love is for real.

If you could only guess,
Without you my life is such a mess.
If my feelings could be put into words,
For eternity I will be yours.

If you only knew how much I love thee.
The only way I could make you see.
Is to tell you, I love you.

Deborah K York
OH, TO QUIT

To my loving husband, Steve. Who has tried and just can't quit.

I'm telling myself I'm going to quit.
Just as I'm reaching for another stick.
I know I can do it as I'm puffing away.
I'll finish this pack and I won't sway.

I find myself pacing the floor.
Feeling like this is really a bore!
Maybe I'll hold it just in any hand.
This will be easy, I won't start again.

My wife tells me, "It's in control!"
It's been a day and I got to get a hold.
I've yelled at the kids and snapped at my wife.
But if I go back, it has my life.

So let me tell you something that's bold.
Keeping it up will leave you cold!
But as for me; I lost the fight.
I bought a new pack; "Hey mister, got a light?!"

Louise Suiter Yates
FALLEN SPARROW
You have fallen little sparrow
But have no fear of your tomorrow,
For God will strengthen your wing
And give you a new song to sing.
Through all your grief and despair
There is one who still cares;
Our BLESSED SAVIOR is the life,
He will ease your hurt and strife.

Little sparrow do look upward,
God's love is the mighty vanguard,
He will lift your spirits again
And help you to bear the pain.

Debbie S Yost
LOVE IS LIKE THE SUNSHINE

This poem is dedicated to my loving husband, Jerry.

Love is like the
Sunshine
It may not always shine
Through the clouds
But it is always
There.

Rachel Young
I MOVED TO A TOWN

I moved to a town, it's a new
place for me
It stirred up some old, long
ago memories
Nostalgia can make you feel so alone
Funny, now that I'm here, I feel
like I'm home

I moved to a town, where
everything's changed
Yet the streets and the trees, they all
seem the same
I once thought I knew what
living meant
Though I felt awfully tired,
my energy spent

Now I'm a real person
Since I moved to this town
My face has a name
My smile has no frown

I walk in the park
My life's changing, I know
When I look in the fireplace
My heart's all aglow

I moved to this town, not
knowing for sure
If I could fit in where the land
is so pure
The wind calls my name, and
the stars fill my eyes
I sense a belonging my heart
can't deny

Judith Yakes
SOLUTIONS

For Don. My Solution for a happy life.

What is wrong? What can it be?
Our children are lost, and so are we.
Our world's gone mad, or so it seems.
They took away God, and smothered
our dreams.
Hidden amongst us, These powers
that be.
They thrive on greed and self, and
strangle mercy.
Ignoring the noble sacrifice made,
and ground hard won.
The blood and tears of the innocents,
drawn from the black barrel of the
gun.
Are all these lives sacrificed to have
been for naught?
Or the love of home, honor and
justice for which they fought.
Have we all been so blind, was it so
hard to see?
How these things have so
underminded humanity.
A human majority can turn this black
tide.
The apathy eroding humanity's pride.
Turn the faces of evil, so it is they
who must hide.
When all good stands together, their
intent to deride.
When light overtakes darkness, and
to each of us comes.
One heartbeat unites us, and sounds
the distant thunder of drums.
From a spark to an ember, from
ember to flame.
The solution's so simple and LOVE
is its name.

Rebekah Dawn Young
A NEW YEAR

A year has gone by.
Many things have been done.
I've been places, seen things,
Where could I have begun?
Now I look to the future,
And remember the past.
A new year has come.
I must face it. Alas!

Betsy Yohannan
A YOUNG CIVILIAN'S PRAYER

The world is made up of so many,
That there's just no way to count;
The way it was in the beginning—it's
so different now, there's no doubt.
Every part of the world has its
problems—a couple, a few, or so.
Each day something new occurs and
the results we'll never know.
So many out there are starving,
hoping for a loaf of bread;
While on the other side there's
always fighting and many people we
find dead.
There's no more peace in this nation;
not one country is together,
This life seems to drag on, going on
forever and ever.
Sometimes we find airplane crashes,
even murders going in on action
There's just such a number of things,
yet for the heathen it's such an
attraction
One day this all will end and
hopefully the world will no longer
fall;
For whatever happened to the saying
of one nation under God indivisible,
with liberty and justice for all.
As they say, every nine seconds a
child is being born
I just wish the children wouldn't have
to see this and mourn.
Abortions, broken families, suicides,
and so the list goes on;
Sometimes that's just too much for
some that wish they too were
long dead and gone.
There's just so many things that
happen
Yet for some until it happens to them,
they don't stop nappin'
But since I know there's a God who
listens—to Him each and every day I
pray,
Please, oh please, oh please Lord,
please help us find a way.

Lorie Yeater
THIS ONE IS FOR YOU

To Gary; This poem is for you, for all your support & love that you have given me. So Honey; This one is for you my dear. Love, Lorie.

This letter is for you,
My dear;
For all the times that we have shared;
With memories of laughter and tears;
And lots of cheers;
For the lonely times;
Even though you were so near;
You've shown me happiness;
You've shown me love and patience;
All this takes a little time;
We've talked of our dreams;
We're making our dreams come true;
But yet we still stay so near;
So thank you dear;
With all the happiness from my heart;
That all of this;
Does make you so dear!

Jessica Yankow
MIXED EMOTIONS

To Mrs. Amendola, Not Just A Teacher, But A Friend.

Isn't that what life is all about?
Happy, sad, angry, mad,
Broken heart, no heart.
Are we boyfriend and girlfriend or
are we just friends?
Sometimes people try too long and
hard to love someone.
What's the point of loving someone
if it's all heartache?
It's all talk but no action
Sometimes it seems that feelings for
someone else come hard for some
people.

Susan Bird Yastrzemsky
TANGLED WEBS

The sun grew dark in days of old
When youth was full of crooked
smiles;
And I began to hide behind the glitter
Of laughter—masking the weeping
child.

Always waiting for better times,
When pain would flee awhile;
Forever hiding from the storms—
alone—
My walls—my safe denial.

The sun eclipsed in middle years
Death stalked me — shadowed my
life.
Until I reached that bitter step
When reality became my eternal
strife.

I passed a moment filled with pain—
Emerged triumphant from the
shadows.
At last I see the tangled webs —
Imprisoned no longer — a smile that
glows.

Mrs Maurice C Yepsen
IN UNISON ALL YEAR ROUND

The Cheerleading and Pom-Pon Squads practice and practice to make sure each cheer, each movement, each motion, each step, each sound is in unison all year round.

The dedication and cooperation these squads portray makes us realize these young people are an asset to their families,
schools, teams, and the rest of the community, in every way. They are a tribute; they do work hard. Maybe we should send
them an appraisal card!

These Cheerleading and Pom-Pon Squads love and enjoy performing at all the football and basketball games. I only wish I could list all their names. Each cheer, each movement, each motion, each step, each sound is in unison all year round.

Anna Young (Age 14)
MEMORIES

Memories of you and myself,
Memories of my teddy bear at night.
Memories of photographs, old dolls,
and stray cats I constantly brought
home.
Memories of rainy days, reading
mysteries, and sipping hot chocolate.
Memories of friends old and new.
Memories of the fish I forget to feed.
Memories of the hugs I needed and
still need.
Memories of times to laugh and times
to cry,
Memories of life as it goes by.

Virginia Yardley
DELICATE PRAISE

You looked deep within
my heart to find
Someone I had hidden
safely inside

You fought to release
who You knew I could be
Good against bad
You always believed

You listened with love
to all I would say
You cared for each thought
I was not afraid

You've helped me to know
through Your delicate praise
In Your arms I've grown
to discover my way

With You I became
whom I'd always dreamed
Safe in Your love
I was free . . .

Nicole Pankowski
MY SWEET

I am the huntress, you the prey,
I give the commands and you obey,
Overpowering, devouring is my love
for you,
Running is useless, I will only
pursue,
I will not let another man tear my
heart in two,
To keep your love there's nothing I
wouldn't do,
All that is needed is your total
submission,
Don't talk, move or think without my
permission,
It's true there are many fish in the
sea,
But you, my sweet, will love only
me.

Daisy Parrado
DRUG ADDICTION

To my husband, Peter, whose hard work on Friendly Warning inspired me to write this poem. I hope Friendly Warning will one day be a reality!

The world of drug addiction
is not one of fiction.
It may someday lead to man's
extinction.

Its poisonous tentacles
spread far and near.
Its random selection is
something to fear.

The purest lives are contaminated.
The end effects are not over-rated.

Age is not the first criteria.
Drug addiction kills as does
diphtheria.

In hidden valleys,
In hidden alleys,
In many places,
and in bright faces,
Drug addiction is not fiction.
It may someday lead to man's extinction.

Colleen McLafferty
FROST
Quietly creeping
Over land,
You leave behind
A shimmering trail
Linger in trees
Adorning branches
With diamond beads
And glittering bangles

And then descending
On panes of glass,
You etch designs
Of delicate lace
And lofty spires
Glazed with silver.

Doris Hand Rex
IT'S A BEAUTIFUL DAY TO PRAISE THE LORD
It's a beautiful day to praise the Lord,
It's a beautiful day to praise His Name,
The sun is shining and the sky is blue,
All of God's creation says, "I love you."

The birds are singing and the grass is green,
And the waters move gently along,
A more beautiful picture has never been seen,
My heart is bursting with song.

So I will praise the Lord with all my heart,
I will praise Him with all of my soul,
For there is none other more worthy of praise,
For He has cleansed me and made me whole!

Virginia Lee Price
A DAY SUCH AS THIS
A rose lifted its face to the morning sun
That had been kissed by the velvety dew.
I passed by the rose, and thought of your face,
And wished that I could kiss you.

The sun shone warm and sweet and good
On the lawn so cool and so green.
I thought of your brow, when kissed by a breeze—
(Only I could know what I mean.)

I hear the song that a songbird sings,
As he calls to his mate on the nest.
I thought of the laughter that bubbles over
And makes me stand out from the rest.

I felt the breezes as they went on their way,
And caressed the petals of the rose.
Why do I love you on a day such as this?
God and myself only know.

Hazel M Halgren
MAN'S REAL DWELLING PLACE
I strolled to the mountains, determined to try,
To scale its great height once more ere I die
My mind was recalling sweet memories of yore
'til unto my body, its strength did restore
I fairly seemed living, as in days long gone by
When there wasn't a hill that seemed any too high
An, 'tis strange how the mind's eye can picture so clear
I almost did fancy that echo I'd hear
It seemed to be saying, "Oh where do you live?"
I really felt queerly, my strength seemed to give
My body was trembling now with emotion
For that echo my heart held a lingering devotion
My childhood voice seemed to ring in my ears
It still was distinct, unmarred by the years
Uncanny! those words of that echo I hear
Were meant for my soul, not alone for my ear
They revealed unto me a man's dwelling place
The home of all men, regardless of race
So, back to that home, I shall hurry and live
Life is not hopeless, my best I shall give
Man lives in the Mind, I just now have found
He buries his deeds in its hallowed ground
Memory's the fruit of the deeds planted there
So plan your life wisely and live it with care

Patricia A Henderson
THE STRONG HAND OF FATE
One minute she bounced along Third Avenue,
Eyeing all there was to be seen
. . . and seeing more.
Then the sunshine turned to rain.

"It doesn't matter," she tipped out of nowhere.
But the raindrops kept coming
Until they slid down her cheeks
. . . along with the tears.

She laughed out loud, deep and strong,
. . . and a little evil.
Because she knew it was better this way,
. . . to laugh rather than cry.

The next time she bounced along Third Avenue,
It really didn't matter.
And time after time, whenever she chose,
It . . . really . . . didn't . . . matter.

She still eyed all there was to be seen
. . . she still saw more;
But the sunshine
. . . thank God . . .
Never . . . again . . . turned to rain!

Tom Hale
MY YELLOW CANARY
My canary was yellow,
He was a handsome fellow.

He sang with such a shrill,
My heart got such a thrill.

I whistled, he whistled back.
There was nothing that my canary lacked.

One day his voice did not ring,
I did not hear him sing.

He looked at me as if to say,
I am leaving you today.

I whistled, I heard no whistle back.
There was something that was lacked.

I took my canary outside,
And buried him, and cried.

I heard a small still voice,
It said, "Rejoice, Rejoice."

It was an angel from up above,
He whistled back his love.

I knew that my canary was there,
He was with the angel somewhere.

I whistled, I heard a whistle back.
There was nothing that my canary lacked.

Elenore M Hall
THIS OLD HOUSE
For one hundred years, this old house stood.
Made of cement, mortar and wood,
Square nails and rough-hewn pine,
Loving hands created a home so fine.

Below a meandering creek is seen,
With stalwart oak, pines and green.
Serene, peaceful, quiet too.
God's handiwork is visible to you.

Laughter, tears this house has known.
Here many generations have grown.
From babies through teens they grow,
And this old house has marks to show.

This old house is staunch and proud,
Sitting below a billowing cloud.
One hundred years have come and gone,
Bringing with it laughter, sadness and song.

Johnny A Holcomb
GET OUT OF MY LIFE
Get out of my life
That's where it's at
Pain, foolishness, hurt and crying
I feel like I'm dying
But it's all hidden
Express it
I just can't
Price? Could be
Sorrow? For sure
Sorrow for all the things I held so dear
I say they're gone
But the sorrow is they never were
I thought the sacrifice for one thing
But in reality it was for nothing
So gather the emotions if you really care
And on this paper let your feelings air
Don't hurt those who are so dear and so unaware
And yourself with raw nerves exposed
Get it intact
Get it controlled
Put it way under to never surface again
You only hurt yourself
You only hurt them
Out of my life you say?
Yeah—it's better this way.

Diane K Hoover
LOVE AGAINST FLESH
Breasts against back
Pelvis pressed to rear
I raise up to nibble on his ear.

Reaching over for his hand,
Pressing tight against my man.
I send my love through to him
Could this be just a whim!

No, this love is strong
Greater than we
It is the state in which
I choose to be!

Arvely E Ficker
NEWLYWEDS
As you walk down the aisle
Think of the miles
That you will walk together
Remember the love
That comes from above
That will help you
In all kinds of weather

As you start your new life
As husband and wife
I'm sure that you will find
The important thing
That you can bring
Is to be considerate and kind

They'll be ups and downs
As everyone has found
Who has walked down
The road before you
But the farther you go
The more you will know
That love is the tie that binds you

Lurline (Billie) Freeman
THE BOUT
A jaybird awoke me this morning
Such chattering I never have heard
I don't see how so much noise could
come from the voice of one bird.

I raised my head from my pillow
To see what the fuss was about
On the ground, with feathers all ruffled
A sparrow and jay had a bout.

"Thief, thief" screamed the blue jay
The sparrow, "Cheap, cheap"
I never learned who won the battle
for I turned over and went back
to sleep!

Andrew Faltonson
MOURNING CLOUDS
Clean is the air when the morning comes.
With its brisk and refreshened feeling.
Thunderclouds raise their spacious mists.
And play with the children's minds

below.
LOOK UP! See the skies all dark.
Yet the sun peeks its fiery eye at you.
Particles of man's own luxuries.
Smother and bury your fungus cities.
A dark forboding cloak, pollution's dagger sinks deep.
Stark realizations leave nightmares in our sleep.
Warm was my bed when the morning came.
With the window curtains waving in the breeze.
Satin sheets flung loosely across your breasts.
As my mind and body regain that sentience glow.
Sounds of cries all begging forgivence, never to be heard from again.
Sounds of falling buildings in the distance, forever to be fallen.
Soundly stripped of man's own essence, severed from the family tree.
Sounds of the angels I ask acceptance, "Please God, let me be me!"

Diane M Foster
LOVE

I love you more as time goes on
And your love for me must be
just as strong
Because our life together will be
just as long
As our hearts are together
through eternity!!

Joseph Howe
SAILS OF THOUGHTS

Thanks for the special times and support . . . Lee Bolt.

Your eyes are so kind, time seems, to stand for your love for mankind you strive to understand, to give a piece of yourself, unselfishly.

But do not the waves of one's thoughts, begin to wash over the top, and the bottom begins to be the top . . .

I can see the paint beginning to wear, for it is time for you to rest.

I have more love for you than yourself, and can see the strongest of men begins to weaken . . .

Once just a child to learn, and now one to teach, take care and let your sails bring you to your port.

Jacqueline H Harris
CANDLELIGHT OF LOVE

To: Thomas Alan Stewart — who blew the candle out!

Light a candle and sit it down beside me,
Sit with your face near the flame so I can see . . .
All the sparkles in your eyes,
Feel . . .
All the love in your heart, and,
In my mind hear our song.
Because Babe I feel it won't be there
For long.
So if it's true — block me from the light,
Pray I make it through the long, lonely night.
And if I'm right — please help, give me no
Doubt,
Just stand up, turn around and
Blow the candle out!

Deanna Ferrell
I CANNOT BE YOUR SON

I know what it would be like to be your son.
Football, baseball oh, so much fun;
We'd cheer together, maybe even share a beer together.
But, I cannot be your son.
We can laugh, talk as we walk along our merry way.
We can discuss our futures as we pass the day away.
But I cannot be your son.
I am your daughter.

Steven H Williamson Jr

Steven H Williamson Jr
THE GOOD HARD DAYS

This is dedicated to my wife Esther and family, and in remembrance of my father Steven H. Williamson Sr. Rest in peace. Your loving son.

I was told that I was born in the back of an old storefront
I guess I didn't get much to eat so I grew up a runt.
I've been on my own since the time I was ten,
I've been wheeling and dealing ever since then.
I've felt the cold of old concrete rising from the ground into my cold bare feet . . .
I've walked the streets with holes in my shoes, no matter what anyone says I have paid my dues . . .
Sometimes I'd rob, sometimes I would steal, just to find money to get a meal
They're times when I could borrow just enough money to get food and shelter to last until tomorrow.
But now I've grown wiser in many ways, but I will never forget the good hard days . . .
I no longer have to beg or steal, I have a good job and I can pay for my meals . . . things have changed for me in many ways
But as long as I live, I will never forget the good hard days.

Gemelia Restum
R.S.V.P.

Tooty little cards,
Painted,
Engraved,
Demanding.

Who are you to demand
of me?
Stack them with the
Sale papers,
or discard them.
Speak in English,
and perhaps,
I will reply.

Reta Diane Johnson
REGRETS

I often sit and wonder
Why it didn't work out
But I guess you didn't love me,
Beyond a shadow of a doubt.

I used to be so happy
When we were together
Now I am dreary
And feel like a beggar.

Begging for you,
Pleading for you,
Thinking about you
Like I've never done before.

You were so careful
About what you said and done.
I tried to make you
Feel selfish and dumb.

If I had it to do over again,
I would never have let you into
My heart like I did,
Except as a friend.

Randee Barasch
STACEY'S DREAM

Stacey was a girl from today
Who sat in front of the television
everyday.
Oblivious to her surroundings—
T.V. was her craze.
When her friends came calling,
They always found her in a daze.

Her parents were quite concerned
And tried to keep her away.
But Stacey just sat and sat in front of
the screen.
She never cared what anyone
thought.
It was quite a scene.

They brought in all the doctors and
nurses, too.
Each one concluded that they didn't
know what to do.
No one dared to close the T.V.;
Or remove her from the room.
Everyone knew that this might lead
to her doom.

The next morning her parents looked
for Stacey in her usual seat,
But they didn't know the final
transition was complete.
Stacey was living her fondest dream.
Now you can view her on your T.V.
screen!!Brandy Barish

Matthew John Kosik
LOVE'S SEVEN PART MEMORY

1. My former love is to me my life's greatest joy and tragedy.

2. That is everything a love can possibly be for life is strange when death seems to be the only remedy.

3. But I understand living more now, since my mind is free, from all foreign substance and most of all <u>me</u>.

4. For if my love cheated, and if my love lied, let me look to myself for the reasons why.

5. So now each night before I lay down and sleep, I get down on my knees and pray the Lord keep that love I once knew a long time ago.

6. My former love who was to me, my life's greatest joy and tragedy.

7. So now I can remember how to smile, now I can see, and live life as it goes on today, for yesterday's love is just a memory.

Brandy Barish
FROM MY HEART

Some days are bright
But some are full of fright
For the thought of losing you
Would break my heart in two
I was never good at saying
Exactly how I feel
So believe me now if you will
I love you more everyday
And I hope together we will stay

Jeannie M Johnson
GRADUATION

Today we're together,
tomorrow we're apart,
all we have from yesterday,
is the loving memories in our heart.

Edwin P Spivey
STORM OF LIFE

The clouds creep ever closer and thunder rolls along
Lightning sends a warning to hush life's happy song.
The waves come ever shoreward, crash o'er life's defenses,
winds reach a crescendo, numbs the very senses.

Skies grow ever darker as raging hell breaks loose,
all sense of reason vanish, engulfed in mad abuse.
The thunder now is overhead, storm rolls to and fro,
the whole landscape lit by a senseless sullen glow.

The howls grow ever louder, like souls in hell's torment,
tear at life's foundations, each lull is heaven-sent.
The storm has reached its zenith, cannot get much worse,
the atmosphere is bitter, just like a devil's curse.

Storms like these must damn the soul, kill all trace of love,
please do heed these warnings that come from high above,
beware of all those sudden squalls and that sound of thunder,
when you see the lightning flash don't just sit and wonder.

As storms like these can wreck a house, uplift mighty trees
the storm of life can wreck a home, all love and comfort flee.
So smooth away all sorrow, soothe away all pain,
cast away all quarrels, so they won't storm again.
for storms can grow and fade away, then return another day,
each violent storm must leave a gap, then the strongest chain can snap.

Annessa Bishop
GOOD-BYE

You left me standing there
with a bitter kiss placed upon my lips
and an empty hug.
A hug so empty
that it made a sorrowing echo
when your arms released me.
For the first time
I could not read your expressions
when I needed to know most
what you were thinking . . . feeling.
Everything we shared

went wearily to the back of my mind
when you looked back at me
as you walked down the terminal.
Your look was not one of
"see you later,"
my heart knew it was good-bye.

Marie Hildalgo-Lindeman
THE REALITY
as i open my eyes
a figure appears
in the still darkness of the night . . .
the figure so deceiving;
as i look in its eyes
i sense a peacefulness, contentness,
and at the same time
raging madness and insanity.
is it going to harm me
or is it just going to watch me
from a far distance
with its curious eyes?
somehow i feel a lot of hurts
coming from within it,
as if it was almost human.
pain and confusion seem
to radiate from it.
i take one step to the side
to avoid its cold stares
that will strip me off of
every defense i've got,
and it steps to the side, too.
i let my mouth drop open
and so did its mouth.
i scratch my face
and it does the same.
i pinch myself to make sure
that i am awake,
i suppose it was doing the same.
i blink
and it blinks with me.
all of a sudden
it's friendly!
it has a sense of humor
just like i do.
it laughs with me
and it moves with me.
it knows how to have fun! . . .
but i still feel the pain
it is trying to hide beneath
those innocent laughters.
i still feel the confusion
it is reflecting to me.
it's definitely pain
from a broken love.
i see in front of me
reflecting what is behind me.
i see the figure.
i see me.

Donna Marie Lambeau
LET ME GO
Faces to haunt my mind and wild memories
can't you find someone that's blind
and help him that he can see?
How can I love you when your eyes are closed?
Let me go, we are through, let me go.

Bells are ringing, voices clear
can't you find someone that's deaf
and help him that he can hear?
How can I love you when your ears are closed?
Let me go, this is my song, let me go.

Words to whisper, make each phrase complete
can't you find someone that's mute
and help him that he can speak?
But how can I love you when you do not tell me?
When I know not what is on your mind?
Oh, let me go, because I don't understand.
Let me go.

Dwight A Black
ALL THINGS
Be sensitive and aware of all things,
The changing leaves, and all the beauty it brings.
Seasons unfold revealing mysteries within,
The fragrance of honeysuckle cradled in wind.
The softness of life, the innocent child,
The whispering wind so harmlessly wild.
A friendly smile from someone's face,
The warmth of love a gentle embrace.
All these things are pure and so free,
They're given to people like you and like me.
So share a gift as a bird when it sings,
Be sensitive and aware of all things.

Prashant Singamsetti
SWEET HEART
Your Soul,
is my S.A. Node,
Your beauty
is my A.V. Node,
Your Age
is my Vagus Nerve,
You are my heart.

Your Right eye
is my Tricuspid valve,
Your left eye
mitral valve,
Your Nose and mouth
are my semilunar Valves,
You are my heart.

Your Thorax
is my auricle,
your abdomen
is my ventricle.
Your Right leg
is my pulmonary Artery,
Your left leg
is my Aorta,
Your Upper limbs
are my Sup. & Inf. Venacavae,
Your hair
is my Pulmonary vein,
You are my heart
I am your pericard'ium.

Leona Zinious
ORANGES
Down the steep hill, we slowly drove.
Into the greenness of the orange groves.
The waxy blossoms were white and fair.
Their heady perfume filled the air.

Orange fruit hung in the trees of green
Nature's beauties were displayed to be seen.
Fruit plume with juice, oozed at a bite.
The golden liquid was better, than the sight.

Bonnie Lee Webber
A WALK IN THE WOODS
Did you ever take a walk in the woods,
Way down a flowering path,
And see a beautiful stream,
Where little fishes swim past?
Did you ever take a walk in the woods,
And follow the trail of a deer,
And say to yourself, "How nice it would be,
To have a picnic right here?"

Did you ever take a walk in the woods,
And walk down in a valley deep,
In time to see the violets there,
Awake from their winter's sleep?

Did you ever take a walk in the woods,
To watch all the birds in the trees,
And see all the little animals at play,
And feel a warm spring breeze?

So if you ever take a walk in the woods,
Be sure you always take care,
Remember God made them for everyone,
And they are only ours to share!

Emily Morrison

Emily Morrison
TO DISAPPEAR

To my best friend & husband Richard.

Some days the stream flows gently,
but there are days the rapids run fast,
trying to get somewhere between the
beginning and the past.

You stare wondering how did it get
there, this stream.
You look into a dream,
the rocks cluttered together like
people trying to get out of each
other's way.
The water pushing but no way will
they move or stray.

Like people they stand still,
nothing to do, sink into the sand,
disappear, just as we all will.

Princess Mary
HI, HOW ARE YOU?
"Hi, how are you?" he asked
She longed for someone to ask that.
"Can I help you be free?"
"Take my hand, I'll lead, you'll see."

Never had anyone taken the time,
Now it's he who makes her shine.
Never has her life been so fine,
Now here he is, this gentle man, so very kind.

The touch of his hand, this gentle man,
Conveys his love for her, as only he can.

Their lives have not been without pain and tears,
Yet for him she's there and for her he's always been.
He's held her, hid her from many times of fear,
They've dried each other's tears.

Their friendship has grown to love.

He took her hand, led her, and she saw the freedom he spoke of.

Mildred Grace McCormick
RAINBOW LAND
When you fly away up High,
And there is nothing left but sky.
Do you think that it is you,
Or is it all a dream come true?

Do you look 'way far below,
And think of Earth as much too slow?
For you are Kings in another world,
Where there's no Flag to be unfurled.

No wonder you are very fond,
To wander off, and leave the ground.
When you can go to Rainbow Land,
Where everything is bright, and
grand.

I'll bet you fly over, the
Rainbow Path,
Snatch all the Gold then laugh,
and laugh.
For you are Kings of the
Rainbow Land,
That beings of Earth,
do not understand.

Where dazzling Stars sparkle,
and play,
On the ever great, White Milky Way.
So go, and be Kings, Kings
while you may
Because Rainbow Land
is there to stay.

jy
nature's quandary
passing through the driving rain and storm,
i happened to notice along the shore,
a sight that was far from the norm,
a sight that summoned my curiosity to lure.

it was a day of glory for that wretched god of the sea,
neptune, rising from his throne, in a drunken rage,
casting his subjects in huge swells,
laughing as they flee,
like the bestial medieval lord to his subservient page.

it was not so much this display of power,
that really made me ponder,
but rather the ocean aviators, astray

from their tower,
humbled, docile, watching old
neptune with wonder.

those graceful navigators of flight,
stranded on the shoreline, overcome
with fright,
bold scavengers, casting their catch
against the rocks,
so infamous for stealing your
unguarded luncheon stock.

not a gull in the sky or upon the sea,
wing to wing, they stand alerted,
perched in safety, emanating their
silent plea,
that the wrath of that old sea dog drift
over an ocean deserted.

Jason Goldstein

Jason Goldstein
WE FOUGHT FOR OUR NATIONS
We fought for our nations—
We fought for our lives—
Oh, what a situation—
Of crying and bribes—
Oh, they shut their eyes—
To never return—
That was the secret—
We could never learn.
Oh, our hearts—
Yes, they burn—
The war really turned!
Oh, lesson of ours—
That's all I can say to the Lord!

Jason Goldstein
THE SEASONS
The seasons of winter—
The seasons of snow—
The wilting flower—
The wind in the trees—
A frightful sound!
The sparkling snow on the ground!

Miriam Farquharson
IN THE BEGINNING
'Twas at the beginning as formless,
untilled
Dense darkness kissed watery deep
unfulfilled
Lo! o'er surface waters His Active
Force milled
For creation patterns the MASTER
ONE skilled.
The darkness then scattered, and
light seeped around
Division of waters, up crept the
dry ground
Sweet-grasses and seeds,
vegetation abound
Trees yielding fruit with their kind
all around
Birds wing-spanned sail 'mongst
white clouds on high
Domestic animals graze peacefully
by
Great sea-monsters lurk in waters that
sigh
Wild beasts of the earth roam thither
and nigh
"Now man in our image, we
both now shall make
To tend EDEN's beauty, to care
and to rake"
And lo! as he lonely in slumber—
then awake!
A woman! a rig—helpmate for his
sake.
Oh! such ecstasy flowed at that
happy event!
The BRIDGE to the
BRIDGEGROOM, from heaven was
sent!
Thus in the BEGINNING—it
happened anew
Thus in the BEGINNING—
JEHOVAH GOD knew
He created a pair—and from these,
'we' grew.

June L Farmer
FINAL LEAP
Oh, spacious skies,
so clear and blue.
Until the haze
of smog and glue.

The times of yesteryear,
have changed to a
psychedelic hue.

When we take our sugar cube,
the sky turns to fiery red,
then yellow blue
or is it purple green?

No! I know,
it's Beethoven pink.
Colors are sound,
and carrots go bump in the night.

Pincushions are soft to touch,
and cactus make good beds.
These are our thoughts
'til we make our
Final Leap.

Kellie French
CONQUERED
Mountain ridges
And desert sands,
Connected by bridges
This beautiful land.

It falls at our feet
We'll reach the top
Even with repeat
We'll not step

Together we'll climb
The mountain ridges,
Together we'll walk
The desert sands,
Together we'll cross
The connecting bridges,
Hand in hand
We'll have this beautiful land.

Connie Franklin
KILLING ME SOFTLY
I fight and strive to be the best
In this corporate struggle, yet I'm left
In the middle always, second or third
in quest
Pass me the baton to catch the rest.

My contributions are greater it seems
Recognition, but not part of the team
Covert genocide of my spirit, is this
the aim?
I keep pressing on, yet things never
change.

Laura A Fiore
BONDS OF SYMPATHY
Bitter days
angry chill
Frozen heart
beating still!

Words unsaid
verbal death
Empty voice
frosting breath!

Vacant arms
hollow space
Physical absence
memory of face!

Abrupt conclusion
life melts away
Destiny continues
everyday!

Jamie Frolick
DRUGS
If you think crack is cool,
Then you're just another stoned fool.

I was a kid who was always high,
Until I realized my life was just
passing by.

I always thought I was really cool at
school,
Until I found out how cool drugs
really are.

When you do crack,
You're just another hanger on the
rack.

Drugs are never cheap,
Especially on the street.

Drugs make you steal,
Even make you kill just to get the
high feel.

When I was high,
I never thought I could die.

When I was high all the time,
I never planned on doing any time for
my crime.

Teresa M Fiore
THE COMING
It will not do any longer
to think we are safe, invulnerable.
No, it will not do.
We are not,
as we sometimes think
master creators, masterminds.
So easily it all crumbles away . . .
our creations,
our assurance,
our technology,
our pride—
all bow before another design.
For a little while in the past,
and now here in the present,
we have been the controller—
or more likely allowed a bit of rein.
But feel the temors—those at its
coming
the footsteps of change.

Elizabeth Evans
FEELINGS

To Dave, my husband for all his encouragement and support.

Loneliness is the feeling without you
here
Hope is the feeling when you are near
Love is the feeling I save just for you
Happiness is the feeling when you
are in view
Peace is the feeling when I'm in your
arms
Joy is the feeling when you use your
charms
Tenderness is the feeling we share
between each other
Fear is the feeling we won't always
be together
Blue is the feeling before you came
Sadness if the feeling I'll never take
your name

B A Walter Fletcher
THE LAST MOMENT
There's a growing feeling engrossed
in me
My mind is a throbbing heart, that
hurts with every pulse
I feel deserted, I'm lost
I'm like a ghost town, with only the
creeks as company

I feel like drinking to soothe my
nerves
Or smoke a spliff and float my mind
away
Can I, how can I, when I don't
possess the courage
I'm a dinosaur with a prehistoric
mind,
That has nothing to live for
But merely going through life's
motion

My fingers carry no sensual feelings
As my nerve is like a shattered glass
window
Eyes getting foggy and I'm seeing
quadruplets of objects now
My limbs are buckling, I have to
muster up energy to stand
Heavenly Father, are you calling me
now? So soon!
Oh, is it too late to ask for forgive-
ness of sin?
What a fool I've been!
My eyes are closing, they are as
heavy as lead
It is time, the end is the next moment
I must say good-bye and fare . . .

Mary Anne Cannavan
POETRY AS MUSIC
A mother sings a lullaby
A father recites a verse
A child learns of music
As a baby learns to nurse.

The lessons of life it seems
Have all been set in rhyme
By poets and philosophers
Since the start of time

Every human soul craves music
Primitive nature sounds the toll
Music in our lives is primal
Poetry is Music for the soul.

Jennifer Bosch
FEELINGS
As summer breezes come and go
My heart yearns more for his love
I shiver in a cold sweat
As I lie awake at night
So close to him I can feel his breath
on my face
Yet so distant, so far from his love
Afraid of every word, every whisp of
breath
Scared to say a thing
Frightened that I've come so close
Yet far enough to lose all hope
Has my dream become a reality
Or has reality become more of my
dream

Susan L King
CHINA DOLL
On a shelf sits a little china doll
with a smile upon her face.
Waiting there so patiently
to be removed from her dusty place.
Her face so bright and cheery,
her hair held back with bows.
Her dress made of pink satin,
she was as pretty as a rose.

But her eyes no longer light up,
for she is never taken down.
Her cheeks are no longer rosy,
her face now holds a frown.
For she is no longer cared for
and left on a shelf to lie,
Is a lonely little china doll
with teardrops in her eyes.
Her heart is now broken,
the pieces left to fall.
Alone on a dusty shelf
sits a little china doll.

Lauri L Wucher
GRANDFATHER, THE CLOCK
Once upon a time lived a grandfather clock
a beauty was he who surely could talk.

He lived in a mansion upon a hill
paid for in full by only one bill!

The family he lived with was very kind
they pampered him so which he didn't mind.

On a daily basis with each passing hour
he'd do his job with such great power.

Then one day grandfather missed a bong
the family couldn't tell what went wrong.

They quickly called grandfather's very own doctor
an excellent specialist whose name was Proctor.

After checking Dr. Proctor found a little bug
which quickly he fixed & gave him a hug.

Once again grandfather was just like new
and lived a good life until age 102.

Grandfather the clock went down in family history
& was loved by them with such chemistry.

THE END

Dena Lynn Ebstein
FEAR

To my Dad, Who always helped me through the bad times.

One night while I was asleep
I heard the sound of wooden feet.
I turned around and shook with fear
The thing was coming awfully near.
I got out of bed and ran into the hall
Then I heard my daddy call.
I ran to him without a second to lose,
"Your imagination you shouldn't abuse."
I still was scared, but took his advice
And went to sleep for the rest of the night.

I'm older now, but still may tremble
When I think of "Those feet" my mind assembled.

Janice Wilson
REFLECTION OF MYSELF
Walking in the autumn eve, the air is chilled, the sky is dim
The leaves are crunching neath my feet, a fire glows across the way
I stop and sit at the water's edge and gaze into the lake
But all I see as I look in, is a clear reflection of him.
The summer's over, the fun subsides
It's quiet here in my solitude
The times we shared, the good, the bad
Seem all so long ago
It's time to gather all my thoughts and dream the dreams that make me glad
The love we lost was never ours, we only borrowed time.
We used each other as a stepping stone, to get to the other side.
I'm starting over and when I learn to put the past behind
Next time I gaze into the lake — the reflection will be mine.

Janice Wilson
MY SHIP CAME IN

Dedicated to the treasures of my life, Debbie, Terri and Sandy.

You never stray too far from me
that I can't feel your touch
Your love is all around me and
you are loved so much
You never stray too far from me
so I can't see your tears
My very purpose for being here
is to wash away your fears
You've touched my soul — my life's reward tho time will pass away
The years we've shared, the joys you bring are in my heart to stay
You never stray too far from me
that I can't see your smile
I know we have to part sometime
but just for a little while
You've been my ship bearing life's meaningful pleasures
A ship that has carried all my worldly treasures

Arianne
FILL ME
Sometimes when I look at you, I just love you so much!
I love you so much my very soul hurts and I ache;
My heart feels like bursting and I long for your touch;
The love I feel just overflows, and I feel my insides quake.
I want you so nothing else matters, nothing else will do,
For you become my all-consuming passion and obsession
As reason flies out the window and I become filled with only you
And the love I feel—for you are my most treasured possession.

Karen Richards
IT'S A CAT'S LIFE
What a great, lazy life, it is to be a cat.
Not any cat, but one who has a good home; always a place to stay.
No matter, what time, day or night; you have a place, to come each day.
There's a lot of time to play, and plenty of food, maybe a rat.
I love to smell catnip; I become a kitten, as it buzzes out my head.
I often like to chase my tail, or maybe a spool of thread.
But soon, I'll get tired and my body feels all in.
So I'll find a place, to rest my weary head again.

I share my house with a female cat;
who used to bully me, as a kitten.
Now, I've grown up big, and she's the one who's thin, and oh so frighten.
When we get fed, she eats in a hurry;
while I eat slower and leave a bite.
I'll cover it up and leave, but nothing seems hidden, from her sight.

That makes me so very mad, and so I begin to fight.
But unlikely as it seems, she never gets one bite.
Until she learns, to leave my food alone; even if she does win.
One must keep face, so when it happens; I'll do it all again.

Even though, I'd never trade my life, with any other outdoor cat.
I do wonder, sometimes, the choice of homes I made.
I dream, she'll leave, and I'll be the only pet cat, just suppose.
Or maybe, we could be friends; if miracles can happen, to a pussycat.

Karen Richards
HIS LOVE
He gave me His grace.
He died in my place.

To save me from my misery.
To live my life in harmony.

To show His love for me.
He made His love to share.

To prove I care and my love is true.
He gave me love to give to you.

Liliana E Bathurst
VIOLETS OF NOVEMBER
I marveled when I cast
My eyes on you today

It is November is it not
And yet here you are
Before me
In a field of green
Blooming
As if it were spring
Even more beautiful
More precious
The second time around
Humble little flowers
That you are

I equate myself with you
As I too am blossoming
Late in life's season

Freeing the inner me
Yearning to reach
Its day in the sun

Louise Chapman
THE MAGIC CRYSTAL

To Yayon, this poem is dedicated to you, in appreciation for the Crystal Pendulum that you gave me for my birthday.

On my birthday a couple of years ago,
I received a wonderful gift
From my daughter-in-law, Yayon.

I think I like it even better than a nugget of gold,
For when the rays of the sun shines on its many facets,
I touch it and let it swing back and forth, showing its colors
Of purple, yellow, red and green.

It is then that my magic crystal turns my small square room,
Into a magic fairy land, the color of the rainbow.
Swaying and flashing on the walls and ceiling,
As I sit and watch them sway back and forth, I feel young instead of old.

Sometimes, when the pain is felt so deep,
I think maybe tomorrow it will be a deeper darker sleep,
Then I remember the sunshine, the colors so bright.

I remember my magic crystal,
I think about the one that loves me so true,
It's then I realize I'm not ready for the endless, silent night.

Julie Fitzgibbons
SPIRAL STAIRCASE
Start. you're up so high you get dizzy, but you keep your balance. Step, step, step. You are always going down, sometimes fast, sometimes slow. You never know when you will stop. Some people join you, and along the way they stop. You wait for them, but they tell you to go on, that they'll catch up. They never quite did catch up. But then, you get to the bottom, and other people wait for you. You say no, go ahead, you'll catch up.
You never quite did.

George A Hodge
MAIKA

To my daughter, Maika Kathleen Hodge, from your loving father.

Like the air I breathe, your spirit floats within me
Like a dove flowing on the wings of love, you spread happiness and joy.
Your eyes wonder with innocence and purity, only to capture that which you love, to house in your temple with security.
Your name was placed in the head of a dream, as if it was destiny.
Not only to exist, but to flow forever within those that love you.
Like the river Niger, may your spirit flow forever.
For you have brought light in the soul of darkness.
For you have brought hope to a heart that seemed boundless with no direction.
For you have washed ashore unto an island that was once inhabited by one.
Maika may we always be as one
Like the sun to a beautiful flower
I now will live and watch you grow,
Maika.

Sharon Feldman
CHRISTI

For mom, who taught me that believing in myself meant I was halfway there. You'll always be "the wind beneath my wings" . . .

my worn hands
leathery, but soft on the inside
and She, with one pout or charming smile
looking always as if She's just cried

i cry for myself
on all white sheets
with one black stain
where my goodness and envy meet

they watch Her progress and praise
their sympathy able to choke Her
blinding them, yet worse, blinding me
as i sit listless and in a blur

one night i was in Her room
watching the stars
try to enlighten a waning moon
when She awoke

Her gaunt arms spread far and wide
Her struggling stare filling me up
She pulled me down to Her side
"I love you" She said
As She slipped from me like a satisfied angel

Theodore L Purnell
SUPERBOWL GAMES COME AND GO!

This poem is dedicated on this day, to my loving and loved wife, Betty, sealed with our logo, Hey! Hey!

Games I and II were won by the Green Bay Packers with a total of 68 points—as to the opponents' 24.

True, New York Jets and Kansas City Chiefs won game thrillers III and IV.

Game V, a squeaker, was won by the Colts of Baltimore.

Both game VI and XII, the Dallas Cowboys won, each win was far from a bore.

So be it, VII and VIII were won by the Miami Dolphins in the years 1973 and 4.

Yes, a record, games IX, X, XIII, and XIV belong to the Pittsburgh Steelers, to date, the only winners of four.

It's hard to believe XI and XV went to Oakland, who like Baltimore, to date exists no more.

However, Oakland must be remembered as the first winner of the Pacific shore,

And that games XVI and XIX claimed by San Francisco Forty-Niners, were typically Western to the core.

Another record, game XVII the Washington Redskins won, Playing before a crowd of thousands, 104.

Still another game XVIII won by L.A. Raiders is on record, to date, as having the highest score.

Amen, two years later game XX, the Chicago Bears won beating the Raiders' 38 by a merit 8 points more.

A master game was XXI, which the New York Giants won, It had everything—to make it Superbowl lore.

In Superbowl XXII the Washington Redskins obliterated the Denver Broncos with points and points galore.

In Game XXIII for San Francisco 49ers, it was a practice chore.

Why?—they blew out Denver with a 55-10 score.

Now! What will the year 1990-91 have in store?

I see the Philadelphia Mighty Eagles soar, into the wide complex "door."

Roberto P Iocco
BOMBS OF DEMOCRACY
They build their weapons to destroy us all,
The bombs in the silos awaiting their call.
The generals and presidents make their decisions.
And the great bombs of all lands make their incisions.

Methods to their madness? Anything to gain
They make us believe pleasure, and put us through pain.
The world of millions, so many of us scared
You should come to your senses if you really cared.

I can blow the world up, ten times or more
These insane threats, we choose to ignore
But one day that crazy button will be pushed
And the anger of the world will once again be hushed.

Bruce Modzelewski
DEEP BELOW
Few mortals will ever know,
What the ocean hides below,
Tell me what you feel my friend,
As you look out over this beauty without end,
Out here time is only an emotion,
Like the endless sky and ocean,
A sailor's dream of a distant port,
Or a pirate's greeting of the deadly sort,

Under the waves the galleons sunk free,
But never to be touched by you or me,
The treasures lie on the ocean floor,
Lost forever in an ancient war,
The ships lay on the bottom like an old ghost,
And the shark is a most unlikeable host,
So few mortals will ever know,
What the ocean hides below.

Eleanor Laverne Brown
THE SUMMARY
Will this world be a better place
Because for a span it saw my face;
Or did I take and never give,
Only to exist and never to live?

Is it enough to just pass through
And not some good for others do;
Because each one should be my brother,
Regardless of race or creed or color.

Can I truly say I've lived life well?
What awaits before me — heaven or hell?
Oh, Dear God, this much I know,
Only Your Love can make heaven so!

Let no hate dwell within my breast;
Help me to love my enemy best.
Always before me the nail-scarred hands
And Love enough to fulfill God's Plan.

And if no trace of me I leave behind
Except of love that heals and binds;
To know I've truly loved I'll be content
To face my Creator when this life is spent.

Sol M Velazquez
UNTOLD
Alone I walk in bright places
Echoes of laughter pierce my mind
Why, oh why, was Mother so cruel
When she cursed me with this fate

Alone I dream, as all are bound to dream
Wishing for that which was never to be mine
If only I could, just for a moment
Be one of those admired, adored . . . seen

But no, no, never to be so
For I am not like the rest
Destined to hide, but never telling why
For telling would only bring pain . . . damn this pride

But then, pride is all there is, and how I cherish it
Because they will never know the secrets
My mind and heart guard well
For I love them, like nothing else I know

Violet C Scott
GOD CREATES

To my children—Constance (Bennett) Miller, Karl, William and Peter Bennett.

A newborn baby's tender cry,
An elderly whisper, or a sigh,
Sunlight and moonglow,
A spring shower,
Or winter's snow,
A beautiful flower,
A minute or an hour,
A gentle breeze,
A piercing storm,
Rain drenched fields,
A dew laden morn,
Memorable years,
Lilting laughter and tears,
Meadows and cities
Woodlands and lakes,
Birds and beasts
"Only God creates!"
Give thanks to Him for these and more,
Enjoy and share our wealth galore.

Laura Winter
EMPTY MEMORIES—BROKEN DREAMS
Empty days gone by.
Empty memories
full of lies.
Empty hearts
mistaken to be full.
A meaningless love
taken up too much time.
Scentless roses
full of thorns.

That fake glow in your eyes,
your insincere smile.
A broken dream,
an empty memory.

Jerry Wayne Shetters (Birdy)
THANK YOU GOD
For giving me life
To enjoy the things
I love to do
Some take it for granted
I owe it all to you

Thank you God
For letting me see
Some take it for granted
My eyes are precious to me

Thank you God
For letting me walk
To smell the flowers
Or just to talk

Thank you God
For all my health
Which is more precious
Than a rich man's wealth

But most of all
Thank you God
For letting me love
To really enjoy
All the above

Jerry Wayne Shetters (Birdy)
YOUNG AND FREE OLD AND ALONE
When your youth is gone
What do you have then
Are you all alone
Or do you have a friend

Everything seems all right
When you're young and free
Please don't waste your life
That's what happened to me

Now I'm paying for
Things I used to do
Things I just forgot
Back when I was new

I've been in love
But took it for granted
Now I'm reaping loneliness
All that I have planted

When I was young
I just didn't care
Now I wish I had someone
To always be there

Lyn Russell
UNITY
How do I know you? Have we met before?
Come closer, for I want to know you

some more.
Have you something to share? Have you "tales for to tell?"
I would so like to hear them. And I have some as well.

Where have I seen you? Where did we meet?
Did I give you a quarter on a big city street?
Did we feed birds together in a green forest glade?
Did I ever share with you bread I had made?

Did I once pick you up from the side of the road?
Or was my thumb aloft? Did you lighten my load?
Did we sit down together to converse and to dine?
Did we toast to the future with burgundy wine?

Did we once slide together down hills pure with snow?
Did we swim the dark coral of oceans below?
Did we sing joy together on the town center lawn?
Or march on the capitol one rainy dawn?

Did we plant a new garden in God's ancient earth?
Were you there for the joy of my baby's new birth?
Did we tackle a mountain and hang from its side?
Was it I who was holding your hand as you died?

Kendra S Poirot
THE STRANGER?

Dedicated, with love, to my parents—"Happy Anniversary," Mom & Dad!

Sunken eyes seeking a world of graven doom . . .
Hysterical raging from across the room—

The stranger shrieks and calls his name—
Oh! The anguish of life—the fear of pain!

As if enclosed with no open door
He shuddered and shook while the stranger swore,

Waiting for a saviour to come along . . .
Who can deliver him from the stranger's wrong?

The pain and anguish life may possess—
But, the child still waits for the stranger's caress.

A love/hate relationship is too hard for a child to understand;
It follows him through life while he becomes a man.

And like a plague it carries through—
Begins with the seed of life and starts anew.

Where the danger lies is apparent;
For it's not the child, but instead the parent.

Whom can the stranger be? Ah! No other . . .
Or am I too blind to see? The stranger is his father!

Shirley Ann McCue
AN AWFUL SIGN

To my beloved family, to Marcie, and Don.

God chose them to wear such an awful sign,
etched deep within their anguished minds,
BEWARE!
BEWARE
Ever present the stigma seems to be,
a flashing light upon their brows for all to see.
They are mentally ill.
There is no cure, no magic pill,
that can remove the stigma
they must always bear.
There is no hell upon this earth
that could torture any worse.
The loneliness, the pain,
the agony, the suffering;
it's a feared and irreversible curse.
Like the leper,
shunned and scorned.
Just like Jesus,
The mentally ill are forced to wear
such an awful sign;
BEWARE!
BEWARE!

Rene J Vallee
RESTLESS
Reposed alone I feel the want,
to caress the ghost of you
within my heart;
Your lovely you lingers to haunt,
the eve of another day to start.

Rene J Vallee
TIME
Time, adults curse it for not having enough
Time, children waste it by not knowing enough
Time, man's bouillon to barter for knowledge
Time, woman's rebellion toward her withering age
Time, years wear out and then renew
Time, where do you hide when I need you.

Jeff Stoneking
ORANGE AIR
The poison white tendrils gore me abruptly,
Scraping me away into the endless depths of regret.
I gouge my fingers into the burning wall,
Pounding pounding pounding ceaselessly,
While my eyes witness, in disbelief, my remains
Flushing away into the churching grey sea
Of the past.

My mind is decaying, swirling into the white grey whirlpool
While the vines of the forest char in the flames of the wall.
Brittle, they crumble when siezed, leaving my hands
Coated fresh with promises unobtainable and sweet
Smells unbelievable; the world above remains only a fantasy.
The tendrils tether me to the enflamed surface;
In the crackling orange air I boil.

A laughing face metamorphizes in the dancing flames
Reminding me of my ineptness and paralizing indecision
And hurdles away under the assumption I am comfortable.
I am alone. The engulfing flames disfigure me
Into a state of ugliness and unrecognition.
I plummet forever in the white void, cast out of perception
Of the gaping hands above me.

Lisa M Canino
INNOCENT REBEL
Playfully pouncing were beads of rain
Upon softly dressed windows.
Pastel shadows delicately fell on the textured walls.
I'd eagerly rub crayons on blank pages of imagination,
Proudly making them my own.
Purple was the trees;
Green was the sun;
(At least that's how it was in my book)
Forbidden by the laws of nature and by those of wisdom
Then contentment of simplicity wasn't permitted at all . . .
The wind ripped its claws in the clouded glass
Which bled crystal tears.

Myrna Peeler
SUCCESS
Cheer up, Cheer up, That's the robin's plea
He never gives up and neither should we.
He keeps searching and searching the ground for that worm,
He knows it's there somewhere
Maybe at the next turn.
Now we should remember that robin whenever we're blue,
That if we keep on trying there's no task we can't do,
We must always be determined And true to our cause,
So if we make mistakes we must correct our flaws.
The road to success is long and severe,
But when we reach the top we can stand up and cheer,
Cheer up, cheer up, Like robin red breast,
Should it out loud and clear
Tell the world, we did our best!

Carol Ann Prigge
NEW ENGLAND IN THE MORNING
I see New England in the morning,
Tho my eyes are far beyond it;
And I walk in the shadows
Of the lovely tulip trees.

I see her breathing in the stillness
Of a quiet April morning
Soft mist gently rising
From the meadow's grassy floor.

I feel her beauty in the autumn,
And if I were gone forever;
I know my heart would take me back,
Beneath the golden trees.

My first love and my strongest;
Touched my soul and clings forever.
Your beauty still enthralls me;
Forever I am yours.

Sheri Lynn Davidson
IT'S A LEGACY
Through an endless corridor
of my mind
I wander what I might
find.

Searching for my Destiny
an endless journey
through time.

I'm in a maze
trying to find the
answers to questions untold

In a ever ending quest
I venture on
What lies ahead of
the unknown

In my mind's eye
I see
It's a Legacy

If everything on earth
could talk
It would show man's
life
Which way he walked

It's a mystery

How we
came to be
you and me

It's a Legacy to find
our Destiny.

Betty T Williams
WHEN CHILDREN HEAR THEIR MOTHERS CRY
I know they usually wonder, for what and why.

Why is Mommy crying like that?, is it because she wants Daddy to come back?

Even though when he's here, he only makes her shed more tears.

Always hitting her with all his might, but she won't hit back, she won't fight.

When I am grown up, I will take up the banner, he can't hurt me and it won't matter.

The time has come for him to discover, that I am a man now, hit me and not my MOTHER!

Mike McCormick
DREAMSAIL

To Resa: About to set sail.

What do you give a girl made of dreams
Setting out on the sea of life
You give her a ship of golden beams
With sails shining silver white
Make the skies blue with sunsets of red
And send a calm wind at first light
Put diamonds and moon-dust in the nets
To catch the black rays of night
Then when her spirit rides out dark storms
And her laughter drowns out the rain
Draw her the treasure map of hearts
And sail her back home again.

Steven J McInnes
PASSION STORM
Two silhouettes brush together
Like the softly waving limbs of a weeping willow
A Mist of perspiration runs down

their limbs,
Like raindrops rolling down the leaves,
It gently caresses each limb.
Basking in the enjoyable and refreshing mist;
They slowly build a rhythm like that of rain and thunder,
Building intensely as the thunder grows louder and closer.
Like the limbs of the willow they intertwine one another;
The wind grows stronger and louder, and in an abrupt moment
Like a provoked streak of lightning,
The storm ceases and the rain
STOPS
The mist continues like the dew dripping from the leaves,
It lingers on the limbs no longer waving or brushing together.
For hours they are heavy and limp
And though the rain has ended
They long for the next storm.

Yvette Z Henderson

AIR OF DECEMBER

Like the shade terra cotta at sunset,
Passion is to the eye.

It can capture the warmth cascading down through the whirling
vast
open
space
that is the wind.

The wind blows, north, south, east, and west.
All at once,
it is put up against choice.

I can feel it crying within the sound it makes while
it blows carrying brown, orange, and green
leaves
to
the
ground.

The wind wraps around my body
caressing it as it warmly
crawls into every pore of
my
cold
exposed
skin.

Margaret E Gardner

A PLEASANT GIFT

Always remember poetry & all the work poets do.

You have a gift worth a lot
Worth more than all the money you've got
A pleasant gift, is a wonderful thing
Having it makes you feel like a king
You'll never be able to pay for it
And it's better than any kind of kit
You consider it a pleasant gift
'Cause it really gives you a lift
Thinking of it when you can
Makes you wonder why you're not a man
Having it gives you great fun
And you think of all that's done
You try to pay for that gift
Because it makes you real swift
A pleasant gift is wonderful to you
With it you are never blue
Having it makes you feel good
And you not as hard as wood
You've had that gift a long time
Considering all your days sublime

Otis Van Cecil

WINTER PREPARATION

The trees have lost their luster,
They've begun to wear a frown.
Most now seem to be ashamed
And are all just looking down.

Trees cover their feet with leaves
This fine weather will not last.
Winter will come as always,
With his cold, bone-chilling blast.

But trees are strong and sturdy,
With a bark to keep them warm.
They will withstand the fierceness
Of next winter's coldest storm.

They will sleep through the winter
Dreaming of the coming spring.
When the grass begins to grow
And the birds begin to sing.

These thoughts will give them
comfort,
Make the winter not so long.
Like trees we too are thinking
Of spring and the warbler's song.

But we must all be patient,
Live the seasons as they come.
If we prepare as we should
There is no fear to succumb.

Erda G Bacorn

FICKLE WEATHER

Southwest wind—a balmy breeze?
I beg to differ, if you please.
This could be a Fool's Day joke—
The southwest wind of which I spoke.
But it's no joke, when April's here,
To find we need our winter gear.
Out in the open countryside,
Where back of buildings one can't hide,
Is no place for a casual walk,
Nor standing still for neighbor talk.

Tabitha Summers

WHAT YOU ARE TO ME

There are times when I look up,
I see the stars in the sky.
The lights that are twinkling
Are reflecting in my eyes.
The moon, in all its splendor,
And the spacious sky above
Are miracles of God's greatness
And His never ending love.

My eyes fill with tears
As I begin to fully see.
How gratefully I am blessed
With the love you have for me.
The world in all its beauty
Never could replaced what you do.
Because when you stepped into my life,
A bit of Heaven came into view.

Bunny L Willis

EVERY ROAD HAS A TURN

Every road has a turn,
Each road has a memory,
Memories of happy moments.
Thoughts of you being alone.
Sadness when we are apart,
Not knowing what to say when we are together.

Each road is different,
Every road has a turn.
Memories of being together,
Thoughts of loving you.
Happiness with tender moments,
Not knowing what to do if I had to be without you.
Each and every road I want to travel with you.

Tina DeLuca

LONELY (BY CHOICE)

Now that you've gone and I am on my own
I feel so alone, yet I must go on.

I think of our love, how we were before
Now I look back, wondering what went wrong.

I wonder if you love me, if you miss me, if you care
I never really see you, still I know you're there.

If I ever need you, if I'm ever blue
Just dial your number
That's all I'd have to do

But towards that seventh digit, my fingers tend to fail
It would only mess my head up
Sadness would prevail

So now I sit here lonely, with the sound of my own voice.
And suddenly I remind myself . . .
I am this way by choice.

Fredda Sansom

CHILDHOOD SEEMS BUT A VAGUE DREAM

Childhood seems but a vague dream
When grim maturity wakes us.
The fragile commitments,
The gossamer friendships,
The leafy perceptions
Of Gondol's time
Comprise a consciousness
Not subject to the arbitrary recall
Of the benevolent usurper
Who occupies the throne
Of our existence.

Blanche L Barkow

A BRAND-NEW DAY

Upon the threshold of this day, I wait, I pray before thee, I appreciate, this day a blessing, all brand-new and white, and at its end will still be shiny bright.
That I'll not darken it by word or deed, but let you in this day so kindly lead,
To make it better than the day before, stand close to me, please be my monitor.
That when I open up my mouth to speak, let nothing dark or black from out it leak, but when my mouth that's wide an open door, let you speak out and be my orator.
As for my fellow man that I may see, but for the grace of God goes he not me,
And so indeed keep mind and soul most pure, to know that in your love I am secure.
Now hoping at the end of this white day, you'll find me faultless as I went my way, so when I kneel at night in prayers with love,
You'll know Christ worked through me from up above.

Eric Elam

BEAUTY

You have conferred to me such peace—such serenity,
As never would I have known without you,
That seldom a moment passes when I am not grateful
For the beauty you have entrusted to me.
Even in my most disheartened state,
I accept the most cherished
As being the beauty which you have so often exposed in me,
But not because it is native to me—for it is not,
But simply because it is a reflection—however flat,
However unblossomed—of the beauty in you
That was consequently transferred to me through our love.

Joy Shields

SUE

We met in '77 the day I don't recall. We became the best of friends Jim, Ed, Sue, and I. But things are so different now since you went away. Sue we truly miss you on this November day. It's been a year now since the Angels took you home. Oh, we wish you were here with us, for we loved you so. But we have such sweet memories that will never be forgot. Oh, we really loved you Sue and we miss you a lot.

Your Best Friend
Joy Shields
11/16/89

Theresa M Helmich

THE IRONWORKER

This poem is dedicated to my father, "Delmar J. Morrison-Buzz." A retired ironworker of Local #10, Kansas City, Mo., for over thirty years.

Out of all past and near
through those gray skies to sunny days
we'll always remember
the ironworkers in the skies
with a heart of gold and hands of steel
you're a man of wisdom
who can bend and change with the wind
to soar like a bird above our heads
with no fear coming to mind
the courage and strength of iron
unknown to some of mankind
with knowledge and skills to control
no matter what the reason being
you're a man of honor like a giant
from buildings at your hands to
bridges at your feet
you've traveled afar and near, and always been there
And as time passes by
There's always a thought to remind me of you
Throughout it all with never a doubt
we're always thinking of you
I love you dad
So when the sun goes down it's another day to break at dawn.

Theresa M Helmich

TIME AND SPACE

We are lost in time and space
here life can be cruel among our human race
But the most frightening of all is darkness
It's too dark for me to see
but I can feel the cold
dark loneliness in our human space
As we grow old time passes on
We feel death drawing us near
We fear it, 'fore it becomes our Loss
among our young and elders
In remaining time

space and death encloses within
overtaking the power of mankind's
human race
This is the time and space
within my human world of life.

Valerie Ann Williams
FAREWELL

Dedicated to Caroline Knox.

I'd never thought that you'd never be here, to continue to spread all your love and your good cheer.

I'll always love you like a real sister, heaven only knows how much I'm gonna miss 'ya.

Although I know life goes on, oh how I wish you were here to help me to be strong.

No one knows my pain, no one knows my sorrow—just the thought of you not being here tomorrow.

I don't understand—nor do I ask the question why, "Why did my best buddy have to die?"

You were always special and in my heart I know why. Jesus loved you first and says we all are born to die.

I'll continue to be good, oh how I'll try. For someday, I know, even I will surely die.

When I leave and I'm put to rest, I want it to be known; like you, I did my very best.

I'll let you go now my friend, on this lonely day. There is still so very much I wish I had said before today.

I'll try to live a good life, so I may see you again. I thank God that you were my best friend.

Farewell, farewell and I bid you a goodbye.

Meurice D Williams
PROBLEMS

Dedicated to Peggy Myers, Jennifer Davis, Cynthia D. Williams, Mr. & Mrs. Edward Lofton.

The gripes and groans
to who's right
and who's wrong
to argue
some virtue.

Rather than explain
we'd blame one another
just the same.

Our ups and downs
in our lives many frowns.
Problems we commonly share
you live only once
good or in despair.

One only needs
God within and
their solemn
to end problems.

LaShawn Moore Hart
DIRECTION

To all of my family and friend, who I'm sure will choose the right path.

Looking for direction
no compass as a guide
seeking out my general way
moving with slower stride
carefully balancing options
of which path I should take
down a dark and winding road
unknowingly tempting fate
a sunlit path is also there
a choice is to be made
to take the safe
or unknown road
is the path that's always laid

Deborah Marie Barrow

Deborah Marie Barrow
UPON HER TOES

For Misty Dawn my beautiful daughter. May the light strengthen you always, courage guide you, and faith keep you forever upon your toes. Your Mother.

Arising in the dawn,
The mist on window seal beads on,
The shoulder bare, no covers care,
Inside the blankets warm . . .
Yet cold the heart of hurt disgraced,
Sorrow searching for the longing face,
The tear has found its way . . .

Oh weary chest of silent pain,
This lovely dancer's lost her way, and
Through the weeping window glass,
The forest thick with memories past,
A new tear now escapes . . .
The music plays a lonely song,
The dancer's curtsy begs pardon . . .

Then through the forest, through the pane,
The shining light of morning beams,
Life into her weakened knees . . .
Upon her toes a ray of faith,
Courage dances, her heart changes glances,
With tomorrow a new ballet.

Pamela D Best
ILLUSION

Illusion; it can be seen, in a sense, but not heard
Though it's not really there at all . . .
Floating in the wind like a dove,
full of grace and beauty.
Reach out . . . but you cannot touch it.
Open your eyes . . . but you cannot see it.
Yet . . . it is there—in your mind.
To try to grasp an illusion is a transgression against nature.
It will slowly fade like a mirage in the desert.
. . . slowly dispersing into a timeless wave of sand,
dancing like a marionette controlled by the wisping fingertips
of the wind.

William R Froggett
THE BOX

The box lies buried, all light shut out.

On a little hill, in a little field
Under the bright green grass, lies the box.

It waits and waits for nothing.
All is quiet, no light or sound.
Earth packed in tight, all around the box.

Up above all is living,
Seasons change and change again.
Years pass, the box still sits and waits.

Now and then a memory is summoned,
An inner light then strikes the box.
It answers, but all inside remain dead.

Rotting of course, an old, useless shell,
The precious spirit left long ago,
And now it lives, it soars!

The memory comforts.
While the box still sits, all cold and damp
and waits for nothing.

Mary Ann Luna
TREE OF LIFE

The breeze blows between the leaves
Each leaf a marked story.
Gutsy winds forever blow
For each branch of fame and glory.

Lightly sags and sways the twigs
A budding birth of a leaf.
A day, a month, a year,
A ring around for many cheers.

I am a tree full of strength and height
Of luscious fruit, of wit, of might.
I stretch my branches to reach out toward the sky,
To all who see me, I'll be awake through the nigh.

Sherry M Revalee
FIELDS

To Terri Nelson—who made a faint hope, become a reality.

We sit among the sweet smelling clover,
laughing and giggling over and over.
The sunshine warms us as we play,
wanting it to be like this day after day
Feeling light and carefree like the clouds above
we float along all wrapped up in love
When the day comes to an end
we must go back and pretend
But each and every day thereafter
we will not forget the laughter
When upon a field I come
I'll always remember us in the sun

Hanne Hartmann-Phipps
MY HUSBAND — MY LOVE

Feelings that were true and deep
awoke my heart from its innocent sleep.
How enchanting it was to find a love
so very dear to keep.
Because of you, my soul has soared
to love's golden throne,
and, I will always yearn for you, and you alone.
Without you, there would be no sunshine or laughter.
My life would be incomplete and sad ever-after.
The song in my heart would have an empty, meaningless tone,
for, I love but you, and you alone.

Jesse Gearhart Jr
TRAIN RIDE

Dedicated to my fellow riders on the trip into history: Emily, Steve and Shannon.

His hand was steady on the throttle
As his steaming train roared down the track.
His passengers he meant to coddle
For an easy trip west and then back.

He was the engineer for the trip
And wanted his passengers to please.
He didn't know that an awful slip
Would soon have all of them on their knees.

Just ahead in the forest so green
Loomed a shiny rail starting to crack.
He would have stopped, if he could have seen
And saved his train from the awful wreck.

But that was simply just not to be
On that cold dreary day in October.
Hushed quickly were shouts of joy and glee.
The train jumped high—the ride was over!

Ambulances to the scene soon sped
And carried the riders fast away.
The engineer sadly hung his head
At this sad end of a joyful day.

Teresa Williams
PICTURES OF MOMMA

This poem is dedicated to my mother, Ruth.

Sitting at home alone
By the telephone.
Trying to occupy her mind
And forget the pain inside.
So as I sat
And I watch her.
My memory book filled up,
In my heart.
Oh PICTURES OF MOMMA
Placed in my heart.
The sounds of her crying
Still tears me apart.
If I could take back
The problems she had.
Then maybe my momma
Wouldn't hurt so bad.
Oh she has cried so many times,
And she has heard so many lies.
So as I remember her world all apart,
PICTURES OF MOMMA
Weigh heavy on my heart.

Alicia Wang
THE MISERABLE COUPLE

There once was a man that had a wife,
They lived in a shack and hated their life.
They ate garbage and bugs to stay alive,
They never had a car to drive.
One time they tried committing suicide,
By drowning themselves in the high tide.

They were down at the beach, ready to die,
When the old man's wife had started to cry.
The old man asked, "What's wrong my dearie,"
"Are you crying because your life is so dreary?"
"It doesn't matter now, it'll end before long,"
"Then we'll go to heaven and see the movie, King Kong."
She said, "You know it's not that, don't be silly,"
"It's just that now we'll never see Willy."
The man said, "Our son's happy, just let it be."
"Don't bother him, Mary, he'll find us at sea."
"And when he does, he won't care a bit,"
"But 'cause we left him nothing, he'll throw a fit."
They finally decided to just live their life,
Even if it was torture for him and his wife.

Robert A Williams

A POEM TO CHERRY

To Cherry . . . best of friends.

Time comes and goes, and with it many special people,
like the wind they flow,
learning different ways to feel,
trials and tribulations, give them their pleasant habits,
never letting confusion, turn them rabid,

as laughter springs forth, like a loving geyser,
many others become warm, and join in the laughter,
when happy and content, the air is filled with joy,
never is life spent, like money, on an unneeded toy.

the
end!

Rebecca Amber Walsh

INNOCENT VICTIM

Dedicated to the preservation of Dolphins.

Dolphins, they are so flawless and free,
Like nothing any human could be.

They are mysteries that lie deep beneath the sea,
Yet they are innocent victims and that we do not see.

Their lives are not ours, not ours to spend.
They snag in the tuna nets, though they've done nothing to offend.

I just hope someday for their sake and mine,
That there's peace on our planet and to all we are kind.

Alvin Williams

MY WIFE

This poem is dedicated to Pamela, my darling wife.

If a rose could bloom
And look into the sun
I'd call it my wife
Just for fun
And if the sky could
be so blue
I'd call it your eyes
because I love you
And if the birds could sing so fine
I'd know they would have you in mind
So my love, when you hear a bird
Sing, see rose so red, or sky so blue
Remember I love you.

Jessica E Withers

UNTITLED (ONCE WHEN THE SUN SHONE . . .)

Once when the sun shone
And the sky was blue,
I lived.

Then the rain fell
And the sky became grey—
I died.

Now the snow has fallen,
And its pristine white has recovered the Soul I thought I had lost:
I live again.

Ronna R Hicklin

ANNIVERSARY

For Todd.

You are gentle, you are sweet
You are all I ever thought you'd be
And more
You are the father to the children I adore
We have worked and we have strived
We have completely shared our lives
And through it all I've learned to know
How to trust and how to grow
You'll be my partner till the end
My most enduring special friend
And all because one day in life
We became husband and wife

Joyce Wilson

ON BEING ALONE

For my daughter, Lysa,
Who fills my heart with love.

Don't be afraid of the vast unknown,
Or of a future you can't see,
For life is always up to you,
Make it what you want it to be.

Time spent alone isn't always bad,
It's "you" you'll get to know,
And while happiness is the easy choice,
It's the hurt that makes you grow.

You can do anything that you want to do,
Just remember that Man above.
You'll want Him to know, at the end of your days,
That you did it ALL with love.

When you think of the past, as you'll often do,
Just listen to what I now say.
Keep only the good times locked in your heart,
And blow all of the bad away.

Take all of your days just one at a time,
And know that it's "you" you must please.
You can open any door that blocks your way
For your head and your heart are the keys.

Scott Wyatt

A NUFF IS A NUFF

My life
My dreams
My heart
My feelings
My love
My emotions
Like a dove without wings,
A poet without an inspiration,
A fighter without the urge to fight the endless battle of love and hate—
My life.
Just like a rock in water sinking.
A nuff is a nuff.
For now the dove has hit the ground
And lies there with no chance of survival.

Marie S White

GOD'S BEAUTIFUL WORLD

God's beautiful world is something to enjoy,
It is meant to take care of
And not to destroy.
Day by day different things were made,
The seventh day he rested and prayed.
Miracles abound us all around
Birds of all kinds in cities and town
Creatures and animals large and small
Trees all shapes and some are so tall
It amazes me and makes me think.
He even gives us water to drink.
The sky so blue and stars above
We thank you God for your great love.

William L Woodel Jr

PRECIOUS WAYS

For both of my Daughters, I'll write down this day.
How each one of you is special, In your very own way.
First one for Ashley, learning everything fast.
With cute loving smiles from the present and past.
You're as precious as the flowers, In a meadow topped with dew.
As the morning sun rises, In a sky that is blue.
Second one for Alyssa, with eyes ocean blue.
Tiny curls in your hair, long eyelashes too.
Your skin very soft, like the fur on a bunny.
The faces you make, very cute sometimes funny.
You're as precious as the pedals, that blossom on a long red rose.
On a sunny Springtime morning, as the gentle wind blows.

Donald B Wesley Jr

SHOULD YOU KNOW?

To Cindy J. M. Ivey, my one and only love. Forever, I will always love you.

What is it that you must know?
Knowledge can be as cruel as the psycho's dagger,
Yet sweet as the sight of morning dew.
'Tis like the stars, not seen before the sun has played
For they have their time just as knowledge its moment.
If you can benefit from this knowledge, may you know,
But shall hurt be foreseen, trust your soul to let it be.
So contemplate a moment and judge with care.
Is it necessary for this knowledge to be expressed,
Or tucked away for only the ear of eternity?

Evelyn M Ward

A MOTHER'S CRY FOR AN ABANDONED LOVE

The joy and love that was bound;
Must be lost it can't be found.
Doctors said go home he's fine;
The morning next, I checked to find,
My son so frail and innocent,
Has gone to heaven from which he was sent.
The love and growth we should have shared;
Was taken from us so unfair.
Son, you left me unaware,
Of all the pain, and grief, despair.
The tears I shed alone at night,
Are there for me to hold what's right.
So far away you may be,
My special child you are to me.
Years have passed, there is no now,
I go through the motions anyhow.
A heart so full and motherhood plenty,
Bury a child and come up empty.

Mary E Nowak

MIRROR: SELF-REFLECTION

A pane of glass which when looked upon
Shows but a shadow of one's self.

Look upon it with a critical view,
You'll see only your flaws.

See eyes too wide set, lips too full, waist too thick, hips too broad, teeth that are crooked.

Look upon it with an honest view,
You'll see your positive side as well.

See eyes always bright, full of life.
See lips that are sensuous and soft.

See waist that no longer a child's, still slender,
See hips that are still proportionate.

See a smile that is always ready, warm.

Be not so hard on yourself that a simple
Mirror becomes a dreaded foe.

Look upon it as an impartial friend,
Allowing you a glimpse of both
Flaws and strengths to accept.

Donna Hogancamp-Sierra

Donna Hogancamp-Sierra

UNTIL YOU ARE IN MY ARMS

The thought of your smile,
Though you're gone from my grasp,

The thought of your laughter,
As I watch time slowly pass.
The thought of your gentleness,
Though right now you're not here,
The thought of your touch,
Until you finally appear.
But while you are out of my grasp,
While you are away,
My thoughts are only yours,
Throughout all of the day.
So I will just hold you in my heart,
Until I can hold you in my arms.
Thinking of your eyes, so beautiful to see,
Thinking of your warmth, wanting you near me,
Dreaming of you, when I can see your smile,
Waiting patiently, just a little longer,
Just a little while.
So I will hold you in my heart,
Until I can hold you in my arms.

Marion O'Neil
PERFECTION
What is perfection? You may well ask.
Is it the end result of our struggle for ultimate supremacy?
Oh, what fools we mortals be—to think this is an attainable goal
For such as we.

We are perfection but once in our lifetime — when we are first born
Ere the Angels' wings have stilled in the distance
Are we perfection . . .
Then, as we pass through Heaven's gates and God has forgiven us our sins
Are we perfection . . .

Yet we can do no more in our lifetime than to struggle toward this goal
For to be less than zealous in our quest
Is to be less than honest with ourself.

Marion O'Neil
THOUGHTS
It is December. The crisp clear air
Bites at our noses and our cheeks.
There is a promise in the ring
Of children's voices, soft and sweet.

For soon it will be Christmas day,
And friends greet friends from far and near.
Our burdens lift, our hearts are full
At this especial time of year.

There is a promise in the air
Of better things to come—
Of happiness, and peace on earth
And birth anew, for some.

To share these thoughts, this hope, this love,
The blessings of the season,
With all mankind throughout the world,
Then life would have new meaning.

The children's voices, soft and clear,
The heavenly promise shining through,
The love, the peace—all we hold dear,
This is my gift to you.

It is December . . .

Marion O'Neil
AWAKENING
In the still, small hours of the dawn,
Before the world's awake,
There's a peaceful strangeness over all—
A waiting, for the day to break.

And in that moment, one can feel
So very near to God,
For I believe him very close,
Tidying up, where fools have trod.

He walks the earth in early morn,
To set his Kingdom right,
To ready it for another day,
And make our world more bright.

And while He walks upon the dew,
I wonder at his troubled thoughts,
Of what he thinks of me—and you,
And of the follies man has wrought!

Before I close my eyes at night—
Before I say my last "Amen,"
I hope I've set my house aright,
Before He comes again.

Marion O'Neil
DEVASTATION
The bombs have stilled; the barren fields
Stretch in endless view.
Why, oh why, must these things be?
Now we must start anew,
To build, destroy, and build again,
For what? Futility? What is the answer,
Where does it end? What is our destiny?

Is this to be the fate of man,
This constant hate and fear?
Why, oh why, must man destroy
All that he holds dear?

This world is large enough for all,
But we must work together,
To plant again the barren fields,
And still the bombs forever.

There is one ruler of our world,
Lest we e'er forget,
And we—just puppets on a string,
To do with as HE judges fit!

Together we must build the peace,
There is no other way,
For tomorrow is determined,
By what we do today.

Marion O'Neil
REFLECTION
The night is still, the silver stars
Are dancing up above.
I sit alone, in reverie, watching—waiting—
For you, my love.
You will not come, you cannot come,
For God has taken you from me.
No more to see your tender face,
Or hear your gentle voice,
Or hold your hand and see you smile,
I know this cannot be.
So I must bear the loneliness
That you have left behind,
And be thankful for the memories
That live on in my mind . . .

Roberta Peacock
SEASONS
Summer's nearly gone,
How time passes by
Soon all the flowers
Will wither and die.
Then natures display
of red and gold,
Another reminder of winters cold.
Trees will be bare
Skies will be gray
A nip in the air
Snow's soon on the way.
One thing is certain
Spring will arrive,
All that lay dormant
Will again burst alive.

Roberta Peacock
THE BRIDE

To My Granddaughter Daria.

I watched as she walked down the aisle
A vision to behold,
My thoughts drifted back to another time
When she was only hours old.
I fought and brushed away the tears,
My heart was filled with pride
to see that little girl all grown
Into a blushing bride.
Her aims are high for the goals she pursues
For a happy successful life,
To share with Charles, her husband,
And to be a loving wife.

Love,
"Mimi"

June 18, 1990

Lois Martin

Lois Martin
TIME IS PRECIOUS

Lonnie Lou Moore, a dear niece, I dedicate this poem.

If there's a deed you've left undone
Before the setting of the sun—
Do it now!

If there are words you didn't speak
To soothe a hurt or boost the weak—
Do it now!

If you can make a sick friend well,
Or just a happy story tell—
Do it now!

Time is precious every day—
Make it count in a selfless way.

Mary Hall Williams
SUNSET

I dedicate this poem to Earth's Day. May all people find peace, joy, and beauty, in a wonderful world created by our heavenly Father. He made all things perfect and beautiful until man disobeyed God. May all seek to return to God' earth purity and love and beauty.

I saw the sunset behind,
the budding spring trees.
It seem a mile wide in the breeze!
And oh! It brought to my mind,
How brilliant it did shine, so gay.
In its golden scarlet hue!
As sun was sinking from the day.

I saw the sunset below,
The bubbling, rolling clouds.
It seem to speak words out loud.
And oh! It said "I do bow"
With respect to the earth's light.
Then, its beauty stabbed me,
As sun was hiding from the night.

I saw the sun set its glow,
A shining amber gleam!
So serene, a joy spread its sunbeams,
And oh! It moved so fast and so low.
I saw with my bare eyes delight!
It did express beauty there,
Gold sun was kissing all good night!

Ifeyinwa Ugokwe
PARADISE LOST
Blossoms disrobe sleepily where
Our kisses have
Precipitated warm rainwater
quenches
Your infatuation eyes pooled as
Forgotten marbles rolling listlessly
About torrented main streets clouds
Extinguish internal bonfires lovers
Scurry wordlessly to escape the
Psychological Elements

Debby Lee Underwood
MY FEELINGS, HOPES, AND DREAMS

To my late mother, October Dawn Stevens, who left her heart and soul with me.

My dreams are the things that keep me going
My dreams keep my tears from showing
There's not an hour that goes by that I don't dream
My dreams put all the things I do the way they should seem

My hopes are the things that I dream of
My hopes are being happy and being loved
I'm almost sure my hopes will never come to reality
But if my hopes come true, I'll better my personality

My feelings are the things I can't explain
My feelings are the things noone but me is to blame
The feelings I have come natural, they are things I can't control
I'm not sure if anyone, including me, will ever understand them, but if they do, I won't let go

My feeling, hopes, and dreams are an important part of me
I know they will always be, where I can see
I know there are more things in life than these
But if you could see what I can, then this is the way you would like it to be

Cathy Mack Unterseher
MODERN DAY COWBOY

I dedicate "Modern Day Cowboy" to my "Modern Day Cowboy," Wade. For helping inspire the old west ways in many of my songs/poems. Because of dreams you hold in your heart and dreams we share; as a love of the land. Love Cathy.

He's up every morning, before the crack of dawn.

Louis Lamour book on his bedside, next to his alarm.
Coffee's abrewin'; you can smell it in the air.
He has his morning cup, then to the stables, Dakota's there.

He bridals up Dakota; he rides the open range.
Checks cattle, opens water holes; feeds hay everyday.
Spring, his favorite time of year, his pride shows right through.
As each new calf that he sees born, takes its first step or two.

He's a modern day cowboy, a century behind. Wishing he could go back into time.
Yes, a modern day cowboy, in a world he don't fit in.
Barely makes a living off the land.
But he thanks the Lord each day for what he has.

When night falls in the evening, and he heads to where it's warm,
An old little shanty, in the hills out all alone.
He turns around one final time as he stands upon the porch.
Sees the colors of the sunset, as it descends somewhere far off.

His mind goes to the old days, a campfire's warming blaze.
A cowboy's strumming soft guitar, coyote howling far away.
Stars brightly shining, like a blanket overhead.
His eyes close; he thanks the Lord, for the dreams that he has.
Yes, he thanks the Lord each day for what he has.

Amisha Upadhyaya
JOSEPHINE
Sadly,
I pause before a stream,
pondering at length
the reflection of a figure sheathed.
I realize the deception of the contented face, which hides the turmoil
of
beneath.

My guise is pedestrian as the shack I call home,
With bleak walls that blend into my cadaverous tone.
None can label me inept or foolish
but
None has ever called me suave or pedantic.
My thoughts I long to turn into words
but
Ne'er do they flow freely as Shakespeare's sonnet.
My eyes and hair as dark as the boards which enclose me,
I am not a beast
but
neither am I the beauty

Tired of reality, I wander into a realm, where I reign as Queen,
Inside my soul lies a vision I alone see,
So mystic and beauteous, called JOSEPHINE
Ah, JOSEPHINE!
How many men have you intoxicated as they drink in your beauty?
A nightingale even swells with envy as you sing your melodious tunes so sweetly,
One gaze into your blue eyes and one is forever lost in their magnetic attraction.
Your caressing touch ignites sensations which drive men to the brinks of madness, lost in passion.
With elegance and charming mien,
You are Cupid's master and a woman's epitome.
My mind deceives what my eyes really see,
You are the other side of what I yearn to be.

Kathleen Cabodi
STICKS
They stood there
Where once was forest lush and green
naked—grim reminder of
a moment in time when wild winds blew

and blazing fires ravaged a hillside
of all beauty and left
a field of sticks.
Twisted remnants of
the mighty oaks and pines—
grey twisted sticks.

Michelle Vanderdoes
ALWAYS, BUT NOT FOREVER . . .
As love goes on, it seems to pass.
But who says love will always last.
I'm not asking for no miracle or two.
I just want a love that will be true.
Love may come for awhile and stay.
But after awhile it will go away.
Sometimes love can last for a long time. But not forever, that's just a line.
I just hope next time you cry. You won't ask that question and wonder why.
So next time you say, "I hope we'll always be together."
Remember, love goes on, but not forever . . .

Mike Van Kerckhove
SHUT UP!
I'm in a big black room
With faces on the walls,
They're laughing at me.
I'd like to tell them all
To shut up!

The room gets smaller,
I can't find the door,
As I dwell in my misery,
The faces laugh even more
Shut up!

I want to tell them "Stop!"
But my voice doesn't work,
A force comes over me
As my body starts to jerk

I feel my body rise,
But I'd much rather fall.
I'm being pushed inside
Now I'm only a face on a wall,
And I can't shut up!

Jay Y Vaishnav
DEMOCRACY
A light in all the darkness,
A lantern in the gloom,
A spot of joy, of peace and light,
Warding off impending doom.

A light in all the darkness,
Piercing the evil in the world,
Amidst all the cries of terror,
Is like a flag unfurled.

A flag of golden beauty,
A lantern in your heart,
A spot of joy, of peace, of light,
In which people must play their part.

Corrine A Vonk
A FRIENDSHIP LIKE OURS

A friendship like ours is without pretense or barriers, where no word is without consequence, no pain without compassion.

When time means nothing, and distance is as insignificant as night or day, where a single word sometimes says all there is to say, and our love grows stronger with each passing day.

Where misunderstandings are impossible, and words have no current, where a chance meeting is enough to last a lifetime and heart speaks to heart with a single contact.

I have known good and gentle people in my lifetime, been lashed together by work and space and every circumstance. Yet few of these could invade the privacy of my inner being, no matter their power, or brilliance, or beauty, or wealth. But you were destined to reside there, my friend, by an eternal edict.

Because even before we met—
YOU WERE ALREADY THERE!!

Corrine A Vonk
DID YA EVER . . .
Did ya ever love somebody, but know they didn't care?

Did ya ever feel like cryin', but knew it'd get you nowhere?

Did ya ever look into their eyes and whisper a little prayer;
And did ya ever look inside their heart and wish that you were there?

Did ya ever watch them dancin', when the lights were way down low;
and whisper out "I love you," but never let them know?

If ya ever fall in love, my friend, you'll find it doesn't pay;
It only causes heartache, happens every day.

Don't ever fall in love, my friend, the price you'll pay is high;
If I could choose, between life and death, I think I'd rather die.

So don't ever fall in love, you'll only get hurt when it's through—for you see, my friend, I ought to know, because I fell in love with you.

It's caused me heartache, pain, and grief so my love for you was great but brief; I know I'll never love again because you were it, my man of all men.

Did ya ever say, "I love you" but it never reached my ears? Because if you have, then I'll have loved but not lost, and you'll keep me happy and quiet my fears.

Jerry L Vasil
FEAR

This poem acknowledges the fears of man from birth to death and is dedicated both to the inner courage that lets us continue and to the man who gave me me mine . . . MY DAD.

What things
in darkness hide,
waiting till time is right,
lurking in the shadows cover
till night.
'Tis fear of death
that haunts the dark of night.
In shadows hide the fears of life.
Yes both
in bleakness lurk.
They haunt the human mind
and badger the human soul,
Death
and Life.

Jerry L Vasil
CHANGE OF HEART

I crawled into her lap hurt and angry but, I left happy and wearing a smile . . . This poem is dedicated with love to . . . MY MOTHER.

Anger
harsh and bitter
raging, snarling, lashing
fury, wrath . . . threat . . . tantrum
sulking, pouting, forgiving
warm and friendly
Happiness

Charles Robert Valencia
THE DANCE

To GOD without whom there would be no dance and to Crystal, Robert, James, Marissa and Meghan, who keep me dancing.

Welcome one and all!
For life is a dance
and we each choose our own music.
Some slow;
idealizing each movement.
Wanting the glow to last forever.
Others go fast,
believing each moment must be taken while time allows,
like a comet that burns fast and bright then goes out while in the glory of its heat.
All different.
All the same.
I hope that I might savor a bit of each and know others even as myself.
But for all of us,
fast or slow,
choose the music of your heart
and . . .
Let the dance begin!

Fadie D Vines
THE WAY OF LIFE

Dedicated To; My late brother, Kenneth Earl Vines.

Sitting here in my room. Feeling nothing but gloom.

Looking for a way out. Life gets so hard, it makes you want to shout.
Getting a job is very hard. Especially if you don't do your part.
Kissing butt, is a thing of the past,
And very out of class.
Money makes the world go around,
Without it see what you found.
Sometimes it seems like you're losing your mind.
Looking for an answer that, hard to find.
There only one way out?
Trust in the Lord, And let him hear you shout.
Praise! his name, and see if things are still the same.
And everything that out of reach
Won't be anything for you to seek.
Because with him, You can reach your peak.

Michelle Vaughan
THE AMERICAN DREAM

To my husband Lloyd, and daughter Charlie'; may all your dreams and desires come true!!!!

You grow up believing
In the american dream
And when it's all over
You find out it's a scheme

You work all your life
They take what you've got
Whether given or gotten
Or stolen or bought

You learn to fight back
You learn to be free
You ride in the wind
Where you know you should be

You learn to be quick
And how to be fast
By now you've found out
You're the social outcast

So what do we do
With the ones left true blue
They will be outlaws, and outcasts
Their whole life through

Michelle Vaughan
THE NEED TO BE FREE

To my daughter Charlie' in memory of her father John Beasly Mabe III, misfit dirty John, who is no longer with us due to an unfortunate accident!!!!

The blood that's been spilled
The bills that aren't paid
No matter how hard you fight
You now can't be saved

The wind in your hair
The need to be free
on your bike on the road
is now your destiny

The bikers they come
The bikers they go
How good or how bad
Only a few of us will know

They live their lives hard
They live their lives fast
If you need to check records
Just look at our past

So now at the end
For the ones that are gone
We will love you forever
Your memories will always carry on

Diana G Vazquez
DEDICADO A TI

I dedicate this poem to the very special person who has given me a bond of wonderful gifts and who means so much: MY MOM.

Sólo en tu rostro
puedo mirar
la gracia y el todo
que encontré al caminar.

Cuando sola yo me encontraba
recordé tu luchar
por aquel ideal que tanto anhelaba
tu alma al caminar.

Mi alma se goza en tu presencia!

Tu espléndido mirar
pudo hipnotizar
tan místico, tan único . . . tu encanto:
y estremece mi corazón!

Y al platicar de amor celestial
en la intimidad,
es fácil ver la luz de amor
que alumbra mi mirar.

De tus ojos fluía hacia mí el amor
como un manantial de luz.
Dios me ama; lo sé
y es fácil de creer,
Pues Su amor me diste tú.

Agnes C Vinson
TWILIGHT SHADOWS

This poem is dedicated to my husband, Roy.

Sunset finds the river world aglow in shimmering shades of red and pink and gold.
Shoreline reeds bend in graceful curves responding to a breeze so bold.
Great blue herons, egrets and myriad smaller birds stand in shadowed silhouette;
shrouded and protected by a misty, velvet cloak; giving rise to stories yet untold.
While muted sounds and murmurings kindle ancient longings to be at one with this natural world. It brings a gentle peace to a troubled human soul.

Kara Vorhes
YOU MAY NEVER KNOW

You may never know when someone might die, so say you love them today.

You may never know when someone will leave, so say whatever you have to say.

You may never know when you'll need someone, so be kind to all.

You may never know when you'll need to catch yourself, so be prepared for the fall.

You may never know when you'll need a helping hand, so always be sure to lend one.

You may never know when life will become too serious, so have a little fun.

You may never know what life will hold, so face it with a smile.

You may never know what time will tell; think about it awhile.

Melonie Vicaire
SHADES OF THE SOUL

A flash of light . . .
All the electricity I need
A human neon flowing freely

Shades of the soul

A depth so dark . . .
Like plummeting into Erebus
Pleasure without a landing

Shades of the soul

The calm azure . . .
Blue tides moving me to sea
The hottest blood of the ocean

Shades of the soul

My lover's eyes
Caressing elements of the world
A shadowy meaning of life

In the shades of the soul

Daisy S Urquhart
REVOLVE

This life I'm living
I hope will be
a passing grade
to the next life for me.
If I should have to live
this life over again,
I hope,
it will not be the same,
that I will recognize the mistakes
I've made before
and will not have to live
This life, once more.

Daisy S Urquhart
PONDERING

Love is such a wondrous word.
It is such a hard word,
to explain.
It has often been misused,
here and there.
And again,
and again.

How can you put any
significance to,
a person who says,
I love you.
When you hear
the same person.
Use the same word.
For things and
animals too.

I don't mean to say,
that I like to prey.
On animals, things
and such.
But why use the word
I love about these.
When you could say
I like, very much.

Millicent Vetterlein
THESE BULBS WE POT OR PEBBLE BED

These bulbs we pot or pebble bed
We choose with special reason
To briefly bloom outside their natural season

To flower from some dark solitude
Where contained, shelved and best ignored
We can only wait their greening sword

Yes the gardens dead and numb in snow
A cutting beds a dream we can't revive
But one fragrant face turned sunward will suffice to survive

Oh to hastily flower — to quicken one's growing span
So desirable and wondrous that appears to be
One almost forgets the implicit brevity

And those loves we force like paperwhites?
Already knowing their unhardy ways
They too briefly bring the warmth of spring
To a handful of wintry days

Pegi Johnson

Pegi Johnson
GOLDDIGGER

Why do you say things you do not want to hear?

Why do you criticize people you know nothing about?

Why is money so important to you when you have none of your own?

I feel very sorry for you, because you don't know what it's like to be happy with a riverbed.

You have never taken the time to stop and smell the roses. Everything is rush, rush, rush.

Sometimes, you worry me because you seem so worried about so many trival things.

Racism, poverty, and homelessness are words that aren't part of your vocabulary.

You treasure your safe, little world with the people you have grown up with.

Cristy Vroman
MY LOVE

When everything is said and done
I hope you'll understand,
My Love . . .
is written in the sand.
It comes and goes
As the wind blows,
Sometimes it isn't there at all.
Some say it's lust, some call it love
but it comes and goes like fall.
I don't know just what I want.
Right now it's hard to say.
I know I never meant to hurt you
in any sort of way.

Sometimes my love was very strong,
Sometimes love's flames dwindled—
but I know that when you kissed me
there was a passion that was kindled.

Brenda Viera
SO UNFAIR

Why is life so unfair?
I am so lonely and scared!
If someday I miss you and need you
will you be there?

I feel at the bottom, when I damn
well know I really do deserve the top!

But wishful thinking will never stop
'cause for as long as there's
tomorrow there's a promise for a new
start.

Give me the courage to be able to
fight to overcome the unfairness
that's in each day of my life.

Ann Vandiver
APRIL

Dedicated to my GrandDaughter April, With Love.

April
a month or a
Little Girl.
April the month, full of bloom the art
of color in all its array of beauty, like
a Bride and Groom.
Natural music in the air, from tiny
creatures that God made so fair. The
warmth that touches your most inner
soul, The little Girl April is about to
unfold.

Her eyes full of color an array of
brown, a dancing delight, truly I tell
you, cannot be found.

Her voice soft and tender,
carefully choosing her words, as she
tells you she loves you, Just plain and
simple, no more needs to be heard.
The warmth of her touches your
heart and soul, a grandmother's
feelings has now been told.

April like pie, the apple of my eye,
you're all of the above, Heaven has
sent you for me to love. April, the
month or a Little Girl, they both
make you feel alive, and put your
heart in a Whirl.

Rachael Ann VanAlphen
FEAR FOR LIFE

To Dave Slemp, a special friend.

There he walks the streets alone,
Trying to find his way home.
Lost in the dark with no sign of light.
He doesn't even put up a fight.
Hurting inside as pain builds
stronger, ambition for life he feels
no longer.
Endlessly walking this time alone,
with absolutely nothing to call his
own.
A life taken captive by such a
horrible thing, something that
destroys this human being.
Addicted to pain and suffering inside,
he is no longer able to hide. In all
due time he knows it's just suicide

Tony Vara
ONE SEASON FOLLOWING ANOTHER

Winter is such a beautiful time for
frost on the pumpkin and snow on the
pine.
And little white snowflakes that
cover the land makes our
mountaintops look so grand.

But even though winter must go we
love to see the melting snow,
because soon the spring will warm
the earth with sweet smelling
fragrants and giving new birth.

Once more the land will be colored
with beautiful sights of yellows,
purples and whites.
I love to see the sun shining bright
that prepares us for the warm summer
nights.
As we spend the days lying in the
sun, we think about swimming,
barbecues and good fun.

So now that the summer makes room
for fall, we cover our pools and
deflate the beach balls.
And as we watch the birds fly south,
when springtime comes they'll be
back no doubt.

Celia Volkman
PEACE RETREATS

Whip the whipped! Wipe not their
tears.
Hear not their cries! They drown out
fears.
Step on the conquered! They will rise
no more.
Tyranny stalks at freedom's
door—
Peace trembles— alone, afraid!

Stay the doctor's hand, heal not the
foe,
Feed not the fallen, feel not their
woe.
Rulers reaped ruin, wrought havoc,
despair,
Tread on their people— new loads
to bear.
Peace totters— distraught,
dismayed!

From Hades, abyss of tortured souls
Cadavers rise, rejoicing in their roles.
Conquer again! New weapons in their
hands
Placed there by those who would
not understand.
Peace shudders— withdraws,
betrayed!

Cecily Atyes Varner
THE CHARACTER BOX

I have a character box
It is little and made of
Etched glass and trimmed in brass

You can see the work of
The cotton tape measure while
Just to the right lays a metal
fingernail file

The wire-rimmed glasses show wear
of
The long hours of the crocheting
needle

The tin snuff can sitting silently
simple
As it always seems to sort of
Sit as proudly as the brass thimble

A strand of pearls and a mending
gourd
These are little keepsakes of
My Grandmother who is with the
Lord

LouElla Cook Van Dusen
NO-MAN'S-LAND

If I wandered around the rest of my
days,
Never would I get rid of this awful
craze.

I wandered around town from city to
city,
Never found peace or from anyone
pity.
But you know it matters not,
For when time comes I would have
forgot.

God lend me a hand and strength on
which to stand,
It's been a long time in this
no-man's-land.

Rivers of water may over me roll but
God will care for my soul.

If you tarry in this no-man's-land,
may He who cares hold your hand.

Vanessa De Villava
MY LIFE

I walk in solitude in this dark,
desolate land.
It seems I took a wrong turn.
Now I am trapped in life's maze.
There is nobody to lend me a helping
hand when I stumble.
There is nobody to hear my loudest
cry.
There is nobody to lean on.
Everyday I wonder when the sun will
rise
Or if it will ever rise.
I do not know where to go
But I do know that I will not give up
Until I reach my goal and see the sun
shine.

Margaret McDonnell
LONDON REVERIE

For Mom and Dad, 1968.

Down the rain come
That the rain would come
To bloat and float
This desperate city beyond the realms
of earthen green
That the rain could come
To purge and surge
The stuffy facades and iron bones
Off the land
To wash and swash
The chrome and coil
To mesh it and thresh it
Off the wayfare
In wonderful cascadings
It would travel space—

Become one in the starbound lather
of tenement sediments and concrete
fixtures.
Such upheaval of grit!
The tumbling, fumbling of spitting
gargoyles
The final bombardment of superman
catastrophes
Up and out to the cosmos about.
All this I did dream on a vegetative
day—
In mac and wellingtons I felt the rain
come down on a rainy day town
of jumbled hallucinations and
sunshine expectations.

Margaret McDonnell
STONE RAPTURE

Gray sky at noon
Lacy curtained rain
Reed and cattail in dizzy dance
Your woolen warmth
Exiled the chill of.

An egret's desperate call
The heron's pained wail—
Communion of two voices
From distant shores as.
Warm tea on salted breath
Marshland stones to savor.

R E Vaughn
ASHLEY MICHELLE KAY

God beautified my life one day, when
He let me meet Ashley Kay—
A beautiful child, the sweetest ever,
and I pray our friendship will last
forever—
She dances beautifully I'm told, and
she has a heart of gold—
She likes to draw, and write, and
play, and jump a rope, little Ashley
Kay—
She is a pretty little girl, and I'm
gonna tell the whole wide world—
Just how intelligent she is, and I
praise God, for a child like this—
She's a girl each child could pattern
after, their lives would be filled with
joy and laughter—
She's always friendly, always a
smile, and for a hug I would walk a
mile—
A good little girl is Ashley Kay, and
often she brightens up my day—
She comes to visit now and then,
with her cousin Crystal, and Ashley,
their friend—
And I love to see her come to visit,
but one day soon, I'm going to miss
it—
Because she's fixing to move away,
and I'll be sad, without Ashley
Kay—
But I'll always remember, the good
times we had, just knowing this child
has made me so glad—
And when she moves, I know she
will write, and I'll think of her, each
day and night—
And I'll whisper her name, each day
as I pray, as I've always done, for
Ashley Kay—
And I'll watch for her to return again,
for she'll always be, my special
friend—
And I'm writing this poem, for the
world to see, how much this child is
loved by me—
Well I've said so much, what more
can I say, about my friend, Ashley
Michelle Kay—
But I'll always cherish, our day in the
sun, and praise God for making me
the fortunate one—
God blessed me with her friendship
one day, and I'll always love, little
Ashley Kay—
I love you pretty girl . . . always, and
forever . . . God bless you.

Robin Wright
DREAMLAND
In restful slumber, his body lies next to mine.
The softness of his skin, the warmth when I feel him.
His smile so divine, his breath so sweet, forever he is mine!
He is my knight in shining armour.
Like the sun he brightens my day, and like the stars, shall always follow.
A gift from God, he is heaven-sent
My most prized possession, a gift I will always cherish.
As I slowly fall to rest, his heart calls out to mine.
We glide away, to the dreamland beyond, where—
Dreams are made, and dreams are kept, forever to remember.

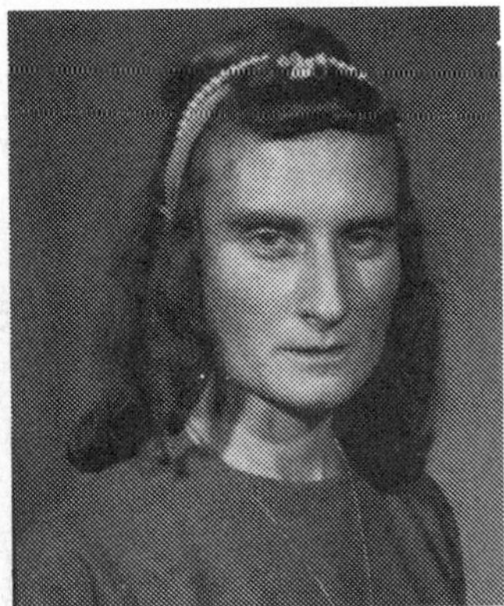

Miss Joan Therese Camp

Miss Joan Therese Camp
OH, IT'S SOMETHING TO BE IRISH

This poem was written by ne'e Frances Elizabeth Loftus, mother of Miss Joan Therese Camp when Frances was a young girl.

Oh, it's something to be Irish,
something whimsical and gay
Though you kill your own ambition
in your contradictory way.
Though you'll never own a house or lot nor ever gain renown.
You have something that's the envy of the richest in the town
For when God breathed the breath of life into the lowly clod,
He smiled, and for the Irish, put a singing in the sod.

George Henry Wiedeman
THE FORGOTTEN MEN OF WARS
Listen to me people, of the world, about our men, that died for us.
They never asked, to go to war, to keep this land, from all, whom do it wrong.
The men that lives, are hurting so, 'cause they are the ones, that needs our love.
So hear their call, for help my friends,
someday you all, could go again,
to face the war's, as they did.
Not to return, ever again, as they were so, clear of mind, than come back, not so fine.

TO ALL SERVICEMEN

Elizabeth A Waters
LISTEN
Listen . . .
Hear the wind sigh through the trees.
Shhh . . . it tells of my lover
yet it teases.
I hear the rhythm, but not the name
never his name.

Alone, I hear it speak
It whispers of pleasures not yet known.
Sweet, tender caresses
Kisses like wine that set my body on fire
Forever burning.
Please, whisper it yet again

The rhythm is enough to set a desire deep within me
I want to caress, touch, love.
I want to strive to reach that one moment of ecstasy, of everlasting joy
Together
with him whose name is on the wind.

Soon he will come.
Until then — I wait alone.

And listen.

Philo Glenn Wooddell
WASHINGTON SQUARE PARK NEW YORK CITY
The ersatz Arch D'Triumphe looms over the bottom of Fifth Avenue like some gaping big mouth with slack problems.

Seemingly, it winks with Downtown wisdom knowing what its entryway beholds.

Yellow-white sun and eventide floodlight hide its callous, weathered corniches.

The iconography of the square is inverted into crystalline fragments,

While Girabaldi, whitewashed, watches wisely the metamorphosed moments.

Representation is rampant.
Patterns become exact.
Sacrosanctity returns.

Living pigment pulsates with colors vibrating off the canvas to Sixth Avenue.

The problematic of all this is easy to ignore.
No one wants an onus of time.
There is no smell. There is nothing.
Why is there a feeling of shallowness in this empty soul that prides itself too often?

Jason Neatrour
MISSING YOU

This poem is dedicated to my true inspiration and future wife to be: Jeri Marie Funderburg.

Sounds of a familiar song are running through my head,
reminding me of times with you,
and things that we have said.

Thoughts of you are always near.
My feelings grow each day.
My heart is now filled with your love;
My mind, with things to say.

I long to be with you now,
and hold you near my heart.
Always may we love each other,
and (in soul) never part.

Penelope Wedgwood
KITTENS
There is a fluffy tangle under the bed.
Some see a kitten, while others
agonize over the threads path.

Marty Wagner
DIAMONDS IN THE SNOW
As I sit here in the window
Looking down below,
I see diamonds,
Diamonds in the snow!
The sky is bright and sunny
and the air is cold and thin.
A good day to be "looking out,"
and better yet for "staying in."
Again my eyes glance downward
To the frosty ground below,
and I see diamonds—
Diamonds glistening in the snow!!

Dorinda White
SWANS
Swans walk gracefully
With their necks held up intelligently.
They move swiftly and joyfully.
They sometimes remind me
Of big white cotton balls
As they waddle down to the water,
Curiously wondering
If they dare to enter the sheets of blue.

Carlos A-Urbina
MY VAGABOND SPIRIT

Dedicated to the memory of my Grandmother, to my Mother, Aunt Flor, Brothers, Sisters, niece, nephew, relatives and best friends David, Thomas, Eric and José Luis.

Sleeps in the deep silence of the sea,
and its voice is heard like the cry of sea gulls,
in the horizon of a maze of sadness and disillusions.
It's the silence in time,
and a stare in blank.

A smile broken within the navy blue flowers.
Flies high above crying mountains,
and its cloth is combined with colors
as the rainbow in faraway worlds,
in valleys of close fantasies.
Discovers looks in every corner,
in plazas of cities, and on the streets
it marches with rhythm of vanities and anxieties.
Sleeps within the rocks,
under a gray roof,
and in the morning it awakes
and it is a free and happy bird.

Pauline Wilson
GOOD-BYE KENNA
Far up on a lonely hill, the snow is softly falling
As a convoy of cars slowly climb the winding road to the top.
In the distance a lonely bird is calling,
As one, by one the cars slowly draw to a stop.
All the family and friends gather around,
The coffin is carried and set upon the ground.
We pray and say our farewells to the one we love,
As you Kenna are in the Lord's home above.
We shall miss you, with all the tears we shed,
May now you have eternal peace ahead.
You were a man who could care,
One who was always ready to share.
You shall always remain in our heart,
As we now must all depart.
Slowly back down the hill we go,
Again it begins to softly snow.
We have said our last good-byes,
As we slowly wipe a tear from our eyes.
You are now in God's hands,
As you said, "You went till you ran out of sand."

C V Williamson
MOMENTS IN TIME

To my darling Jamie, who I will always love.

Those moments in time that we love the most,
Are memories of which we often host.
They grow old with us as we age,
And become yet another paragraph on the page.

My memories of you I keep in my heart,
For in my life they're an integral part.
I call on them when I am sad,
And they never fail to make me glad.

They are not as brilliant as they once were,
For where I stand in your life, I'm not quite sure.
But when I think of you these memories start to flicker.
I feel my heart race and my pulse beat quicker.

The love I have for you never ceases,
As time goes by it just increases.
I love you more than you will ever know,
My feelings for you, I hope, will never cease to show.

Gloria Ward
A RING
Now let me say this about that

You thought I was married
but not wearing a ring
Let me remind you
thoughts don't cost a thing

A ring collects soap
and legitimizes birth
Doesn't make for happiness
or personal worth.

It ain't really your business

if you get my drift
But don't be offended
put off or mifffed

Just remember a ring
is symbolic of things
All personal—all deep
For two people to keep

And then it's all over
symbolic or real

Richard L Webb
THE BORN LOSER

I wake up in the morning very tired,
Go to work to find I'm fired!
I starve from the lack of food,
People say I'm pretty rude?!
I haven't taken a bath in ages,
Cover myself with newspaper pages!
I walk the streets from day to night,
Bumped into a man that wanted to
fight!
I woke up next morning, all covered
with bruises,
I'm what you call a man who loses!

Donna L Wilson
YOU'RE THE ONE I LOVE

I have never loved anyone,
Not until I met you.
You were someone special,
Someone I hardly knew.

Yes, I do love you,
Even more than from the start,
You've taken my love,
My feelings and my heart.

You're the one I love,
And I always will,
I give my life to share with you
For as long as we both shall live.

Mildred R Winters
THE LADY OF TIANANMEN SQUARE

To The Brave Young Patriots.

It lay in abject darkness under the
Oppressor's might,
When the torch was raised in
Tiananmen Square; suffusing it with
light.
Under the heel of tyranny lay the
gloom of deep despair,
A fresh new wind was blowing, and
hope was written there.
A light had pierced the darkness that
set all hearts aflame,
Who holds the torch of freedom high,
Liberty is her name,
The Guardian of those sacred truths;
the Keeper of the Flame.

We watched the brave young
Patriots, their Oppressor they defied,
And we watched in helpless pity as
they for Freedom died.
The bloodstained of the Martyrs; the
numbered of the dead,
There in Tiananmen Square; where
the Patriots' blood ran red.
Courage shone on their faces, fair in
the flower of youth,
They sought not fame and glory; they
sought a right and purer truth.

Long after the Oppressor is gone,
unhonored and unsung;
Their story will be told in every Land
and Tongue.
They long will be remembered afar
from East to West,
The Captive and the Bondman shall
rise and call them blessed.
Their shackles will be broken, the
prisoner from his chains,
And darkness will be lifted o'er a
Land where freedom reigns.

Michael J Tamas

Michael J Tamas
****FRIENDSHIP****

*To all women that I have met; thank you*** Love; M.J.T.*

Is a Priceless Gift; That cannot Be
Bought or Sold.
Its value is far Greater than,
Mountains made of Gold. If You
Should ask Your Higher Power; for a
Gift; Be thankful and Humble.
If, He does not send Gold, Silver,
Pearls or Diamonds; But the Love
and Trust of Friends...
With a Honest Relationship; There is
no need to test Each Other. It is so
wonderful to find someone, Whom I,
Don't need to play games with.
And Lives up to Everything that I,
consider Important, Right and
Beautiful. This is the way that Life is
meant to BE TODAY.
Unconditional Love Is Living...

LOVE, MICHAEL

Carolyn Henderson
HARD TIMES

Dedicated to my loving parents, Alcus & Eddie Payne, both deceased now. My father died on September 19, 1989, and my mother on January 13, 1990.

We lived on a farm in Spearsville
Town
Twenty-two miles going westward
bound.
Dad was hardworking at the age
twenty-three
As time passed on to where he got to
be.
On our farm there was no play for us
Church, work and education, that was
a must.
They struggled through years that
passed
Looked back at their children all
grown at last.
He raised us to work just as he
always did
Following in his footsteps when he
was a kid.
He never had opportunities to go
anywhere
Always had to work before food got
bare.
They never let us go hungry, not a
day
If only a crumb they made a way.
I can say this as much as I can
Alcus Payne was really a
hardworking man.

Christie Williams
THE CREATION OF MAN

Epimetheus being a scatterbrain,
Didn't understand all the rules.
He gave animals all the necessities,
And to humans he was very cruel.

After everything was given to
animals,
And nothing was left for man,
He went to his wise brother
Prometheus,
And said, "Please do what you can."

Prometheus said okay to that,
And from gods he stole some fire,
Thinking he was doing a good deed,
He lost faith in a man he admired.

Well that made Zeus very angry,
And he was going to get him back,
Prometheus was then tied to a rock,
His liver he then did lack.

Prometheus learned his lesson,
And he learned it a very hard way.
That gods are greater than man,
No matter what he would say.

Doris M Weigel
COMMUNION

To my daughter, Kathryn, for her courage and encouragement.

With this day
Let me live
In such a way
As to enhance
My own self-esteem
For others we meet
And pass by
But with myself,
My own true spirit,
I commune eternally . . .

Michael Watson
SAIL ON SAILOR

To My Father:
Mr. G.R. Watson:
May 20th, 1916—January 13th, 1990.

'On a sea of troubled thought' . . .
One small vessel, 'greatly tossed' . . .
A peaceful shore somewhere
behind the cabin's closed door . . .
For so long on the ocean, near beaten
by raging waves and thundering
winds; 'Only to find courage, to raise
his sails and begin again' . . .
No stars to chart his course . . .
One small vessel, 'one worn sailor';
Thinks of a place somewhere ahead.
Of a lighthouse shining bright; 'of a
quiet port', to rest for the night . . .

"So many directions, many more
to choose" . . . Finds him thinking to
himself; "will I ever find you?"

One small vessel, 'one worn
question' . . . A sea gull flying
aimlessly; seems lost with no
direction. 'What has it to live
for? . . . What awaits it, upon another
shore?' . . .
'A simple thought the sailor
pursues'. The Answer, raging inside
his mind; Trying to beat him,
'through each and every line' . . .
Looking over the stern, 'the pages
of the past' . . . Finds him knowing in
himself; 'the past came back at
last' . . .

Sail on Sailor. The weather-worn
gull seems to say; 'Surely in the
distance, there shines a brighter
day . . . Set your sails; Close the book
to your past, lay it upon the
helm' . . .

A song of strength the gull has
learned to sing. "A single gleaming
tear, upon the Sailor's face is
seen" . . .
'The light within his eyes,
somehow lessens the raging tides' . . .

One small vessel, 'Sailing Life's
Troubled Sea' . . .

"Sail on Sailor. Sail on, You're Free"

Patricia A White
A WISH

This poem is dedicated to my lovely daughter Devida, whom I love dearly.

I carry around a wishful dream of
loving someone I've never seen
Imagining him admiring me and
being the woman he wants me to be
Of making love all thru the night
Continuing the love 'til morn day
light
Of sharing laughs and having fun
And taking vacations in the Bermuda
sun
Of having his name 'til death do we
part
Of living our lives as we did from the
start
Of being parents together to share
all the trials our children would bear
Of doing the things that lovers do
Oh! God how I wish my dream
would come true

Yvonne Wathen
LIVING FOR THE WEEKEND

During the week I take to the road.
Hoping this rig will hold up on these
wheels, pulling heavy loads. Many a
mile I put between my family and me
and when it comes to the weekend
home is where I want to be.
Living for the weekend, headed for
home. Spending time with the wife
and kids, tired of being alone.
Putting five into two days is hard to
do, but just like any job it's got good
points and drawbacks too. Out here I
have a sense of freedom that on a
nine-to-five I can't find and then I get
so lonesome and I wonder if I'm not
out of my mind.
Living for the weekend, headed for
home. Spending time with the wife
and kids, tired of being alone.
Many a town and city I've been
through and I feel just like this ole
truck looks, worn and beaten too.
I've put five days in and boss all I'm
asking of you, is give me the
weekend I really need those two.
Living for the weekend, headed for
home. Spending time with the wife
and kids, tired of being alone. Just
living for and looking forward to, the
weekend.

Denise Ann Willis
AS THE SNOW FALLS

As the snow falls, I think of you.
Remembering how much you loved
me when we first met.
As the months have passed your love

for me has weak'en.
We used to always be together, now always an excuse on why we are apart.

As the snow falls, My heart melts thinking of you.
My thoughts remembering how happy you were back then,
That smile on your face —
The sparkle in your eyes.

As the snow falls, I sit and think of you.
Wondering if you will love me like you used to.

As the snow falls, I realize I only have photographs left of you.
Photographs and memories of all the love you once had for me.

As the snow falls,
I still wait for you.

Rick Westover

LIVE IT NOW

Drugs and weapons, war and hate.
Whatever happened to peace sign dreams?
Death and destruction, fear of man.
Whatever happened to bell-bottom jeans?
Why does the best have to lie in the past?
Everything dwindles, everything dies.
Can't they hear our earthly cries?
Slicked back hair and saddle shoes.
Eccentric men like Howard Hughes.
They're all gone. Never to return.
We're in the present,
That's what we must learn.

Denise D Watson

GOODBYE

Goodbye my love, goodbye,
don't make me look back,
as I go.
Let me walk away proudly, holding my head up high.
Don't ask me any questions,
goodbye, my love, goodbye.
Don't wish you knew the answers,
just let me venture on my way,
all I know of this is,
that I simply cannot stay.
I have no explanations,
as to why I cannot be,
the one for you to have,
and hold,
please try dear, just to see.
I'm too tired, you're too scared,
to even want to cry.
My love I just can't stay here,
goodbye my love,
goodbye.

Ida D Wheaton

BEST FRIEND

To Ronnie — My husband of twenty-three years. My companion, My inspiration, My Best Friend.

Every now and then your heart is broken
Seems your world is to an end
You feel like you've been deserted
You need to touch the hand of a FRIEND

You start thinking unpleasant thoughts
That you don't understand
You speak but nobody listens
You need to talk with a FRIEND

Work all day come home tired
And still do the best that you can
But your work is not over
You need to sit and be with a FRIEND

Gone to bed what a relief you say
As you lie close next to your man
You're feeling warm and he is too
You need to be loved by a FRIEND

Awake in the morning start a new day
Knowing by you he'll stand
Leaving the house you realized
Here at home you have your BEST FRIEND!

Jennifer Campanese

Jennifer Campanese

TO THE BEST GRANDMOTHER IN THE WORLD LOVE AND SADNESS

I dedicate this poem to my grandmom. I am old enough now to fully realize the enormous impact she has had upon my life. I thank God for blessing me when he gave me the greatest grandmom in the world.

Why have you gone?
I do not know
You say it's love
But why does it hurt me so

We need you here
You must not stay
Come back to us
Right away!

My love for you is very strong
Why did you go?
It felt like I did something wrong
Come back to us
Before the snow
Put your arms around me
And I promise you
I'll never let you go.
Love You Always,
Jennifer

Linda J Widner

MY FATHER

This poem is dedicated to "Henry Wilson" my father.

My Father is a Blessing
He's given me such Joy
God gave him four daughters
and one precious boy.

My Father is a Teacher
He's taught me what he knew
He's there when I need him
To support me in the bad times too.

My Father is a Strong Man
He's worked hard all his life
To care for his five children
and his very Special Wife.

My Father is so wonderful
He's given me such love
I give thanks each and every day
To the Good Lord up above.

My Father is so precious
I hope you don't get mad
Because I wanted to tell you
You're the World's Greatest Dad.

Eddie Applewhite

Eddie Applewhite

BEAUTY AND THE MIRROR

This poem is dedicated to my beautiful daughter Faness, with all my love.

Oh!
"Precious one"
Clearly I need not introduce myself
For of you
I am truly known
Through endless time of standing alone

I,
"Beauty"
Has found someone
Not pretty
Nor lovely
And far, far from cute.
But beautiful just like me
A twin sister
Of my very own
A twin sister
Indeed.

Sebie D Landers

THE COMMISSION

I said to the artist:
Paint me a lonely tree
Standing robust in greenery
Separate from the family
Of sylvan camaraderie, lonely — for me.
It should stand, bent and twistedly
In wind-whipped, rain-drunk ecstasy.
It should be only for me.
Paint it, please, lonely — for me.

He sent me away that I might not see
As his genius, concentrate, shaped my tree.
I thought of it often as the weeks would flee
Into past ago's lost infinity.
Was he still painting it — lonely — for me?

I said to the artist:
Have you finished the painting and may I see?
"It is done" he informed me, reluctantly,
"And I gave it away to my love because she
had always wanted her own lonely tree."
But I know it is not hers—
it is lonely — for me.

Kenneth Yanow

Kenneth Yanow

LOVING, LOVING, LOVING

I dedicate this poem to my loving wife to be. Joyce, the one I've been waiting for, who brings so much joy into my life.

It was an evening in the winter,
Two paths crossing in the wind,
Like the future and the past,
It all started to begin.
I felt the corners of my world turn,
I knew from now it would never change,
She spoke to me only with her eyes,
It is for her that I wrote this song.

Many dreams come true, and some have a golden lining,
It is this we shall always have, from every day to every year,
From her to me and me to her, like the winter that shines so near,
For us it is only the beginning, I hope that I make this clear.

Lying down, thinking of her, until the night turns into day,
About the woman I love who won my heart, this is what I have to say:

Loving, Loving, Loving; we'll savor it every way,
Loving, Loving, Loving; it is all we need to say,
Loving, Loving, Loving; it can never last too long,
Loving somebody; that is why I wrote this song.

Sebie D Landers
LAUGH

The laugh of love is a passion song
And rare it is, but good.
The laugh at others is a raucous wrong
And always understood.
But if you laugh first at yourself,
And others see this gentle thing,
They will take heart and give you grace
And honor you, remembering
That you are one with them.

Katherine Aguinaldo-Choo
SALUTE TO THE 49ERS

To The Team Of The 80's 4X Superbowl Champions—San Francisco 49ers.

Weeks and weeks of hard-nosed preparation
Make the mistakes, pay the high price
Wait with anticipation.

Thousands flood the streets
Celebrating all the way to the Dome
Forty Niners dominate from the beginning
Bringing the fourth-one home.

High fives to Jerry, Tom and Roger
The team puts on a great show
Fifty-five to ten— final score
Thanks to "Cool-hand" Joe.

Karen Yeisley
WHAT LOVE MEANS TO ME

To Will, And how I found what love means to me.

It means you have someone special
But this kind of special
means a lot to me—
You have to grow with each other
And learn about each other
Sometimes laugh, sometimes cry
But always have that communication
to even try—
For love is a special gift
Of many different things
To many different people
And for many different reasons
Love comes in all sizes and shapes of forms
Big or small
People or things
It just comes together for me.
The different ways of love
Are just so incredible
How I may love thee
Or be loved by thee.

Rusty Hopper
IF I WERE A COLORING BOOK

To My Husband Kenneth W. Hopper.

If I were a coloring book

what would you do?
What color, shade, or hue?
Would you make each part of me,
as only you could see.

color the heart of a man with
gentle, steady hand.
Color a lonely heart so true.
deep inside, color it blue.

Color the soul not unseen,
alive with emotion for you
and me, For the soul is
not dead still it
bleeds, so color it red.

Color my love for you alone
a different shade, so unknown.
Color my love a shade of strong
and when it hurts, color it gone.

Color me now inside out in
rainbow stripes, without doubt.
Pick up your colors, shades, and
hues. If I were a coloring book,
what would you do?

LoAnna C McNew
NEAH BAY

To the wonderful native Americans, who through their perseverance and love of nature, have taught us to appreciate God's world and made our earth a better place to live.

Where the forest meets the ocean,
and the treetops touch the sky.
As I look out o'er the water, there's a teardrop in my eye.
Where the birds fly o'er the ocean,
and they soar into the sky.
How my heart fills with emotion and I feel free enough to fly.
As I look out o'er the valley, and I see the beauty there.
I believe that I belong here, just as the breeze that's in the air.
On the hills and in the valleys, where the beaver roams at will,
There the bear is ever master, and the cougars wander still.
Can it be forever sheltered, could it be that people care?

Must they always just ignore it,
pretending it was never there?
Will we remember all this beauty
when our time has come to pass?
Will it be here for tomorrow, or will destruction come at last?
Shall we call upon tomorrow, for the strength we need today?
To protect the love of beauty, that is found in Neah Bay.
Where the forests meets the ocean,
and the treetops touch the sky.
In my dreams it's here I'll wander,
though today I say goodbye . . .
I'm trying not to cry . . .
Written with Love by—
Bridgett Medeiros
Brenda Hubert
LoAnna McNew

Tiffany Gleaner
BUT IN THE MEANTIME . . .

Dedicated to my mom and dad and to my friends: Lisa W. & Jaime S., and to everyone who loses a good friend.

Left with nothing but a shattered heart,
No one seems to care that all has fallen apart.
Tears fall upon the picture; filled with memories
Nothing's left but heartache; what's left is pain to see.

To face reality is too much to ask;
Friendship is now a thing of the past.
Trust & Love is hard to give, with none in return, it's hard to live

It's over and done; it's time to realize . . .
That everything has to end, but in the meantime . . .

Live for the day, not the time
Your time will come and your heart will find.
Trust & Love may come and make hearts be true . . .
Days and tomorrows will be brighter,
and the sun will shine and the sky . . .
always a faithful blue.

Michael Curtis Johnson
SOMEONE I LOVE!

I've been touched by someone I love. A love that is greater than all other loves. It's made my life new and better than before. A love that's so glorious it shines more and more. My life before this wasn't that good it was sinful and rotten and evil not good. But there came a day I broke down and prayed. I was filled with tears and God understood. He made me feel better. He forgave my sins. He made a Christian all over again. He relit the flame that went out in my heart. God made life worth living, God gave me a new start. I thank the Lord at night in bed and ask Him to teach me and help clear my head. I thank God in all I do even the bad things that I don't like too. God knows much more than anyone could. Because I've been touched by someone I love. A love that comes from only above. God bless you and me and everyone we see. And hope and pray that maybe someday this world will be a better place to be.

Jennifer A Nerowski
SIZZLING SUMMER DAY

Sizzling in the frying pan
Which has flowered pattern print.
The gaze liquid pours on my flesh
Sticking to the bottom.
I heave my burnt body over
to the other side.
Hearing the sounds of the
waves splatt on the rocks
My eyes flickered on a man
with muscles.
My body sprung to glance at
his sunny shine body.
His deep brown hair danced
gracefully in the wind
I lick my red lollipop lips
Every step he took shook my body
He bounced on the blanket
He stiffened and pointed his
finger to me
I crawled like a wild cat
to be tamed
We left our footprints on the
sandy beach
For the water raced between our
toes.

Angelo M Osario
UNTITLED

Sometime the world seems so
Indifferent to the needs of man.
It makes you want to question
Genesis, God and the rest of the clan.
What's the use of all the education & pain.
If you're not part of the establishment
There's no gain
Blackmen, whitemen and those in between.
Are endlessly searching for the fulfillment of life's dreams.
Yet the wars of oppression prejudice and hate.
Assure those individuals of a continued predicted fate.
Perhaps the ensuing years will bring
A balance of sorts.
And the population will benefit from a just court.
Rich man poor man & middle classes of all races have
To consider the masses.
For someday they will be a pot pourri of people
Minus classes.
Somewhere it's written that the meek will inherit the earth.
But what we do now will determine our fate.
The rulers who are for the most part unjust
Will suffer from their position a strategic
Bust.
In the end a barrel like situation will prevail
But by then it won't matter because,
The earth will be everyone's jail.

Pammi Lynne Stewart
HE, ME, OR YOU

I pray this night,
to Jesus above,
may all be right,
in this precious love.

Grant my man kindness,
with a heart sincere,
keep him from blindness,
or occurrences more severe.

Guide his life,
to avoid bad afflictions,
bring no strife,
or terrible addictions.

I pray oh great spirit,
to keep our love true,
let no one go near it,
unless it be he, me, or you.

Pammi Lynne Stewart
MAKES ME SOMETIMES WONDER

I look into the sky,
and see a little star,
I watch a small bird go by,
and wonder if it is traveling far.
I watch a cloud darken,
and pour out lots of rain,
I see a fire sparking,
and admire the bright orange flame.
I feel a soft cool breeze,
on a hot summer day,
I see a little kitten sneeze,
while seeking out its prey.
I smell a sweet fragrance,
brought about colorful flowers.
Oh how my mind does dance,
from all these lovely powers.
It makes me sometimes wonder,
what part I play in life,
do I create my own thunder,
or just avoid all strife?

Pammi Lynne Stewart
DEEP WITHIN
Friendship stands tall,
often above the sky.
It is held by all,
until the day we die.

Its use is grand,
and really fine.
To try and understand
takes plenty of time.

Patience builds love,
from one to another,
It is there to prove,
you can trust each other.

No matter the tears,
or hateful outbursts,
It is all those years,
that settle small squirks.

A friend is found,
in a simple grin,
Love is bound,
From Deep Within.

Pammi Lynne Stewart
EVERY COWBOY
A hat so broad,
and boots so dusty,
there is no fraud,
in a mind so rusty.

Those dirty jeans,
and worn-out shirts,
have torn seams,
but still allow flirts.

Some women love you,
others just turn their heads,
They miss what is true,
in your inner threads.

Arrogance and hate,
are nowhere to be found,
for this is the fate,
of every cowboy around.

Millard R Hall
SENIOR CITIZENS
Senior Citizens are to be respected.
They are to be loved.
They are to be honored.
They are to be wanted.

Senior Citizens are to be listened to.
They are to be treated kindly.
They are to be trusted.
They are to be obeyed.

Senior Citizens are not to be treated
disrespectful.
They are not to be put out to pasture.
They are not to be treated unkindly.
They are not to be left alone.

Senior Citizens can teach you a lot.
They can be helpful.
They can be a joy to be around.
Please love and respect Senior
Citizens.

Christine Davis
WITHOUT YOU IN MY LIFE
Without you in my life I know
the fire wouldn't be.
So with this song for you I give
and everything I bring.
Without you in my life right now
I'd be so lost to see.
So please just say and be glad
to live your life with me.
Without you in my life I think
that I'd just rather die.
Than to give all my love to
some other worthless guy.
So please don't think that I am mad
I know I'm really not.
I really hate to think I love
without you in my life.

Richard D Baxter
RAIN FALLING

To the one I love
Kristin Suzanne Frank

Rain falling
Little drops from Heaven
In the night
I hear your voice calling
I look out my window
And see water dripping off the pane
A tear matches the sight
And you far away drives me insane
Drip, drip
I'm losing my grip
Oh, how these feelings swell
Please, please, my candle is lit
Oh, babe, in love I have fell
Two beads of water collide
And bleed into one
Oh, girl, in you I'll confide
Without you there would be none

Marlee Payne Shaw
THE GIFT OF LOVE
I need your smile to bring happiness
to my life
I need your songs to bring music to
my world
I need your arms to hold me and let
me feel safe
I need your strength to fill my
weakest spots
I need your laughter to add joy to my
soul
I need your trust to allow me to be
strong
I need your support so I'll try even
harder
I need your praise for I want so to
please you
I need your love to make me truly
whole.

There can be no more precious gift
than that of my life
And my love which I choose to share
with you.

Marlee Payne Shaw
ALONE
Where were you when the sun
stopped shining?
I couldn't find you when all the doors
slammed shut.
I didn't feel your loving arms,
I never felt your touch.

Where were you when the world
stopped turning,
My heart beating fearful and wild?
I didn't see you near to me
When my fears were those of a child!

Why do you leave me when it all gets
so rough?
Where do you go to hide?

Forget coming back,
I don't need you.

I'm really quite strong
Inside!

Joseph G Bartholomew
LONE SAGE
I know where the last sage bush in
Monterey grows
Between the cracks down on Cannery
Row
Where once chaparral grew along the
Bay
And the smell of sage blended the
breeze of the day
All around it now stands the
pavements of man

Where once so common, now so rare,
Hardly a person notices it there
Yet it stands out in proud view
To all the passing multitudes
From all around they come to see
Cannery Row as it was and has come
to be

This lone sage is taking its stand
Where once its kind thrived on the
coastal strand
Then man in his earnest to harvest the
world
Paved over the land and nature was
spoiled

The first time I saw it on a ride on my
bike
My spirit soared at the thought and
the sight
Its fragrance on the breeze
Its flowers for the bees

A lost image long gone in living
color
Its outstretched limbs and beyond the
Bay waters

Eleanor Engebretsen
THE ROAD TO PARADISE
There's a road that I know about,
It goes into the woods and never
comes out,
Walking that road brings happiness to
me,
I clear my mind in this tranquility.

There's no hustle, bustle of the street,
No barking dogs that show their
teeth,
No street fights, no honking horns,
I only hear squirrels eating acorns.

Natural noises are what I hear,
There's not a thing out there to fear,
I suppose a logger made this road,
So his wagon could carry out his
load.

I am happy in this silent place,
Where my worries and problems I
can erase,
It's a spot only I know about,
Where I can shut the cruel world out.

Eleanor Engebretsen
MY PICNIC LUNCH
When I was little, I didn't have much,
My biggest thrill was my picnic
lunch,
I'd make a sandwich from some
left-over meat,
Or find some peanut butter and jelly
to eat.

Then to the garden is where I would
head,
I'd pick a tomato, if I had only bread,
I would also pull up a carrot or two,
Just wipe off the dirt is all I'd do.

Then I'd hurry to that cherry tree,
Where dad had made a swing for me,
I'd eat and swing and close my eyes,
And enjoy this moment of paradise.

I never had a camera or a small radio,
And there was no TV then, you
know,
There wasn't any record player to
play,
And the only books were all by Zane
Grey.

You never want what you don't see,
That was the way it was for me,
I was very happy not having much,
My biggest thrill was my picnic
lunch.

Laura Gates Brown
CRESCENDO
Ice-blue filled cauldrons
seem tranquil . . . at peace.
Beneath lies a tension
that longs for release.

Suppressed for a lifetime
it wells up inside,
some dark, deep impression
we think we must hide.

Touched by my current.
Caressed by our wills.
Brown pebbles rushed over,
white foam piques then stills.

What rippled now surges
and finally did crest,
the answers to questions
I now put to rest.

Laura Gates Brown
OUR *H*UMANLY *U*LTIMATE *G*ENTLE *S*QUEEZES
Some got them as children
from husband and wife,
while others express these
as void in their life.

Life's three-letter word
profits more than a few,
when we ask for one
and give away two.

A giver; a taker,
which one is more pleased—
one doing the squeezing
or one being squeezed?

Through bonding of people
we'll nudge, gently shove,
collectively working
toward humanly love.

Once spread universal
our message transcends—
a vision of world peace
and making us friends.

Lawrence E Larkey
WILL-O'-THE WISP SWAMP FIRE

To my wife,
Dana Poston Larkey.

Child of the velvet night
Dance here where once the sycamore
defied
The storm. Here where a frightened
squirrel espied
A grim hunter, eyes bright alight
With that strong lust of kill!

You dart before the moon
Or chase mad bats betwixt gem
brilliant stars;
You startled motorists cruising in
cars
And frighten into flight the loon
With wild cry to break the still.

Across sweet meadowland
You're sheer metoric fire on wind's
wings;
Swiftly you skim the craggy slopes
where sings
The night's songster a golden strand:
"Whip-poor-will, whip-poor-will!"

Despite all this you are
Flight fickle as a bat, wild as the gale
Sweeping from out the stars to kiss
the pale
Moon's face, since never do you dare
Tarry o'er swamp or hill.

Paul and Dorothy Butler and Ruth

Dorothy Wheeler Butler
RECOGNITION

Dedicated to Paul, my husband of 52 years, who managed to give me the experiences which created this poem!

God of the thunder and the lightning,
Roaring with hail and torrents of rain—
Your fiercest storms, however frightening,
Slyly bring quiet and calm again!

God of the winds and waves and sunshine,
Playing our boat at roll and toss;
God of our universe and lifeline —
Hi, You up there, You sure are the Boss!

Robert Schumacher
THE STORM

An angel playing her harp
in the silence of the mist
Tears run down her face as her voice
whispers in the wind

The fire turns to sadness
set in the corner of the violet sky
While crystal drops form
mixing with an emotional tide

A collection of glitter
spreads across the sky
From the anger and pain
which she hides inside

Oceans swell with madness
Howling at the emotions sent
Sending down lines of light
the shores begin to repent

Now the tears cease to fall
and the oceans begin to die
She casts a shadow —
A rainbow from her eyes

Ermal Boone
HOBO

In loving memory to Lonnie & his dog "Hobo."

I wonder why my master went away, he left me here so alone & blue
He never comes home at all any more to play, or hunt or wrestle like he used to do
When I first came to my master a tramp from the road, you know
He took me in with loving kindness fed me and called me "Hobo."
We used to roam these hills my master his friends and me — but now the friends
don't even come no more — They have all forsaken me, you see.
My master's mother moved to the farm, but a part of the family stayed on
I'm torn from this place and her, for what if he comes when I'm gone?
Must I always be so lonely? Can't we go hoot with the owls once more, or hunt the wild buck in his season or beach the canoe on some shore?
What is the meaning of "dying"?
What did they mean when they said (When all was hushed and crying) a "wreck" and "killed" and "dead"?
I get so tired of waiting . . . But once when ill it seemed . . .
The deer and I and my master was crossing this wonderful stream;
A glorious being was waiting with arms outstretched on the shore
Embracing the buck and my master, but to me said: "Wait just a little bit more."
The owls last night in their hooting, told me, "My master was coming no more,"
They said when I start my next crossing his whistle will guide me to shore.

Ruth Adrienne Vance
DEAREST SISTER INA CLAIRE

I wish I could write you a letter dear;
Or hear your lilting voice again by phone.
See your dimpled cheeked smile right here,
Feel your loving welcome when I came home.
How precious was our loyal sisterly love . . .
You were truly special, happy and bright,
Bringing cheerful words, soft as a Dove;
Unforgettable as sunshine, day or night . . .
Friendly secrets we could always share.
Talking our hearts out each visit all day.
You had a beauty that was always there.
How I miss your sparkling personality . . .
I deeply miss you, Dearest Sister Ina Claire.
How lonely now; how I wish for you here!

Ruth Adrienne Vance
THE CHARMS OF PYRAMID LAKE

Looking out over shimmering tranquil blue
And the chisled mountains of Nature's own hue;
Brings us serenity and ever so close-----
To this good old Earth we love the most.
To feel close to Nature, with gifts from the lake,
We'd lose all our ca-res & live for God's sake.
Like we were meant to be, untroubled & serene;
To know the glories of Nature, & warm sun beams.
The charms of cool waters, soothes our cares away.
As I relax, high upon a rock formation this day.

The Fall of the year has a quietness all its own;
After the heat of summer its seeds have grown.
The dry surrounding hills hold secrets untold;
Perhaps even treasures of silver and gold.

Wrapped in meditation, I feel peaceful & blessed
Quietly absorbing life's secrets deep, -----
While the moon is shining, I thankfully sleep.

As the first rays of pink awake with the dawn;
We quickly arise with the first glimpse of morn.
The lake waters are silent, changing hues of blue,
As the pyramid monarch stands silently in view.
This chosen place on earth, her given domain;
Withstanding all seasons, heat, snow or rain.
Fierce winds, lightning or tremors may come & go.
Like a sentinel ever watching the distant shores;
Through ages of changes, even Indian Wars.
These formations will stand and pyramid high,
Appearing in moonlight to reach the sky.
Since all the atmosphere is so calm & serene,
High up on a formation, we may sit and dream.
We cherish this desert, unspoiled by man,
Clean and sandy, baked pure by the summer;
Quietly one can hear the lake waters murmur.
The vastness of this large & deep creation,
Is the outstanding benefit of an Indian Reservation.

Irene G Rozman
THE BOOK
GOLDEN POET AWARD 1987

Dedicated with love to my family.

Have you ever read a book, my friend
One that you wish would never end?
I found that book with characters and theme
Villains and hero, beyond your wildest dream
There is enough hope, joy, faith, love and tears
To last every human being all their years.
As the story unfolds of a Father and Son
The powerful Words said and the Deeds done
Your heart soars with the greatest love story
No other hero can come close to Their glory
Over and over you read the Words and Their name
Until they burn in your heart like a flame.
"What is the name of this book?" you say
"The one you can read day after day?"
This Book I praise so, my friend
'Tis the Bible — the Story without end.

Irene G Rozman
UNCONDITIONAL LOVE
SILVER POET AWARD 1988

God gave us a truth so plain to see,
An example of His love for you and me.
All of His creatures he placed in our care,
Some have feathers, or hides and some have hair,
Some have been gifts, some have been bought,
Some have been adopted, others were caught.
They have one thing in common living with us,
Giving unconditional love and unconditional trust.
They care not if you're thin or fat, rich or poor,
Occasionally smart or sometimes a bore.
As with God, their faith never dims,
Through our accomplishments and through our sins.
Oh! If family and friends would just
Love us — with unconditional love, and unconditional trust.

Irene G Rozman
THE SUNDAY CROSS
GOLDEN POET AWARD 1989

Will you bear my cross for Me, is the question asked of you and me.
We sit in our church pew all proper and prim
Of course we'll bear the cross for Him

Monday	We are asked to help our brother We have our work to do, can't you ask another?
Tuesday	Someone's putting our brother down, None of our affair, we are headed for town.
Wednesday	On our doorstep a poor starving pup Call the police, he will pick him up.
Thursday	We hear crying in the night Go to sleep, someone will soothe their fright.
Friday	Our family we should call and say we care They haven't called us, and fair is fair.
Saturday	Our brother is hurting and needs a friend But we deserve a day off at the hard weeks end.
Sunday	We sit in our church pew all proper and prim Of course, we'll carry the cross for Him.

Irene G Rozman
AMERICA
GOLDEN POET AWARD 1990

America, we are a strong, prosperous nation, so we say;
Yet there are 35 million of our people hungry today.
Little ones without a bed, a meal or a home;
Huddled in a cardboard box just to keep warm.
A mother and father with no more

hope in their eyes;
Big business took their job and home,
their promise of a future all lies.
Can each one of us hold our head up
to other nations today,
And truthfully tell them we are strong
and prosperous in every way?
Other nations honor their elders,
realizing wisdom comes with years;
We leave them lonely, add to their
heartaches and turn our backs on
their tears.
We have taken away the farms from
the farmers who raise our food,
Sold our banks and business to
foreign countries, and call it good.
We are supposed to be united with
"One Nation under God";
Then one person took prayer from us,
showing the path that we trod.
To our children, the hope of our
future, we leave crime sex and dope,
No God in their life and no role
model to follow — we expect them to
cope.
Wake up America and know why
as a Nation
We are not mentioned in the Book
of Revelation!

Vien Phüóng
WAITING FOR ME MY LOVE
Waiting for me my love! Waiting for
me my love!
Don't cry again! Waiting for me my
love!
Although months and years are
longer and longer,
Although rain floods over fields and
rivers,
Waiting for me please!
Waiting for me please!
I will come back home soon my love!
Although your heart is broken into
pieces,
Although the sun burns your smile
without sweetness,
Waiting for me please!
Waiting for me please!
I will come back home soon my love!
Although your eyes are blinded by
your tears,
Although your hairs are turned color
by years,
Waiting for me please!
Waiting for me please!
I will come back home soon my love!
I will come back home with
victorious smile,
I will come back home with my heart
of pride.
Waiting for me my love! Waiting for
me my love!
Don't cry again! Waiting for me my
love!

Vien Phüóng
ONE ROSE FOR YOU
One rose for you,
a newborn baby,
raise your voice loudly,
open your eyes and salute a new life.

One rose for you,
a parentless child,
in whole life, cry more than smile,
and tears are longer than your body.

One rose for you,
an unfortunate lady,
drink cup by cup of whiskey,
and kiss a man, who is not your
lover.

One rose for you,
an unknown soldier,
accept the death as light as a feather,
and sacrifice your life for nation.

And only one rose left for you,
unlucky parents,
are being abused by your children,
on the way to heaven with God.

Lisa Ann Ciolfi
DAUGHTER OF A VIETNAM VETERAN
War is such a terrible waste
It takes the lives of the innocent and
free
Ruins many family dreams
Causes damage that no one sees

Once the purest of a man
Now a soldier told to defend
Puts his life on the line for his
country
In a battle that will never end

A soldier is not a human, he's a
machine
Told to fight for what is right
When doing so in a process that's
wrong
A friend lies dead for this, what a
sight

Cruelty to ones' own kind
In order to stake a claim
Should the families have to suffer
When the heads of the countries are
to blame

So inhuman are the acts we do
In killing we do not solve a bit
We cause more tears and anger
As a relative has been hit

More mind damage then thought
possible
The scars will never go away
The people missing, the body parts
gone
This is the reality that's here to stay.

Brenda Ferrell
JESUS: THE PRICE OF A PEARL
Jesus can change your life, my friend
Jesus is my personal Savior
He can be yours too, for He loves
everyone
He really sees beyond our dreams
He makes a difference in our lives
and hearts
Jesus the price of a pearl!
Yes, Jesus can make your life
happy
If you would only choose to be his
He will gladden your heart
And let your face light up with a
smile
Yes, you can carry your burdens to
Him
Without any questions asked by Him
Jesus the price of a pearl
We can come to the altar one by one
To repent unto Him the
Precious Savior
Then and only then can we be
buried
With Christ in baptism
Let Jesus reign upon
His throne in your heart
For you see Jesus
Is really far more than the
Price of a Pearl

Meg Cassidy
QUIET BIRD
Oh to see,
a cardinal bird, so vivid red,
perching on a tree
watching carefully his world
all around
so quiet and profound,
waiting patiently as other birds
surround
the feed on ground,
and eat so ravenously,
in fear
their seeds will by others
disappear.

Oh to see,
this lovely patient vivid
cardinal bird,
whom God has made for all,
to be seen and be heard.

Miriam Hill Caviness
REFLECTIONS ON A RIVER
How I've missed you, River,
Since I left my place of birth;
To study and to labor,
And to see more of this earth.

Sometimes amid the turmoil
of a hundred sounds and sights,
And, sensing a disharmony,
I've longed for moonlit nights,

When the magic of illusion
Brought the stars down on your
shore,
And I felt a warmth within me,
A serenity once more.

At other times my mind's eye
Caught a glimpse of autumn hours,
When the storm clouds burst upon
you,
As you wrestled with the showers.

Oh, the memory sustains me—
When you clasped hands with the
sun,
And caressed me, swimming, sailing:
The world seemed just begun.

Only He who made us
And this universe designed,
Can understand the reasons
Why our spirits are entwined.

Al Statum

Al Statum
WHEN I AM ALONE

To God, who already knows, with love.

When I am left alone, darkness once again seems to fall across the face of the deep, and bitterness claws its way into the pits of my soul: my faith is gone, my hope shattered, and charity, the pure love from God is held far from my reach. Emptiness settles over me like the hollowness of a vacant tomb and I am left without . . . But thou oh Lord who seeth all things, thou who has suffered all things common to man, looketh upon my loneliness with tender love and mercy. And from a cloud strewn sky a gentle rain begins to wash my soul and I am drawn to walk in the beauty of its wetness. Thou speakest to me in thy thunderings and showeth to me thru the lightnings thine unrelenting tremendous power and I am made to stand in awe of thee . . . I am restored!

Sylvia Noyes
TIME
The years are flyin' by,
They're leaving me behind.
I'm still a child inside,
Held by ties that bind.

Yesterday's a mem'ry,
Tomorrow's just a dream,
Today is but a short time
That's here for you and me.

Yesterday's forgotten,
I can't use it anymore.
Tomorrow waits ahead,
Like an open door.

Today is here for taking,
So I'll live for today,
I'll dream my dreams and
Hope my hopes,
And then go on my way.

Chu-thân

Translated by Chu-thân
UPON MY RETURN
On my return to my thatched cottage
on the old mountain

The orioles were scarce
in the waning spring,
Scattered in a cave, the cherry and
almond flowers were falling.
Only the bamboo trees by the
window did I love,
For my return, their constant shade
of green was still longing.

Mon retour à ma chaumière
à la vieille montagne

Les loriots étaient rare vers la fin
du printemps,
Les fleurs de cerises et d'amandiers,
dans la caverne, s'éparpillaient.
J'aimais seulement le buisson de
bambou à la fenêtre,
Après mon retour, sa constante
verdure soupirait.

A mi vuelta a mis casa de paja
en la vieja montaña

Las oropéndolas eran escasas en la
primavera menguada,

Esparcidas por toda la cueva, flores
de cerozo y almendro caian.
Solo los árboles de bambú
por la ventana yo amaba,
Su tono constante de verde anhelaba
aún mi vuelta.

Translated by Chu-thân
UNTITLED

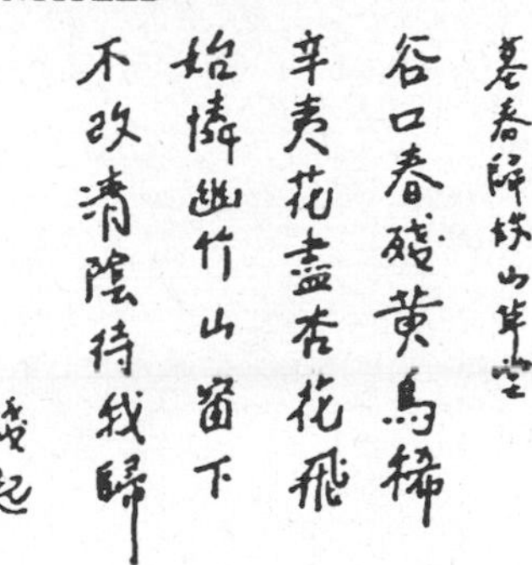
暮春歸故山草堂
谷口春殘黃鳥稀
辛夷花盡杏花飛
始憐幽竹山窗下
不改清陰待我歸
錢起

Mô Xuân Qui Cố Són Tháo Dúóng

Cốc khâu xuân tàn hoàng dìêu hi,
Tân-di hoa tân, hanh hoa phi.
Thị liên u trúc són song ha,
Bất cai thanh âm dai nga qui.

TIÊN KHÓI

Cuối xuân về lều co ó núi xúa

Xuân tàn núi cụ oanh thúa,
Tân-di rung hết, hanh xua bay cung.
Chi thúóng khóm, trúc bên song,
Bóng xanh nào dôi con mong ta về.

CHU THÂN

Tara Emy

Tara Emy
USE A CONDOM
You don't want a baby
You don't want a disease
You just want the pleasure
You just want to please

You always think you're careful
It'll never happen to you
But then when it does
You don't know what to do

Is it really worth risking
Is it worth all the pain
Being so stupid
Is really insane

It's not hard to use
It's no big ordeal
And it doesn't affect
The way that you feel

So when you're raring to go
And your man is erect
Just slip on a condom
It'll really protect.

Melvin L Roberts Sr
PURE SWEET LOVE

To the Queen of my Heart
The Angel in my Life
My Wife.

Well my lady, she has my heart
Even when we are apart
Our life we'll be happy to share
Because we're well aware
Of feelings; calm, peaceful as a dove
Created from our pure, sweet love
Inside of me, she will always have a place
Because thoughts of her occupy all time and space
She picks me up when I am down
As she treats me like I wear a crown
My lady stands at my side
While yet, others take me for a ride
She tells me, "You make me so proud . . .
Everything you do stands out in a crowd!"
You see our love is special to me
As it is so plain to see
Even when I'm tired, all energy spent
I will always have an angel, . . .
HEAVEN SENT!

James Dale Bidwell
WHAT IS THE MEANING OF LOVE
Many people ask what is the meaning of love
one true love is Jesus and God from above,

Love is laughing, crying, sharing pleasures and pain
Love is understanding and compassion with out refrain,

Love is a mixture of good bad happy and sad
Love is full of ups and downs that make you glad or mad,

Love is the most powerful Emotion known to man
Love is also very special and truly grand,

Love is everyone's need and all deserve their share
love is really meaning it when you say I care.

Kim Kapinus
UPON EMERGENCE FROM MY DORMANT STATE
Upon emergence from my dormant state,
I open my arms in welcome to
The newest friendship on the face of the earth,
As I revel in this sublime occurrence,
Be it chance or a strategy of fate.

The locks on the inner chambers of my mind
Have fallen away quietly, of their own accord,
Hidden thoughts freed and floating outward to you.
I know you can sense them and feel them
Perhaps as no one has before.

I open my arms wide to you, my friend,
To share intensities of touch in an embrace.
Arms gathering strength as they fight the letting go
That must take place,
Encircling with urgency, as if the world were coming to an end.

A fingertip taste of some exquisite flavor
That I've not been privileged to sample before
Leaves me hungry, silently screaming for more,
Even as the memory is savored.

Edith Martin
SERENITY
So fair of face,
So full of grace,
A comforting to impart,

To the life of those she meets,
A serenity, a calmness greets,
The one who has seen grief and strife,
In the tribulations of this life.

In the vicissitudes of this world,
Violence is all awhirl,
Such a beauteous spirit is indeed rare,
In an age when nothing is just and fair.

So if happiness to you is unreal,
Remember the Lord Jesus Christ with all zeal,
And follow Him with a new nature,
By His love you too, He'll nurture.

Betty J Sanders
DO YOU

To my wonderful children, Tom, Shirley & Cindy.

Do you love me, do you love me, do you really care?
Do you want me, do you want me, do you want me near?
Could you be real happy in a bungalow,
Out in the meadow where the daisies grow.

Do you love me, do you love me, do you honey lamb?
Shall we go right ahead with the marriage plan?
We'll have some children maybe three or four.
We'll be right there to meet you at the cottage door.

How about it, how about it honey child,
Do you like my planning or does it cramp your style.
You like it fine! you really do honey lamb?
Well slip on my finger that wedding band.

January 14, 1950

Ingrid
THE WATERFALL . . .
In the distance I tried to see myself
By watching this Waterfall
How it Rushes and Gushes
As it Hits once more.

It Twirls and Spins and Ripples
With Rhythm,
A lot like Life wouldn't you say?
You see Life too, has its own Sort of Ways.

We sometime pour out Cold Water
Because of all the Hurt
We, too, take Many Falls,
From the Rushes and Gushes of Life
We Hit Bottom once more.

There are times we're Twirling and Spinning
'Cause Life just isn't Simple
Then there are Tears at times
They're the Tears we Ripple.

But Life goes on like that Waterfall
Does it really Care of all our Grief?
Then I looked much closer,
And seen it had the Strength that We Must Seek
Why go on God only knows how many Years
Spending them like that Waterfall
With Many Cascading Tears.

It Helped Me realize I was So Wrong
Because like this Waterfall
We, too, can Come Out Strong
And Refuse to Hit the Floor
This Time as we Rush and Gush
When we're About to Fall,
We'll Pick Ourself Up, Half-Way there
And Get Up Once More

When We Ripple
Let it be Our Laughter erasing all our Tears
Taking with it our Sorrow and Our Fears
When we Spin and Whirl with Rhythm
Let it be our Song and Dance
I then come out of this Trance

And what I was watching, was it a Trance at all?
Or the Image of Life that we can Face?
Like that Strong, Rushing Waterfall?

. . . Always Stay Strong . . .

Elsie R Thomas
THE SUPREME GIFT
When the Great Creator formed the plan
To give immortality and eternal life to man,
He also gave the ability to love
That man's joy be complete, as designed up above.
Man, by himself, is but one half of a whole,
The woman completes it, to make his life full.
To-gether, they twain, become one flesh,
Their hearts, their souls, completely emeshed.
They give of each other in sickness and health,
They share in trial, in poverty and wealth,
Their secrets, their troubles they confide to each other—
For with held, the precious love gift they will smother.
Encircled in the arms of each other at night
Make the trials of the day well worth the fight.
The touch of the body, the thrill of the kiss—
Consumated love with its heavenly bliss—
Surely the Great Creator planned well,
Love is supreme, a Divine gift, a glorious spell—
When two souls entwine and become as one,
Heaven's on earth, celestial glory has begun.

P Check
A RESTING SPOT FOR US
In the midst of a busy restaurant,
we sit and sip peppermint tea.
It wasn't long ago that we were at
home;
close, comfortable on
the long flowered couch
where it is only a resting spot for us.

As the night got longer, we went into
the car.
It was a cold and clear night,
yet the smile on your face
warmed the air.

We went into our favorite restaurant;
now we sit and converse.
We tell age old stories of
how we were.
Now, nine years later,
we know a glance,
a hand movement—an eye blink
that now tells a story of love.

While we are in this spot indoors,
we drink the herbs that relax us;
soon we'll return to the car,
and come home
in the night air.

Lady Dandelion
I'VE NEVER BEEN A WINNER
I've just always been the average
Jane Doe.
Then I remembered Lady Dandelion
has a meaning you know.
That is something to be very pleased
about.
I keep on appearing so don't count
me out.

Winners are not always the ones who
achieve the most.
Just the one who receives the award
and the special toast.
The one who works and glean even
teases the Brain,
Is maybe the one who becomes
perplexed that acquire the most gain.

We are winners who are privileged to
live to a good age.
We are given more time to inscribe a
better and lasting page.
We are winners who live to make a
better world each day.
We are also winners who remove the
obstacles along our way.

Let us be more like the dandelion
who refuses defeat.
Let us be a plain Joe or Jane, but
encourage those we meet.
Disappointment and discouragement
comes easy to the best of us.
We are all winners who have gained
enough wisdom to not make a fuss.

After all most of us are winners to
some degree.
We are blessed with health, enough
wealth, so Thank God we are free.

Jackie G Gregory
HE MADE ME LISTEN
In the early morning,
As I step outside the door,
I hear the singing of malking birds,
Sounding more beautiful than ever
before.

And in a brief moment of hesitation,
As I hearkened to their singing once
more,
Distinctly, I recall the different tune
variations,
As the small fowls, fly and soar.
Then I'm quickly reminded by the
Master,
How much happier we would be.
If each day we'd sing high Praises,
And proclaim his Majesty.

For if the fowls up in the air,
Soaring high without a care,
Merge to amplify Christ in heaven
above,
Then may we dare, to spread his
wondrous love.

Juanita Willis
GIVE IT TO THE MASTER
If you are burdened and weighed
down with grief;
Give it to the "Master," He's the
giver of peace.

For:

Not one little sparrow shall fall from
a tree,
Not one tear shed that He doesn't see.
Not one broken heart that He cannot
mend,
Not one weary soul will He not
befriend.
Not one promise made that He
doesn't keep;
For you're His lamb, and He cares
for His sheep.

Not one prayer uttered that He
doesn't hear,
Not a burden so heavy that He cannot
bear.
Not a soul cast down that He can't
lift up,
Not a cup too bitter will He have you
sup.
He's rest for the weary, and strength
for the weak;
You're His child, and He cares for
His sheep.

He's eyes for the blind, and truth for
the deceived,
Hope for the dying, and comfort for
the bereaved.
He's God triumphant over death and
the grave,
He has power to cast out, and also to
save.
So if you have a sorrow that is too
deep;
Give it to the "Master,"
He cares for His sheep.

Al Statum

Al Statum
SOLITUDE
I talked to God, He seemed far away.
I cried aloud, He did not answer.
I shouted to Him, He heard me not.
I wept quietly, He spoke to me
gently.
Therefore,
I will never be so manly
As to hold back my tears
In the presence of God.

Anna Ludwiczak-Cadd
CALIFORNIA OAK
California dreams . . .
California oak

A crooked, big tree on the slope of a
dry hill,
With all its strength holds itself in the
little surface of the soil.
With the curved branches, which try
to stop the sun,
Persist forever in its own space on the
stony place.

Thin, hardy leaves tremble in
disorder noise,
As if they didn't know, what is better
for the future.
With the many thousand surfaces
have carried the light hares,
And very busy in their jobs, they
bring us the shadow and air.

The very silent harbor for mosses and
different lichens,
A safe home for the worms and the
mice's burrow in the roots,
This tree exist for the centuries, and
time is going so simple,
And only wooden soul swings silent
inside its body.

With the big branches, like as its
head is in the heaven,
It gives happiness to children, who
play in the shadow with joy,
And creates the happy paradise for
birds and for the squirrels,
And only sometimes asks through the
dreams —
—where are you hurrying, for
what, mankind? . . .

Helen T Dee Ross
UNANSWERED LOVE
Young hearts young minds in
moments decide
Endless torments timeless decisions
we abide
Inner stirrings phases incomplete be
discreet
Restless moments our fate is so thrust
be just
Unfolding fragments unfold stories
be told
Stage the moments to be at hand
Let not this timeless place defeat
Promise—alas—promise—yet not so
bleak
Pass these yearnings pass our love
Thus accept errors delivered with
glistening glove
Taskmaster bent so lean but
unforeseen
Deliver universal dream to part
Hardbound memories innocent tales
Peaceful thoughts fail to hail
Nevermore yearnings feelings so true
Successful achievements act on cue
Loves worth to you dearheart I
extend
Fathom fires end—comprehend and
blend
Behold once more my Love is at your
door
Capture sweetest moments lets adore
lets adore
Multitudes to nights end is clear
Dwindled caressments bliss is now so
near
Cost to cost not this fling upon my
hand I wear your ring.
Unsurpassed ecstasy my Loves voice
I hear.
Once and once again, I but say
Unbend unbend cradled carings erupt
without fear.

Anne J Cope
MY TREASURES

To my loving and most caring family Frances—Jane Marty James & Joseph.

This past Feb 12 I was 93 yrs
I live now in memories
Some happy, some in tears
We were seven sisters
Six were tall
And I the shortest has
Out lived them all
I thank God, for my great joys
Some just grand, others great
And at last just arrived
Is a little "Miss great great"
All help to chase away the tears

Anne J Cope
AMERICAN LEGION AUXILIARY
1st National Convention 1937
New York City

We are proud of you Gold Star
Mother
Blessings on your Silver head
Today the Legion honors you
Mother's of heroes dead

Twenty years ago our Comrades
Marched this avenue
Not a fear nor tear but Victory
Was their only thought in View

Years pass slowly Gold Star Mother
And how brave, you faced it all
Glorious memories of him inspired
you
All his Valor you recall

Lift your face to the skies
Hide the heartache and the sighs
Again we march, his spirit with us
For his sake the tears you'll hush

His sacred memory will shine afar
Oh Mother of the little "gold star"
For in each heart of a Legionaire
In the Oath of remembrance
For those "Over There"

Shirley Avis
WONDERING
Have you ever sat and wondered,
As the days go by.
Why God in heaven put you here,
And why we have to die?

He gave us but a little while
To live here in this place.
To learn to love and care for others
No matter what kind color or race.

He gave us birds and animals,
Trees and flowers too,
He sent them for us to enjoy,
So many not a few.

He gave us rivers, creeks and lakes,
He gave us oceans wide.
He gave us dew, rain and snow
Our waters well supplied.

Thank you Lord for all these things,
We are never grateful enough.
We are always complaining
That things are oh so rough.

Dorothy Morgenthaler
ALONE
Alone there is no wish for tomorrow
Alone there is no hope for today
But as darkness passes over
Do think it might help to pray

The passing weeks & passing months
Make up the passing years
But even time cannot erase
Those lonely, lonely tears.

Nan Treanor Maxey
A BALLAD OF ALASKA
The sand was oily,
The beach was black.
Birds tried to fly
With their wings hanging back.

The fish would be damaged
Their guts full of goo
The rocks would be slippery—no refuge thereto.

A tanker lies crippled, its side busted in.
A captain lies crippled, his gut full of gin.

A corporation bucks the tide in the land.
"All cleaned up" was the theory
As it left the valdez.
"Not our fault. not our fault"
All that gore

Tell that to God and the people
Tell that to God and the land
Tell that to God and the wildlife
Tell all of them that!

No one will believe you
But why should you care?
You've gotten yours
And gone back to your lair!

Generations will suffer
But who gives a damn?

We DO! we all do!

Marjorie H Millett
HORIZONS
This world in which I spend my days
Has bonds that hold me, close and near,
Yet far and free my spirit soars,
As sea gulls sounding high and clear . . .
Unfettered . . . free; but bonds are part
Of love,—in childish words and sighs,
In tiny hands that hold my heart,
And dawn in one small baby's eyes!

On some far shore, there's part of me
That roams horizons strange and new,
That seeks alone a beauty rare,
That finds a freedom given to few—
With smiles and tears and loving arms
My children have imprisoned me—
And in their love my world abounds
With beauty,—limitless and free!

Hector C Borghetty
ITALY
From snow clad Alps once more I see
the fertile plains and sunlit hills
ringing the peaks so wild and free
that beckon to joys of mountain thrills.
Once more I see the tidy farms
mid golden fields and verdant pines
and rising beside the banks of Po,
stately poplars and ancient charms.
Again I see the pure white domes
the winding lanes, and jagged scars,
on mile-high cliffs of Osta's cones
and ever above my friends, the stars
shining so bright to us below.
Though many a day I tread the earth
and see man's vice against his own
Always on high I feel the birth
of hope, for all, that rings so true
and clear as crystal I start anew.

Dawn Nolan

Dawn Nolan
I LOVE THEE LORD
I love Thee Lord
I come to You as a child
Help me find my way
To make life worth while

I love thee Lord
May I serve You fully
Whatever task it may be
No questions will I ask
My pleasure is pleasing Thee

Elizabeth Snyder
WALKING THE NATURE TRAIL
I shall walk the trail again today,
And wonder who I will meet along the way;
Neighbors maybe or friends from town,
They all like to walk the circle 'roun.

Then along nature's trail I go;
The squirrels and rabbits say hello.
I listen to the singing of the birds,
And the crickets also, I think I heard.

The blooming bushes are a sight;
I can walk this trail in spite,
of aching calves and blistery heels.
I'll keep walking and walking, I will.

I'll walk this trail a time or two,
Or maybe three or more I'll do.
I'll not stop until my exercise I've got,
Then I'll go home and rest a lot.

Rose Marie Gillums
MY ARMS ARE EMPTY

Constant care & loving you
All the while — Kevin DeCarlo Holland (my son).

For each of your moments of growth,
growth was swiftly.
I am only the basket that carried you.
You belong to another whom I hope
will adore you,
throughout your life here on earth.

Rose Marie Gillums
BROKEN RELATIONSHIP
I need a kind word with a soothing voice.
Even in marriage there is a great deal of loneliness.

Rose Marie Gillums
HEAVEN OH HEAVEN
All people talk about going there,
Heaven, but they not going to be there.

Rose Marie Gillums
WONDER FROM MOM
You're rise out of sleep, growing,
so swiftly, everything about you,
is preplanned like a garden, so fresh, so ripe,
ok, you are so bright, so full of questionable life,
Just ripe for the touch of life.

Kay L Klipp
MEMORY OF OUR FAMILY
I once had parents,
then the men came and there was torment.

I remember my mother's smiles,
when I was a young child.

My Grandmother old,
with the stories she told.

My sister pretty and thin,
until the men distorted her skin.

My brothers brave and bold,
until the men shot them blank cold.

My father in sincere wisdom,
until they made him go with them.

My uncles gentle and strong,
soon they we're gone.

The friends we had,
when it all went bad.

Tears in mine eyes, Pain in mine soul,
For those men should not have stole.

The blood shed of my family—
is like a motionless sea,

Upon waters,
blood flows deep.

Michael Harmon
THE SWAN

To a fellow poet, Chris Couto,
Thanks for being a friend and believing in me.
I love you pal.

The swan was beautiful
The swan was white.
The swan was graceful
In its lonely flight.

The swan came around
In wet and dry weather.
Sporting an orange beak.
And a pure white feather

To watch the swan
Was to be great fun.
Then it suddenly ended
With the roar of a gun

There was great sorrow
A sit fell through the sky.
It came tumbling down
And I don't know why.

I was full of emotion
In my heart and in my head.
For that once beautiful swan
Is now dead.

Kimberly Marie Porter
MY TWIN AND I
My twin and I don't get along. Yes, I'm human, but I don't know what's wrong. Lord, I don't know why my twin brother hates me. To him, I'm as nice as I can be. It hurts me to know that we can't get along, and to me and my friends, he lets it be known. He fights me constantly and I don't fight back. I think it's a very rude and hideous act.

This has happened every day for the past six years. Lord, what else is there to do — except shed my tears? I've never done anything to acquire his hate. Lord, he even despises the men I date. I'm eighteen and I've had all I can take. If you will, set his mind straight. Lord, you know I love him as well as I, but everything we do is a total lie.

I show him respect and he treats me like a fool. Lord, why is my brother so uncool? I've lived with his hate all my life — please take away my pain and strife.

Lord, you teach us to love and you know I've tried, but, because of Tim, I'm losing my pride. Lord, I feel much better after talking with you because I know the three of us can work it through.

Michaele K McMurphy
CONFUSION
Here I am within myself,
So deeply searching for those emotions
Long forgotten; to dance around
The pain and seek to find the
Emotions that were to die! Why do I seek so?
What is my need? Is it so great that all
Else is but a speck of dust? Am I not
Alone? Tears needing to be shed may
Come, but too quickly all reason flees
Before the invading army of tangled
Emotions . . . no mourning now; just cope
Until . . . No trace of peace remains,
For these emotions so strong can kill the
Bearer before she has breached the walls!
I do what I must to find what was lost within;
Without this I am no better off than before it
All began. Back against the wall . . . yet forward
Looking, will I be able to relieve the exhausting
Confusion . . . and become me?

Patrick Rosati
IT'S FALL IN MINNESOTA
The trees are colored brilliant all around,
a leaf, here and there, floats gently to the ground.
The mornings are brisk, the sky true blue,
the grass is covered with a frosted

dew . . . .
It's fall in Minnesota

The birds have departed from summer nests,
the bear grows sleepy, in winter he rests.
The sky is full of geese in flight,
their perfect formation a thrilling sight . . . .
It's fall in Minnesota

Gray squirrels scurry, looking for food,
sometimes they play, when they're in the mood.
A faint smell of wood smoke wafts thru the air,
someone's fireplace is crackling there . . . .
It's fall in Minnesota

It's now Indian summer, the days are warm,
Mother Nature's last delight before the storm.
It's the time of the year I like the best,
before winter's white coat puts things to rest . . .
It's fall in Minnesota

Ernest L Smith
LES VERSES RHYTHMIQUES
MON PLAN
Quand j'étudie à la nuit,
Le silence descend sur ma chambre.
Je m'assieds et je pense, et puis
La situation grandit un peu sombre.

Il faut que j'écris un poèm;
Ma professeur demande un joli.
La sujet est d'abord un problème,
Mais mon plan est bientôt compris.

D'abord il faut à dormir,
Parce que j'ai un mal de tête.
Mon lit peut allègement fournir,
Mon repos est maintenant complet.

Ensuite je cherche l'inspiration,
Par jouer des disques melodieuses.
Alors il faut prendre mon stylo
Et composer le poème trés doux.

Après toutes ces preparations
A composer un est trés facile.
Mon plan travaille avec raison,
Voici le poème trés gentil.

Marilyn Johnson

Marilyn Johnson
A THOUGHT FOR TODAY
As I sit alone this morning
With many thoughts in mind,
I think of how we grumble
Seems like most the time.
People often make us mad,
We feel jealous, abused and unloved.
We carry chips on our shoulders
For days, for weeks or months.
What good does all this brooding bring?
It just makes us feel sad.
We could try to settle things,
But it seems we'd rather stay mad.
We have no promise of tomorrow.
Today could be our last.
Why not show love towards one another—
And forget bad things in the past.
Yes, we could make things better,
But we tend to make things worse.
Seems we'd rather wear a frown on our face
Than a smile of laughter and love.

Marilyn Johnson
LITTLE BOYS ARE SPECIAL

"I dedicate this poem to Scotty, Brandon, Robert, Justin and Westley, with lots of love." Grandma.

Little boys have high hopes.
They have so many dreams.
Sometimes they get so noisy
They may even make you scream,
But when they say "I love you"
It always warms our hearts.
They love to watch the rising sun
And search for higher stars.
They love to witness laughter
As they pull their greatest pranks.
They tell the cutest stories
While they're sitting in our swing.
They often bring us flowers
With the brightest kind of smiles,
With tender hugs so precious
And a gleam in their eyes.

Mark A Dandurand
IN MEMORY OF MY DEAR MOTHER
Thank you, Lord, for my Mother!

You gave me a Mother who was loving and caring,
One of those people who was always sharing.

You gave me a Mother who was intelligent and sweet,
One who was firm and who made delicious things to eat.

You gave me a Mother who was patient and kind,
One who gave birth to NINE and yet, for others, she still found time.

You gave me a Mother who was faithful and dear,
One who prayed, worked, cried, laughed, played piano, and made good cheer.

You gave me a Mother who had unending love,
That you, Lord, gave her from your home above.

You've taken her now, Lord, and I know she's okay,
Because you take care of those who have faith and pray.

Good-bye for now, Mom; I know you're not far away.
I'm looking forward to being with you again someday.

Your loving son,
Mark A. Dandurand

Mathew S Weski
A JOURNEY
What I want is to prove myself.
If I cannot achieve,
I will make others fail.
Either way it makes me feel like
I move up to a new level.

Initial perception is my cornerstone.
I need to shine like a new toy.
If it means a new mask, a play
on emotions or a crocodile conscience,
it is worth the price.
My presence has to be brief.
They can never know who I really am.

I answer only to myself.
Look what I have.
My soul is crying for something.
The battle with myself never ends.
I am always turning to look around a new corner,
hoping for anew; finding the same nothing.
It is that frustration that seems
to fuel me on.

Jesse Means
WOE'S

This poem is dedicated to my father; Foster Means.

I am all alone in a world of sadness, I wish I had a dream or dad. I don't know the answers; I just guess that having a father would mean everything to me. I can't call my father, because he cannot hear me. I can't see my father, because he is not around. All I wish it could happen, just like a baby being tossed into the air. I want to be a writer of profound sound, so that the world would understand me and hear the moans and cries that are all around. If I could change what is real, then maybe all the sadness in the world would be healed. I know that life goes on when we all start with ourselves endeavor, but when death continues it makes us feel the hell instead of the heaven. There isn't enough love to keep this world free from armaggedon, but when others wonder it makes me feel helpless. If love revolved around each and everyone living, then maybe in heaven we will all be forgiven. I wonder sometimes if it's true to forget the dead and keep on living, because my father is gone and I wish I was with him. I don't wish to be with because of the sadness, but because of the madness that one can face in a day.

Elizabeth Hobbin Hodge
PRIMAVERA
The drastic, picturesque and sometimes cruel changes of winter,
The colourful, nostalgic and gleaning changes of fall,
The enjoyable, warm and gay changes of summer,
All these different phases are necessary and beneficial.
There is a season, however, not only needed but which surpasses all others.
Springtime is when nature stirs and becomes prophetic,
Springtime is when the heart and soul sings and finds a mystic joy.
Springtime is when the blood of life runs in all forms of existence,
When the eyes feast themselves on the sight of rebirth and newness,
When beauty and drama emerge where nothing seemed to exist.
Springtime is when life is renewed, hope and eternity first come into view.

Kim Van Ausdall
SACRIFICE

This poem is dedicated to you—my loving mother and my special friend!

You could have chosen a type of career in life's younger years,
Instead, you gave your life away
to three God given peers.
Oh yes, you could have retired by now with quite a healthy pay,
With benefits and privileges
that never came your way.
I'm sure this thought has crossed your mind as you've lived day to day,
But let's put the two on the scales
of "success" to see which one outweighs.
Your oldest son Mike has been given a gift from our Father above so Holy.
His nature is always seeking to
help the outcast and the lowly.
It's not a burden or chore for him to lay down his life for a friend,
I've heard it said many times of
Mike, "He's there for you, true to the end.
I've always admired Marks ability to love equally the young and the old,
He's never so rushed that he hasn't
time to put his own life on hold.
And give of himself to those who have need; Marks ways are gentle/caring indeed.
I have a compassion deep in my heart, I'm sensitive to others,
You've taught me how to die
to myself, and care more for
my brothers.
I made the choice to give away my life to two young men,
for then they'll see, they'll get
more out of life,
If they give theirs away in the end.

Toyonnia LC Vazquez
I BELIEVE
I believe in the thought, the simple instead of the material. The education of the mind.
I believe in life, the success and the fulfillment of it.
I believe in the intangible, the presence of air, instinct, of god and of nothingness.
I believe in love and in hatred, the power within them, and the fine line which divides them.
I believe in obsession, the power of need, the driven existence.
I believe in death, the sleep, the peace, the journey.
I believe in faith and devotion, the worship, the trust and the loyalty that they create.
I believe in possibilities, anything can

happen, will happen, and has
happened.
I believe in survival, yours, mine,
ours.
You can, you will, you must,
I believe . . .

Doris M Browning

Doris M Browning
CAN I PLEASE BE ME

To my loving husband, who has
inspired me throughout the years.
Ross W. Browning.

When I was very young, I sang in a
band;
I danced and wrote poetry, love
beaches and sand.
A musician, an artist, a traveler was I;
The world was my oyster, chased
rainbows in the sky.
I had no inhibitions, no worries or
fears;
each day was so precious, as it turned
into years.
But something happened along the
way,
exactly when, I cannot say.
When I surrendered my individuality;
I became what I'm not, in reality.
And I try to be, what I cannot be;
for what I am today, is really not me.
So my mind gets confused, when I
play the part;
for the role meant for me, was like at
the start.
Can I please have back, the original
me,
to sing and to dance, and play by the
sea.
To laugh with little children, to have
friends at my door;
to travel again, and paint some more.
Can I just have the role, that I had
from the start;
Then my soul could have a home,
with a happy heart.

Doris M Browning
POWER OF THE MIND
The mind is the most precious gift,
that you could ever own;
No one can take it from you, to you
alone — it does belong.
Such an intricate piece of machinery,
thoughts travel everywhere;
to the past, and plans of the future,
your mind will take you there.

Such a magnificent computer, and so
highly sensitive;
it will only send right back to you,
exactly what you give.
You can feed it with great literature,
you send it to many a school;
Make it wise, strong and great, or
turn it into a fool.

You can neglect and abuse this mind,
but what a foolish thing to do;
For everything you are in life, this
mind has made of you.

You can lead it to creativity, or let it
waste away;
You can accomplish the impossible,
or deny it the time of day.
For like a sponge — so much it is,
absorbs and wants to learn;
And whatever you shall do for it,
you'll get back in return.

For a gift like this, there is no price;
no worldly goods can buy,
and if you're stripped of all you own,
with a mind you can survive.
Your mind can build, invent, create,
make a mark in its life time;
for such a powerful weapon, nothing
equals it, you'll find.
No matter what your age may be, it
will keep you young through time,
while you feed upon its reservoir, and
thank your precious mind.

Diane Lamphere
THERE'S A CALL THAT HAS BEEN SOUNDED
There's a call that has been sounded
and it echoes 'cross the field,
To the ears of those we beckon and
who know that they must yield.

Then stillness where I'm standing in
the dark, wet countryside,
We're awaiting their arrival with both
gates opened wide.

Somewhere, out there, through the
rolling mist,
They'll be coming to us silently, and
their leader will be first.

My ears strain to hear the sound, my
eyes seek to see,
A few more moments pass away and
they will come to me.

Like spirits from another world, they
enter through the fog,
Obedience to our will, along the
paths they plod.

And then they come across the road
and file through the stone,
Glad to find release at last from such
a heavy load.

So I begin my work again, as daily
it's begun,
A couple of hours shall pass away
and then the milking will be done.

Foster Creighton
SPECTRAL BONDAGE
I lie awake so vaguely sane,
Slowly pulled from slumber's snare,
Moonbeam lazers the windowpane,
Is she a dream or my nightmare?

Silently at the foot of my bed
Reaching without in a motionless
drift,
Suspended as though by a single
thread,
Transparent fingers extend with a
sift.

Five years since a December night,
Yuletide stupor with vision impaired,
Crossing the tracks, her scream—that
light!
Sparks and a deafening horn that
blared.
I can faintly hear that whaling cry,
A railspike sinks to the pit of my
soul,
Out in the night as it rushes by
It punctures my heart and my blood
runs cold.

Why does she come to the dark of my
room?
Turning my wits inside-out like a
glove,
Sentenced to life in this nocturnal
doom
Tormented seduction . . . my departed
love.

Viola Allen
THE SILENT INVADERS
The inky blackness of a country night
clings softly,
A velvet blanket wrapping soul and
body in contentment and peace.
Through tiny holes, stars twinkle
brightly
High above in the wide expanse of
space.
Trees dimly outlined appear as
mountains
Ghostly guarding open spaces from
any light which might penetrate
And disturb the solace of this place.
The air, its freshness filling lungs and
nostrils
Gives a heady lightness and a feeling
of well-being.
No wafts of smoke, gases, nor foul
smelling water pierce the air.
The quiet hypnotizes, yet is
deafening to ears
Unaccustomed to the tranquility of
the country.
While a few miles away, as if in a
different world,
The sounds, the lights, and the smells
of the city
Have molded bodies into robot-like
creatures
Who dart around wildly trying to
escape.
How long before the robot-run city
will invade the country;
The woods, the streams which have
for centuries
Stood in silent repose, secure in
peace and serenity?

LorriAnn Wood
I DON'T MISS YOU
I miss moonlit walks on the beach at
night.
I miss romantic talks by candle light.
But I don't miss you.
I may miss the fact of not having
someone there,
I may miss the fact that there's no
one to care,
But I don't miss you.
I don't like being alone at night by
myself.
I don't like staring at the empty
picture frames on my shelf.
I don't like the fact that sometimes I
miss you.
I don't like the fact that you're seeing
someone new.
No matter what I feel I keep it hidden
within.
Looking for new love so I can begin
again.
I've been hurt before, but not
anymore.
I'm scared yes, but I won't shut my
door.
I'll be smarter in love less likely to
burn,
I'll just wait in line until it's my turn.
So I'll miss those moonlit walks,
So I'll miss those romantic talks,
So I'll miss not having someone
there,
I'll miss not having someone to care,
But I won't miss you.

Trudy Van Riper
APOLLO TRAGEDY
In the '67 Apollo tragedy
Three men lost their lives.
Brave men those Astronauts,
Grisson, Chaffee and White.

Fire both friend and deadly foe,
Broke with the inferno of hell;
There alone at the rocket's top
These men faced death well.

No man can give more
Than his life in dedication,
In paving the way for others
For so great a nation.

This is a job that must be done,
If the world is to live without strife.
These men gave their all,
Grisson, Chaffee and White.

Never a rocket leaves the pad
To soar the space of sky
Without the spirit of these three,
Grisson, Chaffee and White.

James Clemens Jr
THE TICK OF TIME
As I sit by the bed and watch you so
soundly sleep,
I dread the quietness of future years
but knowing these memories
will always keep.

I've wanted to be with you on the
darkest nights and chase away your
fears.
To tell you everything will be alright
as I wiped away your tears.

But in the quietness I can hear the
tomorrow so slowly tick away.
Wishing I could stop the clock that
will rob us of today.

It seems like yesterday when I first
heard your tiny cry.
Now a voice has took its place as the
years have gone by.

The rugs are not in disarray where
you would lie and go to sleep.
Now they are worn ragged with the
years as you have stopped to wipe
your feet.

So someday as you pass this room
and I lie upon this bed,
Will you stop to take the time and
hear the tick I now dread.

Christopher G Moran
STOP THE FIGHTING
You talk about the power,
as if it were the last hour.
For some of us, it is.

We blame all our problems on the
white man,
but when the pressures on we don't
take a stand.
He has helped us, fight each other.
He benefits from the winner and
condemns the loser.

We praise the ones who make it,
We help the ones who fake it,
As we ignore the ones who can't take
it.

The world sees us as a dying race, as they set the pace.
The watch us separate ourselves.
Whether we are fighting for our colors, Our turf,
Or in the business world proving our worth.

The battle continues. I wonder what's on today's menu.
They see us as the nation's poor
as they put stronger locks on their door.

And another brother dies, Another mother cries.
I share these tears and these fears
I cannot explain, the pain that comes over and over again.
To know that people hate me because of the color of my skin.

Joseph M Baniukiewicz Jr
WAKE ME UP

To E. L. F. for waking me.

How much we learn from ourselves
the art of self-indulgence
we slow at redlights,
race on yellow
and go on green,
running in circles so fast
sometimes it's hard to catch your breath.
Night eats up the day light
It's autumn, leaves turn from shadows of green,
living under false pretenses.
So much changes as we get older—
hundreds of nights, following days
reaching towards heaven, and alone once again
where is equality
you can't just pass through here, it's life, don't ya know
where everyone has an answer to old questions—
not one new.
So we believe in something.
If we didn't know each other, and by chance we met,
would you look into my eyes?
do you recognize me this way
morning comes, the sun is rising
awakening the into is disappearing
this is a dream
wake me up.

Julie Sanders
A CHRISTMAS POEM
Hold your head up, my dear son
And try to smile through this day
Put some warmth within your heart
Don't you know it's Christmas Day?
For those around you know you're sad
And that's no way to be
Come celebrate the birth of Christ with me.

Do my eyes deceive me?
Or do I see some tears?
Come to me my little one.
And sit beside me, here
Just because you didn't get
The gift you thought you should
Your meaning of Christmas is misunderstood.

You have so many toys this year
Most of them ignored
With each year brings a longer list
You're still not satisfied, you're bored
So many kids do without
And have reasons to be sad
What makes you think you have it bad?

You've lost the simple point of giving
And the feeling that it brings
Let's pray to God and give him thanks
For what we have and everything
How love can show a warming side
Especially when it's shared
Why not give your priceless gift of love and care?

Carlton E Rollings Jr
THE STRUGGLE
She tries so hard to be a wondrous wife;
But, alas, and withal,
Her depressive past doth lurk and irk the way to cure.
Then more depression compounds the hurt of failing.

I've often asked (To no one; to someone; the wind):
"Why must she suffer (this soaring spirit)?
Is life's circumstance so unfair, unkind;
To punish those who try their hardest?"

To be, or not —
These questions dominate the mind
Of this wife of mine.
Life's cooking pressure is more than she can bear.

I must steady the shambled nerves;
But how long can this go on?
I clarify, null-ify;
But can we move on from here?

The future knows the end —
To the struggle.

Noble Morton Singer with Wife and Great Granddaughter

Noble Morton Singer
REFLECTIONS OF AN EIGHTY YEAR OLD GREAT GRANDFATHER

To my lovely wife, Tillie my beautiful daughter, and my son-in-law. My grandson and his charming wife. My two great granddaughters Kelly-Ann and Nicole Lee. My grandson Steven and his wife Jennifer.

I am eighty to-day.
I would like very much to say,
That I would love to celebrate
My nintieth,
In this same wonderful way,
The beautiful people here
Have made it a most
Unforgettable day.

To my daughter and son-in-law,
Allen and Rénee,
I have this to say.
You have made me very, very
Happy and tremendously proud,
All your accomplishments make
You stand heads above the
Crowd.

To my Grandsons, Stephen and Larry
Each of whom married a beautiful
And caring wife,
I wish them good fortune, good
Health, Good luck
May they experience the
Great pleasures that
Come with the good life.

To my Great Grand Daughters,
Kelly Ann and Nicole Lee
The cutest and prettiest
Youngsters you'll ever see,
Through the many years yet to come
May all their troubles add
Up to none.

To my wife who' shared the
Pleasures, the adversities,
The cares and the strife,
Truly she is a shining star
In the galaxy of life

I was very happy to see
Murray and Faye
And very glad that we
Could share this memorable day
In the game of life, each one
Of us won,
Because my daughter is happily married
To your son.

John W Gibler
TWO LITTLE PEOPLE

Two nice kids, And Folks
USAF Captain And Mrs Lance Ray.

There's a petite miss named Katie
Who is living in old Cheyenne,
She's quite a fine little lady
With ready smile and cheeks of tan.

Her young brother is Jordan Ray
And quite a boy in his own right,
Who keeps busy throughout the day
And until his bedtime at night.

She rides around on her new bike
While singing her favorite song,
With short legs pedaling his trike
Jordan strives to race along.

Each evening these two take a walk
Their golden retriever in tow,
With many laughs and lots of talk
Until back to their home they must go.

As the years roll by in their world
Life's many bridges to be spanned,
With their battle flags all unfurled
They will most proudly take
their stand.

Nancy M Barath
WITHIN MY HEART

To My Beloved and Precious Mother (Mommy) I love and miss you dearly.

Within my heart
I hold many precious thoughts
Memories of Happiness
Memories of Sadness
As time goes on
My feelings go on
My heart seems to get weaker
Instead of stronger
Yet within my heart
each day is filled with
God's ways
Until my passing days
My memories and feelings
will always be cherished
Nothing will ever perish
Within my heart.

Nancy M Barath
GOD'S COUNTLESS WAYS

To Dr. Alfred R. Lorenz
A person with Great Wisdom, Knowledge and Understanding.
Minister of Grace Presbyterian Church.

This poem begins with God's Countless Ways
It has no end
for it is eternal just as his Magistic Ways

The Rain from heaven that falls upon the earth like our human tears
Sand is like the grains of life that has covered the earth for countless years.
Stars are the eyes in heaven that searches for human compassion for miles and miles
The sun that gives warmth and light our rays of our smiles.
Clouds are like people moving about
Darknest are shadows of passed life that surrounds the earth
Wind is like a breath that reaches out into the universe
Snowflakes are like humans there are no two alike.
Trees are like people for they too have roots of life.
You see I can go on and on
One cannot begin to count the Ways
there is no end to
God's Countless Ways.

Alan Dean Openshaw
JENNY—THAT INSPIRATIONAL FRIEND

To Jenny
My Special Friend
With Love
Alan Dean Openshaw.

Jenny — You give inspirational and loving friendship

Jenny — I will always and forever hold you dear to my heart

Jenny — The sound of your voice lifts spirits and to me your presence gives me a small piece of heaven

No matter how long or far away you are, your friendship brings me peace of mind because when you return to my mind, heaven is a little nearer

Charles M Roberts
HAPPINESS
I sought for happiness
Among the sun and stars
Where the wild seas roll
I found it not.
As mute I stood—fear overwhelmed
My soul
But when I shared with
One in need
I found happiness indeed

Gina Marie Lanute
IN A DAZE, BLUE AND BEAUTIFUL
In a daze, blue and beautiful:
Your darkness holds me in captivity.
I whirl around and catch a glimpse of your world
I knock; but you will not let me in.
I can only peer through your windows, but your shades are drawn halfway.

I want to share my world with you, no need to look through my windows.
My door is open for you to come in; for I trust enough in a person
To give them a fair chance: until they throw a rock through my window,
Then I pass judgement, and stand firm on my ground.

I can only hope you believe enough in yourself to know when to open
The door.
For the right person could be knocking:
And you would never know.

Warren Fenner
EARTH BIRTH

To the memory of my beloved wife Eda, companion and friend.

While on my way one, fine, Spring day,
A daffodil I did see bud;
It looked so grim . . . this her, or him,
Just lying still there, in the mud.

The daffodil waited until
The teasing sun warmed up the soil,
Then raised its head from wintry bed,
While Earth assisted flower's toil.

As Time dragged by the bud did try
Though, there beside it snow did lay;
Then mouse, I saw, helped dig with paw,
Till Ides Of March chased her away.

"Oh wondrous Spring, what joy you bring,
Today I watched the Earth give birth;
March winds, abreast, bud's strength did test,
But brave bud thrived, wet-nursed by Earth."

Cathy Wilson Katz
ANGER
I give you hell, to equal our being.
Are you grateful.
Can my camaraderie be dealt with.
Or have I gone too far . . .

The mutation of my soul,
has been your gift to me.
I return to you with pleasure,
The Justice . . .

Cathy Wilson Katz
TO MY FRIEND
You nurtured a rose.
Then bestowed it on me.
Just like my soul.
How gracious you be . . .

I envision your arms.
As the petals extend.
What a nice reminder.
I love my friend . . .

The stem is exposed.
There is no pain.
You taught me clearly.
All is born again . . .

Cathy Wilson Katz
FORGIVENESS
I am so inclined to bask in your genius.
The glow from thou's radiance, blind me.
I am reminded of thee's saintliness.
I am inadequate . . .

Thee hath given me insecurity.
I pass it on to mine.
I live in blind confusion.
Is my pain justified . . .

In my journey, a higher power.
I begin to understand.
You performed in your best capacity.
And me, in mine . . .

I forsake my greed for pity.
I endure the change.
Contentment is my reward.
Mother is our name . . .

Cathy Wilson Katz
COMPASSION
Enter my sanctum, fellow mortal.
I shall be familiar.

Embrace my consciousness.
I shall stroke your soul.

Relinquish your anger.
I shall teach you to sob.

Now sleep in my arms, for when you wake.
I shall let you go.

Today we made a difference . . .

Cathy Wilson Katz
DETATCHMENT
'Twas mine own err.
That hath made me into this cowardly, sometimes lion.
How'd dare I emerge into the life of thou's unwary soul.
Thou maketh me happy. Thou giveth me peace.
I demanded . . .

I envelop my pride.
For thou could not giveth, what I must find.
Behold. The rapture of my being I imbibe.
The wretched storm hath ceased. I free thee of my satan.
I wish thee well . . .

Cathy Wilson Katz
DESPAIR
Mine swollen eyes are but only a memory.
Mine broken heart an interim in time.
Is there peace for thou in my departure.
Or only in my mind . . .

I leave thee to thine own world.
I free thee of my unholiness.
Is there peace for me in my departure.
Or ungodly loneliness . . .

Cathy Wilson Katz
DEFIANCE
You are a lord. Swill is your audience.
You challenge its existence.
It challenges yours.
Who will rein.
The demons ???

You vaunt, I am the master.
Control is my middle name.
Although you try, you cannot get out.
Your audience has rend you lame.
The demons enter . . .

With teeth like machetes, the demons sneer.
You pompously return the pain.
Your glass held high, A drink to victory.
For they will not win this game.
The audience steals your soul . . .

Infantile cries is what we hear.
Relegation has become your fate.
You shrink inside your armor.
God takes you home, It's late.
You've won ???

Cathy Wilson Katz
BROKEN SPIRIT
As I look high. I see a lie.
A bogus sky. Can you tell me why . . .

I see no sun. How come no one.
Has my life begun. Why can't I run . . .

Unseen birds. Empty words.
Am I absurd. I cannot be heard . . .

There is no rain. I feel no pain.
Someone explain. I don't like this game . . .

Do I appear. Or am I mere.
Why can't I veer. A token tear . . .

With head hung down. A look around.
My face — A frown. There lies my crown . . .

Here in this cell. I cannot rebel.
I expel. No more thoughts to tell . . .

Cathy Wilson Katz
HATE
I scorn your pathetic existence.
Yet I extend my extremities.
You exhaust my energy.
I despise . . .

You call to me in your desperation.
I extend my heart.
You devour it.
I despise . . .

You enter my soul.
You find no one there.
You stole my fantasies.
I despise . . .

In these words, I see denial.
I have let you rape my being.
I blame the wrong child . . .

Joseph H Smith
TWO HEARTS
A silent cry of loneliness
Enters my dream,
A dream of solitude
Of endless search
That has made me weary,
I reach out
To find the key
That will turn my cry
Into a soft melody,
A song of golden tune
Of love reborn,
It is a birth of twins
Of two hearts
That beat as one
That dream as one.

Joseph H Smith
POKER HEART
You play a dangerous game my love,
A game of many chances.
You may win, lose or come up draw,
In any of your romances.
To sit and watch while others play,
is for the shy and lonely.
You must play the game my precious love,
until you find your one and only.

Sarah Griffith
A LITTLE FRIEND
When I was just a wee little lad,
an imaginative friend I had
whom I would see when I felt gloomy or sad.

This little guy would pop out of nowhere,
when I, too amazed to do anything but stare
would say, "Hi!" "How's everything doing down there?"

My friend and I, oh, we would play and sing.
Why, together we would do almost everything.

We would laugh & run until the day was done,
and then it was time to say goodbye
to this red-headed, rosy-cheeked little guy.

Sherry Ann Valiton
OCEAN
A dim light stretches over the sky.
Misty fog rides on incoming waves.
Sea gulls become airborne, soaring high,
The shore, just beginning to awake.

Edge of the sun rests on the water.
Reflections of light cover the bay.
Movement begins out of the stillness,
Time, transforming night into day.

Silence breaks, as waves crash on the sand.
All traces of the night have now gone.
The sun, how it performs such miracles,
All alone, on the shore, at dawn.

Karen Correll Wilke
AGONIES OF WAR
The indecisions and attainable chaos,
of world leaders,
Have created decades of wars.
These men are the blood seekers of hordes,
Of our babies and youth.

Oh! God! Why?
We can only look to the sky.
To close our eyes with a mere cry.
To cherish our grief
For it may become very brief.
We fear the destruction of humanity.

We hope for our entity
In the Final War,
It will close our door.

Bill and Loree Ford and Tim

Loree Ford
IT'S GONE
It's gone—
That weather-beaten, old shingled house,
That stood beside the road—
A landmark of its era,
To our family, a treasured abode;

A source of speculation
For the curious passer by;
(As the years rolled on, tangled surroundings
Offended the critical eye.)

For the adventurous pilferer,
A source of rich reward;
A shelter for the transients;
A hide-out for the bored.

The gaping door, torn open
By their unscrupulous hands,
Exposed a woeful wreckage,
Made worthless by their bands.

Yes, it's gone—
The shingled house
That stood beside the road,
Dismantled by those remembering
Lives lived in a different mode.

Shawnna S Kramer
PETE JONES

To my Grandfather, Pete Jones, a grandfather that each and every grandkid should have. Thanks, Grandpa Pete, for giving all of us unusual sight to see life's beauties.

"You've got big hands, Son.
Dig into life.
Grow some values you can eat.
Root out the stink weeds."
Pete softly weaves our lives;
Adding red and blue thread before
Gently placing those within his long reach
Up where he thinks we belong.

"You've got a heart of gold, Son.
Don't be afraid to thump or caress.
Keep your promises.
Find the good when others can't."
Pete lets life become good in its time;
People he can help walk tall and laugh deep.

"Teach me now, Grandpa.
Tell me how to die right."
Heart weakened and hands swollen,
Pete blankly stares down at hospital nothing.
Tubes in place, Pete fails to teach me God's mercy.

Shawnna S Kramer
THE EMPTY BOTTLE
Desperately, Uncle Doug tried
Befriending me once a summer.

I wanted it but
Older summers I saw what he was:
Rotten teeth and bent back
Bounding to each hacking cough.

Maybe, I figured, he wanted to stop:
Stop the losing
Stop the pain of living.

Last summer was hot
And he was sick with
Gin, vodka, Old Crow
Bourbon and Pain:
Yelling, pounding the chair,
Wanting to shoot someone.

Dead cigarette and empty bottle clutched,
Uncle Doug pleaded for my skin cleanser
With alcohol and called me by my
Granny Zephyr's
Name.

Angle H Williams
A DAY IN THE LIFE OF A NASCAR DRIVER
Come one, come all to today's race,
They're not moving along at a slow pace.

This crowd isn't bored,
Leading the pack are three Fords.

Just when you think he can't,
Here comes Harry Gant!

There they were Cope and Rudd at the line,
Unfortunately, they both got a fine.

They were sent back one lap,
But Rudd's going to put himself back on the map,

Just as everyone gave up hope,
From the back of the pack here comes Cope!

Did you know that after the race all the crews,
Go out to get some brews.

At turn four a blown tire,
Oh no! Schrader's on fire!

The winner of today's race, Ricky Rudd!
Congratulations, great driving Bud!!!

Stephani Fordham
DO YOU BELIEVE?

To every lost soul in search of a meaningful life.

Do you believe in Jesus Christ?
Do you believe He sacrificed . . .
His own life . . . to save your soul
Do you believe in God above?
Do you believe He sent His love . . .
Through His Son . . . to make you whole
Do you believe Christ paid the cost?
Bore all our sins nailed on the cross
So we can live . . . eternally
Do you believe . . . like I believe?

Angle H Williams
A DAY AT THE TRACK
It was a perfect sunny day,
The race was in its way.

The stands were full with cheering fans,
A hush came about as everyone looked at turn one.

Elliott and Earnhardt had crashed,
And Cope was mashed.

The caution flag flew,
The ambulance lights and siren blew.

Elliott and Earnhardt were alright,
Then on pitrow a fight.

While the fight was breaking up,
Allison was receiving his trophy cup!

ALLISON HAD WON THE RACE!!

Onnalinda Vitalini
WELCOME
This message of love goes out to all.
WE will help you when you fall.
When you need a shoulder or a helping hand.
WE will do for you whatever we can.

Need a hug, how about a joke, or just want to talk?
Call US, we'll take a ride, just sit, or perhaps go for a walk.
To us this is love: being there and caring.
Open arms, open minds, & hearts for sharing.

Who are WE and US with all this love to give?
YOU are: for without it you cannot truly live
So open your hearts, give a hug, put a smile on your face.
Love someone: Welcome to the Human Race.

Onnalinda Vitalini
WE CAN'T FORGET— WE MUST GO ON
Today is your birthday—but I can't give you anything—not even a card.
We aren't baking your favorite 'Whoppie cake'—Oh Lord this is so hard.
I can't hold you in my arms and congratulate you on another year.
Can you see us or feel what's in our hearts even though you're not here?

You left us so suddenly—without warning you were gone from our world.
One by one the pain, loneliness and self-pity—along with other confusing emotions unfurled.

We are left here in reality to cope with whatever comes our way.
Looking to each other for support and comfort—taking it day by day.
Often to the outside world we smile and our words are lighthearted . . .
but don't be disillusioned.
Secretly in our home we release our grief for you, our dearly
departed . . . and try to sort through the confusion.

There are many memories of you we cherish and will always carry.
Your drive was such that you would never tarry.
For those who knew you well, having you here was a pleasure.
And I for one, in reminiscing, will relish the treasure.

There are no answers to all the "WHYS" we've asked.
Our time on this earth is a mystery—never to be unmasked.
Slowly we move on with life's daily chores.
Waiting to see what's behind all the unopened doors.

Linda Verdalette
REFLECTION OF MY FATHER'S EYES

To Elias my husband with all my love and admiration . . . Linda.

I see the love of God in your eyes
White lily fair . . .

I feel His love abide in your heart
And meet His glory there.

Countenance of radiance; grace abounds
Tender beauty rare.

Oh, the love of Jesus His son
Depth beyond compare . . .

Burning, dwelling within your eyes
His witness that you share.

Roscoe D Miller (Rocky Dee)
IT WILL ALWAYS BE YOU!
It will always be you,
When I dream a dream;
It will always be you,
In each little scheme.
If you wonder how I know,
Well, my heart tells me so.
It will always be you.

I will always see you,
When I have a vision.
It will always be you;
For every little reason.
You're always there,
In every thing that I do;
Oh Darling, my Darling,
It will always be you.

You are always there,
In times of distress.
You are always near,
In times of loneliness.
You wonder how I know,
Well my heart tells me so.
It will always be you.

You seem to be,
In every thought of mine;
You're always so sweet,
So considerate and kind;
You lift me up when I'm feeling blue,
I know my Darling;
It will always be you!

loleka
MAKE UP AND TASTE THE WAKE UP
Impress thoughts of passion
Express feelings of compassion

Impress thoughts of purity
Express feelings of security

Impress thoughts of cleanliness
Express feelings of godliness

Make up and taste the wake up!

loleka
A NEED TO ESCAPE
Here I am caught up in a jam:
—Too weak to fight
—Too proud to lose
—Too scared to scram

What am I to do?
—My family is a bit confused
—My friends are nowhere to find
—My lover is stubborn as hell

We are guilty of the #1 crime . . .
—There is nowhere to run
—There is no place to hide
—There is no room for pride
. . . We are all gamblers of time!

I feel a need to escape . . .
—I am tired of being held prisoner
—I have no more room for pain
—I must set myself free
. . . From being a victim of rape

Ida R Sheffron

Ida R Sheffron
ME WITHOUT YOU

To my loving son Ron, who's always there for me—Right on!!!

Like An Infant Without Its Mom
Or A Lad Without His Dad
That's Me Without You!!
Like A Beautiful Sunset
Hidden From View
Or A Magnificent Rainbow
Minus Its Hues
That's Me Without You!!
Like Baseball Without A Bat
Or Thinking "Thin"
When One Is "Fat"
Like A Mystery Without
A "Who Done It"
Or a Government Without
Qualified Personnel To Run It
That's Me Without You!!!
Where Is This Shangra La
To Which Each Of Us Can Flee?
Perhaps To Find The
Right You And
The Right Me?

Sara Hausner
MIDSUMMER'S NIGHTMARE
Wet
Dry
Drops cold on my nose.
Bach
And screeching cockatiels
Inside the house
A wall apart
Where a stranger is cursing
Loudly and softly
My name.

I owe her nothing
But owe her everything.
Little pleases or can soothe
The flow of angry grunts
That drip from her mouth
And drown her
And her family
In a soaking misery.

Sara Hausner
AT THE ROASTERY
Pretty rows of brilliant pastries,
Faces distant enough and
Coffee scalding delicious, hot
On my tongue. I'd like to remain
Invisible, but between sips
Look up for a familiar smile.

Old memories renewed on a stool
still warm
from my last visit a year ago.Table
still sticky
From my chocolate powder foam two
years ago.
I got high, down in the back room
three years ago.
Twinkling faces of yesterdays, they
are pressing
against my window pained, misted
eyes.
The steam of the coffee in my
other hand is
squeezing out tears inside the walls
of my face.

Secret, shh, be quiet and
Invisible; I can delight, dancing,
Twirling with my pen in ballpoint
Ballroom embracing conversation.
I am returning, turning, turning.

Laurie Habets
PASTEL SHADES
Pastel shades and Wedgewood Skies
First light of loving in your eyes,
soon to fade then to flee,
Leaving me alone with me.
It's too late for me to run,
What's said is said,
What's done is done.
When I'm with you I find release,
For loving, laughter, joy and peace.
I'm lost in a dream with you so near.
Your leaving me is what I fear.
Reflecting the sweetness from your
eyes,
I say I love you but echoes die.
I hold you close, then let you go,
Echoes die but the love still grows.

Kelley J T Long
I BARE MY SOUL
I wish I were a tree
for children on me could swing
Laughter below and laughter above
Within my limbs they've filled with
love.

As seasons come and seasons go
Leaves of color change, brilliance,
does show
A pile of leaves at my feet
See the children frolic and play
'tis sweet
Winter bares her cold frosty desire
To keep my warmth shed of leaves
even higher
I bare my soul my naked self
For all to see time has changed itself

With first breath green is alive
A thrust of new leaves spring has
arrived
Flowers for those who love and share
Carve a heart, with arrow too,
to show they
care
Warmer days children play
I with my branches a full display
Blankets under baskets and food
within
Lay in the shade, whisper of wind,
through limbs,
. . . listen
Children have grown and left their
home
Quiet still calm and all alone
Wind blown leaves scatter over the
grass
Echoes the laughter from way in the
past
The wind as it whistles through my
leaves
Tichles the old swing it begins to
weave
Memories and wishes . . . , I deny my
rings
Until that day a little girl came to
swing.

Dianne Joyce Gage
TO MY SON

Dedicated to my sons, Frank and Christopher Stricker.

There once was a girl that no one
loved
so God sent her a boy from up above.
She held him close and cared for him
but for her it still looked dim.
She loved him deep, she loved him
strong
but she still didn't feel like she
belonged.
She told him she loved him without a
doubt
but he just wanted her out.
This is my son I love so deep
if only I knew how his love to keep.
I try hard to show I care
but there is no help anywhere.
All I wanted is for him to know
all my love I try to show.
I don't think he knows how much I
need to keep in touch
I did my best to raise him right
but he thought I wanted to fight.
I want happiness for him and for me
this I hope I will get to see.
My nights are short, my days are
long
I wish we could get along.

Dianne Joyce Gage
A KISS
A kiss can make your love come out
but if you take your kiss away
it will hurt everyday.
So bring your kisses back to me
and see how happy you make me.
Your kisses make the birds sing
they make me happy about
everything.
They make me happy you are close
but they make me love you the most.

Joyce Dianne Gage
I NEED YOUR KISSES
I need your kisses, I need your love
I need all of the up above.
I need you, do you need me?
Please show me so I can see.
A kiss from you makes me shine so
bright
it makes me feel alright.
I need your kiss just to smile
it keeps me going for a while.
I need your kiss to shelter pain
with your kiss there is no rain.
I need your kiss to bring sight to me
as your kiss lights up me.
Your kiss brings everything to me
can't you see how much you mean to
me?
If you are blind and cannot see
just bring your kiss here to me.
I will show you how to see.
Oh how happy you will make me.

Dianne Joyce Gage
I AM NOT STRONG
I am not strong like everyone thinks I
am
I am not strong like everyone expects
me to be.
I am weak if only they could see.
I need someone to love me,
I need someone to care.
I need someone with whom to share.
I need someone who will always be
there.
There to hold me not to scold me.
Someone to trust through all the dust.
I need love I can count on being there
without a care.
I need you to always be there.

Dianne Joyce Gage
WHEN GOD FOUND YOU
When God found you, He thought of
me
He knew you would set me free.
Free from pain and sorrow at last
God knew you and I would last.
God gave us the chance to work
things out
He knew we would without a doubt.
God gave us love to share
He knew we would care.
God wants His children to stay
together
even through stormy weather.
So let's make God happy and do this
right
let's make God happy and do not
fight.
Let's be good to God and stay
together
no matter what they say.
Because God doesn't want us to go
astray
so let's love each other all the way.

Dianne Joyce Gage
GLAD TO BE YOUR WIFE
I care about you with all the love in
my heart
I feel like you have been with me
from the start
Your kisses are sweet like a
rewarding treat
I feel all your love from my head to
my feet
Oh how glad I am, "you" I got to
meet
Your touch is caring your thoughts
are sharing
I need you in my life
I am so glad you made me your wife
So thank you again for everything
As you make my heart sing
But most of all thanks for being you
and you alone
Because of you it's love I've known
All my love I give to you
So you know with my love what to
do

Dianne Joyce Gage
CAN'T HE SEE HE HAS LEFT A SCAR?
Why does he want to leave when she
loves him so much?
She would do anything just for his
touch
To her he is her whole world her
reason to go on
Her reason to belong, the feeling is so
strong
She knows he is right for her,
because he lights up her life for her
I know God has sent him to be with
me
Oh, why can't he see he is right for
me?
There must be a reason for this man
to want to go

But will I ever know?
He has decided to stay, oh thank God I will pray
But now she is scared it will happen again
She is afraid to let him in
Afraid he will go and hurt her more her heart is oh so sore
But she still loves him deep and within
She wishes his love she could keep in
She loves him deep and within surely this cannot be a sin
She needs him and wants him without a doubt
But she is afraid he will just walk out
I pray to God to bring him back to me
Can't he see how much he needs me?
Because I love him today and I love him tomorrow
And I love him through pain and I love him through sorrow
I love him everyday and I love him tomorrow
I love him close and I love him far
Can't he see he has left a scar?

Dianne Joyce Gage
HOLD ME

So hold me close, hold me tight.
And I will feel good tonight.
I feel good in your arms
when I can see and feel your loving charms.
Your arms reach for me to hold me close
this is what I need the most.
I need you, do you need me?
All your love helps me see
see the good and the bad.
I can't stand it when you stay mad.

Dianne Joyce Gage
WHAT WOULD GOD SAY?

Dedicated to my husband Eddie D. Gage.

There once was a man that needed love
I was sure he was sent from up above
There was a look of happiness and love in his eyes
that no one could disguise.
I felt his loneliness and distress
I loved him to my best.
There could never be another
to make me feel like when we were with one another.
I still need this man more than any other.
All I ask is a chance to make things right
I think a love like this is worth a fight.
If you both believe this is right
I think everything will turn out alright.
It's easy to go and hard to stay
but what would God stay?

Donna Die Joia
THEOLOGY OF FRIENDS

As people come and go in and out of my life,
I've never met one that's touched me so deeply, as you have;
That my heart is heavy, and totally adorned with thoughts of you,
Questionable as to where to fit you into this busy life of mine;
Friends we may be, nothing more, nothing less;
As life has restrictions, which I live by, and would never betray anyone that I love . . .

Donna Die Joia
A DAY IN JUNE

To my Family with love who makes my days of June possible and worthwhile.

The most beautiful sight I've ever seen,
Is sitting here on the terrace, looking out through the screen;
An occasional squirrel may pass on by,
Collecting pecans, looking agile against the sky;
The birds are singing their natural tune,
As they do in the month of June,
The Hummingbirds race over to feed,
Flying bullet like, with their great speed;
The sun is shining through the trees,
As I enjoy an occasional breeze,
What better way to spend my time,
Than sitting here and making rhyme . . .

Iola E Denniston
THE GOLDEN ANNIVERSARY

To my husband Earl.

We've had fifty years of wedded bliss
With our share of struggle and strife.

But there were so many happy times
With much fun and laughter in our life.

We had our ups, we had our downs
But we always seemed to bounce back

Somehow with the guidance of God and friends
We got back on the right track

We've now reached a half-century mark
I hope we have many more good years
And may we be as happy as a lark.

Don Elbert Conley
SEPTEMBER SONG

It was in the Autumn of the year. The leaves on the trees had turned to gold and brown . . . and you left me standing beneath the old Acacia tree calling out your name.

It was not so long ago when your eyes filled with joy when you would first see me. Love, tell me that you will come again. My heart still does a dance when our eyes meet. Do not turn and walk away from me—leaving me feeling cold and drawn up against the wind alone. Tell me something on this earth in the arena of man is real and lasts for more than just a little while.

This is the tree that has carved in its bark, John loves Jeannie, for everyone to see. It was not so long ago, my love, when you held me oh so close and you said, murmuring in my ear, I love you John, and, I always will.

Come once again, my love, to the arms that once held you on so tight—the arms that long to hold nobody but you. It is cold in the night—and I am so alone. I love you . . .

Don Elbert Conley
LOOKS LIKE THE BLUES

Baby, it's the blues tonight
can't stand the wind blowing thru the window
had too many cigarettes—taste bad
woman's gone/can't you hear
what I'm saying: looks like the blues tonight.

Ashtray's need dumping
wine bottles ought to be dumped in the trash
Baby, can't you hear what I'm sayin'
Can't stand the sight or the sound of the night:
looks like the blues tonight

Wasn't long ago you shared this place with me
I see your smiling face
I hear the laughing sound of your voice
I can't stand being without you
Can't you hear what I'm sayin'/looks like the blues tonight.

Sharon Rainwater

Sharon Rainwater
MANSION OF MEMORIES

To My Mother, Mrs. Doris Minor, Our Eternal Rose in My Mansion of Memories.

In our mansion of memories is a beautiful place,
An estate of great wealth, I don't want to escape
Overlooking a garden of splendor and grace
Are beautiful flowers that our hearts embrace
What beautiful fragrance come from this place
The sweet smell of memories in our garden estate
The pathways are lined with thoughts that will last
Thoughts of laughing and music and card games of past
Our mansion of memories such a beautiful place
Was built by a woman we wish to imitate
She built it with hardship, it took all her life
But she finished it even with all of the strife
From foundation to roof top she carefully planned
The blue print was taken from God's master plan
The curtains were lined with what looked like lace
And through the windows one could see her smiling face
Yes in our mansion of memories is a beautiful place
An estate of great wealth we don't want to escape
And a woman who forever will be in our hearts
In our mansion of memories we will never be apart

Emma A Williams
TO NIPPY

Today, I went a visiting, oh, not too far away
But to a nearby nursing home, where folk enter
Just to stay, maybe for weeks, maybe for months
My thoughts were on a dear old man, ninety-one today
Imagine! ninety-one long years of smiles, of rants & raves.
For "Nippy" is his pet name, a short & stocky son of a gun
Who charmed or irritated as the case may be.
But whose many years caught up with him.
As I looked & smiled & kissed his face, I thought of years gone by—
When he, a rascal sure as fate, would toast the world
And with these words "Eight bells & all's well"
Pass my door each night at eight.
That happy chap with ne'er a care, ne'er dreamed he'd end up there,
But still, as I bent down to whisper "Goodbye Nippy"
He took my hand & gently kissed my fingers.
That was Nippy's way of saying "Good bye," he doesn't talk much any more.
He kisses the fingers of those he loves, the rest get a grunt or a scowl,
Ninety-one today, I hope I don't reach ninety-one
And lay there like a log, that's only two years hence, I fear
A few months later, I read these words
For Nippy is no longer here!

Barbara Wicklander
DEPRESSION

It is a physical thing
Covering me like a blanket
Touching me like an unwanted caress

It is much stronger today
Sneaking up behind me
I struggle against it.

It leaves me for a moment
Then beckons back
Like a lost and lonely friend

Barbara Wicklander
PAIN

The sun is breaking over the snow
It is all about to end
As the snow melts so does my pain
It has been a long winter.

Jodie M Rahn
THE VOICE

A little voice inside me says.
Go pursue your fondest wishes,
Yet everytime I try, I find,
A sink full of dirty dishes,
And clothes to wash, kids to bathe,
Beds that could use a-changing,
Walls to clean, shirts to mend,
Closets that need re-arranging.

Buy some groceries, fix the meals,
And pay the paper boy,
Take out the trash, mow the lawn,
I'm like a wind-up toy,
So little voice, please shut-up,

I've got to mop the floor,
I don't have time to listen,
Oh no,—someone's at the door,
"Yes, Sir, the lady of the house,
is in, and standing right here,
Now what'd you say, I don't believe,
You're awarding me,—
HOMEMAKER OF THE YEAR?"

Ahna Marcantognini
WHAT DREAM?
living without money
the green tinge of possession
people die—friends, lovers, family
leaving dreams, dreamers and
dreaming
security to fulfill a dream when age
is clear and death is near
retire, old, wrinkled
memory fading
what was I saving for?
what dream, what dream?
working young fighting shoving
up down around and round
invisible art
visible fear
dead
no need to save
no need to care.

Dolores Gray
RESIGNATION
Heart throbs and tears are blended
With sighs as deep as seas,
The moon and night are sorrowing,
I hear their sob in the breeze.
You've gone and left a shadow
Of remembrance 'cross my brain:
It haunts me like a spirit
I've tried to lose—in vain,
And so I've left off trying
Because I've lived a lot,
I'll forget my idle crying
And glory in my thought!

Louis J Warmoth
HE WAITS FOR ME
I Hear No Sounds Behind Me, But I
Know He's Lurking There.
He Quickly Stept In Behind Me,
When He Saw I Did Not Care.
He Knows That I've Been Waiting,
For Love To Call My Own.
I Know That He's Been Watching,
But No Love E'er Was Shown.

He Knows That I've Been Praying,
For Love To Come My Way.
I Know That He's Still Dreaming,
For Me To Make His Day.
I Look Right Then Look Left, But,
No Love In Sight I See.
I'll Continue Down This Road,
Knowing Reaper Waits For Me.

I Know He Will Embrace Me, Like
Written In Years Of Yore.
He Waits For Me To Enter, Like I've
Tried In Times Before.
This Time No One Is Watching, Or
They Really Do Not Care.
There Are Even Some Who'd Wish,
I'd Make My Journey There.

Ones I Love Are Standing, Looking
At Another Path They See,
So Now I Say, Grim Reaper, Step
Up, And Softly Embody Me.
You Can Never Steal My Love, My
Love, You Can Never Take,
But Now My Love I Offer, Grim
Reaper, As Your Day I Make.

I Could Fight And Beat You, If I
Fought You, Upon This Day,
But No Love Is There Watching,
So I'll Embody You This Way.
You Just Stand There Facing Me,
Pointing At Me Your Knife,
And I Will Then Jump Upon You,
Forcing You To Take My Life.

Louis J Warmoth
RED, WHITE, OR BLUE?
The Red, The White, Or The Color
Blue.
What True Meaning have They,
I Ask You?

Is Red The Blood, Color Which We
Shed?
Is White The Color, Of Our
Wounded Bed?

Calling On Blue Angels, A Ring Or
Band,
Should I Change The Oar, Calling It
And?

Now The Pyramid, Or Family, You
Now See.
The Guardian Angel, Together With
Thee.

Red And White Can Destroy, From
The Blue.
Only Men Of Earth, Renew Mother
For You.

Restoring Our Faith, When United
As One,
Showing The World, FATHER'S
Will Be Done.

Next Time You See, Before You
OLD GLORY,
Go Into Your Past, Know The Whole
Story.

See Your FATHER, HIS SON, Or
HOLY GHOST.
Believe In The Secret Three, I Now
Toast.

Louis J Warmoth
THE OLD TOM CAT
The Stories I've Told, It's Seems, To
Be Most Profound.
The Plane Glorified, Misther Chance,
Never Left The Ground.
She Was The One, Who Only, Nearly
Took My Light.
She Was Married To, Old Tom Cat,
Who Lead The Fight.

Old Tom Was Meant, To Be, A
Strong Leader For Men.
On His Solid Green Side, A Yellow
Cat, Hid Fighters Within.
The Law Of Averages Say, Before
Twenty, A Fighter Will Die.
Old Tom Flew Two Hundred,
Straight Through, The Enemy Sky.

After Two Hundred His Uncle,
Ordered Tom, To Come Home.
We Need You To Sell War Bonds,
Then Rest In A Dome.
Old Tom Lead The Invasion, His
Spot, Showing Enemy Light.
Bombers Of Different Color,
Followed, Showing Father's Might.

Misther Chance Showed Only, A
Bakini, Tom Showed The Red,
Blue Angels Then Followed, Making
Everything Look Dead.
Red And White Can Destroy
Anything, Striking From The Blue,
But Men Of The Earth, Must Return,
Rebuilding Mother For You.

Old Tom Had One Flaw, His Orders
Came, Through Men In Satin.
He Slew His Own Brother One Day,
Orders, From One Called Patton.
Patton's Telegram Stated, He Was
Sorry, He entered The Spot.
He Crossed The Line Of Our Love, A
Spot, He Had Forgot.

Louis J Warmoth
THE POET
The Poet Is A Person, Who Possess
Vision.
He May See The Future, But Not The
Reason.
He Can See The Die, Know What's
Being Cast,
And Tell You A Story, That'll Come
To Past.

Looking At A Rosebud, He'll See
The Bloom.
Looking At A Problem, He'll See
The Doom.
He'll Tell A Story, A Message He'll
Send.
A Word Of Warning, Of What's
Round The Bend.

Sometimes You'll Listen, And
Sometimes See,
What's Waiting Up Ahead, For You
And For Me.
You May Think Him Smart, Or
Think He's Dumb,
But The Story He Tells, The Ending
Will Come.

A GOD Given Gift, Resting Within
His Head,
Tells Him At Night, While Sleeping
In Bed.
Traveling Into His Past, He Studies
The Way.
Returning Next Morning, He Knows
Of Today.

History Repeats Itself, All Poets Now
Know.
They Study Our Lives, Knowing
Where They Go.
No Matter What Story, Or Tale You
May Bear,
I'll Swear To You, I've Already Been
There.

Raymond Clarke
TO BE THREE

To my granddaughter—
Teresa O'Brien.

You are the three in my sixty-three
years.
You are the joy in my three score and
more.
You are the third generation of me.
You are the love of my children's
love life.
You are the hope of your family's
peers.
You are the result your mother's
strife bore.
You are the faith your parents had in
He.
You are the child borne by your
father's wife.
I am your pop-pop; you are my
Puppa.
I am the father of your mother, dear.
I am the bone in your mom-mom's
zuppa.
I am the walk partner whose voice
you hear.
I am the faith He gave from up
above.
I wish you HAPPY BIRTHDAY!
All my love!

Raymond Clarke
FORTY YEARS TOGETHER
Forty years seems like forty days my
dear.
You are now as you were then, my
darling.
My better half you always are, to me.
Your faith and love have calmed my
anxious heart.
You have filled my days with the
song I hear,
The ring of life shines like the bird
"starling"!
My nights bloom full of all my love
of thee.
Our whole family shows you did
your part.
The dawn of marriage was the light
of life new.
The days of life echoed our beam of
love.
The rays of faith blessed you with
mother's hue.
The joy of children, twice blessed
from above.
Happy Anniversary! Forty bye!
The road to forty more before we die.

Raymond Clarke
A STRING OF PEARLS
THE PEARLS OF LIFE . . .
Are the parthenons of the soul.
THE PEARLS OF WISDOM . . .
Are the pyramids of the mind.
THE PEARLS OF LOVE . . .
Are the gems of the heart.
A MOTHER'S LOVE . . .
Is like a string of pearls:
Full of life, strung with wisdom,
And worn with infinite love.

Wayne B Cooper
OUR LOVE

Dedication—Paula Julie Abdul.

I love you precious Paula at five foot
two
When I return from heaven, let's say
I do,
You're like Gene Kelly and Singing
in The Rain
How about a shower of blessings
from God and Wayne,
Our love is coming together in a big
rush rush
Let's tell the world and not keep it
hush hush,
You're blessed with outer beauty and
inner beauty too
Our love is from above, I know that
to be true,
In God's eyes we are woman and
man
United together for his perfect plan,
You've had enough proposals to
make your heart sing
My proposal was like a diet coke, it's
the real thing,
The Lord will send you to me when
the time is right
it could be any day now, possibly at
night,
Blessings greater than fame and
money, you own
You belong to God and me, you're
not alone,
Although I'm six feet tall, we do see
eye to eye
You're the only girl for me and I'm
your only guy,
We will share our loaves and fishes
each day
And tell the whole world, Jesus is the
way,

Our love is Godly love; that's the best
Our love has past each and every test,
Paula I'm waiting for you to enter my life
As my friend, woman, lover and wife.

Carol Boly
ELVIS
Elvis Presley, you are gone, but I still love you anyway.
And this song must carry on.
I need to know you were my first choice.
I need to hear your tender voice.
I Love you so much, it hurts me so.
You are a big movie star, the biggest, and the best.
You used to sing, and make people laugh, smile and cry.
God Bless you Elvis.
You sing as high as the mountains.
And as low as the valley.
God Bless you Elvis.

Bertha Jane Hawkins
FATHER'S TO LOVE
Every father is here to love
God made them everyone—
Fathers live—some gone on to the Promise Land—
God took a rib from man; made a help mate—a woeman—
They made love; helped each other.
Wasn't long until man—had a son—a daughter
And brother—this is how it all began.
I don't know what a woeman—would do without a man?
Because my dad is my father—head of the family—
And my mother's keeper—God made all kinds—
Gave them a trade—Some are laborers—
Some are carpenters—some are reepers—
"Every father is here to love"
—But mine sleeps in the shade.

Ann Herwitz
BUTTERFLY LOVE
From out of nowhere, you came—
To play with my heart,
And capture my love.
Flames of love engulf me,
To the greatest heights I soar.
The love I gave with no restraint,
Like a butterfly you sipped,
And drained the nectar from my life.
A butterfly you are,
Sipping from flower to flower,
Stabbing a thousand death blows,
To my tortured bleeding heart,
And crashing down upon me
From the euphoria and ecstasy,
Crumbling beyond repair,
Amoung the embers of yesterday,
To live and dream amoung my memories.

Wanda Annette Pack
LITTLE RED BOOTS
Little Red Boots on,—
That gleam in her eye;
A little shock of bright blond hair,
Hardly enough for a ribbon to tie.

I can almost hear her laughing,
As she bounces on Granddad's knee.
Her red ruffled dress flying,
As if riding a pony in the breeze.

My baby so carefree and happy.
My baby so cuddly and sweet.
I can still see these Little Red Boots,
On her tiny little feet!

Barbara Luster
THE CROSS OF SHAME
O'What A Shame, To Nail Him.
O'What A Shame, To Hang Him.
In Bearing Such Shame—For Our Sins,
He Hung There & Died—Only To Rise Again.
Saying To One, Saying To All,
REPENT YE! REPENT ALL!
For The Fall Shall Be Great,
Of The Large & The Small
Those That Do-Not Heed The Call
Of The Father To us all.
Come Ye, "Seek My Face,"
Surely You Shall Be Saved
I Bored The Cross
And You're Saved By Grace.
O'What A Shame, He Beared
They Nailed Him To The Cross
"Hung Him There"
Pierced His Side—With Thorns On His Head,
They Hung Him There—For "All" To Mock
They Left Him Hanging There.

Barbara Luster
CLOUD BURST
Everyone Looks For That, Beam Of Light—
Beneath The Cloud,
I Look For The Cloud
Everyone Prays For A Sunny Day,
I Look For The Rain.
When It Rains
I think Of God's Tears,
Pouring Down From Heaven
For His Children "In" Wickedness & Sin—
Dominated By Satan's Lust & Greed,
Never To harken To Our Father's Heed.
YES! Everyone Looks For The Sun Shiny Day,
I Look For The Cloud.
After The Burst Of Clouds
Comes The Rain—After The Rain,
"A Rain Bow's In The Sky;"
I See My Silver Lining
I Know The Sun Will Shine
Once More & Again.

Connie Williams

Connie Williams
MY FUTURE
With love to my children & grandchildren & future grandchildren.

I love my children
I love my grandchildren
More than life will ever know
They are my life blood
They are my future
With them I live forever
Without them I am dead forever

Ms Dorothy J Hamilton
HAPPY, HAPPY, MORNING!
For: All my folks—Psm. 118 Vs. 24.

HAPPY, HAPPY Morning Haulm Culm Cottage,
HAPPY, HAPPY Morning—hot, Nutritious Cottage,
There's No Incantation, No Hoo-doo, Voo-doo;
Under Yonder Calumet or war bonnet
Enough, 'tis no sonnet—
Decalogue—those

tablets of stone shall never, never be overthrown,
Now, the Cream, of the elite of the teaching team chatting so merrily by serene stream in
Aramaic—no way Prosaic, much Mosaic, never, hardly ever algebraic.

Ms Dorothy J Hamilton
THE KNIGHT WHOSE ARMOR DIDN'T SQUEAK
The Chief is dead. It is with deep regret we announce the passing of the Rt. Hon. Charles MacLean, the Lord of Duart and Morvern, Knight of the Thistle, Knight of the British Empire, Twenty-seventh Chief of Clan Gillean, on the 8th of February A.D. 1990. Long live the Chief.

Did you ever hear of "The Knight Whose Armor Didn't Squeak"?
They say he like to play hide-and-seek
At least 4 or 5 times a week
After every joust, Crusade and tournament triumph
He and his children and friends would gambol and frolic
and galumph, galumph, galumph.

One autumn day as umbrellas and gamp signalled a day dreary, cold and damp
From a manor mansion door with Crepe of purple purfle
Casket drape of velvet with much accolade of "Funeral March"
From icy mount windy blast to sun-drenched desert parch
Eulogy from young hearts—we bid farewell with praise and laud
Our Knight is now at home with The Angels and God;
As always, any day of the week
He's will always be "The Knight Whose Armor Didn't Squeak!"

Ms Dorothy J Hamilton
ALWAYS AVOID!
Always, Avoid, Avoid a Humanoid Dendroid
Always, Avoid, Avoid a Defective Detective
Skulking Around Piers Socked in with fog whichever towns,
Cities or dorps various horrors of corpse!
Skulking Around Wharfs not exactly looking for "The Seven Dwarfs"
Even Loch Ness Monster what a hoax for tourists wherever we rove—tentacles with spectacles?
Maybe akin to Disney's Production of "The Monster of Strawberry Cove"
Always Avoid any "Orange Ogopogo,"
Lavender "Loup-garou"
KRAKEN,
or Mauve
Susquatch, be not mistaken
Viewing with your Lorgnette, ne'er forget
Always avoid

Ms Dorothy J Hamilton
Fergus MacErc
From DALRIADA, Antrim to Argyll—
disembogue
With his stylish, surprising, winsome, Irish brogue—
No pirate, no buccaneer, no privateer, No renegade rogue;
From armor-bearer to armor-wearer—(1 Chr. 10:40)
his regalia naturally vogue!
Fergus MacErc, Christian Irish Chieftain
Was he off the ilk of Gilgamesh or Cuchulain—No bilk
Or a Milesian—your decision!?
His gnomonic clock of classic design
Bound to stand the tests of time;
He founded Scotland's Royal House 503 A.D.
That giant forerunner of the Stuart dynasty!

Ms Dorothy J Hamilton
WALPURGIS NIGHT!
(maybe sounds better to the tune of "Silent Night!")

(800 B.C. to 800 A.D.)

Walpurgis Night
Unholy Night,
Everything's Wrong
Nothing right,

Queen Semiramis with her son "Prince Nimrod"
With praises only for his father "Baal" the sun god,
We're singing all righteousness shall cease
We demand War not Peace!

(Semiramis declared Nimrod was a virgin birth—Dc. 25—and he married his mother!)

(Babylonian legend) not myth or fable!
even transmitted by Atlantic Cable!

Ms Dorothy J Hamilton
ORDERS OF ANGELS!
Orders of Angels 9—so Divine!?
Cherubim and Seraphim surround HIM
Yes, so Divine!
If you look in your Bible—
You'll very certainly be liable
To see names of Archangels 3
Gabriel, Michael, and Raphael
Who ever fight with all their might
Against Lucifer and His Hordes of Hell
All together Archangels 7 guiding
God's people straight to HEAVEN,

(Orders of Angels—
Seraphs, Cherubs, Thrones, Dominions, Virtues, Powers, Principalities, Archangels & Angels!)

Ms Dorothy J Hamilton
BRIMSTONE
Burning stone
Returning stone
Instant evil-churning stone
Monstrous evil-churning stone
Sulfureous stone
Toxic stone
Often caustic stone
Netherworld, underworld
Encircled by the River Styx—
surrounded by the Devil's
evil Flicks!*
and (Tricks)
St. Elmo—Oh, No!!
that riverboat it was all for SHOW!
*(Silent movies—Nickelodeon)

Ms Dorothy J Hamilton
RUDOLF!
Since Rudolf has become a Celebrity
Quite often has been said
His popularity's gone
Straight to his head
Whenever he doesn't get
what he wants immediately
he blows his fuse!
When the Yuletide rolls
around hope it blows
and snows
Goodness knows what
might happen
If Rudolf ever decides
to blow his nose!

Ms Dorothy J Hamilton
BALTHAZAR, CASPAR AND MELCHIOR?
These 3 of pencel we
need not at any length
dwell,
If they ever knocked at your
door would you immediately
meet the floor?
In their quest? Why,
by prophet bards foretold!
The Age of Gold was
foretold and with the
argentic idea
Joseph of Arimathea with
next to no help from Kerioth
We can say both, maybe
all 3, or mangered house did see!

Ms Dorothy J Hamilton
HOBGOBLIN HALL
WHEN Jack-o-Lanterns gleam,
Witches, warlocks, ghouls scream,
Moon and stars icily glistering,
Witches and Phantoms sistering!
Along the mansion's broad hall-way
There's a masquerading you
would find most corposant
Bells chiming, there's even
a tintinnabulation
sensation
As icicles form such a fine
line
With a hoot, howl, yawp
and then stop—Friends,
As St. Elmo's fire descends—
The Dragon all serpentine
and furry
Whizzes by in such a
hurry as hobgoblins,
scurry every which
way
He's headed for "THE Wagon"
for a go at "THE Flagon"
A Drunken Dypsomaniac
about to reside in yonder
coffin—a reminder that
so often "Hobgoblin Hall"
has made them take the fall.
His Lunatic maniac ravings
with his cravings for
debauchery put "The Dragon"
in the Funeral Wagon.

Ms Dorothy J Hamilton
MOOSE AND GOOSE GOT LOOSE!
(The Canadian Moose And Goose)
For a variation of this
versification
There is no drouth of
abuse and criminal
excuse
Of how that situation
came about
north or south!
There's a fouth and routh
even by word of mouth
That our Canada Moose and
Goose got loose, they were on
the giggle juice and
someone took dead aim and
they got the blame!

Ms Dorothy J Hamilton
ARCH-BISHOP ANSELM
He of helmet and pelmet
not strolling by hearth
and garth but seated 'neath
trusty oak and elm, with the
soverign who was so great at the
helm of "The Ship of State,"
Strumming on his harmonium,
along came Ladies Bea and
Pelar Gonium;
To get their poppy 'broidered copy
of "The Benedictus"—exact
copies from his own hand—
at royal Command? Yes,
indeed poppy 'broidered copies
and lest we pass by without
noting that they were by
Anselm personally blest!

Ms Dorothy J Hamilton
REMEMBRANCE!!
Red poppies—blood red poppies
Each one wind-blown, copies from
the
* Master's Illumined Hands;
Each one wind-blown, copies from
the
Master's Illuminated Lands; in
Bygone days of World War I Angels
of Mons (Blgm.)
Ready to
Attack—allies forced "The Enemy"
back;
Now we see "Flander's Field"
(fate) future sealed,
Crosses, crosses interspersed with
floral tribute
Each one wind-blown, copies from
the Master's Hands, "The
Foe"—Mute—Pandemonium's
Pawns!

*Lord God Almighty!

Ms Dorothy J Hamilton
THOSE AMAZING CREATURES

The Stork	with fan shaped
The Turtle	plumage and
The Crane	misty, diaphanous
The Peacocks	wings and
The Serpents	such things;
The Cockatrices	turquoise
The Dragons	tortoise, such timorous creatures
Jrmh. 8:17	with many distinctive,
Jrmh. 9:11	fascinating and varied features;
&	AMAZING Paraphrasing
Genesis 1.	of "The Fifth Day!"
Dtnmy. 14 1-18	What of "Vulture Culture?"

Ms Dorothy J Hamilton
BRIGHTEN THE CORNER WHERE YOU ARE
God's watching O'er us whether
near or far
Sun with evening and morning
STAR
Brighten The Corner Where You
Are!
Over Horizons Autumn's Setting
Sun—The God—
The One;
No Angels Singing, No Jubilant
bells ringing, Yes
Zinging and pinging for
Our Island Universe's Shore
guess where
Over "The Rainbow" and "The
Equator"
World Ranger—no stranger whether
earth, Betelgeuse,—whether
Hyksos or Peasant—dine on
bustard,
pheasant, custard and no mayo
no
mustard.

Ms Dorothy J Hamilton
NARWHAL OR NON-MONSTER
Whether "look out below"—
Geronimo or
"Narwhal" or "Lochness
Monster"
'Tis the season to be jolly with
eringo oh sea holly;
way down
Below in "Davey Jones" Locker
(J.P.)
or
That arm of the sea—what
Maritime scenery by 1993!
Sea food with the accompaniment
of "The Maritime Hymn" Rhythm
with
Lighting from "Star Fish"
so swank, so surish.
As you enjoy Maritime railway
Atlantis travel under "The English
Channel!"
Whether floral arrangements from:
"Frond, Kelp and Pankton"
You'll have a lichen for
various shades of decor—
Chartreuse, puce, purple, orange
and mauve
So, on and on and on
NARWHAL For Sale!

Ms Dorothy J Hamilton
NO NAME BIERS!
From 969 years to a mere
120 years
So many of Longevity each
whose name in Gns. 5-9
appears!
Gave untold benefits to
mankind
Theirs no no-name biers!
Such empathy with humanity.

Methuselah	969
Jared	962
Noah	950
Adam	930
Seth	912
Cainan	910
Enos	905
Malaleel	895
Enoch	365
Moses	120

Ms Dorothy J Hamilton
MEMORY LANE
Down "Memory Lane" we travel
again and again
Life's melodious, meaningful,
often time melancholy
refrain;
A constant reminder—follow
God's commandments—Acts 7:35
of "THE
Bush" burning as "The
Decalogue" page was turning—
Save yourself and others
much pain and strain;
By our ever mindful example—
don't dismantle—be really alive—
as there's everything fine and
rewarding to gain!

Ms Dorothy J Hamilton
MOTHER BARNES
Mother Barnes—
Aquarius or Sagittarius,
Jukes or Kallikaks,
Mazzaroth or Zodiacs,
Hyksos or Planxty
Airs—these or those,
With her 6th sense,
no pretense—
one most surely dares
To heed and hearken
not harangue and harp;
She from 1800-1890
in Athens Ontario
known as
"the Little Witch of
Hog's Hollow!"
A
Buoyant/Clairvoyant!

Ms Dorothy J Hamilton
TAKE AN ETERNAL BOW!
Catherine Lundy—of that
Bealltainn Lane
Tending those grieved and
teary, even fatigued weary,
warriors of 1812
With whatever weapons—sabre,
musket, axe or helve
With prayers of Thanksgiving

and praise with many a
proud voice would raise
You'd hear—, "Lunêtre, Fenestra,
Église, École and such
as these!
Content to tend those military
giants with strength and
encouragement—with a
cooling spring breeze salutations
glister
and praise to our Canadian Sister!
great gratitude to:
Duchess D'Auigillon
C.1630—like Percivate
She responsible for
first N.(orth) A.(merican)
Hospital;
from Zebec to Quebec
and now some of her
heroic Canadian sisters—
each a
Glister Sister:

Abigail Becker—praise bedecker
C.1850 (Ont.) (often time weary
that ship-wreck—on Lake Erie,
Alys Bryant—1913

Alys Bryant—C.1913 (B.C.)—1913
aviatrix with stellar fix so valiant
and self-reliant! That was Alys
Bryant!

Laura Secord—C.1814 (Ont.)—With
one accord heroine blessed by our
Heavenly Lord.

Posthuma Simcoe C.1800's (Ont.)—
"The Lady of the Lake" no
mistake!?
(Lake Simcoe is near Orillia)
Yes—she married Ontario's 1st
Lt./Governor—you know,
Ontario's
Posthuma Simcoe!

Kathy M Manley
LIFE LONG FRIENDS
Reflecting back on my tender age,
I identified who made me the
person I am.
Beginning with mistakes I made
during premature adulthood,
Reasonable punishments were set
in my life.
Learning the hard way, I finally
realized they were right.
Although I came close to doing the
worst, they always seemed to
understand.
Open ears and communication led
us through the pain.

Time after time, I brought them days
of anguish.
Friendships going sour, boyfriends
causing crises,
other friends' family problems,
and my usual day to day
irritability.
Making my troubles theirs, they
would walk through fire for me.

Open arms and a shoulder to cry on
helped me through my miseries.
Up until all hours of the night with
me,
my heartaches became part of
them.
In their own special way, they always
tried their hardest
to shield me from all the hurt and
pain.

Molding my values, giving me high
morals,
Believing in me, and building my
confidence,
They provided me with my
excellence.
Giving me the most they could and
sticking with me through good and
bad . . .
My parents became my BEST
FRIENDS!

Ms Dorothy J Hamilton
WHO IS?
Who is The Universe's Olympian—
is he Raphael—Spanish
banish or is vanish?
Should
Aramaic language of a
silver/golden age!
Space Travel,
Selah, Selah! Selah!
Mene, Mene, Tekel Upharsin—
Plaister of Paris,
Eloi, Eloi, Lama Sabachthani
Tibetan Monk of China, that is,
Abba! Tabitha Cumi!
Ephphatha! Rabboni!
That's a feather in his hat and they
called it "Macaroni."
HALLELUJAH!
You trudge thru mountains
from Wales to Alaska
Juneau how for the Glory Star
Is—"The Wizard of Oz" is not
Show Biz

Ms Dorothy J Hamilton
WHO'S WHO?
Eboracums, Caernarvons, Snowdons
There's a lot you know & they
know we Ott-tu-doo,
There's a gnashing, crashing
wail and cry out from
the Cosmos-sky of
blue is
Heaven's domain with Kraal and
swaddling band (Job 38:9)
Not in vain Knights Graal and
Cup, goblet and skaal
Each and every land with their
village and tillage—"Skoal" is our
goal!

Rebecca A Shaw

Rebecca A Shaw
HER TAXIED HEART

To Him: Thanks for the evocation of hearts delight, of precious moments of illusive beautiful memories.

His eyes, exhilarate and capture . . .
that—tenacity which makes her
breathing labored;
as, in a frolicked heart-beat paralyzed
by rapture.
Surmounting pleasure obligates—
disarrays . . .
solidifies the heart and mind as one.
Captured and imbued, his intoxifying
eyes have won.
She separates her despair, a unit of
duplicity, to shun.
Her men's sana lies, lamenting while
it was his to mien.

Cognizant reality . . . more content!
"The pain is less, says she,
I now should know of heart-less
minds, because of the pain in my
mind-less heart.
His eyes, HIS EYES, my God . . .
those endearing lies!"
Now, she never peers into that
two-faced place;
that doublet concealing vacuum,
that tears her heart and lies,
rips it from its caged space,
guiles it to her sleeve; wiles it
there . . .
His—pace—her—heart—must—
race . . .

Rebecca A Shaw
CREATIVITY UNITED

To artists of all forms. Thank you for making life a tolerable existence.

Poetry, like abstract art, is literature
a labyrinth complexity, remotely
tiered.

It's music beats to different hearts,
the purpose and interpretation to
endear

As ears take in the beauty,
In mind's eye a painter's palette does
appear.

A sacrosanct choir of star-dust,
sprinkles joy upon those near.

The conductor's gift, an adagio for
you and I,
engulfing emptiness, and blanking
out the tears.

A gift of love—a love of gift.
Wrapped so translucent, all
encompassed to appear.

The artist, eases his midnight sorrow,
as we relate our own, he holds us
near.

Born a canvas of white, our senses of
hue and value,
we keep adding to the spectrum, until
our end is here.

A pristine sharing of truth and
beauty,
rendered for contentment, crystal
clear.

Guy Swanson
CHRISTMAS MORNING
It's Christmas! It's Christmas! Oh
boy what fun!
Oh look! Oh look! what they got for
their son.
The thing I wanted most of all,
The thing that was big and so very
tall—
Not a toy train and not a sweet cane,
Not a toy horse and not a red
Porsche,
But the thing I'll love,
and the thing I'll cherish—
The thing that I'll never ever share—
Is my new giant teddy bear.

Sonyia A Stone
MY FRIEND

Dedicated to my daughter Kristen for her compassion and love for all God's creatures.

I had a friend who was quiet and shy
did not say much and never asked
why.

She was loyal and faithful and for
that I have always been grateful.

She was strong and lasting through
all my times, good and bad, happy
and sad but most important you see
she was there just for me.

My secrets we shared, and there were
many but I never feared that she
would tell any.

She trusted me so to do what was
right I hope she knows I did try
with all my might.

Our friendship was for seventeen
years then came true all of my fears.
Her eyes dimmed and then I knew it
wouldn't be long, my friend would
be gone.

Soon after I laid my little dog to rest,
and although she's not around any
longer this friend of mine, her
blessing of love she left behind.

Kathryn Vernon
GRANDPARENT
To be a grandparent can be a lot of
fun,
You get to love a lot when they are
young,
Spoiled as they may become
grandchild is a lot of fun,
Sunshine comes in their smile as they
are with you awhile,
Cranky they can be when not sitting
on your knee,
Their language changes many a word
some you have never heard,
Friendly and bright they're the
bestest buddy of your life,
You watch them grow,
See them change and learn,
Onto bigger and better they go, but
always to be a grandchild,
Not a sister, niece or a 2nd. cousin,
but forever my grandchild

Rebecca L Davis
YOU ARE
You are my light when I have
darkness
and my joy when I am sad.

You are the sunshine that brightens
my day
and the moon that guides my night.

You are the happiness that chases my tears away
and the laughter to replace my frown.

You are my blanket when I am insecure
and my crutch when I need support.

You are my hope when I have doubt
and my vision when I need motivation.

You are my fire when I am cold
and my food when I need nutrition.

You are my knight in armour when I need to be rescued
and my bodyguard when I need protection.

You are my love when I feel hate.

You are my friend when I'm alone.

You are my everything when I have nothing.

You are my life,
my dream,
my fantasy.

John B Walters

John B Walters
WHAT IS LIFE

Dedicated to Ada Black.

Life is like waking up in the morning and thanking God for another day.
Life is like seeing the sun shine through your window for the first time.
Life is like someone you care about.
Life is like going to your job and enjoying it.
Life is like going through the woods and seeing the animals running free.
Life is like seeing your friends and neighbors with a smile on their face.
Life is like driving through the countryside just you and your family.
Life is just being yourself.

Roselle G Broeckel
EASTER "MOURN"
To those of you who Easter morn
Share not with us the first of dawn
When God's bright sun bids us again.
Awake! Proclaim our faith anew.
You in the cause your young hearts gave
Your hopes, your dreams, your life your all
To help a world to better be
A circle of true humanity
Where men will live, not have to die
To understand the reason why
Rest in belief we too shall try to
Make an earthly paradise

Margie Adamson
THE STREETS ARE HOME TO PEOPLE
Take time to see the people;
Take time to feel their pain
Look into their faces and you will find you gain . . .
The joy of helping others
And ease their hurting souls
Reach deep into your own heart
And share that "Pot of Gold."

THE STREETS ARE HOME TO PEOPLE

The streets are home to people
who've lost their place to live . . .
It's time we reach inside us and ask them to forgive—
Our years of never caring or looking in their eyes—
The streets are home to people
Please do not let them die.

For the joy we bring to others
No measure can be named
So share their weary hearts
and ever feel their pain

For the joy we bring to others
No measure can be named
Let's stop and see the roses
And even smell the rain

For love it is the answer
Yes love it is the gold
These riches shared among us
Helps keep away the cold.

The streets are home to people
who've lost their place to live . . .
It's time we reach inside us and ask them to forgive
Our years of never caring or looking in their eyes—
The streets are home to people
Please do not let them die.

Take time to smell the roses and even taste the rain,
Lift your arms to others and help to ease their pain—
For they are all around us, people young and old
Gather up your courage and share their weary load . . .

The love you give to others, no measure can be named—
Share their weary heart and even feel their pain . . .
Love it is the answer
Love it is the gold
These riches shared amoung us helps keep away the cold.

Lord, today you led us to look into the face of a beautiful man whose steel-blue eyes were stonecold from the streets; wrapped in plastic, he waited for nothing. Would he accept our pitiful offer of a few coins? Only from someplace deep in his troubled heart would he help to ease my troubled heart by saying — YES.

Lord, today you answered the rhetorical question: Am I my brothers keeper? --- Yes; and he is mine . . .

Tilly Van Norman
SAMSON
At school the teacher asked this question,
What is your most valued possession?

I gave the question a lot of thought
Of things I'd been given, things I had bought.
The one that means the most to me
Is Samson, my little red leppie;

When Dad brought him for me to feed
He was so little, in so much need,

His little legs were not quite right
Something about him was not quite bright;
For the first ten days he couldn't even see
For everything he depended on me.

I brushed him, fed him kept him warm
Did all I could to keep him from harm.

All the other leppies Dad brought home
Have all grown up, out on the range they roam
Samson is different in so many ways
He stays around the barnyard to spend his days,

I pet him and hug him and feed him grain
He still has problems and that gives me pain . . .

He has so many problems you see
But I love him and he loves me.

Dionne Frey
REMEMBER
He is a man
Of few words
But many thoughts.
He will be alone forever
In his heart;
Even when he is
With another.
Since I can never
Give him my heart,
I will give him
Something to
Remember me by.
And with his
Guitar slung over
His shoulder
He walks alone,
Yet never alone;
For the strings on
His guitar are
The strings of my heart.

Larry Johnson

Larry Johnson
mae west again
the best in the west
to me struts my moll
in her jet- black fishnets
here she comes! on the beach
in the sack
and back to the highway stretching
the squeeze from a blonde who needs much dough
and gallons of creamy water
to quench her thirsty
donut smile

from a bakery mold
sweet and tartly rolled
her bust would burst
courts wide open
and fill them full of lead,
tossing down all jurys
with the motion of her head

mae west again!

Larry Johnson
CHARMING RHAPSODY
Angels! i do beckon thee to hear these words of power—
Michele is my candle when darkness doth devour

She gives comfort when lances of havoc reign
aimed for Achilles' heel—still my beast remains untamed
unseen by the useless eyes of shame and will rest in glory
when dealt a fearsome, ruthless game

Michele doth clothe me in armour
of circles unbroken, pendants and chants
as we sacrifice grains of sand
swirling within the century glass.
with our moonlight dance
the blustery stars conceived in heaven
have never known such a fiery romance
as Angels bless our love with Seven,
brushing Michele's hair with silvery stardust
as i kiss her raspberry lips
the sacred hour following eleven . . .
12 and her rainbow eyes become my wishing well
both yielding freely
to the charming rhapsody of Cupid's magic spell!

Larry Johnson
sea wings
feathers part the wind that sweeps the sea
down below the fishing boats anchor before dusk
and porpoises high above hear the signal of my plea
let the wells wash over me: save me from eternal dust

wings are for the seafaring souls of yesteryore
voodoo handed down to flocks that dream of no remorse
to fly on beyond jaws of death alive no more
to anchor in the peaceful cove and never stray from course

must i fly alone thru the distant veil beyond?
the sirens harp and whales ballet upon thrashing wave again, again
in answer the shards of glaciers fell at once
sunken fathomless depths below and lost in secret caves

Pricilla Brown
IT'S SIMPLE

To Father Mother & my three girls Lila, Oprah, Chanae.

Sure I can write a poem
It's as easy as 123
Every line I write rhythm

And a poet I will be

Sometime you sit talking to yourself
Then wonder is you really need help
That's not insane as you suppose
'Cause loneliness leaves only
yourself to hold.

To daydream you tamed something
wild
The thought alone makes u smile
From Cartoon Carnival to Whoopi
Goldberg
Or something funny you've seen or
heard

I can think of big words to say
Not knowing a meaning in any way
Instead I'll keep it simple for you
And write a poem which is easy to do

Calvin D Hoffman
COLE PARK

To Julie, my wife, whose gentle love I treasure.

Darkened waters on the rocks
In broken rhythm
Lap and splash,
Reflecting sombre heaven.

A lonely paper cup,
The water at its lip,
Eludes the danger deep
And bobs away in laughing sips.

I wonder when a wave will break
And leap its rim
And sink it to the deep
As refuse on the bottom dim.

Here and there a seagull
Swims in the sky
And flaps and dips
And snatches something floating by;

And lifts again,
And like a mobile on a string
It hangs; then glides
And screams at unknown things.

Nonie Ann Ingalls
SLOW DOWN

To my Father, my Friend. A man whose love and guidance has been an important part of my life. This poem, my promise to you because I Love You.

The old man sighed,
The child cried,
No one even tried.
To understand or ask,
Why Sir what's the matter?
So he could reply,
My how things have changed!
No one stopped long enough
To tell the little one
Her socks didn't match.

Slow down,
Don't be in such a hurry.
The old man has a story to tell.
The little one wants to learn.

Slow down,
Before the old man's story
Can never be told
And the little one just doesn't care.

Phyllis Jean Jones
DOLLARS AND GOOD SENSE

Dedicated to all who survive on Social Security as I do! With love your Sister in Christ.

I don't have many dollars, but I have
many friends,
and I have peace of mind at dusk,
when my day ends.
Each day I read God's word, then I
kneel and pray, for wisdom to help
family and friends along their way.
I used to pray for dollars, think how
rich I'd like to be,
then I realized riches, would only
change the inner me.
It's taken many years to learn, it's
what's inside that counts,
you can't measure people, with dollar
sign amounts.
Mere money couldn't buy the love
my family has for me,
living in this circle of love, is how I
always want to be.
Dollars are necessary, as they help to
pay our bills,
but can never hold the answer to all
society's ills.
So love comes first, I place money in
past tense,
yes love for all, next we all need
common sense,
yet, when we haven't any money, life
gets pretty tense.
Wouldn't it be great to have both
dollars and good sense.

Dorothy B Ponczek
BAHIA HONDA

It is so extreme, the beauty I have
seen
Nowhere is the quiet so intense
As on this beach.
From it I can watch the sun set,
As it flashes its brilliance
Across the gulf waters.

The warmth engulfs my body
And draws me closer to the sand.
I can see the bridge in the distance,
but I can't hear it.
I disappear within myself and feel
what you feel

At once I am the bird on the horizon
And the Anglefish off the reef.
The tireless fisherman drawing his
nets,
And the child saying its prayers in the
Keys.

Too soon I am jolted
And become, once again, me.
But so as never to forget this
moment,
I give it to you now,
A piece of my soul,
embodying the world.

Sonia Hixon
CONSIDER LIFE AS A SCHOOL, A FARM AND A RIVER

To Richard,
My patient, loving husband.

When life's problems, and upside
downs knock the wind out of you,
and you're flat on the ground, take a
while to recuperate,
but get up, even with a slow start.

Things are not always as bad as they
seem.
You can cope! With perseverance,
courage and hope.

A school because we must learn from
our mistakes,
don't be doubtful of everyone and
everything.
There is some good left in the world.

A river because all of life's problems
are really stepping stones.
So no matter how many times you
must groan, your life is still the only
life you own.

Don't worry about failing;
broken-hearts and bruised pride.
Experience life and live it! Because
in fact, There's really no place to
hide.

Do your thing whatever that may be,
No one's life is ever easy.
A few tears help, the seed of life to
grow.
And the loving "you" helps to bring
it to harvest.

Much later you will notice, that with
God's help,
You've farmed the best crop yet.

Herbert L Carter
THE KING AND I

The King and I walk hand in hand
On my road to the Promised Land.

His Signs I see, from time to time
And His Love is ever Sublime.

He foretells of many perils that await
As the many blindly grope for
their fate.

Many are they who would assail
But the Will of the Lord shall
prevail.

Though I am weak, in Him am I
strong
And in His Love, I am never
wrong.

I may ever a pauper be
My Riches await in Eternity.

His Spirit is above all other
That I may be as His Brother.

He raises me to the Heights Supreme
And fills me with the Eternal
Dream.

Herbert L Carter
VOWS

One dost toss aside the ring of love
As though there is no God above.

Is there no sacred vow
That bonds the heart forever now?

Vows in Truth are made Above
They will bring Eternal Love.

Though my world is empty now
To the Lord I have a Vow.

Celestial Heights do I seek to roam
There dwell upon the Ethereal
Throne.

The Lord hast prepared my Place
And I shall not pass without a
Trace.

The pen has etched as in Words of
Stone
That all may seek and Atone.

Makest thou a Sacred Vow
Find the Way to keep it now.

Prayer will seal it True
'Til there shall come the New.

Hold dear thy Love that all may
know
Both shall share the same Halo.

Herbert L Carter
TO MY LOVE

I bring a precious gift to you
A heart that will be forever true.

As a treasure from above
It brings all my love.

Keep it not lightly now
For I have made the Vow.

I shall honor thee in many ways
And hold dear thy love always.

I am thine alone
And for my failings, I atone.

I am lost without thee
For my love is unto Eternity.

A Vow, I will never break
Honor will never be forsake.

My heart, once given
Is ever unto Heaven.

Herbert L Carter
HIS HALIDOM

A-top the highest mountain
Upon the shining sea
There exists a Holy Place
Wherever I may be.

The soul reaches out
In prayer each day
That the Lord will answer
And lead me in His Way.

I am cloaked in His Robe
And steeped in His Love
Angels sing His Praise
Always from Above.

My destiny is in the stars
Man cannot erase
The Angel watches o'er me
That I may see His Face.

Comes the New Dawn
And all life's work is done
I shall exalt in His Grace
And revel Forever in His Halidom.

Ada Kantor
AND THEN LIFE BECOMES A CHERRY

To my sister LANA, whom I love dearly.

Dreams were meant to be broken
And life can be a bitch,
But you can collect the tokens,
And buy yourself a treat.
Anything you want, you can get,
If you are willing to forgive and
forget.
If you are willing to pay the shilling
You may also get the top billing.
Money, Money, Money!!
That's all it takes.
If you collect a lot,
And hit the Jack Pot,
Then your life becomes a cherry!!!

Ada Kantor
SHOULD I . . . ?

Am I pretty? Am I fat?
Do you think I'm too flat?
Do you find me boring?
Should I smile more, be jolly?
Should I act holy, or rebellious?
Should I listen to Beethoven, or to
Beetles?
Should I read King Lear, or the
Shining?
Should I jog a mile, do aerobics?
Tuck my buttocks,
Find a job, make more bucks?
Or should I stay home and be a cute
hostess?
Should I talk with vulgarity,
Or should I memorize the dictionary?
Tell me, What should I do,
To be like you, and make you like
me,
Or is that impossible, and highly
unlikely?

Ada Kantor
WAR

Missiles flying,
People dying,
Mother's crying,
Father's gone to war.
Children frightened of the bullets
Headed for the door,
Begging: "MISTER, PLEASE
DON'T HURT US ANY MORE,
WE'RE THE CHILDREN OF THE
FUTURE
HEAR OUR VOICES AND OUR
PLEA:
'STOP THE FIGHTING, START
UNITING,'
THAT'S THE ESSENCE OF OUR
DREAMS!!!!"

Helen C Shallcross
REFLECTIONS

Beauteous splendor in Rocky mountains.

There is a beauteous splendor, high in
the mountains
Where voices and noise are lost in the
silence of God's wondrous world
Where land and horizon meet in a
marriage
To a cosmic beyond all
comprehension

Birds find their sanctuary in leaves
that never fall
Stars abound in the inestimable
galaxies
The moon plays hid and seek with
the lowering sun

Then dawn creeps in with rainbow
colors
Never to be recorded by camera's eye
And aromas that titilate the senses,
Awakening wonder
Filling the spirit and soul to depths
unfathomable

Ah, that man should search and find
and sense
The gloriousness of God's nature
High in the high clarity of air, purity
in soul and mind
Seared of all frustrations, cleansed
for another day

Elizabeth Eugenia Kapp
OUR HOUSE

To my father, Carl, who supported and furnished our house. And to Julia, my mother, who truly made it into a home.

Our house is large with fourteen
rooms
A garden in the rear
A wide front door the hallway
grooms
And greets those who appear

Five porches lead within or out
Depending on your view
The house is tall and wide and stout
And readily welcomes you

Enclosed by cellar cool and attic
stocked
With toys and treasures old
Our house stands out along our block
As quite well-kept we're told

Cream columns grace the front
facade
Two benches greet our guests
And offer them a quiet place
To pause, relax, and rest

Shrubs and arbors do the house
surround
We see them back and front
Hedges and ivy grow along the
ground
Where squirrels and rabbits hunt

The house within gives warmth to all
The rooms so full of things
Reminding us of days of old
And happiest memories brings

Wine cellar holding colored flasks
Red lamps in rooms do glow
Walls in flowered paper bask
Especially the yellow rose

The silver service newly cleaned
Prints by Currier and Ives
Long bannister with circular bend
Down which we all did slide

Orientals cover most all floors
Which shine so from shellac
One always smells the lemon oil
And freshly polished wax

Three fireplaces warm our home
In the kitchen homemade soup
Heats up atop our old gas stove
To soothe our hungry group

In the music room of pink and blue
We'd often meet to chat
And hear a quite familiar tune
With drink from golden glass

Red block adorns the table bright
With festive Christmas plates
And candles lit we'd all arrive
To dine no less than eight

Our house we know is old and so
May not forever be
But in our minds it's always there
Aglow for us to see.

Elizabeth Eugenia Kapp
EDGAR COTTAGE

There is a place 'long Lavallette's
shore
A cottage small and yet secure
'Gainst ocean wind and rising tide
A summer haunt where Edgars abide

Bare wood retained in natural state
Place where guests may sleep in late
Then rise to walk along the sand
And view the ocean just at hand

Peace and quiet are always there
Relaxation in a porch rocking chair
Deep sleep in an iron attic bed
Sea wave sounds to gently nod the
head

And like its owner Mistress Liz
The cottage strong yet gentle is
Welcoming and warm to all its guests
Yet preserving needed quiet rest

Never a phone may dare there ring
Disturbing chat or slumbering
Or rest next to the fireplace warm
In gold/green room of comfort
charm

Somehow the air and atmosphere
Create happy good-natured cheer
One wouldn't dare there to complain
Or ever feel an ache or pain

Umbrella'd picnics in the sand
Seafood suppers really grand
Rice, tomatoes — spinach too
Followed up with beauteous fruit

(Always the food tastes better there
Perhaps since spiced with ocean air)
Long strolls along a wooden walk
And in the evening abundant good
talk

By day a lot of splashing fun
A swim to cool from summer sun
With life preservers red and green
And Skol or favorite sun screen

An outdoor shower overhead
Helping sticky sand to shed
Then predinner race along the water
Getting trousers wetter than they
ought

With sunburned bodies oh but good
And too stuffed from plenteous food
Tossed and tumbled pumpkinheads
Would climb nodding into bed

By eight o'clock the guests would go
Hesitantly and really quite slow
For how they dreaded so to leave
'Twas all too short but perfect
reprieve

Belongings passing back and forth
A cake for Liz and rolls for Jude
Favorite ritual of giving
Silly seeming but relieving

The boys would race away the cars
Huffing, stretching legs and arms
'Til they left around the bend
Signaling sacred Sunday's end

The cottage sturdy on Avenue Kerr
To visitors offers strong an elixir
Way afar from the city's throng
It utters just a sea breeze song.

Elizabeth Eugenia Kapp
KAOKES

Above the shores of Susquehanna
Was a Walden called The Creek
Where all the relatives of Irma
Would for many summers meet

They met there at Camp Kaokes
Where they'd fish and swim and eat
At night they'd hear the frog and
crickets
Just before they'd doze toward sleep

The sounds of katydid and hoot owl
Would prevail the trees around
The whippoorwill with haunting call
And the water rushing down—

Over the dam and round behind
The cottage neat and white above
Which housed the whole Kaokes
tribe
And was their favorite summer love

The Kapps, the Kestys, Sobers and
Owens
Did for many years meet there
Crossroad for their comings and
goings
A haven truly, really rare

Lying on the dock in sun
Or skipping stones across the creek
Always they had heaps of fun
As they would after treasure seek

Arrowheads along the shore and
Fossil stones and snake skins on
The lower level of the dam
Where they would try an echo song

The smell of sun on wooden boat
Of fragrant grasses and of trees
The sight of birches on the shore
And water rippling from the breeze

All these the tribesmen knew and
more
Of pleasures at this summer place
They'd canoe and swiftly dip their
oar
And round the islands they would
race

To the jungle they would go
Well up beyond Arbutis Park
And see the lily-pod and toad
And bats above as it grew dark

Evenings they'd gather on the porch
For pinochle and Chinese checkers
The children settled on the couch
Would read by oil lamp to each other

When time would come the pump to
prime
And then to go on up the stair
The stars into their eyes would shine
On the porch for sleeping there

When morning came they all would
wake
And gathering chamber pots in hand
To house of moon and star would
take
Then brush their teeth on birmbank
land

And now that cottage, Camp Kaokes
Where traveling tribesmen came to
rest
Did move away amidst great protest
For there were those who thought it
best

But many tribesmen so remember
That 'tis said the place lives on
And as each summer nears
September
Still they hear the "jig-o-rum" song!

Elizabeth Eugenia Kapp
ADVICE FROM THE MAID

Polish the door knob
Sweep the steps
A mighty man enters within

All do be quiet
Show him respect
Be sure not to bother him

He is our strength
He is the master
He is in charge of us all

He was willing
To learn and seek after
What was needed for him to walk tall

Don't ask questions
Unless you are asked
His time is the greatest in value

Let him be free
To finish his tasks
Don't disturb him unless you're
allowed

Make his life easy
For higher deeds
And if he appears not to attend—

To our matters important
He still answers our needs
And will look after us well in the end

Be charming, polite
Don't stay in his way
And be sure not to tarry too long

For he will be restless
Toward the next day
So shorten your violin song

Oft' in a hurry
A slight bit abrupt
He soon might ask you to leave

Please do not worry
Tho' he might interrupt
It's not for you to grieve

Walk very lightly
Tiptoe if you must
And quietly close the door

Where he is concerned
All must be hushed
Calm is what he's looking for

When his labor is through
The curtains he'll part
The heavy doors will slide wide

He'll enter the room
You'll jump up with a start
No more lying down on your side

He may seem busy
Too much so to care
And you must curb your laughter

But if you're distressed
He will be there
The first to ask what's the matter

He'll listen if he must
But make no mistake
He'll like you best if you're good

'Tho don't be afraid
Even tho' you might shake
If he had to understand you he could

Polish the door knob
Sweep the steps
He's nearly ready to come in

Now if you look closely
Tho' you may not expect
You'll see 'neath his mustache a grin.

Elizabeth Eugenia Kapp
OLD SUMMER HOUSES
Old summer houses
With white wicker chairs
Wide screened in porches
And creaking wooden stairs

The paint gently peeling
From off outer walls
Adds intrigue charming
To view inner halls

Chintz prints and pastels
And the faint scent of damp
Perhaps when day darkens
A kerosene lamp

There may be houses
Close to the shore
Of a river, a lake
Or near an ocean roar

Or in a wooded area
Where birds and creatures fly
Or alongside a mountain—
Companion of sky

Mansion or cottage
It makes not a diff—
Whether lawns are overgrown
Well-manicured or clipped

What is it about them
You might wonder friend
That brings about changes
And fences does mend

Ladies and gentlemen
The guests all become
Yet still remain capable
Of being a chum

Good manners, respect
Contagious good fun
Is it simply the presence
Of an abundance of sun?

Perhaps as in nature
There's a keeping in tune
A prelude to fall
For guests to be groomed

The sounds are so clear
And precise in the air
While still part of the whole
They're individually there

A call to a friend
A slamming screen door
Court with ball bouncing
A creak of the oar

Feet shuffling 'long
A dusty worn path
Or bare on the floor padding
En route to the bath

The rustling of curtains
Insects lazy humming
(The season of heaven
Must surely be summer)

But those old summer houses
Alone must remain
Throughout dismal winter
'Til spring comes again

Those vacant old houses
Their scenes, scents and sounds
Stay patiently waiting
For summer to come 'round

And when it arrives
Those houses are there
With yard gates wide open
To welcome and share

Whether rambling and rich
Or rustic and small
Those old summer houses
Show comfort to all

Old summer houses
Offering warmth like a friend
Do sadden us softly
When summer must end.

Kristen E Smith
FRIENDSHIP
I have something, but I'm really not sure if what I have,
Is what I want and if it's what I want how do I get it?
And if I get it what do I do with it?
It's mine
so why am I sad?
Because it isn't what I think.
It isn't love,
It's FRIENDSHIP
and it's just what I wanted.

Eric Bryant
INTO VIEW
I believe that there not an
Endless End,
the progress of utilization with
Human resource,
It's like the perpetual that all we
must lend,
And percipercate of the world
voice.

Almost always situation are in
your favor,
When you extrapolate before
others,
It's because of your
behavior,
That tend you to go much
further.

Thought of ideas in the
past,
Have a generation on
society,
I think that we have found the answer
at last,
And it comes in all varieties.

Some react in a familiar
way,
Which have not yet been
visualized,
The production of wave form happen
every day,
A retrospective may have been
syncronized.

Gloria Smith
WHEN I'M WITH YOU
The times I'm with you have to go uncounted like the stars in the sky, the waves in the ocean and the grains of sand on the beach.
Each time produces anxiousness for more tender moments and confidence in knowing these times won't hardly cease.

With this in mind, I look forward to more times of you and I sharing great pleasures.
It's kind of exciting, these moments going by uncounted, not to mention unmeasured.

Ruth M Syftestad
AS WE WALK
The pebbles on the highway
Are stepping stones we take
To woodland, field and snow capped mount,
To river, stream or lake.

And often on to foreign shores;
In winter, to warmer lands.
And sometimes even heavenward
As we travel in His hands.

Yes, the pebbles on the highway
Take us here and there alike,
As our thoughts and voices mingle
When we take our morning hike.

C J Owens
**YOU'RE ALWAYS THERE—
IN THE BACK OF MY MIND**
Always there in the back of my mind
I still remember our lovely garden
Of love with colors of a kind
I had not seen before or yet again

Always there in the back of my mind
I came to you incapable then
Of escaping your love to find
That kind not found before or yet again

Could you now know and believe this too
That once my love for you was true
And when the dewy past we knew
Was all gone, I tried so hard to tell you

About all my sorrow, but honey
The words did not come too easily
My memories are still the ones of the kind
I had not known before or yet again, sincerely
(So I will always keep them, in the back of my mind).

Jacqueline Daniels
HOPE
Through all the years, the hard times and the tears
there in the shadows of my life came a wounderous flash of light
and it set me free I said set me free
My soul is alive now so full of love
for the one who inspired me
to go on go fourth you can make it no matter how rough
oh yeah that's what he told me I'll get by
No need to worry he stands by me
right there beside me Oh my only love my wounderous light who let me see all that is right
Through his eyes I shall look
No more shadows darkening my path
all my tomorrows shall be bright
and my tears there just for joy I can't go wrong to love to live to be FREE

Jennifer Johnson
SKELETONS
Locked up tight
Are secrets of a past
To never be revealed.
In this secret hiding
Place are dreams and fears,
Forever to be sealed.
From the public's eye
The doubts are gone
And only to them seems,
A perfect world
Of an unbroken heart
And always-fulfilled dreams.

Loraine Greene
REINCARNATION
This can't be all—our constant fear
Is, "What's the point—why are we here?"

Life's span is brief—there must be more
To this adventure than some distant shore!

And so we try to analyze;
We study, dream and fantasize.

Life's brevity we will defy;
The sting of DEATH we must decry!

Is there a chance as some believe,
That FATE will final pain reprieve?

Vicissitudes of life are real;
A second time has great appeal!

Eternal life for which we yearn—
A fleeting myth; the pages turn.

As babes to mothers fiercely cling,
We cherish life, though knells will ring!

If REBIRTH is the master plan,
The truth remains unknown to man.

Janice L David
DREAMS AND GOALS

This poem is dedicated to my wonderful children, Chad and Melanie.

We all have our own dreams and goals.
We make our own choices of people in our lives who will play the biggest roles.
These dreams and goals will change over the years.
With these changes, there will be many fears.

The challenges we face will test our strength and weakness.
We may get the feeling that we will have to settle for less.
Sometimes it's easier to just give up when we are so full of doubt.
It takes patience enough to realize that there will always be another route.

We question our inner self to see who's really in control.
There will be a battle of emotions and it will take its toll.
Can we control our own destiny and fulfill our dreams?
This is a question that continually comes up, or so it seems.

We hear people tell us, "Never give up on your dreams."
Sometimes it can be a matter of choosing the right teams.
Be a winner, they say.
You can always find the way.

The emotional strains we put ourselves through,
The many changes that came as we grew,
The sacrifices that were made to reach those goals,
It is all worth it and it came from our hearts and our souls.

Harriet Smith Copp
THE BIBLE AND THE UMBRELLA

To God who gives me everything — including my poetry! To my wonderful son, Harry Copp, and to Pat Newell for encouragement.

I have read the Bible many times —
A dozen — perhaps more,
And each time that I read it,
I learn more than before.

So often, down a chapter,
I will realize that I,
Did not remember what I'd read,
Back, I'd go again — and try!

For if you let your mind stray;
There's not much you can gain,
It's like taking an umbrella,
And then standing in the rain!

In order to make use of it,
You must open it real wide,
Just as you should your wandering mind,
To the book and what's inside!

For if you don't know what you've read
And of this knowledge gain;
Just like a closed umbrella;
It can't shield you from the rain!

Harriet Smith Copp
WHERE THE WILD WIND ROARS

To God first — then to my son Bill Copp and his wife Allison. With special love always.

Dear God, let me dream that I can fly
Up thru the blue, where the moon rides high; —
Up, up, and away where the wild winds roar,
Where the eagles glide and dip and soar,
Then tumble about and beg for more!

Let me gather the stars in the dead of night,
And dance on the "Milky Way," so light,
That my feet will carry in fancy flight,
Wherever my dream will have me be,
Where the moon hangs high and the wind blows free!

Then, when my dream comes to an end —
On the gentle wave of a breeze, please send —
Me back to the earth, where I may tend,
To every day tasks, and the mundane chores,
Back from my dream, where the wild wind roars!

Harriet Smith Copp
OH, HOW I BASK IN HIS LOVE

To God, first and always and to my dearest and oldest friends — Winnie Smith, Wealthy Schoenhofen, Dr. Sally Stickel — Last, but not least, my lovely friend Holly Freedman.

When I speak to God — up in Heaven
Our Lord, who looks down from above —
His light reaches out to embrace me;
And, oh, how I bask in His love!

Whenever I ask Him for something. —
He'll say, "Just pass Me your cup!"
And then without fanfare or praises,
I'll find, to the brim, it's filled up!

There are times when I ask about Jesus; —
With patience, He'll always reply,
"Just dry all your tears now, and I will explain,
Why My dear son, had to die!

Yes, He took on the sins of all mankind,
He knew that His task was to pay,
For the dastardly deeds of the wicked,
Those who would throw Him away!"

Still, I wonder sometimes what He's thinking,
As He hands out His gifts from above; —
When His light shines on me, I'm so happy I'm free,
And, oh, how I bask in His love!

Marc and Linda

Ann Muscarello
MY CHILD, MY LOVE

This is dedicated to my children, Marc and Linda, whom I love dearly.

When you were in my tummy,
My love for you grew and grew.
Life was so sunny
Because I knew I would have you,
My child, my love.

When you came out,
What a beautiful sight!
I began to shout
With pure delight.
My child, my love.

You belong to me,
And you're all mine.
Cute as you can be,
Sweet as a Valentine.
My child, my love.

Mine to love,
And mine to hold.
Sometimes to kiss,
Sometimes to scold.
My child, my love.

As I sit back
And watch you play,
My heart bursts with joy.
Then to myself I say,
My child, my love.

Now I see you grow,
The way all children do.
And in my mind I know,
I will always love you.
My child, my love.

Brooke Buchanan (Age 10)
YOUR STORMY LOVE

crack of lightning
crashing of thunder
stormy windy nights
in the mid of summer

as the rain falls
i think of you
and of that love we shared
all night through

and when you left
i fell apart
with nothing else
but a broken heart

your love is lightning
your kiss is thunder
our love fell apart
in the mid of summer

come back to me
where you belong
for your thunder
is so very strong

Debbie Allen
I MISS YOU

This poem is dedicated to Nina Joyce Epler Allen, I love you Mom!!!

God had a reason for taking you away
And one day I hope to know why
Since he took away a special person
The day he chose for you to die.

Although I have no memories of you
And you are no longer here
You're always in my heart and mind
And one day we'll reunite there

I'm living my life as I think you'd want
And I hope from up there you're proud
Of who I am, and what I've become
For I'm doing it in the name of love.

Mom, each day of my life I think of you
And wish that you could be here
Sharing with me all my joys and pains
Because I miss you, and want you near.

Donald C Beach
WITHOUT ME

The wind whispers through the trees —
Amongst the leaves as though to say,
"Without me, there would be no breeze."

The sun writes with rays upon the earth —
Breaking the dawn as though to say,
"Without me, day would have no birth."

The rain inks with water onto the ground —
Flowing along streams as though to say,
"Without me, life could not abound."

The heart draws with desires across the mind —
Sketching its feelings as though to say,
"Without me, love you'll never find!"

Edith E Avila
A TEAR FROM THE HEART

I can't understand why you left me
I am a lonely girl filled with tears
I sit and wonder about you
I tell myself I shouldn't cry
Tears don't make up sadness!

When I met you, you brought me a smile
You were my happiness
You were all I ever thought about
And all I ever talked about.

I had you, you were once all mine
I belonged to you
And you belonged to me
It was me and you
Us two together
How I wish it would last forever.

Now you went your own way
And you left me a frown
The only good thing I have are memories
Inside my heart cries for you
I miss you so, with all my heart
Forever my heart will have a place for you.
To me there may be substitutes
But never one like you.

I love you always
and most of all I miss you so!

Frederick D Clark
WIFE POEM

A wife poem is the flower of her patience
sprung from the rich, deep soil of her strength.
It blossoms sweet and ripe like fresh star fruit
giving renewed life to weakened limbs and heart.
It is a thing that springs from her courage
and radiates like a polished crown jewel.

Frederick D Clark
LIVES
For African-American Youth
A dark child's life is sometimes a vision of thorns,
prickly and tangled, sprouting from the cracked soil of frustration.
It sometimes is a diamond rough,
precious but unpolished,
buried deep in the bowls of the heat.
It is a life crimson and grey,
sometimes gutted like tenement hulls.
A dark child's life is sometimes a festival
with colored ribbons streaming on the shoulders of the wind.
It sometimes is a life of cellar silence, damp
and musty in moments of fear.
A dark child's life is a magnificent thing,
multi-colored and brilliant and raging like the sea.

Karen Walker Stumpf
THE BUTTERFLY
(A METAMORPHIS)
My heart was young,
Light with touches of spring.
The world around me;
Fanciful, daring, unspoiled.
Nothing could stop me!
A ravenous hunger for life.

My heart grew heavy,
Filled with burdensome duties.
Many voices pushed and pulled.
I wrapped myself up in my cocoon
To shut the world out,
But change would not leave me alone.
I pushed against it,
But with it
I found new growth.

My heart carried a song
As the chrysalis burst open
And there,
Unfolded a magnificent butterfly.

Karen Walker Stumpf
WINTER SOLITUDE
Ruffled snow lies on lazy hillsides
crusted hard, entombing earth.
White organdy, its beauty lingers
though man longs for Spring's rebirth.

Naked trees stand tall against ashen sky
cast stenciled shadows across frozen lace.
Quiet solitude sings to no one here
as honeyed sun rises to warm this place.

Gail J VanWart
MOTHER'S THOUGHTS
When the distant patter of little feet
Run through her memory,
Of distant times in days gone by
Which only memories can see,
She pauses from her daily chores
For a little while . . .
And she alone appreciates
The reasons for her smile.

Since seasons only come to go,
There's nothing else she can do . . .
When there's no more Goldie Locks,
No more Little Boy Blue . . .
But to reminisce from time to time
When she thinks of you.
Wouldn't it be nice
If she was sure
You thought about her too?

Jeanne T Mancini
TOO LATE
When I was young I thought the world would be
Forever waiting for ever-youthful me
To fill a promised place in grand design,
A place I had no doubt would soon be mine.
But I took too long to grow into my fate,
And the impatient world decided not to wait.

Michele A Page
ALL CONSUMING EARTH

To my husband Daniel who gives me confidence.

There is so much we could all say
Concerning where we all stay,
Yes, earth is alive with a heartbeat
Breathing in all we dare feed it to eat.
The heart of earth is ticking away
Unable to digest all that we lay
Far beneath the earth's surface at the core,
Can it not take it all in beyond the shore?

All consuming man, greedy to build,
Streets are now paved, dumps are all filled.
We're racing too fast beyond the beat
Yes, all are guilty of filling the street.

Where do we turn, and to whom do we go?
Is there an answer? We all need to know.
Cleanse the earth with fire, wash it with snow.
God almighty the creator of all will show.

All consuming God teach us your way
This earth is nearly unfit for us all to stay.
We humble ourselves, and seek your face
Teach us all to clean up this earth, our place.

Michele A Page
A MOTHER'S LOVE

I dedicate this to my dear mother and my dear mother in law. Lucretia Cutcher and MaryJane Page.

A mother's love is like the center of a wheel
Spinning consistently around,
Her children surrounding on either side
Which she's sustained by each warm meal.

She's like the binding stitch in time
All things hold fast to her,
Without as such, her strength and touch
All else would be out of rhyme.

She meets the need before she's asked
Always one step ahead.
She sees on the inside to the heart
Things that cannot be masked.

She takes her stand with confidence and grace,
Strength in a time of weakness.
Giving of herself all she has,
No one can take her place.

She wants to be there for every need,
And rightly so she is,
Then in return for all she's sown
She'll reap love, we've all agreed.

Carol Schaefer
DAWN OF LIFE
The fiery ball rose from the hill,
Illuminating the earth below,
Signaling the dawn of a new day.
Despite the moon's determination,
The sun persisted and won the battle
For daylight and time for activity.
The crimson sky shimmered with color,
And birds awoke, flying toward the horizon.

The new day is upon the world,
Morning comes more quickly each day.
It seems time passes so rapidly.
Each new dawn represents aging
Gently reminding one how fragile life is,
And giving forth its beauty,
Shares daily the promise of happiness,
And the gift of life we share.

Karen Walker Stumpf
GRANDMA'S QUILT
Moving quickly her fingers make
Tiny stitches as the needle
Weaves in and out.
Now and then, a pricked finger.
Blood staining the thread.
Her life has been like the quilt.
Each patch a new event.
Love for a man,
Birth of a child,
Good times, hard times,
A prick staining the thread.
Children and family,
Smaller patches around the edge.
Each stitch a busy day.
Laced through the years are
Tears, smiles, fears and joy.
With head bent in prayer,
She binds together her quilt of life.

Index

A

D

E

F

G

H

K

L

M

N

S

U

V

Y

Z